MR. MINT

NUMBER 1

MAJOR PURCHASES:

FIND I Purchaser of over $400,000 worth of Gem-Mint high-number series of 1952 Topps cards.

FIND II Purchaser of over $400,000 worth of 1954 & 1955 Topps and Bowman unopened boxes in Paris, Tennessee.

FIND III Purchaser of over $125,000 worth of rare vintage World Series press pins.

Purchaser of the Kansas City Bowman Find of over $125,000 in catalog value.
Purchaser of $385,000 Topps and Bowmans in the ABC Collectables Find in Moline, Illinois.
Purchaser of $400,000 of the Hit King Marketing 500 Homerun print and baseball buyout.
Purchaser of Manny's Baseball Land over $400,000 worth of yearbooks, World Series & All-Star programs in the original boxes.
Purchaser of over $11 Million in old cards in the past three years. New card sales not included.
Purchaser of Baseball Cards Unlimited. Over $250,000 worth of unopened cases and new sets.

"Featured with an 8 page spread in the July 4th, 1988 issue of Sports Illustrated."

"Appeared nationally on ABC's Good Morning America with Joan Junden and Joel Siegel."

PRESS CREDENTIALS:

Feature stories in such fine National magazines as Sports Illustrated February 1989, Money Magazine, Forbes Magazine, New York Magazine, Baseball Today, A.C. Delco's In Tune Magazine, Northwest Airlines Magazine, Globe, and in addition, major daily newspapers such as: New York Times, New York Post, Philadelphia Times, New York Daily News, New Jersey's Bergen Record, St. Petersburg Times, L.A. Times, USA Today, Honolulu Advertiser, Star Ledger, Patterson News, and mentioned in hundreds of other baseball card related articles across the country.
Has appeared on National Television shows as: Good Morning America, CBS Sports, ESPN, NBC's Game of the Week, ABC Nightline, FNN, CBS News Network, Rod Michaud's Sports Talk, Home Shopping Network, CNBC, Channel 5's Good Day New York, NBC's Sunday A.M. and major radio shows on such stations as The Art Rust Show, WABC, WFAN, WCBS and WNBC affiliates.

THE NO. 1 BUYER

in the hobby invites you to consider the above when selling your collectables

ALAN ROSEN - MR. MINT
70 I Chestnut Ridge Road
Montvale, NJ 07645
FAX (201) 307-1653
(201) 307-0700

SCD's Largest Advertiser

CLASSIC REPRINTS

COLLECTOR'S ALERT

There is a T-206 reprint set offered for sale by another advertiser at a price lower than ours.

These cards from the other company were rejected by a company who commissioned them to be made because of the extremely poor reproductive quality and totally dissimilar typesetting of the names.

Send us a stamped, self-addressed envelope and we will send you, free of charge, a sample of each set.

Our price per set is $39.95. Decide for yourself. If not satisfied, send it back for full refund.

By the way, our set is complete with 524 cards. Their's is 523 cards. Our set has the rare Doyle card.

PRESS RELEASE - IMMEDIATE RELEASE FREE FREE KEN GRIFFEY JR. CARDS

Card Collector's Company proudly announces that it is producing a Ken Griffey Jr. Boyhood Set to commemorate Ken's Rookie season. This 16 card set will be given out free to our customers. For every $10.00 worth of merchandise that you order we will send you a card. $50.00 we will send you ½ a set. For $100.00 we will send you a free set.

1933 GOUDEY REPRINT SET

240 cards in full color with the backs faithfully reproduced. This classic set contains 4 different Babe Ruth Cards, 2 Lou Gehrigs and the rare Napoleon Lajoie. Other greats in the set Mel Ott, B. Terry, Cronin, Hornsby, Gehringer, Gomez, Grove, Ruffing, Speaker, both Waners, Maranville. The list goes on and on.

BONUS

Bonus offer good until January 3, 1990. With every set that you order we will send you free the following 1933 Reprints: 4 Babe Ruth, 2 Gehrig and 1 Napolean Lajoie.

1 Set $32.95
5 Sets 125.00
10 Sets 219.00

9 Pocket plastic sheets designed for 1933 Goudey Cards .... .22 each

1915 CRACKER JACK REPRINT SET

Great 176 Card Set

To find an original MT set is close to impossible. This set contains Shoeless Joe Jackson, Ty Cobb, Christy Mathewson, Honus Wagner, Walter Johnson, Tris Speaker, John McGraw, Lajoie, Connie Mack and on and on and on.

1 Set .... $24.00 5 Sets 91.00
10 Sets 159.00

9 Pocket plastic sheets available at . .22 each

The Lou Gehrig Postcard Set

- 10 Full Color Cards
- Limited printing 5000 sets
- Traces Lou's historic career
- Shots of Babe Ruth and Joe D. in the background

1 Set .... $8.00 10 Sets 65.00

Also available. Set of 10 silk cachets, first day issue, postmarked June 10, 1989 at Cooperstown. All 10 pictures on the postcard set are on these 1st Day Covers.

Complete Set $25.00
1 Cachet our choice 3.00

DEALER DISCOUNT

Order 5 of the same set listed on this page and you may have a 35% discount. This offer DOES NOT apply to the T-206, the Bowman 52 Set, and the Bowman 49.

THE MONSTER IS HERE

The classic Tobacco card set, nicknamed "The Monster", recognized as the most popular card set ever issued.
The great T-206 set, all 523 cards, originally issued 1909-1911, has been carefully reprinted in full color, fine detail, and in original size.
Set includes such famous cards as the rare Wagner, Maglie error, Plank, 4 Ty Cobbs and almost 100 other Hall of Famers.
An original set today would cost over $150,000.
You can enjoy it now for only $39.95.
All orders will be filled on a 1st come, 1st served basis.
Dealer Special - 5 Sets for $130.00

Historic Allen And Ginter "Large Card Set"

- 1880's Set 6 card set
- Full color Tobacco Card Set With Great Artwork Of The Period On Both Sides Of The Card.

1 Set .... **$3.95** 5 Sets **15.95**
10 Sets **23.95**

NEW

1900 Turn of the century British Golfers Reprint Set - 50 cards. Size of T-206 - very collectible. See what our English Friends contributed to card collecting

Only $7.99

15 card T206 Hall of Famers Set:

Includes Wagner, Magee, Error, Plank and four Ty Cobbs.

One set $5.95 10 sets $32.95

T206 Plastic Sheet Sale

Each sheet is 15 pockets
Price per sheet 22¢.
These sheets should be used to display the T206 set

1949 BOWMAN REPRINT SET

Complete set $24.95

- Set contains 240 cards
- First Bowman Color Set
- Includes Rookie Cards of J. Robinson, D. Snider, G. Hodges, R. Campanella, and the only Bowman card of the legendary Satchell Paige.

Just In — 1952 REDMAN REPRINT

Set 52 cards

1 Set .... $19.95 10 Sets $115.00
5 Sets .... 64.95 25 Sets 250.00

1948 BOWMAN FOOTBALL REPRINT SET

108 Cards of the Greats of the ERA only $19.95

1904 WG2 Fan Craze National League Reprint 48 Cards Set inlcudes Wagner, Chance, McGraw, Bresnahan, Young.

1 set 6.95

1904 WG2 American League Fan Craze Reprint 51 Cards Set Includes Nap Lajoie, Ed Plank, Cy Young, Connie Mack, Chief Bender and Billy Keeler.

1 set 6.95

CLASSIC REPRINT (T-201)

MECCA DOUBLE FOLDER SET

Made in 1911, one of the first sets to have statistics.

One hundred players on fifty cards. All cards are die cut, and when they are folded over you get a new player with the background and legs of the first player.

Quite a creative idea. Topps copied this concept in their 1955 Double-header Set.

Set includes Cobb, Baker, Collins, Wheat, Huggins, Chance.

Complete Set $14.95

1887 LONE JACK REPRINT SET

13 Card Sepia Set of the 1886 World Champion St. Louis Browns

$4.99 per set

N172 OLD JUDGE TYPE SET REPRINT - SERIES 1

$5.00 plus postage & handling

The N172 Old Judge issue by the Goodwin Company was one of the original, and most significant, baseball card sets ever issued. The mid-1880s issue contains at least 2300 different poses. While no one has amassed the entire set (new cards are being discovered each year), there are many "types" of Old Judge poses. The 20-card reprint set contains a number of these types of Old Judge cards. Each card is marked "reprint".

1940 PLAY BALL REPRINT SET

All Cards Black And White And The Same Size As The Originals

SERIES 1 (#1-45)
Includes Joe DiMaggio, Tommy Henrich, Lefty Gomez, Bill Dickey, Red Ruffing, Ted Williams, Hank Greenberg, Charlie Gehringer **$5.00**

SERIES 2 (#46-90)
Includes Earl Averill, Van Lingo Mungo, Carl Hubbell, Mel Ott 5.00

SERIES 3 (#91-135)
Includes Walter Johnson, Grover Cleveland Alexander, Joe Cronin, Connie Mack, Jimmy Foxx, Chuck Klein, Lloyd Waner, Paul Waner, Waite Hoyt, Arky Vaughn, Bucky Harris 5.00

Series 4 (#136-180)
Includes Nap Lajoie, Mickey Cochrane, George Sisler, Max Carey, Frank Baker, Heinie Manush, Christy Mathewson, Johnny Evers, Chief Bender, Harry Heilmann, Tris Speaker, Honus Wagner, Frankie Frisch, Casey Stengel 5.00

SERIES 5
(60 cards-high numbers)
(#181-240) Includes "Shoeless Joe" Jackson, Tony Lazzeri, Wee Willie Keeler, John J. McGraw, Frank Chance, Goose Goslin, Red Faber, Pie Traynor, Hugh Jennings 8.00

Complete set of all 240 cards Series #1-#5 $25.00

**Dealer Special
5 Complete Sets Of All 5 Series - 240 Cards
Each Set $85.00**

1941 PLAY BALL Reprint Set — Full Color

72 cards includes Joe DiMaggio, T. Williams, B. Dickey, Pee Wee Reese 1 set - $8.95, 5 sets - $30.00, 10 sets **$14.95**

1941 GOUDEY REPRINT SET

$8.00 plus postage & handling
Specify background color desired

One set each of the four background colors
$30.00 plus postage & handling

This 33 card set was the last baseball card set made by the Goudey Gum Company. The blank backed cards themselves are black & white photos with a colored background. The background colors are red, blue, yellow or green; therefore, an astronomical number of possibilities for color-variation sets using the basic 33 cards exist. Hall of Famers Carl Hubbell and Mel Ott highlight this set along with card numbers 21 to 25, considered scarcer in the original issue.

JOHNSTON COOKIE REPRINT COLOR SETS OF MILWAUKEE BRAVES

1953 - 25 cards **$8.00**
1954 - 35 cards **9.00**
1955 - 35 cards **9.00**
All three sets **23.00**

1951 BOWMAN REPRINT SET

Complete Set of 324 Cards

Set includes:

Mickey Mantle (Rookie Card), Pee Wee Reese, Phil Rizzuto, Gil Hodges, Whitey Ford, Robin Roberts, Joe Garagiola, Casey Stengel, Bill Dickey, Yogi Berra, Duke Snider, Roy Campanella, Bob Feller, Warren Spahn, Ted Williams

Original Set Now Worth Over **$10,000.00**

• All cards the same size as the original Bowman 1951's. The set captures the beautiful artwork and detail of each card. All cards are made by the STATE OF THE ART "Diamond Vue" process. There are only four printing presses in the United States that can produce these cards. The final product is awesome and something that you will be proud to add to your collection. All cards in full color with a rich lacquer finish. You will be impressed! Each set comes in a special collectors box.

1 Set $39.95
10 Sets $275.00
25 Sets $560.00

1948 BOWMAN REPRINT SET

Complete Set of 48 Cards
- **All Cards Are Black And White**
- **The Same Size As The Original 1948's**

Complete Set of all 48 Cards **$6.95**
Dealers Special 10 Sets **$37.50**

Includes Rookie Cards of: Yogi Berra, Stan Musial, Phil Rizzuto, Enos Slaughter, Warren Spahn, Red Schoendienst, Ralph Kiner, Marty Marion

Includes Superstars such as: Bob Feller, Johnny Mize, Hank Sauer, Ewell Blackwell, Tommy Henrich, Bobby Thomson

1935 NATIONAL CHICLE FOOTBALL CARD SET

$5.00

"The" classic football card set of all time features the two most valuable football cards in existence — Knute Rockne and Bronco Nagurski. The 36-card set features the National Chicle art-deco style which has contributed to the lasting popularity of the set.

1949 Bowman Pacific Coast League Reprint Set. 36 full color cards $6.95.

1939 PLAY BALL REPRINT SET SERIES 1

$8.00 plus postage & handling

This first series of the 1939 Play Ball reprint set includes the first 55 cards in the set. The stars in this series include Joe DiMaggio, Bill Dickey, Red Ruffing, Bobby Doerr, Rick Ferrell, Lefty Gomez and Charlie Gehringer. The black and white cards have been reproduced at original size and can be housed by Style 9PB plastic sheets. All cards are marked "reprint".

NEW REPRINT

1913 T-200 FATIMA TEAM CARDS

16 Card Set Only **$5.99**

1936 GOUDEY GAME REPRINT SET

$5.00 plus postage & handling

This 25-card black & white set features Hall of Famers Mickey Cochrane, Kiki Cuyler, Rick Ferrell, Lefty Gomez, Hank Greenberg, Chuck Klein and Paul Waner. The backs contain short narratives of the players and "game" situations (hence the nickname of the set).

1933 GOUDEY SPORT KINGS

(48 cards) .. **$9.00**

Includes Babe Ruth, Ty Cobb, Carl Hubbell, football players Red Grange, Jim Thorpe, and Knute Rockne, boxers Jack Dempsey and Gene Tunney and many other "SPORTS KINGS!"

1935 GOUDEY

$7.00

This 36-card set, commonly called the Goudey 4-in-1 or Goudey Puzzle set, features four players per card with red or blue borders separating the players. Ruth, Dean, Foxx, Klein and many other Hall of Famers are included.

1938 GOUDEY HEADS UP

$7.00

This unusual, and extremely popular, 48-card set features the first gum cards of Joe DiMaggio and Bob Feller. Of the 48 cards, 14 feature Hall of Famers.

1933 GOUDEY REPRINT SUPER SET

7 cards, 4 different Babe Ruths, 2 Gehrigs, 1 N. Lajoie

1 Set $4.95
10 Sets 24.95

1934 GOUDEY

$15.00

(96 Cards) includes 2 Lou Gehrig cards, Jimmy Foxx, Dizzy Dean, Lefty and rare high number series

1934-1936 DIAMOND STARS

$15.00

The entire set of 108 cards, including the difficult-to-obtain high numbers are reproduced superbly in this reprint edition. More than 25 Hall of Famers Foxx, Grove, Greenberg, Hornsby, and most of the greats of the period are contained within this set

1952 BOWMAN REPRINT IN UNCUT SHEETS

• 1952 Bowman Baseball Reprint • Set in 4 Uncut Sheets • Complete Set of All 252 Cards • Plus a Bonus 36 Cards Including Extra Cards of Mickey Mantle, Willie Mays and Stan Musial • Each Sheet Measures a Full 20 Inches by 28 Inches • Suitable For Framing • Perfect Centerpiece Display For Your Private Sports Den!

Only **$119.95** postpaid (No postage and handling charge on this item)

1954 DAN DEE POTATO CHIPS

Reprint set full color 29 cards includes superstars of era Doby, Feller, Hodges, Mantle, Rizzuto and other greats **$9.95**

1913 JOE BARKER NATIONAL GAME REPRINT
52 cards
You can actually play the game. Includes 2 Cobbs, Shoeless Joe, Wagner, W. Johnson, and Tinker. Only **$6.95**

AMERICAN CARD CATALOG

The American Card Catalog (ACC) is available with the original text reprinted exactly as it appears in the last edition (1960) along with the original catalog price.

This book is the most important reference guide (nicknamed the "Bible") to collecting baseball and all types of cards (bubble gum, candies, tobacco, advertising cards, etc.) that were known from pre 1850 on.

The numbering system continues to be of great reference value. This is where you get the familiar designations from, such as T-206, R-333 and E-90. You can now get your copy of this historic publication for $9.95

NEW! HOME RUN DERBY REPRINT SET

- Set of 19 Baseball Sluggers.
- Produced in 1959 by American Motors to publicize a T.V. program.
- All cards are black and white and blank backed.
- Set includes: Mantle, Aaron, Banks, Hodges, Mays, Killebrew, and Snider.

Complete Set **$5.95**

NEW! NEW LANDMARK REPRINT

CARD COLLECTOR'S COMPANY is proud to announce that we have reprinted the 1887 and 1888 Allen and Ginter baseball cards as well as the 1888 Goodwins. These cards were the first baseball cards of individual players in full color. They are the forerunners of the T cards at the turn of the century. These three sets include Hall of Famers: Anson, Bennett, Brouthers, Keefe, Kelly, and Ward.

Front and back of all these cards have been reprinted. Complete set of 24 cards (10 cards from 1887 A&G, 6 cards from 1888 A&G, and 8 cards from 1888 Goodwin).

All for **$5.95**

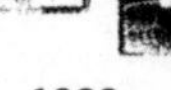

1933 GOUDEY PREMIUM

A fine Goudey effort to establish their BB cards. Large 4 card set with Gold Border. Set includes Ruth, A.L. All Stars 1933, N.L. All Stars 1933, World Champs 1933.

Set **$3.95**

1954 WILSON WEINER REPRINT SET

$8.00 plus postage & handling

This 20-card set is one of the more valuable of the 1950s meat card issues. The set contains the currently most valuable Ted Williams card plus cards of Roy Campanella, Bob Feller, Gil Hodges, Enos Slaughter and Nellie Fox. The full-color cards have been scaled down to standard size.

NEW REPRINT

1954 Red Heart Dog Food Set
33 Card Set

Includes Mantle, D. Snider, Spahn, Lemon and other stars of the 1950's.

$9.95

NEGRO LEAGUE BASEBALL SET

115 cards from 1898 to 1946.

Classic B/W shots.

Set **$9.95**

RICHARD GELMAN
Wholesale Prices Available For Multiple Purchases.

American Express

Card Collectors' Co.

**105 West 77 Street
New York City, NY 10024
212-873-6999
FAX: 212-873-4016**

Watch our weekly Baseball Card TV show. Every Monday 7:30-8:00 PM. On Manhattan Cable TV channel 23. Call our special TV telephone number 212-213-8785 if you would like to sponsor this show in your area.

Postage & Handling.
Please add $3.00 per total order unless otherwise stated.

New York State residents add sales tax.

Visit our store, open 7 days 12-7 p.m. • CALL TOLL FREE FOR ORDERS ONLY 1-800-822-0028

standard catalog of

second edition

BASEBALL CARDS

the most comprehensive price guide ever published!

Jeff Kurowski, Editor

Special Consultants

Dan Albaugh
Bill Bossert
John Brigandi
Dwight Chapin
Larry Fritsch
Dick Goddard
Don Harrison
(Minor Leagues Section)
Rob Lifson
Mark Mac Rae
Bill Mendel
John Spalding

Library of Congress Catalog Number: 88-80850
ISBN: 0-87341-138-2

ACKNOWLEDGEMENTS

Dozens of individuals have made countless valuable contributions which have been incorporated into the *Standard Catalog of Baseball Cards.* While all cannot be acknowledged, special appreciation is extended to the following principal contributors who have exhibited a special dedication by creating, revising or verifying listings and technical data, reviewing market valuations or loaning cards for photography.

Johnny Adams, Jr.
Ken Agona
(Sports Cards Plus)
Gary Agostino
Lisa Albano
Mark Anker
Steve Applebaum
John Beisiegel
Karen Bell
Cathy Black
Mike Bodner
Brian Boston
Mike Boyd
Lou Brown
Dan Bruner
(The Card King)
Greg Bussineau
(Superior Sports Cards)
Billy Caldwell
(Packman)
Len Caprisecca
Tony Carrafiell
(Delco Sports Cards)
Lee Champion
Dwight Chapin
Chriss Christiansen
Shane Cohen
(Grand Slam Sports Collectibles)
Charles Conlon
Eric Cooper
(All Star Cards)
Bryan Couling
Clyde Cripe
Jim Cumpton
Robert Curtiss
Tom Daniels
(T&J Sports Cards)
Tom Day
(Major League Marketing)
Dick DeCourcy
(Georgia Music & Sports)
Mike Del Gado
(All American Sportscards)
Larry Dluhy
(Texas Trading Cards)
John Dorsey
Curtis Earl
Steve Ellingboe
Joe Esposito
(B&E Collectibles)
Doak Ewing
Shirley Eross
(Hobbyrama Sports By Eross)
David Festberg
(Baseball and Hobby Shop)
Jay Finglass
Nick Flaviano
Jeff Fritsch
Richard Galasso
Tom Galic
Tony Galovich
(American Card Exchange)
Frank Giffune
Richard Gilkeson
Bill Goodwin
Jack Goodman
Audre Gold
(Au Sports Memorabilia)
Mike Gordon
Howard Gordon
Bob Gray
Paul Green
Wayne Grove
(First Base)
Gerry Guenther
Don Guilbert
Tom Guilfoile
David Hall
Joel Hall
Walter Hall
(Hall's Nostalgia)
Gary Hamilton
Tom Harbin
Rick Hawksley
Herbert Hecht
Bill Henderson
Gregg Hitesman
Jack Horkan
Jim Horne
Ron Hosmer
Marvin Huck
Robert Jacobsen
Donn Jennings
Scott Jensen
LouAnne Johnson
(Baseball Card News)
Jim Johnston
Stewart Jones
Larry Jordon
Judy Kay
(Kay's Baseball Cards)
Allan Kaye
Michael Keedy
Mark Kemmerle
Rick Keplinger
John King
John Kittleson
(Sports Collectibles)
Bob Koehler
David Kohler
Steve Lacasse
Lee Lasseigne
William Lawrence
Morley Leeking
Don Lepore
Rod Lethbridge
Paul Lewicki
Neil Lewis
(Leaf, Inc.)
Howie Levy
(Blue Chip Sportscard)
Ken & Norman Liss
(Topps, Inc.)
Jeff Litteral
Paul Marchant
Bill Mastro
Jay McCracken
(Upper Deck)
Tony McLaughlin
Don McPherson
John Mehlin
Blake Meyer
(Lone Star Sportcard Co.)
Dick Millerd
Minnesota Sports Collectibles
Keith Mitchell
J.A. Monaco
Joe Morano
Brian Morris
Mike Mowery
Peter Muldavin
Mark Murphy
(The Baseball Card "Kid")
Vincent Murray
(Fleer Corp.)
David Musser
(D.M.B.'s Baseball Cards)
Steve Myland
Frank Nagy
Chuck Nobriga
Mark Nochta
Wayne Nochta
Keith Olbermann
Joe Pasternack
(Card Collectors Co.)
Marty Perry
Tom Pfirrman
(Baseball Card Corner)
Dan Piepenbrok
(Uneeda Hobbie)
Stan Pietruska
(Pro Sports Investments)
Paul Pollard
Ed Ransom
Fred Rapoport
(Yesterday's Heroes)
Tom Reid
Bob Richardson
Gavin Riley
Ron Ritzler
Mike Rodell
Mike Rogers
Chris Ronan
Rocky Rosato
Alan Rosen
John Rumierz
Bob Rund
Jon Sands
(Howard's Coin Shop)
Kevin Savage
(The Sports Gallery)
Stephen Schauer
Dave Schwartz
(Dave's Sportscards)
Robert Scott
Corey Shanus
Dan Shedrick
(Major League Marketing)
Max Silberman
Barry Sloate
Joe Smith
Mark Soltan
Kevin Spears
Gene Speranza
David Spivack
Don Steinbach
(Sports Collectors Store)
Dan Stickney
Larry Stone
Doug Stultz
Joe Szeremet
Erik Teller
K.J. Terplak
Dick Tinsley
Bud Tompkins
(Minnesota Connection)
Scott Torrey
Rich Unruh
Jack Urban
Joe Valle
(Cardboard Dreams)
Pete Waldman
Eric Waller
Gary Walter
Ken Weimer
Dale Weselowski
(Ab D. Cards of Winnipeg)
E.C. Wharton-Tigar
Chris Williams
Charles Williamson
Kit Young
Ted Zanidakis

standard catalog of

BASEBALL CARDS

The most comprehensive price guide ever published

INTRODUCTORY NOTE

The 2nd edition of the Standard Catalog of Baseball Cards is an updated version of the first edition released in 1988. Future editions will contain additional regional sets, minor league issues and collector issues once those checklists have been substantiated.

Readers should be aware that attempts were made to include as many sets issued in 1990 as possible. However, due to late releases, production deadlines, or a lack of established prices, some 1990 sets are not listed.

BASEBALL CARD HISTORY

In 1887 – exactly 100 years ago – the first nationally distributed baseball cards were issued by Goodwin & Co., of New York City. The 1½" x 2½" cards featured posed studio photographs glued to stiff cardboard. They were inserted into cigarette packages with such exotic brand names as Old Judge, Gypsy Queen and Dog's Head. Poses were formal, with artificial backgrounds and bare-handed players fielding balls suspended on strings to simulate action.

Then, as now, baseball cards were intended to stimulate product sales. what could be more American than using the diamond heroes of the national pastime to gain an edge on the competition? It is a tradition that has continued virtually unbroken for a century.

Following Goodwin's lead a year later, competitors began issuing baseball cards with their cigarettes, using full-color lithography to bring to life painted portraits of the era's top players.

After a few short years of intense competition, the cigarette industry's leading firms formed a monopoly and cornered the market. By the mid-1890s, there was little competition, and no reason to issue baseball cards. The first great period of baseball card issues came to an end.

The importing of Turkish tobaccos in the years just prior to 1910 created a revolution in American smoking habits. with dozens of new firms entering the market, the idea of using baseball cards to boost sales was revived.

In the years from 1909-1912, dozens of different sets of cards were produced to be given away in cigarette packages. There was greater than ever variety in sizes, shapes and designs, from the extremely popular 1½" x 2⅝" color-lithographed set of 500+ players which collectors call T206, to the large (5" x 8") Turkey Red brand cards. There were double-folders, featuring two players on the same card, and triple-folders, which had two player portraits and an action scene. Gold ink and embossed designs were also tried to make each competing company's cards attractive and popular.

It was this era that saw the issue of the "King of Baseball Cards," the T206 Honus Wagner card, worth $75,000.

The zeal with which America's youngsters pursued their fathers, uncles, and neighbors for cigarette cards in the years just prior to World War I convinced the nation's confectioners that baseball cards could also be used to boost candy sales.

While baseball cards had been produced by candy companies on a limited basis as far back as the 1880s, by the early 1920s, the concept was being widely used in the industry. The highly competitive caramel business was a major force in this new marketing strategy, offering a baseball card in each package of candy. Not to be outdone, Cracker Jack began including baseball cards in each box. The 1914-1915 Cracker Jack cards are important because they were the most popular of the candy cards to include players from a short-lived third major league, the Federal League.

Generally, candy cards of the era were not as colorful or well-printed as the earlier tobacco cards, due to shortage of paper and ink-making ingredients caused by World War I.

The association of bubble gum and baseball cards is a phenomenon of only the past half-century. In the early 1930s, techniques were developed using rubber tree products to give the elasticity necessary for blowing bubbles.

During ths era that standard method of selling a slab of bubble gum and a baseball card in a colorfully wax-wrapped 1¢ package was developed. Bubble gum – and baseball cards – production in this era was centered in Massachusetts, where National Chicle Company (Cambridge) and Goudey Gum Company (Boston) were headquartered.

Most bubble gum cards produced in the early 1930s featured a roughly square (about 2½") format, with players depicted in colorful paintings. For the first time, considerable attention was paid to the backs of the cards, where biographical details, career highlights and past season statistics were presented.

In 1939, a new company entered the baseball card market – Gum, Inc., of Philadelphia. Its "Play Ball" gum was the major supplier of baseball cards until 1941, when World War II caused a shortage of the materials necessary both for the production of bubble gum and the printing of baseball cards.

Three years after the end of World War II baseball cards returned on a national scale, with two companies competing for the bubble gum market. In Philadelphia, the former Gum, Inc., reappeared on the market as Bowman Gum, Inc.

Bowman's first baseball card set appeared in 1948, very similar in format to the cards which had existed prior to the war, black and white player photos on nearly square (2" x 2½") cardboard. The '48 Bowman effort was modest, with only 48 cards. The following year, color was added to the photos. For 1950, Bowman replaced the re-rouched photos with original color painting of players, many of which were repeated a year later in the 1951 issue. Also new for 1951 was a larger card size, 2" x 3⅛."

Bowman had little national competition in this era,. In 1948-1949,. Leaf Gum in Chicago produced a 98-card set that is the only bubble gum issue of the era to include a Joe DiMaggio card.

While Bowman dominated the post-war era through 1951, in that year Topps began production of its first baseball cards, issuing three different small sets of cards and serving warning that it was going to become a major force in the baseball card field.

In 1952, Brooklyn-based Topps entered the baseball card market in a big way. Not only was its 407-card set the largest single-year issue ever produced, but its 2⅝" x 3¾" format was the largest-size baseball card ever offered for over-the-counter sale. Other innovations in Topps' premiere issue for 1952 included the first-ever use of team logos in card design, and on the back of the card, the first use of line statistics to document the player's previous year and career performance. By contrast, Bowman's set for 1952 remained in the smaller format, had 72 fewer cards and showed little change in design from 1951.

Just as clearly as Topps won the 1952 baseball card battle, Bowman came back in 1953 with what is often considered the finest baseball card set ever produced. For the first time ever, actual color photographs were reproduced on baseball cards in Bowman's 160-card set. To allow the full impact of the new technology, there were no other design elements on the front of the card and Bowman adopted a larger format, 2½" x 3¾."

And so the competition went for five years, each company trying to gain an edge by signing players to exclusive contracts and creating new and exciting card designs each year. Gradually, Topps become the dominant force in the baseball card market. In late 1955, Bowman admitted defeat and the company was sold to Topps.

Baseball cards entered a new era in 1957. After years of intense competition, Topps enjoyed a virtual monopoly that was rarely seriously challenged in the next 25 years. One such challenge in the opening years of the 1960s came from Post cereal, which from 1961-1963 issued 200-card sets on the backs of its cereal boxes.

In 1957, Topps' baseball cards were issued in a new size – 2½" x 3½" – that would become the industry-wide standard that prevails to this day. It was also that year that Topps first used full-color photographs for its cards, rather than paintings or re-touched black and white photos. Another innovation in the 1947 set was the introduction of complete major and/or minor league statistics on the card backs. This feature quickly became a favorite with youngsters and provided fuel for endless schoolyard debates about whether one player was better than another.

In the ensuing five years, major league baseball underwent monumental changes. In 1958, The Giants and Dodgers left New York for California. In 1961-1962 expansion came to the major leagues, with new teams springing up from coast to coast and border to border.

The Topps baseball cards of the era preserve those days when modern baseball was in its formative stages.

In 1963, for the first time in seven years, it looked as if there might once again be two baseball card issues to choose from. After three years of issuing "old-timers" cards sets, Fleer issued a 66-card set of current players. Topps took Fleer to court, where the validity of Topps' exclusive contracts with baseball players to appear on bubble gum cards was upheld. It was the last major challenge to Topps for nearly 20 years.

The 1960s offered baseball card collecting at its traditional finest. Youngsters would wait and worry through the long winter, watching candy store shelves for the first appearance of the brightly colored 5¢ card packs in the spring. A cry of, "They're in!" could empty a playground in seconds as youngsters rushed to the counter store to see what design innovations Topps had come up with for the new year. Then, periodically through the summer, new series would be released, offering a new challenge to complete. As the season wore down, fewer and fewer stores carried the final few series, and it became a real struggle to complete the "high numbers" from a given year's set. But it was all part of the fun of buying baseball cards in the 1960s.

The early 1970s brought some important changes to the baseball card scene. The decade's first two Topps' issues were stunning in that the traditional white border was dropped in favor of gray in 1970, and black in 1971. In 1972, Topps' card design was absolutely psychedelic, with brightly colored frames around the player photos, and comic book typography popping out all over. The design for the 1973 cards was more traditional, but the photos were not. Instead of close-up portraits or posed "action" shots, many cards in the 1973 Topps set featured actual game action photos. Unfortunately, too many of those photos made it hard to tell which player was which, and the set was roundly panned by collectors.

But most significantly, 1973 marked the last year in which baseball cards were issued by series through the course of the summer. On the positive side, this eliminated the traditionally scarce "high numbers" produced toward the end of the season. On the negative side, it meant players who had been traded in the pre-season could no longer be shown in their "correct" uniforms, and outstanding new players had to wait a full year before their rookie cards would debut.

This marketing change made a significant impact on the hobby and helped spur a tremendous growth period in the late 1970s. By offering all of its cards at once, Topps made it easy for baseball card dealers to offer complete sets early in the year. Previously, collectors had to either assemble their sets by buying packs of cards, or wait until all series had been issued to buy a set from a dealer. It was in this era that many of today's top baseball card dealers got their start or made the switch to baseball cards as a full-time business.

During this era, the first significant national competition to Topps' baseball card monopoly in many years was introduced. Hostess bakery products company began distributing baseball cards printed on the bottoms of packages of its snack cakes, while the Kellogg's company distributed simulated 3-D cards in boxes of its cereals. The eagerness with which collectors

gobbled up these issues showed that the hobby was ready for a period of unprecendented growth.

The baseball card hobby literally boomed in 1981. A Federal court broke Topps' monopoly on the issue of baseball cards with bubble gum and Fleer of Philadelphia and Donruss of Memphis, entered the field as the first meaningful competition in nearly 20 years.

That same year also marked a beginning of the resurgence in the number of regional baseball card issues. Over the next few years, dozens of such sets came onto the market, helping to boost sales of everything from snack cakes to soda pop and police public relations. By 1984, more than half of the teams in the major leagues were issuing some type of baseball cards on a regional basis. The hobby had not enjoyed such diversity of issue since the mid-1950s.

While yet another court decision cost Fleer and Donruss the right to sell their baseball cards with bubble gum, both companies remained in the market and gained strength.

Topps' major contribution in this era was the introduction of annual "Traded" sets which offered cards of the year's new rookies as well as cards of traded players in their "correct" uniforms.

The mid-1980s showed continued strong growth in the number of active baseball card collectors, as well as the number of new baseball card issues. Topps, still the industry's leader, expanded the number and variety of its baseball issues with many different test issues and on-going specialty sets, including oversize cards, 3-D plastic cards, metal "cards" and much more.

After three years of over-production of its baseball card sets, Donruss, in 1984, significantly limited the number of cards printed, creating a situation in which demand exceeded supply, causing the value of Donruss cards to rise above Topps for the first time.

In 1984, Fleer followed Topps' lead and produced a season's-end "Update" set. Because the quantity of sets printed was extremely limited, and because it contains many of today's hottest young players, the 1984 Fleer Update set has become the most valuable baseball card issue produced in recent times.

In 1986, a fourth company joined the baseball "card wars." Called "Sportflics," the cards were produced by a subsidiary of the Wrigley Gum company, and featured three different photos on each card in a simulated 3-D effect. For 1987, a fourth national baseball card set called Score entered the scene.

Baseball card collecting entered its second century in 1987. In 1989, Upper Deck entered the card market with its first issue. With more collectors amd more new cards than ever before, 1990 looks like another growth year for baseball cards.

HOW TO USE THIS CATALOG

This catalog has been uniquely designed to serve the needs of both beginning and advanced collectors. It provides a comprehensive guide to more than 100 years of baseball card issues, arranged so that even the most novice collector can consult it with confidence and erase.

The following explanations summarize the general practices used in preparing this catalog's listings. However, because of specialized requirements which may vary from card set to card set, these must not be considered ironclad. Where these standards have been set aside, appropriate notations are incorporated.

ARRANGEMENT

Because the most important feature in identifying, and pricing, a baseball card is its set of origin, this catalog has been alphabetically arranged according to the name by which the set is mostly popularly known to collectors.

Those sets that were issued for more than one year are then listed chronologically, from earliest to most recent.

Within each set, the cards are listed by their designated card number, or in the absence of card numbers, alphabetically according to the last name of the player pictured.

IDENTIFICATION

While most modern baseball cards are well identified on front, back or both, as to date and issuer, such has not always been the case. In general, the back of the card is more useful in identifying the set of origin than the front. The issuer or sponsor's name will usually appear on the back since, after all, baseball cards were first issued as a promotional item to stimulate sales of other products. As often as not, that issuer's name is the name by which the set is known to collectors and under which it will be found listed in this catalog.

Virtually every set listed in this catalog is accompanied by a photograph of a representative card. If all else fails, a comparison of an unknown card with the photos in this book will usually produce a match.

As a special feature, each set listed in this catalog has been cross-indexed by its date of issue. This will allow identification in some difficult cases since a baseball card's general age, if not specific year of issue, can usually be fixed by studying the biographical or statistical information on the back of the card. The last year mentioned in either bio or stats is usually the year which preceded the year of issue.

PHOTOGRAPHS

A photograph of the front and back of at least one representative card from virtually every set listed in this catalog has been incorporated into the listings to aid in identification.

Photographs have been printed in reduced size. The actual

size of cards in each set is given in the introductory text preceding its listing.

DATING

The dating of baseball cards by year of issue on the front or back of the card itself is a relatively new phenomenon. In most cases, to accurately determine a date of issue for an unidentified card, it must be studied for clues. As mentioned, the biography, career summary or statistics on the back of the card are the best way to pinpoint a year of issue. In most cases, the year of issue will be the year after the last season mentioned on the card.

Luckily for today's collector, earlier generations have done much of the research in determining year of issue for those cards which bear no clues. The painstaking task of matching players' listed and/or pictured team against their career records often allowed an issue date to be determined.

In some cases, particular card sets were issued over a period of more than one calendar year, but since they are collected together as a single set, their specific year of issue is not important. Such sets will be listed with their complete known range of issue years, as 1909-1911 T206, or 1948-1949 Leaf, etc.

NUMBERING

While many baseball card issues as far back as the 1880s have contained card numbers assigned by the issuer, to facilitate the collecting of a complete set, the practice has by no means been universal. Even today, not every set bears card numbers.

Logically, those baseball cards which were numbered by their manufacturer are presented in that numerical order within the listings of this catalog. The many unnumbered issues, however, have been assigned *Standard Catalog of Baseball Cards* numbers to facilitate their universal identication within the hobby, especially when buying and selling by mail. In all cases, numbers which have been assigned, or which otherwise do not appear on the card through error or by design, are shown in this catalog within parentheses. In virtually all cases, unless a more natural system suggested itself by the unique nature of a particular set, the assignment of Standard Catalog of Baseball Cards numbers by the cataloging staff has been done by alphabetical arrangement of the player's last names or the card's principal title.

Significant collectible variations of any particular card are noted within the listings by the application of a suffix letter within parentheses.

NAMES

The identification of a player by full name on the front of his baseball card has been a common practice only since the 1920s. Prior to that, the player's last name and team were the more usual information found on the card front.

As a standard practice, the listings in the Standard Catalog of Baseball Cards present the player's name exactly as it appears on the front of the card, if his full name is given there. If the player's full name only appears on the back, rather than the front, of the card, the listing corresponds to that designation.

In cases where only the player's last name is given on the card, the cataloging staff has included the first name by which he was most often known for ease of identification.

Cards which contain misspelled first or last name, or even wrong initials, will have included in their listings the incorrect information, with a correction accompanying in parentheses. This extends, also, to cases where the name on the card does not correspond to the player actually pictured.

GRADING

It is necessary that some sort of card grading standard be used so that buyer and seller (especially when dealing by mail) may reach an informed agreement on the value of a card. Each card set's listings are priced in the three grades of preservation in which those cards are most commonly encountered in the day to day buying and selling of the hobby marketplace.

Older cards are listed in grades of Near Mint (NR MT), Excellent (EX) and Very Good (VG), reflecting the basic fact that few cards were able to survive for 25, 50 or even 100 years in a close semblance to the condition of their issue. The pricing of cards in these three conditions will allow readers to accurately price cards which fall in intermediate grades, such as EX-MT, or VG-EX.

More recent issues, which have been preserved in top condition in considerable number, are listed in the grades of Mint (MT), Near Mint and Excellent, reflective of the fact that there exists in the current market little or no demand for cards of the recent past in grades below Excellent.

In general, although grades below Very Good are not priced in this catalog, close approximations of low-grade card values may figured on the following formula; Good condition cards are valued at about 50% of VG price, with Fair cards priced about 50% of Good. Cards in Poor condition have no market value except in the cases of the rarest and most expensive cards. In such cases, value has to be negotiated individually.

For the benefit of the reader, we present herewith the grading guide which was originally formulated by *Baseball Cards* magazine and *Sports Collectors Digest* in 1981, and has been continually refined since that time. These grading definitions have been used in the pricing of cards in this catalog, but they are by no means a universally accepted grading standard. The potential buyer of a baseball card should keep that in mind when encountering cards of nominally the same grade, but at a price which diffes widely from that quoted in this book.

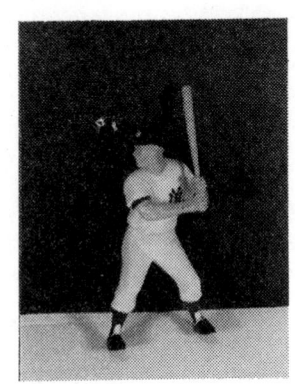

Ultimately, the collector, himself, must formulate his own personal grading standards in deciding whether cards available for purchase meet the needs of his own collection.

No collector or dealer is required to adhere to the grading standards presented herewith – or to any other published grading standards — but all are invited to do so. The editor of the *Standard Catalog of Baseball Cards* is eager to work toward the development of a standardized system of card grading that will be consistent with the realities of the hobby marketplace. Contact the editor.

Mint (MT): A perfect card. Well-centered, with parallel borders which appear equal to the naked eye. Four sharp, square corners. No creases, edge dents, surface scratches, paper flaws, loss of luster, yellowing or fading, regardless of age. No imperfectly printed card – out of register, badly cut or ink-flawed – or card stained by contact with gum, wax or other substances can be considered truly Mint, even if new out of the pack.

Near Mint (NR MT): A nearly perfect card. At first glance, a Near Mint card appears perfect; upon closer examination, however, a minor flaw will be discovered. On well-centered cards, three of the four corners must be perfectly sharp; only one corner showing a minor imperfection upon close inspection. A slightly off-center card with one or more borders being noticeably unequal – but still present – would also fit this grade.

Excellent (EX): Corners are still fairly sharp with only moderate wear. Card borders may be off center. No creases. No gum, wax or product stains, front or back. Surfaces may show slight loss of luster from rubbing across other cards.

Very Good (VG): Shows obvious handling. Corners rounded and/or pehaps showing minor creases. Other minor creases may be visible. Surfaces may exhibit loss of luster, but all printing is intact. May show gum, wax or other packaging stains. No major creases, tape marks or extraneous markings or writing. Exhibits honest wear.

Good (G): A well-worn card, but exhibits no intentional damage or abuse. May have major or multiple creases. Corners rounded well beyond the border.

Fair: Shows excessive wear, along with damage or abuse. Will show all of the wear characteristics of a Good card, along with such damage as thumb tack holes in or near margins, evidence of having been taped or pasted, perhaps small tears around the edges, or creases so heavy as to break the cardboard. Backs may show minor added pen or pencil writing, or be missing small bits of paper. Still, a basically complete card.

Poor: A card that has been tortured to death. Corners or other areas may be torn off. Card may have been trimmed, show holes from paper punch or have been used for BB gun practice. Front may have extraneous pen or pencil writing, or other defacement. Major portions of front or back design may be missing. Not a pretty sight.

In addition to these seven widely-used grading terms, collectors will often encounter intermediate grades, such as VG-EX (Very Good to Excellent), EX-MT (Excellent to Mint), or NR MT-MT (Near Mint to Mint). Persons who describe a card with such grades are usually trying to convey that the card has all the characteristics of the lower grade, with enough of the higher grade to merit mention. Such cards are usually priced at a point midway between the two grades.

VALUATIONS

Values quoted in this book represent the current retail market and are compiled from recommendations provided and verified through the authors' day to day involvement in the publication of the hobby's leading advertising periodicals, as well as the input of specialized consultants.

It should be stressed, however, that this book is intended to serve only as an aid in evaluating cards; actual market conditions are constantly changing. This is especially true of the cards of current players, whose on-field performance during the course of a season can greatly affect the value of their cards – upwards or downwards.

Publication of this catalog is not intended as a solicitation to buy or sell the listed cards by the editor, publishers or contributors.

Again, the values listed here are retail prices; what a collector can expect to pay when buying a card from a dealer. The wholesale price; that which a collector can expect to receive from a dealer when selling cards will be significantly lower. Most dealers operate on a 100% mark-up, generally paying about 50% of a card's retail value. On some high-demand cards, dealers will pay up to 75% or even 100% or more of retail value, anticipating continued price increases. Conversely, for many low-demand cards, such as common players' cards of recent years, dealers may pay 25% or even less of retail.

It should also be noted that with several hundred thousand valuations quoted in this book, there are bound to be a few compilation or typographical errors which will creep into the final product; a fact readers should remember if they encounter a listing at a fraction of, or several times, the card's actual current retail price. The editor welcomes the correction of any such errors discovered. Write: *Standard Catalog of Baseball Cards,* 700 E. State St., Iola, WI 54990.

SETS

Collectors may note that the complete set prices for newer issues quoted in these listings are usually significantly lower than the total of the value of the individual cards which comprise the set.

This reflects two factors in the baseball card market. First, a seller is often willing to take a lower composite price for a complete set as a "volume discount," and to avoid inventorying a large number of common player or other lower-demand cards.

Second, to a degree, the value of common cards can be said to be inflated as a result of having a built-in overhead charge to justify the dealer's time in sorting cards, carrying them in stock and filling orders. This accounts for the fact that even brand new baseball cards, which cost the dealer around ½¢ apiece when bought in bulk, carry individual price tags of 3¢ or higher.

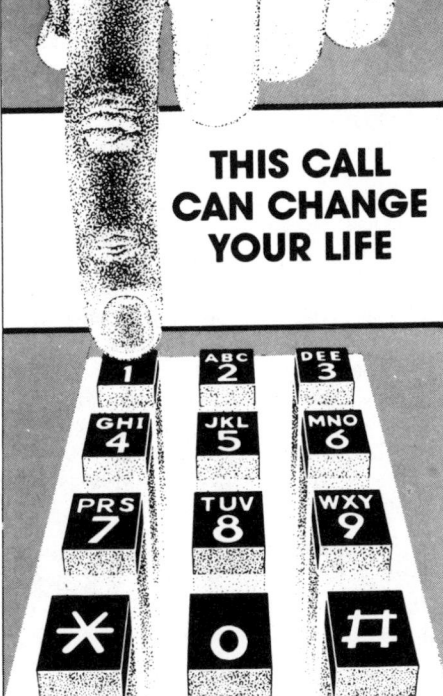

ERRORS/VARIATIONS

It is often hard for the beginning collector to understand that an error on a baseball card, in and of itself, does not usually add premium value to that card. It is usually only when the correcting of an error in a subsequent printing creates a variation that premium value attaches to an error.

Minor errors such as wrong stats or personal data, misspellings, inconsistencies, etc. – usually affecting the back of the card – are very common, especially in recent years. Unless a corrected variation was also printed, these errors are not noted in the listings of this book because they are not generally perceived by collectors to have premium value.

On the other hand, major effort has been expended to include the most complete listings ever for collectible variation cards. Many scarce and valuable variations – dozens of them never before cataloged – are included in these listings because they are widely collected and often have significant premium value.

COUNTERFEITS/REPRINTS

As the value of baseball cards has risen in the past 10-20 years, certain cards and sets have become too expensive for the average collector to obtain. This, along with changes in the technology of color printing, have given rise to increasing numbers of counterfeit and reprint cards.

While both terms describe essentially the same thing – a modern copy which attempts to duplicate as closely as possible an original baseball card – there are differences which are important to the collector.

Generally, a counterfeit is made with the intention of deceiving somebody into believing it is genuine, and thus paying large amounts of money for it. The counterfeiter takes every pain to try to make his fakes look as authentic as possible. In recent years, the 1963 Pete Rose, 1984 Donruss Don Mattingly and more than 30 superstar cards of the late 1960s-early 1980s have been counterfeited – all were quickly detected because of the differences in quality of cardboard on which they were printed.

A reprint, on the other hand, while it may have been made to look as close as possible to an original card, is made with the intention of allowing collectors to buy them as substitues for cards they may never be otherwise able to afford. The big difference is that a reprint is generally marked as such, usually on the back of the card. In other cases, like the Topps 1952 reprint set, the replicas are printed in a size markedly different from the originals.

Collectors should be aware, however, that unscrupulous persons will sometimes cut off or otherwise obliterate the distinguishing word – "Reprint," "Copy," – or modern copyright date on the back of a reprint card in an attempt to pass it as genuine.

A collector's best defense against reprints and counterfeits is to acquire a knowledge of the "look" and "feel" of genuine baseball cards of various eras and issues.

UNLISTED CARDS

Readers who have cards or sets which are not covered in this edition are invited to correspond with the editor for purposes of adding to the compilation work now in progress. Address: *Standard Catalog of Baseball Cards,* 700 E. State St., Iola, WI 54990.

Contributions will be acknowledged in future editions.

NEW ISSUES

Because new baseball cards are being issued all the time, the cataloging of them remains an on-going challenge. The editor will attempt to keep abreast of new issues so that they may be added to future editions of this book.

Readers are invited to submit news of new issues, especially limited-edition or regionally issued cards to the editor. Address: *Standard Catalog of Baseball Cards,* 700 E. State St., Iola, WI 54990

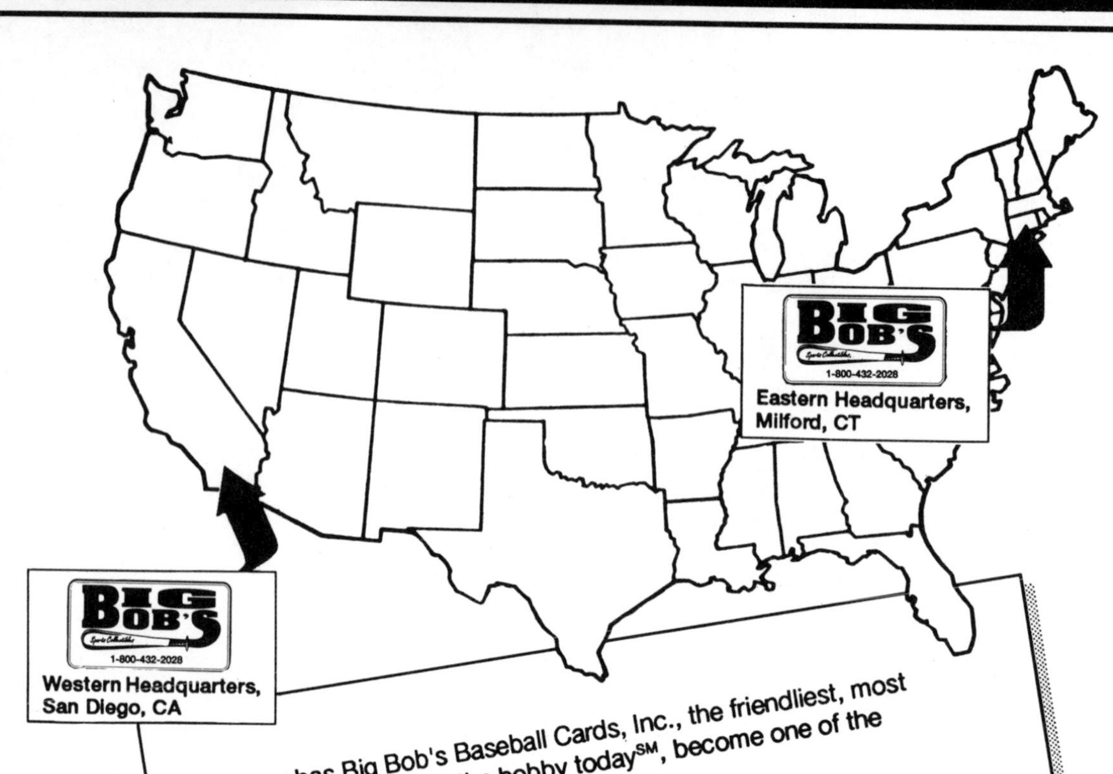

How has Big Bob's Baseball Cards, Inc., the friendliest, most courteous dealer in the hobby today℠, become one of the *biggest* dealers in the business?

It's no secret, really.... We offer sports card and memorabilia collectors from coast to coast and around the world a level of service and selection designed to turn first-time customers into regulars. That's been our philosophy from the beginning, and it's the driving force behind our tremendous growth. Call our toll-free 800 number and see for yourself how friendly our sales representatives are! (And make an order while you're at it, to see how responsive we are to your needs.)

You see, our business is a family business. We enjoy our work and we hope it shows. We feel fortunate to be employed in a hobby as fun and rewarding as sports collectibles. It's not often you find an occupation that so effectively blends business and pleasure. So we appreciate your patronage, and try our best to keep you, our customers, satisfied.

If our growth so far is a reflection of that commitment, then we must be doing a good job of it. Because Big Bob's continues to grow. In fact, we're now offering qualified individuals a chance to join us. If you've ever dreamed of turning your hobby into a full-time business, then I encourage you to call for information. You may have what it takes to own your own Big Bob's Sports Collectibles franchise. See our ad on the following page.

Sincerely,

Big Bob Amato

"Big Bob" Amato
1-800-432-2028

1970 Action Cartridge

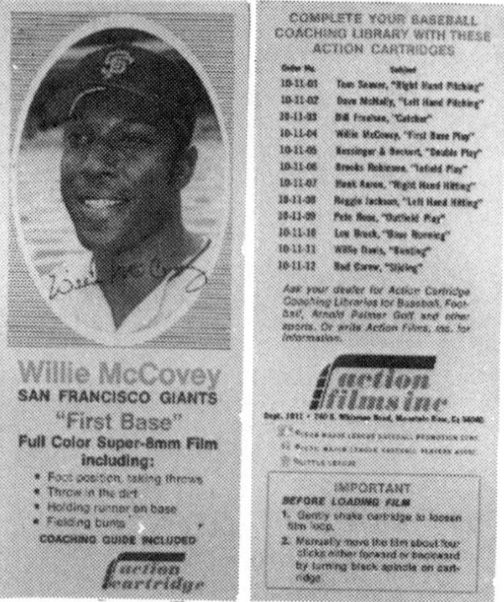

This set of boxes with baseball players' pictures on them was issued by Action Films Inc. of Mountain View, Calif., in 1970-71. The boxes, measuring 2-5/8" by 6" by 1" deep, contained 8mm film cartridges of various professional athletes demonstrating playing tips. The movie series include 12 baseball players. (Other sports represented were football, golf, tennis, hockey and skiing.) The movie cartridges are occasionally collected today, as are the boxes, which feature attractive, color player portraits. The photos appear inside an oval and include a facsimile autograph. The values listed are for complete boxes (without the movie cartridge).

		NR MT	EX	VG
Complete Set:		450.00	225.00	135.00
Common Player:		7.50	3.75	2.50
1	Tom Seaver	40.00	20.00	12.50
2	Dave McNally	7.50	3.75	2.50
3	Bill Freehan	7.50	3.75	2.50
4	Willie McCovey	25.00	12.50	7.00
5	Glenn Beckert, Don Kessinger	7.50	3.75	2.50
6	Brooks Robinson	40.00	20.00	12.50
7	Hank Aaron	75.00	37.50	25.00
8	Reggie Jackson	75.00	37.50	25.00
9	Pete Rose	125.00	67.00	35.00
10	Lou Brock	25.00	12.50	7.00
11	Willie Davis	7.50	3.75	2.50
12	Rod Carew	30.00	15.00	9.00

1983 Affiliated Food Rangers

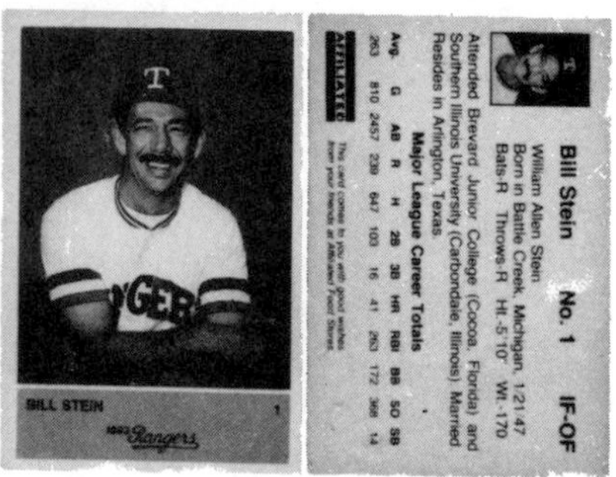

This 28-card set, featuring the Texas Rangers, was issued as a promotion by the Affiliated Food Stores chain of Arlington, Texas, late during the 1983 baseball season. Complete sets were given out free to youngsters 13 and under at the 9/3/83 Rangers game. The cards measure 2-3/8" by 3-1/2" and feature a full-color photo on the front. Also on the front, located inside a blue box, is the player's name, uniform number, and the words "1983 Rangers." The card backs contain a small player photo plus biographical and statistical information, along with the Affiliated logo and a brief promotional message. A total of 10,000 sets were reportedly printed. Cards are numbered by the players' uniform numbers in the checklist that follows.

		MT	NR MT	EX
Complete Set:		7.00	5.25	2.75
Common Player:		.10	.08	.04
1	Bill Stein	.10	.08	.04
2	Mike Richardt	.10	.08	.04
3	Wayne Tolleson	.10	.08	.04
5	Billy Sample	.10	.08	.04
6	Bobby Jones	.10	.08	.04
7	Bucky Dent	.30	.25	.12
8	Bobby Johnson	.10	.08	.04
9	Pete O'Brien	.70	.50	.30
10	Jim Sundberg	.20	.15	.08
11	Doug Rader	.10	.08	.04
12	Dave Hostetler	.10	.08	.04
14	Larry Biittner	.10	.08	.04
15	Larry Parrish	.35	.25	.14
17	Mickey Rivers	.20	.15	.08
21	Odell Jones	.10	.08	.04
24	Dave Schmidt	.15	.11	.06
25	Buddy Bell	.50	.40	.20
26	George Wright	.10	.08	.04
28	Frank Tanana	.20	.15	.08
29	John Butcher	.10	.08	.04
32	Jon Matlack	.15	.11	.06
40	Rick Honeycutt	.15	.11	.06
41	Dave Tobik	.10	.08	.04
44	Danny Darwin	.15	.11	.06
46	Jim Anderson	.10	.08	.04
48	Mike Smithson	.10	.08	.04
49	Charlie Hough	.35	.25	.14
---	Coaching Staff (Rich Donnelly, Glenn Ezell, Merv Rettenmund, Dick Such, Wayne Terwilliger)	.10	.08	.04

1910 All Star Base-Ball

Issued circa 1910, this rare 12-card set was issued by candy maker J.H. Dockman & Son. The cards, measuring approximately 1-7/8" by 3-3/8", were printed on the front and back of boxes of candy sold as "All Star Base-Ball Package." There are two players on each box - one on the front, the other on the back - but the cards consist of crude drawings that actually bear no resemblance to the player named below the drawing.

		NR MT	EX	VG
Complete Set:		1400.00	700.00	400.00
Common Player:		60.00	30.00	15.00
(1)	Heinie Beckendorf	60.00	30.00	15.00
(2)	Roger Bresnahan	100.00	50.00	30.00
(3)	Al Burch	60.00	30.00	15.00
(4)	Frank Chance	125.00	67.00	37.00
(5)	Wid Conroy	60.00	30.00	15.00
(6)	Jack Coombs	60.00	30.00	15.00
(7)	George Gibson	60.00	30.00	15.00
(8)	Dick Hoblitzel	60.00	30.00	15.00
(9)	Johnny Kling	60.00	30.00	15.00
(10)	Frank LaPorte	60.00	30.00	15.00
(11)	Connie Mack	175.00	87.00	52.00
(12)	Christy Mathewson	250.00	125.00	75.00
(13)	Matty McIntyre	60.00	30.00	15.00
(14)	Jimmy Sheckard	60.00	30.00	15.00
(15)	Al Schweitzer	60.00	30.00	15.00
(16)	Harry Wolter	60.00	30.00	15.00

Definitions for grading conditions are located in the Introduction section at the front of this book.

1987 Allstate Insurance

This 6-card set was the second promotional series of baseball cards created by Allstate Insurance graphic artist Ray Lending for internal use by the company. Modeled after the famous "Diamond Stars" from the 1930s, this set features full-color player portraits of legendary sluggers. "Life Grand Slam" (the promotion theme) is printed beneath the player portrait and the player's name appears in an upper corner. Black and white backs provide personal information, player profiles and career highlights. 15,000 sets of the cards were distributed, although only a few filtered into the collecting hobby. Cards measure 2-3/4" by 3-5/8" in size. Full-color 22" x 28" reproductions of the cards in this set were produced in poster format.

		MT	NR MT	EX
Complete Set:		15.00	11.00	5.50
Common Player:		1.50	1.25	.60
(1)	Hank Aaron	2.50	2.00	1.00
(2)	Joe DiMaggio	2.50	2.00	1.00
(3)	Jimmie Foxx	1.50	1.25	.60
(4)	Lou Gehrig	2.50	2.00	1.00
(5)	Babe Ruth	3.00	2.25	1.25
(6)	Ted Williams	2.50	2.00	1.00

1962 American Tract Society

These full-color cards, which carry religious messages on the back, were issued in 1962 by the American Tract Society, an interdenominational, non-sectarian publisher of Christain literature in the United States since 1825. Known as "Tracards", the cards measure 2-3/4" by 3-1/2" and feature attractive photographs on the fronts. The set includes religious scenes along with photos of various celebrities and sports stars, including baseball players Felipe Alou, Bobby Richardson, Jerry Kindall and Al Worthington. (There are two poses each of Alou and Kindall.) The backs carry rather lengthy, first-person religious testimonials from the players. The cards are numbered on the back in the lower right corner.

		NR MT	EX	VG
Complete Set:		20.00	10.00	6.00
Common Player:		4.00	2.00	1.25
43	Bobby Richardson	7.00	3.50	2.00
51a	Jerry Kindall (portrait to chest)	4.00	2.00	1.25
51b	Jerry Kindall (kneeling with bat)	4.00	2.00	1.25
52a	Felipe Alou (kneeling on one knee)	5.00	2.50	.50
52b	Felipe Alou (batting, full length)	5.00	2.50	.50
66	Al Worthington	4.00	2.00	1.25

1989 Ames 20/20 Club

This 33-card set was produced by Topps for the Ames toy store chain. As its name implies, the special boxed set highlights members of the 20/20 club, players who have recorded 20 home runs and 20 stolen bases in the same season. The glossy cards feature action or posed photos on the front with the player's name at the top and "Ames 20/20 Club" along the bottom. The Topps logo appears in the upper right corner.

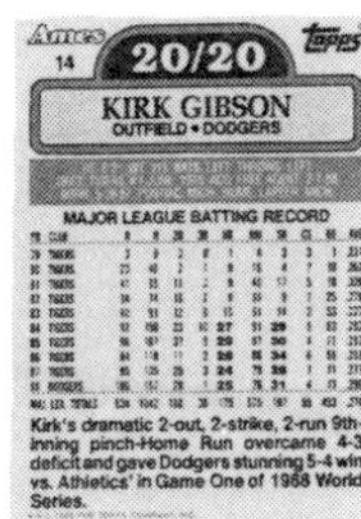

		MT	NR MT	EX
Complete Set:		5.00	3.75	2.00
Common Player:		.09	.07	.04
1	Jesse Barfield	.09	.07	.04
2	Kevin Bass	.09	.07	.04
3	Don Baylor	.09	.07	.04
4	George Bell	.12	.09	.05
5	Barry Bonds	.12	.09	.05
6	Phil Bradley	.09	.07	.04
7	Ellis Burks	.40	.30	.15
8	Jose Canseco	.70	.50	.30
9	Joe Carter	.15	.11	.06
10	Kal Daniels	.09	.07	.04
11	Eric Davis	.40	.30	.15
12	Mike Davis	.09	.07	.04
13	Andre Dawson	.12	.09	.05
14	Kirk Gibson	.09	.07	.04
15	Pedro Guerrero	.12	.09	.05
16	Rickey Henderson	.50	.40	.20
17	Bo Jackson	.80	.60	.30
18	Howard Johnson	.20	.15	.08
19	Jeffrey Leonard	.09	.07	.04
20	Kevin McReynolds	.12	.09	.05
21	Dale Murphy	.09	.07	.04
22	Dwayne Murphy	.09	.07	.04
23	Dave Parker	.12	.09	.05
24	Kirby Puckett	.50	.40	.20
25	Juan Samuel	.09	.07	.04
26	Ryne Sandberg	.20	.15	.08
27	Mike Schmidt	.80	.60	.30
28	Darryl Strawberry	.25	.20	.10
29	Alan Trammell	.09	.07	.04
30	Andy Van Slyke	.09	.07	.04
31	Devon White	.09	.07	.04
32	Dave Winfield	.12	.09	.05
33	Robin Yount	.30	.25	.12

1955 Armour Coins

In 1955, Armour inserted a plastic "coin" in their packages of hot dogs. A raised profile of a ballplayer is on the front of each coin along with the player's name, position, birthplace and date, batting and throwing preference, and 1954 hitting or pitching record. The coins, which measure 1-1/2" in diameter and are unnumbered, came in a variety of colors. Common colors are aqua, dark blue, light green, orange, red and yellow. Scarce colors are black, pale blue, lime green, very dark green, gold, pale orange, pink, silver, and tan. Scarce colors are double the value of the coins listed in the checklist that follows. Twenty-four different players are included in the set. Variations can be found for the Kuenn and Mantle coins. The Kuenn coin comes with the letters in his name bunched closely together (condensed) or spread apart (spaced). The Mantle coin can be found with his last name spelled correctly or misspelled "Mantel." The complete set price includes the two variations.

		NR MT	EX	VG
Complete Set:		900.00	450.00	270.00
Common Player:		12.00	6.00	3.50
(1)	John "Johnny" Antonelli	15.00	7.50	4.50
(2)	Larry "Yogi" Berra	50.00	25.00	15.00
(3)	Delmar "Del" Crandall	15.00	7.50	4.50
(4)	Lawrence "Larry" Doby	18.00	9.00	5.50
(5)	James "Jim" Finigan	12.00	6.00	3.50
(6)	Edward "Whitey" Ford	50.00	25.00	15.00
(7)	James "Junior" Gilliam	20.00	10.00	6.00
(8)	Harvey "Kitten" Haddix	12.00	6.00	3.50
(9)	Ranson "Randy" Jackson (name actually Ransom)	20.00	10.00	6.00
(10)	Jack "Jackie" Jensen	18.00	9.00	5.50
(11)	Theodore "Ted" Kluszewski	18.00	9.00	5.50
(12a)	Harvey E. Kuenn (spaced letters in name)	25.00	12.50	7.50
(12b)	Harvey E. Kuenn (condensed letters in name)	40.00	20.00	12.00
(13a)	Charles "Mickey" Mantel (incorrect spelling)	120.00	60.00	35.00
(13b)	Charles "Mickey" Mantle (correct spelling)	375.00	182.00	115.00
(14)	Donald "Don" Mueller	20.00	10.00	6.00
(15)	Harold "Pee Wee" Reese	30.00	15.00	9.00
(16)	Allie P. Reynolds	18.00	9.00	5.50
(17)	Albert "Flip" Rosen	18.00	9.00	5.50
(18)	Curtis "Curt" Simmons	12.00	6.00	3.50
(19)	Edwin "Duke" Snider	60.00	30.00	18.00
(20)	Warren Spahn	35.00	17.50	10.50
(21)	Frank J. Thomas	35.00	17.50	10.50
(22)	Virgil "Fire" Trucks	12.00	6.00	3.50
(23)	Robert "Bob" Turley	18.00	9.00	5.50
(24)	James "Mickey" Vernon	12.00	6.00	3.50

1959 Armour Coins

After a three-year layoff, Armour once again inserted plastic baseball "coins" into their hot dog packages. The coins retained their 1-1/2" size but did not include as much detailed information as in 1955. Missing from the coins' backs is information such as birthplace and date, team, and batting and throwing preference. The fronts contain the player's name and, unlike 1955, only the team nickname is given. The set consists of 20 coins which come in a myriad of colors. Common colors are navy blue, royal blue, dark green, orange, red, and pale yellow. Scarce colors are pale blue, cream, grey-green, pale green, dark or light pink, pale red, tan, and translucent coins of any color with or without multi-colored flecks in the plastic mix. Scarce colors are double the value listed for coins in the checklist that follows. In 1959, Armour had a write-in offer of ten coins for one dollar. The same ten players were part of the write-in offer, accounting for why half of the coins in the set are much more plentiful than the other.

		NR MT	EX	VG
Complete Set:		400.00	200.00	125.00
Common Player:		7.00	3.50	2.00
(1)	Hank Aaron	35.00	17.50	10.50
(2)	John Antonelli	15.00	7.50	4.50
(3)	Richie Ashburn	15.00	7.50	4.50
(4)	Ernie Banks	40.00	20.00	12.00
(5)	Don Blasingame	7.00	3.50	2.00
(6)	Bob Cerv	7.00	3.50	2.00
(7)	Del Crandall	15.00	7.50	4.50
(8)	Whitey Ford	35.00	17.50	10.50
(9)	Nellie Fox	12.00	6.00	3.50
(10)	Jackie Jensen	25.00	12.50	7.50
(11)	Harvey Kuenn	15.00	7.50	4.50
(12)	Frank Malzone	7.00	3.50	2.00
(13)	Johnny Podres	15.00	7.50	4.50
(14)	Frank Robinson	18.00	9.00	5.50
(15)	Roy Sievers	7.00	3.50	2.00
(16)	Bob Skinner	7.00	3.50	2.00
(17)	Frank Thomas	15.00	9.00	4.50
(18)	Gus Triandos	7.00	3.50	2.00
(19)	Bob Turley	18.00	9.00	5.50
(20)	Mickey Vernon	15.00	9.00	4.50

1960 Armour Coins

The 1960 Armour coin issue is identical in number and style to the 1959 set. The unnumbered coins, which measure 1-1/2" in diameter, once again came in a variety of colors. Common colors for 1960 are dark blue, light blue, dark green, light green, red-orange, dark red, and light yellow. Scarce colors are aqua, grey-blue, cream, tan, and dark yellow. Scarce colors are double the value of the coins in the checklist that follows. The Daley coin is very scarce, although it is not exactly known why. Theories for the scarcity center on broken printing molds, contract disputes, and that the coin was only inserted in a test product that quickly proved to be unsuccessful. As in 1959, a mail-in offer for ten free coins was made available by Armour. The set price for the 1960 Armour set does not include the three more difficult variations.

		NR MT	EX	VG
Complete Set:		1200.00	600.00	350.00
Common Player:		7.00	3.50	2.00
(1a)	Hank Aaron (Braves)	35.00	17.50	10.50
(1b)	Hank Aaron (Milwaukee Braves)	70.00	35.00	21.00
(2)	Bob Allison	12.00	6.00	3.50
(3)	Ernie Banks	12.00	6.00	3.50
(4)	Ken Boyer	10.00	5.00	3.00
(5)	Rocky Colavito	12.00	6.00	3.50
(6)	Gene Conley	10.00	5.00	3.00
(7)	Del Crandall	10.00	5.00	3.00
(8)	Bud Daley	750.00	375.00	225.00
(9a)	Don Drysdale (L.A condensed)	20.00	10.00	6.00
(9b)	Don Drysdale (space between L. and A.)	25.00	12.50	7.50
(10)	Whitey Ford	15.00	7.50	4.50
(11)	Nellie Fox	10.00	5.00	3.00
(12)	Al Kaline	25.00	12.50	7.50
(13a)	Frank Malzone (Red Sox)	7.00	3.50	2.00
(13b)	Frank Malzone (Boston Red Sox)	25.00	12.50	7.50
(14)	Mickey Mantle	80.00	40.00	25.00
(15)	Ed Mathews	25.00	12.50	7.50
(16)	Willie Mays	40.00	20.00	12.00
(17)	Vada Pinson	10.00	5.00	3.00
(18)	Dick Stuart	10.00	5.00	3.00
(19)	Gus Triandos	7.00	3.50	2.00
(20)	Early Wynn	20.00	10.00	6.00

1986 Ault Foods Blue Jays

The Ault Foods Blue Jays set is comprised of 24 full-color stickers. Designed to be placed in a special album, the stickers measure 2" by 3" in size. The attractive album measures 9" by 12" and is printed on glossy stock. While the stickers carry no information except for the player's last name and uniform number, the 20-page album contains extensive personal and statistical information about each of the 24 players.

		MT	NR MT	EX
Complete Set:		40.00	30.00	15.00
Common Player:		.60	.45	.25
Album:		5.00	3.75	2.00
1	Tony Fernandez	4.00	3.00	1.50
5	Rance Mulliniks	.60	.45	.25
7	Damaso Garcia	.60	.45	.25
11	George Bell	5.00	3.75	2.00
12	Ernie Whitt	.90	.70	.35
13	Buck Martinez	.60	.45	.25
15	Lloyd Moseby	1.25	.90	.50
16	Garth Iorg	.60	.45	.25
17	Kelly Gruber	2.00	1.50	.80
18	Jim Clancy	.90	.70	.35
22	Jimmy Key	2.00	1.50	.80
23	Cecil Fielder	2.00	1.50	.80
25	Steve Davis	.60	.45	.25
26	Willie Upshaw	.90	.70	.35
29	Jesse Barfield	1.75	1.25	.70
31	Jim Acker	.60	.45	.25
33	Doyle Alexander	.90	.70	.35
36	Bill Caudill	.60	.45	.25
37	Dave Stieb	2.50	2.00	1.00
39	Don Gordon	.60	.45	.25
44	Cliff Johnson	.60	.45	.25
46	Gary Lavelle	.60	.45	.25
50	Tom Henke	1.25	.90	.50
53	Dennis Lamp	.60	.45	.25

1914 B18 Blankets

These 5-1/4" flannels were issued in 1914 with

several popular brands of tobacco. The flannels, whose ACC designation is B18, picked up the nickname blankets because many of the square pieces of cloth were sewn together to form pillow covers or bed spreads. Different color combinations on the flannels exist for all ten teams included in the set. The complete set price in the checklist that follows does not include higher priced variations.

		NR MT	EX	VG
	Complete Set:	3500.00	1750.00	1050.
	Common Player:	15.00	7.50	4.50
(1a)	Babe Adams (purple pennants)	30.00	15.00	9.00
(1b)	Babe Adams (red pennants)	35.00	17.50	10.50
(2a)	Sam Agnew (purple basepaths)	30.00	15.00	9.00
(2b)	Sam Agnew (red basepaths)	35.00	17.50	10.50
(3a)	Eddie Ainsmith (green pennants)	15.00	7.50	4.50
(3b)	Eddie Ainsmith (brown pennants)	15.00	7.50	4.50
(4a)	Jimmy Austin (purple basepaths)	30.00	15.00	9.00
(4b)	Jimmy Austin (red basepaths)	35.00	17.50	10.50
(5a)	Del Baker (white infield)	15.00	7.50	4.50
(5b)	Del Baker (brown infield)	60.00	30.00	18.00
(5c)	Del Baker (red infield)	250.00	125.00	75.00
(6a)	Johnny Bassler (purple pennants)	30.00	15.00	9.00
(6b)	Johnny Bassler (yellow pennants)	60.00	30.00	18.00
(7a)	Paddy Bauman (Baumann) (white infield)	15.00	7.50	4.50
(7b)	Paddy Bauman (Baumann) (brown infield)	60.00	30.00	18.00
(7c)	Paddy Bauman (Baumann) (red infield)	250.00	125.00	75.00
(8a)	Luke Boone (blue infield)	15.00	7.50	4.50
(8b)	Luke Boone (green infield)	15.00	7.50	4.50
(9a)	George Burns (brown basepaths)	15.00	7.50	4.50
(9b)	George Burns (green basepaths)	15.00	7.50	4.50
(10a)	Tioga George Burns (white infield)	15.00	7.50	4.50
(10b)	Tioga George Burns (brown infield)	60.00	30.00	18.00
(11a)	Max Carey (purple pennants)	50.00	25.00	15.00
(11b)	Max Carey (red pennants)	65.00	32.00	19.50
(12a)	Marty Cavanaugh (Kavanagh) (white infield)	15.00	7.50	4.50
(12b)	Marty Cavanaugh (Kavanagh) (brown infield)	70.00	35.00	21.00
(12c)	Marty Cavanaugh (Kavanagh) (red infield)	250.00	125.00	75.00
(12d)	Marty Kavanaugh (Kavanagh)	15.00	7.50	4.50
(13a)	Frank Chance (green infield)	40.00	20.00	12.00
(13b)	Frank Chance (brown pennants, blue infield)	40.00	20.00	12.00
(13c)	Frank Chance (yellow pennants, blue infield)	250.00	125.00	75.00
(14a)	Ray Chapman (purple pennants)	30.00	15.00	9.00
(14b)	Ray Chapman (yellow pennants)	60.00	30.00	18.00
(15a)	Ty Cobb (white infield)	250.00	125.00	75.00
(15b)	Ty Cobb (brown infield)	400.00	200.00	125.00
(15c)	Ty Cobb (red infield)	2000.00	1000.00	300.00
(16a)	King Cole (blue infield)	15.00	7.50	4.50
(16b)	King Cole (green infield)	15.00	7.50	4.50
(17a)	Joe Connolly (white infield)	15.00	7.50	4.50
(17b)	Joe Connolly (brown infield)	60.00	30.00	18.00
(18a)	Harry Coveleski (white infield)	15.00	7.50	4.50
(18b)	Harry Coveleski (brown infield)	60.00	30.00	18.00
(19a)	George Cutshaw (blue infield)	15.00	7.50	4.50
(19b)	George Cutshaw (green infield)	15.00	7.50	4.50
(20a)	Jake Daubert (blue infield)	20.00	10.00	6.00
(20b)	Jake Daubert (green infield)	20.00	10.00	6.00
(21a)	Ray Demmitt (white infield)	15.00	7.50	4.50
(21b)	Ray Demmitt (brown infield)	60.00	30.00	18.00
(22a)	Bill Doak (purple pennants)	30.00	15.00	9.00
(22b)	Bill Doak (yellow pennants)	60.00	30.00	18.00
(23a)	Cozy Dolan (purple pennants)	30.00	15.00	9.00
(23b)	Cozy Dolan (yellow pennants)	60.00	30.00	18.00
(24a)	Larry Doyle (brown basepaths)	18.00	9.00	5.50
(24b)	Larry Doyle (green basepaths)	18.00	9.00	5.50
(25a)	Art Fletcher (brown basepaths)	15.00	7.50	4.50
(25b)	Art Fletcher (green basepaths)	15.00	7.50	4.50
(26a)	Eddie Foster (brown pennants)	15.00	7.50	4.50
(26b)	Eddie Foster (green pennants)	15.00	7.50	4.50
(27a)	Del Gainor (white infield)	15.00	7.50	4.50
(27b)	Del Gainor (brown infield)	60.00	30.00	18.00
(28a)	Chick Gandil (brown pennants)	20.00	10.00	6.00
(28b)	Chick Gandil (green pennants)	20.00	10.00	6.00
(29a)	George Gibson (purple pennants)	30.00	15.00	9.00
(29b)	George Gibson (red pennants)	35.00	17.50	10.50
(30a)	Hank Gowdy (white infield)	15.00	7.50	4.50
(30b)	Hank Gowdy (brown infield)	60.00	30.00	18.00
(30c)	Hank Gowdy (red infield)	250.00	125.00	75.00
(31a)	Jack Graney (purple pennants)	30.00	15.00	9.00
(31b)	Jack Graney (yellow pennants)	60.00	30.00	18.00
(32a)	Eddie Grant (brown basepaths)	15.00	7.50	4.50
(32b)	Eddie Grant (green basepaths)	15.00	7.50	4.50
(33a)	Tommy Griffith (white infield, green pennants)	15.00	7.50	4.50
(33b)	Tommy Griffith (white infield, red pennants)	250.00	125.00	75.00
(33c)	Tommy Griffith (brown infield)	60.00	30.00	18.00
(34a)	Earl Hamilton (purple basepaths)	30.00	15.00	9.00
(34b)	Earl Hamilton (red basepaths)	35.00	17.50	10.50
(35a)	Roy Hartzell (blue infield)	15.00	7.50	4.50
(35b)	Roy Hartzell (green infield)	15.00	7.50	4.50
(36a)	Miller Huggins (purple pennants)	50.00	25.00	15.00
(36b)	Miller Huggins (yellow pennants)	100.00	50.00	30.00
(37a)	John Hummel (brown infield)	15.00	7.50	4.50
(37b)	John Hummel (green infield)	15.00	7.50	4.50
(38a)	Ham Hyatt (purple pennants)	30.00	15.00	9.00
(38b)	Ham Hyatt (red pennants)	35.00	17.50	10.50
(39a)	Shoeless Joe Jackson (purple pennants)	400.00	200.00	125.00
(39b)	Shoeless Joe Jackson (yellow pennants)	450.00	225.00	135.00
(40a)	Bill James (white infield)	15.00	7.50	4.50
(40b)	Bill James (brown infield)	60.00	30.00	18.00
(41a)	Walter Johnson (brown pennants)	250.00	125.00	75.00
(41b)	Walter Johnson (green pennants)	250.00	125.00	75.00
(42a)	Ray Keating (blue infield)	15.00	7.50	4.50
(42b)	Ray Keating (green infield)	15.00	7.50	4.50
(43a)	Joe Kelley (Kelly) (purple pennants)	50.00	25.00	15.00
(43b)	Joe Kelley (Kelly) (red pennants)	65.00	32.00	19.50
(44a)	Ed Konetchy (purple pennants)	30.00	15.00	9.00
(44b)	Ed Konetchy (red pennants)	35.00	17.50	10.50
(45a)	Nemo Leibold (purple pennants)	30.00	15.00	9.00
(45b)	Nemo Leibold (yellow pennants)	60.00	30.00	18.00
(46a)	Fritz Maisel (blue infield)	15.00	7.50	4.50
(46b)	Fritz Maisel (green infield)	15.00	7.50	4.50
(47a)	Les Mann (white infield)	15.00	7.50	4.50
(47b)	Les Mann (brown infield)	50.00	25.00	15.00
(48a)	Rabbit Maranville (white infield)	45.00	22.00	13.50
(48b)	Rabbit Maranville (brown infield)	125.00	62.00	40.00
(48c)	Rabbit Maranville (red infield)	300.00	150.00	90.00
(49a)	Bill McAllister (McAllester) (purple pennants)	30.00	15.00	9.00
(49b)	Bill McAllister (McAllester) (red pennants)	35.00	17.50	10.50
(50a)	George McBride (brown pennants)	15.00	7.50	4.50
(50b)	George McBride (green pennants)	15.00	7.50	4.50
(51a)	Chief Meyers (brown basepaths)	15.00	7.50	4.50
(51b)	Chief Meyers (green basepaths)	15.00	7.50	4.50
(52a)	Clyde Milan (brown pennants)	15.00	7.50	4.50
(52b)	Clyde Milan (green pennants)	15.00	7.50	4.50
(53a)	Dots Miller (purple pennants)	30.00	15.00	9.00
(53b)	Dots Miller (yellow pennants)	60.00	30.00	18.00
(54a)	Otto Miller (blue infield)	15.00	7.50	4.50
(54b)	Otto Miller (green infield)	15.00	7.50	4.50
(55a)	Willie Mitchell (purple pennants)	30.00	15.00	9.00
(55b)	Willie Mitchell (yellow pennants)	60.00	30.00	18.00
(56a)	Danny Moeller (brown pennants)	15.00	7.50	4.50
(56b)	Danny Moeller (green pennants)	15.00	7.50	4.50
(57a)	Ray Morgan (brown pennants)	15.00	7.50	4.50
(57b)	Ray Morgan (green pennants)	15.00	7.50	4.50
(58a)	George Moriarty (white infield)	15.00	7.50	4.50
(58b)	Geroge Moriarty (brown infield)	60.00	30.00	18.00
(58c)	Geroge Moriarty (red infield)	250.00	125.00	75.00
(59a)	Mike Mowrey (purple pennants)	30.00	15.00	9.00
(59b)	Mike Mowrey (red pennants)	35.00	17.50	10.50
(60a)	Red Murray (brown basepaths)	15.00	7.50	4.50
(60b)	Red Murray (green basepaths)	15.00	7.50	4.50
(61a)	Ivy Olson (purple pennants)	30.00	15.00	9.00
(61b)	Ivy Olson (yellow pennants)	60.00	30.00	18.00
(62a)	Steve O'Neill (purple pennants)	30.00	15.00	9.00
(62b)	Steve O'Neill (red pennants)	60.00	30.00	18.00
(63a)	Marty O'Toole (purple pennants)	30.00	15.00	9.00
(63b)	Marty O'Toole (red pennants)	35.00	17.50	10.50
(64a)	Roger Peckinpaugh (blue infield)	18.00	9.00	5.50
(64b)	Roger Peckinpaugh (green infield)	18.00	9.00	5.50
(65a)	Hub Perdue (white infield)	15.00	7.50	4.50
(65b)	Hub Perdue (brown infield)	60.00	30.00	18.00
(66a)	Del Pratt (purple pennants)	30.00	15.00	9.00
(66b)	Del Pratt (yellow pennants)	35.00	17.50	10.50
(67a)	Hank Robinson (purple pennants)	30.00	15.00	9.00
(67b)	Hank Robinson (yellow pennants)	60.00	30.00	18.00
(68a)	Nap Rucker (blue infield)	15.00	7.50	4.50
(68b)	Nap Rucker (green infield)	15.00	7.50	4.50
(69a)	Slim Sallee (purple pennants)	30.00	15.00	9.00
(69b)	Slim Sallee (yellow pennants)	60.00	30.00	18.00
(70a)	Howard Shanks (brown pennants)	15.00	7.50	4.50
(70b)	Howard Shanks (green pennants)	15.00	7.50	4.50
(71a)	Burt Shotton (purple basepaths)	30.00	15.00	9.00
(71b)	Burt Shotton (red basepaths)	35.00	17.50	10.50
(72a)	Red Smith (blue infield)	15.00	7.50	4.50
(72b)	Red Smith (green infield)	15.00	7.50	4.50
(73a)	Fred Snodgrass (brown basepaths)	18.00	9.00	5.50
(73b)	Fred Snodgrass (green basepaths)	18.00	9.00	5.50
(74a)	Bill Steele (purple pennants)	30.00	15.00	9.00
74b	Bill Steele (yellow pennants)	60.00	30.00	18.00
(75a)	Casey Stengel (blue infield)	70.00	35.00	21.00
(75b)	Casey Stengel (green infield)	70.00	35.00	21.00
(76a)	Jeff Sweeney (blue infield)	15.00	7.50	4.50
(76b)	Jeff Sweeney (green infield)	15.00	7.50	4.50
(77a)	Jeff Tesreau (brown basepaths)	15.00	7.50	4.50
(77b)	Jeff Tesreau (green basepaths)	15.00	7.50	4.50
(78a)	Terry Turner (purple pennants)	30.00	15.00	9.00
(78b)	Terry Turner (yellow pennants)	60.00	30.00	18.00
(79a)	Lefty Tyler (white infield)	15.00	7.50	4.50
(79b)	Lefty Tyler (brown infield)	60.00	30.00	18.00
(79c)	Lefty Tyler (red infield)	250.00	125.00	75.00
(80a)	Jim Viox (purple pennants)	30.00	15.00	9.00
(80b)	Jim Viox (red pennants)	35.00	17.50	10.50
(81a)	Bull Wagner (blue infield)	15.00	7.50	4.50
(81b)	Bull Wagner (green infield)	15.00	7.50	4.50
(82a)	Bobby Wallace (purple basepaths)	50.00	25.00	15.00
(82b)	Bobby Wallace (red basepaths)	60.00	30.00	18.00
(83a)	Dee Walsh (purple basepaths)	30.00	15.00	9.00
(83b)	Dee Walsh (red basepaths)	35.00	17.50	10.50
(84a)	Jimmy Walsh (blue infield)	15.00	7.50	4.50
(84b)	Jimmy Walsh (green infield)	15.00	7.50	4.50
(85a)	Bert Whaling (white infield)	15.00	7.50	4.50
(85b)	Bert Whaling (brown infield)	60.00	30.00	18.00
(85c)	Bert Whaling (red infield)	250.00	125.00	75.00
(86a)	Zach Wheat (blue infield)	50.00	25.00	15.00
(86b)	Zach Wheat (green infield)	50.00	25.00	15.00
(87a)	Possum Whitted (purple pennants)	30.00	15.00	9.00
(87b)	Possum Whitted (yellow pennants)	60.00	30.00	18.00
(88a)	Gus Williams (purple basepaths)	30.00	15.00	9.00
(88b)	Gus Williams (red basepaths)	35.00	17.50	10.50
(89a)	Owen Wilson (purple pennants)	30.00	15.00	9.00
(89b)	Owen Wilson (yellow pennants)	60.00	30.00	18.00
(90a)	Hooks Wiltse (brown basepaths)	15.00	7.50	4.50
(90b)	Hooks Wiltse (green basepaths)	15.00	7.50	4.50

1916 BF2 Felt Pennants

Issued circa 1916, this unnumbered set consists of 94 felt pennants with a small black and white player photo glued to each one. The triangular pennants measure approximately 8-1/4" long, while the photos are 1-3/4" by 1-1/4" and appear to be identical to photos used for The Sporting News issues of the same period. The pennants list the player's name and team.

		NR MT	EX	VG
	Complete Set:	7500.00	3750.00	2250.
	Common Player:	40.00	20.00	12.00
(1)	Grover Alexander	125.00	62.00	37.00
(2)	Jimmy Archer	40.00	20.00	12.00

		NR MT	EX	VG
(3)	Home Run Baker	125.00	62.00	37.00
(4)	Dave Bancroft	60.00	30.00	18.00
(5)	Jack Barry	40.00	20.00	12.00
(6)	Chief Bender	125.00	62.00	37.00
(7)	Joe Benz	40.00	20.00	12.00
(8)	Mordecai Brown	100.00	50.00	30.00
(9)	George J. Burns	40.00	20.00	12.00
(10)	Donie Bush	40.00	20.00	12.00
(11)	Hick Cady	40.00	20.00	12.00
(12)	Max Carey	40.00	20.00	12.00
(13)	Ray Chapman	50.00	25.00	15.00
(14)	Ty Cobb	500.00	250.00	150.00
(15)	Eddie Collins	125.00	62.00	37.00
(16)	Shano Collins	40.00	20.00	12.00
(17)	Commy Comiskey	125.00	62.00	37.00
(18)	Harry Coveleskie (Coveleski)	40.00	20.00	12.00
(19)	Gavvy Cravath	45.00	22.00	13.50
(20)	Sam Crawford	100.00	50.00	30.00
(21)	Jake Daubert	45.00	22.00	13.50
(22)	Josh Devore	40.00	20.00	12.00
(23)	Red Dooin	40.00	20.00	12.00
(24)	Larry Doyle	40.00	20.00	12.00
(25)	Jean Dubuc	40.00	20.00	12.00
(26)	Johnny Evers	125.00	62.00	37.00
(27)	Red Faber	100.00	50.00	30.00
(28)	Eddie Foster	40.00	20.00	12.00
(29)	Del Gainer (Gainor)	40.00	20.00	12.00
(30)	Chick Gandil	50.00	25.00	15.00
(31)	Joe Gedeon	40.00	20.00	12.00
(32)	Hank Gowdy	40.00	20.00	12.00
(33)	Earl Hamilton	40.00	20.00	12.00
(34)	Claude Hendrix	40.00	20.00	12.00
(35)	Buck Herzog	40.00	20.00	12.00
(36)	Harry Hooper	60.00	30.00	18.00
(37)	Miller Huggins	60.00	30.00	18.00
(38)	Shoeless Joe Jackson	500.00	250.00	150.00
(39)	Seattle Bill James	40.00	20.00	12.00
(40)	Hugh Jennings	60.00	30.00	18.00
(41)	Walter Johnson	300.00	150.00	90.00
(42)	Fielder Jones	40.00	20.00	12.00
(43)	Joe Judge	40.00	20.00	12.00
(44)	Benny Kauff	40.00	20.00	12.00
(45)	Bill Killefer	40.00	20.00	12.00
(46)	Nap Lajoie	200.00	100.00	60.00
(47)	Jack Lapp	40.00	20.00	12.00
(48)	Doc Lavan	40.00	20.00	12.00
(49)	Jimmy Lavender	40.00	20.00	12.00
(50)	Dutch Leonard	40.00	20.00	12.00
(51)	Duffy Lewis	40.00	20.00	12.00
(52)	Hans Lobert	40.00	20.00	12.00
(53)	Fred Luderus	40.00	20.00	12.00
(54)	Connie Mack	150.00	75.00	45.00
(55)	Sherry Magee	45.00	22.00	13.50
(56)	Al Mamaux	40.00	20.00	12.00
(57)	Rabbit Maranville	100.00	50.00	30.00
(58)	Rube Marquard	100.00	50.00	30.00
(59)	George McBride	40.00	20.00	12.00
(60)	John McGraw	75.00	37.00	22.00
(61)	Stuffy McInnes (McInnis)	40.00	20.00	12.00
(62)	Fred Merkle	45.00	22.00	13.50
(63)	Chief Meyers	40.00	20.00	12.00
(64)	Clyde Milan	40.00	20.00	12.00
(65)	Otto Miller	40.00	20.00	12.00
(66)	Pat Moran	40.00	20.00	12.00
(67)	Ray Morgan	40.00	20.00	12.00
(68)	Guy Morton	40.00	20.00	12.00
(69)	Eddie Murphy	40.00	20.00	12.00
(70)	Rube Oldring	40.00	20.00	12.00
(71)	Dode Paskert	40.00	20.00	12.00
(72)	Wally Pipp	60.00	30.00	18.00
(73)	Pants Rowland	40.00	20.00	12.00
(74)	Nap Rucker	40.00	20.00	12.00
(75)	Dick Rudolph	40.00	20.00	12.00
(76)	Reb Russell	40.00	20.00	12.00
(77)	Vic Saier	40.00	20.00	12.00
(78)	Slim Sallee	40.00	20.00	12.00
(79)	Ray Schalk	100.00	50.00	30.00
(80)	Wally Schang	40.00	20.00	12.00
(81)	Wildfire Schulte	40.00	20.00	12.00
(82)	Jim Scott	40.00	20.00	12.00
(83)	George Sisler	125.00	62.00	37.00
(84)	George Stallings	40.00	20.00	12.00
(85)	Oscar Stanage	40.00	20.00	12.00
(86)	Jeff Tesreau	40.00	20.00	12.00
(87)	Joe Tinker	125.00	62.00	37.00
(88)	Lefty Tyler	40.00	20.00	12.00
(89)	Hippo Vaughn	40.00	20.00	12.00
(90)	Bobby Veach	40.00	20.00	12.00
(91)	Honus Wagner	300.00	150.00	90.00
(92)	Ed Walsh	100.00	50.00	30.00
(93)	Buck Weaver	60.00	30.00	18.00
(94)	Ivy Wingo	40.00	20.00	12.00
(95)	Joe Wood	50.00	25.00	15.00
(96)	Ralph Young	40.00	20.00	12.00
(97)	Heinie Zimmerman	40.00	20.00	12.00

1936-37 BF3 Felt Pennants - Type I

The checklist for this obscure set of felt pennants issued circa 1936-1937 is not complete, and new examples are still being reported. The pennants do not carry any manufacturer's name and their method of distribution is not certain, although it is believed they were issued as a premium with candy or gum. The pennants vary in size slightly but generally measure approximately 2-1/2" by 4-1/2" and were issued in various styles and colors, including red, yellow, white, blue, green, purple, black and brown. Most of the printing is white, although some pennants have been found with red or black printing, and the same pennant is often found in more than one color combination. The pennants feature both individual players and teams, including some minor league clubs. Advanced collectors have categorized the BF3 pennants into the following 11 design types, depending on what elements are included on the pennant: Type I: Player's name and figure. Type II: Player's name, team nickname and figure. Type III: Player's name and team nickname. Type IV: Team nickname and figure. Type V: Team nickname with emblem. Type VI: Team nickname only. Type VII: Player's name and team nickname on two-tailed pennant displayed inside the BF3 pennant. Type VIII: Player's name, year, and team nickname on ball. Type IX: Player's name, year on ball and team nickname. Type X: Team nickname and year. Type XI: Minor league and team.

	NR MT	EX	VG
Complete Set:	4000.00	2000.00	1250.
Common Player: Type I	15.00	7.50	4.50
Common Player: Type II	15.00	7.50	4.50
Common Player: Type III	15.00	7.50	4.50
Common Team: Type IV	15.00	7.50	4.50
Common Team: Type V	15.00	7.50	4.50
Common Team: Type VI	15.00	7.50	4.50
Common Player: Type VII	15.00	7.50	4.50
Common Player: Type VIII	15.00	7.50	4.50
Common Player: Type IX	15.00	7.50	4.50
Common Team: Type X	15.00	7.50	4.50
Common Team: Type XI	15.00	7.50	4.50

		NR MT	EX	VG
(1)	Luke Appling (batting)	25.00	12.50	7.50
(2)	Wally Berger (fielding)	15.00	7.50	4.50
(3)	Zeke Bonura (fielding ground ball)	15.00	7.50	4.50
(4)	Dolph Camilli (fielding)	15.00	7.50	4.50
(5)	Ben Chapman (batting)	15.00	7.50	4.50
(6)	Mickey Cochrane (catching)	25.00	12.50	7.50
(7)	Rip Collins (batting)	15.00	7.50	4.50
(8)	Joe Cronin (batting)	25.00	12.50	7.50
(9)	Kiki Cuyler (running)	25.00	12.50	7.50
(10)	Dizzy Dean (pitching)	40.00	20.00	12.50
(11)	Frank Demaree (batting)	15.00	7.50	4.50
(12)	Paul Derringer (pitching)	15.00	7.50	4.50
(13)	Bill Dickey (catching)	35.00	17.50	10.50
(14)	Jimmy Dykes (fielding)	15.00	7.50	4.50
(15)	Bob Feller (pitching)	35.00	17.50	10.50
(16)	Wes Ferrell (running)	15.00	7.50	4.50
(17)	Jimmy Foxx (batting)	35.00	17.50	10.50
(18)	Larry French (batting)	15.00	7.50	4.50
(19)	Franky Frisch (running)	25.00	12.50	7.50
(20)	Lou Gehrig (fielding at 1st base)	90.00	45.00	27.50
(21)	Charles Gehringer (running)	25.00	12.50	7.50
(22)	Lefty Gomez (pitching)	25.00	12.50	7.50
(23)	Goose Goslin (batting)	25.00	12.50	7.50
(24)	Hank Greenberg (fielding)	25.00	12.50	7.50
(25)	Charlie Grimm (running)	18.00	9.00	5.50
(26)	Lefty Grove (pitching)	25.00	12.50	7.50
(27)	Gabby Hartnett (catching)	25.00	12.50	7.50
(28)	Rollie Hemsley (catching)	15.00	7.50	4.50
(29)	Billy Herman (fielding at 1st base)	25.00	12.50	7.50
(30)	Frank Higgins (fielding)	15.00	7.50	4.50
(31)	Rogers Hornsby (batting)	25.00	12.50	7.50
(32)	Carl Hubbell (pitching)	25.00	12.50	7.50
(33)	Chuck Klein (throwing)	25.00	12.50	7.50
(34)	Tony Lazzeri (batting)	15.00	7.50	4.50
(35)	Hank Leiber (fielding ground ball)	15.00	7.50	4.50
(36)	Ernie Lombardi (catching)	25.00	12.50	7.50
(37)	Al Lopez (throwing)	25.00	12.50	7.50
(38)	Gus Mancuso (running)	15.00	7.50	4.50
(39)	Heinie Manush (batting)	25.00	12.50	7.50
(40)	Pepper Martin (batting)	18.00	9.00	5.50
(41)	Joe McCarthy (kneeling)	25.00	12.50	7.50
(42)	Wally Moses (running)	15.00	7.50	4.50
(43)	Van Mungo (standing)	15.00	7.50	4.50
(44)	Mel Ott (throwing)	35.00	17.50	10.50
(45)	Schoolboy Rowe (pitching)	18.00	9.00	5.50
(46)	Babe Ruth (batting)	150.00	75.00	45.00
(47)	George Selkirk (batting)	15.00	7.50	4.50
(48)	Luke Sewell (sliding)	15.00	7.50	4.50
(49)	Joe Stripp (batting)	15.00	7.50	4.50
(50)	Hal Trosky (fielding)	15.00	7.50	4.50
(51)	Floyd Vaughan (running, script signature)	25.00	12.50	7.50
(52)	Floyd Vaughan (running, not script signature)	25.00	12.50	7.50
(53)	Paul Waner (batting)	25.00	12.50	7.50
(54)	Lon Warneke (pitching)	15.00	7.50	4.50
(55)	Jimmy Wilson (fielding ground ball)	15.00	7.50	4.50
(56)	Joe Vosmik (running)	15.00	7.50	4.50

1936-37 BF3 Felt Pennants - Type II

		NR MT	EX	VG
(1)	Luke Appling (batting)	25.00	12.50	7.50
(2)	Zeke Bonura (batting)	15.00	7.50	4.50
(3)	Dolph Camilli (batting)	15.00	7.50	4.50
(4)	Dizzy Dean (batting)	40.00	20.00	12.50
(5)	Frank Demaree (batting)	15.00	7.50	4.50
(6)	Bob Feller (pitching)	40.00	20.00	12.50
(7)	Wes Ferrell (throwing)	15.00	7.50	4.50
(8)	Frank Frisch (fielding)	25.00	12.50	7.50
(9)	Lou Gehrig (batting)	90.00	45.00	27.50
(10)	Lou Gehrig (fielding)	90.00	45.00	27.50
(11)	Hank Greenberg (throwing)	25.00	12.50	7.50
(12)	Charlie Grimm (fielding)	12.00	6.00	3.50
(13)	Charlie Grimm (throwing)	12.00	6.00	3.50
(14)	Lefty Grove (pitching)	25.00	12.50	7.50
(15)	Gabby Hartnett (batting)	25.00	12.50	7.50
(16)	Billy Herman (batting)	25.00	12.50	7.50
(17)	Tony Lazzeri (running)	20.00	10.00	6.00
(18)	Tony Lazzeri (throwing)	20.00	10.00	6.00
(19)	Hank Leiber (batting)	15.00	7.50	4.50
(20)	Ernie Lombardi (batting)	25.00	12.50	7.50
(21)	Ducky Medwick (batting)	25.00	12.50	7.50
(22)	Joe Stripp (batting)	15.00	7.50	4.50
(23)	Floyd Vaughan (batting)	25.00	12.50	7.50
(24)	Joe Vosmik (throwing)	15.00	7.50	4.50
(25)	Paul Waner (batting)	25.00	12.50	7.50
(26)	Lon Warneke (batting)	15.00	7.50	4.50
(27)	Lon Warneke (pitching)	15.00	7.50	4.50

1936-37 BF3 Felt Pennants - Type III

		NR MT	EX	VG
(1)	Zeke Bonura	15.00	7.50	4.50
(2)	Dolph Camilli	15.00	7.50	4.50
(3)	Ben Chapman	15.00	7.50	4.50
(4)	Dizzy Dean	40.00	20.00	12.50
(5)	Bill Dickey	35.00	17.50	10.50
(6)	Joe DiMaggio (name in script)	100.00	50.00	30.00
(7)	Bob Feller (name in script)	35.00	17.50	10.50
(8)	Wes Ferrell	15.00	7.50	4.50
(9)	Lou Gehrig (name in script)	100.00	50.00	30.00
(10)	Charles Gehringer	25.00	12.50	7.50
(11)	Lefty Grove	25.00	12.50	7.50
(12)	Billy Herman (name in script)	25.00	12.50	7.50
(13)	Carl Hubbell	25.00	12.50	7.50
(14)	Chuck Klein	25.00	12.50	7.50
(15)	Tony Lazzeri	20.00	10.00	6.00
(16)	Al Lopez	25.00	12.50	7.50
(17)	Johnny Marcum	15.00	7.50	4.50
(18)	Pepper Martin	15.00	7.50	4.50
(19)	Van Lingo Mungo	15.00	7.50	4.50
(20)	Schoolboy Rowe	15.00	7.50	4.50
(21)	George Selkirk	15.00	7.50	4.50
(22)	Bill Terry	25.00	12.50	7.50
(23)	Hal Trosky	15.00	7.50	4.50
(24)	Floyd Vaughan	25.00	12.50	7.50
(25)	Lon Warneke	15.00	7.50	4.50

1936-37 BF3 Felt Pennants - Type IV

		NR MT	EX	VG
(1)	Athletics (fielder)	15.00	7.50	4.50
(2)	Browns (catcher)	15.00	7.50	4.50
(3)	Cubs (batter)	15.00	7.50	4.50
(4)	Dodgers (batter)	15.00	7.50	4.50
(5)	Dodgers (fielder)	15.00	7.50	4.50
(6)	Giants (standing by base)	15.00	7.50	4.50
(7)	Giants (two players)	15.00	7.50	4.50
(8)	Phillies (pitcher)	15.00	7.50	4.50
(9)	Reds (batter)	15.00	7.50	4.50
(10)	Reds (pitcher)	15.00	7.50	4.50
(11)	White Sox (batter)	15.00	7.50	4.50
(12)	White Sox (catcher)	15.00	7.50	4.50
(13)	White Sox (pitcher)	15.00	7.50	4.50
(14)	Yankees (batter)	25.00	12.50	7.50
(15)	Yankees (fielding ball, from waist up)	25.00	12.50	7.50

1936-37 BF3 Felt Pennants - Type V

		NR MT	EX	VG
(1)	Athletics (bat)	15.00	7.50	4.50
(2)	Athletics (elephant)	15.00	7.50	4.50
(3)	Bees (bee)	15.00	7.50	4.50
(4)	Browns (bat)	15.00	7.50	4.50
(5)	Cardinals (bat)	15.00	7.50	4.50
(6)	Cardinals (cardinal)	15.00	7.50	4.50
(7)	Cardinals (four birds flying)	15.00	7.50	4.50
(8)	Cubs (cub)	15.00	7.50	4.50
(9)	Cubs (cub's head)	15.00	7.50	4.50
(10)	Dodgers (ball, bat and glove)	15.00	7.50	4.50
(11)	Dodgers (ball)	15.00	7.50	4.50
(12)	Indians (Indian)	15.00	7.50	4.50
(13)	Indians (Indian's head)	15.00	7.50	4.50
(14)	Indians (Indian's head with hat)	15.00	7.50	4.50
(15)	Phillies (Liberty Bell)	15.00	7.50	4.50
(16)	Pirates (skull and crossbones)	15.00	7.50	4.50
(17)	Red Sox (ball and bat)	15.00	7.50	4.50
(18)	Red Sox (bat)	15.00	7.50	4.50
(19)	Reds (ball)	15.00	7.50	4.50
(20)	Senators (bat)	15.00	7.50	4.50
(21)	Senators (Capitol building)	15.00	7.50	4.50
(22)	Tigers (cap)	15.00	7.50	4.50
(23)	Tigers (tiger)	15.00	7.50	4.50

1936-37 BF3 Felt Pennants - Type VI

		NR MT	EX	VG
(1)	Cardinals	15.00	7.50	4.50

(2)	Cubs	15.00	7.50	4.50
(3)	Dodgers	15.00	7.50	4.50
(4)	Giants	15.00	7.50	4.50
(5)	Indians	15.00	7.50	4.50
(6)	Phillies (Phillies on spine)	15.00	7.50	4.50
(7)	Pirates (Pirates on spine)	15.00	7.50	4.50
(8)	Pirates (no Pirates on spine)	15.00	7.50	4.50
(9)	Yankees	25.00	12.50	7.50

1936-37BF3
Felt Pennants - Type VII

		NR MT	EX	VG
(1)	Earl Grace	15.00	7.50	4.50
(2)	Al Lopez	25.00	12.50	7.50

1936-37 BF3
Felt Pennants - Type VIII

		NR MT	EX	VG
(1)	Larry French	15.00	7.50	4.50

1936-37 BF3
Felt Pennants - Type IX

		NR MT	EX	VG
(1)	Clay Bryant	15.00	7.50	4.50
(2)	Tex Carleton	15.00	7.50	4.50
(3)	Phil Cavaretta (Cavarretta)	15.00	7.50	4.50
(4)	Irving Cherry	15.00	7.50	4.50
(5)	Ripper Collins	15.00	7.50	4.50
(6)	Curt Davis	15.00	7.50	4.50
(7)	Vince DiMaggio	18.00	9.00	5.50
(8)	Frank Demaree	15.00	7.50	4.50
(9)	Wes Flowers	15.00	7.50	4.50
(10)	Larry French	15.00	7.50	4.50
(11)	Linus Frey	15.00	7.50	4.50
(12)	Augie Galan	15.00	7.50	4.50
(13)	Charlie Grimm	18.00	9.00	5.50
(14)	Stan Hack	15.00	7.50	4.50
(15)	Gabby Hartnett	25.00	12.50	7.50
(16)	Billy Herman	25.00	12.50	7.50
(17)	Walt Higbee	15.00	7.50	4.50
(18)	Billy Jurges	15.00	7.50	4.50
(19)	Andy Lotshaw	15.00	7.50	4.50
(20)	Henry Majeski	15.00	7.50	4.50
(21)	Joe Marty	15.00	7.50	4.50
(22)	Tony Piet	15.00	7.50	4.50
(23)	Chas. Root	15.00	7.50	4.50
(24)	Tuck Stainback	15.00	7.50	4.50

Felt Pennants - Type X

		NR MT	EX	VG
(1)	Yankees (1936 Champions)	25.00	12.50	7.50

1936-37 BF3
Felt Pennants - Type XI

		NR MT	EX	VG
(1)	Barons, (Southern Association)	15.00	7.50	4.50
(2)	Bears (International League)	15.00	7.50	4.50
(3)	Blues (American Association)	15.00	7.50	4.50
(4)	Brewers (American Association)	15.00	7.50	4.50
(5)	Chicks (Southern Association)	15.00	7.50	4.50
(6)	Colonels (American Association)	15.00	7.50	4.50
(7)	Giants (International League)	15.00	7.50	4.50
(8)	Maple Leafs (International League)	15.00	7.50	4.50
(9)	Millers (American Association)	15.00	7.50	4.50
(10)	Mud Hens (American Association)	15.00	7.50	4.50
(11)	Orioles (International League)	15.00	7.50	4.50
(12)	Red Birds (American Association)	15.00	7.50	4.50
(13)	Saints (American Association)	15.00	7.50	4.50
(14)	Smokies (Southern Association)	15.00	7.50	4.50
(15)	Travelers (Southern Association)	15.00	7.50	4.50

1948 Babe Ruth Story

The Philadelphia Gum Co., in 1948, created a card set about the movie "The Babe Ruth Story", which starred William Bendix and Claire Trevor. The set, whose American Card Catalog designation is R421, contains 28 black and white, numbered cards which measure 2" by 2-1/2". The Babe Ruth Story set was originally intended to consist of sixteen cards. Twelve additional cards (#'s 17-28) were added when Ruth died before the release of the film. The card backs include a offer for an autographed photo of William Bendix, starring as the Babe, for five Swell Bubble Gum wrappers and five cents.

	NR MT	EX	VG
Complete Set:	1000.00	500.00	300.00
Common Player: 1-16	12.00	6.00	3.50
Common Player: 17-28	35.00	17.50	10.50

		NR MT	EX	VG
1	"The Babe Ruth Story" In The Making	75.00	38.00	23.00
2	Bat Boy Becomes the Babe... William Bendix	12.00	6.00	3.50
3	Claire Hodgson...Claire Trevor	12.00	6.00	3.50
4	Babe Ruth and Claire Hodgson	12.00	6.00	3.50
5	Brother Matthias...Charles Bickford	12.00	6.00	3.50
6	Phil Conrad...Sam Levene	12.00	6.00	3.50
7	Night Club Singer...Gertrude Niesen	12.00	6.00	3.50
8	Baseball's Famous Deal...Jack Dunn (William Frawley)	12.00	6.00	3.50
9	Mr. & Mrs. Babe Ruth	12.00	6.00	3.50
10	Babe Ruth, Claire Ruth, and Brother Matthias	12.00	6.00	3.50
11	Babe Ruth and Miller Huggins (Fred Lightner)	12.00	6.00	3.50
12	Babe Ruth At Bed Of Ill Boy Johnny Sylvester (Gregory Marshall)	12.00	6.00	3.50
13	Sylvester Family Listening To Game	12.00	6.00	3.50
14	"When A Feller Needs a Friend" (With Dog At Police Station)	12.00	6.00	3.50
15	Dramatic Home Run	12.00	6.00	3.50
16	The Homer That Set the Record (#60)	12.00	6.00	3.50
17	"The Slap That Started Baseball's Famous Career"	35.00	17.50	10.50
18	The Babe Plays Santa Claus	35.00	17.50	10.50
19	Meeting Of Owner And Manager	35.00	17.50	10.50
20	"Broken Window Paid Off"	35.00	17.50	10.50
21	Babe In A Crowd Of Autograph Collectors	35.00	17.50	10.50
22	Charley Grimm And William Bendix	35.00	17.50	10.50
23	Ted Lyons And William Bendix	50.00	25.00	15.00
24	Lefty Gomez, William Bendix, And Bucky Harris	50.00	25.00	15.00
25	Babe Ruth and William Bendix	100.00	50.00	30.00
26	Babe Ruth And William Bendix	100.00	50.00	30.00
27	Babe Ruth And Claire Trevor	100.00	50.00	30.00
28	William Bendix, Babe Ruth, And Claire Trevor	100.00	50.00	30.00

1986 Baltimore Orioles Team Issue

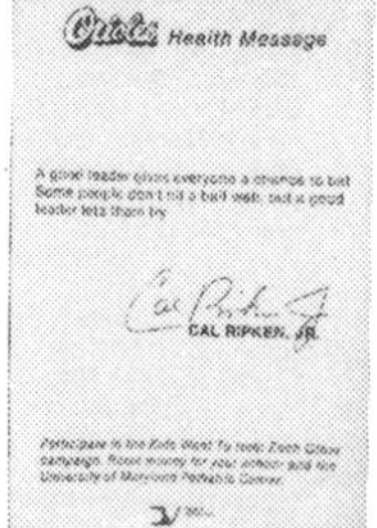

	MT	NR MT	EX
Complete Set:	10.00	7.50	4.00
Common Player:	.15	.11	.06

		MT	NR MT	EX
(1)	Don Aase	.15	.11	.06
(2a)	Mike Boddicker (message begins "I always...")	.40	.30	.15
(2b)	Mike Boddicker (message begins "They call...")	.40	.30	.15
(3)	Storm Davis	.20	.15	.08
(4a)	Rick Dempsey (message begins "I always...")	.15	.11	.06
(4b)	Rick Dempsey (message begins "In baseball...")	.15	.11	.06
(5)	Ken Dixon	.15	.11	.06
(6)	Jim Dwyer	.15	.11	.06
(7a)	Mike Flanagan (message begins "I know...")	.20	.15	.08
(7b)	Mike Flanagan (message begins "It's a...")	.20	.15	.08
(8)	Lee Lacy	.15	.11	.06
(9a)	Fred Lynn (message begins "I need...")	.35	.25	.14
(9b)	Fred Lynn (message begins "There are...")	.35	.25	.14
(10a)	Dennis Martinez	.30	.25	.12
(11)	Tippy Martinez	.15	.11	.06
(12)	Scott McGregor	.20	.15	.08
(13a)	Eddie Murray (message begins "Do you...")	.90	.70	.35
(13b)	Eddie Murray (message begins "During my...")	.90	.70	.35
(13c)	Eddie Murray (message begins "You can't...")	.90	.70	.35
(14a)	Floyd Rayford (message begins "I always...")	.15	.11	.06
(14b)	Floyd Rayford (message begins "I had...")	.15	.11	.06
(15)	Cal Ripken, Jr. (message begins "A good...")	1.25	.90	.50
(15b)	Cal Ripken, Jr. (message begins "Drinking ...")	1.25	.90	.50
(15c)	Cal Ripken, Jr. (message begins "To hit...")	1.25	.90	.50
(16a)	Larry Sheets (message begins "As a...")	.25	.20	.10
(16b)	Larry Sheets (message begins "There is...")	.25	.20	.10
(17)	John Shelby	.15	.11	.06
(18)	Earl Weaver	.35	.25	.14
(19)	Alan Wiggins	.15	.11	.06
(20)	Mike Young	.20	.15	.08

1911 Baseball Bats

Issued circa 1911, cards in this rare 47-card issue were printed on the back panel of "Baseball Bats" penny candy. The cards themselves measure approximately 1-3/8" by 2-3/8" and feature a black and white player photo surrounded by an orange or white border. The player's name and team are printed in small, black capital letters near the bottom of the photo.

	NR MT	EX	VG
Complete Set:	7500.	3750.	2250.
Common Player:	100.00	50.00	30.00

		NR MT	EX	VG
(1)	Red Ames	100.00	50.00	30.00
(2)	Home Run Baker	175.00	87.00	52.00
(3)	Jack Barry	100.00	50.00	30.00
4	Ginger Beaumont	175.00	87.00	52.00
(5)	Chief Bender	175.00	87.00	52.00
(6)	Al Bridwell	100.00	50.00	30.00
(7)	Mordecai Brown	175.00	87.00	52.00
(8)	Bill Corrigan (Carrigan)	100.00	50.00	30.00
(9)	Frank Chance	150.00	75.00	45.00
(10)	Hal Chase	125.00	62.00	37.00
(11)	Ed Cicotte	125.00	62.00	37.00
(12)	Fred Clark (Clarke)	175.00	87.00	52.00
(13)	Ty Cobb	700.00	350.00	200.00
(14)	King Cole	100.00	50.00	30.00
(15)	Eddie Collins	200.00	100.00	60.00
(16)	Sam Crawford	175.00	87.00	52.00
(17)	Lou Criger	100.00	50.00	30.00
(18)	Harry Davis	100.00	50.00	30.00
(19)	Jim Delehanty	100.00	50.00	30.00
(20)	Art Devlin	100.00	50.00	30.00
(21)	Josh Devore	100.00	50.00	30.00
(22)	Wild Bill Donovan	100.00	50.00	30.00
(23)	Larry Doyle	110.00	55.00	33.00
(24)	Johnny Evers	175.00	87.00	52.00
(25)	John Flynn	100.00	50.00	30.00
26	George Gibson	175.00	87.00	52.00
(27)	Solly Hoffman (Hofman)	100.00	50.00	30.00
(28)	Walter Johnson	300.00	150.00	90.00
(29)	Johnny Kling	100.00	50.00	30.00
(30)	Nap Lajoie	250.00	125.00	75.00
(31)	Matty McIntyre	100.00	50.00	30.00
(32)	Fred Merkle	110.00	55.00	33.00
(33)	Tom Needham	100.00	50.00	30.00
(34)	Rube Oldring	100.00	50.00	30.00
(35)	Wildfire Schulte	100.00	50.00	30.00
(36)	Cy Seymour	100.00	50.00	30.00
(37)	Jimmy Sheckard	100.00	50.00	30.00
(38)	Tris Speaker	225.00	112.00	67.00
(39)	Oscar Stanage (batting - front view)	100.00	50.00	30.00
(40)	Oscar Stanage (batting - side view)	100.00	50.00	30.00
(41)	Ira Thomas	100.00	50.00	30.00
(42)	Joe Tinker	175.00	87.00	52.00
(43)	Heinie Wagner	100.00	50.00	30.00
(44)	Honus Wagner	350.00	175.00	100.00
(45)	Ed Walsh	175.00	87.00	52.00
(46)	Art Wilson	100.00	50.00	30.00
(47)	Owen Wilson	100.00	50.00	30.00

Definitions for grading conditions are located in the Introduction section at the front of this book.

NOTE: A card number in parentheses ( ) indicates the set is unnumbered.

1988 Baseball Immortals

One of the most popular of the "collectors' issues", this set is produced with the permission of Major League Baseball by Renata Galasso Inc. and TCMA. The set features players in the Baseball Hall of Fame and was first issued in 1980. Each year since 1980 the set has been updated to include new inductees. The cards measure 2-1/2" by 3-1/2" and have colorful borders. The card fronts include the player's name, position and year of induction. The backs feature a short biography and a trivia question. The photos used are color; most players who were active before 1950 have colored black and white photos. The designation "first printing" appears on all cards issued 1981 and after.

		MT	NR MT	EX
	Complete Set:	12.00	9.00	4.75
	Common Player:	.03	.02	.01
1	Babe Ruth	.20	.15	.08
2	Ty Cobb	.15	.11	.06
3	Walter Johnson	.07	.05	.03
4	Christy Mathewson	.07	.05	.03
5	Honus Wagner	.07	.05	.03
6	Morgan Bulkeley	.03	.02	.01
7	Ban Johnson	.03	.02	.01
8	Larry Lajoie	.05	.04	.02
9	Connie Mack	.05	.04	.02
10	John McGraw	.05	.04	.02
11	Tris Speaker	.05	.04	.02
12	George Wright	.03	.02	.01
13	Cy Young	.08	.06	.04
14	Grover Alexander	.05	.04	.02
15	Alexander Cartwright	.03	.02	.01
16	Henry Chadwick	.03	.02	.01
17	Cap Anson	.05	.04	.02
18	Eddie Collins	.05	.04	.02
19	Charles Comiskey	.03	.02	.01
20	Candy Cummings	.03	.02	.01
21	Buck Ewing	.03	.02	.01
22	Lou Gehrig	.15	.11	.06
23	Willie Keeler	.03	.02	.01
24	Hoss Radbourne	.03	.02	.01
25	George Sisler	.05	.04	.02
26	Albert Spalding	.03	.02	.01
27	Rogers Hornsby	.07	.05	.03
28	Judge Landis	.03	.02	.01
29	Roger Bresnahan	.03	.02	.01
30	Dan Brouthers	.03	.02	.01
31	Fred Clarke	.03	.02	.01
32	James Collins	.03	.02	.01
33	Ed Delahanty	.03	.02	.01
34	Hugh Duffy	.03	.02	.01
35	Hughie Jennings	.03	.02	.01
36	Mike "King" Kelly	.03	.02	.01
37	James O'Rourke	.03	.02	.01
38	Wilbert Robinson	.03	.02	.01
39	Jesse Burkett	.03	.02	.01
40	Frank Chance	.03	.02	.01
41	Jack Chesbro	.03	.02	.01
42	John Evers	.03	.02	.01
43	Clark Griffith	.03	.02	.01
44	Thomas McCarthy	.03	.02	.01
45	Joe McGinnity	.03	.02	.01
46	Eddie Plank	.03	.02	.01
47	Joe Tinker	.03	.02	.01
48	Rube Waddell	.03	.02	.01
49	Ed Walsh	.03	.02	.01
50	Mickey Cochrane	.05	.04	.02
51	Frankie Frisch	.03	.02	.01
52	Lefty Grove	.05	.04	.02
53	Carl Hubbell	.05	.04	.02
54	Herb Pennock	.03	.02	.01
55	Pie Traynor	.03	.02	.01
56	Three Finger Brown	.03	.02	.01
57	Charlie Gehringer	.05	.04	.02
58	Kid Nichols	.03	.02	.01
59	Jimmie Foxx	.07	.05	.03
60	Mel Ott	.05	.04	.02
61	Harry Heilmann	.03	.02	.01
62	Paul Waner	.03	.02	.01
63	Ed Barrow	.03	.02	.01
64	Chief Bender	.03	.02	.01
65	Tom Connolly	.03	.02	.01
66	Dizzy Dean	.07	.05	.03
67	Bill Klem	.03	.02	.01
68	Al Simmons	.03	.02	.01
69	Bobby Wallace	.03	.02	.01
70	Harry Wright	.03	.02	.01
71	Bill Dickey	.05	.04	.02
72	Rabbit Maranville	.03	.02	.01
73	Bill Terry	.05	.04	.02
74	Home Run Baker	.03	.02	.01
75	Joe DiMaggio	.10	.08	.04
76	Gabby Hartnett	.03	.02	.01
77	Ted Lyons	.03	.02	.01
78	Ray Schalk	.03	.02	.01
79	Dazzy Vance	.03	.02	.01
80	Joe Cronin	.05	.04	.02
81	Hank Greenberg	.05	.04	.02
82	Sam Crawford	.03	.02	.01
83	Joe McCarthy	.03	.02	.01
84	Zack Wheat	.03	.02	.01
85	Max Carey	.03	.02	.01
86	Billy Hamilton	.03	.02	.01
87	Bob Feller	.07	.05	.03
88	Bill McKechnie	.03	.02	.01
89	Jackie Robinson	.10	.08	.04
90	Edd Roush	.03	.02	.01
91	John Clarkson	.03	.02	.01
92	Elmer Flick	.03	.02	.01
93	Sam Rice	.03	.02	.01
94	Eppa Rixey	.03	.02	.01
95	Luke Appling	.03	.02	.01
96	Red Faber	.03	.02	.01
97	Burleigh Grimes	.03	.02	.01
98	Miller Huggins	.03	.02	.01
99	Tim Keefe	.03	.02	.01
100	Heinie Manush	.03	.02	.01
101	John Ward	.03	.02	.01
102	Pud Galvin	.03	.02	.01
103	Casey Stengel	.07	.05	.03
104	Ted Williams	.10	.08	.04
105	Branch Rickey	.03	.02	.01
106	Red Ruffing	.03	.02	.01
107	Lloyd Waner	.03	.02	.01
108	Kiki Cuyler	.03	.02	.01
109	Goose Goslin	.03	.02	.01
110	Joe (Ducky) Medwick	.03	.02	.01
111	Roy Campanella	.07	.05	.03
112	Stan Coveleski	.03	.02	.01
113	Waite Hoyt	.03	.02	.01
114	Stan Musial	.10	.08	.04
115	Lou Boudreau	.03	.02	.01
116	Earle Combs	.03	.02	.01
117	Ford Frick	.03	.02	.01
118	Jesse Haines	.03	.02	.01
119	Dave Bancroft	.03	.02	.01
120	Jake Beckley	.03	.02	.01
121	Chick Hafey	.03	.02	.01
122	Harry Hooper	.03	.02	.01
123	Joe Kelley	.03	.02	.01
124	Rube Marquard	.03	.02	.01
125	Satchel Paige	.05	.04	.02
126	George Weiss	.03	.02	.01
127	Yogi Berra	.07	.05	.03
128	Josh Gibson	.03	.02	.01
129	Lefty Gomez	.05	.04	.02
130	Will Harridge	.03	.02	.01
131	Sandy Koufax	.07	.05	.03
132	Buck Leonard	.03	.02	.01
133	Early Wynn	.03	.02	.01
134	Ross Youngs	.03	.02	.01
135	Roberto Clemente	.10	.08	.04
136	Billy Evans	.03	.02	.01
137	Monte Irvin	.03	.02	.01
138	George Kelly	.03	.02	.01
139	Warren Spahn	.07	.05	.03
140	Mickey Welch	.03	.02	.01
141	Cool Papa Bell	.03	.02	.01
142	Jim Bottomley	.03	.02	.01
143	Jocko Conlan	.03	.02	.01
144	Whitey Ford	.03	.02	.01
145	Mickey Mantle	.15	.11	.08
146	Sam Thompson	.03	.02	.01
147	Earl Averill	.03	.02	.01
148	Bucky Harris	.03	.02	.01
149	Billy Herman	.03	.02	.01
150	Judy Johnson	.03	.02	.01
151	Ralph Kiner	.05	.04	.02
152	Oscar Charleston	.03	.02	.01
153	Roger Connor	.03	.02	.01
154	Cal Hubbard	.03	.02	.01
155	Bob Lemon	.03	.02	.01
156	Fred Lindstrom	.03	.02	.01
157	Robin Roberts	.03	.02	.01
158	Ernie Banks	.05	.04	.02
159	Martin Dihigo	.03	.02	.01
160	John Henry Lloyd	.03	.02	.01
161	Al Lopez	.03	.02	.01
162	Amos Rusie	.03	.02	.01
163	Joe Sewell	.03	.02	.01
164	Addie Joss	.03	.02	.01
165	Larry MacPhail	.03	.02	.01
166	Eddie Mathews	.03	.02	.01
167	Warren Giles	.03	.02	.01
168	Willie Mays	.15	.11	.06
169	Hack Wilson	.03	.02	.01
170	Duke Snider	.07	.05	.03
171	Al Kaline	.05	.04	.02
172	Chuck Klein	.03	.02	.01
173	Tom Yawkey	.03	.02	.01
174	Bob Gibson	.05	.04	.02
175	Rube Foster	.03	.02	.01
176	Johnny Mize	.03	.02	.01
177	Hank Aaron	.15	.11	.06
178	Frank Robinson	.05	.04	.02
179	Happy Chandler	.03	.02	.01
180	Travis Jackson	.03	.02	.01
181	Brooks Robinson	.05	.04	.02
182	Juan Marichal	.03	.02	.01
183	George Kell	.03	.02	.01
184	Walter Alston	.03	.02	.01
185	Harmon Killebrew	.05	.04	.02
186	Luis Aparicio	.03	.02	.01
187	Don Drysdale	.05	.04	.02
188	Pee Wee Reese	.05	.04	.02
189	Rick Ferrell	.03	.02	.01
190	Willie McCovey	.05	.04	.02
191	Ernie Lombardi	.03	.02	.01
192	Bobby Doerr	.03	.02	.01
193	Arky Vaughan	.03	.02	.01
194	Enos Slaughter	.03	.02	.01
195	Lou Brock	.05	.04	.02
196	Hoyt Wilhelm	.03	.02	.01
197	Billy Williams	.03	.02	.01
198	"Catfish" Hunter	.03	.02	.01
199	Ray Dandridge	.03	.02	.01

1987 Baseball Super Stars Discs

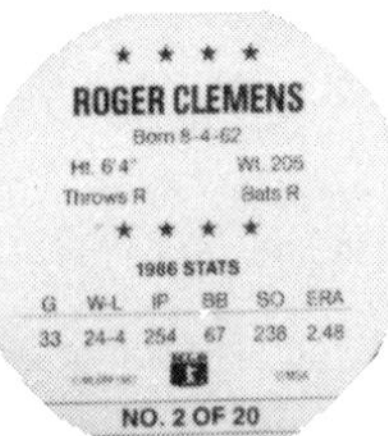

Produced by Mike Schecter and Associates, the "Baseball Super Stars" disc set was released as part of a promotion for various brands of iced tea mixes in many parts of the country. Among the brands participating in the promotion were Acme, Alpha Beta, Bustelo, Key, King Kullen, Lady Lee, Our Own and Weis. The discs were issued in three-part folding panels with each disc measuring 2-1/2" in diameter. The disc fronts feature a full-color photo inside a bright yellow border. Two player discs were included in each panel along with a coupon disc offering either an uncut press sheet of the set or a facsimile autographed ball.

		MT	NR MT	EX
	Complete Panel Set:	9.00	6.75	3.50
	Complete Singles Set:	4.00	3.00	1.50
	Common Panel:	.25	.20	.10
	Common Single Player:	.05	.04	.02
Panel		.90	.70	.35
1	Darryl Strawberry	.20	.15	.08
2	Roger Clemens	.30	.25	.12
Panel		.35	.25	.14
3	Ron Darling	.05	.04	.02
4	Keith Hernandez	.10	.08	.04
Panel		1.25	.90	.50
5	Tony Pena	.05	.04	.02
6	Don Mattingly	.70	.50	.30
Panel		.90	.70	.35
7	Eric Davis	.35	.25	.14
8	Gary Carter	.08	.06	.03
Panel		.80	.60	.30
9	Dave Winfield	.12	.09	.05
10	Wally Joyner	.20	.15	.08
Panel		.50	.40	.20
11	Mike Schmidt	.25	.20	.10
12	Robby Thompson	.05	.04	.02
Panel		.90	.70	.35
13	Wade Boggs	.35	.25	.14
14	Cal Ripken Jr.	.15	.11	.06
Panel		.90	.70	.35
15	Dale Murphy	.15	.11	.06
16	Tony Gwynn	.15	.11	.06
Panel		1.75	1.25	.70
17	Jose Canseco	.70	.50	.30
18	Rickey Henderson	.30	.25	.12
Panel		.25	.20	.10
19	Lance Parrish	.08	.06	.03
20	Dave Righetti	.08	.06	.03

1988 Baseball Super Stars Discs

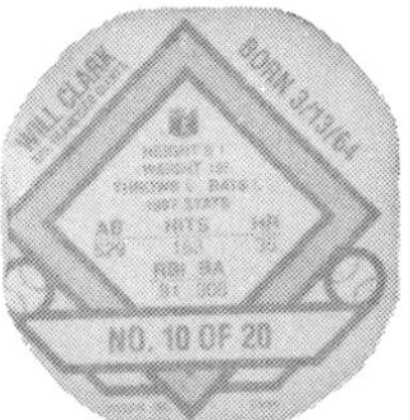

The "Second Annual Collector's Edition" of Baseball Super Stars Discs is very similar to the 1987 issue. A set of 20 discs (2-1/2" diameter) featuring full-color baseball player photos was inserted in specially marked cannisters of iced tea and fruit drinks. Each triple-fold insert consists of 2 player discs and one redemption card. Player discs are bright blue, yellow, red and green with a diamond design framing the player closeup. The player name appears upper left, the set logo appears upper right. Personalized disc series were issued for Tetley, Weis, Key Food and A&P supermarkets (untitled series were also sold at Lucky, Skaggs, Alpha Beta, Acme King Kullen, Laneco and Krasdale stores). The series name (i.e. Weis Winners) is printed below the player photo.

		MT	NR MT	EX
	Complete Panel Set:	8.00	6.00	3.25
	Complete Singles Set:	3.00	2.25	1.25
	Common Panel:	.60	.45	.25
	Common Single Player:	.05	.04	.02
Panel		1.00	.70	.40
1	Wade Boggs	.35	.25	.14
2	Ellis Burks	.20	.15	.08
Panel		1.25	.90	.50
3	Don Mattingly	.70	.50	.30
4	Mark McGwire	.25	.20	.10

Panel		.70	.50	.30
5	Matt Nokes	.10	.08	.04
6	Kirby Puckett	.30	.25	.12
Panel		.80	.60	.30
7	Billy Ripken	.05	.04	.02
8	Kevin Seitzer	.15	.11	.06
Panel		.90	.70	.35
9	Roger Clemens	.30	.25	.12
10	Will Clark	.50	.40	.20
Panel		.80	.60	.30
11	Vince Coleman	.10	.08	.04
12	Eric Davis	.30	.25	.12
Panel		.70	.50	.30
13	Dave Magadan	.05	.04	.02
14	Dale Murphy	.15	.11	.06
Panel		.80	.60	.30
15	Benito Santiago	.15	.11	.06
16	Mike Schmidt	.30	.25	.12
Panel		.60	.45	.25
17	Darryl Strawberry	.20	.15	.08
18	Steve Bedrosian	.05	.04	.02
Panel		.80	.60	.30
19	Dwight Gooden	.20	.15	.08
20	Fernando Valenzuela	.08	.06	.03

1934 Batter-Up

National Chicle's 192-card "Batter-Up" set was issued from 1934 through 1936. The blank-backed cards are die-cut, enabling collectors of the era to fold the top of the card over so that it could stand upright on its own support. The cards can be found in black and white or a variety of color tints. Card numbers 1-80 measure 2-3/8" by 3-1/4" in size, while the high-numbered cards (#'s 81-192) measure 1/4" smaller in width. The high-numbered cards are significantly more difficult to find than the lower numbers. The set's ACC designation is R318.

		NR MT	EX	VG
Complete Set:		35000.00	15000.00	7000.
Common Player: 1-80		75.00	35.00	15.00
Common Player: 81-192		150.00	70.00	25.00
1	Wally Berger	150.00	50.00	15.00
2	Ed Brandt	75.00	35.00	15.00
3	Al Lopez	150.00	70.00	25.00
4	Dick Bartell	75.00	35.00	15.00
5	Carl Hubbell	200.00	100.00	35.00
6	Bill Terry	200.00	100.00	35.00
7	Pepper Martin	75.00	35.00	15.00
8	Jim Bottomley	150.00	70.00	25.00
9	Tommy Bridges	75.00	35.00	15.00
10	Rick Ferrell	125.00	50.00	15.00
11	Ray Benge	75.00	35.00	15.00
12	Wes Ferrell	75.00	35.00	15.00
13	Bill Cissell	75.00	35.00	15.00
14	Pie Traynor	175.00	80.00	30.00
15	Roy Mahaffey	75.00	35.00	15.00
16	Chick Hafey	150.00	75.00	25.00
17	Lloyd Waner	150.00	75.00	25.00
18	Jack Burns	75.00	35.00	15.00
19	Buddy Myer	75.00	35.00	15.00
20	Bob Johnson	75.00	35.00	15.00
21	Arky Vaughn (Vaughan)	125.00	55.00	28.00
22	Red Rolfe	75.00	35.00	15.00
23	Lefty Gomez	250.00	125.00	40.00
24	Earl Averill	125.00	55.00	20.00
25	Mickey Cochrane	150.00	75.00	30.00
26	Van Mungo	75.00	35.00	15.00
27	Mel Ott	275.00	125.00	50.00
28	Jimmie Foxx	300.00	150.00	50.00
29	Jimmy Dykes	75.00	35.00	15.00
30	Bill Dickey	275.00	125.00	55.00
31	Lefty Grove	250.00	125.00	35.00
32	Joe Cronin	150.00	75.00	28.00
33	Frankie Frisch	200.00	100.00	35.00
34	Al Simmons	150.00	70.00	25.00
35	Rogers Hornsby	400.00	200.00	75.00
36	Ted Lyons	175.00	80.00	25.00
37	Rabbit Maranville	175.00	80.00	25.00
38	Jimmie Wilson	75.00	35.00	15.00
39	Willie Kamm	75.00	35.00	15.00
40	Bill Hallahan	75.00	35.00	15.00
41	Gus Suhr	75.00	35.00	15.00
42	Charlie Gehringer	250.00	125.00	40.00
43	Joe Heving	75.00	35.00	15.00
44	Adam Comorosky	75.00	35.00	15.00
45	Tony Lazzeri	150.00	70.00	25.00
46	Sam Leslie	75.00	35.00	15.00
47	Bob Smith	75.00	35.00	15.00
48	Willis Hudlin	75.00	35.00	15.00
49	Carl Reynolds	75.00	35.00	15.00
50	Fred Schulte	75.00	35.00	15.00
51	Cookie Lavagetto	75.00	35.00	15.00
52	Hal Schumacher	75.00	35.00	15.00
53	Doc Cramer	75.00	35.00	15.00
54	Si Johnson	75.00	35.00	15.00
55	Ollie Bejma	75.00	35.00	15.00
56	Sammy Byrd	75.00	35.00	15.00
57	Hank Greenberg	250.00	125.00	40.00
58	Bill Knickerbocker	75.00	35.00	15.00
59	Billy Urbanski	75.00	35.00	15.00
60	Ed Morgan	75.00	35.00	15.00
61	Eric McNair	75.00	35.00	15.00
62	Ben Chapman	75.00	35.00	15.00
63	Roy Johnson	75.00	35.00	15.00
64	"Dizzy" Dean	650.00	300.00	100.00
65	Zeke Bonura	75.00	35.00	15.00
66	Firpo Marberry	75.00	35.00	15.00
67	Gus Mancuso	75.00	35.00	15.00
68	Joe Vosmik	75.00	35.00	15.00
69	Earl Grace	75.00	35.00	15.00
70	Tony Piet	75.00	35.00	15.00
71	Rollie Hemsley	75.00	35.00	15.00
72	Fred Fitzsimmons	75.00	35.00	15.00
73	Hack Wilson	300.00	150.00	50.00
74	Chick Fullis	75.00	35.00	15.00
75	Fred Frankhouse	75.00	35.00	15.00
76	Ethan Allen	75.00	35.00	15.00
77	Heinie Manush	125.00	50.00	18.00
78	Rip Collins	75.00	35.00	15.00
79	Tony Cuccinello	75.00	35.00	15.00
80	Joe Kuhel	75.00	35.00	15.00
81	Thomas Bridges	150.00	70.00	25.00
82	Clinton Brown	150.00	70.00	25.00
83	Albert Blanche	150.00	70.00	25.00
84	"Boze" Berger	150.00	70.00	25.00
85	Goose Goslin	400.00	200.00	65.00
86	Vernon Gomez	550.00	275.00	110.00
87	Joe Glen (Glenn)	150.00	70.00	25.00
88	"Cy" Blanton	150.00	70.00	25.00
89	Tom Carey	150.00	70.00	25.00
90	Ralph Birkhofer	150.00	70.00	25.00
91	Frank Gabler	150.00	70.00	25.00
92	Dick Coffman	150.00	70.00	25.00
93	Ollie Bejma	150.00	70.00	25.00
94	Leroy Earl Parmalee	150.00	70.00	25.00
95	Carl Reynolds	150.00	70.00	25.00
96	Ben Cantwell	150.00	70.00	25.00
97	Curtis Davis	150.00	70.00	25.00
98	Wallace Moses, Billy Webb	150.00	70.00	25.00
99	Ray Benge	150.00	70.00	25.00
100	"Pie" Traynor	400.00	200.00	75.00
101	Phil. Cavarretta	150.00	70.00	25.00
102	"Pep" Young	150.00	70.00	25.00
103	Willis Hudlin	150.00	70.00	25.00
104	Mickey Haslin	150.00	70.00	25.00
105	Oswald Bluege	150.00	70.00	25.00
106	Paul Andrews	150.00	70.00	25.00
107	Edward A. Brandt	150.00	70.00	25.00
108	Dan Taylor	150.00	70.00	25.00
109	Thornton T. Lee	150.00	70.00	25.00
110	Hal Schumacher	150.00	70.00	25.00
111	Minter Hayes, Ted Lyons	500.00	250.00	125.00
112	Odell Hale	150.00	70.00	25.00
113	Earl Averill	300.00	150.00	50.00
114	Italo Chelini	150.00	70.00	25.00
115	Ivy Andrews, Jim Bottomley	500.00	250.00	125.00
116	Bill Walker	150.00	70.00	25.00
117	Bill Dickey	550.00	275.00	115.00
118	Gerald Walker	150.00	70.00	25.00
119	Ted Lyons	300.00	150.00	50.00
120	Elden Auker (Eldon)	150.00	70.00	25.00
121	Wild Bill Hallahan	150.00	70.00	25.00
122	Freddy Lindstrom	350.00	175.00	65.00
123	Oral C. Hildebrand	150.00	70.00	25.00
124	Luke Appling	350.00	175.00	65.00
125	"Pepper" Martin	175.00	80.00	30.00
126	Rick Ferrell	350.00	175.00	65.00
127	Ival Goodman	150.00	70.00	25.00
128	Joe Kuhel	150.00	70.00	25.00
129	Ernest Lombardi	350.00	175.00	65.00
130	Charles Gehringer	500.00	250.00	100.00
131	Van L. Mungo	175.00	80.00	30.00
132	Larry French	150.00	70.00	25.00
133	"Buddy" Myer	150.00	70.00	25.00
134	Mel Harder	150.00	70.00	25.00
135	Augie Galan	150.00	70.00	25.00
136	"Gabby" Hartnett	350.00	175.00	65.00
137	Stan Hack	150.00	70.00	25.00
138	Billy Herman	350.00	175.00	65.00
139	Bill Jurges	150.00	70.00	25.00
140	Bill Lee	150.00	70.00	25.00
141	"Zeke" Bonura	150.00	70.00	25.00
142	Tony Piet	150.00	70.00	25.00
143	Paul Dean	250.00	125.00	50.00
144	Jimmy Foxx	700.00	300.00	115.00
145	Joe Medwick	350.00	175.00	65.00
146	Rip Collins	150.00	70.00	25.00
147	Melo Almada	150.00	70.00	25.00
148	Allan Cooke	150.00	70.00	25.00
149	Moe Berg	150.00	70.00	25.00
150	Adolph Camilli	150.00	70.00	25.00
151	Oscar Melillo	150.00	70.00	25.00
152	Bruce Campbell	150.00	70.00	25.00
153	Lefty Grove	600.00	275.00	115.00
154	John Murphy	150.00	70.00	25.00
155	Luke Sewell	150.00	70.00	25.00
156	Leo Durocher	350.00	175.00	65.00
157	Lloyd Waner	350.00	175.00	65.00
158	Guy Bush	150.00	70.00	25.00
159	Jimmy Dykes	150.00	70.00	25.00
160	Steve O'Neill	150.00	70.00	25.00
161	Gen. Crowder	150.00	70.00	25.00
162	Joe Cascarella	150.00	70.00	25.00
163	"Bud" Hafey	150.00	70.00	25.00
164	"Gilly" Campbell	150.00	70.00	25.00
165	Ray Hayworth	150.00	70.00	25.00
166	Frank Demaree	150.00	70.00	25.00
167	John Babich	150.00	70.00	25.00
168	Marvin Owen	150.00	70.00	25.00
169	Ralph Kress	150.00	70.00	25.00
170	"Mule" Haas	150.00	70.00	25.00
171	Frank Higgins	150.00	70.00	25.00
172	Walter Berger	150.00	70.00	25.00
173	Frank Frisch	400.00	200.00	75.00
174	Wess Ferrell (Wes)	150.00	70.00	25.00
175	Pete Fox	150.00	70.00	25.00
176	John Vergez	150.00	70.00	25.00
177	William Rogell	150.00	70.00	25.00
178	"Don" Brennan	150.00	70.00	25.00
179	James Bottomley	250.00	125.00	50.00
180	Travis Jackson	350.00	175.00	65.00
181	Robert Rolfe	175.00	80.00	30.00
182	Frank Crosetti	275.00	135.00	50.00
183	Joe Cronin	350.00	175.00	65.00
184	"Schoolboy" Rowe	175.00	80.00	30.00
185	"Chuck" Klein	350.00	175.00	65.00
186	Lon Warneke	150.00	70.00	25.00
187	Gus Suhr	150.00	70.00	25.00
188	Ben Chapman	200.00	90.00	30.00
189	Clint. Brown	180.00	85.00	35.00
190	Paul Derringer	250.00	125.00	40.00
191	John Burns	300.00	150.00	45.00
192	John Broaca	500.00	200.00	100.00

1959 Bazooka

The 1959 Bazooka set, consisting of 23 full-color, unnumbered cards, was issued on boxes of Bazooka one-cent bubble gum. The individually wrapped pieces of Bazooka gum were produced by Topps Chewing Gum. The blank-backed cards measure 2-13/16" by 4-15/16". Nine cards were first issued, with 14 being added to the set later. The nine more plentiful cards are #'s 1, 5, 8, 9, 14, 15, 16, 17 and 22. Complete boxes would command 75 percent over the prices in the checklist that follows.

		NR MT	EX	VG
Complete Set:		8000.	4000.	2500.
Common Player:		125.00	62.00	37.00
(1a)	Hank Aaron (name in white)	600.00	300.00	180.00
(1b)	Hank Aaron (name in yellow)	600.00	300.00	180.00
(2)	Richie Ashburn	400.00	200.00	120.00
(3)	Ernie Banks	600.00	300.00	180.00
(4)	Ken Boyer	300.00	150.00	90.00
(5)	Orlando Cepeda	200.00	100.00	60.00
(6)	Bob Cerv	200.00	100.00	60.00
(7)	Rocco Colavito	450.00	225.00	135.00
(8)	Del Crandall	125.00	62.00	37.00
(9)	Jim Davenport	125.00	62.00	37.00
(10)	Don Drysdale	650.00	325.00	210.00
(11)	Nellie Fox	350.00	175.00	105.00
(12)	Jackie Jensen	250.00	125.00	75.00
(13)	Harvey Kuenn	250.00	125.00	75.00
(14)	Mickey Mantle	1800.	900.00	550.00
(15)	Willie Mays	450.00	225.00	135.00
(16)	Bill Mazeroski	150.00	75.00	45.00
(17)	Roy McMillan	125.00	62.00	37.00
(18)	Billy Pierce	200.00	100.00	60.00
(19)	Roy Sievers	200.00	100.00	60.00
(20)	Duke Snider	800.00	400.00	250.00
(21)	Gus Triandos	200.00	100.00	60.00
(22)	Bob Turley	125.00	62.00	37.00
(23)	Vic Wertz	200.00	100.00	60.00

1960 Bazooka

Three-card panels were found on the bottoms of Bazooka bubble gum boxes in 1960. The blank-backed set is comprised of 36 cards with the card number located at the bottom of each full-color card. The individual cards measure 1-13/16" by

2-3/4"; the panels measure 2-3/4" by 5-1/2" in size. Prices, in the checklist that follows, are given for complete panels and individual cards.

		NR MT	EX	VG
Complete Panel Set:		1500.	750.00	450.00
Complete Singles Set:		1000.	500.00	300.00
Common Panel:		75.00	37.00	22.00
Common Single Player:		5.00	2.50	1.50
Panel		90.00	45.00	27.00
1	Ernie Banks	50.00	25.00	15.00
2	Bud Daley	5.00	2.50	1.50
3	Wally Moon	5.00	2.50	1.50
Panel		125.00	62.00	37.00
4	Hank Aaron	80.00	40.00	25.00
5	Milt Pappas	10.00	5.00	3.00
6	Dick Stuart	10.00	5.00	3.00
Panel		200.00	100.00	60.00
7	Bob Clemente	90.00	45.00	27.00
8	Yogi Berra	50.00	25.00	15.00
9	Ken Boyer	12.00	6.00	3.50
Panel		75.00	38.00	23.00
10	Orlando Cepeda	15.00	7.50	4.50
11	Gus Triandos	10.00	5.00	3.00
12	Frank Malzone	10.00	5.00	3.00
Panel		80.00	40.00	25.00
13	Willie Mays	60.00	30.00	18.00
14	Camilo Pascual	5.00	2.50	1.50
15	Bob Cerv	5.00	2.50	1.50
Panel		90.00	45.00	27.00
16	Vic Power	5.00	2.50	1.50
17	Larry Sherry	5.00	2.50	1.50
18	Al Kaline	50.00	25.00	15.00
Panel		100.00	50.00	30.00
19	Warren Spahn	40.00	20.00	12.50
20	Harmon Killebrew	30.00	15.00	9.00
21	Jackie Jensen	12.00	6.00	3.50
Panel		115.00	57.00	34.00
22	Luis Aparicio	25.00	12.50	7.50
23	Gil Hodges	30.00	15.00	9.00
24	Richie Ashburn	30.00	15.00	9.00
Panel		100.00	50.00	30.00
25	Nellie Fox	30.00	15.00	9.00
26	Robin Roberts	30.00	15.00	9.00
27	Joe Cunningham	5.00	2.50	1.50
Panel		100.00	50.00	30.00
28	Early Wynn	25.00	12.50	7.50
29	Frank Robinson	50.00	25.00	15.00
30	Rocky Colavito	15.00	7.50	4.50
Panel		450.00	225.00	135.00
31	Mickey Mantle	250.00	125.00	75.00
32	Glen Hobbie	5.00	2.50	1.50
33	Roy McMillan	5.00	2.50	1.50
Panel		75.00	37.00	22.00
34	Harvey Kuenn	12.00	6.00	3.50
35	Johnny Antonelli	5.00	2.50	1.50
36	Del Crandall	10.00	5.00	3.00

1961 Bazooka

TED KLUSZEWSKI
LOS ANGELES ANGELS 1st base
NO. 18 OF 36 CARDS

Similar in design to the 1960 Bazooka set, the 1961 edition consists of 36 cards issued in panels of three on the bottom of Bazooka bubble gum boxes. The full-color cards, which measure 1-13/16" by 2-3/4" individually and 2-3/4" by 5-1/2" as panels, are numbered 1 through 36. The backs are blank.

		NR MT	EX	VG
Complete Panel Set:		1200.	600.00	350.00
Complete Singles Set:		700.00	350.00	200.00
Common Panel:		60.00	30.00	18.00
Common Single Player:		5.00	2.50	1.50
Panel		400.00	200.00	120.00
1	Art Mahaffey	10.00	5.00	3.00
2	Mickey Mantle	250.00	125.00	75.00
3	Ron Santo	12.00	6.00	3.50
Panel		80.00	40.00	24.00
4	Bud Daley	5.00	2.50	1.50
5	Roger Maris	70.00	35.00	21.00
6	Eddie Yost	5.00	2.50	1.50
Panel		65.00	32.00	19.50
7	Minnie Minoso	12.00	6.00	3.50
8	Dick Groat	12.00	6.00	3.50
9	Frank Malzone	10.00	5.00	3.00
Panel		70.00	35.00	21.00
10	Dick Donovan	5.00	2.50	1.50
11	Ed Mathews	30.00	15.00	9.00
12	Jim Lemon	5.00	2.50	1.50
Panel		60.00	30.00	18.00
13	Chuck Estrada	5.00	2.50	1.50
14	Ken Boyer	12.00	6.00	3.50
15	Harvey Kuenn	12.00	6.00	3.50
Panel		60.00	30.00	18.00
16	Ernie Broglio	5.00	2.50	1.50
17	Rocky Colavito	15.00	7.50	4.50
18	Ted Kluszewski	15.00	7.50	4.50
Panel		250.00	125.00	75.00
19	Ernie Banks	75.00	38.00	23.00
20	Al Kaline	75.00	38.00	23.00
21	Ed Bailey	5.00	2.50	1.50
Panel		75.00	37.00	22.00
22	Jim Perry	5.00	2.50	1.50
23	Willie Mays	70.00	35.00	21.00
24	Bill Mazeroski	12.00	6.00	3.50
Panel		70.00	35.00	21.00
25	Gus Triandos	5.00	2.50	1.50
26	Don Drysdale	25.00	12.50	7.50
27	Frank Herrera	10.00	5.00	3.00
Panel		70.00	35.00	21.00
28	Earl Battey	5.00	2.50	1.50
29	Warren Spahn	35.00	17.50	10.50
30	Gene Woodling	10.00	5.00	3.00
Panel		60.00	30.00	18.00
31	Frank Robinson	35.00	17.50	10.50
32	Pete Runnels	10.00	5.00	3.00
33	Woodie Held	5.00	2.50	1.50
Panel		65.00	32.00	19.50
34	Norm Larker	5.00	2.50	1.50
35	Luis Aparicio	20.00	10.00	6.00
36	Bill Tuttle	5.00	2.50	1.50

1962 Bazooka

In 1962, Bazooka increased the size of its set to 45 full-color cards. The set is unnumbered and was issued in panels of three on the bottoms of bubble gum boxes. The individual cards measure 1-13/16" by 2-3/4" in size, whereas the panels are 2-3/4" by 5-1/2". In the checklist that follows the cards have been numbered by panel using the name of the player who appears on the left side of the panel. Panel #'s 1-3, 31-33 and 43-45 were issued in much shorter supply and command a higher price.

		NR MT	EX	VG
Complete Panel Set:		3000.	1500.	900.00
Complete Singles Set:		1500.	750.00	450.00
Common Panel:		30.00	15.00	9.00
Common Single Player:		8.00	4.00	2.50
Panel		1000.	500.00	300.00
(1)	Bob Allison	150.00	75.00	45.00
(2)	Ed Mathews	350.00	175.00	105.00
(3)	Vada Pinson	150.00	75.00	45.00
Panel		50.00	25.00	15.00
(4)	Earl Battey	8.00	4.00	2.50
(5)	Warren Spahn	30.00	15.00	9.00
(6)	Lee Thomas	8.00	4.00	2.50
Panel		40.00	20.00	12.00
(7)	Orlando Cepeda	15.00	7.50	4.50
(8)	Woodie Held	8.00	4.00	2.50
(9)	Bob Aspromonte	8.00	4.00	2.50
Panel		100.00	50.00	30.00
(10)	Dick Howser	10.00	5.00	3.00
(11)	Bob Clemente	50.00	25.00	15.00
(12)	Al Kaline	30.00	15.00	9.00
Panel		80.00	40.00	24.00
(13)	Joey Jay	8.00	4.00	2.50
(14)	Roger Maris	40.00	20.00	12.00
(15)	Frank Howard	15.00	7.50	4.50
Panel		70.00	35.00	21.00
(16)	Sandy Koufax	50.00	25.00	15.00
(17)	Jim Gentile	8.00	4.00	2.50
(18)	Johnny Callison	10.00	5.00	3.00
Panel		30.00	15.00	9.00
(19)	Jim Landis	8.00	4.00	2.50
(20)	Ken Boyer	12.00	6.00	3.50
(21)	Chuck Schilling	8.00	4.00	2.50
Panel		450.00	225.00	135.00
(22)	Art Mahaffey	10.00	5.00	3.00
(23)	Mickey Mantle	200.00	100.00	60.00
(24)	Dick Stuart	10.00	5.00	3.00
Panel		80.00	40.00	24.00
(25)	Ken McBride	8.00	4.00	2.50
(26)	Frank Robinson	35.00	17.50	10.50
(27)	Gil Hodges	25.00	12.50	7.50
Panel		100.00	50.00	30.00
(28)	Milt Pappas	10.00	5.00	3.00
(29)	Hank Aaron	70.00	35.00	21.00
(30)	Luis Aparicio	20.00	10.00	6.00
Panel		1000.	500.00	300.00
(31)	Johnny Romano	150.00	75.00	45.00
(32)	Ernie Banks	450.00	225.00	135.00
(33)	Norm Siebern	150.00	75.00	45.00
Panel		40.00	20.00	12.00
(34)	Ron Santo	12.00	6.00	3.50
(35)	Norm Cash	10.00	5.00	3.00
(36)	Jim Piersall	10.00	5.00	3.00
Panel		70.00	35.00	21.00
(37)	Don Schwall	8.00	4.00	2.50
(38)	Willie Mays	50.00	25.00	15.00
(39)	Norm Larker	8.00	4.00	2.50
Panel		70.00	35.00	21.00
(40)	Bill White	10.00	5.00	3.00
(41)	Whitey Ford	30.00	15.00	9.00
(42)	Rocky Colavito	15.00	7.50	4.50
Panel		1000.	500.00	300.00
(43)	Don Zimmer	200.00	100.00	60.00
(44)	Harmon Killebrew	300.00	150.00	90.00
(45)	Gene Woodling	150.00	75.00	45.00

1963 Bazooka

FRANK ROBINSON
CINN. REDS OF
NO. 31 OF 36 CARDS

The 1963 Bazooka issue reverted back to a 12-panel, 36-card set, but saw a change in the size of the cards. Individual cards measure 1-9/16" by 2-1/2", while panels are 2-1/2" by 4-11/16" in size. The card design was altered also, with the player's name, team and position situated in a white oval space at the bottom of the card. The full-color, blank-backed set is numbered 1-36. Five Bazooka All-Time Greats cards were inserted in each box of bubble gum.

		NR MT	EX	VG
Complete Panel Set:		1200.	600.00	350.00
Complete Singles Set:		650.00	325.00	200.00
Common Panel:		30.00	15.00	9.00
Common Single Player:		5.00	2.50	1.50
Panel		400.00	200.00	120.00
1	Mickey Mantle (batting righty)	250.00	125.00	75.00
2	Bob Rodgers	5.00	2.50	1.50
3	Ernie Banks	40.00	20.00	12.50
Panel		50.00	25.00	15.00
4	Norm Siebern	5.00	2.50	1.50
5	Warren Spahn (portrait)	30.00	15.00	9.00
6	Bill Mazeroski	10.00	5.00	3.00
Panel		115.00	57.00	34.00
7	Harmon Killebrew (batting)	30.00	15.00	9.00
8	Dick Farrell (portrait)	5.00	2.50	1.50
9	Hank Aaron (glove in front)	60.00	30.00	17.50
Panel		150.00	75.00	45.00
10	Dick Donovan	5.00	2.50	1.50
11	Jim Gentile (batting)	5.00	2.50	1.50
12	Willie Mays (bat in front)	75.00	38.00	23.00
Panel		70.00	35.00	21.00
13	Camilo Pascual (hands at waist)	5.00	2.50	1.50
14	Bob Clemente (portrait)	50.00	25.00	15.00
15	Johnny Callison (wearing pinstripe uniform)	8.00	4.00	2.50
Panel		175.00	87.00	52.00
16	Carl Yastrzemski (kneeling)	90.00	45.00	27.00
17	Don Drysdale	70.00	35.00	20.00
18	Johnny Romano (portrait)	5.00	2.50	1.50
Panel		30.00	15.00	9.00
19	Al Jackson	8.00	4.00	2.50
20	Ralph Terry	8.00	4.00	2.50
21	Bill Monbouquette	5.00	2.50	1.50
Panel		95.00	47.00	28.00
22	Orlando Cepeda	15.00	7.50	4.50
23	Stan Musial	50.00	25.00	15.00
24	Floyd Robinson (no pinstripes on uniform)	5.00	2.50	1.50
Panel		30.00	15.00	9.00
25	Chuck Hinton (batting)	5.00	2.50	1.50
26	Bob Purkey	5.00	2.50	1.50
27	Ken Hubbs	12.00	6.00	3.50
Panel		60.00	30.00	18.00
28	Bill White	8.00	4.00	2.50
29	Ray Herbert	5.00	2.50	1.50
30	Brooks Robinson (glove in front)	35.00	17.50	10.50
Panel		60.00	30.00	18.00
31	Frank Robinson (batting, uniform number doesn't show)	50.00	25.00	15.00
32	Lee Thomas	5.00	2.50	1.50
33	Rocky Colavito (Detroit)	10.00	5.00	3.00
Panel		60.00	30.00	18.00
34	Al Kaline (kneeling)	35.00	17.50	10.50
35	Art Mahaffey	5.00	2.50	1.50
36	Tommy Davis (batting follow-thru)			

1963 Bazooka All-Time Greats

Consisting of 41 cards, the Bazooka All-Time

18 CONNIE MACK
Mgr. Phila. Ath.
BORN: DECEMBER 22, 1862
HOME: E. BROOKFIELD, MASS.
One of baseball's greatest managers, Connie Mack held the reins of the Athletics for 50 seasons, from 1901 through 1950. Through that span, Connie brought many pennant flags to the city of brotherly love. During his playing days, he was a catcher for several ballclubs. Although he never compiled a high batting average, Connie's knowledge of the sport helped him become a great strategist. The name of Connie Mack will always be held in high esteem in baseball circles.
©T.C.G. PRINTED IN U.S.A.

Greats set was issued as inserts (5 per box) in boxes of Bazooka bubble gum. A black and white head-shot of the player is placed inside a gold plaque within a white border. The card backs have black print on white and white and yellow and contain a brief biography of the player. The numbered cards measure 1-9/16" by 2-1/2" in size. The cards can be found with silver fronts instead of gold. The silver are worth double the values listed in the following checklist.

		NR MT	EX	VG
Complete Set:		200.00	100.00	60.00
Common Player:		2.50	1.25	.70
1	Joe Tinker	3.50	1.75	1.00
2	Harry Heilmann	2.50	1.25	.70
3	Jack Chesbro	3.00	1.50	.90
4	Christy Mathewson	5.00	2.50	1.50
5	Herb Pennock	3.00	1.50	.90
6	Cy Young	6.00	3.00	1.75
7	Big Ed Walsh	2.50	1.25	.70
8	Nap Lajoie	3.50	1.75	1.00
9	Eddie Plank	2.50	1.25	.70
10	Honus Wagner	8.00	4.00	2.50
11	Chief Bender	3.00	1.50	.90
12	Walter Johnson	8.00	4.00	2.50
13	Three-Fingered Brown	2.50	1.25	.70
14	Rabbit Maranville	3.00	1.50	.90
15	Lou Gehrig	25.00	12.50	7.50
16	Ban Johnson	2.50	1.25	.70
17	Babe Ruth	40.00	20.00	12.00
18	Connie Mack	5.00	2.50	1.50
19	Hank Greenberg	3.50	1.75	1.00
20	John McGraw	3.50	1.75	1.00
21	Johnny Evers	2.50	1.25	.70
22	Al Simmons	2.50	1.25	.70
23	Jimmy Collins	2.50	1.25	.70
24	Tris Speaker	3.50	1.75	1.00
25	Frank Chance	2.50	1.25	.70
26	Fred Clarke	2.50	1.25	.70
27	Wilbert Robinson	2.50	1.25	.70
28	Dazzy Vance	2.50	1.25	.70
29	Pete Alexander	3.50	1.75	1.00
30	Judge Landis	2.50	1.25	.70
31	Wee Willie Keeler	2.50	1.25	.70
32	Rogers Hornsby	5.00	2.50	1.50
33	Hugh Duffy	2.50	1.25	.70
34	Mickey Cochrane	3.50	1.75	1.00
35	Ty Cobb	25.00	12.50	7.50
36	Mel Ott	3.50	1.75	1.00
37	Clark Griffith	2.50	1.25	.70
38	Ted Lyons	2.50	1.25	.70
39	Cap Anson	3.50	1.75	1.00
40	Bill Dickey	3.50	1.75	1.00
41	Eddie Collins	3.50	1.75	1.00

1964 Bazooka

The 1964 Bazooka set is identical in design and size to the previous year's effort. However, different photographs were used from year to year by Topps, issuer of Bazooka bubble gum. The 1964 set consists of 36 full-color, blank-backed cards numbered 1 through 36. Individual cards measure 1-9/16" by 2-1/2"; three-card panels measure 2-1/2" by 4-11/16". Sheets of ten full-color baseball stamps were inserted in each box of bubble gum.

		NR MT	EX	VG
Complete Panel Set:		1200.00	600.00	350.00
Complete Singles Set:		600.00	300.00	180.00
Common Panel:		25.00	12.50	7.50
Common Single Player:		5.00	2.50	1.50
Panel		220.00	110.00	66.00
1	Mickey Mantle (portrait)	175.00	87.00	52.00
2	Dick Groat	8.00	4.00	2.50
3	Steve Barber	5.00	2.50	1.50
Panel		40.00	20.00	12.00
4	Ken McBride	5.00	2.50	1.50
5	Warren Spahn (head to waist shot)	30.00	15.00	9.00
6	Bob Friend	6.00	3.00	1.75
Panel		115.00	57.00	34.00
7	Harmon Killebrew (portrait)	30.00	15.00	9.00
8	Dick Farrell (hands above head)	5.00	2.50	1.50
9	Hank Aaron (glove to left)	70.00	35.00	20.00
Panel		70.00	35.00	21.00
10	Rich Rollins	5.00	2.50	1.50
11	Jim Gentile (portrait)	5.00	2.50	1.50
12	Willie Mays (looking to left)	50.00	25.00	15.00
Panel		70.00	35.00	21.00
13	Camilo Pascual (pitching follow-thru)	5.00	2.50	1.50
14	Bob Clemente (throwing)	50.00	25.00	15.00
15	Johnny Callison (batting, screen showing)	8.00	4.00	2.50
Panel		75.00	37.00	22.00
16	Carl Yastrzemski (batting)	50.00	25.00	15.00
17	Billy Williams (kneeling)	25.00	12.50	7.50
18	Johnny Romano (batting)	5.00	2.50	1.50
Panel		55.00	27.00	16.50
19	Jim Maloney	5.00	2.50	1.50
20	Norm Cash	8.00	4.00	2.50
21	Willie McCovey	30.00	15.00	9.00
Panel		25.00	12.50	7.50
22	Jim Fregosi (batting)	6.00	3.00	1.75
23	George Altman	5.00	2.50	1.50
24	Floyd Robinson (wearing pinstripe uniform)	5.00	2.50	1.50
Panel		25.00	12.50	7.50
25	Chuck Hinton (portrait)	5.00	2.50	1.50
26	Ron Hunt (batting)	8.00	4.00	2.50
27	Gary Peters (pitching)	5.00	2.50	1.50
Panel		60.00	30.00	18.00
28	Dick Ellsworth	5.00	2.50	1.50
29	Elston Howard (holding bat)	12.00	6.00	3.50
30	Brooks Robinson (kneeling with glove)	30.00	15.00	9.00
Panel		110.00	55.00	33.00
31	Frank Robinson (uniforn number shows)	40.00	20.00	12.00
32	Sandy Koufax (glove in front)	50.00	25.00	15.00
33	Rocky Colavito (Kansas City)	10.00	5.00	3.00
Panel		65.00	32.00	19.50
34	Al Kaline (holding two bats)	30.00	15.00	9.00
35	Ken Boyer (head to waist shot)	10.00	5.00	3.00
36	Tommy Davis (batting)	8.00	4.00	2.50

1964 Bazooka Stamps

Occasionally mislabeled "Topps Stamps," the 1964 Bazooka Stamps set was produced by Topps, but was found only in boxes of 1¢ Bazooka bubble gum. Issued in sheets of ten, 100 color stamps make up the set. Each stamp measures 1" by 1-1/2" in size. While the stamps are not individually numbered, the sheets are numbered one through ten. The stamps are commonly found as complete sheets of ten and are priced in that fashion in the checklist that follows.

		NR MT	EX	VG
Complete Sheet Set:		400.00	200.00	125.00
Common Sheet:		15.00	7.50	4.50
1	Max Alvis, Ed Charles, Dick Ellsworth, Jimmie Hall, Frank Malzone, Milt Pappas, Vada Pinson, Tony Taylor, Pete Ward, Bill White	15.00	7.50	4.50
2	Bob Aspromonte, Larry Jackson, Willie Mays, Al McBean, Bill Monbouquette, Bobby Richardson, Floyd Robinson, Frank Robinson, Norm Siebern, Don Zimmer	40.00	20.00	12.00
3	Ernie Banks, Bob Clemente, Curt Flood, Jesse Gonder, Woody Held, Don Lock, Dave Nicholson, Joe Pepitone, Brooks Robinson, Carl Yastrzemski	60.00	30.00	18.00
4	Hank Aguirre, Jim Grant, Harmon Killebrew, Jim Maloney, Juan Marichal, Bill Mazeroski, Juan Pizarro, Boog Powell, Ed Roebuck, Ron Santo	30.00	15.00	9.00
5	Jim Bouton, Norm Cash, Orlando Cepeda, Tommy Harper, Chuck Hinton, Albie Pearson, Ron Perranoski, Dick Radatz, Johnny Romano, Carl Willey	18.00	9.00	5.50
6	Steve Barber, Jim Fregosi, Tony Gonzalez, Mickey Mantle, Jim O'Toole, Gary Peters, Rich Rollins, Warren Spahn, Dick Stuart, Joe Torre	125.00	62.00	37.00
7	Felipe Alou, George Altman, Ken Boyer, Rocky Colavito, Jim Davenport, Tommy Davis, Bill Freehan, Bob Friend, Ken Johnson, Billy Moran	18.00	9.00	5.50
8	Earl Battey, Ernie Broglio, Johnny Callison, Donn Clendenon, Don Drysdale, Jim Gentile, Elston Howard, Claude Osteen, Billy Williams, Hal Woodeshick	25.00	12.50	7.50
9	Hank Aaron, Jack Baldschun, Wayne Causey, Moe Drabowsky, Dick Groat, Frank Howard, Al Jackson, Jerry Lumpe, Ken McBride, Rusty Staub	40.00	20.00	12.00
10	Ray Culp, Vic Davalillo, Dick Farrell, Ron Hunt, Al Kaline, Sandy Koufax, Ed Mathews, Willie McCovey, Camilo Pascual, Lee Thomas	50.00	25.00	15.00

1965 Bazooka

The 1965 Bazooka set is identical to the 1963 and 1964 sets. Different players were added each year and different photographs were used for those players being included again. Individual cards cut from the boxes measure 1-9/16" by 2-1/2". Complete three-card panels measure 2-1/2" by 4-11/16". Thirty-six full-color, blank-backed, num- bered cards comprise the set. Prices are given for individual cards and complete panels in the checklist that follows.

		NR MT	EX	VG
Complete Panel Set:		1100.00	550.00	325.00
Complete Singles Set:		600.00	300.00	180.00
Common Panel:		25.00	12.50	7.50
Common Single Player:		5.00	2.50	1.50
Panel		225.00	115.00	70.00
1	Mickey Mantle (batting lefty)	175.00	87.00	52.00
2	Larry Jackson	5.00	2.50	1.50
3	Chuck Hinton	5.00	2.50	1.50
Panel		30.00	15.00	9.00
4	Tony Oliva	10.00	5.00	3.00
5	Dean Chance	5.00	2.50	1.50
6	Jim O'Toole	5.00	2.50	1.50
Panel		95.00	47.00	28.00
7	Harmon Killebrew (bat on shoulder)	25.00	12.50	7.50
8	Pete Ward	5.00	2.50	1.50
9	Hank Aaron (batting)	50.00	25.00	15.00
Panel		70.00	35.00	21.00
10	Dick Radatz	5.00	2.50	1.50
11	Boog Powell	10.00	5.00	3.00
12	Willie Mays (looking down)	40.00	20.00	12.00
Panel		65.00	32.00	19.50
13	Bob Veale	5.00	2.50	1.50
14	Bob Clemente (batting)	40.00	20.00	12.00
15	Johnny Callison (batting, no screen in background)	8.00	4.00	2.50
Panel		45.00	22.00	13.50
16	Joe Torre	8.00	4.00	2.50
17	Billy Williams (batting)	20.00	10.00	6.00
18	Bob Chance	5.00	2.50	1.50
Panel		30.00	15.00	9.00
19	Bob Aspromonte	5.00	2.50	1.50
20	Joe Christopher	5.00	2.50	1.50
21	Jim Bunning	12.00	6.00	3.50
Panel		70.00	35.00	21.00
22	Jim Fregosi (portrait)	8.00	4.00	2.50
23	Bob Gibson	25.00	12.50	7.50
24	Juan Marichal	20.00	10.00	6.00
Panel		25.00	12.50	7.50
25	Dave Wickersham	5.00	2.50	1.50
26	Ron Hunt (throwing)	8.00	4.00	2.50
27	Gary Peters (portrait)	5.00	2.50	1.50
Panel		70.00	35.00	21.00
28	Ron Santo	10.00	5.00	3.00
29	Elston Howard (with glove)	12.00	6.00	3.50
30	Brooks Robinson (portrait)	30.00	15.00	9.00
Panel		95.00	47.00	28.00
31	Frank Robinson (portrait)	35.00	17.50	10.50
32	Sandy Koufax (hands over head)	40.00	20.00	12.00
33	Rocky Colavito (Cleveland)	10.00	5.00	3.00
Panel		60.00	30.00	18.00

		NR MT	EX	VG
34	Al Kaline (portrait)	30.00	15.00	9.00
35	Ken Boyer (portrait)	10.00	5.00	3.00
36	Tommy Davis (fielding)	8.00	4.00	2.50

1966 Bazooka

The 1966 Bazooka set was increased to 48 cards. Issued in panels of three on the bottoms of boxes of bubble gum, the full-color cards are blank-backed and numbered. Individual cards measure 1-9/16" by 2-1/2", whereas panels measure 2-1/2" by 4-11/16".

	NR MT	EX	VG
Complete Panel Set:	1500.00	750.00	450.00
Complete Singles Set:	800.00	400.00	250.00
Common Panel:	25.00	12.50	7.50
Common Single Player:	5.00	2.50	1.50

		NR MT	EX	VG
Panel		65.00	32.00	19.50
1	Sandy Koufax	40.00	20.00	12.00
2	Willie Horton	6.00	3.00	1.75
3	Frank Howard	8.00	4.00	2.50
Panel		40.00	20.00	12.00
4	Richie Allen	10.00	5.00	3.00
5	Mel Stottlemyre	8.00	4.00	2.50
6	Tony Conigliaro	15.00	7.50	4.50
Panel		250.00	125.00	70.00
7	Mickey Mantle	175.00	87.00	52.00
8	Leon Wagner	5.00	2.50	1.50
9	Ed Kranepool	6.00	3.00	1.75
Panel		70.00	35.00	21.00
10	Juan Marichal	20.00	10.00	6.00
11	Harmon Killebrew	25.00	12.50	7.50
12	Johnny Callison	6.00	3.00	1.75
Panel		55.00	27.00	16.50
13	Roy McMillan	5.00	2.50	1.50
14	Willie McCovey	25.00	12.50	7.50
15	Rocky Colavito	10.00	5.00	3.00
Panel		65.00	32.00	19.50
16	Willie Mays	40.00	20.00	12.00
17	Sam McDowell	8.00	4.00	2.50
18	Vern Law	6.00	3.00	1.75
Panel		50.00	25.00	15.00
19	Jim Fregosi	6.00	3.00	1.75
20	Ron Fairly	6.00	3.00	1.75
21	Bob Gibson	25.00	12.50	7.50
Panel		70.00	35.00	21.00
22	Carl Yastrzemski	40.00	20.00	12.00
23	Bill White	8.00	4.00	2.50
24	Bob Aspromonte	5.00	2.50	1.50
Panel		55.00	27.00	16.50
25	Dean Chance (California)	5.00	2.50	1.50
26	Bob Clemente	40.00	20.00	12.00
27	Tony Cloninger	5.00	2.50	1.50
Panel		70.00	35.00	21.00
28	Curt Blefary	5.00	2.50	1.50
29	Milt Pappas	5.00	2.50	1.50
30	Hank Aaron	50.00	25.00	15.00
Panel		60.00	30.00	18.00
31	Jim Bunning	12.00	6.00	3.50
32	Frank Robinson (portrait)	30.00	15.00	9.00
33	Bill Skowron	8.00	4.00	2.50
Panel		60.00	30.00	18.00
34	Brooks Robinson	30.00	15.00	9.00
35	Jim Wynn	6.00	3.00	1.75
36	Joe Torre	8.00	4.00	2.50
Panel		145.00	72.00	43.00
37	Jim Grant	5.00	2.50	1.50
38	Pete Rose	90.00	45.00	27.50
39	Ron Santo	10.00	5.00	3.00
Panel		60.00	30.00	18.00
40	Tom Tresh	8.00	4.00	2.50
41	Tony Oliva	10.00	5.00	3.00
42	Don Drysdale	25.00	12.50	7.50
Panel		25.00	12.50	7.50
43	Pete Richert	5.00	2.50	1.50
44	Bert Campaneris	8.00	4.00	2.50
45	Jim Maloney	5.00	2.50	1.50
Panel		70.00	35.00	21.00
46	Al Kaline	30.00	15.00	9.00
47	Eddie Fisher	5.00	2.50	1.50
48	Billy Williams	20.00	10.00	6.00

1967 Bazooka

The 1967 Bazooka set is identical in design to the Bazooka sets of 1964-1966. Issued in panels of three on the bottoms of bubble gum boxes, the set is made up of 48 full-color, blank-backed,

numbered cards. Individual cards measure 1-9/16" by 2-1/2"; complete panels measure 2-1/2" by 4-11/16" in size.

	NR MT	EX	VG
Complete Panel Set:	1400.00	700.00	425.00
Complete Singles Set:	775.00	387.00	232.00
Common Panel:	25.00	12.50	7.50
Common Single Player:	5.00	2.50	1.50

		NR MT	EX	VG
Panel		25.00	12.50	7.50
1	Rick Reichardt	5.00	2.50	1.50
2	Tommy Agee	5.00	2.50	1.50
3	Frank Howard	8.00	4.00	2.50
Panel		35.00	17.50	10.50
4	Richie Allen	10.00	5.00	3.00
5	Mel Stottlemyre	8.00	4.00	2.50
6	Tony Conigliaro	15.00	7.50	4.50
Panel		225.00	110.00	70.00
7	Mickey Mantle	175.00	87.00	52.00
8	Leon Wagner	5.00	2.50	1.50
9	Gary Peters	5.00	2.50	1.50
Panel		70.00	35.00	21.00
10	Juan Marichal	20.00	10.00	6.00
11	Harmon Killebrew	25.00	12.50	7.50
12	Johnny Callison	6.00	3.00	1.75
Panel		50.00	25.00	15.00
13	Denny McLain	12.00	6.00	3.50
14	Willie McCovey	25.00	12.50	7.50
15	Rocky Colavito	10.00	5.00	3.00
Panel		65.00	32.00	19.50
16	Willie Mays	40.00	20.00	12.00
17	Sam McDowell	6.00	3.00	1.75
18	Jim Kaat	12.00	6.00	3.50
Panel		50.00	25.00	15.00
19	Jim Fregosi	6.00	3.00	1.75
20	Ron Fairly	6.00	3.00	1.75
21	Bob Gibson	25.00	12.50	7.50
Panel		70.00	35.00	21.00
22	Carl Yastrzemski	40.00	20.00	12.00
23	Bill White	6.00	3.00	1.75
24	Bob Aspromonte	5.00	2.50	1.50
Panel		60.00	30.00	18.00
25	Dean Chance (Minnesota)	5.00	2.50	1.50
26	Bob Clemente	40.00	20.00	12.00
27	Tony Cloninger	5.00	2.50	1.50
Panel		70.00	35.00	21.00
28	Curt Blefary	5.00	2.50	1.50
29	Phil Regan	5.00	2.50	1.50
30	Hank Aaron	50.00	25.00	15.00
Panel		60.00	30.00	18.00
31	Jim Bunning	12.00	6.00	3.50
32	Frank Robinson (batting)	25.00	12.50	7.50
33	Ken Boyer	10.00	5.00	3.00
Panel		60.00	30.00	18.00
34	Brooks Robinson	30.00	15.00	9.00
35	Jim Wynn	6.00	3.00	1.75
36	Joe Torre	8.00	4.00	2.50
Panel		140.00	70.00	42.00
37	Tommy Davis	6.00	3.00	1.75
38	Pete Rose	90.00	45.00	27.00
39	Ron Santo	10.00	5.00	3.00
Panel		60.00	30.00	18.00
40	Tom Tresh	8.00	4.00	2.50
41	Tony Oliva	10.00	5.00	3.00
42	Don Drysdale	25.00	12.50	7.50
Panel		25.00	12.50	7.50
43	Pete Richert	5.00	2.50	1.50
44	Bert Campaneris	6.00	3.00	1.75
45	Jim Maloney	5.00	2.50	1.50
Panel		70.00	35.00	21.00
46	Al Kaline	30.00	15.00	9.00
47	Matty Alou	6.00	3.00	1.75
48	Billy Williams	20.00	10.00	6.00

1968 Bazooka

The design of the 1968 Bazooka set is radically different from previous years. The player cards are situated on the sides of the boxes with the box back containing "Tipps From The Topps." Four unnum- bered player cards, measuring 1-1/4" by 3-1/8", are featured on each box. The box back includes a small player photo plus illustrated tips on various aspects of the game of baseball. The boxes are numbered 1-15 on the top panels. There are 56 different player cards in the set, with four of the cards (Agee, Drysdale, Rose, Santo) being used twice to round out the set of fifteen boxes.

	NR MT	EX	VG
Complete Box Set:	3000.00	1500.00	900.00
Complete Singles Set:	1800.00	900.00	550.00
Common Box:	110.00	55.00	33.00

		NR MT	EX	VG
Common Single Player:		5.00	2.50	1.50
Box		175.00	87.00	52.00
Maury Wills (Bunting)		20.00	10.00	6.00
(1)	Clete Boyer	9.00	4.50	2.75
(2)	Paul Casanova	7.00	3.50	2.00
(3)	Al Kaline	30.00	15.00	9.00
(4)	Tom Seaver	70.00	35.00	21.00
Box		150.00	75.00	45.00
2	Carl Yastrzemski (Batting)	50.00	25.00	15.00
(5)	Matty Alou	9.00	4.50	2.75
(6)	Bill Freehan	9.00	4.50	2.75
(7)	Jim Hunter	20.00	10.00	6.00
(8)	Jim Lefebvre	7.00	3.50	2.00
Box		110.00	55.00	33.00
3	Bert Campaneris (Stealing bases)	20.00	10.00	6.00
(9)	Bobby Knoop	7.00	3.50	2.00
(10)	Tim McCarver	12.00	6.00	3.50
(11)	Frank Robinson	25.00	12.50	7.50
(12)	Bob Veale	7.00	3.50	2.00
Box		90.00	45.00	27.00
4	Maury Wills (Sliding)	20.00	10.00	6.00
(13)	Joe Azcue	7.00	3.50	2.00
(14)	Tony Conigliaro	15.00	7.50	4.50
(15)	Ken Holtzman	9.00	4.50	2.75
(16)	Bill White	9.00	4.50	2.75
Box		150.00	75.00	45.00
5	Julian Javier (The Double Play)	20.00	10.00	6.00
(17)	Hank Aaron	50.00	25.00	15.00
(18)	Juan Marichal	20.00	10.00	6.00
(19)	Joe Pepitone	12.00	6.00	3.50
(20)	Rico Petrocelli	9.00	4.50	2.75
Box		175.00	87.00	52.00
6	Orlando Cepeda (Playing 1st Base)	25.00	12.50	7.50
(21)	Tommie Agee	5.00	2.50	1.50
(22)	Don Drysdale	10.00	5.00	3.00
(23)	Pete Rose	70.00	35.00	21.00
(24)	Ron Santo	5.00	2.50	1.50
Box		110.00	55.00	33.00
7	Bill Mazeroski (Playing 2nd Base)	20.00	10.00	6.00
(25)	Jim Bunning	12.00	6.00	3.50
(26)	Frank Howard	12.00	6.00	3.50
(27)	John Roseboro	9.00	4.50	2.75
(28)	George Scott	9.00	4.50	2.75
Box		150.00	75.00	45.00
8	Brooks Robinson (Playing 3rd Base)	50.00	25.00	15.00
(29)	Tony Gonzalez	7.00	3.50	2.00
(30)	Willie Horton	9.00	4.50	2.75
(31)	Harmon Killebrew	25.00	12.50	7.50
(32)	Jim McGlothlin	7.00	3.50	2.00
Box		110.00	55.00	33.00
9	Jim Fregosi (Playing Shortstop)	20.00	10.00	6.00
(33)	Max Alvis	7.00	3.50	2.00
(34)	Bob Gibson	20.00	10.00	6.00
(35)	Tony Oliva	12.00	6.00	3.50
(36)	Vada Pinson	12.00	6.00	3.50
Box		110.00	55.00	33.00
10	Joe Torre (Catching)	25.00	12.50	7.50
(37)	Dean Chance	7.00	3.50	2.00
(38)	Tommy Davis	9.00	4.50	2.75
(39)	Ferguson Jenkins	15.00	7.50	4.50
(40)	Rick Monday	9.00	4.50	2.75
Box		275.00	137.00	82.00
11	Jim Lonborg (Pitching)	25.00	12.50	7.50
(41)	Curt Flood	9.00	4.50	2.75
(42)	Joel Horlen	7.00	3.50	2.00
(43)	Mickey Mantle	125.00	62.00	37.00
(44)	Jim Wynn	7.00	3.50	2.00
Box		150.00	75.00	45.00
12	Mike McCormick (Fielding the Pitcher's Position)	20.00	10.00	6.00
(45)	Bob Clemente	40.00	20.00	12.00
(46)	Al Downing	9.00	4.50	2.75
(47)	Don Mincher	7.00	3.50	2.00
(48)	Tony Perez	15.00	7.50	4.50
Box		175.00	87.00	52.00
13	Frank Crosetti (Coaching)	35.00	17.50	10.50
(49)	Rod Carew	40.00	20.00	12.00
(50)	Willie McCovey	25.00	12.50	7.50
(51)	Ron Swoboda	7.00	3.50	2.00
(52)	Earl Wilson	7.00	3.50	2.00
Box		150.00	75.00	45.00
14	Willie Mays (Playing the Outfield)	50.00	25.00	15.00
(53)	Richie Allen	12.00	6.00	3.50
(54)	Gary Peters	7.00	3.50	2.00
(55)	Rusty Staub	10.00	5.00	3.00

		NR MT	EX	VG
(56)	Billy Williams	20.00	10.00	6.00
Box		175.00	87.00	52.00
15	Lou Brock (Base Running)	40.00	20.00	12.00
(57)	Tommie Agee	5.00	2.50	1.50
(58)	Don Drysdale	10.00	5.00	3.00
(59)	Pete Rose	70.00	35.00	21.00
(60)	Ron Santo	5.00	2.50	1.50

1969 Bazooka

Issued over a two-year span, the 1969-70 Bazooka set utilized the box bottom and sides. The box bottom, entitled "Baseball Extra," features an historic event in baseball. The bottom panels are numbered 1 through 12. Two "All-Time Great" cards were located on each side of the box. These cards are not numbered and have no distinct borders. Individual cards measure 1-1/4" by 3-1/8"; the "Baseball Extra" panels measure 3" by 6-1/4". The prices in the checklist that follows are for complete boxes only. Cards/panels cut from the boxes have a greatly reduced value - 25 per cent of the complete box prices for all cut pieces.

		NR MT	EX	VG
Complete Box Set:		200.00	100.00	60.00
Common Box:		10.00	5.00	3.00
1	No-Hit Duel By Toney And Vaughn (Mordecai Brown, Ty Cobb, Willie Keeler, Eddie Plank)	15.00	7.50	4.50
2	Alexander Conquers Yanks (Rogers Hornsby, Ban Johnson, Walter Johnson, Al Simmons)	10.00	5.00	3.00
3	Yanks Lazzeri Sets A.L. Hit Record (Hugh Duffy, Lou Gehrig, Tris Speaker, Joe Tinker)	15.00	7.50	4.50
4	Home Run Almost Hit Out Of Stadium (Grover Alexander, Chief Bender, Christy Mathewson, Cy Young)	10.00	5.00	3.00
5	Four Consecutive Homers By Gehrig (Frank Chance, Mickey Cochrane, John McGraw, Babe Ruth)	30.00	15.00	9.00
6	No-Hit Game By Walter Johnson (Johnny Evers, Walter Johnson, John McGraw, Cy Young)	10.00	5.00	3.00
7	Twelve RBI's By Bottomley (Ty Cobb, Eddie Collins, Johnny Evers, Lou Gehrig)	20.00	10.00	6.00
8	Ty Ties Record (Mickey Cochrane, Eddie Collins, Met Ott, Honus Wagner)	10.00	5.00	3.00
9	Babe Ruth Hits Three Homers In Game (Cap Anson, Jack Chesbro, Al Simmons, Tris Speaker)	25.00	12.50	7.50
10	Calls Shot In Series Game (Nap Lajoie, Connie Mack, Rabbit Maranville, Ed Walsh)	25.00	12.50	7.50
11	Ruth's 60th Homer Sets New Record (Frank Chance, Nap Lajoie, Mel Ott, Joe Tinker)	25.00	12.50	7.50
12	Double Shutout By Ed Reulbach (Rogers Hornsby, Rabbit Maranville, Christy Mathewson, Honus Wagner)	10.00	5.00	3.00

1971 Bazooka

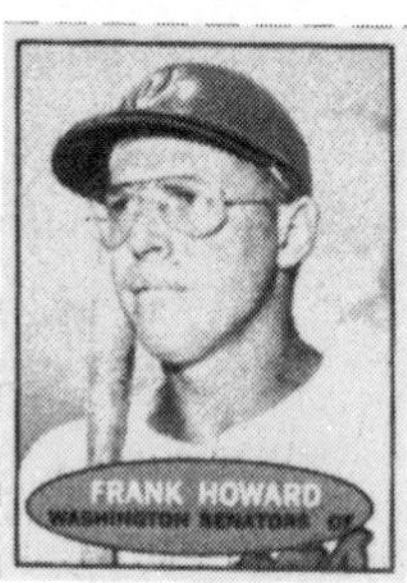

This Bazooka set was issued in 1971, consisting of 36 full-color, blank-backed, unnumbered cards. Issued in panels of three on the bottoms of Bazooka bubble gum boxes, individual cards measure 2" by 2-5/8" whereas complete panels measure 2-5/8" by 5-5/16". In the checklist that follows, the cards have been numbered by panel using the name of the player who appears on the left portion of the panel.

		NR MT	EX	VG
Complete Panel Set:		325.00	162.00	97.00
Complete Singles Set:		190.00	95.00	57.00
Common Panel:		10.00	5.00	3.00
Common Single Player:		1.25	.60	.40
1	Panel	30.00	15.00	9.00
(1)	Tommie Agee	1.25	.60	.40
(2)	Harmon Killebrew	7.00	3.50	2.00
2	Panel	40.00	20.00	12.00
(3)	Reggie Jackson	20.00	10.00	6.00
3	Panel	25.00	12.50	7.50
(4)	Bert Campaneris	1.25	.60	.40
4	Panel	25.00	12.50	7.50
(5)	Pete Rose	25.00	12.50	7.50
5	Panel	15.00	7.50	4.50
(6)	Orlando Cepeda	3.00	1.50	.90
6	Panel	30.00	15.00	9.00
(7)	Rico Carty	2.00	1.00	.60
7	Panel	15.00	7.50	4.50
(8)	Johnny Bench	20.00	10.00	6.00
8	Panel	30.00	15.00	9.00
(9)	Tommy Harper	1.25	.60	.40
9	Panel	15.00	7.50	4.50
(10)	Bill Freehan	2.00	1.00	.60
10	Panel	10.00	5.00	3.00
(11)	Roberto Clemente	20.00	10.00	6.00
11	Panel	30.00	15.00	9.00
(12)	Claude Osteen	1.25	.60	.40
12	Panel	15.00	7.50	4.50
(13)	Jim Fregosi	2.00	1.00	.60
(14)	Billy Williams	6.00	3.00	1.75
(15)	Dave McNally	1.25	.60	.40
(16)	Randy Hundley	1.25	.60	.40
(17)	Willie Mays	20.00	10.00	4.50
(18)	Jim Hunter	6.00	3.00	1.75
(19)	Juan Marichal	6.00	3.00	1.75
(20)	Frank Howard	3.00	1.50	.90
(21)	Bill Melton	1.25	.60	.40
(22)	Willie McCovey	7.00	3.50	2.00
(23)	Carl Yastrzemski	12.00	6.00	3.50
(24)	Clyde Wright	1.25	.60	.40
(25)	Jim Merritt	1.25	.60	.40
(26)	Luis Aparicio	6.00	3.00	1.75
(27)	Bobby Murcer	3.00	1.50	.90
(28)	Rico Petrocelli	2.00	1.00	.60
(29)	Sam McDowell	2.00	1.00	.60
(30)	Clarence Gaston	1.25	.60	.40
(31)	Brooks Robinson	6.50	3.25	2.00
(32)	Hank Aaron	20.00	10.00	4.50
(33)	Larry Dierker	1.25	.60	.40
(34)	Rusty Staub	2.00	1.00	.60
(35)	Bob Gibson	7.00	3.50	2.00
(36)	Amos Otis	1.25	.60	.40

1971 Bazooka Numbered Set

The 1971 Bazooka numbered set is a proof set produced by the company after the unnumbered set was released. The set is comprised of 48 cards as opposed to the 36 cards which make up the unnumbered set. Issued in panels of three, the nine cards not found in the unnumbered set are #'s 1-3, 13-15 and 43-45. All other cards are identical to those found in the unnumbered set. The cards, which measure 2" by 2-5/8", contain full-color photos and are blank-backed.

		NR MT	EX	VG
Complete Panel Set:		1000.	500.00	300.00
Complete Singles Set:		550.00	275.00	165.00
Common Panel:		10.00	5.00	3.00
Common Single Player:		2.00	1.00	.60
Panel		150.00	75.00	45.00
1	Tim McCarver	15.00	7.50	4.50
2	Frank Robinson	45.00	23.00	13.50
3	Bill Mazeroski	15.00	7.50	4.50
Panel		45.00	22.00	13.50
4	Willie McCovey	12.00	6.00	3.50
5	Carl Yastrzemski	20.00	10.00	6.00
6	Clyde Wright	2.00	1.00	.60
Panel		20.00	10.00	6.00
7	Jim Merritt	2.00	1.00	.60
8	Luis Aparicio	9.00	4.50	2.75
9	Bobby Murcer	5.00	2.50	1.50
Panel		10.00	5.00	3.00
10	Rico Petrocelli	3.00	1.50	.90
11	Sam McDowell	3.00	1.50	.90
12	Clarence Gaston	2.00	1.00	.60
Panel		150.00	75.00	45.00
13	Ferguson Jenkins	20.00	10.00	6.00
14	Al Kaline	45.00	23.00	13.50
15	Ken Harrelson	15.00	7.50	4.50
Panel		45.00	22.00	13.50
16	Tommie Agee	2.00	1.00	.60
17	Harmon Killebrew	12.00	6.00	3.50
18	Reggie Jackson	20.00	10.00	6.00
Panel		20.00	10.00	6.00
19	Juan Marichal	9.00	4.50	2.75
20	Frank Howard	5.00	2.50	1.50
21	Bill Melton	2.00	1.00	.60
Panel		55.00	27.00	16.50
22	Brooks Robinson	15.00	7.50	4.50
23	Hank Aaron	30.00	15.00	9.00
24	Larry Dierker	2.00	1.00	.60
Panel		20.00	10.00	6.00
25	Jim Fregosi	3.00	1.50	.90
26	Billy Williams	10.00	5.00	3.00
27	Dave McNally	2.00	1.00	.60
Panel		30.00	15.00	9.00
28	Rico Carty	3.00	1.50	.90
29	Johnny Bench	18.00	9.00	5.50
30	Tommy Harper	2.00	1.00	.60
Panel		60.00	30.00	18.00
31	Bert Campaneris	2.00	1.00	.60
32	Pete Rose	35.00	17.50	10.50
33	Orlando Cepeda	6.00	3.00	1.75
Panel		45.00	22.00	13.50
34	Maury Wills	6.00	3.00	1.75
35	Tom Seaver	20.00	10.00	6.00
36	Tony Oliva	6.00	3.00	1.75
Panel		30.00	15.00	9.00
37	Bill Freehan	3.00	1.50	.90
38	Roberto Clemente	25.00	12.50	7.50
39	Claude Osteen	2.00	1.00	.60
Panel		20.00	10.00	6.00
40	Rusty Staub	3.00	1.50	.90
41	Bob Gibson	10.00	5.00	3.00
42	Amos Otis	2.00	1.00	.60
Panel		125.00	62.00	37.00
43	Jim Wynn	10.00	5.00	3.00
44	Rich Allen	18.00	9.00	5.50
45	Tony Conigliaro	10.00	5.00	3.00
Panel		40.00	20.00	12.00
46	Randy Hundley	2.00	1.00	.60
47	Willie Mays	30.00	15.00	9.00
48	Jim Hunter	9.00	4.50	2.75

1988 Bazooka

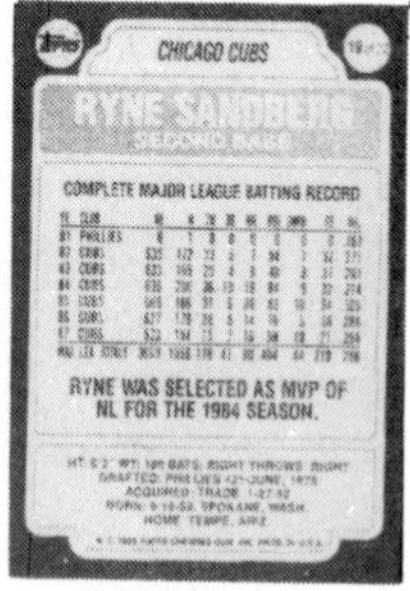

This 22-card set from Topps marks the first Bazooka issue since 1971. Full-color player photos are bordered in white, with the player name printed on a red, white and blue bubble gum box in the lower right corner. Flip sides are also red, white and blue, printed vertically. A large, but faint, Bazooka logo backs the Topps baseball logo, team name, card number, player's name and position, followed by batting records, personal information and brief career highlights. Cards were sold inside specially marked 59¢ and 79¢ Bazooka gum and candy boxes, one card per box.

		MT	NR MT	EX
Complete Set:		10.00	7.50	4.00
Common Player:		.20	.15	.08
1	George Bell	.25	.20	.10
2	Wade Boggs	.90	.70	.35
3	Jose Canseco	1.25	.90	.50
4	Roger Clemens	.60	.45	.25
5	Vince Coleman	.20	.15	.08
6	Eric Davis	.60	.45	.25
7	Tony Fernandez	.20	.15	.08
8	Dwight Gooden	.60	.45	.25
9	Tony Gwynn	.40	.30	.15
10	Wally Joyner	.40	.30	.15
11	Don Mattingly	2.00	1.50	.80
12	Willie McGee	.20	.15	.08
13	Mark McGwire	.90	.70	.35
14	Kirby Puckett	.50	.40	.20
15	Tim Raines	.30	.25	.12
16	Dave Righetti	.20	.15	.08
17	Cal Ripken	.35	.25	.14
18	Juan Samuel	.20	.15	.08
19	Ryne Sandberg	.30	.25	.12
20	Benny Santiago	.20	.15	.08
21	Darryl Strawberry	.60	.45	.25
22	Todd Worrell	.20	.15	.08

1989 Bazooka

This 22-card set marks the second consecutive year Bazooka has issued following a 17-year absence. Full color action and posed player shots are bordered by a white frame. Other features of this standard-size includes a "Shining Stars" logo across the top, a yellow stripe enclosing the player's name at the bottom, and the Topps/Bazooka logo in the bottom right corner. Flip sides are printed in red and blue, and contain a large but faint Bazooka logo, the Topps baseball logo, card number, team name, player's name and position, followed by batting or pitching records, personal information and brief highlights. Topps produced this 22-card set in 1989 to be included (one card per box) in specially-marked boxes of its Bazooka brand bubblegum. The player photos have the words "Shining Star" along the top, while the player's name appears along the bottom of the card, along with the Topps Bazooka logo in the lower right corner. The cards are numbered alphabetically.

		MT	NR MT	EX
Complete Set:		7.00	5.25	2.75
Common Player:		.15	.11	.06
1	Tim Belcher	.20	.15	.08
2	Damon Berryhill	.15	.11	.06
3	Wade Boggs	.80	.60	.30
4	Jay Buhner	.15	.11	.06
5	Jose Canseco	.80	.60	.30
6	Vince Coleman	.15	.11	.06
7	Cecil Espy	.15	.11	.06
8	Dave Gallagher	.15	.11	.06
9	Ron Gant	.15	.11	.06
10	Kirk Gibson	.15	.11	.06
11	Paul Gibson	.15	.11	.06
12	Mark Grace	.60	.45	.25
13	Tony Gwynn	.35	.25	.14
14	Rickey Henderson	.40	.30	.15
15	Orel Hershiser	.25	.20	.10
16	Gregg Jefferies	.50	.40	.20
17	Ricky Jordan	.25	.20	.10
18	Chris Sabo	.15	.11	.06
19	Gary Sheffield	.50	.40	.20
20	Darryl Strawberry	.50	.40	.20
21	Frank Viola	.20	.15	.08
22	Walt Weiss	.15	.11	.06

1958 Bell Brand Dodgers

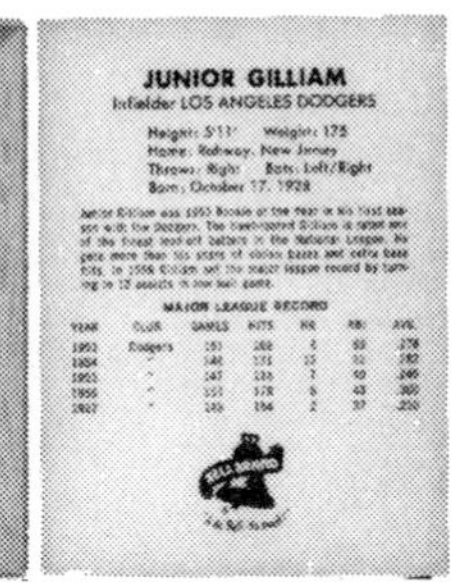

Celebrating the Dodgers first year of play in Los Angeles, Bell Brand inserted ten different unnumbered cards in their bags of potato chips and corn chips. The cards, which measure 3" by 4", have a sepia-colored photo inside a 1/4" green woodgrain border. The card backs feature statistical and biographical information and include the Bell Brand logo. Roy Campanella is included in the set despite a career-ending car wreck that prevented him from ever playing in Los Angeles.

		NR MT	EX	VG
Complete Set:		1000.00	500.00	300.00
Common Player:		35.00	17.50	10.50
1	Roy Campanella	125.00	56.00	35.00
2	Gino Cimoli	100.00	50.00	30.00
3	Don Drysdale	90.00	45.00	27.00
4	Junior Gilliam	35.00	17.50	10.50
5	Gil Hodges	90.00	45.00	27.00
6	Sandy Koufax	125.00	56.00	35.00
7	Johnny Podres	100.00	50.00	30.00
8	Pee Wee Reese	90.00	45.00	27.00
9	Duke Snider	250.00	125.00	75.00
10	Don Zimmer	35.00	17.50	10.50

1960 Bell Brand Dodgers

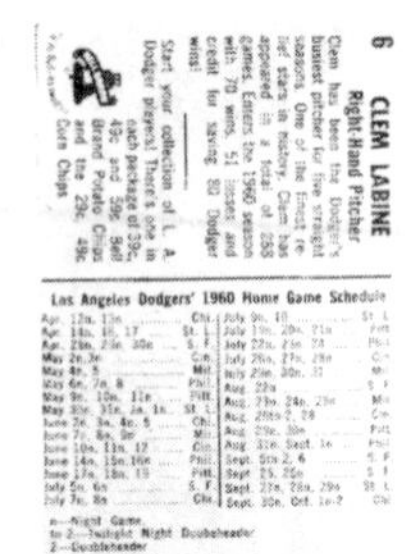

Bell Brand returned with a baseball card set in 1960 that was entirely different in style to their previous effort. The cards, which measure 2-1/2" by 3-1/2", feature beautiful, full-color photos. The backs carry a short player biography, the 1960 Dodgers home schedule, and the Bell Brand logo. Twenty different numbered cards were inserted in various size bags of potato chips and corn chips. Although sealed in cellophane, the cards were still subject to grease stains. Cards #'s 6, 12 and 18 are the scarcest in the set.

		NR MT	EX	VG
Complete Set:		700.00	350.00	210.00
Common Player:		15.00	7.50	4.50
1	Norm Larker	15.00	7.50	4.50
2	Duke Snider	70.00	35.00	21.00
3	Danny McDevitt	15.00	7.50	4.50
4	Jim Gilliam	18.00	9.00	5.50
5	Rip Repulski	15.00	7.50	4.50
6	Clem Labine	90.00	45.00	27.00
7	John Roseboro	15.00	7.50	4.50
8	Carl Furillo	18.00	9.00	5.50
9	Sandy Koufax	100.00	50.00	30.00
10	Joe Pignatano	15.00	7.50	4.50
11	Chuck Essegian	15.00	7.50	4.50
12	John Klippstein	80.00	40.00	25.00
13	Ed Roebuck	15.00	7.50	4.50
14	Don Demeter	15.00	7.50	4.50
15	Roger Craig	30.00	15.00	9.00
16	Stan Williams	15.00	7.50	4.50
17	Don Zimmer	18.00	9.00	5.50
18	Walter Alston	100.00	50.00	30.00
19	Johnny Podres	18.00	9.00	5.50
20	Maury Wills	30.00	15.00	9.00

1961 Bell Brand Dodgers

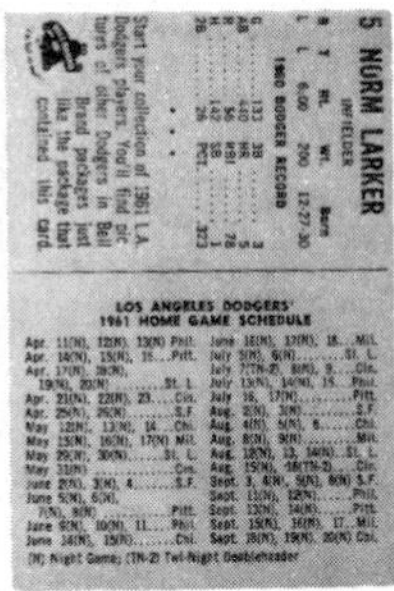

The 1961 Bell Brand set is identical in format to the previous year, although printed on thinner stock. Cards can be distinguished from the 1960 set by the 1961 schedule on the backs. The cards, which measure 2-7/16" by 3-1/2", are numbered by the player's uniform number. Twenty different cards were inserted into various size potato chip and corn chip packages, each card being sealed in a cellophane wrapper.

		NR MT	EX	VG
Complete Set:		375.00	185.00	110.00
Common Player:		12.00	6.00	3.50
3	Willie Davis	15.00	7.50	4.50
4	Duke Snider	50.00	30.00	15.00
5	Norm Larker	12.00	6.00	3.50
8	John Roseboro	12.00	6.00	3.50
9	Wally Moon	12.00	6.00	3.50
11	Bob Lillis	12.00	6.00	3.50
12	Tom Davis	12.00	6.00	3.50
14	Gil Hodges	25.00	12.50	7.50
16	Don Demeter	12.00	6.00	3.50
19	Jim Gilliam	15.00	7.50	4.50
22	John Podres	15.00	7.50	4.50
24	Walter Alston	25.00	12.50	7.50
30	Maury Wills	25.00	12.50	7.50
32	Sandy Koufax	80.00	40.00	25.00
34	Norm Sherry	12.00	6.00	3.50
37	Ed Roebuck	12.00	6.00	3.50
38	Roger Craig	15.00	7.50	4.50
40	Stan Williams	12.00	6.00	3.50
43	Charlie Neal	12.00	6.00	3.50
51	Larry Sherry	12.00	6.00	3.50

1962 Bell Brand Dodgers

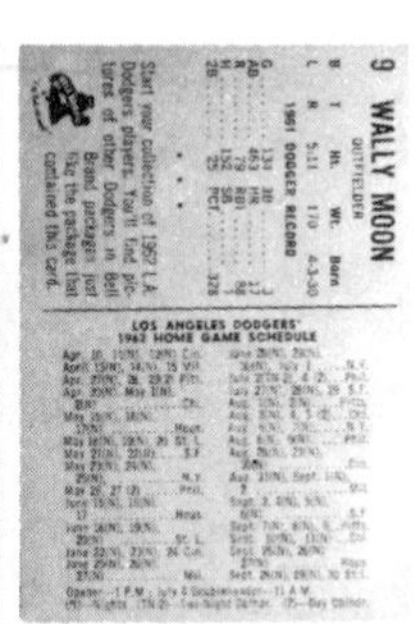

The 1962 Bell Brand set is identical in style to the previous two years and cards can be distinguished by the 1962 Dodgers schedule on the back. The set consists of 20 cards, each measuring 2-7/16" by 3- 1/2" and numbered by the player's uniform number. Printed on glossy stock, the 1962 set was less susceptible to grease stains.

		NR MT	EX	VG
Complete Set:		375.00	185.00	110.00
Common Player:		12.00	6.00	3.50
3	Willie Davis	15.00	7.50	4.50
4	Duke Snider	50.00	30.00	15.00
6	Ron Fairly	12.00	6.00	3.50
8	John Roseboro	12.00	6.00	3.50
9	Wally Moon	12.00	6.00	3.50
12	Tom Davis	12.00	6.00	3.50
16	Ron Perranoski	12.00	6.00	3.50
19	Jim Gilliam	15.00	7.50	4.50
20	Daryl Spencer	12.00	6.00	3.50
22	John Podres	15.00	7.50	4.50
24	Walter Alston	25.00	12.50	7.50
25	Frank Howard	15.00	7.50	4.50
30	Maury Wills	25.00	12.50	7.50
32	Sandy Koufax	80.00	40.00	25.00
34	Norm Sherry	12.00	6.00	3.50
37	Ed Roebuck	12.00	6.00	3.50
40	Stan Williams	12.00	6.00	3.50
51	Larry Sherry	12.00	6.00	3.50
53	Don Drysdale	35.00	17.50	10.50
56	Lee Walls	12.00	6.00	3.50

1951 Berk Ross

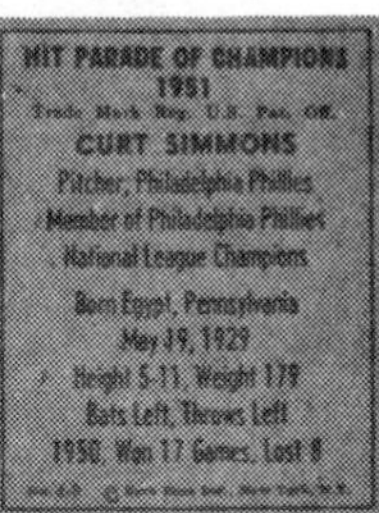

Entitled "Hit Parade of Champions," the 1951 Berk Ross set features 72 stars of various sports. The cards, which measure 2-1/16" by 2-1/2" and have tinted color photographs, were issued in boxes containing two-card panels. The issue is divided into four subsets with the first ten players of each series being baseball players. Only the baseball players are listed in the checklist that follows. Complete panels are valued 50 per cent higher than the sum of the individual cards.

		NR MT	EX	VG
Complete Set:		1100.	550.00	330.00
Common Player:		12.00	6.00	3.50
1-1	Al Rosen	20.00	10.00	6.00

		NR MT	EX	VG
1-2	Bob Lemon	20.00	10.00	6.00
1-3	Phil Rizzuto	50.00	25.00	15.00
1-4	Hank Bauer	25.00	12.50	7.50
1-5	Billy Johnson	13.00	6.50	4.00
1-6	Jerry Coleman	13.00	6.50	4.00
1-7	Johnny Mize	30.00	15.00	7.50
1-8	Dom DiMaggio	25.00	12.50	7.50
1-9	Richie Ashburn	15.00	7.50	4.50
1-10	Del Ennis	13.00	6.50	4.00
2-1	Stan Musial	300.00	150.00	90.00
2-2	Warren Spahn	25.00	12.50	7.50
2-3	Tommy Henrich	15.00	7.50	4.50
2-4	Larry "Yogi" Berra	200.00	100.00	60.00
2-5	Joe DiMaggio	400.00	200.00	120.00
2-6	Bobby Brown	15.00	7.50	4.50
2-7	Granville Hamner	12.00	6.00	3.50
2-8	Willie Jones	12.00	6.00	3.50
2-9	Stanley Lopata	12.00	6.00	3.50
2-10	Mike Goliat	12.00	6.00	3.50
3-1	Ralph Kiner	30.00	15.00	9.00
3-2	Billy Goodman	12.00	6.00	3.50
3-3	Allie Reynolds	15.00	7.50	4.50
3-4	Vic Raschi	15.00	7.50	4.50
3-5	Joe Page	13.00	6.50	4.00
3-6	Eddie Lopat	15.00	7.50	4.50
3-7	Andy Seminick	12.00	6.00	3.50
3-8	Dick Sisler	12.00	6.00	3.50
3-9	Eddie Waitkus	12.00	6.00	3.50
3-10	Ken Heintzelman	12.00	6.00	3.50
4-1	Gene Woodling	15.00	7.50	4.50
4-2	Cliff Mapes	13.00	6.50	4.00
4-3	Fred Sanford	13.00	6.50	4.00
4-4	Tommy Bryne	13.00	6.50	4.00
4-5	Eddie (Whitey) Ford	125.00	62.00	37.00
4-6	Jim Konstanty	13.00	6.50	4.00
4-7	Russ Meyer	12.00	6.00	3.50
4-8	Robin Roberts	30.00	15.00	9.00
4-9	Curt Simmons	13.00	6.50	4.00
4-10	Sam Jethroe	30.00	15.00	9.00

1952 Berk Ross

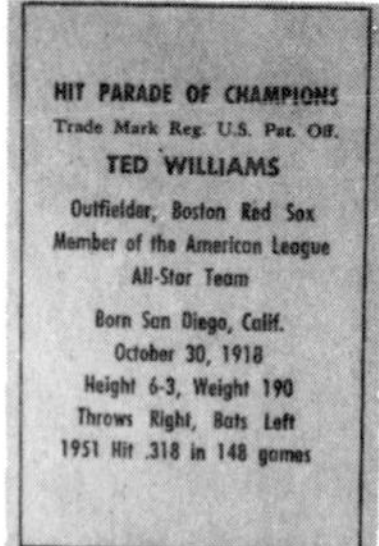

Although the card size is different (2" by 3"), the style of the fronts and backs of the 1952 Berk Ross set is similar to the previous year's effort. Seventy-two unnumbered cards make up the set. Rizzuto is included twice in the set and the Blackwell and Fox cards have transposed backs. The cards were issued individually rather than as two-card panels like in 1951.

		NR MT	EX	VG
Complete Set:		4000.	2000.	1175.
Common Player:		12.00	6.00	3.50
(1)	Richie Ashburn	30.00	15.00	9.00
(2)	Hank Bauer	18.00	9.00	5.50
(3)	Larry "Yogi" Berra	100.00	50.00	30.00
(4)	Ewell Blackwell (photo actually Nelson Fox)	18.00	9.00	5.50
(5)	Bobby Brown	18.00	9.00	5.50
(6)	Jim Busby	12.00	6.00	3.50
(7)	Roy Campanella	125.00	56.00	35.00
(8)	Chico Carrasquel	12.00	6.00	3.50
(9)	Jerry Coleman	15.00	7.50	4.50
(10)	Joe Collins	15.00	7.50	4.50
(11)	Alvin Dark	15.00	7.50	4.50
(12)	Dom DiMaggio	18.00	9.00	5.50
(13)	Joe DiMaggio	700.00	350.00	200.00
(14)	Larry Doby	18.00	9.00	5.50
(15)	Bobby Doerr	35.00	17.50	10.50
(16)	Bob Elliot (Elliott)	12.00	6.00	3.50
(17)	Del Ennis	10.00	5.00	3.00
(18)	Ferris Fain	12.00	6.00	3.50
(19)	Bob Feller	75.00	38.00	23.00
(20)	Nelson Fox (photo actually Ewell Blackwell)	18.00	9.00	5.50
(21)	Ned Garver	12.00	6.00	3.50
(22)	Clint Hartung	12.00	6.00	3.50
(23)	Jim Hearn	12.00	6.00	3.50
(24)	Gil Hodges	50.00	30.00	15.00
(25)	Monte Irvin	30.00	15.00	9.00
(26)	Larry Jansen	12.00	6.00	3.50
(27)	George Kell	25.00	12.50	7.50
(28)	Sheldon Jones	12.00	6.00	3.50
(29)	Monte Kennedy	12.00	6.00	3.50
(30)	Ralph Kiner	40.00	20.00	12.00
(31)	Dave Koslo	12.00	6.00	3.50
(32)	Bob Kuzava	15.00	7.50	4.50
(33)	Bob Lemon	30.00	15.00	9.00
(34)	Whitey Lockman	12.00	6.00	3.50
(35)	Eddie Lopat	18.00	9.00	5.50
(36)	Sal Maglie	15.00	7.50	4.50
(37)	Mickey Mantle	1000.	500.00	300.00
(38)	Billy Martin	50.00	30.00	15.00
(39)	Willie Mays	500.00	250.00	150.00
(40)	Gil McDougal (McDougald)	18.00	9.00	5.50

		MT	NR MT	EX
(41)	Orestes Minoso	15.00	7.50	4.50
(42)	Johnny Mize	40.00	20.00	12.00
(43)	Tom Morgan	15.00	7.50	4.50
(44)	Don Mueller	12.00	6.00	3.50
(45)	Stan Musial	400.00	200.00	120.00
(46)	Don Newcombe	18.00	9.00	5.50
(47)	Ray Noble	12.00	6.00	3.50
(48)	Joe Ostrowski	15.00	7.50	4.50
(49)	Mel Parnell	12.00	6.00	3.50
(50)	Vic Raschi	18.00	9.00	5.50
(51)	Pee Wee Reese	65.00	33.00	20.00
(52)	Allie Reynolds	18.00	9.00	5.50
(53)	Bill Rigney	10.00	5.00	3.00
(54)	Phil Rizzuto (bunting)	55.00	28.00	16.50
(55)	Phil Rizzuto (swinging)	55.00	28.00	16.50
(56)	Robin Roberts	30.00	15.00	9.00
(57)	Eddie Robinson	12.00	6.00	3.50
(58)	Jackie Robinson	200.00	100.00	60.00
(59)	Elwin "Preacher" Roe	15.00	7.50	4.50
(60)	Johnny Sain	15.00	7.50	4.50
(61)	Albert "Red" Schoendienst	30.00	15.00	9.00
(62)	Duke Snider	125.00	56.00	35.00
(63)	George Spencer	12.00	6.00	3.50
(64)	Eddie Stanky	15.00	7.50	4.50
(65)	Henry Thompson	12.00	6.00	3.50
(66)	Bobby Thomson	18.00	9.00	5.50
(67)	Vic Wertz	10.00	5.00	3.00
(68)	Waldon Westlake	12.00	6.00	3.50
(69)	Wes Westrum	10.00	5.00	3.00
(70)	Ted Williams	400.00	200.00	120.00
(71)	Gene Woodling	18.00	9.00	5.50
(72)	Gus Zernial	12.00	6.00	3.50

1911 Big Eater

This very rare set was issued circa 1911 and includes only members of the Pacific Coast League Sacramento Solons. The black and white cards measure 2-1/8" by 4" and feature action photos. The lower part of the card contains a three-line caption that includes the player's last name, team designation (abbreviated to "Sac'to), and the promotional line: "He Eats 'Big Eaters'." (Although the exact origin is undetermined, it is believed that "Big Eaters" were a candy novelty.)

		NR MT	EX	VG
Complete Set:		3000.00	1500.00	900.00
Common Player:		125.00	62.00	37.00
(1)	Arellanes	125.00	62.00	37.00
(2)	Baum	125.00	62.00	37.00
(3)	Byram	125.00	62.00	37.00
(4)	Danzig	125.00	62.00	37.00
(5)	Fitzgerald	125.00	62.00	37.00
(6)	Gaddy	125.00	62.00	37.00
(7)	Heister	125.00	62.00	37.00
(8)	Hunt	125.00	62.00	37.00
(9)	Kerns	125.00	62.00	37.00
(10)	LaLonge	125.00	62.00	37.00
(11)	Lerchen	125.00	62.00	37.00
(12)	Lewis	125.00	62.00	37.00
(13)	Mahoney	125.00	62.00	37.00
(14)	Nebinger	125.00	62.00	37.00
(15)	O'Rourke	125.00	62.00	37.00
(16)	Shinn	125.00	62.00	37.00
(17)	Thomas	125.00	62.00	37.00
(18)	Thompson	125.00	62.00	37.00
(19)	Thornton	125.00	62.00	37.00
(20)	Van Buren	125.00	62.00	37.00

1986 Big League Chew

The 1986 Big Leauge Chew set consists of 12 cards featuring the players who have hit 500 or more career home runs. The cards, which measure 2-1/2" by 3-1/2", were inserted in specially marked packages of Big League Chew, the shredded bubble gum developed by former major leaguer Jim Bouton. The set is entitled "Home Run Legends" and was available through a write-in offer on the package. Recent-day players in the set are shown in color photos, while the

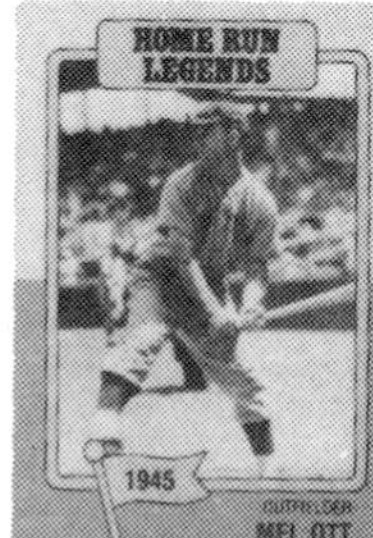

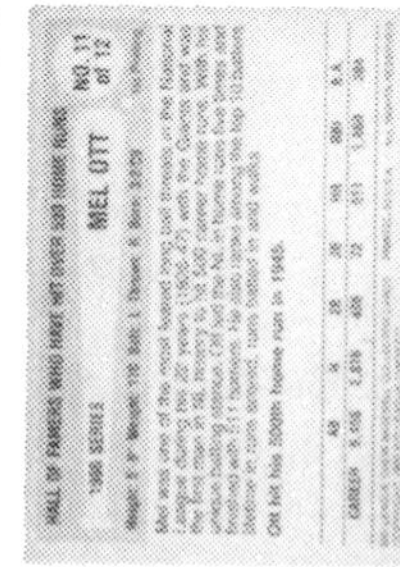

older sluggers are pictured in black and white.

		MT	NR MT	EX
Complete Set:		6.00	4.50	2.50
Common Player:		.35	.25	.14
1	Hank Aaron	.60	.45	.25
2	Babe Ruth	.80	.60	.30
3	Willie Mays	.60	.45	.25
4	Frank Robinson	.35	.25	.14
5	Harmon Killebrew	.35	.25	.14
6	Mickey Mantle	1.25	.90	.50
7	Jimmie Foxx	.35	.25	.14
8	Ted Williams	.70	.50	.30
9	Ernie Banks	.35	.25	.14
10	Eddie Mathews	.35	.25	.14
11	Mel Ott	.35	.25	.14
12	500-HR Group Card	.50	.40	.20

1987 Boardwalk And Baseball

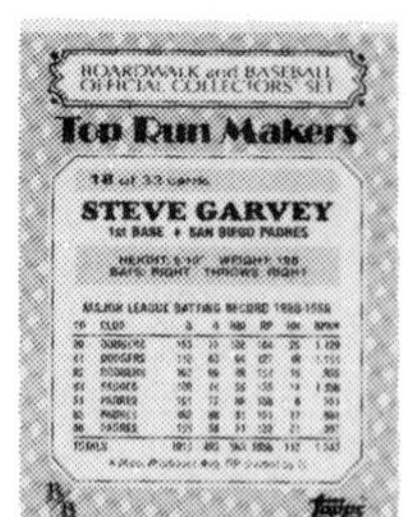

The 33-card "Top Run Makers" set was produced by Topps for distribution by the recreation amusement park "Boardwalk and Baseball," located near Orlando, Fla. The cards, which measure 2-1/2" by 3-1/2", feature fronts which contain full-color player photos and the park's logo (B/B). The card backs are printed in black and pink on white stock and offer personal data and career statistics. The set was issued in a specially designed box.

		MT	NR MT	EX
Complete Set:		7.00	5.25	2.75
Common Player:		.09	.07	.04
1	Mike Schmidt	.50	.40	.20
2	Eddie Murray	.35	.25	.14
3	Dale Murphy	.40	.30	.15
4	Dave Winfield	.30	.25	.12
5	Jim Rice	.30	.25	.12
6	Cecil Cooper	.12	.09	.05
7	Dwight Evans	.15	.11	.06
8	Rickey Henderson	.40	.30	.15
9	Robin Yount	.35	.25	.14
10	Andre Dawson	.25	.20	.10
11	Gary Carter	.35	.25	.14
12	Keith Hernandez	.30	.25	.12
13	George Brett	.40	.30	.15
14	Bill Buckner	.09	.07	.04
15	Tony Armas	.09	.07	.04
16	Harold Baines	.15	.11	.06
17	Don Baylor	.12	.09	.05
18	Steve Garvey	.35	.25	.14
19	Lance Parrish	.20	.15	.08
20	Dave Parker	.15	.11	.06
21	Buddy Bell	.09	.07	.04
22	Cal Ripken	.40	.30	.15
23	Bob Horner	.12	.09	.05
24	Tim Raines	.30	.25	.12
25	Jack Clark	.15	.11	.06
26	Leon Durham	.09	.07	.04
27	Pedro Guerrero	.15	.11	.06
28	Kent Hrbek	.15	.11	.06
29	Kirk Gibson	.20	.15	.08
30	Ryne Sandberg	.40	.30	.15
31	Wade Boggs	1.00	.70	.40
32	Don Mattingly	1.75	1.25	.70
33	Darryl Strawberry	.60	.45	.25

1987 Bohemian Hearth

Bohemian Hearth Bread Company of San Diego

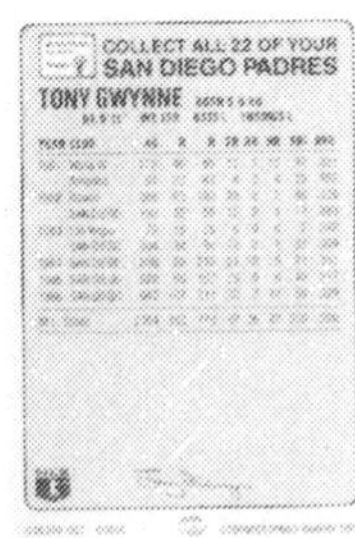

issued a 22-card set highlighting the San Diego Padres. Produced in conjunction with Mike Schechter Associates, the cards are the standard 2-1/2" by 3-1/2" size. The card fronts contain a full-color photo encompassed by a yellow border. The Bohemian Hearth Bread logo is located in the upper left corner of the card. The card backs are printed in light brown ink on a cream color card stock and carry player personal and statistical information.

		MT	NR MT	EX
Complete Set:		50.00	37.50	20.00
Common Player:		.50	.40	.20
1	Garry Templeton	1.25	.90	.50
4	Jose Cora	.60	.45	.25
5	Randy Ready	.50	.40	.20
6	Steve Garvey	5.00	3.75	2.00
7	Kevin Mitchell	6.00	4.50	2.50
8	John Kruk	3.75	2.75	1.50
9	Benito Santiago	8.00	6.00	3.25
10	Larry Bowa	1.00	.70	.40
11	Tim Flannery	.50	.40	.20
14	Carmelo Martinez	.80	.60	.30
16	Marvell Wynne	.50	.40	.20
19	Tony Gwynn	12.00	9.00	4.75
21	James Steels	.50	.40	.20
22	Stan Jefferson	1.00	.70	.40
30	Eric Show	1.00	.70	.40
31	Ed Whitson	1.00	.70	.40
34	Storm Davis	1.00	.70	.40
37	Craig Lefferts	.80	.60	.30
40	Andy Hawkins	1.00	.70	.40
41	Lance McCullers	.80	.60	.30
43	Dave Dravecky	1.75	1.25	.70
54	Rich Gossage	2.25	1.75	.90

1947 Bond Bread

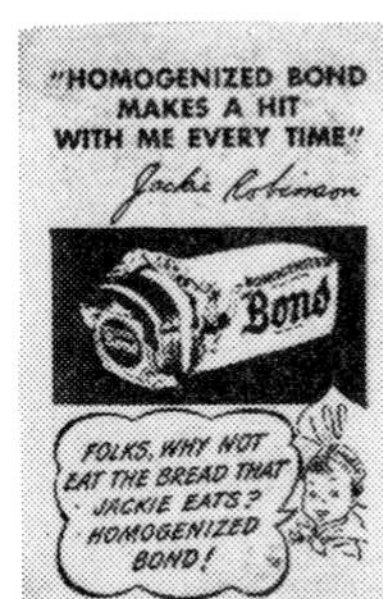

The major league's first black player, Jackie Robinson, was featured in a 13-card set issued by Bond Bread in 1947. The cards, which measure 2-1/4" by 3-1/2", are black and white photos of Robinson in various action and portrait poses. The unnumbered cards bear three different backs which contain advertising for Bond Bread. Four of the 13 cards make use of a horizontal format. Card #6 in the checklist below is believed to have been issued in greater quantities and perhaps was a promotional card. The back of this card is the only one in the set containing a short biography of Jackie. The ACC designation for the set is D302.

		NR MT	EX	VG
Complete Set:		4500.00	2250.00	1350.
Common Player:		250.00	125.00	75.00
(1)	Batting (awaiting pitch)	375.00	187.00	112.00
(2)	Batting Follow-Thru (white shirtsleeves)	375.00	187.00	112.00
(3)	Batting Follow-Thru (no shirtsleeves)	375.00	187.00	112.00
(4)	Leaping (scoreboard in background)	375.00	187.00	112.00
(5)	Leaping (no scoreboard)	375.00	187.00	112.00
(6)	Portrait (facsimile autograph)	250.00	125.00	75.00
(7)	Portrait (holding glove in air)	375.00	187.00	112.00
(8)	Running (down the baseline)	375.00	187.00	112.00
(9)	Running (about to catch ball)	375.00	187.00	112.00
(10)	Sliding (umpire in picture)	375.00	187.00	112.00
(11)	Stretching For Throw (ball in glove)	375.00	187.00	112.00
(12)	Stretching For Throw (no ball visible)	375.00	187.00	112.00
(13)	Throwing (ball in hand)	375.00	187.00	112.00

1984 Borden's Stickers Reds

This regional set of eight Reds stickers was issued by Borden Dairy in the Cincinnati area in 1984. Originally issued in two perforated sheets of four stickers each, the individual stickers measure 2-1/2" by 3-7/8", while a full sheet measures 5-1/2" by 8". The colorful stickers feature a player photo surrounded by a bright red border with the Reds logo and the Borden logo in the corners. The backs display coupons for Borden dairy products. The set is numbered according to the players' uniform numbers.

		MT	NR MT	EX
Complete Panel Set:		25.00	20.00	10.00
Complete Singles Set:		18.00	13.50	7.25
Common Player:		.50	.40	.20
Panel		4.00	3.00	1.50
2	Gary Redus	.50	.40	.20
20	Eddie Milner	.50	.40	.20
24	Tony Perez	1.00	.70	.40
46	Jeff Russell	.80	.60	.30
Panel		20.00	15.00	8.00
16	Ron Oester	.50	.40	.20
36	Mario Soto	.60	.45	.25
39	Dave Parker	1.00	.70	.40
44	Eric Davis	15.00	11.00	6.00

1948 Bowman

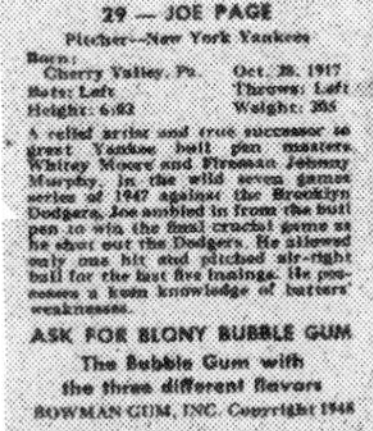

Bowman Gum Co.'s premiere set was produced in 1948, making it one of the first major issues of the post-war period. Forty-eight black and white cards comprise the set, with each card measuring 2-1/16" by 2-1/2" in size. The card backs, printed in black ink on grey stock, include the card number and the player's name, team, position, and a short biography. Twelve cards (#'s 7, 8, 13, 16, 20, 22, 24, 26, 29, 30 and 34) were printed in short supply when they were removed from the 36-card printing sheet to make room for the set's high numbers (#'s 37-48). These 24 cards command a higher price than the remaining cards in the set.

		NR MT	EX	VG
Complete Set:		2900.00	1450.00	875.00
Common Player: 1-36		18.00	9.00	5.50
Common Player: 37-48		25.00	12.50	7.50
1	Bob Elliott	80.00	9.00	5.00
2	Ewell (The Whip) Blackwell	25.00	12.50	7.50
3	Ralph Kiner	125.00	60.00	40.00
4	Johnny Mize	75.00	38.00	23.00
5	Bob Feller	150.00	75.00	45.00
6	*Larry (Yogi) Berra*	450.00	225.00	135.00
7	Pete (Pistol Pete) Reiser	40.00	20.00	12.00
8	Phil (Scooter) Rizzuto	200.00	100.00	60.00
9	Walker Cooper	18.00	9.00	5.50
10	Buddy Rosar	18.00	9.00	5.50
11	Johnny Lindell	18.00	9.00	5.50
12	Johnny Sain	25.00	12.50	7.50
13	Willard Marshall	30.00	15.00	9.00
14	Allie Reynolds	30.00	15.00	9.00
15	Eddie Joost	18.00	9.00	5.50
16	Jack Lohrke	30.00	15.00	9.00
17	Enos (Country) Slaughter	80.00	40.00	24.00
18	Warren Spahn	225.00	112.00	70.00
19	Tommy (The Clutch) Henrich	25.00	12.50	7.50
20	Buddy Kerr	30.00	15.00	9.00
21	Ferris Fain	15.00	7.50	4.50
22	Floyd (Bill) Bevins (Bevens)	40.00	20.00	12.00
23	Larry Jansen	18.00	9.00	5.50
24	Emil (Dutch) Leonard	30.00	15.00	9.00
25	Barney McCoskey (McCosky)	18.00	9.00	5.50
26	Frank Shea	40.00	20.00	12.00
27	Sid Gordon	18.00	9.00	5.50
28	Emil (The Antelope) Verban	30.00	15.00	9.00
29	Joe Page	40.00	20.00	12.00
30	"Whitey" Lockman	30.00	15.00	9.00
31	Bill McCahan	18.00	9.00	5.50
32	Bill Rigney	15.00	7.50	4.50
33	Bill (The Bull) Johnson	18.00	9.00	5.50
34	Sheldon (Available) Jones	30.00	15.00	9.00
35	George (Snuffy) Stirnweiss	18.00	9.00	5.50
36	Stan Musial	600.00	275.00	190.00
37	Clint Hartung	25.00	12.50	7.50
38	Al "Red" Schoendienst	100.00	50.00	30.00
39	Augie Galan	25.00	12.50	7.50
40	Marty Marion	50.00	25.00	15.00
41	Rex Barney	25.00	12.50	7.50
42	Ray Poat	25.00	12.50	7.50
43	Bruce Edwards	25.00	12.50	7.50
44	Johnny Wyrostek	25.00	12.50	7.50
45	Hank Sauer	25.00	12.50	7.50
46	Herman Wehmeier	25.00	12.50	7.50
47	Bobby Thomson	50.00	30.00	15.00
48	George "Dave" Koslo	50.00	8.00	5.00

1949 Bowman

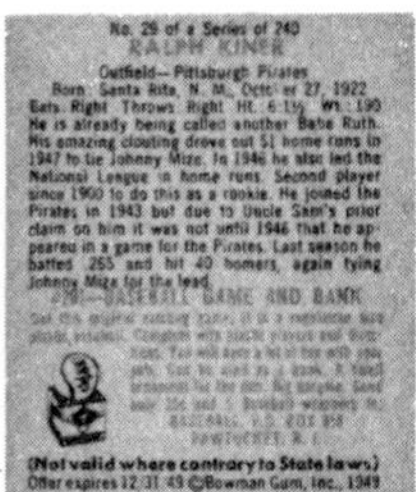

In 1949, Bowman increased the size of its issue to 240 numbered cards. The cards, which measure 2-1/16" by 2-1/2", are black and white photos overprinted with various pastel colors. Beginning with card #109 in the set, Bowman inserted the player's names on the card fronts. Twelve cards (#'s 4, 78, 83, 85, 88, 98, 109, 124, 127, 132 and 143), which were produced in the first four series of printings, were reprinted in the seventh series with either a card front or back modification. These variations are noted in the checklist that follows. Card #'s 1-3 and 5-73 can be found with either white or grey backs. The complete set of value in the following checklist does not include the higher priced variation cards.

		NR MT	EX	VG
Complete Set:		15000.00	7500.00	4500.
Common Player: 1-36		10.00	5.00	3.00
Common Player: 37-73		12.00	6.00	3.50
Common Player: 74-144		10.00	5.00	3.00
Common Player: 145-240		75.00	37.00	22.00
1	Vernon Bickford	75.00	7.50	3.00
2	Carroll "Whitey" Lockman	15.00	5.00	3.00
3	Bob Porterfield	15.00	7.50	4.50
4a	Jerry Priddy (no name on front)	12.00	6.00	3.50
4b	Jerry Priddy (name on front)	40.00	20.00	12.00
5	Hank Sauer	10.00	5.00	3.00
6	Phil Cavarretta	12.00	6.00	3.50
7	Joe Dobson	10.00	5.00	3.00
8	Murry Dickson	10.00	5.00	3.00
9	Ferris Fain	12.00	6.00	3.50
10	Ted Gray	10.00	5.00	3.00
11	Lou Boudreau	50.00	25.00	15.00
12	Cass Michaels	10.00	5.00	3.00
13	Bob Chesnes	10.00	5.00	3.00
14	*Curt Simmons*	25.00	12.50	7.50
15	Ned Garver	10.00	5.00	3.00
16	Al Kozar	10.00	5.00	3.00
17	Earl Torgeson	10.00	5.00	3.00
18	Bobby Thomson	25.00	12.50	7.50
19	*Bobby Brown*	35.00	17.50	10.50
20	Gene Hermanski	12.00	6.00	3.50
21	Frank Baumholtz	10.00	5.00	3.00
22	Harry "P-Nuts" Lowrey	10.00	5.00	3.00
23	Bobby Doerr	75.00	37.00	22.00
24	Stan Musial	450.00	225.00	135.00
25	Carl Scheib	10.00	5.00	3.00
26	George Kell	50.00	25.00	15.00
27	Bob Feller	125.00	60.00	40.00
28	Don Kolloway	10.00	5.00	3.00

		NR MT	EX	VG
29	Ralph Kiner	75.00	37.00	22.00
30	Andy Seminick	10.00	5.00	3.00
31	Dick Kokos	10.00	5.00	3.00
32	Eddie Yost	10.00	5.00	3.00
33	Warren Spahn	125.00	60.00	40.00
34	Dave Koslo	10.00	5.00	3.00
35	Vic Raschi	20.00	10.00	6.00
36	Harold "Peewee" Reese	150.00	60.00	38.00
37	John Wyrostek	12.00	6.00	3.50
38	Emil "The Antelope" Verban	12.00	6.00	3.50
39	Bill Goodman	12.00	6.00	3.50
40	George "Red" Munger	12.00	6.00	3.50
41	Lou Brissie	12.00	6.00	3.50
42	Walter "Hoot" Evers	12.00	6.00	3.50
43	Dale Mitchell	12.00	6.00	3.50
44	Dave Philley	12.00	6.00	3.50
45	Wally Westlake	12.00	6.00	3.50
46	*Robin Roberts*	175.00	87.00	50.00
47	Johnny Sain	18.00	9.00	5.50
48	Willard Marshall	12.00	6.00	3.50
49	Frank Shea	18.00	9.00	5.50
50	Jackie Robinson	700.00	350.00	200.00
51	Herman Wehmeier	12.00	6.00	3.50
52	Johnny Schmitz	12.00	6.00	3.50
53	Jack Kramer	12.00	6.00	3.50
54	Marty "Slats" Marion	16.00	8.00	4.75
55	Eddie Joost	12.00	6.00	3.50
56	Pat Mullin	12.00	6.00	3.50
57	Gene Bearden	12.00	6.00	3.50
58	Bob Elliott	12.00	6.00	3.50
59	Jack "Lucky" Lohrke	12.00	6.00	3.50
60	Larry "Yogi" Berra	300.00	150.00	90.00
61	Rex Barney	14.00	7.00	4.25
62	Grady Hatton	12.00	6.00	3.50
63	Andy Pafko	14.00	7.00	4.25
64	Dom "The Little Professor" DiMaggio	25.00	12.50	7.50
65	Enos "Country" Slaughter	75.00	37.00	22.00
66	Elmer Valo	12.00	6.00	3.50
67	Alvin Dark	20.00	10.00	6.00
68	Sheldon "Available" Jones	12.00	6.00	3.50
69	Tommy "The Clutch" Henrich	25.00	12.50	7.50
70	Carl Furillo	50.00	25.00	15.00
71	Vern "Junior" Stephens	12.00	6.00	3.50
72	Tommy Holmes	14.00	7.00	4.25
73	Billy Cox	14.00	7.00	4.25
74	Tom McBride	10.00	5.00	3.00
75	Eddie Mayo	10.00	5.00	3.00
76	Bill Nicholson	10.00	5.00	3.00
77	Ernie (Jumbo and Tiny) Bonham	10.00	5.00	3.00
78a	Sam Zoldak (no name on front)	12.00	6.00	3.50
78b	Sam Zoldak (name on front)	40.00	20.00	12.00
79	Ron Northey	10.00	5.00	3.00
80	Bill McCahan	10.00	5.00	3.00
81	Virgil "Red" Stallcup	10.00	5.00	3.00
82	Joe Page	16.00	8.00	4.75
83a	Bob Scheffing (no name on front)	12.00	6.00	3.50
83b	Bob Scheffing (name on front)	40.00	20.00	12.00
84	*Roy Campanella*	600.00	300.00	175.00
85a	Johnny "Big John" Mize (no name on front)	75.00	37.00	22.00
85b	Johnny "Big John" Mize (name on front)	110.00	50.00	28.00
86	Johnny Pesky	12.00	6.00	3.50
87	Randy Gumpert	10.00	5.00	3.00
88a	Bill Salkeld (no name on front)	12.00	6.00	3.50
88b	Bill Salkeld (name on front)	40.00	20.00	12.00
89	Mizell "Whitey" Platt	10.00	5.00	3.00
90	Gil Coan	10.00	5.00	3.00
91	Dick Wakefield	10.00	5.00	3.00
92	Willie "Puddin-Head" Jones	10.00	5.00	3.00
93	Ed Stevens	10.00	5.00	3.00
94	James "Mickey" Vernon	12.00	6.00	3.50
95	Howie Pollett	10.00	5.00	3.00
96	Taft Wright	10.00	5.00	3.00
97	Danny Litwhiler	10.00	5.00	3.00
98a	Phil Rizzuto (no name on front)	80.00	40.00	24.00
98b	Phil Rizzuto (name on front)	200.00	100.00	60.00
99	Frank Gustine	10.00	5.00	3.00
100	Gil Hodges	175.00	87.00	52.00
101	Sid Gordon	10.00	5.00	3.00
102	Stan Spence	10.00	5.00	3.00
103	Joe Tipton	10.00	5.00	3.00
104	Ed Stanky	12.00	6.00	3.50
105	Bill Kennedy	10.00	5.00	3.00
106	Jake Early	10.00	5.00	3.00
107	Eddie Lake	10.00	5.00	3.00
108	Ken Heintzelman	10.00	5.00	3.00
109a	Ed Fitzgerald (Fitz Gerald) (script name on back)	12.00	6.00	3.50
109b	Ed Fitzgerald (Fitz Gerald) (printed name on back)	40.00	20.00	12.00
110	Early Wynn	90.00	45.00	27.00
111	Al "Red" Schoendienst	75.00	37.00	22.00
112	Sam Chapman	10.00	5.00	3.00
113	Ray Lamanno	10.00	5.00	3.00
114	Allie Reynolds	30.00	15.00	9.00
115	Emil "Dutch" Leonard	10.00	5.00	3.00
116	Joe Hatten	12.00	6.00	3.50
117	Walker Cooper	10.00	5.00	3.00
118	Sam Mele	10.00	5.00	3.00
119	Floyd Baker	10.00	5.00	3.00
120	Cliff Fannin	10.00	5.00	3.00
121	Mark Christman	10.00	5.00	3.00
122	George Vico	10.00	5.00	3.00
123	Johnny Blatnick	10.00	5.00	3.00
124a	Danny Murtaugh (script name on back)	12.00	6.00	3.50
124b	Danny Murtaugh (printed name on back)	40.00	20.00	12.00
125	Ken Keltner	12.00	6.00	3.50
126a	Al Brazle (script name on back)	12.00	6.00	3.50
126b	Al Brazle (printed name on back)	40.00	20.00	12.00
127a	Henry "Heeney" Majeski (script name on back)	12.00	6.00	3.50
127b	Henry "Heeney" Majeski (printed name on back)	40.00	20.00	12.00
128	Johnny Vander Meer	16.00	8.00	4.75
129	Bill "The Bull" Johnson	16.00	8.00	4.75
130	Harry "The Hat" Walker	12.00	6.00	3.50
131	Paul Lehner	10.00	5.00	3.00
132a	Al Evans (script name on back)	12.00	6.00	3.50
132b	Al Evans (printed name on back)	40.00	20.00	12.00
133	Aaron Robinson	10.00	5.00	3.00
134	Hank Borowy	10.00	5.00	3.00
135	Stan Rojek	10.00	5.00	3.00
136	Henry "Hank" Edwards	10.00	5.00	3.00
137	Ted Wilks	10.00	5.00	3.00
138	Warren "Buddy" Rosar	10.00	5.00	3.00
139	Hank "Bow-Wow" Arft	10.00	5.00	3.00
140	Rae Scarborough (Ray)	10.00	5.00	3.00
141	Ulysses "Tony" Lupien	10.00	5.00	3.00
142	Eddie Waitkus	10.00	5.00	3.00
143a	Bob Dillinger (script name on back)	12.00	6.00	3.50
143b	Bob Dillinger (printed name on back)	40.00	20.00	12.00
144	Milton "Mickey" Haefner	10.00	5.00	3.00
145	Sylvester "Blix" Donnelly	75.00	37.00	22.00
146	Myron "Mike" McCormick	55.00	27.00	16.50
147	Elmer "Bert" Singleton	75.00	37.00	22.00
148	Bob Swift	75.00	37.00	22.00
149	Roy Partee	55.00	27.00	16.50
150	Alfred "Allie" Clark	75.00	37.00	22.00
151	Maurice "Mickey" Harris	75.00	37.00	22.00
152	Clarence Maddern	75.00	37.00	22.00
153	Phil Masi	75.00	37.00	22.00
154	Clint Hartung	75.00	37.00	22.00
155	Fermin "Mickey" Guerra	75.00	37.00	22.00
156	Al "Zeke" Zarilla	75.00	37.00	22.00
157	Walt Masterson	75.00	37.00	22.00
158	Harry "The Cat" Brecheen	75.00	37.00	22.00
159	Glen Moulder	75.00	37.00	22.00
160	Jim Blackburn	75.00	37.00	22.00
161	John "Jocko" Thompson	75.00	37.00	22.00
162	Elwin "Preacher" Roe	125.00	56.00	35.00
163	Clyde McCullough	75.00	37.00	22.00
164	Vic Wertz	55.00	27.00	16.50
165	George "Snuffy" Stirnweiss	75.00	37.00	22.00
166	Mike Tresh	75.00	37.00	22.00
167	Boris "Babe" Martin	75.00	37.00	22.00
168	Doyle Lade	75.00	37.00	22.00
169	Jeff Heath	75.00	37.00	22.00
170	Bill Rigney	55.00	27.00	16.50
171	Dick Fowler	75.00	37.00	22.00
172	Eddie Pellagrini	75.00	37.00	22.00
173	Eddie Stewart	75.00	37.00	22.00
174	Terry Moore	55.00	27.00	16.50
175	Luke Appling	100.00	45.00	27.00
176	Ken Raffensberger	75.00	37.00	22.00
177	Stan Lopata	75.00	37.00	22.00
178	Tommy Brown	55.00	27.00	16.50
179	Hugh Casey	55.00	27.00	16.50
180	Connie Berry	75.00	37.00	22.00
181	Gus Niarhos	75.00	37.00	22.00
182	Hal Peck	75.00	37.00	22.00
183	Lou Stringer	75.00	37.00	22.00
184	Bob Chipman	75.00	37.00	22.00
185	Pete Reiser	55.00	27.00	16.50
186	John "Buddy" Kerr	75.00	37.00	22.00
187	Phil Marchildon	75.00	37.00	22.00
188	Karl Drews	75.00	37.00	22.00
189	Earl Wooten	75.00	37.00	22.00
190	Jim Hearn	75.00	37.00	22.00
191	Joe Haynes	75.00	37.00	22.00
192	Harry Gumbert	75.00	37.00	22.00
193	Ken Trinkle	75.00	37.00	22.00
194	Ralph Branca	100.00	45.00	27.00
195	Eddie Bockman	75.00	37.00	22.00
196	Fred Hutchinson	55.00	27.00	16.50
197	Johnny Lindell	75.00	37.00	22.00
198	Steve Gromek	75.00	37.00	22.00
199	Cecil "Tex" Hughson	75.00	37.00	22.00
200	Jess Dobernic	75.00	37.00	22.00
201	Sibby Sisti	75.00	37.00	22.00
202	Larry Jansen	75.00	37.00	22.00
203	Barney McCosky	75.00	37.00	22.00
204	Bob Savage	75.00	37.00	22.00
205	Dick Sisler	75.00	37.00	22.00
206	Bruce Edwards	55.00	27.00	16.50
207	Johnny "Hippity" Hopp	75.00	37.00	22.00
208	Paul "Dizzy" Trout	55.00	27.00	16.50
209	Charlie "King Kong" Keller	90.00	45.00	27.00
210	Joe "Flash" Gordon	55.00	27.00	16.50
211	Dave "Boo" Ferris	75.00	37.00	22.00
212	Ralph Hamner	75.00	37.00	22.00
213	Charles "Red" Barrett	75.00	37.00	22.00
214	*Richie Ashburn*	500.00	250.00	150.00
215	Kirby Higbe	75.00	37.00	22.00
216	Lynwood "Schoolboy" Rowe	75.00	37.00	22.00
217	Marino Pieretti	75.00	37.00	22.00
218	Dick Kryhoski	75.00	37.00	22.00
219	Virgil "Fire" Trucks	55.00	27.00	16.50
220	Johnny McCarthy	75.00	37.00	22.00
221	Bob Muncrief	75.00	37.00	22.00
222	Alex Kellner	75.00	37.00	22.00
223	Bob Hoffman (Hofman)	75.00	37.00	22.00
224	*Leroy "Satchel" Paige*	1100.00	440.00	275.00
225	*Gerry Coleman*	90.00	45.00	27.00
226	Edwin "Duke" Snider	900.00	360.00	225.00
227	Fritz Ostermueller	75.00	37.00	22.00
228	Jackie Mayo	75.00	37.00	22.00
229	Ed Lopat	125.00	60.00	40.00
230	Augie Galan	75.00	37.00	22.00
231	Earl Johnson	75.00	37.00	22.00
232	George McQuinn	75.00	37.00	22.00
233	*Larry Doby*	125.00	56.00	35.00
234	Truett "Rip" Sewell	55.00	27.00	16.50
235	Jim Russell	75.00	37.00	22.00
236	Fred Sanford	75.00	37.00	22.00
237	Monte Kennedy	75.00	37.00	22.00
238	Bob Lemon	225.00	112.00	67.00
239	Frank McCormick	75.00	37.00	22.00
240	Norman "Babe" Young (photo actually Bobby Young)	100.00	45.00	27.00

1949 Bowman

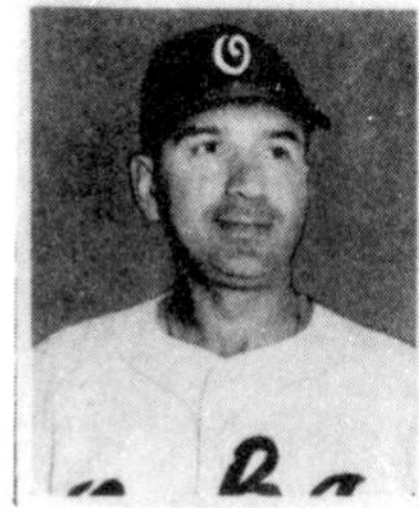

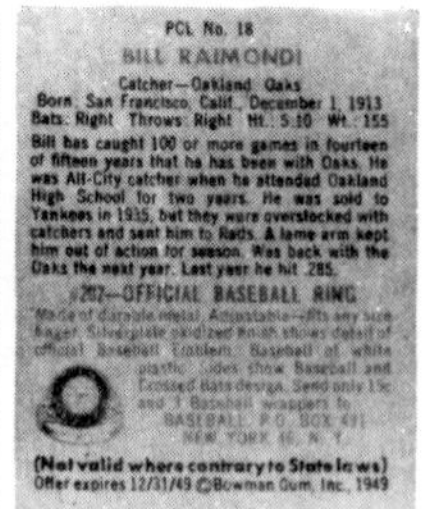

One of the scarcest issues of the post-war period, the 1949 Bowman PCL set was issued only on the West Coast. Like the 1949 Bowman regular issue, the cards contain black and white photos overprinted with various pastel colors. Thirty-six cards, which measure 2-1/16" by 2-1/2", make up the set. It is believed that the cards may have been issued only in sheets and not sold in gum packs.

		NR MT	EX	VG
Complete Set:		6000.00	3000.00	1750.
Common Player:		150.00	75.00	45.00
1	Lee Anthony	150.00	75.00	45.00
2	George Metkovich	150.00	75.00	45.00
3	Ralph Hodgin	150.00	75.00	45.00
4	George Woods	150.00	75.00	45.00
5	Xavier Rescigno	150.00	75.00	45.00
6	Mickey Grasso	150.00	75.00	45.00
7	Johnny Rucker	150.00	75.00	45.00
8	Jack Brewer	150.00	75.00	45.00
9	Dom D'Allessandro	150.00	75.00	45.00
10	Charlie Gassaway	150.00	75.00	45.00
11	Tony Freitas	150.00	75.00	45.00
12	Gordon Maltzberger	150.00	75.00	45.00
13	John Jensen	150.00	75.00	45.00
14	Joyner White	150.00	75.00	45.00
15	Harvey Storey	150.00	75.00	45.00
16	Dick Lajeski	150.00	75.00	45.00
17	Albie Glossop	150.00	75.00	45.00
18	Bill Raimondi	150.00	75.00	45.00
19	Ken Holcombe	150.00	75.00	45.00
20	Don Ross	150.00	75.00	45.00
21	Pete Coscarart	150.00	75.00	45.00
22	Tony York	150.00	75.00	45.00
23	Jake Mooty	150.00	75.00	45.00
24	Charles Adams	150.00	75.00	45.00
25	Les Scarsella	150.00	75.00	45.00
26	Joe Marty	150.00	75.00	45.00
27	Frank Kelleher	150.00	75.00	45.00
28	Lee Handley	150.00	75.00	45.00
29	Herman Besse	150.00	75.00	45.00
30	John Lazor	150.00	75.00	45.00
31	Eddie Malone	150.00	75.00	45.00
32	Maurice Van Robays	150.00	75.00	45.00
33	Jim Tabor	150.00	75.00	45.00
34	Gene Handley	150.00	75.00	45.00
35	Tom Seats	150.00	75.00	45.00
36	Ora Burnett	150.00	75.00	45.00

1950 Bowman

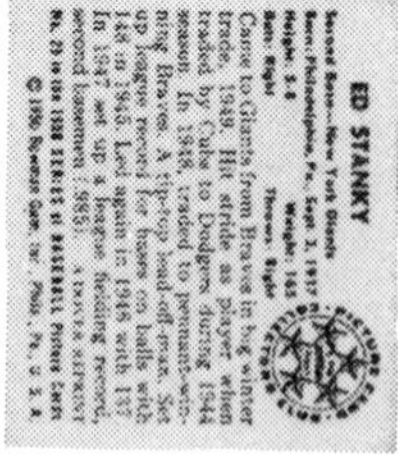

The quality of the 1950 Bowman issue showed a marked improvement over the company's previous efforts. The cards are beautiful color art reproduc- tions of actual photographs and measure 2-1/16" by 2-1/2" in size. The card backs include the same type of information as found in the previous year's issue but are designed in a horizontal format. Cards found in the first two series of the set (#'s 1-72) are the scarcest in the issue. The backs of the final 72 cards in the set (#'s 181-252) can be found with or without the copyright line at the bottom of the card, the "without" version being the less common.

	NR MT	EX	VG
Complete Set:	8000.00	4000.00	2500.

		NR MT	EX	VG
Common Player: 1-72		45.00	22.00	13.50
Common Player: 73-252		15.00	7.50	4.50
1	Mel Parnell	225.00	25.00	8.00
2	Vern Stephens	40.00	20.00	12.50
3	Dom DiMaggio	50.00	25.00	15.00
4	Gus Zernial	45.00	22.00	13.50
5	Bob Kuzava	45.00	22.00	13.50
6	Bob Feller	150.00	75.00	45.00
7	Jim Hegan	45.00	22.00	13.50
8	George Kell	70.00	35.00	21.00
9	Vic Wertz	45.00	22.00	13.50
10	Tommy Henrich	40.00	20.00	12.00
11	Phil Rizzuto	125.00	60.00	35.00
12	Joe Page	30.00	15.00	9.00
13	Ferris Fain	45.00	22.00	13.50
14	Alex Kellner	45.00	22.00	13.50
15	Al Kozar	45.00	22.00	13.50
16	*Roy Sievers*	30.00	15.00	9.00
17	Sid Hudson	45.00	22.00	13.50
18	Eddie Robinson	45.00	22.00	13.50
19	Warren Spahn	150.00	75.00	45.00
20	Bob Elliott	45.00	22.00	13.50
21	Harold Reese	150.00	60.00	38.00
22	Jackie Robinson	600.00	300.00	175.00
23	*Don Newcombe*	80.00	40.00	24.00
24	Johnny Schmitz	45.00	22.00	13.50
25	Hank Sauer	45.00	22.00	13.50
26	Grady Hatton	45.00	22.00	13.50
27	Herman Wehmeier	45.00	22.00	13.50
28	Bobby Thomson	50.00	25.00	15.00
29	Ed Stanky	45.00	22.00	13.50
30	Eddie Waitkus	45.00	22.00	13.50
31	Del Ennis	45.00	22.00	13.50
32	Robin Roberts	100.00	50.00	30.00
33	Ralph Kiner	90.00	45.00	27.00
34	Murry Dickson	45.00	22.00	13.50
35	Enos Slaughter	80.00	40.00	25.00
36	Eddie Kazak	45.00	22.00	13.50
37	Luke Appling	50.00	25.00	15.00
38	Bill Wight	45.00	22.00	13.50
39	Larry Doby	50.00	25.00	15.00
40	Bob Lemon	50.00	25.00	15.00
41	Walter "Hoot" Evers	45.00	22.00	13.50
42	Art Houtteman	45.00	22.00	13.50
43	Bobby Doerr	50.00	25.00	15.00
44	Joe Dobson	45.00	22.00	13.50
45	Al "Zeke" Zarilla	45.00	22.00	13.50
46	Larry "Yogi" Berra	350.00	175.00	100.00
47	Jerry Coleman	35.00	17.50	10.50
48	Leland "Lou" Brissie	45.00	22.00	13.50
49	Elmer Valo	45.00	22.00	13.50
50	Dick Kokos	45.00	22.00	13.50
51	Ned Garver	45.00	22.00	13.50
52	Sam Mele	45.00	22.00	13.50
53	Clyde Vollmer	45.00	22.00	13.50
54	Gil Coan	45.00	22.00	13.50
55	John "Buddy" Kerr	45.00	22.00	13.50
56	*Del Crandell (Crandall)*	45.00	23.00	13.50
57	Vernon Bickford	45.00	22.00	13.50
58	Carl Furillo	45.00	23.00	13.50
59	Ralph Branca	45.00	23.00	13.50
60	Andy Pafko	22.00	11.00	6.50
61	Bob Rush	45.00	22.00	13.50
62	Ted Kluszewski	50.00	25.00	15.00
63	Ewell Blackwell	22.00	11.00	6.50
64	Alvin Dark	45.00	23.00	13.50
65	Dave Koslo	45.00	22.00	13.50
66	Larry Jansen	45.00	22.00	13.50
67	Willie Jones	45.00	22.00	13.50
68	Curt Simmons	45.00	22.00	13.50
69	Wally Westlake	45.00	22.00	13.50
70	Bob Chesnes	45.00	22.00	13.50
71	Al Schoendienst	75.00	38.00	23.00
72	Howie Pollet	45.00	22.00	13.50
73	Willard Marshall	15.00	7.50	4.50
74	*Johnny Antonelli*	15.00	7.50	4.50
75	Roy Campanella	250.00	100.00	63.00
76	Rex Barney	12.00	6.00	3.50
77	Edwin "Duke" Snider	225.00	100.00	60.00
78	Mickey Owen	15.00	7.50	4.50
79	Johnny Vander Meer	12.00	6.00	3.50
80	Howard Fox	15.00	7.50	4.50
81	Ron Northey	15.00	7.50	4.50
82	Carroll Lockman	15.00	7.50	4.50
83	Sheldon Jones	15.00	7.50	4.50
84	Richie Ashburn	75.00	38.00	23.00
85	Ken Heintzelman	15.00	7.50	4.50
86	Stan Rojek	15.00	7.50	4.50
87	Bill Werle	15.00	7.50	4.50
88	Marty Marion	12.00	6.00	3.50
89	George Munger	15.00	7.50	4.50
90	Harry Brecheen	12.00	6.00	3.50
91	Cass Michaels	15.00	7.50	4.50
92	Hank Majeski	15.00	7.50	4.50
93	Gene Bearden	15.00	7.50	4.50
94	Lou Boudreau	40.00	20.00	12.00
95	Aaron Robinson	15.00	7.50	4.50
96	Virgil "Fire" Trucks	12.00	6.00	3.50
97	Maurice McDermott	15.00	7.50	4.50
98	Ted Williams	550.00	230.00	144.00
99	Billy Goodman	15.00	7.50	4.50
100	Vic Raschi	20.00	10.00	6.00
101	Bobby Brown	20.00	10.00	6.00
102	Billy Johnson	15.00	7.50	4.50
103	Eddie Joost	15.00	7.50	4.50
104	Sam Chapman	15.00	7.50	4.50
105	Bob Dillinger	15.00	7.50	4.50
106	Cliff Fannin	15.00	7.50	4.50
107	Sam Dente	15.00	7.50	4.50
108	Rae Scarborough (Ray)	15.00	7.50	4.50
109	Sid Gordon	15.00	7.50	4.50
110	Tommy Holmes	12.00	6.00	3.50
111	Walker Cooper	15.00	7.50	4.50
112	Gil Hodges	80.00	40.00	24.00
113	Gene Hermanski	12.00	6.00	3.50
114	Wayne Terwilliger	15.00	7.50	4.50
115	Roy Smalley	15.00	7.50	4.50
116	Virgil "Red" Stallcup	15.00	7.50	4.50
117	Bill Rigney	12.00	6.00	3.50
118	Clint Hartung	15.00	7.50	4.50
119	Dick Sisler	15.00	7.50	4.50
120	John Thompson	15.00	7.50	4.50
121	Andy Seminick	15.00	7.50	4.50
122	Johnny Hopp	15.00	7.50	4.50
123	Dino Restelli	15.00	7.50	4.50
124	Clyde McCullough	15.00	7.50	4.50
125	Del Rice	15.00	7.50	4.50
126	Al Brazle	15.00	7.50	4.50
127	Dave Philley	15.00	7.50	4.50
128	Phil Masi	15.00	7.50	4.50
129	Joe "Flash" Gordon	12.00	6.00	3.50
130	Dale Mitchell	15.00	7.50	4.50
131	Steve Gromek	15.00	7.50	4.50
132	James Vernon	12.00	6.00	3.50
133	Don Kolloway	15.00	7.50	4.50
134	Paul "Dizzy" Trout	12.00	6.00	3.50
135	Pat Mullin	15.00	7.50	4.50
136	Warren Rosar	15.00	7.50	4.50
137	Johnny Pesky	12.00	6.00	3.50
138	Allie Reynolds	45.00	22.00	13.50
139	Johnny Mize	60.00	30.00	18.00
140	Pete Suder	15.00	7.50	4.50
141	Joe Coleman	15.00	7.50	4.50
142	*Sherman Lollar*	12.00	6.00	3.50
143	Eddie Stewart	15.00	7.50	4.50
144	Al Evans	15.00	7.50	4.50
145	Jack Graham	15.00	7.50	4.50
146	Floyd Baker	15.00	7.50	4.50
147	*Mike Garcia*	12.00	6.00	3.50
148	Early Wynn	60.00	30.00	18.00
149	Bob Swift	15.00	7.50	4.50
150	George Vico	15.00	7.50	4.50
151	Fred Hutchinson	12.00	6.00	3.50
152	Ellis Kinder	15.00	7.50	4.50
153	Walt Masterson	15.00	7.50	4.50
154	Gus Niarhos	15.00	7.50	4.50
155	Frank "Spec" Shea	15.00	7.50	4.50
156	Fred Sanford	15.00	7.50	4.50
157	Mike Guerra	15.00	7.50	4.50
158	Paul Lehner	15.00	7.50	4.50
159	Joe Tipton	15.00	7.50	4.50
160	Mickey Harris	15.00	7.50	4.50
161	Sherry Robertson	15.00	7.50	4.50
162	Eddie Yost	15.00	7.50	4.50
163	Earl Torgeson	15.00	7.50	4.50
164	Sibby Sisti	15.00	7.50	4.50
165	Bruce Edwards	12.00	6.00	3.50
166	Joe Hatten	12.00	6.00	3.50
167	Elwin Roe	45.00	22.00	13.50
168	Bob Scheffing	15.00	7.50	4.50
169	Hank Edwards	15.00	7.50	4.50
170	Emil Leonard	15.00	7.50	4.50
171	Harry Gumbert	15.00	7.50	4.50
172	Harry Lowrey	15.00	7.50	4.50
173	Lloyd Merriman	15.00	7.50	4.50
174	Henry Thompson	15.00	7.50	4.50
175	Monte Kennedy	15.00	7.50	4.50
176	Sylvester Donnelly	15.00	7.50	4.50
177	Hank Borowy	15.00	7.50	4.50
178	Eddy Fitzgerald (Fitz Gerald)	15.00	7.50	4.50
179	Charles Diering	15.00	7.50	4.50
180	Harry Walker	12.00	6.00	3.50
181	Marino Pieretti	15.00	7.50	4.50
182	Sam Zoldak	15.00	7.50	4.50
183	Mickey Haefner	15.00	7.50	4.50
184	Randy Gumpert	15.00	7.50	4.50
185	Howie Judson	15.00	7.50	4.50
186	Ken Keltner	12.00	6.00	3.50
187	Lou Stringer	15.00	7.50	4.50
188	Earl Johnson	15.00	7.50	4.50
189	Owen Friend	15.00	7.50	4.50
190	Ken Wood	15.00	7.50	4.50
191	Dick Starr	15.00	7.50	4.50
192	Bob Chipman	15.00	7.50	4.50
193	Harold "Pete" Reiser	12.00	6.00	3.50
194	Billy Cox	15.00	7.50	4.50
195	Phil Cavaretta (Cavarretta)	12.00	6.00	3.50
196	Doyle Lade	15.00	7.50	4.50
197	Johnny Wyrostek	15.00	7.50	4.50
198	Danny Litwhiler	15.00	7.50	4.50
199	Jack Kramer	15.00	7.50	4.50
200	Kirby Higbe	15.00	7.50	4.50
201	Pete Castiglione	15.00	7.50	4.50
202	Cliff Chambers	15.00	7.50	4.50
203	Danny Murtaugh	12.00	6.00	3.50
204	Granville Hamner	15.00	7.50	4.50
205	Mike Goliat	15.00	7.50	4.50
206	Stan Lopata	15.00	7.50	4.50
207	Max Lanier	15.00	7.50	4.50
208	Jim Hearn	15.00	7.50	4.50
209	Johnny Lindell	15.00	7.50	4.50
210	Ted Gray	15.00	7.50	4.50
211	Charlie Keller	15.00	7.50	4.50
212	Gerry Priddy	15.00	7.50	4.50
213	Carl Scheib	15.00	7.50	4.50
214	Dick Fowler	15.00	7.50	4.50
215	Ed Lopat	20.00	10.00	6.00
216	Bob Porterfield	15.00	7.50	4.50
217	Casey Stengel	110.00	55.00	30.00
218	Cliff Mapes	15.00	7.50	4.50
219	*Hank Bauer*	60.00	30.00	17.50
220	Leo Durocher	50.00	25.00	15.00
221	Don Mueller	15.00	7.50	4.50
222	Bobby Morgan	12.00	6.00	3.50
223	Jimmy Russell	12.00	6.00	3.50
224	Jack Banta	12.00	6.00	3.50
225	Eddie Sawyer	15.00	7.50	4.50
226	Jim Konstanty	12.00	6.00	3.50
227	Bob Miller	15.00	7.50	4.50
228	Bill Nicholson	15.00	7.50	4.50
229	Frank Frisch	40.00	20.00	12.00
230	Bill Serena	15.00	7.50	4.50
231	Preston Ward	15.00	7.50	4.50
232	*Al "Flip" Rosen*	40.00	20.00	12.00
233	Allie Clark	15.00	7.50	4.50
234	*Bobby Shantz*	20.00	10.00	6.00
235	Harold Gilbert	15.00	7.50	4.50
236	Bob Cain	15.00	7.50	4.50
237	Bill Salkeld	15.00	7.50	4.50
238	Vernal Jones	15.00	7.50	4.50
239	Bill Howerton	15.00	7.50	4.50
240	Eddie Lake	15.00	7.50	4.50
241	Neil Berry	15.00	7.50	4.50
242	Dick Kryhoski	15.00	7.50	4.50
243	Johnny Groth	15.00	7.50	4.50
244	Dale Coogan	15.00	7.50	4.50
245	Al Papai	15.00	7.50	4.50
246	*Walt Dropo*	12.00	6.00	3.50
247	Irv Noren	15.00	7.50	4.50
248	*Sam Jethroe*	12.00	6.00	3.50
249	George Stirnweiss	15.00	7.50	4.50
250	Ray Coleman	15.00	7.50	4.50
251	John Lester Moss	15.00	5.00	3.00
252	Billy DeMars	70.00	7.50	3.00

1951 Bowman

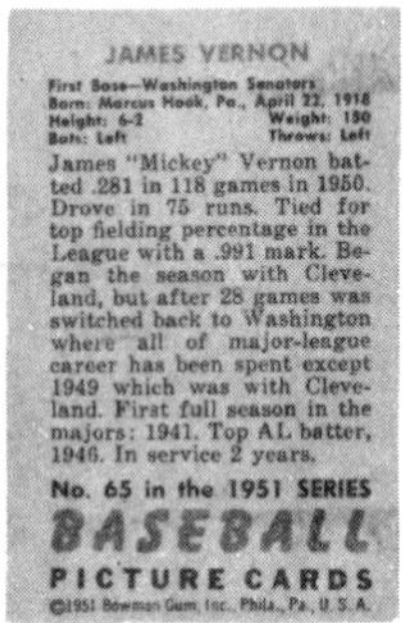
JAMES VERNON

First Base—Washington Senators
Born: Marcus Hook, Pa., April 22, 1918
Height: 6-2 Weight: 180
Bats: Left Throws: Left

James "Mickey" Vernon batted .281 in 118 games in 1950. Drove in 75 runs. Tied for top fielding percentage in the League with a .991 mark. Began the season with Cleveland, but after 28 games was switched back to Washington where all of major-league career has been spent except 1949 which was with Cleveland. First full season in the majors: 1941. Top AL batter, 1946. In service 2 years.

No. 65 in the 1951 SERIES
BASEBALL
PICTURE CARDS
©1951 Bowman Gum, Inc., Phila., Pa., U.S.A.

In 1951, Bowman increased the numbers of cards in its set for the third consecutive year when it issued 324 cards. The cards are, like 1950, color art reproductions of actual photographs but now measured 2-1/16" by 3-1/8" in size. The player's name is situated in a small, black box on the card front. Several of the card fronts are enlargements of the 1950 version. The high-numbered series of the set (#'s 253-324), which includes the rookie cards of Mantle and Mays, are the scarcest of the issue.

		NR MT	EX	VG
Complete Set:		17000.00	8500.00	4300.
Common Player: 1-36		12.00	6.00	3.50
Common Player: 37-252		10.00	5.00	3.00
Common Player: 253-324		40.00	20.00	12.00
1	*Ed Ford*	1500.00	500.00	300.00
2	Larry "Yogi" Berra	450.00	225.00	135.00
3	Robin Roberts	70.00	35.00	20.00
4	Del Ennis	12.00	6.00	3.50
5	Dale Mitchell	12.00	6.00	3.50
6	Don Newcombe	30.00	15.00	9.00
7	Gil Hodges	65.00	33.00	20.00
8	Paul Lehner	12.00	6.00	3.50
9	Sam Chapman	12.00	6.00	3.50
10	Al "Red" Schoendienst	60.00	30.00	18.00
11	George "Red" Munger	12.00	6.00	3.50
12	Hank Majeski	12.00	6.00	3.50
13	Ed Stanky	15.00	7.50	4.50
14	Alvin Dark	18.00	9.00	5.50
15	Johnny Pesky	15.00	7.50	4.50
16	Maurice McDermott	12.00	6.00	3.50
17	Pete Castiglione	12.00	6.00	3.50
18	Gil Coan	12.00	6.00	3.50
19	Sid Gordon	12.00	6.00	3.50
20	Del Crandall	15.00	7.50	4.50
21	George "Snuffy" Stirnweiss	12.00	6.00	3.50
22	Hank Sauer	12.00	6.00	3.50
23	Walter "Hoot" Evers	12.00	6.00	3.50
24	Ewell Blackwell	15.00	7.50	4.50
25	Vic Raschi	20.00	10.00	6.00
26	Phil Rizzuto	75.00	38.00	23.00
27	Jim Konstanty	12.00	6.00	3.50
28	Eddie Waitkus	12.00	6.00	3.50
29	Allie Clark	12.00	6.00	3.50
30	Bob Feller	100.00	50.00	30.00
31	Roy Campanella	275.00	137.00	82.00
32	Duke Snider	225.00	100.00	60.00
33	Bob Hooper	12.00	6.00	3.50
34	Marty Marion	15.00	7.50	4.50
35	Al Zarilla	12.00	6.00	3.50
36	Joe Dobson	12.00	6.00	3.50
37	Whitey Lockman	10.00	5.00	3.00
38	Al Evans	10.00	5.00	3.00
39	Ray Scarborough	10.00	5.00	3.00
40	*Dave "Gus" Bell*	12.00	6.00	3.50
41	Eddie Yost	12.00	6.00	3.50
42	Vern Bickford	10.00	5.00	3.00
43	Billy DeMars	10.00	5.00	3.00
44	Roy Smalley	10.00	5.00	3.00
45	Art Houtteman	10.00	5.00	3.00
46	George Kell	50.00	25.00	15.00
47	Grady Hatton	10.00	5.00	3.00
48	Ken Raffensberger	10.00	5.00	3.00
49	Jerry Coleman	15.00	7.50	4.50
50	Johnny Mize	50.00	25.00	15.00
51	Andy Seminick	10.00	5.00	3.00
52	Dick Sisler	10.00	5.00	3.00
53	Bob Lemon	40.00	20.00	12.00
54	Ray Boone	12.00	6.00	3.50
55	Gene Hermanski	12.00	6.00	3.50
56	Ralph Branca	30.00	15.00	9.00
57	Alex Kellner	10.00	5.00	3.00
58	Enos Slaughter	50.00	25.00	15.00
59	Randy Gumpert	10.00	5.00	3.00
60	Alfonso Carrasquel	10.00	5.00	3.00
61	Jim Hearn	10.00	5.00	3.00
62	Lou Boudreau	50.00	25.00	15.00
63	Bob Dillinger	10.00	5.00	3.00

		NR MT	EX	VG
64	Bill Werle	10.00	5.00	3.00
65	Mickey Vernon	12.00	6.00	3.50
66	Bob Elliott	10.00	5.00	3.00
67	Roy Sievers	12.00	6.00	3.50
68	Dick Kokos	10.00	5.00	3.00
69	Johnny Schmitz	10.00	5.00	3.00
70	Ron Northey	10.00	5.00	3.00
71	Jerry Priddy	10.00	5.00	3.00
72	Lloyd Merriman	10.00	5.00	3.00
73	Tommy Byrne	15.00	7.50	4.50
74	Billy Johnson	15.00	7.50	4.50
75	Russ Meyer	10.00	5.00	3.00
76	Stan Lopata	10.00	5.00	3.00
77	Mike Goliat	10.00	5.00	3.00
78	Early Wynn	50.00	25.00	15.00
79	Jim Hegan	10.00	5.00	3.00
80	Harold "Peewee" Reese	125.00	56.00	35.00
81	Carl Furillo	25.00	12.50	7.50
82	Joe Tipton	10.00	5.00	3.00
83	Carl Scheib	10.00	5.00	3.00
84	Barney McCosky	10.00	5.00	3.00
85	Eddie Kazak	10.00	5.00	3.00
86	Harry Brecheen	12.00	6.00	3.50
87	Floyd Baker	10.00	5.00	3.00
88	Eddie Robinson	10.00	5.00	3.00
89	Henry Thompson	10.00	5.00	3.00
90	Dave Koslo	10.00	5.00	3.00
91	Clyde Vollmer	10.00	5.00	3.00
92	Vern "Junior" Stephens	12.00	6.00	3.50
93	Danny O'Connell	10.00	5.00	3.00
94	Clyde McCullough	10.00	5.00	3.00
95	Sherry Robertson	10.00	5.00	3.00
96	Sandalio Consuegra	10.00	5.00	3.00
97	Bob Kuzava	10.00	5.00	3.00
98	Willard Marshall	10.00	5.00	3.00
99	Earl Torgeson	10.00	5.00	3.00
100	Sherman Lollar	12.00	6.00	3.50
101	Owen Friend	10.00	5.00	3.00
102	Emil "Dutch" Leonard	10.00	5.00	3.00
103	Andy Pafko	12.00	6.00	3.50
104	Virgil "Fire" Trucks	12.00	6.00	3.50
105	Don Kolloway	10.00	5.00	3.00
106	Pat Mullin	10.00	5.00	3.00
107	Johnny Wyrostek	10.00	5.00	3.00
108	Virgil Stallcup	10.00	5.00	3.00
109	Allie Reynolds	25.00	12.50	7.50
110	Bobby Brown	25.00	12.50	7.50
111	Curt Simmons	12.00	6.00	3.50
112	Willie Jones	10.00	5.00	3.00
113	Bill "Swish" Nicholson	10.00	5.00	3.00
114	Sam Zoldak	10.00	5.00	3.00
115	Steve Gromek	10.00	5.00	3.00
116	Bruce Edwards	12.00	6.00	3.50
117	Eddie Miksis	12.00	6.00	3.50
118	Preacher Roe	25.00	12.50	7.50
119	Eddie Joost	10.00	5.00	3.00
120	Joe Coleman	10.00	5.00	3.00
121	Gerry Staley	10.00	5.00	3.00
122	Joe Garagiola	125.00	62.00	37.00
123	Howie Judson	10.00	5.00	3.00
124	Gus Niarhos	10.00	5.00	3.00
125	Bill Rigney	12.00	6.00	3.50
126	Bobby Thomson	25.00	12.50	7.50
127	Sal Maglie	40.00	20.00	12.00
128	Ellis Kinder	10.00	5.00	3.00
129	Matt Batts	10.00	5.00	3.00
130	Tom Saffell	10.00	5.00	3.00
131	Cliff Chambers	10.00	5.00	3.00
132	Cass Michaels	10.00	5.00	3.00
133	Sam Dente	10.00	5.00	3.00
134	Warren Spahn	90.00	45.00	27.00
135	Walker Cooper	10.00	5.00	3.00
136	Ray Coleman	10.00	5.00	3.00
137	Dick Starr	10.00	5.00	3.00
138	Phil Cavarretta	12.00	6.00	3.50
139	Doyle Lade	10.00	5.00	3.00
140	Eddie Lake	10.00	5.00	3.00
141	Fred Hutchinson	12.00	6.00	3.50
142	Aaron Robinson	10.00	5.00	3.00
143	Ted Kluszewski	25.00	12.50	7.50
144	Herman Wehmeier	10.00	5.00	3.00
145	Fred Sanford	15.00	7.50	4.50
146	Johnny Hopp	15.00	7.50	4.50
147	Ken Heintzelman	10.00	5.00	3.00
148	Granny Hamner	10.00	5.00	3.00
149	Emory "Bubba" Church	10.00	5.00	3.00
150	Mike Garcia	12.00	6.00	3.50
151	Larry Doby	20.00	10.00	6.00
152	Cal Abrams	12.00	6.00	3.50
153	Rex Barney	12.00	6.00	3.50
154	Pete Suder	10.00	5.00	3.00
155	Lou Brissie	10.00	5.00	3.00
156	Del Rice	10.00	5.00	3.00
157	Al Brazle	10.00	5.00	3.00
158	Chuck Diering	10.00	5.00	3.00
159	Eddie Stewart	10.00	5.00	3.00
160	Phil Masi	10.00	5.00	3.00
161	Wes Westrum	12.00	6.00	3.50
162	Larry Jansen	10.00	5.00	3.00
163	Monte Kennedy	10.00	5.00	3.00
164	Bill Wight	10.00	5.00	3.00
165	Ted Williams	500.00	250.00	150.00
166	Stan Rojek	10.00	5.00	3.00
167	Murry Dickson	10.00	5.00	3.00
168	Sam Mele	10.00	5.00	3.00
169	Sid Hudson	10.00	5.00	3.00
170	Sibby Sisti	10.00	5.00	3.00
171	Buddy Kerr	10.00	5.00	3.00
172	Ned Garver	10.00	5.00	3.00
173	Hank Arft	10.00	5.00	3.00
174	Mickey Owen	10.00	5.00	3.00
175	Wayne Terwilliger	10.00	5.00	3.00
176	Vic Wertz	12.00	6.00	3.50
177	Charlie Keller	12.00	6.00	3.50
178	Ted Gray	10.00	5.00	3.00
179	Danny Litwhiler	10.00	5.00	3.00
180	Howie Fox	10.00	5.00	3.00
181	Casey Stengel	80.00	40.00	25.00
182	Tom Ferrick	15.00	7.50	4.50
183	Hank Bauer	25.00	12.50	7.50
184	Eddie Sawyer	10.00	5.00	3.00
185	Jimmy Bloodworth	10.00	5.00	3.00
186	Richie Ashburn	50.00	25.00	15.00
187	Al "Flip" Rosen	20.00	10.00	6.00
188	*Roberto Avila*	12.00	6.00	3.50
189	Erv Palica	12.00	6.00	3.50
190	Joe Hatten	12.00	6.00	3.50
191	Billy Hitchcock	10.00	5.00	3.00
192	Hank Wyse	10.00	5.00	3.00
193	Ted Wilks	10.00	5.00	3.00
194	Harry "Peanuts" Lowrey	10.00	5.00	3.00
195	Paul Richards	15.00	7.50	4.50
196	Bill Pierce	15.00	7.50	4.50
197	Bob Cain	10.00	5.00	3.00
198	*Monte Irvin*	80.00	40.00	25.00
199	Sheldon Jones	10.00	5.00	3.00
200	Jack Kramer	10.00	5.00	3.00
201	Steve O'Neill	10.00	5.00	3.00
202	Mike Guerra	10.00	5.00	3.00
203	*Vernon Law*	15.00	7.50	4.50
204	Vic Lombardi	10.00	5.00	3.00
205	Mickey Grasso	10.00	5.00	3.00
206	Conrado Marrero	10.00	5.00	3.00
207	Billy Southworth	10.00	5.00	3.00
208	Blix Donnelly	10.00	5.00	3.00
209	Ken Wood	10.00	5.00	3.00
210	Les Moss	10.00	5.00	3.00
211	Hal Jeffcoat	10.00	5.00	3.00
212	Bob Rush	10.00	5.00	3.00
213	Neil Berry	10.00	5.00	3.00
214	Bob Swift	10.00	5.00	3.00
215	Kent Peterson	10.00	5.00	3.00
216	Connie Ryan	10.00	5.00	3.00
217	Joe Page	15.00	7.50	4.50
218	Ed Lopat	25.00	12.50	7.50
219	Gene Woodling	25.00	12.50	7.50
220	Bob Miller	10.00	5.00	3.00
221	Dick Whitman	10.00	5.00	3.00
222	Thurman Tucker	10.00	5.00	3.00
223	Johnny Vander Meer	20.00	10.00	6.00
224	Billy Cox	15.00	7.50	4.50
225	Dan Bankhead	15.00	7.50	4.50
226	Jimmy Dykes	15.00	7.50	4.50
227	Bobby Schantz (Shantz)	15.00	7.50	4.50
228	Cloyd Boyer	10.00	5.00	3.00
229	Bill Howerton	10.00	5.00	3.00
230	Max Lanier	10.00	5.00	3.00
231	Luis Aloma	10.00	5.00	3.00
232	Nelson Fox	80.00	40.00	25.00
233	Leo Durocher	50.00	25.00	15.00
234	Clint Hartung	10.00	5.00	3.00
235	Jack "Lucky" Lohrke	10.00	5.00	3.00
236	Warren "Buddy" Rosar	10.00	5.00	3.00
237	Billy Goodman	10.00	5.00	3.00
238	Pete Reiser	15.00	7.50	4.50
239	Bill MacDonald	10.00	5.00	3.00
240	Joe Haynes	10.00	5.00	3.00
241	Irv Noren	10.00	5.00	3.00
242	Sam Jethroe	15.00	7.50	4.50
243	John Antonelli	15.00	7.50	4.50
244	Cliff Fannin	10.00	5.00	3.00
245	John Berardino	15.00	7.50	4.50
246	Bill Serena	10.00	5.00	3.00
247	Bob Ramazotti	10.00	5.00	3.00
248	*Johnny Klippstein*	15.00	7.50	4.50
249	Johnny Groth	10.00	5.00	3.00
250	Hank Borowy	10.00	5.00	3.00
251	Willard Ramsdell	10.00	5.00	3.00
252	Homer "Dixie" Howell	10.00	5.00	3.00
253	*Mickey Mantle*	4500.00	2300.00	1350.
254	*Jackie Jensen*	80.00	40.00	24.00
255	Milo Candini	40.00	20.00	12.00
256	Ken Silvestri	40.00	20.00	12.00
257	Birdie Tebbetts	40.00	20.00	12.00
258	*Luke Easter*	45.00	22.00	13.50
259	Charlie Dressen	45.00	22.00	13.50
260	Carl Erskine	90.00	45.00	27.00
261	Wally Moses	40.00	20.00	12.00
262	Gus Zernial	40.00	20.00	12.00
263	Howie Pollett (Pollet)	40.00	20.00	12.00
264	Don Richmond	40.00	20.00	12.00
265	Steve Bilko	40.00	20.00	12.00
266	Harry Dorish	40.00	20.00	12.00
267	Ken Holcombe	40.00	20.00	12.00
268	Don Mueller	40.00	20.00	12.00
269	Ray Noble	40.00	20.00	12.00
270	Willard Nixon	40.00	20.00	12.00
271	Tommy Wright	40.00	20.00	12.00
272	Billy Meyer	40.00	20.00	12.00
273	Danny Murtaugh	45.00	22.00	13.50
274	George Metkovich	40.00	20.00	12.00
275	Bucky Harris	60.00	30.00	18.00
276	Frank Quinn	40.00	20.00	12.00
277	Roy Hartsfield	40.00	20.00	12.00
278	Norman Roy	40.00	20.00	12.00
279	Jim Delsing	40.00	20.00	12.00
280	Frank Overmire	40.00	20.00	12.00
281	Al Widmar	40.00	20.00	12.00
282	Frank Frisch	60.00	30.00	18.00
283	Walt Dubiel	40.00	20.00	12.00
284	Gene Bearden	40.00	20.00	12.00
285	Johnny Lipon	40.00	20.00	12.00
286	Bob Usher	40.00	20.00	12.00
287	Jim Blackburn	40.00	20.00	12.00
288	Bobby Adams	40.00	20.00	12.00
289	Cliff Mapes	45.00	22.00	13.50
290	Bill Dickey	175.00	70.00	44.00
291	Tommy Henrich	60.00	30.00	18.00
292	Eddie Pellagrini	40.00	20.00	12.00
293	Ken Johnson	40.00	20.00	12.00
294	Jocko Thompson	40.00	20.00	12.00
295	Al Lopez	65.00	33.00	20.00
296	Bob Kennedy	40.00	20.00	12.00
297	Dave Philley	40.00	20.00	12.00
298	Joe Astroth	40.00	20.00	12.00
299	Clyde King	45.00	22.00	13.50
300	Hal Rice	40.00	20.00	12.00
301	Tommy Glaviano	40.00	20.00	12.00
302	Jim Busby	40.00	20.00	12.00
303	Marv Rotblatt	40.00	20.00	12.00
304	Allen Gettel	40.00	20.00	12.00
305	*Willie Mays*	1550.00	575.00	350.00
306	*Jim Piersall*	80.00	40.00	24.00
307	Walt Masterson	40.00	20.00	12.00
308	Ted Beard	40.00	20.00	12.00
309	Mel Queen	40.00	20.00	12.00
310	Erv Dusak	40.00	20.00	12.00
311	Mickey Harris	40.00	20.00	12.00
312	Gene Mauch	50.00	30.00	15.00
313	Ray Mueller	40.00	20.00	12.00
314	Johnny Sain	50.00	25.00	15.00
315	Zack Taylor	40.00	20.00	12.00
316	Duane Pillette	40.00	20.00	12.00
317	*Forrest Burgess*	50.00	25.00	15.00
318	Warren Hacker	40.00	20.00	12.00
319	Red Rolfe	40.00	20.00	12.00
320	Hal White	40.00	20.00	12.00
321	Earl Johnson	40.00	20.00	12.00
322	Luke Sewell	40.00	20.00	12.00
323	*Joe Adcock*	60.00	28.00	16.50
324	Johnny Pramesa	90.00	20.00	12.00

1952 Bowman

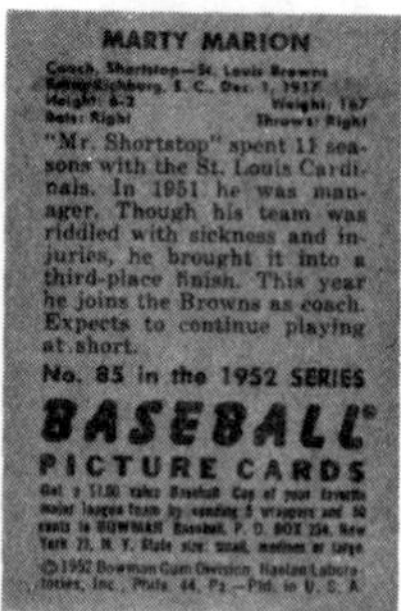

Bowman reverted back to a 252-card set in 1952, but retained the card size (2-1/16" by 3-1/8") employed the preceding year. The cards, which are color art reproductions of actual photographs, feature a facsimile autograph on the fronts. Artwork for 15 cards that were never issued was uncovered several years ago and a set featuring those cards was subsequently made available to the collecting public.

		NR MT	EX	VG
Complete Set:		8000.00	4000.00	2500.
Common Player: 1-36		12.00	6.00	3.50
Common Player: 37-216		10.00	5.00	3.00
Common Player: 217-252		20.00	10.00	6.00
1	Larry "Yogi" Berra	600.00	85.00	38.00
2	Bobby Thomson	30.00	10.00	6.00
3	Fred Hutchinson	14.00	7.00	4.25
4	Robin Roberts	50.00	25.00	15.00
5	*Orestes Minoso*	50.00	25.00	15.00
6	Virgil "Red" Stallcup	12.00	6.00	3.50
7	Mike Garcia	14.00	7.00	4.25
8	Harold "Pee Wee" Reese	150.00	60.00	38.00
9	Vern Stephens	12.00	6.00	3.50
10	Bob Hooper	12.00	6.00	3.50
11	Ralph Kiner	45.00	23.00	13.50
12	Max Surkont	12.00	6.00	3.50
13	Cliff Mapes	12.00	6.00	3.50
14	Cliff Chambers	12.00	6.00	3.50
15	Sam Mele	12.00	6.00	3.50
16	Omar Lown	12.00	6.00	3.50
17	Ed Lopat	25.00	12.50	7.50
18	Don Mueller	12.00	6.00	3.50
19	Bob Cain	12.00	6.00	3.50
20	Willie Jones	12.00	6.00	3.50
21	Nelson Fox	40.00	20.00	12.00
22	Willard Ramsdell	12.00	6.00	3.50
23	Bob Lemon	45.00	23.00	13.50
24	Carl Furillo	20.00	10.00	6.00
25	Maurice McDermott	12.00	6.00	3.50
26	Eddie Joost	12.00	6.00	3.50
27	Joe Garagiola	70.00	35.00	20.00
28	Roy Hartsfield	12.00	6.00	3.50
29	Ned Garver	12.00	6.00	3.50
30	Al "Red" Schoendienst	50.00	30.00	15.00
31	Eddie Yost	12.00	6.00	3.50
32	Eddie Miksis	12.00	6.00	3.50
33	*Gil McDougald*	40.00	20.00	12.00
34	Al Dark	16.00	8.00	4.75
35	Gran Hamner	12.00	6.00	3.50
36	Cass Michaels	12.00	6.00	3.50
37	Vic Raschi	18.00	9.00	5.50
38	Whitey Lockman	10.00	5.00	3.00
39	Vic Wertz	12.00	6.00	3.50
40	Emory Church	10.00	5.00	3.00
41	Chico Carrasquel	10.00	5.00	3.00
42	Johnny Wyrostek	10.00	5.00	3.00
43	Bob Feller	80.00	40.00	25.00
44	Roy Campanella	175.00	70.00	44.00
45	Johnny Pesky	12.00	6.00	3.50
46	Carl Scheib	10.00	5.00	3.00
47	Pete Castiglione	10.00	5.00	3.00
48	Vern Bickford	10.00	5.00	3.00
49	Jim Hearn	10.00	5.00	3.00
50	Gerry Staley	10.00	5.00	3.00
51	Gil Coan	10.00	5.00	3.00
52	Phil Rizzuto	55.00	27.00	16.50
53	Richie Ashburn	40.00	20.00	12.00
54	Billy Pierce	12.00	6.00	3.50
55	Ken Raffensberger	10.00	5.00	3.00
56	Clyde King	12.00	6.00	3.50
57	Clyde Vollmer	10.00	5.00	3.00
58	Hank Majeski	10.00	5.00	3.00
59	Murray Dickson (Murry)	10.00	5.00	3.00
60	Sid Gordon	10.00	5.00	3.00

		NR MT	EX	VG
61	Tommy Byrne	10.00	5.00	3.00
62	Joe Presko	10.00	5.00	3.00
63	Irv Noren	10.00	5.00	3.00
64	Roy Smalley	10.00	5.00	3.00
65	Hank Bauer	20.00	10.00	6.00
66	Sal Maglie	20.00	10.00	6.00
67	Johnny Groth	10.00	5.00	3.00
68	Jim Busby	10.00	5.00	3.00
69	Joe Adcock	12.00	6.00	3.50
70	Carl Erskine	18.00	9.00	5.50
71	Vernon Law	12.00	6.00	3.50
72	Earl Torgeson	10.00	5.00	3.00
73	Jerry Coleman	18.00	9.00	5.50
74	Wes Westrum	12.00	6.00	3.50
75	George Kell	40.00	20.00	12.00
76	Del Ennis	12.00	6.00	3.50
77	Eddie Robinson	10.00	5.00	3.00
78	Lloyd Merriman	10.00	5.00	3.00
79	Lou Brissie	10.00	5.00	3.00
80	Gil Hodges	60.00	30.00	15.00
81	Billy Goodman	10.00	5.00	3.00
82	Gus Zernial	10.00	5.00	3.00
83	Howie Pollet	10.00	5.00	3.00
84	Sam Jethroe	10.00	5.00	3.00
85	Marty Marion	12.00	6.00	3.50
86	Cal Abrams	12.00	6.00	3.50
87	Mickey Vernon	12.00	6.00	3.50
88	Bruce Edwards	10.00	5.00	3.00
89	Billy Hitchcock	10.00	5.00	3.00
90	Larry Jansen	10.00	5.00	3.00
91	Don Kolloway	10.00	5.00	3.00
92	Eddie Waitkus	10.00	5.00	3.00
93	Paul Richards	12.00	6.00	3.50
94	Luke Sewell	10.00	5.00	3.00
95	Luke Easter	12.00	6.00	3.50
96	Ralph Branca	18.00	9.00	5.50
97	Willard Marshall	10.00	5.00	3.00
98	Jimmy Dykes	12.00	6.00	3.50
99	Clyde McCullough	10.00	5.00	3.00
100	Sibby Sisti	10.00	5.00	3.00
101	Mickey Mantle	1400.00	560.00	280.00
102	Peanuts Lowrey	10.00	5.00	3.00
103	Joe Haynes	10.00	5.00	3.00
104	Hal Jeffcoat	10.00	5.00	3.00
105	Bobby Brown	18.00	9.00	5.50
106	Randy Gumpert	10.00	5.00	3.00
107	Del Rice	10.00	5.00	3.00
108	George Metkovich	10.00	5.00	3.00
109	Tom Morgan	15.00	7.50	4.50
110	Max Lanier	10.00	5.00	3.00
111	Walter "Hoot" Evers	10.00	5.00	3.00
112	Forrest "Smokey" Burgess	12.00	6.00	3.50
113	Al Zarilla	10.00	5.00	3.00
114	Frank Hiller	10.00	5.00	3.00
115	Larry Doby	20.00	10.00	6.00
116	Duke Snider	150.00	75.00	45.00
117	Bill Wight	10.00	5.00	3.00
118	Ray Murray	10.00	5.00	3.00
119	Bill Howerton	10.00	5.00	3.00
120	Chet Nichols	10.00	5.00	3.00
121	Al Corwin	10.00	5.00	3.00
122	Billy Johnson	10.00	5.00	3.00
123	Sid Hudson	10.00	5.00	3.00
124	George Tebbetts	10.00	5.00	3.00
125	Howie Fox	10.00	5.00	3.00
126	Phil Cavarretta	12.00	6.00	3.50
127	Dick Sisler	10.00	5.00	3.00
128	Don Newcombe	20.00	10.00	6.00
129	Gus Niarhos	10.00	5.00	3.00
130	Allie Clark	10.00	5.00	3.00
131	Bob Swift	10.00	5.00	3.00
132	Dave Cole	10.00	5.00	3.00
133	Dick Kryhoski	10.00	5.00	3.00
134	Al Brazle	10.00	5.00	3.00
135	Mickey Harris	10.00	5.00	3.00
136	Gene Hermanski	10.00	5.00	3.00
137	Stan Rojek	10.00	5.00	3.00
138	Ted Wilks	10.00	5.00	3.00
139	Jerry Priddy	10.00	5.00	3.00
140	Ray Scarborough	10.00	5.00	3.00
141	Hank Edwards	10.00	5.00	3.00
142	Early Wynn	45.00	23.00	13.50
143	Sandalio Consuegra	10.00	5.00	3.00
144	Joe Hatten	10.00	5.00	3.00
145	Johnny Mize	50.00	30.00	15.00
146	Leo Durocher	40.00	20.00	12.00
147	Marlin Stuart	10.00	5.00	3.00
148	Ken Heintzelman	10.00	5.00	3.00
149	Howie Judson	10.00	5.00	3.00
150	Herman Wehmeier	10.00	5.00	3.00
151	Al "Flip" Rosen	18.00	9.00	5.50
152	Billy Cox	12.00	6.00	3.50
153	Fred Hatfield	10.00	5.00	3.00
154	Ferris Fain	12.00	6.00	3.50
155	Billy Meyer	10.00	5.00	3.00
156	Warren Spahn	80.00	40.00	24.00
157	Jim Delsing	10.00	5.00	3.00
158	Bucky Harris	30.00	15.00	9.00
159	Dutch Leonard	10.00	5.00	3.00
160	Eddie Stanky	12.00	6.00	3.50
161	Jackie Jensen	25.00	12.50	7.50
162	Monte Irvin	40.00	20.00	12.00
163	Johnny Lipon	10.00	5.00	3.00
164	Connie Ryan	10.00	5.00	3.00
165	Saul Rogovin	10.00	5.00	3.00
166	Bobby Adams	10.00	5.00	3.00
167	Bob Avila	10.00	5.00	3.00
168	Preacher Roe	25.00	12.50	7.50
169	Walt Dropo	10.00	5.00	3.00
170	Joe Astroth	10.00	5.00	3.00
171	Mel Queen	10.00	5.00	3.00
172	Ebba St. Claire	10.00	5.00	3.00
173	Gene Bearden	10.00	5.00	3.00
174	Mickey Grasso	10.00	5.00	3.00
175	Ransom Jackson	10.00	5.00	3.00
176	Harry Brecheen	12.00	6.00	3.50
177	Gene Woodling	18.00	9.00	5.50
178	Dave Williams	10.00	5.00	3.00
179	Pete Suder	10.00	5.00	3.00
180	Eddie Fitzgerald (Fitz Gerald)	10.00	5.00	3.00
181	Joe Collins	15.00	7.50	4.50
182	Dave Koslo	10.00	5.00	3.00
183	Pat Mullin	10.00	5.00	3.00
184	Curt Simmons	12.00	6.00	3.50
185	Eddie Stewart	10.00	5.00	3.00
186	Frank Smith	10.00	5.00	3.00
187	Jim Hegan	10.00	5.00	3.00
188	Charlie Dressen	15.00	7.50	4.50
189	Jim Piersall	18.00	9.00	5.50
190	Dick Fowler	10.00	5.00	3.00
191	*Bob Friend*	15.00	7.50	4.50
192	John Cusick	10.00	5.00	3.00
193	Bobby Young	10.00	5.00	3.00
194	Bob Porterfield	10.00	5.00	3.00
195	Frank Baumholtz	10.00	5.00	3.00
196	Stan Musial	450.00	225.00	135.00
197	Charlie Silvera	15.00	7.50	4.50
198	Chuck Diering	10.00	5.00	3.00
199	Ted Gray	10.00	5.00	3.00
200	Ken Silvestri	10.00	5.00	3.00
201	Ray Coleman	10.00	5.00	3.00
202	Harry Perkowski	10.00	5.00	3.00
203	Steve Gromek	10.00	5.00	3.00
204	Andy Pafko	12.00	6.00	3.50
205	Walt Masterson	10.00	5.00	3.00
206	Elmer Valo	10.00	5.00	3.00
207	George Strickland	10.00	5.00	3.00
208	Walker Cooper	10.00	5.00	3.00
209	Dick Littlefield	10.00	5.00	3.00
210	Archie Wilson	10.00	5.00	3.00
211	Paul Minner	10.00	5.00	3.00
212	Solly Hemus	10.00	5.00	3.00
213	Monte Kennedy	10.00	5.00	3.00
214	Ray Boone	12.00	6.00	3.50
215	Sheldon Jones	10.00	5.00	3.00
216	Matt Batts	10.00	5.00	3.00
217	Casey Stengel	125.00	56.00	35.00
218	Willie Mays	800.00	400.00	250.00
219	Neil Berry	25.00	12.50	7.50
220	Russ Meyer	25.00	12.50	7.50
221	Lou Kretlow	25.00	12.50	7.50
222	Homer "Dixie" Howell	25.00	12.50	7.50
223	Harry Simpson	25.00	12.50	7.50
224	Johnny Schmitz	27.00	13.50	8.00
225	Del Wilber	25.00	12.50	7.50
226	Alex Kellner	25.00	12.50	7.50
227	Clyde Sukeforth	25.00	12.50	7.50
228	Bob Chipman	25.00	12.50	7.50
229	Hank Arft	25.00	12.50	7.50
230	Frank Shea	25.00	12.50	7.50
231	Dee Fondy	25.00	12.50	7.50
232	Enos Slaughter	60.00	30.00	18.00
233	Bob Kuzava	32.00	16.00	9.50
234	Fred Fitzsimmons	25.00	12.50	7.50
235	Steve Souchock	25.00	12.50	7.50
236	Tommy Brown	25.00	12.50	7.50
237	Sherman Lollar	27.00	13.50	8.00
238	*Roy McMillan*	27.00	13.50	8.00
239	Dale Mitchell	25.00	12.50	7.50
240	*Billy Loes*	35.00	17.50	10.50
241	Mel Parnell	27.00	13.50	8.00
242	Everett Kell	25.00	12.50	7.50
243	George "Red" Munger	25.00	12.50	7.50
244	*Lew Burdette*	50.00	30.00	15.00
245	George Schmees	25.00	12.50	7.50
246	Jerry Snyder	25.00	12.50	7.50
247	John Pramesa	25.00	12.50	7.50
248	Bill Werle	25.00	12.50	7.50
249	Henry Thompson	25.00	12.50	7.50
250	Ivan Delock	25.00	12.50	7.50
251	Jack Lohrke	32.00	12.50	7.50
252	Frank Crosetti	125.00	30.00	15.00

1953 Bowman Color

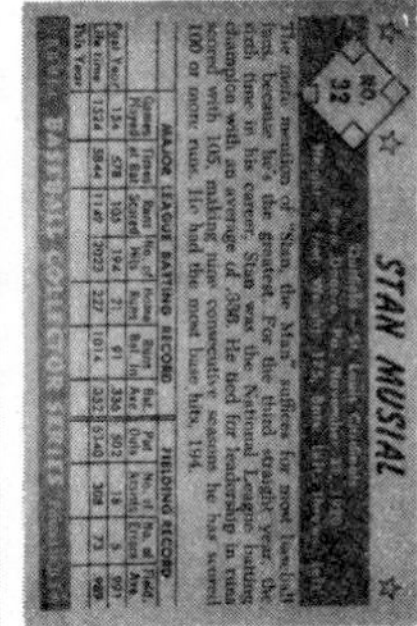

The first set of current major league players featuring actual color photographs, the 160-card 1953 Bowman Color set remains one of the most popular issues of the post-war era. The set is greatly appreciated for its uncluttered look; card fronts that contain no names, teams or facsimile autographs. Bowman increased the size of their cards to a 2-1/2" by 3-3/4" size in order to better compete with Topps Chewing Gum. Bowman copied an idea from the 1952 Topps set and developed card backs that gave player career and previous year statistics. The high- numbered cards (#'s 113-160) are the scarcest of the set, with #'s 113-128 being exceptionally difficult to find.

	NR MT	EX	VG
Complete Set:	12000.00	6000.00	3500.
Common Player: 1-112	35.00	17.50	10.50
Common Player: 113-128	50.00	25.00	15.00
Common Player: 129-160	35.00	17.50	10.50

		NR MT	EX	VG
1	Davey Williams	110.00	15.00	9.00
2	Vic Wertz	50.00	25.00	15.00
3	Sam Jethroe	35.00	17.50	10.50
4	Art Houtteman	35.00	17.50	10.50
5	Sid Gordon	35.00	17.50	10.50
6	Joe Ginsberg	35.00	17.50	10.50
7	Harry Chiti	35.00	17.50	10.50
8	Al Rosen	50.00	25.00	15.00
9	Phil Rizzuto	80.00	40.00	24.00
10	Richie Ashburn	75.00	38.00	23.00
11	Bobby Shantz	35.00	17.50	10.50
12	Carl Erskine	50.00	25.00	15.00
13	Gus Zernial	35.00	17.50	10.50
14	Billy Loes	35.00	17.50	10.50
15	Jim Busby	35.00	17.50	10.50
16	Bob Friend	35.00	17.50	10.50
17	Gerry Staley	35.00	17.50	10.50
18	Nelson Fox	60.00	30.00	18.00
19	Al Dark	35.00	17.50	10.50
20	Don Lenhardt	35.00	17.50	10.50
21	Joe Garagiola	60.00	30.00	18.00
22	Bob Porterfield	35.00	17.50	10.50
23	Herman Wehmeier	35.00	17.50	10.50
24	Jackie Jensen	35.00	17.50	10.50
25	Walter "Hoot" Evers	35.00	17.50	10.50
26	Roy McMillan	35.00	17.50	10.50
27	Vic Raschi	50.00	25.00	15.00
28	Forrest "Smoky" Burgess	35.00	17.50	10.50
29	Roberto Avila	35.00	17.50	10.50
30	Phil Cavarretta	35.00	17.50	10.50
31	Jimmy Dykes	35.00	17.50	10.50
32	Stan Musial	400.00	160.00	100.00
33	Harold "Peewee" Reese	250.00	125.00	70.00
34	Gil Coan	35.00	17.50	10.50
35	Maury McDermott	35.00	17.50	10.50
36	Orestes Minoso	50.00	25.00	15.00
37	Jim Wilson	35.00	17.50	10.50
38	Harry Byrd	35.00	17.50	10.50
39	Paul Richards	35.00	17.50	10.50
40	Larry Doby	50.00	25.00	15.00
41	Sammy White	35.00	17.50	10.50
42	Tommy Brown	35.00	17.50	10.50
43	Mike Garcia	35.00	17.50	10.50
44	Hank Bauer, Yogi Berra, Mickey Mantle	400.00	200.00	120.00
45	Walt Dropo	35.00	17.50	10.50
46	Roy Campanella	275.00	137.00	82.00
47	Ned Garver	35.00	17.50	10.50
48	Hank Sauer	35.00	17.50	10.50
49	Eddie Stanky	35.00	17.50	10.50
50	Lou Kretlow	35.00	17.50	10.50
51	Monte Irvin	45.00	23.00	13.50
52	Marty Marion	35.00	17.50	10.50
53	Del Rice	35.00	17.50	10.50
54	Chico Carrasquel	35.00	17.50	10.50
55	Leo Durocher	65.00	33.00	20.00
56	Bob Cain	35.00	17.50	10.50
57	Lou Boudreau	50.00	25.00	15.00
58	Willard Marshall	35.00	17.50	10.50
59	Mickey Mantle	1200.00	500.00	300.00
60	Granny Hamner	35.00	17.50	10.50
61	George Kell	50.00	25.00	15.00
62	Ted Kluszewski	50.00	25.00	15.00
63	Gil McDougald	50.00	25.00	15.00
64	Curt Simmons	35.00	17.50	10.50
65	Robin Roberts	60.00	30.00	17.50
66	Mel Parnell	35.00	17.50	10.50
67	Mel Clark	35.00	17.50	10.50
68	Allie Reynolds	50.00	25.00	15.00
69	Charlie Grimm	35.00	17.50	10.50
70	Clint Courtney	35.00	17.50	10.50
71	Paul Minner	35.00	17.50	10.50
72	Ted Gray	35.00	17.50	10.50
73	Billy Pierce	35.00	17.50	10.50
74	Don Mueller	35.00	17.50	10.50
75	Saul Rogovin	35.00	17.50	10.50
76	Jim Hearn	35.00	17.50	10.50
77	Mickey Grasso	35.00	17.50	10.50
78	Carl Furillo	50.00	25.00	15.00
79	Ray Boone	35.00	17.50	10.50
80	Ralph Kiner	60.00	30.00	18.00
81	Enos Slaughter	60.00	30.00	18.00
82	Joe Astroth	35.00	17.50	10.50
83	Jack Daniels	35.00	17.50	10.50
84	Hank Bauer	50.00	25.00	15.00
85	Solly Hemus	35.00	17.50	10.50
86	Harry Simpson	35.00	17.50	10.50
87	Harry Perkowski	35.00	17.50	10.50
88	Joe Dobson	35.00	17.50	10.50
89	Sandalio Consuegra	35.00	17.50	10.50
90	Joe Nuxhall	35.00	17.50	10.50
91	Steve Souchock	35.00	17.50	10.50
92	Gil Hodges	100.00	45.00	27.00
93	Billy Martin, Phil Rizzuto	200.00	100.00	60.00
94	Bob Addis	35.00	17.50	10.50
95	Wally Moses	35.00	17.50	10.50
96	Sal Maglie	35.00	17.50	10.50
97	Eddie Mathews	125.00	62.00	40.00
98	Hector Rodriquez	35.00	17.50	10.50
99	Warren Spahn	125.00	62.00	37.00
100	Bill Wight	35.00	17.50	10.50
101	Al "Red" Schoendienst	70.00	35.00	21.00
102	Jim Hegan	35.00	17.50	10.50
103	Del Ennis	35.00	17.50	10.50
104	Luke Easter	35.00	17.50	10.50
105	Eddie Joost	35.00	17.50	10.50
106	Ken Raffensberger	35.00	17.50	10.50
107	Alex Kellner	35.00	17.50	10.50
108	Bobby Adams	35.00	17.50	10.50
109	Ken Wood	35.00	17.50	10.50
110	Bob Rush	35.00	17.50	10.50
111	Jim Dyck	35.00	17.50	10.50
112	Toby Atwell	35.00	17.50	10.50
113	Karl Drews	50.00	25.00	15.00
114	Bob Feller	250.00	100.00	63.00
115	Cloyd Boyer	50.00	25.00	15.00
116	Eddie Yost	50.00	25.00	15.00
117	Duke Snider	500.00	225.00	150.00
118	Billy Martin	275.00	137.00	82.00
119	Dale Mitchell	50.00	25.00	15.00
120	Marlin Stuart	50.00	25.00	15.00
121	Yogi Berra	475.00	190.00	119.00
122	Bill Serena	50.00	25.00	15.00

		NR MT	EX	VG
123	Johnny Lipon	50.00	25.00	15.00
124	Charlie Dressen	45.00	23.00	13.50
125	Fred Hatfield	50.00	25.00	15.00
126	Al Corwin	50.00	25.00	15.00
127	Dick Kryhoski	50.00	25.00	15.00
128	Whitey Lockman	50.00	25.00	15.00
129	Russ Meyer	50.00	25.00	15.00
130	Cass Michaels	35.00	17.50	10.50
131	Connie Ryan	35.00	17.50	10.50
132	Fred Hutchinson	50.00	25.00	15.00
133	Willie Jones	35.00	17.50	10.50
134	Johnny Pesky	50.00	25.00	15.00
135	Bobby Morgan	50.00	25.00	15.00
136	Jim Bridewesser	40.00	20.00	12.00
137	Sam Dente	35.00	17.50	10.50
138	Bubba Church	35.00	17.50	10.50
139	Pete Runnels	50.00	25.00	15.00
140	Alpha Brazle	35.00	17.50	10.50
141	Frank "Spec" Shea	35.00	17.50	10.50
142	Larry Miggins	35.00	17.50	10.50
143	Al Lopez	60.00	30.00	18.00
144	Warren Hacker	35.00	17.50	10.50
145	George Shuba	50.00	25.00	15.00
146	Early Wynn	125.00	62.00	40.00
147	Clem Koshorek	35.00	17.50	10.50
148	Billy Goodman	35.00	17.50	10.50
149	Al Corwin	35.00	17.50	10.50
150	Carl Scheib	35.00	17.50	10.50
151	Joe Adcock	40.00	20.00	12.00
152	Clyde Vollmer	35.00	17.50	10.50
153	Ed "Whitey" Ford	500.00	225.00	150.00
154	Omar "Turk" Lown	35.00	17.50	10.50
155	Allie Clark	35.00	17.50	10.50
156	Max Surkont	35.00	17.50	10.50
157	Sherman Lollar	50.00	25.00	15.00
158	Howard Fox	35.00	17.50	10.50
159	Mickey Vernon (Photo actually Floyd Baker)	40.00	17.50	10.50
160	Cal Abrams	100.00	17.50	9.00

1953 Bowman

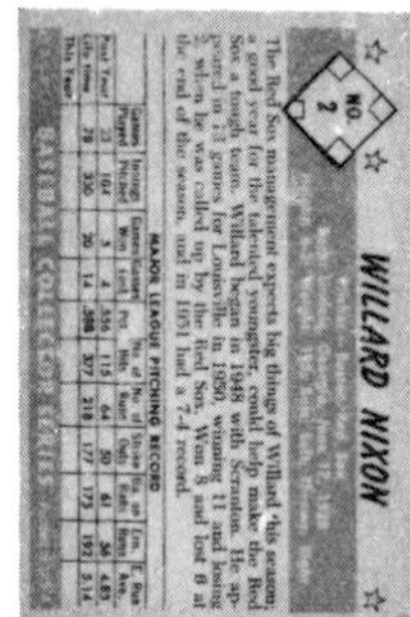

The 1953 Bowman Black and White set is similar in all respects to the 1953 Bowman Color set, except that it lacks color. Purportedly, high costs in producing the color series forced Bowman to issue the set in black and white. Sixty-four cards, which measure 2-1/2" by 3-3/4", comprise the set.

		NR MT	EX	VG
Complete Set:		2200.00	880.00	440.00
Common Player:		30.00	15.00	9.00
1	Gus Bell	100.00	45.00	27.00
2	Willard Nixon	32.00	11.00	6.50
3	Bill Rigney	27.00	13.50	8.00
4	Pat Mullin	30.00	15.00	9.00
5	Dee Fondy	30.00	15.00	9.00
6	Ray Murray	30.00	15.00	9.00
7	Andy Seminick	30.00	15.00	9.00
8	Pete Suder	30.00	15.00	9.00
9	Walt Masterson	30.00	15.00	9.00
10	Dick Sisler	30.00	15.00	9.00
11	Dick Gernert	30.00	15.00	9.00
12	Randy Jackson	30.00	15.00	9.00
13	Joe Tipton	30.00	15.00	9.00
14	Bill Nicholson	30.00	15.00	9.00
15	Johnny Mize	110.00	50.00	28.00
16	Stu Miller	30.00	15.00	9.00
17	Virgil Trucks	27.00	13.50	8.00
18	Billy Hoeft	30.00	15.00	9.00
19	Paul LaPalme	30.00	15.00	9.00
20	Eddie Robinson	30.00	15.00	9.00
21	Clarence "Bud" Podbielan	30.00	15.00	9.00
22	Matt Batts	30.00	15.00	9.00
23	Wilmer Mizell	30.00	15.00	9.00
24	Del Wilber	30.00	15.00	9.00
25	John Sain	50.00	25.00	15.00
26	Preacher Roe	50.00	25.00	15.00
27	Bob Lemon	90.00	45.00	27.00
28	Hoyt Wilhelm	100.00	50.00	28.00
29	Sid Hudson	30.00	15.00	9.00
30	Walker Cooper	30.00	15.00	9.00
31	Gene Woodling	40.00	20.00	12.00
32	Rocky Bridges	30.00	15.00	9.00
33	Bob Kuzava	32.00	16.00	9.50
34	Ebba St. Clair (St. Claire)	30.00	15.00	9.00
35	Johnny Wyrostek	30.00	15.00	9.00
36	Jim Piersall	40.00	20.00	12.00
37	Hal Jeffcoat	30.00	15.00	9.00
38	Dave Cole	30.00	15.00	9.00
39	Casey Stengel	300.00	150.00	90.00
40	Larry Jansen	30.00	15.00	9.00
41	Bob Ramazotti	30.00	15.00	9.00
42	Howie Judson	30.00	15.00	9.00
43	Hal Bevan	30.00	15.00	9.00
44	Jim Delsing	30.00	15.00	9.00
45	Irv Noren	32.00	16.00	9.50
46	Bucky Harris	55.00	28.00	16.50
47	Jack Lohrke	30.00	15.00	9.00
48	Steve Ridzik	30.00	15.00	9.00
49	Floyd Baker	30.00	15.00	9.00
50	Emil "Dutch" Leonard	30.00	15.00	9.00
51	Lou Burdette	40.00	20.00	12.00
52	Ralph Branca	40.00	20.00	12.00
53	Morris Martin	30.00	15.00	9.00
54	Bill Miller	32.00	16.00	9.50
55	Don Johnson	30.00	15.00	9.00
56	Roy Smalley	30.00	15.00	9.00
57	Andy Pafko	30.00	15.00	9.00
58	Jim Konstanty	30.00	15.00	9.00
59	Duane Pillette	30.00	15.00	9.00
60	Billy Cox	30.00	15.00	9.00
61	Tom Gorman	32.00	16.00	9.50
62	Keith Thomas	30.00	15.00	9.00
63	Steve Gromek	27.00	11.00	6.50
64	Andy Hansen	45.00	13.50	6.50

1954 Bowman

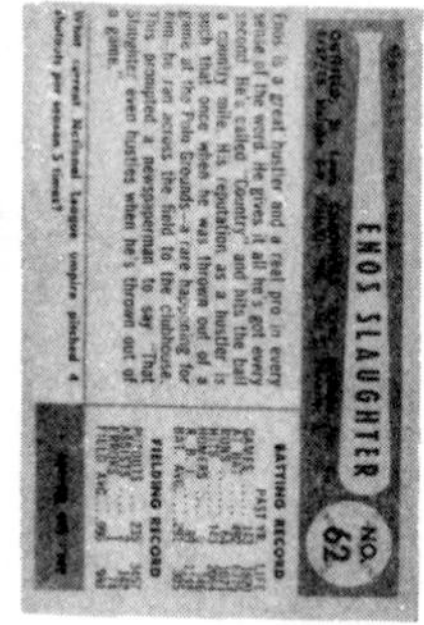

Bowman's 1954 set consists of 224 full-color cards that measure 2-1/2" by 3-3/4". It is believed that contractual problems caused the pulling of card #66 (Ted Williams) from the set, creating one of the most sought-after scarcities of the post-war era. The Williams card was replaced by Jim Piersall (who is also #210) in subsequent print runs. The set contains over 40 variations, most involving statistical errors on the card backs that were corrected. Neither variation carries a premium value as both varieties appear to have been printed in equal amounts. The complete set price that follows does not include all variations or #66 Williams.

		NR MT	EX	VG
Complete Set:		4000.00	2000.00	1200.
Common Player: 1-224		7.00	3.50	2.00
1	Phil Rizzuto	150.00	60.00	38.00
2	Jack Jensen	10.00	5.00	3.00
3	Marion Fricano	7.00	3.50	2.00
4	Bob Hooper	7.00	3.50	2.00
5	William Hunter	7.00	3.50	2.00
6	Nelson Fox	15.00	7.50	4.50
7	Walter Dropo	7.00	3.50	2.00
8	James F. Busby	7.00	3.50	2.00
9	Dave Williams	7.00	3.50	2.00
10	Carl Daniel Erskine	10.00	5.00	3.00
11	Sid Gordon	7.00	3.50	2.00
12a	Roy McMillan (551/1290 At Bat)	6.00	3.00	1.75
12b	Roy McMillan (557/1296 At Bat)	6.00	3.00	1.75
13	Paul Minner	7.00	3.50	2.00
14	Gerald Staley	7.00	3.50	2.00
15	Richie Ashburn	25.00	12.50	7.50
16	Jim Wilson	7.00	3.50	2.00
17	Tom Gorman	8.00	4.00	2.50
18	Walter "Hoot" Evers	7.00	3.50	2.00
19	Bobby Shantz	7.00	3.50	2.00
20	Artie Houtteman	7.00	3.50	2.00
21	Victor Wertz	6.00	3.00	1.75
22a	Sam Mele (213/1661 Putouts)	6.00	3.00	1.75
22b	Sam Mele (217/1665 Putouts)	6.00	3.00	1.75
23	*Harvey Kuenn*	25.00	12.50	7.50
24	Bob Porterfield	7.00	3.50	2.00
25a	Wes Westrum (1.000/.987 Field Avg.)	6.00	3.00	1.75
25b	Wes Westrum (.982/.986 Field Avg.)	6.00	3.00	1.75
26a	Billy Cox (1.000/.960 Field Avg.)	7.00	3.50	2.00
26b	Billy Cox (.972/.960 Field Avg.)	7.00	3.50	2.00
27	Richard Roy Cole	7.00	3.50	2.00
28a	Jim Greengrass (Birthplace Addison, N.J.)	6.00	3.00	1.75
28b	Jim Greengrass (Birthplace Addison, N.Y.)	6.00	3.00	1.75
29	Johnny Klippstein	7.00	3.50	2.00
30	Delbert Rice Jr.	7.00	3.50	2.00
31	"Smoky" Burgess	6.00	3.00	1.75
32	Del Crandall	6.00	3.00	1.75
33a	Victor Raschi (no traded line)	10.00	5.00	3.00
33b	Victor Raschi (with traded line)	25.00	12.50	7.50
34	Sammy White	7.00	3.50	2.00
35a	Eddie Joost (quiz answer is 8)	6.00	3.00	1.75
35b	Eddie Joost (quiz answer is 33)	6.00	3.00	1.75
36	George Strickland	7.00	3.50	2.00
37	Dick Kokos	7.00	3.50	2.00
38a	Orestes Minoso (.895/.961 Field Avg.)	8.00	4.00	2.50
38b	Orestes Minoso (.963/.963 Field Avg.)	8.00	4.00	2.50
39	Ned Garver	7.00	3.50	2.00
40	Gil Coan	7.00	3.50	2.00
41a	Alvin Dark (.986/.960 Field Avg.)	8.00	4.00	2.50
41b	Alvin Dark (.968/.960 Field Avg.)	8.00	4.00	2.50
42	Billy Loes	7.00	3.50	2.00
43a	Robert B. Friend (20 shutouts in quiz question)	7.00	3.50	2.00
43b	Robert B. Friend (16 shutouts in quiz question)	7.00	3.50	2.00
44	Harry Perkowski	7.00	3.50	2.00
45	Ralph Kiner	40.00	20.00	12.00
46	Eldon Repulski	7.00	3.50	2.00
47a	Granville Hamner (.970/.953 Field Avg.)	6.00	3.00	1.75
47b	Granville Hamner (.953/.951 Field Avg.)	6.00	3.00	1.75
48	Jack Dittmer	7.00	3.50	2.00
49	Harry Byrd	8.00	4.00	2.50
50	George Kell	25.00	12.50	7.50
51	Alex Kellner	7.00	3.50	2.00
52	Myron N. Ginsberg	7.00	3.50	2.00
53a	Don Lenhardt (.969/.984 Field Avg.)	6.00	3.00	1.75
53b	Don Lenhardt (.966/.983 Field Avg.)	6.00	3.00	1.75
54	Alfonso Carrasquel	7.00	3.50	2.00
55	Jim Delsing	7.00	3.50	2.00
56	Maurice M. McDermott	7.00	3.50	2.00
57	Hoyt Wilhelm	25.00	12.50	7.50
58	"Pee Wee" Reese	50.00	30.00	15.00
59	Robert D. Schultz	7.00	3.50	2.00
60	Fred Baczewski	7.00	3.50	2.00
61a	Eddie Miksis (.954/.962 Field Avg.)	6.00	3.00	1.75
61b	Eddie Miksis (.954/.961 Field Avg.)	6.00	3.00	1.75
62	Enos Slaughter	25.00	12.50	7.50
63	Earl Torgeson	7.00	3.50	2.00
64	Ed Mathews	40.00	20.00	12.00
65	Mickey Mantle	675.00	325.00	175.00
66a	Ted Williams	3000.00	1500.00	900.00
66b	Jimmy Piersall	90.00	45.00	27.00
67a	Carl Scheib (.306 Pct. with two lines under bio)	6.00	3.00	1.75
67b	Carl Scheib (.306 Pct. with one line under bio)	6.00	3.00	1.75
67c	Carl Scheib (.300 Pct.)	6.00	3.00	1.75
68	Bob Avila	6.00	3.00	1.75
69	Clinton Courtney	7.00	3.50	2.00
70	Willard Marshall	7.00	3.50	2.00
71	Ted Gray	7.00	3.50	2.00
72	Ed Yost	7.00	3.50	2.00
73	Don Mueller	7.00	3.50	2.00
74	James Gilliam	10.00	5.00	3.00
75	Max Surkont	7.00	3.50	2.00
76	Joe Nuxhall	6.00	3.00	1.75
77	Bob Rush	7.00	3.50	2.00
78	Sal A. Yvars	7.00	3.50	2.00
79	Curt Simmons	6.00	3.00	1.75
80a	John Logan (106 Runs)	6.00	3.00	1.75
80b	John Logan (100 Runs)	6.00	3.00	1.75
81a	Jerry Coleman (1.000/.975 Field Avg.)	8.00	4.00	2.50
81b	Jerry Coleman (.952/.975 Field Avg.)	8.00	4.00	2.50
82a	Bill Goodman (.965/.986 Field Avg.)	6.00	3.00	1.75
82b	Bill Goodman (.972/.985 Field Avg.)	6.00	3.00	1.75
83	Ray Murray	7.00	3.50	2.00
84	Larry Doby	8.00	4.00	2.50
85a	Jim Dyck (.926/.956 Field Avg.)	6.00	3.00	1.75
85b	Jim Dyck (.947/.960 Field Avg.)	6.00	3.00	1.75
86	Harry Dorish	7.00	3.50	2.00
87	Don Lund	7.00	3.50	2.00
88	Tommy Umphlett	7.00	3.50	2.00
89	Willie May (Mays)	300.00	120.00	75.00
90	Roy Campanella	150.00	60.00	38.00
91	Cal Abrams	7.00	3.50	2.00
92	Kenneth David Raffensberger	7.00	3.50	2.00
93a	Bill Serena (.983/.966 Field Avg.)	6.00	3.00	1.75
93b	Bill Serena (.977/.966 Field Avg.)	6.00	3.00	1.75
94a	Solly Hemus (476/1343 Assists)	6.00	3.00	1.75
94b	Solly Hemus (477/1343 Assists)	6.00	3.00	1.75
95	Robin Roberts	25.00	12.50	7.50
96	Joe Adcock	7.00	3.50	2.00
97	Gil McDougald	12.00	6.00	3.50
98	Ellis Kinder	7.00	3.50	2.00
99a	Peter Suder (.985/.974 Field Avg.)	6.00	3.00	1.75
99b	Peter Suder (.978/.974 Field Avg.)	6.00	3.00	1.75
100	Mike Garcia	6.00	3.00	1.75
101	*Don James Larsen*	30.00	15.00	9.00
102	Bill Pierce	6.00	3.00	1.75
103a	Stephen Souchock (144/1192 Putouts)	6.00	3.00	1.75
103b	Stephen Souchock (147/1195 Putouts)	6.00	3.00	1.75
104	Frank Spec Shea	7.00	3.50	2.00
105a	Sal Maglie (quiz answer is 8)	7.00	3.50	2.00
105b	Sal Maglie (quiz answer is 1904)	7.00	3.50	2.00
106	"Clem" Labine	7.00	3.50	2.00

		NR MT	EX	VG
107	Paul E. LaPalme	7.00	3.50	2.00
108	Bobby Adams	7.00	3.50	2.00
109	Roy Smalley	7.00	3.50	2.00
110	Al Schoendienst	30.00	15.00	9.00
111	Murry Monroe Dickson	7.00	3.50	2.00
112	Andy Pafko	6.00	3.00	1.75
113	Allie Reynolds	12.00	6.00	3.50
114	Willard Nixon	7.00	3.50	2.00
115	Don Bollweg	7.00	3.50	2.00
116	Luscious Luke Easter	7.00	3.50	2.00
117	Dick Kryhoski	7.00	3.50	2.00
118	Robert R. Boyd	7.00	3.50	2.00
119	Fred Hatfield	7.00	3.50	2.00
120	Mel Hoderlein	7.00	3.50	2.00
121	Ray Katt	7.00	3.50	2.00
122	Carl Furillo	15.00	7.50	4.50
123	Toby Atwell	7.00	3.50	2.00
124a	Gus Bell (15/27 Errors)	6.00	3.00	1.75
124b	Gus Bell (11/26 Errors)	6.00	3.00	1.75
125	Warren Hacker	7.00	3.50	2.00
126	Cliff Chambers	7.00	3.50	2.00
127	Del Ennis	6.00	3.00	1.75
128	Ebba St Claire	7.00	3.50	2.00
129	Hank Bauer	15.00	7.50	4.50
130	Milt Bolling	7.00	3.50	2.00
131	Joe Astroth	7.00	3.50	2.00
132	Bob Feller	70.00	35.00	21.00
133	Duane Pillette	7.00	3.50	2.00
134	Luis Aloma	7.00	3.50	2.00
135	Johnny Pesky	6.00	3.00	1.75
136	Clyde Vollmer	7.00	3.50	2.00
137	Elmer N. Corwin Jr.	7.00	3.50	2.00
138a	Gil Hodges (.993/.991 Field Avg.)	50.00	25.00	15.00
138b	Gil Hodges (.992/.991 Field Avg.)	55.00	28.00	16.50
139a	Preston Ward (.961/.992 Field Avg.)	6.00	3.00	1.75
139b	Preston Ward (.990/.992 Field Avg.)	6.00	3.00	1.75
140a	Saul Rogovin (7-12 Won/Lost with 2 Strikeouts)	6.00	3.00	1.75
140b	Saul Rogovin (7-12 Won/Lost with 62 Strikeouts)	6.00	3.00	1.75
140c	Saul Rogovin (8-12 Won/Lost)	6.00	3.00	1.75
141	Joe Garagiola	35.00	17.50	10.50
142	Al Brazle	7.00	3.50	2.00
143	Puddin Head Jones	7.00	3.50	2.00
144	Ernie Johnson	7.00	3.50	2.00
145a	Billy Martin (.985/.983 Field Avg.)	40.00	20.00	12.00
145b	Billy Martin (.983/.982 Field Avg.)	40.00	20.00	12.00
146	Dick Gernert	7.00	3.50	2.00
147	Joe DeMaestri	7.00	3.50	2.00
148	Dale Mitchell	7.00	3.50	2.00
149	Bob Young	7.00	3.50	2.00
150	Cass Michaels	7.00	3.50	2.00
151	Patrick J. Mullin	7.00	3.50	2.00
152	Mickey Vernon	6.00	3.00	1.75
153a	Whitey Lockman (100/331 Assists)	6.00	3.00	1.75
153b	Whitey Lockman (102/333 Assists)	6.00	3.00	1.75
154	Don Newcombe	15.00	7.50	4.50
155	*Frank J. Thomas*	6.00	3.00	1.75
156a	Everett Lamar Bridges (320/467 Assists)	6.00	3.00	1.75
156b	Everett Lamar Bridges (328/475 Assists)	6.00	3.00	1.75
157	Omar Lown	7.00	3.50	2.00
158	Stu Miller	7.00	3.50	2.00
159	John Lindell	7.00	3.50	2.00
160	Danny O'Connell	7.00	3.50	2.00
161	Yogi Berra	125.00	62.00	37.00
162	Ted Lepcio	7.00	3.50	2.00
163a	Dave Philley (152 Games with no traded line)	7.00	3.50	2.00
163b	Dave Philley (152 Games with traded line)	25.00	12.50	7.50
163c	Dave Philley (157 Games with traded line)	7.00	3.50	2.00
164	Early "Gus" Wynn	35.00	17.50	10.50
165	Johnny Groth	7.00	3.50	2.00
166	Sandalio Consuegra	7.00	3.50	2.00
167	Bill Hoeft	7.00	3.50	2.00
168	Edward Fitzgerald (Fitz Gerald)	7.00	3.50	2.00
169	Larry Jansen	7.00	3.50	2.00
170	Edwin D. Snider	125.00	62.00	40.00
171	Carlos Bernier	7.00	3.50	2.00
172	Andy Seminick	7.00	3.50	2.00
173	Dee V. Fondy Jr.	7.00	3.50	2.00
174a	Peter Paul Castiglione (.966/.959 Field Avg.)	6.00	3.00	1.75
174b	Peter Paul Castiglione (.970/.959 Field Avg.)	6.00	3.00	1.75
175	Melvin E. Clark	7.00	3.50	2.00
176	Vernon Bickford	7.00	3.50	2.00
177	Edward Ford	75.00	38.00	23.00
178	Del Wilber	7.00	3.50	2.00
179a	Morris Martin (44 ERA)	6.00	3.00	1.75
179b	Morris Martin (4.44 ERA)	6.00	3.00	1.75
180	Joe Tipton	7.00	3.50	2.00
181	Lester Moss	7.00	3.50	2.00
182	Sherman Lollar	6.00	3.00	1.75
183	Matt Batts	7.00	3.50	2.00
184	Mickey Grasso	7.00	3.50	2.00
185a	*Daryl Spencer* (.941/.944 Field Avg.)	6.00	3.00	1.75
185b	*Daryl Spencer* (.933/.936 Field Avg.)	6.00	3.00	1.75
186	Russell Meyer	7.00	3.50	2.00
187	Verne Law (Vern)	6.00	3.00	1.75
188	Frank Smith	7.00	3.50	2.00
189	Ransom Jackson	7.00	3.50	2.00
190	Joe Presko	7.00	3.50	2.00
191	Karl A. Drews	7.00	3.50	2.00
192	Selva L. Burdette	7.00	3.50	2.00
193	Eddie Robinson	8.00	4.00	2.50
194	Sid Hudson	7.00	3.50	2.00
195	Bob Cain	7.00	3.50	2.00
196	Bob Lemon	30.00	15.00	9.00
197	Lou Kretlow	7.00	3.50	2.00
198	Virgil Trucks	6.00	3.00	1.75
199	Steve Gromek	7.00	3.50	2.00
200	C. Marrero	7.00	3.50	2.00
201	Bob Thomson	7.00	3.50	2.00
202	George Shuba	7.00	3.50	2.00
203	Vic Janowicz	7.00	3.50	2.00
204	Jack Collum	7.00	3.50	2.00
205	Hal Jeffcoat	7.00	3.50	2.00
206	Steve Bilko	7.00	3.50	2.00
207	Stan Lopata	7.00	3.50	2.00
208	Johnny Antonelli	6.00	3.00	1.75
209	Gene Woodling (photo reversed)	10.00	5.00	3.00
210	Jimmy Piersall	10.00	5.00	3.00
211	Alfred James Robertson Jr.	7.00	3.50	2.00
212a	Owen L. Friend (.964/.957 Field Avg.)	6.00	3.00	1.75
212b	Owen L. Friend (.967/.958 Field Avg.)	6.00	3.00	1.75
213	Dick Littlefield	7.00	3.50	2.00
214	Ferris Fain	6.00	3.00	1.75
215	Johnny Bucha	7.00	3.50	2.00
216a	Jerry Snyder (.988/.988 Field Avg.)	6.00	3.00	1.75
216b	Jerry Snyder (.968/.968 Field Avg.)	6.00	3.00	1.75
217a	Henry Thompson (.956/.951 Field Avg.)	6.00	3.00	1.75
217b	Henry Thompson (.958/.952 Field Avg.)	6.00	3.00	1.75
218	Preacher Roe	10.00	5.00	3.00
219	Hal Rice	7.00	3.50	2.00
220	Hobie Landrith	7.00	3.50	2.00
221	Frank Baumholtz	7.00	3.50	2.00
222	Memo Luna	7.00	3.50	2.00
223	Steve Ridzik	7.00	2.50	1.50
224	William Bruton	30.00	9.00	4.00

1955 Bowman

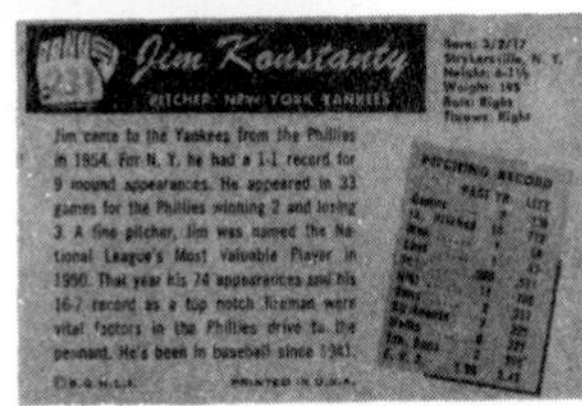

Bowman produced its final baseball card set in 1955, a popular issue which has player photographs placed inside a television set design. The set consists of 320 cards that measure 2-1/2" by 3-3/4" in size. The high-numbered cards (#'s 225-320) are scarcest in the set and include 31 umpire cards.

		NR MT	EX	VG
	Complete Set:	4500.00	2300.00	1350.
	Common Player: 1-224	5.00	2.50	1.50
	Common Player: 225-320	15.00	7.50	4.50
1	Hoyt Wilhelm	100.00	20.00	6.00
2	Al Dark	15.00	7.50	4.50
3	Joe Coleman	5.00	2.50	1.50
4	Eddie Waitkus	5.00	2.50	1.50
5	Jim Robertson	5.00	2.50	1.50
6	Pete Suder	5.00	2.50	1.50
7	Gene Baker	5.00	2.50	1.50
8	Warren Hacker	5.00	2.50	1.50
9	Gil McDougald	10.00	5.00	3.00
10	Phil Rizzuto	40.00	20.00	12.00
11	Billy Bruton	5.00	2.50	1.50
12	Andy Pafko	6.00	3.00	1.75
13	Clyde Vollmer	5.00	2.50	1.50
14	Gus Keriazakos	5.00	2.50	1.50
15	*Frank Sullivan*	6.00	3.00	1.75
16	Jim Piersall	7.00	3.50	2.00
17	Del Ennis	6.00	3.00	1.75
18	Stan Lopata	5.00	2.50	1.50
19	Bobby Avila	5.00	2.50	1.50
20	Al Smith	5.00	2.50	1.50
21	Don Hoak	7.00	3.50	2.00
22	Roy Campanella	100.00	50.00	30.00
23	Al Kaline	100.00	50.00	30.00
24	Al Aber	5.00	2.50	1.50
25	Orestes "Minnie" Minoso	10.00	5.00	3.00
26	Virgil Trucks	6.00	3.00	1.75
27	Preston Ward	5.00	2.50	1.50
28	Dick Cole	5.00	2.50	1.50
29	Al "Red" Schoendienst	30.00	15.00	10.50
30	Bill Sarni	5.00	2.50	1.50
31	Johnny Temple	5.00	2.50	1.50
32	Wally Post	5.00	2.50	1.50
33	Nelson Fox	18.00	9.00	5.50
34	Clint Courtney	5.00	2.50	1.50
35	Bill Tuttle	5.00	2.50	1.50
36	Wayne Belardi	5.00	2.50	1.50
37	Harold "Pee Wee" Reese	60.00	30.00	18.00
38	Early Wynn	20.00	10.00	6.00
39	Bob Darnell	6.00	3.00	1.75
40	Vic Wertz	6.00	3.00	1.75
41	Mel Clark	5.00	2.50	1.50
42	Bob Greenwood	5.00	2.50	1.50
43	Bob Buhl	6.00	3.00	1.75
44	Danny O'Connell	5.00	2.50	1.50
45	Tom Umphlett	5.00	2.50	1.50
46	Mickey Vernon	6.00	3.00	1.75
47	Sammy White	5.00	2.50	1.50
48a	Milt Bolling (Frank Bolling back)	6.00	3.00	1.75
48b	Milt Bolling (Milt Bolling back)	15.00	7.50	4.50
49	Jim Greengrass	5.00	2.50	1.50
50	Hobie Landrith	5.00	2.50	1.50
51	Elvin Tappe	5.00	2.50	1.50
52	Hal Rice	5.00	2.50	1.50
53	Alex Kellner	5.00	2.50	1.50
54	Don Bollweg	5.00	2.50	1.50
55	Cal Abrams	5.00	2.50	1.50
56	Billy Cox	5.00	2.50	1.50
57	Bob Friend	6.00	3.00	1.75
58	Frank Thomas	5.00	2.50	1.50
59	Ed "Whitey" Ford	60.00	30.00	18.00
60	Enos Slaughter	20.00	10.00	6.00
61	Paul LaPalme	5.00	2.50	1.50
62	Royce Lint	5.00	2.50	1.50
63	Irv Noren	8.00	4.00	2.50
64	Curt Simmons	6.00	3.00	1.75
65	*Don Zimmer*	25.00	12.50	7.50
66	George Shuba	6.00	3.00	1.75
67	Don Larsen	15.00	7.50	4.50
68	*Elston Howard*	25.00	12.50	7.50
69	Bill Hunter	8.00	4.00	2.50
70	Lou Burdette	7.00	3.50	2.00
71	Dave Jolly	5.00	2.50	1.50
72	Chet Nichols	5.00	2.50	1.50
73	Eddie Yost	5.00	2.50	1.50
74	Jerry Snyder	5.00	2.50	1.50
75	Brooks Lawrence	5.00	2.50	1.50
76	Tom Poholsky	5.00	2.50	1.50
77	Jim McDonald	5.00	2.50	1.50
78	Gil Coan	5.00	2.50	1.50
79	Willie Miranda	5.00	2.50	1.50
80	Lou Limmer	5.00	2.50	1.50
81	Bob Morgan	5.00	2.50	1.50
82	Lee Walls	5.00	2.50	1.50
83	Max Surkont	5.00	2.50	1.50
84	George Freese	5.00	2.50	1.50
85	Cass Michaels	5.00	2.50	1.50
86	Ted Gray	5.00	2.50	1.50
87	Randy Jackson	5.00	2.50	1.50
88	Steve Bilko	5.00	2.50	1.50
89	Lou Boudreau	20.00	10.00	6.00
90	Art Ditmar	5.00	2.50	1.50
91	Dick Marlowe	5.00	2.50	1.50
92	George Zuverink	5.00	2.50	1.50
93	Andy Seminick	5.00	2.50	1.50
94	Hank Thompson	5.00	2.50	1.50
95	Sal Maglie	10.00	5.00	3.00
96	Ray Narleski	5.00	2.50	1.50
97	John Podres	15.00	7.50	4.50
98	James "Junior" Gilliam	15.00	7.50	4.50
99	Jerry Coleman	8.00	4.00	2.50
100	Tom Morgan	8.00	4.00	2.50
101a	Don Johnson (Ernie Johnson (Braves) on front)	6.00	3.00	1.75
101b	Don Johnson (Don Johnson (Orioles) on front)	15.00	7.50	4.50
102	Bobby Thomson	8.00	4.00	2.50
103	Eddie Mathews	30.00	15.00	9.00
104	Bob Porterfield	5.00	2.50	1.50
105	Johnny Schmitz	5.00	2.50	1.50
106	Del Rice	5.00	2.50	1.50
107	Solly Hemus	5.00	2.50	1.50
108	Lou Kretlow	5.00	2.50	1.50
109	Vern Stephens	5.00	2.50	1.50
110	Bob Miller	5.00	2.50	1.50
111	Steve Ridzik	5.00	2.50	1.50
112	Gran Hamner	5.00	2.50	1.50
113	Bob Hall	5.00	2.50	1.50
114	Vic Janowicz	5.00	2.50	1.50
115	Roger Bowman	5.00	2.50	1.50
116	Sandalio Consuegra	5.00	2.50	1.50
117	Johnny Groth	5.00	2.50	1.50
118	Bobby Adams	5.00	2.50	1.50
119	Joe Astroth	5.00	2.50	1.50
120	Ed Burtschy	5.00	2.50	1.50
121	Rufus Crawford	5.00	2.50	1.50
122	Al Corwin	5.00	2.50	1.50
123	Marv Grissom	5.00	2.50	1.50
124	Johnny Antonelli	6.00	3.00	1.75
125	Paul Giel	5.00	2.50	1.50
126	Billy Goodman	5.00	2.50	1.50
127	Hank Majeski	5.00	2.50	1.50
128	Mike Garcia	6.00	3.00	1.75
129	Hal Naragon	5.00	2.50	1.50
130	Richie Ashburn	15.00	7.50	4.50
131	Willard Marshall	5.00	2.50	1.50
132a	Harvey Kueen (incorrect spelling on back)	7.00	3.50	2.00
132b	Harvey Kuenn (correct spelling on back)	30.00	15.00	9.00
133	Charles King	5.00	2.50	1.50
134	Bob Feller	55.00	28.00	16.50
135	Lloyd Merriman	5.00	2.50	1.50
136	Rocky Bridges	5.00	2.50	1.50
137	Bob Talbot	5.00	2.50	1.50
138	Davey Williams	5.00	2.50	1.50
139	Billy & Bobby Shantz	7.00	3.50	2.00
140	Bobby Shantz	6.00	3.00	1.75
141	Wes Westrum	6.00	3.00	1.75
142	Rudy Regalado	5.00	2.50	1.50
143	Don Newcombe	8.00	4.00	2.50
144	Art Houtteman	5.00	2.50	1.50
145	Bob Nieman	5.00	2.50	1.50
146	Don Liddle	5.00	2.50	1.50
147	Sam Mele	5.00	2.50	1.50

		NR MT	EX	VG
148	Bob Chakales	5.00	2.50	1.50
149	Cloyd Boyer	5.00	2.50	1.50
150	Bill Klaus	5.00	2.50	1.50
151	Jim Brideweser	5.00	2.50	1.50
152	Johnny Klippstein	5.00	2.50	1.50
153	Eddie Robinson	8.00	4.00	2.50
154	*Frank Lary*	7.00	3.50	2.00
155	Gerry Staley	5.00	2.50	1.50
156	Jim Hughes	6.00	3.00	1.75
157a	Ernie Johnson (Don Johnson (Orioles) picture on front)	6.00	3.00	1.75
157b	Ernie Johnson (Ernie Johnson (Braves) picture on front)	15.00	7.50	4.50
158	Gil Hodges	40.00	20.00	12.00
159	Harry Byrd	5.00	2.50	1.50
160	Bill Skowron	15.00	7.50	4.50
161	Matt Batts	5.00	2.50	1.50
162	Charlie Maxwell	5.00	2.50	1.50
163	Sid Gordon	5.00	2.50	1.50
164	Toby Atwell	5.00	2.50	1.50
165	Maurice McDermott	5.00	2.50	1.50
166	Jim Busby	5.00	2.50	1.50
167	Bob Grim	8.00	4.00	2.50
168	Larry "Yogi" Berra	75.00	38.00	23.00
169	Carl Furillo	15.00	7.50	4.50
170	Carl Erskine	8.00	4.00	2.50
171	Robin Roberts	20.00	10.00	6.00
172	Willie Jones	5.00	2.50	1.50
173	Al "Chico" Carrasquel	5.00	2.50	1.50
174	Sherman Lollar	6.00	3.00	1.75
175	Wilmer Shantz	5.00	2.50	1.50
176	Joe DeMaestri	5.00	2.50	1.50
177	Willard Nixon	5.00	2.50	1.50
178	Tom Brewer	5.00	2.50	1.50
179	Hank Aaron	200.00	100.00	60.00
180	Johnny Logan	5.00	2.50	1.50
181	Eddie Miksis	5.00	2.50	1.50
182	Bob Rush	5.00	2.50	1.50
183	Ray Katt	5.00	2.50	1.50
184	Willie Mays	200.00	100.00	60.00
185	Vic Raschi	6.00	3.00	1.75
186	Alex Grammas	5.00	2.50	1.50
187	Fred Hatfield	5.00	2.50	1.50
188	Ned Garver	5.00	2.50	1.50
189	Jack Collum	5.00	2.50	1.50
190	Fred Baczewski	5.00	2.50	1.50
191	Bob Lemon	25.00	12.50	7.50
192	George Strickland	5.00	2.50	1.50
193	Howie Judson	5.00	2.50	1.50
194	Joe Nuxhall	6.00	3.00	1.75
195a	Erv Palica (no traded line on back)	7.00	3.50	2.00
195b	Erv Palica (traded line on back)	25.00	12.50	7.50
196	Russ Meyer	6.00	3.00	1.75
197	Ralph Kiner	30.00	15.00	9.00
198	Dave Pope	5.00	2.50	1.50
199	Vernon Law	6.00	3.00	1.75
200	Dick Littlefield	5.00	2.50	1.50
201	Allie Reynolds	15.00	7.50	4.50
202	Mickey Mantle	400.00	175.00	100.00
203	Steve Gromek	5.00	2.50	1.50
204a	*Frank Bolling* (Milt Bolling back)	6.00	3.00	1.75
204b	*Frank Bolling* (Frank Bolling back)	20.00	10.00	6.00
205	Eldon "Rip" Repulski	5.00	2.50	1.50
206	Ralph Beard	5.00	2.50	1.50
207	Frank Shea	5.00	2.50	1.50
208	Eddy Fitzgerald (Fitz Gerald)	5.00	2.50	1.50
209	Forrest "Smoky" Burgess	6.00	3.00	1.75
210	Earl Torgeson	5.00	2.50	1.50
211	John "Sonny" Dixon	5.00	2.50	1.50
212	Jack Dittmer	5.00	2.50	1.50
213	George Kell	25.00	12.50	7.50
214	Billy Pierce	6.00	3.00	1.75
215	Bob Kuzava	5.00	2.50	1.50
216	Preacher Roe	6.00	3.00	1.75
217	Del Crandall	6.00	3.00	1.75
218	Joe Adcock	6.00	3.00	1.75
219	Whitey Lockman	5.00	2.50	1.50
220	Jim Hearn	5.00	2.50	1.50
221	Hector "Skinny" Brown	5.00	2.50	1.50
222	Russ Kemmerer	5.00	2.50	1.50
223	Hal Jeffcoat	5.00	2.50	1.50
224	Dee Fondy	5.00	2.50	1.50
225	Paul Richards	11.00	5.50	3.25
226	W.F. McKinley (umpire)	15.00	7.50	4.50
227	Frank Baumholtz	10.00	5.00	3.00
228	John M. Phillips	10.00	5.00	3.00
229	Jim Brosnan	11.00	5.50	3.25
230	Al Brazle	10.00	5.00	3.00
231	Jim Konstanty	15.00	7.50	4.50
232	Birdie Tebbetts	10.00	5.00	3.00
233	Bill Serena	10.00	5.00	3.00
234	Dick Bartell	10.00	5.00	3.00
235	J.A. Paparella (umpire)	15.00	7.50	4.50
236	Murray Dickson (Murry)	10.00	5.00	3.00
237	Johnny Wyrostek	10.00	5.00	3.00
238	Eddie Stanky	11.00	5.50	3.25
239	Edwin A. Rommel (umpire)	15.00	7.50	4.50
240	Billy Loes	11.00	5.50	3.25
241	John Pesky	11.00	5.50	3.25
242	Ernie Banks	350.00	175.00	100.00
243	Gus Bell	11.00	5.50	3.25
244	Duane Pillette	10.00	5.00	3.00
245	Bill Miller	10.00	5.00	3.00
246	Hank Bauer	25.00	12.50	7.50
247	Dutch Leonard	10.00	5.00	3.00
248	Harry Dorish	10.00	5.00	3.00
249	Billy Gardner	10.00	5.00	3.00
250	Larry Napp (umpire)	15.00	7.50	4.50
251	Stan Jok	10.00	5.00	3.00
252	Roy Smalley	10.00	5.00	3.00
253	Jim Wilson	10.00	5.00	3.00
254	Bennett Flowers	10.00	5.00	3.00
255	Pete Runnels	11.00	5.50	3.25
256	Owen Friend	10.00	5.00	3.00
257	Tom Alston	10.00	5.00	3.00
258	John W. Stevens (umpire)	15.00	7.50	4.50
259	*Don Mossi*	15.00	7.50	4.50
260	Edwin H. Hurley (umpire)	15.00	7.50	4.50
261	Walt Moryn	11.00	5.50	3.25

		NR MT	EX	VG
262	Jim Lemon	11.00	5.50	3.25
263	Eddie Joost	10.00	5.00	3.00
264	Bill Henry	10.00	5.00	3.00
265	Albert J. Barlick (umpire)	70.00	35.00	20.00
266	Mike Fornieles	10.00	5.00	3.00
267	George (Jim) Honochick (umpire)	60.00	30.00	18.00
268	Roy Lee Hawes	10.00	5.00	3.00
269	Joe Amalfitano	10.00	5.00	3.00
270	Chico Fernandez	11.00	5.50	3.25
271	Bob Hooper	10.00	5.00	3.00
272	John Flaherty (umpire)	15.00	7.50	4.50
273	Emory "Bubba" Church	10.00	5.00	3.00
274	Jim Delsing	10.00	5.00	3.00
275	William T. Grieve (umpire)	15.00	7.50	4.50
276	Ivan Delock	10.00	5.00	3.00
277	Ed Runge (umpire)	15.00	7.50	4.50
278	*Charles Neal*	15.00	7.50	4.50
279	Hank Soar (umpire)	15.00	7.50	4.50
280	Clyde McCullough	10.00	5.00	3.00
281	Charles Berry (umpire)	15.00	7.50	4.50
282	Phil Cavarretta	11.00	5.50	3.25
283	Nestor Chylak (umpire)	15.00	7.50	4.50
284	William A. Jackowski (umpire)	15.00	7.50	4.50
285	Walt Dropo	11.00	5.50	3.25
286	Frank E. Secory (umpire)	15.00	7.50	4.50
287	Ron Mrozinski	10.00	5.00	3.00
288	Dick Smith	10.00	5.00	3.00
289	Arthur J. Gore (umpire)	15.00	7.50	4.50
290	Hershell Freeman	10.00	5.00	3.00
291	Frank Dascoli (umpire)	15.00	7.50	4.50
292	Marv Blaylock	10.00	5.00	3.00
293	Thomas D. Gorman (umpire)	15.00	7.50	4.50
294	Wally Moses	10.00	5.00	3.00
295	E. Lee Ballanfant (umpire)	15.00	7.50	4.50
296	*Bill Virdon*	25.00	12.50	7.50
297	L.R. "Dusty" Boggess (umpire)	15.00	7.50	4.50
298	Charlie Grimm	15.00	7.50	4.50
299	Lonnie Warneke (umpire)	15.00	7.50	4.50
300	Tommy Byrne	14.00	7.00	4.25
301	William R. Engeln (umpire)	15.00	7.50	4.50
302	*Frank Malzone*	15.00	7.50	4.50
303	J.B. "Jocko" Conlan (umpire)	75.00	37.00	22.00
304	Harry Chiti	10.00	5.00	3.00
305	Frank Umont (umpire)	15.00	7.50	4.50
306	Bob Cerv	15.00	7.50	4.50
307	R.A. "Babe" Pinelli (umpire)	15.00	7.50	4.50
308	Al Lopez	35.00	17.50	10.50
309	Hal H. Dixon (umpire)	15.00	7.50	4.50
310	Ken Lehman	11.00	5.50	3.25
311	Lawrence J. Goetz (umpire)	15.00	7.50	4.50
312	Bill Wight	10.00	5.00	3.00
313	A.J. Donatelli (umpire)	15.00	7.50	4.50
314	Dale Mitchell	10.00	5.00	3.00
315	Cal Hubbard (umpire)	70.00	35.00	20.00
316	Marion Fricano	10.00	5.00	3.00
317	Wm. R. Summers (umpire)	15.00	7.50	4.50
318	Sid Hudson	10.00	5.00	3.00
319	Albert B. Schroll	15.00	7.50	4.50
320	George D. Susce, Jr.	50.00	6.00	3.50

1989 Bowman

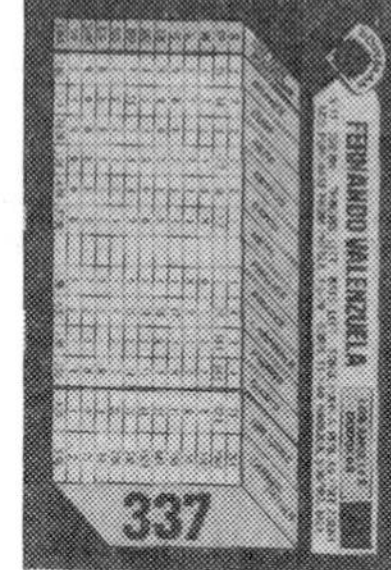

Topps, which purchased the Bowman Co. back in 1955, revived the Bowman name in 1989, issuing a 484-card set modeled after the 1953 Bowman cards. The cards are 2-1/2" by 3-3/4", slightly larger than a current standard-sized card. The fronts contain a full-color player photo, with facsimile autograph on the bottom and the Bowman logo in an upper corner. The unique card backs include a breakdown of the player's stats against each team in his league. A series of "Hot Rookie Stars" highlight the set. The cards were distributed in both wax packs and rack packs. Each pack included a special reproduction of a classic Bowman card with a sweepstakes on the back. The special cards said "reprint" on the front.

		MT	NR MT	EX
	Complete Set:	22.00	16.50	9.00
	Common Player:	.03	.02	.01
1	Oswald Peraza	.05	.04	.02
2	Brian Holton	.05	.04	.02
3	Jose Bautista	.05	.04	.02
4	Pete Harnisch	.10	.08	.04
5	Dave Schmidt	.03	.02	.01
6	Gregg Olson	.60	.45	.25
7	Jeff Ballard	.10	.08	.04
8	Bob Melvin	.03	.02	.01
9	Cal Ripken	.20	.15	.08
10	Randy Milligan	.08	.06	.03
11	Juan Bell	.15	.11	.06
12	Billy Ripken	.05	.04	.02
13	Jim Trabor	.03	.02	.01
14	Pete Stanicek	.03	.02	.01
15	Steve Finley	.20	.15	.08
16	Larry Sheets	.03	.02	.01
17	Phil Bradley	.05	.04	.02
18	Brady Anderson	.10	.08	.04
19	Lee Smith	.03	.02	.01
20	Tom Fischer	.15	.11	.06
21	Mike Boddicker	.03	.02	.01
22	Rob Murphy	.03	.02	.01
23	Wes Gardner	.03	.02	.01
24	John Dopson	.10	.08	.04
25	Bob Stanley	.03	.02	.01
26	Roger Clemens	.20	.15	.08
27	Rich Gedman	.03	.02	.01
28	Marty Barrett	.03	.02	.01
29	Luis Rivera	.03	.02	.01
30	Jody Reed	.05	.04	.02
31	Nick Esasky	.05	.04	.02
32	Wade Boggs	.40	.30	.15
33	Jim Rice	.10	.08	.04
34	Mike Greenwell	.40	.30	.15
35	Dwight Evans	.15	.11	.06
36	Ellis Burks	.25	.20	.10
37	Chuck Finley	.05	.04	.02
38	Kirk McCaskill	.05	.04	.02
39	Jim Abbott	1.75	1.25	.70
40	Bryan Harvey	.05	.04	.02
41	Bert Blyleven	.08	.06	.03
42	Mike Witt	.03	.02	.01
43	Bob McClure	.03	.02	.01
44	Bill Schroeder	.03	.02	.01
45	Lance Parrish	.05	.04	.02
46	Dick Schofield	.03	.02	.01
47	Wally Joyner	.10	.08	.04
48	Jack Howell	.03	.02	.01
49	Johnny Ray	.03	.02	.01
50	Chili Davis	.05	.04	.02
51	Tony Armas	.03	.02	.01
52	Claudell Washington	.03	.02	.01
53	Brian Downing	.03	.02	.01
54	Devon White	.10	.08	.04
55	Bobby Thigpen	.08	.06	.03
56	Bill Long	.03	.02	.01
57	Jerry Reuss	.03	.02	.01
58	Shawn Hillegas	.03	.02	.01
59	Melido Perez	.05	.04	.02
60	Jeff Bittiger	.05	.04	.02
61	Jack McDowell	.03	.02	.01
62	Carlton Fisk	.10	.08	.04
63	Steve Lyons	.03	.02	.01
64	Ozzie Guillen	.05	.04	.02
65	Robin Ventura	.70	.50	.30
66	Fred Manrique	.03	.02	.01
67	Dan Pasqua	.03	.02	.01
68	Ivan Calderon	.03	.02	.01
69	Ron Kittle	.03	.02	.01
70	Daryl Boston	.03	.02	.01
71	Dave Gallagher	.05	.04	.02
72	Harold Baines	.08	.06	.03
73	Charles Nagy	.20	.15	.08
74	John Farrell	.03	.02	.01
75	Kevin Wickander	.25	.20	.10
76	Greg Swindell	.15	.11	.06
77	Mike Walker	.15	.11	.06
78	Doug Jones	.05	.04	.02
79	Rich Yett	.03	.02	.01
80	Tom Candiotti	.03	.02	.01
81	Jesse Orosco	.03	.02	.01
82	Bud Black	.03	.02	.01
83	Andy Allanson	.03	.02	.01
84	Pete O'Brien	.05	.04	.02
85	Jerry Browne	.05	.04	.02
86	Brook Jacoby	.03	.02	.01
87	Mark Lewis	.50	.40	.20
88	Luis Aguayo	.03	.02	.01
89	Cory Snyder	.05	.04	.02
90	Oddibe McDowell	.05	.04	.02
91	Joe Carter	.15	.11	.06
92	Frank Tanana	.03	.02	.01
93	Jack Morris	.03	.02	.01
94	Doyle Alexander	.03	.02	.01
95	Steve Searcy	.08	.06	.03
96	Randy Bockus	.05	.04	.02
97	Jeff Robinson	.05	.04	.02
98	Mike Henneman	.05	.04	.02
99	Paul Gibson	.03	.02	.01
100	Frank Williams	.03	.02	.01
101	Matt Nokes	.05	.04	.02
102	Rico Brogna	.15	.11	.06
103	Lou Whitaker	.08	.06	.03
104	Al Pedrique	.03	.02	.01
105	Alan Trammell	.05	.04	.02
106	Chris Brown	.03	.02	.01
107	Pat Sheridan	.03	.02	.01
108	Gary Pettis	.03	.02	.01
109	Keith Moreland	.03	.02	.01
110	Mel Stottlemyre, Jr.	.15	.11	.06
111	Bret Saberhagen	.10	.08	.04
112	Floyd Bannister	.03	.02	.01
113	Jeff Montgomery	.05	.04	.02
114	Steve Farr	.05	.04	.02
115	Tom Gordon	.80	.60	.30
116	Charlie Leibrandt	.03	.02	.01
117	Mark Gubicza	.08	.06	.03
118	Mike MacFarlane	.03	.02	.01
119	Bob Boone	.05	.04	.02
120	Kurt Stillwell	.05	.04	.02
121	George Brett	.15	.11	.06
122	Frank White	.05	.04	.02
123	Kevin Seitzer	.08	.06	.03
124	Willie Wilson	.03	.02	.01
125	Pat Tabler	.03	.02	.01
126	Bo Jackson	.90	.70	.35
127	Hugh Walker	.20	.15	.08
128	Danny Tartabull	.05	.04	.02
129	Teddy Higuera	.08	.06	.03
130	Don August	.03	.02	.01
131	Juan Nieves	.03	.02	.01

		MT	NR MT	EX
132	Mike Birkbeck	.03	.02	.01
133	Dan Plesac	.05	.04	.02
134	Chris Bosio	.05	.04	.02
135	Bill Wegman	.03	.02	.01
136	Chuck Crim	.03	.02	.01
137	B.J. Surhoff	.05	.04	.02
138	Joey Meyer	.03	.02	.01
139	Dale Sveum	.03	.02	.01
140	Paul Molitor	.08	.06	.03
141	Jim Gantner	.03	.02	.01
142	Gary Sheffield	1.00	.70	.40
143	Greg Brock	.03	.02	.01
144	Robin Yount	.25	.20	.10
145	Glenn Braggs	.03	.02	.01
146	Rob Deer	.03	.02	.01
147	Fred Toliver	.03	.02	.01
148	Jeff Reardon	.03	.02	.01
149	Allan Anderson	.05	.04	.02
150	Frank Viola	.15	.11	.06
151	Shane Rawley	.03	.02	.01
152	Juan Berenguer	.03	.02	.01
153	Johnny Ard	.20	.15	.08
154	Tim Laudner	.03	.02	.01
155	Brian Harper	.03	.02	.01
156	Al Newman	.03	.02	.01
157	Kent Hrbek	.08	.06	.03
158	Gary Gaetti	.08	.06	.03
159	Wally Backman	.03	.02	.01
160	Gene Larkin	.03	.02	.01
161	Greg Gagne	.03	.02	.01
162	Kirby Puckett	.35	.25	.14
163	Danny Gladden	.03	.02	.01
164	Randy Bush	.03	.02	.01
165	Dave LaPoint	.03	.02	.01
166	Andy Hawkins	.03	.02	.01
167	Dave Righetti	.05	.04	.02
168	Lance McCullers	.03	.02	.01
169	Jimmy Jones	.03	.02	.01
170	Al Leiter	.03	.02	.01
171	John Candelaria	.03	.02	.01
172	Don Slaught	.03	.02	.01
173	Jamie Quirk	.03	.02	.01
174	Rafael Santana	.03	.02	.01
175	Mike Pagliarulo	.03	.02	.01
176	Don Mattingly	.90	.70	.35
177	Ken Phelps	.03	.02	.01
178	Steve Sax	.08	.06	.03
179	Dave Winfield	.20	.15	.08
180	Stan Jefferson	.03	.02	.01
181	Rickey Henderson	.40	.30	.15
182	Bob Brower	.03	.02	.01
183	Roberto Kelly	.10	.08	.04
184	Curt Young	.03	.02	.01
185	Gene Nelson	.03	.02	.01
186	Bob Welch	.03	.02	.01
187	Rick Honeycutt	.03	.02	.01
188	Dave Stewart	.08	.06	.03
189	Mike Moore	.08	.06	.03
190	Dennis Eckersley	.08	.06	.03
191	Eric Plunk	.03	.02	.01
192	Storm Davis	.03	.02	.01
193	Terry Steinbach	.10	.08	.04
194	Ron Hassey	.03	.02	.01
195	Stan Royer	.15	.11	.06
196	Walt Weiss	.15	.11	.06
197	Mark McGwire	.40	.30	.15
198	Carney Lansford	.08	.06	.03
199	Glenn Hubbard	.03	.02	.01
200	Dave Henderson	.05	.04	.02
201	Jose Canseco	1.50	1.25	.60
202	Dave Parker	.05	.04	.02
203	Scott Bankhead	.05	.04	.02
204	Tom Niedenfuer	.03	.02	.01
205	Mark Langston	.15	.11	.06
206	Erik Hanson	.15	.11	.06
207	Mike Jackson	.03	.02	.01
208	Dave Valle	.03	.02	.01
209	Scott Bradley	.03	.02	.01
210	Harold Reynolds	.08	.06	.03
211	Tino Martinez	1.00	.70	.40
212	Rich Renteria	.03	.02	.01
213	Rey Quinones	.03	.02	.01
214	Jim Presley	.03	.02	.01
215	Alvin Davis	.10	.08	.04
216	Edgar Martinez	.03	.02	.01
217	Darnell Coles	.03	.02	.01
218	Jeffrey Leonard	.08	.06	.04
219	Jay Buhner	.03	.02	.01
220	Ken Griffey, Jr.	5.00	3.75	2.00
221	Drew Hall	.03	.02	.01
222	Bobby Witt	.03	.02	.01
223	Jamie Moyer	.03	.02	.01
224	Charlie Hough	.03	.02	.01
225	Nolan Ryan	.70	.50	.30
226	Jeff Russell	.05	.04	.02
227	Jim Sundberg	.03	.02	.01
228	Julio Franco	.15	.11	.06
229	Buddy Bell	.03	.02	.01
230	Scott Fletcher	.03	.02	.01
231	Jeff Kunkel	.03	.02	.01
232	Steve Buechele	.03	.02	.01
233	Monty Fariss	.25	.20	.10
234	Rick Leach	.03	.02	.01
235	Ruben Sierra	.40	.30	.15
236	Cecil Espy	.05	.04	.02
237	Rafael Palmeiro	.10	.08	.04
238	Pete Incaviglia	.03	.02	.01
239	Dave Steib	.05	.04	.02
240	Jeff Musselman	.03	.02	.01
241	Mike Flanagan	.03	.02	.01
242	Todd Stottlemyre	.05	.04	.02
243	Jimmy Key	.05	.04	.02
244	Tony Castillo	.10	.08	.04
245	Alex Sanchez	.05	.04	.02
246	Tom Henke	.03	.02	.01
247	John Cerutti	.03	.02	.01
248	Ernie Whitt	.03	.02	.01
249	Bob Brenly	.03	.02	.01
250	Rance Mulliniks	.03	.02	.01
251	Kelly Gruber	.10	.08	.04
252	Ed Sprague	.20	.15	.08
253	Fred McGriff	.40	.30	.15
254	Tony Fernandez	.08	.06	.03

		MT	NR MT	EX
255	Tom Lawless	.03	.02	.01
256	George Bell	.10	.08	.04
257	Jesse Barfield	.05	.04	.02
258	Sandy Alomar	.20	.15	.08
259	Ken Griffey	.30	.25	.12
260	Cal Ripken, Sr.	.15	.11	.06
261	Mel Stottlemyre	.15	.11	.06
262	Zane Smith	.03	.02	.01
263	Charlie Puleo	.03	.02	.01
264	Derek Lilliquist	.15	.11	.06
265	Paul Assenmacher	.03	.02	.01
266	John Smoltz	.60	.45	.25
267	Tom Glavine	.10	.08	.04
268	Steve Avery	1.00	.70	.40
269	Pete Smith	.05	.04	.02
270	Jody Davis	.03	.02	.01
271	Bruce Benedict	.03	.02	.01
272	Andres Thomas	.03	.02	.01
273	Gerald Perry	.05	.04	.02
274	Ron Gant	.05	.04	.02
275	Darrell Evans	.03	.02	.01
276	Dale Murphy	.08	.06	.03
277	Dion James	.03	.02	.01
278	Lonnie Smith	.08	.06	.03
279	Geronimo Berroa	.05	.04	.02
280	Steve Wilson	.20	.15	.08
281	Rick Suctcliffe	.05	.04	.02
282	Kevin Coffman	.03	.02	.01
283	Mitch Williams	.10	.08	.04
284	Greg Maddux	.05	.04	.02
285	Paul Kilgus	.03	.02	.01
286	Mike Harkey	.10	.08	.04
287	Lloyd McClendon	.05	.04	.02
288	Damon Berryhill	.05	.04	.02
289	Ty Griffin	.60	.45	.25
290	Ryne Sandberg	.15	.11	.06
291	Mark Grace	1.00	.70	.40
292	Curt Wilkerson	.03	.02	.01
293	Vance Law	.03	.02	.01
294	Shawon Dunston	.08	.06	.04
295	Jerome Walton	2.25	1.75	.90
296	Mitch Webster	.03	.02	.01
297	Dwight Smith	1.50	1.25	.60
298	Andre Dawson	.15	.11	.06
299	Jeff Sellers	.03	.02	.01
300	Jose Rijo	.05	.04	.02
301	John Franco	.05	.04	.02
302	Rick Mahler	.03	.02	.01
303	Ron Robinson	.03	.02	.01
304	Danny Jackson	.03	.02	.01
305	Rob Dibble	.08	.06	.04
306	Tom Browning	.03	.02	.01
307	Bo Diaz	.03	.02	.01
308	Manny Trillo	.03	.02	.01
309	Chris Sabo	.15	.11	.06
310	Ron Oester	.03	.02	.01
311	Barry Larkin	.15	.11	.06
312	Todd Benzinger	.05	.04	.02
313	Paul O'Neil	.05	.04	.02
314	Kal Daniels	.05	.04	.02
315	Joel Youngblood	.03	.02	.01
316	Eric Davis	.25	.20	.10
317	Dave Smith	.05	.04	.03
318	Mark Portugal	.03	.02	.01
319	Brian Meyer	.03	.02	.01
320	Jim Deshaies	.05	.04	.02
321	Juan Agosto	.03	.02	.01
322	Mike Scott	.10	.08	.04
323	Rick Rhoden	.03	.02	.01
324	Jim Clancy	.03	.02	.01
325	Larry Andersen	.03	.02	.01
326	Alex Trevino	.03	.02	.01
327	Alan Ashby	.03	.02	.01
328	Craig Reynolds	.03	.02	.01
329	Bill Doran	.03	.02	.01
330	Rafael Ramirez	.03	.02	.01
331	Glenn Davis	.10	.08	.04
332	Willie Ansley	.35	.25	.14
333	Gerald Young	.03	.02	.01
334	Cameron Drew	.10	.08	.04
335	Jay Howell	.05	.04	.03
336	Tim Belcher	.05	.04	.03
337	Fernando Valenzuela	.05	.04	.03
338	Ricky Horton	.03	.02	.01
339	Tim Leary	.03	.02	.01
340	Bill Bene	.15	.11	.06
341	Orel Hershiser	.20	.15	.08
342	Mike Scioscia	.05	.04	.02
343	Rick Dempsey	.03	.02	.01
344	Willie Randolph	.03	.02	.01
345	Alfredo Griffin	.03	.02	.01
346	Eddie Murray	.08	.06	.03
347	Mickey Hatcher	.03	.02	.01
348	Mike Sharperson	.03	.02	.01
349	John Shelby	.03	.02	.01
350	Mike Marshall	.03	.02	.01
351	Kirk Gibson	.05	.04	.02
352	Mike Davis	.03	.02	.01
353	Bryn Smith	.03	.02	.01
354	Pascual Perez	.03	.02	.01
355	Kevin Gross	.03	.02	.01
356	Andy McGaffigan	.03	.02	.01
357	Brian Holman	.05	.04	.02
358	Dave Wainhouse	.20	.15	.08
359	Denny Martinez	.03	.02	.01
360	Tim Burke	.03	.02	.01
361	Nelson Santovenia	.08	.06	.04
362	Tim Wallach	.05	.04	.02
363	Spike Owen	.03	.02	.01
364	Rex Hudler	.03	.02	.01
365	Andres Galarraga	.08	.06	.03
366	Otis Nixon	.03	.02	.01
367	Hubie Brooks	.03	.02	.01
368	Mike Aldrete	.03	.02	.01
369	Rock Raines	.08	.06	.03
370	Dave Martinez	.03	.02	.01
371	Bob Ojeda	.03	.02	.01
372	Ron Darling	.05	.04	.02
373	Wally Whitehurst	.20	.15	.08
374	Randy Myers	.05	.04	.02
375	David Cone	.05	.04	.02
376	Doc Gooden	.25	.20	.10
377	Sid Fernandez	.05	.04	.02

		MT	NR MT	EX
378	Dave Proctor	.20	.15	.08
379	Gary Carter	.03	.02	.01
380	Keith Miller	.05	.04	.02
381	Gregg Jefferies	1.25	.90	.50
382	Tim Teufel	.03	.02	.01
383	Kevin Elster	.03	.02	.01
384	Dave Magadan	.03	.02	.01
385	Keith Hernandez	.05	.04	.02
386	Mookie Wilson	.05	.04	.02
387	Darryl Strawberry	.40	.30	.15
388	Kevin McReynolds	.10	.08	.04
389	Mark Carreon	.05	.04	.02
390	Jeff Parrett	.05	.04	.02
391	Mike Maddux	.03	.02	.01
392	Don Carman	.03	.02	.01
393	Bruce Ruffin	.03	.02	.01
394	Ken Howell	.03	.02	.01
395	Steve Bedrosian	.05	.04	.02
396	Floyd Youmans	.03	.02	.01
397	Larry McWilliams	.03	.02	.01
398	Pat Combs	.40	.30	.15
399	Steve Lake	.03	.02	.01
400	Dickie Thon	.03	.02	.01
401	Ricky Jordan	.35	.25	.14
402	Mike Schmidt	.60	.45	.25
403	Tom Herr	.03	.02	.01
404	Chris James	.03	.02	.01
405	Juan Samuel	.08	.06	.03
406	Von Hayes	.08	.06	.03
407	Ron Jones	.15	.11	.06
408	Curt Ford	.03	.02	.01
409	Bob Walk	.03	.02	.01
410	Jeff Robinson	.03	.02	.01
411	Jim Gott	.03	.02	.01
412	Scott Medvin	.03	.02	.01
413	John Smiley	.03	.02	.01
414	Bob Kipper	.03	.02	.01
415	Brian Fisher	.03	.02	.01
416	Doug Drabek	.03	.02	.01
417	Mike Lavalliere	.03	.02	.01
418	Ken Oberkfell	.03	.02	.01
419	Sid Bream	.03	.02	.01
420	Austin Manahan	.20	.15	.08
421	Jose Lind	.03	.02	.01
422	Bobby Bonilla	.10	.08	.04
423	Glenn Wilson	.03	.02	.01
424	Andy Van Slyke	.10	.08	.04
425	Gary Redus	.03	.02	.01
426	Barry Bonds	.10	.08	.04
427	Don Heinkel	.03	.02	.01
428	Ken Dayley	.03	.02	.01
429	Todd Worrell	.05	.04	.02
430	Brad DuVall	.20	.15	.08
431	Jose DeLeon	.03	.02	.01
432	Joe Magrane	.10	.08	.04
433	John Ericks	.20	.15	.08
434	Frank DiPino	.03	.02	.01
435	Tony Pena	.05	.04	.02
436	Ozzie Smith	.08	.06	.03
437	Terry Pendleton	.03	.02	.01
438	Jose Oquendo	.03	.02	.01
439	Tim Jones	.05	.04	.02
440	Pedro Guerrero	.10	.08	.04
441	Milt Thompson	.03	.02	.01
442	Willie McGee	.05	.04	.02
443	Vince Coleman	.05	.04	.02
444	Tom Brunansky	.05	.04	.02
445	Walt Terrell	.03	.02	.01
446	Eric Show	.03	.02	.01
447	Mark Davis	.10	.08	.04
448	Andy Benes	1.00	.70	.40
449	Eddie Whitson	.03	.02	.01
450	Dennis Rasmussen	.03	.02	.01
451	Bruce Hurst	.03	.02	.01
452	Pat Clements	.03	.02	.01
453	Benito Santiago	.10	.08	.04
454	Sandy Alomar, Jr.	.60	.45	.25
455	Garry Templeton	.03	.02	.01
456	Jack Clark	.05	.04	.02
457	Tim Flannery	.03	.02	.01
458	Roberto Alomar	.80	.60	.30
459	Camelo Martinez	.03	.02	.01
460	John Kruk	.03	.02	.01
461	Tony Gwynn	.20	.15	.08
462	Jerald Clark	.05	.04	.02
463	Don Robinson	.03	.02	.01
464	Craig Lefferts	.03	.02	.01
465	Kelly Downs	.03	.02	.01
466	Rick Rueschel	.05	.04	.02
467	Scott Garrelts	.03	.02	.01
468	Wil Tejada	.03	.02	.01
469	Kirt Manwaring	.10	.08	.04
470	Terry Kennedy	.03	.02	.01
471	Jose Uribe	.03	.02	.01
472	Royce Clayton	.20	.15	.08
473	Robby Thompson	.05	.04	.02
474	Kevin Mitchell	.80	.60	.30
475	Ernie Riles	.03	.02	.01
476	Will Clark	1.00	.70	.40
477	Donnell Nixon	.03	.02	.01
478	Candy Maldonado	.03	.02	.01
479	Tracy Jones	.03	.02	.01
480	Brett Butler	.05	.04	.02
481	Checklist	.05	.04	.02
482	Checklist	.05	.04	.02
483	Checklist	.05	.04	.02
484	Checklist	.05	.04	.02

1954 Briggs Meats

The Briggs Meat set was issued over a two-year span (1953-54) and features 26 players from the Washington Senators and 12 from the New York City area baseball teams. The set was issued in two-card panels on hot dog packages sold in the Washington, D.C. vicinity. The color cards, which are blank-backed and measure 2-1/4" by 3-1/2", are printed on waxed cardboard. The style of the

Senators cards in the set differs from that of the New York players. Poses for the New York players can also be found on cards in the 1954 Dan-Dee Potato Chips and 1953-1955 Stahl-Meyer Franks sets.

		NR MT	EX	VG
Complete Set		8000.00	4000.00	2500.
Common Player		100.00	50.00	30.00
(1)	Hank Bauer	150.00	75.00	45.00
(2)	James Busby	100.00	50.00	30.00
(3)	Tommy Byrne	100.00	50.00	30.00
(4)	John Dixon	100.00	50.00	30.00
(5)	Carl Erskine	150.00	75.00	45.00
(6)	Edward Fitzgerald (Fitz Gerald)	100.00	50.00	30.00
(7)	Newton Grasso	100.00	50.00	30.00
(8)	Melvin Hoderlein	100.00	50.00	30.00
(9)	Gil Hodges	250.00	125.00	75.00
(10)	Monte Irvin	175.00	87.00	52.00
(11)	Whitey Lockman	100.00	50.00	30.00
(12)	Mickey Mantle	2200.00	1100.00	660.00
(13)	Conrado Marrero	100.00	50.00	30.00
(14)	Walter Masterson	100.00	50.00	30.00
(15)	Carmen Mauro	100.00	50.00	30.00
(16)	Willie Mays	1000.00	500.00	300.00
(17)	Mickey McDermott	100.00	50.00	30.00
(18)	Gil McDougald	150.00	75.00	45.00
(19)	Julio Moreno	100.00	50.00	30.00
(20)	Don Mueller	100.00	50.00	30.00
(21)	Don Newcombe	150.00	75.00	45.00
(22)	Robert Oldis	100.00	50.00	30.00
(23)	Erwin Porterfield	100.00	50.00	30.00
(24)	Phil Rizzuto	250.00	125.00	75.00
(25)	James Runnels	100.00	50.00	30.00
(26)	John Schmitz	100.00	50.00	30.00
(27)	Angel Scull	100.00	50.00	30.00
(28)	Frank Shea	100.00	50.00	30.00
(29)	Albert Sima	100.00	50.00	30.00
(30)	Duke Snider	500.00	250.00	150.00
(31)	Charles Stobbs	100.00	50.00	30.00
(32)	Willard Terwilliger	100.00	50.00	30.00
(33)	Joe Tipton	100.00	50.00	30.00
(34)	Thomas Umphlett	100.00	50.00	30.00
(35)	Gene Verble	100.00	50.00	30.00
(36)	James Vernon	125.00	62.00	37.00
(37)	Clyde Volmer (Vollmer)	100.00	50.00	30.00
(38)	Edward Yost	100.00	50.00	30.00

1977 Burger King Yankees

The first Topps-produced set for Burger King restaurants was issued in the New York area in 1977 and featured the A.L. champion New York Yankees. Twenty-two players plus an unnumbered checklist were issued at the beginning of the promotion with card #23 (Lou Piniella) being added to the set at a later date. The Piniella card was issued in limited quantities. The cards, numbered 1 through 23, are 2-1/2" by 3-1/2" in size and have fronts identical to the regular 1977 Topps set except for the following numbers: 2, 6, 7, 13, 14, 15, 17, 20 and 21. These cards feature different poses or major picture- cropping variations. It should be noted that very minor cropping variations between the regular Topps sets and the Burger King issues exist throughout the years the sets were produced.

		NR MT	EX	VG
Complete Set:		50.00	25.00	15.00
Common Player:		.30	.15	.09
1	Yankees Team (Billy Martin)	1.25	.60	.40
2	Thurman Munson	7.00	3.50	2.00
3	Fran Healy	.30	.15	.09
4	Jim Hunter	2.00	1.00	.60
5	Ed Figueroa	.30	.15	.09
6	Don Gullett	.70	.35	.20
7	Mike Torrez	.70	.35	.20
8	Ken Holtzman	.50	.25	.15
9	Dick Tidrow	.30	.15	.09
10	Sparky Lyle	.50	.25	.15
11	Ron Guidry	1.25	.60	.40
12	Chris Chambliss	.50	.25	.15
13	Willie Randolph	.80	.40	.25
14	Bucky Dent	.80	.40	.25
15	Graig Nettles	1.25	.60	.40
16	Fred Stanley	.30	.15	.09
17	Reggie Jackson	8.00	4.00	2.50
18	Mickey Rivers	.50	.25	.15
19	Roy White	.50	.25	.15
20	Jim Wynn	.70	.35	.20
21	Paul Blair	.70	.35	.20
22	Carlos May	.30	.15	.09
23	Lou Piniella	25.00	12.50	7.50
---	Checklist	.10	.05	.03

1978 Burger King Astros

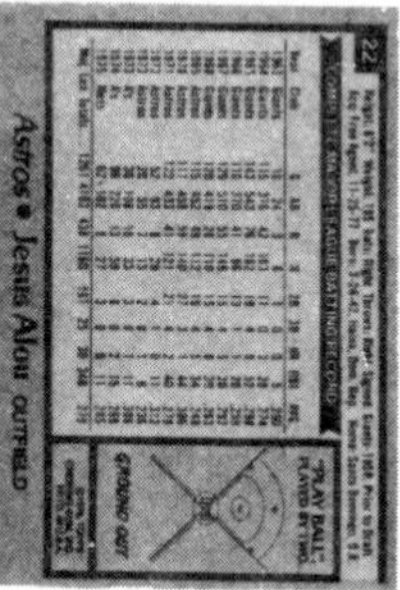

Burger King restaurants in the Houston area distributed a Topps-produced 23-card set showcasing the Astros in 1978. The cards are standard size (2-1/2" by 3-1/2") and are numbered 1 through 22. The checklist card is unnumbered. The card fronts are identical to the regular 1978 Topps set with the exception of card numbers 21 and 22, which have different poses. Although not noted in the following checklist, it should be remembered that very minor picture-cropping variations between the regular Topps issues and the 1977-1980 Burger King sets do exist.

		NR MT	EX	VG
Complete Set:		12.00	6.00	3.50
Common Player:		.30	.15	.09
1	Bill Virdon	.50	.25	.15
2	Joe Ferguson	.30	.15	.09
3	Ed Herrmann	.30	.15	.09
4	J.R. Richard	.60	.30	.20
5	Joe Niekro	.60	.30	.20
6	Floyd Bannister	.70	.35	.20
7	Joaquin Andujar	.60	.30	.20
8	Ken Forsch	.40	.20	.12
9	Mark Lemongello	.30	.15	.09
10	Joe Sambito	.40	.20	.12
11	Gene Pentz	.30	.15	.09
12	Bob Watson	.40	.20	.12
13	Julio Gonzalez	.30	.15	.09
14	Enos Cabell	.40	.20	.12
15	Roger Metzger	.30	.15	.09
16	Art Howe	.60	.30	.20
17	Jose Cruz	.80	.40	.25
18	Cesar Cedeno	.80	.40	.25
19	Terry Puhl	.40	.20	.12
20	Wilbur Howard	.30	.15	.09
21	Dave Bergman	.60	.30	.20
22	Jesus Alou	.60	.30	.20
---	Checklist	.04	.02	.01

1978 Burger King Rangers

Issued by Burger King restaurants in the Dallas-Fort Worth area, this 23-card Topps-produced set features the Texas Rangers. The cards are standard size (2-1/2" by 3-1/2") and are identical in style to the regular 1978 Topps set with the following exceptions: #'s 5, 8, 10, 12, 17, 21 and 22. An unnumbered checklist card was included with the set.

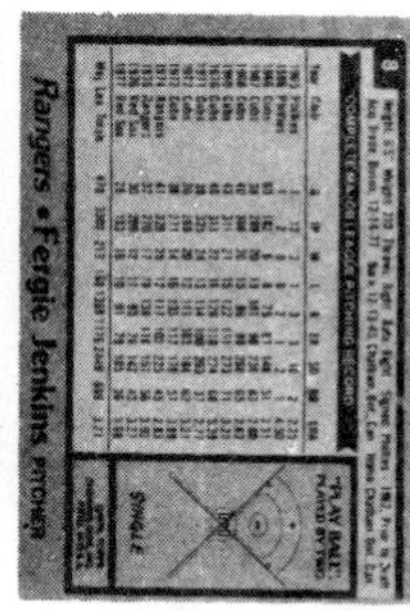

		NR MT	EX	VG
Complete Set:		12.00	6.00	3.50
Common Player:		.30	.15	.09
1	Billy Hunter	.30	.15	.09
2	Jim Sundberg	.50	.25	.15
3	John Ellis	.30	.15	.09
4	Doyle Alexander	.50	.25	.15
5	Jon Matlack	.60	.30	.20
6	Dock Ellis	.30	.15	.09
7	George Medich	.30	.15	.09
8	Fergie Jenkins	1.25	.60	.40
9	Len Barker	.30	.15	.09
10	Reggie Cleveland	.60	.30	.20
11	Mike Hargrove	.40	.20	.12
12	Bump Wills	.60	.30	.20
13	Toby Harrah	.50	.25	.15
14	Bert Campaneris	.50	.25	.15
15	Sandy Alomar	.30	.15	.09
16	Kurt Bevacqua	.30	.15	.09
17	Al Oliver	1.00	.50	.30
18	Juan Beniquez	.30	.15	.09
19	Claudell Washington	.50	.25	.15
20	Richie Zisk	.40	.20	.12
21	John Lowenstein	.60	.30	.20
22	Bobby Thompson	.60	.30	.20
---	Checklist	.04	.02	.01

Definitions for grading conditions are located in the Introduction section at the front of this book.

1978 Burger King Tigers

Rookie cards of Morris, Trammell and Whitaker make the Topps-produced 1978 Burger King Detroit Tigers issue the most popular of the BK sets. Twenty-two player cards and an unnumbered checklist make up the set which was issued in the Detroit area. The cards measure 2-1/2" by 3-1/2", aruue ideuuntical to the regular 1978 Topps issue with the following exceptions - card #'s 6, 7, 8, 13, 15 and 16. Collectors are reminded that numerous minor picture-cropping variations between the regular Topps issues and the Burger King sets appear from the 1977 through 1980. These minor variations are not noted in the following checklist.

		NR MT	EX	VG
Complete Set:		60.00	30.00	18.00
Common Player:		.40	.20	.12
1	Ralph Houk	.40	.20	.12
2	Milt May	.40	.20	.12
3	John Wockenfuss	.40	.20	.12
4	Mark Fidrych	1.00	.50	.30
5	Dave Rozema	.40	.20	.12
6	Jack Billingham	.40	.20	.12
7	Jim Slaton	.40	.20	.12
8	Jack Morris	12.00	6.00	3.50
9	John Hiller	.50	.25	.15
10	Steve Foucault	.40	.20	.12
11	Milt Wilcox	.40	.20	.12
12	Jason Thompson	.50	.25	.15
13	Lou Whitaker	12.00	6.00	3.50
14	Aurelio Rodriguez	.40	.20	.12
15	Alan Trammell	20.00	10.00	6.00
16	Steve Dillard	.40	.20	.12
17	Phil Mankowski	.40	.20	.12
18	Steve Kemp	.50	.25	.15
19	Ron LeFlore	.50	.25	.15
20	Tim Corcoran	.40	.20	.12
21	Mickey Stanley	.40	.20	.12
22	Rusty Staub	1.00	.50	.30
---)	Checklist	.10	.05	.03

1978 Burger King Yankees

Produced by Topps for Burger King outlets in the New York area for the second year in a row,

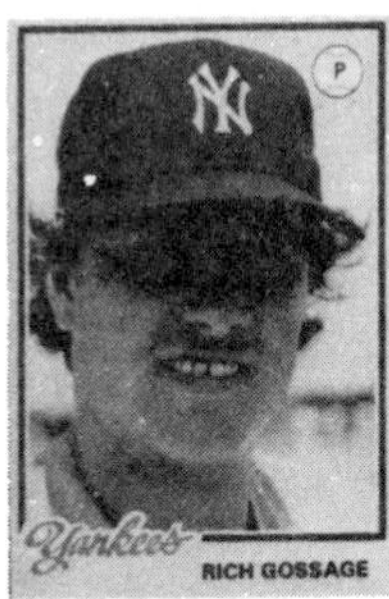

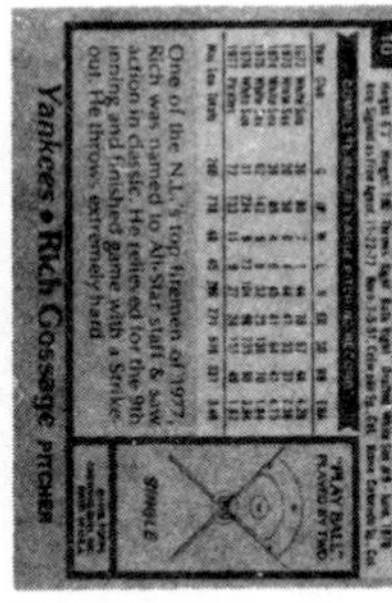

the 1978 Yankees set contains 22 cards plus an unnumbered checklist. The cards are numbered 1 through 22 and are the standard size of 2-1/2" by 3-1/2". The cards feature the same pictures found in the regular 1978 Topps set except for numbers 10, 11 and 16. Only those variations containing different poses or major picture-cropping differences are noted. Numerous minor picture-cropping variations, that are very insignificant in nature, exist between the regular Topps sets and the Burger King issues of 1977-1980.

		NR MT	EX	VG
	Complete Set:	12.00	6.00	3.50
	Common Player:	.30	.15	.09
1	Billy Martin	.80	.40	.25
2	Thurman Munson	3.00	1.50	.90
3	Cliff Johnson	.30	.15	.09
4	Ron Guidry	1.25	.60	.40
5	Ed Figueroa	.30	.15	.09
6	Dick Tidrow	.30	.15	.09
7	Jim Hunter	1.00	.50	.30
8	Don Gullett	.30	.15	.09
9	Sparky Lyle	.50	.25	.15
10	Rich Gossage	1.25	.60	.40
11	Rawly Eastwick	.70	.35	.20
12	Chris Chambliss	.50	.25	.15
13	Willie Randolph	.50	.25	.15
14	Graig Nettles	.80	.40	.25
15	Bucky Dent	.50	.25	.15
16	Jim Spencer	.70	.35	.20
17	Fred Stanley	.30	.15	.09
18	Lou Piniella	.80	.40	.25
19	Roy White	.50	.25	.15
20	Mickey Rivers	.50	.25	.15
21	Reggie Jackson	4.00	2.00	1.25
22	Paul Blair	.30	.15	.09
---	Checklist	.04	.02	.01

1979 Burger King Phillies

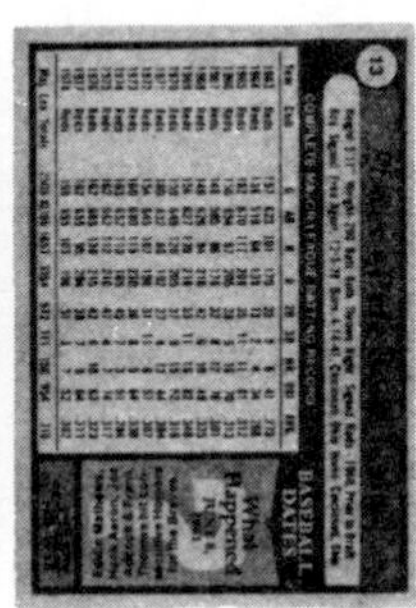

Twenty-two Philadelphia Phillies players are featured in the 1979 Burger King issue given out in the Philadelphia area. The Topps-produced set, whose cards measure 2-1/2" by 3-1/2", also includes an unnumbered checklist. The cards are identical to the regular 1979 Topps set except in seven instances. Card numbers 1, 11, 12, 13, 14, 17 and 22 have different poses. Very minor picture- cropping variations between the regular Topps issues and the Burger King sets can be found throughout the four years the cards were produced, but only those variations featuring major changes are noted in the following checklist.

		NR MT	EX	VG
	Complete Set:	10.00	5.00	3.00
	Common Player:	.20	.10	.06
1	Danny Ozark	.60	.30	.20
2	Bob Boone	.60	.30	.20
3	Tim McCarver	.60	.30	.20
4	Steve Carlton	2.50	1.25	.70
5	Larry Christenson	.20	.10	.06
6	Dick Ruthven	.20	.10	.06
7	Ron Reed	.20	.10	.06
8	Randy Lerch	.20	.10	.06
9	Warren Brusstar	.20	.10	.06
10	Tug McGraw	.40	.20	.12
11	Nino Espinosa	.60	.30	.20
12	Doug Bird	.20	.10	.06
13	Pete Rose	4.00	1.25	.90
14	Manny Trillo	.60	.30	.20
15	Larry Bowa	.50	.25	.15
16	Mike Schmidt	4.00	2.00	1.25
17	Pete Mackanin	.60	.30	.20
18	Jose Cardenal	.20	.10	.06
19	Greg Luzinski	.40	.20	.12
20	Garry Maddox	.30	.15	.09
21	Bake McBride	.20	.10	.06
22	Greg Gross	.20	.10	.06
---	Checklist	.04	.02	.01

1979 Burger King Yankees

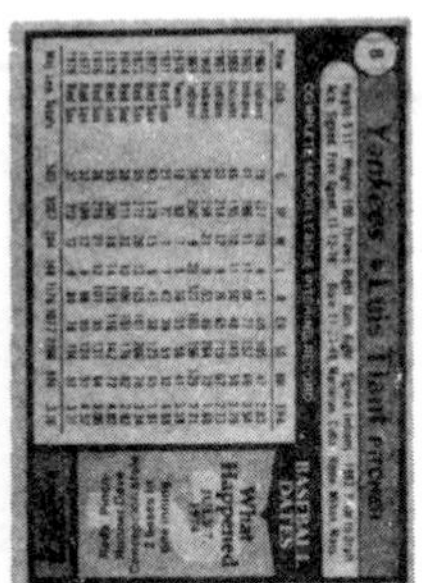

The New York Yankees were featured in a Topps-produced Burger King set for the third consecutive year in 1979. Once again, 22 numbered player cards and an unnumbered checklist made up the set. The cards, which measure 2-1/2" by 3-1/2", are identical to the 1979 Topps regular set except for card numbers 4, 8, 9 and 22 which included new poses. Only different poses or major picture-cropping variations between the regular Topps set and the Burger King issue are recognized in the checklist that follows. Numerous minor picture cropping variations between the regular Topps issue and the Burger King sets of 1977-1980 exist.

		NR MT	EX	VG
	Complete Set:	10.00	5.00	3.00
	Common Player:	.30	.15	.09
1	Yankees Team (Bob Lemon)	.50	.25	.15
2	Thurman Munson	2.00	1.00	.60
3	Cliff Johnson	.30	.15	.09
4	Ron Guidry	1.25	.60	.40
5	Jay Johnstone	.40	.20	.12
6	Jim Hunter	.90	.45	.25
7	Jim Beattie	.30	.15	.09
8	Luis Tiant	.80	.40	.25
9	Tommy John	1.00	.50	.30
10	Rich Gossage	.90	.45	.25
11	Ed Figueroa	.30	.15	.09
12	Chris Chambliss	.50	.25	.15
13	Willie Randolph	.50	.25	.15
14	Bucky Dent	.50	.25	.15
15	Graig Nettles	.70	.35	.20
16	Fred Stanley	.30	.15	.09
17	Jim Spencer	.30	.15	.09
18	Lou Piniella	.70	.35	.20
19	Roy White	.50	.25	.15
20	Mickey Rivers	.50	.25	.15
21	Reggie Jackson	3.00	1.50	.90
22	Juan Beniquez	.30	.15	.09
---	Checklist	.04	.02	.01

1980 Burger King Phillies

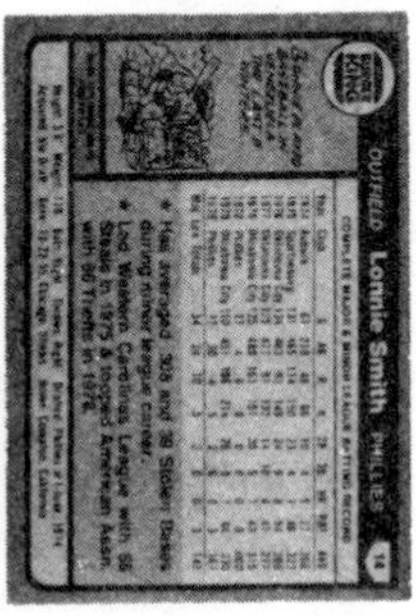

Philadelphia-area Burger King outlets issued a 23- card set featuring the Phillies for the second in a row in 1980. The Topps-produced set, whose cards measure 2-1/2" by 3-1/2", contains 22 player cards and an unnumbered checklist. The card fronts are identical in design to the regular 1980 Topps sets with the following exceptions - card numbers 1, 3, 8, 14 and 22 feature new poses. Collectors should note that very minor picture-cropping variations between the regular Topps issues and the Burger King sets exist in all years. Those minor differences are not noted in the checklist that follows. The 1980 Burger King sets were the first to include the Burger King logo on the card backs.

		NR MT	EX	VG
	Complete Set:	7.00	3.50	2.00
	Common Player:	.15	.08	.05
1	Dallas Green	.50	.25	.15
2	Bob Boone	.25	.13	.08
3	Keith Moreland	.60	.30	.20
4	Pete Rose	2.75	1.50	.80
5	Manny Trillo	.20	.10	.06
6	Mike Schmidt	2.75	1.50	.80
7	Larry Bowa	.40	.20	.12
8	John Vukovich	.50	.25	.15
9	Bake McBride	.15	.08	.05
10	Garry Maddox	.20	.10	.06
11	Greg Luzinski	.30	.15	.09
12	Greg Gross	.15	.08	.05
13	Del Unser	.15	.08	.05
14	Lonnie Smith	.50	.25	.15
15	Steve Carlton	1.25	.60	.40
16	Larry Christenson	.15	.08	.05
17	Nino Espinosa	.15	.08	.05
18	Randy Lerch	.15	.08	.05
19	Dick Ruthven	.15	.08	.05
20	Tug McGraw	.30	.15	.09
21	Ron Reed	.15	.08	.05
22	Kevin Saucier	.50	.25	.15
---	Checklist	.04	.02	.01

1980 Burger King Pitch, Hit & Run

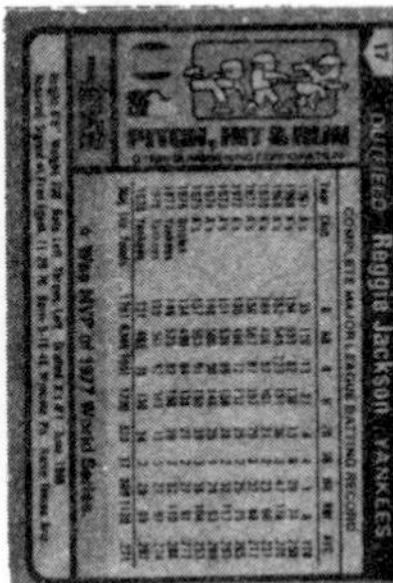

In 1980, Burger King issued, in conjunction with its "Pitch, Hit & Run" promotion, a Topps-produced 34-card set featuring pitchers (card #'s 1-11), hitters (#'s 12-22), and base stealers (#'s 23-33). The card fronts, which carry the Burger King logo, are identical in nature to the regular 1980 Topps set except for numbers 1, 4, 5, 7, 9, 10, 16, 17, 18, 22, 23, 27, 28, 29 and 30, which feature different poses. The cards, which are numbered 1 through 33, measure 2-1/2" by 3-1/2" in size. An unnumbered checklist was included with the set.

		NR MT	EX	VG
	Complete Set:	18.00	9.00	5.50
	Common Player:	.20	.10	.06
1	Vida Blue	.50	.25	.15
2	Steve Carlton	1.00	.50	.30
3	Rollie Fingers	.30	.15	.09
4	Ron Guidry	.70	.35	.20
5	Jerry Koosman	.40	.20	.12
6	Phil Niekro	.40	.20	.12
7	Jim Palmer	1.25	.60	.40
8	J.R. Richard	.20	.10	.06
9	Nolan Ryan	3.00	1.50	.90
10	Tom Seaver	1.25	.60	.40
11	Bruce Sutter	.25	.13	.08
12	Don Baylor	.25	.13	.08
13	George Brett	1.25	.60	.40
14	Rod Carew	.90	.45	.25
15	George Foster	.25	.13	.08
16	Keith Hernandez	.90	.45	.25
17	Reggie Jackson	2.25	1.25	.70
18	Fred Lynn	.70	.35	.20
19	Dave Parker	.40	.20	.12
20	Jim Rice	.80	.40	.25
21	Pete Rose	2.50	1.25	.70
22	Dave Winfield	1.25	.60	.40
23	Bobby Bonds	.40	.20	.12
24	Enos Cabell	.20	.10	.06
25	Cesar Cedeno	.20	.10	.06
26	Julio Cruz	.20	.10	.06
27	Ron LeFlore	.40	.20	.12
28	Dave Lopes	.40	.20	.12
29	Omar Moreno	.40	.20	.12
30	Joe Morgan	1.00	.50	.30
31	Bill North	.20	.10	.06
32	Frank Taveras	.20	.10	.06
33	Willie Wilson	.25	.13	.08
---	Checklist	.04	.02	.01

1982 Burger King Braves

A set consisting of 27 "Collector Lids" featuring the Atlanta Braves was issued by Burger King restaurants in 1982. The lids, which measure 3-5/8" in diameter, were placed on a special Coca-Cola cup which listed the scores of the Braves' season-opening 13-game win streak. A black and white photo plus the player's name, position, height, weight, and 1981 statistics are found on the lid front. The unnumbered, blank-backed lids also contain logos for Burger King, Coca-Cola, and the Major League Baseball Players Association.

		MT	NR MT	EX
Complete Set:		40.00	30.00	16.00
Common Player:		1.00	.70	.40
(1)	Steve Bedrosian	2.50	2.00	1.00
(2)	Bruce Benedict	1.00	.70	.40
(3)	Tommy Boggs	1.00	.70	.40
(4)	Brett Butler	2.50	2.00	1.00
(5)	Rick Camp	1.00	.70	.40
(6)	Chris Chambliss	1.25	.90	.50
(7)	Ken Dayley	1.00	.70	.40
(8)	Gene Garber	1.00	.70	.40
(9)	Preston Hanna	1.00	.70	.40
(10)	Terry Harper	1.00	.70	.40
(11)	Bob Horner	3.00	2.25	1.25
(12)	Al Hrabosky	1.25	.90	.50
(13)	Glenn Hubbard	1.00	.70	.40
(14)	Randy Johnson	1.00	.70	.40
(15)	Rufino Linares	1.00	.70	.40
(16)	Rick Mahler	1.50	1.25	.60
(17)	Larry McWilliams	1.00	.70	.40
(18)	Dale Murphy	12.00	9.00	4.75
(19)	Phil Niekro	5.00	3.75	2.00
(20)	Biff Pocoroba	1.00	.70	.40
(21)	Rafael Ramirez	1.00	.70	.40
(22)	Jerry Royster	1.00	.70	.40
(23)	Ken Smith	1.00	.70	.40
(24)	Bob Walk	1.00	.70	.40
(25)	Claudell Washington	1.25	.90	.50
(26)	Bob Watson	1.00	.70	.40
(27)	Larry Whisenton	1.00	.70	.40

1982 Burger King Indians

The 1982 Burger King Indians set was sponsored by WUAB-TV and Burger Kings in the Cleveland vicinity. The cards' green borders encompass a large yellow area which contains a black and white photo plus a baseball tip. Manager Dave Garcia and his four coaches provide the baseball hints. The cards, which measure 3" x 5", are unnumbered and blank-backed.

		MT	NR MT	EX
Complete Set:		10.00	7.50	4.00
Common Player:		.70	.50	.30
(1)	Dave Garcia (Be In The Game)	.70	.50	.30
(2)	Dave Garcia (Sportsmanship)	.70	.50	.30
(3)	Johnny Goryl (Rounding The Bases)	.70	.50	.30
(4)	Johnny Goryl (3rd Base Running)	.70	.50	.30
(5)	Tom McCraw (Follow Thru)	.70	.50	.30
(6)	Tom McCraw (Selecting A Bat)	.70	.50	.30
(7)	Tom McCraw (Watch The Ball)	.70	.50	.30
(8)	Mel Queen (Master One Pitch)	.70	.50	.30
(9)	Mel Queen (Warm Up)	.70	.50	.30
(10)	Dennis Sommers (Get Down On A Ground Ball)	.70	.50	.30
(11)	Dennis Sommers (Protect Your Fingers)	.70	.50	.30
(12)	Dennis Sommers (Tagging First Base)	.70	.50	.30

1986 Burger King

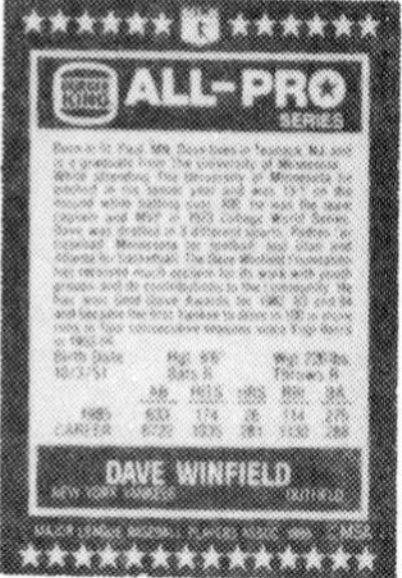

Burger King restaurants in the Pennsylvania and New Jersey areas issued a 20-card set entitled "All-Pro Series". The cards were issued with the purchase of a Whopper sandwich and came in folded panels of two cards each, along with a coupon card. The card fronts feature a color photo and contain the player's name, team and position plus the Burger King logo. Due to a licensing problem, the team insignias on the players' caps were airbrushed away. The card backs feature black print on white stock and contain brief biographical and statistical information.

		MT	NR MT	EX
Complete Panel Set		10.00	7.50	4.00
Complete Singles Set		6.00	4.50	2.50
Common Panel		.75	.60	.30
Common Single Player		.10	.08	.04
Panel		.70	.50	.30
1	Tony Pena	.10	.08	.04
2	Dave Winfield	.20	.15	.08
Panel		2.00	1.50	.80
3	Fernando Valenzuela	.20	.15	.08
4	Pete Rose	.50	.40	.20
Panel		1.50	1.25	.60
5	Mike Schmidt	1.00	.70	.40
6	Steve Carlton	.30	.25	.12
Panel		.70	.50	.30
7	Glenn Wilson	.10	.08	.04
8	Jim Rice	.20	.15	.08
Panel		2.50	2.00	1.00
9	Wade Boggs	.80	.60	.30
10	Juan Samuel	.10	.08	.04
Panel		1.50	1.25	.60
11	Dale Murphy	.40	.30	.15
12	Reggie Jackson	.30	.25	.12
Panel		1.25	.90	.50
13	Kirk Gibson	.20	.15	.08
14	Eddie Murray	.30	.25	.12
Panel		1.00	.70	.40
15	Cal Ripken, Jr.	.30	.25	.12
16	Willie McGee	.10	.08	.04
Panel		1.75	1.25	.70
17	Dwight Gooden	.50	.40	.20
18	Steve Garvey	.25	.20	.10
Panel		3.00	2.25	1.25
19	Don Mattingly	1.50	1.25	.60
20	George Brett	.40	.30	.15

1987 Burger King

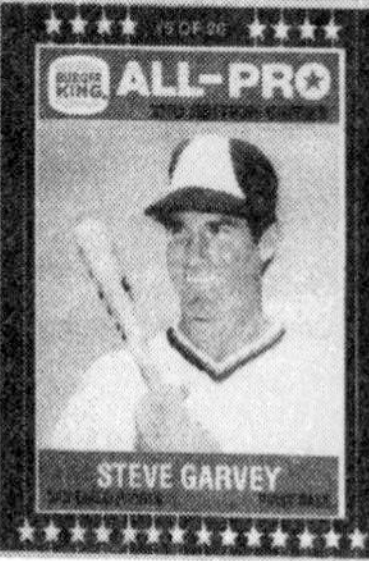

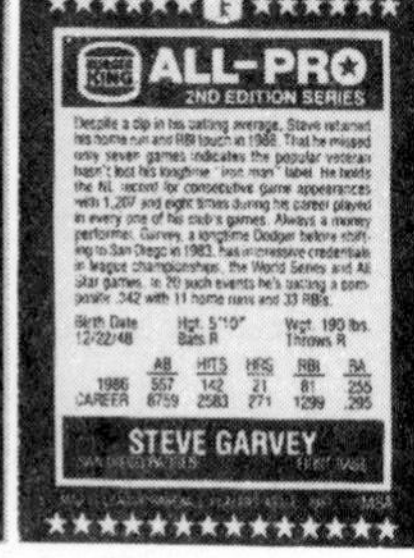

The 1987 Burger King "All-Pro 2nd Edition Series" set was part of a giveaway promotion at participating Burger King restaurants. The set is comprised of 20 players on ten different panels. The cards measure 2-1/2" by 3-1/2" each with a three-card panel (includes a coupon card) measuring 7-5/8" by 3-1/2". The card fronts feature a full-color photo and the Burger King logo surrounded by a blue stars-and-stripes border. The backs contain black print on white stock and carry a brief player biography and 1986 career statistics. The set was produced by Mike Schecter Associates and, as with many MSA issues, all team insignias were airbrushed away.

		MT	NR MT	EX
Complete Panel Set:		7.00	5.25	2.75
Complete Singles Set:		4.00	3.00	1.50
Common Panel:		.25	.20	.10
Common Single Player:		.05	.04	.02
Panel		1.25	.90	.50
1	Wade Boggs	.40	.30	.15
2	Gary Carter	.15	.11	.06
Panel		1.00	.70	.40
3	Will Clark	.50	.40	.20
4	Roger Clemens	.20	.15	.08
Panel		.50	.40	.20
5	Steve Garvey	.15	.11	.06
6	Ron Darling	.08	.06	.03
Panel		.25	.20	.10
7	Pedro Guerrero	.08	.06	.03
8	Von Hayes	.05	.04	.02
Panel		.60	.45	.25
9	Rickey Henderson	.25	.20	.10
10	Keith Hernandez	.12	.09	.05
Panel		.60	.45	.25
11	Wally Joyner	.20	.15	.08
12	Mike Krukow	.05	.04	.02
Panel		1.75	1.25	.70
13	Don Mattingly	6.00	4.50	2.50
14	Ozzie Smith	.08	.06	.03
Panel		.50	.40	.20
15	Tony Pena	.05	.04	.02
16	Jim Rice	.15	.11	.06
Panel		.80	.60	.30
17	Ryne Sandberg	.25	.20	.10
18	Mike Schmidt	.40	.30	.15
Panel		.80	.60	.30
19	Darryl Strawberry	.12	.09	.05
20	Fernando Valenzuela	.20	.15	.08

1933 Butter Cream

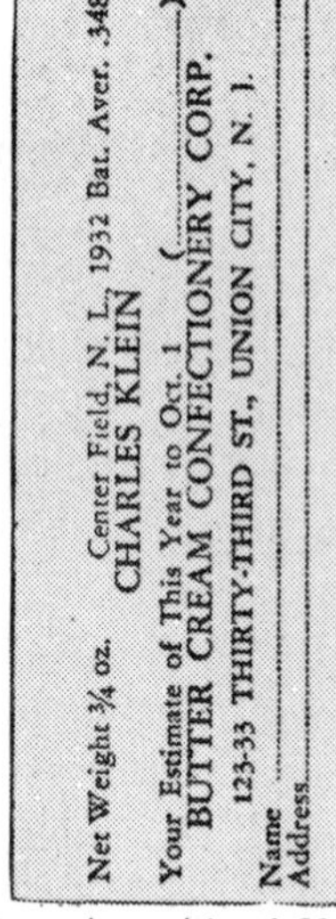

The 1933 Butter Cream set consists of 30 unnumbered, black and white cards which measure 1-1/4" by 3-1/2" in size. The card backs feature a contest sponsored by the Butter Cream Confectionary Corp. in which the collector was to estimate the players' statistics by a specific date. Two different backs are known: 1) Estimate through Sept. 1 and no company address, and 2) Estimate through Oct. 1 with the Butter Cream address. The ACC designation for the set is R306.

		NR MT	EX	VG
Complete Set:		10000.	5000.	3000.
Common Player:		225.00	112.00	67.00
(1)	Earl Averill	350.00	175.00	105.00
(2)	Ed. Brandt	225.00	112.00	67.00
(3)	Guy T. Bush	225.00	112.00	67.00
(4)	Gordon Cochrane	400.00	200.00	120.00
(5)	Joe Cronin	400.00	200.00	120.00
(6)	George Earnshaw	225.00	112.00	67.00
(7)	Wesley Ferrell	225.00	112.00	67.00
(8)	"Jimmy" E. Foxx	600.00	300.00	175.00
(9)	Frank C. Frisch	400.00	200.00	120.00
(10)	Charles M. Gelbert	225.00	112.00	67.00

		NR MT	EX	VG
(11)	"Lefty" Robert M. Grove	450.00	225.00	135.00
(12)	Leo Charles Hartnett	350.00	175.00	105.00
(13)	"Babe" Herman	225.00	112.00	67.00
(14)	Charles Klein	350.00	175.00	105.00
(15)	Ray Kremer	225.00	112.00	67.00
(16)	Fred C. Linstrom (Lindstrom)	350.00	175.00	105.00
(17)	Ted A. Lyons	350.00	175.00	105.00
(18)	"Pepper" John L. Martin	225.00	112.00	67.00
(19)	Robert O'Farrell	225.00	112.00	67.00
(20)	Ed. A. Rommel	225.00	112.00	67.00
(21)	Charles Root	225.00	112.00	67.00
(22)	Harold "Muddy" Ruel (Herold)	225.00	112.00	67.00
23	Babe Ruth	1500.	750.00	450.00
(24)	"Al" Simmons	350.00	175.00	105.00
(25)	"Bill" Terry	400.00	200.00	120.00
(26)	George E. Uhle	225.00	112.00	67.00
(27)	Lloyd J. Waner	350.00	175.00	105.00
(28)	Paul G. Waner	350.00	175.00	105.00
(29)	"Hack" Wilson	350.00	175.00	105.00
(30)	Glen. Wright	225.00	112.00	67.00

1912 C46

JOHN WHITE
Buffalo.

John White, left-fielder, Buffalo International League Club, was born in Indianapolis and learned the game there. White has been in the Eastern (now International) League over fifteen years, being with Toronto and Buffalo. He has been traded several times between these two Clubs. He is a right hander and bats both right and left handed. He hit .272 for 105 games and fielded .975.

BASEBALL SERIES No. 4

This minor league set, issued in 1912 by the Imperial Tobacco Company, is the only tobacco baseball set issued in Canada. Designated as C46 in the American Card Catalog, each sepia-toned card measures 1-1/2" by 2-5/8" and features a distinctive card design that pictures the player inside an oval surrounded by a simulated woodgrain background featuring a bat, ball and glove in the borders. The player's last name appears in capital letters in a panel beneath the oval. (An exception is the card of James Murray, whose caption includes both first and last names.) The backs include the player's name and team at the top, followed by a brief biography. The 90 subjects in the set are members of the eight teams in the Eastern League (Rochester, Toronto, Buffalo, Newark, Providence, Baltimore, Montreal and Jersey City), even though the card backs refer to it as the International League. Although a minor league issue, the C46 set contains many players with major league experience, including Hall of Famers Joe Kelley and Joe "Iron Man" McGinnity.

		NR MT	EX	VG
	Complete Set:	4000.00	2000.00	1200.
	Common Player:	35.00	17.50	10.50
1	William O'Hara	100.00	50.00	30.00
2	James McGinley	50.00	25.00	15.00
3	"Frenchy" LeClaire	35.00	17.50	10.50
4	John White	35.00	17.50	10.50
5	James Murray	35.00	17.50	10.50
6	Joe Ward	35.00	17.50	10.50
7	"Whitey" Alperman	35.00	17.50	10.50
8	"Natty" Nattress	35.00	17.50	10.50
9	Fred Sline	35.00	17.50	10.50
10	Royal Rock	35.00	17.50	10.50
11	Ray Demmitt	35.00	17.50	10.50
12	"Butcher Boy" Schmidt	35.00	17.50	10.50
13	Samuel Frock	35.00	17.50	10.50
14	Fred Burchell	35.00	17.50	10.50
15	Jack Kelley	35.00	17.50	10.50
16	Frank Barberich	35.00	17.50	10.50
17	Frank Corridon	35.00	17.50	10.50
18	"Doc" Adkins	35.00	17.50	10.50
19	Jack Dunn	35.00	17.50	10.50
20	James Walsh	35.00	17.50	10.50
21	Charles Hanford	35.00	17.50	10.50
22	Dick Rudolph	35.00	17.50	10.50
23	Curt Elston	35.00	17.50	10.50
24	Silton	35.00	17.50	10.50
25	Charlie French	35.00	17.50	10.50
26	John Ganzel	35.00	17.50	10.50
27	Joe Kelley	100.00	50.00	30.00
28	Benny Meyers	35.00	17.50	10.50
29	George Schirm	35.00	17.50	10.50
30	William Purtell	35.00	17.50	10.50
31	Bayard Sharpe	35.00	17.50	10.50
32	Tony Smith	35.00	17.50	10.50
33	John Lush	35.00	17.50	10.50
34	William Collins	35.00	17.50	10.50
35	Art Phelan	35.00	17.50	10.50
36	Edward Phelps	35.00	17.50	10.50
37	"Rube" Vickers	35.00	17.50	10.50
38	Cy Seymour	35.00	17.50	10.50
39	"Shadow" Carroll	35.00	17.50	10.50
40	Jake Gettman	35.00	17.50	10.50
41	Luther Taylor	35.00	17.50	10.50
42	Walter Justis	35.00	17.50	10.50
43	Robert Fisher	35.00	17.50	10.50
44	Fred Parent	35.00	17.50	10.50
45	James Dygert	35.00	17.50	10.50
46	Johnnie Butler	35.00	17.50	10.50
47	Fred Mitchell	35.00	17.50	10.50
48	Heinie Batch	35.00	17.50	10.50
49	Michael Corcoran	35.00	17.50	10.50
50	Edward Doescher	35.00	17.50	10.50
51	Wheeler	35.00	17.50	10.50
52	Elijah Jones	35.00	17.50	10.50
53	Fred Truesdale	35.00	17.50	10.50
54	Fred Beebe	35.00	17.50	10.50
55	Louis Brockett	35.00	17.50	10.50
56	Wells	35.00	17.50	10.50
57	"Lew" McAllister	35.00	17.50	10.50
58	Ralph Stroud	35.00	17.50	10.50
59	Manser	35.00	17.50	10.50
60	"Ducky" Holmes	35.00	17.50	10.50
61	Rube Dessau	35.00	17.50	10.50
62	Fred Jacklitsch	35.00	17.50	10.50
63	Graham	35.00	17.50	10.50
64	Noah Henline	35.00	17.50	10.50
65	"Chick" Gandil	50.00	25.00	15.00
66	Tom Hughes	35.00	17.50	10.50
67	Joseph Delehanty	35.00	17.50	10.50
68	Pierce	35.00	17.50	10.50
69	Gaunt	35.00	17.50	10.50
70	Edward Fitzpatrick	35.00	17.50	10.50
71	Wyatt Lee	35.00	17.50	10.50
72	John Kissinger	35.00	17.50	10.50
73	William Malarkey	35.00	17.50	10.50
74	William Byers	35.00	17.50	10.50
75	George Simmons	35.00	17.50	10.50
76	Daniel Moeller	35.00	17.50	10.50
77	Joseph McGinnity	100.00	50.00	30.00
78	Alex Hardy	35.00	17.50	10.50
79	Bob Holmes	35.00	17.50	10.50
80	William Baxter	35.00	17.50	10.50
81	Edward Spencer	35.00	17.50	10.50
82	Bradley Kocher	35.00	17.50	10.50
83	Robert Shaw	35.00	17.50	10.50
84	Joseph Yeager	35.00	17.50	10.50
85	Carlo	35.00	17.50	10.50
86	William Abstein	35.00	17.50	10.50
87	Tim Jordan	35.00	17.50	10.50
88	Dick Breen	35.00	17.50	10.50
89	Tom McCarty	50.00	25.00	15.00
90	Ed Curtis	100.00	50.00	30.00

1985 CBS Radio Sports

CONNECT WITH BASEBALL'S GAME-OF-THE-WEEK ON CBS RADIO SPORTS

Dick Stockton Announce Team

Broadcasting Stats

STOCKTON is a veteran sportscaster who has covered almost every type of athletic event since his CBS Radio Network debut in 1979. He spent four seasons providing pre-game and play-by-play coverage of the Network's NFL games and has previously served as anchor of "Sports Spectacular" on the CBS Television Network. He is also a play-by-play commentator on NBA and NFL games for CBS Sports.

As part of a promotion for its radio Game of the Week broadcasts, CBS issued a six-card set in 1985 picturing network announcers, including former major leaguer Johnny Bench. The cards are the standard 2-1/2" by 3-1/2" and were sent to CBS affiliate stations only. The fronts of the full-color cards picture the announcers in CBS Radio Sports baseball-style uniforms.

		MT	NR MT	EX
	Complete Set:	30.00	22.00	12.00
	Common Player:	2.00	1.50	.80
(1)	Johnny Bench	12.00	9.00	4.75
(2)	Brent Musburger	6.00	4.50	2.50
(3)	Lindsey Nelson	4.00	3.00	1.50
(4)	John Rooney	2.00	1.50	.80
(5)	Dick Stockton	3.00	2.25	1.25
(6)	Bill White	6.00	4.50	2.50

1986 CBS Radio Sports

For the second consecutive year, CBS Radio

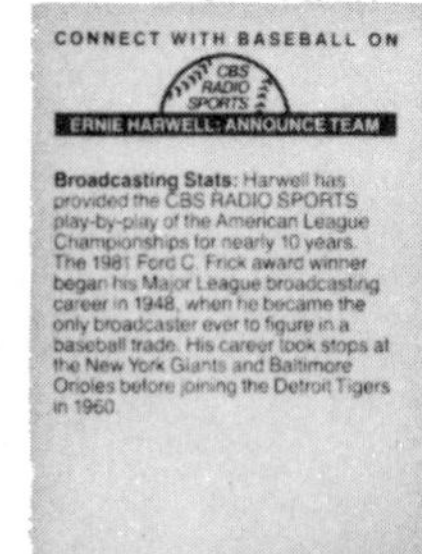

Sports issued a five-card set featuring announcers used by the network for the Game of the Week and post-season broadcasts. The cards, which were included in a custom-designed wrapper, were sent to CBS radio affiliates as part of a promotion for the Game of the Week. The color cards measure 2-1/2" by 3-1/2" in size.

		MT	NR MT	EX
	Complete Set:	20.00	15.00	8.00
	Common Player:	2.00	1.50	.80
(1)	Sparky Anderson	8.00	6.00	3.25
(2)	Jack Buck	4.00	3.00	1.50
(3)	Howard David	2.00	1.50	.80
(4)	Ernie Harwell	5.00	3.75	2.00
(5)	Ted Robinson	2.00	1.50	.80

1985 Cain's

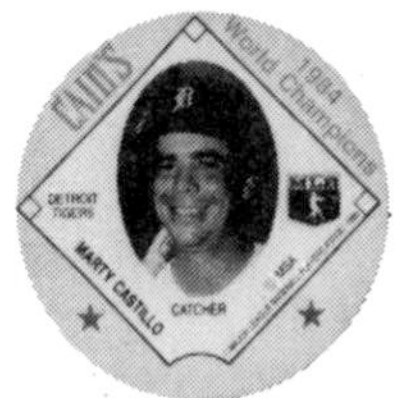

This 20-card set commemorating the 1984 World champion Tigers was issued by Cain's Potato Chips in the Michigan area in 1985. The yellow-bordered, unnumbered cards measure 2-3/4" in diameter and feature full-color oval photos inside a diamond. The word "Cain's" appears in the upper left corner, while the player's name appears in the lower left with his position directly below the photo. The words "1984 World Champions" are printed in the upper right corner. The backs include 1984 statistics. The cards were inserted in bags of potato chips.

		MT	NR MT	EX
	Complete Set:	40.00	30.00	16.00
	Common Player:	1.00	.70	.40
(1)	Doug Bair	1.00	.70	.40
(2)	Juan Berenguer	1.00	.70	.40
(3)	Dave Bergman	1.00	.70	.40
(4)	Tom Brookens	1.00	.70	.40
(5)	Marty Castillo	1.00	.70	.40
(6)	Darrell Evans	2.75	2.00	1.00
(7)	Barbaro Garbey	1.00	.70	.40
(8)	Kirk Gibson	3.50	2.75	1.50
(9)	John Grubb	1.00	.70	.40
(10)	Willie Hernandez	1.50	1.25	.60
(11)	Larry Herndon	1.50	1.25	.60
(12)	Chet Lemon	1.50	1.25	.60
(13)	Aurelio Lopez	1.00	.70	.40
(14)	Jack Morris	3.50	2.75	1.50
(15)	Lance Parrish	3.50	2.75	1.50
(16)	Dan Petry	1.50	1.25	.60
(17)	Bill Scherrer	1.00	.70	.40
(18)	Alan Trammell	4.00	3.00	1.50
(19)	Lou Whitaker	3.50	2.75	1.50
(20)	Milt Wilcox	1.00	.70	.40

1986 Cain's

For the second year in a row, player discs of the Detroit Tigers were found in boxes of Cain's Potato Chips sold in the Detroit area. Twenty discs make up the set which is branded as a "1986 Annual Collectors' Edition." The discs, which measure 2-3/4" in diameter, have fronts which contain a color photo plus the player's name, team and position. The Cain's logo and the Major League Baseball Players Association's logo also appear. The backs, which display black print on white stock, contain player information plus the card number.

		MT	NR MT	EX
Complete Set:		40.00	30.00	16.00
Common Player:		1.00	.70	.40
1	Tom Brookens	1.00	.70	.40
2	Willie Hernandez	1.50	1.25	.60
3	Dave Bergman	1.00	.70	.40
4	Lou Whitaker	3.50	2.75	1.50
5	Dave LaPoint	1.00	.70	.40
6	Lance Parrish	3.50	2.75	1.50
7	Randy O'Neal	1.00	.70	.40
8	Nelson Simmons	1.00	.70	.40
9	Larry Herndon	1.00	.70	.40
10	Doug Flynn	1.00	.70	.40
11	Jack Morris	3.50	2.75	1.50
12	Dan Petry	1.00	.70	.40
13	Walt Terrell	1.00	.70	.40
14	Chet Lemon	1.50	1.25	.60
15	Frank Tanana	1.50	1.25	.60
16	Kirk Gibson	4.00	3.00	1.50
17	Darrell Evans	2.75	2.00	1.00
18	Dave Collins	1.00	.70	.40
19	John Grubb	1.00	.70	.40
20	Alan Trammell	4.00	3.00	1.50

1987 Cain's

Player discs of the Detroit Tigers were inserted in boxes of Cain's Potato Chips for the third consecutive year. The 1987 edition is made up of 20 round cards, each measuring 2-3/4" in diameter. The discs, which were packaged in a cellophane wrapper, feature a full-color photo surrounded by an orange border. The backs are printed in red on white stock. The set was produced by Mike Schecter and Associates.

		MT	NR MT	EX
Complete Set:		20.00	15.00	8.00
Common Player:		.60	.45	.25
1	Tom Brookens	.60	.45	.25
2	Darnell Coles	.75	.60	.30
3	Mike Heath	.60	.45	.25
4	Dave Bergman	.60	.45	.25
5	Dwight Lowry	.60	.45	.25
6	Darrell Evans	1.25	.90	.50
7	Alan Trammell	2.75	2.00	1.00
8	Lou Whitaker	2.00	1.50	.80
9	Kirk Gibson	2.75	2.00	1.00
10	Chet Lemon	.75	.60	.30
11	Larry Herndon	.60	.45	.25
12	John Grubb	.60	.45	.25
13	Willie Hernandez	.75	.60	.30
14	Jack Morris	2.00	1.50	.80
15	Dan Petry	.60	.45	.25
16	Walt Terrell	.60	.45	.25
17	Mark Thurmond	.60	.45	.25
18	Pat Sheridan	.60	.45	.25
19	Eric King	.75	.60	.30
20	Frank Tanana	.75	.60	.30

1989 Cap'n Crunch

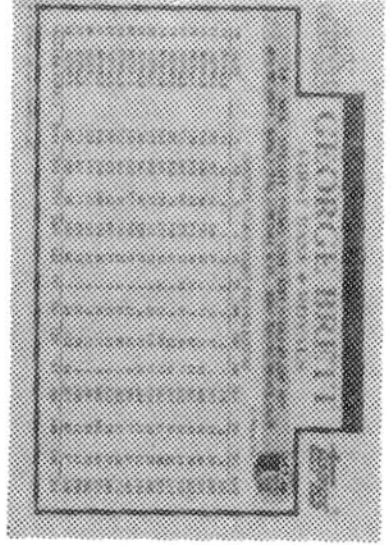

This 22-card set was produced by Topps for Cap'n Crunch cereal boxes. Two cards and a stick of gum were included in each cereal box while the offer was active. The fronts of these 2-1/2" by 3-1/2" cards feature red, white and blue borders. The card backs are horizontal and feature lifetime statistics. The set was not offered in any complete set deal.

		MT	NR MT	EX
Complete Set:		15.00	11.00	6.00
Common Player:		.50	.40	.20
1	Jose Canseco	1.00	.70	.40
2	Kirk Gibson	.50	.40	.20
3	Orel Hershiser	.70	.50	.30
4	Frank Viola, Frank Viola	.70	.50	.30
5	Tony Gwynn	.70	.50	.30
6	Cal Ripken	.70	.50	.30
7	Darryl Strawberry	.80	.60	.30
8	Don Mattingly	.90	.70	.40
9	George Brett	.60	.45	.25
10	Andre Dawson	.60	.45	.25
11	Dale Murphy	.60	.45	.25
12	Alan Trammell	.50	.40	.20
13	Eric Davis	.80	.60	.30
14	Jack Clark	.50	.40	.20
15	Eddie Murray	.50	.40	.20
16	Mike Schmidt	1.00	.70	.40
17	Dwight Gooden	.80	.60	.30
18	Roger Clemens	.80	.60	.30
19	Will Clark	1.00	.70	.40
20	Kirby Puckett	.80	.60	.30
21	Robin Yount	.70	.50	.30
22	Mark McGwire	.80	.60	.30

1970 Carl Aldana Orioles

Little is known about the distribution or origin of this 12-card regional set, which was available in 1970 in the Baltimore area. Measuring 3-1/4" by 2-1/8", the unnumbered cards picture members of the Baltimore Orioles and include two poses of Brooks Robinson. The cards feature line drawings of the players surrounded by a plain border. The player's last name appears below the portrait sketch. The set was named after Carl Aldana, who supplied the artwork for the cards.

		NR MT	EX	VG
Complete Set:		45.00	23.00	13.50
Common Player:		1.25	.60	.40
(1)	Mark Belanger	2.00	1.00	.60
(2)	Paul Blair	2.00	1.00	.60
(3)	Mike Cuellar	2.00	1.00	.60
(4)	Ellie Hendricks	1.25	.60	.40
(5)	Dave Johnson	3.00	1.50	.90
(6)	Dave McNally	2.25	1.25	.70
(7)	Jim Palmer	10.00	5.00	3.00
(8)	Boog Powell	3.00	1.50	.90
(9)	Brooks Robinson (diving - face showing)	10.00	5.00	3.00
(10)	Brooks Robinson (diving - back showing)	10.00	5.00	3.00
(11)	Frank Robinson	10.00	5.00	3.00
(12)	Earl Weaver	2.25	1.25	.70

1984 Cereal Series

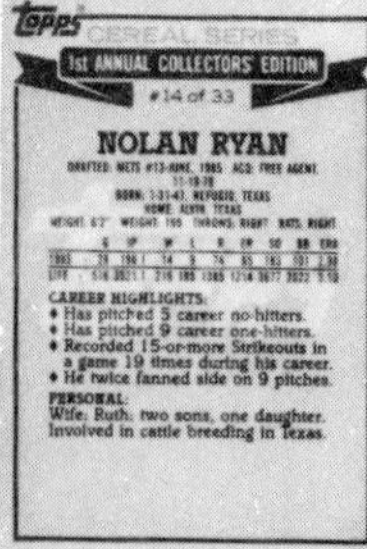

The Topps-produced 1984 Cereal Series set is identical to the Ralston Purina set from the same year in nearly all aspects. On the card fronts the words "Ralston Purina Company" were replaced by "Cereal Series" and Topps logos were substituted for Ralston checkerboard logos. The set is comprised of 33 cards, each measuring 2-1/2" by 3-1/2." The cards were inserted in unmarked boxes of Chex brand cereals.

		MT	NR MT	EX
Complete Set		13.00	9.75	5.25
Common Player		.20	.15	.08
1	Eddie Murray	.50	.40	.20
2	Ozzie Smith	.30	.25	.12
3	Ted Simmons	.20	.15	.08
4	Pete Rose	1.00	.70	.40
5	Greg Luzinski	.20	.15	.08
6	Andre Dawson	.50	.40	.20
7	Dave Winfield	.50	.40	.20
8	Tom Seaver	.50	.40	.20
9	Jim Rice	.50	.40	.20
10	Fernando Valenzuela	.40	.30	.15
11	Wade Boggs	1.75	1.25	.70
12	Dale Murphy	.90	.70	.35
13	George Brett	.90	.70	.35
14	Nolan Ryan	1.00	.70	.40
15	Rickey Henderson	.80	.60	.30
16	Steve Carlton	.50	.40	.20
17	Rod Carew	.60	.45	.25
18	Steve Garvey	.50	.40	.20
19	Reggie Jackson	.60	.45	.25
20	Dave Concepcion	.20	.15	.08
21	Robin Yount	.60	.45	.25
22	Mike Schmidt	1.00	.70	.40
23	Jim Palmer	1.00	.70	.40
24	Bruce Sutter	.20	.15	.08
25	Dan Quisenberry	.20	.15	.08
26	Bill Madlock	.20	.15	.08
27	Cecil Cooper	.20	.15	.08
28	Gary Carter	.30	.25	.12
29	Fred Lynn	.30	.25	.12
30	Pedro Guerrero	.30	.25	.12
31	Ron Guidry	.30	.25	.12
32	Keith Hernandez	.40	.30	.15
33	Carlton Fisk	.30	.25	.12

1987 Champion Phillies

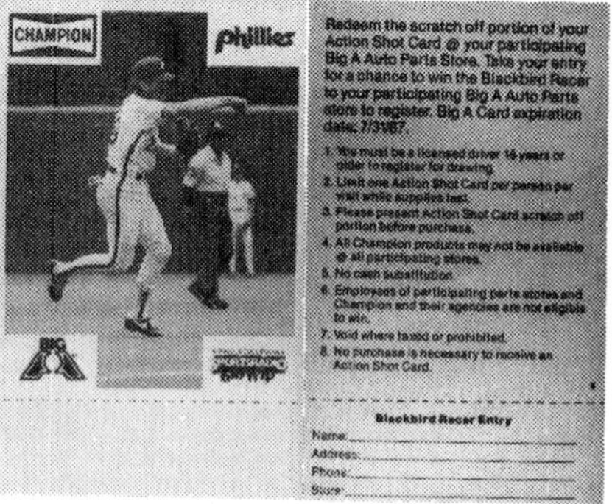

This four card set is interesting in that the players are not identified on the card fronts or backs. The full-color cards, which measure 2-3/4" by 4-5/16", were produced by the Champion Spark Plug Co. as part of a contest held at participating Big A, Car Quest and Pep Boys auto parts stores. Entrants were advised to return the scratch-off coupon portion of the card for a chance to win a Blackbird Racer. Each card contains a scratch-off portion which may have contained an instant prize. Each card can be found with either a Big A, Car Quest or Pep Boys logo in the lower left corner on the card front. The contest was also sponsored in part by the Philadelphia Phillies and radio station WIP.

		MT	NR MT	EX
Complete Set:		18.00	13.50	7.25
Common Player:		1.00	.70	.40
(1)	Von Hayes (glove on knee)	3.00	2.25	1.25
(2)	Steve Jeltz (#30 on uniform)	1.00	.70	.40
(3)	Juan Samuel (laying on base)	3.50	2.75	1.50
(4)	Mike Schmidt (making throw)	12.00	9.00	4.75

1932 Charles Denby Cigars Cubs

Actually a series of postcards, this Chicago Cubs set issued by the Charles Denby Company in 1932 is the last known tobacco issue produced before World War II. The cards are a standard postcard size (5-1/4" by 3-3/8") and feature a glossy black and white player photo with a

facsimile autograph. In typical postcard style, the back of the card is divided in half, with a printed player profile on the left and room for the mailing address on the right. The back also includes an advertisement for Charles Denby Cigars, the mild five-cent cigar "for men who like to inhale". Only five different subjects have been reported to date, but there is speculation that more probably exist.

		NR MT	EX	VG
Complete Set:		450.00	225.00	135.00
Common Player:		75.00	37.00	22.00
(1)	Elwood English	75.00	37.00	22.00
(2)	Charles J. Grimm	100.00	50.00	30.00
(3)	William Herman	150.00	75.00	45.00
(4)	William F. Jurges	75.00	37.00	22.00
(5)	Lonnie Warneke	75.00	37.00	22.00

1988 Chef Boyardee

This uncut sheet of 24 cards highlights 12 American and 12 National League players. Full-color player closeup photos are printed beneath a red, white and blue "1988 1st Annual Collector's Edition" header. The player name, team and position appear beneath his photo. Card backs are printed in blue ink on a red background and include biographical information, stats and career highlights including acquisition date and draft date/choice number. The set was produced by American Home Food Products for exclusive distribution via a mail-in offer involving proofs of purchase from the company's Chef Boyardee products.

		MT	NR MT	EX
Complete Uncut Sheet:		25.00	18.50	10.00
Complete Singles Set:		20.00	15.00	8.00
Common Single Player:		.50	.40	.20
1	Mark McGwire	2.50	2.00	1.00
2	Eric Davis	1.75	1.25	.70
3	Jack Morris	.50	.40	.20
4	George Bell	.75	.60	.30
5	Ozzie Smith	.50	.40	.20
6	Tony Gwynn	1.00	.70	.40
7	Cal Ripken, Jr.	1.00	.70	.40
8	Todd Worrell	.50	.40	.20
9	Larry Parrish	.50	.40	.20
10	Gary Carter	.70	.50	.30
11	Ryne Sandberg	.75	.60	.30
12	Keith Hernandez	.60	.45	.25
13	Kirby Puckett	1.25	.90	.50
14	Mike Schmidt	1.75	1.25	.70
15	Frank Viola	.50	.40	.20
16	Don Mattingly	3.00	2.25	1.25
17	Dale Murphy	.90	.70	.35
18a	Andre Dawson (1987 team is Expos)	.75	.60	.30
18b	Andre Dawson (1987 team is Cubs)	.75	.60	.30
19	Mike Scott	.50	.40	.20
20	Rickey Henderson	1.25	.90	.50
21	Jim Rice	.75	.60	.30
22	Wade Boggs	2.00	1.50	.80
23	Roger Clemens	1.75	1.25	.70
24	Fernando Valenzuela	.75	.60	.30

1985 Circle K

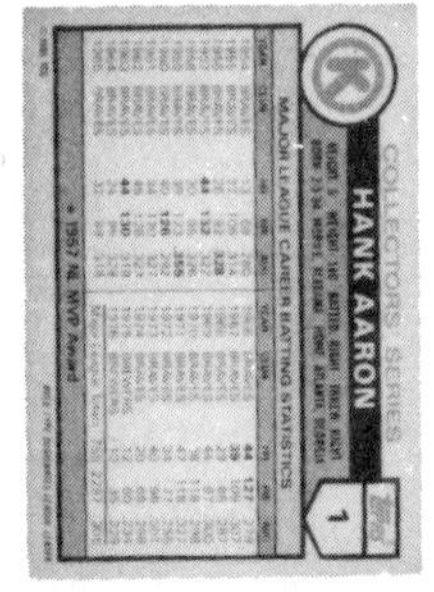

Produced by Topps for Circle K stores, this 33-card set is entitled "Baseball All Time Home Run Kings". The cards, which measure 2-1/2" by 3-1/2", are numbered on the back according to the player's position on the all-time career home run list. Joe DiMaggio, who ranked 31st, was not included in the set. The set is skip-numbered from 30 to 32. The glossy card fronts contain the player's name in the lower left corner and feature a color photo, although black and white photos were utilized for a few of the homer kings who played before 1960. The card backs have blue and red print on white stock and contain the player's career batting statistics. The set was issued with a specially designed box.

		MT	NR MT	EX
Complete Set:		10.00	7.50	4.00
Common Player:		.15	.11	.06
1	Hank Aaron	.60	.45	.25
2	Babe Ruth	1.25	.90	.50
3	Willie Mays	.60	.45	.25
4	Frank Robinson	.25	.20	.10
5	Harmon Killebrew	.25	.20	.10
6	Mickey Mantle	2.00	1.50	.80
7	Jimmie Foxx	.25	.20	.10
8	Willie McCovey	.25	.20	.10
9	Ted Williams	.70	.50	.30
10	Ernie Banks	.25	.20	.10
11	Eddie Mathews	.25	.20	.10
12	Mel Ott	.20	.15	.08
13	Reggie Jackson	.40	.30	.15
14	Lou Gehrig	.70	.50	.30
15	Stan Musial	.60	.45	.25
16	Willie Stargell	.20	.15	.08
17	Carl Yastrzemski	.50	.40	.20
18	Billy Williams	.20	.15	.08
19	Mike Schmidt	.40	.30	.15
20	Duke Snider	.40	.30	.15
21	Al Kaline	.25	.20	.10
22	Johnny Bench	.35	.25	.14
23	Frank Howard	.15	.11	.06
24	Orlando Cepeda	.15	.11	.06
25	Norm Cash	.15	.11	.06
26	Dave Kingman	.15	.11	.06
27	Rocky Colavito	.15	.11	.06
28	Tony Perez	.15	.11	.06
29	Gil Hodges	.20	.15	.08
30	Ralph Kiner	.20	.15	.08
32	Johnny Mize	.20	.15	.08
33	Yogi Berra	.35	.25	.14
34	Lee May	.15	.11	.06

1969 Citgo Coins

The 20-player set of small (about 1" in diameter) metal coins was issued by Citgo in 1969 to commemorate professional baseball's 100th anniversary. The brass-coated coins, susceptible to oxidation, display the player in a crude portrait with his name across the top. The backs honor the 100th anniversary of pro ball. The coins are unnumbered but are generally checklisted according to numbers that appear on a display card which was available from Citgo by mail.

		NR MT	EX	VG
Complete Set:		60.00	30.00	18.00
Common Player:		1.00	.50	.30
1	Denny McLain	1.25	.60	.40
2	Dave McNally	1.00	.50	.30
3	Jim Lonborg	1.00	.50	.30
4	Harmon Killebrew	5.00	2.50	1.50
5	Mel Stottlemyre	1.00	.50	.30
6	Willie Horton	1.00	.50	.30
7	Jim Fregosi	1.00	.50	.30
8	Rico Petrocelli	1.00	.50	.30
9	Stan Bahnsen	1.00	.50	.30
10	Frank Howard	1.25	.60	.40
11	Joe Torre	1.25	.60	.40
12	Jerry Koosman	1.00	.50	.30
13	Ron Santo	1.00	.50	.30
14	Pete Rose	20.00	10.00	6.00
15	Rusty Staub	1.00	.50	.30
16	Henry Aaron	15.00	7.50	4.50
17	Richie Allen	1.25	.60	.40
18	Ron Swoboda	1.00	.50	.30
19	Willie McCovey	5.00	2.50	1.50
20	Jim Bunning	2.00	1.00	.60

1987 Classic Major

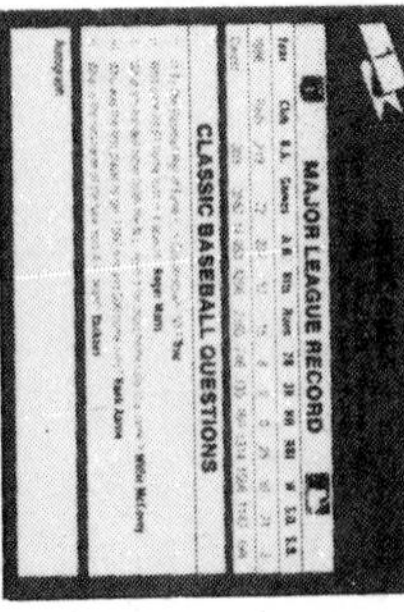

The "Classic Major League Baseball Board Game" set consists of 100 full-color cards which were used to play the game. Game participants were required to answer trivia questions found on the backs of the cards. The attractive cards measure 2 1/2" by 3 1/2" and are printed on glossy card stock. The card backs carry the player's career statistics besides the Classic Baseball Questions. The game was produced by Game Time, Ltd. of Marietta, Ga., and sold for $19.95 in most retail outlets.

		MT	NR MT	EX
Complete Set:		125.00	90.00	50.00
Common Player:		.10	.08	.04
1	Pete Rose	1.00	.70	.40
2	Len Dykstra	.30	.25	.12
3	Darryl Strawberry	.80	.60	.30
4	Keith Hernandez	.40	.30	.15
5	Gary Carter	.50	.40	.20
6	Wally Joyner	1.00	.70	.40
7	Andres Thomas	.15	.11	.06
8	Pat Dodson	.15	.11	.06
9	Kirk Gibson	.30	.25	.12
10	Don Mattingly	3.00	2.25	1.25
11	Dave Winfield	.40	.30	.15
12	Rickey Henderson	.60	.45	.25
13	Dan Pasqua	.15	.11	.06
14	Don Baylor	.15	.11	.06
15	Bo Jackson	60.00	45.00	25.00
16	Pete Incaviglia	.60	.45	.25
17	Kevin Bass	.10	.08	.04
18	Barry Larkin	.40	.30	.15
19	Dave Magadan	.40	.30	.15
20	Steve Sax	.20	.15	.08
21	Eric Davis	1.25	.90	.50
22	Mike Pagliarulo	.15	.11	.06
23	Fred Lynn	.20	.15	.08
24	Reggie Jackson	.50	.40	.20
25	Larry Parrish	.10	.08	.04
26	Tony Gwynn	.60	.45	.25
27	Steve Garvey	.40	.30	.15
28	Glenn Davis	.20	.15	.08
29	Tim Raines	.40	.30	.15
30	Vince Coleman	.20	.15	.08
31	Willie McGee	.15	.11	.06
32	Ozzie Smith	.80	.60	.30
33	Dave Parker	.20	.15	.08
34	Tony Pena	.10	.08	.04
35	Ryne Sandberg	.80	.60	.30
36	Brett Butler	.10	.08	.04
37	Dale Murphy	.70	.50	.30
38	Bob Horner	.15	.11	.06
39	Pedro Guerrero	.25	.20	.10
40	Brook Jacoby	.15	.11	.06
41	Carlton Fisk	.20	.15	.08
42	Harold Baines	.15	.11	.06
43	Rob Deer	.10	.08	.04
44	Robin Yount	1.00	.70	.40
45	Paul Molitor	.20	.15	.08
46	Jose Canseco	10.00	7.50	4.00
47	George Brett	.70	.50	.30
48	Jim Presley	.15	.11	.06
49	Rich Gedman	.10	.08	.04
50	Lance Parrish	.20	.15	.08
51	Eddie Murray	.50	.40	.20
52	Cal Ripken, Jr.	.60	.45	.25
53	Kent Hrbek	.25	.20	.10
54	Gary Gaetti	.20	.15	.08
55	Kirby Puckett	.90	.70	.35
56	George Bell	.40	.30	.15
57	Tony Fernandez	.20	.15	.08
58	Jesse Barfield	.15	.11	.06

		MT	NR MT	EX
59	Jim Rice	.40	.30	.15
60	Wade Boggs	1.25	.90	.50
61	Marty Barrett	.10	.08	.04
62	Mike Schmidt	1.25	.90	.50
63	Von Hayes	.15	.11	.06
64	Jeff Leonard	.10	.08	.04
65	Chris Brown	.15	.11	.06
66	Dave Smith	.10	.08	.04
67	Mike Krukow	.10	.08	.04
68	Ron Guidry	.20	.15	.08
69	Rob Woodward	.15	.11	.06
70	Rob Murphy	.15	.11	.06
71	Andres Galarraga	.25	.20	.10
72	Dwight Gooden	1.25	.90	.50
73	Bob Ojeda	.10	.08	.04
74	Sid Fernandez	.15	.11	.06
75	Jesse Orosco	.10	.08	.04
76	Roger McDowell	.15	.11	.06
77	John Tutor (Tudor)	.15	.11	.06
78	Tom Browning	.15	.11	.06
79	Rick Aguilera	.10	.08	.04
80	Lance McCullers	.15	.11	.06
81	Mike Scott	.20	.15	.08
82	Nolan Ryan	2.00	1.50	.80
83	Bruce Hurst	.15	.11	.06
84	Roger Clemens	1.00	.70	.40
85	Oil Can Boyd	.10	.08	.04
86	Dave Righetti	.20	.15	.08
87	Dennis Rasmussen	.10	.08	.04
88	Bret Saberhagan (Saberhagen)	.35	.25	.14
89	Mark Langston	.35	.25	.14
90	Jack Morris	.15	.11	.06
91	Fernando Valenzuela	.25	.20	.10
92	Orel Hershiser	.35	.25	.14
93	Rick Honeycutt	.10	.08	.04
94	Jeff Reardon	.15	.11	.06
95	John Habyan	.10	.08	.04
96	Goose Gossage	.15	.11	.06
97	Todd Worrell	.20	.15	.08
98	Floyd Youmans	.10	.08	.04
99	Don Aase	.10	.08	.04
100	John Franco	.15	.11	.06

1987 Classic Baseball

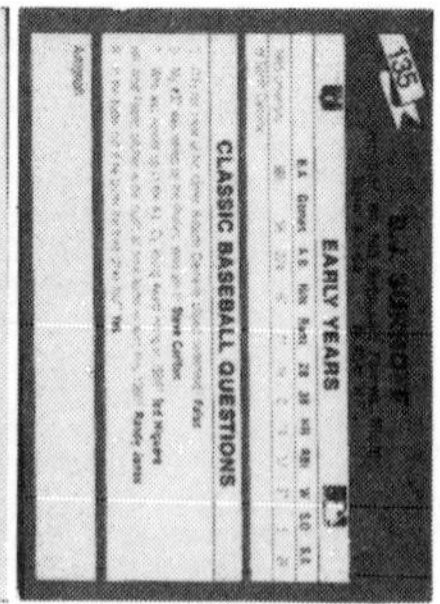

Game Time, Ltd. of Marietta, Ga., issued as an update to their Classic Baseball Board Game a 50-card set entitled "Travel Edition." The cards measure 2-1/2" by 3-1/2" and feature the same outstanding quality characteristic of the first release. Numbered from 101 to 150, the "Travel Edition" is an extension of the original set. Besides updating player trades and showcasing rookies, the set offers several highlights from the 1987 season, including Andre Dawson's beaning. All new trivia questions are contained on the card backs.

		MT	NR MT	EX
	Complete Set:	15.00	11.00	6.00
	Common Player:	.08	.06	.03
101	Mike Schmidt	1.25	.90	.50
102	Eric Davis	1.00	.70	.40
103	Pete Rose	.70	.50	.30
104	Don Mattingly	2.75	2.00	1.00
105	Wade Boggs	1.50	1.25	.60
106	Dale Murphy	.70	.50	.30
107	Glenn Davis	.20	.15	.08
108	Wally Joyner	1.00	.70	.40
109	Bo Jackson	2.00	1.50	.80
110	Cory Snyder	.60	.45	.25
111	Jim Lindeman	.15	.11	.06
112	Kirby Puckett	.90	.70	.35
113	Barry Bonds	.50	.40	.20
114	Roger Clemens	.70	.50	.30
115	Oddibe McDowell	.08	.06	.03
116	Bret Saberhagen	.30	.25	.12
117	Joe Magrane	.30	.25	.12
118	Scott Fletcher	.08	.06	.03
119	Mark McLemore	.08	.06	.03
120	Who Me? (Joe Niekro)	.25	.20	.10
121	Mark McGwire	2.00	1.50	.80
122	Darryl Strawberry	.80	.60	.30
123	Mike Scott	.20	.15	.08
124	Andre Dawson	.50	.40	.20
125	Jose Canseco	2.00	1.50	.80
126	Kevin McReynolds	.25	.20	.10
127	Joe Carter	.20	.15	.08
128	Casey Candaele	.08	.06	.03
129	Matt Nokes	1.00	.70	.40
130	Kal Daniels	.60	.45	.25
131	Pete Incaviglia	.60	.45	.25
132	Benito Santiago	.60	.45	.25
133	Barry Larkin	.60	.45	.25
134	Gary Pettis	.08	.06	.03
135	B.J. Surhoff	.60	.45	.25
136	Juan Nieves	.15	.11	.06
137	Jim Deshaies	.15	.11	.06
138	Pete O'Brien	.15	.11	.06
139	Kevin Seitzer	1.25	.90	.50
140	Devon White	.70	.50	.30
141	Rob Deer	.08	.06	.03
142	Kurt Stillwell	.25	.20	.10
143	Edwin Correa	.08	.06	.03
144	Dion James	.08	.06	.03
145	Danny Tartabull	.40	.30	.15
146	Jerry Browne	.08	.06	.03
147	Ted Higuera	.15	.11	.06
148	Jack Clark	.20	.15	.08
149	Ruben Sierra	.90	.70	.35
150	McGwire/Davis (Eric Davis, Mark McGwire)	1.25	.90	.50

1988 Classic Baseball

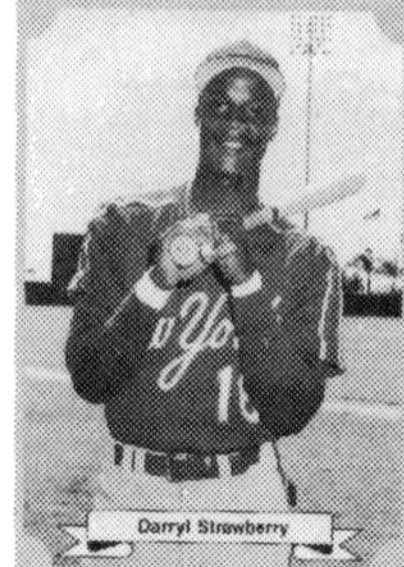

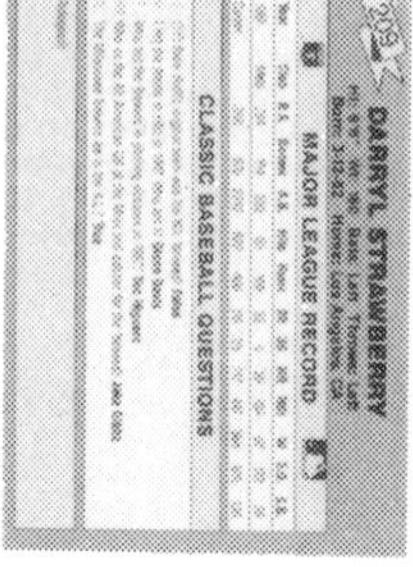

This 50-card set, numbered 201-250, was produced for use with the travel edition of Game Time's Classic Baseball Board Game. Two cards in the set feature two players: Davis/Murphy and McGwire/Mattingly. A follow-up to the first edition in 1987, the 1988 Blue was designed for use with the 1988 Red Series (151-200). Blue Series card fronts have blue borders, a yellow classic logo in the upper left corner and a black and beige player name banner beneath the photo. The card backs are printed in blue on white and include the player name, personal info, major league records, a baseball question and space for the player autograph. Classic card series are sold via hobby dealers and retail toy stores nationwide. Game Time Ltd., the set's producer, was purchased by Scoreboard of Cherry Hill, N.J. in 1988.

		MT	NR MT	EX
	Complete Set:	16.00	12.00	6.50
	Common Player:	.15	.11	.06
201	Davis/Murphy (Eric Davis, Dale Murphy)	.40	.30	.15
202	B.J. Surhoff	.15	.11	.06
203	John Kruk	.20	.15	.08
204	Sam Horn	.15	.11	.06
205	Jack Clark	.25	.20	.10
206	Wally Joyner	.70	.50	.30
207	Matt Nokes	.50	.40	.20
208	Bo Jackson	2.00	1.50	.80
209	Darryl Strawberry	.80	.60	.30
210	Ozzie Smith	.25	.20	.10
211	Don Mattingly	2.00	1.50	.80
212	Mark McGwire	1.25	.90	.50
213	Eric Davis	1.00	.70	.40
214	Wade Boggs	1.50	1.25	.60
215	Dale Murphy	.70	.50	.30
216	Andre Dawson	.30	.25	.12
217	Roger Clemens	.70	.50	.30
218	Kevin Seitzer	.60	.45	.25
219	Benito Santiago	.30	.25	.12
220	Tony Gwynn	.50	.40	.20
221	Mike Scott	.20	.15	.08
222	Steve Bedrosian	.15	.11	.06
223	Vince Coleman	.25	.20	.10
224	Rick Sutcliffe	.15	.11	.06
225	Will Clark	2.00	1.50	.80
226	Pete Rose	.80	.60	.30
227	Mike Greenwell	1.00	.70	.40
228	Ken Caminiti	.15	.11	.06
229	Ellis Burks	.80	.60	.30
230	Dave Magadan	.15	.11	.06
231	Alan Trammell	.30	.25	.12
232	Paul Molitor	.25	.20	.10
233	Gary Gaetti	.25	.20	.10
234	Rickey Henderson	.60	.45	.25
235	Danny Tartabull	.40	.30	.15
236	Bobby Bonilla	.25	.20	.10
237	Mike Dunne	.20	.15	.08
238	Al Leiter	.70	.50	.30
239	John Farrell	.30	.25	.12
240	Joe Magrane	.15	.11	.06
241	Mike Henneman	.15	.11	.06
242	George Bell	.40	.30	.15
243	Gregg Jefferies	1.50	1.25	.60
244	Jay Buhner	.40	.30	.15
245	Todd Benzinger	.30	.25	.12
246	Matt Williams	.30	.25	.12
247	McGwire/Mattingly (Don Mattingly, Mark McGwire) (no card number on back)	1.50	1.25	.60
248	George Brett	.70	.50	.30
249	Jimmy Key	.20	.15	.08
250	Mark Langston	.20	.15	.08

1988 Classic Baseball

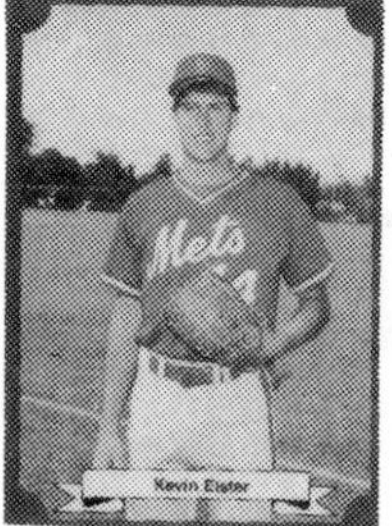

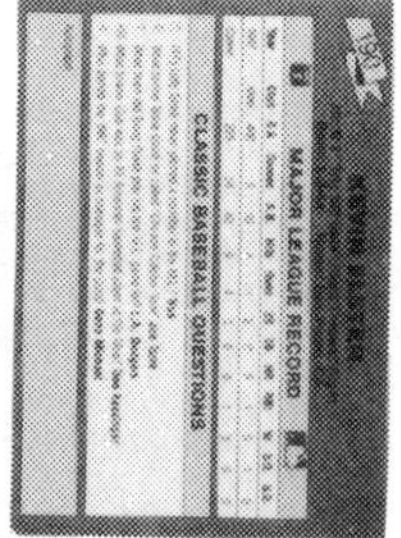

This 50-card set, numbered 151-200, was produced for use with the travel edition of Game Time's Classic Baseball Board Game. Special cards in the set include a McGwire/Mattingly, an instruction card with McGwire/Canseco, and three different cards featuring Phil Niekro (in different uniforms). A follow-up to the first edition in 1987, the 1988 Red Series was designed for use with the 1988 Blue Series (#'s 201-250). Red Series card fronts have red borders, a yellow Classic logo in the upper left corner and a black and beige player name banner beneath the photo. The card backs are printed in red and pink on white and include the player name, personal info, major league records, a baseball question and space for the player autograph. Classic card series were sold via hobby dealers and retail toy stores nationwide. Game Time Ltd., the set's producer, was purchased by Scoreboard of Cherry Hill, N.J. in 1988.

		MT	NR MT	EX
	Complete Set:	13.00	9.75	5.25
	Common Player:	.08	.06	.03
151	Don Mattingly, Mark McGwire,	2.00	1.50	.80
152	Don Mattingly	2.00	1.50	.80
153	Mark McGwire	.50	.40	.20
154	Eric Davis	.50	.40	.20
155	Wade Boggs	1.25	.90	.50
156	Dale Murphy	.50	.40	.20
157	Andre Dawson	.25	.20	.10
158	Roger Clemens	.50	.40	.20
159	Kevin Seitzer	.25	.20	.10
160	Benito Santiago	.25	.20	.10
161	Kal Daniels	.25	.20	.10
162	John Kruk	.25	.20	.10
163	Bill Ripken	.08	.06	.03
164	Kirby Puckett	.50	.40	.20
165	Jose Canseco	1.50	1.25	.60
166	Matt Nokes	.25	.20	.10
167	Mike Schmidt	1.00	.70	.40
168	Tim Raines	.25	.20	.10
169	Ryne Sandberg	.25	.20	.10
170	Dave Winfield	.25	.20	.10
171	Dwight Gooden	.70	.50	.30
172	Bret Saberhagen	.20	.15	.08
173	Willie McGee	.08	.06	.03
174	Jack Morris	.08	.06	.03
175	Jeff Leonard	.08	.06	.03
176	Cal Ripken, Jr.	.25	.20	.10
177	Pete Incaviglia	.08	.06	.03
178	Devon White	.25	.20	.10
179	Nolan Ryan	3.00	2.25	1.25
180	Ruben Sierra	.70	.50	.25
181	Todd Worrell	.08	.06	.03
182	Glenn Davis	.25	.20	.10
183	Frank Viola	.25	.20	.10
184	Cory Snyder	.40	.30	.15
185	Tracy Jones	.08	.06	.03
186	Terry Steinbach	.70	.50	.25
187	Julio Franco	.15	.11	.06
188	Larry Sheets	.08	.06	.03
189	John Marzano	.08	.06	.03
190	Kevin Elster	.08	.06	.03
191	Vincente Palacios	.08	.06	.03
192	Kent Hrbek	.25	.20	.10
193	Eric Bell	.25	.20	.10
194	Kelly Downs	.08	.06	.03
195	Jose Lind	.10	.08	.04
196	Dave Stewart	.15	.11	.06
197	Jose canseco, Mark McGwire,	2.00	1.50	.80
198	Phil Niekro	.25	.20	.10
199	Phil Niekro	.25	.20	.10
200	Phil Niekro	.25	.20	.10

1989 Classic Baseball

This 100-card set was released by The Score Board to accompany trivia board games. Cards numbered 1-100 correlate with the 1989 Classic Baseball Game, while cards numbered 101-150 belong to the 1989 Classic Travel Series No. 1. The card fronts display full-color photos with the Classic Baseball logo in the upper left corner. The

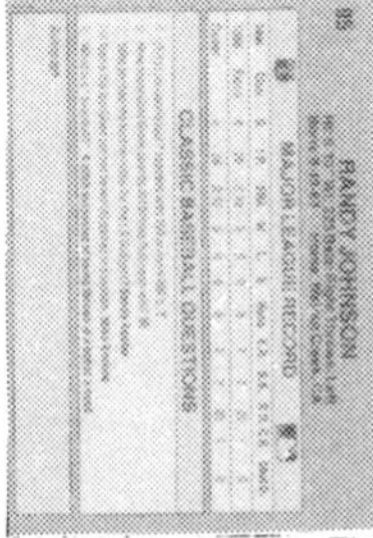

player's name appears beneath the photo. The flip side includes the card number in the upper left, personal information, and the player's major league record in a boxed area. Another boxed area below the record presents five trivia questions. The lower border of the flip side provides an autograph space. The Classic card series was sold by retail stores and hobby dealers nationwide.

		MT	NR MT	EX
Complete Set:		30.00	22.50	12.00
Common Player:		.08	.06	.03
1	Orel Hershiser	.30	.25	.12
2	Wade Boggs	1.00	.70	.30
3	Jose Canseco	1.75	1.25	.70
4	Mark McGwire	1.00	.70	.30
5	Don Mattingly	1.25	.90	.50
6	Gregg Jefferies	1.00	.70	.40
7	Dwight Gooden	.60	.45	.25
8	Darryl Strawberry	.40	.30	.15
9	Eric Davis	.50	.40	.20
10	Joey Meyer	.08	.06	.03
11	Joe Carter	.15	.11	.06
12	Paul Molitor	.15	.11	.06
13	Mark Grace	2.00	1.50	.80
14	Kurt Stillwell	.08	.06	.03
15	Kirby Puckett	1.00	.70	.30
16	Keith Miller	.08	.06	.03
17	Glenn Davis	.15	.11	.06
18	Will Clark	2.00	1.50	.80
19	Cory Snyder	.15	.11	.06
20	Jose Lind	.08	.06	.03
21	Andres Thomas	.08	.06	.03
22	Dave Smith	.08	.06	.03
23	Mike Scott	.15	.11	.06
24	Kevin McReynolds	.20	.15	.08
25	B.J. Surhoff	.20	.15	.08
26	Mackey Sasser	.08	.06	.03
27	Chad Kreuter	.30	.25	.12
28	Hal Morris	.30	.25	.12
29	Wally Joyner	.40	.30	.15
30	Tony Gwynn	.40	.30	.15
31	Kevin Mitchell	1.75	1.25	.70
32	Dave Winfield	.25	.20	.10
33	Billy Bean	.08	.06	.03
34	Steve Bedrosian	.08	.06	.03
35	Ron Gant	.08	.06	.03
36	Len Dykstra	.08	.06	.03
37	Andre Dawson	.20	.15	.08
38	Brett Butler	.20	.15	.08
39	Rob Deer	.08	.06	.03
40	Tommy John	.08	.06	.03
41	Gary Gaetti	.20	.15	.08
42	Tim Raines	.20	.15	.08
43	George Bell	.20	.15	.08
44	Dwight Evans	.20	.15	.08
45	Denny Martinez	.08	.06	.03
46	Andres Galarraga	.20	.15	.08
47	George Brett	.40	.30	.15
48	Mike Schmidt	1.00	.70	.30
49	Dave Steib	.20	.15	.08
50	Rickey Henderson	.50	.40	.20
51	Craig Biggio	1.00	.70	.30
52	Mark Lemke	.25	.20	.10
53	Chris Sabo	.60	.45	.25
54	Jeff Treadway	.15	.11	.06
55	Kent Hrbek	.15	.11	.06
56	Cal Ripken, Jr.	.25	.20	.10
57	Tim Belcher	.15	.11	.06
58	Ozzie Smith	.40	.30	.15
59	Keith Hernandez	.20	.15	.08
60	Pedro Guerrero	.20	.15	.08
61	Greg Swindell	.25	.20	.10
62	Bret Saberhagen	.40	.30	.15
63	John Tudor	.08	.06	.03
64	Gary Carter	.15	.11	.06
65	Kevin Seitzer	.20	.15	.08
66	Jesse Barfield	.20	.15	.08
67	Luis Medina	.35	.25	.14
68	Walt Weiss	.35	.25	.14
69	Terry Steinbach	.60	.45	.25
70	Barry Larkin	.30	.25	.12
71	Pete Rose	1.00	.70	.30
72	Luis Salazar	.08	.06	.03
73	Benito Santiago	.40	.30	.15
74	Kal Daniels	.20	.15	.08
75	Kevin Elster	.08	.06	.03
76	Rob Dibble	.15	.11	.06
77	Bobby Witt	.08	.06	.03
78	Steve Searcy	.25	.20	.10
79	Sandy Alomar	2.00	1.50	.80
80	Chili Davis	.20	.15	.08
81	Alvin Davis	.20	.15	.08
82	Charlie Leibrandt	.08	.06	.03
83	Robin Yount	1.00	.70	.30
84	Mark Carreon	.25	.20	.10
85	Pascual Perez	.08	.06	.03
86	Dennis Rasmussen	.08	.06	.03
87	Ernie Riles	.08	.06	.03
88	Melido Perez	.20	.15	.08
89	Doug Jones	.08	.06	.03
90	Dennis Eckersley	.15	.11	.06
91	Bob Welch	.15	.11	.06
92	Bob Milacki	.35	.25	.14
93	Jeff Robinson	.15	.11	.06
94	Mike Henneman	.15	.11	.06
95	Randy Johnson	.40	.30	.15
96	Ron Jones	.40	.30	.15
97	Jack Armstrong	.08	.06	.03
98	Willie McGee	.08	.06	.03
99	Ryne Sandberg	.40	.30	.15
100	David Cone / Danny Jackson	.70	.50	.25
101	Gary Sheffield	1.00	.70	.30
102	Wade Boggs	1.00	.70	.30
103	Jose Canseco	1.25	.90	.50
104	Mark McGwire	1.25	.90	.50
105	Orel Hershiser	.30	.25	.12
106	Don Mattingly	1.25	.90	.50
107	Dwight Gooden	.70	.50	.30
108	Darryl Strawberry	.40	.30	.15
109	Eric Davis	.40	.30	.15
110	Bam Bam Meulens	1.00	.70	.30
111	Andy Van Slyke	.20	.15	.08
112	Al Leiter	.08	.06	.03
113	Matt Nokes	.35	.25	.14
114	Mike Krukow	.08	.06	.03
115	Tony Fernandez	.25	.20	.10
116	Fred McGriff	.70	.50	.25
117	Barry Bonds	.25	.20	.10
118	Gerald Perry	.08	.06	.03
119	Roger Clemens	.40	.30	.15
120	Kirk Gibson	.12	.09	.05
121	Greg Maddux	.30	.25	.12
122	Bo Jackson	1.25	.90	.50
123	Danny Jackson	.08	.06	.03
124	Dale Murphy	.20	.15	.08
125	David Cone	.35	.25	.14
126	Tom Browning	.15	.11	.06
127	Roberto Alomar	.50	.40	.20
128	Alan Trammell	.15	.11	.06
129	Rickey Jordan	.40	.30	.15
130	Ramon Martinez	.50	.40	.20
131	Ken Griffey, Jr.	3.00	2.25	1.25
132	Gregg Olson	.80	.60	.30
133	Carlos Quintana	.35	.25	.14
134	Dave West	.60	.45	.25
135	Cameron Drew	.30	.25	.12
136	Ted Higuera	.25	.20	.20
137	Sil Campusano	.20	.15	.08
138	Mark Gubicza	.20	.15	.08
139	Mike Boddicker	.08	.06	.03
140	Paul Gibson	.08	.06	.03
141	Jose Rijo	.15	.11	.06
142	John Costello	.08	.06	.03
143	Cecil Espy	.08	.06	.03
144	Frank Viola	.25	.20	.10
145	Erik Hanson	.25	.20	.10
146	Juan Samuel	.08	.06	.03
147	Harold Reynolds	.15	.11	.06
148	Joe Magrane	.15	.11	.06
149	Mike Greenwell	.70	.50	.30
150	Darryl Strawberry / Will Clark	1.50	1.25	.60

1989 Classic Update

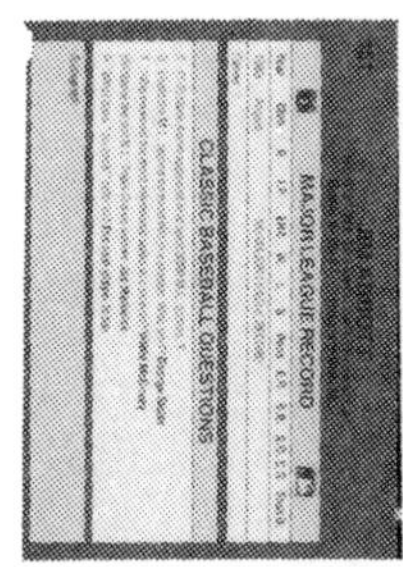

Numbered from 151-200, this 50-card set features rookies and traded players with their new teams. The cards are purple and gray and were sold as part of a board game with baseball trivia questions.

		MT	NR MT	EX
Complete Set:		15.00	11.00	6.00
Common Player:		.05	.04	.02
151	Jim Abbott	1.50	1.25	.60
152	Ellis Burks	.30	.25	.12
153	Mike Schmidt	1.00	.70	.30
154	Gregg Jefferies	.50	.40	.20
155	Mark Grace	.30	.25	.12
156	Jerome Walton	2.25	1.75	.90
157	Bo Jackson	1.00	.70	.40
158	Jack Clark	.05	.04	.02
159	Tom Glavine	.10	.08	.04
160	Eddie Murray	.10	.08	.04
161	John Dopson	.05	.04	.02
162	Ruben Sierra	.35	.25	.14
163	Rafael Palmeiro	.20	.15	.08
164	Nolan Ryan	1.00	.70	.30
165	Barry Larkin	.20	.15	.08
166	Tommy Herr	.05	.04	.02
167	Roberto Kelly	.25	.20	.10
168	Glenn Davis	.10	.08	.04
169	Glenn Braggs	.05	.04	.02
170	Juan Bell	.30	.25	.12
171	Todd Burns	.05	.04	.02
172	Derek Lilliquist	.10	.08	.04
173	Orel Hershiser	.20	.15	.08
174	John Smoltz	.60	.45	.25
175	Ozzie Guillen / Ellis Burks	.30	.25	.12
176	Kirby Puckett	.50	.40	.20
177	Robin Ventura	.80	.60	.30
178	Allan Anderson	.05	.04	.02
179	Steve Sax	.05	.04	.02
180	Will Clark	.80	.60	.30
181	Mike Devereaux	.05	.04	.02
182	Tom Gordon	1.00	.70	.40
183	Rob Murphy	.05	.04	.02
184	Pete O'Brien	.05	.04	.02
185	Cris Carpenter	.10	.08	.04
186	Tom Brunansky	.05	.04	.02
187	Bob Boone	.05	.04	.02
188	Lou Whitaker	.05	.04	.02
189	Dwight Gooden	.30	.25	.12
190	Mark McGwire	.40	.30	.15
191	John Smiley	.05	.04	.02
192	Tommy Gregg	.05	.04	.02
193	Ken Griffey, Jr.	2.50	2.00	1.00
194	Bruce Hurst	.05	.04	.02
195	Greg Swindell	.20	.15	.08
196	Nelson Liriano	.05	.04	.02
197	Randy Myers	.05	.04	.02
198	Kevin Mitchell	.70	.50	.30
199	Dante Bichette	.10	.08	.04
200	Deion Sanders	1.00	.70	.40

1990 Classic Baseball

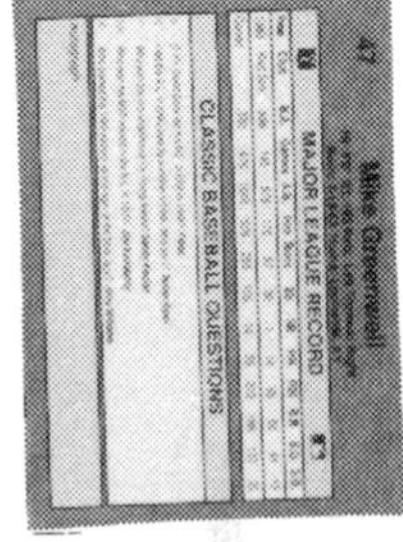

Classic Baseball returned in 1990 with another 150-card set. The cards were again sold as part of a baseball trivia game, and each game included a box designed to store all the cards in the set.

		MT	NR MT	EX
Complete Set:		20.00	15.00	8.00
Common Player:		.05	.04	.02
1	Nolan Ryan	.70	.50	.30
2	Bo Jackson	.80	.60	.30
3	Gregg Olson	.30	.25	.12
4	Tom Gordon	.50	.40	.20
5	Robin Ventura	.80	.60	.30
6	Will Clark	.50	.40	.20
7	Ruben Sierra	.20	.15	.08
8	Mark Grace	.30	.25	.12
9	Luis de los Santos	.05	.04	.02
10	Bernie Williams	1.00	.70	.40
11	Eric Davis	.10	.08	.04
12	Carney Lansford	.05	.04	.02
13	John Smoltz	.10	.08	.04
14	Gary Sheffield	.60	.45	.25
15	Kent Merker	.40	.30	.15
16	Don Mattingly	.50	.40	.20
17	Tony Gwynn	.15	.11	.06
18	Ozzie Smith	.05	.04	.02
19	Fred McGriff	.25	.20	.10
20	Ken Griffey, Jr.	2.00	1.50	.80
21a	Deion Sanders ("Prime Time")	12.00	9.00	4.75
21b	Deion Sanders (Deion "Prime Time" Sanders)	1.50	1.25	.60
22	Jose Canseco	.50	.40	.20
23	Mitch Williams	.20	.15	.08
24	Cal Ripken, Jr.	.10	.08	.04
25	Bob Geren	.20	.15	.08
26	Wade Boggs	.15	.11	.06
27	Ryne Sandberg	.15	.11	.06
28	Kirby Puckett	.30	.25	.12
29	Mike Scott	.05	.04	.02
30	Dwight Smith	.80	.60	.30
31	Craig Worthington	.10	.08	.04
32	Ricky Jordan	.15	.11	.06
33	Darryl Strawberry	.10	.08	.04
34	Jerome Walton	1.25	.90	.50
35	John Olerud	2.50	2.00	1.00
36	Tom Glavine	.05	.04	.02
37	Rickey Henderson	.30	.25	.12
38	Rolando Roomes	.10	.08	.04
39	Mickey Tettleton	.10	.08	.04
40	Jim Abbott	.90	.70	.35
41	Dave Righetti	.05	.04	.02
42	Mike LaValliere	.05	.04	.02
43	Rob Dibble	.05	.04	.02
44	Pete Harnisch	.10	.08	.04
45	Jose Offerman	2.00	1.50	.80
46	Walt Weiss	.05	.04	.02
47	Mike Greenwell	.25	.20	.10
48	Barry Larkin	.10	.08	.04
49	Dave Gallagher	.05	.04	.02
50	Junior Felix	.60	.45	.25
51	Roger Clemens	.10	.08	.04
52	Lonnie Smith	.05	.04	.02
53	Jerry Browne	.05	.04	.02
54	Greg Briley	.25	.20	.10
55	Delino Desheilds	1.25	.90	.50
56	Carmelo Martinez	.05	.04	.02

		MT	NR MT	EX
57	Craig Biggio	.20	.15	.08
58	Dwight Gooden	.15	.11	.06
59a	Bo Jackson, Ruben Sierra, Mark McGwire (Bo, Ruben, Mark)	8.00	6.00	3.25
59b	Bo Jackson, Ruben Sierra, Mark McGwire (A.L. Fence Busters)	.60	.45	.25
60	Greg Vaughn	1.00	.70	.40
61	Roberto Alomar	.10	.08	.04
62	Steve Bedrosian	.05	.04	.02
63	Devon White	.05	.04	.02
64	Kevin Mitchell	.40	.30	.15
65	Marquis Grissom	1.00	.70	.40
66	Brian Holman	.05	.04	.02
67	Julio Franco	.10	.08	.04
68	Dave West	.10	.08	.04
69	Harold Baines	.10	.08	.04
70	Eric Anthony	1.00	.70	.40
71	Glenn Davis	.05	.04	.02
72	Mark Langston	.15	.11	.06
73	Matt Williams	.25	.20	.10
74	Rafael Palmeiro	.05	.04	.02
75	Pete Rose, Jr.	1.00	.70	.40
76	Ramon Martinez	.20	.15	.08
77	Dwight Evans	.10	.08	.04
78	Mackey Sasser	.05	.04	.02
79	Mike Schooler	.05	.04	.02
80	Dennis Cook	.10	.08	.04
81	Orel Hershiser	.20	.15	.08
82	Barry Bonds	.10	.08	.04
83	Geronimo Berroa	.10	.08	.04
84	George Bell	.10	.08	.04
85	Andre Dawson	.10	.08	.04
86	John Franco	.05	.04	.02
87a	Will Clark, Tony Gwynn (Clark/Gwynn)	7.00	5.25	2.75
87b	Will Clark, Tony Gwynn (N.L. Hit Kings)	.40	.30	.15
88	Glenallen Hill	.35	.25	.14
89	Jeff Ballard	.10	.08	.04
90	Todd Zeile	1.75	1.25	.70
91	Frank Viola	.15	.11	.06
92	Ozzie Guillen	.05	.04	.02
93	Jeff Leonard	.05	.04	.02
94	Dave Smith	.05	.04	.02
95	Dave Parker	.10	.08	.04
96	Jose Gonzalez	1.00	.70	.40
97	Dave Steib	.05	.04	.02
98	Charlie Hayes	.15	.11	.06
99	Jesse Barfield	.05	.04	.02
100	Joey Belle	.80	.60	.30
101	Jeff Reardon	.05	.04	.02
102	Bruce Hurst	.05	.04	.02
103	Luis Medina	.05	.04	.02
104	Mike Moore	.10	.08	.04
105	Vince Coleman	.10	.08	.04
106	Alan Trammell	.10	.08	.04
107	Randy Myers	.05	.04	.02
108	Frank Tanana	.05	.04	.02
109	Craig Lefferts	.05	.04	.02
110	John Wetteland	.30	.25	.12
111	Chris Gwynn	.10	.08	.04
112	Mark Carreon	.10	.08	.04
113	Von Hayes	.05	.04	.02
114	Doug Jones	.05	.04	.02
115	Andres Galarraga	.10	.08	.04
116	Carlton Fisk	.10	.08	.04
117	Paul O'Neill	.05	.04	.02
118	Tim Raines	.10	.08	.04
119	Tom Brunansky	.05	.04	.02
120	Andy Benes	.70	.50	.30
121	Mark Portugal	.05	.04	.02
122	Willie Randolph	.05	.04	.02
123	Jeff Blauser	.05	.04	.02
124	Don August	.05	.04	.02
125	Chuck Cary	.05	.04	.02
126	John Smiley	.05	.04	.02
127	Terry Mullholland	.05	.04	.02
128	Harold Reynolds	.05	.04	.02
129	Hubie Brooks	.05	.04	.02
130	Ben McDonald	1.75	1.25	.70
131	Kevin Ritz	.20	.15	.08
132	Luis Quinones	.05	.04	.02
133	Bam Bam Meulens	.20	.15	.08
134	Bill Spiers	.20	.15	.08
135	Andy Hawkins	.05	.04	.02
136	Alvin Davis	.10	.08	.04
137	Lee Smith	.05	.04	.02
138	Joe Carter	.10	.08	.04
139	Bret Saberhagen	.10	.08	.04
140	Sammy Sosa	.70	.50	.30
141	Matt Nokes	.05	.04	.02
142	Bert Blyleven	.10	.08	.04
143	Bobby Bonilla	.10	.08	.04
144	Howard Johnson	.10	.08	.04
145	Joe Magrane	.05	.04	.02
146	Pedro Guerrero	.10	.08	.04
147	Robin Yount	.35	.25	.14
148	Dan Gladden	.05	.04	.02
149	Steve Sax	.10	.08	.04
150a	Will Clark, Kevin Mitchell (Clark/Mitchell)	6.00	4.50	2.50
150b	Will Clark, Kevin Mitchell (Bay Bombers)	.50	.40	.20

1990 Classic Series II

Like in previous years, Classic released a 50-card second series set for use with its baseball trivia game. Unlike the 1989 update set, the 1990 Classic Series II set is numbered 1-50 with a "T" designation accompanying the card number. The cards measure 2-1/2" by 3-1/2" and are designed after the original 1990 Classic cards. Series II cards have pink borders with a blue design, while the cards from the regular issue feature the opposite color combination. The cards are issued in a complete Series II set form.

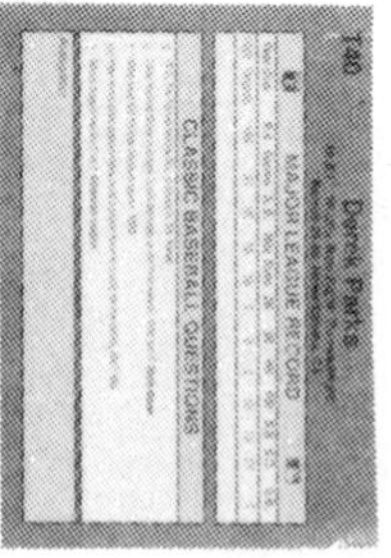

		MT	NR MT	EX
	Complete Set:	9.00	6.75	3.50
	Common Player:	.05	.04	.02
1	Gregg Jefferies	.25	.20	.10
2	Steve Adkins	.50	.40	.20
3	Sandy Alomar, Jr.	.25	.20	.10
4	Steve Avery	.35	.25	.14
5	Mike Blowers	.20	.15	.08
6	George Brett	.05	.04	.02
7	Tom Browning	.05	.04	.02
8	Ellis Burks	.10	.08	.04
9	Joe Carter	.10	.08	.04
10	Jerald Clark	.10	.08	.04
11	"Hot Corners"	.40	.30	.15
12	Pat Combs	.25	.20	.10
13	Scott Cooper	.25	.20	.10
14	Mark Davis	.05	.04	.02
15	Storm Davis	.05	.04	.02
16	Larry Walker	.10	.08	.04
17	Brian DuBois	.10	.08	.04
18	Len Dykstra	.10	.08	.04
19	John Franco	.10	.08	.04
20	Kirk Gibson	.05	.04	.02
21	Juan Gonzalez	.50	.40	.20
22	Tommy Greene	.15	.11	.06
23	Kent Hrbek	.05	.04	.02
24	Mike Huff	.30	.25	.12
25	Bo Jackson	1.25	.90	.50
26	Nolan Knows Bo	3.50	2.75	1.50
27	Roberto Kelly	.05	.04	.02
28	Mark Langston	.10	.08	.04
29	Ray Lankford	.80	.60	.30
30	Kevin Maas	.25	.20	.10
31	Julio Machado	.15	.11	.06
32	Greg Maddux	.05	.04	.02
33	Mark McGwire	.15	.11	.06
34	Paul Molitor	.05	.04	.02
35	Hal Morris	.10	.08	.04
36	Dale Murphy	.05	.04	.02
37	Eddie Murray	.05	.04	.02
38	Jaime Navarro	.10	.08	.04
39	Dean Palmer	.15	.11	.06
40	Derek Parks	.30	.25	.12
41	Bobby Rose	.20	.15	.08
42	Wally Joyner	.05	.04	.02
43	Chris Sabo	.05	.04	.02
44	Benito Santiago	.05	.04	.02
45	Mike Stanton	.10	.08	.04
46	Terry Steinbach	.05	.04	.02
47	Dave Stewart	.05	.04	.02
48	Greg Swindell	.05	.04	.02
49	Jose Vizcaino	.15	.11	.06
50	"Royal Flush"	.25	.20	.10

1989 Cleveland Indians

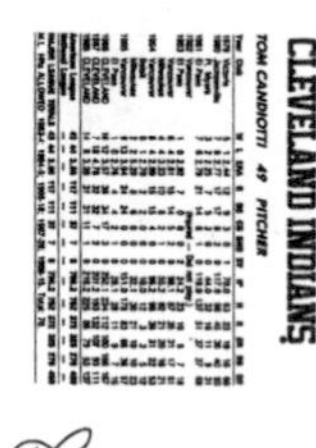

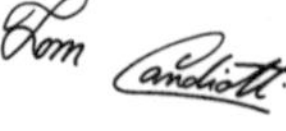

The Cleveland Indians released this oversized (2-3/4" by 4-1/2") 28-card set in 1989. The cards feature a full-color player photo on the front with the "Tribe" logo in the upper left corner. Card backs include major and minor league statistics and a facsimile autograph.

		MT	NR MT	EX
	Complete Set:	6.00	4.50	2.50
	Common Player:	.20	.15	.08
(1)	Doc Edwards	.20	.15	.08
(2)	Joel Skinner	.20	.15	.08
(3)	Andy Allanson	.20	.15	.08
(4)	Tom Candiotti	.20	.15	.08
(5)	Doug Jones	.20	.15	.08
(6)	Keith Atherton	.20	.15	.08
(7)	Rich Yett	.20	.15	.08
(8)	John Farrell	.20	.15	.08
(9)	Rod Nichols	.20	.15	.08
(10)	Joe Skalski	.30	.25	.12
(11)	Pete O'Brien	.30	.25	.12
(12)	Jerry Browne	.30	.25	.12
(13)	Brook Jacoby	.30	.25	.12
(14)	Felix Fermin	.20	.15	.08
(15)	Bud Black	.20	.15	.08
(16)	Brad Havens	.20	.15	.08
(17)	Greg Swindell	.40	.30	.15
(18)	Scott Bailes	.20	.15	.08
(19)	Jesse Orosco	.20	.15	.08
(20)	Oddibe McDowell	.30	.25	.12
(21)	Joe Carter	.50	.40	.20
(22)	Cory Snyder	.40	.30	.15
(23)	Louie Medina	.25	.20	.10
(24)	Dave Clark	.25	.20	.10
(25)	Brad Komminsk	.20	.15	.08
(26)	Luis Aguayo	.20	.15	.08
(27)	Pat Keedy	.25	.20	.10
(28)	Tribe Coaches	.20	.15	.08

1981 Coca-Cola

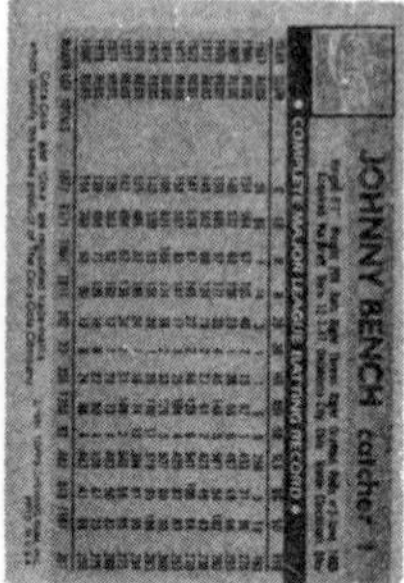

In 1981, Topps produced for Coca-Cola 12-card sets for 11 various American and National League teams. The sets include 11 player cards and one unnumbered header card. The card fronts, which measure 2-1/2" by 3-1/2", are identical in style to the 1981 Topps regular issue save for the Coca-Cola logo. The backs differ only from the '81 Topps regular set in that they are numbered 1-11 and carry the Coca-Cola trademark and copyright line. The backs of the header cards contain an offer for 132-card uncut sheets of 1981 Topps baseball cards.

		MT	NR MT	EX
	Complete Set:	30.00	22.00	12.50
	Common Player:	.06	.05	.02
1	Tom Burgmeier	.06	.05	.02
2	Dennis Eckersley	.15	.11	.06
3	Dwight Evans	.60	.45	.25
4	Bob Stanley	.10	.08	.04
5	Glenn Hoffman	.06	.05	.02
6	Carney Lansford	.20	.15	.08
7	Frank Tanana	.10	.08	.04
8	Tony Perez	.20	.15	.08
9	Jim Rice	.80	.60	.30
10	Dave Stapleton	.06	.05	.02
11	Carl Yastrzemski	2.00	1.50	.80
---	Header Card	.03	.02	.01
1	Tim Blackwell	.06	.05	.02
2	Bill Buckner	.15	.11	.06
3	Ivan DeJesus	.06	.05	.02
4	Leon Durham	.15	.11	.06
5	Steve Henderson	.06	.05	.02
6	Mike Krukow	.10	.08	.04
7	Ken Reitz	.06	.05	.02
8	Rick Reuschel	.15	.11	.06
9	Scot Thompson	.06	.05	.02
10	Dick Tidrow	.06	.05	.02
11	Mike Tyson	.06	.05	.02
---	Header Card	.03	.02	.01
1	Britt Burns	.10	.08	.04
2	Todd Cruz	.06	.05	.02
3	Rich Dotson	.20	.15	.08
4	Jim Essian	.06	.05	.02
5	Ed Farmer	.06	.05	.02
6	Lamar Johnson	.06	.05	.02
7	Ron LeFlore	.10	.08	.04
8	Chet Lemon	.10	.08	.04
9	Bob Molinaro	.06	.05	.02
10	Jim Morrison	.06	.05	.02
11	Wayne Nordhagen	.06	.05	.02
---	Header Card	.03	.02	.01
1	Johnny Bench	2.00	1.50	.80
2	Dave Collins	.10	.08	.04
3	Dave Concepcion	.15	.11	.06
4	Dan Driessen	.10	.08	.04
5	George Foster	.25	.20	.10
6	Ken Griffey	.15	.11	.06
7	Tom Hume	.06	.05	.02
8	Ray Knight	.10	.08	.04
9	Ron Oester	.06	.05	.02
10	Tom Seaver	1.25	.90	.50
11	Mario Soto	.10	.08	.04
---	Header Card	.03	.02	.01
1	Champ Summers	.06	.05	.02
2	Al Cowens	.06	.05	.02
3	Rich Hebner	.06	.05	.02
4	Steve Kemp	.10	.08	.04
5	Aurelio Lopez	.06	.05	.02
6	Jack Morris	.35	.25	.14
7	Lance Parrish	.35	.25	.14
8	Johnny Wockenfuss	.06	.05	.02

#	Player	MT	NR MT	EX
9	Alan Trammell	1.00	.70	.40
10	Lou Whitaker	1.00	.70	.40
11	Kirk Gibson	1.00	.70	.40
---	Header Card	.03	.02	.01
1	Alan Ashby	.06	.05	.02
2	Cesar Cedeno	.15	.11	.06
3	Jose Cruz	.15	.11	.06
4	Art Howe	.06	.05	.02
5	Rafael Landestoy	.06	.05	.02
6	Joe Niekro	.15	.11	.06
7	Terry Puhl	.06	.05	.02
8	J.R. Richard	.15	.11	.06
9	Nolan Ryan	3.00	2.25	1.25
10	Joe Sambito	.06	.05	.02
11	Don Sutton	.35	.25	.14
---	Header Card	.03	.02	.01
1	Willie Aikens	.06	.05	.02
2	George Brett	1.50	1.25	.60
3	Larry Gura	.06	.05	.02
4	Dennis Leonard	.06	.05	.02
5	Hal McRae	.15	.11	.06
6	Amos Otis	.10	.08	.04
7	Dan Quisenberry	.15	.11	.06
8	U.L. Washington	.06	.05	.02
9	John Wathan	.10	.08	.04
10	Frank White	.10	.08	.04
11	Willie Wilson	.15	.11	.06
---	Header Card	.03	.02	.01
1	Neil Allen	.06	.05	.02
2	Doug Flynn	.06	.05	.02
3	Dave Kingman	.15	.11	.06
4	Randy Jones	.06	.05	.02
5	Pat Zachry	.06	.05	.02
6	Lee Mazzilli	.10	.08	.04
7	Rusty Staub	.15	.11	.06
8	Craig Swan	.06	.05	.02
9	Frank Taveras	.06	.05	.02
10	Alex Trevino	.06	.05	.02
11	Joel Youngblood	.06	.05	.02
---	Header Card	.03	.02	.01
1	Bob Boone	.30	.25	.12
2	Larry Bowa	.15	.11	.06
3	Steve Carlton	1.00	.70	.40
4	Greg Luzinski	.15	.11	.06
5	Garry Maddox	.10	.08	.04
6	Bake McBride	.06	.05	.02
7	Tug McGraw	.15	.11	.06
8	Pete Rose	2.00	1.50	.80
9	Mike Schmidt	2.25	1.75	.90
10	Lonnie Smith	.15	.11	.06
11	Manny Trillo	.06	.05	.02
---	Header Card	.03	.02	.01
1	Jim Bibby	.06	.05	.02
2	John Candelaria	.10	.08	.04
3	Mike Easler	.10	.08	.04
4	Tim Foli	.06	.05	.02
5	Phil Garner	.06	.05	.02
6	Bill Madlock	.15	.11	.06
7	Omar Moreno	.06	.05	.02
8	Ed Ott	.06	.05	.02
9	Dave Parker	.35	.25	.14
10	Willie Stargell	1.00	.70	.40
11	Kent Tekulve	.10	.08	.04
---	Header Card	.03	.02	.01
1	Bob Forsch	.10	.08	.04
2	George Hendrick	.10	.08	.04
3	Keith Hernandez	.50	.40	.20
4	Tom Herr	.15	.11	.06
5	Sixto Lezcano	.06	.05	.02
6	Ken Oberkfell	.06	.05	.02
7	Darrell Porter	.10	.08	.04
8	Tony Scott	.06	.05	.02
9	Lary Sorensen	.06	.05	.02
10	Bruce Sutter	.15	.11	.06
11	Garry Templeton	.10	.08	.04
---	Header Card	.03	.02	.01

1982 Coca-Cola/Brigham's

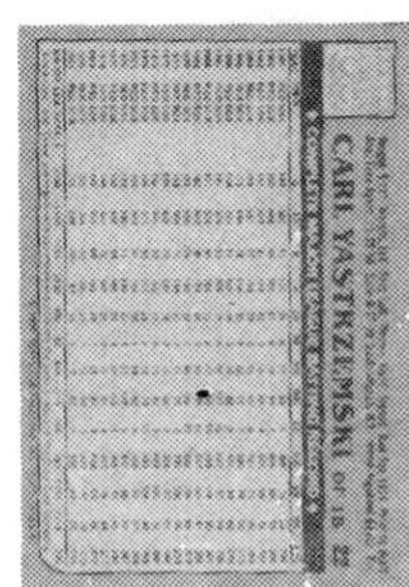

Coca-Cola, in conjunction with Brigham's Ice Cream stores, issued a 23-card set in the Boston area featuring Red Sox players. The Topps-produced cards, which measure 2-1/2" by 3-1/2", are identical in style to the regular 1982 Topps set but contain the Coca-Cola and Brigham's logos in the corners. The cards were distributed in three-card cello packs, including an unnumbered header card.

#	Player	MT	NR MT	EX
	Complete Set:	6.00	4.50	2.50
	Common Player:	.08	.06	.03
1	Gary Allenson	.08	.06	.03
2	Tom Burgmeier	.08	.06	.03
3	Mark Clear	.15	.11	.06
4	Steve Crawford	.08	.06	.03
5	Dennis Eckersley	.30	.25	.12
6	Dwight Evans	.80	.60	.30
7	Rich Gedman	.30	.25	.12
8	Garry Hancock	.08	.06	.03
9	Glen Hoffman (Glenn)	.08	.06	.03
10	Carney Lansford	.20	.15	.08
11	Rick Miller	.08	.06	.03
12	Reid Nichols	.08	.06	.03
13	Bob Ojeda	.20	.15	.08
14	Tony Perez	.30	.25	.12
15	Chuck Rainey	.08	.06	.03
16	Jerry Remy	.08	.06	.03
17	Jim Rice	.80	.60	.30
18	Bob Stanley	.15	.11	.06
19	Dave Stapleton	.08	.06	.03
20	Mike Torrez	.08	.06	.03
21	John Tudor	.30	.25	.12
22	Carl Yastrzemski	2.00	1.50	.80
---	Header Card	.05	.04	.02

1982 Coca-Cola Reds

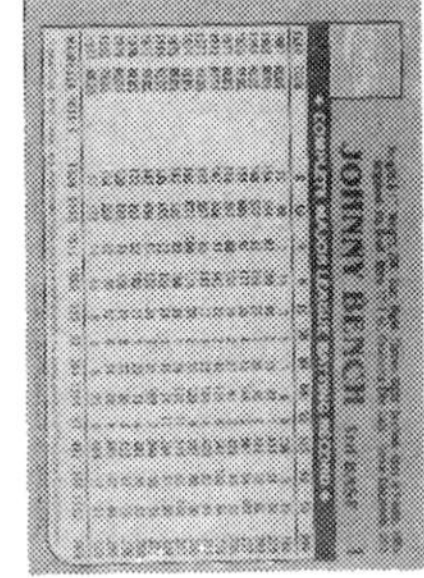

Produced by Topps for Coca-Cola, the set consists of 23 cards featuring the Cincinnati Reds and was distributed in the Cincinnati area. The cards, which are 2-1/2" by 3-1/2" in size, are identical in design to the regular 1982 Topps set but have a Coca-Cola logo on the front and red backs. An unnumbered header card is included in the set.

#	Player	MT	NR MT	EX
	Complete Set:	7.00	5.25	2.75
	Common Player:	.08	.06	.03
1	Johnny Bench	2.00	1.50	.80
2	Bruce Berenyi	.08	.06	.03
3	Larry Biittner	.08	.06	.03
4	Cesar Cedeno	.15	.11	.06
5	Dave Concepcion	.25	.20	.10
6	Dan Driessen	.15	.11	.06
7	Greg Harris	.08	.06	.03
8	Paul Householder	.08	.06	.03
9	Tom Hume	.08	.06	.03
10	Clint Hurdle	.08	.06	.03
11	Jim Kern	.08	.06	.03
12	Wayne Krenchicki	.08	.06	.03
13	Rafael Landestoy	.08	.06	.03
14	Charlie Leibrandt	.15	.11	.06
15	Mike O'Berry	.08	.06	.03
16	Ron Oester	.08	.06	.03
17	Frank Pastore	.08	.06	.03
18	Joe Price	.08	.06	.03
19	Tom Seaver	2.00	1.50	.80
20	Mario Soto	.15	.11	.06
21	Alex Trevino	.08	.06	.03
22	Mike Vail	.08	.06	.03
---	Header Card	.04	.03	.02

1985 Coca-Cola White Sox

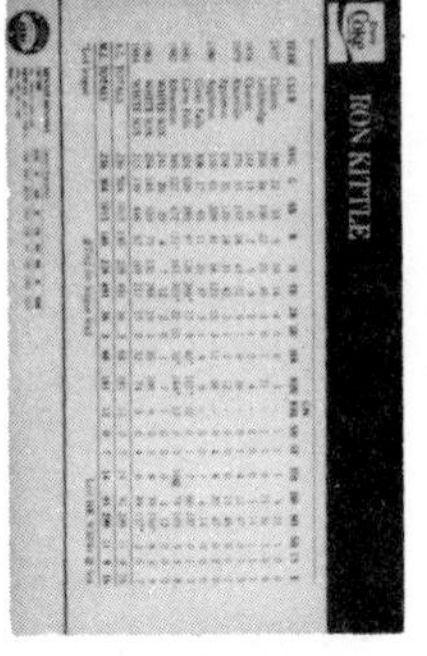

Featuring past and present White Sox players, the cards in this set were given out on Tuesday night home games. The cards, which measure 2-5/8" by 4-1/8", contain a color photo of a current Sox member. A red box at the bottom of the card carries the team logo, the player's name, uniform number and position, plus a small oval portrait of a past Sox player. The card backs contain the Coca-Cola logo and the lifetime hitting or pitching statistics for the current and past player. The set is numbered in the checklist that follows by the player's uniform number with the last three cards being unnumbered. Complete sets were available through a fan club offer found in White Sox programs.

#	Player	MT	NR MT	EX
	Complete Set:	14.00	10.50	5.50
	Common Player:	.25	.20	.10
	Oscar Gamble (Zeke Bonura)	.25	.20	.10
1	Scott Fletcher (Luke Appling)	.40	.30	.15
3	Harold Baines (Bill Melton)	.80	.60	.30
5	Luis Salazar (Chico Carrasquel)	.25	.20	.10
7	Marc Hill (Sherm Lollar)	.25	.20	.10
8	Daryl Boston (Jim Landis)	.25	.20	.10
10	Tony LaRussa (Al Lopez)	.40	.30	.15
12	Julio Cruz (Nellie Fox)	.40	.30	.15
13	Ozzie Guillen (Luis Aparicio)	.80	.60	.30
17	Jerry Hairston (Smoky Burgess)	.25	.20	.10
20	Joe DeSa (Carlos May)	.25	.20	.10
22	Joel Skinner (J.C. Martin)	.25	.20	.10
23	Rudy Law (Bill Skowron)	.25	.20	.10
24	Floyd Bannister (Red Faber)	.35	.25	.14
29	Greg Walker (Dick Allen)	.70	.50	.30
30	Gene Nelson (Early Wynn)	.35	.25	.14
32	Tim Hulett (Pete Ward)	.25	.20	.10
34	Richard Dotson (Ed Walsh)	.35	.25	.14
37	Dan Spillner (Thornton Lee)	.25	.20	.10
40	Britt Burns (Gary Peters)	.25	.20	.10
41	Tom Seaver (Ted Lyons)	.80	.60	.30
42	Ron Kittle (Minnie Minoso)	.40	.30	.15
43	Bob James (Hoyt Wilhelm)	.40	.30	.15
44	Tom Paciorek (Eddie Collins)	.35	.25	.14
46	Tim Lollar (Billy Pierce)	.25	.20	.10
50	Juan Agosto (Wilbur Wood)	.25	.20	.10
72	Carlton Fisk (Ray Schalk)	.70	.50	.30
---	Comiskey Park	.50	.40	.20
---	Ribbie and Roobarb (mascots)	.25	.20	.10
---	Nancy Faust (organist)	.25	.20	.10

1986 Coca-Cola White Sox

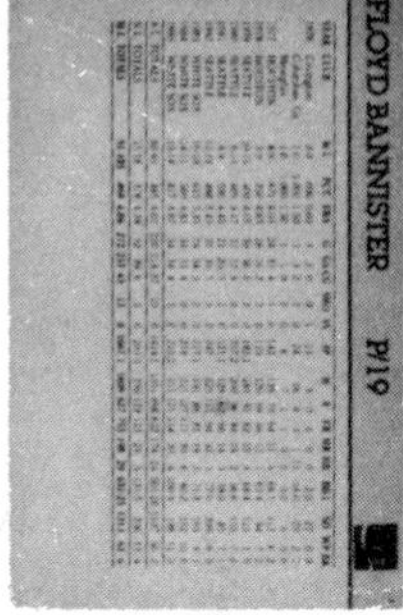

For the second year in a row, Coca-Cola, in conjunction with the Chicago White Sox, issued a 30-card set. As in 1985, cards were given out at the park on Tuesday night games. Full sets were again available through a fan club offer found in the White Sox program. The cards, which measure 2-5/8" by 4-1/8", feature 25 players plus other White Sox personnel. The card fronts feature a color photo (an action shot in most instances) and a white bar at the bottom. A black and white bat with "SOX" shown on the barrel is located within the white bar, along with the player's name, position and uniform number. The white and grey backs with black print include the Coca-Cola trademark. Lifetime statistics are shown on all player cards, but there is no personal information such as height, weight or age. The non-player cards are blank-backed save for the name and logo at the top. The cards in the checklist that follows are numbered by the players' uniform numbers, with the last five cards of the set being unnumbered.

#	Player	MT	NR MT	EX
	Complete Set:	12.00	9.00	4.75
	Common Player:	.25	.20	.10
1	Wayne Tolleson	.25	.20	.10
3	Harold Baines	.60	.45	.25
7	Marc Hill	.25	.20	.10
8	Daryl Boston	.25	.20	.10
12	Julio Cruz	.25	.20	.10
13	Ozzie Guillen	.45	.35	.20
17	Jerry Hairston	.25	.20	.10
19	Floyd Bannister	.35	.25	.14
20	Reid Nichols	.25	.20	.10
22	Joel Skinner	.25	.20	.10
24	Dave Schmidt	.25	.20	.10
26	Bobby Bonilla	.70	.50	.30
29	Greg Walker	.40	.30	.15
30	Gene Nelson	.25	.20	.10

		MT	NR MT	EX
32	Tim Hulett	.25	.20	.10
33	Neil Allen	.25	.20	.10
34	Richard Dotson	.35	.25	.14
40	Joe Cowley	.25	.20	.10
41	Tom Seaver	.70	.50	.30
42	Ron Kittle	.35	.25	.14
43	Bob James	.25	.20	.10
44	John Cangelosi	.35	.25	.14
50	Juan Agosto	.25	.20	.10
52	Joel Davis	.25	.20	.10
72	Carlton Fisk	.50	.40	.20
---	Ribbie & Roobarb (mascots)	.25	.20	.10
---	Nancy Faust (organist)	.25	.20	.10
---	Ken "Hawk" Harrelson	.30	.25	.12
---	Tony LaRussa	.30	.25	.12
---	Minnie Minoso	.30	.25	.12

1987 Coca-Cola Tigers

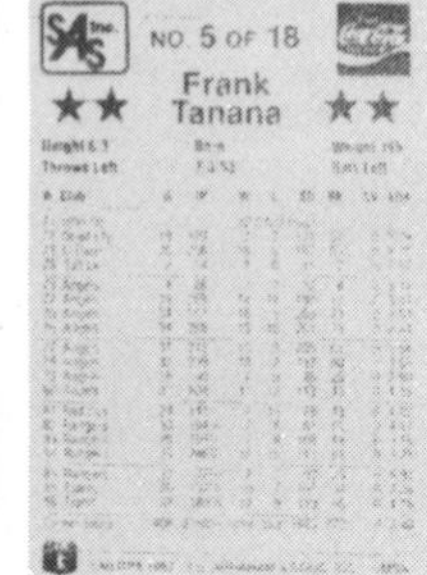

Coca-Cola and S. Abraham & Sons, Inc. issued a set of 18 baseball cards featuring members of the Detroit Tigers. The set is comprised of six four-part folding panels. Each panel includes three player cards (each 2-1/2" by 3-1/2") and one team logo card. A bright yellow border surrounds the full-color photo. The backs are designed on a vertical format and contain personal data and career statistics. The set was produced by Mike Schecter and Associates.

		MT	NR MT	EX
	Complete Set:	6.00	4.50	2.50
	Complete Singles Set:	2.00	1.50	.80
	Common Panel:	.60	.45	.25
	Common Single Player:	.05	.04	.02
Panel		1.25	.90	.50
1	Kirk Gibson	.50	.40	.20
2	Larry Herndon	.08	.06	.03
3	Walt Terrell	.10	.08	.04
Panel		1.25	.90	.50
4	Alan Trammell	.50	.40	.20
5	Frank Tanana	.10	.08	.04
6	Pat Sheridan	.05	.04	.02
Panel		.90	.70	.35
7	Jack Morris	.30	.25	.12
8	Mike Heath	.05	.04	.02
9	Dave Bergman	.05	.04	.02
Panel		.60	.45	.25
10	Chet Lemon	.10	.08	.04
11	Dwight Lowry	.08	.06	.03
12	Dan Petry	.10	.08	.04
Panel		.80	.60	.30
13	Darrell Evans	.20	.15	.08
14	Darnell Coles	.10	.08	.04
15	Willie Hernandez	.10	.08	.04
Panel		1.00	.70	.40
16	Lou Whitaker	.30	.25	.12
17	Tom Brookens	.05	.04	.02
18	John Grubb	.05	.04	.02

1987 Coca-Cola White Sox

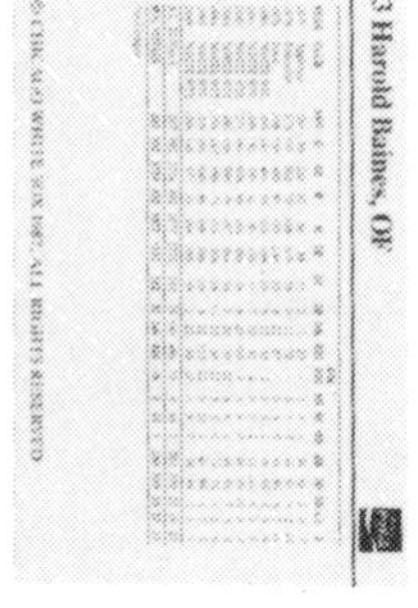

The Chicago White Sox Fan Club, in conjunction with Coca-Cola, offered members a set of 30 trading cards. For the $10 membership fee, fans received the set plus additional fan club gifts and privileges. The cards, which measure 2-5/8" by 4", feature full-color photos inside a blue and red border. The backs include the player's name, position, uniform number and statistics. The Coca-Cola logo is also included on the card backs.

		MT	NR MT	EX
	Complete Set:	12.00	9.00	4.75
	Common Player:	.25	.20	.10
1	Jerry Royster	.25	.20	.10
3	Harold Baines	.60	.45	.25
5	Ron Karkovice	.30	.25	.12
8	Daryl Boston	.25	.20	.10
10	Fred Manrique	.30	.25	.12
12	Steve Lyons	.25	.20	.10
13	Ozzie Guillen	.40	.30	.15
14	Russ Morman	.30	.25	.12
15	Donnie Hill	.25	.20	.10
16	Jim Fregosi	.30	.25	.12
17	Jerry Hairston	.25	.20	.10
19	Floyd Bannister	.35	.25	.14
21	Gary Redus	.25	.20	.10
22	Ivan Calderon	.40	.30	.15
25	Ron Hassey	.25	.20	.10
26	Jose DeLeon	.30	.25	.12
29	Greg Walker	.40	.30	.15
32	Tim Hulett	.25	.20	.10
33	Neil Allen	.25	.20	.10
34	Rich Dotson	.35	.25	.14
36	Ray Searage	.25	.20	.10
37	Bobby Thigpen	.40	.30	.15
40	Jim Winn	.25	.20	.10
43	Bob James	.25	.20	.10
50	Joel McKeon	.25	.20	.10
52	Joel Davis	.25	.20	.10
72	Carlton Fisk	.50	.40	.20
---	Ribbie & Roobarb (mascots)	.25	.20	.10
---	Nancy Faust (organist)	.25	.20	.10
---	Minnie Minoso	.30	.25	.12

1988 Coca-Cola Padres

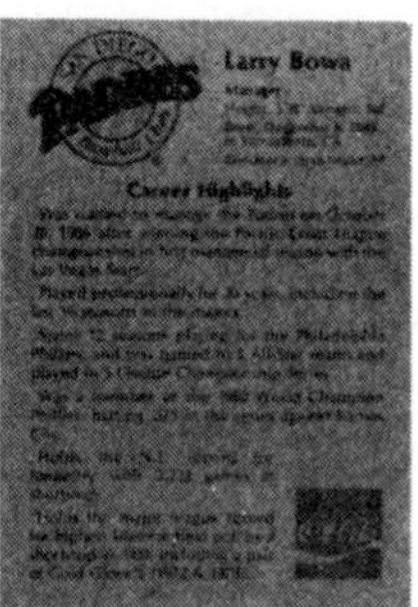

A 20-card team set sponsored by Coca-Cola was designed as part of the San Diego Padres Junior Fan Club promotion for 1988. This set was distributed as a nine-card starter sheet, with 11 additional single cards handed out during the team's home games. The standard-size cards feature full-color player photos framed by a black and orange border. The player's name is printed above the photo; uniform number and position appear lower right. A large Padres logo curves upward from the lower left corner. Card backs are brown on white and include the Padres logo upper left opposite the player's name and personal information. Career highlights and 1987 stats appear in the center of the card back above the Coca-Cola and Junior Padres Fan Club logos.

		MT	NR MT	EX
	Complete Set:	35.00	25.00	13.00
	Common Player:	.50	.40	.20
Panel				
1	Garry Templeton	.75	.60	.30
5	Randy Ready	.50	.40	.20
10	Larry Bowa	.75	.60	.30
11	Tim Flannery	.50	.40	.20
35	Chris Brown	.75	.60	.30
45	Jimmy Jones	1.00	.70	.40
48	Mark Davis	.50	.40	.20
55	Mark Grant	.50	.40	.20
---	20th Anniversary Logo Card	.10	.08	.04
Singles				
7	Keith Moreland	1.00	.70	.40
8	John Kruk	2.25	1.75	.90
9	Benito Santiago	3.25	2.50	1.25
14	Carmelo Martinez	1.00	.70	.40
15	Jack McKeon	1.00	.70	.40
19	Tony Gwynn	9.00	6.75	3.50
22	Stan Jefferson	1.00	.70	.40
27	Mark Parent	2.00	1.50	.80
30	Eric Show	1.50	1.25	.60
31	Ed Whitson	1.00	.70	.40
41	Lance McCullers	1.25	.90	.50
51	Greg Booker	1.00	.70	.40

1988 Coca-Cola White Sox

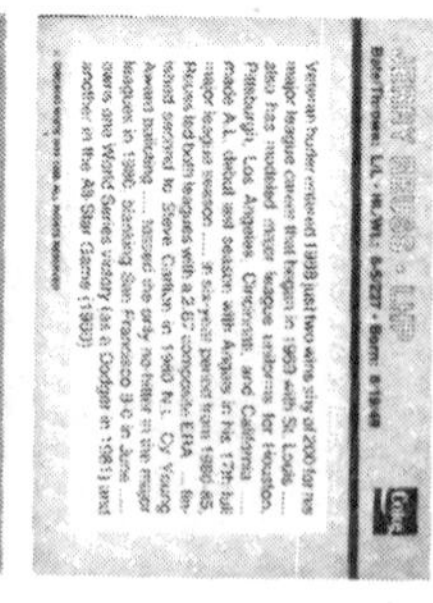

Part of a fan club membership package, this unnumbered 30-card set features full-color photos of 27 players, the team mascot, team organist and Comiskey Park. Cards have a bright red border, with the team logo in the lower left corner of the photo. A large player name fills the bottom border. Card backs are printed in black on grey and white and include player name, personal info and career summary. The set was included in the $10 membership package, with a portion of the cost going to the ChiSox Kids Charity.

		MT	NR MT	EX
	Complete Set:	8.00	6.00	3.25
	Common Player:	.20	.15	.08
(1)	Harold Baines	.50	.40	.20
(2)	Daryl Boston	.20	.15	.08
(3)	Ivan Calderon	.30	.25	.12
(4)	John Davis	.20	.15	.08
(5)	Jim Fregosi	.25	.20	.10
(6)	Carlton Fisk	.40	.30	.15
(7)	Ozzie Guillen	.30	.25	.12
(8)	Donnie Hill	.20	.15	.08
(9)	Rick Horton	.20	.15	.08
(10)	Lance Johnson	.30	.25	.12
(11)	Dave LaPoint	.20	.15	.08
(12)	Bill Long	.25	.20	.10
(13)	Steve Lyons	.20	.15	.08
(14)	Jack McDowell	.40	.30	.15
(15)	Fred Manrique	.20	.15	.08
(16)	Minnie Minoso	.25	.20	.10
(17)	Dan Pasqua	.30	.25	.12
(18)	John Pawlowski	.25	.20	.10
(19)	Melido Perez	.40	.30	.15
(20)	Billy Pierce	.25	.20	.10
(21)	Gary Redus	.20	.15	.08
(22)	Jerry Reuss	.25	.20	.10
(23)	Mark Salas	.20	.15	.08
(24)	Jose Segura	.30	.25	.12
(25)	Bobby Thigpen	.25	.20	.10
(26)	Greg Walker	.30	.25	.12
(27)	Kenny Williams	.30	.25	.12
(28)	Nancy Faust (organist)	.20	.15	.08
(29)	Ribbie & Roobarb (mascots)	.20	.15	.08
(30)	Comiskey Park	.40	.30	.15

1989 Coca-Cola Padres

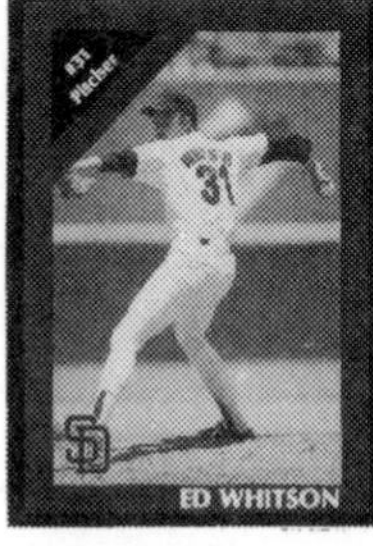

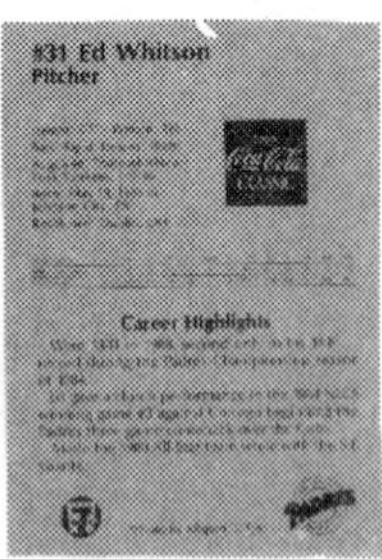

This 20-card set is part of the Junior Padres Fan Club membership package. Members receive a 9-card starter set printed on one large perforated sheet. Additional cards are distributed to kids at specially designated games (free admission for kids). Card fronts feature an orange-and-brown double border, with a bright orange Padres logo printed lower left. Player uniform number and position are printed diagonally across the upper right corner, with the player's name in large block letters along the bottom border.

		MT	NR MT	EX
	Complete Set:	30.00	22.00	12.00
	Common Player:	.50	.40	.30
Panel				
1	Garry Templeton	.70	.50	.30

		MT	NR MT	EX
5	Randy Ready	.50	.40	.20
12	Roberto Alomar	1.00	.70	.40
14	Carmelo Martinez	.50	.40	.20
15	Jack McKeon	.50	.40	.20
30	Eric Show	.50	.40	.20
31	Ed Whitson	.50	.40	.20
43	Dennis Rasmussen	.50	.40	.20
---	Logo Card	.10	.08	.04
Singles				
6	Luis Salazar	1.00	.70	.40
9	Benito Santiago	3.00	2.25	1.25
10	Leon Roberts	1.00	.70	.40
11	Tim Flannery	1.00	.70	.40
18	Chris James	2.00	1.50	.80
19	Tony Gwynn	7.00	5.25	2.75
25	Jack Clark	3.00	2.25	1.25
27	Mark Parent	2.00	1.50	.80
35	Walt Terrell	1.00	.70	.40
47	Bruce Hurst	2.00	1.50	.80
48	Mark Davis	3.00	2.25	1.25
55	Mark Grant	1.00	.70	.30

1989 Coca-Cola White Sox

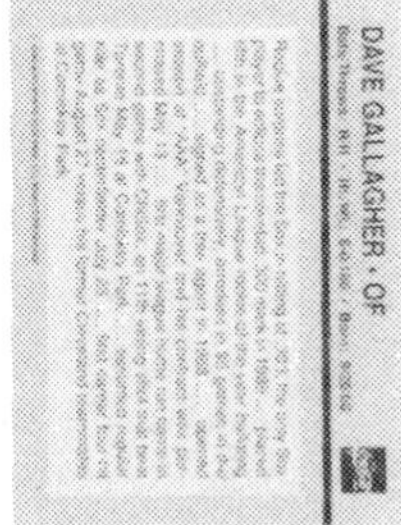

For the fifth straight year, Coca-Cola sponsored a set of cards featuring the Chicago White Sox. The 30-card set was distributed to fans attending a special promotional day at Comiskey Park and was also available by mail to members of the ChiSox fan club. The fronts of the cards feature a red, white and blue color scheme and include a pair of crossed bats. "White Sox" appears along the top, while the name and position are in the lower right, and a pennant proclaiming "Chicago's American Pastime" is just below the photo. The horizontal backs include player biographies, other data, special facts about Comiskey Park and the Coca-Cola logo.

		MT	NR MT	EX
Complete Set:		7.00	5.25	2.75
Common Player:		.20	.15	.08
1	New Comiskey Park, 1991	.40	.30	.15
2	Comiskey Park	.40	.30	.15
3	Jeff Torborg	.20	.15	.08
4	Coaching Staff	.20	.15	.08
5	Harold Baines	.50	.40	.20
6	Daryl Boston	.20	.15	.08
7	Ivan Calderon	.30	.25	.12
8	Carlton Fisk	.40	.30	.15
9	Dave Gallagher	.30	.25	.12
10	Ozzie Guillen	.30	.25	.12
11	Shawn Hillegas	.20	.15	.08
12	Barry Jones	.20	.15	.08
13	Ron Karkovice	.20	.15	.08
14	Eric King	.20	.15	.08
15	Ron Kittle	.30	.25	.12
16	Bill Long	.20	.15	.08
17	Steve Lyons	.20	.15	.08
18	Donn Pall	.20	.15	.08
19	Dan Pasqua	.30	.25	.12
20	Ken Patterson	.20	.15	.08
21	Melido Perez	.30	.25	.12
22	Jerry Reuss	.25	.20	.10
23	Billy Jo Robidoux	.20	.15	.08
24	Steve Rosenberg	.20	.15	.08
25	Jeff Schaefer	.25	.20	.10
26	Bobby Thigpen	.25	.20	.10
27	Greg Walker	.25	.20	.10
28	Eddie Williams	.25	.20	.10
29	Nancy Faust, organist	.20	.15	.08
30	Minnie Minoso	.20	.15	.08

1914 Cracker Jack

The 1914 Cracker Jack set, whose ACC designation is E145-1, is one of the most popular of the "E" card sets and features baseball stars from the American, National and Federal Leagues. The cards, which measure 2-1/4" by 3" and are printed on thin stock, were found in boxes of Cracker Jack. The 1914 issue consists of 144 cards with tinted color photographs on a red background. The numbered backs feature a short biography plus an advertisement. The advertising on the low-numbered cards in the set indicate that 10 million cards were issued, while the high-numbered cards boast that 15 million were printed.

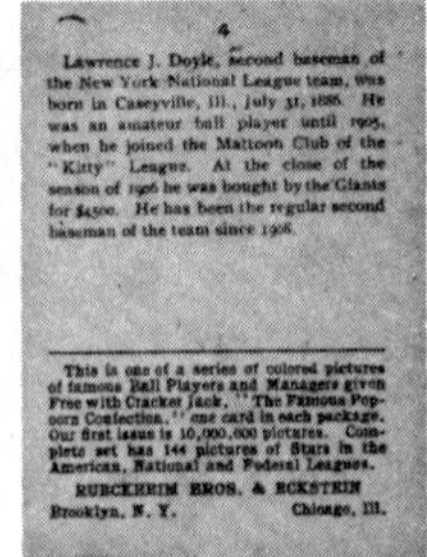

		NR MT	EX	VG
Complete Set:		75000.00	30000.00	15000.
Common Player:		175.00	87.00	52.00
1	Otto Knabe	750.00	275.00	125.00
2	Home Run Baker	900.00	400.00	175.00
3	Joe Tinker	700.00	300.00	125.00
4	Larry Doyle	175.00	87.00	52.00
5	Ward Miller	175.00	87.00	52.00
6	Eddie Plank	1000.00	450.00	200.00
7	Eddie Collins	600.00	275.00	125.00
8	Rube Oldring	175.00	87.00	52.00
9	Artie Hoffman (Hofman)	175.00	87.00	52.00
10	Stuffy McInnis	175.00	87.00	52.00
11	George Stovall	175.00	87.00	52.00
12	Connie Mack	700.00	300.00	125.00
13	Art Wilson	175.00	87.00	52.00
14	Sam Crawford	400.00	175.00	75.00
15	Reb Russell	175.00	87.00	52.00
16	Howie Camnitz	175.00	87.00	52.00
17a	Roger Bresnahan (no number on back)	600.00	275.00	125.00
17b	Roger Bresnahan (number on back)	600.00	275.00	125.00
18	Johnny Evers	550.00	250.00	100.00
19	Chief Bender	600.00	275.00	125.00
20	Cy Falkenberg	175.00	87.00	52.00
21	Heinie Zimmerman	175.00	87.00	52.00
22	Smoky Joe Wood	175.00	87.00	52.00
23	Charles Comiskey	600.00	275.00	125.00
24	George Mullen (Mullin)	175.00	87.00	52.00
25	Mike Simon	175.00	87.00	52.00
26	Jim Scott	175.00	87.00	52.00
27	Bill Carrigan	175.00	87.00	52.00
28	Jack Barry	175.00	87.00	52.00
29	Vean Gregg	175.00	87.00	52.00
30	Ty Cobb	6500.00	3000.00	1500.
31	Heinie Wagner	175.00	87.00	52.00
32	Mordecai Brown	500.00	250.00	100.00
33	Amos Strunk	175.00	87.00	52.00
34	Ira Thomas	175.00	87.00	52.00
35	Harry Hooper	550.00	250.00	100.00
36	Ed Walsh	600.00	275.00	125.00
37	Grover C. Alexander	800.00	375.00	150.00
38	Red Dooin	175.00	87.00	52.00
39	Chick Gandil	175.00	87.00	52.00
40	Jimmy Austin	175.00	87.00	52.00
41	Tommy Leach	175.00	87.00	52.00
42	Al Bridwell	175.00	87.00	52.00
43	Rube Marquard	550.00	250.00	100.00
44	Jeff Tesreau	175.00	87.00	52.00
45	Fred Luderus	175.00	87.00	52.00
46	Bob Groom	175.00	87.00	52.00
47	Josh Devore	175.00	87.00	52.00
48	Harry Lord	375.00	175.00	75.00
49	Dots Miller	175.00	87.00	52.00
50	John Hummell (Hummel)	175.00	87.00	52.00
51	Nap Rucker	175.00	87.00	52.00
52	Zach Wheat	550.00	250.00	100.00
53	Otto Miller	175.00	87.00	52.00
54	Marty O'Toole	175.00	87.00	52.00
55	Dick Hoblitzel (Hoblitzell)	175.00	87.00	52.00
56	Clyde Milan	175.00	87.00	52.00
57	Walter Johnson	2500.00	1200.00	500.00
58	Wally Schang	175.00	87.00	52.00
59	Doc Gessler	175.00	87.00	52.00
60	Rollie Zeider	500.00	200.00	100.00
61	Ray Schalk	500.00	200.00	100.00
62	Jay Cashion	500.00	200.00	100.00
63	Babe Adams	175.00	87.00	52.00
64	Jimmy Archer	175.00	87.00	52.00
65	Tris Speaker	1000.00	500.00	200.00
66	Nap Lajoie	1250.00	600.00	250.00
67	Doc Crandall	175.00	87.00	52.00
68	Honus Wagner	2800.00	1400.00	600.00
69	John McGraw	900.00	450.00	200.00
70	Fred Clarke	450.00	200.00	100.00
71	Chief Meyers	175.00	87.00	52.00
72	Joe Boehling	175.00	87.00	52.00
73	Max Carey	400.00	185.00	78.00
74	Frank Owens	175.00	87.00	52.00
75	Miller Huggins	500.00	225.00	100.00
76	Claude Hendrix	175.00	87.00	52.00
77	Hughie Jennings	550.00	250.00	100.00
78	Fred Merkle	175.00	87.00	52.00
79	Ping Bodie	175.00	87.00	52.00
80	Ed Reulbach	175.00	87.00	52.00
81	Jim Delehanty (Delahanty)	175.00	87.00	52.00
82	Gavvy Cravath	175.00	87.00	52.00
83	Russ Ford	175.00	87.00	52.00
84	Elmer Knetzer	175.00	87.00	52.00
85	Buck Herzog	175.00	87.00	52.00
86	Burt Shotten	175.00	87.00	52.00
87	Hick Cady	175.00	87.00	52.00
88	Christy Mathewson	2000.00	900.00	400.00
89	Larry Cheney	175.00	87.00	52.00
90	Frank Smith	175.00	87.00	52.00
91	Roger Peckinpaugh	175.00	87.00	52.00
92	Al Demaree	175.00	87.00	52.00
93	Del Pratt	600.00	250.00	100.00
94	Eddie Cicotte	275.00	125.00	75.00
95	Ray Keating	175.00	87.00	52.00
96	Beals Becker	175.00	87.00	52.00
97	Rube Benton	175.00	87.00	52.00
98	Frank Laporte (LaPorte)	175.00	87.00	52.00
99	Frank Chance	1900.00	900.00	400.00
100	Tom Seaton	175.00	87.00	52.00
101	Wildfire Schulte	175.00	87.00	52.00
102	Ray Fisher	175.00	87.00	52.00
103	Shoeless Joe Jackson	7500.00	3500.00	1500.
104	Vic Saier	175.00	87.00	52.00
105	Jimmy Lavender	175.00	87.00	52.00
106	Joe Birmingham	175.00	87.00	52.00
107	Tom Downey	175.00	87.00	52.00
108	Sherry Magee	175.00	87.00	52.00
109	Fred Blanding	175.00	87.00	52.00
110	Bob Bescher	175.00	87.00	52.00
111	Nixey Callahan	600.00	250.00	100.00
112	Jeff Sweeney	175.00	87.00	52.00
113	George Suggs	175.00	87.00	52.00
114	George Moriarity (Moriarty)	175.00	87.00	52.00
115	Ad Brennan	175.00	87.00	52.00
116	Rollie Zeider	175.00	87.00	52.00
117	Ted Easterly	175.00	87.00	52.00
118	Ed Konetchy	175.00	87.00	52.00
119	George Perring	175.00	87.00	52.00
120	Mickey Doolan	175.00	87.00	52.00
121	Hub Perdue	175.00	87.00	52.00
122	Donie Bush	175.00	87.00	52.00
123	Slim Sallee	175.00	87.00	52.00
124	Earle Moore (Earl)	175.00	87.00	52.00
125	Bert Niehoff	175.00	87.00	52.00
126	Walter Blair	175.00	87.00	52.00
127	Butch Schmidt	175.00	87.00	52.00
128	Steve Evans	175.00	87.00	52.00
129	Ray Caldwell	175.00	87.00	52.00
130	Ivy Wingo	175.00	87.00	52.00
131	George Baumgardner	175.00	87.00	52.00
132	Les Nunamaker	175.00	87.00	52.00
133	Branch Rickey	600.00	250.00	100.00
134	Armando Marsans	175.00	87.00	52.00
135	Bill Killifer (Killefer)	175.00	87.00	52.00
136	Rabbit Maranville	450.00	200.00	80.00
137	Bill Rariden	175.00	87.00	52.00
138	Hank Gowdy	175.00	87.00	52.00
139	Rebel Oakes	175.00	87.00	52.00
140	Danny Murphy	175.00	87.00	52.00
141	Cy Barger	175.00	87.00	52.00
142	Gene Packard	175.00	87.00	52.00
143	Jake Daubert	175.00	87.00	52.00
144	Jimmy Walsh	500.00	200.00	80.00

1915 Cracker Jack

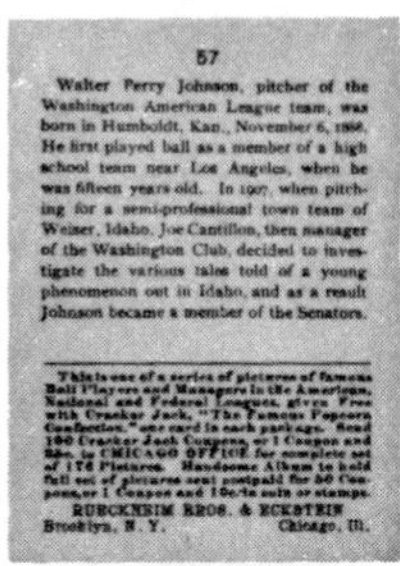

The 1915 Cracker Jack set (E145-2) is a re-issue of the 1914 edition with some card additions and deletions, team designation changes, and new poses. A total of 176 cards comprise the set. The deletions involve card #'s 48, 60, 62, 99 and 111. Cards can be distinguished as either 1914 or 1915 by the backs. The advertising on the backs of the 1914 cards call the set complete at 144 pictures, while the 1915 version notes 176 pictures. A complete set and an album were available from the company.

		NR MT	EX	VG
Complete Set:		62500.00	27000.00	16500
Common Player: 1-144		125.00	62.00	37.00
Common Player: 145-176		175.00	75.00	40.00
1	Otto Knabe	600.00	250.00	100.00
2	Home Run Baker	750.00	350.00	150.00
3	Joe Tinker	600.00	275.00	125.00
4	Larry Doyle	125.00	62.00	37.00
5	Ward Miller	125.00	62.00	37.00
6	Eddie Plank	750.00	350.00	150.00
7	Eddie Collins	550.00	250.00	125.00
8	Rube Oldring	125.00	62.00	37.00
9	Artie Hoffman (Hofman)	125.00	62.00	37.00
10	Stuffy McInnis	125.00	62.00	37.00
11	George Stovall	125.00	62.00	37.00
12	Connie Mack	500.00	225.00	100.00
13	Art Wilson	125.00	62.00	37.00
14	Sam Crawford	450.00	200.00	90.00
15	Reb Russell	125.00	62.00	37.00
16	Howie Camnitz	125.00	62.00	37.00
17	Roger Bresnahan	500.00	225.00	100.00
18	Johnny Evers	500.00	225.00	100.00
19	Chief Bender	400.00	175.00	65.00
20	Cy Falkenberg	125.00	62.00	37.00
21	Heinie Zimmerman	125.00	62.00	37.00
22	Smoky Joe Wood	125.00	62.00	37.00
23	Charles Comiskey	500.00	225.00	100.00
24	George Mullen (Mullin)	125.00	62.00	37.00
25	Mike Simon	125.00	62.00	37.00
26	Jim Scott	125.00	62.00	37.00
27	Bill Carrigan	125.00	62.00	37.00

		NR MT	EX	VG
28	Jack Barry	125.00	62.00	37.00
29	Vean Gregg	125.00	62.00	37.00
30	Ty Cobb	5000.00	2500.00	1500.
31	Heinie Wagner	125.00	62.00	37.00
32	Mordecai Brown	450.00	225.00	100.00
33	Amos Strunk	125.00	62.00	37.00
34	Ira Thomas	125.00	62.00	37.00
35	Harry Hooper	450.00	225.00	100.00
36	Ed Walsh	450.00	225.00	100.00
37	Grover C. Alexander	700.00	325.00	135.00
38	Red Dooin	125.00	62.00	37.00
39	Chick Gandil	125.00	62.00	37.00
40	Jimmy Austin	125.00	62.00	37.00
41	Tommy Leach	125.00	62.00	37.00
42	Al Bridwell	125.00	62.00	37.00
43	Rube Marquard	500.00	225.00	100.00
44	Jeff Tesreau	125.00	62.00	37.00
45	Fred Luderus	125.00	62.00	37.00
46	Bob Groom	125.00	62.00	37.00
47	Josh Devore	125.00	62.00	37.00
48	Steve O'Neill	125.00	62.00	37.00
49	Dots Miller	125.00	62.00	37.00
50	John Hummell (Hummel)	125.00	62.00	37.00
51	Nap Rucker	125.00	62.00	37.00
52	Zach Wheat	500.00	225.00	100.00
53	Otto Miller	125.00	62.00	37.00
54	Marty O'Toole	125.00	62.00	37.00
55	Dick Hoblitzel (Hoblitzell)	125.00	62.00	37.00
56	Clyde Milan	125.00	62.00	37.00
57	Walter Johnson	1800.00	900.00	350.00
58	Wally Schang	125.00	62.00	37.00
59	Doc Gessler	125.00	62.00	37.00
60	Oscar Dugey	125.00	62.00	37.00
61	Ray Schalk	400.00	200.00	85.00
62	Willie Mitchell	125.00	62.00	37.00
63	Babe Adams	125.00	62.00	37.00
64	Jimmy Archer	125.00	62.00	37.00
65	Tris Speaker	950.00	450.00	200.00
66	Nap Lajoie	1000.00	500.00	225.00
67	Doc Crandall	125.00	62.00	37.00
68	Honus Wagner	2000.00	900.00	400.00
69	John McGraw	750.00	375.00	200.00
70	Fred Clarke	400.00	180.00	75.00
71	Chief Meyers	125.00	62.00	37.00
72	Joe Boehling	125.00	62.00	37.00
73	Max Carey	375.00	165.00	70.00
74	Frank Owens	125.00	62.00	37.00
75	Miller Huggins	450.00	200.00	90.00
76	Claude Hendrix	125.00	62.00	37.00
77	Hughie Jennings	450.00	200.00	90.00
78	Fred Merkle	125.00	62.00	37.00
79	Ping Bodie	125.00	62.00	37.00
80	Ed Reulbach	125.00	62.00	37.00
81	Jim Delehanty (Delahanty)	125.00	62.00	37.00
82	Gavvy Cravath	125.00	62.00	37.00
83	Russ Ford	125.00	62.00	37.00
84	Elmer Knetzer	125.00	62.00	37.00
85	Buck Herzog	125.00	62.00	37.00
86	Burt Shotten	125.00	62.00	37.00
87	Hick Cady	125.00	62.00	37.00
88	Christy Mathewson	1500.00	750.00	300.00
89	Larry Cheney	125.00	62.00	37.00
90	Frank Smith	125.00	62.00	37.00
91	Roger Peckinpaugh	125.00	62.00	37.00
92	Al Demaree	125.00	62.00	37.00
93	Del Pratt	125.00	62.00	37.00
94	Eddie Cicotte	125.00	62.00	37.00
95	Ray Keating	125.00	62.00	37.00
96	Beals Becker	125.00	62.00	37.00
97	Rube Benton	125.00	62.00	37.00
98	Frank Laporte (LaPorte)	125.00	62.00	37.00
99	Hal Chase	450.00	225.00	100.00
100	Tom Seaton	125.00	62.00	37.00
101	Wildfire Schulte	125.00	62.00	37.00
102	Ray Fisher	125.00	62.00	37.00
103	Shoeless Joe Jackson	6000.00	3000.00	1500.
104	Vic Saier	125.00	62.00	37.00
105	Jimmy Lavender	125.00	62.00	37.00
106	Joe Birmingham	125.00	62.00	37.00
107	Tom Downey	125.00	62.00	37.00
108	Sherry Magee	125.00	62.00	37.00
109	Fred Blanding	125.00	62.00	37.00
110	Bob Bescher	125.00	62.00	37.00
111	Herbie Moran	125.00	62.00	37.00
112	Jeff Sweeney	125.00	62.00	37.00
113	George Suggs	125.00	62.00	37.00
114	George Moriarity (Moriarty)	125.00	62.00	37.00
115	Ad Brennan	125.00	62.00	37.00
116	Rollie Zeider	125.00	62.00	37.00
117	Ted Easterly	125.00	62.00	37.00
118	Ed Konetchy	125.00	62.00	37.00
119	George Perring	125.00	62.00	37.00
120	Mickey Doolan	125.00	62.00	37.00
121	Hub Perdue	125.00	62.00	37.00
122	Donie Bush	125.00	62.00	37.00
123	Slim Sallee	125.00	62.00	37.00
124	Earle Moore (Earl)	125.00	62.00	37.00
125	Bert Niehoff	125.00	62.00	37.00
126	Walter Blair	125.00	62.00	37.00
127	Butch Schmidt	125.00	62.00	37.00
128	Steve Evans	125.00	62.00	37.00
129	Ray Caldwell	125.00	62.00	37.00
130	Ivy Wingo	125.00	62.00	37.00
131	George Baumgardner	125.00	62.00	37.00
132	Les Nunamaker	125.00	62.00	37.00
133	Branch Rickey	500.00	200.00	90.00
134	Armando Marsans	125.00	62.00	37.00
135	Bill Killifer (Killefer)	125.00	62.00	37.00
136	Rabbit Maranville	400.00	180.00	80.00
137	Bill Rariden	125.00	62.00	37.00
138	Hank Gowdy	125.00	62.00	37.00
139	Rebel Oakes	125.00	62.00	37.00
140	Danny Murphy	125.00	62.00	37.00
141	Cy Barger	125.00	62.00	37.00
142	Gene Packard	125.00	62.00	37.00
143	Jake Daubert	125.00	62.00	37.00
144	Jimmy Walsh	125.00	62.00	37.00
145	Ted Cather	175.00	75.00	40.00
146	Lefty Tyler	175.00	75.00	40.00
147	Lee Magee	175.00	75.00	40.00
148	Owen Wilson	175.00	75.00	40.00
149	Hal Janvrin	175.00	75.00	40.00
150	Doc Johnston	175.00	75.00	40.00
151	Possum Whitted	175.00	75.00	40.00
152	George McQuillen (McQuillan)	175.00	75.00	40.00
153	Bill James	175.00	75.00	40.00
154	Dick Rudolph	175.00	75.00	40.00
155	Joe Connolly	175.00	75.00	40.00
156	Jean Dubuc	175.00	75.00	40.00
157	George Kaiserling	175.00	75.00	40.00
158	Fritz Maisel	175.00	75.00	40.00
159	Heinie Groh	175.00	75.00	40.00
160	Benny Kauff	175.00	75.00	40.00
161	Edd Rousch (Roush)	400.00	200.00	85.00
162	George Stallings	175.00	75.00	40.00
163	Bert Whaling	175.00	75.00	40.00
164	Bob Shawkey	175.00	75.00	40.00
165	Eddie Murphy	175.00	75.00	40.00
166	Bullet Joe Bush	200.00	100.00	45.00
167	Clark Griffith	550.00	250.00	100.00
168	Vin Campbell	175.00	75.00	40.00
169	Ray Collins	175.00	75.00	40.00
170	Hans Lobert	175.00	75.00	40.00
171	Earl Hamilton	175.00	75.00	40.00
172	Erskine Mayer	175.00	75.00	40.00
173	Tilly Walker	175.00	75.00	40.00
174	Bobby Veach	175.00	75.00	40.00
175	Joe Benz	350.00	175.00	75.00
176	Hippo Vaughn	500.00	250.00	100.00

1982 Cracker Jack

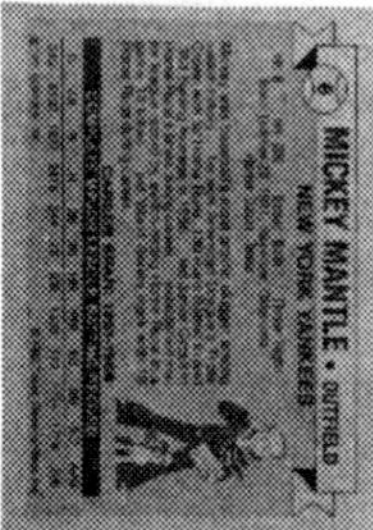

The Topps-produced 1982 Cracker Jack set was issued to promote the first "Old Timers Baseball Classic," held in Washington, D.C. Sixteen cards comprise the set which was issued in two sheets of eight cards, plus an advertising card located in the center. The individual cards are 2-1/2" by 3-1/2" in size with the complete sheets measuring 7-1/2" by 10-1/2". Card #'s 1-8 feature American League players with #'s 9-16 being former National League stars. The card fronts feature a full-color photo inside a Cracker Jack border. The backs contain the Cracker Jack logo plus a short player biography and his lifetime pitching or batting record. Complete sheets were available through a write-in offer.

		MT	NR MT	EX
Complete Panel Set:		8.00	6.00	3.25
Complete Singles Set:		3.50	2.75	1.50
Common Single Player:		.05	.04	.02
Panel		5.00	3.75	2.00
1	Larry Doby	.05	.04	.02
2	Bob Feller	.10	.08	.04
3	Whitey Ford	.10	.08	.04
4	Al Kaline	.10	.08	.04
5	Harmon Killebrew	.10	.08	.04
6	Mickey Mantle	1.75	1.25	.70
7	Tony Oliva	.05	.04	.02
8	Brooks Robinson	.10	.08	.04
Panel		3.50	2.75	1.50
9	Hank Aaron	1.00	.70	.40
10	Ernie Banks	.10	.08	.04
11	Ralph Kiner	.10	.08	.04
12	Eddie Mathews	.10	.08	.04
13	Willie Mays	.80	.60	.30
14	Robin Roberts	.10	.08	.04
15	Duke Snider	.10	.08	.04
16	Warren Spahn	.10	.08	.04
---	Advertising Card	.02	.02	.01

1976 Crane Potato Chips

This unnumbered 70-card set of player discs was issued with Crane Potato Chips in 1976. The front of the discs are designed to look like a baseball with the player's portrait in the center and his name, position and team beneath. The Crane name appears on both the front and the back of the discs, making the issue easy to identify.

		NR MT	EX	VG
Complete Set:		18.00	9.00	5.50
Common Player:		.10	.05	.03
(1)	Henry Aaron	1.25	.60	.40
(2)	Johnny Bench	.80	.40	.25
(3)	Vida Blue	.12	.06	.04
(4)	Larry Bowa	.12	.06	.04
(5)	Lou Brock	.60	.30	.20
(6)	Jeff Burroughs	.10	.05	.03
(7)	John Candelaria	.12	.06	.04
(8)	Jose Cardenal	.10	.05	.03
(9)	Rod Carew	.80	.40	.25
(10)	Steve Carlton	.80	.40	.25
(11)	Dave Cash	.10	.05	.03
(12)	Cesar Cedeno	.12	.06	.04
(13)	Ron Cey	.12	.06	.04
(14)	Carlton Fisk	.40	.20	.12
(15)	Tito Fuentes	.10	.05	.03
(16)	Steve Garvey	.70	.35	.20
(17)	Ken Griffey	.12	.06	.04
(18)	Don Gullett	.10	.05	.03
(19)	Willie Horton	.10	.05	.03
(20)	Al Hrabosky	.10	.05	.03
(21)	Catfish Hunter	.50	.25	.15
(22)	Reggie Jackson	1.00	.50	.30
(23)	Randy Jones	.10	.05	.03
(24)	Jim Kaat	.15	.08	.05
(25)	Don Kessinger	.10	.05	.03
(26)	Dave Kingman	.15	.08	.05
(27)	Jerry Koosman	.12	.06	.04
(28)	Mickey Lolich	.15	.08	.05
(29)	Greg Luzinski	.15	.08	.05
(30)	Fred Lynn	.20	.10	.06
(31)	Bill Madlock	.15	.08	.05
(32)	Carlos May	.10	.05	.03
(33)	John Mayberry	.10	.05	.03
(34)	Bake McBride	.10	.05	.03
(35)	Doc Medich	.10	.05	.03
(36)	Andy Messersmith	.10	.05	.03
(37)	Rick Monday	.12	.06	.04
(38)	John Montefusco	.10	.05	.03
(39)	Jerry Morales	.10	.05	.03
(40)	Joe Morgan	.40	.20	.12
(41)	Thurman Munson	.40	.20	.12
(42)	Bobby Murcer	.12	.06	.04
(43)	Al Oliver	.15	.08	.05
(44)	Jim Palmer	.60	.30	.20
(45)	Dave Parker	.20	.10	.06
(46)	Tony Perez	.20	.10	.06
(47)	Jerry Reuss	.12	.06	.04
(48)	Brooks Robinson	.70	.35	.20
(49)	Frank Robinson	.70	.35	.20
(50)	Steve Rogers	.10	.05	.03
(51)	Pete Rose	1.25	.60	.40
(52)	Nolan Ryan	1.25	.60	.40
(53)	Manny Sanguillen	.10	.05	.03
(54)	Mike Schmidt	1.00	.50	.30
(55)	Tom Seaver	1.00	.50	.30
(56)	Ted Simmons	.15	.08	.05
(57)	Reggie Smith	.12	.06	.04
(58)	Willie Stargell	.60	.30	.20
(59)	Rusty Staub	.15	.08	.05
(60)	Rennie Stennett	.10	.05	.03
(61)	Don Sutton	.20	.10	.06
(62)	Andy Thornton	.12	.06	.04
(63)	Luis Tiant	.15	.08	.05
(64)	Joe Torre	.12	.06	.04
(65)	Mike Tyson	.10	.05	.03
(66)	Bob Watson	.10	.05	.03
(67)	Wilbur Wood	.10	.05	.03
(68)	Jimmy Wynn	.10	.05	.03
(69)	Carl Yastrzemski	1.00	.50	.30
(70)	Richie Zisk	.10	.05	.03

1914 D303 General Baking

Issued in 1914 by the General Baking Company, these unnumbered cards measure 1-1/2" by 2-3/4". The player photos and fronts of the cards are identical to the E106 set, but the D303 cards are easily identified by the advertisement for General Baking on the back.

		NR MT	EX	VG
Complete Set:		9000.00	4500.00	2750.
Common Player:		80.00	40.00	24.00
(1)	Jack Barry	80.00	40.00	24.00
(2)	Chief Bender (blue background)	200.00	100.00	60.00
(3)	Chief Bender (green background)	200.00	100.00	60.00
(4a)	Bob Bescher (New York)	80.00	40.00	24.00
(4b)	Bob Bescher (St. Louis)	80.00	40.00	24.00

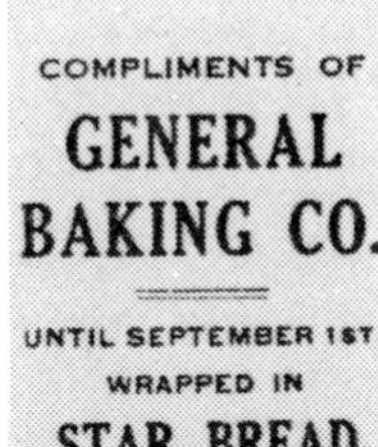

		NR MT	EX	VG
(5)	Roger Bresnahan	200.00	100.00	60.00
(6)	Al Bridwell	80.00	40.00	24.00
(7)	Donie Bush	80.00	40.00	24.00
(8)	Hal Chase (catching)	90.00	45.00	27.00
(9)	Hal Chase (portrait)	90.00	45.00	27.00
(10)	Ty Cobb (batting, front view)	900.00	450.00	275.00
(11)	Ty Cobb (batting, side view)	900.00	450.00	275.00
(12)	Eddie Collins	200.00	100.00	60.00
(13)	Sam Crawford	200.00	100.00	60.00
(14)	Ray Demmitt	80.00	40.00	24.00
(15)	Wild Bill Donovan	80.00	40.00	24.00
(16)	Red Dooin	80.00	40.00	24.00
(17)	Mickey Doolan	80.00	40.00	24.00
(18)	Larry Doyle	80.00	40.00	24.00
(19)	Clyde Engle	80.00	40.00	24.00
(20)	Johnny Evers	200.00	100.00	60.00
(21)	Art Fromme	80.00	40.00	24.00
(22)	George Gibson (catching, back view)	80.00	40.00	24.00
(23)	George Gibson (catching, front view)	80.00	40.00	24.00
(24)	Roy Hartzell	80.00	40.00	24.00
(25)	Fred Jacklitsch	80.00	40.00	24.00
(26)	Hugh Jennings	200.00	100.00	60.00
(27)	Otto Knabe	80.00	40.00	24.00
(28)	Nap Lajoie	300.00	150.00	90.00
(29)	Hans Lobert	80.00	40.00	24.00
(30)	Rube Marquard	200.00	100.00	60.00
(31)	Christy Mathewson	500.00	250.00	150.00
(32)	John McGraw	250.00	125.00	75.00
(33)	George McQuillan	80.00	40.00	24.00
(34)	Dots Miller	80.00	40.00	24.00
(35)	Danny Murphy	80.00	40.00	24.00
(36)	Rebel Oakes	80.00	40.00	24.00
(37a)	Eddie Plank (no position on front)	200.00	100.00	60.00
(37b)	Eddie Plank (position on front)	200.00	100.00	60.00
(38)	Germany Schaefer	80.00	40.00	24.00
(39)	Boss Smith (Schmidt)	80.00	40.00	24.00
(40)	Tris Speaker	250.00	125.00	75.00
(41)	Oscar Stanage	80.00	40.00	24.00
(42)	George Stovall	80.00	40.00	24.00
(43)	Jeff Sweeney	80.00	40.00	24.00
(44)	Joe Tinker (batting)	200.00	100.00	60.00
(45)	Joe Tinker (portrait)	200.00	100.00	60.00
(46)	Honus Wagner (batting)	500.00	225.00	150.00
(47)	Honus Wagner (throwing)	500.00	225.00	150.00
(48)	Hooks Wiltse	80.00	40.00	24.00
(49)	Heinie Zimmerman	80.00	40.00	24.00

1911 D304 General Baking

BETTER BREAD
FOR BUFFALO
BUY
BRUNNERS
Butter Krust
BUSTER BROWN
PEERLESS
FAMILY
THERE ARE 25 SUBJECTS
IN THIS SET
ONE WITH EACH LOAF OF THE
ABOVE BREADS.
G.B.C.
102

This unnumbered 25-card set, issued in 1911, is similar in design to the tobacco and candy company issues of the same period, but is different in size, measuring 1-3/4" by 2-1/2". The fronts of the cards feature a color lithograph with the player's name and team below in capital letters. The backs advertise various breads produced by the General Baking Company in the Buffalo, N.Y. area. The bottom of the back notes that "There are 25 subjects in this set/One with each loaf of the above breads."

		NR MT	EX	VG
	Complete Set:	4000.00	2000.00	1200.
	Common Player:	50.00	25.00	15.00
(1)	J. Frank Baker	125.00	62.00	37.00
(2)	Jack Barry	50.00	25.00	15.00
(3)	George Bell	50.00	25.00	15.00
(4)	Charles Bender	125.00	62.00	37.00
(5)	Frank Chance	125.00	62.00	37.00
(6)	Hal Chase	75.00	38.00	23.00
(7)	Ty Cobb	800.00	400.00	250.00
(8)	Eddie Collins	125.00	62.00	37.00
(9)	Otis Crandall	50.00	25.00	15.00
(10)	Sam Crawford	125.00	62.00	37.00
(11)	John Evers	125.00	62.00	37.00
(12)	Arthur Fletcher	50.00	25.00	15.00
(13)	Charles Herzog	50.00	25.00	15.00
(14)	M. Kelly	50.00	25.00	15.00
(15)	Napoleon Lajoie	200.00	100.00	60.00
(16)	Rube Marquard	125.00	62.00	37.00
(17)	Christy Mathewson	375.00	187.00	115.00
(18)	Fred Merkle	50.00	25.00	15.00
(19)	"Chief" Meyers	50.00	25.00	15.00
(20)	Marty O'Toole	50.00	25.00	15.00
(21)	Nap. Rucker	50.00	25.00	15.00
(22)	Arthur Shafer	50.00	25.00	15.00
(23)	Fred Tenny (Tenney)	50.00	25.00	15.00
(24)	Honus Wagner	500.00	250.00	150.00
(25)	Cy Young	325.00	162.00	97.00

1954 Dan-Dee Potato Chips

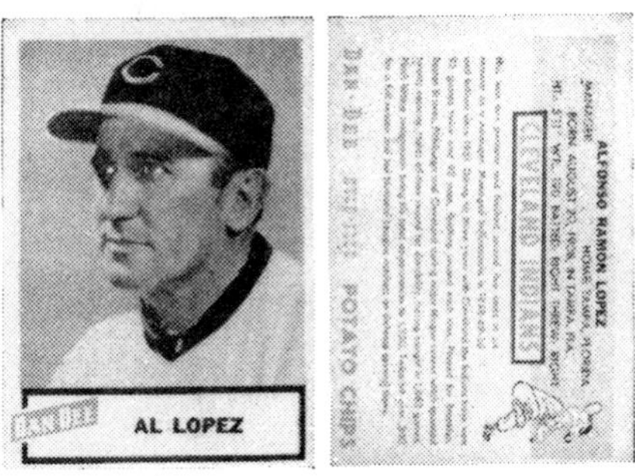

Issued in bags of potato chips, the cards in this 29-card set are commonly found with grease stains despite their waxed surface. The unnumbered cards, which measure 2-1/2" by 3-5/8", feature full-color photos. The card backs contain player statistical and biographical information. The set consists mostly of players from the Indians and Pirates. Photos of the Yankees players were also used for the Briggs Meats and Stahl-Meyer Franks sets. Cooper and Smith are the scarcest cards in the set.

		NR MT	EX	VG
	Complete Set	4500.00	2250.00	1350.
	Common Player	60.00	30.00	18.00
(1)	Bob Avila	60.00	30.00	18.00
(2)	Hank Bauer	80.00	40.00	24.00
(3)	Walker Cooper	350.00	175.00	105.00
(4)	Larry Doby	90.00	45.00	27.00
(5)	Luke Easter	60.00	30.00	18.00
(6)	Bob Feller	200.00	100.00	60.00
(7)	Bob Friend	60.00	30.00	18.00
(8)	Mike Garcia	60.00	30.00	18.00
(9)	Sid Gordon	60.00	30.00	18.00
(10)	Jim Hegan	60.00	30.00	18.00
(11)	Gil Hodges	150.00	75.00	45.00
(12)	Art Houtteman	60.00	30.00	18.00
(13)	Monte Irvin	90.00	45.00	27.00
(14)	Paul LaPalm (LaPalme)	60.00	30.00	18.00
(15)	Bob Lemon	110.00	55.00	33.00
(16)	Al Lopez	90.00	45.00	27.00
(17)	Mickey Mantle	1500.00	750.00	450.00
(18)	Dale Mitchell	60.00	30.00	18.00
(19)	Phil Rizzuto	125.00	62.00	37.00
(20)	Curtis Roberts	60.00	30.00	18.00
(21)	Al Rosen	80.00	40.00	24.00
(22)	Red Schoendienst	110.00	55.00	33.00
(23)	Paul Smith	450.00	225.00	135.00
(24)	Duke Snider	225.00	112.00	67.00
(25)	George Strickland	60.00	30.00	18.00
(26)	Max Surkont	60.00	30.00	18.00
(27)	Frank Thomas	125.00	62.00	37.00
(28)	Wally Westlake	60.00	30.00	18.00
(29)	Early Wynn	110.00	55.00	33.00

1987 David Berg Hot Dogs Cubs

Changing sponsors from Gatorade to David Berg Pure Beef Hot Dogs, the Chicago Cubs handed out a 26-card set of baseball cards to fans attending the July 29th game at Wrigley Field. The cards are printed in full-color on white stock and measure 2-7/8" by 4-1/4" in size. The set is numbered by the players' uniform numbers. The card backs contain player personal and statistical information, plus a full-color picture of a David

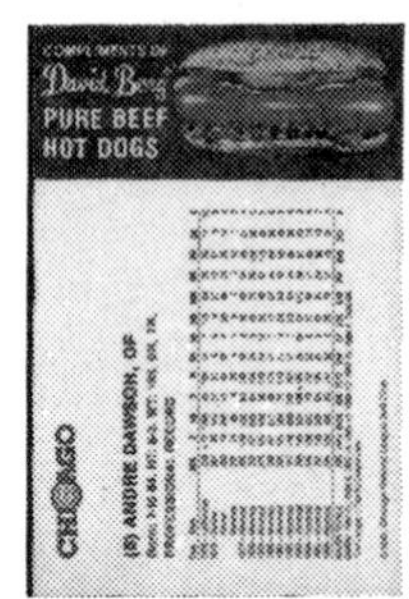

Berg hot dog in a bun with all the garnishings. The set marked the sixth consecutive year the Cubs held a baseball card giveaway promotion.

		MT	NR MT	EX
	Complete Set:	10.00	7.50	4.00
	Common Player:	.15	.11	.06
1	Dave Martinez	.50	.40	.20
4	Gene Michael	.15	.11	.06
6	Keith Moreland	.30	.25	.12
7	Jody Davis	.30	.25	.12
8	Andre Dawson	1.00	.70	.40
10	Leon Durham	.30	.25	.12
11	Jim Sundberg	.15	.11	.06
12	Shawon Dunston	.60	.45	.25
19	Manny Trillo	.15	.11	.06
20	Bob Dernier	.15	.11	.06
21	Scott Sanderson	.15	.11	.06
22	Jerry Mumphrey	.15	.11	.06
23	Ryne Sandberg	2.00	1.50	.80
24	Brian Dayett	.15	.11	.06
29	Chico Walker	.15	.11	.06
31	Greg Maddux	.70	.50	.30
33	Frank DiPino	.15	.11	.06
34	Steve Trout	.20	.15	.08
36	Gary Matthews	.20	.15	.08
37	Ed Lynch	.15	.11	.06
39	Ron Davis	.15	.11	.06
40	Rick Sutcliffe	.70	.50	.30
46	Lee Smith	.30	.25	.12
47	Dickie Noles	.15	.11	.06
49	Jamie Moyer	.20	.15	.08
---	The Coaching Staff (Johnny Oates, Jim Snyder, Herm Starrette, John Vukovich, Billy Williams)	.15	.11	.06

1988 David Berg Hot Dogs Cubs

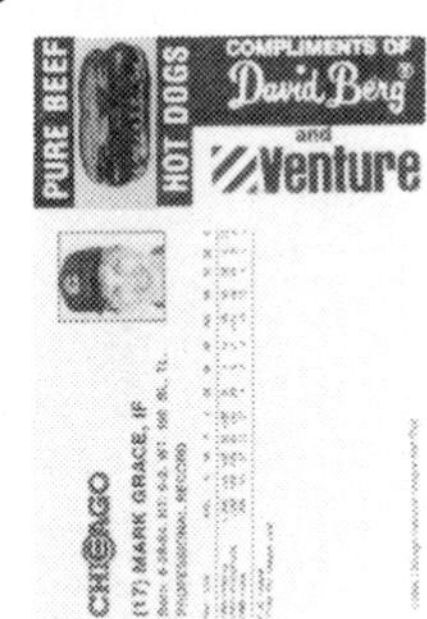

This oversized (2-7/8" by 4-1/2") set of 26 cards was distributed to fans at Wrigley Field on August 24th. The set includes cards for the manager and coaching staff, as well as players. Full-color action photos are framed in red and blue on a white background. The backs feature small black and white player close-ups, colorful team logos, statistics and sponsor logos (David Berg Hot Dogs and Venture Store Restaurants). The numbers in the following checklist refer to players' uniforms.

		MT	NR MT	EX
	Complete Set:	11.00	8.25	4.50
	Common Player:	.15	.11	.06
2	Vance Law	.15	.11	.06
4	Don Zimmer	.15	.11	.06
7	Jody Davis	.30	.25	.12
8	Andre Dawson	1.00	.70	.40
9	Damon Berryhill	.80	.60	.30
12	Shawon Dunston	.60	.45	.25
17	Mark Grace	3.00	2.25	1.25
18	Angel Salazar	.15	.11	.06
19	Manny Trillo	.15	.11	.06
21	Scott Sanderson	.15	.11	.06
22	Jerry Mumphrey	.15	.11	.06
23	Ryne Sandberg	2.00	1.50	.80
24	Gary Varsho	.40	.30	.15
25	Rafael Palmeiro	1.25	.90	.50
28	Mitch Webster	.15	.11	.06
30	Darrin Jackson	.40	.30	.15

		MT	NR MT	EX
31	Greg Maddux	.70	.50	.30
32	Calvin Schiraldi	.20	.15	.08
33	Frank DiPino	.15	.11	.06
37	Pat Perry	.15	.11	.06
40	Rick Sutcliffe	.70	.50	.30
41	Jeff Pico	.50	.40	.20
45	Al Nipper	.15	.11	.06
49	Jamie Moyer	.20	.15	.08
50	Les Lancaster	.15	.11	.06
54	Rich Gossage	.70	.50	.30
---	Joe Altobelli, Chuck Cottier, Larry Cox, Jose Martinez, Dick Pole	.15	.11	.06

1933 Delong

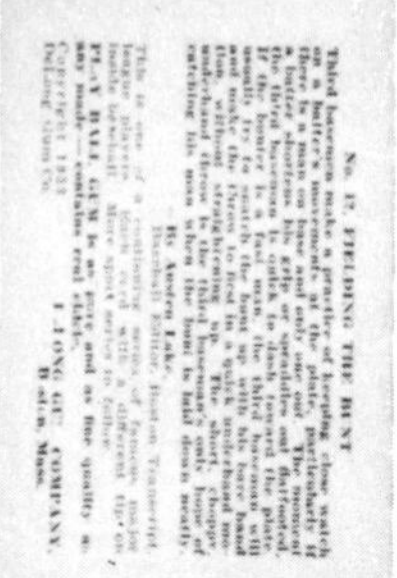

The DeLong Gum Company of Boston, Mass. was among the first to sell baseball cards with gum. It issued a set of 24 cards in 1933, the same year the Goudey Gum Co. issued its premiere set, making both companies pioneers in the field. The DeLong cards measure 2" by 3" and feature black and white player photos on a color background. The photos show the players in various action poses and positions them in the middle of a miniature stadium setting so that they appear to be giant in size. Most of the cards in the set are vertically designed, but a few are horizontal. The backs of the cards, written by Austen Lake, editor of the Boston Transcript, contain a series of sports tips to help youngsters become better ballplayers. Lake later wrote the tips that appeared on the backs of the Diamond Stars cards issued by National Chicle from 1934-1936. The ACC designation for this set is R333. The checklist below gives the players' names exactly as they appear on the fronts of the cards.

		NR MT	EX	VG
	Complete Set:	9500.00	4250.00	2750.
	Common Player:	175.00	87.00	52.00
1	"Marty" McManus	200.00	100.00	60.00
2	Al Simmons	275.00	137.00	75.00
3	Oscar Melillo	175.00	87.00	52.00
4	William (Bill) Terry	400.00	200.00	125.00
5	Charlie Gehringer	400.00	200.00	125.00
6	Gordon (Mickey) Cochrane	400.00	200.00	125.00
7	Lou Gehrig	3000.00	1500.00	800.00
8	Hazen S. (Kiki) Cuyler	300.00	150.00	90.00
9	Bill Urbanski	175.00	87.00	52.00
10	Frank J. (Lefty) O'Doul	200.00	100.00	60.00
11	Freddie Lindstrom	250.00	125.00	70.00
12	Harold (Pie) Traynor	300.00	150.00	90.00
13	"Rabbit" Maranville	300.00	150.00	90.00
14	Vernon "Lefty" Gomez	300.00	150.00	90.00
15	Riggs Stephenson	175.00	87.00	52.00
16	Lon Warneke	175.00	87.00	52.00
17	Pepper Martin	200.00	100.00	60.00
18	Jimmy Dykes	175.00	87.00	52.00
19	Chick Hafey	300.00	150.00	90.00
20	Joe Vosmik	175.00	87.00	52.00
21	Jimmy Foxx	600.00	300.00	175.00
22	Charles (Chuck) Klein	300.00	150.00	90.00
23	Robert (Lefty) Grove	500.00	250.00	150.00
24	"Goose" Goslin	300.00	150.00	90.00

1909 Derby Cigars

Although there is no advertising on these cards to indicate their origin, it is generally accepted that this 1909 set was issued by Derby Cigars, a product of the American Tobacco Co. A dozen different subjects, all members of the New York Giants, have been found. Much uncertainty still surrounds this obscure set, but it is believed that the cards, which measure 1-3/4" by 2-3/4", were inserted in boxes of Derby "Little Cigars." The cards feature a player portrait inside an oval with the player's name and position at the bottom.

		NR MT	EX	VG
	Complete Set:	800.00	400.00	250.00
	Common Player:	40.00	20.00	12.00
(1)	Josh Devore	40.00	20.00	12.00
(2)	Larry Doyle	50.00	25.00	15.00
(3)	Art Fletcher	40.00	20.00	12.00
(4)	Buck Herzog	40.00	20.00	12.00
(5)	Rube Marquard	100.00	50.00	30.00
(6)	Christy Mathewson	200.00	100.00	60.00
(7)	Fred Merkle	50.00	25.00	15.00
(8)	Chief Meyers	40.00	20.00	12.00
(9)	Red Murray	40.00	20.00	12.00
(10)	John McGraw	100.00	50.00	30.00
(11)	Fred Snodgrass	50.00	25.00	15.00
(12)	Hooks Wiltse	40.00	20.00	12.00

1934-36 Diamond Stars

DIAMOND STARS, No. 9

Fielding Tips—The Catcher's Throw

Issued from 1934 through 1936, the Diamond Stars set (ACC designation R327) consists of 108 cards. Produced by National Chicle, the numbered cards measure 2-3/8" by 2-7/8" and are color art reproductions of actual photographs. The year of issue can be determined by the player's statistics found on the reverse of the card. The backs feature either a player biography or a baseball playing tip. Some cards can be found with either green or blue printing on the backs. Artwork for 12 cards that were never issued was uncovered several years ago and a set featuring those cards was subsequently made available to the collecting public. The complete set price does not include the higher priced variations.

		NR MT	EX	VG
	Complete Set:	20000.	95000.	6000.
	Common Player: 1-31	90.00	45.00	27.00
	Common Player: 32-72	70.00	35.00	21.00
	Common Player: 73-84	75.00	38.00	23.00
	Common Player: 85-96	125.00	62.00	37.00
	Common Player: 97-108	300.00	150.00	90.00
1a	"Lefty" Grove (1934 green back)	1300.00	650.00	390.00
1b	"Lefty" Grove (1935 green back)	1300.00	650.00	390.00
2a	Al Simmons (1934 green back)	200.00	100.00	60.00
2b	Al Simmons (1935 green back)	200.00	100.00	60.00
2c	Al Simmons (1936 blue back)	225.00	112.00	67.00
3a	"Rabbit" Maranville (1934 green back)	100.00	50.00	30.00
3b	"Rabbit" Maranville (1935 green back)	100.00	50.00	30.00
4a	"Buddy" Myer (1934 green back)	90.00	45.00	27.00
4b	"Buddy" Myer (1935 green back)	90.00	45.00	27.00
4c	"Buddy" Myer (1936 blue back)	90.00	45.00	27.00
5a	Tom Bridges (1934 green back)	90.00	45.00	27.00
5b	Tom Bridges (1935 green back)	90.00	45.00	27.00
5c	Tom Bridges (1936 blue back)	90.00	45.00	27.00
6a	Max Bishop (1934 green back)	90.00	45.00	27.00
6b	Max Bishop (1935 green back)	90.00	45.00	27.00
7a	Lew Fonseca (1934 green back)	90.00	45.00	27.00
7b	Lew Fonseca (1935 green back)	90.00	45.00	27.00
8a	Joe Vosmik (1934 green back)	90.00	45.00	27.00
8b	Joe Vosmik (1935 green back)	90.00	45.00	27.00
8c	Joe Vosmik (1936 blue back)	90.00	45.00	27.00
9a	"Mickey" Cochrane (1934 green back)	225.00	112.00	67.00
9b	"Mickey" Cochrane (1935 green back)	225.00	112.00	67.00
9c	"Mickey" Cochrane (1936 blue back)	225.00	112.00	67.00
10a	Roy Mahaffey (1934 green back)	90.00	45.00	27.00
10b	Roy Mahaffey (1935 green back)	90.00	45.00	27.00
10c	Roy Mahaffey (1936 blue back)	90.00	45.00	27.00
11a	Bill Dickey (1934 green back)	275.00	137.00	82.00
11b	Bill Dickey (1935 green back)	275.00	137.00	82.00
12a	"Dixie" Walker (1934 green back)	90.00	45.00	27.00
12b	"Dixie" Walker (1935 green back)	90.00	45.00	27.00
12c	"Dixie" Walker (1936 blue back)	90.00	45.00	27.00
13a	George Blaeholder (1934 green back)	90.00	45.00	27.00
13b	George Blaeholder (1935 green back)	90.00	45.00	27.00
14a	Bill Terry (1934 green back)	110.00	55.00	33.00
14b	Bill Terry (1935 green back)	110.00	55.00	33.00
15a	Dick Bartell (1934 green back)	90.00	45.00	27.00
15b	Dick Bartell (1935 green back)	90.00	45.00	27.00
16a	Lloyd Waner (1934 green back)	125.00	62.00	37.00
16b	Lloyd Waner (1935 green back)	125.00	62.00	37.00
16c	Lloyd Waner (1936 blue back)	125.00	62.00	37.00
17a	Frankie Frisch (1934 green back)	110.00	55.00	33.00
17b	Frankie Frisch (1935 green back)	110.00	55.00	33.00
18a	"Chick" Hafey (1934 green back)	100.00	50.00	30.00
18b	"Chick" Hafey (1935 green back)	100.00	50.00	30.00
19a	Van Mungo (1934 green back)	90.00	45.00	27.00
19b	Van Mungo (1935 green back)	90.00	45.00	27.00
20a	"Shanty" Hogan (1934 green back)	90.00	45.00	27.00
20b	"Shanty" Hogan (1935 green back)	90.00	45.00	27.00
21a	Johnny Vergez (1934 green back)	90.00	45.00	27.00
21b	Johnny Vergez (1935 green back)	90.00	45.00	27.00
22a	Jimmy Wilson (1934 green back)	90.00	45.00	27.00
22b	Jimmy Wilson (1935 green back)	90.00	45.00	27.00
22c	Jimmy Wilson (1936 blue back)	90.00	45.00	27.00
23a	Bill Hallahan (1934 green back)	90.00	45.00	27.00
23b	Bill Hallahan (1935 green back)	90.00	45.00	27.00
24a	"Sparky" Adams (1934 green back)	90.00	45.00	27.00
24b	"Sparky" Adams (1935 green back)	90.00	45.00	27.00
25	Walter Berger	100.00	50.00	30.00
26a	"Pepper" Martin (1935 green back)	100.00	50.00	30.00
26b	"Pepper" Martin (1936 blue back)	100.00	50.00	30.00
27	"Pie" Traynor	225.00	112.00	67.00
28	"Al" Lopez	225.00	112.00	67.00
29	Robert Rolfe	90.00	45.00	27.00
30a	"Heinie" Manush (1935 green back)	125.00	62.00	37.00
30b	"Heinie" Manush (1936 blue back)	150.00	75.00	45.00
31a	"Kiki" Cuyler (1935 green back)	125.00	62.00	37.00
31b	"Kiki" Cuyler (1936 blue back)	125.00	62.00	37.00
32	Sam Rice	125.00	62.00	37.00
33	"Schoolboy" Rowe	90.00	45.00	27.00
34	Stanley Hack	90.00	45.00	27.00
35	Earle Averill	125.00	62.00	37.00
36a	Earnie Lombardi	200.00	100.00	60.00
36b	Ernie Lombardi	150.00	75.00	45.00
37	"Billie" Urbanski	70.00	35.00	21.00
38	Ben Chapman	90.00	45.00	27.00
39	Carl Hubbell	110.00	55.00	33.00
40	"Blondy" Ryan	70.00	35.00	21.00
41	Harvey Hendrick	70.00	35.00	21.00
42	Jimmy Dykes	90.00	45.00	27.00
43	Ted Lyons	100.00	50.00	30.00
44	Rogers Hornsby	300.00	150.00	90.00
45	"Jo Jo" White	70.00	35.00	21.00
46	"Red" Lucas	70.00	35.00	21.00
47	Cliff Bolton	70.00	35.00	21.00
48	"Rick" Ferrell	125.00	62.00	37.00
49	"Buck" Jordan	70.00	35.00	21.00
50	"Mel" Ott	275.00	137.00	82.00
51	John Whitehead	70.00	35.00	21.00
52	George Stainback	70.00	35.00	21.00
53	Oscar Melillo	70.00	35.00	21.00
54a	"Hank" Greenburg	400.00	200.00	120.00
54b	"Hank" Greenberg	250.00	125.00	75.00
55	Tony Cuccinello	70.00	35.00	21.00

		NR MT	EX	VG
56	"Gus" Suhr	70.00	35.00	21.00
57	"Cy" Blanton	70.00	35.00	21.00
58	Glenn Myatt	70.00	35.00	21.00
59	Jim Bottomley	125.00	62.00	37.00
60	Charley "Red" Ruffing	100.00	50.00	30.00
61	"Billie" Werber	70.00	35.00	21.00
62	Fred M. Frankhouse	70.00	35.00	21.00
63	"Stonewall" Jackson	125.00	62.00	37.00
64	Jimmie Foxx	300.00	150.00	90.00
65	"Zeke" Bonura	70.00	35.00	21.00
66	"Ducky" Medwick	100.00	50.00	30.00
67	Marvin Owen	70.00	35.00	21.00
68	"Sam" Leslie	70.00	35.00	21.00
69	Earl Grace	70.00	35.00	21.00
70	"Hal" Trosky	70.00	35.00	21.00
71	"Ossie" Bluege	70.00	35.00	21.00
72	"Tony" Piet	70.00	35.00	21.00
73a	"Fritz" Ostermueller (1935 green back)	75.00	38.00	23.00
73b	"Fritz" Ostermueller (1935 blue back)	75.00	38.00	23.00
73c	"Fritz" Ostermueller (1936 blue back)	75.00	38.00	23.00
74a	Tony Lazzeri (1935 green back)	125.00	62.00	37.00
74b	Tony Lazzeri (1935 blue back)	125.00	62.00	37.00
74c	Tony Lazzeri (1936 blue back)	125.00	62.00	37.00
75a	Irving Burns (1935 green back)	75.00	38.00	23.00
75b	Irving Burns (1935 blue back)	75.00	38.00	23.00
75c	Irving Burns (1936 blue back)	75.00	38.00	23.00
76a	Bill Rogell (1935 green back)	75.00	38.00	23.00
76b	Bill Rogell (1935 blue back)	75.00	38.00	23.00
76c	Bill Rogell (1936 blue back)	75.00	38.00	23.00
77a	Charlie Gehringer (1935 green back)	150.00	75.00	45.00
77b	Charlie Gehringer (1935 blue back)	150.00	75.00	45.00
77c	Charlie Gehringer (1936 blue back)	150.00	75.00	45.00
78a	Joe Kuhel (1935 green back)	75.00	38.00	23.00
78b	Joe Kuhel (1935 blue back)	75.00	38.00	23.00
78c	Joe Kuhel (1936 blue back)	75.00	38.00	23.00
79a	Willis Hudlin (1935 green back)	75.00	38.00	23.00
79b	Willis Hudlin (1935 blue back)	75.00	38.00	23.00
79c	Willis Hudlin (1936 blue back)	75.00	38.00	23.00
80a	Louis Chiozza (1935 green back)	75.00	38.00	23.00
80b	Louis Chiozza (1935 blue back)	75.00	38.00	23.00
80c	Louis Chiozza (1936 blue back)	75.00	38.00	23.00
81a	Bill DeLancey (1935 green back)	75.00	38.00	23.00
81b	Bill DeLancey (1935 blue back)	75.00	38.00	23.00
81c	Bill DeLancey (1936 blue back)	75.00	38.00	23.00
82a	John Babich (1935 green back)	100.00	50.00	30.00
82b	John Babich (1935 blue back)	100.00	50.00	30.00
82c	John Babich (1936 blue back)	100.00	50.00	30.00
83a	Paul Waner (1935 green back)	200.00	100.00	60.00
83b	Paul Waner (1935 blue back)	200.00	100.00	60.00
83c	Paul Waner (1936 blue back)	200.00	100.00	60.00
84a	Sam Byrd (1935 green back)	75.00	38.00	23.00
84b	Sam Byrd (1935 blue back)	75.00	38.00	23.00
84c	Sam Byrd (1936 blue back)	75.00	38.00	23.00
85	Julius Solters	125.00	62.00	37.00
86	Frank Crosetti	200.00	100.00	60.00
87	Steve O'Neil (O'Neill)	125.00	62.00	37.00
88	Geo. Selkirk	100.00	50.00	30.00
89	Joe Stripp	125.00	62.00	37.00
90	Ray Hayworth	125.00	62.00	37.00
91	Bucky Harris	150.00	75.00	45.00
92	Ethan Allen	125.00	62.00	37.00
93	Alvin Crowder	125.00	62.00	37.00
94	Wes Ferrell	125.00	62.00	37.00
95	Luke Appling	275.00	137.00	82.00
96	Lew Riggs	125.00	62.00	37.00
97	"Al" Lopez	500.00	250.00	150.00
98	"Schoolboy" Rowe	300.00	150.00	90.00
99	"Pie" Traynor	600.00	300.00	180.00
100	Earle Averill (Earl)	500.00	250.00	150.00
101	Dick Bartell	300.00	150.00	90.00
102	Van Mungo	300.00	150.00	90.00
103	Bill Dickey	800.00	400.00	250.00
104	Robert Rolfe	300.00	150.00	90.00
105	"Ernie" Lombardi	500.00	250.00	150.00
106	"Red" Lucas	300.00	150.00	90.00
107	Stanley Hack	300.00	150.00	90.00
108	Walter Berger	350.00	175.00	105.00

1924 Diaz Cigarettes

Because they were printed in Cuba and feature only pitchers, the 1924 Diaz Cigarette cards are among the rarest and most intriguing of all tobacco issues. Produced in Havana for the Diaz brand, the black and white cards measure 1-3/4" by 2-1/2" and were printed on a glossy-type stock. The player's name and position are listed at the bottom of the card, while his team and league appear at the top. According to the card backs, printed in Spanish, the set consists of 136

cards - all major league pitchers. But to date only the 12 cards checklisted here have been discovered.

		NR MT	EX	VG
Complete Set:		3500.00	1750.00	1050.
Common Player:		225.00	112.00	67.00
2	Waite C. Hoyt	400.00	200.00	120.00
12	Curtis Fullerton	225.00	112.00	67.00
14	George Walberg	225.00	112.00	67.00
40	A. Wilbur Cooper	225.00	112.00	67.00
51	Roy Meeker	225.00	112.00	67.00
58	Sam Gray	225.00	112.00	67.00
96	Philip B. Weinart	225.00	112.00	67.00
105	Hubert F. Pruett	225.00	112.00	67.00
121	Bert Cole	225.00	112.00	67.00
---	Leslie J. Bush	225.00	112.00	67.00
---	Wm. Piercy	225.00	112.00	67.00
---	Arnold E. Stone	225.00	112.00	67.00

1937 Dixie Lids

This unnumbered set of Dixie cup ice cream lids was issued in 1937 and consists of 24 different lids, although only six picture sports stars - four of whom are baseball stars. The lids are found in two different sizes, either 2-11/16" in diameter or 2-5/16" in diameter. The 1937 Dixie Lids were printed in black or dark red. The lids must have the small tab still intact to command top value.

		NR MT	EX	VG
Complete Set:		400.00	200.00	120.00
Common Player:		75.00	38.00	23.00
(1)	Charles Gehringer	100.00	50.00	30.00
(2)	Charles ("Gabby") Hartnett	100.00	50.00	30.00
(3)	Carl Hubbell	125.00	62.00	37.00
(4)	Joe Medwick	75.00	38.00	23.00

1937 Dixie Lids Premiums

Issued as a premium offer in conjunction with the 1937 Dixie lids, this unnumbered set of color 8" by 10" pictures was printed on heavy paper and features the same subjects as the Dixie Lids set. The 1937 Dixie premiums have a distinctive dark green band along the left margin containing the player's name. The back has smaller photos of the player in action with a large star at the top and a player write-up.

		NR MT	EX	VG
Complete Set:		400.00	200.00	120.00
Common Player:		75.00	38.00	23.00
(1)	Charles Gehringer	100.00	50.00	30.00
(2)	Charles (Gabby) Hartnett	100.00	50.00	30.00
(3)	Carl Hubbell	125.00	62.00	37.00
(4)	Joe (Ducky) Medwick	75.00	38.00	23.00

1938 Dixie Lids

Similar to its set of the previous year, the 1938 Dixie Lids set is a 24-subject set that includes six sports stars - four of whom are baseball players. The lids are found in two sizes, either 2 11/16" in diameter or 2-5/16" in diameter. The 1938 Dixie lids are printed in blue ink. Dixie lids must have the small tab still intact to command top value.

		NR MT	EX	VG
Complete Set:		350.00	175.00	105.00
Common Player:		50.00	25.00	15.00
(1)	Bob Feller	100.00	50.00	30.00
(2)	Jimmie Foxx	100.00	50.00	30.00
(3)	Carl Hubbell	100.00	50.00	30.00
(4)	Wally Moses	50.00	25.00	15.00

1938 Dixie Lids Premiums

Issued in conjunction with the 1938 Dixie cup lids, this unnumbered set of 8" x 10" pictures contains the same subjects and is printed on heavy paper. The 1938 Dixie Lids Premiums have a light green border surrounding the entire picture with the player's name to the left. The back contains smaller photos of the player in action with his name in script at the top and a short write-up.

		NR MT	EX	VG
Complete Set:		300.00	150.00	90.00
Common Player:		50.00	25.00	15.00
(1)	Bob Feller	100.00	50.00	30.00
(2)	Jimmy Foxx	75.00	37.00	22.00
(3)	Carl Hubbell	75.00	37.00	22.00
(4)	Wally Moses	50.00	25.00	15.00

1952 Dixie Lids

After a 14-year break, another Dixie lid set, featuring 24 baseball players, appeared in 1952. The unnumbered lids measure 2-11/16" in diameter and were printed with a blue tint. The

Dixie lids of the 1950s can be distinguished from earlier issues because the bottom of the photo is squared off to accomodate the player's name. Dixie lids must contain the small tab to command top value.

		NR MT	EX	VG
Complete Set:		3500.00	1750.00	1050.
Common Player:		135.00	67.00	40.00
(1)	Richie Ashburn	175.00	87.00	52.00
(2)	Tommy Byrne	135.00	67.00	40.00
(3)	Chico Carrasquel	135.00	67.00	40.00
(4)	Pete Castiglione	135.00	67.00	40.00
(5)	Walker Cooper	135.00	67.00	40.00
(6)	Billy Cox	135.00	67.00	40.00
(7)	Ferris Fain	135.00	67.00	40.00
(8)	Bobby Feller	250.00	125.00	75.00
(9)	Nelson Fox	175.00	87.00	52.00
(10)	Monte Irvin	200.00	100.00	60.00
(11)	Ralph Kiner	200.00	100.00	60.00
(12)	Cass Michaels	135.00	67.00	40.00
(13)	Don Mueller	135.00	67.00	40.00
(14)	Mel Parnell	135.00	67.00	40.00
(15)	Allie Reynolds	175.00	87.00	52.00
(16)	Preacher Roe	175.00	87.00	52.00
(17)	Connie Ryan	135.00	67.00	40.00
(18)	Hank Sauer	135.00	67.00	40.00
(19)	Al Schoendienst	175.00	87.00	52.00
(20)	Andy Seminick	135.00	67.00	40.00
(21)	Bobby Shantz	150.00	75.00	45.00
(22)	Enos Slaughter	200.00	100.00	60.00
(23)	Virgil Trucks	135.00	67.00	40.00
(24)	Gene Woodling	150.00	75.00	45.00

1952 Dixie Lids Premiums

This unnumbered set of 24 player photos was issued as a premium in conjunction with the 1952 Dixie cup lids and features the same subjects. The player's team and facsimile autograph appear along the bottom of the 8" by 10" blank-backed photo, which was printed on heavy paper. The 1952 Dixie premiums show the player's 1951 season statistics in the lower right corner.

		NR MT	EX	VG
Complete Set:		550.00	275.00	165.00
Common Player:		25.00	12.50	7.50
(1)	Richie Ashburn	30.00	15.00	9.00
(2)	Tommy Byrne	25.00	12.50	7.50
(3)	Chico Carrasquel	25.00	12.50	7.50
(4)	Pete Castiglione	25.00	12.50	7.50
(5)	Walker Cooper	25.00	12.50	7.50
(6)	Billy Cox	25.00	12.50	7.50
(7)	Ferris Fain	25.00	12.50	7.50
(8)	Bob Feller	75.00	37.00	22.00
(9)	Nelson Fox	30.00	15.00	9.00
(10)	Monte Irvin	40.00	20.00	12.00
(11)	Ralph Kiner	45.00	22.00	13.50
(12)	Cass Michaels	25.00	12.50	7.50
(13)	Don Mueller	25.00	12.50	7.50
(14)	Mel Parnell	25.00	12.50	7.50
(15)	Allie Reynolds	30.00	15.00	9.00
(16)	Preacher Roe	30.00	15.00	9.00
(17)	Connie Ryan	25.00	12.50	7.50
(18)	Hank Sauer	25.00	12.50	7.50
(19)	Al Schoendienst	30.00	15.00	9.00
(20)	Andy Seminick	25.00	12.50	7.50
(21)	Bobby Shantz	30.00	15.00	9.00
(22)	Enos Slaughter	45.00	22.00	13.50
(23)	Virgil Trucks	25.00	12.50	7.50
(24)	Gene Woodling	30.00	15.00	9.00

1953 Dixie Lids

The 1953 Dixie Lids set again consists of 24 unnumbered players and is identical in design to the 1953 set. Each lid measures 2-11/16"in diameter and must include the small tab to command top value.

		NR MT	EX	VG
Complete Set:		1500.00	750.00	450.00
Common Player:		35.00	17.50	10.50
(1)	Richie Ashburn	40.00	20.00	12.00
(2)	Chico Carrasquel	35.00	17.50	10.50
(3)	Billy Cox	35.00	17.50	10.50
(4)	Ferris Fain	35.00	17.50	10.50
(5)	Nelson Fox	40.00	20.00	12.00
(6a)	Sid Gordon (Boston)	70.00	35.00	20.00
(6b)	Sid Gordon (Milwaukee)	35.00	17.50	10.50
(7)	Warren Hacker	35.00	17.50	10.50
(8)	Monte Irvin	60.00	30.00	18.00
(9)	Jackie Jensen	40.00	20.00	12.00
(10a)	Ralph Kiner (Pittsburgh)	100.00	50.00	30.00
(10b)	Ralph Kiner (Chicago)	60.00	30.00	18.00
(11)	Ted Kluszewski	40.00	20.00	12.00
(12)	Bob Lemon	60.00	30.00	18.00
(13)	Don Mueller	35.00	17.50	10.50
(14)	Mel Parnell	35.00	17.50	10.50
(15)	Jerry Priddy	35.00	17.50	10.50
(16)	Allie Reynolds	40.00	20.00	12.00
(17)	Preacher Roe	40.00	20.00	12.00
(18)	Hank Sauer	35.00	17.50	10.50
(19)	Al Schoendienst	40.00	20.00	12.00
(20)	Bobby Shantz	40.00	20.00	12.00
(21)	Enos Slaughter	60.00	30.00	18.00
(22a)	Warren Spahn (Boston)	125.00	62.00	37.00
(22b)	Warren Spahn (Milwaukee)	75.00	38.00	23.00
(23a)	Virgil Trucks (Chicago)	75.00	38.00	23.00
(23b)	Virgil Trucks (St. Louis)	35.00	17.50	10.50
(24)	Gene Woodling	40.00	20.00	12.00

1953 Dixie Lids Premiums

This set of 24 8" by 10" photos was issued as a premium in conjunction with the 1953 Dixie Lids set and includes the same subjects. The player's team and facsimile autograph are at the bottom of the unnumbered, blank-backed photos. His 1952 season stats are shown in the lower right corner.

		NR MT	EX	VG
Complete Set:		600.00	300.00	175.00
Common Player:		18.00	9.00	5.50
(1)	Richie Ashburn	20.00	10.00	6.00
(2)	Chico Carrasquel	18.00	9.00	5.50
(3)	Billy Cox	18.00	9.00	5.50
(4)	Ferris Fain	18.00	9.00	5.50
(5)	Nelson Fox	20.00	10.00	6.00
(6)	Sid Gordon	18.00	9.00	5.50
(7)	Warren Hacker	18.00	9.00	5.50
(8)	Monte Irvin	25.00	12.50	7.50
(9)	Jack Jensen	25.00	12.50	7.50
(10)	Ralph Kiner	30.00	15.00	9.00
(11)	Ted Kluszewski	20.00	10.00	6.00
(12)	Bob Lemon	30.00	15.00	9.00
(13)	Don Mueller	18.00	9.00	5.50
(14)	Mel Parnell	18.00	9.00	5.50
(15)	Jerry Priddy	18.00	9.00	5.50
(16)	Allie Reynolds	20.00	10.00	6.00
(17)	Preacher Roe	20.00	10.00	6.00
(18)	Hank Sauer	18.00	9.00	5.50
(19)	Al Schoendienst	20.00	10.00	6.00
(20)	Bobby Shantz	18.00	9.00	5.50
(21)	Enos Slaughter	30.00	15.00	9.00
(22)	Warren Spahn	40.00	20.00	12.00
(23)	Virgil Trucks	18.00	9.00	5.50
(24)	Gene Woodling	20.00	10.00	6.00

1954 Dixie Lids

The 1954 Dixie Lids set consists of 18 players, and the lids are usually found with a gray tint. The lids usually measure 2-11/16" in diameter, although two other sizes also exist (2-1/4" in diameter and 3-3/16" in diameter), which are valued at about twice the prices listed. The 1953 Dixie Lids are similar to earlier issues, except they carry an offer for a "3-D Starviewer" around the outside edge. The small tabs must be attached to command top value. The lids are unnumbered.

		NR MT	EX	VG
Complete Set:		500.00	250.00	150.00
Common Player:		20.00	10.00	6.00
(1)	Richie Ashburn	25.00	12.50	7.50
(2)	Clint Courtney	20.00	10.00	6.00
(3)	Sid Gordon	20.00	10.00	6.00
(4)	Billy Hoeft	20.00	10.00	6.00
(5)	Monte Irvin	35.00	17.50	10.50
(6)	Jackie Jensen	25.00	12.50	7.50
(7)	Ralph Kiner	40.00	20.00	12.00
(8)	Ted Kluszewski	25.00	12.50	7.50
(9)	Gil McDougald	25.00	12.50	7.50
(10)	Minny Minoso	25.00	12.50	7.50
(11)	Danny O'Connell	20.00	10.00	6.00
(12)	Mel Parnell	20.00	10.00	6.00
(13)	Preacher Roe	25.00	12.50	7.50
(14)	Al Rosen	25.00	12.50	7.50
(15)	Al Schoendienst	25.00	12.50	7.50
(16)	Enos Slaughter	40.00	20.00	12.00
(17)	Gene Woodling	25.00	12.50	7.50
(18)	Gus Zernial	20.00	10.00	6.00

1988 Domino's Pizza Tigers

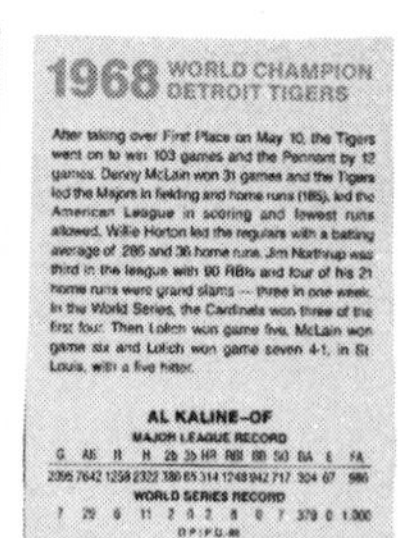

Domino's Pizza produced a 28-card set commemorating the 20th anniversary of the 1968 World Champion Detroit Tigers. The cards were given away at an Old Timers Game at Tiger Stadium in 1988. The cards, which measure 2-1/2" by 3-1/2", feature black and white photos semi-surrounded by a two-stripe band. The stripes on the card's left side are the same color (red and light blue) as the Domino's Pizza logo in the upper corner. The stripes on the card's right side match the colors of the Tigers logo (red and dark blue). The backs of all the cards (except for Ernie Harwell) contain a brief summary of the Tigers' 1968 season. Located at the bottom on the card backs are the players' major league records through 1968 plus their 1968 World Series statistics.

		MT	NR MT	EX
Complete Set:		11.00	8.25	4.50
Common Player:		.20	.15	.08
(1)	Gates Brown	.30	.25	.12
(2)	Norm Cash	.90	.70	.35
(3)	Wayne Comer	.20	.15	.08
(4)	Pat Dobson	.20	.15	.08
(5)	Bill Freehan	.60	.45	.25
(6)	John Hiller	.30	.25	.12
(7)	Ernie Harwell (announcer)	.20	.15	.08
(8)	Willie Horton	.60	.45	.25
(9)	Al Kaline	1.50	1.25	.60
(10)	Fred Lasher	.20	.15	.08
(11)	Mickey Lolich	.90	.70	.35
(12)	Tom Matchick	.20	.15	.08
(13)	Ed Mathews	.90	.70	.35
(14)	Dick McAuliff (McAuliffe)	.40	.30	.15
(15)	Denny McLain	1.00	.70	.40
(16)	Don McMahon	.20	.15	.08
(17)	Jim Northrup	.40	.30	.15
(18)	Ray Oyler	.20	.15	.08
(19)	Daryl Patterson	.20	.15	.08
(20)	Jim Price	.20	.15	.08
(21)	Joe Sparma	.20	.15	.08
(22)	Mickey Stanley	.40	.30	.15
(23)	Dick Tracewski	.20	.15	.08
(24)	Jon Warden	.20	.15	.08
(25)	Don Wert	.20	.15	.08
(26)	Earl Wilson	.20	.15	.08
(27)	Header Card	.20	.15	.08
(28)	Coupon Card	.20	.15	.08

1981 Donruss

The Donruss Co. of Memphis, Tenn., produced its premiere baseball card issue in 1981 with a set

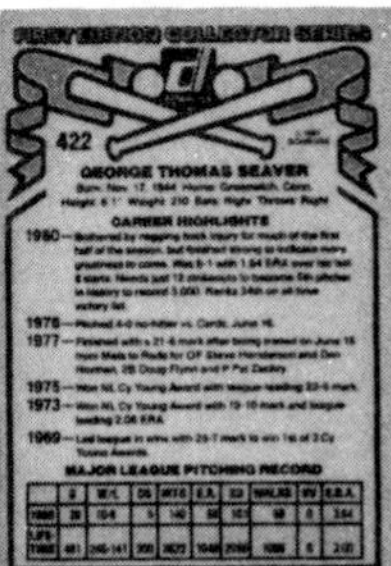

that consisted of 600 numbered cards and five unnumbered checklists. The cards, which measure 2-1/2" by 3-1/2", are printed on thin stock. The card fronts contain the Donruss logo plus the year of issue. The card backs are designed on a vertical format and have black print on red and white. The set, entitled "First Edition Collector Series," contains nearly 40 variations, those being first-printing errors that were corrected in a subsequent print run. The cards were issued in gum wax packs, with hobby dealer sales being coordinated by TCMA of Amawalk, N.Y. The complete set price does not include the higher priced variations.

		MT	NR MT	EX
Complete Set:		40.00	30.00	15.00
Common Player:		.06	.05	.02
1	Ozzie Smith	.50	.40	.20
2	Rollie Fingers	.25	.20	.10
3	Rick Wise	.08	.06	.03
4	Gene Richards	.06	.05	.02
5	Alan Trammell	.40	.30	.15
6	Tom Brookens	.08	.06	.03
7a	Duffy Dyer (1980 Avg. .185)	1.00	.70	.40
7b	Duffy Dyer (1980 Avg. 185)	.10	.08	.04
8	Mark Fidrych	.08	.06	.03
9	Dave Rozema	.06	.05	.02
10	Ricky Peters	.06	.05	.02
11	Mike Schmidt	1.50	1.25	.60
12	Willie Stargell	.40	.30	.15
13	Tim Foli	.06	.05	.02
14	Manny Sanguillen	.06	.05	.02
15	Grant Jackson	.06	.05	.02
16	Eddie Solomon	.06	.05	.02
17	Omar Moreno	.06	.05	.02
18	Joe Morgan	.60	.45	.25
19	Rafael Landestoy	.06	.05	.02
20	Bruce Bochy	.06	.05	.02
21	Joe Sambito	.06	.05	.02
22	Manny Trillo	.08	.06	.03
23a	*Dave Smith* (incomplete box around stats)	1.00	.70	.40
23b	*Dave Smith* (complete box around stats)	.30	.25	.12
24	Terry Puhl	.06	.05	.02
25	Bump Wills	.06	.05	.02
26a	John Ellis (Danny Walton photo - with bat)	1.25	.90	.50
26b	John Ellis (John Ellis photo - with glove)	.10	.08	.04
27	Jim Kern	.06	.05	.02
28	Richie Zisk	.08	.06	.03
29	John Mayberry	.08	.06	.03
30	Bob Davis	.06	.05	.02
31	Jackson Todd	.06	.05	.02
32	Al Woods	.06	.05	.02
33	Steve Carlton	.80	.60	.30
34	Lee Mazzilli	.08	.06	.03
35	John Stearns	.06	.05	.02
36	Roy Jackson	.06	.05	.02
37	Mike Scott	.70	.50	.30
38	Lamar Johnson	.06	.05	.02
39	Kevin Bell	.06	.05	.02
40	Ed Farmer	.06	.05	.02
41	Ross Baumgarten	.06	.05	.02
42	Leo Sutherland	.06	.05	.02
43	Dan Meyer	.06	.05	.02
44	Ron Reed	.06	.05	.02
45	Mario Mendoza	.06	.05	.02
46	Rick Honeycutt	.06	.05	.02
47	Glenn Abbott	.06	.05	.02
48	Leon Roberts	.06	.05	.02
49	Rod Carew	.60	.45	.25
50	Bert Campaneris	.10	.08	.04
51a	Tom Donahue (incorrect spelling)	1.00	.70	.40
51b	Tom Donohue (Donohue on front)	.10	.08	.04
52	Dave Frost	.06	.05	.02
53	Ed Halicki	.06	.05	.02
54	Dan Ford	.06	.05	.02
55	Garry Maddox	.10	.08	.04
56a	Steve Garvey ("Surpassed 25 HR..." on back)	1.75	1.25	.70
56b	Steve Garvey ("Surpassed 21 HR..." on back)	.60	.45	.25
57	Bill Russell	.08	.06	.03
58	Don Sutton	.30	.25	.12
59	Reggie Smith	.10	.08	.04
60	Rick Monday	.10	.08	.04
61	Ray Knight	.10	.08	.04
62	Johnny Bench	.80	.60	.30
63	Mario Soto	.08	.06	.03
64	Doug Bair	.06	.05	.02
65	George Foster	.20	.15	.08
66	Jeff Burroughs	.08	.06	.03
67	Keith Hernandez	.40	.30	.15
68	Tom Herr	.10	.08	.04
69	Bob Forsch	.08	.06	.03
70	John Fulgham	.06	.05	.02
71a	Bobby Bonds (lifetime HR 986)	1.00	.70	.40
71b	Bobby Bonds (lifetime HR 326)	.15	.11	.06
72a	Rennie Stennett ("...breaking broke leg..." on back)	1.00	.70	.40
72b	Rennie Stennett ("...breaking leg..." on back)	.10	.08	.04
73	Joe Strain	.06	.05	.02
74	Ed Whitson	.06	.05	.02
75	Tom Griffin	.06	.05	.02
76	Bill North	.06	.05	.02
77	Gene Garber	.06	.05	.02
78	Mike Hargrove	.06	.05	.02
79	Dave Rosello	.06	.05	.02
80	Ron Hassey	.06	.05	.02
81	Sid Monge	.06	.05	.02
82a	*Joe Charboneau* ("For some reason, Phillies..." on back)	1.00	.70	.40
82b	*Joe Charboneau* ("Phillies..." on back)	.12	.09	.05
83	Cecil Cooper	.15	.11	.06
84	Sal Bando	.10	.08	.04
85	Moose Haas	.06	.05	.02
86	Mike Caldwell	.06	.05	.02
87a	Larry Hisle ("...Twins with 28 RBI." on back)	1.00	.70	.40
87b	Larry Hisle ("...Twins with 28 HR" on back)	.10	.08	.04
88	Luis Gomez	.06	.05	.02
89	Larry Parrish	.10	.08	.04
90	Gary Carter	.40	.30	.15
91	*Bill Gullickson*	.15	.11	.06
92	Fred Norman	.06	.05	.02
93	Tommy Hutton	.06	.05	.02
94	Carl Yastrzemski	.80	.60	.30
95	Glenn Hoffman	.06	.05	.02
96	Dennis Eckersley	.12	.09	.05
97a	Tom Burgmeier (Throws: Right)	1.00	.70	.40
97b	Tom Burgmeier (Throws: Left)	.10	.08	.04
98	Win Remmerswaal	.06	.05	.02
99	Bob Horner	.12	.09	.05
100	George Brett	.80	.60	.30
101	Dave Chalk	.06	.05	.02
102	Dennis Leonard	.08	.06	.03
103	Renie Martin	.06	.05	.02
104	Amos Otis	.08	.06	.03
105	Graig Nettles	.15	.11	.06
106	Eric Soderholm	.06	.05	.02
107	Tommy John	.20	.15	.08
108	Tom Underwood	.06	.05	.02
109	Lou Piniella	.12	.09	.05
110	Mickey Klutts	.06	.05	.02
111	Bobby Murcer	.10	.08	.04
112	Eddie Murray	.70	.50	.30
113	Rick Dempsey	.08	.06	.03
114	Scott McGregor	.08	.06	.03
115	Ken Singleton	.10	.08	.04
116	Gary Roenicke	.06	.05	.02
117	Dave Revering	.06	.05	.02
118	Mike Norris	.06	.05	.02
119	Rickey Henderson	5.00	3.75	2.00
120	Mike Heath	.06	.05	.02
121	Dave Cash	.06	.05	.02
122	Randy Jones	.08	.06	.03
123	Eric Rasmussen	.06	.05	.02
124	Jerry Mumphrey	.06	.05	.02
125	Richie Hebner	.06	.05	.02
126	Mark Wagner	.06	.05	.02
127	Jack Morris	.30	.25	.12
128	Dan Petry	.08	.06	.03
129	Bruce Robbins	.06	.05	.02
130	Champ Summers	.06	.05	.02
131a	Pete Rose ("...see card 251." on back)	2.25	1.75	.90
131b	Pete Rose ("...see card 371." on back)	1.25	.90	.50
132	Willie Stargell	.40	.30	.15
133	Ed Ott	.06	.05	.02
134	Jim Bibby	.06	.05	.02
135	Bert Blyleven	.12	.09	.05
136	Dave Parker	.30	.25	.12
137	Bill Robinson	.06	.05	.02
138	Enos Cabell	.06	.05	.02
139	Dave Bergman	.06	.05	.02
140	J R Richard	.10	.08	.04
141	Ken Forsch	.06	.05	.02
142	Larry Bowa	.15	.11	.06
143	Frank LaCorte (photo actually Randy Niemann)	.06	.05	.02
144	Dennis Walling	.06	.05	.02
145	Buddy Bell	.12	.09	.05
146	Ferguson Jenkins	.20	.15	.08
147	Danny Darwin	.06	.05	.02
148	John Grubb	.06	.05	.02
149	Alfredo Griffin	.08	.06	.03
150	Jerry Garvin	.06	.05	.02
151	*Paul Mirabella*(FC)	.10	.08	.04
152	Rick Bosetti	.06	.05	.02
153	Dick Ruthven	.06	.05	.02
154	Frank Taveras	.06	.05	.02
155	Craig Swan	.06	.05	.02
156	*Jeff Reardon*	.90	.70	.35
157	Steve Henderson	.06	.05	.02
158	Jim Morrison	.06	.05	.02
159	Glenn Borgmann	.06	.05	.02
160	*Lamarr Hoyt (LaMarr)*	.10	.08	.04
161	Rich Wortham	.06	.05	.02
162	Thad Bosley	.06	.05	.02
163	Julio Cruz	.06	.05	.02
164a	Del Unser (no 3B in stat heads)	1.00	.70	.40
164b	Del Unser (3B in stat heads)	.10	.08	.04
165	Jim Anderson	.06	.05	.02
166	Jim Beattie	.06	.05	.02
167	Shane Rawley	.10	.08	.04
168	Joe Simpson	.06	.05	.02
169	Rod Carew	.70	.50	.30
170	Fred Patek	.06	.05	.02
171	Frank Tanana	.10	.08	.04
172	Alfredo Martinez	.06	.05	.02
173	Chris Knapp	.06	.05	.02
174	Joe Rudi	.10	.08	.04
175	Greg Luzinski	.15	.11	.06
176	Steve Garvey	.50	.40	.20
177	Joe Ferguson	.06	.05	.02
178	Bob Welch	.12	.09	.05
179	Dusty Baker	.10	.08	.04
180	Rudy Law	.06	.05	.02
181	Dave Concepcion	.15	.11	.06
182	Johnny Bench	.50	.40	.20
183	Mike LaCoss	.06	.05	.02
184	Ken Griffey	.12	.09	.05
185	Dave Collins	.08	.06	.03
186	Brian Asselstine	.06	.05	.02
187	Garry Templeton	.10	.08	.04
188	Mike Phillips	.06	.05	.02
189	Pete Vukovich	.08	.06	.03
190	John Urrea	.06	.05	.02
191	Tony Scott	.06	.05	.02
192	Darrell Evans	.12	.09	.05
193	Milt May	.06	.05	.02
194	Bob Knepper	.08	.06	.03
195	Randy Moffitt	.06	.05	.02
196	Larry Herndon	.08	.06	.03
197	Rick Camp	.06	.05	.02
198	Andre Thornton	.10	.08	.04
199	Tom Veryzer	.06	.05	.02
200	Gary Alexander	.06	.05	.02
201	Rick Waits	.06	.05	.02
202	Rick Manning	.06	.05	.02
203	Paul Molitor	.20	.15	.08
204	Jim Gantner	.08	.06	.03
205	Paul Mitchell	.06	.05	.02
206	Reggie Cleveland	.06	.05	.02
207	Sixto Lezcano	.06	.05	.02
208	Bruce Benedict	.06	.05	.02
209	Rodney Scott	.06	.05	.02
210	John Tamargo	.06	.05	.02
211	Bill Lee	.08	.06	.03
212	Andre Dawson	.50	.40	.20
213	Rowland Office	.06	.05	.02
214	Carl Yastrzemski	1.00	.70	.40
215	Jerry Remy	.06	.05	.02
216	Mike Torrez	.08	.06	.03
217	Skip Lockwood	.06	.05	.02
218	Fred Lynn	.20	.15	.08
219	Chris Chambliss	.08	.06	.03
220	Willie Aikens	.06	.05	.02
221	John Wathan	.08	.06	.03
222	Dan Quisenberry	.15	.11	.06
223	Willie Wilson	.15	.11	.06
224	Clint Hurdle	.06	.05	.02
225	Bob Watson	.08	.06	.03
226	Jim Spencer	.06	.05	.02
227	Ron Guidry	.25	.20	.10
228	Reggie Jackson	.90	.70	.35
229	Oscar Gamble	.08	.06	.03
230	Jeff Cox	.06	.05	.02
231	Luis Tiant	.12	.09	.05
232	Rich Dauer	.06	.05	.02
233	Dan Graham	.06	.05	.02
234	Mike Flanagan	.10	.08	.04
235	John Lowenstein	.06	.05	.02
236	Benny Ayala	.06	.05	.02
237	Wayne Gross	.06	.05	.02
238	Rick Langford	.06	.05	.02
239	Tony Armas	.10	.08	.04
240a	Bob Lacy (incorrect spelling)	1.00	.70	.40
240b	Bob Lacey (correct spelling)	.10	.08	.04
241	Gene Tenace	.08	.06	.03
242	Bob Shirley	.06	.05	.02
243	Gary Lucas	.08	.06	.03
244	Jerry Turner	.06	.05	.02
245	John Wockenfuss	.06	.05	.02
246	Stan Papi	.06	.05	.02
247	Milt Wilcox	.06	.05	.02
248	Dan Schatzeder	.06	.05	.02
249	Steve Kemp	.08	.06	.03
250	Jim Lentine	.06	.05	.02
251	Pete Rose	1.00	.70	.40
252	Bill Madlock	.12	.09	.05
253	Dale Berra	.06	.05	.02
254	Kent Tekulve	.08	.06	.03
255	Enrique Romo	.06	.05	.02
256	Mike Easler	.08	.06	.03
257	Chuck Tanner	.06	.05	.02
258	Art Howe	.06	.05	.02
259	Alan Ashby	.06	.05	.02
260	Nolan Ryan	2.00	1.50	.80
261a	Vern Ruhle (Ken Forsch photo - head shot)	1.25	.90	.50
261b	Vern Ruhle (Vern Ruhle photo - waist to head shot)	.10	.08	.04
262	Bob Boone	.10	.08	.04
263	Cesar Cedeno	.12	.09	.05
264	Jeff Leonard	.12	.09	.05
265	Pat Putnam	.06	.05	.02
266	Jon Matlack	.08	.06	.03
267	Dave Rajsich	.06	.05	.02
268	Billy Sample	.06	.05	.02
269	*Damaso Garcia*	.10	.08	.04
270	Tom Buskey	.06	.05	.02
271	Joey McLaughlin	.06	.05	.02
272	Barry Bonnell	.06	.05	.02
273	Tug McGraw	.10	.08	.04
274	Mike Jorgensen	.06	.05	.02
275	Pat Zachry	.06	.05	.02
276	Neil Allen	.08	.06	.03
277	Joel Youngblood	.06	.05	.02
278	Greg Pryor	.06	.05	.02
279	*Britt Burns*	.10	.08	.04
280	*Rich Dotson*	.35	.25	.14
281	Chet Lemon	.08	.06	.03
282	Rusty Kuntz	.06	.05	.02
283	Ted Cox	.06	.05	.02
284	Sparky Lyle	.10	.08	.04
285	Larry Cox	.06	.05	.02
286	Floyd Bannister	.10	.08	.04
287	Byron McLaughlin	.06	.05	.02
288	Rodney Craig	.06	.05	.02
289	Bobby Grich	.10	.08	.04
290	Dickie Thon	.08	.06	.03
291	Mark Clear	.06	.05	.02

		MT	NR MT	EX
292	Dave Lemanczyk	.06	.05	.02
293	Jason Thompson	.06	.05	.02
294	Rick Miller	.06	.05	.02
295	Lonnie Smith	.08	.06	.03
296	Ron Cey	.12	.09	.05
297	Steve Yeager	.06	.05	.02
298	Bobby Castillo	.06	.05	.02
299	Manny Mota	.08	.06	.03
300	Jay Johnstone	.08	.06	.03
301	Dan Driessen	.08	.06	.03
302	Joe Nolan	.06	.05	.02
303	Paul Householder	.06	.05	.02
304	Harry Spilman	.06	.05	.02
305	Cesar Geronimo	.06	.05	.02
306a	Gary Mathews (Mathews on front)	1.25	.90	.50
306b	Gary Matthews (Matthews on front)	.10	.08	.04
307	Ken Reitz	.06	.05	.02
308	Ted Simmons	.12	.09	.05
309	John Littlefield	.06	.05	.02
310	George Frazier	.06	.05	.02
311	Dane Iorg	.06	.05	.02
312	Mike Ivie	.06	.05	.02
313	Dennis Littlejohn	.06	.05	.02
314	Gary LaVelle (Lavelle)	.06	.05	.02
315	Jack Clark	.25	.20	.10
316	Jim Wohlford	.06	.05	.02
317	Rick Matula	.06	.05	.02
318	Toby Harrah	.08	.06	.03
319a	Dwane Kuiper (Dwane on front)	1.00	.70	.40
319b	Duane Kuiper (Duane on front)	.10	.08	.04
320	Len Barker	.08	.06	.03
321	Victor Cruz	.06	.05	.02
322	Dell Alston	.06	.05	.02
323	Robin Yount	1.25	.90	.50
324	Charlie Moore	.06	.05	.02
325	Lary Sorensen	.06	.05	.02
326a	Gorman Thomas ("...30-HR mark 4th..." on back)	1.25	.90	.50
326b	Gorman Thomas ("...30-HR mark 3rd..." on back)	.10	.08	.04
327	Bob Rodgers	.08	.06	.03
328	Phil Niekro	.30	.25	.12
329	Chris Speier	.06	.05	.02
330a	Steve Rodgers (Rodgers on front)	1.00	.70	.40
330b	Steve Rogers (Rogers on front)	.10	.08	.04
331	Woodie Fryman	.08	.06	.03
332	Warren Cromartie	.06	.05	.02
333	Jerry White	.06	.05	.02
334	Tony Perez	.20	.15	.08
335	Carlton Fisk	.50	.40	.20
336	Dick Drago	.06	.05	.02
337	Steve Renko	.06	.05	.02
338	Jim Rice	.50	.40	.20
339	Jerry Royster	.06	.05	.02
340	Frank White	.10	.08	.04
341	Jamie Quirk	.06	.05	.02
342a	Paul Spittorff (Spittorff on front)	1.00	.70	.40
342b	Paul Splittorff (Splittorff on front)	.08	.06	.03
343	Marty Pattin	.06	.05	.02
344	Pete LaCock	.06	.05	.02
345	Willie Randolph	.10	.08	.04
346	Rick Cerone	.06	.05	.02
347	Rich Gossage	.20	.15	.08
348	Reggie Jackson	.70	.50	.30
349	Ruppert Jones	.06	.05	.02
350	Dave McKay	.06	.05	.02
351	Yogi Berra	.15	.11	.06
352	Doug Decinces (DeCinces)	.10	.08	.04
353	Jim Palmer	.70	.50	.30
354	Tippy Martinez	.06	.05	.02
355	Al Bumbry	.08	.06	.03
356	Earl Weaver	.10	.08	.04
357a	Bob Picciolo (Bob on front)	1.00	.70	.40
357b	Rob Picciolo (Rob on front)	.10	.08	.04
358	Matt Keough	.06	.05	.02
359	Dwayne Murphy	.08	.06	.03
360	Brian Kingman	.06	.05	.02
361	Bill Fahey	.06	.05	.02
362	Steve Mura	.06	.05	.02
363	Dennis Kinney	.06	.05	.02
364	Dave Winfield	.50	.40	.20
365	Lou Whitaker	.40	.30	.15
366	Lance Parrish	.35	.25	.14
367	Tim Corcoran	.06	.05	.02
368	Pat Underwood	.06	.05	.02
369	Al Cowens	.06	.05	.02
370	Sparky Anderson	.10	.08	.04
371	Pete Rose	1.00	.70	.40
372	Phil Garner	.08	.06	.03
373	Steve Nicosia	.06	.05	.02
374	John Candelaria	.10	.08	.04
375	Don Robinson	.08	.06	.03
376	Lee Lacy	.06	.05	.02
377	John Milner	.06	.05	.02
378	Craig Reynolds	.06	.05	.02
379a	Luis Pujois (Pujois on front)	1.00	.70	.40
379b	Luis Pujols (Pujols on front)	.10	.08	.04
380	Joe Niekro	.12	.09	.05
381	Joaquin Andujar	.10	.08	.04
382	*Keith Moreland*	.35	.25	.14
383	Jose Cruz	.12	.09	.05
384	Bill Virdon	.06	.05	.02
385	Jim Sundberg	.08	.06	.03
386	Doc Medich	.06	.05	.02
387	Al Oliver	.15	.11	.06
388	Jim Norris	.06	.05	.02
389	Bob Bailor	.06	.05	.02
390	Ernie Whitt	.08	.06	.03
391	Otto Velez	.06	.05	.02
392	Roy Howell	.06	.05	.02
393	*Bob Walk*	.25	.20	.10
394	Doug Flynn	.06	.05	.02
395	Pete Falcone	.06	.05	.02
396	Tom Hausman	.06	.05	.02
397	Elliott Maddox	.06	.05	.02
398	Mike Squires	.06	.05	.02
399	Marvis Foley	.06	.05	.02
400	Steve Trout	.06	.05	.02
401	Wayne Nordhagen	.06	.05	.02
402	Tony Larussa (LaRussa)	.08	.06	.03
403	Bruce Bochte	.06	.05	.02
404	Bake McBride	.06	.05	.02
405	Jerry Narron	.06	.05	.02
406	Rob Dressler	.06	.05	.02
407	Dave Heaverlo	.06	.05	.02
408	Tom Paciorek	.06	.05	.02
409	Carney Lansford	.10	.08	.04
410	Brian Downing	.10	.08	.04
411	Don Aase	.06	.05	.02
412	Jim Barr	.06	.05	.02
413	Don Baylor	.12	.09	.05
414	Jim Fregosi	.08	.06	.03
415	Dallas Green	.08	.06	.03
416	Dave Lopes	.10	.08	.04
417	Jerry Reuss	.10	.08	.04
418	Rick Sutcliffe	.20	.15	.08
419	Derrel Thomas	.06	.05	.02
420	Tommy LaSorda (Lasorda)	.10	.08	.04
421	*Charlie Leibrandt*	.30	.25	.12
422	Tom Seaver	.60	.45	.25
423	Ron Oester	.06	.05	.02
424	Junior Kennedy	.06	.05	.02
425	Tom Seaver	.60	.45	.25
426	Bobby Cox	.06	.05	.02
427	*Leon Durham*	.20	.15	.08
428	Terry Kennedy	.08	.06	.03
429	Silvio Martinez	.06	.05	.02
430	George Hendrick	.08	.06	.03
431	Red Schoendienst	.08	.06	.03
432	John LeMaster	.06	.05	.02
433	Vida Blue	.12	.09	.05
434	John Montefusco	.08	.06	.03
435	Terry Whitfield	.06	.05	.02
436	Dave Bristol	.06	.05	.02
437	Dale Murphy	.90	.70	.35
438	Jerry Dybzinski	.06	.05	.02
439	Jorge Orta	.06	.05	.02
440	Wayne Garland	.06	.05	.02
441	Miguel Dilone	.06	.05	.02
442	Dave Garcia	.06	.05	.02
443	Don Money	.06	.05	.02
444a	Buck Martinez (photo reversed)	1.00	.70	.40
444b	Buck Martinez (photo correct)	.10	.08	.04
445	Jerry Augustine	.06	.05	.02
446	Ben Oglivie	.08	.06	.03
447	Jim Slaton	.06	.05	.02
448	Doyle Alexander	.10	.08	.04
449	Tony Bernazard	.06	.05	.02
450	Scott Sanderson	.06	.05	.02
451	Dave Palmer	.06	.05	.02
452	Stan Bahnsen	.06	.05	.02
453	Dick Williams	.06	.05	.02
454	Rick Burleson	.08	.06	.03
455	Gary Allenson	.06	.05	.02
456	Bob Stanley	.06	.05	.02
457a	*John Tudor* (lifetime W/L 9.7)	1.50	1.25	.60
457b	*John Tudor* (lifetime W/L 9-7)	1.00	.70	.40
458	Dwight Evans	.15	.11	.06
459	Glenn Hubbard	.08	.06	.03
460	U L Washington	.06	.05	.02
461	Larry Gura	.06	.05	.02
462	Rich Gale	.06	.05	.02
463	Hal McRae	.10	.08	.04
464	Jim Frey	.06	.05	.02
465	Bucky Dent	.10	.08	.04
466	Dennis Werth	.06	.05	.02
467	Ron Davis	.08	.06	.03
468	Reggie Jackson	.70	.50	.30
469	Bobby Brown	.06	.05	.02
470	*Mike Davis*	.25	.20	.10
471	Gaylord Perry	.30	.25	.12
472	Mark Belanger	.08	.06	.03
473	Jim Palmer	.70	.50	.30
474	Sammy Stewart	.06	.05	.02
475	Tim Stoddard	.06	.05	.02
476	Steve Stone	.08	.06	.03
477	Jeff Newman	.06	.05	.02
478	Steve McCatty	.06	.05	.02
479	Billy Martin	.12	.09	.05
480	Mitchell Page	.06	.05	.02
481	Cy Young 1980 (Steve Carlton)	.35	.25	.14
482	Bill Buckner	.12	.09	.05
483a	Ivan DeJesus (lifetime hits 702)	1.00	.70	.40
483b	Ivan DeJesus (lifetime hits 642)	.10	.08	.04
484	Cliff Johnson	.06	.05	.02
485	Lenny Randle	.06	.05	.02
486	Larry Milbourne	.06	.05	.02
487	Roy Smalley	.06	.05	.02
488	John Castino	.06	.05	.02
489	Ron Jackson	.06	.05	.02
490a	Dave Roberts (1980 highlights begins "Showed pop...")	1.00	.70	.40
490b	Dave Roberts (1980 highlights begins "Declared himself...")	.10	.08	.04
491	MVP (George Brett)	.60	.45	.25
492	Mike Cubbage	.06	.05	.02
493	Rob Wilfong	.06	.05	.02
494	Danny Goodwin	.06	.05	.02
495	Jose Morales	.06	.05	.02
496	Mickey Rivers	.08	.06	.03
497	Mike Edwards	.06	.05	.02
498	Mike Sadek	.06	.05	.02
499	Lenn Sakata	.06	.05	.02
500	Gene Michael	.06	.05	.02
501	Dave Roberts	.06	.05	.02
502	Steve Dillard	.06	.05	.02
503	Jim Essian	.06	.05	.02
504	Rance Mulliniks	.06	.05	.02
505	Darrell Porter	.08	.06	.03
506	Joe Torre	.08	.06	.03
507	Terry Crowley	.06	.05	.02
508	Bill Travers	.06	.05	.02
509	Nelson Norman	.06	.05	.02
510	Bob McClure	.06	.05	.02
511	*Steve Howe*	.10	.08	.04
512	Dave Rader	.06	.05	.02
513	Mick Kelleher	.06	.05	.02
514	Kiko Garcia	.06	.05	.02
515	Larry Biittner	.06	.05	.02
516a	Willie Norwood (1980 highlights begins "Spent most...")	1.00	.70	.40
516b	Willie Norwood (1980 highlights begins "Traded to...")	.10	.08	.04
517	Bo Diaz	.08	.06	.03
518	Juan Beniquez	.06	.05	.02
519	Scot Thompson	.06	.05	.02
520	Jim Tracy	.06	.05	.02
521	Carlos Lezcano	.06	.05	.02
522	Joe Amalfitano	.06	.05	.02
523	Preston Hanna	.06	.05	.02
524a	Ray Burris (1980 highlights begins "Went on...")	1.00	.70	.40
524b	Ray Burris (1980 highlights begins "Drafted by...")	.10	.08	.04
525	Broderick Perkins	.06	.05	.02
526	Mickey Hatcher	.08	.06	.03
527	John Goryl	.06	.05	.02
528	Dick Davis	.06	.05	.02
529	Butch Wynegar	.06	.05	.02
530	Sal Butera	.06	.05	.02
531	Jerry Koosman	.10	.08	.04
532a	Jeff Zahn (Geoff) (1980 highlights begins "Was 2nd in...")	1.00	.70	.40
532b	Jeff Zahn (Geoff) (1980 highlights begins "Signed a 3 year...")	.10	.08	.04
533	Dennis Martinez	.08	.06	.03
534	Gary Thomasson	.06	.05	.02
535	Steve Macko	.06	.05	.02
536	Jim Kaat	.15	.11	.06
537	Best Hitters (George Brett, Rod Carew)	1.50	1.25	.60
538	*Tim Raines*	5.00	3.75	2.00
539	Keith Smith	.06	.05	.02
540	Ken Macha	.06	.05	.02
541	Burt Hooton	.08	.06	.03
542	Butch Hobson	.06	.05	.02
543	Bill Stein	.06	.05	.02
544	Dave Stapleton	.06	.05	.02
545	Bob Pate	.06	.05	.02
546	Doug Corbett	.06	.05	.02
547	Darrell Jackson	.06	.05	.02
548	Pete Redfern	.06	.05	.02
549	Roger Erickson	.06	.05	.02
550	Al Hrabosky	.08	.06	.03
551	Dick Tidrow	.06	.05	.02
552	Dave Ford	.06	.05	.02
553	Dave Kingman	.15	.11	.06
554a	Mike Vail (1980 highlights begins "After...")	1.00	.70	.40
554b	Mike Vail (1980 highlights begins "Traded...")	.10	.08	.04
555a	Jerry Martin (1980 highlights begins "Overcame...")	1.00	.70	.40
555b	Jerry Martin (1980 highlights begins "Traded...")	.10	.08	.04
556a	Jesus Figueroa (1980 highlights begins "Had...")	1.00	.70	.40
556b	Jesus Figueroa (1980 highlights begins "Traded...")	.10	.08	.04
557	Don Stanhouse	.06	.05	.02
558	Barry Foote	.06	.05	.02
559	Tim Blackwell	.06	.05	.02
560	Bruce Sutter	.15	.11	.06
561	Rick Reuschel	.10	.08	.04
562	Lynn McGlothen	.06	.05	.02
563a	Bob Owchinko (1980 highlights begins "Traded...")	1.00	.70	.40
563b	Bob Owchinko (1980 highlights begins "Involved...")	.10	.08	.04
564	John Verhoeven	.06	.05	.02
565	Ken Landreaux	.06	.05	.02
566a	Glen Adams (Glen on front)	1.00	.70	.40
566b	Glenn Adams (Glenn on front)	.10	.08	.04
567	Hosken Powell	.06	.05	.02
568	Dick Noles	.06	.05	.02
569	*Danny Ainge*	.25	.20	.10
570	Bobby Mattick	.06	.05	.02
571	Joe LeFebvre (Lefebvre)	.06	.05	.02
572	Bobby Clark	.06	.05	.02
573	Dennis Lamp	.06	.05	.02
574	Randy Lerch	.06	.05	.02
575	*Mookie Wilson*	.60	.45	.25
576	Ron LeFlore	.08	.06	.03
577	Jim Dwyer	.06	.05	.02
578	Bill Castro	.06	.05	.02
579	Greg Minton	.06	.05	.02
580	Mark Littell	.06	.05	.02
581	Andy Hassler	.06	.05	.02
582	Dave Stieb	.20	.15	.08
583	Ken Oberkfell	.06	.05	.02
584	Larry Bradford	.06	.05	.02
585	Fred Stanley	.06	.05	.02
586	Bill Caudill	.06	.05	.02
587	Doug Capilla	.06	.05	.02
588	George Riley	.06	.05	.02
589	Willie Hernandez	.10	.08	.04
590	MVP (Mike Schmidt)	.80	.60	.30
591	Cy Young 1980 (Steve Stone)	.08	.06	.03
592	Rick Sofield	.06	.05	.02
593	Bombo Rivera	.06	.05	.02
594	Gary Ward	.08	.06	.03
595a	Dave Edwards (1980 highlights begins "Sidelined...")	1.00	.70	.40
595b	Dave Edwards (1980 highlights begins "Traded...")	.10	.08	.04
596	Mike Proly	.06	.05	.02
597	Tommy Boggs	.06	.05	.02
598	Greg Gross	.06	.05	.02
599	Elias Sosa	.06	.05	.02
600	Pat Kelly	.06	.05	.02
---a	Checklist 1-120 (51 Tom Donohue)	2.00	1.50	.80
---b	Checklist 1-120 (51 Tom Donahue)	.10	.08	.04
---	Checklist 121-240	.06	.05	.02
---a	Checklist 241-360 (306 Gary Mathews)	.70	.50	.30
---b	Checklist 241-360 (306 Gary Matthews)	.10	.08	.04
---a	Checklist 361-480 (379 Luis Pujois)	.70	.50	.30

		MT	NR MT	EX
---b	Checklist 361-480 (379 Luis Pujols)	.10	.08	.04
---a	Checklist 481-600 (566 Glen Adams)	.70	.50	.30
---b	Checklist 481-600 (566 Glenn Adams)	.10	.08	.04

1982 Donruss

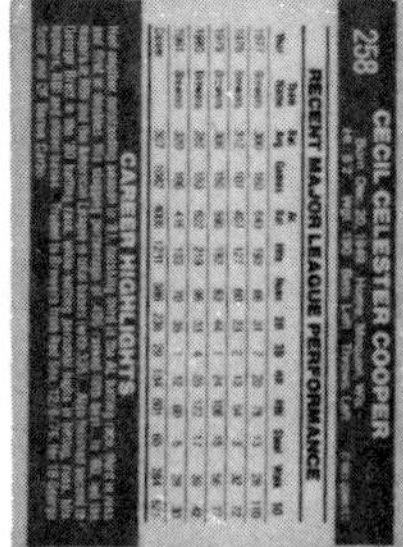

Using card stock thicker than the previous year, Donruss issued a 660-card set which includes 653 numbered cards and seven unnumbered checklists. The cards, which measure 2-1/2" by 3-1/2", were sold with puzzle pieces rather than gum as a result of a lawsuit by Topps. The puzzle pieces (three pieces on one card per pack) feature Babe Ruth. The first 26 cards of the set, entitled Diamond Kings, showcase the artwork of Dick Perez of Perez-Steele Galleries. The card fronts display the Donruss logo and the year of issue. The card backs have black and blue ink on white stock and include the player's career highlights. The complete set price does not include the higher priced variations.

		MT	NR MT	EX
	Complete Set:	40.00	30.00	15.00
	Common Player:	.06	.05	.02
1	Pete Rose (DK)	1.50	1.25	.60
2	Gary Carter (DK)	.50	.40	.20
3	Steve Garvey (DK)	.50	.40	.20
4	Vida Blue (DK)	.12	.09	.05
5a	Alan Trammel (DK) (name incorrect)	1.50	1.25	.60
5b	Alan Trammell (DK) (name correct)	.40	.30	.15
6	Len Barker (DK)	.08	.06	.03
7	Dwight Evans (DK)	.15	.11	.06
8	Rod Carew (DK)	.50	.40	.20
9	George Hendrick (DK)	.08	.06	.03
10	Phil Niekro (DK)	.30	.25	.12
11	Richie Zisk (DK)	.08	.06	.03
12	Dave Parker (DK)	.30	.25	.12
13	Nolan Ryan (DK)	1.00	.70	.40
14	Ivan DeJesus (DK)	.08	.06	.03
15	George Brett (DK)	.70	.50	.30
16	Tom Seaver (DK)	.50	.40	.20
17	Dave Kingman (DK)	.15	.11	.06
18	Dave Winfield (DK)	.50	.40	.20
19	Mike Norris (DK)	.08	.06	.03
20	Carlton Fisk (DK)	.25	.20	.10
21	Ozzie Smith (DK)	.20	.15	.08
22	Roy Smalley (DK)	.08	.06	.03
23	Buddy Bell (DK)	.12	.09	.05
24	Ken Singleton (DK)	.10	.08	.04
25	John Mayberry (DK)	.08	.06	.03
26	Gorman Thomas (DK)	.10	.08	.04
27	Earl Weaver	.10	.08	.04
28	Rollie Fingers	.20	.15	.08
29	Sparky Anderson	.10	.08	.04
30	Dennis Eckersley	.12	.09	.05
31	Dave Winfield	.50	.40	.20
32	Burt Hooton	.08	.06	.03
33	Rick Waits	.06	.05	.02
34	George Brett	.70	.50	.30
35	Steve McCatty	.06	.05	.02
36	Steve Rogers	.08	.06	.03
37	Bill Stein	.06	.05	.02
38	Steve Renko	.06	.05	.02
39	Mike Squires	.06	.05	.02
40	George Hendrick	.08	.06	.03
41	Bob Knepper	.08	.06	.03
42	Steve Carlton	.50	.40	.20
43	Larry Biittner	.06	.05	.02
44	Chris Welsh	.06	.05	.02
45	Steve Nicosia	.06	.05	.02
46	Jack Clark	.25	.20	.10
47	Chris Chambliss	.08	.06	.03
48	Ivan DeJesus	.06	.05	.02
49	Lee Mazzilli	.08	.06	.03
50	Julio Cruz	.06	.05	.02
51	Pete Redfern	.06	.05	.02
52	Dave Stieb	.12	.09	.05
53	Doug Corbett	.06	.05	.02
54	*Jorge Bell*(FC)	7.00	5.25	2.75
55	Joe Simpson	.06	.05	.02
56	Rusty Staub	.10	.08	.04
57	Hector Cruz	.06	.05	.02
58	Claudell Washington(FC)	.10	.08	.04
59	Enrique Romo	.06	.05	.02
60	Gary Lavelle	.06	.05	.02
61	Tim Flannery	.06	.05	.02
62	Joe Nolan	.06	.05	.02
63	Larry Bowa	.15	.11	.06
64	Sixto Lezcano	.06	.05	.02
65	Joe Sambito	.06	.05	.02
66	Bruce Kison	.06	.05	.02
67	Wayne Nordhagen	.06	.05	.02
68	Woodie Fryman	.08	.06	.03
69	Billy Sample	.06	.05	.02
70	Amos Otis	.08	.06	.03
71	Matt Keough	.06	.05	.02
72	Toby Harrah	.08	.06	.03
73	*Dave Righetti*(FC)	2.00	1.50	.80
74	Carl Yastrzemski	.80	.60	.30
75	Bob Welch	.12	.09	.05
76a	Alan Trammel (name incorrect)	1.25	.90	.50
76b	Alan Trammell (name correct)	.40	.30	.15
77	Rick Dempsey	.08	.06	.03
78	Paul Molitor	.20	.15	.08
79	Dennis Martinez	.08	.06	.03
80	Jim Slaton	.06	.05	.02
81	Champ Summers	.06	.05	.02
82	Carney Lansford	.08	.06	.03
83	Barry Foote	.06	.05	.02
84	Steve Garvey	.50	.40	.20
85	Rick Manning	.06	.05	.02
86	John Wathan	.08	.06	.03
87	Brian Kingman	.06	.05	.02
88	Andre Dawson	.40	.30	.15
89	Jim Kern	.06	.05	.02
90	Bobby Grich	.10	.08	.04
91	Bob Forsch	.08	.06	.03
92	Art Howe	.06	.05	.02
93	Marty Bystrom	.06	.05	.02
94	Ozzie Smith	.20	.15	.08
95	Dave Parker	.30	.25	.12
96	Doyle Alexander	.10	.08	.04
97	Al Hrabosky	.08	.06	.03
98	Frank Taveras	.06	.05	.02
99	Tim Blackwell	.06	.05	.02
100	Floyd Bannister	.10	.08	.04
101	Alfredo Griffin	.08	.06	.03
102	Dave Engle	.06	.05	.02
103	Mario Soto	.08	.06	.03
104	Ross Baumgarten	.06	.05	.02
105	Ken Singleton	.10	.08	.04
106	Ted Simmons	.12	.09	.05
107	Jack Morris	.30	.25	.12
108	Bob Watson	.08	.06	.03
109	Dwight Evans	.15	.11	.06
110	Tom Lasorda	.10	.08	.04
111	Bert Blyleven	.12	.09	.05
112	Dan Quisenberry	.15	.11	.06
113	Rickey Henderson	2.00	1.50	.80
114	Gary Carter	.35	.25	.14
115	Brian Downing	.10	.08	.04
116	Al Oliver	.15	.11	.06
117	LaMarr Hoyt	.06	.05	.02
118	Cesar Cedeno	.12	.09	.05
119	Keith Moreland	.10	.08	.04
120	Bob Shirley	.06	.05	.02
121	Terry Kennedy	.08	.06	.03
122	Frank Pastore	.06	.05	.02
123	Gene Garber	.06	.05	.02
124	Tony Pena(FC)	.25	.20	.10
125	Allen Ripley	.06	.05	.02
126	Randy Martz	.06	.05	.02
127	Richie Zisk	.08	.06	.03
128	Mike Scott	.15	.11	.06
129	Lloyd Moseby(FC)	.20	.15	.08
130	Rob Wilfong	.06	.05	.02
131	Tim Stoddard	.06	.05	.02
132	Gorman Thomas	.10	.08	.04
133	Dan Petry	.08	.06	.03
134	Bob Stanley	.06	.05	.02
135	Lou Piniella	.12	.09	.05
136	Pedro Guerrero(FC)	.70	.50	.30
137	Len Barker	.08	.06	.03
138	Richard Gale	.06	.05	.02
139	Wayne Gross	.06	.05	.02
140	*Tim Wallach*(FC)	1.50	1.25	.60
141	Gene Mauch	.08	.06	.03
142	Doc Medich	.06	.05	.02
143	Tony Bernazard	.06	.05	.02
144	Bill Virdon	.06	.05	.02
145	John Littlefield	.06	.05	.02
146	Dave Bergman	.06	.05	.02
147	Dick Davis	.06	.05	.02
148	Tom Seaver	.60	.45	.25
149	Matt Sinatro	.06	.05	.02
150	Chuck Tanner	.06	.05	.02
151	Leon Durham	.08	.06	.03
152	Gene Tenace	.08	.06	.03
153	Al Bumbry	.08	.06	.03
154	Mark Brouhard	.06	.05	.02
155	Rick Peters	.06	.05	.02
156	Jerry Remy	.06	.05	.02
157	Rick Reuschel	.10	.08	.04
158	Steve Howe	.08	.06	.03
159	Alan Bannister	.06	.05	.02
160	U L Washington	.06	.05	.02
161	Rick Langford	.06	.05	.02
162	Bill Gullickson	.08	.06	.03
163	Mark Wagner	.06	.05	.02
164	Geoff Zahn	.06	.05	.02
165	Ron LeFlore	.08	.06	.03
166	Dane Iorg	.06	.05	.02
167	Joe Niekro	.12	.09	.05
168	Pete Rose	1.00	.70	.40
169	Dave Collins	.08	.06	.03
170	Rick Wise	.08	.06	.03
171	Jim Bibby	.06	.05	.02
172	Larry Herndon	.08	.06	.03
173	Bob Horner	.12	.09	.05
174	Steve Dillard	.06	.05	.02
175	Mookie Wilson	.12	.09	.05
176	Dan Meyer	.06	.05	.02
177	Fernando Arroyo	.06	.05	.02
178	Jackson Todd	.06	.05	.02
179	Darrell Jackson	.06	.05	.02
180	Al Woods	.06	.05	.02
181	Jim Anderson	.06	.05	.02
182	Dave Kingman	.15	.11	.06
183	Steve Henderson	.06	.05	.02
184	Brian Asselstine	.06	.05	.02
185	Rod Scurry	.06	.05	.02
186	Fred Breining	.06	.05	.02
187	Danny Boone	.06	.05	.02
188	Junior Kennedy	.06	.05	.02
189	Sparky Lyle	.10	.08	.04
190	Whitey Herzog	.08	.06	.03
191	Dave Smith	.10	.08	.04
192	Ed Ott	.06	.05	.02
193	Greg Luzinski	.15	.11	.06
194	Bill Lee	.08	.06	.03
195	Don Zimmer	.06	.05	.02
196	Hal McRae	.12	.09	.05
197	Mike Norris	.06	.05	.02
198	Duane Kuiper	.06	.05	.02
199	Rick Cerone	.06	.05	.02
200	Jim Rice	.40	.30	.15
201	Steve Yeager	.06	.05	.02
202	Tom Brookens	.06	.05	.02
203	Jose Morales	.06	.05	.02
204	Roy Howell	.06	.05	.02
205	Tippy Martinez	.06	.05	.02
206	Moose Haas	.06	.05	.02
207	Al Cowens	.06	.05	.02
208	Dave Stapleton	.06	.05	.02
209	Bucky Dent	.10	.08	.04
210	Ron Cey	.12	.09	.05
211	Jorge Orta	.06	.05	.02
212	Jamie Quirk	.06	.05	.02
213	Jeff Jones	.06	.05	.02
214	Tim Raines	1.00	.70	.40
215	Jon Matlack	.08	.06	.03
216	Rod Carew	.50	.40	.20
217	Jim Kaat	.15	.11	.06
218	Joe Pittman	.06	.05	.02
219	Larry Christenson	.06	.05	.02
220	Juan Bonilla	.06	.05	.02
221	Mike Easler	.08	.06	.03
222	Vida Blue	.12	.09	.05
223	Rick Camp	.06	.05	.02
224	Mike Jorgensen	.06	.05	.02
225	*Jody Davis*(FC)	.30	.25	.12
226	Mike Parrott	.06	.05	.02
227	Jim Clancy	.08	.06	.03
228	Hosken Powell	.06	.05	.02
229	Tom Hume	.06	.05	.02
230	Britt Burns	.06	.05	.02
231	Jim Palmer	.70	.50	.30
232	Bob Rodgers	.08	.06	.03
233	Milt Wilcox	.06	.05	.02
234	Dave Revering	.06	.05	.02
235	Mike Torrez	.08	.06	.03
236	Robert Castillo	.06	.05	.02
237	*Von Hayes*(FC)	1.25	.90	.50
238	Renie Martin	.06	.05	.02
239	Dwayne Murphy	.08	.06	.03
240	Rodney Scott	.06	.05	.02
241	Fred Patek	.06	.05	.02
242	Mickey Rivers	.08	.06	.03
243	Steve Trout	.06	.05	.02
244	Jose Cruz	.12	.09	.05
245	Manny Trillo	.08	.06	.03
246	Lary Sorensen	.06	.05	.02
247	Dave Edwards	.06	.05	.02
248	Dan Driessen	.08	.06	.03
249	Tommy Boggs	.06	.05	.02
250	Dale Berra	.06	.05	.02
251	Ed Whitson	.06	.05	.02
252	*Lee Smith*(FC)	.70	.50	.30
253	Tom Paciorek	.06	.05	.02
254	Pat Zachry	.06	.05	.02
255	Luis Leal	.06	.05	.02
256	John Castino	.06	.05	.02
257	Rich Dauer	.06	.05	.02
258	Cecil Cooper	.15	.11	.06
259	Dave Rozema	.06	.05	.02
260	John Tudor	.15	.11	.06
261	Jerry Mumphrey	.06	.05	.02
262	Jay Johnstone	.08	.06	.03
263	Bo Diaz	.08	.06	.03
264	Dennis Leonard	.08	.06	.03
265	Jim Spencer	.06	.05	.02
266	John Milner	.06	.05	.02
267	Don Aase	.06	.05	.02
268	Jim Sundberg	.08	.06	.03
269	Lamar Johnson	.06	.05	.02
270	Frank LaCorte	.06	.05	.02
271	Barry Evans	.06	.05	.02
272	Enos Cabell	.06	.05	.02
273	Del Unser	.06	.05	.02
274	George Foster	.20	.15	.08
275	*Brett Butler*(FC)	.80	.60	.30
276	Lee Lacy	.06	.05	.02
277	Ken Reitz	.06	.05	.02
278	Keith Hernandez	.40	.30	.15
279	Doug DeCinces	.10	.08	.04
280	Charlie Moore	.06	.05	.02
281	Lance Parrish	.35	.25	.14
282	Ralph Houk	.08	.06	.03
283	Rich Gossage	.20	.15	.08
284	Jerry Reuss	.10	.08	.04
285	Mike Stanton	.06	.05	.02
286	Frank White	.10	.08	.04
287	Bob Owchinko	.06	.05	.02
288	Scott Sanderson	.06	.05	.02
289	Bump Wills	.06	.05	.02
290	Dave Frost	.06	.05	.02
291	Chet Lemon	.08	.06	.03
292	Tito Landrum	.06	.05	.02
293	Vern Ruhle	.06	.05	.02
294	Mike Schmidt	1.00	.90	.50
295	Sam Mejias	.06	.05	.02
296	Gary Lucas	.06	.05	.02
297	John Candelaria	.10	.08	.04
298	Jerry Martin	.06	.05	.02
299	Dale Murphy	.90	.70	.35
300	Mike Lum	.06	.05	.02
301	Tom Hausman	.06	.05	.02
302	Glenn Abbott	.06	.05	.02
303	Roger Erickson	.06	.05	.02
304	Otto Velez	.06	.05	.02
305	Danny Goodwin	.06	.05	.02
306	John Mayberry	.08	.06	.03
307	Lenny Randle	.06	.05	.02

		MT	NR MT	EX
308	Bob Bailor	.06	.05	.02
309	Jerry Morales	.06	.05	.02
310	Rufino Linares	.06	.05	.02
311	Kent Tekulve	.08	.06	.03
312	Joe Morgan	.50	.40	.20
313	John Urrea	.06	.05	.02
314	Paul Householder	.06	.05	.02
315	Garry Maddox	.10	.08	.04
316	Mike Ramsey	.06	.05	.02
317	Alan Ashby	.06	.05	.02
318	Bob Clark	.06	.05	.02
319	Tony LaRussa	.08	.06	.03
320	Charlie Lea	.08	.06	.03
321	Danny Darwin	.06	.05	.02
322	Cesar Geronimo	.06	.05	.02
323	Tom Underwood	.06	.05	.02
324	Andre Thornton	.10	.08	.04
325	Rudy May	.06	.05	.02
326	Frank Tanana	.10	.08	.04
327	Davey Lopes	.10	.08	.04
328	Richie Hebner	.06	.05	.02
329	Mike Flanagan	.10	.08	.04
330	Mike Caldwell	.06	.05	.02
331	Scott McGregor	.08	.06	.03
332	Jerry Augustine	.06	.05	.02
333	Stan Papi	.06	.05	.02
334	Rick Miller	.06	.05	.02
335	Graig Nettles	.15	.11	.06
336	Dusty Baker	.10	.08	.04
337	Dave Garcia	.06	.05	.02
338	Larry Gura	.06	.05	.02
339	Cliff Johnson	.06	.05	.02
340	Warren Cromartie	.06	.05	.02
341	Steve Comer	.06	.05	.02
342	Rick Burleson	.08	.06	.03
343	John Martin	.06	.05	.02
344	Craig Reynolds	.06	.05	.02
345	Mike Proly	.06	.05	.02
346	Ruppert Jones	.06	.05	.02
347	Omar Moreno	.06	.05	.02
348	Greg Minton	.06	.05	.02
349	*Rick Mahler*(FC)	.25	.20	.10
350	Alex Trevino	.06	.05	.02
351	Mike Krukow	.08	.06	.03
352a	Shane Rawley (Jim Anderson photo - shaking hands)	1.25	.90	.50
352b	Shane Rawley (correct photo - kneeling)	.15	.11	.06
353	Garth Iorg	.06	.05	.02
354	Pete Mackanin	.06	.05	.02
355	Paul Moskau	.06	.05	.02
356	Richard Dotson	.10	.08	.04
357	Steve Stone	.08	.06	.03
358	Larry Hisle	.08	.06	.03
359	Aurelio Lopez	.06	.05	.02
360	Oscar Gamble	.08	.06	.03
361	Tom Burgmeier	.06	.05	.02
362	Terry Forster	.08	.06	.03
363	Joe Charboneau	.08	.06	.03
364	Ken Brett	.08	.06	.03
365	Tony Armas	.10	.08	.04
366	Chris Speier	.06	.05	.02
367	Fred Lynn	.20	.15	.08
368	Buddy Bell	.12	.09	.05
369	Jim Essian	.06	.05	.02
370	Terry Puhl	.06	.05	.02
371	Greg Gross	.06	.05	.02
372	Bruce Sutter	.15	.11	.06
373	Joe Lefebvre	.06	.05	.02
374	Ray Knight	.10	.08	.04
375	Bruce Benedict	.06	.05	.02
376	Tim Foli	.06	.05	.02
377	Al Holland	.06	.05	.02
378	Ken Kravec	.06	.05	.02
379	Jeff Burroughs	.08	.06	.03
380	Pete Falcone	.06	.05	.02
381	Ernie Whitt	.08	.06	.03
382	Brad Havens	.06	.05	.02
383	Terry Crowley	.06	.05	.02
384	Don Money	.06	.05	.02
385	Dan Schatzeder	.06	.05	.02
386	Gary Allenson	.06	.05	.02
387	Yogi Berra	.15	.11	.06
388	Ken Landreaux	.06	.05	.02
389	Mike Hargrove	.06	.05	.02
390	Darryl Motley	.06	.05	.02
391	Dave McKay	.06	.05	.02
392	Stan Bahnsen	.06	.05	.02
393	Ken Forsch	.06	.05	.02
394	Mario Mendoza	.06	.05	.02
395	Jim Morrison	.06	.05	.02
396	Mike Ivie	.06	.05	.02
397	Broderick Perkins	.06	.05	.02
398	Darrell Evans	.15	.11	.06
399	Ron Reed	.06	.05	.02
400	Johnny Bench	.60	.45	.25
401	*Steve Bedrosian*(FC)	.80	.60	.30
402	Bill Robinson	.06	.05	.02
403	Bill Buckner	.12	.09	.05
404	Ken Oberkfell	.06	.05	.02
405	*Cal Ripken, Jr.*(FC)	9.00	6.75	3.50
406	Jim Gantner	.08	.06	.03
407	Kirk Gibson(FC)	1.50	1.25	.60
408	Tony Perez	.20	.15	.08
409	Tommy John	.20	.15	.08
410	*Dave Stewart*(FC)	4.00	3.00	1.50
411	Dan Spillner	.06	.05	.02
412	Willie Aikens	.06	.05	.02
413	Mike Heath	.06	.05	.02
414	Ray Burris	.06	.05	.02
415	Leon Roberts	.06	.05	.02
416	*Mike Witt*(FC)	.70	.50	.30
417	Bobby Molinaro	.06	.05	.02
418	Steve Braun	.06	.05	.02
419	Nolan Ryan	2.00	1.50	.80
420	Tug McGraw	.12	.09	.05
421	Dave Concepcion	.12	.09	.05
422a	Juan Eichelberger (Gary Lucas photo - white player)	1.25	.90	.50
422b	Juan Eichelberger (correct photo - black player)	.08	.06	.03
423	Rick Rhoden	.10	.08	.04
424	Frank Robinson	.12	.09	.05

		MT	NR MT	EX
425	Eddie Miller	.06	.05	.02
426	Bill Caudill	.06	.05	.02
427	Doug Flynn	.06	.05	.02
428	Larry Anderson (Andersen)	.06	.05	.02
429	Al Williams	.06	.05	.02
430	Jerry Garvin	.06	.05	.02
431	Glenn Adams	.06	.05	.02
432	Barry Bonnell	.06	.05	.02
433	Jerry Narron	.06	.05	.02
434	John Stearns	.06	.05	.02
435	Mike Tyson	.06	.05	.02
436	Glenn Hubbard	.08	.06	.03
437	Eddie Solomon	.06	.05	.02
438	Jeff Leonard	.10	.08	.04
439	Randy Bass	.06	.05	.02
440	Mike LaCoss	.06	.05	.02
441	Gary Matthews	.10	.08	.04
442	Mark Littell	.06	.05	.02
443	Don Sutton	.30	.25	.12
444	John Harris	.06	.05	.02
445	Vada Pinson	.08	.06	.03
446	Elias Sosa	.06	.05	.02
447	Charlie Hough	.10	.08	.04
448	Willie Wilson	.15	.11	.06
449	Fred Stanley	.06	.05	.02
450	Tom Veryzer	.06	.05	.02
451	Ron Davis	.06	.05	.02
452	Mark Clear	.06	.05	.02
453	Bill Russell	.08	.06	.03
454	Lou Whitaker	.40	.30	.15
455	Dan Graham	.06	.05	.02
456	Reggie Cleveland	.06	.05	.02
457	Sammy Stewart	.06	.05	.02
458	Pete Vuckovich	.08	.06	.03
459	John Wockenfuss	.06	.05	.02
460	Glenn Hoffman	.06	.05	.02
461	Willie Randolph	.10	.08	.04
462	Fernando Valenzuela(FC)	.80	.60	.30
463	Ron Hassey	.06	.05	.02
464	Paul Splittorff	.06	.05	.02
465	Rob Picciolo	.06	.05	.02
466	Larry Parrish	.10	.08	.04
467	Johnny Grubb	.06	.05	.02
468	Dan Ford	.06	.05	.02
469	Silvio Martinez	.06	.05	.02
470	Kiko Garcia	.06	.05	.02
471	Bob Boone	.10	.08	.04
472	Luis Salazar	.08	.06	.03
473	Randy Niemann	.06	.05	.02
474	Tom Griffin	.06	.05	.02
475	Phil Niekro	.30	.25	.12
476	Hubie Brooks(FC)	.25	.20	.10
477	Dick Tidrow	.06	.05	.02
478	Jim Beattie	.06	.05	.02
479	Damaso Garcia	.06	.05	.02
480	Mickey Hatcher	.08	.06	.03
481	Joe Price	.06	.05	.02
482	Ed Farmer	.06	.05	.02
483	Eddie Murray	.60	.45	.25
484	Ben Oglivie	.08	.06	.03
485	Kevin Saucier	.06	.05	.02
486	Bobby Murcer	.10	.08	.04
487	Bill Campbell	.06	.05	.02
488	Reggie Smith	.10	.08	.04
489	Wayne Garland	.06	.05	.02
490	Jim Wright	.06	.05	.02
491	Billy Martin	.12	.09	.05
492	Jim Fanning	.06	.05	.02
493	Don Baylor	.12	.09	.05
494	Rick Honeycutt	.06	.05	.02
495	Carlton Fisk	.50	.40	.20
496	Denny Walling	.06	.05	.02
497	Bake McBride	.06	.05	.02
498	Darrell Porter	.08	.06	.03
499	Gene Richards	.06	.05	.02
500	Ron Oester	.06	.05	.02
501	*Ken Dayley*(FC)	.20	.15	.08
502	Jason Thompson	.06	.05	.02
503	Milt May	.06	.05	.02
504	Doug Bird	.06	.05	.02
505	Bruce Bochte	.06	.05	.02
506	Neil Allen	.06	.05	.02
507	Joey McLaughlin	.06	.05	.02
508	Butch Wynegar	.06	.05	.02
509	Gary Roenicke	.06	.05	.02
510	Robin Yount	1.50	1.25	.60
511	Dave Tobik	.06	.05	.02
512	*Rich Gedman*(FC)	.35	.25	.14
513	*Gene Nelson*(FC)	.12	.09	.05
514	Rick Monday	.10	.08	.04
515	Miguel Dilone	.06	.05	.02
516	Clint Hurdle	.06	.05	.02
517	Jeff Newman	.06	.05	.02
518	Grant Jackson	.06	.05	.02
519	Andy Hassler	.06	.05	.02
520	Pat Putnam	.06	.05	.02
521	Greg Pryor	.06	.05	.02
522	Tony Scott	.06	.05	.02
523	Steve Mura	.06	.05	.02
524	Johnnie LeMaster	.06	.05	.02
525	Dick Ruthven	.06	.05	.02
526	John McNamara	.06	.05	.02
527	Larry McWilliams	.06	.05	.02
528	*Johnny Ray*(FC)	.70	.50	.30
529	*Pat Tabler*(FC)	.60	.45	.25
530	Tom Herr	.10	.08	.04
531a	San Diego Chicken (trademark symbol on front)	1.25	.90	.50
531b	San Diego Chicken (no trademark symbol)	.50	.40	.20
532	Sal Butera	.06	.05	.02
533	Mike Griffin	.06	.05	.02
534	Kelvin Moore	.06	.05	.02
535	Reggie Jackson	.60	.45	.25
536	Ed Romero	.06	.05	.02
537	Derrel Thomas	.06	.05	.02
538	Mike O'Berry	.06	.05	.02
539	Jack O'Connor	.06	.05	.02
540	*Bob Ojeda*(FC)	.50	.40	.20
541	Roy Lee Jackson	.06	.05	.02
542	Lynn Jones	.06	.05	.02
543	Gaylord Perry	.30	.25	.12
544a	Phil Garner (photo reversed)	1.25	.90	.50

		MT	NR MT	EX
544b	Phil Garner (photo correct)	.10	.08	.04
545	Garry Templeton	.10	.08	.04
546	Rafael Ramirez(FC)	.10	.08	.04
547	Jeff Reardon	.20	.15	.08
548	Ron Guidry	.25	.20	.10
549	*Tim Laudner*(FC)	.25	.20	.10
550	John Henry Johnson	.06	.05	.02
551	Chris Bando	.06	.05	.02
552	Bobby Brown	.06	.05	.02
553	Larry Bradford	.06	.05	.02
554	*Scott Fletcher*(FC)	.30	.25	.12
555	Jerry Royster	.06	.05	.02
556	Shooty Babbitt	.06	.05	.02
557	*Kent Hrbek*(FC)	3.00	2.25	1.25
558	Yankee Winners (Ron Guidry, Tommy John)	.15	.11	.06
559	Mark Bomback	.06	.05	.02
560	Julio Valdez	.06	.05	.02
561	Buck Martinez	.06	.05	.02
562	*Mike Marshall*(FC)	1.50	1.25	.60
563	Rennie Stennett	.06	.05	.02
564	Steve Crawford	.06	.05	.02
565	Bob Babcock	.06	.05	.02
566	Johnny Podres	.08	.06	.03
567	Paul Serna	.06	.05	.02
568	Harold Baines(FC)	.80	.60	.30
569	Dave LaRoche	.06	.05	.02
570	Lee May	.08	.06	.03
571	Gary Ward(FC)	.10	.08	.04
572	John Denny	.06	.05	.02
573	Roy Smalley	.06	.05	.02
574	*Bob Brenly*(FC)	.20	.15	.08
575	Bronx Bombers (Reggie Jackson, Dave Winfield)	.40	.30	.15
576	Luis Pujols	.06	.05	.02
577	Butch Hobson	.06	.05	.02
578	Harvey Kuenn	.08	.06	.03
579	Cal Ripken, Sr.	.08	.06	.03
580	Juan Berenguer	.08	.06	.03
581	Benny Ayala	.06	.05	.02
582	Vance Law(FC)	.15	.11	.06
583	*Rick Leach*(FC)	.12	.09	.05
584	George Frazier	.06	.05	.02
585	Phillies Finest (Pete Rose, Mike Schmidt)	.70	.50	.30
586	Joe Rudi	.10	.08	.04
587	Juan Beniquez	.06	.05	.02
588	*Luis DeLeon*(FC)	.08	.06	.03
589	Craig Swan	.06	.05	.02
590	Dave Chalk	.06	.05	.02
591	Billy Gardner	.06	.05	.02
592	Sal Bando	.08	.06	.03
593	Bert Campaneris	.10	.08	.04
594	Steve Kemp	.08	.06	.03
595a	Randy Lerch (Braves)	1.25	.90	.50
595b	Randy Lerch (Brewers)	.08	.06	.03
596	Bryan Clark	.06	.05	.02
597	Dave Ford	.06	.05	.02
598	Mike Scioscia(FC)	.20	.15	.08
599	John Lowenstein	.06	.05	.02
600	Rene Lachmann (Lachemann)	.06	.05	.02
601	Mick Kelleher	.06	.05	.02
602	Ron Jackson	.06	.05	.02
603	Jerry Koosman	.10	.08	.04
604	Dave Goltz	.08	.06	.03
605	Ellis Valentine	.06	.05	.02
606	Lonnie Smith	.08	.06	.03
607	Joaquin Andujar	.08	.06	.03
608	Garry Hancock	.06	.05	.02
609	Jerry Turner	.06	.05	.02
610	Bob Bonner	.06	.05	.02
611	Jim Dwyer	.06	.05	.02
612	Terry Bulling	.06	.05	.02
613	Joel Youngblood	.06	.05	.02
614	Larry Milbourne	.06	.05	.02
615	Phil Roof (Gene)	.06	.05	.02
616	Keith Drumright	.06	.05	.02
617	Dave Rosello	.06	.05	.02
618	Rickey Keeton	.06	.05	.02
619	Dennis Lamp	.06	.05	.02
620	Sid Monge	.06	.05	.02
621	Jerry White	.06	.05	.02
622	*Luis Aguayo*(FC)	.10	.08	.04
623	Jamie Easterly	.06	.05	.02
624	*Steve Sax*(FC)	3.00	2.25	1.25
625	Dave Roberts	.06	.05	.02
626	Rick Bosetti	.06	.05	.02
627	*Terry Francona*(FC)	.10	.08	.04
628	Pride of the Reds (Johnny Bench, Tom Seaver)	.35	.25	.14
629	Paul Mirabella	.06	.05	.02
630	Rance Mulliniks	.06	.05	.02
631	Kevin Hickey	.06	.05	.02
632	Reid Nichols	.06	.05	.02
633	Dave Geisel	.06	.05	.02
634	Ken Griffey	.12	.09	.05
635	Bob Lemon	.10	.08	.04
636	Orlando Sanchez	.06	.05	.02
637	Bill Almon	.06	.05	.02
638	Danny Ainge	.12	.09	.05
639	Willie Stargell	.40	.30	.15
640	Bob Sykes	.06	.05	.02
641	Ed Lynch	.06	.05	.02
642	John Ellis	.06	.05	.02
643	Fergie Jenkins	.15	.11	.06
644	Lenn Sakata	.06	.05	.02
645	Julio Gonzales	.06	.05	.02
646	Jesse Orosco(FC)	.15	.11	.06
647	Jerry Dybzinski	.06	.05	.02
648	Tommy Davis	.08	.06	.03
649	Ron Gardenhire	.06	.05	.02
650	Felipe Alou	.08	.06	.03
651	Harvey Haddix	.08	.06	.03
652	Willie Upshaw(FC)	.15	.11	.06
653	Bill Madlock	.12	.09	.05
---a	Checklist 1-26 DK (5 Trammel)	.70	.50	.30
---b	Checklist 1-26 DK (5 Trammell)	.08	.06	.03
---	Checklist 27-130	.06	.05	.02
---	Checklist 131-234	.06	.05	.02
---	Checklist 235-338	.06	.05	.02
---	Checklist 339-442	.06	.05	.02

		MT	NR MT	EX
---	Checklist 443-544	.06	.05	.02
---	Checklist 545-653	.06	.05	.02

1983 Donruss

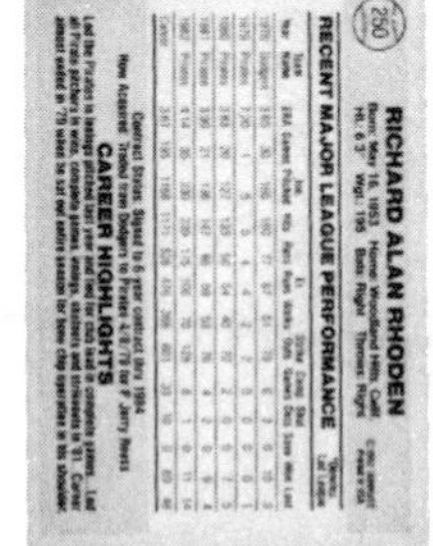

The 1983 Donruss set consists of 653 numbered cards plus seven unnumbered checklists. The cards, which measure 2-1/2" by 3-1/2", were issued with puzzle pieces (three pieces on one card per pack) that feature Ty Cobb. The first 26 cards in the set were once again the Diamond Kings series. The card fronts display the Donruss logo and the year of issue. The card backs have black print on yellow and white and include statistics, career highlights, and the player's contract status. (DK) in the checklist that follows indicates cards which belong to the Diamond Kings series.

		MT	NR MT	EX
	Complete Set:	70.00	52.00	27.00
	Common Player:	.06	.05	.02
1	Fernando Valenzuela (DK)	.40	.30	.15
2	Rollie Fingers (DK)	.20	.15	.08
3	Reggie Jackson (DK)	.50	.40	.20
4	Jim Palmer (DK)	.40	.30	.15
5	Jack Morris (DK)	.30	.25	.12
6	George Foster (DK)	.20	.15	.08
7	Jim Sundberg (DK)	.08	.06	.03
8	Willie Stargell (DK)	.40	.30	.15
9	Dave Stieb (DK)	.12	.09	.05
10	Joe Niekro (DK)	.12	.09	.05
11	Rickey Henderson (DK)	.60	.45	.25
12	Dale Murphy (DK)	.80	.60	.30
13	Toby Harrah (DK)	.08	.06	.03
14	Bill Buckner (DK)	.12	.09	.05
15	Willie Wilson (DK)	.15	.11	.06
16	Steve Carlton (DK)	.40	.30	.15
17	Ron Guidry (DK)	.25	.20	.10
18	Steve Rogers (DK)	.08	.06	.03
19	Kent Hrbek (DK)	.40	.30	.15
20	Keith Hernandez (DK)	.40	.30	.15
21	Floyd Bannister (DK)	.10	.08	.04
22	Johnny Bench (DK)	.40	.30	.15
23	Britt Burns (DK)	.08	.06	.03
24	Joe Morgan (DK)	.30	.25	.12
25	Carl Yastrzemski (DK)	.80	.60	.30
26	Terry Kennedy (DK)	.08	.06	.03
27	Gary Roenicke	.06	.05	.02
28	Dwight Bernard	.06	.05	.02
29	Pat Underwood	.06	.05	.02
30	Gary Allenson	.06	.05	.02
31	Ron Guidry	.25	.20	.10
32	Burt Hooton	.08	.06	.03
33	Chris Bando	.06	.05	.02
34	Vida Blue	.12	.09	.05
35	Rickey Henderson	1.00	.70	.40
36	Ray Burris	.06	.05	.02
37	John Butcher	.06	.05	.02
38	Don Aase	.06	.05	.02
39	Jerry Koosman	.10	.08	.04
40	Bruce Sutter	.15	.11	.06
41	Jose Cruz	.12	.09	.05
42	Pete Rose	1.00	.70	.40
43	Cesar Cedeno	.12	.09	.05
44	Floyd Chiffer	.06	.05	.02
45	Larry McWilliams	.06	.05	.02
46	Alan Fowlkes	.06	.05	.02
47	Dale Murphy	.90	.70	.35
48	Doug Bird	.06	.05	.02
49	Hubie Brooks	.12	.09	.05
50	Floyd Bannister	.10	.08	.04
51	Jack O'Connor	.06	.05	.02
52	Steve Senteney	.06	.05	.02
53	*Gary Gaetti*(FC)	4.00	3.00	1.50
54	Damaso Garcia	.06	.05	.02
55	Gene Nelson	.06	.05	.02
56	Mookie Wilson	.10	.08	.04
57	Allen Ripley	.06	.05	.02
58	Bob Horner	.12	.09	.05
59	Tony Pena	.10	.08	.04
60	Gary Lavelle	.06	.05	.02
61	Tim Lollar	.06	.05	.02
62	Frank Pastore	.06	.05	.02
63	Garry Maddox	.10	.08	.04
64	Bob Forsch	.08	.06	.03
65	Harry Spilman	.06	.05	.02
66	Geoff Zahn	.06	.05	.02
67	Salome Barojas	.06	.05	.02
68	David Palmer	.06	.05	.02
69	Charlie Hough	.10	.08	.04
70	Dan Quisenberry	.15	.11	.06
71	Tony Armas	.10	.08	.04
72	Rick Sutcliffe	.12	.09	.05

		MT	NR MT	EX
73	Steve Balboni(FC)	.15	.11	.06
74	Jerry Remy	.06	.05	.02
75	Mike Scioscia	.08	.06	.03
76	John Wockenfuss	.06	.05	.02
77	Jim Palmer	.70	.50	.30
78	Rollie Fingers	.20	.15	.08
79	Joe Nolan	.06	.05	.02
80	Pete Vuckovich	.08	.06	.03
81	Rick Leach	.06	.05	.02
82	Rick Miller	.06	.05	.02
83	Graig Nettles	.15	.11	.06
84	Ron Cey	.12	.09	.05
85	Miguel Dilone	.06	.05	.02
86	John Wathan	.08	.06	.03
87	Kelvin Moore	.06	.05	.02
88a	Byrn Smith (first name incorrect)	.90	.70	.35
88b	Bryn Smith (first name correct)	.08	.06	.03
89	Dave Hostetler	.06	.05	.02
90	Rod Carew	.50	.40	.20
91	Lonnie Smith	.08	.06	.03
92	Bob Knepper	.08	.06	.03
93	Marty Bystrom	.06	.05	.02
94	Chris Welsh	.06	.05	.02
95	Jason Thompson	.06	.05	.02
96	Tom O'Malley	.06	.05	.02
97	Phil Niekro	.30	.25	.12
98	Neil Allen	.06	.05	.02
99	Bill Buckner	.12	.09	.05
100	*Ed VandeBerg (Vande Berg)*(FC)	.10	.08	.04
101	Jim Clancy	.08	.06	.03
102	Robert Castillo	.06	.05	.02
103	Bruce Berenyi	.06	.05	.02
104	Carlton Fisk	.40	.30	.15
105	Mike Flanagan	.10	.08	.04
106	Cecil Cooper	.15	.11	.06
107	Jack Morris	.30	.25	.12
108	Mike Morgan(FC)	.12	.09	.05
109	Luis Aponte	.06	.05	.02
110	Pedro Guerrero	.25	.20	.10
111	Len Barker	.08	.06	.03
112	Willie Wilson	.15	.11	.06
113	Dave Beard	.06	.05	.02
114	Mike Gates	.06	.05	.02
115	Reggie Jackson	.50	.40	.20
116	George Wright	.06	.05	.02
117	Vance Law	.08	.06	.03
118	Nolan Ryan	1.50	1.25	.60
119	Mike Krukow	.08	.06	.03
120	Ozzie Smith	.20	.15	.08
121	Broderick Perkins	.06	.05	.02
122	Tom Seaver	.50	.40	.20
123	Chris Chambliss	.08	.06	.03
124	Chuck Tanner	.06	.05	.02
125	Johnnie LeMaster	.06	.05	.02
126	*Mel Hall*(FC)	.50	.40	.20
127	Bruce Bochte	.06	.05	.02
128	*Charlie Puleo*(FC)	.12	.09	.05
129	Luis Leal	.06	.05	.02
130	John Pacella	.06	.05	.02
131	Glenn Gulliver	.06	.05	.02
132	Don Money	.06	.05	.02
133	Dave Rozema	.06	.05	.02
134	Bruce Hurst(FC)	.25	.20	.10
135	Rudy May	.06	.05	.02
136	Tom LaSorda (Lasorda)	.10	.08	.04
137	Dan Spillner (photo actually Ed Whitson)	.06	.05	.02
138	Jerry Martin	.06	.05	.02
139	Mike Norris	.06	.05	.02
140	Al Oliver	.15	.11	.06
141	Daryl Sconiers	.06	.05	.02
142	Lamar Johnson	.06	.05	.02
143	Harold Baines	.15	.11	.06
144	Alan Ashby	.06	.05	.02
145	Garry Templeton	.10	.08	.04
146	Al Holland	.06	.05	.02
147	Bo Diaz	.08	.06	.03
148	Dave Concepcion	.12	.09	.05
149	Rick Camp	.06	.05	.02
150	Jim Morrison	.06	.05	.02
151	Randy Martz	.06	.05	.02
152	Keith Hernandez	.40	.30	.15
153	John Lowenstein	.06	.05	.02
154	Mike Caldwell	.06	.05	.02
155	Milt Wilcox	.06	.05	.02
156	Rich Gedman	.08	.06	.03
157	Rich Gossage	.20	.15	.08
158	Jerry Reuss	.10	.08	.04
159	Ron Hassey	.06	.05	.02
160	Larry Gura	.06	.05	.02
161	Dwayne Murphy	.08	.06	.03
162	Woodie Fryman	.08	.06	.03
163	Steve Comer	.06	.05	.02
164	Ken Forsch	.06	.05	.02
165	Dennis Lamp	.06	.05	.02
166	David Green	.06	.05	.02
167	Terry Puhl	.06	.05	.02
168	Mike Schmidt	.80	.60	.30
169	*Eddie Milner*(FC)	.10	.08	.04
170	John Curtis	.06	.05	.02
171	Don Robinson	.08	.06	.03
172	Richard Gale	.06	.05	.02
173	Steve Bedrosian	.12	.09	.05
174	Willie Hernandez	.08	.06	.03
175	Ron Gardenhire	.06	.05	.02
176	Jim Beattie	.06	.05	.02
177	Tim Laudner	.08	.06	.03
178	Buck Martinez	.06	.05	.02
179	Kent Hrbek	1.25	.90	.50
180	Alfredo Griffin	.08	.06	.03
181	Larry Andersen	.06	.05	.02
182	Pete Falcone	.06	.05	.02
183	Jody Davis	.10	.08	.04
184	Glenn Hubbard	.08	.06	.03
185	Dale Berra	.06	.05	.02
186	Greg Minton	.06	.05	.02
187	Gary Lucas	.06	.05	.02
188	Dave Van Gorder	.06	.05	.02
189	Bob Dernier(FC)	.10	.08	.04
190	*Willie McGee*(FC)	1.00	.70	.40
191	Dickie Thon	.08	.06	.03

		MT	NR MT	EX
192	Bob Boone	.10	.08	.04
193	Britt Burns	.06	.05	.02
194	Jeff Reardon	.12	.09	.05
195	Jon Matlack	.08	.06	.03
196	*Don Slaught*(FC)	.20	.15	.08
197	Fred Stanley	.06	.05	.02
198	Rick Manning	.06	.05	.02
199	Dave Righetti	.25	.20	.10
200	Dave Stapleton	.06	.05	.02
201	Steve Yeager	.06	.05	.02
202	Enos Cabell	.06	.05	.02
203	Sammy Stewart	.06	.05	.02
204	Moose Haas	.06	.05	.02
205	Lenn Sakata	.06	.05	.02
206	Charlie Moore	.06	.05	.02
207	Alan Trammell	.40	.30	.15
208	Jim Rice	.40	.30	.15
209	Roy Smalley	.06	.05	.02
210	Bill Russell	.08	.06	.03
211	Andre Thornton	.10	.08	.04
212	Willie Aikens	.06	.05	.02
213	Dave McKay	.06	.05	.02
214	Tim Blackwell	.06	.05	.02
215	Buddy Bell	.12	.09	.05
216	Doug DeCinces	.10	.08	.04
217	Tom Herr	.10	.08	.04
218	Frank LaCorte	.06	.05	.02
219	Steve Carlton	.50	.40	.20
220	Terry Kennedy	.08	.06	.03
221	Mike Easler	.08	.06	.03
222	Jack Clark	.25	.20	.10
223	Gene Garber	.06	.05	.02
224	Scott Holman	.06	.05	.02
225	Mike Proly	.06	.05	.02
226	Terry Bulling	.06	.05	.02
227	Jerry Garvin	.06	.05	.02
228	Ron Davis	.06	.05	.02
229	Tom Hume	.06	.05	.02
230	Marc Hill	.06	.05	.02
231	Dennis Martinez	.08	.06	.03
232	Jim Gantner	.08	.06	.03
233	Larry Pashnick	.06	.05	.02
234	Dave Collins	.08	.06	.03
235	Tom Burgmeier	.06	.05	.02
236	Ken Landreaux	.06	.05	.02
237	John Denny	.06	.05	.02
238	Hal McRae	.12	.09	.05
239	Matt Keough	.06	.05	.02
240	Doug Flynn	.06	.05	.02
241	Fred Lynn	.20	.15	.08
242	Billy Sample	.06	.05	.02
243	Tom Paciorek	.06	.05	.02
244	Joe Sambito	.06	.05	.02
245	Sid Monge	.06	.05	.02
246	Ken Oberkfell	.06	.05	.02
247	Joe Pittman (photo actually Juan Eichelberger)	.06	.05	.02
248	Mario Soto	.08	.06	.03
249	Claudell Washington	.08	.06	.03
250	Rick Rhoden	.10	.08	.04
251	Darrell Evans	.15	.11	.06
252	Steve Henderson	.06	.05	.02
253	Manny Castillo	.06	.05	.02
254	Craig Swan	.06	.05	.02
255	Joey McLaughlin	.06	.05	.02
256	Pete Redfern	.06	.05	.02
257	Ken Singleton	.10	.08	.04
258	Robin Yount	.80	.60	.30
259	Elias Sosa	.06	.05	.02
260	Bob Ojeda	.12	.09	.05
261	Bobby Murcer	.10	.08	.04
262	*Candy Maldonado*(FC)	.50	.40	.20
263	Rick Waits	.06	.05	.02
264	Greg Pryor	.06	.05	.02
265	Bob Owchinko	.06	.05	.02
266	Chris Speier	.06	.05	.02
267	Bruce Kison	.06	.05	.02
268	Mark Wagner	.06	.05	.02
269	Steve Kemp	.10	.08	.04
270	Phil Garner	.08	.06	.03
271	Gene Richards	.06	.05	.02
272	Renie Martin	.06	.05	.02
273	Dave Roberts	.06	.05	.02
274	Dan Driessen	.08	.06	.03
275	Rufino Linares	.06	.05	.02
276	Lee Lacy	.06	.05	.02
277	*Ryne Sandberg*(FC)	12.00	9.00	4.75
278	Darrell Porter	.08	.06	.03
279	Cal Ripken	1.00	.70	.40
280	Jamie Easterly	.06	.05	.02
281	Bill Fahey	.06	.05	.02
282	Glenn Hoffman	.06	.05	.02
283	Willie Randolph	.10	.08	.04
284	Fernando Valenzuela	.30	.25	.12
285	Alan Bannister	.06	.05	.02
286	Paul Splittorff	.06	.05	.02
287	Joe Rudi	.10	.08	.04
288	Bill Gullickson	.06	.05	.02
289	Danny Darwin	.06	.05	.02
290	Andy Hassler	.06	.05	.02
291	Ernesto Escarrega	.06	.05	.02
292	Steve Mura	.06	.05	.02
293	Tony Scott	.06	.05	.02
294	Manny Trillo	.08	.06	.03
295	Greg Harris(FC)	.08	.06	.03
296	Luis DeLeon	.06	.05	.02
297	Kent Tekulve	.08	.06	.03
298	Atlee Hammaker(FC)	.12	.09	.05
299	Bruce Benedict	.06	.05	.02
300	Fergie Jenkins	.15	.11	.06
301	Dave Kingman	.15	.11	.06
302	Bill Caudill	.06	.05	.02
303	John Castino	.06	.05	.02
304	Ernie Whitt	.08	.06	.03
305	Randy Johnson	.06	.05	.02
306	Garth Iorg	.06	.05	.02
307	Gaylord Perry	.30	.25	.12
308	Ed Lynch	.06	.05	.02
309	Keith Moreland	.08	.06	.03
310	Rafael Ramirez	.06	.05	.02
311	Bill Madlock	.12	.09	.05
312	Milt May	.06	.05	.02
313	John Montefusco	.06	.05	.02

#	Player	MT	NR MT	EX
314	Wayne Krenchicki	.06	.05	.02
315	George Vukovich	.06	.05	.02
316	Joaquin Andujar	.08	.06	.03
317	Craig Reynolds	.06	.05	.02
318	Rick Burleson	.08	.06	.03
319	Richard Dotson	.10	.08	.04
320	Steve Rogers	.08	.06	.03
321	Dave Schmidt(FC)	.10	.08	.04
322	*Bud Black*(FC)	.20	.15	.08
323	Jeff Burroughs	.08	.06	.03
324	Von Hayes	.15	.11	.06
325	Butch Wynegar	.06	.05	.02
326	Carl Yastrzemski	.80	.60	.30
327	Ron Roenicke	.06	.05	.02
328	*Howard Johnson*(FC)	10.00	7.50	4.00
329	Rick Dempsey	.08	.06	.03
330a	Jim Slaton (one yellow box on back)	.70	.50	.30
330b	Jim Slaton (two yellow boxes on back)	.08	.06	.03
331	Benny Ayala	.06	.05	.02
332	Ted Simmons	.12	.09	.05
333	Lou Whitaker	.40	.30	.15
334	Chuck Rainey	.06	.05	.02
335	Lou Piniella	.12	.09	.05
336	Steve Sax	.30	.25	.12
337	Toby Harrah	.08	.06	.03
338	George Brett	.70	.50	.30
339	Davey Lopes	.10	.08	.04
340	Gary Carter	.40	.30	.15
341	John Grubb	.06	.05	.02
342	Tim Foli	.06	.05	.02
343	Jim Kaat	.15	.11	.06
344	Mike LaCoss	.06	.05	.02
345	Larry Christenson	.06	.05	.02
346	Juan Bonilla	.06	.05	.02
347	Omar Moreno	.06	.05	.02
348	Charles Davis(FC)	.20	.15	.08
349	Tommy Boggs	.06	.05	.02
350	Rusty Staub	.10	.08	.04
351	Bump Wills	.06	.05	.02
352	Rick Sweet	.06	.05	.02
353	*Jim Gott*(FC)	.20	.15	.08
354	Terry Felton	.06	.05	.02
355	Jim Kern	.06	.05	.02
356	Bill Almon	.06	.05	.02
357	Tippy Martinez	.06	.05	.02
358	Roy Howell	.06	.05	.02
359	Dan Petry	.08	.06	.03
360	Jerry Mumphrey	.06	.05	.02
361	Mark Clear	.06	.05	.02
362	Mike Marshall	.20	.15	.08
363	Lary Sorensen	.06	.05	.02
364	Amos Otis	.08	.06	.03
365	Rick Langford	.06	.05	.02
366	Brad Mills	.06	.05	.02
367	Brian Downing	.10	.08	.04
368	Mike Richardt	.06	.05	.02
369	Aurelio Rodriguez	.08	.06	.03
370	Dave Smith	.08	.06	.03
371	Tug McGraw	.12	.09	.05
372	Doug Bair	.06	.05	.02
373	Ruppert Jones	.06	.05	.02
374	Alex Trevino	.06	.05	.02
375	Ken Dayley	.06	.05	.02
376	Rod Scurry	.06	.05	.02
377	Bob Brenly(FC)	.08	.06	.03
378	Scot Thompson	.06	.05	.02
379	Julio Cruz	.06	.05	.02
380	John Stearns	.06	.05	.02
381	Dale Murray	.06	.05	.02
382	*Frank Viola*(FC)	4.00	3.00	1.50
383	Al Bumbry	.08	.06	.03
384	Ben Oglivie	.08	.06	.03
385	Dave Tobik	.06	.05	.02
386	Bob Stanley	.06	.05	.02
387	Andre Robertson	.06	.05	.02
388	Jorge Orta	.06	.05	.02
389	Ed Whitson	.06	.05	.02
390	Don Hood	.06	.05	.02
391	Tom Underwood	.06	.05	.02
392	Tim Wallach	.20	.15	.08
393	Steve Renko	.06	.05	.02
394	Mickey Rivers	.08	.06	.03
395	Greg Luzinski	.12	.09	.05
396	Art Howe	.06	.05	.02
397	Alan Wiggins	.06	.05	.02
398	Jim Barr	.06	.05	.02
399	Ivan DeJesus	.06	.05	.02
400	*Tom Lawless*(FC)	.08	.06	.03
401	Bob Walk	.08	.06	.03
402	Jimmy Smith	.06	.05	.02
403	Lee Smith	.15	.11	.06
404	George Hendrick	.08	.06	.03
405	Eddie Murray	.60	.45	.25
406	Marshall Edwards	.06	.05	.02
407	Lance Parrish	.35	.25	.14
408	Carney Lansford	.08	.06	.03
409	Dave Winfield	.40	.30	.15
410	Bob Welch	.12	.09	.05
411	Larry Milbourne	.06	.05	.02
412	Dennis Leonard	.08	.06	.03
413	Dan Meyer	.06	.05	.02
414	Charlie Lea	.06	.05	.02
415	Rick Honeycutt	.06	.05	.02
416	Mike Witt	.15	.11	.06
417	Steve Trout	.06	.05	.02
418	Glenn Brummer	.06	.05	.02
419	Denny Walling	.06	.05	.02
420	Gary Matthews	.10	.08	.04
421	Charlie Liebrandt (Leibrandt)	.08	.06	.03
422	Juan Eichelberger	.06	.05	.02
423	*Matt Guante (Cecilio)*(FC)	.15	.11	.06
424	Bill Laskey	.06	.05	.02
425	Jerry Royster	.06	.05	.02
426	Dickie Noles	.06	.05	.02
427	George Foster	.15	.11	.06
428	*Mike Moore*(FC)	1.50	1.25	.60
429	Gary Ward	.08	.06	.03
430	Barry Bonnell	.06	.05	.02
431	Ron Washington	.06	.05	.02
432	Rance Mulliniks	.06	.05	.02
433	Mike Stanton	.06	.05	.02
434	Jesse Orosco	.10	.08	.04
435	Larry Bowa	.12	.09	.05
436	Biff Pocoroba	.06	.05	.02
437	Johnny Ray	.12	.09	.05
438	Joe Morgan	.30	.25	.12
439	*Eric Show*(FC)	.30	.25	.12
440	Larry Biittner	.06	.05	.02
441	Greg Gross	.06	.05	.02
442	Gene Tenace	.08	.06	.03
443	Danny Heep	.06	.05	.02
444	Bobby Clark	.06	.05	.02
445	Kevin Hickey	.06	.05	.02
446	Scott Sanderson	.06	.05	.02
447	Frank Tanana	.10	.08	.04
448	Cesar Geronimo	.06	.05	.02
449	Jimmy Sexton	.06	.05	.02
450	Mike Hargrove	.06	.05	.02
451	Doyle Alexander	.10	.08	.04
452	Dwight Evans	.15	.11	.06
453	Terry Forster	.08	.06	.03
454	Tom Brookens	.06	.05	.02
455	Rich Dauer	.06	.05	.02
456	Rob Picciolo	.06	.05	.02
457	Terry Crowley	.06	.05	.02
458	Ned Yost	.06	.05	.02
459	Kirk Gibson	.40	.30	.15
460	Reid Nichols	.06	.05	.02
461	Oscar Gamble	.08	.06	.03
462	Dusty Baker	.10	.08	.04
463	Jack Perconte	.06	.05	.02
464	Frank White	.10	.08	.04
465	Mickey Klutts	.06	.05	.02
466	Warren Cromartie	.06	.05	.02
467	Larry Parrish	.10	.08	.04
468	Bobby Grich	.10	.08	.04
469	Dane Iorg	.06	.05	.02
470	Joe Niekro	.12	.09	.05
471	Ed Farmer	.06	.05	.02
472	Tim Flannery	.06	.05	.02
473	Dave Parker	.30	.25	.12
474	Jeff Leonard	.10	.08	.04
475	Al Hrabosky	.08	.06	.03
476	Ron Hodges	.06	.05	.02
477	Leon Durham	.08	.06	.03
478	Jim Essian	.06	.05	.02
479	Roy Lee Jackson	.06	.05	.02
480	Brad Havens	.06	.05	.02
481	Joe Price	.06	.05	.02
482	Tony Bernazard	.06	.05	.02
483	Scott McGregor	.08	.06	.03
484	Paul Molitor	.20	.15	.08
485	Mike Ivie	.06	.05	.02
486	Ken Griffey	.12	.09	.05
487	Dennis Eckersley	.12	.09	.05
488	Steve Garvey	.40	.30	.15
489	Mike Fischlin	.06	.05	.02
490	U.L. Washington	.06	.05	.02
491	Steve McCatty	.06	.05	.02
492	Roy Johnson	.06	.05	.02
493	Don Baylor	.12	.09	.05
494	Bobby Johnson	.06	.05	.02
495	Mike Squires	.06	.05	.02
496	Bert Roberge	.06	.05	.02
497	Dick Ruthven	.06	.05	.02
498	Tito Landrum	.06	.05	.02
499	Sixto Lezcano	.06	.05	.02
500	Johnny Bench	.40	.30	.15
501	Larry Whisenton	.06	.05	.02
502	Manny Sarmiento	.06	.05	.02
503	Fred Breining	.06	.05	.02
504	Bill Campbell	.06	.05	.02
505	Todd Cruz	.06	.05	.02
506	Bob Bailor	.06	.05	.02
507	Dave Stieb	.12	.09	.05
508	Al Williams	.06	.05	.02
509	Dan Ford	.06	.05	.02
510	Gorman Thomas	.10	.08	.04
511	Chet Lemon	.08	.06	.03
512	Mike Torrez	.08	.06	.03
513	Shane Rawley	.10	.08	.04
514	Mark Belanger	.08	.06	.03
515	Rodney Craig	.06	.05	.02
516	Onix Concepcion	.06	.05	.02
517	Mike Heath	.06	.05	.02
518	Andre Dawson	.35	.25	.14
519	Luis Sanchez	.06	.05	.02
520	Terry Bogener	.06	.05	.02
521	Rudy Law	.06	.05	.02
522	Ray Knight	.10	.08	.04
523	Joe Lefebvre	.06	.05	.02
524	Jim Wohlford	.06	.05	.02
525	*Julio Franco*(FC)	4.00	3.00	1.50
526	Ron Oester	.06	.05	.02
527	Rick Mahler	.08	.06	.03
528	Steve Nicosia	.06	.05	.02
529	Junior Kennedy	.06	.05	.02
530a	Whitey Herzog (one yellow box on back)	.70	.50	.30
530b	Whitey Herzog (two yellow boxes on back)	.10	.08	.04
531a	Don Sutton (blue frame around photo)	1.00	.70	.40
531b	Don Sutton (green frame around photo)	.30	.25	.12
532	Mark Brouhard	.06	.05	.02
533a	Sparky Anderson (one yellow box on back)	.70	.50	.30
533b	Sparky Anderson (two yellow boxes on back)	.10	.08	.04
534	Roger LaFrancois	.06	.05	.02
535	George Frazier	.06	.05	.02
536	Tom Niedenfuer	.08	.06	.03
537	Ed Glynn	.06	.05	.02
538	Lee May	.08	.06	.03
539	Bob Kearney	.06	.05	.02
540	Tim Raines	.35	.25	.14
541	Paul Mirabella	.06	.05	.02
542	Luis Tiant	.12	.09	.05
543	Ron LeFlore	.08	.06	.03
544	*Dave LaPoint*(FC)	.30	.25	.12
545	Randy Moffitt	.06	.05	.02
546	Luis Aguayo	.06	.05	.02
547	Brad Lesley	.06	.05	.02
548	Luis Salazar	.06	.05	.02
549	John Candelaria	.10	.08	.04
550	Dave Bergman	.06	.05	.02
551	Bob Watson	.08	.06	.03
552	Pat Tabler	.10	.08	.04
553	Brent Gaff	.06	.05	.02
554	Al Cowens	.06	.05	.02
555	Tom Brunansky(FC)	.25	.20	.10
556	Lloyd Moseby	.12	.09	.05
557a	Pascual Perez (Twins)(FC)	.90	.70	.35
557b	Pascual Perez (Braves)(FC)	.15	.11	.06
558	Willie Upshaw	.08	.06	.03
559	Richie Zisk	.08	.06	.03
560	Pat Zachry	.06	.05	.02
561	Jay Johnstone	.08	.06	.03
562	Carlos Diaz	.06	.05	.02
563	John Tudor	.10	.08	.04
564	Frank Robinson	.12	.09	.05
565	Dave Edwards	.06	.05	.02
566	Paul Householder	.06	.05	.02
567	Ron Reed	.06	.05	.02
568	Mike Ramsey	.06	.05	.02
569	Kiko Garcia	.06	.05	.02
570	Tommy John	.20	.15	.08
571	Tony LaRussa	.08	.06	.03
572	Joel Youngblood	.06	.05	.02
573	*Wayne Tolleson*(FC)	.12	.09	.05
574	Keith Creel	.06	.05	.02
575	Billy Martin	.12	.09	.05
576	Jerry Dybzinski	.06	.05	.02
577	Rick Cerone	.06	.05	.02
578	Tony Perez	.20	.15	.08
579	*Greg Brock*(FC)	.35	.25	.14
580	*Glen Wilson (Glenn)*(FC)	.35	.25	.14
581	Tim Stoddard	.06	.05	.02
582	Bob McClure	.06	.05	.02
583	Jim Dwyer	.06	.05	.02
584	Ed Romero	.06	.05	.02
585	Larry Herndon	.08	.06	.03
586	*Wade Boggs*(FC)	18.00	13.50	7.25
587	Jay Howell(FC)	.15	.11	.06
588	Dave Stewart	.15	.11	.06
589	Bert Blyleven	.12	.09	.05
590	Dick Howser	.06	.05	.02
591	Wayne Gross	.06	.05	.02
592	Terry Francona	.06	.05	.02
593	Don Werner	.06	.05	.02
594	Bill Stein	.06	.05	.02
595	Jesse Barfield(FC)	.70	.50	.30
596	Bobby Molinaro	.06	.05	.02
597	Mike Vail	.06	.05	.02
598	*Tony Gwynn*(FC)	13.00	9.75	5.25
599	Gary Rajsich	.06	.05	.02
600	Jerry Ujdur	.06	.05	.02
601	Cliff Johnson	.06	.05	.02
602	Jerry White	.06	.05	.02
603	Bryan Clark	.06	.05	.02
604	Joe Ferguson	.06	.05	.02
605	Guy Sularz	.06	.05	.02
606a	Ozzie Virgil (green frame around photo)(FC)	.90	.70	.35
606b	Ozzie Virgil (orange frame around photo)(FC)	.08	.06	.03
607	Terry Harper(FC)	.06	.05	.02
608	Harvey Kuenn	.08	.06	.03
609	Jim Sundberg	.08	.06	.03
610	Willie Stargell	.40	.30	.15
611	Reggie Smith	.10	.08	.04
612	Rob Wilfong	.06	.05	.02
613	Niekro Brothers (Joe Niekro, Phil Niekro)	.15	.11	.06
614	Lee Elia	.06	.05	.02
615	Mickey Hatcher	.08	.06	.03
616	Jerry Hairston	.06	.05	.02
617	John Martin	.06	.05	.02
618	Wally Backman(FC)	.15	.11	.06
619	*Storm Davis*(FC)	.50	.40	.20
620	Alan Knicely	.06	.05	.02
621	John Stuper	.06	.05	.02
622	Matt Sinatro	.06	.05	.02
623	*Gene Petralli*(FC)	.15	.11	.06
624	Duane Walker	.06	.05	.02
625	Dick Williams	.06	.05	.02
626	Pat Corrales	.06	.05	.02
627	Vern Ruhle	.06	.05	.02
628	Joe Torre	.08	.06	.03
629	Anthony Johnson	.06	.05	.02
630	Steve Howe	.08	.06	.03
631	Gary Woods	.06	.05	.02
632	Lamarr Hoyt (LaMarr)	.06	.05	.02
633	Steve Swisher	.06	.05	.02
634	Terry Leach(FC)	.12	.09	.05
635	Jeff Newman	.06	.05	.02
636	Brett Butler	.10	.08	.04
637	Gary Gray	.06	.05	.02
638	Lee Mazzilli	.08	.06	.03
639a	Ron Jackson (A's)	18.00	13.50	7.25
639b	Ron Jackson (Angels - green frame around photo)	.90	.70	.35
639c	Ron Jackson (Angels - red frame around photo)	.20	.15	.08
640	Juan Beniquez	.06	.05	.02
641	Dave Rucker	.06	.05	.02
642	Luis Pujols	.06	.05	.02
643	Rick Monday	.10	.08	.04
644	Hosken Powell	.06	.05	.02
645	San Diego Chicken	.20	.15	.08
646	Dave Engle	.06	.05	.02
647	Dick Davis	.06	.05	.02
648	MVP's (Vida Blue, Joe Morgan, Frank Robinson)	.15	.11	.06
649	Al Chambers	.06	.05	.02
650	Jesus Vega	.06	.05	.02
651	Jeff Jones	.06	.05	.02
652	Marvis Foley	.06	.05	.02
653	Ty Cobb Puzzle	.06	.05	.02
---a	Dick Perez/DK Checklist (no word "Checklist" on back)	.70	.50	.30
---b	Dick Perez/DK Checklist (word "Checklist" on back)	.08	.06	.03
---	Checklist 27-130	.06	.05	.02
---	Checklist 131-234	.06	.05	.02
---	Checklist 235-338	.06	.05	.02

		MT	NR MT	EX
---	Checklist 339-442	.06	.05	.02
---	Checklist 443-546	.06	.05	.02
---	Checklist 547-653	.06	.05	.02

1983 Donruss Action All-Stars

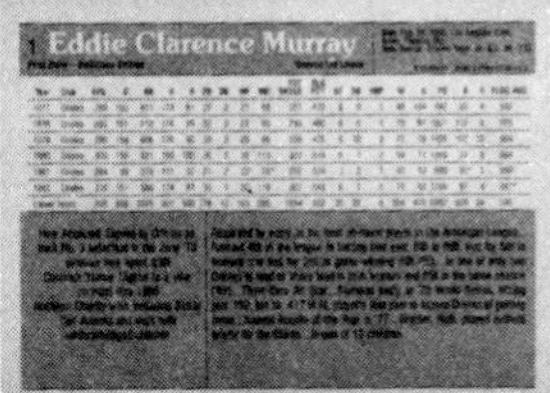

The cards in this 60-card set are designed on a horizontal format and contain a large close-up photo of the player on the left and a smaller action photo on the right. The cards, which measure 3-1/2" by 5", have deep red borders and contain the Donruss logo and the year of issue. The card backs have black print on red and white and contain various statistical and biographical information. The cards were sold with puzzle pieces (three pieces on one card per pack) that feature Mickey Mantle.

		MT	NR MT	EX
Complete Set:		6.50	5.00	3.00
Common Player:		.10	.08	.04
1	Eddie Murray	.30	.25	.12
2	Dwight Evans	.15	.11	.06
3a	Reggie Jackson (red covers part of statistics on back)	.35	.25	.14
3b	Reggie Jackson (red does not cover any statistics on back)	.35	.25	.14
4	Greg Luzinski	.12	.09	.05
5	Larry Herndon	.10	.08	.04
6	Al Oliver	.12	.09	.05
7	Bill Buckner	.10	.08	.04
8	Jason Thompson	.10	.08	.04
9	Andre Dawson	.20	.15	.08
10	Greg Minton	.10	.08	.04
11	Terry Kennedy	.10	.08	.04
12	Phil Niekro	.20	.15	.08
13	Willie Wilson	.12	.09	.05
14	Johnny Bench	.35	.25	.14
15	Ron Guidry	.15	.11	.06
16	Hal McRae	.10	.08	.04
17	Damaso Garcia	.10	.08	.04
18	Gary Ward	.10	.08	.04
19	Cecil Cooper	.12	.09	.05
20	Keith Hernandez	.25	.20	.10
21	Ron Cey	.12	.09	.05
22	Rickey Henderson	.50	.40	.20
23	Nolan Ryan	1.00	.70	.40
24	Steve Carlton	.30	.25	.12
25	John Stearns	.10	.08	.04
26	Jim Sundberg	.10	.08	.04
27	Joaquin Andujar	.10	.08	.04
28	Gaylord Perry	.15	.11	.06
29	Jack Clark	.15	.11	.06
30	Bill Madlock	.12	.09	.05
31	Pete Rose	.35	.25	.14
32	Mookie Wilson	.10	.08	.04
33	Rollie Fingers	.15	.11	.06
34	Lonnie Smith	.10	.08	.04
35	Tony Pena	.10	.08	.04
36	Dave Winfield	.30	.25	.12
37	Tim Lollar	.10	.08	.04
38	Rod Carew	.30	.25	.12
39	Toby Harrah	.10	.08	.04
40	Buddy Bell	.10	.08	.04
41	Bruce Sutter	.12	.09	.05
42	George Brett	.40	.30	.15
43	Carlton Fisk	.35	.25	.14
44	Carl Yastrzemski	.40	.30	.15
45	Dale Murphy	.30	.25	.12
46	Bob Horner	.12	.09	.05
47	Dave Concepcion	.12	.09	.05
48	Dave Stieb	.12	.09	.05
49	Kent Hrbek	.20	.15	.08
50	Lance Parrish	.15	.11	.06
51	Joe Niekro	.12	.09	.05
52	Cal Ripken Jr.	.35	.25	.14
53	Fernando Valenzuela	.12	.09	.05
54	Rickie Zisk	.10	.08	.04
55	Leon Durham	.10	.08	.04
56	Robin Yount	.40	.30	.15
57	Mike Schmidt	.70	.50	.30
58	Gary Carter	.15	.11	.06
59	Fred Lynn	.15	.11	.06
60	Checklist	.10	.08	.04

1983 Donruss Hall of Fame Heroes

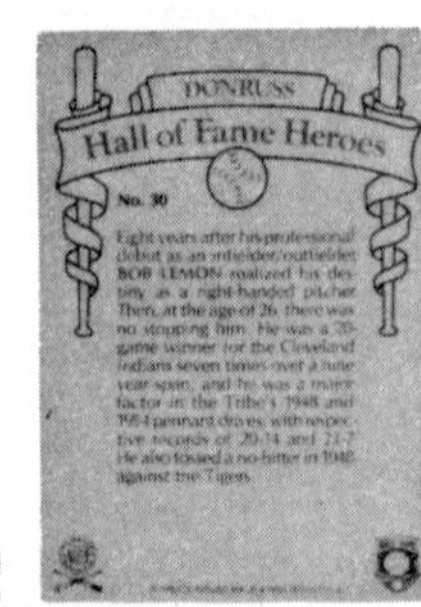

The artwork of Dick Perez is featured in the 44-card Donruss Hall of Fame Heroes set issued in 1983. The standard-size cards (2-1/2" by 3-1/2") were available in wax packs that contained eight cards plus a Mickey Mantle puzzle piece card (three pieces on one card per pack). The backs, which display red and blue print on white stock, contain a short player biograpical sketch derived from the Hall of Fame yearbook. The numbered set consists of 44 player cards, a Mantle puzzle card, and a checklist.

		MT	NR MT	EX
Complete Set:		6.00	4.50	2.50
Common Player:		.05	.04	.02
1	Ty Cobb	.50	.40	.20
2	Walter Johnson	.15	.11	.06
3	Christy Mathewson	.15	.11	.06
4	Josh Gibson	.10	.08	.04
5	Honus Wagner	.15	.11	.06
6	Jackie Robinson	.30	.25	.12
7	Mickey Mantle	1.00	.70	.40
8	Luke Appling	.05	.04	.02
9	Ted Williams	.50	.40	.20
10	Johnny Mize	.15	.11	.06
11	Satchel Paige	.15	.11	.06
12	Lou Boudreau	.15	.11	.06
13	Jimmie Foxx	.15	.11	.06
14	Duke Snider	.50	.40	.20
15	Monte Irvin	.15	.11	.06
16	Hank Greenberg	.15	.11	.06
17	Roberto Clemente	.20	.15	.08
18	Al Kaline	.30	.25	.12
19	Frank Robinson	.30	.25	.12
20	Joe Cronin	.09	.07	.04
21	Burleigh Grimes	.05	.04	.02
22	The Waner Brothers (Lloyd Waner, Paul Waner)	.09	.07	.04
23	Grover Alexander	.09	.07	.04
24	Yogi Berra	.30	.25	.12
25	James Bell	.05	.04	.02
26	Bill Dickey	.09	.07	.04
27	Cy Young	.15	.11	.06
28	Charlie Gehringer	.09	.07	.04
29	Dizzy Dean	.15	.11	.06
30	Bob Lemon	.15	.11	.06
31	Red Ruffing	.05	.04	.02
32	Stan Musial	.50	.40	.20
33	Carl Hubbell	.15	.11	.06
34	Hank Aaron	.50	.40	.20
35	John McGraw	.09	.07	.04
36	Bob Feller	.30	.25	.12
37	Casey Stengel	.15	.11	.06
38	Ralph Kiner	.15	.11	.06
39	Roy Campanella	.15	.11	.06
40	Mel Ott	.09	.07	.04
41	Robin Roberts	.15	.11	.06
42	Early Wynn	.15	.11	.06
43	Mickey Mantle Puzzle Card	.09	.07	.04
---	Checklist	.09	.07	.04

1984 Donruss

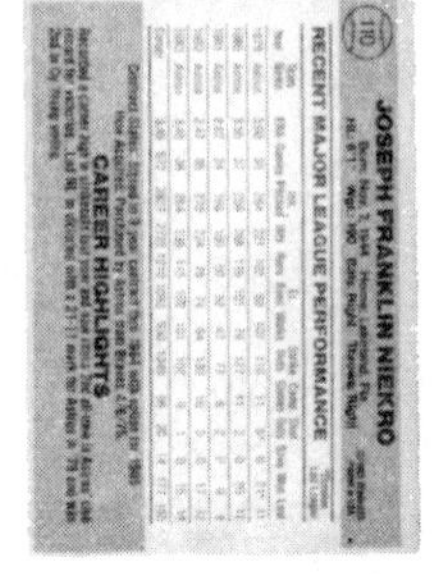

The 1984 Donruss set consists of 651 numbered cards, seven unnumbered checklists and two "Living Legends" cards (designated A and B). The A and B cards were issued only in wax packs and not available to hobby dealers purchasing vending sets. The card fronts differ in style from the previous years, however the Donruss logo and year of issue are still included. The card backs have black print on green and white and are identical in format to the preceding year. The standard-size cards (2-1/2" by 3-1/2") were issued with a 63-piece puzzle of Duke Snider. A limited print run of the issue by Donruss has caused the set to escalate in price in recent years. The complete set price in the checklist that follows does not include the higher priced variations. Cards marked with (DK) or (RR) in the checklist refer to the Diamond Kings and Rated Rookies subsets.

		MT	NR MT	EX
Complete Set:		300.00	225.00	125.00
Common Player:		.10	.08	.04
1a	Robin Yount (DK) (Perez-Steel on back)	.80	.60	.30
1b	Robin Yount (DK) (Perez-Steele on back)	1.50	1.25	.60
2a	Dave Concepcion (DK) (Perez-Steel on back)	.30	.25	.12
2b	Dave Concepcion (DK) (Perez-Steele on back)	.60	.45	.25
3a	Dwayne Murphy (DK) (Perez-Steel on back)	.25	.20	.10
3b	Dwayne Murphy (DK) (Perez-Steele on back)	.60	.45	.25
4a	John Castino (DK) (Perez-Steel on back)	.20	.15	.08
4b	John Castino (DK) (Perez-Steele on back)	.60	.45	.25
5a	Leon Durham (DK) (Perez-Steel on back)	.25	.20	.10
5b	Leon Durham (DK) (Perez-Steele on back)	.60	.45	.25
6a	Rusty Staub (DK) (Perez-Steel on back)	.30	.25	.12
6b	Rusty Staub (DK) (Perez-Steele on back)	.60	.45	.25
7a	Jack Clark (DK) (Perez-Steel on back)	.40	.30	.15
7b	Jack Clark (DK) (Perez-Steele on back)	.80	.60	.30
8a	Dave Dravecky (DK) (Perez-Steel on back)	.25	.20	.10
8b	Dave Dravecky (DK) (Perez-Steele on back)	.60	.45	.25
9a	Al Oliver (DK) (Perez-Steel on back)	.35	.25	.14
9b	Al Oliver (DK) (Perez-Steele on back)	.70	.50	.30
10a	Dave Righetti (DK) (Perez-Steel on back)	.40	.30	.15
10b	Dave Righetti (DK) (Perez-Steele on back)	.80	.60	.30
11a	Hal McRae (DK) (Perez-Steel on back)	.30	.25	.12
11b	Hal McRae (DK) (Perez-Steele on back)	.60	.45	.25
12a	Ray Knight (DK) (Perez-Steel on back)	.25	.20	.10
12b	Ray Knight (DK) (Perez-Steele on back)	.60	.45	.25
13a	Bruce Sutter (DK) (Perez-Steel on back)	.35	.25	.14
13b	Bruce Sutter (DK) (Perez-Steele on back)	.70	.50	.30
14a	Bob Horner (DK) (Perez-Steel on back)	.40	.30	.15
14b	Bob Horner (DK) (Perez-Steele on back)	.80	.60	.30
15a	Lance Parrish (DK) (Perez-Steel on back)	.60	.45	.25
15b	Lance Parrish (DK) (Perez-Steele on back)	1.25	.90	.50
16a	Matt Young (DK) (Perez-Steel on back)	.25	.20	.10
16b	Matt Young (DK) (Perez-Steele on back)	.60	.45	.25
17a	Fred Lynn (DK) (Perez-Steel on back)	.35	.25	.14
17b	Fred Lynn (DK) (Perez-Steele on back)	.70	.50	.30
18a	Ron Kittle (DK) (Perez-Steel on back)(FC)	.35	.25	.14
18b	Ron Kittle (DK) (Perez-Steele on back)(FC)	.70	.50	.30
19a	Jim Clancy (DK) (Perez-Steel on back)	.25	.20	.10
19b	Jim Clancy (DK) (Perez-Steele on back)	.60	.45	.25
20a	Bill Madlock (DK) (Perez-Steele on back)	.30	.25	.12
20b	Bill Madlock (DK) (Perez-Steele on back)	.60	.45	.25
21a	Larry Parrish (DK) (Perez-Steel on back)	.30	.25	.12
21b	Larry Parrish (DK) (Perez-Steele on back)	.60	.45	.25
22a	Eddie Murray (DK) (Perez-Steel on back)	1.25	.90	.50
22b	Eddie Murray (DK) (Perez-Steele on back)	2.50	2.00	1.00
23a	Mike Schmidt (DK) (Perez-Steel on back)	1.25	.90	.50
23b	Mike Schmidt (DK) (Perez-Steele on back)	2.50	2.00	1.00
24a	Pedro Guerrero (DK) (Perez-Steel on back)	.50	.40	.20
24b	Pedro Guerrero (DK) (Perez-Steele on back)	1.00	.70	.40
25a	Andre Thornton (DK) (Perez-Steel on back)	.30	.25	.12
25b	Andre Thornton (DK) (Perez-Steele on back)	.60	.45	.25
26a	Wade Boggs (DK) (Perez-Steel on back)	3.75	2.75	1.50

		MT	NR MT	EX
26b	Wade Boggs (DK) (Perez-Steele on back)	5.00	3.75	2.00
27	*Joel Skinner (RR)*(FC)	.20	.15	.08
28	Tom Dunbar (RR)	.10	.08	.04
29a	Mike Stenhouse (RR) (no number on back)	.15	.11	.06
29b	Mike Stenhouse (RR) (29 on back)	8.00	6.00	3.25
30a	*Ron Darling* (no number on back)(FC)	6.00	4.50	2.50
30b	*Ron Darling* (30 on back)(FC)	20.00	15.00	8.00
31	*Dion James (RR)*(FC)	.40	.30	.15
32	*Tony Fernandez (RR)*(FC)	8.00	6.00	3.25
33	Angel Salazar (RR)	.10	.08	.04
34	*Kevin McReynolds (RR)*(FC)	12.00	9.00	4.75
35	*Dick Schofield (RR)*(FC)	.40	.30	.15
36	*Brad Komminsk (RR)*(FC)	.15	.11	.06
37	*Tim Teufel (RR)*(FC)	.40	.30	.15
38	Doug Frobel (RR)	.10	.08	.04
39	*Greg Gagne (RR)*(FC)	.50	.40	.20
40	Mike Fuentes (RR)	.10	.08	.04
41	*Joe Carter (RR)*(FC)	15.00	11.00	6.00
42	Mike Brown (RR)	.10	.08	.04
43	Mike Jeffcoat (RR)	.10	.08	.04
44	*Sid Fernandez (RR)*(FC)	6.00	4.50	2.50
45	Brian Dayett (RR)	.10	.08	.04
46	Chris Smith (RR)	.10	.08	.04
47	Eddie Murray	1.25	.90	.50
48	Robin Yount	2.00	1.50	.80
49	Lance Parrish	.50	.40	.20
50	Jim Rice	.90	.70	.35
51	Dave Winfield	.90	.70	.35
52	Fernando Valenzuela	.70	.50	.30
53	George Brett	1.50	1.25	.60
54	Rickey Henderson	3.00	2.00	1.00
55	Gary Carter	.80	.60	.30
56	Buddy Bell	.20	.15	.08
57	Reggie Jackson	1.25	.90	.50
58	Harold Baines	.25	.20	.10
59	Ozzie Smith	.25	.20	.10
60	Nolan Ryan	3.50	2.75	1.50
61	Pete Rose	2.50	2.00	1.00
62	Ron Oester	.10	.08	.04
63	Steve Garvey	.90	.70	.35
64	Jason Thompson	.10	.08	.04
65	Jack Clark	.35	.25	.14
66	Dale Murphy	1.50	1.25	.60
67	Leon Durham	.12	.09	.05
68	*Darryl Strawberry*(FC)	35.00	27.00	15.00
69	Richie Zisk	.12	.09	.05
70	Kent Hrbek	.60	.45	.25
71	Dave Stieb	.25	.20	.10
72	Ken Schrom	.10	.08	.04
73	George Bell	1.75	1.25	.70
74	John Moses	.15	.11	.06
75	Ed Lynch	.10	.08	.04
76	Chuck Rainey	.10	.08	.04
77	Biff Pocoroba	.10	.08	.04
78	Cecilio Guante	.10	.08	.04
79	Jim Barr	.10	.08	.04
80	Kurt Bevacqua	.10	.08	.04
81	Tom Foley	.10	.08	.04
82	Joe Lefebvre	.10	.08	.04
83	*Andy Van Slyke*(FC)	4.00	3.00	1.50
84	Bob Lillis	.10	.08	.04
85	Rick Adams	.10	.08	.04
86	Jerry Hairston	.10	.08	.04
87	Bob James	.10	.08	.04
88	Joe Altobelli	.10	.08	.04
89	Ed Romero	.10	.08	.04
90	John Grubb	.10	.08	.04
91	John Henry Johnson	.10	.08	.04
92	Juan Espino	.10	.08	.04
93	Candy Maldonado	.20	.15	.08
94	Andre Thornton	.20	.15	.08
95	Onix Concepcion	.10	.08	.04
96	*Don Hill*(FC)	.20	.15	.08
97	Andre Dawson	.60	.45	.25
98	Frank Tanana	.15	.11	.06
99	*Curt Wilkerson*(FC)	.15	.11	.06
100	Larry Gura	.10	.08	.04
101	Dwayne Murphy	.12	.09	.05
102	Tom Brennan	.10	.08	.04
103	Dave Righetti	.40	.30	.15
104	Steve Sax	.30	.25	.12
105	Dan Petry	.12	.09	.05
106	Cal Ripken	1.50	1.25	.60
107	Paul Molitor	.35	.25	.14
108	Fred Lynn	.35	.25	.14
109	Neil Allen	.10	.08	.04
110	Joe Niekro	.20	.15	.08
111	Steve Carlton	1.00	.70	.40
112	Terry Kennedy	.15	.11	.06
113	Bill Madlock	.20	.15	.08
114	Chili Davis	.15	.11	.06
115	Jim Gantner	.12	.09	.05
116	Tom Seaver	1.00	.70	.40
117	Bill Buckner	.20	.15	.08
118	Bill Caudill	.10	.08	.04
119	Jim Clancy	.15	.11	.06
120	John Castino	.10	.08	.04
121	Dave Concepcion	.20	.15	.08
122	Greg Luzinski	.20	.15	.08
123	Mike Boddicker(FC)	.20	.15	.08
124	Pete Ladd	.10	.08	.04
125	Juan Berenguer	.10	.08	.04
126	John Montefusco	.10	.08	.04
127	Ed Jurak	.10	.08	.04
128	Tom Niedenfuer	.12	.09	.05
129	Bert Blyleven	.30	.25	.12
130	Bud Black	.12	.09	.05
131	Gorman Heimueller	.10	.08	.04
132	Dan Schatzeder	.10	.08	.04
133	Ron Jackson	.10	.08	.04
134	*Tom Henke*(FC)	.90	.70	.35
135	Kevin Hickey	.10	.08	.04
136	Mike Scott	.30	.25	.12
137	Bo Diaz	.12	.09	.05
138	Glenn Brummer	.10	.08	.04
139	Sid Monge	.10	.08	.04

		MT	NR MT	EX
140	Rich Gale	.10	.08	.04
141	Brett Butler	.15	.11	.06
142	Brian Harper	.10	.08	.04
143	John Rabb	.10	.08	.04
144	Gary Woods	.10	.08	.04
145	Pat Putnam	.10	.08	.04
146	*Jim Acker*(FC)	.15	.11	.06
147	Mickey Hatcher	.12	.09	.05
148	Todd Cruz	.10	.08	.04
149	Tom Tellmann	.10	.08	.04
150	John Wockenfuss	.10	.08	.04
151	Wade Boggs	12.00	9.00	4.75
152	Don Baylor	.20	.15	.08
153	Bob Welch	.20	.15	.08
154	Alan Bannister	.10	.08	.04
155	Willie Aikens	.10	.08	.04
156	Jeff Burroughs	.12	.09	.05
157	Bryan Little	.10	.08	.04
158	Bob Boone	.15	.11	.06
159	Dave Hostetler	.10	.08	.04
160	Jerry Dybzinski	.10	.08	.04
161	Mike Madden	.10	.08	.04
162	Luis DeLeon	.10	.08	.04
163	Willie Hernandez	.15	.11	.06
164	Frank Pastore	.10	.08	.04
165	Rick Camp	.10	.08	.04
166	Lee Mazzilli	.12	.09	.05
167	Scot Thompson	.10	.08	.04
168	Bob Forsch	.12	.09	.05
169	Mike Flanagan	.15	.11	.06
170	Rick Manning	.10	.08	.04
171	Chet Lemon	.12	.09	.05
172	Jerry Remy	.10	.08	.04
173	Ron Guidry	.35	.25	.14
174	Pedro Guerrero	.50	.40	.20
175	Willie Wilson	.25	.20	.10
176	Carney Lansford	.20	.15	.08
177	Al Oliver	.30	.25	.12
178	Jim Sundberg	.12	.09	.05
179	Bobby Grich	.20	.15	.08
180	Richard Dotson	.20	.15	.08
181	Joaquin Andujar	.12	.09	.05
182	Jose Cruz	.20	.15	.08
183	Mike Schmidt	4.00	3.00	1.50
184	*Gary Redus*(FC)	.30	.25	.12
185	Garry Templeton	.15	.11	.06
186	Tony Pena	.20	.15	.08
187	Greg Minton	.10	.08	.04
188	Phil Niekro	.50	.40	.20
189	Ferguson Jenkins	.30	.25	.12
190	Mookie Wilson	.15	.11	.06
191	Jim Beattie	.10	.08	.04
192	Gary Ward	.12	.09	.05
193	Jesse Barfield	.40	.30	.15
194	Pete Filson	.10	.08	.04
195	Roy Lee Jackson	.10	.08	.04
196	Rick Sweet	.10	.08	.04
197	Jesse Orosco	.15	.11	.06
198	*Steve Lake*(FC)	.12	.09	.05
199	Ken Dayley	.10	.08	.04
200	Manny Sarmiento	.10	.08	.04
201	Mark Davis(FC)	.25	.20	.10
202	Tim Flannery	.10	.08	.04
203	Bill Scherrer	.10	.08	.04
204	Al Holland	.10	.08	.04
205	David Von Ohlen	.10	.08	.04
206	Mike LaCoss	.10	.08	.04
207	Juan Beniquez	.10	.08	.04
208	*Juan Agosto*(FC)	.20	.15	.08
209	Bobby Ramos	.10	.08	.04
210	Al Bumbry	.12	.09	.05
211	Mark Brouhard	.10	.08	.04
212	Howard Bailey	.10	.08	.04
213	Bruce Hurst	.20	.15	.08
214	Bob Shirley	.10	.08	.04
215	Pat Zachry	.10	.08	.04
216	Julio Franco	.25	.20	.10
217	Mike Armstrong	.10	.08	.04
218	Dave Beard	.10	.08	.04
219	Steve Rogers	.12	.09	.05
220	John Butcher	.10	.08	.04
221	*Mike Smithson*(FC)	.20	.15	.08
222	Frank White	.20	.15	.08
223	Mike Heath	.10	.08	.04
224	Chris Bando	.10	.08	.04
225	Roy Smalley	.10	.08	.04
226	Dusty Baker	.20	.15	.08
227	Lou Whitaker	.60	.45	.25
228	John Lowenstein	.10	.08	.04
229	Ben Oglivie	.12	.09	.05
230	Doug DeCinces	.15	.11	.06
231	Lonnie Smith	.12	.09	.05
232	Ray Knight	.15	.11	.06
233	Gary Matthews	.20	.15	.08
234	Juan Bonilla	.10	.08	.04
235	Rod Scurry	.10	.08	.04
236	Atlee Hammaker	.10	.08	.04
237	Mike Caldwell	.10	.08	.04
238	Keith Hernandez	.80	.60	.30
239	Larry Bowa	.25	.20	.10
240	Tony Bernazard	.10	.08	.04
241	Damaso Garcia	.10	.08	.04
242	Tom Brunansky	.35	.25	.14
243	Dan Driessen	.12	.09	.05
244	Ron Kittle(FC)	.30	.25	.12
245	Tim Stoddard	.10	.08	.04
246	Bob Gibson	.10	.08	.04
247	Marty Castillo	.10	.08	.04
248	*Don Mattingly*(FC)	100.00	75.00	40.00
249	Jeff Newman	.10	.08	.04
250	*Alejandro Pena*(FC)	.40	.30	.15
251	Toby Harrah	.12	.09	.05
252	Cesar Geronimo	.10	.08	.04
253	Tom Underwood	.10	.08	.04
254	Doug Flynn	.10	.08	.04
255	Andy Hassler	.10	.08	.04
256	Odell Jones	.10	.08	.04
257	Rudy Law	.10	.08	.04
258	Harry Spilman	.10	.08	.04
259	Marty Bystrom	.10	.08	.04
260	Dave Rucker	.10	.08	.04
261	Ruppert Jones	.10	.08	.04
262	Jeff Jones	.10	.08	.04

		MT	NR MT	EX
263	*Gerald Perry*(FC)	1.50	1.25	.60
264	Gene Tenace	.12	.09	.05
265	Brad Wellman	.10	.08	.04
266	Dickie Noles	.10	.08	.04
267	Jamie Allen	.10	.08	.04
268	Jim Gott	.15	.11	.06
269	Ron Davis	.10	.08	.04
270	Benny Ayala	.10	.08	.04
271	Ned Yost	.10	.08	.04
272	Dave Rozema	.10	.08	.04
273	Dave Stapleton	.10	.08	.04
274	Lou Piniella	.20	.15	.08
275	Jose Morales	.10	.08	.04
276	Brod Perkins	.10	.08	.04
277	Butch Davis	.10	.08	.04
278	*Tony Phillips*(FC)	.20	.15	.08
279	Jeff Reardon	.25	.20	.10
280	Ken Forsch	.10	.08	.04
281	*Pete O'Brien*(FC)	1.50	1.25	.60
282	Tom Paciorek	.10	.08	.04
283	Frank LaCorte	.10	.08	.04
284	Tim Lollar	.10	.08	.04
285	Greg Gross	.10	.08	.04
286	Alex Trevino	.10	.08	.04
287	Gene Garber	.10	.08	.04
288	Dave Parker	.50	.40	.20
289	Lee Smith	.20	.15	.08
290	Dave LaPoint	.15	.11	.06
291	*John Shelby*(FC)	.35	.25	.14
292	Charlie Moore	.10	.08	.04
293	Alan Trammell	.60	.45	.25
294	Tony Armas	.20	.15	.08
295	Shane Rawley	.20	.15	.08
296	Greg Brock	.15	.11	.06
297	Hal McRae	.20	.15	.08
298	Mike Davis	.12	.09	.05
299	Tim Raines	.80	.60	.30
300	Bucky Dent	.15	.11	.06
301	Tommy John	.35	.25	.14
302	Carlton Fisk	.50	.40	.20
303	Darrell Porter	.12	.09	.05
304	Dickie Thon	.12	.09	.05
305	Garry Maddox	.12	.09	.05
306	Cesar Cedeno	.20	.15	.08
307	Gary Lucas	.10	.08	.04
308	Johnny Ray	.20	.15	.08
309	Andy McGaffigan	.10	.08	.04
310	Claudell Washington	.12	.09	.05
311	Ryne Sandberg	4.00	3.00	1.50
312	George Foster	.30	.25	.12
313	*Spike Owen*(FC)	.30	.25	.12
314	Gary Gaetti	.90	.70	.35
315	Willie Upshaw	.12	.09	.05
316	Al Williams	.10	.08	.04
317	Jorge Orta	.10	.08	.04
318	Orlando Mercado	.10	.08	.04
319	*Junior Ortiz*(FC)	.12	.09	.05
320	Mike Proly	.10	.08	.04
321	Randy Johnson	.10	.08	.04
322	Jim Morrison	.10	.08	.04
323	Max Venable	.10	.08	.04
324	Tony Gwynn	6.00	4.50	2.50
325	Duane Walker	.10	.08	.04
326	Ozzie Virgil	.10	.08	.04
327	Jeff Lahti	.10	.08	.04
328	*Bill Dawley*(FC)	.12	.09	.05
329	Rob Wilfong	.10	.08	.04
330	Marc Hill	.10	.08	.04
331	Ray Burris	.10	.08	.04
332	Allan Ramirez	.10	.08	.04
333	Chuck Porter	.10	.08	.04
334	Wayne Krenchicki	.10	.08	.04
335	Gary Allenson	.10	.08	.04
336	*Bob Meacham*(FC)	.20	.15	.08
337	Joe Beckwith	.10	.08	.04
338	Rick Sutcliffe	.25	.20	.10
339	*Mark Huismann*(FC)	.15	.11	.06
340	*Tim Conroy*(FC)	.15	.11	.06
341	Scott Sanderson	.10	.08	.04
342	Larry Biittner	.10	.08	.04
343	Dave Stewart	.20	.15	.08
344	Darryl Motley	.10	.08	.04
345	*Chris Codiroli*(FC)	.12	.09	.05
346	Rick Behenna	.10	.08	.04
347	Andre Robertson	.10	.08	.04
348	Mike Marshall	.25	.20	.10
349	Larry Herndon	.12	.09	.05
350	Rich Dauer	.10	.08	.04
351	Cecil Cooper	.25	.20	.10
352	Rod Carew	.90	.70	.35
353	Willie McGee	.40	.30	.15
354	Phil Garner	.12	.09	.05
355	Joe Morgan	.60	.45	.25
356	Luis Salazar	.10	.08	.04
357	John Candelaria	.20	.15	.08
358	Bill Laskey	.10	.08	.04
359	Bob McClure	.10	.08	.04
360	Dave Kingman	.30	.25	.12
361	Ron Cey	.20	.15	.08
362	*Matt Young*(FC)	.20	.15	.08
363	Lloyd Moseby	.20	.15	.08
364	Frank Viola	1.25	.90	.50
365	Eddie Milner	.10	.08	.04
366	Floyd Bannister	.20	.15	.08
367	Dan Ford	.10	.08	.04
368	Moose Haas	.10	.08	.04
369	Doug Bair	.10	.08	.04
370	*Ray Fontenot*(FC)	.12	.09	.05
371	Luis Aponte	.10	.08	.04
372	Jack Fimple	.10	.08	.04
373	*Neal Heaton*(FC)	.20	.15	.08
374	Greg Pryor	.10	.08	.04
375	Wayne Gross	.10	.08	.04
376	Charlie Lea	.10	.08	.04
377	Steve Lubratich	.10	.08	.04
378	Jon Matlack	.12	.09	.05
379	Julio Cruz	.10	.08	.04
380	John Mizerock	.10	.08	.04
381	*Kevin Gross*(FC)	.40	.30	.15
382	Mike Ramsey	.10	.08	.04
383	Doug Gwosdz	.10	.08	.04
384	Kelly Paris	.10	.08	.04
385	Pete Falcone	.10	.08	.04

		MT	NR MT	EX
386	Milt May	.10	.08	.04
387	Fred Breining	.10	.08	.04
388	*Craig Lefferts*(FC)	.25	.20	.10
389	Steve Henderson	.10	.08	.04
390	Randy Moffitt	.10	.08	.04
391	Ron Washington	.10	.08	.04
392	Gary Roenicke	.10	.08	.04
393	*Tom Candiotti*(FC)	.30	.25	.12
394	Larry Pashnick	.10	.08	.04
395	Dwight Evans	.30	.25	.12
396	Goose Gossage	.40	.30	.15
397	Derrel Thomas	.10	.08	.04
398	Juan Eichelberger	.10	.08	.04
399	Leon Roberts	.10	.08	.04
400	Davey Lopes	.15	.11	.06
401	Bill Gullickson	.10	.08	.04
402	Geoff Zahn	.10	.08	.04
403	Billy Sample	.10	.08	.04
404	Mike Squires	.10	.08	.04
405	Craig Reynolds	.10	.08	.04
406	Eric Show	.15	.11	.06
407	John Denny	.10	.08	.04
408	Dann Bilardello	.10	.08	.04
409	Bruce Benedict	.10	.08	.04
410	Kent Tekulve	.12	.09	.05
411	Mel Hall	.20	.15	.08
412	John Stuper	.10	.08	.04
413	Rick Dempsey	.12	.09	.05
414	Don Sutton	.50	.40	.20
415	Jack Morris	.50	.40	.20
416	John Tudor	.20	.15	.08
417	Willie Randolph	.20	.15	.08
418	Jerry Reuss	.15	.11	.06
419	Don Slaught	.10	.08	.04
420	Steve McCatty	.10	.08	.04
421	Tim Wallach	.25	.20	.10
422	Larry Parrish	.20	.15	.08
423	Brian Downing	.20	.15	.08
424	Britt Burns	.10	.08	.04
425	David Green	.10	.08	.04
426	Jerry Mumphrey	.12	.09	.05
427	Ivan DeJesus	.10	.08	.04
428	Mario Soto	.12	.09	.05
429	Gene Richards	.10	.08	.04
430	Dale Berra	.10	.08	.04
431	Darrell Evans	.25	.20	.10
432	Glenn Hubbard	.12	.09	.05
433	Jody Davis	.15	.11	.06
434	Danny Heep	.10	.08	.04
435	*Ed Nunez*(FC)	.20	.15	.08
436	Bobby Castillo	.10	.08	.04
437	Ernie Whitt	.12	.09	.05
438	Scott Ullger	.10	.08	.04
439	Doyle Alexander	.15	.11	.06
440	Domingo Ramos	.10	.08	.04
441	Craig Swan	.10	.08	.04
442	Warren Brusstar	.10	.08	.04
443	Len Barker	.12	.09	.05
444	Mike Easler	.12	.09	.05
445	Renie Martin	.10	.08	.04
446	*Dennis Rasmussen*(FC)	.70	.50	.30
447	Ted Power(FC)	.15	.11	.06
448	*Charlie Hudson*(FC)	.25	.20	.10
449	*Danny Cox*(FC)	.70	.50	.30
450	Kevin Bass(FC)	.30	.25	.12
451	Daryl Sconiers	.10	.08	.04
452	Scott Fletcher	.12	.09	.05
453	Bryn Smith	.10	.08	.04
454	Jim Dwyer	.10	.08	.04
455	Rob Picciolo	.10	.08	.04
456	Enos Cabell	.10	.08	.04
457	*Dennis "Oil Can" Boyd*(FC)	.50	.40	.20
458	Butch Wynegar	.10	.08	.04
459	Burt Hooton	.12	.09	.05
460	Ron Hassey	.10	.08	.04
461	*Danny Jackson*(FC)	2.50	2.00	1.00
462	Bob Kearney	.10	.08	.04
463	Terry Francona	.10	.08	.04
464	Wayne Tolleson	.10	.08	.04
465	Mickey Rivers	.12	.09	.05
466	John Wathan	.12	.09	.05
467	Bill Almon	.10	.08	.04
468	George Vukovich	.10	.08	.04
469	Steve Kemp	.15	.11	.06
470	Ken Landreaux	.10	.08	.04
471	Milt Wilcox	.10	.08	.04
472	Tippy Martinez	.10	.08	.04
473	Ted Simmons	.20	.15	.08
474	Tim Foli	.10	.08	.04
475	George Hendrick	.12	.09	.05
476	Terry Puhl	.10	.08	.04
477	Von Hayes	.25	.20	.10
478	Bobby Brown	.10	.08	.04
479	Lee Lacy	.10	.08	.04
480	Joel Youngblood	.10	.08	.04
481	Jim Slaton	.10	.08	.04
482	*Mike Fitzgerald*(FC)	.20	.15	.08
483	Keith Moreland	.12	.09	.05
484	Ron Roenicke	.10	.08	.04
485	Luis Leal	.10	.08	.04
486	Bryan Oelkers	.10	.08	.04
487	Bruce Berenyi	.10	.08	.04
488	LaMarr Hoyt	.10	.08	.04
489	Joe Nolan	.10	.08	.04
490	Marshall Edwards	.10	.08	.04
491	*Mike Laga*(FC)	.12	.09	.05
492	Rick Cerone	.10	.08	.04
493	Mike Miller (Rick)	.10	.08	.04
494	Rick Honeycutt	.10	.08	.04
495	Mike Hargrove	.10	.08	.04
496	Joe Simpson	.10	.08	.04
497	*Keith Atherton*(FC)	.25	.20	.10
498	Chris Welsh	.10	.08	.04
499	Bruce Kison	.10	.08	.04
500	Bob Johnson	.10	.08	.04
501	Jerry Koosman	.15	.11	.06
502	Frank DiPino	.10	.08	.04
503	Tony Perez	.40	.30	.15
504	Ken Oberkfell	.10	.08	.04
505	*Mark Thurmond*(FC)	.12	.09	.05
506	Joe Price	.10	.08	.04
507	Pascual Perez	.15	.11	.06
508	*Marvell Wynne*(FC)	.25	.20	.10

		MT	NR MT	EX
509	Mike Krukow	.12	.09	.05
510	Dick Ruthven	.10	.08	.04
511	Al Cowens	.10	.08	.04
512	Cliff Johnson	.10	.08	.04
513	*Randy Bush*(FC)	.20	.15	.08
514	Sammy Stewart	.10	.08	.04
515	*Bill Schroeder*(FC)	.25	.20	.10
516	Aurelio Lopez	.10	.08	.04
517	Mike Brown	.10	.08	.04
518	Graig Nettles	.35	.25	.14
519	Dave Sax	.10	.08	.04
520	Gerry Willard	.10	.08	.04
521	Paul Splittorff	.10	.08	.04
522	Tom Burgmeier	.10	.08	.04
523	Chris Speier	.10	.08	.04
524	Bobby Clark	.10	.08	.04
525	George Wright	.10	.08	.04
526	Dennis Lamp	.10	.08	.04
527	Tony Scott	.10	.08	.04
528	Ed Whitson	.10	.08	.04
529	Ron Reed	.10	.08	.04
530	Charlie Puleo	.10	.08	.04
531	Jerry Royster	.10	.08	.04
532	Don Robinson	.12	.09	.05
533	Steve Trout	.10	.08	.04
534	Bruce Sutter	.30	.25	.12
535	Bob Horner	.20	.15	.08
536	Pat Tabler	.15	.11	.06
537	Chris Chambliss	.12	.09	.05
538	Bob Ojeda	.15	.11	.06
539	Alan Ashby	.10	.08	.04
540	Jay Johnstone	.12	.09	.05
541	Bob Dernier	.10	.08	.04
542	*Brook Jacoby*(FC)	1.25	.90	.50
543	U.L. Washington	.10	.08	.04
544	Danny Darwin	.10	.08	.04
545	Kiko Garcia	.10	.08	.04
546	Vance Law	.12	.09	.05
547	Tug McGraw	.20	.15	.08
548	Dave Smith	.12	.09	.05
549	Len Matuszek	.10	.08	.04
550	Tom Hume	.10	.08	.04
551	Dave Dravecky	.15	.11	.06
552	Rick Rhoden	.15	.11	.06
553	Duane Kuiper	.10	.08	.04
554	Rusty Staub	.20	.15	.08
555	Bill Campbell	.10	.08	.04
556	Mike Torrez	.12	.09	.05
557	Dave Henderson(FC)	.25	.20	.10
558	Len Whitehouse	.10	.08	.04
559	Barry Bonnell	.10	.08	.04
560	Rick Lysander	.10	.08	.04
561	Garth Iorg	.10	.08	.04
562	Bryan Clark	.10	.08	.04
563	Brian Giles	.10	.08	.04
564	Vern Ruhle	.10	.08	.04
565	Steve Bedrosian	.20	.15	.08
566	Larry McWilliams	.10	.08	.04
567	Jeff Leonard	.15	.11	.06
568	Alan Wiggins	.10	.08	.04
569	*Jeff Russell*(FC)	.25	.20	.10
570	Salome Barojas	.10	.08	.04
571	Dane Iorg	.10	.08	.04
572	Bob Knepper	.15	.11	.06
573	Gary Lavelle	.10	.08	.04
574	Gorman Thomas	.15	.11	.06
575	Manny Trillo	.12	.09	.05
576	Jim Palmer	.70	.50	.30
577	Dale Murray	.10	.08	.04
578	Tom Brookens	.10	.08	.04
579	Rich Gedman	.15	.11	.06
580	*Bill Doran*(FC)	1.25	.90	.50
581	Steve Yeager	.10	.08	.04
582	Dan Spillner	.10	.08	.04
583	Dan Quisenberry	.15	.11	.06
584	Rance Mulliniks	.10	.08	.04
585	Storm Davis	.15	.11	.06
586	Dave Schmidt	.10	.08	.04
587	Bill Russell	.12	.09	.05
588	*Pat Sheridan*(FC)	.20	.15	.08
589	Rafael Ramirez	.10	.08	.04
590	Bud Anderson	.10	.08	.04
591	George Frazier	.10	.08	.04
592	*Lee Tunnell*(FC)	.12	.09	.05
593	Kirk Gibson	.60	.45	.25
594	Scott McGregor	.12	.09	.05
595	Bob Bailor	.10	.08	.04
596	Tom Herr	.20	.15	.08
597	Luis Sanchez	.10	.08	.04
598	Dave Engle	.10	.08	.04
599	*Craig McMurtry*(FC)	.15	.11	.06
600	Carlos Diaz	.10	.08	.04
601	Tom O'Malley	.10	.08	.04
602	*Nick Esasky*(FC)	3.75	2.75	1.50
603	Ron Hodges	.10	.08	.04
604	Ed Vande Berg	.10	.08	.04
605	Alfredo Griffin	.12	.09	.05
606	Glenn Hoffman	.10	.08	.04
607	Hubie Brooks	.20	.15	.08
608	Richard Barnes (photo actually Neal Heaton)	.10	.08	.04
609	*Greg Walker*(FC)	.60	.45	.25
610	Ken Singleton	.20	.15	.08
611	Mark Clear	.10	.08	.04
612	Buck Martinez	.10	.08	.04
613	Ken Griffey	.15	.11	.06
614	Reid Nichols	.10	.08	.04
615	*Doug Sisk*(FC)	.12	.09	.05
616	Bob Brenly	.10	.08	.04
617	Joey McLaughlin	.10	.08	.04
618	Glenn Wilson	.12	.09	.05
619	Bob Stoddard	.10	.08	.04
620	Len Sakata (Lenn)	.10	.08	.04
621	*Mike Young*(FC)	.25	.20	.10
622	John Stefero	.10	.08	.04
623	*Carmelo Martinez*(FC)	.30	.25	.12
624	Dave Bergman	.10	.08	.04
625	Runnin' Reds (David Green, Willie McGee, Lonnie Smith, Ozzie Smith)	.30	.25	.12
626	Rudy May	.10	.08	.04
627	Matt Keough	.10	.08	.04
628	*Jose DeLeon*(FC)	.80	.60	.30
629	Jim Essian	.10	.08	.04

		MT	NR MT	EX
630	*Darnell Coles*(FC)	.35	.25	.14
631	Mike Warren	.10	.08	.04
632	Del Crandall	.10	.08	.04
633	Dennis Martinez	.12	.09	.05
634	Mike Moore	.12	.09	.05
635	Lary Sorensen	.10	.08	.04
636	Ricky Nelson	.10	.08	.04
637	Omar Moreno	.10	.08	.04
638	Charlie Hough	.15	.11	.06
639	Dennis Eckersley	.25	.20	.10
640	*Walt Terrell*(FC)	.40	.30	.15
641	Denny Walling	.10	.08	.04
642	*Dave Anderson*(FC)	.20	.15	.08
643	*Jose Oquendo*(FC)	.25	.20	.10
644	Bob Stanley	.10	.08	.04
645	Dave Geisel	.10	.08	.04
646	*Scott Garrelts*(FC)	.90	.70	.35
647	*Gary Pettis*(FC)	.40	.30	.15
648	Duke Snider Puzzle Card	.10	.08	.04
649	Johnnie LeMaster	.10	.08	.04
650	Dave Collins	.12	.09	.05
651	San Diego Chicken	.25	.20	.10
---a	Checklist 1-26 DK (Perez-Steel on back)	.12	.09	.05
---b	Checklist 1-26 DK (Perez-Steele on back)	.40	.30	.15
---	Checklist 27-130	.10	.08	.04
---	Checklist 131-234	.10	.08	.04
---	Checklist 235-338	.10	.08	.04
---	Checklist 339-442	.10	.08	.04
---	Checklist 443-546	.10	.08	.04
---	Checklist 547-651	.10	.08	.04
---A	Living Legends (Rollie Fingers, Gaylord Perry)	2.75	2.00	1.00
---B	Living Legends (Johnny Bench, Carl Yastrzemski)	5.00	3.75	2.00

1984 Donruss Action All-Stars

Full-color photos on the card fronts and backs make the 1984 Donruss Action All-Stars set somewhat unusual. The fronts contain a large action photo plus the Donruss logo and year of issue inside a deep red border. The top half of the card backs feature a close-up photo with the bottom portion containing biographical and statistical information. The cards, which measure 3-1/2" by 5", were sold with Ted Williams puzzle pieces.

		MT	NR MT	EX
Complete Set:		7.00	5.25	2.75
Common Player:		.09	.07	.04
1	Gary Lavelle	.09	.07	.04
2	Willie McGee	.15	.11	.06
3	Tony Pena	.09	.07	.04
4	Lou Whitaker	.15	.11	.06
5	Robin Yount	.35	.25	.14
6	Doug DeCinces	.09	.07	.04
7	John Castino	.09	.07	.04
8	Terry Kennedy	.09	.07	.04
9	Rickey Henderson	.50	.40	.20
10	Bob Horner	.12	.09	.05
11	Harold Baines	.15	.11	.06
12	Buddy Bell	.09	.07	.04
13	Fernando Valenzuela	.12	.09	.05
14	Nolan Ryan	1.00	.70	.40
15	Andre Thornton	.09	.07	.04
16	Gary Redus	.09	.07	.04
17	Pedro Guerrero	.15	.11	.06
18	Andre Dawson	.20	.15	.08
19	Dave Stieb	.12	.09	.05
20	Cal Ripken	.35	.25	.14
21	Ken Griffey	.12	.09	.05
22	Wade Boggs	1.00	.70	.40
23	Keith Hernandez	.25	.20	.10
24	Steve Carlton	.30	.25	.12
25	Hal McRae	.12	.09	.05
26	John Lowenstein	.09	.07	.04
27	Fred Lynn	.15	.11	.06
28	Bill Buckner	.09	.07	.04
29	Chris Chambliss	.09	.07	.04
30	Richie Zisk	.09	.07	.04
31	Jack Clark	.15	.11	.06
32	George Hendrick	.09	.07	.04
33	Bill Madlock	.12	.09	.05
34	Lance Parrish	.15	.11	.06
35	Paul Molitor	.15	.11	.06
36	Reggie Jackson	.35	.25	.14
37	Kent Hrbek	.20	.15	.08
38	Steve Garvey	.20	.15	.08
39	Carney Lansford	.09	.07	.04
40	Dale Murphy	.30	.25	.12
41	Greg Luzinski	.12	.09	.05

		MT	NR MT	EX
42	Larry Parrish	.09	.07	.04
43	Ryne Sandberg	.25	.20	.10
44	Dickie Thon	.09	.07	.04
45	Bert Blyleven	.12	.09	.05
46	Ron Oester	.09	.07	.04
47	Dusty Baker	.09	.07	.04
48	Steve Rogers	.09	.07	.04
49	Jim Clancy	.09	.07	.04
50	Eddie Murray	.15	.11	.06
51	Ron Guidry	.15	.11	.06
52	Jim Rice	.15	.11	.06
53	Tom Seaver	.30	.25	.12
54	Pete Rose	.30	.25	.12
55	George Brett	.40	.30	.15
56	Dan Quisenberry	.09	.07	.04
57	Mike Schmidt	.60	.45	.25
58	Ted Simmons	.12	.09	.05
59	Dave Righetti	.15	.11	.06
60	Checklist	.09	.07	.04

1984 Donruss Champions

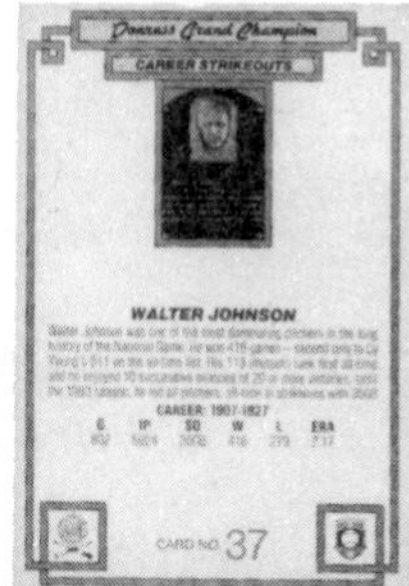

The 60-card Donruss Champions set includes ten Hall of Famers, forty-nine current players and one numbered checklist. The ten Hall of Famers' cards (called Grand Champions) feature the artwork of Dick Perez, while cards of the current players (called Champions) are color photos. The cards measure 3-1/2" by 5". The Grand Champions represent hallmarks of excellence in various statistical categories, while the Champions are the leaders among active players in each category. The ten Grand Champion cards are #'s 1, 8, 14, 20, 26, 31, 37, 43, 50 and 55. The cards were issued with Duke Snider puzzle pieces.

		MT	NR MT	EX
Complete Set:		6.50	5.00	3.00
Common Player:		.07	.05	.03
1	Babe Ruth	.60	.45	.25
2	George Foster	.10	.08	.04
3	Dave Kingman	.10	.08	.04
4	Jim Rice	.10	.08	.04
5	Gorman Thomas	.10	.08	.04
6	Ben Oglivie	.07	.05	.03
7	Jeff Burroughs	.07	.05	.03
8	Hank Aaron	.35	.25	.14
9	Reggie Jackson	.30	.25	.12
10	Carl Yastrzemski	.50	.40	.20
11	Mike Schmidt	.50	.40	.20
12	Graig Nettles	.14	.11	.06
13	Greg Luzinski	.10	.08	.04
14	Ted Williams	1.00	.70	.40
15	George Brett	.35	.25	.14
16	Wade Boggs	.50	.40	.20
17	Hal McRae	.10	.08	.04
18	Bill Buckner	.10	.08	.04
19	Eddie Murray	.10	.08	.04
20	Rogers Hornsby	.14	.11	.06
21	Rod Carew	.20	.15	.08
22	Bill Madlock	.10	.08	.04
23	Lonnie Smith	.07	.05	.03
24	Cecil Cooper	.10	.08	.04
25	Ken Griffey	.10	.08	.04
26	Ty Cobb	.40	.30	.15
27	Pete Rose	.40	.30	.15
28	Rusty Staub	.10	.08	.04
29	Tony Perez	.10	.08	.04
30	Al Oliver	.10	.08	.04
31	Cy Young	.14	.11	.06
32	Gaylord Perry	.14	.11	.06
33	Ferguson Jenkins	.10	.08	.04
34	Phil Niekro	.14	.11	.06
35	Jim Palmer	.30	.25	.12
36	Tommy John	.10	.08	.04
37	Walter Johnson	.20	.15	.08
38	Steve Carlton	.25	.20	.10
39	Nolan Ryan	.50	.40	.20
40	Tom Seaver	.25	.20	.10
41	Don Sutton	.14	.11	.06
42	Bert Blyleven	.10	.08	.04
43	Frank Robinson	.35	.25	.14
44	Joe Morgan	.25	.20	.10
45	Rollie Fingers	.14	.11	.06
46	Keith Hernandez	.10	.08	.04
47	Robin Yount	.50	.40	.20
48	Cal Ripken	.25	.20	.10
49	Dale Murphy	.35	.25	.14
50	Mickey Mantle	1.00	.70	.40
51	Johnny Bench	.50	.40	.20
52	Carlton Fisk	.30	.25	.12
53	Tug McGraw	.10	.08	.04
54	Paul Molitor	.10	.08	.04
55	Carl Hubbell	.14	.11	.06
56	Steve Garvey	.15	.11	.06
57	Dave Parker	.14	.11	.06
58	Gary Carter	.15	.11	.06
59	Fred Lynn	.14	.11	.06
60	Checklist	.10	.08	.04

1985 Donruss

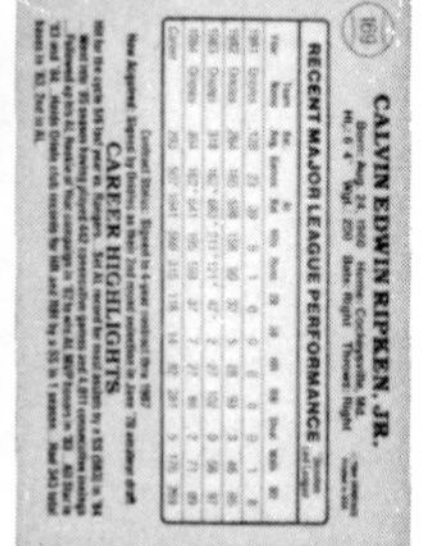

The black-bordered 1985 Donruss set includes 653 numbered cards and seven unnumbered checklists. Displaying the artwork of Dick Perez for the fourth consecutive year, card #'s 1-26 feature the Diamond Kings series. Donruss, realizing the hobby craze over rookie cards, included a Rated Rookies subset (card #'s 27-46). The cards, which are the standard size of 2-1/2" by 3-1/2", were issued with a Lou Gehrig puzzle. The backs of the cards have black print on yellow and white. The complete set price does not include the higher priced variations. (DK) and (RR) refer to the Diamond Kings and Rated Rookies subsets.

		MT	NR MT	EX
Complete Set:		150.00	125.00	60.00
Common Player:		.08	.06	.03
1	Ryne Sandberg (DK)	.60	.45	.25
2	Doug DeCinces (DK)	.10	.08	.04
3	Rich Dotson (DK)	.12	.09	.05
4	Bert Blyleven (DK)	.15	.11	.06
5	Lou Whitaker (DK)	.30	.25	.12
6	Dan Quisenberry (DK)	.15	.11	.06
7	Don Mattingly (DK)	6.00	4.50	2.50
8	Carney Lansford (DK)	.10	.08	.04
9	Frank Tanana (DK)	.12	.09	.05
10	Willie Upshaw (DK)	.10	.08	.04
11	Claudell Washington (DK)	.10	.08	.04
12	Mike Marshall (DK)	.20	.15	.08
13	Joaquin Andujar (DK)	.10	.08	.04
14	Cal Ripken, Jr. (DK)	.60	.45	.25
15	Jim Rice (DK)	.50	.40	.20
16	Don Sutton (DK)	.30	.25	.12
17	Frank Viola (DK)	.15	.11	.06
18	Alvin Davis (DK)(FC)	.60	.45	.25
19	Mario Soto (DK)	.10	.08	.04
20	Jose Cruz (DK)	.12	.09	.05
21	Charlie Lea (DK)	.10	.08	.04
22	Jesse Orosco (DK)	.10	.08	.04
23	Juan Samuel (DK)(FC)	.40	.30	.15
24	Tony Pena (DK)	.12	.09	.05
25	Tony Gwynn (DK)	.50	.40	.20
26	Bob Brenly (DK)	.10	.08	.04
27	*Danny Tartabull (RR)*(FC)	6.00	4.50	2.50
28	*Mike Bielecki (RR)*(FC)	.15	.11	.06
29	*Steve Lyons (RR)*(FC)	.20	.15	.08
30	*Jeff Reed (RR)*(FC)	.15	.11	.06
31	Tony Brewer (RR)	.08	.06	.03
32	*John Morris (RR)*(FC)	.15	.11	.06
33	*Daryl Boston (RR)*(FC)	.25	.20	.10
34	Alfonso Pulido (RR)	.08	.06	.03
35	*Steve Kiefer (RR)*(FC)	.10	.08	.04
36	*Larry Sheets (RR)*(FC)	.50	.40	.20
37	*Scott Bradley (RR)*(FC)	.25	.20	.10
38	*Calvin Schiraldi (RR)*(FC)	.30	.25	.12
39	*Shawon Dunston (RR)*(FC)	3.00	2.25	1.25
40	Charlie Mitchell (RR)	.08	.06	.03
41	*Billy Hatcher (RR)*(FC)	.70	.50	.30
42	Russ Stephans (RR)	.08	.06	.03
43	Alejandro Sanchez (RR)	.08	.06	.03
44	*Steve Jeltz (RR)*(FC)	.15	.11	.06
45	*Jim Traber (RR)*(FC)	.30	.25	.12
46	Doug Loman (RR)	.08	.06	.03
47	Eddie Murray	.60	.45	.25
48	Robin Yount	.80	.60	.30
49	Lance Parrish	.30	.25	.12
50	Jim Rice	.50	.40	.20
51	Dave Winfield	.50	.40	.20
52	Fernando Valenzuela	.35	.25	.14
53	George Brett	.70	.50	.30
54	Dave Kingman	.15	.11	.06
55	Gary Carter	.40	.30	.15
56	Buddy Bell	.12	.09	.05
57	Reggie Jackson	.60	.45	.25
58	Harold Baines	.20	.15	.08
59	Ozzie Smith	.20	.15	.08
60	Nolan Ryan	1.75	1.25	.70
61	Mike Schmidt	1.75	1.25	.70
62	Dave Parker	.35	.25	.14
63	Tony Gwynn	1.50	1.25	.60
64	Tony Pena	.12	.09	.05
65	Jack Clark	.25	.20	.10
66	Dale Murphy	.80	.60	.30
67	Ryne Sandberg	.80	.60	.30
68	Keith Hernandez	.40	.30	.15
69	*Alvin Davis*(FC)	4.00	3.00	1.50
70	Kent Hrbek	.30	.25	.12
71	Willie Upshaw	.10	.08	.04
72	Dave Engle	.08	.06	.03
73	Alfredo Griffin	.10	.08	.04
74a	Jack Perconte (last line of highlights begins "Batted .346...")	.10	.08	.04
74b	Jack Perconte (last line of highlights begins "Led the...")	1.25	.90	.50
75	Jesse Orosco	.10	.08	.04
76	Jody Davis	.12	.09	.05
77	Bob Horner	.12	.09	.05
78	Larry McWilliams	.08	.06	.03
79	Joel Youngblood	.08	.06	.03
80	Alan Wiggins	.08	.06	.03
81	Ron Oester	.08	.06	.03
82	Ozzie Virgil	.08	.06	.03
83	*Ricky Horton*(FC)	.35	.25	.14
84	Bill Doran	.12	.09	.05
85	Rod Carew	.50	.40	.20
86	LaMarr Hoyt	.08	.06	.03
87	Tim Wallach	.15	.11	.06
88	Mike Flanagan	.12	.09	.05
89	Jim Sundberg	.10	.08	.04
90	Chet Lemon	.10	.08	.04
91	Bob Stanley	.08	.06	.03
92	Willie Randolph	.12	.09	.05
93	Bill Russell	.10	.08	.04
94	Julio Franco	.15	.11	.06
95	Dan Quisenberry	.12	.09	.05
96	Bill Caudill	.08	.06	.03
97	Bill Gullickson	.08	.06	.03
98	Danny Darwin	.08	.06	.03
99	Curtis Wilkerson	.08	.06	.03
100	Bud Black	.08	.06	.03
101	Tony Phillips	.08	.06	.03
102	Tony Bernazard	.08	.06	.03
103	Jay Howell	.10	.08	.04
104	Burt Hooton	.10	.08	.04
105	Milt Wilcox	.08	.06	.03
106	Rich Dauer	.08	.06	.03
107	Don Sutton	.35	.25	.14
108	Mike Witt	.15	.11	.06
109	Bruce Sutter	.15	.11	.06
110	Enos Cabell	.08	.06	.03
111	John Denny	.08	.06	.03
112	Dave Dravecky	.10	.08	.04
113	Marvell Wynne	.08	.06	.03
114	Johnnie LeMaster	.08	.06	.03
115	Chuck Porter	.08	.06	.03
116	John Gibbons	.08	.06	.03
117	Keith Moreland	.10	.08	.04
118	Darnell Coles	.12	.09	.05
119	Dennis Lamp	.08	.06	.03
120	Ron Davis	.08	.06	.03
121	Nick Esasky	.10	.08	.04
122	Vance Law	.10	.08	.04
123	Gary Roenicke	.08	.06	.03
124	Bill Schroeder	.08	.06	.03
125	Dave Rozema	.08	.06	.03
126	Bobby Meacham	.08	.06	.03
127	Marty Barrett(FC)	.25	.20	.10
128	*R.J. Reynolds*(FC)	.30	.25	.12
129	Ernie Camacho	.08	.06	.03
130	Jorge Orta	.08	.06	.03
131	Lary Sorensen	.08	.06	.03
132	Terry Francona	.08	.06	.03
133	Fred Lynn	.25	.20	.10
134	Bobby Jones	.08	.06	.03
135	Jerry Hairston	.08	.06	.03
136	Kevin Bass	.12	.09	.05
137	Garry Maddox	.08	.06	.03
138	Dave LaPoint	.10	.08	.04
139	Kevin McReynolds	1.00	.70	.40
140	Wayne Krenchicki	.08	.06	.03
141	Rafael Ramirez	.08	.06	.03
142	Rod Scurry	.08	.06	.03
143	Greg Minton	.08	.06	.03
144	Tim Stoddard	.08	.06	.03
145	Steve Henderson	.08	.06	.03
146	George Bell	.50	.40	.20
147	Dave Meier	.08	.06	.03
148	Sammy Stewart	.08	.06	.03
149	Mark Brouhard	.08	.06	.03
150	Larry Herndon	.10	.08	.04
151	Oil Can Boyd	.10	.08	.04
152	Brian Dayett	.08	.06	.03
153	Tom Niedenfuer	.10	.08	.04
154	Brook Jacoby	.15	.11	.06
155	Onix Concepcion	.08	.06	.03
156	Tim Conroy	.08	.06	.03
157	*Joe Hesketh*(FC)	.15	.11	.06
158	Brian Downing	.12	.09	.05
159	Tommy Dunbar	.08	.06	.03
160	Marc Hill	.08	.06	.03
161	Phil Garner	.10	.08	.04
162	Jerry Davis	.08	.06	.03
163	Bill Campbell	.08	.06	.03
164	*John Franco*(FC)	2.00	1.50	.80
165	Len Barker	.10	.08	.04
166	*Benny Distefano*(FC)	.10	.08	.04
167	George Frazier	.08	.06	.03
168	Tito Landrum	.08	.06	.03
169	Cal Ripken	.60	.45	.25
170	Cecil Cooper	.15	.11	.06
171	Alan Trammell	.40	.30	.15
172	Wade Boggs	5.50	4.25	2.25
173	Don Baylor	.15	.11	.06
174	Pedro Guerrero	.30	.25	.12
175	Frank White	.12	.09	.05
176	Rickey Henderson	1.00	.70	.40
177	Charlie Lea	.08	.06	.03
178	Pete O'Brien	.20	.15	.08
179	Doug DeCinces	.12	.09	.05
180	Ron Kittle	.12	.09	.05
181	George Hendrick	.10	.08	.04
182	Joe Niekro	.12	.09	.05
183	Juan Samuel(FC)	.60	.45	.25

		MT	NR MT	EX
184	Mario Soto	.10	.08	.04
185	Goose Gossage	.25	.20	.10
186	Johnny Ray	.15	.11	.06
187	Bob Brenly	.08	.06	.03
188	Craig McMurtry	.08	.06	.03
189	Leon Durham	.10	.08	.04
190	*Dwight Gooden*(FC)	14.00	10.50	5.00
191	Barry Bonnell	.08	.06	.03
192	Tim Teufel	.12	.09	.05
193	Dave Stieb	.15	.11	.06
194	Mickey Hatcher	.08	.06	.03
195	Jesse Barfield	.25	.20	.10
196	Al Cowens	.08	.06	.03
197	Hubie Brooks	.12	.09	.05
198	Steve Trout	.08	.06	.03
199	Glenn Hubbard	.08	.06	.03
200	Bill Madlock	.15	.11	.06
201	*Jeff Robinson*(FC)	.35	.25	.14
202	Eric Show	.10	.08	.04
203	Dave Concepcion	.15	.11	.06
204	Ivan DeJesus	.08	.06	.03
205	Neil Allen	.08	.06	.03
206	Jerry Mumphrey	.08	.06	.03
207	Mike Brown	.08	.06	.03
208	Carlton Fisk	.40	.30	.15
209	Bryn Smith	.08	.06	.03
210	Tippy Martinez	.08	.06	.03
211	Dion James	.10	.08	.04
212	Willie Hernandez	.10	.08	.04
213	Mike Easler	.10	.08	.04
214	Ron Guidry	.30	.25	.12
215	Rick Honeycutt	.08	.06	.03
216	Brett Butler	.12	.09	.05
217	Larry Gura	.08	.06	.03
218	Ray Burris	.08	.06	.03
219	Steve Rogers	.10	.08	.04
220	Frank Tanana	.12	.09	.05
221	Ned Yost	.08	.06	.03
222	*Bret Saberhagen*	10.00	7.50	4.00
223	Mike Davis	.10	.08	.04
224	Bert Blyleven	.15	.11	.06
225	Steve Kemp	.10	.08	.04
226	Jerry Reuss	.10	.08	.04
227	Darrell Evans	.15	.11	.06
228	Wayne Gross	.08	.06	.03
229	Jim Gantner	.10	.08	.04
230	Bob Boone	.10	.08	.04
231	Lonnie Smith	.10	.08	.04
232	Frank DiPino	.08	.06	.03
233	Jerry Koosman	.12	.09	.05
234	Graig Nettles	.20	.15	.08
235	John Tudor	.12	.09	.05
236	John Rabb	.08	.06	.03
237	Rick Manning	.08	.06	.03
238	Mike Fitzgerald	.08	.06	.03
239	Gary Matthews	.12	.09	.05
240	*Jim Presley*(FC)	1.00	.70	.40
241	Dave Collins	.10	.08	.04
242	Gary Gaetti	.30	.25	.12
243	Dann Bilardello	.08	.06	.03
244	Rudy Law	.08	.06	.03
245	John Lowenstein	.08	.06	.03
246	Tom Tellmann	.08	.06	.03
247	Howard Johnson	1.75	1.25	.70
248	Ray Fontenot	.08	.06	.03
249	Tony Armas	.12	.09	.05
250	Candy Maldonado	.12	.09	.05
251	*Mike Jeffcoat*(FC)	.10	.08	.04
252	Dane Iorg	.08	.06	.03
253	Bruce Bochte	.08	.06	.03
254	Pete Rose	1.25	.90	.50
255	Don Aase	.08	.06	.03
256	George Wright	.08	.06	.03
257	Britt Burns	.08	.06	.03
258	Mike Scott	.20	.15	.08
259	Len Matuszek	.08	.06	.03
260	Dave Rucker	.08	.06	.03
261	Craig Lefferts	.10	.08	.04
262	*Jay Tibbs*(FC)	.20	.15	.08
263	Bruce Benedict	.08	.06	.03
264	Don Robinson	.10	.08	.04
265	Gary Lavelle	.08	.06	.03
266	Scott Sanderson	.08	.06	.03
267	Matt Young	.08	.06	.03
268	Ernie Whitt	.10	.08	.04
269	Houston Jimenez	.08	.06	.03
270	*Ken Dixon*(FC)	.12	.09	.05
271	Peter Ladd	.08	.06	.03
272	Juan Berenguer	.08	.06	.03
273	*Roger Clemens*(FC)	14.00	10.50	5.50
274	Rick Cerone	.08	.06	.03
275	Dave Anderson	.08	.06	.03
276	George Vukovich	.08	.06	.03
277	Greg Pryor	.08	.06	.03
278	Mike Warren	.08	.06	.03
279	Bob James	.08	.06	.03
280	Bobby Grich	.12	.09	.05
281	*Mike Mason*(FC)	.12	.09	.05
282	Ron Reed	.08	.06	.03
283	Alan Ashby	.08	.06	.03
284	Mark Thurmond	.08	.06	.03
285	Joe Lefebvre	.08	.06	.03
286	Ted Power	.08	.06	.03
287	Chris Chambliss	.10	.08	.04
288	Lee Tunnell	.08	.06	.03
289	Rich Bordi	.08	.06	.03
290	Glenn Brummer	.08	.06	.03
291	Mike Boddicker	.12	.09	.05
292	Rollie Fingers	.25	.20	.10
293	Lou Whitaker	.40	.30	.15
294	Dwight Evans	.15	.11	.06
295	Don Mattingly	16.00	12.00	6.50
296	Mike Marshall	.15	.11	.06
297	Willie Wilson	.15	.11	.06
298	Mike Heath	.08	.06	.03
299	Tim Raines	.50	.40	.20
300	Larry Parrish	.12	.09	.05
301	Geoff Zahn	.08	.06	.03
302	Rich Dotson	.12	.09	.05
303	David Green	.08	.06	.03
304	Jose Cruz	.12	.09	.05
305	Steve Carlton	.50	.40	.20
306	Gary Redus	.10	.08	.04
307	Steve Garvey	.50	.40	.20

		MT	NR MT	EX
308	Jose DeLeon	.10	.08	.04
309	Randy Lerch	.08	.06	.03
310	Claudell Washington	.10	.08	.04
311	Lee Smith	.12	.09	.05
312	Darryl Strawberry	4.00	3.00	1.50
313	Jim Beattie	.08	.06	.03
314	John Butcher	.08	.06	.03
315	Damaso Garcia	.10	.08	.04
316	Mike Smithson	.08	.06	.03
317	Luis Leal	.08	.06	.03
318	Ken Phelps(FC)	.25	.20	.10
319	Wally Backman	.10	.08	.04
320	Ron Cey	.12	.09	.05
321	Brad Komminsk	.08	.06	.03
322	Jason Thompson	.08	.06	.03
323	*Frank Williams*(FC)	.20	.15	.08
324	Tim Lollar	.08	.06	.03
325	*Eric Davis*(FC)	20.00	15.00	8.00
326	Von Hayes	.12	.09	.05
327	Andy Van Slyke	.40	.30	.15
328	Craig Reynolds	.08	.06	.03
329	Dick Schofield	.10	.08	.04
330	Scott Fletcher	.10	.08	.04
331	Jeff Reardon	.15	.11	.06
332	Rick Dempsey	.10	.08	.04
333	Ben Oglivie	.10	.08	.04
334	Dan Petry	.10	.08	.04
335	Jackie Gutierrez	.08	.06	.03
336	Dave Righetti	.25	.20	.10
337	Alejandro Pena	.10	.08	.04
338	Mel Hall	.10	.08	.04
339	Pat Sheridan	.08	.06	.03
340	Keith Atherton	.08	.06	.03
341	David Palmer	.08	.06	.03
342	Gary Ward	.10	.08	.04
343	Dave Stewart	.15	.11	.06
344	*Mark Gubicza*(FC)	2.00	1.50	.80
345	Carney Lansford	.12	.09	.05
346	Jerry Willard	.08	.06	.03
347	Ken Griffey	.12	.09	.05
348	*Franklin Stubbs*(FC)	.30	.25	.12
349	Aurelio Lopez	.08	.06	.03
350	Al Bumbry	.10	.08	.04
351	Charlie Moore	.08	.06	.03
352	Luis Sanchez	.08	.06	.03
353	Darrell Porter	.10	.08	.04
354	Bill Dawley	.08	.06	.03
355	Charlie Hudson	.10	.08	.04
356	Garry Templeton	.10	.08	.04
357	Cecilio Guante	.08	.06	.03
358	Jeff Leonard	.12	.09	.05
359	Paul Molitor	.20	.15	.08
360	Ron Gardenhire	.08	.06	.03
361	Larry Bowa	.12	.09	.05
362	Bob Kearney	.08	.06	.03
363	Garth Iorg	.08	.06	.03
364	Tom Brunansky	.15	.11	.06
365	Brad Gulden	.08	.06	.03
366	Greg Walker	.12	.09	.05
367	Mike Young	.10	.08	.04
368	Rick Waits	.08	.06	.03
369	Doug Bair	.08	.06	.03
370	Bob Shirley	.08	.06	.03
371	Bob Ojeda	.12	.09	.05
372	Bob Welch	.15	.11	.06
373	Neal Heaton	.08	.06	.03
374	Danny Jackson (photo actually Steve Farr)	.80	.60	.30
375	Donnie Hill	.08	.06	.03
376	Mike Stenhouse	.08	.06	.03
377	Bruce Kison	.08	.06	.03
378	Wayne Tolleson	.08	.06	.03
379	Floyd Bannister	.12	.09	.05
380	Vern Ruhle	.08	.06	.03
381	Tim Corcoran	.08	.06	.03
382	Kurt Kepshire	.08	.06	.03
383	Bobby Brown	.08	.06	.03
384	Dave Van Gorder	.08	.06	.03
385	Rick Mahler	.08	.06	.03
386	Lee Mazzilli	.10	.08	.04
387	Bill Laskey	.08	.06	.03
388	Thad Bosley	.08	.06	.03
389	Al Chambers	.08	.06	.03
390	Tony Fernandez	.50	.40	.20
391	Ron Washington	.08	.06	.03
392	Bill Swaggerty	.08	.06	.03
393	Bob Gibson	.08	.06	.03
394	Marty Castillo	.08	.06	.03
395	Steve Crawford	.08	.06	.03
396	Clay Christiansen	.08	.06	.03
397	Bob Bailor	.08	.06	.03
398	Mike Hargrove	.08	.06	.03
399	Charlie Leibrandt	.10	.08	.04
400	Tom Burgmeier	.08	.06	.03
401	Razor Shines	.08	.06	.03
402	Rob Wilfong	.08	.06	.03
403	Tom Henke	.12	.09	.05
404	Al Jones	.08	.06	.03
405	Mike LaCoss	.08	.06	.03
406	Luis DeLeon	.08	.06	.03
407	Greg Gross	.08	.06	.03
408	Tom Hume	.08	.06	.03
409	Rick Camp	.08	.06	.03
410	Milt May	.08	.06	.03
411	*Henry Cotto*(FC)	.20	.15	.08
412	Dave Von Ohlen	.08	.06	.03
413	Scott McGregor	.10	.08	.04
414	Ted Simmons	.15	.11	.06
415	Jack Morris	.30	.25	.12
416	Bill Buckner	.15	.11	.06
417	Butch Wynegar	.08	.06	.03
418	Steve Sax	.25	.20	.10
419	Steve Balboni	.10	.08	.04
420	Dwayne Murphy	.10	.08	.04
421	Andre Dawson	.30	.25	.12
422	Charlie Hough	.10	.08	.04
423	Tommy John	.25	.20	.10
424a	Tom Seaver (Floyd Bannister photo - throwing left)	.80	.60	.30
424b	Tom Seaver (correct photo - throwing right)	7.00	5.25	2.75
425	Tom Herr	.12	.09	.05
426	Terry Puhl	.08	.06	.03
427	Al Holland	.08	.06	.03

		MT	NR MT	EX
428	Eddie Milner	.08	.06	.03
429	Terry Kennedy	.10	.08	.04
430	John Candelaria	.12	.09	.05
431	Manny Trillo	.10	.08	.04
432	Ken Oberkfell	.08	.06	.03
433	Rick Sutcliffe	.15	.11	.06
434	Ron Darling	.70	.50	.30
435	Spike Owen	.10	.08	.04
436	Frank Viola	.25	.20	.10
437	Lloyd Moseby	.12	.09	.05
438	*Kirby Puckett*(FC)	25.00	20.00	10.00
439	Jim Clancy	.10	.08	.04
440	Mike Moore	.08	.06	.03
441	Doug Sisk	.08	.06	.03
442	Dennis Eckersley	.15	.11	.06
443	Gerald Perry	.25	.20	.10
444	Dale Berra	.08	.06	.03
445	Dusty Baker	.10	.08	.04
446	Ed Whitson	.08	.06	.03
447	Cesar Cedeno	.12	.09	.05
448	*Rick Schu*(FC)	.20	.15	.08
449	Joaquin Andujar	.10	.08	.04
450	*Mark Bailey*(FC)	.12	.09	.05
451	*Ron Romanick*(FC)	.12	.09	.05
452	Julio Cruz	.08	.06	.03
453	Miguel Dilone	.08	.06	.03
454	Storm Davis	.12	.09	.05
455	Jaime Cocanower	.08	.06	.03
456	Barbaro Garbey	.12	.09	.05
457	Rich Gedman	.12	.09	.05
458	Phil Niekro	.30	.25	.12
459	Mike Scioscia	.10	.08	.04
460	Pat Tabler	.10	.08	.04
461	Darryl Motley	.08	.06	.03
462	Chris Codoroli (Codiroli)	.08	.06	.03
463	Doug Flynn	.08	.06	.03
464	Billy Sample	.08	.06	.03
465	Mickey Rivers	.10	.08	.04
466	John Wathan	.10	.08	.04
467	Bill Krueger	.08	.06	.03
468	Andre Thornton	.12	.09	.05
469	Rex Hudler	.12	.09	.05
470	*Sid Bream*(FC)	.50	.40	.20
471	Kirk Gibson	.40	.30	.15
472	John Shelby	.10	.08	.04
473	Moose Haas	.08	.06	.03
474	Doug Corbett	.08	.06	.03
475	Willie McGee	.35	.25	.14
476	Bob Knepper	.10	.08	.04
477	Kevin Gross	.12	.09	.05
478	Carmelo Martinez	.10	.08	.04
479	Kent Tekulve	.10	.08	.04
480	Chili Davis	.12	.09	.05
481	Bobby Clark	.08	.06	.03
482	Mookie Wilson	.12	.09	.05
483	Dave Owen	.08	.06	.03
484	Ed Nunez	.08	.06	.03
485	Rance Mulliniks	.08	.06	.03
486	Ken Schrom	.08	.06	.03
487	Jeff Russell	.08	.06	.03
488	Tom Paciorek	.08	.06	.03
489	Dan Ford	.08	.06	.03
490	Mike Caldwell	.08	.06	.03
491	Scottie Earl	.08	.06	.03
492	*Jose Rijo*(FC)	.70	.50	.30
493	Bruce Hurst	.15	.11	.06
494	Ken Landreaux	.08	.06	.03
495	Mike Fischlin	.08	.06	.03
496	Don Slaught	.08	.06	.03
497	Steve McCatty	.08	.06	.03
498	Gary Lucas	.08	.06	.03
499	Gary Pettis	.10	.08	.04
500	Marvis Foley	.08	.06	.03
501	Mike Squires	.08	.06	.03
502	*Jim Pankovitz*(FC)	.15	.11	.06
503	Luis Aguayo	.08	.06	.03
504	Ralph Citarella	.08	.06	.03
505	Bruce Bochy	.08	.06	.03
506	Bob Owchinko	.08	.06	.03
507	Pascual Perez	.10	.08	.04
508	Lee Lacy	.08	.06	.03
509	Atlee Hammaker	.08	.06	.03
510	Bob Dernier	.08	.06	.03
511	Ed Vande Berg	.08	.06	.03
512	Cliff Johnson	.08	.06	.03
513	Len Whitehouse	.08	.06	.03
514	Dennis Martinez	.10	.08	.04
515	Ed Romero	.08	.06	.03
516	Rusty Kuntz	.08	.06	.03
517	Rick Miller	.08	.06	.03
518	Dennis Rasmussen	.15	.11	.06
519	Steve Yeager	.08	.06	.03
520	Chris Bando	.08	.06	.03
521	U.L. Washington	.08	.06	.03
522	*Curt Young*(FC)	.40	.30	.15
523	Angel Salazar	.08	.06	.03
524	Curt Kaufman	.08	.06	.03
525	Odell Jones	.08	.06	.03
526	Juan Agosto	.08	.06	.03
527	Denny Walling	.08	.06	.03
528	Andy Hawkins(FC)	.20	.15	.08
529	Sixto Lezcano	.08	.06	.03
530	Skeeter Barnes	.08	.06	.03
531	Randy Johnson	.08	.06	.03
532	Jim Morrison	.08	.06	.03
533	Warren Brusstar	.08	.06	.03
534a	*Jeff Pendleton* (first name incorrect)(FC)	.85	.60	.35
534b	*Terry Pendleton* (first name correct)(FC)	3.00	2.25	1.25
535	Vic Rodriguez	.08	.06	.03
536	Bob McClure	.08	.06	.03
537	Dave Bergman	.08	.06	.03
538	Mark Clear	.08	.06	.03
539	*Mike Pagliarulo*(FC)	1.00	.70	.40
540	Terry Whitfield	.08	.06	.03
541	Joe Beckwith	.08	.06	.03
542	Jeff Burroughs	.10	.08	.04
543	Dan Schatzeder	.08	.06	.03
544	Donnie Scott	.08	.06	.03
545	Jim Slaton	.08	.06	.03
546	Greg Luzinski	.12	.09	.05
547	*Mark Salas*(FC)	.15	.11	.06
548	Dave Smith	.10	.08	.04

		MT	NR MT	EX
549	John Wockenfuss	.08	.06	.03
550	Frank Pastore	.08	.06	.03
551	Tim Flannery	.08	.06	.03
552	Rick Rhoden	.12	.09	.05
553	Mark Davis	.08	.06	.03
554	*Jeff Dedmon*(FC)	.15	.11	.06
555	Gary Woods	.08	.06	.03
556	Danny Heep	.08	.06	.03
557	*Mark Langston*(FC)	7.00	5.25	2.75
558	Darrell Brown	.08	.06	.03
559	*Jimmy Key*(FC)	1.50	1.25	.60
560	Rick Lysander	.08	.06	.03
561	Doyle Alexander	.12	.09	.05
562	Mike Stanton	.08	.06	.03
563	Sid Fernandez	.50	.40	.20
564	Richie Hebner	.08	.06	.03
565	Alex Trevino	.08	.06	.03
566	Brian Harper	.08	.06	.03
567	*Dan Gladden*(FC)	.60	.45	.25
568	Luis Salazar	.08	.06	.03
569	Tom Foley	.08	.06	.03
570	Larry Andersen	.08	.06	.03
571	Danny Cox	.12	.09	.05
572	Joe Sambito	.08	.06	.03
573	Juan Beniquez	.08	.06	.03
574	Joel Skinner	.08	.06	.03
575	*Randy St. Claire*(FC)	.15	.11	.06
576	Floyd Rayford	.08	.06	.03
577	Roy Howell	.08	.06	.03
578	John Grubb	.08	.06	.03
579	Ed Jurak	.08	.06	.03
580	John Montefusco	.08	.06	.03
581	*Orel Hershiser*(FC)	12.00	9.00	4.75
582	*Tom Waddell*(FC)	.08	.06	.03
583	Mark Huismann	.08	.06	.03
584	Joe Morgan	.30	.25	.12
585	Jim Wohlford	.08	.06	.03
586	Dave Schmidt	.08	.06	.03
587	*Jeff Kunkel*(FC)	.12	.09	.05
588	Hal McRae	.12	.09	.05
589	Bill Almon	.08	.06	.03
590	Carmen Castillo(FC)	.10	.08	.04
591	Omar Moreno	.08	.06	.03
592	*Ken Howell*(FC)	.20	.15	.08
593	Tom Brookens	.08	.06	.03
594	Joe Nolan	.08	.06	.03
595	Willie Lozado	.08	.06	.03
596	*Tom Nieto*(FC)	.12	.09	.05
597	Walt Terrell	.10	.08	.04
598	Al Oliver	.15	.11	.06
599	Shane Rawley	.12	.09	.05
600	*Denny Gonzalez*(FC)	.10	.08	.04
601	*Mark Grant*(FC)	.15	.11	.06
602	Mike Armstrong	.08	.06	.03
603	George Foster	.15	.11	.06
604	Davey Lopes	.10	.08	.04
605	Salome Barojas	.08	.06	.03
606	Roy Lee Jackson	.08	.06	.03
607	Pete Filson	.08	.06	.03
608	Duane Walker	.08	.06	.03
609	Glenn Wilson	.10	.08	.04
610	*Rafael Santana*(FC)	.20	.15	.08
611	Roy Smith	.08	.06	.03
612	Ruppert Jones	.08	.06	.03
613	Joe Cowley(FC)	.08	.06	.03
614	*Al Nipper* (photo actually Mike Brown)(FC)	.20	.15	.08
615	Gene Nelson	.08	.06	.03
616	Joe Carter	1.50	1.25	.60
617	Ray Knight	.12	.09	.05
618	Chuck Rainey	.08	.06	.03
619	Dan Driessen	.10	.08	.04
620	Daryl Sconiers	.08	.06	.03
621	Bill Stein	.08	.06	.03
622	Roy Smalley	.08	.06	.03
623	Ed Lynch	.08	.06	.03
624	*Jeff Stone*(FC)	.15	.11	.06
625	Bruce Berenyi	.08	.06	.03
626	Kelvin Chapman	.08	.06	.03
627	Joe Price	.08	.06	.03
628	Steve Bedrosian	.12	.09	.05
629	Vic Mata	.08	.06	.03
630	Mike Krukow	.10	.08	.04
631	*Phil Bradley*(FC)	.90	.70	.35
632	Jim Gott	.08	.06	.03
633	Randy Bush	.08	.06	.03
634	*Tom Browning*(FC)	2.00	1.50	.80
635	Lou Gehrig Puzzle Card	.08	.06	.03
636	Reid Nichols	.08	.06	.03
637	*Dan Pasqua*(FC)	.60	.45	.25
638	German Rivera	.08	.06	.03
639	*Don Schulze*(FC)	.10	.08	.04
640a	Mike Jones (last line of highlights begins "Was 11-7...")	.10	.08	.04
640b	Mike Jones (last line of highlights begins "Spent some ...")	1.25	.90	.50
641	Pete Rose	1.25	.90	.50
642	*Wade Rowdon*(FC)	.10	.08	.04
643	Jerry Narron	.08	.06	.03
644	*Darrell Miller*(FC)	.15	.11	.06
645	*Tim Hulett*(FC)	.15	.11	.06
646	Andy McGaffigan	.08	.06	.03
647	Kurt Bevacqua	.08	.06	.03
648	*John Russell*(FC)	.20	.15	.08
649	*Ron Robinson*(FC)	.25	.20	.10
650	Donnie Moore(FC)	.08	.06	.03
651a	Two for the Title (Don Mattingly, Dave Winfield) (player names in yellow)	3.00	2.25	1.25
651b	Two for the Title (Don Mattingly, Dave Winfield) (player names in white)	6.00	4.50	2.50
652	Tim Laudner	.08	.06	.03
653	*Steve Farr*(FC)	.35	.25	.14
---	Checklist 1-26 DK	.08	.06	.03
---	Checklist 27-130	.08	.06	.03
---	Checklist 131-234	.08	.06	.03
---	Checklist 235-338	.08	.06	.03
---	Checklist 339-442	.08	.06	.03
---	Checklist 443-546	.08	.06	.03
---	Checklist 547-653	.08	.06	.03

NOTE: A card number in parentheses ( ) indicates the set is unnumbered.

1985 Donruss Action All-Stars

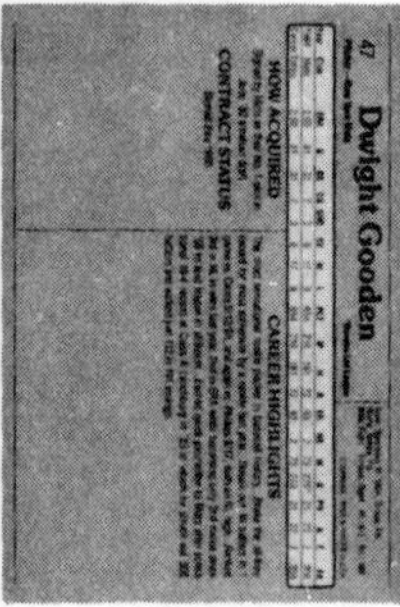

In 1985, Donruss issued an Action All-Stars set for the third consecutive year. The card fronts feature an action photo with an inset head-shot of the player inside a black border with grey boxes through it. The card backs have black print on blue and white and include statistical and biographical information. The cards were issued with a Lou Gehrig puzzle.

		MT	NR MT	EX
Complete Set:		8.00	6.00	3.25
Common Player:		.09	.07	.04
1	Tim Raines	.35	.25	.14
2	Jim Gantner	.09	.07	.04
3	Mario Soto	.09	.07	.04
4	Spike Owen	.09	.07	.04
5	Lloyd Moseby	.12	.09	.05
6	Damaso Garcia	.09	.07	.04
7	Cal Ripken	.35	.25	.14
8	Dan Quisenberry	.09	.07	.04
9	Eddie Murray	.12	.09	.05
10	Tony Pena	.09	.07	.04
11	Buddy Bell	.09	.07	.04
12	Dave Winfield	.30	.25	.12
13	Ron Kittle	.12	.09	.05
14	Rich Gossage	.12	.09	.05
15	Dwight Evans	.15	.11	.06
16	Al Davis	.15	.11	.06
17	Mike Schmidt	.40	.30	.15
18	Pascual Perez	.09	.07	.04
19	Tony Gwynn	.30	.25	.12
20	Nolan Ryan	.50	.40	.20
21	Robin Yount	.50	.40	.20
22	Mike Marshall	.12	.09	.05
23	Brett Butler	.09	.07	.04
24	Ryne Sandberg	.25	.20	.10
25	Dale Murphy	.40	.30	.15
26	George Brett	.40	.30	.15
27	Jim Rice	.15	.11	.06
28	Ozzie Smith	.15	.11	.06
29	Larry Parrish	.09	.07	.04
30	Jack Clark	.15	.11	.06
31	Manny Trillo	.09	.07	.04
32	Dave Kingman	.12	.09	.05
33	Geoff Zahn	.09	.07	.04
34	Pedro Guerrero	.15	.11	.06
35	Dave Parker	.20	.15	.08
36	Rollie Fingers	.15	.11	.06
37	Fernando Valenzuela	.12	.09	.05
38	Wade Boggs	1.00	.70	.40
39	Reggie Jackson	.30	.25	.12
40	Kent Hrbek	.20	.15	.08
41	Keith Hernandez	.25	.20	.10
42	Lou Whitaker	.15	.11	.06
43	Tom Herr	.09	.07	.04
44	Alan Trammell	.20	.15	.08
45	Butch Wynegar	.09	.07	.04
46	Leon Durham	.09	.07	.04
47	Dwight Gooden	1.50	1.25	.60
48	Don Mattingly	2.00	1.50	.80
49	Phil Niekro	.20	.15	.08
50	Johnny Ray	.09	.07	.04
51	Doug DeCinces	.09	.07	.04
52	Willie Upshaw	.09	.07	.04
53	Lance Parrish	.15	.11	.06
54	Jody Davis	.09	.07	.04
55	Steve Carlton	.30	.25	.12
56	Juan Samuel	.09	.07	.04
57	Gary Carter	.12	.09	.05
58	Harold Baines	.15	.11	.06
59	Eric Show	.09	.07	.04
60	Checklist	.09	.07	.04

1985 Donruss Box Panels

In 1985, Donruss placed on the bottoms of their wax pack boxes a four-card panel which included three player cards and a Lou Gehrig puzzle card. The player cards, numbered PC 1 through PC 3, have backs identical to the regular 1985 Donruss issue. The card fronts are identical in design to the regular issue, but carry different picture poses.

	MT	NR MT	EX
Complete Panel Set:	6.50	5.00	3.00
Complete Singles Set:	4.50	3.50	1.50
Common Single Player:	.10	.08	.04

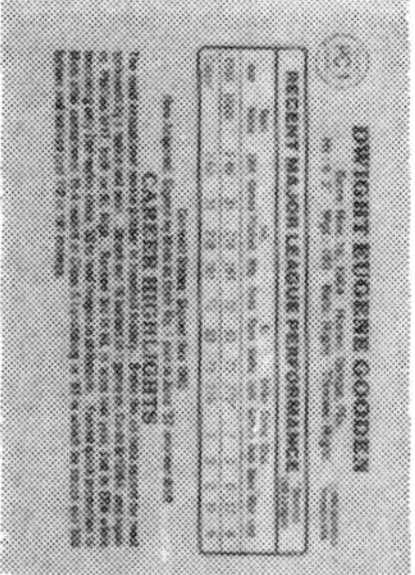

		MT	NR MT	EX
Panel		6.50	5.00	3.00
1	Dwight Gooden	4.00	3.00	1.50
2	Ryne Sanberg	.50	.40	.20
3	Ron Kittle	.10	.08	.04
---	Lou Gehrig Puzzle Card	.05	.04	.02

1985 Donruss Diamond Kings Supers

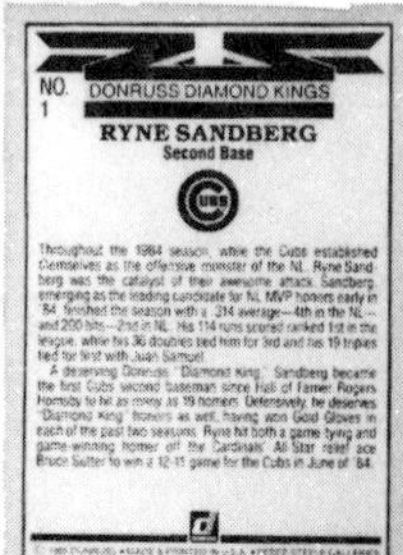

The 1985 Donruss Diamond Kings Supers are enlarged versions of the Diamond Kings card (#'s 1-26) in the regular 1985 Donruss set. The cards measure 4-15/16" by 6-3/4". The Diamond Kings series features the artwork of Dick Perez. Twenty- eight cards make up the set - 26 DK cards, an unnumbered checklist, and an unnumbered Dick Perez card. The back of the Perez card contains a brief history of Dick Perez and the Perez-Steele Galleries. The set could be obtained through a write-in offer found on the wrappers of the regular issue wax packs.

		MT	NR MT	EX
Complete Set:		11.00	8.25	4.50
Common Player:		.20	.15	.08
1	Ryne Sandberg	.60	.45	.25
2	Doug DeCinces	.20	.15	.08
3	Richard Dotson	.20	.15	.08
4	Bert Blyleven	.25	.20	.10
5	Lou Whitaker	.30	.25	.12
6	Dan Quisenberry	.20	.15	.08
7	Don Mattingly	4.50	3.25	1.75
8	Carney Lansford	.20	.15	.08
9	Frank Tanana	.20	.15	.08
10	Willie Upshaw	.20	.15	.08
11	Claudell Washington	.20	.15	.08
12	Mike Marshall	.25	.20	.10
13	Joaquin Andujar	.20	.15	.08
14	Cal Ripken, Jr.	.50	.40	.20
15	Jim Rice	.35	.25	.14
16	Don Sutton	.30	.25	.12
17	Frank Viola	.35	.25	.14
18	Alvin Davis	.30	.25	.12
19	Mario Soto	.20	.15	.08
20	Jose Cruz	.20	.15	.08
21	Charlie Lea	.20	.15	.08
22	Jesse Orosco	.20	.15	.08
23	Juan Samuel	.20	.15	.08
24	Tony Pena	.20	.15	.08
25	Tony Gwynn	.40	.30	.15
26	Bob Brenly	.20	.15	.08
---	Checklist	.12	.09	.05
---	Dick Perez (DK artist)	.12	.09	.05

1985 Donruss Highlights

Designed in the style of the regular 1985 Donruss set, this issue features the Player of the Month in the major leagues plus highlight cards of special baseball events and milestones that occurred during the 1985 season. Fifty-six cards, including an unnumbered checklist, comprise the set which was available only through hobby dealers. The cards measure 2-1/2" by 3-1/2" and have glossy fronts. The last two cards in the set feature Donruss' picks for the A.L. and N.L. Rookies of the Year. The set was issued in a

Pete Rose
Breaks Ty Cobb's all-time hit record
Sept. 11

NO. 40

specially designed box.

		MT	NR MT	EX
Complete Set:		24.00	18.00	9.50
Common Player:		.12	.09	.05
1	Sets Opening Day Record (Tom Seaver)	.40	.30	.15
2	Establishes A.L. Save Mark (Rollie Fingers)	.15	.11	.06
3	A.L. Player of the Month - April (Mike Davis)	.12	.09	.05
4	A.L. Pitcher of the Month - April (Charlie Leibrandt)	.12	.09	.05
5	N.L. Player of the Month - April (Dale Murphy)	.40	.30	.15
6	N.L. Pitcher of the Month - April (Fernando Valenzuela)	.12	.09	.05
7	N.L. Shortstop Record (Larry Bowa)	.12	.09	.05
8	Joins Reds 2000 Hit Club (Dave Concepcion)	.12	.09	.05
9	Eldest Grand Slammer (Tony Perez)	.15	.11	.06
10	N.L. Career Run Leader (Pete Rose)	1.25	.90	.50
11	A.L. Player of the Month - May (George Brett)	.90	.70	.35
12	A.L. Pitcher of the Month - May (Dave Stieb)	.12	.09	.05
13	N.L. Player of the Month - May (Dave Parker)	.20	.15	.08
14	N.L. Pitcher of the Month - May (Andy Hawkins)	.12	.09	.05
15	Records 11th Straight Win (Andy Hawkins)	.12	.09	.05
16	Two Homers In First Inning (Von Hayes)	.15	.11	.06
17	A.L. Player of the Month - June (Rickey Henderson)	1.00	.70	.40
18	A.L. Pitcher of the Month - June (Jay Howell)	.12	.09	.05
19	N.L. Player of the Month - June (Pedro Guerrero)	.20	.15	.08
20	N.L. Pitcher of the Month - June (John Tudor)	.12	.09	.05
21	Marathon Game Iron Men (Gary Carter, Keith Hernandez)	.35	.25	.14
22	Records 4000th K (Nolan Ryan)	1.25	.90	.50
23	All-Star Game MVP (LaMarr Hoyt)	.12	.09	.05
24	1st Ranger To Hit For Cycle (Oddibe McDowell)	.40	.30	.15
25	A.L. Player of the Month - July (George Brett)	.90	.70	.35
26	A.L. Pitcher of the Month - July (Bret Saberhagen)	1.50	1.25	.60
27	N.L. Player of the Month - July (Keith Hernandez)	.35	.25	.14
28	N.L. Pitcher of the Month - July (Fernando Valenzuela)	.12	.09	.05
29	Record Setting Base Stealers (Vince Coleman, Willie McGee)	.80	.60	.30
30	Notches 300th Career Win (Tom Seaver)	.35	.25	.14
31	Strokes 3000th Hit (Rod Carew)	.40	.30	.15
32	Establishes Met Record (Dwight Gooden)	2.25	1.75	.90
33	Achieves Strikeout Milestone (Dwight Gooden)	2.25	1.75	.90
34	Explodes For 9 RBI (Eddie Murray)	.70	.50	.30
35	A.L. Career Hbp Leader (Don Baylor)	.15	.11	.06
36	A.L. Player of the Month - August (Don Mattingly)	3.25	2.50	1.25
37	A.L. Pitcher of the Month - August (Dave Righetti)	.20	.15	.08
38	N.L. Player of the Month (Willie McGee)	.20	.15	.08
39	N.L. Pitcher of the Month - August (Shane Rawley)	.12	.09	.05
40	Ty-Breaking Hit (Pete Rose)	.90	.70	.35
41	Hits 3 Hrs Drives In 8 Runs (Andre Dawson)	.20	.15	.08
42	Sets Yankee Theft Mark (Rickey Henderson)	1.00	.70	.40
43	20 Wins In Rookie Season (Tom Browning)	.35	.25	.14
44	Yankee Milestone For Hits (Don Mattingly)	3.25	2.50	1.25
45	A.L. Player of the Month - September (Don Mattingly)	3.25	2.50	1.25
46	A.L. Pitcher of the Month - September (Charlie Leibrandt)	.12	.09	.05
47	N.L. Player of the Month - September (Gary Carter)	.12	.09	.05
48	N.L. Pitcher of the Month - September (Dwight Gooden)	2.25	1.75	.90
49	Major League Record Setter (Wade Boggs)	2.00	1.50	.80
50	Hurls Shutout For 300th Win (Phil Niekro)	.30	.25	.12
51	Venerable HR King (Darrell Evans)	.15	.11	.06
52	N.L. Switch-hitting Record (Willie McGee)	.20	.15	.08
53	Equals DiMaggio Feat (Dave Winfield)	.30	.25	.12
54	Donruss N.L. Rookie of the Year (Vince Coleman)	2.25	1.75	.90
55	Donruss A.L. Rookie of the Year (Ozzie Guillen)	.50	.40	.20
---	Checklist	.20	.15	.08

1985 Donruss Sluggers

In much the same manner as the first Bazooka cards were issued in 1959, this eight-player set from Donruss consists of cards which formed the bottom panel of a box of bubble gum. When cut off the box, cards measure 3-1/2" by 6-1/2", with blank backs. Players are pictured on the cards in paintings done by Dick Perez.

		MT	NR MT	EX
Complete Set:		8.00	6.00	3.25
Common Player:		.60	.45	.25
1	Babe Ruth	1.50	1.25	.60
2	Ted Williams	1.00	.70	.40
3	Lou Gehrig	1.00	.70	.40
4	Johnny Mize	.60	.45	.25
5	Stan Musial	1.00	.70	.40
6	Mickey Mantle	3.00	2.25	1.25
7	Hank Aaron	1.00	.70	.40
8	Frank Robinson	.70	.50	.30

1986 Donruss

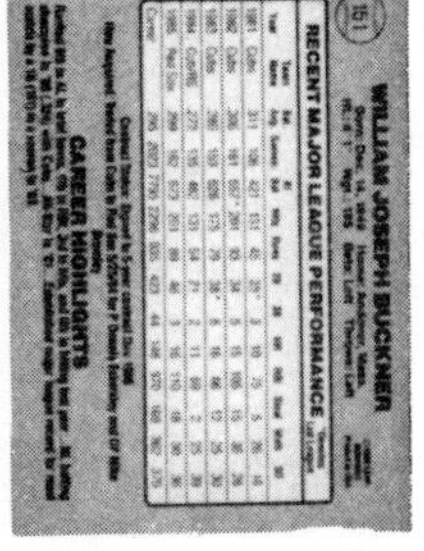

In 1986, Donruss issued a 660-card set which included 653 numbered cards and seven unnumbered checklists. The cards, which measure 2-1/2" by 3-1/2", have fronts that feature blue borders and backs that have black print on blue and white. For the fifth year in a row, the first 26 cards in the set are Diamond Kings. The Rated Rookies subset (card #'s 27-46) appears once again. The cards were distributed with a Hank Aaron puzzle. The complete set price does not include the higher priced variations. In the checklist that follows, (DK) and (RR) refer to the Diamond Kings and Rated Rookies series.

		MT	NR MT	EX
Complete Set:		150.00	110.00	60.00
Common Player:		.06	.05	.02
1	Kirk Gibson (DK)	.30	.25	.12
2	Goose Gossage (DK)	.20	.15	.08
3	Willie McGee (DK)	.15	.11	.06
4	George Bell (DK)	.30	.25	.12
5	Tony Armas (DK)	.10	.08	.04
6	Chili Davis (DK)	.10	.08	.04
7	Cecil Cooper (DK)	.12	.09	.05
8	Mike Boddicker (DK)	.10	.08	.04
9	Davey Lopes (DK)	.10	.08	.04
10	Bill Doran (DK)	.12	.09	.05
11	Bret Saberhagen (DK)	.25	.20	.10
12	Brett Butler (DK)	.10	.08	.04
13	Harold Baines (DK)	.15	.11	.06
14	Mike Davis (DK)	.10	.08	.04
15	Tony Perez (DK)	.15	.11	.06
16	Willie Randolph (DK)	.12	.09	.05
17	Bob Boone (DK)	.10	.08	.04
18	Orel Hershiser (DK)	1.00	.70	.40
19	Johnny Ray (DK)	.12	.09	.05
20	Gary Ward (DK)	.10	.08	.04
21	Rick Mahler (DK)	.08	.06	.03
22	Phil Bradley (DK)	.20	.15	.08
23	Jerry Koosman (DK)	.12	.09	.05
24	Tom Brunansky (DK)	.15	.11	.06
25	Andre Dawson (DK)	.30	.25	.12
26	Dwight Gooden (DK)	1.00	.70	.40
27	*Kal Daniels (RR)*(FC)	3.75	2.75	1.50
28	*Fred McGriff (RR)*(FC)	16.00	12.00	6.50
29	*Cory Snyder (RR)*(FC)	3.00	2.25	1.25
30	*Jose Guzman (RR)*(FC)	.30	.25	.12
31	*Ty Gainey (RR)*(FC)	.10	.08	.04
32	*Johnny Abrego (RR)*(FC)	.08	.06	.03
33a	*Andres Galarraga (RR)* (no accent mark above "e" in Andres on back)(FC)	4.00	3.00	1.50
33b	*Andres Galarraga (RR)* (accent mark above "e" in Andres on back)(FC)	5.00	3.75	2.00
34	*Dave Shipanoff (RR)*(FC)	.08	.06	.03
35	*Mark McLemore (RR)*(FC)	.20	.15	.08
36	*Marty Clary (RR)*(FC)	.08	.06	.03
37	*Paul O'Neill (RR)*(FC)	1.50	1.25	.60
38	Danny Tartabull (RR)	.80	.60	.30
39	*Jose Canseco (RR)*(FC)	100.00	75.00	40.00
40	*Juan Nieves (RR)*(FC)	.30	.25	.12
41	*Lance McCullers (RR)*(FC)	.35	.25	.14
42	*Rick Surhoff (RR)*(FC)	.08	.06	.03
43	*Todd Worrell (RR)*(FC)	1.00	.70	.40
44	*Bob Kipper (RR)*(FC)	.20	.15	.08
45	*John Habyan (RR)*(FC)	.15	.11	.06
46	*Mike Woodard (RR)*(FC)	.10	.08	.04
47	Mike Boddicker	.10	.08	.04
48	Robin Yount	.90	.70	.35
49	Lou Whitaker	.30	.25	.12
50	"Oil Can" Boyd	.08	.06	.03
51	Rickey Henderson	.60	.45	.25
52	Mike Marshall	.15	.11	.06
53	George Brett	.50	.40	.20
54	Dave Kingman	.15	.11	.06
55	Hubie Brooks	.10	.08	.04
56	*Oddibe McDowell*(FC)	.35	.25	.14
57	Doug DeCinces	.10	.08	.04
58	Britt Burns	.06	.05	.02
59	Ozzie Smith	.15	.11	.06
60	Jose Cruz	.10	.08	.04
61	Mike Schmidt	.50	.40	.20
62	Pete Rose	.80	.60	.30
63	Steve Garvey	.40	.30	.15
64	Tony Pena	.10	.08	.04
65	Chili Davis	.10	.08	.04
66	Dale Murphy	.60	.45	.25
67	Ryne Sandberg	.40	.30	.15
68	Gary Carter	.35	.25	.14
69	Alvin Davis	.30	.25	.12
70	Kent Hrbek	.25	.20	.10
71	George Bell	.30	.25	.12
72	Kirby Puckett	4.50	3.25	1.50
73	Lloyd Moseby	.10	.08	.04
74	Bob Kearney	.06	.05	.02
75	Dwight Gooden	3.00	2.25	1.25
76	Gary Matthews	.10	.08	.04
77	Rick Mahler	.06	.05	.02
78	Benny Distefano	.06	.05	.02
79	Jeff Leonard	.08	.06	.03
80	Kevin McReynolds	.30	.25	.12
81	Ron Oester	.06	.05	.02
82	John Russell	.06	.05	.02
83	Tommy Herr	.10	.08	.04
84	Jerry Mumphrey	.06	.05	.02
85	Ron Romanick	.06	.05	.02
86	Daryl Boston	.08	.06	.03
87	Andre Dawson	.30	.25	.12
88	Eddie Murray	.40	.30	.15
89	Dion James	.08	.06	.03
90	Chet Lemon	.08	.06	.03
91	Bob Stanley	.06	.05	.02
92	Willie Randolph	.10	.08	.04
93	Mike Scioscia	.08	.06	.03
94	Tom Waddell	.06	.05	.02
95	Danny Jackson	.30	.25	.12
96	Mike Davis	.08	.06	.03
97	Mike Fitzgerald	.06	.05	.02
98	Gary Ward	.08	.06	.03
99	Pete O'Brien	.10	.08	.04
100	Bret Saberhagen	.40	.30	.15
101	Alfredo Griffin	.08	.06	.03
102	Brett Butler	.08	.06	.03
103	Ron Guidry	.20	.15	.08
104	Jerry Reuss	.08	.06	.03
105	Jack Morris	.30	.25	.12
106	Rick Dempsey	.08	.06	.03
107	Ray Burris	.06	.05	.02
108	Brian Downing	.10	.08	.04
109	Willie McGee	.15	.11	.06
110	Bill Doran	.10	.08	.04
111	Kent Tekulve	.08	.06	.03
112	Tony Gwynn	.40	.30	.15
113	Marvell Wynne	.06	.05	.02
114	David Green	.06	.05	.02
115	Jim Gantner	.08	.06	.03
116	George Foster	.15	.11	.06
117	Steve Trout	.06	.05	.02
118	Mark Langston	.30	.25	.12
119	Tony Fernandez	.20	.15	.08
120	John Butcher	.06	.05	.02

		MT	NR MT	EX
121	Ron Robinson	.08	.06	.03
122	Dan Spillner	.06	.05	.02
123	Mike Young	.06	.05	.02
124	Paul Molitor	.15	.11	.06
125	Kirk Gibson	.35	.25	.14
126	Ken Griffey	.12	.09	.05
127	Tony Armas	.08	.06	.03
128	*Mariano Duncan*(FC)	.15	.11	.06
129	Mr. Clutch (Pat Tabler)	.08	.06	.03
130	Frank White	.10	.08	.04
131	Carney Lansford	.10	.08	.04
132	Vance Law	.08	.06	.03
133	Dick Schofield	.06	.05	.02
134	Wayne Tolleson	.06	.05	.02
135	Greg Walker	.10	.08	.04
136	Denny Walling	.06	.05	.02
137	Ozzie Virgil	.06	.05	.02
138	Ricky Horton	.08	.06	.03
139	LaMarr Hoyt	.06	.05	.02
140	Wayne Krenchicki	.06	.05	.02
141	Glenn Hubbard	.06	.05	.02
142	Cecilio Guante	.06	.05	.02
143	Mike Krukow	.08	.06	.03
144	Lee Smith	.10	.08	.04
145	Edwin Nunez	.06	.05	.02
146	Dave Stieb	.12	.09	.05
147	Mike Smithson	.06	.05	.02
148	Ken Dixon	.06	.05	.02
149	Danny Darwin	.06	.05	.02
150	Chris Pittaro	.06	.05	.02
151	Bill Buckner	.12	.09	.05
152	Mike Pagliarulo	.20	.15	.08
153	Bill Russell	.08	.06	.03
154	Brook Jacoby	.10	.08	.04
155	Pat Sheridan	.06	.05	.02
156	*Mike Gallego*(FC)	.15	.11	.06
157	Jim Wohlford	.06	.05	.02
158	Gary Pettis	.06	.05	.02
159	Toby Harrah	.08	.06	.03
160	Richard Dotson	.10	.08	.04
161	Bob Knepper	.08	.06	.03
162	Dave Dravecky	.08	.06	.03
163	Greg Gross	.06	.05	.02
164	Eric Davis	3.50	2.75	1.50
165	Gerald Perry	.15	.11	.06
166	Rick Rhoden	.10	.08	.04
167	Keith Moreland	.08	.06	.03
168	Jack Clark	.20	.15	.08
169	Storm Davis	.10	.08	.04
170	Cecil Cooper	.12	.09	.05
171	Alan Trammell	.35	.25	.14
172	Roger Clemens	4.00	3.00	1.50
173	Don Mattingly	6.00	4.50	2.50
174	Pedro Guerrero	.20	.15	.08
175	Willie Wilson	.12	.09	.05
176	Dwayne Murphy	.08	.06	.03
177	Tim Raines	.40	.30	.15
178	Larry Parrish	.10	.08	.04
179	Mike Witt	.10	.08	.04
180	Harold Baines	.15	.11	.06
181	*Vince Coleman*(FC)	2.00	1.50	.80
182	*Jeff Heathcock*(FC)	.10	.08	.04
183	Steve Carlton	.40	.30	.15
184	Mario Soto	.08	.06	.03
185	Goose Gossage	.20	.15	.08
186	Johnny Ray	.12	.09	.05
187	Dan Gladden	.08	.06	.03
188	Bob Horner	.12	.09	.05
189	Rick Sutcliffe	.12	.09	.05
190	Keith Hernandez	.35	.25	.14
191	Phil Bradley	.20	.15	.08
192	Tom Brunansky	.12	.09	.05
193	Jesse Barfield	.20	.15	.08
194	Frank Viola	.20	.15	.08
195	Willie Upshaw	.08	.06	.03
196	Jim Beattie	.06	.05	.02
197	Darryl Strawberry	3.00	2.25	1.25
198	Ron Cey	.10	.08	.04
199	Steve Bedrosian	.12	.09	.05
200	Steve Kemp	.08	.06	.03
201	Manny Trillo	.08	.06	.03
202	Garry Templeton	.08	.06	.03
203	Dave Parker	.25	.20	.10
204	John Denny	.06	.05	.02
205	Terry Pendleton	.15	.11	.06
206	Terry Puhl	.06	.05	.02
207	Bobby Grich	.10	.08	.04
208	*Ozzie Guillen*(FC)	.50	.40	.20
209	Jeff Reardon	.12	.09	.05
210	Cal Ripken Jr.	.50	.40	.20
211	Bill Schroeder	.06	.05	.02
212	Dan Petry	.08	.06	.03
213	Jim Rice	.40	.30	.15
214	Dave Righetti	.20	.15	.08
215	Fernando Valenzuela	.35	.25	.14
216	Julio Franco	.12	.09	.05
217	Darryl Motley	.06	.05	.02
218	Dave Collins	.08	.06	.03
219	Tim Wallach	.12	.09	.05
220	George Wright	.06	.05	.02
221	Tommy Dunbar	.06	.05	.02
222	Steve Balboni	.08	.06	.03
223	Jay Howell	.08	.06	.03
224	Joe Carter	.25	.20	.10
225	Ed Whitson	.06	.05	.02
226	Orel Hershiser	1.25	.90	.50
227	Willie Hernandez	.08	.06	.03
228	Lee Lacy	.06	.05	.02
229	Rollie Fingers	.20	.15	.08
230	Bob Boone	.08	.06	.03
231	Joaquin Andujar	.08	.06	.03
232	Craig Reynolds	.06	.05	.02
233	Shane Rawley	.10	.08	.04
234	Eric Show	.08	.06	.03
235	Jose DeLeon	.08	.06	.03
236	*Jose Uribe*(FC)	.25	.20	.10
237	Moose Haas	.06	.05	.02
238	Wally Backman	.08	.06	.03
239	Dennis Eckersley	.12	.09	.05
240	Mike Moore	.06	.05	.02
241	Damaso Garcia	.06	.05	.02
242	Tim Teufel	.06	.05	.02
243	Dave Concepcion	.12	.09	.05
244	Floyd Bannister	.10	.08	.04
245	Fred Lynn	.20	.15	.08
246	Charlie Moore	.06	.05	.02
247	Walt Terrell	.08	.06	.03
248	Dave Winfield	.40	.30	.15
249	Dwight Evans	.12	.09	.05
250	*Dennis Powell*(FC)	.10	.08	.04
251	Andre Thornton	.10	.08	.04
252	Onix Concepcion	.06	.05	.02
253	Mike Heath	.06	.05	.02
254a	David Palmer (2B on front)	.06	.05	.02
254b	David Palmer (P on front)	1.00	.70	.40
255	Donnie Moore	.06	.05	.02
256	Curtis Wilkerson	.06	.05	.02
257	Julio Cruz	.06	.05	.02
258	Nolan Ryan	.70	.50	.30
259	Jeff Stone	.06	.05	.02
260a	John Tudor (1981 Games is .18)	.10	.08	.04
260b	John Tudor (1981 Games is 18)	1.00	.70	.40
261	Mark Thurmond	.06	.05	.02
262	Jay Tibbs	.06	.05	.02
263	Rafael Ramirez	.06	.05	.02
264	Larry McWilliams	.06	.05	.02
265	Mark Davis	.06	.05	.02
266	Bob Dernier	.06	.05	.02
267	Matt Young	.06	.05	.02
268	Jim Clancy	.08	.06	.03
269	Mickey Hatcher	.06	.05	.02
270	Sammy Stewart	.06	.05	.02
271	Bob Gibson	.06	.05	.02
272	Nelson Simmons	.06	.05	.02
273	Rich Gedman	.10	.08	.04
274	Butch Wynegar	.06	.05	.02
275	Ken Howell	.06	.05	.02
276	Mel Hall	.08	.06	.03
277	Jim Sundberg	.08	.06	.03
278	Chris Codiroli	.06	.05	.02
279	*Herman Winningham*(FC)	.15	.11	.06
280	Rod Carew	.40	.30	.15
281	Don Slaught	.06	.05	.02
282	Scott Fletcher	.08	.06	.03
283	Bill Dawley	.06	.05	.02
284	Andy Hawkins	.06	.05	.02
285	Glenn Wilson	.08	.06	.03
286	Nick Esasky	.08	.06	.03
287	Claudell Washington	.08	.06	.03
288	Lee Mazzilli	.08	.06	.03
289	Jody Davis	.10	.08	.04
290	Darrell Porter	.08	.06	.03
291	Scott McGregor	.08	.06	.03
292	Ted Simmons	.12	.09	.05
293	Aurelio Lopez	.06	.05	.02
294	Marty Barrett	.10	.08	.04
295	Dale Berra	.06	.05	.02
296	Greg Brock	.08	.06	.03
297	Charlie Leibrandt	.08	.06	.03
298	Bill Krueger	.06	.05	.02
299	Bryn Smith	.06	.05	.02
300	Burt Hooton	.08	.06	.03
301	*Stu Cliburn*(FC)	.12	.09	.05
302	Luis Salazar	.06	.05	.02
303	Ken Dayley	.06	.05	.02
304	Frank DiPino	.06	.05	.02
305	Von Hayes	.10	.08	.04
306a	Gary Redus (1983 2B is .20)	.08	.06	.03
306b	Gary Redus (1983 2B is 20)	1.00	.70	.40
307	Craig Lefferts	.06	.05	.02
308	Sam Khalifa	.06	.05	.02
309	Scott Garrelts	.06	.05	.02
310	Rick Cerone	.06	.05	.02
311	Shawon Dunston	.20	.15	.08
312	Howard Johnson	.12	.09	.05
313	Jim Presley	.15	.11	.06
314	Gary Gaetti	.25	.20	.10
315	Luis Leal	.06	.05	.02
316	Mark Salas	.06	.05	.02
317	Bill Caudill	.06	.05	.02
318	Dave Henderson	.10	.08	.04
319	Rafael Santana	.06	.05	.02
320	Leon Durham	.08	.06	.03
321	Bruce Sutter	.15	.11	.06
322	Jason Thompson	.06	.05	.02
323	Bob Brenly	.06	.05	.02
324	Carmelo Martinez	.08	.06	.03
325	Eddie Milner	.06	.05	.02
326	Juan Samuel	.15	.11	.06
327	Tom Nieto	.06	.05	.02
328	Dave Smith	.08	.06	.03
329	*Urbano Lugo*(FC)	.08	.06	.03
330	Joel Skinner	.06	.05	.02
331	Bill Gullickson	.06	.05	.02
332	Floyd Rayford	.06	.05	.02
333	Ben Oglivie	.08	.06	.03
334	Lance Parrish	.30	.25	.12
335	Jackie Gutierrez	.06	.05	.02
336	Dennis Rasmussen	.12	.09	.05
337	Terry Whitfield	.06	.05	.02
338	Neal Heaton	.06	.05	.02
339	Jorge Orta	.06	.05	.02
340	Donnie Hill	.06	.05	.02
341	Joe Hesketh	.06	.05	.02
342	Charlie Hough	.10	.08	.04
343	Dave Rozema	.06	.05	.02
344	Greg Pryor	.06	.05	.02
345	*Mickey Tettleton*(FC)	.80	.60	.30
346	George Vukovich	.06	.05	.02
347	Don Baylor	.12	.09	.05
348	Carlos Diaz	.06	.05	.02
349	Barbaro Garbey	.06	.05	.02
350	Larry Sheets	.12	.09	.05
351	*Ted Higuera*(FC)	1.25	.90	.50
352	Juan Beniquez	.06	.05	.02
353	Bob Forsch	.08	.06	.03
354	Mark Bailey	.06	.05	.02
355	Larry Andersen	.06	.05	.02
356	Terry Kennedy	.08	.06	.03
357	Don Robinson	.08	.06	.03
358	Jim Gott	.06	.05	.02
359	*Earnest Riles*(FC)	.20	.15	.08
360	*John Christensen*(FC)	.10	.08	.04
361	Ray Fontenot	.06	.05	.02
362	Spike Owen	.06	.05	.02
363	Jim Acker	.06	.05	.02
364a	Ron Davis (last line in highlights ends with "...in May.")	.08	.06	.03
364b	Ron Davis (last line in highlights ends with "...relievers (9).")	1.00	.70	.40
365	Tom Hume	.06	.05	.02
366	Carlton Fisk	.25	.20	.10
367	Nate Snell	.06	.05	.02
368	Rick Manning	.06	.05	.02
369	Darrell Evans	.15	.11	.06
370	Ron Hassey	.06	.05	.02
371	Wade Boggs	2.50	2.00	1.00
372	Rick Honeycutt	.06	.05	.02
373	Chris Bando	.06	.05	.02
374	Bud Black	.06	.05	.02
375	Steve Henderson	.06	.05	.02
376	Charlie Lea	.06	.05	.02
377	Reggie Jackson	.40	.30	.15
378	Dave Schmidt	.06	.05	.02
379	Bob James	.06	.05	.02
380	Glenn Davis(FC)	4.00	3.00	1.50
381	Tim Corcoran	.06	.05	.02
382	Danny Cox	.10	.08	.04
383	Tim Flannery	.06	.05	.02
384	Tom Browning	.20	.15	.08
385	Rick Camp	.06	.05	.02
386	Jim Morrison	.06	.05	.02
387	Dave LaPoint	.08	.06	.03
388	Davey Lopes	.08	.06	.03
389	Al Cowens	.06	.05	.02
390	Doyle Alexander	.10	.08	.04
391	Tim Laudner	.06	.05	.02
392	Don Aase	.06	.05	.02
393	Jaime Cocanower	.06	.05	.02
394	Randy O'Neal(FC)	.08	.06	.03
395	Mike Easler	.08	.06	.03
396	Scott Bradley	.06	.05	.02
397	Tom Niedenfuer	.08	.06	.03
398	Jerry Willard	.06	.05	.02
399	Lonnie Smith	.08	.06	.03
400	Bruce Bochte	.06	.05	.02
401	Terry Francona	.06	.05	.02
402	Jim Slaton	.06	.05	.02
403	Bill Stein	.06	.05	.02
404	Tim Hulett	.06	.05	.02
405	Alan Ashby	.06	.05	.02
406	Tim Stoddard	.06	.05	.02
407	Garry Maddox	.08	.06	.03
408	Ted Power	.06	.05	.02
409	Len Barker	.08	.06	.03
410	Denny Gonzalez	.06	.05	.02
411	George Frazier	.06	.05	.02
412	Andy Van Slyke	.15	.11	.06
413	Jim Dwyer	.06	.05	.02
414	Paul Householder	.06	.05	.02
415	Alejandro Sanchez	.06	.05	.02
416	Steve Crawford	.06	.05	.02
417	Dan Pasqua	.15	.11	.06
418	Enos Cabell	.06	.05	.02
419	Mike Jones	.06	.05	.02
420	Steve Kiefer	.06	.05	.02
421	*Tim Burke*(FC)	.30	.25	.12
422	Mike Mason	.06	.05	.02
423	Ruppert Jones	.06	.05	.02
424	Jerry Hairston	.06	.05	.02
425	Tito Landrum	.06	.05	.02
426	Jeff Calhoun	.06	.05	.02
427	*Don Carman*(FC)	.30	.25	.12
428	Tony Perez	.15	.11	.06
429	Jerry Davis	.06	.05	.02
430	Bob Walk	.06	.05	.02
431	Brad Wellman	.06	.05	.02
432	Terry Forster	.08	.06	.03
433	Billy Hatcher	.10	.08	.04
434	Clint Hurdle	.06	.05	.02
435	*Ivan Calderon*(FC)	.50	.40	.20
436	Pete Filson	.06	.05	.02
437	Tom Henke	.08	.06	.03
438	Dave Engle	.06	.05	.02
439	Tom Filer	.06	.05	.02
440	Gorman Thomas	.10	.08	.04
441	*Rick Aguilera*(FC)	.25	.20	.10
442	Scott Sanderson	.06	.05	.02
443	Jeff Dedmon	.06	.05	.02
444	*Joe Orsulak*(FC)	.15	.11	.06
445	Atlee Hammaker	.06	.05	.02
446	Jerry Royster	.06	.05	.02
447	Buddy Bell	.10	.08	.04
448	Dave Rucker	.06	.05	.02
449	Ivan DeJesus	.06	.05	.02
450	Jim Pankovits	.06	.05	.02
451	Jerry Narron	.06	.05	.02
452	Bryan Little	.06	.05	.02
453	Gary Lucas	.06	.05	.02
454	Dennis Martinez	.08	.06	.03
455	Ed Romero	.06	.05	.02
456	*Bob Melvin*(FC)	.12	.09	.05
457	Glenn Hoffman	.06	.05	.02
458	Bob Shirley	.06	.05	.02
459	Bob Welch	.12	.09	.05
460	Carmen Castillo	.06	.05	.02
461	Dave Leeper	.06	.05	.02
462	*Tim Birtsas*(FC)	.12	.09	.05
463	Randy St. Claire	.06	.05	.02
464	Chris Welsh	.06	.05	.02
465	Greg Harris	.06	.05	.02
466	Lynn Jones	.06	.05	.02
467	Dusty Baker	.08	.06	.03
468	Roy Smith	.06	.05	.02
469	Andre Robertson	.06	.05	.02
470	Ken Landreaux	.06	.05	.02
471	Dave Bergman	.06	.05	.02
472	Gary Roenicke	.06	.05	.02
473	Pete Vuckovich	.08	.06	.03
474	*Kirk McCaskill*(FC)	.35	.25	.14
475	Jeff Lahti	.06	.05	.02
476	Mike Scott	.20	.15	.08
477	*Darren Daulton*(FC)	.12	.09	.05
478	Graig Nettles	.15	.11	.06
479	Bill Almon	.06	.05	.02
480	Greg Minton	.06	.05	.02
481	Randy Ready(FC)	.10	.08	.04

		MT	NR MT	EX
482	*Lenny Dykstra*(FC)	1.25	.90	.50
483	Thad Bosley	.06	.05	.02
484	*Harold Reynolds*(FC)	.60	.45	.25
485	Al Oliver	.12	.09	.05
486	Roy Smalley	.06	.05	.02
487	John Franco	.15	.11	.06
488	Juan Agosto	.06	.05	.02
489	Al Pardo	.06	.05	.02
490	*Bill Wegman*(FC)	.25	.20	.10
491	Frank Tanana	.10	.08	.04
492	*Brian Fisher*(FC)	.30	.25	.12
493	Mark Clear	.06	.05	.02
494	Len Matuszek	.06	.05	.02
495	Ramon Romero	.06	.05	.02
496	John Wathan	.08	.06	.03
497	Rob Picciolo	.06	.05	.02
498	U.L. Washington	.06	.05	.02
499	John Candelaria	.10	.08	.04
500	Duane Walker	.06	.05	.02
501	Gene Nelson	.06	.05	.02
502	John Mizerock	.06	.05	.02
503	Luis Aguayo	.06	.05	.02
504	Kurt Kepshire	.06	.05	.02
505	Ed Wojna	.06	.05	.02
506	Joe Price	.06	.05	.02
507	*Milt Thompson*(FC)	.30	.25	.12
508	Junior Ortiz	.06	.05	.02
509	Vida Blue	.10	.08	.04
510	Steve Engel	.06	.05	.02
511	Karl Best	.06	.05	.02
512	*Cecil Fielder*(FC)	3.00	2.25	1.25
513	Frank Eufemia	.06	.05	.02
514	Tippy Martinez	.06	.05	.02
515	*Billy Robidoux*(FC)	.10	.08	.04
516	Bill Scherrer	.06	.05	.02
517	Bruce Hurst	.12	.09	.05
518	Rich Bordi	.06	.05	.02
519	Steve Yeager	.06	.05	.02
520	Tony Bernazard	.06	.05	.02
521	Hal McRae	.10	.08	.04
522	Jose Rijo	.10	.08	.04
523	*Mitch Webster*(FC)	.25	.20	.10
524	*Jack Howell*(FC)	.35	.25	.14
525	Alan Bannister	.06	.05	.02
526	Ron Kittle	.10	.08	.04
527	Phil Garner	.08	.06	.03
528	Kurt Bevacqua	.06	.05	.02
529	Kevin Gross	.08	.06	.03
530	Bo Diaz	.08	.06	.03
531	Ken Oberkfell	.06	.05	.02
532	Rick Reuschel	.10	.08	.04
533	Ron Meridith	.06	.05	.02
534	Steve Braun	.06	.05	.02
535	Wayne Gross	.06	.05	.02
536	Ray Searage	.06	.05	.02
537	Tom Brookens	.06	.05	.02
538	Al Nipper	.06	.05	.02
539	Billy Sample	.06	.05	.02
540	Steve Sax	.20	.15	.08
541	Dan Quisenberry	.10	.08	.04
542	Tony Phillips	.06	.05	.02
543	*Floyd Youmans*(FC)	.30	.25	.12
544	*Steve Buechele*(FC)	.25	.20	.10
545	Craig Gerber	.06	.05	.02
546	Joe DeSa	.06	.05	.02
547	Brian Harper	.06	.05	.02
548	Kevin Bass	.10	.08	.04
549	Tom Foley	.06	.05	.02
550	Dave Van Gorder	.06	.05	.02
551	Bruce Bochy	.06	.05	.02
552	R.J. Reynolds	.08	.06	.03
553	*Chris Brown*(FC)	.20	.15	.08
554	Bruce Benedict	.06	.05	.02
555	Warren Brusstar	.06	.05	.02
556	Danny Heep	.06	.05	.02
557	Darnell Coles	.08	.06	.03
558	Greg Gagne	.08	.06	.03
559	Ernie Whitt	.08	.06	.03
560	Ron Washington	.06	.05	.02
561	Jimmy Key	.15	.11	.06
562	Billy Swift(FC)	.15	.11	.06
563	Ron Darling	.15	.11	.06
564	Dick Ruthven	.06	.05	.02
565	Zane Smith(FC)	.15	.11	.06
566	Sid Bream	.10	.08	.04
567a	Joel Youngblood (P on front)	.08	.06	.03
567b	Joel Youngblood (IF on front)	1.00	.70	.40
568	Mario Ramirez	.06	.05	.02
569	Tom Runnells	.06	.05	.02
570	Rick Schu	.06	.05	.02
571	Bill Campbell	.06	.05	.02
572	Dickie Thon	.08	.06	.03
573	Al Holland	.06	.05	.02
574	Reid Nichols	.06	.05	.02
575	Bert Roberge	.06	.05	.02
576	Mike Flanagan	.10	.08	.04
577	Tim Leary(FC)	.35	.25	.14
578	Mike Laga	.06	.05	.02
579	Steve Lyons	.06	.05	.02
580	Phil Niekro	.30	.25	.12
581	Gilberto Reyes	.06	.05	.02
582	Jamie Easterly	.06	.05	.02
583	Mark Gubicza	.12	.09	.05
584	*Stan Javier*(FC)	.15	.11	.06
585	Bill Laskey	.06	.05	.02
586	Jeff Russell	.06	.05	.02
587	Dickie Noles	.06	.05	.02
588	Steve Farr	.08	.06	.03
589	*Steve Ontiveros*(FC)	.15	.11	.06
590	Mike Hargrove	.06	.05	.02
591	Marty Bystrom	.06	.05	.02
592	Franklin Stubbs	.08	.06	.03
593	Larry Herndon	.08	.06	.03
594	Bill Swaggerty	.06	.05	.02
595	Carlos Ponce	.06	.05	.02
596	*Pat Perry*(FC)	.12	.09	.05
597	Ray Knight	.08	.06	.03
598	*Steve Lombardozzi*(FC)	.15	.11	.06
599	Brad Havens	.06	.05	.02
600	*Pat Clements*(FC)	.12	.09	.05
601	Joe Niekro	.12	.09	.05
602	Hank Aaron Puzzle Card	.06	.05	.02
603	*Dwayne Henry*(FC)	.10	.08	.04
604	Mookie Wilson	.10	.08	.04
605	Buddy Biancalana	.06	.05	.02
606	Rance Mulliniks	.06	.05	.02
607	Alan Wiggins	.06	.05	.02
608	Joe Cowley	.06	.05	.02
609a	Tom Seaver (green stripes around name)	.40	.30	.15
609b	Tom Seaver (yellow stripes around name)	2.00	1.50	.80
610	Neil Allen	.06	.05	.02
611	Don Sutton	.30	.25	.12
612	*Fred Toliver*(FC)	.15	.11	.06
613	Jay Baller	.06	.05	.02
614	Marc Sullivan	.06	.05	.02
615	John Grubb	.06	.05	.02
616	Bruce Kison	.06	.05	.02
617	Bill Madlock	.12	.09	.05
618	Chris Chambliss	.08	.06	.03
619	Dave Stewart	.12	.09	.05
620	Tim Lollar	.06	.05	.02
621	Gary Lavelle	.06	.05	.02
622	Charles Hudson	.06	.05	.02
623	*Joel Davis*(FC)	.08	.06	.03
624	*Joe Johnson*(FC)	.08	.06	.03
625	Sid Fernandez	.12	.09	.05
626	Dennis Lamp	.06	.05	.02
627	Terry Harper	.06	.05	.02
628	Jack Lazorko	.06	.05	.02
629	*Roger McDowell*(FC)	.60	.45	.25
630	Mark Funderburk	.06	.05	.02
631	Ed Lynch	.06	.05	.02
632	Rudy Law	.06	.05	.02
633	*Roger Mason*(FC)	.08	.06	.03
634	*Mike Felder*(FC)	.15	.11	.06
635	Ken Schrom	.06	.05	.02
636	Bob Ojeda	.08	.06	.03
637	Ed Vande Berg	.06	.05	.02
638	Bobby Meacham	.06	.05	.02
639	Cliff Johnson	.06	.05	.02
640	Garth Iorg	.06	.05	.02
641	Dan Driessen	.08	.06	.03
642	Mike Brown	.06	.05	.02
643	John Shelby	.06	.05	.02
644	Ty-Breaking Hit (Pete Rose)	.50	.40	.20
645	Knuckle Brothers (Joe Niekro, Phil Niekro)	.15	.11	.06
646	Jesse Orosco	.08	.06	.03
647	*Billy Beane*(FC)	.06	.05	.02
648	Cesar Cedeno	.10	.08	.04
649	Bert Blyleven	.15	.11	.06
650	Max Venable	.06	.05	.02
651	Fleet Feet (Vince Coleman, Willie McGee)	.35	.25	.14
652	Calvin Schiraldi	.08	.06	.03
653	King of Kings (Pete Rose)	.70	.50	.30
---	Checklist 1-26 DK	.06	.05	.02
---a	Checklist 27-130 (45 is Beane)	.08	.06	.03
---b	Checklist 27-130 (45 is Habyan)	.60	.45	.25
---	Checklist 131-234	.06	.05	.02
---	Checklist 235-338	.06	.05	.02
---	Checklist 339-442	.06	.05	.02
---	Checklist 443-546	.06	.05	.02
---	Checklist 547-653	.06	.05	.02

1986 Donruss All-Stars

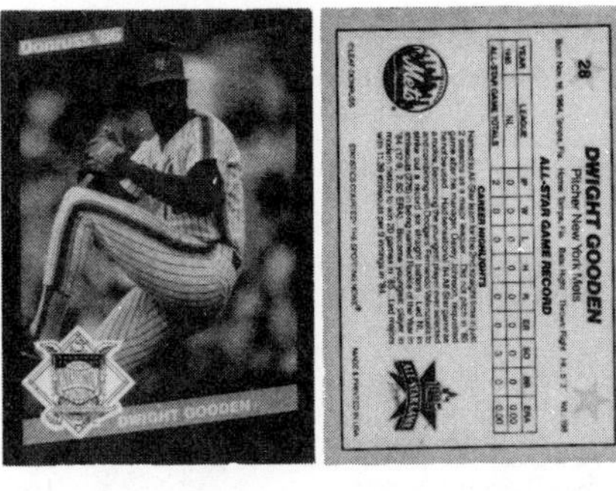

Issued in conjunction with the 1986 Donruss Pop-Ups set, the Donruss All-Stars set consists of 60 cards that measure 3-1/2" by 5". Fifty-nine players involved in the 1985 All-Star game plus an unnumbered checklist comprise the set. The card fronts have the same blue border found on the regular 1986 Donruss issue. Retail packs included one Pop-up card, three All-Star cards and one Hank Aaron puzzle card.

	MT	NR MT	EX
Complete Set:	6.00	4.50	2.50
Common Player:	.09	.07	.04

		MT	NR MT	EX
1	Tony Gwynn	.30	.25	.12
2	Tommy Herr	.09	.07	.04
3	Steve Garvey	.30	.25	.12
4	Dale Murphy	.40	.30	.15
5	Darryl Strawberry	.50	.40	.20
6	Graig Nettles	.12	.09	.05
7	Terry Kennedy	.09	.07	.04
8	Ozzie Smith	.15	.11	.06
9	LaMarr Hoyt	.09	.07	.04
10	Rickey Henderson	.50	.40	.20
11	Lou Whitaker	.15	.11	.06
12	George Brett	.40	.30	.15
13	Eddie Murray	.12	.09	.05
14	Cal Ripken, Jr.	.35	.25	.14
15	Dave Winfield	.25	.20	.10
16	Jim Rice	.12	.09	.05
17	Carlton Fisk	.15	.11	.06
18	Jack Morris	.15	.11	.06
19	Jose Cruz	.09	.07	.04
20	Tim Raines	.25	.20	.10
21	Nolan Ryan	.50	.40	.20
22	Tony Pena	.09	.07	.04
23	Jack Clark	.15	.11	.06
24	Dave Parker	.15	.11	.06
25	Tim Wallach	.12	.09	.05
26	Ozzie Virgil	.09	.07	.04
27	Fernando Valenzuela	.12	.09	.05
28	Dwight Gooden	.60	.45	.25
29	Glenn Wilson	.09	.07	.04
30	Garry Templeton	.09	.07	.04
31	Goose Gossage	.12	.09	.05
32	Ryne Sandberg	.25	.20	.10
33	Jeff Reardon	.12	.09	.05
34	Pete Rose	.35	.25	.14
35	Scott Garrelts	.09	.07	.04
36	Willie McGee	.12	.09	.05
37	Ron Darling	.12	.09	.05
38	Dick Williams	.09	.07	.04
39	Paul Molitor	.15	.11	.06
40	Damaso Garcia	.09	.07	.04
41	Phil Bradley	.12	.09	.05
42	Dan Petry	.09	.07	.04
43	Willie Hernandez	.09	.07	.04
44	Tom Brunansky	.12	.09	.05
45	Alan Trammell	.20	.15	.08
46	Donnie Moore	.09	.07	.04
47	Wade Boggs	.90	.70	.35
48	Ernie Whitt	.09	.07	.04
49	Harold Baines	.15	.11	.06
50	Don Mattingly	2.00	1.50	.80
51	Gary Ward	.09	.07	.04
52	Bert Blyleven	.12	.09	.05
53	Jimmy Key	.12	.09	.05
54	Cecil Cooper	.12	.09	.05
55	Dave Stieb	.12	.09	.05
56	Rich Gedman	.09	.07	.04
57	Jay Howell	.09	.07	.04
58	Sparky Anderson	.09	.07	.04
59	Minneapolis Metrodome	.09	.07	.04
---	Checklist	.09	.07	.04

1986 Donruss Box Panels

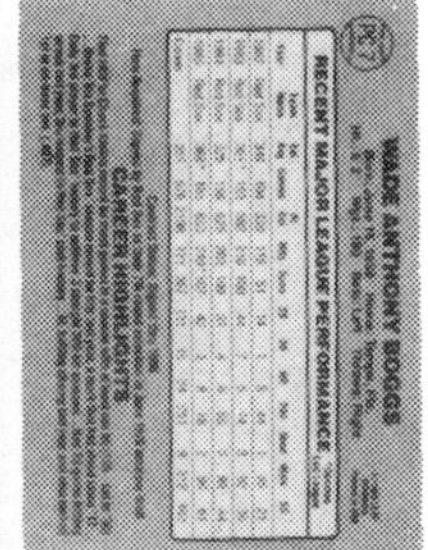

For the second year in a row, Donruss placed baseball cards on the bottom of their wax and cello pack boxes. The cards, which come four to a panel, are the standard 2-1/2" by 3-1/2" in size. With numbering that begins where Donruss left off in 1985, cards PC 4 through PC 6 were found on boxes of regular Donruss issue wax packs. Cards PC 7 through PC 9 were found on boxes of the 1986 All- Star/Pop-up packs. An unnumbered Hank Aaron puzzle card was included on each box.

		MT	NR MT	EX
Complete Panel Set:		5.00	3.75	2.00
Complete Singles Set:		3.00	2.25	1.25
Common Single Player:		.15	.11	.06
Panel		1.00	.70	.40
4	Kirk Gibson	.35	.25	.14
5	Willie Hernandez	.15	.11	.06
6	Doug DeCinces	.15	.11	.06
---	Aaron Puzzle Card	.04	.03	.02
Panel		4.00	3.00	1.50
7	Wade Boggs	2.00	1.50	.80
8	Lee Smith	.15	.11	.06
9	Cecil Cooper	.20	.15	.08
---	Aaron Puzzle Card	.04	.03	.02

1986 Donruss Diamond Kings Supers

Donruss produced a set of giant-size Diamond Kings in 1986 for the second year in a row. The cards, which measure 4-11/6" by 6-3/4", are enlarged versions of the 26 Diamond Kings cards found in the regular 1986 Donruss set. Featuring the artwork of Dick Perez, the set consists of 28 cards - 26 DKs, an unnumbered checklist and an unnumbered Pete Rose "King of Kings" card.

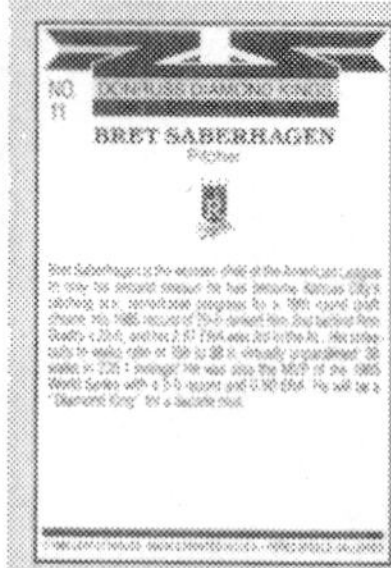

	MT	NR MT	EX
Complete Set:	11.00	8.25	4.50
Common Player:	.20	.15	.08

No.	Player	MT	NR MT	EX
1	Kirk Gibson	.50	.40	.20
2	Goose Gossage	.30	.25	.12
3	Willie McGee	.30	.25	.12
4	George Bell	.30	.25	.12
5	Tony Armas	.20	.15	.08
6	Chili Davis	.20	.15	.08
7	Cecil Cooper	.25	.20	.10
8	Mike Boddicker	.20	.15	.08
9	Davey Lopes	.20	.15	.08
10	Bill Doran	.25	.20	.10
11	Bret Saberhagen	.70	.50	.30
12	Brett Butler	.20	.15	.08
13	Harold Baines	.30	.25	.12
14	Mike Davis	.20	.15	.08
15	Tony Perez	.25	.20	.10
16	Willie Randolph	.25	.20	.10
18	Orel Hershiser	1.00	.70	.40
19	Johnny Ray	.25	.20	.10
20	Gary Ward	.20	.15	.08
21	Rick Mahler	.20	.15	.08
22	Phil Bradley	.30	.25	.12
23	Jerry Koosman	.20	.15	.08
24	Tom Brunansky	.25	.20	.10
25	Andre Dawson	.35	.25	.14
26	Dwight Gooden	1.50	1.25	.60
---	Checklist	.15	.11	.06
---	King of Kings (Pete Rose)	1.50	1.25	.60

1986 Donruss Highlights

Dale Murphy
National League Player of the Month
August

Dale Murphy, a two-time National League Most Valuable Player, brought a streak of four straight 100-RBI seasons into 1986. As the season moved on into August, it appeared as if Murphy might have trouble making that five in a row. Nevertheless, the Atlanta Braves' centerfielder made a determined effort to reach his goal when he accumulated 30 RBI in 29 games in August. Over that span, Murphy batted .337 (35-for-104) with 9 doubles, 2 triples and 10 home runs. That performance was good enough to earn him the National League's Player of the Month honor for the sixth time in his career.

NO. 41

Donruss, for the second year in a row, issued a 56- card highlights set which featured cards of the A.L. and N.L. Player of the Month plus significant events that took place during the 1986 season. The cards, which measure 2-1/2" by 3-1/2" in size, are similar in design to the regular 1986 Donruss set but have a gold border instead of blue. A "Highlights" logo appears in the lower left corner of each card front. The card backs are designed on a vertical format and feature black print on a yellow background. As in 1985, the set includes Donruss' picks for the Rookies of the Year awards. A new feature was three cards honoring the 1986 Hall of Fame inductees. The set, available only through hobby dealers, was issued in a specially designed box.

	MT	NR MT	EX
Complete Set:	10.00	7.50	4.00
Common Player:	.10	.08	.04

No.	Card	MT	NR MT	EX
1	Homers In First At-Bat (Will Clark)	2.00	1.50	.80
2	Oakland Milestone For Strikeouts (Jose Rijo)	.10	.08	.04
3	Royals' All-Time Hit Man (George Brett)	.20	.15	.08
4	Phillies RBI Leader (Mike Schmidt)	.30	.25	.12
5	KKKKKKKKKKKKKKKKKKKK (Roger Clemens)	.75	.55	.20
6	A.L. Pitcher of the Month-April (Roger Clemens)	.50	.40	.20
7	A.L. Player of the Month-April (Kirby Puckett)	.50	.40	.20
8	N.L. Pitcher of the Month-April (Dwight Gooden)	.50	.40	.20
9	N.L. Player of the Month-April (Johnny Ray)	.10	.08	.04
10	Eclipses Mantle HR Record (Reggie Jackson)	.25	.20	.10
11	First Five Hit Game of Career (Wade Boggs)	.50	.40	.20
12	A.L. Pitcher of the Month-May (Don Aase)	.10	.08	.04
13	A.L. Player of the Month-May (Wade Boggs)	.50	.40	.20
14	N.L. Pitcher of the Month-May (Jeff Reardon)	.15	.11	.06
15	N.L. Player of the Month-May (Hubie Brooks)	.10	.08	.04
16	Notches 300th Career Win (Don Sutton)	.10	.08	.04
17	Starts Season 14-0 (Roger Clemens)	.50	.40	.20
18	A.L. Pitcher of the Month-June (Roger Clemens)	.50	.40	.20
19	A.L. Player of the Month-June (Kent Hrbek)	.10	.08	.04
20	N.L. Pitcher of the Month-June (Rick Rhoden)	.10	.08	.04
21	N.L. Player of the Month-June (Kevin Bass)	.10	.08	.04
22	Blasts 4 HRS in 1 Game (Bob Horner)	.10	.08	.04
23	Starting All Star Rookie (Wally Joyner)	.50	.40	.20
24	Starts 3rd Straight All Star Game (Darryl Strawberry)	.25	.20	.10
25	Ties All Star Game Record (Fernando Valenzuela)	.10	.08	.04
26	All Star Game MVP (Roger Clemens)	.50	.40	.20
27	A.L. Pitcher of the Month-July (Jack Morris)	.10	.08	.04
28	A.L. Player of the Month-July (Scott Fletcher)	.10	.08	.04
29	N.L. Pitcher of the Month-July (Todd Worrell)	.25	.20	.10
30	N.L. PLayer of the Month-July (Eric Davis)	.40	.30	.15
31	Records 3000th Strikeout (Bert Blyleven)	.15	.11	.06
32	1986 Hall of Fame Inductee (Bobby Doerr)	.15	.11	.06
33	1986 Hall of Fame Inductee (Ernie Lombardi)	.15	.11	.06
34	1986 Hall of Fame Inductee (Willie McCovey)	.20	.15	.08
35	Notches 4000th K (Steve Carlton)	.25	.20	.10
36	Surpasses DiMaggio Record (Mike Schmidt)	.40	.30	.15
37	Records 3rd "Quadruple Double" (Juan Samuel)	.10	.08	.04
38	A.L. Pitcher of the Month-August (Mike Witt)	.10	.08	.04
39	A.L. Player of the Month-August (Doug DeCinces)	.10	.08	.04
40	N.L. Pitcher of the Month-August (Bill Gullickson)	.10	.08	.04
41	N.L. Player of the Month-August (Dale Murphy)	.20	.15	.08
42	Sets Tribe Offensive Record (Joe Carter)	.25	.20	.10
43	Longest HR In Royals Stadium (Bo Jackson)	2.00	1.50	.80
44	Majors 1st No-Hitter In 2 Years (Joe Cowley)	.10	.08	.04
45	Sets M.L. Strikeout Record (Jim Deshaies)	.15	.11	.06
46	No Hitter Clinches Division (Mike Scott)	.10	.08	.04
47	A.L. Pitcher of the Month-September (Bruce Hurst)	.10	.08	.04
48	A.L. Player of the Month-September (Don Mattingly)	1.00	.70	.40
49	N.L. Pitcher of the Month-September (Mike Krukow)	.10	.08	.04
50	N.L. Player of the Month-September (Steve Sax)	.10	.08	.04
51	A.L. Record For Steals By A Rookie (John Cangelosi)	.10	.08	.04
52	Shatters M.L. Save Mark (Dave Righetti)	.10	.08	.04
53	Yankee Record For Hits & Doubles (Don Mattingly)	1.00	.70	.40
54	Donruss N.L. Rookie of the Year (Todd Worrell)	.25	.20	.10
55	Donruss A.L. Rookie of the Year (Jose Canseco)	3.00	2.25	1.25
56	Highlight Checklist	.10	.08	.04

1986 Donruss Pop-Ups

Issued in conjunction with the 1986 Donruss All-Stars set, the Donruss Pop-Ups (18 unnumbered cards) feature the 1985 All-Star Game starting lineups. The cards, which measure 2-1/2" by 5", are die-cut and fold out to form a three-dimensional stand-up card. The background for the cards is the Minneapolis Metrodome, site of the 1985 All-Star Game. Retail packs included one Pop-Up card, three All-Star cards and one Hank Aaron puzzle card.

	MT	NR MT	EX
Complete Set:	5.00	3.75	2.00
Common Player:	.20	.15	.08

No.	Player	MT	NR MT	EX
(1)	George Brett	.60	.45	.25
(2)	Carlton Fisk	.30	.25	.12
(3)	Steve Garvey	.20	.15	.08
(4)	Tony Gwynn	.50	.40	.20
(5)	Rickey Henderson	.50	.40	.20
(6)	Tommy Herr	.20	.15	.08
(7)	LaMarr Hoyt	.20	.15	.08
(8)	Terry Kennedy	.20	.15	.08
(9)	Jack Morris	.20	.15	.08
(10)	Dale Murphy	.30	.25	.12
(11)	Eddie Murray	.20	.15	.08
(12)	Graig Nettles	.20	.15	.08
(13)	Jim Rice	.20	.15	.08
(14)	Cal Ripken Jr.	.50	.40	.20
(15)	Ozzie Smith	.30	.25	.12
(16)	Darryl Strawberry	.70	.50	.30
(17)	Lou Whitaker	.30	.25	.12
(18)	Dave Winfield	.30	.25	.12

1986 Donruss Rookies

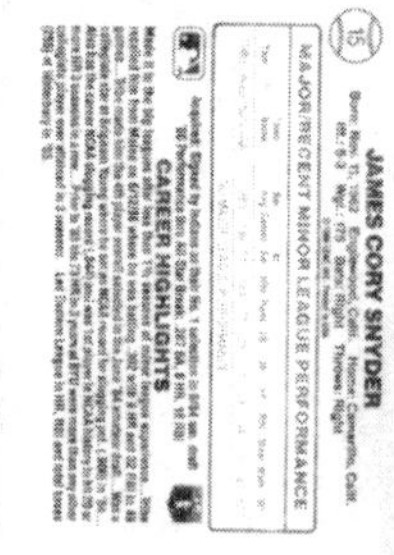

Entitled "The Rookies," this 56-card set includes the top 55 rookies of 1986 plus an unnumbered checklist. The cards, which measure 2-1/2" by 3-1/2", are similar to the format used for the 1986 Donruss regular issue, except that the borders are green rather than blue. Several of the rookies who had cards in the regular 1986 Donruss set appear again in "The Rookies" set. The sets, which were only available through hobby dealers, came in a specially designed box.

	MT	NR MT	EX
Complete Set:	50.00	37.00	20.00
Common Player:	.15	.11	.06

No.	Player	MT	NR MT	EX
1	Wally Joyner(FC)	3.75	2.75	1.50
2	Tracy Jones(FC)	.50	.40	.20
3	Allan Anderson(FC)	.40	.30	.15
4	Ed Correa(FC)	.25	.20	.10
5	Reggie Williams	.20	.15	.08
6	Charlie Kerfeld(FC)	.15	.11	.06
7	Andres Galarraga	.80	.60	.30
8	Bob Tewksbury(FC)	.15	.11	.06
9	Al Newman	.15	.11	.06
10	Andres Thomas(FC)	.40	.30	.15
11	Barry Bonds(FC)	2.00	1.50	.80
12	Juan Nieves	.15	.11	.06
13	Mark Eichhorn(FC)	.25	.20	.10
14	Dan Plesac(FC)	.40	.30	.15
15	Cory Snyder	1.75	1.25	.70
16	Kelly Gruber	.50	.40	.20
17	Kevin Mitchell(FC)	8.00	6.00	3.25
18	Steve Lombardozzi	.15	.11	.06
19	Mitch Williams	.60	.45	.25
20	John Cerutti(FC)	.25	.20	.10
21	Todd Worrell	.50	.40	.20
22	Jose Canseco	15.00	11.00	6.00
23	Pete Incaviglia(FC)	.80	.60	.30
24	Jose Guzman	.25	.20	.10
25	Scott Bailes(FC)	.25	.20	.10
26	Greg Mathews(FC)	.25	.20	.10
27	Eric King(FC)	.20	.15	.08
28	Paul Assenmacher	.20	.15	.08
29	Jeff Sellers	.25	.20	.10
30	Bobby Bonilla(FC)	2.00	1.50	.80
31	Doug Drabek(FC)	.50	.40	.20
32	Will Clark(FC)	15.00	11.00	6.00
33	Bip Roberts	.15	.11	.06
34	Jim Deshaies(FC)	.25	.20	.10
35	Mike Lavalliere (LaValliere)(FC)	.30	.25	.12

		MT	NR MT	EX
36	Scott Bankhead(FC)	.20	.15	.08
37	Dale Sveum(FC)	.25	.20	.10
38	Bo Jackson(FC)	12.00	9.00	4.75
39	Rob Thompson(FC)	.50	.40	.20
40	Eric Plunk(FC)	.20	.15	.08
41	Bill Bathe	.15	.11	.06
42	John Kruk(FC)	.40	.30	.15
43	Andy Allanson(FC)	.20	.15	.08
44	Mark Portugal	.15	.11	.06
45	Danny Tartabull	1.00	.70	.40
46	Bob Kipper	.15	.11	.06
47	Gene Walter	.15	.11	.06
48	Rey Quinonez	.15	.11	.06
49	Bobby Witt(FC)	.40	.30	.15
50	Bill Mooneyham	.15	.11	.06
51	John Cangelosi(FC)	.20	.15	.08
52	Ruben Sierra(FC)	8.00	6.00	3.35
53	Rob Woodward	.15	.11	.06
54	Ed Hearn	.15	.11	.06
55	Joel McKeon	.15	.11	.06
56	Checklist 1-56	.05	.04	.02

1987 Donruss

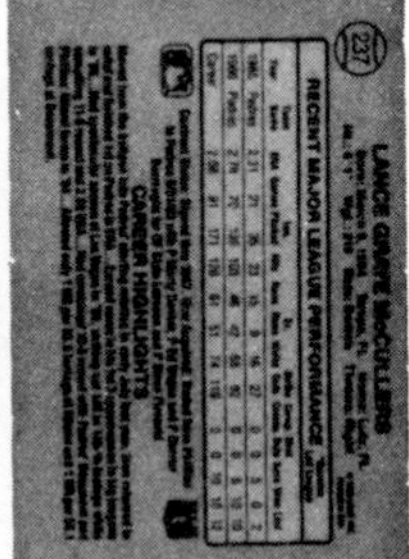

The 1987 Donruss set consists of 660 numbered cards, each measuring 2-1/2" by 3-1/2" in size. Full color photos are surrounded by a bold black border separated by two narrow bands of yellow which enclose a brown area filled with baseballs. The player's name, team and team logo appear on the card fronts along with the words "Donruss '87." The card backs are designed on a horizontal format and contain black print on a yellow and white background. The backs are very similar to those in previous years' sets. Backs of cards issued in wax and rack packs face to the left when turned over, while those issued in vending sets face to the right.

	MT	NR MT	EX
Complete Set:	80.00	60.00	32.50
Common Player:	.05	.04	.02

		MT	NR MT	EX
1	Wally Joyner (DK)	1.25	.90	.50
2	Roger Clemens (DK)	.70	.50	.30
3	Dale Murphy (DK)	.40	.30	.15
4	Darryl Strawberry (DK)	.40	.30	.15
5	Ozzie Smith (DK)	.12	.09	.05
6	Jose Canseco (DK)	2.00	1.50	.80
7	Charlie Hough (DK)	.07	.05	.03
8	Brook Jacoby (DK)	.10	.08	.04
9	Fred Lynn (DK)	.12	.09	.05
10	Rick Rhoden (DK)	.10	.08	.04
11	Chris Brown (DK)	.10	.08	.04
12	Von Hayes (DK)	.10	.08	.04
13	Jack Morris (DK)	.20	.15	.08
14a	Kevin McReynolds (DK) ("Donruss Diamond Kings" in white band on back)	1.25	.90	.50
14b	Kevin McReynolds (DK) ("Donruss Diamond Kings" in yellow band on back)	.20	.15	.08
15	George Brett (DK)	.40	.30	.15
16	Ted Higuera (DK)	.20	.15	.08
17	Hubie Brooks (DK)	.10	.08	.04
18	Mike Scott (DK)	.12	.09	.05
19	Kirby Puckett (DK)	.25	.20	.10
20	Dave Winfield (DK)	.25	.20	.10
21	Lloyd Moseby (DK)	.10	.08	.04
22a	Eric Davis (DK) ("Donruss Diamond Kings" in white band on back)	3.00	2.25	1.25
22b	Eric Davis (DK) ("Donruss Diamond Kings" in yellow band on back)	1.00	.70	.40
23	Jim Presley (DK)	.12	.09	.05
24	Keith Moreland (DK)	.07	.05	.03
25a	Greg Walker (DK) ("Donruss Diamond Kings" in white band on back)	1.25	.90	.50
25b	Greg Walker (DK) ("Donruss Diamond Kings" in yellow band on back)	.10	.08	.04
26	Steve Sax (DK)	.12	.09	.05
27	Checklist 1-27	.05	.04	.02
28	*B.J. Surhoff (RR)*(FC)	.70	.50	.30
29	*Randy Myers (RR)*(FC)	.70	.50	.30
30	*Ken Gerhart (RR)*(FC)	.15	.11	.06
31	Benito Santiago (RR)(FC)	2.25	1.75	.90
32	*Greg Swindell (RR)*(FC)	1.25	.90	.50
33	*Mike Birkbeck (RR)*(FC)	.20	.15	.08
34	*Terry Steinbach (RR)*(FC)	1.00	.70	.40
35	*Bo Jackson (RR)*	12.00	9.00	4.75
36	*Greg Maddux (RR)*(FC)	1.25	.90	.50
37	*Jim Lindeman (RR)*(FC)	.15	.11	.06
38	*Devon White (RR)*(FC)	1.00	.70	.40
39	*Eric Bell (RR)*(FC)	.12	.09	.05
40	*Will Fraser (RR)*(FC)	.20	.15	.08
41	*Jerry Browne (RR)*(FC)	.60	.45	.25
42	*Chris James (RR)*(FC)	.70	.50	.30
43	*Rafael Palmeiro (RR)*(FC)	2.25	1.75	.90
44	*Pat Dodson (RR)*(FC)	.12	.09	.05
45	*Duane Ward (RR)*(FC)	.20	.15	.08
46	*Mark McGwire (RR)*(FC)	8.00	6.00	3.25
47	*Bruce Fields (RR)* (photo actually Darnell Coles)(FC)	.10	.08	.04
48	Eddie Murray	.35	.25	.14
49	Ted Higuera	.20	.15	.08
50	Kirk Gibson	.25	.20	.10
51	Oil Can Boyd	.07	.05	.03
52	Don Mattingly	2.50	2.00	1.00
53	Pedro Guerrero	.15	.11	.06
54	George Brett	.40	.30	.15
55	Jose Rijo	.07	.05	.03
56	Tim Raines	.30	.25	.12
57	*Ed Correa*	.15	.11	.06
58	Mike Witt	.10	.08	.04
59	Greg Walker	.10	.08	.04
60	Ozzie Smith	.15	.11	.06
61	Glenn Davis	.35	.25	.14
62	Glenn Wilson	.07	.05	.03
63	Tom Browning	.10	.08	.04
64	Tony Gwynn	.35	.25	.14
65	R.J. Reynolds	.07	.05	.03
66	*Will Clark*	12.00	9.00	4.75
67	Ozzie Virgil	.05	.04	.02
68	Rick Sutcliffe	.12	.09	.05
69	Gary Carter	.30	.25	.12
70	Mike Moore	.05	.04	.02
71	Bert Blyleven	.12	.09	.05
72	Tony Fernandez	.12	.09	.05
73	Kent Hrbek	.15	.11	.06
74	Lloyd Moseby	.10	.08	.04
75	Alvin Davis	.12	.09	.05
76	Keith Hernandez	.25	.20	.10
77	Ryne Sandberg	.35	.25	.14
78	Dale Murphy	.40	.30	.15
79	Sid Bream	.07	.05	.03
80	Chris Brown	.07	.05	.03
81	Steve Garvey	.25	.20	.10
82	Mario Soto	.07	.05	.03
83	Shane Rawley	.07	.05	.03
84	Willie McGee	.12	.09	.05
85	Jose Cruz	.10	.08	.04
86	Brian Downing	.07	.05	.03
87	Ozzie Guillen	.10	.08	.04
88	Hubie Brooks	.10	.08	.04
89	Cal Ripken	.35	.25	.14
90	Juan Nieves	.07	.05	.03
91	Lance Parrish	.20	.15	.08
92	Jim Rice	.30	.25	.12
93	Ron Guidry	.15	.11	.06
94	Fernando Valenzuela	.25	.20	.10
95	*Andy Allanson*	.15	.11	.06
96	Willie Wilson	.12	.09	.05
97	Jose Canseco	10.00	7.50	4.00
98	Jeff Reardon	.10	.08	.04
99	*Bobby Witt*	.35	.25	.14
100	Checklist 28-133	.05	.04	.02
101	Jose Guzman	.10	.08	.04
102	Steve Balboni	.07	.05	.03
103	Tony Phillips	.05	.04	.02
104	Brook Jacoby	.10	.08	.04
105	Dave Winfield	.30	.25	.12
106	Orel Hershiser	.40	.30	.15
107	Lou Whitaker	.25	.20	.10
108	Fred Lynn	.15	.11	.06
109	Bill Wegman	.07	.05	.03
110	Donnie Moore	.05	.04	.02
111	Jack Clark	.15	.11	.06
112	Bob Knepper	.07	.05	.03
113	Von Hayes	.10	.08	.04
114	Leon "Bip" Roberts	.05	.04	.02
115	Tony Pena	.08	.06	.03
116	Scott Garrelts	.05	.04	.02
117	Paul Molitor	.15	.11	.06
118	Darryl Strawberry	.60	.45	.25
119	Shawon Dunston	.10	.08	.04
120	Jim Presley	.10	.08	.04
121	Jesse Barfield	.20	.15	.08
122	Gary Gaetti	.15	.11	.06
123	*Kurt Stillwell*	.50	.40	.20
124	Joel Davis	.05	.04	.02
125	Mike Boddicker	.07	.05	.03
126	Robin Yount	.50	.40	.20
127	Alan Trammell	.25	.20	.10
128	Dave Righetti	.15	.11	.06
129	Dwight Evans	.12	.09	.05
130	Mike Scioscia	.07	.05	.03
131	Julio Franco	.10	.08	.04
132	Bret Saberhagen	.25	.20	.10
133	Mike Davis	.07	.05	.03
134	Joe Hesketh	.05	.04	.02
135	*Wally Joyner*	1.75	1.25	.70
136	Don Slaught	.05	.04	.02
137	Daryl Boston	.05	.04	.02
138	Nolan Ryan	.70	.50	.30
139	Mike Schmidt	.50	.40	.20
140	Tommy Herr	.10	.08	.04
141	Garry Templeton	.07	.05	.03
142	Kal Daniels	.80	.60	.30
143	Billy Sample	.05	.04	.02
144	Johnny Ray	.10	.08	.04
145	*Rob Thompson*	.30	.25	.12
146	Bob Dernier	.05	.04	.02
147	Danny Tartabull	.25	.20	.10
148	Ernie Whitt	.07	.05	.03
149	Kirby Puckett	1.50	1.25	.60
150	Mike Young	.05	.04	.02
151	Ernest Riles	.05	.04	.02
152	Frank Tanana	.07	.05	.03
153	Rich Gedman	.10	.08	.04
154	Willie Randolph	.10	.08	.04
155a	Bill Madlock (name in brown band)	.12	.09	.05
155b	Bill Madlock (name in red band)	.70	.50	.30
156a	Joe Carter (name in brown band)	.15	.11	.06
156b	Joe Carter (name in red band)	.70	.50	.30
157	Danny Jackson	.15	.11	.06
158	Carney Lansford	.10	.08	.04
159	Bryn Smith	.05	.04	.02
160	Gary Pettis	.05	.04	.02
161	Oddibe McDowell	.10	.08	.04
162	*John Cangelosi*	.12	.09	.05
163	Mike Scott	.15	.11	.06
164	Eric Show	.07	.05	.03
165	Juan Samuel	.12	.09	.05
166	Nick Esasky	.07	.05	.03
167	Zane Smith	.07	.05	.03
168	Mike Brown	.05	.04	.02
169	Keith Moreland	.07	.05	.03
170	John Tudor	.10	.08	.04
171	Ken Dixon	.05	.04	.02
172	Jim Gantner	.07	.05	.03
173	Jack Morris	.20	.15	.08
174	Bruce Hurst	.10	.08	.04
175	Dennis Rasmussen	.10	.08	.04
176	Mike Marshall	.12	.09	.05
177	Dan Quisenberry	.07	.05	.03
178	Eric Plunk(FC)	.10	.08	.04
179	Tim Wallach	.12	.09	.05
180	Steve Buechele	.07	.05	.03
181	Don Sutton	.20	.15	.08
182	Dave Schmidt	.05	.04	.02
183	Terry Pendleton	.10	.08	.04
184	*Jim Deshaies*	.35	.25	.14
185	Steve Bedrosian	.12	.09	.05
186	Pete Rose	.60	.45	.25
187	Dave Dravecky	.07	.05	.03
188	Rick Reuschel	.10	.08	.04
189	Dan Gladden	.05	.04	.02
190	Rick Mahler	.05	.04	.02
191	Thad Bosley	.05	.04	.02
192	Ron Darling	.15	.11	.06
193	Matt Young	.05	.04	.02
194	Tom Brunansky	.10	.08	.04
195	Dave Stieb	.12	.09	.05
196	Frank Viola	.15	.11	.06
197	Tom Henke	.07	.05	.03
198	Karl Best	.05	.04	.02
199	Dwight Gooden	.90	.70	.35
200	Checklist 134-239	.05	.04	.02
201	Steve Trout	.05	.04	.02
202	Rafael Ramirez	.05	.04	.02
203	Bob Walk	.05	.04	.02
204	Roger Mason	.05	.04	.02
205	Terry Kennedy	.07	.05	.03
206	Ron Oester	.05	.04	.02
207	John Russell	.05	.04	.02
208	*Greg Mathews*	.20	.15	.08
209	Charlie Kerfeld	.10	.08	.04
210	Reggie Jackson	.35	.25	.14
211	Floyd Bannister	.10	.08	.04
212	Vance Law	.07	.05	.03
213	Rich Bordi	.05	.04	.02
214	*Dan Plesac*	.35	.25	.14
215	Dave Collins	.07	.05	.03
216	Bob Stanley	.05	.04	.02
217	Joe Niekro	.10	.08	.04
218	Tom Niedenfuer	.07	.05	.03
219	Brett Butler	.07	.05	.03
220	Charlie Leibrandt	.07	.05	.03
221	Steve Ontiveros	.05	.04	.02
222	Tim Burke	.05	.04	.02
223	Curtis Wilkerson	.05	.04	.02
224	*Pete Incaviglia*	.60	.45	.25
225	Lonnie Smith	.07	.05	.03
226	Chris Codiroli	.05	.04	.02
227	*Scott Bailes*	.20	.15	.08
228	Rickey Henderson	.35	.25	.14
229	Ken Howell	.05	.04	.02
230	Darnell Coles	.07	.05	.03
231	Don Aase	.05	.04	.02
232	Tim Leary	.07	.05	.03
233	Bob Boone	.07	.05	.03
234	Ricky Horton	.07	.05	.03
235	Mark Bailey	.05	.04	.02
236	Kevin Gross	.07	.05	.03
237	Lance McCullers	.07	.05	.03
238	Cecilio Guante	.05	.04	.02
239	Bob Melvin	.05	.04	.02
240	Billy Jo Robidoux	.05	.04	.02
241	Roger McDowell	.12	.09	.05
242	Leon Durham	.07	.05	.03
243	Ed Nunez	.05	.04	.02
244	Jimmy Key	.12	.09	.05
245	Mike Smithson	.05	.04	.02
246	Bo Diaz	.07	.05	.03
247	Carlton Fisk	.20	.15	.08
248	Larry Sheets	.08	.06	.03
249	*Juan Castillo*(FC)	.10	.08	.04
250	*Eric King*	.25	.20	.10
251	*Doug Drabek*	.40	.30	.15
252	Wade Boggs	1.50	1.25	.60
253	Mariano Duncan	.05	.04	.02
254	Pat Tabler	.07	.05	.03
255	Frank White	.10	.08	.04
256	Alfredo Griffin	.07	.05	.03
257	Floyd Youmans	.07	.05	.03
258	Rob Wilfong	.05	.04	.02
259	Pete O'Brien	.10	.08	.04
260	Tim Hulett	.05	.04	.02
261	Dickie Thon	.07	.05	.03
262	Darren Daulton	.05	.04	.02
263	Vince Coleman	.25	.20	.10
264	Andy Hawkins	.05	.04	.02
265	Eric Davis	1.25	.90	.50
266	*Andres Thomas*	.25	.20	.10
267	*Mike Diaz*(FC)	.15	.11	.06
268	Chili Davis	.07	.05	.03
269	Jody Davis	.07	.05	.03
270	Phil Bradley	.12	.09	.05
271	George Bell	.25	.20	.10
272	Keith Atherton	.05	.04	.02
273	Storm Davis	.10	.08	.04
274	Rob Deer(FC)	.20	.15	.08
275	Walt Terrell	.07	.05	.03
276	Roger Clemens	1.75	1.25	.70
277	Mike Easler	.07	.05	.03
278	Steve Sax	.15	.11	.06
279	Andre Thornton	.07	.05	.03
280	Jim Sundberg	.07	.05	.03

#	Player	MT	NR MT	EX
281	Bill Bathe	.05	.04	.02
282	Jay Tibbs	.05	.04	.02
283	Dick Schofield	.05	.04	.02
284	Mike Mason	.05	.04	.02
285	Jerry Hairston	.05	.04	.02
286	Bill Doran	.10	.08	.04
287	Tim Flannery	.05	.04	.02
288	Gary Redus	.05	.04	.02
289	John Franco	.10	.08	.04
290	*Paul Assenmacher*	.15	.11	.06
291	Joe Orsulak	.05	.04	.02
292	Lee Smith	.10	.08	.04
293	Mike Laga	.05	.04	.02
294	Rick Dempsey	.07	.05	.03
295	Mike Felder	.05	.04	.02
296	Tom Brookens	.05	.04	.02
297	Al Nipper	.05	.04	.02
298	Mike Pagliarulo	.10	.08	.04
299	Franklin Stubbs	.07	.05	.03
300	Checklist 240-345	.05	.04	.02
301	Steve Farr	.05	.04	.02
302	*Bill Mooneyham*	.10	.08	.04
303	Andres Galarraga	.25	.20	.10
304	Scott Fletcher	.07	.05	.03
305	Jack Howell	.07	.05	.03
306	*Russ Morman*(FC)	.10	.08	.04
307	Todd Worrell	.20	.15	.08
308	Dave Smith	.07	.05	.03
309	Jeff Stone	.05	.04	.02
310	Ron Robinson	.05	.04	.02
311	Bruce Bochy	.05	.04	.02
312	Jim Winn	.05	.04	.02
313	Mark Davis	.05	.04	.02
314	Jeff Dedmon	.05	.04	.02
315	*Jamie Moyer*(FC)	.20	.15	.08
316	Wally Backman	.07	.05	.03
317	Ken Phelps	.07	.05	.03
318	Steve Lombardozzi	.05	.04	.02
319	Rance Mulliniks	.05	.04	.02
320	Tim Laudner	.05	.04	.02
321	*Mark Eichhorn*	.15	.11	.06
322	*Lee Guetterman*	.15	.11	.06
323	Sid Fernandez	.12	.09	.05
324	Jerry Mumphrey	.05	.04	.02
325	David Palmer	.05	.04	.02
326	Bill Almon	.05	.04	.02
327	Candy Maldonado	.07	.05	.03
328	*John Kruk*	.30	.25	.12
329	John Denny	.05	.04	.02
330	Milt Thompson	.07	.05	.03
331	*Mike LaValliere*	.25	.20	.10
332	Alan Ashby	.05	.04	.02
333	Doug Corbett	.05	.04	.02
334	*Ron Karkovice*(FC)	.10	.08	.04
335	Mitch Webster	.07	.05	.03
336	Lee Lacy	.05	.04	.02
337	*Glenn Braggs*(FC)	.30	.25	.12
338	Dwight Lowry	.05	.04	.02
339	Don Baylor	.12	.09	.05
340	Brian Fisher	.07	.05	.03
341	*Reggie Williams*	.10	.08	.04
342	Tom Candiotti	.05	.04	.02
343	Rudy Law	.05	.04	.02
344	Curt Young	.07	.05	.03
345	Mike Fitzgerald	.05	.04	.02
346	*Ruben Sierra*	7.00	5.25	2.75
347	*Mitch Williams*	.60	.45	.25
348	Jorge Orta	.05	.04	.02
349	Mickey Tettleton	.10	.08	.04
350	Ernie Camacho	.05	.04	.02
351	Ron Kittle	.10	.08	.04
352	Ken Landreaux	.05	.04	.02
353	Chet Lemon	.07	.05	.03
354	John Shelby	.05	.04	.02
355	Mark Clear	.05	.04	.02
356	Doug DeCinces	.07	.05	.03
357	Ken Dayley	.05	.04	.02
358	Phil Garner	.05	.04	.02
359	Steve Jeltz	.05	.04	.02
360	Ed Whitson	.05	.04	.02
361	*Barry Bonds*	2.00	1.50	.80
362	Vida Blue	.10	.08	.04
363	Cecil Cooper	.12	.09	.05
364	Bob Ojeda	.07	.05	.03
365	Dennis Eckersley	.12	.09	.05
366	Mike Morgan	.05	.04	.02
367	Willie Upshaw	.07	.05	.03
368	*Allan Anderson*(FC)	.25	.20	.10
369	Bill Gullickson	.07	.05	.03
370	*Bobby Thigpen*(FC)	.30	.25	.12
371	Juan Beniquez	.05	.04	.02
372	Charlie Moore	.05	.04	.02
373	Dan Petry	.07	.05	.03
374	Rod Scurry	.05	.04	.02
375	Tom Seaver	.40	.30	.15
376	Ed Vande Berg	.05	.04	.02
377	Tony Bernazard	.05	.04	.02
378	Greg Pryor	.05	.04	.02
379	Dwayne Murphy	.07	.05	.03
380	Andy McGaffigan	.05	.04	.02
381	Kirk McCaskill	.07	.05	.03
382	Greg Harris	.05	.04	.02
383	Rich Dotson	.07	.05	.03
384	Craig Reynolds	.05	.04	.02
385	Greg Gross	.05	.04	.02
386	Tito Landrum	.05	.04	.02
387	Craig Lefferts	.05	.04	.02
388	Dave Parker	.20	.15	.08
389	Bob Horner	.10	.08	.04
390	Pat Clements	.05	.04	.02
391	Jeff Leonard	.07	.05	.03
392	Chris Speier	.05	.04	.02
393	John Moses	.05	.04	.02
394	Garth Iorg	.05	.04	.02
395	Greg Gagne	.05	.04	.02
396	Nate Snell	.05	.04	.02
397	*Bryan Clutterbuck*(FC)	.10	.08	.04
398	Darrell Evans	.12	.09	.05
399	Steve Crawford	.05	.04	.02
400	Checklist 346-451	.05	.04	.02
401	*Phil Lombardi*(FC)	.10	.08	.04
402	Rick Honeycutt	.05	.04	.02
403	Ken Schrom	.05	.04	.02
404	Bud Black	.05	.04	.02
405	Donnie Hill	.05	.04	.02
406	Wayne Krenchicki	.05	.04	.02
407	*Chuck Finley*(FC)	.20	.15	.08
408	Toby Harrah	.07	.05	.03
409	Steve Lyons	.05	.04	.02
410	Kevin Bass	.10	.08	.04
411	Marvell Wynne	.05	.04	.02
412	Ron Roenicke	.05	.04	.02
413	*Tracy Jones*	.25	.20	.10
414	Gene Garber	.05	.04	.02
415	Mike Bielecki	.05	.04	.02
416	Frank DiPino	.05	.04	.02
417	Andy Van Slyke	.12	.09	.05
418	Jim Dwyer	.05	.04	.02
419	Ben Oglivie	.07	.05	.03
420	Dave Bergman	.05	.04	.02
421	Joe Sambito	.05	.04	.02
422	*Bob Tewksbury*	.12	.09	.05
423	Len Matuszek	.05	.04	.02
424	*Mike Kingery*(FC)	.15	.11	.06
425	Dave Kingman	.12	.09	.05
426	*Al Newman*	.07	.05	.03
427	Gary Ward	.07	.05	.03
428	Ruppert Jones	.05	.04	.02
429	Harold Baines	.15	.11	.06
430	Pat Perry	.05	.04	.02
431	Terry Puhl	.05	.04	.02
432	Don Carman	.07	.05	.03
433	Eddie Milner	.05	.04	.02
434	LaMarr Hoyt	.05	.04	.02
435	Rick Rhoden	.10	.08	.04
436	Jose Uribe	.07	.05	.03
437	Ken Oberkfell	.05	.04	.02
438	Ron Davis	.05	.04	.02
439	Jesse Orosco	.07	.05	.03
440	Scott Bradley	.05	.04	.02
441	Randy Bush	.05	.04	.02
442	*John Cerutti*	.20	.15	.08
443	Roy Smalley	.05	.04	.02
444	Kelly Gruber	.90	.70	.35
445	Bob Kearney	.05	.04	.02
446	*Ed Hearn*	.10	.08	.04
447	Scott Sanderson	.05	.04	.02
448	Bruce Benedict	.05	.04	.02
449	Junior Ortiz	.05	.04	.02
450	*Mike Aldrete*	.25	.20	.10
451	Kevin McReynolds	.15	.11	.06
452	*Rob Murphy*(FC)	.20	.15	.08
453	Kent Tekulve	.07	.05	.03
454	Curt Ford(FC)	.07	.05	.03
455	Davey Lopes	.07	.05	.03
456	Bobby Grich	.10	.08	.04
457	Jose DeLeon	.07	.05	.03
458	Andre Dawson	.20	.15	.08
459	Mike Flanagan	.07	.05	.03
460	*Joey Meyer*(FC)	.25	.20	.10
461	*Chuck Cary*(FC)	.10	.08	.04
462	Bill Buckner	.10	.08	.04
463	Bob Shirley	.05	.04	.02
464	*Jeff Hamilton*(FC)	.30	.25	.12
465	Phil Niekro	.20	.15	.08
466	Mark Gubicza	.12	.09	.05
467	Jerry Willard	.05	.04	.02
468	*Bob Sebra*(FC)	.10	.08	.04
469	Larry Parrish	.10	.08	.04
470	Charlie Hough	.07	.05	.03
471	Hal McRae	.10	.08	.04
472	*Dave Leiper*(FC)	.10	.08	.04
473	Mel Hall	.07	.05	.03
474	Dan Pasqua	.10	.08	.04
475	Bob Welch	.10	.08	.04
476	Johnny Grubb	.05	.04	.02
477	Jim Traber	.07	.05	.03
478	*Chris Bosio*(FC)	.40	.30	.15
479	Mark McLemore	.07	.05	.03
480	John Morris	.05	.04	.02
481	Billy Hatcher	.07	.05	.03
482	Dan Schatzeder	.05	.04	.02
483	Rich Gossage	.15	.11	.06
484	Jim Morrison	.05	.04	.02
485	Bob Brenly	.05	.04	.02
486	Bill Schroeder	.05	.04	.02
487	Mookie Wilson	.10	.08	.04
488	*Dave Martinez*(FC)	.25	.20	.10
489	Harold Reynolds	.10	.08	.04
490	Jeff Hearron	.05	.04	.02
491	Mickey Hatcher	.05	.04	.02
492	*Barry Larkin*(FC)	3.50	2.75	1.50
493	Bob James	.05	.04	.02
494	John Habyan	.05	.04	.02
495	*Jim Adduci*(FC)	.07	.05	.03
496	Mike Heath	.05	.04	.02
497	Tim Stoddard	.05	.04	.02
498	Tony Armas	.07	.05	.03
499	Dennis Powell	.05	.04	.02
500	Checklist 452-557	.05	.04	.02
501	Chris Bando	.05	.04	.02
502	*David Cone*(FC)	2.75	2.00	1.00
503	Jay Howell	.07	.05	.03
504	Tom Foley	.05	.04	.02
505	*Ray Chadwick*(FC)	.10	.08	.04
506	*Mike Loynd*(FC)	.15	.11	.06
507	Neil Allen	.05	.04	.02
508	Danny Darwin	.05	.04	.02
509	Rick Schu	.05	.04	.02
510	Jose Oquendo	.05	.04	.02
511	Gene Walter	.07	.05	.03
512	*Terry McGriff*(FC)	.12	.09	.05
513	Ken Griffey	.10	.08	.04
514	Benny Distefano	.05	.04	.02
515	*Terry Mulholland*(FC)	.12	.09	.05
516	Ed Lynch	.05	.04	.02
517	Bill Swift	.05	.04	.02
518	Manny Lee(FC)	.07	.05	.03
519	Andre David	.05	.04	.02
520	Scott McGregor	.07	.05	.03
521	Rick Manning	.05	.04	.02
522	Willie Hernandez	.07	.05	.03
523	Marty Barrett	.10	.08	.04
524	Wayne Tolleson	.05	.04	.02
525	*Jose Gonzalez*(FC)	.15	.11	.06
526	Cory Snyder	.70	.50	.30
527	Buddy Biancalana	.05	.04	.02
528	Moose Haas	.05	.04	.02
529	*Wilfredo Tejada*(FC)	.10	.08	.04
530	Stu Cliburn	.05	.04	.02
531	*Dale Mohorcic*(FC)	.20	.15	.08
532	Ron Hassey	.05	.04	.02
533	Ty Gainey	.05	.04	.02
534	Jerry Royster	.05	.04	.02
535	*Mike Maddux*(FC)	.20	.15	.08
536	Ted Power	.05	.04	.02
537	Ted Simmons	.12	.09	.05
538	*Rafael Belliard*(FC)	.12	.09	.05
539	Chico Walker	.05	.04	.02
540	Bob Forsch	.07	.05	.03
541	John Stefero	.05	.04	.02
542	*Dale Sveum*	.20	.15	.08
543	Mark Thurmond	.05	.04	.02
544	*Jeff Sellers*	.20	.15	.08
545	Joel Skinner	.05	.04	.02
546	Alex Trevino	.05	.04	.02
547	*Randy Kutcher*(FC)	.10	.08	.04
548	Joaquin Andujar	.07	.05	.03
549	*Casey Candaele*(FC)	.15	.11	.06
550	Jeff Russell	.05	.04	.02
551	John Candelaria	.10	.08	.04
552	Joe Cowley	.05	.04	.02
553	Danny Cox	.07	.05	.03
554	Denny Walling	.05	.04	.02
555	*Bruce Ruffin*(FC)	.20	.15	.08
556	Buddy Bell	.10	.08	.04
557	*Jimmy Jones*(FC)	.20	.15	.08
558	*Bobby Bonilla*	2.25	1.75	.90
559	Jeff Robinson	.07	.05	.03
560	Ed Olwine	.05	.04	.02
561	*Glenallen Hill*(FC)	1.75	1.25	.70
562	Lee Mazzilli	.07	.05	.03
563	Mike Brown	.05	.04	.02
564	George Frazier	.05	.04	.02
565	*Mike Sharperson*(FC)	.10	.08	.04
566	*Mark Portugal*	.10	.08	.04
567	Rick Leach	.05	.04	.02
568	Mark Langston	.12	.09	.05
569	Rafael Santana	.05	.04	.02
570	Manny Trillo	.07	.05	.03
571	Cliff Speck	.05	.04	.02
572	Bob Kipper	.05	.04	.02
573	*Kelly Downs*(FC)	.30	.25	.12
574	*Randy Asadoor*(FC)	.10	.08	.04
575	*Dave Magadan*(FC)	.35	.25	.14
576	*Marvin Freeman*(FC)	.12	.09	.05
577	Jeff Lahti	.05	.04	.02
578	Jeff Calhoun	.05	.04	.02
579	Gus Polidor(FC)	.07	.05	.03
580	Gene Nelson	.05	.04	.02
581	Tim Teufel	.05	.04	.02
582	Odell Jones	.05	.04	.02
583	Mark Ryal	.05	.04	.02
584	Randy O'Neal	.05	.04	.02
585	*Mike Greenwell*(FC)	9.00	6.75	3.50
586	Ray Knight	.07	.05	.03
587	*Ralph Bryant*(FC)	.12	.09	.05
588	Carmen Castillo	.05	.04	.02
589	Ed Wojna	.05	.04	.02
590	Stan Javier	.05	.04	.02
591	*Jeff Musselman*(FC)	.20	.15	.08
592	*Mike Stanley*(FC)	.20	.15	.08
593	Darrell Porter	.07	.05	.03
594	*Drew Hall*(FC)	.20	.15	.08
595	*Rob Nelson*(FC)	.10	.08	.04
596	Bryan Oelkers	.05	.04	.02
597	*Scott Nielsen*(FC)	.10	.08	.04
598	*Brian Holton*(FC)	.20	.15	.08
599	*Kevin Mitchell*	6.00	4.50	2.50
600	Checklist 558-660	.05	.04	.02
601	Jackie Gutierrez	.05	.04	.02
602	*Barry Jones*(FC)	.12	.09	.05
603	Jerry Narron	.05	.04	.02
604	Steve Lake	.05	.04	.02
605	Jim Pankovits	.05	.04	.02
606	Ed Romero	.05	.04	.02
607	Dave LaPoint	.07	.05	.03
608	Don Robinson	.07	.05	.03
609	Mike Krukow	.07	.05	.03
610	*Dave Valle*(FC)	.12	.09	.05
611	Len Dykstra	.30	.25	.12
612	Roberto Clemente Puzzle Card	.05	.04	.02
613	Mike Trujillo(FC)	.05	.04	.02
614	Damaso Garcia	.05	.04	.02
615	Neal Heaton	.05	.04	.02
616	Juan Berenguer	.05	.04	.02
617	Steve Carlton	.25	.20	.10
618	Gary Lucas	.05	.04	.02
619	Geno Petralli	.05	.04	.02
620	Rick Aguilera	.07	.05	.03
621	Fred McGriff	3.00	2.25	1.25
622	Dave Henderson	.10	.08	.04
623	*Dave Clark*(FC)	.20	.15	.08
624	Angel Salazar	.05	.04	.02
625	Randy Hunt	.05	.04	.02
626	John Gibbons	.05	.04	.02
627	*Kevin Brown*(FC)	.07	.05	.03
628	Bill Dawley	.05	.04	.02
629	Aurelio Lopez	.05	.04	.02
630	Charlie Hudson	.05	.04	.02
631	Ray Soff	.05	.04	.02
632	*Ray Hayward*(FC)	.12	.09	.05
633	Spike Owen	.05	.04	.02
634	Glenn Hubbard	.05	.04	.02
635	*Kevin Elster*(FC)	.40	.30	.15
636	Mike LaCoss	.05	.04	.02
637	Dwayne Henry	.05	.04	.02
638	*Rey Quinones*	.15	.11	.06
639	Jim Clancy	.07	.05	.03
640	Larry Andersen	.05	.04	.02
641	Calvin Schiraldi	.05	.04	.02
642	*Stan Jefferson*(FC)	.25	.20	.10
643	Marc Sullivan	.05	.04	.02
644	Mark Grant	.05	.04	.02
645	Cliff Johnson	.05	.04	.02
646	Howard Johnson	.10	.08	.04
647	Dave Sax	.05	.04	.02
648	Dave Stewart	.12	.09	.05

		MT	NR MT	EX
649	Danny Heep	.05	.04	.02
650	Joe Johnson	.05	.04	.02
651	*Bob Brower*(FC)	.20	.15	.08
652	Rob Woodward	.07	.05	.03
653	John Mizerock	.05	.04	.02
654	*Tim Pyznarski*(FC)	.10	.08	.04
655	*Luis Aquino*(FC)	.10	.08	.04
656	Mickey Brantley(FC)	.10	.08	.04
657	Doyle Alexander	.07	.05	.03
658	Sammy Stewart	.05	.04	.02
659	Jim Acker	.05	.04	.02
660	Pete Ladd	.05	.04	.02

1987 Donruss All-Stars

Issued in conjunction with the Donruss Pop-Ups set for the second consecutive year, the 1987 Donruss All-Stars set consists of 59 players (plus a checklist) who were selected to the 1986 All-Star Game. Measuring 3-1/2" by 5" in size, the card fronts feature black borders and American or National League logos. Included on the backs are the player's career highlights and All-Star Game statistics. Retail packs included one pop-Up card, three All-Star cards and one Roberto Clemente puzzle.

		MT	NR MT	EX
	Complete Set:	6.00	4.50	2.50
	Common Player:	.09	.07	.04
1	Wally Joyner	1.00	.70	.40
2	Dave Winfield	.25	.20	.10
3	Lou Whitaker	.15	.11	.06
4	Kirby Puckett	.50	.40	.20
5	Cal Ripken, Jr.	.30	.25	.12
6	Rickey Henderson	.50	.40	.20
7	Wade Boggs	.80	.60	.30
8	Roger Clemens	.50	.40	.20
9	Lance Parrish	.09	.07	.04
10	Dick Howser	.09	.07	.04
11	Keith Hernandez	.10	.08	.04
12	Darryl Strawberry	.50	.40	.20
13	Ryne Sandberg	.25	.20	.10
14	Dale Murphy	.40	.30	.15
15	Ozzie Smith	.15	.11	.06
16	Tony Gwynn	.30	.25	.12
17	Mike Schmidt	.40	.30	.15
18	Dwight Gooden	.60	.45	.25
19	Gary Carter	.15	.11	.06
20	Whitey Herzog	.09	.07	.04
21	Jose Canseco	1.25	.90	.50
22	John Franco	.09	.07	.04
23	Jesse Barfield	.12	.09	.05
24	Rick Rhoden	.09	.07	.04
25	Harold Baines	.15	.11	.06
26	Sid Fernandez	.12	.09	.05
27	George Brett	.40	.30	.15
28	Steve Sax	.15	.11	.06
29	Jim Presley	.12	.09	.05
30	Dave Smith	.09	.07	.04
31	Eddie Murray	.10	.08	.04
32	Mike Scott	.12	.09	.05
33	Don Mattingly	2.00	1.50	.80
34	Dave Parker	.15	.11	.06
35	Tony Fernandez	.15	.11	.06
36	Tim Raines	.25	.20	.10
37	Brook Jacoby	.12	.09	.05
38	Chili Davis	.09	.07	.04
39	Rich Gedman	.09	.07	.04
40	Kevin Bass	.09	.07	.04
41	Frank White	.09	.07	.04
42	Glenn Davis	.15	.11	.06
43	Willie Hernandez	.09	.07	.04
44	Chris Brown	.09	.07	.04
45	Jim Rice	.10	.08	.04
46	Tony Pena	.09	.07	.04
47	Don Aase	.09	.07	.04
48	Hubie Brooks	.09	.07	.04
49	Charlie Hough	.09	.07	.04
50	Jody Davis	.09	.07	.04
51	Mike Witt	.09	.07	.04
52	Jeff Reardon	.12	.09	.05
53	Ken Schrom	.09	.07	.04
54	Fernando Valenzuela	.10	.08	.04
55	Dave Righetti	.15	.11	.06
56	Shane Rawley	.09	.07	.04
57	Ted Higuera	.12	.09	.05
58	Mike Krukow	.09	.07	.04
59	Lloyd Moseby	.09	.07	.04
60	Checklist	.09	.07	.04

1987 Donruss Box Panels

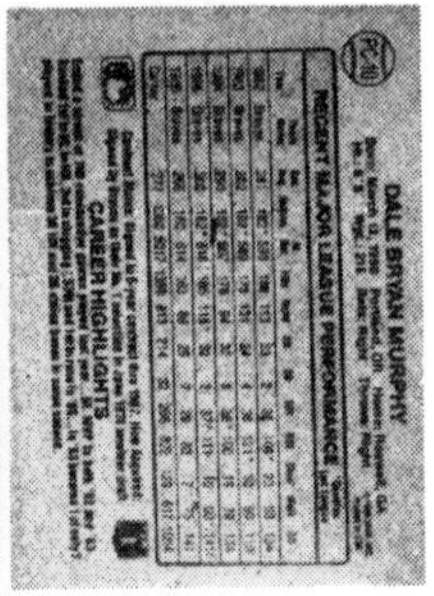

Continuing with an idea they initiated in 1985, Donruss once again placed baseball cards on the bottoms of their retail boxes. The cards, which are 2-1/2" by 3-1/2" in size, come four to a panel with each panel containing an unnumbered Roberto Clemente puzzle card. With numbering that begins where Donruss left off in 1986, cards PC 10 through PC 12 were found on boxes of Donruss regular issue wax packs. Cards PC 13 through PC 15 were located on boxes of the 1987 All-Star/Pop-Up packs.

		MT	NR MT	EX
	Complete Panel Set:	6.00	4.50	2.50
	Complete Singles Set:	3.00	2.25	1.25
	Common Single Player:	.15	.11	.06
	Panel	4.00	3.00	1.50
10	Dale Murphy	.50	.40	.20
11	Jeff Reardon	.20	.15	.08
12	Jose Canseco	2.00	1.50	.80
---	Roberto Clemente Puzzle Card	.04	.03	.02
	Panel	2.25	1.75	.90
13	Mike Scott	.20	.15	.08
14	Roger Clemens	1.00	.70	.40
15	Mike Krukow	.15	.11	.06
---	Roberto Clemente Puzzle Card	.04	.03	.02

1987 Donruss Diamond Kings Supers

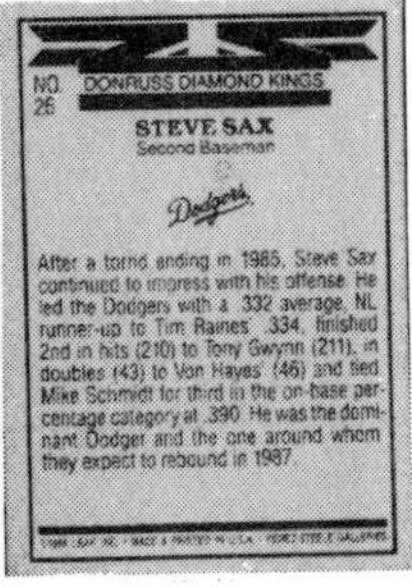

For a third straight baseball card season, Donruss produced a set of enlarged size Diamond Kings. The cards, which measure 4-11/16" by 6-3/4", are giant versions of the Diamond Kings subset found in the regular 1987 Donruss set. The 28-card set, which features the artwork of Dick Perez, contains 26 player cards, a checklist and a Roberto Clemente puzzle card. The set was available through a mail-in offer for $9.50 plus three wrappers.

		MT	NR MT	EX
	Complete Set:	10.00	7.50	4.00
	Common Player:	.20	.15	.08
1	Wally Joyner	1.25	.90	.50
2	Roger Clemens	1.00	.70	.40
3	Dale Murphy	.70	.50	.30
4	Darryl Strawberry	.90	.70	.35
5	Ozzie Smith	.30	.25	.12
6	Jose Canseco	2.00	1.50	.80
7	Charlie Hough	.20	.15	.08
8	Brook Jacoby	.20	.15	.08
9	Fred Lynn	.20	.15	.08
10	Rick Rhoden	.20	.15	.08
11	Chris Brown	.25	.20	.10
12	Von Hayes	.25	.20	.10
13	Jack Morris	.20	.15	.08
14	Kevin McReynolds	.35	.25	.14
15	George Brett	.70	.50	.30
16	Ted Higuera	.20	.15	.08
17	Hubie Brooks	.20	.15	.08
18	Mike Scott	.20	.15	.08
19	Kirby Puckett	.90	.70	.35
20	Dave Winfield	.30	.25	.12
21	Lloyd Moseby	.20	.15	.08

		MT	NR MT	EX
22	Eric Davis	.90	.70	.35
23	Jim Presley	.25	.20	.10
24	Keith Moreland	.20	.15	.08
25	Greg Walker	.20	.15	.08
26	Steve Sax	.30	.25	.12
27	Checklist	.15	.11	.06
---	Roberto Clemente Puzzle Card	.15	.11	.06

1987 Donruss Highlights

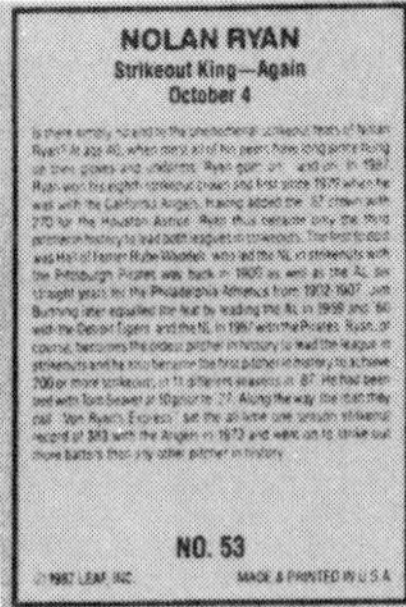

For a third consecutive year, Donruss produced a 56-card set which highlighted the special events of the 1987 baseball season. The cards, which measure 2-1/2" by 3-1/2", have a front design similar to the regular 1987 Donruss set. A blue border and the "Highlights" logo are the significant differences. The card backs feature black print on a white background and include the date the event took place plus the particulars about it. As in the past, the set includes Donruss' picks for the A.L. and N.L. Rookies of the Year. The set was issued in a specially designed box and was available only through hobby dealers.

		MT	NR MT	EX
	Complete Set:	8.00	6.00	3.25
	Common Player:	.10	.08	.04
1	First No-Hitter For Brewers (Juan Nieves)	.15	.11	.06
2	Hits 500th Homer (Mike Schmidt)	.40	.30	.15
3	N.L. Player of the Month - April (Eric Davis)	.50	.40	.20
4	N.L. Pitcher of the Month - April (Sid Fernandez)	.10	.08	.04
5	A.L. Player of the Month - April (Brian Downing)	.10	.08	.04
6	A.L. Pitcher of the Month - April (Bret Saberhagen)	.30	.25	.12
7	Free Agent Holdout Returns (Tim Raines)	.25	.20	.10
8	N.L. Player of the Month - May (Eric Davis)	.50	.40	.20
9	N.L. Pitcher of the Month - May (Steve Bedrosian)	.15	.11	.06
10	A.L. Player of the Month - May (Larry Parrish)	.10	.08	.04
11	A.L. Pitcher of the Month - May (Jim Clancy)	.10	.08	.04
12	N.L. Player of the Month - June (Tony Gwynn)	.30	.25	.12
13	N.L. Pitcher of the Month - June (Orel Hershiser)	.25	.20	.10
14	A.L. Player of the Month - June (Wade Boggs)	.80	.60	.30
15	A.L. Pitcher of the Month - June (Steve Ontiveros)	.10	.08	.04
16	All Star Game Hero (Tim Raines)	.25	.20	.10
17	Consecutive Game Homer Streak (Don Mattingly)	1.00	.70	.40
18	1987 Hall of Fame Inductee (Jim "Catfish" Hunter)	.20	.15	.08
19	1987 Hall of Fame Inductee (Ray Dandridge)	.10	.08	.04
20	1987 Hall of Fame Inductee (Billy Williams)	.20	.15	.08
21	N.L. Player of the Month - July (Bo Diaz)	.10	.08	.04
22	N.L. Pitcher of the Month - July (Floyd Youmans)	.10	.08	.04
23	A.L. Player of the Month - July (Don Mattingly)	1.00	.70	.40
24	A.L. Pitcher of the Month - July (Frank Viola)	.20	.15	.08
25	Strikes Out 4 Batters In 1 Inning (Bobby Witt)	.15	.11	.06
26	Ties A.L. 9-Inning Game Hit Mark (Kevin Seitzer)	.50	.40	.20
27	Sets Rookie Home Run Record (Mark McGwire)	1.25	.90	.50
28	Sets Cubs' 1st Year Homer Mark (Andre Dawson)	.20	.15	.08
29	Hits In 39 Straight Games (Paul Molitor)	.15	.11	.06
30	Record Weekend (Kirby Puckett)	.50	.40	.20
31	N.L. Player of the Month - August (Andre Dawson)	.20	.15	.08
32	N.L. Pitcher of the Month - August (Doug Drabek)	.10	.08	.04

		MT	NR MT	EX
33	A.L. Player of the Month - August (Dwight Evans)	.15	.11	.06
34	A.L. Pitcher of the Month - August (Mark Langston)	.25	.20	.10
35	100 RBI In 1st 2 Major League Seasons (Wally Joyner)	.40	.30	.15
36	100 SB In 1st 3 Major League Seasons (Vince Coleman)	.20	.15	.08
37	Orioles' All Time Homer King (Eddie Murray)	.10	.08	.04
38	Ends Consecutive Innings Streak (Cal Ripken)	.30	.25	.12
39	Blue Jays Hit Record 10 Homers In 1 Game (Rob Ducey, Fred McGriff, Ernie Whitt)	.50	.40	.20
40	Equal A's RBI Marks (Jose Canseco, Mark McGwire)	2.50	2.00	1.00
41	Sets All-Time Catching Record (Bob Boone)	.10	.08	.04
42	Sets Mets' One-Season HR Mark (Darryl Strawberry)	.50	.40	.20
43	N.L.'s All-Time Switch Hit HR King (Howard Johnson)	.15	.11	.06
44	Five Straight 200-Hit Seasons (Wade Boggs)	.80	.60	.30
45	Eclipses Rookie Game Hitting Streak (Benito Santiago)	.40	.30	.15
46	Eclipses Jackson's A's HR Record (Mark McGwire)	1.25	.90	.50
47	13th Rookie To Collect 200 Hits (Kevin Seitzer)	.50	.40	.20
48	Sets Slam Record (Don Mattingly)	1.00	.70	.40
49	N.L. Player of the Month - September (Darryl Strawberry)	.50	.40	.20
50	N.L. Pitcher of the Month - September (Pascual Perez)	.10	.08	.04
51	A.L. Player of the Month - September (Alan Trammell)	.20	.15	.08
52	A.L. Pitcher of the Month - September (Doyle Alexander)	.10	.08	.04
53	Strikeout King - Again (Nolan Ryan)	1.00	.70	.40
54	Donruss A.L. Rookie of the Year (Mark McGwire)	1.25	.90	.50
55	Donruss N.L. Rookie of the Year (Benito Santiago)	.40	.30	.15
56	Highlight Checklist	.10	.08	.04

1987 Donruss Opening Day

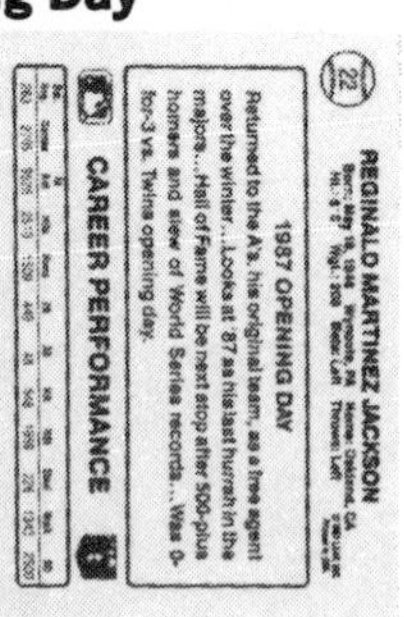

The Donruss Opening Day set includes all players in major league baseball's starting lineups on the opening day of the 1987 baseball season. Cards in the 272-piece set measure 2-1/2" by 3-1/2" and have a glossy coating. The card fronts are identical in design to the regular Donruss set, but new photos were utilized and the fronts contain maroon borders as opposed to black. The backs carry black printing on white and yellow and carry a brief player biography plus the player's career statistics. The set was packaged in a sturdy 15" by 5" by 2" box with a clear acetate lid.

		MT	NR MT	EX
Complete Set:		20.00	15.00	8.00
Common Player:		.05	.04	.02
1	Doug DeCinces	.07	.05	.03
2	Mike Witt	.12	.09	.05
3	George Hendrick	.07	.05	.03
4	Dick Schofield	.05	.04	.02
5	Devon White	.50	.40	.20
6	Butch Wynegar	.05	.04	.02
7	Wally Joyner	.75	.55	.30
8	Mark McLemore	.05	.04	.02
9	Brian Downing	.07	.05	.03
10	Gary Pettis	.05	.04	.02
11	Bill Doran	.07	.05	.03
12	Phil Garner	.05	.04	.02
13	Jose Cruz	.07	.05	.03
14	Kevin Bass	.07	.05	.03
15	Mike Scott	.12	.09	.05
16	Glenn Davis	.15	.11	.06
17	Alan Ashby	.05	.04	.02
18	Billy Hatcher	.07	.05	.03
19	Craig Reynolds	.05	.04	.02
20	Carney Lansford	.07	.05	.03
21	Mike Davis	.05	.04	.02
22	Reggie Jackson	.30	.25	.12
23	Mickey Tettleton	.07	.05	.03
24	Jose Canseco	1.75	1.25	.70
25	Rob Nelson	.05	.04	.02
26	Tony Phillips	.05	.04	.02
27	Dwayne Murphy	.05	.04	.02
28	Alfredo Griffin	.07	.05	.03
29	Curt Young	.05	.04	.02
30	Willie Upshaw	.05	.04	.02
31	Mike Sharperson	.05	.04	.02
32	Rance Mulliniks	.05	.04	.02
33	Ernie Whitt	.05	.04	.02
34	Jesse Barfield	.12	.09	.05
35	Tony Fernandez	.12	.09	.05
36	Lloyd Moseby	.07	.05	.03
37	Jimmy Key	.10	.08	.04
38	Fred McGriff	1.50	1.25	.60
39	George Bell	.25	.20	.10
40	Dale Murphy	.40	.30	.15
41	Rick Mahler	.05	.04	.02
42	Ken Griffey	.07	.05	.03
43	Andres Thomas	.10	.08	.04
44	Dion James	.05	.04	.02
45	Ozzie Virgil	.05	.04	.02
46	Ken Oberkfell	.05	.04	.02
47	Gary Roenicke	.05	.04	.02
48	Glenn Hubbard	.05	.04	.02
49	Bill Schroeder	.05	.04	.02
50	Greg Brock	.07	.05	.03
51	Billy Jo Robidoux	.05	.04	.02
52	Glenn Braggs	.12	.09	.05
53	Jim Gantner	.05	.04	.02
54	Paul Molitor	.15	.11	.06
55	Dale Sveum	.15	.11	.06
56	Ted Higuera	.12	.09	.05
57	Rob Deer	.07	.05	.03
58	Robin Yount	.35	.25	.14
59	Jim Lindeman	.10	.08	.04
60	Vince Coleman	.15	.11	.06
61	Tommy Herr	.07	.05	.03
62	Terry Pendleton	.07	.05	.03
63	John Tudor	.10	.08	.04
64	Tony Pena	.07	.05	.03
65	Ozzie Smith	.15	.11	.06
66	Tito Landrum	.05	.04	.02
67	Jack Clark	.15	.11	.06
68	Bob Dernier	.05	.04	.02
69	Rick Sutcliffe	.10	.08	.04
70	Andre Dawson	.20	.15	.08
71	Keith Moreland	.07	.05	.03
72	Jody Davis	.07	.05	.03
73	Brian Dayett	.05	.04	.02
74	Leon Durham	.07	.05	.03
75	Ryne Sandberg	.25	.20	.10
76	Shawon Dunston	.20	.15	.08
77	Mike Marshall	.10	.08	.04
78	Bill Madlock	.07	.05	.03
79	Orel Hershiser	.30	.25	.12
80	Mike Ramsey	.05	.04	.02
81	Ken Landreaux	.05	.04	.02
82	Mike Scioscia	.05	.04	.02
83	Franklin Stubbs	.07	.05	.03
84	Mariano Duncan	.05	.04	.02
85	Steve Sax	.15	.11	.06
86	Mitch Webster	.07	.05	.03
87	Reid Nichols	.05	.04	.02
88	Tim Wallach	.10	.08	.04
89	Floyd Youmans	.07	.05	.03
90	Andres Galarraga	.25	.20	.10
91	Hubie Brooks	.07	.05	.03
92	Jeff Reed	.05	.04	.02
93	Alonzo Powell	.05	.04	.02
94	Vance Law	.05	.04	.02
95	Bob Brenly	.05	.04	.02
96	Will Clark	2.00	1.50	.80
97	Chili Davis	.07	.05	.03
98	Mike Krukow	.05	.04	.02
99	Jose Uribe	.05	.04	.02
100	Chris Brown	.07	.05	.03
101	Rob Thompson	.10	.08	.04
102	Candy Maldonado	.07	.05	.03
103	Jeff Leonard	.07	.05	.03
104	Tom Candiotti	.05	.04	.02
105	Chris Bando	.05	.04	.02
106	Cory Snyder	.30	.25	.12
107	Pat Tabler	.07	.05	.03
108	Andre Thornton	.07	.05	.03
109	Joe Carter	.25	.20	.10
110	Tony Bernazard	.05	.04	.02
111	Julio Franco	.10	.08	.04
112	Brook Jacoby	.10	.08	.04
113	Brett Butler	.07	.05	.03
114	Donnell Nixon	.05	.04	.02
115	Alvin Davis	.12	.09	.05
116	Mark Langston	.25	.20	.10
117	Harold Reynolds	.07	.05	.03
118	Ken Phelps	.05	.04	.02
119	Mike Kingery	.10	.08	.04
120	Dave Valle	.07	.05	.03
121	Rey Quinones	.07	.05	.03
122	Phil Bradley	.12	.09	.05
123	Jim Presley	.12	.09	.05
124	Keith Hernandez	.12	.09	.05
125	Kevin McReynolds	.12	.09	.05
126	Rafael Santana	.05	.04	.02
127	Bob Ojeda	.07	.05	.03
128	Darryl Strawberry	.60	.45	.25
129	Mookie Wilson	.07	.05	.03
130	Gary Carter	.15	.11	.06
131	Tim Teufel	.05	.04	.02
132	Howard Johnson	.20	.15	.08
133	Cal Ripken	.30	.25	.12
134	Rick Burleson	.05	.04	.02
135	Fred Lynn	.12	.09	.05
136	Eddie Murray	.15	.11	.06
137	Ray Knight	.07	.05	.03
138	Alan Wiggins	.05	.04	.02
139	John Shelby	.05	.04	.02
140	Mike Boddicker	.07	.05	.03
141	Ken Gerhart	.07	.05	.03
142	Terry Kennedy	.07	.05	.03
143	Steve Garvey	.30	.25	.12
144	Marvell Wynne	.05	.04	.02
145	Kevin Mitchell	1.50	1.25	.60
146	Tony Gwynn	.35	.25	.14
147	Joey Cora	.10	.08	.04
148	Benito Santiago	.60	.45	.25
149	Eric Show	.07	.05	.03
150	Garry Templeton	.07	.05	.03
151	Carmelo Martinez	.05	.04	.02
152	Von Hayes	.10	.08	.04
153	Lance Parrish	.10	.08	.04
154	Milt Thompson	.07	.05	.03
155	Mike Easler	.05	.04	.02
156	Juan Samuel	.10	.08	.04
157	Steve Jeltz	.05	.04	.02
158	Glenn Wilson	.05	.04	.02
159	Shane Rawley	.07	.05	.03
160	Mike Schmidt	.40	.30	.15
161	Andy Van Slyke	.10	.08	.04
162	Johnny Ray	.07	.05	.03
163a	Barry Bonds (dark jersey, photo actually Johnny Ray)	125.00	94.00	50.00
163b	Barry Bonds (white jersey, correct photo)	.15	.11	.06
164	Junior Ortiz	.05	.04	.02
165	Rafael Belliard	.05	.04	.02
166	Bob Patterson	.05	.04	.02
167	Bobby Bonilla	.15	.11	.06
168	Sid Bream	.07	.05	.03
169	Jim Morrison	.05	.04	.02
170	Jerry Browne	.10	.08	.04
171	Scott Fletcher	.05	.04	.02
172	Ruben Sierra	1.50	1.25	.60
173	Larry Parrish	.07	.05	.03
174	Pete O'Brien	.07	.05	.03
175	Pete Incaviglia	.35	.25	.14
176	Don Slaught	.05	.04	.02
177	Oddibe McDowell	.10	.08	.04
178	Charlie Hough	.07	.05	.03
179	Steve Buechele	.05	.04	.02
180	Bob Stanley	.05	.04	.02
181	Wade Boggs	1.00	.70	.40
182	Jim Rice	.10	.08	.04
183	Bill Buckner	.07	.05	.03
184	Dwight Evans	.10	.08	.04
185	Spike Owen	.05	.04	.02
186	Don Baylor	.10	.08	.04
187	Marc Sullivan	.05	.04	.02
188	Marty Barrett	.07	.05	.03
189	Dave Henderson	.07	.05	.03
190	Bo Diaz	.05	.04	.02
191	Barry Larkin	.90	.70	.35
192	Kal Daniels	.25	.20	.10
193	Terry Francona	.05	.04	.02
194	Tom Browning	.07	.05	.03
195	Ron Oester	.05	.04	.02
196	Buddy Bell	.07	.05	.03
197	Eric Davis	.60	.45	.25
198	Dave Parker	.15	.11	.06
199	Steve Balboni	.05	.04	.02
200	Danny Tartabull	.30	.25	.12
201	Ed Hearn	.05	.04	.02
202	Buddy Biancalana	.05	.04	.02
203	Danny Jackson	.05	.04	.02
204	Frank White	.08	.06	.03
205	Bo Jackson	2.00	1.50	.80
206	George Brett	.40	.30	.15
207	Kevin Seitzer	1.50	1.25	.60
208	Willie Wilson	.10	.08	.04
209	Orlando Mercado	.05	.04	.02
210	Darrell Evans	.07	.05	.03
211	Larry Herndon	.05	.04	.02
212	Jack Morris	.15	.11	.06
213	Chet Lemon	.07	.05	.03
214	Mike Heath	.05	.04	.02
215	Darnell Coles	.07	.05	.03
216	Alan Trammell	.20	.15	.08
217	Terry Harper	.05	.04	.02
218	Lou Whitaker	.15	.11	.06
219	Gary Gaetti	.15	.11	.06
220	Tom Nieto	.05	.04	.02
221	Kirby Puckett	.80	.60	.30
222	Tom Brunansky	.10	.08	.04
223	Greg Gagne	.05	.04	.02
224	Dan Gladden	.07	.05	.03
225	Mark Davidson	.07	.05	.03
226	Bert Blyleven	.10	.08	.04
227	Steve Lombardozzi	.05	.04	.02
228	Kent Hrbek	.15	.11	.06
229	Gary Redus	.05	.04	.02
230	Ivan Calderon	.10	.08	.04
231	Tim Hulett	.05	.04	.02
232	Carlton Fisk	.15	.11	.06
233	Greg Walker	.07	.05	.03
234	Ron Karkovice	.05	.04	.02
235	Ozzie Guillen	.07	.05	.03
236	Harold Baines	.12	.09	.05
237	Donnie Hill	.05	.04	.02
238	Rich Dotson	.07	.05	.03
239	Mike Pagliarulo	.10	.08	.04
240	Joel Skinner	.05	.04	.02
241	Don Mattingly	1.50	1.25	.60
242	Gary Ward	.05	.04	.02
243	Dave Winfield	.20	.15	.08
244	Dan Pasqua	.10	.08	.04
245	Wayne Tolleson	.05	.04	.02
246	Willie Randolph	.07	.05	.03
247	Dennis Rasmussen	.07	.05	.03
248	Rickey Henderson	.30	.25	.12
249	Angels Logo/Checklist	.05	.04	.02
250	Astros Logo/Checklist	.05	.04	.02
251	Athletics Logo/Checklist	.05	.04	.02
252	Blue Jays Logo/Checklist	.05	.04	.02
253	Braves Logo/Checklist	.05	.04	.02
254	Brewers Logo/Checklist	.05	.04	.02
255	Cardinals Logo/Checklist	.05	.04	.02
256	Dodgers Logo/Checklist	.05	.04	.02
257	Expos Logo/Checklist	.05	.04	.02
258	Giants Logo/Checklist	.05	.04	.02
259	Indians Logo/Checklist	.05	.04	.02
260	Mariners Logo/Checklist	.05	.04	.02
261	Orioles Logo/Checklist	.05	.04	.02
262	Padres Logo/Checklist	.05	.04	.02
263	Phillies Logo/Checklist	.05	.04	.02
264	Pirates Logo/Checklist	.05	.04	.02
265	Rangers Logo/Checklist	.05	.04	.02
266	Red Sox Logo/Checklist	.05	.04	.02
267	Reds Logo/Checklist	.05	.04	.02
268	Royals Logo/Checklist	.05	.04	.02

		MT	NR MT	EX
269	Tigers Logo/Checklist	.05	.04	.02
270	Twins Logo/Checklist	.05	.04	.02
271	White Sox-Cubs Logos/Checklist	.05	.04	.02
272	Yankees-Mets Logos/Checklist	.05	.04	.02

1987 Donruss Pop-Ups

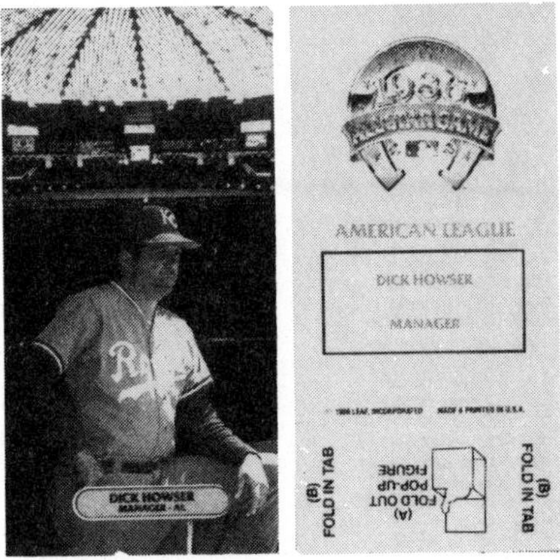

For the second straight year, Donruss released in conjunction with its All-Stars issue a set of cards designed to fold out to form a three-dimensional stand-up card. Consisting of 20 cards, as opposed to the previous year's 18, the 1987 Donruss Pop-Ups set contains players selected to the 1986 All-Star Game. Background for the 2-1/2" by 5" cards is the Houston Astrodome, site of the 1986 mid-summer classic. Retail packs included one Pop-Up card, three All-Star cards and one Roberto Clemente puzzle card.

		MT	NR MT	EX
	Complete Set:	5.00	3.75	2.00
	Common Player:	.20	.15	.08
(1)	Wade Boggs	1.00	.70	.40
(2)	Gary Carter	.25	.20	.10
(3)	Roger Clemens	.80	.60	.30
(4)	Dwight Gooden	.80	.60	.30
(5)	Tony Gwynn	.50	.40	.20
(6)	Rickey Henderson	.75	.55	.30
(7)	Keith Hernandez	.25	.20	.10
(8)	Whitey Herzog	.20	.15	.08
(9)	Dick Howser	.20	.15	.08
(10)	Wally Joyner	.50	.40	.20
(11)	Dale Murphy	.60	.45	.25
(12)	Lance Parrish	.20	.15	.08
(13)	Kirby Puckett	.75	.55	.30
(14)	Cal Ripken	.50	.40	.20
(15)	Ryne Sandberg	.40	.30	.15
(16)	Mike Schmidt	.60	.45	.25
(17)	Ozzie Smith	.30	.25	.12
(18)	Darryl Strawberry	.50	.40	.20
(19)	Lou Whitaker	.20	.15	.08
(20)	Dave Winfield	.30	.25	.12

1987 Donruss Rookies

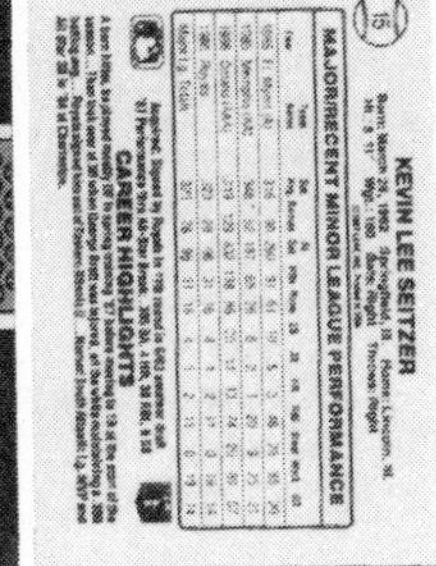

As they did in 1986, Donruss issued a 56-card set highlighting the major league's most promising rookies. The cards are the standard 2-1/2" by 3-1/2" size and are identical in design to the regular Donruss issue. The card fronts have green borders as opposed to the black found in the regular issue and carry the words "The Rookies" in the lower left portion of the card. The set came housed in a specially designed box and was available only through hobby dealers.

		MT	NR MT	EX
	Complete Set:	20.00	15.00	8.00
	Common Player:	.10	.08	.04
1	Mark McGwire	3.00	2.25	1.25
2	Eric Bell	.10	.08	.04
3	Mark Williamson(FC)	.15	.11	.06
4	Mike Greenwell	3.25	2.50	1.25
5	Ellis Burks(FC)	2.75	2.00	1.00
6	DeWayne Buice(FC)	.20	.15	.08
7	Mark Mclemore (McLemore)	.10	.08	.04
8	Devon White	.50	.40	.20
9	Willie Fraser	.15	.11	.06
10	Lester Lancaster(FC)	.15	.11	.06
11	Ken Williams(FC)	.20	.15	.08
12	Matt Nokes(FC)	.70	.50	.30
13	Jeff Robinson(FC)	.40	.30	.15
14	Bo Jackson	4.00	3.00	1.50
15	Kevin Seitzer(FC)	1.00	.70	.40
16	Billy Ripken(FC)	.25	.20	.10
17	B.J. Surhoff	.20	.15	.08
18	Chuck Crim(FC)	.15	.11	.06
19	Mike Birbeck	.10	.08	.04
20	Chris Bosio	.10	.08	.04
21	Les Straker(FC)	.20	.15	.08
22	Mark Davidson(FC)	.15	.11	.06
23	Gene Larkin(FC)	.35	.25	.14
24	Ken Gerhart	.15	.11	.06
25	Luis Polonia(FC)	.35	.25	.14
26	Terry Steinbach	.25	.20	.10
27	Mickey Brantley	.10	.08	.04
28	Mike Stanley	.20	.15	.08
29	Jerry Browne	.10	.08	.04
30	Todd Benzinger(FC)	.60	.45	.25
31	Fred McGriff	2.00	1.50	.80
32	Mike Henneman(FC)	.30	.25	.12
33	Casey Candaele	.10	.08	.04
34	Dave Magadan	.25	.20	.10
35	David Cone	1.00	.70	.40
36	Mike Jackson(FC)	.20	.15	.08
37	John Mitchell(FC)	.20	.15	.08
38	Mike Dunne(FC)	.25	.20	.10
39	John Smiley(FC)	.40	.30	.15
40	Joe Magrane(FC)	1.25	.90	.50
41	Jim Lindeman	.10	.08	.04
42	Shane Mack(FC)	.25	.20	.10
43	Stan Jefferson	.10	.08	.04
44	Benito Santiago	.60	.45	.25
45	Matt Williams(FC)	3.25	2.50	1.25
46	Dave Meads(FC)	.20	.15	.08
47	Rafael Palmeiro	.70	.50	.30
48	Bill Long(FC)	.20	.15	.08
49	Bob Brower	.10	.08	.04
50	James Steels(FC)	.15	.11	.06
51	Paul Noce(FC)	.15	.11	.06
52	Greg Maddux	.60	.45	.25
53	Jeff Musselman	.15	.11	.06
54	Brian Holton	.15	.11	.06
55	Chuck Jackson(FC)	.20	.15	.08
56	Checklist 1-56	.10	.08	.04

1988 Donruss

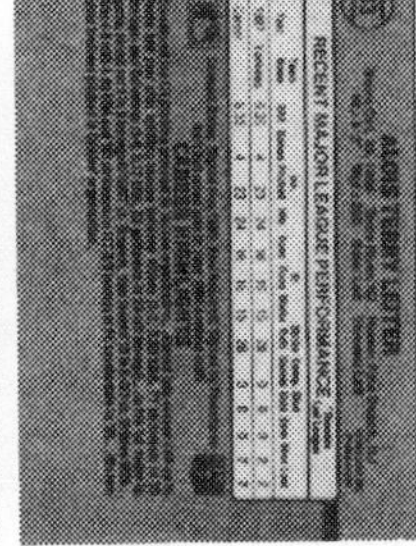

The 1988 Donruss set consists of 660 cards, each measuring 2-1/2" by 3-1/2" in size. The card fronts feature a full-color photo surrounded by a colorful border - alternating stripes of black, red, black, blue, black, blue, black, red and black (in that order), separated by soft-focus edges and airbrushed fades. The player's name and position appear in a red band at the bottom of the card. The Donruss logo is situated in the upper left corner of the card, while the team logo is located in the lower right corner. For the seventh consecutive season, Donruss included a subset of "Diamond Kings" cards (#'s 1-27) in the issue. And for the fifth straight year, Donruss incorporated their highly popular "Rated Rookies" (card #'s 28-47) with the set.

		MT	NR MT	EX
	Complete Set:	28.00	21.00	12.00
	Common Player	.05	.04	.02
1	Mark McGwire (DK)	.70	.50	.30
2	Tim Raines (DK)	.25	.20	.10
3	Benito Santiago (DK)	.30	.25	.12
4	Alan Trammell (DK)	.25	.20	.10
5	Danny Tartabull (DK)	.20	.15	.08
6	Ron Darling (DK)	.12	.09	.05
7	Paul Molitor (DK)	.12	.09	.05
8	Devon White (DK)	.20	.15	.08
9	Andre Dawson (DK)	.20	.15	.08
10	Julio Franco (DK)	.10	.08	.04
11	Scott Fletcher (DK)	.07	.05	.03
12	Tony Fernandez (DK)	.12	.09	.05
13	Shane Rawley (DK)	.07	.05	.03
14	Kal Daniels (DK)	.20	.15	.08
15	Jack Clark (DK)	.15	.11	.06
16	Dwight Evans (DK)	.12	.09	.05
17	Tommy John (DK)	.15	.11	.06
18	Andy Van Slyke (DK)	.15	.11	.06
19	Gary Gaetti (DK)	.12	.09	.05
20	Mark Langston (DK)	.10	.08	.04
21	Will Clark (DK)	.80	.60	.30
22	Glenn Hubbard (DK)	.07	.05	.03
23	Billy Hatcher (DK)	.07	.05	.03
24	Bob Welch (DK)	.10	.08	.04
25	Ivan Calderon (DK)	.10	.08	.04
26	Cal Ripken, Jr. (DK)	.35	.25	.14
27	Checklist 1-27	.05	.04	.02
28	*Mackey Sasser* (RR)(FC)	.20	.15	.08
29	*Jeff Treadway* (RR)(FC)	.40	.30	.15
30	*Mike Campbell* (RR)(FC)	.25	.20	.10
31	*Lance Johnson* (RR)(FC)	.40	.30	.15
32	*Nelson Liriano* (RR)(FC)	.25	.20	.10
33	Shawn Abner (RR)(FC)	.20	.15	.08
34	*Roberto Alomar* (RR)(FC)	2.00	1.50	.80
35	*Shawn Hillegas* (RR)(FC)	.25	.20	.10
36	Joey Meyer (RR)	.20	.15	.08
37	Kevin Elster (RR)	.30	.25	.12
38	*Jose Lind* (RR)(FC)	.30	.25	.12
39	*Kirt Manwaring* (RR)(FC)	.35	.25	.14
40	*Mark Grace* (RR)(FC)	7.00	5.25	2.75
41	*Jody Reed* (RR)(FC)	.50	.40	.20
42	*John Farrell* (RR)(FC)	.35	.25	.14
43	*Al Leiter* (RR)(FC)	.20	.15	.08
44	*Gary Thurman* (RR)(FC)	.20	.15	.18
45	*Vicente Palacios* (RR)(FC)	.20	.15	.08
46	*Eddie Williams* (RR)(FC)	.25	.20	.10
47	*Jack McDowell* (RR)(FC)	.30	.25	.12
48	Ken Dixon	.05	.04	.02
49	Mike Birkbeck	.07	.05	.03
50	Eric King	.07	.05	.03
51	Roger Clemens	.80	.60	.30
52	Pat Clements	.05	.04	.02
53	Fernando Valenzuela	.25	.20	.10
54	Mark Gubicza	.12	.09	.05
55	Jay Howell	.07	.05	.03
56	Floyd Youmans	.05	.04	.02
57	Ed Correa	.05	.04	.02
58	*DeWayne Buice*	.15	.11	.06
59	Jose DeLeon	.07	.05	.03
60	Danny Cox	.07	.05	.03
61	Nolan Ryan	.50	.40	.20
62	Steve Bedrosian	.12	.09	.05
63	Tom Browning	.10	.08	.04
64	Mark Davis	.05	.04	.02
65	R.J. Reynolds	.05	.04	.02
66	Kevin Mitchell	.60	.45	.25
67	Ken Oberkfell	.05	.04	.02
68	Rick Sutcliffe	.10	.08	.04
69	Dwight Gooden	.60	.45	.25
70	Scott Bankhead	.07	.05	.03
71	Bert Blyleven	.12	.09	.05
72	Jimmy Key	.10	.08	.04
73	*Les Straker*	.15	.11	.06
74	Jim Clancy	.07	.05	.03
75	Mike Moore	.05	.04	.02
76	Ron Darling	.12	.09	.05
77	Ed Lynch	.05	.04	.02
78	Dale Murphy	.40	.30	.15
79	Doug Drabek	.07	.05	.03
80	Scott Garrelts	.05	.04	.02
81	Ed Whitson	.05	.04	.02
82	Rob Murphy	.07	.05	.03
83	Shane Rawley	.07	.05	.03
84	Greg Mathews	.07	.05	.03
85	Jim Deshaies	.07	.05	.03
86	Mike Witt	.07	.05	.03
87	Donnie Hill	.05	.04	.02
88	Jeff Reed	.05	.04	.02
89	Mike Boddicker	.07	.05	.03
90	Ted Higuera	.10	.08	.04
91	Walt Terrell	.07	.05	.03
92	Bob Stanley	.05	.04	.02
93	Dave Righetti	.15	.11	.06
94	Orel Hershiser	.25	.20	.10
95	Chris Bando	.05	.04	.02
96	Bret Saberhagen	.15	.11	.06
97	Curt Young	.07	.05	.03
98	Tim Burke	.05	.04	.02
99	Charlie Hough	.07	.05	.03
100a	Checklist 28-137	.05	.04	.02
100b	Checklist 28-133	.10	.08	.04
101	Bobby Witt	.10	.08	.04
102	George Brett	.40	.30	.15
103	Mickey Tettleton	.25	.20	.10
104	Scott Bailes	.07	.05	.03
105	Mike Pagliarulo	.10	.08	.04
106	Mike Scioscia	.07	.05	.03
107	Tom Brookens	.05	.04	.02
108	Ray Knight	.07	.05	.03
109	Dan Plesac	.10	.08	.04
110	Wally Joyner	.40	.30	.15
111	Bob Forsch	.07	.05	.03
112	Mike Scott	.12	.09	.05
113	Kevin Gross	.07	.05	.03
114	Benito Santiago	.35	.25	.14
115	Bob Kipper	.05	.04	.02
116	Mike Krukow	.07	.05	.03
117	Chris Bosio	.07	.05	.03
118	Sid Fernandez	.10	.08	.04
119	Jody Davis	.07	.05	.03
120	Mike Morgan	.05	.04	.02
121	Mark Eichhorn	.07	.05	.03
122	Jeff Reardon	.10	.08	.04
123	John Franco	.10	.08	.04
124	Richard Dotson	.07	.05	.03
125	Eric Bell	.05	.04	.02
126	Juan Nieves	.07	.05	.03
127	Jack Morris	.20	.15	.08
128	Rick Rhoden	.07	.05	.03
129	Rich Gedman	.07	.05	.03
130	Ken Howell	.05	.04	.02
131	Brook Jacoby	.10	.08	.04
132	Danny Jackson	.12	.09	.05
133	Gene Nelson	.05	.04	.02

		MT	NR MT	EX
134	Neal Heaton	.05	.04	.02
135	Willie Fraser	.05	.04	.02
136	Jose Guzman	.07	.05	.03
137	Ozzie Guillen	.07	.05	.03
138	Bob Knepper	.07	.05	.03
139	*Mike Jackson*	.20	.15	.08
140	*Joe Magrane*	.60	.45	.25
141	Jimmy Jones	.07	.05	.03
142	Ted Power	.05	.04	.02
143	Ozzie Virgil	.05	.04	.02
144	*Felix Fermin*(FC)	.15	.11	.06
145	Kelly Downs	.10	.08	.04
146	Shawon Dunston	.10	.08	.04
147	Scott Bradley	.05	.04	.02
148	Dave Stieb	.10	.08	.04
149	Frank Viola	.15	.11	.06
150	Terry Kennedy	.07	.05	.03
151	Bill Wegman	.05	.04	.02
152	*Matt Nokes*	.60	.45	.25
153	Wade Boggs	1.00	.70	.40
154	Wayne Tolleson	.05	.04	.02
155	Mariano Duncan	.05	.04	.02
156	Julio Franco	.10	.08	.04
157	Charlie Leibrandt	.07	.05	.03
158	Terry Steinbach	.10	.08	.04
159	Mike Fitzgerald	.05	.04	.02
160	Jack Lazorko	.05	.04	.02
161	Mitch Williams	.07	.05	.03
162	Greg Walker	.07	.05	.03
163	Alan Ashby	.05	.04	.02
164	Tony Gwynn	.35	.25	.14
165	Bruce Ruffin	.07	.05	.03
166	Ron Robinson	.05	.04	.02
167	Zane Smith	.07	.05	.03
168	Junior Ortiz	.05	.04	.02
169	Jamie Moyer	.07	.05	.03
170	Tony Pena	.07	.05	.03
171	Cal Ripken	.35	.25	.14
172	B.J. Surhoff	.12	.09	.05
173	Lou Whitaker	.25	.20	.10
174	*Ellis Burks*	1.75	1.25	.70
175	Ron Guidry	.15	.11	.06
176	Steve Sax	.15	.11	.06
177	Danny Tartabull	.20	.15	.08
178	Carney Lansford	.10	.08	.04
179	Casey Candaele	.05	.04	.02
180	Scott Fletcher	.07	.05	.03
181	Mark McLemore	.05	.04	.02
182	Ivan Calderon	.10	.08	.04
183	Jack Clark	.15	.11	.06
184	Glenn Davis	.15	.11	.06
185	Luis Aguayo	.05	.04	.02
186	Bo Diaz	.07	.05	.03
187	Stan Jefferson	.07	.05	.03
188	Sid Bream	.07	.05	.03
189	Bob Brenly	.05	.04	.02
190	Dion James	.07	.05	.03
191	Leon Durham	.07	.05	.03
192	Jesse Orosco	.07	.05	.03
193	Alvin Davis	.12	.09	.05
194	Gary Gaetti	.12	.09	.05
195	Fred McGriff	.40	.30	.15
196	Steve Lombardozzi	.05	.04	.02
197	Rance Mulliniks	.05	.04	.02
198	Rey Quinones	.05	.04	.02
199	Gary Carter	.25	.20	.10
200a	Checklist 138-247	.05	.04	.02
200b	Checklist 134-239	.10	.08	.04
201	Keith Moreland	.07	.05	.03
202	Ken Griffey	.07	.05	.03
203	*Tommy Gregg*(FC)	.25	.20	.10
204	Will Clark	1.25	.90	.50
205	John Kruk	.10	.08	.04
206	Buddy Bell	.07	.05	.03
207	Von Hayes	.07	.05	.03
208	Tommy Herr	.07	.05	.03
209	Craig Reynolds	.05	.04	.02
210	Gary Pettis	.05	.04	.02
211	Harold Baines	.12	.09	.05
212	Vance Law	.07	.05	.03
213	Ken Gerhart	.07	.05	.03
214	Jim Gantner	.05	.04	.02
215	Chet Lemon	.07	.05	.03
216	Dwight Evans	.12	.09	.05
217	Don Mattingly	1.50	1.25	.60
218	Franklin Stubbs	.07	.05	.03
219	Pat Tabler	.07	.05	.03
220	Bo Jackson	1.25	.90	.50
221	Tony Phillips	.05	.04	.02
222	Tim Wallach	.10	.08	.04
223	Ruben Sierra	.60	.45	.25
224	Steve Buechele	.05	.04	.02
225	Frank White	.07	.05	.03
226	Alfredo Griffin	.07	.05	.03
227	Greg Swindell	.20	.15	.08
228	Willie Randolph	.07	.05	.03
229	Mike Marshall	.12	.09	.05
230	Alan Trammell	.25	.20	.10
231	Eddie Murray	.35	.25	.14
232	Dale Sveum	.07	.05	.03
233	Dick Schofield	.05	.04	.02
234	Jose Oquendo	.05	.04	.02
235	Bill Doran	.07	.05	.03
236	Milt Thompson	.05	.04	.02
237	Marvell Wynne	.05	.04	.02
238	Bobby Bonilla	.15	.11	.06
239	Chris Speier	.05	.04	.02
240	Glenn Braggs	.10	.08	.04
241	Wally Backman	.07	.05	.03
242	Ryne Sandberg	.30	.25	.12
243	Phil Bradley	.10	.08	.04
244	Kelly Gruber	.05	.04	.02
245	Tom Brunansky	.10	.08	.04
246	Ron Oester	.05	.04	.02
247	Bobby Thigpen	.10	.08	.04
248	Fred Lynn	.15	.11	.06
249	Paul Molitor	.12	.09	.05
250	Darrell Evans	.10	.08	.04
251	Gary Ward	.07	.05	.03
252	Bruce Hurst	.10	.08	.04
253	Bob Welch	.10	.08	.04
254	Joe Carter	.12	.09	.05
255	Willie Wilson	.10	.08	.04
256	Mark McGwire	1.25	.90	.50

		MT	NR MT	EX
257	Mitch Webster	.07	.05	.03
258	Brian Downing	.07	.05	.03
259	Mike Stanley	.10	.08	.04
260	Carlton Fisk	.20	.15	.08
261	Billy Hatcher	.07	.05	.03
262	Glenn Wilson	.07	.05	.03
263	Ozzie Smith	.15	.11	.06
264	Randy Ready	.05	.04	.02
265	Kurt Stillwell	.10	.08	.04
266	David Palmer	.05	.04	.02
267	Mike Diaz	.07	.05	.03
268	Rob Thompson	.07	.05	.03
269	Andre Dawson	.20	.15	.08
270	Lee Guetterman	.05	.04	.02
271	Willie Upshaw	.07	.05	.03
272	Randy Bush	.05	.04	.02
273	Larry Sheets	.07	.05	.03
274	Rob Deer	.07	.05	.03
275	Kirk Gibson	.20	.15	.08
276	Marty Barrett	.07	.05	.03
277	Rickey Henderson	.35	.25	.14
278	Pedro Guerrero	.15	.11	.06
279	Brett Butler	.07	.05	.03
280	Kevin Seitzer	.80	.60	.30
281	Mike Davis	.07	.05	.03
282	Andres Galarraga	.15	.11	.06
283	Devon White	.30	.25	.12
284	Pete O'Brien	.07	.05	.03
285	Jerry Hairston	.05	.04	.02
286	Kevin Bass	.07	.05	.03
287	Carmelo Martinez	.07	.05	.03
288	Juan Samuel	.12	.09	.05
289	Kal Daniels	.20	.15	.08
290	Albert Hall	.05	.04	.02
291	Andy Van Slyke	.12	.09	.05
292	Lee Smith	.10	.08	.04
293	Vince Coleman	.20	.15	.08
294	Tom Niedenfuer	.07	.05	.03
295	Robin Yount	.30	.25	.12
296	*Jeff Robinson*	.40	.30	.15
297	*Todd Benzinger*	.40	.30	.15
298	Dave Winfield	.30	.25	.12
299	Mickey Hatcher	.05	.04	.02
300a	Checklist 248-357	.05	.04	.02
300b	Checklist 240-345	.10	.08	.04
301	Bud Black	.05	.04	.02
302	Jose Canseco	2.50	2.00	1.00
303	Tom Foley	.05	.04	.02
304	Pete Incaviglia	.15	.11	.06
305	Bob Boone	.07	.05	.03
306	*Bill Long*	.20	.15	.08
307	Willie McGee	.12	.09	.05
308	*Ken Caminiti*(FC)	.30	.25	.12
309	Darren Daulton	.05	.04	.02
310	Tracy Jones	.12	.09	.05
311	Greg Booker	.07	.05	.03
312	Mike LaValliere	.07	.05	.03
313	Chili Davis	.07	.05	.03
314	Glenn Hubbard	.05	.04	.02
315	*Paul Noce*	.10	.08	.04
316	Keith Hernandez	.20	.15	.08
317	Mark Langston	.12	.09	.05
318	Keith Atherton	.05	.04	.02
319	Tony Fernandez	.12	.09	.05
320	Kent Hrbek	.15	.11	.06
321	John Cerutti	.07	.05	.03
322	Mike Kingery	.05	.04	.02
323	Dave Magadan	.12	.09	.05
324	Rafael Palmeiro	.40	.30	.15
325	Jeff Dedmon	.05	.04	.02
326	Barry Bonds	.12	.09	.05
327	Jeffrey Leonard	.07	.05	.03
328	Tim Flannery	.05	.04	.02
329	Dave Concepcion	.07	.05	.03
330	Mike Schmidt	.50	.40	.20
331	Bill Dawley	.05	.04	.02
332	Larry Andersen	.05	.04	.02
333	Jack Howell	.07	.05	.03
334	*Ken Williams*	.20	.15	.08
335	Bryn Smith	.05	.04	.02
336	*Billy Ripken*	.25	.20	.10
337	Greg Brock	.07	.05	.03
338	Mike Heath	.05	.04	.02
339	Mike Greenwell	1.25	.90	.50
340	Claudell Washington	.07	.05	.03
341	Jose Gonzalez	.05	.04	.02
342	Mel Hall	.07	.05	.03
343	Jim Eisenreich	.07	.05	.03
344	Tony Bernazard	.05	.04	.02
345	Tim Raines	.25	.20	.10
346	Bob Brower	.07	.05	.03
347	Larry Parrish	.07	.05	.03
348	Thad Bosley	.05	.04	.02
349	Dennis Eckersley	.12	.09	.05
350	Cory Snyder	.20	.15	.08
351	Rick Cerone	.05	.04	.02
352	John Shelby	.05	.04	.02
353	Larry Herndon	.05	.04	.02
354	John Habyan	.05	.04	.02
355	*Chuck Crim*	.12	.09	.05
356	Gus Polidor	.05	.04	.02
357	Ken Dayley	.05	.04	.02
358	Danny Darwin	.05	.04	.02
359	Lance Parrish	.15	.11	.06
360	*James Steels*	.12	.09	.05
361	*Al Pedrique*(FC)	.15	.11	.06
362	Mike Aldrete	.07	.05	.03
363	Juan Castillo	.05	.04	.02
364	Len Dykstra	.10	.08	.04
365	Luis Quinones	.05	.04	.02
366	Jim Presley	.10	.08	.04
367	Lloyd Moseby	.07	.05	.03
368	Kirby Puckett	.50	.40	.25
369	Eric Davis	.80	.60	.30
370	Gary Redus	.05	.04	.02
371	Dave Schmidt	.05	.04	.02
372	Mark Clear	.05	.04	.02
373	Dave Bergman	.05	.04	.02
374	Charles Hudson	.05	.04	.02
375	Calvin Schiraldi	.05	.04	.02
376	Alex Trevino	.05	.04	.02
377	Tom Candiotti	.05	.04	.02
378	Steve Farr	.05	.04	.02

		MT	NR MT	EX
379	Mike Gallego	.05	.04	.02
380	Andy McGaffigan	.05	.04	.02
381	Kirk McCaskill	.07	.05	.03
382	Oddibe McDowell	.07	.05	.03
383	Floyd Bannister	.07	.05	.03
384	Denny Walling	.05	.04	.02
385	Don Carman	.07	.05	.03
386	Todd Worrell	.10	.08	.04
387	Eric Show	.07	.05	.03
388	Dave Parker	.20	.15	.08
389	Rick Mahler	.05	.04	.02
390	*Mike Dunne*	.25	.20	.08
391	Candy Maldonado	.07	.05	.03
392	Bob Dernier	.05	.04	.02
393	Dave Valle	.05	.04	.02
394	Ernie Whitt	.07	.05	.03
395	Juan Berenguer	.05	.04	.02
396	Mike Young	.05	.04	.02
397	Mike Felder	.05	.04	.02
398	Willie Hernandez	.07	.05	.03
399	Jim Rice	.30	.25	.12
400a	Checklist 358-467	.05	.04	.02
400b	Checklist 346-451	.10	.08	.04
401	Tommy John	.15	.11	.06
402	Brian Holton	.07	.05	.03
403	Carmen Castillo	.05	.04	.02
404	Jamie Quirk	.05	.04	.02
405	Dwayne Murphy	.07	.05	.03
406	*Jeff Parrett*(FC)	.25	.20	.10
407	Don Sutton	.20	.15	.08
408	Jerry Browne	.07	.05	.03
409	Jim Winn	.05	.04	.02
410	Dave Smith	.07	.05	.03
411	*Shane Mack*	.15	.11	.06
412	Greg Gross	.05	.04	.02
413	Nick Esasky	.07	.05	.03
414	Damaso Garcia	.05	.04	.02
415	Brian Fisher	.07	.05	.03
416	Brian Dayett	.05	.04	.02
417	Curt Ford	.05	.04	.02
418	*Mark Williamson*	.12	.09	.05
419	Bill Schroeder	.05	.04	.02
420	*Mike Henneman*	.25	.20	.10
421	*John Marzano*(FC)	.25	.20	.10
422	Ron Kittle	.07	.05	.03
423	Matt Young	.05	.04	.02
424	Steve Balboni	.07	.05	.03
425	*Luis Polonia*	.25	.20	.10
426	Randy St. Claire	.05	.04	.02
427	Greg Harris	.05	.04	.02
428	Johnny Ray	.07	.05	.03
429	Ray Searage	.05	.04	.02
430	Ricky Horton	.07	.05	.03
431	*Gerald Young*(FC)	.35	.25	.14
432	Rick Schu	.05	.04	.02
433	Paul O'Neill	.07	.05	.03
434	Rich Gossage	.15	.11	.06
435	John Cangelosi	.05	.04	.02
436	Mike LaCoss	.05	.04	.02
437	Gerald Perry	.10	.08	.04
438	Dave Martinez	.07	.05	.03
439	Darryl Strawberry	.35	.25	.14
440	John Moses	.05	.04	.02
441	Greg Gagne	.05	.04	.02
442	Jesse Barfield	.12	.09	.05
443	George Frazier	.05	.04	.02
444	Garth Iorg	.05	.04	.02
445	Ed Nunez	.05	.04	.02
446	Rick Aguilera	.05	.04	.02
447	Jerry Mumphrey	.05	.04	.02
448	Rafael Ramirez	.05	.04	.02
449	*John Smiley*	.35	.25	.14
450	Atlee Hammaker	.05	.04	.02
451	Lance McCullers	.07	.05	.03
452	Guy Hoffman(FC)	.07	.05	.03
453	Chris James	.12	.09	.05
454	Terry Pendleton	.07	.05	.03
455	*Dave Meads*	.15	.11	.06
456	Bill Buckner	.10	.08	.04
457	*John Pawlowski*(FC)	.10	.08	.04
458	Bob Sebra	.05	.04	.02
459	Jim Dwyer	.05	.04	.02
460	*Jay Aldrich*(FC)	.12	.09	.05
461	Frank Tanana	.07	.05	.03
462	Oil Can Boyd	.07	.05	.03
463	Dan Pasqua	.10	.08	.04
464	*Tim Crews*(FC)	.15	.11	.06
465	Andy Allanson	.07	.05	.03
466	*Bill Pecota*(FC)	.15	.11	.06
467	Steve Ontiveros	.05	.04	.02
468	Hubie Brooks	.10	.08	.04
469	*Paul Kilgus*(FC)	.20	.15	.08
470	Dale Mohorcic	.05	.04	.02
471	Dan Quisenberry	.07	.05	.03
472	Dave Stewart	.10	.08	.04
473	Dave Clark	.07	.05	.03
474	Joel Skinner	.05	.04	.02
475	Dave Anderson	.05	.04	.02
476	Dan Petry	.07	.05	.03
477	*Carl Nichols*(FC)	.12	.09	.05
478	Ernest Riles	.05	.04	.02
479	George Hendrick	.07	.05	.03
480	John Morris	.05	.04	.02
481	*Manny Hernandez*(FC)	.10	.08	.04
482	Jeff Stone	.05	.04	.02
483	Chris Brown	.07	.05	.03
484	Mike Bielecki	.05	.04	.02
485	Dave Dravecky	.07	.05	.03
486	Rick Manning	.05	.04	.02
487	Bill Almon	.05	.04	.02
488	Jim Sundberg	.07	.05	.03
489	Ken Phelps	.07	.05	.03
490	Tom Henke	.07	.05	.03
491	Dan Gladden	.05	.04	.02
492	Barry Larkin	.40	.30	.15
493	*Fred Manrique*(FC)	.15	.11	.06
494	Mike Griffin	.05	.04	.02
495	*Mark Knudson*(FC)	.10	.08	.04
496	Bill Madlock	.10	.08	.04
497	Tim Stoddard	.05	.04	.02
498	*Sam Horn*(FC)	.30	.25	.12
499	*Tracy Woodson*(FC)	.15	.11	.06
500a	Checklist 468-577	.05	.04	.02

		MT	NR MT	EX
500b	Checklist 452-557	.10	.08	.04
501	Ken Schrom	.05	.04	.02
502	Angel Salazar	.05	.04	.02
503	Eric Plunk	.05	.04	.02
504	Joe Hesketh	.05	.04	.02
505	Greg Minton	.05	.04	.02
506	Geno Petralli	.05	.04	.02
507	Bob James	.05	.04	.02
508	*Robbie Wine*(FC)	.12	.09	.05
509	Jeff Calhoun	.05	.04	.02
510	Steve Lake	.05	.04	.02
511	Mark Grant	.05	.04	.02
512	Frank Williams	.05	.04	.02
513	*Jeff Blauser*(FC)	.30	.25	.12
514	Bob Walk	.05	.04	.02
515	Craig Lefferts	.05	.04	.02
516	Manny Trillo	.07	.05	.03
517	Jerry Reed	.05	.04	.02
518	Rick Leach	.05	.04	.02
519	*Mark Davidson*	.12	.09	.05
520	*Jeff Ballard*(FC)	.35	.25	.14
521	*Dave Stapleton*(FC)	.10	.08	.04
522	Pat Sheridan	.05	.04	.02
523	Al Nipper	.05	.04	.02
524	Steve Trout	.05	.04	.02
525	Jeff Hamilton	.07	.05	.03
526	*Tommy Hinzo*(FC)	.15	.11	.06
527	Lonnie Smith	.07	.05	.03
528	*Greg Cadaret*(FC)	.20	.15	.08
529	Rob McClure (Bob)	.05	.04	.02
530	Chuck Finley	.10	.08	.04
531	Jeff Russell	.05	.04	.02
532	Steve Lyons	.05	.04	.02
533	Terry Puhl	.05	.04	.02
534	*Eric Nolte*(FC)	.15	.11	.06
535	Kent Tekulve	.07	.05	.03
536	*Pat Pacillo*(FC)	.15	.11	.06
537	Charlie Puleo	.05	.04	.02
538	*Tom Prince*(FC)	.15	.11	.06
539	Greg Maddux	.15	.11	.06
540	Jim Lindeman	.07	.05	.03
541	*Pete Stanicek*(FC)	.25	.20	.10
542	Steve Kiefer	.05	.04	.02
543	Jim Morrison	.05	.04	.02
544	Spike Owen	.05	.04	.02
545	*Jay Buhner*(FC)	.30	.25	.12
546	*Mike Devereaux*(FC)	.30	.25	.12
547	Jerry Don Gleaton	.05	.04	.02
548	Jose Rijo	.07	.05	.03
549	Dennis Martinez	.05	.04	.02
550	Mike Loynd	.05	.04	.02
551	Darrell Miller	.05	.04	.02
552	Dave LaPoint	.07	.05	.03
553	John Tudor	.10	.08	.04
554	*Rocky Childress*(FC)	.12	.09	.05
555	*Wally Ritchie*(FC)	.15	.11	.06
556	Terry McGriff	.05	.04	.02
557	Dave Leiper	.05	.04	.02
558	Jeff Robinson	.07	.05	.03
559	Jose Uribe	.05	.04	.02
560	Ted Simmons	.10	.08	.04
561	*Lester Lancaster*	.15	.11	.06
562	*Keith Miller*(FC)	.25	.20	.10
563	Harold Reynolds	.07	.05	.03
564	*Gene Larkin*	.20	.15	.08
565	Cecil Fielder	.70	.50	.30
566	Roy Smalley	.05	.04	.02
567	Duane Ward	.07	.05	.03
568	*Bill Wilkinson*(FC)	.15	.11	.06
569	Howard Johnson	.10	.08	.04
570	Frank DiPino	.05	.04	.02
571	*Pete Smith*(FC)	.20	.15	.08
572	Darnell Coles	.07	.05	.03
573	Don Robinson	.07	.05	.03
574	Rob Nelson	.05	.04	.02
575	Dennis Rasmussen	.10	.08	.04
576	Steve Jeltz (photo actually Juan Samuel)	.05	.04	.02
577	*Tom Pagnozzi*(FC)	.15	.11	.06
578	Ty Gainey	.05	.04	.02
579	Gary Lucas	.05	.04	.02
580	Ron Hassey	.05	.04	.02
581	Herm Winningham	.05	.04	.02
582	*Rene Gonzales*(FC)	.15	.11	.06
583	Brad Komminsk	.05	.04	.02
584	Doyle Alexander	.07	.05	.03
585	Jeff Sellers	.07	.05	.03
586	Bill Gullickson	.05	.04	.02
587	Tim Belcher(FC)	.50	.40	.20
588	*Doug Jones*(FC)	.40	.30	.15
589	*Melido Perez*(FC)	.30	.25	.12
590	Rick Honeycutt	.05	.04	.02
591	Pascual Perez	.07	.05	.03
592	Curt Wilkerson	.05	.04	.02
593	Steve Howe	.07	.05	.03
594	*John Davis*(FC)	.20	.15	.08
595	Storm Davis	.10	.08	.04
596	Sammy Stewart	.05	.04	.02
597	Neil Allen	.05	.04	.02
598	Alejandro Pena	.07	.05	.03
599	Mark Thurmond	.05	.04	.02
600a	Checklist 578-BC26	.05	.04	.02
600b	Checklist 558-660	.10	.08	.04
601	*Jose Mesa*(FC)	.20	.15	.08
602	*Don August*(FC)	.25	.20	.10
603	Terry Leach	.10	.08	.04
604	*Tom Newell*(FC)	.20	.15	.08
605	*Randall Byers*(FC)	.20	.15	.08
606	Jim Gott	.05	.04	.02
607	Harry Spilman	.05	.04	.02
608	John Candelaria	.07	.05	.03
609	*Mike Brumley*(FC)	.20	.15	.08
610	Mickey Brantley	.07	.05	.03
611	*Jose Nunez*(FC)	.25	.20	.10
612	Tom Nieto	.05	.04	.02
613	Rick Reuschel	.10	.08	.04
614	Lee Mazzilli	.12	.09	.05
615	*Scott Lusader*(FC)	.20	.15	.08
616	Bobby Meacham	.05	.04	.02
617	Kevin McReynolds	.15	.11	.06
618	Gene Garber	.05	.04	.02
619	*Barry Lyons*(FC)	.15	.11	.06
620	Randy Myers	.10	.08	.04
621	Donnie Moore	.05	.04	.02
622	Domingo Ramos	.05	.04	.02
623	Ed Romero	.05	.04	.02
624	*Greg Myers*(FC)	.25	.20	.10
625	Ripken Baseball Family (Billy Ripken, Cal Ripken, Jr., Cal Ripken, Sr.)	.15	.11	.06
626	Pat Perry	.05	.04	.02
627	Andres Thomas	.10	.08	.04
628	*Matt Williams*	1.00	.70	.40
629	*Dave Hengel*(FC)	.20	.15	.08
630	Jeff Musselman	.07	.05	.03
631	Tim Laudner	.05	.04	.02
632	Bob Ojeda	.07	.05	.03
633	Rafael Santana	.05	.04	.02
634	*Wes Gardner*(FC)	.25	.20	.10
635	*Roberto Kelly*(FC)	1.00	.70	.40
636	Mike Flanagan	.12	.09	.05
637	*Jay Bell*(FC)	.40	.30	.15
638	Bob Melvin	.05	.04	.02
639	*Damon Berryhill*(FC)	.40	.30	.15
640	*David Wells*(FC)	.25	.20	.10
641	Stan Musial Puzzle Card	.05	.04	.02
642	Doug Sisk	.05	.04	.02
643	*Keith Hughes*(FC)	.20	.15	.08
644	*Tom Glavine*(FC)	.40	.30	.15
645	Al Newman	.05	.04	.02
646	Scott Sanderson	.05	.04	.02
647	Scott Terry	.10	.08	.04
648	Tim Teufel	.12	.09	.05
649	Garry Templeton	.12	.09	.05
650	Manny Lee	.05	.04	.02
651	Roger McDowell	.10	.08	.04
652	Mookie Wilson	.15	.11	.06
653	David Cone	.70	.50	.30
654	*Ron Gant*(FC)	.40	.30	.15
655	Joe Price	.12	.09	.05
656	George Bell	.25	.20	.10
657	*Gregg Jefferies*(FC)	5.00	3.75	2.00
658	*Todd Stottlemyre*(FC)	.50	.40	.20
659	*Geronimo Berroa*(FC)	.25	.20	.10
660	Jerry Royster	.12	.09	.05

1988 Donruss All-Stars

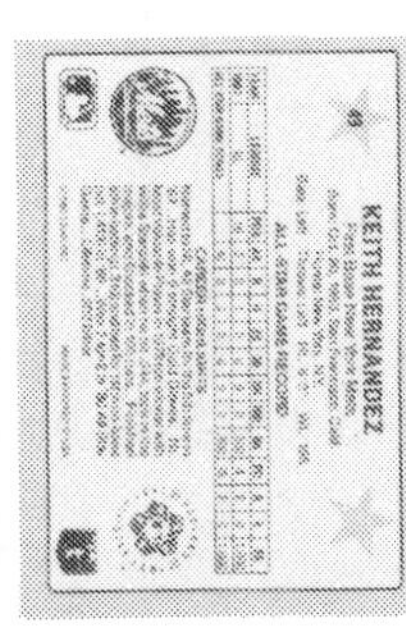

For the third consecutive year, this set of 64 cards featuring major league All-Stars was marketed in conjunction with Donruss Pop-Ups. The 1988 issue included a major change - the cards were reduced in size from 3-1/2" x 5" to a standard 2-1/2" x 3-1/2". The set features players from the 1987 All-Star Game starting lineup. Card fronts feature full-color photos, framed in blue, black and white, with a Donruss logo upper left. Player name and position appear in a red banner below the photo, along with the appropriate National or American League logo. All-Stars card backs include player stats and All-Star Game record. In 1988, All-Stars cards were distributed in individual packages containing three All-Stars, one Pop-Up and three Donruss puzzle pieces.

		MT	NR MT	EX
	Complete Set:	8.00	6.00	3.25
	Common Player:	.09	.07	.04
1	Don Mattingly	2.00	1.50	.80
2	Dave Winfield	.25	.20	.10
3	Willie Randolph	.09	.07	.04
4	Rickey Henderson	.50	.40	.20
5	Cal Ripken, Jr.	.30	.25	.12
6	George Bell	.20	.15	.08
7	Wade Boggs	.80	.60	.30
8	Bret Saberhagen	.15	.11	.06
9	Terry Kennedy	.09	.07	.04
10	John McNamara	.09	.07	.04
11	Jay Howell	.09	.07	.04
12	Harold Baines	.12	.09	.05
13	Harold Reynolds	.09	.07	.04
14	Bruce Hurst	.09	.07	.04
15	Kirby Puckett	.50	.40	.20
16	Matt Nokes	.20	.15	.08
17	Pat Tabler	.09	.07	.04
18	Dan Plesac	.12	.09	.05
19	Mark McGwire	1.00	.70	.40
20	Mike Witt	.09	.07	.04
21	Larry Parrish	.09	.07	.04
22	Alan Trammell	.20	.15	.08
23	Dwight Evans	.12	.09	.05
24	Jack Morris	.12	.09	.05
25	Tony Fernandez	.12	.09	.05
26	Mark Langston	.20	.15	.08
27	Kevin Seitzer	.40	.30	.15
28	Tom Henke	.09	.07	.04
29	Dave Righetti	.12	.09	.05
30	Oakland Coliseum	.09	.07	.04
31	Top Vote Getter (Wade Boggs)	.60	.45	.25
32	Checklist 1-32	.09	.07	.04
33	Jack Clark	.15	.11	.06
34	Darryl Strawberry	.40	.30	.15
35	Ryne Sandberg	.20	.15	.08
36	Andre Dawson	.20	.15	.08
37	Ozzie Smith	.15	.11	.06
38	Eric Davis	.50	.40	.20
39	Mike Schmidt	.80	.60	.30
40	Mike Scott	.12	.09	.05
41	Gary Carter	.12	.09	.05
42	Davey Johnson	.09	.07	.04
43	Rick Sutcliffe	.12	.09	.05
44	Willie McGee	.12	.09	.05
45	Hubie Brooks	.09	.07	.04
46	Dale Murphy	.40	.30	.15
47	Bo Diaz	.09	.07	.04
48	Pedro Guerrero	.15	.11	.06
49	Keith Hernandez	.15	.11	.06
50	Ozzie Virgil	.09	.07	.04
51	Tony Gwynn	.25	.20	.10
52	Rick Reuschel	.12	.09	.05
53	John Franco	.12	.09	.05
54	Jeffrey Leonard	.09	.07	.04
55	Juan Samuel	.15	.11	.06
56	Orel Hershiser	.20	.15	.08
57	Tim Raines	.20	.15	.08
58	Sid Fernandez	.12	.09	.05
59	Tim Wallach	.12	.09	.05
60	Lee Smith	.09	.07	.04
61	Steve Bedrosian	.12	.09	.05
62	MVP (Tim Raines)	.20	.15	.08
63	Top Vote Getter (Ozzie Smith)	.15	.11	.06
64	Checklist 33-64	.09	.07	.04

1988 Donruss Baseball's Best

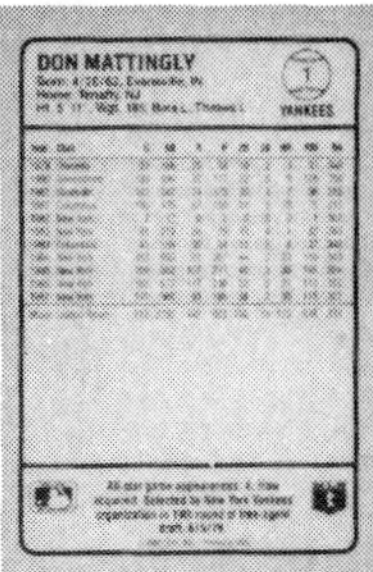

The design of this 336-card set (2-1/2" by 3-1/2") is similar to the regular 1988 Donruss issue with the exception of the borders which are orange, instead of blue. Full-color player photos are framed by the Donruss logo upper left, team logo lower right and a bright red and white player name that spans the bottom margin. The backs are black and white, framed by a yellow border, and include personal information, year-by-year stats and major league totals. This set was packaged in a bright red cardboard box (10" x 11" x 12") that contained six individually shrink-wrapped packs of 56 cards. Donruss marketed the set via retail chain outlets including Walgreens, Venture, Wall-Mart, Ben Frank- lin, Shopko, Super X, Target, McCrory's, Osco, Woolworth and J.C. Murphy.

		MT	NR MT	EX
	Complete Set:	21.00	16.00	8.50
	Common Player:	.05	.04	.02
1	Don Mattingly	1.50	1.25	.60
2	Ron Gant	.10	.08	.04
3	Bob Boone	.05	.04	.02
4	Mark Grace	1.50	1.25	.60
5	Andy Allanson	.05	.04	.02
6	Kal Daniels	.12	.09	.05
7	Floyd Bannister	.07	.05	.03
8	Alan Ashby	.05	.04	.02
9	Marty Barrett	.07	.05	.03
10	Tim Belcher	.10	.08	.04
11	Harold Baines	.12	.09	.05
12	Hubie Brooks	.07	.05	.03
13	Doyle Alexander	.07	.05	.03
14	Gary Carter	.15	.11	.06
15	Glenn Braggs	.07	.05	.03
16	Steve Bedrosian	.07	.05	.03
17	Barry Bonds	.15	.11	.06
18	Bert Blyleven	.10	.08	.04
19	Tom Brunansky	.10	.08	.04
20	John Candelaria	.07	.05	.03
21	Shawn Abner	.15	.11	.06
22	Jose Canseco	1.25	.90	.50
23	Brett Butler	.07	.05	.03
24	Scott Bradley	.05	.04	.02
25	Ivan Calderon	.10	.08	.04
26	Rich Gossage	.10	.08	.04
27	Brian Downing	.07	.05	.03
28	Jim Rice	.10	.08	.04
29	Dion James	.05	.04	.02
30	Terry Kennedy	.07	.05	.03
31	George Bell	.10	.08	.04
32	Scott Fletcher	.05	.04	.02
33	Bobby Bonilla	.15	.11	.06
34	Tim Burke	.05	.04	.02

		MT	NR MT	EX
35	Darrell Evans	.07	.05	.03
36	Mike Davis	.05	.04	.02
37	Shawon Dunston	.15	.11	.06
38	Kevin Bass	.07	.05	.03
39	George Brett	.40	.30	.15
40	David Cone	.25	.20	.10
41	Ron Darling	.10	.08	.04
42	Roberto Alomar	.20	.15	.08
43	Dennis Eckersley	.10	.08	.04
44	Vince Coleman	.15	.11	.06
45	Sid Bream	.07	.05	.03
46	Gary Gaetti	.12	.09	.05
47	Phil Bradley	.12	.09	.05
48	Jim Clancy	.05	.04	.02
49	Jack Clark	.15	.11	.06
50	Mike Krukow	.05	.04	.02
51	Henry Cotto	.05	.04	.02
52	Rich Dotson	.07	.05	.03
53	Jim Gantner	.05	.04	.02
54	John Franco	.07	.05	.03
55	Pete Incaviglia	.12	.09	.05
56	Joe Carter	.20	.15	.08
57	Roger Clemens	.70	.50	.30
58	Gerald Perry	.10	.08	.04
59	Jack Howell	.05	.04	.02
60	Vance Law	.05	.04	.02
61	Jay Bell	.07	.05	.03
62	Eric Davis	.70	.50	.30
63	Gene Garber	.05	.04	.02
64	Glenn Davis	.12	.09	.05
65	Wade Boggs	1.00	.70	.40
66	Kirk Gibson	.20	.15	.08
67	Carlton Fisk	.15	.11	.06
68	Casey Candaele	.05	.04	.02
69	Mike Heath	.05	.04	.02
70	Kevin Elster	.15	.11	.06
71	Greg Brock	.07	.05	.03
72	Don Carman	.05	.04	.02
73	Doug Drabek	.07	.05	.03
74	Greg Gagne	.05	.04	.02
75	Danny Cox	.07	.05	.03
76	Rickey Henderson	.60	.45	.25
77	Chris Brown	.07	.05	.03
78	Terry Steinbach	.15	.11	.06
79	Will Clark	1.00	.70	.40
80	Mickey Brantley	.05	.04	.02
81	Ozzie Guillen	.07	.05	.03
82	Greg Maddux	.12	.09	.05
83	Kirk McCaskill	.05	.04	.02
84	Dwight Evans	.10	.08	.04
85	Ozzie Virgil	.05	.04	.02
86	Mike Morgan	.05	.04	.02
87	Tony Fernandez	.10	.08	.04
88	Jose Guzman	.05	.04	.02
89	Mike Dunne	.12	.09	.05
90	Andres Galarraga	.15	.11	.06
91	Mike Henneman	.10	.08	.04
92	Alfredo Griffin	.07	.05	.03
93	Rafael Palmeiro	.12	.09	.05
94	Jim Deshaies	.07	.05	.03
95	Mark Gubicza	.07	.05	.03
96	Dwight Gooden	.70	.50	.30
97	Howard Johnson	.25	.20	.10
98	Mark Davis	.05	.04	.02
99	Dave Stewart	.10	.08	.04
100	Joe Magrane	.12	.09	.05
101	Brian Fisher	.07	.05	.03
102	Kent Hrbek	.15	.11	.06
103	Kevin Gross	.05	.04	.02
104	Tom Henke	.07	.05	.03
105	Mike Pagliarulo	.10	.08	.04
106	Kelly Downs	.10	.08	.04
107	Alvin Davis	.12	.09	.05
108	Willie Randolph	.07	.05	.03
109	Rob Deer	.07	.05	.03
110	Bo Diaz	.05	.04	.02
111	Paul Kilgus	.10	.08	.04
112	Tom Candiotti	.05	.04	.02
113	Dale Murphy	.40	.30	.15
114	Rick Mahler	.05	.04	.02
115	Wally Joyner	.40	.30	.15
116	Ryne Sandberg	.25	.20	.10
117	John Farrell	.12	.09	.05
118	Nick Esasky	.05	.04	.02
119	Bo Jackson	.90	.70	.35
120	Bill Doran	.07	.05	.03
121	Ellis Burks	.70	.50	.30
122	Pedro Guerrero	.12	.09	.05
123	Dave LaPoint	.05	.04	.02
124	Neal Heaton	.05	.04	.02
125	Willie Hernandez	.05	.04	.02
126	Roger McDowell	.07	.05	.03
127	Ted Higuera	.10	.08	.04
128	Von Hayes	.10	.08	.04
129	Mike LaValliere	.07	.05	.03
130	Dan Gladden	.07	.05	.03
131	Willie McGee	.12	.09	.05
132	Al Lieter	.20	.15	.08
133	Mark Grant	.05	.04	.02
134	Bob Welch	.07	.05	.03
135	Dave Dravecky	.05	.04	.02
136	Mark Langston	.10	.08	.04
137	Dan Pasqua	.10	.08	.04
138	Rick Sutcliffe	.12	.09	.05
139	Dan Petry	.05	.04	.02
140	Rich Gedman	.07	.05	.03
141	Ken Griffey	.07	.05	.03
142	Eddie Murray	.10	.08	.04
143	Jimmy Key	.10	.08	.04
144	Dale Mohoric	.05	.04	.02
145	Jose Lind	.15	.11	.06
146	Dennis Martinez	.05	.04	.02
147	Chet Lemon	.07	.05	.03
148	Orel Hershiser	.20	.15	.08
149	Dave Martinez	.07	.05	.03
150	Billy Hatcher	.07	.05	.03
151	Charlie Leibrandt	.07	.05	.03
152	Keith Hernandez	.10	.08	.04
153	Kevin McReynolds	.12	.09	.05
154	Tony Gwynn	.30	.25	.12
155	Stan Javier	.05	.04	.02
156	Tony Pena	.07	.05	.03
157	Andy Van Slyke	.10	.08	.04
158	Gene Larkin	.07	.05	.03

		MT	NR MT	EX
159	Chris James	.10	.08	.04
160	Fred McGriff	.50	.40	.20
161	Rick Rhoden	.07	.05	.03
162	Scott Garrelts	.05	.04	.02
163	Mike Campbell	.12	.09	.05
164	Dave Righetti	.12	.09	.05
165	Paul Molitor	.15	.11	.06
166	Danny Jackson	.10	.08	.04
167	Pete O'Brien	.07	.05	.03
168	Julio Franco	.10	.08	.04
169	Mark McGwire	1.00	.70	.40
170	Zane Smith	.07	.05	.03
171	Johnny Ray	.07	.05	.03
172	Lester Lancaster	.07	.05	.03
173	Mel Hall	.05	.04	.02
174	Tracy Jones	.12	.09	.05
175	Kevin Seitzer	.35	.25	.14
176	Bob Knepper	.07	.05	.03
177	Mike Greenwell	.60	.45	.25
178	Mike Marshall	.10	.08	.04
179	Melido Perez	.15	.11	.06
180	Tim Raines	.30	.25	.12
181	Jack Morris	.12	.09	.05
182	Darryl Strawberry	.60	.45	.25
183	Robin Yount	.35	.25	.14
184	Lance Parrish	.15	.11	.06
185	Darnell Coles	.07	.05	.03
186	Kirby Puckett	.40	.30	.15
187	Terry Pendleton	.07	.05	.03
188	Don Slaught	.05	.04	.02
189	Jimmy Jones	.07	.05	.03
190	Dave Parker	.12	.09	.05
191	Mike Aldrete	.07	.05	.03
192	Mike Moore	.05	.04	.02
193	Greg Walker	.07	.05	.03
194	Calvin Schiraldi	.07	.05	.03
195	Dick Schofield	.05	.04	.02
196	Jody Reed	.25	.20	.10
197	Pete Smith	.10	.08	.04
198	Cal Ripken	.30	.25	.12
199	Lloyd Moseby	.07	.05	.03
200	Ruben Sierra	.25	.20	.10
201	R.J. Reynolds	.07	.05	.03
202	Bryn Smith	.05	.04	.02
203	Gary Pettis	.05	.04	.02
204	Steve Sax	.12	.09	.05
205	Frank DiPino	.05	.04	.02
206	Mike Scott	.12	.09	.05
207	Kurt Stillwell	.12	.09	.05
208	Mookie Wilson	.07	.05	.03
209	Lee Mazzilli	.05	.04	.02
210	Lance McCullers	.07	.05	.03
211	Rick Honeycutt	.05	.04	.02
212	John Tudor	.10	.08	.04
213	Jim Gott	.05	.04	.02
214	Frank Viola	.12	.09	.05
215	Juan Samuel	.10	.08	.04
216	Jesse Barfield	.12	.09	.05
217	Claudell Washington	.05	.04	.02
218	Rick Reuschel	.07	.05	.03
219	Jim Presley	.10	.08	.04
220	Tommy John	.12	.09	.05
221	Dan Plesac	.10	.08	.04
222	Barry Larkin	.20	.15	.08
223	Mike Stanley	.07	.05	.03
224	Cory Snyder	.25	.20	.10
225	Andre Dawson	.20	.15	.08
226	Ken Oberkfell	.05	.04	.02
227	Devon White	.20	.15	.08
228	Jamie Moyer	.05	.04	.02
229	Brook Jacoby	.10	.08	.04
230	Rob Murphy	.10	.08	.04
231	Bret Saberhagen	.20	.15	.08
232	Nolan Ryan	.50	.40	.20
233	Bruce Hurst	.10	.08	.04
234	Jesse Orosco	.07	.05	.03
235	Bobby Thigpen	.07	.05	.03
236	Pascual Perez	.05	.04	.02
237	Matt Nokes	.20	.15	.08
238	Bob Ojeda	.07	.05	.03
239	Joey Meyer	.07	.05	.03
240	Shane Rawley	.07	.05	.03
241	Jeff Robinson	.07	.05	.03
242	Jeff Reardon	.10	.08	.04
243	Ozzie Smith	.15	.11	.06
244	Dave Winfield	.30	.25	.12
245	John Kruk	.12	.09	.05
246	Carney Lansford	.07	.05	.03
247	Candy Maldonado	.07	.05	.03
248	Ken Phelps	.05	.04	.02
249	Ken Williams	.10	.08	.04
250	Al Nipper	.05	.04	.02
251	Mark McLemore	.05	.04	.02
252	Lee Smith	.07	.05	.03
253	Albert Hall	.05	.04	.02
254	Billy Ripken	.15	.11	.06
255	Kelly Gruber	.05	.04	.02
256	Charlie Hough	.07	.05	.03
257	John Smiley	.07	.05	.03
258	Tim Wallach	.10	.08	.04
259	Frank Tanana	.07	.05	.03
260	Mike Scioscia	.05	.04	.02
261	Damon Berryhill	.10	.08	.04
262	Dave Smith	.07	.05	.03
263	Willie Wilson	.10	.08	.04
264	Len Dykstra	.07	.05	.03
265	Randy Myers	.10	.08	.04
266	Keith Moreland	.07	.05	.03
267	Eric Plunk	.05	.04	.02
268	Todd Worrell	.10	.08	.04
269	Bob Walk	.05	.04	.02
270	Keith Atherton	.05	.04	.02
271	Mike Schmidt	.40	.30	.15
272	Mike Flanagan	.07	.05	.03
273	Rafael Santana	.05	.04	.02
274	Rob Thompson	.10	.08	.04
275	Rey Quinones	.05	.04	.02
276	Cecilio Guante	.05	.04	.02
277	B.J. Surhoff	.15	.11	.06
278	Chris Sabo	.80	.60	.30
279	Mitch Williams	.07	.05	.03
280	Greg Swindell	.10	.08	.04
281	Alan Trammell	.20	.15	.08
282	Storm Davis	.07	.05	.03

		MT	NR MT	EX
283	Chuck Finley	.05	.04	.02
284	Dave Stieb	.10	.08	.04
285	Scott Bailes	.05	.04	.02
286	Larry Sheets	.07	.05	.03
287	Danny Tartabull	.20	.15	.08
288	Checklist	.05	.04	.02
289	Todd Benzinger	.15	.11	.06
290	John Shelby	.05	.04	.02
291	Steve Lyons	.05	.04	.02
292	Mitch Webster	.05	.04	.02
293	Walt Terrell	.05	.04	.02
294	Pete Stanicek	.12	.09	.05
295	Chris Bosio	.05	.04	.02
296	Milt Thompson	.07	.05	.03
297	Fred Lynn	.12	.09	.05
298	Juan Berenguer	.05	.04	.02
299	Ken Dayley	.05	.04	.02
300	Joel Skinner	.05	.04	.02
301	Benito Santiago	.30	.25	.12
302	Ron Hassey	.05	.04	.02
303	Jose Uribe	.05	.04	.02
304	Harold Reynolds	.07	.05	.03
305	Dale Sveum	.07	.05	.03
306	Glenn Wilson	.05	.04	.02
307	Mike Witt	.07	.05	.03
308	Ron Robinson	.05	.04	.02
309	Denny Walling	.05	.04	.02
310	Joe Orsulak	.05	.04	.02
311	David Wells	.10	.08	.04
312	Steve Buechele	.05	.04	.02
313	Jose Oquendo	.05	.04	.02
314	Floyd Youmans	.07	.05	.03
315	Lou Whitaker	.12	.09	.05
316	Fernando Valenzuela	.12	.09	.05
317	Mike Boddicker	.07	.05	.03
318	Gerald Young	.15	.11	.06
319	Frank White	.07	.05	.03
320	Bill Wegman	.05	.04	.02
321	Tom Niedenfuer	.05	.04	.02
322	Ed Whitson	.05	.04	.02
323	Curt Young	.05	.04	.02
324	Greg Mathews	.10	.08	.04
325	Doug Jones	.07	.05	.03
326	Tommy Herr	.07	.05	.03
327	Kent Tekulve	.07	.05	.03
328	Rance Mulliniks	.05	.04	.02
329	Checklist	.05	.04	.02
330	Craig Lefferts	.05	.04	.02
331	Franklin Stubbs	.07	.05	.03
332	Rick Cerone	.05	.04	.02
333	Dave Schmidt	.05	.04	.02
334	Larry Parrish	.07	.05	.03
335	Tom Browning	.07	.05	.03
336	Checklist	.05	.04	.02

1988 Donruss Diamond Kings Supers

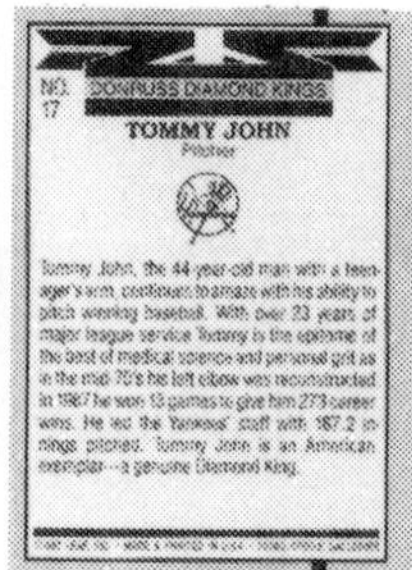

This 28-card set (including the checklist) marks the fourth edition of Donruss' super-size (5"x7") set. These cards, exact duplicates of the 1988 Diamond Kings that feature player portraits by Dick Perez, have a red, blue and black striped border. A gold Diamond Kings banner curves above the player portrait and a matching oval name banner is printed below. Each card features a large player closeup and a smaller full-figure inset on a split background that is white at the top and striped with multi-colors on the lower portion. Card backs are black and white with a blue border and contain the card number, DK logo, player name, team logo and a paragraph style career summary. A 12-piece Stan Musial puzzle was also included with the purchase of the super-size set which was marketed via a mail-in offer printed on Donruss wrappers.

		MT	NR MT	EX
Complete Set:		10.00	7.50	4.00
Common Player:		.20	.15	.08
1	Mark McGwire	1.25	.90	.50
2	Tim Raines	.30	.25	.12
3	Benito Santiago	.30	.25	.12
4	Alan Trammell	.30	.25	.12
5	Danny Tartabull	.35	.25	.14
6	Ron Darling	.30	.25	.12
7	Paul Molitor	.30	.25	.12
8	Devon White	.35	.25	.14
9	Andre Dawson	.30	.25	.12
10	Julio Franco	.25	.20	.10
11	Scott Fletcher	.20	.15	.08
12	Tony Fernandez	.30	.25	.12
13	Shane Rawley	.20	.15	.08
14	Kal Daniels	.30	.25	.12

		MT	NR MT	EX
15	Jack Clark	.30	.25	.12
16	Dwight Evans	.25	.20	.10
17	Tommy John	.25	.20	.10
18	Andy Van Slyke	.25	.20	.10
19	Gary Gaetti	.30	.25	.12
20	Mark Langston	.35	.25	.14
21	Will Clark	1.50	1.25	.60
22	Glenn Hubbard	.20	.15	.08
23	Billy Hatcher	.20	.15	.08
24	Bob Welch	.20	.15	.08
25	Ivan Calderon	.20	.15	.08
26	Cal Ripken, Jr.	.60	.45	.25
27	Checklist	.20	.15	.08
641	Stan Musial Puzzle Card	.20	.15	.08

1988 Donruss MVP

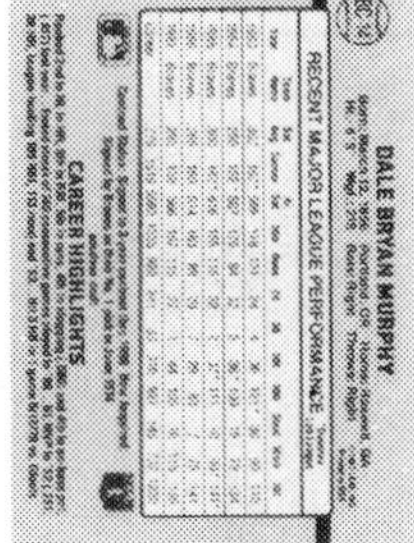

This 26-card set of standard-size player cards replaced the Donruss box-bottom cards in 1988. Instead of box-bottoms, the bonus cards (numbered BC-1 through BC-26) were randomly inserted in Donruss wax or rack packs. Cards feature the company's choice of Most Valuable Player for each major league team and are titled "Donruss MVP." The MVP cards were not included in the factory-collated sets. Card fronts carry the same basic red-blue-black flowing border design as the 1988 Donruss basic 660-card issue (with the exception of the Donruss MVP logo). Card backs are the same as the regular issue, except for the numbering system.

		MT	NR MT	EX
Complete Set:		8.00	6.00	3.25
Common Player:		.15	.11	.06
1	Cal Ripken	.30	.25	.12
2	Eric Davis	.50	.40	.20
3	Paul Molitor	.20	.15	.08
4	Mike Schmidt	.35	.25	.14
5	Ivan Calderon	.15	.11	.06
6	Tony Gwynn	.30	.25	.12
7	Wade Boggs	.75	.55	.30
8	Andy Van Slyke	.15	.11	.06
9	Joe Carter	.25	.20	.10
10	Andre Dawson	.25	.20	.10
11	Alan Trammell	.25	.20	.10
12	Mike Scott	.15	.11	.06
13	Wally Joyner	.25	.20	.10
14	Dale Murphy	.35	.25	.14
15	Kirby Puckett	.50	.40	.30
16	Pedro Guerrero	.20	.15	.08
17	Kevin Seitzer	.50	.40	.30
18	Tim Raines	.25	.20	.10
19	George Bell	.25	.20	.10
20	Darryl Strawberry	.50	.40	.30
21	Don Mattingly	1.50	1.25	.60
22	Ozzie Smith	.20	.15	.08
23	Mark McGwire	1.00	.70	.40
24	Will Clark	.90	.70	.35
25	Alvin Davis	.15	.11	.06
26	Ruben Sierra	.35	.25	.14

1988 Donruss Pop-Ups

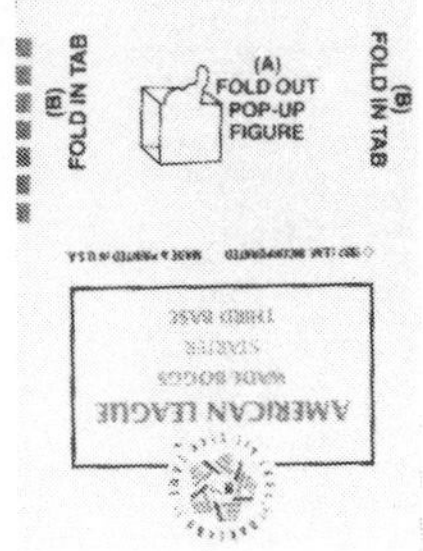

Donruss introduced its Pop-Up cards in 1986. The first two annual issues featured 2-1/2" x 5" cards. In 1988, Donruss reduced the size of the Pop-Ups cards to a standard 2-1/2"x 3-1/2". The 1988 set includes 20 cards that fold out so that the upper portion of the player stands upright, giving a three-dimensional effect. Pop-ups feature players from the All-Star Game starting lineup. Card fronts feature full-color photos, with the player's name, team and position printed in black on a yellow banner near the bottom of the card front. As in previous issues, the card backs contain only the player's name, league and position. Pop-Ups were distributed in individual packages containing one Pop-Up, three puzzle pieces and three All-Star cards.

		MT	NR MT	EX
Complete Set:		4.00	3.00	1.50
Common Player:		.15	.11	.06
(1)	George Bell	.20	.15	.08
(2)	Wade Boggs	.75	.55	.30
(3)	Gary Carter	.20	.15	.08
(4)	Jack Clark	.20	.15	.08
(5)	Eric Davis	.50	.40	.20
(6)	Andre Dawson	.20	.15	.08
(7)	Rickey Henderson	.50	.40	.20
(8)	Davey Johnson	.15	.11	.06
(9)	Don Mattingly	1.00	.70	.40
(10)	Terry Kennedy	.15	.11	.06
(11)	John McNamara	.15	.11	.06
(12)	Willie Randolph	.15	.11	.06
(13)	Cal Ripken, Jr.	.50	.40	.20
(14)	Bret Saberhagen	.35	.25	.14
(15)	Ryne Sandberg	.40	.30	.15
(16)	Mike Schmidt	.60	.45	.25
(17)	Mike Scott	.15	.11	.06
(18)	Ozzie Smith	.20	.15	.08
(19)	Darryl Strawberry	.50	.40	.20
(20)	Dave Winfield	.25	.20	.10

1988 Donruss Rookies

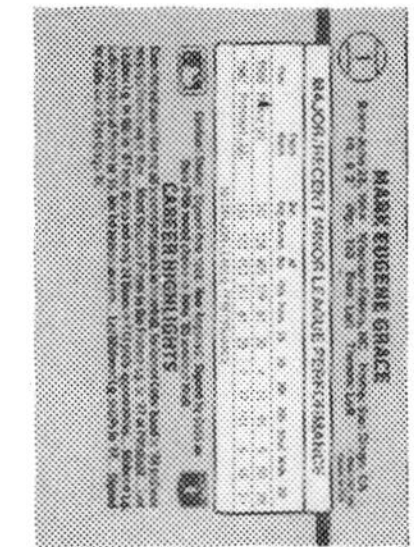

For the third consecutive year, Donruss issued this 56-card boxed set highlighting current rookies. The complete set includes a checklist and a 15-piece Stan Musial Diamond Kings puzzle. As in previous years, the set is similar to the company's basic issue, with the exception of the logo and border color. Card fronts feature red, green and black-striped borders, with a red-and-white player name printed in the lower left corner beneath the full-color photo. "The Rookies" logo is printed in red, white and black in the lower right corner. The card backs are printed in black on bright aqua and include personal data, recent performance stats and major league totals, as well as 1984-88 year-by-year minor league stats. The cards are the standard 2-1/2" by 3-1/2" size.

		MT	NR MT	EX
Complete Set:		12.00	9.00	4.75
Common Player:		.10	.08	.04
1	Mark Grace	6.00	4.50	2.50
2	Mike Campbell	.10	.08	.04
3	Todd Frowirth(FC)	.20	.15	.08
4	Dave Stapleton	.10	.08	.04
5	Shawn Abner	.15	.11	.06
6	Jose Cecena(FC)	.25	.20	.10
7	Dave Gallagher(FC)	.25	.20	.10
8	Mark Parent(FC)	.25	.20	.10
9	Cecil Espy(FC)	.15	.11	.06
10	Pete Smith	.10	.08	.04
11	Jay Buhner	.20	.15	.08
12	Pat Borders(FC)	.30	.25	.12
13	Doug Jennings(FC)	.25	.20	.10
14	Brady Anderson(FC)	.40	.30	.15
15	Pete Stanicek	.15	.11	.06
16	Roberto Kelly	.40	.30	.15
17	Jeff Treadway	.15	.11	.06
18	Walt Weiss(FC)	.90	.70	.35
19	Paul Gibson(FC)	.20	.15	.08
20	Tim Crews	.10	.08	.04
21	Melido Perez	.15	.11	.06
22	Steve Peters(FC)	.20	.15	.08
23	Craig Worthington(FC)	.70	.50	.30
24	John Trautwein(FC)	.15	.11	.06
25	DeWayne Vaughn(FC)	.15	.11	.06
26	David Wells	.10	.08	.04
27	Al Leiter	.30	.25	.12
28	Tim Belcher	.20	.15	.08
29	Johnny Paredes(FC)	.20	.15	.08
30	Chris Sabo(FC)	1.75	1.25	.70
31	Damon Berryhill	.25	.20	.10
32	Randy Milligan(FC)	.20	.15	.08
33	Gary Thurman	.20	.15	.08
34	Kevin Elster	.20	.15	.08
35	Roberto Alomar	.80	.60	.30
36	Edgar Martinez(FC)	.80	.60	.30
37	Todd Stottlemyre	.15	.11	.06
38	Joey Meyer	.15	.11	.06
39	Carl Nichols	.10	.08	.04
40	Jack McDowell	.15	.11	.06
41	Jose Bautista(FC)	.20	.15	.08
42	Sil Campusano(FC)	.25	.20	.10
43	John Dopson(FC)	.20	.15	.08
44	Jody Reed	.35	.25	.14
45	Darrin Jackson(FC)	.20	.15	.08
46	Mike Capel(FC)	.20	.15	.08
47	Ron Gant	.20	.15	.08
48	John Davis	.10	.08	.04
49	Kevin Coffman(FC)	.15	.11	.06
50	Cris Carpenter(FC)	.35	.25	.14
51	Mackey Sasser	.10	.08	.04
52	Luis Alicea(FC)	.25	.20	.10
53	Bryan Harvey(FC)	.30	.25	.12
54	Steve Ellsworth(FC)	.15	.11	.06
55	Mike Macfarlane(FC)	.25	.20	.10
56	Checklist 1-56	.10	.08	.04

1989 Donruss

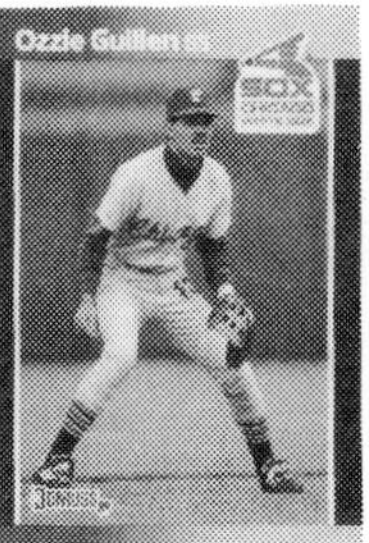

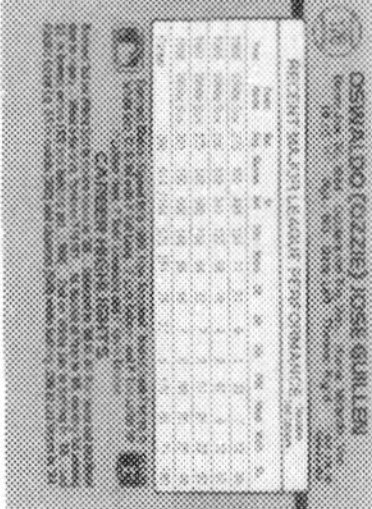

This basic annual issue consists of 660 standard- size (2-1/2" by 3-1/2") cards, including 26 Diamond Kings portrait cards and 20 Rated Rookies cards. Top and bottom borders of the cards are printed in a variety of colors that fade from dark to light (i.e. dark blue to light purple, bright red to pale yellow). A white-lettered player name is printed across the top margin. The team logo appears upper right and the Donruss logo lower left. A black stripe and thin white line make up the vertical side borders. The black outer stripe has a special varnish that gives a faintly visible filmstrip texture to the border. The backs (horizontal format) are printed in orange and black, similar to the 1988 design, with personal info, recent stats and major league totals. Team logo sticker cards (22 total) and Warren Spahn puzzle cards (63 total) are included in individual wax packs of cards.

		MT	NR MT	EX
Complete Set:		25.00	20.00	10.00
Common Player:		.04	.03	.02
1	Mike Greenwell (DK)	.40	.30	.15
2	Bobby Bonilla (DK)	.12	.09	.05
3	Pete Incaviglia (DK)	.12	.09	.05
4	Chris Sabo (DK)	.25	.20	.10
5	Robin Yount (DK)	.25	.20	.10
6	Tony Gwynn (DK)	.35	.25	.14
7	Carlton Fisk (DK)	.12	.09	.05
8	Cory Snyder (DK)	.15	.11	.06
9	David Cone (DK)	.35	.25	.14
10	Kevin Seitzer (DK)	.25	.20	.10
11	Rick Reuschel (DK)	.10	.08	.04
12	Johnny Ray (DK)	.10	.08	.04
13	Dave Schmidt (DK)	.08	.06	.03
14	Andres Galarraga (DK)	.15	.11	.06
15	Kirk Gibson (DK)	.20	.15	.08
16	Fred McGriff (DK)	.25	.20	.10
17	Mark Grace (DK)	1.25	.90	.50
18	Jeff Robinson (DK)	.12	.09	.05
19	Vince Coleman (DK)	.20	.15	.08
20	Dave Henderson (DK)	.10	.08	.04
21	Harold Reynolds (DK)	.08	.06	.03
22	Gerald Perry (DK)	.10	.08	.04
23	Frank Viola (DK)	.15	.11	.06
24	Steve Bedrosian (DK)	.10	.08	.04
25	Glenn Davis (DK)	.15	.11	.06
26	Don Mattingly (DK)	1.25	.90	.50
27	Checklist 1-27	.04	.03	.02
28	*Sandy Alomar, Jr.* (RR)(FC)	1.75	1.25	.70
29	*Steve Searcy* (RR)(FC)	.20	.15	.08
30	*Cameron Drew* (RR)(FC)	.20	.15	.08
31	*Gary Sheffield* (RR)(FC)	1.75	1.25	.70
32	*Erik Hanson* (RR)(FC)	.35	.25	.14
33	*Ken Griffey, Jr.* (RR)(FC)	8.00	6.00	3.25
34	*Greg Harris* (RR)(FC)	.30	.25	.12
35	*Gregg Jefferies* (RR)	1.75	1.25	.70
36	*Luis Medina* (RR)(FC)	.30	.25	.12
37	*Carlos Quintana* (RR)	.50	.40	.20
38	*Felix Jose* (RR)(FC)	.30	.25	.12
39	*Cris Carpenter* (RR)(FC)	.35	.25	.14
40	*Ron Jones* (RR)(FC)	.35	.25	.14
41	*Dave West* (RR)(FC)	.60	.45	.25

		MT	NR MT	EX
42	*Randy Johnson* (RR)(FC)	.40	.30	.15
43	*Mike Harkey* (RR)(FC)	.40	.30	.15
44	*Pete Harnisch* (RR)(FC)	.30	.25	.12
45	*Tom Gordon* (RR)(FC)	1.00	.70	.40
46	*Gregg Olson* (RR)(FC)	1.25	.90	.50
47	*Alex Sanchez* (RR)(FC)	.25	.20	.10
48	Ruben Sierra	.50	.40	.20
49	Rafael Palmeiro	.25	.20	.10
50	Ron Gant	.10	.08	.04
51	Cal Ripken, Jr.	.30	.25	.12
52	Wally Joyner	.20	.15	.08
53	Gary Carter	.20	.15	.08
54	Andy Van Slyke	.12	.09	.05
55	Robin Yount	.25	.20	.10
56	Pete Incaviglia	.10	.08	.04
57	Greg Brock	.06	.05	.02
58	Melido Perez	.08	.06	.03
59	Craig Lefferts	.04	.03	.02
60	Gary Pettis	.04	.03	.02
61	Danny Tartabull	.15	.11	.06
62	Guillermo Hernandez	.06	.05	.02
63	Ozzie Smith	.12	.09	.05
64	Gary Gaetti	.12	.09	.05
65	Mark Davis	.04	.03	.02
66	Lee Smith	.08	.06	.03
67	Dennis Eckersley	.10	.08	.04
68	Wade Boggs	.90	.70	.35
69	Mike Scott	.10	.08	.04
70	Fred McGriff	.50	.40	.20
71	Tom Browning	.08	.06	.03
72	Claudell Washington	.06	.05	.02
73	Mel Hall	.06	.05	.02
74	Don Mattingly	1.00	.70	.40
75	Steve Bedrosian	.08	.06	.03
76	Juan Samuel	.10	.08	.04
77	Mike Scioscia	.06	.05	.02
78	Dave Righetti	.12	.09	.05
79	Alfredo Griffin	.06	.05	.02
80	Eric Davis	.40	.30	.15
81	Juan Berenguer	.04	.03	.02
82	Todd Worrell	.08	.06	.03
83	Joe Carter	.12	.09	.05
84	Steve Sax	.12	.09	.05
85	Frank White	.06	.05	.02
86	John Kruk	.06	.05	.02
87	Rance Mulliniks	.04	.03	.02
88	Alan Ashby	.04	.03	.02
89	Charlie Leibrandt	.06	.05	.02
90	Frank Tanana	.06	.05	.02
91	Jose Canseco	1.50	1.25	.60
92	Barry Bonds	.12	.09	.05
93	Harold Reynolds	.06	.05	.02
94	Mark McLemore	.04	.03	.02
95	Mark McGwire	.60	.45	.25
96	Eddie Murray	.25	.20	.10
97	Tim Raines	.25	.20	.10
98	Rob Thompson	.06	.05	.02
99	Kevin McReynolds	.12	.09	.05
100	Checklist 28-137	.04	.03	.02
101	Carlton Fisk	.20	.15	.08
102	Dave Martinez	.06	.05	.02
103	Glenn Braggs	.06	.05	.02
104	Dale Murphy	.30	.25	.12
105	Ryne Sandberg	.25	.20	.10
106	Dennis Martinez	.06	.05	.02
107	Pete O'Brien	.06	.05	.02
108	Dick Schofield	.04	.03	.02
109	Henry Cotto	.04	.03	.02
110	Mike Marshall	.12	.09	.05
111	Keith Moreland	.06	.05	.02
112	Tom Brunansky	.10	.08	.04
113	Kelly Gruber	.04	.03	.02
114	Brook Jacoby	.08	.06	.03
115	*Keith Brown*(FC)	.20	.15	.08
116	Matt Nokes	.15	.11	.06
117	Keith Hernandez	.20	.15	.08
118	Bob Forsch	.06	.05	.02
119	Bert Blyleven	.10	.08	.04
120	Willie Wilson	.08	.06	.03
121	Tommy Gregg	.08	.06	.03
122	Jim Rice	.25	.20	.10
123	Bob Knepper	.06	.05	.02
124	Danny Jackson	.12	.09	.05
125	Eric Plunk	.04	.03	.02
126	Brian Fisher	.06	.05	.02
127	Mike Pagliarulo	.08	.06	.03
128	Tony Gwynn	.30	.25	.12
129	Lance McCullers	.06	.05	.02
130	Andres Galarraga	.15	.11	.06
131	Jose Uribe	.04	.03	.02
132	Kirk Gibson	.20	.15	.08
133	David Palmer	.04	.03	.02
134	R.J. Reynolds	.04	.03	.02
135	Greg Walker	.06	.05	.02
136	Kirk McCaskill	.06	.05	.02
137	Shawon Dunston	.08	.06	.03
138	Andy Allanson	.04	.03	.02
139	Rob Murphy	.04	.03	.02
140	Mike Aldrete	.06	.05	.02
141	Terry Kennedy	.06	.05	.02
142	Scott Fletcher	.06	.05	.02
143	Steve Balboni	.06	.05	.02
144	Bret Saberhagen	.12	.09	.05
145	Ozzie Virgil	.04	.03	.02
146	Dale Sveum	.06	.05	.02
147	Darryl Strawberry	.35	.25	.14
148	Harold Baines	.10	.08	.04
149	George Bell	.25	.20	.10
150	Dave Parker	.12	.09	.05
151	Bobby Bonilla	.12	.09	.05
152	Mookie Wilson	.06	.05	.02
153	Ted Power	.04	.03	.02
154	Nolan Ryan	.35	.25	.14
155	Jeff Reardon	.08	.06	.03
156	Tim Wallach	.08	.06	.03
157	Jamie Moyer	.04	.03	.02
158	Rich Gossage	.10	.08	.04
159	Dave Winfield	.25	.20	.10
160	Von Hayes	.08	.06	.03
161	Willie McGee	.10	.08	.04
162	Rich Gedman	.06	.05	.02
163	Tony Pena	.06	.05	.02
164	Mike Morgan	.04	.03	.02

		MT	NR MT	EX
165	Charlie Hough	.06	.05	.02
166	Mike Stanley	.04	.03	.02
167	Andre Dawson	.20	.15	.08
168	Joe Boever(FC)	.04	.03	.02
169	Pete Stanicek	.08	.06	.03
170	Bob Boone	.06	.05	.02
171	Ron Darling	.10	.08	.04
172	Bob Walk	.04	.03	.02
173	Rob Deer	.06	.05	.02
174	Steve Buechele	.04	.03	.02
175	Ted Higuera	.08	.06	.03
176	Ozzie Guillen	.06	.05	.02
177	Candy Maldonado	.06	.05	.02
178	Doyle Alexander	.06	.05	.02
179	Mark Gubicza	.10	.08	.04
180	Alan Trammell	.15	.11	.06
181	Vince Coleman	.15	.11	.06
182	Kirby Puckett	.30	.25	.12
183	Chris Brown	.06	.05	.02
184	Marty Barrett	.06	.05	.02
185	Stan Javier	.04	.03	.02
186	Mike Greenwell	.60	.45	.25
187	Billy Hatcher	.06	.05	.02
188	Jimmy Key	.08	.06	.03
189	Nick Esasky	.06	.05	.02
190	Don Slaught	.04	.03	.02
191	Cory Snyder	.15	.11	.06
192	John Candelaria	.06	.05	.02
193	Mike Schmidt	.40	.30	.15
194	Kevin Gross	.06	.05	.02
195	John Tudor	.08	.06	.03
196	Neil Allen	.04	.03	.02
197	Orel Hershiser	.25	.20	.10
198	Kal Daniels	.15	.11	.06
199	Kent Hrbek	.15	.11	.06
200	Checklist 138-247	.04	.03	.02
201	Joe Magrane	.08	.06	.03
202	Scott Bailes	.04	.03	.02
203	Tim Belcher	.10	.08	.04
204	George Brett	.30	.25	.12
205	Benito Santiago	.12	.09	.05
206	Tony Fernandez	.10	.08	.04
207	Gerald Young	.10	.08	.04
208	Bo Jackson	.80	.60	.30
209	Chet Lemon	.06	.05	.02
210	Storm Davis	.08	.06	.03
211	Doug Drabek	.06	.05	.02
212	Mickey Brantley (photo actually Nelson Simmons)	.04	.03	.02
213	Devon White	.10	.08	.04
214	Dave Stewart	.08	.06	.03
215	Dave Schmidt	.04	.03	.02
216	Bryn Smith	.04	.03	.02
217	Brett Butler	.06	.05	.02
218	Bob Ojeda	.06	.05	.02
219	*Steve Rosenberg*(FC)	.20	.15	.08
220	Hubie Brooks	.08	.06	.03
221	B.J. Surhoff	.08	.06	.03
222	Rick Mahler	.04	.03	.02
223	Rick Sutcliffe	.08	.06	.03
224	Neal Heaton	.04	.03	.02
225	Mitch Williams	.06	.05	.02
226	Chuck Finley	.08	.06	.03
227	Mark Langston	.10	.08	.04
228	Jesse Orosco	.06	.05	.02
229	Ed Whitson	.04	.03	.02
230	Terry Pendleton	.08	.06	.03
231	Lloyd Moseby	.06	.05	.02
232	Greg Swindell	.10	.08	.04
233	John Franco	.08	.06	.03
234	Jack Morris	.15	.11	.06
235	Howard Johnson	.08	.06	.03
236	Glenn Davis	.12	.09	.05
237	Frank Viola	.12	.09	.05
238	Kevin Seitzer	.25	.20	.10
239	Gerald Perry	.08	.06	.03
240	Dwight Evans	.10	.08	.04
241	Jim Deshaies	.04	.03	.02
242	Bo Diaz	.06	.05	.02
243	Carney Lansford	.06	.05	.02
244	Mike LaValliere	.06	.05	.02
245	Rickey Henderson	.35	.25	.14
246	Roberto Alomar	.25	.20	.10
247	Jimmy Jones	.04	.03	.02
248	Pascual Perez	.06	.05	.02
249	Will Clark	.80	.60	.30
250	Fernando Valenzuela	.15	.11	.06
251	Shane Rawley	.06	.05	.02
252	Sid Bream	.06	.05	.02
253	Steve Lyons	.04	.03	.02
254	Brian Downing	.06	.05	.02
255	Mark Grace	1.50	1.25	.60
256	Tom Candiotti	.04	.03	.02
257	Barry Larkin	.20	.15	.08
258	Mike Krukow	.06	.05	.02
259	Billy Ripken	.06	.05	.02
260	Cecilio Guante	.04	.03	.02
261	Scott Bradley	.04	.03	.02
262	Floyd Bannister	.06	.05	.02
263	Pete Smith	.08	.06	.03
264	Jim Gantner	.04	.03	.02
265	Roger McDowell	.08	.06	.03
266	Bobby Thigpen	.08	.06	.03
267	Jim Clancy	.06	.05	.02
268	Terry Steinbach	.08	.06	.03
269	Mike Dunne	.08	.06	.03
270	Dwight Gooden	.50	.40	.20
271	Mike Heath	.04	.03	.02
272	Dave Smith	.06	.05	.02
273	Keith Atherton	.04	.03	.02
274	Tim Burke	.04	.03	.02
275	Damon Berryhill	.12	.09	.05
276	Vance Law	.06	.05	.02
277	Rich Dotson	.06	.05	.02
278	Lance Parrish	.15	.11	.06
279	Denny Walling	.04	.03	.02
280	Roger Clemens	.50	.40	.20
281	Greg Mathews	.06	.05	.02
282	Tom Niedenfuer	.06	.05	.02
283	Paul Kilgus	.10	.08	.04
284	Jose Guzman	.08	.06	.03
285	Calvin Schiraldi	.04	.03	.02
286	Charlie Puleo	.04	.03	.02

		MT	NR MT	EX
287	Joe Orsulak	.04	.03	.02
288	Jack Howell	.06	.05	.02
289	Kevin Elster	.08	.06	.03
290	Jose Lind	.10	.08	.04
291	Paul Molitor	.12	.09	.05
292	Cecil Espy	.08	.06	.03
293	Bill Wegman	.04	.03	.02
294	Dan Pasqua	.08	.06	.03
295	Scott Garrelts	.04	.03	.02
296	Walt Terrell	.06	.05	.02
297	Ed Hearn	.04	.03	.02
298	Lou Whitaker	.20	.15	.08
299	Ken Dayley	.04	.03	.02
300	Checklist 248-357	.04	.03	.02
301	Tommy Herr	.06	.05	.02
302	Mike Brumley	.06	.05	.02
303	Ellis Burks	.60	.45	.25
304	Curt Young	.06	.05	.02
305	Jody Reed	.10	.08	.04
306	Bill Doran	.06	.05	.02
307	David Wells	.06	.05	.02
308	Ron Robinson	.04	.03	.02
309	Rafael Santana	.04	.03	.02
310	Julio Franco	.10	.08	.04
311	Jack Clark	.15	.11	.06
312	Chris James	.08	.06	.03
313	Milt Thompson	.04	.03	.02
314	John Shelby	.04	.03	.02
315	Al Leiter	.15	.11	.06
316	Mike Davis	.06	.05	.02
317	*Chris Sabo*	.50	.40	.20
318	Greg Gagne	.04	.03	.02
319	Jose Oquendo	.04	.03	.02
320	John Farrell	.10	.08	.04
321	Franklin Stubbs	.04	.03	.02
322	Kurt Stillwell	.06	.05	.02
323	Shawn Abner	.10	.08	.04
324	Mike Flanagan	.06	.05	.02
325	Kevin Bass	.06	.05	.02
326	Pat Tabler	.06	.05	.02
327	Mike Henneman	.08	.06	.03
328	Rick Honeycutt	.04	.03	.02
329	John Smiley	.10	.08	.04
330	Rey Quinones	.04	.03	.02
331	Johnny Ray	.06	.05	.02
332	Bob Welch	.08	.06	.03
333	Larry Sheets	.06	.05	.02
334	Jeff Parrett	.08	.06	.03
335	Rick Reuschel	.08	.06	.03
336	Randy Myers	.10	.08	.04
337	Ken Williams	.06	.05	.02
338	Andy McGaffigan	.04	.03	.02
339	Joey Meyer	.08	.06	.03
340	Dion James	.04	.03	.02
341	Les Lancaster	.06	.05	.02
342	Tom Foley	.04	.03	.02
343	Geno Petralli	.04	.03	.02
344	Dan Petry	.06	.05	.02
345	Alvin Davis	.12	.09	.05
346	Mickey Hatcher	.04	.03	.02
347	Marvell Wynne	.04	.03	.02
348	Danny Cox	.06	.05	.02
349	Dave Stieb	.08	.06	.03
350	Jay Bell	.06	.05	.02
351	Jeff Treadway	.10	.08	.04
352	Luis Salazar	.04	.03	.02
353	Lenny Dykstra	.08	.06	.03
354	Juan Agosto	.04	.03	.02
355	Gene Larkin	.10	.08	.04
356	Steve Farr	.04	.03	.02
357	Paul Assenmacher	.04	.03	.02
358	Todd Benzinger	.12	.09	.05
359	Larry Andersen	.04	.03	.02
360	Paul O'Neill	.04	.03	.02
361	Ron Hassey	.04	.03	.02
362	Jim Gott	.04	.03	.02
363	Ken Phelps	.06	.05	.02
364	Tim Flannery	.04	.03	.02
365	Randy Ready	.04	.03	.02
366	*Nelson Santovenia*(FC)	.30	.25	.12
367	Kelly Downs	.08	.06	.03
368	Danny Heep	.04	.03	.02
369	Phil Bradley	.08	.06	.03
370	Jeff Robinson	.06	.05	.02
371	Ivan Calderon	.06	.05	.02
372	Mike Witt	.06	.05	.02
373	Greg Maddux	.10	.08	.04
374	Carmen Castillo	.04	.03	.02
375	Jose Rijo	.06	.05	.02
376	Joe Price	.04	.03	.02
377	R.C. Gonzalez	.04	.03	.02
378	Oddibe McDowell	.06	.05	.02
379	Jim Presley	.06	.05	.02
380	Brad Wellman	.04	.03	.02
381	Tom Glavine	.10	.08	.04
382	Dan Plesac	.08	.06	.03
383	Wally Backman	.06	.05	.02
384	*Dave Gallagher*	.25	.20	.10
385	Tom Henke	.06	.05	.02
386	Luis Polonia	.06	.05	.02
387	Junior Ortiz	.04	.03	.02
388	David Cone	.35	.25	.14
389	Dave Bergman	.04	.03	.02
390	Danny Darwin	.04	.03	.02
391	Dan Gladden	.04	.03	.02
392	*John Dopson*	.25	.20	.10
393	Frank DiPino	.04	.03	.02
394	Al Nipper	.04	.03	.02
395	Willie Randolph	.06	.05	.02
396	Don Carman	.06	.05	.02
397	Scott Terry	.06	.05	.02
398	Rick Cerone	.04	.03	.02
399	Tom Pagnozzi	.06	.05	.02
400	Checklist 358-467	.04	.03	.02
401	Mickey Tettleton	.08	.06	.03
402	Curtis Wilkerson	.04	.03	.02
403	Jeff Russell	.04	.03	.02
404	Pat Perry	.04	.03	.02
405	*Jose Alvarez*(FC)	.15	.11	.06
406	Rick Schu	.04	.03	.02
407	*Sherman Corbett*(FC)	.15	.11	.06
408	Dave Magadan	.10	.08	.04
409	Bob Kipper	.04	.03	.02

		MT	NR MT	EX
410	Don August	.08	.06	.03
411	Bob Brower	.04	.03	.02
412	Chris Bosio	.04	.03	.02
413	Jerry Reuss	.06	.05	.02
414	Atlee Hammaker	.04	.03	.02
415	Jim Walewander(FC)	.06	.05	.02
416	*Mike Macfarlane*	.20	.15	.08
417	Pat Sheridan	.04	.03	.02
418	Pedro Guerrero	.15	.11	.06
419	Allan Anderson	.06	.05	.02
420	*Mark Parent*	.20	.15	.08
421	Bob Stanley	.04	.03	.02
422	Mike Gallego	.04	.03	.02
423	Bruce Hurst	.08	.06	.03
424	Dave Meads	.04	.03	.02
425	Jesse Barfield	.10	.08	.04
426	*Rob Dibble*(FC)	.40	.30	.15
427	Joel Skinner	.04	.03	.02
428	Ron Kittle	.06	.05	.02
429	Rick Rhoden	.08	.06	.03
430	Bob Dernier	.04	.03	.02
431	Steve Jeltz	.04	.03	.02
432	Rick Dempsey	.06	.05	.02
433	Roberto Kelly	.10	.08	.04
434	Dave Anderson	.04	.03	.02
435	Herm Winningham	.04	.03	.02
436	Al Newman	.04	.03	.02
437	Jose DeLeon	.06	.05	.02
438	Doug Jones	.10	.08	.04
439	Brian Holton	.06	.05	.02
440	Jeff Montgomery(FC)	.06	.05	.02
441	Dickie Thon	.04	.03	.02
442	Cecil Fielder	.04	.03	.02
443	*John Fishel*(FC)	.20	.15	.08
444	Jerry Don Gleaton	.04	.03	.02
445	*Paul Gibson*	.15	.11	.06
446	Walt Weiss	.40	.30	.15
447	Glenn Wilson	.06	.05	.02
448	Mike Moore	.04	.03	.02
449	Chili Davis	.06	.05	.02
450	Dave Henderson	.08	.06	.03
451	*Jose Bautista*	.20	.15	.08
452	Rex Hudler	.04	.03	.02
453	Bob Brenly	.04	.03	.02
454	Mackey Sasser	.06	.05	.02
455	Daryl Boston	.04	.03	.02
456	Mike Fitzgerald	.04	.03	.02
457	Jeffery Leonard	.06	.05	.02
458	Bruce Sutter	.08	.06	.03
459	Mitch Webster	.06	.05	.02
460	Joe Hesketh	.04	.03	.02
461	Bobby Witt	.08	.06	.03
462	Stew Cliburn	.04	.03	.02
463	Scott Bankhead	.04	.03	.02
464	*Ramon Martinez*(FC)	.50	.40	.20
465	Dave Leiper	.04	.03	.02
466	*Luis Alicea*	.20	.15	.08
467	John Cerutti	.06	.05	.02
468	Ron Washington	.04	.03	.02
469	Jeff Reed	.04	.03	.02
470	Jeff Robinson	.12	.09	.05
471	Sid Fernandez	.08	.06	.03
472	Terry Puhl	.04	.03	.02
473	Charlie Lea	.04	.03	.02
474	*Israel Sanchez*(FC)	.15	.11	.06
475	Bruce Benedict	.04	.03	.02
476	Oil Can Boyd	.06	.05	.02
477	Craig Reynolds	.04	.03	.02
478	Frank Williams	.04	.03	.02
479	Greg Cadaret	.10	.08	.04
480	*Randy Kramer*(FC)	.15	.11	.06
481	*Dave Eiland*(FC)	.20	.15	.08
482	Eric Show	.06	.05	.02
483	Garry Templeton	.06	.05	.02
484	Wallace Johnson(FC)	.04	.03	.02
485	Kevin Mitchell	.60	.45	.25
486	Tim Crews	.06	.05	.02
487	Mike Maddux	.04	.03	.02
488	Dave LaPoint	.06	.05	.02
489	Fred Manrique	.06	.05	.02
490	Greg Minton	.04	.03	.02
491	*Doug Dascenzo*(FC)	.25	.20	.10
492	Willie Upshaw	.06	.05	.02
493	*Jack Armstrong*(FC)	.90	.70	.35
494	Kirt Manwaring	.10	.08	.04
495	Jeff Ballard	.06	.05	.02
496	Jeff Kunkel	.04	.03	.02
497	Mike Campbell	.08	.06	.03
498	Gary Thurman	.10	.08	.04
499	Zane Smith	.06	.05	.02
500	Checklist 468-577	.04	.03	.02
501	Mike Birkbeck	.04	.03	.02
502	Terry Leach	.04	.03	.02
503	Shawn Hillegas	.06	.05	.02
504	Manny Lee	.04	.03	.02
505	*Doug Jennings*	.20	.15	.08
506	Ken Oberkfell	.04	.03	.02
507	Tim Teufel	.04	.03	.02
508	Tom Brookens	.04	.03	.02
509	Rafael Ramirez	.04	.03	.02
510	Fred Toliver	.04	.03	.02
511	*Brian Holman*(FC)	.40	.30	.15
512	Mike Bielecki	.04	.03	.02
513	*Jeff Pico*(FC)	.25	.20	.10
514	Charles Hudson	.04	.03	.02
515	Bruce Ruffin	.04	.03	.02
516	Larry McWilliams	.04	.03	.02
517	Jeff Sellers	.04	.03	.02
518	*John Costello*(FC)	.20	.15	.08
519	*Brady Anderson*	.35	.25	.14
520	Craig McMurtry	.04	.03	.02
521	Ray Hayward	.08	.06	.03
522	Drew Hall	.08	.06	.03
523	*Mark Lemke*(FC)	.20	.15	.08
524	*Oswald Peraza*(FC)	.20	.15	.08
525	*Bryan Harvey*	.25	.20	.10
526	Rick Aguilera	.04	.03	.02
527	Tom Prince	.06	.05	.02
528	Mark Clear	.04	.03	.02
529	Jerry Browne	.04	.03	.02
530	Juan Castillo	.04	.03	.02
531	Jack McDowell	.08	.06	.03
532	Chris Speier	.04	.03	.02
533	Darrell Evans	.08	.06	.03

		MT	NR MT	EX
534	Luis Aquino	.04	.03	.02
535	Eric King	.04	.03	.02
536	*Ken Hill*(FC)	.25	.20	.10
537	Randy Bush	.04	.03	.02
538	Shane Mack	.06	.05	.02
539	Tom Bolton(FC)	.06	.05	.02
540	Gene Nelson	.04	.03	.02
541	Wes Gardner	.06	.05	.02
542	Ken Caminiti	.06	.05	.02
543	Duane Ward	.04	.03	.02
544	*Norm Charlton*(FC)	.20	.15	.08
545	*Hal Morris*(FC)	.20	.15	.08
546	Rich Yett(FC)	.04	.03	.02
547	*Hensley Meulens*(FC)	.60	.45	.25
548	Greg Harris	.04	.03	.02
549	Darren Daulton	.04	.03	.02
550	Jeff Hamilton	.06	.05	.02
551	Luis Aguayo	.04	.03	.02
552	Tim Leary	.06	.05	.02
553	Ron Oester	.04	.03	.02
554	Steve Lombardozzi	.04	.03	.02
555	*Tim Jones*(FC)	.15	.11	.06
556	Bud Black	.04	.03	.02
557	Alejandro Pena	.04	.03	.02
558	*Jose DeJesus*(FC)	.15	.11	.06
559	Dennis Rasmussen	.08	.06	.03
560	*Pat Borders*	.20	.15	.08
561	*Craig Biggio*(FC)	.90	.70	.35
562	*Luis de los Santos*(FC)	.20	.15	.08
563	Fred Lynn	.10	.08	.04
564	*Todd Burns*(FC)	.30	.25	.12
565	Felix Fermin	.06	.05	.02
566	Darnell Coles	.06	.05	.02
567	Willie Fraser	.04	.03	.02
568	Glenn Hubbard	.04	.03	.02
569	*Craig Worthington*	.50	.40	.20
570	*Johnny Paredes*	.20	.15	.08
571	Don Robinson	.04	.03	.02
572	Barry Lyons	.04	.03	.02
573	Bill Long	.06	.05	.02
574	Tracy Jones	.10	.08	.04
575	Juan Nieves	.06	.05	.02
576	Andres Thomas	.06	.05	.02
577	*Rolando Roomes*(FC)	.35	.25	.14
578	Luis Rivera(FC)	.04	.03	.02
579	*Chad Kreuter*(FC)	.20	.15	.08
580	Tony Armas	.06	.05	.02
581	Jay Buhner	.10	.08	.04
582	Ricky Horton	.06	.05	.02
583	Andy Hawkins	.04	.03	.02
584	*Sil Campusano*	.20	.15	.08
585	Dave Clark	.06	.05	.02
586	*Van Snider*(FC)	.20	.15	.08
587	Todd Frohwirth(FC)	.06	.05	.02
588	Warren Spahn Puzzle Card	.04	.03	.02
589	*William Brennan*(FC)	.20	.15	.08
590	*German Gonzalez*(FC)	.20	.15	.08
591	Ernie Whitt	.06	.05	.02
592	Jeff Blauser	.08	.06	.03
593	Spike Owen	.04	.03	.02
594	Matt Williams	.10	.08	.04
595	Lloyd McClendon(FC)	.04	.03	.02
596	Steve Ontiveros	.04	.03	.02
597	*Scott Medvin*(FC)	.20	.15	.08
598	*Hipolito Pena*(FC)	.15	.11	.06
599	*Jerald Clark*(FC)	.25	.20	.10
600a	Checklist 578-BC26 (#635 is Kurt Schilling)	.15	.11	.06
600b	Checklist 578-BC26 (#635 is Curt Schilling)	.06	.05	.02
601	Carmelo Martinez	.04	.03	.02
602	Mike LaCoss	.04	.03	.02
603	Mike Devereaux	.15	.11	.06
604	*Alex Madrid*(FC)	.15	.11	.06
605	Gary Redus	.04	.03	.02
606	Lance Johnson	.06	.05	.02
607	*Terry Clark*(FC)	.15	.11	.06
608	Manny Trillo	.04	.03	.02
609	*Scott Jordan*(FC)	.15	.11	.06
610	Jay Howell	.06	.05	.02
611	*Francisco Melendez*(FC)	.25	.20	.10
612	Mike Boddicker	.06	.05	.02
613	Kevin Brown	.20	.15	.08
614	Dave Valle	.04	.03	.02
615	Tim Laudner	.04	.03	.02
616	*Andy Nezelek*(FC)	.20	.15	.08
617	Chuck Crim	.04	.03	.02
618	Jack Savage(FC)	.10	.08	.04
619	Adam Peterson(FC)	.10	.08	.04
620	Todd Stottlemyre	.10	.08	.04
621	*Lance Blankenship*(FC)	.25	.20	.10
622	*Miguel Garcia*(FC)	.15	.11	.06
623	Keith Miller	.06	.05	.02
624	*Ricky Jordan*(FC)	1.50	1.25	.60
625	Ernest Riles	.04	.03	.02
626	John Moses	.04	.03	.02
627	Nelson Liriano	.06	.05	.02
628	Mike Smithson	.04	.03	.02
629	Scott Sanderson	.04	.03	.02
630	Dale Mohorcic	.04	.03	.02
631	Marvin Freeman	.04	.03	.02
632	Mike Young	.04	.03	.02
633	Dennis Lamp	.04	.03	.02
634	*Dante Bichette*(FC)	.35	.25	.14
635	*Curt Schilling*(FC)	.15	.11	.06
636	*Scott May*(FC)	.15	.11	.06
637	*Mike Schooler*(FC)	.35	.25	.14
638	Rick Leach	.04	.03	.02
639	*Tom Lampkin*(FC)	.15	.11	.06
640	*Brian Meyer*(FC)	.15	.11	.06
641	Brian Harper	.04	.03	.02
642	*John Smoltz*(FC)	.70	.50	.30
643	40/40 Club (Jose Canseco)	.80	.60	.30
644	Bill Schroeder	.04	.03	.02
645	*Edgar Martinez*	.40	.30	.15
646	*Dennis Cook*(FC)	.50	.40	.20
647	Barry Jones	.04	.03	.02
648	59 and Counting (Orel Hershiser)	.15	.11	.06
649	*Rod Nichols*(FC)	.15	.11	.06
650	Jody Davis	.06	.05	.02
651	*Bob Milacki*(FC)	.25	.20	.10
652	Mike Jackson	.06	.05	.02

		MT	NR MT	EX
653	*Derek Lilliquist*(FC)	.35	.25	.14
654	Paul Mirabella	.04	.03	.02
655	Mike Diaz	.06	.05	.02
656	Jeff Musselman	.06	.05	.02
657	Jerry Reed	.04	.03	.02
658	*Kevin Blankenship*(FC)	.20	.15	.08
659	Wayne Tolleson	.04	.03	.02
660	*Eric Hetzel*(FC)	.20	.15	.08

1989 Donruss All-Stars

For the fourth consecutive year in conjunction with the Pop-Ups, Donruss featured a 64-card set with players from the 1988 All-Star Game. The card fronts include a red- to-gold fade or gold-to-red fade border and blue vertical side borders. The top border features the player's name and position along with the "Donruss 89" logo. Each full-color player photo is highlighted by a thin white line and includes a league logo in the lower right corner. Card backs reveal an orange-gold border and black and white printing. The player's ID and personal information is displayed with a gold star on both sides. The star in the left corner includes the card number. 1988 All-Star game statistics and run totals follow along with a career highlights feature surrounded by the team, All-Star Game MLB, MLBPA, and Leaf Inc. logos. The All-Stars were distributed in wax packages containing five All-Stars, one Pop-Up, and one three-piece Warren Spahn puzzle card.

		MT	NR MT	EX
Complete Set:		8.00	6.00	3.25
Common Player:		.09	.07	.04
1	Mark McGwire	.80	.60	.30
2	Jose Canseco	1.00	.70	.40
3	Paul Molitor	.12	.09	.05
4	Rickey Henderson	.30	.25	.12
5	Cal Ripken, Jr.	.30	.25	.12
6	Dave Winfield	.20	.15	.08
7	Wade Boggs	.80	.60	.30
8	Frank Viola	.15	.11	.06
9	Terry Steinbach	.15	.11	.06
10	Tom Kelly	.09	.07	.04
11	George Brett	.12	.09	.05
12	Doyle Alexander	.09	.07	.04
13	Gary Gaetti	.12	.09	.05
14	Roger Clemens	.25	.20	.10
15	Mike Greenwell	.25	.20	.10
16	Dennis Eckersley	.12	.09	.05
17	Carney Lansford	.09	.07	.04
18	Mark Gubicza	.09	.07	.04
19	Tim Laudner	.09	.07	.04
20	Doug Jones	.09	.07	.04
21	Don Mattingly	1.50	1.25	.60
22	Dan Plesac	.12	.09	.05
23	Kirby Puckett	.30	.25	.12
24	Jeff Reardon	.09	.07	.04
25	Johnny Ray	.09	.07	.04
26	Jeff Russell	.09	.07	.04
27	Harold Reynolds	.09	.07	.04
28	Dave Stieb	.09	.07	.04
29	Kurt Stillwell	.09	.07	.04
30	Jose Canseco	1.25	.90	.50
31	Terry Steinbach	.15	.11	.06
32	AL Checklist	.09	.07	.05
33	Will Clark	1.25	.90	.50
34	Darryl Strawberry	.60	.45	.25
35	Ryne Sandberg	.20	.15	.08
36	Andre Dawson	.20	.15	.08
37	Ozzie Smith	.20	.15	.08
38	Vince Coleman	.15	.11	.06
39	Bobby Bonilla	.15	.11	.06
40	Dwight Gooden	.40	.30	.15
41	Gary Carter	.10	.08	.04
42	Whitey Herzog	.09	.07	.05
43	Shawon Dunston	.09	.07	.05
44	David Cone	.12	.09	.05
45	Andres Galarraga	.12	.09	.05
46	Mark Davis	.12	.09	.05
47	Barry Larkin	.12	.09	.05
48	Kevin Gross	.09	.07	.04
49	Vance Law	.09	.07	.04
50	Orel Hershiser	.20	.15	.08
51	Willie McGee	.09	.07	.04
52	Danny Jackson	.09	.07	.04
53	Rafael Palmeiro	.09	.07	.04
54	Bob Knepper	.09	.07	.04
55	Lance Parrish	.09	.07	.04
56	Greg Maddux	.20	.15	.08
57	Gerald Perry	.09	.07	.04
58	Bob Walk	.09	.07	.04

		MT	NR MT	EX
59	Chris Sabo	.12	.09	.04
60	Todd Worrell	.12	.09	.04
61	Andy Van Slyke	.12	.09	.04
62	Ozzie Smith	.20	.15	.08
63	Riverfront Stadium	.09	.07	.04
64	NL Checklist	.09	.07	.04

1989 Donruss Baseball's Best

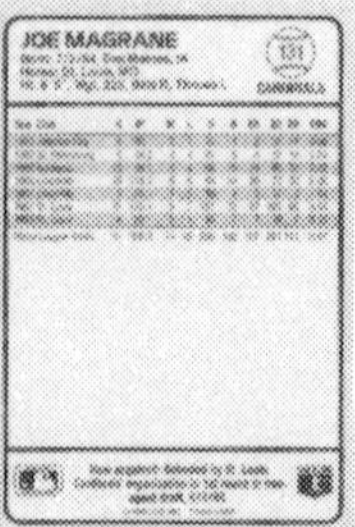

For the second consecutive year, Donruss issued a "Baseball's Best" set in 1989 to highlight the game's top players. The special 336-card set was packaged in a special box and was sold at various retail chains nationwide following the conclusion of the 1989 baseball season. The cards are styled after the regular 1989 Donruss set with green borders and a glossy finish. The set included a Warren Spahn puzzle.

	MT	NR MT	EX
Complete Set:	18.00	13.50	7.25
Common Player:	.05	.04	.02

		MT	NR MT	EX
1	Don Mattingly	2.00	1.50	.80
2	Tom Glavine	.08	.06	.03
3	Bert Blyleven	.08	.06	.03
4	Andre Dawson	.10	.08	.04
5	Pete O'Brien	.05	.04	.02
6	Eric Davis	.70	.50	.30
7	George Brett	.10	.08	.04
8	Glenn Davis	.10	.08	.04
9	Ellis Burks	.50	.40	.20
10	Kirk Gibson	.08	.06	.03
11	Carlton Fisk	.08	.06	.03
12	Andres Galarraga	.08	.06	.03
13	Alan Trammell	.06	.05	.02
14	Dwight Gooden	.60	.45	.25
15	Paul Molitor	.10	.08	.04
16	Roger McDowell	.05	.04	.02
17	Doug Drabek	.05	.04	.02
18	Kent Hrbek	.08	.06	.03
19	Vince Coleman	.08	.06	.03
20	Steve Sax	.08	.06	.03
21	Roberto Alomar	.30	.25	.12
22	Carney Lansford	.06	.05	.02
23	Will Clark	1.50	1.25	.60
24	Alvin Davis	.08	.06	.03
25	Bobby Thigpen	.08	.06	.03
26	Ryne Sandberg	.25	.20	.10
27	Devon White	.08	.06	.03
28	Mike Greenwell	.40	.30	.15
29	Dale Murphy	.10	.08	.04
30	Jeff Ballard	.10	.08	.04
31	Kelly Gruber	.08	.06	.03
32	Julio Franco	.07	.05	.03
33	Bobby Bonilla	.15	.11	.06
34	Tim Wallach	.05	.04	.02
35	Lou Whitaker	.07	.05	.03
36	Jay Howell	.07	.05	.03
37	Greg Maddux	.30	.25	.12
38	Bill Doran	.07	.05	.03
39	Danny Tartabull	.12	.09	.05
40	Darryl Strawberry	.50	.40	.20
41	Ron Darling	.10	.08	.06
42	Tony Gwynn	.30	.25	.12
43	Mark McGwire	.80	.60	.30
44	Ozzie Smith	.15	.11	.06
45	Andy Van Slyke	.12	.09	.05
46	Juan Berenguer	.05	.04	.02
47	Von Hayes	.08	.06	.03
48	Tony Fernandez	.12	.09	.05
49	Eric Plunk	.05	.04	.02
50	Ernest Riles	.05	.04	.02
51	Harold Reynolds	.07	.05	.03
52	Andy Hawkins	.06	.05	.02
53	Robin Yount	.35	.25	.14
54	Danny Jackson	.06	.05	.02
55	Nolan Ryan	.40	.30	.15
56	Joe Carter	.12	.09	.05
57	Jose Canseco	1.00	.70	.40
58	Jody Davis	.05	.04	.02
59	Lance Parrish	.06	.05	.02
60	Mitch Williams	.15	.11	.06
61	Brook Jacoby	.06	.05	.02
62	Tom Browning	.10	.08	.06
63	Kurt Stillwell	.06	.05	.02
64	Rafael Ramirez	.05	.04	.02
65	Roger Clemens	.50	.40	.20
66	Mike Scioscia	.07	.05	.02
67	Dave Gallagher	.07	.05	.02
68	Mark Langston	.15	.11	.06
69	Chet Lemon	.06	.05	.02
70	Kevin McReynolds	.25	.20	.10
71	Rob Deer	.06	.05	.02
72	Tommy Herr	.07	.05	.03
73	Barry Bonds	.12	.09	.05
74	Frank Viola	.15	.11	.06
75	Pedro Guerrero	.15	.11	.06
76	Dave Righetti	.07	.05	.03
77	Bruce Hurst	.08	.06	.03
78	Rickey Henderson	.40	.30	.15
79	Robby Thompson	.08	.06	.03
80	Randy Johnson	.25	.20	.10
81	Harold Baines	.12	.09	.05
82	Calvin Schiraldi	.05	.04	.02
83	Kirk McCaskill	.05	.04	.02
84	Lee Smith	.07	.05	.03
85	John Smoltz	.25	.20	.10
86	Mickey Tettleton	.20	.15	.08
87	Jimmy Key	.08	.06	.03
88	Rafael Palmeiro	.10	.08	.04
89	Sid Bream	.05	.04	.02
90	Dennis Martinez	.05	.04	.02
91	Frank Tanana	.05	.04	.02
92	Eddie Murray	.15	.11	.06
93	Shawon Dunston	.15	.11	.06
94	Mike Scott	.10	.08	.04
95	Bret Saberhagen	.25	.20	.10
96	David Cone	.20	.15	.08
97	Kevin Elster	.05	.04	.02
98	Jack Clark	.20	.15	.08
99	Dave Stewart	.20	.15	.08
100	Jose Oquendo	.06	.05	.02
101	Jose Lind	.05	.04	.02
102	Gary Gaetti	.12	.09	.05
103	Ricky Jordan	.25	.20	.10
104	Fred McGriff	.50	.40	.20
105	Don Slaught	.05	.04	.02
106	Jose Uribe	.05	.04	.02
107	Jeffrey Leonard	.07	.05	.02
108	Lee Guetterman	.05	.04	.02
109	Chris Bosio	.08	.06	.03
110	Barry Larkin	.15	.11	.06
111	Ruben Sierra	.30	.25	.12
112	Greg Swindell	.12	.09	.05
113	Gary Sheffield	.90	.70	.40
114	Lonnie Smith	.10	.08	.04
115	Chili Davis	.08	.06	.03
116	Damon Berryhill	.08	.06	.03
117	Tom Candiotti	.05	.04	.02
118	Kal Daniels	.10	.08	.04
119	Mark Gubicza	.10	.08	.04
120	Jim Deshaies	.08	.06	.03
121	Dwight Evans	.10	.08	.04
122	Mike Morgan	.05	.04	.02
123	Dan Pasqua	.05	.04	.02
124	Bryn Smith	.07	.05	.03
125	Doyle Alexander	.07	.05	.03
126	Howard Johnson	.25	.20	.10
127	Chuck Crim	.07	.05	.03
128	Darren Daulton	.05	.04	.02
129	Jeff Robinson	.08	.06	.03
130	Kirby Puckett	.50	.40	.20
131	Joe Magrane	.10	.08	.04
132	Jesse Barfield	.07	.05	.03
133	Mark Davis (Photo actually Dave Leiper)	.25	.20	.10
134	Dennis Eckersley	.10	.08	.04
135	Mike Krukow	.05	.04	.02
136	Jay Buhner	.10	.08	.04
137	Ozzie Guillen	.08	.06	.03
138	Rick Sutcliffe	.12	.09	.05
139	Wally Joyner	.25	.20	.10
140	Wade Boggs	1.00	.70	.40
141	Jeff Treadway	.08	.06	.05
142	Cal Ripken	.30	.25	.12
143	Dave Steib	.10	.08	.04
144	Pete Incaviglia	.07	.05	.03
145	Bob Walk	.05	.04	.02
146	Nelson Santovenia	.10	.08	.04
147	Mike Heath	.05	.04	.02
148	Willie Randolph	.08	.06	.03
149	Paul Kilgus	.05	.04	.02
150	Billy Hatcher	.07	.05	.03
151	Steve Farr	.05	.04	.02
152	Gregg Jefferies	1.00	.70	.40
153	Randy Myers	.06	.05	.02
154	Garry Templeton	.06	.05	.02
155	Walt Weiss	.10	.08	.04
156	Terry Pendleton	.10	.08	.04
157	John Smiley	.08	.06	.03
158	Greg Gagne	.05	.04	.02
159	Lenny Dykstra	.08	.06	.03
160	Nelson Liriano	.05	.04	.02
161	Alvaro Espinosa	.70	.50	.30
162	Rick Reuschel	.08	.06	.03
163	Omar Vizquel	.35	.25	.14
164	Clay Parker	.15	.11	.06
165	Dan Plesac	.06	.05	.02
166	John Franco	.06	.05	.02
167	Scott Fletcher	.06	.05	.02
168	Cory Snyder	.12	.09	.05
169	Bo Jackson	1.00	.70	.40
170	Tommy Gregg	.08	.06	.03
171	Jim Abbott	1.25	.90	.50
172	Jerome Walton	1.75	1.25	.70
173	Doug Jones	.06	.05	.02
174	Todd Benzinger	.08	.06	.03
175	Frank White	.08	.06	.03
176	Craig Biggio	.20	.15	.08
177	John Dopson	.10	.08	.06
178	Alfredo Griffin	.06	.05	.02
179	Melido Perez	.06	.05	.02
180	Tim Burke	.06	.05	.02
181	Matt Nokes	.10	.08	.04
182	Gary Carter	.10	.08	.04
183	Ted Higuera	.08	.06	.03
184	Ken Howell	.05	.04	.02
185	Rey Quinones	.05	.04	.02
186	Wally Backman	.07	.05	.03
187	Tom Brunansky	.07	.05	.03
188	Steve Balboni	.05	.04	.02
189	Marvell Wynne	.05	.04	.02
190	Dave Henderson	.08	.06	.03
191	Don Robinson	.05	.04	.02
192	Ken Griffey, Jr.	1.50	1.25	.60
193	Ivan Calderon	.05	.04	.02
194	Mike Bielecki	.07	.05	.03
195	Johnny Ray	.07	.05	.03
196	Rob Murphy	.05	.04	.02
197	Andres Thomas	.05	.04	.02
198	Phil Bradley	.06	.05	.02
199	Junior Felix	.70	.50	.30
200	Jeff Russell	.08	.06	.03
201	Mike LaValliere	.05	.04	.02
202	Kevin Gross	.06	.05	.02
203	Keith Moreland	.06	.05	.02
204	Mike Marshall	.06	.05	.02
205	Dwight Smith	.90	.70	.40
206	Jim Clancy	.05	.04	.02
207	Kevin Seitzer	.10	.08	.04
208	Keith Hernandez	.10	.08	.04
209	Bob Ojeda	.06	.05	.02
210	Ed Whitson	.06	.05	.02
211	Tony Phillips	.06	.05	.02
212	Milt Thompson	.05	.04	.02
213	Randy Kramer	.05	.04	.02
214	Randy Bush	.05	.04	.02
215	Randy Ready	.05	.04	.02
216	Duane Ward	.05	.04	.02
217	Jimmy Jones	.05	.04	.02
218	Scott Garrelts	.08	.06	.03
219	Scott Bankhead	.10	.08	.04
220	Lance McCullers	.06	.05	.02
221	B.J. Surhoff	.06	.05	.02
222	Chris Sabo	.06	.05	.02
223	Steve Buechele	.06	.05	.02
224	Joel Skinner	.05	.04	.02
225	Orel Hershiser	.15	.11	.06
226	Derek Lilliquist	.10	.08	.06
227	Claudell Washington	.08	.06	.05
228	Lloyd McClendon	.10	.08	.04
229	Felix Fermin	.05	.04	.02
230	Paul O'Neill	.08	.06	.03
231	Charlie Leibrandt	.05	.04	.02
232	Dave Smith	.06	.05	.02
233	Bob Stanley	.05	.04	.02
234	Tim Belcher	.15	.11	.06
235	Eric King	.05	.04	.02
236	Spike Owen	.05	.04	.02
237	Mike Henneman	.05	.04	.02
238	Juan Samuel	.06	.05	.02
239	Greg Brock	.06	.05	.02
240	John Kruk	.06	.05	.02
241	Glenn Wilson	.06	.05	.02
242	Jeff Reardon	.06	.05	.02
243	Todd Worrell	.08	.06	.03
244	Dave LaPoint	.05	.04	.02
245	Walt Terrell	.05	.04	.02
246	Mike Moore	.08	.06	.03
247	Kelly Downs	.05	.04	.02
248	Dave Valle	.05	.04	.02
249	Ron Kittle	.06	.05	.04
250	Steve Wilson	.10	.08	.04
251	Dick Schofield	.05	.04	.02
252	Marty Barrett	.06	.05	.02
253	Dion James	.06	.05	.02
254	Bob Milacki	.10	.08	.04
255	Ernie Whitt	.06	.05	.02
256	Kevin Brown	.08	.06	.03
257	R.J. Reynolds	.05	.04	.02
258	Tim Raines	.10	.08	.04
259	Frank Williams	.05	.04	.02
260	Jose Gonzalez	.05	.04	.02
261	Mitch Webster	.05	.04	.02
262	Ken Caminiti	.07	.05	.03
263	Bob Boone	.07	.05	.03
264	Dave Magadan	.07	.05	.03
265	Rick Aguilera	.05	.04	.02
266	Chris James	.05	.04	.02
267	Bob Welch	.07	.05	.03
268	Ken Dayley	.05	.04	.02
269	Junior Ortiz	.05	.04	.02
270	Allan Anderson	.08	.06	.03
271	Steve Jeltz	.05	.04	.02
272	George Bell	.10	.08	.04
273	Roberto Kelly	.10	.08	.04
274	Brett Butler	.07	.05	.03
275	Mike Schooler	.07	.05	.02
276	Ken Phelps	.05	.04	.02
277	Glenn Braggs	.06	.05	.02
278	Jose Rijo	.06	.05	.02
279	Bobby Witt	.06	.05	.02
280	Jerry Browne	.06	.05	.02
281	Kevin Mitchell	.70	.50	.30
282	Craig Worthington	.30	.25	.12
283	Greg Minton	.05	.04	.02
284	Nick Esasky	.07	.05	.03
285	John Farrell	.05	.04	.02
286	Rick Mahler	.05	.04	.02
287	Tom Gordon	.60	.45	.25
288	Gerald Young	.05	.04	.02
289	Jody Reed	.08	.06	.03
290	Jeff Hamilton	.05	.04	.02
291	Gerald Perry	.05	.04	.02
292	Hubie Brooks	.05	.04	.02
293	Bo Diaz	.05	.04	.02
294	Terry Puhl	.05	.04	.02
295	Jim Gantner	.05	.04	.02
296	Jeff Parrett	.05	.04	.02
297	Mike Boddicker	.05	.04	.02
298	Dan Gladden	.05	.04	.02
299	Tony Pena	.07	.05	.03
300	Checklist	.05	.04	.02
301	Tom Henke	.05	.04	.02
302	Pascual Perez	.05	.04	.02
303	Steve Bedrosian	.05	.04	.02
304	Ken Hill	.10	.08	.04
305	Jerry Reuss	.07	.05	.03
306	Jim Eisenreich	.05	.04	.02
307	Jack Howell	.05	.04	.02
308	Rick Cerone	.05	.04	.02
309	Tim Leary	.05	.04	.02
310	Joe Orsulak	.05	.04	.02
311	Jim Dwyer	.05	.04	.02
312	Geno Petralli	.05	.04	.02
313	Rick Honeycutt	.05	.04	.02
314	Tom Foley	.05	.04	.02
315	Kenny Rogers	.10	.08	.04
316	Mike Flanagan	.06	.05	.02
317	Bryan Harvey	.06	.05	.02
318	Billy Ripken	.05	.04	.02
319	Jeff Montgomery	.05	.04	.02

		MT	NR MT	EX
320	Erik Hanson	.12	.09	.05
321	Brian Downing	.06	.05	.02
322	Gregg Olson	.60	.45	.25
323	Terry Steinbach	.12	.09	.05
324	Sammy Sosa	.90	.70	.40
325	Gene Harris	.05	.04	.02
326	Mike Devereaux	.10	.08	.04
327	Dennis Cook	.12	.09	.05
328	David Wells	.08	.06	.03
329	Checklist	.05	.04	.02
330	Kirt Manwaring	.10	.08	.04
331	Jim Presley	.05	.04	.02
332	Checklist	.05	.04	.02
333	Chuck Finley	.05	.04	.02
334	Rob Dibble	.08	.06	.03
335	Cecil Espy	.06	.05	.02
336	Dave Parker	.08	.06	.02

Definitions for grading conditions are located in the Introduction section at the front of this book.

1989 Donruss Grand Slammers

One card from this 12-card set was included in each Donruss cello pack. The featured players all hit grand slams in 1988. The 2-1/2" by 3-1/2" cards feature full color action photos. The card backs feature the story of the player's grand slam. Border variations on the front of the card have been discovered, but the prices are consistent with all forms of the cards.

		MT	NR MT	EX
Complete Set:		5.00	3.75	2.00
Common Player:		.12	.09	.05
1	Jose Canseco	1.25	.90	.50
2	Mike Marshall	.12	.09	.05
3	Walt Weiss	.12	.09	.05
4	Kevin McReynolds	.15	.11	.06
5	Mike Greenwell	.40	.30	.15
6	Dave Winfield	.40	.30	.15
7	Mark McGwire	.70	.50	.30
8	Keith Hernandez	.15	.11	.06
9	Franklin Stubbs	.12	.09	.05
10	Danny Tartabull	.25	.20	.10
11	Jesse Barfield	.15	.11	.06
12	Ellis Burks	.35	.25	.14

1989 Donruss MVP

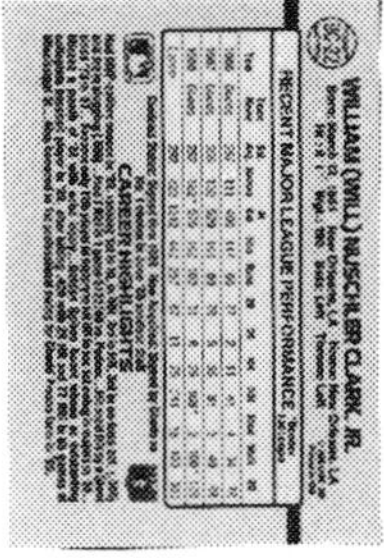

This 26-card set, numbered BC-1 through BC-26, was randomly packed in Donruss wax packs, but were not included in factory sets or other card packs. Players highlighted in this set are selected by Donruss, one player per team. MVP cards feature a variation of the design in the basic Donruss issue, with multi-color upper and lower borders and black side borders. The player name and Donruss '89 logos appear in the upper margin with the team logo appearing lower right. The "MVP" designation in large, bright letters serves as a backdrop for the full-color player photo. The cards measure 2-1/2" by 3-1/2" in size.

		MT	NR MT	EX
Complete Set:		4.00	3.00	1.50
Common Player:		.15	.11	.06
1	Kirby Puckett	.50	.40	.20
2	Mike Scott	.15	.11	.06
3	Joe Carter	.20	.15	.08
4	Orel Hershiser	.25	.20	.10
5	Jose Canseco	.75	.55	.30
6	Darryl Strawberry	.60	.45	.25
7	George Brett	.35	.25	.14
8	Andre Dawson	.25	.20	.10
9	Paul Molitor	.20	.15	.08
10	Andy Van Slyke	.15	.11	.06
11	Dave Winfield	.20	.15	.08
12	Kevin Gross	.15	.11	.06
13	Mike Greenwell	.60	.45	.25
14	Ozzie Smith	.20	.15	.08
15	Cal Ripken	.30	.25	.12
16	Andres Galarraga	.20	.15	.08
17	Alan Trammell	.25	.20	.10
18	Kal Daniels	.20	.15	.08
19	Fred McGriff	.35	.25	.14
20	Tony Gwynn	.30	.25	.12
21	Wally Joyner	.30	.25	.12
22	Will Clark	.75	.55	.30
23	Ozzie Guillen	.15	.11	.06
24	Gerald Perry	.15	.11	.06
25	Alvin Davis	.15	.11	.06
26	Ruben Sierra	.15	.11	.06

1989 Donruss Pop-Ups

This set features the eighteen starters from the 1988 Major League All-Star game. The cards are designed with a perforated outline so each player can be popped out and made to stand upright. On the front side, each player's name, team, and position is featured in an orange-and-yellow rectangle below the borderless full-color photo. Each Pop-Up includes a unique double card, folded over and glued together on the back. The flip side features a red, white, and blue "Cincinnati Reds All-Star Game" logo at the top, a blue-lettered league designation, and the player's name and position in red. The lower portion of the flip side displays illustrated instructions for creating the base of the Pop-Up. The Pop-Ups were marketed in conjunction with All-Star and Warren Spahn Puzzle Cards.

		MT	NR MT	EX
Complete Set:		6.00	4.50	2.50
Common Player:		.20	.15	.08
(1)	Mark McGwire	.70	.50	.30
(2)	Jose Canseco	1.00	.70	.40
(3)	Paul Molitor	.30	.25	.12
(4)	Rickey Henderson	.50	.40	.20
(5)	Cal Ripken, Jr.	.50	.40	.20
(6)	Dave Winfield	.40	.30	.15
(7)	Wade Boggs	1.00	.70	.40
(8)	Frank Viola	.30	.25	.12
(9)	Terry Steinbach	.20	.15	.08
(10)	Tom Kelly	.20	.15	.08
(11)	Will Clark	1.25	.90	.50
(12)	Darryl Strawberry	.70	.50	.30
(13)	Ryne Sandberg	.40	.30	.15
(14)	Andre Dawson	.35	.25	.14
(15)	Ozzie Smith	.30	.25	.12
(16)	Vince Coleman	.30	.25	.12
(17)	Bobby Bonilla	.30	.25	.12
(18)	Dwight Gooden	.50	.40	.20
(19)	Gary Carter	.20	.15	.08
(20)	Whitey Herzog	.20	.15	.08

1989 Donruss Rookies

For the fourth straight year, Donruss issued a 56-card "Rookies" set in 1989. As in previous years, the set is similar in design to the regular Donruss set, except for a new "The Rookies" logo and a green and black border.

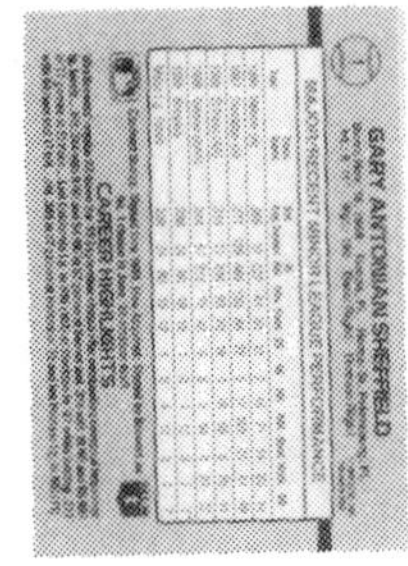

		MT	NR MT	EX
Complete Set:		30.00	22.50	12.50
Common Player:		.10	.08	.04
1	Gary Sheffield	1.00	.70	.40
2	Gregg Jefferies	1.00	.70	.40
3	Ken Griffey, Jr.	6.00	4.50	2.50
4	Tom Gordon	1.00	.70	.40
5	Billy Spiers(FC)	.35	.25	.14
6	Deion Sanders(FC)	1.50	1.25	.60
7	Donn Pall(FC)	.20	.15	.08
8	Steve Carter(FC)	.20	.15	.08
9	Francisco Oliveras(FC)	.15	.11	.06
10	Steve Wilson(FC)	.25	.20	.10
11	Bob Geren(FC)	.40	.30	.15
12	Tony Castillo(FC)	.15	.11	.06
13	Kenny Rogers(FC)	.20	.15	.08
14	Carlos Martinez(FC)	.30	.25	.12
15	Edgar Martinez	.40	.30	.15
16	Jim Abbott(FC)	2.50	2.00	1.00
17	Torey Lovullo(FC)	.20	.15	.08
18	Mark Carreon(FC)	.15	.11	.06
19	Geronimo Berroa	.10	.08	.04
20	Luis Medina	.10	.08	.04
21	Sandy Alomar, Jr.	.50	.40	.20
22	Bob Milacki	.10	.08	.04
23	Joe Girardi(FC)	.30	.25	.12
24	German Gonzalez	.10	.08	.04
25	Craig Worthington	.15	.11	.06
26	Jerome Walton(FC)	4.00	3.00	1.50
27	Gary Wayne(FC)	.20	.15	.08
28	Tim Jones	.10	.08	.04
29	Dante Bichette	.10	.08	.04
30	Alexis Infante(FC)	.15	.11	.06
31	Ken Hill	.10	.08	.04
32	Dwight Smith(FC)	1.50	1.25	.60
33	Luis de los Santos	.10	.08	.04
34	Eric Yelding(FC)	.25	.20	.10
35	Gregg Olson	1.00	.70	.40
36	Phil Stephenson(FC)	.15	.11	.06
37	Ken Patterson(FC)	.15	.11	.06
38	Rick Wrona(FC)	.25	.20	.10
39	Mike Brumley	.10	.08	.04
40	Cris Carpenter	.10	.08	.04
41	Jeff Brantley(FC)	.20	.15	.08
42	Ron Jones	.10	.08	.04
43	Randy Johnson	.10	.08	.04
44	Kevin Brown	.10	.08	.04
45	Ramon Martinez	.60	.45	.25
46	Greg Harris	.10	.08	.04
47	Steve Finley(FC)	.30	.25	.12
48	Randy Kramer	.10	.08	.04
49	Erik Hanson	.10	.08	.04
50	Matt Merullo(FC)	.15	.11	.06
51	Mike Devereaux	.10	.08	.04
52	Clay Parker(FC)	.15	.11	.06
53	Omar Vizquel(FC)	.20	.15	.08
54	Derek Lilliquist	.10	.08	.04
55	Junior Felix(FC)	1.25	.90	.50
56	Checklist	.10	.08	.04

1989 Donruss Traded

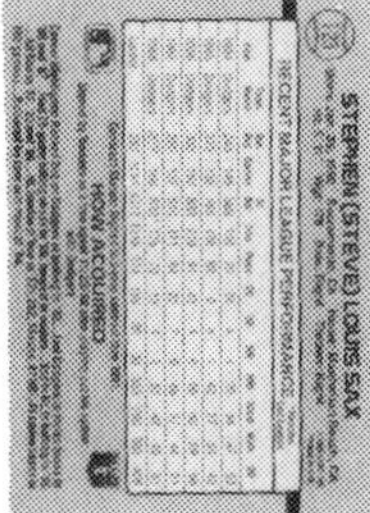

Donruss issued its first "Traded" set in 1989, releasing a 56-card boxed set designed in the same style as the regular 1989 Donruss set. The set included a Stan Musial puzzle card and a checklist.

		MT	NR MT	EX
Complete Set:		6.00	4.50	2.50
Common Player:		.06	.05	.02
1	Jeffrey Leonard	.08	.06	.03
2	Jack Clark	.15	.11	.06
3	Kevin Gross	.06	.05	.02
4	Tommy Herr	.08	.06	.03
5	Bob Boone	.10	.08	.04
6	Rafael Palmeiro	.20	.15	.08
7	John Dopson	.15	.11	.06
8	Willie Randolph	.08	.06	.03
9	Chris Brown	.06	.05	.02
10	Wally Backman	.06	.05	.02

		MT	NR MT	EX
11	Steve Ontiveros	.06	.05	.02
12	Eddie Murray	.30	.25	.12
13	Lance McCullers	.08	.06	.03
14	Spike Owen	.06	.05	.02
15	Rob Murphy	.06	.05	.02
16	Pete O'Brien	.08	.06	.03
17	Ken Williams	.06	.05	.02
18	Nick Esasky	.06	.05	.02
19	Nolan Ryan	1.00	.70	.40
20	Brian Holton	.06	.05	.02
21	Mike Moore	.08	.06	.03
22	Joel Skinner	.06	.05	.02
23	Steve Sax	.15	.11	.06
24	Rick Mahler	.06	.05	.02
25	Mike Aldrete	.06	.05	.02
26	Jesse Orosco	.08	.06	.03
27	Dave LaPoint	.06	.05	.02
28	Walt Terrell	.08	.06	.03
29	Eddie Williams	.08	.06	.03
30	Mike Devereaux	.10	.08	.04
31	Julio Franco	.15	.11	.06
32	Jim Clancy	.06	.05	.02
33	Felix Fermin	.06	.05	.02
34	Curtis Wilkerson	.06	.05	.02
35	Bert Blyleven	.12	.09	.05
36	Mel Hall	.08	.06	.03
37	Eric King	.06	.05	.02
38	Mitch Williams	.12	.09	.05
39	Jamie Moyer	.06	.05	.02
40	Rick Rhoden	.08	.06	.03
41	Phil Bradley	.08	.06	.03
42	Paul Kilgus	.08	.06	.03
43	Milt Thompson	.06	.05	.02
44	Jerry Browne	.08	.06	.03
45	Bruce Hurst	.08	.06	.03
46	Claudell Washington	.08	.06	.03
47	Todd Benzinger	.12	.09	.05
48	Steve Balboni	.06	.05	.02
49	Oddibe McDowell	.08	.06	.03
50	Charles Hudson	.06	.05	.02
51	Ron Kittle	.08	.06	.03
52	Andy Hawkins	.06	.05	.02
53	Tom Brookens	.06	.05	.02
54	Tom Niedenfuer	.06	.05	.02
55	Jeff Parrett	.08	.06	.03
56	Checklist	.06	.05	.02

1990 Donruss

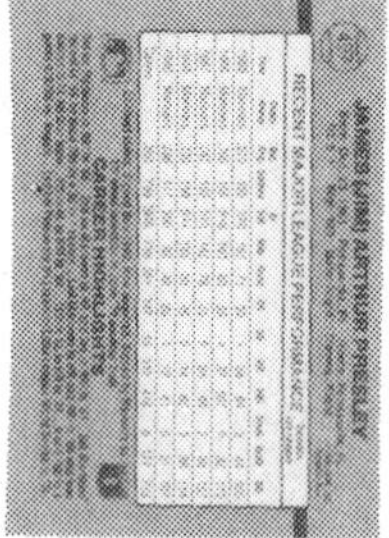

Donruss celebrated its 10th anniversary in the baseball card hobby with a 715-card set in 1990, up from the 660-card sets of previous years. The standard-size cards feature bright red borders with the player's name in script along the top. The 1990 set included 26 "Diamond Kings" and 20 "Rated Rookies," along with a Carl Yastrzemski puzzle.

		MT	NR MT	EX
	Complete Set:	25.00	18.50	10.00
	Common Player:	.04	.03	.02
1	Bo Jackson (DK)	.60	.45	.25
2	Steve Sax (DK)	.12	.09	.05
3a	Ruben Sierra (DK - missing line on top border)	1.25	.90	.50
3b	Ruben Sierra (DK)	.30	.25	.12
4	Ken Griffey, Jr. (DK)	2.00	1.50	.80
5	Mickey Tettleton (DK)	.12	.09	.05
6	Dave Stewart (DK)	.12	.09	.05
7	Jim Deshaies (DK)	.07	.05	.03
8	John Smoltz (DK)	.25	.20	.10
9	Mike Bielecki (DK)	.07	.05	.03
10a	Brian Downing DK (Reverse Negative)	1.75	1.25	.70
10b	Brian Downing DK (Corrected)	.25	.20	.10
11	Kevin Mitchell (DK)	.35	.25	.14
12	Kelly Gruber (DK)	.08	.06	.03
13	Joe Magrane (DK)	.08	.06	.03
14	John Franco (DK)	.08	.06	.03
15	Ozzie Guillen (DK)	.08	.06	.03
16	Lou Whitaker (DK)	.08	.06	.03
17	John Smiley (DK)	.08	.06	.03
18	Howard Johnson (DK)	.30	.25	.12
19	Willie Randolph (DK)	.08	.06	.03
20	Chris Bosio (DK)	.07	.05	.03
21	Tommy Herr (DK)	.07	.05	.03
22	Dan Gladden (DK)	.07	.05	.03
23	Ellis Burks (DK)	.20	.15	.08
24	Pete O'Brien (DK)	.08	.06	.03
25	Bryn Smith (DK)	.07	.05	.03
26	Ed Whitson (DK)	.07	.05	.03
27	Checklist 1-27	.04	.03	.02
28	Robin Ventura (RR)(FC)	.50	.40	.20
29	*Todd Zeile* (RR)(FC)	1.75	1.25	.70
30	Sandy Alomar, Jr. (RR)	.30	.25	.12
31	*Kent Mercker* (RR)(FC)	.30	.25	.12
32	*Ben McDonald* (RR)(FC)	2.00	1.50	.80
33a	*Juan Gonzalez RR* (Reverse Negative)(FC)	4.00	3.00	1.50
33b	*Juan Gonzalez RR* (Corrected)(FC)	.60	.45	.25
34	*Eric Anthony* (RR)(FC)	2.00	1.50	.80
35	*Mike Fetters* (RR)(FC)	.20	.15	.08
36	*Marquis Grissom* (RR)(FC)	1.00	.70	.40
37	*Greg Vaughn* (RR)(FC)	1.25	.90	.50
38	*Brian Dubois* (RR)(FC)	.25	.20	.10
39	Steve Avery (RR)(FC)	.50	.40	.20
40	*Mark Gardner* (RR)(FC)	.20	.15	.08
41	Andy Benes (RR)(FC)	.60	.45	.25
42	*Delino Deshields* (RR)(FC)	.80	.60	.30
43	*Scott Coolbaugh* (RR)(FC)	.30	.25	.12
44	*Pat Combs* (RR)(FC)	.50	.40	.20
45	Alex Sanchez (RR)	.15	.11	.06
46	*Kelly Mann* (RR)(FC)	.25	.20	.10
47	*Julio Machado* (RR)(FC)	.30	.25	.12
48	Pete Incaviglia	.05	.04	.02
49	Shawon Dunston	.07	.05	.03
50	Jeff Treadway	.05	.04	.02
51	Jeff Ballard	.10	.08	.04
52	Claudell Washington	.08	.06	.03
53	Juan Samuel	.10	.08	.04
54	John Smiley	.08	.06	.03
55	Rob Deer	.06	.05	.02
56	Geno Petralli	.04	.03	.02
57	Chris Bosio	.10	.08	.04
58	Carlton Fisk	.12	.09	.05
59	Kirt Manwaring	.10	.08	.04
60	Chet Lemon	.06	.05	.02
61	Bo Jackson	.60	.45	.25
62	Doyle Alexander	.05	.04	.02
63	Pedro Guerrero	.12	.09	.05
64	Allan Anderson	.07	.05	.03
65	Greg Harris	.07	.05	.03
66	Mike Greenwell	.25	.20	.10
67	Walt Weiss	.08	.06	.03
68	Wade Boggs	.30	.25	.12
69	Jim Clancy	.04	.03	.02
70	*Junior Felix*	.40	.30	.15
71	Barry Larkin	.12	.09	.05
72	Dave LaPoint	.05	.04	.02
73	Joel Skinner	.04	.03	.02
74	Jesse Barfield	.08	.06	.03
75	Tommy Herr	.08	.06	.03
76	Ricky Jordan	.20	.15	.08
77	Eddie Murray	.15	.11	.06
78	Steve Sax	.10	.08	.04
79	Tim Belcher	.10	.08	.04
80	Danny Jackson	.06	.05	.02
81	Kent Hrbek	.10	.08	.04
82	Milt Thompson	.05	.04	.02
83	Brook Jacoby	.07	.05	.03
84	Mike Marshall	.08	.06	.03
85	Kevin Seitzer	.12	.09	.05
86	Tony Gwynn	.15	.11	.06
87	Dave Steib	.08	.06	.03
88	Dave Smith	.06	.05	.02
89	Bret Saberhagen	.15	.11	.06
90	Alan Trammell	.10	.08	.04
91	Tony Phillips	.05	.04	.03
92	Doug Drabek	.05	.04	.03
93	Jeffrey Leonard	.09	.07	.04
94	Wally Joyner	.15	.11	.06
95	Carney Lansford	.09	.07	.04
96	Cal Ripken	.15	.11	.06
97	Andres Galarraga	.15	.11	.06
98	Kevin Mitchell	.30	.25	.12
99	Howard Johnson	.15	.11	.06
100	Checklist	.04	.03	.02
101	Melido Perez	.07	.05	.03
102	Spike Owen	.05	.04	.02
103	Paul Molitor	.10	.08	.04
104	Geronimo Berroa	.06	.05	.02
105	Ryne Sandberg	.15	.11	.06
106	Bryn Smith	.06	.05	.02
107	Steve Buechele	.04	.03	.02
108	Jim Abbott	.60	.45	.25
109	Alvin Davis	.10	.08	.04
110	Lee Smith	.05	.04	.02
111	Roberto Alomar	.15	.11	.06
112	Rick Reuschel	.09	.07	.04
113	Kelly Gruber	.09	.07	.04
114	Joe Carter	.09	.07	.04
115	Jose Rijo	.06	.05	.02
116	Greg Minton	.04	.03	.02
117	Bob Ojeda	.04	.03	.02
118	Glenn Davis	.08	.06	.03
119	Jeff Reardon	.05	.04	.02
120	Kurt Stillwell	.05	.04	.02
121	John Smoltz	.15	.11	.06
122	Dwight Evans	.08	.06	.03
123	Eric Yelding	.08	.06	.03
124	John Franco	.05	.04	.02
125	Jose Canseco	.70	.50	.30
126	Barry Bonds	.15	.11	.06
127	Lee Guetterman	.04	.03	.02
128	Jack Clark	.10	.08	.04
129	Dave Valle	.04	.03	.02
130	Hubie Brooks	.05	.04	.02
131	Ernest Riles	.04	.03	.02
132	Mike Morgan	.04	.03	.02
133	Steve Jeltz	.04	.03	.02
134	Jeff Robinson	.05	.04	.02
135	Ozzie Guillen	.05	.04	.02
136	Chili Davis	.06	.05	.02
137	Mitch Webster	.04	.03	.02
138	Jerry Browne	.06	.05	.02
139	Bo Diaz	.04	.03	.02
140	Robby Thompson	.07	.05	.03
141	Craig Worthington	.09	.07	.04
142	Julio Franco	.09	.07	.04
143	Brian Holman	.05	.04	.02
144	George Brett	.10	.08	.04
145	Tom Glavine	.10	.08	.04
146	Robin Yount	.20	.15	.08
147	Gary Carter	.06	.05	.02
148	Ron Kittle	.06	.05	.02
149	Tony Fernandez	.07	.05	.03
150	Dave Stewart	.07	.05	.03
151	Gary Gaetti	.07	.05	.03
152	Kevin Elster	.04	.03	.02
153	Gerald Perry	.05	.04	.02
154	Jesse Orosco	.05	.04	.02
155	Wally Backman	.05	.04	.02
156	Dennis Martinez	.05	.04	.02
157	Rick Sutcliffe	.08	.06	.03
158	Greg Maddux	.12	.09	.05
159	Andy Hawkins	.05	.04	.02
160	John Kruk	.05	.04	.02
161	Jose Oquendo	.05	.04	.02
162	John Dopson	.08	.06	.03
163	Joe Magrane	.08	.06	.03
164	Billy Ripken	.04	.03	.02
165	Fred Manrique	.04	.03	.02
166	Nolan Ryan	.25	.20	.10
167	Damon Berryhill	.06	.05	.02
168	Dale Murphy	.09	.07	.04
169	Mickey Tettleton	.08	.06	.03
170	Kirk McCaskill	.05	.04	.02
171	Dwight Gooden	.15	.11	.06
172	Jose Lind	.04	.03	.02
173	B.J. Surhoff	.07	.05	.03
174	Ruben Sierra	.15	.11	.06
175	Dan Plesac	.08	.06	.03
176	Dan Pasqua	.05	.04	.02
177	Kelly Downs	.05	.04	.02
178	Matt Nokes	.08	.06	.03
179	Luis Aquino	.04	.03	.02
180	Frank Tanana	.04	.03	.02
181	Tony Pena	.07	.05	.03
182	Dan Gladden	.05	.04	.02
183	Bruce Hurst	.05	.04	.02
184	Roger Clemens	.20	.15	.08
185	Mark McGwire	.30	.25	.12
186	Rob Murphy	.04	.03	.02
187	Jim Deshaies	.06	.05	.02
188	Fred McGriff	.20	.15	.08
189	Rob Dibble	.06	.05	.02
190	Don Mattingly	.90	.70	.35
191	Felix Fermin	.04	.03	.02
192	Roberto Kelly	.08	.06	.03
193	Dennis Cook	.08	.06	.03
194	Darren Daulton	.04	.03	.02
195	Alfredo Griffin	.05	.04	.02
196	Eric Plunk	.05	.04	.02
197	Orel Hershiser	.20	.15	.08
198	Paul O'Neil	.07	.05	.03
199	Randy Bush	.04	.03	.02
200	Checklist	.04	.03	.02
201	Ozzie Smith	.10	.08	.04
202	Pete O'Brien	.06	.05	.02
203	Jay Howell	.06	.05	.02
204	Mark Gibicza	.08	.06	.03
205	Ed Whitson	.04	.03	.02
206	George Bell	.09	.07	.04
207	Mike Scott	.09	.07	.04
208	Charlie Leibrandt	.04	.03	.02
209	Mike Heath	.04	.03	.02
210	Dennis Eckersley	.09	.07	.04
211	Mike LaValliere	.04	.03	.02
212	Darnell Coles	.04	.03	.02
213	Lance Parrish	.07	.05	.03
214	Mike Moore	.07	.05	.03
215	*Steve Finley*	.20	.15	.08
216	Tim Raines	.09	.07	.04
217	Scott Garrelts	.06	.05	.02
218	Kevin McReynolds	.09	.07	.04
219	Dave Gallagher	.08	.06	.03
220	Tim Wallach	.08	.06	.03
221	Chuck Crim	.04	.03	.02
222	Lonnie Smith	.08	.06	.03
223	Andre Dawson	.10	.08	.04
224	Nelson Santovenia	.07	.05	.03
225	Rafael Palmeiro	.07	.05	.03
226	Devon White	.07	.05	.03
227	Harold Reynolds	.07	.05	.03
228	Ellis Burks	.15	.11	.06
229	Mark Parent	.04	.03	.02
230	Will Clark	.60	.45	.25
231	Jimmy Key	.08	.06	.03
232	John Farrell	.04	.03	.02
233	Eric Davis	.30	.25	.12
234	Johnny Ray	.05	.04	.02
235	Darryl Strawberry	.30	.25	.12
236	Bill Doran	.05	.04	.02
237	Greg Gagne	.05	.04	.02
238	Jim Eisenreich	.04	.03	.02
239	Tommy Gregg	.06	.05	.02
240	Marty Barrett	.05	.04	.02
241	Rafael Ramirez	.05	.04	.02
242	Chris Sabo	.07	.05	.03
243	Dave Henderson	.07	.05	.03
244	Andy Van Slyke	.07	.05	.03
245	Alvaro Espinoza	.10	.07	.04
246	Garry Templeton	.06	.05	.02
247	Gene Harris	.04	.03	.02
248	Kevin Gross	.05	.04	.02
249	Brett Butler	.09	.07	.04
250	Willie Randolph	.07	.05	.03
251	Roger McDowell	.05	.04	.02
252	Rafael Belliard	.04	.03	.02
253	Steve Rosenberg	.04	.03	.02
254	Jack Howell	.04	.03	.02
255	Marvell Wynne	.04	.03	.02
256	Tom Candiotti	.05	.04	.02
257	Todd Benzinger	.05	.04	.02
258	Don Robinson	.04	.03	.02
259	Phil Bradley	.08	.06	.03
260	Cecil Espy	.05	.04	.02
261	Scott Bankhead	.05	.04	.02
262	Frank White	.07	.05	.03
263	Andres Thomas	.05	.04	.02
264	Glenn Braggs	.05	.04	.02
265	David Cone	.10	.08	.04
266	Bobby Thigpen	.07	.05	.03
267	Nelson Liriano	.04	.03	.02
268	Terry Steinbach	.09	.07	.04
269	Kirby Puckett	.30	.25	.12
270	Gregg Jefferies	.40	.30	.15
271	Jeff Blauser	.05	.04	.02
272	Cory Snyder	.07	.05	.03
273	Roy Smith	.05	.04	.02

		MT	NR MT	EX
274	Tom Foley	.04	.03	.02
275	Mitch Williams	.09	.07	.04
276	Paul Kilgus	.04	.03	.02
277	Don Slaught	.04	.03	.02
278	Von Hayes	.08	.06	.03
279	Vince Coleman	.10	.08	.04
280	Mike Boddicker	.05	.04	.02
281	Ken Dayley	.04	.03	.02
282	Mike Devereaux	.07	.05	.03
283	*Kenny Rogers*	.09	.07	.04
284	Jeff Russell	.07	.05	.04
285	*Jerome Walton*	1.00	.70	.40
286	Derek Lilliquist	.08	.06	.03
287	Joe Orsulak	.04	.03	.02
288	Dick Schofield	.04	.03	.02
289	Ron Darling	.09	.07	.04
290	Bobby Bonilla	.10	.07	.04
291	Jim Gantner	.05	.04	.02
292	Bobby Witt	.05	.04	.02
293	Greg Brock	.05	.04	.02
294	Ivan Calderon	.05	.04	.02
295	Steve Bedrosian	.06	.05	.02
296	Mike Henneman	.06	.05	.02
297	Tom Gordon	.25	.20	.10
298	Lou Whitaker	.08	.06	.03
299	Terry Pendleton	.07	.05	.03
300	Checklist	.04	.03	.02
301	Juan Berenguer	.04	.03	.02
302	Mark Davis	.09	.07	.05
303	Nick Esasky	.09	.07	.05
304	Rickey Henderson	.15	.11	.06
305	Rick Cerone	.04	.03	.02
306	Craig Biggio	.15	.11	.06
307	Duane Ward	.04	.03	.02
308	Tom Browning	.07	.05	.03
309	Walt Terrell	.05	.04	.02
310	Greg Swindell	.10	.08	.04
311	Dave Righetti	.07	.05	.03
312	Mike Maddux	.04	.03	.02
313	Lenny Dykstra	.07	.05	.03
314	Jose Gonzalez	.08	.06	.03
315	Steve Balboni	.04	.03	.02
316	Mike Scioscia	.07	.05	.02
317	Ron Oester	.04	.03	.02
318	*Gary Wayne*	.09	.07	.04
319	Todd Worrell	.06	.05	.02
320	Doug Jones	.05	.04	.02
321	Jeff Hamilton	.05	.04	.02
322	Danny Tartabull	.09	.07	.04
323	Chris James	.05	.04	.02
324	Mike Flanagan	.05	.04	.02
325	Gerald Young	.05	.04	.02
326	Bob Boone	.09	.07	.04
327	Frank Williams	.04	.03	.02
328	Dave Parker	.09	.07	.04
329	Sid Bream	.04	.03	.02
330	Mike Schooler	.06	.05	.02
331	Bert Blyleven	.08	.06	.03
332	Bob Welch	.07	.05	.03
333	Bob Milacki	.06	.05	.02
334	Tim Burke	.05	.04	.02
335	Jose Uribe	.05	.04	.02
336	Randy Myers	.05	.04	.02
337	Eric King	.04	.03	.02
338	Mark Langston	.12	.09	.05
339	Ted Higuera	.08	.06	.03
340	Oddibe McDowell	.06	.05	.02
341	Lloyd McClendon	.07	.05	.03
342	Pascual Perez	.05	.04	.02
343	Kevin Brown	.08	.06	.03
344	Chuck Finley	.05	.04	.02
345	Erik Hanson	.09	.07	.05
346	Rich Gedman	.05	.04	.02
347	Bip Roberts	.10	.08	.04
348	Matt Williams	.20	.15	.08
349	Tom Henke	.05	.04	.02
350	Brad Komminsk	.05	.04	.02
351	Jeff Reed	.04	.03	.02
352	Brian Downing	.05	.04	.02
353	Frank Viola	.09	.07	.04
354	Terry Puhl	.05	.04	.02
355	Brian Harper	.05	.04	.02
356	Steve Farr	.05	.04	.02
357	Joe Boever	.05	.04	.02
358	Danny Heep	.04	.03	.02
359	Larry Andersen	.04	.03	.02
360	Rolando Roomes	.10	.08	.04
361	Mike Gallego	.05	.04	.02
362	Bob Kipper	.04	.03	.02
363	Clay Parker	.07	.05	.03
364	Mike Pagliarulo	.05	.04	.02
365	Ken Griffey, Jr.	2.25	1.75	.90
366	Rex Hudler	.04	.03	.02
367	Pat Sheridan	.04	.03	.02
368	Kirk Gibson	.09	.07	.04
369	Jeff Parrett	.05	.04	.02
370	Bob Walk	.05	.04	.02
371	Ken Patterson	.04	.03	.02
372	Bryan Harvey	.05	.04	.02
373	Mike Bielecki	.07	.05	.03
374	*Tom Magrann*(FC)	.20	.15	.08
375	Rick Mahler	.05	.04	.02
376	Craig Lefferts	.05	.04	.02
377	Gregg Olson	.20	.15	.08
378	Jamie Moyer	.04	.03	.02
379	Randy Johnson	.09	.07	.04
380	Jeff Montgomery	.06	.05	.02
381	Marty Clary	.06	.05	.02
382	*Bill Spiers*	.15	.11	.06
383	Dave Magadan	.06	.05	.02
384	*Greg Hibbard*(FC)	.20	.15	.08
385	Ernie Whitt	.05	.04	.02
386	Rick Honeycutt	.04	.03	.02
387	Dave West	.08	.06	.03
388	Keith Hernandez	.07	.05	.03
389	Jose Alvarez	.04	.03	.02
390	*Joey Belle*(FC)	.60	.45	.25
391	Rick Aguilera	.05	.04	.02
392	Mike Fitzgerald	.04	.03	.02
393	*Dwight Smith*	.80	.60	.30
394	*Steve Wilson*	.09	.07	.04
395	*Bob Geren*	.20	.15	.08
396	Randy Ready	.04	.03	.02
397	Ken Hill	.07	.05	.03

		MT	NR MT	EX
398	Jody Reed	.05	.04	.02
399	Tom Brunansky	.07	.05	.03
400	Checklist	.04	.03	.02
401	Rene Gonzales	.04	.03	.02
402	Harold Baines	.09	.07	.04
403	Cecilio Guante	.04	.03	.02
404	Joe Girardi	.15	.11	.06
405	*Sergio Valdez*(FC)	.20	.15	.08
406	Mark Williamson	.04	.03	.02
407	Glenn Hoffman	.04	.03	.02
408	*Jeff Innis*(FC)	.10	.08	.04
409	Randy Kramer	.04	.03	.02
410	Charlie O'Brien(FC)	.04	.03	.02
411	Charlie Hough	.06	.05	.02
412	Gus Polidor	.04	.03	.02
413	Ron Karkovice	.04	.03	.02
414	Trevor Wilson(FC)	.07	.05	.03
415	*Kevin Ritz*(FC)	.20	.15	.08
416	Gary Thurman	.04	.03	.02
417	Jeff Robinson	.04	.03	.02
418	Scott Terry	.05	.04	.02
419	Tim Laudner	.04	.03	.02
420	Dennis Rasmussen	.04	.03	.02
421	Luis Rivera	.04	.03	.02
422	Jim Corsi(FC)	.07	.05	.03
423	Dennis Lamp	.04	.03	.02
424	Ken Caminiti	.06	.05	.02
425	David Wells	.06	.05	.02
426	Norm Charlton	.09	.07	.04
427	*Deion Sanders*	.70	.50	.30
428	Dion James	.05	.04	.02
429	Chuck Cary	.05	.04	.02
430	Ken Howell	.04	.03	.02
431	Steve Lake	.04	.03	.02
432	Kal Daniels	.09	.07	.04
433	Lance McCullers	.05	.04	.02
434	Lenny Harris(FC)	.10	.08	.04
435	*Scott Scudder*(FC)	.20	.15	.08
436	Gene Larkin	.04	.03	.02
437	Dan Quisenberry	.05	.04	.02
438	*Steve Olin*(FC)	.15	.11	.06
439	Mickey Hatcher	.05	.04	.02
440	Willie Wilson	.05	.04	.02
441	Mark Grant	.05	.04	.02
442	Mookie Wilson	.07	.05	.03
443	Alex Trevino	.04	.03	.02
444	Pat Tabler	.05	.04	.02
445	Dave Bergman	.04	.03	.02
446	Todd Burns	.05	.04	.02
447	R.J. Reynolds	.04	.03	.02
448	Jay Buhner	.08	.06	.03
449	*Lee Stevens*(FC)	.20	.15	.08
450	Ron Hassey	.04	.03	.02
451	Bob Melvin	.04	.03	.02
452	Dave Martinez	.05	.04	.02
453	*Greg Litton*(FC)	.25	.20	.10
454	Mark Carreon	.10	.07	.04
455	Scott Fletcher	.05	.04	.02
456	Otis Nixon	.04	.03	.02
457	*Tony Fossas*(FC)	.10	.08	.04
458	John Russell	.04	.03	.02
459	Paul Assenmacher	.04	.03	.02
460	Zane Smith	.04	.03	.02
461	*Jack Daugherty*	.20	.15	.08
462	*Rich Monteleone*(FC)	.15	.11	.06
463	Greg Briley(FC)	.25	.20	.10
464	Mike Smithson	.04	.03	.02
465	Benito Santiago	.09	.07	.04
466	*Jeff Brantley*	.10	.08	.04
467	Jose Nunez	.07	.05	.03
468	Scott Bailes	.04	.03	.02
469	Ken Griffey	.06	.05	.02
470	Bob McClure	.04	.03	.02
471	Mackey Sasser	.04	.03	.02
472	Glenn Wilson	.04	.03	.02
473	*Kevin Tapani*(FC)	.30	.25	.15
474	Bill Buckner	.05	.04	.02
475	Ron Gant	.05	.04	.02
476	Kevin Romine(FC)	.05	.04	.02
477	Juan Agosto	.04	.03	.02
478	Herm Winningham	.04	.03	.02
479	Storm Davis	.05	.04	.02
480	Jeff King(FC)	.09	.07	.04
481	*Kevin Mmahat*(FC)	.25	.20	.10
482	Carmelo Martinez	.05	.04	.02
483	*Omar Vizquel*	.10	.08	.04
484	Jim Dwyer	.04	.03	.02
485	Bob Knepper	.04	.03	.02
486	Dave Anderson	.04	.03	.02
487	Ron Jones	.09	.07	.04
488	Jay Bell	.05	.04	.02
489	*Sammy Sosa*(FC)	.60	.45	.25
490	*Kent Anderson*(FC)	.15	.11	.06
491	Domingo Ramos	.04	.03	.02
492	Dave Clark	.05	.04	.02
493	Tim Birtsas	.04	.03	.02
494	Ken Oberkfell	.04	.03	.02
495	Larry Sheets	.04	.03	.02
496	Jeff Kunkel	.04	.03	.02
497	Jim Presley	.04	.03	.02
498	Mike Macfarlane	.04	.03	.02
499	Pete Smith	.05	.04	.02
500	Checklist	.04	.03	.02
501	Gary Sheffield	.40	.30	.15
502	*Terry Bross*(FC)	.20	.15	.08
503	*Jerry Kutzler*(FC)	.20	.15	.08
504	Lloyd Moseby	.05	.04	.02
505	Curt Young	.04	.03	.02
506	Al Newman	.04	.03	.02
507	Keith Miller	.04	.03	.02
508	*Mike Stanton*(FC)	.20	.15	.08
509	Rich Yett	.04	.03	.02
510	*Tim Drummond*(FC)	.20	.15	.08
511	Joe Hesketh	.04	.03	.02
512	*Rick Wrona*	.10	.08	.04
513	Luis Salazar	.04	.03	.02
514	Hal Morris	.06	.05	.02
515	Terry Mullholland	.07	.05	.03
516	John Morris	.05	.04	.02
517	Carlos Quintana	.08	.06	.03
518	Frank DiPino	.04	.03	.02
519	Randy Milligan	.06	.05	.02
520	Chad Kreuter	.07	.05	.03
521	Mike Jeffcoat	.04	.03	.02

		MT	NR MT	EX
522	Mike Harkey	.10	.08	.04
523	Andy Nezelek	.07	.05	.03
524	Dave Schmidt	.04	.03	.02
525	Tony Armas	.04	.03	.02
526	Barry Lyons	.04	.03	.02
527	*Rick Reed*(FC)	.20	.15	.08
528	Jerry Reuss	.06	.05	.02
529	*Dean Palmer*(FC)	.70	.50	.30
530	*Jeff Peterek*(FC)	.20	.15	.08
531	*Carlos Martinez*	.20	.15	.08
532	Atlee Hammaker	.05	.04	.02
533	Mike Brumley	.04	.03	.02
534	Terry Leach	.04	.03	.02
535	*Doug Strange*(FC)	.20	.15	.08
536	Jose DeLeon	.05	.04	.02
537	Shane Rawley	.05	.04	.02
538	Joey Cora(FC)	.10	.08	.04
539	Eric Hetzel	.08	.06	.03
540	Gene Nelson	.04	.03	.02
541	Wes Gardner	.04	.03	.02
542	Mark Portugal	.04	.03	.02
543	Al Leiter	.05	.04	.02
544	Jack Armstrong	.04	.03	.02
545	Greg Cadaret	.04	.03	.02
546	Rod Nichols	.04	.03	.02
547	Luis Polonia	.05	.04	.02
548	Charlie Hayes(FC)	.15	.11	.06
549	Dickie Thon	.04	.03	.02
550	Tim Crews	.04	.03	.02
551	Dave Winfield	.20	.15	.08
552	Mike Davis	.04	.03	.02
553	Ron Robinson	.04	.03	.02
554	Carmen Castillo	.04	.03	.02
555	John Costello	.04	.03	.02
556	Bud Black	.04	.03	.02
557	Rick Dempsey	.04	.03	.02
558	Jim Acker	.04	.03	.02
559	Eric Show	.06	.05	.02
560	Pat Borders	.06	.05	.02
561	Danny Darwin	.04	.03	.02
562	*Rick Luecken*(FC)	.20	.15	.08
563	Edwin Nunez	.05	.04	.02
564	Felix Jose	.09	.07	.04
565	John Cangelosi	.04	.03	.02
566	Billy Swift	.04	.03	.02
567	Bill Schroeder	.04	.03	.02
568	Stan Javier	.04	.03	.02
569	Jim Traber	.04	.03	.02
570	Wallace Johnson	.04	.03	.02
571	Donell Nixon	.04	.03	.02
572	Sid Fernandez	.08	.06	.03
573	Lance Johnson	.09	.07	.04
574	Andy McGaffigan	.04	.03	.02
575	Mark Knudson	.04	.03	.02
576	*Tommy Greene*(FC)	.25	.20	.10
577	Mark Grace	.25	.20	.10
578	*Larry Walker*(FC)	.25	.20	.10
579	Mike Stanley	.04	.03	.02
580	Mike Witt	.05	.04	.02
581	Scott Bradley	.04	.03	.02
582	Greg Harris	.07	.05	.03
583	Kevin Hickey	.04	.03	.02
584	Lee Mazzilli	.04	.03	.02
585	Jeff Pico	.04	.03	.02
586	*Joe Oliver*(FC)	.40	.30	.15
587	Willie Fraser	.04	.03	.02
588	Puzzle Card	.04	.03	.02
589	Kevin Bass	.06	.05	.03
590	John Moses	.04	.03	.02
591	Tom Pagnozzi	.04	.03	.02
592	*Tony Castillo*	.10	.08	.04
593	Jerald Clark	.06	.05	.03
594	Dan Schatzeder	.04	.03	.02
595	Luis Quinones	.04	.03	.02
596	Pete Harnisch	.08	.06	.03
597	Gary Redus	.04	.03	.02
598	Mel Hall	.05	.04	.02
599	Rick Schu	.04	.03	.02
600	Checklist	.04	.03	.02
601	Mike Kingery	.04	.03	.02
602	Terry Kennedy	.04	.03	.02
603	Mike Sharperson	.06	.05	.02
604	Don Carman	.04	.03	.02
605	Jim Gott	.05	.04	.03
606	Donn Pall	.05	.04	.03
607	Rance Mulliniks	.04	.03	.02
608	Curt Wilkerson	.04	.03	.02
609	Mike Felder	.04	.03	.02
610	Guillermo Hernandez	.04	.03	.02
611	Candy Maldonado	.05	.04	.02
612	Mark Thurmond	.04	.03	.02
613	Rick Leach	.04	.03	.02
614	Jerry Reed	.04	.03	.02
615	Franklin Stubbs	.05	.04	.02
616	Billy Hatcher	.05	.04	.02
617	Don August	.05	.04	.02
618	Tim Teufel	.04	.03	.02
619	Shawn Hillegas	.04	.03	.02
620	Manny Lee	.04	.03	.02
621	Gary Ward	.05	.04	.02
622	*Mark Guthrie*(FC)	.20	.15	.08
623	Jeff Musselman	.05	.04	.02
624	Mark Lemke	.07	.05	.03
625	Fernando Valenzuela	.07	.05	.03
626	*Paul Sorrento*(FC)	.20	.15	.08
627	Glenallen Hill	.20	.15	.08
628	Les Lancaster	.05	.04	.03
629	Vance Law	.04	.03	.02
630	Randy Velarde(FC)	.10	.08	.04
631	Todd Frohwirth	.04	.03	.02
632	Willie McGee	.06	.05	.02
633	Oil Can Boyd	.06	.05	.02
634	Cris Carpenter	.09	.07	.04
635	Brian Holton	.04	.03	.02
636	Tracy Jones	.05	.04	.02
637	Terry Steinbach (AS)	.09	.07	.04
638	Brady Anderson	.09	.07	.04
639	Jack Morris	.06	.05	.02
640	*Jaime Navarro*(FC)	.20	.15	.08
641	Darrin Jackson	.05	.04	.02
642	*Mike Dyer*(FC)	.20	.15	.08
643	Mike Schmidt	.40	.30	.15
644	Henry Cotto	.04	.03	.02
645	John Cerutti	.05	.04	.02

		MT	NR MT	EX
646	*Francisco Cabrera*(FC)	.40	.30	.15
647	Scott Sanderson	.05	.04	.02
648	Brian Meyer	.05	.04	.02
649	Ray Searage	.05	.04	.02
650a	Bo Jackson AS (Recent Major League Performance on back)	3.00	2.25	1.25
650b	Bo Jackson AS (Corrected)	.50	.40	.20
651	Steve Lyons	.04	.03	.02
652	Mike LaCoss	.04	.03	.02
653	Ted Power	.04	.03	.02
654	Howard Johnson (AS)	.20	.15	.08
655	*Mauro Gozzo*(FC)	.15	.11	.06
656	*Mike Blowers*(FC)	.30	.25	.12
657	Paul Gibson	.05	.04	.02
658	Neal Heaton	.05	.04	.02
659a	5000 K (Nolan Ryan) (King card number 665 back)	12.00	9.00	4.75
659b	5000 K (Nolan Ryan) (Corrected)	1.00	.70	.40
660a	Harold Baines (AS - recent major league performance on back)	5.00	3.75	2.00
660b	Harold Baines (AS - line through star on front-incorrect back)	15.00	11.00	6.00
660c	Harold Baines (AS - Incorrect front and back)	15.00	11.00	6.00
660d	Harold Baines (AS - Corrected)	.10	.08	.04
661	Gary Pettis	.05	.04	.02
662	*Clint Zavaras*(FC)	.20	.15	.08
663	Rick Reuschel	.08	.06	.03
664	Alejandro Pena	.05	.04	.02
665a	King of Kings (Nolan Ryan) (5000 K card number 659 back)	12.00	9.00	4.75
665b	King of Kings (Nolan Ryan) (Corrected)	1.00	.70	.40
666	Ricky Horton	.04	.03	.02
667	Curt Schilling	.06	.05	.02
668	Bill Landrum(FC)	.05	.04	.02
669	Todd Stottlemyre	.05	.04	.02
670	Tim Leary	.05	.04	.02
671	*John Wetteland*(FC)	.25	.20	.10
672	Calvin Schiraldi	.04	.03	.02
673	Ruben Sierra (AS)	.09	.07	.04
674	Pedro Guerrero (AS)	.09	.07	.04
675	Ken Phelps	.04	.03	.02
676	Cal Ripken (AS)	.09	.07	.04
677	Denny Walling	.04	.03	.02
678	Goose Gossage	.04	.03	.02
679	*Gary Mielke*(FC)	.20	.15	.08
680	Bill Bathe	.04	.03	.02
681	Tom Lawless	.04	.03	.02
682	*Xavier Hernandez*(FC)	.20	.15	.08
683	Kirby Puckett (AS)	.09	.07	.04
684	Mariano Duncan	.05	.04	.02
685	Ramon Martinez	.10	.08	.04
686	Tim Jones	.05	.04	.02
687	Tom Filer	.04	.03	.02
688	Steve Lombardozzi	.04	.03	.02
689	*Bernie Williams*(FC)	.50	.40	.20
690	*Chip Hale*(FC)	.25	.20	.10
691	*Beau Allred*(FC)	.40	.30	.15
692	Ryne Sandberg (AS)	.09	.07	.04
693	*Jeff Huson*(FC)	.25	.20	.10
694	Curt Ford	.04	.03	.02
695	Eric Davis (AS)	.09	.07	.04
696	Scott Lusader	.05	.04	.02
697	Mark McGwire (AS)	.09	.07	.04
698	*Steve Cummings*(FC)	.20	.15	.08
699	*George Canale*(FC)	.20	.15	.08
700	Checklist	.04	.03	.02
701	Julio Franco (AS)	.09	.07	.04
702	*Dave Johnson*(FC)	.10	.08	.04
703	Dave Stewart (AS)	.08	.06	.03
704	*Dave Justice*(FC)	.25	.20	.10
705	Tony Gwynn (AS)	.09	.07	.04
706	Greg Myers	.06	.05	.02
707	Will Clark (AS)	.15	.11	.06
708	Benito Santiago (AS)	.08	.06	.03
709	Larry McWilliams	.04	.03	.02
710	Ozzie Smith (AS)	.08	.06	.03
711	*John Olerud*(FC)	2.75	2.00	1.00
712	Wade Boggs (AS)	.09	.07	.04
713	*Gary Eave*(FC)	.15	.11	.06
714	Bob Tewksbury	.05	.04	.02
715	Kevin Mitchell (AS)	.09	.07	.04
716	A. Bartlett Giamatti	1.25	.90	.50

1990 Donruss MVP

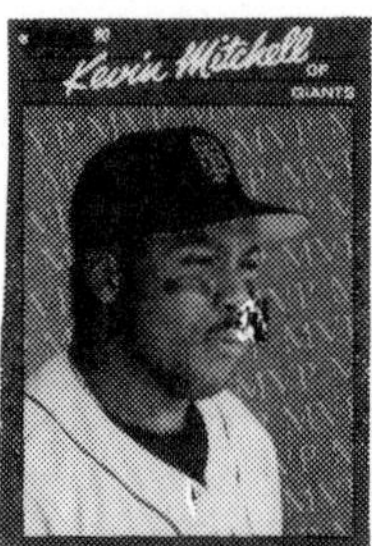

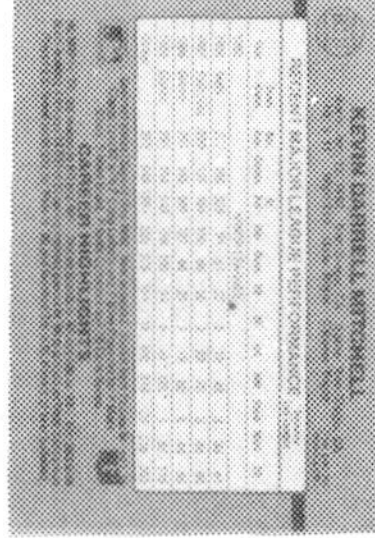

This special 26-card set includes one player from each Major League team. Numbered BC-1 (the "BC" stands for "Bonus Card") through BC-26, the cards from this set were randomly packed in 1990 Donruss wax packs and were not available in factory sets or other types of packaging. The red-bordered cards are similar in design to the regular 1990 Donruss set, except the player photos are set against a special background made up of the "MVP" logo.

		MT	NR MT	EX
Complete Set:		4.00	3.00	1.50
Common Player:		.08	.06	.03
1	Bo Jackson	.30	.25	.12
2	Howard Johnson	.10	.08	.04
3	Dave Stewart	.08	.06	.03
4	Tony Gwynn	.15	.11	.06
5	Orel Hershiser	.10	.08	.04
6	Pedro Guerrero	.10	.08	.04
7	Tim Raines	.10	.08	.04
8	Kirby Puckett	.30	.25	.12
9	Alvin Davis	.08	.06	.03
10	Ryne Sandberg	.10	.08	.04
11	Kevin Mitchell	.20	.15	.08
12a	John Smoltz (photo of Tom Glavine)	5.00	3.75	2.00
12b	John Smoltz (corrected)	.40	.30	.15
13	George Bell	.10	.08	.04
14	Julio Franco	.10	.08	.04
15	Paul Molitor	.10	.08	.04
16	Bobby Bonilla	.12	.09	.05
17	Mike Greenwell	.30	.25	.12
18	Cal Ripken	.30	.25	.12
19	Carlton Fisk	.12	.09	.05
20	Chili Davis	.08	.06	.03
21	Glenn Davis	.10	.08	.04
22	Steve Sax	.10	.08	.04
23	Eric Davis	.30	.25	.12
24	Greg Swindell	.08	.06	.03
25	Von Hayes	.08	.06	.03
26	Alan Trammell	.10	.08	.04

1986 Dorman's Cheese

Found in specially-marked packages of Dorman's American Cheese Singles, the Dorman's set consists of ten two-card panels of baseball superstars. Labeled as a "Super Star Limited Edition" set, the panels measure 1-1/2" by 2" each and have a perforation line in the center. The fronts contain a color photo along with the Dorman's logo and the player's name, team and position. Due to a lack of proper licensing, all team insignias have been airbrushed from the players' caps. The backs of the cards contain brief player statistics.

		MT	NR MT	EX
Complete Panel Set:		30.00	22.00	12.00
Complete Singles Set:		12.00	9.00	4.75
Common Panel:		1.25	.90	.50
Common Single Player:		.15	.11	.06
Panel		2.00	1.50	.80
(1)	George Brett	.50	.40	.20
(2)	Jack Morris	.15	.11	.06
Panel		2.00	1.50	.80
(3)	Gary Carter	.30	.25	.12
(4)	Cal Ripken	.40	.30	.15
Panel		2.00	1.50	.80
(5)	Dwight Gooden	.60	.45	.25
(6)	Kent Hrbek	.20	.15	.08
Panel		3.00	1.50	.90
(7)	Rickey Henderson	.40	.30	.15
(8)	Mike Schmidt	.80	.60	.30
Panel		2.00	1.50	.80
(9)	Keith Hernandez	.30	.25	.12
(10)	Dale Murphy	.50	.40	.20
Panel		2.00	1.50	.80
(11)	Reggie Jackson	.40	.30	.15
(12)	Eddie Murray	.40	.30	.15
Panel		4.00	3.00	1.50
(13)	Don Mattingly	1.00	.70	.40
(14)	Ryne Sandberg	.30	.25	.12
Panel		1.25	.90	.50
(15)	Willie McGee	.15	.11	.06
(16)	Robin Yount	.30	.25	.12
Panel		2.25	1.75	.90
(17)	Rick Sutcliff (Sutcliffe)	.15	.11	.06
(18)	Wade Boggs	.80	.60	.30
Panel		1.50	1.25	.60
(19)	Dave Winfield	.40	.30	.15
(20)	Jim Rice	.20	.15	.10

1941 Double Play

Issued by Gum, Inc., this set includes 75 numbered cards (two consecutive numbers per card) featuring 150 baseball players. The cards, which are blank-backed and measure 2-1/2" by 3-1/8", contain sepia-tone photos of two players. Action and portrait poses are found in the set, with card designs on either a vertical or horizontal format. The last fifty cards are the scarcest of the set. Cards cut to form two single cards have little value.

		NR MT	EX	VG
Complete Set:		6500.00	3300.00	2000.
Common Player: 1-100		35.00	17.50	10.50
Common Player: 101-150		50.00	25.00	15.00
1	Larry French			
2	Vance Page	75.00	38.50	23.00
3	Billy Herman			
4	Stanley Hack	50.00	25.00	15.00
5	Linus Frey			
6	John Vander Meer	45.00	23.00	13.50
7	Paul Derringer			
8	Bucky Walters	35.00	17.50	10.50
9	Frank McCormick			
10	Bill Werber	35.00	17.50	10.50
11	Jimmy Ripple			
12	Ernie Lombardi	60.00	30.00	18.00
13	Alex Kampouris			
14	John Wyatt	35.00	17.50	10.50
15	Mickey Owen			
16	Paul Waner	60.00	30.00	18.00
17	Harry Lavagetto			
18	Harold Reiser	45.00	22.00	13.50
19	Jimmy Wasdell			
20	Dolph Camilli	45.00	22.00	13.50
21	Dixie Walker			
22	Ducky Medwick	60.00	30.00	18.00
23	Harold Reese			
24	Kirby Higbe	225.00	112.00	70.00
25	Harry Danning			
26	Cliff Melton	35.00	17.50	10.50
27	Harry Gumbert			
28	Burgess Whitehead	35.00	17.50	10.50
29	Joe Orengo			
30	Joe Moore	35.00	17.50	10.50
31	Mel Ott			
32	Babe Young	90.00	45.00	27.00
33	Lee Handley			
34	Arky Vaughan	60.00	30.00	18.00
35	Bob Klinger			
36	Stanley Brown	35.00	17.50	10.50
37	Terry Moore			
38	Gus Mancuso	35.00	17.50	10.50
39	Johnny Mize			
40	Enos Slaughter	100.00	50.00	30.00
41	John Cooney			
42	Sibby Sisti	35.00	17.50	10.50
43	Max West			
44	Carvel Rowell	35.00	17.50	10.50
45	Dan Litwhiler			
46	Merrill May	35.00	17.50	10.50
47	Frank Hayes			
48	Al Brancato	35.00	17.50	10.50
49	Bob Johnson			
50	Bill Nagel	35.00	17.50	10.50
51	Buck Newsom			
52	Hank Greenberg	90.00	45.00	27.00
53	Barney McCosky			
54	Charley Gehringer	90.00	45.00	27.00
55	Pinky Higgins			
56	Dick Bartell	35.00	17.50	10.50
57	Ted Williams			
58	Jim Tabor	550.00	280.00	165.00
59	Joe Cronin			
60	Jimmy Foxx	175.00	90.00	50.00
61	Lefty Gomez			
62	Phil Rizzuto	250.00	125.00	70.00
63	Joe DiMaggio			
64	Charley Keller	675.00	340.00	210.00
65	Red Rolfe			
66	Bill Dickey	125.00	62.00	37.00
67	Joe Gordon			
68	Red Ruffing	75.00	37.00	22.00
69	Mike Tresh			
70	Luke Appling	60.00	30.00	18.00
71	Moose Solters			
72	John Rigney	35.00	17.50	10.50
73	Buddy Meyer			
74	Ben Chapman	35.00	17.50	10.50
75	Cecil Travis			
76	George Case	35.00	17.50	10.50
77	Joe Krakauskas			
78	Bob Feller	150.00	75.00	45.00
79	Ken Keltner			
80	Hal Trosky	35.00	17.50	10.50
81	Ted Williams			
82	Joe Cronin	600.00	300.00	175.00
83	Joe Gordon			
84	Charley Keller	45.00	22.00	13.50

		NR MT	EX	VG
85	Hank Greenberg			
86	Red Ruffing	90.00	45.00	27.00
87	Hal Trosky			
88	George Case	35.00	17.50	10.50
89	Mel Ott			
90	Burgess Whitehead	90.00	45.00	27.00
91	Harry Danning			
92	Harry Gumbert	35.00	17.50	10.50
93	Babe Young			
94	Cliff Melton	35.00	17.50	10.50
95	Jimmy Ripple			
96	Bucky Walters	35.00	17.50	10.50
97	Stanley Hack			
98	Bob Klinger	35.00	17.50	10.50
99	Johnny Mize			
100	Dan Litwhiler	60.00	30.00	20.00
101	Dominic Dallessandro			
102	Augie Galan	50.00	25.00	15.00
103	Bill Lee			
104	Phil Cavarretta	50.00	25.00	15.00
105	Lefty Grove			
106	Bobby Doerr	150.00	70.00	45.00
107	Frank Pytlak			
108	Dom DiMaggio	60.00	30.00	20.00
109	Gerald Priddy			
110	John Murphy	60.00	30.00	20.00
111	Tommy Henrich			
112	Marius Russo	75.00	37.00	22.00
113	Frank Crosetti			
114	John Sturm	75.00	37.00	22.00
115	Ival Goodman			
116	Myron McCormick	50.00	25.00	15.00
117	Eddie Joost			
118	Ernest Koy	50.00	25.00	15.00
119	Lloyd Waner			
120	Henry Majeski	75.00	37.00	22.00
121	Buddy Hassett			
122	Eugene Moore	50.00	25.00	15.00
123	Nick Etten			
124	John Rizzo	50.00	25.00	15.00
125	Sam Chapman			
126	Wally Moses	50.00	25.00	15.00
127	John Babich			
128	Richard Siebert	50.00	25.00	15.00
129	Nelson Potter			
130	Benny McCoy	50.00	25.00	15.00
131	Clarence Campbell			
132	Louis Boudreau	75.00	37.00	22.00
133	Rolly Hemsley			
134	Mel Harder	50.00	25.00	15.00
135	Gerald Walker			
136	Joe Heving	50.00	25.00	15.00
137	John Rucker			
138	Ace Adams	50.00	25.00	15.00
139	Morris Arnovich			
140	Carl Hubbell	125.00	62.00	37.00
141	Lew Riggs			
142	Leo Durocher	75.00	37.00	22.00
143	Fred Fitzsimmons			
144	Joe Vosmik	50.00	25.00	15.00
145	Frank Crespi			
146	Jim Brown	50.00	25.00	15.00
147	Don Heffner			
148	Harland Clift (Harlond)	50.00	25.00	15.00
149	Debs Garms			
150	Elbert Fletcher	80.00	40.00	24.00

1950 Drake's

Entitled "TV Baseball Series", the 1950 Drake's Bakeries set pictures 36 different players on a television screen format. The cards, which measure 2-1/2" by 2-1/2", contain black and white photos surrounded by a black border. The card backs carry a player biography plus an advertisement advising collectors to look for the cards in packages of Oatmeal or Jumble cookies. The ACC designation for the set is D358.

		NR MT	EX	VG
	Complete Set:	5000.00	3000.00	1500.
	Common Player:	50.00	25.00	15.00
1	Elwin "Preacher" Roe	100.00	50.00	30.00
2	Clint Hartung	50.00	25.00	15.00
3	Earl Torgeson	50.00	25.00	15.00
4	Leland "Lou" Brissie	50.00	25.00	15.00
5	Edwin "Duke" Snider	350.00	175.00	100.00
6	Roy Campanella	400.00	200.00	125.00
7	Sheldon "Available" Jones	50.00	25.00	15.00
8	Carroll "Whitey" Lockman	50.00	25.00	15.00
9	Bobby Thomson	80.00	40.00	25.00
10	Dick Sisler	50.00	25.00	15.00
11	Gil Hodges	200.00	100.00	60.00
12	Eddie Waitkus	50.00	25.00	15.00
13	Bobby Doerr	150.00	75.00	45.00
14	Warren Spahn	225.00	125.00	70.00
15	John "Buddy" Kerr	50.00	25.00	15.00
16	Sid Gordon	50.00	25.00	15.00
17	Willard Marshall	50.00	25.00	15.00
18	Carl Furillo	90.00	45.00	25.00
19	Harold "Pee Wee" Reese	300.00	150.00	90.00
20	Alvin Dark	70.00	35.00	20.00
21	Del Ennis	50.00	25.00	15.00
22	Ed Stanky	70.00	35.00	20.00
23	Tommy "Old Reliable" Henrich	90.00	45.00	25.00
24	Larry "Yogi" Berra	400.00	200.00	125.00
25	Phil "Scooter" Rizzuto	275.00	150.00	100.00
26	Jerry Coleman	70.00	35.00	20.00
27	Joe Page	70.00	35.00	20.00
28	Allie Reynolds	90.00	45.00	25.00
29	Ray Scarborough	50.00	25.00	15.00
30	George "Birdie" Tebbetts	50.00	25.00	15.00
31	Maurice "Lefty" McDermott	50.00	25.00	15.00
32	Johnny Pesky	70.00	35.00	20.00
33	Dom "Little Professor" DiMaggio	80.00	40.00	25.00
34	Vern "Junior" Stephens	50.00	25.00	15.00
35	Bob Elliott	50.00	25.00	15.00
36	Enos "Country" Slaughter	225.00	112.00	70.00

1981 Drake's

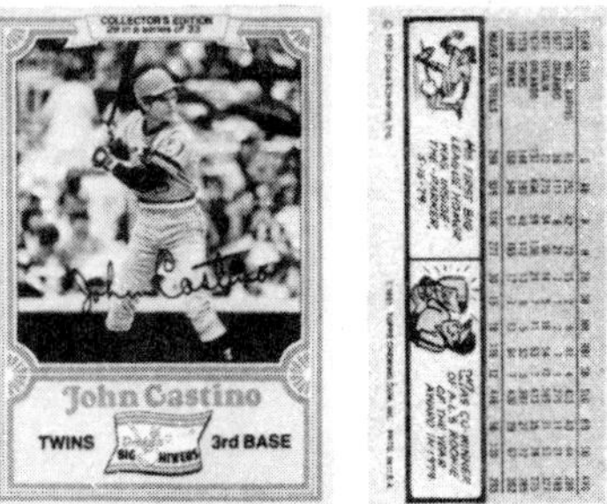

Producing their first baseball card set since 1950, Drake Bakeries, in conjunction with Topps, issued a 33-card set entitled "Big Hitters." The cards, which are the standard 2-1/2" by 3-1/2" in size, feature 19 American League and 14 National League sluggers. Full-color photos, containing a facsimile autograph, are positioned in red frames for A.L. players and blue frames for N.L. hitters. The player's name, team, position, and the Drake's logo are also included on the card fronts. The card backs, which are similar to the regular 1981 Topps issue, contain the card number (1-33), statistical and biographical informa- tion, and the Drake's logo.

		MT	NR MT	EX
	Complete Set:	7.00	5.25	2.75
	Common Player:	.12	.09	.05
1	Carl Yastrzemski	.70	.50	.30
2	Rod Carew	.50	.40	.20
3	Pete Rose	1.00	.70	.40
4	Dave Parker	.25	.20	.10
5	George Brett	.70	.50	.30
6	Eddie Murray	.50	.40	.20
7	Mike Schmidt	1.00	.70	.40
8	Jim Rice	.45	.35	.20
9	Fred Lynn	.25	.20	.10
10	Reggie Jackson	.60	.45	.25
11	Steve Garvey	.45	.35	.20
12	Ken Singleton	.12	.09	.05
13	Bill Buckner	.12	.09	.05
14	Dave Winfield	.50	.40	.20
15	Jack Clark	.30	.25	.12
16	Cecil Cooper	.20	.15	.08
17	Bob Horner	.20	.15	.08
18	George Foster	.20	.15	.08
19	Dave Kingman	.20	.15	.08
20	Cesar Cedeno	.12	.09	.05
21	Joe Charboneau	.12	.09	.05
22	George Hendrick	.12	.09	.05
23	Gary Carter	.45	.35	.20
24	Al Oliver	.20	.15	.08
25	Bruce Bochte	.12	.09	.05
26	Jerry Mumphrey	.12	.09	.05
27	Steve Kemp	.12	.09	.05
28	Bob Watson	.12	.09	.05
29	John Castino	.12	.09	.05
30	Tony Armas	.12	.09	.05
31	John Mayberry	.12	.09	.05
32	Carlton Fisk	.30	.25	.12
33	Lee Mazzilli	.12	.09	.05

1982 Drake's

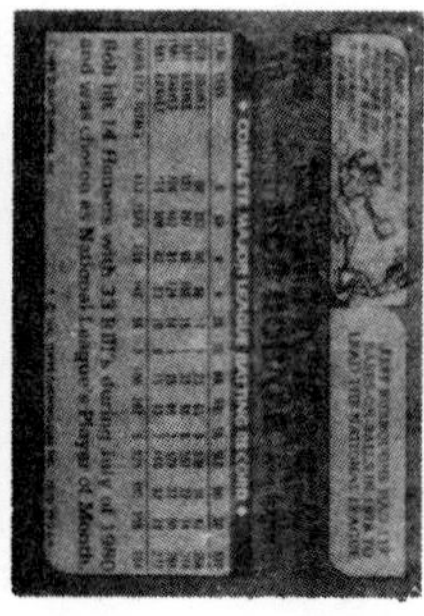

Drake Bakeries produced, in conjunction with Topps, a "2nd Annual Collectors' Edition" in 1982. Thirty-three standard-size cards (2-1/2" by 3-1/2") make up the set. Like the previous year, the set is entitled "Big Hitters" and is comprised of 19 American League players and 14 from the National League. The card fronts have a mounted photo appearance and contain a facsimile autograph. The player's name, team, position, and the Drake's logo also are located on the fronts. The card backs, other than being numbered 1-33 and containing a Drake's copyright line, are identical to the regular 1982 Topps issue.

		MT	NR MT	EX
	Complete Set:	9.00	6.75	3.50
	Common Player:	.12	.09	.05
1	Tony Armas	.12	.09	.05
2	Buddy Bell	.20	.15	.08
3	Johnny Bench	.50	.40	.20
4	George Brett	.70	.50	.30
5	Bill Buckner	.12	.09	.05
6	Rod Carew	.50	.40	.20
7	Gary Carter	.45	.35	.20
8	Jack Clark	.30	.25	.12
9	Cecil Cooper	.20	.15	.08
10	Jose Cruz	.12	.09	.05
11	Dwight Evans	.20	.15	.08
12	Carlton Fisk	.30	.25	.12
13	George Foster	.20	.15	.08
14	Steve Garvey	.45	.35	.20
15	Kirk Gibson	.40	.30	.15
16	Mike Hargrove	.12	.09	.05
17	George Hendrick	.12	.09	.05
18	Bob Horner	.20	.15	.08
19	Reggie Jackson	.60	.45	.25
20	Terry Kennedy	.12	.09	.05
21	Dave Kingman	.20	.15	.08
22	Greg Luzinski	.20	.15	.08
23	Bill Madlock	.20	.15	.08
24	John Mayberry	.12	.09	.05
25	Eddie Murray	.50	.40	.20
26	Graig Nettles	.20	.15	.08
27	Jim Rice	.45	.35	.20
28	Pete Rose	1.00	.70	.40
29	Mike Schmidt	1.00	.70	.40
30	Ken Singleton	.12	.09	.05
31	Dave Winfield	.50	.40	.20
32	Butch Wynegar	.12	.09	.05
33	Richie Zisk	.12	.09	.05

1983 Drake's

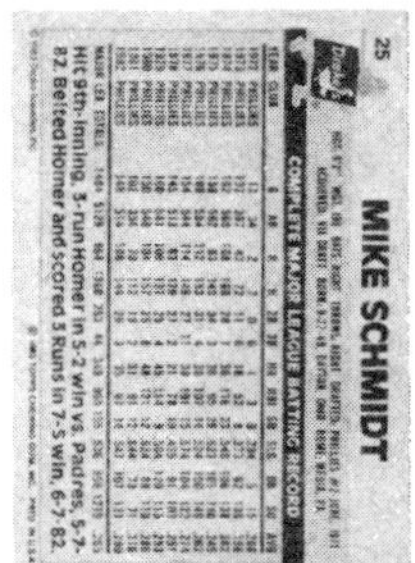

Seventeen American League and 16 National League "Big Hitters" make up the 33-card "3rd Annual Collectors' Edition" set issued by Drake Bakeries in 1983. The Topps-produced set contains 33 cards which measure 2-1/2" by 3-1/2" in size. The card fronts are somewhat similar in design to the previous year's set. The backs are identical to the 1983 Topps regular issue except for being numbered 1-33 and containing a Drake's logo and copyright line.

		MT	NR MT	EX
	Complete Set:	7.00	5.25	2.75
	Common Player:	.12	.09	.05
1	Don Baylor	.20	.15	.08
2	Bill Buckner	.12	.09	.05
3	Rod Carew	.50	.40	.20
4	Gary Carter	.45	.35	.20
5	Jack Clark	.25	.20	.10
6	Cecil Cooper	.20	.15	.08
7	Dwight Evans	.20	.15	.08
8	George Foster	.20	.15	.08
9	Pedro Guerrero	.25	.20	.10
10	George Hendrick	.12	.09	.05
11	Bob Horner	.20	.15	.08
12	Reggie Jackson	.60	.45	.25
13	Steve Kemp	.12	.09	.05
14	Dave Kingman	.20	.15	.08
15	Bill Madlock	.20	.15	.08

		MT	NR MT	EX
16	Gary Matthews	.12	.09	.05
17	Hal McRae	.12	.09	.05
18	Dale Murphy	.70	.50	.30
19	Eddie Murray	.50	.40	.20
20	Ben Oglivie	.12	.09	.05
21	Al Oliver	.20	.15	.08
22	Jim Rice	.45	.35	.20
23	Cal Ripken	.60	.45	.25
24	Pete Rose	1.00	.70	.40
25	Mike Schmidt	1.00	.70	.40
26	Ken Singleton	.12	.09	.05
27	Gorman Thomas	.12	.09	.05
28	Jason Thompson	.12	.09	.05
29	Mookie Wilson	.10	.08	.04
30	Willie Wilson	.20	.15	.08
31	Dave Winfield	.50	.40	.20
32	Carl Yastrzemski	.70	.50	.30
33	Robin Yount	.40	.30	.15

1984 Drake's

For the fourth year in a row, Drake Bakeries issued a 33-card "Big Hitters" set. The 1984 edition, produced again by Topps, includes 17 National League players and 16 from the American League. As in all previous years, the card fronts feature the player in a batting pose. The backs are identical to the 1984 Topps regular issue except for being numbered 1-33 and carrying the Drake's logo and copyright line. The cards are the standard size 2-1/2" by 3-1/2".

		MT	NR MT	EX
Complete Set:		8.00	6.00	3.25
Complete Set:		.12	.09	.05
1	Don Baylor	.20	.15	.08
2	Wade Boggs	1.25	.90	.50
3	George Brett	.70	.50	.30
4	Bill Buckner	.12	.09	.05
5	Rod Carew	.50	.40	.20
6	Gary Carter	.45	.35	.20
7	Ron Cey	.12	.09	.05
8	Cecil Cooper	.20	.15	.08
9	Andre Dawson	.35	.25	.14
10	Steve Garvey	.45	.35	.20
11	Pedro Guerrero	.25	.20	.10
12	George Hendrick	.12	.09	.05
13	Keith Hernandez	.40	.30	.15
14	Bob Horner	.20	.15	.08
15	Reggie Jackson	.60	.45	.25
16	Steve Kemp	.12	.09	.05
17	Ron Kittle	.20	.15	.08
18	Greg Luzinski	.20	.15	.08
19	Fred Lynn	.20	.15	.08
20	Bill Madlock	.20	.15	.08
21	Gary Matthews	.12	.09	.05
22	Dale Murphy	.70	.50	.30
23	Eddie Murray	.50	.40	.20
24	Al Oliver	.20	.15	.08
25	Jim Rice	.45	.35	.20
26	Cal Ripken	.60	.45	.25
27	Pete Rose	1.00	.70	.40
28	Mike Schmidt	1.00	.70	.40
29	Darryl Strawberry	1.25	.90	.50
30	Alan Trammell	.30	.25	.12
31	Mookie Wilson	.12	.09	.05
32	Dave Winfield	.50	.40	.20
33	Robin Yount	.40	.30	.15

1985 Drake's

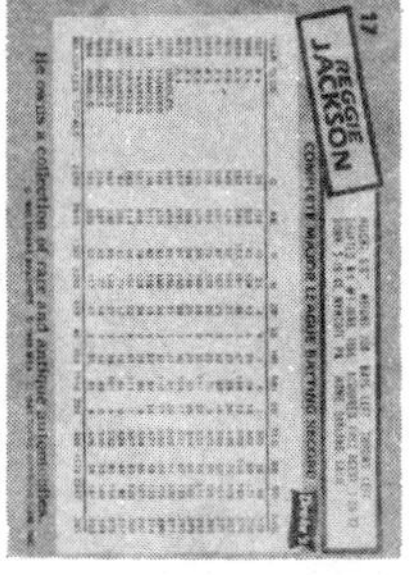

The "5th Annual Collectors' Edition" set produced by Topps for Drake Bakeries consists of 33 "Big Hitters" and 11 "Super Pitchers." The new "Super Pitchers" feature increased the set's size from the usual 33 cards to 44. The cards, which measure 2-1/2" by 3-1/2", show the player in either a batting or pitching pose. The backs differ only from the regular 1985 Topps issue in that they are numbered 1-44 and carry the Drake's logo.

		MT	NR MT	EX
Complete Set:		13.00	9.75	5.25
Commmon Player:		.12	.09	.05
1	Tony Armas	.12	.09	.05
2	Harold Baines	.20	.15	.08
3	Don Baylor	.20	.15	.08
4	George Brett	.70	.50	.30
5	Gary Carter	.45	.35	.20
6	Ron Cey	.12	.09	.05
7	Jose Cruz	.12	.09	.05
8	Alvin Davis	.25	.20	.10
9	Chili Davis	.12	.09	.05
10	Dwight Evans	.20	.15	.08
11	Steve Garvey	.45	.35	.20
12	Kirk Gibson	.35	.25	.14
13	Pedro Guerrero	.25	.20	.10
14	Tony Gwynn	.60	.45	.25
15	Keith Hernandez	.40	.30	.15
16	Kent Hrbek	.35	.25	.14
17	Reggie Jackson	.60	.45	.25
18	Gary Matthews	.12	.09	.05
19	Don Mattingly	2.25	1.75	.90
20	Dale Murphy	.70	.50	.30
21	Eddie Murray	.45	.35	.20
22	Dave Parker	.20	.15	.08
23	Lance Parrish	.25	.20	.10
24	Tim Raines	.45	.35	.20
25	Jim Rice	.45	.35	.20
26	Cal Ripken	.60	.45	.25
27	Juan Samuel	.25	.20	.10
28	Ryne Sandberg	.40	.30	.15
29	Mike Schmidt	1.00	.70	.40
30	Darryl Strawberry	.90	.70	.35
31	Alan Trammell	.30	.25	.12
32	Dave Winfield	.50	.40	.20
33	Robin Yount	.40	.30	.15
34	Mike Boddicker	.12	.09	.05
35	Steve Carlton	.40	.30	.15
36	Dwight Gooden	1.50	1.25	.60
37	Willie Hernandez	.12	.09	.05
38	Mark Langston	.20	.15	.08
39	Dan Quisenberry	.12	.09	.05
40	Dave Righetti	.20	.15	.08
41	Tom Seaver	.40	.30	.15
42	Bob Stanley	.12	.09	.05
43	Rick Sutcliffe	.20	.15	.08
44	Bruce Sutter	.20	.15	.08

1986 Drake's

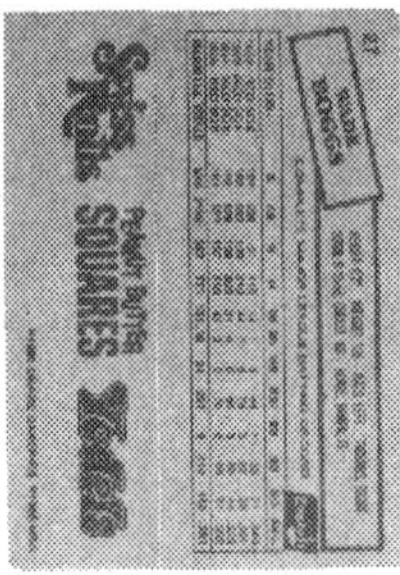

For the sixth year in a row, Drake Bakeries issued a baseball card set. Produced for Drake's by Topps in the past, the 1986 set was not and was available only by buying the actual products the cards were printed on. The cards, which measure 2-1/2" by 3-1/2", were issued in either two-, three-, or four-card panels. Fourteen panels, consisting of 37 different players, comprise the set. The players who make up the set are tabbed as either "Big Hitters" or "Super Pitchers." Logos of various Drake's products can be found on the panel backs. The value of the set is higher when collected in either panel or complete box form.

		MT	NR MT	EX
Complete Panel Set:		40.00	30.00	16.00
Complete Singles Set:		25.00	18.50	10.00
Common Panel:		1.75	1.25	.70
Common Single Player:		.20	.15	.08
Panel		1.75	1.25	.70
1	Gary Carter	.50	.40	.20
2	Dwight Evans	.25	.20	.10
Panel		2.00	1.50	.80
3	Reggie Jackson	.60	.45	.25
4	Dave Parker	.25	.20	.10
Panel		2.00	1.50	.80
5	Rickey Henderson	1.00	.70	.40
6	Pedro Guerrero	.30	.25	.12
Panel		5.00	3.75	2.00
7	Don Mattingly	2.00	1.50	.80
8	Mike Marshall	.25	.20	.10
9	Keith Moreland	.20	.15	.08
Panel		2.00	1.50	.80
10	Keith Hernandez	.40	.30	.15
11	Cal Ripken	.60	.45	.25
Panel		2.25	1.75	.90
12	Dale Murphy	.60	.45	.25
13	Jim Rice	.40	.30	.15
Panel		2.25	1.75	.90
14	George Brett	.60	.45	.25
15	Tim Raines	.50	.40	.20
Panel		2.00	1.50	.80
16	Darryl Strawberry	.80	.60	.30
17	Bill Buckner	.20	.15	.08
Panel		2.75	2.00	1.00
18	Dave Winfield	.50	.40	.20
19	Ryne Sandberg	.40	.30	.15
20	Steve Balboni	.20	.15	.08
21	Tom Herr	.25	.20	.10
Panel		3.75	2.75	1.50
22	Pete Rose	.90	.70	.35
23	Willie McGee	.25	.20	.10
24	Harold Baines	.25	.20	.10
25	Eddie Murray	.50	.40	.20
Panel		4.00	3.00	1.50
26	Mike Schmidt	1.00	.70	.40
27	Wade Boggs	1.25	.90	.50
28	Kirk Gibson	.35	.25	.14
Panel		2.00	1.50	.80
29	Bret Saberhagen	.35	.25	.14
30	John Tudor	.20	.15	.08
31	Orel Hershiser	.40	.30	.15
Panel		2.00	1.50	.80
32	Ron Guidry	.25	.20	.10
33	Nolan Ryan	1.00	.70	.40
34	Dave Stieb	.25	.20	.10
Panel		2.75	2.00	1.00
35	Dwight Gooden	.80	.60	.30
36	Fernando Valenzuela	.35	.25	.14
37	Tom Browning	.25	.20	.10

1987 Drake's

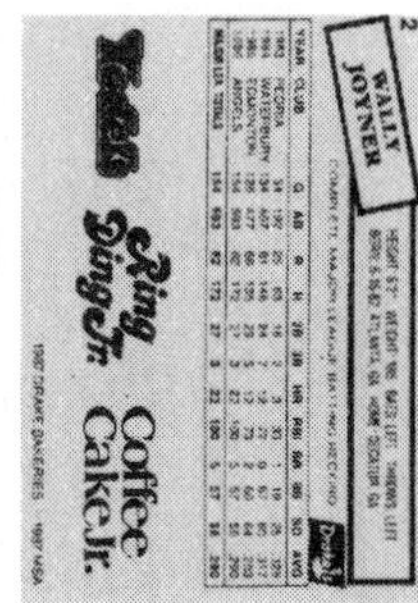

For the seventh consecutive season, Drake Bakeries produced a baseball card set. The cards, which measure 2-1/2" by 3-1/2", were included in either two-, three-, or four-card panels on boxes of various Drake's products distributed in the eastern United States. The set is comprised of 33 cards, with 25 players branded as "Big Hitters" and 8 as "Super Pitchers". The card fronts carry a full-color photo and the Drake's logo surrounded by a brown and yellow border. The backs contain the player's complete major league record.

		MT	NR MT	EX
Complete Panel Set:		40.00	30.00	16.00
Complete Singles Set:		25.00	18.50	10.00
Common Panel:		1.75	1.25	.70
Common Single Player:		.20	.15	.08
Panel		4.00	3.00	1.50
1	Darryl Strawberry	.80	.60	.30
2	Wally Joyner	1.25	.90	.50
Panel		3.75	2.75	1.50
3	Von Hayes	.25	.20	.10
4	Jose Canseco	1.75	1.25	.70
Panel		2.00	1.50	.80
5	Dave Winfield	.50	.40	.20
6	Cal Ripken	.60	.45	.25
Panel		4.50	3.50	1.75
7	Keith Moreland	.20	.15	.08
8	Don Mattingly	2.00	1.50	.80
9	Willie McGee	.25	.20	.10
Panel		2.00	1.50	.80
10	Keith Hernandez	.40	.30	.15
11	Tony Gwynn	.60	.45	.25
Panel		4.25	3.25	1.75
12	Rickey Henderson	1.00	.70	.40
13	Dale Murphy	.60	.45	.25
14	George Brett	.60	.45	.25
15	Jim Rice	.40	.30	.15
Panel		4.00	3.00	1.50
16	Wade Boggs	1.25	.90	.50
17	Kevin Bass	.20	.15	.08
18	Dave Parker	.25	.20	.10
19	Kirby Puckett	.50	.40	.20
Panel		2.00	1.50	.80
20	Gary Carter	.50	.40	.20
21	Ryne Sandberg	.40	.30	.15
22	Harold Baines	.25	.20	.10
Panel		2.75	2.00	1.00
23	Mike Schmidt	1.00	.70	.40
24	Eddie Murray	.50	.40	.20
25	Steve Sax	.25	.20	.10
Panel		1.75	1.25	.70

		MT	NR MT	EX
26	Dwight Gooden	.80	.60	.30
27	Jack Morris	.25	.20	.10
Panel		1.75	1.25	.70
28	Ron Darling	.25	.20	.10
29	Fernando Valenzuela	.35	.25	.14
30	John Tudor	.20	.15	.08
Panel		2.50	2.00	1.00
31	Roger Clemens	.80	.60	.30
32	Nolan Ryan	1.00	.70	.40
33	Mike Scott	.25	.20	.10

1988 Drake's

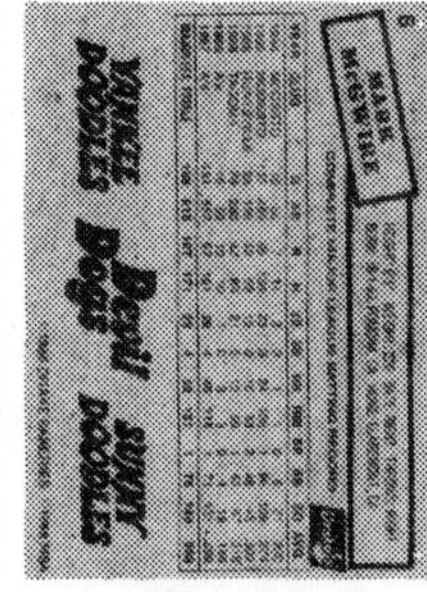

The 8th annual edition of this set includes 33 glossy full-color cards printed on cut-out panels of 2, 3 or 4 cards on Drake's dessert snack boxes. Card fronts have white borders with a large red and blue "Super Pitchers" (6 cards) or "Big Hitters" (27 cards) caption upper left, beside the "8th Annual Collector's Edition label. The Drake logo, player name and team logo are printed in black and include the card number, personal data, batting/pitching record and sponsor logos. Sets were available exclusively on 12 different Drake's packages. To complete the set, collectors had to purchase all 12 products.

		MT	NR MT	EX
Complete Panel Set:		40.00	30.00	16.00
Complete Singles Set:		25.00	18.50	10.00
Common Panel:		1.75	1.25	.70
Common Single Player:		.20	.15	.08
Panel		4.25	3.25	1.75
1	Don Mattingly	2.00	1.50	.80
2	Tim Raines	.50	.40	.20
Panel		3.75	2.75	1.50
3	Darryl Strawberry	.80	.60	.30
4	Wade Boggs	1.25	.90	.50
Panel		3.25	2.50	1.25
5	Keith Hernandez	.40	.30	.15
6	Mark McGwire	1.25	.90	.50
Panel		2.75	2.00	1.00
7	Rickey Henderson	1.00	.70	.40
8	Mike Schmidt	.60	.45	.25
9	Dwight Evans	.25	.20	.10
Panel		1.75	1.25	.70
10	Gary Carter	.50	.40	.20
11	Paul Molitor	.30	.25	.12
Panel		2.75	2.00	1.00
12	Dave Winfield	.50	.40	.20
13	Alan Trammell	.35	.25	.14
14	Tony Gwynn	.50	.40	.20
Panel		2.50	2.00	1.00
15	Dale Murphy	.60	.45	.25
16	Andre Dawson	.30	.25	.12
17	Von Hayes	.20	.15	.08
18	Willie Randolph	.20	.15	.08
Panel		2.00	1.50	.80
19	Kirby Puckett	.50	.40	.20
20	Juan Samuel	.25	.20	.10
21	Eddie Murray	.40	.30	.15
Panel		3.00	2.25	1.25
22	George Bell	.35	.25	.14
23	Larry Sheets	.20	.15	.08
24	Eric Davis	.70	.50	.30
Panel		2.25	1.75	.90
25	Cal Ripken	.60	.45	.25
26	Pedro Guerrero	.25	.20	.10
27	Will Clark	1.75	1.25	.70
Panel		2.00	1.50	.80
28	Dwight Gooden	.80	.60	.30
29	Frank Viola	.25	.20	.10
Panel		3.00	2.25	1.25
30	Roger Clemens	.80	.60	.30
31	Rick Sutcliffe	.20	.15	.08
32	Jack Morris	.25	.20	.10
33	John Tudor	.20	.15	.08

A player's name in *italic* type indicates a rookie card. An (FC) indicates a player's first card for that particular card company.

Definitions for grading conditions are located in the Introduction section at the front of this book.

1909-11 E90-1 American Caramel

The E90-1 set was issued by the American Caramel Co. from 1909 through 1911, with the bulk of the set being produced in the first year. The cards, which measure 1-1/2" by 2-3/4" in size and were issued with sticks of caramel candy, are color reproductions of actual photographs. The card backs state that 100 subjects are included in the set though more actually do exist. There are several levels of scarcity in the set, those levels being mostly determined by the year the cards were issued. Mitchell (Cincinnati), Clarke (Pittsburg), Graham, and Sweeney (Boston) are the most difficult cards in the set to obtain. For the collector's convenience, the players' first names have been added in the checklist that follows. The complete set price includes all variations.

		NR MT	EX	VG
Complete Set:		85000.	35000.	13500.
Common Player:		125.00	62.00	37.00
(1)	Bill Bailey	125.00	62.00	37.00
(2)	Home Run Baker	550.00	220.00	105.00
(3)	Jack Barry	125.00	62.00	37.00
(4)	George Bell	125.00	62.00	37.00
(5)	Harry Bemis	225.00	100.00	50.00
(6)	Chief Bender	450.00	180.00	95.00
(7)	Bob Bescher	175.00	75.00	40.00
(8)	Cliff Blankenship	125.00	62.00	37.00
(9)	John Bliss	125.00	62.00	37.00
(10)	Bill Bradley	125.00	62.00	37.00
(11)	Kitty Bransfield ("P" on shirt)	125.00	62.00	37.00
(12)	Kitty Bransfield (no "P" on shirt)	175.00	75.00	40.00
(13)	Roger Bresnahan	500.00	250.00	125.00
(14)	Al Bridwell	125.00	62.00	37.00
(15)	Buster Brown (Boston)	125.00	62.00	37.00
(16)	Mordecai Brown (Chicago)	650.00	275.00	150.00
(17)	Donie Bush	125.00	62.00	37.00
(18)	John Butler	125.00	62.00	37.00
(19)	Howie Camnitz	125.00	62.00	37.00
(20)	Frank Chance	550.00	225.00	105.00
(21)	Hal Chase	150.00	70.00	30.00
(22a)	Fred Clarke (Philadelphia)	450.00	180.00	95.00
(22b)	Fred Clarke (Pittsburgh)	1500.	750.00	335.00
(23)	Wally Clement	175.00	75.00	40.00
(24)	Ty Cobb	4500.	2000.	900.00
(25)	Eddie Collins	550.00	220.00	105.00
(26)	Sam Crawford	500.00	200.00	100.00
(27)	Frank Corridon	125.00	62.00	37.00
(28)	Lou Criger	125.00	62.00	37.00
(29)	George Davis	125.00	62.00	37.00
(30)	Harry Davis	125.00	62.00	37.00
(31)	Ray Demmitt	375.00	150.00	60.00
(32)	Mike Donlin	125.00	62.00	37.00
(33)	Wild Bill Donovan	125.00	62.00	37.00
(34)	Red Dooin	125.00	62.00	37.00
(35)	Patsy Dougherty	225.00	100.00	50.00
(36)	Hugh Duffy	1800.	900.00	400.00
(37)	Jimmy Dygert	125.00	62.00	37.00
(38)	Rube Ellis	125.00	62.00	37.00
(39)	Clyde Engle	125.00	62.00	37.00
(40)	Art Fromme	450.00	200.00	75.00
(41)	George Gibson (back view)	600.00	250.00	100.00
(42)	George Gibson (front view)	125.00	62.00	37.00
(43)	Peaches Graham	2200.	1000.	600.00
(44)	Eddie Grant	125.00	62.00	37.00
(45)	Dolly Gray	125.00	62.00	37.00
(46)	Bob Groom	125.00	62.00	37.00
(47)	Charley Hall	125.00	62.00	37.00
(48)	Roy Hartzell (fielding)	125.00	62.00	37.00
(49)	Roy Hartzell (batting)	125.00	62.00	37.00
(50)	Heinie Heitmuller	125.00	62.00	37.00
(51)	Harry Howell (follow thru)	125.00	62.00	37.00
(52)	Harry Howell (windup)	175.00	75.00	40.00
(53)	Tex Irwin (Erwin)	125.00	62.00	37.00
(54)	Frank Isbell	125.00	62.00	37.00
(55)	Shoeless Joe Jackson	7500.	3500.	1600.
(56)	Hughie Jennings	500.00	250.00	100.00
(57)	Buck Jordon (Jordan)	125.00	62.00	37.00
(58)	Addie Joss (portrait)	500.00	250.00	100.00
(59)	Addie Joss (pitching)	1650.	825.00	350.00
(60)	Ed Karger	1650.	825.00	350.00
(61a)	Willie Keeler (portrait, pink background)	550.00	225.00	125.00
(61b)	Willie Keeler (portrait, red background)	1650.	825.00	375.00
(62)	Willie Keeler (throwing)	2000.	1000.	500.00
(63)	John Knight	125.00	62.00	37.00
(64)	Harry Krause	125.00	62.00	37.00
(65)	Nap Lajoie	775.00	350.00	175.00
(66)	Tommy Leach (throwing)	125.00	62.00	37.00
(67)	Tommy Leach (batting)	125.00	62.00	37.00
(68)	Sam Leever	125.00	62.00	37.00
(69)	Hans Lobert	1000.	400.00	245.00
(70)	Harry Lumley	125.00	62.00	37.00
(71)	Rube Marquard	500.00	200.00	100.00
(72)	Christy Matthewson (Mathewson)	1000.	500.00	225.00
(73)	Stuffy McInnes (McInnis)	125.00	62.00	37.00
(74)	Harry McIntyre	125.00	62.00	37.00
(75)	Larry McLean	225.00	100.00	40.00
(76)	George McQuillan	125.00	62.00	37.00
(77)	Dots Miller	125.00	62.00	37.00
(78)	Fred Mitchell (New York)	125.00	62.00	37.00
(79)	Mike Mitchell (Cincinnati)	10000.	5000.	2250.
(80)	George Mullin	125.00	62.00	37.00
(81)	Rebel Oakes	125.00	62.00	37.00
(82)	Paddy O'Connor	125.00	62.00	37.00
(83)	Charley O'Leary	125.00	62.00	37.00
(84)	Orval Overall	1000.	475.00	235.00
(85)	Jim Pastorius	125.00	62.00	37.00
(86)	Ed Phelps	125.00	62.00	37.00
(87)	Eddie Plank	900.00	450.00	200.00
(88)	Lew Richie	125.00	62.00	37.00
(89)	Germany Schaefer	125.00	62.00	37.00
(90)	Biff Schlitzer	175.00	75.00	35.00
(91)	Johnny Seigle (Siegle)	225.00	100.00	40.00
(92)	Dave Shean	175.00	75.00	35.00
(93)	Jimmy Sheckard	175.00	75.00	35.00
(94)	Tris Speaker	2000.	900.00	400.00
(95)	Jake Stahl	1650.	825.00	375.00
(96)	Oscar Stanage	125.00	62.00	37.00
(97)	George Stone (no hands visible)	125.00	62.00	37.00
(98)	George Stone (left hand visible)	125.00	62.00	37.00
(99)	George Stovall	125.00	62.00	37.00
(100)	Ed Summers	125.00	62.00	37.00
(101)	Bill Sweeney (Boston)	1800.	900.00	400.00
(102)	Jeff Sweeney (New York)	125.00	62.00	37.00
(103)	Jesse Tannehill (Chicago A.L.)	125.00	62.00	37.00
(104)	Lee Tannehill (Chicago N.L.)	125.00	62.00	37.00
(105)	Fred Tenney	125.00	62.00	37.00
(106)	Ira Thomas (Philadelphia)	125.00	62.00	37.00
(107)	Roy Thomas (Boston)	125.00	62.00	37.00
(108)	Joe Tinker	500.00	225.00	100.00
(109)	Bob Unglaub	125.00	62.00	37.00
(110)	Jerry Upp	125.00	62.00	37.00
(111)	Honus Wagner (batting)	1500.	750.00	300.00
(112)	Honus Wagner (throwing)	1500.	750.00	300.00
(113)	Bobby Wallace	400.00	175.00	90.00
(114)	Ed Walsh	1750.	875.00	500.00
(115)	Vic Willis	125.00	62.00	37.00
(116)	Hooks Wiltse	225.00	100.00	35.00
(117)	Cy Young (Cleveland)	900.00	450.00	225.00
(118)	Cy Young (Boston)	750.00	375.00	200.00

The values quoted are intended to reflect the market price.

1910 E90-2 American Caramel

Closely related to the E90-1 American Caramel set, the E90-2 set consists of 11 cards featuring members of the 1909 champion Pittsburgh Pirates. The cards measure 1-1/2" by 2-3/4" and display a color lithograph on the front with a solid color background of either red, green blue or pink. The player's name and "Pittsburg" appear in blue capital letters in the border beneath the portrait. The backs are identical to those in the E90-1 set, depicting a drawing of a ball, glove and crossed bats with the words "Base Ball Caramels" and a reference to "100 Subjects." The set includes Hall of Famers Honus Wagner and Fred Clarke.

		NR MT	EX	VG
Complete Set:		5000.	2500.	1000.
Common Player:		175.00	87.00	52.00
(1)	Babe Adams	175.00	87.00	52.00
(2)	Fred Clarke	500.00	225.00	100.00
(3)	George Gibson	175.00	87.00	52.00
(4)	Ham Hyatt	175.00	87.00	52.00
(5)	Tommy Leach	175.00	87.00	52.00
(6)	Sam Leever	175.00	87.00	52.00
(7)	Nick Maddox	175.00	87.00	52.00
(8)	Dots Miller	175.00	87.00	52.00
(9)	Deacon Phillippe	175.00	87.00	52.00
(10)	Honus Wagner	2000.	900.00	400.00
(11)	Owen Wilson	175.00	87.00	52.00

1910 E90-3 American Caramel

Schulte, r. f. Cubs

Similar in size (1-1/2" by 2-3/4") and style to the more popular E90-1 set, the E90-3 set was issued by the American Caramel Co. in 1910. The 20-card, color lithograph set includes 11 Chicago Cubs and nine White Sox. The fronts of the cards have a similar design to the E90-1 set, although different photos were used. The backs can be differentiated by two major changes: The bottom of the card indicates the American Caramel Co. of "Chicago," rather than Philadelphia, and the top of the card contains the phrase "All The Star Players," rather than "100 Subjects." The E90-3 cards are generally more scarce than those in the E90-1 set.

		NR MT	EX	VG
Complete Set:		8500.	4000.	2200.
Common Player:		200.00	100.00	60.00
(1)	Jimmy Archer	200.00	100.00	60.00
(2)	Lena Blackburne	200.00	100.00	60.00
(3)	Mordecai Brown	600.00	300.00	150.00
(4)	Frank Chance	900.00	450.00	200.00
(5)	King Cole	200.00	100.00	60.00
(6)	Patsy Dougherty	200.00	100.00	60.00
(7)	Johnny Evers	600.00	300.00	150.00
(8)	Chick Gandil	300.00	150.00	75.00
(9)	Ed Hahn	200.00	100.00	60.00
(10)	Solly Hofman	200.00	100.00	60.00
(11)	Orval Overall	200.00	100.00	60.00
(12)	Fred Payne	200.00	100.00	60.00
(13)	Billy Purtell	200.00	100.00	60.00
(14)	Wildfire Schulte	200.00	100.00	60.00
(15)	Jimmy Sheckard	200.00	100.00	60.00
(16)	Frank Smith	200.00	100.00	60.00
(17)	Harry Steinfeldt	250.00	125.00	50.00
(18)	Joe Tinker	600.00	300.00	150.00
(19)	Ed Walsh	600.00	300.00	150.00
(20)	Rollie Zeider	200.00	100.00	60.00

1908 E91
American Caramel - Set A

Issued by Philadelphia's American Caramel Company from 1908 through 1910, the E91 set of Base Ball Caramels is generally not popular with collectors because the color drawings show "generic" players, rather than actual major leaguers. In other words, the exact same drawing was used to depict two or three different players. For this reason, the set is sometimes referred to as "Fake Design". The player's name, position and team appear below the color drawing on the front of the card. The cards measure approximately 1-1/2" by 2-3/4" and were issued in three separate series. They can be differentiated by their backs, which checklist the cards. Set A

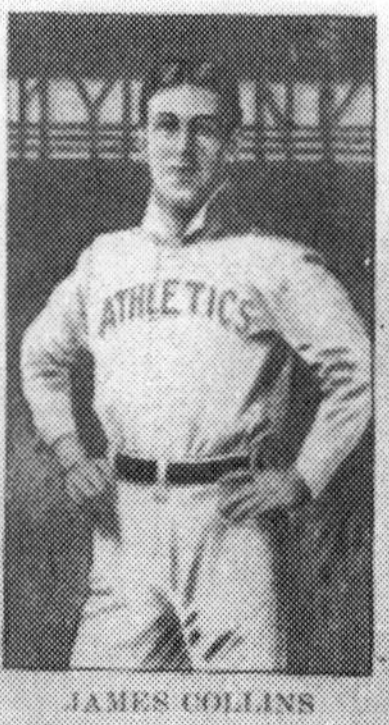

Base Ball Caramels.
THIS CARD IS ONE OF A SET OF THIRTY-THREE BASE BALL PLAYERS, CONSISTING OF NEW YORK, PHILADELPHIA AND CHICAGO BASE BALL TEAMS, ONE OF WHICH IS WRAPPED WITH EVERY BASE BALL CARAMEL.
Manufactured only by the AMERICAN CARAMEL CO

backs list the Athletics in the upper left, the Giants in the upper right and the Cubs below. Set B backs list the Cubs and Athletics on top with the Giants below, and Set C backs list Pittsburg and Washington on top with Boston below. A line indicating the cards were "Manufactured Only by the American Caramel Co." appears at the bottom.

		NR MT	EX	VG
Complete Set:		4500.	2250.	1500.
Common Player:		50.00	25.00	15.00
(1)	Charles Bender	200.00	100.00	35.00
(2)	Roger Bresnahan	200.00	100.00	35.00
(3)	Albert Bridwell	50.00	25.00	15.00
(4)	Mordecai Brown	200.00	100.00	35.00
(5)	Frank Chance	250.00	125.00	40.00
(6)	James Collins	200.00	100.00	35.00
(7)	Harry Davis	50.00	25.00	15.00
(8)	Arthur Devlin	50.00	25.00	15.00
(9)	Michael Donlin	50.00	25.00	15.00
(10)	John Evers	200.00	100.00	35.00
(11)	Frederick L. Hartsel	50.00	25.00	15.00
(12)	John Kling	50.00	25.00	15.00
(13)	Christopher Matthewson (Mathewson)	350.00	175.00	75.00
(14)	Joseph McGinnity	200.00	100.00	35.00
(15)	John J McGraw	250.00	125.00	40.00
(16)	Daniel F Murphy	50.00	25.00	15.00
(17)	Simon Nicholls	50.00	25.00	15.00
(18)	Reuben Oldring	50.00	25.00	15.00
(19)	Orvill Overall (Orval)	50.00	25.00	15.00
(20)	Edward S. Plank	300.00	150.00	60.00
(21)	Edward Reulbach	50.00	25.00	15.00
(22)	James Scheckard (Sheckard)	50.00	25.00	15.00
(23)	Osee Schreckengost (Ossee)	50.00	25.00	15.00
(24)	Ralph O. Seybold	50.00	25.00	15.00
(25)	J. Bentley Seymour	50.00	25.00	15.00
(26)	Daniel Shay	50.00	25.00	15.00
(27)	Frank Shulte (Schulte)	50.00	25.00	15.00
(28)	James Slagle	50.00	25.00	15.00
(29)	Harry Steinfeldt	60.00	30.00	18.00
(30)	Luther H. Taylor	50.00	25.00	15.00
(31)	Fred Tenney	50.00	25.00	15.00
(32)	Joseph B. Tinker	200.00	100.00	35.00
(33)	George Edward Waddell	200.00	100.00	35.00

1909 E-91
American Caramel - Set B

Base Ball Caramels.
THIS CARD IS ONE OF A SET OF THIRTY-THREE BASE BALL PLAYERS, CONSISTING OF CHICAGO, ATHLETICS AND NEW YORK BASE BALL TEAMS, ONE OF WHICH IS WRAPPED WITH EVERY BASE BALL CARAMEL.
Manufactured only by the AMERICAN CARAMEL CO.

		NR MT	EX	VG
Complete Set:		4300.	2100.	1450.
Common Player:		50.00	25.00	15.00
(1)	James Archer	50.00	25.00	15.00
(2)	Frank Baker	200.00	100.00	35.00
(3)	John Barry	50.00	25.00	15.00
(4)	Charles Bender	250.00	125.00	35.00
(5)	Albert Bridwell	50.00	25.00	15.00
(6)	Mordecai Brown	200.00	100.00	35.00
(7)	Frank Chance	250.00	100.00	40.00
(8)	Edw. Collins	200.00	100.00	35.00
(9)	Harry Davis	50.00	25.00	15.00
(10)	Arthur Devlin	50.00	25.00	15.00
(11)	Michael Donlin	50.00	25.00	15.00
(12)	Larry Doyle	50.00	25.00	15.00
(13)	John Evers	200.00	100.00	35.00
(14)	Robt. Ganley	50.00	25.00	15.00
(15)	Frederick L. Hartsel	50.00	25.00	15.00
(16)	Arthur Hoffman (Hofman)	50.00	25.00	15.00
(17)	Harry Krause	50.00	25.00	15.00
(18)	Rich. W. Marquard	200.00	100.00	35.00
(19)	Christopher Matthewson (Mathewson)	350.00	175.00	75.00
(20)	John J. McGraw	250.00	125.00	40.00
(21)	J.T. Meyers	50.00	25.00	15.00
(22)	Dan Murphy	50.00	25.00	15.00
(23)	Jno. J. Murray	50.00	25.00	15.00
(24)	Orvill Overall (Orval)	50.00	25.00	15.00
(25)	Edward S. Plank	300.00	150.00	50.00
(26)	Edward Reulbach	50.00	25.00	15.00
(27)	James Scheckard (Sheckard)	50.00	25.00	15.00
(28)	J. Bentley Seymour	50.00	25.00	15.00
(29)	Harry Steinfeldt	60.00	30.00	18.00
(30)	Frank Shulte (Schulte)	60.00	30.00	18.00
(31)	Fred Tenney	50.00	25.00	15.00
(32)	Joseph B Tinker	200.00	100.00	35.00
(33)	Ira Thomas	50.00	25.00	15.00

1909 E91
American Caramel - Set C

Base Ball Caramels.
THIS CARD IS ONE OF A SET OF THIRTY-THREE BASE BALL PLAYERS, CONSISTING OF PITTSBURG, WASHINGTON AND BOSTON BASE BALL TEAMS, ONE OF WHICH IS WRAPPED WITH EVERY BASE BALL CARAMEL.
Manufactured only by the AMERICAN CARAMEL CO.

		NR MT	EX	VG
Complete Set:		4000.	2000.	1200.
Common Player:		50.00	25.00	15.00
(1)	W.J. Barbeau	50.00	25.00	15.00
(2)	Geo. Brown	50.00	25.00	15.00
(3)	Robt. Check (Charles Chech)	50.00	25.00	15.00
(4)	Fred Clarke	225.00	112.50	37.50
(5)	Wid Conroy	50.00	25.00	15.00
(6)	James Delehanty	50.00	25.00	15.00
(7)	Jon A. Donohue (Donahue)	50.00	25.00	15.00
(8)	P. Donahue	50.00	25.00	15.00
(9)	Geo. Gibson	50.00	25.00	15.00
(10)	Robt. Groom	50.00	25.00	15.00
(11)	Harry Hooper	200.00	100.00	35.00
(12)	Tom Hughes	50.00	25.00	15.00
(13)	Walter Johnson	500.00	225.00	100.00
(14)	Edwin Karger	50.00	25.00	15.00
(15)	Tommy Leach	50.00	25.00	15.00
(16)	Sam'l Leever	50.00	25.00	15.00
(17)	Harry Lord	50.00	25.00	15.00
(18)	Geo. F. McBride	50.00	25.00	15.00
(19)	Ambr. McConnell	50.00	25.00	15.00
(20)	Clyde Milan	50.00	25.00	15.00
(21)	J.B. Miller	50.00	25.00	15.00
(22)	Harry Niles	50.00	25.00	15.00
(23)	Chas. Phillipi (Phillippe)	50.00	25.00	15.00
(24)	T.H. Speaker	350.00	175.00	75.00
(25)	Jacob Stahl	50.00	25.00	15.00
(26)	Chas. E. Street	50.00	25.00	15.00
(27)	Allen Storke	50.00	25.00	15.00
(28)	Robt. Unglaub	50.00	25.00	15.00
(29)	C. Wagner	50.00	25.00	15.00
(30)	Hans Wagner	500.00	250.00	110.00
(31)	Victor Willis	50.00	25.00	15.00
(32)	Owen Wilson	50.00	25.00	15.00
(33)	Jos. Wood	75.00	35.00	18.00

1909 E92 Croft's Candy

		NR MT	EX	VG
Complete Set:		27500.	15000.	6500.
Common Player:		150.00	75.00	45.00
(1)	Jack Barry	450.00	225.00	100.00
(2)	Harry Bemis	150.00	75.00	45.00
(3)	Chief Bender (striped cap)	700.00	325.00	150.00
(4)	Chief Bender (white cap)	450.00	225.00	100.00
(5)	Bill Bergen	150.00	75.00	45.00
(6)	Bob Bescher	150.00	75.00	45.00
(7)	Al Bridwell	150.00	75.00	45.00
(8)	Doc Casey	150.00	75.00	45.00
(9)	Frank Chance	450.00	225.00	100.00
(10)	Hal Chase	200.00	100.00	50.00
(11)	Ty Cobb	4500.	2200.	1000.
(12)	Eddie Collins	850.00	400.00	200.00

		NR MT	EX	VG
(13)	Sam Crawford	400.00	200.00	100.00
(14)	Harry Davis	150.00	75.00	45.00
(15)	Art Devlin	150.00	75.00	45.00
(16)	Wild Bill Donovan	150.00	75.00	45.00
(17)	Red Dooin	350.00	175.00	75.00
(18)	Mickey Doolan	150.00	75.00	45.00
(19)	Patsy Dougherty	150.00	75.00	45.00
(20)	Larry Doyle (throwing)	150.00	75.00	45.00
(21)	Larry Doyle (with bat)	150.00	75.00	45.00
(22)	Johnny Evers	1000.	500.00	200.00
(23)	George Gibson	150.00	75.00	45.00
(24)	Topsy Hartsel	150.00	75.00	45.00
(25)	Fred Jacklitsch	350.00	175.00	75.00
(26)	Hugh Jennings	400.00	200.00	100.00
(27)	Red Kleinow	150.00	75.00	45.00
(28)	Otto Knabe	350.00	175.00	75.00
(29)	Jack Knight	350.00	175.00	75.00
(30)	Nap Lajoie	700.00	350.00	200.00
(31)	Hans Lobert	150.00	75.00	45.00
(32)	Sherry Magee	150.00	75.00	45.00
(33)	Christy Matthewson (Mathewson)	1200.	600.00	275.00
(34)	John McGraw	550.00	275.00	150.00
(35)	Larry McLean	150.00	75.00	45.00
(36)	Dots Miller (batting)	150.00	75.00	45.00
(37)	Dots Miller (fielding)	350.00	175.00	75.00
(38)	Danny Murphy	150.00	75.00	45.00
(39)	Bil O'Hara	150.00	75.00	45.00
(40)	Germany Schaefer	150.00	75.00	45.00
(41)	Admiral Schlei	150.00	75.00	45.00
(42)	Boss Schmidt	150.00	75.00	45.00
(43)	Johnny Seigle (Siegle)	150.00	75.00	45.00
(44)	Dave Shean	150.00	75.00	45.00
(45)	Boss Smith (Schmidt)	150.00	75.00	45.00
(46)	Joe Tinker	450.00	225.00	110.00
(47)	Honus Wagner (batting)	1000.	500.00	275.00
(48)	Honus Wagner (throwing)	1000.	500.00	275.00
(49)	Cy Young	900.00	450.00	250.00
(50)	Heinie Zimmerman	150.00	75.00	45.00

1909 E92 Croft's Cocoa

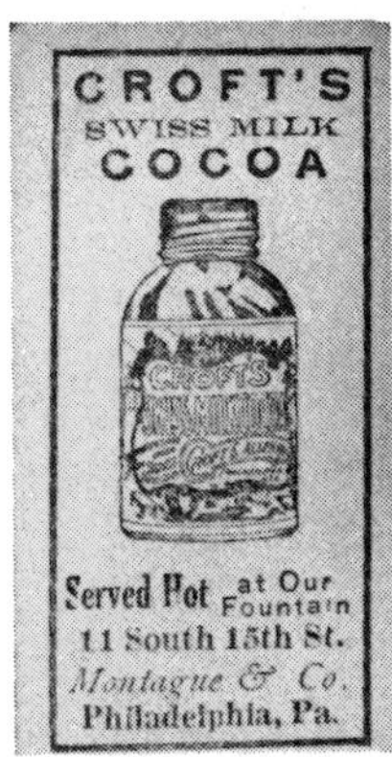

		NR MT	EX	VG
Complete Set:		27500.	15000.	6500.
Common Player:		150.00	75.00	45.00
(1)	Jack Barry	450.00	225.00	100.00
(2)	Harry Bemis	150.00	75.00	45.00
(3)	Chief Bender (striped hat)	700.00	325.00	150.00
(4)	Chief Bender (shite hat)	450.00	225.00	100.00
(5)	Bill Bergen	150.00	75.00	45.00
(6)	Bob Bescher	150.00	75.00	45.00
(7)	Al Bridwell	150.00	75.00	45.00
(8)	Doc Casey	150.00	75.00	45.00
(9)	Frank Chance	450.00	225.00	100.00
(10)	Hal Chase	200.00	100.00	50.00
(11)	Ty Cobb	4500.	2200.	1000.
(12)	Eddie Collins	850.00	400.00	200.00
(13)	Sam Crawford	400.00	200.00	100.00
(14)	Harry Davis	150.00	75.00	45.00
(15)	Art Devlin	150.00	75.00	45.00
(16)	Wild Bill Donovan	150.00	75.00	45.00
(17)	Red Dooin	350.00	175.00	75.00
(18)	Mickey Doolan	150.00	75.00	45.00
(19)	Patsy Dougherty	150.00	75.00	45.00
(20)	Larry Doyle (throwing)	150.00	75.00	45.00
(21)	Larry Doyle (with bat)	150.00	75.00	45.00
(22)	Johnny Evers	1000.	500.00	200.00
(23)	George Gibson	150.00	75.00	45.00
(24)	Topsy Hartsel	150.00	75.00	45.00
(25)	Fred Jacklitsch	350.00	175.00	75.00
(26)	Hugh Jennings	400.00	200.00	100.00
(27)	Red Kleinow	150.00	75.00	45.00
(28)	Otto Knabe	350.00	175.00	75.00
(29)	Jack Knight	350.00	175.00	75.00
(30)	Nap Lajoie	700.00	350.00	200.00
(31)	Hans Lobert	150.00	75.00	45.00
(32)	Sherry Magee	150.00	75.00	30.00
(33)	Christy Matthewson (Mathewson)	1200.	600.00	275.00
(34)	John McGraw	550.00	275.00	150.00
(35)	Larry McLean	150.00	75.00	45.00
(36)	Dots Miller (batting)	150.00	75.00	45.00
(37)	Dots Miller (fielding)	350.00	175.00	75.00
(38)	Danny Murphy	150.00	75.00	45.00
(39)	Bill O'Hara	150.00	75.00	45.00

		NR MT	EX	VG
(40)	Germany Schaefer	150.00	75.00	45.00
(41)	Admiral Schlei	150.00	75.00	45.00
(42)	Boss Schmidt	150.00	75.00	45.00
(43)	Johnny Seigle (Siegle)	150.00	75.00	45.00
(44)	Dave Shean	150.00	75.00	45.00
(45)	Boss Smith (Schmidt)	150.00	75.00	45.00
(46)	Joe Tinker	450.00	225.00	110.00
(47)	Honus Wagner (batting)	1000.	500.00	275.00
(48)	Honus Wagner (throwing)	1000.	500.00	275.00
(49)	Cy Young	900.00	450.00	250.00
(50)	Heinie Zimmerman	150.00	75.00	45.00

1909 E92 Dockman

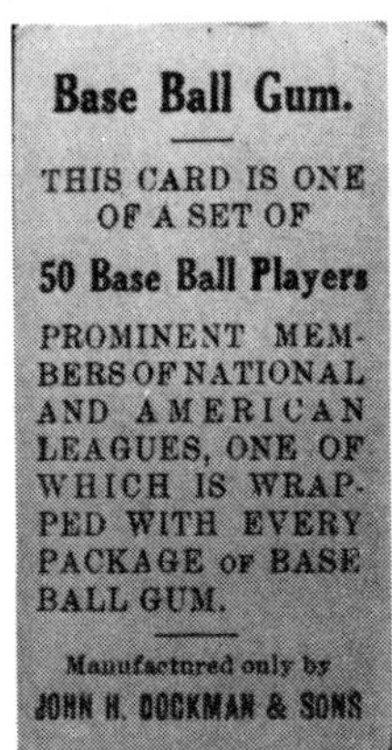

Designated in the American Card Catalog as the E92 set, this 1910 issue which is similar in size (1-1/2" by 2-3/4") and style to the E101 set, could actually be considered four separate sets, depending on the back design. The fronts of the cards are nearly identical to the more popular E90-1 American Caramels set. The four different backs included under the E92 designation advertise Croft's Candy, Croft's Cocoa, Nadja Caramels, and John H. Dockman and Sons Base Ball Gum. The basic set consists of 50 cards picturing 45 different players (five players are shown on two cards each). However, only 40 cards are known to exist with the Dockman back, and eight additional cards have been found only with the Nadja back and are considered very rare.

		NR MT	EX	VG
Complete Set:		13500.	7500.	3000.
Common Player:		125.00	62.00	37.00
(1)	Harry Bemis	125.00	62.00	37.00
(2)	Chief Bender	350.00	175.00	75.00
(3)	Bill Bergen	125.00	62.00	37.00
(4)	Bob Bescher	125.00	62.00	37.00
(5)	Al Bridwell	125.00	62.00	37.00
(6)	Doc Casey	125.00	62.00	37.00
(7)	Frank Chance	350.00	175.00	75.00
(8)	Hal Chase	125.00	50.00	25.00
(9)	Sam Crawford	300.00	150.00	50.00
(10)	Harry Davis	125.00	62.00	37.00
(11)	Art Devlin	125.00	62.00	37.00
(12)	Wild Bill Donovan	125.00	62.00	37.00
(13)	Mickey Doolan	125.00	62.00	37.00
(14)	Patsy Dougherty	125.00	62.00	37.00
(15)	Larry Doyle (throwing)	125.00	62.00	37.00
(16)	Larry Doyle (with bat)	125.00	62.00	37.00
(17)	George Gibson	125.00	62.00	37.00
(18)	Topsy Hartsel	125.00	62.00	37.00
(19)	Hugh Jennings	350.00	175.00	75.00
(20)	Red Kleinow	125.00	62.00	37.00
(21)	Nap Lajoie	500.00	250.00	100.00
(22)	Hans Lobert	125.00	62.00	37.00
(23)	Sherry Magee	125.00	62.00	37.00
(24)	Christy Matthewson (Mathewson)	900.00	450.00	200.00
(25)	John McGraw	400.00	200.00	85.00
(26)	Larry McLean	125.00	62.00	37.00
(27)	Dots Miller	125.00	62.00	37.00
(28)	Danny Murphy	125.00	62.00	37.00
(29)	Bill O'Hara	125.00	62.00	37.00
(30)	Germany Schaefer	125.00	62.00	37.00
(31)	Admiral Schlei	125.00	62.00	37.00
(32)	Boss Schmidt	125.00	62.00	37.00
(33)	Johnny Seigle	125.00	62.00	37.00
(34)	Dave Shean	125.00	62.00	37.00
(35)	Boss Smith (Schmidt)	125.00	62.00	37.00
(36)	Joe Tinker	350.00	175.00	75.00
(37)	Honus Wagner (batting)	700.00	350.00	150.00
(38)	Honus Wagner (throwing)	700.00	350.00	150.00
(39)	Cy Young	600.00	300.00	135.00
(40)	Heinie Zimmerman	125.00	62.00	37.00

1909 E92 Najda

		NR MT	EX	VG
Complete Set:		13500.	7500.	4000.
Common Player:		200.00	100.00	60.00

(1)	Bill Bailey	200.00	100.00	60.00
(2)	Roy Hartzell (batting)	200.00	100.00	60.00
(3)	Roy Hartzell (fielding)	200.00	100.00	60.00
(4)	Harry Howell (ready to pitch)	200.00	100.00	60.00
(5)	Harry Howell (follow-thru)	200.00	100.00	60.00
(6)	Eddie Phelps	200.00	100.00	60.00
(7)	George Stone	200.00	100.00	60.00
(8)	Bobby Wallace	1000.	500.00	200.00
9	Roger Bresnahan	2500.	1250.	500.00
10	Cy Young	3500.	1750.	750.00
11	Rebel Oakes	400.00	200.00	100.00
12	Fred Clarke	2500.	1250.	500.00

1910 E93 Standard Caramel

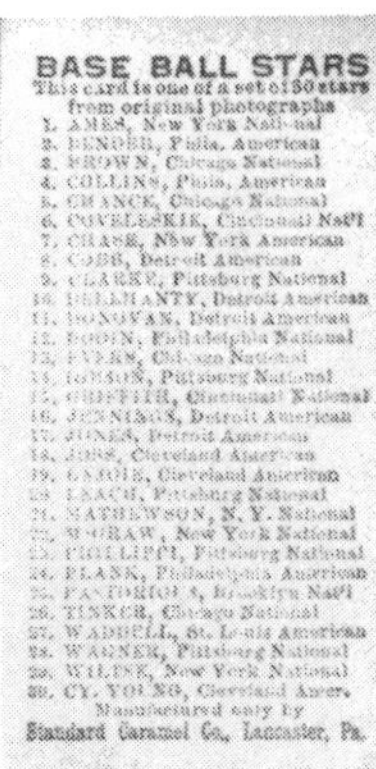

This 30-card set issued in 1910 by Standard Caramel Co. of Lancaster, Pa., is closely related to several other candy sets from this period which share the same format and, in many cases, the same player poses. The cards measure 1-1/2" by 2-3/4" and contain tinted black and white player photos. The back of each card contains an alphabetical checklist of the set plus a line indicating it was manufactured by Standard Caramel Co., Lancaster, Pa. The set carries the ACC designation of E93.

		NR MT	EX	VG
Complete Set:		24000.	10500.	5000.
Common Player:		175.00	87.00	52.00
(1)	Red Ames	175.00	87.00	52.00
(2)	Chief Bender	500.00	225.00	100.00
(3)	Mordecai Brown	500.00	225.00	100.00
(4)	Frank Chance	550.00	250.00	115.00
(5)	Hal Chase	250.00	100.00	50.00
(6)	Fred Clarke	500.00	225.00	100.00
(7)	Ty Cobb	4500.	2000.	1150.
(8)	Eddie Collins	500.00	225.00	100.00
(9)	Harry Coveleskie (Coveleski)	175.00	87.00	52.00
(10)	Jim Delehanty	175.00	87.00	52.00
(11)	Wild Bill Donovan	175.00	87.00	52.00
(12)	Red Dooin	175.00	87.00	52.00
(13)	Johnny Evers	500.00	225.00	100.00
(14)	George Gibson	175.00	87.00	52.00
(15)	Clark Griffith	500.00	225.00	100.00
(16)	Hugh Jennings	500.00	225.00	100.00
(17)	Davy Jones	175.00	87.00	52.00
(18)	Addie Joss	500.00	225.00	100.00
(19)	Nap Lajoie	750.00	350.00	150.00
(20)	Tommy Leach	175.00	87.00	52.00
(21)	Christy Mathewson	1000.	450.00	200.00
(22)	John McGraw	600.00	250.00	115.00
(23)	Jim Pastorious	175.00	87.00	52.00
(24)	Deacon Phillippi (Phillippe)	175.00	87.00	52.00
(25)	Eddie Plank	650.00	300.00	130.00
(26)	Joe Tinker	500.00	225.00	100.00
(27)	Honus Wagner	1500.	700.00	300.00
(28)	Rube Waddell	500.00	225.00	100.00
(29)	Hooks Wiltse	175.00	87.00	52.00
(30)	Cy Young	1000.	450.00	200.00

1911 E94

MAGEE, PHILA. NAT'L

This card is one of a set of Star Base Ball Players' Cards as follows:
MOORE, Philadelphia National
GRANT, Cincinnati National
MURRAY, New York National
BYRNE, Pittsburg National
CRAWFORD, Detroit American
AUSTIN, New York American
"JOE" LAKE, St. Louis National
LOBERT, Philadelphia National
MAGEE, Philadelphia National
"HUGH" JENNINGS, Det. American
DOOLAN, Philadelphia National
"OLD" CY YOUNG, Cleveland Amer.
"HARRY" DAVIS, Phila. American
McGRAW, New York National
"TY" COBB, Detroit American
"TOMMY" LEACH, Pittsburg Nat.
LORD, Chicago American
DOUGHERTY, New York American
LAJOIE, Cleveland American
DEVORE, New York National
CHANCE, Chicago National
CICOTTE, Boston American
BATES, Philadelphia National
"HANS" WAGNER, Pittsburg Nat.
SPEAKER, Boston American
KLEINOW, New York American
BESCHER, Cincinnati National
TURNER, Cleveland American
EVERS, Chicago National
DEVLIN, New York National

This 30-card set, issued in 1911, is nearly identical to several early candy and caramel sets of the same period. The set was apparently issued by the George Close Candy Co. of Cambridge, Mass., however, many of the cards found contain no indication of who produced them. The cards measure 1-1/2" by 2-3/4" and feature tinted black and white player photos. The back of each card, printed in gray, carries a checklist of the 30 cards in the set. Eight different back variations are known to exist. One variation contains just the checklist without any advertising, while seven other variations include overprinted backs advertising various candy products manufactured by the George Close Company. The set carries the ACC designation E94.

		NR MT	EX	VG
Complete Set:		29000.	15000.	6500.
Common Player:		185.00	92.00	55.00
(1)	Jimmy Austin	185.00	92.00	55.00
(2)	Johnny Bates	185.00	92.00	55.00
(3)	Bob Bescher	185.00	92.00	55.00
(4)	Bobby Byrne	185.00	92.00	55.00
(5)	Frank Chance	550.00	225.00	100.00
(6)	Ed Cicotte	225.00	112.50	55.00
(7)	Ty Cobb	4500.	2000.	1000.
(8)	Sam Crawford	500.00	250.00	100.00
(9)	Harry Davis	185.00	92.00	55.00
(10)	Art Devlin	185.00	92.00	55.00
(11)	Josh Devore	185.00	92.00	55.00
(12)	Mickey Doolan	185.00	92.00	55.00
(13)	Patsy Dougherty	185.00	92.00	55.00
(14)	Johnny Evers	500.00	250.00	100.00
(15)	Eddie Grant	185.00	92.00	55.00
(16)	Hugh Jennings	500.00	250.00	100.00
(17)	Kleinow	185.00	92.00	55.00
(18)	Joe Lake	185.00	92.00	55.00
(19)	Nap Lajoie	800.00	400.00	200.00
(20)	Tommy Leach	185.00	92.00	55.00
(21)	Hans Lobert	185.00	92.00	55.00
(22)	Harry Lord	185.00	92.00	55.00
(23)	Sherry Magee	200.00	100.00	50.00
(24)	John McGraw	575.00	287.00	150.00
(25)	Earl Moore	185.00	92.00	55.00
(26)	Red Murray	185.00	92.00	55.00
(27)	Tris Speaker	900.00	450.00	250.00
(28)	Turner	185.00	92.00	55.00
(29)	"Hans" Wagner	1500.	750.00	400.00
(30)	Cy (Old) Young	1000.	500.00	225.00

1909 E95
Philadelphia Caramel

MORGAN, ATHLETICS AMER.

This card is one of a set of
25 BALL PLAYERS
Cards, as follows:
1. WAGNER, Pittsburg National
2. MADDOX, Pittsburg National
3. MERKLE, New York National
4. MORGAN, Athletics American
5. BENDER, Athletics American
6. KRAUSE, Athletics American
7. DEVLIN, New York National
8. McINTYRE, Detroit American
9. COBB, Detroit American
10. WILLETTS, Detroit American
11. CRAWFORD, Detroit Amer.
12. MATTHEWSON, N. Y. Nat'l
13. WILTSE, New York National
14. DOYLE, New York National
15. LEACH, Pittsburg National
16. LORD, Boston American
17. CICOTTE, Boston American
18. CARRIGAN, Boston American
19. WILLIS, Pittsburg National
20. EVERS, Chicago National
21. CHANCE, Chicago National
22. HOFFMAN, Chicago National
23. PLANK, Athletics American
24. COLLINS, Athletics American
25. REULBACH, Chicago Nat'l
Made by
PHILADELPHIA CARAMEL CO.
Camden, New Jersey

Similar in style to the many other early candy and caramel cards, the set designated as E95 by the American Card Catalog is a 25-card issue produced by the Philadelphia Caramel Co. (actually of Camden, N.J.) in 1909. The cards measure approximately 2-5/8" by 1-1/2" and contain a full-color player drawing. The back, which differentiates the set from other similar issues, checklists the 25 players in black ink and displays the Philadelphia Caramel Co. name at the bottom.

		NR MT	EX	VG
Complete Set:		18000.	7500.	4750.
Common Player:		200.00	100.00	60.00
(1)	Chief Bender	500.00	250.00	110.00
(2)	Bill Carrigan	200.00	100.00	60.00
(3)	Frank Chance	550.00	275.00	125.00
(4)	Ed Cicotte	225.00	112.50	65.00
(5)	Ty Cobb	5000.	2500.	210.00
(6)	Eddie Collins	500.00	250.00	135.00
(7)	Sam Crawford	500.00	250.00	135.00
(8)	Art Devlin	200.00	100.00	60.00
(9)	Larry Doyle	200.00	100.00	60.00
(10)	Johnny Evers	500.00	250.00	135.00
(11)	Solly Hoffman (Hofman)	200.00	100.00	60.00
(12)	Harry Krause	200.00	100.00	60.00
(13)	Tommy Leach	200.00	100.00	60.00
(14)	Harry Lord	200.00	100.00	60.00
(15)	Nick Maddox	200.00	100.00	60.00
(16)	Christy Matthewson (Mathewson)	1500.	750.00	350.00
(17)	Matty McIntyre	200.00	100.00	60.00
(18)	Fred Merkle	250.00	125.00	75.00
(19)	Cy Morgan	200.00	100.00	60.00
(20)	Eddie Plank	650.00	325.00	200.00
(21)	Ed Reulbach	200.00	100.00	60.00
(22)	Honus Wagner	1800.	900.00	450.00
(23)	Ed Willetts (Willett)	200.00	100.00	60.00
(24)	Vic Willis	200.00	100.00	60.00
(25)	Hooks Wiltse	200.00	100.00	60.00

1910 E96
Philadelphia Caramel

MULLIN, DETROIT, A. L.

This Card is one of a New Set of
30 BALL PLAYERS
1. DAVIS, Athletics
2. CONNIE MACK, Athletics
3. THOMAS, Athletics
4. BAKER, Athletics
5. DOOIN, Phila. Natl.
6. McQUILLAN, Phila. Natl.
7. KONETCHY, St. Louis Nat'l
8. KARGER, St. Louis Natl.
9. MOWRAY, St. Louis Natl.
10. MURRAY, St. Louis Natl
11. LAJOIE, Cleveland
12. ROSSMAN, Cleveland
13. RUCKER, Brooklyn
14. JENNINGS, Detroit
15. DONOVAN, Detroit
16. DELAHANTY, Detroit
17. MULLIN, Detroit
18. ARRELANES, Boston Am.
19. SPENCER, Boston Am.
20. KLING, Chicago
21. PFISTER, Chicago
22. BROWN, Chicago
23. TINKER, Chicago
24. CLARK, Pittsburg
25. GIBSON, Pittsburg
26. ADAMS, Pittsburg
27. AMES, N. Y. Natl.
28. MARQUARD, N. Y. Natl.
29. HERZOG, N. Y. Natl.
30. MYERS, N. Y. Natl.
Previous Series 25, making total issue 55 Cards.
PHILADELPHIA CARAMEL CO.
Camden, N. J.

This set of 30 subjects, known by the ACC designation E96, was issued in 1910 by the Philadelphia Caramel Co. as a continuation of the E95 set of the previous year. The front design remained the same, but the two issues can be identified by the backs. The backs of the E96 cards are printed in red and carry a checklist of 30 players. There is also a line at the bottom advising "Previous series 25, making total issue 55 cards." Just below that appears "Philadelphia Caramel Co./Camden, N.J."

		NR MT	EX	VG
Complete Set:		11500.	5500.	2750.
Common Player:		200.00	100.00	60.00
(1)	Babe Adams	200.00	100.00	60.00
(2)	Red Ames	200.00	100.00	60.00
(3)	Frank Arrelanes (Arellanes)	200.00	100.00	60.00
(4)	Home Run Baker	550.00	275.00	150.00
(5)	Mordecai Brown	500.00	250.00	100.00
(6)	Fred Clark (Clarke)	500.00	250.00	100.00
(7)	Harry Davis	200.00	100.00	60.00
(8)	Wild Bill Donovan	200.00	100.00	60.00
(9)	Jim Delehanty	200.00	100.00	60.00
(10)	Red Dooin	200.00	100.00	60.00
(11)	George Gibson	200.00	100.00	60.00
(12)	Buck Herzog	200.00	100.00	60.00
(13)	Hugh Jennings	500.00	250.00	100.00
(14)	Ed Karger	200.00	100.00	60.00
(15)	Johnny Kling	200.00	100.00	60.00
(16)	Ed Konetchy	200.00	100.00	60.00
(17)	Nap Lajoie	800.00	400.00	200.00
(18)	Connie Mack	900.00	450.00	215.00
(19)	Rube Marquard	500.00	250.00	100.00
(20)	George McQuillan	200.00	100.00	60.00
(21)	Chief Meyers	200.00	100.00	60.00
(22)	Mike Mowrey	200.00	100.00	60.00
(23)	George Mullin	200.00	100.00	60.00
(24)	Red Murray	200.00	100.00	60.00
(25)	Jack Pfeister (Pfiester)	200.00	100.00	60.00
(26)	Nap Rucker	200.00	100.00	60.00
(27)	Claude Rossman	200.00	100.00	60.00
(28)	Tubby Spencer	200.00	100.00	60.00
(29)	Ira Thomas	200.00	100.00	60.00
(30)	Joe Tinker	500.00	250.00	100.00

1909-10 E97 Briggs

SULLIVAN, BOSTON AMER.

Measuring approximately 1-1/2" by 2-3/4", this 30-card set is nearly identical to several other candy issues of the same period. Designated as E97 in the American Card Catalog, the set was issued in 1909-1910 by C.A. Briggs Co., Lozenge Makers of Boston, Mass.. The front of the card shows a tinted black and white player photo, with the player's last name, position and team printed below. The backs of the cards are printed in brown type and checklist the 30 players in the set alphabetically. The C.A. Briggs Co. name appears at the bottom. Black and white examples of this set have also been found on a thin paper stock with blank backs and are believed to be "proof cards." Four variations are also found in the set. The more expensive variations are not included in the complete set price.

		NR MT	EX	VG
Complete Set:		25000.	10700.	5300.
Common Player:		300.00	150.00	90.00
(1)	Jimmy Austin	300.00	150.00	90.00
(2)	Joe Birmingham	300.00	150.00	90.00
(3)	Bill Bradley	300.00	150.00	90.00
(4)	Kitty Bransfield	300.00	150.00	90.00
(5)	Howie Camnitz	300.00	150.00	90.00
(6)	Bill Carrigan	300.00	150.00	90.00
(7)	Harry Davis	300.00	150.00	90.00
(8)	Josh Devore	300.00	150.00	90.00
(9)	Mickey Doolan	300.00	150.00	90.00
(10)	Bull Durham	300.00	150.00	90.00
(11)	Jimmy Dygert	300.00	150.00	90.00
(12)	Topsy Hartsell (Hartsel)	300.00	150.00	90.00
(13)	Bill Heinchman (Hinchman)	300.00	150.00	90.00
(14)	Charlie Hemphill	300.00	150.00	90.00
(15)	Wee Willie Keeler	1000.	500.00	225.00
(16)	Joe Kelly (Kelley)	900.00	450.00	200.00
(17)	Red Kleinow	300.00	150.00	90.00
(18)	Rube Kroh	300.00	150.00	90.00
(19)	Matty McIntyre	300.00	150.00	90.00
(20)	Amby McConnell	300.00	150.00	90.00
(21)	Chief Meyers	300.00	150.00	90.00
(22)	Earl Moore	300.00	150.00	90.00
(23)	George Mullin	300.00	150.00	90.00
(24)	Red Murray	300.00	150.00	90.00
(25a)	Simon Nichols (Nicholls) (Philadelphia)	550.00	275.00	150.00
(25b)	Simon Nichols (Nicholls) (Cleveland)	300.00	150.00	90.00
(26)	Claude Rossman	300.00	150.00	90.00
(27)	Admiral Schlei	300.00	150.00	90.00
(28a)	Harry Steinfeld (name incorrect)	300.00	150.00	90.00
(28b)	Harry Steinfeldt (name correct)	550.00	275.00	150.00
(29a)	Dennis Sullivan (Chicago)	300.00	150.00	90.00
(29b)	Dennis Sullivan (Boston)	3500.	1500.	675.00
(30a)	Cy. Young (Cleveland)	1800.	900.00	400.00
(30b)	Cy. Young (Boston)	1500.	700.00	325.00

1910 E98

This set of 30 subjects was issued in 1910 and is closely related to several other early candy issues that are nearly identical. The cards measure 1-1/2" by 2-3/4" and feature tinted black and white player photos. THe backs, printed in brown, contain a checklist of the set but no advertising or other information indicating the manufacturer. The set is assigned the designation of E98 by the ACC.

		NR MT	EX	VG
Complete Set:		30000.	13700.	6500.
Common Player:		225.00	112.00	67.00
(1)	Chief Bender	650.00	325.00	200.00
(2)	Roger Bresnahan	650.00	325.00	200.00
(3)	Al Bridwell	225.00	112.00	67.00
(4)	Miner Brown	600.00	300.00	150.00
(5)	Frank Chance	700.00	350.00	215.00

This card is one of a set of the following 30 BALL PLAYERS
1 "CHRISTY" MATHEWSON, N.Y.N.
2 McGRAW, New York National
3 "JOHNNY" KLING, Chicago Nat.
4 CHANCE, Chicago National
5 "HANS" WAGNER, Pittsburg Nat.
6 CLARKE, Pittsburg National
7 BRESNAHAN, St. Louis National
8 HAL CHASE, New York American
9 FORD, New York American
10 "TY" COBB, Detroit American
11 "HUGHEY" JENNINGS, Det. Am.
12 BENDER, Philadelphia American
13 "ED" WALSH, Chicago American
14 "CY" YOUNG, Cleveland American
15 BRIDWELL, New York National
16 "MINER" BROWN, Chicago Nat.
17 MULLIN, Detroit American
18 "CHIEF" MEYERS, N. Y. National
19 VAUGHN, New York American
20 DOOIN, Philadelphia National
21 TENNY, New York National
22 McLEAN, Cincinnati National
23 LAJOIE, Cleveland American
24 TINKER, Chicago National
25 EVERS, Chicago National
26 DAVIS, Philadelphia American
27 COLLINS, Philadelphia American
28 BILL DAHLEN, Brooklyn Nat.
29 CONNIE MACK, Phila. American
30 COOMBS, Philadelphia American

		NR MT	EX	VG
(6)	Hal Chase	300.00	150.00	75.00
(7)	Fred Clarke	650.00	325.00	200.00
(8)	Ty Cobb	5500.	2250.	1500.
(9)	Eddie Collins	600.00	300.00	150.00
(10)	Jack Coombs	250.00	125.00	70.00
(11)	Bill Dahlen	225.00	112.00	67.00
(12)	Harry Davis	225.00	112.00	67.00
(13)	Red Dooin	225.00	112.00	67.00
(14)	Johnny Evers	650.00	325.00	200.00
(15)	Russ Ford	225.00	112.00	67.00
(16)	Hughey Jennings	650.00	325.00	200.00
(17)	Johnny Kling	225.00	112.00	67.00
(18)	Nap Lajoie	1000.	500.00	225.00
(19)	Connie Mack	1000.	500.00	225.00
(20)	Christy Mathewson	1500.	750.00	325.00
(21)	John McGraw	850.00	425.00	240.00
(22)	Larry McLean	225.00	112.00	67.00
(23)	Chief Meyers	225.00	112.00	67.00
(24)	George Mullin	225.00	112.00	67.00
(25)	Fred Tenny (Tenney)	225.00	112.00	67.00
(26)	Joe Tinker	650.00	325.00	200.00
(27)	Hippo Vaughn	225.00	112.00	67.00
(28)	Hans Wagner	2000.	1000.	500.00
(29)	Ed Walsh	700.00	350.00	225.00
(30)	Cy Young	1000.	500.00	250.00

1910 E99 Bishop & Co.

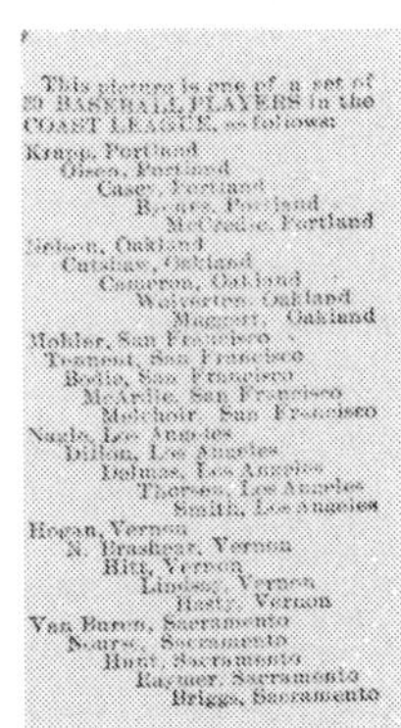

This picture is one of a set of 30 BASEBALL PLAYERS in the COAST LEAGUE, as follows:
Krapp, Portland
Olsen, Portland
Casey, Portland
[illegible], Portland
McCredie, Portland
Nelson, Oakland
Cutshaw, Oakland
Cameron, Oakland
Wolverton, Oakland
Maggert, Oakland
Mohler, San Francisco
Tennant, San Francisco
Bodie, San Francisco
McArdle, San Francisco
Melchoir, San Francisco
Nagle, Los Angeles
Dillon, Los Angeles
Delmas, Los Angeles
Thorsen, Los Angeles
Smith, Los Angeles
Hogan, Vernon
N. Brashear, Vernon
Hitt, Vernon
Lindsay, Vernon
Hasty, Vernon
Van Buren, Sacramento
Nourse, Sacramento
Hunt, Sacramento
Raymer, Sacramento
Briggs, Sacramento

The first of two obscure sets produced by the Los Angeles candy maker Bishop & Co., this 30-card set was issued in 1910 and depicts players from the Pacific Coast League, showing five players from each of the six teams. The cards measure approximately 1-1/2" by 2-3/4" and feature black and white player photos with colored backgrounds (either green, blue, purple or yellow). The player's last name, position and team appear along the bottom. The backs of the cards contain the complete checklist in groups of five, according to team, with each name indented slightly more than the name above. Cards in the 1910 set, which has been designated E99 by the ACC, do not contain the name "Bishop & Company, California" along the bottom on the back.

		NR MT	EX	VG
Complete Set:		10000.	4500.	2500.
Common Player:		250.00	125.00	75.00
(1)	Bodie	350.00	175.00	95.00
(2)	N. Brashear	250.00	125.00	75.00
(3)	Briggs	250.00	125.00	75.00
(4)	Byones (Byrnes)	250.00	125.00	75.00
(5)	Cameron	250.00	125.00	75.00
(6)	Casey	250.00	125.00	75.00
(7)	Cutshaw	250.00	125.00	75.00
(8)	Delmas	250.00	125.00	75.00
(9)	Dillon	250.00	125.00	75.00
(10)	Hasty	250.00	125.00	75.00
(11)	Hitt	250.00	125.00	75.00
(12)	Hap. Hogan	250.00	125.00	75.00
(13)	Hunt	250.00	125.00	75.00
(14)	Krapp	250.00	125.00	75.00
(15)	Lindsay	250.00	125.00	75.00
(16)	McArdle	250.00	125.00	75.00
(17)	McCredie (McCreedle)	250.00	125.00	75.00
(18)	Maggert	250.00	125.00	75.00
(19)	Melchoir	250.00	125.00	75.00
(20)	Mohler	250.00	125.00	75.00
(21)	Nagle	250.00	125.00	75.00
(22)	Nelson	250.00	125.00	75.00
(23)	Nourse	250.00	125.00	75.00
(24)	Olsen	250.00	125.00	75.00
(25)	Raymer	250.00	125.00	75.00
(26)	Smith	250.00	125.00	75.00
(27)	Tennent (Tennant)	250.00	125.00	75.00
(28)	Thorsen	250.00	125.00	75.00
(29)	Van Buren	250.00	125.00	75.00
(30)	Wolverton	250.00	125.00	75.00

1911 E100 Bishop & Co. - Type I

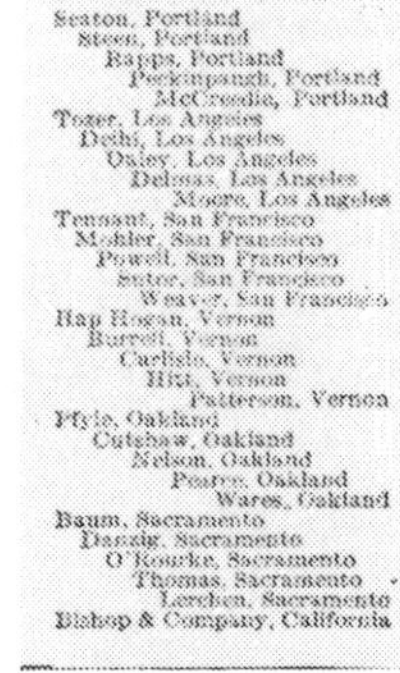

This picture is one of a set of 30 BASEBALL PLAYERS in the COAST LEAGUE, as follows:
Seaton, Portland
Steen, Portland
Rapps, Portland
Peckinpaugh, Portland
McCredie, Portland
Tozer, Los Angeles
Delhi, Los Angeles
Daley, Los Angeles
Delmas, Los Angeles
Moore, Los Angeles
Tennant, San Francisco
Mohler, San Francisco
Powell, San Francisco
Sutor, San Francisco
Weaver, San Francisco
Hap Hogan, Vernon
Burrell, Vernon
Carlisle, Vernon
Hitt, Vernon
Patterson, Vernon
Pfyle, Oakland
Cutshaw, Oakland
Nelson, Oakland
Pearce, Oakland
Wares, Oakland
Baum, Sacramento
Danzig, Sacramento
O'Rourke, Sacramento
Thomas, Sacramento
Lerchen, Sacramento
Bishop & Company, California

		NR MT	EX	VG
Complete Set:		80000.	3700.	1700.
Common Player:		215.00	107.00	64.00
(1)	Spider Baum	215.00	107.00	64.00
(2)	Burrell	215.00	107.00	64.00
(3)	Carlisle	215.00	107.00	64.00
(4)	Cutshaw	215.00	107.00	64.00
(5)	Pete Daley	215.00	107.00	64.00
(6)	Danzig	215.00	107.00	64.00
(7)	Delhi	215.00	107.00	64.00
(8)	Delmas	215.00	107.00	64.00
(9)	Hitt	215.00	107.00	64.00
(10)	Hap Hogan (actually Walter Bray)	215.00	107.00	64.00
(11)	Lerchen	215.00	107.00	64.00
(12)	McCreddie (McCreedie)	215.00	107.00	64.00
(13)	Mohler	215.00	107.00	64.00
(14)	Moore	215.00	107.00	64.00
(15)	Slim Nelson	215.00	107.00	64.00
(16)	P. O'Rourke	215.00	107.00	64.00
(17)	Patterson	215.00	107.00	64.00
(18)	Bunny Pearce	215.00	107.00	64.00
(19)	Peckinpaugh	250.00	125.00	60.00
(20)	Monte Pfyle (Pfyl)	215.00	107.00	64.00
(21)	Powell	215.00	107.00	64.00
(22)	Rapps	215.00	107.00	64.00
(23)	Seaton	215.00	107.00	64.00
(24)	Steen	215.00	107.00	64.00
(25)	Suter	215.00	107.00	64.00
(26)	Tennant	215.00	107.00	64.00
(27)	Thomas	215.00	107.00	64.00
(28)	Tozer	215.00	107.00	64.00
(29)	Clyde Wares	215.00	107.00	64.00
(30)	Weaver	500.00	200.00	100.00

1911 E100 Bishop & Co. - Type II

This 30-card set, designated E100 by the ACC, was issued in 1911 by the California confectioner Bishop & Company of Los Angeles, which had produced a similar set a year earlier. Both sets showcased star players from the Pacific Coast League. The cards measure approximately 1-1/2" by 2-3/4" and feature black and white photos with a background of either green, blue, yellow or red. The backs contain the complete checklist of the set, listing the players in groups of five by team, with one line indented slightly more than the previous one. In addition to the checklist, the 1911 set can be differentiated from the previous year because the line "Bishop & Company, California" appears along the bottom. The Type II E100's are blank-backed and are enlarged Type I photos. Variations have been discovered in recent years for many of the cards in the E100 set. The variations, known as "Type II" have either orange backgrounds or green backgrounds with more tightly cropped photos and blank backs.

		NR MT	EX	VG
Complete Set:		4500.	2000.	1000.
Common Player:		200.00	100.00	60.00
(1)	Burrell	200.00	100.00	60.00
(2)	Danzig	200.00	100.00	60.00
(3)	Delhi	200.00	100.00	60.00
(4)	Hitt	200.00	100.00	60.00
(5)	Lerchen	200.00	100.00	60.00
(6)	McCreddie	200.00	100.00	60.00
(7)	Slim Nelson	200.00	100.00	60.00
(8)	P. O'Rourke	200.00	100.00	60.00
(9)	Patterson	200.00	100.00	60.00
(10)	Bunny Pearce	200.00	100.00	60.00
(11)	Monte Pfyle	200.00	100.00	60.00
(12)	Rapps	200.00	100.00	60.00
(13)	Seaton	200.00	100.00	60.00
(14)	Steen	200.00	100.00	60.00
(15)	Suter	200.00	100.00	60.00
(16)	Tennant	200.00	100.00	60.00
(17)	Weaver	400.00	200.00	100.00

1909 E101

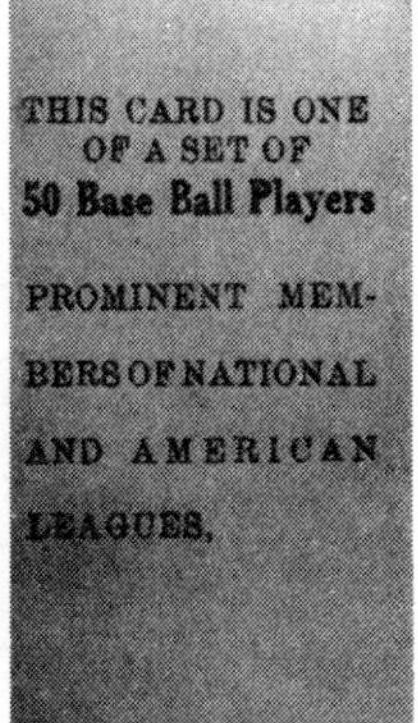

THIS CARD IS ONE OF A SET OF 50 Base Ball Players PROMINENT MEMBERS OF NATIONAL AND AMERICAN LEAGUES.

This 50-card set, issued in 1910, is closely related to the E92 set and is sometimes collected as part of that set. The fronts of the E101 cards are identical to the E92 set, but the back is an "anonymous" one, containing no advertising or any other information regarding the set's sponsor. The backs read simply "This card is one of a set of 50 Base Ball Players/Prominent Members of National and American Leagues."

		NR MT	EX	VG
Complete Set:		32500.	14500.	7500.
Common Player:		175.00	87.00	52.00
(1)	Jack Barry	175.00	87.00	52.00
(2)	Harry Bemis	175.00	87.00	52.00
(3)	Chief Bender (white hat)	600.00	300.00	150.00
(4)	Chief Bender (striped hat)	600.00	300.00	150.00
(5)	Bill Bergen	175.00	87.00	52.00
(6)	Bob Bescher	175.00	87.00	52.00
(7)	Al Bridwell	175.00	87.00	52.00
(8)	Doc Casey	175.00	87.00	52.00
(9)	Frank Chance	650.00	325.00	200.00
(10)	Hal Chase	350.00	175.00	80.00
(11)	Ty Cobb	6000.	3000.	1500.
(12)	Eddie Collins	650.00	325.00	200.00
(13)	Sam Crawford	650.00	325.00	200.00
(14)	Harry Davis	175.00	87.00	52.00
(15)	Art Devlin	175.00	87.00	52.00
(16)	Wild Bill Donovan	175.00	87.00	52.00
(17)	Red Dooin	175.00	87.00	52.00
(18)	Mickey Doolan	175.00	87.00	52.00
(19)	Patsy Dougherty	175.00	87.00	52.00
(20)	Larry Doyle (with bat)	175.00	87.00	52.00

		NR MT	EX	VG
(21)	Larry Doyle (throwing)	175.00	87.00	52.00
(22)	Johnny Evers	600.00	300.00	150.00
(23)	George Gibson	175.00	87.00	52.00
(24)	Topsy Hartsel	175.00	87.00	52.00
(25)	Fred Jacklitsch	175.00	87.00	52.00
(26)	Hugh Jennings	550.00	275.00	115.00
(27)	Red Kleinow	550.00	275.00	115.00
(28)	Otto Knabe	550.00	275.00	115.00
(29)	Jack Knight	550.00	275.00	115.00
(30)	Nap Lajoie	1000.	500.00	250.00
(31)	Hans Lobert	175.00	87.00	52.00
(32)	Sherry Magee	200.00	100.00	50.00
(33)	Christy Matthewson (Mathewson)	1400.	700.00	300.00
(34)	John McGraw	700.00	350.00	175.00
(35)	Larry McLean	175.00	87.00	52.00
(36)	Dots Miller (batting)	175.00	87.00	52.00
(37)	Dots Miller (fielding)	175.00	87.00	52.00
(38)	Danny Murphy	175.00	87.00	52.00
(39)	Bill O'Hara	175.00	87.00	52.00
(40)	Germany Schaefer	175.00	87.00	52.00
(41)	Admiral Schlei	175.00	87.00	52.00
(42)	Boss Schmidt	175.00	87.00	52.00
(43)	Johnny Seigle	175.00	87.00	52.00
(44)	Dave Shean	175.00	87.00	52.00
(45)	Boss Smith (Schmidt)	175.00	87.00	52.00
(46)	Joe Tinker	600.00	300.00	150.00
(47)	Honus Wagner (batting)	2000.	1000.	500.00
(48)	Honus Wagner (throwing)	2000.	1000.	500.00
(49)	Cy Young	1000.	500.00	225.00
(50)	Heinie Zimmerman	175.00	87.00	52.00

1908 E102

Dooin, c. Phila. Nat.

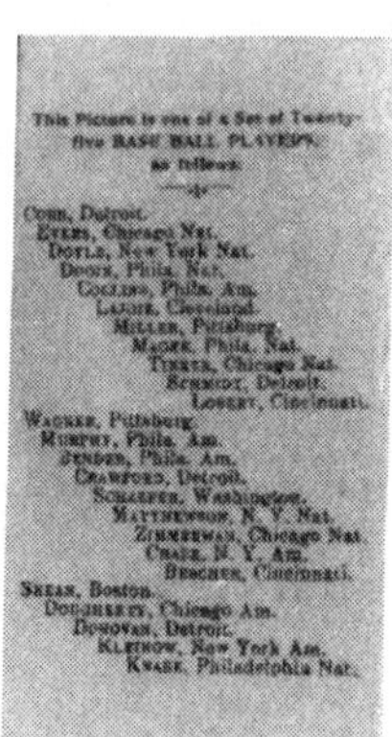
This Picture is one of a Set of Twenty-five BASE BALL PLAYERS, as follows:

Cobb, Detroit.
Evers, Chicago Nat.
Doyle, New York Nat.
Dooin, Phila. Nat.
Collins, Phila. Am.
Lajoie, Cleveland.
Miller, Pittsburg.
Magee, Phila. Nat.
Tinker, Chicago Nat.
Schmidt, Detroit.
Lobert, Cincinnati.
Wagner, Pittsburg.
Murphy, Phila. Am.
Bender, Phila. Am.
Crawford, Detroit.
Schaefer, Washington.
Mathewson, N. Y. Nat.
Zimmerman, Chicago Nat.
Chase, N. Y. Am.
Bescher, Cincinnati.
Shean, Boston.
Dougherty, Chicago Am.
Donovan, Detroit.
Kleinow, New York Am.
Knabe, Philadelphia Nat.

One of many similar early candy card sets, this set - designated as E102 in the American Card Catalog - was distributed around 1910, although the producer of the set is unknown. Measuring approximately 1-1/2" by 2-3/4", the set is almost identical in design to the E101 set and other closely related issues. The set consists of 25 players, which are checklisted on the back of the card. Three of the players have been found in two poses, resulting in 28 different cards. Because there is no advertising on the cards, the set can best be identified by the words - "This Picture is one of a Set of Twenty-five Base Ball Players, as follows" - which appears at the top of the back of each card.

		NR MT	EX	VG
	Complete Set:	25000.	12000.	6000.
	Common Player:	200.00	100.00	60.00
(1)	Chief Bender	600.00	300.00	150.00
(2)	Bob Bescher	200.00	100.00	60.00
(3)	Hal Chase	350.00	175.00	75.00
(4)	Ty Cobb	6250.	2800.	1300.
(5)	Eddie Collins	600.00	300.00	150.00
(6)	Sam Crawford	600.00	300.00	150.00
(7)	Wild Bill Donovan	200.00	100.00	60.00
(8)	Red Dooin	200.00	100.00	60.00
(9)	Patsy Dougherty	200.00	100.00	60.00
(10)	Larry Doyle (batting)	200.00	100.00	60.00
(11)	Larry Doyle (throwing)	200.00	100.00	60.00
(12)	Johnny Evers	600.00	300.00	150.00
(13)	Red Kleinow	200.00	100.00	60.00
(14)	Otto Knabe	200.00	100.00	60.00
(15)	Nap Lajoie	1200.	600.00	275.00
(16)	Hans Lobert	200.00	100.00	60.00
(17)	Sherry Magee	250.00	125.00	60.00
(18)	Christy Matthewson (Mathewson)	1500.	750.00	375.00
(19)	Dots Miller (batting)	200.00	100.00	60.00
(20)	Dots Miller (fielding)	1900.	800.00	450.00
(21)	Danny Murphy	200.00	100.00	60.00
(22)	Germany Schaefer	200.00	100.00	60.00
(23)	Boss Schmidt	200.00	100.00	60.00
(24)	Dave Shean	200.00	100.00	60.00
(25)	Boss Smith (Schmidt)	200.00	100.00	60.00
(26)	Joe Tinker	600.00	300.00	150.00
(27)	Honus Wagner (batting)	2200.	1000.	500.00
(28)	Honus Wagner (fielding)	2200.	1000.	500.00
(29)	Heinie Zimmerman	200.00	100.00	60.00

1910 E103 Williams Caramel

FRED TENNY, 1st B., N. Y.
The Williams Caramel Co. Oxford, Pa.

This 30-card set issued by the Williams Caramel Co. of Oxford, Pa., in 1910 can be differentiated from other similar sets because it was printed on a thin paper stock rather than cardboard. Measuring approximately 1-1/2" by 2-3/4", each card features a player portrait set against a red background. The bottom of the card lists the player's last name, position and team, followed by a line reading "The Williams Caramel Co. Oxford Pa." Nearly all of the photos in the set, which is designated E103 by the ACC, are identical to those in the M116 Sporting Life set.

		NR MT	EX	VG
	Complete Set:	35000.	15700.	6200.
	Common Player:	300.00	150.00	90.00
(1)	Chas. Bender	1000.	500.00	225.00
(2)	Roger Bresnahan	1000.	500.00	225.00
(3)	Mordecai Brown	1000.	500.00	225.00
(4)	Frank Chance	1100.	550.00	235.00
(5)	Hal Chase	500.00	250.00	125.00
(6)	Ty Cobb	7500.	3500.	1500.
(7)	Edward Collins	1000.	500.00	225.00
(8)	Sam Crawford	1000.	500.00	225.00
(9)	Harry Davis	300.00	150.00	90.00
(10)	Arthur Devlin	300.00	150.00	90.00
(11)	William Donovan	300.00	150.00	90.00
(12)	Chas. Dooin	300.00	150.00	90.00
(13)	L. Doyle	300.00	150.00	90.00
(14)	John Ewing	300.00	150.00	90.00
(15)	George Gibson	300.00	150.00	90.00
(16)	Hugh Jennings	1000.	500.00	225.00
(17)	David Jones	300.00	150.00	90.00
(18)	Tim Jordan	300.00	150.00	90.00
(19)	N. Lajoie	1500.	750.00	300.00
(20)	Thomas Leach	300.00	150.00	90.00
(21)	Harry Lord	300.00	150.00	90.00
(22)	Chris. Mathewson	2500.	1200.	500.00
(23)	John McLean	300.00	150.00	90.00
(24)	Geo. W. McQuillan	300.00	150.00	90.00
(25)	Pastorius	300.00	150.00	90.00
(26)	N. Rucker	300.00	150.00	90.00
(27)	Fred Tenny (Tenney)	300.00	150.00	90.00
(28)	Ira Thomas	300.00	150.00	90.00
(29)	Hans Wagner	3500.	1750.	750.00
(30)	Robert Wood	300.00	150.00	90.00

1910 E104 Nadja - Type I

BARRY, ATHLETICS.

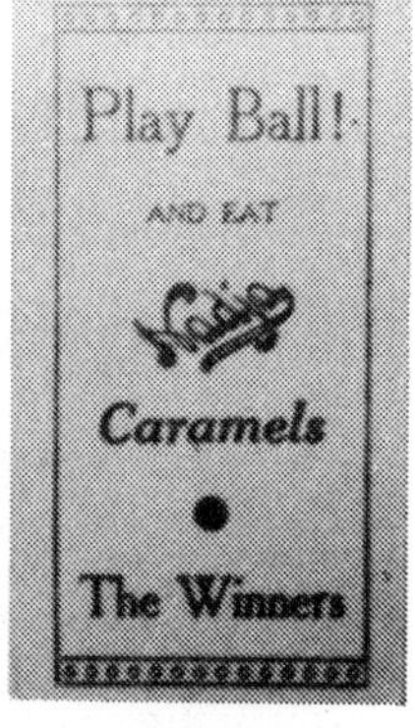

Although advanced collectors usually refer to this set as "Nadjas," because of the ad for Nadja Caramels on some of the backs, examples are also found with blank backs. (In fact, the blank backs are more common.) Issued in 1910-1911, the cards measure 2-5/8" by 1-1/2" and feature player portraits with the player's name and team printed below in blue capital letters. Three distinct types exist. Type I, an 18-card series picturing members of the 1910 World Champion Philadelphia Athletics, is nearly identical in appearance to the T208 Fireside set. Type II is an 11-card series similar to the E90-2 set of Pittsburgh Pirates; and Type III is a 30-card series featuring original artwork. Cards in all three types can be found either with the Nadja back or with blank backs. Collectively, these cards have been designated E104 by the American Card Catalog. Complete set prices for all three types do not include the higher priced variations.

		NR MT	EX	VG
	Complete Set:	6000.	3000.	1750.
	Common Player:	80.00	40.00	24.00
(1a)	Home Run Baker (no "World's Champions" at top)	200.00	100.00	60.00
(1b)	Home Run Baker ("World's Champions" at top)	250.00	125.00	75.00
(2a)	Jack Barry (no "World's Champions" at top)	80.00	40.00	24.00
(2b)	Jack Barry ("World's Champions" at top)	100.00	50.00	30.00
(3a)	Chief Bender (no "World's Champions" at top)	200.00	100.00	60.00
(3b)	Chief Bender ("World's Champions" at top)	250.00	125.00	75.00
(4a)	Eddie Collins (no "World's Champions" at top)	200.00	100.00	60.00
(4b)	Eddie Collins ("World's Champions" at top)	250.00	125.00	75.00
(5a)	Harry Davis (no "World's Champions" at top)	80.00	40.00	24.00
(5b)	Harry Davis ("World's Champions" at top)	100.00	50.00	30.00
(6a)	Jimmy Dygert (no "World's Champions" at top)	80.00	40.00	24.00
(6b)	Jimmy Dygert ("World's Champions" at top)	100.00	50.00	30.00
(6c)	Jimmy Dygert (Nadja ad on back)	100.00	50.00	30.00
(7a)	Topsy Hartsel (no "World's Champions" at top)	80.00	40.00	24.00
(7b)	Topsy Hartel ("World's Champions" at top)	100.00	50.00	30.00
(7c)	Topsy Hartsel (Nadja ad on back)	100.00	50.00	30.00
(8a)	Harry Krause (no "World's Champions" at top)	80.00	40.00	24.00
(8b)	Harry Krause ("World's Champions" at top)	100.00	50.00	30.00
(9a)	Jack Lapp (no "World's Champions" at top)	80.00	40.00	24.00
(9b)	Jack Lapp ("World's Champions" at top)	100.00	50.00	30.00
(10a)	Paddy Livingstone (Livingston) (no "World's Champions" at top)	80.00	40.00	24.00
(10b)	Paddy Livingstone (Livingston) ("World's Champions" at top)	100.00	50.00	30.00
(11a)	Bris Lord (no "World's Champions" at top)	80.00	40.00	24.00
(11b)	Bris Lord ("World's Champions" at top)	100.00	50.00	30.00
(12a)	Connie Mack (no "World's Champions" at top)	250.00	125.00	75.00
(12b)	Connie Mack ("World's Champions" at top)	350.00	175.00	105.00
(12c)	Connie Mack (Nadja ad on back)	350.00	175.00	105.00
(13a)	Cy Morgan (no "World's Champions" at top)	80.00	40.00	24.00
(13b)	Cy Morgan ("World's Champions" at top)	100.00	50.00	30.00
(13c)	Cy Morgan (Nadja ad on back)	100.00	50.00	30.00
(14a)	Danny Murphy (no "World's Champions" at top)	80.00	40.00	24.00
(14b)	Danny Murphy ("World's Champions" at top)	100.00	50.00	30.00
(15a)	Rube Oldring (no "World's Champions" at top)	80.00	40.00	24.00
(15b)	Rube Oldring ("World's Champions" at top)	100.00	50.00	30.00
(16a)	Eddie Plank (no "World's Champions" at top)	200.00	100.00	60.00
(16b)	Eddie Plank ("World's Champions" at top)	250.00	125.00	75.00
(16c)	Eddie Plank (Nadja ad on back)	250.00	125.00	75.00
(17a)	Amos Strunk (no "World's Champions" at top)	80.00	40.00	24.00
(17b)	Amos Strunk ("World's Champions" at top)	100.00	50.00	30.00
(18a)	Ira Thomas (no "World's Champions" at top)	80.00	40.00	24.00
(18b)	Ira Thomas ("World's Champions" at top)	100.00	50.00	30.00

1910 E104 Nadja - Type II

		NR MT	EX	VG
	Complete Set:	4000.	2000.	1200.
	Common Player:	100.00	50.00	30.00
(1a)	Babe Adams (no ad on back)	100.00	50.00	30.00
(1b)	Babe Adams (Nadja ad on back)	100.00	50.00	30.00
(2)	Fred Clarke	250.00	125.00	75.00
(3a)	George Gibson (no ad on back)	100.00	50.00	30.00
(3b)	George Gibson (Nadja ad on back)	100.00	50.00	30.00
(4a)	Ham Hyatt (no ad on back)	100.00	50.00	30.00
(4b)	Ham Hyatt (Nadja ad on back)	100.00	50.00	30.00
(5)	Tommy Leach	100.00	50.00	30.00
(6)	Sam Leever	100.00	50.00	30.00
(7)	Nick Maddox	100.00	50.00	30.00
(8)	Dots Miller	100.00	50.00	30.00

PHILLIPPE, PITTSBURG

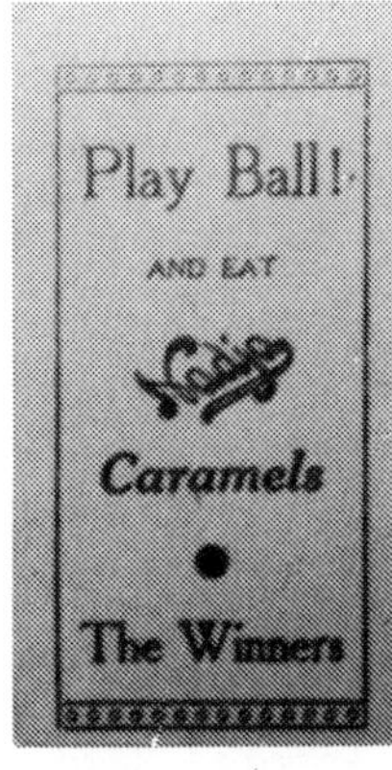

		NR MT	EX	VG
(9)	Deacon Phillippe	100.00	50.00	30.00
(10a)	Honus Wagner (no ad on back)	750.00	375.00	225.00
(10b)	Honus Wagner (Nadja ad on back)	750.00	375.00	225.00
(11a)	Owen Wilson (no ad on back)	100.00	50.00	30.00
(11b)	Owen Wilson (Nadja ad on back)	100.00	50.00	30.00

1910 E104 Nadja - Type III

MOORE, PHILADELPHIA

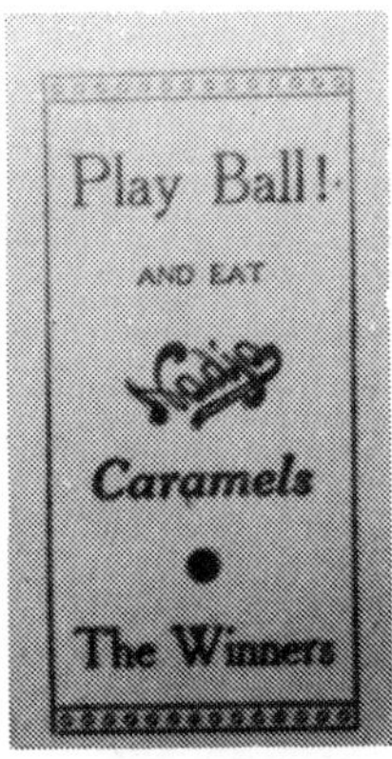

		NR MT	EX	VG
Complete Set:		9000.	4500.	2750.
Common Player:		150.00	75.00	45.00
(1)	Bill Abstein	150.00	75.00	45.00
(2)	Red Ames	150.00	75.00	45.00
(3)	Johnny Bates	150.00	75.00	45.00
(4a)	Kitty Bransfield (blank back)	150.00	75.00	45.00
(4b)	Kitty Bransfield (Nadja back)	200.00	100.00	60.00
(5a)	Al Bridwell (blank back)	150.00	75.00	45.00
(5b)	Al Bridwell (Nadja back)	200.00	100.00	60.00
(6)	Doc Crandall	150.00	75.00	45.00
(7)	Sam Crawford	400.00	200.00	120.00
(8)	Jim Delehanty	150.00	75.00	45.00
(9)	Larry Doyle	150.00	75.00	45.00
(10a)	Eddie Grant (blank back)	150.00	75.00	45.00
(10b)	Eddie Grant (Nadja back)	200.00	100.00	60.00
(11)	Fred Jacklitsch	150.00	75.00	45.00
(12)	Hugh Jennings	400.00	200.00	120.00
(13)	Davy Jones	150.00	75.00	45.00
(14)	Tom Jones	150.00	75.00	45.00
(15a)	Otto Knabe (blank back)	150.00	75.00	45.00
(15b)	Otto Knabe (Nadja back)	200.00	100.00	60.00
(16)	John McGraw	450.00	225.00	135.00
(17)	Matty McIntyre	150.00	75.00	45.00
(18)	Earl Moore	150.00	75.00	45.00
(19)	Pat Moren (Moran)	150.00	75.00	45.00
(20)	George Moriarity	150.00	75.00	45.00
(21)	George Mullin	150.00	75.00	45.00
(22)	Red Murray	150.00	75.00	45.00
(23)	Simon Nicholls	150.00	75.00	45.00
(24)	Charley O'Leary	150.00	75.00	45.00
(25a)	Admiral Schlei (blank back)	150.00	75.00	45.00
(25b)	Admiral Schlei (Nadja back)	200.00	100.00	60.00
(26a)	Cy Seymore (Seymour) (blank back)	150.00	75.00	45.00
(26b)	Cy Seymore (Seymour) (Nadja back)	200.00	100.00	60.00
(27)	Tully Sparks	150.00	75.00	45.00
(28)	Ed Summers	150.00	75.00	45.00
(29a)	Ed Willetts (Willetts) (blank back)	150.00	75.00	45.00
(29b)	Ed Willetts (Willetts) (Nadja back)	200.00	100.00	60.00
(30)	Vic Willis	150.00	75.00	45.00

1910 E105 Mello-Mint

Issued circa 1910 by Smith's Mello-Mint, "The

Evers, 2b. Chicago Nat.

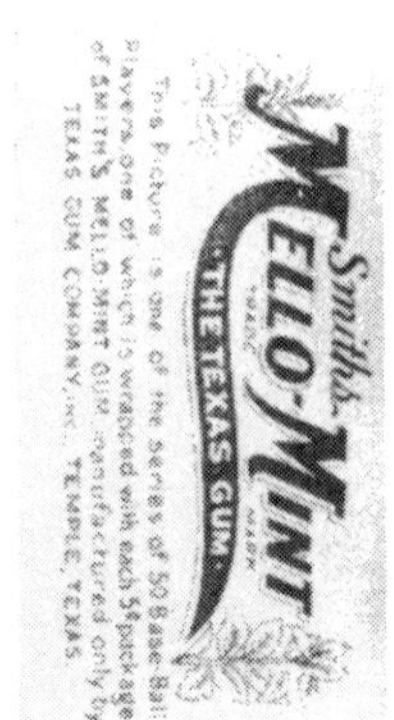

Texas Gum", this set of 50 cards shares the same checklist and artwork as the better known E101 set. The Mello-Mint cards, however, are slightly smaller, measuring approximately 2-5/8" by 1-3/8", and were printed on thin paper, making them difficult to find in top condition. The backs contain an advertisement for Mello-Mint Gum. The set carries an ACC designation of E105.

		NR MT	EX	VG
Complete Set:		15000.	7500.	4500.
Common Player:		125.00	62.00	37.00
(1)	Jack Barry	125.00	62.00	37.00
(2)	Harry Bemis	125.00	62.00	37.00
(3)	Chief Bender (white hat)	300.00	150.00	90.00
(4)	Chief Bender (striped hat)	300.00	150.00	90.00
(5)	Bill Bergen	125.00	62.00	37.00
(6)	Bob Bescher	125.00	62.00	37.00
(7)	Al Bridwell	125.00	62.00	37.00
(8)	Doc Casey	125.00	62.00	37.00
(9)	Frank Chance	400.00	200.00	120.00
(10)	Hal Chase	250.00	125.00	75.00
(11)	Ty Cobb	2000.	1000.	600.00
(12)	Eddie Collins	300.00	150.00	90.00
(13)	Sam Crawford	300.00	150.00	90.00
(14)	Harry Davis	125.00	62.00	37.00
(15)	Art Devlin	125.00	62.00	37.00
(16)	Wild Bill Donovan	125.00	62.00	37.00
(17)	Red Dooin	125.00	62.00	37.00
(18)	Mickey Doolan	125.00	62.00	37.00
(19)	Patsy Dougherty	125.00	62.00	37.00
(20)	Larry Doyle (with bat)	125.00	62.00	37.00
(21)	Larry Doyle (throwing)	125.00	62.00	37.00
(22)	Johnny Evers	300.00	150.00	90.00
(23)	George Gibson	125.00	62.00	37.00
(24)	Topsy Hartsel	125.00	62.00	37.00
(25)	Fred Jacklitsch	125.00	62.00	37.00
(26)	Hugh Jennings	300.00	150.00	90.00
(27)	Red Kleinow	125.00	62.00	37.00
(28)	Otto Knabe	125.00	62.00	37.00
(29)	Jack Knight	125.00	62.00	37.00
(30)	Nap Lajoie	500.00	225.00	150.00
(31)	Hans Lobert	125.00	62.00	37.00
(32)	Sherry Magee	125.00	62.00	37.00
(33)	Christy Matthewson (Mathewson)	600.00	300.00	175.00
(34)	John McGraw	350.00	175.00	105.00
(35)	Larry McLean	125.00	62.00	37.00
(36)	Dots Miller (batting)	125.00	62.00	37.00
(37)	Dots Miller (fielding)	125.00	62.00	37.00
(38)	Danny Murphy	125.00	62.00	37.00
(39)	Bill O'Hara	125.00	62.00	37.00
(40)	Germany Schaefer	125.00	62.00	37.00
(41)	Admiral Schlei	125.00	62.00	37.00
(42)	Boss Schmidt	125.00	62.00	37.00
(43)	Johnny Seigle	125.00	62.00	37.00
(44)	Dave Shean	125.00	62.00	37.00
(45)	Boss Smith (Schmidt)	125.00	62.00	37.00
(46)	Joe Tinker	300.00	150.00	90.00
(47)	Honus Wagner (batting)	800.00	400.00	250.00
(48)	Honus Wagner (throwing)	800.00	400.00	250.00
(49)	Cy Young	500.00	250.00	150.00
(50)	Heinie Zimmerman	125.00	62.00	37.00

1915 E106 American Caramel

Chase, 1b. Buffalo Feds

This card is one of a set of forty-eight leading Baseball Players in the National, American and Federal Leagues. One card is given with every piece of Baseball Caramel manufactured by the
AMERICAN CARAMEL CO.
YORK PA
UNDER THE FAMOUS BRAND OF THE
P. C. W.

This 48-card set, designated E106 by the American Card Catalog, was produced by the American Caramel Company of York, Pa., in 1915 and includes players from the National, American and Federal Leagues. The cards measure 1-1/2" by 2-3/4". The set is related to the E90-1 and E92 sets, from which the artwork is taken. The American Caramel cards, however, have a glossy coating, which makes them very susceptible to cracking. The backs of the cards advise that the card is "one of a set of forty-eight leading Baseball Players" and identifies the American Caramel Co. as the manufacturer.

		NR MT	EX	VG
Complete Set:		40000.	20000.	10000.
Common Player:		275.00	137.00	82.00
(1)	Jack Barry	275.00	137.00	82.00
(2)	Chief Bender (white hat)	700.00	325.00	200.00
(3)	Chief Bender (striped hat)	700.00	325.00	200.00
(4)	Bob Bescher	275.00	137.00	82.00
(5)	Roger Bresnahan	700.00	325.00	200.00
(6)	Al Bridwell	275.00	137.00	82.00
(7)	Donie Bush	275.00	137.00	82.00
(8)	Hal Chase (portrait)	400.00	200.00	120.00
(9)	Hal Chase (catching)	400.00	200.00	120.00
(10)	Ty Cobb (batting, facing front)	6000.	3000.	1200.
(11)	Ty Cobb (batting, facing to side)	6500.	3250.	2000.
(12)	Eddie Collins	600.00	300.00	175.00
(13)	Sam Crawford	600.00	300.00	175.00
(14)	Ray Demmitt	275.00	137.00	82.00
(15)	Wild Bill Donovan	275.00	137.00	82.00
(16)	Red Dooin	275.00	137.00	82.00
(17)	Mickey Doolan	275.00	137.00	82.00
(18)	Larry Doyle	275.00	137.00	82.00
(19)	Clyde Engle	275.00	137.00	82.00
(20)	Johnny Evers	600.00	300.00	175.00
(21)	Art Fromme	275.00	137.00	82.00
(22)	George Gibson (catching, back view)	275.00	137.00	82.00
(23)	George Gibson (catching, front view)	275.00	137.00	82.00
(24)	Roy Hartzell	275.00	137.00	82.00
(25)	Fred Jacklitsch	275.00	137.00	82.00
(26)	Hugh Jennings	600.00	300.00	175.00
(27)	Otto Knabe	275.00	137.00	82.00
(28)	Nap Lajoie	1400.	600.00	250.00
(29)	Hans Lobert	275.00	137.00	82.00
(30)	Rube Marquard	600.00	300.00	175.00
(31)	Christy Matthewson (Mathewson)	1800.	825.00	375.00
(32)	John McGraw	850.00	400.00	250.00
(33)	George McQuillan	275.00	137.00	82.00
(34)	Dots Miller	275.00	137.00	82.00
(35)	Danny Murphy	275.00	137.00	82.00
(36)	Rebel Oakes	275.00	137.00	82.00
(37)	Eddie Plank	900.00	425.00	255.00
(38)	Germany Schaefer	275.00	137.00	82.00
(39)	Tris Speaker	1000.	450.00	225.00
(40)	Oscar Stanage	275.00	137.00	82.00
(41)	George Stovall	275.00	137.00	82.00
(42)	Jeff Sweeney	275.00	137.00	82.00
(43)	Joe Tinker (portrait)	700.00	325.00	200.00
(44)	Joe Tinker (batting)	700.00	325.00	200.00
(45)	Honus Wagner (batting)	3000.	1250.	500.00
(46)	Honus Wagner (throwing)	3000.	1250.	500.00
(47)	Hooks Wiltse	275.00	137.00	82.00
(48)	Heinie Zimmerman	275.00	137.00	82.00

1903 E107
Breisch Williams - Type I

W. GLEASON, 2 B, Phila. N

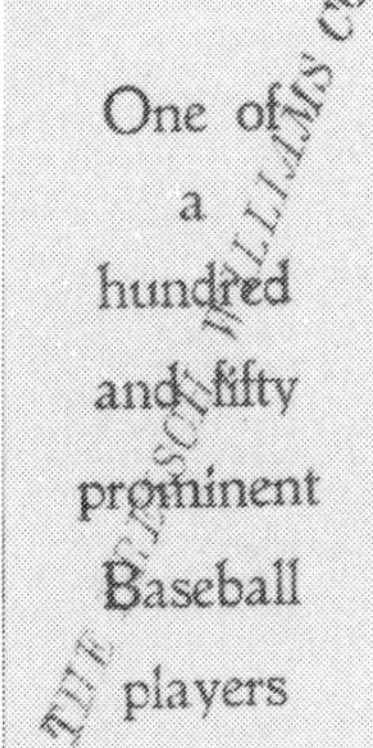

Identified by the American Card Catalog as E107, this circa 1903 set is very significant because it was the first major baseball card set since the days of the Old Judge issues in the 1880s, and it established the pattern for most of the tobacco and candy cards that were to follow over the next two decades. Measuring approximately 1-3/8" by 2-5/8", the cards feature black and white player photos with the name, position and team along the bottom. The back states simply "One of a hundred and fifty prominent Baseball players," although blank-backed varieties of this set are fairly common. Also found have been cards with a diagonal overprint stating "The Breisch-Williams Co." establishing the producer of the set. The Type I set consists of 147 different players although 11 additional variations can be found. The Type III cards are thicker than those in Type I and may have been cut from an advertising piece. The Keeler and Delehanty cards have captions different from those found in Type I. The 11 variations found in Type I are not included in the complete set price. Many of the photos were used in other sets, like T206 and M116 Sporting Life.

		NR MT	EX	VG
Complete Set:		35000.	17500.	10500.
Common Player:		150.00	75.00	45.00
(1a)	John Anderson (New York)	150.00	75.00	45.00
(1b)	John Anderson (St. Louis)	150.00	75.00	45.00
(2)	Jimmy Barret (Barrett)	150.00	75.00	45.00
(3)	Ginger Beaumont	150.00	75.00	45.00
(4)	Fred Beck	150.00	75.00	45.00
(5)	Jake Beckley	400.00	200.00	120.00
(6)	Harry Bemis	150.00	75.00	45.00
(7)	Chief Bender	350.00	175.00	105.00
(8)	Bill Bernhard	150.00	75.00	45.00
(9)	Harry Bey (Bay)	150.00	75.00	45.00
(10)	Bill Bradley	150.00	75.00	45.00
(11)	Fritz Buelow	150.00	75.00	45.00
(12)	Nixey Callahan	150.00	75.00	45.00
(13)	Scoops Carey	350.00	175.00	105.00
(14)	Charley Carr	150.00	75.00	45.00
(15)	Bill Carrick	150.00	75.00	45.00
(16)	Doc Casey	150.00	75.00	45.00
(17)	Frank Chance	350.00	175.00	105.00
(18)	Jack Chesbro	350.00	175.00	105.00
(19)	Boileryard Clark (Clarke)	150.00	75.00	45.00
(20)	Fred Clarke	400.00	200.00	120.00
(21)	Jimmy Collins	400.00	200.00	120.00
(22)	Duff Cooley	150.00	75.00	45.00
(23)	Tommy Corcoran	150.00	75.00	45.00
(24)	Bill Coughlan (Coughlin)	150.00	75.00	45.00
(25)	Lou Criger	150.00	75.00	45.00
(26)	Lave Cross	150.00	75.00	45.00
(27)	Monte Cross	150.00	75.00	45.00
(28)	Bill Dahlen	150.00	75.00	45.00
(29)	Tom Daly	150.00	75.00	45.00
(30)	George Davis	150.00	75.00	45.00
(31)	Harry Davis	150.00	75.00	45.00
(32)	Ed Delehanty	500.00	250.00	150.00
(33)	Gene DeMont (DeMontreville)	150.00	75.00	45.00
(34a)	Pop Dillon (Detroit)	150.00	75.00	45.00
(34b)	Pop Dillon (Brooklyn)	150.00	75.00	45.00
(35)	Bill Dineen (Dinneen)	150.00	75.00	45.00
(36)	Jiggs Donahue	150.00	75.00	45.00
(37)	Mike Donlin	150.00	75.00	45.00
(38)	Patsy Donovan	150.00	75.00	45.00
(39)	Patsy Dougherty	150.00	75.00	45.00
(40)	Klondike Douglass	150.00	75.00	45.00
(41a)	Jack Doyle (Brooklyn)	150.00	75.00	45.00
(41b)	Jack Doyle (Philadelphia)	150.00	75.00	45.00
(42)	Lew Drill	150.00	75.00	45.00
(43)	Jack Dunn	150.00	75.00	45.00
(44a)	Kid Elberfield (Elberfeld) (Detroit)	150.00	75.00	45.00
(44b)	Kid Elberfield (Elberfeld) (no team designation)	150.00	75.00	45.00
(45)	Duke Farrell	150.00	75.00	45.00
(46)	Hobe Ferris	150.00	75.00	45.00
(47)	Elmer Flick	400.00	200.00	120.00
(48)	Buck Freeman	150.00	75.00	45.00
(49)	Bill Freil (Friel)	150.00	75.00	45.00
(50)	Dave Fultz	150.00	75.00	45.00
(51)	Ned Garvin	150.00	75.00	45.00
(52)	Billy Gilbert	150.00	75.00	45.00
(53)	Harry Gleason	150.00	75.00	45.00
(54a)	Kid Gleason (New York)	150.00	75.00	45.00
(54b)	Kid Gleason (Philadelphia)	150.00	75.00	45.00
(55)	John Gochnauer (Gochnaur)	150.00	75.00	45.00
(56)	Danny Green	150.00	75.00	45.00
(57)	Noodles Hahn	150.00	75.00	45.00
(58)	Bill Hallman	150.00	75.00	45.00
(59)	Ned Hanlon	150.00	75.00	45.00
(60)	Dick Harley	150.00	75.00	45.00
(61)	Jack Harper	150.00	75.00	45.00
(62)	Topsy Hartsell (Hartsel)	150.00	75.00	45.00
(63)	Emmet Heidrick	150.00	75.00	45.00
(64)	Charlie Hemphill	150.00	75.00	45.00
(65)	Weldon Henley	150.00	75.00	45.00
(66)	Piano Legs Hickman	150.00	75.00	45.00
(67)	Harry Howell	150.00	75.00	45.00
(68)	Frank Isabel (Isbell)	150.00	75.00	45.00
(69)	Fred Jacklitzch (Jacklitsch)	150.00	75.00	45.00
(70)	Fielder Jones (Chicago)	150.00	75.00	45.00
(71)	Charlie Jones (Boston)	150.00	75.00	45.00
(72)	Addie Joss	400.00	200.00	120.00
(73)	Mike Kahoe	150.00	75.00	45.00
(74)	Wee Willie Keeler	400.00	200.00	120.00
(75)	Joe Kelley	400.00	200.00	120.00
(76)	Brickyard Kennedy	150.00	75.00	45.00
(77)	Frank Kitson	150.00	75.00	45.00
(78a)	Malachi Kittredge (Boston)	150.00	75.00	45.00
(78b)	Malachi Kittredge (Washington)	150.00	75.00	45.00
(79)	Candy LaChance	150.00	75.00	45.00
(80)	Nap Lajoie	700.00	350.00	200.00
(81)	Tommy Leach	150.00	75.00	45.00
(82a)	Watty Lee (Washington)	150.00	75.00	45.00
(82b)	Watty Lee (Pittsburg)	150.00	75.00	45.00
(83)	Sam Leever	150.00	75.00	45.00
(84)	Herman Long	150.00	75.00	45.00
(85a)	Billy Lush (Detroit)	150.00	75.00	45.00
(85b)	Billy Lush (Cleveland)	150.00	75.00	45.00
(86)	Christy Mathewson	1000.	500.00	300.00
(87)	Sport McAllister	150.00	75.00	45.00
(88)	Jack McCarthy	150.00	75.00	45.00
(89)	Barry McCormick	150.00	75.00	45.00
(90)	Ed McFarland (Chicago)	150.00	75.00	45.00
(91)	Herm McFarland (New York)	150.00	75.00	45.00
(92)	Joe McGinnity	400.00	200.00	120.00
(93)	John McGraw	450.00	225.00	135.00
(94)	Deacon McGuire	150.00	75.00	45.00
(95)	Jock Menefee	150.00	75.00	45.00
(96)	Sam Mertes	150.00	75.00	45.00
(97)	Roscoe Miller	150.00	75.00	45.00
(98)	Fred Mitchell	150.00	75.00	45.00
(99)	Earl Moore	150.00	75.00	45.00
(100)	Danny Murphy	150.00	75.00	45.00
(101)	Jack O'Connor	150.00	75.00	45.00
(102)	Al Orth	150.00	75.00	45.00
(103)	Dick Padden	150.00	75.00	45.00
(104)	Freddy Parent	150.00	75.00	45.00
(105)	Roy Patterson	150.00	75.00	45.00
(106)	Heinie Peitz	150.00	75.00	45.00
(107)	Deacon Phillipi (Phillippe)	150.00	75.00	45.00
(108)	Wiley Piatt	150.00	75.00	45.00
(109)	Ollie Pickering	150.00	75.00	45.00
(110)	Eddie Plank	600.00	300.00	175.00
(111a)	Ed Poole (Cincinnati)	150.00	75.00	45.00
(111b)	Ed Poole (Brooklyn)	150.00	75.00	45.00
(112a)	Jack Powell (St. Louis)	150.00	75.00	45.00
(112b)	Jack Powell (New York)	150.00	75.00	45.00
(113)	Mike Powers	150.00	75.00	45.00
(114)	Claude Ritchie (Ritchey)	150.00	75.00	45.00
(115)	Jimmy Ryan	150.00	75.00	45.00
(116)	Ossee Schreckengost	150.00	75.00	45.00
(117)	Kip Selbach	150.00	75.00	45.00
(118)	Socks Seybold	150.00	75.00	45.00
(119)	Jimmy Sheckard	150.00	75.00	45.00
(120)	Ed Siever	150.00	75.00	45.00
(121)	Harry Smith	150.00	75.00	45.00
(122)	Tully Sparks	150.00	75.00	45.00
(123)	Jake Stahl	150.00	75.00	45.00
(124)	Harry Steinfeldt	175.00	87.00	52.00
(125)	Sammy Strang	150.00	75.00	45.00
(126)	Willie Sudhoff	150.00	75.00	45.00
(127)	Joe Sugden	150.00	75.00	45.00
(128)	Billy Sullivan	150.00	75.00	45.00
(129)	Jack Taylor	150.00	75.00	45.00
(130)	Fred Tenney	150.00	75.00	45.00
(131)	Ira Thomas	150.00	75.00	45.00
(132a)	Jack Thoney (Cleveland)	150.00	75.00	45.00
(132b)	Jack Thoney (New York)	150.00	75.00	45.00
(133)	Jack Townsend	150.00	75.00	45.00
(134)	George Van Haltren	150.00	75.00	45.00
(135)	Rube Waddell	400.00	200.00	120.00
(136)	Honus Wagner	1500.	750.00	450.00
(137)	Bobby Wallace	400.00	200.00	120.00
(138)	Jack Warner	150.00	75.00	45.00
(139)	Jimmy Wiggs	150.00	75.00	45.00
(140)	Jimmy Williams	150.00	75.00	45.00
(141)	Vic Willis	150.00	75.00	45.00
(142)	Snake Wiltse	150.00	75.00	45.00
(143)	George Winters (Winter)	150.00	75.00	45.00
(144)	Bob Wood	150.00	75.00	45.00
(145)	Joe Yeager	150.00	75.00	45.00
(146)	Cy Young	800.00	400.00	250.00
(147)	Chief Zimmer	150.00	75.00	45.00

1903 E107 Breisch Williams - Type II

		NR MT	EX	VG
Complete Set:		2250.	1250.	700.00
Common Player:		300.00	150.00	90.00
(1)	Ed Delehanty	450.00	225.00	135.00
(2)	Jack Doyle	300.00	150.00	90.00
(3)	Wee Willie Keeler	450.00	225.00	135.00
(4)	Tommy Leach	300.00	150.00	90.00
(5)	Socks Seybold	300.00	150.00	90.00
(6)	Fred Tenney	300.00	150.00	90.00

1922 E120 American Caramel

One of the most popular of the "E" issues, the 1922 E120 set was produced by the American Caramel Co. in 1922 and distributed with sticks of caramel candy. The unnumbered cards measure 2" by 3-1/2" in size. Cards depicting players from the American League are printed in brown ink on yellow, while the National Leaguers are printed in green on a blue-green background. The card reverses carry team checklists Many of the E120 photos were used in other sets such as E121, W572, W573 and V61.

BOSTON AMERICANS
"RED SOX"
MANAGER—HUGH DUFFY
HERB PENNOCK PITCHER
ELMER MYERS PITCHER
JACK QUINN PITCHER
BEN KARR PITCHER
HAROLD (MUDDY) RUEL CATCHER
AL WALTERS CATCHER
GEORGE BURNS FIRST B. AND O. F.
DERRILL PRATT SECOND BASE
CLARK PITTENGER THIRD BASE
JOE DUGAN INFIELD
NEMO LEIBOLD OUTFIELD
ELMER SMITH OUTFIELD
MIKE MENOSKY OUTFIELD
JOHN (SHANO) COLLINS UTILITY
JOE HARRIS INFIELD AND OUTFIELD

THIS PICTURE IS ONE OF A SERIES OF 240 PICTURES OF BASEBALL STARS—15 PLAYERS IN EACH OF THE 16 MAJOR LEAGUE TEAMS. WE SUPPLY HANDSOME BLANK ALBUMS TO HOLD 120 PICTURES—ONE FOR AMERICAN LEAGUE, ONE FOR NATIONAL LEAGUE—FOR 15 CENTS EACH POSTPAID.

AMERICAN CARAMEL CO.
LANCASTER, PA. YORK, PA.

		NR MT	EX	VG
Complete Set:		15000.	7500.	4500.
Common Player:		35.00	17.50	10.50
(1)	Charles (Babe) Adams	35.00	17.50	10.50
(2)	Eddie Ainsmith	35.00	17.50	10.50
(3)	Vic Aldridge	35.00	17.50	10.50
(4)	Grover C. Alexander	100.00	50.00	30.00
(5)	Jim Bagby	35.00	17.50	10.50
(6)	Frank (Home Run) Baker	100.00	50.00	30.00
(7)	Dave (Beauty) Bancroft	90.00	45.00	27.00
(8)	Walt Barbare	35.00	17.50	10.50
(9)	Turner Barber	35.00	17.50	10.50
(10)	Jess Barnes	35.00	17.50	10.50
(11)	Clyde Barnhart	35.00	17.50	10.50
(12)	John Bassler	35.00	17.50	10.50
(13)	Will Bayne	35.00	17.50	10.50
(14)	Walter (Huck) Betts	35.00	17.50	10.50
(15)	Carson Bigbee	35.00	17.50	10.50
(16)	Lu Blue	35.00	17.50	10.50
(17)	Norman Boeckel	35.00	17.50	10.50
(18)	Sammy Bohne	35.00	17.50	10.50
(19)	George Burns	35.00	17.50	10.50
(20)	George Burns	35.00	17.50	10.50
(21)	"Bullet Joe" Bush	35.00	17.50	10.50
(22)	Leon Cadore	40.00	20.00	12.00
(23)	Marty Callaghan	35.00	17.50	10.50
(24)	Frank Calloway (Callaway)	35.00	17.50	10.50
(25)	Max Carey	90.00	45.00	27.00
(26)	Jimmy Caveney	35.00	17.50	10.50
(27)	Virgil Cheeves	35.00	17.50	10.50
(28)	Vern Clemons	35.00	17.50	10.50
(29)	Ty Cob (Cobb)	600.00	300.00	180.00
(30)	Bert Cole	35.00	17.50	10.50
(31)	Eddie Collins	100.00	50.00	30.00
(32)	John (Shano) Collins	35.00	17.50	10.50
(33)	T.P. (Pat) Collins	35.00	17.50	10.50
(34)	Wilbur Cooper	35.00	17.50	10.50
(35)	Harry Courtney	35.00	17.50	10.50
(36)	Stanley Coveleskie (Coveleski)	90.00	45.00	27.00
(37)	Elmer Cox	35.00	17.50	10.50
(38)	Sam Crane	35.00	17.50	10.50
(39)	Walton Cruise	35.00	17.50	10.50
(40)	Bill Cunningham	35.00	17.50	10.50
(41)	George Cutshaw	35.00	17.50	10.50
(42)	Dave Danforth	35.00	17.50	10.50
(43)	Jake Daubert	35.00	17.50	10.50
(44)	George Dauss	35.00	17.50	10.50
(45)	Frank (Dixie) Davis	35.00	17.50	10.50
(46)	Hank DeBerry	35.00	17.50	10.50
(47)	Albert (Lou) Devormer (DeVormer)	40.00	20.00	12.00
(48)	Bill Doak	35.00	17.50	10.50
(49)	Pete Donohue	35.00	17.50	10.50
(50)	"Shufflin" Phil Douglas	40.00	20.00	12.00
(51)	Joe Dugan	40.00	20.00	12.00
(52)	Louis (Pat) Duncan	35.00	17.50	10.50
(53)	Jimmy Dykes	40.00	20.00	12.00
(54)	Howard Ehmke	40.00	20.00	12.00
(55)	Frank Ellerbe	35.00	17.50	10.50
(56)	Urban (Red) Faber	90.00	45.00	27.00
(57)	Bib Falk (Bibb)	35.00	17.50	10.50
(58)	Dana Fillingim	35.00	17.50	10.50
(59)	Max Flack	35.00	17.50	10.50
(60)	Ira Flagstead	35.00	17.50	10.50
(61)	Art Fletcher	35.00	17.50	10.50
(62)	Horace Ford	35.00	17.50	10.50
(63)	Jack Fournier	35.00	17.50	10.50
(64)	Frank Frisch	100.00	50.00	30.00
(65)	Ollie Fuhrman	35.00	17.50	10.50
(66)	Clarance Galloway	35.00	17.50	10.50
(67)	Larry Gardner	35.00	17.50	10.50
(68)	Walter Gerber	35.00	17.50	10.50
(69)	Ed Gharrity	35.00	17.50	10.50
(70)	John Gillespie	35.00	17.50	10.50
(71)	Chas. (Whitey) Glazner	35.00	17.50	10.50
(72)	Johnny Gooch	35.00	17.50	10.50
(73)	Leon Goslin	90.00	45.00	27.00
(74)	Hank Gowdy	40.00	20.00	12.00
(75)	John Graney	35.00	17.50	10.50
(76)	Tom Griffith	35.00	17.50	10.50
(77)	Burleigh Grimes	90.00	45.00	27.00
(78)	Oscar Ray Grimes	35.00	17.50	10.50
(79)	Charlie Grimm	35.00	17.50	10.50
(80)	Heinie Groh	35.00	17.50	10.50
(81)	Jesse Haines	90.00	45.00	27.00
(82)	Earl Hamilton	35.00	17.50	10.50
(83)	Gene (Bubbles) Hargrave	35.00	17.50	10.50
(84)	Bryan Harris (Harriss)	35.00	17.50	10.50
(85)	Joe Harris	35.00	17.50	10.50
(86)	Stanley Harris	35.00	17.50	10.50
(87)	Chas. (Dowdy) Hartnett	100.00	50.00	30.00
(88)	Bob Hasty	35.00	17.50	10.50
(89)	Joe Hauser	35.00	17.50	10.50
(90)	Clif Heathcote (Cliff)	35.00	17.50	10.50
(91)	Harry Heilmann	90.00	45.00	27.00
(92)	Walter (Butch) Henline	35.00	17.50	10.50
(93)	Clarence (Shovel) Hodge	35.00	17.50	10.50
(94)	Walter Holke	35.00	17.50	10.50
(95)	Charles Hollocher	35.00	17.50	10.50

		NR MT	EX	VG
(96)	Harry Hooper	90.00	45.00	27.00
(97)	Rogers Hornsby	200.00	100.00	60.00
(98)	Waite Hoyt	90.00	45.00	27.00
(99)	Wilbur Hubbell (Wilbert)	35.00	17.50	10.50
(100)	Bernard (Bud) Hungling	35.00	17.50	10.50
(101)	Will Jacobson	35.00	17.50	10.50
(102)	Charlie Jamieson	35.00	17.50	10.50
(103)	Ernie Johnson	35.00	17.50	10.50
(104)	Sylvester Johnson	35.00	17.50	10.50
(105)	Walter Johnson	400.00	200.00	120.00
(106)	Jimmy Johnston	35.00	17.50	10.50
(107)	W.R. (Doc) Johnston	35.00	17.50	10.50
(108)	"Deacon" Sam Jones	40.00	20.00	12.00
(109)	Bob Jones	35.00	17.50	10.50
(110)	Percy Jones	35.00	17.50	10.50
(111)	Joe Judge	35.00	17.50	10.50
(112)	Ben Karr	35.00	17.50	10.50
(113)	Johnny Kelleher	35.00	17.50	10.50
(114)	George Kelly	90.00	45.00	27.00
(115)	Lee King	35.00	17.50	10.50
(116)	Wm (Larry) Kopff (Kopf)	35.00	17.50	10.50
(117)	Marty Krug	35.00	17.50	10.50
(118)	Johnny Lavan	35.00	17.50	10.50
(119)	Nemo Leibold	35.00	17.50	10.50
(120)	Roy Leslie	35.00	17.50	10.50
(121)	George Leverette (Leverett)	35.00	17.50	10.50
(122)	Adolfo Luque	35.00	17.50	10.50
(123)	Walter Mails	35.00	17.50	10.50
(124)	Al Mamaux	35.00	17.50	10.50
(125)	"Rabbit" Maranville	90.00	45.00	27.00
(126)	Cliff Markle	35.00	17.50	10.50
(127)	Richard (Rube) Marquard	100.00	50.00	30.00
(128)	Carl Mays	60.00	30.00	18.00
(129)	Hervey McClellan (Harvey)	35.00	17.50	10.50
(130)	Austin McHenry	35.00	17.50	10.50
(131)	"Stuffy" McInnis	40.00	20.00	12.00
(132)	Martin McManus	35.00	17.50	10.50
(133)	Mike McNally	40.00	20.00	12.00
(134)	Hugh McQuillan	35.00	17.50	10.50
(135)	Lee Meadows	35.00	17.50	10.50
(136)	Mike Menosky	35.00	17.50	10.50
(137)	Bob (Dutch) Meusel	60.00	30.00	18.00
(138)	Emil (Irish) Meusel	35.00	17.50	10.50
(139)	Clyde Milan	35.00	17.50	10.50
(140)	Edmund (Bing) Miller	35.00	17.50	10.50
(141)	Elmer Miller	40.00	20.00	12.00
(142)	Lawrence (Hack) Miller	35.00	17.50	10.50
(143)	Clarence Mitchell	35.00	17.50	10.50
(144)	George Mogridge	35.00	17.50	10.50
(145)	Roy Moore	35.00	17.50	10.50
(146)	John L. Mokan	35.00	17.50	10.50
(147)	John Morrison	35.00	17.50	10.50
(148)	Johnny Mostil	35.00	17.50	10.50
(149)	Elmer Myers	35.00	17.50	10.50
(150)	Hy Myers	35.00	17.50	10.50
(151)	Roliene Naylor (Roleine)	35.00	17.50	10.50
(152)	Earl (Greasy) Neale	60.00	30.00	18.00
(153)	Art Nehf	35.00	17.50	10.50
(154)	Les Nunamaker	35.00	17.50	10.50
(155)	Joe Oeschger	40.00	20.00	12.00
(156)	Bob O'Farrell	35.00	17.50	10.50
(157)	Ivan Olson	35.00	17.50	10.50
(158)	George O'Neil	35.00	17.50	10.50
(159)	Steve O'Neill	35.00	17.50	10.50
(160)	Frank Parkinson	35.00	17.50	10.50
(161)	Roger Peckinpaugh	35.00	17.50	10.50
(162)	Herb Pennock	90.00	45.00	27.00
(163)	Ralph (Cy) Perkins	35.00	17.50	10.50
(164)	Will Pertica	35.00	17.50	10.50
(165)	Jack Peters	35.00	17.50	10.50
(166)	Tom Phillips	35.00	17.50	10.50
(167)	Val Picinich	35.00	17.50	10.50
(168)	Herman Pillette	35.00	17.50	10.50
(169)	Ralph Pinelli	40.00	20.00	12.00
(170)	Wallie Pipp	50.00	25.00	15.00
(171)	Clark Pittenger (Clarke)	35.00	17.50	10.50
(172)	Raymond Powell	35.00	17.50	10.50
(173)	Derrill Pratt	35.00	17.50	10.50
(174)	Jack Quinn	35.00	17.50	10.50
(175)	Joe (Goldie) Rapp	35.00	17.50	10.50
(176)	John Rawlings	35.00	17.50	10.50
(177)	Walter (Dutch) Reuther (Ruether)	35.00	17.50	10.50
(178)	Sam Rice	90.00	45.00	27.00
(179)	Emory Rigney	35.00	17.50	10.50
(180)	Jimmy Ring	35.00	17.50	10.50
(181)	Eppa Rixey	90.00	45.00	27.00
(182)	Charles Robertson	35.00	17.50	10.50
(183)	Ed Rommel	40.00	20.00	12.00
(184)	Eddie Roush	90.00	45.00	27.00
(185)	Harold (Muddy) Ruel (Herold)	35.00	17.50	10.50
(186)	Babe Ruth	1200.	600.00	350.00
(187)	Ray Schalk	90.00	45.00	27.00
(188)	Wallie Schang	40.00	20.00	12.00
(189)	Ray Schmandt	35.00	17.50	10.50
(190)	Walter Schmidt	35.00	17.50	10.50
(191)	Joe Schultz	35.00	17.50	10.50
(192)	Everett Scott	40.00	20.00	12.00
(193)	Henry Severeid	35.00	17.50	10.50
(194)	Joe Sewell	100.00	50.00	30.00
(195)	Howard Shanks	35.00	17.50	10.50
(196)	Bob Shawkey	35.00	17.50	10.50
(197)	Earl Sheely	35.00	17.50	10.50
(198)	Will Sherdel	35.00	17.50	10.50
(199)	Ralph Shinners	35.00	17.50	10.50
(200)	Urban Shocker	35.00	17.50	10.50
(201)	Charles (Chick) Shorten	35.00	17.50	10.50
(202)	George Sisler	125.00	62.00	37.00
(203)	Earl Smith	35.00	17.50	10.50
(204)	Earl Smith	35.00	17.50	10.50
(205)	Elmer Smith	35.00	17.50	10.50
(206)	Jack Smith	35.00	17.50	10.50
(207)	Sherrod Smith	35.00	17.50	10.50
(208)	Colonel Snover	35.00	17.50	10.50
(209)	Frank Snyder	35.00	17.50	10.50
(210)	Al Sothoron	35.00	17.50	10.50
(211)	Bill Southworth	40.00	20.00	12.00
(212)	Tris Speaker	250.00	125.00	75.00
(213)	Arnold Statz	35.00	17.50	10.50
(214)	Milton Stock	35.00	17.50	10.50
(215)	Amos Strunk	35.00	17.50	10.50
(216)	Jim Tierney	35.00	17.50	10.50
(217)	John Tobin	35.00	17.50	10.50
(218)	Fred Toney	35.00	17.50	10.50
(219)	George Toporcer	35.00	17.50	10.50
(220)	Harold (Pie) Traynor	90.00	45.00	27.00
(221)	George Uhle	35.00	17.50	10.50
(222)	Elam Vangilder	35.00	17.50	10.50
(223)	Bob Veach	35.00	17.50	10.50
(224)	Clarence (Tillie) Walker	35.00	17.50	10.50
(225)	Curtis Walker	35.00	17.50	10.50
(226)	Al Walters	35.00	17.50	10.50
(227)	Bill Wambsganss	35.00	17.50	10.50
(228)	Aaron (Erin) Ward	40.00	20.00	12.00
(229)	John Watson	35.00	17.50	10.50
(230)	Frank Welch	35.00	17.50	10.50
(231)	Zach Wheat	100.00	50.00	30.00
(232)	Fred (Cy) Williams	35.00	17.50	10.50
(233)	Kenneth Williams	35.00	17.50	10.50
(234)	Ivy Wingo	35.00	17.50	10.50
(235)	Joe Wood	35.00	17.50	10.50
(236)	Lawrence Woodall	35.00	17.50	10.50
(237)	Russell Wrightstone	35.00	17.50	10.50
(238)	Everett Yaryan	35.00	17.50	10.50
(239)	Ross Young (Youngs)	100.00	50.00	30.00
(240)	J.T. Zachary	35.00	17.50	10.50

1921 E121 American Caramel

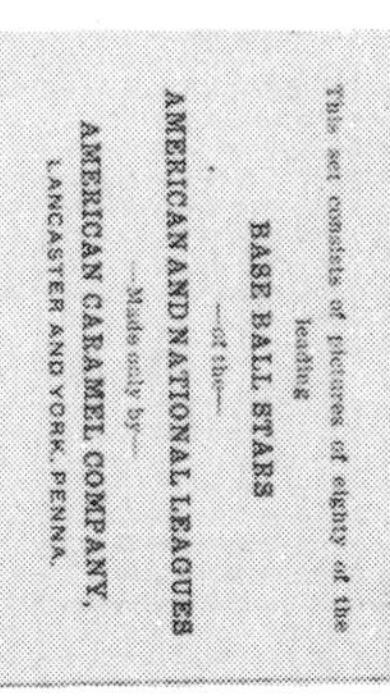

This set consists of pictures of eighty of the
leading
BASE BALL STARS
—of the—
AMERICAN AND NATIONAL LEAGUES
—Made only by—
AMERICAN CARAMEL COMPANY,
LANCASTER AND YORK, PENNA.

Issued circa 1921, the E121 Series of 80 is designated as such because of the card reverses which indicate the player pictured is just one of 80 baseball stars in the set. The figure of 80 supplied by the American Caramel Co. is incorrect as over 100 different pictures do exist. The unnumbered cards, which measure 2" by 3-1/2", feature black and white photos. Two different backs exist for the Series of 80. The common back variation has the first line ending with the word "the," while the scarcer version ends with the word "eighty." The complete set price does not include the variations.

		NR MT	EX	VG
	Complete Set:	10000.	5000.	3000.
	Commmon Player:	25.00	12.50	7.50
(1)	G.C. Alexander (arms above head)	100.00	50.00	30.00
(2)	Grover Alexander	100.00	50.00	30.00
(3)	Jim Bagby	25.00	12.50	7.50
(4a)	J. Franklin Baker	100.00	50.00	30.00
(4b)	Frank Baker	100.00	50.00	30.00
(5)	Dave Bancroft (batting)	80.00	40.00	24.00
(6)	Dave Bancroft (leaping)	80.00	40.00	24.00
(7)	Ping Bodie	25.00	12.50	7.50
(8)	George Burns	25.00	12.50	7.50
(9)	Geo. J. Burns	25.00	12.50	7.50
(10)	Owen Bush	25.00	12.50	7.50
(11)	Max Carey (batting)	80.00	40.00	24.00
(12)	Max Carey (hands at hips)	80.00	40.00	24.00
(13)	Cecil Causey	25.00	12.50	7.50
(14)	Ty Cobb (throwing, looking front)	400.00	200.00	120.00
(15a)	Ty Cobb (throwing, looking right, Mgr. on front)	400.00	200.00	120.00
(15b)	Ty Cobb (throwing, looking right, Manager on front)	400.00	200.00	120.00
(16)	Eddie Collins	100.00	50.00	30.00
(17)	"Rip" Collins	25.00	12.50	7.50
(18)	Jake Daubert	50.00	25.00	15.00
(19)	George Dauss	25.00	12.50	7.50
(20)	Charles Deal (dark uniform)	25.00	12.50	7.50
(21)	Charles Deal (white uniform)	25.00	12.50	7.50
(22)	William Doak	25.00	12.50	7.50
(23)	Bill Donovan	25.00	12.50	7.50
(24)	"Phil" Douglas	50.00	25.00	15.00
(25a)	Johnny Evers (Manager)	80.00	40.00	24.00
(25b)	Johnny Evers (Mgr.)	80.00	40.00	24.00
(26)	Urban Faber (dark uniform)	80.00	40.00	24.00
(27)	Urban Faber (white uniform)	80.00	40.00	24.00
(28)	William Fewster (first name actually Wilson)	25.00	12.50	7.50
(29)	Eddie Foster	25.00	12.50	7.50
(30)	Frank Frisch	70.00	35.00	21.00
(31)	W.L. Gardner	25.00	12.50	7.50
(32a)	Alexander Gaston (no position on front)	25.00	12.50	7.50
(32b)	Alexander Gaston (position on front)	25.00	12.50	7.50
(33)	"Kid" Gleason	25.00	12.50	7.50
(34)	"Mike" Gonzalez	25.00	12.50	7.50
(35)	Hank Gowdy	25.00	12.50	7.50
(36)	John Graney	25.00	12.50	7.50
(37)	Tom Griffith	25.00	12.50	7.50
(38)	Heinie Groh	50.00	25.00	15.00
(39)	Harry Harper	25.00	12.50	7.50
(40)	Harry Heilman (Heilmann)	80.00	40.00	24.00
(41)	Walter Holke (portrait)	25.00	12.50	7.50
(42)	Walter Holke (throwing)	25.00	12.50	7.50
(43)	Charles Hollacher (Hollocher)	25.00	12.50	7.50
(44)	Harry Hooper	80.00	40.00	24.00
(45)	Rogers Hornsby	150.00	75.00	45.00
(46)	Waite Hoyt	80.00	40.00	24.00
(47)	Miller Huggins	80.00	40.00	24.00
(48)	Wm. C. Jacobson	25.00	12.50	7.50
(49)	Hugh Jennings	80.00	40.00	24.00
(50)	Walter Johnson (throwing)	275.00	137.00	82.00
(51)	Walter Johnson (hands at chest)	275.00	137.00	82.00
(52)	James Johnston	25.00	12.50	7.50
(53)	Joe Judge	25.00	12.50	7.50
(54)	George Kelly	80.00	40.00	24.00
(55)	Dick Kerr	25.00	12.50	7.50
(56)	P.J. Kilduff	25.00	12.50	7.50
(57a)	Bill Killifer (incorrect name)	50.00	25.00	15.00
(57b)	Bill Killefer (correct name)	50.00	25.00	15.00
(58)	John Lavan	25.00	12.50	7.50
(59)	"Nemo" Leibold	25.00	12.50	7.50
(60)	Duffy Lewis	50.00	25.00	15.00
(61)	Al. Mamaux	25.00	12.50	7.50
(62)	"Rabbit" Maranville	80.00	40.00	24.00
(63a)	Carl May (incorrect name)	80.00	40.00	24.00
(63b)	Carl Mays (correct name)	50.00	25.00	15.00
(64)	John McGraw	100.00	50.00	30.00
(65)	Jack McInnis	25.00	12.50	7.50
(66)	M.J. McNally	25.00	12.50	7.50
(67)	Emil Muesel (Photo actually Lou DeVormer)	50.00	25.00	15.00
(68)	R. Meusel	40.00	20.00	12.00
(69)	Clyde Milan	25.00	12.50	7.50
(70)	Elmer Miller	25.00	12.50	7.50
(71)	Otto Miller	25.00	12.50	7.50
(72)	Guy Morton	25.00	12.50	7.50
(73)	Eddie Murphy	25.00	12.50	7.50
(74)	"Hy" Myers	25.00	12.50	7.50
(75)	Arthur Nehf	25.00	12.50	7.50
(76)	Steve O'Neill	25.00	12.50	7.50
(77a)	Roger Peckinbaugh (incorrect name)	50.00	25.00	15.00
(77b)	Roger Peckinpaugh (correct name)	50.00	25.00	15.00
(78a)	Jeff Pfeffer (Brooklyn)	25.00	12.50	7.50
(78b)	Jeff Pfeffer (St. Louis)	25.00	12.50	7.50
(79)	Walter Pipp	40.00	20.00	12.00
(80)	Jack Quinn	25.00	12.50	7.50
(81)	John Rawlings	25.00	12.50	7.50
(82)	E.C. Rice	80.00	40.00	24.00
(83)	Eppa Rixey, Jr.	80.00	40.00	24.00
(84)	Robert Roth	25.00	12.50	7.50
(85a)	Ed. Roush (C.F.)	80.00	40.00	24.00
(85b)	Ed. Roush (L.F.)	70.00	35.00	21.00
(86a)	Babe Ruth	700.00	350.00	210.00
(86b)	"Babe" Ruth	700.00	350.00	210.00
(86c)	George Ruth	700.00	350.00	210.00
(87)	"Bill" Ryan	25.00	12.50	7.50
(88)	"Slim" Sallee (glove showing)	25.00	12.50	7.50
(89)	"Slim" Sallee (no glove showing)	25.00	12.50	7.50
(90)	Ray Schalk	80.00	40.00	24.00
(91)	Walter Schang	25.00	12.50	7.50
(92a)	Fred Schupp (name incorrect)	50.00	25.00	15.00
(92b)	Ferd Schupp (name correct)	50.00	25.00	15.00
(93)	Everett Scott	25.00	12.50	7.50
(94)	Hank Severeid	25.00	12.50	7.50
(95)	Robert Shawkey	50.00	25.00	15.00
(96a)	Pat Shea	50.00	25.00	15.00
(96b)	"Pat" Shea	25.00	12.50	7.50
(97)	George Sisler (batting)	70.00	35.00	21.00
(98)	George Sisler (throwing)	70.00	35.00	21.00
(99)	Earl Smith	25.00	12.50	7.50
(100)	Frank Snyder	25.00	12.50	7.50
(101a)	Tris Speaker (Mgr.)	150.00	75.00	45.00
(101b)	Tris Speaker (Manager - large projection)	150.00	75.00	45.00
(101c)	Tris Speaker (Manager - small projection)	150.00	75.00	45.00
(102)	Milton Stock	25.00	12.50	7.50
(103)	Amos Strunk	25.00	12.50	7.50
(104)	Zeb Terry	25.00	12.50	7.50
(105)	Chester Thomas	25.00	12.50	7.50
(106)	Fred Toney (trees in background)	25.00	12.50	7.50
(107)	Fred Toney (no trees in background)	25.00	12.50	7.50
(108)	George Tyler	25.00	12.50	7.50
(109)	Jim Vaughn (dark hat)	25.00	12.50	7.50
(110)	Jim Vaughn (white hat)	25.00	12.50	7.50
(111)	Bob Veach (glove in air)	25.00	12.50	7.50
(112)	Bob Veach (arms crossed)	25.00	12.50	7.50
(113)	Oscar Vitt	25.00	12.50	7.50
(114)	W. Wambsganss (photo actually Fred Coumbe)	50.00	25.00	15.00
(115)	Aaron Ward	25.00	12.50	7.50
(116)	Zach Wheat	100.00	50.00	30.00
(117)	George Whitted	25.00	12.50	7.50
(118)	Fred Williams	50.00	25.00	15.00
(119)	Ivy B. Wingo	25.00	12.50	7.50
(120)	Joe Wood	50.00	25.00	15.00
(121)	"Pep" Young	25.00	12.50	7.50

1922 E121 American Caramel

Produced by the American Caramel Co. circa 1922, the E121 Series of 120 is labeled as such by the company's claim that the set contained 120 subjects. Identical in design to the E121 Series of 80 set except for the card backs, the cards measure 2" by 3-1/2" in size. Numerous variations are found in the set, most involving a change in the player's name, team or position. The complete set price does not include variations.

ELMER SMITH
O. F.—Boston Americans

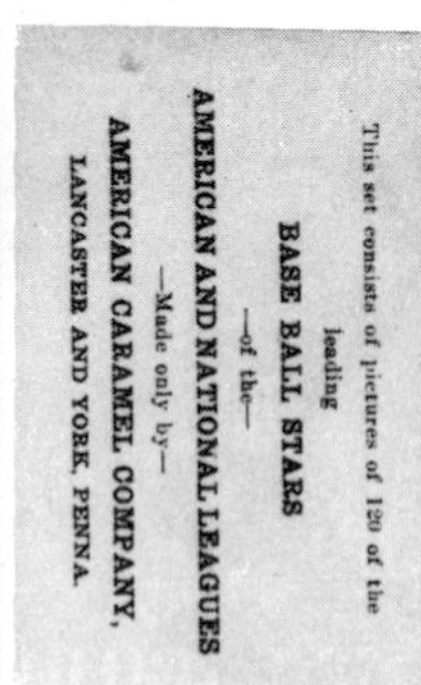

This set consists of pictures of 120 of the
leading
BASE BALL STARS
—of the—
AMERICAN AND NATIONAL LEAGUES
—Made only by—
AMERICAN CARAMEL COMPANY,
LANCASTER AND YORK, PENNA.

		NR MT	EX	VG
Complete Set:		12000.	6000.	3500.
Common Player:		30.00	15.00	9.00
(1)	Chas. "Babe" Adams	30.00	15.00	9.00
(2)	G.C. Alexander	100.00	50.00	30.00
(3)	Jim Bagby	30.00	15.00	9.00
(4)	Dave Bancroft	80.00	40.00	24.00
(5)	Turner Barber	30.00	15.00	9.00
(6a)	Carlson Bigbee (correct name Carson L. Bigbee)	35.00	17.50	10.50
(6b)	Carlson L. Bigbee	30.00	15.00	9.00
(6c)	Corson L. Bigbee	35.00	17.50	10.50
(6d)	L. Bigbee	30.00	15.00	9.00
(7)	"Bullet Joe" Bush	30.00	15.00	9.00
(8)	Max Carey	80.00	40.00	24.00
(9)	Cecil Causey	30.00	15.00	9.00
(10)	Ty Cobb (batting)	400.00	200.00	120.00
(11)	Ty Cobb (throwing)	400.00	200.00	120.00
(12)	Eddie Collins	100.00	50.00	30.00
(13)	A. Wilbur Cooper	30.00	15.00	9.00
(14)	Stanley Coveleskie (Coveleski)	80.00	40.00	24.00
(15)	Dave Danforth	30.00	15.00	9.00
(16)	Jake Daubert	30.00	15.00	9.00
(17)	George Dauss	30.00	15.00	9.00
(18)	"Dixie" Davis	30.00	15.00	9.00
(19)	Lou DeVormer	30.00	15.00	9.00
(20)	William Doak	30.00	15.00	9.00
(21)	Phil Douglas	30.00	15.00	9.00
(22)	Urban Faber	80.00	40.00	24.00
(23)	Bib Falk (Bibb)	30.00	15.00	9.00
(24)	Wm: Fewster (first name actually Wilson)	30.00	15.00	9.00
(25)	Max Flack	30.00	15.00	9.00
(26)	Ira Falgstead (Flagstead)	30.00	15.00	9.00
(27)	Frank Frisch	100.00	50.00	30.00
(28)	W.L. Gardner	30.00	15.00	9.00
(29)	Alexander Gaston	30.00	15.00	9.00
(30)	E.P. Gharrity	30.00	15.00	9.00
(31)	George Gibson	30.00	15.00	9.00
(32)	Chas. "Whitey" Glazner	30.00	15.00	9.00
(33)	"Kid" Gleason	30.00	15.00	9.00
(34)	Hank Gowdy	30.00	15.00	9.00
(35)	John Graney	30.00	15.00	9.00
(36)	Tom Griffith	30.00	15.00	9.00
(37)	Chas. Grimm	35.00	17.50	10.50
(38)	Heine Groh	30.00	15.00	9.00
(39)	Jess Haines	80.00	40.00	24.00
(40)	Harry Harper	30.00	15.00	9.00
(41a)	Harry Heilman (name incorrect)	100.00	50.00	30.00
(41b)	Harry Heilmann (name correct)	80.00	40.00	24.00
(42)	Clarence Hodge	30.00	15.00	9.00
(43)	Walter Holke (portrait)	35.00	17.50	10.50
(44)	Walter Holke (throwing)	30.00	15.00	9.00
(45)	Charles Hollocher	30.00	15.00	9.00
(46)	Harry Hooper	80.00	40.00	24.00
(47a)	Rogers Hornsby (2B.)	150.00	75.00	45.00
(47b)	Rogers Hornsby (O.F.)	150.00	75.00	45.00
(48)	Waite Hoyt	80.00	40.00	24.00
(49)	Miller Huggins	80.00	40.00	24.00
(50)	Walter Johnson	275.00	137.00	82.00
(51)	Joe Judge	30.00	15.00	9.00
(52)	George Kelly	80.00	40.00	24.00
(53)	Dick Kerr	30.00	15.00	9.00
(54)	P.J. Kilduff	30.00	15.00	9.00
(55)	Bill Killifer (Killefer) (batting)	30.00	15.00	9.00
(56)	Bill Killifer (Killefer) (throwing)	30.00	15.00	9.00
(57)	John Lavan	30.00	15.00	9.00
(58)	Walter Mails	30.00	15.00	9.00
(59)	"Rabbit" Maranville	80.00	40.00	24.00
(60)	Elwood Martin	30.00	15.00	9.00
(61)	Carl Mays	35.00	17.50	10.50
(62)	John J. McGraw	125.00	62.00	37.00
(63)	Jack McInnis	30.00	15.00	9.00
(64)	M.J. McNally	30.00	15.00	9.00
(65)	Emil Meusel (photo actually Lou DeVormer)	30.00	15.00	9.00
(66)	R. Meusel	40.00	20.00	12.00
(67)	Clyde Milan	30.00	15.00	9.00
(68)	Elmer Miller	30.00	15.00	9.00
(69)	Otto Miller	30.00	15.00	9.00
(70)	Johnny Mostil	30.00	15.00	9.00
(71)	Eddie Mulligan	30.00	15.00	9.00
(72a)	Hy Myers	30.00	15.00	9.00
(72b)	"Hy" Myers	35.00	17.50	10.50
(73)	Earl Neale	40.00	20.00	12.00
(74)	Arthur Nehf	30.00	15.00	9.00
(75)	Leslie Nunamaker	30.00	15.00	9.00
(76)	Joe Oeschger	30.00	15.00	9.00
(77)	Chas. O'Leary	35.00	17.50	10.50
(78)	Steve O'Neill	30.00	15.00	9.00
(79)	D.B. Pratt	30.00	15.00	9.00
(80a)	John Rawlings (2B.)	30.00	15.00	9.00
(80b)	John Rawlings (Utl.)	30.00	15.00	9.00
(81)	E.S. Rice (intials actually E.C.)	80.00	40.00	24.00
(82)	Eppa J. Rixey	80.00	40.00	24.00
(83)	Eppa Rixey, Jr.	80.00	40.00	24.00
(84)	Wilbert Robinson	80.00	40.00	24.00
(85)	Tom Rogers	30.00	15.00	9.00
(86a)	Ed Rounnel	30.00	15.00	9.00
(86b)	Ed. Rommel	30.00	15.00	9.00
(87)	Ed Roush	80.00	40.00	24.00
(88)	"Muddy" Ruel	30.00	15.00	9.00
(89)	Walter Ruether	30.00	15.00	9.00
(90a)	Babe Ruth (photo montage)	700.00	350.00	210.00
(90b)	"Babe" Ruth (photo montage)	700.00	350.00	210.00
(91a)	Babe Ruth (holding bird)	700.00	350.00	210.00
(91b)	"Babe" Ruth (holding bird)	700.00	350.00	210.00
(92)	"Babe" Ruth (holding ball)	700.00	350.00	210.00
(93)	Bill Ryan	30.00	15.00	9.00
(94)	Ray Schalk (catching)	80.00	40.00	24.00
(95)	Ray Schalk (batting)	80.00	40.00	24.00
(96)	Wally Schang	24.00	12.00	7.25
(97)	Ferd Schupp	35.00	17.50	10.50
(98)	Everett Scott	30.00	15.00	9.00
(99)	Joe Sewell	100.00	50.00	30.00
(100)	Robert Shawkey	30.00	15.00	9.00
(101)	Pat Shea	30.00	15.00	9.00
(102)	Earl Sheely	30.00	15.00	9.00
(103)	Urban Schocker	30.00	15.00	9.00
(104)	George Sisler (batting)	100.00	50.00	30.00
(105)	George Sisler (throwing)	75.00	37.00	22.00
(106)	Earl Smith	30.00	15.00	9.00
(107)	Elmer Smith	30.00	15.00	9.00
(108)	Frank Snyder	30.00	15.00	9.00
(109)	Bill Southworth	30.00	15.00	9.00
(110a)	Tris Speaker (large projection)	150.00	75.00	45.00
(110b)	Tris Speaker (small projection)	150.00	75.00	45.00
(111a)	Milton Stock	35.00	17.50	10.50
(111b)	Milton J. Stock	30.00	15.00	9.00
(112)	Amos Strunk	30.00	15.00	9.00
(113)	Zeb Terry	30.00	15.00	9.00
(114)	Fred Toney	30.00	15.00	9.00
(115)	George Topocer (Toporcer)	30.00	15.00	9.00
(116)	Bob Veach	30.00	15.00	9.00
(117)	Oscar Vitt	30.00	15.00	9.00
(118)	Curtis Walker	30.00	15.00	9.00
(119)	W. Wambsganss (photo actually Fred Coumbe)	30.00	15.00	9.00
(120)	Aaron Ward	30.00	15.00	9.00
(121)	Zach Wheat	40.00	20.00	12.00
(122a)	George Whitted (Pittsburgh)	30.00	15.00	9.00
(122b)	George Whitted (Brooklyn)	30.00	15.00	9.00
(123)	Fred Williams	30.00	15.00	9.00
(124)	Ivy B. Wingo	30.00	15.00	9.00
(125)	Ross Young (Youngs)	100.00	50.00	30.00

1922 E122 American Caramel

"RABBIT" MARANVILLE
S. S.—Pittsburgh Nationals

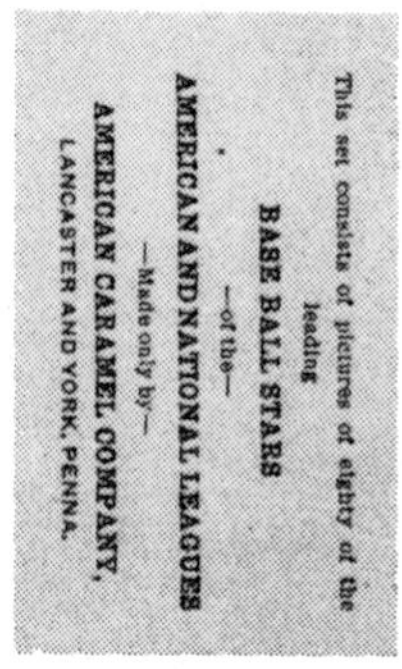

This set consists of pictures of eighty of the
leading
BASE BALL STARS
—of the—
AMERICAN AND NATIONAL LEAGUES
—Made only by—
AMERICAN CARAMEL COMPANY,
LANCASTER AND YORK, PENNA.

Known as E122 in the American Card Catalog, this set is actually a subset of the E121 American Caramel set. The cards are nearly identical to E121's "Series of 80," except the player's name, position and team are printed inside a gray rectangle at the bottom of the card, and the photos have a more coarse appearance.

		NR MT	EX	VG
Complete Set:		7000.	3500.	2100.
Common Player:		40.00	20.00	12.00
(1)	Grover Alexander	125.00	62.00	37.00
(2)	Jim Bagby	40.00	20.00	12.00
(3)	J. Franklin Baker	110.00	55.00	33.00
(4)	Dave Bancroft	110.00	55.00	33.00
(5)	Ping Bodie	40.00	20.00	12.00
(6)	George Burns	40.00	20.00	12.00
(7)	Geo. J. Burns	40.00	20.00	12.00
(8)	Owen Bush	40.00	20.00	12.00
(9)	Max Carey	110.00	55.00	33.00
(10)	Cecil Causey	40.00	20.00	12.00
(11)	Ty Cobb	800.00	400.00	240.00
(12)	Eddie Collins	110.00	55.00	33.00
(13)	Jake Daubert	50.00	25.00	15.00
(14)	George Dauss	40.00	20.00	12.00
(15)	Charles Deal	40.00	20.00	12.00
(16)	William Doak	40.00	20.00	12.00
(17)	Bill Donovan	40.00	20.00	12.00
(18)	Johnny Evers	110.00	55.00	33.00
(19)	Urban Faber	110.00	55.00	33.00
(20)	Eddie Foster	40.00	20.00	12.00
(21)	W.L. Gardner	40.00	20.00	12.00
(22)	"Kid" Gleason	40.00	20.00	12.00
(23)	Hank Gowdy	40.00	20.00	12.00
(24)	John Graney	40.00	20.00	12.00
(25)	Tom Griffith	40.00	20.00	12.00
(26)	Harry Heilman (Heilmann)	110.00	55.00	33.00
(27)	Walter Holke	40.00	20.00	12.00
(28)	Charles Hollacher (Hollocher)	40.00	20.00	12.00
(29)	Harry Hooper	110.00	55.00	33.00
(30)	Rogers Hornsby	200.00	100.00	60.00
(31)	Wm. C. Jacobson	40.00	20.00	12.00
(32)	Walter Johnson	300.00	150.00	90.00
(33)	James Johnston	40.00	20.00	12.00
(34)	Joe Judge	40.00	20.00	12.00
(35)	George Kelly	110.00	55.00	33.00
(36)	Dick Kerr	40.00	20.00	12.00
(37)	P.J. Kilduff	40.00	20.00	12.00
(38)	Bill Killefer	40.00	20.00	12.00
(39)	John Lavan	40.00	20.00	12.00
(40)	Duffy Lewis	40.00	20.00	12.00
(41)	Perry Lipe	40.00	20.00	12.00
(42)	Al. Mamaux	40.00	20.00	12.00
(43)	"Rabbit" Maranville	110.00	55.00	33.00
(44)	Carl May (Mays)	60.00	30.00	18.00
(45)	John McGraw	125.00	62.00	37.00
(46)	Jack McInnis	40.00	20.00	12.00
(47)	Clyde Milan	40.00	20.00	12.00
(48)	Otto Miller	40.00	20.00	12.00
(49)	Guy Morton	40.00	20.00	12.00
(50)	Eddie Murphy	40.00	20.00	12.00
(51)	"Hy" Myers	40.00	20.00	12.00
(52)	Steve O'Neill	40.00	20.00	12.00
(53)	Roger Peckinbaugh (Peckinpaugh)	40.00	20.00	12.00
(54)	Jeff Pfeffer	40.00	20.00	12.00
(55)	Walter Pipp	75.00	37.00	22.00
(56)	E.C. Rice	110.00	55.00	33.00
(57)	Eppa Rixey, Jr.	110.00	55.00	33.00
(58)	Babe Ruth	1000.	500.00	300.00
(59)	"Slim" Sallee	40.00	20.00	12.00
(60)	Ray Schalk	110.00	55.00	33.00
(61)	Walter Schang	40.00	20.00	12.00
(62a)	Fred Schupp (name incorrect)	40.00	20.00	12.00
(62b)	Ferd Schupp (name correct)	40.00	20.00	12.00
(63)	Everett Scott	40.00	20.00	12.00
(64)	Hank Severeid	40.00	20.00	12.00
(65)	George Sisler (batting)	110.00	55.00	33.00
(66)	George Sisler (throwing)	110.00	55.00	33.00
(67)	Tris Speaker	150.00	75.00	45.00
(68)	Milton Stock	40.00	20.00	12.00
(69)	Amos Strunk	40.00	20.00	12.00
(70)	Chester Thomas	40.00	20.00	12.00
(71)	George Tyler	40.00	20.00	12.00
(72)	Jim Vaughn	40.00	20.00	12.00
(73)	Bob Veach	40.00	20.00	12.00
(74)	W. Wambsganss	60.00	30.00	18.00
(75)	Zach Wheat	110.00	55.00	33.00
(76)	Fred Williams	50.00	25.00	15.00
(77)	Ivy B. Wingo	40.00	20.00	12.00
(78)	Joe Wood	60.00	30.00	18.00
(79)	Pep Young	40.00	20.00	12.00

1923 E123 Curtis Ireland

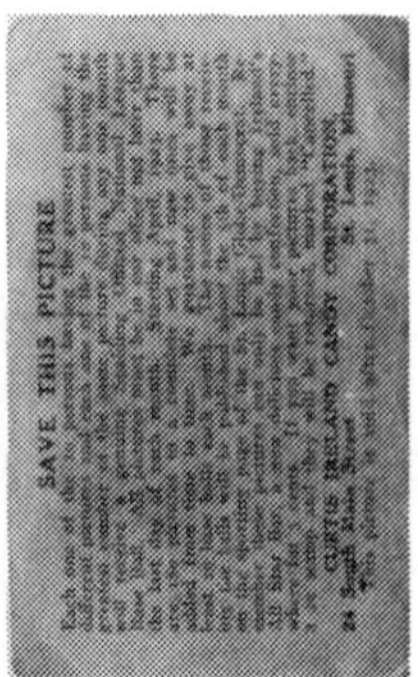

SAVE THIS PICTURE

This set, identified in the ACC as E123, was issued in 1923 by the Curtis Ireland Candy Corporation of St. Louis and was distributed with Ireland's "All Star Bars." Except for the backs, the Ireland set is identical to the Willard Chocolate V100 set of the same year. Measuring 3-1/4" by 2-1/16", the cards feature sepia-toned photos with the player's name in script on the front. The backs advertise a contest which required the collector to mail in the cards in exchange for prizes, which probably explains their relative scarcity today.

		NR MT	EX	VG
Complete Set:		15000.	7500.	4500.
Common Player:		30.00	15.00	9.00
(1)	Chas. B Adams	30.00	15.00	9.00
(2)	Grover C. Alexander	175.00	87.00	52.00
(3)	J.P. Austin	30.00	15.00	9.00
(4)	J.C. Bagby	30.00	15.00	9.00
(5)	J. Franklin Baker	125.00	62.00	37.00
(6)	David J. Bancroft	125.00	62.00	37.00
(7)	Turner Barber	30.00	15.00	9.00
(8)	Jesse L. Barnes	30.00	15.00	9.00
(9)	J.C. Bassler	30.00	15.00	9.00
(10)	L.A. Blue	30.00	15.00	9.00
(11)	Norman D. Boeckel	30.00	15.00	9.00
(12)	F.L. Brazil (Brazill)	30.00	15.00	9.00
(13)	G.H. Burns	30.00	15.00	9.00
(14)	Geo. J. Burns	30.00	15.00	9.00
(15)	Leon Cadore	30.00	15.00	9.00
(16)	Max G. Carey	125.00	62.00	37.00
(17)	Harold G. Carlson	30.00	15.00	9.00
(18)	Lloyd R. Christenberry (Christenbury)	30.00	15.00	9.00
(19)	Vernon J.. Clemons	30.00	15.00	9.00
(20)	T.R. Cobb	800.00	400.00	250.00
(21)	Bert Cole	30.00	15.00	9.00

		NR MT	EX	VG
(22)	John F. Collins	30.00	15.00	9.00
(23)	S. Coveleskie (Coveleski)	125.00	62.00	37.00
(24)	Walton E. Cruise	30.00	15.00	9.00
(25)	G.W. Cutshaw	30.00	15.00	9.00
(26)	Jacob E. Daubert	35.00	17.50	10.50
(27)	Geo. Dauss	30.00	15.00	9.00
(28)	F.T. Davis	30.00	15.00	9.00
(29)	Chas. A. Deal	30.00	15.00	9.00
(30)	William L. Doak	30.00	15.00	9.00
(31)	William E. Donovan	30.00	15.00	9.00
(32)	Hugh Duffy	125.00	62.00	37.00
(33)	J.A. Dugan	35.00	17.50	10.50
(34)	Louis B. Duncan	30.00	15.00	9.00
(35)	James Dykes	35.00	17.50	10.50
(36)	H.J. Ehmke	30.00	15.00	9.00
(37)	F.R. Ellerbe	30.00	15.00	9.00
(38)	E.G. Erickson	30.00	15.00	9.00
(39)	John J. Evers	125.00	62.00	37.00
(40)	U.C. Faber	125.00	62.00	37.00
(41)	B.A. Falk	30.00	15.00	9.00
(42)	Max Flack	30.00	15.00	9.00
(43)	Lee Fohl	30.00	15.00	9.00
(44)	Jacques F. Fournier	30.00	15.00	9.00
(45)	Frank F. Frisch	125.00	62.00	37.00
(46)	C.E. Galloway	30.00	15.00	9.00
(47)	W.C. Gardner	30.00	15.00	9.00
(48)	E.P. Gharrity	30.00	15.00	9.00
(49)	Geo. Gibson	30.00	15.00	9.00
(50)	Wm. Gleason	30.00	15.00	9.00
(51)	William Gleason	30.00	15.00	9.00
(52)	Henry M. Gowdy	30.00	15.00	9.00
(53)	I.M. Griffin	30.00	15.00	9.00
(54)	Griffith	125.00	62.00	37.00
(55)	Burleigh A. Grimes	125.00	62.00	37.00
(56)	Charles J. Grimm	35.00	17.50	10.50
(57)	Jesse J. Haines	125.00	62.00	37.00
(58)	S.R. Harris	125.00	62.00	37.00
(59)	W.B. Harris	30.00	15.00	9.00
(60)	R.K. Hasty	30.00	15.00	9.00
(61)	H.E. Heilman (Heilmann)	125.00	62.00	37.00
(62)	Walter J. Henline	30.00	15.00	9.00
(63)	Walter L. Holke	30.00	15.00	9.00
(64)	Charles J. Hollocher	30.00	15.00	9.00
(65)	H.B. Hooper	125.00	62.00	37.00
(66)	Rogers Hornsby	125.00	62.00	37.00
(67)	W.C. Hoyt	125.00	62.00	37.00
(68)	Miller Huggins	125.00	62.00	37.00
(69)	W.C. Jacobsen (Jacobson)	30.00	15.00	9.00
(70)	C.D. Jamieson	30.00	15.00	9.00
(71)	Ernest Johnson	30.00	15.00	9.00
(72)	W.P. Johnson	400.00	200.00	125.00
(73)	James H. Johnston	30.00	15.00	9.00
(74)	R.W. Jones	30.00	15.00	9.00
(75)	Samuel Pond Jones	30.00	15.00	9.00
(76)	J.I. Judge	30.00	15.00	9.00
(77)	James W. Keenan	30.00	15.00	9.00
(78)	Geo. L. Kelly	125.00	62.00	37.00
(79)	Peter J. Kilduff	30.00	15.00	9.00
(80)	William Killefer	30.00	15.00	9.00
(81)	Lee King	30.00	15.00	9.00
(82)	Ray Kolp	30.00	15.00	9.00
(83)	John Lavan	30.00	15.00	9.00
(84)	H.L. Leibold	30.00	15.00	9.00
(85)	Connie Mack	500.00	250.00	150.00
(86)	J.W. Mails	30.00	15.00	9.00
(87)	Walter J. Maranville	125.00	62.00	37.00
(88)	Richard W. Marquard	125.00	62.00	37.00
(89)	C.W. Mays	35.00	17.50	10.50
(90)	Geo. F. McBride	30.00	15.00	9.00
(91)	H.M. McClellan	30.00	15.00	9.00
(92)	John J. McGraw	450.00	225.00	135.00
(93)	Austin B. McHenry	30.00	15.00	9.00
(94)	J. McInnis	30.00	15.00	9.00
(95)	Douglas McWeeney (McWeeny)	30.00	15.00	9.00
(96)	M. Menosky	30.00	15.00	9.00
(97)	Emil F. Meusel	30.00	15.00	9.00
(98)	R. Meusel	35.00	17.50	10.50
(99)	Henry W. Meyers	30.00	15.00	9.00
(100)	J.C. Milan	30.00	15.00	9.00
(101)	John K. Miljus	30.00	15.00	9.00
(102)	Edmund J. Miller	30.00	15.00	9.00
(103)	Elmer Miller	30.00	15.00	9.00
(104)	Otto L. Miller	30.00	15.00	9.00
(105)	Fred Mitchell	30.00	15.00	9.00
(106)	Geo. Mogridge	30.00	15.00	9.00
(107)	Patrick J. Moran	30.00	15.00	9.00
(108)	John D. Morrison	30.00	15.00	9.00
(109)	J.A. Mostil	30.00	15.00	9.00
(110)	Clarence F. Mueller	30.00	15.00	9.00
(111)	A. Earle Neale	35.00	17.50	10.50
(112)	Joseph Oeschger	30.00	15.00	9.00
(113)	Robert J. O'Farrell	30.00	15.00	9.00
(114)	J.C. Oldham	30.00	15.00	9.00
(115)	I.M. Olson	30.00	15.00	9.00
(116)	Geo. M. O'Neil	30.00	15.00	9.00
(117)	S.F. O'Neill	30.00	15.00	9.00
(118)	Frank J. Parkinson	30.00	15.00	9.00
(119)	Geo. H. Paskert	30.00	15.00	9.00
(120)	R.T. Peckinpaugh	30.00	15.00	9.00
(121)	H.J. Pennock	125.00	62.00	37.00
(122)	Ralph Perkins	30.00	15.00	9.00
(123)	Edw. J. Pfeffer	30.00	15.00	9.00
(124)	W.C. Pipp	250.00	125.00	75.00
(125)	Charles Elmer Ponder	30.00	15.00	9.00
(126)	Raymond R. Powell	30.00	15.00	9.00
(127)	D.B. Pratt	30.00	15.00	9.00
(128)	Joseph Rapp	30.00	15.00	9.00
(129)	John H. Rawlings	30.00	15.00	9.00
(130)	E.S. Rice (should be E.C.)	125.00	62.00	37.00
(131)	Rickey	200.00	100.00	60.00
(132)	James J. Ring	30.00	15.00	9.00
(133)	Eppa J. Rixey	125.00	62.00	37.00
(134)	Davis A. Robertson	30.00	15.00	9.00
(135)	Edwin Rommel	30.00	15.00	9.00
(136)	Edd J. Roush	125.00	62.00	37.00
(137)	Harold Ruel (Herold)	30.00	15.00	9.00
(138)	Allen Russell	30.00	15.00	9.00
(139)	G.H. Ruth	1000.	500.00	300.00
(140)	Wilfred D. Ryan	30.00	15.00	9.00
(141)	Henry F. Sallee	30.00	15.00	9.00
(142)	W.H. Schang	30.00	15.00	9.00
(143)	Raymond H. Schmandt	30.00	15.00	9.00
(144)	Everett Scott	30.00	15.00	9.00
(145)	Henry Severeid	30.00	15.00	9.00
(146)	Jos. W. Sewell	125.00	62.00	37.00
(147)	Howard S. Shanks	30.00	15.00	9.00
(148)	E.H. Sheely	30.00	15.00	9.00
(149)	Ralph Shinners	30.00	15.00	9.00
(150)	U.J. Shocker	30.00	15.00	9.00
(151)	G.H. Sisler	125.00	62.00	37.00
(152)	Earl L. Smith	30.00	15.00	9.00
(153)	Earl S. Smith	30.00	15.00	9.00
(154)	Geo. A. Smith	30.00	15.00	9.00
(155)	J.W. Smith	30.00	15.00	9.00
(156)	Tris E. Speaker	250.00	125.00	75.00
(157)	Arnold Staatz	30.00	15.00	9.00
(158)	J.R. Stephenson	30.00	15.00	9.00
(159)	Milton J. Stock	30.00	15.00	9.00
(160)	John L. Sullivan	30.00	15.00	9.00
(161)	H.F. Tormahlen	30.00	15.00	9.00
(162)	Jas. A. Tierney	30.00	15.00	9.00
(163)	J.T. Tobin	30.00	15.00	9.00
(164)	Jas. L. Vaughn	30.00	15.00	9.00
(165)	R.H. Veach	30.00	15.00	9.00
(166)	C.W. Walker	30.00	15.00	9.00
(167)	A.L. Ward	30.00	15.00	9.00
(168)	Zack D. Wheat	125.00	62.00	37.00
(169)	George B. Whitted	30.00	15.00	9.00
(170)	Irvin K. Wilhelm	30.00	15.00	9.00
(171)	Roy H. Wilkinson	30.00	15.00	9.00
(172)	Fred C. Williams	35.00	17.50	10.50
(173)	K.R. Williams	30.00	15.00	9.00
(174)	Sam'l W. Wilson	30.00	15.00	9.00
(175)	Ivy B. Wingo	30.00	15.00	9.00
(176)	L.W. Witt	30.00	15.00	9.00
(177)	Joseph Wood	35.00	17.50	10.50
(178)	E. Yaryan	30.00	15.00	9.00
(179)	R.S. Young	30.00	15.00	9.00
(180)	Ross Young (Youngs)	125.00	62.00	37.00

1910 E125 American Caramel

Issued circa 1910 by the American Caramel Company, this set of die-cut cards is so rare that it wasn't even known to exist until the late 1960s. Apparently inserted in boxes of caramels, these cards, which are die-cut figures of baseball players, vary in size but are all relatively large - some measuring 7" high and 4" wide. Players from the Athletics, Red Sox, Giants and Pirates are known with a team checklist appearing on the back. According to the checklists, the set would be complete at 41 cards (including two separate poses of Honus Wagner), but to date only about 20 different cards have been found. The set is designated as E125.

		NR MT	EX	VG
Complete Set:		90000.	45000.	27500.
Common Player:		1500.	750.00	450.00
(1)	Babe Adams	1500.	750.00	450.00
(2)	Red Ames	1500.	750.00	450.00
(3)	Home Run Baker	4000.	2000.	1250.
(4)	Jack Barry	1500.	750.00	450.00
(5)	Chief Bender	4000.	2000.	1250.
(6)	Al Bridwell	1500.	750.00	450.00
(7)	Bobby Byrne	1500.	750.00	450.00
(8)	Bill Carrigan	1500.	750.00	450.00
(9)	Ed Cicotte	2500.	1100.	550.00
(10)	Fred Clark (Clarke)	4000.	2000.	1250.
(11)	Eddie Collins	5000.	2500.	1500.
(12)	Harry Davis	1500.	750.00	450.00
(13)	Art Devlin	1500.	750.00	450.00
(14)	Josh Devore	1500.	750.00	450.00
(15)	Larry Doyle	1500.	750.00	450.00
(16)	John Flynn	1500.	750.00	450.00
(17)	George Gibson	1500.	750.00	450.00
(18)	Topsy Hartsell (Hartsel)	1500.	750.00	450.00
(19)	Harry Hooper	4000.	2000.	1250.
(20)	Harry Krause	1500.	750.00	450.00
(21)	Tommy Leach	1500.	750.00	450.00
(22)	Harry Lord	1500.	750.00	450.00
(23)	Christy Mathewson	10000.	4000.	1550.
(24)	Amby McConnell	1500.	750.00	450.00
(25)	Fred Merkle	1500.	750.00	450.00
(26)	Dots Miller	1500.	750.00	450.00
(27)	Danny Murphy	1500.	750.00	450.00
(28)	Red Murray	1500.	750.00	450.00
(29)	Harry Niles	1500.	750.00	450.00
(30)	Rube Oldring	1500.	750.00	450.00
(31)	Eddie Plank	5000.	2000.	750.00
(32)	Cy Seymour	1500.	750.00	450.00
(33)	Tris Speaker	7500.	3000.	1000.
(34)	Jake Stahl	1500.	750.00	450.00
(35)	Ira Thomas	1500.	750.00	450.00
(36)	Heinie Wagner	1500.	750.00	450.00
(37)	Honus Wagner (batting)	12000.	4500.	2000.
(38)	Honus Wagner (throwing)	12000.	4500.	2000.
(39)	Art Wilson	1500.	750.00	450.00
(40)	Owen Wilson	1500.	750.00	450.00
(41)	Hooks Wiltse	1500.	750.00	450.00

1927 E126 American Caramel

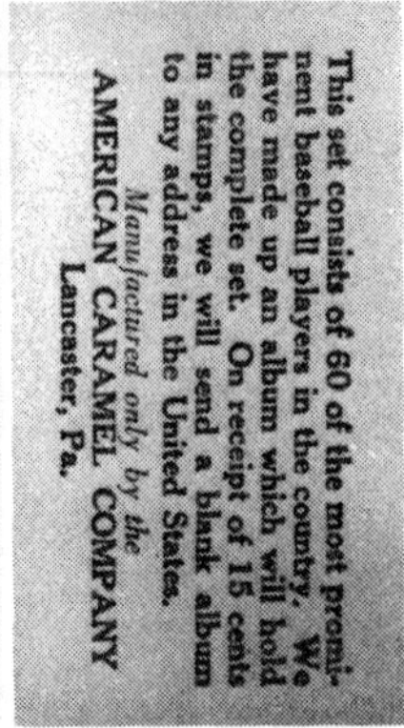
This set consists of 60 of the most prominent baseball players in the country. We have made up an album which will hold the complete set. On receipt of 15 cents in stamps, we will send a blank album to any address in the United States.

Manufactured only by the
AMERICAN CARAMEL COMPANY
Lancaster, Pa.

Issued in 1927 by the American Caramel Company of Lancaster, Pa., this obscure 60-card set was one of the last of the caramel card issues. Measuring 2" by 3-1/4", the cards differ from most sets of the period because they are numbered. The back of each card includes an offer for an album to house the 60-card set which includes players from all 16 major league teams, but to date no such album has been found. The set has been given the designation E126.

		NR MT	EX	VG
Complete Set:		15000.	6200.	3500.
Common Player:		75.00	37.00	22.00
1	John Gooch	200.00	100.00	60.00
2	Clyde L. Barnhart	75.00	37.00	22.00
3	Joe Busch (Bush)	100.00	50.00	30.00
4	Lee Meadows	75.00	37.00	22.00
5	E.T. Cox	75.00	37.00	22.00
6	"Red" Faber	250.00	125.00	50.00
7	Aaron Ward	75.00	37.00	22.00
8	Ray Schalk	250.00	125.00	50.00
9	"Specks" Toporcer ("Specs")	75.00	37.00	22.00
10	Bill Southworth	75.00	37.00	22.00
11	Allen Sothoron	75.00	37.00	22.00
12	Will Sherdel	75.00	37.00	22.00
13	Grover Alexander	350.00	175.00	75.00
14	Jack Quinn	75.00	37.00	22.00
15	C. Galloway	75.00	37.00	22.00
16	"Eddie" Collins	275.00	130.00	50.00
17	"Ty" Cobb	1500.	700.00	250.00
18	Percy Jones	75.00	37.00	22.00
19	Chas. Grimm	100.00	50.00	30.00
20	"Bennie" Karr	75.00	37.00	22.00
21	Charlie Jamieson	75.00	37.00	22.00
22	Sherrod Smith	75.00	37.00	22.00
23	Virgil Cheeves	75.00	37.00	22.00
24	James Ring	75.00	37.00	22.00
25	"Muddy" Ruel	75.00	37.00	22.00
26	Joe Judge	75.00	37.00	22.00
27	Tris Speaker	350.00	175.00	75.00
28	Walter Johnson	600.00	300.00	150.00
29	E.C. "Sam" Rice	250.00	125.00	50.00
30	Hank DeBerry	75.00	37.00	22.00
31	Walter Henline	75.00	37.00	22.00
32	Max Carey	250.00	125.00	50.00
33	Arnold J. Statz	75.00	37.00	22.00
34	Emil Meusel	75.00	37.00	22.00
35	T.P. "Pat" Collins	75.00	37.00	22.00
36	Urban Shocker	75.00	37.00	22.00
37	Bob Shawkey	100.00	50.00	30.00
38	"Babe" Ruth	2500.	1000.	450.00
39	Bob Meusel	100.00	40.00	16.00
40	Alex Ferguson	75.00	37.00	22.00
41	"Stuffy" McInnis	75.00	37.00	22.00
42	"Cy" Williams	100.00	40.00	16.00
43	Russel Wrightstone (Russell)	75.00	37.00	22.00
44	John Tobin	75.00	37.00	22.00
45	Wm. C. Jacobson	75.00	37.00	22.00
46	Bryan "Slim" Harriss	75.00	37.00	22.00
47	Elam Vangilder	75.00	37.00	22.00
48	Ken Williams	75.00	37.00	22.00
49	Geo. R. Sisler	250.00	125.00	50.00
50	Ed Brown	75.00	37.00	22.00
51	Jack Smith	75.00	37.00	22.00
52	Dave Bancroft	250.00	125.00	50.00
53	Larry Woodall	75.00	37.00	22.00
54	Lu Blue	75.00	37.00	22.00
55	Johnny Bassler	75.00	37.00	22.00
56	"Jakie" May	75.00	37.00	22.00

		NR MT	EX	VG
57	Horace Ford	75.00	37.00	22.00
58	"Curt" Walker	75.00	37.00	22.00
59	"Artie" Nehf	75.00	37.00	22.00
60	Geo. Kelly	400.00	175.00	75.00

1916 E135 Collins-McCarthy

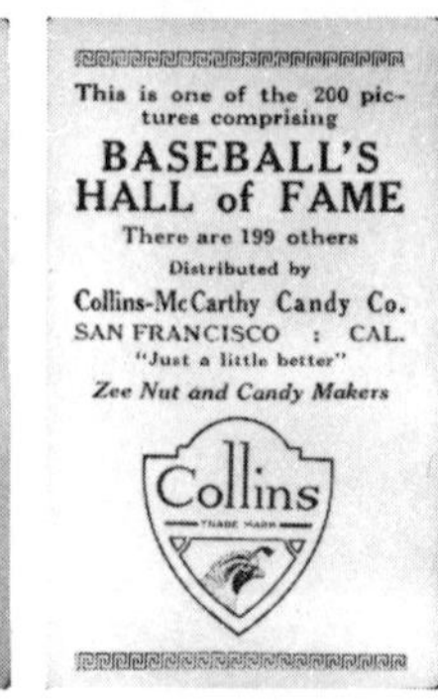

Produced by the Collins-McCarthy Candy Co. of San Francisco, the 200-card, black and white set represents the company's only venture into issuing non-Pacific Coast League players. The cards, which are numbered alphabetically, measure 2" by 3-1/4" in size and are printed on think stock. Though the set is entitled "Baseball's Hall of Fame," many nondescript players appear in the issue. The complete set price does not include the more expensive variations.

		NR MT	EX	VG
	Complete Set:	15000.	7500.	4500.
	Common Player:	35.00	17.50	10.50
1	Sam Agnew	35.00	17.50	10.50
2	Grover Alexander	125.00	62.00	37.00
3	W.S. Alexander (initials actually W.E.)	35.00	17.50	10.50
4	Leon Ames	35.00	17.50	10.50
5	Fred Anderson	35.00	17.50	10.50
6	Ed Appleton	35.00	17.50	10.50
7	Jimmy Archer	35.00	17.50	10.50
8	Jimmy Austin	35.00	17.50	10.50
9	Jim Bagby	35.00	17.50	10.50
10	H.D. Baird	35.00	17.50	10.50
11	J. Franklin Baker	125.00	62.00	37.00
12	Dave Bancroft	125.00	62.00	37.00
13	Jack Barry	35.00	17.50	10.50
14	Joe Benz	35.00	17.50	10.50
15	Al Betzel	35.00	17.50	10.50
16	Ping Bodie	35.00	17.50	10.50
17	Joe Boehling	35.00	17.50	10.50
18	Eddie Burns	35.00	17.50	10.50
19	George Burns	35.00	17.50	10.50
20	Geo. J. Burns	35.00	17.50	10.50
21	Joe Bush	40.00	17.50	10.50
22	Owen Bush	35.00	17.50	10.50
23	Bobby Byrne	35.00	17.50	10.50
24	Forrest Cady	35.00	17.50	10.50
25	Max Carey	125.00	62.00	37.00
26	Ray Chapman	45.00	20.00	12.00
27	Larry Cheney	35.00	17.50	10.50
28	Eddie Cicotte	50.00	22.00	13.50
29	Tom Clarke	35.00	17.50	10.50
30	Ty Cobb	700.00	350.00	210.00
31	Eddie Collins	125.00	62.00	37.00
32	"Shauno" Collins (Shano)	35.00	17.50	10.50
33	Fred Coumbe	35.00	17.50	10.50
34	Harry Coveleskie (Coveleski)	35.00	17.50	10.50
35	Gavvy Cravath	40.00	17.50	10.50
36	Sam Crawford	125.00	62.00	37.00
37	Geo. Cutshaw	35.00	17.50	10.50
38	Jake Daubert	40.00	17.50	10.50
39	Geo. Dauss	35.00	17.50	10.50
40	Charles Deal	35.00	17.50	10.50
41	"Wheezer" Dell	35.00	17.50	10.50
42	William Doak	35.00	17.50	10.50
43	Bill Donovan	35.00	17.50	10.50
44	Larry Doyle	40.00	17.50	10.50
45	Johnny Evers	125.00	62.00	37.00
46	Urban Faber	125.00	62.00	37.00
47	"Hap" Felsch	40.00	22.00	13.50
48	Bill Fischer	35.00	17.50	10.50
49	Ray Fisher	35.00	17.50	10.50
50	Art Fletcher	35.00	17.50	10.50
51	Eddie Foster	35.00	17.50	10.50
52	Jacques Fournier	35.00	17.50	10.50
53	Del Gainer (Gainor)	35.00	17.50	10.50
54	Bert Gallia	35.00	17.50	10.50
55	"Chic" Gandil (Chick)	55.00	22.00	13.50
56	Larry Gardner	35.00	17.50	10.50
57	Joe Gedeon	35.00	17.50	10.50
58	Gus Getz	35.00	17.50	10.50
59	Frank Gilhooley	35.00	17.50	10.50
60	Wm. Gleason	35.00	17.50	10.50
61	M.A. Gonzales (Gonzalez)	35.00	17.50	10.50
62	Hank Gowdy	35.00	17.50	10.50
63	John Graney	35.00	17.50	10.50
64	Tom Griffith	35.00	17.50	10.50
65	Heinie Groh	40.00	17.50	10.50
66	Bob Groom	35.00	17.50	10.50
67	Louis Guisto	35.00	17.50	10.50
68	Earl Hamilton	35.00	17.50	10.50
69	Harry Harper	35.00	17.50	10.50
70	Grover Hartley	35.00	17.50	10.50
71	Harry Heilmann	125.00	62.00	37.00
72	Claude Hendrix	35.00	17.50	10.50
73	Olaf Henriksen	35.00	17.50	10.50
74	John Henry	35.00	17.50	10.50
75	"Buck" Herzog	35.00	17.50	10.50
76a	Hugh High (white stockings, photo actually Claude Williams)	125.00	62.00	37.00
76b	Hugh High (black stockings, correct photo)	40.00	17.50	10.50
77	Dick Hoblitzell	35.00	17.50	10.50
78	Walter Holke	35.00	17.50	10.50
79	Harry Hooper	125.00	62.00	37.00
80	Rogers Hornsby	200.00	100.00	60.00
81	Ivan Howard	35.00	17.50	10.50
82	Joe Jackson	1200.	600.00	350.00
83	Harold Janvrin	35.00	17.50	10.50
84	William James	35.00	17.50	10.50
85	C. Jamieson	35.00	17.50	10.50
86	Hugh Jennings	125.00	62.00	37.00
87	Walter Johnson	400.00	200.00	120.00
88	James Johnston	35.00	17.50	10.50
89	Fielder Jones	35.00	17.50	10.50
90a	Joe Judge (bat on right shoulder, photo actually Ray Morgan)	125.00	62.00	37.00
90b	Joe Judge (bat on left shoulder, correct photo)	40.00	17.50	10.50
91	Hans Lobert	35.00	17.50	10.50
92	Benny Kauff	35.00	17.50	10.50
93	Wm. Killefer Jr.	35.00	17.50	10.50
94	Ed. Konetchy	35.00	17.50	10.50
95	John Lavan	35.00	17.50	10.50
96	Jimmy Lavender	35.00	17.50	10.50
97	"Nemo" Leibold	35.00	17.50	10.50
98	H.B. Leonard	35.00	17.50	10.50
99	Duffy Lewis	40.00	17.50	10.50
100	Tom Long	35.00	17.50	10.50
101	Wm. Louden	35.00	17.50	10.50
102	Fred Luderus	35.00	17.50	10.50
103	Lee Magee	35.00	17.50	10.50
104	Sherwood Magee	40.00	17.50	10.50
105	Al Mamaux	35.00	17.50	10.50
106	Leslie Mann	35.00	17.50	10.50
107	"Rabbit" Maranville	125.00	62.00	37.00
108	Rube Marquard	125.00	62.00	37.00
109	Armando Marsans	35.00	17.50	10.50
110	J. Erskine Mayer	35.00	17.50	10.50
111	George McBride	35.00	17.50	10.50
112	Lew McCarty	35.00	17.50	10.50
113	John J. McGraw	150.00	75.00	45.00
114	Jack McInnis	35.00	17.50	10.50
115	Lee Meadows	35.00	17.50	10.50
116	Fred Merkle	40.00	17.50	10.50
117	"Chief" Meyers	35.00	17.50	10.50
118	Clyde Milan	35.00	17.50	10.50
119	Otto Miller	35.00	17.50	10.50
120	Clarence Mitchell	35.00	17.50	10.50
121a	Ray Morgan (bat on right shoulder, photo actually Joe Judge)	125.00	62.00	37.00
121b	Ray Morgan (bat on left shoulder, correct photo)	40.00	17.50	10.50
122	Guy Morton	35.00	17.50	10.50
123	"Mike" Mowrey	35.00	17.50	10.50
124	Elmer Myers	35.00	17.50	10.50
125	"Hy" Myers	35.00	17.50	10.50
126	A.E. Neale	50.00	20.00	12.00
127	Arthur Nehf	35.00	17.50	10.50
128	J.A. Niehoff	35.00	17.50	10.50
129	Steve O'Neill	35.00	17.50	10.50
130	"Dode" Paskert	35.00	17.50	10.50
131	Roger Peckinpaugh	40.00	17.50	10.50
132	"Pol" Perritt	35.00	17.50	10.50
133	"Jeff" Pfeffer	35.00	17.50	10.50
134	Walter Pipp	80.00	40.00	25.00
135	Derril Pratt (Derrill)	35.00	17.50	10.50
136	Bill Rariden	35.00	17.50	10.50
137	E.C. Rice	125.00	62.00	37.00
138	Wm. A. Ritter (actually Wm. H.)	35.00	17.50	10.50
139	Eppa Rixey	125.00	62.00	37.00
140	Davey Robertson	35.00	17.50	10.50
141	"Bob" Roth	35.00	17.50	10.50
142	Ed. Roush	125.00	62.00	37.00
143	Clarence Rowland	35.00	17.50	10.50
144	Dick Rudolph	35.00	17.50	10.50
145	William Rumler	35.00	17.50	10.50
146a	Reb Russell (pitching follow-thru, photo actually Mellie Wolfgang)	125.00	62.00	37.00
146b	Reb Russell (hands at side, correct photo)	400.00	17.50	10.50
147	"Babe" Ruth	1250.	625.00	400.00
148	Vic Saier	35.00	17.50	10.50
149	"Slim" Sallee	35.00	17.50	10.50
150	Ray Schalk	125.00	62.00	37.00
151	Walter Schang	35.00	17.50	10.50
152	Frank Schulte	35.00	17.50	10.50
153	Ferd Schupp	35.00	17.50	10.50
154	Everett Scott	35.00	17.50	10.50
155	Hank Severeid	35.00	17.50	10.50
156	Howard Shanks	35.00	17.50	10.50
157	Bob Shawkey	40.00	17.50	10.50
158	Jas. Sheckard	35.00	17.50	10.50
159	Ernie Shore	35.00	17.50	10.50
160	C.H. Shorten	35.00	17.50	10.50
161	Burt Shotton	35.00	17.50	10.50
162	Geo. Sisler	125.00	62.00	37.00
163	Elmer Smith	35.00	17.50	10.50
164	J. Carlisle Smith	35.00	17.50	10.50
165	Fred Snodgrass	35.00	17.50	10.50
166	Tris Speaker	200.00	100.00	60.00
167	Oscar Stanage	35.00	17.50	10.50
168	Charles Stengel	300.00	150.00	90.00
169	Milton Stock	35.00	17.50	10.50
170	Amos Strunk	35.00	17.50	10.50
171	"Zeb" Terry	35.00	17.50	10.50
172	"Jeff" Tesreau	35.00	17.50	10.50
173	Chester Thomas	35.00	17.50	10.50
174	Fred Toney	35.00	17.50	10.50
175	Terry Turner	35.00	17.50	10.50
176	George Tyler	35.00	17.50	10.50
177	Jim Vaughn	35.00	17.50	10.50
178	Bob Veach	35.00	17.50	10.50
179	Oscar Vitt	35.00	17.50	10.50
180	Hans Wagner	600.00	300.00	175.00
181	Clarence Walker	35.00	17.50	10.50
182	Jim Walsh	35.00	17.50	10.50
183	Al Walters	35.00	17.50	10.50
184	W. Wambsganss	40.00	17.50	10.50
185	Buck Weaver	50.00	30.00	15.00
186	Carl Weilman	35.00	17.50	10.50
187	Zack Wheat	125.00	62.00	37.00
188	Geo. Whitted	35.00	17.50	10.50
189	Joe Wilhoit	35.00	17.50	10.50
190a	Claude Williams (black stockings, photo actually Hugh High)	125.00	62.00	37.00
190b	Claude Williams (white stockings, correct photo)	50.00	22.00	13.50
191	Fred Williams	40.00	17.50	10.50
192	Art Wilson	35.00	17.50	10.50
193	Lawton Witt	35.00	17.50	10.50
194	Joe Wood	40.00	22.00	13.50
195	William Wortman	35.00	17.50	10.50
196	Steve Yerkes	35.00	17.50	10.50
197	Earl Yingling	35.00	17.50	10.50
198	"Pep" Young (photo actually Ralph Young)	35.00	17.50	10.50
199	Rollie Zeider	35.00	17.50	10.50
200	Henry Zimmerman	35.00	17.50	10.50

1911 E136 Zeenut

Produced for 28 straight years, these Pacific Coast League cards were among the longest-running and most popular baseball issues ever to appear on the West Coast. Issued by the Collins-McCarthy Candy Co. (later known as the Collins-Hencke Candy Co. and then simply the Collins Candy Co.) of San Francisco, Zeenut cards were inserted in boxes of the company's products: Zeenuts, Ruf-Neks and Home Run Kisses. All Zeenut cards issued from 1913 to 1937 included a half-inch coupon at the bottom that could be redeemed for various prizes. Since most of these coupons were removed (and many not too carefully) Zeenuts are difficult to find in top condition today, and only a very small percentage survived with the coupon intact. (The sizes listed in the following descriptions are for cards without coupons.) Over the 28-year span, it is estimated that nearly 3,700 different cards were issued as part of the Zeenuts series, but new discoveries are still being made, and the checklist continues to grow. It is sometimes difficult to differentiate one year from another after 1930. Because it is so rare to find Zeenuts cards with the coupon still attached, values listed are for cards without the coupon. Cards with the coupon still intact will generally command an additional 25-35 percent premium. The first Zeenut cards measure 2-1/8" by 4" and feature a sepia-toned photo on a brown background surrounded by an off-white border. The backs of the cards are blank. Although the 1911 cards did not include the coupon bottom, some cards have been found with punch holes, indicating they may have also been used for premiums. A total of 122 different players have been found.

		NR MT	EX	VG
	Complete Set:	2700.	1350.	800.00
	Common Player:	18.00	9.00	5.50
(1)	Abbott	18.00	9.00	5.50
(2)	Ables	18.00	9.00	5.50
(3a)	Agnew (large pose)	18.00	9.00	5.50
(3b)	Agnew (small pose)	18.00	9.00	5.50
(4a)	Akin (large pose)	18.00	9.00	5.50
(4b)	Akin (small pose)	18.00	9.00	5.50
(5)	Arellanes	18.00	9.00	5.50
(6a)	Arlett (large pose)	18.00	9.00	5.50
(6b)	Arlett (middle size pose)	18.00	9.00	5.50
(6c)	Arlett (small pose)	18.00	9.00	5.50
(7)	Barry	18.00	9.00	5.50
(8)	Baum	18.00	9.00	5.50
(9)	Bernard	18.00	9.00	5.50
(10)	Berry	18.00	9.00	5.50
(11)	Bohen	18.00	9.00	5.50
(12)	Brackenridge	18.00	9.00	5.50

	NR MT	EX	VG
(13) Brashear	18.00	9.00	5.50
(14a) Brown (large pose)	18.00	9.00	5.50
(14b) Brown (small pose)	18.00	9.00	5.50
(15) Browning	18.00	9.00	5.50
(16a) Burrell (large pose)	18.00	9.00	5.50
(16b) Burrell (small pose)	18.00	9.00	5.50
(17) Byram	18.00	9.00	5.50
(18) Carlisle	18.00	9.00	5.50
(19) Carman	18.00	9.00	5.50
(20a) Carson (large pose)	18.00	9.00	5.50
(20b) Carson (middle size pose)	18.00	9.00	5.50
(20c) Carson (small pose)	18.00	9.00	5.50
(21) Castleton	18.00	9.00	5.50
(22) Chadbourne	18.00	9.00	5.50
(23) Christian	18.00	9.00	5.50
(24) Couchman	18.00	9.00	5.50
(25) Coy	18.00	9.00	5.50
(26) Criger	18.00	9.00	5.50
(27) Cutshaw	18.00	9.00	5.50
(28) Daley	18.00	9.00	5.50
(29) Danzig	18.00	9.00	5.50
(30) Delhi	18.00	9.00	5.50
(31a) Delmas (large pose)	18.00	9.00	5.50
(31b) Delmas (small pose)	18.00	9.00	5.50
(32) Dillon	18.00	9.00	5.50
(33a) Discoll (name incorrect)	18.00	9.00	5.50
(33b) Driscoll (name correct)	18.00	9.00	5.50
(34) Dulin	18.00	9.00	5.50
(35) Fanning	18.00	9.00	5.50
(36) Fitzgerald	18.00	9.00	5.50
(37) Flater	18.00	9.00	5.50
(38) French	18.00	9.00	5.50
(39) Fullerton	18.00	9.00	5.50
(40) Gleason	18.00	9.00	5.50
(41) Gregory	18.00	9.00	5.50
(42) Halla	18.00	9.00	5.50
(43) Harkness	18.00	9.00	5.50
(44a) Heitmuller (large pose)	18.00	9.00	5.50
(44b) Heitmuller (small pose)	18.00	9.00	5.50
(45) Henley	18.00	9.00	5.50
(46) Hetling	18.00	9.00	5.50
(47) Hiester	18.00	9.00	5.50
(48a) Hitt (large pose)	18.00	9.00	5.50
(48b) Hitt (small pose)	18.00	9.00	5.50
(50) Hoffman	18.00	9.00	5.50
(51) Hogan	18.00	9.00	5.50
(52a) Holland (large pose)	18.00	9.00	5.50
(52b) Holland (small pose)	18.00	9.00	5.50
(53) Hosp	18.00	9.00	5.50
(54a) Howard (large pose)	18.00	9.00	5.50
(54b) Howard (small pose)	18.00	9.00	5.50
(55) Kane	18.00	9.00	5.50
(56) Kerns	18.00	9.00	5.50
(57) Kilroy	18.00	9.00	5.50
(58) Knight	18.00	9.00	5.50
(59) Koestner	18.00	9.00	5.50
(60) Krueger	18.00	9.00	5.50
(61) Kuhn	18.00	9.00	5.50
(62) LaLonge	18.00	9.00	5.50
(63) Lerchen	18.00	9.00	5.50
(64) Leverenz	18.00	9.00	5.50
(65) Lewis	18.00	9.00	5.50
(66) Lindsay	18.00	9.00	5.50
(67) Lober	18.00	9.00	5.50
(68) Madden	18.00	9.00	5.50
(69) Maggert	18.00	9.00	5.50
(70) Mahoney	18.00	9.00	5.50
(71) Martinoni	18.00	9.00	5.50
(72) McArdle	18.00	9.00	5.50
(73) McCredie	18.00	9.00	5.50
(74) McDonnell	18.00	9.00	5.50
(75a) McKune (large pose)	18.00	9.00	5.50
(75b) McKune (middle size pose)	18.00	9.00	5.50
(75c) McKune (small pose)	18.00	9.00	5.50
(76) Meikle	18.00	9.00	5.50
(77) Melchoir	18.00	9.00	5.50
(78) Metzger	18.00	9.00	5.50
(79) Miller	18.00	9.00	5.50
(80) Mitze	18.00	9.00	5.50
(81) Mohler	18.00	9.00	5.50
(82a) Moore (large pose)	18.00	9.00	5.50
(82b) Moore (small pose)	18.00	9.00	5.50
(83a) Moskiman (lettering size large)	18.00	9.00	5.50
(83b) Moskiman (lettering size small)	18.00	9.00	5.50
(84) Murray	18.00	9.00	5.50
(85) Naylor	18.00	9.00	5.50
(86) Nebinger	18.00	9.00	5.50
(87) Nourse	18.00	9.00	5.50
(88a) Noyes (large pose)	18.00	9.00	5.50
(88b) Noyes (small pose)	18.00	9.00	5.50
(89) O'Rourke	18.00	9.00	5.50
(90) Patterson (Oakland)	18.00	9.00	5.50
(91) Patterson (Vernon)	18.00	9.00	5.50
(92) Pearce	18.00	9.00	5.50
(93) Peckinpaugh	30.00	15.00	9.00
(94) Pernoll	18.00	9.00	5.50
(95) Pfyl	18.00	9.00	5.50
(96) Powell	18.00	9.00	5.50
(97a) Raleigh (large pose)	18.00	9.00	5.50
(97b) Raleigh (small pose)	18.00	9.00	5.50
(98) Rapps	18.00	9.00	5.50
(99) Rodgers	18.00	9.00	5.50
(100a) Ryan (Portland, box around name and team)	25.00	12.50	7.50
(100b) Ryan (Portland, no box around name and team)	18.00	9.00	5.50
(101) Ryan (San Francisco)	18.00	9.00	5.50
(102) Seaton	18.00	9.00	5.50
(103) Shaw	18.00	9.00	5.50
(104) Sheehan	18.00	9.00	5.50
(105) Shinn	18.00	9.00	5.50
106a Smith (Los Angeles, large pose)	18.00	9.00	5.50
(106b) Smith (Los Angeles, small pose)	18.00	9.00	5.50
(107a) Smith (San Francisco, large pose)	18.00	9.00	5.50
(107b) Smith (San Francisco, small pose)	18.00	9.00	5.50
(108) Steen	18.00	9.00	5.50
(109) Stewart	18.00	9.00	5.50
(110a) Stinson (large pose)	18.00	9.00	5.50
(110b) Stinson (small pose)	18.00	9.00	5.50
(111) Sutor	18.00	9.00	5.50
(112) Tennant	18.00	9.00	5.50
(113) Thomas	18.00	9.00	5.50
(114) Thompson	18.00	9.00	5.50
(115) Thornton	18.00	9.00	5.50
(116) Tiedeman	18.00	9.00	5.50
(117) Van Buren	18.00	9.00	5.50
(118) Vitt	18.00	9.00	5.50
(119) Wares	18.00	9.00	5.50
(120) Weaver	75.00	38.00	23.00
(121) Wolverton	18.00	9.00	5.50
(122) Zacher	18.00	9.00	5.50
(123) Zamloch	18.00	9.00	5.50

1912 E136 Home Run Kisses

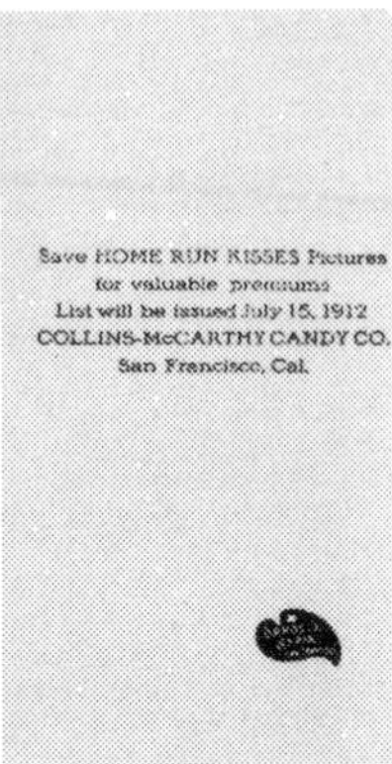

This 90-card set of Pacific Coast League players, known by the ACC designation E136, was produced in 1912 by the San Francisco candy company of Collins-McCarthy. Each card measures a large 2-1/4" by 4 1/4" and features sepia-toned player photos surrounded by an ornate frame. The front of the card has the words "Home Run Kisses" above the player's name. Most cards found are blank-backed, but others exist with a back that advises "Save Home Run Kisses Pictures for Valuable Premiums" along with other details of the Collins-McCarthy promotion.

	NR MT	EX	VG
Complete Set:	7250.	3625.	2250.
Common Player:	80.00	40.00	24.00
(1) Ables	80.00	40.00	24.00
(2) Agnew	80.00	40.00	24.00
(3) Altman	80.00	40.00	24.00
(4) Arrelanes	80.00	40.00	24.00
(5) Auer	80.00	40.00	24.00
(6) Bancroft	175.00	87.00	52.00
(7) Bayless	80.00	40.00	24.00
(8) Berry	80.00	40.00	24.00
(9) Boles	80.00	40.00	24.00
(10) Brashear	80.00	40.00	24.00
(11) Brooks (Los Angeles)	80.00	40.00	24.00
(12) Brooks (Oakland)	80.00	40.00	24.00
(13) Brown	80.00	40.00	24.00
(14) Burrell	80.00	40.00	24.00
(15) Butler	80.00	40.00	24.00
(16) Carlisle	90.00	45.00	27.00
(17) Carson	80.00	40.00	24.00
(18) Castleton	80.00	40.00	24.00
(19) Chadbourne	80.00	40.00	24.00
(20) Check	80.00	40.00	24.00
(21) Core	80.00	40.00	24.00
(22) Corhan	80.00	40.00	24.00
(23) Coy	80.00	40.00	24.00
(24) Daley	80.00	40.00	24.00
(25) Dillon	80.00	40.00	24.00
(26) Doane	80.00	40.00	24.00
(27) Driscoll	90.00	45.00	27.00
(28) Fisher	80.00	40.00	24.00
(29) Flater	80.00	40.00	24.00
(30) Gaddy	80.00	40.00	24.00
(31) Gregg	80.00	40.00	24.00
(32) Gregory	80.00	40.00	24.00
(33) Harkness	80.00	40.00	24.00
(34) Heitmuller	80.00	40.00	24.00
(35) Henley	80.00	40.00	24.00
(36) Hiester	80.00	40.00	24.00
(37) Hoffman	80.00	40.00	24.00
(38) Hogan	80.00	40.00	24.00
(39) Hosp	80.00	40.00	24.00
(40) Howley	80.00	40.00	24.00
(41) Ireland	80.00	40.00	24.00
(42) Johnson	80.00	40.00	24.00
(43) Kane	80.00	40.00	24.00
(44) Klawitter	80.00	40.00	24.00
(45) Kreitz	80.00	40.00	24.00
(46) Krueger	80.00	40.00	24.00
(47) Leard	80.00	40.00	24.00
(48) Leverencz	90.00	45.00	27.00
(49) Lewis	80.00	40.00	24.00
(50) Lindsay	80.00	40.00	24.00
(51) Litschi	80.00	40.00	24.00
(52) Lober	80.00	40.00	24.00
(53) Malarkey	80.00	40.00	24.00
(54) Martinoni	80.00	40.00	24.00
(55) McArdle	80.00	40.00	24.00
(56) McCorry	80.00	40.00	24.00
(57) McDowell	80.00	40.00	24.00
(58) McIver	80.00	40.00	24.00
(59) Metzger	90.00	45.00	27.00
(60) Miller	80.00	40.00	24.00
(61) Mundorf	80.00	40.00	24.00
(62) Nagle	80.00	40.00	24.00
(63) Noyes	80.00	40.00	24.00
(64) Olmstead	80.00	40.00	24.00
(65) O'Rourke	80.00	40.00	24.00
(66) Page	80.00	40.00	24.00
(67) Parkins	80.00	40.00	24.00
(68) Patterson (Oakland)	80.00	40.00	24.00
(69) Patterson (Vernon)	80.00	40.00	24.00
(70) Pernoll	80.00	40.00	24.00
(71) Powell	80.00	40.00	24.00
(72) Price	80.00	40.00	24.00
(73) Raftery	80.00	40.00	24.00
(74) Raleigh	80.00	40.00	24.00
(75) Rogers	80.00	40.00	24.00
(76) Schmidt	80.00	40.00	24.00
(77) Schwenk	80.00	40.00	24.00
(78) Sheehan	80.00	40.00	24.00
(79) Shinn	80.00	40.00	24.00
(80) Slagle	80.00	40.00	24.00
(81) Smith	80.00	40.00	24.00
(82) Stone	80.00	40.00	24.00
(83) Swain	80.00	40.00	24.00
(84) Taylor	80.00	40.00	24.00
(85) Tiedeman	80.00	40.00	24.00
(86) Toner	80.00	40.00	24.00
(87) Tozer	80.00	40.00	24.00
(88) Van Buren	80.00	40.00	24.00
(89) Williams	80.00	40.00	24.00
(90) Zacher	80.00	40.00	24.00

1912 E136 Zeenut

The second series of Zeenut cards measure 2-1/8" by 4-1/8" and featured sepia-toned photographs on a brown background with no border. Most cards have blank backs, but some have been found with printing advising collectors to "Save Zeenut pictures for valuable premiums." The checklist consists of 158 subjects, but more cards are still being discovered.

	NR MT	EX	VG
Complete Set:	2875.	1425.	850.00
Common Player:	18.00	9.00	5.50
(1) Abbott	18.00	9.00	5.50
(2) Ables	18.00	9.00	5.50
(3) Agnew	18.00	9.00	5.50
(4) Altman	18.00	9.00	5.50
(5) Arellanes	18.00	9.00	5.50
(6) Auer	18.00	9.00	5.50
(7) Baker (horizontal pose)	18.00	9.00	5.50
(8) Baker (vertical pose)	18.00	9.00	5.50
(9) Bancroft	50.00	25.00	15.00
(10) Baum	18.00	9.00	5.50
(11) Bayless	18.00	9.00	5.50
(12) Berger	18.00	9.00	5.50
(13) Berry	18.00	9.00	5.50
(14) Bohen	18.00	9.00	5.50
(15) Boles	18.00	9.00	5.50
(16) Bonner			
(17) Boone	18.00	9.00	5.50
(18) Brackenridge	18.00	9.00	5.50
(19) Brashear	18.00	9.00	5.50
(20) Breen			
(21) Brooks (Los Angeles)	18.00	9.00	5.50
(22) Brooks (Oakland)	18.00	9.00	5.50
(23) Brown	18.00	9.00	5.50
(24) Burch	18.00	9.00	5.50
(25) Burrell	18.00	9.00	5.50
(26) Butcher	18.00	9.00	5.50
(27) Butler	18.00	9.00	5.50
(28) Byram	18.00	9.00	5.50
(29) Carlisle	18.00	9.00	5.50
(30) Carson	18.00	9.00	5.50
(31) Castleton	18.00	9.00	5.50
(32) Chadbourne	18.00	9.00	5.50
(33) Chech	18.00	9.00	5.50
(34) Cheek	18.00	9.00	5.50
(35) Christian	18.00	9.00	5.50
(36) Cook	18.00	9.00	5.50
(37) Core	18.00	9.00	5.50
(38) Corhan	18.00	9.00	5.50
(39) Coy	18.00	9.00	5.50
(40) Daley	18.00	9.00	5.50
(41) Delhi	18.00	9.00	5.50
(42) Dillon	18.00	9.00	5.50

		NR MT	EX	VG
(43)	Doane	18.00	9.00	5.50
(44)	Driscoll	18.00	9.00	5.50
(45)	Durbin	18.00	9.00	5.50
(46)	Fanning	18.00	9.00	5.50
(47)	Felts	18.00	9.00	5.50
(48)	Fisher	18.00	9.00	5.50
(49)	Fitzgerald	18.00	9.00	5.50
(50)	Flater	18.00	9.00	5.50
(51)	Frick	18.00	9.00	5.50
(52)	Gaddy	18.00	9.00	5.50
(53)	Gedeon	18.00	9.00	5.50
(54)	Gilligan	18.00	9.00	5.50
(55)	Girot	18.00	9.00	5.50
(56)	Gray	18.00	9.00	5.50
(57)	Gregg	18.00	9.00	5.50
(58)	Gregory	18.00	9.00	5.50
(59)	Halla	18.00	9.00	5.50
(60)	Hamilton (Oakland)	18.00	9.00	5.50
(61)	Hamilton (San Francisco)	18.00	9.00	5.50
(62)	Harkness	18.00	9.00	5.50
(63)	Hartley	18.00	9.00	5.50
(64)	Heitmuller	18.00	9.00	5.50
(65)	Henley	18.00	9.00	5.50
(66)	Hetling (glove open)	18.00	9.00	5.50
(67)	Hetling (glove closed)	18.00	9.00	5.50
(68)	Hiester	18.00	9.00	5.50
(69)	Higginbottom	18.00	9.00	5.50
(70)	Hitt	18.00	9.00	5.50
(71)	Hoffman	18.00	9.00	5.50
(72)	Hogan	18.00	9.00	5.50
(73)	Hosp	18.00	9.00	5.50
(74)	Howard	18.00	9.00	5.50
(75)	Howley	18.00	9.00	5.50
(76)	Ireland	18.00	9.00	5.50
(77)	Jackson	18.00	9.00	5.50
(78)	Johnson	18.00	9.00	5.50
(79)	Kane	18.00	9.00	5.50
(80)	Killilay	18.00	9.00	5.50
(81)	Klawitter	18.00	9.00	5.50
(82)	Knight	18.00	9.00	5.50
(83)	Koestner ("P" visible)	18.00	9.00	5.50
(84)	Koestner (no "P" visible)	18.00	9.00	5.50
(85)	Kreitz	18.00	9.00	5.50
(86)	Krueger	18.00	9.00	5.50
(87)	LaLonge	18.00	9.00	5.50
(88)	Leard	18.00	9.00	5.50
(89)	Leverenz	18.00	9.00	5.50
(90)	Lewis	18.00	9.00	5.50
(91)	Lindsay	18.00	9.00	5.50
(92)	Litschi	18.00	9.00	5.50
(93)	Lober	18.00	9.00	5.50
(94)	Madden	18.00	9.00	5.50
(95)	Mahoney	18.00	9.00	5.50
(96)	Malarkey	18.00	9.00	5.50
(97)	Martinoni	18.00	9.00	5.50
(98)	McArdle	18.00	9.00	5.50
(99)	McAvoy	18.00	9.00	5.50
(100)	McCorrey	18.00	9.00	5.50
(101)	McCredie	18.00	9.00	5.50
(102)	McDonald	18.00	9.00	5.50
(103)	McDowell	18.00	9.00	5.50
(104)	McIver	18.00	9.00	5.50
(105)	Meikle	18.00	9.00	5.50
(106)	Metzger	18.00	9.00	5.50
(107)	Miller (Sacramento)	18.00	9.00	5.50
(108)	Miller (San Francisco)	18.00	9.00	5.50
(109)	Mitze	18.00	9.00	5.50
(110)	Mohler	18.00	9.00	5.50
(111)	Moore	18.00	9.00	5.50
(112)	Mundorf (batting)	18.00	9.00	5.50
(113)	Mundorf (fielding)	18.00	9.00	5.50
(114)	Nagle	18.00	9.00	5.50
(115)	Noyes	18.00	9.00	5.50
(116)	O'Rourke	18.00	9.00	5.50
(117)	Olmstead	18.00	9.00	5.50
(118)	Orr	18.00	9.00	5.50
(119)	Page	18.00	9.00	5.50
(120)	Parkins	18.00	9.00	5.50
(121)	Patterson (Oakland)	18.00	9.00	5.50
(122)	Patterson (Vernon)	18.00	9.00	5.50
(123)	Pernol	18.00	9.00	5.50
(124)	Pope	18.00	9.00	5.50
(125)	Powell	18.00	9.00	5.50
(126)	Price	18.00	9.00	5.50
(127)	Raftery	18.00	9.00	5.50
(128)	Raleigh	18.00	9.00	5.50
(129)	Rapps ("P" visible)	18.00	9.00	5.50
(130)	Rapps (no "P" visible)	18.00	9.00	5.50
(131)	Reidy	18.00	9.00	5.50
(132)	Rodgers	18.00	9.00	5.50
(133)	Rohrer	18.00	9.00	5.50
(134)	Schmidt	18.00	9.00	5.50
(135)	Schwenk	18.00	9.00	5.50
(136)	Sharpe	18.00	9.00	5.50
(137)	Sheehan	18.00	9.00	5.50
(138)	Shinn	18.00	9.00	5.50
(139)	Slagle	18.00	9.00	5.50
(140)	Smith	18.00	9.00	5.50
(141)	Stewart	18.00	9.00	5.50
(142)	Stinson	18.00	9.00	5.50
(143)	Stone	18.00	9.00	5.50
(144)	Sullivan	18.00	9.00	5.50
(145)	Swain	18.00	9.00	5.50
(146)	Taylor	18.00	9.00	5.50
(147)	Temple	18.00	9.00	5.50
(148)	Tiedeman	18.00	9.00	5.50
(149)	Toner	18.00	9.00	5.50
(150)	Tozer	18.00	9.00	5.50
(151)	Van Buren	18.00	9.00	5.50
(152)	Wagner	18.00	9.00	5.50
(153)	Whalen	18.00	9.00	5.50
(154)	Williams (Sacramento)	18.00	9.00	5.50
(155)	Williams (San Francisco)	18.00	9.00	5.50
(156)	Joe Williams	18.00	9.00	5.50
(157)	Wuffli	18.00	9.00	5.50
(158)	Zacher	18.00	9.00	5.50
(159)	Zimmerman	18.00	9.00	5.50

NOTE: A card number in parentheses ( ) indicates the set is unnumbered.

1913 E136 Zeenut

The first year to include the coupon bottom, the 1913 Zeenuts measure 2" by 3-1/4" without the coupon. The sepia-toned photos are printed on a yellow background that contains the words "P.C. League/Season 1913." This series is the only Zeenut set printed prior to 1931 that does not have the words "Zeenuts Series" on the front. The backs of the cards are blank.

		NR MT	EX	VG
Complete Set:		2700.	1350.	800.00
Common Player:		18.00	9.00	5.50
(1)	Abbott	18.00	9.00	5.50
(2)	Ables	18.00	9.00	5.50
(3)	Arelanes	18.00	9.00	5.50
(4)	Arlett	18.00	9.00	5.50
(5)	Baker	18.00	9.00	5.50
(6)	Baum	18.00	9.00	5.50
(7)	Bayless	18.00	9.00	5.50
(8)	Becker	18.00	9.00	5.50
(9)	Berry	18.00	9.00	5.50
(10)	Bliss	18.00	9.00	5.50
(11)	Boles	18.00	9.00	5.50
(12)	Brackenridge	18.00	9.00	5.50
(13)	Brashear	18.00	9.00	5.50
(14)	Brooks	18.00	9.00	5.50
(15)	Byrnes	18.00	9.00	5.50
(16)	Cadreau	18.00	9.00	5.50
(17)	Carlisle	18.00	9.00	5.50
(18)	Carson	18.00	9.00	5.50
(19)	Cartwright	18.00	9.00	5.50
(20)	Chadbourne	18.00	9.00	5.50
(21)	Charles	18.00	9.00	5.50
(22)	Cheek	18.00	9.00	5.50
(23)	Christian	18.00	9.00	5.50
(24)	Clarke	18.00	9.00	5.50
(25)	Clemons	18.00	9.00	5.50
(26)	Cook	18.00	9.00	5.50
(27)	Corhan	18.00	9.00	5.50
(28)	Coy	18.00	9.00	5.50
(29)	Crabb	18.00	9.00	5.50
(30)	Crisp	18.00	9.00	5.50
(31)	Derrick	18.00	9.00	5.50
(32)	DeCanniere	18.00	9.00	5.50
(33)	Dillon	18.00	9.00	5.50
(34)	Doane	18.00	9.00	5.50
(35)	Douglass	18.00	9.00	5.50
(36)	Downs	18.00	9.00	5.50
(37)	Driscoll	18.00	9.00	5.50
(38)	Drucke	18.00	9.00	5.50
(39)	Elliott	18.00	9.00	5.50
(40)	Ellis	18.00	9.00	5.50
(41)	Fanning	18.00	9.00	5.50
(42)	Fisher	18.00	9.00	5.50
(43)	Fitzgerald	18.00	9.00	5.50
(44)	Gardner	18.00	9.00	5.50
(45)	Gill	18.00	9.00	5.50
(46)	Goodwin	18.00	9.00	5.50
(47a)	Gregory (large pose)	18.00	9.00	5.50
(47b)	Gregory (small pose)	18.00	9.00	5.50
(48)	Grey	18.00	9.00	5.50
(49)	Guest	18.00	9.00	5.50
(50)	Hagerman	18.00	9.00	5.50
(51)	Halla	18.00	9.00	5.50
(52)	Hallinan	18.00	9.00	5.50
(53)	Heilmann	100.00	50.00	30.00
(54)	Henley	18.00	9.00	5.50
(55)	Hetling	18.00	9.00	5.50
(56)	Higginbotham	18.00	9.00	5.50
(57)	Hitt	18.00	9.00	5.50
(58)	Hoffman	18.00	9.00	5.50
(59)	Hogan (San Francisco)	18.00	9.00	5.50
(60)	Hogan (Vernon)	18.00	9.00	5.50
(61)	Hosp	18.00	9.00	5.50
(62)	Howard (Los Angeles)	18.00	9.00	5.50
(63)	Howard (San Francisco)	18.00	9.00	5.50
(64)	Hughes	18.00	9.00	5.50
(65)	Jackson	18.00	9.00	5.50
(66)	James	18.00	9.00	5.50
(67)	Johnson	18.00	9.00	5.50
(68)	Johnston	18.00	9.00	5.50
(69)	Kane	18.00	9.00	5.50
(70)	Kaylor	18.00	9.00	5.50
(71)	Kenworthy	18.00	9.00	5.50
(72)	Killilay	18.00	9.00	5.50
(73)	Klawitter	18.00	9.00	5.50
(74)	Koestner	18.00	9.00	5.50
(75)	Kores	18.00	9.00	5.50
(76)	Krapp	18.00	9.00	5.50
(77)	Kreitz	18.00	9.00	5.50
(78)	Krause	18.00	9.00	5.50
(79)	Krueger	18.00	9.00	5.50
(80)	Leard	18.00	9.00	5.50
(81)	Leifield	18.00	9.00	5.50
(82)	Lewis	18.00	9.00	5.50
(83)	Lindsay	18.00	9.00	5.50
(84)	Litschi	18.00	9.00	5.50
(85)	Lively	18.00	9.00	5.50
(86)	Lober	18.00	9.00	5.50
(87)	Lohman	18.00	9.00	5.50
(88)	Maggart	18.00	9.00	5.50
(89)	Malarky	18.00	9.00	5.50
(90)	McArdle	18.00	9.00	5.50
(91)	McCarl	18.00	9.00	5.50
(92)	McCormick	18.00	9.00	5.50
(93)	McCorry	18.00	9.00	5.50
(94)	McCredie	18.00	9.00	5.50
(95)	McDonnell	18.00	9.00	5.50
(96)	Meloan	18.00	9.00	5.50
(97)	Metzger	18.00	9.00	5.50
(98)	Miller	18.00	9.00	5.50
(99)	Mitze	18.00	9.00	5.50
(100)	Moore	18.00	9.00	5.50
(101)	Moran	18.00	9.00	5.50
(102)	Mundorf	18.00	9.00	5.50
(103)	Munsell	18.00	9.00	5.50
(104)	Ness	18.00	9.00	5.50
(105)	O'Rourke	18.00	9.00	5.50
(106)	Overall	18.00	9.00	5.50
(107)	Page	18.00	9.00	5.50
(108)	Parkin	18.00	9.00	5.50
(109)	Patterson	18.00	9.00	5.50
(110)	Pearce	18.00	9.00	5.50
(111)	Pernoll	18.00	9.00	5.50
(112)	Perritt	18.00	9.00	5.50
(113)	Pope	18.00	9.00	5.50
(114)	Pruitt	18.00	9.00	5.50
(115)	Raleigh	18.00	9.00	5.50
(116)	Reitmyer	18.00	9.00	5.50
(117)	Riordan	18.00	9.00	5.50
(118)	Rodgers	18.00	9.00	5.50
(119)	Rogers	18.00	9.00	5.50
(120)	Rohrer	18.00	9.00	5.50
(121)	Ryan	18.00	9.00	5.50
(122)	Schaller	18.00	9.00	5.50
(123)	Schirm	18.00	9.00	5.50
(124)	Schmidt	18.00	9.00	5.50
(125)	Schulz	18.00	9.00	5.50
(126)	Sepulveda	18.00	9.00	5.50
(127)	Shinn	18.00	9.00	5.50
(128)	Spenger	18.00	9.00	5.50
(129)	Stanley	18.00	9.00	5.50
(130)	Stanridge	18.00	9.00	5.50
(131)	Stark	18.00	9.00	5.50
(132)	Sterritt	18.00	9.00	5.50
(133)	Stroud	18.00	9.00	5.50
(134)	Tennant	18.00	9.00	5.50
(135)	Thomas	18.00	9.00	5.50
(136)	Todd	18.00	9.00	5.50
(137)	Tonneman	18.00	9.00	5.50
(138)	Tozer	18.00	9.00	5.50
(139)	Van Buren	18.00	9.00	5.50
(140)	Wagner	18.00	9.00	5.50
(141)	West	18.00	9.00	5.50
(142)	Williams	18.00	9.00	5.50
(143)	Wolverton	18.00	9.00	5.50
(144)	Wotell	18.00	9.00	5.50
(145)	Wuffli	18.00	9.00	5.50
(146)	Young	18.00	9.00	5.50
(147)	Zacher	18.00	9.00	5.50
(148)	Zimmerman	18.00	9.00	5.50

1914 E136 Zeenut

The 1914 Zeenut cards measure 2" by 3-1/2" without the coupon, and feature black and white photos on a gray, borderless background. To date, 146 different poses have been found. The backs are blank.

		NR MT	EX	VG
Complete Set:		2200.	1100.	700.00
Common Player:		15.00	7.50	4.50
(1)	Ables	15.00	7.50	4.50
(2)	Abstein	15.00	7.50	4.50
(3)	Alexander	15.00	7.50	4.50
(4)	Arbogast	15.00	7.50	4.50
(5)	Arlett	15.00	7.50	4.50
(6)	Arrelanes	15.00	7.50	4.50

		NR MT	EX	VG
(7)	Bancroft	75.00	38.00	23.00
(8)	Barham	15.00	7.50	4.50
(9)	Barrenkamp	15.00	7.50	4.50
(10)	Barton	15.00	7.50	4.50
(11)	Baum	15.00	7.50	4.50
(12)	Bayless	15.00	7.50	4.50
(13a)	Bliss (large pose)	15.00	7.50	4.50
(13b)	Bliss (small pose)	15.00	7.50	4.50
(14)	Boles	15.00	7.50	4.50
(15)	Borton	15.00	7.50	4.50
(16)	Brashear	15.00	7.50	4.50
(17)	Brenegan	15.00	7.50	4.50
(18)	Brooks	15.00	7.50	4.50
(19)	Brown	15.00	7.50	4.50
(20)	Butler	15.00	7.50	4.50
(21)	Calvo	15.00	7.50	4.50
(22)	Carlisle	15.00	7.50	4.50
(23)	Cartwright	15.00	7.50	4.50
(24)	Charles	15.00	7.50	4.50
(25)	Chech	15.00	7.50	4.50
(26)	Christian	15.00	7.50	4.50
(27)	Clarke	15.00	7.50	4.50
(28)	Colligan	15.00	7.50	4.50
(29)	Cook	15.00	7.50	4.50
(31)	Coy	15.00	7.50	4.50
(32)	Crabb	15.00	7.50	4.50
(33)	Davis	15.00	7.50	4.50
(34)	Derrick	15.00	7.50	4.50
(35)	Devlin	15.00	7.50	4.50
(36)	DeCannier	15.00	7.50	4.50
(37)	Dillon	15.00	7.50	4.50
(38)	Doane	15.00	7.50	4.50
(39)	Downs	15.00	7.50	4.50
(40)	Ehmke	12.00	6.00	3.50
(41)	Ellis	15.00	7.50	4.50
(42)	Evans	15.00	7.50	4.50
(43)	Fanning	15.00	7.50	4.50
(44)	Fisher	15.00	7.50	4.50
(45)	Fitzgerald	15.00	7.50	4.50
(46)	Fleharty	15.00	7.50	4.50
(47)	Frambach	15.00	7.50	4.50
(48)	Gardner	15.00	7.50	4.50
(49)	Gedeon	15.00	7.50	4.50
(50)	Geyer	15.00	7.50	4.50
(51)	Gianini	15.00	7.50	4.50
(52)	Gregory	15.00	7.50	4.50
(53)	Guest	15.00	7.50	4.50
(54)	Hallinan	15.00	7.50	4.50
(55)	Hannah	15.00	7.50	4.50
(56)	Harkness (batting)	15.00	7.50	4.50
(57)	Haworth (batting)	15.00	7.50	4.50
(58)	Haworth (catching)	15.00	7.50	4.50
(59)	Henderson	15.00	7.50	4.50
(60)	Henley	15.00	7.50	4.50
(61)	Hern	15.00	7.50	4.50
(62)	Hettling	15.00	7.50	4.50
(63)	Higginbotham	15.00	7.50	4.50
(64)	Hitt	15.00	7.50	4.50
(65)	Hogan	15.00	7.50	4.50
(66a)	Hosp (large pose)	15.00	7.50	4.50
(66b)	Hosp (small pose)	15.00	7.50	4.50
(67)	Howard	15.00	7.50	4.50
(68)	Hughes (Los Angeles)	15.00	7.50	4.50
(69)	Hughes (San Francisco)	15.00	7.50	4.50
(70)	Johnson	15.00	7.50	4.50
(71)	Kane	15.00	7.50	4.50
(72)	Kaylor	15.00	7.50	4.50
(73)	Killilay	15.00	7.50	4.50
(74)	Klawitter	15.00	7.50	4.50
(75)	Klepfler	15.00	7.50	4.50
(76)	Kores	15.00	7.50	4.50
(77)	Kramer	15.00	7.50	4.50
(78)	Krause	15.00	7.50	4.50
(79a)	Leard (large pose)	15.00	7.50	4.50
(79b)	Leard (small pose)	15.00	7.50	4.50
(80)	Liefeld	15.00	7.50	4.50
(81)	Litschi	15.00	7.50	4.50
(82)	Lober	15.00	7.50	4.50
(83)	Loomis	15.00	7.50	4.50
(84)	Love	15.00	7.50	4.50
(85)	Lynn	15.00	7.50	4.50
(86)	Maggart	15.00	7.50	4.50
(87)	Malarkey	15.00	7.50	4.50
(88)	Martinoni	15.00	7.50	4.50
(89)	McArdle	15.00	7.50	4.50
(90)	McCredie	15.00	7.50	4.50
(91)	McDonald	15.00	7.50	4.50
(92)	Meek	15.00	7.50	4.50
(93)	Meloan	15.00	7.50	4.50
(94)	Menges	15.00	7.50	4.50
(95)	Metzger	15.00	7.50	4.50
(96)	Middleton	15.00	7.50	4.50
(97)	Mitze	15.00	7.50	4.50
(98)	Mohler	15.00	7.50	4.50
(99)	Moore	15.00	7.50	4.50
(100)	Moran	15.00	7.50	4.50
(101)	Mundorf	15.00	7.50	4.50
(102)	Murphy	15.00	7.50	4.50
(103)	Musser	15.00	7.50	4.50
(104)	Ness	15.00	7.50	4.50
(105)	O'Leary	15.00	7.50	4.50
(106)	Orr	15.00	7.50	4.50
(107)	Page	15.00	7.50	4.50
(108)	Pape	15.00	7.50	4.50
(109)	Parkin	15.00	7.50	4.50
(110a)	Peet (large pose)	15.00	7.50	4.50
(110b)	Peet (small pose)	15.00	7.50	4.50
(111)	Perkins	15.00	7.50	4.50
(112)	Pernoll	15.00	7.50	4.50
(113)	Perritt	15.00	7.50	4.50
(114)	Powell	15.00	7.50	4.50
(115)	Prough	15.00	7.50	4.50
(116)	Pruiett	15.00	7.50	4.50
(117)	Quinlan	15.00	7.50	4.50
(118a)	Raney (incorrect spelling)	15.00	7.50	4.50
(118b)	Ramey (correct spelling)	15.00	7.50	4.50
(119)	Rieger	15.00	7.50	4.50
(120)	Rodgers	15.00	7.50	4.50
(121)	Rogers	15.00	7.50	4.50
(122)	Rohrer	15.00	7.50	4.50
(123)	Ryan	15.00	7.50	4.50
(124)	Ryan	15.00	7.50	4.50
(125)	Sawyer	15.00	7.50	4.50
(126)	Schaller	15.00	7.50	4.50
(127)	Schmidt	15.00	7.50	4.50
(128)	Sepulveda	15.00	7.50	4.50
(129)	Shinn	15.00	7.50	4.50
(130)	Slagle	15.00	7.50	4.50
(131)	Speas	15.00	7.50	4.50
(132)	Stanridge	15.00	7.50	4.50
(133)	Stroud	15.00	7.50	4.50
(134)	Tennant	15.00	7.50	4.50
(135)	Tobin	15.00	7.50	4.50
(136)	Tozer	15.00	7.50	4.50
(137)	Van Buren	15.00	7.50	4.50
(138)	West	15.00	7.50	4.50
(139)	White	15.00	7.50	4.50
(140)	Wolter	15.00	7.50	4.50
(141)	Wolverton	15.00	7.50	4.50
(142)	Yantz	15.00	7.50	4.50
(143)	Young	15.00	7.50	4.50
(144)	Zacher	15.00	7.50	4.50
(145)	Zumwalt	15.00	7.50	4.50

1915 E137 Zeenut

The 1915 Zeenut cards are dated on the front, making identification very easy. They measure 2" by 3-1/8" without the coupon and feature a black and white photo on a light background. To date 141 different cards are known to exist. This year is among the toughest of all Zeenuts to find.

		NR MT	EX	VG
Complete Set:		2600.	1300.	775.00
Common Player:		18.00	9.00	5.50
(1)	Ables	18.00	9.00	5.50
(2)	Abstein	18.00	9.00	5.50
(3)	Alcock	18.00	9.00	5.50
(4)	Arbogast	18.00	9.00	5.50
(5)	Baerwald	18.00	9.00	5.50
(6)	Barbour	18.00	9.00	5.50
(7)	Bates	18.00	9.00	5.50
(8)	Baum	18.00	9.00	5.50
(9)	Bayless	18.00	9.00	5.50
(10)	Beatty	18.00	9.00	5.50
(11)	Beer	18.00	9.00	5.50
(12)	Benham	18.00	9.00	5.50
(13)	Berger	18.00	9.00	5.50
(14)	Beumiller	18.00	9.00	5.50
(15)	Blankenship	18.00	9.00	5.50
(16)	Block	18.00	9.00	5.50
(17)	Bodie	25.00	12.50	7.50
(18)	Boles	18.00	9.00	5.50
(19)	Boyd	18.00	9.00	5.50
(20)	Bromley	18.00	9.00	5.50
(21)	Brown	18.00	9.00	5.50
(22)	Burns	18.00	9.00	5.50
(23)	Carlisle	18.00	9.00	5.50
(24)	Carrisch	18.00	9.00	5.50
(25)	Charles	18.00	9.00	5.50
(26)	Chech	18.00	9.00	5.50
(27)	Christian	18.00	9.00	5.50
(28)	Clarke	18.00	9.00	5.50
(29)	Couch	18.00	9.00	5.50
(30)	Covaleski (Coveleski)	40.00	20.00	12.00
(31)	Daniels	18.00	9.00	5.50
(32)	Davis	18.00	9.00	5.50
(33)	DeCanniere	18.00	9.00	5.50
(34)	Dent	18.00	9.00	5.50
(35)	Derrick	18.00	9.00	5.50
(36)	Dillon	18.00	9.00	5.50
(37)	Doane	18.00	9.00	5.50
(38)	Downs	18.00	9.00	5.50
(39)	Elliott	18.00	9.00	5.50
(40)	F. Elliott	18.00	9.00	5.50
(41)	Ellis	18.00	9.00	5.50
(42)	Evans	18.00	9.00	5.50
(43)	Fanning	18.00	9.00	5.50
(44)	Faye	18.00	9.00	5.50
(45)	Fisher	18.00	9.00	5.50
(46)	Fittery	18.00	9.00	5.50
(47)	Fitzgerald	18.00	9.00	5.50
(48)	Fromme	18.00	9.00	5.50
(49)	Gardiner	18.00	9.00	5.50
(50)	Gedeon	18.00	9.00	5.50
(51)	Gleischmann	18.00	9.00	5.50
(52)	Gregory	18.00	9.00	5.50
(53)	Guest	18.00	9.00	5.50
(54)	Hall	18.00	9.00	5.50
(55)	Halla	18.00	9.00	5.50
(56)	Hallinan	18.00	9.00	5.50
(57)	Hannah	18.00	9.00	5.50
(58)	Harper	18.00	9.00	5.50
(59)	Heilmann	75.00	38.00	23.00
(60)	Henley	18.00	9.00	5.50
(61)	Hetling	18.00	9.00	5.50
(62)	Higginbotham	18.00	9.00	5.50
(63)	Hilliard	18.00	9.00	5.50
(64)	Hitt (winding up)	18.00	9.00	5.50
(65)	Hitt (throwing)	18.00	9.00	5.50
(66)	Hogan	18.00	9.00	5.50
(67)	Hosp	18.00	9.00	5.50
(68)	Howard	18.00	9.00	5.50
(69)	Hughes	18.00	9.00	5.50
(70)	Johnson	18.00	9.00	5.50
(71)	Jones	18.00	9.00	5.50
(72)	Kahler	18.00	9.00	5.50
(73)	Kane	18.00	9.00	5.50
(74)	Karr	18.00	9.00	5.50
(75)	Killilay	18.00	9.00	5.50
(76)	Klawitter	18.00	9.00	5.50
(77)	Koerner	18.00	9.00	5.50
(78)	Krause	18.00	9.00	5.50
(79)	Kuhn	18.00	9.00	5.50
(80)	LaRoy	18.00	9.00	5.50
(81)	Leard	18.00	9.00	5.50
(82)	Lindsay	18.00	9.00	5.50
(83)	Litschi	18.00	9.00	5.50
(84)	Lober	18.00	9.00	5.50
(85)	Love	18.00	9.00	5.50
(86)	Lush	18.00	9.00	5.50
(87)	Maggart	18.00	9.00	5.50
(88)	Malarkey	18.00	9.00	5.50
(89)	Manda	18.00	9.00	5.50
(90)	Marcan	18.00	9.00	5.50
(91)	Martinoni	18.00	9.00	5.50
(92)	McAvoy	18.00	9.00	5.50
(93)	McCredie	18.00	9.00	5.50
(94)	McDonell	18.00	9.00	5.50
(95)	McMullen	75.00	38.00	23.00
(96)	Meek	18.00	9.00	5.50
(97)	Meloan	18.00	9.00	5.50
(98)	Metzger	18.00	9.00	5.50
(99)	Middleton	18.00	9.00	5.50
(100)	Mitchell	18.00	9.00	5.50
(101)	Mitze	18.00	9.00	5.50
(102)	Morgan	18.00	9.00	5.50
(103)	Mundorff	18.00	9.00	5.50
(104)	Murphy	18.00	9.00	5.50
(105)	Ness	18.00	9.00	5.50
(106)	Nutt	18.00	9.00	5.50
(107)	Orr	18.00	9.00	5.50
(108)	Pernoll	18.00	9.00	5.50
(109)	Perritt	18.00	9.00	5.50
(110)	Piercey	18.00	9.00	5.50
(111)	Price	18.00	9.00	5.50
(112)	Prough	18.00	9.00	5.50
(113)	Prueitt	18.00	9.00	5.50
(114)	Purtell	18.00	9.00	5.50
(115)	Reed	18.00	9.00	5.50
(116)	Reisigl	18.00	9.00	5.50
(117)	Remneas	18.00	9.00	5.50
(118)	Risberg	75.00	38.00	23.00
(119)	Rohrer	18.00	9.00	5.50
(120)	Russell	18.00	9.00	5.50
(121)	Ryan (Los Angeles)	18.00	9.00	5.50
(122)	Ryan	18.00	9.00	5.50
(123)	Schaller	18.00	9.00	5.50
(124)	Schmidt	18.00	9.00	5.50
(125)	Scoggins	18.00	9.00	5.50
(126)	Sepulveda	18.00	9.00	5.50
(127)	Shinn	18.00	9.00	5.50
(128)	Smith	18.00	9.00	5.50
(129)	Speas	18.00	9.00	5.50
(130)	Spencer	18.00	9.00	5.50
(132)	Tennant	18.00	9.00	5.50
(133)	Terry	18.00	9.00	5.50
(134)	Tobin	18.00	9.00	5.50
(135)	West	18.00	9.00	5.50
(136)	White	18.00	9.00	5.50
(137)	C. Williams	75.00	38.00	23.00
(138)	J. Williams	18.00	9.00	5.50
(139)	Wolter	18.00	9.00	5.50
(140)	Wolverton	18.00	9.00	5.50
(141)	Zacher	18.00	9.00	5.50

1916 E137 Zeenut

The 1916 Zeenuts measure 2" by 3-1/8" without the coupon and are dated on the front (some cards were misdated 1916, however). The card fronts feature black and white photos on a blue background. There are 144 known subjects. The 1916 series was among the more difficult.

	NR MT	EX	VG
Complete Set:	2200.	1100.	625.00
Common Player:	15.00	7.50	4.50
(1) Autrey	15.00	7.50	4.50
(2) Barbeau	15.00	7.50	4.50
(3) Barry	15.00	7.50	4.50
(4) Bassler	15.00	7.50	4.50
(5) Bates	15.00	7.50	4.50
(6) Baum	15.00	7.50	4.50
(7) Bayless	15.00	7.50	4.50
(8) Beer	15.00	7.50	4.50
(9) Berg	15.00	7.50	4.50
(10) Berger	15.00	7.50	4.50
(11) Blankenship	15.00	7.50	4.50
(12) Block	15.00	7.50	4.50
(13) Bodie	20.00	10.00	6.00
(14) Bohne	15.00	7.50	4.50
(15) Boles	15.00	7.50	4.50
(16) Boyd	15.00	7.50	4.50
(17) Brief	15.00	7.50	4.50
(18) Brooks	15.00	7.50	4.50
(19) Brown	15.00	7.50	4.50
(20) Butler	15.00	7.50	4.50
(21) Callahan	15.00	7.50	4.50
(22) Carrisch	15.00	7.50	4.50
(23) Chance	75.00	38.00	23.00
(24) Claxton	100.00	50.00	30.00
(25) Coffey	15.00	7.50	4.50
(26) Cook	15.00	7.50	4.50
(27) Corbett	15.00	7.50	4.50
(28) Couch	15.00	7.50	4.50
(29) Crandall	15.00	7.50	4.50
(30) Dalton	15.00	7.50	4.50
(31) Davis	15.00	7.50	4.50
(32) Derrick	15.00	7.50	4.50
(33) Doane	15.00	7.50	4.50
(34) Downs	15.00	7.50	4.50
(35) Dugan	15.00	7.50	4.50
(36) Eldred	15.00	7.50	4.50
(37) F. Elliott	15.00	7.50	4.50
(38) H. Elliott	15.00	7.50	4.50
(39) Ellis	15.00	7.50	4.50
(40) Erickson	15.00	7.50	4.50
(41) Fanning	15.00	7.50	4.50
(42) Fisher	15.00	7.50	4.50
(43) Fittery	15.00	7.50	4.50
(44) Fitzgerald	15.00	7.50	4.50
(45) Fromme	15.00	7.50	4.50
(46) Galloway	15.00	7.50	4.50
(47) Gardner	15.00	7.50	4.50
(48) Gay	15.00	7.50	4.50
(49) Gleischmann	15.00	7.50	4.50
(50) Griffith	15.00	7.50	4.50
(51) Griggs	15.00	7.50	4.50
(52) Guisto	15.00	7.50	4.50
(53) Hagerman	15.00	7.50	4.50
(54) Hall	15.00	7.50	4.50
(55) Hallinan	15.00	7.50	4.50
(56) Hannah	15.00	7.50	4.50
(57) Harstadt	15.00	7.50	4.50
(58) Haworth	15.00	7.50	4.50
(59) Hess	15.00	7.50	4.50
(60) Higginbotham	15.00	7.50	4.50
(61) Hitt	15.00	7.50	4.50
(62) Hogg	15.00	7.50	4.50
(63) Hollocher	15.00	7.50	4.50
(64) Horstman	15.00	7.50	4.50
(65) Houck	15.00	7.50	4.50
(66) Howard	15.00	7.50	4.50
(67) Hughes	15.00	7.50	4.50
(68) E. Johnston	15.00	7.50	4.50
(69) G. Johnston	15.00	7.50	4.50
(70) Jones	15.00	7.50	4.50
(71) Kahler	15.00	7.50	4.50
(72) Kane	15.00	7.50	4.50
(73) Kelly	15.00	7.50	4.50
(74) Kenworthy	15.00	7.50	4.50
(75) Klawitter	15.00	7.50	4.50
(76) Klein	15.00	7.50	4.50
(77) Koerner	15.00	7.50	4.50
(78) Krause	15.00	7.50	4.50
(79) Kuhn	15.00	7.50	4.50
(80) Lane	15.00	7.50	4.50
(81) Larsen	15.00	7.50	4.50
(82) Lush	15.00	7.50	4.50
(83) Machold	15.00	7.50	4.50
(84) Maggert	15.00	7.50	4.50
(85) Manser	15.00	7.50	4.50
(86) Martin	15.00	7.50	4.50
(87) Mattick	15.00	7.50	4.50
(88) McCredie	15.00	7.50	4.50
(89) McGaffigan	15.00	7.50	4.50
(90) McLarry	15.00	7.50	4.50
(91) Menges	15.00	7.50	4.50
(92) Middleton	15.00	7.50	4.50
(93) Mitchell	15.00	7.50	4.50
(94) Mitze	15.00	7.50	4.50
(95) Munsell	15.00	7.50	4.50
(96) Murphy	15.00	7.50	4.50
(97) Nixon	15.00	7.50	4.50
(98) Noyes	15.00	7.50	4.50
(99) Nutt	15.00	7.50	4.50
(100) O'Brien	15.00	7.50	4.50
(101) Oldham	15.00	7.50	4.50
(102) Orr	15.00	7.50	4.50
(103) Patterson	15.00	7.50	4.50
(104) Perritt	15.00	7.50	4.50
(105) Prough	15.00	7.50	4.50
(106) Prueitt	15.00	7.50	4.50
(107) Quinlan	15.00	7.50	4.50
(108) Quinn (Portland)	15.00	7.50	4.50
(109) Quinn (Vernon)	15.00	7.50	4.50
(110) Rader	15.00	7.50	4.50
(111) Randall	15.00	7.50	4.50
(112) Rath	15.00	7.50	4.50
(113) Reisegl	15.00	7.50	4.50
(114) Reuther	15.00	7.50	4.50
(115) Risberg	75.00	38.00	23.00
(116) Roche	15.00	7.50	4.50
(117) Ryan	15.00	7.50	4.50
(118) Ryan	15.00	7.50	4.50
(119) Scoggins	15.00	7.50	4.50
(120) Sepulveda	15.00	7.50	4.50
(121) Schaller	15.00	7.50	4.50

	NR MT	EX	VG
(122) Sheehan	15.00	7.50	4.50
(123) Shinn	15.00	7.50	4.50
(124) Smith	15.00	7.50	4.50
(125) Sothoron	15.00	7.50	4.50
(126) Southworth	15.00	7.50	4.50
(127) Speas	15.00	7.50	4.50
(128) Spencer	15.00	7.50	4.50
(129) Standridge	15.00	7.50	4.50
(130) Steen	15.00	7.50	4.50
(131) Stumpf	15.00	7.50	4.50
(132) Vann	15.00	7.50	4.50
(133) Vaughn	15.00	7.50	4.50
(134) Ward	15.00	7.50	4.50
(135) Whalling	15.00	7.50	4.50
(136) Wilie	15.00	7.50	4.50
(137) Williams	15.00	7.50	4.50
(138) Wolverton	15.00	7.50	4.50
(139) Wuffli	15.00	7.50	4.50
(140) Zabel	15.00	7.50	4.50
(141) Zacher	15.00	7.50	4.50
(142) Zimmerman	15.00	7.50	4.50

1917 E137 Zeenut

The 1917 Zeenuts measure 1-3/4" by 3-1/2" and feature black and white photos on a light background. They are dated on the front and have blank backs. An advertising poster has been found listing 119 players (two pose variations brings the total to 121), but to date, six players on the list have not been found.

	NR MT	EX	VG
Complete Set:	1800.	900.00	550.00
Common Player:	15.00	7.50	4.50
(1) Arlett	15.00	7.50	4.50
(2) Arrelanes	15.00	7.50	4.50
(3) Baker (catching)	15.00	7.50	4.50
(4) Baker (throwing)	15.00	7.50	4.50
(5) Baldwin	15.00	7.50	4.50
(6) Bassler	15.00	7.50	4.50
(7) Baum	15.00	7.50	4.50
(8) Beer	15.00	7.50	4.50
(9) Bernhard	15.00	7.50	4.50
(10) Bliss	15.00	7.50	4.50
(11) Boles	15.00	7.50	4.50
(12) Brenton	15.00	7.50	4.50
(13) Brief	15.00	7.50	4.50
(14) Brown	15.00	7.50	4.50
(15) Burns	15.00	7.50	4.50
(16) Callahan	15.00	7.50	4.50
(17) Callan	15.00	7.50	4.50
(18) Calvo	15.00	7.50	4.50
(19) Chadbourne	15.00	7.50	4.50
(20) Chance	75.00	38.00	23.00
(21) Coltrin	15.00	7.50	4.50
(22) Connifer	15.00	7.50	4.50
(23) Corhan	15.00	7.50	4.50
(24) Crandall (Los Angeles)	15.00	7.50	4.50
(25) Crandall (Salt Lake)	15.00	7.50	4.50
(26) Cress	15.00	7.50	4.50
(27) Davis	15.00	7.50	4.50
(28) DeCanniere	15.00	7.50	4.50
(29) Doane	15.00	7.50	4.50
(30) Dougan	15.00	7.50	4.50
(31) Dougherty	15.00	7.50	4.50
(32) Downs	15.00	7.50	4.50
(33) Dubuc	15.00	7.50	4.50
(34) Ellis	15.00	7.50	4.50
(35) Erickson	15.00	7.50	4.50
(36) Evans	15.00	7.50	4.50
(37) Farmer	15.00	7.50	4.50
(38) Fincher	15.00	7.50	4.50
(39) Fisher	15.00	7.50	4.50
(40) Fitzgerald	15.00	7.50	4.50
(41) Fournier	15.00	7.50	4.50
(42) Fromme	15.00	7.50	4.50
(43) Galloway	15.00	7.50	4.50
(44) Gislason	15.00	7.50	4.50
(45) Goodbred	15.00	7.50	4.50
(46) Griggs	15.00	7.50	4.50
(47) Groehling	15.00	7.50	4.50
(48) Hall (Los Angeles)	15.00	7.50	4.50
(49) Hall (San Francisco)	15.00	7.50	4.50
(50) Hannah	15.00	7.50	4.50
(51) Harstad	15.00	7.50	4.50
(52) Helfrich	15.00	7.50	4.50
(53) Hess	15.00	7.50	4.50
(54) Hitt	15.00	7.50	4.50

	NR MT	EX	VG
(55) Hoff	15.00	7.50	4.50
(56) Hollacher	15.00	7.50	4.50
(57) Hollywood	15.00	7.50	4.50
(58) Houck	15.00	7.50	4.50
(59) Howard	15.00	7.50	4.50
(60) Hughes	15.00	7.50	4.50
(61) Johnson	15.00	7.50	4.50
(62) Kilhullen	15.00	7.50	4.50
(63) Killiffer	15.00	7.50	4.50
(64) Koerner	15.00	7.50	4.50
(65) Krause	15.00	7.50	4.50
(66) Lane	15.00	7.50	4.50
(67) Lapan	15.00	7.50	4.50
(68) Leake	15.00	7.50	4.50
(69) Lee	15.00	7.50	4.50
(70) Leverenz	15.00	7.50	4.50
(71) Maggert	15.00	7.50	4.50
(72) Maisel	15.00	7.50	4.50
(73) Mattick	15.00	7.50	4.50
(74) McCreedie	15.00	7.50	4.50
(75) McLarry	15.00	7.50	4.50
(76) Mensor	15.00	7.50	4.50
(77) Meusel	12.00	6.00	3.50
(78) Middleton	15.00	7.50	4.50
(79) Miller (batting)	15.00	7.50	4.50
(80) Miller (throwing)	15.00	7.50	4.50
(81) Mitchell	15.00	7.50	4.50
(82) Mitze	15.00	7.50	4.50
(83) Murphy	15.00	7.50	4.50
(84) Murray	15.00	7.50	4.50
(85) O'Brien	15.00	7.50	4.50
(86) O'Mara	15.00	7.50	4.50
(87) Oldham	15.00	7.50	4.50
(88) Orr	15.00	7.50	4.50
(89) Penelli	15.00	7.50	4.50
(90) Penner	15.00	7.50	4.50
(91) Pick	15.00	7.50	4.50
(92) Prough	15.00	7.50	4.50
(93) Pruiett	15.00	7.50	4.50
(94) Quinlan	15.00	7.50	4.50
(95) Quinn	15.00	7.50	4.50
(96) Rath	15.00	7.50	4.50
(97) Roche	15.00	7.50	4.50
(98) Ryan (Los Angeles)	15.00	7.50	4.50
(99) Ryan (Salt Lake)	15.00	7.50	4.50
(100) Schaller	15.00	7.50	4.50
(101) Schinkle	15.00	7.50	4.50
(102) Schultz	15.00	7.50	4.50
(103) Sheehan	15.00	7.50	4.50
(104) Sheeley	15.00	7.50	4.50
(105) Shinn	15.00	7.50	4.50
(106) Siglin	15.00	7.50	4.50
(107) Simon	15.00	7.50	4.50
(108) Smith	15.00	7.50	4.50
(109) Snyder	15.00	7.50	4.50
(110) Stanridge	15.00	7.50	4.50
(111) Steen	15.00	7.50	4.50
(112) Stovall	15.00	7.50	4.50
(113) Stumpf	15.00	7.50	4.50
(114) Sullivan	15.00	7.50	4.50
(115) Terry	15.00	7.50	4.50
(116) Tobin	15.00	7.50	4.50
(117) Valencia	15.00	7.50	4.50
(118) Vaughn	15.00	7.50	4.50
(119) Whalling	15.00	7.50	4.50
(120) Wilie	15.00	7.50	4.50
(121) Wolverton	15.00	7.50	4.50

1918 E137 Zeenut

The 1918 Zeenuts are among the most distinctive because of their red borders surrounding the photos. They measure 1-3/4" by 3-1/8" and are among the more difficult years to find.

	NR MT	EX	VG
Complete Set:	2000.	1000.	600.00
Common Player:	18.00	9.00	5.50
(1) Alcock	18.00	9.00	5.50
(2) Arkenburg	18.00	9.00	5.50
(3) A. Arlett	18.00	9.00	5.50
(4) Baum	18.00	9.00	5.50
(5) Boles	18.00	9.00	5.50
(6) Borton	18.00	9.00	5.50
(7) Brenton	18.00	9.00	5.50
(8) Bromley	18.00	9.00	5.50
(9) Brooks	18.00	9.00	5.50
(10) Brown	18.00	9.00	5.50
(11) Caldera	18.00	9.00	5.50
(12) Camm	18.00	9.00	5.50

		NR MT	EX	VG
(13)	Chadbourne	18.00	9.00	5.50
(14)	Chappell	18.00	9.00	5.50
(15)	Codington	18.00	9.00	5.50
(16)	Conwright	18.00	9.00	5.50
(17)	Cooper	18.00	9.00	5.50
(18)	Cox	18.00	9.00	5.50
(19)	Crandall (Los Angeles)	18.00	9.00	5.50
(20)	Crandall (Salt Lake)	18.00	9.00	5.50
(21)	Crawford	18.00	9.00	5.50
(22)	Croll	18.00	9.00	5.50
(23)	Davis	18.00	9.00	5.50
(24)	DeVormer	18.00	9.00	5.50
(25)	Dobbs	18.00	9.00	5.50
(26)	Downs	18.00	9.00	5.50
(27)	Dubuc	18.00	9.00	5.50
(28)	Dunn	18.00	9.00	5.50
(29)	Easterly	18.00	9.00	5.50
(30)	Eldred	18.00	9.00	5.50
(31)	Elliot	18.00	9.00	5.50
(32)	Ellis	18.00	9.00	5.50
(33)	Essick	18.00	9.00	5.50
(34)	Farmer	18.00	9.00	5.50
(35)	Fisher	18.00	9.00	5.50
(36)	Fittery	18.00	9.00	5.50
(37)	Forsythe	18.00	9.00	5.50
(38)	Fournier	18.00	9.00	5.50
(39)	Fromme	18.00	9.00	5.50
(40)	Gardner (Oakland)	18.00	9.00	5.50
(41)	Gardner (Sacramento)	18.00	9.00	5.50
(42)	Goldie	18.00	9.00	5.50
(43)	Griggs	18.00	9.00	5.50
(44)	Hawkes	18.00	9.00	5.50
(45)	Hollander	18.00	9.00	5.50
(46)	Hosp	18.00	9.00	5.50
(47)	Howard	18.00	9.00	5.50
(48)	Hummel	18.00	9.00	5.50
(49)	Hunter	18.00	9.00	5.50
(50)	Johnson	18.00	9.00	5.50
(51)	G. Johnson	18.00	9.00	5.50
(52)	Kantlehner	18.00	9.00	5.50
(53)	Killefer	18.00	9.00	5.50
(54)	Koerner	18.00	9.00	5.50
(55)	Konnick	18.00	9.00	5.50
(56)	Kremer	18.00	9.00	5.50
(57)	Lapan	18.00	9.00	5.50
(58)	Leake	18.00	9.00	5.50
(59)	Leathers	18.00	9.00	5.50
(60)	Leifer	18.00	9.00	5.50
(61)	Leverenz	18.00	9.00	5.50
(62)	Llewlyn	18.00	9.00	5.50
(63)	Martin	18.00	9.00	5.50
(64)	McCabe	18.00	9.00	5.50
(65)	McCredie	18.00	9.00	5.50
(66)	McKee	18.00	9.00	5.50
(67)	McNulty	18.00	9.00	5.50
(68)	Mensor	18.00	9.00	5.50
(69)	Middleton	18.00	9.00	5.50
(70)	Miller (Oakland)	18.00	9.00	5.50
(71)	Miller (Salt Lake)	18.00	9.00	5.50
(72)	J. Mitchell	18.00	9.00	5.50
(73)	R. Mitchell	18.00	9.00	5.50
(74)	Mitze	18.00	9.00	5.50
(75)	Moore	18.00	9.00	5.50
(76)	Morton	18.00	9.00	5.50
(77)	Murray	18.00	9.00	5.50
(78)	O'Doul	75.00	38.00	23.00
(79)	Orr	18.00	9.00	5.50
(80)	Pepe	18.00	9.00	5.50
(81)	Pertica	18.00	9.00	5.50
(82)	Phillips	18.00	9.00	5.50
(83)	Pick	18.00	9.00	5.50
(84)	Pinelli	35.00	17.50	10.50
(85)	Prentice	18.00	9.00	5.50
(86)	Prough	18.00	9.00	5.50
(87)	Quinlan	18.00	9.00	5.50
(88)	Ritchie	18.00	9.00	5.50
(89)	Rogers	18.00	9.00	5.50
(90)	Ryan	18.00	9.00	5.50
(91)	Sand	18.00	9.00	5.50
(92)	Shader	18.00	9.00	5.50
(93)	Sheely	18.00	9.00	5.50
(94)	Siglin	18.00	9.00	5.50
(95)	Smale	18.00	9.00	5.50
(96)	Smith	18.00	9.00	5.50
(97)	Smith	18.00	9.00	5.50
(98)	Stanbridge	18.00	9.00	5.50
(99)	Terry	18.00	9.00	5.50
(100)	Valencia	18.00	9.00	5.50
(101)	West	18.00	9.00	5.50
(102)	Wilie	18.00	9.00	5.50
(103)	Williams	18.00	9.00	5.50
(104)	Wisterzill	18.00	9.00	5.50

1919 E137 Zeenut

The 1919-1921 Zeenuts cards were dated on the front and measure 1-3/4" by 3-1/8". They featured borderless, sepia-toned photos. To date, 144 subjects exist in the 1919 series; 151 have been found for 1920; and 168 different subjects have been discovered for 1921 (even though a promotional flier indicates 180 players).

		NR MT	EX	VG
Complete Set:		1450.	725.00	425.00
Common Player:		10.00	5.00	3.00
(1)	Ally	10.00	5.00	3.00
(2)	Fatty Arbuckle	60.00	30.00	18.00
(3)	A. Arlett	10.00	5.00	3.00
(4)	R. Arlett	10.00	5.00	3.00
(5)	Baker	10.00	5.00	3.00
(6)	Baldwin	10.00	5.00	3.00
(7)	Baum	10.00	5.00	3.00
(8)	Beck	10.00	5.00	3.00
(9)	Bigbee	10.00	5.00	3.00
(10)	Blue	10.00	5.00	3.00
(11)	Bohne	10.00	5.00	3.00
(12)	Boles	10.00	5.00	3.00
(13)	Borton	10.00	5.00	3.00
(14)	Bowman	10.00	5.00	3.00
(15)	Brooks	10.00	5.00	3.00
(16)	Brown	10.00	5.00	3.00
(17)	Byler	10.00	5.00	3.00
(18)	Caldera	10.00	5.00	3.00
(19)	Cavaney	10.00	5.00	3.00
(20)	Chadbourne	10.00	5.00	3.00
(21)	Chech	10.00	5.00	3.00
(22)	Church	10.00	5.00	3.00
(23)	Clymer	10.00	5.00	3.00
(24)	Coleman	10.00	5.00	3.00
(25)	Compton	10.00	5.00	3.00
(26)	Conkwright	10.00	5.00	3.00
(27)	Connolly	10.00	5.00	3.00
(28)	Cook	10.00	5.00	3.00
(29)	Cooper (Los Angeles)	10.00	5.00	3.00
(30)	Cooper (Oakland)	10.00	5.00	3.00
(31)	Cooper (Portland)	10.00	5.00	3.00
(32)	Corhan	10.00	5.00	3.00
(33)	Couch	10.00	5.00	3.00
(34)	Cox	10.00	5.00	3.00
(35)	Crandall (Los Angeles)	10.00	5.00	3.00
(36)	Crandall (San Francisco)	10.00	5.00	3.00
(37)	Crespi	10.00	5.00	3.00
(38)	Croll	10.00	5.00	3.00
(39)	Cunningham	10.00	5.00	3.00
(40)	Dawson	10.00	5.00	3.00
(41)	Dell	10.00	5.00	3.00
(42)	DeVormer	10.00	5.00	3.00
(43)	Driscoll	10.00	5.00	3.00
(44)	Eastley	10.00	5.00	3.00
(45)	Edington	10.00	5.00	3.00
(46)	Eldred	10.00	5.00	3.00
(47)	Elliott	10.00	5.00	3.00
(48)	Ellis	10.00	5.00	3.00
(49)	Essick	10.00	5.00	3.00
(50)	Fabrique	10.00	5.00	3.00
(51)	Falkenberg	10.00	5.00	3.00
(52)	Fallentine	10.00	5.00	3.00
(53)	Finneran	10.00	5.00	3.00
(54)	Fisher (Sacramento)	10.00	5.00	3.00
(55)	Fisher (Vernon)	10.00	5.00	3.00
(56)	Fitzgerald	10.00	5.00	3.00
(57)	Flannigan	10.00	5.00	3.00
(58)	Fournier	10.00	5.00	3.00
(59)	French	10.00	5.00	3.00
(60)	Fromme	10.00	5.00	3.00
(61)	Gibson	10.00	5.00	3.00
(62)	Griggs	10.00	5.00	3.00
(63)	Haney	9.00	4.50	2.75
(64)	Harper	10.00	5.00	3.00
(65)	Henkle	10.00	5.00	3.00
(66)	Herr	10.00	5.00	3.00
(67)	Hickey	10.00	5.00	3.00
(68)	High	10.00	5.00	3.00
(69)	Holling	10.00	5.00	3.00
(70)	Hosp	10.00	5.00	3.00
(71)	Houck	10.00	5.00	3.00
(72)	Howard	10.00	5.00	3.00
(73)	Kamm	10.00	5.00	3.00
(74)	Kenworthy	10.00	5.00	3.00
(75)	Killefer	10.00	5.00	3.00
(76)	King	10.00	5.00	3.00
(77)	Koehler	10.00	5.00	3.00
(78)	Koerner	10.00	5.00	3.00
(79)	Kramer (Oakland)	10.00	5.00	3.00
(80)	Kramer (San Francisco)	10.00	5.00	3.00
(81)	Land	10.00	5.00	3.00
(82)	Lane	10.00	5.00	3.00
(83)	Lapan	10.00	5.00	3.00
(84)	Larkin	10.00	5.00	3.00
(85)	Lee	10.00	5.00	3.00
(86)	Long	10.00	5.00	3.00
(87)	Mails	10.00	5.00	3.00
(88)	Mains	10.00	5.00	3.00
(89)	Maisel	10.00	5.00	3.00
(90)	Mathes	10.00	5.00	3.00
(91)	McCredie	10.00	5.00	3.00
(92)	McGaffigan	10.00	5.00	3.00
(93)	McHenry	10.00	5.00	3.00
(94)	McNulty	10.00	5.00	3.00
(95)	Meusel	12.00	6.00	3.50
(96)	Middleton	10.00	5.00	3.00
(97)	Mitchell	10.00	5.00	3.00
(98)	Mitze	10.00	5.00	3.00
(99)	Mulory	10.00	5.00	3.00
(100)	Murphy	10.00	5.00	3.00
(101)	Murray	10.00	5.00	3.00
(102)	Niehoff (Los Angeles)	10.00	5.00	3.00
(103)	Niehoff (Seattle)	10.00	5.00	3.00
(104)	Norse	10.00	5.00	3.00
(105)	Oldham	10.00	5.00	3.00
(106)	Orr	10.00	5.00	3.00
(107)	Penner	10.00	5.00	3.00
(108)	Pennington	10.00	5.00	3.00
(109)	Piercy	10.00	5.00	3.00
(110)	Pinelli	15.00	7.50	4.50
(111)	Prough	10.00	5.00	3.00
(112)	Rader	10.00	5.00	3.00
(113)	Reiger	10.00	5.00	3.00
(114)	Ritchie	10.00	5.00	3.00
(115)	Roach	10.00	5.00	3.00
(116)	Rodgers	10.00	5.00	3.00
(117)	Rumler	10.00	5.00	3.00
(118)	Sands	10.00	5.00	3.00
(119)	Schick	10.00	5.00	3.00
(120)	Schultz	10.00	5.00	3.00
(121)	Scott	10.00	5.00	3.00
(122)	Seaton	10.00	5.00	3.00
(123)	Sheely	10.00	5.00	3.00
(124)	Siglin	10.00	5.00	3.00
(125)	Smith	10.00	5.00	3.00
(126)	Bill Smith	10.00	5.00	3.00
(127)	Snell	10.00	5.00	3.00
(128)	Spangler	10.00	5.00	3.00
(129)	Speas	10.00	5.00	3.00
(130)	Spencer	10.00	5.00	3.00
(131)	Starasenich	10.00	5.00	3.00
(132)	Stumpf	10.00	5.00	3.00
(133)	Sutherland	10.00	5.00	3.00
(134)	Vance	10.00	5.00	3.00
(135)	Walker	10.00	5.00	3.00
(136)	Walsh	10.00	5.00	3.00
(137)	Ware	10.00	5.00	3.00
(138)	Weaver	10.00	5.00	3.00
(139)	Westerzil	10.00	5.00	3.00
(140)	Wilhoit	10.00	5.00	3.00
(141)	Wilie	10.00	5.00	3.00
(142)	Willets	10.00	5.00	3.00
(143)	Zamloch	10.00	5.00	3.00
(144)	Zweifel	10.00	5.00	3.00

1920 E137 Zeenut

		NR MT	EX	VG
Complete Set:		1500.	750.00	450.00
Common Player:		10.00	5.00	3.00
(1)	Adams	10.00	5.00	3.00
(2)	Agnew	10.00	5.00	3.00
(3)	Alcock	10.00	5.00	3.00
(4)	Aldrige	10.00	5.00	3.00
(5)	Andrews	10.00	5.00	3.00
(6)	Anfinson	10.00	5.00	3.00
(7)	A. Arlett	10.00	5.00	3.00
(8)	R. Arlett	9.00	4.50	2.75
(9)	Baker	10.00	5.00	3.00
(10)	Baldwin	10.00	5.00	3.00
(11)	Bassler	10.00	5.00	3.00
(12)	Baum	10.00	5.00	3.00
(13)	Blue	10.00	5.00	3.00
(14)	Bohne	10.00	5.00	3.00
(15)	Brenton	10.00	5.00	3.00
(16)	Bromley (dark hat)	10.00	5.00	3.00
(17)	Bromley (light hat)	10.00	5.00	3.00
(18)	Brown	10.00	5.00	3.00
(19)	Butler	10.00	5.00	3.00
(20)	Caveney	10.00	5.00	3.00
(21)	Chadbourne	10.00	5.00	3.00
(22)	Compton	10.00	5.00	3.00
(23)	Connolly	10.00	5.00	3.00
(24)	Cook	10.00	5.00	3.00
(25)	Corhan	10.00	5.00	3.00
(26)	Cox	10.00	5.00	3.00
(27)	K. Crandall	10.00	5.00	3.00
(28)	O. Crandall	10.00	5.00	3.00
(29)	Crawford	10.00	5.00	3.00
(30)	Cullop	10.00	5.00	3.00
(31)	Cunningham	10.00	5.00	3.00
(32)	DeVitalis	10.00	5.00	3.00
(33)	DeVormer	10.00	5.00	3.00
(34)	Dooley	10.00	5.00	3.00
(35)	Dorman	10.00	5.00	3.00
(36)	Dumovich	10.00	5.00	3.00
(37)	Dylar	10.00	5.00	3.00
(38)	Edington	10.00	5.00	3.00
(39)	Eldred	10.00	5.00	3.00
(40)	Ellis	10.00	5.00	3.00
(41)	Essick	10.00	5.00	3.00
(42)	Fisher	10.00	5.00	3.00
(43)	Fitzgerald	10.00	5.00	3.00
(44)	Fromme	10.00	5.00	3.00
(45)	Gardner	10.00	5.00	3.00
(46)	Gingl ardi	10.00	5.00	3.00
(47)	Gough	10.00	5.00	3.00
(48)	Griggs	10.00	5.00	3.00
(49)	Guisto	10.00	5.00	3.00
(50)	Hamilton	10.00	5.00	3.00
(51)	Hanicy	10.00	5.00	3.00

	NR MT	EX	VG
(52) Hartford	10.00	5.00	3.00
(53) High	10.00	5.00	3.00
(54) Hill	10.00	5.00	3.00
(55) Hodges	10.00	5.00	3.00
(56) Howard	10.00	5.00	3.00
(57) James	.0.00	5.00	3.00
(58) Jenkins	10.00	5.00	3.00
(59) Johnson (Portland)	10.00	5.00	3.00
(60) Johnson (Salt Lake)	10.00	5.00	3.00
(61) Jones	10.00	5.00	3.00
(62) Juney	10.00	5.00	3.00
(63) Kallio	10.00	5.00	3.00
(64) Kamm	10.00	5.00	3.00
(65) Keating	10.00	5.00	3.00
(66) Kenworthy	10.00	5.00	3.00
(67) Killeen	10.00	5.00	3.00
(68) Killefer	10.00	5.00	3.00
(69) Kingdon	10.00	5.00	3.00
(70) Knight	10.00	5.00	3.00
(71) Koehler	10.00	5.00	3.00
(72) Koerner	10.00	5.00	3.00
(73) Kopp	10.00	5.00	3.00
(74) Kremer	10.00	5.00	3.00
(75) Krug	10.00	5.00	3.00
(76) Kunz	10.00	5.00	3.00
(77) Lambert	10.00	5.00	3.00
(78) Lane	10.00	5.00	3.00
(79) Larkin	10.00	5.00	3.00
(80) Leverenz	10.00	5.00	3.00
(81) Long	10.00	5.00	3.00
(82) Love	10.00	5.00	3.00
(83) Maggart	10.00	5.00	3.00
(84) Mails	10.00	5.00	3.00
(85) Maisel	10.00	5.00	3.00
(86) Matterson	10.00	5.00	3.00
(87) Matteson	10.00	5.00	3.00
(88) McAuley	10.00	5.00	3.00
(89) McCredie	10.00	5.00	3.00
(90) McGaffigan	10.00	5.00	3.00
(91) McHenry	10.00	5.00	3.00
(92) McQuaid	10.00	5.00	3.00
(93) Miller	10.00	5.00	3.00
(94) Mitchell	10.00	5.00	3.00
(95) J. Mitchell	10.00	5.00	3.00
(96) Mitchell	10.00	5.00	3.00
(97) Mitze	10.00	5.00	3.00
(98) Moffitt	10.00	5.00	3.00
(99) Mollwitz	10.00	5.00	3.00
(100) Morse	10.00	5.00	3.00
(101) Mulligan	10.00	5.00	3.00
(102) Murphy	10.00	5.00	3.00
(103) Niehoff	10.00	5.00	3.00
(104) Nixon	10.00	5.00	3.00
(105) O'Shaughnessy	10.00	5.00	3.00
(106) Orr	10.00	5.00	3.00
(107) Paull	10.00	5.00	3.00
(108) Penner	10.00	5.00	3.00
(109) Pertica	10.00	5.00	3.00
(110) Peterson	10.00	5.00	3.00
(111) Polson	10.00	5.00	3.00
(112) Prough	10.00	5.00	3.00
(113) Reagan	10.00	5.00	3.00
(114) Reiger	10.00	5.00	3.00
(115) Reilly	10.00	5.00	3.00
(116) Rheinhart	10.00	5.00	3.00
(117) Rodgers	10.00	5.00	3.00
(118) Ross	10.00	5.00	3.00
(119) Rumler	10.00	5.00	3.00
(120) Russell	10.00	5.00	3.00
(121) Sands	10.00	5.00	3.00
(122) Schaller	10.00	5.00	3.00
(123) Schang	10.00	5.00	3.00
(124) Schellenback	10.00	5.00	3.00
(125) Schick	10.00	5.00	3.00
(126) Schorr	10.00	5.00	3.00
(127) Schroeder	10.00	5.00	3.00
(128) Scott	10.00	5.00	3.00
(129) Seaton	10.00	5.00	3.00
(130) Sheely	10.00	5.00	3.00
(131) Siebold	10.00	5.00	3.00
(132) Siglin	10.00	5.00	3.00
(133) Smith	10.00	5.00	3.00
(134) G. Smith	10.00	5.00	3.00
(135) Spellman	10.00	5.00	3.00
(136) Spranger	10.00	5.00	3.00
(137) Stroud	10.00	5.00	3.00
(138) Stumpf	10.00	5.00	3.00
(139) Sullivan	10.00	5.00	3.00
(140) Sutherland	10.00	5.00	3.00
(141) Thurston (dark hat)	10.00	5.00	3.00
(142) Thurston (light hat)	10.00	5.00	3.00
(143) Walsh	10.00	5.00	3.00
(144) Wares	10.00	5.00	3.00
(145) Weaver	10.00	5.00	3.00
(146) Willie	10.00	5.00	3.00
(147) Winn	10.00	5.00	3.00
(148) Wisterzill	10.00	5.00	3.00
(149) Worth	10.00	5.00	3.00
(150) Yelle	10.00	5.00	3.00
(151) Zamlock	10.00	5.00	3.00
(152) Zeider	10.00	5.00	3.00

1921 E137 Zeenut

	NR MT	EX	VG
Complete Set:	1750.	875.00	500.00
Common Player:	10.00	5.00	3.00
(1) Adams	10.00	5.00	3.00
(2) Alcock	10.00	5.00	3.00
(3) Aldridge	10.00	5.00	3.00
(4) Alton	10.00	5.00	3.00
(5) Anfinson	10.00	5.00	3.00
(6) Arlett	9.00	4.50	2.75
(7) Baker	10.00	5.00	3.00
(8) Baldwin	10.00	5.00	3.00
(9) Bates	10.00	5.00	3.00
(10) Berry	10.00	5.00	3.00
(11) Blacholder	10.00	5.00	3.00
(12) Blossom	10.00	5.00	3.00

	NR MT	EX	VG
(13) Bourg	10.00	5.00	3.00
(14) Brinley	10.00	5.00	3.00
(15) Bromley	10.00	5.00	3.00
(16) Brown	10.00	5.00	3.00
(17) Brubaker	10.00	5.00	3.00
(18) Butler	10.00	5.00	3.00
(19) Byler	10.00	5.00	3.00
(20) Carroll	10.00	5.00	3.00
(21) Casey	10.00	5.00	3.00
(22) Cather	10.00	5.00	3.00
(23) Caveney	10.00	5.00	3.00
(24) Chadbourne	10.00	5.00	3.00
(25) Compton	10.00	5.00	3.00
(26) Connel	10.00	5.00	3.00
(27) Cook	10.00	5.00	3.00
(28) Cooper	10.00	5.00	3.00
(29) Couch	10.00	5.00	3.00
(30) Cox	10.00	5.00	3.00
(31) Crandall	10.00	5.00	3.00
(32) Cravath	10.00	5.00	3.00
(33) Crawford	75.00	38.00	23.00
(34) Crumpler	10.00	5.00	3.00
(35) Cunningham	10.00	5.00	3.00
(36) Daley	10.00	5.00	3.00
(37) Dell	10.00	5.00	3.00
(38) Demaree	10.00	5.00	3.00
(39) Douglas	10.00	5.00	3.00
(40) Dumovich	10.00	5.00	3.00
(41) Elliott	10.00	5.00	3.00
(42) Ellis	10.00	5.00	3.00
(43) Ellison	10.00	5.00	3.00
(44) Essick	10.00	5.00	3.00
(45) Faeth	10.00	5.00	3.00
(46) Fisher	10.00	5.00	3.00
(47) Fittery	10.00	5.00	3.00
(48) Fitzgerald	10.00	5.00	3.00
(49) Flaherty	10.00	5.00	3.00
(50) Francis	10.00	5.00	3.00
(51) French	10.00	5.00	3.00
(52) Fromme	10.00	5.00	3.00
(53) Gardner	10.00	5.00	3.00
(54) Geary	10.00	5.00	3.00
(55) Gennin	10.00	5.00	3.00
(56) Gorman	10.00	5.00	3.00
(57) Gould	10.00	5.00	3.00
(58) Griggs	10.00	5.00	3.00
(59) Hale	10.00	5.00	3.00
(60) Hannah	10.00	5.00	3.00
(61) Hansen	10.00	5.00	3.00
(62) Hesse	10.00	5.00	3.00
(63) High	10.00	5.00	3.00
(64) Hughes	10.00	5.00	3.00
(65) Hyatt	10.00	5.00	3.00
(66) Jackson	10.00	5.00	3.00
(67) Jacobs	10.00	5.00	3.00
(68) Jacobs	10.00	5.00	3.00
(69) Jenkins	10.00	5.00	3.00
(70) Johnson	10.00	5.00	3.00
(71) Jones	10.00	5.00	3.00
(72) Jourden	10.00	5.00	3.00
(73) Kallio	10.00	5.00	3.00
(74) Kamm	10.00	5.00	3.00
(75) Kearns	10.00	5.00	3.00
(76) Kelly	10.00	5.00	3.00
(77) Kersten	10.00	5.00	3.00
(78) Kifer	10.00	5.00	3.00
(79) Killefer	10.00	5.00	3.00
(80) King	10.00	5.00	3.00
(81) Kingdon	10.00	5.00	3.00
(82) Knight	10.00	5.00	3.00
(83) Koehler	10.00	5.00	3.00
(84) Kopp	10.00	5.00	3.00
(85) Krause	10.00	5.00	3.00
(86) Kremer	10.00	5.00	3.00
(87) Krug	10.00	5.00	3.00
(88) Kunz	10.00	5.00	3.00
(89) Lane	10.00	5.00	3.00
(90) Leverenz	10.00	5.00	3.00
(91) Lewis	10.00	5.00	3.00
(92) Lindimore	10.00	5.00	3.00
(93) Love	10.00	5.00	3.00
(94) Ludolph	10.00	5.00	3.00
(95) Lynn	10.00	5.00	3.00
(96) Lyons	10.00	5.00	3.00
(97) McAuley	10.00	5.00	3.00
(98) McCredie	10.00	5.00	3.00
(99) McGaffigan	10.00	5.00	3.00
(100) McGraw	10.00	5.00	3.00
(101) McQuaid	10.00	5.00	3.00
(102) Merritt	10.00	5.00	3.00
(103) Middleton	10.00	5.00	3.00
(104) Miller	10.00	5.00	3.00
(105) Mitchell	10.00	5.00	3.00
(106) Mitze	10.00	5.00	3.00
(107) Mollwitz	10.00	5.00	3.00
(108) Morse	10.00	5.00	3.00
(109) Murphy (Seattle)	10.00	5.00	3.00

	NR MT	EX	VG
(110) Murphy (Vernon)	10.00	5.00	3.00
(111) Mustain	10.00	5.00	3.00
(112) Nickels	10.00	5.00	3.00
(113) Niehaus	10.00	5.00	3.00
(114) Niehoff	10.00	5.00	3.00
(115) Nofziger	10.00	5.00	3.00
(116) O'Connell	10.00	5.00	3.00
(117) O'Doul	40.00	20.00	12.00
(118) O'Malia	10.00	5.00	3.00
(119) Oldring	10.00	5.00	3.00
(120) Oliver	10.00	5.00	3.00
(121) Orr	10.00	5.00	3.00
(122) Paton	10.00	5.00	3.00
(123) Penner	10.00	5.00	3.00
(124) Pick	10.00	5.00	3.00
(125) Pillette	10.00	5.00	3.00
(126) Pinelli	10.00	5.00	3.00
(127) Polson	10.00	5.00	3.00
(128) Poole	10.00	5.00	3.00
(129) Prough	10.00	5.00	3.00
(130) Rath	10.00	5.00	3.00
(131) Read	10.00	5.00	3.00
(132) Reinhardt	10.00	5.00	3.00
(133) Rieger	10.00	5.00	3.00
(134) Rogers	10.00	5.00	3.00
(135) Rose (Sacramento)	10.00	5.00	3.00
(136) Rose (Salt Lake)	10.00	5.00	3.00
(137) Ross (Portland)	10.00	5.00	3.00
(138) Ross (Sacramento)	10.00	5.00	3.00
(139) Ryan	10.00	5.00	3.00
(140) Sand	10.00	5.00	3.00
(141) Schick	10.00	5.00	3.00
(142) Schneider	10.00	5.00	3.00
(143) Scott	10.00	5.00	3.00
(144) Shang	10.00	5.00	3.00
(145) Sheehan	10.00	5.00	3.00
(146) Shore	10.00	5.00	3.00
(147) Shorr	10.00	5.00	3.00
(148) Shultis	10.00	5.00	3.00
(149) Siebold	10.00	5.00	3.00
(150) Siglin	10.00	5.00	3.00
(151) Smallwood	10.00	5.00	3.00
(152) Smith	10.00	5.00	3.00
(153) Spencer	10.00	5.00	3.00
(154) Stanage	10.00	5.00	3.00
(155) Statz	10.00	5.00	3.00
(156) Stumph	10.00	5.00	3.00
(157) Thomas	10.00	5.00	3.00
(158) Thurston	10.00	5.00	3.00
(159) Tyrrell	10.00	5.00	3.00
(160) Van Osdoll	10.00	5.00	3.00
(161) Walsh	10.00	5.00	3.00
(162) White	10.00	5.00	3.00
(163) Wilhoit	10.00	5.00	3.00
(164) Wilie	10.00	5.00	3.00
(165) Winn	10.00	5.00	3.00
(166) Wolfer	10.00	5.00	3.00
(167) Yelle	10.00	5.00	3.00
(168) Young	10.00	5.00	3.00
(169) Zeider	10.00	5.00	3.00

1922 E137 Zeenut

The 1922 Zeenuts are dated on the front, measure 1-7/8" by 3-1/8" and feature black and white photos with sepia highlights. There are 162 subjects, and four of them (Koehler, Williams, Gregg and Schneider) have been found with variations in color tones.

	NR MT	EX	VG
Complete Set:	2650.	1325.	750.00
Common Player:	10.00	5.00	3.00
(1) J. Adams	10.00	5.00	3.00
(2) S. Adams	10.00	5.00	3.00
(3) Agnew	10.00	5.00	3.00
(4) Anfinson	10.00	5.00	3.00
(5) Arlett	9.00	4.50	2.75
(6) Baldwin	10.00	5.00	3.00
(7) Barney	10.00	5.00	3.00
(8) Bell	10.00	5.00	3.00
(9) Blaeholder	10.00	5.00	3.00
(10) Bodie	12.00	6.00	3.50
(11) Brenton	10.00	5.00	3.00
(12) Bromley	10.00	5.00	3.00
(13) Brovold	10.00	5.00	3.00
(14) Brown	10.00	5.00	3.00
(15) Brubaker	10.00	5.00	3.00
(16) Burger	10.00	5.00	3.00

		NR MT	EX	VG
(17)	Byler	10.00	5.00	3.00
(18)	Canfield	10.00	5.00	3.00
(19)	Carroll	10.00	5.00	3.00
(20)	Cartwright	10.00	5.00	3.00
(21)	Chadbourne	10.00	5.00	3.00
(22)	Compton	10.00	5.00	3.00
(23)	Connolly	10.00	5.00	3.00
(24)	Cook	10.00	5.00	3.00
(25)	Cooper	10.00	5.00	3.00
(26)	Coumbe	10.00	5.00	3.00
(27)	Cox	10.00	5.00	3.00
(28)	Crandall	10.00	5.00	3.00
(29)	Crumpler	10.00	5.00	3.00
(30)	Cueto	10.00	5.00	3.00
(31)	Dailey	10.00	5.00	3.00
(32)	Daly	10.00	5.00	3.00
(33)	Deal	10.00	5.00	3.00
(34)	Dell	10.00	5.00	3.00
(35)	Doyle	10.00	5.00	3.00
(36)	Dumovich	10.00	5.00	3.00
(37)	Eldred	10.00	5.00	3.00
(38)	Eller	10.00	5.00	3.00
(39)	Elliott	10.00	5.00	3.00
(40)	Ellison	10.00	5.00	3.00
(41)	Essick	10.00	5.00	3.00
(42)	Finneran	10.00	5.00	3.00
(43)	Fittery	10.00	5.00	3.00
(44)	Fitzgerald	10.00	5.00	3.00
(45)	Freeman	10.00	5.00	3.00
(46)	French	10.00	5.00	3.00
(47)	Gardner	10.00	5.00	3.00
(48)	Geary	10.00	5.00	3.00
(49)	Gibson	10.00	5.00	3.00
(50)	Gilder	10.00	5.00	3.00
(51)	Gould	10.00	5.00	3.00
(52)	Gregg	10.00	5.00	3.00
(53)	Gressett	10.00	5.00	3.00
(54)	Griggs	10.00	5.00	3.00
(55)	Hampton	10.00	5.00	3.00
(56)	Hannah	10.00	5.00	3.00
(57)	Hawks	10.00	5.00	3.00
(58)	Henke	10.00	5.00	3.00
(59)	High (Portland)	10.00	5.00	3.00
(60)	High (Vernon)	10.00	5.00	3.00
(61)	Houck	10.00	5.00	3.00
(62)	Howard	10.00	5.00	3.00
(63)	Hughes	10.00	5.00	3.00
(64)	Hyatt	10.00	5.00	3.00
(65)	Jacobs	10.00	5.00	3.00
(66)	James	10.00	5.00	3.00
(67)	Jenkins	10.00	5.00	3.00
(68)	Jones	10.00	5.00	3.00
(69)	Kallio	10.00	5.00	3.00
(70)	Kamm	10.00	5.00	3.00
(71)	Keiser	10.00	5.00	3.00
(72)	Kelly	10.00	5.00	3.00
(73)	Kenworthy	10.00	5.00	3.00
(74)	Kilduff	10.00	5.00	3.00
(75)	Killefer	10.00	5.00	3.00
(76)	Killhullen	10.00	5.00	3.00
(77)	King	10.00	5.00	3.00
(78)	Knight	10.00	5.00	3.00
(79)	Koehler	10.00	5.00	3.00
(80)	Kremer	10.00	5.00	3.00
(81)	Kunz	10.00	5.00	3.00
(82)	Lafayette	10.00	5.00	3.00
(83)	Lane	10.00	5.00	3.00
(84)	Lazzeri	60.00	30.00	18.00
(85)	Lefevre	10.00	5.00	3.00
(86)	D. Lewis	15.00	7.50	4.50
(87)	S. Lewis	10.00	5.00	3.00
(88)	Lindimore	10.00	5.00	3.00
(89)	Locker	10.00	5.00	3.00
(90)	Lyons	10.00	5.00	3.00
(91)	Mack	10.00	5.00	3.00
(92)	Marriott	10.00	5.00	3.00
(93)	May	10.00	5.00	3.00
(94)	McAuley	10.00	5.00	3.00
(95)	McCabe	10.00	5.00	3.00
(96)	McCann	10.00	5.00	3.00
(97)	McCredie	10.00	5.00	3.00
(98)	McNeely	10.00	5.00	3.00
(99)	McQuaid	10.00	5.00	3.00
(100)	Miller	10.00	5.00	3.00
(101)	Mitchell	10.00	5.00	3.00
(102)	Mitze	10.00	5.00	3.00
(103)	Mollwitz	10.00	5.00	3.00
(104)	Monahan	10.00	5.00	3.00
(105)	Murphy (Seattle)	10.00	5.00	3.00
(106)	Murphy (Vernon)	10.00	5.00	3.00
(107)	Niehaus	10.00	5.00	3.00
(108)	O'Connell	10.00	5.00	3.00
(109)	Orr	10.00	5.00	3.00
(110)	Owen	10.00	5.00	3.00
(111)	Pearce	10.00	5.00	3.00
(112)	Pick	10.00	5.00	3.00
(113)	Ponder	10.00	5.00	3.00
(114)	Poole	10.00	5.00	3.00
(115)	Prough	10.00	5.00	3.00
(116)	Read	10.00	5.00	3.00
(117)	Richardson	10.00	5.00	3.00
(118)	Rieger	10.00	5.00	3.00
(119)	Ritchie	10.00	5.00	3.00
(120)	Ross	10.00	5.00	3.00
(121)	Ryan	10.00	5.00	3.00
(122)	Sand	10.00	5.00	3.00
(123)	Sargent	10.00	5.00	3.00
(124)	Sawyer	10.00	5.00	3.00
(125)	Schang	10.00	5.00	3.00
(126)	Schick	10.00	5.00	3.00
(127)	Schneider	10.00	5.00	3.00
(128)	Schorr	10.00	5.00	3.00
(129)	Schulte (Oakland)	10.00	5.00	3.00
(130)	Schulte (Seattle)	10.00	5.00	3.00
(131)	Scott	10.00	5.00	3.00
(132)	See	10.00	5.00	3.00
(133)	Shea	10.00	5.00	3.00
(134)	Sheehan	10.00	5.00	3.00
(135)	Siglin	10.00	5.00	3.00
(136)	Smith	10.00	5.00	3.00
(137)	Soria	10.00	5.00	3.00
(138)	Spencer	10.00	5.00	3.00
(139)	Stanage	10.00	5.00	3.00
(140)	Strand	10.00	5.00	3.00
(141)	Stumpf	10.00	5.00	3.00
(142)	Sullivan	10.00	5.00	3.00
(143)	Sutherland	10.00	5.00	3.00
(144)	Thomas	10.00	5.00	3.00
(145)	Thorpe	1000.	500.00	300.00
(146)	Thurston	10.00	5.00	3.00
(147)	Tobin	10.00	5.00	3.00
(148)	Turner	10.00	5.00	3.00
(149)	Twombly	10.00	5.00	3.00
(150)	Valla	10.00	5.00	3.00
(151)	Vargas	10.00	5.00	3.00
(152)	Viveros	10.00	5.00	3.00
(153)	Wallace	10.00	5.00	3.00
(154)	Walsh	10.00	5.00	3.00
(155)	Wells	10.00	5.00	3.00
(156)	Westersil	10.00	5.00	3.00
(157)	Wheat	10.00	5.00	3.00
(158)	Wilhoit	10.00	5.00	3.00
(159)	Wilie	10.00	5.00	3.00
(160)	Williams	10.00	5.00	3.00
(161)	Yelle	10.00	5.00	3.00
(162)	Zeider	10.00	5.00	3.00

1923 E137 Zeenut

This is the only year that Zeenuts cards were issued in two different sizes. Cards in the "regular" series measure 1-7/8" by 3", feature black and white photos and are dated 1923. A second series, containing just 24 cards (all San Francisco and Oakland players), were actually re-issues of the 1922 series with a "1923" date.

		NR MT	EX	VG
	Complete Set:	2100.	1050.	650.00
	Common Player:	10.00	5.00	3.00
(1)	Agnew (1923 photo)	10.00	5.00	3.00
(2)	Agnew (1922 photo re-dated)	20.00	10.00	6.00
(3)	Alten	10.00	5.00	3.00
(4)	Anderson	10.00	5.00	3.00
(5)	Anfinson	10.00	5.00	3.00
(6)	Arlett	9.00	4.50	2.75
(7)	Baker	10.00	5.00	3.00
(8)	Baldwin	10.00	5.00	3.00
(9)	Barney	10.00	5.00	3.00
(10)	Blake	10.00	5.00	3.00
(11)	Bodie	7.00	3.50	2.00
(12)	Brazil	10.00	5.00	3.00
(13)	Brenton	11.00	5.50	3.25
(14)	Brown (Oakland)	11.00	5.50	3.25
(15)	Brown (Sacramento)	10.00	5.00	3.00
(16)	Brubaker	10.00	5.00	3.00
(17)	Buckley	10.00	5.00	3.00
(18)	Canfield	10.00	5.00	3.00
(19)	Carroll	10.00	5.00	3.00
(20)	Cather	10.00	5.00	3.00
(21)	Chadbourne	10.00	5.00	3.00
(22)	Charvez	10.00	5.00	3.00
(23)	Cochrane	75.00	38.00	23.00
(24)	Colwell	10.00	5.00	3.00
(25)	Compton	10.00	5.00	3.00
(26)	Cook	10.00	5.00	3.00
(27)	Cooper (1923 photo)	10.00	5.00	3.00
(28)	Cooper (1922 photo re-dated)	20.00	10.00	6.00
(29)	Coumbe	10.00	5.00	3.00
(30)	Courtney	10.00	5.00	3.00
(31)	Crandall	10.00	5.00	3.00
(32)	Crane	10.00	5.00	3.00
(33)	Crowder	7.00	3.50	2.00
(34)	Crumpler	10.00	5.00	3.00
(35)	Daly (Los Angeles)	10.00	5.00	3.00
(36)	Daly (Portland)	10.00	5.00	3.00
(37)	Deal	10.00	5.00	3.00
(38)	Doyle	10.00	5.00	3.00
(39)	Duchalsky	10.00	5.00	3.00
(40)	Eckert	10.00	5.00	3.00
(41)	Eldred	10.00	5.00	3.00
(42)	Eley	10.00	5.00	3.00
(43)	Eller	11.00	5.50	3.25
(44)	Ellison (1923 photo)	10.00	5.00	3.00
(45)	Ellison (1922 photo re-dated)	20.00	10.00	6.00
(46)	Essick	10.00	5.00	3.00
(47)	Fittery	10.00	5.00	3.00
(48)	Flashkamper	10.00	5.00	3.00
(49)	Frederick	10.00	5.00	3.00
(50)	French	10.00	5.00	3.00
(51)	Geary (1923 photo)	10.00	5.00	3.00
(52)	Geary (1922 photo re-dated)	20.00	10.00	6.00
(53)	Gilder	10.00	5.00	3.00
(54)	Golvin	10.00	5.00	3.00
(55)	Gorman	10.00	5.00	3.00
(56)	Gould	10.00	5.00	3.00
(57)	Gressett	10.00	5.00	3.00
(58)	Griggs	10.00	5.00	3.00
(59)	Hannah (Los Angeles)	10.00	5.00	3.00
(60)	Hannah (Vernon)	10.00	5.00	3.00
(61)	Hemingway	10.00	5.00	3.00
(62)	Hendryx	10.00	5.00	3.00
(63)	High	10.00	5.00	3.00
(64)	H. High	10.00	5.00	3.00
(65)	Hodge	10.00	5.00	3.00
(66)	Hood	10.00	5.00	3.00
(67)	Houghs	10.00	5.00	3.00
(68)	Howard (1923 photo)	10.00	5.00	3.00
(69)	Howard (1922 photo re-dated)	20.00	10.00	6.00
(70)	Del Howard	10.00	5.00	3.00
(71)	Jacobs	10.00	5.00	3.00
(72)	James	10.00	5.00	3.00
(73)	Johnson	10.00	5.00	3.00
(74)	Johnston	10.00	5.00	3.00
(75)	Jolly	10.00	5.00	3.00
(76)	Jones (Los Angeles)	10.00	5.00	3.00
(77)	Jones (Oakland)	11.00	5.50	3.25
(78)	Jones (Portland)	10.00	5.00	3.00
(79)	Kallio	10.00	5.00	3.00
(80)	Kearns	10.00	5.00	3.00
(81)	Keiser	10.00	5.00	3.00
(82)	Keller	10.00	5.00	3.00
(83)	Kelly (San Francisco)	10.00	5.00	3.00
(84)	Kelly (Seattle)	10.00	5.00	3.00
(85)	Kenna	10.00	5.00	3.00
(86)	Kilduff	10.00	5.00	3.00
(87)	Killifer	10.00	5.00	3.00
(88)	King	10.00	5.00	3.00
(89)	Knight (1923 photo)	10.00	5.00	3.00
(90)	Knight (1922 photo re-dated)	11.00	5.50	3.25
(91)	Koehler	10.00	5.00	3.00
(92)	Kopp	10.00	5.00	3.00
(93)	Krause	10.00	5.00	3.00
(94)	Kremer	10.00	5.00	3.00
(95)	Krug	10.00	5.00	3.00
(96)	Lafayette (1923 photo)	10.00	5.00	3.00
(97)	Lafayette (1922 photo re-dated)	11.00	5.50	3.25
(98)	Lane	10.00	5.00	3.00
(99)	Lefevre	20.00	10.00	6.00
(100)	Leslie	10.00	5.00	3.00
(101)	Levere	10.00	5.00	3.00
(102)	Leverenz	10.00	5.00	3.00
(103)	Lewis	10.00	5.00	3.00
(104)	Lindimore	10.00	5.00	3.00
(105)	Locker	10.00	5.00	3.00
(106)	Lyons	10.00	5.00	3.00
(107)	Maderas	10.00	5.00	3.00
(108)	Mails	10.00	5.00	3.00
(109)	Marriott	20.00	10.00	6.00
(110)	Matzen	10.00	5.00	3.00
(111)	McAuley	10.00	5.00	3.00
(112)	McAuliffe	10.00	5.00	3.00
(113)	McCabe (Los Angeles)	10.00	5.00	3.00
(114)	McCabe (Salt Lake)	10.00	5.00	3.00
(115)	McCann	10.00	5.00	3.00
(116)	McGaffigan	10.00	5.00	3.00
(117)	McGinnis	10.00	5.00	3.00
(118)	McNeilly	10.00	5.00	3.00
(119)	McWeeney	10.00	5.00	3.00
(120)	Middleton	10.00	5.00	3.00
(122)	Mitchell (1923 photo)	10.00	5.00	3.00
(123)	Mitchell (1922 photo re-dated)	20.00	10.00	6.00
(124)	Mitze	11.00	5.50	3.25
(125)	Mulligan	10.00	5.00	3.00
(126)	Murchio	10.00	5.00	3.00
(127)	D. Murphy	10.00	5.00	3.00
(128)	R. Murphy	10.00	5.00	3.00
(129)	Noack	10.00	5.00	3.00
(130)	O'Brien	10.00	5.00	3.00
(131)	Onslow	10.00	5.00	3.00
(132)	Orr	10.00	5.00	3.00
(133)	Pearce	10.00	5.00	3.00
(134)	Penner	10.00	5.00	3.00
(135)	Peters	10.00	5.00	3.00
(136)	Pick	10.00	5.00	3.00
(137)	Pigg	10.00	5.00	3.00
(138)	Plummer	10.00	5.00	3.00
(139)	Ponder	10.00	5.00	3.00
(140)	Poole	10.00	5.00	3.00
(141)	Ramage	10.00	5.00	3.00
(142)	Read (1923 photo)	10.00	5.00	3.00
(143)	Read (1922 photo re-dated)	20.00	10.00	6.00
(144)	Rhyne	10.00	5.00	3.00
(145)	Ritchie	10.00	5.00	3.00
(146)	Robertson	10.00	5.00	3.00
(147)	Rohwer (Sacramento)	10.00	5.00	3.00
(148)	Rohwer (Seattle)	10.00	5.00	3.00
(149)	Ryan	10.00	5.00	3.00
(150)	Sawyer	10.00	5.00	3.00
(151)	Schang	10.00	5.00	3.00
(152)	Schneider	10.00	5.00	3.00
(153)	Schroeder	10.00	5.00	3.00
(154)	Scott	10.00	5.00	3.00
(155)	See	20.00	10.00	6.00
(156)	Shea	10.00	5.00	3.00
(157)	M. Shea	10.00	5.00	3.00
(158)	Spec Shea	10.00	5.00	3.00
(159)	Sheehan	10.00	5.00	3.00
(160)	Shellenback	10.00	5.00	3.00
(161)	Siglin	10.00	5.00	3.00
(162)	Singleton	10.00	5.00	3.00
(163)	Smith	10.00	5.00	3.00
(164)	M.H. Smith	10.00	5.00	3.00
(165)	Stanton	10.00	5.00	3.00
(166)	Strand	10.00	5.00	3.00
(167)	Stumpf	10.00	5.00	3.00
(168)	Sutherland	10.00	5.00	3.00
(169)	Tesar	10.00	5.00	3.00
(170)	Thomas (Los Angeles)	10.00	5.00	3.00
(171)	Thomas (Oakland)	10.00	5.00	3.00
(172)	Tobin	10.00	5.00	3.00
(173)	Twombly	10.00	5.00	3.00
(174)	Valla	10.00	5.00	3.00
(175)	Vargas	11.00	5.50	3.25
(176)	Vitt	10.00	5.00	3.00

	NR MT	EX	VG
(177) Wallace	10.00	5.00	3.00
(178) Walsh (San Francisco)	10.00	5.00	3.00
(179) Walsh (Seattle)	10.00	5.00	3.00
(180) Waner	75.00	38.00	23.00
(181) Wells (Oakland)	10.00	5.00	3.00
(182) Wells (San Francisco)	11.00	5.50	3.25
(183) Welsh	10.00	5.00	3.00
(184) Wilhoit	10.00	5.00	3.00
(185) Wilie (1923 photo)	10.00	5.00	3.00
(186) Wilie (1922 photo re-dated)	11.00	5.50	3.25
(187) Williams	10.00	5.00	3.00
(188) Witzel	10.00	5.00	3.00
(189) Wolfer	10.00	5.00	3.00
(190) Wolverton	10.00	5.00	3.00
(191) Yarrison	10.00	5.00	3.00
(192) Yaryan	10.00	5.00	3.00
(193) Yelle (1923 photo)	10.00	5.00	3.00
(194) Yelle (1922 photo re-dated)	11.00	5.50	3.25
(195) Yellowhorse	9.00	4.50	2.75
(196) Zeider	10.00	5.00	3.00
(1210) Miller			

1924 E137 Zeenut

Zeenut cards in 1924 and 1925 measure 1-3/4" by 2-7/8" and display the date on the front. The cards include a full photographic background. There are 144 subjects known in the 1924 series and 162 known for 1925.

	NR MT	EX	VG
Complete Set:	1500.	750.00	450.00
Common Player:	10.00	5.00	3.00

	NR MT	EX	VG
(1) Adams	10.00	5.00	3.00
(2) Agnew	10.00	5.00	3.00
(3) Arlett	9.00	4.50	2.75
(4) Baker	10.00	5.00	3.00
(5) E. Baldwin	10.00	5.00	3.00
(6) T. Baldwin	10.00	5.00	3.00
(7) Beck	10.00	5.00	3.00
(8) Benton	10.00	5.00	3.00
(9) Bernard	10.00	5.00	3.00
(10) Bigbee	10.00	5.00	3.00
(11) Billings	10.00	5.00	3.00
(12) Blakesly	10.00	5.00	3.00
(13) Brady	10.00	5.00	3.00
(14) Brazil	10.00	5.00	3.00
(15) Brown	10.00	5.00	3.00
(16) Brubaker	10.00	5.00	3.00
(17) Buckley	10.00	5.00	3.00
(18) Burger	10.00	5.00	3.00
(19) Byler	10.00	5.00	3.00
(20) Cadore	10.00	5.00	3.00
(21) Cather	10.00	5.00	3.00
(22) Chadbourne	10.00	5.00	3.00
(23) Christian	10.00	5.00	3.00
(24) Cochrane (Portland)	75.00	38.00	23.00
(25) Cochrane (Sacramento)	10.00	5.00	3.00
(26) Cooper	10.00	5.00	3.00
(27) Coumbe	10.00	5.00	3.00
(28) Cox	10.00	5.00	3.00
(29) Crandall	10.00	5.00	3.00
(30) Daly	10.00	5.00	3.00
(31) Deal	10.00	5.00	3.00
(32) Distel	10.00	5.00	3.00
(33) Durst	10.00	5.00	3.00
(34) Eckert	10.00	5.00	3.00
(35) Eldred	10.00	5.00	3.00
(36) Ellison	10.00	5.00	3.00
(37) Essick	10.00	5.00	3.00
(38) Flashkamper	10.00	5.00	3.00
(39) Foster	10.00	5.00	3.00
(40) Fredericks	10.00	5.00	3.00
(41) Geary	10.00	5.00	3.00
(42) Goebel	10.00	5.00	3.00
(43) Golvin	10.00	5.00	3.00
(44) Gorman	10.00	5.00	3.00
(45) Gould	10.00	5.00	3.00
(46) Gressett	10.00	5.00	3.00
(47) Griffin (San Francisco)	10.00	5.00	3.00
(48) Griffin (Vernon)	10.00	5.00	3.00
(49) Guisto	10.00	5.00	3.00
(50) Gunther	10.00	5.00	3.00
(51) Hall	10.00	5.00	3.00
(52) Hannah	10.00	5.00	3.00
(53) Hendryx	10.00	5.00	3.00
(54) High	10.00	5.00	3.00
(55) Hodge	10.00	5.00	3.00
(56) Hood	10.00	5.00	3.00
(57) Ivan Howard	10.00	5.00	3.00
(58) Hughes (Los Angeles)	10.00	5.00	3.00
(59) Hughes (Sacramento)	10.00	5.00	3.00
(60) Jacobs	10.00	5.00	3.00
(61) James	10.00	5.00	3.00
(62) Jenkins	10.00	5.00	3.00
(63) Johnson	10.00	5.00	3.00
(64) Jones	10.00	5.00	3.00
(65) Keck	10.00	5.00	3.00
(66) Kelley	10.00	5.00	3.00
(67) Kenworthy	10.00	5.00	3.00
(68) Kilduff	10.00	5.00	3.00
(69) Killifer	10.00	5.00	3.00
(70) Kimmick	10.00	5.00	3.00
(71) Kopp	10.00	5.00	3.00
(72) Krause	10.00	5.00	3.00
(73) Krug	10.00	5.00	3.00
(74) Kunz	10.00	5.00	3.00
(75) Lafayette	10.00	5.00	3.00
(76) Lennon	10.00	5.00	3.00
(77) Leptich	10.00	5.00	3.00
(78) Leslie	10.00	5.00	3.00
(79) Leverenz	10.00	5.00	3.00
(80) Lewis	10.00	5.00	3.00
(81) Maderas	10.00	5.00	3.00
(82) Mails	10.00	5.00	3.00
(83) McAuley	10.00	5.00	3.00
(84) McCann	10.00	5.00	3.00
(85) McDowell	10.00	5.00	3.00
(86) McNeely	10.00	5.00	3.00
(87) Menosky	10.00	5.00	3.00
(88) Meyers	10.00	5.00	3.00
(89) Miller	10.00	5.00	3.00
(90) Mitchell	10.00	5.00	3.00
(91) Mulligan	10.00	5.00	3.00
(92) D. Murphy	10.00	5.00	3.00
(93) R. Murphy	10.00	5.00	3.00
(94) Osborne	10.00	5.00	3.00
(95) Paynter	10.00	5.00	3.00
(96) Penner	10.00	5.00	3.00
(97) Peters (Sacramento)	10.00	5.00	3.00
(98) Peters (Salt Lake)	10.00	5.00	3.00
(99) Pick	10.00	5.00	3.00
(100) Pillette	10.00	5.00	3.00
(101) Poole	10.00	5.00	3.00
(102) Prough	10.00	5.00	3.00
(103) Querry	10.00	5.00	3.00
(104) Read	10.00	5.00	3.00
(105) Rhyne	10.00	5.00	3.00
(106) Ritchie	10.00	5.00	3.00
(107) Root	12.00	6.00	3.50
(108) Rowher	10.00	5.00	3.00
(109) Schang	10.00	5.00	3.00
(110) Schneider	10.00	5.00	3.00
(111) Schorr	10.00	5.00	3.00
(112) Schroeder	10.00	5.00	3.00
(113) Scott	10.00	5.00	3.00
(114) Sellers	10.00	5.00	3.00
(115) "Speck" Shay	10.00	5.00	3.00
(116) Shea (Sacramento)	10.00	5.00	3.00
(117) Shea (San Francisco)	10.00	5.00	3.00
(118) Shellenback	10.00	5.00	3.00
(119) Siebold	10.00	5.00	3.00
(120) Siglin	10.00	5.00	3.00
(121) Slade	10.00	5.00	3.00
(122) Smith (Sacramento)	10.00	5.00	3.00
(123) Smith (San Francisco)	10.00	5.00	3.00
(124) Stanton	10.00	5.00	3.00
(125) Tanner	10.00	5.00	3.00
(126) Twomley	10.00	5.00	3.00
(127) Valla	10.00	5.00	3.00
(128) Vargas	10.00	5.00	3.00
(129) Vines	10.00	5.00	3.00
(130) Vitt	10.00	5.00	3.00
(131) Wallace	10.00	5.00	3.00
(132) Walsh	10.00	5.00	3.00
(133) Waner	75.00	38.00	23.00
(134) Warner (fielding)	10.00	5.00	3.00
(135) Warner (throwing)	10.00	5.00	3.00
(136) Welsh	10.00	5.00	3.00
(137) Wetzel	10.00	5.00	3.00
(138) Whalen	10.00	5.00	3.00
(139) Wilhoit	10.00	5.00	3.00
(140) Williams (San Francisco)	10.00	5.00	3.00
(141) Williams (Seattle)	10.00	5.00	3.00
(142) Wolfer	10.00	5.00	3.00
(143) Yelle	10.00	5.00	3.00
(144) Yellowhorse	9.00	4.50	2.75

1925 E137 Zeenut

	NR MT	EX	VG
Complete Set:	1700.	850.00	500.00
Common Player:	10.00	5.00	3.00

	NR MT	EX	VG
(1) Adeylatte	10.00	5.00	3.00
(2) Agnew	10.00	5.00	3.00
(3) Arlett	12.00	6.00	3.50
(4) Bagby	10.00	5.00	3.00
(5) Bahr	10.00	5.00	3.00
(6) Baker	10.00	5.00	3.00
(7) E. Baldwin	10.00	5.00	3.00
(8) Barfoot	10.00	5.00	3.00
(9) Beck	10.00	5.00	3.00
(10) Becker	10.00	5.00	3.00
(11) Blakesley	10.00	5.00	3.00
(12) Boehler	10.00	5.00	3.00
(13) Brady	10.00	5.00	3.00
(14) Brandt	10.00	5.00	3.00
(15) Bratcher	10.00	5.00	3.00
(16) Brazil	10.00	5.00	3.00
(17) Brower	10.00	5.00	3.00
(18) Brown	10.00	5.00	3.00
(19) Brubaker	10.00	5.00	3.00
(20) Bryan	10.00	5.00	3.00
(21) Canfield	10.00	5.00	3.00
(22) W. Canfield	10.00	5.00	3.00
(23) Cather	10.00	5.00	3.00
(24) Chavez	10.00	5.00	3.00
(25) Christain	10.00	5.00	3.00
(26) Cochrane	10.00	5.00	3.00
(27) Connolly	10.00	5.00	3.00
(28) Cook	10.00	5.00	3.00
(29) Cooper	10.00	5.00	3.00
(30) Coumbe	10.00	5.00	3.00
(31) Crandall	10.00	5.00	3.00
(32) Crane	10.00	5.00	3.00
(33) Crockett	10.00	5.00	3.00
(34) Crosby	10.00	5.00	3.00
(35) Cutshaw	10.00	5.00	3.00
(36) Daly	10.00	5.00	3.00
(37) Davis	10.00	5.00	3.00
(38) Deal	10.00	5.00	3.00
(39) Delaney	10.00	5.00	3.00
(40) Dempsey	10.00	5.00	3.00
(41) Dumovich	10.00	5.00	3.00
(42) Eckert	10.00	5.00	3.00
(43) Eldred	10.00	5.00	3.00
(44) Elliott	10.00	5.00	3.00
(45) Ellison	10.00	5.00	3.00
(46) Emmer	10.00	5.00	3.00
(47) Ennis	10.00	5.00	3.00
(48) Essick	10.00	5.00	3.00
(49) Finn	10.00	5.00	3.00
(50) Flowers	10.00	5.00	3.00
(51) Frederick	10.00	5.00	3.00
(52) Fussell	10.00	5.00	3.00
(53) Geary	10.00	5.00	3.00
(54) Gorman	10.00	5.00	3.00
(55) Griffin (San Francisco)	10.00	5.00	3.00
(56) Griffin (Vernon)	10.00	5.00	3.00
(57) Grimes	10.00	5.00	3.00
(58) Guisto	10.00	5.00	3.00
(59) Hannah	10.00	5.00	3.00
(60) Haughy	10.00	5.00	3.00
(61) Hemingway	10.00	5.00	3.00
(62) Hendryx	10.00	5.00	3.00
(63) Herman	15.00	7.50	4.50
(64) High	10.00	5.00	3.00
(65) Hoffman	10.00	5.00	3.00
(66) Hood	10.00	5.00	3.00
(67) Horan	10.00	5.00	3.00
(68) Horton	10.00	5.00	3.00
(69) Howard	10.00	5.00	3.00
(70) Hughes	10.00	5.00	3.00
(71) Hulvey	10.00	5.00	3.00
(72) Hunnefield	10.00	5.00	3.00
(73) Jacobs	10.00	5.00	3.00
(74) James	10.00	5.00	3.00
(75) Keating	10.00	5.00	3.00
(76) Keefe	10.00	5.00	3.00
(77) Kelly	10.00	5.00	3.00
(78) Kilduff	10.00	5.00	3.00
(79) Kohler	10.00	5.00	3.00
(80) Kopp	10.00	5.00	3.00
(81) Krause	10.00	5.00	3.00
(82) Krug	10.00	5.00	3.00
(83) Kunz	10.00	5.00	3.00
(84) Lafayette	10.00	5.00	3.00
(85) Lazzeri	60.00	30.00	18.00
(86) Leslie	10.00	5.00	3.00
(87) Leverenz	10.00	5.00	3.00
(88) Duffy Lewis	15.00	7.50	4.50
(89) Lindemore	10.00	5.00	3.00
(90) Ludolph	10.00	5.00	3.00
(91) Makin	10.00	5.00	3.00
(92) Martin (Sacramento)	10.00	5.00	3.00
(93) Martin (Portland)	10.00	5.00	3.00
(94) McCabe	10.00	5.00	3.00
(95) McCann	10.00	5.00	3.00
(96) McCarren	10.00	5.00	3.00
(97) McDonald	10.00	5.00	3.00
(98) McGinnis (Portland)	10.00	5.00	3.00
(99) McGinnis (Sacramento)	10.00	5.00	3.00
(100) McLaughlin	10.00	5.00	3.00
(101) Milstead	10.00	5.00	3.00
(102) Mitchell	10.00	5.00	3.00
(103) Moudy	10.00	5.00	3.00
(104) Mulcahy	10.00	5.00	3.00
(105) Mulligan	10.00	5.00	3.00
(106) O'Doul	40.00	20.00	12.00
(107) O'Neil	10.00	5.00	3.00
(108) Ortman	10.00	5.00	3.00
(109) Pailey	10.00	5.00	3.00
(110) Paynter	10.00	5.00	3.00
(111) Peery	10.00	5.00	3.00
(112) Penner	10.00	5.00	3.00
(113) Pfeffer	10.00	5.00	3.00
(114) Phillips	10.00	5.00	3.00
(115) Pickering	10.00	5.00	3.00
(116) Piercy	10.00	5.00	3.00
(117) Pillette	10.00	5.00	3.00
(118) Plummer	10.00	5.00	3.00
(119) Ponder	10.00	5.00	3.00
(120) Pruett	10.00	5.00	3.00
(121) Rawlings	10.00	5.00	3.00
(122) Read	10.00	5.00	3.00
(123) Reese	12.00	6.00	3.50

	NR MT	EX	VG
(124) Rhyne	10.00	5.00	3.00
(125) Riconda	10.00	5.00	3.00
(126) Ritchie	10.00	5.00	3.00
(127) Rohwer	10.00	5.00	3.00
(128) Rowland	10.00	5.00	3.00
(129) Ryan	10.00	5.00	3.00
(130) Sandberg	10.00	5.00	3.00
(131) Schang	10.00	5.00	3.00
(132) Shea	10.00	5.00	3.00
(133) M. Shea	10.00	5.00	3.00
(134) Shellenbach	10.00	5.00	3.00
(135) Sherling	10.00	5.00	3.00
(136) Siglin	10.00	5.00	3.00
(137) Slade	10.00	5.00	3.00
(138) Spencer	10.00	5.00	3.00
(139) Steward	10.00	5.00	3.00
(140) Stivers	10.00	5.00	3.00
(141) Suhr	10.00	5.00	3.00
(142) Sutherland	10.00	5.00	3.00
(143) Thomas (Portland)	10.00	5.00	3.00
(144) Thomas (Vernon)	10.00	5.00	3.00
(145) Thompson	10.00	5.00	3.00
(146) Tobin	10.00	5.00	3.00
(147) Twombly	10.00	5.00	3.00
(148) Valla	10.00	5.00	3.00
(149) Vinci	10.00	5.00	3.00
(150) O. Vitt	10.00	5.00	3.00
(151) Wachenfeld	10.00	5.00	3.00
(152) Waner	75.00	38.00	23.00
(153) L. Waner	75.00	38.00	23.00
(154) Warner	10.00	5.00	3.00
(155) Watson	10.00	5.00	3.00
(156) Weinert	10.00	5.00	3.00
(157) Whaley	10.00	5.00	3.00
(158) Whitney	10.00	5.00	3.00
(159) Williams	10.00	5.00	3.00
(160) Winters	10.00	5.00	3.00
(161) Wolfer	10.00	5.00	3.00
(162) Woodring	10.00	5.00	3.00
(163) Yeargin	10.00	5.00	3.00
(164) Yelle	10.00	5.00	3.00

1926 E137 Zeenut

Except for their slightly smaller size (1-3/4" by 2-3/4"), the 1926 Zeenut cards are nearly identical to the previous two years. Considered more difficult than other Zeenuts series of this era, the 1926 set consists of 71 known subjects.

	NR MT	EX	VG
Complete Set:	1800.	900.00	550.00
Common Player:	10.00	5.00	3.00
(1) Agnew	10.00	5.00	3.00
(2) Allen	10.00	5.00	3.00
(3) Alley	10.00	5.00	3.00
(4) Averill	25.00	12.50	7.50
(5) Bagwell	10.00	5.00	3.00
(6) Baker	10.00	5.00	3.00
(7) T. Baldwin	10.00	5.00	3.00
(8) Berry	10.00	5.00	3.00
(9) Bool	10.00	5.00	3.00
(10) Boone	10.00	5.00	3.00
(11) Boyd	10.00	5.00	3.00
(12) Brady	10.00	5.00	3.00
(13) Brazil	10.00	5.00	3.00
(14) Brower	10.00	5.00	3.00
(15) Brubaker	10.00	5.00	3.00
(16) Bryan	10.00	5.00	3.00
(17) Burns	10.00	5.00	3.00
(18) C. Canfield	10.00	5.00	3.00
(19) W. Canfield	10.00	5.00	3.00
(20) Carson	10.00	5.00	3.00
(21) Christian	10.00	5.00	3.00
(22) Cole	10.00	5.00	3.00
(23) Connolly	10.00	5.00	3.00
(24) Cook	10.00	5.00	3.00
(25) Couch	10.00	5.00	3.00
(26) Coumbe	10.00	5.00	3.00
(27) Crockett	10.00	5.00	3.00
(28) Cunningham	10.00	5.00	3.00
(29) Cutshaw	10.00	5.00	3.00
(30) Daglia	10.00	5.00	3.00
(31) Danning	10.00	5.00	3.00
(32) Davis	10.00	5.00	3.00
(33) Delaney	10.00	5.00	3.00
(34) Eckert	10.00	5.00	3.00
(35) Eldred	10.00	5.00	3.00
(36) Elliott	10.00	5.00	3.00
(37) Ellison	10.00	5.00	3.00
(38) Ellsworth	10.00	5.00	3.00
(39) Elsh	10.00	5.00	3.00
(40) Fenton	10.00	5.00	3.00
(41) Finn	10.00	5.00	3.00
(42) Flashkamper	10.00	5.00	3.00
(43) Fowler	10.00	5.00	3.00
(44) Frederick	10.00	5.00	3.00
(45) Freeman	10.00	5.00	3.00
(46) French	10.00	5.00	3.00
(47) Garrison	10.00	5.00	3.00
(48) Geary	10.00	5.00	3.00
(49) Gillespie	10.00	5.00	3.00
(50) Glazner	10.00	5.00	3.00
(51) Gould	10.00	5.00	3.00
(52) Governor	10.00	5.00	3.00
(53) Griffin (Missions)	10.00	5.00	3.00
(54) Griffin (San Francisco)	10.00	5.00	3.00
(55) Guisto	10.00	5.00	3.00
(56) Hamilton	10.00	5.00	3.00
(57) Hannah	10.00	5.00	3.00
(58) Hansen	10.00	5.00	3.00
(59) Hasty	10.00	5.00	3.00
(60) Hemingway	10.00	5.00	3.00
(61) Hendryx	10.00	5.00	3.00
(62) Hickok	10.00	5.00	3.00
(63) Hillis	10.00	5.00	3.00
(64) Hoffman	10.00	5.00	3.00
(65) Hollerson	10.00	5.00	3.00
(66) Holmes	10.00	5.00	3.00
(67) Hood	10.00	5.00	3.00
(68) Howard	10.00	5.00	3.00
(69) Hufft	10.00	5.00	3.00
(70) Hughes	10.00	5.00	3.00
(71) Hulvey	10.00	5.00	3.00
(72) Hurst	10.00	5.00	3.00
(73) R. Jacobs	10.00	5.00	3.00
(74) Jahn	10.00	5.00	3.00
(75) Jenkins	10.00	5.00	3.00
(76) Johnson	10.00	5.00	3.00
(77) Jolly	10.00	5.00	3.00
(78) Jones	10.00	5.00	3.00
(79) Kallio	10.00	5.00	3.00
(80) Keating	10.00	5.00	3.00
(81) Kerr (Hollywood)	10.00	5.00	3.00
(82) Kerr (San Francisco)	10.00	5.00	3.00
(83) Kilduff	10.00	5.00	3.00
(84) Killifer	10.00	5.00	3.00
(85) Knight	10.00	5.00	3.00
(86) Koehler	10.00	5.00	3.00
(87) Kopp	10.00	5.00	3.00
(88) Krause	10.00	5.00	3.00
(89) Krug	10.00	5.00	3.00
(90) Kunz	10.00	5.00	3.00
(91) Lafayette	10.00	5.00	3.00
(92) Lane	10.00	5.00	3.00
(93) Lang	10.00	5.00	3.00
(94) Lary	10.00	5.00	3.00
(95) Leslie	10.00	5.00	3.00
(96) Lindemore	10.00	5.00	3.00
(97) Ludolph	10.00	5.00	3.00
(98) Makin	10.00	5.00	3.00
(99) Mangum	10.00	5.00	3.00
(100) Martin	10.00	5.00	3.00
(101) McCredie	10.00	5.00	3.00
(102) McDowell	10.00	5.00	3.00
(103) McKenry	10.00	5.00	3.00
(104) McLoughlin	10.00	5.00	3.00
(105) McNally	10.00	5.00	3.00
(106) McPhee	10.00	5.00	3.00
(107) Meeker	10.00	5.00	3.00
(108) Metz	10.00	5.00	3.00
(109) Miller	10.00	5.00	3.00
(110) Mitchell (Los Angeles)	10.00	5.00	3.00
(111) Mitchell (San Francisco)	10.00	5.00	3.00
(112) Monroe	10.00	5.00	3.00
(113) Moudy	10.00	5.00	3.00
(114) Mulcahy	10.00	5.00	3.00
(115) Mulligan	10.00	5.00	3.00
(116) Murphy	10.00	5.00	3.00
(117) O'Doul	40.00	20.00	12.50
(118) O'Neill	10.00	5.00	3.00
(119) Oeschger	9.00	4.50	2.75
(120) Oliver	10.00	5.00	3.00
(121) Ortman	10.00	5.00	3.00
(122) Osborn	10.00	5.00	3.00
(123) Paynter	10.00	5.00	3.00
(124) Peters	10.00	5.00	3.00
(125) Pfahler	10.00	5.00	3.00
(126) Pillette	10.00	5.00	3.00
(127) Plummer	10.00	5.00	3.00
(128) Prothro	10.00	5.00	3.00
(129) Pruett	10.00	5.00	3.00
(130) Rachac	10.00	5.00	3.00
(131) Ramsey	10.00	5.00	3.00
(132) Rathjen	10.00	5.00	3.00
(133) Read	10.00	5.00	3.00
(134) Redman	10.00	5.00	3.00
(135) Reese	12.00	6.00	3.50
(136) Rodda	10.00	5.00	3.00
(137) Rohwer	10.00	5.00	3.00
(138) Ryan	10.00	5.00	3.00
(139) Sandberg	10.00	5.00	3.00
(140) Sanders	10.00	5.00	3.00
(141) E. Shea	10.00	5.00	3.00
(142) M. Shea	10.00	5.00	3.00
(143) Sheehan	10.00	5.00	3.00
(144) Shellenbach	10.00	5.00	3.00
(145) Sherlock	10.00	5.00	3.00
(146) Siglin	10.00	5.00	3.00
(147) Slade	10.00	5.00	3.00
(148) E. Smith	10.00	5.00	3.00
(149) M. Smith	10.00	5.00	3.00
(150) Staley	10.00	5.00	3.00
(151) Statz	10.00	5.00	3.00
(152) Stroud	10.00	5.00	3.00
(153) Stuart	10.00	5.00	3.00
(154) Suhr	10.00	5.00	3.00
(155) Swanson	10.00	5.00	3.00
(156) Sweeney	10.00	5.00	3.00
(157) Tadevich	10.00	5.00	3.00
(158) Thomas	10.00	5.00	3.00
(159) Thompson	10.00	5.00	3.00
(160) Tobin	10.00	5.00	3.00
(161) Valla	10.00	5.00	3.00
(162) Vargas	10.00	5.00	3.00
(163) Vinci	10.00	5.00	3.00
(164) Walters	10.00	5.00	3.00
(165) Waner	75.00	38.00	23.00
(166) Weis	10.00	5.00	3.00
(167) Whitney	10.00	5.00	3.00
(168) Williams	10.00	5.00	3.00
(169) Wright	10.00	5.00	3.00
(170) Yelle	10.00	5.00	3.00
(171) Zaeffel	10.00	5.00	3.00
(172) Zoellers	10.00	5.00	3.00

1927 E137 Zeenut

The 1927 Zeenuts are the same size and color as the 1926 issue, except the year is expressed in just two digits (27), a practice that continued through 1930. There are 144 subjects known.

	NR MT	EX	VG
Complete Set:	1500.	750.00	450.00
Common Player:	10.00	5.00	3.00
(1) Agnew	10.00	5.00	3.00
(2) Arlett	12.00	6.00	3.50
(3) Averill	25.00	12.50	7.50
(4) Backer	10.00	5.00	3.00
(5) Bagwell	10.00	5.00	3.00
(6) Baker	10.00	5.00	3.00
(7) D. Baker	10.00	5.00	3.00
(8) Ballenger	10.00	5.00	3.00
(9) Baumgartner	10.00	5.00	3.00
(10) Bigbee	10.00	5.00	3.00
(11) Boehler	10.00	5.00	3.00
(12) Bool	10.00	5.00	3.00
(13) Borreani	10.00	5.00	3.00
(14) Brady	10.00	5.00	3.00
(15) Bratcher	10.00	5.00	3.00
(16) Brett	10.00	5.00	3.00
(17) Brown	10.00	5.00	3.00
(18) Brubaker	10.00	5.00	3.00
(19) Bryan	10.00	5.00	3.00
(20) Callaghan	10.00	5.00	3.00
(21) Caveney	10.00	5.00	3.00
(22) Christian	10.00	5.00	3.00
(23) Cissell	10.00	5.00	3.00
(24) Cook	10.00	5.00	3.00
(25) Cooper (Oakland)	10.00	5.00	3.00
(26) Cooper (Sacramento)	10.00	5.00	3.00
(27) Cox	10.00	5.00	3.00
(28) Cunningham	10.00	5.00	3.00
(29) Daglia	10.00	5.00	3.00
(30) Dickerman	10.00	5.00	3.00
(31) Dumovitch	10.00	5.00	3.00
(32) Eckert	10.00	5.00	3.00
(33) Eldred	10.00	5.00	3.00
(34) Ellison	10.00	5.00	3.00
(35) Fenton	10.00	5.00	3.00
(36) Finn	10.00	5.00	3.00
(37) Fischer	10.00	5.00	3.00
(38) Frederick	10.00	5.00	3.00
(39) French	10.00	5.00	3.00
(40) Fullerton	10.00	5.00	3.00
(41) Geary	10.00	5.00	3.00
(42) Gillespie	10.00	5.00	3.00
(43) Gooch	10.00	5.00	3.00
(44) Gould	10.00	5.00	3.00
(45) Governor	10.00	5.00	3.00
(46) Guisto	10.00	5.00	3.00
(47) Hannah	10.00	5.00	3.00
(48) Hasty	10.00	5.00	3.00
(49) Hemingway	10.00	5.00	3.00
(50) Hoffman	10.00	5.00	3.00
(51) Hood	10.00	5.00	3.00
(52) Hooper	75.00	38.00	23.00
(53) Hudgens	10.00	5.00	3.00
(54) Hufft	10.00	5.00	3.00
(55) Hughes	10.00	5.00	3.00
(56) Jahn	10.00	5.00	3.00
(57) Johnson (Portland)	10.00	5.00	3.00
(58) Johnson (Seals)	10.00	5.00	3.00
(59) Jolly	10.00	5.00	3.00
(60) Jones	10.00	5.00	3.00
(61) Kallio	10.00	5.00	3.00
(62) Keating	10.00	5.00	3.00
(63) Keefe	10.00	5.00	3.00

		NR MT	EX	VG
(64)	Killifer	10.00	5.00	3.00
(65)	Kimmick	10.00	5.00	3.00
(66)	Kinney	10.00	5.00	3.00
(67)	Knight	10.00	5.00	3.00
(68)	Koehler	10.00	5.00	3.00
(69)	Kopp	10.00	5.00	3.00
(70)	Krause	10.00	5.00	3.00
(71)	Krug	10.00	5.00	3.00
(72)	Kunz	10.00	5.00	3.00
(73)	Lary	10.00	5.00	3.00
(74)	Leard	10.00	5.00	3.00
(75)	Lingrel	10.00	5.00	3.00
(76)	Ludolph	10.00	5.00	3.00
(77)	Mails	10.00	5.00	3.00
(78)	Makin	10.00	5.00	3.00
(79)	Martin	10.00	5.00	3.00
(80)	May	10.00	5.00	3.00
(81)	McCabe	10.00	5.00	3.00
(82)	McCurdy	10.00	5.00	3.00
(83)	McDaniel	10.00	5.00	3.00
(84)	McGee	10.00	5.00	3.00
(85)	McLaughlin	10.00	5.00	3.00
(86)	McMurtry	10.00	5.00	3.00
(87)	Metz	10.00	5.00	3.00
(88)	Miljus	10.00	5.00	3.00
(89)	Mitchell	10.00	5.00	3.00
(90)	Monroe	10.00	5.00	3.00
(91)	Moudy	10.00	5.00	3.00
(92)	Mulligan	10.00	5.00	3.00
(93)	Murphy	10.00	5.00	3.00
(94)	O'Brien	10.00	5.00	3.00
(95)	O'Doul	40.00	20.00	12.00
(96)	Oliver	10.00	5.00	3.00
(97)	Osborn	10.00	5.00	3.00
(98)	Parker (Missions, batting)	10.00	5.00	3.00
(99)	Parker (Missions, throwing)	10.00	5.00	3.00
(100)	Parker (Portland)	10.00	5.00	3.00
(101)	Peters	10.00	5.00	3.00
(102)	Pillette	10.00	5.00	3.00
(103)	Ponder	10.00	5.00	3.00
(104)	Prothro	10.00	5.00	3.00
(105)	Rachac	10.00	5.00	3.00
(106)	Ramsey	10.00	5.00	3.00
(107)	Read	10.00	5.00	3.00
(108)	Reese	12.00	6.00	3.50
(109)	Rodda	10.00	5.00	3.00
(110)	Rohwer	10.00	5.00	3.00
(111)	Rose	10.00	5.00	3.00
(112)	Ryan	10.00	5.00	3.00
(113)	Sandberg	10.00	5.00	3.00
(114)	Sanders	10.00	5.00	3.00
(115)	Severeid	10.00	5.00	3.00
(116)	Shea	10.00	5.00	3.00
(117)	Sheehan (Hollywood)	10.00	5.00	3.00
(118)	Sheehan (Seals)	10.00	5.00	3.00
(119)	Sherlock	10.00	5.00	3.00
(120a)	Shinners (date is "1927")	25.00	12.50	7.50
(120b)	Shinners (date is "27")	10.00	5.00	3.00
(121)	Singleton	10.00	5.00	3.00
(122)	Slade	10.00	5.00	3.00
(123)	E. Smith	10.00	5.00	3.00
(124)	Sparks	10.00	5.00	3.00
(125)	Stokes	10.00	5.00	3.00
(126)	J. Storti	10.00	5.00	3.00
(127)	L. Storti	10.00	5.00	3.00
(128)	Strand	10.00	5.00	3.00
(129)	Suhr	10.00	5.00	3.00
(130)	Sunseri	10.00	5.00	3.00
(131)	Swanson	10.00	5.00	3.00
(132)	Tierney	10.00	5.00	3.00
(133)	Valla	10.00	5.00	3.00
(134)	Vargas	10.00	5.00	3.00
(135)	Vitt	10.00	5.00	3.00
(136)	Weinert	10.00	5.00	3.00
(137)	Weis	10.00	5.00	3.00
(138)	Wendell	10.00	5.00	3.00
(139)	Whitney	10.00	5.00	3.00
(140)	Williams	10.00	5.00	3.00
(141)	Guy Williams	10.00	5.00	3.00
(142)	Woodson	10.00	5.00	3.00
(143)	Wright	10.00	5.00	3.00
(144)	Yelle	10.00	5.00	3.00

1928 E137 Zeenut

Zeenut cards from 1928 through 1930 maintain the same size and style as the 1927 series. The 1928 and 1929 series consist of 168 known subjects, while the 1930 series has 186. There are some lettering variations in the 1930 series.

		NR MT	EX	VG
Complete Set:		1700.	850.00	500.00
Common Player:		10.00	5.00	3.00
(1)	Agnew	10.00	5.00	3.00
(2)	Averill	25.00	12.50	7.50
(3)	Backer	10.00	5.00	3.00
(4)	Baker	10.00	5.00	3.00
(5)	Baldwin	10.00	5.00	3.00
(6)	Barfoot	10.00	5.00	3.00
(7)	Bassler	10.00	5.00	3.00
(8)	Berger	10.00	5.00	3.00
(9)	Bigbee (Los Angeles)	10.00	5.00	3.00
(10)	Bigbee (Portland)	10.00	5.00	3.00
(11)	Bodie	12.00	6.00	3.50
(12)	Boehler	10.00	5.00	3.00
(13)	Bool	10.00	5.00	3.00
(14)	Boone	10.00	5.00	3.00
(15)	Borreani	10.00	5.00	3.00
(16)	Bratcher	10.00	5.00	3.00
(17)	Brenzel	10.00	5.00	3.00
(18)	Brubaker	10.00	5.00	3.00
(19)	Bryan	10.00	5.00	3.00
(20)	Burkett	10.00	5.00	3.00
(21)	Camilli	12.00	6.00	3.50
(22)	W. Canfield	10.00	5.00	3.00
(23)	Caveney	10.00	5.00	3.00
(24)	Cohen	10.00	5.00	3.00
(25)	Cook	10.00	5.00	3.00
(26)	Cooper	10.00	5.00	3.00
(27)	Craghead	10.00	5.00	3.00
(28)	Crosetti	20.00	10.00	6.00
(29)	Cunningham	10.00	5.00	3.00
(30)	Daglia	10.00	5.00	3.00
(31)	Davis	10.00	5.00	3.00
(32)	Dean	10.00	5.00	3.00
(33)	Dittmar	10.00	5.00	3.00
(34)	Donovan	10.00	5.00	3.00
(35)	Downs	10.00	5.00	3.00
(36)	Duff	10.00	5.00	3.00
(37)	Eckert	10.00	5.00	3.00
(38)	Eldred	10.00	5.00	3.00
(39)	Ellsworth	10.00	5.00	3.00
(40)	Fenton	10.00	5.00	3.00
(41)	Finn	10.00	5.00	3.00
(42)	Fitterer	10.00	5.00	3.00
(43)	Flynn	10.00	5.00	3.00
(44)	Frazier	10.00	5.00	3.00
(45)	French (Portland)	10.00	5.00	3.00
(46)	French (Sacramento)	10.00	5.00	3.00
(47)	Fullerton	10.00	5.00	3.00
(48)	Gabler	10.00	5.00	3.00
(49)	Gomes	10.00	5.00	3.00
(50)	Gooch	10.00	5.00	3.00
(51)	Gould	10.00	5.00	3.00
(52)	Governor	10.00	5.00	3.00
(53)	Graham ("S" on uniform)	10.00	5.00	3.00
(54)	Graham (no "S" on uniform)	10.00	5.00	3.00
(55)	Guisto	10.00	5.00	3.00
(56)	Hannah	10.00	5.00	3.00
(57)	Hansen	10.00	5.00	3.00
(58)	Harris	10.00	5.00	3.00
(59)	Hasty	10.00	5.00	3.00
(60)	Heath	10.00	5.00	3.00
(61)	Hoffman	10.00	5.00	3.00
(62)	Holling	10.00	5.00	3.00
(63)	Hood	10.00	5.00	3.00
(64)	House	10.00	5.00	3.00
(65)	Howard	10.00	5.00	3.00
(66)	Hudgens	10.00	5.00	3.00
(67)	Hufft	10.00	5.00	3.00
(68)	Hughes	10.00	5.00	3.00
(69)	Hulvey	10.00	5.00	3.00
(70)	Jacobs	10.00	5.00	3.00
(71)	Johnson (Portland)	10.00	5.00	3.00
(72)	Johnson (San Francisco)	10.00	5.00	3.00
(73)	Jolley	10.00	5.00	3.00
(74)	Jones (batting)	10.00	5.00	3.00
(75)	Jones (throwing)	10.00	5.00	3.00
(76)	Kallio	10.00	5.00	3.00
(77)	Keating	10.00	5.00	3.00
(78)	Keefe	10.00	5.00	3.00
(79)	Keesey	10.00	5.00	3.00
(80)	Kerr	10.00	5.00	3.00
(81)	Killifer	10.00	5.00	3.00
(82)	Kinney	10.00	5.00	3.00
(83)	Knight	10.00	5.00	3.00
(84)	Knothe	10.00	5.00	3.00
(85)	Koehler	10.00	5.00	3.00
(86)	Kopp	10.00	5.00	3.00
(87)	Krause	10.00	5.00	3.00
(88)	Krug	10.00	5.00	3.00
(89)	Lary	10.00	5.00	3.00
(90)	LeBourveau	10.00	5.00	3.00
(91)	Lee	10.00	5.00	3.00
(92)	Lombardi	50.00	25.00	15.00
(93)	Mails	10.00	5.00	3.00
(94)	Martin (Missions)	10.00	5.00	3.00
(95)	Martin (Seattle)	10.00	5.00	3.00
(96)	May	10.00	5.00	3.00
(97)	McCabe	10.00	5.00	3.00
(98)	McCrea	10.00	5.00	3.00
(99)	McDaniel	10.00	5.00	3.00
(100)	McLaughlin	10.00	5.00	3.00
(101)	McNulty	10.00	5.00	3.00
(102)	Mellano	10.00	5.00	3.00
(103)	Muesel (Meusel)	9.00	4.50	2.75
(104)	Middleton	10.00	5.00	3.00
(105)	Mishkin	10.00	5.00	3.00
(106)	Mitchell	10.00	5.00	3.00
(107)	Monroe	10.00	5.00	3.00
(108)	Moudy	10.00	5.00	3.00
(109)	Mulcahy	10.00	5.00	3.00
(110)	Muller	10.00	5.00	3.00
(111)	Mulligan	10.00	5.00	3.00
(112)	W. Murphy	10.00	5.00	3.00
(113)	Nance	10.00	5.00	3.00
(114)	Nelson	10.00	5.00	3.00
(115)	Osborn	10.00	5.00	3.00
(116)	Osborne	10.00	5.00	3.00
(117)	Parker	10.00	5.00	3.00
(118)	Peters	10.00	5.00	3.00
(119)	Pillette	10.00	5.00	3.00
(120)	Pinelli	10.00	5.00	3.00
(121)	Plitt	10.00	5.00	3.00
(122)	Ponder	10.00	5.00	3.00
(123)	Rachac	10.00	5.00	3.00
(124)	Read	10.00	5.00	3.00
(125)	Reed	10.00	5.00	3.00
(126)	Reese	12.00	6.00	3.50
(127)	Rego	10.00	5.00	3.00
(128)	Rhodes	10.00	5.00	3.00
(129)	Rhyne	10.00	5.00	3.00
(130)	Rodda	10.00	5.00	3.00
(131)	Rohwer	10.00	5.00	3.00
(132)	Rose	10.00	5.00	3.00
(133)	Roth	10.00	5.00	3.00
(134)	Ruble	10.00	5.00	3.00
(135)	Ryan	10.00	5.00	3.00
(136)	Sandberg	10.00	5.00	3.00
(137)	Schulmerich	10.00	5.00	3.00
(138)	Severeid	10.00	5.00	3.00
(139)	Shea	10.00	5.00	3.00
(140)	Sheely	10.00	5.00	3.00
(141)	Shellenback	10.00	5.00	3.00
(142)	Sherlock	10.00	5.00	3.00
(143)	Sigafoos	10.00	5.00	3.00
(144)	Singleton	10.00	5.00	3.00
(145)	Slade	10.00	5.00	3.00
(146)	Smith	10.00	5.00	3.00
(147)	Sprinz	10.00	5.00	3.00
(148)	Staley	10.00	5.00	3.00
(149)	Suhr	10.00	5.00	3.00
(150)	Sunseri	10.00	5.00	3.00
(151)	Swanson	10.00	5.00	3.00
(152)	Sweeney	10.00	5.00	3.00
(153)	Teachout	10.00	5.00	3.00
(154)	Twombly	10.00	5.00	3.00
(155)	Vargas	10.00	5.00	3.00
(156)	Vinci	10.00	5.00	3.00
(157)	Vitt	10.00	5.00	3.00
(158)	Warhop	10.00	5.00	3.00
(159)	Weathersby	10.00	5.00	3.00
(160)	Weiss	10.00	5.00	3.00
(161)	Welch	10.00	5.00	3.00
(162)	Wera	10.00	5.00	3.00
(163)	Wetzel	10.00	5.00	3.00
(164)	Whitney	10.00	5.00	3.00
(165)	Williams	10.00	5.00	3.00
(166)	Wilson	10.00	5.00	3.00
(167)	Wolfer	10.00	5.00	3.00
(168)	Yerkes	10.00	5.00	3.00

1929 E137 Zeenut

		NR MT	EX	VG
Complete Set:		1700.	850.00	500.00
Common Player:		10.00	5.00	3.00
(1)	Albert	10.00	5.00	3.00
(2)	Almada	10.00	5.00	3.00
(3)	Anderson	10.00	5.00	3.00
(4)	Anton	10.00	5.00	3.00
(5)	Backer	10.00	5.00	3.00
(6)	Baker	10.00	5.00	3.00
(7)	Baldwin	10.00	5.00	3.00
(8)	Barbee	10.00	5.00	3.00
(9)	Barfoot	10.00	5.00	3.00
(10)	Bassler	10.00	5.00	3.00
(11)	Bates	10.00	5.00	3.00
(12)	Berger	10.00	5.00	3.00
(13)	Boehler	10.00	5.00	3.00
(14)	Boone	10.00	5.00	3.00
(15)	Borreani	10.00	5.00	3.00
(16)	Brenzel	10.00	5.00	3.00
(17)	Brooks	10.00	5.00	3.00
(18)	Brubaker	10.00	5.00	3.00
(19)	Bryan	10.00	5.00	3.00
(20)	Burke	10.00	5.00	3.00
(21)	Burkett	10.00	5.00	3.00
(22)	Burns	10.00	5.00	3.00
(23)	Bush	10.00	5.00	3.00
(24)	Butler	10.00	5.00	3.00
(25)	Camilli	12.00	6.00	3.50
(26)	Carlyle	10.00	5.00	3.00
(27)	Carlyle	10.00	5.00	3.00
(28)	Cascarella	10.00	5.00	3.00
(29)	Caveney	10.00	5.00	3.00
(30)	Childs	10.00	5.00	3.00
(31)	Christensen	10.00	5.00	3.00
(32)	Cole	10.00	5.00	3.00
(33)	Collard	10.00	5.00	3.00
(34)	Cooper	10.00	5.00	3.00
(35)	Couch	10.00	5.00	3.00
(36)	Cox	10.00	5.00	3.00
(37)	Craghead	10.00	5.00	3.00
(38)	Crandall	10.00	5.00	3.00
(39)	Cronin	10.00	5.00	3.00
(40)	Crosetti	20.00	10.00	6.00
(41)	Daglia	10.00	5.00	3.00
(42)	Davis	10.00	5.00	3.00
(43)	Dean	10.00	5.00	3.00

		NR MT	EX	VG
(44)	Dittmar	10.00	5.00	3.00
(45)	Donovan	10.00	5.00	3.00
(46)	Dumovich	10.00	5.00	3.00
(47)	Eckardt	10.00	5.00	3.00
(48)	Ellsworth	10.00	5.00	3.00
(49)	Fenton	10.00	5.00	3.00
(50)	Finn	10.00	5.00	3.00
(51)	Fisch	10.00	5.00	3.00
(52)	Flynn	10.00	5.00	3.00
(53)	Frazier	10.00	5.00	3.00
(54)	Freitas	10.00	5.00	3.00
(55)	French	10.00	5.00	3.00
(56)	Gabler	10.00	5.00	3.00
(57)	Glynn	10.00	5.00	3.00
(58)	Gomez	50.00	25.00	15.00
(59)	Gould	10.00	5.00	3.00
(60)	Governor	10.00	5.00	3.00
(61)	Graham	10.00	5.00	3.00
(62)	Hand	10.00	5.00	3.00
(63)	Hannah	10.00	5.00	3.00
(64)	Harris	10.00	5.00	3.00
(65)	Heath	10.00	5.00	3.00
(66)	Heatherly	10.00	5.00	3.00
(67)	Hepting	10.00	5.00	3.00
(68)	Hillis	10.00	5.00	3.00
(69)	Hoffman	10.00	5.00	3.00
(70)	Holling	10.00	5.00	3.00
(71)	Hood	10.00	5.00	3.00
(72)	House	10.00	5.00	3.00
(73)	Howard	10.00	5.00	3.00
(74)	Hubbell	10.00	5.00	3.00
(75)	Hufft	10.00	5.00	3.00
(76)	Hurst	10.00	5.00	3.00
(77)	Jacobs (Los Angeles)	10.00	5.00	3.00
(78)	Jacobs (San Francisco)	10.00	5.00	3.00
(79)	Jahn	10.00	5.00	3.00
(80)	Jeffcoat	10.00	5.00	3.00
(81)	Johnson	10.00	5.00	3.00
(82)	Jolley	10.00	5.00	3.00
(83)	Jones	10.00	5.00	3.00
(84)	Jones	10.00	5.00	3.00
(85)	Kallio	10.00	5.00	3.00
(86)	Kasich	10.00	5.00	3.00
(87)	Keane	10.00	5.00	3.00
(88)	Keating	10.00	5.00	3.00
(89)	Keesey	10.00	5.00	3.00
(90)	Killifer	10.00	5.00	3.00
(91)	Knight	10.00	5.00	3.00
(92)	Knothe	10.00	5.00	3.00
(93)	Knott	10.00	5.00	3.00
(94)	Koehler	10.00	5.00	3.00
(95)	Krasovich	10.00	5.00	3.00
(96)	Krause	10.00	5.00	3.00
(97)	Krug (Hollywood)	10.00	5.00	3.00
(98)	Krug (Los Angeles)	10.00	5.00	3.00
(99)	Kunz	10.00	5.00	3.00
(100)	Langford	10.00	5.00	3.00
(101)	Lee	10.00	5.00	3.00
(102)	Lombardi	50.00	25.00	15.00
(103)	Mahaffey	10.00	5.00	3.00
(104)	Mails	10.00	5.00	3.00
(105)	Maloney	10.00	5.00	3.00
(106)	McCabe	10.00	5.00	3.00
(107)	McDaniel	10.00	5.00	3.00
(108)	McEvoy	10.00	5.00	3.00
(109)	McIssacs	10.00	5.00	3.00
(110)	McQuaid	10.00	5.00	3.00
(111)	Miller	10.00	5.00	3.00
(112)	Monroe	10.00	5.00	3.00
(113)	Muller	10.00	5.00	3.00
(114)	Mulligan	10.00	5.00	3.00
(115)	Nance	10.00	5.00	3.00
(116)	Nelson	10.00	5.00	3.00
(117)	Nevers	10.00	5.00	3.00
(118)	Oana	10.00	5.00	3.00
(119)	Olney	10.00	5.00	3.00
(120)	Ortman	10.00	5.00	3.00
(121)	Osborne	10.00	5.00	3.00
(122)	Ostenberg	10.00	5.00	3.00
(123)	Peters	10.00	5.00	3.00
(124)	Pillette	10.00	5.00	3.00
(125)	Pinelli	12.00	6.50	3.50
(126)	Pipgras	10.00	5.00	3.00
(127)	Plitt	10.00	5.00	3.00
(128)	Polvogt	10.00	5.00	3.00
(129)	Rachac	10.00	5.00	3.00
(130)	Read	10.00	5.00	3.00
(131)	Reed	10.00	5.00	3.00
(132)	Reese	12.00	6.50	3.50
(133)	Rego	10.00	5.00	3.00
(134)	Ritter	10.00	5.00	3.00
(135)	Roberts	10.00	5.00	3.00
(136)	Rodda	10.00	5.00	3.00
(137)	Rodgers	10.00	5.00	3.00
(138)	Rohwer	10.00	5.00	3.00
(139)	Rollings	10.00	5.00	3.00
(140)	Rumler	10.00	5.00	3.00
(141)	Ryan	10.00	5.00	3.00
(142)	Sandberg	10.00	5.00	3.00
(143)	Schino	10.00	5.00	3.00
(144)	Schmidt	10.00	5.00	3.00
(145)	Schulmerich	10.00	5.00	3.00
(146)	Scott	10.00	5.00	3.00
(147)	Severeid	10.00	5.00	3.00
(148)	Shanklin	10.00	5.00	3.00
(149)	Sherlock	10.00	5.00	3.00
(150)	Slade	10.00	5.00	3.00
(151)	Staley	10.00	5.00	3.00
(152)	Statz	10.00	5.00	3.00
(153)	Steinecke	10.00	5.00	3.00
(154)	Suhr	10.00	5.00	3.00
(155)	Taylor	10.00	5.00	3.00
(156)	Thurston	10.00	5.00	3.00
(157)	Tierney	10.00	5.00	3.00
(158)	Tolson	10.00	5.00	3.00
(159)	Tomlin	10.00	5.00	3.00
(160)	Vergez	10.00	5.00	3.00
(161)	Vinci	10.00	5.00	3.00
(162)	Volkman	10.00	5.00	3.00
(163)	Walsh	10.00	5.00	3.00
(164)	Warren	10.00	5.00	3.00
(165)	Webb	10.00	5.00	3.00
(166)	Weustling	10.00	5.00	3.00
(167)	Williams	10.00	5.00	3.00
(168)	Wingo	10.00	5.00	3.00

1930 E137 Zeenut

		NR MT	EX	VG
Complete Set:		1200.	600.00	360.00
Common Player:		10.00	5.00	3.00
(1)	Allington	10.00	5.00	3.00
(2)	Almada	10.00	5.00	3.00
(3)	Andrews	10.00	5.00	3.00
(4)	Anton	10.00	5.00	3.00
(5)	Arlett	12.00	6.00	3.50
(6)	Backer	10.00	5.00	3.00
(7)	Baecht	10.00	5.00	3.00
(8)	Baker	10.00	5.00	3.00
(9)	Baldwin	10.00	5.00	3.00
(10)	Ballou	10.00	5.00	3.00
(11)	Barbee	10.00	5.00	3.00
(12)	Barfoot	10.00	5.00	3.00
(13)	Bassler	10.00	5.00	3.00
(14)	Bates	10.00	5.00	3.00
(15)	Beck	10.00	5.00	3.00
(16)	Boone	10.00	5.00	3.00
(17)	Bowman	10.00	5.00	3.00
(18)	Brannon	10.00	5.00	3.00
(19)	Brenzel	10.00	5.00	3.00
(20)	Brown	10.00	5.00	3.00
(21)	Brubaker	10.00	5.00	3.00
(22)	Brucker	10.00	5.00	3.00
(23)	Bryan	10.00	5.00	3.00
(24)	Burkett	10.00	5.00	3.00
(25)	Burns	10.00	5.00	3.00
(26)	Butler	10.00	5.00	3.00
(27)	Camilli	12.00	6.00	3.50
(28)	Carlyle	10.00	5.00	3.00
(29)	Caster	10.00	5.00	3.00
(30)	Caveney	10.00	5.00	3.00
(31)	Chamberlain	10.00	5.00	3.00
(32)	Chatham	10.00	5.00	3.00
(33)	Childs	10.00	5.00	3.00
(34)	Christensen	10.00	5.00	3.00
(35)	Church	10.00	5.00	3.00
(36)	Cole	10.00	5.00	3.00
(37)	Coleman	10.00	5.00	3.00
(38)	Collins	10.00	5.00	3.00
(39)	Coscarart	10.00	5.00	3.00
(40)	Cox	10.00	5.00	3.00
(41)	Coyle	10.00	5.00	3.00
(42)	Craghead	10.00	5.00	3.00
(43)	Cronin	10.00	5.00	3.00
(44)	Crosetti	20.00	10.00	6.00
(45)	Daglia	10.00	5.00	3.00
(46)	Davis	10.00	5.00	3.00
(47)	Dean	10.00	5.00	3.00
(48)	DeViveiros	10.00	5.00	3.00
(49)	Dittmar	10.00	5.00	3.00
(50)	Donovan	10.00	5.00	3.00
(51)	Douglas	10.00	5.00	3.00
(52)	Dumovich	10.00	5.00	3.00
(53)	Edwards	10.00	5.00	3.00
(54)	Ellsworth	10.00	5.00	3.00
(55)	Falk	10.00	5.00	3.00
(56)	Fisch	10.00	5.00	3.00
(57)	Flynn	10.00	5.00	3.00
(58)	Freitas	10.00	5.00	3.00
(59)	French (Portland)	10.00	5.00	3.00
(60)	French (Sacramento)	10.00	5.00	3.00
(61)	Gabler	10.00	5.00	3.00
(62)	Gaston	10.00	5.00	3.00
(63)	Gazella	10.00	5.00	3.00
(64)	Gould	10.00	5.00	3.00
(65)	Governor	10.00	5.00	3.00
(66)	Green	10.00	5.00	3.00
(67)	Griffin	10.00	5.00	3.00
(68)	Haney	9.00	4.50	2.75
(69)	Hannah	10.00	5.00	3.00
(70)	Harper	10.00	5.00	3.00
(71)	Heath	10.00	5.00	3.00
(72)	Hillis	10.00	5.00	3.00
(73)	Hoag	10.00	5.00	3.00
(74)	Hoffman	10.00	5.00	3.00
(75)	Holland	10.00	5.00	3.00
(76)	Hollerson	10.00	5.00	3.00
(77)	Holling	10.00	5.00	3.00
(78)	Hood	10.00	5.00	3.00
(79)	Horn	10.00	5.00	3.00
(80)	House	10.00	5.00	3.00
(81)	Hubbell	10.00	5.00	3.00
(82)	Hufft	10.00	5.00	3.00
(83)	Hurst	10.00	5.00	3.00
(84)	Jacobs (Los Angeles)	10.00	5.00	3.00
(85)	Jacobs (Oakland)	10.00	5.00	3.00
(86)	Jacobs	10.00	5.00	3.00
(87)	Jahn	10.00	5.00	3.00
(88)	Jeffcoat	10.00	5.00	3.00
(89)	Johns	10.00	5.00	3.00
(90)	Johnson (Portland)	10.00	5.00	3.00
(91)	Johnson (Seattle)	10.00	5.00	3.00
(92)	Joiner	10.00	5.00	3.00
(93)	Kallio	10.00	5.00	3.00
(94)	Kasich	10.00	5.00	3.00
(95)	Keating	10.00	5.00	3.00
(96)	Kelly	10.00	5.00	3.00
(97)	Killifer	10.00	5.00	3.00
(98)	Knight	10.00	5.00	3.00
(99)	Knothe	10.00	5.00	3.00
(100)	Koehler	10.00	5.00	3.00
(101)	Kunz	10.00	5.00	3.00
(102)	Lamanski	10.00	5.00	3.00
(103)	Lawrence	10.00	5.00	3.00
(104)	Lee	10.00	5.00	3.00
(105)	Leishman	10.00	5.00	3.00
(106)	Lelivelt	10.00	5.00	3.00
(107)	Lieber	10.00	5.00	3.00
(108)	Lombardi	50.00	25.00	15.00
(109)	Mails	10.00	5.00	3.00
(110)	Maloney	10.00	5.00	3.00
(111)	Martin	10.00	5.00	3.00
(112)	McDougal	10.00	5.00	3.00
(113)	McLaughlin	10.00	5.00	3.00
(114)	McQuaide	10.00	5.00	3.00
(115)	Mellana	10.00	5.00	3.00
(116)	Miljus ("S" on uniform)	10.00	5.00	3.00
(117)	Miljus ("Seals" on uniform)	10.00	5.00	3.00
(118)	Monroe	10.00	5.00	3.00
(119)	Montgomery	10.00	5.00	3.00
(120)	Moore	10.00	5.00	3.00
(121)	Mulana	10.00	5.00	3.00
(122)	Muller	10.00	5.00	3.00
(123)	Mulligan	10.00	5.00	3.00
(124)	Nelson	10.00	5.00	3.00
(125)	Nevers	10.00	5.00	3.00
(126)	Odell	10.00	5.00	3.00
(127)	Olney	10.00	5.00	3.00
(128)	Osborne	10.00	5.00	3.00
(129)	Page	10.00	5.00	3.00
(130)	Palmisano	10.00	5.00	3.00
(131)	Parker	10.00	5.00	3.00
(132)	Pasedel	10.00	5.00	3.00
(133)	Pearson	10.00	5.00	3.00
(134)	Penebskey	10.00	5.00	3.00
(135)	Perry	10.00	5.00	3.00
(136)	Peters	10.00	5.00	3.00
(137)	Petterson	10.00	5.00	3.00
(138)	H. Pillette	10.00	5.00	3.00
(139)	T. Pillette	10.00	5.00	3.00
(140)	Pinelli	12.00	6.00	3.50
(141)	Pipgrass	10.00	5.00	3.00
(142)	Porter	10.00	5.00	3.00
(143)	Powles	10.00	5.00	3.00
(144)	Read	10.00	5.00	3.00
(145)	Reed	10.00	5.00	3.00
(146)	Rehg	10.00	5.00	3.00
(147)	Ricci	10.00	5.00	3.00
(148)	Roberts	10.00	5.00	3.00
(149)	Rodda	10.00	5.00	3.00
(150)	Rohwer	10.00	5.00	3.00
(151)	Rosenberg	10.00	5.00	3.00
(152)	Rumler	10.00	5.00	3.00
(153)	Ryan	10.00	5.00	3.00
(154)	Schino	10.00	5.00	3.00
(155)	Severeid	10.00	5.00	3.00
(156)	Shanklin	10.00	5.00	3.00
(157)	Sheely	10.00	5.00	3.00
(158)	Sigafoos	10.00	5.00	3.00
(159)	Statz	10.00	5.00	3.00
(160)	Steinbacker	10.00	5.00	3.00
(161)	Stevenson	10.00	5.00	3.00
(162)	Sulik	10.00	5.00	3.00
(163)	Taylor	10.00	5.00	3.00
(164)	Thomas (Sacramento)	10.00	5.00	3.00
(165)	Thomas (San Francisco)	10.00	5.00	3.00
(166)	Trembly	10.00	5.00	3.00
(167)	Turner	10.00	5.00	3.00
(168)	Turpin	10.00	5.00	3.00
(169)	Uhalt	10.00	5.00	3.00
(170)	Vergez	10.00	5.00	3.00
(171)	Vinci	10.00	5.00	3.00
(172)	Vitt	10.00	5.00	3.00
(173)	Wallgren	10.00	5.00	3.00
(174)	Walsh	10.00	5.00	3.00
(175)	Ward	10.00	5.00	3.00
(176)	Warren	10.00	5.00	3.00
(177)	Webb	10.00	5.00	3.00
(178)	Wetzell	10.00	5.00	3.00
(179)	F. Wetzel	10.00	5.00	3.00
(180)	Williams	10.00	5.00	3.00
(181)	Wilson	10.00	5.00	3.00
(182)	Wingo	10.00	5.00	3.00
(183)	Wirts	10.00	5.00	3.00
(184)	Woodall	10.00	5.00	3.00
(185)	Zamlack	10.00	5.00	3.00
(186)	Zinn	10.00	5.00	3.00

1931 E137 Zeenut

Beginning in 1931, Zeenuts cards were no longer dated on the front, and cards without the coupon are very difficult to date. The words "Zeenuts Series" was also dropped from the front and replaced with just the words "Coast League." Zeenut cards in 1931 and 1932 measure 1-3/4" by 2-3/4".

		NR MT	EX	VG
Complete Set:		1200.	600.00	350.00
Common Player:		10.00	5.00	3.00
(1)	Abbott	10.00	5.00	3.00
(2)	Andrews	10.00	5.00	3.00
(3)	Anton	10.00	5.00	3.00
(4)	Backer	10.00	5.00	3.00

		NR MT	EX	VG
(5)	Baker	10.00	5.00	3.00
(6)	Baldwin	10.00	5.00	3.00
(7)	Barbee	10.00	5.00	3.00
(8)	Barton	10.00	5.00	3.00
(9)	Bassler	10.00	5.00	3.00
(10)	Berger (Missions)	10.00	5.00	3.00
(11)	Berger (Portland)	10.00	5.00	3.00
(12)	Biggs	10.00	5.00	3.00
(13)	Bowman	10.00	5.00	3.00
(14)	Brenzel	10.00	5.00	3.00
(15)	Bryan	10.00	5.00	3.00
(16)	Burns	10.00	5.00	3.00
(17)	Camilli	12.00	6.00	3.50
(18)	Campbell	10.00	5.00	3.00
(19)	Carlyle	10.00	5.00	3.00
(20)	Caveney	10.00	5.00	3.00
(21)	Chesterfield	10.00	5.00	3.00
(22)	Cole	10.00	5.00	3.00
(23)	Coleman	10.00	5.00	3.00
(24)	Coscarart	10.00	5.00	3.00
(25)	Crosetti	20.00	10.00	6.00
(26)	Davis	10.00	5.00	3.00
(27)	DeBerry	10.00	5.00	3.00
(28)	Demaree	10.00	5.00	3.00
(29)	Dean	10.00	5.00	3.00
(30)	Delaney	10.00	5.00	3.00
(31)	Dondero	10.00	5.00	3.00
(32)	Donovan	10.00	5.00	3.00
(33)	Douglas	10.00	5.00	3.00
(34)	Ellsworth	10.00	5.00	3.00
(35)	Farrell	10.00	5.00	3.00
(36)	Fenton	10.00	5.00	3.00
(37)	Fitzpatrick	10.00	5.00	3.00
(38)	Flagstead	10.00	5.00	3.00
(39)	Flynn	10.00	5.00	3.00
(40)	Frazier	10.00	5.00	3.00
(41)	Freitas	10.00	5.00	3.00
(42)	French	10.00	5.00	3.00
(43)	Fullerton	10.00	5.00	3.00
(44)	Gabler	10.00	5.00	3.00
(45)	Gazella	10.00	5.00	3.00
(46)	Hale	10.00	5.00	3.00
(47)	Hamilton	10.00	5.00	3.00
(48)	Haney	9.00	4.50	2.75
(49)	Hannah	10.00	5.00	3.00
(50)	Harper	10.00	5.00	3.00
(51)	Henderson	10.00	5.00	3.00
(52)	Herrmann	10.00	5.00	3.00
(53)	Hoffman	10.00	5.00	3.00
(54)	Holland	10.00	5.00	3.00
(55)	Holling	10.00	5.00	3.00
(56)	Hubbell	10.00	5.00	3.00
(57)	Hufft	10.00	5.00	3.00
(58)	Hurst	10.00	5.00	3.00
(59)	Jacobs	10.00	5.00	3.00
(60)	Kallio	10.00	5.00	3.00
(61)	Keating	10.00	5.00	3.00
(62)	Keesey	10.00	5.00	3.00
(63)	Knothe	10.00	5.00	3.00
(64)	Knott	10.00	5.00	3.00
(65)	Kohler	10.00	5.00	3.00
(66)	Lamanski	10.00	5.00	3.00
(67)	Lee	10.00	5.00	3.00
(68)	Lelivelt	10.00	5.00	3.00
(69)	Lieber	10.00	5.00	3.00
(70)	Lipanovic	10.00	5.00	3.00
(71)	McDonald	10.00	5.00	3.00
(72)	McDougall	10.00	5.00	3.00
(73)	McLaughlin	10.00	5.00	3.00
(74)	Monroe	10.00	5.00	3.00
(75)	Moss	10.00	5.00	3.00
(76)	Mulligan	10.00	5.00	3.00
(77)	Ortman	10.00	5.00	3.00
(78)	Orwoll	10.00	5.00	3.00
(79)	Parker	10.00	5.00	3.00
(80)	Penebskey	10.00	5.00	3.00
(81)	H. Pillette	10.00	5.00	3.00
(82)	T. Pillette	10.00	5.00	3.00
(83)	Pinelli	12.00	6.00	3.50
(84)	Pool	10.00	5.00	3.00
(85)	Posedel	10.00	5.00	3.00
(86)	Powers	10.00	5.00	3.00
(87)	Read	10.00	5.00	3.00
(88)	Reese	12.00	6.00	3.50
(89)	Rhiel	10.00	5.00	3.00
(90)	Ricci	10.00	5.00	3.00
(91)	Rohwer	10.00	5.00	3.00
(92)	Ryan	10.00	5.00	3.00
(93)	Schino	10.00	5.00	3.00
(94)	Schulte	10.00	5.00	3.00
(95)	Severeid	10.00	5.00	3.00
(96)	Sharpe	10.00	5.00	3.00
(97)	Shellenback	10.00	5.00	3.00
(98)	Simas	10.00	5.00	3.00
(99)	Steinbacker	10.00	5.00	3.00
(100)	Summa	10.00	5.00	3.00
(101)	Tubbs	10.00	5.00	3.00
(102)	Turner	10.00	5.00	3.00
(103)	Turpin	10.00	5.00	3.00
(104)	Uhalt	10.00	5.00	3.00
(105)	Vinci	10.00	5.00	3.00
(106)	Vitt	10.00	5.00	3.00
(107)	Wade	10.00	5.00	3.00
(108)	Walsh	10.00	5.00	3.00
(109)	Walters	10.00	5.00	3.00
(110)	Wera	10.00	5.00	3.00
(111)	Wetzel	10.00	5.00	3.00
(112)	Williams (Portland)	10.00	5.00	3.00
(113)	Williams (San Francisco)	10.00	5.00	3.00
(114)	Wingo	10.00	5.00	3.00
(115)	Wirts	10.00	5.00	3.00
(116)	Wise	10.00	5.00	3.00
(117)	Woodall	10.00	5.00	3.00
(118)	Yerkes	10.00	5.00	3.00
(119)	Zamlock	10.00	5.00	3.00
(120)	Zinn	10.00	5.00	3.00

1932 E137 Zeenut

		NR MT	EX	VG
Complete Set:		1200.	600.00	350.00
Common Player:		10.00	5.00	3.00
(1)	Abbott	10.00	5.00	3.00
(2)	Almada	10.00	5.00	3.00
(3)	Anton	10.00	5.00	3.00
(4)	Babich	10.00	5.00	3.00
(5)	Backer	10.00	5.00	3.00
(6)	Baker	10.00	5.00	3.00
(7)	Ballou	10.00	5.00	3.00
(8)	Bassler	10.00	5.00	3.00
(9)	Berger	10.00	5.00	3.00
(10)	Blackerby	10.00	5.00	3.00
(11)	Bordagaray	10.00	5.00	3.00
(12)	Brannon	10.00	5.00	3.00
(13)	Briggs	10.00	5.00	3.00
(14)	Brubaker	10.00	5.00	3.00
(15)	Callaghan	10.00	5.00	3.00
(16)	Camilli	12.00	6.00	3.50
(17)	Campbell	10.00	5.00	3.00
(18)	Carlyle	10.00	5.00	3.00
(19)	Caster	10.00	5.00	3.00
(20)	Caveney	10.00	5.00	3.00
(21)	Chamberlain	10.00	5.00	3.00
(22)	Cole	10.00	5.00	3.00
(23)	Collard	10.00	5.00	3.00
(24)	Cook	10.00	5.00	3.00
(25)	Coscarart	10.00	5.00	3.00
(26)	Cox	10.00	5.00	3.00
(27)	Cronin	10.00	5.00	3.00
(28)	Daglia	10.00	5.00	3.00
(29)	Dahlgren	12.00	6.00	3.50
(30)	Davis	10.00	5.00	3.00
(31)	Dean	10.00	5.00	3.00
(32)	Delaney	10.00	5.00	3.00
(33)	Demaree	10.00	5.00	3.00
(34)	Devine	10.00	5.00	3.00
(35)	DeViveiros	10.00	5.00	3.00
(36)	Dittmar	10.00	5.00	3.00
(37)	Donovan	10.00	5.00	3.00
(38)	Ellsworth	10.00	5.00	3.00
(39)	Fitzpatrick	10.00	5.00	3.00
(40)	Frazier	10.00	5.00	3.00
(41)	Freitas	10.00	5.00	3.00
(42)	Garibaldi	10.00	5.00	3.00
(43)	Gaston	10.00	5.00	3.00
(44)	Gazella	10.00	5.00	3.00
(45)	Gillick	10.00	5.00	3.00
(46)	Hafey	10.00	5.00	3.00
(47)	Haney	9.00	4.50	2.75
(48)	Hannah	10.00	5.00	3.00
(49)	Henderson	10.00	5.00	3.00
(50)	Herrmann	10.00	5.00	3.00
(51)	Hipps	10.00	5.00	3.00
(52)	Hofman	10.00	5.00	3.00
(53)	Holland	10.00	5.00	3.00
(54)	House	10.00	5.00	3.00
(55)	Hufft	10.00	5.00	3.00
(56)	Hunt	10.00	5.00	3.00
(57)	Hurst	10.00	5.00	3.00
(58)	Jacobs	10.00	5.00	3.00
(59)	Johns	10.00	5.00	3.00
(60)	Johnson (Missions)	10.00	5.00	3.00
(61)	Johnson (Portland)	10.00	5.00	3.00
(62)	Johnson (Seattle)	10.00	5.00	3.00
(63)	Joiner	10.00	5.00	3.00
(64)	Kallio	10.00	5.00	3.00
(65)	Kasich	10.00	5.00	3.00
(66)	Keesey	10.00	5.00	3.00
(67)	Kelly	10.00	5.00	3.00
(68)	Koehler	10.00	5.00	3.00
(69)	Lee	10.00	5.00	3.00
(70)	Lieber	10.00	5.00	3.00
(71)	Mailho	10.00	5.00	3.00
(72)	Martin (Oakland)	10.00	5.00	3.00
(73)	Martin (San Francisco)	10.00	5.00	3.00
(74)	McNeely	10.00	5.00	3.00
(75)	Miljus	10.00	5.00	3.00
(76)	Monroe	10.00	5.00	3.00
(77)	Mosolf	10.00	5.00	3.00
(78)	Moss	10.00	5.00	3.00
(79)	Muller	10.00	5.00	3.00
(80)	Mulligan	10.00	5.00	3.00
(81)	Oana	10.00	5.00	3.00
(82)	Osborn	10.00	5.00	3.00
(83)	Page	10.00	5.00	3.00
(84)	Penebsky	10.00	5.00	3.00
(85)	H. Pillette	10.00	5.00	3.00
(86)	Pinelli	12.00	6.00	3.50
(87)	Poole	10.00	5.00	3.00
(88)	Quellich	10.00	5.00	3.00
(89)	Read	10.00	5.00	3.00
(90)	Ricci	10.00	5.00	3.00
(91)	Salvo	10.00	5.00	3.00
(92)	Sankey	10.00	5.00	3.00
(93)	Sheehan	10.00	5.00	3.00
(94)	Shellenback	10.00	5.00	3.00
(95)	Sherlock (Hollywood)	10.00	5.00	3.00
(96)	Sherlock (Missions)	10.00	5.00	3.00
(97)	Shores	10.00	5.00	3.00
(98)	Simas	10.00	5.00	3.00
(99)	Statz	10.00	5.00	3.00
(100)	Steinbacker	10.00	5.00	3.00
(101)	Sulik	10.00	5.00	3.00
(102)	Summa	10.00	5.00	3.00
(103)	Thomas	10.00	5.00	3.00
(104)	Uhalt	10.00	5.00	3.00
(105)	Vinci	10.00	5.00	3.00
(106)	Vitt	10.00	5.00	3.00
(107)	Walsh (Missions)	10.00	5.00	3.00
(108)	Walsh (Oakland)	10.00	5.00	3.00
(109)	Walters	10.00	5.00	3.00
(110)	Ward	10.00	5.00	3.00
(111)	Welsh	10.00	5.00	3.00
(112)	Wera	10.00	5.00	3.00
(113)	Williams	10.00	5.00	3.00
(114)	Willoughby	10.00	5.00	3.00
(115)	Wirts	10.00	5.00	3.00
(116)	Wise	10.00	5.00	3.00
(117)	Woodall	10.00	5.00	3.00
(118)	Yde	10.00	5.00	3.00
(119)	Zahniser	10.00	5.00	3.00
(120)	Zamloch	10.00	5.00	3.00

1933 E137 Zeenut

This is the most confusing era for Zeenut cards. The cards in all three years are nearly identical, displaying the words, "Coast League" in a small rectangle (with rounded corners), along with the player's name and team. The photos were black and white (except 1933 Zeenuts have also been found with sepia photos). Because no date appears on the photos, cards from these years are impossible to tell apart without the coupon bottom that lists an expiration date. To date 161 subjects have been found, with some known to exist in all four years. There are cases where the exact same photo was used from one year to the next (sometimes with minor cropping differences). All cards of Joe and Vince DiMaggio have their last name misspelled "DeMaggio."

		NR MT	EX	VG
Complete Set:		475.00	235.00	135.00
Common Player:		10.00	5.00	3.00
(1)	L. Almada	10.00	5.00	3.00
(2)	Anton	10.00	5.00	3.00
(3)	Bassler	10.00	5.00	3.00
(4)	Bonnelly	10.00	5.00	3.00
(5)	Bordagary	10.00	5.00	3.00
(6)	Bottarini	10.00	5.00	3.00
(7)	Brannan	10.00	5.00	3.00
(8)	Brubaker	10.00	5.00	3.00
(9)	Bryan	10.00	5.00	3.00
(10)	Burns	10.00	5.00	3.00
(11)	Camilli	12.00	6.00	3.50
(12)	Chozen	10.00	5.00	3.00

	NR MT	EX	VG
(13) Cole	10.00	5.00	3.00
(14) Cronin	10.00	5.00	3.00
(15) Dahlgren	12.00	6.00	3.50
(16) Donovan	10.00	5.00	3.00
(17) Douglas	10.00	5.00	3.00
(18) Flynn	10.00	5.00	3.00
(19) French	10.00	5.00	3.00
(20) Frietas	10.00	5.00	3.00
(21) Galan	10.00	5.00	3.00
(22) Hofmann	10.00	5.00	3.00
(23) Kelman	10.00	5.00	3.00
(24) Lelivelt	10.00	5.00	3.00
(25) Ludolph	10.00	5.00	3.00
(26) McDonald	10.00	5.00	3.00
(27) McNeely	10.00	5.00	3.00
(28) McQuaid	10.00	5.00	3.00
(29) Moncrief	10.00	5.00	3.00
(30) Nelson	10.00	5.00	3.00
(31) Osborne	10.00	5.00	3.00
(32) Petersen	10.00	5.00	3.00
(33) Reeves	10.00	5.00	3.00
(34) Scott	10.00	5.00	3.00
(35) Shellenback	10.00	5.00	3.00
(36) J. Sherlock	10.00	5.00	3.00
(37) V. Sherlock	10.00	5.00	3.00
(38) Steinbacker	10.00	5.00	3.00
(39) Stine	10.00	5.00	3.00
(40) Strange	10.00	5.00	3.00
(41) Sulik	10.00	5.00	3.00
(42) Sweetland	10.00	5.00	3.00
(43) Uhalt	10.00	5.00	3.00
(44) Vinci	10.00	5.00	3.00
(45) Vitt	10.00	5.00	3.00
(46) Wetzel	10.00	5.00	3.00
(47) Woodall	10.00	5.00	3.00
(48) Zinn	10.00	5.00	3.00

1933 E137 Zeenut Black and White

	NR MT	EX	VG
Complete Set:	4100.	2050.	1100.
Common Player:	10.00	5.00	3.00
(1a) Almada (large pose)	10.00	5.00	3.00
(1b) Almada (small pose)	10.00	5.00	3.00
(2a) Anton (large pose)	10.00	5.00	3.00
(2b) Anton (small pose)	10.00	5.00	3.00
(3) Babich	10.00	5.00	3.00
(4) Backer	10.00	5.00	3.00
(5) Ballou (black stockings)	10.00	5.00	3.00
(6a) Ballou (stockings with band, large pose)	10.00	5.00	3.00
(6b) Ballou (stockings with band, small pose)			
(7) Barath	10.00	5.00	3.00
(8) Beck	10.00	5.00	3.00
(9) C. Beck	10.00	5.00	3.00
(10) W. Beck	10.00	5.00	3.00
(11) Becker	10.00	5.00	3.00
(12) Biongovanni	10.00	5.00	3.00
(13) Blackerby	10.00	5.00	3.00
(14) Blakely	10.00	5.00	3.00
(15) Borja (Sacramento)	10.00	5.00	3.00
(16) Borja (Seals)	10.00	5.00	3.00
(17) Brundin	10.00	5.00	3.00
(18) Carlyle	10.00	5.00	3.00
(19a) Caveney (name incorrect)	10.00	5.00	3.00
(19b) Cavaney (name correct)	10.00	5.00	3.00
(20) Chelini	10.00	5.00	3.00
(21) Cole (with glove)	10.00	5.00	3.00
(22) Cole (no glove)	10.00	5.00	3.00
(23) Connors	10.00	5.00	3.00
(24) Coscarart (Missions)	10.00	5.00	3.00
(25) Coscarart (Seattle)	10.00	5.00	3.00
(26) Cox	10.00	5.00	3.00
(27) Davis	10.00	5.00	3.00
(28) J. DeMaggio (DiMaggio) (batting)	1200.	600.00	350.00
(29) J. DeMaggio (DiMaggio) (throwing)	1200.	600.00	350.00
(30) V. DeMaggio (DiMaggio)	100.00	50.00	30.00
(31) DeViveiros	10.00	5.00	3.00
(32) Densmore	10.00	5.00	3.00
(33) Dittmar	10.00	5.00	3.00
(34) Donovan	10.00	5.00	3.00
(35) Douglas (Oakland)	10.00	5.00	3.00
(36) Douglas (Seals)	10.00	5.00	3.00
(37a) Duggan (large pose)	10.00	5.00	3.00
(37b) Duggan (small pose)	10.00	5.00	3.00
(38) Durst	10.00	5.00	3.00
(39a) Eckhardt (large pose)	10.00	5.00	3.00
(39b) Eckhardt (small pose)	10.00	5.00	3.00
(40) Ellsworth	10.00	5.00	3.00
(41) Fenton	10.00	5.00	3.00
(42) Fitzpatrick	10.00	5.00	3.00
(43) Francovich	10.00	5.00	3.00
(44) Funk	10.00	5.00	3.00
(45a) Garibaldi (large pose)	10.00	5.00	3.00
(45b) Garibaldi (small pose)	10.00	5.00	3.00
(46) Gibson (black sleeves)	10.00	5.00	3.00
(47) Gibson (white sleeves)	10.00	5.00	3.00
(48) Gira	10.00	5.00	3.00
(49) Glaister	10.00	5.00	3.00
(50) Graves	10.00	5.00	3.00
(51a) Hafey (Missions, large pose)	10.00	5.00	3.00
(51b) Hafey (Missions, middle-size pose)	10.00	5.00	3.00
(51c) Hafey (Missions, small pose)	10.00	5.00	3.00
(52) Hafey (Sacramento)	10.00	5.00	3.00
(53) Haid (Oakland)	10.00	5.00	3.00
(54) Haid (Seattle)	10.00	5.00	3.00
(55) Haney	9.00	4.50	2.75
(56a) Hartwig (Sacramento, large pose)	10.00	5.00	3.00
(56b) Hartwig (Sacramento, small pose)	10.00	5.00	3.00
(57) Hartwig (Seals)	10.00	5.00	3.00
(58) Henderson	10.00	5.00	3.00
(59) Herrmann	10.00	5.00	3.00
(60) B. Holder	10.00	5.00	3.00
(61) Holland	10.00	5.00	3.00
(62) Horne	10.00	5.00	3.00
(63) House	10.00	5.00	3.00
(64) Hunt	10.00	5.00	3.00
(65) A.E. Jacobs	10.00	5.00	3.00
(66) Johns	10.00	5.00	3.00
(67) D. Johnson	10.00	5.00	3.00
(68) L. Johnson	10.00	5.00	3.00
(69) Joiner	10.00	5.00	3.00
(70) Jolly, Jorgensen	10.00	5.00	3.00
(71) Joost, Kallio	10.00	5.00	3.00
(74) Kamm	10.00	5.00	3.00
(75) Kampouris	10.00	5.00	3.00
(76) E. Kelly (Oakland)	10.00	5.00	3.00
(77) E. Kelly (Seattle)	10.00	5.00	3.00
(78) Kenna	10.00	5.00	3.00
(79) Kintana	10.00	5.00	3.00
(80) Lahman	10.00	5.00	3.00
(81) Lieber	10.00	5.00	3.00
(82) Ludolph	10.00	5.00	3.00
(83) Mailho	10.00	5.00	3.00
(84a) Mails (large pose)	10.00	5.00	3.00
(84b) Mails (small pose)	10.00	5.00	3.00
(85) Marty (black sleeves)	10.00	5.00	3.00
(86) Marty (white sleeves)	10.00	5.00	3.00
(87) Massuci (different pose)	10.00	5.00	3.00
(88) Masucci (different pose)	10.00	5.00	3.00
(89a) McEvoy (large pose)	10.00	5.00	3.00
(89b) McEvoy (small pose)	10.00	5.00	3.00
(90) McIsaacs	10.00	5.00	3.00
(91) McMullen (Oakland)	10.00	5.00	3.00
(92) McMullen (Seals)	10.00	5.00	3.00
(93) Mitchell	10.00	5.00	3.00
(94a) Monzo (large pose)	10.00	5.00	3.00
(94b) Monzo (small pose)	10.00	5.00	3.00
(95) Mort (throwing)	10.00	5.00	3.00
(96) Mort (batting)	10.00	5.00	3.00
(97a) Muller (Oakland, large pose)	10.00	5.00	3.00
(97b) Muller (Oakland, small pose)	10.00	5.00	3.00
(98) Muller (Seattle)	10.00	5.00	3.00
(99) Mulligan (hands showing)	10.00	5.00	3.00
(100) Mulligan (hands not showing)	10.00	5.00	3.00
(101) Newkirk	10.00	5.00	3.00
(102) Nicholas	10.00	5.00	3.00
(103) Nitcholas	10.00	5.00	3.00
(103a) Norbert (large pose)	10.00	5.00	3.00
(103b) Norbert (small pose)	10.00	5.00	3.00
(105) O'Doul (black sleeves)	40.00	20.00	12.00
(106) O'Doul (white sleeves)	40.00	20.00	12.00
(107) Oglesby	10.00	5.00	3.00
(108) Ostenberg	10.00	5.00	3.00
(109) Outen (throwing)	10.00	5.00	3.00
(110) Outen (batting)	10.00	5.00	3.00
(111) Page (Hollywood)	10.00	5.00	3.00
(112) Page (Seattle)	10.00	5.00	3.00
(113) Palmisano	10.00	5.00	3.00
(114) Parker	10.00	5.00	3.00
(115) Phebus	10.00	5.00	3.00
(116) T. Pillette	10.00	5.00	3.00
(117) Pool	10.00	5.00	3.00
(118) Powers	10.00	5.00	3.00
(119) Quellich	10.00	5.00	3.00
(120) Radonitz	10.00	5.00	3.00
(121a) Raimondi (large pose)	10.00	5.00	3.00
(121b) Raimondi (small pose)	10.00	5.00	3.00
(122a) Reese (large pose)	12.00	6.00	3.50
(122b) Reese (small pose)	12.00	6.00	3.50
(123) Rego	10.00	5.00	3.00
(124) Rhyne (front)	10.00	5.00	3.00
(125) Rosenberg	10.00	5.00	3.00
(126) Salinsen	10.00	5.00	3.00
(127) Salkeld	10.00	5.00	3.00
(128) Salvo	10.00	5.00	3.00
(129) Sever	10.00	5.00	3.00
(130) Sheehan (black sleeves)	10.00	5.00	3.00
(131) Sheehan (white sleeves)	10.00	5.00	3.00
(132a) Sheely (large pose)	10.00	5.00	3.00
(132b) Sheely (small pose)	10.00	5.00	3.00
(134) Sprinz	10.00	5.00	3.00
(135) Starritt	10.00	5.00	3.00
(136) Statz	10.00	5.00	3.00
(137a) Steinbacker (large pose)	10.00	5.00	3.00
(137b) Steinbacker (small pose)	10.00	5.00	3.00
(138) Stewart	10.00	5.00	3.00
(139) Stitzel (Los Angeles)	10.00	5.00	3.00
(140) Stitzel (Missions)	10.00	5.00	3.00
(141) Stitzel (Seals)	10.00	5.00	3.00
(142) Stoneham	10.00	5.00	3.00
(143) Street	10.00	5.00	3.00
(144) Stroner	10.00	5.00	3.00
(145) Stutz	10.00	5.00	3.00
(146) Sulik	10.00	5.00	3.00
(147a) Thurston (Mission)	10.00	5.00	3.00
(147b) Thurston (Missions)	10.00	5.00	3.00
(148) Vitt (Hollywood)	10.00	5.00	3.00
(149) Vitt (Oakland)	10.00	5.00	3.00
(150) Wallgren	10.00	5.00	3.00
(151) Walsh	10.00	5.00	3.00
(152) Walters	10.00	5.00	3.00
(153) West	10.00	5.00	3.00
(154a) Wirts (large pose)	10.00	5.00	3.00
(154b) Wirts (small pose)	10.00	5.00	3.00
(155) Woodall (batting)	10.00	5.00	3.00
(156) Woodall (throwing)	10.00	5.00	3.00
(157) Wright (facing to front)	10.00	5.00	3.00
(158) Wright (facing to left)	10.00	5.00	3.00
(159) Zinn	10.00	5.00	3.00

1937 E137 Zeenut

The 1937 and 1938 Zeenuts are similar to the 1933-1936 issues, except the black rectangle containing the player's name and team has square (rather than rounded) corners. Again, it is difficult to distinguish between the two years. In 1938, Zeenuts eliminated the coupon bottom and began including a separate coupon in the candy package along with the baseball card. The final two years of the Zeenuts issues, the 1937 and 1938 cards, are among the more difficult to find.

	NR MT	EX	VG
Complete Set:	1850.	925.00	525.00
Common Player:	18.00	9.00	5.50
(1) Annunzio	18.00	9.00	5.50
(2) Baker	18.00	9.00	5.50
(3) Ballou	18.00	9.00	5.50
(4) C. Beck			
(5) W. Beck	18.00	9.00	5.50
(6) Bolin	18.00	9.00	5.50
(7) Bongiavanni	18.00	9.00	5.50
(8) Boss	18.00	9.00	5.50
(9) Carson	18.00	9.00	5.50
(10) Clabaugh	12.00	6.00	3.50
(11) Clifford	18.00	9.00	5.50
(12) B. Cole	18.00	9.00	5.50
(13) Coscarart	18.00	9.00	5.50
(14) Cronin	18.00	9.00	5.50
(15) Cullop	18.00	9.00	5.50
(16) Daglia	18.00	9.00	5.50
(17) D. DeMaggio (DiMaggio)	100.00	50.00	30.00
(18) Douglas	18.00	9.00	5.50
(19) Frankovich	18.00	9.00	5.50
(20) Frazier	18.00	9.00	5.50
(21) Fredericks	18.00	9.00	5.50
(22) Freitas	18.00	9.00	5.50
(23) Gabrielson (Oakland)	18.00	9.00	5.50
(24) Gabrielson (Seattle)	18.00	9.00	5.50
(25) Garibaldi	18.00	9.00	5.50
(26) Gibson	18.00	9.00	5.50
(27) Gill	18.00	9.00	5.50
(28) Graves	18.00	9.00	5.50
(29) Guay	18.00	9.00	5.50
(30) Gudat	18.00	9.00	5.50
(31) Haid	18.00	9.00	5.50
(32) Hannah	18.00	9.00	5.50
(33) Hawkins	18.00	9.00	5.50
(34) Herrmann	18.00	9.00	5.50
(35) Holder	18.00	9.00	5.50
(36) Jennings	18.00	9.00	5.50
(37) Judnich	18.00	9.00	5.50
(38) Klinger	18.00	9.00	5.50
(39) Koenig	18.00	9.00	5.50
(40) Koupal	18.00	9.00	5.50
(41) Koy	18.00	9.00	5.50
(42) Lamanski	18.00	9.00	5.50
(43) Leishman (Oakland)	18.00	9.00	5.50
(44) Leishman (Seattle)	18.00	9.00	5.50
(45) G. Lillard	18.00	9.00	5.50
(46) Mann	18.00	9.00	5.50
(47) Marble (Hollywood)	18.00	9.00	5.50
(49) Miller	18.00	9.00	5.50
(50) Mills	18.00	9.00	5.50
(51) Monzo	18.00	9.00	5.50
(52) B. Mort (Hollywood)	18.00	9.00	5.50
(53) B. Mort (Missions)	18.00	9.00	5.50
(54) Muller	18.00	9.00	5.50
(55) Murray	18.00	9.00	5.50
(56) Newsome	18.00	9.00	5.50
(57) Nitcholas	18.00	9.00	5.50
(58) Olds	18.00	9.00	5.50
(59) Orengo	18.00	9.00	5.50
(60) Osborne	18.00	9.00	5.50

		NR MT	EX	VG
(61)	Outen	18.00	9.00	5.50
(62)	C. Outen (Hollywood)	18.00	9.00	5.50
(63)	C. Outen (Missions)	18.00	9.00	5.50
(64)	Pippin	18.00	9.00	5.50
(65)	Powell	18.00	9.00	5.50
(66)	Radonitz	18.00	9.00	5.50
(67)	Raimondi (Oakland)	18.00	9.00	5.50
(68)	Raimondi (San Francisco)	18.00	9.00	5.50
(69)	A. Raimondi	18.00	9.00	5.50
(70)	W. Raimondi	18.00	9.00	5.50
(71)	Rhyne	18.00	9.00	5.50
(72)	Rosenberg (Missions)	18.00	9.00	5.50
(73)	Rosenberg (Portland)	18.00	9.00	5.50
(74)	Sawyer	18.00	9.00	5.50
(75)	Seats	18.00	9.00	5.50
(76)	Sheehan (Oakland)	18.00	9.00	5.50
(77)	Sheehan (San Francisco)	18.00	9.00	5.50
(78)	Shores	18.00	9.00	5.50
(79)	Slade (Hollywood)	18.00	9.00	5.50
(80)	Slade (Missions)	18.00	9.00	5.50
(81)	Sprinz (Missions)	18.00	9.00	5.50
(82)	Sprinz (San Francisco)	18.00	9.00	5.50
(83)	Statz	18.00	9.00	5.50
(84)	Storey	18.00	9.00	5.50
(85)	Stringfellow	18.00	9.00	5.50
(86)	Stutz	18.00	9.00	5.50
(87)	Sweeney	18.00	9.00	5.50
(88)	Thomson	18.00	9.00	5.50
(89)	Tost (Hollywood)	18.00	9.00	5.50
(90)	Tost (Missions)	18.00	9.00	5.50
(91)	Ulrich	18.00	9.00	5.50
(92)	Vergez	18.00	9.00	5.50
(93)	Vezelich	18.00	9.00	5.50
(94)	Vitter (Hollywood)	18.00	9.00	5.50
(95)	Vitter (San Francisco)	18.00	9.00	5.50
(96)	West	18.00	9.00	5.50
(97)	Wilson	18.00	9.00	5.50
(98)	Woodall	18.00	9.00	5.50
(99)	Wright	18.00	9.00	5.50

1927 E210
York Caramel - Type I

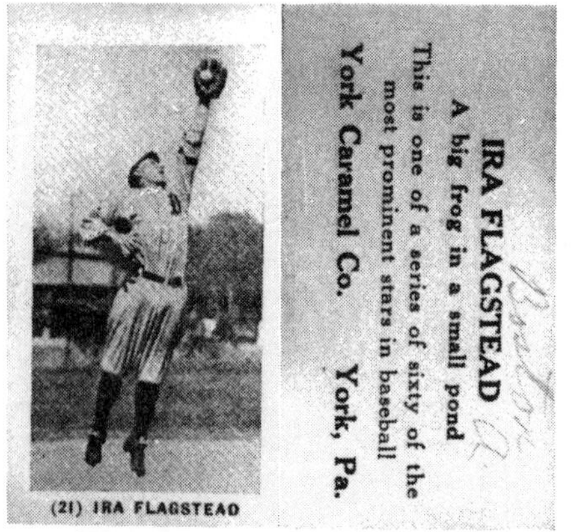
(21) IRA FLAGSTEAD
IRA FLAGSTEAD
A big frog in a small pond
This is one of a series of sixty of the most prominent stars in baseball
York Caramel Co. York, Pa.

Issued in 1927 by the York Caramel Co. of York, Pa., these black and white cards are among the last of the caramel issues. Measuring 1-3/8" by 2-1/2", they are similar in appearance to earlier candy and tobacco cards. The front of the card carries the player's name in capital letters beneath the photo preceded by a number in parenthesis. The back also lists the player's name in capital letters, along with a brief phrase describing him and the line "This is one of a series of sixty of the most prominent stars in baseball." The bottom of the cards reads "York Caramel Co. York, Pa." The set includes several variations and is designated in the ACC as E210. It is closely related to the W502 set of the same year. The E210-2s differ from the E210-1s in that the card stock is close to being glossy as opposed to the dull appearance of E210-1.

		NR MT	EX	VG
Complete Set:		5000.	2500.	1500.
Common Player:		32.00	16.00	9.50
1	Burleigh Grimes	125.00	35.00	21.00
2	Walter Reuther (Ruether)	32.00	16.00	9.50
3	Joe Duggan (Dugan)	40.00	20.00	12.00
4	Red Faber	70.00	35.00	21.00
5	Gabby Hartnett	70.00	35.00	21.00
6	Babe Ruth	1000.	500.00	300.00
7	Bob Meusel	40.00	20.00	12.00
8	Herb Pennock	70.00	35.00	21.00
9	George Burns	32.00	16.00	9.50
10	Joe Sewell	70.00	35.00	21.00
11	George Uhle	32.00	16.00	9.50
12	Bob O'Farrel (O'Farrell)	32.00	16.00	9.50
13	Rogers Hornsby	125.00	62.00	37.00
14	Pie Traynor	70.00	35.00	21.00
15	Clarence Mitchell	32.00	16.00	9.50
16	Eppa Jepha Rixey (Jeptha)	70.00	35.00	21.00
17	Carl Mays	40.00	20.00	12.00
18	Adolph Luque (Adolfo)	32.00	16.00	9.50
19	Dave Bancroft	70.00	35.00	21.00
20	George Kelly	70.00	35.00	21.00
21	Ira Flagstead	32.00	16.00	9.50
22	Harry Heilmann	70.00	35.00	21.00
23	Raymond W. Shalk (Schalk)	70.00	35.00	21.00
24	Johnny Mostil	32.00	16.00	9.50
25	Hack Wilson (photo actually Art Wilson)	70.00	35.00	21.00
26	Tom Zachary	32.00	16.00	9.50
27	Ty Cobb	675.00	337.00	202.00
28	Tris Speaker	90.00	45.00	27.00
29	Ralph Perkins	32.00	16.00	9.50
30	Jess Haines	70.00	35.00	21.00
31	Sherwood Smith (photo actually Jack Coombs)	32.00	16.00	9.50
32	Max Carey	70.00	35.00	21.00
33	Eugene Hargraves	32.00	16.00	9.50
34	Miguel L. Gonzales	32.00	16.00	9.50
35a	Clifton Heathcot (incorrect spelling)	32.00	16.00	9.50
35b	Clifton Heathcote (correct spelling)	32.00	16.00	9.50
36	E.C. (Sam) Rice	70.00	35.00	21.00
37	Earl Sheely	32.00	16.00	9.50
38	Emory E. Rigney	32.00	16.00	9.50
39	Bib A. Falk (Bibb)	32.00	16.00	9.50
40	Nick Altrock	32.00	16.00	9.50
41	Stanley Harris	70.00	35.00	21.00
42	John J. McGraw	80.00	40.00	24.00
43	Wilbert Robinson	70.00	35.00	21.00
44	Grover Alexander	80.00	40.00	24.00
45	Walter Johnson	150.00	75.00	45.00
46	William H. Terry (photo actually Zeb Terry)	90.00	45.00	27.00
47	Edward Collins	70.00	35.00	21.00
48	Marty McManus	32.00	16.00	9.50
49	Leon (Goose) Goslin	70.00	35.00	21.00
50	Frank Frisch	70.00	35.00	21.00
51	Jimmie Dykes	35.00	17.50	10.50
52	Fred (Cy) Williams	35.00	17.50	10.50
53	Eddie Roush	70.00	35.00	21.00
54	George Sisler	70.00	35.00	21.00
55	Ed Rommel	32.00	16.00	9.50
56	Rogers Peckinpaugh (Roger)	35.00	17.50	10.50
57	Stanley Coveleskie (Coveleski)	70.00	35.00	21.00
58	Clarence Gallaway (Galloway)	32.00	16.00	9.50
59	Bob Shawkey	35.00	17.50	10.50
60	John P. McInnis	75.00	16.00	9.50

1927 E210
York Caramel - Type II

(3) JOE DUGAN

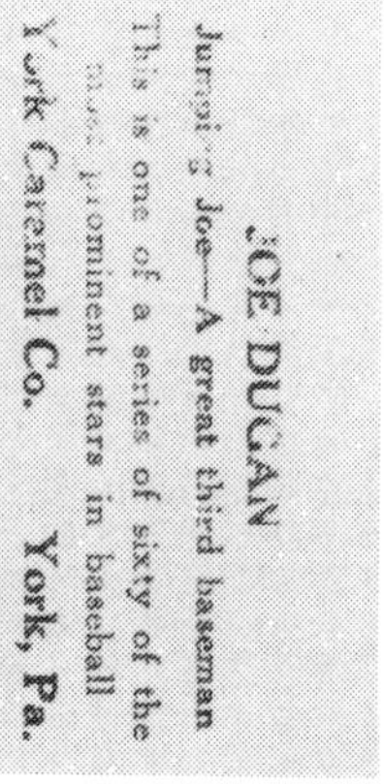
JOE DUGAN
Jumping Joe—A great third baseman
This is one of a series of sixty of the most prominent stars in baseball
York Caramel Co. York, Pa.

		NR MT	EX	VG
Complete Set:		3800.	1900.	1140.
Common Player:		50.00	25.00	15.00
1	Burleigh Grimes	125.00	45.00	27.00
2	Walter Reuther (Ruether)	50.00	25.00	15.00
3	Joe Dugan	60.00	30.00	18.00
6	Babe Ruth	1200.	600.00	360.00
12	Bob O'Farrell	50.00	25.00	15.00
14	Pie Traynor	90.00	45.00	27.00
16	Eppa Rixey	90.00	45.00	27.00
18	Adolfo Luque	50.00	25.00	15.00
22	Harry Heilmann	90.00	45.00	27.00
23	Ray W. Schalk	90.00	45.00	27.00
24	Johnny Mostil	50.00	25.00	15.00
27	Ty Cobb	800.00	400.00	240.00
29	Tony Lazzeri	75.00	37.00	22.00
31	Sherwood Smith (photo actually Jack Coombs)	50.00	25.00	15.00
32	Max Carey	90.00	45.00	27.00
33	Eugene Hargrave (Hargraves)	50.00	25.00	15.00
34	Miguel L. Gonzales	50.00	25.00	15.00
35	Joe Judge	50.00	25.00	15.00
40	Willie Kamm	50.00	25.00	15.00
43	Artie Nehf	50.00	25.00	15.00
46	William H. Terry (photo actually Zeb Terry)	110.00	55.00	33.00
51	Joe Harris	50.00	25.00	15.00
54	George Sisler	90.00	45.00	27.00
55	Ed Rommel	50.00	25.00	15.00
57	Stanley Coveleskie (Coveleski)	90.00	45.00	27.00
58	Lester Bell	75.00	25.00	15.00

1921-23 E220
National Caramel

Issued circa 1921 to 1923, this 120-card set is sometimes confused with the E121 or E122 sets, but is easy to identify because of the words

LARRY GARDNER
3rd.B. Cleveland

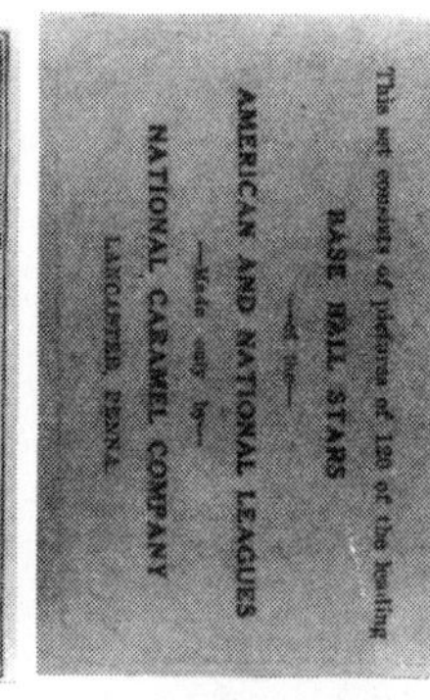
This set consists of pictures of 120 of the leading
BASE BALL STARS
of the
AMERICAN AND NATIONAL LEAGUES
Made only by
NATIONAL CARAMEL COMPANY
LANCASTER, PENNA.

"Made only by National Caramel Company" on the back. It is the only baseball card set issued by National Caramel of Lancaster, Pa. The cards measure 2" by 3-1/4" and feature black and white photos with the player's name, position and team at the bottom. In addition to the line indicating the manufacturer, the backs read "This set consists of pictures of 120 of the leading Base Ball Stars of the American and National Leagues". There are 115 different players included in the set, with five players shown on two cards each. About half of the photos in the set are identical to those used in either the E120 or E121 sets, leading to some confusion regarding the three sets.

		NR MT	EX	VG
Complete Set:		11000.	5500.	3300.
Common Player:		45.00	22.00	13.50
(1)	Charles "Babe" Adams	45.00	22.00	13.50
(2)	G.C. Alexander	150.00	75.00	45.00
(3)	James Austin	45.00	22.00	13.50
(4)	Jim Bagbyk (Bagby)	45.00	22.00	13.50
(5)	Franklin "Home Run Baker"	125.00	62.00	37.00
(6)	Dave Bancroft	125.00	62.00	37.00
(7)	Turner Barber	45.00	22.00	13.50
(8)	George Burns (Cincinnati)	45.00	22.00	13.50
(9)	George Burns (Cleveland)	45.00	22.00	13.50
(10)	Joe Bush	50.00	25.00	15.00
(11)	Leon Cadore	45.00	22.00	13.50
(12)	Max Carey	125.00	62.00	37.00
(13)	Ty Cobb	750.00	375.00	225.00
(14)	Eddie Collins	125.00	62.00	37.00
(15)	John Collins	45.00	22.00	13.50
(16)	Wilbur Cooper	45.00	22.00	13.50
(17)	S. Coveleskie (Coveleski)	125.00	62.00	37.00
(18)	Walton Cruise	45.00	22.00	13.50
(19)	Wm. Cunningham	45.00	22.00	13.50
(20)	George Cutshaw	45.00	22.00	13.50
(21)	Jake Daubert	50.00	25.00	15.00
(22)	Chas. A. Deal	45.00	22.00	13.50
(23)	Bill Doak	45.00	22.00	13.50
(24)	Joe Dugan	60.00	30.00	18.00
(25)	Jimmy Dykes (batting)	50.00	25.00	15.00
(26)	Jimmy Dykes (fielding)	50.00	25.00	15.00
(27)	"Red" Faber	125.00	62.00	37.00
(28)	"Chick" Fewster	45.00	22.00	13.50
(29)	Wilson Fewster	45.00	22.00	13.50
(30)	Ira Flagstead	45.00	22.00	13.50
(31)	Arthur Fletcher	45.00	22.00	13.50
(32)	Frank Frisch	125.00	62.00	37.00
(33)	Larry Gardner	45.00	22.00	13.50
(34)	Walter Gerber	45.00	22.00	13.50
(35)	Charles Glazner	45.00	22.00	13.50
(36)	Hank Gowdy	45.00	22.00	13.50
(37)	J.C. Graney (should be J.G.)	45.00	22.00	13.50
(38)	Tommy Griffith	45.00	22.00	13.50
(39)	Charles Grimm	50.00	25.00	15.00
(40)	Heinie Groh	45.00	22.00	13.50
(41)	Byron Harris	45.00	22.00	13.50
(42)	Sam Harris (Stanley or Bucky)	125.00	62.00	37.00
(43)	Harry Heilman (Heilmann)	125.00	62.00	37.00
(44)	Claude Hendrix	45.00	22.00	13.50
(45)	Walter Henline	45.00	22.00	13.50
(46)	Chas. Hollocher	45.00	22.00	13.50
(47)	Harry Hooper	125.00	62.00	37.00
(48)	Rogers Hornsby	200.00	100.00	60.00
(49)	Waite Hoyt	125.00	62.00	37.00
(50)	Wilbert Hubbell	45.00	22.00	13.50
(51)	Wm. Jacobson	45.00	22.00	13.50
(52)	Walter Johnson	300.00	150.00	90.00
(53)	Jimmy Johnston	45.00	22.00	13.50
(54)	Joe Judge	45.00	22.00	13.50
(55)	Geo. "Bingo" Kelly	125.00	62.00	37.00
(56)	Dick Kerr	45.00	22.00	13.50
(57)	Pete Kilduff (bending)	45.00	22.00	13.50
(58)	Pete Kilduff (leaping)	45.00	22.00	13.50
(59)	Larry Kopf	45.00	22.00	13.50
(60)	H.B. Leonard	45.00	22.00	13.50
(61)	Harry Liebold (Leibold)	45.00	22.00	13.50
(62)	Walter "Buster" Mails ("Duster")	45.00	22.00	13.50
(63)	Walter "Rabbit" Maranville	125.00	62.00	37.00
(64)	Carl Mays	50.00	25.00	15.00
(65)	Lee Meadows	45.00	22.00	13.50
(66)	Bob Meusel	60.00	30.00	18.00
(67)	Emil Meusel	45.00	22.00	13.50
(68)	J.C. Milan	45.00	22.00	13.50
(69)	Earl Neale	60.00	30.00	18.00
(70)	Albert Nehf (Arthur)	45.00	22.00	13.50
(71)	Robert Nehf (Arthur)	45.00	22.00	13.50
(72)	Bernie Neis	45.00	22.00	13.50
(73)	Joe Oeschger	45.00	22.00	13.50
(74)	Robert O'Farrell	45.00	22.00	13.50
(75)	Ivan Olson	45.00	22.00	13.50
(76)	Steve O'Neill	45.00	22.00	13.50

		NR MT	EX	VG
(77)	Geo. Paskert	45.00	22.00	13.50
(78)	Roger Peckinpaugh	50.00	25.00	15.00
(79)	Herb Pennock	125.00	62.00	37.00
(80)	Ralph "Cy" Perkins	45.00	22.00	13.50
(81)	Scott Perry (photo actually Ed Rommel)	45.00	22.00	13.50
(82)	Jeff Pfeffer	45.00	22.00	13.50
(83)	V.J. Picinich	45.00	22.00	13.50
(84)	Walter Pipp	75.00	37.00	22.00
(85)	Derrill Pratt	45.00	22.00	13.50
(86)	Goldie Rapp	45.00	22.00	13.50
(87)	Edgar Rice	125.00	62.00	37.00
(88)	Jimmy Ring	45.00	22.00	13.50
(89)	Eddie Rousch (Roush)	125.00	62.00	37.00
(90)	Babe Ruth	1100.	550.00	330.00
(91)	Raymond Schmandt	45.00	22.00	13.50
(92)	Everett Scott	50.00	25.00	15.00
(93)	Joe Sewell	125.00	62.00	37.00
(94)	Wally Shang (Schang)	45.00	22.00	13.50
(95)	Maurice Shannon	45.00	22.00	13.50
(96)	Bob Shawkey	50.00	25.00	15.00
(97)	Urban Shocker	45.00	22.00	13.50
(98)	George Sisler	125.00	62.00	37.00
(99)	Earl Smith	45.00	22.00	13.50
(100)	John Smith	45.00	22.00	13.50
(101)	Sherrod Smith	45.00	22.00	13.50
(102)	Frank Snyder (crouching)	45.00	22.00	13.50
(103)	Frank Snyder (standing)	45.00	22.00	13.50
(104)	Tris Speaker	150.00	75.00	45.00
(105)	Vernon Spencer	45.00	22.00	13.50
(106)	Chas. "Casey" Stengle (Stengel)	275.00	137.00	82.00
(107)	Milton Stock (batting)	45.00	22.00	13.50
(108)	Milton Stock (fielding)	45.00	22.00	13.50
(109)	James Vaughn	45.00	22.00	13.50
(110)	Robert Veach	45.00	22.00	13.50
(111)	Wm. Wambsgauss (Wambsganss)	50.00	25.00	15.00
(112)	Aaron Ward	45.00	22.00	13.50
(113)	Zach Wheat	125.00	62.00	37.00
(114)	George Whitted (batting)	45.00	22.00	13.50
(115)	George Whitted (fielding)	45.00	22.00	13.50
(116)	Fred C. Williams	50.00	25.00	15.00
(117)	Arthur Wilson	45.00	22.00	13.50
(118)	Ivy Wingo	45.00	22.00	13.50
(119)	Lawton Witt	45.00	22.00	13.50
(120)	"Pep" Young (photo actually Ralph Young)	45.00	22.00	13.50
(121)	Ross Young (Youngs)	125.00	62.00	37.00

1910 E221 Bishop & Co.

A very rare issue, this series of team pictures of clubs in the Pacific Coast League, was distributed by Bishop & Compnay of Los Angeles in 1910. The team photos were printed on a thin, newsprint-type paper that measures an elongated 2-3/4" by 10". Although there were six teams in the PCL at the time, only five clubs have been found - Los Angeles, San Francisco, Portland, Vernon and Oakland. The sixth team, Sacramento, was apparently never issued. The cards indicate that they were issued with five-cent packages of Bishop's Milk Chocolate and that the photos were taken by the Los Angeles Examiner. The black and white team photos are found with either a red or green background. The set has been designated E221.

		NR MT	EX	VG
Complete Set:		4500.	2250.	1350.
Common Team:		900.00	450.00	270.00
(1)	Los Angeles	900.00	450.00	270.00
(2)	Oakland	900.00	450.00	270.00
(3)	Portland	900.00	450.00	270.00
(4)	San Francisco	900.00	450.00	270.00
(5)	Vernon	900.00	450.00	270.00

1910 E222 A.W.H. Caramel

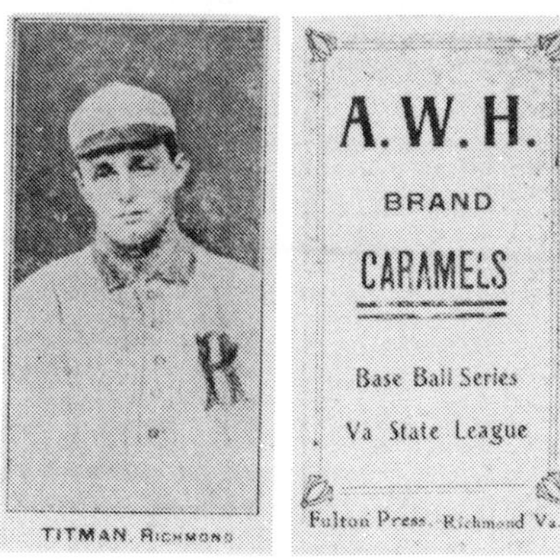

This rare set of cards picturing players from the Virginia League was issued by the A.W.H. Caramel Company in 1910. The cards measure 1-1/2" by 2-3/4" and feature player portraits in either red, black, brown, or blue and white. To date examples of 10 different cards have been found. The set carries the ACC designation of E222. The front of the card displays the player's last name and team below his photo. The back states "A.W.H. Brand Caramels" in large letters with "Base Ball Series/Va. State League" below.

		NR MT	EX	VG
Complete Set:		4500.	2250.	1350.
Common Player:		400.00	200.00	120.00
(1)	Guiheen	400.00	200.00	120.00
(2)	Hooker	400.00	200.00	120.00
(3)	Ison	400.00	200.00	120.00
(4)	McCauley	400.00	200.00	120.00
(5)	Otey	400.00	200.00	120.00
(6)	Revelle	400.00	200.00	120.00
(7)	Ryan	400.00	200.00	120.00
(8)	Shaugnessy	400.00	200.00	120.00
(9)	Sieber	400.00	200.00	120.00
(10)	Smith	400.00	200.00	120.00
(11)	Titman	400.00	200.00	120.00

1888 E223 G & B Chewing Gum

This set, issued with G&B Chewing Gum, is the first baseball card issued with candy or gum and the only 19th Century candy issue. The cards in the G&B set are small, measuring just 1" by 2-1/8". The cards are very similar in design to the August Beck Yum Yum issue (N403) and many of the photos appear have been to borrowed from that set. The player's name and position appear in thin capital letters below the photo, followed by either "National League" or "American League" (actually referring to the American Association.) At the very bottom of the card, the manufacturer, "G&B N.Y." is indicated. (Some of the "National League" cards also include the words "Chewing Gum" after the league designation.) The set has been assigned the ACC number E223.

		NR MT	EX	VG
Complete Set:		70000.	35000.	20000.
Common Player:		500.00	250.00	150.00
(1)	Cap Anson	5000.	2500.	1500.
(2)	Fido Baldwin (bat at side)	500.00	250.00	150.00
(3)	Fido Baldwin (portrait)	700.00	350.00	210.00
(4)	Lady Baldwin (Detroit)	500.00	250.00	150.00
(5)	Stephen Brady	700.00	350.00	210.00
(6)	Bill Brown (portrait)	700.00	350.00	210.00
(7)	Bill Brown (standing)	500.00	250.00	150.00
(8)	Charles Buffington (Buffinton)	500.00	250.00	150.00
(9)	Thomas Burns	700.00	350.00	210.00
(10)	John Clarkson	2000.	1000.	360.00
(11)	John Coleman	700.00	350.00	210.00
(12)	Commy Comiskey	2000.	1000.	600.00
(13)	Roger Connor (batting)	1000.	500.00	300.00
(14)	Roger Connor (portrait)	2000.	1000.	600.00
(15)	Con Daily	700.00	350.00	210.00
(16)	Tom Deasley	700.00	350.00	210.00
(17)	Dude Esterbrook	700.00	350.00	210.00
(18)	Buck Ewing (batting)	1000.	500.00	300.00
(19)	Buck Ewing (portrait)	2000.	1000.	600.00
(20)	Charlie Ferguson	500.00	250.00	150.00
(21)	Silver Flint	700.00	350.00	210.00
(22)	Charlie Getzein	500.00	250.00	150.00
(23)	Will Gleason	500.00	250.00	150.00
(24)	Frank Hankinson	700.00	350.00	210.00
(25)	Pete Hotaling	500.00	250.00	150.00
(26)	Spud Johnson	500.00	250.00	150.00
(27)	Tim Keefe (batting)	1000.	500.00	300.00
(28)	Tim Keefe (throwing)	1000.	500.00	300.00
(29)	Tim Keefe (portrait)	2000.	1000.	600.00
(30)	King Kelly (batting)	1000.	500.00	300.00
(31)	King Kelly (standing by urn)	2500.	1250.	750.00
(32)	Gus Krock	700.00	350.00	210.00
(33)	Connie Mack	2000.	1000.	600.00
(34)	Doggie Miller	500.00	250.00	150.00
(35)	Honest John Morrill	500.00	250.00	150.00
(36)	James Mutrie	700.00	350.00	210.00
(37)	Little Nick Nicoll (Nicol)	700.00	350.00	210.00
(38)	Tip O'Neill	700.00	350.00	210.00
(39)	Orator Jim O'Rourke	2000.	1000.	600.00
(40)	Fred Pfeffer	500.00	250.00	150.00
(41)	Henry Porter	500.00	250.00	150.00
(42)	Danny Richardson (batting)	500.00	250.00	150.00
(43)	Danny Richardson (portrait)	700.00	350.00	210.00
(44)	Chief Roseman	700.00	350.00	210.00
(45)	Jimmy Ryan (portrait)	700.00	350.00	210.00
(46)	Jimmy Ryan (throwing)	500.00	250.00	150.00
(47)	Little Bill Sowders (throwing)	500.00	250.00	150.00
(48)	Marty Sullivan	700.00	350.00	210.00
(49)	Billy Sunday (fielding)	900.00	450.00	275.00
(50)	Billy Sunday (portrait)	1800.	900.00	550.00
(51)	Ezra Sutton	500.00	250.00	150.00
(52)	Silent Mike Tiernan (batting)	500.00	250.00	150.00
(53)	Silent Mike Tiernan (portrait)	700.00	350.00	210.00
(54)	Big Sam Thompson	700.00	350.00	210.00
(55)	Larry Twitchell	700.00	350.00	210.00
(56)	Rip Van Haltren	700.00	350.00	210.00
(57)	Monte Ward	2000.	1000.	600.00
(58)	Smiling Mickey Welch (pitching)	1000.	500.00	300.00
(59)	Smiling Mickey Welch (portrait)	2000.	1000.	600.00
(60)	Curt Welsh (Welch)	700.00	350.00	210.00
(61)	Grasshopper Whitney	700.00	350.00	210.00
(62)	Pete Wood	500.00	250.00	150.00

1914 E224
Texas Tommy - Type I

Little is known about the origin of this 50-card set issued in 1914 and designated as E224 in the American Card Catalog. Measuring 2-3/8" by 3-1/2", the front of the cards feature sepia-toned action photos with the player's name in capital letters and his team below in parenthesis. The back carries a rather lengthy player biography and most cards, although not all, include year-by-year statistics atthe bottom. The words "Texas Tommy" appear at the top, apparently referring to the sponsor of the set, although it is still unclear who or what "Texas Tommy" was, and despite its name, most examples of this set have been found in northern California. There is also a second variety of the set, smaller in size (1-7/8" by 3"), which are borderless pictures with a glossy finish.

		NR MT	EX	VG
Complete Set:		22000.	11000.	6600.
Common Player:		200.00	100.00	60.00
(1)	Jimmy Archer	200.00	100.00	60.00

		NR MT	EX	VG
(2)	Jimmy Austin	200.00	100.00	60.00
(3)	Home Run Baker	600.00	300.00	180.00
(4)	Chief Bender	600.00	300.00	180.00
(5)	Bob Bescher	200.00	100.00	60.00
(6)	Ping Bodie	200.00	100.00	60.00
(7)	Donie Bush	200.00	100.00	60.00
(8)	Bobby Byrne	200.00	100.00	60.00
(9)	Nixey Callanan (Callahan)	200.00	100.00	60.00
(10)	Howie Camnitz	200.00	100.00	60.00
(11)	Frank Chance	650.00	325.00	195.00
(12)	Hal Chase	350.00	175.00	105.00
(13)	Ty Cobb	2000.	1000.	600.00
(14)	Jack Coombs	200.00	100.00	60.00
(15)	Sam Crawford	600.00	300.00	180.00
(16)	Birdie Cree	200.00	100.00	60.00
(17)	Al DeMaree	200.00	100.00	60.00
(18)	Red Dooin	200.00	100.00	60.00
(19)	Larry Doyle	200.00	100.00	60.00
(20)	Johnny Evers	600.00	300.00	180.00
(21)	Vean Gregg	200.00	100.00	60.00
(22)	Bob Harmon	200.00	100.00	60.00
(23)	Shoeless Joe Jackson	2000.	1000.	600.00
(24)	Walter Johnson	850.00	425.00	255.00
(25)	Otto Knabe	200.00	100.00	60.00
(26)	Nap Lajoie	750.00	375.00	225.00
(27)	Harry Lord	200.00	100.00	60.00
(28)	Connie Mack	700.00	350.00	210.00
(29)	Armando Marsans	200.00	100.00	60.00
(30)	Christy Mathewson	800.00	400.00	240.00
(31)	George McBride	200.00	100.00	60.00
(32)	John McGraw	650.00	325.00	195.00
(33)	Stuffy McInnis	200.00	100.00	60.00
(34)	Chief Meyers	200.00	100.00	60.00
(35)	Earl Moore	200.00	100.00	60.00
(36)	Mike Mowrey	200.00	100.00	60.00
(37)	Marty O'Toole	200.00	100.00	60.00
(38)	Eddie Plank	600.00	300.00	180.00
(39)	Bud Ryan	200.00	100.00	60.00
(40)	Tris Speaker	750.00	375.00	225.00
(41)	Jake Stahl	200.00	100.00	60.00
(42)	Oscar Strange (Stanage)	200.00	100.00	60.00
(43)	Bill Sweeney	200.00	100.00	60.00
(44)	Honus Wagner	1000.	500.00	300.00
(45)	Ed Walsh	600.00	300.00	180.00
(46)	Zach Wheat	600.00	300.00	180.00
(47)	Harry Wolter	200.00	100.00	60.00
(48)	Joe Wood	300.00	150.00	90.00
(49)	Steve Yerkes	200.00	100.00	60.00
(50)	Heinie Zimmerman	200.00	100.00	60.00

1914 E224 Texas Tommy - Type II

		NR MT	EX	VG
Complete Set:		7500.	3750.	2250.
Common Player:		250.00	125.00	75.00
(1)	Ping Bodie	250.00	125.00	75.00
(2)	Larry Doyle	250.00	125.00	75.00
(3)	Vean Gregg	250.00	125.00	75.00
(4)	Harry Hooper	600.00	300.00	180.00
(5)	Walter Johnson	850.00	425.00	255.00
(6)	Connie Mack	700.00	350.00	210.00
(7)	Rube Marquard	600.00	300.00	180.00
(8)	Christy Mathewson	750.00	375.00	225.00
(9)	John McGraw	650.00	325.00	195.00
(10)	Chief Meyers	250.00	125.00	75.00
(11)	Jake Stahl	250.00	125.00	75.00
(12)	Honus Wagner	1000.	500.00	300.00
(13)	Joe Wood	275.00	137.00	82.00
(14)	Steve Yerkes	250.00	125.00	75.00

1921 E253

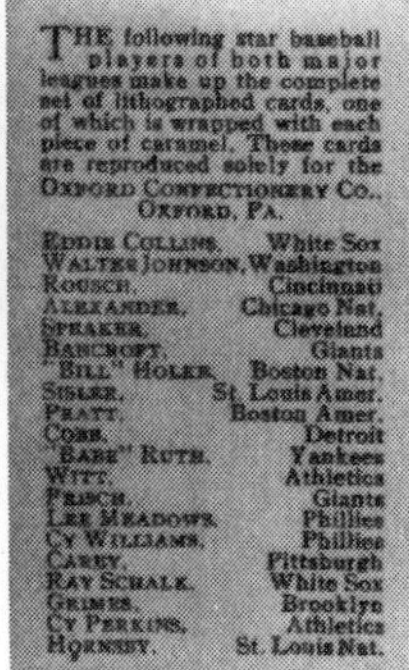

THE following star baseball players of both major leagues make up the complete set of lithographed cards, one of which is wrapped with each piece of caramel. These cards are reproduced solely for the OXFORD CONFECTIONERY CO., OXFORD, PA.

EDDIE COLLINS,	White Sox
WALTER JOHNSON,	Washington
ROUSCH,	Cincinnati
ALEXANDER,	Chicago Nat.
SPEAKER,	Cleveland
BANCROFT,	Giants
"BILL" HOLKE,	Boston Nat.
SISLER,	St. Louis Amer.
PRATT,	Boston Amer.
COBB,	Detroit
"BABE" RUTH,	Yankees
WITT,	Athletics
FRISCH,	Giants
LEE MEADOWS,	Phillies
CY WILLIAMS,	Phillies
CAREY,	Pittsburgh
RAY SCHALK,	White Sox
GRIMES,	Brooklyn
CY PERKINS,	Athletics
HORNSBY,	St. Louis Nat.

Issued in 1921 by Oxford Confectionary of Oxford, Pa., this 20-card set was printed on thin paper and distributed with caramels. Each card measures 1-5/8" by 2-3/4" and features a black and white player photo with the player's name and team printed in a white band along the bottom. The back carries the Oxford Confectionary name and a checklist of the 20 major leaguers in the set, 14 of whom are now in the Hall of Fame. The set is designated as E253 in the ACC.

		NR MT	EX	VG
Complete Set:		5000.	2500.	1500.
Common Player:		60.00	30.00	18.00
(1)	Grover Alexander	175.00	87.00	52.00
(2)	Dave Bancroft	140.00	70.00	42.00
(3)	Max Carey	140.00	70.00	42.00
(4)	Ty Cobb	900.00	450.00	270.00
(5)	Eddie Collins	140.00	70.00	42.00
(6)	Frankie Frisch	140.00	70.00	42.00
(7)	Burleigh Grimes	140.00	70.00	42.00
(8)	"Bill" Holke (Walter)	60.00	30.00	18.00
(9)	Rogers Hornsby	250.00	125.00	75.00
(10)	Walter Johnson	350.00	175.00	105.00
(11)	Lee Meadows	60.00	30.00	18.00
(12)	Cy Perkins	60.00	30.00	18.00
(13)	Derrill Pratt	60.00	30.00	18.00
(14)	Ed Rousch (Roush)	140.00	70.00	42.00
(15)	"Babe" Ruth	1500.	750.00	450.00
(16)	Ray Schalk	140.00	70.00	42.00
(17)	George Sisler	140.00	70.00	42.00
(18)	Tris Speaker	175.00	87.00	52.00
(19)	Cy Williams	60.00	30.00	18.00
(20)	Whitey Witt	60.00	30.00	18.00

1909-11 E254 Colgan's Chips

This unusual set of round cards, each measuring 1-1/2" in diameter, was issued over a three-year period from 1909 to 1911 by the Colgan Gum Company of Louisville, Ky. The cards were printed on paper and inserted in five-cent cannisters of Colgan's Mint Chips and Violet Chips. The borderless cards include a player portrait on the front along with the player's last name, team and league. The back identifies the set as "Stars of the Diamond" and carries advertising for Colgan's Gum. A total of 235 different players were pictured over the three-year period, but because of team changes and other variations, more than 300 different cards exist. The set, designated as E254, is closely related to the E270 Red Border and E270 Tin Tops sets of the same period. The complete set price does not include all variations.

		NR MT	EX	VG
Complete Set:		30000.	13750.	70000.
Common Player:		50.00	25.00	15.00
(1)	Ed Abbaticchio	50.00	25.00	15.00
(2)	Fred Abbott	50.00	25.00	15.00
(3a)	Bill Abstein (Pittsburg)	50.00	25.00	15.00
(3b)	Bill Abstein (Jersey City)	50.00	25.00	15.00
(4)	Babe Adams	50.00	25.00	15.00
(5)	Doc Adkins	50.00	25.00	15.00
(6)	Joe Agler	50.00	25.00	15.00
(7a)	Dave Altizer (Cincinnati)	50.00	25.00	15.00
(7b)	Dave Altizer (Minneapolis)	50.00	25.00	15.00
(8)	Nick Altrock	50.00	25.00	15.00
(9)	Red Ames	50.00	25.00	15.00
(10)	Jimmy Archer	50.00	25.00	15.00
(11a)	Jimmy Austin (New York)	50.00	25.00	15.00
(11b)	Jimmy Austin (St. Louis)	50.00	25.00	15.00
(12a)	Charlie Babb (Memphis)	50.00	25.00	15.00
(12b)	Charlie Babb (Norfolk)	50.00	25.00	15.00
(13)	Baerwald	50.00	25.00	15.00
(14)	Bill Bailey	50.00	25.00	15.00
(15)	Home Run Baker	150.00	75.00	45.00
(16)	Jack Barry	50.00	25.00	15.00
(17a)	Bill Bartley (curved letters)	50.00	25.00	15.00
(17b)	Bill Bartley (horizontal letters)	50.00	25.00	15.00
(18a)	Johnny Bates (Cincinnati)	50.00	25.00	15.00
(18b)	Johnny Bates (Philadelphia, black letters)	50.00	25.00	15.00
(18c)	Johnny Bates (Philadelphia, white letters)	50.00	25.00	15.00
(19)	Dick Bayless	50.00	25.00	15.00
(20a)	Ginger Beaumont (Boston)	50.00	25.00	15.00
(20b)	Ginger Beaumont (Chicago)	50.00	25.00	15.00
(20c)	Ginger Beaumont (St. Paul)	50.00	25.00	15.00
(21)	Beals Becker	50.00	25.00	15.00
(22)	George Bell	50.00	25.00	15.00
(23a)	Harry Bemis (Cleveland)	50.00	25.00	15.00
(23b)	Harry Bemis (Columbus)	50.00	25.00	15.00
(24a)	Heinie Berger (Cleveland)	50.00	25.00	15.00
(24b)	Heinie Berger (Columbus)	50.00	25.00	15.00
(25)	Bob Bescher	50.00	25.00	15.00
(26)	Beumiller	50.00	25.00	15.00
(27)	Joe Birmingham	50.00	25.00	15.00
(28)	Kitty Bransfield	50.00	25.00	15.00
(29)	Roger Bresnahan	150.00	75.00	45.00
(30)	Al Bridwell	50.00	25.00	15.00
(31)	Lew Brockett	50.00	25.00	15.00
(32)	Al Burch	50.00	25.00	15.00
(33a)	Burke (Ft. Wayne)	50.00	25.00	15.00
(33b)	Burke (Indianapolis)	50.00	25.00	15.00
(34)	Donie Bush	50.00	25.00	15.00
(35)	Bill Byers	50.00	25.00	15.00
(36)	Howie Cammitz (Camnitz)	50.00	25.00	15.00
(37a)	Charlie Carr (Indianapolis)	50.00	25.00	15.00
(37b)	Charlie Carr (Utica)	50.00	25.00	15.00
(38)	Frank Chance	175.00	87.00	52.00
(39)	Hal Chase	100.00	50.00	30.00
(40)	Bill Clancy (Clancey)	50.00	25.00	15.00
(41a)	Fred Clarke (Pittsburg)	150.00	75.00	45.00
(41b)	Fred Clarke (Pittsburgh)	150.00	75.00	45.00
(42)	Tommy Clarke (Cincinnati)	50.00	25.00	15.00
(43)	Bill Clymer	50.00	25.00	15.00
(44a)	Ty Cobb (no team on uniform)	1200.	600.00	250.00
(44b)	Ty Cobb (team name on uniform))	1500.	750.00	300.00
(45)	Eddie Collins	150.00	75.00	45.00
(46)	Bunk Congalton	50.00	25.00	15.00
(47)	Wid Conroy	50.00	25.00	15.00
(48)	Ernie Courtney	50.00	25.00	15.00
(49a)	Harry Coveleski (Cincinnati)	50.00	25.00	15.00
(49b)	Harry Coveleski (Chattanooga)	50.00	25.00	15.00
(50)	Doc Crandall	50.00	25.00	15.00
(51)	Gavvy Cravath	60.00	30.00	18.00
(52)	Dode Criss	50.00	25.00	15.00
(53)	Bill Dahlen	50.00	25.00	15.00
(54a)	Jake Daubert (Memphis)	60.00	30.00	18.00
(54b)	Jake Daubert (Brooklyn)	60.00	30.00	18.00
(55)	Harry Davis (Philadelphia)	50.00	25.00	15.00
(56)	Davis (St. Paul)	50.00	25.00	15.00
(57)	Frank Delahanty	50.00	25.00	15.00
(58a)	Ray Demmett (Demmitt) (New York)	50.00	25.00	15.00
(58b)	Ray Demmett (Demmitt) (Montreal)	50.00	25.00	15.00
(58c)	Ray Demmett (Demmitt) (St. Louis)	50.00	25.00	15.00
(59)	Art Devlin	50.00	25.00	15.00
(60)	Wild Bill Donovan	50.00	25.00	15.00
(61)	Mickey Doolin (Doolan)	50.00	25.00	15.00
(62)	Patsy Dougherty	50.00	25.00	15.00
(63)	Tom Downey	50.00	25.00	15.00
(64)	Larry Doyle	50.00	25.00	15.00
(65)	Jack Dunn	50.00	25.00	15.00
(66)	Dick Eagan (Egan)	50.00	25.00	15.00
(67a)	Kid Elberfield (Elberfeld) (Washington)	50.00	25.00	15.00
(67b)	Kid Elberfield (Elberfeld) (New York)	50.00	25.00	15.00
(68)	Rube Ellis	50.00	25.00	15.00
(69a)	Clyde Engle (New York)	50.00	25.00	15.00
(69b)	Clyde Engle (Boston)	50.00	25.00	15.00
(70a)	Steve Evans (curved letters)	50.00	25.00	15.00
(70b)	Steve Evans (horizontal letters)	50.00	25.00	15.00
(71)	Johnny Evers	150.00	75.00	45.00
(72)	Cecil Ferguson	50.00	25.00	15.00
(73)	Hobe Ferris	50.00	25.00	15.00
(74)	Field	50.00	25.00	15.00
(75)	Fitzgerald	50.00	25.00	15.00
(76a)	Patsy Flaherty (Kansas City)	50.00	25.00	15.00
(76b)	Patsy Flaherty (Atlanta)	50.00	25.00	15.00
(77)	Jack Flater	50.00	25.00	15.00
(78a)	Elmer Flick (Cleveland)	150.00	75.00	45.00
(78b)	Elmer Flick (Toledo)	150.00	75.00	45.00
(79a)	James Freck (Frick) (Baltimore)	50.00	25.00	15.00
(79b)	James Freck (Frick) (Toronto)	50.00	25.00	15.00
(80)	Jerry Freeman (photo actually Buck Freeman)	50.00	25.00	15.00
(81)	Art Froome (Fromme)	50.00	25.00	15.00
(82a)	Larry Gardner (Boston)	50.00	25.00	15.00
(82b)	Larry Gardner (New York)	50.00	25.00	15.00
(83)	Harry Gaspar	50.00	25.00	15.00
(84a)	Gus Getz	50.00	25.00	15.00
(84b)	Gus Getz	50.00	25.00	15.00
(85)	George Gibson	50.00	25.00	15.00
(86a)	Moose Grimshaw (Toronto)	50.00	25.00	15.00
(86b)	Moose Grimshaw (Louisville)	50.00	25.00	15.00
(87)	Ed Hahn	50.00	25.00	15.00
(88)	John Halla	50.00	25.00	15.00
(89)	Ed Hally (Holly)	50.00	25.00	15.00
(90)	Charlie Hanford	50.00	25.00	15.00
(91)	Topsy Hartsel	50.00	25.00	15.00
(92a)	Roy Hartzell (St. Louis)	50.00	25.00	15.00
(92b)	Roy Hartzell (New York)	50.00	25.00	15.00
(93)	Weldon Henley	50.00	25.00	15.00
(94)	Harry Hinchman	50.00	25.00	15.00
(95)	Solly Hofman	50.00	25.00	15.00
(96a)	Harry Hooper (Boston Na'l)	150.00	75.00	45.00
(96b)	Harry Hooper (Boston Am. L.)	150.00	75.00	45.00
(97)	Howard	50.00	25.00	15.00
(98a)	Hughes (no team name on uniform)	50.00	25.00	15.00
(98b)	Hughes (team name on uniform)	50.00	25.00	15.00
(99a)	Rudy Hulswilt (St. Louis, name incorrect)	50.00	25.00	15.00
(99b)	Rudy Hulswitt (St. Louis, name correct)	50.00	25.00	15.00
(99c)	Rudy Hulswitt (Chattanooga)	50.00	25.00	15.00
(100)	John Hummel	50.00	25.00	15.00
(101)	George Hunter	50.00	25.00	15.00
(102)	Shoeless Joe Jackson	2500.	1200.	600.00
(103)	Hugh Jennings	150.00	75.00	45.00
(104)	Davy Jones	50.00	25.00	15.00
(105)	Tom Jones	50.00	25.00	15.00
(106a)	Tim Jordon (Jordan) (Brooklyn)	50.00	25.00	15.00
(106b)	Tim Jordon (Jordan) (Atlanta)	50.00	25.00	15.00
(106c)	Tim Jordon (Jordan) (Louisville)	50.00	25.00	15.00
(107)	Addie Joss	200.00	100.00	60.00
(108)	Al Kaiser	50.00	25.00	15.00
(109)	Wee Wille Keeler	150.00	75.00	45.00
(110)	Joe Kelly (Kelley)	150.00	75.00	45.00
(111)	Bill Killefer	50.00	25.00	15.00
(112a)	Ed Killian (Detroit)	50.00	25.00	15.00
(112b)	Ed Killian (Toronto)	50.00	25.00	15.00
(113)	Johnny Kling	50.00	25.00	15.00
(114)	Otto Knabe	50.00	25.00	15.00

	NR MT	EX	VG
(115) Jack Knight	50.00	25.00	15.00
(116) Ed Konetchy	50.00	25.00	15.00
(117) Rube Kroh	50.00	25.00	15.00
(118) James Lafitte	50.00	25.00	15.00
(119) Nap Lajoie	400.00	200.00	90.00
(120) Lakoff	50.00	25.00	15.00
(121) Frank Lange	50.00	25.00	15.00
(122a) Frank LaPorte (St. Louis)	50.00	25.00	15.00
(122b) Frank LaPorte (New York)	50.00	25.00	15.00
(123) Tommy Leach	50.00	25.00	15.00
(124) Jack Lelivelt	50.00	25.00	15.00
(125a) Jack Lewis (Milwaukee)	50.00	25.00	15.00
(125b) Jack Lewis (Indianapolis)	50.00	25.00	15.00
(126a) Vive Lindaman (Boston)	50.00	25.00	15.00
(126b) Vive Lindaman (Louisville)	50.00	25.00	15.00
(126c) Vive Lindaman (Indianapolis)	50.00	25.00	15.00
(127) Bris Lord	50.00	25.00	15.00
(128a) Harry Lord (Boston)	50.00	25.00	15.00
(128b) Harry Lord (Chicago)	50.00	25.00	15.00
(129a) Bill Ludwig (Milwaukee)	50.00	25.00	15.00
(129b) Bill Ludwig (St. Louis)	50.00	25.00	15.00
(130) Madden	50.00	25.00	15.00
(131) Nick Maddox	50.00	25.00	15.00
(132a) Manser (Jersey City)	50.00	25.00	15.00
(132b) Manser (Rochester)	50.00	25.00	15.00
(133) Rube Marquard	150.00	75.00	45.00
(134) Al Mattern	50.00	25.00	15.00
(135) Bill Matthews	50.00	25.00	15.00
(136) George McBride	50.00	25.00	15.00
(137) McCathy	50.00	25.00	15.00
(138) McConnell	50.00	25.00	15.00
(139) Moose McCormick	50.00	25.00	15.00
(140) Dan McGann	50.00	25.00	15.00
(141) Jim McGinley	50.00	25.00	15.00
(142) Iron Man McGinnity	150.00	75.00	45.00
(143a) Matty McIntyre (Detroit)	50.00	25.00	15.00
(143b) Matty McIntyre (Chicago)	50.00	25.00	15.00
(144) Larry McLean	50.00	25.00	15.00
(145) Fred Merkle	60.00	30.00	18.00
(146a) Merritt (Buffalo)	50.00	25.00	15.00
(146b) Merritt (Jersey City)	50.00	25.00	15.00
(147a) Meyer (Newark, name correct)	50.00	25.00	15.00
(147b) Meyers (Newark, name incorrect)	50.00	25.00	15.00
(148) Chief Meyers (New York)	50.00	25.00	15.00
(149) Clyde Milan	50.00	25.00	15.00
(150) Dots Miller	50.00	25.00	15.00
(151) Mike Mitchell	50.00	25.00	15.00
(152) Moran	50.00	25.00	15.00
(153a) Bill Moriarty (Louisville)	50.00	25.00	15.00
(153b) Bill Moriarty (Omaha)	50.00	25.00	15.00
(154) George Moriarty	50.00	25.00	15.00
(155a) George Mullen (name incorrect)	50.00	25.00	15.00
(155b) George Mullin (name correct)	50.00	25.00	15.00
(156a) Simmy Murch (Chattanooga)	50.00	25.00	15.00
(156b) Simmy Murch (Indianapolis)	50.00	25.00	15.00
(157) Danny Murphy	50.00	25.00	15.00
(158a) Red Murray (New York, white letters)	50.00	25.00	15.00
(158b) Red Murray (New York, black letters)	50.00	25.00	15.00
(158c) Red Murray (St. Paul)	50.00	25.00	15.00
(159) Billy Nattress	50.00	25.00	15.00
(160a) Red Nelson (St. Louis)	50.00	25.00	15.00
(160b) Red Nelson (Toledo)	50.00	25.00	15.00
(161) Rebel Oakes	50.00	25.00	15.00
(162) Fred Odwell	50.00	25.00	15.00
(163) O'Rourke	50.00	25.00	15.00
(164a) Al Orth (New York)	50.00	25.00	15.00
(164b) Al Orth (Indianapolis)	50.00	25.00	15.00
(165) Fred Osborn	50.00	25.00	15.00
(166) Orval Overall	50.00	25.00	15.00
(167) Owens	50.00	25.00	15.00
(168) Fred Parent	50.00	25.00	15.00
(169a) Dode Paskert (Cincinnati)	50.00	25.00	15.00
(169b) Dode Paskert (Philadelphia)	50.00	25.00	15.00
(170) Heinie Peitz	50.00	25.00	15.00
(171) Bob Peterson	50.00	25.00	15.00
(172) Jake Pfeister	50.00	25.00	15.00
(173) Deacon Phillipe (Phillippe)	50.00	25.00	15.00
(174a) Ollie Pickering (Louisville)	50.00	25.00	15.00
(174b) Ollie Pickering (Minneapolis)	50.00	25.00	15.00
(174c) Ollie Pickering (Omaha)	50.00	25.00	15.00
(175a) Billy Purtell (Chicago)	50.00	25.00	15.00
(175b) Billy Purtell (Boston)	50.00	25.00	15.00
(176) Bugs Raymond	50.00	25.00	15.00
(177) Pat Regan (Ragan)	50.00	25.00	15.00
(178) Barney Reilly	50.00	25.00	15.00
(179) Duke Reilly (Reilley)	50.00	25.00	15.00
(180) Ed Reulbach	50.00	25.00	15.00
(181) Ritchery	50.00	25.00	15.00
(182) Lou Ritter	50.00	25.00	15.00
(183) Robinson	50.00	25.00	15.00
(184) Rock	50.00	25.00	15.00
(185a) Jack Rowan (Cincinnati)	50.00	25.00	15.00
(185b) Jack Rowan (Philadelphia)	50.00	25.00	15.00
(186) Nap Rucker	50.00	25.00	15.00
(187a) Dick Rudolph (New York)	50.00	25.00	15.00
(187b) Dick Rudolph (Toronto)	50.00	25.00	15.00
(188) Ryan	50.00	25.00	15.00
(189) Slim Sallee	50.00	25.00	15.00
(190a) Bill Schardt (Birmingham)	50.00	25.00	15.00
(190b) Bill Schardt (Milwaukee)	50.00	25.00	15.00
(191) Jimmy Scheckard (Sheckard)	50.00	25.00	15.00
(192a) George Schirm (Birmingham)	50.00	25.00	15.00
(192b) George Schirm (Buffalo)	50.00	25.00	15.00
(193) Larry Schlafly	50.00	25.00	15.00
(194) Wildfire Schulte	50.00	25.00	15.00
(195a) James Seabaugh (looking to left, photo actually Julius Weisman)	50.00	25.00	15.00
(195b) James Seabaugh (looking straight ahead, correct photo)	50.00	25.00	15.00
(196) Selby	50.00	25.00	15.00
(197a) Cy Seymour (New York)	50.00	25.00	15.00
(197b) Cy Seymour (Baltimore)	50.00	25.00	15.00
(198) Hosea Siner	50.00	25.00	15.00
(199) G. Smith	50.00	25.00	15.00
(200a) Sid Smith (Atlanta)	50.00	25.00	15.00
(200b) Sid Smith (Buffalo)	50.00	25.00	15.00
(201) Fred Snodgrass	60.00	30.00	18.00
(202a) Bob Spade (Cincinnati)	50.00	25.00	15.00
(202b) Bob Spade (Newark)	50.00	25.00	15.00
(203a) Tully Sparks (Philadelphia)	50.00	25.00	15.00
(203b) Tully Sparks (Richmond)	50.00	25.00	15.00
(204a) Tris Speaker (Boston Nat'l)	275.00	125.00	55.00
(204b) Tris Speaker (Boston Am.)	275.00	125.00	55.00
(205) Tubby Spencer	50.00	25.00	15.00
(206) Jake Stahl	50.00	25.00	15.00
(207) John Stansberry (Stansbury)	50.00	25.00	15.00
(208) Harry Steinfeldt	35.00	17.50	10.50
(209) George Stone	50.00	25.00	15.00
(210) George Stovall	50.00	25.00	15.00
(211) Gabby Street	50.00	25.00	15.00
(212a) Sullivan (Louisville)	50.00	25.00	15.00
(212b) Sullivan (Omaha)	50.00	25.00	15.00
(213) Ed Summers	50.00	25.00	15.00
(214) Lee Tannehill	50.00	25.00	15.00
(215) Taylor	50.00	25.00	15.00
(216) Joe Tinker	150.00	75.00	45.00
(217) John Titus	50.00	25.00	15.00
(218) Terry Turner	50.00	25.00	15.00
(219a) Bob Unglaub (Washington)	50.00	25.00	15.00
(219b) Bob Unglaub (Lincoln)	50.00	25.00	15.00
(220a) Rube Waddell (St. Louis)	150.00	75.00	45.00
(220b) Rube Waddell (Minneapolis)	150.00	75.00	45.00
(220c) Rube Waddell (Newark)	150.00	75.00	45.00
(221a) Honus Wagner (Pittsburg, curved letters)	900.00	400.00	150.00
(221b) Honus Wagner (Pittsburg, horizontal letters)	900.00	400.00	150.00
(221c) Honus Wagner (Pittsburgh)	900.00	400.00	150.00
(222) Walker	50.00	25.00	15.00
(223) Waller	50.00	25.00	15.00
(224) Clarence Wauner (Wanner)	50.00	25.00	15.00
(225a) Julius Wiesman (name incorrect)	50.00	25.00	15.00
(225b) Julius Weisman (name correct)	50.00	25.00	15.00
(226) Jack White (Buffalo)	50.00	25.00	15.00
(227) Kirby White (Boston)	50.00	25.00	15.00
(228) Ed Willett	50.00	25.00	15.00
(229a) Otto Williams (Indianapolis)	50.00	25.00	15.00
(229b) Otto Williams (Minneapolis)	50.00	25.00	15.00
(230) Owen Wilson	50.00	25.00	15.00
(231) Hooks Wiltse	50.00	25.00	15.00
(232a) Orville Woodruff (Indianapolis)	50.00	25.00	15.00
(232b) Orville Woodruff (Louisville)	50.00	25.00	15.00
(233) Woods	50.00	25.00	15.00
(234) Cy Young	500.00	250.00	135.00
(235) Bill Zimmerman	50.00	25.00	15.00
(236) Heinie Zimmerman	50.00	25.00	15.00

1912 E270 Red Border

This set, issued in 1912 by Colgan Gum Company of Louisville, Ky., is very similar to the E254 Colgan's Chips set. Measuring 1-1/2" in diameter, these round, paper player photos were inserted in cannisters of Colgan's Mint Chips and Violet Chips. They are differentiated from other similar issues by their distinctive red borders and by the back of the cards, which advises collectors to "Send 25 Box Tops" for a photo of the "World's Pennant Winning Team." The set is designated as the E270 Red Border set.

	NR MT	EX	VG
Complete Set:	12000.	6000.	3600.
Common Player:	60.00	30.00	18.00
(1) Ed Abbaticchio	60.00	30.00	18.00
(2) Fred Abbott	60.00	30.00	18.00
(3) Babe Adams	60.00	30.00	18.00
(4) Red Ames	60.00	30.00	18.00
(5) Charlie Babb	60.00	30.00	18.00
(6) Bill Bailey	60.00	30.00	18.00
(7) Home Run Baker	125.00	62.00	37.00
(8) Jack Barry	60.00	30.00	18.00
(9) Johnny Bates	60.00	30.00	18.00
(10) Dick Bayless	60.00	30.00	18.00
(11) Beals Becker	60.00	30.00	18.00
(13) Heinie Berger	60.00	30.00	18.00
(14) Beumiller	60.00	30.00	18.00
(15) Joe Birmingham	60.00	30.00	18.00
(16) Kitty Bransfield	60.00	30.00	18.00
(17) Roger Bresnahan	125.00	62.00	37.00
(18) Lew Brockett	60.00	30.00	18.00
(19) Al Burch	60.00	30.00	18.00
(20) Donie Bush	60.00	30.00	18.00
(21) Bill Byers	60.00	30.00	18.00
(22) Howie Cammitz (Camnitz)	60.00	30.00	18.00
(23) Charlie Carr	60.00	30.00	18.00
(24) Frank Chance	135.00	67.00	40.00
(25) Fred Clarke (Pittsburg)	125.00	62.00	37.00
(26) Tommy Clarke (Cincinnati)	60.00	30.00	18.00
(27) Bill Clymer	60.00	30.00	18.00
(28) Ty Cobb	800.00	400.00	250.00
(29) Eddie Collins	125.00	62.00	37.00
(30) Wid Conroy	60.00	30.00	18.00
(31) Harry Coveleski	60.00	30.00	18.00
(32) Gavvy Cravath	65.00	32.00	19.50
(33) Dode Criss	60.00	30.00	18.00
(34) Harry Davis (Philadelphia)	60.00	30.00	18.00
(35) Davis (St. Paul)	60.00	30.00	18.00
(36) Frank Delahanty	60.00	30.00	18.00
(37) Ray Demmett (Demmitt)	60.00	30.00	18.00
(38) Art Devlin	60.00	30.00	18.00
(39) Wild Bill Donovan	60.00	30.00	18.00
(40) Mickey Doolan	60.00	30.00	18.00
(41) Patsy Dougherty	60.00	30.00	18.00
(42) Tom Downey	60.00	30.00	18.00
(43) Larry Doyle	60.00	30.00	18.00
(44) Jack Dunn	60.00	30.00	18.00
(45) Dick Eagan (Egan)	60.00	30.00	18.00
(46) Kid Elberfield (Elberfeld)	60.00	30.00	18.00
(47) Rube Ellis	60.00	30.00	18.00
(48) Steve Evans	60.00	30.00	18.00
(49) Johnny Evers	125.00	62.00	37.00
(50) Cecil Ferguson	60.00	30.00	18.00
(51) Hobe Ferris	60.00	30.00	18.00
(52) Fitzgerald	60.00	30.00	18.00
(53) Fisher	125.00	62.00	37.00
(54) Elmer Flick	125.00	62.00	37.00
(55) James Freck (Frick)	60.00	30.00	18.00
(56) Art Froome (Fromme)	60.00	30.00	18.00
(57) Harry Gaspar	60.00	30.00	18.00
(58) George Gibson	60.00	30.00	18.00
(59) Moose Grimshaw	60.00	30.00	18.00
(60) John Halla	60.00	30.00	18.00
(61) Ed Hally (Holly)	60.00	30.00	18.00
(62) Charlie Hanford	60.00	30.00	18.00
(63) Topsy Hartsel	60.00	30.00	18.00
(64) Roy Hartzell	60.00	30.00	18.00
(65) Weldon Henley	60.00	30.00	18.00
(66) Harry Hinchman	60.00	30.00	18.00
(67) Solly Hofman	60.00	30.00	18.00
(68) Harry Hooper	125.00	62.00	37.00
(69) Howard	60.00	30.00	18.00
(70) Hughes	60.00	30.00	18.00
(71) Rudy Hulswitt	60.00	30.00	18.00
(72) John Hummel	60.00	30.00	18.00
(73) George Hunter	60.00	30.00	18.00
(74) Hugh Jennings	125.00	62.00	37.00
(75) Davy Jones	60.00	30.00	18.00
(76) Tim Jordon (Jordan)	60.00	30.00	18.00
(77) Bill Killefer	60.00	30.00	18.00
(78) Ed Killian	60.00	30.00	18.00
(79) Otto Knabe	60.00	30.00	18.00
(80) Jack Knight	60.00	30.00	18.00
(81) Ed Konetchy	60.00	30.00	18.00
(82) Rube Kroh	60.00	30.00	18.00
(83) LaCrosse (photo actually Bill Schardt)	60.00	30.00	18.00
(84) Tommy Leach	60.00	30.00	18.00
(85) Jack Lelivelt	60.00	30.00	18.00
(86) Jack Lewis	60.00	30.00	18.00
(87) Vive Lindaman	60.00	30.00	18.00
(88) Bris Lord	60.00	30.00	18.00
(89) Bill Ludwig	60.00	30.00	18.00
(90) Harry Lord	60.00	30.00	18.00
(91) Nick Maddox	60.00	30.00	18.00
(92) Al Mattern	60.00	30.00	18.00
(93) George McBride	60.00	30.00	18.00
(94) McCathy	60.00	30.00	18.00
(95) McConnell	60.00	30.00	18.00
(96) Moose McCormick	60.00	30.00	18.00
(97) Jim McGinley	60.00	30.00	18.00
(98) Iron Man McGinnity	125.00	62.00	37.00
(99) Matty McIntyre	60.00	30.00	18.00
(100) Fred Merkle	65.00	32.00	19.50
(101) Merritt	60.00	30.00	18.00
(102) Chief Meyers	60.00	30.00	18.00
(103) Clyde Milan	60.00	30.00	18.00
(104) Dots Miller	60.00	30.00	18.00
(105) Mike Mitchell	60.00	30.00	18.00
(106) Bill Moriarty (Omaha)	60.00	30.00	18.00
(107) George Moriarty (Detroit)	60.00	30.00	18.00
(108) George Mullen	60.00	30.00	18.00
(109) Simmy Murch	60.00	30.00	18.00
(110) Danny Murphy	60.00	30.00	18.00
(111) Red Murray	60.00	30.00	18.00
(112) Red Nelson	60.00	30.00	18.00
(113) Rebel Oakes	60.00	30.00	18.00
(114) Orval Overall	60.00	30.00	18.00
(115) Owens	60.00	30.00	18.00
(116) Fred Parent	60.00	30.00	18.00
(117) Dode Paskert	60.00	30.00	18.00
(118) Heinie Peitz (Pietz)	60.00	30.00	18.00
(119) Bob Peterson	60.00	30.00	18.00
(120) Ollie Pickering	60.00	30.00	18.00
(121) Bugs Raymond	60.00	30.00	18.00
(122) Pat Regan (Ragan)	60.00	30.00	18.00
(123) Robinson	60.00	30.00	18.00
(124) Rock	60.00	30.00	18.00
(125) Jack Rowan	60.00	30.00	18.00
(126) Nap Rucker	60.00	30.00	18.00
(127) Dick Rudolph	60.00	30.00	18.00
(128) Slim Sallee	60.00	30.00	18.00
(129) Jimmy Scheckard (Sheckard)	60.00	30.00	18.00
(130) George Schirm	60.00	30.00	18.00
(131) Wildfire Schulte	60.00	30.00	18.00
(132) James Seabaugh	60.00	30.00	18.00
(133) Selby	60.00	30.00	18.00
(134) Hosea Siner	60.00	30.00	18.00
(135) Sid Smith	60.00	30.00	18.00
(136) Fred Snodgrass	65.00	32.00	19.50
(137) Bob Spade	60.00	30.00	18.00
(138) Tully Sparks	60.00	30.00	18.00
(139) Tris Speaker	200.00	100.00	60.00
(140) Tubby Spencer	60.00	30.00	18.00
(141) George Stone	60.00	30.00	18.00
(142) George Stovall	60.00	30.00	18.00
(143) Gabby Street	60.00	30.00	18.00
(144) Sullivan (Omaha)	60.00	30.00	18.00
(145) John Sullivan (Louisville)	60.00	30.00	18.00
(146) Ed Summers	60.00	30.00	18.00
(147) Joe Tinker	125.00	62.00	37.00
(148) John Titus	60.00	30.00	18.00
(149) Rube Waddell	125.00	62.00	37.00
(150) Walker	60.00	30.00	18.00
(151) Waller	60.00	30.00	18.00
(152) Julius Wiesman (Weisman)	60.00	30.00	18.00
(153) Jack White	60.00	30.00	18.00
(154) Otto Williams	60.00	30.00	18.00
(155) Hooks Wiltse	60.00	30.00	18.00
(156) Orville Woodruff	60.00	30.00	18.00
(157) Woods	60.00	30.00	18.00
(158) Cy Young	350.00	175.00	105.00
(159) Heinie Zimmerman	60.00	30.00	18.00

1912 E270 Tin Tops

Except for the backs, these round, paper cards (measuring 1-1/2" in diameter) are identical to the E254 Colgan's Chips issue, and were inserted in tin cannisters of Colgan's Mint Chips and Violet Chips. The front contains a player portrait photo along with the player's last name, team and league. The back advises collectors to "Send 25 Tin Tops" and a two-cent stamp to receive a photo of the "World's Pennant Winning Team." The set carries the designation E270 Tin Tops.

		NR MT	EX	VG
	Complete Set:	15000.	7500.	4500.
	Common Player:	70.00	35.00	21.00
(1)	Doc Adkins	70.00	35.00	21.00
(2)	Whitey Alperman	70.00	35.00	21.00
(3a)	Red Ames (New York)	70.00	35.00	21.00
(3b)	Red Ames (Cincinnati)	70.00	35.00	21.00
(4a)	Tommy Atkins (Atlanta)	70.00	35.00	21.00
(4b)	Tommy Atkins (Ft. Wayne)	70.00	35.00	21.00
(5)	Jake Atz	70.00	35.00	21.00
(6)	Jimmy Austin	70.00	35.00	21.00
(7)	Home Run Baker	140.00	70.00	42.00
(8)	Johnny Bates	70.00	35.00	21.00
(9)	Beebe	70.00	35.00	21.00
(10)	Harry Bemis	70.00	35.00	21.00
(11)	Bob Bescher	70.00	35.00	21.00
(12)	Joe Birmingham	70.00	35.00	21.00
(13)	Roger Bresnahan	140.00	70.00	42.00
(14)	George Brown (Browne)	70.00	35.00	21.00
(15)	Al Burch	70.00	35.00	21.00
(16)	Burns	70.00	35.00	21.00
(17)	Donie Bush	70.00	35.00	21.00
(18)	Bobby Byrne	70.00	35.00	21.00
(19)	Nixey Callahan	70.00	35.00	21.00
(20)	Billy Campbell	70.00	35.00	21.00
(21)	Charlie Carr	70.00	35.00	21.00
(22)	Jay Cashion	70.00	35.00	21.00
(23)	Frank Chance	150.00	75.00	45.00
(24)	Hal Chase	110.00	55.00	33.00
(25)	Ed Cicotte	90.00	45.00	27.00
(26)	Clarke (Indianapolis)	70.00	35.00	21.00
(27)	Fred Clarke (Pittsburg)	140.00	70.00	42.00
(28)	Tommy Clarke (Cincinnati)	70.00	35.00	21.00
(29)	Clemons	70.00	35.00	21.00
(30)	Bill Clymer	70.00	35.00	21.00
(31)	Ty Cobb	650.00	325.00	195.00
(32)	Eddie Collins	140.00	70.00	42.00
(33a)	Bunk Congalton (Omaha)	70.00	35.00	21.00
(33b)	Bunk Congalton (Toledo)	70.00	35.00	21.00
(34)	Cook	70.00	35.00	21.00
(35)	Jack Coombs	70.00	35.00	21.00
(36)	Corcoran	70.00	35.00	21.00
(37)	Sam Crawford	140.00	70.00	42.00
(38)	Bert Daniels	70.00	35.00	21.00
(39)	Jake Daubert	80.00	40.00	24.00
(40a)	Josh Devore	70.00	35.00	21.00
(40b)	Josh Devore	70.00	35.00	21.00
(41)	Mike Donlin	70.00	35.00	21.00
(42)	Red Dooin	70.00	35.00	21.00
(43)	Mickey Doolan	70.00	35.00	21.00
(44)	Larry Doyle	70.00	35.00	21.00
(45)	Delos Drake	70.00	35.00	21.00
(46)	Kid Elberfield (Elberfeld)	70.00	35.00	21.00
(47)	Roy Ellam	70.00	35.00	21.00
(48)	Elliott	70.00	35.00	21.00
(49)	Rube Ellis	70.00	35.00	21.00
(50)	Elwert	70.00	35.00	21.00
(51)	Clyde Engle	70.00	35.00	21.00
(52)	Jimmy Esmond	70.00	35.00	21.00
(53)	Steve Evans	70.00	35.00	21.00
(54)	Johnny Evers	140.00	70.00	42.00
(55)	Hobe Ferris	70.00	35.00	21.00
(56)	Russ Ford	70.00	35.00	21.00
(57)	Ed Foster	70.00	35.00	21.00
(58)	Friel	70.00	35.00	21.00
(59)	John Frill	70.00	35.00	21.00
(60)	Art Froome (Fromme)	70.00	35.00	21.00
(61)	Gus Getz	70.00	35.00	21.00
(62)	George Gibson	70.00	35.00	21.00
(63)	Graham	70.00	35.00	21.00
(64a)	Eddie Grant (Cincinnati)	70.00	35.00	21.00
(64b)	Eddie Grant (New York)	70.00	35.00	21.00
(65)	Grief	70.00	35.00	21.00
(66)	Bob Grom (Groom)	70.00	35.00	21.00
(67)	Charlie Hanford	70.00	35.00	21.00
(68)	Topsy Hartsel	70.00	35.00	21.00
(69)	Harry Hinchman	70.00	35.00	21.00
(70)	Dick Hoblitzell	70.00	35.00	21.00
(71)	Happy Hogan (St. Louis)	70.00	35.00	21.00
(72)	Happy Hogan (San Francisco)	70.00	35.00	21.00
(73)	Harry Hooper	140.00	70.00	42.00
(74)	Miller Huggins	140.00	70.00	42.00
(75a)	Hughes (Milwaukee)	70.00	35.00	21.00
(75b)	Hughes (Rochester)	70.00	35.00	21.00
(76)	Rudy Hulswitt	70.00	35.00	21.00
(77)	John Hummel	70.00	35.00	21.00
(78)	Hugh Jennings	140.00	70.00	42.00
(79)	Pete Johns	70.00	35.00	21.00
(80)	Davy Jones	70.00	35.00	21.00
(81)	Tim Jordan	70.00	35.00	21.00
(82)	Bob Keefe	70.00	35.00	21.00
(83)	Wee Willie Keeler	140.00	70.00	42.00
(84)	Joe Kelly (Kelley)	140.00	70.00	42.00
(85)	Bill Killefer	70.00	35.00	21.00
(86)	Ed Killian	70.00	35.00	21.00
(87)	Klipfer	70.00	35.00	21.00
(88)	Otto Knabe	70.00	35.00	21.00
(89)	Jack Knight	70.00	35.00	21.00
(90)	Ed Konetchy	70.00	35.00	21.00
(91)	Paul Krichell	70.00	35.00	21.00
(92)	James Lafitte	70.00	35.00	21.00
(93)	Nap Lajoie	200.00	100.00	60.00
(94)	Frank Lange	70.00	35.00	21.00
(95)	Lee	70.00	35.00	21.00
(96)	Jack Lewis	70.00	35.00	21.00
(97)	Harry Lord	70.00	35.00	21.00
(98)	Johnny Lush	70.00	35.00	21.00
(99)	Madden	70.00	35.00	21.00
(100)	Nick Maddox	70.00	35.00	21.00
(101)	Sherry Magee	80.00	40.00	24.00
(102)	Manser	70.00	35.00	21.00
(103)	McAllister	70.00	35.00	21.00
(104)	McCathy	70.00	35.00	21.00
(105)	McConnell	70.00	35.00	21.00
(106)	Larry McLean	70.00	35.00	21.00
(107)	Fred Merkle	75.00	37.00	22.00
(108)	Chief Meyers	70.00	35.00	21.00
(109)	Miller (Columbus)	70.00	35.00	21.00
(110)	Dots Miller (Pittsburg)	70.00	35.00	21.00
(111)	Clarence Mitchell	70.00	35.00	21.00
(112)	Mike Mitchell	70.00	35.00	21.00
(113)	Roy Mitchell	70.00	35.00	21.00
(114)	Carlton Molesworth	70.00	35.00	21.00
(115)	Herbie Moran	70.00	35.00	21.00
(116)	George Moriarty	70.00	35.00	21.00
(117)	Danny Murphy	70.00	35.00	21.00
(118)	Jim Murray	70.00	35.00	21.00
(119)	Jake Northrop	70.00	35.00	21.00
(120)	Rube Oldring	70.00	35.00	21.00
(121)	Steve O'Neil (O'Neill)	70.00	35.00	21.00
(122)	O'Rourke	70.00	35.00	21.00
(123)	Larry Pape	70.00	35.00	21.00
(124)	Fred Parent	70.00	35.00	21.00
(125)	Perry	70.00	35.00	21.00
(126)	Billy Purtell	70.00	35.00	21.00
(127)	Bill Rariden	70.00	35.00	21.00
(128)	Morrie Rath	70.00	35.00	21.00
(129)	Dick Rudolph	70.00	35.00	21.00
(130)	Bud Ryan	70.00	35.00	21.00
(131)	Slim Sallee	70.00	35.00	21.00
(132)	Ray Schalk	70.00	35.00	21.00
(133)	Jimmy Scheckard (Sheckard)	70.00	35.00	21.00
(134)	Bob Shawkey	70.00	35.00	21.00
(135)	Skeeter Shelton	70.00	35.00	21.00
(136)	Smith (Montreal)	70.00	35.00	21.00
(137a)	Sid Smith (Atlanta)	70.00	35.00	21.00
(137b)	Sid Smith (Newark)	70.00	35.00	21.00
(138)	Fred Snodgrass	70.00	35.00	21.00
(139)	Tris Speaker	175.00	87.00	52.00
(140)	Jake Stahl	70.00	35.00	21.00
(141)	John Stansberry (Stansbury)	70.00	35.00	21.00
(142)	Amos Strunk	70.00	35.00	21.00
(143)	Sullivan	70.00	35.00	21.00
(144)	Harry Swacina	70.00	35.00	21.00
(145)	Bill Sweeney	70.00	35.00	21.00
(146)	Jeff Sweeney	70.00	35.00	21.00
(147)	Taylor	70.00	35.00	21.00
(148)	Jim Thorpe	1000.	500.00	300.00
(149)	Joe Tinker	140.00	70.00	42.00
(150)	John Titus	70.00	35.00	21.00
(151)	Terry Turner	70.00	35.00	21.00
(152)	Bob Unglaub	70.00	35.00	21.00
(153)	Viebahn	70.00	35.00	21.00
(154)	Rube Waddell	140.00	70.00	42.00
(155)	Honus Wagner	500.00	250.00	150.00
(156)	Bobby Wallace	140.00	70.00	42.00
(157)	Ed Walsh	140.00	70.00	42.00
(158)	Jack Warhop	70.00	35.00	21.00
(159)	Zach Wheat	140.00	70.00	42.00
(160)	Kaiser Wilhelm	70.00	35.00	21.00
(161)	Ed Willett	70.00	35.00	21.00
(162)	Owen Wilson	70.00	35.00	21.00
(163)	Hooks Wiltse	70.00	35.00	21.00
(164)	Joe Wood	80.00	40.00	24.00
(165)	Orville Woodruff	70.00	35.00	21.00
(166)	Joe Yeager	70.00	35.00	21.00
(167)	Bill Zimmerman	70.00	35.00	21.00

1910 E271 Darby Chocolates

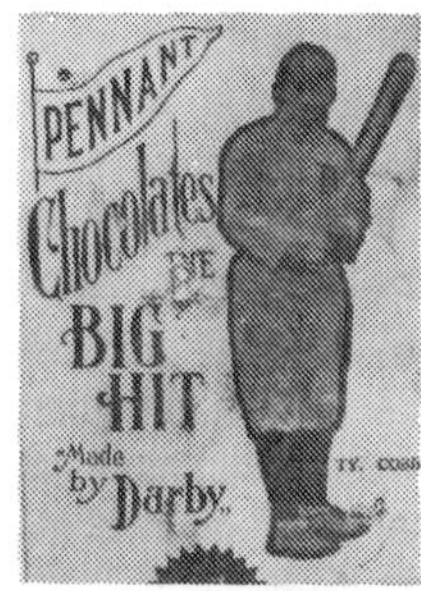

Designated as E271 by the ACC, the 1910 Darby Chocolates cards are among the rarest of all candy cards. The cards were printed on boxes of Darby's "Pennant" Chocolates, two players per box - one on the front of the box, the other on the back. The cards feature black and white player silhouettes outlined with a thick dark line. The cards are accented with orange or green tinting. Most of the 32 known examples of this set were not found until 1982, and there is speculation that the checklist is still not complete.

		NR MT	EX	VG
	Complete Set:	62000.	28500.	16500.
	Common Player:	1250.	625.00	375.00
(1)	Jimmy Archer	1250.	625.00	375.00
(2)	Chief Bender	2200.	1100.	660.00
(3)	"Bob" Bescher	1250.	625.00	375.00
(4)	Roger Bresnahan	2200.	1100.	660.00
(5)	Al Bridwell	1250.	625.00	375.00
(6)	Mordicai Brown (Mordecai)	2200.	1100.	660.00
(7)	"Eddie" Cicotte	650.00	325.00	195.00
(8)	Fred Clark (Clarke)	2200.	1100.	660.00
(9)	Ty. Cobb	4500.	2100.	1500.
(10)	King Cole	1250.	625.00	375.00
(11)	E. Collins	2200.	1100.	660.00
(12)	Wid Conroy	1250.	625.00	375.00
(13)	"Sam" Crawford	2200.	1100.	660.00
(14)	Bill Dahlin (Dahlen)	1250.	625.00	375.00
(15)	Bill Donovan	1250.	625.00	375.00
(16)	"Pat" Dougherty	1250.	625.00	375.00
(17)	Kid Elberfeld	1250.	625.00	375.00
(18)	"Johnny" Evers	2200.	1100.	660.00
(19)	Charlie Herzog	1250.	625.00	375.00
(20)	Walter Johnson	3000.	1500.	650.00
(21)	Ed Konetchy	1250.	625.00	375.00
(22)	Tommy Leach	1250.	625.00	375.00
(23)	Fred Luderous (Luderus)	1250.	625.00	375.00
(24)	"Mike" Mowery	1250.	625.00	375.00
(25)	Jack Powell	1250.	625.00	375.00
(26)	Slim Sallee	1250.	625.00	375.00
(27)	James Scheckard (Sheckard)	1250.	625.00	375.00
(28)	Walter Snodgrass	1250.	625.00	375.00
(29)	"Tris" Speaker	2400.	1200.	575.00
(30)	Charlie Suggs	1250.	625.00	375.00
(31)	Fred Tenney	1250.	625.00	375.00
(32)	"Hans" Wagner	3500.	1750.	750.00

1933 E285 Rittenhouse

Designed to resemble a set of playing cards, this set, issued circa 1933 by the Rittenhouse Candy Company of Philadelphia, carries the ACC designation E285 and is generally considered to be the last of the E-card issues. Each card measures 2-1/4" by 1-7/16" and features a small player photo in the center of the playing card design. The backs of the cards usually consist of just one large letter and were part of a promotion in which collectors were instructed to find enough different letters to spell "Rittenhouse Candy Co." Other backs explaining the contest and the prizes available have also been found. Because it was designed as a deck of playing cards, the set is complete at 52 cards, featuring 46 different players (six are pictured on two cards each). Cards have been found in red, green and blue.

		NR MT	EX	VG
	Complete Set:	5000.	2500.	1500.
	Common Player:	50.00	25.00	15.00
(1)	Dick Bartell	50.00	25.00	15.00
(2)	Walter Berger	50.00	25.00	15.00
(3)	Max Bishop	50.00	25.00	15.00
(4)	James Bottomley	80.00	40.00	24.00
(5)	Fred Brickell	50.00	25.00	15.00
(6)	Sugar Cain	50.00	25.00	15.00
(7)	Ed. Cihocki	50.00	25.00	15.00
(8)	Phil Collins	50.00	25.00	15.00
(9)	Roger Cramer	50.00	25.00	15.00
(10)	Hughie Critz	50.00	25.00	15.00
(11)	Joe Cronin	90.00	45.00	27.00
(12)	Hazen (Kiki) Cuyler	80.00	40.00	24.00
(13)	Geo. Davis	50.00	25.00	15.00
(14)	Spud Davis	50.00	25.00	15.00
(15)	Jimmy Dykes	55.00	27.00	16.50
(16)	George Earnshaw	50.00	25.00	15.00
(17)	Jumbo Elliot	50.00	25.00	15.00
(18)	Lou Finney	50.00	25.00	15.00
(19)	Jimmy Foxx	150.00	75.00	45.00
(20)	Frankie Frisch (3 of Spades)	80.00	40.00	24.00
(21)	Frankie Frisch (7 of Spades)	80.00	40.00	24.00
(22)	Robert (Lefty) Grove	100.00	50.00	30.00
(23)	Mule Haas	50.00	25.00	15.00
(24)	Chick Hafey	80.00	40.00	24.00
(25)	Chas. Leo Hartnett	80.00	40.00	24.00
(26)	Babe Herman	55.00	27.00	16.50
(27)	Wm. Herman	80.00	40.00	24.00
(28)	Kid Higgins	50.00	25.00	15.00
(29)	Rogers Hornsby	125.00	62.00	37.00
(30)	Don Hurst (Jack of Diamonds)	50.00	25.00	15.00
(31)	Don Hurst (6 of Spades)	50.00	25.00	15.00
(32)	Chuck Klein	80.00	40.00	24.00
(33)	Leroy Mahaffey	50.00	25.00	15.00
(34)	Gus Mancuso	50.00	25.00	15.00

		NR MT	EX	VG
(35)	Rabbit McNair	50.00	25.00	15.00
(36)	Bing Miller	50.00	25.00	15.00
(37)	Frank (Lefty) O'Doul	60.00	30.00	18.00
(38)	Mel Ott	110.00	55.00	33.00
(39)	Babe Ruth (Ace of Spades)	650.00	325.00	195.00
(40)	Babe Ruth (King of Clubs)	650.00	325.00	195.00
(41)	Al Simmons	80.00	40.00	24.00
(42)	Bill Terry	90.00	45.00	27.00
(43)	Pie Traynor	80.00	40.00	24.00
(44)	Rube Wallberg (Walberg)	50.00	25.00	15.00
(45)	Lloyd Waner	80.00	40.00	24.00
(46)	Paul Waner	80.00	40.00	24.00
(47)	Lloyd Warner (Waner)	80.00	40.00	24.00
(48)	Paul Warner (Warner)	80.00	40.00	24.00
(49)	Pinkey Whitney	50.00	25.00	15.00
(50)	Dib Williams	50.00	25.00	15.00
(51)	Hack Wilson (9 of Spades)	80.00	40.00	24.00
(52)	Hack Wilson (9 of Clubs)	80.00	40.00	24.00

1910 E286 JuJu Drums

Issued in 1910 with Ju Ju Drum Candy, this extremely rare set of circular baseball cards is very similar in design to the more common Colgan's Chips cards. About the size of a silver dollar (1-7/16" in diameter) the cards display a player photo on the front with the player's name and team printed below in a semi-circle design. The backs carry advertising for Ju Ju Drums. The checklist contains 45 different players to date, but the issue - known as E286 in the American Card Catalog - is so rare that others are likely to exist.

		NR MT	EX	VG
Complete Set:		17000.	8500.	5100.
Common Player:		250.00	125.00	75.00
(1)	Eddie Ainsmith	250.00	125.00	75.00
(2)	Jimmy Austin	250.00	125.00	75.00
(3)	Chief Bender	500.00	250.00	150.00
(4)	Bob Bescher	250.00	125.00	75.00
(5)	Bruno Bloch (Block)	250.00	125.00	75.00
(6)	Frank Burke	250.00	125.00	75.00
(7)	Donie Bush	250.00	125.00	75.00
(8)	Frank Chance	525.00	262.00	157.00
(9)	Harry Cheek	250.00	125.00	75.00
(10)	Ed Cicotte	300.00	150.00	90.00
(11)	Ty Cobb	2000.	1000.	600.00
(12)	King Cole	250.00	125.00	75.00
(13)	Jack Coombs	250.00	125.00	75.00
(14)	Bill Dahlen	250.00	125.00	75.00
(15)	Bert Daniels	250.00	125.00	75.00
(16)	Harry Davis	250.00	125.00	75.00
(17)	Larry Doyle	250.00	125.00	75.00
(18)	Rube Ellis	250.00	125.00	75.00
(19)	Cecil Ferguson	250.00	125.00	75.00
(20)	Russ Ford	250.00	125.00	75.00
(21)	Bob Harnion (Harmon)	250.00	125.00	75.00
(22)	Ham Hyatt	250.00	125.00	75.00
(23)	Red Kellifer (Killifer)	250.00	125.00	75.00
(24)	Art Kruger (Krueger)	250.00	125.00	75.00
(25)	Tommy Leach	250.00	125.00	75.00
(26)	Harry Lumley	250.00	125.00	75.00
(27)	Christy Mathewson	800.00	400.00	240.00
(28)	John McGraw	600.00	300.00	180.00
(29)	Deacon McGuire	250.00	125.00	75.00
(30)	Chief Meyers	250.00	125.00	75.00
(31)	Otto Miller	250.00	125.00	75.00
(32)	Charlie Mullen	250.00	125.00	75.00
(33)	Tom Needham	250.00	125.00	75.00
(34)	Rube Oldring	250.00	125.00	75.00
(35)	Barney Pelty	250.00	125.00	75.00
(36)	Ed Reulbach	250.00	125.00	75.00
(37)	Jack Rowan	250.00	125.00	75.00
(38)	Dave Shean	250.00	125.00	75.00
(39)	Tris Speaker	650.00	325.00	195.00
(40)	Jeff Sweeney	250.00	125.00	75.00
(41)	Honus Wagner	1200.	600.00	360.00
(42)	Ed Walsh	500.00	250.00	150.00
(43)	Kirby White	250.00	125.00	75.00
(44)	Ralph Works	250.00	125.00	75.00
(45)	Elmer Zacher	250.00	125.00	75.00

1912 E300 Plow's Candy

An extremely rare candy issue, cards in this 1912 set measure 3" by 4" and feature sepia-toned photos surrounded by a rather wide border. The player's name and team appear in the border below the photo, while the words "Plow's Candy Collection" appear at the top. The backs are blank. Not even known to exist until the late 1960s, this set has been assigned the designation E300.

		NR MT	EX	VG
Complete Set:		25000.	12500.	7500.
Common Player:		450.00	225.00	135.00
(1)	Babe Adams	450.00	225.00	135.00
(2)	Home Run Baker	750.00	375.00	225.00
(3)	Cy Barger	450.00	225.00	135.00
(4)	Jack Barry	450.00	225.00	135.00
(5)	Johnny Bates	450.00	225.00	135.00
(7)	Joe Benz	450.00	225.00	135.00
(8)	Cy Berger (Barger)	450.00	225.00	135.00
(9)	Roger Bresnahan	750.00	375.00	225.00
(10)	Mordecai Brown	750.00	375.00	225.00
(11)	Donie Bush	450.00	225.00	135.00
(12)	Bobby Byrne	450.00	225.00	135.00
(13)	Nixey Callahan	450.00	225.00	135.00
(14)	Hal Chase	500.00	250.00	150.00
(15)	Fred Clarke	750.00	375.00	225.00
(16)	Ty Cobb	2500.	1250.	750.00
(17)	King Cole	450.00	225.00	135.00
(18)	Eddie Collins	800.00	400.00	240.00
(19)	Jack Coombs	450.00	225.00	135.00
(20)	Bill Dahlen	450.00	225.00	135.00
(21)	Bert Daniels	450.00	225.00	135.00
(22)	Harry Davis	450.00	225.00	135.00
(23)	Jim Delehanty	450.00	225.00	135.00
(24)	Josh Devore	450.00	225.00	135.00
(25)	Wild Bill Donovan	450.00	225.00	135.00
(26)	Red Dooin	450.00	225.00	135.00
(27)	Johnny Evers	750.00	375.00	225.00
(28)	Russ Ford	450.00	225.00	135.00
(29)	Del Gainor	450.00	225.00	135.00
(30)	Vean Gregg	450.00	225.00	135.00
(31)	Bob Harmon	450.00	225.00	135.00
(32)	Arnold Hauser	450.00	225.00	135.00
(33)	Dick Hoblitzelle (Hoblitzell)	450.00	225.00	135.00
(34)	Solly Hofman	450.00	225.00	135.00
(35)	Miller Huggins	750.00	375.00	225.00
(36)	John Hummel	450.00	225.00	135.00
(37)	Walter Johnson	1200.	600.00	360.00
(38)	Johnny Kling	450.00	225.00	135.00
(39)	Nap Lajoie	1000.	500.00	300.00
(40)	Jack Lapp	450.00	225.00	135.00
(41)	Fred Luderus	450.00	225.00	135.00
(42)	Sherry Magee	450.00	225.00	135.00
(43)	Rube Marquard	750.00	375.00	225.00
(44)	Christy Mathewson	1200.	600.00	360.00
(45)	Stuffy McInnes (McInnis)	450.00	225.00	135.00
(46)	Larry McLean	450.00	225.00	135.00
(47)	Fred Merkle	450.00	225.00	135.00
(48)	Cy Morgan	450.00	225.00	135.00
(49)	George Moriarty	450.00	225.00	135.00
(50)	Mike Mowrey	450.00	225.00	135.00
(51)	Chief Myers (Meyers)	450.00	225.00	135.00
(52)	Rube Oldring	450.00	225.00	135.00
(53)	Marty O'Toole	450.00	225.00	135.00
(54)	Nap Rucker	450.00	225.00	135.00
(55)	Slim Sallee	450.00	225.00	135.00
(56)	Boss Schmidt	450.00	225.00	135.00
(57)	Jimmy Sheckard	450.00	225.00	135.00
(58)	Tris Speaker	850.00	425.00	255.00
(59)	Billy Sullivan	450.00	225.00	135.00
(60)	Ira Thomas	450.00	225.00	135.00
(61)	Joe Tinker	750.00	375.00	225.00
(62)	John Titus	450.00	225.00	135.00
(63)	Hippo Vaughan (Vaughn)	450.00	225.00	135.00
(64)	Honus Wagner	1800.	900.00	540.00
(65)	Ed Walsh	750.00	375.00	225.00
(66)	Bob Williams	450.00	225.00	135.00

1889 E.R. Williams Card Game

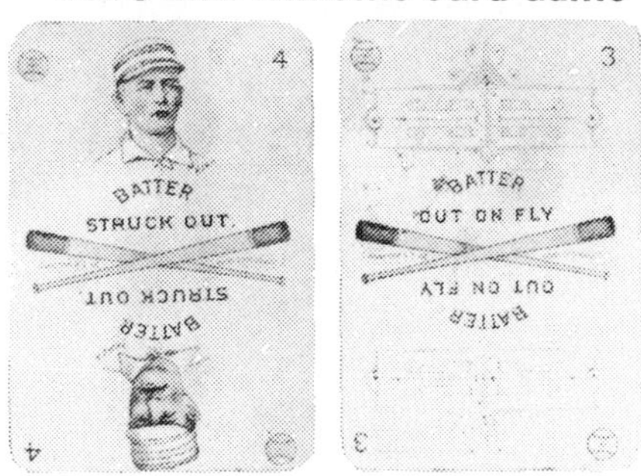

This 1889 set of 52 playing cards came packed in its own box that advertised the set as the "Egerton R. Williams Popular Indoor Base Ball Game." Designed to look like a conventional deck of playing cards, the set included various players from the National League and the American Association. Although the set contains 52 cards (like a typical deck of playing cards) only 19 actually feature color drawings of players. Each of these cards pictures two different players (one at the top and a second at the bottom, separated by sepia-colored crossed bats in the middle), resulting in 38 different players. The remaining 33 cards in the deck are strictly game cards showing a specific baseball play (such as "Batter Out on Fly" or "Two Base Hit," etc.) The cards have green-tinted backs and measure 2-7/16" by 3-1/2". Each one carries an 1889 copyright line by E.R. Williams.

		NR MT	EX	VG
Complete Set:		6000.	3000.	1750.
Common Player:		225.00	112.00	67.00
(1)	Cap Anson, Buck Ewing	700.00	350.00	210.00
(2)	Dan Brouthers, Arlie Latham	375.00	187.00	112.00
(3)	Charles Buffinton, Parisian Bob Carruthers	225.00	112.00	67.00
(4)	Hick Carpenter, Cliff Carroll	225.00	112.00	67.00
(5)	Charles Comiskey, Roger Connor	500.00	250.00	150.00
(6)	Pop Corkhill, Jim Fogarty	225.00	112.00	67.00
(7)	John Clarkson, Tim Keefe	500.00	250.00	150.00
(8)	Jerry Denny, Silent Mike Tiernan	225.00	112.00	67.00
(9)	Dave Foutz, King Kelly	400.00	200.00	120.00
(10)	Pud Galvin, Dave Orr	375.00	187.00	112.00
(11)	Pebbly Jack Glasscock, Foghorn Tucker	225.00	112.00	67.00
(12)	Mike Griffin, Ed McKean	225.00	112.00	67.00
(13)	Dummy Hoy, Long John Reilley (Reilly)	225.00	112.00	67.00
(14)	Arthur Irwin, Ned Williamson	225.00	112.00	67.00
(15)	Silver King, John Tener	225.00	112.00	67.00
(16)	Al Myers, Cub Stricker	225.00	112.00	67.00
(17)	Fred Pfeffer, Chicken Wolf	225.00	112.00	67.00
(18)	Toad Ramsey, Gus Weyhing	225.00	112.00	67.00
(19)	Monte Ward, Curt Welch	375.00	187.00	112.00

1966 East Hills Pirates

Stores in the East Hills Shopping Center, a large mall located in suburban Pittsburgh, distributed cards from this 25-card full-color set in 1966. The cards, which measure 3-1/4" by 4-1/4", are blank-backed and are numbered by the players' uniform numbers. The numbers appear in the lower right corners of the cards.

		NR MT	EX	VG
Complete Set:		35.00	17.50	10.50
Common Player:		.50	.25	.15
3	Harry Walker	.70	.35	.20
7	Bob Bailey	.50	.25	.15
8	Willie Stargell	8.00	4.00	2.50
9	Bill Mazeroski	2.00	1.00	.60
10	Jim Pagliaroni	.50	.25	.15
11	Jose Pagan	.50	.25	.15
12	Jerry May	.50	.25	.15
14	Gene Alley	.60	.30	.20
15	Manny Mota	.80	.40	.25
16	Andy Rodgers	.50	.25	.15
17	Donn Clendenon	.60	.30	.20
18	Matty Alou	.80	.40	.25
19	Pete Mikkelsen	.50	.25	.15
20	Jesse Gonder	.50	.25	.15
21	Bob Clemente	18.00	9.00	5.50
22	Woody Fryman	.60	.30	.20
24	Jerry Lynch	.50	.25	.15
25	Tommie Sisk	.50	.25	.15
26	Roy Face	1.25	.60	.40
28	Steve Blass	.60	.30	.20
32	Vernon Law	1.25	.60	.40
34	Al McBean	.50	.25	.15
39	Bob Veale	.60	.30	.20
43	Don Cardwell	.50	.25	.15
45	Gene Michael	.60	.30	.20

1954 Esskay Hot Dogs Orioles

Measuring 2-1/4" by 3-1/2", the 1954 Esskay Hot Dogs set features the Baltimore Orioles. The unnumbered color cards were issued in panels of two on packages of hot dogs and are usually found with grease stains. The cards have waxed fronts with blank backs on a white stock. Complete boxes of Esskay Hot Dogs are scarce and command a price of 2-3 times greater than the single card values.

	NR MT	EX	VG
Complete Set:	3300.	1650.	990.00

		NR MT	EX	VG
	Common Player:	90.00	45.00	27.00
(1)	Neil Berry	90.00	45.00	27.00
(2)	Michael Blyzka	90.00	45.00	27.00
(3)	Harry Brecheen	90.00	45.00	27.00
(4)	Gil Coan	90.00	45.00	27.00
(5)	Joe Coleman	90.00	45.00	27.00
(6)	Clinton Courtney	90.00	45.00	27.00
(7)	Charles E. Diering	90.00	45.00	27.00
(8)	Jimmie Dykes	100.00	50.00	30.00
(9)	Frank J. Fanovich	90.00	45.00	27.00
(10)	Howard Fox	90.00	45.00	27.00
(11)	Jim Fridley	90.00	45.00	27.00
(12)	Vinicio "Chico" Garcia	90.00	45.00	27.00
(13)	Jehosie Heard	90.00	45.00	27.00
(14)	Darrell Johnson	90.00	45.00	27.00
(15)	Bob Kennedy	90.00	45.00	27.00
(16)	Dick Kokos	90.00	45.00	27.00
(17)	Dave Koslo	90.00	45.00	27.00
(18)	Lou Kretlow	90.00	45.00	27.00
(19)	Richard D. Kryhoski	90.00	45.00	27.00
(20)	Don Larsen	100.00	50.00	30.00
(21)	Donald E. Lenhardt	90.00	45.00	27.00
(22)	Richard Littlefield	90.00	45.00	27.00
(23)	Sam Mele	90.00	45.00	27.00
(24)	Les Moss	90.00	45.00	27.00
(25)	Ray L. Murray	90.00	45.00	27.00
(26a)	"Bobo" Newsom (no stadium lights in background)	125.00	62.00	37.00
(26b)	"Bobo" Newson (stadium lights in background)	125.00	62.00	37.00
(27)	Tom Oliver	90.00	45.00	27.00
(28)	Duane Pillette	90.00	45.00	27.00
(29)	Francis M. Skaff	90.00	45.00	27.00
(30)	Marlin Stuart	90.00	45.00	27.00
(31)	Robert L. Turley	150.00	75.00	45.00
(32)	Eddie Waitkus	90.00	45.00	27.00
(33)	Vic Wertz	110.00	55.00	33.00
(34)	Robert G. Young	90.00	45.00	27.00

1955 Esskay Hot Dogs Orioles

For the second consecutive year, Esskay Meats placed two baseball cards of Orioles players on their boxes of hot dogs. The unnumbered, color cards measure 2-1/4" by 3-1/2" and can be distinguished from the previous year by unwaxed fronts and grey backs. Many of the same photos from 1954 were used with only minor picture-cropping differences

		NR MT	EX	VG
	Complete Set:	2400.	1200.	720.00
	Common Player:	90.00	45.00	27.00
(1)	Cal Abrams	90.00	45.00	27.00
(2)	Robert S. Alexander	90.00	45.00	27.00
(3)	Harry Byrd	90.00	45.00	27.00
(4)	Gil Coan	90.00	45.00	27.00
(5)	Joseph P. Coleman	90.00	45.00	27.00
(6)	William R. Cox	90.00	45.00	27.00
(7)	Charles E. Diering	90.00	45.00	27.00
(8)	Walter A. Evers	90.00	45.00	27.00
(9)	Don Johnson	90.00	45.00	27.00
(10)	Robert D. Kennedy	90.00	45.00	27.00
(11)	Lou Kretlow	90.00	45.00	27.00
(12)	Robert L. Kuzava	90.00	45.00	27.00
(13)	Fred Marsh	90.00	45.00	27.00
(14)	Charles Maxwell	90.00	45.00	27.00
(15)	Jimmie McDonald	90.00	45.00	27.00
(16)	Bill Miller	90.00	45.00	27.00
(17)	Willy Miranda	90.00	45.00	27.00
(18)	Raymond L. Moore	90.00	45.00	27.00
(19)	John Lester Moss	90.00	45.00	27.00
(20)	"Bobo" Newsom	100.00	50.00	30.00
(21)	Duane Pillette	90.00	45.00	27.00
(22)	Edward S. Waitkus	90.00	45.00	27.00
(23)	Harold W. Smith	90.00	45.00	27.00
(24)	Gus Triandos	110.00	55.00	33.00
(25)	Eugene R. Woodling	110.00	55.00	33.00
(26)	Robert G. Young	90.00	45.00	27.00

1921 Exhibits - 1921

The Exhibit Supply Company of Chicago issued the first in a long series of postcard-size baseball cards in 1921. The Exhibit cards were commonly sold in "penny arcade" vending machines. The 1921 series consists of 64 cards and includes four players from each of the 16 major league teams. The cards feature black and white photos with the player's name printed in a fancy script. The player's position and team appear below the name in small, hand-lettered capital letters. American League is designated as "AM.L.," which can help differentiate the 1921 series from future years. Some of the cards contain white borders, while others do not. All have blank backs. There are various spelling errors in the picture legends.

		NR MT	EX	VG
	Complete Set:	2000.00	1000.00	600.00
	Common Player:	15.00	7.50	4.50
(1)	Chas. B. Adams	15.00	7.50	4.50
(2)	Grover C. Alexander	15.00	7.50	4.50
(3)	David Bancroft	30.00	15.00	9.00
(4)	Geo. J. Burns	15.00	7.50	4.50
(5)	Owen Bush	15.00	7.50	4.50
(6)	Max J. Carey	30.00	15.00	9.00
(7)	Ty Cobb	200.00	100.00	60.00
(8)	Eddie T. Collins	30.00	15.00	9.00
(9)	John Collins	15.00	7.50	4.50
(10)	Stanley Coveleskie (Coveleski)	30.00	15.00	9.00
(11)	Walton E. Cruse (Cruise)	15.00	7.50	4.50
(12)	Jacob E. Daubert	18.00	9.00	5.50
(13)	George Dauss	15.00	7.50	4.50
(14)	Charles A. Deal	15.00	7.50	4.50
(15)	Joe A. Dugan	20.00	10.00	6.00
(16)	James Dykes	18.00	9.00	5.50
(17)	U.C. "Red" Faber	30.00	15.00	9.00
(18)	J.F. Fournier	15.00	7.50	4.50
(19)	Frank F. Frisch	30.00	15.00	9.00
(20)	W.L. Gardner	15.00	7.50	4.50
(21)	H.M. "Hank" Gowdy	15.00	7.50	4.50
(22)	Burleigh Grimes	30.00	15.00	9.00
(23)	Heinie Groh	15.00	7.50	4.50
(24)	Jesse Haines	30.00	15.00	9.00
(25)	Sam Harris (Stanley)	30.00	15.00	9.00
(26)	Walter L. Holke	15.00	7.50	4.50
(27)	Charles J. Hollicher (Hollocher)	15.00	7.50	4.50
(28)	Rogers Hornsby	60.00	30.00	18.00
(29)	James H. Johnson (Johnston)	15.00	7.50	4.50
(30)	Walter P. Johnson	100.00	50.00	30.00
(31)	Sam P. Jones	15.00	7.50	4.50
(32)	Geo. L. Kelly	30.00	15.00	9.00
(33)	Dick Kerr	15.00	7.50	4.50
(34)	William L. Killifer	15.00	7.50	4.50
(35)	Ed Konetchy	15.00	7.50	4.50
(36)	John "Doc" Lavan	15.00	7.50	4.50
(37)	Walter J. Maranville	30.00	15.00	9.00
(38)	Carl W. Mays	18.00	9.00	5.50
(39)	J. "Stuffy" McInnis	15.00	7.50	4.50
(40)	Rollie C. Naylor	15.00	7.50	4.50
(41)	A. Earl Neale (Earle)	20.00	10.00	6.00
(42)	Ivan M. Olsen	15.00	7.50	4.50
(43)	S.F. "Steve" O'Neil (O'Neill)	15.00	7.50	4.50
(44)	Robert Peckinpaugh	18.00	9.00	5.50
(45)	Ralph "Cy" Perkins	15.00	7.50	4.50
(46)	Raymond R. Powell	15.00	7.50	4.50
(47)	Joe "Goldie" Rapp	15.00	7.50	4.50
(48)	Edgar S. Rice	30.00	15.00	9.00
(49)	Jimmy Ring	15.00	7.50	4.50
(50)	Geo. H. "Babe" Ruth	400.00	200.00	120.00
(51)	Ray W. Schalk	30.00	15.00	9.00
(52)	Wallie Schang	15.00	7.50	4.50
(53)	Everett Scott	15.00	7.50	4.50
(54)	H.S. Shanks (photo actually Wally Schang)	15.00	7.50	4.50
(55)	Urban Shocker	15.00	7.50	4.50
(56)	Geo. J. Sisler	30.00	15.00	9.00
(57)	Tris Speaker	100.00	50.00	30.00
(58)	John Tobin	15.00	7.50	4.50
(59)	Robt. Veach	15.00	7.50	4.50
(60)	Zack D. Wheat	30.00	15.00	9.00
(61)	Geo. B. Whitted	15.00	7.50	4.50
(62)	Cy Williams	18.00	9.00	5.50
(63)	Kenneth R. Williams	18.00	9.00	5.50
(64)	Ivy B. Wingo	15.00	7.50	4.50

1922 Exhibits - 1922

The Exhibit Supply Company continued the same format in 1922 but doubled the number of cards in the series to 128, including eight players from each team. All but nine of the players who appeared in the 1921 series are pictured in the 1922 set, along with 74 new players. The cards again display black and white photos with blank backs. Some of the photos have white borders. The player's name appears in a plain script with the position and team below in small capital letters. American League is designated as "A.L." Again, there are several spelling errors and incorrect player identifications. In early printings the Earl Smith card actually pictured Brad Kocher. Only the 74 new additions are included in the checklist that follows.

		NR MT	EX	VG
	Complete Set:	1800.00	900.00	550.00
	Common Player:	18.00	9.00	5.50
(1)	J. Frank Baker	35.00	17.50	10.50
(2)	Jin Bagby	18.00	9.00	5.50
(3)	Walter Barbare	18.00	9.00	5.50
(4)	Turner Barber	18.00	9.00	5.50
(5)	John Bassler	18.00	9.00	5.50
(6)	Carlson L. Bigbee (Carson)	18.00	9.00	5.50
(7)	Sam Bohne	18.00	9.00	5.50
(8)	Geo. Burns	18.00	9.00	5.50
(9)	George Burns	18.00	9.00	5.50
(10)	Jeo Bush (Joe)	20.00	10.00	6.00
(11)	Leon Cadore	18.00	9.00	5.50
(12)	Jim Caveney	18.00	9.00	5.50
(13)	Wilbur Cooper	18.00	9.00	5.50
(14)	Dave Danforth	18.00	9.00	5.50
(15)	George Cutshaw	18.00	9.00	5.50
(16)	Bill Doak	18.00	9.00	5.50
(17)	Joe Dugan	25.00	12.50	7.50
(18)	Pat Duncan	18.00	9.00	5.50
(19)	Howard Emke (Ehmke)	18.00	9.00	5.50
(20)	Wm. Evans (umpire)	35.00	17.50	10.50
(21)	Bib Falk (Bibb)	18.00	9.00	5.50
(22)	Dana Fillingin (Fillingim)	18.00	9.00	5.50
(23)	Ira Flagstead	18.00	9.00	5.50
(24)	Fletcher	18.00	9.00	5.50
(25)	Gerber	18.00	9.00	5.50
(26)	Ray Grimes	18.00	9.00	5.50
(27)	Hildebrand (umpire)	18.00	9.00	5.50
(28)	Harry Heilman (Heilmann)	35.00	17.50	10.50
(29)	Wibur Hubbell (Wilbert)	18.00	9.00	5.50
(30)	Bill Jacobson	18.00	9.00	5.50
(31)	E.R. Johnson	18.00	9.00	5.50
(32)	Joe Judge	18.00	9.00	5.50
(33)	Bill Klem (umpire)	35.00	17.50	10.50
(34)	Harry Liebold (Leibold)	18.00	9.00	5.50
(35)	Walter Mails	18.00	9.00	5.50
(36)	Geo. Maisel	18.00	9.00	5.50
(37)	Lee Meadows	18.00	9.00	5.50
(38)	Clyde Milam (Milan)	18.00	9.00	5.50
(39)	Ed (Bing) Miller	18.00	9.00	5.50
(40)	Hack Miller	18.00	9.00	5.50
(41)	Moriarty (umpire)	18.00	9.00	5.50
(42)	Robert Muesel (Meusel)	25.00	12.50	7.50
(43)	Harry Myers	18.00	9.00	5.50
(44)	Arthur Nehf	18.00	9.00	5.50
(45)	Joe Oeschger	18.00	9.00	5.50
(46)	Geo. O'Neil	18.00	9.00	5.50
(47)	Roger Peckinpaugh	20.00	10.00	6.00
(48)	Val Picinich	18.00	9.00	5.50
(49)	Bill Piercy	18.00	9.00	5.50
(50)	Derrill Pratt	18.00	9.00	5.50
(51)	Jack Quinn	18.00	9.00	5.50
(52)	Walter Reuther (Ruether)	18.00	9.00	5.50
(53)	Rigler	18.00	9.00	5.50
(54)	Eppa Rixey	35.00	17.50	10.50
(55)	Chas. Robertson	18.00	9.00	5.50
(56)	Everett Scott	18.00	9.00	5.50
(57)	Earl Sheely	18.00	9.00	5.50
(58)	Earl Smith (portrait)	18.00	9.00	5.50
(59)	Earl Smith (standing) (photo actually Brad Kocher)	18.00	9.00	5.50
(60)	Elmer Smith	18.00	9.00	5.50
(61)	Jack Smith (photo actually Jimmy Smith)	18.00	9.00	5.50
(62)	Sherrod Smith	18.00	9.00	5.50
(63)	Frank Snyder	18.00	9.00	5.50
(64)	Allan Sothoron	18.00	9.00	5.50
(65)	Arnold Statz	18.00	9.00	5.50
(66)	Milton Stock	18.00	9.00	5.50
(67)	James Tierney	18.00	9.00	5.50
(68)	George Toporcer	18.00	9.00	5.50
(69)	Clarence (Tilly) Walker	18.00	9.00	5.50
(70)	Curtis Walker	18.00	9.00	5.50
(71)	Aaron Ward	18.00	9.00	5.50
(72)	Joe Wood	20.00	10.00	6.00
(73)	Moses Yellowhorse	20.00	10.00	6.00
(74)	Ross Young (Youngs)	35.00	17.50	10.50

1923 Exhibits - 1923-1924

The Exhibit cards for 1923 and 1924 are generally collected as a single 128-card series. The format remained basically the same as the previous year, with black and white photos (some surrounded by a white border) and blank backs.

The player's name is again shown in a plain script with the position and team printed below in a small, square-block type style. Many of the same photos were used from previous years, although some are cropped differently, and some players have new team designations, background changes, team emblems removed, borders added or taken away, and other minor changes. Fifty-eight new cards are featured, including 38 players pictured for the first time in an Exhibit set. Only the 58 new cards are included in the checklist that follows.

		NR MT	EX	VG
	Complete Set:	2000.00	1000.00	600.00
	Common Player:	20.00	10.00	6.00
(1)	Clyde Barnhart	20.00	10.00	6.00
(2)	Ray Blades	20.00	10.00	6.00
(3)	James Bottomley	40.00	20.00	12.00
(4)	George Burns	20.00	10.00	6.00
(5)	Dan Clark	20.00	10.00	6.00
(6)	Bill Doak	20.00	10.00	6.00
(7)	Joe Dugan	25.00	12.50	7.50
(8)	Howard J. Ehmke	20.00	10.00	6.00
(9)	Ira Flagstead	20.00	10.00	6.00
(10)	J.F. Fournier	20.00	10.00	6.00
(11)	Howard Freigan (Freigau)	20.00	10.00	6.00
(12)	C.E. Galloway	20.00	10.00	6.00
(13)	Joe Genewich	20.00	10.00	6.00
(14)	Mike Gonzales	20.00	10.00	6.00
(15)	H.M. "Hank" Gowdy	20.00	10.00	6.00
(16)	Charles Grimm	22.00	11.00	6.50
(17)	Heinie Groh	20.00	10.00	6.00
(18)	Chas. L. Harnett (Hartnett)	60.00	30.00	18.00
(19)	George Harper	20.00	10.00	6.00
(20)	Slim Harris (Harriss)	20.00	10.00	6.00
(21)	Clifton Heathcote	20.00	10.00	6.00
(22)	Andy High	20.00	10.00	6.00
(23)	Walter L. Holke	20.00	10.00	6.00
(24)	Charles D. Jamieson	20.00	10.00	6.00
(25)	Willie Kamm	20.00	10.00	6.00
(26)	Tony Kaufmann	20.00	10.00	6.00
(27)	Dudley Lee	20.00	10.00	6.00
(28)	Harry Liebold (Leibold)	20.00	10.00	6.00
(29)	Aldofo Luque	20.00	10.00	6.00
(30)	W.C. (Wid) Matthews	20.00	10.00	6.00
(31)	John J. McGraw	80.00	40.00	24.00
(32)	J. "Stuffy" McInnis	20.00	10.00	6.00
(33)	Johnny Morrison	20.00	10.00	6.00
(34)	John A. Mostil	20.00	10.00	6.00
(35)	J.F. O'Neill (should be S.F.)	20.00	10.00	6.00
(36)	Ernest Padgett	20.00	10.00	6.00
(37)	Val Picinich	20.00	10.00	6.00
(38)	Bill Piercy	20.00	10.00	6.00
(39)	Herman Pillette	20.00	10.00	6.00
(40)	Wallie Pipp	30.00	15.00	9.00
(41)	Raymond R. Powell	20.00	10.00	6.00
(42)	Del. Pratt	20.00	10.00	6.00
(43)	E.E. Rigney	20.00	10.00	6.00
(44)	Eddie Rommel	20.00	10.00	6.00
(45)	Geo. H. "Babe" Ruth	500.00	250.00	150.00
(46)	Muddy Ruel	20.00	10.00	6.00
(47)	J.H. Sand	20.00	10.00	6.00
(48)	Henry Severeid	20.00	10.00	6.00
(49)	Joseph Sewell	70.00	35.00	20.00
(50)	Al. Simmons	40.00	20.00	12.00
(51)	R.E. Smith	20.00	10.00	6.00
(52)	Sherrod Smith	20.00	10.00	6.00
(53)	Casey Stengel	125.00	62.00	37.00
(54)	J.R. Stevenson (Stephenson)	20.00	10.00	6.00
(55)	James Tierney	20.00	10.00	6.00
(56)	Robt. Veach	20.00	10.00	6.00
(57)	L. Woodall	20.00	10.00	6.00
(58)	Russell G. Wrighstone	20.00	10.00	6.00

1925 Exhibits - 1925

The 1925 series of Exhibits contains 128 unnumbered cards, each measuring 3-3/8" by 5-3/8". The player's name (in all capital letters), position and team (along with a line reading "Made in U.S.A.) are printed in a small white box in a lower corner of the card. Most of the photos are vertical, however a few are horizontal. There are several misspellings in the set, and the card of Robert Veach actually pictures Ernest Vache. The cards are listed here in alphabetical order.

		NR MT	EX	VG
	Complete Set:	5500.00	2750.00	1650.
	Common Player:	25.00	12.50	7.50
(1)	Sparky Adams	25.00	12.50	7.50
(2)	Grover C. Alexander	100.00	50.00	30.00
(3)	David Bancroft	45.00	22.00	13.50
(4)	Jesse Barnes	25.00	12.50	7.50
(5)	John Bassler	25.00	12.50	7.50
(6)	Lester Bell	25.00	12.50	7.50
(7)	Lawrence Benton	25.00	12.50	7.50
(8)	Carson Bigbee	25.00	12.50	7.50
(9)	Max Bishop	25.00	12.50	7.50
(10)	Raymond Blates (Blades)	25.00	12.50	7.50
(11)	Oswald Bluege	25.00	12.50	7.50
(12)	James Bottomly (Bottomley)	45.00	22.00	13.50
(13)	Raymond Bressler	25.00	12.50	7.50
(14)	John Brooks	25.00	12.50	7.50
(15)	Maurice Burrus	25.00	12.50	7.50
(16)	Max Carey	45.00	22.00	13.50
(17)	Tyrus Cobb	500.00	250.00	150.00
(18)	Eddie Collins	35.00	17.50	10.50
(19)	Stanley Coveleski	35.00	17.50	10.50
(20)	Hugh M. Critz	25.00	12.50	7.50
(21)	Hazen Cuyler	35.00	17.50	10.50
(22)	George Dauss	25.00	12.50	7.50
(23)	I.M. Davis	25.00	12.50	7.50
(24)	John H. DeBerry	25.00	12.50	7.50
(25)	Decatur	25.00	12.50	7.50
(26)	Peter Donohue	25.00	12.50	7.50
(27)	Charles Dressen	30.00	15.00	9.00
(28)	James J. Dykes	28.00	14.00	8.50
(29)	Howard Ehmke	25.00	12.50	7.50
(30)	Bib Falk (Bibb)	25.00	12.50	7.50
(31)	Wilson Fewster	25.00	12.50	7.50
(32)	Max Flack	25.00	12.50	7.50
(33)	Ira Flagstead	25.00	12.50	7.50
(34)	Jacques F. Fournier	25.00	12.50	7.50
(35)	Howard Freigau	25.00	12.50	7.50
(36)	Frank Frisch	35.00	17.50	10.50
(37)	Henry L. Gehrig	500.00	250.00	150.00
(38)	Joseph Genewich	25.00	12.50	7.50
(39)	Walter Gerber	25.00	12.50	7.50
(40)	Frank Gibson	25.00	12.50	7.50
(41)	Leon Goslin	35.00	17.50	10.50
(42)	George Grantham	25.00	12.50	7.50
(43)	Samuel Gray	25.00	12.50	7.50
(44)	Burleigh A. Grimes	35.00	17.50	10.50
(45)	Charles Grimm	28.00	14.00	8.50
(46)	Heine Groh (Heinie)	25.00	12.50	7.50
(47)	Samuel Hale	25.00	12.50	7.50
(48)	George Harper	25.00	12.50	7.50
(49)	David Harris	25.00	12.50	7.50
(50)	Stanley Harris	45.00	22.00	13.50
(51)	Leo Hartnett	45.00	22.00	13.50
(52)	Nelson Hawks	25.00	12.50	7.50
(53)	Harry Heilmann	45.00	22.00	13.50
(54)	Walter Henline	25.00	12.50	7.50
(55)	Walter Holke	25.00	12.50	7.50
(56)	Harry Hooper	45.00	22.00	13.50
(57)	Rogers Hornsby	90.00	45.00	27.00
(58)	Wilbur Hubbell	25.00	12.50	7.50
(59)	Travis C. Jackson	45.00	22.00	13.50
(60)	William Jacobson	25.00	12.50	7.50
(61)	Charles Jamieson	25.00	12.50	7.50
(62)	James H. Johnson (Johnston)	25.00	12.50	7.50
(63)	Walter Johnson	100.00	50.00	30.00
(64)	Joseph Judge	25.00	12.50	7.50
(65)	Willie Kamm	25.00	12.50	7.50
(66)	Ray Kremer	25.00	12.50	7.50
(67)	Walter Lutzke	25.00	12.50	7.50
(68)	Walter Maranville	45.00	22.00	13.50
(69)	John ("Stuffy") McInnes (McInnis)	25.00	12.50	7.50
(70)	Martin McManus	25.00	12.50	7.50
(71)	Earl McNeely	25.00	12.50	7.50
(72)	Emil Meusel	25.00	12.50	7.50
(73)	Edmund (Bing) Miller (Bing)	25.00	12.50	7.50
(74)	John Mokan	25.00	12.50	7.50
(75)	Clarence Mueller	25.00	12.50	7.50
(76)	Robert W. Muesel (Meusel)	35.00	17.50	10.50
(77)	Glenn Myatt	25.00	12.50	7.50
(78)	Arthur Nehf	25.00	12.50	7.50
(79)	George O'Neil	25.00	12.50	7.50
(80)	Frank O'Rourke	25.00	12.50	7.50
(81)	Ralph Perkins	25.00	12.50	7.50
(82)	Valentine Picinich	25.00	12.50	7.50
(83)	Walter C. Pipp	35.00	17.50	10.50
(84)	John Quinn	25.00	12.50	7.50
(85)	Emory Rigney	25.00	12.50	7.50
(86)	Eppa Rixey	45.00	22.00	13.50
(87)	Edwin Rommel	25.00	12.50	7.50
(88)	Ed Roush	45.00	22.00	13.50
(89)	Harold Ruel (Herold)	25.00	12.50	7.50
(90)	Charles Ruffing	45.00	22.00	13.50
(91)	George H. "Babe" Ruth	600.00	300.00	180.00
(92)	John Sand	25.00	12.50	7.50
(93)	Henry Severid (Severeid)	25.00	12.50	7.50
(94)	Joseph Sewell	45.00	22.00	13.50
(95)	Ray Shalk (Schalk)	45.00	22.00	13.50
(96)	Walter H. Shang (Schang)	25.00	12.50	7.50
(97)	J.R. Shawkey	28.00	14.00	8.50
(98)	Earl Sheely	25.00	12.50	7.50
(99)	William Sherdell (Sherdel)	25.00	12.50	7.50
(100)	Urban J. Shocker	25.00	12.50	7.50
(101)	George Sissler (Sisler)	45.00	22.00	13.50
(102)	Earl Smith	25.00	12.50	7.50
(103)	Sherrod Smith	25.00	12.50	7.50
(104)	Frank Snyder	25.00	12.50	7.50
(105)	Wm. H. Southworth	25.00	12.50	7.50
(106)	Tristram Speaker	55.00	27.00	16.50
(107)	Milton J. Stock	25.00	12.50	7.50
(108)	Homer Summa	25.00	12.50	7.50
(109)	William Terry	60.00	30.00	18.00
(110)	Hollis Thurston	25.00	12.50	7.50
(111)	John Tobin	25.00	12.50	7.50
(112)	Philip Todt	25.00	12.50	7.50
(113)	George Torporcer (Toporcer)	25.00	12.50	7.50
(114)	Harold Traynor	45.00	22.00	13.50
(115)	A.C. "Dazzy" Vance	45.00	22.00	13.50
(116)	Robert Veach	25.00	12.50	7.50
(117)	William Wambsganss	28.00	14.00	8.50
(118)	Aaron Ward	25.00	12.50	7.50
(119)	A.J. Weis	25.00	12.50	7.50
(120)	Frank Welch	25.00	12.50	7.50
(121)	Zack Wheat	45.00	22.00	13.50
(122)	Fred Williams	28.00	14.00	8.50
(123)	Kenneth Williams	28.00	14.00	8.50
(124)	Ernest Wingard	25.00	12.50	7.50
(125)	Ivy Wingo	25.00	12.50	7.50
(126)	Al Wings (Wingo)	25.00	12.50	7.50
(127)	Larry Woodall	25.00	12.50	7.50
(128)	Glen Wright (Glenn)	25.00	12.50	7.50

1926 Exhibits - 1926

The 1926 Exhibit cards are the same size (3-3/8" by 5-3/8") as previous Exhibit issues but are easily distinguished because of their blue-gray color. The set consists of 128 cards, 91 of which are identical to the photos in the 1925 series. The 37 new photos do not include the boxed caption used in 1925. There are several errors in the 1926 set: The photos of Hunnefield and Thomas are transposed; Bischoff's card identifies him as playing for Boston, N.L. (rather than A.L.) and the photo of Galloway is reversed. The cards are unnumbered and are listed here alphabetically.

		NR MT	EX	VG
	Complete Set:	5500.00	2750.00	1650.
	Common Player:	25.00	12.50	7.50
(1)	Sparky Adams	25.00	12.50	7.50
(2)	David Bancroft	45.00	22.00	13.50
(3)	John Bassler	25.00	12.50	7.50
(4)	Lester Bell	25.00	12.50	7.50
(5)	John M. Bentley	25.00	12.50	7.50
(6)	Lawrence Benton	25.00	12.50	7.50
(7)	Carson Bigbee	25.00	12.50	7.50
(8)	George Bischoff	25.00	12.50	7.50
(9)	Max Bishop	25.00	12.50	7.50
(10)	J. Fred Blake	25.00	12.50	7.50
(11)	Ted Blankenship	25.00	12.50	7.50
(12)	Raymond Blates (Blades)	25.00	12.50	7.50
(13)	Lucerne A. Blue (Luzerne)	25.00	12.50	7.50
(14)	Oswald Bluege	25.00	12.50	7.50
(15)	James Bottomly (Bottomley)	45.00	22.00	13.50
(16)	Raymond Bressler	25.00	12.50	7.50
(17)	Geo. H. Burns	25.00	12.50	7.50
(18)	Maurice Burrus	25.00	12.50	7.50
(19)	John Butler	25.00	12.50	7.50
(20)	Max Carey	45.00	22.00	13.50
(21)	Tyrus Cobb	500.00	250.00	150.00
(22)	Eddie Collins	45.00	22.00	13.50
(23)	Patrick T. Collins	25.00	12.50	7.50
(24)	Earl B. Combs (Earle)	45.00	22.00	13.50
(25)	James E. Cooney	25.00	12.50	7.50
(26)	Stanley Coveleski	45.00	22.00	13.50
(27)	Hugh M. Critz	25.00	12.50	7.50
(28)	Hazen Cuyler	45.00	22.00	13.50
(29)	George Dauss	25.00	12.50	7.50
(30)	Peter Donohue	25.00	12.50	7.50
(31)	Charles Dressen	30.00	15.00	9.00
(32)	James J. Dykes	28.00	14.00	8.50
(33)	Bib Falk (Bibb)	25.00	12.50	7.50
(34)	Edward S. Farrell	25.00	12.50	7.50
(35)	Wilson Fewster	25.00	12.50	7.50
(36)	Ira Flagstead	25.00	12.50	7.50
(37)	Howard Freigau	25.00	12.50	7.50
(38)	Bernard Friberg	25.00	12.50	7.50
(39)	Frank Frisch	45.00	22.00	13.50
(40)	Jacques F. Furnier (Fournier)	25.00	12.50	7.50
(41)	Joseph Galloway (Clarence)	25.00	12.50	7.50
(42)	Henry L. Gehrig	500.00	250.00	150.00
(43)	Charles Gehringer	45.00	22.00	13.50
(44)	Joseph Genewich	25.00	12.50	7.50
(45)	Walter Gerber	25.00	12.50	7.50
(46)	Leon Goslin	45.00	22.00	13.50
(47)	George Grantham	25.00	12.50	7.50
(48)	Burleigh A. Grimes	45.00	22.00	13.50
(49)	Charles Grimm	28.00	14.00	8.50
(50)	Fred Haney	28.00	14.00	8.50
(51)	Wm. Hargrave	25.00	12.50	7.50
(52)	George Harper	25.00	12.50	7.50
(53)	Stanley Harris	45.00	22.00	13.50
(54)	Leo Hartnett	45.00	22.00	13.50
(55)	Joseph Hauser	30.00	15.00	9.00
(56)	C.E. Heathcote	25.00	12.50	7.50
(57)	Harry Heilmann	45.00	22.00	13.50
(58)	Walter Henline	25.00	12.50	7.50
(59)	Ramon Herrera	25.00	12.50	7.50
(60)	Andrew A. High	25.00	12.50	7.50
(61)	Rogers Hornsby	100.00	50.00	30.00
(62)	Clarence Huber	25.00	12.50	7.50

		NR MT	EX	VG
(63)	Wm. Hunnefield (photo actually Tommy Thomas)	25.00	12.50	7.50
(64)	William Jacobson	25.00	12.50	7.50
(65)	Walter Johnson	100.00	50.00	30.00
(66)	Joseph Judge	25.00	12.50	7.50
(67)	Willie Kamm	25.00	12.50	7.50
(68)	Ray Kremer	25.00	12.50	7.50
(69)	Anthony Lazzeri	35.00	17.50	10.50
(70)	Frederick Lindstrom	45.00	22.00	13.50
(71)	Walter Lutzke	25.00	12.50	7.50
(72)	John Makan (Mokan)	25.00	12.50	7.50
(73)	Walter Maranville	45.00	22.00	13.50
(74)	Martin McManus	25.00	12.50	7.50
(75)	Earl McNeely	25.00	12.50	7.50
(76)	Hugh A. McQuillan	25.00	12.50	7.50
(77)	Douglas McWeeny	25.00	12.50	7.50
(78)	Oscar Melillo	25.00	12.50	7.50
(79)	Edmund (Bind) Miller (Bing)	25.00	12.50	7.50
(80)	Clarence Mueller	25.00	12.50	7.50
(81)	Robert W. Muesel (Meusel)	35.00	17.50	10.50
(82)	Joseph W. Munson	25.00	12.50	7.50
(83)	Emil Musel (Meusel)	25.00	12.50	7.50
(84)	Glenn Myatt	25.00	12.50	7.50
(85)	Bernie F. Neis	25.00	12.50	7.50
(86)	Robert O'Farrell	25.00	12.50	7.50
(87)	George O'Neil	25.00	12.50	7.50
(88)	Frank O'Rourke	25.00	12.50	7.50
(89)	Ralph Perkins	25.00	12.50	7.50
(90)	Walter C. Pipp	35.00	17.50	10.50
(91)	Emory Rigney	25.00	12.50	7.50
(92)	James J. Ring	25.00	12.50	7.50
(93)	Eppa Rixey	45.00	22.00	13.50
(94)	Edwin Rommel	25.00	12.50	7.50
(95)	Ed. Roush	45.00	22.00	13.50
(96)	Harold Ruel (Herold)	25.00	12.50	7.50
(97)	Charles Ruffing	45.00	22.00	13.50
(98)	Geo. H. "Babe" Ruth	600.00	300.00	180.00
(99)	John Sand	25.00	12.50	7.50
(100)	Joseph Sewell	45.00	22.00	13.50
(101)	Ray Shalk (Schalk)	45.00	22.00	13.50
(102)	J.R. Shawkey	28.00	14.00	8.50
(103)	Earl Sheely	25.00	12.50	7.50
(104)	William Sherdell (Sherdel)	25.00	12.50	7.50
(105)	Urban J. Shocker	25.00	12.50	7.50
(106)	George Sissler (Sisler)	45.00	22.00	13.50
(107)	Earl Smith	25.00	12.50	7.50
(108)	Sherrod Smith	25.00	12.50	7.50
(109)	Frank Snyder	25.00	12.50	7.50
(110)	Tristram Speaker	50.00	25.00	15.00
(111)	Fred Spurgeon	25.00	12.50	7.50
(112)	Homer Summa	25.00	12.50	7.50
(113)	Edward Taylor	25.00	12.50	7.50
(114)	J. Taylor	25.00	12.50	7.50
(115)	William Terry	50.00	25.00	15.00
(116)	Hollis Thurston	25.00	12.50	7.50
(117)	Philip Todt	25.00	12.50	7.50
(118)	George Torporcer (Toporcer)	25.00	12.50	7.50
(119)	Harold Traynor	45.00	22.00	13.50
(120)	Wm. Wambsganss	28.00	14.00	8.50
(121)	John Warner	25.00	12.50	7.50
(122)	Zach Wheat	45.00	22.00	13.50
(123)	Kenneth Williams	28.00	14.00	8.50
(124)	Ernest Wingard	25.00	12.50	7.50
(125)	Fred Wingfield	25.00	12.50	7.50
(126)	Ivy Wingo	25.00	12.50	7.50
(127)	Glen Wright (Glenn)	25.00	12.50	7.50
(128)	Russell Wrightstone	25.00	12.50	7.50

1927 Exhibits - 1927

The Exhibit Supply Company issued a set of 64 cards in 1927, each measuring 3-3/8" by 5-3/8". The set can be differentiated from earlier issues by its light green tint. The player's name and team appear in capital letters in one lower corner, while "Ex. Sup. Co., Chgo." and "Made in U.S.A." appear in the other. All 64 photos used in the 1927 set were borrowed from previous issues, but 13 players are listed with new teams. There are several misspellings and other labeling errors in the set. The unnumbered cards are listed here in alphabetical order.

		NR MT	EX	VG
Complete Set:		3000.00	1500.00	900.00
Common Player:		18.00	9.00	5.50
(1)	Sparky Adams	18.00	9.00	5.50
(2)	Grover C. Alexander	45.00	22.00	13.50
(3)	David Bancroft	35.00	17.50	10.50
(4)	John Bassler	18.00	9.00	5.50
(5)	John M. Bentley (middle initial actually N.)	18.00	9.00	5.50
(6)	Fred Blankenship (Ted)	18.00	9.00	5.50
(7)	James Bottomly (Bottomley)	35.00	17.50	10.50
(8)	Raymond Bressler	18.00	9.00	5.50
(9)	Geo. H. Burns	18.00	9.00	5.50
(10)	John Buttler (Butler)	18.00	9.00	5.50
(11)	Tyrus Cobb	300.00	150.00	90.00
(12)	Eddie Collins	35.00	17.50	10.50
(13)	Hazen Cuyler	35.00	17.50	10.50
(14)	George Daus (Dauss)	18.00	9.00	5.50
(15)	A.R. Decatur	18.00	9.00	5.50
(16)	Wilson Fewster	18.00	9.00	5.50
(17)	Ira Flagstead	18.00	9.00	5.50
(18)	Henry L. Gehrig	300.00	150.00	90.00
(19)	Charles Gehringer	35.00	17.50	10.50
(20)	Joseph Genewich	18.00	9.00	5.50
(21)	Leon Goslin	35.00	17.50	10.50
(22)	Burleigh A. Grimes	35.00	17.50	10.50
(23)	Charles Grimm	20.00	10.00	6.00
(24)	Fred Haney	20.00	10.00	6.00
(25)	Wm. Hargrave	18.00	9.00	5.50
(26)	George Harper	18.00	9.00	5.50
(27)	Leo Hartnett	35.00	17.50	10.50
(28)	Clifton Heathcote	18.00	9.00	5.50
(29)	Harry Heilman (Heillmann)	35.00	17.50	10.50
(30)	Walter Henline	18.00	9.00	5.50
(31)	Andrew High	18.00	9.00	5.50
(32)	Rogers Hornsby	100.00	50.00	30.00
(33)	Wm. Hunnefield (photo actually Tommy Thomas)	18.00	9.00	5.50
(34)	Walter Johnson	100.00	50.00	30.00
(35)	Willie Kamm	18.00	9.00	5.50
(36)	Ray Kremer	18.00	9.00	5.50
(37)	Anthony Lazzeri	30.00	15.00	9.00
(38)	Fredrick Lindstrom (Frederick)	35.00	17.50	10.50
(39)	Walter Lutzke	18.00	9.00	5.50
(40)	John "Stuffy" McInnes (McInnis)	18.00	9.00	5.50
(41)	John Mokan	18.00	9.00	5.50
(42)	Robert W. Muesel (Meusel)	25.00	12.50	7.50
(43)	Glenn Myatt	18.00	9.00	5.50
(44)	Bernie Neis	18.00	9.00	5.50
(45)	Robert O'Farrell	18.00	9.00	5.50
(46)	Walter C. Pipp	30.00	15.00	9.00
(47)	Eppa Rixey	35.00	17.50	10.50
(48)	Harold Ruel (Herold)	18.00	9.00	5.50
(49)	Geo. H. "Babe" Ruth	500.00	250.00	150.00
(50)	Ray Schalk	35.00	17.50	10.50
(51)	George Sissler (Sisler)	35.00	17.50	10.50
(52)	Earl Smith	18.00	9.00	5.50
(53)	Wm. H. Southworth	18.00	9.00	5.50
(54)	Tristam Speaker (Tristram)	100.00	50.00	30.00
(55)	J. Taylor	18.00	9.00	5.50
(56)	Philip Todt	18.00	9.00	5.50
(57)	Harold Traynor	35.00	17.50	10.50
(58)	William Wambsganns (Wambsganss)	20.00	10.00	6.00
(59)	Zach Wheat	35.00	17.50	10.50
(60)	Kenneth Williams	20.00	10.00	6.00
(61)	Ernest Wingard	18.00	9.00	5.50
(62)	Fred Wingfield	18.00	9.00	5.50
(63)	Ivy Wingo	18.00	9.00	5.50
(64)	Russell Wrightstone	18.00	9.00	5.50

1928 Exhibits - 1928

The Exhibit Supply Company switched to a blue tint for the photos in its 64-card set in 1928. There are 36 new photos in the set, including 24 new players. Four players from the previous year are shown with new teams and 24 of the cards are identical to the 1927 series, except for the color of the card. Cards are found with either blank backs or postcard backs. The photos are captioned in the same style as the 1927 set. The set again includes some misspelling and incorrect labels. The cards are unnumbered and are listed here in alphabetical order.

		NR MT	EX	VG
Complete Set:		2750.00	1375.00	800.00
Common Player:		18.00	9.00	5.50
(1)	Grover C. Alexander	70.00	35.00	20.00
(2)	David Bancroft	18.00	9.00	5.50
(3)	Virgil Barnes	18.00	9.00	5.50
(4)	Francis R. Blades	18.00	9.00	5.50
(5)	L.A. Blue	18.00	9.00	5.50
(6)	Edward W. Brown	18.00	9.00	5.50
(7)	Max G. Carey	35.00	17.50	10.50
(8)	Chalmer W. Cissell	18.00	9.00	5.50
(9)	Gordon S. Cochrane	35.00	17.50	10.50
(10)	Pat Collins	18.00	9.00	5.50
(11)	Hugh M. Critz	18.00	9.00	5.50
(12)	Howard Ehmke	18.00	9.00	5.50
(13)	E. English	18.00	9.00	5.50
(14)	Bib Falk (Bibb)	18.00	9.00	5.50
(15)	Ira Flagstead	18.00	9.00	5.50
(16)	Robert Fothergill	18.00	9.00	5.50
(17)	Frank Frisch	35.00	17.50	10.50
(18)	Lou Gehrig	500.00	250.00	150.00
(19)	Leon Goslin	35.00	17.50	10.50
(20)	Eugene Hargrave	18.00	9.00	5.50
(21)	Charles R. Hargraves (Hargreaves)	18.00	9.00	5.50
(22)	Stanley Harris	35.00	17.50	10.50
(23)	Bryan "Slim" Harriss	18.00	9.00	5.50
(24)	Leo Hartnett	35.00	17.50	10.50
(25)	Joseph Hauser	18.00	9.00	5.50
(26)	Fred Hoffman (Hofmann)	18.00	9.00	5.50
(27)	J. Francis Hogan	18.00	9.00	5.50
(28)	Rogers Hornsby	100.00	50.00	30.00
(29)	Chas. Jamieson	18.00	9.00	5.50
(30)	Sam Jones	18.00	9.00	5.50
(31)	Ray Kremer	18.00	9.00	5.50
(32)	Fred Leach	18.00	9.00	5.50
(33)	Fredrick Lindstrom (Frederick)	35.00	17.50	10.50
(34)	Adolph Luque (Adolfo)	18.00	9.00	5.50
(35)	Theodore Lyons	35.00	17.50	10.50
(36)	Harry McCurdy	18.00	9.00	5.50
(37)	Glenn Myatt	18.00	9.00	5.50
(38)	John Ogden (photo actually Warren Ogden)	18.00	9.00	5.50
(39)	James Ring	18.00	9.00	5.50
(40)	A.C. Root (should be C.H.)	18.00	9.00	5.50
(41)	Edd. Roush	35.00	17.50	10.50
(42)	Harold Ruel (Herold)	18.00	9.00	5.50
(43)	Geo. H. "Babe" Ruth	600.00	300.00	180.00
(44)	Henry Sand	18.00	9.00	5.50
(45)	Joseph Sewell	35.00	17.50	10.50
(46)	Walter Shang (Schang)	18.00	9.00	5.50
(47)	Urban J. Shocker	18.00	9.00	5.50
(48)	Al. Simmons	60.00	30.00	18.00
(49)	Earl Smith	18.00	9.00	5.50
(50)	Robert Smith	18.00	9.00	5.50
(51)	Fred Schulte	18.00	9.00	5.50
(52)	Jack Tavener	18.00	9.00	5.50
(53)	J. Taylor	18.00	9.00	5.50
(54)	Philip Todt	18.00	9.00	5.50
(55)	Geo. Uhle	18.00	9.00	5.50
(56)	Arthur "Dazzy" Vance	35.00	17.50	10.50
(57)	Paul Waner	35.00	17.50	10.50
(58)	Earl G. Whitehill (middle intial actually O.)	18.00	9.00	5.50
(59)	Fred Williams	20.00	10.00	6.00
(60)	James Wilson	18.00	9.00	5.50
(61)	L.R. (Hack) Wilson	35.00	17.50	10.50
(62)	Lawrence Woodall	18.00	9.00	5.50
(63)	Glen Wright (Glen)	18.00	9.00	5.50
(64)	William A. Zitzman (Zitzmann)	18.00	9.00	5.50

1928 Exhibits Pacific Coast League

This regional series of 32 cards pictures players from the six California teams in the Pacific Coast League. Like the 1928 major league Exhibits, the PCL cards have a blue tint and are not numbered. They are blank-backed and measure 3-3/8" by 5-3/8". The set includes several misspellings. Cards are occasionally found with a corner clipped, the card corner to be used as a coupon with redemption value.

		NR MT	EX	VG
Complete Set:		1500.00	750.00	450.00
Common Player:		40.00	20.00	12.00
1	"Buzz" Arlett	70.00	35.00	20.00
2	Earl Averill	150.00	75.00	45.00
3	Carl Berger (Walter)	70.00	35.00	20.00
4	"Ping" Bodie	60.00	30.00	18.00
5	Carl Dittmar	40.00	20.00	12.00
6	Jack Fenton	40.00	20.00	12.00
7	Neal "Mickey" Finn (Cornelius)	40.00	20.00	12.00
8	Ray French	40.00	20.00	12.00
9	Tony Governor	40.00	20.00	12.00
10	"Truck" Hannah	40.00	20.00	12.00
11	Mickey Heath	40.00	20.00	12.00
12	Wally Hood	40.00	20.00	12.00

		NR MT	EX	VG
13	"Fuzzy" Hufft	40.00	20.00	12.00
14	Snead Jolly (Smead)	40.00	20.00	12.00
15	Bobby "Ducky" Jones	40.00	20.00	12.00
16	Rudy Kallio	40.00	20.00	12.00
17	Ray Keating	40.00	20.00	12.00
18	Johnny Kerr	40.00	20.00	12.00
19	Harry Krause	40.00	20.00	12.00
20	Lynford H. Larry (Lary)	40.00	20.00	12.00
21	Dudley Lee	40.00	20.00	12.00
22	Walter "Duster" Mails	40.00	20.00	12.00
23	Jimmy Reese	50.00	25.00	15.00
24	"Dusty" Rhodes	40.00	20.00	12.00
25	Hal Rhyne	40.00	20.00	12.00
26	Hank Severied (Severeid)	40.00	20.00	12.00
27	Earl Sheely	40.00	20.00	12.00
28	Frank Shellenback	40.00	20.00	12.00
29	Gordon Slade	40.00	20.00	12.00
30	Hollis Thurston	40.00	20.00	12.00
31	"Babe" Twombly	40.00	20.00	12.00
32	Earl "Tex" Weathersby	40.00	20.00	12.00

1929-30 Exhibits Four-On-One

Although the size of the card remained the same, the Exhibit Supply Company of Chicago began putting four players' pictures on each card in 1929 - a practice that would continue for the next decade. Known as "four-on-one" cards, the players are identified by name and team at the bottom of the photos, which are separated by borders. The 32 cards in the 1929-30 series have postcard backs and were printed in a wide range of color combinations including: black on orange, black on blue, brown on orange, blue on green, black on red, black on white, blue on white, black on yellow, brown on white, brown on yellow and red on yellow. Most of the backs are uncolored, however, cards with a black on red front have been seen with red backs, and cards with blue on yellow fronts have been seen with yellow backs. There are numerous spelling and caption errors in the set, and the player identified as Babe Herman is actually Jesse Petty.

	NR MT	EX	VG
Complete Set:	2500.00	1250.00	750.00
Common Player:	30.00	15.00	9.00
(1) Earl J. Adams, R. Bartell, Earl Sheely, Harold Traynor	45.00	22.00	13.50
(2) Dale Alexander, C. Gehringer, G.F. McManus (should be M.J.), H.F. Rice	45.00	22.00	13.50
(3) Grover C. Alexander, James Bottomly (Bottomley), Frank Frisch, James Wilson	70.00	35.00	20.00
(4) Martin G. Autrey (Autry), Alex Metzler, Carl Reynolds, Alphonse Thomas	30.00	15.00	9.00
(5) Earl Averill, B.A. Falk, K. Holloway, L. Sewell	45.00	22.00	13.50
(6) David Bancroft, Del L. Bisonette (Bissonette), John H. DeBerry, Floyd C. Herman (photo actually Jesse Petty)	45.00	22.00	13.50
(7) C.E. Beck, Leo Hartnett, Rogers Hornsby, L.R. (Hack) Wilson	90.00	45.00	27.00
(8) Ray Benge, Lester L. Sweetland, A.C. Whitney, Cy. Williams	30.00	15.00	9.00
(9) Benny Bengough, Earl B. Coombs (Combs), Waite Hoyt, Anthony Lazzeri	50.00	25.00	15.00
(10) L. Benton, Melvin Ott, Andrew Reese, William Terry	45.00	22.00	13.50
(11) Max Bishop, James Dykes, Samuel Hale, Homer Summa	30.00	15.00	9.00
(12) L.A. Blue, O. Melillo, F.O. Rourke (Frank O'Rourke), F. Schulte	30.00	15.00	9.00
(13) Oswald Bluege, Leon Goslin, Joseph Judge, Harold Ruel (Herold)	45.00	22.00	13.50
(14) Chalmer W. Cissell, John W. Clancy, Willie Kamm, John L. Kerr	30.00	15.00	9.00
(15) Gordon S. Cochrane, Jimmy Foxx, Robert M. Grove, George Haas	100.00	50.00	30.00
(16) Pat Collins, Joe Dugan, Edward Farrel (Farrell), George Sisler	45.00	22.00	13.50
(17) H.M. Critz, G.L. Kelly, V.J. Picinich, W.C. Walker	45.00	22.00	13.50
(18) Nick Cullop, D'Arcy Flowers, Harvey Hendrick, Arthur "Dazzy" Vance	45.00	22.00	13.50
(19) Hazen Cuyler, E. English, C.J. Grimm, C.H. Root	45.00	22.00	13.50
(20) Taylor Douthit, Chas. M. Gilbert (Gelbert), Chas. J. Hafey, Fred G. Haney	45.00	22.00	13.50
(21) Leo Durocher, Henry L. Gehrig, Mark Koenig, Geo. H. "Babe" Ruth	700.00	350.00	200.00
(22) L.A. Fonseca, Carl Lind, J. Sewell, J. Tavener	45.00	22.00	13.50
(23) H.E. Ford, C.F. Lucas, C.A. Pittenger, E.V. Purdy	30.00	15.00	9.00
(24) Bernard Friberg, Donald Hurst, Frank O'Doul, Fresco Thompson	30.00	15.00	9.00
(25) S. Gray, R. Kress, H. Manush, W.H. Shang (Schang)	45.00	22.00	13.50
(26) Charles R. Hargreaves, Ray Kremer, Lloyd Waner, Paul Waner	45.00	22.00	13.50
(27) George Harper, Fred Maguire, Lance Richbourg, Robert Smith	30.00	15.00	9.00
(28) Jack Hayes, Sam P. Jones, Chas. M. Myer, Sam Rice	45.00	22.00	13.50
(29) Harry E. Heilman (Heilmann), C.N. Richardson, M.J. Shea, G.E. Uhle	45.00	22.00	13.50
(30) J.A. Heving, R.R. Reeves (should be R.E.), J. Rothrock, C.H. Ruffing	45.00	22.00	13.50
(31) J.F. Hogan, T.C. Jackson, Fred Lindstrom, J.D. Welsh	45.00	22.00	13.50
(32) W.W. Regan, H. Rhyne, D. Taitt, P.J. Todt	30.00	15.00	9.00

1931-32 Exhibits Four-On-One

The 1931-1932 series issued by the Exhibit Company again consisted of 32 cards, each picturing four players. The series can be differentiated from the previous year by the coupon backs, which list various premiums available (including kazoos, toy pistols and other prizes). The cards again were printed in various color combinations, including: black on green, blue on green, black on orange, black on red, blue on white and black on yellow. There are numerous spelling and caption errors in the series. The Babe Herman/Jesse Petty error of the previous year was still not corrected, and the card of Rick Ferrell not only misspells his name ("Farrel"), but also pictures the wrong player (Edward Farrell).

	NR MT	EX	VG
Complete Set:	3000.00	1500.00	900.00
Common Player:	40.00	20.00	12.00
(1) Earl J. Adams, James Bottomly (Bottomley), Frank Frisch, James Wilson	55.00	27.00	16.50
(2) Dale Alexander, C. Gehringer, G.F. McManus (should be M.J.), G.E. Uhle	55.00	27.00	16.50
(3) L.L. Appling (should be L.B.), Chalmer W. Cissell, Willie Kamm, Ted Lyons	55.00	27.00	16.50
(4) Buzz Arlett, Ray Benge, Chuck Klein, A.C. Whitney	55.00	27.00	16.50
(5) Earl Averill, B.A. Falk, L.A. Fonseca, L. Sewell	55.00	27.00	16.50
(6) Richard Bartell, Bernard Friberg, Donald Hurst, Harry McCurdy	40.00	20.00	12.00
(7) Walter Berger, Fred Maguire, Lance Richbourg, Earl Sheely	40.00	20.00	12.00
(8) Chas. Berry, Robt. Reeves, R.R. Reeves (should be R.E.), J. Rothrock	40.00	20.00	12.00
(9) Del L. Bisonette (Bissonette), Floyd C. Herman (photo - J. Petty), Jack Quinn, Glenn Wright	40.00	20.00	12.00
(10) L.A. Blue, Smead Jolley, Carl Reynolds, Henry Tate	40.00	20.00	12.00
(11) O. Bluege, Joe Judge, Chas. M. Myer, Sam Rice	55.00	27.00	16.50
(12) John Boley, James Dykes, E.J. Miller, Al. Simmons	55.00	27.00	16.50
(13) Gordon S. Chochrane, Jimmy Foxx, Robert M. Grove, George Haas	150.00	75.00	45.00
(14) Adam Comorosky, Gus Suhr, T.J. Thevenow, Harold Traynor	55.00	27.00	16.50
(15) Earl B. Coombs (Combs), W. Dickey, Anthony Lazzeri, H. Pennock	150.00	75.00	45.00
(16) H.M. Critz, J.F. Hogan, T.C. Jackson, Fred Lindstrom	55.00	27.00	16.50
(17) Joe Cronin, H. Manush, F. Marberry, Roy Spencer	55.00	27.00	16.50
(18) Nick Cullop, Les Durocher (Leo), Harry Heilmann, W.C. Walker	55.00	27.00	16.50
(19) Hazen Cuyler, E. English, C.J. Grimm, C.H. Root	55.00	27.00	16.50
(20) Taylor Douthit, Chas. M. Gilbert (Gelbert), Chas. J. Hafey, Bill Hallahan	40.00	20.00	12.00
(21) Richard Farrel (Ferrell), S. Gray, R. Kress, W. Stewart	50.00	25.00	15.00
(22) W. Ferrell, J. Goldman, Hunnefield, Ed Morgan	40.00	20.00	12.00
(23) Fred Fitzsimmons, Robert O'Farrell, Melvin Ott, William Terry	55.00	27.00	16.50
(24) D'Arcy Flowers, Frank O'Doul, Fresco Thompson, Arthur "Dazzy" Vance	55.00	27.00	16.50
(25) H.E. Ford (should be H.H.), Gooch, C.F. Lucas, W. Roettger	40.00	20.00	12.00
(26) E. Funk, W. Hoyt, Mark Koenig, Wallie Schang	55.00	27.00	16.50
(27) Henry L. Gehrig, Lyn Lary, James Reese, Geo. H. "Babe" Ruth	500.00	250.00	150.00
(28) George Grantham, Ray Kremer, Lloyd Waner, Paul Waner	55.00	27.00	16.50
(29) Leon Goslin, O. Melillo, F.O. Rourke (Frank O'Rourke), F. Schulte	55.00	27.00	16.50
(30) Leo Hartnett, Rogers Hornsby, J.R. Stevenson (Stephenson), L.R. (Hack) Wilson	90.00	45.00	27.00
(31) D. MacFayden, H. Rhyne, Bill Sweeney, E.W. Webb	40.00	20.00	12.00
(32) Walter Maranville, Randolph Moore, Alfred Spohrer, J.T. Zachary	55.00	27.00	16.50

1933 Exhibits Four-On-One

The 1933 series of four-on-one Exhibits consists of 16 cards with blank backs. Color combinations include: blue on green, black on orange, black on red, blue on white and black on yellow. Most have a plain, white back, although the black on yellow cards are also found with a yellow back. Most of the pictures used are reprinted from previous series, and there are some spelling and caption errors, including the Richard Ferrell/ Edward Farrell mixup from the previous year. Al Lopez is shown as "Vincent" Lopez.

	NR MT	EX	VG
Complete Set:	2000.00	1000.00	600.00
Common Player:	40.00	20.00	12.00
(1) Earl J. Adams, Frank Frisch, Chas. Gilbert (Gelbert), Bill Hallahan	55.00	27.00	16.50
(2) Earl Averill, W. Ferrell, Ed Morgan, L. Sewell	55.00	27.00	16.50
(3) Richard Bartell, Ray Benge, Donald Hurst, Chuck Klein	55.00	27.00	16.50
(4) Walter Berger, Walter Maranville, Alfred Spohrer, J.T. Zachary	55.00	27.00	16.50
(5) Charles Berry, L.A. Blue, Ted Lyons, Bob Seeds	55.00	27.00	16.50
(6) Chas. Berry, D. MacFayden, H. Rhyne, E.W. Webb	40.00	20.00	12.00
(7) Mickey Cochrane, Jimmy Foxx, Robert M. Grove, Al. Simmons	200.00	100.00	60.00
(8) H.M. Critz, Fred Fitzsimmons, Fred Lindstrom, Robert O'Farrell	55.00	27.00	16.50
(9) W. Dickey, Anthony Lazzeri, H. Pennock, George H. "Babe" Ruth	800.00	400.00	250.00
(10) Taylor Douthit, George Grantham, Chas. J. Hafey, C.F. Lucas	55.00	27.00	16.50
(11) E. English, C.J. Grimm, C.H. Root, J.R. Stevenson (Stephenson)	40.00	20.00	12.00
(12) Richard Farrel (Farrell), Leon Goslin, S. Gray, O. Melillo	55.00	27.00	16.50
(13) C. Gehringer, "Muddy" Ruel, Jonathan Stone (first name - John), G.E. Uhle	55.00	27.00	16.50
(14) Joseph Judge, H. Manush, F. Marberry, Roy Spencer	55.00	27.00	16.50
(15) Vincent Lopez (Al), Frank O'Doul, Arthur "Dazzy" Vance, Glenn Wright	55.00	27.00	16.50
(16) Gus Suhr, Tom J. Thevenow, Lloyd Waner, Paul Waner	55.00	27.00	16.50

1934 Exhibits Four-On-One

This 16-card series issued by the Exhibit Co. in 1934 is again blank-backed and continues the four-on-one format. The 1934 series can be differentiated from previous years by the more subdued color combinations of the cards, which include lighter shades of blue, brown, green and violet - all printed on white card stock. Many new photos were also used in the 1934 series. Of the 64 players included, 25 appear for the first time and another 16 were given new poses. Spelling was improved, but Al Lopez is still identified as "Vincent."

	NR MT	EX	VG
Complete Set:	1750.00	875.00	500.00
Common Player:	30.00	15.00	9.00
(1) Luke Appling, George Earnshaw, Al Simmons, Evar Swanson	45.00	22.00	13.50
(2) Earl Averill, W. Ferrell, Willie Kamm, Frank Pytlak	45.00	22.00	13.50
(3) Richard Bartell, Donald Hurst, Wesley Schulmerich, Jimmy Wilson	30.00	15.00	9.00
(4) Walter Berger, Ed Brandt, Frank Hogan, Bill Urbanski	30.00	15.00	9.00
(5) Jim Bottomley, Chas. J. Hafey, Botchi Lombardi, Tony Piet	45.00	22.00	13.50
(6) Irving Burns, Irving Hadley, Rollie Hemsley, O. Melillo	30.00	15.00	9.00
(7) Bill Cissell, Rick Ferrell, Lefty Grove, Roy Johnson	45.00	22.00	13.50
(8) Mickey Cochrane, C. Gehringer, Goose Goslin, Fred Marberry	70.00	35.00	20.00
(9) George Cramer (Roger), Jimmy Foxx, Frank Higgins, Slug Mahaffey	70.00	35.00	20.00
(10) Joe Cronin, Alvin Crowder, Joe Kuhel, H. Manush	45.00	22.00	13.50
(11) W. Dickey, Lou Gehrig, Vernon Gomez, Geo. H. "Babe" Ruth	800.00	400.00	250.00
(12) E. English, C.J. Grimm, Chas. Klein, Lon Warneke	45.00	22.00	13.50
(13) Frank Frisch, Bill Hallahan, Pepper Martin,			

	NR MT	EX	VG
John Rothrock	45.00	22.00	13.50
(14) Carl Hubbell, Mel Ott, Blondy Ryan, Bill Terry	70.00	35.00	20.00
(15) Leonard Koenecke, Sam Leslie, Vincent Lopez (Al), Glenn Wright	40.00	20.00	12.00
(16) T.J. Thevenow, Pie Traynor, Lloyd Waner, Paul Waner	65.00	33.00	20.00

1935 Exhibits Four-On-One

Continuing with the same four-on-one format, the Exhibit Supply Co. issued another 16-card series in 1935. All cards were printed in a slate-blue color with a plain, blank back. Seventeen of the players included in the 1935 series appear for the first time, while another 11 are shown with new poses. There are several spelling and caption errors. Babe Ruth appears in a regular Exhibit issue for the last time.

	NR MT	EX	VG
Complete Set:	2000.00	1000.00	600.00
Common Player:	30.00	15.00	9.00
(1) Earl Averill, Mel Harder, Willie Kamm, Hal Trosky	45.00	22.00	13.50
(2) Walter Berger, Ed Brandt, Frank Hogan, "Babe" Ruth	500.00	250.00	150.00
(3) Henry Bonura, Jimmy Dykes, Ted Lyons, Al Simmons	45.00	22.00	13.50
(4) Jimmy Bottomley, Paul Derringer, Chas. J. Hafey, Botchi Lombardi	65.00	33.00	20.00
(5) Irving Burns, Rollie Hemsley, O. Melillo, L.N. Newson	30.00	15.00	9.00
(6) Guy Bush, Pie Traynor, Floyd Vaughn (Vaughan), Paul Waner	65.00	33.00	20.00
(7) Mickey Cochrane, C. Gehringer, Goose Goslin, Linwood Rowe (Lynwood)	65.00	33.00	20.00
(8) Phil Collins, John "Blondy" Ryan, Geo. Watkins, Jimmy Wilson	30.00	15.00	9.00
(9) George Cramer (Roger), Jimmy Foxx, Bob Johnson, Slug Mahaffey	65.00	33.00	20.00
(10) Hughie Critz, Carl Hubbell, Mel Ott, Bill Terry	70.00	35.00	21.00
(11) Joe Cronin, Rick Ferrell, Lefty Grove, Billy Werber	65.00	33.00	20.00
(12) Tony Cuccinello, Vincent Lopez (Al), Van Mungo, Dan Taylor	40.00	20.00	12.00
(13) Jerome "Dizzy" Dean, Paul Dean, Frank Frisch, Pepper Martin	150.00	75.00	45.00
(14) W. Dickey, Lou Gehrig, Vernon Gomez, Tony Lazzeri	500.00	250.00	150.00
(15) C.J. Grimm, Gabby Hartnett, Chas. Klein, Lon Warneke	45.00	22.00	13.50
(16) H. Manush, Buddy Meyer (Myer), Fred Schulte, Earl Whitehill	45.00	22.00	13.50

1936 Exhibits Four-On-One

The 1936 series of four-on-one cards again consisted of 16 cards printed in either green or slate blue with plain, blank backs. The series can be differentiated from the previous year's Exhibit cards by the line "PTD. IN U.S.A." at the bottom. Of the 64 players pictured, 16 appear for the first time and another nine are shown in new poses. The series is again marred by several spelling and caption errors.

	NR MT	EX	VG
Complete Set:	1750.00	875.00	500.00
Common Player:	30.00	15.00	9.00
(1) Paul Andrews, Harland Clift (Harlond), Rollie Hemsley, Sammy West	30.00	15.00	9.00
(2) Luke Appling, Henry Bonura, Jimmy Dykes, Ted Lyons	45.00	22.00	13.50
(3) Earl Averill, Mel Harder, Hal Trosky, Joe Vosmik	45.00	22.00	13.50
(4) Walter Berger, Danny MacFayden, Bill Urbanski, Pinky Whitney	30.00	15.00	9.00
(5) Charles Berry, Frank Higgins, Bob Johnson, Puccinelli	30.00	15.00	9.00
(6) Ossie Bluege, Buddy Meyer (Myer), L.N. Newsom, Earl Whitehill	30.00	15.00	9.00
(7) Stan. Bordagaray, Dutch Brandt, Fred Lindstrom, Van Mungo	45.00	22.00	13.50
(8) Guy Bush, Pie Traynor, Floyd Vaughn (Vaughan), Paul Waner	60.00	30.00	18.00
(9) Dolph Camilli, Curt Davis, Johnny Moore, Jimmy Wilson	30.00	15.00	9.00
(10) Mickey Cochrane, C. Gehringer, Goose Goslin, Linwood Rowe (Lynwood)	60.00	30.00	18.00
(11) Joe Cronin, Rick Ferrell, Jimmy Foxx, Lefty Grove	75.00	38.00	23.00
(12) Jerome "Dizzy" Dean, Paul Dean, Frank Frisch, Joe "Ducky" Medwick	150.00	75.00	45.00
(13) Paul Derringer, Babe Herman, Alex Kampouris, Botchi Lombardi	45.00	22.00	13.50
(14) Augie Galan, Gabby Hartnett, Billy Herman, Lon Warneke	45.00	22.00	13.50
(15) Lou Gehrig, Vernon Gomez, Tony Lazzeri, Red Ruffing	500.00	250.00	150.00
(16) Carl Hubbell, Gus Mancuso, Mel Ott, Bill Terry	65.00	33.00	20.00

1937 Exhibits Four-On-One

The 1937 four-on-one Exhibit cards were printed in either green or bright blue. The backs are again blank. The 1937 cards are difficult to distinguish from the 1936 series, because both contain the "PTD. IN U.S.A." line along the bottom. Of the 64 photos, 47 are re-issues from previous series.

	NR MT	EX	VG
Complete Set:	1800.00	900.00	550.00
Common Player:	30.00	15.00	9.00
(1) Earl Averill, Bob Feller, Frank Pytlak, Hal Trosky	75.00	38.00	23.00
(2) Luke Appling, Henry Bonura, Jimmy Dykes, Vernon Kennedy	45.00	22.00	13.50
(3) Walter Berger, Alfonso Lopez, Danny MacFayden, Bill Urbanski	40.00	20.00	12.00
(4) Cy Blanton, Gus Suhr, Floyd Vaughn (Vaughan), Paul Waner	45.00	22.00	13.50
(5) Dolph Camilli, Johnny Moore, Wm. Walters, Pinky Whitney	30.00	15.00	9.00
(6) Harland Clift (Harlond), Rollie Hemsley, Orval Hildebrand (Oral), Sammy West	30.00	15.00	9.00
(7) Mickey Cochrane, C. Gehringer, Goose Goslin, Linwood Rowe (Lynwood)	60.00	30.00	18.00
(8) Joe Cronin, Rick Ferrell, Jimmy Foxx, Lefty Grove	75.00	38.00	23.00
(9) Jerome "Dizzy" Dean, Stuart Martin, Joe "Ducky" Medwick, Lon Warneke	110.00	55.00	33.00
(10) Paul Derringer, Botchi Lombardi, Lew Riggs, Phil Weintraub	45.00	22.00	13.50
(11) Joe DiMaggio, Lou Gehrig, Vernon Gomez, Tony Lazzeri	600.00	300.00	180.00
(12) E. English, Johnny Moore, Van Mungo, Gordon Phelps	30.00	15.00	9.00
(13) Augie Galan, Gabby Hartnett, Billy Herman, Bill Lee	45.00	22.00	13.50
(14) Carl Hubbell, Sam Leslie, Gus. Mancuso, Mel Ott	45.00	22.00	13.50
(15) Bob Johnson, Harry Kelly (Kelley), Wallace Moses, Billy Weber (Werber)	30.00	15.00	9.00
(16) Joe Kuhel, Buddy Meyer (Myer), L.N. Newsom, Jonathan Stone (first name actually John)	30.00	15.00	9.00

1938 Exhibits Four-On-One

The Exhibit Co. used its four-on-one format for the final time in 1938, issuing another 16-card series. The cards feature brown printing on white stock with the line "MADE IN U.S.A." appearing along the bottom. The backs are blank. Twelve players appeared for the first time and three others are shown in new poses. Again, there are several spelling and caption mistakes.

	NR MT	EX	VG
Complete Set:	1800.00	900.00	550.00
Common Player:	35.00	17.50	10.50
(1) Luke Appling, Mike Kreevich, Ted Lyons, L. Sewell	45.00	22.00	13.50
(2) Morris Arnovich, Chas. Klein, Wm. Walters, Pinky Whitney	45.00	22.00	13.50
(3) Earl Averill, Bob Feller, Odell Hale, Hal Trosky	75.00	38.00	23.00
(4) Beau Bell, Harland Clift (Harlond), L.N. Newsom, Sammy West	35.00	17.50	10.50
(5) Cy Blanton, Gus Suhr, Floyd Vaughn (Vaughan), Paul Waner	45.00	22.00	13.50
(6) Tom Bridges, C. Gehringer, Hank Greenberg, Rudy York	45.00	22.00	13.50
(7) Dolph Camilli, Leo Durocher, Van Mungo, Gordon Phelps	40.00	20.00	12.00
(8) Joe Cronin, Jimmy Foxx, Lefty Grove, Joe Vosmik	65.00	33.00	20.00
(9) Tony Cuccinello, Vince DiMaggio, Roy Johnson, Danny MacFayden	35.00	17.50	10.50
(10) Jerome "Dizzy" Dean, Augie Galan, Gabby Hartnett, Billy Herman	100.00	50.00	30.00
(11) Paul Derringer, Ival Goodman, Botchi Lombardi, Lew Riggs	45.00	22.00	13.50
(12) W. Dickey, Joe DiMaggio, Lou Gehrig, Vernon Gomez	700.00	350.00	200.00
(13) Rick Ferrell, W. Ferrell, Buddy Meyer (Myer), Jonathan Stone (first name actually John)	45.00	22.00	13.50
(14) Carl Hubbell, Hank Leiber, Mel Ott, Jim Ripple	60.00	30.00	18.00
(15) Bob Johnson, Harry Kelly (Kelley), Wallace Moses, Billy Weber (Werber)	35.00	17.50	10.50
(16) Stuart Martin, Joe "Ducky" Medwick, Johnny Mize, Lon Warneke	45.00	22.00	13.50

1939-46 Exhibits Salutation

Referred to as "Exhibits" because they were issued by the Exhibit Supply Co. of Chicago, Ill., this group was produced over an 8-year span. They are frequently called "Salutations" because of the personalized greeting found on the card. The black and white cards, which measure 3-3/8" by 5-3/8", are unnumbered and blank-backed. Most exhibits were sold through vending machines for a penny. The complete set price includes all variations.

	NR MT	EX	VG
Complete Set:	4500.00	2250.00	1350.
Common Player:	4.00	2.00	1.25
(1a) Luke Appling ("Made In U.S.A." in left corner)	12.00	6.00	3.50
(1b) Luke Appling ("Made In U.S.A." in right corner)	7.00	3.50	2.00
(2) Earl Averill	375.00	175.00	100.00
(3) Charles "Red" Barrett	4.00	2.00	1.25
(4) Henry "Hank" Borowy	4.00	2.00	1.25
(5) Lou Boudreau	8.00	4.00	2.50
(6) Adolf Camilli	25.00	12.50	7.50
(7) Phil Cavarretta	3.50	1.75	1.00
(8) Harland Clift (Harlond)	12.00	6.00	3.50
(9) Tony Cuccinello	25.00	12.50	7.50
(10) Dizzy Dean	80.00	40.00	24.00
(11) Paul Derringer	4.00	2.00	1.25

		NR MT	EX	VG
(12a)	Bill Dickey ("Made In U.S.A." in left corner)	25.00	12.50	7.50
(12b)	Bill Dickey ("Made In U.S.A." in right corner)	25.00	12.50	7.50
(13)	Joe DiMaggio	35.00	17.50	10.50
(14)	Bob Elliott	4.00	2.00	1.25
(15)	Bob Feller (portrait)	100.00	50.00	30.00
(16)	Bob Feller (pitching)	30.00	15.00	9.00
(17)	Dave Ferriss	4.00	2.00	1.25
(18)	Jimmy Foxx	100.00	50.00	30.00
(19)	Lou Gehrig	700.00	350.00	210.00
(20)	Charlie Gehringer	125.00	56.00	35.00
(21)	Vernon Gomez	180.00	90.00	55.00
(22a)	Joe Gordon (Cleveland)	25.00	12.50	7.50
(22b)	Joe Gordon (New York)	3.50	1.75	1.00
(23)	Hank Greenberg (Truly yours)	20.00	10.00	6.00
(24)	Hank Greenberg (Very truly yours)	80.00	40.00	24.00
(25)	Robert Grove	50.00	25.00	15.00
(26)	Gabby Hartnett	275.00	150.00	80.00
(27)	Buddy Hassett	15.00	7.50	4.50
(28a)	Jeff Heath (large projection)	25.00	12.50	7.50
(28b)	Jeff Heath (small projection)	4.00	2.00	1.25
(29)	Kirby Higbe	15.00	7.50	4.50
(30a)	Tommy Holmes (Yours truly)	4.00	2.00	1.25
(30b)	Tommy Holmes (Sincerely yours)	125.00	60.00	40.00
(31)	Carl Hubbell	25.00	12.50	7.50
(32)	Bob Johnson	15.00	7.50	4.50
(33)	Charles Keller	4.00	2.00	1.25
(34)	Ken Keltner	25.00	12.50	7.50
(35)	Chuck Klein	175.00	90.00	50.00
(36)	Mike Kreevich	80.00	40.00	24.00
(37)	Joe Kuhel	20.00	10.00	6.00
(38)	Bill Lee	20.00	10.00	6.00
(39)	Ernie Lombardi (Cordially)	200.00	100.00	60.00
(40)	Ernie Lombardi (Cordially yours)	8.00	4.00	2.50
(41a)	Martin Marion ("Made in U.S.A." in left corner)	4.00	2.00	1.25
(41b)	Martin Marion ("Made in U.S.A." in right corner)	4.00	2.00	1.25
(42)	Merrill May	20.00	10.00	6.00
(43a)	Frank McCormick ("Made In U.S.A." in left corner)	20.00	10.00	6.00
(43b)	Frank McCormick ("Made In U.S.A." in right corner)	3.50	1.75	1.00
(44a)	George McQuinn ("Made In U.S.A." in left corner)	20.00	10.00	6.00
(44b)	George McQuinn ("Made In U.S.A." in right corner)	3.50	1.75	1.00
(45)	Joe Medwick	30.00	15.00	9.00
(46a)	Johnny Mize ("Made In U.S.A." in left corner)	25.00	12.50	7.50
(46b)	Johnny Mize ("Made In U.S.A." in right corner)	15.00	7.50	4.50
(47)	Hugh Mulcahy	80.00	40.00	24.00
(48)	Hal Newhouser	4.00	2.00	1.25
(49)	Buck Newson (Newsom)	175.00	90.00	50.00
(50)	Louis (Buck) Newsom	4.00	2.00	1.25
(51a)	Mel Ott ("Made In U.S.A." in left corner)	50.00	25.00	15.00
(51b)	Mel Ott ("Made In U.S.A." in right corner)	25.00	12.50	7.50
(52a)	Andy Pafko ("C" on cap)	4.00	2.00	1.25
(52b)	Andy Pafko (plain cap)	4.00	2.00	1.25
(53)	Claude Passeau	3.50	1.75	1.00
(54a)	Howard Pollet ("Made In U.S.A." in left corner)	11.00	5.50	3.25
(54b)	Howard Pollet ("Made In U.S.A." in right corner)	4.00	2.00	1.25
(55a)	Pete Reiser ("Made In U.S.A." in left corner)	80.00	40.00	24.00
(55b)	Pete Reiser ("Made In U.S.A." in right corner)	4.00	2.00	1.25
(56)	Johnny Rizzo	90.00	45.00	27.00
(57)	Glenn Russell	90.00	45.00	27.00
(58)	George Stirnweiss	4.00	2.00	1.25
(59)	Cecil Travis	15.00	7.50	4.50
(60)	Paul Trout	4.00	2.00	1.25
(61)	Johnny Vander Meer	40.00	20.00	12.00
(62)	Arky Vaughn (Vaughan)	20.00	10.00	6.00
(63a)	Fred "Dixie" Walker ("D" on cap)	4.00	2.00	1.25
(63b)	Fred "Dixie" Walker ("D" blanked out)	25.00	12.50	7.50
(64)	"Bucky" Walters	4.00	2.00	1.25
(65)	Lon Warneke	6.50	3.25	2.00
(66)	Ted Williams (#9 shows)	300.00	150.00	90.00
(67)	Ted Williams (#9 not showing)	40.00	20.00	12.00
(68)	Rudy York	4.00	2.00	1.25

1947-66 Exhibits

Called "Exhibits" as they were produced by the Exhibit Supply Co. of Chicago, Ill., this group covers a span of twenty years. Each unnumbered, black and white card, printed on heavy stock, measures 3-3/8" by 5-3/8" and is blank-backed. The Exhibit Supply Co. issued new sets each year, with many players being repeated year after year/ Other players appeared in only one or two years, thereby creating levels of scarcity. Many variations off the same basic pose are found in the group. Those cards are listed in the checklist that follows with an "a", "b", etc. following the assigned card number. The complete set includes all variations

		NR MT	EX	VG
	Complete Set:	4500.00	2250.00	1350.
	Common Player:	3.00	1.50	.90
(1)	Hank Aaron	25.00	12.50	7.50
(2a)	Joe Adcock (script signature)	3.00	1.50	.90
(2b)	Joe Adcock (plain signature)	5.00	2.50	1.50
(3)	Max Alvis	20.00	10.00	6.00
(4)	Johnny Antonelli (Braves)	3.00	1.50	.90
(5)	Johnny Antonelli (Giants)	5.00	2.50	1.50
(6)	Luis Aparicio (portrait)	7.00	3.50	2.00
(7)	Luis Aparicio (batting)	20.00	10.00	6.00
(8)	Luke Appling	7.00	3.50	2.00
(9a)	Ritchie Ashburn (Phillies, first name incorrect)	5.00	2.50	1.50
(9b)	Richie Ashburn (Phillies, first name correct)	7.00	3.50	2.00
(10)	Richie Ashburn (Cubs)	13.00	6.50	4.00
(11)	Bob Aspromonte	3.00	1.50	.90
(12)	Toby Atwell	3.00	1.50	.90
(13)	Ed Bailey (with cap)	5.00	2.50	1.50
(14)	Ed Bailey (no cap)	3.00	1.50	.90
(15)	Gene Baker	3.00	1.50	.90
(16a)	Ernie Banks (bat on shoulder, script signature)	20.00	10.00	6.00
(16b)	Ernie Banks (bat on shoulder, plain signature)	10.00	5.00	3.00
(17)	Ernie Banks (portrait)	20.00	10.00	6.00
(18)	Steve Barber	3.00	1.50	.90
(19)	Earl Battey	5.00	2.50	1.50
(20)	Matt Batts	3.00	1.50	.90
(21a)	Hank Bauer (N.Y. cap)	5.00	2.50	1.50
(21b)	Hank Bauer (plain cap)	7.00	3.50	2.00
(22)	Frank Baumholtz	3.00	1.50	.90
(23)	Gene Bearden	3.00	1.50	.90
(24)	Joe Beggs	12.00	6.00	3.50
(25)	Larry "Yogi" Berra	30.00	15.00	9.00
(26)	Yogi Berra	10.00	5.00	3.00
(27)	Steve Bilko	5.00	2.50	1.50
(28)	Ewell Blackwell (pitching)	7.00	3.50	2.00
(29)	Ewell Blackwell (portrait)	3.00	1.50	.90
(30a)	Don Blasingame (St. Louis cap)	3.00	1.50	.90
(30b)	Don Blasingame (plain cap)	6.00	3.00	1.75
(31)	Ken Boyer	7.00	3.50	2.00
(32)	Ralph Branca	7.00	3.50	2.00
(33)	Jackie Brandt	50.00	25.00	15.00
(34)	Harry Brecheen	3.00	1.50	.90
(35)	Tom Brewer	12.00	6.00	3.50
(36)	Lou Brissie	5.00	2.50	1.50
(37)	Bill Bruton	3.00	1.50	.90
(38)	Lew Burdette (pitching, side view)	3.00	1.50	.90
(39)	Lew Burdette (pitching, front view)	6.00	3.00	1.75
(40)	Johnny Callison	7.00	3.50	2.00
(41)	Roy Campanella	13.00	6.50	4.00
(42)	Chico Carrasquel (portrait)	13.00	6.50	4.00
(43)	Chico Carrasquel (leaping)	3.00	1.50	.90
(44)	George Case	12.00	6.00	3.50
(45)	Hugh Casey	5.00	2.50	1.50
(46)	Norm Cash	7.00	3.50	2.00
(47)	Orlando Cepeda (portrait)	7.00	3.50	2.00
(48)	Orlando Cepeda (batting)	7.00	3.50	2.00
(49a)	Bob Cerv (A's cap)	7.00	3.50	2.00
(49b)	Bob Cerv (plain cap)	16.00	8.00	4.75
(50)	Dean Chance	3.00	1.50	.90
(51)	Spud Chandler	12.00	6.00	3.50
(52)	Tom Cheney	3.00	1.50	.90
(53)	Bubba Church	5.00	2.50	1.50
(54)	Roberto Clemente	25.00	12.50	7.50
(55)	Rocky Colavito (portrait)	25.00	12.50	7.50
(56)	Rocky Colavito (batting)	7.00	3.50	2.00
(57)	Choo Choo Coleman	13.00	6.50	4.00
(58)	Gordy Coleman	20.00	10.00	6.00
(59)	Jerry Coleman	5.00	2.50	1.50
(60)	Mort Cooper	12.00	6.00	3.50
(61)	Walker Cooper	3.00	1.50	.90
(62)	Roger Craig	12.00	6.00	3.50
(63)	Delmar Crandall	3.00	1.50	.90
(64)	Joe Cunningham (batting)	25.00	12.50	7.50
(65)	Joe Cunningham (portrait)	7.00	3.50	2.00
(66)	Guy Curtwright (Curtright)	5.00	2.50	1.50
(67)	Bud Daley	35.00	17.50	10.50
(68a)	Alvin Dark (Braves)	7.00	3.50	2.00
(68b)	Alvin Dark (Giants)	5.00	2.50	1.50
(69)	Alvin Dark (Cubs)	7.00	3.50	2.00
(70)	Murray Dickson (Murry)	5.00	2.50	1.50
(71)	Bob Dillinger	7.00	3.50	2.00
(72)	Dom DiMaggio	18.00	9.00	5.50
(73)	Joe Dobson	7.00	3.50	2.00
(74)	Larry Doby	3.00	1.50	.90
(75)	Bobby Doerr	12.00	6.00	3.50
(76)	Dick Donovan (plain cap)	7.00	3.50	2.00
(77)	Dick Donovan (Sox cap)	4.00	2.00	1.25
(78)	Walter Dropo	3.00	1.50	.90
(79)	Don Drysdale (glove at waist)	25.00	12.50	7.50
(80)	Don Drysdale (portrait)	25.00	12.50	7.50
(81)	Luke Easter	5.00	2.50	1.50
(82)	Bruce Edwards	5.00	2.50	1.50
(83)	Del Ennis	3.00	1.50	.90
(84)	Al Evans	4.50	2.25	1.25
(85)	Walter Evers	3.00	1.50	.90
(86)	Ferris Fain (fielding)	7.00	3.50	2.00
(87)	Ferris Fain (portrait)	3.00	1.50	.90
(88)	Dick Farrell	3.00	1.50	.90
(89)	Ed "Whitey" Ford	15.00	7.50	4.50
(90)	Whitey Ford (pitching)	10.00	5.00	3.00
(91)	Whitey Ford (portrait)	60.00	30.00	17.50
(92)	Dick Fowler	7.00	3.50	2.00
(93)	Nelson Fox	5.00	2.50	1.50
(94)	Tito Francona	3.00	1.50	.90
(95)	Bob Friend	3.00	1.50	.90
(96)	Carl Furillo	7.00	3.50	2.00
(97)	Augie Galan	7.00	3.50	2.00
(98)	Jim Gentile	3.00	1.50	.90
(99)	Tony Gonzalez	3.00	1.50	.90
(100)	Billy Goodman (leaping)	3.00	1.50	.90
(101)	Billy Goodman (batting)	7.00	3.50	2.00
(102)	Ted Greengrass (Jim)	3.00	1.50	.90
(103)	Dick Groat	7.00	3.50	2.00
(104)	Steve Gromek	3.00	1.50	.90
(105)	Johnny Groth	3.00	1.50	.90
(106)	Orval Grove	13.00	6.50	4.00
(107a)	Frank Gustine (Pirates uniform)	5.00	2.50	1.50
(107b)	Frank Gustine (plain uniform)	5.00	2.50	1.50
(108)	Berthold Haas	13.00	6.50	4.00
(109)	Grady Hatton	5.00	2.50	1.50
(110)	Jim Hegan	3.00	1.50	.90
(111)	Tom Henrich	7.00	3.50	2.00
(112)	Ray Herbert	20.00	10.00	6.00
(113)	Gene Hermanski	4.50	2.25	1.25
(114)	Whitey Herzog	7.00	3.50	2.00
(115)	Kirby Higbe	13.00	6.50	4.00
(116)	Chuck Hinton	3.00	1.50	.90
(117)	Don Hoak	13.00	6.50	4.00
(118a)	Gil Hodges ("B" on cap)	9.00	4.50	2.75
(118b)	Gil Hodges ("LA" on cap)	9.00	4.50	2.75
(119)	Johnny Hopp	12.00	6.00	3.50
(120)	Elston Howard	3.00	1.50	.90
(121)	Frank Howard	7.00	3.50	2.00
(122)	Ken Hubbs	35.00	17.50	10.50
(123)	Tex Hughson	12.00	6.00	3.50
(124)	Fred Hutchinson	4.50	2.25	1.25
(125)	Monty Irvin	7.00	3.50	2.00
(126)	Joey Jay	3.00	1.50	.90
(127)	Jackie Jensen	25.00	12.50	7.50
(128)	Sam Jethroe	5.00	2.50	1.50
(129)	Bill Johnson	5.00	2.50	1.50
(130)	Walter Judnich	12.00	6.00	3.50
(131)	Al Kaline (kneeling)	25.00	12.50	7.50
(132)	Al Kaline (portrait)	25.00	12.50	7.50
(133)	George Kell	7.00	3.50	2.00
(134)	Charley Keller	4.50	2.25	1.25
(135)	Alex Kellner	3.00	1.50	.90
(136)	Kenn Keltner (Ken)	5.00	2.50	1.50
(137)	Harmon Killebrew (batting)	25.00	12.50	7.50
(138)	Harmon Killebrew (throwing)	25.00	12.50	7.50
(139)	Harmon Killibrew (Killebrew) (portrait)	25.00	12.50	7.50
(140)	Ellis Kinder	3.00	1.50	.90
(141)	Ralph Kiner	6.00	3.00	1.75
(142)	Billy Klaus	20.00	10.00	6.00
(143)	Ted Kluzewski (Kluszewski) (batting)	5.00	2.50	1.50
(144a)	Ted Kluzewski (Kluszewski) (Pirates uniform)	5.00	2.50	1.50
(144b)	Ted Kluzewski (Kluszewski) (plain uniform)	13.00	6.50	4.00
(145)	Don Kolloway	7.00	3.50	2.00
(146)	Jim Konstanty	5.00	2.50	1.50
(147)	Sandy Koufax	20.00	10.00	6.00
(148)	Ed Kranepool	50.00	25.00	15.00
(149a)	Tony Kubek (light background)	7.00	3.50	2.00
(149b)	Tony Kubek (dark background)	5.00	2.50	1.50
(150a)	Harvey Kuenn ("D" on cap)	12.00	6.00	3.50
(150b)	Harvey Kuenn (plain cap)	13.00	6.50	4.00
(151)	Harvey Kuenn ("SF" on cap)	7.00	3.50	2.00
(152)	Kurowski (Whitey)	4.50	2.25	1.25
(153)	Eddie Lake	5.00	2.50	1.50
(154)	Jim Landis	3.00	1.50	.90
(155)	Don Larsen	3.00	1.50	.90
(156)	Bob Lemon (glove not visible)	7.00	3.50	2.00
(157)	Bob Lemon (glove partially visible)	25.00	12.50	7.50
(158)	Buddy Lewis	12.00	6.00	3.50
(159)	Johnny Lindell	20.00	10.00	6.00
(160)	Phil Linz	20.00	10.00	6.00
(161)	Don Lock	20.00	10.00	6.00
(162)	Whitey Lockman	3.00	1.50	.90
(163)	Johnny Logan	3.00	1.50	.90
(164)	Dale Long ("P" on cap)	3.00	1.50	.90
(165)	Dale Long ("C" on cap)	7.00	3.50	2.00
(166)	Ed Lopat	5.00	2.50	1.50
(167a)	Harry Lowery (name misspelled)	5.00	2.50	1.50
(167b)	Harry Lowrey (name correct)	5.00	2.50	1.50
(168)	Sal Maglie	3.00	1.50	.90
(169)	Art Mahaffey	5.00	2.50	1.50
(170)	Hank Majeski	3.00	1.50	.90
(171)	Frank Malzone	3.00	1.50	.90
(172)	Mickey Mantle (batting, pinstriped uniform)	100.00	50.00	30.00
(173a)	Mickey Mantle (batting, no pinstripes, first name outlined in white)	75.00	38.00	23.00
173b	Mickey Mantle (batting, no pinstripes, first name not outlined in white)	75.00	38.00	23.00
(174)	Mickey Mantle (portrait)	300.00	120.00	75.00
(175)	Martin Marion	7.00	3.50	2.00
(176)	Roger Maris	20.00	10.00	6.00
(177)	Willard Marshall	5.00	2.50	1.50
(178a)	Eddie Matthews (name incorrect)	12.00	6.00	3.50
(178b)	Eddie Mathews (name correct)	13.00	6.50	4.00
(179)	Ed Mayo	5.00	2.50	1.50
(180)	Willie Mays (batting)	18.00	9.00	5.50
(181)	Willie Mays (portrait)	20.00	10.00	6.00
(182)	Bill Mazeroski (portrait)	7.00	3.50	2.00
(183)	Bill Mazeroski (batting)	7.00	3.50	2.00
(184)	Ken McBride	3.00	1.50	.90
(185a)	Barney McCaskey (McCosky)	13.00	6.50	4.00
(185b)	Barney McCoskey (McCosky)	90.00	45.00	27.00

		NR MT	EX	VG
(186)	Lindy McDaniel	3.00	1.50	.90
(187)	Gil McDougald	3.00	1.50	.90
(188)	Albert Mele	13.00	6.50	4.00
(189)	Sam Mele	5.00	2.50	1.50
(190)	Orestes Minoso ("C" on cap)	7.00	3.50	2.00
(191)	Orestes Minoso (Sox on cap)	3.00	1.50	.90
(192)	Dale Mitchell	3.00	1.50	.90
(193)	Wally Moon	7.00	3.50	2.00
(194)	Don Mueller	5.00	2.50	1.50
(195)	Stan Musial (kneeling)	15.00	7.50	4.50
(196)	Stan Musial (batting)	35.00	17.50	10.50
(197)	Charley Neal	18.00	9.00	5.50
(198)	Don Newcombe (shaking hands)	7.00	3.50	2.00
(199a)	Don Newcombe (Dodgers on jacket)	5.00	2.50	1.50
(199b)	Don Newcombe (plain jacket)	5.00	2.50	1.50
(200)	Hal Newhouser	3.00	1.50	.90
(201)	Ron Northey	12.00	6.00	3.50
(202)	Bill O'Dell	3.00	1.50	.90
(203)	Joe Page	12.00	6.00	3.50
(204)	Satchel Paige	35.00	17.50	10.50
(205)	Milt Pappas	3.00	1.50	.90
(206)	Camilo Pascual	3.00	1.50	.90
(207)	Albie Pearson	20.00	10.00	6.00
(208)	Johnny Pesky	3.00	1.50	.90
(209)	Gary Peters	20.00	10.00	6.00
(210)	Dave Philley	3.00	1.50	.90
(211)	Billy Pierce	3.00	1.50	.90
(212)	Jimmy Piersall	16.00	8.00	4.75
(213)	Vada Pinson	7.00	3.50	2.00
(214)	Bob Porterfield	3.00	1.50	.90
(215)	John "Boog" Powell	35.00	17.50	10.50
(216)	Vic Raschi	4.50	2.25	1.25
(217a)	Harold "Peewee" Reese (fielding, ball partially visible)	10.00	5.00	3.00
(217b)	Harold "Peewee" Reese (fielding, ball not visible)	10.00	5.00	3.00
(218)	Del Rice	3.00	1.50	.90
(219)	Bobby Richardson	55.00	28.00	16.50
(220)	Phil Rizzuto	6.00	3.00	1.75
(221a)	Robin Roberts (script signature)	12.00	6.00	3.50
(221b)	Robin Roberts (plain signature)	6.00	3.00	1.75
(222)	Brooks Robinson	25.00	12.50	7.50
(223)	Eddie Robinson	3.00	1.50	.90
(224)	Floyd Robinson	20.00	10.00	6.00
(225)	Frankie Robinson	18.00	9.00	5.50
(226)	Jackie Robinson	30.00	15.00	9.00
(227)	Preacher Roe	4.50	2.25	1.25
(228)	Bob Rogers (Rodgers)	20.00	10.00	6.00
(229)	Richard Rollins	20.00	10.00	6.00
(230)	Pete Runnels	12.00	6.00	3.50
(231)	John Sain	5.00	2.50	1.50
(232)	Ron Santo	6.00	3.00	1.75
(233)	Henry Sauer	5.00	2.50	1.50
(234a)	Carl Sawatski ("M" on cap)	3.00	1.50	.90
(234b)	Carl Sawatski ("P" on cap)	3.00	1.50	.90
(234c)	Carl Sawatski (plain cap)	13.00	6.50	4.00
(235)	Johnny Schmitz	5.00	2.50	1.50
(236a)	Red Schoendeinst (Schoendienst) (fielding, name in white)	5.00	2.50	1.50
(236b)	Red Schoendeinst (Schoendienst) (fielding, name in red-brown)	7.00	3.50	2.00
(237)	Red Schoendinst (Schoendienst) (batting)	3.00	1.50	.90
(238a)	Herb Score ("C" on cap)	5.00	2.50	1.50
(238b)	Herb Score (plain cap)	12.00	6.00	3.50
(239)	Andy Seminick	3.00	1.50	.90
(240)	Rip Sewell	7.00	3.50	2.00
(241)	Norm Siebern	3.00	1.50	.90
(242)	Roy Sievers (batting)	5.00	2.50	1.50
(243a)	Roy Sievers (portrait, "W" on cap, light background)	7.00	3.50	2.00
(243b)	Roy Sievers (portrait, "W" on cap, dark background)	5.00	2.50	1.50
(243c)	Roy Sievers (portrait, plain cap)	4.50	2.25	1.25
(244)	Curt Simmons	5.00	2.50	1.50
(245)	Dick Sisler	5.00	2.50	1.50
(246)	Bill Skowron	5.00	2.50	1.50
(247)	Bill "Moose" Skowron	55.00	28.00	16.50
(248)	Enos Slaughter	7.00	3.50	2.00
(249a)	Duke Snider ("B" on cap)	8.50	4.25	2.50
(249b)	Duke Snider ("LA" on cap)	18.00	9.00	5.50
(250a)	Warren Spahn ("B" on cap)	10.00	5.00	3.00
(250b)	Warren Spahn ("M" on cap)	12.00	6.00	3.50
(251)	Stanley Spence	13.00	6.50	4.00
(252)	Ed Stanky (plain uniform)	5.00	2.50	1.50
(253)	Ed Stanky (Giants uniform)	5.00	2.50	1.50
(254)	Vern Stephens (batting)	5.00	2.50	1.50
(255)	Vern Stephens (portrait)	5.00	2.50	1.50
(256)	Ed Stewart	5.00	2.50	1.50
(257)	Snuffy Stirnweiss	13.00	6.50	4.00
(258)	George "Birdie" Tebbetts	12.00	6.00	3.50
(259)	Frankie Thomas (photo actually Bob Skinner)	25.00	12.50	7.50
(260)	Frank Thomas (portrait)	13.00	6.50	4.00
(261)	Lee Thomas	3.00	1.50	.90
(262)	Bobby Thomson	7.00	3.50	2.00
(263a)	Earl Torgeson (Braves uniform)	3.00	1.50	.90
(263b)	Earl Torgeson (plain uniform)	5.00	2.50	1.50
(264)	Gus Triandos	7.00	3.50	2.00
(265)	Virgil Trucks	3.00	1.50	.90
(266)	Johnny Vandermeer (VanderMeer)	13.00	6.50	4.00
(267)	Emil Verban	7.00	3.50	2.00
(268)	Mickey Vernon (throwing)	3.00	1.50	.90
(269)	Mickey Vernon (batting)	3.00	1.50	.90
(270)	Bill Voiselle	7.00	3.50	2.00
(271)	Leon Wagner	3.00	1.50	.90
(272a)	Eddie Waitkus (throwing, Chicago uniform)	7.00	3.50	2.00
(272b)	Eddie Waitkus (throwing, plain uniform)	5.00	2.50	1.50
(273)	Eddie Waitkus (portrait)	13.00	6.50	4.00
(274)	Dick Wakefield	5.00	2.50	1.50
(275)	Harry Walker	7.00	3.50	2.00
(276)	Bucky Walters	4.50	2.25	1.25
(277)	Pete Ward	25.00	12.50	7.50
(278)	Herman Wehmeier	5.00	2.50	1.50
(279)	Vic Wertz (batting)	3.00	1.50	.90
(280)	Vic Wertz (portrait)	3.00	1.50	.90
(281)	Wally Westlake	5.00	2.50	1.50
(282)	Wes Westrum	13.00	6.50	4.00
(283)	Billy Williams	13.00	6.50	4.00
(284)	Maurice Wills	12.00	6.00	3.50
(285a)	Gene Woodling (script signature)	3.00	1.50	.90
(285b)	Gene Woodling (plain signature)	7.00	3.50	2.00
(286)	Taffy Wright	5.00	2.50	1.50
(287)	Carl Yastrazemski (Yastrzemski)	175.00	90.00	50.00
(288)	Al Zarilla	5.00	2.50	1.50
(289a)	Gus Zernial (script signature)	3.00	1.50	.90
(289b)	Gus Zernial (plain signature)	7.00	3.50	2.00
(290)	Braves Team - 1948	18.00	9.00	5.50
(291)	Dodgers Team - 1949	20.00	10.00	6.00
(292)	Dodgers Team - 1952	20.00	10.00	6.00
(293)	Dodgers Team - 1955	20.00	10.00	6.00
(294)	Dodgers Team - 1956	20.00	10.00	6.00
(295)	Giants Team - 1951	18.00	9.00	5.50
(296)	Giants Team - 1954	18.00	9.00	5.50
(297)	Indians Team - 1948	18.00	9.00	5.50
(298)	Indians Team - 1954	18.00	9.00	5.50
(299)	Phillies Team - 1950	18.00	9.00	5.50
(300)	Yankees Team - 1949	25.00	12.50	7.50
(301)	Yankees Team - 1950	25.00	12.50	7.50
(302)	Yankees Team - 1951	25.00	12.50	7.50
(303)	Yankees Team - 1952	25.00	12.50	7.50
(304)	Yankees Team - 1955	25.00	12.50	7.50
(305)	Yankees Team - 1956	25.00	12.50	7.50

1962 Exhibits Statistic Backs

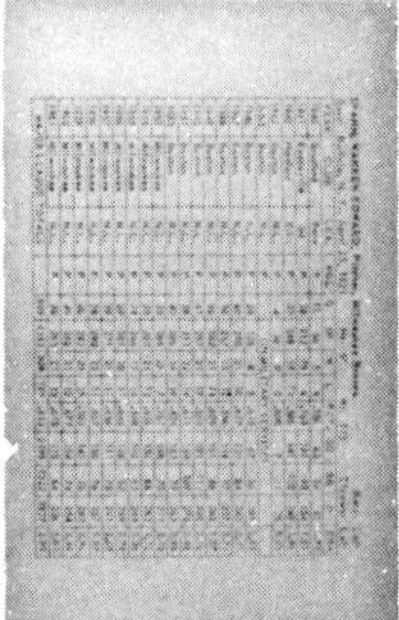

In 1962, the Exhibit Supply Co. added career statistics to the yearly set they produced. The black and white, unnumbered cards measure 3-3/8" by 5-3/8". The statistics found on the back are printed in black or red. The red backs are three times greater in value. The set is comprised of 32 cards.

		NR MT	EX	VG
Complete Set:		350.00	175.00	105.00
Common Player:		3.00	1.50	.90
(1)	Hank Aaron	30.00	15.00	9.00
(2)	Luis Aparicio	4.00	2.00	1.25
(3)	Ernie Banks	7.00	3.50	2.00
(4)	Larry "Yogi" Berra	10.00	5.00	3.00
(5)	Ken Boyer	4.00	2.00	1.25
(6)	Lew Burdette	3.50	1.75	1.00
(7)	Norm Cash	3.50	1.75	1.00
(8)	Orlando Cepeda	3.00	1.50	.90
(9)	Roberto Clemente	30.00	15.00	9.00
(10)	Rocky Colavito	4.00	2.00	1.25
(11)	Ed "Whitey" Ford	7.00	3.50	2.00
(12)	Nelson Fox	3.00	1.50	.90
(13)	Tito Francona	3.00	1.50	.90
(14)	Jim Gentile	3.00	1.50	.90
(15)	Dick Groat	3.50	1.75	1.00
(16)	Don Hoak	3.50	1.75	1.00
(17)	Al Kaline	10.00	5.00	3.00
(18)	Harmon Killebrew	10.00	5.00	3.00
(19)	Sandy Koufax	25.00	12.50	7.50
(20)	Jim Landis	3.00	1.50	.90
(21)	Art Mahaffey	3.00	1.50	.90
(22)	Frank Malzone	3.00	1.50	.90
(23)	Mickey Mantle	60.00	30.00	18.00
(24)	Roger Maris	10.00	5.00	3.00
(25)	Eddie Mathews	5.00	2.50	1.50
(26)	Willie Mays	30.00	15.00	9.00
(27)	Wally Moon	3.50	1.75	1.00
(28)	Stan Musial	30.00	15.00	9.00
(29)	Milt Pappas	3.50	1.75	1.00
(30)	Vada Pinson	4.00	2.00	1.25
(31)	Norm Siebern	3.00	1.50	.90
(32)	Warren Spahn	10.00	5.00	3.00

1963 Exhibits Statistic Backs

The Exhibit Supply Co. issued a 64-card set with career statistics on the backs of the cards in 1963. The unnumbered, black and white cards are printed on thick cardboard and measure 3-3/8" by 5-3/8" in size. The statistics on the back are printed in black.

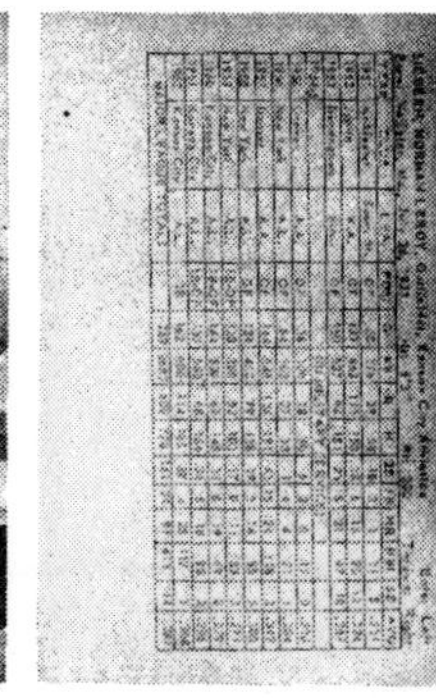

		NR MT	EX	VG
Complete Set:		450.00	225.00	135.00
Common Player:		3.00	1.50	.90
(1)	Hank Aaron	30.00	15.00	9.00
(2)	Luis Aparicio	4.00	2.00	1.25
(3)	Bob Aspromonte	3.00	1.50	.90
(4)	Ernie Banks	18.00	9.00	5.50
(5)	Steve Barber	3.00	1.50	.90
(6)	Earl Battey	3.00	1.50	.90
(7)	Larry "Yogi" Berra	12.00	6.00	3.50
(8)	Ken Boyer	4.00	2.00	1.25
(9)	Lew Burdette	3.50	1.75	1.00
(10)	Johnny Callison	3.50	1.75	1.00
(11)	Norm Cash	3.50	1.75	1.00
(12)	Orlando Cepeda	3.00	1.50	.90
(13)	Dean Chance	3.00	1.50	.90
(14)	Tom Cheney	3.00	1.50	.90
(15)	Roberto Clemente	30.00	15.00	9.00
(16)	Rocky Colavito	4.00	2.00	1.25
(17)	Choo Choo Coleman	3.00	1.50	.90
(18)	Roger Craig	3.50	1.75	1.00
(19)	Joe Cunningham	3.00	1.50	.90
(20)	Don Drysdale	7.00	3.50	2.00
(21)	Dick Farrell	3.00	1.50	.90
(22)	Ed "Whitey" Ford	13.00	6.50	4.00
(23)	Nelson Fox	3.00	1.50	.90
(24)	Tito Francona	3.00	1.50	.90
(25)	Jim Gentile	3.00	1.50	.90
(26)	Tony Gonzalez	3.00	1.50	.90
(27)	Dick Groat	3.50	1.75	1.00
(28)	Ray Herbert	3.00	1.50	.90
(29)	Chuck Hinton	3.00	1.50	.90
(30)	Don Hoak	3.50	1.75	1.00
(31)	Frank Howard	4.00	2.00	1.25
(32)	Ken Hubbs	3.50	1.75	1.00
(33)	Joey Jay	3.00	1.50	.90
(34)	Al Kaline	13.00	6.50	4.00
(35)	Harmon Killebrew	13.00	6.50	4.00
(36)	Sandy Koufax	20.00	10.00	6.00
(37)	Harvey Kuenn	4.00	2.00	1.25
(38)	Jim Landis	3.00	1.50	.90
(39)	Art Mahaffey	3.00	1.50	.90
(40)	Frank Malzone	3.00	1.50	.90
(41)	Mickey Mantle	100.00	50.00	30.00
(42)	Roger Maris	13.00	6.50	4.00
(43)	Eddie Mathews	5.00	2.50	1.50
(44)	Willie Mays	30.00	15.00	9.00
(45)	Bill Mazeroski	4.00	2.00	1.25
(46)	Ken McBride	3.00	1.50	.90
(47)	Wally Moon	3.50	1.75	1.00
(48)	Stan Musial	30.00	15.00	9.00
(49)	Charlie Neal	3.00	1.50	.90
(50)	Bill O'Dell	3.00	1.50	.90
(51)	Milt Pappas	3.50	1.75	1.00
(52)	Camilo Pascual	3.50	1.75	1.00
(53)	Jimmy Piersall	4.00	2.00	1.25
(54)	Vada Pinson	4.00	2.00	1.25
(55)	Brooks Robinson	13.00	6.50	4.00
(56)	Frankie Robinson	13.00	6.50	4.00
(57)	Pete Runnels	3.50	1.75	1.00
(58)	Ron Santo	4.00	2.00	1.25
(59)	Norm Siebern	3.00	1.50	.90
(60)	Warren Spahn	10.00	5.00	3.00
(61)	Lee Thomas	3.00	1.50	.90
(62)	Leon Wagner	3.00	1.50	.90
(63)	Billy Williams	4.00	2.00	1.25
(64)	Maurice Wills	3.00	1.50	.90

1948 Exhibits - Baseball's Great Hall of Fame

Titled "Baseball's Great Hall of Fame," this 32-player set features black and white player photos against a gray background. The photos are accented by Greek columns on either side with brief player information printed at the bottom. The blank-backed cards are unnumbered and are listed here alphabetically. The cards measure 3-3/8" by 5-3/8". Collectors should be aware that 24 of the cards in this set were reprinted on white stock in the mid-1970s.

		NR MT	EX	VG
Complete Set:		500.00	250.00	150.00
Common Player:		3.50	1.75	1.00
(1)	Grover Cleveland Alexander	7.00	3.50	2.00
(2)	Roger Bresnahan	3.50	1.75	1.00
(3)	Frank Chance	4.00	2.00	1.25
(4)	Jack Chesbro	3.50	1.75	1.00
(5)	Fred Clarke	3.50	1.75	1.00
(6)	Ty Cobb	40.00	20.00	12.00
(7)	Mickey Cochrane	4.00	2.00	1.25
(8)	Eddie Collins	3.50	1.75	1.00
(9)	Hugh Duffy	3.50	1.75	1.00
(10)	Johnny Evers	3.50	1.75	1.00
(11)	Frankie Frisch	3.50	1.75	1.00
(12)	Lou Gehrig	40.00	20.00	12.00
(13)	Clark Griffith	3.50	1.75	1.00
(14)	Robert "Lefty" Grove	6.00	3.00	1.75
(15)	Rogers Hornsby	10.00	5.00	3.00
(16)	Carl Hubbell	4.00	2.00	1.25
(17)	Hughie Jennings	3.50	1.75	1.00
(18)	Walter Johnson	15.00	7.50	4.50
(19)	Willie Keeler	3.50	1.75	1.00
(20)	Napolean Lajoie	7.00	3.50	2.00
(21)	Connie Mack	7.00	3.50	2.00
(22)	Christy Matthewson (Mathewson)	15.00	7.50	4.50
(23)	John J. McGraw	4.00	2.00	1.25
(24)	Eddie Plank	3.50	1.75	1.00
(25)	Babe Ruth (batting)	60.00	30.00	18.00
(26)	Babe Ruth (standing with bats)	200.00	100.00	60.00
(27)	George Sisler	4.00	2.00	1.25
(28)	Tris Speaker	7.00	3.50	2.00
(29)	Joe Tinker	3.50	1.75	1.00
(30)	Rube Waddell	3.50	1.75	1.00
(31)	Honus Wagner	15.00	7.50	4.50
(32)	Ed Walsh	3.50	1.75	1.00
(33)	Cy Young	9.00	4.50	2.75

1953 Exhibits - Canadian

This Canadian-issued set consists of 64 cards and includes both major leaguers and players from the Montreal Royals of the International League. The cards are slightly smaller than the U.S. exhibit cards, measuring 3-1/4" by 5-1/4", and are numbered. The blank-backed cards were printed on gray stock. Card numbers 1-32 have a green or red tint, while card numbers 33-64 have a blue or reddish-brown tint.

		NR MT	EX	VG
Complete Set:		1200.00	600.00	350.00
Common Player: 1-32		6.00	3.00	1.75
Common Player: 33-64		4.00	2.00	1.25
1	Preacher Roe	9.00	4.50	2.75
2	Luke Easter	6.00	3.00	1.75
3	Gene Bearden	6.00	3.00	1.75
4	Chico Carrasquel	6.00	3.00	1.75
5	Vic Raschi	9.00	4.50	2.75
6	Monty Irvin	18.00	9.00	5.50
7	Henry Sauer	6.00	3.00	1.75
8	Ralph Branca	9.00	4.50	2.75
9	Ed Stanky	7.00	3.50	2.00
10	Sam Jethroe	6.00	3.00	1.75
11	Larry Doby	7.00	3.50	2.00
12	Hal Newhouser	6.00	3.00	1.75
13	Gil Hodges	25.00	12.50	7.50
14	Harry Brecheen	6.00	3.00	1.75
15	Ed Lopat	9.00	4.50	2.75
16	Don Newcombe	9.00	4.50	2.75
17	Bob Feller	35.00	17.50	10.50
18	Tommy Holmes	6.00	3.00	1.75
19	Jackie Robinson	90.00	45.00	27.00
20	Roy Campanella	90.00	45.00	27.00
21	Harold "Peewee" Reese	30.00	15.00	9.00
22	Ralph Kiner	25.00	12.50	7.50
23	Dom DiMaggio	8.00	4.00	2.50
24	Bobby Doerr	18.00	9.00	5.50
25	Phil Rizzuto	25.00	12.50	7.50
26	Bob Elliott	6.00	3.00	1.75
27	Tom Henrich	9.00	4.50	2.75
28	Joe DiMaggio	300.00	150.00	90.00
29	Harry Lowery (Lowrey)	6.00	3.00	1.75
30	Ted Williams	125.00	62.00	37.00
31	Bob Lemon	20.00	10.00	6.00
32	Warren Spahn	30.00	15.00	9.00
33	Don Hoak	5.00	2.50	1.50
34	Bob Alexander	4.00	2.00	1.25
35	Simmons	4.00	2.00	1.25
36	Steve Lembo	4.00	2.00	1.25
37	Norman Larker	4.50	2.25	1.25
38	Bob Ludwick	4.00	2.00	1.25
39	Walter Moryn	4.00	2.00	1.25
40	Charlie Thompson	4.00	2.00	1.25
41	Ed Roebuck	4.50	2.25	1.25
42	Rose	4.00	2.00	1.25
43	Edmundo Amoros	4.50	2.25	1.25
44	Bob Milliken	4.00	2.00	1.25
45	Art Fabbro	4.00	2.00	1.25
46	Jacobs	4.00	2.00	1.25
47	Mauro	4.00	2.00	1.25
48	Walter Fiala	4.00	2.00	1.25
49	Rocky Nelson	4.00	2.00	1.25
50	Tom La Sorda (Lasorda)	40.00	20.00	12.00
51	Ronnie Lee	4.00	2.00	1.25
52	Hampton Coleman	4.00	2.00	1.25
53	Frank Marchio	4.00	2.00	1.25
54	Sampson	4.00	2.00	1.25
55	Gil Mills	4.00	2.00	1.25
56	Al Ronning	4.00	2.00	1.25
57	Stan Musial	55.00	28.00	16.50
58	Walker Cooper	4.50	2.25	1.25
59	Mickey Vernon	5.00	2.50	1.50
60	Del Ennis	5.00	2.50	1.50
61	Walter Alston	20.00	10.00	6.00
62	Dick Sisler	4.50	2.25	1.25
63	Billy Goodman	4.50	2.25	1.25
64	Alex Kellner	4.00	2.00	1.25

1961 Exhibits - Wrigley Field

Distributed at Chicago's Wrigley Field circa 1961, this 24-card set features members of the Baseball Hall of Fame. The cards measure 3-3/8" by 5-3/8" and include the player's full name along the bottom. They were printed on gray stock and have a postcard back. The set is unnumbered.

		NR MT	EX	VG
Complete Set:		250.00	125.00	75.00
Common Player:		4.00	2.00	1.25
(1)	Grover Cleveland Alexander	6.00	3.00	1.75
(2)	Adrian Constantine Anson	6.00	3.00	1.75
(3)	John Franklin Baker	4.00	2.00	1.25
(4)	Roger Phillip Bresnahan	4.00	2.00	1.25
(5)	Mordecai Peter Brown	4.00	2.00	1.25
(6)	Frank Leroy Chance	5.00	2.50	1.50
(7)	Tyrus Raymond Cobb	30.00	15.00	9.00
(8)	Edward Trowbridge Collins	4.00	2.00	1.25
(9)	James J. Collins	4.00	2.00	1.25
(10)	John Joseph Evers	4.00	2.00	1.25
(11)	Henry Louis Gehrig	30.00	15.00	9.00
(12)	Clark C. Griffith	4.00	2.00	1.25
(13)	Walter Perry Johnson	10.00	5.00	3.00
(14)	Anthony Michael Lazzeri	4.00	2.00	1.25
(15)	James Walter Vincent Maranville	4.00	2.00	1.25
(16)	Christopher Mathewson	10.00	5.00	3.00
(17)	John Joseph McGraw	5.00	2.50	1.50
(18)	Melvin Thomass Ott	5.00	2.50	1.50
(19)	Herbert Jeffries Pennock	4.00	2.00	1.25
(20)	George Herman Ruth	50.00	25.00	15.00
(21)	Aloysius Harry Simmons	4.00	2.00	1.25
(22)	Tristram Speaker	9.00	4.50	2.75
(23)	Joseph B. Tinker	4.00	2.00	1.25
(24)	John Peter Wagner	10.00	5.00	3.00

Definitions for grading conditions are located in the Introduction of this price guide.

M.L. TEAM ADDRESSES

Collectors often request the addresses of M.L. teams so they may direct autograph requests to players. Here they are:

American League

Baltimore Orioles: Memorial Stadium, Baltimore, MD 21218.

Boston Red Sox: Fenway Park, 24 Yawkey Way, Boston, MA 02215.

California Angels: Anaheim Stadium, 2000 State College Blvd., Anaheim, CA 92806.

Chicago White Sox: Comiskey Park, 324 W. 35th St., Chicago, IL 60616.

Cleveland Indians: Boudreau Blvd., Cleveland, OH 44114.

Detroit Tigers: Tiger Stadium, Detroit, MI 48216.

Kansas City Royals: P.O. Box 419969, Kansas City, MO 64141.

Milwaukee Brewers: Milw. County Stadium, Milwaukee, WI 53214.

Minnesota Twins: 501 Chicago Ave. S., Minneapolis, MN 55415.

New York Yankees: Yankee Stadium, Bronx, NY 10451.

Oakland A's: Oakland Alameda Co. Coliseum, P.O. Box 2220, Oakland, CA 94621.

Seattle Mariners: P.O. Box 4100, Seattle, WA 98104.

Texas Rangers: P.O. Box 1111, Arlington, TX 76010.

Toronto Blue Jays: Skydome, 300 The Esplanade West, Suite #3200, Toronto, Ont., Canada M5V 3B3.

National League

Atlanta Braves: P.O. Box 4064, Atlanta, GA 30302.

Chicago Cubs: Wrigley Field, 1060 W. Addison St., Chicago, IL 60613.

Cincinnati Reds: Riverfront Stadium, Cincinnati, OH 45202.

Houston Astros: P.O. Box 288, Houston, TX 77001.

Los Angeles Dodgers: Dodger Stadium, 1000 Elysian Park Ave., L.A., CA 90012.

Montreal Expos: P.O. Box 500, Station M, Montreal, Quebec, Canada H1V 3P2.

New York Mets: Shea Stadium, Flushing, NY 11368.

Philadelphia Phillies: P.O. Box 7575, Philadelphia, PA 19101

Pittsburgh Pirates: Three Rivers Stadium, 600 Stadium Circle, Pittsburgh, PA 15212

St. Louis Cardinals: 250 Stadium Plaza, St. Louis, MO 63102.

San Diego Padres: P.O. Box 2000, San Diego, CA 92120.

San Francisco Giants: Candlestick Park, San Francisco, CA 94124.

1988 Fantastic Sam's

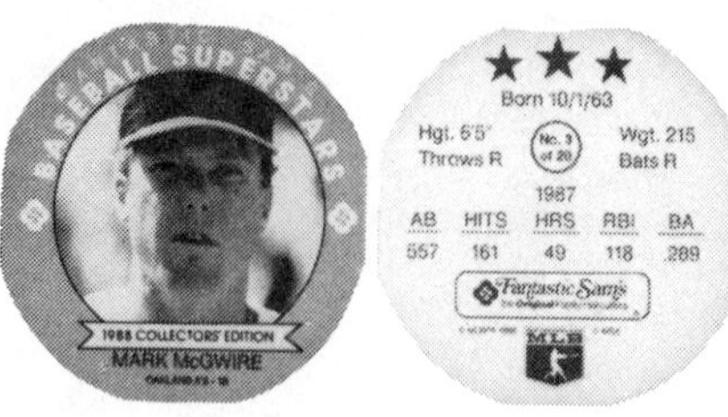

This set of 20 full-color player discs (2-1/2" diameter) was distributed during a Superstar Sweepstakes sponsored by Fantastic Sam's Family Haircutters' 1,800 stores nationwide. Each sweep- stakes card consists of two connected discs (bright orange fronts, white backs) perforated for easy separation. One disc features the baseball player photo, the other carries the sweepstakes logo and a list of prizes. Player discs carry a Fantastic Sam's Baseball Superstars header curved above the photo, with his name, team and position printed in black. The disc backs are black and white and include personal info, card number and 1987 player stats. Sweepstakes discs list contest prizes (Grand Prize was 4 tickets to a 1988 Championship game) on the front and an entry form on the flipside. Below the prize list is a silver scratch-off rectangle which may reveal an instant prize.

		MT	NR MT	EX
Complete Set:		10.00	7.50	4.00
Common Player:		.20	.15	.08
1	Kirby Puckett	.75	.60	.30
2	George Brett	1.00	.70	.40
3	Mark McGwire	1.75	1.25	.70
4	Wally Joyner	1.25	.90	.50
5	Paul Molitor	.20	.15	.08
6	Alan Trammell	.40	.30	.15
7	George Bell	.50	.40	.20
8	Wade Boggs	2.25	1.75	.90
9	Don Mattingly	3.50	2.75	1.50
10	Julio Franco	.20	.15	.08
11	Ozzie Smith	.20	.15	.08
12	Will Clark	.75	.60	.30
13	Dale Murphy	1.00	.70	.40
14	Eric Davis	1.50	1.25	.60
15	Andre Dawson	.50	.40	.20
16	Tim Raines	.60	.45	.25
17	Darryl Strawberry	1.25	.90	.50
18	Tony Gwynn	.75	.60	.30
19	Mike Schmidt	1.50	1.25	.60
20	Pedro Guerrero	.20	.15	.08

1987 Farmland Dairies Mets

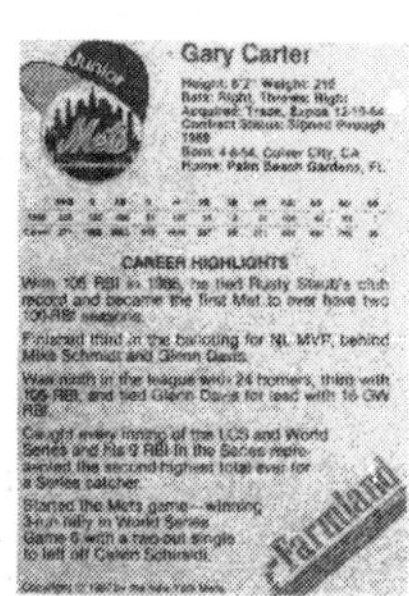

The New York Mets and Farmland Dairies produced a nine-card panel of baseball cards for members of the Junior Mets Club. Members of the club, kids 14 years of age and younger, received the perforated panel as part of a package featuring gifts and special privileges. The cards are the standard 2-1/2" by 3-1/2" with fronts containing a full-color photo encompassed by a blue border. The backs are designed on a vertical format and have player statistics and career highlights. The Farmland Dairies and Junior Mets Club logos are also carried on the card backs.

		MT	NR MT	EX
Complete Panel Set:		15.00	11.00	6.00
Complete Singles Set:		6.00	4.50	2.50
Common Single Player:		.25	.20	.10
Panel		12.00	9.00	4.75
1	Mookie Wilson	.25	.20	.10
4	Len Dykstra	.50	.40	.20
8	Gary Carter	.70	.50	.30
12	Ron Darling	.40	.30	.15
18	Darryl Strawberry	1.25	.90	.50
19	Bob Ojeda	.25	.20	.10
22	Kevin McReynolds	.40	.30	.15
42	Roger McDowell	.35	.25	.14
---	Team Card	.25	.20	.10

1988 Farmland Dairies Mets

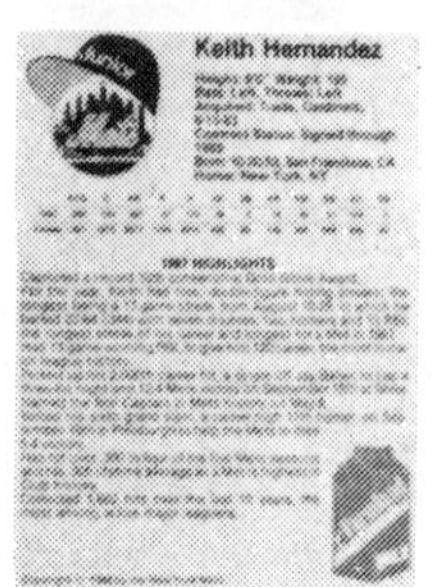

Part of the Junior Mets Fan Club membership package, this set of 9 standard size cards was printed on a single panel. Card fronts feature full-color action shots framed in orange and blue. A white player name runs across the top border, with a large team logo, uniform number and position printed below the photo. Card backs are blue on brown and include personal data, stats and 1987 season highlights. The set was offered to fans 14 years and younger for a $6 fan club membership fee, with a $1 discount for those who sent in two proofs of purchase from Farmland Dairies milk cartons.

		MT	NR MT	EX
Complete Panel Set:		15.00	11.00	6.00
Complete Singles Set:		6.00	4.50	2.50
Common Single Player:		.25	.20	.10
Panel		12.00	9.00	4.75
8	Gary Carter	.70	.50	.30
16	Dwight Gooden	1.25	.90	.50
17	Keith Hernandez	.60	.45	.25
18	Darryl Strawberry	1.25	.90	.50
20	Howard Johnson	.70	.50	.30
21	Kevin Elster	.35	.25	.14
42	Roger McDowell	.25	.20	.10
48	Randy Myers	.35	.25	.14

1939 Father & Son Shoes Phillies

Chuck Klein, outfielder, Phillies
Compliments Father & Son Shoes

This 25-card set featuring members of the Phillies was distributed in the Philadelphia area in 1939 by Father & Son Shoes stores. The unnumbered black and white cards measure 3" by 4". The player's name, position and team (Phillies) appear below the photo, along with the line "Compliments of Fathers & Son Shoes." The backs are blank. The only player of note in the set is Hall of Famer Chuck Klein.

		NR MT	EX	VG
Complete Set:		700.00	350.00	200.00
Common Player:		35.00	17.50	10.50
(1)	Morrie Arnovich	35.00	17.50	10.50
(2)	Earl Brucker	35.00	17.50	10.50
(3)	George Caster	35.00	17.50	10.50
(4)	Spud Davis	35.00	17.50	10.50
(5)	Gantenbein	35.00	17.50	10.50
(6)	Bob Johnson	45.00	22.00	13.50
(7)	Merrill May	35.00	17.50	10.50
(8)	Claude Passeau	35.00	17.50	10.50
(9)	Sam Chapman	35.00	17.50	10.50
(10)	Chuck Klein	125.00	62.00	37.00
(11)	Herschel Martin	35.00	17.50	10.50
(12)	Wally Moses	45.00	22.00	13.50
(13)	Hugh Mulcahy	35.00	17.50	10.50
(14)	Skeeter Newsome	35.00	17.50	10.50
(15)	George Scharien	35.00	17.50	10.50
(16)	Dick Siebert	35.00	17.50	10.50

1951 Fischer Baking Labels

This set of end-labels from loaves of bread consists of 32 player photos, each measuring approximately 2-3/4" square. The labels include the player's name, team and position, along with a few words about him. The bakery's slogan "Bread For Energy" appears in a dark band along the bottom. The set, which is unnumbered, was distributed in the Northeast.

		NR MT	EX	VG
Complete Set:		2250.00	1125.00	700.00
Common Player:		60.00	30.00	18.00
(1)	Vern Bickford	60.00	30.00	18.00
(2)	Ralph Branca	65.00	32.00	19.50
(3)	Harry Brecheen	60.00	30.00	18.00
(4)	"Chico" Carrasquel	60.00	30.00	18.00
(5)	Cliff Chambers	60.00	30.00	18.00
(6)	"Hoot" Evers	60.00	30.00	18.00
(7)	Ned Garver	60.00	30.00	18.00
(8)	Billy Goodman	60.00	30.00	18.00
(9)	Gil Hodges	90.00	45.00	27.00
(10)	Larry Jansen	60.00	30.00	18.00
(11)	Willie Jones	60.00	30.00	18.00
(12)	Eddie Joost	60.00	30.00	18.00
(13)	George Kell	85.00	42.00	25.00
(14)	Alex Kellner	60.00	30.00	18.00
(15)	Ted Kluszewski	70.00	35.00	21.00
(16)	Jim Konstanty	60.00	30.00	18.00
(17)	Bob Lemon	85.00	42.00	25.00
(18)	Cass Michaels	60.00	30.00	18.00
(19)	Johnny Mize	85.00	42.00	25.00
(20)	Irv Noren	60.00	30.00	18.00
(21)	Joe Page	65.00	32.00	19.50
(22)	Andy Pafko	65.00	32.00	19.50
(23)	Mel Parnell	60.00	30.00	18.00
(24)	Johnny Sain	65.00	32.00	19.50
(25)	"Red" Schoendienst	70.00	35.00	21.00
(26)	Roy Sievers	60.00	30.00	18.00
(27)	Roy Smalley	60.00	30.00	18.00
(28)	Herman Wehmeier	60.00	30.00	18.00
(29)	Bill Werle	60.00	30.00	18.00
(30)	Wes Westrum	60.00	30.00	18.00
(31)	Early Wynn	85.00	42.00	25.00
(32)	Gus Zernial	60.00	30.00	18.00

1959 Fleer Ted Williams

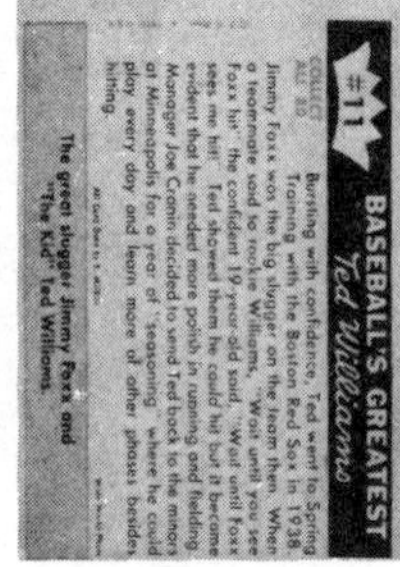

This 80-card 1959 Fleer set tells of the life of baseball great Ted Williams, from his childhood years up to 1958. The full-color cards measure 2-1/2" by 3-1/2" in size and make use of both horizontal and vertical formats. The card backs, all designed horizontally, contain a continuing biography of Williams. Card #68 was withdrawn from the set early in production and is scarce. Counterfeit cards of #68 have been produced and can be distinguished by a cross-hatch pattern which appears over the photo on the card fronts.

	NR MT	EX	VG
Complete Set:	700.00	350.00	200.00
Common Player:	3.00	1.50	.90

		NR MT	EX	VG
1	The Early Years	15.00	7.50	4.50
2	Ted's Idol - Babe Ruth	15.00	7.50	4.50
3	Practice Makes Perfect	3.00	1.50	.90
4	1934 - Ted Learns The Fine Points	3.00	1.50	.90
5	Ted's Fame Spreads - 1935-36	3.00	1.50	.90
6	Ted Turns Professional	3.00	1.50	.90
7	1936 - From Mound To Plate	3.00	1.50	.90
8	1937 - First Full Season	3.00	1.50	.90
9	1937 - First Step To The Majors	3.00	1.50	.90
10	1938 - Gunning As A Pastime	3.00	1.50	.90
11	1938 - First Spring Training	4.00	2.00	1.25
12	1939 - Burning Up The Minors	3.00	1.50	.90
13	1939 - Ted Shows He Will Stay	3.00	1.50	.90
14	Outstanding Rookie of 1939	3.00	1.50	.90
15	1940 - Williams Licks Sophomore Jinx	3.00	1.50	.90
16	1941 - Williams' Greatest Year	3.00	1.50	.90
17	1941 - How Ted Hit .400	3.00	1.50	.90
18	1941 - All-Star Hero	3.00	1.50	.90
19	1942 - Ted Wins Triple Crown	3.00	1.50	.90
20	1942 - On To Naval Training	3.00	1.50	.90
21	1943 - Honors For Williams	3.00	1.50	.90
22	1944 - Ted Solos	3.00	1.50	.90
23	1944 - Williams Wins His Wings	3.00	1.50	.90
24	1945 - Sharpshooter	3.00	1.50	.90
25	1945 - Ted Is Discharged	3.00	1.50	.90
26	1946 - Off To A Flying Start	3.00	1.50	.90
27	July 9, 1946 - One Man Show	3.00	1.50	.90
28	July 14, 1946 - The Williams Shift	3.00	1.50	.90
29	July 21, 1946, Ted Hits For The Cycle	3.00	1.50	.90
30	1946 - Beating The Williams Shift	3.00	1.50	.90
31	Oct. 1946 - Sox Lose The Series	3.00	1.50	.90
32	1946 - Most Valuable Player	3.00	1.50	.90
33	1947 - Another Triple Crown For Ted	3.00	1.50	.90
34	1947 - Ted Sets Runs-Scored Record	3.00	1.50	.90
35	1948 - The Sox Miss The Pennant	3.00	1.50	.90
36	1948 - Banner Year For Ted	3.00	1.50	.90
37	1949 - Sox Miss Out Again	3.00	1.50	.90
38	1949 - Power Rampage	3.00	1.50	.90
39	1950 - Great Start	4.50	2.25	1.25
40	July 11, 1950 - Ted Crashes Into Wall	3.00	1.50	.90
41	1950 - Ted Recovers	3.00	1.50	.90
42	1951 - Williams Slowed By Injury	3.00	1.50	.90
43	1951 - Leads Outfielders In Double Plays	3.00	1.50	.90
44	1952 - Back To The Marines	3.00	1.50	.90
45	1952 - Farewell To Baseball?	3.00	1.50	.90
46	1952 - Ready For Combat	3.00	1.50	.90
47	1953 - Ted Crash Lands Jet	3.00	1.50	.90
48	July 14, 1953 - Ted Returns	3.00	1.50	.90
49	1953 - Smash Return	3.00	1.50	.90
50	March 1954 - Spring Injury	3.00	1.50	.90
51	May 16, 1954 - Ted Is Patched Up	3.00	1.50	.90
52	1954 - Ted's Comeback	3.00	1.50	.90
53	1954 - Ted's Comeback Is A Sucess	3.00	1.50	.90
54	Dec. 1954, Fisherman Ted Hooks a Big One	3.00	1.50	.90
55	1955 - Ted Decides Retirement Is "No Go"	3.00	1.50	.90
56	1956 - Ted Reaches 400th Homer,	3.00	1.50	.90
58	1957 - Williams Hits .388	3.00	1.50	.90
59	1957 - Hot September For Ted	3.00	1.50	.90
60	1957 - More Records For Ted	3.00	1.50	.90
61	1957 - Outfielder Ted	3.00	1.50	.90
62	1958 - 6th Batting Title For Ted	3.00	1.50	.90
63	Ted's All-Star Record	3.00	1.50	.90
64	1958 - Daughter And Famous Daddy	3.00	1.50	.90
65	August 30, 1958	3.00	1.50	.90
66	1958 - Powerhouse	3.00	1.50	.90
67	Two Famous Fisherman	4.50	2.25	1.25
68	Jan. 23, 1959 - Ted Signs For 1959	450.00	225.00	135.00
69	A Future Ted Williams?	3.00	1.50	.90
70	Ted Williams & Jim Thorpe	4.50	2.25	1.25
71	Ted's Hitting Fundamentals #1	3.00	1.50	.90
72	Ted's Hitting Fundamentals #2	3.00	1.50	.90
73	Ted's Hitting Fundamentals #3	3.00	1.50	.90
74	Here's How!	3.00	1.50	.90
75	Williams' Value To Red Sox	7.00	3.50	2.00
76	Ted's Remarkable "On Base" Record	3.00	1.50	.90
77	Ted Relaxes	3.00	1.50	.90
78	Honors For Williams	3.00	1.50	.90
79	Where Ted Stands	3.00	1.50	.90
80	Ted's Goals For 1959	7.00	3.50	2.00

1960 Fleer

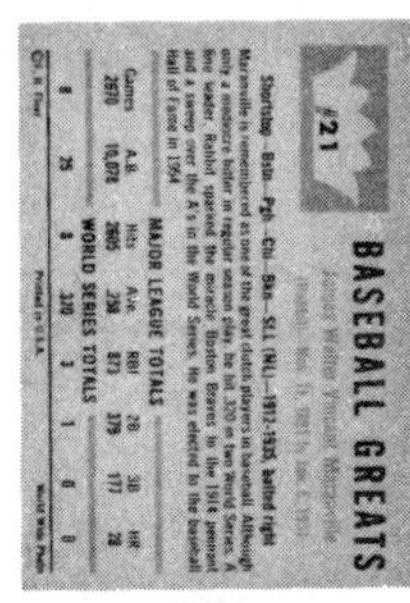

The 1960 Fleer Baseball Greats set consists of 79 cards of the game's top players from the past. (The set does include a card of Ted Williams, who was in his final major league season). The cards are standard size (2-1/2" by 3-1/2") and feature color photos inside blue, green, red or yellow borders. The card backs carry a short player biography plus career hitting or pitching statistics. Cards with a Pepper Martin back (#80), but with another player pictured on the front are in existence.

		NR MT	EX	VG
	Complete Set:	275.00	137.00	82.00
	Common Player:	1.75	.90	.50
1	Nap Lajoie	8.00	4.00	2.50
2	Christy Mathewson	6.00	3.00	1.75
3	Babe Ruth	45.00	23.00	13.50
4	Carl Hubbell	2.00	1.00	.60
5	Grover Cleveland Alexander	3.00	1.50	.90
6	Walter Johnson	6.00	3.00	1.75
7	Chief Bender	1.75	.90	.50
8	Roger Bresnahan	1.75	.90	.50
9	Mordecai Brown	1.75	.90	.50
10	Tris Speaker	2.00	1.00	.60
11	Arky Vaughan	1.75	.90	.50
12	Zack Wheat	1.75	.90	.50
13	George Sisler	2.00	1.00	.60
14	Connie Mack	3.00	1.50	.90
15	Clark Griffith	1.75	.90	.50
16	Lou Boudreau	1.75	.90	.50
17	Ernie Lombardi	1.75	.90	.50
18	Heinie Manush	1.75	.90	.50
19	Marty Marion	1.75	.90	.50
20	Eddie Collins	2.00	1.00	.60
21	Rabbit Maranville	1.75	.90	.50
22	Joe Medwick	1.75	.90	.50
23	Ed Barrow	1.75	.90	.50
24	Mickey Cochrane	2.00	1.00	.60
25	Jimmy Collins	1.75	.90	.50
26	Bob Feller	7.00	3.50	2.00
27	Luke Appling	1.75	.90	.50
28	Lou Gehrig	20.00	10.00	6.00
29	Gabby Hartnett	1.75	.90	.50
30	Chuck Klein	1.75	.90	.50
31	Tony Lazzeri	1.75	.90	.50
32	Al Simmons	1.75	.90	.50
33	Wilbert Robinson	1.75	.90	.50
34	Sam Rice	1.75	.90	.50
35	Herb Pennock	1.75	.90	.50
36	Mel Ott	2.00	1.00	.60
37	Lefty O'Doul	1.75	.90	.50
38	Johnny Mize	2.00	1.00	.60
39	Bing Miller	1.75	.90	.50
40	Joe Tinker	1.75	.90	.50
41	Frank Baker	1.75	.90	.50
42	Ty Cobb	20.00	10.00	6.00
43	Paul Derringer	1.75	.90	.50
44	Cap Anson	2.00	1.00	.60
45	Jim Bottomley	1.75	.90	.50
46	Eddie Plank	1.75	.90	.50
47	Cy Young	3.50	1.75	1.00
48	Hack Wilson	1.75	.90	.50
49	Ed Walsh	1.75	.90	.50
50	Frank Chance	1.75	.90	.50
51	Dazzy Vance	1.75	.90	.50
52	Bill Terry	2.00	1.00	.60
53	Jimmy Foxx	3.00	1.50	.90
54	Lefty Gomez	2.00	1.00	.60
55	Branch Rickey	1.75	.90	.50
56	Ray Schalk	1.75	.90	.50
57	Johnny Evers	1.75	.90	.50
58	Charlie Gehringer	2.00	1.00	.60
59	Burleigh Grimes	1.75	.90	.50
60	Lefty Grove	2.00	1.00	.60
61	Rube Waddell	1.75	.90	.50
62	Honus Wagner	6.00	3.00	1.75
63	Red Ruffing	1.75	.90	.50
64	Judge Landis	1.75	.90	.50
65	Harry Heilmann	1.75	.90	.50
66	John McGraw	2.00	1.00	.60
67	Hughie Jennings	1.75	.90	.50
68	Hal Newhouser	1.75	.90	.50
69	Waite Hoyt	1.75	.90	.50
70	Bobo Newsom	1.75	.90	.50
71	Earl Averill	1.75	.90	.50
72	Ted Williams	35.00	17.50	10.50
73	Warren Giles	1.75	.90	.50
74	Ford Frick	1.75	.90	.50
75	Ki Ki Cuyler	1.75	.90	.50
76	Paul Waner	1.75	.90	.50
77	Pie Traynor	1.75	.90	.50
78	Lloyd Waner	1.75	.90	.50
79	Ralph Kiner	6.00	3.00	1.75

1961 Fleer

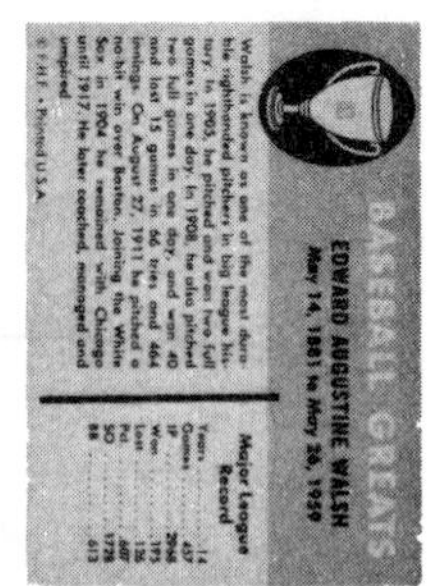

Over a two-year period, Fleer issued another set utilizing the Baseball Greats theme. The 154-card set was issued in two series and features a color player portrait against a color background. The player's name is located in a pennant set at the bottom of the card. The card backs feature orange and black on white stock and contain player biographical and statistical information. The cards measure 2-1/2" by 3-1/2" in size. The second series cards (#'s 89-154) were issued in 1962.

		NR MT	EX	VG
	Complete Set:	550.00	275.00	165.00
	Common Player: 1-88	1.75	.90	.50
	Common Player: 89-154	3.00	1.50	.90
1	Baker, Cobb, Wheat/Checklist	20.00	10.00	6.00
2	G.C. Alexander	3.00	1.50	.90
3	Nick Altrock	1.75	.90	.50
4	Cap Anson	2.00	1.00	.60
5	Earl Averill	1.75	.90	.50
6	Home Run Baker	1.75	.90	.50
7	Dave Bancroft	1.75	.90	.50
8	Chief Bender	1.75	.90	.50
9	Jim Bottomley	1.75	.90	.50
10	Roger Bresnahan	1.75	.90	.50
11	Mordecai Brown	1.75	.90	.50
12	Max Carey	1.75	.90	.50
13	Jack Chesbro	1.75	.90	.50
14	Ty Cobb	20.00	10.00	6.00
15	Mickey Cochrane	2.00	1.00	.60
16	Eddie Collins	2.00	1.00	.60
17	Earle Combs	1.75	.90	.50
18	Charles Comiskey	1.75	.90	.50
19	Ki Ki Cuyler	1.75	.90	.50
20	Paul Derringer	1.75	.90	.50
21	Howard Ehmke	1.75	.90	.50
22	Billy Evans	1.75	.90	.50
23	Johnny Evers	1.75	.90	.50
24	Red Faber	1.75	.90	.50
25	Bob Feller	4.00	2.00	1.25
26	Wes Ferrell	1.75	.90	.50
27	Lew Fonseca	1.75	.90	.50
28	Jimmy Foxx	3.00	1.50	.90
29	Ford Frick	1.75	.90	.50
30	Frankie Frisch	2.00	1.00	.60
31	Lou Gehrig	20.00	10.00	6.00
32	Charlie Gehringer	2.00	1.00	.60
33	Warren Giles	1.75	.90	.50
34	Lefty Gomez	2.00	1.00	.60
35	Goose Goslin	1.75	.90	.50
36	Clark Griffith	1.75	.90	.50
37	Burleigh Grimes	1.75	.90	.50
38	Lefty Grove	1.50	.70	.45
39	Chick Hafey	1.75	.90	.50
40	Jesse Haines	1.75	.90	.50
41	Gabby Hartnett	1.75	.90	.50
42	Harry Heilmann	1.75	.90	.50
43	Rogers Hornsby	3.00	1.50	.90
44	Waite Hoyt	1.75	.90	.50
45	Carl Hubbell	1.50	.70	.45
46	Miller Huggins	1.75	.90	.50
47	Hughie Jennings	1.75	.90	.50
48	Ban Johnson	1.75	.90	.50
49	Walter Johnson	3.00	1.50	.90
50	Ralph Kiner	2.00	1.00	.60
51	Chuck Klein	1.75	.90	.50
52	Johnny Kling	1.75	.90	.50
53	Judge Landis	1.75	.90	.50
54	Tony Lazzeri	1.75	.90	.50
55	Ernie Lombardi	1.75	.90	.50
56	Dolf Luque	1.75	.90	.50
57	Heinie Manush	1.75	.90	.50
58	Marty Marion	1.75	.90	.50
59	Christy Mathewson	2.50	1.25	.70
60	John McGraw	2.00	1.00	.60
61	Joe Medwick	1.75	.90	.50
62	Bing Miller	1.75	.90	.50
63	Johnny Mize	2.00	1.00	.60
64	Johnny Mostil	1.75	.90	.50
65	Art Nehf	1.75	.90	.50
66	Hal Newhouser	1.75	.90	.50
67	Bobo Newsom	1.75	.90	.50
68	Mel Ott	1.50	.70	.45

		NR MT	EX	VG
69	Allie Reynolds	1.75	.90	.50
70	Sam Rice	1.75	.90	.50
71	Eppa Rixey	1.75	.90	.50
72	Edd Roush	1.75	.90	.50
73	Schoolboy Rowe	1.75	.90	.50
74	Red Ruffing	1.75	.90	.50
75	Babe Ruth	45.00	23.00	13.50
76	Joe Sewell	1.75	.90	.50
77	Al Simmons	1.75	.90	.50
78	George Sisler	2.00	1.00	.60
79	Tris Speaker	1.50	.70	.45
80	Fred Toney	1.75	.90	.50
81	Dazzy Vance	1.75	.90	.50
82	Jim Vaughn	1.75	.90	.50
83	Big Ed Walsh	1.75	.90	.50
84	Lloyd Waner	1.75	.90	.50
85	Paul Waner	1.75	.90	.50
86	Zach Wheat	1.75	.90	.50
87	Hack Wilson	1.75	.90	.50
88	Jimmy Wilson	1.75	.90	.50
89	Sisler & Traynor/Checklist	20.00	10.00	6.00
90	Babe Adams	3.00	1.50	.90
91	Dale Alexander	3.00	1.50	.90
92	Jim Bagby	3.00	1.50	.90
93	Ossie Bluege	3.00	1.50	.90
94	Lou Boudreau	4.00	2.00	1.25
95	Tommy Bridges	3.00	1.50	.90
96	Donnie Bush (Donie)	3.00	1.50	.90
97	Dolph Camilli	3.00	1.50	.90
98	Frank Chance	4.00	2.00	1.25
99	Jimmy Collins	3.00	1.50	.90
100	Stanley Coveleskie (Coveleski)	3.00	1.50	.90
101	Hughie Critz	3.00	1.50	.90
102	General Crowder	3.00	1.50	.90
103	Joe Dugan	3.00	1.50	.90
104	Bibb Falk	3.00	1.50	.90
105	Rick Ferrell	3.00	1.50	.90
106	Art Fletcher	3.00	1.50	.90
107	Dennis Galehouse	3.00	1.50	.90
108	Chick Galloway	3.00	1.50	.90
109	Mule Haas	3.00	1.50	.90
110	Stan Hack	3.00	1.50	.90
111	Bump Hadley	3.00	1.50	.90
112	Billy Hamilton	3.00	1.50	.90
113	Joe Hauser	3.00	1.50	.90
114	Babe Herman	3.00	1.50	.90
115	Travis Jackson	3.00	1.50	.90
116	Eddie Joost	3.00	1.50	.90
117	Addie Joss	3.00	1.50	.90
118	Joe Judge	3.00	1.50	.90
119	Joe Kuhel	3.00	1.50	.90
120	Nap Lajoie	6.00	3.00	1.75
121	Dutch Leonard	3.00	1.50	.90
122	Ted Lyons	3.00	1.50	.90
123	Connie Mack	6.00	3.00	1.75
124	Rabbit Maranville	3.00	1.50	.90
125	Fred Marberry	3.00	1.50	.90
126	Iron Man McGinnity	3.00	1.50	.90
127	Oscar Melillo	3.00	1.50	.90
128	Ray Mueller	3.00	1.50	.90
129	Kid Nichols	3.00	1.50	.90
130	Lefty O'Doul	3.00	1.50	.90
131	Bob O'Farrell	3.00	1.50	.90
132	Roger Peckinpaugh	3.00	1.50	.90
133	Herb Pennock	3.00	1.50	.90
134	George Pipgras	3.00	1.50	.90
135	Eddie Plank	3.00	1.50	.90
136	Ray Schalk	3.00	1.50	.90
137	Hal Schumacher	3.00	1.50	.90
138	Luke Sewell	3.00	1.50	.90
139	Bob Shawkey	3.00	1.50	.90
140	Riggs Stephenson	3.00	1.50	.90
141	Billy Sullivan	3.00	1.50	.90
142	Bill Terry	5.00	2.50	1.50
143	Joe Tinker	2.75	1.50	.80
144	Pie Traynor	4.00	2.00	1.25
145	George Uhle	3.00	1.50	.90
146	Hal Troskey (Trosky)	3.00	1.50	.90
147	Arky Vaughan	3.00	1.50	.90
148	Johnny Vander Meer	3.00	1.50	.90
149	Rube Waddell	3.00	1.50	.90
150	Honus Wagner	20.00	10.00	6.00
151	Dixie Walker	3.00	1.50	.90
152	Ted Williams	45.00	23.00	13.50
153	Cy Young	8.00	4.00	2.50
154	Ross Young (Youngs)	6.00	3.00	1.75

1963 Fleer

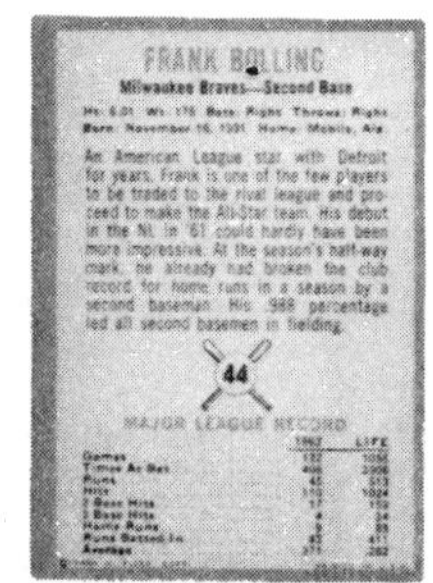

A lawsuit by Topps stopped Fleer's 1963 set at one series of 66 cards. Issued with a cookie rather than gum, the set features color photos of current players. The card backs include statistical information for 1962 and career plus a brief player biography. The cards, which measure 2-1/2" by 3-1/2", are numbered 1-66. An unnumbered checklist was issued with the set and is included in the complete set price in the checklist that follows. The checklist and #46 Adcock are scarce.

		NR MT	EX	VG
	Complete Set:	800.00	400.00	250.00
	Common Player:	5.00	2.50	1.50
1	Steve Barber	10.00	2.00	1.25
2	Ron Hansen	5.00	2.50	1.50
3	Milt Pappas	2.25	1.25	.70
4	Brooks Robinson	30.00	15.00	9.00
5	Willie Mays	75.00	38.00	23.00
6	Lou Clinton	5.00	2.50	1.50
7	Bill Monbouquette	5.00	2.50	1.50
8	Carl Yastrzemski	75.00	38.00	23.00
9	Ray Herbert	5.00	2.50	1.50
10	Jim Landis	5.00	2.50	1.50
11	Dick Donovan	5.00	2.50	1.50
12	Tito Francona	5.00	2.50	1.50
13	Jerry Kindall	5.00	2.50	1.50
14	Frank Lary	2.25	1.25	.70
15	Dick Howser	2.50	1.25	.70
16	Jerry Lumpe	5.00	2.50	1.50
17	Norm Siebern	5.00	2.50	1.50
18	Don Lee	5.00	2.50	1.50
19	Albie Pearson	5.00	2.50	1.50
20	Bob Rodgers	2.25	1.25	.70
21	Leon Wagner	5.00	2.50	1.50
22	Jim Kaat	6.00	3.00	1.75
23	Vic Power	5.00	2.50	1.50
24	Rich Rollins	5.00	2.50	1.50
25	Bobby Richardson	5.00	2.50	1.50
26	Ralph Terry	2.50	1.25	.70
27	Tom Cheney	2.25	1.25	.70
28	Chuck Cottier	5.00	2.50	1.50
29	Jimmy Piersall	2.50	1.25	.70
30	Dave Stenhouse	5.00	2.50	1.50
31	Glen Hobbie	5.00	2.50	1.50
32	Ron Santo	6.00	3.00	1.75
33	Gene Freese	5.00	2.50	1.50
34	Vada Pinson	6.00	3.00	1.75
35	Bob Purkey	5.00	2.50	1.50
36	Joe Amalfitano	5.00	2.50	1.50
37	Bob Aspromonte	5.00	2.50	1.50
38	Dick Farrell	5.00	2.50	1.50
39	Al Spangler	5.00	2.50	1.50
40	Tommy Davis	2.50	1.25	.70
41	Don Drysdale	20.00	10.00	6.00
42	Sandy Koufax	80.00	40.00	24.00
43	Maury Wills	30.00	15.00	9.00
44	Frank Bolling	5.00	2.50	1.50
45	Warren Spahn	30.00	15.00	9.00
46	Joe Adcock	100.00	45.00	27.00
47	Roger Craig	4.00	2.00	1.25
48	Al Jackson	2.25	1.25	.70
49	Rod Kanehl	2.25	1.25	.70
50	Ruben Amaro	5.00	2.50	1.50
51	John Callison	2.25	1.25	.70
52	Clay Dalrymple	5.00	2.50	1.50
53	Don Demeter	5.00	2.50	1.50
54	Art Mahaffey	5.00	2.50	1.50
55	"Smoky" Burgess	2.25	1.25	.70
56	Roberto Clemente	75.00	38.00	23.00
57	Elroy Face	2.25	1.25	.70
58	Vernon Law	2.25	1.25	.70
59	Bill Mazeroski	6.00	3.00	1.75
60	Ken Boyer	6.00	3.00	1.75
61	Bob Gibson	25.00	12.50	7.50
62	Gene Oliver	5.00	2.50	1.50
63	Bill White	2.75	1.50	.80
64	Orlando Cepeda	5.00	2.50	1.50
65	Jimmy Davenport	5.00	2.50	1.50
66	Billy O'Dell	6.00	3.00	1.75
---	Checklist 1-66	325.00	130.00	81.00

1981 Fleer

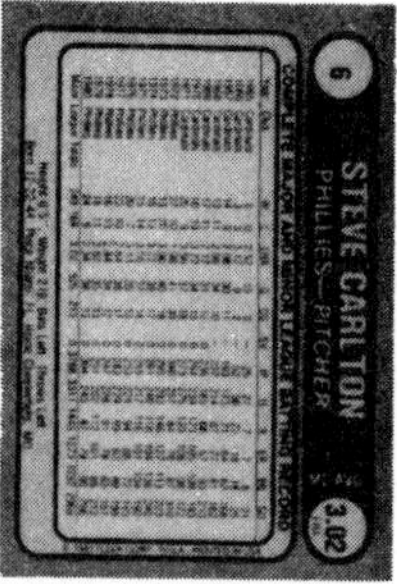

For the first time in 18 years, Fleer issued a baseball card set featuring current players. Fleer's 660-card effort included numerous errors in the first printing run which were subsequently corrected in additional runs. The cards, which measure 2-1/2" by 3-1/2", are numbered alphabetically by team. The card fronts feature a full-color photo inside a border which is color-coded by team. The card backs have black, grey and yellow ink on white stock and carry player statistical information. The player's batting average or earned run average is located in a circle in the upper right corner of the card. The complete set price in the checklist that follows does not include the higher priced variations.

		MT	NR MT	EX
	Complete Set:	40.00	30.00	15.00
	Common Player:	.06	.05	.02
1	Pete Rose	1.75	1.25	.70
2	Larry Bowa	.15	.11	.06
3	Manny Trillo	.08	.06	.03
4	Bob Boone	.10	.08	.04
5a	Mike Schmidt (portrait)	1.25	.90	.50
5b	Mike Schmidt (batting)	.90	.70	.35
6a	Steve Carlton ("Lefty" on front)	1.00	.70	.40
6b	Steve Carlton (Pitcher of the Year on front, date 1066 on back)	.60	.45	.25
6c	Steve Carlton (Pitcher of the Year on front, date 1966 on back)	2.00	1.50	.80
7a	Tug McGraw (Game Saver on front)	.50	.40	.20
7b	Tug McGraw (Pitcher on front)	.12	.09	.05
8	Larry Christenson	.06	.05	.02
9	Bake McBride	.06	.05	.02
10	Greg Luzinski	.15	.11	.06
11	Ron Reed	.06	.05	.02
12	Dickie Noles	.06	.05	.02
13	*Keith Moreland*	.35	.25	.14
14	*Bob Walk*	.25	.20	.10
15	Lonnie Smith	.08	.06	.03
16	Dick Ruthven	.06	.05	.02
17	Sparky Lyle	.10	.08	.04
18	Greg Gross	.06	.05	.02
19	Garry Maddox	.10	.08	.04
20	Nino Espinosa	.06	.05	.02
21	George Vukovich	.06	.05	.02
22	John Vukovich	.06	.05	.02
23	Ramon Aviles	.06	.05	.02
24a	Kevin Saucier (Ken Saucier on back)	.15	.11	.06
24b	Kevin Saucier (Kevin Saucier on back)	.70	.50	.30
25	Randy Lerch	.06	.05	.02
26	Del Unser	.06	.05	.02
27	Tim McCarver	.15	.11	.06
28a	George Brett (batting)	1.25	.90	.50
28b	George Brett (portrait)	.90	.70	.35
29a	Willie Wilson (portrait)	.60	.45	.25
29b	Willie Wilson (batting)	.15	.11	.06
30	Paul Splittorff	.06	.05	.02
31	Dan Quisenberry	.15	.11	.06
32a	Amos Otis (batting)	.50	.40	.20
32b	Amos Otis (portrait)	.10	.08	.04
33	Steve Busby	.08	.06	.03
34	U.L. Washington	.06	.05	.02
35	Dave Chalk	.06	.05	.02
36	Darrell Porter	.08	.06	.03
37	Marty Pattin	.06	.05	.02
38	Larry Gura	.06	.05	.02
39	Renie Martin	.06	.05	.02
40	Rich Gale	.06	.05	.02
41a	Hal McRae (dark blue "Royals" on front)	.40	.30	.15
41b	Hal McRae (light blue "Royals" on front)	.10	.08	.04
42	Dennis Leonard	.08	.06	.03
43	Willie Aikens	.06	.05	.02
44	Frank White	.10	.08	.04
45	Clint Hurdle	.06	.05	.02
46	John Wathan	.08	.06	.03
47	Pete LaCock	.06	.05	.02
48	Rance Mulliniks	.06	.05	.02
49	Jeff Twitty	.06	.05	.02
50	Jamie Quirk	.06	.05	.02
51	Art Howe	.06	.05	.02
52	Ken Forsch	.06	.05	.02
53	Vern Ruhle	.06	.05	.02
54	Joe Niekro	.12	.09	.05
55	Frank LaCorte	.06	.05	.02
56	J.R. Richard	.10	.08	.04
57	Nolan Ryan	2.00	1.50	.80
58	Enos Cabell	.06	.05	.02
59	Cesar Cedeno	.12	.09	.05
60	Jose Cruz	.12	.09	.05
61	Bill Virdon	.06	.05	.02
62	Terry Puhl	.06	.05	.02
63	Joaquin Andujar	.10	.08	.04
64	Alan Ashby	.06	.05	.02
65	Joe Sambito	.06	.05	.02
66	Denny Walling	.06	.05	.02
67	Jeff Leonard	.12	.09	.05
68	Luis Pujols	.06	.05	.02
69	Bruce Bochy	.06	.05	.02
70	Rafael Landestoy	.06	.05	.02
71	*Dave Smith*	.30	.25	.12
72	*Danny Heep*	.10	.08	.04
73	Julio Gonzalez	.06	.05	.02
74	Craig Reynolds	.06	.05	.02
75	Gary Woods	.06	.05	.02
76	Dave Bergman	.06	.05	.02
77	Randy Niemann	.06	.05	.02
78	Joe Morgan	.60	.45	.25
79a	Reggie Jackson (portrait)	1.00	.70	.40
79b	Reggie Jackson (batting)	.75	.60	.30
80	Bucky Dent	.10	.08	.04
81	Tommy John	.20	.15	.08
82	Luis Tiant	.12	.09	.05
83	Rick Cerone	.06	.05	.02
84	Dick Howser	.06	.05	.02
85	Lou Piniella	.12	.09	.05
86	Ron Davis	.08	.06	.03
87a	Graig Nettles (Craig on back)	12.00	9.00	4.75
87b	Graig Nettles (Graig on back)	.30	.25	.12
88	Ron Guidry	.25	.20	.10
89	Rich Gossage	.20	.15	.08
90	Rudy May	.06	.05	.02
91	Gaylord Perry	.30	.25	.12
92	Eric Soderholm	.06	.05	.02
93	Bob Watson	.08	.06	.03
94	Bobby Murcer	.10	.08	.04
95	Bobby Brown	.06	.05	.02
96	Jim Spencer	.06	.05	.02
97	Tom Underwood	.06	.05	.02
98	Oscar Gamble	.08	.06	.03
99	Johnny Oates	.06	.05	.02
100	Fred Stanley	.06	.05	.02
101	Ruppert Jones	.06	.05	.02
102	Dennis Werth	.06	.05	.02

		MT	NR MT	EX
103	Joe Lefebvre	.06	.05	.02
104	Brian Doyle	.06	.05	.02
105	Aurelio Rodriguez	.08	.06	.03
106	Doug Bird	.06	.05	.02
107	Mike Griffin	.06	.05	.02
108	Tim Lollar	.06	.05	.02
109	Willie Randolph	.10	.08	.04
110	Steve Garvey	.50	.40	.20
111	Reggie Smith	.10	.08	.04
112	Don Sutton	.30	.25	.12
113	Burt Hooton	.08	.06	.03
114a	Davy Lopes (Davey) (no finger on back)	.10	.08	.04
114b	Davy Lopes (Davey) (small finger on back)	1.00	.70	.40
115	Dusty Baker	.10	.08	.04
116	Tom Lasorda	.10	.08	.04
117	Bill Russell	.08	.06	.03
118	Jerry Reuss	.10	.08	.04
119	Terry Forster	.08	.06	.03
120a	Robert Welch (Bob Welch on back)	.20	.15	.08
120b	Robert Welch (Robert Welch on back)	1.00	.70	.40
121	Don Stanhouse	.06	.05	.02
122	Rick Monday	.10	.08	.04
123	Derrel Thomas	.06	.05	.02
124	Joe Ferguson	.06	.05	.02
125	Rick Sutcliffe	.20	.15	.08
126a	Ron Cey (no finger on back)	.12	.09	.05
126b	Ron Cey (small finger on back)	1.00	.70	.40
127	Dave Goltz	.08	.06	.03
128	Jay Johnstone	.08	.06	.03
129	Steve Yeager	.06	.05	.02
130	Gary Weiss	.06	.05	.02
131	*Mike Scioscia*	.60	.45	.25
132	Vic Davalillo	.08	.06	.03
133	Doug Rau	.06	.05	.02
134	Pepe Frias	.06	.05	.02
135	Mickey Hatcher	.08	.06	.03
136	*Steve Howe*	.10	.08	.04
137	Robert Castillo	.06	.05	.02
138	Gary Thomasson	.06	.05	.02
139	Rudy Law	.06	.05	.02
140	*Fernand Valenzuela (Fernando)*	4.00	3.00	1.50
141	Manny Mota	.08	.06	.03
142	Gary Carter	.40	.30	.15
143	Steve Rogers	.08	.06	.03
144	Warren Cromartie	.06	.05	.02
145	Andre Dawson	.40	.30	.15
146	Larry Parrish	.10	.08	.04
147	Rowland Office	.06	.05	.02
148	Ellis Valentine	.06	.05	.02
149	Dick Williams	.06	.05	.02
150	*Bill Gullickson*	.15	.11	.06
151	Elias Sosa	.06	.05	.02
152	John Tamargo	.06	.05	.02
153	Chris Speier	.06	.05	.02
154	Ron LeFlore	.08	.06	.03
155	Rodney Scott	.06	.05	.02
156	Stan Bahnsen	.06	.05	.02
157	Bill Lee	.08	.06	.03
158	Fred Norman	.06	.05	.02
159	Woodie Fryman	.08	.06	.03
160	Dave Palmer	.06	.05	.02
161	Jerry White	.06	.05	.02
162	Roberto Ramos	.06	.05	.02
163	John D'Acquisto	.06	.05	.02
164	Tommy Hutton	.06	.05	.02
165	*Charlie Lea*	.12	.09	.05
166	Scott Sanderson	.06	.05	.02
167	Ken Macha	.06	.05	.02
168	Tony Bernazard	.06	.05	.02
169	Jim Palmer	.70	.50	.30
170	Steve Stone	.08	.06	.03
171	Mike Flanagan	.10	.08	.04
172	Al Bumbry	.08	.06	.03
173	Doug DeCinces	.10	.08	.04
174	Scott McGregor	.08	.06	.03
175	Mark Belanger	.08	.06	.03
176	Tim Stoddard	.06	.05	.02
177a	Rick Dempsey (no finger on front)	.10	.08	.04
177b	Rick Dempsey (small finger on front)	1.00	.70	.40
178	Earl Weaver	.10	.08	.04
179	Tippy Martinez	.06	.05	.02
180	Dennis Martinez	.08	.06	.03
181	Sammy Stewart	.06	.05	.02
182	Rich Dauer	.06	.05	.02
183	Lee May	.08	.06	.03
184	Eddie Murray	.70	.50	.30
185	Benny Ayala	.06	.05	.02
186	John Lowenstein	.06	.05	.02
187	Gary Roenicke	.06	.05	.02
188	Ken Singleton	.10	.08	.04
189	Dan Graham	.06	.05	.02
190	Terry Crowley	.06	.05	.02
191	Kiko Garcia	.06	.05	.02
192	Dave Ford	.06	.05	.02
193	Mark Corey	.06	.05	.02
194	Lenn Sakata	.06	.05	.02
195	Doug DeCinces	.10	.08	.04
196	Johnny Bench	.60	.45	.25
197	Dave Concepcion	.15	.11	.06
198	Ray Knight	.10	.08	.04
199	Ken Griffey	.12	.09	.05
200	Tom Seaver	.70	.50	.30
201	Dave Collins	.08	.06	.03
202	George Foster	.20	.15	.08
203	Junior Kennedy	.06	.05	.02
204	Frank Pastore	.06	.05	.02
205	Dan Driessen	.08	.06	.03
206	Hector Cruz	.06	.05	.02
207	Paul Moskau	.06	.05	.02
208	*Charlie Leibrandt*	.30	.25	.12
209	Harry Spilman	.06	.05	.02
210	*Joe Price*	.12	.09	.05
211	Tom Hume	.06	.05	.02
212	Joe Nolan	.06	.05	.02
213	Doug Bair	.06	.05	.02
214	Mario Soto	.08	.06	.03
215a	Bill Bonham (no finger on back)	.08	.06	.03
215b	Bill Bonham (small finger on back)	1.00	.70	.40
216a	George Foster (Slugger on front)	.25	.20	.10
216b	George Foster (Outfield on front)	.20	.15	.08
217	Paul Householder	.06	.05	.02
218	Ron Oester	.06	.05	.02
219	Sam Mejias	.06	.05	.02
220	Sheldon Burnside	.06	.05	.02
221	Carl Yastrzemski	1.00	.70	.40
222	Jim Rice	.50	.40	.20
223	Fred Lynn	.20	.15	.08
224	Carlton Fisk	.50	.40	.20
225	Rick Burleson	.08	.06	.03
226	Dennis Eckersley	.12	.09	.05
227	Butch Hobson	.06	.05	.02
228	Tom Burgmeier	.06	.05	.02
229	Garry Hancock	.06	.05	.02
230	Don Zimmer	.06	.05	.02
231	Steve Renko	.06	.05	.02
232	Dwight Evans	.15	.11	.06
233	Mike Torrez	.08	.06	.03
234	Bob Stanley	.06	.05	.02
235	Jim Dwyer	.06	.05	.02
236	Dave Stapleton	.06	.05	.02
237	Glenn Hoffman	.06	.05	.02
238	Jerry Remy	.06	.05	.02
239	Dick Drago	.06	.05	.02
240	Bill Campbell	.06	.05	.02
241	Tony Perez	.20	.15	.08
242	Phil Niekro	.30	.25	.12
243	Dale Murphy	.90	.70	.35
244	Bob Horner	.12	.09	.05
245	Jeff Burroughs	.08	.06	.03
246	Rick Camp	.06	.05	.02
247	Bob Cox	.06	.05	.02
248	Bruce Benedict	.06	.05	.02
249	Gene Garber	.06	.05	.02
250	Jerry Royster	.06	.05	.02
251a	Gary Matthews (no finger on back)	.12	.09	.05
251b	Gary Matthews (small finger on back)	1.00	.70	.40
252	Chris Chambliss	.08	.06	.03
253	Luis Gomez	.06	.05	.02
254	Bill Nahorodny	.06	.05	.02
255	Doyle Alexander	.10	.08	.04
256	Brian Asselstine	.06	.05	.02
257	Biff Pocoroba	.06	.05	.02
258	Mike Lum	.06	.05	.02
259	Charlie Spikes	.06	.05	.02
260	Glenn Hubbard	.08	.06	.03
261	Tommy Boggs	.06	.05	.02
262	Al Hrabosky	.08	.06	.03
263	Rick Matula	.06	.05	.02
264	Preston Hanna	.06	.05	.02
265	Larry Bradford	.06	.05	.02
266	*Rafael Ramirez*	.20	.15	.08
267	Larry McWilliams	.06	.05	.02
268	Rod Carew	.70	.50	.30
269	Bobby Grich	.10	.08	.04
270	Carney Lansford	.10	.08	.04
271	Don Baylor	.12	.09	.05
272	Joe Rudi	.10	.08	.04
273	Dan Ford	.06	.05	.02
274	Jim Fregosi	.08	.06	.03
275	Dave Frost	.06	.05	.02
276	Frank Tanana	.10	.08	.04
277	Dickie Thon	.08	.06	.03
278	Jason Thompson	.06	.05	.02
279	Rick Miller	.06	.05	.02
280	Bert Campaneris	.10	.08	.04
281	Tom Donohue	.06	.05	.02
282	Brian Downing	.10	.08	.04
283	Fred Patek	.06	.05	.02
284	Bruce Kison	.06	.05	.02
285	Dave LaRoche	.06	.05	.02
286	Don Aase	.06	.05	.02
287	Jim Barr	.06	.05	.02
288	Alfredo Martinez	.06	.05	.02
289	Larry Harlow	.06	.05	.02
290	Andy Hassler	.06	.05	.02
291	Dave Kingman	.15	.11	.06
292	Bill Buckner	.12	.09	.05
293	Rick Reuschel	.10	.08	.04
294	Bruce Sutter	.15	.11	.06
295	Jerry Martin	.06	.05	.02
296	Scot Thompson	.06	.05	.02
297	Ivan DeJesus	.06	.05	.02
298	Steve Dillard	.06	.05	.02
299	Dick Tidrow	.06	.05	.02
300	Randy Martz	.06	.05	.02
301	Lenny Randle	.06	.05	.02
302	Lynn McGlothen	.06	.05	.02
303	Cliff Johnson	.06	.05	.02
304	Tim Blackwell	.06	.05	.02
305	Dennis Lamp	.06	.05	.02
306	Bill Caudill	.06	.05	.02
307	Carlos Lezcano	.06	.05	.02
308	Jim Tracy	.06	.05	.02
309	Doug Capilla	.06	.05	.02
310	Willie Hernandez	.10	.08	.04
311	Mike Vail	.06	.05	.02
312	Mike Krukow	.08	.06	.03
313	Barry Foote	.06	.05	.02
314	Larry Biittner	.06	.05	.02
315	Mike Tyson	.06	.05	.02
316	Lee Mazzilli	.08	.06	.03
317	John Stearns	.06	.05	.02
318	Alex Trevino	.06	.05	.02
319	Craig Swan	.06	.05	.02
320	Frank Taveras	.06	.05	.02
321	Steve Henderson	.06	.05	.02
322	Neil Allen	.08	.06	.03
323	Mark Bomback	.06	.05	.02
324	Mike Jorgensen	.06	.05	.02
325	Joe Torre	.08	.06	.03
326	Elliott Maddox	.06	.05	.02
327	Pete Falcone	.06	.05	.02
328	Ray Burris	.06	.05	.02
329	Claudell Washington	.08	.06	.03
330	Doug Flynn	.06	.05	.02
331	Joel Youngblood	.06	.05	.02
332	Bill Almon	.06	.05	.02
333	Tom Hausman	.06	.05	.02
334	Pat Zachry	.06	.05	.02
335	*Jeff Reardon*	.70	.50	.30
336	*Wally Backman*	.35	.25	.14
337	Dan Norman	.06	.05	.02
338	Jerry Morales	.06	.05	.02
339	Ed Farmer	.06	.05	.02
340	Bob Molinaro	.06	.05	.02
341	Todd Cruz	.06	.05	.02
342a	*Britt Burns* (no finger on front)	.20	.15	.08
342b	*Britt Burns* (small finger on front)	1.00	.70	.40
343	Kevin Bell	.06	.05	.02
344	Tony LaRussa	.08	.06	.03
345	Steve Trout	.06	.05	.02
346	*Harold Baines*	2.50	2.00	1.00
347	Richard Wortham	.06	.05	.02
348	Wayne Nordhagen	.06	.05	.02
349	Mike Squires	.06	.05	.02
350	Lamar Johnson	.06	.05	.02
351	Rickey Henderson	5.00	3.75	2.00
352	Francisco Barrios	.06	.05	.02
353	Thad Bosley	.06	.05	.02
354	Chet Lemon	.08	.06	.03
355	Bruce Kimm	.06	.05	.02
356	*Richard Dotson*	.35	.25	.14
357	Jim Morrison	.06	.05	.02
358	Mike Proly	.06	.05	.02
359	Greg Pryor	.06	.05	.02
360	Dave Parker	.30	.25	.12
361	Omar Moreno	.06	.05	.02
362a	Kent Tekulve (1071 Waterbury on back)	.15	.11	.06
362b	Kent Tekulve (1971 Waterbury on back)	.70	.50	.30
363	Willie Stargell	.40	.30	.15
364	Phil Garner	.08	.06	.03
365	Ed Ott	.06	.05	.02
366	Don Robinson	.08	.06	.03
367	Chuck Tanner	.06	.05	.02
368	Jim Rooker	.06	.05	.02
369	Dale Berra	.06	.05	.02
370	Jim Bibby	.06	.05	.02
371	Steve Nicosia	.06	.05	.02
372	Mike Easler	.08	.06	.03
373	Bill Robinson	.06	.05	.02
374	Lee Lacy	.06	.05	.02
375	John Candelaria	.10	.08	.04
376	Manny Sanguillen	.06	.05	.02
377	Rick Rhoden	.10	.08	.04
378	Grant Jackson	.06	.05	.02
379	Tim Foli	.06	.05	.02
380	*Rod Scurry*	.08	.06	.03
381	Bill Madlock	.12	.09	.05
382a	Kurt Bevacqua (photo reversed, backwards "P" on cap)	.15	.11	.06
382b	Kurt Bevacqua (correct photo)	.70	.50	.30
383	Bert Blyleven	.12	.09	.05
384	Eddie Solomon	.06	.05	.02
385	Enrique Romo	.06	.05	.02
386	John Milner	.06	.05	.02
387	Mike Hargrove	.06	.05	.02
388	Jorge Orta	.06	.05	.02
389	Toby Harrah	.08	.06	.03
390	Tom Veryzer	.06	.05	.02
391	Miguel Dilone	.06	.05	.02
392	Dan Spillner	.06	.05	.02
393	Jack Brohamer	.06	.05	.02
394	Wayne Garland	.06	.05	.02
395	Sid Monge	.06	.05	.02
396	Rick Waits	.06	.05	.02
397	*Joe Charboneau*	.10	.08	.04
398	Gary Alexander	.06	.05	.02
399	Jerry Dybzinski	.06	.05	.02
400	Mike Stanton	.06	.05	.02
401	Mike Paxton	.06	.05	.02
402	Gary Gray	.06	.05	.02
403	Rick Manning	.06	.05	.02
404	Bo Diaz	.08	.06	.03
405	Ron Hassey	.06	.05	.02
406	Ross Grimsley	.06	.05	.02
407	Victor Cruz	.06	.05	.02
408	Len Barker	.08	.06	.03
409	Bob Bailor	.06	.05	.02
410	Otto Velez	.06	.05	.02
411	Ernie Whitt	.08	.06	.03
412	Jim Clancy	.08	.06	.03
413	Barry Bonnell	.06	.05	.02
414	Dave Stieb	.20	.15	.08
415	*Damaso Garcia*	.10	.08	.04
416	John Mayberry	.08	.06	.03
417	Roy Howell	.06	.05	.02
418	*Dan Ainge*	.25	.20	.10
419a	Jesse Jefferson (Pirates on back)	.10	.08	.04
419b	Jesse Jefferson (Blue Jays on back)	.50	.40	.20
420	Joey McLaughlin	.06	.05	.02
421	*Lloyd Moseby*	.70	.50	.30
422	Al Woods	.06	.05	.02
423	Garth Iorg	.06	.05	.02
424	Doug Ault	.06	.05	.02
425	*Ken Schrom*	.06	.05	.02
426	Mike Willis	.06	.05	.02
427	Steve Braun	.06	.05	.02
428	Bob Davis	.06	.05	.02
429	Jerry Garvin	.06	.05	.02
430	Alfredo Griffin	.08	.06	.03
431	Bob Mattick	.06	.05	.02
432	Vida Blue	.12	.09	.05
433	Jack Clark	.25	.20	.10
434	Willie McCovey	.40	.30	.15
435	Mike Ivie	.06	.05	.02
436a	Darrel Evans (Darrel on front)	.15	.11	.06
436b	Darrell Evans (Darrell on front)	.70	.50	.30
437	Terry Whitfield	.06	.05	.02
438	Rennie Stennett	.06	.05	.02
439	John Montefusco	.08	.06	.03
440	Jim Wohlford	.06	.05	.02
441	Bill North	.06	.05	.02
442	Milt May	.06	.05	.02
443	Max Venable	.06	.05	.02

		MT	NR MT	EX
444	Ed Whitson	.06	.05	.02
445	*Al Holland*	.08	.06	.03
446	Randy Moffitt	.06	.05	.02
447	Bob Knepper	.08	.06	.03
448	Gary Lavelle	.06	.05	.02
449	Greg Minton	.06	.05	.02
450	Johnnie LeMaster	.06	.05	.02
451	Larry Herndon	.08	.06	.03
452	Rich Murray	.06	.05	.02
453	Joe Pettini	.06	.05	.02
454	Allen Ripley	.06	.05	.02
455	Dennis Littlejohn	.06	.05	.02
456	Tom Griffin	.06	.05	.02
457	Alan Hargesheimer	.06	.05	.02
458	Joe Strain	.06	.05	.02
459	Steve Kemp	.08	.06	.03
460	Sparky Anderson	.10	.08	.04
461	Alan Trammell	.40	.30	.15
462	Mark Fidrych	.08	.06	.03
463	Lou Whitaker	.40	.30	.15
464	Dave Rozema	.06	.05	.02
465	Milt Wilcox	.06	.05	.02
466	Champ Summers	.06	.05	.02
467	Lance Parrish	.35	.25	.14
468	Dan Petry	.08	.06	.03
469	Pat Underwood	.06	.05	.02
470	Rick Peters	.06	.05	.02
471	Al Cowens	.06	.05	.02
472	John Wockenfuss	.06	.05	.02
473	Tom Brookens	.08	.06	.03
474	Richie Hebner	.06	.05	.02
475	Jack Morris	.30	.25	.12
476	Jim Lentine	.06	.05	.02
477	Bruce Robbins	.06	.05	.02
478	Mark Wagner	.06	.05	.02
479	Tim Corcoran	.06	.05	.02
480a	Stan Papi (Pitcher on front)	.15	.11	.06
480b	Stan Papi (Shortstop on front)	.70	.50	.30
481	*Kirk Gibson*	3.75	2.75	1.50
482	Dan Schatzeder	.06	.05	.02
483	Amos Otis	.70	.50	.30
484	Dave Winfield	.50	.40	.20
485	Rollie Fingers	.25	.20	.10
486	Gene Richards	.06	.05	.02
487	Randy Jones	.08	.06	.03
488	Ozzie Smith	.40	.30	.15
489	Gene Tenace	.08	.06	.03
490	Bill Fahey	.06	.05	.02
491	John Curtis	.06	.05	.02
492	Dave Cash	.06	.05	.02
493a	Tim Flannery (photo reversed, batting righty)	.15	.11	.06
493b	Tim Flannery (photo correct, batting lefty)	.70	.50	.30
494	Jerry Mumphrey	.06	.05	.02
495	Bob Shirley	.06	.05	.02
496	Steve Mura	.06	.05	.02
497	Eric Rasmussen	.06	.05	.02
498	Broderick Perkins	.06	.05	.02
499	Barry Evans	.06	.05	.02
500	Chuck Baker	.06	.05	.02
501	*Luis Salazar*	.15	.11	.06
502	Gary Lucas	.08	.06	.03
503	Mike Armstrong	.06	.05	.02
504	Jerry Turner	.06	.05	.02
505	Dennis Kinney	.06	.05	.02
506	Willy Montanez (Willie)	.06	.05	.02
507	Gorman Thomas	.10	.08	.04
508	Ben Oglivie	.08	.06	.03
509	Larry Hisle	.08	.06	.03
510	Sal Bando	.10	.08	.04
511	Robin Yount	1.25	.90	.50
512	Mike Caldwell	.06	.05	.02
513	Sixto Lezcano	.06	.05	.02
514a	Jerry Augustine (Billy Travers photo)	.15	.11	.06
514b	Billy Travers (correct name with photo)	.70	.50	.30
515	Paul Molitor	.20	.15	.08
516	Moose Haas	.06	.05	.02
517	Bill Castro	.06	.05	.02
518	Jim Slaton	.06	.05	.02
519	Lary Sorensen	.06	.05	.02
520	Bob McClure	.06	.05	.02
521	Charlie Moore	.06	.05	.02
522	Jim Gantner	.08	.06	.03
523	Reggie Cleveland	.06	.05	.02
524	Don Money	.06	.05	.02
525	Billy Travers	.06	.05	.02
526	Buck Martinez	.06	.05	.02
527	Dick Davis	.06	.05	.02
528	Ted Simmons	.12	.09	.05
529	Garry Templeton	.10	.08	.04
530	Ken Reitz	.06	.05	.02
531	Tony Scott	.06	.05	.02
532	Ken Oberkfell	.06	.05	.02
533	Bob Sykes	.06	.05	.02
534	Keith Smith	.06	.05	.02
535	John Littlefield	.06	.05	.02
536	Jim Kaat	.15	.11	.06
537	Bob Forsch	.08	.06	.03
538	Mike Phillips	.06	.05	.02
539	*Terry Landrum*	.10	.08	.04
540	*Leon Durham*	.20	.15	.08
541	Terry Kennedy	.08	.06	.03
542	George Hendrick	.08	.06	.03
543	Dane Iorg	.06	.05	.02
544	Mark Littell (photo actually Jeff Little)	.06	.05	.02
545	Keith Hernandez	.40	.30	.15
546	Silvio Martinez	.06	.05	.02
547a	Pete Vuckovich (photo actually Don Hood)	.15	.11	.06
547b	Don Hood (correct name with photo)	.70	.50	.30
548	Bobby Bonds	.10	.08	.04
549	Mike Ramsey	.06	.05	.02
550	Tom Herr	.10	.08	.04
551	Roy Smalley	.06	.05	.02
552	Jerry Koosman	.10	.08	.04
553	Ken Landreaux	.06	.05	.02
554	John Castino	.06	.05	.02
555	Doug Corbett	.06	.05	.02
556	Bombo Rivera	.06	.05	.02

		MT	NR MT	EX
557	Ron Jackson	.06	.05	.02
558	Butch Wynegar	.06	.05	.02
559	Hosken Powell	.06	.05	.02
560	Pete Redfern	.06	.05	.02
561	Roger Erickson	.06	.05	.02
562	Glenn Adams	.06	.05	.02
563	Rick Sofield	.06	.05	.02
564	Geoff Zahn	.06	.05	.02
565	Pete Mackanin	.06	.05	.02
566	Mike Cubbage	.06	.05	.02
567	Darrell Jackson	.06	.05	.02
568	Dave Edwards	.06	.05	.02
569	Rob Wilfong	.06	.05	.02
570	Sal Butera	.06	.05	.02
571	Jose Morales	.06	.05	.02
572	Rick Langford	.06	.05	.02
573	Mike Norris	.06	.05	.02
574	Rickey Henderson	4.00	3.00	1.50
575	Tony Armas	.10	.08	.04
576	Dave Revering	.06	.05	.02
577	Jeff Newman	.06	.05	.02
578	Bob Lacey	.06	.05	.02
579	Brian Kingman (photo actually Alan Wirth)	.06	.05	.02
580	Mitchell Page	.06	.05	.02
581	Billy Martin	.12	.09	.05
582	Rob Picciolo	.06	.05	.02
583	Mike Heath	.06	.05	.02
584	Mickey Klutts	.06	.05	.02
585	Orlando Gonzalez	.06	.05	.02
586	*Mike Davis*	.25	.20	.10
587	Wayne Gross	.06	.05	.02
588	Matt Keough	.06	.05	.02
589	Steve McCatty	.06	.05	.02
590	Dwayne Murphy	.08	.06	.03
591	Mario Guerrero	.06	.05	.02
592	Dave McKay	.06	.05	.02
593	Jim Essian	.06	.05	.02
594	Dave Heaverlo	.06	.05	.02
595	Maury Wills	.10	.08	.04
596	Juan Beniquez	.06	.05	.02
597	Rodney Craig	.06	.05	.02
598	Jim Anderson	.06	.05	.02
599	Floyd Bannister	.10	.08	.04
600	Bruce Bochte	.06	.05	.02
601	Julio Cruz	.06	.05	.02
602	Ted Cox	.06	.05	.02
603	Dan Meyer	.06	.05	.02
604	Larry Cox	.06	.05	.02
605	Bill Stein	.06	.05	.02
606	Steve Garvey	.50	.40	.20
607	Dave Roberts	.06	.05	.02
608	Leon Roberts	.06	.05	.02
609	Reggie Walton	.06	.05	.02
610	Dave Edler	.06	.05	.02
611	Larry Milbourne	.06	.05	.02
612	Kim Allen	.06	.05	.02
613	Mario Mendoza	.06	.05	.02
614	Tom Paciorek	.06	.05	.02
615	Glenn Abbott	.06	.05	.02
616	Joe Simpson	.06	.05	.02
617	Mickey Rivers	.08	.06	.03
618	Jim Kern	.06	.05	.02
619	Jim Sundberg	.08	.06	.03
620	Richie Zisk	.08	.06	.03
621	Jon Matlack	.08	.06	.03
622	Ferguson Jenkins	.20	.15	.08
623	Pat Corrales	.06	.05	.02
624	Ed Figueroa	.06	.05	.02
625	Buddy Bell	.12	.09	.05
626	Al Oliver	.15	.11	.06
627	Doc Medich	.06	.05	.02
628	Bump Wills	.06	.05	.02
629	Rusty Staub	.10	.08	.04
630	Pat Putnam	.06	.05	.02
631	John Grubb	.06	.05	.02
632	Danny Darwin	.06	.05	.02
633	Ken Clay	.06	.05	.02
634	Jim Norris	.06	.05	.02
635	John Butcher	.06	.05	.02
636	Dave Roberts	.06	.05	.02
637	Billy Sample	.06	.05	.02
638	Carl Yastrzemski	.80	.60	.30
639	Cecil Cooper	.15	.11	.06
640	Mike Schmidt	2.00	1.50	.80
641a	Checklist 1-50 (41 Hal McRae)	.10	.08	.04
641b	Checklist 1-50 (41 Hal McRae Double Threat)	.40	.30	.15
642	Checklist 51-109	.06	.05	.02
643	Checklist 110-168	.06	.05	.02
644a	Checklist 169-220 (202 George Foster)	.10	.08	.04
644b	Checklist 169-220 (202 George Foster "Slugger")	.40	.30	.15
645a	Triple Threat (Larry Bowa, Pete Rose, Mike Schmidt) (no number on back)	1.00	.70	.40
645b	Triple Threat (Larry Bowa, Pete Rose, Mike Schmidt) (645 on back)	2.00	1.50	.80
646	Checklist 221-267	.06	.05	.02
647	Checklist 268-315	.06	.05	.02
648	Checklist 316-359	.06	.05	.02
649	Checklist 360-408	.06	.05	.02
650	Reggie Jackson	1.50	1.25	.60
651	Checklist 409-458	.06	.05	.02
652a	Checklist 459-509 (483 Aurelio Lopez)	.10	.08	.04
652b	Checklist 459-506 (no 483)	.40	.30	.15
653	Willie Wilson	1.00	.70	.40
654a	Checklist 507-550 (514 Jerry Augustine)	.10	.08	.04
654b	Checklist 507-550 (514 Billy Travers)	.40	.30	.15
655	George Brett	2.00	1.50	.80
656	Checklist 551-593	.06	.05	.02
657	Tug McGraw	1.00	.70	.40
658	Checklist 594-637	.06	.05	.02
659a	Checklist 640-660 (last number on front is 551)	.10	.08	.04
659b	Checklist 640-660 (last number on front is 483)	.40	.30	.15
660a	Steve Carlton (date 1066 on back)	1.00	.70	.40
660b	Steve Carlton (date 1966 on back)	2.00	1.50	.80

1981 Fleer Star Stickers

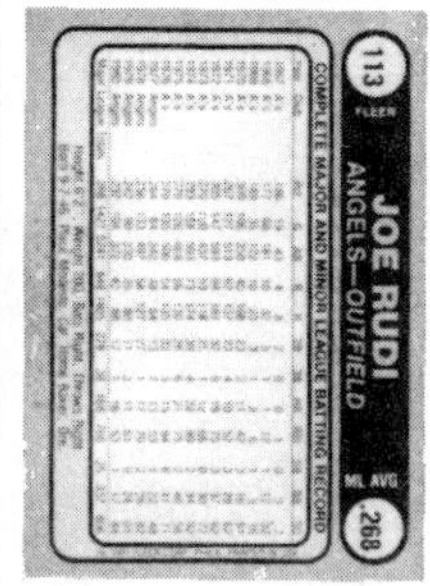

The 128-card 1981 Fleer Star Sticker set was designed for the card fronts to be peeled away from the cardboard backs. The card obverses feature color photos with blue and yellow trim. The card backs are identical in design to the regular 1981 Fleer set except for color and numbering. The set contains three unnumbered checklist cards whose fronts depict Reggie Jackson (#'s 1-42), George Brett (#'s 43-83) and Mike Schmidt (#'s 84-125). The cards, which are the standard 2-1/2" by 3-1/2", were issued in gum wax packs.

		MT	NR MT	EX
	Complete Set	50.00	37.00	20.00
	Common Player	.10	.08	.04
1	Steve Garvey	1.00	.70	.40
2	Ron LeFlore	.10	.08	.04
3	Ron Cey	.25	.20	.10
4	Dave Revering	.10	.08	.04
5	Tony Armas	.15	.11	.06
6	Mike Norris	.10	.08	.04
7	Steve Kemp	.15	.11	.06
8	Bruce Bochte	.10	.08	.04
9	Mike Schmidt	3.00	2.25	1.25
10	Scott McGregor	.10	.08	.04
11	Buddy Bell	.20	.15	.08
12	Carney Lansford	.20	.15	.08
13	Carl Yastrzemski	3.50	2.75	1.50
14	Ben Oglivie	.10	.08	.04
15	Willie Stargell	3.00	2.25	1.25
16	Cecil Cooper	.15	.11	.06
17	Gene Richards	.10	.08	.04
18	Jim Kern	.10	.08	.04
19	Jerry Koosman	.15	.11	.06
20	Larry Bowa	.20	.15	.08
21	Kent Tekulve	.15	.11	.06
22	Dan Driessen	.10	.08	.04
23	Phil Niekro	1.00	.70	.40
24	Dan Quisenberry	.30	.25	.12
25	Dave Winfield	1.00	.70	.40
26	Dave Parker	1.00	.70	.40
27	Rick Langford	.10	.08	.04
28	Amos Otis	.15	.11	.06
29	Bill Buckner	.15	.11	.06
30	Al Bumbry	.10	.08	.04
31	Bake McBride	.10	.08	.04
32	Mickey Rivers	.10	.08	.04
33	Rick Burleson	.10	.08	.04
34	Dennis Eckersley	.25	.20	.10
35	Cesar Cedeno	.20	.15	.08
36	Enos Cabell	.10	.08	.04
37	Johnny Bench	3.00	2.25	1.25
38	Robin Yount	3.00	2.25	1.25
39	Mark Belanger	.10	.08	.04
40	Rod Carew	1.00	.70	.40
41	George Foster	.40	.30	.15
42	Lee Mazzilli	.15	.11	.06
43	Triple Threat (Larry Bowa, Pete Rose, Mike Schmidt)	2.00	1.50	.80
44	J.R. Richard	.15	.11	.06
45	Lou Piniella	.30	.25	.12
46	Ken Landreaux	.10	.08	.04
47	Rollie Fingers	1.00	.70	.40
48	Joaquin Andujar	.10	.08	.04
49	Tom Seaver	3.00	2.25	1.25
50	Bobby Grich	.20	.15	.08
51	Jon Matlack	.10	.08	.04
52	Jack Clark	.25	.20	.10
53	Jim Rice	.25	.20	.10
54	Rickey Henderson	3.00	2.25	1.25
55	Roy Smalley	.10	.08	.04
56	Mike Flanagan	.15	.11	.06
57	Steve Rogers	.10	.08	.04
58	Carlton Fisk	.60	.45	.25
59	Don Sutton	1.00	.70	.40
60	Ken Griffey	.20	.15	.08
61	Burt Hooton	.10	.08	.04
62	Dusty Baker	.20	.15	.08
63	Vida Blue	.25	.20	.10
64	Al Oliver	.30	.25	.12
65	Jim Bibby	.10	.08	.04
66	Tony Perez	1.00	.70	.40
67	Davy Lopes (Davey)	.15	.11	.06
68	Bill Russell	.15	.11	.06
69	Larry Parrish	.20	.15	.08
70	Garry Maddox	.15	.11	.06
71	Phil Garner	.15	.11	.06
72	Graig Nettles	.35	.25	.14

		MT	NR MT	EX
73	Gary Carter	1.00	.70	.40
74	Pete Rose	3.00	2.25	1.25
75	Greg Luzinski	.30	.25	.12
76	Ron Guidry	.25	.20	.10
77	Gorman Thomas	.15	.11	.06
78	Jose Cruz	.20	.15	.08
79	Bob Boone	.15	.11	.06
80	Bruce Sutter	.35	.25	.14
81	Chris Chambliss	.15	.11	.06
82	Paul Molitor	.60	.45	.25
83	Tug McGraw	.25	.20	.10
84	Ferguson Jenkins	.40	.30	.15
85	Steve Carlton	1.25	.90	.50
86	Miguel Dilone	.10	.08	.04
87	Reggie Smith	.20	.15	.08
88	Rick Cerone	.10	.08	.04
89	Alan Trammell	1.00	.70	.40
90	Doug DeCinces	.20	.15	.08
91	Sparky Lyle	.15	.11	.06
92	Warren Cromartie	.10	.08	.04
93	Rick Reuschel	.25	.20	.10
94	Larry Hisle	.10	.08	.04
95	Paul Splittorff	.10	.08	.04
96	Manny Trillo	.10	.08	.04
97	Frank White	.20	.15	.08
98	Fred Lynn	.25	.20	.10
99	Bob Horner	.15	.11	.06
100	Omar Moreno	.10	.08	.04
101	Dave Concepcion	.20	.15	.08
102	Larry Gura	.10	.08	.04
103	Ken Singleton	.20	.15	.08
104	Steve Stone	.15	.11	.06
105	Richie Zisk	.10	.08	.04
106	Willie Wilson	.40	.30	.15
107	Willie Randolph	.20	.15	.08
108	Nolan Ryan	1.25	.90	.50
109	Joe Morgan	1.00	.70	.40
110	Bucky Dent	.20	.15	.08
111	Dave Kingman	.40	.30	.15
112	John Castino	.10	.08	.04
113	Joe Rudi	.20	.15	.08
114	Ed Farmer	.10	.08	.04
115	Reggie Jackson	3.00	2.25	1.25
116	George Brett	1.00	.70	.40
117	Eddie Murray	.25	.20	.10
118	Rich Gossage	.25	.20	.10
119	Dale Murphy	1.00	.70	.40
120	Ted Simmons	.15	.11	.06
121	Tommy John	.25	.20	.10
122	Don Baylor	.30	.25	.12
123	Andre Dawson	1.00	.70	.40
124	Jim Palmer	3.00	2.25	1.25
125	Garry Templeton	.20	.15	.08
---	Reggie Jackson/Checklist 1-42	3.00	2.25	1.25
---	George Brett/Checklist 43-83	3.00	2.25	1.25
---	Mike Schmidt/Checklist 84-125	3.00	2.25	1.25

1982 Fleer

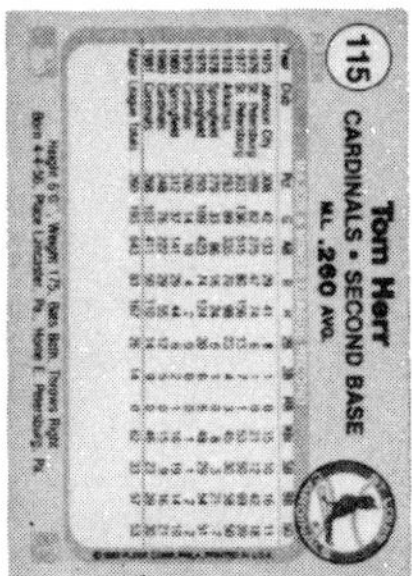

Fleer's 1982 set did not match the quality of the previous year's effort. Many of the photos in the set are blurred and have muddied backgrounds. The cards, which measure 2-1/2" by 3-1/2", feature color photos surrounded by a border frame which is color-coded by team. The card backs are blue, white, and yellow and contain the player's team logo plus the logos of Major League Baseball and the Major League Baseball Players Association. Due to a lawsuit by Topps, Fleer was forced to issue the set with team logo stickers rather than gum. The complete set price does not include the higher priced variations.

		MT	NR MT	EX
Complete Set:		40.00	30.00	15.00
Common Player:		.06	.05	.02
1	Dusty Baker	.10	.08	.04
2	Robert Castillo	.06	.05	.02
3	Ron Cey	.12	.09	.05
4	Terry Forster	.08	.06	.03
5	Steve Garvey	.50	.40	.20
6	Dave Goltz	.08	.06	.03
7	Pedro Guerrero(FC)	.60	.45	.25
8	Burt Hooton	.08	.06	.03
9	Steve Howe	.08	.06	.03
10	Jay Johnstone	.08	.06	.03
11	Ken Landreaux	.06	.05	.02
12	Davey Lopes	.10	.08	.04
13	*Mike Marshall*(FC)	1.50	1.25	.60
14	Bobby Mitchell	.06	.05	.02
15	Rick Monday	.10	.08	.04
16	*Tom Niedenfuer*(FC)	.20	.15	.08
17	*Ted Power*(FC)	.20	.15	.08
18	Jerry Reuss	.10	.08	.04
19	Ron Roenicke	.06	.05	.02
20	Bill Russell	.08	.06	.03
21	*Steve Sax*(FC)	3.00	2.25	1.25
22	Mike Scioscia	.08	.06	.03
23	Reggie Smith	.10	.08	.04
24	*Dave Stewart*(FC)	4.00	3.00	1.50
25	Rick Sutcliffe	.15	.11	.06
26	Derrel Thomas	.06	.05	.02
27	Fernando Valenzuela	.60	.45	.25
28	Bob Welch	.12	.09	.05
29	Steve Yeager	.06	.05	.02
30	Bobby Brown	.06	.05	.02
31	Rick Cerone	.06	.05	.02
32	Ron Davis	.06	.05	.02
33	Bucky Dent	.10	.08	.04
34	Barry Foote	.06	.05	.02
35	George Frazier	.06	.05	.02
36	Oscar Gamble	.08	.06	.03
37	Rich Gossage	.20	.15	.08
38	Ron Guidry	.25	.20	.10
39	Reggie Jackson	.60	.45	.25
40	Tommy John	.20	.15	.08
41	Rudy May	.06	.05	.02
42	Larry Milbourne	.06	.05	.02
43	Jerry Mumphrey	.06	.05	.02
44	Bobby Murcer	.10	.08	.04
45	*Gene Nelson*	.12	.09	.05
46	Graig Nettles	.15	.11	.06
47	Johnny Oates	.06	.05	.02
48	Lou Piniella	.12	.09	.05
49	Willie Randolph	.10	.08	.04
50	Rick Reuschel	.10	.08	.04
51	Dave Revering	.06	.05	.02
52	*Dave Righetti*(FC)	2.00	1.50	.80
53	Aurelio Rodriguez	.08	.06	.03
54	Bob Watson	.08	.06	.03
55	Dennis Werth	.06	.05	.02
56	Dave Winfield	.50	.40	.20
57	Johnny Bench	.60	.45	.25
58	Bruce Berenyi	.06	.05	.02
59	Larry Biittner	.06	.05	.02
60	Scott Brown	.06	.05	.02
61	Dave Collins	.08	.06	.03
62	Geoff Combe	.06	.05	.02
63	Dave Concepcion	.12	.09	.05
64	Dan Driessen	.08	.06	.03
65	Joe Edelen	.06	.05	.02
66	George Foster	.20	.15	.08
67	Ken Griffey	.12	.09	.05
68	Paul Householder	.06	.05	.02
69	Tom Hume	.06	.05	.02
70	Junior Kennedy	.06	.05	.02
71	Ray Knight	.10	.08	.04
72	Mike LaCoss	.06	.05	.02
73	Rafael Landestoy	.06	.05	.02
74	Charlie Leibrandt	.10	.08	.04
75	Sam Mejias	.06	.05	.02
76	Paul Moskau	.06	.05	.02
77	Joe Nolan	.06	.05	.02
78	Mike O'Berry	.06	.05	.02
79	Ron Oester	.06	.05	.02
80	Frank Pastore	.06	.05	.02
81	Joe Price	.06	.05	.02
82	Tom Seaver	.60	.45	.25
83	Mario Soto	.08	.06	.03
84	Mike Vail	.06	.05	.02
85	Tony Armas	.10	.08	.04
86	Shooty Babitt	.06	.05	.02
87	Dave Beard	.06	.05	.02
88	Rick Bosetti	.06	.05	.02
89	Keith Drumright	.06	.05	.02
90	Wayne Gross	.06	.05	.02
91	Mike Heath	.06	.05	.02
92	Rickey Henderson	1.00	.70	.40
93	Cliff Johnson	.06	.05	.02
94	Jeff Jones	.06	.05	.02
95	Matt Keough	.06	.05	.02
96	Brian Kingman	.06	.05	.02
97	Mickey Klutts	.06	.05	.02
98	Rick Langford	.06	.05	.02
99	Steve McCatty	.06	.05	.02
100	Dave McKay	.06	.05	.02
101	Dwayne Murphy	.08	.06	.03
102	Jeff Newman	.06	.05	.02
103	Mike Norris	.06	.05	.02
104	Bob Owchinko	.06	.05	.02
105	Mitchell Page	.06	.05	.02
106	Rob Picciolo	.06	.05	.02
107	Jim Spencer	.06	.05	.02
108	Fred Stanley	.06	.05	.02
109	Tom Underwood	.06	.05	.02
110	Joaquin Andujar	.08	.06	.03
111	Steve Braun	.06	.05	.02
112	Bob Forsch	.08	.06	.03
113	George Hendrick	.08	.06	.03
114	Keith Hernandez	.40	.30	.15
115	Tom Herr	.10	.08	.04
116	Dane Iorg	.06	.05	.02
117	Jim Kaat	.15	.11	.06
118	Tito Landrum	.06	.05	.02
119	Sixto Lezcano	.06	.05	.02
120	Mark Littell	.06	.05	.02
121	John Martin	.06	.05	.02
122	Silvio Martinez	.06	.05	.02
123	Ken Oberkfell	.06	.05	.02
124	Darrell Porter	.08	.06	.03
125	Mike Ramsey	.06	.05	.02
126	Orlando Sanchez	.06	.05	.02
127	Bob Shirley	.06	.05	.02
128	Lary Sorensen	.06	.05	.02
129	Bruce Sutter	.15	.11	.06
130	Bob Sykes	.06	.05	.02
131	Garry Templeton	.10	.08	.04
132	Gene Tenace	.08	.06	.03
133	Jerry Augustine	.06	.05	.02
134	Sal Bando	.08	.06	.03
135	Mark Brouhard	.06	.05	.02
136	Mike Caldwell	.06	.05	.02
137	Reggie Cleveland	.06	.05	.02
138	Cecil Cooper	.15	.11	.06
139	Jamie Easterly	.06	.05	.02
140	Marshall Edwards	.06	.05	.02
141	Rollie Fingers	.20	.15	.08
142	Jim Gantner	.08	.06	.03
143	Moose Haas	.06	.05	.02
144	Larry Hisle	.08	.06	.03
145	Roy Howell	.06	.05	.02
146	Rickey Keeton	.06	.05	.02
147	Randy Lerch	.06	.05	.02
148	Paul Molitor	.20	.15	.08
149	Don Money	.06	.05	.02
150	Charlie Moore	.06	.05	.02
151	Ben Oglivie	.08	.06	.03
152	Ted Simmons	.12	.09	.05
153	Jim Slaton	.06	.05	.02
154	Gorman Thomas	.10	.08	.04
155	Robin Yount	1.25	.90	.50
156	Pete Vukovich	.08	.06	.03
157	Benny Ayala	.06	.05	.02
158	Mark Belanger	.08	.06	.03
159	Al Bumbry	.08	.06	.03
160	Terry Crowley	.06	.05	.02
161	Rich Dauer	.06	.05	.02
162	Doug DeCinces	.10	.08	.04
163	Rick Dempsey	.08	.06	.03
164	Jim Dwyer	.06	.05	.02
165	Mike Flanagan	.10	.08	.04
166	Dave Ford	.06	.05	.02
167	Dan Graham	.06	.05	.02
168	Wayne Krenchicki	.06	.05	.02
169	John Lowenstein	.06	.05	.02
170	Dennis Martinez	.08	.06	.03
171	Tippy Martinez	.06	.05	.02
172	Scott McGregor	.08	.06	.03
173	Jose Morales	.06	.05	.02
174	Eddie Murray	.60	.45	.25
175	Jim Palmer	.40	.30	.15
176	*Cal Ripken, Jr.*(FC)	9.00	6.75	3.50
177	Gary Roenicke	.06	.05	.02
178	Lenn Sakata	.06	.05	.02
179	Ken Singleton	.10	.08	.04
180	Sammy Stewart	.06	.05	.02
181	Tim Stoddard	.06	.05	.02
182	Steve Stone	.08	.06	.03
183	Stan Bahnsen	.06	.05	.02
184	Ray Burris	.06	.05	.02
185	Gary Carter	.35	.25	.14
186	Warren Cromartie	.06	.05	.02
187	Andre Dawson	.40	.30	.15
188	*Terry Francona*(FC)	.10	.08	.04
189	Woodie Fryman	.08	.06	.03
190	Bill Gullickson	.08	.06	.03
191	Grant Jackson	.06	.05	.02
192	Wallace Johnson	.06	.05	.02
193	Charlie Lea	.06	.05	.02
194	Bill Lee	.08	.06	.03
195	Jerry Manuel	.06	.05	.02
196	Brad Mills	.06	.05	.02
197	John Milner	.06	.05	.02
198	Rowland Office	.06	.05	.02
199	David Palmer	.06	.05	.02
200	Larry Parrish	.10	.08	.04
201	Mike Phillips	.06	.05	.02
202	Tim Raines	1.50	1.25	.60
203	Bobby Ramos	.06	.05	.02
204	Jeff Reardon	.20	.15	.08
205	Steve Rogers	.08	.06	.03
206	Scott Sanderson	.06	.05	.02
207	Rodney Scott (photo actually Tim Raines)	.10	.08	.04
208	Elias Sosa	.06	.05	.02
209	Chris Speier	.06	.05	.02
210	*Tim Wallach*(FC)	1.50	1.25	.60
211	Jerry White	.06	.05	.02
212	Alan Ashby	.06	.05	.02
213	Cesar Cedeno	.12	.09	.05
214	Jose Cruz	.12	.09	.05
215	Kiko Garcia	.06	.05	.02
216	Phil Garner	.08	.06	.03
217	Danny Heep	.06	.05	.02
218	Art Howe	.06	.05	.02
219	Bob Knepper	.08	.06	.03
220	Frank LaCorte	.06	.05	.02
221	Joe Niekro	.12	.09	.05
222	Joe Pittman	.06	.05	.02
223	Terry Puhl	.06	.05	.02
224	Luis Pujols	.06	.05	.02
225	Craig Reynolds	.06	.05	.02
226	J.R. Richard	.10	.08	.04
227	Dave Roberts	.06	.05	.02
228	Vern Ruhle	.06	.05	.02
229	Nolan Ryan	2.00	1.50	.80
230	Joe Sambito	.06	.05	.02
231	Tony Scott	.06	.05	.02
232	Dave Smith	.10	.08	.04
233	Harry Spilman	.06	.05	.02
234	Don Sutton	.30	.25	.12
235	Dickie Thon	.08	.06	.03
236	Denny Walling	.06	.05	.02
237	Gary Woods	.06	.05	.02
238	*Luis Aguayo*(FC)	.10	.08	.04
239	Ramon Aviles	.06	.05	.02
240	Bob Boone	.10	.08	.04
241	Larry Bowa	.15	.11	.06
242	Warren Brusstar	.06	.05	.02
243	Steve Carlton	.50	.40	.20
244	Larry Christenson	.06	.05	.02
245	Dick Davis	.06	.05	.02
246	Greg Gross	.06	.05	.02
247	Sparky Lyle	.10	.08	.04
248	Garry Maddox	.10	.08	.04
249	Gary Matthews	.10	.08	.04
250	Bake McBride	.06	.05	.02
251	Tug McGraw	.12	.09	.05
252	Keith Moreland	.10	.08	.04
253	Dickie Noles	.06	.05	.02
254	Mike Proly	.06	.05	.02
255	Ron Reed	.06	.05	.02
256	Pete Rose	1.00	.70	.40
257	Dick Ruthven	.06	.05	.02
258	Mike Schmidt	1.00	.70	.40
259	Lonnie Smith	.08	.06	.03
260	Manny Trillo	.08	.06	.03
261	Del Unser	.06	.05	.02
262	George Vukovich	.06	.05	.02
263	Tom Brookens	.06	.05	.02

		MT	NR MT	EX
264	George Cappuzzello	.06	.05	.02
265	Marty Castillo	.06	.05	.02
266	Al Cowens	.06	.05	.02
267	Kirk Gibson	.70	.50	.30
268	Richie Hebner	.06	.05	.02
269	Ron Jackson	.06	.05	.02
270	Lynn Jones	.06	.05	.02
271	Steve Kemp	.08	.06	.03
272	*Rick Leach*(FC)	.12	.09	.05
273	Aurelio Lopez	.06	.05	.02
274	Jack Morris	.30	.25	.12
275	Kevin Saucier	.06	.05	.02
276	Lance Parrish	.35	.25	.14
277	Rick Peters	.06	.05	.02
278	Dan Petry	.08	.06	.03
279	David Rozema	.06	.05	.02
280	Stan Papi	.06	.05	.02
281	Dan Schatzeder	.06	.05	.02
282	Champ Summers	.06	.05	.02
283	Alan Trammell	.40	.30	.15
284	Lou Whitaker	.40	.30	.15
285	Milt Wilcox	.06	.05	.02
286	John Wockenfuss	.06	.05	.02
287	Gary Allenson	.06	.05	.02
288	Tom Burgmeier	.06	.05	.02
289	Bill Campbell	.06	.05	.02
290	Mark Clear	.06	.05	.02
291	Steve Crawford	.06	.05	.02
292	Dennis Eckersley	.12	.09	.05
293	Dwight Evans	.15	.11	.06
294	*Rich Gedman*(FC)	.35	.25	.14
295	Garry Hancock	.06	.05	.02
296	Glenn Hoffman	.06	.05	.02
297	Bruce Hurst(FC)	.30	.25	.12
298	Carney Lansford	.08	.06	.03
299	Rick Miller	.06	.05	.02
300	Reid Nichols	.06	.05	.02
301	*Bob Ojeda*(FC)	.50	.40	.20
302	Tony Perez	.20	.15	.08
303	Chuck Rainey	.06	.05	.02
304	Jerry Remy	.06	.05	.02
305	Jim Rice	.40	.30	.15
306	Joe Rudi	.10	.08	.04
307	Bob Stanley	.06	.05	.02
308	Dave Stapleton	.06	.05	.02
309	Frank Tanana	.10	.08	.04
310	Mike Torrez	.08	.06	.03
311	John Tudor(FC)	.25	.20	.10
312	Carl Yastrzemski	.80	.60	.30
313	Buddy Bell	.12	.09	.05
314	Steve Comer	.06	.05	.02
315	Danny Darwin	.06	.05	.02
316	John Ellis	.06	.05	.02
317	John Grubb	.06	.05	.02
318	Rick Honeycutt	.06	.05	.02
319	Charlie Hough	.10	.08	.04
320	Ferguson Jenkins	.15	.11	.06
321	John Henry Johnson	.06	.05	.02
322	Jim Kern	.06	.05	.02
323	Jon Matlack	.08	.06	.03
324	Doc Medich	.06	.05	.02
325	Mario Mendoza	.06	.05	.02
326	Al Oliver	.15	.11	.06
327	Pat Putnam	.06	.05	.02
328	Mickey Rivers	.08	.06	.03
329	Leon Roberts	.06	.05	.02
330	Billy Sample	.06	.05	.02
331	Bill Stein	.06	.05	.02
332	Jim Sundberg	.08	.06	.03
333	Mark Wagner	.06	.05	.02
334	Bump Wills	.06	.05	.02
335	Bill Almon	.06	.05	.02
336	Harold Baines	.30	.25	.12
337	Ross Baumgarten	.06	.05	.02
338	Tony Bernazard	.06	.05	.02
339	Britt Burns	.06	.05	.02
340	Richard Dotson	.10	.08	.04
341	Jim Essian	.06	.05	.02
342	Ed Farmer	.06	.05	.02
343	Carlton Fisk	.50	.40	.20
344	Kevin Hickey	.06	.05	.02
345	Lamarr Hoyt (LaMarr)	.06	.05	.02
346	Lamar Johnson	.06	.05	.02
347	Jerry Koosman	.10	.08	.04
348	Rusty Kuntz	.06	.05	.02
349	Dennis Lamp	.06	.05	.02
350	Ron LeFlore	.08	.06	.03
351	Chet Lemon	.08	.06	.03
352	Greg Luzinski	.15	.11	.06
353	Bob Molinaro	.06	.05	.02
354	Jim Morrison	.06	.05	.02
355	Wayne Nordhagen	.06	.05	.02
356	Greg Pryor	.06	.05	.02
357	Mike Squires	.06	.05	.02
358	Steve Trout	.06	.05	.02
359	Alan Bannister	.06	.05	.02
360	Len Barker	.08	.06	.03
361	Bert Blyleven	.12	.09	.05
362	Joe Charboneau	.08	.06	.03
363	John Denny	.06	.05	.02
364	Bo Diaz	.08	.06	.03
365	Miguel Dilone	.06	.05	.02
366	Jerry Dybzinski	.06	.05	.02
367	Wayne Garland	.06	.05	.02
368	Mike Hargrove	.06	.05	.02
369	Toby Harrah	.08	.06	.03
370	Ron Hassey	.06	.05	.02
371	*Von Hayes*(FC)	1.25	.90	.50
372	Pat Kelly	.06	.05	.02
373	Duane Kuiper	.06	.05	.02
374	Rick Manning	.06	.05	.02
375	Sid Monge	.06	.05	.02
376	Jorge Orta	.06	.05	.02
377	Dave Rosello	.06	.05	.02
378	Dan Spillner	.06	.05	.02
379	Mike Stanton	.06	.05	.02
380	Andre Thornton	.10	.08	.04
381	Tom Veryzer	.06	.05	.02
382	Rick Waits	.06	.05	.02
383	Doyle Alexander	.10	.08	.04
384	Vida Blue	.12	.09	.05
385	Fred Breining	.06	.05	.02
386	Enos Cabell	.06	.05	.02
387	Jack Clark	.25	.20	.10
388	Darrell Evans	.15	.11	.06
389	Tom Griffin	.06	.05	.02
390	Larry Herndon	.08	.06	.03
391	Al Holland	.06	.05	.02
392	Gary Lavelle	.06	.05	.02
393	Johnnie LeMaster	.06	.05	.02
394	Jerry Martin	.06	.05	.02
395	Milt May	.06	.05	.02
396	Greg Minton	.06	.05	.02
397	Joe Morgan	.50	.40	.20
398	Joe Pettini	.06	.05	.02
399	Alan Ripley	.06	.05	.02
400	Billy Smith	.06	.05	.02
401	Rennie Stennett	.06	.05	.02
402	Ed Whitson	.06	.05	.02
403	Jim Wohlford	.06	.05	.02
404	Willie Aikens	.06	.05	.02
405	George Brett	.70	.50	.30
406	Ken Brett	.08	.06	.03
407	Dave Chalk	.06	.05	.02
408	Rich Gale	.06	.05	.02
409	Cesar Geronimo	.06	.05	.02
410	Larry Gura	.06	.05	.02
411	Clint Hurdle	.06	.05	.02
412	Mike Jones	.06	.05	.02
413	Dennis Leonard	.08	.06	.03
414	Renie Martin	.06	.05	.02
415	Lee May	.08	.06	.03
416	Hal McRae	.12	.09	.05
417	Darryl Motley	.06	.05	.02
418	Rance Mulliniks	.06	.05	.02
419	Amos Otis	.08	.06	.03
420	*Ken Phelps*(FC)	.50	.40	.20
421	Jamie Quirk	.06	.05	.02
422	Dan Quisenberry	.15	.11	.06
423	Paul Splittorff	.06	.05	.02
424	U.L. Washington	.06	.05	.02
425	John Wathan	.08	.06	.03
426	Frank White	.10	.08	.04
427	Willie Wilson	.15	.11	.06
428	Brian Asselstine	.06	.05	.02
429	Bruce Benedict	.06	.05	.02
430	Tom Boggs	.06	.05	.02
431	Larry Bradford	.06	.05	.02
432	Rick Camp	.06	.05	.02
433	Chris Chambliss	.08	.06	.03
434	Gene Garber	.06	.05	.02
435	Preston Hanna	.06	.05	.02
436	Bob Horner	.12	.09	.05
437	Glenn Hubbard	.08	.06	.03
438a	Al Hrabosky (All Hrabosky, 5'1" on back)	20.00	15.00	8.00
438b	Al Hrabosky (Al Hrabosky, 5'1" on back)	1.25	.90	.50
438c	Al Hrabosky (Al Hrabosky, 5'10" on back)	.35	.25	.14
439	Rufino Linares	.06	.05	.02
440	*Rick Mahler*(FC)	.25	.20	.10
441	Ed Miller	.06	.05	.02
442	John Montefusco	.08	.06	.03
443	Dale Murphy	.90	.70	.35
444	Phil Niekro	.30	.25	.12
445	Gaylord Perry	.30	.25	.12
446	Biff Pocoroba	.06	.05	.02
447	Rafael Ramirez	.08	.06	.03
448	Jerry Royster	.06	.05	.02
449	Claudell Washington	.08	.06	.03
450	Don Aase	.06	.05	.02
451	Don Baylor	.12	.09	.05
452	Juan Beniquez	.06	.05	.02
453	Rick Burleson	.08	.06	.03
454	Bert Campaneris	.10	.08	.04
455	Rod Carew	.50	.40	.20
456	Bob Clark	.06	.05	.02
457	Brian Downing	.10	.08	.04
458	Dan Ford	.06	.05	.02
459	Ken Forsch	.06	.05	.02
460	Dave Frost	.06	.05	.02
461	Bobby Grich	.10	.08	.04
462	Larry Harlow	.06	.05	.02
463	John Harris	.06	.05	.02
464	Andy Hassler	.06	.05	.02
465	Butch Hobson	.06	.05	.02
466	Jesse Jefferson	.06	.05	.02
467	Bruce Kison	.06	.05	.02
468	Fred Lynn	.20	.15	.08
469	Angel Moreno	.06	.05	.02
470	Ed Ott	.06	.05	.02
471	Fred Patek	.06	.05	.02
472	Steve Renko	.06	.05	.02
473	*Mike Witt*(FC)	.70	.50	.30
474	Geoff Zahn	.06	.05	.02
475	Gary Alexander	.06	.05	.02
476	Dale Berra	.06	.05	.02
477	Kurt Bevacqua	.06	.05	.02
478	Jim Bibby	.06	.05	.02
479	John Candelaria	.10	.08	.04
480	Victor Cruz	.06	.05	.02
481	Mike Easler	.08	.06	.03
482	Tim Foli	.06	.05	.02
483	Lee Lacy	.06	.05	.02
484	Vance Law(FC)	.12	.09	.05
485	Bill Madlock	.12	.09	.05
486	Willie Montanez	.06	.05	.02
487	Omar Moreno	.06	.05	.02
488	Steve Nicosia	.06	.05	.02
489	Dave Parker	.30	.25	.12
490	Tony Pena(FC)	.25	.20	.10
491	Pascual Perez(FC)	.15	.11	.06
492	*Johnny Ray*(FC)	.70	.50	.30
493	Rick Rhoden	.10	.08	.04
494	Bill Robinson	.06	.05	.02
495	Don Robinson	.08	.06	.03
496	Enrique Romo	.06	.05	.02
497	Rod Scurry	.06	.05	.02
498	Eddie Solomon	.06	.05	.02
499	Willie Stargell	.40	.30	.15
500	Kent Tekulve	.08	.06	.03
501	Jason Thompson	.06	.05	.02
502	Glenn Abbott	.06	.05	.02
503	Jim Anderson	.06	.05	.02
504	Floyd Bannister	.10	.08	.04
505	Bruce Bochte	.06	.05	.02
506	Jeff Burroughs	.08	.06	.03
507	Bryan Clark	.06	.05	.02
508	Ken Clay	.06	.05	.02
509	Julio Cruz	.06	.05	.02
510	Dick Drago	.06	.05	.02
511	Gary Gray	.06	.05	.02
512	Dan Meyer	.06	.05	.02
513	Jerry Narron	.06	.05	.02
514	Tom Paciorek	.06	.05	.02
515	Casey Parsons	.06	.05	.02
516	Lenny Randle	.06	.05	.02
517	Shane Rawley	.10	.08	.04
518	Joe Simpson	.06	.05	.02
519	Richie Zisk	.08	.06	.03
520	Neil Allen	.06	.05	.02
521	Bob Bailor	.06	.05	.02
522	Hubie Brooks(FC)	.25	.20	.10
523	Mike Cubbage	.06	.05	.02
524	Pete Falcone	.06	.05	.02
525	Doug Flynn	.06	.05	.02
526	Tom Hausman	.06	.05	.02
527	Ron Hodges	.06	.05	.02
528	Randy Jones	.08	.06	.03
529	Mike Jorgensen	.06	.05	.02
530	Dave Kingman	.15	.11	.06
531	Ed Lynch	.06	.05	.02
532	Mike Marshall	.10	.08	.04
533	Lee Mazzilli	.08	.06	.03
534	Dyar Miller	.06	.05	.02
535	Mike Scott(FC)	.60	.45	.25
536	Rusty Staub	.10	.08	.04
537	John Stearns	.06	.05	.02
538	Craig Swan	.06	.05	.02
539	Frank Taveras	.06	.05	.02
540	Alex Trevino	.06	.05	.02
541	Ellis Valentine	.06	.05	.02
542	Mookie Wilson(FC)	.15	.11	.06
543	Joel Youngblood	.06	.05	.02
544	Pat Zachry	.06	.05	.02
545	Glenn Adams	.06	.05	.02
546	Fernando Arroyo	.06	.05	.02
547	John Verhoeven	.06	.05	.02
548	Sal Butera	.06	.05	.02
549	John Castino	.06	.05	.02
550	Don Cooper	.06	.05	.02
551	Doug Corbett	.06	.05	.02
552	Dave Engle	.06	.05	.02
553	Roger Erickson	.06	.05	.02
554	Danny Goodwin	.06	.05	.02
555a	Darrell Jackson (black cap)	1.00	.70	.40
555b	Darrell Jackson (red cap with emblem)	.10	.08	.04
555c	Darrell Jackson (red cap, no emblem)	.25	.20	.10
556	Pete Mackanin	.06	.05	.02
557	Jack O'Connor	.06	.05	.02
558	Hosken Powell	.06	.05	.02
559	Pete Redfern	.06	.05	.02
560	Roy Smalley	.06	.05	.02
561	Chuck Baker	.06	.05	.02
562	Gary Ward	.08	.06	.03
563	Rob Wilfong	.06	.05	.02
564	Al Williams	.06	.05	.02
565	Butch Wynegar	.06	.05	.02
566	Randy Bass	.06	.05	.02
567	Juan Bonilla	.06	.05	.02
568	Danny Boone	.06	.05	.02
569	John Curtis	.06	.05	.02
570	Juan Eichelberger	.06	.05	.02
571	Barry Evans	.06	.05	.02
572	Tim Flannery	.06	.05	.02
573	Ruppert Jones	.06	.05	.02
574	Terry Kennedy	.08	.06	.03
575	Joe Lefebvre	.06	.05	.02
576a	John Littlefield (pitching lefty)	150.00	105.00	60.00
576b	John Littlefield (pitching righty)	.08	.06	.03
577	Gary Lucas	.06	.05	.02
578	Steve Mura	.06	.05	.02
579	Broderick Perkins	.06	.05	.02
580	Gene Richards	.06	.05	.02
581	Luis Salazar	.06	.05	.02
582	Ozzie Smith	.20	.15	.08
583	John Urrea	.06	.05	.02
584	Chris Welsh	.06	.05	.02
585	Rick Wise	.08	.06	.03
586	Doug Bird	.06	.05	.02
587	Tim Blackwell	.06	.05	.02
588	Bobby Bonds	.10	.08	.04
589	Bill Buckner	.12	.09	.05
590	Bill Caudill	.06	.05	.02
591	Hector Cruz	.06	.05	.02
592	*Jody Davis*(FC)	.30	.25	.12
593	Ivan DeJesus	.06	.05	.02
594	Steve Dillard	.06	.05	.02
595	Leon Durham	.08	.06	.03
596	Rawly Eastwick	.06	.05	.02
597	Steve Henderson	.06	.05	.02
598	Mike Krukow	.08	.06	.03
599	Mike Lum	.06	.05	.02
600	Randy Martz	.06	.05	.02
601	Jerry Morales	.06	.05	.02
602	Ken Reitz	.06	.05	.02
603a	*Lee Smith* (Cubs logo reversed on back)(FC)	1.25	.90	.50
603b	*Lee Smith* (Cubs logo correct)(FC)	.60	.45	.25
604	Dick Tidrow	.06	.05	.02
605	Jim Tracy	.06	.05	.02
606	Mike Tyson	.06	.05	.02
607	Ty Waller	.06	.05	.02
608	Danny Ainge	.12	.09	.05
609	*Jorge Bell*(FC)	7.00	5.25	2.75
610	Mark Bomback	.06	.05	.02
611	Barry Bonnell	.06	.05	.02
612	Jim Clancy	.08	.06	.03
613	Damaso Garcia	.06	.05	.02
614	Jerry Garvin	.06	.05	.02
615	Alfredo Griffin	.08	.06	.03
616	Garth Iorg	.06	.05	.02
617	Luis Leal	.06	.05	.02
618	Ken Macha	.06	.05	.02
619	John Mayberry	.08	.06	.03
620	Joey McLaughlin	.06	.05	.02
621	Lloyd Moseby	.12	.09	.05

		MT	NR MT	EX
622	Dave Stieb	.12	.09	.05
623	Jackson Todd	.06	.05	.02
624	Willie Upshaw(FC)	.15	.11	.06
625	Otto Velez	.06	.05	.02
626	Ernie Whitt	.08	.06	.03
627	Al Woods	.06	.05	.02
628	1981 All-Star Game	.08	.06	.03
629	All-Star Infielders (Bucky Dent, Frank White)	.10	.08	.04
630	Big Red Machine (Dave Concepcion, Dan Driessen, George Foster)	.15	.11	.06
631	Top N.L. Relief Pitcher (Bruce Sutter)	.15	.11	.06
632	Steve & Carlton (Steve Carlton, Carlton Fisk)	.25	.20	.10
633	3000th Game, May 25, 1981 (Carl Yastrzemski)	.35	.25	.14
634	Dynamic Duo (Johnny Bench, Tom Seaver)	.30	.25	.12
635	West Meets East (Gary Carter, Fernando Valenzuela)	.30	.25	.12
636a	N.L. Strikeout King (Fernando Valenzuela) ("...led he National League...")	1.00	.70	.40
636b	N.L. Strikeout King (Fernando Valenzuela) ("...led the National League...")	.50	.40	.20
637	1981 Home Run King (Mike Schmidt)	.40	.30	.15
638	N.L. All-Stars (Gary Carter, Dave Parker)	.25	.20	.10
639	Perfect Game! (Len Barker, Bo Diaz)	.08	.06	.03
640	Pete & Re-Pete (Pete Rose, Pete Rose, Jr.)	1.25	.90	.50
641	Phillies' Finest (Steve Carlton, Mike Schmidt, Lonnie Smith)	.50	.40	.20
642	Red Sox Reunion (Dwight Evans, Fred Lynn)	.15	.11	.06
643	1981 Most Hits, Most Runs (Rickey Henderson)	.35	.25	.14
644	Most Saves 1981 A.L. (Rollie Fingers)	.15	.11	.06
645	Most 1981 Wins (Tom Seaver)	.25	.20	.10
646a	Yankee Powerhouse (Reggie Jackson, Dave Winfield) (comma after "outfielder" on back)	1.25	.90	.50
646b	Yankee Powerhouse (Reggie Jackson, Dave Winfield) (no comma after "oufielder")	.60	.45	.25
647	Checklist 1-56	.06	.05	.02
648	Checklist 57-109	.06	.05	.02
649	Checklist 110-156	.06	.05	.02
650	Checklist 157-211	.06	.05	.02
651	Checklist 212-262	.06	.05	.02
652	Checklist 263-312	.06	.05	.02
653	Checklist 313-358	.06	.05	.02
654	Checklist 359-403	.06	.05	.02
655	Checklist 404-449	.06	.05	.02
656	Checklist 450-501	.06	.05	.02
657	Checklist 502-544	.06	.05	.02
658	Checklist 545-585	.06	.05	.02
659	Checklist 586-627	.06	.05	.02
660	Checklist 628-646	.06	.05	.02

1982 Fleer Stamps

each measuring 2-1/2" by 1-13/16". Originally issued in perforated strips of 10, the full-color stamps are numbered in the lower left corner and were designed to be placed in an album, also available from Fleer. Six of the stamps feature two players each.

	MT	NR MT	EX
Complete Set:	12.00	9.00	4.75
Common Player:	.03	.02	.01
Stamp Album:	1.50	1.25	.60

		MT	NR MT	EX
1	Fernando Valenzuela	.15	.11	.06
2	Rick Monday	.04	.03	.02
3	Ron Cey	.06	.05	.02
4	Dusty Baker	.04	.03	.02
5	Burt Hooton	.04	.03	.02
6	Pedro Guerrero	.12	.09	.05
7	Jerry Reuss	.06	.05	.02
8	Bill Russell	.04	.03	.02
9	Steve Garvey	.20	.15	.08
10	Davey Lopes	.04	.03	.02
11	Tom Seaver	.25	.20	.10
12	George Foster	.08	.06	.03
13	Frank Pastore	.03	.02	.01
14	Dave Collins	.03	.02	.01
15	Dave Concepcion	.06	.05	.02
16	Ken Griffey	.08	.06	.03
17	Johnny Bench	.03	.02	.01
18	Ray Knight	.04	.03	.02
19	Mario Soto	.04	.03	.02
20	Ron Oester	.03	.02	.01
21	Ken Oberkfell	.03	.02	.01
22	Bob Forsch	.03	.02	.01
23	Keith Hernandez	.15	.11	.06
24	Dane Iorg	.03	.02	.01
25	George Hendrick	.04	.03	.02
26	Gene Tenace	.03	.02	.01
27	Garry Templeton	.06	.05	.02
28	Bruce Sutter	.08	.06	.03
29	Darrell Porter	.03	.02	.01
30	Tom Herr	.06	.05	.02
31	Tim Raines	.20	.15	.08
32	Chris Speier	.03	.02	.01
33	Warren Cromartie	.03	.02	.01
34	Larry parrish	.04	.03	.02
35	Andre Dawson	.15	.11	.06
36	Steve Rogers	.03	.02	.01
37	Jeff Reardon	.08	.06	.03
38	Rodney Scott	.03	.02	.01
39	Gary Carter	.20	.15	.08
40	Scott Sanderson	.03	.02	.01
41	Cesar Cedeno	.06	.05	.02
42	Nolan Ryan	.20	.15	.08
43	Don Sutton	.12	.09	.05
44	Terry Puhl	.03	.02	.01
45	Joe Niekro	.06	.05	.02
46	Tony Scott	.03	.02	.01
47	Joe Sambito	.03	.02	.01
48	Art Howe	.03	.02	.01
49	Bob Knepper	.06	.05	.02
50	Jose Cruz	.04	.03	.02
51	Pete Rose	.40	.30	.15
52	Dick Ruthven	.03	.02	.01
53	Mike Schmidt	.30	.25	.12
54	Steve Carlton	.20	.15	.08
55	Tug McGraw	.08	.06	.03
56	Larry Bowa	.08	.06	.03
57	Garry Maddox	.04	.03	.02
58	Gary Matthews	.04	.03	.02
59	Manny Trillo	.04	.03	.02
60	Lonnie Smith	.03	.02	.01
61	Vida Blue	.08	.06	.03
62	Milt May	.03	.02	.01
63	Joe Morgan	.12	.09	.05
64	Enos Cabell	.03	.02	.01
65	Jack Clark	.10	.08	.04
66	Caudell Washington	.04	.03	.02
67	Gaylord Perry	.15	.11	.06
68	Phil Niekro	.15	.11	.06
69	Bob Horner	.08	.06	.03
70	Chris Chambliss	.04	.03	.02
71	Dave Parker	.12	.09	.05
72	Tony Pena	.06	.05	.02
73	Kent Tekulve	.04	.03	.02
74	Mike Easler	.04	.03	.02
75	Tim Foli	.03	.02	.01
76	Willie Stargell	.20	.15	.08
77	Bill Madlock	.06	.05	.02
78	Jim Bibby	.03	.02	.01
79	Omar Moreno	.03	.02	.01
80	Lee Lacy	.03	.02	.01
81	Hubie Brooks	.06	.05	.02
82	Rusty Staub	.06	.05	.02
83	Ellis Valentine	.03	.02	.01
84	Neil Allen	.03	.02	.01
85	Dave Kingman	.08	.06	.03
86	Mookie Wilson	.04	.03	.02
87	Doug Flynn	.03	.02	.01
88	Pat Zachry	.03	.02	.01
89	John Stearns	.03	.02	.01
90	Lee Mazzilli	.04	.03	.02
91	Ken Reitz	.03	.02	.01
92	Mike Krukow	.03	.02	.01
93	Jerry Morales	.03	.02	.01
94	Leon Durham	.06	.05	.02
95	Ivan DeJesus	.03	.02	.01
96	Bill Buckner	.06	.05	.02
97	Jim Tracy	.03	.02	.01
98	Steve Henderson	.03	.02	.01
99	Dick Tidrow	.03	.02	.01
100	Mike Tyson	.03	.02	.01
101	Ozzie Smith	.08	.06	.03
102	Ruppert Jones	.03	.02	.01
103	Broderick Perkins	.03	.02	.01
104	Gene Richrds	.03	.02	.01
105	Terry Kennedy	.04	.03	.02
106	Jim Bibby, Willie Stargell	.12	.09	.05
107	Larry Bowa, Pete Rose	.25	.20	.10
108	Warren Spahn, Fernando Valenzuela	.15	.11	.06
109	Dave Concepcion, Pete Rose	.25	.20	.10
110	Reggie Jackson, Dave Winfield	.20	.15	.08
111	Tom Lasorda, Fernando Valenzuela	.10	.08	.04
112	Reggie Jackson	.30	.25	.12
113	Dave Winfield	.20	.15	.08
114	Lou Piniella	.08	.06	.03
115	Tommy John	.10	.08	.04
116	Rich Gossage	.10	.08	.04
117	Ron Davis	.03	.02	.01
118	Rick Cerone	.03	.02	.01
119	Graig Nettles	.08	.06	.03
120	Ron Guidry	.08	.06	.03
121	Willie Randolph	.06	.05	.02
122	Dwayne Murphy	.03	.02	.01
123	Rickey Henderson	.25	.20	.10
124	Wayne Gross	.03	.02	.01
125	Mike Norris	.03	.02	.01
126	Rick Langford	.03	.02	.01
127	Jim Spencer	.03	.02	.01
128	Tony Armas	.03	.02	.01
129	Matt Keough	.03	.02	.01
130	Jeff Jones	.03	.02	.01
131	Steve McCatty	.03	.02	.01
132	Rollie Fingers	.10	.08	.04
133	Jim Gantner	.03	.02	.01
134	Gorman Thomas	.04	.03	.02
135	Robin Yount	.15	.11	.06
136	Paul Molitor	.10	.08	.04
137	Ted Simmons	.08	.06	.03
138	Ben Oglivie	.04	.03	.02
139	Moose Haas	.03	.02	.01
140	Cecil Cooper	.08	.06	.03
141	Pete Vuckovich	.04	.03	.02
142	Doug DeCinces	.04	.03	.02
143	Jim Palmer	.15	.11	.06
144	Steve Stone	.06	.05	.02
145	Mike Flanagan	.04	.03	.02
146	Rick Dempsey	.03	.02	.01
147	Al Bumbry	.03	.02	.01
148	Mark Belanger	.04	.03	.02
149	Scott McGregor	.04	.03	.02
150	Ken Singleton	.06	.05	.02
151	Eddie Murray	.25	.20	.10
152	Lance Parrish	.12	.09	.05
153	David Rozema	.03	.02	.01
154	Champ Summers	.03	.02	.01
155	Alan Trammell	.15	.11	.06
156	Lou Whitaker	.10	.08	.04
157	Milt Wilcox	.03	.02	.01
158	Kevin Saucier	.03	.02	.01
159	Jack Morris	.12	.09	.05
160	Steve Kemp	.04	.03	.02
161	Kirk Gibson	.12	.09	.05
162	Carl Yastrzemski	.35	.25	.14
163	Jim Rice	.20	.15	.08
164	Carney Lansford	.06	.05	.02
165	Dennis Eckersley	.06	.05	.02
166	Mike Torrez	.03	.02	.01
167	Dwight Evans	.08	.06	.03
168	Glenn Hoffman	.03	.02	.01
169	Bob Stanley	.03	.02	.01
170	Tony Perez	.08	.06	.03
171	Jerry Remy	.03	.02	.01
172	Buddy Bell	.06	.05	.02
173	Ferguson Jenkins	.08	.06	.03
174	Mickey Rivers	.04	.03	.02
175	Bump Wills	.03	.02	.01
176	Jon Matlack	.03	.02	.01
177	Steve Comer	.03	.02	.01
178	Al Oliver	.06	.05	.02
179	Bill Stein	.03	.02	.01
180	Pat Putnam	.03	.02	.01
181	Jim Sundberg	.03	.02	.01
182	Ron Leflore	.03	.02	.01
183	Carlton Fisk	.12	.09	.05
184	Harold Baines	.10	.08	.04
185	Bill Almon	.03	.02	.01
186	Richard Dotson	.04	.03	.02
187	Greg Luzinski	.08	.06	.03
188	Mike Squires	.03	.02	.01
189	Britt Burns	.03	.02	.01
190	Lamarr Hoyt	.03	.02	.01
191	Chet Lemon	.04	.03	.02
192	Joe Charboneau	.04	.03	.02
193	Toby Harrah	.03	.02	.01
194	John Denny	.03	.02	.01
195	Rick Manning	.03	.02	.01
196	Miguel Dilone	.03	.02	.01
197	Bo Diaz	.03	.02	.01
198	Mike Hargrove	.03	.02	.01
199	Bert Blyleven	.10	.08	.04
200	Len Barker	.03	.02	.01
201	Andre Thornton	.04	.03	.02
202	George Brett	.30	.25	.12
203	U.L. Washington	.03	.02	.01
204	Dan Quisenberry	.06	.05	.02
205	Larry Gura	.03	.02	.01
206	Willie Aikens	.03	.02	.01
207	Willie Wilson	.08	.06	.03
208	Dennis Leonard	.03	.02	.01
209	Frank White	.06	.05	.02
210	Hal McRae	.06	.05	.02
211	Amos Otis	.04	.03	.02
212	Don Aase	.03	.02	.01
213	Butch Hobson	.03	.02	.01
214	Fred Lynn	.10	.08	.04
215	Brian Downing	.04	.03	.02
216	Dan Ford	.03	.02	.01
217	Rod Carew	.25	.20	.10
218	Bobby Grich	.06	.05	.02
219	Rick Burleson	.03	.02	.01
220	Don Baylor	.10	.08	.04
221	Ken Forsch	.03	.02	.01
222	Bruce Bochte	.03	.02	.01
223	Richie Zisk	.03	.02	.01
224	Tom Paciorek	.03	.02	.01
225	Julio Cruz	.03	.02	.01
226	Jeff Burroughs	.03	.02	.01
227	Doug Corbett	.03	.02	.01
228	Roy Smalley	.03	.02	.01
229	Gary Ward	.03	.02	.01
230	John Castino	.03	.02	.01
231	Rob Wilfong	.03	.02	.01
232	Dave Stieb	.06	.05	.02
233	Otto Velez	.03	.02	.01
234	Damaso Garcia	.03	.02	.01
235	John Mayberry	.03	.02	.01
236	Alfredo Griffin	.06	.05	.02
237	Ted Williams, Carl Yastrzemski	.35	.25	.14
238	Rick Cerone, Graig Nettles	.04	.03	.02
239	Buddy Bell, George Brett	.15	.11	.06
240	Steve Carlton, Jim Kaat	.12	.09	.05
241	Steve Carlton, Dave Parker	.12	.09	.05
242	Ron Davis, Nolan Ryan	.10	.08	.04

1983 Fleer

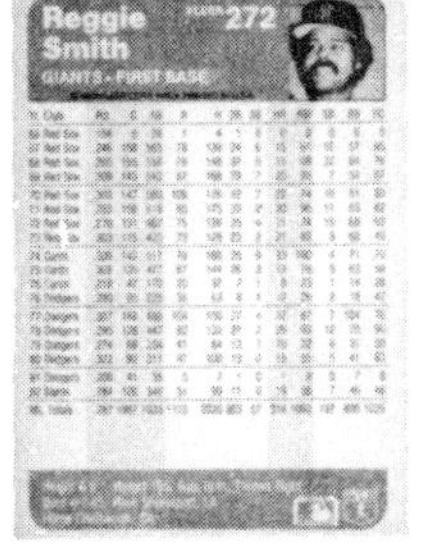

The 1983 Fleer set features color photos set inside a light brown border. The cards are the standard size of 2-1/2" by 3-1/2". A team logo is located at the card bottom and the word "Fleer" is found at the top. The card backs are designed on a vertical format and include a small black and white photo of the player along with biographical and statistical information. The reverses are done in two shades of brown on white stock. The set was issued with team logo stickers.

	MT	NR MT	EX
Complete Set:	60.00	40.00	25.00
Common Player:	.06	.05	.02

		MT	NR MT	EX
1	Joaquin Andujar	.08	.06	.03
2	Doug Bair	.06	.05	.02
3	Steve Braun	.06	.05	.02
4	Glenn Brummer	.06	.05	.02
5	Bob Forsch	.08	.06	.03
6	David Green	.06	.05	.02
7	George Hendrick	.08	.06	.03
8	Keith Hernandez	.40	.30	.15
9	Tom Herr	.10	.08	.04
10	Dane Iorg	.06	.05	.02
11	Jim Kaat	.15	.11	.06
12	Jeff Lahti	.06	.05	.02
13	Tito Landrum	.06	.05	.02
14	*Dave LaPoint*(FC)	.30	.25	.12
15	*Willie McGee*(FC)	1.00	.70	.40
16	Steve Mura	.06	.05	.02
17	Ken Oberkfell	.06	.05	.02
18	Darrell Porter	.08	.06	.03
19	Mike Ramsey	.06	.05	.02
20	Gene Roof	.06	.05	.02
21	Lonnie Smith	.08	.06	.03
22	Ozzie Smith	.20	.15	.08
23	John Stuper	.06	.05	.02
24	Bruce Sutter	.15	.11	.06
25	Gene Tenace	.08	.06	.03
26	Jerry Augustine	.06	.05	.02
27	Dwight Bernard	.06	.05	.02
28	Mark Brouhard	.06	.05	.02
29	Mike Caldwell	.06	.05	.02
30	Cecil Cooper	.15	.11	.06
31	Jamie Easterly	.06	.05	.02
32	Marshall Edwards	.06	.05	.02
33	Rollie Fingers	.20	.15	.08
34	Jim Gantner	.08	.06	.03
35	Moose Haas	.06	.05	.02
36	Roy Howell	.06	.05	.02
37	Peter Ladd	.06	.05	.02
38	Bob McClure	.06	.05	.02
39	Doc Medich	.06	.05	.02
40	Paul Molitor	.20	.15	.08
41	Don Money	.06	.05	.02
42	Charlie Moore	.06	.05	.02
43	Ben Oglivie	.08	.06	.03
44	Ed Romero	.06	.05	.02
45	Ted Simmons	.12	.09	.05
46	Jim Slaton	.06	.05	.02
47	Don Sutton	.30	.25	.12
48	Gorman Thomas	.10	.08	.04
49	Pete Vuckovich	.08	.06	.03
50	Ned Yost	.06	.05	.02
51	Robin Yount	.70	.50	.30
52	Benny Ayala	.06	.05	.02
53	Bob Bonner	.06	.05	.02
54	Al Bumbry	.08	.06	.03
55	Terry Crowley	.06	.05	.02
56	*Storm Davis*(FC)	.50	.40	.20
57	Rich Dauer	.06	.05	.02
58	Rick Dempsey	.08	.06	.03
59	Jim Dwyer	.06	.05	.02
60	Mike Flanagan	.10	.08	.04
61	Dan Ford	.06	.05	.02
62	Glenn Gulliver	.06	.05	.02
63	John Lowenstein	.06	.05	.02
64	Dennis Martinez	.08	.06	.03
65	Tippy Martinez	.06	.05	.02
66	Scott McGregor	.08	.06	.03
67	Eddie Murray	.60	.45	.25
68	Joe Nolan	.06	.05	.02
69	Jim Palmer	.50	.40	.20
70	Cal Ripken, Jr.	1.75	1.25	.70
71	Gary Roenicke	.06	.05	.02
72	Lenn Sakata	.06	.05	.02
73	Ken Singleton	.10	.08	.04
74	Sammy Stewart	.06	.05	.02
75	Tim Stoddard	.06	.05	.02
76	Don Aase	.06	.05	.02
77	Don Baylor	.12	.09	.05
78	Juan Beniquez	.06	.05	.02
79	Bob Boone	.10	.08	.04
80	Rick Burleson	.08	.06	.03
81	Rod Carew	.50	.40	.20
82	Bobby Clark	.06	.05	.02
83	Doug Corbett	.06	.05	.02
84	John Curtis	.06	.05	.02
85	Doug DeCinces	.10	.08	.04
86	Brian Downing	.10	.08	.04
87	Joe Ferguson	.06	.05	.02
88	Tim Foli	.06	.05	.02
89	Ken Forsch	.06	.05	.02
90	Dave Goltz	.08	.06	.03
91	Bobby Grich	.10	.08	.04
92	Andy Hassler	.06	.05	.02
93	Reggie Jackson	.50	.40	.20
94	Ron Jackson	.06	.05	.02
95	Tommy John	.20	.15	.08
96	Bruce Kison	.06	.05	.02
97	Fred Lynn	.20	.15	.08
98	Ed Ott	.06	.05	.02
99	Steve Renko	.06	.05	.02
100	Luis Sanchez	.06	.05	.02
101	Rob Wilfong	.06	.05	.02
102	Mike Witt	.15	.11	.06
103	Geoff Zahn	.06	.05	.02
104	Willie Aikens	.06	.05	.02
105	Mike Armstrong	.06	.05	.02
106	Vida Blue	.12	.09	.05
107	*Bud Black*(FC)	.20	.15	.08
108	George Brett	.70	.50	.30
109	Bill Castro	.06	.05	.02
110	Onix Concepcion	.06	.05	.02
111	Dave Frost	.06	.05	.02
112	Cesar Geronimo	.06	.05	.02
113	Larry Gura	.06	.05	.02
114	Steve Hammond	.06	.05	.02
115	Don Hood	.06	.05	.02
116	Dennis Leonard	.08	.06	.03
117	Jerry Martin	.06	.05	.02
118	Lee May	.08	.06	.03
119	Hal McRae	.12	.09	.05
120	Amos Otis	.08	.06	.03
121	Greg Pryor	.06	.05	.02
122	Dan Quisenberry	.15	.11	.06
123	*Don Slaught*(FC)	.20	.15	.08
124	Paul Splittorff	.06	.05	.02
125	U.L. Washington	.06	.05	.02
126	John Wathan	.08	.06	.03
127	Frank White	.10	.08	.04
128	Willie Wilson	.15	.11	.06
129	Steve Bedrosian(FC)	.35	.25	.14
130	Bruce Benedict	.06	.05	.02
131	Tommy Boggs	.06	.05	.02
132	Brett Butler(FC)	.15	.11	.06
133	Rick Camp	.06	.05	.02
134	Chris Chambliss	.08	.06	.03
135	Ken Dayley(FC)	.10	.08	.04
136	Gene Garber	.06	.05	.02
137	Terry Harper	.06	.05	.02
138	Bob Horner	.12	.09	.05
139	Glenn Hubbard	.08	.06	.03
140	Rufino Linares	.06	.05	.02
141	Rick Mahler	.08	.06	.03
142	Dale Murphy	.90	.70	.35
143	Phil Niekro	.30	.25	.12
144	Pascual Perez	.08	.06	.03
145	Biff Pocoroba	.06	.05	.02
146	Rafael Ramirez	.06	.05	.02
147	Jerry Royster	.06	.05	.02
148	Ken Smith	.06	.05	.02
149	Bob Walk	.08	.06	.03
150	Claudell Washington	.08	.06	.03
151	Bob Watson	.08	.06	.03
152	Larry Whisenton	.06	.05	.02
153	Porfirio Altamirano	.06	.05	.02
154	Marty Bystrom	.06	.05	.02
155	Steve Carlton	.50	.40	.20
156	Larry Christenson	.06	.05	.02
157	Ivan DeJesus	.06	.05	.02
158	John Denny	.06	.05	.02
159	Bob Dernier(FC)	.10	.08	.04
160	Bo Diaz	.08	.06	.03
161	Ed Farmer	.06	.05	.02
162	Greg Gross	.06	.05	.02
163	Mike Krukow	.08	.06	.03
164	Garry Maddox	.10	.08	.04
165	Gary Matthews	.10	.08	.04
166	Tug McGraw	.12	.09	.05
167	Bob Molinaro	.06	.05	.02
168	Sid Monge	.06	.05	.02
169	Ron Reed	.06	.05	.02
170	Bill Robinson	.06	.05	.02
171	Pete Rose	1.00	.70	.40
172	Dick Ruthven	.06	.05	.02
173	Mike Schmidt	.80	.60	.30
174	Manny Trillo	.08	.06	.03
175	Ozzie Virgil(FC)	.10	.08	.04
176	George Vukovich	.06	.05	.02
177	Gary Allenson	.06	.05	.02
178	Luis Aponte	.06	.05	.02
179	*Wade Boggs*(FC)	18.00	13.50	7.25
180	Tom Burgmeier	.06	.05	.02
181	Mark Clear	.06	.05	.02
182	Dennis Eckersley	.12	.09	.05
183	Dwight Evans	.15	.11	.06
184	Rich Gedman	.08	.06	.03
185	Glenn Hoffman	.06	.05	.02
186	Bruce Hurst	.10	.08	.04
187	Carney Lansford	.08	.06	.03
188	Rick Miller	.06	.05	.02
189	Reid Nichols	.06	.05	.02
190	Bob Ojeda	.12	.09	.05
191	Tony Perez	.20	.15	.08
192	Chuck Rainey	.06	.05	.02
193	Jerry Remy	.06	.05	.02
194	Jim Rice	.40	.30	.15
195	Bob Stanley	.06	.05	.02
196	Dave Stapleton	.06	.05	.02
197	Mike Torrez	.08	.06	.03
198	John Tudor	.10	.08	.04
199	Julio Valdez	.06	.05	.02
200	Carl Yastrzemski	.70	.50	.30
201	Dusty Baker	.10	.08	.04
202	Joe Beckwith	.06	.05	.02
203	*Greg Brock*(FC)	.35	.25	.14
204	Ron Cey	.12	.09	.05
205	Terry Forster	.08	.06	.03
206	Steve Garvey	.40	.30	.15
207	Pedro Guerrero	.25	.20	.10
208	Burt Hooton	.08	.06	.03
209	Steve Howe	.08	.06	.03
210	Ken Landreaux	.06	.05	.02
211	Mike Marshall	.20	.15	.08
212	*Candy Maldonado*(FC)	.50	.40	.20
213	Rick Monday	.10	.08	.04
214	Tom Niedenfuer	.10	.08	.04
215	Jorge Orta	.06	.05	.02
216	Jerry Reuss	.10	.08	.04
217	Ron Roenicke	.06	.05	.02
218	Vicente Romo	.06	.05	.02
219	Bill Russell	.08	.06	.03
220	Steve Sax	.30	.25	.12
221	Mike Scioscia	.08	.06	.03
222	Dave Stewart	.15	.11	.06
223	Derrel Thomas	.06	.05	.02
224	Fernando Valenzuela	.30	.25	.12
225	Bob Welch	.12	.09	.05
226	Ricky Wright	.06	.05	.02
227	Steve Yeager	.06	.05	.02
228	Bill Almon	.06	.05	.02
229	Harold Baines	.15	.11	.06
230	Salome Barojas	.06	.05	.02
231	Tony Bernazard	.06	.05	.02
232	Britt Burns	.06	.05	.02
233	Richard Dotson	.10	.08	.04
234	Ernesto Escarrega	.06	.05	.02
235	Carlton Fisk	.30	.25	.12
236	Jerry Hairston	.06	.05	.02
237	Kevin Hickey	.06	.05	.02
238	LaMarr Hoyt	.06	.05	.02
239	Steve Kemp	.10	.08	.04
240	Jim Kern	.06	.05	.02
241	*Ron Kittle*(FC)	.70	.50	.30
242	Jerry Koosman	.10	.08	.04
243	Dennis Lamp	.06	.05	.02
244	Rudy Law	.06	.05	.02
245	Vance Law	.08	.06	.03
246	Ron LeFlore	.08	.06	.03
247	Greg Luzinski	.12	.09	.05
248	Tom Paciorek	.06	.05	.02
249	Aurelio Rodriguez	.08	.06	.03
250	Mike Squires	.06	.05	.02
251	Steve Trout	.06	.05	.02
252	Jim Barr	.06	.05	.02
253	Dave Bergman	.06	.05	.02
254	Fred Breining	.06	.05	.02
255	Bob Brenly(FC)	.08	.06	.03
256	Jack Clark	.25	.20	.10
257	Chili Davis(FC)	.20	.15	.08
258	Darrell Evans	.15	.11	.06
259	Alan Fowlkes	.06	.05	.02
260	Rich Gale	.06	.05	.02
261	Atlee Hammaker(FC)	.12	.09	.05
262	Al Holland	.06	.05	.02
263	Duane Kuiper	.06	.05	.02
264	Bill Laskey	.06	.05	.02
265	Gary Lavelle	.06	.05	.02
266	Johnnie LeMaster	.06	.05	.02
267	Renie Martin	.06	.05	.02
268	Milt May	.06	.05	.02
269	Greg Minton	.06	.05	.02
270	Joe Morgan	.40	.30	.15
271	Tom O'Malley	.06	.05	.02
272	Reggie Smith	.10	.08	.04
273	Guy Sularz	.06	.05	.02
274	Champ Summers	.06	.05	.02
275	Max Venable	.06	.05	.02
276	Jim Wohlford	.06	.05	.02
277	Ray Burris	.06	.05	.02
278	Gary Carter	.35	.25	.14
279	Warren Cromartie	.06	.05	.02
280	Andre Dawson	.35	.25	.14
281	Terry Francona	.06	.05	.02
282	Doug Flynn	.06	.05	.02
283	Woody Fryman	.08	.06	.03
284	Bill Gullickson	.06	.05	.02
285	Wallace Johnson	.06	.05	.02
286	Charlie Lea	.06	.05	.02
287	Randy Lerch	.06	.05	.02
288	Brad Mills	.06	.05	.02
289	Dan Norman	.06	.05	.02
290	Al Oliver	.15	.11	.06
291	David Palmer	.06	.05	.02
292	Tim Raines	.35	.25	.14
293	Jeff Reardon	.12	.09	.05
294	Steve Rogers	.08	.06	.03
295	Scott Sanderson	.06	.05	.02
296	Dan Schatzeder	.06	.05	.02
297	Bryn Smith	.08	.06	.03
298	Chris Speier	.06	.05	.02
299	Tim Wallach	.20	.15	.08
300	Jerry White	.06	.05	.02
301	Joel Youngblood	.06	.05	.02
302	Ross Baumgarten	.06	.05	.02
303	Dale Berra	.06	.05	.02
304	John Candelaria	.10	.08	.04
305	Dick Davis	.06	.05	.02
306	Mike Easler	.08	.06	.03
307	Richie Hebner	.06	.05	.02
308	Lee Lacy	.06	.05	.02
309	Bill Madlock	.12	.09	.05
310	Larry McWilliams	.06	.05	.02
311	John Milner	.06	.05	.02
312	Omar Moreno	.06	.05	.02
313	Jim Morrison	.06	.05	.02
314	Steve Nicosia	.06	.05	.02
315	Dave Parker	.30	.25	.12
316	Tony Pena	.10	.08	.04
317	Johnny Ray	.12	.09	.05
318	Rick Rhoden	.10	.08	.04
319	Don Robinson	.08	.06	.03
320	Enrique Romo	.06	.05	.02
321	Manny Sarmiento	.06	.05	.02
322	Rod Scurry	.06	.05	.02
323	Jim Smith	.06	.05	.02
324	Willie Stargell	.40	.30	.15
325	Jason Thompson	.06	.05	.02
326	Kent Tekulve	.08	.06	.03
327a	Tom Brookens (narrow (1/4") brown box at bottom on back)	.30	.25	.12
327b	Tom Brookens (wide (1 1/4") brown box at bottom on back)	.08	.06	.03
328	Enos Cabell	.06	.05	.02
329	Kirk Gibson	.40	.30	.15
330	Larry Herndon	.08	.06	.03
331	Mike Ivie	.06	.05	.02
332	*Howard Johnson*(FC)	10.00	7.50	4.00
333	Lynn Jones	.06	.05	.02
334	Rick Leach	.06	.05	.02
335	Chet Lemon	.08	.06	.03
336	Jack Morris	.30	.25	.12
337	Lance Parrish	.35	.25	.14
338	Larry Pashnick	.06	.05	.02
339	Dan Petry	.08	.06	.03
340	Dave Rozema	.06	.05	.02
341	Dave Rucker	.06	.05	.02
342	Elias Sosa	.06	.05	.02
343	Dave Tobik	.06	.05	.02
344	Alan Trammell	.40	.30	.15
345	Jerry Turner	.06	.05	.02
346	Jerry Ujdur	.06	.05	.02
347	Pat Underwood	.06	.05	.02
348	Lou Whitaker	.40	.30	.15
349	Milt Wilcox	.06	.05	.02
350	*Glenn Wilson*(FC)	.35	.25	.14
351	John Wockenfuss	.06	.05	.02
352	Kurt Bevacqua	.06	.05	.02

		MT	NR MT	EX
353	Juan Bonilla	.06	.05	.02
354	Floyd Chiffer	.06	.05	.02
355	Luis DeLeon	.06	.05	.02
356	*Dave Dravecky*(FC)	.80	.60	.30
357	Dave Edwards	.06	.05	.02
358	Juan Eichelberger	.06	.05	.02
359	Tim Flannery	.06	.05	.02
360	*Tony Gwynn*(FC)	13.00	9.75	5.25
361	Ruppert Jones	.06	.05	.02
362	Terry Kennedy	.08	.06	.03
363	Joe Lefebvre	.06	.05	.02
364	Sixto Lezcano	.06	.05	.02
365	Tim Lollar	.06	.05	.02
366	Gary Lucas	.06	.05	.02
367	John Montefusco	.06	.05	.02
368	Broderick Perkins	.06	.05	.02
369	Joe Pittman	.06	.05	.02
370	Gene Richards	.06	.05	.02
371	Luis Salazar	.06	.05	.02
372	*Eric Show*(FC)	.30	.25	.12
373	Garry Templeton	.10	.08	.04
374	Chris Welsh	.06	.05	.02
375	Alan Wiggins	.06	.05	.02
376	Rick Cerone	.06	.05	.02
377	Dave Collins	.08	.06	.03
378	Roger Erickson	.06	.05	.02
379	George Frazier	.06	.05	.02
380	Oscar Gamble	.08	.06	.03
381	Goose Gossage	.20	.15	.08
382	Ken Griffey	.12	.09	.05
383	Ron Guidry	.25	.20	.10
384	Dave LaRoche	.06	.05	.02
385	Rudy May	.06	.05	.02
386	John Mayberry	.08	.06	.03
387	Lee Mazzilli	.08	.06	.03
388	Mike Morgan(FC)	.12	.09	.05
389	Jerry Mumphrey	.06	.05	.02
390	Bobby Murcer	.10	.08	.04
391	Graig Nettles	.15	.11	.06
392	Lou Piniella	.12	.09	.05
393	Willie Randolph	.10	.08	.04
394	Shane Rawley	.10	.08	.04
395	Dave Righetti	.25	.20	.10
396	Andre Robertson	.06	.05	.02
397	Roy Smalley	.06	.05	.02
398	Dave Winfield	.40	.30	.15
399	Butch Wynegar	.06	.05	.02
400	Chris Bando	.06	.05	.02
401	Alan Bannister	.06	.05	.02
402	Len Barker	.08	.06	.03
403	Tom Brennan	.06	.05	.02
404	*Carmelo Castillo*(FC)	.12	.09	.05
405	Miguel Dilone	.06	.05	.02
406	Jerry Dybzinski	.06	.05	.02
407	Mike Fischlin	.06	.05	.02
408	Ed Glynn (photo actually Bud Anderson)	.06	.05	.02
409	Mike Hargrove	.06	.05	.02
410	Toby Harrah	.08	.06	.03
411	Ron Hassey	.06	.05	.02
412	Von Hayes	.15	.11	.06
413	Rick Manning	.06	.05	.02
414	Bake McBride	.06	.05	.02
415	Larry Milbourne	.06	.05	.02
416	Bill Nahorodny	.06	.05	.02
417	Jack Perconte	.06	.05	.02
418	Lary Sorensen	.06	.05	.02
419	Dan Spillner	.06	.05	.02
420	Rick Sutcliffe	.12	.09	.05
421	Andre Thornton	.10	.08	.04
422	Rick Waits	.06	.05	.02
423	Eddie Whitson	.06	.05	.02
424	Jesse Barfield(FC)	.60	.45	.25
425	Barry Bonnell	.06	.05	.02
426	Jim Clancy	.08	.06	.03
427	Damaso Garcia	.06	.05	.02
428	Jerry Garvin	.06	.05	.02
429	Alfredo Griffin	.08	.06	.03
430	Garth Iorg	.06	.05	.02
431	Roy Lee Jackson	.06	.05	.02
432	Luis Leal	.06	.05	.02
433	Buck Martinez	.06	.05	.02
434	Joey McLaughlin	.06	.05	.02
435	Lloyd Moseby	.12	.09	.05
436	Rance Mulliniks	.06	.05	.02
437	Dale Murray	.06	.05	.02
438	Wayne Nordhagen	.06	.05	.02
439	*Gene Petralli*(FC)	.15	.11	.06
440	Hosken Powell	.06	.05	.02
441	Dave Stieb	.12	.09	.05
442	Willie Upshaw	.08	.06	.03
443	Ernie Whitt	.08	.06	.03
444	Al Woods	.06	.05	.02
445	Alan Ashby	.06	.05	.02
446	Jose Cruz	.12	.09	.05
447	Kiko Garcia	.06	.05	.02
448	Phil Garner	.08	.06	.03
449	Danny Heep	.06	.05	.02
450	Art Howe	.06	.05	.02
451	Bob Knepper	.08	.06	.03
452	Alan Knicely	.06	.05	.02
453	Ray Knight	.10	.08	.04
454	Frank LaCorte	.06	.05	.02
455	Mike LaCoss	.06	.05	.02
456	Randy Moffitt	.06	.05	.02
457	Joe Niekro	.12	.09	.05
458	Terry Puhl	.06	.05	.02
459	Luis Pujols	.06	.05	.02
460	Craig Reynolds	.06	.05	.02
461	Bert Roberge	.06	.05	.02
462	Vern Ruhle	.06	.05	.02
463	Nolan Ryan	1.25	.90	.50
464	Joe Sambito	.06	.05	.02
465	Tony Scott	.06	.05	.02
466	Dave Smith	.08	.06	.03
467	Harry Spilman	.06	.05	.02
468	Dickie Thon	.08	.06	.03
469	Denny Walling	.06	.05	.02
470	Larry Andersen	.06	.05	.02
471	Floyd Bannister	.10	.08	.04
472	Jim Beattie	.06	.05	.02
473	Bruce Bochte	.06	.05	.02
474	Manny Castillo	.06	.05	.02
475	Bill Caudill	.06	.05	.02

		MT	NR MT	EX
476	Bryan Clark	.06	.05	.02
477	Al Cowens	.06	.05	.02
478	Julio Cruz	.06	.05	.02
479	Todd Cruz	.06	.05	.02
480	Gary Gray	.06	.05	.02
481	Dave Henderson(FC)	.20	.15	.08
482	*Mike Moore*(FC)	1.25	.90	.50
483	Gaylord Perry	.30	.25	.12
484	Dave Revering	.06	.05	.02
485	Joe Simpson	.06	.05	.02
486	Mike Stanton	.06	.05	.02
487	Rick Sweet	.06	.05	.02
488	*Ed Vande Berg*(FC)	.10	.08	.04
489	Richie Zisk	.08	.06	.03
490	Doug Bird	.06	.05	.02
491	Larry Bowa	.12	.09	.05
492	Bill Buckner	.12	.09	.05
493	Bill Campbell	.06	.05	.02
494	Jody Davis	.10	.08	.04
495	Leon Durham	.08	.06	.03
496	Steve Henderson	.06	.05	.02
497	Willie Hernandez	.08	.06	.03
498	Ferguson Jenkins	.15	.11	.06
499	Jay Johnstone	.08	.06	.03
500	Junior Kennedy	.06	.05	.02
501	Randy Martz	.06	.05	.02
502	Jerry Morales	.06	.05	.02
503	Keith Moreland	.08	.06	.03
504	Dickie Noles	.06	.05	.02
505	Mike Proly	.06	.05	.02
506	Allen Ripley	.06	.05	.02
507	*Ryne Sandberg*(FC)	12.00	9.00	4.75
508	Lee Smith	.15	.11	.06
509	Pat Tabler(FC)	.15	.11	.06
510	Dick Tidrow	.06	.05	.02
511	Bump Wills	.06	.05	.02
512	Gary Woods	.06	.05	.02
513	Tony Armas	.10	.08	.04
514	Dave Beard	.06	.05	.02
515	Jeff Burroughs	.08	.06	.03
516	John D'Acquisto	.06	.05	.02
517	Wayne Gross	.06	.05	.02
518	Mike Heath	.06	.05	.02
519	Rickey Henderson	.70	.50	.30
520	Cliff Johnson	.06	.05	.02
521	Matt Keough	.06	.05	.02
522	Brian Kingman	.06	.05	.02
523	Rick Langford	.06	.05	.02
524	Davey Lopes	.10	.08	.04
525	Steve McCatty	.06	.05	.02
526	Dave McKay	.06	.05	.02
527	Dan Meyer	.06	.05	.02
528	Dwayne Murphy	.08	.06	.03
529	Jeff Newman	.06	.05	.02
530	Mike Norris	.06	.05	.02
531	Bob Owchinko	.06	.05	.02
532	Joe Rudi	.10	.08	.04
533	Jimmy Sexton	.06	.05	.02
534	Fred Stanley	.06	.05	.02
535	Tom Underwood	.06	.05	.02
536	Neil Allen	.06	.05	.02
537	Wally Backman	.08	.06	.03
538	Bob Bailor	.06	.05	.02
539	Hubie Brooks	.12	.09	.05
540	Carlos Diaz	.06	.05	.02
541	Pete Falcone	.06	.05	.02
542	George Foster	.15	.11	.06
543	Ron Gardenhire	.06	.05	.02
544	Brian Giles	.06	.05	.02
545	Ron Hodges	.06	.05	.02
546	Randy Jones	.08	.06	.03
547	Mike Jorgensen	.06	.05	.02
548	Dave Kingman	.15	.11	.06
549	Ed Lynch	.06	.05	.02
550	Jesse Orosco(FC)	.15	.11	.06
551	Rick Ownbey	.06	.05	.02
552	*Charlie Puleo*(FC)	.12	.09	.05
553	Gary Rajsich	.06	.05	.02
554	Mike Scott	.15	.11	.06
555	Rusty Staub	.10	.08	.04
556	John Stearns	.06	.05	.02
557	Craig Swan	.06	.05	.02
558	Ellis Valentine	.06	.05	.02
559	Tom Veryzer	.06	.05	.02
560	Mookie Wilson	.10	.08	.04
561	Pat Zachry	.06	.05	.02
562	Buddy Bell	.12	.09	.05
563	John Butcher	.06	.05	.02
564	Steve Comer	.06	.05	.02
565	Danny Darwin	.06	.05	.02
566	Bucky Dent	.10	.08	.04
567	John Grubb	.06	.05	.02
568	Rick Honeycutt	.06	.05	.02
569	Dave Hostetler	.06	.05	.02
570	Charlie Hough	.10	.08	.04
571	Lamar Johnson	.06	.05	.02
572	Jon Matlack	.08	.06	.03
573	Paul Mirabella	.06	.05	.02
574	Larry Parrish	.10	.08	.04
575	Mike Richardt	.06	.05	.02
576	Mickey Rivers	.08	.06	.03
577	Billy Sample	.06	.05	.02
578	*Dave Schmidt*(FC)	.10	.08	.04
579	Bill Stein	.06	.05	.02
580	Jim Sundberg	.08	.06	.03
581	Frank Tanana	.10	.08	.04
582	Mark Wagner	.06	.05	.02
583	George Wright	.06	.05	.02
584	Johnny Bench	.40	.30	.15
585	Bruce Berenyi	.06	.05	.02
586	Larry Biittner	.06	.05	.02
587	Cesar Cedeno	.12	.09	.05
588	Dave Concepcion	.12	.09	.05
589	Dan Driessen	.08	.06	.03
590	Greg Harris(FC)	.08	.06	.03
591	Ben Hayes	.06	.05	.02
592	Paul Householder	.06	.05	.02
593	Tom Hume	.06	.05	.02
594	Wayne Krenchicki	.06	.05	.02
595	Rafael Landestoy	.06	.05	.02
596	Charlie Leibrandt	.08	.06	.03
597	*Eddie Milner*(FC)	.10	.08	.04
598	Ron Oester	.06	.05	.02
599	Frank Pastore	.06	.05	.02

		MT	NR MT	EX
600	Joe Price	.06	.05	.02
601	Tom Seaver	.50	.40	.20
602	Bob Shirley	.06	.05	.02
603	Mario Soto	.08	.06	.03
604	Alex Trevino	.06	.05	.02
605	Mike Vail	.06	.05	.02
606	Duane Walker	.06	.05	.02
607	Tom Brunansky(FC)	.25	.20	.10
608	Bobby Castillo	.06	.05	.02
609	John Castino	.06	.05	.02
610	Ron Davis	.06	.05	.02
611	Lenny Faedo	.06	.05	.02
612	Terry Felton	.06	.05	.02
613	*Gary Gaetti*(FC)	4.00	3.00	1.50
614	Mickey Hatcher	.08	.06	.03
615	Brad Havens	.06	.05	.02
616	Kent Hrbek(FC)	.80	.60	.30
617	Randy Johnson	.06	.05	.02
618	Tim Laudner(FC)	.12	.09	.05
619	Jeff Little	.06	.05	.02
620	Bob Mitchell	.06	.05	.02
621	Jack O'Connor	.06	.05	.02
622	John Pacella	.06	.05	.02
623	Pete Redfern	.06	.05	.02
624	Jesus Vega	.06	.05	.02
625	*Frank Viola*(FC)	4.00	3.00	1.50
626	Ron Washington	.06	.05	.02
627	Gary Ward	.08	.06	.03
628	Al Williams	.06	.05	.02
629	Red Sox All-Stars (Mark Clear, Dennis Eckersley, Carl Yastrzemski)	.25	.20	.10
630	300 Career Wins (Terry Bulling, Gaylord Perry)	.15	.11	.06
631	Pride of Venezuela (Dave Concepcion, Manny Trillo)	.10	.08	.04
632	All-Star Infielders (Buddy Bell, Robin Yount)	.15	.11	.06
633	Mr. Vet & Mr. Rookie (Kent Hrbek, Dave Winfield)	.25	.20	.10
634	Fountain of Youth (Pete Rose, Willie Stargell)	.40	.30	.15
635	Big Chiefs (Toby Harrah, Andre Thornton)	.08	.06	.03
636	"Smith Bros." (Lonnie Smith, Ozzie Smith)	.10	.08	.04
637	Base Stealers' Threat (Gary Carter, Bo Diaz)	.15	.11	.06
638	All-Star Catchers (Gary Carter, Carlton Fisk)	.20	.15	.08
639	The Silver Shoe (Rickey Henderson)	.30	.25	.12
640	Home Run Threats (Reggie Jackson, Ben Oglivie)	.25	.20	.10
641	Two Teams - Same Day (Joel Youngblood)	.08	.06	.03
642	Last Perfect Game (Len Barker, Ron Hassey)	.08	.06	.03
643	Blue (Vida Blue)	.10	.08	.04
644	Black & (Bud Black)	.10	.08	.04
645	Power (Reggie Jackson)	.30	.25	.12
646	Speed & (Rickey Henderson)	.30	.25	.12
647	Checklist 1-51	.06	.05	.02
648	Checklist 52-103	.06	.05	.02
649	Checklist 104-152	.06	.05	.02
650	Checklist 153-200	.06	.05	.02
651	Checklist 201-251	.06	.05	.02
652	Checklist 252-301	.06	.05	.02
653	Checklist 302-351	.06	.05	.02
654	Checklist 352-399	.06	.05	.02
655	Checklist 400-444	.06	.05	.02
656	Checklist 445-489	.06	.05	.02
657	Checklist 490-535	.06	.05	.02
658	Checklist 536-583	.06	.05	.02
659	Checklist 584-628	.06	.05	.02
660	Checklist 629-646	.06	.05	.02

1983 Fleer Stamps

The 1983 Fleer Stamp set consists of 288 stamps, including 224 player stamps and 64 team logo stamps. They were originally issued on four different sheets of 72 stamps each (checklisted below) and in "Vend-A-Stamp" dispensers of 18 stamps each. Sixteen different dispenser strips were needed to complete the set (strips 1-4 comprise Sheet 1; strips 5-8 comprise Sheet 2; strips 9-12 comprise Sheet 3; and strips 13-16 comprise Sheet 4.)

	MT	NR MT	EX
Complete Sheet Set:	7.00	5.25	2.75
Complete Vend-A-Stamp Set:	7.00	5.25	2.75
Common Sheet:	1.75	1.25	.70
Common Stamp Dispenser:	.25	.20	.10
Common Single Stamp:	.01	.01	

1 Sheet 1 (A's Logo, Angels Logo, Astros Logo, Cardinals Logo, Cubs Logo, Dodgers Logo, Expos Logo, Giants Logo, Indians Logo, Mets Logo, Orioles Logo, Phillies Logo, Pirates Logo, Red Sox Logo, Twins

		MT	NR MT	EX
	Logo, White Sox Logo, Neil Allen, Harold Baines, Buddy Bell, Dale Berra, Wade Boggs, George Brett, Bill Buckner, Jack Clark, Dave Concepcion, Warren Cromartie, Doug DeCinces, Luis DeLeon, Brian Downing, Dan Driessen, Mike Flanagan, Bob Forsch, Ken Forsch, Toby Harrah, Keith Hernandez, Steve Howe, Reggie Jackson, Ruppert Jones, Ray Knight, Gary Lavelle, Ron LeFlore, Davey Lopes, Lee Mazzilli, Bob McClure, Tug McGraw, Paul Molitor, Rick Monday, John Montefusco, Gaylord Perry, Dan Quisenberry, Ron Reed, Rick Rhoden, Ron Roenicke, Jerry Royster, Mike Schmidt, Roy Smalley, Reggie Smith, Mario Soto, Chris Speier, Willie Stargell, Rick Sutcliffe, Don Sutton, Craig Swan, Kent Tekulve, Dick Tidrow, Willie Upshaw, Fernando Valenzuela, U.L. Washington, Bump Wills, Dave Winfield, Robin Yount, Pat Zachry)	1.75	1.25	.70
2	Sheet 2 (Angels Logo, Astros Logo, Braves Logo, Cardinals Logo, Dodgers Logo, Expos Logo, Indians Logo, Mariners Logo, Mets Logo, Phillies Logo, Pirates Logo, Rangers Logo, Reds Logo, Royals Logo, Tigers Logo, Yankees Logo, Willie Aikens, Bob Bailor, Dusty Baker, Floyd Bannister, Len Barker, Hubie Brooks, Tom Brunansky, Chris Chambliss, Mark Clear, Andre Dawson, Bo Diaz, Dennis Eckersley, Rollie Fingers, George Foster, Goose Gossage, Ken Griffey, Ron Guidry, Rickey Henderson, Bob Horner, Lamarr Hoyt (LaMarr), Tom Hume, Garth Iorg, Tommy John, Sixto Lezcano, Fred Lynn, John Matlack (Jon), Scott McGregor, Eddie Milner, Greg Minton, Joe Morgan, Steve Mura, Dwayne Murphy, Ken Oberkfell, Ben Oglivie, Al Oliver, Jim Palmer, Lance Parrish, Larry Parrish, Lou Piniella, Tim Raines, Rafael Ramirez, Jeff Reardon, Jerry Reuss, Jim Rice, Pete Rose, Tom Seaver, Eric Show, Jim Sundberg, Bruce Sutter, Gorman Thomas, Jason Thompson, Tom Underwood, Mookie Wilson, Willie Wilson, John Wockenfuss, Carl Yastrzemski)	1.75	1.25	.70
3	Sheet 3 (A's Logo, Angels Logo, Blue Jays Logo, Braves Logo, Brewers Logo, Dodgers Logo, Giants Logo, Indians Logo, Mariners Logo, Orioles Logo, Padres Logo, Reds Logo, Royals Logo, Tigers Logo, Twins Logo, White Sox Logo, Alan Ashby, Dave Beard, Jim Beattie, Johnny Bench, Larry Biittner, Bob Boone, Rod Carew, Gary Carter, Bobby Castillo, Bill Caudill, Cecil Cooper, Mike Easler, Dwight Evans, Carlton Fisk, Gene Garber, Damaso Garcia, Larry Herndon, Al Holland, Burt Hooton, Art Howe, Kent Hrbek, Jerry Koosman, Duane Kuiper, Bill Laskey, Dennis Leonard, Garry Maddox, Bill Madlock, Rick Manning, Hal McRae, Keith Moreland, Jerry Mumphrey, Eddie Murray, Joe Niekro, Phil Niekro, Amos Otis, Darrell Porter, Johnny Ray, Mike Richardt, Cal Ripken, Jr, Steve Rogers, Nolan Ryan, Manny Sarmiento, Steve Sax, Ted Simmons, Ken Singleton, Bob Stanley, Rusty Staub, Dave Stieb, Dickie Thon, Andre Thornton, Manny Trillo, John Tudor, Ed Vande Berg, Bob Watson, Frank White, Milt Wilcox)	1.75	1.25	.70
4	Sheet 4 (Blue Jays Logo, Braves Logo, Brewers Logo, Cubs Logo, Expos Logo, Giants Logo, Padres Logo, Phillies Logo, Pirates Logo, Rangers Logo, Red Sox Logo, Reds Logo, Royals Logo, Twins Logo, White Sox Logo, Yankees Logo, Joaquin Andujar, Don Baylor, Vida Blue, Bruce Bochte, Larry Bowa, Al Bumbry, Jeff Burroughs, Enos Cabell, Steve Carlton, Cesar Cedeno, Rick Cerone, Ron Cey, Larry Christenson, Jim Clancy, Jose Cruz, Danny Darwin, Rich Dauer, Ron Davis, Ivan DeJesus, Leon Durham, Phil Garner, Steve Garvey, John Grubb, Atlee Hammaker, Mike Hargrove, Tom Herr, Ferguson Jenkins, Steve Kemp, Bruce Kison, Ken Landreaux, Carney Lansford, Charlie Lea, John Lowenstein, Greg Luzinski, Dennis Martinez, Tippy Martinez, Randy Martz, Gary Matthews, Milt May, Dale Murphy, Graig Nettles, Tom Paciorek, Dave Parker, Tony Pena, Hosken Powell, Willie Randolph, Lonnie Smith, Ozzie Smith, Dan Spillner, Ellis Valentine, Pete Vuckovich, Gary Ward, Claudell Washington, Lou Whitaker, Al Williams, Richie Zisk)	1.75	1.25	.70

1983 Fleer Stickers

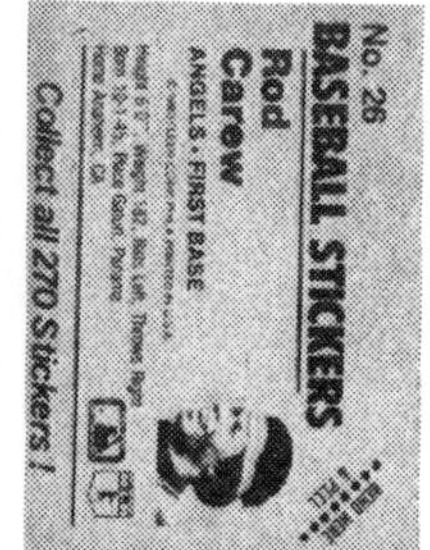

This 270-sticker set consists of both player stickers and team logo stickers, all measuring 1-13/16" by 2-1/2". The player stickers are numbered on the back. The front features a full-color photo surrounded by a blue border with two stars at the top. The 1983 Fleer stickers were issued in strips of ten player stickers plus two team logo stickers. The 26 logo stickers have been assigned numbers 271 through 296.

		MT	NR MT	EX
Complete Set:		18.00	13.50	7.25
Common Player:		.03	.02	.01
1	Bruce Sutter	.08	.06	.03
2	Willie McGee	.08	.06	.03
3	Darrell Porter	.03	.02	.01
4	Lonnie Smith	.03	.02	.01
5	Dane Iorg	.03	.02	.01
6	Keith Hernandez	.15	.11	.06
7	Joaquin Andujar	.04	.03	.02
8	Ken Oberkfell	.03	.02	.01
9	John Stuper	.03	.02	.01
10	Ozzie Smith	.10	.08	.04
11	Bob Forsch	.03	.02	.01
12	Jim Gantner	.03	.02	.01
13	Rollie Fingers	.10	.08	.04
14	Pete Vuckovich	.03	.02	.01
15	Ben Oglivie	.04	.03	.02
16	Don Sutton	.10	.08	.04
17	Bob McClure	.03	.02	.01
18	Robin Yount	.15	.11	.06
19	Paul Molitor	.10	.08	.04
20	Gorman Thomas	.06	.05	.02
21	Mike Caldwell	.03	.02	.01
22	Ted Simmons	.06	.05	.02
23	Cecil Cooper	.08	.06	.03
24	Steve Renko	.03	.02	.01
25	Tommy John	.08	.06	.03
26	Rod Carew	.25	.20	.10
27	Bruce Kison	.03	.02	.01
28	Ken Forsch	.03	.02	.01
29	Geoff Zahn	.03	.02	.01
30	Doug DiCinces	.06	.05	.02
31	Fred Lynn	.10	.08	.04
32	Reggie Jackson	.25	.20	.10
33	Don Baylor	.08	.06	.03
34	Bob Boone	.04	.03	.02
35	Brian Downing	.04	.03	.02
36	Goose Gossage	.08	.06	.03
37	Roy Smalley	.03	.02	.01
38	Graig Nettles	.06	.05	.02
39	Dave Winfield	.20	.15	.08
40	Lee Mazzilli	.04	.03	.02
41	Jerry Mumphrey	.03	.02	.01
42	Dave Collins	.03	.02	.01
43	Rick Cerone	.03	.02	.01
44	Willie Randolph	.06	.05	.02
45	Lou Piniella	.06	.05	.02
46	Ken Griffey	.06	.05	.02
47	Ron Guidry	.10	.08	.04
48	Jack Clark	.08	.06	.03
49	Reggie Smith	.06	.05	.02
50	Atlee Hammaker	.03	.02	.01
51	Fred Breining	.03	.02	.01
52	Gary Lavelle	.03	.02	.01
53	Chili Davis	.06	.05	.02
54	Greg Minton	.03	.02	.01
55	Joe Morgan	.12	.09	.05
56	Al Holland	.03	.02	.01
57	Bill Laskey	.03	.02	.01
58	Duane Kuiper	.03	.02	.01
59	Tom Burgmeier	.03	.02	.01
60	Carl Yastrzemski	.35	.25	.14
61	Mark Clear	.03	.02	.01
62	Mike Torrez	.03	.02	.01
63	Dennis Eckersley	.06	.05	.02
64	Wade Boggs	.75	.60	.30
65	Bob Stanley	.03	.02	.01
66	Jim Rice	.20	.15	.08
67	Carney Lansford	.06	.05	.02
68	Jerry Remy	.03	.02	.01
69	Dwight Evans	.08	.06	.03
70	John Candelaria	.06	.05	.02
71	Bill Madlock	.06	.05	.02
72	Dave Parker	.10	.08	.04
73	Kent Tekulve	.04	.03	.02
74	Tony Pena	.06	.05	.02
75	Manny Sarmiento	.03	.02	.01
76	Johnny Ray	.06	.05	.02
77	Dale Berra	.03	.02	.01
78	Lee Lacy	.03	.02	.01
79	Jason Thompson	.03	.02	.01
80	Mike Easler	.04	.03	.02
81	Willie Stargell	.20	.15	.08
82	Rick Camp	.03	.02	.01
83	Bob Watson	.03	.02	.01
84	Bob Horner	.08	.06	.03
85	Rafael Ramirez	.03	.02	.01
86	Chris Chambliss	.04	.03	.02
87	Gene Garber	.03	.02	.01
88	Claudell Washington	.04	.03	.02
89	Steve Bedrosian	.06	.05	.02
90	Dale Murphy	.30	.25	.12
91	Phil Niekro	.10	.08	.04
92	Jerry Royster	.03	.02	.01
93	Bob Walk	.03	.02	.01
94	Frank White	.06	.05	.02
95	Dennis Leonard	.03	.02	.01
96	Vida Blue	.06	.05	.02
97	U.L. Washington	.03	.02	.01
98	George Brett	.30	.25	.12
99	Amos Otis	.04	.03	.02
100	Dan Quisenberry	.06	.05	.02
101	Willie Aikens	.03	.02	.01
102	Hal McRae	.06	.05	.02
103	Larry Gura	.03	.02	.01
104	Willie Wilson	.06	.05	.02
105	Damaso Garcia	.03	.02	.01
106	Hosken Powell	.03	.02	.01
107	Joey McLaughlin	.03	.02	.01
108	Jim Clancy	.03	.02	.01
109	Barry Bonnell	.03	.02	.01
110	Garth Lorg	.03	.02	.01
111	Dave Stieb	.06	.05	.02
112	Fernando Valenzuela	.15	.11	.06
113	Steve Garvey	.20	.15	.08
114	Rick Monday	.04	.03	.02
115	Burt Hooton	.03	.02	.01
116	Bill Russell	.04	.03	.02
117	Pedro Guerrero	.12	.09	.05
118	Steve Sax	.08	.06	.03
119	Steve Howe	.04	.03	.02
120	Ken Landreaux	.03	.02	.01
121	Dusty Baker	.04	.03	.02
122	Ron Cey	.06	.05	.02
123	Jerry Reuss	.06	.05	.02
124	Bump Wills	.03	.02	.01
125	Keith Moreland	.06	.05	.02
126	Dick Tidrow	.03	.02	.01
127	Bill Campbell	.03	.02	.01
128	Larry Bowa	.06	.05	.02
129	Randy Martz	.03	.02	.01
130	Ferguson Jenkins	.06	.05	.02
131	Leon Durham	.04	.03	.02
132	Bill Buckner	.06	.05	.02
133	Ron Davis	.03	.02	.01
134	Jack O'Connor	.03	.02	.01
135	Kent Hrbek	.10	.08	.04
136	Gary Ward	.03	.02	.01
137	Al Williams	.03	.02	.01
138	Tom Brunansky	.06	.05	.02
139	Bobby Castillo	.03	.02	.01
140	Dusty Baker, Dale Murphy	.20	.15	.08
141	Nolan Ryan	.10	.08	.04
142	Lee Lacey, Omar Moreno	.03	.02	.01
143	Al Oliver, Pete Rose	.40	.30	.15
144	Ricky Henderson	.25	.20	.10
145	Ray Knight, Pete Rose, Mike Schmidt	.40	.30	.15
146	Hal McRae, Ben Oglivie	.06	.05	.02
147	Tom Hume, Ray Knight	.04	.03	.02
148	Buddy Bell, Carlton Fisk	.06	.05	.02
149	Steve Kemp	.04	.03	.02
150	Rudy Law	.03	.02	.01
151	Ron LeFlore	.04	.03	.02
152	Jerry Koosman	.04	.03	.02
153	Carlton Fisk	.12	.09	.05
154	Salome Barojas	.03	.02	.01
155	Harold Baines	.10	.08	.04
156	Britt Burns	.03	.02	.01
157	Tom Paciorek	.03	.02	.01
158	Greg Luzinski	.06	.05	.02
159	LaMarr Hoyt	.03	.02	.01
160	George Wright	.03	.02	.01
161	Danny Darwin	.03	.02	.01
162	Lamar Johnson	.03	.02	.01
163	Charlie Hough	.04	.03	.02
164	Buddy Bell	.06	.05	.02
165	John Matlack (Jon)	.04	.03	.02
166	Billy Sample	.03	.02	.01
167	John Grubb	.03	.02	.01
168	Larry Parrish	.06	.05	.02
169	Ivan DeJesus	.03	.02	.01
170	Mike Schmidt	.30	.25	.12
171	Tug McGraw	.06	.05	.02
172	Ron Reed	.03	.02	.01
173	Garry Maddox	.04	.03	.02
174	Pete Rose	.40	.30	.15
175	Manny Trillo	.04	.03	.02
176	Steve Carlton	.20	.15	.08
177	Bo Diaz	.04	.03	.02
178	Gary Matthews	.04	.03	.02
179	Bill Caudill	.03	.02	.01
180	Ed Vande Berg	.03	.02	.01
181	Gaylord Perry	.12	.09	.05
182	Floyd Bannister	.04	.03	.02
183	Richie Zisk	.04	.03	.02
184	Al Cowens	.03	.02	.01
185	Bruce Bochte	.03	.02	.01
186	Jeff Burroughs	.04	.03	.02
187	Dave Beard	.03	.02	.01
188	Davey Lopes	.04	.03	.02
189	Dwayne Murphy	.04	.03	.02
190	Rick Langford	.03	.02	.01
191	Tom Underwood	.03	.02	.01
192	Rickey Henderson	.25	.20	.10
193	Mike Flanagan	.06	.05	.02
194	Scott McGregor	.04	.03	.02
195	Ken Singleton	.06	.05	.02
196	Rich Dauer	.03	.02	.01
197	John Lowenstein	.03	.02	.01
198	Cal Ripken, Jr.	.25	.20	.10
199	Dennis Martinez	.04	.03	.02
200	Jim Palmer	.15	.11	.06
201	Tippy Martinez	.03	.02	.01
202	Eddie Murray	.25	.20	.10
203	Al Bumbry	.03	.02	.01
204	Dickie Thon	.03	.02	.01
205	Phil Garner	.03	.02	.01
206	Jose Cruz	.04	.03	.02
207	Nolan Ryan	.15	.11	.06
208	Ray Knight	.04	.03	.02
209	Terry Puhl	.03	.02	.01
210	Joe Niekro	.06	.05	.02
211	Art Howe	.03	.02	.01
212	Alan Ashby	.03	.02	.01
213	Tom Hume	.03	.02	.01
214	Johnny Bench	.25	.20	.10
215	Larry Biittner	.03	.02	.01
216	Mario Soto	.04	.03	.02
217	Dan Driessen	.04	.03	.02
218	Tom Seaver	.20	.15	.08
219	Dave Concepcion	.06	.05	.02
220	Wayne Krenchicki	.03	.02	.01
221	Cesar Cedeno	.06	.05	.02
222	Ruppert Jones	.03	.02	.01
223	Terry Kennedy	.04	.03	.02
224	Luis DeLeon	.03	.02	.01
225	Eric Show	.04	.03	.02
226	Tim Flannery	.03	.02	.01
227	Garry Templeton	.04	.03	.02
228	Tim Lollar	.03	.02	.01
229	Sixto Lezcano	.03	.02	.01
230	Bob Bailor	.03	.02	.01
231	Craig Swan	.03	.02	.01
232	Dave Kingman	.06	.05	.02

		MT	NR MT	EX
233	Mookie Wilson	.04	.03	.02
234	John Stearns	.03	.02	.01
235	Ellis Valentine	.03	.02	.01
236	Neil Allen	.03	.02	.01
237	Pat Zachry	.03	.02	.01
238	Rusty Staub	.06	.05	.02
239	George Foster	.06	.05	.02
240	Rick Sutcliffe	.06	.05	.02
241	Andre Thornton	.04	.03	.02
242	Mike Hargrove	.03	.02	.01
243	Dan Spillner	.03	.02	.01
244	Lary Sorensen	.03	.02	.01
245	Len Barker	.03	.02	.01
246	Rick Manning	.03	.02	.01
247	Toby Harrah	.04	.03	.02
248	Milt Wilcox	.03	.02	.01
249	Lou Whitaker	.10	.08	.04
250	Tom Brookens	.03	.02	.01
251	Chet Lemon	.04	.03	.02
252	Jack Morris	.12	.09	.05
253	Alan Trammell	.15	.11	.06
254	John Wockenfuss	.03	.02	.01
255	Lance Parrish	.12	.09	.05
256	Larry Herndon	.03	.02	.01
257	Chris Speier	.03	.02	.01
258	Woody Fryman	.03	.02	.01
259	Scott Sanderson	.03	.02	.01
260	Steve Rogers	.03	.02	.01
261	Warren Cromartie	.03	.02	.01
262	Gary Carter	.20	.15	.08
263	Bill Gullickson	.03	.02	.01
264	Andre Dawson	.15	.11	.06
265	Tim Raines	.20	.15	.08
266	Charlie Lea	.03	.02	.01
267	Jeff Reardon	.06	.05	.02
268	Al Oliver	.06	.05	.02
269	George Hendrick	.04	.03	.02
270	John Montefusco	.03	.02	.01
(271)	A's Logo	.03	.02	.01
(272)	Angels Logo	.03	.02	.01
(273)	Astros Logo	.03	.02	.01
(274)	Blue Jays Logo	.03	.02	.01
(275)	Braves Logo	.03	.02	.01
(276)	Brewers Logo	.03	.02	.01
(277)	Cardinals Logo	.03	.02	.01
(278)	Cubs Logo	.03	.02	.01
(279)	Dodgers Logo	.03	.02	.01
(280)	Expos Logo	.03	.02	.01
(281)	Giants Logo	.03	.02	.01
(282)	Indians Logo	.03	.02	.01
(283)	Mariners Logo	.03	.02	.01
(284)	Mets Logo	.03	.02	.01
(285)	Orioles Logo	.03	.02	.01
(286)	Padres Logo	.03	.02	.01
(287)	Phillies Logo	.03	.02	.01
(288)	Pirates Logo	.03	.02	.01
(289)	Rangers Logo	.03	.02	.01
(290)	Red Sox Logo	.03	.02	.01
(291)	Reds Logo	.03	.02	.01
(292)	Royals Logo	.03	.02	.01
(293)	Tigers Logo	.03	.02	.01
(294)	Twins Logo	.03	.02	.01
(295)	Yankees Logo	.03	.02	.01
(296)	White Sox Logo	.03	.02	.01

1984 Fleer

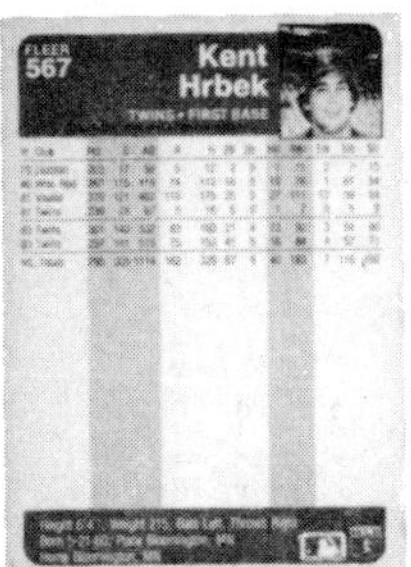

The 1984 Fleer set contained 660 cards for the fourth consecutive year. The cards, which measure 2-1/2" by 3-1/2", feature a color photo surrounded by four white borders and two blue stripes. The top stripe contains the word "Fleer" with the lower carrying the player's name. The card backs contain a small black and white photo of the player and are done in blue ink on white stock. The set was issued with team logo stickers.

		MT	NR MT	EX
	Complete Set:	125.00	90.00	50.00
	Common Player:	.08	.06	.03
1	*Mike Boddicker*(FC)	.20	.15	.08
2	Al Bumbry	.10	.08	.04
3	Todd Cruz	.08	.06	.03
4	Rich Dauer	.08	.06	.03
5	Storm Davis	.12	.09	.05
6	Rick Dempsey	.10	.08	.04
7	Jim Dwyer	.08	.06	.03
8	Mike Flanagan	.12	.09	.05
9	Dan Ford	.08	.06	.03
10	John Lowenstein	.08	.06	.03
11	Dennis Martinez	.10	.08	.04
12	Tippy Martinez	.08	.06	.03
13	Scott McGregor	.10	.08	.04
14	Eddie Murray	.60	.45	.25
15	Joe Nolan	.08	.06	.03
16	Jim Palmer	.40	.30	.15
17	Cal Ripken, Jr.	.90	.70	.35
18	Gary Roenicke	.08	.06	.03
19	Lenn Sakata	.08	.06	.03
20	*John Shelby*(FC)	.25	.20	.10
21	Ken Singleton	.12	.09	.05
22	Sammy Stewart	.08	.06	.03
23	Tim Stoddard	.08	.06	.03
24	Marty Bystrom	.08	.06	.03
25	Steve Carlton	.50	.40	.20
26	Ivan DeJesus	.08	.06	.03
27	John Denny	.08	.06	.03
28	Bob Dernier	.08	.06	.03
29	Bo Diaz	.10	.08	.04
30	Kiko Garcia	.08	.06	.03
31	Greg Gross	.08	.06	.03
32	*Kevin Gross*(FC)	.35	.25	.14
33	Von Hayes	.15	.11	.06
34	Willie Hernandez	.12	.09	.05
35	Al Holland	.08	.06	.03
36	*Charles Hudson*(FC)	.20	.15	.08
37	Joe Lefebvre	.08	.06	.03
38	Sixto Lezcano	.08	.06	.03
39	Garry Maddox	.10	.08	.04
40	Gary Matthews	.12	.09	.05
41	Len Matuszek	.08	.06	.03
42	Tug McGraw	.12	.09	.05
43	Joe Morgan	.40	.30	.15
44	Tony Perez	.20	.15	.08
45	Ron Reed	.08	.06	.03
46	Pete Rose	1.00	.70	.40
47	*Juan Samuel*(FC)	3.50	2.75	1.50
48	Mike Schmidt	2.25	1.75	.90
49	Ozzie Virgil	.08	.06	.03
50	*Juan Agosto*(FC)	.15	.11	.06
51	Harold Baines	.25	.20	.10
52	Floyd Bannister	.12	.09	.05
53	Salome Barojas	.08	.06	.03
54	Britt Burns	.08	.06	.03
55	Julio Cruz	.08	.06	.03
56	Richard Dotson	.12	.09	.05
57	Jerry Dybzinski	.08	.06	.03
58	Carlton Fisk	.30	.25	.12
59	Scott Fletcher(FC)	.15	.11	.06
60	Jerry Hairston	.08	.06	.03
61	Kevin Hickey	.08	.06	.03
62	Marc Hill	.08	.06	.03
63	LaMarr Hoyt	.08	.06	.03
64	Ron Kittle	.15	.11	.06
65	Jerry Koosman	.12	.09	.05
66	Dennis Lamp	.08	.06	.03
67	Rudy Law	.08	.06	.03
68	Vance Law	.10	.08	.04
69	Greg Luzinski	.12	.09	.05
70	Tom Paciorek	.08	.06	.03
71	Mike Squires	.08	.06	.03
72	Dick Tidrow	.08	.06	.03
73	*Greg Walker*(FC)	.45	.35	.20
74	Glenn Abbott	.08	.06	.03
75	Howard Bailey	.08	.06	.03
76	Doug Bair	.08	.06	.03
77	Juan Berenguer	.08	.06	.03
78	Tom Brookens	.08	.06	.03
79	Enos Cabell	.08	.06	.03
80	Kirk Gibson	.40	.30	.15
81	John Grubb	.08	.06	.03
82	Larry Herndon	.10	.08	.04
83	Wayne Krenchicki	.08	.06	.03
84	Rick Leach	.08	.06	.03
85	Chet Lemon	.10	.08	.04
86	Aurelio Lopez	.08	.06	.03
87	Jack Morris	.30	.25	.12
88	Lance Parrish	.35	.25	.14
89	Dan Petry	.10	.08	.04
90	Dave Rozema	.08	.06	.03
91	Alan Trammell	.40	.30	.15
92	Lou Whitaker	.40	.30	.15
93	Milt Wilcox	.08	.06	.03
94	Glenn Wilson	.10	.08	.04
95	John Wockenfuss	.08	.06	.03
96	Dusty Baker	.12	.09	.05
97	Joe Beckwith	.08	.06	.03
98	Greg Brock	.12	.09	.05
99	Jack Fimple	.08	.06	.03
100	Pedro Guerrero	.35	.25	.14
101	Rick Honeycutt	.08	.06	.03
102	Burt Hooton	.10	.08	.04
103	Steve Howe	.12	.09	.05
104	Ken Landreaux	.08	.06	.03
105	Mike Marshall	.15	.11	.06
106	Rick Monday	.10	.08	.04
107	Jose Morales	.08	.06	.03
108	Tom Niedenfuer	.10	.08	.04
109	*Alejandro Pena*(FC)	.30	.25	.12
110	Jerry Reuss	.12	.09	.05
111	Bill Russell	.10	.08	.04
112	Steve Sax	.20	.15	.08
113	Mike Scioscia	.10	.08	.04
114	Derrel Thomas	.08	.06	.03
115	Fernando Valenzuela	.40	.30	.15
116	Bob Welch	.15	.11	.06
117	Steve Yeager	.08	.06	.03
118	Pat Zachry	.08	.06	.03
119	Don Baylor	.15	.11	.06
120	Bert Campaneris	.12	.09	.05
121	Rick Cerone	.08	.06	.03
122	*Ray Fontenot*(FC)	.10	.08	.04
123	George Frazier	.08	.06	.03
124	Oscar Gamble	.10	.08	.04
125	Goose Gossage	.25	.20	.10
126	Ken Griffey	.12	.09	.05
127	Ron Guidry	.30	.25	.12
128	Jay Howell(FC)	.15	.11	.06
129	Steve Kemp	.10	.08	.04
130	Matt Keough	.08	.06	.03
131	*Don Mattingly*(FC)	50.00	37.50	20.00
132	John Montefusco	.08	.06	.03
133	Omar Moreno	.08	.06	.03
134	Dale Murray	.08	.06	.03
135	Graig Nettles	.20	.15	.08
136	Lou Piniella	.15	.11	.06
137	Willie Randolph	.12	.09	.05
138	Shane Rawley	.12	.09	.05
139	Dave Righetti	.25	.20	.10
140	Andre Robertson	.08	.06	.03
141	Bob Shirley	.08	.06	.03
142	Roy Smalley	.08	.06	.03
143	Dave Winfield	.40	.30	.15
144	Butch Wynegar	.08	.06	.03
145	*Jim Acker*(FC)	.12	.09	.05
146	Doyle Alexander	.12	.09	.05
147	Jesse Barfield	.25	.20	.10
148	Jorge Bell	1.00	.70	.40
149	Barry Bonnell	.08	.06	.03
150	Jim Clancy	.10	.08	.04
151	Dave Collins	.10	.08	.04
152	*Tony Fernandez*(FC)	6.00	4.50	2.50
153	Damaso Garcia	.08	.06	.03
154	Dave Geisel	.08	.06	.03
155	Jim Gott(FC)	.10	.08	.04
156	Alfredo Griffin	.10	.08	.04
157	Garth Iorg	.08	.06	.03
158	Roy Lee Jackson	.08	.06	.03
159	Cliff Johnson	.08	.06	.03
160	Luis Leal	.08	.06	.03
161	Buck Martinez	.08	.06	.03
162	Joey McLaughlin	.08	.06	.03
163	Randy Moffitt	.08	.06	.03
164	Lloyd Moseby	.12	.09	.05
165	Rance Mulliniks	.08	.06	.03
166	Jorge Orta	.08	.06	.03
167	Dave Stieb	.15	.11	.06
168	Willie Upshaw	.10	.08	.04
169	Ernie Whitt	.10	.08	.04
170	Len Barker	.10	.08	.04
171	Steve Bedrosian	.12	.09	.05
172	Bruce Benedict	.08	.06	.03
173	Brett Butler	.10	.08	.04
174	Rick Camp	.08	.06	.03
175	Chris Chambliss	.10	.08	.04
176	Ken Dayley	.08	.06	.03
177	Pete Falcone	.08	.06	.03
178	Terry Forster	.10	.08	.04
179	Gene Garber	.08	.06	.03
180	Terry Harper	.08	.06	.03
181	Bob Horner	.12	.09	.05
182	Glenn Hubbard	.10	.08	.04
183	Randy Johnson	.08	.06	.03
184	*Craig McMurtry*(FC)	.12	.09	.05
185	Donnie Moore(FC)	.10	.08	.04
186	Dale Murphy	1.00	.70	.40
187	Phil Niekro	.30	.25	.12
188	Pascual Perez	.10	.08	.04
189	Biff Pocoroba	.08	.06	.03
190	Rafael Ramirez	.08	.06	.03
191	Jerry Royster	.08	.06	.03
192	Claudell Washington	.10	.08	.04
193	Bob Watson	.10	.08	.04
194	Jerry Augustine	.08	.06	.03
195	Mark Brouhard	.08	.06	.03
196	Mike Caldwell	.08	.06	.03
197	*Tom Candiotti*(FC)	.25	.20	.10
198	Cecil Cooper	.15	.11	.06
199	Rollie Fingers	.25	.20	.10
200	Jim Gantner	.10	.08	.04
201	Bob Gibson	.08	.06	.03
202	Moose Haas	.08	.06	.03
203	Roy Howell	.08	.06	.03
204	Pete Ladd	.08	.06	.03
205	Rick Manning	.08	.06	.03
206	Bob McClure	.08	.06	.03
207	Paul Molitor	.20	.15	.08
208	Don Money	.08	.06	.03
209	Charlie Moore	.08	.06	.03
210	Ben Oglivie	.10	.08	.04
211	Chuck Porter	.08	.06	.03
212	Ed Romero	.08	.06	.03
213	Ted Simmons	.15	.11	.06
214	Jim Slaton	.08	.06	.03
215	Don Sutton	.30	.25	.12
216	Tom Tellmann	.08	.06	.03
217	Pete Vuckovich	.10	.08	.04
218	Ned Yost	.08	.06	.03
219	Robin Yount	1.25	.90	.50
220	Alan Ashby	.08	.06	.03
221	Kevin Bass(FC)	.20	.15	.08
222	Jose Cruz	.12	.09	.05
223	*Bill Dawley*(FC)	.10	.08	.04
224	Frank DiPino	.08	.06	.03
225	*Bill Doran*(FC)	.70	.60	.30
226	Phil Garner	.10	.08	.04
227	Art Howe	.08	.06	.03
228	Bob Knepper	.10	.08	.04
229	Ray Knight	.12	.09	.05
230	Frank LaCorte	.08	.06	.03
231	Mike LaCoss	.08	.06	.03
232	Mike Madden	.08	.06	.03
233	Jerry Mumphrey	.08	.06	.03
235	Terry Puhl	.08	.06	.03
236	Luis Pujols	.08	.06	.03
237	Craig Reynolds	.08	.06	.03
238	Vern Ruhle	.08	.06	.03
239	Nolan Ryan	2.50	2.00	1.00
240	Mike Scott	.20	.15	.08
241	Tony Scott	.08	.06	.03
242	Dave Smith	.10	.08	.04
243	Dickie Thon	.10	.08	.04
244	Denny Walling	.08	.06	.03
245	Dale Berra	.08	.06	.03
246	Jim Bibby	.08	.06	.03
247	John Candelaria	.12	.09	.05
248	*Jose DeLeon*(FC)	.50	.40	.20
249	Mike Easler	.10	.08	.04
250	Cecilio Guante(FC)	.10	.08	.04
251	Richie Hebner	.08	.06	.03
252	Lee Lacy	.08	.06	.03
253	Bill Madlock	.12	.09	.05
254	Milt May	.08	.06	.03
255	Lee Mazzilli	.10	.08	.04
256	Larry McWilliams	.08	.06	.03
257	Jim Morrison	.08	.06	.03
258	Dave Parker	.30	.25	.12
259	Tony Pena	.12	.09	.05
260	Johnny Ray	.12	.09	.05
261	Rick Rhoden	.12	.09	.05
262	Don Robinson	.10	.08	.04
263	Manny Sarmiento	.08	.06	.03
264	Rod Scurry	.08	.06	.03

		MT	NR MT	EX
265	Kent Tekulve	.10	.08	.04
266	Gene Tenace	.10	.08	.04
267	Jason Thompson	.08	.06	.03
268	*Lee Tunnell*(FC)	.10	.08	.04
269	*Marvell Wynne*(FC)	.20	.15	.08
270	Ray Burris	.08	.06	.03
271	Gary Carter	.40	.30	.15
272	Warren Cromartie	.08	.06	.03
273	Andre Dawson	.35	.25	.14
274	Doug Flynn	.08	.06	.03
275	Terry Francona	.08	.06	.03
276	Bill Gullickson	.08	.06	.03
277	Bob James	.08	.06	.03
278	Charlie Lea	.08	.06	.03
279	Bryan Little	.08	.06	.03
280	Al Oliver	.20	.15	.08
281	Tim Raines	.40	.30	.15
282	Bobby Ramos	.08	.06	.03
283	Jeff Reardon	.15	.11	.06
284	Steve Rogers	.10	.08	.04
285	Scott Sanderson	.08	.06	.03
286	Dan Schatzeder	.08	.06	.03
287	Bryn Smith	.08	.06	.03
288	Chris Speier	.08	.06	.03
289	Manny Trillo	.10	.08	.04
290	Mike Vail	.08	.06	.03
291	Tim Wallach	.15	.11	.06
292	Chris Welsh	.08	.06	.03
293	Jim Wohlford	.08	.06	.03
294	Kurt Bevacqua	.08	.06	.03
295	Juan Bonilla	.08	.06	.03
296	Bobby Brown	.08	.06	.03
297	Luis DeLeon	.08	.06	.03
298	Dave Dravecky	.10	.08	.04
299	Tim Flannery	.08	.06	.03
300	Steve Garvey	.50	.40	.20
301	Tony Gwynn	2.00	1.50	.80
302	*Andy Hawkins*(FC)	.40	.30	.15
303	Ruppert Jones	.08	.06	.03
304	Terry Kennedy	.10	.08	.04
305	Tim Lollar	.08	.06	.03
306	Gary Lucas	.08	.06	.03
307	*Kevin McReynolds*(FC)	7.00	5.25	2.75
308	Sid Monge	.08	.06	.03
309	Mario Ramirez	.08	.06	.03
310	Gene Richards	.08	.06	.03
311	Luis Salazar	.08	.06	.03
312	Eric Show	.12	.09	.05
313	Elias Sosa	.08	.06	.03
314	Garry Templeton	.12	.09	.05
315	*Mark Thurmond*(FC)	.10	.08	.04
316	Ed Whitson	.08	.06	.03
317	Alan Wiggins	.08	.06	.03
318	Neil Allen	.08	.06	.03
319	Joaquin Andujar	.10	.08	.04
320	Steve Braun	.08	.06	.03
321	Glenn Brummer	.08	.06	.03
322	Bob Forsch	.10	.08	.04
323	David Green	.08	.06	.03
324	George Hendrick	.10	.08	.04
325	Tom Herr	.12	.09	.05
326	Dane Iorg	.08	.06	.03
327	Jeff Lahti	.08	.06	.03
328	Dave LaPoint	.10	.08	.04
329	Willie McGee	.35	.25	.14
330	Ken Oberkfell	.08	.06	.03
331	Darrell Porter	.10	.08	.04
332	Jamie Quirk	.08	.06	.03
333	Mike Ramsey	.08	.06	.03
334	Floyd Rayford	.08	.06	.03
335	Lonnie Smith	.10	.08	.04
336	Ozzie Smith	.20	.15	.08
337	John Stuper	.08	.06	.03
338	Bruce Sutter	.20	.15	.08
339	*Andy Van Slyke*(FC)	3.00	2.25	1.25
340	Dave Von Ohlen	.08	.06	.03
341	Willie Aikens	.08	.06	.03
342	Mike Armstrong	.08	.06	.03
343	Bud Black	.10	.08	.04
344	George Brett	.70	.50	.30
345	Onix Concepcion	.08	.06	.03
346	Keith Creel	.08	.06	.03
347	Larry Gura	.08	.06	.03
348	Don Hood	.08	.06	.03
349	Dennis Leonard	.10	.08	.04
350	Hal McRae	.12	.09	.05
351	Amos Otis	.12	.09	.05
352	Gaylord Perry	.30	.25	.12
353	Greg Pryor	.08	.06	.03
354	Dan Quisenberry	.12	.09	.05
355	Steve Renko	.08	.06	.03
356	Leon Roberts	.08	.06	.03
357	*Pat Sheridan*(FC)	.15	.11	.06
358	Joe Simpson	.08	.06	.03
359	Don Slaught	.08	.06	.03
360	Paul Splittorff	.08	.06	.03
361	U.L. Washington	.08	.06	.03
362	John Wathan	.10	.08	.04
363	Frank White	.12	.09	.05
364	Willie Wilson	.15	.11	.06
365	Jim Barr	.08	.06	.03
366	Dave Bergman	.08	.06	.03
367	Fred Breining	.08	.06	.03
368	Bob Brenly	.08	.06	.03
369	Jack Clark	.25	.20	.10
370	Chili Davis	.12	.09	.05
371	Mark Davis(FC)	.20	.15	.08
372	Darrell Evans	.15	.11	.06
373	Atlee Hammaker	.08	.06	.03
374	Mike Krukow	.10	.08	.04
375	Duane Kuiper	.08	.06	.03
376	Bill Laskey	.08	.06	.03
377	Gary Lavelle	.08	.06	.03
378	Johnnie LeMaster	.08	.06	.03
379	Jeff Leonard	.12	.09	.05
380	Randy Lerch	.08	.06	.03
381	Renie Martin	.08	.06	.03
382	Andy McGaffigan	.08	.06	.03
383	Greg Minton	.08	.06	.03
384	Tom O'Malley	.08	.06	.03
385	Max Venable	.08	.06	.03
386	Brad Wellman	.08	.06	.03
387	Joel Youngblood	.08	.06	.03
388	Gary Allenson	.08	.06	.03
389	Luis Aponte	.08	.06	.03
390	Tony Armas	.12	.09	.05
391	Doug Bird	.08	.06	.03
392	Wade Boggs	7.00	5.25	2.75
393	*Dennis Boyd*(FC)	.35	.25	.14
394	Mike Brown	.08	.06	.03
395	Mark Clear	.08	.06	.03
396	Dennis Eckersley	.15	.11	.06
397	Dwight Evans	.20	.15	.08
398	Rich Gedman	.10	.08	.04
399	Glenn Hoffman	.08	.06	.03
400	Bruce Hurst	.15	.11	.06
401	John Henry Johnson	.08	.06	.03
402	Ed Jurak	.08	.06	.03
403	Rick Miller	.08	.06	.03
404	Jeff Newman	.08	.06	.03
405	Reid Nichols	.08	.06	.03
406	Bob Ojeda	.12	.09	.05
407	Jerry Remy	.08	.06	.03
408	Jim Rice	.40	.30	.15
409	Bob Stanley	.08	.06	.03
410	Dave Stapleton	.08	.06	.03
411	John Tudor	.12	.09	.05
412	Carl Yastrzemski	.80	.60	.30
413	Buddy Bell	.12	.09	.05
414	Larry Biittner	.08	.06	.03
415	John Butcher	.08	.06	.03
416	Danny Darwin	.08	.06	.03
417	Bucky Dent	.12	.09	.05
418	Dave Hostetler	.08	.06	.03
419	Charlie Hough	.12	.09	.05
420	Bobby Johnson	.08	.06	.03
421	Odell Jones	.08	.06	.03
422	Jon Matlack	.10	.08	.04
423	*Pete O'Brien*(FC)	1.00	.70	.40
424	Larry Parrish	.12	.09	.05
425	Mickey Rivers	.10	.08	.04
426	Billy Sample	.08	.06	.03
427	Dave Schmidt	.08	.06	.03
428	*Mike Smithson*(FC)	.15	.11	.06
429	Bill Stein	.08	.06	.03
430	Dave Stewart	.15	.11	.06
431	Jim Sundberg	.10	.08	.04
432	Frank Tanana	.12	.09	.05
433	Dave Tobik	.08	.06	.03
434	Wayne Tolleson(FC)	.10	.08	.04
435	George Wright	.08	.06	.03
436	Bill Almon	.08	.06	.03
437	*Keith Atherton*(FC)	.20	.15	.08
438	Dave Beard	.08	.06	.03
439	Tom Burgmeier	.08	.06	.03
440	Jeff Burroughs	.10	.08	.04
441	*Chris Codiroli*(FC)	.10	.08	.04
442	*Tim Conroy*(FC)	.12	.09	.05
443	Mike Davis	.10	.08	.04
444	Wayne Gross	.08	.06	.03
445	Garry Hancock	.08	.06	.03
446	Mike Heath	.08	.06	.03
447	Rickey Henderson	1.50	1.25	.60
448	*Don Hill*(FC)	.15	.11	.06
449	Bob Kearney	.08	.06	.03
450	Bill Krueger	.08	.06	.03
451	Rick Langford	.08	.06	.03
452	Carney Lansford	.12	.09	.05
453	Davey Lopes	.10	.08	.04
454	Steve McCatty	.08	.06	.03
455	Dan Meyer	.08	.06	.03
456	Dwayne Murphy	.10	.08	.04
457	Mike Norris	.08	.06	.03
458	Ricky Peters	.08	.06	.03
459	*Tony Phillips*(FC)	.15	.11	.06
460	Tom Underwood	.08	.06	.03
461	Mike Warren	.08	.06	.03
462	Johnny Bench	.80	.60	.30
463	Bruce Berenyi	.08	.06	.03
464	Dann Bilardello	.08	.06	.03
465	Cesar Cedeno	.12	.09	.05
466	Dave Concepcion	.15	.11	.06
467	Dan Driessen	.10	.08	.04
468	*Nick Esasky*(FC)	3.00	2.25	1.25
469	Rich Gale	.08	.06	.03
470	Ben Hayes	.08	.06	.03
471	Paul Householder	.08	.06	.03
472	Tom Hume	.08	.06	.03
473	Alan Knicely	.08	.06	.03
474	Eddie Milner	.08	.06	.03
475	Ron Oester	.08	.06	.03
476	Kelly Paris	.08	.06	.03
477	Frank Pastore	.08	.06	.03
478	Ted Power	.10	.08	.04
479	Joe Price	.08	.06	.03
480	Charlie Puleo	.08	.06	.03
481	*Gary Redus*(FC)	.25	.20	.10
482	Bill Scherrer	.08	.06	.03
483	Mario Soto	.10	.08	.04
484	Alex Trevino	.08	.06	.03
485	Duane Walker	.08	.06	.03
486	Larry Bowa	.15	.11	.06
487	Warren Brusstar	.08	.06	.03
488	Bill Buckner	.15	.11	.06
489	Bill Campbell	.08	.06	.03
490	Ron Cey	.12	.09	.05
491	Jody Davis	.10	.08	.04
492	Leon Durham	.10	.08	.04
493	Mel Hall(FC)	.20	.15	.08
494	Ferguson Jenkins	.20	.15	.08
495	Jay Johnstone	.10	.08	.04
496	*Craig Lefferts*(FC)	.20	.15	.08
497	*Carmelo Martinez*(FC)	.25	.20	.10
498	Jerry Morales	.08	.06	.03
499	Keith Moreland	.10	.08	.04
500	Dickie Noles	.08	.06	.03
501	Mike Proly	.08	.06	.03
502	Chuck Rainey	.08	.06	.03
503	Dick Ruthven	.08	.06	.03
504	Ryne Sandberg	2.50	2.00	1.00
505	Lee Smith	.15	.11	.06
506	Steve Trout	.08	.06	.03
507	Gary Woods	.08	.06	.03
508	Juan Beniquez	.08	.06	.03
509	Bob Boone	.10	.08	.04
510	Rick Burleson	.10	.08	.04
511	Rod Carew	.50	.40	.20
512	Bobby Clark	.08	.06	.03
513	John Curtis	.08	.06	.03
514	Doug DeCinces	.12	.09	.05
515	Brian Downing	.12	.09	.05
516	Tim Foli	.08	.06	.03
517	Ken Forsch	.08	.06	.03
518	Bobby Grich	.12	.09	.05
519	Andy Hassler	.08	.06	.03
520	Reggie Jackson	.80	.60	.30
521	Ron Jackson	.08	.06	.03
522	Tommy John	.25	.20	.10
523	Bruce Kison	.08	.06	.03
524	Steve Lubratich	.08	.06	.03
525	Fred Lynn	.25	.20	.10
526	*Gary Pettis*(FC)	.25	.20	.10
527	Luis Sanchez	.08	.06	.03
528	Daryl Sconiers	.08	.06	.03
529	Ellis Valentine	.08	.06	.03
530	Rob Wilfong	.08	.06	.03
531	Mike Witt	.15	.11	.06
532	Geoff Zahn	.08	.06	.03
533	Bud Anderson	.08	.06	.03
534	Chris Bando	.08	.06	.03
535	Alan Bannister	.08	.06	.03
536	Bert Blyleven	.20	.15	.08
537	Tom Brennan	.08	.06	.03
538	Jamie Easterly	.08	.06	.03
539	Juan Eichelberger	.08	.06	.03
540	Jim Essian	.08	.06	.03
541	Mike Fischlin	.08	.06	.03
542	Julio Franco(FC)	1.75	1.25	.70
543	Mike Hargrove	.08	.06	.03
544	Toby Harrah	.10	.08	.04
545	Ron Hassey	.08	.06	.03
546	*Neal Heaton*(FC)	.15	.11	.06
547	Bake McBride	.08	.06	.03
548	Broderick Perkins	.08	.06	.03
549	Lary Sorensen	.08	.06	.03
550	Dan Spillner	.08	.06	.03
551	Rick Sutcliffe	.15	.11	.06
552	Pat Tabler	.10	.08	.04
553	Gorman Thomas	.10	.08	.04
554	Andre Thornton	.12	.09	.05
555	George Vukovich	.08	.06	.03
556	Darrell Brown	.08	.06	.03
557	Tom Brunansky	.20	.15	.08
558	*Randy Bush*(FC)	.15	.11	.06
559	Bobby Castillo	.08	.06	.03
560	John Castino	.08	.06	.03
561	Ron Davis	.08	.06	.03
562	Dave Engle	.08	.06	.03
563	Lenny Faedo	.08	.06	.03
564	Pete Filson	.08	.06	.03
565	Gary Gaetti	.60	.45	.25
566	Mickey Hatcher	.10	.08	.04
567	Kent Hrbek	.40	.30	.15
568	Rusty Kuntz	.08	.06	.03
569	Tim Laudner	.08	.06	.03
570	Rick Lysander	.08	.06	.03
571	Bobby Mitchell	.08	.06	.03
572	Ken Schrom	.08	.06	.03
573	Ray Smith	.08	.06	.03
574	*Tim Teufel*(FC)	.30	.25	.12
575	Frank Viola	.80	.60	.30
576	Gary Ward	.10	.08	.04
577	Ron Washington	.08	.06	.03
578	Len Whitehouse	.08	.06	.03
579	Al Williams	.08	.06	.03
580	Bob Bailor	.08	.06	.03
581	Mark Bradley	.08	.06	.03
582	Hubie Brooks	.15	.11	.06
583	Carlos Diaz	.08	.06	.03
584	George Foster	.20	.15	.08
585	Brian Giles	.08	.06	.03
586	Danny Heep	.08	.06	.03
587	Keith Hernandez	.40	.30	.15
588	Ron Hodges	.08	.06	.03
589	Scott Holman	.08	.06	.03
590	Dave Kingman	.15	.11	.06
591	Ed Lynch	.08	.06	.03
592	*Jose Oquendo*(FC)	.15	.11	.06
593	Jesse Orosco	.10	.08	.04
594	*Junior Ortiz*(FC)	.10	.08	.04
595	Tom Seaver	.50	.40	.20
596	*Doug Sisk*(FC)	.10	.08	.04
597	Rusty Staub	.12	.09	.05
598	John Stearns	.08	.06	.03
599	*Darryl Strawberry*(FC)	25.00	20.00	10.00
600	Craig Swan	.08	.06	.03
601	*Walt Terrell*(FC)	.30	.25	.12
602	Mike Torrez	.10	.08	.04
603	Mookie Wilson	.12	.09	.05
604	Jamie Allen	.08	.06	.03
605	Jim Beattie	.08	.06	.03
606	Tony Bernazard	.08	.06	.03
607	Manny Castillo	.08	.06	.03
608	Bill Caudill	.08	.06	.03
609	Bryan Clark	.08	.06	.03
610	Al Cowens	.08	.06	.03
611	Dave Henderson	.12	.09	.05
612	Steve Henderson	.08	.06	.03
613	Orlando Mercado	.08	.06	.03
614	Mike Moore	.10	.08	.04
615	Ricky Nelson	.08	.06	.03
616	*Spike Owen*(FC)	.20	.15	.08
617	Pat Putnam	.08	.06	.03
618	Ron Roenicke	.08	.06	.03
619	Mike Stanton	.08	.06	.03
620	Bob Stoddard	.08	.06	.03
621	Rick Sweet	.08	.06	.03
622	Roy Thomas	.08	.06	.03
623	Ed Vande Berg	.08	.06	.03
624	*Matt Young*(FC)	.15	.11	.06
625	Richie Zisk	.10	.08	.04
626	'83 All-Star Game Record Breaker (Fred Lynn)	.12	.09	.05
627	'83 All-Star Game Record Breaker (Manny Trillo)	.10	.08	.04
628	N.L. Iron Man (Steve Garvey)	.20	.15	.08
629	A.L. Batting Runner-Up (Rod Carew)	.25	.20	.10
630	A.L. Batting Champion (Wade Boggs)	.60	.45	.25
631	Letting Go Of The Raines (Tim Raines)	.20	.15	.08

		MT	NR MT	EX
632	Double Trouble (Al Oliver)	.10	.08	.04
633	All-Star Second Base (Steve Sax)	.15	.11	.06
634	All-Star Shortstop (Dickie Thon)	.10	.08	.04
635	Ace Firemen (Tippy Martinez, Dan Quisenberry)	.10	.08	.04
636	Reds Reunited (Joe Morgan, Tony Perez, Pete Rose)	.50	.40	.20
637	Backstop Stars (Bob Boone, Lance Parrish)	.15	.11	.06
638	The Pine Tar Incident, 7/24/83 (George Brett, Gaylord Perry)	.30	.25	.12
639	1983 No-Hitters (Bob Forsch, Dave Righetti, Mike Warren)	.10	.08	.04
640	Retiring Superstars (Johnny Bench, Carl Yastrzemski)	.80	.60	.30
641	Going Out In Style (Gaylord Perry)	.15	.11	.06
642	300 Club & Strikeout Record (Steve Carlton)	.20	.15	.08
643	The Managers (Joe Altobelli, Paul Owens)	.10	.08	.04
644	The MVP (Rick Dempsey)	.10	.08	.04
645	The Rookie Winner (Mike Boddicker)(FC)	.12	.09	.05
646	The Clincher (Scott McGregor)	.10	.08	.04
647	Checklist: Orioles/Royals (Joe Altobelli)	.08	.06	.03
648	Checklist: Phillies/Giants (Paul Owens)	.08	.06	.03
649	Checklist: White Sox/Red Sox (Tony LaRussa)	.08	.06	.03
650	Checklist: Tigers/Rangers (Sparky Anderson)	.08	.06	.03
651	Checklist: Dodgers/A's (Tom Lasorda)	.08	.06	.03
652	Checklist: Yankees/Reds (Billy Martin)	.08	.06	.03
653	Checklist: Blue Jays/Cubs (Bobby Cox)	.08	.06	.03
654	Checklist: Braves/Angels (Joe Torre)	.08	.06	.03
655	Checklist: Brewers/Indians (Rene Lachemann)	.08	.06	.03
656	Checklist: Astros/Twins (Bob Lillis)	.08	.06	.03
657	Checklist: Pirates/Mets (Chuck Tanner)	.08	.06	.03
658	Checklist: Expos/Mariners (Bill Virdon)	.08	.06	.03
659	Checklist: Padres/Specials (Dick Williams)	.08	.06	.03
660	Checklist: Cardinals/Specials (Whitey Herzog)	.08	.06	.03

1984 Fleer Stickers

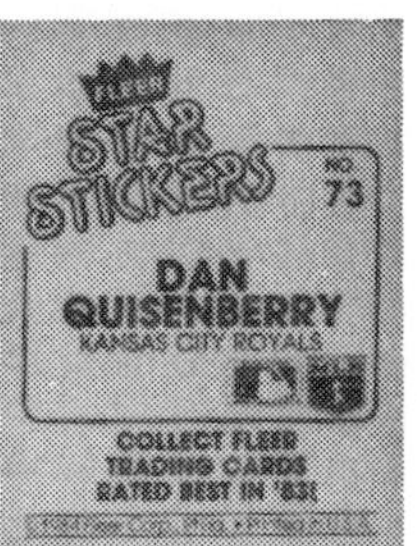

This 126-sticker set was designed to be housed in a special collector's album that was organized according to various league leader categories, resulting in some players being pictured on more than one sticker. Each full-color sticker measures 2-1/2" by 1-15/16" and is framed with a beige border. The stickers, which were sold in packs of six, are numbered on the back.

		MT	NR MT	EX
	Complete Set:	12.00	9.00	4.75
	Common Player:	.03	.02	.01
	Sticker Album:	1.00	.70	.40
1	Dickie Thon	.03	.02	.01
2	Ken Landreaux	.03	.02	.01
3	Darrell Evans	.06	.05	.02
4	Harold Baines	.10	.08	.04
5	Dave Winfield	.20	.15	.08
6	Bill Madlock	.06	.05	.02
7	Lonnie Smith	.03	.02	.01
8	Jose Cruz	.04	.03	.02
9	George Hendrick	.04	.03	.02
10	Ray Knight	.04	.03	.02
11	Wade Boggs	.40	.30	.15
12	Rod Carew	.25	.20	.10
13	Lou Whitaker	.10	.08	.04
14	Alan Trammell	.15	.11	.06
15	Cal Ripken, Jr.	.25	.20	.10
16	Mike Schmidt	.30	.25	.12
17	Dale Murphy	.30	.25	.12
18	Andre Dawson	.15	.11	.06
19	Pedro Guerrero	.12	.09	.05
20	Jim Rice	.20	.15	.08
21	Tony Armas	.03	.02	.01
22	Ron Kittle	.04	.03	.02
23	Eddie Murray	.25	.20	.10
24	Jose Cruz	.04	.03	.02
25	Andre Dawson	.15	.11	.06
26	Rafael Ramirez	.03	.02	.01
27	Al Oliver	.06	.05	.02
28	Wade Boggs	.40	.30	.15
29	Cal Ripken, Jr.	.25	.20	.10
30	Lou Whitaker	.10	.08	.04
31	Cecil Cooper	.08	.06	.03
32	Dale Murphy	.30	.25	.12
33	Andre Dawson	.15	.11	.06
34	Pedro Guerrero	.12	.09	.05
35	Mike Schmidt	.30	.25	.12
36	George Brett	.30	.25	.12
37	Jim Rice	.20	.15	.08
38	Eddie Murray	.25	.20	.10
39	Carlton Fisk	.12	.09	.05
40	Rusty Staub	.06	.05	.02
41	Duane Walker	.03	.02	.01
42	Steve Braun	.03	.02	.01
43	Kurt Bevacqua	.03	.02	.01
44	Hal McRae	.06	.05	.02
45	Don Baylor	.10	.08	.04
46	Ken Singleton	.06	.05	.02
47	Greg Luzinski	.08	.06	.03
48	Mike Schmidt	.30	.25	.12
49	Keith Hernandez	.15	.11	.06
50	Dale Murphy	.30	.25	.12
51	Tim Raines	.20	.15	.08
52	Wade Boggs	.40	.30	.15
53	Rickey Henderson	.25	.20	.10
54	Rod Carew	.25	.20	.10
55	Ken Singleton	.06	.05	.02
56	John Denny	.03	.02	.01
57	John Candelaria	.04	.03	.02
58	Larry McWilliams	.03	.02	.01
59	Pascual Perez	.04	.03	.02
60	Jesse Orosco	.04	.03	.02
61	Moose Haas	.03	.02	.01
62	Richard Dotson	.04	.03	.02
63	Mike Flanagan	.04	.03	.02
64	Scott McGregor	.04	.03	.02
65	Atlee Hammaker	.03	.02	.01
66	Rick Honeycutt	.03	.02	.01
67	Lee Smith	.06	.05	.02
68	Al Holland	.03	.02	.01
69	Greg Minton	.03	.02	.01
70	Bruce Sutter	.08	.06	.03
71	Jeff Reardon	.08	.06	.03
72	Frank DiPino	.03	.02	.01
73	Dan Quisenberry	.06	.05	.02
74	Bob Stanley	.03	.02	.01
75	Ron Davis	.03	.02	.01
76	Bill Caudill	.03	.02	.01
77	Peter Ladd	.03	.02	.01
78	Steve Carlton	.20	.15	.08
79	Mario Soto	.04	.03	.02
80	Larry McWilliams	.03	.02	.01
81	Fernando Valenzuela	.15	.11	.06
82	Nolan Ryan	.20	.15	.08
83	Jack Morris	.12	.09	.05
84	Floyd Bannister	.04	.03	.02
85	Dave Stieb	.06	.05	.02
86	Dave Righetti	.12	.09	.05
87	Rick Sutcliffe	.08	.06	.03
88	Tim Raines	.20	.15	.08
89	Alan Wiggins	.03	.02	.01
90	Steve Sax	.10	.08	.04
91	Mookie Wilson	.04	.03	.02
92	Rickey Henderson	.25	.20	.10
93	Rudy Law	.03	.02	.01
94	Willie Wilson	.08	.06	.03
95	Julio Cruz	.03	.02	.01
96	Johnny Bench	.30	.25	.12
97	Carl Yastrzemski	.35	.25	.14
98	Gaylord Perry	.15	.11	.06
99	Pete Rose	.40	.30	.15
100	Joe Morgan	.12	.09	.05
101	Steve Carlton	.20	.15	.08
102	Jim Palmer	.15	.11	.06
103	Rod Carew	.25	.20	.10
104	Darryl Strawberry	.35	.25	.14
105	Craig McMurtry	.03	.02	.01
106	Mel Hall	.03	.02	.01
107	Lee Tunnell	.03	.02	.01
108	Bill Dawley	.03	.02	.01
109	Ron Kittle	.04	.03	.02
110	Mike Boddicker	.04	.03	.02
111	Julio Franco	.08	.06	.03
112	Daryl Sconiers	.03	.02	.01
113	Neal Heaton	.03	.02	.01
114	John Shelby	.03	.02	.01
115	Rick Dempsey	.03	.02	.01
116	John Lowenstein	.03	.02	.01
117	Jim Dwyer	.03	.02	.01
118	Bo Diaz	.03	.02	.01
119	Pete Rose	.40	.30	.15
120	Joe Morgan	.12	.09	.05
121	Gary Matthews	.04	.03	.02
122	Garry Maddox	.04	.03	.02
123	Paul Owens	.03	.02	.01
124	Tom Lasorda	.06	.05	.02
125	Joe Altobelli	.03	.02	.01
126	Tony LaRussa	.03	.02	.01

1984 Fleer Update

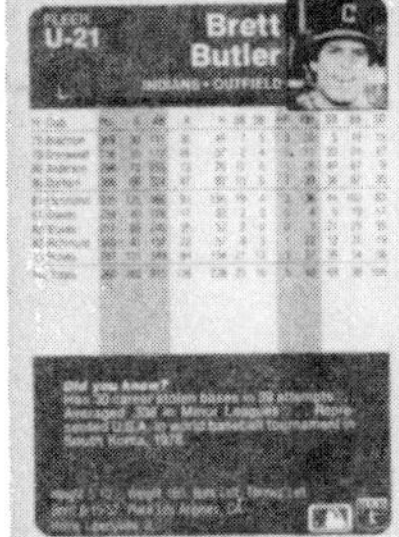

Following the lead of Topps, Fleer issued near the end of the baseball season a 132-card set to update player trades and include rookies not depicted in the regular issue. The cards, which measure 2-1/2" by 3-1/2", are identical in design to the regular issue but are numbered U-1 through U-132. Available to the collecting public only through hobby dealers, the set was printed in limited quantities and has escalated in price quite rapidly the past several years. The set was issued with team logo stickers in a specially designed box.

		MT	NR MT	EX
	Complete Set:	475.00	325.00	175.00
	Common Player:	.15	.11	.06
1	Willie Aikens	.15	.11	.06
2	Luis Aponte	.15	.11	.06
3	Mark Bailey(FC)	.20	.15	.08
4	Bob Bailor	.15	.11	.06
5	Dusty Baker	.30	.25	.12
6	Steve Balboni(FC)	.40	.30	.15
7	Alan Bannister	.15	.11	.06
8	Marty Barrett(FC)	3.00	2.25	1.25
9	Dave Beard	.15	.11	.06
10	Joe Beckwith	.15	.11	.06
11	Dave Bergman	.15	.11	.06
12	Tony Bernazard	.15	.11	.06
13	Bruce Bochte	.15	.11	.06
14	Barry Bonnell	.15	.11	.06
15	Phil Bradley(FC)	4.00	3.00	1.50
16	Fred Breining	.15	.11	.06
17	Mike Brown	.15	.11	.06
18	Bill Buckner	.50	.40	.20
19	Ray Burris	.15	.11	.06
20	John Butcher	.15	.11	.06
21	Brett Butler	.30	.25	.12
22	Enos Cabell	.15	.11	.06
23	Bill Campbell	.15	.11	.06
24	Bill Caudill	.15	.11	.06
25	Bobby Clark	.15	.11	.06
26	Bryan Clark	.15	.11	.06
27	Roger Clemens(FC)	90.00	67.00	35.00
28	Jaime Cocanower	.15	.11	.06
29	Ron Darling(FC)	12.00	9.00	4.75
30	Alvin Davis(FC)	12.00	9.00	4.75
31	Bob Dernier	.15	.11	.06
32	Carlos Diaz	.15	.11	.06
33	Mike Easler	.20	.15	.08
34	Dennis Eckersley	.80	.60	.30
35	Jim Essian	.15	.11	.06
36	Darrell Evans	.60	.45	.25
37	Mike Fitzgerald(FC)	.20	.15	.08
38	Tim Foli	.15	.11	.06
39	John Franco(FC)	7.00	5.25	2.75
40	George Frazier	.15	.11	.06
41	Rich Gale	.15	.11	.06
42	Barbaro Garbey	.20	.15	.08
43	Dwight Gooden(FC)	80.00	60.00	33.00
44	Goose Gossage	1.00	.70	.40
45	Wayne Gross	.15	.11	.06
46	Mark Gubicza(FC)	10.00	7.50	4.00
47	Jackie Gutierrez	.15	.11	.06
48	Toby Harrah	.20	.15	.08
49	Ron Hassey	.15	.11	.06
50	Richie Hebner	.15	.11	.06
51	Willie Hernandez	.40	.30	.15
52	Ed Hodge	.15	.11	.06
53	Ricky Horton(FC)	.70	.50	.30
54	Art Howe	.15	.11	.06
55	Dane Iorg	.15	.11	.06
56	Brook Jacoby(FC)	2.25	1.75	.90
57	Dion James(FC)	.40	.30	.15
58	Mike Jeffcoat(FC)	.20	.15	.08
59	Ruppert Jones	.15	.11	.06
60	Bob Kearney	.15	.11	.06
61	Jimmy Key(FC)	6.00	4.50	2.50
62	Dave Kingman	.70	.50	.30
63	Brad Komminsk(FC)	.20	.15	.08
64	Jerry Koosman	.50	.40	.20
65	Wayne Krenchicki	.15	.11	.06
66	Rusty Kuntz	.15	.11	.06
67	Frank LaCorte	.15	.11	.06
68	Dennis Lamp	.15	.11	.06
69	Tito Landrum	.15	.11	.06
70	Mark Langston(FC)	30.00	22.00	12.00
71	Rick Leach	.15	.11	.06
72	Craig Lefferts(FC)	.30	.25	.12
73	Gary Lucas	.15	.11	.06
74	Jerry Martin	.15	.11	.06
75	Carmelo Martinez	.30	.25	.12
76	Mike Mason(FC)	.20	.15	.08
77	Gary Matthews	.30	.25	.12
78	Andy McGaffigan	.15	.11	.06
79	Joey McLaughlin	.15	.11	.06
80	Joe Morgan	4.00	3.00	1.50
81	Darryl Motley	.15	.11	.06
82	Graig Nettles	1.50	1.25	.60
83	Phil Niekro	2.50	2.00	1.00
84	Ken Oberkfell	.15	.11	.06
85	Al Oliver	.80	.60	.30
86	Jorge Orta	.15	.11	.06
87	Amos Otis	.30	.25	.12
88	Bob Owchinko	.15	.11	.06
89	Dave Parker	2.00	1.50	.80
90	Jack Perconte	.15	.11	.06
91	Tony Perez	1.50	1.25	.60
92	Gerald Perry(FC)	2.25	1.75	.90
93	Kirby Puckett(FC)	150.00	110.00	60.00
94	Shane Rawley	.35	.30	.14
95	Floyd Rayford	.15	.11	.06
96	Ron Reed	.20	.15	.08
97	R.J. Reynolds(FC)	.90	.70	.35
98	Gene Richards	.15	.11	.06
99	Jose Rijo(FC)	2.50	2.00	1.00
100	Jeff Robinson(FC)	1.00	.70	.40
101	Ron Romanick(FC)	.20	.15	.08
102	Pete Rose	25.00	18.50	10.00
103	Bret Saberhagen(FC)	40.00	30.00	15.00
104	Scott Sanderson	.15	.11	.06
105	Dick Schofield(FC)	.40	.30	.15

		MT	NR MT	EX
106	Tom Seaver	10.00	7.50	4.00
107	Jim Slaton	.15	.11	.06
108	Mike Smithson	.20	.15	.08
109	Lary Sorensen	.15	.11	.06
110	Tim Stoddard	.15	.11	.06
111	Jeff Stone(FC)	.30	.25	.12
112	Champ Summers	.15	.11	.06
113	Jim Sundberg	.20	.15	.08
114	Rick Sutcliffe	.80	.60	.30
115	Craig Swan	.15	.11	.06
116	Derrel Thomas	.15	.11	.06
117	Gorman Thomas	.35	.30	.14
118	Alex Trevino	.15	.11	.06
119	Manny Trillo	.20	.15	.08
120	John Tudor	.60	.45	.25
121	Tom Underwood	.15	.11	.06
122	Mike Vail	.15	.11	.06
123	Tom Waddell(FC)	.15	.11	.06
124	Gary Ward	.20	.15	.08
125	Terry Whitfield	.15	.11	.06
126	Curtis Wilkerson	.15	.11	.06
127	Frank Williams(FC)	.35	.25	.14
128	Glenn Wilson	.25	.20	.10
129	John Wockenfuss	.15	.11	.06
130	Ned Yost	.15	.11	.06
131	Mike Young(FC)	.35	.25	.14
132	Checklist 1-132	.15	.11	.06

1985 Fleer

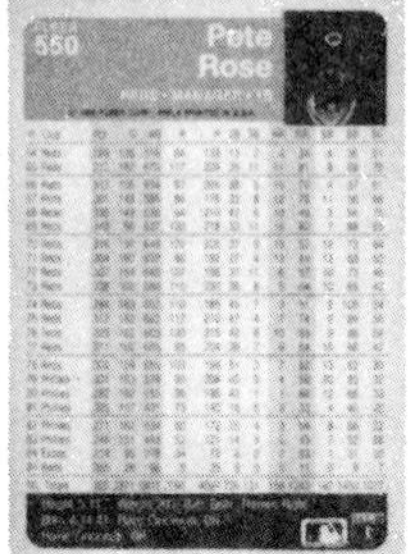

The 1985 Fleer set consists of 660 cards, each measuring 2-1/2" by 3-1/2" in size. The card fronts feature a color photo plus the player's team logo and the word "Fleer." The photos have a color-coded frame which corresponds to the player's team. A grey border surrounds the color-coded frame. The card backs are similar in design to the previous two years, but have two shades of red and black ink on white stock. For the fourth consecutive year, Fleer included special cards and team checklists in the set. Also incorporated in a set for the first time were ten "Major League Prospect" cards, each featuring two rookie hopefuls. The set was issued with team logo stickers.

	MT	NR MT	EX
Complete Set:	125.00	90.00	50.00
Common Player:	.06	.05	.02

		MT	NR MT	EX
1	Doug Bair	.06	.05	.02
2	Juan Berenguer	.06	.05	.02
3	Dave Bergman	.06	.05	.02
4	Tom Brookens	.06	.05	.02
5	Marty Castillo	.06	.05	.02
6	Darrell Evans	.12	.09	.05
7	Barbaro Garbey	.12	.09	.05
8	Kirk Gibson	.35	.25	.14
9	John Grubb	.06	.05	.02
10	Willie Hernandez	.08	.06	.03
11	Larry Herndon	.08	.06	.03
12	Howard Johnson	1.75	1.25	.70
13	Ruppert Jones	.06	.05	.02
14	Rusty Kuntz	.06	.05	.02
15	Chet Lemon	.08	.06	.03
16	Aurelio Lopez	.06	.05	.02
17	Sid Monge	.06	.05	.02
18	Jack Morris	.25	.20	.10
19	Lance Parrish	.30	.25	.12
20	Dan Petry	.08	.06	.03
21	Dave Rozema	.06	.05	.02
22	Bill Scherrer	.06	.05	.02
23	Alan Trammell	.35	.25	.14
24	Lou Whitaker	.35	.25	.14
25	Milt Wilcox	.06	.05	.02
26	Kurt Bevacqua	.06	.05	.02
27	*Greg Booker*(FC)	.15	.11	.06
28	Bobby Brown	.06	.05	.02
29	Luis DeLeon	.06	.05	.02
30	Dave Dravecky	.08	.06	.03
31	Tim Flannery	.06	.05	.02
32	Steve Garvey	.40	.30	.15
33	Goose Gossage	.20	.15	.08
34	Tony Gwynn	1.50	1.25	.60
35	Greg Harris	.06	.05	.02
36	Andy Hawkins	.08	.06	.03
37	Terry Kennedy	.08	.06	.03
38	Craig Lefferts	.08	.06	.03
39	Tim Lollar	.06	.05	.02
40	Carmelo Martinez	.08	.06	.03
41	Kevin McReynolds	1.00	.70	.40
42	Graig Nettles	.15	.11	.06
43	Luis Salazar	.06	.05	.02
44	Eric Show	.08	.06	.03
45	Garry Templeton	.08	.06	.03
46	Mark Thurmond	.06	.05	.02
47	Ed Whitson	.06	.05	.02
48	Alan Wiggins	.06	.05	.02
49	Rich Bordi	.06	.05	.02
50	Larry Bowa	.12	.09	.05
51	Warren Brusstar	.06	.05	.02
52	Ron Cey	.10	.08	.04
53	*Henry Cotto*(FC)	.15	.11	.06
54	Jody Davis	.10	.08	.04
55	Bob Dernier	.06	.05	.02
56	Leon Durham	.08	.06	.03
57	Dennis Eckersley	.12	.09	.05
58	George Frazier	.06	.05	.02
59	Richie Hebner	.06	.05	.02
60	Dave Lopes	.08	.06	.03
61	Gary Matthews	.10	.08	.04
62	Keith Moreland	.08	.06	.03
63	Rick Reuschel	.10	.08	.04
64	Dick Ruthven	.06	.05	.02
65	Ryne Sandberg	.50	.40	.20
66	Scott Sanderson	.06	.05	.02
67	Lee Smith	.10	.08	.04
68	Tim Stoddard	.06	.05	.02
69	Rick Sutcliffe	.12	.09	.05
70	Steve Trout	.06	.05	.02
71	Gary Woods	.06	.05	.02
72	Wally Backman	.08	.06	.03
73	Bruce Berenyi	.06	.05	.02
74	Hubie Brooks	.10	.08	.04
75	Kelvin Chapman	.06	.05	.02
76	Ron Darling	1.25	.90	.50
77	Sid Fernandez(FC)	1.00	.70	.40
78	Mike Fitzgerald	.08	.06	.03
79	George Foster	.15	.11	.06
80	Brent Gaff	.06	.05	.02
81	Ron Gardenhire	.06	.05	.02
82	*Dwight Gooden*	10.00	7.50	4.00
83	Tom Gorman	.06	.05	.02
84	Danny Heep	.06	.05	.02
85	Keith Hernandez	.30	.25	.12
86	Ray Knight	.10	.08	.04
87	Ed Lynch	.06	.05	.02
88	Jose Oquendo	.08	.06	.03
89	Jesse Orosco	.08	.06	.03
90	*Rafael Santana*(FC)	.20	.15	.08
91	Doug Sisk	.06	.05	.02
92	Rusty Staub	.12	.09	.05
93	Darryl Strawberry	4.00	3.00	1.50
94	Walt Terrell	.08	.06	.03
95	Mookie Wilson	.10	.08	.04
96	Jim Acker	.06	.05	.02
97	Willie Aikens	.06	.05	.02
98	Doyle Alexander	.10	.08	.04
99	Jesse Barfield	.25	.20	.10
100	George Bell	.50	.40	.20
101	Jim Clancy	.08	.06	.03
102	Dave Collins	.08	.06	.03
103	Tony Fernandez	.35	.25	.14
104	Damaso Garcia	.06	.05	.02
105	Jim Gott	.06	.05	.02
106	Alfredo Griffin	.08	.06	.03
107	Garth Iorg	.06	.05	.02
108	Roy Lee Jackson	.06	.05	.02
109	Cliff Johnson	.06	.05	.02
110	*Jimmy Key*	1.00	.70	.40
111	Dennis Lamp	.06	.05	.02
112	Rick Leach	.06	.05	.02
113	Luis Leal	.06	.05	.02
114	Buck Martinez	.06	.05	.02
115	Lloyd Moseby	.10	.08	.04
116	Rance Mulliniks	.06	.05	.02
117	Dave Stieb	.12	.09	.05
118	Willie Upshaw	.08	.06	.03
119	Ernie Whitt	.08	.06	.03
120	Mike Armstrong	.06	.05	.02
121	Don Baylor	.12	.09	.05
122	Marty Bystrom	.06	.05	.02
123	Rick Cerone	.06	.05	.02
124	Joe Cowley(FC)	.06	.05	.02
125	Brian Dayett(FC)	.06	.05	.02
126	Tim Foli	.06	.05	.02
127	Ray Fontenot	.06	.05	.02
128	Ken Griffey	.10	.08	.04
129	Ron Guidry	.25	.20	.10
130	Toby Harrah	.08	.06	.03
131	Jay Howell	.08	.06	.03
132	Steve Kemp	.08	.06	.03
133	Don Mattingly	12.00	9.00	4.75
134	Bobby Meacham	.06	.05	.02
135	John Montefusco	.06	.05	.02
136	Omar Moreno	.06	.05	.02
137	Dale Murray	.06	.05	.02
138	Phil Niekro	.25	.20	.10
139	*Mike Pagliarulo*(FC)	.90	.70	.35
140	Willie Randolph	.10	.08	.04
141	Dennis Rasmussen(FC)	.30	.25	.12
142	Dave Righetti	.20	.15	.08
143	*Jose Rijo*	.50	.40	.20
144	Andre Robertson	.06	.05	.02
145	Bob Shirley	.06	.05	.02
146	Dave Winfield	.35	.25	.14
147	Butch Wynegar	.06	.05	.02
148	Gary Allenson	.06	.05	.02
149	Tony Armas	.10	.08	.04
150	Marty Barrett	.20	.15	.08
151	Wade Boggs	3.75	2.75	1.50
152	Dennis Boyd	.10	.08	.04
153	Bill Buckner	.12	.09	.05
154	Mark Clear	.06	.05	.02
155	*Roger Clemens*	12.00	9.00	4.75
156	Steve Crawford	.06	.05	.02
157	Mike Easler	.08	.06	.03
158	Dwight Evans	.12	.09	.05
159	Rich Gedman	.10	.08	.04
160	Jackie Gutierrez	.06	.05	.02
161	Bruce Hurst	.12	.09	.05
162	John Henry Johnson	.06	.05	.02
163	Rick Miller	.06	.05	.02
164	Reid Nichols	.06	.05	.02
165	*Al Nipper*(FC)	.15	.11	.06
166	Bob Ojeda	.10	.08	.04
167	Jerry Remy	.06	.05	.02
168	Jim Rice	.35	.25	.14
169	Bob Stanley	.06	.05	.02
170	Mike Boddicker	.10	.08	.04
171	Al Bumbry	.08	.06	.03
172	Todd Cruz	.06	.05	.02
173	Rich Dauer	.06	.05	.02
174	Storm Davis	.10	.08	.04
175	Rick Dempsey	.08	.06	.03
176	Jim Dwyer	.06	.05	.02
177	Mike Flanagan	.10	.08	.04
178	Dan Ford	.06	.05	.02
179	Wayne Gross	.06	.05	.02
180	John Lowenstein	.06	.05	.02
181	Dennis Martinez	.08	.06	.03
182	Tippy Martinez	.06	.05	.02
183	Scott McGregor	.08	.06	.03
184	Eddie Murray	.50	.40	.20
185	Joe Nolan	.06	.05	.02
186	Floyd Rayford	.06	.05	.02
187	Cal Ripken, Jr.	.50	.40	.20
188	Gary Roenicke	.06	.05	.02
189	Lenn Sakata	.06	.05	.02
190	John Shelby	.08	.06	.03
191	Ken Singleton	.08	.06	.03
192	Sammy Stewart	.06	.05	.02
193	Bill Swaggerty	.06	.05	.02
194	Tom Underwood	.06	.05	.02
195	Mike Young	.12	.09	.05
196	Steve Balboni	.08	.06	.03
197	Joe Beckwith	.06	.05	.02
198	Bud Black	.06	.05	.02
199	George Brett	.50	.40	.20
200	Onix Concepcion	.06	.05	.02
201	*Mark Gubicza*	1.75	1.25	.70
202	Larry Gura	.06	.05	.02
203	Mark Huismann(FC)	.06	.05	.02
204	Dane Iorg	.06	.05	.02
205	Danny Jackson(FC)	1.00	.70	.40
206	Charlie Leibrandt	.08	.06	.03
207	Hal McRae	.10	.08	.04
208	Darryl Motley	.06	.05	.02
209	Jorge Orta	.06	.05	.02
210	Greg Pryor	.06	.05	.02
211	Dan Quisenberry	.10	.08	.04
212	*Bret Saberhagen*	8.00	6.00	3.25
213	Pat Sheridan	.06	.05	.02
214	Don Slaught	.06	.05	.02
215	U.L. Washington	.06	.05	.02
216	John Wathan	.08	.06	.03
217	Frank White	.10	.08	.04
218	Willie Wilson	.12	.09	.05
219	Neil Allen	.06	.05	.02
220	Joaquin Andujar	.08	.06	.03
221	Steve Braun	.06	.05	.02
222	Danny Cox(FC)	.20	.20	.10
223	Bob Forsch	.08	.06	.03
224	David Green	.06	.05	.02
225	George Hendrick	.08	.06	.03
226	Tom Herr	.10	.08	.04
227	*Ricky Horton*	.30	.25	.12
228	Art Howe	.06	.05	.02
229	Mike Jorgensen	.06	.05	.02
230	Kurt Kepshire	.06	.05	.02
231	Jeff Lahti	.06	.05	.02
232	Tito Landrum	.06	.05	.02
233	Dave LaPoint	.08	.06	.03
234	Willie McGee	.30	.25	.12
235	*Tom Nieto*(FC)	.10	.08	.04
236	*Terry Pendleton*(FC)	.70	.50	.30
237	Darrell Porter	.08	.06	.03
238	Dave Rucker	.06	.05	.02
239	Lonnie Smith	.08	.06	.03
240	Ozzie Smith	.15	.11	.06
241	Bruce Sutter	.12	.09	.05
242	Andy Van Slyke	.35	.25	.14
243	Dave Von Ohlen	.06	.05	.02
244	Larry Andersen	.06	.05	.02
245	Bill Campbell	.06	.05	.02
246	Steve Carlton	.40	.30	.15
247	Tim Corcoran	.06	.05	.02
248	Ivan DeJesus	.06	.05	.02
249	John Denny	.06	.05	.02
250	Bo Diaz	.08	.06	.03
251	Greg Gross	.06	.05	.02
252	Kevin Gross	.10	.08	.04
253	Von Hayes	.12	.09	.05
254	Al Holland	.06	.05	.02
255	Charles Hudson	.08	.06	.03
256	Jerry Koosman	.10	.08	.04
257	Joe Lefebvre	.06	.05	.02
258	Sixto Lezcano	.06	.05	.02
259	Garry Maddox	.10	.08	.04
260	Len Matuszek	.06	.05	.02
261	Tug McGraw	.10	.08	.04
262	Al Oliver	.12	.09	.05
263	Shane Rawley	.10	.08	.04
264	Juan Samuel	.30	.25	.12
265	Mike Schmidt	1.00	.70	.40
266	*Jeff Stone*	.12	.09	.05
267	Ozzie Virgil	.06	.05	.02
268	Glenn Wilson	.08	.06	.03
269	John Wockenfuss	.06	.05	.02
270	Darrell Brown	.06	.05	.02
271	Tom Brunansky	.12	.09	.05
272	Randy Bush	.06	.05	.02
273	John Butcher	.06	.05	.02
274	Bobby Castillo	.06	.05	.02
275	Ron Davis	.06	.05	.02
276	Dave Engle	.06	.05	.02
277	Pete Filson	.06	.05	.02
278	Gary Gaetti	.25	.20	.10
279	Mickey Hatcher	.06	.05	.02
280	Ed Hodge	.06	.05	.02
281	Kent Hrbek	.25	.20	.10
282	Houston Jimenez	.06	.05	.02
283	Tim Laudner	.06	.05	.02
284	Rick Lysander	.06	.05	.02
285	Dave Meier	.06	.05	.02
286	*Kirby Puckett*	20.00	15.00	8.00
287	Pat Putnam	.06	.05	.02
288	Ken Schrom	.06	.05	.02
289	Mike Smithson	.06	.05	.02
290	Tim Teufel	.08	.06	.03
291	Frank Viola	.20	.15	.08
292	Ron Washington	.06	.05	.02
293	Don Aase	.06	.05	.02
294	Juan Beniquez	.06	.05	.02

#	Player	MT	NR MT	EX
295	Bob Boone	.08	.06	.03
296	Mike Brown	.06	.05	.02
297	Rod Carew	.40	.30	.15
298	Doug Corbett	.06	.05	.02
299	Doug DeCinces	.10	.08	.04
300	Brian Downing	.10	.08	.04
301	Ken Forsch	.06	.05	.02
302	Bobby Grich	.10	.08	.04
303	Reggie Jackson	.40	.30	.15
304	Tommy John	.20	.15	.08
305	Curt Kaufman	.06	.05	.02
306	Bruce Kison	.06	.05	.02
307	Fred Lynn	.20	.15	.08
308	Gary Pettis	.08	.06	.03
309	*Ron Romanick*	.10	.08	.04
310	Luis Sanchez	.06	.05	.02
311	Dick Schofield	.12	.09	.05
312	Daryl Sconiers	.06	.05	.02
313	Jim Slaton	.06	.05	.02
314	Derrel Thomas	.06	.05	.02
315	Rob Wilfong	.06	.05	.02
316	Mike Witt	.12	.09	.05
317	Geoff Zahn	.06	.05	.02
318	Len Barker	.08	.06	.03
319	Steve Bedrosian	.12	.09	.05
320	Bruce Benedict	.06	.05	.02
321	Rick Camp	.06	.05	.02
322	Chris Chambliss	.08	.06	.03
323	*Jeff Dedmon*(FC)	.12	.09	.05
324	Terry Forster	.08	.06	.03
325	Gene Garber	.06	.05	.02
326	*Albert Hall*(FC)	.15	.11	.06
327	Terry Harper	.06	.05	.02
328	Bob Horner	.12	.09	.05
329	Glenn Hubbard	.06	.05	.02
330	Randy Johnson	.06	.05	.02
331	Brad Komminsk	.06	.05	.02
332	Rick Mahler	.06	.05	.02
333	Craig McMurtry	.06	.05	.02
334	Donnie Moore	.06	.05	.02
335	Dale Murphy	.60	.45	.25
336	Ken Oberkfell	.06	.05	.02
337	Pascual Perez	.08	.06	.03
338	Gerald Perry	.35	.25	.14
339	Rafael Ramirez	.06	.05	.02
340	Jerry Royster	.06	.05	.02
341	Alex Trevino	.06	.05	.02
342	Claudell Washington	.08	.06	.03
343	Alan Ashby	.06	.05	.02
344	*Mark Bailey*	.10	.08	.04
345	Kevin Bass	.10	.08	.04
346	Enos Cabell	.06	.05	.02
347	Jose Cruz	.10	.08	.04
348	Bill Dawley	.06	.05	.02
349	Frank DiPino	.06	.05	.02
350	Bill Doran	.12	.09	.05
351	Phil Garner	.08	.06	.03
352	Bob Knepper	.08	.06	.03
353	Mike LaCoss	.06	.05	.02
354	Jerry Mumphrey	.06	.05	.02
355	Joe Niekro	.10	.08	.04
356	Terry Puhl	.06	.05	.02
357	Craig Reynolds	.06	.05	.02
358	Vern Ruhle	.06	.05	.02
359	Nolan Ryan	.60	.45	.25
360	Joe Sambito	.06	.05	.02
361	Mike Scott	.15	.11	.06
362	Dave Smith	.08	.06	.03
363	*Julio Solano*(FC)	.08	.06	.03
364	Dickie Thon	.08	.06	.03
365	Denny Walling	.06	.05	.02
366	Dave Anderson	.06	.05	.02
367	Bob Bailor	.06	.05	.02
368	Greg Brock	.08	.06	.03
369	Carlos Diaz	.06	.05	.02
370	Pedro Guerrero	.25	.20	.10
371	*Orel Hershiser*(FC)	10.00	7.50	4.00
372	Rick Honeycutt	.06	.05	.02
373	Burt Hooton	.08	.06	.03
374	*Ken Howell*(FC)	.15	.11	.06
375	Ken Landreaux	.08	.06	.03
376	Candy Maldonado	.10	.08	.04
377	Mike Marshall	.15	.11	.06
378	Tom Niedenfuer	.08	.06	.03
379	Alejandro Pena	.08	.06	.03
380	Jerry Reuss	.08	.06	.03
381	*R.J. Reynolds*	.25	.20	.10
382	German Rivera	.06	.05	.02
383	Bill Russell	.08	.06	.03
384	Steve Sax	.20	.15	.08
385	Mike Scioscia	.08	.06	.03
386	*Franklin Stubbs*(FC)	.25	.20	.10
387	Fernando Valenzuela	.35	.25	.14
388	Bob Welch	.12	.09	.05
389	Terry Whitfield	.06	.05	.02
390	Steve Yeager	.06	.05	.02
391	Pat Zachry	.06	.05	.02
392	Fred Breining	.06	.05	.02
393	Gary Carter	.35	.25	.14
394	Andre Dawson	.30	.25	.12
395	Miguel Dilone	.06	.05	.02
396	Dan Driessen	.08	.06	.03
397	Doug Flynn	.06	.05	.02
398	Terry Francona	.06	.05	.02
399	Bill Gullickson	.06	.05	.02
400	Bob James	.06	.05	.02
401	Charlie Lea	.06	.05	.02
402	Bryan Little	.06	.05	.02
403	Gary Lucas	.06	.05	.02
404	David Palmer	.06	.05	.02
405	Tim Raines	.35	.25	.14
406	Mike Ramsey	.06	.05	.02
407	Jeff Reardon	.12	.09	.05
408	Steve Rogers	.08	.06	.03
409	Dan Schatzeder	.06	.05	.02
410	Bryn Smith	.06	.05	.02
411	Mike Stenhouse	.06	.05	.02
412	Tim Wallach	.12	.09	.05
413	Jim Wohlford	.06	.05	.02
414	Bill Almon	.06	.05	.02
415	Keith Atherton	.06	.05	.02
416	Bruce Bochte	.06	.05	.02
417	Tom Burgmeier	.06	.05	.02
418	Ray Burris	.06	.05	.02

#	Player	MT	NR MT	EX
419	Bill Caudill	.06	.05	.02
420	Chris Codiroli	.06	.05	.02
421	Tim Conroy	.06	.05	.02
422	Mike Davis	.08	.06	.03
423	Jim Essian	.06	.05	.02
424	Mike Heath	.06	.05	.02
425	Rickey Henderson	.50	.40	.20
426	Donnie Hill	.06	.05	.02
427	Dave Kingman	.15	.11	.06
428	Bill Krueger	.06	.05	.02
429	Carney Lansford	.10	.08	.04
430	Steve McCatty	.06	.05	.02
431	Joe Morgan	.30	.25	.12
432	Dwayne Murphy	.08	.06	.03
433	Tony Phillips	.06	.05	.02
434	Lary Sorensen	.06	.05	.02
435	Mike Warren	.06	.05	.02
436	*Curt Young*(FC)	.35	.25	.14
437	Luis Aponte	.06	.05	.02
438	Chris Bando	.06	.05	.02
439	Tony Bernazard	.06	.05	.02
440	Bert Blyleven	.15	.11	.06
441	Brett Butler	.10	.08	.04
442	Ernie Camacho	.06	.05	.02
443	Joe Carter(FC)	3.50	2.75	1.50
444	Carmelo Castillo	.06	.05	.02
445	Jamie Easterly	.06	.05	.02
446	*Steve Farr*(FC)	.30	.25	.12
447	Mike Fischlin	.06	.05	.02
448	Julio Franco	.12	.09	.05
449	Mel Hall	.08	.06	.03
450	Mike Hargrove	.06	.05	.02
451	Neal Heaton	.06	.05	.02
452	Brook Jacoby	.30	.25	.12
453	*Mike Jeffcoat*	.08	.06	.03
454	*Don Schulze*(FC)	.08	.06	.03
455	Roy Smith	.06	.05	.02
456	Pat Tabler	.08	.06	.03
457	Andre Thornton	.10	.08	.04
458	George Vukovich	.06	.05	.02
459	Tom Waddell	.06	.05	.02
460	Jerry Willard	.06	.05	.02
461	Dale Berra	.06	.05	.02
462	John Candelaria	.10	.08	.04
463	Jose DeLeon	.08	.06	.03
464	Doug Frobel	.06	.05	.02
465	Cecilio Guante	.06	.05	.02
466	Brian Harper	.06	.05	.02
467	Lee Lacy	.06	.05	.02
468	Bill Madlock	.12	.09	.05
469	Lee Mazzilli	.08	.06	.03
470	Larry McWilliams	.06	.05	.02
471	Jim Morrison	.06	.05	.02
472	Tony Pena	.10	.08	.04
473	Johnny Ray	.12	.09	.05
474	Rick Rhoden	.10	.08	.04
475	Don Robinson	.08	.06	.03
476	Rod Scurry	.06	.05	.02
477	Kent Tekulve	.08	.06	.03
478	Jason Thompson	.06	.05	.02
479	John Tudor	.10	.08	.04
480	Lee Tunnell	.06	.05	.02
481	Marvell Wynne	.06	.05	.02
482	Salome Barojas	.06	.05	.02
483	Dave Beard	.06	.05	.02
484	Jim Beattie	.06	.05	.02
485	Barry Bonnell	.06	.05	.02
486	*Phil Bradley*	.90	.70	.35
487	Al Cowens	.06	.05	.02
488	*Alvin Davis*	3.00	2.25	1.25
489	Dave Henderson	.10	.08	.04
490	Steve Henderson	.06	.05	.02
491	Bob Kearney	.06	.05	.02
492	*Mark Langston*	4.00	3.00	1.50
493	Larry Milbourne	.06	.05	.02
494	Paul Mirabella	.06	.05	.02
495	Mike Moore	.06	.05	.02
496	Edwin Nunez(FC)	.08	.06	.03
497	Spike Owen	.08	.06	.03
498	Jack Perconte	.06	.05	.02
499	Ken Phelps	.10	.08	.04
500	*Jim Presley*(FC)	1.00	.70	.40
501	Mike Stanton	.06	.05	.02
502	Bob Stoddard	.06	.05	.02
503	Gorman Thomas	.10	.08	.04
504	Ed Vande Berg	.06	.05	.02
505	Matt Young	.06	.05	.02
506	Juan Agosto	.06	.05	.02
507	Harold Baines	.15	.11	.06
508	Floyd Bannister	.10	.08	.04
509	Britt Burns	.06	.05	.02
510	Julio Cruz	.06	.05	.02
511	Richard Dotson	.10	.08	.04
512	Jerry Dybzinski	.06	.05	.02
513	Carlton Fisk	.30	.25	.12
514	Scott Fletcher	.08	.06	.03
515	Jerry Hairston	.06	.05	.02
516	Marc Hill	.06	.05	.02
517	LaMarr Hoyt	.06	.05	.02
518	Ron Kittle	.10	.08	.04
519	Rudy Law	.06	.05	.02
520	Vance Law	.08	.06	.03
521	Greg Luzinski	.10	.08	.04
522	Gene Nelson	.06	.05	.02
523	Tom Paciorek	.06	.05	.02
524	Ron Reed	.06	.05	.02
525	Bert Roberge	.06	.05	.02
526	Tom Seaver	.40	.30	.15
527	Roy Smalley	.06	.05	.02
528	Dan Spillner	.06	.05	.02
529	Mike Squires	.06	.05	.02
530	Greg Walker	.12	.09	.05
531	Cesar Cedeno	.10	.08	.04
532	Dave Concepcion	.12	.09	.05
533	*Eric Davis*(FC)	18.00	13.50	7.25
534	Nick Esasky	.08	.06	.03
535	Tom Foley	.06	.05	.02
536	*John Franco*	1.00	.70	.40
537	Brad Gulden	.06	.05	.02
538	Tom Hume	.06	.05	.02
539	Wayne Krenchicki	.06	.05	.02
540	Andy McGaffigan	.06	.05	.02
541	Eddie Milner	.06	.05	.02
542	Ron Oester	.06	.05	.02

#	Player	MT	NR MT	EX
543	Bob Owchinko	.06	.05	.02
544	Dave Parker	.25	.20	.10
545	Frank Pastore	.06	.05	.02
546	Tony Perez	.15	.11	.06
547	Ted Power	.06	.05	.02
548	Joe Price	.06	.05	.02
549	Gary Redus	.08	.06	.03
550	Pete Rose	1.00	.70	.40
551	Jeff Russell(FC)	.10	.08	.04
552	Mario Soto	.08	.06	.03
553	*Jay Tibbs*(FC)	.15	.11	.06
554	Duane Walker	.06	.05	.02
555	Alan Bannister	.06	.05	.02
556	Buddy Bell	.12	.09	.05
557	Danny Darwin	.06	.05	.02
558	Charlie Hough	.08	.06	.03
559	Bobby Jones	.06	.05	.02
560	Odell Jones	.06	.05	.02
561	*Jeff Kunkel*(FC)	.10	.08	.04
562	*Mike Mason*	.10	.08	.04
563	Pete O'Brien	.12	.09	.05
564	Larry Parrish	.10	.08	.04
565	Mickey Rivers	.08	.06	.03
566	Billy Sample	.06	.05	.02
567	Dave Schmidt	.06	.05	.02
568	Donnie Scott	.06	.05	.02
569	Dave Stewart	.12	.09	.05
570	Frank Tanana	.10	.08	.04
571	Wayne Tolleson	.06	.05	.02
572	Gary Ward	.08	.06	.03
573	Curtis Wilkerson	.08	.06	.03
574	George Wright	.06	.05	.02
575	Ned Yost	.06	.05	.02
576	Mark Brouhard	.06	.05	.02
577	Mike Caldwell	.06	.05	.02
578	Bobby Clark	.06	.05	.02
579	Jaime Cocanower	.06	.05	.02
580	Cecil Cooper	.15	.11	.06
581	Rollie Fingers	.20	.15	.08
582	Jim Gantner	.08	.06	.03
583	Moose Haas	.06	.05	.02
584	Dion James	.12	.09	.05
585	Pete Ladd	.06	.05	.02
586	Rick Manning	.06	.05	.02
587	Bob McClure	.06	.05	.02
588	Paul Molitor	.15	.11	.06
589	Charlie Moore	.06	.05	.02
590	Ben Oglivie	.08	.06	.03
591	Chuck Porter	.06	.05	.02
592	*Randy Ready*(FC)	.20	.15	.08
593	Ed Romero	.06	.05	.02
594	Bill Schroeder(FC)	.10	.08	.04
595	Ray Searage	.06	.05	.02
596	Ted Simmons	.12	.09	.05
597	Jim Sundberg	.08	.06	.03
598	Don Sutton	.30	.25	.12
599	Tom Tellmann	.06	.05	.02
600	Rick Waits	.06	.05	.02
601	Robin Yount	.70	.50	.30
602	Dusty Baker	.08	.06	.03
603	Bob Brenly	.06	.05	.02
604	Jack Clark	.20	.15	.08
605	Chili Davis	.10	.08	.04
606	Mark Davis	.06	.05	.02
607	*Dan Gladden*(FC)	.50	.40	.20
608	Atlee Hammaker	.06	.05	.02
609	Mike Krukow	.08	.06	.03
610	Duane Kuiper	.06	.05	.02
611	Bob Lacey	.06	.05	.02
612	Bill Laskey	.06	.05	.02
613	Gary Lavelle	.06	.05	.02
614	Johnnie LeMaster	.06	.05	.02
615	Jeff Leonard	.10	.08	.04
616	Randy Lerch	.06	.05	.02
617	Greg Minton	.06	.05	.02
618	Steve Nicosia	.06	.05	.02
619	Gene Richards	.06	.05	.02
620	*Jeff Robinson*	.30	.25	.12
621	Scot Thompson	.06	.05	.02
622	Manny Trillo	.08	.06	.03
623	Brad Wellman	.06	.05	.02
624	*Frank Williams*	.15	.11	.06
625	Joel Youngblood	.06	.05	.02
626	Ripken-In-Action (Cal Ripken)	.30	.25	.12
627	Schmidt-In-Action (Mike Schmidt)	.30	.25	.12
628	Giving the Signs (Sparky Anderson)	.08	.06	.03
629	A.L. Pitcher's Nightmare (Rickey Henderson, Dave Winfield)	.30	.25	.12
630	N.L. Pitcher's Nightmare (Ryne Sandberg, Mike Schmidt)	.30	.25	.12
631	N.L. All-Stars (Gary Carter, Steve Garvey, Ozzie Smith, Darryl Strawberry)	.30	.25	.12
632	All-Star Game Winning Battery (Gary Carter, Charlie Lea)	.15	.11	.06
633	N.L. Pennant Clinchers (Steve Garvey, Goose Gossage)	.20	.15	.08
634	N.L. Rookie Phenoms (Dwight Gooden, Juan Samuel)	1.00	.70	.40
635	Toronto's Big Guns (Willie Upshaw)	.08	.06	.03
636	Toronto's Big Guns (Lloyd Moseby)	.08	.06	.03
637	Holland (Al Holland)	.08	.06	.03
638	Tunnell (Lee Tunnell)	.08	.06	.03
639	500th Homer (Reggie Jackson)	.30	.25	.12
640	4,000th Hit (Pete Rose)	.50	.40	.20
641	Father & Son (Cal Ripken, Jr., Cal Ripken, Sr.)	.30	.25	.12
642	Cubs Team	.08	.06	.03
643	1984's Two Perfect Games & One No Hitter (Jack Morris, David Palmer, Mike Witt)	.15	.11	.06
644	Major League Prospect (Willie Lozado, Vic Mata)	.06	.05	.02
645	Major League Prospect (*Kelly Gruber, Randy O'Neal*)(FC)	2.75	2.00	1.00
646	Major League Prospect (*Jose Roman, Joel Skinner*)(FC)	.12	.09	.05
647	Major League Prospect (*Steve Kiefer, Danny Tartabull*)(FC)	5.00	3.75	2.00

		MT	NR MT	EX
648	Major League Prospect *(Rob Deer, Alejandro Sanchez)*(FC)	1.50	1.25	.60
649	Major League Prospect *(Shawon Dunston, Bill Hatcher)*(FC)	2.75	2.00	1.00
650	Major League Prospect *(Mike Bielecki, Ron Robinson)*(FC)	.30	.25	.12
651	Major League Prospect *(Zane Smith, Paul Zuvella)*(FC)	.35	.25	.14
652	Major League Prospect *(Glenn Davis, Joe Hesketh)*(FC)	10.00	7.50	4.00
653	Major League Prospect *(Steve Jeltz, John Russell)*(FC)	.20	.15	.08
654	Checklist 1-95	.06	.05	.02
655	Checklist 96-195	.06	.05	.02
656	Checklist 196-292	.06	.05	.02
657	Checklist 293-391	.06	.05	.02
658	Checklist 392-481	.06	.05	.02
659	Checklist 482-575	.06	.05	.02
660	Checklist 576-660	.06	.05	.02

1985 Fleer Limited Edition

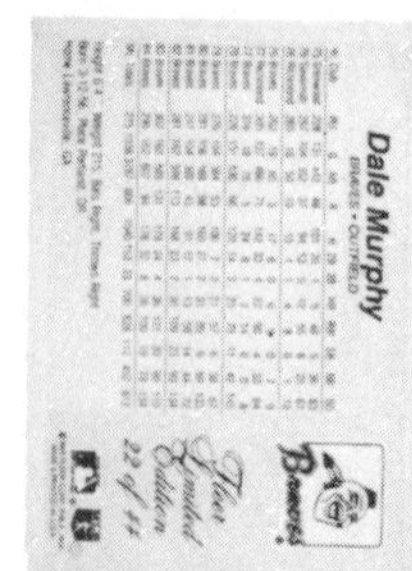

The 1985 Fleer Limited Edition 44-card set was distributed through McCrory's, J.J. Newbury, McClellan, Kress, YDC, and Green stores. The cards, which are the standard 2-1/2" by 3-1/2" size, have full-color photos inside a red and yellow frame. The card backs are set in black type against two different shades of yellow and contain the player's personal and statistical information. The set was issued in a specially designed box which carried the complete checklist for the set on the back. Six team logo stickers were also included with the set.

		MT	NR MT	EX
Complete Set:		8.00	6.00	3.25
Common Player:		.05	.04	.02
1	Buddy Bell	.07	.05	.03
2	Bert Blyleven	.10	.08	.04
3	Wade Boggs	.70	.50	.30
4	George Brett	.30	.25	.12
5	Rod Carew	.30	.25	.12
6	Steve Carlton	.25	.20	.10
7	Alvin Davis	.20	.15	.08
8	Andre Dawson	.15	.11	.06
9	Steve Garvey	.25	.20	.10
10	Goose Gossage	.12	.09	.05
11	Tony Gwynn	.40	.30	.15
12	Keith Hernandez	.20	.15	.08
13	Kent Hrbek	.15	.11	.06
14	Reggie Jackson	.30	.25	.12
15	Dave Kingman	.10	.08	.04
16	Ron Kittle	.07	.05	.03
17	Mark Langston	.25	.20	.10
18	Jeff Leonard	.05	.04	.02
19	Bill Madlock	.07	.05	.03
20	Don Mattingly	1.50	1.25	.60
21	Jack Morris	.15	.11	.06
22	Dale Murphy	.30	.25	.12
23	Eddie Murray	.25	.20	.10
24	Tony Pena	.07	.05	.03
25	Dan Quisenberry	.07	.05	.03
26	Tim Raines	.25	.20	.10
27	Jim Rice	.25	.20	.10
28	Cal Ripken, Jr.	.30	.25	.12
29	Pete Rose	.60	.45	.25
30	Nolan Ryan	.70	.50	.30
31	Ryne Sandberg	.20	.15	.08
32	Steve Sax	.15	.11	.06
33	Mike Schmidt	.50	.40	.20
34	Tom Seaver	.50	.40	.20
35	Ozzie Smith	.12	.09	.05
36	Mario Soto	.05	.04	.02
37	Dave Stieb	.10	.08	.04
38	Darryl Strawberry	.60	.45	.25
39	Rick Sutcliffe	.10	.08	.04
40	Alan Trammell	.20	.15	.08
41	Willie Upshaw	.05	.04	.02
42	Fernando Valenzuela	.20	.15	.08
43	Dave Winfield	.25	.20	.10
44	Robin Yount	.50	.40	.20

1985 Fleer Stickers

The 1985 Fleer sticker set consists of 126 player stickers, each measuring 2-1/2" by 1-15/16". Numbered on the back, the stickers were designed to be put in a special album.

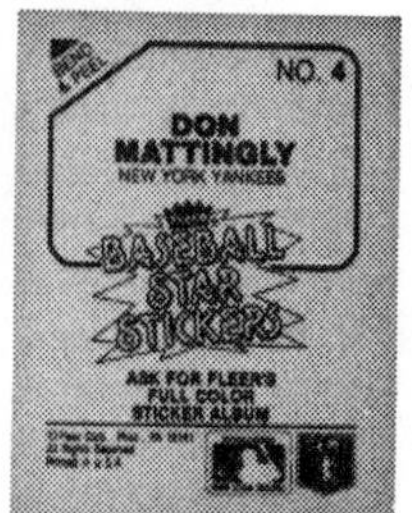

		MT	NR MT	EX
Complete Set:		15.00	11.00	6.00
Common Player:		.03	.02	.01
Sticker Album:		1.00	.70	.40
1	Pete Rose	.40	.30	.15
2	Pete Rose	.30	.25	.12
3	Pete Rose	.30	.25	.12
4	Don Mattingly	.90	.70	.35
5	Dave Winfield	.20	.15	.08
6	Wade Boggs	.50	.40	.20
7	Buddy Bell	.06	.05	.02
8	Tony Gwynn	.25	.20	.10
9	Lee Lacy	.03	.02	.01
10	Chili Davis	.06	.05	.02
11	Ryne Sandberg	.15	.11	.06
12	Tony Armas	.04	.03	.02
13	Jim Rice	.20	.15	.08
14	Dave Kingman	.06	.05	.02
15	Alvin Davis	.12	.09	.05
16	Gary Carter	.20	.15	.08
17	Mike Schmidt	.30	.25	.12
18	Dale Murphy	.30	.25	.12
19	Ron Cey	.06	.05	.02
20	Eddie Murray	.25	.20	.10
21	Harold Baines	.10	.08	.04
22	Kirk Gibson	.15	.11	.06
23	Jim Rice	.20	.15	.08
24	Gary Matthews	.06	.05	.02
25	Keith Hernandez	.15	.11	.06
26	Gary Carter	.20	.15	.08
27	George Hendrick	.04	.03	.02
28	Tony Armas	.04	.03	.02
29	Dave Kingman	.06	.05	.02
30	Dwayne Murphy	.04	.03	.02
31	Lance Parrish	.12	.09	.05
32	Andre Thornton	.04	.03	.02
33	Dale Murphy	.30	.25	.12
34	Mike Schmidt	.30	.25	.12
35	Gary Carter	.20	.15	.08
36	Darryl Strawberry	.30	.25	.12
37	Don Mattingly	.90	.70	.35
38	Larry Parrish	.04	.03	.02
39	George Bell	.20	.15	.08
40	Dwight Evans	.06	.05	.02
41	Cal Ripken, Jr.	.25	.20	.10
42	Tim Raines	.20	.15	.08
43	Johnny Ray	.06	.05	.02
44	Juan Samuel	.08	.06	.03
45	Ryne Sandberg	.15	.11	.06
46	Mike Easler	.04	.03	.02
47	Andre Thornton	.04	.03	.02
48	Dave Kingman	.06	.05	.02
49	Don Baylor	.08	.06	.03
50	Rusty Staub	.06	.05	.02
51	Steve Braun	.03	.02	.01
52	Kevin Bass	.06	.05	.02
53	Greg Gross	.03	.02	.01
54	Rickey Henderson	.25	.20	.10
55	Dave Collins	.03	.02	.01
56	Brett Butler	.04	.03	.02
57	Gary Pettis	.04	.03	.02
58	Tim Raines	.20	.15	.08
59	Juan Samuel	.08	.06	.03
60	Alan Wiggins	.03	.02	.01
61	Lonnie Smith	.03	.02	.01
62	Eddie Murray	.25	.20	.10
63	Eddie Murray	.25	.20	.10
64	Eddie Murray	.25	.20	.10
65	Eddie Murray	.25	.20	.10
66	Eddie Murray	.25	.20	.10
67	Eddie Murray	.25	.20	.10
68	Tom Seaver	.20	.15	.08
69	Tom Seaver	.20	.15	.08
70	Tom Seaver	.20	.15	.08
71	Tom Seaver	.20	.15	.08
72	Tom Seaver	.20	.15	.08
73	Tom Seaver	.20	.15	.08
74	Mike Schmidt	.30	.25	.12
75	Mike Schmidt	.30	.25	.12
76	Mike Schmidt	.30	.25	.12
77	Mike Schmidt	.30	.25	.12
78	Mike Schmidt	.30	.25	.12
79	Mike Schmidt	.30	.25	.12
80	Mike Boddicker	.04	.03	.02
81	Bert Blyleven	.08	.06	.03
82	Jack Morris	.12	.09	.05
83	Dan Petry	.04	.03	.02
84	Frank Viola	.06	.05	.02
85	Joaquin Andujar	.04	.03	.02
86	Mario Soto	.04	.03	.02
87	Dwight Gooden	.60	.45	.25
88	Joe Niekro	.06	.05	.02
89	Rick Sutcliffe	.08	.06	.03
90	Mike Boddicker	.04	.03	.02
91	Dave Stieb	.06	.05	.02
92	Bert Blyleven	.08	.06	.03
93	Phil Niekro	.12	.09	.05
94	Alejandro Pena	.03	.02	.01
95	Dwight Gooden	.60	.45	.25
96	Orel Hershiser	.15	.11	.06
97	Rick Rhoden	.04	.03	.02
98	John Candelaria	.04	.03	.02
99	Dan Quisenberry	.06	.05	.02
100	Bil Caudill	.03	.02	.01
101	Willie Hernandez	.04	.03	.02
102	Dave Righetti	.10	.08	.04
103	Ron Davis	.03	.02	.01
104	Bruce Sutter	.08	.06	.03
105	Lee Smith	.06	.05	.02
106	Jesse Orosco	.04	.03	.02
107	Al Holland	.03	.02	.01
108	Goose Gossage	.08	.06	.03
109	Mark Langston	.10	.08	.04
110	Dave Stieb	.06	.05	.02
111	Mike Witt	.06	.05	.02
112	Bert Blyleven	.08	.06	.03
113	Dwight Gooden	.60	.45	.25
114	Fernando Valenzuela	.15	.11	.06
115	Nolan Ryan	.15	.11	.06
116	Mario Soto	.04	.03	.02
117	Ron Darling	.08	.06	.03
118	Dan Gladden	.04	.03	.02
119	Jeff Stone	.04	.03	.02
120	John Franco	.06	.05	.02
121	Barbaro Garbey	.03	.02	.01
122	Kirby Puckett	.20	.15	.08
123	Roger Clemens	.60	.45	.25
124	Bret Saberhagen	.20	.15	.08
125	Sparky Anderson	.03	.02	.01
126	Dick Williams	.03	.02	.01

1985 Fleer Update

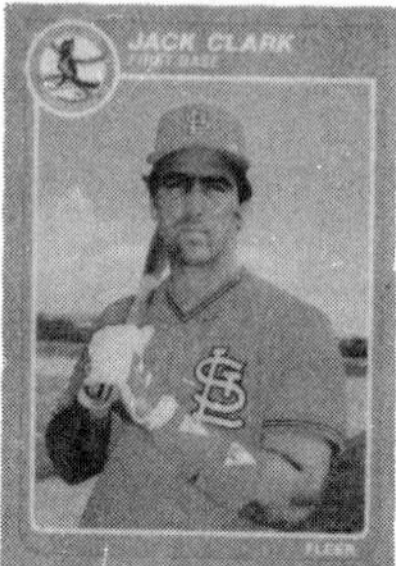

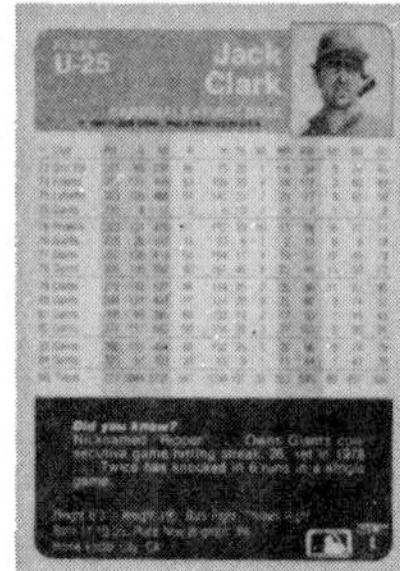

For the second straight year, Fleer issued a 132- card update set. The cards, which measure 2-1/2" by 3-1/2", portray players on their new teams and also includes rookies not depicted in the regular issue. The cards are identical in design to the 1985 Fleer set but are numbered U-1 through U-132. The set was issued with team logo stickers in a specially designed box and was available only through hobby dealers.

		MT	NR MT	EX
Complete Set:		16.00	12.00	6.50
Common Player:		.10	.08	.04
1	Don Aase	.15	.11	.06
2	Bill Almon	.10	.08	.04
3	Dusty Baker	.15	.11	.06
4	Dale Berra	.10	.08	.04
5	Karl Best(FC)	.10	.08	.04
6	Tim Birtsas(FC)	.20	.15	.08
7	Vida Blue	.20	.15	.08
8	Rich Bordi	.10	.08	.04
9	Daryl Boston(FC)	.20	.15	.08
10	Hubie Brooks	.20	.15	.08
11	Chris Brown(FC)	.25	.20	.10
12	Tom Browning(FC)	1.25	.90	.50
13	Al Bumbry	.10	.08	.04
14	Tim Burke(FC)	.50	.40	.20
15	Ray Burris	.10	.08	.04
16	Jeff Burroughs	.15	.11	.06
17	Ivan Calderon(FC)	.60	.45	.25
18	Jeff Calhoun	.10	.08	.04
19	Bill Campbell	.10	.08	.04
20	Don Carman(FC)	.40	.30	.15
21	Gary Carter	.80	.60	.30
22	Bobby Castillo	.10	.08	.04
23	Bill Caudill	.10	.08	.04
24	Rick Cerone	.10	.08	.04
25	Jack Clark	.35	.25	.14
26	Pat Clements(FC)	.20	.15	.08
27	Stewart Cliburn(FC)	.15	.11	.06
28	Vince Coleman(FC)	4.00	3.00	1.50
29	Dave Collins	.15	.11	.06
30	Fritz Connally	.10	.08	.04
31	Henry Cotto(FC)	.20	.15	.08
32	Danny Darwin	.15	.11	.06
33	Darren Daulton(FC)	.20	.15	.08
34	Jerry Davis	.10	.08	.04
35	Brian Dayett	.10	.08	.04
36	Ken Dixon(FC)	.10	.08	.04
37	Tommy Dunbar	.10	.08	.04
38	Mariano Duncan(FC)	.20	.15	.08
39	Bob Fallon	.10	.08	.04
40	Brian Fisher(FC)	.40	.30	.15
41	Mike Fitzgerald	.10	.08	.04
42	Ray Fontenot	.10	.08	.04
43	Greg Gagne(FC)	.35	.25	.14
44	Oscar Gamble	.15	.11	.06
45	Jim Gott	.10	.08	.04
46	David Green	.10	.08	.04
47	Alfredo Griffin	.15	.11	.06
48	Ozzie Guillen(FC)	1.25	.90	.50
49	Toby Harrah	.15	.11	.06
50	Ron Hassey	.10	.08	.04
51	Rickey Henderson	2.00	1.50	.80
52	Steve Henderson	.10	.08	.04
53	George Hendrick	.15	.11	.06
54	Teddy Higuera(FC)	2.25	1.75	.90
55	Al Holland	.10	.08	.04

		MT	NR MT	EX
56	Burt Hooton	.15	.11	.06
57	Jay Howell	.15	.11	.06
58	LaMarr Hoyt	.10	.08	.04
59	Tim Hulett(FC)	.20	.15	.08
60	Bob James	.10	.08	.04
61	Cliff Johnson	.10	.08	.04
62	Howard Johnson	2.25	1.75	.90
63	Ruppert Jones	.10	.08	.04
64	Steve Kemp	.15	.11	.06
65	Bruce Kison	.10	.08	.04
66	Mike LaCoss	.15	.11	.06
67	Lee Lacy	.15	.11	.06
68	Dave LaPoint	.20	.15	.08
69	Gary Lavelle	.10	.08	.04
70	Vance Law	.15	.11	.06
71	Manny Lee(FC)	.20	.15	.08
72	Sixto Lezcano	.10	.08	.04
73	Tim Lollar	.10	.08	.04
74	Urbano Lugo(FC)	.15	.11	.06
75	Fred Lynn	.30	.25	.12
76	Steve Lyons(FC)	.15	.11	.06
77	Mickey Mahler	.10	.08	.04
78	Ron Mathis(FC)	.10	.08	.04
79	Len Matuszek	.10	.08	.04
80	Oddibe McDowell(FC)	.80	.60	.30
81	Roger McDowell(FC)	.90	.70	.35
82	Donnie Moore	.10	.08	.04
83	Ron Musselman	.10	.08	.04
84	Al Oliver	.25	.20	.10
85	Joe Orsulak(FC)	.20	.15	.08
86	Dan Pasqua(FC)	.50	.40	.20
87	Chris Pittaro(FC)	.10	.08	.04
88	Rick Reuschel	.20	.15	.08
89	Earnie Riles(FC)	.20	.15	.08
90	Jerry Royster	.10	.08	.04
91	Dave Rozema	.10	.08	.04
92	Dave Rucker	.10	.08	.04
93	Vern Ruhle	.10	.08	.04
94	Mark Salas(FC)	.20	.15	.08
95	Luis Salazar	.10	.08	.04
96	Joe Sambito	.10	.08	.04
97	Billy Sample	.10	.08	.04
98	Alex Sanchez	.10	.08	.04
99	Calvin Schiraldi(FC)	.25	.20	.10
100	Rick Schu(FC)	.20	.15	.08
101	Larry Sheets(FC)	.50	.40	.20
102	Ron Shepherd	.10	.08	.04
103	Nelson Simmons(FC)	.10	.08	.04
104	Don Slaught	.10	.08	.04
105	Roy Smalley	.15	.11	.06
106	Lonnie Smith	.15	.11	.06
107	Nate Snell(FC)	.10	.08	.04
108	Lary Sorensen	.10	.08	.04
109	Chris Speier	.10	.08	.04
110	Mike Stenhouse	.10	.08	.04
111	Tim Stoddard	.10	.08	.04
112	John Stuper	.10	.08	.04
113	Jim Sundberg	.15	.11	.06
114	Bruce Sutter	.25	.20	.10
115	Don Sutton	.60	.45	.25
116	Bruce Tanner(FC)	.10	.08	.04
117	Kent Tekulve	.15	.11	.06
118	Walt Terrell	.15	.11	.06
119	Mickey Tettleton(FC)	1.25	.90	.50
120	Rich Thompson	.10	.08	.04
121	Louis Thornton(FC)	.10	.08	.04
122	Alex Trevino	.10	.08	.04
123	John Tudor	.30	.25	.12
124	Jose Uribe(FC)	.25	.20	.10
125	Dave Valle(FC)	.20	.15	.08
126	Dave Von Ohlen	.10	.08	.04
127	Curt Wardle	.10	.08	.04
128	U.L. Washington	.10	.08	.04
129	Ed Whitson	.10	.08	.04
130	Herm Winningham(FC)	.20	.15	.08
131	Rich Yett(FC)	.15	.11	.06
132	Checklist	.10	.08	.04

1986 Fleer

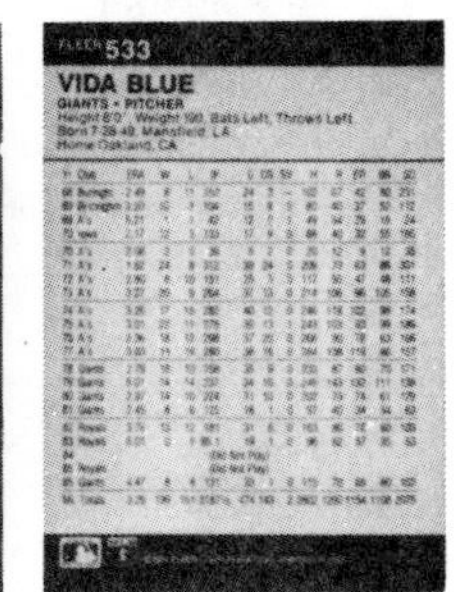

The 1986 Fleer set contains 660 color photos, with each card measuring 2-1/2" by 3-1/2" in size. The card fronts include the word "Fleer," the player's team logo, and a player picture enclosed by a dark blue border. The card reverses are minus the black and white photo that was included in past Fleer efforts. Player biographical and statistical information appear in black and yellow ink on white stock. As in 1985, Fleer devoted ten cards, entitled "Major League Prospects," to twenty promising rookie players. The 1986 set, as in the previous four years, was issued with team logo stickers.

	MT	NR MT	EX
Complete Set:	90.00	67.00	35.00

		MT	NR MT	EX
	Common Player:	.06	.05	.02
1	Steve Balboni	.08	.06	.03
2	Joe Beckwith	.06	.05	.02
3	Buddy Biancalana	.06	.05	.02
4	Bud Black	.06	.05	.02
5	George Brett	.50	.40	.20
6	Onix Concepcion	.06	.05	.02
7	Steve Farr	.08	.06	.03
8	Mark Gubicza	.12	.09	.05
9	Dane Iorg	.06	.05	.02
10	Danny Jackson	.20	.15	.08
11	Lynn Jones	.06	.05	.02
12	Mike Jones	.06	.05	.02
13	Charlie Leibrandt	.08	.06	.03
14	Hal McRae	.10	.08	.04
15	Omar Moreno	.06	.05	.02
16	Darryl Motley	.06	.05	.02
17	Jorge Orta	.06	.05	.02
18	Dan Quisenberry	.08	.06	.03
19	Bret Saberhagen	1.50	1.25	.60
20	Pat Sheridan	.06	.05	.02
21	Lonnie Smith	.08	.06	.03
22	Jim Sundberg	.08	.06	.03
23	John Wathan	.08	.06	.03
24	Frank White	.10	.08	.04
25	Willie Wilson	.12	.09	.05
26	Joaquin Andujar	.08	.06	.03
27	Steve Braun	.06	.05	.02
28	Bill Campbell	.06	.05	.02
29	Cesar Cedeno	.10	.08	.04
30	Jack Clark	.20	.15	.08
31	*Vince Coleman*	1.75	1.25	.70
32	Danny Cox	.10	.08	.04
33	Ken Dayley	.06	.05	.02
34	Ivan DeJesus	.06	.05	.02
35	Bob Forsch	.08	.06	.03
36	Brian Harper	.06	.05	.02
37	Tom Herr	.10	.08	.04
38	Ricky Horton	.08	.06	.03
39	Kurt Kepshire	.06	.05	.02
40	Jeff Lahti	.06	.05	.02
41	Tito Landrum	.06	.05	.02
42	Willie McGee	.15	.11	.06
43	Tom Nieto	.06	.05	.02
44	Terry Pendleton	.15	.11	.06
45	Darrell Porter	.08	.06	.03
46	Ozzie Smith	.15	.11	.06
47	John Tudor	.10	.08	.04
48	Andy Van Slyke	.15	.11	.06
49	*Todd Worrell*(FC)	.90	.70	.35
50	Jim Acker	.06	.05	.02
51	Doyle Alexander	.10	.08	.04
52	Jesse Barfield	.20	.15	.08
53	George Bell	.30	.25	.12
54	Jeff Burroughs	.08	.06	.03
55	Bill Caudill	.06	.05	.02
56	Jim Clancy	.08	.06	.03
57	Tony Fernandez	.20	.15	.08
58	Tom Filer	.06	.05	.02
59	Damaso Garcia	.06	.05	.02
60	Tom Henke(FC)	.15	.11	.06
61	Garth Iorg	.06	.05	.02
62	Cliff Johnson	.06	.05	.02
63	Jimmy Key	.15	.11	.06
64	Dennis Lamp	.06	.05	.02
65	Gary Lavelle	.06	.05	.02
66	Buck Martinez	.06	.05	.02
67	Lloyd Moseby	.10	.08	.04
68	Rance Mulliniks	.06	.05	.02
69	Al Oliver	.10	.08	.04
70	Dave Stieb	.12	.09	.05
71	Louis Thornton	.06	.05	.02
72	Willie Upshaw	.08	.06	.03
73	Ernie Whitt	.08	.06	.03
74	*Rick Aguilera*(FC)	.25	.20	.10
75	Wally Backman	.08	.06	.03
76	Gary Carter	.25	.20	.10
77	Ron Darling	.15	.11	.06
78	*Len Dykstra*(FC)	1.25	.90	.50
79	Sid Fernandez	.12	.09	.05
80	George Foster	.15	.11	.06
81	Dwight Gooden	2.00	1.50	.80
82	Tom Gorman	.06	.05	.02
83	Danny Heep	.06	.05	.02
84	Keith Hernandez	.30	.25	.12
85	Howard Johnson	.12	.09	.05
86	Ray Knight	.08	.06	.03
87	Terry Leach	.08	.06	.03
88	Ed Lynch	.06	.05	.02
89	*Roger McDowell*(FC)	.60	.45	.25
90	Jesse Orosco	.08	.06	.03
91	Tom Paciorek	.06	.05	.02
92	Ronn Reynolds	.06	.05	.02
93	Rafael Santana	.06	.05	.02
94	Doug Sisk	.06	.05	.02
95	Rusty Staub	.10	.08	.04
96	Darryl Strawberry	2.00	1.50	.80
97	Mookie Wilson	.10	.08	.04
98	Neil Allen	.06	.05	.02
99	Don Baylor	.12	.09	.05
100	Dale Berra	.06	.05	.02
101	Rich Bordi	.06	.05	.02
102	Marty Bystrom	.06	.05	.02
103	Joe Cowley	.06	.05	.02
104	*Brian Fisher*	.30	.25	.12
105	Ken Griffey	.10	.08	.04
106	Ron Guidry	.20	.15	.08
107	Ron Hassey	.06	.05	.02
108	Rickey Henderson	.40	.30	.15
109	Don Mattingly	4.00	3.00	1.50
110	Bobby Meacham	.06	.05	.02
111	John Montefusco	.06	.05	.02
112	Phil Niekro	.25	.20	.10
113	Mike Pagliarulo	.20	.15	.08
114	Dan Pasqua	.20	.15	.08
115	Willie Randolph	.10	.08	.04
116	Dave Righetti	.20	.15	.08
117	Andre Robertson	.06	.05	.02
118	Billy Sample	.06	.05	.02
119	Bob Shirley	.06	.05	.02
120	Ed Whitson	.06	.05	.02
121	Dave Winfield	.30	.25	.12
122	Butch Wynegar	.06	.05	.02

		MT	NR MT	EX
123	Dave Anderson	.06	.05	.02
124	Bob Bailor	.06	.05	.02
125	Greg Brock	.08	.06	.03
126	Enos Cabell	.06	.05	.02
127	Bobby Castillo	.06	.05	.02
128	Carlos Diaz	.06	.05	.02
129	*Mariano Duncan*	.15	.11	.06
130	Pedro Guerrero	.20	.15	.08
131	Orel Hershiser	1.25	.90	.50
132	Rick Honeycutt	.06	.05	.02
133	Ken Howell	.06	.05	.02
134	Ken Landreaux	.06	.05	.02
135	Bill Madlock	.12	.09	.05
136	Candy Maldonado	.10	.08	.04
137	Mike Marshall	.15	.11	.06
138	Len Matuszek	.06	.05	.02
139	Tom Niedenfuer	.08	.06	.03
140	Alejandro Pena	.08	.06	.03
141	Jerry Reuss	.08	.06	.03
142	Bill Russell	.08	.06	.03
143	Steve Sax	.20	.15	.08
144	Mike Scioscia	.08	.06	.03
145	Fernando Valenzuela	.30	.25	.12
146	Bob Welch	.12	.09	.05
147	Terry Whitfield	.06	.05	.02
148	Juan Beniquez	.06	.05	.02
149	Bob Boone	.08	.06	.03
150	John Candelaria	.10	.08	.04
151	Rod Carew	.30	.25	.12
152	*Stewart Cliburn*(FC)	.12	.09	.05
153	Doug DeCinces	.10	.08	.04
154	Brian Downing	.08	.06	.03
155	Ken Forsch	.06	.05	.02
156	Craig Gerber	.06	.05	.02
157	Bobby Grich	.10	.08	.04
158	George Hendrick	.08	.06	.03
159	Al Holland	.06	.05	.02
160	Reggie Jackson	.35	.25	.14
161	Ruppert Jones	.06	.05	.02
162	*Urbano Lugo*	.08	.06	.03
163	*Kirk McCaskill*(FC)	.35	.25	.14
164	Donnie Moore	.06	.05	.02
165	Gary Pettis	.06	.05	.02
166	Ron Romanick	.06	.05	.02
167	Dick Schofield	.06	.05	.02
168	Daryl Sconiers	.06	.05	.02
169	Jim Slaton	.06	.05	.02
170	Don Sutton	.25	.20	.10
171	Mike Witt	.10	.08	.04
172	Buddy Bell	.10	.08	.04
173	Tom Browning	.30	.25	.12
174	Dave Concepcion	.12	.09	.05
175	Eric Davis	3.00	2.25	1.25
176	Bo Diaz	.08	.06	.03
177	Nick Esasky	.08	.06	.03
178	John Franco	.12	.09	.05
179	Tom Hume	.06	.05	.02
180	Wayne Krenchicki	.06	.05	.02
181	Andy McGaffigan	.06	.05	.02
182	Eddie Milner	.06	.05	.02
183	Ron Oester	.06	.05	.02
184	Dave Parker	.20	.15	.08
185	Frank Pastore	.06	.05	.02
186	Tony Perez	.15	.11	.06
187	Ted Power	.08	.06	.03
188	Joe Price	.06	.05	.02
189	Gary Redus	.06	.05	.02
190	Ron Robinson	.08	.06	.03
191	Pete Rose	.70	.50	.30
192	Mario Soto	.08	.06	.03
193	John Stuper	.06	.05	.02
194	Jay Tibbs	.06	.05	.02
195	Dave Van Gorder	.06	.05	.02
196	Max Venable	.06	.05	.02
197	Juan Agosto	.06	.05	.02
198	Harold Baines	.15	.11	.06
199	Floyd Bannister	.10	.08	.04
200	Britt Burns	.06	.05	.02
201	Julio Cruz	.06	.05	.02
202	*Joel Davis*(FC)	.08	.06	.03
203	Richard Dotson	.10	.08	.04
204	Carlton Fisk	.30	.25	.12
205	Scott Fletcher	.08	.06	.03
206	*Ozzie Guillen*	.70	.50	.30
207	Jerry Hairston	.06	.05	.02
208	Tim Hulett	.08	.06	.03
209	Bob James	.06	.05	.02
210	Ron Kittle	.10	.08	.04
211	Rudy Law	.06	.05	.02
212	Bryan Little	.06	.05	.02
213	Gene Nelson	.06	.05	.02
214	Reid Nichols	.06	.05	.02
215	Luis Salazar	.06	.05	.02
216	Tom Seaver	.40	.30	.15
217	Dan Spillner	.06	.05	.02
218	Bruce Tanner	.06	.05	.02
219	Greg Walker	.10	.08	.04
220	Dave Wehrmeister	.06	.05	.02
221	Juan Berenguer	.06	.05	.02
222	Dave Bergman	.06	.05	.02
223	Tom Brookens	.06	.05	.02
224	Darrell Evans	.12	.09	.05
225	Barbaro Garbey	.06	.05	.02
226	Kirk Gibson	.30	.25	.12
227	John Grubb	.06	.05	.02
228	Willie Hernandez	.08	.06	.03
229	Larry Herndon	.08	.06	.03
230	Chet Lemon	.08	.06	.03
231	Aurelio Lopez	.06	.05	.02
232	Jack Morris	.20	.15	.08
233	Randy O'Neal	.06	.05	.02
234	Lance Parrish	.20	.15	.08
235	Dan Petry	.08	.06	.03
236	Alex Sanchez	.06	.05	.02
237	Bill Scherrer	.06	.05	.02
238	Nelson Simmons	.06	.05	.02
239	Frank Tanana	.10	.08	.04
240	Walt Terrell	.08	.06	.03
241	Alan Trammell	.30	.25	.12
242	Lou Whitaker	.30	.25	.12
243	Milt Wilcox	.06	.05	.02
244	Hubie Brooks	.10	.08	.04
245	*Tim Burke*(FC)	.30	.25	.12
246	Andre Dawson	.20	.15	.08

		MT	NR MT	EX
247	Mike Fitzgerald	.06	.05	.02
248	Terry Francona	.06	.05	.02
249	Bill Gullickson	.06	.05	.02
250	Joe Hesketh	.06	.05	.02
251	Bill Laskey	.06	.05	.02
252	Vance Law	.08	.06	.03
253	Charlie Lea	.06	.05	.02
254	Gary Lucas	.06	.05	.02
255	David Palmer	.06	.05	.02
256	Tim Raines	.30	.25	.12
257	Jeff Reardon	.12	.09	.05
258	Bert Roberge	.06	.05	.02
259	Dan Schatzeder	.06	.05	.02
260	Bryn Smith	.06	.05	.02
261	Randy St. Claire(FC)	.08	.06	.03
262	Scot Thompson	.06	.05	.02
263	Tim Wallach	.12	.09	.05
264	U.L. Washington	.06	.05	.02
265	*Mitch Webster*(FC)	.25	.20	.10
266	*Herm Winningham*	.15	.11	.06
267	*Floyd Youmans*(FC)	.30	.25	.12
268	Don Aase	.06	.05	.02
269	Mike Boddicker	.08	.06	.03
270	Rich Dauer	.06	.05	.02
271	Storm Davis	.10	.08	.04
272	Rick Dempsey	.08	.06	.03
273	Ken Dixon	.06	.05	.02
274	Jim Dwyer	.06	.05	.02
275	Mike Flanagan	.10	.08	.04
276	Wayne Gross	.06	.05	.02
277	Lee Lacy	.06	.05	.02
278	Fred Lynn	.20	.15	.08
279	Tippy Martinez	.06	.05	.02
280	Dennis Martinez	.08	.06	.03
281	Scott McGregor	.08	.06	.03
282	Eddie Murray	.40	.30	.15
283	Floyd Rayford	.06	.05	.02
284	Cal Ripken, Jr.	.40	.30	.15
285	Gary Roenicke	.06	.05	.02
286	Larry Sheets	.20	.15	.08
287	John Shelby	.06	.05	.02
288	Nate Snell	.06	.05	.02
289	Sammy Stewart	.06	.05	.02
290	Alan Wiggins	.06	.05	.02
291	Mike Young	.06	.05	.02
292	Alan Ashby	.06	.05	.02
293	Mark Bailey	.06	.05	.02
294	Kevin Bass	.10	.08	.04
295	Jeff Calhoun	.06	.05	.02
296	Jose Cruz	.10	.08	.04
297	Glenn Davis	.70	.50	.30
298	Bill Dawley	.06	.05	.02
299	Frank DiPino	.06	.05	.02
300	Bill Doran	.10	.08	.04
301	Phil Garner	.08	.06	.03
302	*Jeff Heathcock*(FC)	.10	.08	.04
303	*Charlie Kerfeld*(FC)	.15	.11	.06
304	Bob Knepper	.08	.06	.03
305	Ron Mathis	.06	.05	.02
306	Jerry Mumphrey	.06	.05	.02
307	Jim Pankovits	.06	.05	.02
308	Terry Puhl	.06	.05	.02
309	Craig Reynolds	.06	.05	.02
310	Nolan Ryan	.50	.40	.20
311	Mike Scott	.15	.11	.06
312	Dave Smith	.08	.06	.03
313	Dickie Thon	.08	.06	.03
314	Denny Walling	.06	.05	.02
315	Kurt Bevacqua	.06	.05	.02
316	Al Bumbry	.06	.05	.02
317	Jerry Davis	.06	.05	.02
318	Luis DeLeon	.06	.05	.02
319	Dave Dravecky	.08	.06	.03
320	Tim Flannery	.06	.05	.02
321	Steve Garvey	.30	.25	.12
322	Goose Gossage	.20	.15	.08
323	Tony Gwynn	.40	.30	.15
324	Andy Hawkins	.06	.05	.02
325	LaMarr Hoyt	.06	.05	.02
326	Roy Lee Jackson	.06	.05	.02
327	Terry Kennedy	.08	.06	.03
328	Craig Lefferts	.06	.05	.02
329	Carmelo Martinez	.08	.06	.03
330	*Lance McCullers*(FC)	.25	.20	.10
331	Kevin McReynolds	.30	.25	.12
332	Graig Nettles	.15	.11	.06
333	Jerry Royster	.06	.05	.02
334	Eric Show	.08	.06	.03
335	Tim Stoddard	.06	.05	.02
336	Garry Templeton	.08	.06	.03
337	Mark Thurmond	.06	.05	.02
338	Ed Wojna	.06	.05	.02
339	Tony Armas	.08	.06	.03
340	Marty Barrett	.10	.08	.04
341	Wade Boggs	2.25	1.75	.90
342	Dennis Boyd	.08	.06	.03
343	Bill Buckner	.12	.09	.05
344	Mark Clear	.06	.05	.02
345	Roger Clemens	3.00	2.25	1.25
346	Steve Crawford	.06	.05	.02
347	Mike Easler	.08	.06	.03
348	Dwight Evans	.12	.09	.05
349	Rich Gedman	.10	.08	.04
350	Jackie Gutierrez	.06	.05	.02
351	Glenn Hoffman	.06	.05	.02
352	Bruce Hurst	.12	.09	.05
353	Bruce Kison	.06	.05	.02
354	Tim Lollar	.06	.05	.02
355	Steve Lyons	.08	.06	.03
356	Al Nipper	.08	.06	.03
357	Bob Ojeda	.08	.06	.03
358	Jim Rice	.30	.25	.12
359	Bob Stanley	.06	.05	.02
360	Mike Trujillo	.06	.05	.02
361	Thad Bosley	.06	.05	.02
362	Warren Brusstar	.06	.05	.02
363	Ron Cey	.10	.08	.04
364	Jody Davis	.10	.08	.04
365	Bob Dernier	.06	.05	.02
366	Shawon Dunston	.15	.11	.06
367	Leon Durham	.08	.06	.03
368	Dennis Eckersley	.12	.09	.05
369	Ray Fontenot	.06	.05	.02
370	George Frazier	.06	.05	.02

		MT	NR MT	EX
371	Bill Hatcher	.10	.08	.04
372	Dave Lopes	.08	.06	.03
373	Gary Matthews	.10	.08	.04
374	Ron Meredith	.06	.05	.02
375	Keith Moreland	.08	.06	.03
376	Reggie Patterson	.06	.05	.02
377	Dick Ruthven	.06	.05	.02
378	Ryne Sandberg	.40	.30	.15
379	Scott Sanderson	.06	.05	.02
380	Lee Smith	.10	.08	.04
381	Lary Sorensen	.06	.05	.02
382	Chris Speier	.06	.05	.02
383	Rick Sutcliffe	.12	.09	.05
384	Steve Trout	.06	.05	.02
385	Gary Woods	.06	.05	.02
386	Bert Blyleven	.15	.11	.06
387	Tom Brunansky	.12	.09	.05
388	Randy Bush	.06	.05	.02
389	John Butcher	.06	.05	.02
390	Ron Davis	.06	.05	.02
391	Dave Engle	.06	.05	.02
392	Frank Eufemia	.06	.05	.02
393	Pete Filson	.06	.05	.02
394	Gary Gaetti	.20	.15	.08
395	Greg Gagne	.10	.08	.04
396	Mickey Hatcher	.06	.05	.02
397	Kent Hrbek	.20	.15	.08
398	Tim Laudner	.06	.05	.02
399	Rick Lysander	.06	.05	.02
400	Dave Meier	.06	.05	.02
401	Kirby Puckett	3.75	2.75	1.50
402	Mark Salas	.08	.06	.03
403	Ken Schrom	.06	.05	.02
404	Roy Smalley	.06	.05	.02
405	Mike Smithson	.06	.05	.02
406	Mike Stenhouse	.06	.05	.02
407	Tim Teufel	.06	.05	.02
408	Frank Viola	.15	.11	.06
409	Ron Washington	.06	.05	.02
410	Keith Atherton	.06	.05	.02
411	Dusty Baker	.08	.06	.03
412	*Tim Birtsas*	.12	.09	.05
413	Bruce Bochte	.06	.05	.02
414	Chris Codiroli	.06	.05	.02
415	Dave Collins	.08	.06	.03
416	Mike Davis	.08	.06	.03
417	Alfredo Griffin	.08	.06	.03
418	Mike Heath	.06	.05	.02
419	Steve Henderson	.06	.05	.02
420	Donnie Hill	.06	.05	.02
421	Jay Howell	.08	.06	.03
422	Tommy John	.20	.15	.08
423	Dave Kingman	.15	.11	.06
424	Bill Krueger	.06	.05	.02
425	Rick Langford	.06	.05	.02
426	Carney Lansford	.10	.08	.04
427	Steve McCatty	.06	.05	.02
428	Dwayne Murphy	.08	.06	.03
429	*Steve Ontiveros*(FC)	.12	.09	.05
430	Tony Phillips	.06	.05	.02
431	Jose Rijo	.10	.08	.04
432	*Mickey Tettleton*	.90	.70	.35
433	Luis Aguayo	.06	.05	.02
434	Larry Andersen	.06	.05	.02
435	Steve Carlton	.30	.25	.12
436	*Don Carman*	.30	.25	.12
437	Tim Corcoran	.06	.05	.02
438	*Darren Daulton*	.12	.09	.05
439	John Denny	.06	.05	.02
440	Tom Foley	.06	.05	.02
441	Greg Gross	.06	.05	.02
442	Kevin Gross	.08	.06	.03
443	Von Hayes	.10	.08	.04
444	Charles Hudson	.06	.05	.02
445	Garry Maddox	.08	.06	.03
446	Shane Rawley	.10	.08	.04
447	Dave Rucker	.06	.05	.02
448	John Russell	.06	.05	.02
449	Juan Samuel	.12	.09	.05
450	Mike Schmidt	.50	.40	.20
451	Rick Schu	.08	.06	.03
452	Dave Shipanoff	.06	.05	.02
453	Dave Stewart	.12	.09	.05
454	Jeff Stone	.06	.05	.02
455	Kent Tekulve	.08	.06	.03
456	Ozzie Virgil	.06	.05	.02
457	Glenn Wilson	.08	.06	.03
458	Jim Beattie	.06	.05	.02
459	Karl Best	.06	.05	.02
460	Barry Bonnell	.06	.05	.02
461	Phil Bradley	.20	.15	.08
462	*Ivan Calderon*	.40	.30	.15
463	Al Cowens	.06	.05	.02
464	Alvin Davis	.30	.25	.12
465	Dave Henderson	.10	.08	.04
466	Bob Kearney	.06	.05	.02
467	Mark Langston	.30	.25	.12
468	Bob Long	.06	.05	.02
469	Mike Moore	.06	.05	.02
470	Edwin Nunez	.06	.05	.02
471	Spike Owen	.06	.05	.02
472	Jack Perconte	.06	.05	.02
473	Jim Presley	.15	.11	.06
474	Donnie Scott	.06	.05	.02
475	Bill Swift(FC)	.12	.09	.05
476	Danny Tartabull	.50	.40	.20
477	Gorman Thomas	.10	.08	.04
478	Roy Thomas	.06	.05	.02
479	Ed Vande Berg	.06	.05	.02
480	Frank Wills	.06	.05	.02
481	Matt Young	.06	.05	.02
482	Ray Burris	.06	.05	.02
483	Jaime Cocanower	.06	.05	.02
484	Cecil Cooper	.12	.09	.05
485	Danny Darwin	.06	.05	.02
486	Rollie Fingers	.20	.15	.08
487	Jim Gantner	.08	.06	.03
488	Bob Gibson	.06	.05	.02
489	Moose Haas	.06	.05	.02
490	*Teddy Higuera*	1.00	.70	.40
491	Paul Householder	.06	.05	.02
492	Pete Ladd	.06	.05	.02
493	Rick Manning	.06	.05	.02
494	Bob McClure	.06	.05	.02

		MT	NR MT	EX
495	Paul Molitor	.15	.11	.06
496	Charlie Moore	.06	.05	.02
497	Ben Oglivie	.08	.06	.03
498	Randy Ready	.06	.05	.02
499	*Earnie Riles*	.20	.15	.08
500	Ed Romero	.06	.05	.02
501	Bill Schroeder	.06	.05	.02
502	Ray Searage	.06	.05	.02
503	Ted Simmons	.12	.09	.05
504	Pete Vuckovich	.08	.06	.03
505	Rick Waits	.06	.05	.02
506	Robin Yount	.30	.25	.12
507	Len Barker	.08	.06	.03
508	Steve Bedrosian	.12	.09	.05
509	Bruce Benedict	.06	.05	.02
510	Rick Camp	.06	.05	.02
511	Rick Cerone	.06	.05	.02
512	Chris Chambliss	.08	.06	.03
513	Jeff Dedmon	.06	.05	.02
514	Terry Forster	.08	.06	.03
515	Gene Garber	.06	.05	.02
516	Terry Harper	.06	.05	.02
517	Bob Horner	.12	.09	.05
518	Glenn Hubbard	.06	.05	.02
519	*Joe Johnson*(FC)	.08	.06	.03
520	Brad Komminsk	.06	.05	.02
521	Rick Mahler	.06	.05	.02
522	Dale Murphy	.50	.40	.20
523	Ken Oberkfell	.06	.05	.02
524	Pascual Perez	.08	.06	.03
525	Gerald Perry	.12	.09	.05
526	Rafael Ramirez	.06	.05	.02
527	*Steve Shields*(FC)	.12	.09	.05
528	Zane Smith	.10	.08	.04
529	Bruce Sutter	.12	.09	.05
530	*Milt Thompson*(FC)	.30	.25	.12
531	Claudell Washington	.08	.06	.03
532	Paul Zuvella	.06	.05	.02
533	Vida Blue	.10	.08	.04
534	Bob Brenly	.06	.05	.02
535	*Chris Brown*	.20	.15	.08
536	Chili Davis	.10	.08	.04
537	Mark Davis	.06	.05	.02
538	Rob Deer	.12	.09	.05
539	Dan Driessen	.08	.06	.03
540	Scott Garrelts	.08	.06	.03
541	Dan Gladden	.08	.06	.03
542	Jim Gott	.06	.05	.02
543	David Green	.06	.05	.02
544	Atlee Hammaker	.06	.05	.02
545	Mike Jeffcoat	.06	.05	.02
546	Mike Krukow	.08	.06	.03
547	Dave LaPoint	.08	.06	.03
548	Jeff Leonard	.08	.06	.03
549	Greg Minton	.06	.05	.02
550	Alex Trevino	.06	.05	.02
551	Manny Trillo	.08	.06	.03
552	*Jose Uribe*	.20	.15	.08
553	Brad Wellman	.06	.05	.02
554	Frank Williams	.06	.05	.02
555	Joel Youngblood	.06	.05	.02
556	Alan Bannister	.06	.05	.02
557	Glenn Brummer	.06	.05	.02
558	*Steve Buechele*(FC)	.20	.15	.08
559	*Jose Guzman*(FC)	.30	.25	.12
560	Toby Harrah	.08	.06	.03
561	Greg Harris	.06	.05	.02
562	*Dwayne Henry*(FC)	.10	.08	.04
563	Burt Hooton	.08	.06	.03
564	Charlie Hough	.08	.06	.03
565	Mike Mason	.06	.05	.02
566	*Oddibe McDowell*	.30	.25	.12
567	Dickie Noles	.06	.05	.02
568	Pete O'Brien	.10	.08	.04
569	Larry Parrish	.10	.08	.04
570	Dave Rozema	.06	.05	.02
571	Dave Schmidt	.06	.05	.02
572	Don Slaught	.06	.05	.02
573	Wayne Tolleson	.06	.05	.02
574	Duane Walker	.06	.05	.02
575	Gary Ward	.08	.06	.03
576	Chris Welsh	.06	.05	.02
577	Curtis Wilkerson	.06	.05	.02
578	George Wright	.06	.05	.02
579	Chris Bando	.06	.05	.02
580	Tony Bernazard	.06	.05	.02
581	Brett Butler	.08	.06	.03
582	Ernie Camacho	.06	.05	.02
583	Joe Carter	.20	.15	.08
584	Carmello Castillo (Carmelo)	.06	.05	.02
585	Jamie Easterly	.06	.05	.02
586	Julio Franco	.10	.08	.04
587	Mel Hall	.08	.06	.03
588	Mike Hargrove	.06	.05	.02
589	Neal Heaton	.06	.05	.02
590	Brook Jacoby	.10	.08	.04
591	*Otis Nixon*(FC)	.12	.09	.05
592	Jerry Reed	.06	.05	.02
593	Vern Ruhle	.06	.05	.02
594	Pat Tabler	.08	.06	.03
595	Rich Thompson	.06	.05	.02
596	Andre Thornton	.08	.06	.03
597	Dave Von Ohlen	.06	.05	.02
598	George Vukovich	.06	.05	.02
599	Tom Waddell	.06	.05	.02
600	Curt Wardle	.06	.05	.02
601	Jerry Willard	.06	.05	.02
602	Bill Almon	.06	.05	.02
603	Mike Bielecki	.08	.06	.03
604	Sid Bream	.10	.08	.04
605	Mike Brown	.06	.05	.02
606	*Pat Clements*	.12	.09	.05
607	Jose DeLeon	.08	.06	.03
608	Denny Gonzalez	.06	.05	.02
609	Cecilio Guante	.06	.05	.02
610	Steve Kemp	.08	.06	.03
611	Sam Khalifa	.06	.05	.02
612	Lee Mazzilli	.08	.06	.03
613	Larry McWilliams	.06	.05	.02
614	Jim Morrison	.06	.05	.02
615	*Joe Orsulak*	.15	.11	.06
616	Tony Pena	.10	.08	.04
617	Johnny Ray	.10	.08	.04
618	Rick Reuschel	.10	.08	.04

#	Player	MT	NR MT	EX
619	R.J. Reynolds	.08	.06	.03
620	Rick Rhoden	.10	.08	.04
621	Don Robinson	.08	.06	.03
622	Jason Thompson	.06	.05	.02
623	Lee Tunnell	.06	.05	.02
624	Jim Winn	.06	.05	.02
625	Marvell Wynne	.06	.05	.02
626	Gooden In Action (Dwight Gooden)	.50	.40	.20
627	Mattingly In Action (Don Mattingly)	1.25	.90	.50
628	4,192! (Pete Rose)	.50	.40	.20
629	3,000 Career Hits (Rod Carew)	.20	.15	.08
630	300 Career Wins (Phil Niekro, Tom Seaver)	.20	.15	.08
631	Ouch! (Don Baylor)	.08	.06	.03
632	Instant Offense (Tim Raines, Darryl Strawberry)	.30	.25	.12
633	Shortstops Supreme (Cal Ripken, Jr., Alan Trammell)	.30	.25	.12
634	Boggs & "Hero" (Wade Boggs, George Brett)	.60	.45	.25
635	Braves Dynamic Duo (Bob Horner, Dale Murphy)	.30	.25	.12
636	Cardinal Ignitors (Vince Coleman, Willie McGee)	.35	.25	.14
637	Terror on the Basepaths (Vince Coleman)	.35	.25	.14
638	Charlie Hustle & Dr. K (Dwight Gooden, Pete Rose)	.70	.50	.30
639	1984 and 1985 A.L. Batting Champs (Wade Boggs, Don Mattingly)	1.75	1.25	.70
640	N.L. West Sluggers (Steve Garvey, Dale Murphy, Dave Parker)	.30	.25	.12
641	Staff Aces (Dwight Gooden, Fernando Valenzuela)	.40	.30	.15
642	Blue Jay Stoppers (Jimmy Key, Dave Stieb)	.10	.08	.04
643	A.L. All-Star Backstops (Carlton Fisk, Rich Gedman)	.10	.08	.04
644	Major League Prospect *(Benito Santiago, Gene Walter)*(FC)	5.00	3.75	2.00
645	Major League Prospect *(Colin Ward, Mike Woodard)*(FC)	.10	.08	.04
646	Major League Prospect *(Kal Daniels, Paul O'Neill)*(FC)	4.00	3.00	1.50
647	Major League Prospect *(Andres Galarraga, Fred Toliver)*(FC)	4.00	3.00	1.50
648	Major League Prospect *(Curt Ford, Bob Kipper)*(FC)	.25	.20	.10
649	Major League Prospect *(Jose Canseco, Eric Plunk)*(FC)	50.00	37.00	20.00
650	Major League Prospect *(Mark McLemore, Gus Polidor)*(FC)	.20	.15	.08
651	Major League Prospect *(Mickey Brantley, Rob Woodward)*(FC)	.35	.25	.14
652	Major League Prospect *(Mark Funderburk, Billy Joe Robidoux)*(FC)	.10	.08	.04
653	Major League Prospect *(Cecil Fielder, Cory Snyder)*(FC)	7.00	5.25	2.75
654	Checklist 1-97	.06	.05	.02
655	Checklist 98-196	.06	.05	.02
656	Checklist 197-291	.06	.05	.02
657	Checklist 292-385	.06	.05	.02
658	Checklist 386-482	.06	.05	.02
659	Checklist 483-578	.06	.05	.02
660	Checklist 579-660	.06	.05	.02

1986 Fleer All Star Team

Fleer's choices for a major league All-Star team make up this 12-card set. The cards, which measure 2-1/2" by 3-1/2", were randomly inserted in 35¢ wax packs and 59¢ cello packs. The card fronts have a color photo set against a bright red background for A.L. players or a bright blue background for N.L. players. The card backs feature the player's career highlights set in white type against a red and blue background.

		MT	NR MT	EX
Complete Set:		20.00	15.00	8.00
Common Player:		.60	.45	.25
1	Don Mattingly	6.00	4.50	2.50
2	Tom Herr	.60	.45	.25
3	George Brett	2.00	1.50	.80
4	Gary Carter	1.00	.70	.40
5	Cal Ripken, Jr.	1.75	1.25	.70
6	Dave Parker	.75	.60	.30
7	Rickey Henderson	2.50	2.00	1.00
8	Pedro Guerrero	.75	.60	.30
9	Dan Quisenberry	.60	.45	.25
10	Dwight Gooden	4.00	3.00	1.50
11	Gorman Thomas	.60	.45	.25
12	John Tudor	.60	.45	.25

1986 Fleer Baseball's Best

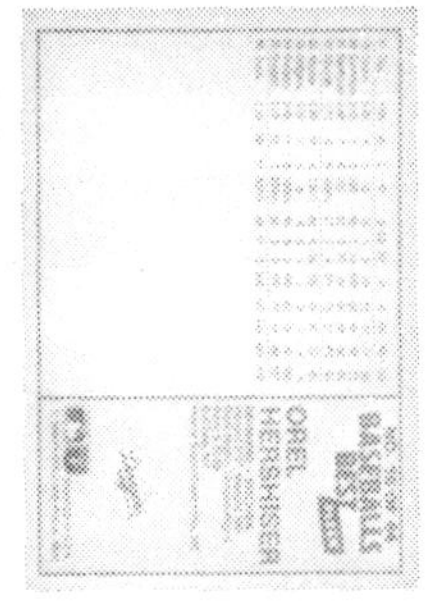

The 1986 Fleer Baseball's Best set consists of 44 cards and was produced for the McCrory's store chain and their affiliated stores. Subtitled "Sluggers vs. Pitchers," the set contains 22 each of the game's best hitters and pitchers. The cards, which measure 2-1/2" by 3-1/2", have color photos depicting an action pose. The backs are done in blue and red ink on white stock and carry the player's personal and statistical information. The sets were issued in a specially designed box with six team logo stickers.

		MT	NR MT	EX
Complete Set:		7.00	5.25	2.75
Common Player:		.05	.04	.02
1	Bert Blyleven	.10	.08	.04
2	Wade Boggs	1.00	.70	.40
3	George Brett	.30	.25	.12
4	Tom Browning	.15	.11	.06
5	Jose Canseco	3.50	2.75	1.50
6	Will Clark	1.50	1.25	.60
7	Roger Clemens	.70	.50	.30
8	Alvin Davis	.10	.08	.04
9	Julio Franco	.10	.08	.04
10	Kirk Gibson	.20	.15	.08
11	Dwight Gooden	1.00	.70	.40
12	Goose Gossage	.12	.09	.05
13	Pedro Guerrero	.15	.11	.06
14	Ron Guidry	.12	.09	.05
15	Tony Gwynn	.25	.20	.10
16	Orel Hershiser	.20	.15	.08
17	Kent Hrbek	.15	.11	.06
18	Reggie Jackson	.25	.20	.10
19	Wally Joyner	.50	.40	.20
20	Charlie Leibrandt	.05	.04	.02
21	Don Mattingly	1.50	1.25	.60
22	Willie McGee	.12	.09	.05
23	Jack Morris	.15	.11	.06
24	Dale Murphy	.30	.25	.12
25	Eddie Murray	.25	.20	.10
26	Jeff Reardon	.07	.05	.03
27	Rick Reuschel	.07	.05	.03
28	Cal Ripken, Jr	.30	.25	.12
29	Pete Rose	.60	.45	.25
30	Nolan Ryan	.50	.40	.20
31	Bret Saberhagen	.15	.11	.06
32	Ryne Sandberg	.20	.15	.08
33	Mike Schmidt	.30	.25	.12
34	Tom Seaver	.25	.20	.10
35	Bryn Smith	.05	.04	.02
36	Mario Soto	.05	.04	.02
37	Dave Stieb	.10	.08	.04
38	Darryl Strawberry	.40	.30	.15
39	Rick Sutcliffe	.10	.08	.04
40	John Tudor	.10	.08	.04
41	Fernando Valenzuela	.20	.15	.08
42	Bobby Witt	.15	.11	.06
43	Mike Witt	.07	.05	.03
44	Robin Yount	.35	.25	.14

1986 Fleer Box Panels

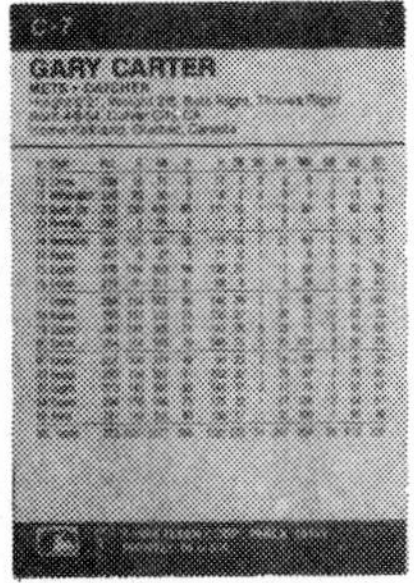

Picking up on a Donruss idea, Fleer issued eight cards in panels of four on the bottoms of the wax and cello pack boxes. The cards are numbered C-1 through C-8 and are 2-1/2" by 3-1/2", with a complete panel measuring 5" by 7-1/8" in size. Included in the eight cards are six player cards and two team logo/checklist cards.

		MT	NR MT	EX
Complete Panel Set:		4.00	3.00	1.50
Complete Singles Set:		1.75	1.25	.70
Common Single Player:		.20	.15	.08
Panel		2.75	2.00	1.00
1	Royals Logo/Checklist	.05	.04	.02
2	George Brett	.60	.45	.25
3	Ozzie Guillen	.40	.30	.15
4	Dale Murphy	.60	.45	.25
Panel		1.50	1.25	.60
5	Cardinals Logo/Checklist	.05	.04	.02
6	Tom Browning	.20	.15	.08
7	Gary Carter	.35	.25	.14
8	Carlton Fisk	.20	.15	.08

1986 Fleer Future Hall of Famers

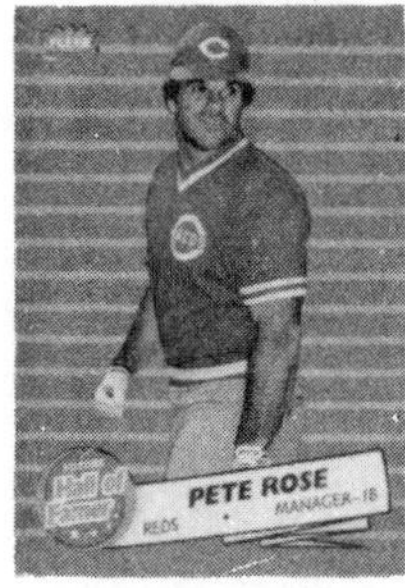

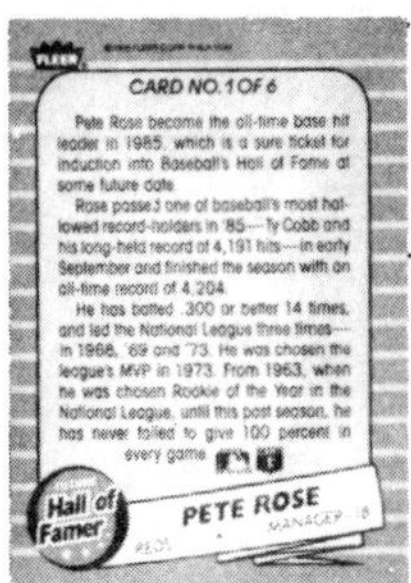

The 1986 Fleer Future Hall of Famers set is comprised of six players Fleer felt would gain eventual entrance into the Baseball Hall of Fame. The cards are the standard 2-1/2" by 3-1/2" in size and were randomly inserted in three-pack cello packs. The card fronts feature a player photo set against a blue background with horizontal light blue stripes. The card backs are printed in black on a blue background and feature player highlights in paragraph form.

		MT	NR MT	EX
Complete Set:		10.00	7.50	4.00
Common Player:		1.50	1.25	.60
1	Pete Rose	1.50	1.25	.60
2	Steve Carlton	1.50	1.25	.60
3	Tom Seaver	1.50	1.25	.60
4	Rod Carew	1.50	1.25	.60
5	Nolan Ryan	2.00	1.50	.80
6	Reggie Jackson	1.50	1.25	.60

1986 Fleer League Leaders

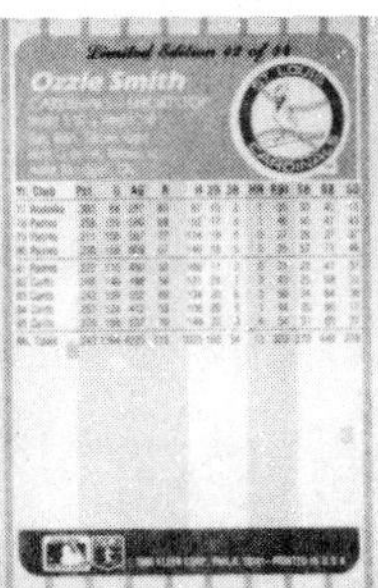

Fleer's 1986 "League Leaders" set features 44 of the game's top players and was issued through the Walgreens drug store chain. The card fronts contain a color photo and feature the player's name, team and postition in a blue band near the bottom of the card. The words "League Leaders" appear in a red band at the top of the card. The background for the card fronts is alternating blue and white stripes. The card backs are printed in blue, red and white and carry the player's statistical information and team logo. The cards are the standard 2-1/2" by 3-1/2" size. The set was issued in a special cardboard box, along with six team logo stickers.

		MT	NR MT	EX
Complete Set:		8.00	6.00	3.00
Common Player:		.05	.04	.02
1	Wade Boggs	1.00	.70	.40
2	George Brett	.30	.25	.12
3	Jose Canseco	3.50	2.75	1.50
4	Rod Carew	.30	.25	.12
5	Gary Carter	.25	.20	.10
6	Jack Clark	.12	.09	.05
7	Vince Coleman	.60	.45	.25
8	Jose Cruz	.05	.04	.02

		MT	NR MT	EX
9	Alvin Davis	.10	.08	.04
10	Mariano Duncan	.05	.04	.02
11	Leon Durham	.05	.04	.02
12	Carlton Fisk	.15	.11	.06
13	Julio Franco	.10	.08	.04
14	Scott Garrelts	.05	.04	.02
15	Steve Garvey	.25	.20	.10
16	Dwight Gooden	1.00	.70	.40
17	Ozzie Guillen	.10	.08	.04
18	Willie Hernandez	.05	.04	.02
19	Bob Horner	.07	.05	.03
20	Kent Hrbek	.15	.11	.06
21	Charlie Leibrandt	.05	.04	.02
22	Don Mattingly	1.50	1.25	.60
23	Oddibe McDowell	.12	.09	.05
24	Willie McGee	.10	.08	.04
25	Keith Moreland	.05	.04	.02
26	Lloyd Moseby	.07	.05	.03
27	Dale Murphy	.30	.25	.12
28	Phil Niekro	.15	.11	.06
29	Joe Orsulak	.05	.04	.02
30	Dave Parker	.12	.09	.05
31	Lance Parrish	.15	.11	.06
32	Kirby Puckett	.70	.50	.30
33	Tim Raines	.25	.20	.10
34	Earnie Riles	.07	.05	.03
35	Cal Ripken, Jr.	.30	.25	.12
36	Pete Rose	.60	.45	.25
37	Bret Saberhagen	.15	.11	.06
38	Juan Samuel	.10	.08	.04
39	Ryne Sandberg	.20	.15	.08
40	Tom Seaver	.25	.20	.10
41	Lee Smith	.07	.05	.03
42	Ozzie Smith	.12	.09	.05
43	Dave Stieb	.10	.08	.04
44	Robin Yount	.35	.25	.12

1986 Fleer Limited Edition

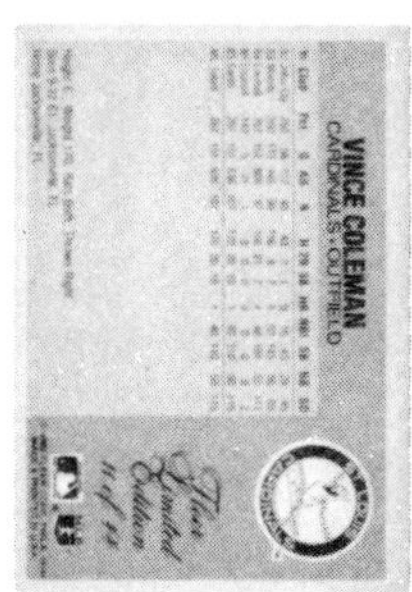

Produced for the McCrory's store chain and their affiliates for the second year in a row, the 1986 Fleer Limited Edition set contains 44 cards. The cards, which are the standard 2-1/2" by 3-1/2" size, have color photos enclosed by green, red and yellow trim. The card backs carry black print on two shades of red. The set was issued in a special cardboard box, along with six team logo stickers.

		MT	NR MT	EX
Complete Set:		7.00	5.25	2.75
Common Player:		.05	.04	.02
1	Doyle Alexander	.05	.04	.02
2	Joaquin Andujar	.05	.04	.02
3	Harold Baines	.12	.09	.05
4	Wade Boggs	1.00	.70	.40
5	Phil Bradley	.12	.09	.05
6	George Brett	.30	.25	.12
7	Hubie Brooks	.07	.05	.03
8	Chris Brown	.12	.09	.05
9	Tom Brunansky	.10	.08	.04
10	Gary Carter	.25	.20	.10
11	Vince Coleman	.60	.45	.25
12	Cecil Cooper	.07	.05	.03
13	Jose Cruz	.05	.04	.02
14	Mike Davis	.05	.04	.02
15	Carlton Fisk	.15	.11	.06
16	Julio Franco	.10	.08	.04
17	Damaso Garcia	.05	.04	.02
18	Rich Gedman	.05	.04	.02
19	Kirk Gibson	.20	.15	.08
20	Dwight Gooden	1.00	.70	.40
21	Pedro Guerrero	.15	.11	.06
22	Tony Gwynn	.25	.20	.10
23	Rickey Henderson	.50	.40	.20
24	Orel Hershiser	.20	.15	.08
25	LaMarr Hoyt	.05	.04	.02
26	Reggie Jackson	.30	.25	.12
27	Don Mattingly	1.50	1.25	.60
28	Oddibe McDowell	.12	.09	.05
29	Willie McGee	.10	.08	.04
30	Paul Molitor	.12	.09	.05
31	Dale Murphy	.30	.25	.12
32	Eddie Murray	.25	.20	.10
33	Dave Parker	.12	.09	.05
34	Tony Pena	.07	.05	.03
35	Jeff Reardon	.07	.05	.03
36	Cal Ripken, Jr.	.30	.25	.12
37	Pete Rose	.60	.45	.25
38	Bret Saberhagen	.15	.11	.06
39	Juan Samuel	.10	.08	.04
40	Ryne Sandberg	.20	.15	.08
41	Mike Schmidt	.30	.25	.12
42	Lee Smith	.07	.05	.03
43	Don Sutton	.12	.09	.05
44	Lou Whitaker	.15	.11	.06

1986 Fleer Mini

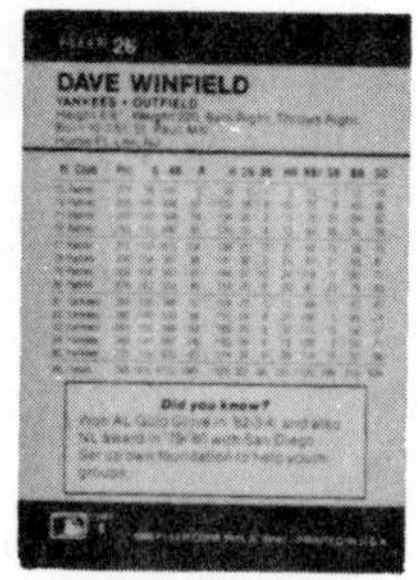

Fleer's 1986 "Classic Miniatures" set contains 120 cards that measure 1-13/16" by 2-9/16" in size. The design of the high-gloss cards is identical to the regular 1986 Fleer set but the player photos are entirely different. The set, which was issued in a specially designed box along with 18 team logo stickers, was available to the collecting public only through hobby dealers.

		MT	NR MT	EX
Complete Set:		12.00	9.00	5.00
Common Player:		.05	.04	.02
1	George Brett	.30	.25	.12
2	Dan Quisenberry	.07	.05	.03
3	Bret Saberhagen	.15	.11	.06
4	Lonnie Smith	.05	.04	.02
5	Willie Wilson	.10	.08	.04
6	Jack Clark	.12	.09	.05
7	Vince Coleman	.50	.40	.20
8	Tom Herr	.07	.05	.03
9	Willie McGee	.10	.08	.04
10	Ozzie Smith	.12	.09	.05
11	John Tudor	.07	.05	.03
12	Jesse Barfield	.12	.09	.05
13	George Bell	.20	.15	.08
14	Tony Fernandez	.10	.08	.04
15	Damaso Garcia	.05	.04	.02
16	Dave Stieb	.07	.05	.03
17	Gary Carter	.20	.15	.08
18	Ron Darling	.10	.08	.04
19	Dwight Gooden	.60	.45	.25
20	Keith Hernandez	.20	.15	.08
21	Darryl Strawberry	.50	.40	.20
22	Ron Guidry	.15	.11	.06
23	Rickey Henderson	.30	.25	.12
24	Don Mattingly	1.75	1.25	.70
25	Dave Righetti	.12	.09	.05
26	Dave Winfield	.20	.15	.08
27	Mariano Duncan	.07	.05	.03
28	Pedro Guerrero	.12	.09	.05
29	Bill Madlock	.10	.08	.04
30	Mike Marshall	.10	.08	.04
31	Fernando Valenzuela	.10	.08	.04
32	Reggie Jackson	.30	.25	.12
33	Gary Pettis	.05	.04	.02
34	Ron Romanick	.05	.04	.02
35	Don Sutton	.12	.09	.05
36	Mike Witt	.07	.05	.03
37	Buddy Bell	.07	.05	.03
38	Tom Browning	.10	.08	.04
39	Dave Parker	.12	.09	.05
40	Pete Rose	.60	.45	.25
41	Mario Soto	.05	.04	.02
42	Harold Baines	.12	.09	.05
43	Carlton Fisk	.15	.11	.06
44	Ozzie Guillen	.12	.09	.05
45	Ron Kittle	.07	.05	.03
46	Tom Seaver	.20	.15	.08
47	Kirk Gibson	.20	.15	.08
48	Jack Morris	.15	.11	.06
49	Lance Parrish	.15	.11	.06
50	Alan Trammell	.20	.15	.08
51	Lou Whitaker	.15	.11	.06
52	Hubie Brooks	.07	.05	.03
53	Andre Dawson	.15	.11	.06
54	Tim Raines	.20	.15	.08
55	Bryn Smith	.05	.04	.02
56	Tim Wallach	.10	.08	.04
57	Mike Boddicker	.05	.04	.02
58	Eddie Murray	.25	.20	.10
59	Cal Ripken	.30	.25	.12
60	John Shelby	.05	.04	.02
61	Mike Young	.05	.04	.02
62	Jose Cruz	.07	.05	.03
63	Glenn Davis	.15	.11	.06
64	Phil Garner	.05	.04	.02
65	Nolan Ryan	.50	.40	.20
66	Mike Scott	.12	.09	.05
67	Steve Garvey	.20	.15	.08
68	Goose Gossage	.12	.09	.05
69	Tony Gwynn	.25	.20	.10
70	Andy Hawkins	.05	.04	.02
71	Garry Templeton	.05	.04	.02
72	Wade Boggs	1.00	.70	.40
73	Roger Clemens	1.00	.70	.40
74	Dwight Evans	.12	.09	.05
75	Rich Gedman	.05	.04	.02
76	Jim Rice	.20	.15	.08
77	Shawon Dunston	.10	.08	.04
78	Leon Durham	.05	.04	.02
79	Keith Moreland	.05	.04	.02
80	Ryne Sandberg	.20	.15	.08
81	Rick Sutcliffe	.10	.08	.04
82	Bert Blyleven	.12	.09	.05
83	Tom Brunansky	.10	.08	.04
84	Kent Hrbek	.15	.11	.06
85	Kirby Puckett	.70	.50	.30
86	Bruce Bochte	.05	.04	.02
87	Jose Canseco	3.50	2.75	1.50
88	Mike Davis	.05	.04	.02
89	Jay Howell	.07	.05	.03
90	Dwayne Murphy	.05	.04	.02
91	Steve Carlton	.20	.15	.08
92	Von Hayes	.10	.08	.04
93	Juan Samuel	.12	.09	.05
94	Mike Schmidt	.30	.25	.12
95	Glenn Wilson	.05	.04	.02
96	Phil Bradley	.10	.08	.04
97	Alvin Davis	.10	.08	.04
98	Jim Presley	.10	.08	.04
99	Danny Tartabull	.15	.11	.06
100	Cecil Cooper	.10	.08	.04
101	Paul Molitor	.12	.09	.05
102	Earnie Riles	.07	.05	.03
103	Robin Yount	.30	.25	.12
104	Bob Horner	.10	.08	.04
105	Dale Murphy	.30	.25	.12
106	Bruce Sutter	.10	.08	.04
107	Claudell Washington	.05	.04	.02
108	Chris Brown	.12	.09	.05
109	Chili Davis	.05	.04	.02
110	Scott Garrelts	.05	.04	.02
111	Oddibe McDowell	.12	.09	.05
112	Pete O'Brien	.07	.05	.03
113	Gary Ward	.05	.04	.02
114	Brett Butler	.05	.04	.02
115	Julio Franco	.10	.08	.04
116	Brook Jacoby	.10	.08	.04
117	Mike Brown	.05	.04	.02
118	Joe Orsulak	.05	.04	.02
119	Tony Pena	.07	.05	.03
120	R.J. Reynolds	.05	.04	.02

1986 Fleer Star Stickers

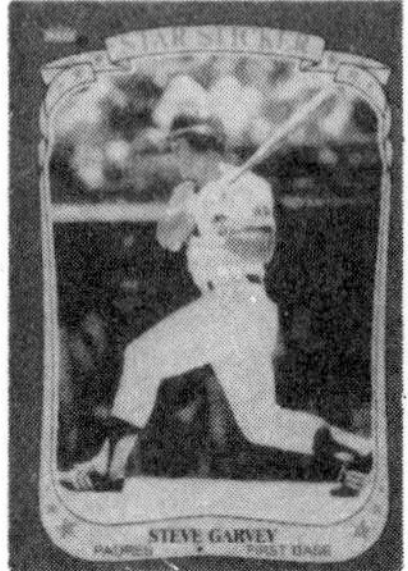

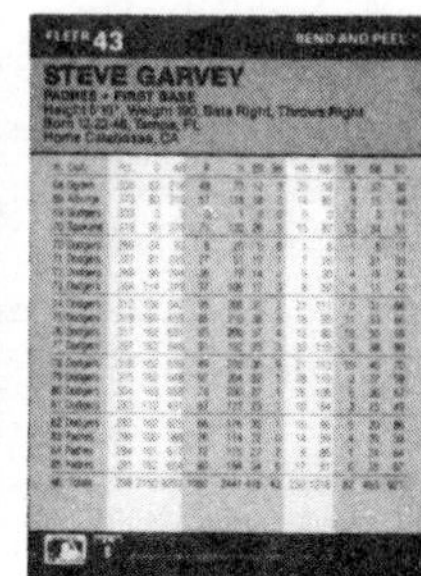

After a five-year layoff, Fleer once again produced a Star Sticker set. The cards, which measure 2-1/2" by 3-1/2", have color photos inside dark maroon borders. The card backs are identical to the 1986 regular issue except for the 1-132 numbering system and blue ink instead of yellow. The words "Bend and Peel" are found in the upper right corner of the card backs. Card #132 is a multi-player card featuring Dwight Gooden and Dale Murphy on the front and a complete checklist for the set on the reverse. The cards were sold in wax packs with team logo stickers.

		MT	NR MT	EX
Complete Set		25.00	20.00	10.00
Common Player		.05	.04	.02
1	Harold Baines	.20	.15	.08
2	Jesse Barfield	.20	.15	.08
3	Don Baylor	.12	.09	.05
4	Juan Beniquez	.05	.04	.02
5	Tim Birtsas	.08	.06	.03
6	Bert Blyleven	.15	.11	.06
7	Bruce Bochte	.05	.04	.02
8	Wade Boggs	1.00	.70	.40
9	Dennis Boyd	.12	.09	.05
10	Phil Bradley	.20	.15	.08
11	George Brett	.50	.40	.20
12	Hubie Brooks	.12	.09	.05
13	Chris Brown	.45	.35	.20
14	Tom Browning	.15	.11	.06
15	Tom Brunansky	.15	.11	.06
16	Bill Buckner	.10	.08	.04
17	Britt Burns	.05	.04	.02
18	Brett Butler	.08	.06	.03
19	Jose Canseco	3.50	2.75	1.50
20	Rod Carew	.40	.30	.15
21	Steve Carlton	.40	.30	.15
22	Don Carman	.20	.15	.08
23	Gary Carter	.40	.30	.15
24	Jack Clark	.20	.15	.08
25	Vince Coleman	.70	.50	.30
26	Cecil Cooper	.15	.11	.06
27	Jose Cruz	.10	.08	.04
28	Ron Darling	.20	.15	.08
29	Alvin Davis	.20	.15	.08
30	Jody Davis	.08	.06	.03
31	Mike Davis	.05	.04	.02
32	Andre Dawson	.25	.20	.10
33	Mariano Duncan	.10	.08	.04
34	Shawon Dunston	.15	.11	.06
35	Leon Durham	.08	.06	.03
36	Darrell Evans	.12	.09	.05
37	Tony Fernandez	.15	.11	.06
38	Carlton Fisk	.20	.15	.08
39	John Franco	.10	.08	.04
40	Julio Franco	.12	.09	.05
41	Damaso Garcia	.05	.04	.02

		MT	NR MT	EX
42	Scott Garrelts	.05	.04	.02
43	Steve Garvey	.25	.20	.10
44	Rich Gedman	.10	.08	.04
45	Kirk Gibson	.30	.25	.12
46	Dwight Gooden	.90	.70	.35
47	Pedro Guerrero	.20	.15	.08
48	Ron Guidry	.20	.15	.08
49	Ozzie Guillen	.30	.25	.12
50	Tony Gwynn	.40	.30	.15
51	Andy Hawkins	.08	.06	.03
52	Von Hayes	.12	.09	.05
53	Rickey Henderson	1.00	.70	.40
54	Tom Henke	.12	.09	.05
55	Keith Hernandez	.35	.25	.14
56	Willie Hernandez	.05	.04	.02
57	Tom Herr	.10	.08	.04
58	Orel Hershiser	.30	.25	.12
59	Teddy Higuera	.60	.45	.25
60	Bob Horner	.12	.09	.05
61	Charlie Hough	.08	.06	.03
62	Jay Howell	.08	.06	.03
63	LaMarr Hoyt	.05	.04	.02
64	Kent Hrbek	.30	.25	.12
65	Reggie Jackson	.50	.40	.20
66	Bob James	.05	.04	.02
67	Dave Kingman	.12	.09	.05
68	Ron Kittle	.12	.09	.05
69	Charlie Leibrandt	.08	.06	.03
70	Fred Lynn	.25	.20	.10
71	Mike Marshall	.20	.15	.08
72	Don Mattingly	2.25	1.75	.90
73	Oddibe McDowell	.25	.20	.10
74	Willie McGee	.20	.15	.08
75	Scott McGregor	.05	.04	.02
76	Paul Molitor	.20	.15	.08
77	Donnie Moore	.05	.04	.02
78	Keith Moreland	.08	.06	.03
79	Jack Morris	.25	.20	.10
80	Dale Murphy	.40	.30	.15
81	Eddie Murray	.50	.40	.20
82	Phil Niekro	.25	.20	.10
83	Joe Orsulak	.10	.08	.04
84	Dave Parker	.25	.20	.10
85	Lance Parrish	.25	.20	.10
86	Larry Parrish	.08	.06	.03
87	Tony Pena	.10	.08	.04
88	Gary Pettis	.05	.04	.02
89	Jim Presley	.15	.11	.06
90	Kirby Puckett	1.00	.70	.40
91	Dan Quisenberry	.12	.09	.05
92	Tim Raines	.35	.25	.14
93	Johnny Ray	.10	.08	.04
94	Jeff Reardon	.10	.08	.04
95	Rick Reuschel	.10	.08	.04
96	Jim Rice	.15	.11	.06
97	Dave Righetti	.20	.15	.08
98	Earnie Riles	.12	.09	.05
99	Cal Ripken, Jr.	.60	.45	.25
100	Ron Romanick	.05	.04	.02
101	Pete Rose	1.00	.70	.40
102	Nolan Ryan	1.00	.70	.40
103	Bret Saberhagen	.25	.20	.10
104	Mark Salas	.05	.04	.02
105	Juan Samuel	.15	.11	.06
106	Ryne Sandberg	.70	.50	.30
107	Mike Schmidt	1.00	.70	.40
108	Mike Scott	.15	.11	.06
109	Tom Seaver	.30	.25	.12
110	Bryn Smith	.05	.04	.02
111	Dave Smith	.05	.04	.02
112	Lee Smith	.10	.08	.04
113	Ozzie Smith	.20	.15	.08
114	Mario Soto	.05	.04	.02
115	Dave Stieb	.12	.09	.05
116	Darryl Strawberry	1.00	.70	.40
117	Bruce Sutter	.10	.08	.04
118	Garry Templeton	.08	.06	.03
119	Gorman Thomas	.08	.06	.03
120	Andre Thornton	.10	.08	.04
121	Allan Trammell	.20	.15	.08
122	John Tudor	.12	.09	.05
123	Fernando Valenzuela	.30	.25	.12
124	Frank Viola	.20	.15	.08
125	Gary Ward	.05	.04	.02
126	Lou Whitaker	.25	.20	.10
127	Frank White	.10	.08	.04
128	Glenn Wilson	.08	.06	.03
129	Willie Wilson	.15	.11	.06
130	Dave Winfield	.40	.30	.15
131	Robin Yount	.35	.25	.14
132	Dwight Gooden, Dale Murphy/Checklist	1.25	.90	.50

1986 Fleer Star Stickers Box Panel

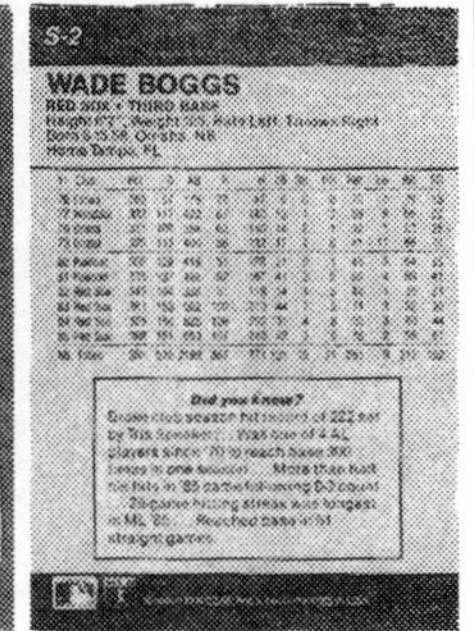

Four cards, numbered S-1 through S-4, were placed on the bottoms of 1986 Fleer Star Stickers wax pack boxes. The cards are nearly identical in format to the regular issue sticker cards. Individual cards measure 2-1/2" by 3-1/2" in size, while a complete panel of four measures 5" by 7-1/8".

		MT	NR MT	EX
Complete Panel Set:		3.00	2.25	1.25
Complete Singles Set:		1.50	1.25	.60
Common Single Player:		.30	.25	.12
Panel		3.00	2.25	1.25
1	Dodgers Logo	.05	.04	.02
2	Wade Boggs	1.00	.70	.40
3	Steve Garvey	.30	.25	.12
4	Dave Winfield	.30	.25	.12

1986 Fleer Update

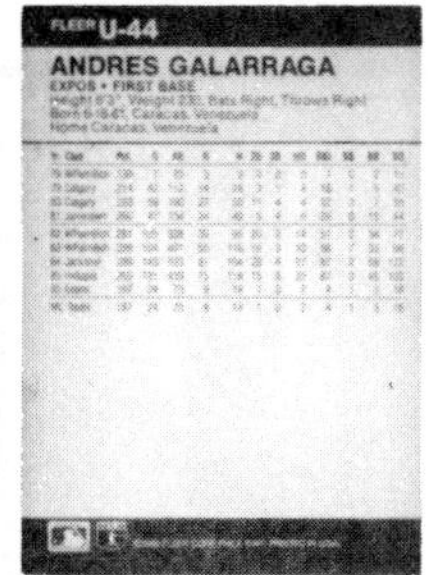

Issued near the end of the baseball season, the 1986 Fleer Update set consists of 132 cards numbered U-1 through U-132. The cards, which measure 2-1/2" by 3-1/2" in size, are identical in design to the regular 1986 Fleer set. The purpose of the set is to update player trades and include new players not depicted in the regular issue. The set was issued with team logo stickers in a specially designed box and was available only through hobby dealers.

		MT	NR MT	EX
Complete Set:		35.00	27.00	15.00
Common Player:		.08	.06	.03
1	Mike Aldrete(FC)	.35	.25	.14
2	Andy Allanson(FC)	.20	.15	.08
3	Neil Allen	.08	.06	.03
4	Joaquin Andujar	.10	.08	.04
5	Paul Assenmacher(FC)	.20	.15	.08
6	Scott Bailes(FC)	.25	.20	.10
7	Jay Baller(FC)	.15	.11	.06
8	Scott Bankhead(FC)	.20	.15	.08
9	Bill Bathe(FC)	.08	.06	.03
10	Don Baylor	.15	.11	.06
11	Billy Beane(FC)	.08	.06	.03
12	Steve Bedrosian	.15	.11	.06
13	Juan Beniquez	.08	.06	.03
14	Barry Bonds(FC)	2.00	1.50	.80
15	Bobby Bonilla(FC)	2.00	1.50	.80
16	Rich Bordi	.08	.06	.03
17	Bill Campbell	.08	.06	.03
18	Tom Candiotti	.08	.06	.03
19	John Cangelosi(FC)	.20	.15	.08
20	Jose Canseco	12.00	9.00	4.75
21	Chuck Cary(FC)	.15	.11	.06
22	Juan Castillo(FC)	.10	.08	.04
23	Rick Cerone	.08	.06	.03
24	John Cerutti(FC)	.25	.20	.10
25	Will Clark(FC)	15.00	11.00	6.00
26	Mark Clear	.08	.06	.03
27	Darnell Coles(FC)	.15	.11	.06
28	Dave Collins	.10	.08	.04
29	Tim Conroy	.08	.06	.03
30	Ed Correa(FC)	.20	.15	.08
31	Joe Cowley	.08	.06	.03
32	Bill Dawley	.08	.06	.03
33	Rob Deer	.15	.11	.06
34	John Denny	.08	.06	.03
35	Jim DeShaies (Deshaies)(FC)	.25	.20	.10
36	Doug Drabek(FC)	.35	.25	.14
37	Mike Easler	.12	.09	.05
38	Mark Eichhorn(FC)	.20	.15	.08
39	Dave Engle	.08	.06	.03
40	Mike Fischlin	.08	.06	.03
41	Scott Fletcher	.15	.11	.06
42	Terry Forster	.12	.09	.05
43	Terry Francona	.08	.06	.03
44	Andres Galarraga	.90	.70	.35
45	Lee Guetterman(FC)	.20	.15	.08
46	Bill Gullickson	.08	.06	.03
47	Jackie Gutierrez	.08	.06	.03
48	Moose Haas	.08	.06	.03
49	Billy Hatcher	.15	.11	.06
50	Mike Heath	.08	.06	.03
51	Guy Hoffman(FC)	.10	.08	.04
52	Tom Hume	.08	.06	.03
53	Pete Incaviglia(FC)	.50	.40	.20
54	Dane Iorg	.08	.06	.03
55	Chris James(FC)	.60	.45	.25
56	Stan Javier(FC)	.25	.20	.10
57	Tommy John	.20	.15	.08
58	Tracy Jones(FC)	.40	.30	.15
59	Wally Joyner(FC)	2.50	2.00	1.00
60	Wayne Krenchicki	.08	.06	.03
61	John Kruk(FC)	.40	.30	.15
62	Mike LaCoss	.08	.06	.03
63	Pete Ladd	.08	.06	.03
64	Dave LaPoint	.15	.11	.06
65	Mike LaValliere(FC)	.30	.25	.12
66	Rudy Law	.08	.06	.03
67	Dennis Leonard	.10	.08	.04
68	Steve Lombardozzi(FC)	.20	.15	.08
69	Aurelio Lopez	.08	.06	.03
70	Mickey Mahler	.08	.06	.03
71	Candy Maldonado	.15	.11	.06
72	Roger Mason(FC)	.10	.08	.04
73	Greg Mathews(FC)	.25	.20	.10
74	Andy McGaffigan	.08	.06	.03
75	Joel McKeon(FC)	.12	.09	.05
76	Kevin Mitchell(FC)	7.00	5.25	2.75
77	Bill Mooneyham(FC)	.12	.09	.05
78	Omar Moreno	.08	.06	.03
79	Jerry Mumphrey	.08	.06	.03
80	Al Newman(FC)	.12	.09	.05
81	Phil Niekro	.40	.30	.15
82	Randy Niemann	.08	.06	.03
83	Juan Nieves(FC)	.20	.15	.08
84	Bob Ojeda	.12	.09	.05
85	Rick Ownbey	.08	.06	.03
86	Tom Paciorek	.08	.06	.03
87	David Palmer	.08	.06	.03
88	Jeff Parrett(FC)	.25	.20	.10
89	Pat Perry(FC)	.15	.11	.06
90	Dan Plesac(FC)	.35	.25	.14
91	Darrell Porter	.12	.09	.05
92	Luis Quinones(FC)	.12	.09	.05
93	Rey Quinonez(FC)	.20	.15	.08
94	Gary Redus	.10	.08	.04
95	Jeff Reed(FC)	.12	.09	.05
96	Bip Roberts(FC)	.08	.06	.03
97	Billy Joe Robidoux	.12	.09	.05
98	Gary Roenicke	.08	.06	.03
99	Ron Roenicke	.08	.06	.03
100	Angel Salazar	.08	.06	.03
101	Joe Sambito	.08	.06	.03
102	Billy Sample	.08	.06	.03
103	Dave Schmidt	.08	.06	.03
104	Ken Schrom	.08	.06	.03
105	Ruben Sierra(FC)	7.00	5.25	2.75
106	Ted Simmons	.20	.15	.08
107	Sammy Stewart	.08	.06	.03
108	Kurt Stillwell(FC)	.30	.25	.12
109	Dale Sveum(FC)	.25	.20	.10
110	Tim Teufel	.08	.06	.03
111	Bob Tewksbury(FC)	.12	.09	.05
112	Andres Thomas(FC)	.25	.20	.10
113	Jason Thompson	.08	.06	.03
114	Milt Thompson	.12	.09	.05
115	Rob Thompson(FC)	.40	.30	.15
116	Jay Tibbs	.08	.06	.03
117	Fred Toliver	.12	.09	.05
118	Wayne Tolleson	.08	.06	.03
119	Alex Trevino	.08	.06	.03
120	Manny Trillo	.10	.08	.04
121	Ed Vande Berg	.08	.06	.03
122	Ozzie Virgil	.08	.06	.03
123	Tony Walker(FC)	.08	.06	.03
124	Gene Walter	.12	.09	.05
125	Duane Ward(FC)	.20	.15	.08
126	Jerry Willard	.08	.06	.03
127	Mitch Williams(FC)	.60	.45	.25
128	Reggie Williams(FC)	.20	.15	.08
129	Bobby Witt(FC)	.50	.40	.20
130	Marvell Wynne	.08	.06	.03
131	Steve Yeager	.08	.06	.03
132	Checklist	.08	.06	.03

1987 Fleer

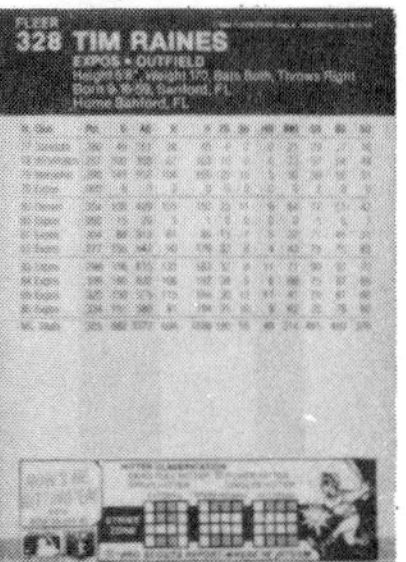

The 1987 Fleer set consists of 660 cards, each measuring 2-1/2" by 3-1/2". The card fronts feature an attractive blue and white border. The player's name and position appears in the upper left corner of the card. The player's team logo is located in the lower right corner. The card backs are done in blue, red and white and contain an innovative "Pro Scouts Report" feature which lists the hitter's or pitcher's batting and pitching strengths. For the third year in a row, Fleer included its "Major League Prospects" subset. Fleer produced a glossy-finish Collectors Edition set which came housed in a specially-designed tin box. It was speculated that 100,000 of the glossy sets were produced. After experiencing a dramatic drop in price during 1987, the glossy set now sells for only a few dollars more than the regular issue.

	MT	NR MT	EX
Complete Set:	100.00	75.00	40.00
Common Player:	.06	.05	.02

		MT	NR MT	EX
1	Rick Aguilera	.08	.06	.03
2	Richard Anderson	.06	.05	.02
3	Wally Backman	.08	.06	.03
4	Gary Carter	.25	.20	.10
5	Ron Darling	.15	.11	.06
6	Len Dykstra	.20	.15	.08
7	*Kevin Elster*(FC)	.50	.40	.20
8	Sid Fernandez	.12	.09	.05
9	Dwight Gooden	.90	.70	.35
10	*Ed Hearn*(FC)	.10	.08	.04
11	Danny Heep	.06	.05	.02
12	Keith Hernandez	.25	.20	.10
13	Howard Johnson	.10	.08	.04
14	Ray Knight	.08	.06	.03
15	Lee Mazzilli	.08	.06	.03
16	Roger McDowell	.12	.09	.05
17	*Kevin Mitchell*	9.00	6.75	3.50
18	Randy Niemann	.06	.05	.02
19	Bob Ojeda	.08	.06	.03
20	Jesse Orosco	.08	.06	.03
21	Rafael Santana	.06	.05	.02
22	Doug Sisk	.06	.05	.02
23	Darryl Strawberry	1.00	.70	.40
24	Tim Teufel	.06	.05	.02
25	Mookie Wilson	.10	.08	.04
26	Tony Armas	.08	.06	.03
27	Marty Barrett	.10	.08	.04
28	Don Baylor	.12	.09	.05
29	Wade Boggs	1.50	1.25	.60
30	Oil Can Boyd	.08	.06	.03
31	Bill Buckner	.10	.08	.04
32	Roger Clemens	1.50	1.25	.60
33	Steve Crawford	.06	.05	.02
34	Dwight Evans	.12	.09	.05
35	Rich Gedman	.10	.08	.04
36	Dave Henderson	.10	.08	.04
37	Bruce Hurst	.10	.08	.04
38	Tim Lollar	.06	.05	.02
39	Al Nipper	.06	.05	.02
40	Spike Owen	.06	.05	.02
41	Jim Rice	.30	.25	.12
42	Ed Romero	.06	.05	.02
43	Joe Sambito	.06	.05	.02
44	Calvin Schiraldi	.10	.08	.04
45	Tom Seaver	.40	.30	.15
46	*Jeff Sellers*(FC)	.20	.15	.08
47	Bob Stanley	.06	.05	.02
48	Sammy Stewart	.06	.05	.02
49	Larry Andersen	.06	.05	.02
50	Alan Ashby	.06	.05	.02
51	Kevin Bass	.10	.08	.04
52	Jeff Calhoun	.06	.05	.02
53	Jose Cruz	.10	.08	.04
54	Danny Darwin	.06	.05	.02
55	Glenn Davis	.30	.25	.12
56	*Jim Deshaies*	.25	.20	.10
57	Bill Doran	.10	.08	.04
58	Phil Garner	.06	.05	.02
59	Billy Hatcher	.08	.06	.03
60	Charlie Kerfeld	.06	.05	.02
61	Bob Knepper	.08	.06	.03
62	Dave Lopes	.08	.06	.03
63	Aurelio Lopez	.06	.05	.02
64	Jim Pankovits	.06	.05	.02
65	Terry Puhl	.06	.05	.02
66	Craig Reynolds	.06	.05	.02
67	Nolan Ryan	1.00	.70	.40
68	Mike Scott	.15	.11	.06
69	Dave Smith	.08	.06	.03
70	Dickie Thon	.08	.06	.03
71	Tony Walker	.06	.05	.02
72	Denny Walling	.06	.05	.02
73	Bob Boone	.08	.06	.03
74	Rick Burleson	.08	.06	.03
75	John Candelaria	.10	.08	.04
76	Doug Corbett	.06	.05	.02
77	Doug DeCinces	.08	.06	.03
78	Brian Downing	.08	.06	.03
79	*Chuck Finley*(FC)	.15	.11	.06
80	Terry Forster	.08	.06	.03
81	Bobby Grich	.10	.08	.04
82	George Hendrick	.08	.06	.03
83	Jack Howell(FC)	.10	.08	.04
84	Reggie Jackson	.35	.25	.14
85	Ruppert Jones	.06	.05	.02
86	*Wally Joyner*	2.50	2.00	1.00
87	Gary Lucas	.06	.05	.02
88	Kirk McCaskill	.08	.06	.03
89	Donnie Moore	.06	.05	.02
90	Gary Pettis	.06	.05	.02
91	Vern Ruhle	.06	.05	.02
92	Dick Schofield	.06	.05	.02
93	Don Sutton	.20	.15	.08
94	Rob Wilfong	.06	.05	.02
95	Mike Witt	.10	.08	.04
96	*Doug Drabek*	.50	.40	.20
97	Mike Easler	.08	.06	.03
98	Mike Fischlin	.06	.05	.02
99	Brian Fisher	.08	.06	.03
100	Ron Guidry	.15	.11	.06
101	Rickey Henderson	.50	.40	.20
102	Tommy John	.20	.15	.08
103	Ron Kittle	.10	.08	.04
104	Don Mattingly	3.00	2.25	1.25
105	Bobby Meacham	.06	.05	.02
106	Joe Niekro	.10	.08	.04
107	Mike Pagliarulo	.10	.08	.04
108	Dan Pasqua	.10	.08	.04
109	Willie Randolph	.10	.08	.04
110	Dennis Rasmussen	.10	.08	.04
111	Dave Righetti	.15	.11	.06
112	Gary Roenicke	.06	.05	.02
113	Rod Scurry	.06	.05	.02
114	Bob Shirley	.06	.05	.02
115	Joel Skinner	.06	.05	.02
116	Tim Stoddard	.06	.05	.02
117	*Bob Tewksbury*	.12	.09	.05
118	Wayne Tolleson	.06	.05	.02
119	Claudell Washington	.08	.06	.03
120	Dave Winfield	.30	.25	.12
121	Steve Buechele	.08	.06	.03
122	*Ed Correa*	.15	.11	.06
123	Scott Fletcher	.08	.06	.03
124	Jose Guzman	.10	.08	.04
125	Toby Harrah	.08	.06	.03
126	Greg Harris	.06	.05	.02
127	Charlie Hough	.08	.06	.03
128	*Pete Incaviglia*	.60	.45	.25
129	Mike Mason	.06	.05	.02
130	Oddibe McDowell	.10	.08	.04
131	*Dale Mohorcic*(FC)	.20	.15	.08
132	Pete O'Brien	.10	.08	.04
133	Tom Paciorek	.06	.05	.02
134	Larry Parrish	.08	.06	.03
135	Geno Petralli	.06	.05	.02
136	Darrell Porter	.08	.06	.03
137	Jeff Russell	.06	.05	.02
138	*Ruben Sierra*	12.00	9.00	4.75
139	Don Slaught	.06	.05	.02
140	Gary Ward	.08	.06	.03
141	Curtis Wilkerson	.06	.05	.02
142	*Mitch Williams*	.60	.45	.25
143	*Bobby Witt*	.35	.25	.14
144	Dave Bergman	.06	.05	.02
145	Tom Brookens	.06	.05	.02
146	Bill Campbell	.06	.05	.02
147	*Chuck Cary*	.10	.08	.04
148	Darnell Coles	.08	.06	.03
149	Dave Collins	.08	.06	.03
150	Darrell Evans	.12	.09	.05
151	Kirk Gibson	.25	.20	.10
152	John Grubb	.06	.05	.02
153	Willie Hernandez	.08	.06	.03
154	Larry Herndon	.08	.06	.03
155	*Eric King*	.25	.20	.10
156	Chet Lemon	.08	.06	.03
157	Dwight Lowry	.06	.05	.02
158	Jack Morris	.20	.15	.08
159	Randy O'Neal	.06	.05	.02
160	Lance Parrish	.20	.15	.08
161	Dan Petry	.08	.06	.03
162	Pat Sheridan	.06	.05	.02
163	Jim Slaton	.06	.05	.02
164	Frank Tanana	.08	.06	.03
165	Walt Terrell	.08	.06	.03
166	Mark Thurmond	.06	.05	.02
167	Alan Trammell	.25	.20	.10
168	Lou Whitaker	.25	.20	.10
169	Luis Aguayo	.06	.05	.02
170	Steve Bedrosian	.12	.09	.05
171	Don Carman	.10	.08	.04
172	Darren Daulton	.06	.05	.02
173	Greg Gross	.06	.05	.02
174	Kevin Gross	.08	.06	.03
175	Von Hayes	.10	.08	.04
176	Charles Hudson	.06	.05	.02
177	Tom Hume	.06	.05	.02
178	Steve Jeltz	.06	.05	.02
179	*Mike Maddux*(FC)	.20	.15	.08
180	Shane Rawley	.08	.06	.03
181	Gary Redus	.06	.05	.02
182	Ron Roenicke	.06	.05	.02
183	*Bruce Ruffin*(FC)	.20	.15	.08
184	John Russell	.06	.05	.02
185	Juan Samuel	.12	.09	.05
186	Dan Schatzeder	.06	.05	.02
187	Mike Schmidt	.60	.45	.25
188	Rick Schu	.06	.05	.02
189	Jeff Stone	.06	.05	.02
190	Kent Tekulve	.08	.06	.03
191	Milt Thompson	.08	.06	.03
192	Glenn Wilson	.08	.06	.03
193	Buddy Bell	.10	.08	.04
194	Tom Browning	.10	.08	.04
195	Sal Butera	.06	.05	.02
196	Dave Concepcion	.12	.09	.05
197	Kal Daniels	.80	.60	.30
198	Eric Davis	1.50	1.25	.60
199	John Denny	.06	.05	.02
200	Bo Diaz	.08	.06	.03
201	Nick Esasky	.08	.06	.03
202	John Franco	.10	.08	.04
203	Bill Gullickson	.06	.05	.02
204	*Barry Larkin*(FC)	6.00	4.50	2.50
205	Eddie Milner	.06	.05	.02
206	*Rob Murphy*(FC)	.20	.15	.08
207	Ron Oester	.06	.05	.02
208	Dave Parker	.20	.15	.08
209	Tony Perez	.15	.11	.06
210	Ted Power	.06	.05	.02
211	Joe Price	.06	.05	.02
212	Ron Robinson	.06	.05	.02
213	Pete Rose	.60	.45	.25
214	Mario Soto	.08	.06	.03
215	*Kurt Stillwell*	.50	.40	.20
216	Max Venable	.06	.05	.02
217	Chris Welsh	.06	.05	.02
218	*Carl Willis*(FC)	.10	.08	.04
219	Jesse Barfield	.15	.11	.06
220	George Bell	.25	.20	.10
221	Bill Caudill	.06	.05	.02
222	*John Cerutti*	.20	.15	.08
223	Jim Clancy	.08	.06	.03
224	*Mark Eichhorn*	.15	.11	.06
225	Tony Fernandez	.12	.09	.05
226	Damaso Garcia	.06	.05	.02
227	Kelly Gruber	.30	.25	.12
228	Tom Henke	.08	.06	.03
229	Garth Iorg	.06	.05	.02
230	Cliff Johnson	.06	.05	.02
231	Joe Johnson	.06	.05	.02
232	Jimmy Key	.12	.09	.05
233	Dennis Lamp	.06	.05	.02
234	Rick Leach	.06	.05	.02
235	Buck Martinez	.06	.05	.02
236	Lloyd Moseby	.10	.08	.04
237	Rance Mulliniks	.06	.05	.02
238	Dave Stieb	.12	.09	.05
239	Willie Upshaw	.08	.06	.03
240	Ernie Whitt	.08	.06	.03
241	*Andy Allanson*	.15	.11	.06
242	*Scott Bailes*	.20	.15	.08
243	Chris Bando	.06	.05	.02
244	Tony Bernazard	.06	.05	.02
245	John Butcher	.06	.05	.02
246	Brett Butler	.08	.06	.03
247	Ernie Camacho	.06	.05	.02
248	Tom Candiotti	.06	.05	.02
249	Joe Carter	.25	.20	.10
250	Carmen Castillo	.06	.05	.02
251	Julio Franco	.10	.08	.04
252	Mel Hall	.08	.06	.03
253	Brook Jacoby	.10	.08	.04
254	Phil Niekro	.20	.15	.08
255	Otis Nixon	.06	.05	.02
256	Dickie Noles	.06	.05	.02
257	Bryan Oelkers	.06	.05	.02
258	Ken Schrom	.06	.05	.02
259	Don Schulze	.06	.05	.02
260	Cory Snyder	.70	.50	.30
261	Pat Tabler	.08	.06	.03
262	Andre Thornton	.08	.06	.03
263	*Rich Yett*(FC)	.12	.09	.05
264	*Mike Aldrete*	.25	.20	.10
265	Juan Berenguer	.06	.05	.02
266	Vida Blue	.10	.08	.04
267	Bob Brenly	.06	.05	.02
268	Chris Brown	.08	.06	.03
269	*Will Clark*	35.00	27.00	15.00
270	Chili Davis	.08	.06	.03
271	Mark Davis	.06	.05	.02
272	*Kelly Downs*(FC)	.30	.25	.12
273	Scott Garrelts	.06	.05	.02
274	Dan Gladden	.06	.05	.02
275	Mike Krukow	.08	.06	.03
276	*Randy Kutcher*(FC)	.10	.08	.04
277	Mike LaCoss	.06	.05	.02
278	Jeff Leonard	.08	.06	.03
279	Candy Maldonado	.08	.06	.03
280	Roger Mason	.06	.05	.02
281	Bob Melvin(FC)	.08	.06	.03
282	Greg Minton	.06	.05	.02
283	Jeff Robinson	.08	.06	.03
284	Harry Spilman	.06	.05	.02
285	*Rob Thompson*	.35	.25	.14
286	Jose Uribe	.08	.06	.03
287	Frank Williams	.06	.05	.02
288	Joel Youngblood	.06	.05	.02
289	Jack Clark	.15	.11	.06
290	Vince Coleman	.25	.20	.10
291	Tim Conroy	.06	.05	.02
292	Danny Cox	.08	.06	.03
293	Ken Dayley	.06	.05	.02
294	Curt Ford	.06	.05	.02
295	Bob Forsch	.08	.06	.03
296	Tom Herr	.10	.08	.04
297	Ricky Horton	.08	.06	.03
298	Clint Hurdle	.06	.05	.02
299	Jeff Lahti	.06	.05	.02
300	Steve Lake	.06	.05	.02
301	Tito Landrum	.06	.05	.02
302	*Mike LaValliere*	.25	.20	.10
303	*Greg Mathews*(FC)	.20	.15	.08
304	Willie McGee	.12	.09	.05
305	Jose Oquendo	.06	.05	.02
306	Terry Pendleton	.10	.08	.04
307	Pat Perry	.08	.06	.03
308	Ozzie Smith	.15	.11	.06
309	Ray Soff	.06	.05	.02
310	John Tudor	.10	.08	.04
311	Andy Van Slyke	.12	.09	.05
312	Todd Worrell	.20	.15	.08
313	Dann Bilardello	.06	.05	.02
314	Hubie Brooks	.10	.08	.04
315	Tim Burke	.06	.05	.02
316	Andre Dawson	.20	.15	.08
317	Mike Fitzgerald	.06	.05	.02
318	Tom Foley	.06	.05	.02
319	Andres Galarraga	.40	.30	.15
320	Joe Hesketh	.06	.05	.02
321	Wallace Johnson	.06	.05	.02
322	Wayne Krenchicki	.06	.05	.02
323	Vance Law	.08	.06	.03
324	Dennis Martinez	.08	.06	.03
325	Bob McClure	.06	.05	.02
326	Andy McGaffigan	.06	.05	.02
327	*Al Newman*	.08	.06	.03
328	Tim Raines	.30	.25	.12
329	Jeff Reardon	.10	.08	.04
330	*Luis Rivera*(FC)	.10	.08	.04
331	*Bob Sebra*(FC)	.10	.08	.04
332	Bryn Smith	.06	.05	.02
333	Jay Tibbs	.06	.05	.02
334	Tim Wallach	.12	.09	.05
335	Mitch Webster	.08	.06	.03
336	Jim Wohlford	.06	.05	.02
337	Floyd Youmans	.08	.06	.03
338	*Chris Bosio*(FC)	.40	.30	.15
339	*Glenn Braggs*(FC)	.40	.30	.15
340	Rick Cerone	.06	.05	.02
341	Mark Clear	.06	.05	.02
342	*Bryan Clutterbuck*(FC)	.10	.08	.04
343	Cecil Cooper	.12	.09	.05
344	Rob Deer	.10	.08	.04
345	Jim Gantner	.08	.06	.03
346	Ted Higuera	.20	.15	.08
347	John Henry Johnson	.06	.05	.02
348	Tim Leary(FC)	.30	.25	.12
349	Rick Manning	.06	.05	.02
350	Paul Molitor	.15	.11	.06
351	Charlie Moore	.06	.05	.02
352	Juan Nieves	.10	.08	.04
353	Ben Oglivie	.08	.06	.03
354	*Dan Plesac*	.35	.25	.14
355	Ernest Riles	.06	.05	.02
356	Billy Joe Robidoux	.06	.05	.02
357	Bill Schroeder	.06	.05	.02
358	*Dale Sveum*	.20	.15	.08
359	Gorman Thomas	.10	.08	.04
360	Bill Wegman(FC)	.10	.08	.04
361	Robin Yount	.40	.30	.15
362	Steve Balboni	.08	.06	.03
363	*Scott Bankhead*	.30	.25	.12
364	Buddy Biancalana	.06	.05	.02
365	Bud Black	.06	.05	.02
366	George Brett	.40	.30	.15
367	Steve Farr	.06	.05	.02
368	Mark Gubicza	.12	.09	.05
369	*Bo Jackson*	20.00	15.00	8.00
370	Danny Jackson	.15	.11	.06
371	*Mike Kingery*	.15	.11	.06
372	Rudy Law	.06	.05	.02

		MT	NR MT	EX
373	Charlie Leibrandt	.08	.06	.03
374	Dennis Leonard	.08	.06	.03
375	Hal McRae	.10	.08	.04
376	Jorge Orta	.06	.05	.02
377	Jamie Quirk	.06	.05	.02
378	Dan Quisenberry	.08	.06	.03
379	Bret Saberhagen	.30	.25	.12
380	Angel Salazar	.06	.05	.02
381	Lonnie Smith	.08	.06	.03
382	Jim Sundberg	.08	.06	.03
383	Frank White	.10	.08	.04
384	Willie Wilson	.12	.09	.05
385	Joaquin Andujar	.08	.06	.03
386	Doug Bair	.06	.05	.02
387	Dusty Baker	.08	.06	.03
388	Bruce Bochte	.06	.05	.02
389	Jose Canseco	12.00	9.00	4.75
390	Chris Codiroli	.06	.05	.02
391	Mike Davis	.08	.06	.03
392	Alfredo Griffin	.08	.06	.03
393	Moose Haas	.06	.05	.02
394	Donnie Hill	.06	.05	.02
395	Jay Howell	.08	.06	.03
396	Dave Kingman	.12	.09	.05
397	Carney Lansford	.10	.08	.04
398	*David Leiper*(FC)	.12	.09	.05
399	*Bill Mooneyham*	.10	.08	.04
400	Dwayne Murphy	.08	.06	.03
401	Steve Ontiveros	.06	.05	.02
402	Tony Phillips	.06	.05	.02
403	Eric Plunk	.08	.06	.03
404	Jose Rijo	.08	.06	.03
405	*Terry Steinbach*(FC)	.90	.70	.35
406	Dave Stewart	.12	.09	.05
407	Mickey Tettleton	.06	.05	.02
408	Dave Von Ohlen	.06	.05	.02
409	Jerry Willard	.06	.05	.02
410	Curt Young	.08	.06	.03
411	Bruce Bochy	.06	.05	.02
412	Dave Dravecky	.08	.06	.03
413	Tim Flannery	.06	.05	.02
414	Steve Garvey	.25	.20	.10
415	Goose Gossage	.15	.11	.06
416	Tony Gwynn	.35	.25	.14
417	Andy Hawkins	.06	.05	.02
418	LaMarr Hoyt	.06	.05	.02
419	Terry Kennedy	.08	.06	.03
420	*John Kruk*	.35	.25	.14
421	Dave LaPoint	.08	.06	.03
422	Craig Lefferts	.06	.05	.02
423	Carmelo Martinez	.08	.06	.03
424	Lance McCullers	.08	.06	.03
425	Kevin McReynolds	.15	.11	.06
426	Graig Nettles	.12	.09	.05
427	Bip Roberts	.06	.05	.02
428	Jerry Royster	.06	.05	.02
429	Benito Santiago	1.25	.90	.50
430	Eric Show	.08	.06	.03
431	Bob Stoddard	.06	.05	.02
432	Garry Templeton	.08	.06	.03
433	Gene Walter	.06	.05	.02
434	Ed Whitson	.06	.05	.02
435	Marvell Wynne	.06	.05	.02
436	Dave Anderson	.06	.05	.02
437	Greg Brock	.08	.06	.03
438	Enos Cabell	.06	.05	.02
439	Mariano Duncan	.06	.05	.02
440	Pedro Guerrero	.15	.11	.06
441	Orel Hershiser	.40	.30	.15
442	Rick Honeycutt	.06	.05	.02
443	Ken Howell	.06	.05	.02
444	Ken Landreaux	.06	.05	.02
445	Bill Madlock	.12	.09	.05
446	Mike Marshall	.12	.09	.05
447	Len Matuszek	.06	.05	.02
448	Tom Niedenfuer	.08	.06	.03
449	Alejandro Pena	.08	.06	.03
450	Dennis Powell(FC)	.08	.06	.03
451	Jerry Reuss	.08	.06	.03
452	Bill Russell	.08	.06	.03
453	Steve Sax	.15	.11	.06
454	Mike Scioscia	.08	.06	.03
455	Franklin Stubbs	.08	.06	.03
456	Alex Trevino	.06	.05	.02
457	Fernando Valenzuela	.25	.20	.10
458	Ed Vande Berg	.06	.05	.02
459	Bob Welch	.10	.08	.04
460	*Reggie Williams*	.10	.08	.04
461	Don Aase	.06	.05	.02
462	Juan Beniquez	.06	.05	.02
463	Mike Boddicker	.08	.06	.03
464	Juan Bonilla	.06	.05	.02
465	Rich Bordi	.06	.05	.02
466	Storm Davis	.10	.08	.04
467	Rick Dempsey	.08	.06	.03
468	Ken Dixon	.06	.05	.02
469	Jim Dwyer	.06	.05	.02
470	Mike Flanagan	.08	.06	.03
471	Jackie Gutierrez	.06	.05	.02
472	Brad Havens	.06	.05	.02
473	Lee Lacy	.06	.05	.02
474	Fred Lynn	.15	.11	.06
475	Scott McGregor	.08	.06	.03
476	Eddie Murray	.35	.25	.14
477	Tom O'Malley	.06	.05	.02
478	Cal Ripken, Jr.	.35	.25	.14
479	Larry Sheets	.08	.06	.03
480	John Shelby	.06	.05	.02
481	Nate Snell	.06	.05	.02
482	Jim Traber(FC)	.10	.08	.04
483	Mike Young	.06	.05	.02
484	Neil Allen	.06	.05	.02
485	Harold Baines	.15	.11	.06
486	Floyd Bannister	.10	.08	.04
487	Daryl Boston	.08	.06	.03
488	Ivan Calderon	.12	.09	.05
489	*John Cangelosi*	.12	.09	.05
490	Steve Carlton	.25	.20	.10
491	Joe Cowley	.06	.05	.02
492	Julio Cruz	.06	.05	.02
493	Bill Dawley	.06	.05	.02
494	Jose DeLeon	.08	.06	.03
495	Richard Dotson	.08	.06	.03
496	Carlton Fisk	.15	.11	.06

		MT	NR MT	EX
497	Ozzie Guillen	.10	.08	.04
498	Jerry Hairston	.06	.05	.02
499	Ron Hassey	.06	.05	.02
500	Tim Hulett	.06	.05	.02
501	Bob James	.06	.05	.02
502	Steve Lyons	.06	.05	.02
503	*Joel McKeon*	.10	.08	.04
504	Gene Nelson	.06	.05	.02
505	Dave Schmidt	.06	.05	.02
506	Ray Searage	.06	.05	.02
507	*Bobby Thigpen*(FC)	.35	.25	.14
508	Greg Walker	.10	.08	.04
509	Jim Acker	.06	.05	.02
510	Doyle Alexander	.08	.06	.03
511	*Paul Assenmacher*	.15	.11	.06
512	Bruce Benedict	.06	.05	.02
513	Chris Chambliss	.08	.06	.03
514	Jeff Dedmon	.06	.05	.02
515	Gene Garber	.06	.05	.02
516	Ken Griffey	.10	.08	.04
517	Terry Harper	.06	.05	.02
518	Bob Horner	.10	.08	.04
519	Glenn Hubbard	.06	.05	.02
520	Rick Mahler	.06	.05	.02
521	Omar Moreno	.06	.05	.02
522	Dale Murphy	.40	.30	.15
523	Ken Oberkfell	.06	.05	.02
524	Ed Olwine	.06	.05	.02
525	David Palmer	.06	.05	.02
526	Rafael Ramirez	.06	.05	.02
527	Billy Sample	.06	.05	.02
528	Ted Simmons	.12	.09	.05
529	Zane Smith	.08	.06	.03
530	Bruce Sutter	.12	.09	.05
531	*Andres Thomas*	.25	.20	.10
532	Ozzie Virgil	.06	.05	.02
533	*Allan Anderson*(FC)	.25	.20	.10
534	Keith Atherton	.06	.05	.02
535	Billy Beane	.06	.05	.02
536	Bert Blyleven	.12	.09	.05
537	Tom Brunansky	.10	.08	.04
538	Randy Bush	.06	.05	.02
539	George Frazier	.06	.05	.02
540	Gary Gaetti	.15	.11	.06
541	Greg Gagne	.06	.05	.02
542	Mickey Hatcher	.06	.05	.02
543	Neal Heaton	.06	.05	.02
544	Kent Hrbek	.15	.11	.06
545	Roy Lee Jackson	.06	.05	.02
546	Tim Laudner	.06	.05	.02
547	Steve Lombardozzi	.10	.08	.04
548	*Mark Portugal*(FC)	.10	.08	.04
549	Kirby Puckett	2.25	1.75	.90
550	Jeff Reed	.08	.06	.03
551	Mark Salas	.06	.05	.02
552	Roy Smalley	.06	.05	.02
553	Mike Smithson	.06	.05	.02
554	Frank Viola	.15	.11	.06
555	Thad Bosley	.06	.05	.02
556	Ron Cey	.10	.08	.04
557	Jody Davis	.08	.06	.03
558	Ron Davis	.06	.05	.02
559	Bob Dernier	.06	.05	.02
560	Frank DiPino	.06	.05	.02
561	Shawon Dunston	.10	.08	.04
562	Leon Durham	.08	.06	.03
563	Dennis Eckersley	.12	.09	.05
564	Terry Francona	.06	.05	.02
565	Dave Gumpert	.06	.05	.02
566	Guy Hoffman	.08	.06	.03
567	Ed Lynch	.06	.05	.02
568	Gary Matthews	.10	.08	.04
569	Keith Moreland	.08	.06	.03
570	*Jamie Moyer*(FC)	.20	.15	.08
571	Jerry Mumphrey	.06	.05	.02
572	Ryne Sandberg	.30	.25	.12
573	Scott Sanderson	.06	.05	.02
574	Lee Smith	.10	.08	.04
575	Chris Speier	.06	.05	.02
576	Rick Sutcliffe	.12	.09	.05
577	Manny Trillo	.08	.06	.03
578	Steve Trout	.06	.05	.02
579	Karl Best	.06	.05	.02
580	Scott Bradley(FC)	.08	.06	.03
581	Phil Bradley	.12	.09	.05
582	Mickey Brantley	.08	.06	.03
583	Mike Brown	.06	.05	.02
584	Alvin Davis	.12	.09	.05
585	*Lee Guetterman*(FC)	.15	.11	.06
586	Mark Huismann	.06	.05	.02
587	Bob Kearney	.06	.05	.02
588	Pete Ladd	.06	.05	.02
589	Mark Langston	.12	.09	.05
590	Mike Moore	.06	.05	.02
591	Mike Morgan	.06	.05	.02
592	John Moses	.06	.05	.02
593	Ken Phelps	.08	.06	.03
594	Jim Presley	.10	.08	.04
595	*Rey Quinonez (Quinones)*	.15	.11	.06
596	Harold Reynolds	.15	.11	.06
597	Billy Swift	.06	.05	.02
598	Danny Tartabull	.25	.20	.10
599	Steve Yeager	.06	.05	.02
600	Matt Young	.06	.05	.02
601	Bill Almon	.06	.05	.02
602	*Rafael Belliard*(FC)	.12	.09	.05
603	Mike Bielecki	.06	.05	.02
604	*Barry Bonds*	2.75	2.00	1.00
605	*Bobby Bonilla*	3.25	2.50	1.25
606	Sid Bream	.08	.06	.03
607	Mike Brown	.06	.05	.02
608	Pat Clements	.06	.05	.02
609	*Mike Diaz*(FC)	.15	.11	.06
610	Cecilio Guante	.06	.05	.02
611	*Barry Jones*(FC)	.12	.09	.05
612	Bob Kipper	.06	.05	.02
613	Larry McWilliams	.06	.05	.02
614	Jim Morrison	.06	.05	.02
615	Joe Orsulak	.06	.05	.02
616	Junior Ortiz	.06	.05	.02
617	Tony Pena	.08	.06	.03
618	Johnny Ray	.10	.08	.04
619	Rick Reuschel	.10	.08	.04
620	R.J. Reynolds	.06	.05	.02

		MT	NR MT	EX
621	Rick Rhoden	.10	.08	.04
622	Don Robinson	.08	.06	.03
623	Bob Walk	.06	.05	.02
624	Jim Winn	.06	.05	.02
625	Youthful Power (Jose Canseco, Pete Incaviglia)	.70	.50	.30
626	300 Game Winners (Phil Niekro, Don Sutton)	.12	.09	.05
627	A.L. Firemen (Don Aase, Dave Righetti)	.08	.06	.03
628	Rookie All-Stars (Jose Canseco, Wally Joyner)	2.00	1.50	.80
629	Magic Mets (Gary Carter, Sid Fernandez, Dwight Gooden, Keith Hernandez, Darryl Strawberry)	.60	.45	.25
630	N.L. Best Righties (Mike Krukow, Mike Scott)	.08	.06	.03
631	Sensational Southpaws (John Franco, Fernando Valenzuela)	.10	.08	.04
632	Count 'Em (Bob Horner)	.08	.06	.03
633	A.L. Pitcher's Nightmare (Jose Canseco, Kirby Puckett, Jim Rice)	1.50	1.25	.60
634	All Star Battery (Gary Carter, Roger Clemens)	.25	.20	.10
635	4,000 Strikeouts (Steve Carlton)	.12	.09	.05
636	Big Bats At First Sack (Glenn Davis, Eddie Murray)	.20	.15	.08
637	On Base (Wade Boggs, Keith Hernandez)	.35	.25	.14
638	Sluggers From Left Side (Don Mattingly, Darryl Strawberry)	.90	.70	.35
639	Former MVP's (Dave Parker, Ryne Sandberg)	.12	.09	.05
640	Dr. K. & Super K (Roger Clemens, Dwight Gooden)	.50	.40	.20
641	A.L. West Stoppers (Charlie Hough, Mike Witt)	.08	.06	.03
642	Doubles & Triples (Tim Raines, Juan Samuel)	.12	.09	.05
643	Outfielders With Punch (Harold Baines, Jesse Barfield)	.10	.08	.04
644	Major League Prospects *(Dave Clark, Greg Swindell)*(FC)	2.50	2.00	1.00
645	Major League Prospects *(Ron Karkovice, Russ Morman)*(FC)	.12	.09	.05
646	Major League Prospects *(Willie Fraser, Devon White)*(FC)	1.75	1.25	.70
647	Major League Prospects *(Jerry Browne, Mike Stanley)*(FC)	.60	.45	.25
648	Major League Prospects *(Phil Lombardi, Dave Magadan)*(FC)	.80	.60	.30
649	Major League Prospects *(Ralph Bryant, Jose Gonzalez)*(FC)	.20	.15	.08
650	Major League Prospects *(Randy Asadoor, Jimmy Jones)*(FC)	.20	.15	.08
651	Major League Prospects *(Marvin Freeman, Tracy Jones)*	.25	.20	.10
652	Major League Prospects *(Kevin Seitzer,* John Stefero)(FC)	4.50	3.50	1.75
653	Major League Prospects *(Steve Fireovid, Rob Nelson)*(FC)	.10	.08	.04
654	Checklist 1-95	.06	.05	.02
655	Checklist 96-192	.06	.05	.02
656	Checklist 193-288	.06	.05	.02
657	Checklist 289-384	.06	.05	.02
658	Checklist 385-483	.06	.05	.02
659	Checklist 484-578	.06	.05	.02
660	Checklist 579-660	.06	.05	.02

1987 All Star Team

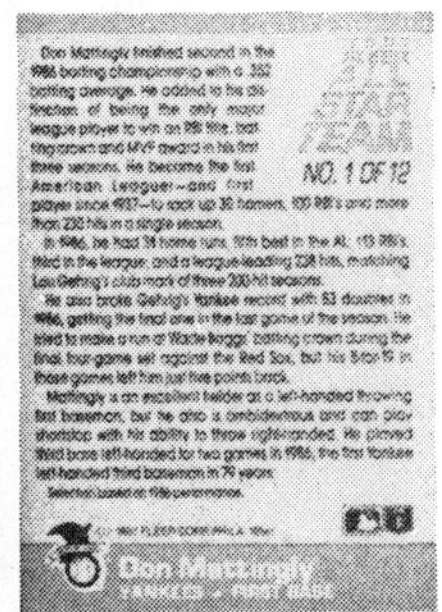

As in 1986, Fleer All Star Team cards were randomly inserted in Fleer wax and cello packs. Twelve cards, each measuring the standard 2-1/2" by 3-1/2", comprise the set. The card fronts feature a full-color player photo set against a gray background for American League players and a black background for National Leaguers. Card backs are printed in black, red and white and feature a lengthy player biography. Fleer's choices for a major league All-Star team is once again the theme for the set.

		MT	NR MT	EX
Complete Set:		18.00	13.50	7.25
Common Player:		.60	.45	.25
1	Don Mattingly	5.00	3.75	2.00
2	Gary Carter	1.00	.70	.40
3	Tony Fernandez	.75	.60	.30
4	Steve Sax	.75	.60	.30
5	Kirby Puckett	3.00	2.25	1.25
6	Mike Schmidt	2.00	1.50	.80

		MT	NR MT	EX
7	Mike Easler	.60	.45	.25
8	Todd Worrell	.75	.60	.30
9	George Bell	1.00	.70	.40
10	Fernando Valenzuela	1.00	.70	.40
11	Roger Clemens	2.25	1.75	.90
12	Tim Raines	1.25	.90	.50

1987 Fleer Award Winner

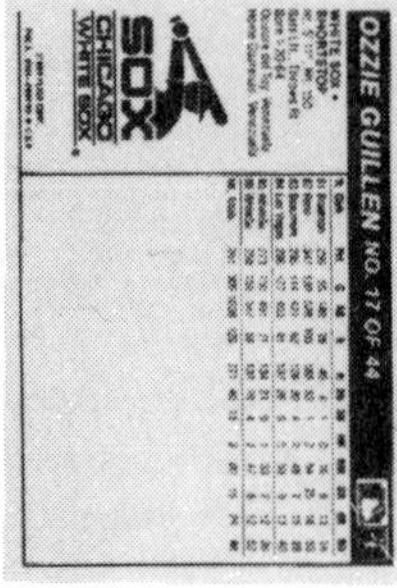

The 1987 Fleer Award Winners boxed set was prepared by Fleer for distribution by 7-Eleven stores. The cards, which measure 2-1/2" by 3-1/2", feature players who have won various major league awards during their careers. The card fronts contain full-color photos surrounded by a yellow border. The name of the award the player won is printed at the bottom of the card in an oval-shaped band designed to resemble a metal nameplate on a trophy. Card backs, printed in black, yellow and white, include lifetime major and minor league statistics along with typical personal information. Each boxed set contained six team logo stickers.

		MT	NR MT	EX
Complete Set:		6.00	4.50	2.50
Common Player:		.05	.04	.02
1	Marty Barrett	.07	.05	.03
2	George Bell	.20	.15	.08
3	Bert Blyleven	.10	.08	.04
4	Bob Boone	.05	.04	.02
5	John Candelaria	.05	.04	.02
6	Jose Canseco	1.50	1.25	.60
7	Gary Carter	.25	.20	.10
8	Joe Carter	.25	.20	.10
9	Roger Clemens	.50	.40	.20
10	Cecil Cooper	.10	.08	.04
11	Eric Davis	.60	.45	.25
12	Tony Fernandez	.10	.08	.04
13	Scott Fletcher	.05	.04	.02
14	Bob Forsch	.05	.04	.02
15	Dwight Gooden	.50	.40	.20
16	Ron Guidry	.12	.09	.05
17	Ozzie Guillen	.07	.05	.03
18	Bill Gullickson	.05	.04	.02
19	Tony Gwynn	.25	.20	.10
20	Bob Knepper	.05	.04	.02
21	Ray Knight	.05	.04	.02
22	Mark Langston	.20	.15	.08
23	Candy Maldonado	.05	.04	.02
24	Don Mattingly	1.25	.90	.50
25	Roger McDowell	.07	.05	.03
26	Dale Murphy	.30	.25	.12
27	Dave Parker	.12	.09	.05
28	Lance Parrish	.15	.11	.06
29	Gary Pettis	.05	.04	.02
30	Kirby Puckett	.70	.50	.40
31	Johnny Ray	.07	.05	.03
32	Dave Righetti	.12	.09	.05
33	Cal Ripken, Jr.	.30	.25	.12
34	Bret Saberhagen	.15	.11	.06
35	Ryne Sandberg	.20	.15	.08
36	Mike Schmidt	.30	.25	.12
37	Mike Scott	.12	.09	.05
38	Ozzie Smith	.12	.09	.05
39	Robbie Thompson	.10	.08	.04
40	Fernando Valenzuela	.20	.15	.08
41	Mitch Webster	.05	.04	.02
42	Frank White	.07	.05	.03
43	Mike Witt	.07	.05	.03
44	Todd Worrell	.15	.11	.06

1987 Fleer Baseball All Stars

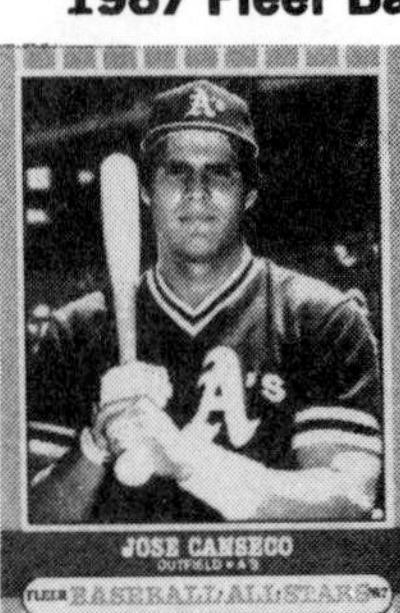

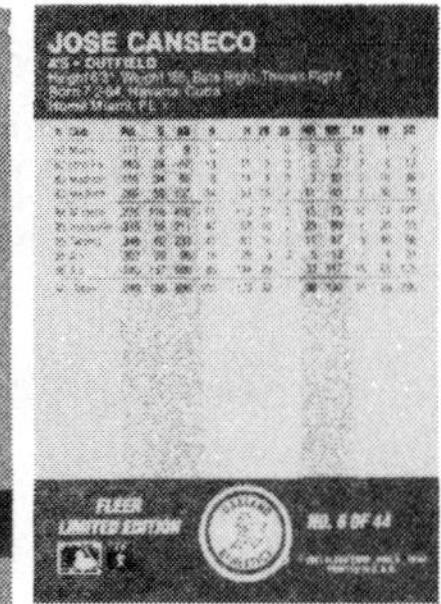

Produced by Fleer for exclusive distribution through Ben Franklin stores, the "Baseball All Stars" set is comprised of 44 cards which are the standard 2-1/2" by 3-1/2" size. The cards have full-color photos surrounded by a bright red border with white pinstripes at the top and bottom. The card backs are printed in blue, white and dark red and include complete major and minor league statistics. The set was issued in a special cardboard box.

		MT	NR MT	EX
Complete Set:		7.00	5.25	2.75
Common Player:		.05	.04	.02
1	Harold Baines	.10	.08	.04
2	Jesse Barfield	.12	.09	.05
3	Wade Boggs	1.00	.70	.40
4	Dennis "Oil Can" Boyd	.05	.04	.02
5	Scott Bradley	.05	.04	.02
6	Jose Canseco	1.50	1.25	.60
7	Gary Carter	.25	.20	.10
8	Joe Carter	.25	.20	.10
9	Mark Clear	.05	.04	.02
10	Roger Clemens	.50	.40	.20
11	Jose Cruz	.05	.04	.02
12	Chili Davis	.07	.05	.03
13	Jody Davis	.05	.04	.02
14	Rob Deer	.05	.04	.02
15	Brian Downing	.05	.04	.02
16	Sid Fernandez	.07	.05	.03
17	John Franco	.07	.05	.03
18	Andres Galarraga	.15	.11	.06
19	Dwight Gooden	.50	.40	.20
20	Tony Gwynn	.25	.20	.10
21	Charlie Hough	.05	.04	.02
22	Bruce Hurst	.10	.08	.04
23	Wally Joyner	.70	.50	.30
24	Carney Lansford	.05	.04	.02
25	Fred Lynn	.12	.09	.05
26	Don Mattingly	1.50	1.25	.60
27	Willie McGee	.10	.08	.04
28	Jack Morris	.15	.11	.06
29	Dale Murphy	.30	.25	.12
30	Bob Ojeda	.07	.05	.03
31	Tony Pena	.07	.05	.03
32	Kirby Puckett	.70	.50	.30
33	Dan Quisenberry	.07	.05	.03
34	Tim Raines	.25	.20	.10
35	Willie Randolph	.07	.05	.03
36	Cal Ripken, Jr.	.25	.20	.10
37	Pete Rose	.50	.40	.20
38	Nolan Ryan	.50	.40	.20
39	Juan Samuel	.10	.08	.04
40	Mike Schmidt	.30	.25	.12
41	Ozzie Smith	.12	.09	.05
42	Andres Thomas	.10	.08	.04
43	Fernando Valenzuela	.20	.15	.08
44	Mike Witt	.07	.05	.03

1987 Fleer Baseball's Best

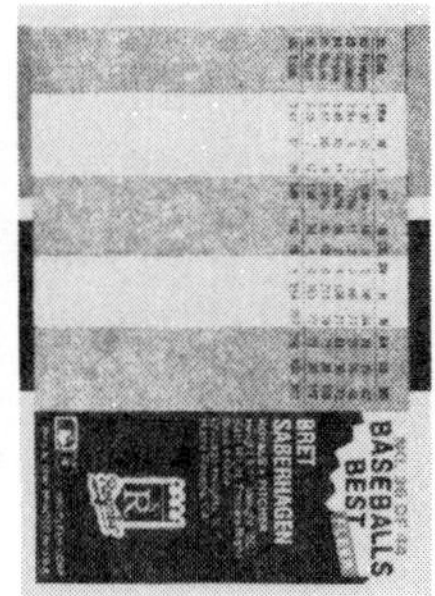

For a second straight baseball card season, Fleer produced for McCrory's stores and their affiliates a 44-card "Baseball's Best" set. Subtitled "Sluggers vs. Pitchers," 28 everyday players and 16 pitchers are featured. The card design is nearly identical to the previous year's effort. The cards, which measure 2-1/2" by 3-1/2", were housed in a specially designed box along with six team logo stickers.

		MT	NR MT	EX
Complete Set:		6.00	4.50	2.50
Common Player:		.05	.04	.02
1	Kevin Bass	.07	.05	.03
2	Jesse Barfield	.12	.09	.05
3	George Bell	.20	.15	.08
4	Wade Boggs	1.00	.70	.40
5	Sid Bream	.05	.04	.02
6	George Brett	.30	.25	.12
7	Ivan Calderon	.10	.08	.04
8	Jose Canseco	1.50	1.25	.60
9	Jack Clark	.12	.09	.05
10	Roger Clemens	.50	.40	.20
11	Eric Davis	.50	.40	.20
12	Andre Dawson	.15	.11	.06
13	Sid Fernandez	.07	.05	.03
14	John Franco	.07	.05	.03
15	Dwight Gooden	.50	.40	.20
16	Pedro Guerrero	.15	.11	.06
17	Tony Gwynn	.25	.20	.10
18	Rickey Henderson	.30	.25	.12
19	Tom Henke	.05	.04	.02
20	Ted Higuera	.10	.08	.04
21	Pete Incaviglia	.30	.25	.12
22	Wally Joyner	.50	.40	.20
23	Jeff Leonard	.05	.04	.02
24	Joe Magrane	.15	.11	.06
25	Don Mattingly	1.50	1.25	.60
26	Mark McGwire	1.50	1.25	.60
27	Jack Morris	.15	.11	.06
28	Dale Murphy	.30	.25	.12
29	Dave Parker	.12	.09	.05
30	Ken Phelps	.05	.04	.02
31	Kirby Puckett	.70	.50	.30
32	Tim Raines	.25	.20	.10
33	Jeff Reardon	.10	.08	.04
34	Dave Righetti	.12	.09	.05
35	Cal Ripken, Jr.	.30	.25	.12
36	Bret Saberhagen	.15	.11	.06
37	Mike Schmidt	.30	.25	.12
38	Mike Scott	.12	.09	.05
39	Kevin Seitzer	.50	.40	.20
40	Darryl Strawberry	.40	.30	.15
41	Rick Sutcliffe	.10	.08	.04
42	Pat Tabler	.05	.04	.02
43	Fernando Valenzuela	.10	.08	.04
44	Mike Witt	.07	.05	.03

1987 Fleer Baseball's Exciting Stars

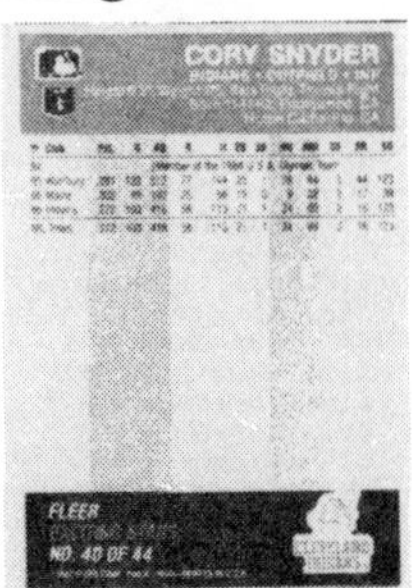

Another entry into the Fleer lineup of individual boxed sets, the "Baseball's Exciting Stars" set was produced by Fleer for Cumberland Farms stores. The card fronts feature a red, white and blue border with the words "Exciting Stars" printed in yellow at the top. The backs are printed in red and blue and carry complete major and minor league statistics. Included with the boxed set of 44 cards were six team logo stickers.

		MT	NR MT	EX
Complete Set:		7.00	5.25	2.75
Common Player:		.05	.04	.02
1	Don Aase	.05	.04	.02
2	Rick Aguilera	.07	.05	.03
3	Jesse Barfield	.12	.09	.05
4	Wade Boggs	1.00	.70	.40
5	Dennis "Oil Can" Boyd	.05	.04	.02
6	Sid Bream	.07	.05	.03
7	Jose Canseco	1.50	1.25	.60
8	Steve Carlton	.25	.20	.10
9	Gary Carter	.25	.20	.10
10	Will Clark	1.00	.70	.40
11	Roger Clemens	.40	.30	.15
12	Danny Cox	.07	.05	.03
13	Alvin Davis	.10	.08	.04
14	Eric Davis	.50	.40	.20
15	Rob Deer	.07	.05	.03
16	Brian Downing	.05	.04	.02
17	Gene Garber	.05	.04	.02
18	Steve Garvey	.25	.20	.10
19	Dwight Gooden	.50	.40	.20
20	Mark Gubicza	.10	.08	.04
21	Mel Hall	.05	.04	.02
22	Terry Harper	.05	.04	.02
23	Von Hayes	.10	.08	.04
24	Rickey Henderson	.60	.45	.25
25	Tom Henke	.05	.04	.02
26	Willie Hernandez	.05	.04	.02
27	Ted Higuera	.10	.08	.04
28	Rick Honeycutt	.05	.04	.02
29	Kent Hrbek	.15	.11	.06
30	Wally Joyner	.60	.45	.25
31	Charlie Kerfeld	.05	.04	.02
32	Fred Lynn	.12	.09	.05
33	Don Mattingly	1.50	1.25	.60
34	Tim Raines	.25	.20	.10
35	Dennis Rasmussen	.07	.05	.03
36	Johnny Ray	.07	.05	.03
37	Jim Rice	.20	.15	.08
38	Pete Rose	.50	.40	.20
39	Lee Smith	.07	.05	.03
40	Cory Snyder	.25	.20	.10
41	Darryl Strawberry	.40	.30	.15
42	Kent Tekulve	.05	.04	.02
43	Willie Wilson	.10	.08	.04
44	Bobby Witt	.12	.09	.05

1987 Fleer Baseball's Game Winners

The 1987 Fleer "Baseball's Game Winners" boxed set of 44 cards was produced for distribution through Bi-Mart Discount Drug,

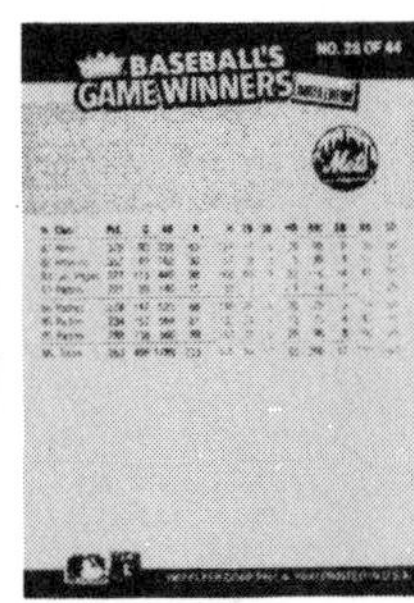

Pay'n-Save, Mott's 5 & 10, M.E. Moses, and Winn's stores. The cards, which measure 2-1/2" by 3-1/2", have a light blue border with the player's name and game winning RBI or games won statistics in a yellow oval band at the top of the card. Below the full-color player photo is the name of the set in blue, yellow and red. Included with the boxed set were six team logo stickers.

		MT	NR MT	EX
Complete Set:		5.00	3.75	2.00
Common Player:		.05	.04	.02
1	Harold Baines	.10	.08	.04
2	Don Baylor	.10	.08	.04
3	George Bell	.20	.15	.08
4	Tony Bernazard	.05	.04	.02
5	Wade Boggs	1.00	.70	.40
6	George Brett	.40	.30	.15
7	Hubie Brooks	.07	.05	.03
8	Jose Canseco	1.00	.70	.40
9	Gary Carter	.20	.15	.08
10	Roger Clemens	.40	.30	.15
11	Eric Davis	.50	.40	.20
12	Glenn Davis	.15	.11	.06
13	Shawon Dunston	.07	.05	.03
14	Mark Eichhorn	.10	.08	.04
15	Gary Gaetti	.12	.09	.05
16	Steve Garvey	.25	.20	.10
17	Kirk Gibson	.20	.15	.08
18	Dwight Gooden	.50	.40	.20
19	Von Hayes	.07	.05	.03
20	Willie Hernandez	.07	.05	.03
21	Ted Higuera	.10	.08	.04
22	Wally Joyner	.80	.60	.30
23	Bob Knepper	.05	.04	.02
24	Mike Krukow	.05	.04	.02
25	Jeff Leonard	.05	.04	.02
26	Don Mattingly	1.50	1.25	.60
27	Kirk McCaskill	.07	.05	.03
28	Kevin McReynolds	.12	.09	.05
29	Jim Morrison	.05	.04	.02
30	Dale Murphy	.30	.25	.12
31	Pete O'Brien	.07	.05	.03
32	Bob Ojeda	.07	.05	.03
33	Larry Parrish	.05	.04	.02
34	Ken Phelps	.05	.04	.02
35	Dennis Rasmussen	.07	.05	.03
36	Ernest Riles	.07	.05	.03
37	Cal Ripken, Jr.	.30	.25	.12
38	Ron Robinson	.05	.04	.02
39	Steve Sax	.15	.11	.06
40	Mike Schmidt	.30	.25	.12
41	John Tudor	.07	.05	.03
42	Fernando Valenzuela	.20	.15	.08
43	Mike Witt	.07	.05	.03
44	Curt Young	.05	.04	.02

1987 Fleer Baseball's Hottest Stars

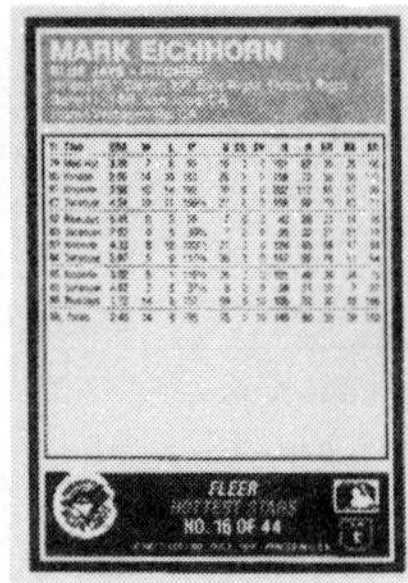

The "Baseball's Hottest Stars" 44-card set was produced by Fleer for the Revco Drug Store chain. Measuring the standard 2-1/2" by 3-1/2", the cards feature full-color photos surrounded by a red, white and blue border. The player's name, position and team appear in a blue band at the bottom of the card. Card backs are printed in red, white and black and contain the player's lifetime professional statistics. The set was housed in a special cardboard box with six team logo stickers.

		MT	NR MT	EX
Complete Set:		7.00	5.25	2.75
Common Player:		.05	.04	.02
1	Joaquin Andujar	.05	.04	.02
2	Harold Baines	.10	.08	.04
3	Kevin Bass	.07	.05	.03
4	Don Baylor	.10	.08	.04
5	Barry Bonds	.20	.15	.08
6	George Brett	.30	.25	.12
7	Tom Brunansky	.10	.08	.04
8	Brett Butler	.05	.04	.02
9	Jose Canseco	1.50	1.25	.60
10	Roger Clemens	.50	.40	.20
11	Ron Darling	.10	.08	.04
12	Eric Davis	.50	.40	.20
13	Andre Dawson	.15	.11	.06
14	Doug DeCinces	.05	.04	.02
15	Leon Durham	.07	.05	.03
16	Mark Eichhorn	.10	.08	.04
17	Scott Garrelts	.05	.04	.02
18	Dwight Gooden	.50	.40	.20
19	Dave Henderson	.05	.04	.02
20	Rickey Henderson	.50	.40	.20
21	Keith Hernandez	.15	.11	.06
22	Ted Higuera	.10	.08	.04
23	Bob Horner	.07	.05	.03
24	Pete Incaviglia	.40	.30	.15
25	Wally Joyner	.50	.40	.20
26	Mark Langston	.07	.05	.03
27	Don Mattingly	1.75	1.25	.70
28	Dale Murphy	.30	.25	.12
29	Kirk McCaskill	.07	.05	.03
30	Willie McGee	.10	.08	.04
31	Dave Righetti	.12	.09	.05
32	Pete Rose	.40	.30	.15
33	Bruce Ruffin	.15	.11	.06
34	Steve Sax	.15	.11	.06
35	Mike Schmidt	.30	.25	.12
36	Larry Sheets	.10	.08	.04
37	Eric Show	.07	.05	.03
38	Dave Smith	.05	.04	.02
39	Cory Snyder	.25	.20	.10
40	Frank Tanana	.05	.04	.02
41	Alan Trammell	.20	.15	.08
42	Reggie Williams	.07	.05	.03
43	Mookie Wilson	.07	.05	.03
44	Todd Worrell	.15	.11	.06

1987 Fleer Box Panels

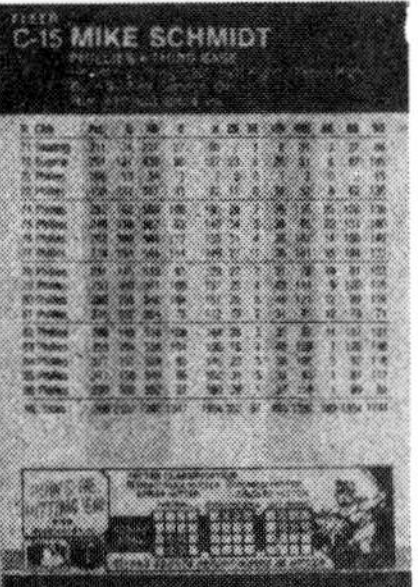

For the second straight year, Fleer produced a special set of cards designed to stimulate sales of their wax and cello pack boxes. In 1987, Fleer issued 16 cards in panels of four on the bottoms of retail boxes. The cards are numbered C-1 through C-16 and are 2-1/2" by 3-1/2" in size. The cards have the same design as the regular issue set with the player photos and card numbers being different.

		MT	NR MT	EX
Complete Panel Set:		8.00	6.00	3.25
Complete Singles Set:		3.50	2.75	1.50
Common Panel:		2.25	1.75	.90
Common Single Player:		.20	.15	.08
Panel		2.50	2.00	1.00
1	Mets Logo	.05	.04	.02
6	Keith Hernandez	.30	.25	.12
8	Dale Murphy	.60	.45	.25
14	Ryne Sandberg	.30	.25	.12
Panel		2.25	1.75	.90
2	Jesse Barfield	.20	.15	.08
3	George Brett	.60	.45	.25
5	Red Sox Logo	.05	.04	.02
11	Kirby Puckett	.30	.25	.12
Panel		2.75	2.00	1.00
4	Dwight Gooden	.80	.60	.30
9	Astros Logo	.05	.04	.02
10	Dave Parker	.25	.20	.10
15	Mike Schmidt	.60	.45	.25
Panel		2.75	2.00	1.00
7	Wally Joyner	1.00	.70	.40
12	Dave Righetti	.20	.15	.08
13	Angels Logo	.05	.04	.02
16	Robin Yount	.25	.20	.10

1987 Fleer '86 World Series

Fleer issued a set of 12 cards highlighting the 1986 World Series between the Boston Red Sox and New York Mets. The sets were available only with Fleer factory-packaged sets of 660 regular issue cards. The cards, which are the standard 2-1/2" by 3-1/2" size, have either horizontal or

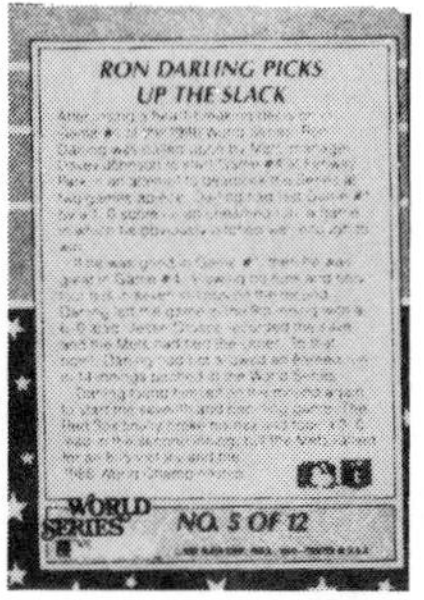

vertical formats. The fronts are bordered in red, white and blue stars and stripes with a thin gold frame around the photo. The backs are printed in red and blue ink on white stock and include information regarding the photo on the card fronts.

		MT	NR MT	EX
Complete Set:		6.00	4.50	2.50
Common Player:		.50	.40	.20
1	Left-Hand Finesse Beats Mets (Bruce Hurst)	.50	.40	.20
2	Hernandez And Boggs (Wade Boggs, Keith Hernandez)	1.00	.70	.40
3	Roger Clemens	.70	.50	.30
4	Clutch Hitting (Gary Carter)	.50	.40	.20
5	Darling Picks Up The Slack (Ron Darling)	.50	.40	.20
6	.433 Series Batting Average (Marty Barrett)	.50	.40	.20
7	Dwight Gooden	.70	.50	.30
8	Strategy At Work	.50	.40	.20
9	Dewey! (Dwight Evans)	.50	.40	.20
10	One Strike From Boston Victory (Dave Henderson, Spike Owen)	.50	.40	.20
11	Series Home Run Duo (Ray Knight, Darryl Strawberry)	.50	.40	.20
12	Series M.V.P. (Ray Knight)	.50	.40	.20

1987 Fleer Headliners

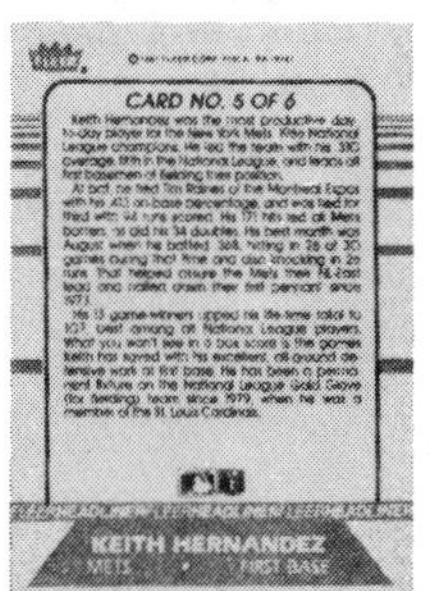

A continuation of the 1986 Future Hall of Famers idea, Fleer encountered legal problems with using the Hall of Fame name and abated them by entitling the set "Headliners." The cards, which are the standard 2-1/2" by 3-1/2" size, were randomly inserted in three-pack cello packs. Card fronts feature a player photo set against a beige background with bright red stripes. The card backs are printed in black, red and gray and offer a brief biography with an emphasis on the player's performance during the 1986 season.

		MT	NR MT	EX
Complete Set:		10.00	7.50	4.00
Common Player:		1.00	.70	.40
1	Wade Boggs	2.25	1.75	.90
2	Jose Canseco	3.00	2.25	1.25
3	Dwight Gooden	1.50	1.25	.60
4	Rickey Henderson	2.00	1.50	.80
5	Keith Hernandez	1.00	.70	.40
6	Jim Rice	1.00	.70	.40

1987 Fleer League Leaders

For the second year in a row, Fleer produced a 44- card "League Leaders" set for Walgreens. The card fronts feature a border style which is identical to that used in 1986. However, an elliptical shaped full-color player photo is placed diagonally on the front. "1987 Fleer League Leaders" appears in the upper left corner of the front although nowhere on the card does it state in which pitching, hitting or fielding department was the player a league leader. The card backs are printed in red and blue on white stock. The cards in the boxed set are the standard 2-1/2" by 3-1/2" size.

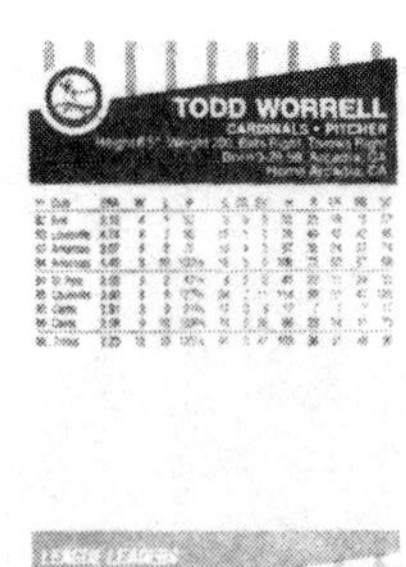

		MT	NR MT	EX
Complete Set:		5.00	3.75	2.00
Common Player:		.05	.04	.02
1	Jesse Barfield	.12	.09	.05
2	Mike Boddicker	.07	.05	.03
3	Wade Boggs	1.00	.70	.40
4	Phil Bradley	.10	.08	.04
5	George Brett	.30	.25	.12
6	Hubie Brooks	.07	.05	.03
7	Chris Brown	.07	.05	.03
8	Jose Canseco	.70	.50	.30
9	Joe Carter	.12	.09	.05
10	Roger Clemens	.40	.30	.15
11	Vince Coleman	.15	.11	.06
12	Joe Cowley	.05	.04	.02
13	Kal Daniels	.20	.15	.08
14	Glenn Davis	.15	.11	.06
15	Jody Davis	.07	.05	.03
16	Darrell Evans	.07	.05	.03
17	Dwight Evans	.10	.08	.04
18	John Franco	.07	.05	.03
19	Julio Franco	.10	.08	.04
20	Dwight Gooden	.40	.30	.15
21	Goose Gossage	.12	.09	.05
22	Tom Herr	.07	.05	.03
23	Ted Higuera	.10	.08	.04
24	Bob Horner	.07	.05	.03
25	Pete Incaviglia	.40	.30	.15
26	Wally Joyner	.40	.30	.15
27	Dave Kingman	.10	.08	.04
28	Don Mattingly	1.75	1.25	.70
29	Willie McGee	.10	.08	.04
30	Donnie Moore	.05	.04	.02
31	Keith Moreland	.05	.04	.02
32	Eddie Murray	.25	.20	.10
33	Mike Pagliarulo	.10	.08	.04
34	Larry Parrish	.05	.04	.02
35	Tony Pena	.07	.05	.03
36	Kirby Puckett	.50	.40	.20
37	Pete Rose	.50	.40	.20
38	Juan Samuel	.12	.09	.05
39	Ryne Sandberg	.20	.15	.08
40	Mike Schmidt	.30	.25	.12
41	Darryl Strawberry	.40	.30	.15
42	Greg Walker	.07	.05	.03
43	Bob Welch	.07	.05	.03
44	Todd Worrell	.12	.09	.05

1987 Fleer Limited Edition

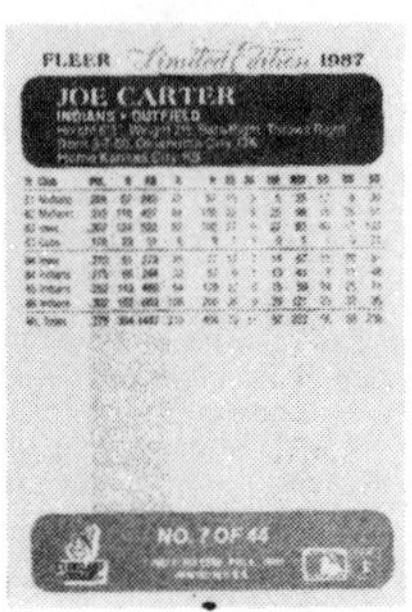

For the third straight year, Fleer produced a Limited Edition set for the McCrory's store chain and their affiliates. The cards are the standard 2-1/2" by 3-1/2" size and feature light blue borders at the top and bottom and a diagonal red and white border running along both sides. The set was issued in a specially prepared cardboard box, along with six team logo stickers.

		MT	NR MT	EX
Complete Set:		5.00	3.75	2.00
Common Player:		.05	.04	.02
1	Floyd Bannister	.05	.04	.02
2	Marty Barrett	.07	.05	.03
3	Steve Bedrosian	.10	.08	.04
4	George Bell	.20	.15	.08
5	George Brett	.30	.25	.12
6	Jose Canseco	1.00	.70	.40
7	Joe Carter	.12	.09	.05
8	Will Clark	1.00	.70	.40
9	Roger Clemens	.40	.30	.15
10	Vince Coleman	.15	.11	.06
11	Glenn Davis	.15	.11	.06
12	Mike Davis	.05	.04	.02
13	Len Dykstra	.07	.05	.03
14	John Franco	.07	.05	.03
15	Julio Franco	.10	.08	.04
16	Steve Garvey	.25	.20	.10
17	Kirk Gibson	.20	.15	.08
18	Dwight Gooden	.40	.30	.15
19	Tony Gwynn	.25	.20	.10
20	Keith Hernandez	.20	.15	.08
21	Teddy Higuera	.10	.08	.04
22	Kent Hrbek	.15	.11	.06
23	Wally Joyner	.50	.40	.20
24	Mike Krukow	.05	.04	.02
25	Mike Marshall	.10	.08	.04
26	Don Mattingly	1.00	.70	.40
27	Oddibe McDowell	.10	.08	.04
28	Jack Morris	.15	.11	.06
29	Lloyd Moseby	.07	.05	.03
30	Dale Murphy	.30	.25	.12
31	Eddie Murray	.25	.20	.10
32	Tony Pena	.07	.05	.03
33	Jim Presley	.10	.08	.04
34	Jeff Reardon	.10	.08	.04
35	Jim Rice	.20	.15	.08
36	Pete Rose	.40	.30	.15
37	Mike Schmidt	.30	.25	.12
38	Mike Scott	.12	.09	.05
39	Lee Smith	.07	.05	.03
40	Lonnie Smith	.05	.04	.02
41	Gary Ward	.05	.04	.02
42	Dave Winfield	.25	.20	.10
43	Todd Worrell	.12	.09	.05
44	Robin Yount	.20	.15	.08

1987 Fleer Mini

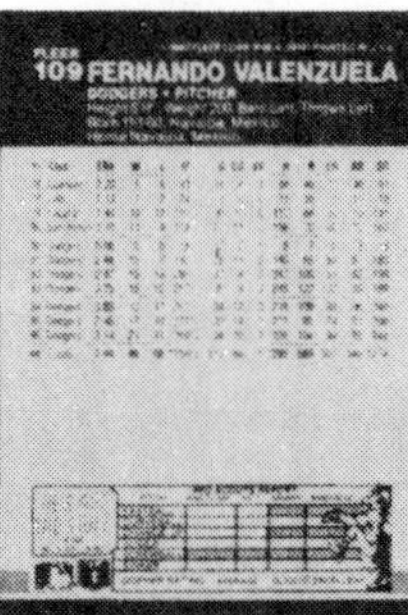

Continuing with an idea originated the previous year, the Fleer "Classic Miniatures" set consists of 120 cards that measure 1-13/16" by 2-9/16" in size. The cards are identical in design to the regular issue set produced by Fleer, but use completely different photos. The set was issued in a specially prepared collectors box along with 18 team logo stickers. The Fleer Mini set was available only through hobby dealers.

		MT	NR MT	EX
Complete Set:		8.00	6.00	3.25
Common Player:		.05	.04	.02
1	Don Aase	.05	.04	.02
2	Joaquin Andujar	.05	.04	.02
3	Harold Baines	.12	.09	.05
4	Jesse Barfield	.12	.09	.05
5	Kevin Bass	.05	.04	.02
6	Don Baylor	.10	.08	.04
7	George Bell	.20	.15	.08
8	Tony Bernazard	.05	.04	.02
9	Bert Blyleven	.12	.09	.05
10	Wade Boggs	1.00	.70	.40
11	Phil Bradley	.10	.08	.04
12	Sid Bream	.05	.04	.02
13	George Brett	.30	.25	.12
14	Hubie Brooks	.07	.05	.03
15	Chris Brown	.07	.05	.03
16	Tom Candiotti	.05	.04	.02
17	Jose Canseco	1.50	1.25	.60
18	Gary Carter	.20	.15	.08
19	Joe Carter	.12	.09	.05
20	Roger Clemens	.60	.45	.25
21	Vince Coleman	.15	.11	.06
22	Cecil Cooper	.10	.08	.04
23	Ron Darling	.10	.08	.04
24	Alvin Davis	.10	.08	.04
25	Chili Davis	.05	.04	.02
26	Eric Davis	.80	.60	.30
27	Glenn Davis	.15	.11	.06
28	Mike Davis	.05	.04	.02
29	Doug DeCinces	.05	.04	.02
30	Rob Deer	.07	.05	.03
31	Jim Deshaies	.10	.08	.04
32	Bo Diaz	.05	.04	.02
33	Richard Dotson	.07	.05	.03
34	Brian Downing	.05	.04	.02
35	Shawon Dunston	.07	.05	.03
36	Mark Eichhorn	.10	.08	.04
37	Dwight Evans	.12	.09	.05
38	Tony Fernandez	.10	.08	.04
39	Julio Franco	.10	.08	.04
40	Gary Gaetti	.12	.09	.05
41	Andres Galarraga	.15	.11	.06
42	Scott Garrelts	.05	.04	.02
43	Steve Garvey	.20	.15	.08
44	Kirk Gibson	.20	.15	.08
45	Dwight Gooden	.60	.45	.25
46	Ken Griffey	.07	.05	.03
47	Mark Gubicza	.10	.08	.04
48	Ozzie Guillen	.07	.05	.03
49	Bill Gullickson	.05	.04	.02
50	Tony Gwynn	.25	.20	.10
51	Von Hayes	.10	.08	.04
52	Rickey Henderson	.50	.40	.20
53	Keith Hernandez	.15	.11	.06
54	Willie Hernandez	.05	.04	.02
55	Ted Higuera	.10	.08	.04
56	Charlie Hough	.05	.04	.02
57	Kent Hrbek	.15	.11	.06
58	Pete Incaviglia	.40	.30	.15
59	Wally Joyner	.80	.60	.30
60	Bob Knepper	.07	.05	.03
61	Mike Krukow	.05	.04	.02
62	Mark Langston	.10	.08	.04
63	Carney Lansford	.07	.05	.03
64	Jim Lindeman	.12	.09	.05
65	Bill Madlock	.10	.08	.04
66	Don Mattingly	1.75	1.25	.70
67	Kirk McCaskill	.05	.04	.02
68	Lance McCullers	.10	.08	.04
69	Keith Moreland	.05	.04	.02
70	Jack Morris	.15	.11	.06
71	Jim Morrison	.05	.04	.02
72	Lloyd Moseby	.07	.05	.03
73	Jerry Mumphrey	.05	.04	.02
74	Dale Murphy	.30	.25	.12
75	Eddie Murray	.25	.20	.10
76	Pete O'Brien	.07	.05	.03
77	Bob Ojeda	.07	.05	.03
78	Jesse Orosco	.05	.04	.02
79	Dan Pasqua	.10	.08	.04
80	Dave Parker	.12	.09	.05
81	Larry Parrish	.05	.04	.02
82	Jim Presley	.10	.08	.04
83	Kirby Puckett	.50	.40	.20
84	Dan Quisenberry	.07	.05	.03
85	Tim Raines	.20	.15	.08
86	Dennis Rasmussen	.07	.05	.03
87	Johnny Ray	.07	.05	.03
88	Jeff Reardon	.07	.05	.03
89	Jim Rice	.20	.15	.08
90	Dave Righetti	.12	.09	.05
91	Earnest Riles	.05	.04	.02
92	Cal Ripken, Jr.	.30	.25	.12
93	Ron Robinson	.05	.04	.02
94	Juan Samuel	.12	.09	.05
95	Ryne Sandberg	.20	.15	.08
96	Steve Sax	.15	.11	.06
97	Mike Schmidt	.30	.25	.12
98	Ken Schrom	.05	.04	.02
99	Mike Scott	.12	.09	.05
100	Ruben Sierra	1.50	1.25	.60
101	Lee Smith	.07	.05	.03
102	Ozzie Smith	.12	.09	.05
103	Cory Snyder	.20	.15	.08
104	Kent Tekulve	.05	.04	.02
105	Andres Thomas	.10	.08	.04
106	Rob Thompson	.10	.08	.04
107	Alan Trammell	.20	.15	.08
108	John Tudor	.07	.05	.03
109	Fernando Valenzuela	.20	.15	.08
110	Greg Walker	.07	.05	.03
111	Mitch Webster	.05	.04	.02
112	Lou Whitaker	.15	.11	.06
113	Frank White	.07	.05	.03
114	Reggie Williams	.10	.08	.04
115	Glenn Wilson	.05	.04	.02
116	Willie Wilson	.10	.08	.04
117	Dave Winfield	.20	.15	.08
118	Mike Witt	.07	.05	.03
119	Todd Worrell	.12	.09	.05
120	Floyd Youmans	.05	.04	.02

1987 Fleer Record Setters

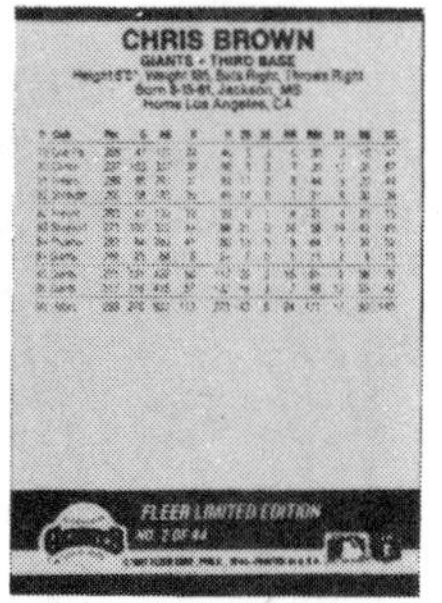

Produced by Fleer for the Eckerd Drug chain, the 1987 Fleer Record Setters set contains 44 cards that measure the standard 2-1/2" by 3-1/2" size. Although the set is titled "Record Setters," the actual records the players have set is not specified anywhere on the cards. Given that several players included in the set were young prospects, a better title for those cards might have been "Possible Record Setters." The set came housed in a special cardboard box with six team logo stickers.

		MT	NR MT	EX
Complete Set:		5.00	3.75	2.00
Common Player:		.05	.04	.02
1	George Brett	.30	.25	.12
2	Chris Brown	.07	.05	.03
3	Jose Canseco	1.00	.70	.40
4	Roger Clemens	.40	.30	.15
5	Alvin Davis	.10	.08	.04

		MT	NR MT	EX
6	Shawon Dunston	.07	.05	.03
7	Tony Fernandez	.10	.08	.04
8	Carlton Fisk	.12	.09	.05
9	Gary Gaetti	.10	.08	.04
10	Gene Garber	.05	.04	.02
11	Rich Gedman	.05	.04	.02
12	Dwight Gooden	.40	.30	.15
13	Ozzie Guillen	.07	.05	.03
14	Bill Gullickson	.05	.04	.02
15	Billy Hatcher	.07	.05	.03
16	Orel Hershiser	.20	.15	.08
17	Wally Joyner	.70	.50	.30
18	Ray Knight	.05	.04	.02
19	Craig Lefferts	.05	.04	.02
20	Don Mattingly	1.75	1.25	.70
21	Kevin Mitchell	.70	.50	.30
22	Lloyd Moseby	.07	.05	.03
23	Dale Murphy	.30	.25	.12
24	Eddie Murray	.25	.20	.10
25	Phil Niekro	.15	.11	.06
26	Ben Oglivie	.05	.04	.02
27	Jesse Orosco	.05	.04	.02
28	Joe Orsulak	.05	.04	.02
29	Larry Parrish	.05	.04	.02
30	Tim Raines	.25	.20	.10
31	Shane Rawley	.07	.05	.03
32	Dave Righetti	.12	.09	.05
33	Pete Rose	.40	.30	.15
34	Steve Sax	.15	.11	.06
35	Mike Schmidt	.30	.25	.12
36	Mike Scott	.12	.09	.05
37	Don Sutton	.12	.09	.05
38	Alan Trammell	.20	.15	.08
39	John Tudor	.10	.08	.04
40	Gary Ward	.05	.04	.02
41	Lou Whitaker	.15	.11	.06
42	Willie Wilson	.10	.08	.04
43	Todd Worrell	.15	.11	.06
44	Floyd Youmans	.10	.08	.04

1987 Fleer Star Stickers

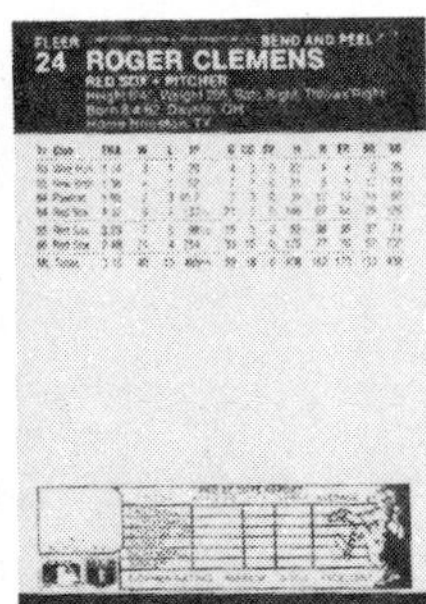

The 1987 Fleer Star Stickers set contains 132 cards which become stickers if the back is bent and peeled off. As in the previous year, the card backs are identical, save the numbering system, to the regular issue cards. The cards measure 2-1/2" by 3-1/2" and were sold in wax packs with team logo stickers. The fronts have a green border with a red and white banner wrapped across the upper left corner and the sides. The backs are printed in green and yellow.

		MT	NR MT	EX
	Complete Set:	23.00	17.00	9.25
	Common Player:	.05	.04	.02
1	Don Aase	.05	.04	.02
2	Harold Baines	.20	.15	.08
3	Floyd Bannister	.08	.06	.03
4	Jesse Barfield	.20	.15	.08
5	Marty Barrett	.10	.08	.04
6	Kevin Bass	.10	.08	.04
7	Don Baylor	.12	.09	.05
8	Steve Bedrosian	.15	.11	.06
9	George Bell	.35	.25	.14
10	Bert Blyleven	.15	.11	.06
11	Mike Boddicker	.08	.06	.03
12	Wade Boggs	1.75	1.25	.70
13	Phil Bradley	.15	.11	.06
14	Sid Bream	.08	.06	.03
15	George Brett	.70	.50	.30
16	Hubie Brooks	.10	.08	.04
17	Tom Brunansky	.15	.11	.06
18	Tom Candiotti	.05	.04	.02
19	Jose Canseco	2.00	1.50	.80
20	Gary Carter	.40	.30	.15
21	Joe Carter	.20	.15	.08
22	Will Clark	2.00	1.50	.80
23	Mark Clear	.05	.04	.02
24	Roger Clemens	.90	.70	.35
25	Vince Coleman	.25	.20	.10
26	Jose Cruz	.10	.08	.04
27	Ron Darling	.20	.15	.08
28	Alvin Davis	.20	.15	.08
29	Chili Davis	.10	.08	.04
30	Eric Davis	1.00	.70	.40
31	Glenn Davis	.20	.15	.08
32	Mike Davis	.05	.04	.02
33	Andre Dawson	.25	.20	.10
34	Doug DeCinces	.08	.06	.03
35	Brian Downing	.08	.06	.03
36	Shawon Dunston	.12	.09	.05
37	Mark Eichhorn	.12	.09	.05
38	Dwight Evans	.15	.11	.06
39	Tony Fernandez	.15	.11	.06
40	Bob Forsch	.05	.04	.02
41	John Franco	.10	.08	.04
42	Julio Franco	.12	.09	.05
43	Gary Gaetti	.20	.15	.08
44	Gene Garber	.05	.04	.02
45	Scott Garrelts	.05	.04	.02
46	Steve Garvey	.40	.30	.15
47	Kirk Gibson	.30	.25	.12
48	Dwight Gooden	.90	.70	.35
49	Ken Griffey	.10	.08	.04
50	Ozzie Guillen	.10	.08	.04
51	Bill Gullickson	.05	.04	.02
52	Tony Gwynn	.40	.30	.15
53	Mel Hall	.08	.06	.03
54	Greg Harris	.05	.04	.02
55	Von Hayes	.12	.09	.05
56	Rickey Henderson	.70	.50	.30
57	Tom Henke	.10	.08	.04
58	Keith Hernandez	.35	.25	.14
59	Willie Hernandez	.05	.04	.02
60	Ted Higuera	.20	.15	.08
61	Bob Horner	.12	.09	.05
62	Charlie Hough	.08	.06	.03
63	Jay Howell	.08	.06	.03
64	Kent Hrbek	.30	.25	.12
65	Bruce Hurst	.12	.09	.05
66	Pete Incaviglia	.60	.45	.25
67	Bob James	.05	.04	.02
68	Wally Joyner	.50	.40	.20
69	Mike Krukow	.05	.04	.02
70	Mark Langston	.15	.11	.06
71	Carney Lansford	.08	.06	.03
72	Fred Lynn	.25	.20	.10
73	Bill Madlock	.12	.09	.05
74	Don Mattingly	2.00	1.50	.80
75	Kirk McCaskill	.05	.04	.02
76	Lance McCullers	.12	.09	.05
77	Oddibe McDowell	.15	.11	.06
78	Paul Molitor	.20	.15	.08
79	Keith Moreland	.08	.06	.03
80	Jack Morris	.25	.20	.10
81	Jim Morrison	.05	.04	.02
82	Jerry Mumphrey	.05	.04	.02
83	Dale Murphy	.70	.50	.30
84	Eddie Murray	.50	.40	.20
85	Ben Oglivie	.05	.04	.02
86	Bob Ojeda	.10	.08	.04
87	Jesse Orosco	.08	.06	.03
88	Dave Parker	.25	.20	.10
89	Larry Parrish	.08	.06	.03
90	Tony Pena	.10	.08	.04
91	Jim Presley	.15	.11	.06
92	Kirby Puckett	.70	.50	.30
93	Dan Quisenberry	.12	.09	.05
94	Tim Raines	.35	.25	.14
95	Dennis Rasmussen	.10	.08	.04
96	Shane Rawley	.08	.06	.03
97	Johnny Ray	.10	.08	.04
98	Jeff Reardon	.10	.08	.04
99	Jim Rice	.35	.25	.14
100	Dave Righetti	.20	.15	.08
101	Cal Ripken, Jr.	.60	.45	.25
102	Pete Rose	1.00	.70	.40
103	Nolan Ryan	1.25	.90	.50
104	Juan Samuel	.15	.11	.06
105	Ryne Sandberg	.35	.25	.14
106	Steve Sax	.20	.15	.08
107	Mike Schmidt	1.25	.90	.50
108	Mike Scott	.15	.11	.06
109	Dave Smith	.05	.04	.02
110	Lee Smith	.10	.08	.04
111	Lonnie Smith	.05	.04	.02
112	Ozzie Smith	.20	.15	.08
113	Cory Snyder	.50	.40	.20
114	Darryl Strawberry	.70	.50	.30
115	Don Sutton	.25	.20	.10
116	Kent Tekulve	.08	.06	.03
117	Gorman Thomas	.08	.06	.03
118	Alan Trammell	.30	.25	.12
119	John Tudor	.12	.09	.05
120	Fernando Valenzuela	.12	.09	.05
121	Bob Welch	.12	.09	.05
122	Lou Whitaker	.25	.20	.10
123	Frank White	.10	.08	.04
124	Reggie Williams	.12	.09	.05
125	Willie Wilson	.15	.11	.06
126	Dave Winfield	.40	.30	.15
127	Mike Witt	.10	.08	.04
128	Todd Worrell	.25	.20	.10
129	Curt Young	.08	.06	.03
130	Robin Yount	.30	.25	.12
131	Jose Canseco, Don Mattingly/Checklist	2.50	2.00	1.00

1987 Fleer Star Stickers Box Panels

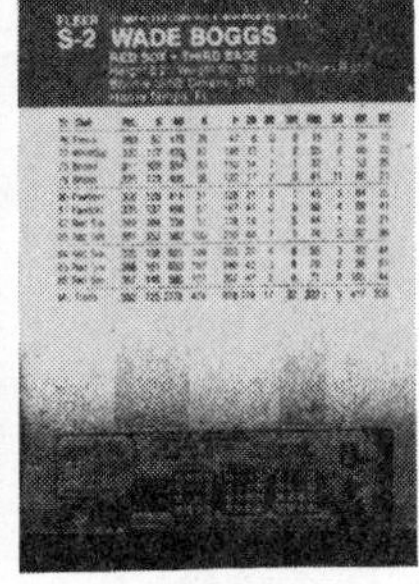

Fleer issued on the bottoms of their Fleer Star Stickers wax pack boxes six player cards plus two team logo/checklist cards. The cards, which measure 2-1/2" by 3-1/2", are numbered S-1 through S-8. The cards are identical in design to the Star Stickers.

		MT	NR MT	EX
	Complete Panel Set:	6.50	5.00	2.50
	Complete Singles Set:	3.25	2.50	1.25
	Common Single Player:	.15	.11	.06
	Panel	5.75	4.25	2.25
2	Wade Boggs	1.00	.70	.40
3	Bert Blyleven	.20	.15	.08
6	Phillies Logo	.05	.04	.02
8	Don Mattingly	2.00	1.50	.80
	Panel	1.00	.70	.40
1	Tigers Logo	.05	.04	.02
4	Jose Cruz	.15	.11	.06
5	Glenn Davis	.20	.15	.08
7	Bob Horner	.15	.11	.06

1987 Fleer Update

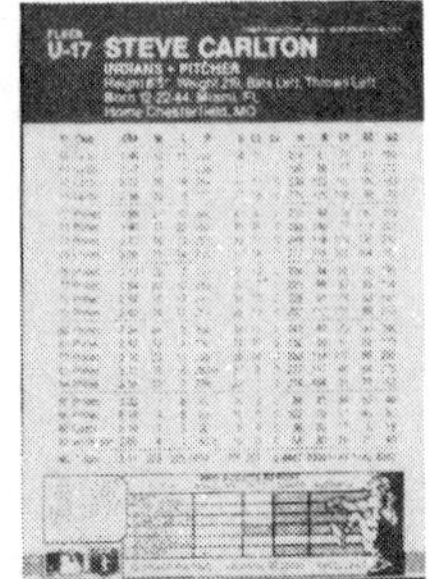

Fleer followed suit on a Topps idea in 1984 and began producing "Update" sets. The 1987 edition brings the regular Fleer set to date by including traded players and hot rookies. The cards measure 2-1/2" by 3-1/2" and are housed in a specially designed box with 25 team logo stickers. As a companion to the glossy-coated Fleer Collectors Edition set, Fleer produced a special edition Update set in its own tin box. Values of the glossy-coated cards are only a few dollars more than the regular Update cards.

		MT	NR MT	EX
	Complete Set:	18.00	13.50	7.25
	Common Player:	.06	.05	.02
1	Scott Bankhead	.08	.06	.03
2	Eric Bell(FC)	.15	.11	.06
3	Juan Beniquez	.06	.05	.02
4	Juan Berenguer	.06	.05	.02
5	Mike Birkbeck(FC)	.20	.15	.08
6	Randy Bockus(FC)	.15	.11	.06
7	Rod Booker(FC)	.15	.11	.06
8	Thad Bosley	.06	.05	.02
9	Greg Brock	.10	.08	.04
10	Bob Brower(FC)	.15	.11	.06
11	Chris Brown	.12	.09	.05
12	Jerry Browne	.15	.11	.06
13	Ralph Bryant	.10	.08	.04
14	DeWayne Buice(FC)	.20	.15	.08
15	Ellis Burks(FC)	2.50	2.00	1.00
16	Casey Candaele(FC)	.15	.11	.06
17	Steve Carlton	.30	.25	.12
18	Juan Castillo	.08	.06	.03
19	Chuck Crim(FC)	.15	.11	.06
20	Mark Davidson(FC)	.20	.15	.08
21	Mark Davis	.06	.05	.02
22	Storm Davis	.12	.09	.05
23	Bill Dawley	.06	.05	.02
24	Andre Dawson	.40	.30	.15
25	Brian Dayett	.06	.05	.02
26	Rick Dempsey	.08	.06	.03
27	Ken Dowell(FC)	.15	.11	.06
28	Dave Dravecky	.10	.08	.04
29	Mike Dunne(FC)	.35	.25	.14
30	Dennis Eckersley	.20	.15	.08
31	Cecil Fielder	1.00	.70	.40
32	Brian Fisher	.10	.08	.04
33	Willie Fraser	.10	.08	.04
34	Ken Gerhart(FC)	.15	.11	.06
35	Jim Gott	.06	.05	.02
36	Dan Gladden	.06	.05	.02
37	Mike Greenwell(FC)	3.50	2.75	1.50
38	Cecilio Guante	.06	.05	.02
39	Albert Hall	.06	.05	.02
40	Atlee Hammaker	.06	.05	.02
41	Mickey Hatcher	.06	.05	.02
42	Mike Heath	.06	.05	.02
43	Neal Heaton	.06	.05	.02
44	Mike Henneman(FC)	.30	.25	.12
45	Guy Hoffman	.06	.05	.02
46	Charles Hudson	.06	.05	.02
47	Chuck Jackson(FC)	.20	.15	.08
48	Mike Jackson(FC)	.20	.15	.08
49	Reggie Jackson	.50	.40	.20
50	Chris James	.35	.25	.14
51	Dion James	.12	.09	.05
52	Stan Javier	.06	.05	.02
53	Stan Jefferson(FC)	.20	.15	.08
54	Jimmy Jones	.10	.08	.04
55	Tracy Jones	.20	.15	.08
56	Terry Kennedy	.08	.06	.03
57	Mike Kingery	.08	.06	.03
58	Ray Knight	.10	.08	.04

		MT	NR MT	EX
59	Gene Larkin(FC)	.40	.30	.15
60	Mike LaValliere	.12	.09	.05
61	Jack Lazorko(FC)	.06	.05	.02
62	Terry Leach	.06	.05	.02
63	Rick Leach	.06	.05	.02
64	Craig Lefferts	.06	.05	.02
65	Jim Lindeman(FC)	.15	.11	.06
66	Bill Long(FC)	.20	.15	.08
67	Mike Loynd(FC)	.15	.11	.06
68	Greg Maddux(FC)	.90	.70	.35
69	Bill Madlock	.15	.11	.06
70	Dave Magadan	.25	.20	.10
71	Joe Magrane(FC)	1.00	.70	.40
72	Fred Manrique(FC)	.20	.15	.08
73	Mike Mason	.06	.05	.02
74	Lloyd McClendon(FC)	.15	.11	.06
75	Fred McGriff(FC)	2.50	2.00	1.00
76	Mark McGwire(FC)	3.50	2.75	1.50
77	Mark McLemore	.06	.05	.02
78	Kevin McReynolds	.30	.25	.12
79	Dave Meads(FC)	.15	.11	.06
80	Greg Minton	.06	.05	.02
81	John Mitchell(FC)	.15	.11	.06
82	Kevin Mitchell	2.00	1.50	.80
83	John Morris	.06	.05	.02
84	Jeff Musselman(FC)	.25	.20	.10
85	Randy Myers(FC)	.60	.45	.25
86	Gene Nelson	.06	.05	.02
87	Joe Niekro	.10	.08	.04
88	Tom Nieto	.06	.05	.02
89	Reid Nichols	.06	.05	.02
90	Matt Nokes(FC)	.60	.45	.25
91	Dickie Noles	.06	.05	.02
92	Edwin Nunez	.06	.05	.02
93	Jose Nunez(FC)	.25	.20	.10
94	Paul O'Neill	.10	.08	.04
95	Jim Paciorek(FC)	.06	.05	.02
96	Lance Parrish	.20	.15	.08
97	Bill Pecota(FC)	.20	.15	.08
98	Tony Pena	.12	.09	.05
99	Luis Polonia(FC)	.30	.25	.12
100	Randy Ready	.06	.05	.02
101	Jeff Reardon	.15	.11	.06
102	Gary Redus	.08	.06	.03
103	Rick Rhoden	.10	.08	.04
104	Wally Ritchie(FC)	.15	.11	.06
105	Jeff Robinson(FC)	.40	.30	.15
106	Mark Salas	.06	.05	.02
107	Dave Schmidt	.06	.05	.02
108	Kevin Seitzer	.80	.60	.30
109	John Shelby	.06	.05	.02
110	John Smiley(FC)	.40	.30	.15
111	Lary Sorenson	.06	.05	.02
112	Chris Speier	.06	.05	.02
113	Randy St. Claire	.06	.05	.02
114	Jim Sundberg	.08	.06	.03
115	B.J. Surhoff(FC)	.50	.40	.20
116	Greg Swindell	.50	.40	.20
117	Danny Tartabull	.35	.25	.14
118	Dorn Taylor(FC)	.12	.09	.05
119	Lee Tunnell	.06	.05	.02
120	Ed Vande Berg	.06	.05	.02
121	Andy Van Slyke	.20	.15	.08
122	Gary Ward	.06	.05	.02
123	Devon White	.35	.25	.14
124	Alan Wiggins	.06	.05	.02
125	Bill Wilkinson(FC)	.15	.11	.06
126	Jim Winn	.06	.05	.02
127	Frank Williams	.06	.05	.02
128	Ken Williams(FC)	.20	.15	.08
129	Matt Williams(FC)	3.00	2.25	1.25
130	Herm Winningham	.06	.05	.02
131	Matt Young	.06	.05	.02
132	Checklist 1-132	.06	.05	.02

1988 Fleer

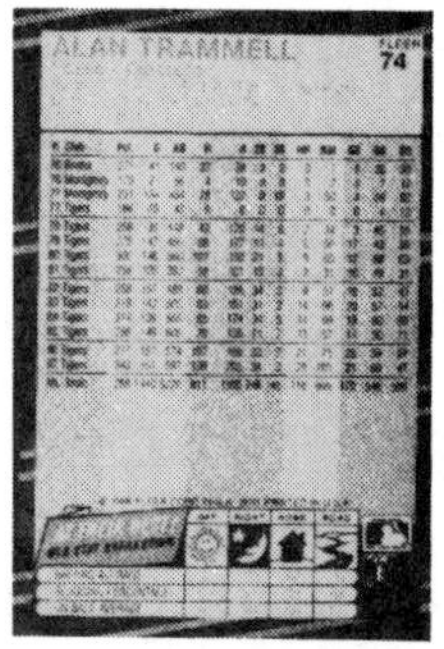

A clean, uncluttered look was the trademark of the 660-card 1988 Fleer set. The cards, which are the standard 2-1/2" by 3-1/2", feature blue and red diagonal lines set inside a white border. The player name and position are located on a slant in the upper left corner of the card. The player's team logo appears in the upper right corner. Below the player photo a blue and red band with the word "Fleer" appears. The backs of the cards include the card number, player personal information, and career statistics, plus a new feature called "At Their Best." This feature graphically shows a player's pitching or hitting statistics for home and road games and how he fared during day games as opposed to night contests. The set includes 19 special cards (#'s 622-640) and 12 "Major League Prospects" cards (#'s 641-653).

		MT	NR MT	EX
	Complete Set:	40.00	30.00	15.00
	Common Player:	.06	.05	.02
1	Keith Atherton	.06	.05	.02
2	Don Baylor	.10	.08	.04
3	Juan Berenguer	.06	.05	.02
4	Bert Blyleven	.12	.09	.05
5	Tom Brunansky	.10	.08	.04
6	Randy Bush	.06	.05	.02
7	Steve Carlton	.25	.20	.10
8	*Mark Davidson*(FC)	.12	.09	.05
9	George Frazier	.06	.05	.02
10	Gary Gaetti	.15	.11	.06
11	Greg Gagne	.06	.05	.02
12	Dan Gladden	.06	.05	.02
13	Kent Hrbek	.15	.11	.06
14	*Gene Larkin*	.20	.15	.08
15	Tim Laudner	.06	.05	.02
16	Steve Lombardozzi	.06	.05	.02
17	Al Newman	.06	.05	.02
18	Joe Niekro	.08	.06	.03
19	Kirby Puckett	.50	.40	.20
20	Jeff Reardon	.10	.08	.04
21a	Dan Schatzader (incorrect spelling)	.40	.30	.15
21b	Dan Schatzeder (correct spelling)	.06	.05	.02
22	Roy Smalley	.06	.05	.02
23	Mike Smithson	.06	.05	.02
24	*Les Straker*(FC)	.15	.11	.06
25	Frank Viola	.15	.11	.06
26	Jack Clark	.15	.11	.06
27	Vince Coleman	.20	.15	.08
28	Danny Cox	.08	.06	.03
29	Bill Dawley	.06	.05	.02
30	Ken Dayley	.06	.05	.02
31	Doug DeCinces	.08	.06	.03
32	Curt Ford	.06	.05	.02
33	Bob Forsch	.08	.06	.03
34	David Green	.06	.05	.02
35	Tom Herr	.08	.06	.03
36	Ricky Horton	.08	.06	.03
37	*Lance Johnson*(FC)	.40	.30	.15
38	Steve Lake	.06	.05	.02
39	Jim Lindeman	.10	.08	.04
40	*Joe Magrane*	.60	.45	.25
41	Greg Mathews	.08	.06	.03
42	Willie McGee	.12	.09	.05
43	John Morris	.06	.05	.02
44	Jose Oquendo	.06	.05	.02
45	Tony Pena	.08	.06	.03
46	Terry Pendleton	.08	.06	.03
47	Ozzie Smith	.15	.11	.06
48	John Tudor	.10	.08	.04
49	Lee Tunnell	.06	.05	.02
50	Todd Worrell	.10	.08	.04
51	Doyle Alexander	.08	.06	.03
52	Dave Bergman	.06	.05	.02
53	Tom Brookens	.06	.05	.02
54	Darrell Evans	.10	.08	.04
55	Kirk Gibson	.20	.15	.08
56	Mike Heath	.06	.05	.02
57	*Mike Henneman*	.25	.20	.10
58	Willie Hernandez	.08	.06	.03
59	Larry Herndon	.06	.05	.02
60	Eric King	.08	.06	.03
61	Chet Lemon	.08	.06	.03
62	*Scott Lusader*(FC)	.20	.15	.08
63	Bill Madlock	.10	.08	.04
64	Jack Morris	.20	.15	.08
65	Jim Morrison	.06	.05	.02
66	*Matt Nokes*	.50	.40	.20
67	Dan Petry	.08	.06	.03
68a	*Jeff Robinson* (Born 12-13-60 on back)	1.25	.90	.50
68b	*Jeff Robinson* (Born 12/14/61 on back)	.40	.30	.15
69	Pat Sheridan	.06	.05	.02
70	Nate Snell	.06	.05	.02
71	Frank Tanana	.08	.06	.03
72	Walt Terrell	.08	.06	.03
73	Mark Thurmond	.06	.05	.02
74	Alan Trammell	.25	.20	.10
75	Lou Whitaker	.25	.20	.10
76	Mike Aldrete	.08	.06	.03
77	Bob Brenly	.06	.05	.02
78	Will Clark	3.25	2.50	1.25
79	Chili Davis	.08	.06	.03
80	Kelly Downs	.10	.08	.04
81	Dave Dravecky	.08	.06	.03
82	Scott Garrelts	.06	.05	.02
83	Atlee Hammaker	.06	.05	.02
84	Dave Henderson	.10	.08	.04
85	Mike Krukow	.08	.06	.03
86	Mike LaCoss	.06	.05	.02
87	Craig Lefferts	.06	.05	.02
88	Jeff Leonard	.08	.06	.03
89	Candy Maldonado	.08	.06	.03
90	Ed Milner	.06	.05	.02
91	Bob Melvin	.06	.05	.02
92	Kevin Mitchell	1.25	.90	.50
93	*Jon Perlman*(FC)	.12	.09	.05
94	Rick Reuschel	.10	.08	.04
95	Don Robinson	.08	.06	.03
96	Chris Speier	.06	.05	.02
97	Harry Spilman	.06	.05	.02
98	Robbie Thompson	.08	.06	.03
99	Jose Uribe	.06	.05	.02
100	*Mark Wasinger*(FC)	.15	.11	.06
101	*Matt Williams*	2.50	2.00	1.00
102	Jesse Barfield	.15	.11	.06
103	George Bell	.25	.20	.10
104	Juan Beniquez	.06	.05	.02
105	John Cerutti	.08	.06	.03
106	Jim Clancy	.08	.06	.03
107	*Rob Ducey*(FC)	.15	.11	.06
108	Mark Eichhorn	.08	.06	.03
109	Tony Fernandez	.12	.09	.05
110	Cecil Fielder	.70	.50	.30
111	Kelly Gruber	.35	.25	.14
112	Tom Henke	.08	.06	.03
113	Garth Iorq (Iorg)	.06	.05	.02
114	Jimmy Key	.10	.08	.04
115	Rick Leach	.06	.05	.02
116	Manny Lee	.08	.06	.03
117	*Nelson Liriano*(FC)	.25	.20	.10
118	*Fred McGriff*	2.00	1.50	.80
119	Lloyd Moseby	.08	.06	.03
120	Rance Mulliniks	.06	.05	.02
121	Jeff Musselman	.10	.08	.04
122	*Jose Nunez*	.25	.20	.10
123	Dave Stieb	.10	.08	.04
124	Willie Upshaw	.08	.06	.03
125	Duane Ward(FC)	.08	.06	.03
126	Ernie Whitt	.08	.06	.03
127	Rick Aguilera	.06	.05	.02
128	Wally Backman	.08	.06	.03
129	*Mark Carreon*(FC)	.12	.09	.05
130	Gary Carter	.25	.20	.10
131	David Cone(FC)	1.25	.90	.50
132	Ron Darling	.12	.09	.05
133	Len Dykstra	.10	.08	.04
134	Sid Fernandez	.10	.08	.04
135	Dwight Gooden	.60	.45	.25
136	Keith Hernandez	.20	.15	.08
137	*Gregg Jefferies*(FC)	5.00	3.75	2.00
138	Howard Johnson	.10	.08	.04
139	Terry Leach	.06	.05	.02
140	*Barry Lyons*(FC)	.15	.11	.06
141	Dave Magadan	.12	.09	.05
142	Roger McDowell	.10	.08	.04
143	Kevin McReynolds	.15	.11	.06
144	*Keith Miller*(FC)	.25	.20	.10
145	*John Mitchell*(FC)	.20	.15	.08
146	Randy Myers	.15	.11	.06
147	Bob Ojeda	.08	.06	.03
148	Jesse Orosco	.08	.06	.03
149	Rafael Santana	.06	.05	.02
150	Doug Sisk	.06	.05	.02
151	Darryl Strawberry	.35	.25	.14
152	Tim Teufel	.06	.05	.02
153	Gene Walter	.06	.05	.02
154	Mookie Wilson	.08	.06	.03
155	*Jay Aldrich*(FC)	.12	.09	.05
156	Chris Bosio	.08	.06	.03
157	Glenn Braggs	.10	.08	.04
158	Greg Brock	.08	.06	.03
159	Juan Castillo	.06	.05	.02
160	Mark Clear	.06	.05	.02
161	Cecil Cooper	.10	.08	.04
162	*Chuck Crim*	.12	.09	.05
163	Rob Deer	.08	.06	.03
164	Mike Felder	.06	.05	.02
165	Jim Gantner	.06	.05	.02
166	Ted Higuera	.10	.08	.04
167	Steve Kiefer	.06	.05	.02
168	Rick Manning	.06	.05	.02
169	Paul Molitor	.12	.09	.05
170	Juan Nieves	.08	.06	.03
171	Dan Plesac	.10	.08	.04
172	Earnest Riles	.06	.05	.02
173	Bill Schroeder	.06	.05	.02
174	*Steve Stanicek*(FC)	.15	.11	.06
175	B.J. Surhoff	.20	.15	.08
176	Dale Sveum	.08	.06	.03
177	Bill Wegman	.06	.05	.02
178	Robin Yount	.30	.25	.12
179	Hubie Brooks	.10	.08	.04
180	Tim Burke	.06	.05	.02
181	Casey Candaele	.06	.05	.02
182	Mike Fitzgerald	.06	.05	.02
183	Tom Foley	.06	.05	.02
184	Andres Galarraga	.15	.11	.06
185	Neal Heaton	.06	.05	.02
186	Wallace Johnson	.06	.05	.02
187	Vance Law	.08	.06	.03
188	Dennis Martinez	.08	.06	.03
189	Bob McClure	.06	.05	.02
190	Andy McGaffigan	.06	.05	.02
191	Reid Nichols	.06	.05	.02
192	Pascual Perez	.08	.06	.03
193	Tim Raines	.25	.20	.10
194	Jeff Reed	.06	.05	.02
195	Bob Sebra	.06	.05	.02
196	Bryn Smith	.06	.05	.02
197	Randy St. Claire	.06	.05	.02
198	Tim Wallach	.10	.08	.04
199	Mitch Webster	.08	.06	.03
200	Herm Winningham	.06	.05	.02
201	Floyd Youmans	.06	.05	.02
202	*Brad Arnsberg*(FC)	.15	.11	.06
203	Rick Cerone	.06	.05	.02
204	Pat Clements	.06	.05	.02
205	Henry Cotto	.06	.05	.02
206	Mike Easler	.08	.06	.03
207	Ron Guidry	.15	.11	.06
208	Bill Gullickson	.06	.05	.02
209	Rickey Henderson	.35	.25	.14
210	Charles Hudson	.06	.05	.02
211	Tommy John	.15	.11	.06
212	*Roberto Kelly*(FC)	1.25	.90	.50
213	Ron Kittle	.08	.06	.03
214	Don Mattingly	1.50	1.25	.60
215	Bobby Meacham	.06	.05	.02
216	Mike Pagliarulo	.10	.08	.04
217	Dan Pasqua	.10	.08	.04
218	Willie Randolph	.08	.06	.03
219	Rick Rhoden	.08	.06	.03
220	Dave Righetti	.15	.11	.06
221	Jerry Royster	.06	.05	.02
222	Tim Stoddard	.06	.05	.02
223	Wayne Tolleson	.06	.05	.02
224	Gary Ward	.08	.06	.03
225	Claudell Washington	.08	.06	.03
226	Dave Winfield	.30	.25	.12
227	Buddy Bell	.08	.06	.03
228	Tom Browning	.10	.08	.04
229	Dave Concepcion	.08	.06	.03
230	Kal Daniels	.20	.15	.08
231	Eric Davis	.80	.60	.30
232	Bo Diaz	.08	.06	.03
233	Nick Esasky	.08	.06	.03
234	John Franco	.10	.08	.04
235	Guy Hoffman	.06	.05	.02
236	Tom Hume	.06	.05	.02
237	Tracy Jones	.12	.09	.05
238	*Bill Landrum*(FC)	.10	.08	.04
239	Barry Larkin	.40	.30	.15
240	Terry McGriff(FC)	.06	.05	.02

		MT	NR MT	EX
241	Rob Murphy	.08	.06	.03
242	Ron Oester	.06	.05	.02
243	Dave Parker	.20	.15	.08
244	Pat Perry	.06	.05	.02
245	Ted Power	.06	.05	.02
246	Dennis Rasmussen	.10	.08	.04
247	Ron Robinson	.06	.05	.02
248	Kurt Stillwell	.10	.08	.04
249	*Jeff Treadway*(FC)	.40	.30	.15
250	Frank Williams	.06	.05	.02
251	Steve Balboni	.08	.06	.03
252	Bud Black	.06	.05	.02
253	Thad Bosley	.06	.05	.02
254	George Brett	.40	.30	.15
255	*John Davis*(FC)	.20	.15	.08
256	Steve Farr	.06	.05	.02
257	Gene Garber	.06	.05	.02
258	Jerry Gleaton	.06	.05	.02
259	Mark Gubicza	.12	.09	.05
260	Bo Jackson	3.25	2.50	1.25
261	Danny Jackson	.12	.09	.05
262	*Ross Jones*(FC)	.12	.09	.05
263	Charlie Leibrandt	.08	.06	.03
264	*Bill Pecota*	.15	.11	.06
265	*Melido Perez*(FC)	.30	.25	.12
266	Jamie Quirk	.06	.05	.02
267	Dan Quisenberry	.08	.06	.03
268	Bret Saberhagen	.15	.11	.06
269	Angel Salazar	.06	.05	.02
270	Kevin Seitzer	.70	.50	.30
271	Danny Tartabull	.20	.15	.08
272	*Gary Thurman*(FC)	.20	.15	.08
273	Frank White	.08	.06	.03
274	Willie Wilson	.10	.08	.04
275	Tony Bernazard	.06	.05	.02
276	Jose Canseco	2.75	2.00	1.00
277	Mike Davis	.08	.06	.03
278	Storm Davis	.10	.08	.04
279	Dennis Eckersley	.12	.09	.05
280	Alfredo Griffin	.08	.06	.03
281	Rick Honeycutt	.06	.05	.02
282	Jay Howell	.08	.06	.03
283	Reggie Jackson	.50	.40	.20
284	Dennis Lamp	.06	.05	.02
285	Carney Lansford	.10	.08	.04
286	Mark McGwire	2.00	1.50	.80
287	Dwayne Murphy	.08	.06	.03
288	Gene Nelson	.06	.05	.02
289	Steve Ontiveros	.06	.05	.02
290	Tony Phillips	.06	.05	.02
291	Eric Plunk	.06	.05	.02
292	*Luis Polonia*	.25	.20	.10
293	*Rick Rodriguez*(FC)	.12	.09	.05
294	Terry Steinbach	.10	.08	.04
295	Dave Stewart	.10	.08	.04
296	Curt Young	.08	.06	.03
297	Luis Aguayo	.06	.05	.02
298	Steve Bedrosian	.12	.09	.05
299	Jeff Calhoun	.06	.05	.02
300	Don Carman	.08	.06	.03
301	*Todd Frohwirth*(FC)	.20	.15	.08
302	Greg Gross	.06	.05	.02
303	Kevin Gross	.08	.06	.03
304	Von Hayes	.08	.06	.03
305	*Keith Hughes*(FC)	.20	.15	.08
306	*Mike Jackson*	.20	.15	.08
307	Chris James	.20	.15	.08
308	Steve Jeltz	.06	.05	.02
309	Mike Maddux	.07	.05	.03
310	Lance Parrish	.15	.11	.06
311	Shane Rawley	.08	.06	.03
312	*Wally Ritchie*	.15	.11	.06
313	Bruce Ruffin	.08	.06	.03
314	Juan Samuel	.12	.09	.05
315	Mike Schmidt	.50	.40	.20
316	Rick Schu	.06	.05	.02
317	Jeff Stone	.06	.05	.02
318	Kent Tekulve	.08	.06	.03
319	Milt Thompson	.06	.05	.02
320	Glenn Wilson	.08	.06	.03
321	Rafael Belliard	.06	.05	.02
322	Barry Bonds	.12	.09	.05
323	Bobby Bonilla	.15	.11	.06
324	Sid Bream	.08	.06	.03
325	John Cangelosi	.06	.05	.02
326	Mike Diaz	.08	.06	.03
327	Doug Drabek	.08	.06	.03
328	*Mike Dunne*	.25	.20	.10
329	Brian Fisher	.08	.06	.03
330	*Brett Gideon*(FC)	.12	.09	.05
331	Terry Harper	.06	.05	.02
332	Bob Kipper	.06	.05	.02
333	Mike LaValliere	.08	.06	.03
334	*Jose Lind*(FC)	.30	.25	.12
335	Junior Ortiz	.06	.05	.02
336	*Vicente Palacios*(FC)	.20	.15	.08
337	*Bob Patterson*(FC)	.12	.09	.05
338	*Al Pedrique*(FC)	.15	.11	.06
339	R.J. Reynolds	.06	.05	.02
340	*John Smiley*	.35	.25	.14
341	Andy Van Slyke	.12	.09	.05
342	Bob Walk	.06	.05	.02
343	Marty Barrett	.08	.06	.03
344	*Todd Benzinger*(FC)	.40	.30	.15
345	Wade Boggs	1.00	.70	.40
346	*Tom Bolton*(FC)	.15	.11	.06
347	Oil Can Boyd	.08	.06	.03
348	*Ellis Burks*	1.75	1.25	.70
349	Roger Clemens	.60	.45	.25
350	Steve Crawford	.06	.05	.02
351	Dwight Evans	.12	.09	.05
352	*Wes Gardner*(FC)	.25	.20	.10
353	Rich Gedman	.08	.06	.03
354	Mike Greenwell	2.00	1.50	.80
355	*Sam Horn*(FC)	.30	.25	.12
356	Bruce Hurst	.10	.08	.04
357	*John Marzano*(FC)	.20	.15	.08
358	Al Nipper	.06	.05	.02
359	Spike Owen	.06	.05	.02
360	*Jody Reed*(FC)	.50	.40	.20
361	Jim Rice	.30	.25	.12
362	Ed Romero	.06	.05	.02
363	Kevin Romine(FC)	.08	.06	.03
364	Joe Sambito	.06	.05	.02

		MT	NR MT	EX
365	Calvin Schiraldi	.06	.05	.02
366	Jeff Sellers	.08	.06	.03
367	Bob Stanley	.06	.05	.02
368	Scott Bankhead	.06	.05	.02
369	Phil Bradley	.10	.08	.04
370	Scott Bradley	.06	.05	.02
371	Mickey Brantley	.06	.05	.02
372	*Mike Campbell*(FC)	.25	.20	.10
373	Alvin Davis	.12	.09	.05
374	Lee Guetterman	.06	.05	.02
375	*Dave Hengel*(FC)	.20	.15	.08
376	Mike Kingery	.06	.05	.02
377	Mark Langston	.12	.09	.05
378	*Edgar Martinez*(FC)	1.25	.90	.50
379	Mike Moore	.06	.05	.02
380	Mike Morgan	.06	.05	.02
381	John Moses	.06	.05	.02
382	*Donnell Nixon*(FC)	.20	.15	.08
383	Edwin Nunez	.06	.05	.02
384	Ken Phelps	.08	.06	.03
385	Jim Presley	.10	.08	.04
386	Rey Quinones	.06	.05	.02
387	Jerry Reed	.06	.05	.02
388	Harold Reynolds	.08	.06	.03
389	Dave Valle	.08	.06	.03
390	*Bill Wilkinson*	.15	.11	.06
391	Harold Baines	.12	.09	.05
392	Floyd Bannister	.08	.06	.03
393	Daryl Boston	.06	.05	.02
394	Ivan Calderon	.10	.08	.04
395	Jose DeLeon	.08	.06	.03
396	Richard Dotson	.08	.06	.03
397	Carlton Fisk	.20	.15	.08
398	Ozzie Guillen	.08	.06	.03
399	Ron Hassey	.06	.05	.02
400	Donnie Hill	.06	.05	.02
401	Bob James	.06	.05	.02
402	Dave LaPoint	.08	.06	.03
403	*Bill Lindsey*(FC)	.12	.09	.05
404	*Bill Long*(FC)	.20	.15	.08
405	Steve Lyons	.06	.05	.02
406	*Fred Manrique*	.15	.11	.06
407	*Jack McDowell*(FC)	.25	.20	.10
408	Gary Redus	.06	.05	.02
409	Ray Searage	.06	.05	.02
410	Bobby Thigpen	.10	.08	.04
411	Greg Walker	.08	.06	.03
412	*Kenny Williams*	.20	.15	.08
413	Jim Winn	.06	.05	.02
414	Jody Davis	.08	.06	.03
415	Andre Dawson	.20	.15	.08
416	Brian Dayett	.06	.05	.02
417	Bob Dernier	.06	.05	.02
418	Frank DiPino	.06	.05	.02
419	Shawon Dunston	.10	.08	.04
420	Leon Durham	.08	.06	.03
421	*Les Lancaster*(FC)	.20	.15	.08
422	Ed Lynch	.06	.05	.02
423	Greg Maddux	.35	.25	.14
424	Dave Martinez(FC)	.07	.05	.03
425a	Keith Moreland (bunting, photo actually Jody Davis)	3.50	2.75	1.50
425b	Keith Moreland (standing upright, correct photo)	.08	.06	.03
426	Jamie Moyer	.08	.06	.03
427	Jerry Mumphrey	.06	.05	.02
428	*Paul Noce*(FC)	.10	.08	.04
429	Rafael Palmeiro(FC)	.70	.50	.30
430	Wade Rowdon(FC)	.08	.06	.03
431	Ryne Sandberg	.25	.20	.10
432	Scott Sanderson	.06	.05	.02
433	Lee Smith	.10	.08	.04
434	Jim Sundberg	.08	.06	.03
435	Rick Sutcliffe	.10	.08	.04
436	Manny Trillo	.08	.06	.03
437	Juan Agosto	.06	.05	.02
438	Larry Andersen	.06	.05	.02
439	Alan Ashby	.06	.05	.02
440	Kevin Bass	.08	.06	.03
441	*Ken Caminiti*(FC)	.35	.25	.14
442	*Rocky Childress*(FC)	.12	.09	.05
443	Jose Cruz	.08	.06	.03
444	Danny Darwin	.06	.05	.02
445	Glenn Davis	.15	.11	.06
446	Jim Deshaies	.08	.06	.03
447	Bill Doran	.08	.06	.03
448	Ty Gainey	.06	.05	.02
449	Billy Hatcher	.08	.06	.03
450	Jeff Heathcock	.06	.05	.02
451	Bob Knepper	.08	.06	.03
452	*Rob Mallicoat*(FC)	.12	.09	.05
453	*Dave Meads*	.15	.11	.06
454	Craig Reynolds	.06	.05	.02
455	Nolan Ryan	.50	.40	.20
456	Mike Scott	.12	.09	.05
457	Dave Smith	.08	.06	.03
458	Denny Walling	.06	.05	.02
459	*Robbie Wine*(FC)	.12	.09	.05
460	*Gerald Young*(FC)	.35	.25	.14
461	Bob Brower	.08	.06	.03
462a	Jerry Browne (white player, photo actually Bob Brower)	3.50	2.75	1.50
462b	Jerry Browne (black player, correct photo)	.08	.06	.03
463	Steve Buechele	.06	.05	.02
464	Edwin Correa	.06	.05	.02
465	*Cecil Espy*(FC)	.30	.25	.12
466	Scott Fletcher	.08	.06	.03
467	Jose Guzman	.08	.06	.03
468	Greg Harris	.06	.05	.02
469	Charlie Hough	.08	.06	.03
470	Pete Incaviglia	.15	.11	.06
471	*Paul Kilgus*(FC)	.20	.15	.08
472	Mike Loynd	.08	.06	.03
473	Oddibe McDowell	.08	.06	.03
474	Dale Mohorcic	.08	.06	.03
475	Pete O'Brien	.08	.06	.03
476	Larry Parrish	.08	.06	.03
477	Geno Petralli	.06	.05	.02
478	Jeff Russell	.06	.05	.02
479	Ruben Sierra	.70	.50	.30
480	Mike Stanley	.08	.06	.03
481	Curtis Wilkerson	.06	.05	.02
482	Mitch Williams	.08	.06	.03

		MT	NR MT	EX
483	Bobby Witt	.10	.08	.04
484	Tony Armas	.08	.06	.03
485	Bob Boone	.08	.06	.03
486	Bill Buckner	.10	.08	.04
487	*DeWayne Buice*	.15	.11	.06
488	Brian Downing	.08	.06	.03
489	Chuck Finley	.06	.05	.02
490	Willie Fraser	.06	.05	.02
491	Jack Howell	.08	.06	.03
492	Ruppert Jones	.06	.05	.02
493	Wally Joyner	.40	.30	.15
494	Jack Lazorko	.06	.05	.02
495	Gary Lucas	.06	.05	.02
496	Kirk McCaskill	.08	.06	.03
497	Mark McLemore	.06	.05	.02
498	Darrell Miller	.06	.05	.02
499	Greg Minton	.06	.05	.02
500	Donnie Moore	.06	.05	.02
501	Gus Polidor	.06	.05	.02
502	Johnny Ray	.08	.06	.03
503	Mark Ryal(FC)	.06	.05	.02
504	Dick Schofield	.06	.05	.02
505	Don Sutton	.20	.15	.08
506	Devon White	.25	.20	.10
507	Mike Witt	.08	.06	.03
508	Dave Anderson	.06	.05	.02
509	Tim Belcher(FC)	.60	.45	.25
510	Ralph Bryant	.06	.05	.02
511	*Tim Crews*(FC)	.15	.11	.06
512	*Mike Devereaux*(FC)	.30	.25	.12
513	Mariano Duncan	.06	.05	.02
514	Pedro Guerrero	.15	.11	.06
515	Jeff Hamilton(FC)	.12	.09	.05
516	Mickey Hatcher	.06	.05	.02
517	Brad Havens	.06	.05	.02
518	Orel Hershiser	.25	.20	.10
519	*Shawn Hillegas*(FC)	.20	.15	.08
520	Ken Howell	.06	.05	.02
521	Tim Leary	.08	.06	.03
522	Mike Marshall	.12	.09	.05
523	Steve Sax	.15	.11	.06
524	Mike Scioscia	.08	.06	.03
525	Mike Sharperson(FC)	.06	.05	.02
526	John Shelby	.06	.05	.02
527	Franklin Stubbs	.08	.06	.03
528	Fernando Valenzuela	.20	.15	.08
529	Bob Welch	.10	.08	.04
530	Matt Young	.06	.05	.02
531	Jim Acker	.06	.05	.02
532	Paul Assenmacher	.06	.05	.02
533	*Jeff Blauser*(FC)	.25	.20	.10
534	*Joe Boever*(FC)	.25	.20	.10
535	Martin Clary(FC)	.06	.05	.02
536	*Kevin Coffman*(FC)	.12	.09	.05
537	Jeff Dedmon	.06	.05	.02
538	*Ron Gant*(FC)	.70	.50	.30
539	*Tom Glavine*(FC)	.40	.30	.15
540	Ken Griffey	.08	.06	.03
541	Al Hall	.06	.05	.02
542	Glenn Hubbard	.06	.05	.02
543	Dion James	.08	.06	.03
544	Dale Murphy	.40	.30	.15
545	Ken Oberkfell	.06	.05	.02
546	David Palmer	.06	.05	.02
547	Gerald Perry	.10	.08	.04
548	Charlie Puleo	.06	.05	.02
549	Ted Simmons	.10	.08	.04
550	Zane Smith	.08	.06	.03
551	Andres Thomas	.08	.06	.03
552	Ozzie Virgil	.06	.05	.02
553	Don Aase	.06	.05	.02
554	*Jeff Ballard*(FC)	.35	.25	.14
555	Eric Bell	.08	.06	.03
556	Mike Boddicker	.08	.06	.03
557	Ken Dixon	.06	.05	.02
558	Jim Dwyer	.06	.05	.02
559	Ken Gerhart	.08	.06	.03
560	*Rene Gonzales*(FC)	.15	.11	.06
561	Mike Griffin	.06	.05	.02
562	John Hayban (Habyan)	.06	.05	.02
563	Terry Kennedy	.08	.06	.03
564	Ray Knight	.08	.06	.03
565	Lee Lacy	.06	.05	.02
566	Fred Lynn	.15	.11	.06
567	Eddie Murray	.35	.25	.14
568	Tom Niedenfuer	.08	.06	.03
569	*Bill Ripken*(FC)	.25	.20	.10
570	Cal Ripken, Jr.	.35	.25	.14
571	Dave Schmidt	.06	.05	.02
572	Larry Sheets	.08	.06	.03
573	*Pete Stanicek*(FC)	.15	.11	.06
574	*Mark Williamson*(FC)	.12	.09	.05
575	Mike Young	.06	.05	.02
576	Shawn Abner(FC)	.20	.15	.08
577	Greg Booker	.06	.05	.02
578	Chris Brown	.08	.06	.03
579	*Keith Comstock*(FC)	.12	.09	.05
580	*Joey Cora*(FC)	.12	.09	.05
581	Mark Davis	.06	.05	.02
582	Tim Flannery	.06	.05	.02
583	Goose Gossage	.15	.11	.06
584	Mark Grant	.06	.05	.02
585	Tony Gwynn	.35	.25	.14
586	Andy Hawkins	.06	.05	.02
587	Stan Jefferson	.10	.08	.04
588	Jimmy Jones	.08	.06	.03
589	John Kruk	.10	.08	.04
590	*Shane Mack*(FC)	.20	.15	.08
591	Carmelo Martinez	.08	.06	.03
592	Lance McCullers	.08	.06	.03
593	*Eric Nolte*(FC)	.15	.11	.06
594	Randy Ready	.06	.05	.02
595	Luis Salazar	.06	.05	.02
596	Benito Santiago	.35	.25	.14
597	Eric Show	.08	.06	.03
598	Garry Templeton	.08	.06	.03
599	Ed Whitson	.06	.05	.02
600	Scott Bailes	.08	.06	.03
601	Chris Bando	.06	.05	.02
602	*Jay Bell*(FC)	.30	.25	.12
603	Brett Butler	.08	.06	.03
604	Tom Candiotti	.06	.05	.02
605	Joe Carter	.12	.09	.05
606	Carmen Castillo	.06	.05	.02

		MT	NR MT	EX
607	*Brian Dorsett*(FC)	.15	.11	.06
608	*John Farrell*(FC)	.35	.25	.14
609	Julio Franco	.10	.08	.04
610	Mel Hall	.08	.06	.03
611	*Tommy Hinzo*(FC)	.15	.11	.06
612	Brook Jacoby	.10	.08	.04
613	*Doug Jones*(FC)	.40	.30	.15
614	Ken Schrom	.06	.05	.02
615	Cory Snyder	.20	.15	.08
616	Sammy Stewart	.06	.05	.02
617	Greg Swindell	.25	.20	.10
618	Pat Tabler	.08	.06	.03
619	Ed Vande Berg	.06	.05	.02
620	*Eddie Williams*(FC)	.20	.15	.08
621	Rich Yett	.06	.05	.02
622	Slugging Sophomores (Wally Joyner, Cory Snyder)	.35	.25	.14
623	Dominican Dynamite (George Bell, Pedro Guerrero)	.12	.09	.05
624	Oakland's Power Team (Jose Canseco, Mark McGwire)	1.25	.90	.50
625	Classic Relief (Dan Plesac, Dave Righetti)	.08	.06	.03
626	All Star Righties (Jack Morris, Bret Saberhagen, Mike Witt)	.10	.08	.04
627	Game Closers (Steve Bedrosian, John Franco)	.08	.06	.03
628	Masters of the Double Play (Ryne Sandberg, Ozzie Smith)	.12	.09	.05
629	Rookie Record Setter (Mark McGwire)	1.00	.70	.40
630	Changing the Guard in Boston (Todd Benzinger, Ellis Burks, Mike Greenwell)	1.00	.70	.40
631	N.L. Batting Champs (Tony Gwynn, Tim Raines)	.15	.11	.06
632	Pitching Magic (Orel Hershiser, Mike Scott)	.12	.09	.05
633	Big Bats At First (Mark McGwire, Pat Tabler)	.60	.45	.25
634	Hitting King and the Thief (Vince Coleman, Tony Gwynn)	.12	.09	.05
635	A.L. Slugging Shortstops (Tony Fernandez, Cal Ripken, Jr., Alan Trammell)	.15	.11	.06
636	Tried and True Sluggers (Gary Carter, Mike Schmidt)	.20	.15	.08
637	Crunch Time (Eric Davis, Darryl Strawberry)	.70	.50	.30
638	A.L. All Stars (Matt Nokes, Kirby Puckett)	.20	.15	.08
639	N.L. All Stars (Keith Hernandez, Dale Murphy)	.20	.15	.08
640	The "O's" Brothers (Bill Ripken, Cal Ripken, Jr.)	.12	.09	.05
641	Major League Prospects *(Mark Grace, Darrin Jackson)*(FC)	12.00	9.00	4.75
642	Major League Prospects *(Damon Berryhill, Jeff Montgomery)*(FC)	1.00	.70	.40
643	Major League Prospects *(Felix Fermin, Jessie Reid)*(FC)	.20	.15	.08
644	Major League Prospects *(Greg Myers, Greg Tabor)*(FC)	.20	.15	.08
645	Major League Prospects *(Jim Eppard,* Joey Meyer)(FC)	.25	.20	.10
646	Major League Prospects *(Adam Peterson, Randy Velarde)*(FC)	.30	.25	.12
647	Major League Prospects *(Chris Gwynn, Peter Smith)*(FC)	.40	.30	.15
648	Major League Prospects *(Greg Jelks, Tom Newell)*(FC)	.25	.20	.10
649	Major League Prospects *(Mario Diaz, Clay Parker)*(FC)	.25	.20	.10
650	Major League Prospects *(Jack Savage, Todd Simmons)*(FC)	.25	.20	.10
651	Major League Prospects *(John Burkett, Kirt Manwaring)*(FC)	.50	.40	.20
652	Major League Prospects *(Dave Otto, Walt Weiss)*(FC)	1.00	.70	.40
653	Major League Prospects *(Randell Byers (Randall), Jeff King)*(FC)	.25	.20	.10
654a	Checklist 1-101 (21 is Schatzader)	.10	.08	.04
654b	Checklist 1-101 (21 is Schatzeder)	.06	.05	.02
655	Checklist 102-201	.06	.05	.02
656	Checklist 202-296	.06	.05	.02
657	Checklist 297-390	.06	.05	.02
658	Checklist 391-483	.06	.05	.02
659	Checklist 484-575	.06	.05	.02
660	Checklist 576-660	.06	.05	.02

1988 Fleer All Star Team

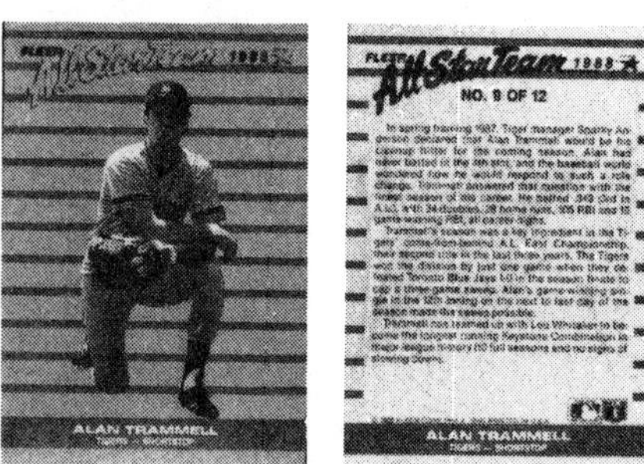

For the third consecutive year, Fleer randomly inserted All Star Team cards in their wax and cello packs. Twelve cards make up the set, each card measuring 2-1/2" by 3-1/2" in size. Players chosen for the set are Fleer's choices for a major league All-Star team.

		MT	NR MT	EX
Complete Set:		16.00	12.00	6.50
Common Player:		.60	.45	.25
1	Matt Nokes	.75	.60	.30
2	Tom Henke	.60	.45	.25
3	Ted Higuera	.60	.45	.25
4	Roger Clemens	2.25	1.75	.90
5	George Bell	1.00	.70	.40
6	Andre Dawson	1.00	.70	.40
7	Eric Davis	2.25	1.75	.90
8	Wade Boggs	3.25	2.50	1.25
9	Alan Trammell	1.00	.70	.40
10	Juan Samuel	.75	.60	.30
11	Jack Clark	.75	.60	.30
12	Paul Molitor	.75	.60	.30

1988 Fleer Award Winners

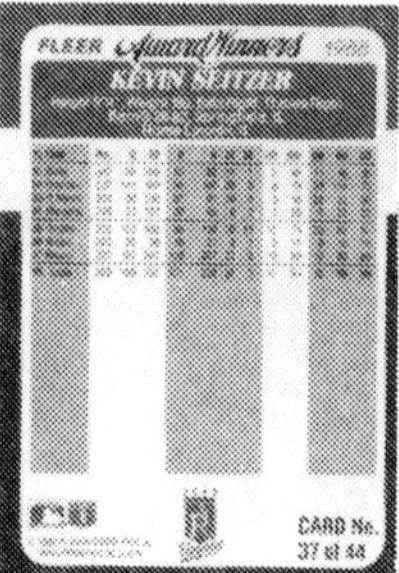

This limited edition 44-card boxed set of 1987 award-winning player cards also includes six team logo sticker cards. Red, white, blue and yellow bands border the sharp, full-color player photos printed below a "Fleer Award Winners 1988" banner. The player's name and award are printed beneath the photo. Flip sides are red, white and blue and list personal information, career data, team logo and card number. This set was sold exclusively at 7-11 stores nationwide.

		MT	NR MT	EX
Complete Set:		7.00	5.25	2.75
Common Player:		.05	.04	.02
1	Steve Bedrosian	.10	.08	.04
2	George Bell	.20	.15	.08
3	Wade Boggs	1.25	.90	.50
4	Jose Canseco	1.25	.90	.50
5	Will Clark	.50	.40	.20
6	Roger Clemens	.40	.30	.15
7	Kal Daniels	.20	.15	.08
8	Eric Davis	.50	.40	.20
9	Andre Dawson	.15	.11	.06
10	Mike Dunne	.10	.08	.04
11	Dwight Evans	.10	.08	.04
12	Carlton Fisk	.15	.11	.06
13	Julio Franco	.07	.05	.03
14	Dwight Gooden	.40	.30	.15
15	Pedro Guerrero	.15	.11	.06
16	Tony Gwynn	.25	.20	.10
17	Orel Hershiser	.20	.15	.08
18	Tom Henke	.05	.04	.02
19	Ted Higuera	.10	.08	.04
20	Charlie Hough	.05	.04	.02
21	Wally Joyner	.30	.25	.12
22	Jimmy Key	.07	.05	.03
23	Don Mattingly	1.25	.90	.50
24	Mark McGwire	1.25	.90	.50
25	Paul Molitor	.12	.09	.05
26	Jack Morris	.12	.09	.05
27	Dale Murphy	.30	.25	.12
28	Terry Pendleton	.05	.04	.02
29	Kirby Puckett	.70	.50	.30
30	Tim Raines	.25	.20	.10
31	Jeff Reardon	.07	.05	.03
32	Harold Reynolds	.05	.04	.02
33	Dave Righetti	.12	.09	.05
34	Benito Santiago	.25	.20	.10
35	Mike Schmidt	.30	.25	.12
36	Mike Scott	.10	.08	.04
37	Kevin Seitzer	.60	.45	.25
38	Larry Sheets	.07	.05	.03
39	Ozzie Smith	.15	.11	.06
40	Darryl Strawberry	.40	.30	.15
41	Rick Sutcliffe	.10	.08	.04
42	Danny Tartabull	.12	.09	.05
43	Alan Trammell	.15	.11	.06
44	Tim Wallach	.10	.08	.04

1988 Fleer Baseball All Stars

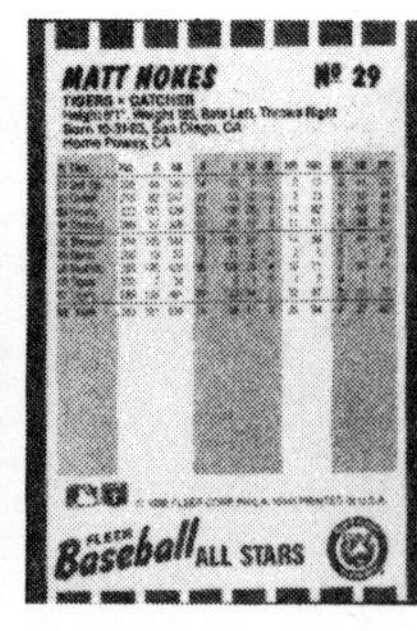

This limited edition 44-card boxed set features excellent photography of major league All-Stars. The standard-size cards feature a sporty bright blue- and yellow-striped background. The player name is printed in white across the upper left front corner. "Fleer Baseball 88 All Stars" appears on a yellow band beneath the photo. Card backs feature a blue- and white-striped design with a yellow highlighted section at the top that contains the player name, card number, team, position and personal data, followed by lifetime career stats. Fleer All Stars are cello-wrapped in blue and yellow striped boxes with checklist backs. The set includes six team logo sticker cards that feature black and white aerial shots of major league ballparks. The set was marketed exclusively by Ben Franklin stores.

		MT	NR MT	EX
Complete Set:		6.00	4.50	2.50
Common Player:		.05	.04	.02
1	George Bell	.20	.15	.08
2	Wade Boggs	1.00	.70	.40
3	Bobby Bonilla	.12	.09	.05
4	George Brett	.30	.25	.12
5	Jose Canseco	1.00	.70	.40
6	Jack Clark	.15	.11	.06
7	Will Clark	1.00	.70	.40
8	Roger Clemens	.40	.30	.15
9	Eric Davis	.50	.40	.20
10	Andre Dawson	.15	.11	.06
11	Julio Franco	.07	.05	.03
12	Dwight Gooden	.40	.30	.15
13	Tony Gwynn	.25	.20	.10
14	Orel Hershiser	.20	.15	.08
15	Teddy Higuera	.10	.08	.04
16	Charlie Hough	.05	.04	.02
17	Kent Hrbek	.15	.11	.06
18	Bruce Hurst	.10	.08	.04
19	Wally Joyner	.30	.25	.12
20	Mark Langston	.10	.08	.04
21	Dave LaPoint	.05	.04	.02
22	Candy Maldonado	.05	.04	.02
23	Don Mattingly	1.00	.70	.40
24	Roger McDowell	.07	.05	.03
25	Mark McGwire	1.00	.70	.40
26	Jack Morris	.12	.09	.05
27	Dale Murphy	.30	.25	.12
28	Eddie Murray	.20	.15	.08
29	Matt Nokes	.30	.25	.12
30	Kirby Puckett	.70	.50	.30
31	Tim Raines	.25	.20	.10
32	Willie Randolph	.07	.05	.03
33	Jeff Reardon	.07	.05	.03
34	Nolan Ryan	.50	.40	.20
35	Juan Samuel	.10	.08	.04
36	Mike Schmidt	.30	.25	.12
37	Mike Scott	.10	.08	.04
38	Kevin Seitzer	.60	.45	.25
39	Ozzie Smith	.15	.11	.06
40	Darryl Strawberry	.40	.30	.15
41	Rick Sutcliffe	.10	.08	.04
42	Alan Trammell	.15	.11	.06
43	Tim Wallach	.10	.08	.04
44	Dave Winfield	.20	.15	.08

1988 Fleer Baseball MVP

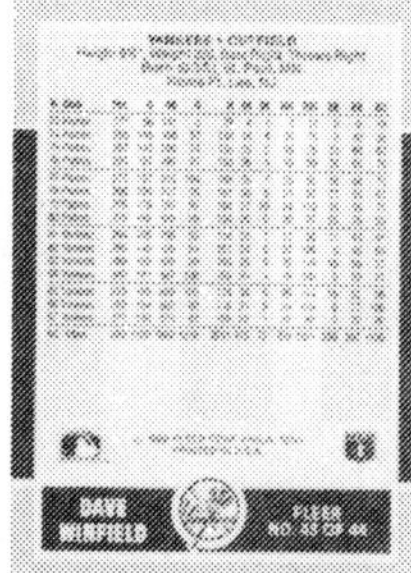

This boxed set of 44 standard-size cards and six team logo stickers was produced by Fleer for exclusive distribution at Toys "R" Us stores. This premiere edition features full-color player photos framed by a yellow and blue border. The player's name is printed in red below and to the left of the photo; team and position are printed in black in the lower right corner. The "Fleer Baseball MVP" logo appears bottom center. Card backs are yellow and blue on a white background. The player's team, position and personal data are followed by stats, logo and a blue banner bearing the player's name, team logo and card number. The six sticker cards feature black and white stadium photos on the backs.

		MT	NR MT	EX
Complete Set:		7.00	5.25	2.75
Common Player:		.05	.04	.02
1	George Bell	.20	.15	.08
2	Wade Boggs	1.00	.70	.40
3	Jose Canseco	1.00	.70	.40
4	Ivan Calderon	.07	.05	.03
5	Will Clark	1.00	.70	.40
6	Roger Clemens	.40	.30	.15
7	Vince Coleman	.15	.11	.06
8	Eric Davis	.50	.40	.20
9	Andre Dawson	.15	.11	.06
10	Dave Dravecky	.05	.04	.02
11	Mike Dunne	.10	.08	.04
12	Dwight Evans	.10	.08	.04
13	Sid Fernandez	.07	.05	.03
14	Tony Fernandez	.10	.08	.04
15	Julio Franco	.07	.05	.03
16	Dwight Gooden	.40	.30	.15
17	Tony Gwynn	.25	.20	.10
18	Ted Higuera	.10	.08	.04
19	Charlie Hough	.05	.04	.02
20	Wally Joyner	.30	.25	.12
21	Mark Langston	.10	.08	.04
22	Don Mattingly	1.25	.90	.50
23	Mark McGwire	1.00	.70	.40
24	Jack Morris	.12	.09	.05
25	Dale Murphy	.30	.25	.12
26	Kirby Puckett	.50	.40	.20
27	Tim Raines	.25	.20	.10
28	Willie Randolph	.07	.05	.03
29	Ryne Sandberg	.20	.15	.08
30	Benito Santiago	.25	.20	.10
31	Mike Schmidt	.30	.25	.12
32	Mike Scott	.10	.08	.04
33	Kevin Seitzer	.60	.45	.25
34	Larry Sheets	.07	.05	.03
35	Ozzie Smith	.15	.11	.06
36	Dave Stewart	.10	.08	.04
37	Darryl Strawberry	.40	.30	.15
38	Rick Sutcliffe	.10	.08	.04
39	Alan Trammell	.15	.11	.06
40	Fernando Valenzuela	.20	.15	.08
41	Frank Viola	.12	.09	.05
42	Tim Wallach	.10	.08	.04
43	Dave Winfield	.20	.15	.08
44	Robin Yount	.25	.20	.10

1988 Fleer Baseball's Best

This boxed set of 44 standard-size cards (2-1/2" by 3-1/2") and six team logo stickers is the third annual issue from Fleer highlighting the best major league sluggers and pitchers. Five additional player cards were printed on retail display box bottoms, along with a checklist logo card (numbered C-1 through C-6). Full-color player photos are framed by a green border that fades to yellow. A red (slugger) or blue (pitcher) player name is printed beneath the photo. The card backs are printed in green on a white background with yellow highlights. Card number, player name and personal info appear in a green vertical box on the left-hand side of the card back with a yellow cartoon-style team logo overprinted across a stats chart on the right. This set was produced by Fleer for exclusive distribution by McCrory's stores (McCrory, McClellan, J.J. Newberry, H.L. Green, TG&Y).

		MT	NR MT	EX
Complete Set:		5.00	3.75	2.00
Common Player:		.05	.04	.02
1	George Bell	.20	.15	.08
2	Wade Boggs	1.00	.70	.40
3	Bobby Bonilla	.12	.09	.05
4	Tom Brunansky	.10	.08	.04
5	Ellis Burks	1.00	.70	.40
6	Jose Canseco	1.00	.70	.40
7	Joe Carter	.12	.09	.05
8	Will Clark	1.00	.70	.40
9	Roger Clemens	.40	.30	.15
10	Eric Davis	.50	.40	.20
11	Glenn Davis	.12	.09	.05
12	Andre Dawson	.15	.11	.06
13	Dennis Eckersley	.07	.05	.03
14	Andres Galarraga	.15	.11	.06
15	Dwight Gooden	.40	.30	.15
16	Pedro Guerrero	.15	.11	.06
17	Tony Gwynn	.25	.20	.10
18	Orel Hershiser	.20	.15	.08
19	Ted Higuera	.10	.08	.04
20	Pete Incaviglia	.12	.09	.05
21	Danny Jackson	.10	.08	.04
22	Doug Jennings	.07	.05	.03
23	Mark Langston	.10	.08	.04
24	Dave LaPoint	.05	.04	.02
25	Mike LaValliere	.07	.05	.03
26	Don Mattingly	1.00	.70	.40
27	Mark McGwire	1.00	.70	.40
28	Dale Murphy	.30	.25	.12
29	Ken Phelps	.05	.04	.02
30	Kirby Puckett	.50	.40	.20
31	Johnny Ray	.05	.04	.02
32	Jeff Reardon	.07	.05	.03
33	Dave Righetti	.12	.09	.05
34	Cal Ripkin, Jr. (Ripken)	.30	.25	.12
35	Chris Sabo	.90	.70	.35
36	Mike Schmidt	.30	.25	.12
37	Mike Scott	.10	.08	.04
38	Kevin Seitzer	.60	.45	.25
39	Dave Stewart	.10	.08	.04
40	Darryl Strawberry	.40	.30	.15
41	Greg Swindell	.10	.08	.04
42	Frank Tanana	.05	.04	.02
43	Dave Winfield	.20	.15	.08
44	Todd Worrell	.10	.08	.04

1988 Fleer Baseball's Best Box Panels

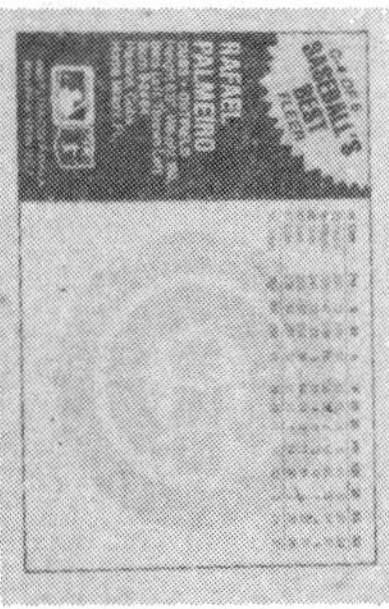

Six cards were placed on the bottoms of retail boxes of the Fleer 44-card Baseball's Best boxed sets in 1988. The cards, which measure 2-1/2" by 3-1/2", are identical in design to cards found in the 44-card set. The cards are numbered C-1 through C-6 and were produced by Fleer for distribution by McCrory stores and its affiliates.

		MT	NR MT	EX
Complete Panel Set:		1.50	1.25	.60
Complete Singles Set:		.90	.70	.35
Common Single Player:		.15	.11	.06
Panel		1.50	1.25	.60
1	Ron Darling	.20	.15	.08
2	Rickey Henderson	.40	.30	.15
3	Carney Lansford	.15	.11	.06
4	Rafael Palmeiro	.20	.15	.08
5	Frank Viola	.20	.15	.08
6	Twins Logo	.05	.04	.02

1988 Fleer Baseball's Exciting Stars

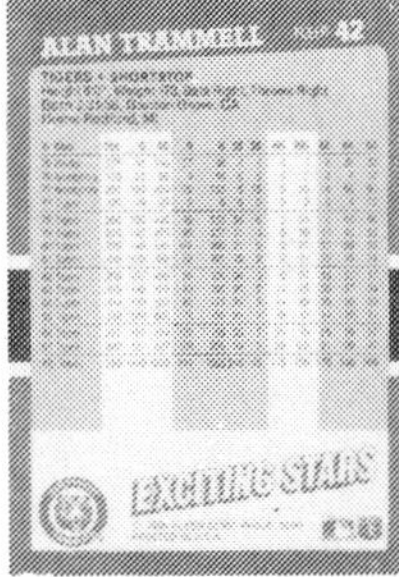

This 44-card limited-edition boxed set showcases star major leaguers. Player photos are slanted upwards to the right, framed by a blue border with a red and white bar stripe across the middle. The player's name is printed in white above the photo. "Baseball's Exciting Stars" is printed in red and yellow across the bottom margin, following the upward slant of the photo. Fleer's logo appears lower right intersecting a white baseball bearing the number "88." Card backs are numbered and printed in red, white and blue. The set was packaged in a checklist box, with six team logo sticker cards featuring black and white stadium photos on the flip sides. Exciting Stars was distributed via Cumberland Farm stores throughout the northeastern U.S. and Florida.

		MT	NR MT	EX
Complete Set:		6.00	4.50	2.50
Common Player:		.05	.04	.02
1	Harold Baines	.10	.08	.04
2	Kevin Bass	.07	.05	.03
3	George Bell	.20	.15	.08
4	Wade Boggs	1.00	.70	.40
5	Mickey Brantley	.05	.04	.02
6	Sid Bream	.05	.04	.02
7	Jose Canseco	1.00	.70	.40
8	Jack Clark	.15	.11	.06
9	Will Clark	1.00	.70	.40
10	Roger Clemens	.40	.30	.15
11	Vince Coleman	.15	.11	.06
12	Eric Davis	.50	.40	.20
13	Andre Dawson	.15	.11	.06
14	Julio Franco	.07	.05	.03
15	Dwight Gooden	.40	.30	.15
16	Mike Greenwell	.70	.50	.30
17	Tony Gwynn	.25	.20	.10
18	Von Hayes	.07	.05	.03
19	Tom Henke	.05	.04	.02
20	Orel Hershiser	.20	.15	.08
21	Teddy Higuera	.10	.08	.04
22	Brook Jacoby	.07	.05	.03
23	Wally Joyner	.30	.25	.12
24	Jimmy Key	.07	.05	.03
25	Don Mattingly	1.00	.70	.40
26	Mark McGwire	1.00	.70	.40
27	Jack Morris	.12	.09	.05
28	Dale Murphy	.30	.25	.12
29	Matt Nokes	.30	.25	.12
30	Kirby Puckett	.50	.40	.20
31	Tim Raines	.25	.20	.10
32	Ryne Sandberg	.20	.15	.08
33	Benito Santiago	.25	.20	.10
34	Mike Schmidt	.30	.25	.12
35	Mike Scott	.10	.08	.04
36	Kevin Seitzer	.60	.45	.25
37	Larry Sheets	.07	.05	.03
38	Ruben Sierra	.12	.09	.05
39	Darryl Strawberry	.40	.30	.15
40	Ozzie Smith	.15	.11	.06
41	Danny Tartabull	.10	.08	.04
42	Alan Trammell	.15	.11	.06
43	Fernando Valenzuela	.20	.15	.08
44	Devon White	.20	.15	.08

1988 Fleer Baseball's Hottest Stars

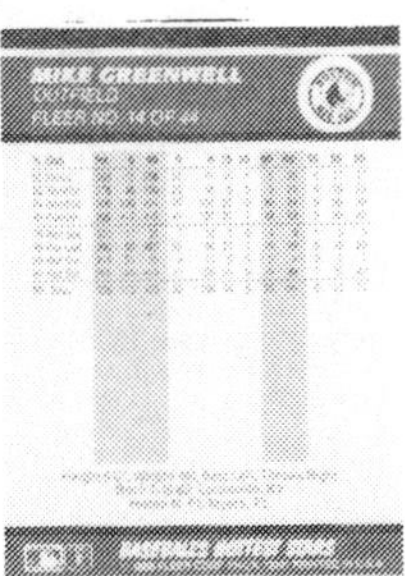

This boxed set of 44 standard-size player cards and six team logo sticker cards was produced by Fleer for exclusive distribution at Revco drug stores nation- wide. Card fronts feature full-color photos of players representing every major league team. Photos are framed in red, orange and yellow, with a blue and white player name printed across the bottom of the card front. A flaming baseball logo bearing the words "Hottest Stars" appears in the lower left corner of the player photo. Card backs are red, white and blue. The player's name, position, card number and team logo are printed across the top section, followed by a stats box, personal data, batting and throwing preferences. The set also includes six team logo sticker cards with flipside stadium photos in black and white.

		MT	NR MT	EX
Complete Set:		6.00	4.50	2.50
Common Player:		.05	.04	.02
1	George Bell	.20	.15	.08
2	Wade Boggs	1.00	.70	.40
3	Bobby Bonilla	.12	.09	.05
4	George Brett	.30	.25	.12
5	Jose Canseco	1.00	.70	.40
6	Will Clark	1.00	.70	.40
7	Roger Clemens	.40	.30	.15
8	Eric Davis	.50	.40	.20
9	Andre Dawson	.15	.11	.06
10	Tony Fernandez	.10	.08	.04
11	Julio Franco	.07	.05	.03
12	Gary Gaetti	.10	.08	.04
13	Dwight Gooden	.40	.30	.15
14	Mike Greenwell	.70	.50	.30
15	Tony Gwynn	.25	.20	.10
16	Rickey Henderson	.50	.40	.20
17	Keith Hernandez	.15	.11	.06
18	Tom Herr	.07	.05	.03
19	Orel Hershiser	.20	.15	.08
20	Ted Higuera	.10	.08	.04
21	Wally Joyner	.30	.25	.12
22	Jimmy Key	.07	.05	.03
23	Mark Langston	.10	.08	.04
24	Don Mattingly	1.25	.90	.50
25	Jack McDowell	.20	.15	.08
26	Mark McGwire	1.00	.70	.40
27	Kevin Mitchell	.50	.40	.20

		MT	NR MT	EX
28	Jack Morris	.12	.09	.05
29	Dale Murphy	.30	.25	.12
30	Kirby Puckett	.50	.40	.20
31	Tim Raines	.25	.20	.10
32	Shane Rawley	.05	.04	.02
33	Benito Santiago	.25	.20	.10
34	Mike Schmidt	.30	.25	.12
35	Mike Scott	.10	.08	.04
36	Kevin Seitzer	.60	.45	.25
37	Larry Sheets	.07	.05	.03
38	Ruben Sierra	.50	.40	.20
39	Dave Smith	.05	.04	.02
41	Darryl Strawberry	.40	.30	.15
42	Rick Sutcliffe	.10	.08	.04
43	Pat Tabler	.05	.04	.02
44	Alan Trammell	.15	.11	.06

1988 Fleer Box Panels

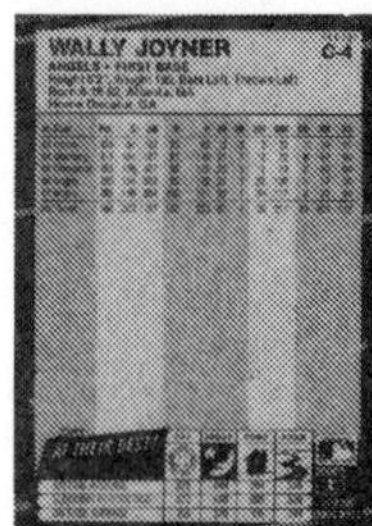

Fleer's third annual box-bottom issue once again included 16 full-color trading cards printed on the bottoms of four different wax and cello pack retail display boxes. Each box contains three player cards and one team logo card. Player cards follow the same design as the basic 1988 Fleer issue - full-color player photo, name upper left, team logo upper right, Fleer logo lower right. Card fronts feature a blue and red striped border, with a thin white line framing the photo. Card backs are printed in blue and red and include personal information and statistics. Standard-size, the cards are numbered C-1 through C-16.

		MT	NR MT	EX
Complete Panel Set:		6.25	4.75	2.50
Complete Singles Set:		2.50	2.00	1.00
Common Panel:		1.25	.90	.50
Common Single Player:		.15	.11	.06
Panel		2.00	1.50	.80
1	Cardinals Logo	.05	.04	.02
11	Mike Schmidt	.60	.45	.25
14	Dave Stewart	.15	.11	.06
15	Tim Wallach	.20	.15	.08
Panel		1.25	.90	.50
2	Dwight Evans	.15	.11	.06
8	Shane Rawley	.15	.11	.06
10	Ryne Sandberg	.30	.25	.12
13	Tigers Logo	.05	.04	.02
Panel		2.75	2.00	1.00
3	Andres Galarraga	.25	.20	.10
6	Dale Murphy	.60	.45	.25
9	Giants Logo	.05	.04	.02
12	Kevin Seitzer	.80	.60	.30
Panel		2.25	1.75	.90
4	Wally Joyner	.60	.45	.25
5	Twins Logo	.05	.04	.02
7	Kirby Puckett	.40	.30	.15
16	Todd Worrell	.20	.15	.08

1988 Fleer '87 World Series

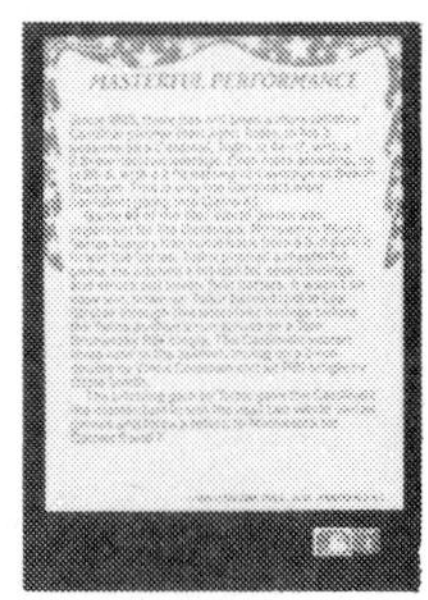

Highlights of the 1987 Series are captured in this full-color insert set found only in Fleer's regular 660-card factory sealed sets. This second World Series edition by Fleer features cards framed in red, with a blue and white starred bunting draped over the upper edges of the photo and a brief photo caption printed on a yellow band across the lower border. Numbered card backs are red, white and blue and include a description of the action pictured on the front, with stats for the Series.

		MT	NR MT	EX
Complete Set:		4.00	3.00	1.50
Common Player:		.30	.25	.12
1	"Grand" Hero In Game 1 (Dan Gladden)	.30	.25	.12
2	The Cardinals "Bush" Whacked (Randy Bush, Tony Pena)	.30	.25	.12
3	Masterful Performance Turns Momentum (John Tudor)	.30	.25	.12
4	The Wizard (Ozzie Smith)	.35	.25	.14
5	Throw Smoke! (Tony Pena, Todd Worrell)	.35	.25	.14
6	Cardinal Attack - Disruptive Speed (Vince Coleman)	.40	.30	.15
7	Herr's Wallop (Dan Driessen, Tom Herr)	.30	.25	.12
8	Kirby's Bat Comes Alive in Game 6 (Kirby Puckett)	1.00	.70	.40
9	Hrbek's Slam Forces Game 7 (Kent Hrbek)	.30	.25	.12
10	Herr, Out At First? (Rich Hacker (coach), Tom Herr, Lee Weyer (umpire))	.30	.25	.12
11	Game 7's Play At The Plate (Don Baylor, Dave Phillips (umpire))	.30	.25	.12
12	Series MVP with 16 K's (Frank Viola)	.35	.25	.14

1988 Fleer Headliners

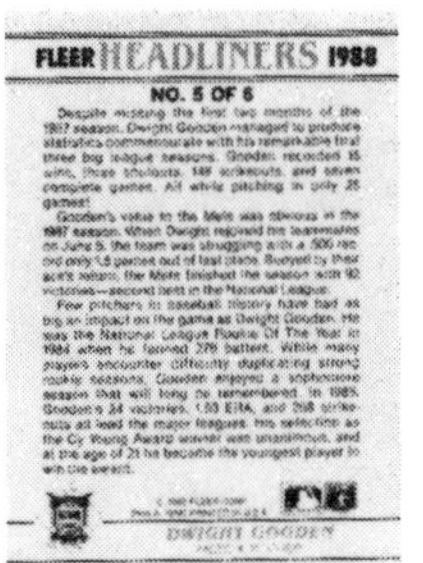

This six-card special set was inserted in Fleer three-packs, sold by retail outlets and hobby dealers nationwide. The card fronts feature crisp full-color player cut-outs printed on a grey and white USA Today-style sports page. "Fleer Headliners 1988" is printed in black and red on a white banner across the top of the card, both front and back. A similar white banner across the card bottom bears the black and white National or American League logo and a red player/team name. Card backs are black on grey with red accents and include the card number and a three-paragraph career summary.

		MT	NR MT	EX
Complete Set:		8.00	6.00	3.25
Common Player:		1.00	.70	.40
1	Don Mattingly	3.00	2.25	1.25
2	Mark McGwire	2.00	1.50	.80
3	Jack Morris	1.00	.70	.40
4	Darryl Strawberry	1.50	1.25	.60
5	Dwight Gooden	1.50	1.25	.60
6	Tim Raines	1.25	.90	.50

1988 Fleer League Leaders

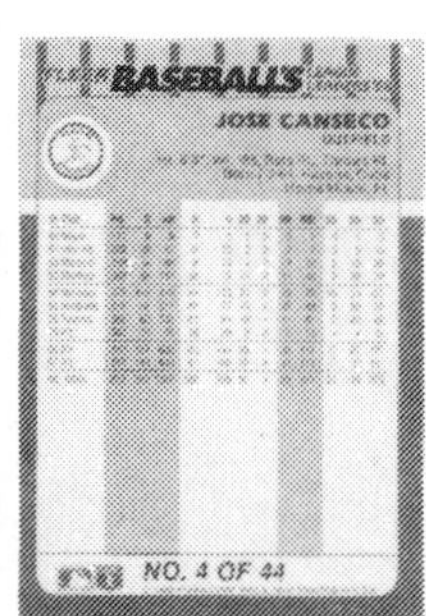

This 44-card boxed set is the third annual limited edition set from Fleer highlighting leading players. The 1988 edition contains the same type of information, front and back, as the previous sets, with a new color scheme and design. Card fronts have bright blue borders, solid on the lower portion, striped on the upper, with a gold bar separating the two sections. "Fleer's Baseball's League Leaders '88" headlines the card face. The full-color player photo is centered above a yellow player name banner. The numbered card backs are blue, pink and white, and contain player stats and personal notes. Six team logo sticker cards, with flipside black and white photos of ballparks, accompany this set which was marketed exclusively by Walgreen drug stores.

		MT	NR MT	EX
Complete Set:		6.00	4.50	2.50
Common Player:		.05	.04	.02
1	George Bell	.20	.15	.08
2	Wade Boggs	1.00	.70	.40
3	Ivan Calderon	.07	.05	.03
4	Jose Canseco	1.00	.70	.40
5	Will Clark	1.00	.70	.40
6	Roger Clemens	.40	.30	.15
7	Vince Coleman	.15	.11	.06
8	Eric Davis	.50	.40	.20
9	Andre Dawson	.15	.11	.06
10	Bill Doran	.07	.05	.03
11	Dwight Evans	.10	.08	.04
12	Julio Franco	.07	.05	.03
13	Gary Gaetti	.10	.08	.04
14	Andres Galarraga	.15	.11	.06
15	Dwight Gooden	.40	.30	.15
16	Tony Gwynn	.25	.20	.10
17	Tom Henke	.05	.04	.02
18	Keith Hernandez	.20	.15	.08
19	Orel Hershiser	.20	.15	.08
20	Ted Higuera	.10	.08	.04
21	Kent Hrbek	.15	.11	.06
22	Wally Joyner	.30	.25	.12
23	Jimmy Key	.07	.05	.03
24	Mark Langston	.10	.08	.04
25	Don Mattingly	1.00	.70	.40
26	Mark McGwire	1.00	.70	.40
27	Paul Molitor	.12	.09	.05
28	Jack Morris	.12	.09	.05
29	Dale Murphy	.30	.25	.12
30	Kirby Puckett	.50	.40	.20
31	Tim Raines	.25	.20	.10
32	Rick Rueschel	.07	.05	.03
33	Bret Saberhagen	.15	.11	.06
34	Benito Santiago	.25	.20	.10
35	Mike Schmidt	.30	.25	.12
36	Mike Scott	.10	.08	.04
37	Kevin Seitzer	.60	.45	.25
38	Larry Sheets	.07	.05	.03
39	Ruben Sierra	.50	.40	.20
40	Darryl Strawberry	.40	.30	.15
41	Rick Sutcliffe	.10	.08	.04
42	Alan Trammell	.15	.11	.06
43	Andy Van Slyke	.10	.08	.04
44	Todd Worrell	.10	.08	.04

1988 Fleer Mini

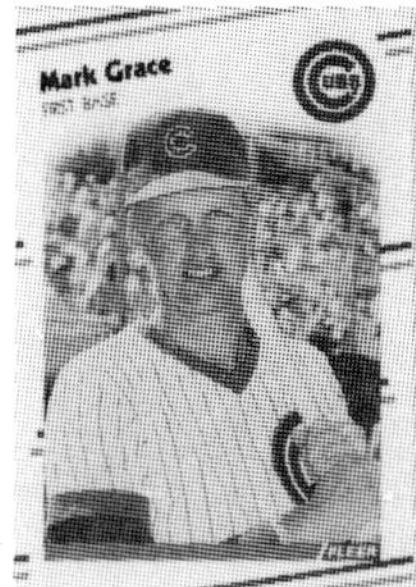

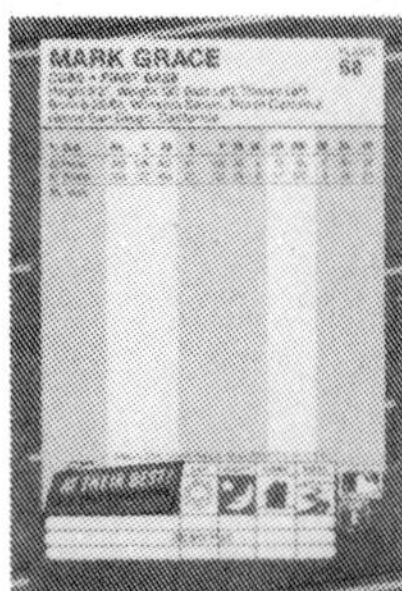

This third annual issue of miniatures (1-7/8" by 2-5/8") includes 120 high-gloss cards featuring new photos, not copies from the regular issue, although the card designs are identical. Card fronts have white borders, with red and blue striping and a bright color band beneath the photo leading to a blue Fleet logo lower right. The player name is printed upper left; the full-color team logo appears upper right. Card backs are red, white and blue and include personal data, yearly career stats and a stats breakdown of batting average, slugging percentage and on-base average, listed for day, night, home and road games. Card backs are numbered in alphabetical order by teams which are also listed alphabetically. The set includes 18 team logo stickers with black and white aerial stadium photos on the flip sides.

		MT	NR MT	EX
Complete Set:		11.00	8.25	4.50
Common Player:		.05	.04	.02
1	Eddie Murray	.25	.20	.10
2	Dave Schmidt	.05	.04	.02
3	Larry Sheets	.07	.05	.03
4	Wade Boggs	1.00	.70	.40
5	Roger Clemens	.60	.45	.25
6	Dwight Evans	.12	.09	.05
7	Mike Greenwell	1.00	.70	.40
8	Sam Horn	.20	.15	.08
9	Lee Smith	.07	.05	.03
10	Brian Downing	.05	.04	.02
11	Wally Joyner	.30	.25	.12
12	Devon White	.10	.08	.04
13	Mike Witt	.07	.05	.03
14	Ivan Calderon	.07	.05	.03
15	Ozzie Guillen	.07	.05	.03
16	Jack McDowell	.20	.15	.08
17	Kenny Williams	.12	.09	.05
18	Joe Carter	.20	.15	.08
19	Julio Franco	.10	.08	.04
20	Pat Tabler	.05	.04	.02
21	Doyle Alexander	.05	.04	.02
22	Jack Morris	.15	.11	.06

		MT	NR MT	EX
23	Matt Nokes	.30	.25	.12
24	Walt Terrell	.05	.04	.02
25	Alan Trammell	.20	.15	.08
26	Bret Saberhagen	.15	.11	.06
27	Kevin Seitzer	.60	.45	.25
28	Danny Tartabull	.15	.11	.06
29	Gary Thurman	.20	.15	.08
30	Ted Higuera	.10	.08	.04
31	Paul Molitor	.12	.09	.05
32	Dan Plesac	.10	.08	.04
33	Robin Yount	.25	.20	.10
34	Gary Gaetti	.12	.09	.05
35	Kent Hrbek	.15	.11	.06
36	Kirby Puckett	.50	.40	.20
37	Jeff Reardon	.07	.05	.03
38	Frank Viola	.12	.09	.05
39	Jack Clark	.12	.09	.05
40	Rickey Henderson	.50	.40	.20
41	Don Mattingly	1.75	1.25	.70
42	Willie Randolph	.05	.04	.02
43	Dave Righetti	.12	.09	.05
44	Dave Winfield	.20	.15	.08
45	Jose Canseco	1.50	1.25	.60
46	Mark McGwire	1.00	.70	.40
47	Dave Parker	.12	.09	.05
48	Dave Stewart	.07	.05	.03
49	Walt Weiss	.60	.45	.25
50	Bob Welch	.07	.05	.03
51	Mickey Brantley	.05	.04	.02
52	Mark Langston	.10	.08	.04
53	Harold Reynolds	.07	.05	.03
54	Scott Fletcher	.05	.04	.02
55	Charlie Hough	.05	.04	.02
56	Pete Incaviglia	.12	.09	.05
57	Larry Parrish	.05	.04	.02
58	Ruben Sierra	.35	.25	.14
59	George Bell	.20	.15	.08
60	Mark Eichhorn	.05	.04	.02
61	Tony Fernandez	.10	.08	.04
62	Tom Henke	.05	.04	.02
63	Jimmy Key	.07	.05	.03
64	Dion James	.05	.04	.02
65	Dale Murphy	.30	.25	.12
66	Zane Smith	.05	.04	.02
67	Andre Dawson	.15	.11	.06
68	Mark Grace	1.75	1.25	.70
69	Jerry Mumphrey	.05	.04	.02
70	Ryne Sandberg	.20	.15	.08
71	Rick Sutcliffe	.10	.08	.04
72	Kal Daniels	.12	.09	.05
73	Eric Davis	.70	.50	.30
74	John Franco	.07	.05	.03
75	Ron Robinson	.05	.04	.02
76	Jeff Treadway	.20	.15	.08
77	Kevin Bass	.07	.05	.03
78	Glenn Davis	.15	.11	.06
79	Nolan Ryan	.50	.40	.20
80	Mike Scott	.12	.09	.05
81	Dave Smith	.05	.04	.02
82	Kirk Gibson	.20	.15	.08
83	Pedro Guerrero	.12	.09	.05
84	Orel Hershiser	.20	.15	.08
85	Steve Sax	.15	.11	.06
86	Fernando Valenzuela	.15	.11	.06
87	Tim Burke	.05	.04	.02
88	Andres Galarraga	.15	.11	.06
89	Neal Heaton	.05	.04	.02
90	Tim Raines	.20	.15	.08
91	Tim Wallach	.10	.08	.04
92	Dwight Gooden	.60	.45	.25
93	Keith Hernandez	.15	.11	.06
94	Gregg Jefferies	2.00	1.50	.80
95	Howard Johnson	.10	.08	.04
96	Roger McDowell	.05	.04	.02
97	Darryl Strawberry	.50	.40	.20
98	Steve Bedrosian	.10	.08	.04
99	Von Hayes	.10	.08	.04
100	Shane Rawley	.05	.04	.02
101	Juan Samuel	.12	.09	.05
102	Mike Schmidt	.30	.25	.12
103	Bobby Bonilla	.15	.11	.06
104	Mike Dunne	.07	.05	.03
105	Andy Van Slyke	.10	.08	.04
106	Vince Coleman	.15	.11	.06
107	Bob Horner	.07	.05	.03
108	Willie McGee	.10	.08	.04
109	Ozzie Smith	.12	.09	.05
110	John Tudor	.07	.05	.03
111	Todd Worrell	.10	.08	.04
112	Tony Gwynn	.25	.20	.10
113	John Kruk	.12	.09	.05
114	Lance McCullers	.05	.04	.02
115	Benito Santiago	.15	.11	.06
116	Will Clark	.30	.25	.12
117	Jeff Leonard	.05	.04	.02
118	Candy Maldonado	.05	.04	.02
119	Rick Rueschel	.07	.05	.03
120	Don Robinson	.05	.04	.02

1988 Fleer Record Setters

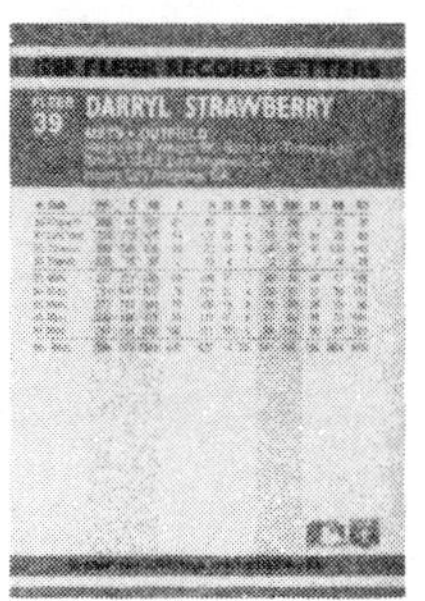

For the second consecutive year, Fleer Corp. issued this special limited-edition 44-card set for exclusive distribution by Eckerd Drug stores. Cards are standard-size with red and blue borders framing the full-color player photos. A "1988 Fleer Record Setters" headline is printed on a yellow strip above the player's photo. The player's name, team and position appear beneath the pose. Card backs list personal information and career stats in red and blue ink on a white background. Each 44-card set comes cello-wrapped in a checklist box that contains six additional cards with peel-off team logo stickers. The sticker cards feature black and white aerial photos of major league ballparks, along with stadium statistics such as field size, seating capacity and date of the first game played.

		MT	NR MT	EX
	Complete Set:	5.00	3.75	2.00
	Common Player:	.05	.04	.02
1	Jesse Barfield	.10	.08	.04
2	George Bell	.20	.15	.08
3	Wade Boggs	1.00	.70	.40
4	Jose Canseco	1.00	.70	.40
5	Jack Clark	.15	.11	.06
6	Will Clark	1.00	.70	.40
7	Roger Clemens	.40	.30	.15
8	Alvin Davis	.10	.08	.04
9	Eric Davis	.50	.40	.20
10	Andre Dawson	.15	.11	.06
11	Mike Dunne	.10	.08	.04
12	John Franco	.07	.05	.03
13	Julio Franco	.07	.05	.03
14	Dwight Gooden	.40	.30	.15
15	Mark Gubicza	.07	.05	.03
16	Ozzie Guillen	.07	.05	.03
17	Tony Gwynn	.25	.20	.10
18	Orel Hershiser	.20	.15	.08
19	Teddy Higuera	.10	.08	.04
20	Howard Johnson	.07	.05	.03
21	Wally Joyner	.30	.25	.12
22	Jimmy Key	.07	.05	.03
23	Jeff Leonard	.05	.04	.02
24	Don Mattingly	1.25	.90	.50
25	Mark McGwire	1.00	.70	.40
26	Jack Morris	.12	.09	.05
27	Dale Murphy	.30	.25	.12
28	Larry Parrish	.05	.04	.02
29	Kirby Puckett	.50	.40	.20
30	Tim Raines	.25	.20	.10
31	Harold Reynolds	.07	.05	.03
32	Dave Righetti	.12	.09	.05
33	Cal Ripken, Jr.	.30	.25	.12
34	Benito Santiago	.25	.20	.10
35	Mike Schmidt	.30	.25	.12
36	Mike Scott	.10	.08	.04
37	Kevin Seitzer	.60	.45	.25
38	Ozzie Smith	.12	.09	.05
39	Darryl Strawberry	.40	.30	.15
40	Rick Sutcliffe	.10	.08	.04
41	Alan Trammell	.15	.11	.06
42	Frank Viola	.12	.09	.05
43	Mitch Williams	.05	.04	.02
44	Todd Worrell	.10	.08	.04

1988 Fleer Star Stickers

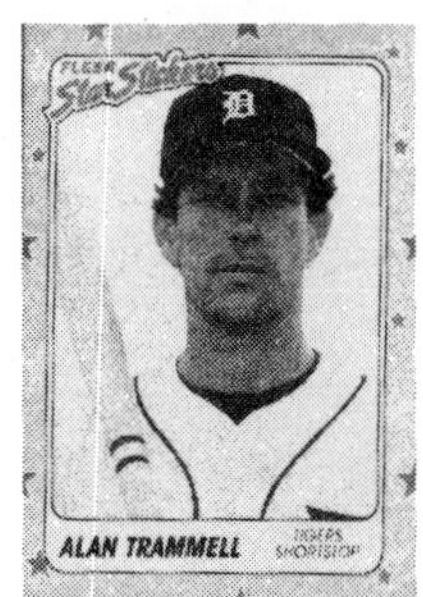

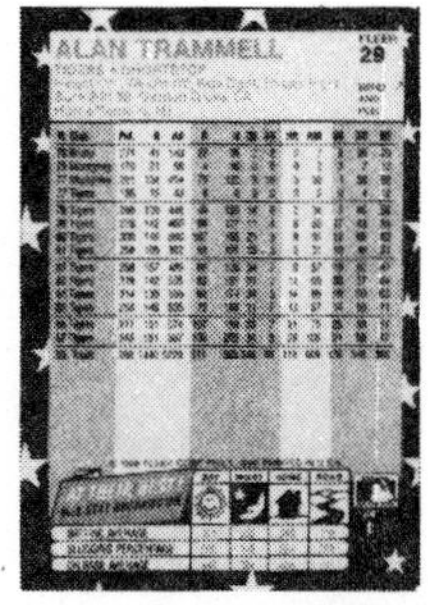

This set of 132 standard-size sticker cards (including a checklist card) features exclusive player photos, different from those in the Fleer regular issue. Card fronts have light gray borders sprinkled with multi-colored stars. The "Fleer Star Stickers" logo appears upper left, player names are printed beneath the photos. Card backs are printed in red, gray and black on white and include personal data and a breakdown of pitching and batting stats into day, night, home and road categories. Cards were marketed in two different display boxes that feature six players and two team logos from Fleer's 1988 Limited Edition box-bottom set.

		MT	NR MT	EX
	Complete Set:	18.00	13.50	7.25
	Common Player:	.05	.04	.02
1	Mike Boddicker	.08	.06	.03
2	Eddie Murray	.50	.40	.20
3	Cal Ripken, Jr.	.60	.45	.25
4	Larry Sheets	.15	.11	.06
5	Wade Boggs	1.75	1.25	.70
6	Ellis Burks	1.00	.70	.40
7	Roger Clemens	.90	.70	.35
8	Dwight Evans	.15	.11	.06
9	Mike Greenwell	1.00	.70	.40
10	Bruce Hurst	.12	.09	.05
11	Brian Downing	.08	.06	.03
12	Wally Joyner	.60	.45	.25
13	Mike Witt	.10	.08	.04
14	Ivan Calderon	.12	.09	.05
15	Jose DeLeon	.05	.04	.02
16	Ozzie Guillen	.15	.11	.06
17	Bobby Thigpen	.10	.08	.04
18	Joe Carter	.20	.15	.08
19	Julio Franco	.12	.09	.05
20	Brook Jacoby	.12	.09	.05
21	Cory Snyder	.40	.30	.15
22	Pat Tabler	.10	.08	.04
23	Doyle Alexander	.08	.06	.03
24	Kirk Gibson	.30	.25	.12
25	Mike Henneman	.20	.15	.08
26	Jack Morris	.25	.20	.10
27	Matt Nokes	.60	.45	.25
28	Walt Terrell	.05	.04	.02
29	Alan Trammell	.30	.25	.12
30	George Brett	.70	.50	.30
31	Charlie Leibrandt	.05	.04	.02
32	Bret Saberhagen	.25	.20	.10
33	Kevin Seitzer	.70	.50	.30
34	Danny Tartabull	.25	.20	.10
35	Frank White	.10	.08	.04
36	Rob Deer	.10	.08	.04
37	Ted Higuera	.15	.11	.06
38	Paul Molitor	.20	.15	.08
39	Dan Plesac	.12	.09	.05
40	Robin Yount	.30	.25	.12
41	Bert Blyleven	.15	.11	.06
42	Tom Brunansky	.15	.11	.06
43	Gary Gaetti	.20	.15	.08
44	Kent Hrbek	.30	.25	.12
45	Kirby Puckett	.50	.40	.20
46	Jeff Reardon	.10	.08	.04
47	Frank Viola	.15	.11	.06
48	Don Mattingly	2.00	1.50	.80
49	Mike Pagliarulo	.12	.09	.05
50	Willie Randolph	.08	.06	.03
51	Rick Rhoden	.08	.06	.03
52	Dave Righetti	.20	.15	.08
53	Dave Winfield	.40	.30	.15
54	Jose Canseco	2.00	1.50	.80
55	Carney Lansford	.08	.06	.03
56	Mark McGwire	1.25	.90	.50
57	Dave Stewart	.12	.09	.05
58	Curt Young	.08	.06	.03
59	Alvin Davis	.15	.11	.06
60	Mark Langston	.15	.11	.06
61	Ken Phelps	.05	.04	.02
62	Harold Reynolds	.10	.08	.04
63	Scott Fletcher	.05	.04	.02
64	Charlie Hough	.08	.06	.03
65	Pete Incaviglia	.25	.20	.10
66	Oddibe McDowell	.10	.08	.04
67	Pete O'Brien	.10	.08	.04
68	Larry Parrish	.08	.06	.03
69	Ruben Sierra	.25	.20	.10
70	Jesse Barfield	.12	.09	.05
71	George Bell	.25	.20	.10
72	Tony Fernandez	.12	.09	.05
73	Tom Henke	.10	.08	.04
74	Jimmy Key	.12	.09	.05
75	Lloyd Moseby	.10	.08	.04
76	Dion James	.05	.04	.02
77	Dale Murphy	.70	.50	.30
78	Zane Smith	.08	.06	.03
79	Andre Dawson	.25	.20	.10
80	Ryne Sandberg	.35	.25	.14
81	Rick Sutcliffe	.15	.11	.06
82	Kal Daniels	.25	.20	.10
83	Eric Davis	.80	.60	.30
84	John Franco	.10	.08	.04
85	Kevin Bass	.10	.08	.04
86	Glenn Davis	.20	.15	.08
87	Bill Doran	.10	.08	.04
88	Nolan Ryan	.50	.40	.20
89	Mike Scott	.15	.11	.06
90	Dave Smith	.05	.04	.02
91	Pedro Guerrero	.20	.15	.08
92	Orel Hershiser	.35	.25	.14
93	Steve Sax	.20	.15	.08
94	Fernando Valenzuela	.35	.25	.14
95	Tim Burke	.05	.04	.02
96	Andres Galarraga	.20	.15	.08
97	Tim Raines	.35	.25	.14
98	Tim Wallach	.12	.09	.05
99	Mitch Webster	.05	.04	.02
100	Ron Darling	.20	.15	.08
101	Sid Fernandez	.10	.08	.04
102	Dwight Gooden	.90	.70	.35
103	Keith Hernandez	.30	.25	.12
104	Howard Johnson	.12	.09	.05
105	Roger McDowell	.10	.08	.04
106	Darryl Strawberry	.70	.50	.30
107	Steve Bedrosian	.12	.09	.05
108	Von Hayes	.12	.09	.05
109	Shane Rawley	.08	.06	.03
110	Juan Samuel	.15	.11	.06
111	Mike Schmidt	.70	.50	.30
112	Milt Thompson	.05	.04	.02
113	Sid Bream	.08	.06	.03
114	Bobby Bonilla	.20	.15	.08
115	Mike Dunne	.15	.11	.06
116	Andy Van Slyke	.12	.09	.05
117	Vince Coleman	.25	.20	.10
118	Willie McGee	.15	.11	.06
119	Terry Pendleton	.10	.08	.04
120	Ozzie Smith	.20	.15	.08
121	John Tudor	.12	.09	.05
122	Todd Worrell	.20	.15	.08
123	Tony Gwynn	.40	.30	.15
124	John Kruk	.20	.15	.08
125	Benito Santiago	.30	.25	.12
126	Will Clark	1.00	.70	.40
127	Dave Dravecky	.05	.04	.02
128	Jeff Leonard	.05	.04	.02
129	Candy Maldonado	.05	.04	.02

		MT	NR MT	EX
130	Rick Rueschel	.10	.08	.04
131	Don Robinson	.05	.04	.02
132	Checklist	.05	.04	.02

1988 Fleer Star Stickers Box Panel

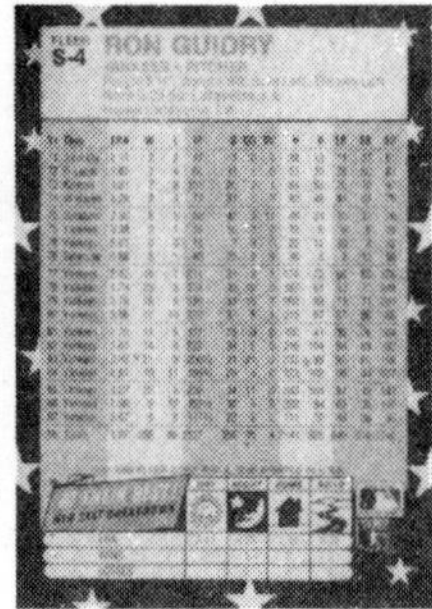

This set of eight box-bottom cards was printed on two different retail display boxes. Six players and two team logo sticker cards are included in the set, three player photos and one team photo per box. The full-color player photos are exclusively limited to the Fleer Star Sticker set. The cards, which measure 2-1/2" by 3-1/2", have a light gray border sprinkled with multi-color stars. The backs are printed in navy blue and red.

		MT	NR MT	EX
Complete Panel Set:		3.50	2.75	1.50
Complete Singles Set:		1.75	1.25	.70
Common Singles Player:		.15	.11	.06
Panel		2.50	2.00	1.00
1	Eric Davis, Mark McGwire	.70	.50	.30
3	Kevin Mitchell	.50	.40	.20
5	Rickey Henderson	.50	.40	.20
7	Tigers Logo	.05	.04	.02
Panel		1.25	.90	.50
2	Gary Carter	.35	.25	.14
4	Ron Guidry	.20	.15	.08
6	Don Baylor	.15	.11	.06
8	Giants Logo	.05	.04	.02

1988 Fleer Superstars

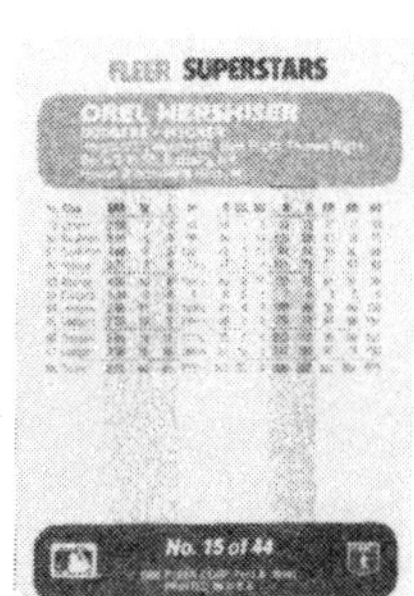

This is the fourth edition of Fleer's 44-card boxed set produced for distribution by McCrory's (1985-87 issues were simply titled "Fleer Limited Edition"). The Superstars standard-size card set features full-color player photos framed by red, white and blue striped top and bottom borders. "Fleer 1988" is printed in an elongated yellow oval banner above the photo. A pale yellow rectangle below the photo carries the player's name and team logo. Card fronts have a semi-glossy slightly textured finish. Card backs are red and blue on white and include card numbers, personal data and statistics. Six team logo sticker cards are also included in this set which was marketed in red, white and blue boxes with checklist backs. Boxed sets were sold exclusively at McCrory's stores and its affiliates.

		MT	NR MT	EX
Complete Set:		5.00	3.75	2.00
Common Player:		.05	.04	.02
1	Steve Bedrosian	.10	.08	.04
2	George Bell	.20	.15	.08
3	Wade Boggs	1.00	.70	.40
4	Barry Bonds	.12	.09	.05
5	Jose Canseco	1.00	.70	.40
6	Joe Carter	.12	.09	.05
7	Jack Clark	.15	.11	.06
8	Will Clark	1.00	.70	.40
9	Roger Clemens	.40	.30	.15
10	Alvin Davis	.10	.08	.04
11	Eric Davis	.50	.40	.20
12	Glenn Davis	.12	.09	.05
13	Andre Dawson	.15	.11	.06
14	Dwight Gooden	.40	.30	.15
15	Orel Hershiser	.20	.15	.08
16	Teddy Higuera	.10	.08	.04
17	Kent Hrbek	.15	.11	.06
18	Wally Joyner	.30	.25	.12
19	Jimmy Key	.07	.05	.03
20	John Kruk	.10	.08	.04
21	Jeff Leonard	.05	.04	.02
22	Don Mattingly	1.75	1.25	.70
23	Mark McGwire	1.00	.70	.40
24	Kevin McReynolds	.12	.09	.05
25	Dale Murphy	.30	.25	.12
26	Matt Nokes	.30	.25	.12
27	Terry Pendleton	.05	.04	.02
28	Kirby Puckett	.50	.40	.20
29	Tim Raines	.25	.20	.10
30	Rick Rhoden	.07	.05	.03
31	Cal Ripken, Jr.	.30	.25	.12
32	Benito Santiago	.25	.20	.10
33	Mike Schmidt	.30	.25	.12
34	Mike Scott	.10	.08	.04
35	Kevin Seitzer	.60	.45	.25
36	Ruben Sierra	.25	.20	.10
37	Cory Snyder	.12	.09	.05
38	Darryl Strawberry	.40	.30	.15
39	Rick Sutcliffe	.10	.08	.04
40	Danny Tartabull	.12	.09	.05
41	Alan Trammell	.15	.11	.06
42	Ken Williams	.07	.05	.03
43	Mike Witt	.07	.05	.03
44	Robin Yount	.15	.11	.06

1988 Fleer Update

This 132-card update set (numbered U-1 through U-132 and 2-1/2" by 3-1/2") features traded veterans and rookies in a mixture of full-color action shots and close-ups, framed by white borders with red and blue stripes. Player name and position appear upper left, printed on an upward slant leading into the team logo, upper right. A bright stripe in a variety of colors (blue, red, green, yellow) edges the bottom of the photo and leads into the Fleer logo at lower right. The backs are red, white and blue-grey and include personal info, along with yearly and "At Their Best" (day, night, home, road) stats charts. The set was packaged in white cardboard boxes with red and blue stripes. A glossy-coated edition of the update set was issued in its own tin box and is valued at two times greater than the regular issue.

		MT	NR MT	EX
Complete Set:		13.00	9.75	5.25
Common Player:		.06	.05	.02
1	Jose Bautista(FC)	.20	.15	.08
2	Joe Orsulak	.06	.05	.02
3	Doug Sisk	.06	.05	.02
4	Craig Worthington(FC)	.70	.50	.30
5	Mike Boddicker	.08	.06	.03
6	Rick Cerone	.06	.05	.02
7	Larry Parrish	.08	.06	.03
8	Lee Smith	.10	.08	.04
9	Mike Smithson	.06	.05	.02
10	John Trautwein(FC)	.15	.11	.06
11	Sherman Corbett(FC)	.15	.11	.06
12	Chili Davis	.10	.08	.04
13	Jim Eppard	.08	.06	.03
14	Bryan Harvey(FC)	.30	.25	.12
15	John Davis	.08	.06	.03
16	Dave Gallagher(FC)	.25	.20	.10
17	Ricky Horton	.08	.06	.03
18	Dan Pasqua	.10	.08	.04
19	Melido Perez	.12	.09	.05
20	Jose Segura(FC)	.15	.11	.06
21	Andy Allanson	.08	.06	.03
22	Jon Perlman	.06	.05	.02
23	Domingo Ramos	.06	.05	.02
24	Rick Rodriguez	.08	.06	.03
25	Willie Upshaw	.10	.08	.04
26	Paul Gibson(FC)	.15	.11	.06
27	Don Heinkel(FC)	.15	.11	.06
28	Ray Knight	.08	.06	.03
29	Gary Pettis	.08	.06	.03
30	Luis Salazar	.06	.05	.02
31	Mike MacFarlane (Macfarlane)(FC)	.20	.15	.08
32	Jeff Montgomery	.08	.06	.03
33	Ted Power	.06	.05	.02
34	Israel Sanchez(FC)	.15	.11	.06
35	Kurt Stillwell	.10	.08	.04
36	Pat Tabler	.08	.06	.03
37	Don August(FC)	.20	.15	.08
38	Darryl Hamilton(FC)	.15	.11	.06
39	Jeff Leonard	.08	.06	.03
40	Joey Meyer	.15	.11	.06
41	Allan Anderson	.10	.08	.04
42	Brian Harper	.06	.05	.02
43	Tom Herr	.10	.08	.04
44	Charlie Lea	.06	.05	.02
45	John Moses	.06	.05	.02
46	John Candelaria	.10	.08	.04
47	Jack Clark	.15	.11	.06
48	Richard Dotson	.10	.08	.04
49	Al Leiter(FC)	.25	.20	.10
50	Rafael Santana	.06	.05	.02
51	Don Slaught	.06	.05	.02
52	Todd Burns(FC)	.25	.20	.10
53	Dave Henderson	.10	.08	.04
54	Doug Jennings(FC)	.15	.11	.06
55	Dave Parker	.12	.09	.05
56	Walt Weiss	.60	.45	.25
57	Bob Welch	.10	.08	.04
58	Henry Cotto	.06	.05	.02
59	Marion Diaz (Mario)	.08	.06	.03
60	Mike Jackson	.06	.05	.02
61	Bill Swift	.06	.05	.02
62	Jose Cecena(FC)	.15	.11	.06
63	Ray Hayward(FC)	.08	.06	.03
64	Jim Steels(FC)	.08	.06	.03
65	Pat Borders(FC)	.20	.15	.08
66	Sil Campusano(FC)	.25	.20	.10
67	Mike Flanagan	.10	.08	.04
68	Todd Stottlemyre(FC)	.30	.25	.12
69	David Wells(FC)	.08	.06	.03
70	Jose Alvarez(FC)	.15	.11	.06
71	Paul Runge	.06	.05	.02
72	Cesar Jimenez (German)(FC)	.15	.11	.06
73	Pete Smith	.08	.06	.03
74	John Smoltz(FC)	1.50	1.25	.60
75	Damon Berryhill	.10	.08	.04
76	Goose Gossage	.15	.11	.06
77	Mark Grace	6.00	4.50	2.50
78	Darrin Jackson	.08	.06	.03
79	Vance Law	.08	.06	.03
80	Jeff Pico(FC)	.20	.15	.08
81	Gary Varsho(FC)	.20	.15	.08
82	Tim Birtsas	.06	.05	.02
83	Rob Dibble(FC)	.40	.30	.15
84	Danny Jackson	.15	.11	.06
85	Paul O'Neill	.08	.06	.03
86	Jose Rijo	.08	.06	.03
87	Chris Sabo(FC)	2.25	1.75	.90
88	John Fishel(FC)	.15	.11	.06
89	Craig Biggio(FC)	1.25	.90	.50
90	Terry Puhl	.06	.05	.02
91	Rafael Ramirez	.06	.05	.02
92	Louie Meadows(FC)	.15	.11	.06
93	Kirk Gibson(FC)	.15	.11	.06
94	Alfredo Griffin	.08	.06	.03
95	Jay Howell	.08	.06	.03
96	Jesse Orosco	.08	.06	.03
97	Alejandro Pena	.08	.06	.03
98	Tracy Woodson(FC)	.10	.08	.04
99	John Dopson(FC)	.25	.20	.10
100	Brian Holman(FC)	.35	.25	.14
101	Rex Hudler(FC)	.08	.06	.03
102	Jeff Parrett(FC)	.10	.08	.04
103	Nelson Santovenia(FC)	.40	.30	.15
104	Kevin Elster	.12	.09	.05
105	Jeff Innis(FC)	.20	.15	.08
106	Mackey Sasser(FC)	.10	.08	.04
107	Phil Bradley	.10	.08	.04
108	Danny Clay(FC)	.15	.11	.06
109	Greg Harris	.06	.05	.02
110	Ricky Jordan(FC)	2.75	2.00	1.00
111	David Palmer	.06	.05	.02
112	Jim Gott	.06	.05	.02
113	Tommy Gregg (photo actually Randy Milligan)(FC)	.10	.08	.04
114	Barry Jones	.06	.05	.02
115	Randy Milligan(FC)	.10	.08	.04
116	Luis Alicea(FC)	.15	.11	.06
117	Tom Brunansky	.12	.09	.05
118	John Costello(FC)	.15	.11	.06
119	Jose DeLeon	.08	.06	.03
120	Bob Horner	.10	.08	.04
121	Scott Terry(FC)	.10	.08	.04
122	Roberto Alomar(FC)	2.50	2.00	1.00
123	Dave Leiper	.06	.05	.02
124	Keith Moreland	.08	.06	.03
125	Mark Parent(FC)	.20	.15	.08
126	Dennis Rasmussen	.10	.08	.04
127	Randy Bockus	.06	.05	.02
128	Brett Butler	.08	.06	.03
129	Donell Nixon	.06	.05	.02
130	Earnest Riles	.06	.05	.02
131	Roger Samuels(FC)	.15	.11	.06
132	Checklist	.06	.05	.02

1989 Fleer

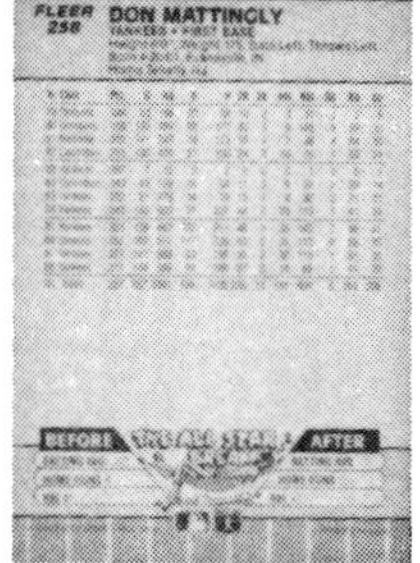

This set includes 660 standard-size cards and was issued with 45 team logo stickers. Individual card fronts feature a grey and white striped background with full-color player photos framed by a bright line of color that slants upward to the right. The set also includes two subsets: 15 Major League Prospects and 12 SuperStar Specials. A special bonus set of 12 All-Star Team cards was randomly inserted in individual wax packs of 15 cards. The last seven cards in the set are checklists, with players listed alphabetically by teams.

	MT	NR MT	EX
Complete Set:	28.00	21.00	12.00
Common Player:	.05	.04	.02

		MT	NR MT	EX
1	Don Baylor	.10	.08	.04
2	*Lance Blankenship*(FC)	.25	.20	.10
3	*Todd Burns*	.30	.25	.12
4	Greg Cadaret(FC)	.07	.05	.03
5	Jose Canseco	1.50	1.25	.60
6	Storm Davis	.10	.08	.04
7	Dennis Eckersley	.12	.09	.05
8	Mike Gallego(FC)	.05	.04	.02
9	Ron Hassey	.05	.04	.02
10	Dave Henderson	.10	.08	.04
11	Rick Honeycutt	.05	.04	.02
12	Glenn Hubbard	.05	.04	.02
13	Stan Javier	.05	.04	.02
14	*Doug Jennings*	.20	.15	.08
15	*Felix Jose*(FC)	.30	.25	.12
16	Carney Lansford	.07	.05	.03
17	Mark McGwire	.70	.50	.30
18	Gene Nelson	.05	.04	.02
19	Dave Parker	.12	.09	.05
20	Eric Plunk	.05	.04	.02
21	Luis Polonia	.07	.05	.03
22	Terry Steinbach	.10	.08	.04
23	Dave Stewart	.10	.08	.04
24	Walt Weiss	.30	.25	.12
25	Bob Welch	.10	.08	.04
26	Curt Young	.07	.05	.03
27	Rick Aguilera	.05	.04	.02
28	Wally Backman	.07	.05	.03
29	Mark Carreon	.07	.05	.03
30	Gary Carter	.20	.15	.08
31	David Cone	.40	.30	.15
32	Ron Darling	.12	.09	.05
33	Len Dykstra	.10	.08	.04
34	Kevin Elster	.10	.08	.04
35	Sid Fernandez	.10	.08	.04
36	Dwight Gooden	.50	.40	.20
37	Keith Hernandez	.25	.20	.10
38	Gregg Jefferies	1.75	1.25	.70
39	Howard Johnson	.10	.08	.04
40	Terry Leach	.05	.04	.02
41	Dave Magadan	.10	.08	.04
42	Bob McClure	.05	.04	.02
43	Roger McDowell	.10	.08	.04
44	Kevin McReynolds	.15	.11	.06
45	Keith Miller	.10	.08	.04
46	Randy Myers	.10	.08	.04
47	Bob Ojeda	.07	.05	.03
48	Mackey Sasser	.07	.05	.03
49	Darryl Strawberry	.40	.30	.15
50	Tim Teufel	.05	.04	.02
51	*Dave West*(FC)	.60	.45	.25
52	Mookie Wilson	.07	.05	.03
53	Dave Anderson	.05	.04	.02
54	Tim Belcher	.10	.08	.04
55	Mike Davis	.07	.05	.03
56	Mike Devereaux	.15	.11	.06
57	Kirk Gibson	.20	.15	.08
58	Alfredo Griffin	.07	.05	.03
59	Chris Gwynn	.12	.09	.05
60	Jeff Hamilton	.07	.05	.03
61a	Danny Heep (Home: San Antonio, TX)	1.00	.70	.40
61b	Danny Heep (Home: Lake Hills, TX)	.05	.04	.02
62	Orel Hershiser	.25	.20	.10
63	Brian Holton(FC)	.07	.05	.03
64	Jay Howell	.07	.05	.03
65	Tim Leary	.07	.05	.03
66	Mike Marshall	.12	.09	.05
67	*Ramon Martinez*(FC)	1.25	.90	.50
68	Jesse Orosco	.07	.05	.03
69	Alejandro Pena	.07	.05	.03
70	Steve Sax	.15	.11	.06
71	Mike Scioscia	.07	.05	.03
72	Mike Sharperson	.05	.04	.02
73	John Shelby	.05	.04	.02
74	Franklin Stubbs	.05	.04	.02
75	John Tudor	.10	.08	.04
76	Fernando Valenzuela	.20	.15	.08
77	Tracy Woodson	.10	.08	.04
78	Marty Barrett	.07	.05	.03
79	Todd Benzinger	.12	.09	.05
80	Mike Boddicker	.07	.05	.03
81	Wade Boggs	.80	.60	.30
82	"Oil Can" Boyd	.07	.05	.03
83	Ellis Burks	.60	.45	.25
84	Rick Cerone	.05	.04	.02
85	Roger Clemens	.50	.40	.20
86	*Steve Curry*(FC)	.20	.15	.08
87	Dwight Evans	.10	.08	.04
88	Wes Gardner	.07	.05	.03
89	Rich Gedman	.07	.05	.03
90	Mike Greenwell	.70	.50	.30
91	Bruce Hurst	.10	.08	.04
92	Dennis Lamp	.05	.04	.02
93	Spike Owen	.05	.04	.02
94	Larry Parrish	.07	.05	.03
95	*Carlos Quintana*(FC)	.50	.40	.20
96	Jody Reed	.12	.09	.05
97	Jim Rice	.25	.20	.10
98a	Kevin Romine (batting follow-thru, photo actually Randy Kutcher)	.50	.40	.20
98b	Kevin Romine (arms crossed on chest, correct photo)	.60	.45	.25
99	Lee Smith	.10	.08	.04
100	Mike Smithson	.05	.04	.02
101	Bob Stanley	.05	.04	.02
102	Allan Anderson	.07	.05	.03
103	Keith Atherton	.05	.04	.02
104	Juan Berenguer	.05	.04	.02
105	Bert Blyleven	.12	.09	.05
106	*Eric Bullock*(FC)	.15	.11	.06
107	Randy Bush	.05	.04	.02
108	John Christensen(FC)	.05	.04	.02
109	Mark Davidson	.07	.05	.03
110	Gary Gaetti	.15	.11	.06
111	Greg Gagne	.05	.04	.02
112	Dan Gladden	.05	.04	.02
113	*German Gonzalez*(FC)	.20	.15	.08
114	Brian Harper	.05	.04	.02
115	Tom Herr	.07	.05	.03
116	Kent Hrbek	.20	.15	.08
117	Gene Larkin	.10	.08	.04
118	Tim Laudner	.05	.04	.02
119	Charlie Lea	.05	.04	.02
120	Steve Lombardozzi	.05	.04	.02
121a	John Moses (Home: Phoenix, AZ)	1.00	.70	.40
121b	John Moses (Home: Tempe, AZ)	.05	.04	.02
122	Al Newman	.05	.04	.02
123	Mark Portugal	.05	.04	.02
124	Kirby Puckett	.35	.25	.14
125	Jeff Reardon	.10	.08	.04
126	Fred Toliver	.05	.04	.02
127	Frank Viola	.15	.11	.06
128	Doyle Alexander	.07	.05	.03
129	Dave Bergman	.05	.04	.02
130a	Tom Brookens (Mike Heath stats on back)	2.25	1.75	.90
130b	Tom Brookens (correct stats on back)	.30	.25	.12
131	*Paul Gibson*	.15	.11	.06
132a	Mike Heath (Tom Brookens stats on back)	2.25	1.75	.90
132b	Mike Heath (correct stats on back)	.30	.25	.12
133	*Don Heinkel*	.15	.11	.06
134	Mike Henneman	.10	.08	.04
135	Guillermo Hernandez	.07	.05	.03
136	Eric King	.05	.04	.02
137	Chet Lemon	.07	.05	.03
138	Fred Lynn	.10	.08	.04
139	Jack Morris	.15	.11	.06
140	Matt Nokes	.20	.15	.08
141	Gary Pettis	.05	.04	.02
142	Ted Power	.05	.04	.02
143	Jeff Robinson	.12	.09	.05
144	Luis Salazar	.05	.04	.02
145	*Steve Searcy*(FC)	.30	.25	.12
146	Pat Sheridan	.05	.04	.02
147	Frank Tanana	.07	.05	.03
148	Alan Trammell	.20	.15	.08
149	Walt Terrell	.07	.05	.03
150	Jim Walewander(FC)	.07	.05	.03
151	Lou Whitaker	.20	.15	.08
152	Tim Birtsas	.05	.04	.02
153	Tom Browning	.10	.08	.04
154	*Keith Brown*(FC)	.20	.15	.08
155	*Norm Charlton*(FC)	.25	.20	.10
156	Dave Concepcion	.10	.08	.04
157	Kal Daniels	.15	.11	.06
158	Eric Davis	.50	.40	.20
159	Bo Diaz	.07	.05	.03
160	*Rob Dibble*	.50	.40	.20
161	Nick Esasky	.07	.05	.03
162	John Franco	.10	.08	.04
163	Danny Jackson	.15	.11	.06
164	Barry Larkin	.25	.20	.10
165	Rob Murphy	.05	.04	.02
166	Paul O'Neill	.05	.04	.02
167	Jeff Reed	.05	.04	.02
168	Jose Rijo	.07	.05	.03
169	Ron Robinson	.05	.04	.02
170	*Chris Sabo*	1.00	.70	.40
171	*Candy Sierra*(FC)	.15	.11	.06
172	*Van Snider*(FC)	.20	.15	.08
173	Jeff Treadway	.12	.09	.05
174	Frank Williams	.05	.04	.02
175	Herm Winningham	.05	.04	.02
176	Jim Adduci(FC)	.05	.04	.02
177	Don August	.10	.08	.04
178	Mike Birkbeck	.05	.04	.02
179	Chris Bosio	.05	.04	.02
180	Glenn Braggs	.07	.05	.03
181	Greg Brock	.07	.05	.03
182	Mark Clear	.05	.04	.02
183	Chuck Crim	.05	.04	.02
184	Rob Deer	.07	.05	.03
185	Tom Filer	.05	.04	.02
186	Jim Gantner	.05	.04	.02
187	*Darryl Hamilton*	.15	.11	.06
188	Ted Higuera	.10	.08	.04
189	Odell Jones	.05	.04	.02
190	Jeffrey Leonard	.07	.05	.03
191	Joey Meyer	.10	.08	.04
192	Paul Mirabella	.05	.04	.02
193	Paul Molitor	.15	.11	.06
194	Charlie O'Brien(FC)	.07	.05	.03
195	Dan Plesac	.10	.08	.04
196	*Gary Sheffield*(FC)	1.75	1.25	.70
197	B.J. Surhoff	.10	.08	.04
198	Dale Sveum	.07	.05	.03
199	Bill Wegman	.05	.04	.02
200	Robin Yount	.25	.20	.10
201	Rafael Belliard	.05	.04	.02
202	Barry Bonds	.12	.09	.05
203	Bobby Bonilla	.12	.09	.05
204	Sid Bream	.07	.05	.03
205	Benny Distefano(FC)	.05	.04	.02
206	Doug Drabek	.07	.05	.03
207	Mike Dunne	.10	.08	.04
208	Felix Fermin	.07	.05	.03
209	Brian Fisher	.07	.05	.03
210	Jim Gott	.05	.04	.02
211	Bob Kipper	.05	.04	.02
212	Dave LaPoint	.07	.05	.03
213	Mike LaValliere	.07	.05	.03
214	Jose Lind	.10	.08	.04
215	Junior Ortiz	.05	.04	.02
216	Vicente Palacios	.07	.05	.03
217	Tom Prince(FC)	.10	.08	.04
218	Gary Redus	.05	.04	.02
219	R.J. Reynolds	.05	.04	.02
220	Jeff Robinson	.07	.05	.03
221	John Smiley	.12	.09	.05
222	Andy Van Slyke	.12	.09	.05
223	Bob Walk	.05	.04	.02
224	Glenn Wilson	.07	.05	.03
225	Jesse Barfield	.10	.08	.04
226	George Bell	.25	.20	.10
227	*Pat Borders*	.25	.20	.10
228	John Cerutti	.07	.05	.03
229	Jim Clancy	.07	.05	.03
230	Mark Eichhorn	.07	.05	.03
231	Tony Fernandez	.12	.09	.05
232	Cecil Fielder	.05	.04	.02
233	Mike Flanagan	.07	.05	.03
234	Kelly Gruber	.05	.04	.02
235	Tom Henke	.07	.05	.03
236	Jimmy Key	.10	.08	.04
237	Rick Leach	.05	.04	.02
238	Manny Lee	.05	.04	.02
239	Nelson Liriano	.07	.05	.03
240	Fred McGriff	.50	.40	.20
241	Lloyd Moseby	.07	.05	.03
242	Rance Mulliniks	.05	.04	.02
243	Jeff Musselman	.07	.05	.03
244	Dave Stieb	.10	.08	.04
245	Todd Stottlemyre	.10	.08	.04
246	Duane Ward	.05	.04	.02
247	David Wells	.10	.08	.04
248	Ernie Whitt	.07	.05	.03
249	Luis Aguayo	.05	.04	.02
250a	Neil Allen (Home: Sarasota, FL)	1.50	1.25	.60
250b	Neil Allen (Home: Syosset, NY)	.05	.04	.02
251	John Candelaria	.07	.05	.03
252	Jack Clark	.15	.11	.06
253	Richard Dotson	.07	.05	.03
254	Rickey Henderson	.35	.25	.14
255	Tommy John	.12	.09	.05
256	Roberto Kelly	.20	.15	.08
257	Al Leiter	.15	.11	.06
258	Don Mattingly	1.50	1.25	.60
259	Dale Mohorcic	.05	.04	.02
260	*Hal Morris*(FC)	.20	.15	.08
261	Scott Nielsen(FC)	.10	.08	.04
262	Mike Pagliarulo	.10	.08	.04
263	*Hipolito Pena*(FC)	.15	.11	.06
264	Ken Phelps	.07	.05	.03
265	Willie Randolph	.07	.05	.03
266	Rick Rhoden	.07	.05	.03
267	Dave Righetti	.12	.09	.05
268	Rafael Santana	.05	.04	.02
269	Steve Shields(FC)	.07	.05	.03
270	Joel Skinner	.05	.04	.02
271	Don Slaught	.05	.04	.02
272	Claudell Washington	.07	.05	.03
273	Gary Ward	.07	.05	.03
274	Dave Winfield	.30	.25	.12
275	Luis Aquino(FC)	.05	.04	.02
276	Floyd Bannister	.07	.05	.03
277	George Brett	.35	.25	.14
278	Bill Buckner	.10	.08	.04
279	*Nick Capra*(FC)	.20	.15	.08
280	*Jose DeJesus*(FC)	.15	.11	.06
281	Steve Farr	.05	.04	.02
282	Jerry Gleaton	.05	.04	.02
283	Mark Gubicza	.10	.08	.04
284	*Tom Gordon*(FC)	1.50	1.25	.60
285	Bo Jackson	1.00	.70	.40
286	Charlie Leibrandt	.07	.05	.03
287	*Mike Macfarlane*	.20	.15	.08
288	Jeff Montgomery	.07	.05	.03
289	Bill Pecota	.07	.05	.03
290	Jamie Quirk	.05	.04	.02
291	Bret Saberhagen	.15	.11	.06
292	Kevin Seitzer	.30	.25	.12
293	Kurt Stillwell	.07	.05	.03
294	Pat Tabler	.07	.05	.03
295	Danny Tartabull	.20	.15	.08
296	Gary Thurman	.12	.09	.05
297	Frank White	.07	.05	.03
298	Willie Wilson	.10	.08	.04
299	Roberto Alomar	.50	.40	.20
300	*Sandy Alomar, Jr.*(FC)	1.75	1.25	.70
301	Chris Brown	.07	.05	.03
302	Mike Brumley(FC)	.07	.05	.03
303	Mark Davis	.05	.04	.02
304	Mark Grant	.05	.04	.02
305	Tony Gwynn	.35	.25	.14
306	*Greg Harris*(FC)	.30	.25	.12
307	Andy Hawkins	.05	.04	.02
308	Jimmy Jones	.05	.04	.02
309	John Kruk	.07	.05	.03
310	Dave Leiper	.05	.04	.02
311	Carmelo Martinez	.05	.04	.02
312	Lance McCullers	.07	.05	.03
313	Keith Moreland	.07	.05	.03
314	Dennis Rasmussen	.10	.08	.04
315	Randy Ready	.05	.04	.02
316	Benito Santiago	.15	.11	.06
317	Eric Show	.07	.05	.03
318	Todd Simmons	.10	.08	.04
319	Garry Templeton	.07	.05	.03
320	Dickie Thon	.05	.04	.02
321	Ed Whitson	.05	.04	.02
322	Marvell Wynne	.05	.04	.02
323	Mike Aldrete	.07	.05	.03
324	Brett Butler	.07	.05	.03
325	Will Clark	.80	.60	.30
326	Kelly Downs	.10	.08	.04
327	Dave Dravecky	.07	.05	.03
328	Scott Garrelts	.05	.04	.02
329	Atlee Hammaker	.05	.04	.02
330	*Charlie Hayes*(FC)	.30	.25	.12
331	Mike Krukow	.07	.05	.03
332	Craig Lefferts	.05	.04	.02
333	Candy Maldonado	.07	.05	.03
334	Kirt Manwaring	.10	.08	.04
335	Bob Melvin	.05	.04	.02
336	Kevin Mitchell	.60	.45	.25
337	Donell Nixon	.05	.04	.02
338	*Tony Perezchica*(FC)	.15	.11	.06
339	Joe Price	.05	.04	.02
340	Rick Reuschel	.10	.08	.04

		MT	NR MT	EX
341	Earnest Riles	.05	.04	.02
342	Don Robinson	.05	.04	.02
343	Chris Speier	.05	.04	.02
344	Robby Thompson	.07	.05	.03
345	Jose Uribe	.05	.04	.02
346	Matt Williams	.12	.09	.05
347	*Trevor Wilson*(FC)	.15	.11	.06
348	Juan Agosto	.05	.04	.02
349	Larry Andersen	.05	.04	.02
350	Alan Ashby	.05	.04	.02
351	Kevin Bass	.07	.05	.03
352	Buddy Bell	.07	.05	.03
353	*Craig Biggio*	.90	.70	.35
354	Danny Darwin	.05	.04	.02
355	Glenn Davis	.25	.20	.10
356	Jim Deshaies	.05	.04	.02
357	Bill Doran	.07	.05	.03
358	*John Fishel*	.20	.15	.08
359	Billy Hatcher	.07	.05	.03
360	Bob Knepper	.07	.05	.03
361	*Louie Meadows*	.15	.11	.06
362	Dave Meads	.05	.04	.02
363	Jim Pankovits	.05	.04	.02
364	Terry Puhl	.05	.04	.02
365	Rafael Ramirez	.05	.04	.02
366	Craig Reynolds	.05	.04	.02
367	Mike Scott	.12	.09	.05
368	Nolan Ryan	.40	.30	.15
369	Dave Smith	.07	.05	.03
370	Gerald Young	.12	.09	.05
371	Hubie Brooks	.10	.08	.04
372	Tim Burke	.05	.04	.02
373	*John Dopson*	.25	.20	.10
374	Mike Fitzgerald	.05	.04	.02
375	Tom Foley	.05	.04	.02
376	Andres Galarraga	.15	.11	.06
377	Neal Heaton	.05	.04	.02
378	Joe Hesketh	.05	.04	.02
379	*Brian Holman*	.35	.25	.14
380	Rex Hudler	.05	.04	.02
381	*Randy Johnson*(FC)	.40	.30	.15
382	Wallace Johnson	.05	.04	.02
383	Tracy Jones	.10	.08	.04
384	Dave Martinez	.07	.05	.03
385	Dennis Martinez	.07	.05	.03
386	Andy McGaffigan	.05	.04	.02
387	Otis Nixon	.05	.04	.02
388	*Johnny Paredes*(FC)	.20	.15	.08
389	Jeff Parrett	.10	.08	.04
390	Pascual Perez	.07	.05	.03
391	Tim Raines	.25	.20	.10
392	Luis Rivera	.05	.04	.02
393	*Nelson Santovenia*	.25	.20	.10
394	Bryn Smith	.05	.04	.02
395	Tim Wallach	.10	.08	.04
396	Andy Allanson	.05	.04	.02
397	*Rod Allen*	.15	.11	.06
398	Scott Bailes	.05	.04	.02
399	Tom Candiotti	.05	.04	.02
400	Joe Carter	.12	.09	.05
401	Carmen Castillo	.05	.04	.02
402	Dave Clark	.07	.05	.03
403	John Farrell	.10	.08	.04
404	Julio Franco	.10	.08	.04
405	Don Gordon	.05	.04	.02
406	Mel Hall	.07	.05	.03
407	Brad Havens	.05	.04	.02
408	Brook Jacoby	.10	.08	.04
409	Doug Jones	.12	.09	.05
410	*Jeff Kaiser*(FC)	.15	.11	.06
411	*Luis Medina*(FC)	.30	.25	.12
412	Cory Snyder	.15	.11	.06
413	Greg Swindell	.12	.09	.05
414	*Ron Tingley*(FC)	.15	.11	.06
415	Willie Upshaw	.07	.05	.03
416	Ron Washington	.05	.04	.02
417	Rich Yett	.05	.04	.02
418	Damon Berryhill	.12	.09	.05
419	Mike Bielecki	.05	.04	.02
420	*Doug Dascenzo*(FC)	.30	.25	.12
421	Jody Davis	.07	.05	.03
422	Andre Dawson	.20	.15	.08
423	Frank DiPino	.05	.04	.02
424	Shawon Dunston	.10	.08	.04
425	"Goose" Gossage	.12	.09	.05
426	Mark Grace	2.00	1.50	.80
427	*Mike Harkey*(FC)	.30	.25	.12
428	Darrin Jackson	.07	.05	.03
429	Les Lancaster	.07	.05	.03
430	Vance Law	.07	.05	.03
431	Greg Maddux	.12	.09	.05
432	Jamie Moyer	.05	.04	.02
433	Al Nipper	.05	.04	.02
434	Rafael Palmeiro	.15	.11	.06
435	Pat Perry	.05	.04	.02
436	*Jeff Pico*	.25	.20	.10
437	Ryne Sandberg	.25	.20	.10
438	Calvin Schiraldi	.05	.04	.02
439	Rick Sutcliffe	.10	.08	.04
440	Manny Trillo	.05	.04	.02
441	*Gary Varsho*	.20	.15	.08
442	Mitch Webster	.07	.05	.03
443	*Luis Alicea*	.20	.15	.08
444	Tom Brunansky	.12	.09	.05
445	Vince Coleman	.15	.11	.06
446	*John Costello*	.20	.15	.08
447	Danny Cox	.07	.05	.03
448	Ken Dayley	.05	.04	.02
449	Jose DeLeon	.07	.05	.03
450	Curt Ford	.05	.04	.02
451	Pedro Guerrero	.15	.11	.06
452	Bob Horner	.10	.08	.04
453	*Tim Jones*(FC)	.15	.11	.06
454	Steve Lake	.05	.04	.02
455	Joe Magrane	.10	.08	.04
456	Greg Mathews	.07	.05	.03
457	Willie McGee	.12	.09	.05
458	Larry McWilliams	.05	.04	.02
459	Jose Oquendo	.05	.04	.02
460	Tony Pena	.07	.05	.03
461	Terry Pendleton	.10	.08	.04
462	*Steve Peters*(FC)	.15	.11	.06
463	Ozzie Smith	.15	.11	.06
464	Scott Terry	.08	.06	.03
465	Denny Walling	.05	.04	.02
466	Todd Worrell	.10	.08	.04
467	Tony Armas	.07	.05	.03
468	*Dante Bichette*(FC)	.30	.25	.12
469	Bob Boone	.07	.05	.03
470	*Terry Clark*(FC)	.15	.11	.06
471	Stew Cliburn(FC)	.05	.04	.02
472	*Mike Cook*(FC)	.15	.11	.06
473	*Sherman Corbett*	.15	.11	.06
474	Chili Davis	.07	.05	.03
475	Brian Downing	.07	.05	.03
476	Jim Eppard	.07	.05	.03
477	Chuck Finley	.05	.04	.02
478	Willie Fraser	.05	.04	.02
479	*Bryan Harvey*	.25	.20	.10
480	Jack Howell	.07	.05	.03
481	Wally Joyner	.25	.20	.10
482	Jack Lazorko	.05	.04	.02
483	Kirk McCaskill	.07	.05	.03
484	Mark McLemore	.05	.04	.02
485	Greg Minton	.05	.04	.02
486	Dan Petry	.07	.05	.03
487	Johnny Ray	.07	.05	.03
488	Dick Schofield	.05	.04	.02
489	Devon White	.12	.09	.05
490	Mike Witt	.07	.05	.03
491	Harold Baines	.12	.09	.05
492	Daryl Boston	.05	.04	.02
493	Ivan Calderon	.07	.05	.03
494	Mike Diaz	.07	.05	.03
495	Carlton Fisk	.20	.15	.08
496	*Dave Gallagher*	.25	.20	.10
497	Ozzie Guillen	.07	.05	.03
498	Shawn Hillegas	.07	.05	.03
499	Lance Johnson	.07	.05	.03
500	Barry Jones	.05	.04	.02
501	Bill Long	.07	.05	.03
502	Steve Lyons	.05	.04	.02
503	Fred Manrique	.07	.05	.03
504	Jack McDowell	.10	.08	.04
505	*Donn Pall*	.20	.15	.08
506	Kelly Paris	.05	.04	.02
507	Dan Pasqua	.10	.08	.04
508	*Ken Patterson*	.20	.15	.08
509	Melido Perez	.10	.08	.04
510	Jerry Reuss	.07	.05	.03
511	Mark Salas	.05	.04	.02
512	Bobby Thigpen	.10	.08	.04
513	Mike Woodard	.05	.04	.02
514	Bob Brower	.05	.04	.02
515	Steve Buechele	.05	.04	.02
516	*Jose Cecena*	.15	.11	.06
517	Cecil Espy	.07	.05	.03
518	Scott Fletcher	.07	.05	.03
519	Cecilio Guante	.05	.04	.02
520	Jose Guzman	.10	.08	.04
521	Ray Hayward	.05	.04	.02
522	Charlie Hough	.07	.05	.03
523	Pete Incaviglia	.12	.09	.05
524	Mike Jeffcoat	.05	.04	.02
525	Paul Kilgus	.10	.08	.04
526	*Chad Kreuter*(FC)	.20	.15	.08
527	Jeff Kunkel	.05	.04	.02
528	Oddibe McDowell	.07	.05	.03
529	Pete O'Brien	.07	.05	.03
530	Geno Petralli	.05	.04	.02
531	Jeff Russell	.05	.04	.02
532	Ruben Sierra	.50	.40	.20
533	Mike Stanley	.05	.04	.02
534	Ed Vande Berg	.05	.04	.02
535	Curtis Wilkerson	.05	.04	.02
536	Mitch Williams	.07	.05	.03
537	Bobby Witt	.10	.08	.04
538	Steve Balboni	.07	.05	.03
539	Scott Bankhead	.05	.04	.02
540	Scott Bradley	.05	.04	.02
541	Mickey Brantley	.05	.04	.02
542	Jay Buhner(FC)	.10	.08	.04
543	Mike Campbell	.10	.08	.04
544	Darnell Coles	.07	.05	.03
545	Henry Cotto	.05	.04	.02
546	Alvin Davis	.12	.09	.05
547	Mario Diaz	.07	.05	.03
548	*Ken Griffey, Jr.*(FC)	10.00	7.50	4.00
549	*Erik Hanson*(FC)	.30	.25	.12
550	Mike Jackson	.07	.05	.03
551	Mark Langston	.10	.08	.04
552	Edgar Martinez	.20	.15	.08
553	*Bill McGuire*(FC)	.15	.11	.06
554	Mike Moore	.05	.04	.02
555	Jim Presley	.07	.05	.03
556	Rey Quinones	.05	.04	.02
557	Jerry Reed	.05	.04	.02
558	Harold Reynolds	.07	.05	.03
559	*Mike Schooler*(FC)	.35	.25	.14
560	Bill Swift	.05	.04	.02
561	Dave Valle	.05	.04	.02
562	Steve Bedrosian	.10	.08	.04
563	Phil Bradley	.10	.08	.04
564	Don Carman	.07	.05	.03
565	Bob Dernier	.05	.04	.02
566	Marvin Freeman	.05	.04	.02
567	Todd Frohwirth	.07	.05	.03
568	Greg Gross	.05	.04	.02
569	Kevin Gross	.07	.05	.03
570	Greg Harris	.05	.04	.02
571	Von Hayes	.10	.08	.04
572	Chris James	.10	.08	.04
573	Steve Jeltz	.05	.04	.02
574	*Ron Jones*(FC)	.35	.25	.14
575	*Ricky Jordan*	1.50	1.25	.60
576	Mike Maddux	.05	.04	.02
577	David Palmer	.05	.04	.02
578	Lance Parrish	.15	.11	.06
579	Shane Rawley	.07	.05	.03
580	Bruce Ruffin	.05	.04	.02
581	Juan Samuel	.12	.09	.05
582	Mike Schmidt	.50	.40	.20
583	Kent Tekulve	.07	.05	.03
584	Milt Thompson	.05	.04	.02
585	*Jose Alvarez*	.15	.11	.06
586	Paul Assenmacher	.05	.04	.02
587	Bruce Benedict	.05	.04	.02
588	Jeff Blauser	.10	.08	.04
589	*Terry Blocker*(FC)	.15	.11	.06
590	Ron Gant	.12	.09	.05
591	Tom Glavine	.10	.08	.04
592	Tommy Gregg	.10	.08	.04
593	Albert Hall	.05	.04	.02
594	Dion James	.05	.04	.02
595	Rick Mahler	.05	.04	.02
596	Dale Murphy	.40	.30	.15
597	Gerald Perry	.10	.08	.04
598	Charlie Puleo	.05	.04	.02
599	Ted Simmons	.10	.08	.04
600	Pete Smith	.10	.08	.04
601	Zane Smith	.07	.05	.03
602	*John Smoltz*	.60	.45	.25
603	Bruce Sutter	.10	.08	.04
604	Andres Thomas	.07	.05	.03
605	Ozzie Virgil	.05	.04	.02
606	*Brady Anderson*(FC)	.35	.25	.14
607	Jeff Ballard	.07	.05	.03
608	*Jose Bautista*	.20	.15	.08
609	Ken Gerhart	.07	.05	.03
610	Terry Kennedy	.07	.05	.03
611	Eddie Murray	.30	.25	.12
612	Carl Nichols(FC)	.10	.08	.04
613	Tom Niedenfuer	.07	.05	.03
614	Joe Orsulak	.05	.04	.02
615	*Oswaldo Peraza (Oswald)*(FC)	.20	.15	.08
616a	Bill Ripken (obscenity on bat)	25.00	19.00	10.00
616b	Bill Ripken (obscenity on bat scrawled out in black)	20.00	15.00	8.00
616c	Bill Ripken (obscenity on bat blocked out in black)	1.00	.70	.40
616d	Bill Ripken (obscenity on bat whiteout)	35.00	27.50	15.00
617	Cal Ripken, Jr.	.35	.25	.14
618	Dave Schmidt	.05	.04	.02
619	Rick Schu	.05	.04	.02
620	Larry Sheets	.07	.05	.03
621	Doug Sisk	.05	.04	.02
622	Pete Stanicek	.10	.08	.04
623	Mickey Tettleton	.05	.04	.02
624	Jay Tibbs	.05	.04	.02
625	Jim Traber	.07	.05	.03
626	Mark Williamson	.07	.05	.03
627	*Craig Worthington*	.40	.30	.15
628	Speed and Power (Jose Canseco)	.80	.60	.30
629	Pitcher Perfect (Tom Browning)	.10	.08	.04
630	Like Father - Like Sons (Roberto Alomar, Sandy Alomar, Jr.)	.40	.30	.15
631	N.L. All-Stars (Will Clark, Rafael Palmeiro)	.40	.30	.15
632	Homeruns Coast to Coast (Will Clark, Darryl Strawberry)	.30	.25	.12
633	Hot Corner's - Hot Hitters (Wade Boggs, Carney Lansford)	.40	.30	.15
634	Triple A's (Jose Canseco, Mark McGwire, Terry Steinbach)	.60	.45	.25
635	Dual Heat (Mark Davis, Dwight Gooden)	.20	.15	.08
636	N.L. Pitching Power (David Cone, Danny Jackson)	.15	.11	.06
637	Cannon Arms (Bobby Bonilla, Chris Sabo)	.20	.15	.08
638	Double Trouble (Andres Galarraga, Gerald Perry)	.10	.08	.04
639	Power Center (Eric Davis, Kirby Puckett)	.30	.25	.12
640	Major League Prospects *(Cameron Drew, Steve Wilson)*(FC)	.25	.20	.10
641	Major League Prospects *(Kevin Brown, Kevin Reimer)*(FC)	.40	.30	.15
642	Major League Prospects *(Jerald Clark, Brad Pounders)*(FC)	.30	.25	.12
643	Major League Prospects *(Mike Capel, Drew Hall)*(FC)	.25	.20	.10
644	Major League Prospects *(Joe Girardi, Rolando Roomes)*(FC)	.50	.40	.20
645	Major League Prospects *(Marty Brown, Lenny Harris)*(FC)	.30	.25	.12
646	Major League Prospects *(Luis de los Santos, Jim Campbell)*(FC)	.30	.15	.08
647	Major League Prospects *(Miguel Garcia, Randy Kramer)*(FC)	.25	.20	.10
648	Major League Prospects *(Torey Lovullo, Robert Palacios)*(FC)	.25	.20	.10
649	Major League Prospects *(Jim Corsi, Bob Milacki)*(FC)	.25	.20	.10
650	Major League Prospects *(Grady Hall, Mike Rochford)*(FC)	.25	.20	.10
651	Major League Prospects *(Vance Lovelace, Terry Taylor)*(FC)	.25	.20	.10
652	Major League Prospects *(Dennis Cook, Ken Hill)*(FC)	.60	.45	.25
653	Major League Prospects *(Scott Service, Shane Turner)*(FC)	.25	.20	.10
654	Checklist 1-101	.05	.04	.02
655	Checklist 102-200	.05	.04	.02
656	Checklist 201-298	.05	.04	.02
657	Checklist 299-395	.05	.04	.02
658	Checklist 396-490	.05	.04	.02
659	Checklist 491-584	.05	.04	.02
660	Checklist 585-660	.05	.04	.02

1989 Fleer All Star Team

This special 12-card set represents Fleer's choices for its 1989 Major League All-Star Team. For the fourth consecutive year, Fleer inserted the special cards randomly inside their regular 1989 wax and cello packs. The cards feature two player photos set against a green background with the "1989 Fleer All Star Team" logo bannered across the top, and the player's name, position and team in the lower left corner. The backs contain a several-paragraph player profile.

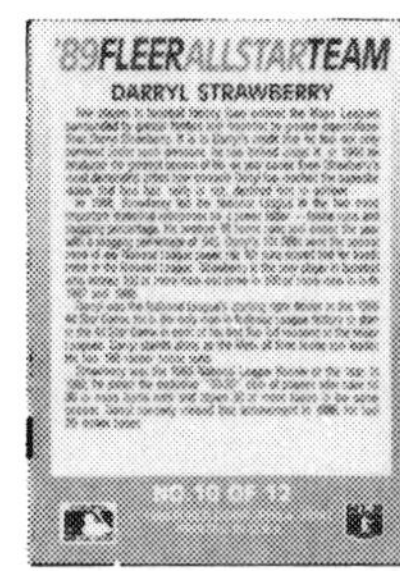

		MT	NR MT	EX
Complete Set:		13.00	9.75	5.25
Common Player:		.50	.40	.20
1	Bobby Bonilla	.60	.45	.25
2	Jose Canseco	2.00	1.50	.80
3	Will Clark	2.50	2.00	1.00
4	Dennis Eckersley	.50	.40	.20
5	Julio Franco	.60	.45	.25
6	Mike Greenwell	1.00	.70	.40
7	Orel Hershiser	1.00	.70	.40
8	Paul Molitor	.70	.50	.30
9	Mike Scioscia	.50	.40	.20
10	Darryl Strawberry	1.25	.90	.50
11	Alan Trammell	1.00	.70	.40
12	Frank Viola	.80	.60	.30

1989 Fleer Baseball All Stars

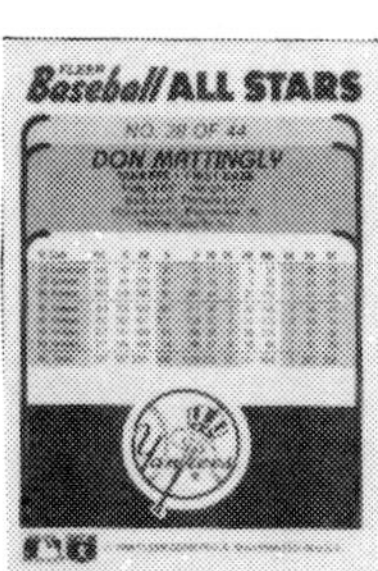

This specially-boxed set was produced by Fleer for the Ben Franklin store chain. The full-color player photos are surrounded by a border of pink and yellow vertical bands. "Fleer Baseball All-Stars" appears along the top in red, white and blue. The set was sold in a box with a checklist on the back.

		MT	NR MT	EX
Complete Set:		4.00	3.00	1.50
Common Player:		.05	.04	.02
1	Doyle Alexander	.05	.04	.02
2	George Bell	.12	.09	.05
3	Wade Boggs	.70	.50	.30
4	Bobby Bonilla	.08	.06	.04
5	Jose Canseco	.80	.60	.30
6	Will Clark	.90	.70	.35
7	Roger Clemens	.30	.25	.12
8	Vince Coleman	.15	.11	.06
9	David Cone	.15	.11	.06
10	Mark Davis	.08	.06	.03
11	Andre Dawson	.10	.08	.04
12	Dennis Eckersley	.08	.06	.03
13	Andres Galarraga	.12	.09	.05
14	Kirk Gibson	.12	.09	.05
15	Dwight Gooden	.30	.25	.12
16	Mike Greenwell	.70	.50	.30
17	Mark Gubicza	.08	.06	.03
18	Ozzie Guillen	.05	.04	.02
19	Tony Gwynn	.20	.15	.08
20	Rickey Henderson	.15	.08	.04
21	Orel Hershiser	.20	.15	.08
22	Danny Jackson	.05	.04	.02
23	Doug Jones	.05	.04	.02
24	Ricky Jordan	.50	.40	.20
25	Bob Knepper	.05	.04	.02
26	Barry Larkin	.20	.15	.08
27	Vance Law	.05	.04	.02
28	Don Mattingly	1.00	.70	.40
29	Mark McGwire	.80	.60	.30
30	Paul Molitor	.08	.06	.02
31	Gerald Perry	.05	.04	.02
32	Kirby Puckett	.35	.25	.12
33	Johnny Ray	.05	.04	.02
34	Harold Reynolds	.08	.06	.03
35	Cal Ripken, Jr.	.15	.11	.06
36	Don Robinson	.05	.04	.02
37	Ruben Sierra	.30	.25	.12
38	Dave Smith	.05	.04	.02
39	Darryl Strawberry	.35	.25	.14
40	Dave Steib	.08	.06	.03
41	Alan Trammell	.15	.11	.06
42	Andy Van Slyke	.10	.08	.04
43	Frank Viola	.15	.11	.06
44	Dave Winfield	.15	.11	.06

1989 Fleer Baseball MVP

Filled with superstars, this 44-card boxed set was produced by Fleer in 1989 for the Toys 'R' Us chain. The fronts of the cards are designed in a yellow and green color scheme and include a "Fleer Baseball MVP" logo above the color player photo. The backs are printed in shades of green and yellow and include biographical notes and stats. The set was issued in a special box with a checklist on the back.

		MT	NR MT	EX
Complete Set:		3.75	2.75	1.50
Common Player:		.05	.04	.02
1	Steve Bedrosian	.05	.04	.02
2	George Bell	.12	.09	.05
3	Wade Boggs	.70	.50	.30
4	George Brett	.15	.11	.06
5	Hubie Brooks	.05	.04	.02
6	Jose Canseco	.90	.70	.35
7	Will Clark	.90	.70	.35
8	Roger Clemens	.30	.25	.12
9	Eric Davis	.20	.15	.08
10	Glenn Davis	.12	.09	.05
11	Andre Dawson	.12	.09	.05
12	Andres Galarraga	.12	.09	.05
13	Kirk Gibson	.15	.11	.06
14	Dwight Gooden	.30	.25	.12
15	Mark Grace	.25	.20	.10
16	Mike Greenwell	.50	.40	.20
17	Tony Gwynn	.20	.15	.08
18	Bryan Harvey	.05	.04	.02
19	Orel Hershiser	.25	.20	.10
20	Ted Higuera	.07	.05	.03
21	Danny Jackson	.05	.04	.02
22	Mike Jackson	.05	.04	.02
23	Doug Jones	.05	.04	.02
24	Greg Maddux	.07	.05	.03
25	Mike Marshall	.05	.04	.02
26	Don Mattingly	1.00	.70	.40
27	Fred McGriff	.30	.25	.12
28	Mark McGwire	.80	.60	.30
29	Kevin McReynolds	.15	.11	.06
30	Jack Morris	.05	.04	.02
31	Gerald Perry	.05	.04	.02
32	Kirby Puckett	.35	.25	.12
33	Chris Sabo	.20	.15	.08
34	Mike Scott	.12	.09	.05
35	Ruben Sierra	.25	.20	.10
36	Darryl Strawberry	.35	.25	.12
37	Danny Tartabull	.09	.07	.04
38	Bobby Thigpen	.09	.07	.04
39	Alan Trammell	.15	.11	.06
40	Andy Van Slyke	.12	.09	.05
41	Frank Viola	.12	.09	.05
42	Walt Weiss	.20	.15	.08
43	Dave Winfield	.15	.11	.06
44	Todd Worrell	.07	.05	.03

1989 Fleer Baseball's Exciting Stars

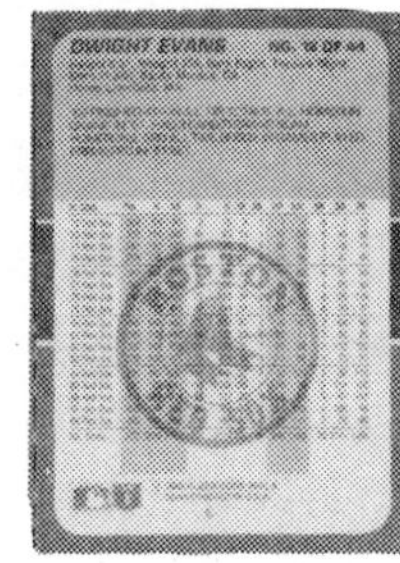

Sold exclusively in Cumberland Farm stores, this 44-card boxed set pictures the game's top stars. The card fronts feature a color player photo surrounded by a blue border with "Baseball's Exciting Stars" along the top. The cards were were numbered alphabetically and packed in a special box with a complete checklist on the back.

		MT	NR MT	EX
Complete Set:		4.00	3.00	1.50
Common Player:		.05	.04	.02
1	Harold Baines	.07	.05	.03
2	Wade Boggs	.70	.50	.30
3	Jose Canseco	.90	.70	.35
4	Joe Carter	.12	.09	.05
5	Will Clark	.90	.70	.35
6	Roger Clemens	.30	.25	.12
7	Vince Coleman	.15	.11	.06
8	David Cone	.15	.11	.06
9	Eric Davis	.20	.15	.08
10	Glenn Davis	.15	.11	.06
11	Andre Dawson	.12	.09	.05
12	Dwight Evans	.09	.07	.04
13	Andres Galarraga	.12	.09	.05
14	Kirk Gibson	.12	.09	.05
15	Dwight Gooden	.30	.25	.12
16	Jim Gott	.05	.04	.02
17	Mark Grace	.30	.25	.12
18	Mike Greenwell	.70	.50	.30
19	Mark Gibicza	.07	.05	.03
20	Tony Gwynn	.20	.15	.08
21	Rickey Henderson	.20	.15	.08
22	Tom Henke	.05	.04	.02
23	Mike Henneman	.05	.04	.02
24	Orel Hershiser	.25	.20	.10
25	Danny Jackson	.05	.04	.02
26	Gregg Jefferies	.80	.60	.30
27	Ricky Jordan	.60	.45	.25
28	Wally Joyner	.15	.11	.06
29	Mark Langston	.15	.11	.06
30	Tim Leary	.05	.04	.02
31	Don Mattingly	1.00	.70	.40
32	Mark McGwire	.80	.60	.30
33	Dale Murphy	.15	.11	.06
34	Kirby Puckett	.35	.25	.14
35	Chris Sabo	.30	.25	.12
36	Kevin Seitzer	.15	.11	.06
37	Ruben Sierra	.30	.25	.12
38	Ozzie Smith	.15	.11	.06
39	Dave Stewart	.07	.05	.03
40	Darryl Strawberry	.35	.25	.14
41	Alan Trammell	.15	.11	.06
42	Frank Viola	.15	.11	.06
43	Dave Winfield	.15	.11	.06
44	Robin Yount	.15	.11	.06

1989 Fleer Box Panels

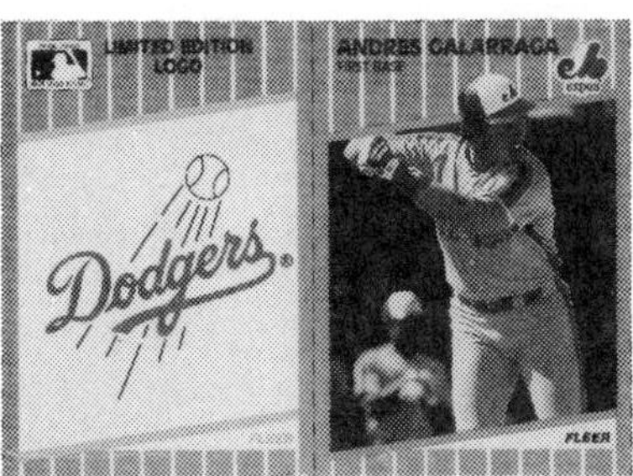

For the fourth consecutive year, Fleer issued a series of cards on the bottom panels of its regular 1989 wax pack boxes. The 28-card set includes 20 players and eight team logo cards, all designed in the identical style of the regular 1989 Fleer set. The box-bottom cards were randomly printed, four cards (three player cards and one team logo) on each bottom panel. The cards were numbered from C-1 to C-28.

		MT	NR MT	EX
Complete Panel Set:		6.00	4.50	2.50
Complete Singles Set:		3.00	2.25	1.25
Common Single Player:		.15	.11	.06
1	Mets Logo	5.00	.04	.02
2	Wade Boggs	.40	.30	.15
3	George Brett	.25	.20	.10
4	Jose Canseco	.50	.40	.20
5	A's Logo	.05	.04	.02
6	Will Clark	.50	.40	.20
7	David Cone	.50	.40	.20
8	Andres Galarraga	.25	.20	.10
9	Dodgers Logo	.05	.04	.02
10	Kirk Gibson	.15	.11	.06
11	Mike Greenwell	.25	.20	.10
12	Tony Gwynn	.25	.20	.10
13	Tigers Logo	.05	.04	.02
14	Orel Hershiser	.20	.15	.08
15	Danny Jackson	.15	.11	.06
16	Wally Joyner	.50	.40	.20
17	Red Sox Logo	.05	.04	.02
18	Yankees Logo	.05	.04	.02
19	Fred McGriff	.60	.45	.25
20	Kirby Puckett	.30	.25	.12
21	Chris Sabo	.15	.11	.06
22	Kevin Seitzer	.30	.25	.12
23	Pirates Logo	.05	.04	.02
24	Astros Logo	.05	.04	.02
25	Darryl Strawberry	.40	.30	.15
26	Alan Trammell	.20	.15	.08
27	Andy Van Slyke	.25	.20	.10
28	Frank Viola	.20	.15	.08

1989 Fleer '88 World Series

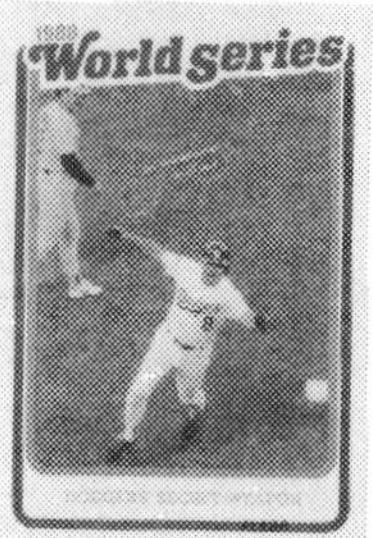

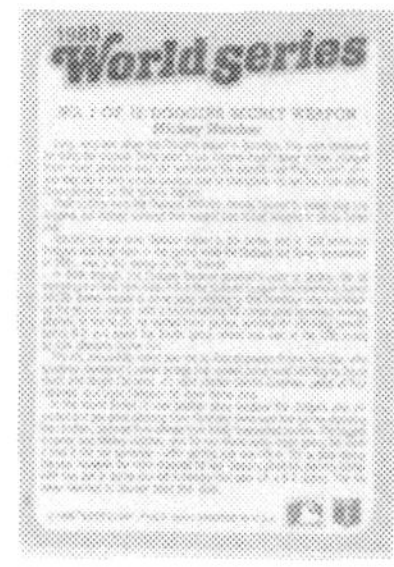

This 12-card set, which depicts highlights of the 1988 World Series, was included as a special sub-set with the regular factory-collated Fleer set. It was not available as individual cards in wax packs, cello packs or any other form.

		MT	NR MT	EX
Complete Set:		3.00	2.25	1.25
Common Player:		.25	.20	.10
1	Dodgers' Secret Weapon (Mickey Hatcher)	.25	.20	.10
2	Rookie Starts Series (Tim Belcher)	.35	.25	.14
3	Canseco Slams L.A. (Jose Canseco)	.40	.30	.20
4	Dramatic Comeback (Mike Scioscia)	.25	.20	.10
5	Gibson Steals The Show (Kirk Gibson)	.40	.30	.15
6	"Bulldog" (Orel Hershiser)	.30	.25	.12
7	One Swing, Three RBI's (Mike Marshall)	.25	.20	.10
8	Game-Winning Home Run (Mark McGwire)	.40	.30	.15
9	Sax's Speed Wins Game 4 (Steve Sax)	.25	.20	.10
10	Series Caps Award-Winning Year (Walt Weiss)	.25	.20	.10
11	The M.V.P. And His Shutout Magic (Orel Hershiser)	.35	.25	.14
12	Dodger Blue, World Champs	.25	.20	.10

1989 Fleer For the Record

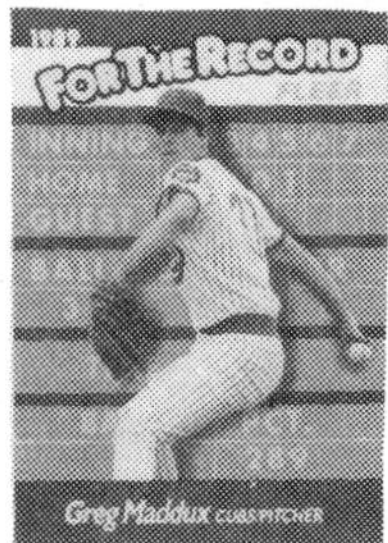

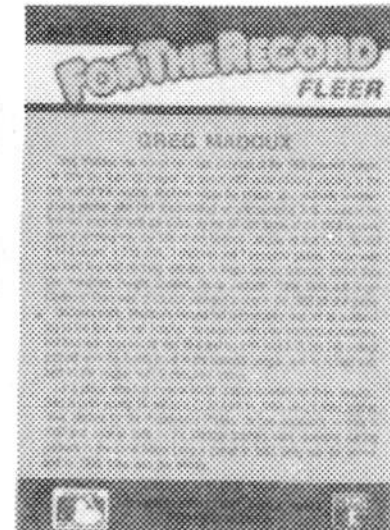

Fleer's "For the Record" set features six players and their achievements from 1988. Fronts of the standard 2-1/2" by 3-1/2" cards feature a full color photo of the player set against a red background. The words "For the Record" appear in blue script at the top of the card and the players name on the bottom, printed in white type. Card backs are grey and describe individual accomplishments. The cards were distributed randomly in rack packs.

		MT	NR MT	EX
Complete Set:		5.00	3.75	2.00
Common Player:		.80	.60	.30
1	Wade Boggs	1.25	.90	.60
2	Roger Clemens	1.00	.70	.40
3	Andres Galarraga	.80	.60	.30
4	Kirk Gibson	.80	.60	.30
5	Greg Maddux	1.00	.70	.40
6	Don Mattingly	1.75	1.25	.80

1989 Fleer Heroes of Baseball

This 44-card boxed set was produced by Fleer for the Woolworth store chain. The fronts of the cards are designed in a red and blue color scheme and feature full-color photos that fade into a soft focus on all edges. "Fleer Heroes of Baseball" appears just above the player's name, team and position at the bottom of the card. The set is numbered alphabetically and was packaged in a special box with a checklist on the back.

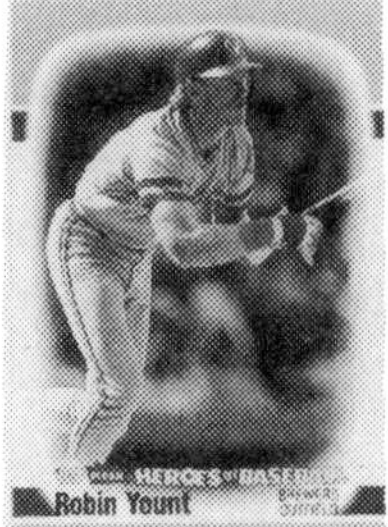

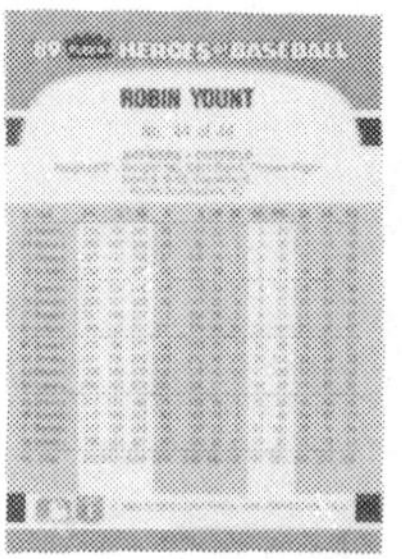

		MT	NR MT	EX
Complete Set:		3.75	2.75	1.50
Common Player:		.05	.04	.02
1	George Bell	.12	.09	.05
2	Wade Boggs	.70	.50	.30
3	Barry Bonds	.12	.09	.05
4	Tom Brunansky	.08	.06	.03
5	Jose Canseco	.90	.70	.35
6	Joe Carter	.12	.09	.05
7	Will Clark	.90	.70	.35
8	Roger Clemens	.30	.25	.12
9	David Cone	.15	.11	.06
10	Eric Davis	.40	.30	.15
11	Glenn Davis	.12	.09	.05
12	Andre Dawson	.12	.09	.05
13	Dennis Eckersley	.07	.05	.03
14	John Franco	.05	.04	.02
15	Gary Gaetti	.12	.09	.05
16	Andres Galarraga	.15	.11	.06
17	Kirk Gibson	.12	.09	.05
18	Dwight Gooden	.30	.25	.12
19	Mike Greenwell	.50	.40	.20
20	Tony Gwynn	.25	.20	.10
21	Bryan Harvey	.05	.04	.02
22	Orel Hershiser	.20	.15	.08
23	Ted Higuera	.07	.05	.03
24	Danny Jackson	.05	.04	.02
25	Ricky Jordan	.40	.30	.15
26	Don Mattingly	1.00	.70	.40
27	Fred McGriff	.30	.25	.12
28	Mark McGwire	.60	.45	.25
29	Kevin McReynolds	.15	.11	.06
30	Gerald Perry	.05	.04	.02
31	Kirby Puckett	.30	.25	.12
32	Johnny Ray	.05	.04	.02
33	Harold Reynolds	.05	.04	.02
34	Cal Ripken, Jr.	.15	.11	.06
35	Ryne Sandberg	.15	.11	.06
36	Kevin Seitzer	.15	.11	.06
37	Ruben Sierra	.30	.25	.12
38	Darryl Strawberry	.30	.25	.12
39	Bobby Thigpen	.05	.04	.02
40	Alan Trammell	.12	.09	.05
41	Andy Van Slyke	.10	.08	.04
42	Frank Viola	.15	.11	.06
43	Dave Winfield	.15	.11	.06
44	Robin Yount	.20	.15	.08

1989 Fleer League Leaders

Another of the various small, boxed sets issued by Fleer, the 44-card "League Leaders" set was produced for Walgreen stores. The standard-size cards feature color photos on the front surrounded by a red border with "Fleer League Leaders" across the top. The player's name, team and position appear in a yellow band at the bottom. The backs include player stats and data and the team logo. The cards are numbered alphabetically and packaged in a special box that includes the full checklist on the back.

		MT	NR MT	EX
Complete Set:		4.00	3.00	1.50
Common Player:		.05	.04	.02
1	Allan Anderson	.05	.04	.02
2	Wade Boggs	.70	.50	.30
3	Jose Canseco	.90	.70	.35
4	Will Clark	.90	.70	.35
5	Roger Clemens	.30	.25	.12
6	Vince Coleman	.15	.11	.06
7	David Cone	.15	.11	.06
8	Kal Daniels	.12	.09	.05
9	Chili Davis	.05	.04	.02
10	Eric Davis	.20	.15	.08
11	Glenn Davis	.15	.11	.06
12	Andre Dawson	.12	.09	.05
13	John Franco	.05	.04	.02
14	Andres Galarraga	.12	.09	.05
15	Kirk Gibson	.12	.09	.05
16	Dwight Gooden	.30	.25	.12
17	Mark Grace	.30	.25	.12
18	Mike Greenwell	.60	.45	.25
19	Tony Gwynn	.20	.15	.08
20	Orel Hershiser	.25	.20	.10
21	Pete Incaviglia	.05	.04	.02
22	Danny Jackson	.05	.04	.02
23	Gregg Jefferies	.90	.70	.35
24	Joe Magrane	.09	.07	.05
25	Don Mattingly	1.00	.70	.40
26	Fred McGriff	.30	.25	.12
27	Mark McGwire	.80	.60	.30
28	Dale Murphy	.15	.11	.06
29	Dan Plesac	.07	.05	.03
30	Kirby Puckett	.40	.30	.15
31	Harold Reynolds	.12	.09	.05
32	Cal Ripken, Jr.	.15	.11	.06
33	Jeff Robinson	.05	.04	.02
34	Mike Scott	.12	.09	.05
35	Ozzie Smith	.15	.09	.05
36	Dave Stewart	.07	.05	.03
37	Darryl Strawberry	.30	.25	.12
38	Greg Swindell	.15	.11	.06
39	Bobby Thigpen	.08	.06	.03
40	Alan Trammell	.12	.09	.05
41	Andy Van Slyke	.12	.09	.05
42	Frank Viola	.12	.09	.05
43	Dave Winfield	.12	.09	.05
44	Robin Yount	.20	.15	.08

1989 Fleer Superstars

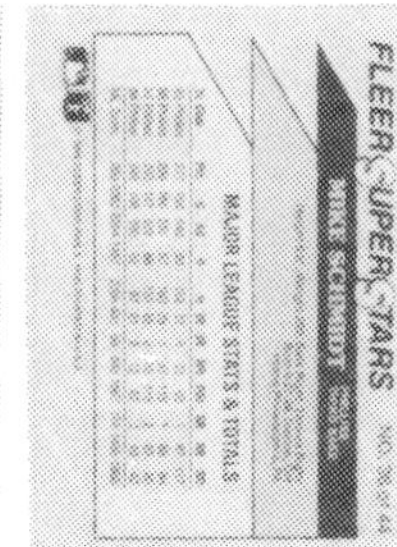

This 44-card boxed set was produced by Fleer for the McCrory store chain. The cards are the standard 2-1/2" by 3-1/2" and the full-color player photos are outlined in red with a tan-and-white striped border. The player's name, position and team logo appear at the bottom of the card. The backs carry yellow and white stripes and include the Fleer "SuperStars" logo, player stats and biographical information. The cards are numbered alphabetically and packaged in a special box that includes a checklist on the back.

		MT	NR MT	EX
Complete Set:		4.00	3.00	1.50
Common Player:		.05	.04	.02
1	Roberto Alomar	.20	.15	.08
2	Harold Baines	.12	.09	.05
3	Tim Belcher	.12	.09	.05
4	Wade Boggs	.70	.50	.30
5	George Brett	.15	.11	.06
6	Jose Canseco	.90	.70	.35
7	Gary Carter	.05	.04	.02
8	Will Clark	.90	.70	.35
9	Roger Clemens	.30	.25	.12
10	Kal Daniels	.15	.11	.06
11	Eric Davis	.20	.15	.08
12	Andre Dawson	.12	.09	.05
13	Tony Fernandez	.12	.09	.05
14	Scott Fletcher	.05	.04	.02
15	Andres Galarraga	.15	.11	.06
16	Kirk Gibson	.15	.11	.06
17	Dwight Gooden	.30	.25	.12
18	Jim Gott	.05	.04	.02
19	Mark Grace	.30	.25	.12
20	Mike Greenwell	.50	.40	.20
21	Tony Gwynn	.20	.15	.08
22	Rickey Henderson	.20	.15	.08
23	Orel Hershiser	.20	.15	.08
24	Ted Higuera	.07	.05	.02
25	Gregg Jefferies	.90	.70	.35
26	Wally Joyner	.15	.11	.06
27	Mark Langston	.15	.11	.06
28	Greg Maddux	.15	.11	.06
29	Don Mattingly	1.00	.70	.40
30	Fred McGriff	.30	.25	.12
31	Mark McGwire	.80	.60	.30
32	Dan Plesac	.09	.07	.04
33	Kirby Puckett	.30	.25	.12
34	Jeff Reardon	.05	.04	.02
35	Chris Sabo	.12	.09	.05
36	Mike Schmidt	.25	.20	.10
37	Mike Scott	.10	.08	.04
38	Cory Snyder	.10	.08	.04
39	Darryl Strawberry	.30	.25	.12
40	Alan Trammell	.12	.09	.05
41	Frank Viola	.12	.09	.05
42	Walt Weiss	.12	.09	.05
43	Dave Winfield	.12	.09	.05
44	Todd Worrell	.05	.04	.02

1989 Fleer Update

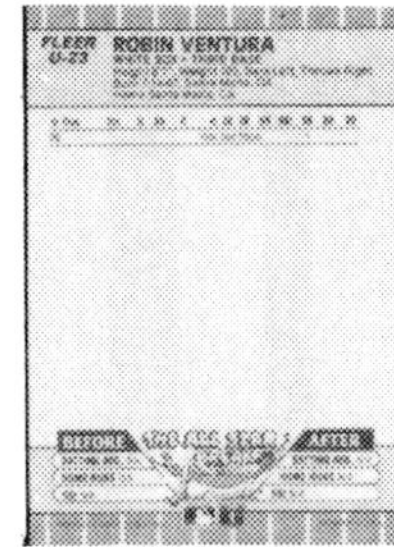

Fleer produced its sixth consecutive "Update" set in 1989 to supplement the company's regular set. As in the past, the set consisted of 132 cards (numbered U-1 through U-132) that were sold by hobby dealers in special collector's boxes.

		MT	NR MT	EX
Complete Set:		20.00	15.00	8.00
Common Player:		.06	.05	.02
1	Phil Bradley	.06	.05	.02
2	Mike Devereaux	.10	.08	.04
3	Steve Finley(FC)	.30	.25	.12
4	Kevin Hickey	.06	.05	.02
5	Brian Holton	.06	.05	.02
6	Bob Milacki	.20	.15	.08
7	Randy Milligan	.10	.08	.04
8	John Dopson	.15	.11	.06
9	Nick Esasky	.10	.08	.04
10	Rob Murphy	.06	.05	.02
11	Jim Abbott(FC)	2.25	1.75	.90
12	Bert Blyleven	.06	.05	.02
13	Jeff Manto(FC)	.30	.25	.12
14	Bob McClure	.06	.05	.02
15	Lance Parrish	.06	.05	.02
16	Lee Stevens(FC)	.30	.25	.12
17	Claudell Washington	.06	.05	.02
18	Mark Davis	.06	.05	.02
19	Eric King	.06	.05	.02
20	Ron Kittle	.06	.05	.02
21	Matt Merullo(FC)	.25	.20	.10
22	Steve Rosenberg(FC)	.08	.06	.03
23	Robin Ventura(FC)	1.50	1.25	.60
24	Keith Atherton	.06	.05	.02
25	Joey Belle(FC)	1.25	.90	.50
26	Jerry Browne	.06	.05	.02
27	Felix Fermin	.06	.05	.02
28	Brad Komminsk	.06	.05	.02
29	Pete O'Brien	.06	.05	.02
30	Mike Brumley	.06	.05	.02
31	Tracy Jones	.06	.05	.02
32	Mike Schwabe(FC)	.30	.25	.12
33	Gary Ward	.06	.05	.02
34	Frank Williams	.06	.05	.02
35	Kevin Appier(FC)	.20	.15	.08
36	Bob Boone	.06	.05	.02
37	Luis de los Santos	.10	.08	.04
38	Jim Eisenreich(FC)	.06	.05	.02
39	Jaime Navarro(FC)	.30	.25	.12
40	Bill Spiers(FC)	.40	.30	.15
41	Greg Vaughn(FC)	3.00	2.25	1.25
42	Randy Veres(FC)	.20	.15	.08
43	Wally Backman	.06	.05	.02
44	Shane Rawley	.06	.05	.02
45	Steve Balboni	.06	.05	.02
46	Jesse Barfield	.06	.05	.02
47	Alvaro Espinosa(FC)	.30	.25	.12
48	Bob Geren(FC)	.40	.30	.15
49	Mel Hall	.06	.05	.02
50	Andy Hawkins	.06	.05	.02
51	Hensley Meulens(FC)	.50	.40	.20
52	Steve Sax	.15	.11	.06
53	Deion Sanders(FC)	1.00	.70	.40
54	Rickey Henderson	.40	.30	.15
55	Mike Moore	.10	.08	.04
56	Tony Phillips	.06	.05	.02
57	Greg Briley(FC)	1.00	.70	.40
58	Gene Harris	.10	.08	.04
59	Randy Johnson	.08	.06	.03
60	Jeffrey Leonard	.06	.05	.02
61	Dennis Powell	.06	.05	.02
62	Omar Vizquel(FC)	.30	.25	.12
63	Kevin Brown	.08	.06	.03
64	Julio Franco	.15	.11	.06
65	Jamie Moyer	.06	.05	.02
66	Rafael Palmeiro	.15	.11	.06
67	Nolan Ryan	1.75	1.25	.70
68	Francisco Cabrera(FC)	.30	.25	.12
69	Junior Felix(FC)	1.25	.90	.50
70	Al Leiter	.06	.05	.02
71	Alex Sanchez(FC)	.20	.15	.08
72	Geronimo Berroa(FC)	.08	.06	.03
73	Derek Lilliquist(FC)	.20	.15	.08
74	Lonnie Smith	.10	.08	.04
75	Jeff Treadway	.06	.05	.02
76	Paul Kilgus	.06	.05	.02
77	Lloyd McClendon	.25	.20	.10
78	Scott Sanderson	.06	.05	.02
79	Dwight Smith(FC)	1.50	1.25	.60
80	Jerome Walton(FC)	3.00	2.25	1.25
81	Mitch Williams	.20	.15	.08
82	Steve Wilson	.25	.20	.10
83	Todd Benzinger	.06	.05	.02
84	Ken Griffey	.20	.15	.08
85	Rick Mahler	.06	.05	.02
86	Rolando Roomes	.20	.15	.08
87	Scott Scudder(FC)	.30	.25	.12
88	Jim Clancy	.06	.05	.02
89	Rick Rhoden	.06	.05	.02
90	Dan Schatzeder	.06	.05	.02
91	Mike Morgan	.06	.05	.02
92	Eddie Murray	.20	.15	.08
93	Willie Randolph	.06	.05	.02
94	Ray Searage	.06	.05	.02
95	Mike Aldrete	.06	.05	.02
96	Kevin Gross	.06	.05	.02
97	Mark Langston	.15	.11	.06
98	Spike Owen	.06	.05	.02
99	Zane Smith	.06	.05	.02
100	Don Aase	.06	.05	.02
101	Barry Lyons	.06	.05	.02
102	Juan Samuel	.06	.05	.02
103	Wally Whitehurst(FC)	.20	.15	.08
104	Dennis Cook	.25	.20	.10
105	Lenny Dykstra	.06	.05	.02
106	Charlie Hayes(FC)	.10	.08	.04
107	Tommy Herr	.06	.05	.02
108	Ken Howell	.06	.05	.02
109	John Kruk	.06	.05	.02
110	Roger McDowell	.06	.05	.02
111	Terry Mulholland(FC)	.06	.05	.02
112	Jeff Parrett	.06	.05	.02
113	Neal Heaton	.06	.05	.02
114	Jeff King	.10	.08	.04
115	Randy Kramer	.06	.05	.02
116	Bill Landrum	.06	.05	.02
117	Cris Carpenter(FC)	.25	.20	.10
118	Eric King	.06	.05	.02
119	Ken Hill	.15	.11	.06
120	Dan Quisenberry	.06	.05	.02
121	Milt Thompson	.06	.05	.02
122	Todd Zeile(FC)	3.00	2.25	1.25
123	Jack Clark	.10	.08	.04
124	Bruce Hurst	.06	.05	.02
125	Mark Parent	.06	.05	.02
126	Bip Roberts	.06	.05	.02
127	Jeff Brantley(FC)	.25	.20	.10
128	Terry Kennedy	.06	.05	.02
129	Mike LaCoss	.06	.05	.02
130	Greg Litton(FC)	.25	.20	.10
131	Mike Schmidt	2.00	1.50	.80
132	Checklist	.06	.05	.02

1990 Fleer

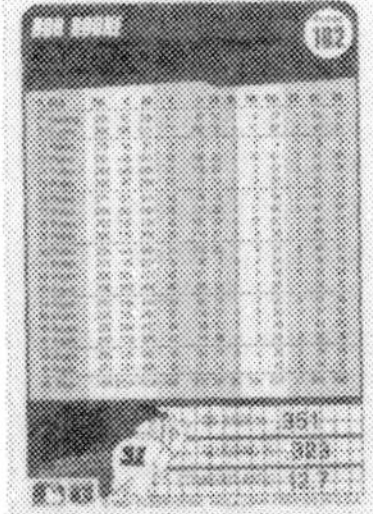

Fleer's 1990 set, its 10th consecutive baseball card offering, again consisted of 660 cards numbered by team. The fronts of the cards feature mostly action photos surrounded by one of several different color bands and a white border. The "Fleer '90" logo appears in the upper left corner, while the team logo is the upper right. The player's name and position are printed in a flowing banner below the photo. The set includes various special cards, including a series of "Major League Prospects," Players of the Decade, team checklist cards and a series of multi-player cards. The backs include complete career stats, player data, and a special "Vital Signs" section showing on-base percentage, slugging percentage, etc. for batters; and strikeout and walk ratios, opposing batting averages, etc. for pitchers.

		MT	NR MT	EX
Complete Set:		22.00	16.50	8.75
Common Player:		.05	.04	.02
1	Lance Blankenship	.07	.05	.03
2	Todd Burns	.06	.05	.02
3	Jose Canseco	.60	.45	.25
4	Jim Corsi	.09	.07	.04
5	Storm Davis	.06	.05	.02
6	Dennis Eckersley	.12	.09	.05
7	Mike Gallego	.06	.05	.02
8	Ron Hassey	.05	.04	.02
9	Dave Henderson	.10	.08	.06
10	Rickey Henderson	.30	.25	.12
11	Rick Honeycutt	.05	.04	.02
12	Stan Javier	.05	.04	.02
13	Felix Jose	.12	.09	.05
14	Carney Lansford	.07	.05	.03
15	Mark McGwire	.70	.50	.30
16	Mike Moore	.10	.08	.04
17	Gene Nelson	.05	.04	.02
18	Dave Parker	.12	.09	.05
19	Tony Phillips	.05	.04	.02
20	Terry Steinbach	.10	.08	.06
21	Dave Stewart	.10	.08	.06
22	Walt Weiss	.10	.08	.06
23	Bob Welch	.06	.05	.03
24	Curt Young	.05	.04	.02
25	Paul Assenmacher	.05	.04	.02
26	Damon Berryhill	.10	.08	.04
27	Mike Bielecki	.10	.08	.04
28	Kevin Blankenship	.07	.05	.03
29	Andre Dawson	.12	.09	.05
30	Shawon Dunston	.09	.07	.04
31	Joe Girardi	.20	.15	.08
32	Mark Grace	.25	.20	.10
33	Mike Harkey	.12	.09	.05
34	Paul Kilgus	.05	.04	.02
35	Les Lancaster	.06	.05	.02
36	Vance Law	.05	.04	.02
37	Greg Maddux	.10	.08	.04
38	Lloyd McClendon	.10	.08	.04
39	Jeff Pico	.05	.04	.02
40	Ryne Sandberg	.15	.11	.06
41	Scott Sanderson	.05	.04	.02
42	Dwight Smith	.70	.50	.30
43	Rick Sutcliffe	.08	.06	.03
44	*Jerome Walton*	1.00	.70	.40
45	Mitch Webster	.05	.04	.02
46	Curt Wilkerson	.05	.04	.02
47	*Dean Wilkins*(FC)	.25	.20	.10
48	Mitch Williams	.08	.06	.03
49	Steve Wilson	.15	.11	.06
50	Steve Bedrosian	.06	.05	.02
51	*Mike Benjamin*(FC)	.35	.25	.14
52	*Jeff Brantley*	.12	.09	.05
53	Brett Butler	.07	.05	.03
54	Will Clark	.50	.40	.20
55	Kelly Downs	.05	.04	.02
56	Scott Garrelts	.09	.07	.04
57	Atlee Hammaker	.05	.04	.02
58	Terry Kennedy	.05	.04	.02
59	Mike LaCoss	.05	.04	.02
60	Craig Lefferts	.06	.05	.02
61	*Greg Litton*	.25	.20	.10
62	Candy Maldonado	.06	.05	.02
63	Kirt Manwaring	.09	.07	.04
64	*Randy McCament*(FC)	.20	.15	.08
65	Kevin Mitchell	.30	.25	.12
66	Donell Nixon	.05	.04	.02
67	Ken Oberkfell	.05	.04	.02
68	Rick Reuschel	.09	.07	.04
69	Ernest Riles	.05	.04	.02
70	Don Robinson	.05	.04	.02
71	Pat Sheridan	.05	.04	.02
72	Chris Speier	.05	.04	.02
73	Robby Thompson	.07	.05	.03
74	Jose Uribe	.06	.05	.02
75	Matt Williams	.20	.15	.08
76	George Bell	.10	.08	.04
77	Pat Borders	.07	.05	.03
78	John Cerutti	.05	.04	.02
79	*Junior Felix*	.80	.60	.30
80	Tony Fernandez	.09	.07	.04
81	Mike Flanagan	.05	.04	.02
82	*Mauro Gozzo*(FC)	.20	.15	.08
83	Kelly Gruber	.07	.05	.03
84	Tom Henke	.05	.04	.02
85	Jimmy Key	.07	.05	.03
86	Manny Lee	.05	.04	.02
87	Nelson Liriano	.05	.04	.02
88	Lee Mazzilli	.05	.04	.02
89	Fred McGriff	.25	.20	.10
90	Lloyd Moseby	.06	.05	.02
91	Rance Mulliniks	.05	.04	.02
92	Alex Sanchez	.15	.11	.06
93	Dave Steib	.09	.07	.05
94	Todd Stottlemyre	.09	.07	.05
95	Duane Ward	.05	.04	.02
96	David Wells	.05	.04	.02
97	Ernie Whitt	.06	.05	.02
98	Frank Wills	.05	.04	.02
99	Mookie Wilson	.09	.07	.04
100	*Kevin Appier*(FC)	.25	.20	.10
101	Luis Aquino	.05	.04	.02
102	Bob Boone	.07	.05	.03
103	George Brett	.15	.11	.06
104	Jose DeJesus	.08	.06	.03
105	Luis de los Santos	.08	.06	.03
106	Jim Eisenreich	.05	.04	.02
107	Steve Farr	.05	.04	.02
108	Tom Gordon	.50	.40	.20
109	Mark Gubicza	.09	.07	.04
110	Bo Jackson	.35	.25	.14
111	Terry Leach	.05	.04	.02
112	Charlie Leibrandt	.05	.04	.02
113	*Rick Luecken*(FC)	.25	.20	.10
114	Mike Macfarlane	.05	.04	.02
115	Jeff Montgomery	.06	.05	.03
116	Bret Saberhagen	.10	.08	.04
117	Kevin Seitzer	.10	.08	.04
118	Kurt Stillwell	.06	.05	.02
119	Pat Tabler	.05	.04	.02
121	Gary Thurman	.05	.04	.02
122	Frank White	.07	.05	.03
123	Willie Wilson	.06	.05	.03
124	*Matt Winters*(FC)	.20	.15	.08
125	Jim Abbott	.90	.70	.35
126	Tony Armas	.05	.04	.02
127	Dante Bichette	.09	.07	.04
128	Bert Blyleven	.09	.07	.04
129	Chili Davis	.06	.05	.02
130	Brian Downing	.06	.05	.02
131	*Mike Fetters*(FC)	.35	.25	.12
132	Chuck Finley	.06	.05	.02
133	Willie Fraser	.05	.04	.02
134	Bryan Harvey	.05	.04	.02
135	Jack Howell	.05	.04	.02
136	Wally Joyner	.10	.08	.04
137	*Jeff Manto*	.20	.15	.08
138	Kirk McCaskill	.06	.05	.02
139	Bob McClure	.05	.04	.02
140	Greg Minton	.05	.04	.02
141	Lance Parrish	.07	.05	.02
142	Dan Petry	.05	.04	.02
143	Johnny Ray	.05	.04	.02
144	Dick Schofield	.06	.05	.02
145	*Lee Stevens*	.30	.25	.12
146	Claudell Washington	.06	.05	.02
147	Devon White	.08	.06	.03
148	Mike Witt	.06	.05	.02
149	Roberto Alomar	.10	.08	.04
150	Sandy Alomar, Jr.	.40	.30	.15
151	Andy Benes(FC)	1.00	.70	.40
152	Jack Clark	.06	.05	.02
153	Pat Clements	.05	.04	.02
154	Joey Cora	.15	.11	.06

		MT	NR MT	EX
155	Mark Davis	.09	.07	.04
156	Mark Grant	.05	.04	.02
157	Tony Gwynn	.25	.20	.10
158	Greg Harris	.10	.08	.04
159	Bruce Hurst	.06	.05	.02
160	Darrin Jackson	.05	.04	.02
161	Chris James	.06	.05	.02
162	Carmelo Martinez	.06	.05	.02
163	Mike Pagliarulo	.06	.05	.02
164	Mark Parent	.05	.04	.02
165	Dennis Rasmussen	.05	.04	.02
166	Bip Roberts	.08	.06	.03
167	Benito Santiago	.12	.09	.05
168	Calvin Schiraldi	.05	.04	.02
169	Eric Show	.06	.05	.02
170	Garry Templeton	.06	.05	.02
171	Ed Whitson	.06	.05	.02
172	Brady Anderson	.07	.05	.03
173	Jeff Ballard	.07	.05	.03
174	Phil Bradley	.07	.05	.03
175	Mike Devereaux	.07	.05	.03
176	*Steve Finley*	.20	.15	.08
177	Pete Harnisch(FC)	.10	.08	.04
178	Kevin Hickey	.10	.08	.04
179	Brian Holton	.05	.04	.02
180	*Ben McDonald*(FC)	2.25	1.75	.90
181	Bob Melvin	.05	.04	.02
182	Bob Milacki	.07	.05	.03
183	Randy Milligan	.06	.05	.02
184	Gregg Olson(FC)	.60	.45	.25
185	Joe Orsulak	.05	.04	.02
186	Bill Ripken	.05	.04	.02
187	Cal Ripken, Jr.	.15	.11	.06
188	Dave Schmidt	.05	.04	.02
189	Larry Sheets	.05	.04	.02
190	Mickey Tettleton	.08	.06	.03
191	Mark Thurmond	.05	.04	.02
192	Jay Tibbs	.05	.04	.02
193	Jim Traber	.05	.04	.02
194	Mark Williamson	.05	.04	.02
195	Craig Worthington	.15	.11	.06
196	Don Aase	.05	.04	.02
197	*Blaine Beatty*(FC)	.35	.25	.12
198	Mark Carreon	.10	.08	.04
199	Gary Carter	.06	.05	.02
200	David Cone	.10	.08	.04
201	Ron Darling	.07	.05	.03
202	Kevin Elster	.05	.04	.02
203	Sid Fernandez	.09	.07	.04
204	Dwight Gooden	.20	.15	.08
205	Keith Hernandez	.06	.05	.02
206	*Jeff Innis*	.15	.11	.06
207	Gregg Jefferies	.50	.40	.20
208	Howard Johnson	.15	.11	.06
209	Barry Lyons	.05	.04	.02
210	Dave Magadan	.06	.05	.02
211	Kevin McReynolds	.07	.05	.03
212	Jeff Musselman	.05	.04	.02
213	Randy Myers	.06	.05	.02
214	Bob Ojeda	.06	.05	.02
215	Juan Samuel	.06	.05	.02
216	Mackey Sasser	.05	.04	.02
217	Darryl Strawberry	.25	.20	.10
218	Tim Teufel	.05	.04	.02
219	Frank Viola	.10	.08	.04
220	Juan Agosto	.05	.04	.02
221	Larry Anderson	.05	.04	.02
222	*Eric Anthony*(FC)	2.00	1.50	.80
223	Kevin Bass	.08	.06	.03
224	Craig Biggio	.10	.08	.04
225	Ken Caminiti	.06	.05	.02
226	Jim Clancy	.05	.04	.02
227	Danny Darwin	.05	.04	.02
228	Glenn Davis	.09	.07	.04
229	Jim Deshaies	.07	.05	.02
230	Bill Doran	.06	.05	.02
231	Bob Forsch	.05	.04	.02
233	Terry Puhl	.05	.04	.02
234	Rafael Ramirez	.05	.04	.02
235	Rick Rhoden	.05	.04	.02
236	Dan Schatzeder	.05	.04	.02
237	Mike Scott	.08	.06	.03
238	Dave Smith	.06	.05	.02
239	Alex Trevino	.05	.04	.02
240	Glenn Wilson	.05	.04	.02
241	Gerald Young	.05	.04	.02
242	Tom Brunansky	.07	.05	.03
243	Cris Carpenter	.10	.08	.04
244	*Alex Cole*(FC)	.25	.20	.10
245	Vince Coleman	.10	.08	.04
246	John Costello	.05	.04	.02
247	Ken Dayley	.05	.04	.02
248	Jose DeLeon	.06	.05	.02
249	Frank DiPino	.05	.04	.02
250	Pedro Guerrero	.09	.07	.04
251	Ken Hill	.09	.07	.04
252	Joe Magrane	.09	.07	.04
253	Willie McGee	.06	.05	.02
254	John Morris	.05	.04	.02
255	Jose Oquendo	.06	.05	.02
256	Tony Pena	.06	.05	.02
257	Terry Pendleton	.06	.05	.02
258	Ted Power	.05	.04	.02
259	Dan Quisenberry	.05	.04	.02
260	Ozzie Smith	.09	.07	.04
261	Scott Terry	.06	.05	.02
262	Milt Thompson	.05	.04	.02
263	Denny Walling	.05	.04	.02
264	Todd Worrell	.06	.05	.02
265	*Todd Zeile*	2.00	1.50	.80
266	Marty Barrett	.05	.04	.02
267	Mike Boddicker	.05	.04	.02
268	Wade Boggs	.40	.30	.15
269	Ellis Burks	.35	.25	.12
270	Rick Cerone	.05	.04	.02
271	Roger Clemens	.25	.20	.10
272	John Dopson	.06	.05	.02
273	Nick Esasky	.07	.05	.03
274	Dwight Evans	.09	.07	.05
275	Wes Gardner	.05	.04	.02
276	Rich Gedman	.05	.04	.02
277	Mike Greenwell	.50	.40	.20
278	Danny Heep	.05	.04	.02
279	Eric Hetzel	.10	.08	.04
280	Dennis Lamp	.05	.04	.02
281	Rob Murphy	.05	.04	.02
282	Joe Price	.05	.04	.02
283	Carlos Quintana	.10	.07	.04
284	Jody Reed	.06	.05	.02
285	Luis Rivera	.05	.04	.02
286	Kevin Romine	.05	.04	.02
287	Lee Smith	.05	.04	.02
288	Mike Smithson	.05	.04	.02
289	Bob Stanley	.05	.04	.02
290	Harold Baines	.09	.07	.04
291	Kevin Brown	.09	.07	.04
292	Steve Buechele	.05	.04	.02
293	*Scott Coolbaugh*(FC)	.35	.25	.14
294	*Jack Daugherty*(FC)	.25	.20	.10
295	Cecil Espy	.06	.05	.02
296	Julio Franco	.07	.05	.03
297	*Juan Gonzalez*(FC)	.80	.60	.30
298	Cecilio Guante	.05	.04	.02
299	Drew Hall	.05	.04	.02
300	Charlie Hough	.06	.05	.02
301	Pete Incaviglia	.08	.06	.03
302	Mike Jeffcoat	.05	.04	.02
303	Chad Kreuter	.08	.06	.03
304	Jeff Kunkel	.05	.04	.02
305	Rick Leach	.05	.04	.02
306	Fred Manrique	.05	.04	.02
307	Jamie Moyer	.06	.05	.02
308	Rafael Palmeiro	.07	.05	.02
309	Geno Petralli	.05	.04	.02
310	Kevin Reimer	.10	.08	.06
311	*Kenny Rogers*(FC)	.20	.15	.08
312	Jeff Russell	.06	.05	.02
313	Nolan Ryan	.50	.40	.20
314	Ruben Sierra	.15	.11	.06
315	Bobby Witt	.05	.04	.02
316	Chris Bosio	.07	.05	.02
317	Glenn Braggs	.07	.05	.02
318	Greg Brock	.05	.04	.02
319	Chuck Crim	.05	.04	.02
320	Rob Deer	.06	.05	.02
321	Mike Felder	.05	.04	.02
322	Tom Filer	.05	.04	.02
323	*Tony Fossas*(FC)	.10	.08	.04
324	Jim Gantner	.06	.05	.02
325	Darryl Hamilton	.08	.06	.03
326	Ted Higuera	.08	.06	.03
327	Mark Knudson(FC)	.10	.08	.04
328	Bill Krueger	.05	.04	.02
329	*Tim McIntosh*(FC)	.25	.20	.10
330	Paul Molitor	.08	.06	.03
331	*Jaime Navarro*	.20	.15	.08
332	Charlie O'Brien	.05	.04	.02
333	*Jeff Peterek*(FC)	.25	.20	.10
334	Dan Plesac	.07	.05	.03
335	Jerry Reuss	.06	.05	.02
336	Gary Sheffield	.40	.30	.15
337	*Bill Spiers*	.35	.25	.12
338	B.J. Surhoff	.07	.05	.02
339	*Greg Vaughn*	2.00	1.50	.80
340	Robin Yount	.20	.15	.08
341	Hubie Brooks	.06	.05	.02
342	Tim Burke	.06	.05	.02
343	Mike Fitzgerald	.05	.04	.02
344	Tom Foley	.05	.04	.02
345	Andres Galarraga	.15	.11	.06
346	Damaso Garcia	.05	.04	.02
347	*Marquis Grissom*(FC)	1.00	.70	.40
348	Kevin Gross	.06	.05	.02
349	Joe Hesketh	.05	.04	.02
350	*Jeff Huson*(FC)	.25	.20	.10
351	Wallace Johnson	.05	.04	.02
352	Mark Langston	.15	.11	.06
353	Dave Martinez	.06	.05	.02
354	Dennis Martinez	.06	.05	.02
355	Andy McGaffigan	.05	.04	.02
356	Otis Nixon	.05	.04	.02
357	Spike Owen	.05	.04	.02
358	Pascual Perez	.06	.05	.02
359	Tim Raines	.10	.08	.04
360	Nelson Santovenia	.10	.08	.04
361	Bryn Smith	.06	.05	.02
362	Zane Smith	.05	.04	.02
363	*Larry Walker*(FC)	.25	.20	.10
364	Tim Wallach	.06	.05	.02
365	Rick Aguilera	.05	.04	.02
366	Allan Anderson	.06	.05	.02
367	Wally Backman	.06	.05	.02
368	Doug Baker(FC)	.08	.06	.03
369	Juan Berenguer	.05	.04	.02
370	Randy Bush	.05	.04	.02
371	Carmen Castillo	.05	.04	.02
372	*Mike Dyer*(FC)	.15	.11	.06
373	Gary Gaetti	.07	.05	.03
374	Greg Gagne	.05	.04	.02
375	Dan Gladden	.05	.04	.02
376	German Gonzalez	.05	.04	.02
377	Brian Harper	.06	.05	.02
378	Kent Hrbek	.10	.08	.04
379	Gene Larkin	.05	.04	.02
380	Tim Laudner	.05	.04	.02
381	John Moses	.05	.04	.02
382	Al Newman	.05	.04	.02
383	Kirby Puckett	.40	.30	.15
384	Shane Rawley	.06	.05	.02
385	Jeff Reardon	.06	.05	.02
386	Roy Smith	.05	.04	.02
387	*Gary Wayne*(FC)	.15	.11	.06
388	Dave West	.25	.20	.10
389	Tim Belcher	.12	.09	.05
390	Tim Crews	.05	.04	.02
391	Mike Davis	.05	.04	.02
392	Rick Dempsey	.05	.04	.02
393	Kirk Gibson	.09	.07	.04
394	Jose Gonzalez	.05	.04	.02
395	Alfredo Griffin	.06	.05	.02
396	Jeff Hamilton	.06	.05	.02
397	Lenny Harris	.10	.08	.06
398	Mickey Hatcher	.05	.04	.02
399	Orel Hershiser	.12	.09	.05
400	Jay Howell	.06	.05	.02
401	Mike Marshall	.06	.05	.02
402	Ramon Martinez	.20	.15	.08
403	Mike Morgan	.05	.04	.02
404	Eddie Murray	.10	.08	.04
405	Alejandro Pena	.05	.04	.02
406	Willie Randolph	.08	.06	.03
407	Mike Scioscia	.06	.05	.02
408	Ray Searage	.05	.04	.02
409	Fernando Valenzuela	.07	.05	.03
410	*Jose Vizcaino*(FC)	.35	.25	.14
411	*John Wetteland*(FC)	.40	.30	.15
412	Jack Armstrong	.05	.04	.02
413	Todd Benzinger	.07	.05	.03
414	Tim Birtsas	.05	.04	.02
415	Tom Browning	.07	.05	.03
416	Norm Charlton	.08	.06	.03
417	Eric Davis	.20	.15	.08
418	Rob Dibble	.15	.11	.06
419	John Franco	.07	.05	.03
420	Ken Griffey, Sr.	.07	.05	.03
421	*Chris Hammond*(FC)	.25	.20	.10
422	Danny Jackson	.06	.05	.02
423	Barry Larkin	.15	.11	.06
424	Tim Leary	.06	.05	.02
425	Rick Mahler	.05	.04	.02
426	*Joe Oliver*(FC)	.30	.25	.12
427	Paul O'Neill	.07	.05	.03
428	Luis Quinones	.05	.04	.02
429	Jeff Reed	.05	.04	.02
430	Jose Rijo	.07	.05	.03
431	Ron Robinson	.05	.04	.02
432	Rolando Roomes	.10	.08	.04
433	Chris Sabo	.15	.11	.06
434	*Scott Scudder*	.30	.25	.12
435	Herm Winningham	.05	.04	.02
436	Steve Balboni	.05	.04	.02
437	Jesse Barfield	.08	.06	.03
438	*Mike Blowers*(FC)	.25	.20	.10
439	Tom Brookens	.05	.04	.02
440	Greg Cadaret	.05	.04	.02
441	Alvaro Espinoza	.25	.20	.10
442	*Bob Geren*	.25	.20	.10
443	Lee Guetterman	.05	.04	.02
444	Mel Hall	.06	.05	.02
445	Andy Hawkins	.06	.05	.02
446	Roberto Kelly	.15	.11	.06
447	Don Mattingly	.80	.60	.30
448	Lance McCullers	.05	.04	.02
449	Hensley Meulens	.35	.25	.14
450	Dale Mohorcic	.05	.04	.02
451	Clay Parker	.10	.07	.04
452	Eric Plunk	.05	.04	.02
453	Dave Righetti	.07	.05	.03
454	*Deion Sanders*	.50	.40	.20
455	Steve Sax	.07	.05	.03
456	Don Slaught	.05	.04	.02
457	Walt Terrell	.05	.04	.02
458	Dave Winfield	.15	.11	.06
459	Jay Bell	.05	.04	.02
460	Rafael Belliard	.05	.04	.02
461	Barry Bonds	.10	.08	.04
462	Bobby Bonilla	.10	.08	.04
463	Sid Bream	.05	.04	.02
464	Benny Distefano	.06	.05	.02
465	Doug Drabek	.06	.05	.02
466	Jim Gott	.06	.05	.02
467	Billy Hatcher	.06	.05	.02
468	Neal Heaton	.06	.05	.02
469	Jeff King	.20	.15	.08
470	Bob Kipper	.05	.04	.02
471	Randy Kramer	.05	.04	.02
472	Bill Landrum	.06	.05	.02
473	Mike LaValliere	.06	.05	.02
474	Jose Lind	.06	.05	.02
475	Junior Ortiz	.05	.04	.02
476	Gary Redus	.05	.04	.02
477	*Rick Reed*(FC)	.20	.15	.08
478	R.J. Reynolds	.05	.04	.02
479	Jeff Robinson	.05	.04	.02
480	John Smiley	.07	.05	.03
481	Andy Van Slyke	.09	.07	.04
482	Bob Walk	.06	.05	.04
483	Andy Allanson	.05	.04	.02
484	Scott Bailes	.05	.04	.02
485	*Joey Belle*	.70	.50	.30
486	Bud Black	.05	.04	.02
487	Jerry Browne	.07	.05	.03
488	Tom Candiotti	.05	.04	.02
489	Joe Carter	.08	.06	.03
490	David Clark	.06	.05	.02
491	John Farrell	.06	.05	.02
492	Felix Fermin	.05	.04	.02
493	Brook Jacoby	.06	.05	.02
494	Dion James	.06	.05	.02
495	Doug Jones	.06	.05	.02
496	Brad Komminsk	.05	.04	.02
497	Rod Nichols	.05	.04	.02
498	Pete O'Brien	.07	.05	.03
499	*Steve Olin*(FC)	.35	.25	.12
500	Jesse Orosco	.05	.04	.02
501	Joel Skinner	.05	.04	.02
502	Cory Snyder	.09	.07	.04
503	Greg Swindell	.10	.08	.04
504	Rich Yett	.05	.04	.02
505	Scott Bankhead	.07	.05	.03
506	Scott Bradley	.05	.04	.02
507	Greg Briley	.20	.15	.08
508	Jay Buhner	.07	.05	.03
509	Darnell Coles	.05	.04	.02
510	Keith Comstock	.05	.04	.02
511	Henry Cotto	.05	.04	.02
512	Alvin Davis	.12	.09	.05
513	Ken Griffey, Jr.	2.00	1.50	.80
514	Erik Hanson	.20	.15	.08
515	Gene Harris	.15	.11	.06
516	Brian Holman	.07	.05	.03
517	Mike Jackson	.05	.04	.02
518	Randy Johnson	.15	.11	.06
519	Jeffrey Leonard	.08	.06	.03
520	Edgar Martinez	.10	.08	.04
521	Dennis Powell	.05	.04	.02
522	Jim Presley	.06	.05	.02
523	Jerry Reed	.05	.04	.02
524	Harold Reynolds	.07	.05	.03
525	Mike Schooler	.06	.05	.04
526	Bill Swift	.05	.04	.02
527	David Valle	.05	.04	.02

		MT	NR MT	EX
528	*Omar Vizquel*	.20	.15	.08
529	Ivan Calderon	.06	.05	.02
530	Carlton Fisk	.10	.08	.04
531	Scott Fletcher	.06	.05	.02
532	Dave Gallagher	.09	.07	.04
533	Ozzie Guillen	.07	.05	.03
534	*Greg Hibbard*(FC)	.15	.11	.06
535	Shawn Hillegas	.05	.04	.02
536	Lance Johnson	.07	.05	.03
537	Eric King	.05	.04	.02
538	Ron Kittle	.07	.05	.02
539	Steve Lyons	.05	.04	.02
540	Carlos Martinez	.15	.11	.06
541	*Tom McCarthy*(FC)	.10	.07	.04
542	*Matt Merullo*	.25	.20	.10
543	Donn Pall	.05	.04	.02
544	Dan Pasqua	.06	.05	.02
545	Ken Patterson	.06	.05	.02
546	Melido Perez	.07	.05	.03
547	Steve Rosenberg	.07	.05	.03
548	*Sammy Sosa*(FC)	.50	.40	.20
549	Bobby Thigpen	.07	.05	.03
550	Robin Ventura	1.00	.90	.50
551	Greg Walker	.06	.05	.02
552	Don Carman	.05	.04	.02
553	*Pat Combs*(FC)	.50	.40	.20
554	Dennis Cook	.20	.15	.08
555	Darren Daulton	.05	.04	.02
556	Lenny Dykstra	.07	.05	.03
557	Curt Ford	.05	.04	.02
558	Charlie Hayes	.10	.08	.04
559	Von Hayes	.07	.05	.03
560	Tom Herr	.06	.05	.02
561	Ken Howell	.05	.04	.02
562	Steve Jeltz	.05	.04	.02
563	Ron Jones	.15	.11	.06
564	Ricky Jordan	.35	.25	.14
565	John Kruk	.07	.05	.03
566	Steve Lake	.05	.04	.02
567	Roger McDowell	.06	.05	.02
568	Terry Mulholland	.05	.04	.02
569	Dwayne Murphy	.05	.04	.02
570	Jeff Parrett	.06	.05	.02
571	Randy Ready	.05	.04	.02
572	Bruce Ruffin	.05	.04	.02
573	Dickie Thon	.05	.04	.02
574	Jose Alvarez	.05	.04	.02
575	Geronimo Berroa	.06	.05	.03
576	Jeff Blauser	.05	.04	.02
577	Joe Boever	.07	.05	.03
578	Marty Clary	.05	.04	.02
579	Jody Davis	.05	.04	.02
580	Mark Eichhorn	.05	.04	.02
581	Darrell Evans	.06	.05	.02
582	Ron Gant	.06	.05	.02
583	Tom Glavine	.09	.07	.04
584	*Tommy Greene*(FC)	.40	.30	.15
585	Tommy Gregg	.10	.07	.04
586	*David Justice*(FC)	.35	.25	.14
587	Mark Lemke(FC)	.10	.08	.04
588	Derek Lilliquist	.10	.08	.04
589	Oddibe McDowell	.07	.05	.03
590	*Kent Mercker*(FC)	.40	.30	.15
591	Dale Murphy	.15	.11	.06
592	Gerald Perry	.06	.05	.02
593	Lonnie Smith	.06	.05	.02
594	Pete Smith	.07	.05	.03
595	John Smoltz	.15	.11	.06
596	*Mike Stanton*(FC)	.35	.25	.14
597	Andres Thomas	.06	.05	.02
598	Jeff Treadway	.06	.05	.02
599	Doyle Alexander	.06	.05	.02
600	Dave Bergman	.05	.04	.02
601	*Brian Dubois*(FC)	.35	.25	.14
602	Paul Gibson	.06	.05	.02
603	Mike Heath	.05	.04	.02
604	Mike Henneman	.07	.05	.03
605	Guillermo Hernandez	.05	.04	.02
606	*Shawn Holman*(FC)	.20	.15	.08
607	Tracy Jones	.09	.07	.04
608	Chet Lemon	.06	.05	.02
609	Fred Lynn	.06	.05	.02
610	Jack Morris	.07	.05	.02
611	Matt Nokes	.10	.08	.04
612	Gary Pettis	.05	.04	.02
613	*Kevin Ritz*(FC)	.15	.11	.06
614	Jeff Robinson	.07	.05	.03
615	Steve Searcy	.10	.08	.04
616	Frank Tanana	.06	.05	.02
617	Alan Trammell	.09	.07	.04
618	Gary Ward	.05	.04	.02
619	Lou Whitaker	.09	.07	.04
620	Frank Williams	.05	.04	.02
621a	Players Of The Decade - 1980 (George Brett) (10 .390 hitting seasons)	4.00	3.00	1.50
621b	Players Of The Decade - 1980 (George Brett) (10 .300 hitting seasons)	.50	.40	.20
622	Players Of The Decade - 1981 (Fernando Valenzuela)	.20	.15	.08
623	Players Of The Decade - 1982 (Dale Murphy)	.25	.20	.10
624a	Players Of The Decade - 1983 (Cal Ripkin, Jr.)	1.00	.70	.40
624b	Players Of The Decade - 1983 (Cal Ripken, Jr.)	.25	.20	.10
625	Players Of The Decade - 1984 (Ryne Sandberg)	.25	.20	.10
626	Players Of The Decade - 1985 (Don Mattingly)	.50	.40	.20
627	Players Of The Decade - 1986 (Roger Clemens)	.25	.20	.10
628	Players Of The Decade - 1987 (George Bell)	.20	.15	.08
629	Players Of The Decade - (Jose Canseco)	.60	.45	.25
630a	Players Of The Decade - 1989 (Will Clark) (total bases (32))	5.00	3.75	2.00
630b	Players Of The Decade - 1989 (Will Clark) (total bases (321))	.60	.45	.25
631	Game Savers	.10	.08	.04
632	Boston Igniters	.10	.08	.04
633	The Starter & Stopper	.10	.08	.04
634	League's Best Shortstops	.10	.08	.04
635	Human Dynamos	.10	.08	.04
636	300 Strikeout Club	.10	.08	.04
637	The Dynamic Duo	.10	.08	.04
638	A.L. All Stars	.10	.08	.04
639	N.L. East Rivals	.10	.08	.04
640	*Rudy Seanez, Colin Charland*(FC)	.20	.15	.08
641	*George Canale, Kevin Maas*(FC)	.20	.15	.08
642	*Kelly Mann, Dave Hansen*(FC)	.30	.25	.12
643	*Greg Smith, Stu Tate*(FC)	.20	.15	.08
644	*Tom Drees, Dan Howitt*(FC)	.20	.15	.08
645	*Mike Roesler, Derrick May*(FC)	.25	.20	.10
646	*Scott Hemond, Mark Gardner*(FC)	.25	.20	.10
647	*John Orton, Scott Leuis*(FC)	.20	.15	.08
648	*Rich Monteleone, Dana Williams*(FC)	.15	.11	.06
649	*Mike Huff, Steve Frey*(FC)	.20	.15	.08
650	*Chuck McElroy, Moises Alou*(FC)	.40	.30	.15
651	*Bobby Rose, Mike Hartley*(FC)	.25	.20	.10
652	*Matt Kinzer, Wayne Edwards*(FC)	.25	.20	.10
653	*Delino Deshields, Jason Grimsley*(FC)	1.00	.70	.40
654	Athletics, Cubs, Giants & Blue Jays (Checklist)	.05	.04	.03
655	Royals, Angels, Padres & Orioles (Checklist)	.05	.04	.03
656	Mets, Astros, Cardinals & Red Sox (Checklist)	.05	.04	.03
657	Rangers, Brewers, Expos & Twins (Checklist)	.05	.04	.03
658	Dodgers, Reds, Yankees & Pirates (Checklist)	.05	.04	.03
659	Indians, Mariners, White Sox & Phillies (Checklist)	.05	.04	.03
660	Braves, Tigers & Special Cards (Checklist)	.05	.04	.03

1990 Fleer '89 World Series

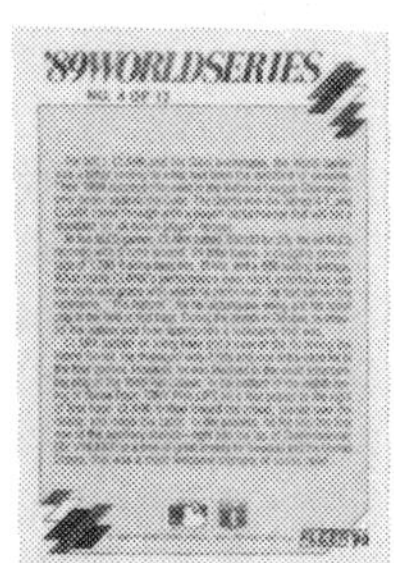

This 12-card set, which depicts highlights of the 1989 World Series, was included as a special sub-set with the regular factory-collated Fleer set. Ironically, single World Series cards were discovered in cello and three-packs. This was not intended to happen. Fronts of the 2-1/2" by 3-1/2" cards feature full color photos set against a white background with a red and blue "'89 World Series" banner. The card backs are pink and white and describe the events of the 1989 FALL Classic.

	MT	NR MT	EX
Complete Set:	3.00	2.25	1.25
Common Player:	.20	.15	.08

		MT	NR MT	EX
1	The Final Piece To The Puzzle (Mike Moore)	.20	.15	.08
2	The National League M.V.P. (Kevin Mitchell)	.30	.25	.12
3	Game Two's Crushing Blow	.20	.15	.08
4	Clark Pwers The Giants Into The Series (Will Clark)	.35	.25	.14
5	Canseco Crushed World Series Slump (Jose Canseco)	.40	.30	.15
6	Great leather In The Field	.20	.15	.08
7	Game One And A's Break Out On Top	.20	.15	.08
8	Oakland's M.V.P. (Dave Stewart)	.25	.20	.10
9	Parker's Bat Produces Power (Dave Parker)	.20	.15	.08
10	World Series Record Book Game 3	.20	.15	.08
11	Swipes Championship Series Records (Rickey Henderson)	.35	.25	.14
12	Oakland A's - Baseball's Best In '89	.25	.20	.10

1990 Fleer League Standouts

Fleer's "League Standouts" set features six of baseball's top players. The cards were distributed randomly in Fleer three-packs. The card fronts feature full color photos with a six dimensional effect. An attractive black and gold frame borders the photo. The card backs are yellow and describe the player's iuuuundividual accomplishments. The cards measure 2-1/2" by 3-1/2" in size.

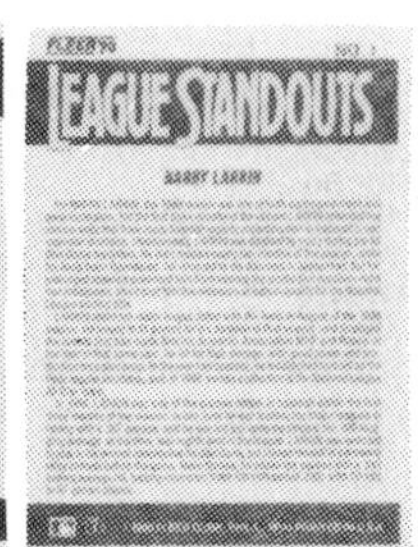

		MT	NR MT	EX
Complete Set:		4.00	3.00	1.50
Common Player:		.50	.40	.20
1	Barry Larkin	.50	.40	.20
2	Mark Grace	.50	.40	.20
3	Don Mattingly	1.00	.70	.40
4	Darryl Strawberry	.60	.45	.25
5	Jose Canseco	1.00	.70	.40
6	Wade Boggs	.60	.45	.25

1887 Four Base Hits

Although the exact origin of this set is still in doubt, the Four Base Hits cards are among the rarest and most sought after of all 19th century tobacco issues. There is some speculation that the cards, measuring 2-1/4" by 3-7/8", were produced by Charles Gross & Co. because of their similarity to the Kalamazoo Bats issues, but there is also some evidence to support the theory that they were issued by August Beck & Co., producer of the Yum Yum set. The Four Base Hits cards feature sepia-toned photos with the player's name and position below the picture, and the words "Smoke Four Base Hits. Four For 10 Cents." along the bottom. The card labeled "Daily" is a double error. The name should have been spelled "Daly," but the card actually pictures Billy Sunday.

		NR MT	EX	VG
Complete Set:		27500.	13750.	8250.
Common Player:		2000.	1000.	600.00
(1)	Tido Daily (Daly)	2000.	1000.	600.00
(2)	Buck Ewing	3500.	1750.	1050.
(3)	Pete Gillespie	2000.	1000.	600.00
(4)	Frank Hankinson	2000.	1000.	600.00
(5)	King Kelly	4000.	2000.	1200.
(6)	Al Mays	2000.	1000.	600.00
(7)	Jim Mutrie	2000.	1000.	600.00
(8)	Chief Roseman	2000.	1000.	600.00
(9)	Marty Sullivan	2000.	1000.	600.00
(10)	Rip Van Haltren	2000.	1000.	600.00
(11)	Mickey Welch	3500.	1750.	1050.

1963 French Bauer Milk Caps

This regional set of cardboard milk bottle caps was issued in the Cincinnati area in 1963 and features 30 members of the Cincinnati Reds. The unnumbered, blank-backed cards are approximately 1-1/4" in diameter and feature rather crude drawings of the players with their names in script alongside the artwork and the words "Visit Beautiful Crosley Field/See The Reds in Action" along the outside. An album was issued to house the set.

		NR MT	EX	VG
Complete Set:		600.00	300.00	180.00
Common Player:		5.00	2.50	1.50
Album:		100.00	50.00	10.00
(1)	Don Blasingame	5.00	2.50	1.50
(2)	Leo Cardenas	5.00	2.50	1.50
(3)	Gordon Coleman	5.00	2.50	1.50
(4)	Wm. O. DeWitt	5.00	2.50	1.50
(5)	John Edwards	5.00	2.50	1.50
(6)	Jesse Gonder	5.00	2.50	1.50
(7)	Tommy Harper	5.00	2.50	1.50
(8)	Bill Henry	5.00	2.50	1.50
(9)	Fred Hutchinson	8.00	4.00	2.50
(10)	Joey Jay	5.00	2.50	1.50
(11)	Eddie Kasko	5.00	2.50	1.50
(12)	Marty Keough	5.00	2.50	1.50
(13)	Jim Maloney	8.00	4.00	2.50
(14)	Joe Nuxhall	8.00	4.00	2.50
(15)	Reggie Otero	5.00	2.50	1.50
(16)	Jim O'Toole	5.00	2.50	1.50
(17)	Jim Owens	5.00	2.50	1.50
(18)	Vada Pinson	18.00	9.00	5.50
(19)	Bob Purkey	5.00	2.50	1.50
(20)	Frank Robinson	70.00	35.00	21.00
(21)	Dr. Richard Rohde	5.00	2.50	1.50
(22)	Pete Rose	250.00	125.00	75.00
(23)	Ray Shore	5.00	2.50	1.50
(24)	Dick Sisler	5.00	2.50	1.50
(25)	Bob Skinner	5.00	2.50	1.50
(26)	John Tsitorius	5.00	2.50	1.50
(27)	Jim Turner	5.00	2.50	1.50
(28)	Ken Walters	5.00	2.50	1.50
(29)	Al Worthington	5.00	2.50	1.50
(30)	Dom Zanni	5.00	2.50	1.50

1987 French/Bray Orioles

8 CAL RIPKEN, IF
Compliments of
FRENCH/BRAY, INC.

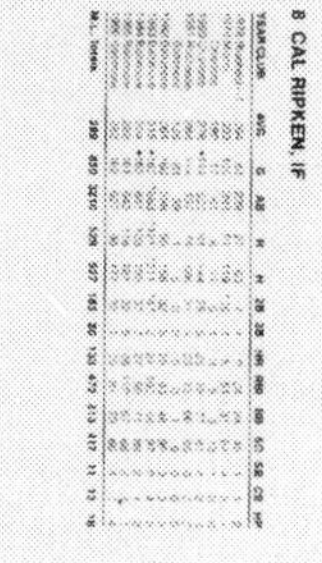

The Baltimore Orioles and French Bray, Inc. issued a baseball card set to be handed out to fans in attendance at Memorial Stadium on July 26th. Thirty perforated, detachable cards were printed within a three-panel fold-out piece measuring 9-1/2" by 11-1/4". The card fronts feature full-color player photos surrounded by an orange border. The French/Bray logo appears on the card front. The backs are of simple design, containing only the player's name, uniform number, position and professional record.

		MT	NR MT	EX
Complete Set:		10.00	7.50	4.00
Common Player:		.15	.11	.06
2	Alan Wiggins	.15	.11	.06
3	Bill Ripken	.80	.60	.30
6	Floyd Rayford	.15	.11	.06
7	Cal Ripken, Sr.	.15	.11	.06
8	Cal Ripken	1.75	1.25	.70
9	Jim Dwyer	.15	.11	.06
10	Terry Crowley	.15	.11	.06
15	Terry Kennedy	.20	.15	.08
16	Scott McGregor	.20	.15	.08
18	Larry Sheets	.50	.40	.20
19	Fred Lynn	.50	.40	.20
20	Frank Robinson	.40	.30	.15
24	Dave Schmidt	.15	.11	.06
25	Ray Knight	.20	.15	.08
27	Lee Lacy	.15	.11	.06
31	Mark Wiley	.15	.11	.06
32	Mark Williamson	.30	.25	.12
33	Eddie Murray	1.50	1.25	.60
38	Ken Gerhart	.50	.40	.20
39	Ken Dixon	.15	.11	.06
40	Jimmy Williams	.15	.11	.06
42	Mike Griffin	.15	.11	.06
43	Mike Young	.20	.15	.08
44	Elrod Hendricks	.15	.11	.06
45	Eric Bell	.30	.25	.12
46	Mike Flanagan	.25	.20	.10
49	Tom Niedenfuer	.20	.15	.08
52	Mike Boddicker	.25	.20	.10
54	John Habyan	.15	.11	.06
57	Tony Arnold	.15	.11	.06

1988 French/Bray Orioles

48 JOSE BAUTISTA, RHS
Compliments of
FRENCH BRAY, INC.

French-Bray sponsored a full-color brochure that was distributed to fans during an in-stadium promotion. A blue and orange front cover features inset photos of the Orioles in action on the upper left in a filmstrip motif. To the right is the Orioles logo and their 1988 slogan, "You Gotta Be There" above a baseball glove and ball. The 3-panel foldout measures approximately 9-1/2" by 11-1/4" and includes a team photo on the inside cover, with two perforated pages of individual cards featuring players, coaches and the team manager. Individual cards measure 2-1/4" by 3-1/8", with close-ups framed in white with an orange accent line. The player name and sponsor logo are printed beneath the photo. The black and white backs are numbered by player uniform and provide career stats. Additional copies of the brochure were made available from the Orioles Baseball Store following the free giveaway.

		MT	NR MT	EX
Complete Set:		8.00	6.00	3.25
Common Player:		.15	.11	.06
2	Don Buford	.15	.11	.06
6	Joe Orsulak	.15	.11	.06
7	Bill Ripken	.40	.30	.15
8	Cal Ripken	1.75	1.25	.70
9	Jim Dwyer	.15	.11	.06
10	Terry Crowley	.15	.11	.06
12	Mike Morgan	.15	.11	.06
14	Mickey Tettleton	.15	.11	.06
15	Terry Kennedy	.20	.15	.08
17	Pete Stanicek	.60	.45	.25
18	Larry Sheets	.40	.30	.15
19	Fred Lynn	.50	.40	.20
20	Frank Robinson	.40	.30	.15
23	Ozzie Peraza	.40	.30	.15
24	Dave Schmidt	.15	.11	.06
25	Rich Schu	.15	.11	.06
28	Jim Traber	.25	.20	.10
31	Herm Starrette	.15	.11	.06
33	Eddie Murray	1.50	1.25	.60
34	Jeff Ballard	.30	.25	.12
38	Ken Gerhart	.30	.25	.12
40	Minnie Mendoza	.15	.11	.06
41	Don Aase	.20	.15	.08
44	Elrod Hendricks	.15	.11	.06
47	John Hart	.15	.11	.06
48	Jose Bautista	.30	.25	.12
49	Tom Niedenfuer	.20	.15	.08
52	Mike Boddicker	.25	.20	.10
53	Jay Tibbs	.15	.11	.06
88	Rene Gonzales	.30	.25	.12

1989 French/Bray Orioles

This 32-card Baltimore Orioles team set was co-sponsored by French-Bray and the Wilcox Walter Furlong Paper Co., and was distributed as an in-stadium promotion to fans attending the May 12, 1989, Orioles game. Smaller than standard size, the cards measure 2-1/4" by 3" and feature a full-color player photo with number, name and position below. The backs, done in black and white, include brief player data and complete major and minor league stats.

		MT	NR MT	EX
Complete Set:		8.00	6.00	3.25
Common Player:		.15	.11	.06
3	Bill Ripken	.30	.25	.12
6	Joe Orsulak	.15	.11	.06
7	Cal Ripken, Sr.	.15	.11	.06
8	Cal Ripken, Jr.	1.75	1.25	.70
9	Brady Anderson	.20	.15	.08
10	Steve Finley	.80	.60	.30
11	Craig Worthington	.50	.40	.20
12	Mike Devereaux	.20	.15	.08
14	Mickey Tettleton	.20	.15	.08
15	Randy Milligan	.15	.11	.06
16	Phil Bradley	.20	.15	.08
18	Bob Milacki	.20	.15	.08
19	Larry Sheets	.15	.11	.06
20	Frank Robinson	.40	.30	.15
21	Mark Thurmond	.15	.11	.06
23	Kevin Hickey	.15	.11	.06
24	Dave Schmidt	.15	.11	.06
28	Jim Traber	.20	.15	.08
29	Jeff Ballard	.30	.25	.12
30	Gregg Olson	1.50	1.25	.60
31	Al Jackson	.15	.11	.06
32	Mark Williamson	.15	.11	.06
36	Bob Melvin	.15	.11	.06
37	Brian Holton	.15	.11	.06
40	Tom McCraw	.15	.11	.06
42	Pete Harnisch	.35	.25	.14
43	Fransisco Melendez	.20	.15	.08
44	Elrod Hendricks	.15	.11	.06
46	Johnny Oates	.15	.11	.06
48	Jose Bautista	.20	.15	.08
88	Rene Gonzales	.25	.20	.10

1928 Fro-joy

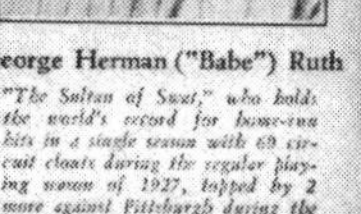

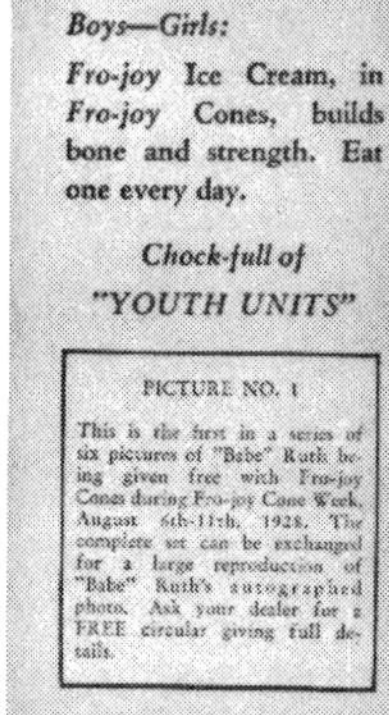

Boys—Girls:
Fro-joy Ice Cream, in Fro-joy Cones, builds bone and strength. Eat one every day.
Chock-full of
"YOUTH UNITS"
PICTURE NO. 1
This is the first in a series of six pictures of "Babe" Ruth being given free with Fro-joy Cones during Fro-joy Cone Week, August 6th-11th, 1928. The complete set can be exchanged for a large reproduction of "Babe" Ruth's autographed photo. Ask your dealer for a FREE circular giving full details.

Capitalizing on the extreme popularity of Babe Ruth, this six-card set was given away with Fro-joy Cones during the August 6-11, 1928 Fro-joy Cone Week. The cards, which measure 2-1/16" by 4" in size, contain black and white photos designed on either a horizontal or vertical format. The card fronts also contain a caption with a few sentences explaining the photo. The card backs contain advertising for Fro-joy Ice Cream and Cones.

		NR MT	EX	VG
Complete Set:		850.00	425.00	255.00
Common Player:		100.00	50.00	30.00
1	George Herman ("Babe")	150.00	75.00	45.00
2	Look Out, Mr. Pitcher!	150.00	75.00	45.00
3	"Babe" Ruth's Grip!	100.00	50.00	30.00
4	Ruth is a Crack Fielder	150.00	75.00	45.00
5	Bang! The Babe Lines Out!	150.00	75.00	45.00
6	When The "Babe" Comes Home	150.00	75.00	45.00

1985 Fun Food Buttons

Fun Foods of Little Silver, N.J. issued a set of 133 full-color metal pins in 1985. The buttons, which are 1-1/4" in diameter and have a "safety pin" back, have bright borders which correspond to the player's team colors. The button backs are numbered and contain the player's 1984 batting or earned run average. The buttons were available as complete sets through hobby dealers and were also distributed in packs (three buttons per pack) through retail stores.

		MT	NR MT	EX
Complete Set:		25.00	20.00	10.00
Common Player:		.10	.08	.04
1	Dave Winfield	.40	.30	.15
2	Lance Parrish	.25	.20	.10
3	Gary Carter	.35	.25	.14
4	Pete Rose	1.50	1.25	.60
5	Jim Rice	.35	.25	.14
6	George Brett	.60	.45	.25
7	Fernando Valenzuela	.30	.25	.12
8	Darryl Strawberry	.70	.50	.30
9	Steve Garvey	.35	.25	.14
10	Rollie Fingers	.20	.15	.08
11	Mike Schmidt	1.25	.90	.50
12	Kent Tekulve	.10	.08	.04
13	Ryne Sandberg	.40	.30	.15
14	Bruce Sutter	.15	.11	.06
15	Tom Seaver	.30	.25	.12
16	Reggie Jackson	.70	.50	.30
17	Rickey Henderson	.70	.50	.30
18	Mark Langston	.35	.25	.14
19	Jack Clark	.20	.15	.08
20	Willie Randolph	.15	.11	.06
21	Kirk Gibson	.30	.25	.12
22	Andre Dawson	.30	.25	.12
23	Dave Concepcion	.15	.11	.06
24	Tony Armas	.10	.08	.04
25	Dan Quisenberry	.10	.08	.04
26	Pedro Guerrero	.25	.20	.10
27	Dwight Gooden	2.00	1.50	.80
28	Tony Gwynn	.40	.30	.15
29	Robin Yount	.70	.50	.30
30	Steve Carlton	1.00	.70	.40
31	Bill Madlock	.15	.11	.06
32	Rick Sutcliffe	.15	.11	.06
33	Willie McGee	.20	.15	.08
34	Greg Luzinski	.15	.11	.06
35	Rod Carew	.40	.30	.15
36	Dave Kingman	.15	.11	.06
37	Alvin Davis	.40	.30	.15
38	Chili Davis	.15	.11	.06
39	Don Baylor	.15	.11	.06
40	Alan Trammell	.30	.25	.12
41	Tim Raines	.35	.25	.14
42	Cesar Cedeno	.15	.11	.06
43	Wade Boggs	1.75	1.25	.70
44	Frank White	.15	.11	.06
45	Steve Sax	.25	.20	.10
46	George Foster	.15	.11	.06
47	Terry Kennedy	.10	.08	.04
48	Cecil Cooper	.15	.11	.06
49	John Denny	.10	.08	.04
50	John Candelaria	.10	.08	.04
51	Jody Davis	.10	.08	.04
52	George Hendrick	.10	.08	.04
53	Ron Kittle	.15	.11	.06
54	Fred Lynn	.20	.15	.08
55	Carney Lansford	.10	.08	.04
56	Gorman Thomas	.10	.08	.04
57	Manny Trillo	.10	.08	.04
58	Steve Kemp	.10	.08	.04
59	Jack Morris	.20	.15	.08
60	Dan Petry	.10	.08	.04
61	Mario Soto	.10	.08	.04
62	Dwight Evans	.20	.15	.08
63	Hal McRae	.10	.08	.04
64	Mike Marshall	.15	.11	.06
65	Mookie Wilson	.15	.11	.06
66	Graig Nettles	.15	.11	.06
67	Ben Oglivie	.10	.08	.04
68	Juan Samuel	.20	.15	.08
69	Johnny Ray	.15	.11	.06
70	Gary Matthews	.15	.11	.06
71	Ozzie Smith	.20	.15	.08
72	Carlton Fisk	.20	.15	.08
73	Doug DeCinces	.10	.08	.04
74	Joe Morgan	.60	.45	.25
75	Dave Stieb	.15	.11	.06
76	Buddy Bell	.15	.11	.06
77	Don Mattingly	2.50	2.00	1.00
78	Lou Whitaker	.25	.20	.10
79	Willie Hernandez	.10	.08	.04
80	Dave Parker	.20	.15	.08
81	Bob Stanley	.10	.08	.04
82	Willie Wilson	.15	.11	.06
83	Orel Hershiser	.70	.50	.30
84	Rusty Staub	.15	.11	.06
85	Goose Gossage	.20	.15	.08
86	Don Sutton	.25	.20	.10
87	Al Holland	.10	.08	.04
88	Tony Pena	.15	.11	.06
89	Ron Cey	.15	.11	.06
90	Joaquin Andujar	.10	.08	.04
91	LaMarr Hoyt	.10	.08	.04
92	Tommy John	.20	.15	.08
93	Dwayne Murphy	.10	.08	.04
94	Willie Upshaw	.10	.08	.04
95	Gary Ward	.10	.08	.04
96	Ron Guidry	.20	.15	.08
97	Chet Lemon	.10	.08	.04
98	Aurelio Lopez	.10	.08	.04
99	Tony Perez	.20	.15	.08
100	Bill Buckner	.15	.11	.06
101	Mike Hargrove	.10	.08	.04
102	Scott McGregor	.10	.08	.04
103	Dale Murphy	.60	.45	.25
104	Keith Hernandez	.35	.25	.14
105	Paul Molitor	.20	.15	.08
106	Bert Blyleven	.15	.11	.06
107	Leon Durham	.10	.08	.04
108	Lee Smith	.15	.11	.06
109	Nolan Ryan	1.25	.90	.50
110	Harold Baines	.15	.11	.06
111	Kent Hrbek	.25	.20	.10
112	Ron Davis	.10	.08	.04
113	George Bell	.30	.25	.12
114	Charlie Hough	.10	.08	.04
115	Phil Niekro	.25	.20	.10
116	Dave Righetti	.20	.15	.08
117	Darrell Evans	.15	.11	.06
118	Cal Ripken, Jr.	.60	.45	.25
119	Eddie Murray	.45	.35	.20
120	Storm Davis	.10	.08	.04
121	Mike Boddicker	.10	.08	.04
122	Bob Horner	.15	.11	.06
123	Chris Chambliss	.10	.08	.04
124	Ted Simmons	.15	.11	.06
125	Andre Thornton	.15	.11	.06
126	Larry Bowa	.15	.11	.06
127	Bob Dernier	.10	.08	.04
128	Joe Niekro	.15	.11	.06
129	Jose Cruz	.15	.11	.06
130	Tom Brunansky	.20	.15	.08
131	Gary Gaetti	.25	.20	.10
132	Lloyd Moseby	.15	.11	.06
133	Frank Tanana	.10	.08	.04

1983 Gardner's Brewers

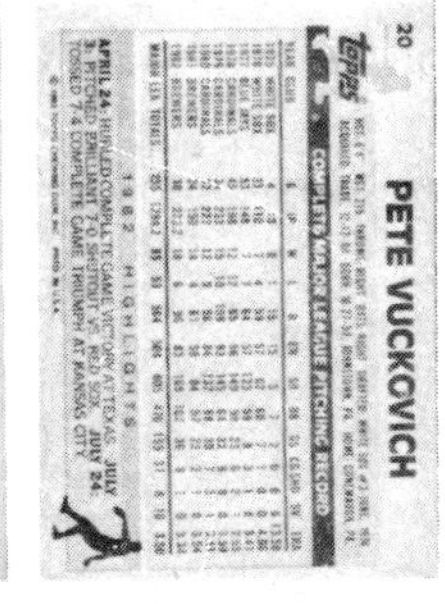

Topps produced in 1983 for Gardner's Bakery of Madison, Wisconsin, a 22-card set featuring the American League champion Milwaukee Brewers. The cards, which measure 2-1/2" by 3-1/2", have colorful fronts which contain the player's name, team and position plus the Brewers and Gardner's logos. The card backs are identical to the regular Topps issue but are numbered 1-22. The cards were inserted in specially marked packages of Gardner's bread products and were susceptible to grease stains.

		MT	NR MT	EX
Complete Set		25.00	18.50	10.00
Common Player		.50	.40	.20
1	Harvey Kuenn	.70	.50	.30
2	Dwight Bernard	.50	.40	.20
3	Mark Brouhard	.50	.40	.20
4	Mike Caldwell	.50	.40	.20
5	Cecil Cooper	1.25	.90	.50
6	Marshall Edwards	.50	.40	.20
7	Rollie Fingers	4.00	3.00	1.50
8	Jim Gantner	.70	.50	.30
9	Moose Haas	.50	.40	.20
10	Bob McClure	.50	.40	.20
11	Paul Molitor	4.00	3.00	1.50
12	Don Money	.50	.40	.20
13	Charlie Moore	.50	.40	.20
14	Ben Oglivie	.60	.45	.25
15	Ed Romero	.50	.40	.20
16	Ted Simmons	.90	.70	.35
17	Jim Slaton	.50	.40	.20
18	Don Sutton	2.00	1.50	.80
19	Gorman Thomas	.70	.50	.30
20	Pete Vuckovich	.70	.50	.30
21	Ned Yost	.50	.40	.20
22	Robin Yount	7.00	5.25	2.75

1984 Gardner's Brewers

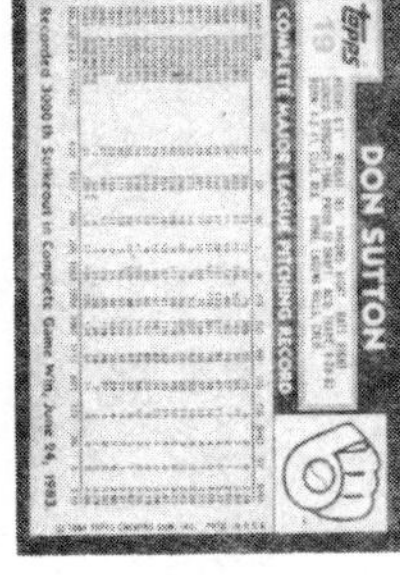

For the second straight year, Gardner's Bakery inserted baseball cards featuring the Milwaukee Brewers with their bread products. The 22-card set, entitled "1984 Series II," have multi-colored fronts that include the Brewers and Gardner's logos. The card backs are identical to the regular 1984 Topps issue except for the 1-22 numbering system. The Topps-produced cards are the standard 2-1/2" by 3-1/2" size. The cards are sometimes found with grease stains, resulting from contact with the bread.

		MT	NR MT	EX
Complete Set:		20.00	15.00	8.00
Common Player:		.50	.40	.20
1	Rene Lachemann	.50	.40	.20
2	Mark Brouhard	.50	.40	.20
3	Mike Caldwell	.50	.40	.20
4	Bobby Clark	.50	.40	.20
5	Cecil Cooper	1.00	.70	.40
6	Rollie Fingers	2.00	1.50	.80
7	Jim Gantner	.70	.50	.30
8	Moose Haas	.50	.40	.20
9	Roy Howell	.50	.40	.20
10	Pete Ladd	.50	.40	.20
11	Rick Manning	.50	.40	.20
12	Bob McClure	.50	.40	.20
13	Paul Molitor	2.00	1.50	.80
14	Charlie Moore	.50	.40	.20
15	Ben Oglivie	.60	.45	.25
16	Ed Romero	.50	.40	.20
17	Ted Simmons	.80	.60	.30
18	Jim Sundberg	.50	.40	.20
19	Don Sutton	1.25	.90	.50
20	Tom Tellmann	.50	.40	.20
21	Pete Vuckovich	.60	.45	.25
22	Robin Yount	5.00	3.75	2.00

1985 Gardner's Brewers

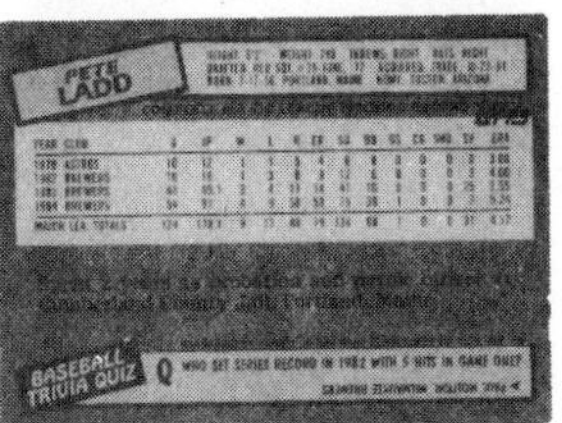

Gardner's Bakery issued a 22-card set featuring the Milwaukee Brewers for the third consecutive year in 1985. The set was produced by Topps and is designed in a horizontal format. The card fronts feature color photos inside blue, red and yellow frames. The player's name and position are placed in orange boxes to the right of the photo and are accompanied by the Brewers and Gardner's logos. The card backs are identical in design to the regular 1985 Topps set but are blue rather than green and are numbered 1- 22. The cards, which were inserted in specially marked bread products, are often found with grease stains.

		MT	NR MT	EX
Complete Set:		15.00	11.00	6.00
Common Player:		.35	.25	.14
1	George Bamberger	.35	.25	.14
2	Mark Brouhard	.35	.25	.14
3	Bob Clark	.35	.25	.14
4	Jaime Cocanower	.35	.25	.14
5	Cecil Cooper	.90	.70	.35
6	Rollie Fingers	1.25	.90	.50
7	Jim Gantner	.50	.40	.20
8	Moose Haas	.35	.25	.14
9	Dion James	.70	.50	.30
10	Pete Ladd	.35	.25	.14
11	Rick Manning	.35	.25	.14
12	Bob McClure	.35	.25	.14
13	Paul Molitor	1.50	1.25	.60
14	Charlie Moore	.35	.25	.14
15	Ben Oglivie	.50	.40	.20
16	Chuck Porter	.35	.25	.14
17	Ed Romero	.35	.25	.14
18	Bill Schroeder	.35	.25	.14
19	Ted Simmons	.70	.50	.30
20	Tom Tellmann	.35	.25	.14
21	Pete Vuckovich	.50	.40	.20
22	Robin Yount	4.00	3.00	1.50

1989 Gardners Brewers

Returning after a three-year hiatus, Gardner's Bread of Madison, Wis., issued a 15-card Milwaukee Brewers set in 1989. The blue and white-bordered cards are the standard size and feature posed portrait photos with all Brewer logos airbrushed from the players' caps. The Gardner's logo appears at the top of the card, while the player's name is below the photo. The set, which was produced in conjunction with Mike Schechter Associates, was issued with loaves of bread or packages of buns, one card per package.

		MT	NR MT	EX
Complete Set:		5.00	3.75	2.00
Common Player:		.10	.08	.04
1	Paul Molitor	1.00	.70	.40
2	Robin Yount	1.25	.90	.50
3	Jim Gantner	.25	.20	.10
4	Rob Deer	.25	.20	.10
5	B.J. Surhoff	.25	.20	.10
6	Dale Sveum	.20	.15	.08
7	Ted Higuera	.25	.20	.10
8	Dan Plesac	.25	.20	.10
9	Bill Wegman	.15	.11	.06
10	Juan Nieves	.15	.11	.06
11	Greg Brock	.20	.15	.08
12	Glenn Braggs	.25	.20	.10
13	Joey Meyer	.15	.11	.06
14	Ernest Riles	.10	.08	.04
15	Don August	.15	.11	.06

1986 Gatorade Cubs

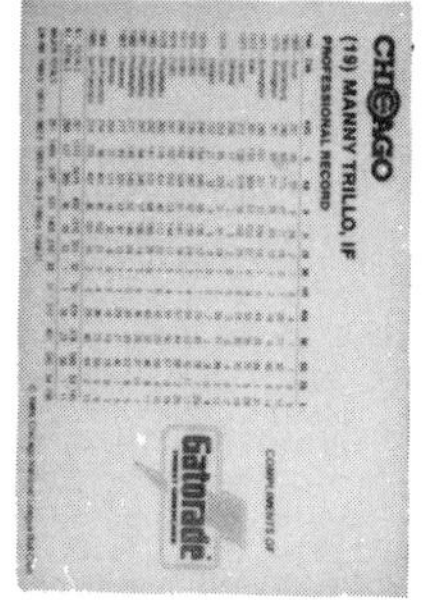

Gatorade sponsored this 28-card set which was given away at the July 17, 1986 Cubs game. The cards measure 2-7/8" by 4-1/4" and feature color photos set inside red and white frames. The Cubs logo appears at the top of the card in blue and red. The card backs include statistical information and the Gatorade logo. This set marked the fifth consecutive year the Cubs had held a baseball card giveaway promotion.

		MT	NR MT	EX
Complete Set:		9.00	6.75	3.50
Common Player:		.10	.08	.04
4	Gene Michael	.10	.08	.04
6	Keith Moreland	.30	.25	.12
7	Jody Davis	.30	.25	.12
10	Leon Durham	.30	.25	.12
11	Ron Cey	.30	.25	.12
12	Shawon Dunston	.80	.60	.30
15	Davey Lopes	.25	.20	.10
16	Terry Francona	.10	.08	.04
18	Steve Christmas	.10	.08	.04
19	Manny Trillo	.15	.11	.06
20	Bob Dernier	.10	.08	.04
21	Scott Sanderson	.10	.08	.04
22	Jerry Mumphrey	.10	.08	.04
23	Ryne Sandberg	2.00	1.50	.80
27	Thad Bosley	.10	.08	.04
28	Chris Speier	.10	.08	.04
29	Steve Lake	.10	.08	.04
31	Ray Fontenot	.10	.08	.04
34	Steve Trout	.20	.15	.08
36	Gary Matthews	.30	.25	.12
39	George Frazier	.10	.08	.04
40	Rick Sutcliffe	.70	.50	.30
43	Dennis Eckersley	.40	.30	.15
46	Lee Smith	.35	.25	.14
48	Jay Baller	.15	.11	.06
49	Jamie Moyer	.35	.25	.14
50	Guy Hoffman	.10	.08	.04
---	The Coaching Staff (Ruben Amaro, Billy Connors, Johnny Oates, John Vuckovich, Billy Williams)	.15	.11	.06

1987 Gatorade Indians

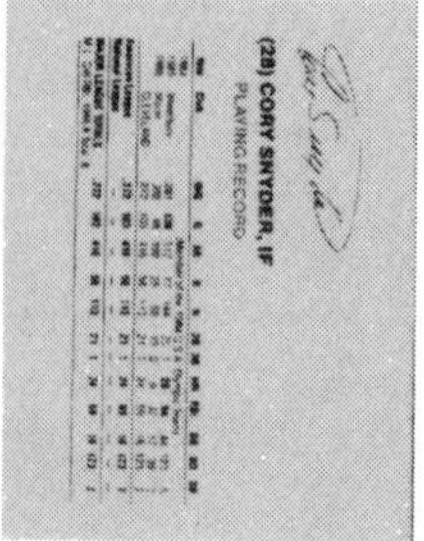

For the second year in a row, the Cleveland Indians gave out a perforated set of baseball cards to fans attending the Team Photo/Baseball Card Day promotion. Sponsored by Gatorade, the individual cards measure 2-1/2" by 3-1/8". The fronts contain a full-color photo surrounded by a red frame inside a white border. The player's name, uniform number and the Gatorade logo are also on the fronts. The card backs are printed in black, blue and red and carry a facsimile autograph and the player's playing record.

		MT	NR MT	EX
Complete Set:		8.00	5.00	2.50
Common Player:		.10	.05	.02
2	Brett Butler	.20	.25	.12
4	Tony Bernazard	.10	.09	.05
6	Andy Allanson	.15	.09	.05
7	Pat Corrales	.10	.09	.05
8	Carmen Castillo	.10	.05	.02
10	Pat Tabler	.20	.20	.10
11	Jamie Easterly	.10	.05	.02
12	Dave Clark	.20	.15	.08
13	Ernie Camacho	.10	.05	.02
14	Julio Franco	.40	.30	.15
17	Junior Noboa	.10	.15	.08
18	Ken Schrom	.10	.08	.04
20	Otis Nixon	.15	.05	.02
21	Greg Swindell	.80	.45	.25
22	Frank Wills	.10	.05	.02
23	Chris Bando	.10	.05	.02
24	Rick Dempsey	.15	.09	.05
26	Brook Jacoby	.60	.30	.15
27	Mel Hall	.30	.25	.12
28	Cory Snyder	.90	.70	.35
29	Andre Thornton	.30	.25	.12
30	Joe Carter	.80	.45	.25
35	Phil Niekro	.40	.30	.15
36	Ed Vande Berg	.10	.05	.02
42	Rich Yett	.10	.05	.02
43	Scott Bailes	.40	.30	.15
46	Doug Jones	.40	.15	.08
49	Tom Candiotti	.20	.09	.05
54	Tom Waddell	.10	.05	.02
---	Manager and Coaching Staff (Jack Aker, Bobby Bonds, Pat Corrales, Doc Edwards, Johnny Goryl)	.10	.05	.02

NOTE: A card number in parentheses () indicates the card set is unnumbered.

1988 Gatorade Indians

This 3-panel foldout was sponsored by Gatorade for distribution during an in-stadium giveaway. The white cover includes four game day photos. One panel of the 9-1/2" by 11-1/4" glossy full-color brochure features a team photo (with checklist), two panels consist of 30 perforated baseball cards (2-1/4" by 3") featuring team members. Posed close-up photos are framed in red on a white background. The player's name and uniform number are printed below the photo. The card backs are printed in red, blue and black on white. A facsimile autograph appears at the top right portion of the card back, opposite the player uniform number, name and position. Both major and minor league stats are listed.

		MT	NR MT	EX
Complete Set:		8.00	6.00	3.25
Common Player:		.10	.08	.04
2	Tom Spencer	.10	.08	.04
6	Andy Allanson	.15	.11	.06
7	Luis Issac	.10	.08	.04
8	Carmen Castillo	.10	.08	.04
9	Charlie Manuel	.10	.08	.04
10	Pat Tabler	.20	.15	.08
11	Doug Jones	.30	.25	.12
14	Julio Franco	.40	.30	.15
15	Ron Washington	.10	.08	.04
16	Jay Bell	.20	.15	.08
17	Bill Laskey	.10	.08	.04
20	Willie Upshaw	.20	.15	.08
21	Greg Swindell	.80	.60	.30
23	Chris Bando	.10	.08	.04
25	Dave Clark	.15	.11	.06
26	Brook Jacoby	.60	.45	.25
27	Mel Hall	.30	.25	.12
28	Cory Snyder	.80	.60	.30
30	Joe Carter	.80	.60	.30
31	Dan Schatzeder	.10	.08	.04
32	Doc Edwards	.10	.08	.04
33	Ron Kittle	.25	.20	.10
35	Mark Wiley	.10	.08	.04
42	Rich Yett	.10	.08	.04
43	Scott Bailes	.20	.15	.08
45	Johnny Goryl	.10	.08	.04
47	Jeff Kaiser	.10	.08	.04
49	Tom Candiotti	.20	.15	.08
50	Jeff Dedmon	.10	.08	.04
52	John Farrell	.40	.30	.15

1985 General Mills Stickers

General Mills of Canada inserted a panel of two baseball stickers, in a cellophane wrapper, in each box of Cheerios in 1985. The full-color sticker panels, which measure 2-3/8" by 3-3/4" in size, feature 30 popular players. The stickers are blank-backed and unnumbered and contain the player's name, team and position in both English and French. The General Mills logo appears at the top of each sticker. Curiously, all team insignias on the players' uniforms and hats have been airbrushed off.

	MT	NR MT	EX
Complete Set:	15.00	11.00	6.00
Common Panel:	.60	.45	.25
Panel	.80	.60	.30
(1) Gary Carter			
(2) Tom Brunansky			
Panel	.80	.60	.30
(3) Gary Carter			
(4) Dave Stieb			
Panel	1.00	.70	.40
(5) Andre Dawson			
(6) Alvin Davis			
Panel	1.25	.90	.50
(7) Steve Garvey			
(8) George Bell			
Panel	1.00	.70	.40
(9) Steve Garvey			
(10) Jim Rice			
Panel	.80	.60	.30
(11) Jeff Leonard			
(12) Eddie Murray			
Panel	1.50	1.25	.60
(13) Dale Murphy			
(14) Robin Yount			
Panel	.90	.70	.35
(15) Terry Puhl			
(16) Reggie Jackson			
Panel	.60	.45	.25
(17) Johnny Ray			
(18) Lou Whitaker			
Panel	.80	.60	.30
(19) Ryne Sandberg			
(20) Mike Hargrove			
Panel	1.75	1.25	.70
(21) Mike Schmidt			
(22) George Brett			
Panel	1.00	.70	.40
(23) Ozzie Smith			
(24) Dave Winfield			

	MT	NR MT	EX
Panel	.60	.45	.25
(25) Mario Soto			
(26) Carlton Fisk			
Panel	.70	.50	.30
(27) Fernando Valenzuela			
(28) Dwayne Murphy			

1986 General Mills Booklets

In 1986, General Mills of Canada inserted six different "Baseball Players Booklets" in specially marked boxes of Cheerios. Ten different players are featured in each booklet, with statistics for the 1985 season being in both English and French. The booklet, when opened fully, measures 3-3/4" by 15". Also included in the booklet is a contest sponsored by Petro-Canada service stations to win a day with a major league player at his 1987 spring training site in Florida. Team insignias have been airbrushed off the players' uniforms and caps.

	MT	NR MT	EX
Complete Set:	15.00	11.00	6.00
Common Booklet:	1.25	.90	.50
1 A.L. East (Wade Boggs, Kirk Gibson, Rickey Henderson, Don Mattingly, Jack Morris, Lance Parrish, Jim Rice, Dave Righetti, Cal Ripken, Lou Whitaker)	3.75	2.75	1.50
2 A.L. West (Harold Baines, Phil Bradley, George Brett, Carlton Fisk, Ozzie Guillen, Kent Hrbek, Reggie Jackson, Dan Quisenberry, Bret Saberhagen, Frank White)	2.00	1.50	.80
3 Toronto Blue Jays (Jesse Barfield, George Bell, Bill Caudill, Tony Fernandez, Damaso Garcia, Lloyd Moseby, Rance Mulliniks, Dave Stieb, Willie Upshaw, Ernie Whitt)	1.75	1.25	.70
4 N.L. East (Gary Carter, Jack Clark, George Foster, Dwight Gooden, Gary Matthews, Willie McGee, Ryne Sandberg, Mike Schmidt, Lee Smith, Ozzie Smith)	3.25	2.50	1.25
5 N.L. West (Dave Concepcion, Pedro Guerrero, Terry Kennedy, Dale Murphy, Graig Nettles, Dave Parker, Tony Perez, Steve Sax, Bruce Sutter, Fernando Valenzuela)	2.00	1.50	.80
6 Montreal Expos (Hubie Brooks, Andre Dawson, Mike Fitzgerald, Vance Law, Tim Raines, Jeff Reardon, Bryn Smith, Jason Thompson, Tim Wallach, Mitch Webster)	1.25	.90	.50

1987 General Mills Booklets

For a second straight year, General Mills of Canada inserted one of six different "Baseball Super-Stars Booklets" in specially marked boxes of Cheerios and Honey Nut Cheerios cereal. Each booklet contains ten full-color photos for a total of 60 players. The booklets, when completely unfolded, measure 15" by 3-3/4". Written in both English and French, the set was produced by Mike Schecter and Associates. All team insignias have been airbrushed away.

	MT	NR MT	EX
Complete Set:	15.00	11.00	6.00
Common Booklet:	1.25	.90	.50
1 Toronto Blue Jays (Jesse Barfield, George Bell, Tony Fernandez, Kelly Gruber, Tom Henke, Jimmy Key, Lloyd Moseby, Dave Stieb, Willie Upshaw, Ernie Whitt)	1.75	1.25	.70
2 A.L. East (Wade Boggs, Roger Clemens, Kirk Gibson, Rickey Henderson, Don Mattingly, Jack Morris, Eddie Murray, Pat Tabler, Dave Winfield, Robin Yount)	3.75	2.75	1.50
3 A.L. West (Phil Bradley, George Brett, Jose Canseco, Carlton Fisk, Reggie Jackson, Wally Joyner, Kirk McCaskill, Larry Parrish, Kirby Puckett, Dan Quisenberry)	3.50	2.75	1.50
4 Montreal Expos (Hubie Brooks, Mike Fitzgerald, Andres Galarraga, Vance Law, Andy McGaffigan, Bryn Smith, Jason Thompson, Tim Wallach, Mitch Webster, Floyd Youmans)	1.25	.90	.50
5 N.L. East (Gary Carter, Dwight Gooden, Keith Hernandez, Willie McGee, Tim Raines, R.J. Reynolds, Ryne Sandberg, Mike Schmidt, Ozzie Smith, Darryl Strawberry)	3.25	2.50	1.25
6 N.L. West (Kevin Bass, Chili Davis, Bill Doran, Pedro Guerrero, Tony Gwynn, Dale Murphy, Dave Parker, Steve Sax, Mike Scott, Fernando Valenzuela)	3.00	2.25	1.25

1933 George C. Miller

Charles Ruffing, Pitcher

The George C. Miller & Co. of Boston, Mass. issued a 32-card set in 1933. The set, which received limited distribution, consists of 16 National League and 16 American League players. The cards are color art reproductions of actual photographs and measure 2-3/8" by 2-7/8" in size. Two distinct variations can be found for each card in the set. Two different typefaces were used, one being much smaller than the other. The most substantial difference is "R" and "L" being used for the "Bats/Throws" information on one version, while the other spells out "Right" and "Left." Collectors were advised on the card backs to collect all 32 cards and return them for prizes. The cards, with a cancellation at the bottom, were returned to the collector with the prize. Two forms of cancellation were used; one involved the complete trimming of the bottom one-quarter of the card, the other a series of diamond-shaped punch holes. Cancelled cards have a significantly decreased value.

	NR MT	EX	VG
Complete Set:	14500.	7250.	4350.
Common Player:	250.00	125.00	75.00
(1) Dale Alexander	250.00	125.00	75.00
(2) "Ivy" Paul Andrews	2500.	1250.	750.00
(3) Earl Averill	400.00	200.00	120.00
(4) Dick Bartell	250.00	125.00	75.00
(5) Walter Berger	250.00	125.00	75.00
(6) Jim Bottomley	400.00	200.00	120.00
(7) Joe Cronin	500.00	250.00	150.00
(8) Jerome "Dizzy" Dean	800.00	400.00	240.00
(9) William Dickey	600.00	300.00	180.00
(10) Jimmy Dykes	250.00	125.00	75.00
(11) Wesley Ferrell	250.00	125.00	75.00
(12) Jimmy Foxx	600.00	300.00	180.00
(13) Frank Frisch	450.00	225.00	135.00
(14) Charlie Gehringer	450.00	225.00	135.00
(15) Leon "Goose" Goslin	400.00	200.00	120.00
(16) Charlie Grimm	250.00	125.00	75.00
(17) Bob "Lefty" Grove	500.00	250.00	150.00
(18) Charles "Chick" Hafey	400.00	200.00	120.00
(19) Ray Hayworth	250.00	125.00	75.00
(20) Charles "Chuck" Klein	400.00	200.00	120.00
(21) Walter "Rabbit" Maranville	400.00	200.00	120.00
(22) Oscar Melillo	250.00	125.00	75.00
(23) Frank "Lefty" O'Doul	250.00	125.00	75.00
(24) Melvin Ott	500.00	250.00	150.00
(25) Carl Reynolds	250.00	125.00	75.00
(26) Charles Ruffing	400.00	200.00	120.00
(27) Al Simmons	400.00	200.00	120.00
(28) Joe Stripp	250.00	125.00	75.00
(29) Bill Terry	450.00	225.00	135.00
(30) Lloyd Waner	400.00	200.00	120.00
(31) Paul Waner	400.00	200.00	120.00
(32) Lonnie Warneke	250.00	125.00	75.00

A player's name in *italic* type indicates a rookie card. An (FC) indicates a player's first card for that particular card company.

1928 George Ruth Candy Co.

When you have a complete set of 6 (six) Pictures Nos. 1, 2, 3, 4, 5 and 6, send them to The Geo. H. Ruth Candy Co., Cleveland, Ohio, and you will receive a Baseball with Babe Ruth's genuine signature on it FREE OF CHARGE.

This obscure six-card set, issued circa 1928, features sepia-toned photos of Babe Ruth, and, according to the back of the cards, was actually issued by the Geo. H. Ruth Candy Co. The cards measure 1-7/8" by 4" and picture Ruth during a 1924 promotional West Coast tour and in scenes from the movie "Babe Comes Home." The cards are numbered and include photo captions at the bottom. The backs of the card contain an offer to exchange the six cards for an autographed baseball, which may explain their scarcity today.

	NR MT	EX	VG
Complete Set:	4500.	2250.	1350.
Common Player:	750.00	375.00	225.00
1 "Babe" Ruth (King of them all. Home Run Candy Bar. His Candy Helped Him.)	750.00	375.00	225.00
2 "Babe" Ruth (Knocked out 60 Home Runs in 1927. His Candy Helped Him.)	750.00	375.00	225.00
3 "Babe" Ruth (The only player who broke his own record. His Candy Helped Him.)	750.00	375.00	225.00
4 "Babe" Ruth (The Popular Bambino eating his Home Run Candy. His Candy Helped Him.)	750.00	375.00	225.00
5 "Babe" Ruth (A favorite with the Kiddies. Babe Ruth's Own Candy.)	750.00	375.00	225.00
6 "Babe" Ruth (The King of Swat. Babe Ruth's Own Candy.)	750.00	375.00	225.00

1953 Glendale Hot Dogs Tigers

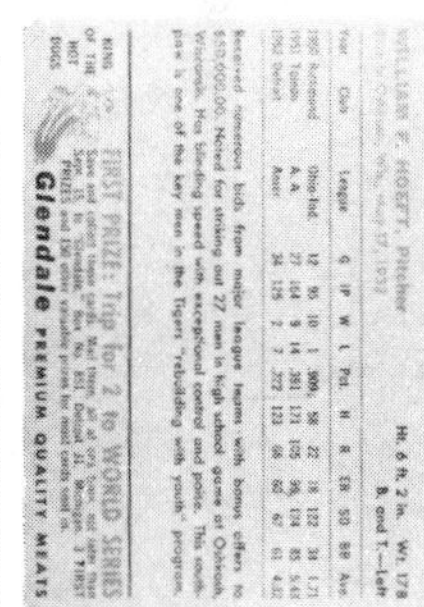

Glendale Meats issued these unnumbered, full-color cards (2-5/8" by 3-3/4") in packages of hot dogs. Featuring Detroit Tigers players, the card fronts contain a player picture plus the player's name, a facsimile autograph, and the Tigers logo. The card reverses carry player statistical and biographical information plus an offer for a trip for two to the World Series. Collectors were advised to mail all the cards they had saved to Glendale Meats. The World Series trip plus 150 other prizes were to be given to the individuals sending in the most cards. As with most cards issued with food products, quality- condition cards are tough to find because of the cards' susceptibilty to stains. The Houtteman card is extremely scarce.

	NR MT	EX	VG
Complete Set:	5300.	2650.	1590.
Common Player:	100.00	50.00	30.00
(1) Matt Batts	100.00	50.00	30.00
(2) Johnny Bucha	100.00	50.00	30.00
(3) Frank Carswell	100.00	50.00	30.00

		NR MT	EX	VG
(4)	Jim Delsing	100.00	50.00	30.00
(5)	Walt Dropo	100.00	50.00	30.00
(6)	Hal Erickson	100.00	50.00	30.00
(7)	Paul Foytack	100.00	50.00	30.00
(8)	Owen Friend	125.00	62.00	37.00
(9)	Ned Garver	100.00	50.00	30.00
(10)	Joe Ginsberg	350.00	175.00	105.00
(11)	Ted Gray	100.00	50.00	30.00
(12)	Fred Hatfield	100.00	50.00	30.00
(13)	Ray Herbert	125.00	62.00	37.00
(14)	Bill Hitchcock	100.00	50.00	30.00
(15)	Bill Hoeft	275.00	137.00	82.00
(16)	Art Houtteman	2000.	1000.	600.00
(17)	Milt Jordan	200.00	100.00	60.00
(18)	Harvey Kuenn	225.00	112.00	67.00
(19)	Don Lund	100.00	50.00	30.00
(20)	Dave Madison	100.00	50.00	30.00
(21)	Dick Marlowe	100.00	50.00	30.00
(22)	Pat Mullin	100.00	50.00	30.00
(23)	Bob Neiman	100.00	50.00	30.00
(24)	Johnny Pesky	125.00	62.00	37.00
(25)	Jerry Priddy	100.00	50.00	30.00
(26)	Steve Souchock	100.00	50.00	30.00
(27)	Russ Sullivan	100.00	50.00	30.00
(28)	Bill Wight	200.00	100.00	60.00

1934 Gold Medal Flour

This set of 12 unnumbered, blank-backed cards was issued by Gold Medal Flour to commemorate the 1934 World Series. The cards, which measure 3-1/4" by 5-3/8", feature members of the Detroit Tigers and the St. Louis Cardinals, who were participants in the '34 World Series.

		NR MT	EX	VG
Complete Set:		400.00	200.00	120.00
Common Player:		20.00	10.00	6.00
(1)	Tommy Bridges	20.00	10.00	6.00
(2)	Mickey Cochrane	40.00	20.00	12.00
(3)	Dizzy Dean	80.00	40.00	25.00
(4)	Paul Dean	25.00	12.50	7.50
(5)	Frank Frisch	40.00	20.00	12.00
(6)	"Goose" Goslin	40.00	20.00	12.00
(7)	William Hallahan	20.00	10.00	6.00
(8)	Fred Marberry	20.00	10.00	6.00
(9)	John "Pepper" Martin	25.00	12.50	7.50
(10)	Joe Medwick	40.00	20.00	12.00
(11)	William Rogell	20.00	10.00	6.00
(12)	"Jo Jo" White	20.00	10.00	6.00

1961 Golden Press

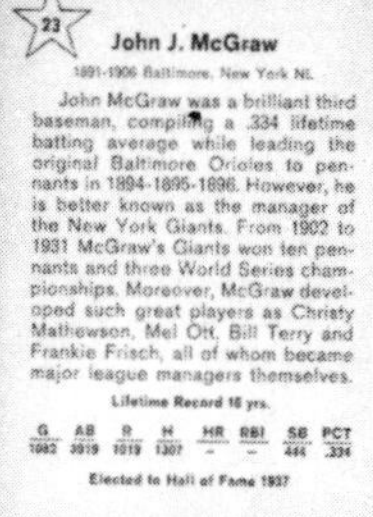

The 1961 Golden Press set features 33 players, all enshrined in the Baseball Hall of Fame. The full color cards measure 2-1/2" by 3-1/2" and came in a booklet with perforations so that they could be easily removed. Full books with the cards intact would command 50 percent over the set price in the checklist that follows. Card numbers 1-3 and 28-33 are slightly higher in price as they were located on the book's front and back covers, making them more susceptible to scuffing and wear.

		NR MT	EX	VG
Complete Set:		65.00	33.00	20.00
Common Player:		.50	.25	.15
1	Mel Ott	1.50	.70	.45
2	Grover Cleveland Alexander	1.50	.70	.45
3	Babe Ruth	18.00	9.00	5.50
4	Hank Greenberg	1.25	.60	.40
5	Bill Terry	.75	.40	.25
6	Carl Hubbell	.75	.40	.25
7	Rogers Hornsby	1.75	.90	.50
8	Dizzy Dean	5.00	2.50	1.50
9	Joe DiMaggio	12.00	6.00	3.50
10	Charlie Gehringer	.75	.40	.25
11	Gabby Hartnett	.50	.25	.15
12	Mickey Cochrane	.75	.40	.25
13	George Sisler	.75	.40	.25
14	Joe Cronin	.75	.40	.25
15	Pie Traynor	.50	.25	.15
16	Lou Gehrig	12.00	6.00	3.50
17	Lefty Grove	.90	.45	.25
18	Chief Bender	.50	.25	.15
19	Frankie Frisch	.75	.40	.25
20	Al Simmons	.50	.25	.15
21	Home Run Baker	.50	.25	.15
22	Jimmy Foxx	1.75	.90	.50
23	John McGraw	.90	.45	.25
24	Christy Mathewson	2.50	1.25	.70
25	Ty Cobb	12.00	6.00	3.50
26	Dazzy Vance	.50	.25	.15
27	Bill Dickey	.90	.45	.25
28	Eddie Collins	.75	.40	.25
29	Walter Johnson	3.00	1.50	.90
30	Tris Speaker	1.50	.70	.45
31	Nap Lajoie	1.50	.70	.45
32	Honus Wagner	3.00	1.50	.90
33	Cy Young	3.00	1.50	.90

1933 Goudey

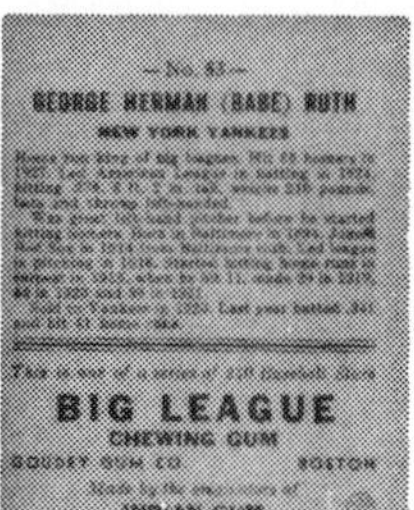

Goudey Gum Co.'s first baseball card issue was their 240-card effort in 1933. The cards are color art reproductions of either portrait or action photos. The numbered cards measure 2-3/8" by 2-7/8" in size and carry a short player biography on the reverses. Card #106 (Napoleon Lajoie) is listed in the set though it was not actually issued until 1934. The card is very scarce and is unique in that it carries a 1934 design obverse and a 1933 reverse. The ACC designation for the set is R319.

		NR MT	EX	VG
Complete Set w/o Lajoie:		80000.	40000.	25000.
Common Player: 1-40		150.00	75.00	45.00
Common Player: 41-44		75.00	37.00	22.00
Common Player: 45-52		150.00	75.00	45.00
Common Player: 53-240		75.00	37.00	22.00
1	Benny Bengough	8500.	1750.	1050.
2	Arthur (Dazzy) Vance	750.00	250.00	75.00
3	Hugh Critz	150.00	75.00	45.00
4	Henry "Heinie" Schuble	150.00	75.00	45.00
5	Floyd (Babe) Herman	200.00	80.00	35.00
6a	Jimmy Dykes (age is 26 in bio)	200.00	80.00	35.00
6b	Jimmy Dykes (age is 36 in bio)	200.00	80.00	35.00
7	Ted Lyons	350.00	175.00	75.00
8	Roy Johnson	150.00	75.00	45.00
9	Dave Harris	150.00	75.00	45.00
10	Glenn Myatt	150.00	75.00	45.00
11	Billy Rogell	150.00	75.00	45.00
12	George Pipgras	175.00	75.00	30.00
13	Lafayette Thompson	150.00	75.00	25.00
14	Henry Johnson	150.00	75.00	45.00
15	Victor Sorrell	150.00	75.00	45.00
16	George Blaeholder	150.00	75.00	45.00
17	Watson Clark	150.00	75.00	45.00
18	Herold (Muddy) Ruel	150.00	75.00	45.00
19	Bill Dickey	750.00	300.00	100.00
20	Bill Terry	425.00	200.00	75.00
21	Phil Collins	150.00	75.00	45.00
22	Harold (Pie) Traynor	500.00	250.00	100.00
23	Hazen (Ki-Ki) Cuyler	550.00	250.00	100.00
24	Horace Ford	150.00	75.00	45.00
25	Paul Waner	600.00	300.00	100.00
26	Chalmer Cissell	150.00	75.00	45.00
27	George Connally	150.00	75.00	45.00
28	Dick Bartell	200.00	75.00	45.00
29	Jimmy Foxx	1000.	500.00	150.00
30	Frank Hogan	150.00	75.00	45.00
31	Tony Lazzeri	350.00	150.00	50.00
32	John (Bud) Clancy	150.00	75.00	45.00
33	Ralph Kress	150.00	75.00	45.00
34	Bob O'Farrell	150.00	75.00	45.00
35	Al Simmons	500.00	225.00	90.00
36	Tommy Thevenow	150.00	75.00	45.00
37	Jimmy Wilson	150.00	75.00	45.00
38	Fred Brickell	150.00	75.00	45.00
39	Mark Koenig	150.00	75.00	45.00

		NR MT	EX	VG
40	Taylor Douthit	150.00	75.00	45.00
41	Gus Mancuso	75.00	37.00	22.00
42	Eddie Collins	275.00	125.00	50.00
43	Lew Fonseca	85.00	40.00	20.00
44	Jim Bottomley	255.00	110.00	35.00
45	Larry Benton	150.00	75.00	45.00
46	Ethan Allen	150.00	75.00	45.00
47	Henry "Heinie" Manush	350.00	150.00	50.00
48	Marty McManus	150.00	75.00	45.00
49	Frank Frisch	500.00	225.00	90.00
50	Ed Brandt	150.00	75.00	45.00
51	Charlie Grimm	200.00	100.00	30.00
52	Andy Cohen	150.00	75.00	45.00
53	George Herman (Babe) Ruth	5200.	2000.	1200.
54	Ray Kremer	75.00	37.00	22.00
55	Perce (Pat) Malone	75.00	37.00	22.00
56	Charlie Ruffing	350.00	150.00	45.00
57	Earl Clark	75.00	37.00	22.00
58	Frank (Lefty) O'Doul	100.00	50.00	22.00
59	Edmund (Bing) Miller	75.00	37.00	22.00
60	Waite Hoyt	300.00	150.00	45.00
61	Max Bishop	75.00	37.00	22.00
62	"Pepper" Martin	125.00	60.00	22.00
63	Joe Cronin	275.00	125.00	50.00
64	Burleigh Grimes	300.00	150.00	50.00
65	Milton Gaston	75.00	37.00	22.00
66	George Grantham	75.00	37.00	22.00
67	Guy Bush	75.00	37.00	22.00
68	Horace Lisenbee	75.00	37.00	22.00
69	Randy Moore	75.00	37.00	22.00
70	Floyd (Pete) Scott	75.00	37.00	22.00
71	Robert J. Burke	75.00	37.00	22.00
72	Owen Carroll	75.00	37.00	22.00
73	Jesse Haines	250.00	125.00	45.00
74	Eppa Rixey	250.00	125.00	45.00
75	Willie Kamm	75.00	37.00	22.00
76	Gordon (Mickey) Cochrane	375.00	150.00	60.00
77	Adam Comorosky	75.00	37.00	22.00
78	Jack Quinn	75.00	37.00	22.00
79	Urban (Red) Faber	250.00	125.00	45.00
80	Clyde Manion	75.00	37.00	22.00
81	Sam Jones	85.00	40.00	25.00
82	Dibrell Williams	75.00	37.00	22.00
83	Pete Jablonowski	150.00	75.00	45.00
84	Glenn Spencer	75.00	37.00	22.00
85	John Henry "Heinie" Sand	75.00	37.00	22.00
86	Phil Todt	75.00	37.00	22.00
87	Frank O'Rourke	75.00	37.00	22.00
88	Russell Rollings	75.00	37.00	22.00
89	Tris Speaker	400.00	200.00	70.00
90	Jess Petty	75.00	37.00	22.00
91	Tom Zachary	75.00	37.00	22.00
92	Lou Gehrig	3500.	1500.	1000.
93	John Welch	75.00	37.00	22.00
94	Bill Walker	75.00	37.00	22.00
95	Alvin Crowder	75.00	37.00	22.00
96	Willis Hudlin	75.00	37.00	22.00
97	Joe Morrissey	75.00	37.00	22.00
98	Walter Berger	75.00	37.00	22.00
99	Tony Cuccinello	75.00	37.00	22.00
100	George Uhle	90.00	45.00	22.00
101	Richard Coffman	75.00	37.00	22.00
102	Travis C. Jackson	250.00	125.00	45.00
103	Earl Combs (Earle)	275.00	130.00	45.00
104	Fred Marberry	75.00	37.00	22.00
105	Bernie Friberg	75.00	37.00	22.00
106	Napoleon (Larry) Lajoie	30000.	13500.	7500.
107	Henry (Heinie) Manush	275.00	125.00	45.00
108	Joe Kuhel	75.00	37.00	22.00
109	Joe Cronin	250.00	125.00	45.00
110	Leon "Goose" Goslin	275.00	130.00	45.00
111	Monte Weaver	75.00	37.00	22.00
112	Fred Schulte	75.00	37.00	22.00
113	Oswald Bluege	75.00	37.00	22.00
114	Luke Sewell	75.00	37.00	22.00
115	Cliff Heathcote	75.00	37.00	22.00
116	Eddie Morgan	75.00	37.00	22.00
117	Walter (Rabbit) Maranville	250.00	125.00	45.00
118	Valentine J. (Val) Picinich	75.00	37.00	22.00
119	Rogers Hornsby	650.00	300.00	100.00
120	Carl Reynolds	75.00	37.00	22.00
121	Walter Stewart	75.00	37.00	22.00
122	Alvin Crowder	75.00	37.00	22.00
123	Jack Russell	75.00	37.00	22.00
124	Earl Whitehill	75.00	37.00	22.00
125	Bill Terry	300.00	135.00	60.00
126	Joe Moore	75.00	37.00	22.00
127	Melvin Ott	400.00	175.00	60.00
128	Charles (Chuck) Klein	300.00	150.00	50.00
129	Harold Schumacher	90.00	40.00	20.00
130	Fred Fitzsimmons	75.00	37.00	22.00
131	Fred Frankhouse	75.00	37.00	22.00
132	Jim Elliott	75.00	37.00	22.00
133	Fred Lindstrom	250.00	125.00	45.00
134	Edgar (Sam) Rice	275.00	130.00	45.00
135	Elwood (Woody) English	75.00	37.00	22.00
136	Flint Rhem	75.00	37.00	22.00
137	Fred (Red) Lucas	75.00	37.00	22.00
138	Herb Pennock	275.00	125.00	45.00
139	Ben Cantwell	75.00	37.00	22.00
140	Irving (Bump) Hadley	75.00	37.00	22.00
141	Ray Benge	75.00	37.00	22.00
142	Paul Richards	125.00	60.00	25.00
143	Glenn Wright	85.00	40.00	22.00
144	George Herman (Babe) Ruth	4400.	1750.	1050.
145	George Walberg	75.00	37.00	22.00
146	Walter Stewart	75.00	37.00	22.00
147	Leo Durocher	200.00	90.00	45.00
148	Eddie Farrell	75.00	37.00	22.00
149	George Herman (Babe) Ruth	4500.	2000.	1200.
150	Ray Kolp	75.00	37.00	22.00
151	D'Arcy (Jake) Flowers	75.00	37.00	22.00
152	James (Zack) Taylor	75.00	37.00	22.00
153	Charles (Buddy) Myer	75.00	37.00	22.00
154	Jimmy Foxx	500.00	225.00	75.00
155	Joe Judge	75.00	37.00	22.00
156	Danny Macfayden (MacFayden)	100.00	50.00	27.00
157	Sam Byrd	100.00	50.00	27.00
158	Morris (Moe) Berg	85.00	40.00	22.00
159	Oswald Bluege	75.00	37.00	22.00
160	Lou Gehrig	3500.	1500.	800.00
161	Al Spohrer	75.00	37.00	22.00
162	Leo Mangum	75.00	37.00	22.00

		NR MT	EX	VG
163	Luke Sewell	75.00	37.00	22.00
164	Lloyd Waner	250.00	125.00	45.00
165	Joe Sewell	300.00	125.00	45.00
166	Sam West	75.00	37.00	22.00
167	Jack Russell	75.00	37.00	22.00
168	Leon (Goose) Goslin	300.00	150.00	45.00
169	Al Thomas	75.00	37.00	22.00
170	Harry McCurdy	75.00	37.00	22.00
171	Charley Jamieson	75.00	37.00	22.00
172	Billy Hargrave	75.00	37.00	22.00
173	Roscoe Holm	75.00	37.00	22.00
174	Warren (Curley) Ogden	75.00	37.00	22.00
175	Dan Howley	75.00	37.00	22.00
176	John Ogden	75.00	37.00	22.00
177	Walter French	75.00	37.00	22.00
178	Jackie Warner	75.00	37.00	22.00
179	Fred Leach	75.00	37.00	22.00
180	Eddie Moore	75.00	37.00	22.00
181	George Herman (Babe) Ruth	4500.	1850.	990.00
182	Andy High	75.00	37.00	22.00
183	George Walberg	75.00	37.00	22.00
184	Charley Berry	75.00	37.00	22.00
185	Bob Smith	75.00	37.00	22.00
186	John Schulte	75.00	37.00	22.00
187	Henry (Heinie) Manush	300.00	150.00	45.00
188	Rogers Hornsby	550.00	250.00	105.00
189	Joe Cronin	300.00	150.00	45.00
190	Fred Schulte	75.00	37.00	22.00
191	Ben Chapman	125.00	60.00	27.00
192	Walter Brown	125.00	60.00	27.00
193	Lynford Lary	125.00	60.00	27.00
194	Earl Averill	250.00	125.00	45.00
195	Evar Swanson	75.00	37.00	22.00
196	Leroy Mahaffey	75.00	37.00	22.00
197	Richard (Rick) Ferrell	225.00	110.00	45.00
198	Irving (Jack) Burns	75.00	37.00	22.00
199	Tom Bridges	80.00	40.00	22.00
200	Bill Hallahan	75.00	37.00	22.00
201	Ernie Orsatti	75.00	37.00	22.00
202	Charles Leo (Gabby) Hartnett	250.00	125.00	45.00
203	Lonnie Warneke	75.00	37.00	22.00
204	Jackson Riggs Stephenson	125.00	60.00	27.00
205	Henry (Heinie) Meine	75.00	37.00	22.00
206	Gus Suhr	75.00	37.00	22.00
207	Melvin Ott	400.00	200.00	45.00
208	Byrne (Bernie) James	75.00	37.00	22.00
209	Adolfo Luque	75.00	37.00	22.00
210	Virgil Davis	75.00	37.00	22.00
211	Lewis (Hack) Wilson	400.00	200.00	45.00
212	Billy Urbanski	75.00	37.00	22.00
213	Earl Adams	75.00	37.00	22.00
214	John Kerr	75.00	37.00	22.00
215	Russell Van Atta	90.00	45.00	27.00
216	Vernon Gomez	350.00	175.00	45.00
217	Frank Crosetti	250.00	125.00	45.00
218	Wesley Ferrell	100.00	50.00	22.00
219	George (Mule) Haas	75.00	37.00	22.00
220	Robert (Lefty) Grove	600.00	300.00	105.00
221	Dale Alexander	75.00	37.00	22.00
222	Charley Gehringer	350.00	175.00	67.00
223	Jerome (Dizzy) Dean	900.00	425.00	225.00
224	Frank Demaree	75.00	37.00	22.00
225	Bill Jurges	75.00	37.00	22.00
226	Charley Root	90.00	45.00	22.00
227	Bill Herman	275.00	125.00	45.00
228	Tony Piet	75.00	37.00	22.00
229	Floyd Vaughan	300.00	150.00	45.00
230	Carl Hubbell	350.00	175.00	67.00
231	Joe Moore	75.00	37.00	22.00
232	Frank (Lefty) O'Doul	90.00	45.00	22.00
233	Johnny Vergez	75.00	37.00	22.00
234	Carl Hubbell	325.00	150.00	67.00
235	Fred Fitzsimmons	75.00	37.00	22.00
236	George Davis	75.00	37.00	22.00
237	Gus Mancuso	75.00	37.00	22.00
238	Hugh Critz	75.00	37.00	22.00
239	Leroy Parmelee	150.00	75.00	27.00
240	Harold Schumacher	550.00	150.00	15.00

1934 Goudey

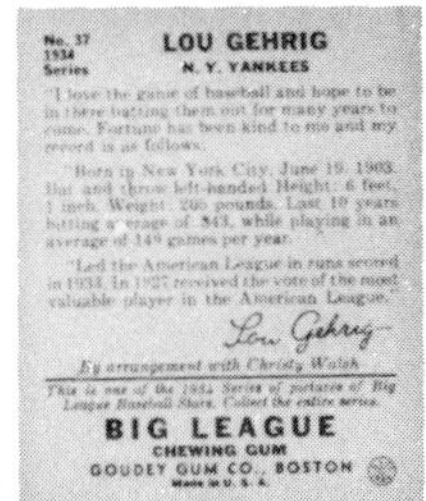

The 1934 Goudey set contains 96 cards (2-3/8" by 2-7/8") that feature color art reproductions of actual photographs. The card fronts have two different designs; one featuring a small head-shot photo of Lou Gehrig with the words "Lou Gehrig says..." inside a blue band, while the other design carries a "Chuck Klein says..." and also has his photo. The card backs contain a short player biography that appears to have been written by Gehrig or Klein. The ACC designation for the set is R320.

	NR MT	EX	VG
Complete Set:	25000.	12500.	7500.
Common Player:	75.00	37.00	22.00
Common Player: 49-72	90.00	45.00	27.00
Common Player: 73-96	275.00	137.00	82.00

		NR MT	EX	VG
1	Jimmy Foxx	1000.	250.00	125.00
2	Gordon (Mickey) Cochrane	250.00	125.00	75.00
3	Charlie Grimm	70.00	35.00	21.00
4	Elwood (Woody) English	75.00	37.00	22.00
5	Ed Brandt	75.00	37.00	22.00
6	Jerome (Dizzy) Dean	700.00	350.00	210.00
7	Leo Durocher	200.00	100.00	60.00
8	Tony Piet	75.00	37.00	22.00
9	Ben Chapman	90.00	45.00	27.00
10	Charles (Chuck) Klein	200.00	100.00	60.00
11	Paul Waner	200.00	100.00	60.00
12	Carl Hubbell	250.00	125.00	75.00
13	Frank Frisch	200.00	100.00	60.00
14	Willie Kamm	75.00	37.00	22.00
15	Alvin Crowder	75.00	37.00	22.00
16	Joe Kuhel	75.00	37.00	22.00
17	Hugh Critz	75.00	37.00	22.00
18	Henry (Heinie) Manush	200.00	100.00	60.00
19	Robert (Lefty) Grove	350.00	175.00	105.00
20	Frank Hogan	75.00	37.00	22.00
21	Bill Terry	250.00	125.00	75.00
22	Floyd Vaughan	200.00	100.00	60.00
23	Charley Gehringer	110.00	55.00	33.00
24	Ray Benge	75.00	37.00	22.00
25	Roger Cramer	75.00	37.00	22.00
26	Gerald Walker	75.00	37.00	22.00
27	Luke Appling	200.00	100.00	60.00
28	Ed. Coleman	75.00	37.00	22.00
29	Larry French	75.00	37.00	22.00
30	Julius Solters	75.00	37.00	22.00
31	Baxter Jordan	75.00	37.00	22.00
32	John (Blondy) Ryan	75.00	37.00	22.00
33	Frank (Don) Hurst	75.00	37.00	22.00
34	Charles (Chick) Hafey	200.00	100.00	60.00
35	Ernie Lombardi	200.00	100.00	60.00
36	Walter (Huck) Betts	75.00	37.00	22.00
37	Lou Gehrig	3100.	1550.	930.00
38	Oral Hildebrand	75.00	37.00	22.00
39	Fred Walker	75.00	37.00	22.00
40	John Stone	75.00	37.00	22.00
41	George Earnshaw	75.00	37.00	22.00
42	John Allen	90.00	45.00	27.00
43	Dick Porter	75.00	37.00	22.00
44	Tom Bridges	55.00	27.00	16.50
45	Oscar Melillo	75.00	37.00	22.00
46	Joe Stripp	75.00	37.00	22.00
47	John Frederick	75.00	37.00	22.00
48	James (Tex) Carleton	75.00	37.00	22.00
49	Sam Leslie	90.00	45.00	27.00
50	Walter Beck	90.00	45.00	27.00
51	Jim (Rip) Collins	90.00	45.00	27.00
52	Herman Bell	90.00	45.00	27.00
53	George Watkins	90.00	45.00	27.00
54	Wesley Schulmerich	90.00	45.00	27.00
55	Ed Holley	90.00	45.00	27.00
56	Mark Koenig	90.00	45.00	27.00
57	Bill Swift	90.00	45.00	27.00
58	Earl Grace	90.00	45.00	27.00
59	Joe Mowry	90.00	45.00	27.00
60	Lynn Nelson	90.00	45.00	27.00
61	Lou Gehrig	3100.	1550.	930.00
62	Henry Greenberg	350.00	175.00	105.00
63	Minter Hayes	90.00	45.00	27.00
64	Frank Grube	90.00	45.00	27.00
65	Cliff Bolton	90.00	45.00	27.00
66	Mel Harder	90.00	45.00	27.00
67	Bob Weiland	90.00	45.00	27.00
68	Bob Johnson	90.00	45.00	27.00
69	John Marcum	90.00	45.00	27.00
70	Ervin (Pete) Fox	90.00	45.00	27.00
71	Lyle Tinning	90.00	45.00	27.00
72	Arndt Jorgens	45.00	22.00	13.50
73	Ed Wells	275.00	137.00	82.00
74	Bob Boken	275.00	137.00	82.00
75	Bill Werber	275.00	137.00	82.00
76	Hal Trosky	275.00	137.00	82.00
77	Joe Vosmik	275.00	137.00	82.00
78	Frank (Pinkey) Higgins	275.00	137.00	82.00
79	Eddie Durham	275.00	137.00	82.00
80	Marty McManus	275.00	137.00	82.00
81	Bob Brown	275.00	137.00	82.00
82	Bill Hallahan	275.00	137.00	82.00
83	Jim Mooney	275.00	137.00	82.00
84	Paul Derringer	300.00	150.00	90.00
85	Adam Comorosky	275.00	137.00	82.00
86	Lloyd Johnson	275.00	137.00	82.00
87	George Darrow	275.00	137.00	82.00
88	Homer Peel	275.00	137.00	82.00
89	Linus Frey	275.00	137.00	82.00
90	Hazen (Ki-Ki) Cuyler	450.00	225.00	135.00
91	Dolph Camilli	275.00	137.00	82.00
92	Steve Larkin	275.00	137.00	82.00
93	Fred Ostermueller	275.00	137.00	82.00
94	Robert A. (Red) Rolfe	350.00	175.00	105.00
95	Myril Hoag	300.00	150.00	90.00
96	Jim DeShong	600.00	150.00	90.00

1935 Goudey

The 1935 Goudey set features four players from the same team on one card. Thirty-six card fronts make up the set with numerous front/back combinations existing. The card backs form nine different puzzles: 1) Tigers Team, 2) Chuck Klein, 3) Frankie Frisch, 4) Mickey Cochrane, 5) Joe Cronin, 6) Jimmy Foxx, 7) Al Simmons, 8) Indians Team, and 9) Senators Team. The cards, which measure 2-3/8" by 2-7/8", have an ACC designation of R321.

	NR MT	EX	VG
Complete Set:	5200.	2600.	1350.
Common Player:	70.00	35.00	21.00

		NR MT	EX	VG
(1)	Sparky Adams, Jim Bottomley, Adam Comorosky, Tony Piet	100.00	50.00	30.00
(2)	Ethan Allen, Fred Brickell, Bubber Jonnard, Hack Wilson	100.00	50.00	30.00
(3)	Johnny Allen, Jimmie Deshong (DeShong), Red Rolfe, Dixie Walker	70.00	35.00	21.00
(4)	Luke Appling, Jimmie Dykes, George Earnshaw, Luke Sewell	100.00	50.00	30.00
(5)	Earl Averill, Oral Hildebrand, Willie Kamm, Hal Trosky	100.00	50.00	30.00
(6)	Dick Bartell, Hughie Critz, Gus Mancuso, Mel Ott	70.00	35.00	21.00
(7)	Ray Benge, Fred Fitzsimmons, Mark Koenig, Tom Zachary	70.00	35.00	21.00
(8)	Larry Benton, Ben Cantwell, Flint Rhem, Al Spohrer	70.00	35.00	21.00
(9)	Charlie Berry, Bobby Burke, Red Kress, Dazzy Vance	100.00	50.00	30.00
(10)	Max Bishop, Bill Cissell, Joe Cronin, Carl Reynolds	125.00	62.00	37.00
(11)	George Blaeholder, Dick Coffman, Oscar Melillo, Sammy West	70.00	35.00	21.00
(12)	Cy Blanton, Babe Herman, Tom Padden, Gus Suhr	70.00	35.00	21.00
(13)	Zeke Bonura, Mule Haas, Jackie Hayes, Ted Lyons	100.00	50.00	30.00
(14)	Jim Bottomley, Adam Comorosky, Willis Hudlin, Glenn Myatt	100.00	50.00	30.00
(15)	Ed Brandt, Fred Frankhouse, Shanty Hogan, Gene Moore	70.00	35.00	21.00
(16)	Ed Brandt, Rabbit Maranville, Marty McManus, Babe Ruth	1200.	600.00	360.00
(17)	Tommy Bridges, Mickey Cochrane, Charlie Gehringer, Billy Rogell	175.00	87.00	52.00
(18)	Jack Burns, Frank Grube, Rollie Hemsley, Bob Weiland	70.00	35.00	21.00
(19)	Guy Bush, Waite Hoyt, Lloyd Waner, Paul Waner	150.00	75.00	45.00
(20)	Sammy Byrd, Danny MacFayden, Pepper Martin, Bob O'Farrell	70.00	35.00	21.00
(21)	Gilly Campbell, Ival Goodman, Alex Kampouris, Billy Meyers (Myers)	70.00	35.00	21.00
(22)	Tex Carleton, Dizzy Dean, Frankie Frisch, Ernie Orsatti	300.00	150.00	90.00
(23)	Watty Clark, Lonny Frey, Sam Leslie, Joe Stripp	70.00	35.00	21.00
(24)	Mickey Cochrane, Willie Kamm, Muddy Ruel, Al Simmons	150.00	75.00	45.00
(25)	Ed Coleman, Doc Cramer, Bob Johnson, Johnny Marcum	70.00	35.00	21.00
(26)	General Crowder, Goose Goslin, Firpo Marberry, Heinie Schuble	100.00	50.00	30.00
(27)	Kiki Cuyler, Woody English, Burleigh Grimes, Chuck Klein	70.00	35.00	21.00
(28)	Bill Dickey, Tony Lazzeri, Pat Malone, Red Ruffing	225.00	112.00	67.00
(29)	Rick Ferrell, Wes Ferrell, Fritz Ostermueller, Bill Werber	100.00	50.00	30.00
(30)	Pete Fox, Hank Greenberg, Schoolboy Rowe, Gee Walker	150.00	75.00	45.00
(31)	Jimmie Foxx, Pinky Higgins, Roy Mahaffey, Dib Williams	225.00	112.00	67.00
(32)	Bump Hadley, Lyn Lary, Heinie Manush, Monte Weaver	100.00	50.00	30.00
(33)	Mel Harder, Bill Knickerbocker, Lefty Stewart, Joe Vosmik	70.00	35.00	21.00
(34)	Travis Jackson, Gus Mancuso, Hal Schumacher, Bill Terry	175.00	87.00	52.00
(35)	Joe Kuhel, Buddy Meyer (Myer), John Stone, Earl Whitehill	70.00	35.00	21.00
(36)	Red Lucas, Tommy Thevenow, Pie Traynor, Glenn Wright	100.00	50.00	30.00

1936 Goudey

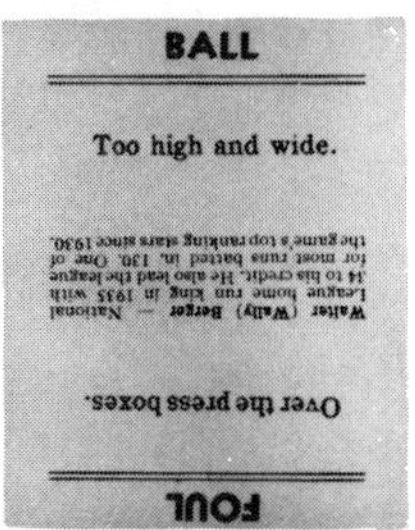

The 1936 Goudey set consists of 25 black and white cards, each measuring 2-3/8" by 2-7/8". A facsimile autograph is positioned on the card fronts. The card backs contain a brief player biography and were to be used by collectors to play a baseball game. Different game situations (out, single, double, etc.) are given on each card. Numerous front/back exist in the set. The ACC designation for the set is R322.

		NR MT	EX	VG
Complete Set:		2500.	1250.	750.00
Common Player:		50.00	25.00	15.00
(1)	Walter Berger	55.00	28.00	16.50
(2)	Henry Bonura	50.00	25.00	15.00
(3)	Stan Bordagaray	50.00	25.00	15.00
(4)	Bill Brubaker	50.00	25.00	15.00
(5)	Dolph Camilli	55.00	27.00	16.50
(6)	Clydell Castleman	50.00	25.00	15.00
(7)	"Mickey" Cochrane	200.00	100.00	60.00
(8)	Joe Coscarart	50.00	25.00	15.00
(9)	Frank Crosetti	100.00	50.00	30.00
(10)	"Kiki" Cuyler	125.00	62.00	37.00
(11)	Paul Derringer	55.00	27.00	16.50
(12)	Jimmy Dykes	55.00	27.00	16.50
(13)	"Rick" Ferrell	125.00	62.00	37.00
(14)	"Lefty" Gomez	250.00	125.00	75.00
(15)	Hank Greenberg	250.00	125.00	75.00
(16)	"Bucky" Harris	125.00	62.00	37.00
(17)	"Rolly" Hemsley	50.00	25.00	15.00
(18)	Frank Higgins	50.00	25.00	15.00
(19)	Oral Hildebrand	50.00	25.00	15.00
(20)	"Chuck" Klein	150.00	75.00	45.00
(21)	"Pepper" Martin	55.00	27.00	16.50
(22)	"Buck" Newsom	55.00	27.00	16.50
(23)	Joe Vosmik	50.00	25.00	15.00
(24)	Paul Waner	150.00	75.00	45.00
(25)	Bill Werber	50.00	25.00	15.00

1938 Goudey

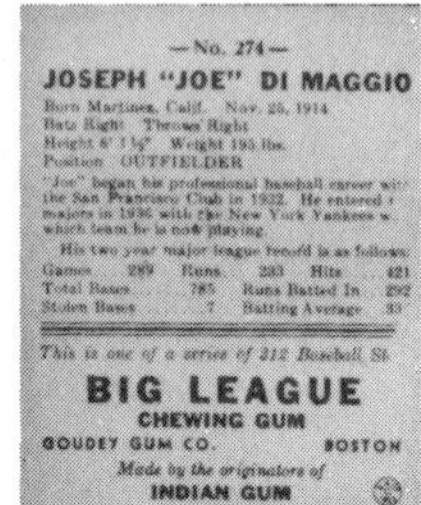

Sometimes referred to as the Goudey Heads-Up set, this issue begins numbering (#241) where the 1933 Goudey set left off. On the card fronts, a photo is used for the player's head with the body being a cartoon drawing. Twenty-four different players are pictured twice in the set. Card #'s 241-264 feature plain backgrounds on the card fronts. Card #'s 265- 288 contain the same basic design and photo but include small drawings and comments within the background. The card backs contain player statistical and biographical information. The ACC designation for the issue is R323.

		NR MT	EX	VG
Complete Set:		18000.	9000.	5500.
Common Player: 241-264		125.00	62.00	37.00
Common Player: 265-288		150.00	75.00	45.00
241	Charlie Gehringer	700.00	200.00	100.00
242	Ervin Fox	125.00	62.00	37.00
243	Joe Kuhel	125.00	62.00	37.00
244	Frank DeMaree	125.00	62.00	37.00
245	Frank Pytlak	125.00	62.00	37.00
246	Ernie Lombardi	200.00	100.00	60.00
247	Joe Vosmik	125.00	62.00	37.00
248	Dick Bartell	125.00	62.00	37.00
249	Jimmy Foxx	500.00	250.00	150.00
250	Joe DiMaggio	3500.	1750.	1000.
251	Bump Hadley	150.00	75.00	45.00
252	Zeke Bonura	125.00	62.00	37.00
253	Hank Greenberg	350.00	175.00	100.00
254	Van Lingle Mungo	150.00	75.00	45.00
255	Julius Solters	125.00	62.00	37.00
256	Vernon Kennedy	125.00	62.00	37.00
257	Al Lopez	135.00	67.00	40.00
258	Bobby Doerr	150.00	75.00	45.00
259	Bill Werber	125.00	62.00	37.00
260	Rudy York	150.00	75.00	45.00
261	Rip Radcliff	125.00	62.00	37.00
262	Joe Ducky Medwick	225.00	125.00	70.00
263	Marvin Owen	125.00	62.00	37.00
264	Bob Feller	550.00	280.00	165.00
265	Charlie Gehringer	400.00	200.00	125.00
266	Ervin Fox	150.00	75.00	45.00
267	Joe Kuhel	150.00	75.00	45.00
268	Frank DeMaree	150.00	75.00	45.00
269	Frank Pytlak	150.00	75.00	45.00
270	Ernie Lombardi	225.00	112.00	67.00
271	Joe Vosmik	150.00	75.00	45.00
272	Dick Bartell	150.00	75.00	45.00
273	Jimmy Foxx	550.00	280.00	165.00
274	Joe DiMaggio	3000.	1500.	900.00
275	Bump Hadley	150.00	75.00	45.00
276	Zeke Bonura	150.00	75.00	45.00
277	Hank Greenberg	400.00	200.00	125.00
278	Van Lingle Mungo	110.00	55.00	33.00
279	Julius Solters	150.00	75.00	45.00
280	Vernon Kennedy	150.00	75.00	45.00
281	Al Lopez	225.00	125.00	70.00
282	Bobby Doerr	225.00	125.00	70.00
283	Bill Werber	150.00	75.00	45.00
284	Rudy York	150.00	75.00	45.00
285	Rip Radcliff	150.00	75.00	45.00
286	Joe Ducky Medwick	250.00	125.00	70.00
287	Marvin Owen	150.00	75.00	45.00
288	Bob Feller	700.00	350.00	20.00

1941 Goudey

Goudey Gum Co.'s last set was issued in 1941. The cards, which measure 2-3/8" by 2-7/8" in size, contain black and white photos set against blue, green, red or yellow backgrounds. The player's name, team and position plus the card number are situated in a box at the bottom of the card. The card reverses are blank. The ACC designation for the set is R324.

		NR MT	EX	VG
Complete Set:		3200.	1600.	950.00
Common Player:		50.00	25.00	15.00
1	Hugh Mulcahy	100.00	50.00	30.00
2	Harlond Clift	50.00	25.00	15.00
3	Louis Chiozza	50.00	25.00	15.00
4	Warren (Buddy) Rosar	36.00	18.00	11.00
5	George McQuinn	50.00	25.00	15.00
6	Emerson Dickman	50.00	25.00	15.00
7	Wayne Ambler	50.00	25.00	15.00
8	Bob Muncrief	50.00	25.00	15.00
9	Bill Dietrich	50.00	25.00	15.00
10	Taft Wright	50.00	25.00	15.00
11	Don Heffner	50.00	25.00	15.00
12	Fritz Ostermueller	50.00	25.00	15.00
13	Frank Hayes	50.00	25.00	15.00
14	John (Jack) Kramer	50.00	25.00	15.00
15	Dario Lodigiani	50.00	25.00	15.00
16	George Case	50.00	25.00	15.00
17	Vito Tamulis	50.00	25.00	15.00
18	Whitlow Wyatt	50.00	25.00	15.00
19	Bill Posedel	50.00	25.00	15.00
20	Carl Hubbell	175.00	90.00	50.00
21	Harold Warstler	175.00	90.00	50.00
22	Joe Sullivan	250.00	125.00	70.00
23	Norman (Babe) Young	175.00	90.00	50.00
24	Stanley Andrews	250.00	125.00	70.00
25	Morris Arnovich	175.00	90.00	50.00
26	Elburt Fletcher	50.00	25.00	15.00
27	Bill Crouch	60.00	30.00	18.00
28	Al Todd	50.00	25.00	15.00
29	Debs Garms	50.00	25.00	15.00
30	Jim Tobin	50.00	25.00	15.00
31	Chester Ross	50.00	25.00	15.00
32	George Coffman	60.00	30.00	18.00
33	Mel Ott	275.00	150.00	80.00

1981 Granny Goose

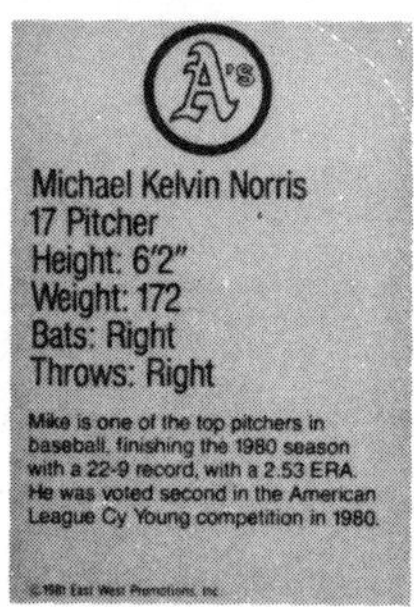

The 1981 Granny Goose set features the Oakland A's. The cards, which measure 2-1/2" by 3-1/2" in size, were issued in bags of potato chips and are sometimes found with grease stains. The cards have full color fronts with the print done in the team's green and yellow colors. The backs contain the A's logo and a short player biography. The Revering card was withdrawn from the set shortly after he was traded and is in shorter supply than the rest of the cards in the set. The cards are numbered in the checklist that follows by the player's uniform number.

		MT	NR MT	EX
Complete Set:		90.00	67.00	36.00
Common Player:		2.00	1.50	.80
1	Billy Martin	10.00	7.50	4.00
2	Mike Heath	2.00	1.50	.80
5	Jeff Newman	2.00	1.50	.80
6	Mitchell Page	2.00	1.50	.80
8	Rob Picciolo	2.00	1.50	.80
10	Wayne Gross	5.00	3.75	2.00
13	Dave Revering	45.00	34.00	18.00
17	Mike Norris	2.00	1.50	.80
20	Tony Armas	4.00	3.00	1.50
21	Dwayne Murphy	3.00	2.25	1.25
22	Rick Langford	2.00	1.50	.80
27	Matt Keough	2.00	1.50	.80
35	Rickey Henderson	20.00	15.00	8.00
39	Dave McKay	2.00	1.50	.80
54	Steve McCatty	2.00	1.50	.80

1982 Granny Goose

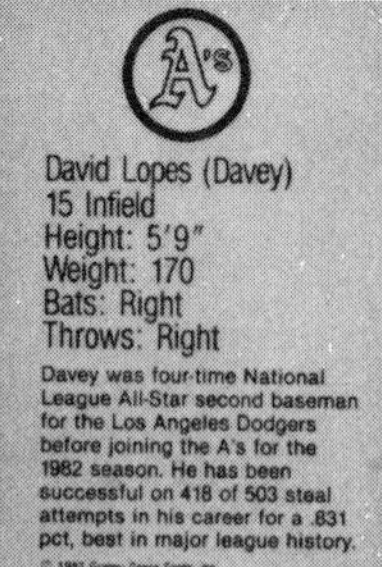

Granny Goose repeated its promotion from the previous year and issued another set featuring the Oakland A's. The cards, which measure 2-1/2" by 3-1/2", were distributed in two fashions - in bags of potato chips and at Fan Appreciation Day at Oakland-Alameda Coliseum. The cards are identical in design to the 1981 set and can be distinguished from it by the date on the copyright on the bottom of the card reverse. The cards are numbered in the checklist that follows by the player's uniform number.

		MT	NR MT	EX
Complete Set:		15.00	11.00	6.00
Common Player:		.40	.30	.15
1	Billy Martin	2.00	1.50	.80
2	Mike Heath	.40	.30	.15
5	Jeff Newman	.40	.30	.15
8	Rob Picciolo	.40	.30	.15
10	Wayne Gross	.40	.30	.15
11	Fred Stanley	.40	.30	.15
15	Davey Lopes	.80	.60	.30
17	Mike Norris	.40	.30	.15
20	Tony Armas	1.00	.70	.40
21	Dwayne Murphy	.60	.45	.25
22	Rick Langford	.40	.30	.15
27	Matt Keough	.40	.30	.15
35	Rickey Henderson	7.00	5.25	2.75
44	Cliff Johnson, Jr.	.40	.30	.15
54	Steve McCatty	.40	.30	.15

1983 Granny Goose

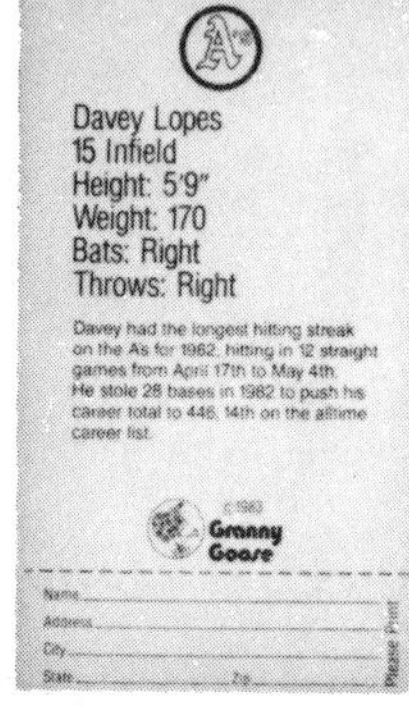

For the third consecutive year, Granny Goose issued a set of baseball cards featuring the Oakland A's. The cards were issued with or without a detachable coupon found at the bottom of each card. Issued in bags of potato chips were the coupon cards, which contain a scratch-off section offering prizes. The cards without the coupon section were given away to fans at Oakland-Alameda Coliseum on July 3, 1983. Cards with the detachable coupon command a 50 per cent premium over the coupon-less variety. The cards in the following checklist are numbered by the player's uniform number.

		MT	NR MT	EX
Complete Set		12.00	9.00	4.75
Common Player		.40	.30	.15
2	Mike Heath	.40	.30	.15
4	Carney Lansford	1.00	.70	.40
10	Wayne Gross	.40	.30	.15

		MT	NR MT	EX
14	Steve Boros	.40	.30	.15
15	Davey Lopes	.80	.60	.30
16	Mike Davis	.80	.60	.30
17	Mike Norris	.40	.30	.15
21	Dwayne Murphy	.60	.45	.25
22	Rick Langford	.40	.30	.15
27	Matt Keough	.40	.30	.15
31	Tom Underwood	.40	.30	.15
33	Dave Beard	.40	.30	.15
35	Rickey Henderson	7.00	5.25	2.75
39	Tom Burgmeier	.40	.30	.15
54	Steve McCatty	.40	.30	.15

1887 Gypsy Queens

The 1887 Gypsy Queen set is very closely related to the N172 Old Judge set and employs the same poses. The Gypsy Queens are easily identified by the words "Gypsy Queen" along the top of the cards. A line near the bottom lists the player's name, position and team, followed by an 1887 copyright line and words "Cigarettes" and "Goodwin & Co. N.Y." Although the checklist is still considered incomplete, 133 different poses have been discovered so far. Collectors should be aware that the Gypsy Queens were issued in two distinct sizes, the more common version measuring 1-1/2" by 2-1/2" (same as Old Judge) and a larger size measuring 2" by 3-1/2" which are considered extremely rare. The large Gypsy Queens are identical in format to the smaller size.

		NR MT	EX	VG
Complete Set:		1250.	50000.	20000.
Common Player:		350.00	150.00	50.00
(1)	Tug Arundel	350.00	150.00	50.00
(2)	Fido Baldwin	350.00	150.00	50.00
(3)	Samuel Barkley (fielding)	350.00	150.00	50.00
(4)	Samuel Barkley (tagging player)	350.00	150.00	50.00
(5)	Handsome Boyle	350.00	150.00	50.00
(6)	Dan Brouthers (looking at ball)	1000.	500.00	190.00
(7)	Dan Brouthers (looking to right)	1000.	500.00	190.00
(8a)	California Brown (New York, throwing, large size)	4500.	2000.	900.00
(8b)	California Brown (New York, throwing, small size)	350.00	150.00	50.00
(9)	California Brown (New York, wearing mask)	350.00	150.00	50.00
(10)	Thomas Brown (Pittsburg, catching)	350.00	150.00	50.00
(11)	Thomas Brown (Pittsburg, with bat)	350.00	150.00	50.00
(12)	Black Jack Burdock	350.00	150.00	50.00
(13)	Watch Burnham	350.00	150.00	50.00
(14)	Doc Bushong	350.00	150.00	50.00
(15)	Patsy Cahill	350.00	150.00	50.00
(16)	Frederick Carroll	350.00	150.00	50.00
(17)	Parisian Bob Caruthers	350.00	150.00	50.00
(18)	Jack Clements (hands on knees)	350.00	150.00	50.00
(19)	Jack Clements (with bat)	350.00	150.00	50.00
(20)	John Coleman	350.00	150.00	50.00
(21)	Commy Comiskey	1000.	500.00	190.00
(22a)	Roger Connor (large size)	7500.	3000.	1250.
(22b)	Roger Connor (small size)	1000.	500.00	190.00
(23)	Dick Conway	350.00	150.00	50.00
(24)	Larry Corcoran	350.00	150.00	50.00
(25)	Samuel Crane (fielding)	350.00	150.00	50.00
(26)	Samuel Crane (with bat)	350.00	150.00	50.00
(27)	Edward Dailey	350.00	150.00	50.00
(28)	Abner Dalrymple	350.00	150.00	50.00
(29)	Dell Darling	350.00	150.00	50.00
(30)	Pat Dealey (bat at side)	350.00	150.00	50.00
(31)	Pat Dealey (bat on right shoulder)	350.00	150.00	50.00
(32)	Jerry Denny (catching)	350.00	150.00	50.00
(33)	Jerry Denny (with bat)	350.00	150.00	50.00
(34)	Jim Donnelly	350.00	150.00	50.00
(35)	Mike Dorgan	350.00	150.00	50.00
(36)	Buck Ewing (large size)	7500.	3000.	1250.
(37)	Buck Ewing (small size)	1000.	500.00	190.00
(38)	Jack Farrell (bat at side)	350.00	150.00	50.00
(39)	Jack Farrell (bat in air)	350.00	150.00	50.00
(40)	Jack Farrell (fielding)	350.00	150.00	50.00
(41)	Jack Farrell (hands on thighs)	350.00	150.00	50.00
(42)	Charlie Ferguson (hands at chest)	350.00	150.00	50.00
(43)	Charlie Ferguson (tagging player)	350.00	150.00	50.00
(44)	Charlie Ferguson (with bat)	350.00	150.00	50.00
(45)	Jocko Fields (catching)	350.00	150.00	50.00
(46)	Jocko Fields (throwing)	350.00	150.00	50.00
(47)	Dave Foutz	350.00	150.00	50.00
(48)	Honest John Gaffney	350.00	150.00	50.00
(49)	Pud Galvin (with bat)	1000.	500.00	190.00
(50)	Pud Galvin (without bat)	1000.	500.00	190.00
(51)	Emil Geiss (hands above waist)	350.00	150.00	50.00
(52)	Emil Geiss (right hand extended)	350.00	150.00	50.00
(53)	Barney Gilligan	350.00	150.00	50.00
(54)	Pebbly Jack Glasscock (hands on knees)	350.00	150.00	50.00
(55)	Pebbly Jack Glasscock (throwing)	350.00	150.00	50.00
(56)	Pebbly Jack Glasscock (with bat)	350.00	150.00	50.00
(57)	Will Gleason	350.00	150.00	50.00
(58)	Piano Legs Gore (fielding)	350.00	150.00	50.00
(59)	Piano Legs Gore (hand at head level)	350.00	150.00	50.00
(60)	Ed Greer	350.00	150.00	50.00
(61)	Tom Gunning (stooping to catch low ball on left)	350.00	150.00	50.00
(62)	Tom Gunning (bending, hands by right knee)	350.00	150.00	50.00
(63)	Ned Hanlon (catching)	350.00	150.00	50.00
(64)	Ned Hanlon (with bat)	350.00	150.00	50.00
(65)	Pa Harkins (hands above waist)	350.00	150.00	50.00
(66)	Pa Harkins (throwing)	350.00	150.00	50.00
(67)	Egyptian Healey	350.00	150.00	50.00
(68)	Paul Hines	350.00	150.00	50.00
(69)	Joe Hornung	350.00	150.00	50.00
(70)	Nat Hudson	350.00	150.00	50.00
(71)	Cutrate Irwin	350.00	150.00	50.00
(72)	Dick Johnston (catching)	350.00	150.00	50.00
(73)	Dick Johnston (with bat)	350.00	150.00	50.00
(74a)	Tim Keefe (pitching, hands at chest, large size)	7500.	3000.	1250.
(74b)	Tim Keefe (pitching, hands at chest, small size)	1000.	500.00	190.00
(75)	Tim Keefe (pitching, hands above waist, facing front)	1000.	500.00	190.00
(76)	Tim Keefe (right hand extended at head level)	1000.	500.00	190.00
(77)	Tim Keefe (with bat)	1000.	500.00	190.00
(78)	King Kelly (catching)	1200.	550.00	200.00
(79)	King Kelly (portrait)	1200.	550.00	200.00
(80a)	King Kelly (with bat, large size)	7500.	3000.	1250.
(80b)	King Kelly (with bat, small size)	1200.	550.00	200.00
(81)	Rudy Kemmler	350.00	150.00	50.00
(82)	Bill Krieg (catching)	350.00	150.00	50.00
(83)	Bill Krieg (with bat)	350.00	150.00	50.00
(84)	Arlie Latham	350.00	150.00	50.00
(85)	Mike Mattimore (hands above head)	350.00	150.00	50.00
(86)	Mike Mattimore (hands at neck)	350.00	150.00	50.00
(87)	Tommy McCarthy (catching)	1000.	500.00	190.00
(88)	Tommy McCarthy (with bat)	1000.	500.00	190.00
(89)	Bill McClellan	350.00	150.00	50.00
(90)	Jim McCormick	350.00	150.00	50.00
(91)	Jack McGeachy	350.00	150.00	50.00
(92)	Deacon McGuire	350.00	150.00	50.00
(93)	George Myers (Indianapolis, stooping)	350.00	150.00	50.00
(94)	George Myers (Indianapolis, with bat)	350.00	150.00	50.00
(95)	Al Myers (Washington)	350.00	150.00	50.00
(96)	Little Nick Nicol	350.00	150.00	50.00
(97)	Hank O'Day (ball in hand)	350.00	150.00	50.00
(98)	Hank O'Day (with bat)	350.00	150.00	50.00
(99)	Tip O'Neill	350.00	150.00	50.00
(100)	George Pinkney	350.00	150.00	50.00
(101)	Hardy Richardson (Detroit)	350.00	150.00	50.00
(102)	Danny Richardson (New York, large size)	4500.	2000.	900.00
(103)	Danny Richardson (New York, small size)	350.00	150.00	50.00
(104)	Yank Robinson	350.00	150.00	50.00
(105)	Jack Rowe	350.00	150.00	50.00
(106)	Emmett Seery (arms folded)	350.00	150.00	50.00
(107)	Emmett Seery (ball in hands)	350.00	150.00	50.00
(108)	Emmett Seery (catching)	350.00	150.00	50.00
(109)	George Shoch	350.00	150.00	50.00
(110)	Otto Shomberg (Schomberg)	350.00	150.00	50.00
(111)	Pap Smith	350.00	150.00	50.00
(112)	Cannonball Stemmyer (Stemmeyer) (pitching)	350.00	150.00	50.00
(113)	Cannonball Stemmyer (Stemmeyer) (with bat)	350.00	150.00	50.00
(114)	Ezra Sutton (with bat)	350.00	150.00	50.00
(115)	Big Sam Thompson (arms folded)	1000.	500.00	190.00
(116)	Big Sam Thompson (bat at side)	1000.	500.00	190.00
(117)	Big Sam Thompson (swinging at ball)	1000.	500.00	190.00
(118)	Silent Mike Tiernan (large size)	4500.	2000.	900.00
(119)	Stephen Toole	350.00	150.00	50.00
(120)	Larry Twitchell (hands by chest)	350.00	150.00	50.00
(121)	Larry Twitchell (right hand extended)	350.00	150.00	50.00
(122)	Chris Von Der Ahe	350.00	150.00	50.00
(123)	Monte Ward (large size)	7500.	3000.	1250.
(124)	Curt Welch	350.00	150.00	50.00
(125)	Art Whitney (Pittsburg, bending)	350.00	150.00	50.00
(126)	Art Whitney (Pittsburg, with bat)	350.00	150.00	50.00
(127)	Grasshopper Whitney (Washington)	350.00	150.00	50.00
(128)	Medoc Wise	350.00	150.00	50.00
(129)	George "Dandy" Wood	350.00	150.00	50.00

A player's name in *italic* type indicates a rookie card. An (FC) indicates a player's first card for that particular card company.

1910 H801-7
Old Mill Cabinets

Similar in size and style to the more popular T3 Turkey Red cabinet cards of the same period, the Old Mill cabinets are much scarcer and picture fewer players. Issued in 1910 as a premium by Old Mill Cigarettes, these minor league cards measure approximately 5-3/8" by 7-5/8". Unlike the Turkey Reds, which feature full-color lithographs, the Old Mill cabinet cards picture the players in black and white photos surrounded by a wide tan border. The player's last name is printed in black in the lower left corner, while his team designation appears in the lower right corner. The backs of the cards carry an advertisement for Old Mill cigarettes. There are 29 known subjects in the set, all players from the old Virginia League. Only two of them (Enos Kirkpatrick and Clarence Munson) ever reached the major leagues. Twenty-five of the 29 players were also featured in the second series of the T-210 set, a massive 640-card set also issued by Old Mill Cigarettes the same year. The Old Mill cabinet cards carry the ACC designation H801-7.

		NR MT	EX	VG
Complete Set:		8700.	4350.	2610.
Common Player:		300.00	150.00	90.00
(1)	Bentley	300.00	150.00	90.00
(2)	Bowen	300.00	150.00	90.00
(3)	Brazille (Brazell)	300.00	150.00	90.00
(4)	Bush (Busch)	300.00	150.00	90.00
(5)	Bussey	300.00	150.00	90.00
(6)	Cross	300.00	150.00	90.00
(7)	Derrick	300.00	150.00	90.00
(8)	Doane	300.00	150.00	90.00
(9)	Doyle	300.00	150.00	90.00
(10)	Fox	300.00	150.00	90.00
(11)	Griffin	300.00	150.00	90.00
(12)	Hearn	300.00	150.00	90.00
(13)	Hooker	300.00	150.00	90.00
(14)	Kirkpatrick	300.00	150.00	90.00
(15)	Laughlin	300.00	150.00	90.00
(16)	McKevitt	300.00	150.00	90.00
(17)	Munson	300.00	150.00	90.00
(18)	Noojn (Noojin)	300.00	150.00	90.00
(19)	O'Halloran	300.00	150.00	90.00
(20)	Pressly	300.00	150.00	90.00
(21)	Revelle	300.00	150.00	90.00
(22)	A. Smith	300.00	150.00	90.00
(23)	Spratt	300.00	150.00	90.00
(24)	Simmons	300.00	150.00	90.00
(25)	Titman	300.00	150.00	90.00
(26)	Walters	300.00	150.00	90.00
(27)	Wallace	300.00	150.00	90.00
(28)	Weherell (Wehrell)	300.00	150.00	90.00
(29)	Woolums	300.00	150.00	90.00

1886 H812 New York Baseball Club

This extremely rare 19th Century baseball card issue can be classified under the general category of "trade" cards, a popular advertising vehicle of the period. The cards measure 3" by 4-3/4" and feature blue line drawings of members of the "New York Base Ball Club," which is printed along the top. As was common with this type of trade card, the bottom was left blank to accomodate various messages. The known examples of this set carry ads for local tobacco merchants, and the player portraits are all based on the photographs used in the N167 Goodwin set. The cards, which have been assigned an ACC designation of H812, are printed on thin paper rather than cardboard.

		NR MT	EX	VG
Complete Set:		34000.	17000.	10200.
Common Player:		3000.	1500.	900.00
(1)	T. Dealsey	3000.	1500.	900.00
(2)	M. Dorgan	3000.	1500.	900.00
(3)	T. Esterbrook	3000.	1500.	900.00
(4)	W. Ewing	5500.	2750.	1650.
(5)	J. Gerhardt	3000.	1500.	900.00
(6)	J. O'Rourke	5500.	2750.	1650.
(7)	D. Richardson	3000.	1500.	900.00
(8)	M. Welch	5500.	2750.	1650.

1887 H891 Tobin Lithographs

The Tobin lithographs, measuring 3" by 4-1/2", were typical of the various "trade" cards that were popular advertising vehicles in the late 19th Century. Found in both black and white and color, the Tobin "lithos" include 10 cards depicting caricature action drawings of popular baseball players of the 1887-1888 era. Each cartoon-like drawing is accompanied by a colorful caption along with the player's name in parenthesis below. The team affiliation is printed in the upper left corner, while a large space in the upper right corner was left blank to accomodate advertising messages. As a result, Tobin cards have been found with this space displaying ads for various cigarettes and other products or left blank. Similarly, the backs of the cards are also found either blank or with advertising. The set takes its name from the manufacturer, whose name ("Tobin N.Y.") appears in the lower right corner of each card.

		NR MT	EX	VG
Complete Set:		2750.	1375.	825.00
Common Player:		200.00	100.00	60.00
(1)	"Go It Old Boy" (Ed Andrews)	200.00	100.00	60.00
(2)	"Oh, Come Off!" (Cap Anson)	500.00	250.00	150.00
(3)	"Watch Me Soak it" (Dan Brouthers)	300.00	150.00	90.00
(4)	"Not Onto It" (Charlie Ferguson)	200.00	100.00	60.00
(5)	"Struck By A Cyclone" (Pebbly Jack Glasscock)	200.00	100.00	60.00
(6)	"An Anxious Moment" (Paul Hines)	200.00	100.00	60.00
(7)	"Where'l You Have It?" (Tim Keefe)	300.00	150.00	90.00
(8)	"The Flower Of The Flock" (Our Own Kelly)	300.00	150.00	90.00
(9)	"A Slide For Home" (Jim M'Cormick) (McCormick)	200.00	100.00	60.00
(10)	"Ain't It A Daisy?" (Smiling Mickey Welch)	300.00	150.00	90.00

1949 Hage's Dairy

Hage's Dairy of California began a three-year run of regional baseball cards featuring Pacific Coast Legaue players in 1949. Despite being produced by the local dairy, the cards were actually distributed inside popcorn boxes at the concession stand in Lane Field Park, home of the P.C.L. San Diego Padres. The 1949 set, like the following two years, was printed on a thin stock measuring 2-5/8" by 3-1/8". The checklist consists of 105 different cards, including several different poses for some of the players. Cards were continually being added or withdrawn to reflect roster changes on the minor league clubs. The Hage's sets were dominated by San Diego players, but also included representatives from the seven other P.C.L. teams. The 1949 cards can be found in four different tints - sepia, green, blue, and black and white. The unnumbered cards have blank backs. The player's name and team appear inside a box on the front of the card, and the 1949 cards can be dated by the large (quarter-inch) type used for the team names, which are sometimes referred to by city and other times by nickname.

		NR MT	EX	VG
Complete Set:		2750.	1375.	825.00
Common Player:		25.00	12.50	7.50
(1)	"Buster" Adams	25.00	12.50	7.50
(2)	"Red" Adams	25.00	12.50	7.50
(3)	Lee Anthony	25.00	12.50	7.50
(4)	Rinaldo Ardizoia	25.00	12.50	7.50
(5)	Del Baker	25.00	12.50	7.50
(6)	Ed Basinski	25.00	12.50	7.50
(7)	Jim Baxes	25.00	12.50	7.50
(8)	Heinz Becker	25.00	12.50	7.50
(9)	Herman Besse	25.00	12.50	7.50
(10)	Tom Bridges	30.00	15.00	9.00
(11)	Gene Brocker	25.00	12.50	7.50
(12)	Ralph Bucton	25.00	12.50	7.50
(13)	Mickey Burnett	25.00	12.50	7.50
(14)	Dain Clay (pose)	25.00	12.50	7.50
(15)	Dain Clay (batting)	25.00	12.50	7.50
(16)	Dain Corriden, Jim Reese	25.00	12.50	7.50
(17)	Pete Coscarart	25.00	12.50	7.50
(18)	Dom Dallessandro	25.00	12.50	7.50
(19)	Con Dempsey	25.00	12.50	7.50
(20)	Vince DiBiasi	25.00	12.50	7.50
(21)	Luke Easter (batting stance)	30.00	15.00	9.00
(22)	Luke Easter (batting follow thru)	30.00	15.00	9.00
(23)	Ed Fernandez	25.00	12.50	7.50
(24)	Les Fleming	25.00	12.50	7.50
(25)	Jess Flores	25.00	12.50	7.50
(26)	Cecil Garriott	25.00	12.50	7.50
(27)	Charles Gassaway	25.00	12.50	7.50
(28)	Mickey Grasso	25.00	12.50	7.50
(29)	Will Hafey (pitching)	25.00	12.50	7.50
(30)	Will Hafey (pose)	25.00	12.50	7.50
(31)	"Jeep" Handley	25.00	12.50	7.50
(32)	"Bucky" Harris (pose)	40.00	20.00	12.00
(33)	"Bucky" Harris (shouting)	40.00	20.00	12.00
(34)	Roy Helser	25.00	12.50	7.50
(35)	Lloyd Hittle	25.00	12.50	7.50
(36)	Ralph Hodgin	25.00	12.50	7.50
(37)	Leroy Jarvis	25.00	12.50	7.50
(38)	John Jensen	25.00	12.50	7.50
(39)	Al Jurisich	25.00	12.50	7.50
(40)	Herb Karpel	25.00	12.50	7.50
(41)	Frank Kelleher	25.00	12.50	7.50
(42)	Bill Kelly	25.00	12.50	7.50
(43)	Bob Kelly	25.00	12.50	7.50
(44)	Frank Kerr	25.00	12.50	7.50
(45)	Thomas Kipp	25.00	12.50	7.50
(46)	Al Lien	25.00	12.50	7.50
(47)	Lyman Linde (pose)	25.00	12.50	7.50
(48)	Lyman Linde (pitching)	25.00	12.50	7.50
(49)	Dennis Luby	25.00	12.50	7.50
(50)	"Red" Lynn	25.00	12.50	7.50
(51)	Pat Malone	25.00	12.50	7.50
(52)	Billy Martin	75.00	38.00	23.00
(53)	Joe Marty	25.00	12.50	7.50
(54)	Cliff Melton	25.00	12.50	7.50
(55)	Steve Mesner	25.00	12.50	7.50
(56)	Leon Mohr	25.00	12.50	7.50
(57)	"Butch" Moran	25.00	12.50	7.50
(58)	Glen Moulder	25.00	12.50	7.50
(59)	Steve Nagy	25.00	12.50	7.50
(60)	Roy Nicely	25.00	12.50	7.50
(61)	Walt Nothe	25.00	12.50	7.50
(62)	John O'Neill	25.00	12.50	7.50
(63)	"Pluto" Oliver	25.00	12.50	7.50
(64)	Al Olsen (pose)	25.00	12.50	7.50
(65)	Al Olsen (throwing)	25.00	12.50	7.50
(66)	Johnny Ostrowski	25.00	12.50	7.50
(67)	Ray Partee	25.00	12.50	7.50
(68)	Bill Raimondi	25.00	12.50	7.50
(69)	Bill Ramsey	25.00	12.50	7.50
(70)	Len Ratto	25.00	12.50	7.50
(71)	Xavier Rescigno	25.00	12.50	7.50
(72)	John Ritchey (batting)	25.00	12.50	7.50
(73)	John Ritchey (catching)	25.00	12.50	7.50
(74)	Mickey Rocco	25.00	12.50	7.50
(75)	John Rucker	25.00	12.50	7.50
(76)	Clarence Russell	25.00	12.50	7.50
(77)	Jack Salverson	25.00	12.50	7.50
(78)	Bill Schuster	25.00	12.50	7.50
(79)	Tom Seats	25.00	12.50	7.50
(80)	Neil Sheridan	25.00	12.50	7.50
(81)	Vince Shupe	25.00	12.50	7.50
(82)	Joe Sprinz	25.00	12.50	7.50
(83)	Chuck Stevens	25.00	12.50	7.50
(84)	Harvey Storey	25.00	12.50	7.50
(85)	Jim Tabor (Sacramento)	25.00	12.50	7.50
(86)	Jim Tabor (Seattle)	25.00	12.50	7.50
(87)	"Junior" Thompson	25.00	12.50	7.50
(88)	Arky Vaughn	45.00	22.00	13.50
(89)	Jackie Warner	25.00	12.50	7.50
(90)	Jim Warner	25.00	12.50	7.50
(91)	Dick Wenner	25.00	12.50	7.50
(92)	Max West (pose)	25.00	12.50	7.50
(93)	Max West (batting swing)	25.00	12.50	7.50
(94)	Max West (batting follow-thru)	25.00	12.50	7.50
(95)	Hank Weyse	25.00	12.50	7.50
(96)	"Fuzzy" White	25.00	12.50	7.50
(97)	Jo Jo White	25.00	12.50	7.50
(98)	Artie Wilson	25.00	12.50	7.50
(99)	Bill Wilson	25.00	12.50	7.50
(100)	Bobbie Wilson (pose)	25.00	12.50	7.50
(101)	Bobbie Wilson (pitching)	25.00	12.50	7.50
(102)	"Pinky" Woods	25.00	12.50	7.50
(103)	Tony York	25.00	12.50	7.50
(104)	Del Young	25.00	12.50	7.50
(105)	Frank Zak	25.00	12.50	7.50

1950 Hage's Dairy

The 1950 P.C.L. set from Hage's Dairy was similar in design and size (2-5/8" by 3-1/8") to the previous year and was again distributed in popcorn boxes at the San Diego stadium. The 1950 set is found with either a blank back or a back containing an advertisement for Hage's Ice Cream, "Your Favorite Brand". The advertising backs also contain the player's name and brief 1949 statistics at the bottom. There are 126 different cards in the 1950 set, including different poses for some of the players. Again, Padres dominate the unnumbered set with lesser representation from the other P.C.L. clubs. For the 1950 edition all team names are referred to by city (no nicknames) and the typeface is smaller.

		NR MT	EX	VG
Complete Set:		2500.	1250.	750.00
Common Player:		18.00	9.00	5.50
(1)	"Buster" Adams (kneeling)	18.00	9.00	5.50
(2a)	"Buster" Adams (batting follow-thru, with inscription)	18.00	9.00	5.50
(2b)	"Buster" Adams (batting follow-thru, no inscription)	18.00	9.00	5.50
(2c)	"Buster" Adams (batting follow-thru, body to left)	18.00	9.00	5.50
3a	"Buster" Adams (batting stance, caption box touching waist)	18.00	9.00	5.50
(3b)	"Buster" Adams (batting stance, caption box not touching waist)	18.00	9.00	5.50
(4)	"Red" Adams	18.00	9.00	5.50
(5)	Dewey Adkins (photo actually Albie Glossop) •	18.00	9.00	5.50
(6)	Rinaldo Ardizoia	18.00	9.00	5.50
(7)	Jose Bache	18.00	9.00	5.50
(8a)	Del Baker, Jim Reese (bat visible at lower right)	18.00	9.00	5.50
(8b)	Del Baker, Jim Reese (no bat visible)	18.00	9.00	5.50
(9)	George Bamberger	18.00	9.00	5.50
(10)	Richard Barrett	18.00	9.00	5.50
(11)	Frank Baumholtz	25.00	12.50	7.50
(12)	Henry Behrman	18.00	9.00	5.50
(13)	Bill Bevens	25.00	12.50	7.50
(14)	Ernie Bickhaus	18.00	9.00	5.50
(15)	Bill Burgher (pose)	18.00	9.00	5.50
(16)	Bill Burgher (catching)	18.00	9.00	5.50
(17)	Mark Christman	18.00	9.00	5.50
(18)	Clint Conaster	18.00	9.00	5.50
(19)	Herb Conyers (fielding)	18.00	9.00	5.50
(20)	Herb Conyers (batting)	18.00	9.00	5.50
(21)	Jim Davis	18.00	9.00	5.50
(22)	Ted Del Guercio	18.00	9.00	5.50
(23)	Vince DiBiasi	18.00	9.00	5.50
(24)	Jess Dobernic	18.00	9.00	5.50
(25)	"Red" Embree (pose)	18.00	9.00	5.50
(26)	"Red" Embree (pitching)	18.00	9.00	5.50
(27)	Elbie Fletcher	18.00	9.00	5.50
(28)	Guy Fletcher	18.00	9.00	5.50
(29)	Tony Freitas	18.00	9.00	5.50
(30)	Denny Galehouse	18.00	9.00	5.50
(31)	Jack Graham (pose, looking to left)	18.00	9.00	5.50
(32)	Jack Graham (pose, looking straight ahead)	18.00	9.00	5.50
(33)	Jack Graham (batting swing)	18.00	9.00	5.50
(34)	Jack Graham (batting stance)	18.00	9.00	5.50
(35)	Orval Grove	18.00	9.00	5.50
(36)	Lee Handley	18.00	9.00	5.50
(37)	Ralph Hodgin	18.00	9.00	5.50
(38)	Don Johnson	18.00	9.00	5.50
(39)	Al Jurisich (pose)	18.00	9.00	5.50
(40)	Al Jurisich (pitching wind-up)	18.00	9.00	5.50
(41)	Al Jurisich (pitching follow-thru)	18.00	9.00	5.50
(42)	Bill Kelly	18.00	9.00	5.50
(43)	Frank Kerr	18.00	9.00	5.50
(44)	Tom Kipp (pose)	18.00	9.00	5.50
(45)	Tom Kipp (pitching)	18.00	9.00	5.50
(46)	Mel Knezovich	18.00	9.00	5.50
(47)	Red Kress	18.00	9.00	5.50
(48)	Dario Lodigiani	18.00	9.00	5.50
(49)	Dennis Luby (pose)	18.00	9.00	5.50
(50)	Dennis Luby (throwing)	18.00	9.00	5.50
(51)	Al Lyons	18.00	9.00	5.50
(52)	Clarence Maddern	18.00	9.00	5.50
(53)	Joe Marty	18.00	9.00	5.50
(54)	Bob McCall	18.00	9.00	5.50
(55)	Cal McIrvin	18.00	9.00	5.50
(56)	Orestes Minoso (batting follow-thru)	40.00	20.00	12.00
(57)	Orestes Minoso (bunting)	40.00	20.00	12.00
(58)	Leon Mohr	18.00	9.00	5.50

		NR MT	EX	VG
(59)	Dee Moore (batting)	18.00	9.00	5.50
(60)	Dee Moore (catching)	18.00	9.00	5.50
(61)	Jim Moran	18.00	9.00	5.50
(62)	Glen Moulder	18.00	9.00	5.50
(63)	Milt Neilsen (pose)	18.00	9.00	5.50
(64)	Milt Neilsen (batting)	18.00	9.00	5.50
(65)	Milt Neilsen (throwing)	18.00	9.00	5.50
(66)	Rube Novotney	18.00	9.00	5.50
(67)	Al Olsen	18.00	9.00	5.50
(68)	Manny Perez	18.00	9.00	5.50
(69)	Bill Raemondi (Raimondi)	18.00	9.00	5.50
(70)	Len Ratto	18.00	9.00	5.50
(71)	Mickey Rocco	18.00	9.00	5.50
(72)	Marv Rotblatt	18.00	9.00	5.50
(73)	Lynwood Rowe (pose)	25.00	12.50	7.50
(74)	Lynwood Rowe (pitching)	25.00	12.50	7.50
(75)	Clarence Russell	18.00	9.00	5.50
(76)	Hal Saltzman (pitching follow-thru)	18.00	9.00	5.50
(77)	Hal Saltzman (pitching wind-up)	18.00	9.00	5.50
(78)	Hal Saltzman (pitching, leg in air)	18.00	9.00	5.50
(79)	Bob Savage (pose)	18.00	9.00	5.50
(80)	Bob Savage (pitching)	18.00	9.00	5.50
(81)	Charlie Schanz	18.00	9.00	5.50
(82)	Bill Schuster	18.00	9.00	5.50
(83)	Neil Sheridan	18.00	9.00	5.50
(84)	Harry Simpson (batting swing)	18.00	9.00	5.50
(85)	Harry Simpson (batting stance)	18.00	9.00	5.50
(86)	Harry Simpson (batting stance, close up)	18.00	9.00	5.50
(87)	Harry Simpson (batting follow-thru)	18.00	9.00	5.50
(88)	Elmer Singleton	18.00	9.00	5.50
(89)	Al Smith (pose)	18.00	9.00	5.50
(90)	Al Smith (batting stance)	18.00	9.00	5.50
(91)	Al Smith (fielding)	18.00	9.00	5.50
(92)	Alphonse Smith (glove above knee)	18.00	9.00	5.50
(93)	Alphonse Smith (glove below knee)	18.00	9.00	5.50
(94)	Steve Souchock	18.00	9.00	5.50
(95)	Jim Steiner	18.00	9.00	5.50
(96)	Harvey Storey (batting stance)	18.00	9.00	5.50
(97)	Harvey Storey (swinging bat)	18.00	9.00	5.50
(98)	Harvey Storey (throwing)	18.00	9.00	5.50
(99)	Harvey Storey (fielding, ball in glove)	18.00	9.00	5.50
(100)	Max Surkont	18.00	9.00	5.50
(101)	Jim Tabor	18.00	9.00	5.50
(102)	Forrest Thompson	18.00	9.00	5.50
(103)	Mike Tresh (pose)	18.00	9.00	5.50
(104)	Mike Tresh (catching)	18.00	9.00	5.50
(105)	Kenny Washington	18.00	9.00	5.50
(106)	Bill Waters (pose)	18.00	9.00	5.50
(107)	Bill Waters (pitching)	18.00	9.00	5.50
(108)	Roy Welmaker (pose)	18.00	9.00	5.50
(109)	Roy Welmaker (pitching)	18.00	9.00	5.50
(110)	Max West (pose)	18.00	9.00	5.50
(111)	Max West (batting stance)	18.00	9.00	5.50
(112)	Max West (kneeling)	18.00	9.00	5.50
(113)	Max West (batting follow-thru)	18.00	9.00	5.50
(114)	Al White	18.00	9.00	5.50
(115)	"Whitey" Wietelmann (pose)	18.00	9.00	5.50
(116)	"Whitey" Wietelmann (bunting)	18.00	9.00	5.50
(117)	"Whitey" Wietelmann (batting stance)	18.00	9.00	5.50
(118)	"Whitey" Wietelmann (throwing)	18.00	9.00	5.50
(119)	Bobbie Wilson	18.00	9.00	5.50
(120)	Bobby Wilson	18.00	9.00	5.50
(121)	Roy Zimmerman	18.00	9.00	5.50
(122)	George Zuverink	18.00	9.00	5.50

1951 Hage's Dairy

The final year of the Hage's P.C.L. issues saw the set reduced to 52 different unnumbered cards, all but 12 of them Padres. The set also includes six cards of Cleveland Indians players, which were issued during an exhibition series with the major league club, and six cards picturing members of the Hollywood Stars. No other P.C.L. teams are represented. The cards maintained the same size and style of the previous two years but were printed in more color tints, including blue, green, burgundy, gold, gray and sepia (but not black and white). The 1951 cards have blank backs and were again distributed in popcorn boxes at the San Diego stadium. The 1951 cards are the most common of the three sets issued by Hage's Dairy. The Indians and Stars players were issued in lesser quantities than the Padres, however, and command a higher value.

		NR MT	EX	VG
	Complete Set:	1000.	500.00	300.00
	Common Player:	15.00	7.50	4.50
(1)	"Buster" Adams	15.00	7.50	4.50
(2)	Del Baker	15.00	7.50	4.50
(3)	Ray Boone	25.00	12.50	7.50
(4)	Russ Christopher	15.00	7.50	4.50
(5)	Allie Clark	25.00	12.50	7.50
(6)	Herb Conyers	15.00	7.50	4.50
(7)	"Red" Embree (pitching, foot in air)	15.00	7.50	4.50
(8)	"Red" Embree (pitching, hands up)	15.00	7.50	4.50
(9)	Jess Flores	25.00	12.50	7.50
(10)	Murray Franklin	25.00	12.50	7.50
(11)	Jack Graham (portrait)	15.00	7.50	4.50
(12)	Jack Graham (batting)	15.00	7.50	4.50
(13)	Gene Handley	25.00	12.50	7.50
(14)	Charles Harris	15.00	7.50	4.50
(15)	Sam Jones (pitching, hands back)	15.00	7.50	4.50
(16)	Sam Jones (pitching, hands up)	15.00	7.50	4.50
(17)	Sam Jones (pitching, leg in air)	15.00	7.50	4.50
(18)	Al Jurisich	15.00	7.50	4.50
(19)	Frank Kerr (batting)	15.00	7.50	4.50
(20)	Frank Kerr (catching)	15.00	7.50	4.50
(21)	Dick Kinaman	15.00	7.50	4.50
(22)	Clarence Maddern (batting)	15.00	7.50	4.50
(23)	Clarence Maddern (fielding)	15.00	7.50	4.50
(24)	Harry Malmberg (bunting)	15.00	7.50	4.50
(25)	Harry Malmberg (batting follow-thru)	15.00	7.50	4.50
(26)	Harry Malmberg (fielding)	15.00	7.50	4.50
(27)	Gordon Maltzberger	25.00	12.50	7.50
(28)	Al Olsen (Cleveland)	25.00	12.50	7.50
(29)	Al Olsen (San Diego)	15.00	7.50	4.50
(30)	Jimmy Reese (clapping)	18.00	9.00	5.50
(31)	Jimmy Reese (hands on knees)	18.00	9.00	5.50
(32)	Al Rosen	45.00	22.00	13.50
(33)	Joe Rowell	15.00	7.50	4.50
(34)	Mike Sandlock	25.00	12.50	7.50
(35)	George Schmees	25.00	12.50	7.50
(36)	Charlie Sipple	15.00	7.50	4.50
(37)	Harvey Storey (batting follow-thru)	15.00	7.50	4.50
(38)	Harvey Storey (batting stance)	15.00	7.50	4.50
(39)	Harvey Storey (fielding)	15.00	7.50	4.50
(40)	Jack Tobin	15.00	7.50	4.50
(41)	Frank Tornay	15.00	7.50	4.50
(42)	Thurman Tucker	15.00	7.50	4.50
(43)	Ben Wade	25.00	12.50	7.50
(44)	Roy Welmaker	15.00	7.50	4.50
(45)	Leroy Wheat	15.00	7.50	4.50
(46)	Don White	15.00	7.50	4.50
(47)	"Whitey" Wietelman (batting)	15.00	7.50	4.50
(48)	"Whitey" Wietelman (fielding)	15.00	7.50	4.50
(49)	Bobby Wilson (batting)	15.00	7.50	4.50
(50)	Bobby Wilson (fielding)	15.00	7.50	4.50
(51)	Tony York	15.00	7.50	4.50
(52)	George Zuverink	25.00	12.50	7.50

1989 Hills Team MVP's

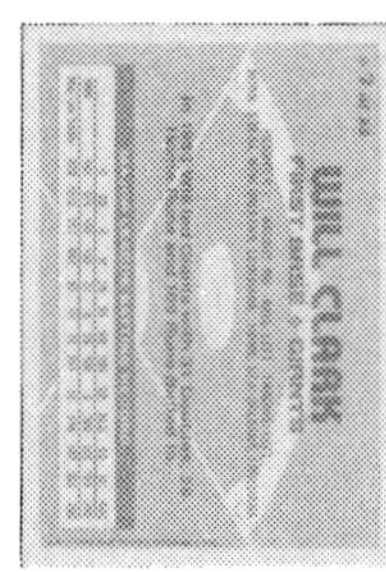

This high-gloss, 33-card boxed set of superstars was produced by Topps for the Hills department store chain. The words "Hills Team MVP's" appear above the player photos, while the player's name and team are printed below. The front of the card carries a red, white and blue color scheme with yellow and gold accents. The horizontal backs include player data set against a green playing field background.

		MT	NR MT	EX
	Complete Set:	2.75	2.00	1.00
	Common Player:	.05	.04	.02
1	Harold Baines	.05	.04	.02
2	Wade Boggs	.30	.25	.12
3	George Brett	.09	.07	.04
4	Tom Brunansky	.05	.04	.02
5	Jose Canseco	.35	.25	.14
6	Joe Carter	.05	.04	.02
7	Will Clark	.35	.25	.12
8	Roger Clemens	.10	.08	.04
9	Dave Cone	.05	.04	.02
10	Glenn Davis	.05	.04	.02
11	Andre Dawson	.09	.07	.04
12	Dennis Eckersley	.09	.07	.04
13	Andres Galarraga	.10	.08	.06
14	Kirk Gibson	.06	.05	.02
15	Mike Greenwell	.15	.11	.06
16	Tony Gwynn	.15	.11	.06
17	Orel Hershiser	.09	.07	.03
18	Danny Jackson	.05	.04	.02
19	Mark Langston	.09	.07	.04
20	Fred McGriff	.10	.08	.04
21	Dale Murphy	.06	.05	.04
22	Eddie Murray	.06	.05	.04
23	Kirby Puckett	.25	.20	.10
24	Johnny Ray	.05	.04	.02
25	Juan Samuel	.05	.04	.02
26	Ruben Sierra	.15	.11	.06
27	Dave Stewart	.05	.04	.02
28	Darryl Strawberry	.20	.15	.08
29	Allan Trammell	.06	.05	.02
30	Andy Van Slyke	.05	.04	.02
31	Frank Viola	.06	.05	.02
32	Dave Winfield	.06	.05	.02
33	Robin Yount	.09	.07	.03

1958 Hires Root Beer Test Set

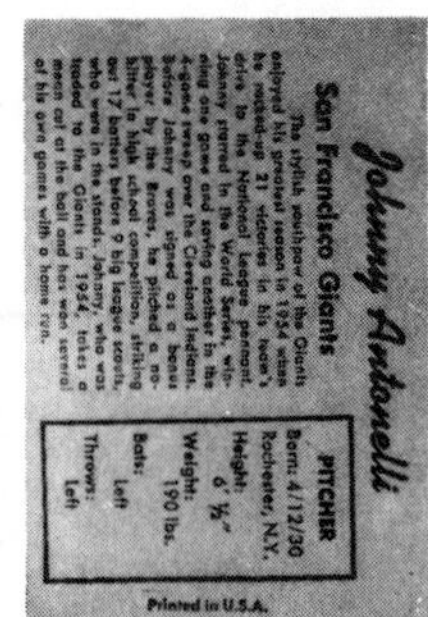

Among the scarcest of the regional issues of the late 1950s is the eight-card test issue which preceded the Hires Root Beer set of 66 cards. Probably issued in a very limited area in the Northeast, the test cards differ from the regular issue in that they have sepia-toned, rather than color pictures, which are set against plain yellow or orange backgrounds (much like the 1958 Topps), instead of viewed through a knothole. Like the regular Hires cards, the 2-5/16" by 3-1/2" cards were issued with an attached wedge-shaped tab of like size. The tab offered membership in Hires baseball fan club, and served to hold the card into the carton of bottled root beer with which it was given away. Values quoted here are for cards with tabs. Cards without tabs would be valued approximately 50 per cent lower.

		NR MT	EX	VG
	Complete Set:	1500.	750.00	450.00
	Common Player:	125.00	60.00	40.00
(1)	Johnny Antonelli	150.00	75.00	45.00
(2)	Jim Busby	125.00	60.00	40.00
(3)	Chico Fernandez	125.00	60.00	40.00
(4)	Bob Friend	150.00	75.00	45.00
(5)	Vern Law	150.00	75.00	45.00
(6)	Stan Lopata	125.00	60.00	40.00
(7)	Willie Mays	550.00	280.00	165.00
(8)	Al Pilarcik	125.00	60.00	40.00

1958 Hires Root Beer

Like most baseball cards issued with a tab in the 1950s, the Hires cards are extremely scarce today in their original form. The basic card was attached to a wedge-shaped tab that served the dual purpose of offering a fan club membership and of holding the card into the cardboard carton of soda bottles with which it was distributed. The card itself measures 2- 5/16" by 3-1/2". The tab extends for another 3-1/2". Numbering of the Hires set begins at 10 and goes through 76, with card #69 never issued, making a set complete at 66 cards. Values given below are for cards with tabs. Cards without tabs would be valued approximately 50 per cent lower.

		NR MT	EX	VG
	Complete Set:	2500.	1250.	700.00
	Common Player:	25.00	12.50	7.50
10	Richie Ashburn	150.00	40.00	25.00

		NR MT	EX	VG
11	Chico Carrasquel	25.00	12.50	7.50
12	Dave Philley	25.00	12.50	7.50
13	Don Newcombe	28.00	14.00	8.50
14	Wally Post	25.00	12.50	7.50
15	Rip Repulski	25.00	12.50	7.50
16	Chico Fernandez	25.00	12.50	7.50
17	Larry Doby	28.00	14.00	8.50
18	Hector Brown	25.00	12.50	7.50
19	Danny O'Connell	25.00	12.50	7.50
20	Granny Hamner	25.00	12.50	7.50
21	Dick Groat	30.00	15.00	9.00
22	Ray Narleski	25.00	12.50	7.50
23	Pee Wee Reese	100.00	50.00	30.00
24	Bob Friend	30.00	15.00	9.00
25	Willie Mays	275.00	150.00	80.00
26	Bob Nieman	25.00	12.50	7.50
27	Frank Thomas	25.00	12.50	7.50
28	Curt Simmons	30.00	15.00	9.00
29	Stan Lopata	25.00	12.50	7.50
30	Bob Skinner	25.00	12.50	7.50
31	Ron Kline	25.00	12.50	7.50
32	Willie Miranda	25.00	12.50	7.50
33	Bob Avila	25.00	12.50	7.50
34	Clem Labine	30.00	15.00	9.00
35	Ray Jablonski	25.00	12.50	7.50
36	Bill Mazeroski	28.00	14.00	8.50
37	Billy Gardner	25.00	12.50	7.50
38	Pete Runnels	30.00	15.00	9.00
39	Jack Sanford	25.00	12.50	7.50
40	Dave Sisler	25.00	12.50	7.50
41	Don Zimmer	30.00	15.00	9.00
42	Johnny Podres	28.00	14.00	8.50
43	Dick Farrell	25.00	12.50	7.50
44	Hank Aaron	275.00	150.00	80.00
45	Bill Virdon	30.00	15.00	9.00
46	Bobby Thomson	30.00	15.00	9.00
47	Willard Nixon	25.00	12.50	7.50
48	Billy Loes	25.00	12.50	7.50
49	Hank Sauer	25.00	12.50	7.50
50	Johnny Antonelli	30.00	15.00	9.00
51	Daryl Spencer	25.00	12.50	7.50
52	Ken Lehman	25.00	12.50	7.50
53	Sammy White	25.00	12.50	7.50
54	Charley Neal	25.00	12.50	7.50
55	Don Drysdale	80.00	40.00	24.00
56	Jack Jensen	28.00	14.00	8.50
57	Ray Katt	25.00	12.50	7.50
58	Franklin Sullivan	25.00	12.50	7.50
59	Roy Face	30.00	15.00	9.00
60	Willie Jones	25.00	12.50	7.50
61	Duke Snider	125.00	62.00	37.00
62	Whitey Lockman	25.00	12.50	7.50
63	Gino Cimoli	30.00	15.00	9.00
64	Marv Grissom	25.00	12.50	7.50
65	Gene Baker	25.00	12.50	7.50
66	George Zuverink	25.00	12.50	7.50
67	Ted Kluszewski	28.00	14.00	8.50
68	Jim Busby	25.00	12.50	7.50
69	Not Issued			
70	Curt Barclay	25.00	12.50	7.50
71	Hank Foiles	25.00	12.50	7.50
72	Gene Stephens	25.00	12.50	7.50
73	Al Worthington	25.00	12.50	7.50
74	Al Walker	25.00	12.50	7.50
75	Bob Boyd	25.00	12.50	7.50
76	Al Pilarcik	30.00	9.00	5.50

1959 Home Run Derby

This 20-card unnumbered set was produced by American Motors to publicize the Home Run Derby television program. The cards measure approximate- ly 3-1/4" by 5-1/4" and feature black and white player photos on black-backed white stock. The player name and team are printed beneath the photo. This set was reprinted (and marked as such) in 1988 by Card Collectors' Company of New York.

		NR MT	EX	VG
	Complete Set:	3500.	1750.	1050.
	Common Player:	50.00	25.00	15.00
(1)	Hank Aaron	400.00	200.00	125.00
(2)	Bob Allison	60.00	30.00	18.00
(3)	Ernie Banks	250.00	125.00	70.00
(4)	Ken Boyer	100.00	50.00	30.00
(5)	Bob Cerv	60.00	30.00	18.00
(6)	Rocky Colavito	100.00	50.00	30.00
(7)	Gil Hodges	150.00	75.00	45.00
(8)	Jackie Jensen	100.00	50.00	30.00
(9)	Al Kaline	250.00	125.00	70.00
(10)	Harmon Killebrew	200.00	100.00	60.00
(11)	Jim Lemon	60.00	30.00	18.00
(12)	Mickey Mantle	1200.	600.00	400.00
(13)	Ed Mathews	225.00	125.00	70.00
(14)	Willie Mays	450.00	225.00	112.00
(15)	Wally Post	60.00	30.00	18.00
(16)	Frank Robinson	225.00	125.00	70.00
(17)	Mark Scott (host)	100.00	50.00	30.00
(18)	Duke Snider	350.00	175.00	105.00
(19)	Dick Stuart	60.00	30.00	18.00
(20)	Gus Triandos	60.00	30.00	18.00

1947 Homogenized Bond Bread

Issued by Homogenized Bond Bread in 1947, this set consists of 48 unnumbered black and white cards, each measuring 2-1/4" by 3-1/2". Of the 48 cards, 44 are baseball players. The remaining four cards picture boxers. The cards are usually found with rounded corners, although cards with square corners are also known to exist. The set contains both portrait and action photos, and features the player's facsimile autograph on the front.

		NR MT	EX	VG
	Complete Set:	600.00	300.00	175.00
	Common Player:	4.00	2.00	1.25
(1)	Rex Barney	4.00	2.00	1.25
(2)	Larry Berra	40.00	20.00	12.00
(3)	Ewell Blackwell	4.00	2.00	1.25
(4)	Lou Boudreau	8.00	4.00	2.50
(5)	Ralph Branca	8.00	4.00	2.50
(6)	Harry Brecheen	4.00	2.00	1.25
(7)	Dom DiMaggio	8.00	4.00	2.50
(8)	Joe DiMaggio	100.00	50.00	30.00
(9)	Bobbie Doerr (Bobby)	8.00	4.00	2.50
(10)	Bruce Edwards	4.00	2.00	1.25
(11)	Bob Elliott	4.00	2.00	1.25
(12)	Del Ennis	4.00	2.00	1.25
(13)	Bob Feller	15.00	7.50	4.50
(14)	Carl Furillo	8.00	4.00	2.50
(15)	Cid Gordon (Sid)	4.00	2.00	1.25
(16)	Joe Gordon	4.00	2.00	1.25
(17)	Joe Hatten	4.00	2.00	1.25
(18)	Gil Hodges	25.00	12.50	7.50
(19)	Tommy Holmes	4.00	2.00	1.25
(20)	Larry Janson (Jansen)	4.00	2.00	1.25
(21)	Sheldon Jones	4.00	2.00	1.25
(22)	Edwin Joost	4.00	2.00	1.25
(23)	Charlie Keller	8.00	4.00	2.50
(24)	Ken Keltner	4.00	2.00	1.25
(25)	Buddy Kerr	4.00	2.00	1.25
(26)	Ralph Kiner	8.00	4.00	2.50
(27)	John Lindell	4.00	2.00	1.25
(28)	Whitey Lockman	4.00	2.00	1.25
(29)	Willard Marshall	4.00	2.00	1.25
(30)	Johnny Mize	8.00	4.00	2.50
(31)	Stan Musial	40.00	20.00	12.00
(32)	Andy Pafko	4.00	2.00	1.25
(33)	Johnny Pesky	4.00	2.00	1.25
(34)	Pee Wee Reese	40.00	20.00	12.00
(35)	Phil Rizzuto	15.00	7.50	4.50
(36)	Aaron Robinson	4.00	2.00	1.25
(37)	Jackie Robinson	60.00	30.00	18.00
(38)	John Sain	5.00	2.50	1.50
(39)	Enos Slaughter	8.00	4.00	2.50
(40)	Vern Stephens	4.00	2.00	1.25
(41)	George Tebbetts	4.00	2.00	1.25
(42)	Bob Thomson	8.00	4.00	2.50
(43)	Johnny Vandermeer (VanderMeer)	8.00	4.00	2.50
(44)	Ted Williams	40.00	20.00	12.00

1975 Hostess

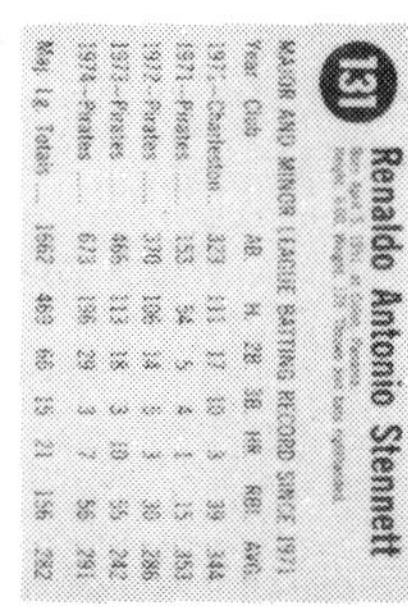

The first of what would become five annual issues, the 1975 Hostess set consists of 50 three-card panels which formed the bottom of boxes of family-size snack cake products. Unlike many similar issues, the Hostess cards do not share common borders, so it was possible to cut them neatly and evenly from the box. Well-cut single cards measure 2-1/4" by 3-1/4", while a three-card panel measures 7-1/4" by 3-1/4". Because some of the panels were issued on packages of less popular snack cakes, they are somewhat scarcer today. Since the hobby was quite well- developed when the Hostess cards were first issued, there is no lack of complete panels. Even unused complete boxes are available today. Some of the photos in this issue also appear on Topps cards of the era.

		NR MT	EX	VG
	Complete Panel Set:	350.00	175.00	105.00
	Complete Singles Set:	150.00	75.00	45.00
	Common Panel:	2.50	1.25	.70
	Common Single Player:	.40	.20	.12
Panel 1		2.50	1.25	.70
1	Bobby Tolan	.40	.20	.12
2	Cookie Rojas	.40	.20	.12
3	Darrell Evans	.70	.35	.20
Panel 2		5.50	2.75	1.75
4	Sal Bando	.50	.25	.15
5	Joe Morgan	2.00	1.00	.60
6	Mickey Lolich	.60	.30	.20
Panel 3		4.00	2.00	1.25
7	Don Sutton	1.50	.70	.45
8	Bill Melton	.40	.20	.12
9	Tim Foli	.40	.20	.12
Panel 4		5.00	2.50	1.50
10	Joe Lahoud	.40	.20	.12
11a	Bert Hooten (incorrect spelling)	1.50	.70	.45
11b	Burt Hooton (correct spelling)	1.50	.70	.45
12	Paul Blair	.40	.20	.12
Panel 5		2.50	1.25	.70
13	Jim Barr	.40	.20	.12
14	Toby Harrah	.50	.25	.15
15	John Milner	.40	.20	.12
Panel 6		3.50	1.75	1.00
16	Ken Holtzman	.50	.25	.15
17	Cesar Cedeno	.50	.25	.15
18	Dwight Evans	.90	.45	.25
Panel 7		7.50	3.75	2.25
19	Willie McCovey	3.00	1.50	.90
20	Tony Oliva	.70	.35	.20
21	Manny Sanguillen	.40	.20	.12
Panel 8		8.00	4.00	2.50
22	Mickey Rivers	.50	.25	.15
23	Lou Brock	3.00	1.50	.90
24	Craig Nettles	.90	.45	.25
Panel 9		3.00	1.50	.90
25	Jimmy Wynn	.50	.25	.15
26	George Scott	.50	.25	.15
27	Greg Luzinski	.50	.25	.15
Panel 10		20.00	10.00	6.00
28	Bert Campaneris	.50	.25	.15
29	Pete Rose	8.00	4.00	2.50
30	Buddy Bell	.50	.25	.15
Panel 11		2.50	1.25	.70
31	Gary Matthews	.50	.25	.15
32	Fred Patek	.40	.20	.12
33	Mike Lum	.40	.20	.12
Panel 12		2.50	1.25	.70
34	Ellie Rodriguez	.40	.20	.12
35	Milt May	.40	.20	.12
36	Willie Horton	.50	.25	.15
Panel 13		10.00	5.00	3.00
37	Dave Winfield	4.50	2.25	1.25
38	Tom Grieve	.40	.20	.12
39	Barry Foote	.40	.20	.12
Panel 14		2.50	1.25	.70
40	Joe Rudi	.50	.25	.15
41	Bake McBride	.40	.20	.12
42	Mike Cuellar	.50	.25	.15
Panel 15		2.50	1.25	.70
43	Garry Maddox	.50	.25	.15
44	Carlos May	.40	.20	.12
45	Bud Harrelson	.40	.20	.12
Panel 16		15.00	7.50	4.50
46	Dave Chalk	.40	.20	.12
47	Dave Concepcion	.50	.25	.15
48	Carl Yastrzemski	6.50	3.25	2.00
Panel 17		9.00	4.50	2.75
49	Steve Garvey	4.00	2.00	1.25
50	Amos Otis	.50	.25	.15
51	Rickey Reuschel	.50	.25	.15
Panel 18		3.75	2.00	1.25
52	Rollie Fingers	1.25	.60	.40
53	Bob Watson	.40	.20	.12
54	John Ellis	.40	.20	.12
Panel 19		9.50	4.75	2.75
55	Bob Bailey	.40	.20	.12
56	Rod Carew	4.00	2.00	1.25
57	Richie Hebner	.40	.20	.12
Panel 20		10.00	5.00	3.00
58	Nolan Ryan	4.00	2.00	1.25
59	Reggie Smith	.50	.25	.15

	NR MT	EX	VG
60 Joe Coleman	.40	.20	.12
Panel 21	10.00	5.00	3.00
61 Ron Cey	.50	.25	.15
62 Darrell Porter	.50	.25	.15
63 Steve Carlton	4.00	2.00	1.25
Panel 22	2.50	1.25	.70
64 Gene Tenace	.40	.20	.12
65 Jose Cardenal	.40	.20	.12
66 Bill Lee	.40	.20	.12
Panel 23	2.50	1.25	.70
67 Dave Lopes	.50	.25	.15
68 Wilbur Wood	.50	.25	.15
69 Steve Renko	.40	.20	.12
Panel 24	3.00	1.50	.90
70 Joe Torre	.50	.25	.15
71 Ted Sizemore	.40	.20	.12
72 Bobby Grich	.50	.25	.15
Panel 25	11.00	5.50	3.25
73 Chris Speier	.40	.20	.12
74 Bert Blyleven	.70	.35	.20
75 Tom Seaver	4.50	2.25	1.25
Panel 26	2.50	1.25	.70
76 Nate Colbert	.40	.20	.12
77 Don Kessinger	.40	.20	.12
78 George Medich	.40	.20	.12
Panel 27	23.00	11.50	7.00
79 Andy Messersmith	.70	.35	.20
80 Robin Yount	9.00	4.50	2.75
81 Al Oliver	1.50	.70	.45
Panel 28	18.00	9.00	5.50
82 Bill Singer	.50	.25	.15
83 Johnny Bench	6.00	3.00	1.75
84 Gaylord Perry	3.00	1.50	.90
Panel 29	5.00	2.50	1.50
85 Dave Kingman	1.25	.60	.40
86 Ed Herrmann	.50	.25	.15
87 Ralph Garr	.60	.30	.20
Panel 30	23.00	11.50	7.00
88 Reggie Jackson	9.00	4.50	2.75
89a Doug Radar (incorrect spelling)	2.00	1.00	.60
89b Doug Rader (correct spelling)	2.00	1.00	.60
90 Elliott Maddox	.50	.25	.15
Panel 31	3.50	1.75	1.00
91 Bill Russell	.60	.30	.20
92 John Mayberry	.50	.25	.15
93 Dave Cash	.50	.25	.15
Panel 32	5.00	2.50	1.50
94 Jeff Burroughs	.60	.30	.20
95 Ted Simmons	1.25	.60	.40
96 Joe Decker	.50	.25	.15
Panel 33	10.00	5.00	3.00
97 Bill Buckner	1.00	.50	.30
98 Bobby Darwin	.50	.25	.15
99 Phil Niekro	3.50	1.75	1.00
Panel 34	3.00	1.50	.90
100 Mike Sundberg (Jim)	.50	.25	.15
101 Greg Gross	.40	.20	.12
102 Luis Tiant	.70	.35	.20
Panel 35	2.50	1.25	.70
103 Glenn Beckert	.40	.20	.12
104 Hal McRae	.50	.25	.15
105 Mike Jorgensen	.40	.20	.12
Panel 36	2.50	1.25	.70
106 Mike Hargrove	.40	.20	.12
107 Don Gullett	.40	.20	.12
108 Tito Fuentes	.40	.20	.12
Panel 37	3.50	1.75	1.00
109 John Grubb	.40	.20	.12
110 Jim Kaat	.90	.45	.25
111 Felix Millan	.40	.20	.12
Panel 38	2.50	1.25	.70
112 Don Money	.40	.20	.12
113 Rick Monday	.50	.25	.15
114 Dick Bosman	.40	.20	.12
Panel 39	3.50	1.75	1.00
115 Roger Metzger	.40	.20	.12
116 Fergie Jenkins	.90	.45	.25
117 Dusky Baker	.50	.25	.15
Panel 40	10.00	5.00	3.00
118 Billy Champion	.50	.25	.15
119 Bob Gibson	3.50	1.75	1.00
120 Bill Freehan	.80	.40	.25
Panel 41	2.50	1.25	.70
121 Cesar Geronimo	.40	.20	.12
122 Jorge Orta	.40	.20	.12
123 Cleon Jones	.40	.20	.12
Panel 42	10.50	5.25	3.25
124 Steve Busby	.40	.20	.12
125a Bill Madlock (Pitcher)	2.00	1.00	.60
125b Bill Madlock (Third Base)	2.00	1.00	.60
126 Jim Palmer	2.75	1.50	.80
Panel 43	4.25	2.25	1.25
127 Tony Perez	1.00	.50	.30
128 Larry Hisle	.40	.20	.12
129 Rusty Staub	.70	.35	.20
Panel 44	20.00	10.00	6.00
130 Hank Aaron	9.00	4.50	2.75
131 Rennie Stennett	.50	.25	.15
132 Rico Petrocelli	.70	.35	.20
Panel 45	16.00	8.00	4.75
133 Mike Schmidt	6.00	3.00	1.75
134 Sparky Lyle	.50	.25	.15
135 Willie Stargell	3.00	1.50	.90
Panel 46	7.00	3.50	2.00
136 Ken Henderson	.40	.20	.12
137 Willie Montanez	.40	.20	.12
138 Thurman Munson	2.50	1.25	.70
Panel 47	2.50	1.25	.70
139 Richie Zisk	.40	.20	.12
140 Geo. Hendricks (Hendrick)	.50	.25	.15
141 Bobby Murcer	.50	.25	.15
Panel 48	10.00	5.00	3.00
142 Lee May	.50	.25	.15
143 Carlton Fisk	1.00	.50	.30
144 Brooks Robinson	3.50	1.75	1.00
Panel 49	2.50	1.25	.70
145 Bobby Bonds	.50	.25	.15
146 Gary Sutherland	.40	.20	.12
147 Oscar Gamble	.40	.20	.12
Panel 50	6.00	3.00	1.75
148 Jim Hunter	2.50	1.25	.70
149 Tug McGraw	.50	.25	.15
150 Dave McNally	.50	.25	.15

1975 Hostess Twinkies

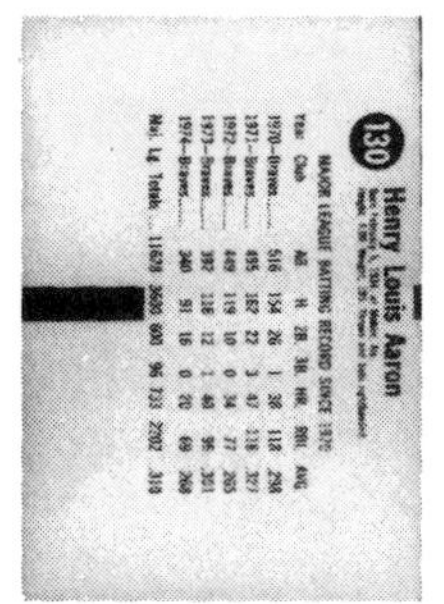

Believed to have been issued only in the Western states, and on a limited basis at that, the 1975 Hostess Twinkie set features 60 of the cards from the "regular" Hostess set of that year. The cards were issued one per pack with the popular snack cake. Card #'s 1-36 are a direct pick-up from the Hostess set, while the remaining 24 cards in the set were selected from the more popular names in the remainder of the Hostess issue - with an emphasis on West Coast players. Thus, after card #36, the '75 Twinkie cards are skip-numbered from 40-136. In identical 2-1/4" by 3-1/4" size, the Twinkie cards differ from the Hostess issue only in the presence of small black bars at top and bottom center of the back of the card. Values quoted are for full bottom panels.

	NR MT	EX	VG
Complete Set:	175.00	87.00	52.00
Common Player:	.90	.45	.25
1 Bobby Tolan	.90	.45	.25
2 Cookie Rojas	.90	.45	.25
3 Darrell Evans	2.00	1.00	.60
4 Sal Bando	1.25	.60	.40
5 Joe Morgan	5.00	2.50	1.50
6 Mickey Lolich	2.00	1.00	.60
7 Don Sutton	4.50	2.25	1.25
8 Bill Melton	.90	.45	.25
9 Tim Foli	.90	.45	.25
10 Joe Lahoud	.90	.45	.25
11 Bert Hooten (Burt Hooton)	1.25	.60	.40
12 Paul Blair	.90	.45	.25
13 Jim Barr	.90	.45	.25
14 Toby Harrah	.90	.45	.25
15 John Milner	.90	.45	.25
16 Ken Holtzman	1.00	.50	.30
17 Cesar Cedeno	1.25	.60	.40
18 Dwight Evans	3.00	1.50	.90
19 Willie McCovey	7.00	3.50	2.00
20 Tony Oliva	2.00	1.00	.60
21 Manny Sanguillen	.90	.45	.25
22 Mickey Rivers	.90	.45	.25
23 Lou Brock	6.50	3.25	2.00
24 Graig Nettles	3.00	1.50	.90
25 Jim Wynn	.90	.45	.25
26 George Scott	.90	.45	.25
27 Greg Luzinski	1.25	.60	.40
28 Bert Campaneris	1.25	.60	.40
29 Pete Rose	20.00	10.00	6.00
30 Buddy Bell	1.75	.90	.50
31 Gary Matthews	1.25	.60	.40
32 Fred Patek	.90	.45	.25
33 Mike Lum	.90	.45	.25
34 Ellie Rodriguez	.90	.45	.25
35 Milt May (photo actually Lee May)	1.25	.60	.40
36 Willie Horton	.90	.45	.25
40 Joe Rudi	1.25	.60	.40
43 Garry Maddox	.90	.45	.25
46 Dave Chalk	.90	.45	.25
49 Steve Garvey	10.00	5.00	3.00
52 Rollie Fingers	4.00	2.00	1.25
58 Nolan Ryan	10.00	5.00	3.00
61 Ron Cey	1.50	.70	.45
64 Gene Tenace	.90	.45	.25
65 Jose Cardenal	.90	.45	.25
67 Dave Lopes	1.25	.60	.40
68 Wilbur Wood	.90	.45	.25
73 Chris Speier	.90	.45	.25
77 Don Kessinger	.90	.45	.25
79 Andy Messersmith	.90	.45	.25
80 Robin Yount	15.00	7.50	4.50
82 Bill Singer	.90	.45	.25
103 Glenn Beckert	.90	.45	.25
110 Jim Kaat	2.50	1.25	.70
112 Don Money	.90	.45	.25
113 Rick Monday	1.25	.60	.40
122 Jorge Orta	.90	.45	.25
125 Bill Madlock	2.25	1.25	.70
130 Hank Aaron	15.00	7.50	4.50
136 Ken Henderson	.90	.45	.25

1976 Hostess

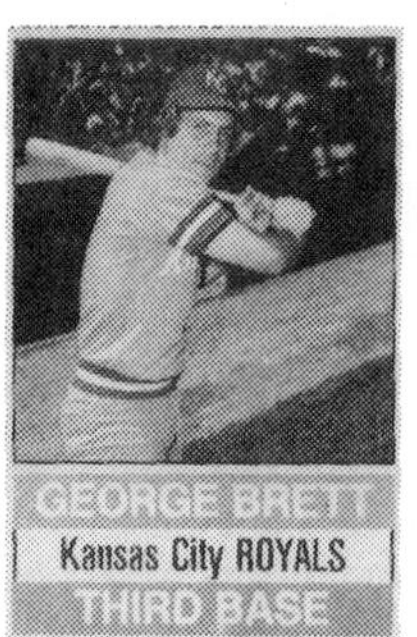

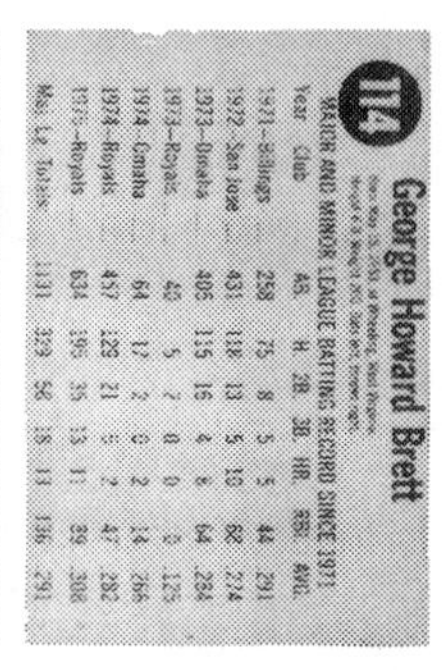

The second of five annual Hostess issues, the 1976 cards carried a "Bicentennial" color theme, with red, white and blue stripes at the bottom of the 2-1/4" by 3-1/4" cards. Like other Hostess issues, the cards were printed in panels of three as the bottom of family-size boxes of snack cake products. This leads to a degree of scarcity for some of the 150 cards in the set; those which were found on less-popular brands. A well-trimmed three-card panel measures 7-1/4" by 3-1/4" size. Some of the photos used in the 1976 Hostess set can also be found on Topps issues of the era.

	NR MT	EX	VG
Complete Panel Set:	350.00	175.00	105.00
Complete Singles Set:	175.00	87.00	52.00
Common Panel:	2.50	1.25	.70
Common Single Player:	.40	.20	.12
Panel 1	11.75	6.00	3.50
1 Fred Lynn	1.25	.60	.40
2 Joe Morgan	2.00	1.00	.60
3 Phil Niekro	2.25	1.25	.70
Panel 2	4.50	2.25	1.25
4 Gaylord Perry	1.75	.90	.50
5 Bob Watson	.40	.20	.12
6 Bill Freehan	.50	.25	.15
Panel 3	6.50	3.25	2.00
7 Lou Brock	3.00	1.50	.90
8 Al Fitzmorris	.40	.20	.12
9 Rennie Stennett	.40	.20	.12
Panel 4	9.00	4.50	2.75
10 Tony Oliva	.70	.35	.20
11 Robin Yount	4.00	2.00	1.25
12 Rick Manning	.40	.20	.12
Panel 5	3.50	1.75	1.00
13 Bobby Grich	.50	.25	.15
14 Terry Forster	.40	.20	.12
15 Dave Kingman	.70	.35	.20
Panel 6	7.00	3.50	2.00
16 Thurman Munson	2.50	1.25	.70
17 Rick Reuschel	.50	.25	.15
18 Bobby Bonds	.50	.25	.15
Panel 7	9.50	4.75	2.75
19 Steve Garvey	4.00	2.00	1.25
20 Vida Blue	.50	.25	.15
21 Dave Rader	.40	.20	.12
Panel 8	9.00	4.50	2.75
22 Johnny Bench	4.00	2.00	1.25
23 Luis Tiant	.50	.25	.15
24 Darrell Evans	.70	.35	.20
Panel 9	2.50	1.25	.70
25 Larry Dierker	.40	.20	.12
26 Willie Horton	.50	.25	.15
27 John Ellis	.40	.20	.12
Panel 10	3.00	1.50	.90
28 Al Cowens	.40	.20	.12
29 Jerry Reuss	.50	.25	.15
30 Reggie Smith	.50	.25	.15
Panel 11	13.00	6.50	4.00
31 Bobby Darwin	.50	.25	.15
32 Fritz Peterson	.50	.25	.15
33 Rod Carew	6.00	3.00	1.75
Panel 12	21.00	10.50	6.25
34 Carlos May	.50	.25	.15
35 Tom Seaver	6.00	3.00	1.75
36 Brooks Robinson	5.00	2.50	1.50
Panel 13	2.50	1.25	.70
37 Jose Cardenal	.40	.20	.12
38 Ron Blomberg	.40	.20	.12
39 Lee Stanton	.40	.20	.12
Panel 14	2.50	1.25	.70
40 Dave Cash	.40	.20	.12
41 John Montefusco	.40	.20	.12
42 Bob Tolan	.40	.20	.12
Panel 15	2.50	1.25	.70
43 Carl Morton	.40	.20	.12
44 Rick Burleson	.50	.25	.15
45 Don Gullett	.40	.20	.12
Panel 16	2.50	1.25	.70
46 Vern Ruhle	.40	.20	.12
47 Cesar Cedeno	.50	.25	.15
48 Toby Harrah	.50	.25	.15
Panel 17	6.00	3.00	1.75
49 Willie Stargell	3.00	1.50	.90
50 Al Hrabosky	.40	.20	.12
51 Amos Otis	.50	.25	.15
Panel 18	2.50	1.25	.70
52 Bud Harrelson	.50	.25	.15
53 Jim Hughes	.40	.20	.12
54 George Scott	.50	.25	.15
Panel 19	9.50	4.75	2.75
55 Mike Vail	.50	.25	.15
56 Jim Palmer	4.00	2.00	1.25
57 Jorge Orta	.80	.40	.25
Panel 20	3.50	1.75	1.00
58 Chris Chambliss	.80	.40	.25
59 Dave Chalk	.50	.25	.15
60 Ray Burris	.50	.25	.15
Panel 21	14.00	7.00	4.25
61 Bert Campaneris	.80	.40	.25
62 Gary Carter	6.00	3.00	1.75
63 Ron Cey	.90	.45	.25
Panel 22	28.00	14.00	8.50
64 Carlton Fisk	2.00	1.00	.60

	NR MT	EX	VG
65 Marty Perez	.50	.25	.15
66 Pete Rose	10.00	5.00	3.00
Panel 23	3.50	1.75	1.00
67 Roger Metzger	.50	.25	.15
68 Jim Sundberg	.60	.30	.20
69 Ron LeFlore	.60	.30	.20
Panel 24	3.50	1.75	1.00
70 Ted Sizemore	.50	.25	.15
71 Steve Busby	.50	.25	.15
72 Manny Sanguillen	.50	.25	.15
Panel 25	5.00	2.50	1.50
73 Larry Hisle	.60	.30	.20
74 Pete Broberg	.50	.25	.15
75 Boog Powell	1.25	.60	.40
Panel 26	6.50	3.25	2.00
76 Ken Singleton	.80	.40	.25
77 Rich Gossage	2.00	1.00	.60
78 Jerry Grote	.50	.25	.15
Panel 27	16.00	8.00	4.75
79 Nolan Ryan	6.00	3.00	1.75
80 Rick Monday	.70	.35	.20
81 Graig Nettles	1.25	.60	.40
Panel 28	18.00	9.00	5.50
82 Chris Speier	.40	.20	.12
83 Dave Winfield	4.00	2.00	1.25
84 Mike Schmidt	6.00	3.00	1.75
Panel 29	4.00	2.00	1.25
85 Buzz Capra	.40	.20	.12
86 Tony Perez	1.00	.50	.30
87 Dwight Evans	.90	.45	.25
Panel 30	2.50	1.25	.70
88 Mike Hargrove	.40	.20	.12
89 Joe Coleman	.40	.20	.12
90 Greg Gross	.40	.20	.12
Panel 31	2.50	1.25	.70
91 John Mayberry	.40	.20	.12
92 John Candelaria	.50	.25	.15
93 Bake McBride	.40	.20	.12
Panel 32	15.00	7.50	4.50
94 Hank Aaron	7.00	3.50	2.00
95 Buddy Bell	.50	.25	.15
96 Steve Braun	.40	.20	.12
Panel 33	2.50	1.25	.70
97 Jon Matlack	.40	.20	.12
98 Lee May	.50	.25	.15
99 Wilbur Wood	.50	.25	.15
Panel 34	4.00	2.00	1.25
100 Bill Madlock	.90	.45	.25
101 Frank Tanana	.50	.25	.15
102 Mickey Rivers	.50	.25	.15
Panel 35	3.75	2.00	1.25
103 Mike Ivie	.40	.20	.12
104 Rollie Fingers	1.25	.60	.40
105 Dave Lopes	.50	.25	.15
Panel 36	3.50	1.75	1.00
106 George Foster	.90	.45	.25
107 Denny Doyle	.40	.20	.12
108 Earl Williams	.40	.20	.12
Panel 37	2.50	1.25	.70
109 Tom Veryzer	.40	.20	.12
110 J.R. Richard	.50	.25	.15
111 Jeff Burroughs	.40	.20	.12
Panel 38	14.00	7.00	4.25
112 Al Oliver	.90	.45	.25
113 Ted Simmons	.80	.40	.25
114 Geroge Brett	5.00	2.50	1.50
Panel 39	3.00	1.50	.90
115 Frank Duffy	.40	.20	.12
116 Bert Blyleven	.80	.40	.25
117 Darrell Porter	.50	.25	.15
Panel 40	2.50	1.25	.70
118 Don Baylor	.70	.35	.20
119 Bucky Dent	.50	.25	.15
120 Felix Millan	.40	.20	.12
Panel 41	2.50	1.25	.70
121 Mike Cuellar	.50	.25	.15
122 Gene Tenace	.40	.20	.12
123 Bobby Murcer	.50	.25	.15
Panel 42	7.00	3.50	2.00
124 Willie McCovey	3.00	1.50	.90
125 Greg Luzinski	.50	.25	.15
126 Larry Parrish	.50	.25	.15
Panel 43	10.00	5.00	3.00
127 Jim Rice	4.00	2.00	1.25
128 Dave Concepcion	.50	.25	.15
129 Jim Wynn	.50	.25	.15
Panel 44	2.50	1.25	.70
130 Tom Grieve	.40	.20	.12
131 Mike Cosgrove	.40	.20	.12
132 Dan Meyer	.40	.20	.12
Panel 45	5.00	2.50	1.50
133 Dave Parker	1.50	.70	.45
134 Don Kessinger	.40	.20	.12
135 Hal McRae	.50	.25	.15
Panel 46	4.00	2.00	1.25
136 Don Money	.70	.35	.20
137 Dennis Eckersley	.90	.45	.25
138 Fergie Jenkins	.80	.40	.25
Panel 47	4.00	2.00	1.25
139 Mike Torrez	.40	.20	.12
140 Jerry Morales	.40	.20	.12
141 Jim Hunter	1.25	.60	.40
Panel 48	2.50	1.25	.70
142 Gary Matthews	.50	.25	.15
143 Randy Jones	.40	.20	.12
144 Mike Jorgensen	.40	.20	.12
Panel 49	13.00	6.50	4.00
145 Larry Bowa	.60	.30	.20
146 Reggie Jackson	5.00	2.50	1.50
147 Steve Yeager	.40	.20	.12
Panel 50	15.00	7.50	4.50
148 Dave May	.40	.20	.12
149 Carl Yastrzemski	6.50	3.25	2.00
150 Cesar Geronimo	.40	.20	.12

A player's name in *italic* type indicates a rookie card. An (FC) indicates a player's first card for that particular card company.

1976 Hostess Twinkies

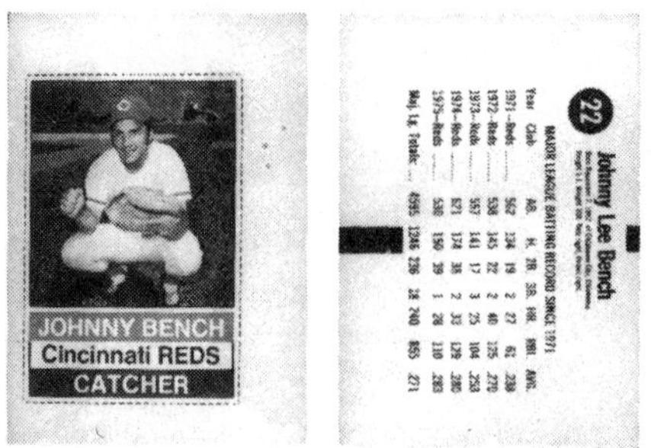

The 60 cards in this regionally-issued (West Coast only) set closely parallel the first 60 cards in the numerical sequence of the "regular" 1976 Hostess issue. The singular difference is the appearance on the back of a black band toward the center of the card at top and bottom. Also unlike the three-card panels of the regular Hostess issue, the 2-1/4" by 3-1/4" Twinkie cards were issued singly, as the cardboard stiffener for the cellophane-wrapped snack cakes. Values quoted are for complete bottom panels.

	NR MT	EX	VG
Complete Set:	175.00	87.00	52.00
Common Player:	.90	.45	.25
1 Fred Lynn	3.00	1.50	.90
2 Joe Morgan	5.00	2.50	1.50
3 Phil Niekro	4.50	2.25	1.25
4 Gaylord Perry	5.00	2.50	1.50
5 Bob Watson	.90	.45	.25
6 Bill Freehan	1.25	.60	.40
7 Lou Brock	7.00	3.50	2.00
8 Al Fitzmorris	.90	.45	.25
9 Rennie Stennett	.90	.45	.25
10 Tony Oliva	2.00	1.00	.60
11 Robin Yount	7.00	3.50	2.00
12 Rick Manning	.90	.45	.25
13 Bobby Grich	1.25	.60	.40
14 Terry Forster	.90	.45	.25
15 Dave Kingman	2.00	1.00	.60
16 Thurman Munson	6.50	3.25	2.00
17 Rick Reuschel	1.25	.60	.40
18 Bobby Bonds	1.25	.60	.40
19 Steve Garvey	10.00	5.00	3.00
20 Vida Blue	1.75	.90	.50
21 Dave Rader	.90	.45	.25
22 Johnny Bench	10.00	5.00	3.00
23 Luis Tiant	1.50	.70	.45
24 Darrell Evans	2.00	1.00	.60
25 Larry Dierker	.90	.45	.25
26 Willie Horton	.90	.45	.25
27 John Ellis	.90	.45	.25
28 Al Cowens	.90	.45	.25
29 Jerry Reuss	1.25	.60	.40
30 Reggie Smith	1.25	.60	.40
31 Bobby Darwin	.90	.45	.25
32 Fritz Peterson	.90	.45	.25
33 Rod Carew	10.00	5.00	3.00
34 Carlos May	.90	.45	.25
35 Tom Seaver	10.00	5.00	3.00
36 Brooks Robinson	9.00	4.50	2.75
37 Jose Cardenal	.90	.45	.25
38 Ron Blomberg	.90	.45	.25
39 Lee Stanton	.90	.45	.25
40 Dave Cash	.90	.45	.25
41 John Montefusco	.90	.45	.25
42 Bob Tolan	.90	.45	.25
43 Carl Morton	.90	.45	.25
44 Rick Burleson	.90	.45	.25
45 Don Gullett	.90	.45	.25
46 Vern Ruhle	.90	.45	.25
47 Cesar Cedeno	1.25	.60	.40
48 Toby Harrah	.90	.45	.25
49 Willie Stargell	7.00	3.50	2.00
50 Al Hrabosky	.90	.45	.25
51 Amos Otis	.90	.45	.25
52 Bud Harrelson	.90	.45	.25
53 Jim Hughes	.90	.45	.25
54 George Scott	.90	.45	.25
55 Mike Vail	.90	.45	.25
56 Jim Palmer	7.00	3.50	2.00
57 Jorge Orta	.90	.45	.25
58 Chris Chambliss	1.25	.60	.40
59 Dave Chalk	.90	.45	.25
60 Ray Burris	.90	.45	.25

1977 Hostess

The third of five consecutive annual issues, the 1977 Hostess cards retained the same card size 2-1/4" by 3-1/4", set size - 150 cards, and mode of issue - three cards on a 7-1/4" by 3-1/4" panel, as the previous two efforts. Because they were issued as the bottom panel of snack cake boxes, and because some brands of Hostess products were more popular than others, certain cards in the set are scarcer than others.

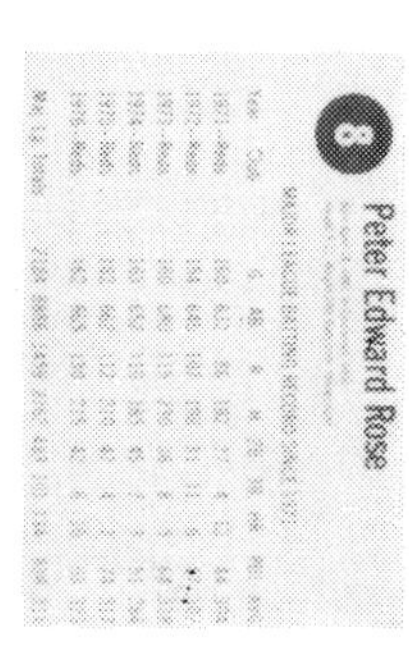

	NR MT	EX	VG
Complete Panel Set:	325.00	162.00	97.00
Complete Singles Set:	175.00	87.00	52.00
Common Panel:	2.50	1.25	.70
Common Single Player:	.40	.20	.12
Panel 1	18.00	9.00	5.50
1 Jim Palmer	2.75	1.50	.80
2 Joe Morgan	2.00	1.00	.60
3 Reggie Jackson	5.00	2.50	1.50
Panel 2	23.00	11.50	7.00
4 Carl Yastrzemski	6.00	3.00	1.75
5 Thurman Munson	2.50	1.25	.70
6 Johnny Bench	4.00	2.00	1.25
Panel 3	32.00	16.00	9.50
7 Tom Seaver	3.00	1.50	.90
8 Pete Rose	8.00	4.00	2.50
9 Rod Carew	4.00	2.00	1.25
Panel 4	2.50	1.25	.70
10 Luis Tiant	.60	.30	.20
11 Phil Garner	.50	.25	.15
12 Sixto Lezcano	.40	.20	.12
Panel 5	2.50	1.25	.70
13 Mike Torrez	.40	.20	.12
14 Dave Lopes	.50	.25	.15
15 Doug DeCinces	.50	.25	.15
Panel 6	2.50	1.25	.70
16 Jim Spencer	.40	.20	.12
17 Hal McRae	.50	.25	.15
18 Mike Hargrove	.40	.20	.12
Panel 7	4.50	2.25	1.25
19 Willie Montanez	.50	.25	.15
20 Roger Metzger	.50	.25	.15
21 Dwight Evans	1.50	.70	.45
Panel 8	10.00	5.00	3.00
22 Steve Rogers	.50	.25	.15
23 Jim Rice	4.00	2.00	1.25
24 Pete Falcone	.50	.25	.15
Panel 9	9.00	4.50	2.75
25 Greg Luzinski	.90	.45	.25
26 Randy Jones	.50	.25	.15
27 Willie Stargell	3.00	1.50	.90
Panel 10	3.50	1.75	1.00
28 John Hiller	.50	.25	.15
29 Bobby Murcer	.70	.35	.20
30 Rick Monday	.70	.35	.20
Panel 11	9.00	4.50	2.75
31 John Montefusco	.50	.25	.15
32 Lou Brock	4.00	2.00	1.25
33 Bill North	.50	.25	.15
Panel 12	32.00	16.00	9.50
34 Robin Yount	4.00	2.00	1.25
35 Steve Garvey	5.00	2.50	1.50
36 George Brett	8.00	4.00	2.50
Panel 13	3.50	1.75	1.00
37 Toby Harrah	.70	.35	.20
38 Jerry Royster	.50	.25	.15
39 Bob Watson	.60	.30	.20
Panel 14	9.50	4.75	2.75
40 George Foster	.90	.45	.25
41 Gary Carter	3.50	1.75	1.00
42 John Denny	.40	.20	.12
Panel 15	18.00	9.00	5.50
43 Mike Schmidt	5.00	2.50	1.50
44 Dave Winfield	3.75	2.00	1.25
45 Al Oliver	.90	.45	.25
Panel 16	3.00	1.50	.90
46 Mark Fidrych	.60	.30	.20
47 Larry Herndon	.50	.25	.15
48 Dave Goltz	.40	.20	.12
Panel 17	3.50	1.75	1.00
49 Jerry Morales	.40	.20	.12
50 Ron LeFlore	.50	.25	.15
51 Fred Lynn	.90	.45	.25
Panel 18	3.50	1.75	1.00
52 Vida Blue	.50	.25	.15
53 Rick Manning	.40	.20	.12
54 Bill Buckner	.70	.35	.20
Panel 19	2.50	1.25	.70
55 Lee May	.50	.25	.15
56 John Mayberry	.40	.20	.12
57 Darrel Chaney	.40	.20	.12
Panel 20	3.50	1.75	1.00
58 Cesar Cedeno	.50	.25	.15
59 Ken Griffey	.50	.25	.15
60 Dave Kingman	.80	.40	.25
Panel 21	3.50	1.75	1.00
61 Ted Simmons	.80	.40	.25
62 Larry Bowa	.50	.25	.15
63 Frank Tanana	.50	.25	.15
Panel 22	2.50	1.25	.70
64 Jason Thompson	.40	.20	.12
65 Ken Brett	.40	.20	.12
66 Roy Smalley	.40	.20	.12
Panel 23	2.50	1.25	.70
67 Ray Burris	.40	.20	.12
68 Rick Burleson	.40	.20	.12
69 Buddy Bell	.50	.25	.15
Panel 24	5.00	2.50	1.50
70 Don Sutton	2.00	1.00	.60
71 Mark Belanger	.40	.20	.12
72 Dennis Leonard	.40	.20	.12
Panel 25	5.00	2.50	1.50
73 Gaylord Perry	1.50	.70	.45

		NR MT	EX	VG
74	Dick Ruthven	.40	.20	.12
75	Jose Cruz	.50	.25	.15
Panel 26		4.25	2.25	1.25
76	Cesar Geronimo	.40	.20	.12
77	Jerry Koosman	.50	.25	.15
78	Garry Templeton	.80	.40	.25
Panel 27		10.00	5.00	3.00
79	Jim Hunter	1.25	.60	.40
80	John Candelaria	.50	.25	.15
81	Nolan Ryan	3.50	1.75	1.00
Panel 28		2.50	1.25	.70
82	Rusty Staub	.50	.25	.15
83	Jim Barr	.40	.20	.12
84	Butch Wynegar	.50	.25	.15
Panel 29		2.50	1.25	.70
85	Jose Cardenal	.40	.20	.12
86	Claudell Washington	.50	.25	.15
87	Bill Travers	.40	.20	.12
Panel 30		2.50	1.25	.70
88	Rick Waits	.40	.20	.12
89	Ron Cey	.50	.25	.15
90	Al Bumbry	.40	.20	.12
Panel 31		2.50	1.25	.70
91	Bucky Dent	.50	.25	.15
92	Amos Otis	.50	.25	.15
93	Tom Grieve	.40	.20	.12
Panel 32		2.50	1.25	.70
94	Enos Cabell	.40	.20	.12
95	Dave Concepcion	.50	.25	.15
96	Felix Millan	.40	.20	.12
Panel 33		2.50	1.25	.70
97	Bake McBride	.40	.20	.12
98	Chris Chambliss	.50	.25	.15
99	Butch Metzger	.40	.20	.12
Panel 34		2.50	1.25	.70
100	Rennie Stennett	.40	.20	.12
101	Dave Roberts	.40	.20	.12
102	Lyman Bostock	.50	.25	.15
Panel 35		3.50	1.75	1.00
103	Rick Reuschel	.50	.25	.15
104	Carlton Fisk	1.00	.50	.30
105	Jim Slaton	.40	.20	.12
Panel 36		2.50	1.25	.70
106	Dennis Eckersley	.60	.30	.20
107	Ken Singleton	.50	.25	.15
108	Ralph Garr	.40	.20	.12
Panel 37		8.00	4.00	2.50
109	Freddie Patek	.50	.25	.15
110	Jim Sundberg	.60	.30	.20
111	Phil Niekro	3.25	1.75	1.00
Panel 38		3.50	1.75	1.00
112	J.R. Richard	.70	.35	.20
113	Gary Nolan	.50	.25	.15
114	Jon Matlack	.60	.30	.20
Panel 39		20.00	10.00	6.00
115	Keith Hernandez	4.00	2.00	1.25
116	Graig Nettles	.70	.35	.20
117	Steve Carlton	4.50	2.25	1.25
Panel 40		6.50	3.25	2.00
118	Bill Madlock	1.50	.70	.45
119	Jerry Reuss	.80	.40	.25
120	Aurelio Rodriguez	.50	.25	.15
Panel 41		3.50	1.75	1.00
121	Dan Ford	.50	.25	.15
122	Ray Fosse	.50	.25	.15
123	George Hendrick	.70	.35	.20
Panel 42		2.50	1.25	.70
124	Alan Ashby	.40	.20	.12
125	Joe Lis	.40	.20	.12
126	Sal Bando	.50	.25	.15
Panel 43		4.00	2.00	1.25
127	Richie Zisk	.50	.25	.15
128	Rich Gossage	.90	.45	.25
129	Don Baylor	.60	.30	.20
Panel 44		2.50	1.25	.70
130	Dave McKay	.40	.20	.12
131	Bob Grich	.50	.25	.15
132	Dave Pagan	.40	.20	.12
Panel 45		2.50	1.25	.70
133	Dave Cash	.40	.20	.12
134	Steve Braun	.40	.20	.12
135	Dan Meyer	.40	.20	.12
Panel 46		4.25	2.25	1.25
136	Bill Stein	.40	.20	.12
137	Rollie Fingers	1.50	.70	.45
138	Brian Downing	.50	.25	.15
Panel 47		2.50	1.25	.70
139	Bill Singer	.40	.20	.12
140	Doyle Alexander	.50	.25	.15
141	Gene Tenace	.40	.20	.12
Panel 48		2.50	1.25	.70
142	Gary Matthews	.50	.25	.15
143	Don Gullett	.40	.20	.12
144	Wayne Garland	.40	.20	.12
Panel 49		2.50	1.25	.70
145	Pete Broberg	.40	.20	.12
146	Joe Rudi	.50	.25	.15
147	Glenn Abbott	.40	.20	.12
Panel 50		2.50	1.25	.70
148	George Scott	.50	.25	.15
149	Bert Campaneris	.50	.25	.15
150	Andy Messersmith	.50	.25	.15

1977 Hostess Twinkies

The 1977 Hostess Twinkie issue, at 150 different cards, is the largest of the single-panel Twinkie sets. It is also the most obscure. The cards, which measure 2-1/4" by 3-1/4", but are part of a larger panel, were found not only with Twinkies, but with Hostess Cupcakes as well. Card #'s 1-30 and 111-150 are Twinkies panels and #'s 31-135 are Cupcakes panels. Complete Cupcakes panels are approximately 2-1/4" by 4-1/2" in size, while complete Twinkies panels measure 3-1/8" by 4-1/4". The photos used in the set are identical to those in the 1977 Hostess three-card panel set. The main difference is the appearance of a black band at the center of the card back. The values quoted in the checklist that follows are for complete bottom panels.

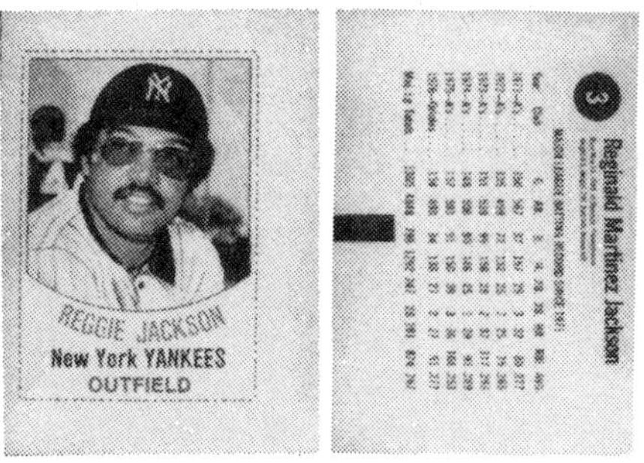

		NR MT	EX	VG
Complete Set:		325.00	162.00	97.00
Common Player:		.80	.40	.25
1	Jim Palmer	6.00	3.00	1.75
2	Joe Morgan	4.00	2.00	1.25
3	Reggie Jackson	10.00	5.00	3.00
4	Carl Yastrzemski	12.00	6.00	3.50
5	Thurman Munson	5.00	2.50	1.50
6	Johnny Bench	8.00	4.00	2.50
7	Tom Seaver	7.00	3.50	2.00
8	Pete Rose	15.00	7.50	4.50
9	Rod Carew	8.00	4.00	2.50
10	Luis Tiant	1.00	.50	.30
11	Phil Garner	.80	.40	.25
12	Sixto Lezcano	.80	.40	.25
13	Mike Torrez	.80	.40	.25
14	Dave Lopes	1.00	.50	.30
15	Doug DeCinces	1.00	.50	.30
16	Jim Spencer	.80	.40	.25
17	Hal McRae	1.00	.50	.30
18	Mike Hargrove	.80	.40	.25
19	Willie Montanez	.80	.40	.25
20	Roger Metzger	.80	.40	.25
21	Dwight Evans	2.00	1.00	.60
22	Steve Rogers	.80	.40	.25
23	Jim Rice	6.00	3.00	1.75
24	Pete Falcone	.80	.40	.25
25	Greg Luzinski	1.50	.70	.45
26	Randy Jones	.80	.40	.25
27	Willie Stargell	6.00	3.00	1.75
28	John Hiller	.80	.40	.25
29	Bobby Murcer	1.25	.60	.40
30	Rick Monday	1.00	.50	.30
31	John Montefusco	.80	.40	.25
32	Lou Brock	6.00	3.00	1.75
33	Bill North	.80	.40	.25
34	Robin Yount	6.00	3.00	1.75
35	Steve Garvey	7.00	3.50	2.00
36	George Brett	10.00	5.00	3.00
37	Toby Harrah	.80	.40	.25
38	Jerry Royster	.80	.40	.25
39	Bob Watson	1.00	.50	.30
40	George Foster	1.75	.90	.50
41	Gary Carter	7.00	3.50	2.00
42	John Denny	.80	.40	.25
43	Mike Schmidt	9.00	4.50	2.75
44	Dave Winfield	7.00	3.50	2.00
45	Al Oliver	1.75	.90	.50
46	Mark Fidrych	1.50	.70	.45
47	Larry Herndon	1.00	.50	.30
48	Dave Goltz	.80	.40	.25
49	Jerry Morales	.80	.40	.25
50	Ron LeFlore	1.00	.50	.30
51	Fred Lynn	1.75	.90	.50
52	Vida Blue	1.00	.50	.30
53	Rick Manning	.80	.40	.25
54	Bill Buckner	1.50	.70	.45
55	Lee May	1.00	.50	.30
56	John Mayberry	.80	.40	.25
57	Darrel Chaney	.80	.40	.25
58	Cesar Cedeno	1.25	.60	.40
59	Ken Griffey	1.25	.60	.40
60	Dave Kingman	1.75	.90	.50
61	Ted Simmons	1.50	.70	.45
62	Larry Bowa	1.25	.60	.40
63	Frank Tanana	1.00	.50	.30
64	Jason Thompson	.80	.40	.25
65	Ken Brett	.80	.40	.25
66	Roy Smalley	.80	.40	.25
67	Ray Burris	.80	.40	.25
68	Rick Burleson	.80	.40	.25
69	Buddy Bell	1.25	.60	.40
70	Don Sutton	3.50	1.75	1.00
71	Mark Belanger	.80	.40	.25
72	Dennis Leonard	.80	.40	.25
73	Gaylord Perry	4.00	2.00	1.25
74	Dick Ruthven	.80	.40	.25
75	Jose Cruz	1.25	.60	.40
76	Cesar Geronimo	.80	.40	.25
77	Jerry Koosman	1.25	.60	.40
78	Garry Templeton	2.50	1.25	.70
79	Jim Hunter	4.00	2.00	1.25
80	John Candelaria	1.00	.50	.30
81	Nolan Ryan	7.00	3.50	2.00
82	Rusty Staub	1.50	.70	.45
83	Jim Barr	.80	.40	.25
84	Butch Wynegar	1.00	.50	.30
85	Jose Cardenal	.80	.40	.25
86	Claudell Washington	1.00	.50	.30
87	Bill Travers	.80	.40	.25
88	Rick Waits	.80	.40	.25
89	Ron Cey	1.25	.60	.40
90	Al Bumbry	.80	.40	.25
91	Bucky Dent	1.00	.50	.30
92	Amos Otis	1.00	.50	.30
93	Tom Grieve	.80	.40	.25
94	Enos Cabell	.80	.40	.25
95	Dave Concepcion	1.25	.60	.40
96	Felix Millan	.80	.40	.25
97	Bake McBride	.80	.40	.25
98	Chris Chambliss	1.00	.50	.30
99	Butch Metzger	.80	.40	.25
100	Rennie Stennett	.80	.40	.25
101	Dave Roberts	.80	.40	.25
102	Lyman Bostock	1.00	.50	.30
103	Rick Reuschel	1.00	.50	.30
104	Carlton Fisk	2.25	1.25	.70
105	Jim Slaton	.80	.40	.25
106	Dennis Eckersley	1.25	.60	.40
107	Ken Singleton	1.00	.50	.30
108	Ralph Garr	.80	.40	.25
109	Freddie Patek	.80	.40	.25
110	Jim Sundberg	.80	.40	.25
111	Phil Niekro	3.50	1.75	1.00
112	J. R. Richard	1.00	.50	.30
113	Gary Nolan	.80	.40	.25
114	Jon Matlack	.80	.40	.25
115	Keith Hernandez	5.00	2.50	1.50
116	Graig Nettles	2.00	1.00	.60
117	Steve Carlton	7.00	3.50	2.00
118	Bill Madlock	1.50	.70	.45
119	Jerry Reuss	1.00	.50	.30
120	Aurelio Rodriguez	.80	.40	.25
121	Dan Ford	.80	.40	.25
122	Ray Fosse	.80	.40	.25
123	George Hendrick	1.00	.50	.30
124	Alan Ashby	.80	.40	.25
125	Joe Lis	.80	.40	.25
126	Sal Bando	1.00	.50	.30
127	Richie Zisk	1.00	.50	.30
128	Rich Gossage	1.75	.90	.50
129	Don Baylor	1.50	.70	.45
130	Dave McKay	.80	.40	.25
131	Bob Grich	1.00	.50	.30
132	Dave Pagan	.80	.40	.25
133	Dave Cash	.80	.40	.25
134	Steve Braun	.80	.40	.25
135	Dan Meyer	.80	.40	.25
136	Bill Stein	.80	.40	.25
137	Rollie Fingers	3.00	1.50	.90
138	Brian Downing	1.00	.50	.30
139	Bill Singer	.80	.40	.25
140	Doyle Alexander	1.00	.50	.30
141	Gene Tenace	1.00	.50	.30
142	Gary Matthews	1.00	.50	.30
143	Don Gullett	.80	.40	.25
144	Wayne Garland	.80	.40	.25
145	Pete Broberg	.80	.40	.25
146	Joe Rudi	1.00	.50	.30
147	Glenn Abbott	.80	.40	.25
148	George Scott	1.00	.50	.30
149	Bert Campaneris	1.25	.60	.40
150	Andy Messersmith	1.00	.50	.30

1978 Hostess

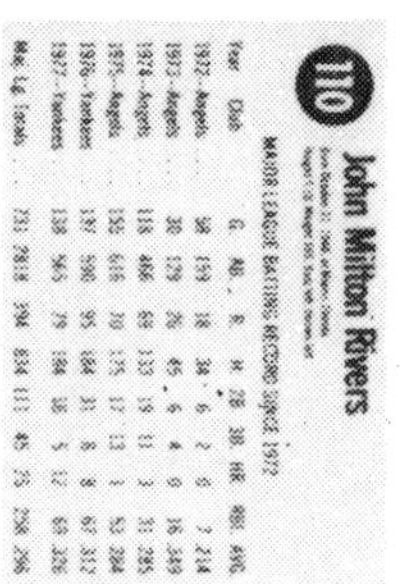

Other than the design on the front of the card, there was little different about the 1978 Hostess cards from the three years' issues which had preceded it, or the one which followed. The 2-1/4" by 3-1/4" cards were printed in panels of three (7-1/4" by 3-1/4") as the bottom of family-sized boxes of snake cakes. The 1978 set was again complete at 150 cards. Like other years of Hostess issues, there are scarcities within the 1978 set that are the result of those panels having been issued with less-popular brands of snack cakes.

		NR MT	EX	VG
Complete Panel:		300.00	150.00	90.00
Complete Singles Set:		175.00	87.00	52.00
Common Panel:		2.50	1.25	.70
Common Single Player:		.40	.20	.12
Panel 1		4.00	2.00	1.25
1	Butch Hobson	.40	.20	.12
2	George Foster	.90	.45	.25
3	Bob Forsch	.50	.25	.15
Panel 2		5.00	2.50	1.50
4	Tony Perez	1.00	.50	.30
5	Bruce Sutter	.90	.45	.25
6	Hal McRae	.50	.25	.15
Panel 3		6.00	3.00	1.75
7	Tommy John	1.50	.70	.45
8	Greg Luzinski	.50	.25	.15
9	Enos Cabell	.40	.20	.12
Panel 4		7.00	3.50	2.00
10	Doug DeCinces	.50	.25	.15
11	Willie Stargell	3.00	1.50	.90
12	Ed Halicki	.40	.20	.12
Panel 5		2.50	1.25	.70
13	Larry Hisle	.40	.20	.12

No.	Player	NR MT	EX	VG
14	Jim Slaton	.40	.20	.12
15	Buddy Bell	.50	.25	.15
Panel 6		2.50	1.25	.70
16	Earl Williams	.40	.20	.12
17	Glenn Abbott	.40	.20	.12
18	Dan Ford	.40	.20	.12
Panel 7		2.50	1.25	.70
19	Gary Mathews	.50	.25	.15
20	Eric Soderholm	.40	.20	.12
21	Bump Wills	.40	.20	.12
Panel 8		7.00	3.50	2.00
22	Keith Hernandez	2.50	1.25	.70
23	Dave Cash	.40	.20	.12
24	George Scott	.50	.25	.15
Panel 9		15.00	7.50	4.50
25	Ron Guidry	1.50	.70	.45
26	Dave Kingman	.80	.40	.25
27	George Brett	5.00	2.50	1.50
Panel 10		3.50	1.75	1.00
28	Bob Watson	.50	.25	.15
29	Bob Boone	.70	.35	.20
30	Reggie Smith	.70	.35	.20
Panel 11		20.00	10.00	6.00
31	Eddie Murray	10.00	5.00	3.00
32	Gary Lavelle	.50	.25	.15
33	Rennie Stennett	.50	.25	.15
Panel 12		3.50	1.75	1.00
34	Duane Kuiper	.50	.25	.15
35	Sixto Lezcano	.50	.25	.15
36	Dave Rozema	.50	.25	.15
Panel 13		3.50	1.75	1.00
37	Butch Wynegar	.50	.25	.15
38	Mitchell Page	.50	.25	.15
39	Bill Stein	.50	.25	.15
Panel 14		2.50	1.25	.70
40	Elliott Maddox	.40	.20	.12
41	Mike Hargrove	.40	.20	.12
42	Bobby Bonds	.50	.25	.15
Panel 15		15.00	7.50	4.50
43	Garry Templeton	.80	.40	.25
44	Johnny Bench	4.00	2.00	1.25
45	Jim Rice	4.00	2.00	1.25
Panel 16		13.00	6.50	4.00
46	Bill Buckner	.80	.40	.25
47	Reggie Jackson	5.00	2.50	1.50
48	Freddie Patek	.40	.20	.12
Panel 17		8.50	4.25	2.50
49	Steve Carlton	3.50	1.75	1.00
50	Cesar Cedeno	.50	.25	.15
51	Steve Yeager	.40	.20	.12
Panel 18		3.50	1.75	1.00
52	Phil Garner	.50	.25	.15
53	Lee May	.50	.25	.15
54	Darrell Evans	.70	.35	.20
Panel 19		2.50	1.25	.70
55	Steve Kemp	.50	.25	.15
56	Dusty Baker	.50	.25	.15
57	Ray Fosse	.40	.20	.12
Panel 20		2.50	1.25	.70
58	Manny Sanguillen	.40	.20	.12
59	Tom Johnson	.40	.20	.12
60	Lee Stanton	.40	.20	.12
Panel 21		10.00	5.00	3.00
61	Jeff Burroughs	.40	.20	.12
62	Bobby Grich	.50	.25	.15
63	Dave Winfield	4.00	2.00	1.25
Panel 22		3.50	1.75	1.00
64	Dan Driessen	.50	.25	.15
65	Ted Simmons	.80	.40	.25
66	Jerry Remy	.40	.20	.12
Panel 23		2.50	1.25	.70
67	Al Cowens	.40	.20	.12
68	Sparky Lyle	.50	.25	.15
69	Manny Trillo	.50	.25	.15
Panel 24		5.00	2.50	1.50
70	Don Sutton	1.50	.70	.45
71	Larry Bowa	.50	.25	.15
72	Jose Cruz	.50	.25	.15
Panel 25		8.00	4.00	2.50
73	Willie McCovey	3.00	1.50	.90
74	Bert Blyleven	.70	.35	.20
75	Ken Singleton	.50	.25	.15
Panel 26		2.50	1.25	.70
76	Bill North	.40	.20	.12
77	Jason Thompson	.40	.20	.12
78	Dennis Eckersley	.50	.25	.15
Panel 27		2.50	1.25	.70
79	Jim Sundberg	.50	.25	.15
80	Jerry Koosman	.50	.25	.15
81	Bruce Bochte	.40	.20	.12
Panel 28		8.50	4.25	2.50
82	George Hendrick	.50	.25	.15
83	Nolan Ryan	3.50	1.75	1.00
84	Roy Howell	.40	.20	.12
Panel 29		5.50	2.75	1.75
85	Butch Metzger	.40	.20	.12
86	George Medich	.40	.20	.12
87	Joe Morgan	2.00	1.00	.60
Panel 30		3.00	1.50	.90
88	Dennis Leonard	.50	.25	.15
89	Willie Randolph	.50	.25	.15
90	Bobby Murcer	.50	.25	.15
Panel 31		3.00	1.50	.90
91	Rick Manning	.40	.20	.12
92	J.R. Richard	.50	.25	.15
93	Ron Cey	.60	.30	.20
Panel 32		2.50	1.25	.70
94	Sal Bando	.50	.25	.15
95	Ron LeFlore	.50	.25	.15
96	Dave Goltz	.40	.20	.12
Panel 33		2.50	1.25	.70
97	Dan Meyer	.40	.20	.12
98	Chris Chambliss	.50	.25	.15
99	Biff Pocoroba	.40	.20	.12
Panel 34		2.50	1.25	.70
100	Oscar Gamble	.40	.20	.12
101	Frank Tanana	.50	.25	.15
102	Lenny Randle	.40	.20	.12
Panel 35		2.50	1.25	.70
103	Tommy Hutton	.40	.20	.12
104	John Candelaria	.50	.25	.15
105	Jorge Orta	.40	.20	.12
Panel 36		3.00	1.50	.90
106	Ken Reitz	.40	.20	.12
107	Bill Campbell	.40	.20	.12
108	Dave Concepcion	.70	.35	.20
Panel 37		2.50	1.25	.70
109	Joe Ferguson	.40	.20	.12
110	Mickey Rivers	.50	.25	.15
111	Paul Splittorff	.40	.20	.12
Panel 38		12.00	6.00	3.50
112	Davey Lopes	.50	.25	.15
113	Mike Schmidt	5.00	2.50	1.50
114	Joe Rudi	.50	.25	.15
Panel 39		7.00	3.50	2.00
115	Milt May	.40	.20	.12
116	Jim Palmer	3.00	1.50	.90
117	Bill Madlock	.70	.35	.20
Panel 40		2.50	1.25	.70
118	Roy Smalley	.40	.20	.12
119	Cecil Cooper	.50	.25	.15
120	Rick Langford	.40	.20	.12
Panel 41		5.75	3.00	1.75
121	Ruppert Jones	.40	.20	.12
122	Phil Niekro	2.25	1.25	.70
123	Toby Harrah	.50	.25	.15
Panel 42		2.50	1.25	.70
124	Chet Lemon	.50	.25	.15
125	Gene Tenace	.40	.20	.12
126	Steve Henderson	.40	.20	.12
Panel 43		20.00	10.00	6.00
127	Mike Torrez	.40	.20	.12
128	Pete Rose	8.00	4.00	2.50
129	John Denny	.50	.25	.15
Panel 44		4.00	2.00	1.25
130	Darrell Porter	.50	.25	.15
131	Rick Reuschel	.50	.25	.15
132	Graig Nettles	.90	.45	.25
Panel 45		4.50	2.25	1.25
133	Garry Maddox	.50	.25	.15
134	Mike Flanagan	.50	.25	.15
135	Dave Parker	1.25	.60	.40
Panel 46		7.50	3.75	2.25
136	Terry Whitfield	.40	.20	.12
137	Wayne Garland	.40	.20	.12
138	Robin Yount	3.00	1.50	.90
Panel 47		12.00	6.00	3.50
139	Gaylord Perry	2.50	1.25	.70
140	Rod Carew	4.00	2.00	1.25
141	Wayne Gross	.40	.20	.12
Panel 48		5.00	2.50	1.50
142	Barry Bonnell	.40	.20	.12
143	Willie Montanez	.40	.20	.12
144	Rollie Fingers	1.75	.90	.50
Panel 49		12.00	6.00	3.50
145	Bob Bailor	.40	.20	.12
146	Tom Seaver	3.50	1.75	1.00
147	Thurman Munson	2.50	1.25	.70
Panel 50		8.00	4.00	2.50
148	Lyman Bostock	.50	.25	.15
149	Gary Carter	3.50	1.75	1.00
150	Ron Blomberg	.40	.20	.12

1979 Hostess

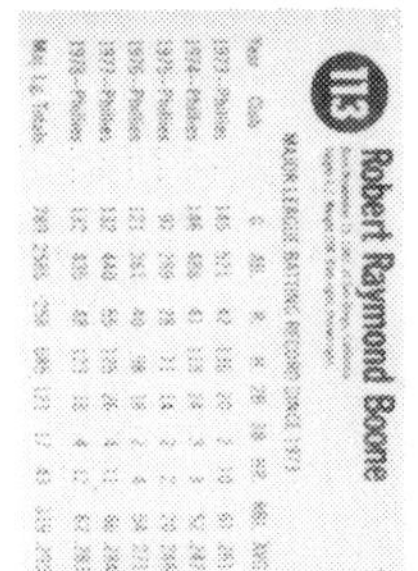

The last of five consecutive annual issues, the 1979 Hostess set retained the 150-card set size, 2-1/4" by 3-1/4" single-card size and 7-1/4" by 3-1/4" three-card panel format from the previous years. The cards were printed as the bottom panel on family-size boxes of Hostess snack cakes. Some panels, which were printed on less-popular brands, are somewhat scarcer today than the rest of the set. Like all Hostess issues, because the hobby was in a well-developed state at the time of issue, the 1979s survive today in complete panels and complete unused boxes, for collectors who like original packaging.

	NR MT	EX	VG
Complete Panel Set:	325.00	162.00	97.00
Complete Singles Set:	175.00	87.00	52.00
Common Panel:	2.50	1.25	.70
Common Single Player:	.40	.20	.12

No.	Player	NR MT	EX	VG
Panel 1		9.50	4.75	2.75
1	John Denny	.40	.20	.12
2	Jim Rice	4.00	2.00	1.25
3	Doug Bair	.40	.20	.12
Panel 2		2.50	1.25	.70
4	Darrell Porter	.50	.25	.15
5	Ross Grimsley	.40	.20	.12
6	Bobby Murcer	.50	.25	.15
Panel 3		18.00	9.00	5.50
7	Lee Mazzilli	.50	.25	.15
8	Steve Garvey	4.00	2.00	1.25
9	Mike Schmidt	5.00	2.50	1.50
Panel 4		6.50	3.25	2.00
10	Terry Whitfield	.40	.20	.12
11	Jim Palmer	3.00	1.50	.90
12	Omar Moreno	.40	.20	.12
Panel 5		2.50	1.25	.70
13	Duane Kuiper	.40	.20	.12
14	Mike Caldwell	.40	.20	.12
15	Steve Kemp	.50	.25	.15
Panel 6		2.50	1.25	.70
16	Dave Goltz	.40	.20	.12
17	Mitchell Page	.40	.20	.12
18	Bill Stein	.40	.20	.12
Panel 7		2.50	1.25	.70
19	Gene Tenace	.40	.20	.12
20	Jeff Burroughs	.40	.20	.12
21	Francisco Barrios	.40	.20	.12
Panel 8		8.00	4.00	2.50
22	Mike Torrez	.40	.20	.12
23	Ken Reitz	.40	.20	.12
24	Gary Carter	3.50	1.75	1.00
Panel 9		8.00	4.00	2.50
25	Al Hrabosky	.50	.25	.15
26	Thurman Munson	2.50	1.25	.70
27	Bill Buckner	.80	.40	.25
Panel 10		5.00	2.50	1.50
28	Ron Cey	.90	.45	.25
29	J.R. Richard	.70	.35	.20
30	Greg Luzinski	.90	.45	.25
Panel 11		5.00	2.50	1.50
31	Ed Ott	.50	.25	.15
32	Denny Martinez	.50	.25	.15
33	Darrell Evans	1.25	.60	.40
Panel 12		2.50	1.25	.70
34	Ron LeFlore	.50	.25	.15
35	Rick Waits	.40	.20	.12
36	Cecil Cooper	.50	.25	.15
Panel 13		9.50	4.75	2.75
37	Leon Roberts	.40	.20	.12
38	Rod Carew	4.00	2.00	1.25
39	John Henry Johnson	.40	.20	.12
Panel 14		2.50	1.25	.70
40	Chet Lemon	.50	.25	.15
41	Craig Swan	.40	.20	.12
42	Gary Matthews	.50	.25	.15
Panel 15		3.50	1.75	1.00
43	Lamar Johnson	.40	.20	.12
44	Ted Simmons	.80	.40	.25
45	Ken Griffey	.50	.25	.15
Panel 16		4.00	2.00	1.25
46	Freddie Patek	.40	.20	.12
47	Frank Tanana	.50	.25	.15
48	Rich Gossage	1.25	.60	.40
Panel 17		2.50	1.25	.70
49	Burt Hooton	.40	.20	.12
50	Ellis Valentine	.40	.20	.12
51	Ken Forsch	.40	.20	.12
Panel 18		5.00	2.50	1.50
52	Bob Knepper	.50	.25	.15
53	Dave Parker	1.50	.70	.45
54	Doug DeCinces	.50	.25	.15
Panel 19		8.00	4.00	2.50
55	Robin Yount	3.00	1.50	.90
56	Rusty Staub	.80	.40	.25
57	Gary Alexander	.40	.20	.12
Panel 20		2.50	1.25	.70
58	Julio Cruz	.40	.20	.12
59	Matt Keough	.40	.20	.12
60	Roy Smalley	.40	.20	.12
Panel 21		10.00	5.00	3.00
61	Joe Morgan	2.50	1.25	.70
62	Phil Niekro	2.50	1.25	.70
63	Don Baylor	.80	.40	.25
Panel 22		10.00	5.00	3.00
64	Dwight Evans	.90	.45	.25
65	Tom Seaver	4.00	2.00	1.25
66	George Hendrick	.50	.25	.15
Panel 23		14.00	7.00	4.25
67	Rick Reuschel	.50	.25	.15
68	Geroge Brett	6.00	3.00	1.75
69	Lou Piniella	.80	.40	.25
Panel 24		8.50	4.25	2.50
70	Enos Cabell	.40	.20	.12
71	Steve Carlton	3.50	1.75	1.00
72	Reggie Smith	.50	.25	.15
Panel 25		4.00	2.00	1.25
73	Rick Dempsey	.50	.25	.15
74	Vida Blue	.80	.40	.25
75	Phil Garner	.70	.35	.20
Panel 26		3.50	1.75	1.00
76	Rick Manning	.50	.25	.15
77	Mark Fidrych	.80	.40	.25
78	Mario Guerrero	.50	.25	.15
Panel 27		5.00	2.50	1.50
79	Bob Stinson	.50	.25	.15
80	Al Oliver	1.25	.60	.40
81	Doug Flynn	.50	.25	.15
Panel 28		6.00	3.00	1.75
82	John Mayberry	.40	.20	.12
83	Gaylord Perry	2.50	1.25	.70
84	Joe Rudi	.50	.25	.15
Panel 29		3.50	1.75	1.00
85	Dave Concepcion	.70	.35	.20
86	John Candelaria	.50	.25	.15
87	Pete Vuckovich	.50	.25	.15
Panel 30		5.00	2.50	1.50
88	Ivan DeJesus	.40	.20	.12
89	Ron Guidry	1.50	.70	.45
90	Hal McRae	.50	.25	.15
Panel 31		5.50	2.75	1.75
91	Cesar Cedeno	.50	.25	.15
92	Don Sutton	2.00	1.00	.60
93	Andre Thornton	.50	.25	.15
Panel 32		2.50	1.25	.70
94	Roger Erickson	.40	.20	.12
95	Larry Hisle	.40	.20	.12
96	Jason Thompson	.40	.20	.12
Panel 33		7.50	3.75	2.25
97	Jim Sundberg	.50	.25	.15
98	Bob Horner	3.00	1.50	.90
99	Ruppert Jones	.40	.20	.12
Panel 34		8.50	4.25	2.50
100	Willie Montanez	.40	.20	.12
101	Nolan Ryan	3.50	1.75	1.00
102	Ozzie Smith	.70	.35	.20
Panel 35		7.50	3.75	2.25
103	Eric Soderholm	.40	.20	.12
104	Willie Stargell	3.00	1.50	.90

	NR MT	EX	VG
105 Bob Bailor	.40	.20	.12
Panel 36	9.00	4.50	2.75
106 Carlton Fisk	1.25	.60	.40
107 George Foster	.90	.45	.25
108 Keith Hernandez	2.50	1.25	.70
Panel 37	4.00	2.00	1.25
109 Dennis Leonard	.50	.25	.15
110 Graig Nettles	.90	.45	.25
111 Jose Cruz	.50	.25	.15
Panel 38	3.50	1.75	1.00
112 Bobby Grich	.50	.25	.15
113 Bob Boone	.50	.25	.15
114 Dave Lopes	.50	.25	.15
Panel 39	15.00	7.50	4.50
115 Eddie Murray	4.50	2.25	1.25
116 Jack Clark	.90	.45	.25
117 Lou Whitaker	.50	.25	.15
Panel 40	10.00	5.00	3.00
118 Miguel Dilone	.40	.20	.12
119 Sal Bando	.50	.25	.15
120 Reggie Jackson	4.50	2.25	1.25
Panel 41	14.00	7.00	4.25
121 Dale Murphy	7.00	3.50	2.00
122 Jon Matlack	.40	.20	.12
123 Bruce Bochte	.40	.20	.12
Panel 42	9.00	4.50	2.75
124 John Stearns	.40	.20	.12
125 Dave Winfield	3.50	1.75	1.00
126 Jorge Orta	.40	.20	.12
Panel 43	9.00	4.50	2.75
127 Garry Templeton	.70	.35	.20
128 Johnny Bench	4.00	2.00	1.25
129 Butch Hobson	.40	.20	.12
Panel 44	4.50	2.25	1.25
130 Bruce Sutter	1.25	.60	.40
131 Bucky Dent	.50	.25	.15
132 Amos Otis	.50	.25	.15
Panel 45	3.50	1.75	1.00
133 Bert Blyleven	.70	.35	.20
134 Larry Bowa	.50	.25	.15
135 Ken Singleton	.50	.25	.15
Panel 46	3.50	1.75	1.00
136 Sixto Lezcano	.40	.20	.12
137 Roy Howell	.40	.20	.12
138 Bill Madlock	.80	.40	.25
Panel 47	2.50	1.25	.70
139 Dave Revering	.40	.20	.12
140 Richie Zisk	.50	.25	.15
141 Butch Wynegar	.50	.25	.15
Panel 48	18.00	9.00	5.50
142 Alan Ashby	.40	.20	.12
143 Sparky Lyle	.50	.25	.15
144 Pete Rose	8.00	4.00	2.50
Panel 49	4.00	2.00	1.25
145 Dennis Eckersley	.60	.30	.20
146 Dave Kingman	.80	.40	.25
147 Buddy Bell	.60	.30	.20
Panel 50	2.50	1.25	.70
148 Mike Hargrove	.40	.20	.12
149 Jerry Koosman	.50	.25	.15
150 Toby Harrah	.50	.25	.15

1985 Hostess Braves

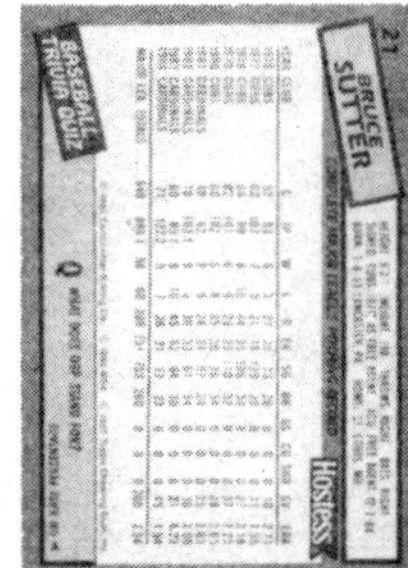

After a five-year hiatus, Hostess returned to the production of baseball cards in 1985 with an Atlanta Braves team set. The 22 cards in the set were printed by Topps and inserted into packages of snack cake products, three cello-wrapped player cards and a header card per box. The 2-1/2" by 3-1/2" cards share a common back design with the regular-issue Topps cards of 1985.

		MT	NR MT	EX
Complete Set:		10.00	7.50	4.00
Common Player:		.35	.25	.14
1	Eddie Haas	.35	.25	.14
2	Len Barker	.35	.25	.14
3	Steve Bedrosian	.90	.70	.35
4	Bruce Benedict	.35	.25	.14
5	Rick Camp	.35	.25	.14
6	Rick Cerone	.35	.25	.14
7	Chris Chambliss	.40	.30	.15
8	Terry Forster	.35	.25	.14
9	Gene Garber	.35	.25	.14
10	Albert Hall	.50	.40	.20
11	Bob Horner	.70	.50	.30
12	Glenn Hubbard	.35	.25	.14
13	Brad Komminsk	.35	.25	.14
14	Rick Mahler	.40	.30	.15
15	Craig McMurtry	.35	.25	.14
16	Dale Murphy	2.00	1.50	.80
17	Ken Oberkfell	.40	.30	.15
18	Pascual Perez	.40	.30	.15
19	Gerald Perry	1.50	1.25	.60
20	Rafael Ramirez	.35	.25	.14
21	Bruce Sutter	.50	.40	.20
22	Claudell Washington	.40	.30	.15
---	Header Card	.10	.08	.04

1987 Hostess Stickers

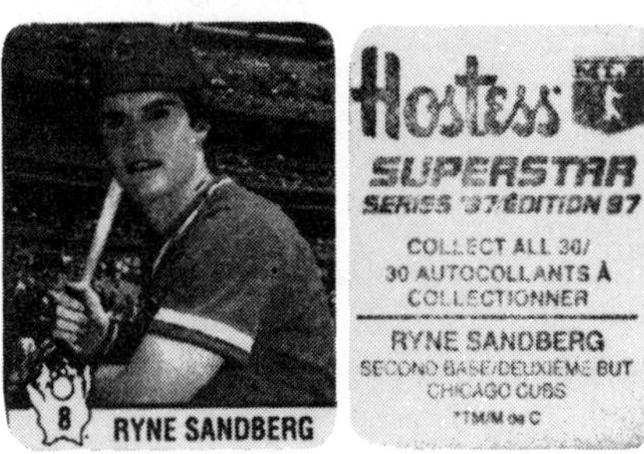

Hostess of Canada issued a 30-card set of stickers in specially marked bags of potato chips. One sticker, measuring 1-3/4" by 1-3/8" in size, was found in each bag. The stickers have full-color fronts with the player's name appearing in black type in a white band. The Hostess logo and the sticker number are also included on the fronts. The backs are written in both English and French and contain the player's name, position and team.

		MT	NR MT	EX
Complete Set:		25.00	18.50	10.00
Common Player:		.20	.15	.08
1	Jesse Barfield	.35	.25	.14
2	Ernie Whitt	.20	.15	.08
3	George Bell	1.00	.70	.40
4	Hubie Brooks	.20	.15	.08
5	Tim Wallach	.35	.25	.14
6	Floyd Youmans	.20	.15	.08
7	Dale Murphy	1.50	1.25	.60
8	Ryne Sandberg	1.00	.70	.40
9	Eric Davis	2.00	1.50	.80
10	Mike Scott	.35	.25	.14
11	Fernando Valenzuela	.75	.60	.30
12	Gary Carter	1.00	.70	.40
13	Mike Schmidt	1.50	1.25	.60
14	Tony Pena	.20	.15	.08
15	Ozzie Smith	.60	.45	.25
16	Tony Gwynn	1.25	.90	.50
17	Mike Krukow	.20	.15	.08
18	Eddie Murray	1.25	.90	.50
19	Wade Boggs	2.25	1.75	.90
20	Wally Joyner	2.00	1.50	.80
21	Harold Baines	.35	.25	.14
22	Brook Jacoby	.35	.25	.14
23	Lou Whitaker	.50	.40	.20
24	George Brett	1.50	1.25	.60
25	Robin Yount	.75	.60	.30
26	Kirby Puckett	1.25	.90	.50
27	Don Mattingly	3.50	2.75	1.50
28	Jose Canseco	3.00	2.25	1.25
29	Phil Bradley	.35	.25	.14
30	Pete O'Brien	.20	.15	.08

1988 Hostess

The Expos and Blue Jays are showcased in this set of 24 discs (1-1/2" diameter). Full-color head shots are framed in white, surrounded by red stars. A yellow-banner "1988 Collectors Edition" label is printed (English and French) beneath the photo, followed by the player's name in black. Numbered disc backs are bilingual, blue and white, and include player name and stats. This set was distributed inside Hostess potato chip packages sold in Canada.

		MT	NR MT	EX
Complete Panel Set:		12.00	9.00	4.75
Complete Singles Set:		7.00	5.25	2.75
Common Panel:		.75	.60	.30
Common Single Player:		.25	.20	.10
Panel		.90	.70	.35
1	Mitch Webster	.25	.20	.10
20	Lloyd Moseby	.40	.30	.15
Panel		.90	.70	.35
2	Tim Burke	.25	.20	.10
23	Tom Henke	.40	.30	.15
Panel		.80	.60	.30
3	Tom Foley	.25	.20	.10
13	Jim Clancy	.30	.25	.12
Panel		.75	.60	.30
4	Herm Winningham	.25	.20	.10
14	Rance Mulliniks	.25	.20	.10
Panel		1.25	.90	.50
5	Hubie Brooks	.40	.30	.15
24	Jimmy Key	.60	.45	.25
Panel		1.00	.70	.40
6	Mike Fitzgerald	.25	.20	.10
17	Dave Stieb	.60	.45	.25
Panel		2.25	1.75	.90
7	Tim Wallach	.70	.50	.30
15	Fred McGriff	1.00	.70	.40
Panel		2.25	1.75	.90
8	Andres Galarraga	1.00	.70	.40
21	Tony Fernandez	.70	.50	.30
Panel		.80	.60	.30
9	Floyd Youmans	.30	.25	.12
18	Mark Eichhorn	.30	.25	.12
Panel		1.00	.70	.40
10	Neal Heaton	.25	.20	.10
19	Jesse Barfield	.70	.50	.30
Panel		2.00	1.50	.80
11	Tim Raines	1.25	.90	.50
16	Ernie Whitt	.25	.20	.10
Panel		1.75	1.25	.70
12	Casey Candaele	.25	.20	.10
22	George Bell	1.00	.70	.40

1953 Hunter Wieners Cardinals

From the great era of the regionally issued hot dog cards in the mid-1950s, the 1953 Hunter wieners set of St. Louis Cardinals is certainly among the rarest today. Originally issued in two-card panels, the cards are most often found as 2-1/4" by 3-1/4" singles today when they can be found at all. The cards feature a light blue facsimile autograph printed over the stat box at the bottom. They are blank-backed.

		NR MT	EX	VG
Complete Set:		2300.	1150.	650.00
Common Player:		60.00	30.00	18.00
(1)	Steve Bilko	60.00	30.00	18.00
(2)	Alpha Brazle	60.00	30.00	18.00
(3)	Cloyd Boyer	60.00	30.00	18.00
(4)	Cliff Chambers	60.00	30.00	18.00
(5)	Michael Clark	60.00	30.00	18.00
(6)	Jack Crimian	60.00	30.00	18.00
(7)	Lester Fusselman	60.00	30.00	18.00
(8)	Harvey Haddix	65.00	33.00	20.00
(9)	Solly Hemus	60.00	30.00	18.00
(10)	Ray Jablonski	60.00	30.00	18.00
(11)	William Johnson	60.00	30.00	18.00
(12)	Harry Lowrey	60.00	30.00	18.00
(13)	Lawrence Miggins	60.00	30.00	18.00
(14)	Stuart Miller	60.00	30.00	18.00
(15)	Wilmer Mizell	60.00	30.00	18.00
(16)	Stanley Musial	600.00	300.00	175.00
(17)	Joseph Presko	60.00	30.00	18.00
(18)	Delbert Rice	60.00	30.00	18.00
(19)	Harold Rice	60.00	30.00	18.00
(20)	Willard Schmidt	60.00	30.00	18.00
(21)	Albert Schoendienst	100.00	50.00	30.00
(22)	Richard Sisler	60.00	30.00	18.00
(23)	Enos Slaughter	150.00	75.00	45.00
(24)	Gerald Staley	60.00	30.00	18.00
(25)	Edward Stanky	70.00	35.00	21.00
(26)	John Yuhas	60.00	30.00	18.00

1954 Hunter Wieners Cardinals

A nearly impossible set to complete today by virtue of the method of its issue, the 1954 Hunter hot dog set essentially features what would traditionally be the front and back of a normal baseball card on two different cards. The "front," containing a color photo of one of 30 St. Louis Cardinals has a box at bottom challenging the collector to name him and quote his stats. The "back" features cartoon Cardinals in action, and contains the answers. However, because both parts were printed on a single panel, and because most of the back (non-picture) panels were thrown away years ago, it is an impossible challenge to complete a '54 Hunter set today. There is no back printing on the 2-1/4" by 3-1/2" cards.

		NR MT	EX	VG
Complete Set:		3900.	1950.	1170.
Common Player:		60.00	30.00	18.00
(1)	Tom Alston	60.00	30.00	18.00
(2)	Steve Bilko	60.00	30.00	18.00
(3)	Al Brazle	60.00	30.00	18.00
(4)	Tom Burgess	60.00	30.00	18.00
(5)	Cot Deal	60.00	30.00	18.00
(6)	Alex Grammas	60.00	30.00	18.00
(7)	Harvey Haddix	60.00	30.00	18.00
(8)	Solly Hemus	60.00	30.00	18.00
(9)	Ray Jablonski	60.00	30.00	18.00
(10)	Royce Lint	60.00	30.00	18.00
(11)	Peanuts Lowrey	60.00	30.00	18.00
(12)	Memo Luna	60.00	30.00	18.00
(13)	Stu Miller	60.00	30.00	18.00
(14)	Stan Musial	600.00	300.00	180.00
(15)	Tom Poholsky	60.00	30.00	18.00
(16)	Bill Posedel	60.00	30.00	18.00
(17)	Joe Presko	60.00	30.00	18.00
(18)	Vic Raschi	60.00	30.00	18.00
(19)	Dick Rand	60.00	30.00	18.00
(20)	Rip Repulski	60.00	30.00	18.00
(21)	Del Rice	60.00	30.00	18.00
(22)	John Riddle	60.00	30.00	18.00
(23)	Mike Ryba	60.00	30.00	18.00
(24)	Red Schoendienst	100.00	50.00	30.00
(25)	Dick Schofield	100.00	50.00	30.00
(26)	Eddie Stanky	110.00	55.00	33.00
(27)	Enos Slaughter	150.00	75.00	45.00
(28)	Gerry Staley	60.00	30.00	18.00
(29)	Ed Yuhas	60.00	30.00	18.00
(30)	Sal Yvars	60.00	30.00	18.00

1955 Hunter Wieners Cardinals

The 1955 team set of St. Louis Cardinals, included with packages of Hunter hot dogs, features the third format change in three years of issue. For 1955, the cards were printed in a tall, narrow 2" by 4-3/4" format, two to a panel. The cards featured both a posed action photo and a portrait photo, along with a facsimile autograph and brief biographical data on the front. There is no back printing, as the cards were part of the wrapping for packages of hot dogs.

		NR MT	EX	VG
Complete Set:		3200.	1600.	1500.
Common Player:		75.00	37.00	22.00
(1)	Thomas Edison Alston	75.00	37.00	22.00
(2)	Kenton Lloyd Boyer	225.00	112.00	67.00
(3)	Harry Lewis Elliott	75.00	37.00	22.00
(4)	John Edward Faszholz	75.00	37.00	22.00
(5)	Joseph Filmore Frazier	75.00	37.00	22.00
(6)	Alexander Pete Grammas	75.00	37.00	22.00
(7)	Harvey Haddix	125.00	62.00	37.00
(8)	Solly Joseph Hemus	75.00	37.00	22.00
(9)	Lawrence Curtis Jackson	75.00	37.00	22.00
(10)	Tony R. Jacobs	75.00	37.00	22.00
(11)	Gordon Bassett Jones	75.00	37.00	22.00
(12)	Paul Edmore LaPalme	75.00	37.00	22.00
(13)	Brooks Ulysses Lawrence	75.00	37.00	22.00
(14)	Wallace Wade Moon	125.00	62.00	37.00
(15)	Stanley Frank Musial	1000.	500.00	300.00
(16)	Thomas George Poholsky	75.00	37.00	22.00
(17)	William John Posedel	75.00	37.00	22.00
(18)	Victor Angelo John Raschi	75.00	37.00	22.00
(19)	Eldon John Repulski	75.00	37.00	22.00
(20)	Delbert Rice	75.00	37.00	22.00
(21)	John Ludy Riddle	75.00	37.00	22.00
(22)	William F. Sarni	75.00	37.00	22.00
(23)	Albert Fred Schoendienst	175.00	87.00	52.00
(24)	Richard John Schofield (actually John Richard)	75.00	37.00	22.00
(25)	Frank Thomas Smith	75.00	37.00	22.00
(26)	Edward R. Stanky	125.00	62.00	37.00
(27)	Bobby Gene Tiefenauer	75.00	37.00	22.00
(28)	William Charles Virdon	175.00	87.00	52.00
(29)	Frederick E. Walker	75.00	37.00	22.00
(30)	Floyd Lewis Woolridge	75.00	37.00	22.00

1982 Hygrade Expos

This 24-card Montreal Expos team set was the object of intense collector speculation when it was first issued. Single cello-wrapped cards were included in packages of Hygrade luncheon meat in the province of Quebec only. Until a mail-in offer for the complete set appeared later in the season, the set was selling for as high as $50. It remains a relatively scarce issue today. The 2" by 3" cards are printed on heavy paper, with round corners. Backs are printed only in French, and contain an offer for an album to house the set.

		MT	NR MT	EX
Complete Set:		40.00	30.00	16.00
Common Player:		1.00	.70	.40
Album:		6.00	4.50	2.50
0	Al Oliver	2.25	1.75	.90
4	Chris Speier	1.00	.70	.40
5	John Milner	1.00	.70	.40
6	Jim Fanning	1.00	.70	.40
8	Gary Carter	7.00	5.25	2.75
10	Andre Dawson	5.00	3.75	2.00
11	Frank Tavaras (Taveras)	1.00	.70	.40
16	Terry Francona	1.25	.90	.50
17	Tim Blackwell	1.00	.70	.40
18	Jerry White	1.00	.70	.40
20	Bob James	1.25	.90	.50
21	Scott Sanderson	1.00	.70	.40
24	Brad Mills	1.00	.70	.40
29	Tim Wallach	3.00	2.25	1.25
30	Tim Raines	7.00	5.25	2.75
34	Bill Gullickson	1.25	.90	.50
35	Woodie Fryman	1.00	.70	.40
38	Bryn Smith	1.50	1.25	.60
41	Jeff Reardon	2.00	1.50	.80
44	Dan Norman	1.00	.70	.40
45	Steve Rogers	1.25	.90	.50
48	Ray Burris	1.00	.70	.40
49	Warren Cromartie	1.00	.70	.40
53	Charlie Lea	1.00	.70	.40

Definitions for grading conditions are located in the Introduction section at the front of this book.

1976 Icee Drinks Reds

Issued in 1976 in the Cincinnati area by Icee Drinks, this 12-card set of circular cards features members of the Cincinnati Reds. The cards measure approximately 2" in diameter with the bottom of the disc squared off. The cards are unnumbered.

		NR MT	EX	VG
Complete Set:		25.00	12.50	7.50
Common Player:		.40	.20	.12
(1)	Johnny Bench	6.00	3.00	1.75
(2)	Dave Concepcion	1.25	.60	.40
(3)	Rawley Eastwick	.40	.20	.12
(4)	George Foster	1.25	.60	.40
(5)	Cesar Geronimo	.40	.20	.12
(6)	Ken Griffey	1.25	.60	.40
(7)	Don Gullett	.70	.35	.20
(8)	Will McEnaney	.40	.20	.12
(9)	Joe Morgan	5.00	2.50	1.50
(10)	Gary Nolan	.40	.20	.12
(11)	Tony Perez	1.50	.70	.45
(12)	Pete Rose	8.00	4.00	2.50

1984 Jarvis Press Rangers

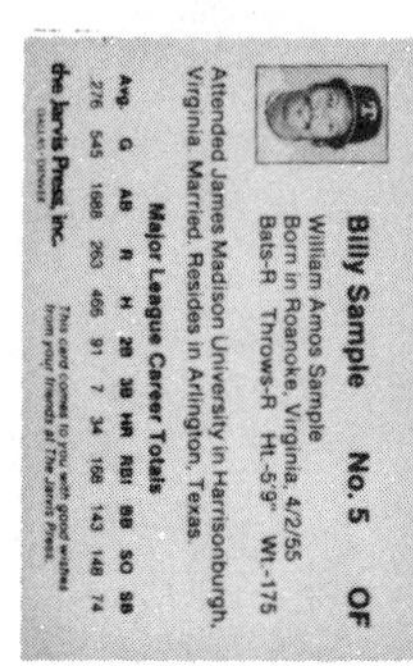

For its second annual "Baseball Card Day" game promotional set, the Rangers picked up a new sponsor, Jarvis Press of Dallas. The 30 cards in the set include 27 players, the manager, trainer and a group card of the coaches. Cards measure 2-3/8" by 3-1/2". Color game-action photos make up the card fronts. Backs, printed in black and white, include a portrait photo of the player. A source close to the promotion indicated 10,000 sets were produced.

		MT	NR MT	EX
Complete Set:		6.00	4.50	2.50
Common Player:		.12	.09	.05
1	Bill Stein	.12	.09	.05
2	Alan Bannister	.12	.09	.05
3	Wayne Tolleson	.12	.09	.05
5	Billy Sample	.12	.09	.05
6	Bobby Jones	.12	.09	.05
7	Ned Yost	.12	.09	.05
9	Pete O'Brien	.50	.40	.20
11	Doug Rader	.12	.09	.05
13	Tommy Dunbar	.12	.09	.05
14	Jim Anderson	.12	.09	.05
15	Larry Parrish	.30	.25	.12
16	Mike Mason	.12	.09	.05

		MT	NR MT	EX
17	Mickey Rivers	.20	.15	.08
19	Curtis Wilkerson	.12	.09	.05
20	Jeff Kunkel	.12	.09	.05
21	Odell Jones	.12	.09	.05
24	Dave Schmidt	.15	.11	.06
25	Buddy Bell	.50	.40	.20
26	George Wright	.12	.09	.05
28	Frank Tanana	.20	.15	.08
30	Marv Foley	.12	.09	.05
31	Dave Stewart	.40	.30	.15
32	Gary Ward	.20	.15	.08
36	Dickie Noles	.12	.09	.05
43	Donnie Scott	.12	.09	.05
44	Danny Darwin	.15	.11	.06
49	Charlie Hough	.30	.25	.12
53	Joey McLaughlin	.12	.09	.05
---	Coaching Staff (Rich Donnelly, Glenn Ezell, Merv Rettenmund, Dick Such, Wayne Terwilliger)	.12	.09	.05
---	Trainer (Bill Zeigler)	.12	.09	.05

1958 Jay Publishing 5x7 Photos -Type I

JOHN CALLISON, Philadelphia Phillies

The name "Picture Packs" has been used to describe this massive series of 5" by 7" black and white player photos issued by Jay Publishing's Big League Books division over the eight-year period from 1958-1965. The company also produced yearbooks for various major league teams during the same period, and many of the photos used in the yearbooks also appear in the Picture Packs sets. The Picture Packs were sold by teams, each set consisting of 12 player photos with his name and team at the bottom. The Picture Packs were available by mail, at the ballparks and in stores. They were sold in either plain brown or white envelopes, or in clear plastic. Most were printed on a glossy, slick paper stock, although the quality of the paper may vary from team to team and year to year. The photos were issued anonymously, with no indication of the producer or year of issue, making it nearly impossible to checklist the sets completely. It is known that two different types were issued, based on the typeface used in the captions. Type I photos, issued from 1958 through 1961, were printed with a sans-serif-style typeface, while Type II photos, issued from 1962 through 1965, used a serif typeface. Attempts to thoroughly checklist the Picture Packs began only recently. To date nearly 1,500 different poses have been found, but more may exist.

		NR MT	EX	VG
	Complete Set:	1200.	600.00	350.00
	Common Player:	.75	.40	.25
(1)	Henry Aaron (Outfielder)	10.00	5.00	3.00
(2)	Henry Aaron (batting)	10.00	5.00	3.00
(3)	Hank Aaron (portrait, pose to neck)	10.00	5.00	3.00
(4)	Joe Adcock (portrait, pose to waist)	1.25	.60	.40
(5)	Joe Adcock (batting, pose to chest)	1.25	.60	.40
(6)	Joseph Adcock (Infielder, portrait, pose to neck)	1.25	.60	.40
(7)	Bob Allison (portrait, pose to neck)	1.00	.50	.30
(8)	Bob Allison (batting, pose to chest)	1.00	.50	.30
(9)	Bob Allison (batting, pose to chest, scored background)	1.00	.50	.30
(10)	Felipe Alou (kneeling, pose to waist, arms crossed)	1.00	.50	.30
(11)	Walter Alston (portrait, pose to neck)	1.75	.90	.50
(12)	George Altman (portrait, pose to chest)	.75	.40	.25
(13)	Ruben Amaro (batting, pose to chest, dark background)	.75	.40	.25
(14)	Ruben Amaro (batting, pose to chest, light background)	.75	.40	.25
(15)	Bob Anderson (portrait, pose to chest)	.75	.40	.25
(16)	Bob Anderson (pitching)	.75	.40	.25
(17)	Harry Anderson (Phillies, portrait, pose to neck)	.75	.40	.25
(18)	Harry Anderson (Philadelphia Phillies, portrait, pose to chest)	.75	.40	.25
(19)	John Antonelli (Giants, pitching)	1.00	.50	.30
(20)	John Antonelli (portrait, pose to neck)	1.00	.50	.30
(21)	John Antonelli (Indians, pitching)	1.00	.50	.30
(22)	Luis Aparicio (portrait, pose to chest)	2.00	1.00	.60
(23)	Luis Aparicio (ready to throw)	2.00	1.00	.60
(24)	Luis Aparicio (portrait, pose to neck)	2.00	1.00	.60
(25)	Richie Ashburn (Phillies, portrait, pose to neck)	1.75	.90	.50
(26)	Richie Ashburn (Philadelphia Phillies, portrait, pose to waist)	1.75	.90	.50
(27)	Richie Asburn (Ashburn) (Cubs, portrait, pose to neck)	1.75	.90	.50
(28)	Richie Ashburn (Cubs, portrait, pose to waist)	1.75	.90	.50
(29)	Ken Aspromonte (portrait, pose to chest)	.75	.40	.25
(30)	Ed Bailey (portrait, pose to chest)	.75	.40	.25
(31)	Ed Bailey (batting, pose to waist)	.75	.40	.25
(32)	Ed Bailey (portrait, pose to neck, smile)	.75	.40	.25
(33)	Ed Bailey (portrait, pose to neck, no smile)	6.00	3.00	1.75
(34)	Ernie Banks (portrait, pose to neck)	6.00	3.00	1.75
(35)	Ernie Banks (portrait, pose to chest)	6.00	3.00	1.75
(36)	Curt Barclay (pitching, pitcher's follow through)	.75	.40	.25
(37)	Earl Battey (portrait, pose to neck)	.75	.40	.25
(38)	Earl Battey (catching, crouching)	.75	.40	.25
(39)	Hank Bauer (Yankees, portrait, pose to neck)	1.25	.60	.40
(40)	Hank Bauer (AThletics, portrait, pose to neck)	1.00	.50	.30
(41)	Hank Bauer (batting)	1.00	.50	.30
(42)	Frank Baumann (portrait, pose to waist, glove)	.75	.40	.25
(43)	Jim Baumer (batting, pose to chest)	.75	.40	.25
(44)	Julio Becquer (portrait, pose to chest)	.75	.40	.25
(45)	Julio Becquer (kneeling, holding bat)	.75	.40	.25
(46)	Gus Bell (portrait, pose to neck)	.75	.40	.25
(47)	Gus Bell (hands on knees)	.75	.40	.25
(48)	Lou Berberet (portrait, pose to chest)	.75	.40	.25
(49)	Larry Berra (portrait, pose to neck)	7.00	3.50	2.00
(50)	Yogi Berra (batting, pose to waist)	7.00	3.50	2.00
(51)	Reno Bertoia (kneeling, holding bat)	.75	.40	.25
(52)	Reno Bertoia (fielding, Detroit uniform)	.75	.40	.25
(53)	Steve Bilko (portrait, pose to chest)	.75	.40	.25
(54)	Steve Bilko (portrait, pose to neck)	.75	.40	.25
(55)	Don Blasingame (bunting)	.75	.40	.25
(56)	Don Blasingame (fielding)	.75	.40	.25
(57)	Don Blasingame (portrait, pose to neck)	.75	.40	.25
(58)	Frank Bolling (Braves, portrait, pose to chest)	.75	.40	.25
(59)	Frank Bolling (Tigers, portrait, pose to chest)	.75	.40	.25
(60)	Steve Boros (portrait, pose to chest)	.75	.40	.25
(61)	Ed Bouchee (portrait, pose to waist, Philadelphia uniform)	.75	.40	.25
(62)	Ed Bouchee (portrait, pose to chest)	.75	.40	.25
(63)	Bob Bowman (portrait, pose to neck)	.75	.40	.25
(64)	Bob Boyd (portrait, pose to neck)	.75	.40	.25
(65)	Bob Boyd (Orioles, portrait, pose to chest)	.75	.40	.25
(66)	Bob Boyd (Athletics, portrait, pose to chest)	.75	.40	.25
(67)	Cletus Boyer (Cletis) (kneeling, holding bat)	1.00	.50	.30
(68)	Ken Boyer (portrait, pose to neck)	1.50	.70	.45
(69)	Ken Boyer (portrait, pose to chest)	1.50	.70	.45
(70)	Jackie Brandt (Giants, portrait, pose to chest)	.75	.40	.25
(71)	Jackie Brandt (batting)	.75	.40	.25
(72)	Jackie Brandt (Orioles, portrait, pose to chest, dark background)	.75	.40	.25
(73)	Jackie Brandt (Orioles, portrait, pose to chest, light background)	.75	.40	.25
(74)	Marv Breeding (batting, pose to chest)	.75	.40	.25
(75)	Eddie Bressoud (fielding)	.75	.40	.25
(76)	Tom Brewer (portrait, pose to chest)	.75	.40	.25
(77)	Tom Brewer (portrait, pose to neck)	.75	.40	.25
(78)	Fritz Brickell (portrait, pose to chest)	.75	.40	.25
(79)	Rocky Bridges (portrait, pose to chest)	.75	.40	.25
(80)	Rocky Bridges (portrati, pose to neck)	.75	.40	.25
(81)	Harry Bright (portrait, pose to chest)	.75	.40	.25
(82)	Ernie Broglio (portrait, pose to chest)	.75	.40	.25
(83)	Jim Brosman (Brosnan) (portrait, pose to chest)	.75	.40	.25
(84)	Jim Brosnan (portrait, pose to neck)	.75	.40	.25
(85)	Dick Brown (catching, crouching)	.75	.40	.25
(86)	Bill Bruton (portrait, pose to chest)	.75	.40	.25
(87)	Billy Bruton (portrait, pose to waist)	.75	.40	.25
(88)	Billy Bruton (fielding, leaping)	.75	.40	.25
(89)	Don Buddin (portrait, pose to neck)	.75	.40	.25
(90)	Don Buddin (portrait, pose to chest)	.75	.40	.25
(91)	Don Buddin (fielding)	.75	.40	.25
(92)	Bob Buhl (portrait, pose to neck)	.75	.40	.25
(93)	Bob Buhl (pitching, pitcher's follow through)	.75	.40	.25
(94)	Jim Bunning (portrait, pose to chest)	1.50	.70	.45
(95)	Lewis Burdette (Pitcher, portrait, pose to neck)	1.00	.50	.30
(96)	Lou Burdette (portrait, pose to chest)	1.00	.50	.30
(97)	Lou Burdette (pitching)	1.00	.50	.30
(98)	"Smokey" Burgess (portrait, pose to neck)	1.00	.50	.30
(99)	Forrest "Smokey" Burgess (portrait, pose to chest)	1.00	.50	.30
(100)	Smokey Burgess (sitting, 3 bats)	1.00	.50	.30
(101)	Smokey Burgess (portrait, pose to chest)	1.00	.50	.30
(102)	Jim Busby (portrait, pose to neck)	.75	.40	.25
(103)	John Callison (White Sox, portrait, pose to neck)	1.00	.50	.30
(104)	John Callison (batting, pose to neck)	1.00	.50	.30
(105)	John Callison (Phillies, batting, pose to chest, 2 bats)	1.00	.50	.30
(106)	Roy Campanella (Catcher, portrait, pose to neck)	5.00	2.50	1.50
(107)	Andy Carey (portrait, pose to neck)	.75	.40	.25
(108)	Andy Carey (portrait, pose to waist)	.75	.40	.25
(109)	Chico Carrasquel (portrait, pose to chest)	.75	.40	.25
(110)	Jerry Casale (portrait, pose to chest)	.75	.40	.25
(111)	Jerry Casale (pitching)	.75	.40	.25
(112)	Norm Cash (portrait, pose to chest)	1.00	.50	.30
(113)	Orlando Cepeda (standing, 4 bats)	1.50	.70	.45
(114)	Bob Cerv (portrait, pose to chest)	.75	.40	.25
(115)	Bob Cerv (portrait, pose to neck)	.75	.40	.25
(116)	Bob Cerv (batting, pose to waist)	.75	.40	.25
(117)	Harry Chiti (catching, crouching)	.75	.40	.25
(118)	Gino Cimoli (outfielder, portrait, pose to neck)	.75	.40	.25
(119)	Gino Cimoli (portrait, pose to chest)	.75	.40	.25
(120)	Gino Cimoli (Cardinals, portrait, pose to neck)	.75	.40	.25
(121)	Roberto Clemente (portrait, pose to neck)	5.00	2.50	1.50
(122)	Roberto Clemente (batting, pose to chest)	5.00	2.50	1.50
(123)	Roberto Clemente (portrait, pose to chest)	5.00	2.50	1.50
(124)	Truman Clevenger (portrait, pose to chest)	.75	.40	.25
(125)	Truman Clevenger (pitching, pitcher's follow through)	.75	.40	.25
(126)	Jim Coker (catching, crouching)	.75	.40	.25
(127)	Rocco "Rocky" Colavito (batting)	1.25	.60	.40
(128)	Rocky Colavito (portrait, pose to chest, glove)	1.25	.60	.40
(129)	Rocky Colavito (hands on knees)	1.25	.60	.40
(130)	Gordon Coleman (batting, pose to chest)	.75	.40	.25
(131)	Billy Consolo (fielding)	.75	.40	.25
(132)	Chuck Cottier (throwing)	.75	.40	.25
(133)	Chuck Cottier (portrait, pose to chest, photo reversed)	.75	.40	.25
(134)	Clint Courtney (portrait, pose to neck, dark background)	.75	.40	.25
(135)	Clint Courtney (portrait, pose to neck, light background)	.75	.40	.25
(136)	John Covington (Outfield, batting, pose to neck)	.75	.40	.25
(137)	Wes Covington (batting)	.75	.40	.25
(138)	Wes Covington (kneeling, holding bat)	.75	.40	.25
(139)	Harry Craft (kneeling, pose to knees)	.75	.40	.25
(140)	Harry Craft (portrait, pose to neck)	.75	.40	.25
(141)	Roger Craig (portrait, pose to chest)	1.00	.50	.30
(142)	Del Crandall (batting, pose to waist)	1.00	.50	.30
(143)	Del Crandall (portrait, pose to neck)	1.00	.50	.30
(144)	Delmar Crandall (Catcher, portrait, pose to neck)	1.00	.50	.30
(145)	George Crowe (portrait, pose to neck)	.75	.40	.25
(146)	Joe Cunningham (portrait, pose to neck)	.75	.40	.25
(147)	Joe Cunningham (batting)	.75	.40	.25
(148)	Bud Daley (portrait, pose to chest)	.75	.40	.25
(149)	Bud Daley (pitching)	.75	.40	.25
(150)	Pete Daley (kneeling, pose to knees)	.75	.40	.25
(151)	Benny Daniels (portrait, pose to chest, hands over head)	.75	.40	.25

	NR MT	EX	VG
(152) Al Dark (batting, pose to chest)	1.25	.60	.40
(153) Alvin Dark (Cardinals, portrait, pose to chest)	1.25	.60	.40
(154) Alvin Dark (Manager-Giants, portrait, pose to chest)	1.00	.50	.30
(155) Jim Davenport (throwing)	.75	.40	.25
(156) Jim Davenport (fielding, glove out)	.75	.40	.25
(157) Jim Davenport (fielding, low ball)	.75	.40	.25
(158) Ike Delock (portrait, pose to chest, light background)	.75	.40	.25
(159) Ivan Delock (portrait, pose to chest, dark background)	.75	.40	.25
(160) Bobby Del Greco (portrait, pose to chest)	.75	.40	.25
(161) Don Demeter (portrait, pose to waist)	.75	.40	.25
(162) Joe DeMaestri (batting, pose to waist)	.75	.40	.25
(163) Murray Dickson (Murry) (pitching, pitcher's follow through, pose to waist)	.75	.40	.25
(164) Art Ditmar (pitching, pitcher's follow through, pose to knees)	.75	.40	.25
(165) Dan Dobbek (portrait, pose to neck)	.75	.40	.25
(166) Dan Dobbek (kneeling, holding bat)	.75	.40	.25
(167) Dick Donovan (portrait, pose to neck)	.75	.40	.25
(168) Dick Donovan (portrait, pose to chest)	.75	.40	.25
(169) Dick Donovan (portrait, pose to chest, glove)	.75	.40	.25
(170) Dutch Dotterer (batting, pose to waist)	.75	.40	.25
(171) Moe Drabowski (Drabowsky) (portrait, pose to chest)	.75	.40	.25
(172) Charlie Dressen (portrait, pose to chest)	.75	.40	.25
(173) Don Drysdale (pitcher, portrait, pose to neck)	2.50	1.25	.70
(174) Don Drysdale (portrait, pose to neck)	2.50	1.25	.70
(175) Don Drysdale (portrait, pose to chest)	2.50	1.25	.70
(176) Jimmy Dykes (portrait, pose to chest)	.75	.40	.25
(177) Bob Elliott (portrait, pose to neck)	.75	.40	.25
(178) Dick Ellsworth (portrait, pose to waist, arms crossed)	.75	.40	.25
(179) Don Elston (portrait, pose to neck)	.75	.40	.25
(180) Del Ennis (portrait, pose to neck)	.75	.40	.25
(181) Chuck Estrada (pitching, pose to knees)	.75	.40	.25
(182) Roy Face (portrait, pose to chest)	1.00	.50	.30
(183) Roy Face (portrait, pose to neck)	1.00	.50	.30
(184) Dick Farrell (Phillies, portrait, pose to neck)	.75	.40	.25
(185) Dick Farrell (Philadelphia Phillies, portrait, pose to neck, glove)	.75	.40	.25
(186) Dick Farrell (portrait, pose to chest)	.75	.40	.25
(187) Chico Fernandez (portrait, pose to neck)	.75	.40	.25
(188) Chico Fernandez (portrait, pose to chest)	.75	.40	.25
(189) Jack Fisher (portrait, pose to chest)	.75	.40	.25
(190) Jack Fisher (pitching, pitcher's follow through)	.75	.40	.25
(191) Ed FitzGerald (portrait, pose to neck)	.75	.40	.25
(192) Curt Flood (portrait, pose to neck)	1.25	.60	.40
(193) Curt Flood (portrait, pose to waist)	1.25	.60	.40
(194) Hank Foiles (portrait, pose to neck)	.75	.40	.25
(195) Hank Foiles (kneeling, holding bat)	.75	.40	.25
(196) Whitey Ford (portrait, pose to neck)	5.00	2.50	1.50
(197) Whitey Ford (portrait, pose to chest)	5.00	2.50	1.50
(198) Nellie Fox (ready to throw)	1.75	.90	.50
(199) Nelson Fox (portrait, pose to neck)	1.75	.90	.50
(200) Nelson Fox (portrait, pose to waist, "S" visible)	1.75	.90	.50
(201) Nelson Fox (portrait, pose to chest," Sox" visible)	1.75	.90	.50
(202) Paul Foytack (portrait, pose to chest)	.75	.40	.25
(203) Tito Francona (batting, pose to chest)	.75	.40	.25
(204) Tito Francona (portrait, pose to neck)	.75	.40	.25
(205) Gene Freese (portrait, pose to neck)	.75	.40	.25
(206) Gene Freeze (portrait, pose to chest)	.75	.40	.25
(207) Bob Friend (portrait, pose to neck)	1.00	.50	.30
(208) Bob Friend (pitching, pitcher's follow through)	1.00	.50	.30
(209) Bob Friend (portrait, pose to chest, "P" on helmet)	1.00	.50	.30
(210) Bob Friend (portrait, pose to neck, no "P" on cap)	1.00	.50	.30
(211) Carl Furillo (Outfielder, portrait, pose to neck)	1.50	.70	.45
(212) Carl Furillo (portrait, pose to neck)	1.50	.70	.45
(213) Billy Gardner (portrait, pose to neck)	.75	.40	.25
(214) Billy Gardner (portrait, pose to chest)	.75	.40	.25
(215) William (Billy) Gardner (portrait, pose to neck)	.75	.40	.25
(216) Ned Garver (portrait, pose to chest)	.75	.40	.25
(217) Ned Garver (pitching, pitcher's follow through)	.75	.40	.25
(218) Ned Garver (pitching, hands over head)	.75	.40	.25
(219) Gary Geiger (portrait, pose to chest)	.75	.40	.25
(220) Jim Gentile (kneeling, holding bat)	.75	.40	.25
(221) Jim Gentile (portrait, pose to chest)	.75	.40	.25
(222) Dick Gernert (portrait, pose to neck)	.75	.40	.25
(223) Dick Gernert (portrait, pose to chest)	.75	.40	.25
(224) Paul Giel (portrait, pose to neck)	.75	.40	.25
(225) Bob Giggie (pitching, pitcher's follow through)	.75	.40	.25
(226) Junior Gilliam (portrait, pose to neck)	1.25	.60	.40
(227) Junior Gilliam (portrait, pose to chest)	1.25	.60	.40
(228) Reuben Gomez (portrait, pose to neck)	.75	.40	.25
(229) Ruben Gomez (portrait, pose to chest)	.75	.40	.25
(230) Bill Goodman (portrait, pose to neck)	.75	.40	.25
(231) Bill Goodman (portrait, pose to chest)	.75	.40	.25
(232) Joe Gordon (portrait, pose to chest)	.75	.40	.25
(233) Alex Grammas (portrait, pose to neck)	.75	.40	.25
(234) Jim Grant (pitching, pitcher's follow through, to knee)	.75	.40	.25
(235) Jim Grant (pitching, pitcher's follow through, left leg visible)	.75	.40	.25
(236) Dallas Green (portrait, pose to neck, hands over head)	.75	.40	.25
(237) Gene Green (portrait, pose to neck)	.75	.40	.25
(238) Jerry "Pumpsie" Green (portrait, pose to chest)	.75	.40	.25
(239) Lenny Green (portraint, pose to neck)	.75	.40	.25
(240) Lenny Green (portrait, pose to chest)	.75	.40	.25
(241) Bob Grim (pitching, pitcher's follow through)	.75	.40	.25
(242) Dick Groat (portrait, pose to neck)	1.25	.60	.40
(243) Dick Groat (portrait, pose to chest, light background)	1.25	.60	.40
(244) Dick Groat (portrait, pose to neck, dark background)	1.25	.60	.40
(245) Dick Groat (kneeling, holding bat)	1.25	.60	.40
(246) Harvey Haddix (portrait, pose to neck)	1.00	.50	.30
(247) Harvey Haddix (portrait, pose to chest)	1.00	.50	.30
(248) Granny Hammer (portrait, pose to neck)	.75	.40	.25
(249) Harry Hanebrink (portrait, pose to waist, MILW uniform)	.75	.40	.25
(250) Fred Haney (portrait, pose to neck)	.75	.40	.25
(251) Ron Hansen (portrait, pose to chest)	.75	.40	.25
(252) Ron Hansen (fielding)	.75	.40	.25
(253) Bill Harrell (portrait, pose to chest)	.75	.40	.25
(254) Jack Harshman (portrait, pose to chest)	.75	.40	.25
(255) Robert Hazel (Hazle) (outfielder, portrait, pose to neck)	.75	.40	.25
(256) Woody Held (batting, pose to waist)	.75	.40	.25
(257) Woody Held (portrait, pose to neck)	.75	.40	.25
(258) Solly Hemus (portrait, pose to chest)	.75	.40	.25
(259) Ray Herbert (pitching, pitcher's follow through)	.75	.40	.25
(260) Ray Herbert (portrait, pose to chest, "A" on cap)	.75	.40	.25
(261) Ray Herbert (portrait, pose to neck, no "A" on cap)	.75	.40	.25
(262) Frank Herrera (portrait, pose to neck, glove)	.75	.40	.25
(263) Pancho Herrera (portrait, pose to waist, glove)	.75	.40	.25
(264) Whitey Herzog (Orioles, portrait, pose to chest)	1.25	.60	.40
(265) Whitey Herzog (Athletics, portrait, pose to chest)	1.25	.60	.40
(266) Mike Higgins (portrait, pose to neck)	.75	.40	.25
(267) Mike Higgins (portrait, pose to chest, one ear showing)	.75	.40	.25
(268) Mike Higgins (portrait, pose to chest, two ears showing)	.75	.40	.25
(269) Don Hoak (portrait, pose to neck)	.75	.40	.25
(270) Don Hoak (portrait, pose to neck)	.75	.40	.25
(271) Don Hoak (portrait, pose to waist)	.75	.40	.25
(272) Glen Hobbie (portrait, pose to neck)	.75	.40	.25
(273) Gil Hodges (first base, portrait, pose to neck)	2.75	1.50	.80
(274) Gil Hodges (portrait, pose to neck)	2.75	1.50	.80
(275) Jay Hook (portrait, pose to neck)	.75	.40	.25
(276) Ralph Houk (portrait, pose to chest)	1.00	.50	.30
(277) Frank House (portrait, pose to neck)	.75	.40	.25
(278) Elston Howard (portrait, pose to chest)	1.50	.70	.45
(279) Elston Howard (batting, pose to chest)	1.50	.70	.45
(280) Frank Howard (batting, pose to waist)	1.50	.70	.45
(281) Fred Hutchinson (portrait, pose to neck)	.75	.40	.25
(282) Fred Hutchinson (portrait, pose to chest)	.75	.40	.25
(283) Dick Hyde (portrait, pose to chest)	.75	.40	.25
(284) Dick Hyde (pitching, pitcher's follow through to, pose to thighs)	.75	.40	.25
(285) Larry Jackson (portrait, pose to neck)	.75	.40	.25
(286) Larry Jackson (portrait, pose to chest)	.75	.40	.25
(287) Julian Javier (portrait, pose to chest)	.75	.40	.25
(288) Joey Jay, Joey Jay (portrait, pose to neck)	.75	.40	.25
(289) Joey Jay (pitching)	.75	.40	.25
(291) Joey Jay (Reds, pitching, pitcher's follow through)	.75	.40	.25
(292) Hal Jeffcoat (portrait, portrait to neck)	.75	.40	.25
(293) Jack Jensen (portrait, pose to neck)	1.25	.60	.40
(294) Jackie Jensen (portrait, pose to chest)	1.25	.60	.40
(295) Jackie Jensen (sitting, pose to knees)	1.25	.60	.40
(296) Bob Johnson (fielding)	.75	.40	.25
(297) Connie Johnson (portrait, pose to neck)	.75	.40	.25
(298) Sam Jones (portrait, pose to waist, trophy, St. Louis uniform)	.75	.40	.25
(299) Sam Jones (pitching)	.75	.40	.25
(300) Sam Jones (portrait, pose to neck)	.75	.40	.25
(301) Willie Jones (batting, pose to chest)	.75	.40	.25
(302) Bill Jurges (portrait, pose to waist)	.75	.40	.25
(303) Al Kaline (portrait, pose to chest)	6.00	3.00	1.75
(304) Al Kaline (kneeling, holding bat)	6.00	3.00	1.75
(305) Eddie Kasco (Kasko) (batting, pose to chest)	.75	.40	.25
(306) Eddie Kasko (portrait, pose to neck)	.75	.40	.25
(307) Marty Keough (portrait, pose to chest)	.75	.40	.25
(308) Harmon Killebrew (portrait, pose to chest)	3.25	1.75	1.00
(309) Harmon Killebrew (kneeling, holding bat)	3.25	1.75	1.00
(310) Harmon Killebrew (batting, pose to waist)	3.25	1.75	1.00
(311) Jerry Kindall (portrait, pose to chest)	.75	.40	.25
(312) Willie Kirkland (kneeling, five bats)	.75	.40	.25
(313) Willie Kirkland (portrait, pose to chest)	.75	.40	.25
(314) Willie Kirkland (batting)	.75	.40	.25
(315) Willie Kirkland (portrait, pose to chest)	.75	.40	.25
(316) Ronald Kline (portrait, pose to neck)	.75	.40	.25
(317) Ronnie Kline (Pirates, portrait, pose to chest)	.75	.40	.25
(318) Ronnie Kline (Cardinals, portrait, pose to chest)	.75	.40	.25
(319) Ted Kluszewksi (kneeling, holding bat)	1.50	.70	.45
(320) Ted Kluszewski (batting, pose to chest)	1.50	.70	.45
(321) Ted Kluzewski (Kluszewski) (portrait, pose to chest)	1.50	.70	.45
(322) Steve Korcheck (batting, pose to chest)	.75	.40	.25
(323) Jack Kralick (portrait, pose to neck)	.75	.40	.25
(324) Tony Kubek (fielding)	1.50	.70	.45
(325) Tony Kubek (portrait, pose to neck "NY" cap)	1.50	.70	.45
(326) Tony Kubek (portrait, pose to neck, "NY" not visible on cap)	1.50	.70	.45
(327) John Kucks (pitching)	.75	.40	.25
(328) Johnny Kucks (portrait, pose to neck)	.75	.40	.25
(329) Harvey Kuenn (Indians, portrait, pose to chest)	1.00	.50	.30
(330) Harvey Kuenn (Giants, portrait, pose to chest)	1.00	.50	.30
(331) Clem Labine (Pitcher, portrait, pose to neck)	.75	.40	.25
(332) Clem Labine (portrait, pose to neck)	.75	.40	.25
(333) Jim Landis (portrait, pose to chest)	.75	.40	.25
(334) Jim Landis (batting)	.75	.40	.25
(335) Hobie Landrith (catching, crouching)	.75	.40	.25
(336) Norm Larker (portrait, pose to chest)	.75	.40	.25
(337) Don Larsen (portrait, pose to neck)	1.25	.60	.40
(338) Don Larsen (pitching, pitcher's follow through)	1.00	.50	.30
(339) Frank Lary (portrait, pose to waist, arms crossed, one hand showing)	.75	.40	.25
(340) Frank Lary (portrait, pose to waist, arms crossed, both hands showing)	.75	.40	.25
(341) Barry Latman (portrait, pose to chest, W. SOX uniform)	.75	.40	.25

	NR MT	EX	VG
(342) Cookie Lavagetto (portrait, pose to chest)	.75	.40	.25
(343) Harry Lavagetto (portrait, pose to neck)	.75	.40	.25
(344) Harry Lavagetto (portrait, pose to chest)	.75	.40	.25
(345) Vern Law (portrait, pose to chest)	1.00	.50	.30
(346) Brooks Lawrence (portrait, pose to neck)	.75	.40	.25
(347) Don Lee (portrait, pose to neck)	.75	.40	.25
(348) Jim Lemon (portrait, pose to neck)	.75	.40	.25
(349) Jim Lemon (kneeling, holding bat)	.75	.40	.25
(350) Jim Lemon (portrait, pose to chest)	.75	.40	.25
(351) Jim Lemon (batting, pose to chest)	.75	.40	.25
(352) Bobbie Locke (pitching, pitcher's follow through)	.75	.40	.25
(353) Carroll (Whitey) Lockman (portrait, pose to chest)	.75	.40	.25
(354) Whitey Lockman (fielding)	.75	.40	.25
(355) Billy Loes (portrait, pose to neck)	.75	.40	.25
(356) John Logan (Infielder, portrait, pose to chest)	.75	.40	.25
(357) Johnny Logan (batting, pose to waist)	.75	.40	.25
(358) Sherman Lollar (portrait, pose to neck)	.75	.40	.25
(359) Sherman Lollar (portrait, pose to chest)	.75	.40	.25
(360) Sherman Lollar (kneeling, two bats)	.75	.40	.25
(361) Dale Long (portrait, pose to neck)	.75	.40	.25
(362) Stan Lopata (batting in cage)	.75	.40	.25
(363) Stan Lopata (portrait, pose to chest)	.75	.40	.25
(364) Stan Lopata (batting)	.75	.40	.25
(365) Stan Lopata (portrait, pose to neck)	.75	.40	.25
(366) Al Lopez (portrait, pose to chest, jacket)	1.50	.70	.45
(367) Al Lopez (portrait, pose to chest, no jacket)	1.50	.70	.45
(368) Hector Lopez (Athletics, batting, pose to waist)	.75	.40	.25
(369) Hector Lopez (fielding)	.75	.40	.25
(370) Hector Lopez (Yankees, batting)	1.00	.50	.30
(371) Jerry Lumpe (portrait, pose to neck)	.75	.40	.25
(372) Jerry Lumpe (portrait, pose to chest)	.75	.40	.25
(373) Jerry Lumpe (fielding)	.75	.40	.25
(374) Jerry Lynch (portrait, pose to chest, one ear showing)	.75	.40	.25
(375) Jerry Lynch (portrait, pose to chest, two ears showing)	.75	.40	.25
(376) Art Mahaffey (portrait, pose to chest, glove)	.75	.40	.25
(377) Bob Malkmus (portrait, pose to chest, glove)	.75	.40	.25
(378) Frank Malzone (portrait, pose to neck)	.75	.40	.25
(379) Frank Malzone (portrait, pose to chest, smile)	.75	.40	.25
(380) Frank Malzone (portrait, pose to chest, no smile)	.75	.40	.25
(381) Frank Malzone (batting, pose to thighs)	.75	.40	.25
(382) Felix Mantilla (portrait, pose to neck)	.75	.40	.25
(383) Felix Mantilla (fielding)	.75	.40	.25
(384) Mickey Mantle (portrait, pose to neck)	15.00	7.50	4.50
(385) Mickey Mantle (batting, pose to chest)	15.00	7.50	4.50
(386) Juan Marichal (pitching, pose to waist, hands over head)	2.50	1.25	.70
(387) Roger Maris (batting, pose to chest)	5.00	2.50	1.50
(388) Roger Maris (kneeling, holding bat)	5.00	2.50	1.50
(389) Roger Maris (portrait, pose to neck)	5.00	2.50	1.50
(390) Eddie Mathews (kneeling, holding bat, glove)	3.25	1.75	1.00
(391) Eddie Mathews (kneeling, holding bat, no glove)	3.25	1.75	1.00
(392) Edwin Mathews (Infielder, portrait, pose to chest)	3.25	1.75	1.00
(393) Gene Mauch (portrait, pose to chest)	.75	.40	.25
(394) Charlie Maxwell (portrait, pose to chest)	.75	.40	.25
(395) Charlie Maxwell (kneeling, holding bat)	.75	.40	.25
(396) Lee Maye (batting, pose to waist)	.75	.40	.25
(397) Willie Mays (leaping)	10.00	5.00	3.00
(398) Willie Mays (fielding)	10.00	5.00	3.00
(399) Willie Mays (batting, pose to waist)	10.00	5.00	3.00
(400) Willie Mays (batting)	10.00	5.00	3.00
(401) Bill Mazeroski (Pirates, portrait, pose to neck)	1.25	.60	.40
(402) Bill Mazeroski (Pittsburgh Pirates, portrait, pose to neck)	1.25	.60	.40
(403) Bill Mazeroski (portrait, pose to chest)	1.25	.60	.40
(404) Mike McCormick (pitching)	.75	.40	.25
(405) Mike McCormick (pitching, pose to waist)	.75	.40	.25
(406) Willie McCovey (kneeling, pose to waist, five bats)	3.25	1.75	1.00
(407) Lindy McDaniel (portrait, pose to neck)	.75	.40	.25
(408) Lindy McDaniel (portrait, pose to chest)	.75	.40	.25
(409) Von McDaniel (portrait, pose to chest)	.75	.40	.25
(410) Gil McDougald (portrait, pose to neck)	1.25	.60	.40
(411) Don McMahon (portrait, pose to waist)	.75	.40	.25
(412) Don McMahon (pitching, pitcher's follow through)	.75	.40	.25
(413) Donald McMahon (pitcher, portrait, pose to neck)	.75	.40	.25
(414) Roy McMillan (portrait, pose to neck, glasses)	.75	.40	.25
(415) Roy McMillan (portrait, pose to neck, no glasses)	.75	.40	.25
(416) Roy McMillan (throwing, pose to knees)	.75	.40	.25
(417) Roman Mejias (portrait, pose to neck)	.75	.40	.25
(418) Stu Miller (portrait, pose to chest)	.75	.40	.25
(419) Stu Miller (pitching, pitcher's follow through)	.75	.40	.25
(420) Minnie Minoso (batting,)	1.25	.60	.40
(421) Orestes Minoso (portrait, pose to chest)	1.25	.60	.40
(422) Willy Miranda (portrait, pose to neck)	.75	.40	.25
(423) Wilmer Mizell (portrait, pose to neck)	.75	.40	.25
(424) Bill Monbouquette (portrait, pose to chest)	.75	.40	.25
(425) Wally Moon (Cardinals, portrait, pose to neck)	.75	.40	.25
(426) Wally Moon (portrait, pose to waist)	.75	.40	.25
(427) Wally Moon (Dodgers, portrait, pose to neck)	.75	.40	.25
(428) Ray Moore (portrait, pose to neck)	.75	.40	.25
(429) Seth Morehead (standing, pose to knees)	.75	.40	.25
(430) Tom Morgan (portrait, pose to chest)	.75	.40	.25
(431) Walt Moryn (portrait, pose to chest)	.75	.40	.25
(432) Don Mossi (portrait, pose to chest)	.75	.40	.25
(433) Billy Muffett (portrait, pose to chest)	.75	.40	.25
(434) Danny Murtaugh (portrait, pose to neck)	.75	.40	.25
(435) Danny Murtaugh (portrait, pose to chest, one ear showing)	.75	.40	.25
(436) Danny Murtaugh (portrait, pose to chest, two ears showing)	.75	.40	.25
(437) Stan Musial (portrait, pose to neck)	10.00	5.00	3.00
(438) Stan Musial (portrait, pose to waist)	10.00	5.00	3.00
(439) Ray Narleski (portrait, pose to chest)	.75	.40	.25
(440) Charley Neal (Infielder, portrait, pose to neck)	.75	.40	.25
(441) Charlie Neal (portrait, pose to neck)	.75	.40	.25
(442) Charlie Neal (portrait, pose to chest)	.75	.40	.25
(443) Don Newcombe (Pitcher, portrait, pose to neck)	1.50	.70	.45
(444) Don Newcombe (portrait, pose to neck)	1.00	.50	.30
(445) Don Newcombe (pitching, hands over head)	1.00	.50	.30
(446) Bob Nieman (Orioles, portrait, pose to neck)	.75	.40	.25
(447) Bob Nieman (portrait, pose to chest)	.75	.40	.25
(448) Bob Nieman (Cardinals, portrait, pose to neck)	.75	.40	.25
(449) Russ Nixon (portrait, pose to chest)	.75	.40	.25
(450) Russ Nixon (batting, pose to waist)	.75	.40	.25
(451) Don Nottebart (portrait, pose to chest)	.75	.40	.25
(452) Joe Nuxhall (pitching, pitcher's follow through)	1.00	.50	.30
(453) Joe Nuxhall (portrait, pose to neck)	1.00	.50	.30
(454) Danny O'Connell (portrait, pose to neck)	.75	.40	.25
(455) Bill Odell (O'Dell) (portrait, pose to neck)	.75	.40	.25
(456) Billy O'Dell (portrait, pose to chest)	.75	.40	.25
(457) Claude Osteen (portrait, pose to waist, glove)	.75	.40	.25
(458) Jim O'Toole (portrait, pose to neck)	.75	.40	.25
(459) Jim O'Toole (portrait, pose to chest)	.75	.40	.25
(460) Jim Owens (pitching, pitcher's follow through)	.75	.40	.25
(461) Andrew Pafko (outfielder, portrait, pose to neck)	1.00	.50	.30
(462) Andy Pafko (batting, pose to waist)	1.00	.50	.30
(463) Jim Pagliaroni (catching, crouching)	.75	.40	.25
(464) Milt Pappas (pitching, pitcher's follow through)	1.00	.50	.30
(465) Milt Pappas (portrait, pose to chest, dark background)	1.00	.50	.30
(466) Milt Pappas (portrait, pose to chest, light background)	1.00	.50	.30
(467) Camilo Pascual (portrait, pose to neck, light background)	1.00	.50	.30
(468) Camilo Pascual (pitching)	1.00	.50	.30
(469) Camilo Pascual (portrait, pose to neck, dark background)	1.00	.50	.30
(470) Camilo Pasqual (Pascual) (portrait, pose to neck)	1.00	.50	.30
(471) Albie Pearson (portrait, pose to chest)	.75	.40	.25
(472) Albie Pearson (portrait, pose to neck, "W" on cap)	.75	.40	.25
(473) Albie Pearson (portrait, pose to neck, "W" not visible on cap)	.75	.40	.25
(474) Orlando Pena (batting, pose to waist)	.75	.40	.25
(475) Bubba Phillips (hands on knees)	.75	.40	.25
(476) Bubba Phillips (batting, pose to waist)	.75	.40	.25
(477) Bubba Phillips (portrait, pose to chest)	.75	.40	.25
(478) Bill Pierce (portrait, pose to neck)	1.00	.50	.30
(479) Billy Pierce (portrait, pose to chest)	1.00	.50	.30
(480) Billy Pierce (pitching, hands over head)	1.00	.50	.30
(481) Jim Piersall (portrait, pose to neck)	1.25	.60	.40
(482) Jim Piersall (batting, pose to chest)	1.25	.60	.40
(483) Jimmy Piersall (batting, pose to chest)	1.25	.60	.40
(484) Joe Pignatano (portrait, pose to chest)	.75	.40	.25
(485) Al Pilarcik (portrait, pose to neck)	.75	.40	.25
(486) Vada Pinson (portrait, pose to neck)	1.25	.60	.40
(487) Vada Pinson (batting, pose to waist)	1.25	.60	.40
(488) Juan Pizzarro (Pizarro) (pitching)	.75	.40	.25
(489) Herb Plews (batting, pose to waist)	.75	.40	.25
(490) Herb Plews (portrait, pose to neck)	.75	.40	.25
(491) Johnny Podres (Pitcher, portrait, pose to neck)	1.25	.60	.40
(492) Johnny Podres (portrait, pose to neck)	1.25	.60	.40
(493) Johnny Podres (portrait, pose to chest)	1.25	.60	.40
(494) Arnie Portocarrero (portrait, pose to chest)	.75	.40	.25
(495) Wally Post (portrait, pose to waist)	.75	.40	.25
(496) Wally Post (batting, pose to waist)	.75	.40	.25
(497) Vic Power (batting, pose to waist)	.75	.40	.25
(498) Vic Power (batting, head shot)	.75	.40	.25
(499) Vic Power (fielding, pose to knees)	.75	.40	.25
(500) Bob Purkey (portrait, pose to neck)	.75	.40	.25
(501) Pedro Ramos (portrait, pose to chest, hands over head)	.75	.40	.25
(502) Pedro Ramos (Senators, portrait, pose to neck, dark background)	.75	.40	.25
(503) Pedro Ramos (portrait, pose to neck, light background)	.75	.40	.25
(504) Pedro Ramos (Twins, portrait, pose to neck)	.75	.40	.25
(505) Pee Wee Reese (Infielder, portrait, pose to neck)	5.00	2.50	1.50
(506) Rip Repulski (portrait, pose to neck)	.75	.40	.25
(507) Rip Repulski (portrait, pose to neck)	.75	.40	.25
(508) Paul Richards (portrait, pose to neck)	.75	.40	.25
(509) Paul Richards (portrait, pose to chest, Orioles uniform)	.75	.40	.25
(510) Paul Richards (portrait, pose to chest, Baltimore uniform)	.75	.40	.25
(511) Bobby Richardson (batting,)	1.50	.70	.45
(512) Bobby Richardson (fielding)	1.50	.70	.45
(513) Bill Rigney (portrait, pose to chest)	.75	.40	.25
(514) Jim Rivera (portrait, pose to neck)	.75	.40	.25
(515) Mel Roach (throwing)	.75	.40	.25
(516) Robin Roberts (portrait, pose to neck)	2.50	1.25	.70
(517) Robin Roberts (pitching, hands on knees)	2.50	1.25	.70
(518) Robin Roberts (portrait, pose to chest)	2.50	1.25	.70
(519) Brooks Robinson (portrait, pose to chest)	6.00	3.00	1.75
(520) Brooks Robinson (fielding)	6.00	3.00	1.75
(521) Frank Robinson (portrait, pose to neck)	3.25	1.75	1.00
(522) Frank Robinson (portrait, pose to chest)	3.25	1.75	1.00
(523) Frank Robinson (batting, pose to waist)	3.25	1.75	1.00
(524) John Romano (portrait, pose to chest, W. Sox uniform)	.75	.40	.25
(525) John Romano (portrait, pose to chest, Indians uniform)	.75	.40	.25
(526) John Roseboro (portrait, pose to neck)	.75	.40	.25
(527) John Roseboro (portrait, pose to chest)	.75	.40	.25
(528) Pete Runnells (Runnels) (portrait, pose to neck)	.75	.40	.25
(529) Pete Runnels (portrait, pose to chest)	.75	.40	.25
(530) Pete Runnels (batting, pose to knees)	.75	.40	.25
(531) Bob Rush (pitching)	.75	.40	.25
(532) Ron Samford (kneeling, holding bat)	.75	.40	.25
(533) Jack Sandford (Sanford) (portrait, pose to neck)	.75	.40	.25
(534) Jack Sanford (pitching)	.75	.40	.25

	NR MT	EX	VG
(535) Jack Sanford (pitching, pitcher's follow through)	.75	.40	.25
(536) Ron Santo (portrait, pose to chest)	1.25	.60	.40
(537) Hank Sauer (batting,)	.75	.40	.25
(538) Hank Sauer (hands on knees)	.75	.40	.25
(539) Eddie Sawyer (portrait, pose to chest)	.75	.40	.25
(540) Bob Schmidt (catching, crouching)	.75	.40	.25
(541) Bob Schmidt (catching, throwing mask)	.75	.40	.25
(542) Bob Schmidt (portrait, pose to neck)	.75	.40	.25
(543) Albert Schoendienst (infielder, batting, pose to neck)	1.50	.70	.45
(544) Red Schoendienst (portrait, pose to neck)	1.50	.70	.45
(545) Red Schoendienst (throwing)	1.50	.70	.45
(546) Don Schwall (pitching, pitcher's follow through)	.75	.40	.25
(547) Ray Semproch (portrait, pose to chest)	.75	.40	.25
(548) Bobby Shantz (portrait, pose to neck)	1.00	.50	.30
(549) Bob Shaw (portrait, pose to neck)	.75	.40	.25
(550) Bob Sheffing (portrait, pose to chest)	.75	.40	.25
(551) Larry Sherry (portrait, pose to chest)	.75	.40	.25
(552) Chuck Shilling (portrait, pose to chest)	.75	.40	.25
(553) Norm Siebern (portrait, pose to chest)	.75	.40	.25
(554) Norm Siebern (throwing)	.75	.40	.25
(555) Roy Sievers (Senators, portrait, pose to neck)	1.00	.50	.30
(556) Roy Sievers (batting, pose to waist)	1.00	.50	.30
(557) Roy Sievers (White Sox, portrait, pose to neck)	1.00	.50	.30
(558) Roy Sievers (batting, pose to chest)	1.00	.50	.30
(559) Curt Simmons (portrait, pose to neck)	1.00	.50	.30
(560) Curt Simmons (portrait, pose to chest)	1.00	.50	.30
(561) Bob Skinner (Pirates, portrait, pose to neck)	.75	.40	.25
(562) Bob Skinner (Pittsburgh Pirates, portrait, pose to neck)	.75	.40	.25
(563) Bob Skinner (portrait, pose to thighs, five bats)	.75	.40	.25
(564) Bob Skinner (batting, pose to chest)	.75	.40	.25
(565) Bill Skowron (portrait, pose to neck)	1.50	.70	.45
(566) Bill Skowron (batting, pose to waist)	1.50	.70	.45
(567) Al Smith (portrait, pose to neck)	.75	.40	.25
(568) Al Smith (portrait, pose to chest)	.75	.40	.25
(569) Al Smith (kneeling, holding bat)	.75	.40	.25
(570) Hal Smith (portrait, pose to neck)	.75	.40	.25
(571) Hal Smith (catching, pose to waist)	.75	.40	.25
(572) Hal Smith (batting)	.75	.40	.25
(573) Hal Smith (batting, head shot)	.75	.40	.25
(574) Mayo Smith (portrait, pose to neck)	.75	.40	.25
(575) Duke Snider (Outfielder, portrait, pose to neck)	7.00	3.50	2.00
(576) Duke Snider (portrait, pose to neck)	7.00	3.50	2.00
(577) Duke Snider (portrait, pose to chest)	7.00	3.50	2.00
(578) Russ Snyder (portrait, pose to chest)	.75	.40	.25
(579) Warren Spahn (Pitcher, portrait, pose to neck)	3.00	1.50	.90
(580) Warren Spahn (portrait, pose to neck)	3.00	1.50	.90
(581) Warren Spahn (pitching)	3.00	1.50	.90
(582) Daryl Spencer (fielding)	.75	.40	.25
(583) Daryl Spencer (throwing)	.75	.40	.25
(584) Daryl Spencer (portrait, pose to neck)	.75	.40	.25
(585) Daryl Spencer (portrait, pose to chest)	.75	.40	.25
(586) Gerry Staley (fielding)	.75	.40	.25
(587) Casey Stengel (portrait, pose to neck)	5.00	2.50	1.50
(588) Gene Stephens (batting, pose to chest)	.75	.40	.25
(589) Gene Stephens (portrait, pose to chest)	.75	.40	.25
(590) R.C. Stevens (portrait, pose to chest)	.75	.40	.25
(591) Chuck Stobbs (pitching, pitcher's follow through)	.75	.40	.25
(592) George Strickland (kneeling, holding bat)	.75	.40	.25
(593) Dick Stuart (portrait, pose to neck, no team designation)	.75	.40	.25
(594) Dick Stuart (batting, pose to chest)	.75	.40	.25
(595) Dick Stuart (kneeling, holding bat)	.75	.40	.25
(596) Dick Stuart (portrait, pose to neck, Pirates)	.75	.40	.25
(597) Tom Sturdivant (portrait, pose to neck)	.75	.40	.25
(598) Tom Sturdivant (portrait, pose to chest)	.75	.40	.25
(599) Frank Sullivan (portrait, pose to neck)	.75	.40	.25
(600) Frank Sullivan (portrait, pose to chest)	.75	.40	.25
(601) Haywood Sullivan (Red Sox, portrait, pose to chest)	.75	.40	.25
(602) Haywood Sullivan (Athletics, portrait, pose to chest)	.75	.40	.25
(603) Willie Tasby (batting, pose to chest)	.75	.40	.25
(604) Willie Tasby (Orioles, portrait, pose to chest)	.75	.40	.25
(605) Willie Tasby (Senators, portrait, pose to chest)	.75	.40	.25
(606) Sam Taylor (portrait, pose to neck)	.75	.40	.25
(607) Tony Taylor (portrait, pose to chest)	.75	.40	.25
(608) Tony Taylor (batting, pose to chest)	.75	.40	.25
(609) "Birdie" Tebbetts (portrait, pose to neck)	.75	.40	.25
(610) John Temple (kneeling, holding bat)	.75	.40	.25
(611) Johnny Temple (portrait, pose to neck)	.75	.40	.25
(612) Johnny Temple (kneeling, holding bat)	.75	.40	.25
(613) Ralph Terry (pitching, pitcher's follow through)	.75	.40	.25
(614) Ralph Terry (pitching, pitcher's follow through, pose to knees)	.75	.40	.25
(615) Moe Thacker (portrait, pose to chest)	.75	.40	.25
(616) Frank Thomas (batting, pose to waist)	.75	.40	.25
(617) Frank Thomas (batting, pose to chest)	.75	.40	.25
(618) Frank Thomas (portrait, pose to neck)	.75	.40	.25
(619) Bobby Thomson (batting, pose to waist, two bats)	1.00	.50	.30
(620) Fay Throneberry (Faye) (batting, pose to chest)	.75	.40	.25
(621) Faye Throneberry (portrait, pose to chest)	.75	.40	.25
(622) Marv Throneberry (throwing)	1.00	.50	.30
(623) Marv Throneberry (portrait, pose to chest)	1.00	.50	.30
(624) Dick Tomanek (pitching, pitcher's follow through)	.75	.40	.25
(625) Frank Torre (portrait, pose to neck)	.75	.40	.25
(626) Frank Torre (fielding)	.75	.40	.25
(627) Gus Triandos (portrait, pose to neck)	.75	.40	.25
(628) Gus Triandos (portrait, pose to chest)	.75	.40	.25
(629) Gus Triandos (catching)	.75	.40	.25
(630) Bob Trowbridge (portrait, pose to waist)	.75	.40	.25
(631) Virgil Trucks (pitching, pitcher's follow through)	1.00	.50	.30
(632) Bob Turley (pitching, pitcher's follow through)	1.00	.50	.30
(633) Bob Turley (portrait, pose to neck, one ear showing)	1.00	.50	.30
(634) Bob Turley (portrait, pose to neck, two ears showing)	1.00	.50	.30
(635) Bill Tuttle (portrait, pose to neck, "A" on cap)	.75	.40	.25
(636) Bill Tuttle (portrait, pose to neck, no "A" on cap)	.75	.40	.25
(637) Bill Tuttle (batting, "KC" on cap)	.75	.40	.25
(638) Bill Tuttle (batting, "A" on cap)	.75	.40	.25
(639) Jack Urban (pitching, pitcher's follow through, pose to knees)	.75	.40	.25
(640) Coot Veal (batting, pose to thighs)	.75	.40	.25
(641) Mickey Vernon (portrait, pose to waist)	1.00	.50	.30
(642) Zorro Versalles (portrait, pose to neck)	.75	.40	.25
(643) Bill Virdon (portrait, pose to neck)	1.00	.50	.30
(644) Bill Virdon (kneeling, holding bat)	1.00	.50	.30
(645) Bill Virdon (batting, pose to chest)	1.00	.50	.30
(646) Jerry Walker (pitching, pitcher's follow through)	.75	.40	.25
(647) Jerry Walker (portrait, pose to chest, tower background)	.75	.40	.25
(648) Jerry Walker (portrait, pose to chest, no tower)	.75	.40	.25
(649) Lee Walls (portrait, pose to neck)	.75	.40	.25
(650) Ken Walters (portrait, pose to neck)	.75	.40	.25
(651) Vic Wertz (portrait, pose to chest)	1.00	.50	.30
(652) Vic Wertz (batting, pose to chest)	1.00	.50	.30
(653) Bill White (portrait, pose to neck)	1.00	.50	.30
(654) Bill White (portrait, pose to chest)	1.00	.50	.30
(655) Sam White (portrait, pose to neck)	.75	.40	.25
(656) Sammy White (portrait, pose to chest)	.75	.40	.25
(657) Hoyt Wilhelm (portrait, pose to chest)	2.00	1.00	.60
(658) James (Hoyt) Wilhelm (portrait, pose to chest)	2.00	1.00	.60
(659) Carl Willey (portrait, pose to neck)	.75	.40	.25
(660) Dick Williams (throwing)	1.00	.50	.30
(661) Stan Williams (portrait, pose to chest)	.75	.40	.25
(662) Ted Williams (batting, pose to neck)	7.00	3.50	2.00
(663) Ted Williams (batting, pose to chest)	7.00	3.50	2.00
(664) Maury Wills (portrait, pose to waist)	1.50	.70	.45
(665) Jim Wilson (portrait, pose to neck)	.75	.40	.25
(666) Gene Woodling (portrait, pose to chest)	1.00	.50	.30
(667) Gene Woodling (portrait, pose to chest)	1.00	.50	.30
(668) Al Worthington (portrait, pose to neck)	.75	.40	.25
(669) Early Wynn (portrait, pose to neck)	2.50	1.25	.70
(670) Early Wynn (portrait, pose to chest)	2.50	1.25	.70
(671) Early Wynn (fielding)	2.50	1.25	.70
(672) Carl Yastrzemski (portrait, pose to chest)	10.00	5.00	3.00
(673) Ed Yost (kneeling, pose to waist)	.75	.40	.25
(674) Ed Yost (portrait, pose to chest)	.75	.40	.25
(675) Eddie Yost (portrait, pose to neck)	.75	.40	.25
(676) Norm Zauchin (portrait, pose to neck)	.75	.40	.25
(677) Don Zimmer (portrait, pose to neck)	1.00	.50	.30
(678) Don Zimmer (portrait, pose to chest)	1.00	.50	.30
(679) Jerry Zimmerman (portrait, pose to chest)	.75	.40	.25
(680) George Zuverink (portrait, pose to neck)	.75	.40	.25
(681) Marion Zipfel (fielding)	.75	.40	.25

1962 Jay Publishing 5x7 Photos -Type II

JOHN CALLISON, Philadelphia Phillies

	NR MT	EX	VG
Complete Set:	1500.	750.00	450.00
Common Player:	.75	.40	.25
(1) Hank Aaron (batting, pose to chest)	10.00	5.00	3.00
(2) Hank Aaron (batting)	10.00	5.00	3.00
(3) Hank Aaron (kneeling, holding bat)	10.00	5.00	3.00
(4) Tommy Aaron (fielding)	.75	.40	.25
(5) Jerry Adair (batting, pose to chest," B" on cap)	.75	.40	.25
(6) Jerry Adair (batting, pose to chest, bird on cap)	.75	.40	.25
(7) Joe Adcock (Braves, portrait, pose to waist)	1.25	.60	.40
(8) Joe Adcock (batting, pose to chest)	1.25	.60	.40
(9) Joe Adcock (Indians, portrait, pose to waist)	1.25	.60	.40
(10) Joe Adcock (batting, pose to neck)	1.25	.60	.40
(11) Hank Aguirre (pitching)	.75	.40	.25
(12) Hank Aguirre (portrait, pose to waist, glove)	.75	.40	.25
(13) Bernie Allen (batting, pose to waist)	.75	.40	.25
(14) Bernie Allen (fielding)	.75	.40	.25
(15) Bob Allison (batting, pose to chest, plain uniform)	1.00	.50	.30
(16) Bob Allison (batting, pose to chest, towers in background)	1.00	.50	.30
(17) Bob Allison (batting, pose to chest, wire background)	1.00	.50	.30
(18) Bob Allison (kneeling, holding bat)	1.00	.50	.30
(19) Felipe Alou (portrait, pose to neck)	1.00	.50	.30
(20) Felipe Alou (batting, pose to thighs)	1.00	.50	.30
(21) Jesus Alou (kneeling, pose to waist)	.75	.40	.25
(22) Matty Alou (portrait, pose to chest)	1.00	.50	.30
(23) Walt Alston (portrait, pose to neck)	1.75	.90	.50
(24) Walt Alston (portrait, pose to chest, dark background)	1.75	.90	.50
(25) Walt Alston (portrait, pose to chest, light background)	1.75	.90	.50
(26) George Altman (portrait, pose to chest, dark background)	.75	.40	.25
(27) George Altman (portrait, pose to chest, light background)	.75	.40	.25
(28) Max Alvis (portrait, pose to chest)	.75	.40	.25
(29) Max Alvis (batting, pose to chest)	.75	.40	.25
(30) Joe Amalfitano (portrait, pose to chest)	.75	.40	.25

	NR MT	EX	VG
(31) Ruben Amaro (batting, pose to chest)	.75	.40	.25
(32) Bob Anderson (portrait, pose to chest)	.75	.40	.25
(33) Luis Aparicio (fielding)	2.00	1.00	.60
(34) Luis Aparicio (batting, pose to chest," B" on cap)	2.00	1.00	.60
(35) Luis Aparicio (batting, pose to chest, bird on cap)	2.00	1.00	.60
(36) Luis Aparicio (kneeling, pose to waist)	2.00	1.00	.60
(37) George Arrigo (Jerry) (portrait, pose to waist)	.75	.40	.25
(38) Luis Arroyo (pitching, pitcher's follow through)	1.00	.50	.30
(39) Bob Aspromonte (portrait, pose to chest)	.75	.40	.25
(40) Bob Aspromonte (batting, pose to chest)	.75	.40	.25
(41) Earl Averill (batting, pose to chest)	.75	.40	.25
(42) Joe Azcue (batting, pose to chest)	.75	.40	.25
(43) Jim Archer (pitching, pitcher's follow through)	.75	.40	.25
(44) Bob Bailey (batting, pose to chest)	.75	.40	.25
(45) Bob Bailey (kneeling, holding bat)	.75	.40	.25
(46) Ed Bailey (catching, lifting mask)	.75	.40	.25
(47) Jack Baldschun (portrait, pose to chest)	.75	.40	.25
(48) Jack Baldschun (portrait, pose to chest, hands over head)	.75	.40	.25
(49) Ernie Banks (fielding)	6.00	3.00	1.75
(50) Ernie Banks (portrait, pose to waist)	6.00	3.00	1.75
(51) Ernie Banks (batting, pose to chest)	6.00	3.00	1.75
(52) Steve Barber (pitching, pose to chest, hands over head)	.75	.40	.25
(53) Steve Barber (portrait, pose to chest)	.75	.40	.25
(54) Steve Barber (pitching, pitcher's follow through)	.75	.40	.25
(55) Norm Bass (portrait, pose to chest)	.75	.40	.25
(56) Norm Bass (portrait, pose to waist, glove)	.75	.40	.25
(57) Earl Battey (batting, pose to chest)	.75	.40	.25
(58) Earl Battey (catching, crouching)	.75	.40	.25
(59) Hank Bauer (portrait, pose to chest)	.75	.40	.25
(60) Frank Baumann (pitching, pitcher's follow through)	.75	.40	.25
(61) Larry Bearnarth (pitching, pitcher's follow through)	.75	.40	.25
(62) Bo Belinsky (portrait, pose to chest)	1.00	.50	.30
(63) Gary Bell (portrait, pose to chest)	.75	.40	.25
(64) Gary Bell (pitching)	.75	.40	.25
(65) Gus Bell (portrait, pose to chest)	.75	.40	.25
(66) Gus Bell (batting, pose to waist)	.75	.40	.25
(67) Dennis Bennett (portrait, pose to chest)	.75	.40	.25
(68) Yogi Berra (Manager, portrait, pose to chest)	7.00	3.50	2.00
(69) Yogi Berra (portrait, pose to chest)	7.00	3.50	2.00
(70) Yogi Berra (batting, pose to thighs)	7.00	3.50	2.00
(71) Dick Bertell (portrait, pose to waist, Cubs uniform)	.75	.40	.25
(72) Dick Bertell (portrait, pose to chest, Chicago uniform)	.75	.40	.25
(73) Steve Bilko (batting, pose to chest)	.75	.40	.25
(74) John Blanchard (batting, pose to chest)	1.00	.50	.30
(75) Don Blasingame (portrait, pose to chest)	.75	.40	.25
(76) Don Blasingame (batting, pose to chest)	.75	.40	.25
(77) Wade Blasingame (pitching, pitcher's follow through)	.75	.40	.25
(78) Frank Bolling (batting, pose to chest)	.75	.40	.25
(79) Frank Bolling (fielding, throwing)	.75	.40	.25
(80) Frank Bolling (kneeling, holding bat)	.75	.40	.25
(81) Steve Boros (kneeling, holding bat)	.75	.40	.25
(82) Jim Bouton (pitching, pitcher's follow through)	1.25	.60	.40
(83) Sam Bowens (batting, pose to chest)	.75	.40	.25
(84) Clete Boyer (fielding)	1.00	.50	.30
(85) Clete Boyer (batting, pose to chest, bat tilted)	1.00	.50	.30
(86) Cletis Boyer (batting, pose to chest, bat vertical)	1.00	.50	.30
(87) Ken Boyer (portrait, pose to chest)	1.50	.70	.45
(88) Ken Boyer (fielding)	1.50	.70	.45
(89) Ken Boyer (kneeling, holding bat)	1.50	.70	.45
(90) Bobbie Bragan (portrait, pose to waist, looks left)	.75	.40	.25
(91) Bobbie Bragan (portrait, pose to waist, looks right)	.75	.40	.25
(92) Jackie Brandt (kneeling, holding bat)	.75	.40	.25
(93) Jackie Brandt (batting, pose to waist)	.75	.40	.25
(94) Jackie Brandt (hands on knees)	.75	.40	.25
(95) Marv Breeding (kneeling, holding bat)	.75	.40	.25
(96) Ed Bressoud (portrait, pose to chest)	.75	.40	.25
(97) Ed Bressoud (batting, pose to thighs)	.75	.40	.25
(98) Ed Bressoud (kneeling, pose to knees, arms crossed)	.75	.40	.25
(99) Ed Brinkman (portrait, pose to chest)	.75	.40	.25
(100) Lou Brock (portrait, pose to chest, dark background)	5.00	2.50	1.50
(101) Lou Brock (portrait, pose to waist, light background)	5.00	2.50	1.50
(102) Ernie Broglio (pitching, pitcher's follow through)	.75	.40	.25
(103) Ernie Broglio (pitching, pose to waist, one ear showing)	.75	.40	.25
(104) Ernie Broglio (pitching, pose to waist, two ears showing)	.75	.40	.25
(105) Ernie Broglio (portrait, pose to chest)	.75	.40	.25
(106) Jim Brosnan (portrait, pose to chest, hands over head)	.75	.40	.25
(107) Jim Brosnan (pitching, pitcher's follow through)	.75	.40	.25
(108) Dick Brown (portrait, pose to waist, glove)	.75	.40	.25
(109) Hector (Skinny) Brown (portrait, pose to chest)	.75	.40	.25
(110) Larry Brown (portrait, pose to chest)	.75	.40	.25
(111) Bob Bruce (pitching, pose to chest, hands over head)	.75	.40	.25
(112) Bob Bruce (portrait, pose to chest)	.75	.40	.25
(113) Mike Brumley (portrait, pose to chest)	.75	.40	.25
(114) Bill Bruton (kneeling, holding bat)	.75	.40	.25
(115) Bill Bryan (batting, pose to chest)	.75	.40	.25
(116) Don Buddin (portrait, pose to chest)	.75	.40	.25
(117) Bob Buhl (pitching)	.75	.40	.25
(118) Bob Buhl (portrait, pose to waist, cage background)	.75	.40	.25
(119) Bob Buhl (portrait, pose to neck, hook background)	.75	.40	.25
(120) Bob Buhl (portrait, pose to chest, bleacher background)	.75	.40	.25
(121) Wally Bunker (pitching, pose to waist)	.75	.40	.25
(122) Jim Bunning (portrait, pose to chest)	1.75	.90	.50
(123) Jim Bunning (pitching, pitcher's follow through)	1.75	.90	.50
(124) Jim Bunning (kneeling, pose to knees, arms crossed)	1.75	.90	.50
(125) Lew Burdette (pitching, photo reversed)	1.00	.50	.30
(126) Lew Burdette (portrait, pose to thighs, glove)	1.00	.50	.30
(127) Lou Burdette (pitching)	1.00	.50	.30
(128) Lou Burdette (portrait, pose to chest)	1.00	.50	.30
(129) Smokey Burgess (kneeling)	1.00	.50	.30
(130) Pete Burnside (pitching)	.75	.40	.25
(131) Larry Burright (portrait, pose to chest)	.75	.40	.25
(132) Cecil Butler (pitching, pitcher's follow through)	.75	.40	.25
(133) John Callison (batting, pose to chest)	1.00	.50	.30
(134) John Callison (batting, pose to neck)	1.00	.50	.30
(135) Chris Cannizzaro (batting, pose to chest)	.75	.40	.25
(136) Leo Cardenas (fielding)	.75	.40	.25
(137) Leo Cardenas (batting, pose to waist)	.75	.40	.25
(138) Don Cardwell (portrait, pose to chest)	.75	.40	.25
(139) Duke Carmel (portrait, pose to chest)	.75	.40	.25
(140) Camilio Carreon (Camilo) (batting, pose to chest)	.75	.40	.25
(141) Camilio Carreon (Camilo) (portrait, pose to chest)	.75	.40	.25
(142) Norm Cash (batting, pose to chest)	1.00	.50	.30
(143) Norm Cash (kneeling, holding bat)	1.00	.50	.30
(144) Norm Cash (fielding)	1.00	.50	.30
(145) Norm Cash (hands on knees)	1.00	.50	.30
(146) Wayne Causey (kneeling, holding bat)	.75	.40	.25
(147) Wayne Causey (portrait, pose to chest, stripe uniform)	.75	.40	.25
(148) Wayne Causey (portrait, pose to chest, vest uniform)	.75	.40	.25
(149) Orlando Cepeda (kneeling, pose to waist)	1.50	.70	.45
(150) Orlando Cepeda (portrait, pose to chest, one ear showing)	1.50	.70	.45
(151) Orlando Cepeda (portrait, pose to chest, two ears showing)	1.50	.70	.45
(152) Orlando Cepeda (batting, pose to chest)	1.50	.70	.45
(153) Elio Chacon (portrait, pose to waist)	.75	.40	.25
(154) Dean Chance (pitching, pitcher's follow through, wrist over glove)	.75	.40	.25
(155) Dean Chance (pitching, pitcher's follow through, hand over glove)	.75	.40	.25
(156) Dean Chance (portrait, pose to chest)	.75	.40	.25
(157) Ed Charles (batting, pose to chest, striped uniform)	.75	.40	.25
(158) Ed Charles (batting, pose to chest, vest uniform)	.75	.40	.25
(159) Tom Cheney (pitching, pitcher's follow through)	.75	.40	.25
(160) Tom Cheney (portrait, pose to chest, hands over head, picture is Osteen)	.75	.40	.25
(161) Frank Cipriani (batting, pose to waist)	.75	.40	.25
(162) Galen Cisco (pitching, pose to knees)	.75	.40	.25
(163) Roberto Clemente (batting, pose to chest, cap)	8.00	4.00	2.50
(164) Roberto Clemente (batting, pose to chest, helmet)	8.00	4.00	2.50
(165) Donn Clendenon (batting, pose to waist)	.75	.40	.25
(166) Donn Clendenon (batting, pose to chest)	.75	.40	.25
(167) Donn Clendenon (portrait, pose to chest)	.75	.40	.25
(168) Lou Clinton (portrait, pose to chest)	.75	.40	.25
(169) Lou Clinton (Red Sox, batting, pose to chest)	.75	.40	.25
(170) Lou Clinton (Angels, batting, pose to chest)	.75	.40	.25
(171) Tony Cloninger (pitching, hands over head)	.75	.40	.25
(172) Tony Cloninger (portrait, pose to chest)	.75	.40	.25
(173) Rocky Colavito (hands on knees)	1.25	.60	.40
(174) Rocky Colavito (batting, pose to chest)	1.25	.60	.40
(175) Choo Choo Coleman (portrait, pose to waist, glove)	.75	.40	.25
(176) Gordy Coleman (batting, pose to chest)	.75	.40	.25
(177) Gordy Coleman (fielding)	.75	.40	.25
(178) Tony Conigliaro (portrait, pose to waist, glove)	1.00	.50	.30
(179) Gene Conley (portrait, pose to chest)	.75	.40	.25
(180) Jim Constable (pitching, pitcher's follow through)	.75	.40	.25
(181) Chuck Cottier (kneeling, holding bat)	.75	.40	.25
(182) Chuck Cottier (batting, pose to chest)	.75	.40	.25
(183) Wes Covington (batting, pose to waist)	.75	.40	.25
(184) Harry Craft (portrait, pose to chest, Colts uniform)	.75	.40	.25
(185) Harry Craft (portrait, pose to chest, Houston uniform)	.75	.40	.25
(186) Roger Craig (portrait, pose to waist)	1.00	.50	.30
(187) Roger Craig (pitching, pitcher's follow through)	1.00	.50	.30
(188) Del Crandall (portrait, pose to chest)	1.00	.50	.30
(189) Del Crandall (kneeling, bats)	1.00	.50	.30
(190) Del Crandall (catching, crouching)	1.00	.50	.30
(191) Del Crandall (catching, crouching, throwing)	1.00	.50	.30
(192) Del Crandall (kneeling, pose to waist)	1.00	.50	.30
(193) Joe Cunningham (portrait, pose to chest)	.75	.40	.25
(194) Joe Cunningham (batting, pose to chest)	.75	.40	.25
(195) Jack Curtis (portrait, pose to chest)	.75	.40	.25
(196) Bill Dailey (pitching, pose to chest, hands over head)	.75	.40	.25
(197) Bud Daley (portrait, pose to chest, glove)	.75	.40	.25
(198) Clay Dalrymple (batting, pose to chest)	.75	.40	.25
(199) Clay Dalrymple (portrait, pose to chest)	.75	.40	.25
(200) Bennie Daniels (pitching, pitcher's follow through)	.75	.40	.25
(201) Bennie Daniels (portrait, pose to waist, glove)	.75	.40	.25
(202) Alvin Dark (kneeling, pose to waist)	1.00	.50	.30
(203) Alvin Dark (portriat, pose to chest)	1.00	.50	.30
(204) Alvin Dark (sitting)	1.00	.50	.30
(205) Jose Davalillo (Vic) (portrait, pose to waist)	.75	.40	.25
(206) Jose Davalillo (Vic) (batting, pose to neck)	.75	.40	.25
(207) Jose Davalillo (Vic) (batting, pose to chest)	.75	.40	.25
(208) Jim Davenport (fielding)	.75	.40	.25
(209) Jim Davenport (fielding, over bag)	.75	.40	.25
(210) Jim Davenport (portrait, pose to chest, San Francisco uniform)	.75	.40	.25
(211) Jim Davenport (portrait, pose to chest, Giants uniform)	.75	.40	.25
(212) Tom Davis (batting, pose to waist)	1.00	.50	.30
(213) Tom Davis (portrait, pose to chest)	1.00	.50	.30
(214) Willie Davis (batting, pose to chest)	1.00	.50	.30
(215) Willie Davis (hands on knees)	1.00	.50	.30
(216) Mike de la Hoz (portrait, pose to waist, arms crossed)	.75	.40	.25
(217) Charlie Dees (portrait, pose to chest)	.75	.40	.25
(218) Ike Delock (sitting, pose to knees)	.75	.40	.25
(219) Don Demeter (portrait, pose to chest)	.75	.40	.25
(220) Don Demeter (batting, pose to chest)	.75	.40	.25
(221) Dick Donovan (portrait, pose to chest)	.75	.40	.25

	NR MT	EX	VG
(222) Dick Donovan (pitching, pitcher's follow through, pose to knees)	.75	.40	.25
(223) Dick Donovan (crouching)	.75	.40	.25
(224) Al Downing (portrait, pose to chest)	1.00	.50	.30
(225) Al Downing (pitching, pitcher's follow through)	1.00	.50	.30
(226) Moe Drabowski (Drabowsky) (portrait, pose to chest)	.75	.40	.25
(227) Chuck Dressen (kneeling, pose to knees)	.75	.40	.25
(228) Chuck Dressen (portrait, pose to chest)	.75	.40	.25
(229) Don Drysdale (portrait, pose to chest, two ears showing)	2.50	1.25	.70
(230) Don Drysdale (portrait, pose to chest, one ear showing)	2.50	1.25	.70
(231) Ryne Duran (Duren) (pitching, pitcher's follow through)	1.00	.50	.30
(232) Doc Edwards (kneeling, holding bat)	.75	.40	.25
(233) Sammy Ellis (portrait, pose to chest)	.75	.40	.25
(234) Dick Ellsworth (portrait, pose to chest, Cubs uniform)	.75	.40	.25
(235) Dick Ellsworth (portrait, pose to waist, Chicago)	.75	.40	.25
(236) Don Elston (portrait, pose to waist, arms crossed)	.75	.40	.25
(237) Sam Esposito (portrait, pose to chest)	.75	.40	.25
(238) Chuck Estrada (pitching, pitcher's follow through)	.75	.40	.25
(239) Chuck Estrada (pitching, pose to knees)	.75	.40	.25
(240) Roy Face (portrait, pose to chest, pole background)	1.00	.50	.30
(241) Roy Face (portrait, pose to chest, no pole)	1.00	.50	.30
(242) Ron Fairley (Fairly) (batting, pose to chest, tower in background)	.75	.40	.25
(243) Ron Fairly (portrait, pose to chest, #6 visible)	.75	.40	.25
(244) Ron Fairly (batting, pose to chest, no tower)	.75	.40	.25
(245) Ron Fairly (portrait, pose to waist)	.75	.40	.25
(246) Dick Farrell (portrait, pose to chest, Colts uniform)	.75	.40	.25
(247) Dick Farrell (portrait, pose to chest, Houston uniform)	.75	.40	.25
(248) Dick Farrell (portrait, pose to chest, glove)	.75	.40	.25
(249) Bill Faul (portrait, pose to chest)	.75	.40	.25
(250) Chico Fernandez (batting, pose to chest)	.75	.40	.25
(251) Hank Fischer (pitching, pitcher's follow through)	.75	.40	.25
(252) Bill Fisher (Fischer) (pitching, pitcher's follow through)	.75	.40	.25
(253) Jack Fisher (kneeling, pose to waist, arms crossed)	.75	.40	.25
(254) Curt Flood (portrait, pose to chest)	1.25	.60	.40
(255) Curt Flood (hands on knees, background shows two men on left and one on right)	1.25	.60	.40
(256) Curt Flood (hands on knees, background shows two men on left and none on right)	1.25	.60	.40
(257) Curt Flood (hands on knees, background shows one man on left and none on right)	1.25	.60	.40
(258) Whitey Ford (portrait, pose to chest)	5.00	2.50	1.50
(259) Whitey Ford (pitching, pose to knees)	5.00	2.50	1.50
(260) Whitey Ford (kneeling, pose to waist, arms crossed)	5.00	2.50	1.50
(261) Nellie Fox (portrait, pose to chest)	1.75	.90	.50
(262) Nellie Fox (portrait, pose to neck)	1.75	.90	.50
(263) Nellie Fox (fielding)	1.75	.90	.50
(264) Paul Foytack (pitching, hands over head)	.75	.40	.25
(265) Tito Francona (batting, pose to waist)	.75	.40	.25
(266) Tito Francona (hands on knees)	.75	.40	.25
(267) Herman Franks (portrait, pose to chest)	.75	.40	.25
(268) Bill Freehan (kneeling, holding bat)	1.00	.50	.30
(269) Bill Freehan (portrait, pose to waist, arms crossed)	1.00	.50	.30
(270) Jim Fregosi (portrait, pose to chest)	1.00	.50	.30
(271) Jim Fregosi (batting, pose to chest)	1.00	.50	.30
(272) Bob Friend (pitching, pitcher's follow through)	1.00	.50	.30
(273) Bob Friend (portrait, pose to chest)	1.00	.50	.30
(274) Frank Funk (pitching, pitcher's follow through)	.75	.40	.25
(275) Gary Geiger (portrait, pose to chest)	.75	.40	.25
(276) Gary Geiger (batting, pose to waist)	.75	.40	.25
(277) Jim Gentile (kneeling, holding bat)	.75	.40	.25
(278) Jim Gentile (batting, pose to chest)	.75	.40	.25
(279) Jim Gentile (batting, pose to waist)	.75	.40	.25
(280) Jim Gentile (kneeling, pose to waist, arms crossed)	.75	.40	.25
(281) Bob Gibson (portrait, pose to chest)	2.50	1.25	.70
(282) Bob Gibson (pitching, pitcher's follow through)	2.50	1.25	.70
(283) Bob Gibson (pitching, pose to knees)	2.50	1.25	.70
(284) Jim Gilliam (portrait, pose to chest, clouds)	1.25	.60	.40
(285) Jim Gilliam (portrait, pose to chest, no clouds)	1.25	.60	.40
(286) Jim Gilliam (batting, pose to waist)	1.50	.70	.45
(287) Jess Gonder (batting, pose to chest)	1.25	.60	.40
(288) Jesse Gonder (portrait, pose to chest)	.75	.40	.25
(289) Tony Gonzalez (hands on knees)	.75	.40	.25
(290) Jim Grant (portrait, pose to thighs, glove)	.75	.40	.25
(291) Jim Grant (pitching, pitcher's follow through, fuzzy background)	.75	.40	.25
(292) Jim Grant (pitching, pitcher's follow through, stands in background)	.75	.40	.25
(293) Eli Grba (pitching, pitcher's follow through)	.75	.40	.25
(294) Dallas Green (pitching, pose to chest, hands over head)	.75	.40	.25
(295) Dallas Green (pitching, pitcher's follow through)	.75	.40	.25
(296) Dick Green (batting, pose to waist)	.75	.40	.25
(297) Lenny Green (kneeling, holding bat)	.75	.40	.25
(298) Dick Groat (kneeling, holding bat)	1.25	.60	.40
(299) Dick Groat (kneeling, holding bat)	1.25	.60	.40
(300) Dick Groat (batting, pose to waist)	1.25	.60	.40
(301) Harvey Haddox (Haddix) (pitching, pitcher's follow through)	1.00	.50	.30
(302) Jimmie Hall (portrait, pose to chest)	.75	.40	.25
(303) Tom Haller (catching, crouching)	.75	.40	.25
(304) Tom Haller (catching, throwing)	.75	.40	.25
(305) Tom Haller (portrait, pose to chest, Giants uniform)	.75	.40	.25
(306) Tom Haller (portrait, pose to chest, San Francisco uniform)	.75	.40	.25
(307) Ken Hamlin (portrait, pose to chest)	.75	.40	.25
(308) Ron Hansen (batting, pose to waist)	.75	.40	.25
(309) Ron Hansen (fielding)	.75	.40	.25
(310) Ron Hansen (kneeling, holding bat)	.75	.40	.25
(311) Carroll Hardy (batting)	.75	.40	.25
(312) Tim Harkness (fielding)	.75	.40	.25
(313) Tommy Harper (hands on knees)	.75	.40	.25
(314) Ken Harrelson (batting, pose to chest)	1.00	.50	.30
(315) Ken Harrelson (portrait, pose to chest)	1.00	.50	.30
(316) Woody Held (batting, pose to waist)	.75	.40	.25
(317) Woody Held (portrait, pose to chest)	.75	.40	.25
(318) Bob Hendley (portrait, pose to chest)	.75	.40	.25
(319) Bob Hendley (pitching, pitcher's follow through)	.75	.40	.25
(320) Ron Henry (batting, pose to chest)	.75	.40	.25
(321) Ray Herbert (pitching, pitcher's follow through)	.75	.40	.25
(322) Ron Herbert (pitching)	.75	.40	.25
(323) Billy Herman (portrait, pose to chest)	1.50	.70	.45
(324) Mike Hershberger (kneeling, holding bat)	.75	.40	.25
(325) Mike Hershberger (portrait, pose to chest, arms crossed)	.75	.40	.25
(326) Whitey Herzog (portrait, pose to chest)	1.25	.60	.40
(327) Jim Hickman (batting, pose to chest)	.75	.40	.25
(328) Jim Hickman (kneeling, pose to knees)	.75	.40	.25
(329) Mike Higgins (portrait, pose to chest)	.75	.40	.25
(330) Chuck Hiller (batting, pose to chest)	.75	.40	.25
(331) Chuck Hiller (portrait, pose to chest, Giants uniform)	.75	.40	.25
(332) Chuck Hiller (portrait, pose to chest, San Francisco uniform)	.75	.40	.25
(333) Chuck Hinton (batting, pose to chest)	.75	.40	.25
(334) Chuck Hinton (portrait, pose to chest)	.75	.40	.25
(335) Chuck Hinton (portrait, pose to waist)	.75	.40	.25
(336) Billy Hitchcock (portrait, pose to chest)	.75	.40	.25
(337) Don Hoak (kneeling, holding bat)	.75	.40	.25
(338) Don Hoak (batting, pose to chest)	.75	.40	.25
(339) Glen Hobbie (portrait, pose to chest)	.75	.40	.25
(340) Gil Hodges (portrait, pose to chest, dark background)	1.50	.70	.45
(341) Gil Hodges (portrait, pose to chest, light background)	1.50	.70	.45
(342) Gil Hodges (portrait, pose to waist)	2.75	1.50	.80
(343) Gil Hodges (batting, pose to chest)	2.75	1.50	.80
(344) Jay Hook (portrait, pose to waist)	.75	.40	.25
(345) Jay Hook (pitching, pose to knees)	[illegible]	.40	.25
(346) Joel Horlen (pitching, pose to chest, hands over head)	.75	.40	.25
(347) Ralph Houk (portrait, pose to chest, Mgr. on front)	1.00	.50	.30
(348) Ralph Houk (portrait, pose to chest, Manager on front)	1.00	.50	.30
(349) Elston Howard (batting, pose to waist)	1.50	.70	.45
(350) Elston Howard (kneeling, holding bat, pose to knees)	1.50	.70	.45
(351) Elston Howard (catching, crouching)	1.50	.70	.45
(352) Frank Howard (batting, pose to thighs)	1.50	.70	.45
(353) Frank Howard (kneeling, holding bat to thigh)	1.50	.70	.45
(354) Frank Howard (kneeling, holding bat, tower background)	1.50	.70	.45
(355) Frank Howard (portrait, pose to chest)	1.50	.70	.45
(356) Dick Howser (portrait, pose to chest)	1.00	.50	.30
(357) Ken Hubbs (portrait, pose to chest)	1.00	.50	.30
(358) Ken Hunt (portrait, pose to chest)	.75	.40	.25
(359) Ken Hunt (batting, pose to chest)	.75	.40	.25
(360) Ron Hunt (batting, pose to waist)	.75	.40	.25
(361) Ron Hunt (fielding)	.75	.40	.25
(362) Fred Hutchinson (portrait, pose to chest)	.75	.40	.25
(363) Al Jackson (portrait, pose to chest)	.75	.40	.25
(364) Al Jackson (pitching, pitcher's follow through)	.75	.40	.25
(365) Larry Jackson (portrait, pose to waist, tank in background)	.75	.40	.25
(366) Larry Jackson (Cardinals, portrait, pose to chest, mouth closed)	.75	.40	.25
(367) Larry Jackson (Cubs, portrait, pose to neck, mouth open)	.75	.40	.25
(368) Larry Jackson (portrait, pose to neck)	.75	.40	.25
(369) Charlie James (fielding)	.75	.40	.25
(370) Julian Javier (batting, pose to waist)	.75	.40	.25
(371) Julian Javier (portrait, pose to chest)	.75	.40	.25
(372) Joey Jay (portrait, pose to chest)	.75	.40	.25
(373) Joey Jay (pitching, pitcher's follow through)	.75	.40	.25
(374) Manny Jiminez (Jimenez) (portrait, pose to chest)	.75	.40	.25
(375) Manny Jiminez (Jimenez) (kneeling, holding bat)	.75	.40	.25
(376) Manny Jiminez (Jimenez) (batting, pose to waist)	.75	.40	.25
(377) Bob Johnson (batting, pose to waist)	.75	.40	.25
(378) Ken Johnson (portrait, pose to chest)	.75	.40	.25
(379) Mack Jones (batting)	.75	.40	.25
(380) Mack Jones (batting, pose to chest)	.75	.40	.25
(381) Jim Kaat (pitching, pitcher's follow through)	1.50	.70	.45
(382) Jim Kaat (portrait, pose to waist, glove)	1.50	.70	.45
(383) Al Kaline (portrait, pose to chest)	6.00	3.00	1.75
(384) Al Kaline (hands on knees)	6.00	3.00	1.75
(385) Al Kaline (batting, pose to chest)	6.00	3.00	1.75
(386) Rod Kanehl (batting, pose to chest, bat straight up)	.75	.40	.25
(387) Rod Kanehl (batting, pose to chest, bat angled)	.75	.40	.25
(388) Eddie Kasko (batting, pose to chest)	.75	.40	.25
(389) John Keane (portrait, pose to waist)	.75	.40	.25
(390) John Keane (standing)	.75	.40	.25
(391) Johnny Keane (portrait, pose to waist)	.75	.40	.25
(392) Russ Kemmerer (pitching, pose to knees)	.75	.40	.25
(393) Bob Kennedy (portrait, pose to chest)	.75	.40	.25
(394) Bob Kennedy (kneeling, holding bat)	.75	.40	.25
(395) John Kennedy (batting, pose to waist)	.75	.40	.25
(396) Marty Keough (batting, pose to chest)	.75	.40	.25
(397) Marty Keough (hands on knees)	.75	.40	.25
(398) Harmon Killebrew (batting, pose to chest)	3.25	1.75	1.00
(399) Harmon Killebrew (portrait, pose to chest)	3.25	1.75	1.00
(400) Jim King (batting, pose to chest)	.75	.40	.25
(401) Jim King (portrait, pose to chest)	.75	.40	.25
(402) Willie Kirkland (Indians, batting, pose to waist)	.75	.40	.25
(403) Willie Kirkland (Orioles, batting, pose to waist)	.75	.40	.25
(404) Ron Kline (pitching, pitcher's follow through)	.75	.40	.25
(405) Ted Kluszewski (batting, pose to chest)	1.50	.70	.45
(406) Bob Knoop (portrait, pose to chest)	.75	.40	.25
(407) Sandy Koufax (portrait, pose to waist, arms crossed)	7.00	3.50	2.00
(408) Sandy Koufax (portrait, pose to chest, smiling)	7.00	3.50	2.00
(409) Sandy Koufax (portrait, pose to chest, palm trees in background)	7.00	3.50	2.00

	NR MT	EX	VG
(410) Jack Kralick (pitching, pitcher's follow through)	.75	.40	.25
(411) Jim Kralick (portrait, pose to chest)	.75	.40	.25
(412) John Kralick (pitching, pitcher's follow through)	.75	.40	.25
(413) Ed Kranepool (batting, pose to chest)	.75	.40	.25
(414) Tony Kubek (fielding)	1.50	.70	.45
(415) Tony Kubek (batting)	1.50	.70	.45
(416) Harvey Kuenn (portrait, pose to chest, Giants uniform)	1.00	.50	.30
(417) Harvey Kuenn (portrait, pose to chest, San Francisco uniform)	1.00	.50	.30
(418) Marty Kutyna (pitching, pitcher's follow through)	.75	.40	.25
(419) Jim Landis (batting)	.75	.40	.25
(420) Jim Landis (kneeling, holding bat)	.75	.40	.25
(421) Jim Landis (kneeling, pose to knees, arms crossed)	.75	.40	.25
(422) Jim Landis (hands on knees)	.75	.40	.25
(423) Hobie Landrith (batting)	.75	.40	.25
(424) Don Landrum (fielding)	.75	.40	.25
(425) Norm Larker (portrait, pose to chest)	.75	.40	.25
(426) Norm Larker (fielding)	.75	.40	.25
(427) Frank Lary (pitching, pitcher's follow through)	.75	.40	.25
(428) Barry Latman (portrait)	.75	.40	.25
(429) Barry Latman (pitching)	.75	.40	.25
(430) Charlie Lau (batting)	.75	.40	.25
(431) Vern Law (portrait)	1.00	.50	.30
(432) Vernon Law (pitching)	1.00	.50	.30
(433) Don Lee (pitching)	.75	.40	.25
(434) Don Lee (portrait)	.75	.40	.25
(435) Denny Lemaster (pitching, pitcher's follow through)	.75	.40	.25
(436) Denny Lemaster (pitching, pose to knees)	.75	.40	.25
(437) Jim Lemon (batting)	.75	.40	.25
(438) Don Leppert (batting)	.75	.40	.25
(439) Bob Lillis (batting)	.75	.40	.25
(440) Don Lock (portrait, pose to chest, light background)	.75	.40	.25
(441) Don Lock (portrait, pose to chest, dark background, Senators in block letters)	.75	.40	.25
(442) Don Lock (portrait, pose to waist, dark background, Senators in script)	.75	.40	.25
(443) Sherm Lollar (kneeling)	.75	.40	.25
(444) Sherm Lollar (portrait)	.75	.40	.25
(445) Ed Lopat (portrait)	1.00	.50	.30
(446) Al Lopez (portrait)	1.50	.70	.45
(447) Al Lopez (portrait, pose to chest, jacket has top of "S" visible)	1.50	.70	.45
(448) Al Lopez (portrait, pose to chest, jacket has "S" and part of "O" visible)	1.50	.70	.45
(449) Jerry Lumpe (batting, pose to waist)	.75	.40	.25
(450) Jerry Lumpe (kneeling, pose to thighs)	.75	.40	.25
(451) Jerry Lumpe (batting, pose to chest)	.75	.40	.25
(452) Jerry Lynch (portrait, pose to chest)	.75	.40	.25
(453) Art Mahaffey (portrait)	.75	.40	.25
(454) Art Mahaffey (pitching)	.75	.40	.25
(455) Roman Majias (portrait)	.75	.40	.25
(456) Jim Maloney (pitching)	.75	.40	.25
(457) Frank Malzone (batting, pose to chest, one ear showing)	.75	.40	.25
(458) Frank Malzone (batting, pose to chest, two ears showing)	.75	.40	.25
(459) Frank Malzone (portrait)	.75	.40	.25
(460) Felix Mantilla (portrait, pose to neck, one ear showing)	.75	.40	.25
(461) Felix Mantilla (portrait, pose to chest, two ears showing)	.75	.40	.25
(462) Felix Mantilla (portrait, pose to waist)	.75	.40	.25
(463) Mickey Mantle (portrait)	15.00	7.50	4.50
(464) Mickey Mantle (batting, pose to chest, one ear showing)	15.00	7.50	4.50
(465) Mickey Mantle (batting, pose to chest, two ears showing)	15.00	7.50	4.50
(466) Juan Marichal (portrait, pose to waist, hands over head)	2.50	1.25	.70
(467) Juan Marichal (pitching)	2.50	1.25	.70
(468) Juan Marichal (portrait, pose to chest)	2.50	1.25	.70
(469) Roger Maris (kneeling)	8.00	4.00	2.50
(470) Roger Maris (batting, pose to chest, one ear showing)	8.00	4.00	2.50
(471) Roger Maris (batting, pose to chest, two ears showing)	.75	.40	.25
(472) J.C. Martin (batting, pose to waist)	.75	.40	.25
(473) Joe Martin (batting, pose to waist)	.75	.40	.25
(474) Eddie Mathews (batting)	3.25	1.75	1.00
(475) Eddie Mathews (batting, pose to waist)	3.25	1.75	1.00
(476) Eddie Mathews (kneeling)	3.25	1.75	1.00
(477) Gene Mauch (portrait, pose to knees, one ear showing)	1.00	.50	.30
(478) Gene Mauch (portrait, pose to knees, two ears showing)	1.00	.50	.30
(479) Gene Mauch (portrait, pose to chest)	1.00	.50	.30
(480) Dal Maxvill (fielding)	.75	.40	.25
(481) Charley Maxwell (batting)	.75	.40	.25
(482) Lee Maye (portrait, pose to chest, holding bat)	.75	.40	.25
(483) Lee Maye (portrait, pose to chest, no bat)	.75	.40	.25
(484) Lee Maye (fielding)	.75	.40	.25
(485) Willie Mays (portrait, pose to neck)	10.00	5.00	3.00
(486) Willie Mays (portrait, pose to chest)	10.00	5.00	3.00
(487) Willie Mays (kneeling)	10.00	5.00	3.00
(488) Willie Mays (hat, pose to waist)	10.00	5.00	3.00
(489) Bill Mazeroski (portrait)	1.25	.60	.40
(490) Bill Mazeroski (batting)	1.25	.60	.40
(491) Bill Mazeroski (fielding)	1.25	.60	.40
(492) Ken McBride (portrait)	.75	.40	.25
(493) Ken McBride (pitching)	.75	.40	.25
(494) Tim McCarver (portrait)	1.25	.60	.40
(495) Tim McCarver (catching)	1.25	.60	.40
(496) Joe McClain (pitching)	.75	.40	.25
(497) Mike McCormick (pitching)	.75	.40	.25
(498) Willie McCovey (portrait)	3.25	1.75	1.00
(499) Willie McCovey (batting)	3.25	1.75	1.00
(500) Willie McCovey (kneeling)	3.25	1.75	1.00
(501) Tom McCraw (batting)	.75	.40	.25
(502) Lindy McDaniel (portrait, pose to chest, Chicago uniform)	.75	.40	.25
(503) Lindy McDaniel (portrait, pose to chest, Cubs uniform)	.75	.40	.25
(504) Lindy McDaniel (Cardinals, portrait, pose to chest)	.75	.40	.25
(505) Sam McDowell (portrait, pose to chest)	1.00	.50	.30
(506) Mel McGaha (portrait, pose to waist, holding bat)	.75	.40	.25
(507) Mel McGaha (portrait, pose to chest)	.75	.40	.25
(508) Roy McMillan (fielding)	.75	.40	.25
(509) Roy McMillan (batting)	.75	.40	.25
(510) Roy McMillan (portrait)	.75	.40	.25
(511) Ken McMullen (portrait)	.75	.40	.25
(512) Sam Mele (portrait)	.75	.40	.25
(513) Dennis Menke (Denis) (throwing)	.75	.40	.25
(514) Dennis Menke (Denis) (portrait, pose to neck)	.75	.40	.25
(515) Bob Miller (portrait)	.75	.40	.25
(516) Stu Miller (pitching)	.75	.40	.25
(517) Minnie Minoso (batting)	1.25	.60	.40
(518) Bill Monbouquette (pitching, pitcher's follow through)	.75	.40	.25
(519) Bill Monbouquette (kneeling, pose to knees)	.75	.40	.25
(520) William Monbouquette (kneeling, pose to knees)	.75	.40	.25
(521) Wally Moon (batting)	.75	.40	.25
(522) Wally Moon (portrait)	.75	.40	.25
(523) Billy Moran (batting)	.75	.40	.25
(524) Tom Morgan (portrait)	.75	.40	.25
(525) Don Mossi (portrait)	.75	.40	.25
(526) Manny Mota (portrait)	1.00	.50	.30
(527) Danny Murtaugh (portrait)	.75	.40	.25
(528) Stan Musial (fielding)	10.00	5.00	3.00
(529) Stan Musial (kneeling)	10.00	5.00	3.00
(530) Don McMahon (pitching)	.75	.40	.25
(531) Buster Narum (portrait)	.75	.40	.25
(532) Charlie Neal (batting)	.75	.40	.25
(533) Fred Newman (portrait)	.75	.40	.25
(534) Dave Nicholson (kneeling, pose to waist, holding bat)	.75	.40	.25
(535) Dave Nicholson (hands on knees)	.75	.40	.25
(536) Phil Niekro (pitching)	2.25	1.25	.70
(537) Bob Nieman (hands on knees)	.75	.40	.25
(538) Russ Nixon (batting)	.75	.40	.25
(539) Joe Nuxhall (portrait)	1.00	.50	.30
(540) Danny O'Connell (batting)	.75	.40	.25
(541) Billy O'Dell (portrait)	.75	.40	.25
(542) Billy O'Dell (Giants, pitching, pitcher's follow through)	.75	.40	.25
(543) Billy O'Dell (pitching)	.75	.40	.25
(544) Billy O'Dell (Braves, pitching, pitcher's follow through)	.75	.40	.25
(545) Jim O'Toole (portrait)	.75	.40	.25
(546) Jim O'Toole (pitching)	.75	.40	.25
(547) Tony Oliva (batting)	2.00	1.00	.60
(548) Gene Oliver (batting)	.75	.40	.25
(549) Nate Oliver (batting)	.75	.40	.25
(550) John Orsino (batting, pose to waist, one ear showing)	.75	.40	.25
(551) John Orsino (batting, pose to waist, two ears showing)	.75	.40	.25
(552) John Orsino (kneeling, pose to waist)	.75	.40	.25
(553) Phil Ortega (portrait)	.75	.40	.25
(554) Dan Osinski (portrait, pose to neck)	.75	.40	.25
(555) Dan Osinski (portrait, pose to chest)	.75	.40	.25
(556) Claude Osteen (portrait, pose to waist, glove)	.75	.40	.25
(557) Claude Osteen (portrait, pose to chest)	.75	.40	.25
(558) Claude Osteen (pitching, pose to knees) (photo actally Tom Cheney)	.75	.40	.25
(559) Jose Pagan (portrait, pose to chest, Giants uniform)	.75	.40	.25
(560) Jose Pagan (portrait, pose to chest, San Francisco uniform)	.75	.40	.25
(561) Jose Pagan (portrait, pose to waist)	.75	.40	.25
(562) Jose Pagan (fielding)	.75	.40	.25
(563) James Pagliaroni (portrait, pose to chest)	.75	.40	.25
(564) Jim Pagliaroni (portrait, pose to waist)	.75	.40	.25
(565) Milt Pappas (pitching, pose to chest, hands over head)	1.00	.50	.30
(566) Milt Pappas (pitching, pitcher's follow through, stands empty)	1.00	.50	.30
(567) Milt Pappas (pitching, pitcher's follow through, people in stands)	1.00	.50	.30
(568) Camilo Pascual (pitching, pitcher's follow through)	1.00	.50	.30
(569) Camilo Pascual (pitching, pose to knees, glove at knee)	1.00	.50	.30
(570) Camilo Pascual (pitching, pose to waist, glove in front)	1.00	.50	.30
(571) Don Pavletich (batting)	.75	.40	.25
(572) Albie Pearson (hands on knees)	.75	.40	.25
(573) Albie Pearson (kneeling, holding bat)	.75	.40	.25
(574) Jim Pendleton (batting)	.75	.40	.25
(575) Joe Pepitone (portrait)	1.25	.60	.40
(576) Joe Pepitone (batting)	1.25	.60	.40
(577) Gaylord Perry (kneeling, pose to waist, holding bat)	2.25	1.25	.70
(578) Johnny Pesky (portrait, pose to chest)	.75	.40	.25
(579) Johnny Pesky (portrait, pose to waist, arms crossed)	.75	.40	.25
(580) Gary Peters (kneeling)	.75	.40	.25
(581) Gary Peters (pitching)	.75	.40	.25
(582) Bubba Phillips (kneeling)	.75	.40	.25
(583) Bubba Phillips (hands on knees)	.75	.40	.25
(584) Ron Piche (portrait)	.75	.40	.25
(585) Billy Pierce (pitching)	1.00	.50	.30
(586) Billy Pierce (portrait)	1.00	.50	.30
(587) Jim Piersall (hands on knees)	1.25	.60	.40
(588) Vada Pinson (batting, pose to waist, tower in background)	1.25	.60	.40
(589) Vada Pinson (batting, pose to chest, stands in background)	.75	.40	.25
(590) Juan Pizzaro (pitching, pose to waist)	.75	.40	.25
(591) Juan Pizzaro (pitching, pitcher's follow through)	.75	.40	.25
(592) John Podres (portrait)	1.25	.60	.40
(593) John Podres (pitching)	1.25	.60	.40
(594) Leo Posada (batting)	.75	.40	.25
(595) Wally Post (batting)	.75	.40	.25
(596) Boog Powell (portrait)	1.50	.70	.45
(597) Boog Powell (batting)	1.50	.70	.45
(598) Vic Power (batting, pose to chest)	.75	.40	.25
(599) Vic Power (kneeling, holding bat)	.75	.40	.25
(600) Vic Power (batting, pose to waist)	.75	.40	.25
(601) Bob Purkey (pitching)	.75	.40	.25
(602) Bob Purkey (kneeling)	.75	.40	.25
(603) Mel Queen (batting, pose to waist)	.75	.40	.25
(604) Dick Radatz (portrait, pose to neck)	.75	.40	.25
(605) Dick Radatz (portrait, pose to chest, two players in background)	.75	.40	.25
(606) Dick Radatz (portrait, pose to chest, sky in background)	.75	.40	.25
(607) Ed Rakow (portrait, pose to chest)	.75	.40	.25
(608) Ed Rakow (kneeling, pose to knees, arms crossed)	.75	.40	.25
(609) Ed Rakow (portrait, pose to chest)	.75	.40	.25
(610) Pedro Ramos (standing)	.75	.40	.25
(611) Merritt Ranew (batting)	.75	.40	.25
(612) Claude Raymond (pitching)	.75	.40	.25
(613) Phil Regan (portrait)	.75	.40	.25
(614) Phil Regan (pitching)	.75	.40	.25
(615) Ken Retzer (batting)	.75	.40	.25
(616) Ken Retzer (kneeling)	.75	.40	.25
(617) Paul Richards (portrait)	.75	.40	.25
(618) Bobby Richardson (fielding)	1.50	.70	.45
(619) Robby Richardson (portrait)	1.50	.70	.45
(620) Pete Richert (portrait)	.75	.40	.25
(621) Bill Rigney (portrait, pose to chest, one ear showing)	.75	.40	.25
(622) Bill Rigney (portrait, pose to chest, two ears showing)	.75	.40	.25
(623) Mike Roarke (catching)	.75	.40	.25
(624) Robin Roberts (pitching)	2.50	1.25	.70
(625) Robin Roberts (kneeling)	2.50	1.25	.70
(626) Brooks Robinson (batting, pose to chest)	6.00	3.00	1.75
(627) Brooks Robinson (kneeling, pose to waist, "B" on cap)	6.00	3.00	1.75
(628) Brooks Robinson (kneeling, holding bat, bird on cap)	6.00	3.00	1.75
(629) Earl Robinson (hands on knees)	.75	.40	.25
(630) Floyd Robinson (kneeling, holding bat)	.75	.40	.25
(631) Floyd Robinson (batting, pose to chest, mouth open)	.75	.40	.25
(632) Floyd Robinson (batting, pose to chest, mouth closed)	.75	.40	.25
(633) Frank Robinson (batting, pose to thigh)	3.25	1.75	1.00
(634) Frank Robinson (kneeling, holding bat)	3.25	1.75	1.00
(635) Andre Rodgers (portrait, pose to chest, Chicago uniform)	.75	.40	.25
(636) Andre Rodgers (portrait, pose to waist, Cubs uniform)	.75	.40	.25
(637) Bob Rodgers (portrait)	1.00	.50	.30
(638) Bob Rodgers (batting)	1.00	.50	.30
(639) Ed Roebuck (pitching, pose to chest, hands over head)	.75	.40	.25
(640) Rich Rollins (fielding)	.75	.40	.25
(641) Rich Rollins (batting)	.75	.40	.25
(642) John Romano (batting, pose to waist)	.75	.40	.25
(643) John Romano (batting, pose to chest)	.75	.40	.25
(644) Pete Rose (portrait)	10.00	5.00	3.00
(645) Pete Rose (kneeling)	10.00	5.00	3.00
(646) John Roseboro (portrait)	.75	.40	.25
(647) John Roseboro (catching)	.75	.40	.25
(648) Don Rudolph (pitching, pose to knees, glove on knee)	.75	.40	.25
(649) Don Rudolph (pitching, pitcher's follow through, picture is Stenhouse)	.75	.40	.25
(650) Pete Runnels (portrait, pose to chest)	.75	.40	.25
(651) Pete Runnels (portrait, pose to chest)	.75	.40	.25
(652) Pete Runnels (portrait, pose to neck)	.75	.40	.25

	NR MT	EX	VG
(653) Ray Sadecki (pitching, pitcher's follow through, glasses)	.75	.40	.25
(654) Ray Sadecki (pitching, pitcher's follow through, no glasses)	.75	.40	.25
(655) Bob Sadowski (portrait, pose to neck)	.75	.40	.25
(656) Amado Samuel (fielding, horizontal)	.75	.40	.25
(657) Jack Sanford (pitching)	.75	.40	.25
(658) Jack Sanford (pitching, pitcher's follow through)	.75	.40	.25
(659) Jack Sanford (pitching, pose to chest)	.75	.40	.25
(660) Ron Santo (portrait, pose to chest, teeth apart)	1.25	.60	.40
(661) Ron Santo (portrait, pose to chest, teeth together)	1.25	.60	.40
(662) Ron Santo (portrait, pose to waist, tank in background)	1.25	.60	.40
(663) Ron Santo (kneeling, holding bat)	.75	.40	.25
(664) Bob Scheffing (portrait, pose to chest)	.75	.40	.25
(665) Bob Sheffing (Scheffing) (portrait, pose to chest)	.75	.40	.25
(666) Charles Schilling (portrait, pose to chest)	.75	.40	.25
(667) Chuck Schilling (batting, pose to waist)	.75	.40	.25
(668) Chuck Schilling (batting, pose to chest)	.75	.40	.25
(669) Bob Schmidt (batting, pose to chest)	.75	.40	.25
(670) Red Schoendienst (portrait, pose to knees)	1.75	.90	.50
(671) Dick Schofield (batting, stands in background)	.75	.40	.25
(672) Dick Schofield (batting, screen in background)	.75	.40	.25
(673) Barney Schultz (portrait, pose to waist, arms crossed)	.75	.40	.25
(674) Don Schwall (portrait, pose to chest)	.75	.40	.25
(675) Diego Segui (portrait, pose to chest)	.75	.40	.25
(676) Mike Shannon (batting, pose to waist)	.75	.40	.25
(677) Bob Shaw (portrait, pose to chest)	.75	.40	.25
(678) Bob Shaw (pitching, pitcher's follow through)	.75	.40	.25
(679) Larry Sherry (portrait, pose to chest)	.75	.40	.25
(680) Chris Short (portrait, pose to chest)	.75	.40	.25
(681) Chris Short (pitching, pitcher's follow through)	.75	.40	.25
(682) Norm Siebern (batting, pose to waist)	.75	.40	.25
(683) Norm Siebern (portrait, pose to chest)	.75	.40	.25
(684) Norm Siebern (batting, pose to chest)	.75	.40	.25
(685) Roy Sievers (kneeling, holding bat)	1.00	.50	.30
(686) Roy Sievers (portrait, pose to chest)	1.00	.50	.30
(687) Roy Sievers (batting, pose to chest)	1.00	.50	.30
(688) Curt Simmons (portrait, pose to chest)	1.00	.50	.30
(689) Curt Simmons (portrait, pose to chest, glove)	1.00	.50	.30
(690) Dick Sisler (portrait, pose to chest)	.75	.40	.25
(691) Bob Skinner (batting, pose to waist)	.75	.40	.25
(692) Bill Skowron (Yankees, kneeling, holding bat)	1.50	.70	.45
(693) Bill Skowron (White Sox, kneeling, holding bat)	.75	.40	.25
(694) Ed Sadowski (batting, pose to waist)	.75	.40	.25
(695) Al Smith (White Sox, kneeling, holding bat)	.75	.40	.25
(696) Al Smith (Indians, kneeling, holding bat)	.75	.40	.25
(697) Hal Smith (portrait, pose to chest)	.75	.40	.25
(698) Hal Smith (batting, pose to chest)	.75	.40	.25
(699) Duke Snider (batting, pose to waist)	7.00	3.50	2.00
(700) Duke Snider (batting)	7.00	3.50	2.00
(701) Duke Snider (portrait, pose to chest)	7.00	3.50	2.00
(702) Russ Snyder (portrait, pose to chest)	.75	.40	.25
(703) Warren Spahn (pitching)	3.00	1.50	.90
(704) Warren Spahn (pitching, pitcher's follow through)	3.00	1.50	.90
(705) Warren Spahn (kneeling, pose to knees, glove)	3.00	1.50	.90
(706) Al Spangler (portrait, pose to chest)	.75	.40	.25
(707) Al Spangler (batting, pose to chest)	.75	.40	.25
(708) Tracy Stallard (portrait, pose to waist, arms crossed)	.75	.40	.25
(709) Willie Stargell (portrait, pose to waist)	3.00	1.50	.90
(710) Willie Stargell (hands on knees)	3.00	1.50	.90
(711) Casey Stengel (portrait, pose to chest)	5.00	2.50	1.50
(712) Dave Stenhouse (pitching, pitcher's follow through) (picture is actually Don Rudolph)	.75	.40	.25
(713) Jim Stewart (batting, pose to waist)	.75	.40	.25
(714) Dick Stigman (pitching, pitcher's follow through, arm down)	.75	.40	.25
(715) Dick Stigman (pitching, pitcher's follow through, arm bent)	.75	.40	.25
(716) Mel Stottlemeyer (Stottlemyre) (portrait, pose to waist)	1.25	.60	.40
(717) Dick Stuart (portrait, pose to chest)	.75	.40	.25
(718) Dick Stuart (batting, pose to neck)	.75	.40	.25
(719) Dick Stuart (Pirates, batting, pose to chest)	.75	.40	.25
(720) Dick Stuart (batting, pose to waist)	.75	.40	.25
(721) Dick Stuart (Red Sox, batting, pose to chest)	.75	.40	.25
(722) Frank Sullivan (portrait, pose to chest, glove)	.75	.40	.25
(723) Hay Sullivan (portrait, pose to waist, arms crossed)	.75	.40	.25
(724) Haywood Sullivan (batting, pose to chest)	.75	.40	.25
(725) Rusty Staub (portrait, pose to chest)	1.25	.60	.40
(726) Wes Stock (pitching, pitcher's follow through)	.75	.40	.25
(727) Wes Stock (kneeling, pose to waist, arms crossed)	.75	.40	.25
(728) Fred Talbot (portrait, pose to chest, arms crossed)	.75	.40	.25
(729) Jose Tartabull (portrait, pose to waist, arms crossed)	.75	.40	.25
(730) Jose Tartabull (batting, pose to chest)	.75	.40	.25
(731) Willie Tasby (batting, pose to waist)	.75	.40	.25
(732) Sam Taylor (portrait, pose to chest, stripe uniform)	.75	.40	.25
(733) Sam Taylor (portrait, pose to chest, plain uniform)	.75	.40	.25
(734) Tony Taylor (batting, pose to chest, 1 ear)	.75	.40	.25
(735) Tony Taylor (batting, pose to chest, 2 ears)	.75	.40	.25
(736) Birdie Tebbets (portrait, pose to neck)	.75	.40	.25
(737) Birdie Tebbetts (arms crossed on knees)	.75	.40	.25
(738) George "Birdie" Tebbetts (portrait, pose to chest)	.75	.40	.25
(739) Johnny Temple (portrait, pose to chest)	.75	.40	.25
(740) Ralph Terry (pitching, pitcher's follow through)	1.00	.50	.30
(741) Ralph Terry (portrait, pose to neck)	.75	.40	.25
(742) Frank Thomas (portrait, pose to chest)	.75	.40	.25
(743) Frank Thomas (batting, pose to chest)	.75	.40	.25
(744) George Thomas (portrait, pose to chest)	.75	.40	.25
(745) Lee Thomas (portrait, pose to chest)	.75	.40	.25
(746) Lee Thomas (batting, pose to chest, two ears)	.75	.40	.25
(747) Lee Thomas (batting, pose to waist, one ear showing)	.75	.40	.25
(748) Marv Throneberry (portrait, pose to chest)	1.00	.50	.30
(749) Luis Tiant (portrait, pose to neck)	1.50	.70	.45
(750) Bob Tillman (batting, pose to chest, one ear showing)	.75	.40	.25
(751) Bob Tillman (batting, pose to chest, two ears showing)	.75	.40	.25
(752) Joe Torre (batting)	1.50	.70	.45
(753) Joe Torre (portrait, pose to chest, no "M" seen on cap)	1.50	.70	.45
(754) Joe Torre (portrait, pose to chest, sky in background)	1.50	.70	.45
(755) Joe Torre (portrait, pose to chest, stands in background)	1.50	.70	.45
(756) Dick Tracewksi (portrait, pose to chest)	.75	.40	.25
(757) Tom Tresh (fielding)	1.00	.50	.30
(758) Tom Tresh (portrait, pose to chest)	1.00	.50	.30
(759) Tom Tresh (batting, pose to waist)	1.00	.50	.30
(760) Gus Triandos (catching, crouching)	.75	.40	.25
(761) Gus Triandos (batting, pose to waist)	.75	.40	.25
(762) Gus Triandos (kneeling, holding bat)	.75	.40	.25
(763) Bob Uecker (catching, crouching)	3.00	1.50	.90
(764) Jose Valdivielso (batting, pose to waist)	.75	.40	.25
(765) Bob Veale (portrait, pose to chest)	.75	.40	.25
(766) Mickey Vernon (standing)	1.00	.50	.30
(767) Zorro Versalles (batting, pose to chest)	.75	.40	.25
(768) Zorro Versalles (fielding, left leg extended)	.75	.40	.25
(769) Zorro Versalles (fielding, legs spaced evenly)	.75	.40	.25
(770) Dave Vineyard (portrait, pose to chest)	.75	.40	.25
(771) Bill Virdon (batting, pose to waist, screen in background)	1.00	.50	.30
(772) Bill Virdon (batting, pose to chest, dark background)	1.00	.50	.30
(773) Leon Wagner (hands on knees)	.75	.40	.25
(774) Leon Wagner (portrait, pose to waist)	.75	.40	.25
(775) Harry Walker (portrait, pose to chest, arms crossed)	.75	.40	.25
(776) Jerry Walker (portrait, pose to waist, glove)	.75	.40	.25
(777) Jerry Walker (pitching)	.75	.40	.25
(778) Ken Walter (batting, pose to chest)	.75	.40	.25
(779) Pete Ward (fielding)	.75	.40	.25
(780) Pete Ward (kneeling, holding bat)	.75	.40	.25
(781) Carl Warwick (batting, pose to chest)	.75	.40	.25
(782) Carl Warwick (batting, pose to the chest)	.75	.40	.25
(783) Bill White (portrait, pose to chest)	1.00	.50	.30
(784) Bill White (batting, pose to chest)	1.00	.50	.30
(785) Carl Willey (pitching)	.75	.40	.25
(786) Carlton Willey (pitching, pose to chest, hands over head)	.75	.40	.25
(787) Billy Williams (portrait, pose to waist, fence background)	2.50	1.25	.70
(788) Billy Williams (portrait, pose to waist, arms crossed)	2.50	1.25	.70
(789) Billy Williams (portrait, pose to chest, dark background)	2.50	1.25	.70
(790) Hoyt Williams (Wilhelm) (pitching)	2.00	1.00	.60
(791) Stan Williams (portrait, pose to chest)	.75	.40	.25
(792) Maury Wills (portrait, pose to chest)	1.50	.70	.45
(793) Maury Wills (batting, pose to waist)	1.50	.70	.45
(794) Maury Wills (batting, pose to waist, photo reversed)	1.50	.70	.45
(795) Earl Wilson (portrait, pose to waist)	.75	.40	.25
(796) Bob Wine (fielding)	.75	.40	.25
(797) Bob Wine (portrait, pose to chest)	.75	.40	.25
(798) Jake Wood (batting, pose to chest)	.75	.40	.25
(799) Jake Wood (fielding)	.75	.40	.25
(800) Hal Woodeshick (portrait, pose to chest)	.75	.40	.25
(801) Gene Woodling (batting, pose to waist)	1.00	.50	.30
(802) Early Wynn (pitching)	2.50	1.25	.70
(803) Jim Wynn (portrait, pose to chest)	.75	.40	.25
(804) Carl Yastrzemski (batting)	10.00	5.00	3.00
(805) Carl Yastrzemski (portrait, pose to chest, Red Sox uniform)	10.00	5.00	3.00
(806) Carl Yastrzemski (portrait, pose to chest, Boston uniform)	10.00	5.00	3.00
(807) Carl Yastrzemski (batting, pose to waist, one ear showing)	10.00	5.00	3.00
(808) Carl Yastrzemski (batting, pose to waist, two ears showing)	10.00	5.00	3.00
(809) Eddie Yost (batting, pose to chest)	.75	.40	.25
(810) Don Zimmer (batting, pose to chest)	1.00	.50	.30
(811) Marion Zipfel (fielding)	.75	.40	.25

Definitions for grading conditions are located in the Introduction section at the front of this book.

1986 Jays Potato Chips

One of a handful of round baseball cards produced for inclusion in boxes of potato chips on a regional basis in 1986, the Jays set of 2-7/8" discs is believed to be the scarcest of the type. The 20 cards in the issue include the most popular Milwaukee Brewers and Chicago Cubs and White Sox players; the set having been distributed in the southern Wisconsin- northern Illinois area. Like many of the recent sets produced by Mike Schecter Associates, the '86 Jays cards feature player photos on which the team logos have been airbrushed off the caps.

		MT	NR MT	EX
Complete Set:		25.00	18.50	10.00
Common Player:		.60	.45	.25
(1)	Harold Baines	1.25	.90	.50
(2)	Cecil Cooper	1.00	.70	.40
(3)	Jody Davis	.75	.60	.30
(4)	Bob Dernier	.60	.45	.25
(5)	Richard Dotson	.75	.60	.30
(6)	Shawon Dunston	1.00	.70	.40
(7)	Carlton Fisk	1.50	1.25	.60
(8)	Jim Gantner	.60	.45	.25
(9)	Ozzie Guillen	.90	.70	.35
(10)	Teddy Higuera	1.75	1.25	.70
(11)	Ron Kittle	.75	.60	.30
(12)	Paul Molitor	1.50	1.25	.60
(13)	Keith Moreland	.75	.60	.30
(14)	Ernie Riles	.75	.60	.30
(15)	Ryne Sandberg	2.50	2.00	1.00
(16)	Tom Seaver	2.00	1.50	.80
(17)	Lee Smith	.90	.70	.35
(18)	Rick Sutcliffe	.90	.70	.35
(19)	Greg Walker	.90	.70	.35
(20)	Robin Yount	2.00	1.50	.80

1962 Jell-O

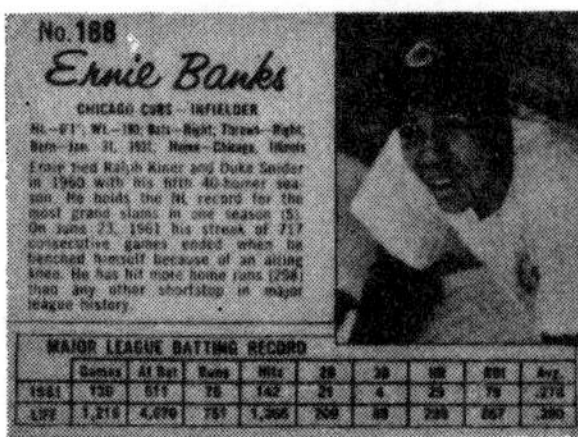

Virtually identical in content to the 1962 Post cereal cards, the '62 Jell-O set of 197 was only issued in the Midwest. Players and card numbers are identical in the two sets, except Brooks Robinson (#29), Ted Kluszewski (#82) and Smoky Burgess (#176) were not issued in the Jell-O version. The Jell-O cards are easy to distinguish from the Post of that year by the absence of the red oval Post logo and red or blue border around the stat box. Cards which have been neatly trimmed from the box which they were printed will measure 3-1/2" by 2-1/2".

		NR MT	EX	VG
Complete Set:		4300.	2150.	1290.
Common Player:		6.00	3.00	1.75
1	Bill Skowron	20.00	10.00	6.00
2	Bobby Richardson	20.00	10.00	6.00
3	Cletis Boyer	10.00	5.00	3.00
4	Tony Kubek	15.00	7.50	4.50
5	Mickey Mantle	600.00	300.00	180.00
6	Roger Maris	100.00	50.00	30.00
7	Yogi Berra	60.00	30.00	18.00
8	Elston Howard	15.00	7.50	4.50
9	Whitey Ford	40.00	20.00	12.00
10	Ralph Terry	10.00	5.00	3.00
11	John Blanchard	7.00	3.50	2.00
12	Luis Arroyo	7.00	3.50	2.00
13	Bill Stafford	20.00	10.00	6.00
14	Norm Cash	10.00	5.00	3.00
15	Jake Wood	6.00	3.00	1.75
16	Steve Boros	6.00	3.00	1.75
17	Chico Fernandez	6.00	3.00	1.75
18	Billy Bruton	6.00	3.00	1.75
19	Ken Aspromonte	6.00	3.00	1.75
20	Al Kaline	40.00	20.00	12.00
21	Dick Brown	6.00	3.00	1.75
22	Frank Lary	7.00	3.50	2.00
23	Don Mossi	7.00	3.50	2.00
24	Phil Regan	6.00	3.00	1.75
25	Charley Maxwell	6.00	3.00	1.75
26	Jim Bunning	15.00	7.50	4.50
27	Jim Gentile	7.00	3.50	2.00
28	Marv Breeding	6.00	3.00	1.75
29	Not Issued			
30	Ron Hansen	6.00	3.00	1.75
31	Jackie Brandt	20.00	10.00	6.00
32	Dick Williams	7.00	3.50	2.00
33	Gus Triandos	7.00	3.50	2.00
34	Milt Pappas	7.00	3.50	2.00
35	Hoyt Wilhelm	25.00	12.50	7.50
36	Chuck Estrada	6.00	3.00	1.75
37	Vic Power	6.00	3.00	1.75
38	Johnny Temple	6.00	3.00	1.75
39	Bubba Phillips	20.00	10.00	6.00
40	Tito Francona	7.00	3.50	2.00
41	Willie Kirkland	6.00	3.00	1.75
42	John Romano	6.00	3.00	1.75
43	Jim Perry	10.00	5.00	3.00
44	Woodie Held	6.00	3.00	1.75
45	Chuck Essegian	6.00	3.00	1.75
46	Roy Sievers	7.00	3.50	2.00
47	Nellie Fox	15.00	7.50	4.50
48	Al Smith	6.00	3.00	1.75
49	Luis Aparicio	25.00	12.50	7.50
50	Jim Landis	6.00	3.00	1.75
51	Minnie Minoso	10.00	5.00	3.00
52	Andy Carey	20.00	10.00	6.00
53	Sherman Lollar	7.00	3.50	2.00
54	Bill Pierce	7.00	3.50	2.00
55	Early Wynn	25.00	12.50	7.50
56	Chuck Schilling	20.00	10.00	6.00
57	Pete Runnels	7.00	3.50	2.00
58	Frank Malzone	7.00	3.50	2.00
59	Don Buddin	10.00	5.00	3.00
60	Gary Geiger	6.00	3.00	1.75
61	Carl Yastrzemski	200.00	100.00	60.00
62	Jackie Jensen	20.00	10.00	6.00
63	Jim Pagliaroni	20.00	10.00	6.00
64	Don Schwall	6.00	3.00	1.75
65	Dale Long	7.00	3.50	2.00
66	Chuck Cottier	10.00	5.00	3.00
67	Billy Klaus	20.00	10.00	6.00
68	Coot Veal	6.00	3.00	1.75
69	Marty Keough	35.00	17.50	10.50
70	Willie Tasby	35.00	17.50	10.50
71	Gene Woodling	7.00	3.50	2.00
72	Gene Green	35.00	17.50	10.50
73	Dick Donovan	10.00	5.00	3.00
74	Steve Bilko	10.00	5.00	3.00
75	Rocky Bridges	20.00	10.00	6.00
76	Eddie Yost	10.00	5.00	3.00
77	Leon Wagner	10.00	5.00	3.00
78	Albie Pearson	10.00	5.00	3.00
79	Ken Hunt	10.00	5.00	3.00
80	Earl Averill	35.00	17.50	10.50
81	Ryne Duren	10.00	5.00	3.00
82	Not Issued			
83	Bob Allison	7.00	3.50	2.00
84	Billy Martin	15.00	7.50	4.50
85	Harmon Killebrew	35.00	17.50	10.50
86	Zorro Versalles	7.00	3.50	2.00
87	Lennie Green	20.00	10.00	6.00
88	Bill Tuttle	6.00	3.00	1.75
89	Jim Lemon	7.00	3.50	2.00
90	Earl Battey	20.00	10.00	6.00
91	Camilo Pascual	7.00	3.50	2.00
92	Norm Siebern	10.00	5.00	3.00
93	Jerry Lumpe	10.00	5.00	3.00
94	Dick Howser	10.00	5.00	3.00
95	Gene Stephens	35.00	17.50	10.50
96	Leo Posada	10.00	5.00	3.00
97	Joe Pignatano	10.00	5.00	3.00
98	Jim Archer	10.00	5.00	3.00
99	Haywood Sullivan	20.00	10.00	6.00
100	Art Ditmar	10.00	5.00	3.00
101	Gil Hodges	35.00	17.50	10.50
102	Charlie Neal	10.00	5.00	3.00
103	Daryl Spencer	10.00	5.00	3.00
104	Maury Wills	20.00	10.00	6.00
105	Tommy Davis	10.00	5.00	3.00
106	Willie Davis	10.00	5.00	3.00
107	John Roseboro	35.00	17.50	10.50
108	John Podres	10.00	5.00	3.00
109	Sandy Koufax	80.00	40.00	24.00
110	Don Drysdale	50.00	25.00	15.00
111	Larry Sherry	20.00	10.00	6.00
112	Jim Gilliam	20.00	10.00	6.00
113	Norm Larker	35.00	17.50	10.50
114	Duke Snider	70.00	35.00	21.00
115	Stan Williams	20.00	10.00	6.00
116	Gordon Coleman	70.00	35.00	21.00
117	Don Blasingame	20.00	10.00	6.00
118	Gene Freese	35.00	17.50	10.50
119	Ed Kasko	35.00	17.50	10.50
120	Gus Bell	20.00	10.00	6.00
121	Vada Pinson	10.00	5.00	3.00
122	Frank Robinson	35.00	17.50	10.50
123	Bob Purkey	10.00	5.00	3.00
124	Joey Jay	10.00	5.00	3.00
125	Jim Brosnan	10.00	5.00	3.00
126	Jim O'Toole	10.00	5.00	3.00
127	Jerry Lynch	10.00	5.00	3.00
128	Wally Post	10.00	5.00	3.00
129	Ken Hunt	10.00	5.00	3.00
130	Jerry Zimmerman	10.00	5.00	3.00
131	Willie McCovey	35.00	17.50	10.50
132	Jose Pagan	20.00	10.00	6.00
133	Felipe Alou	10.00	5.00	3.00
134	Jim Davenport	10.00	5.00	3.00
135	Harvey Kuenn	10.00	5.00	3.00
136	Orlando Cepeda	15.00	7.50	4.50
137	Ed Bailey	10.00	5.00	3.00
138	Sam Jones	10.00	5.00	3.00
139	Mike McCormick	10.00	5.00	3.00
140	Juan Marichal	40.00	20.00	12.00
141	Jack Sanford	10.00	5.00	3.00
142	Willie Mays	125.00	62.00	37.00
143	Stu Miller	70.00	35.00	21.00
144	Joe Amalfitano	10.00	5.00	3.00
145	Joe Adcock	10.00	5.00	3.00
146	Frank Bolling	6.00	3.00	1.75
147	Ed Mathews	35.00	17.50	10.50
148	Roy McMillan	7.00	3.50	2.00
149	Hank Aaron	125.00	62.00	37.00
150	Gino Cimoli	20.00	10.00	6.00
151	Frank Thomas	7.00	3.50	2.00
152	Joe Torre	10.00	5.00	3.00
153	Lou Burdette	10.00	5.00	3.00
154	Bob Buhl	7.00	3.50	2.00
155	Carlton Willey	6.00	3.00	1.75
156	Lee Maye	18.00	9.00	5.50
157	Al Spangler	35.00	17.50	10.50
158	Bill White	35.00	17.50	10.50
159	Ken Boyer	15.00	7.50	4.50
160	Joe Cunningham	10.00	5.00	3.00
161	Carl Warwick	10.00	5.00	3.00
162	Carl Sawatski	6.00	3.00	1.75
163	Lindy McDaniel	6.00	3.00	1.75
164	Ernie Broglio	10.00	5.00	3.00
165	Larry Jackson	6.00	3.00	1.75
166	Curt Flood	15.00	7.50	4.50
167	Curt Simmons	35.00	17.50	10.50
168	Alex Grammas	20.00	10.00	6.00
169	Dick Stuart	7.00	3.50	2.00
170	Bill Mazeroski	20.00	10.00	6.00
171	Don Hoak	10.00	5.00	3.00
172	Dick Groat	10.00	5.00	3.00
173	Roberto Clemente	125.00	62.00	37.00
174	Bob Skinner	20.00	10.00	6.00
175	Bill Virdon	35.00	17.50	10.50
176	Not Issued			
177	Elroy Face	10.00	5.00	3.00
178	Bob Friend	7.00	3.50	2.00
179	Vernon Law	20.00	10.00	6.00
180	Harvey Haddix	35.00	17.50	10.50
181	Hal Smith	20.00	10.00	6.00
182	Ed Bouchee	20.00	10.00	6.00
183	Don Zimmer	7.00	3.50	2.00
184	Ron Santo	10.00	5.00	3.00
185	Andre Rodgers	6.00	3.00	1.75
186	Richie Ashburn	15.00	7.50	4.50
187	George Altman	6.00	3.00	1.75
188	Ernie Banks	35.00	17.50	10.50
189	Sam Taylor	6.00	3.00	1.75
190	Don Elston	6.00	3.00	1.75
191	Jerry Kindall	20.00	10.00	6.00
192	Pancho Herrera	6.00	3.00	1.75
193	Tony Taylor	6.00	3.00	1.75
194	Ruben Amaro	20.00	10.00	6.00
195	Don Demeter	6.00	3.00	1.75
196	Bobby Gene Smith	6.00	3.00	1.75
197	Clay Dalrymple	6.00	3.00	1.75
198	Robin Roberts	25.00	12.50	7.50
199	Art Mahaffey	6.00	3.00	1.75
200	John Buzhardt	6.00	3.00	1.75

1963 Jell-O

Like the other Post and Jell-O issues of the era, the '63 Jell-O set includes many scarce cards; primarily those which were printed as the backs of less popular brands and sizes of the gelatin dessert. Slightly smaller than the virtually identical Post cereal cards of the same year, the 200 cards in the Jell-O issue measure 3-3/8" by 2-1/2". The easiest way to distinguish 1963 Jell-O cards from Post cards is by the red line that separates the 1962 stats from the lifetime stats. On Post cards, the line extends almost all the way to the side borders, on the Jell-O cards, the line begins and ends much closer to the stats.

		NR MT	EX	VG
Complete Set:		2700.	1350.	810.00
Common Player:		2.00	1.00	.60
1	Vic Power	2.50	1.25	.70
2	Bernie Allen	20.00	10.00	6.00
3	Zoilo Versalles	20.00	10.00	6.00
4	Rich Rollins	2.00	1.00	.60
5	Harmon Killebrew	8.00	4.00	2.50
6	Lenny Green	20.00	10.00	6.00
7	Bob Allison	3.00	1.50	.90
8	Earl Battey	15.00	7.50	4.50
9	Camilo Pascual	2.50	1.25	.70
10	Jim Kaat	35.00	17.50	10.50
11	Jack Kralick	2.00	1.00	.60
12	Bill Skowron	20.00	10.00	6.00
13	Bobby Richardson	5.00	2.50	1.50
14	Cletis Boyer	2.50	1.25	.70
15	Mickey Mantle	200.00	100.00	60.00
16	Roger Maris	20.00	10.00	6.00
17	Yogi Berra	20.00	10.00	6.00
18	Elston Howard	20.00	10.00	6.00
19	Whitey Ford	10.00	5.00	3.00
20	Ralph Terry	2.25	1.25	.70
21	John Blanchard	15.00	7.50	4.50
22	Bill Stafford	20.00	10.00	6.00
23	Tom Tresh	2.50	1.25	.70
24	Steve Bilko	2.00	1.00	.60
25	Bill Moran	2.00	1.00	.60
26	Joe Koppe	2.00	1.00	.60
27	Felix Torres	2.00	1.00	.60
28	Leon Wagner	2.50	1.25	.70
29	Albie Pearson	2.00	1.00	.60
30	Lee Thomas	2.00	1.00	.60
31	Bob Rodgers	20.00	10.00	6.00
32	Dean Chance	1.50	.70	.45
33	Ken McBride	20.00	10.00	6.00
34	George Thomas	20.00	10.00	6.00
35	Joe Cunningham	20.00	10.00	6.00
36	Nelson Fox	5.00	2.50	1.50
37	Luis Aparicio	6.00	3.00	1.75
38	Al Smith	2.00	1.00	.60
39	Floyd Robinson	2.00	1.00	.60
40	Jim Landis	2.00	1.00	.60
41	Charlie Maxwell	2.00	1.00	.60
42	Sherman Lollar	2.25	1.25	.70
43	Early Wynn	6.00	3.00	1.75
44	Juan Pizarro	20.00	10.00	6.00
45	Ray Herbert	20.00	10.00	6.00
46	Norm Cash	3.50	1.75	1.00
47	Steve Boros	20.00	10.00	6.00
48	Dick McAuliffe	2.25	1.25	.70
49	Bill Bruton	2.25	1.25	.70
50	Rocky Colavito	5.00	2.50	1.50
51	Al Kaline	12.00	6.00	3.50
52	Dick Brown	20.00	10.00	6.00
53	Jim Bunning	5.00	2.50	1.50
54	Hank Aguirre	2.00	1.00	.60
55	Frank Lary	20.00	10.00	6.00
56	Don Mossi	20.00	10.00	6.00
57	Jim Gentile	2.25	1.25	.70
58	Jackie Brandt	2.00	1.00	.60
59	Brooks Robinson	15.00	7.50	4.50
60	Ron Hansen	2.00	1.00	.60

		NR MT	EX	VG
61	Jerry Adair	55.00	27.00	16.50
62	John Powell	3.50	1.75	1.00
63	Russ Snyder	20.00	10.00	6.00
64	Steve Barber	2.00	1.00	.60
65	Milt Pappas	20.00	10.00	6.00
66	Robin Roberts	6.00	3.00	1.75
67	Tito Francona	2.25	1.25	.70
68	Jerry Kindall	20.00	10.00	6.00
69	Woodie Held	2.25	1.25	.70
70	Bubba Phillips	2.00	1.00	.60
71	Chuck Essegian	2.00	1.00	.60
72	Willie Kirkland	20.00	10.00	6.00
73	Al Luplow	2.00	1.00	.60
74	Ty Cline	20.00	10.00	6.00
75	Dick Donovan	2.00	1.00	.60
76	John Romano	2.00	1.00	.60
77	Pete Runnels	2.25	1.25	.70
78	Ed Bressoud	20.00	10.00	6.00
79	Frank Malzone	2.25	1.25	.70
80	Carl Yastrzemski	70.00	35.00	21.00
81	Gary Geiger	2.00	1.00	.60
82	Lou Clinton	20.00	10.00	6.00
83	Earl Wilson	2.50	1.25	.70
84	Bill Monbouquette	2.50	1.25	.70
85	Norm Siebern	2.50	1.25	.70
86	Jerry Lumpe	2.50	1.25	.70
87	Manny Jimenez	2.00	1.00	.60
88	Gino Cimoli	2.00	1.00	.60
89	Ed Charles	55.00	27.00	16.50
90	Ed Rakow	2.00	1.00	.60
91	Bob Del Greco	20.00	10.00	6.00
92	Haywood Sullivan	20.00	10.00	6.00
93	Chuck Hinton	2.00	1.00	.60
94	Ken Retzer	20.00	10.00	6.00
95	Harry Bright	20.00	10.00	6.00
96	Bob Johnson	2.00	1.00	.60
97	Dave Stenhouse	20.00	10.00	6.00
98	Chuck Cottier	2.25	1.25	.70
99	Tom Cheney	2.00	1.00	.60
100	Claude Osteen	20.00	10.00	6.00
101	Orlando Cepeda	5.00	2.50	1.50
102	Charley Hiller	20.00	10.00	6.00
103	Jose Pagan	20.00	10.00	6.00
104	Jim Davenport	2.00	1.00	.60
105	Harvey Kuenn	3.50	1.75	1.00
106	Willie Mays	60.00	30.00	18.00
107	Felipe Alou	3.00	1.50	.90
108	Tom Haller	2.25	1.25	.70
109	Juan Marichal	6.00	3.00	1.75
110	Jack Sanford	2.25	1.25	.70
111	Bill O'Dell	2.00	1.00	.60
112	Willie McCovey	90.00	45.00	27.00
113	Lee Walls	20.00	10.00	6.00
114	Jim Gilliam	20.00	10.00	6.00
115	Maury Wills	5.00	2.50	1.50
116	Ron Fairly	2.25	1.25	.70
117	Tommy Davis	3.00	1.50	.90
118	Duke Snider	9.00	4.50	2.75
119	Willie Davis	3.00	1.50	.90
120	John Roseboro	2.25	1.25	.70
121	Sandy Koufax	20.00	10.00	6.00
122	Stan Williams	20.00	10.00	6.00
123	Don Drysdale	9.00	4.50	2.75
124	Daryl Spencer	2.00	1.00	.60
125	Gordy Coleman	2.00	1.00	.60
126	Don Blasingame	20.00	10.00	6.00
127	Leo Cardenas	2.00	1.00	.60
128	Eddie Kasko	20.00	10.00	6.00
129	Jerry Lynch	2.00	1.00	.60
130	Vada Pinson	4.00	2.00	1.25
131	Frank Robinson	9.00	4.50	2.75
132	John Edwards	20.00	10.00	6.00
133	Joey Jay	2.00	1.00	.60
134	Bob Purkey	2.00	1.00	.60
135	Marty Keough	55.00	27.00	16.50
136	Jim O'Toole	20.00	10.00	6.00
137	Dick Stuart	2.25	1.25	.70
138	Bill Mazeroski	3.50	1.75	1.00
139	Dick Groat	3.00	1.50	.90
140	Don Hoak	2.25	1.25	.70
141	Bob Skinner	2.25	1.25	.70
142	Bill Virdon	3.00	1.50	.90
143	Roberto Clemente	60.00	30.00	18.00
144	Smoky Burgess	3.00	1.50	.90
145	Bob Friend	2.25	1.25	.70
146	Al McBean	20.00	10.00	6.00
147	ElRoy Face	3.00	1.50	.90
148	Joe Adcock	3.50	1.75	1.00
149	Frank Bolling	2.00	1.00	.60
150	Roy McMillan	2.00	1.00	.60
151	Eddie Mathews	8.00	4.00	2.50
152	Hank Aaron	60.00	30.00	18.00
153	Del Crandall	20.00	10.00	6.00
154	Bob Shaw	2.00	1.00	.60
155	Lew Burdette	3.50	1.75	1.00
156	Joe Torre	20.00	10.00	6.00
157	Tony Cloninger	35.00	17.50	10.50
158	Bill White	2.50	1.25	.70
159	Julian Javier	20.00	10.00	6.00
160	Ken Boyer	4.00	2.00	1.25
161	Julio Gotay	20.00	10.00	6.00
162	Curt Flood	3.00	1.50	.90
163	Charlie James	35.00	17.50	10.50
164	Gene Oliver	20.00	10.00	6.00
165	Ernie Broglio	2.00	1.00	.60
166	Bob Gibson	60.00	30.00	18.00
167	Lindy McDaniel	20.00	10.00	6.00
168	Ray Washburn	2.00	1.00	.60
169	Ernie Banks	12.00	6.00	3.50
170	Ron Santo	3.50	1.75	1.00
171	George Altman	2.00	1.00	.60
172	Billy Williams	60.00	30.00	18.00
173	Andre Rodgers	20.00	10.00	6.00
174	Ken Hubbs	3.00	1.50	.90
175	Don Landrum	20.00	10.00	6.00
176	Dick Bertell	20.00	10.00	6.00
177	Roy Sievers	2.50	1.25	.70
178	Tony Taylor	20.00	10.00	6.00
179	John Callison	2.50	1.25	.70
180	Don Demeter	2.00	1.00	.60
181	Tony Gonzalez	20.00	10.00	6.00
182	Wes Covington	20.00	10.00	6.00
183	Art Mahaffey	2.00	1.00	.60
184	Clay Dalrymple	2.00	1.00	.60
185	Al Spangler	2.00	1.00	.60
186	Roman Mejias	2.00	1.00	.60
187	Bob Aspromonte	50.00	25.00	15.00
188	Norm Larker	2.00	1.00	.60
189	Johnny Temple	2.00	1.00	.60
190	Carl Warwick	20.00	10.00	6.00
191	Bob Lillis	20.00	10.00	6.00
192	Dick Farrell	50.00	25.00	15.00
193	Gil Hodges	8.00	4.00	2.50
194	Marv Throneberry	3.00	1.50	.90
195	Charlie Neal	20.00	10.00	6.00
196	Frank Thomas	2.25	1.25	.70
197	Richie Ashburn	5.00	2.50	1.50
198	Felix Mantilla	20.00	10.00	6.00
199	Rod Kanehl	20.00	10.00	6.00
200	Roger Craig	20.00	10.00	6.00

1986 Jiffy Pop

One of the scarcer of the 1986 "regionals," the 20- card Jiffy Pop issue was inserted in packages of heat-and-eat popcorn. A production of Mike Schecter Associates, the 2-7/8" round discs feature 20 popular stars, many in the same pictures found in other '86 regionals. Like other MSA issues, caps have had the team logos erased, allowing Jiffy Pop to avoid having to pay a licensing fee to the teams.

		MT	NR MT	EX
Complete Set:		40.00	30.00	16.00
Common Player:		1.00	.70	.40
1	Jim Rice	1.75	1.25	.70
2	Wade Boggs	3.50	2.75	1.50
3	Lance Parrish	1.00	.70	.40
4	George Brett	2.50	2.00	1.00
5	Robin Yount	1.75	1.25	.70
6	Don Mattingly	6.00	4.50	2.50
7	Dave Winfield	2.00	1.50	.80
8	Reggie Jackson	2.25	1.75	.90
9	Cal Ripken	2.25	1.75	.90
10	Eddie Murray	2.00	1.50	.80
11	Pete Rose	3.50	2.75	1.50
12	Ryne Sandberg	1.75	1.25	.70
13	Nolan Ryan	1.50	1.25	.60
14	Fernando Valenzuela	1.25	.90	.50
15	Willie McGee	1.00	.70	.40
16	Dale Murphy	2.50	2.00	1.00
17	Mike Schmidt	2.50	2.00	1.00
18	Steve Garvey	2.00	1.50	.80
19	Gary Carter	2.00	1.50	.80
20	Dwight Gooden	3.00	2.25	1.25

1987 Jiffy Pop

For the second year in a row, Jiffy Pop inserted baseball discs in their packages of popcorn. The full-color discs measure 2-7/8" in diameter and were produced by Mike Schecter Associates of Cos Cob, Conn. Titled "2nd Annual Collectors' Edition," the card fronts feature player photos with all team insignias airbrushed away. Information on the backs of the discs are printed in bright red on white stock. Die-cut press sheets containing all 20 discs were available via a mail-in offer.

		MT	NR MT	EX
Complete Set:		40.00	30.00	16.00
Common Player:		1.00	.70	.40
1	Ryne Sandberg	1.75	1.25	.70
2	Dale Murphy	2.50	2.00	1.00
3	Jack Morris	1.00	.70	.40
4	Keith Hernandez	1.50	1.25	.60
5	George Brett	2.50	2.00	1.00
6	Don Mattingly	6.00	4.50	2.50
7	Ozzie Smith	1.00	.70	.40
8	Cal Ripken	2.25	1.75	.90
9	Dwight Gooden	3.00	2.25	1.25
10	Pedro Guerrero	1.00	.70	.40
11	Lou Whitaker	1.00	.70	.40
12	Roger Clemens	3.00	2.25	1.25
13	Lance Parrish	1.00	.70	.40
14	Rickey Henderson	2.25	1.75	.90
15	Fernando Valenzuela	1.25	.90	.50
16	Mike Schmidt	2.50	2.00	1.00
17	Darryl Strawberry	2.75	2.00	1.00
18	Mike Scott	1.00	.70	.40
19	Jim Rice	2.75	2.00	1.00
20	Wade Boggs	3.50	2.75	1.50

1988 Jiffy Pop

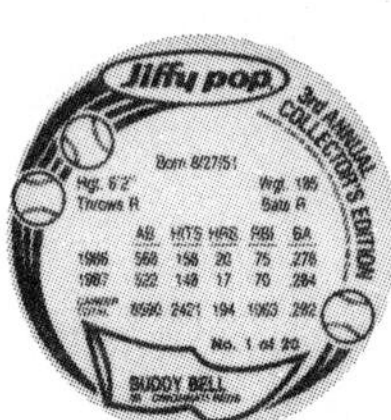

This 20-disc set is the third Jiffy Pop issue spotlighting leading players. Discs are 2-/12" in diameter, with a semi-gloss finish, and feature full-color closeups on white stock. Team logos have been airbrushed off the player's caps. The Jiffy Pop logo appears in red at the top of the disc; a banner running across the bottom encloses a "1988" and player name, also in red. The circular border is blue, with two large baseballs streaking toward the top logo. A third baseball appears lower right under the curved label "3rd Annual Collector's Edition." Dsic backs are white, with dark blue lettering, and contain player information and disc number.

		MT	NR MT	EX
Complete Set:		25.00	18.50	10.00
Common Player:		.75	.60	.30
1	Buddy Bell	.75	.60	.30
2	Wade Boggs	3.50	2.75	1.50
3	Gary Carter	1.50	1.25	.60
4	Jack Clark	1.00	.70	.40
5	Will Clark	1.50	1.25	.60
6	Roger Clemens	2.25	1.75	.90
7	Vince Coleman	1.00	.70	.40
8	Andre Dawson	1.25	.90	.50
9	Keith Hernandez	1.25	.90	.50
10	Kent Hrbek	1.25	.90	.50
11	Wally Joyner	1.50	1.25	.60
12	Paul Molitor	1.00	.70	.40
13	Eddie Murray	1.50	1.25	.60
14	Tim Raines	1.50	1.25	.60
15	Bret Saberhagen	1.25	.90	.50
16	Alan Trammell	1.25	.90	.50
17	Ozzie Virgil	.75	.60	.30
18	Tim Wallach	.75	.60	.30
19	Dave Winfield	1.50	1.25	.60
20	Robin Yount	1.25	.90	.50

1973 Johnny Pro Orioles

This regional set of large (4-1/2" by 7-1/4,) die-cut cards was issued by Johnny Pro Enterprises Inc. of Baltimore and features only Orioles. The cards were designed to be punched out and folded to make baseball player figures that can stand up. The full-color die-cut figures appear against a green background. The card's are numbered according to the player's uniform number, which appears in a white box along with his name and position. The backs are blank. Three players (Robinson, Grich, and Palmer) appear in two poses each, and cards of Orlando Pena were not die-cut. Values listed are for complete cards not punched out.

	NR MT	EX	VG
Complete Set:	60.00	30.00	18.00
Common Player:	.50	.25	.15

		NR MT	EX	VG
1	Al Bumbry	.50	.25	.15
2	Rich Coggins	.50	.25	.15
3a	Bobby Grich (batting)	1.00	.50	.30
3b	Bobby Grich (fielding)	1.00	.50	.30
4	Earl Weaver	1.00	.50	.30
5a	Brooks Robinson (batting)	8.00	4.00	2.50
5b	Brooks Robinson (fielding)	8.00	4.00	2.50
6	Paul Blair	.70	.35	.20
7	Mark Belanger	.70	.35	.20
8	Andy Etchebarren	.50	.25	.15
10	Elrod Hendricks	.50	.25	.15
11	Terry Crowley	.50	.25	.15
12	Tommy Davis	.70	.35	.20
13	Doyle Alexander	.70	.35	.20
14	Merv Rettenmund	.50	.25	.15
15	Frank Baker	.50	.25	.15
19	Dave McNally	1.00	.50	.30
21	Larry Brown	.50	.25	.15
22a	Jim Palmer (follow-through)	6.00	3.00	1.75
22b	Jim Palmer (wind-up)	6.00	3.00	1.75
23	Grant Jackson	.50	.25	.15
25	Don Baylor	3.00	1.50	.90
26	Boog Powell	3.00	1.50	.90
27	Orlando Pena	6.00	3.00	1.75
32	Earl Williams	.50	.25	.15
34	Bob Reynolds	.50	.25	.15
35	Mike Cuellar	1.50	.70	.40
39	Eddie Watt	.50	.25	.15

1973 Johnny Pro Phillies

Although slightly smaller (3-1/4" by 7-1/8") and featuring members of the Phillies, this set is very similar to the Johnny Pro Orioles set of the same year. The full-color die-cut player figures are set against a white background. Again, the set is numbered according to the player's uniform number. The values listed are for complete cards.

	NR MT	EX	VG
Complete Set:	125.00	62.00	37.00
Common Player:	1.00	.50	.30

		NR MT	EX	VG
8	Bob Boone	4.00	2.00	1.25
10	Larry Bowa	3.00	1.50	.90
16	Dave Cash	1.00	.50	.30
19	Greg Luzinski	3.00	1.50	.90
20	Mike Schmidt	100.00	50.00	30.00
22	Mike Anderson	1.00	.50	.30
24	Bill Robinson	1.00	.50	.30
25	Del Unser	1.00	.50	.30
27	Willie Montanez	1.00	.50	.30
32	Steve Carlton	15.00	7.50	4.50
37	Ron Schueler	1.00	.50	.30
41	Jim Lonborg	2.00	1.00	.60

A player's name in *italic* type indicates a rookie card. An (FC) indicates a player's first card for that particular card company.

1953 Johnston Cookies Braves

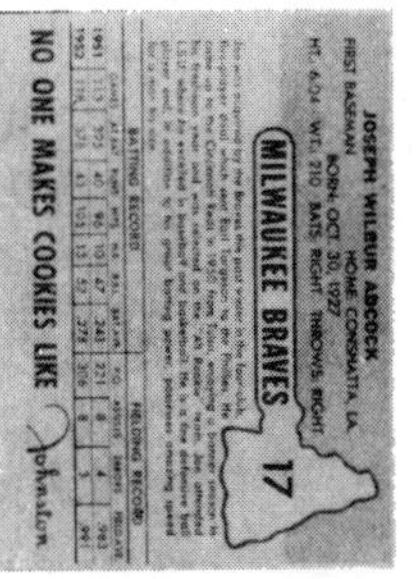

The first and most common of three annual issues, the '53 Johnston's were inserted into boxes of cookies on a regional basis. Complete sets were also available from the company, whose factory sits in the shadow of Milwaukee County Stadium. While at first glance appearing to be color photos, the pictures on the 25 cards in the set are actually well-done colorizations of black and white photos. Cards measure 2-9/16" by 3-5/8". Write-ups on the backs were "borrowed" from the Braves' 1953 yearbook.

	NR MT	EX	VG
Complete Set:	325.00	175.00	100.00
Common Player:	8.00	4.00	2.50

		NR MT	EX	VG
1	Charlie Grimm	10.00	5.00	3.00
2	John Antonelli	10.00	5.00	3.00
3	Vern Bickford	8.00	4.00	2.50
4	Bob Buhl	10.00	5.00	3.00
5	Lew Burdette	15.00	7.50	4.50
6	Dave Cole	8.00	4.00	2.50
7	Ernie Johnson	8.00	4.00	2.50
8	Dave Jolly	8.00	4.00	2.50
9	Don Liddle	8.00	4.00	2.50
10	Warren Spahn	45.00	23.00	13.50
11	Max Surkont	8.00	4.00	2.50
12	Jim Wilson	8.00	4.00	2.50
13	Sibby Sisti	8.00	4.00	2.50
14	Walker Cooper	8.00	4.00	2.50
15	Del Crandall	12.00	6.00	3.50
16	Ebba St. Claire	8.00	4.00	2.50
17	Joe Adcock	12.00	6.00	3.50
18	George Crowe	8.00	4.00	2.50
19	Jack Dittmer	8.00	4.00	2.50
20	Johnny Logan	10.00	5.00	3.00
21	Ed Mathews	45.00	23.00	13.50
22	Bill Bruton	10.00	5.00	3.00
23	Sid Gordon	8.00	4.00	2.50
24	Andy Pafko	10.00	5.00	3.00
25	Jim Pendleton	8.00	4.00	2.50

1954 Johnston Cookies Braves

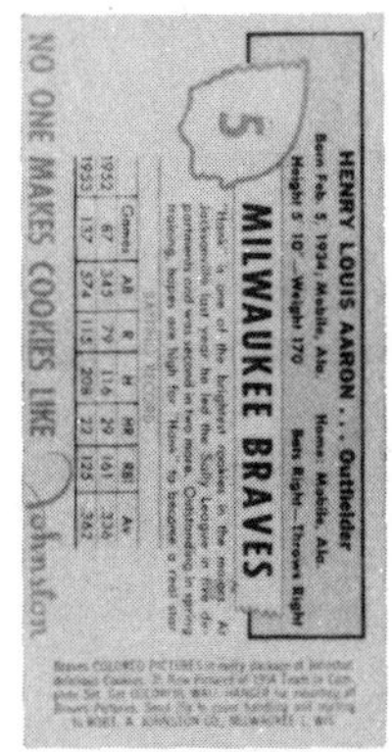

In its second of three annual issues, Johnston's increased the number of cards in its 1954 Braves issue to 35, and switched to an unusual size, a narrow format, 2" by 3-7/8". Besides the players and managers, the '54 set also includes unnumbered cards of the team trainer and equipment manager. Other cards are numbered by uniform number. After his early-season injury (which gave Hank Aaron a chance to play regularly), Bobby Thomson's card was withdrawn, accounting for its scarcity and high value. A cardboard wall-hanging display into which cards could be inserted was available as a premium offer.

	NR MT	EX	VG
Complete Set:	1000.	500.00	300.00
Common Player:	10.00	5.00	3.00

		NR MT	EX	VG
1	Del Crandall	15.00	7.50	4.50
3	Jim Pendleton	10.00	5.00	3.00
4	Danny O'Connell	10.00	5.00	3.00
5	Henry Aaron	400.00	200.00	125.00
6	Jack Dittmer	10.00	5.00	3.00
9	Joe Adcock	15.00	7.50	4.50
10	Robert Buhl	15.00	7.50	4.50
11	Phillip Paine (Phillips)	10.00	5.00	3.00
12	Ben Johnson	10.00	5.00	3.00
13	Sibby Sisti	10.00	5.00	3.00
15	Charles Gorin	10.00	5.00	3.00
16	Chet Nichols	10.00	5.00	3.00
17	Dave Jolly	10.00	5.00	3.00
19	Jim Wilson	10.00	5.00	3.00
20	Ray Crone	10.00	5.00	3.00
21	Warren Spahn	55.00	28.00	16.50
22	Gene Conley	9.00	4.50	2.75
23	Johnny Logan	12.00	6.00	3.50
24	Charlie White	10.00	5.00	3.00
27	George Metkovich	10.00	5.00	3.00
28	John Cooney	10.00	5.00	3.00
29	Paul Burris	10.00	5.00	3.00
31	Wm. Walters	10.00	5.00	3.00
32	Ernest T. Johnson	10.00	5.00	3.00
33	Lew Burdette	18.00	9.00	5.50
34	Bob Thomson	175.00	87.00	52.00
35	Robert Keely	10.00	5.00	3.00
38	Billy Bruton	10.00	5.00	3.00
40	Charles Grimm	10.00	5.00	3.00
41	Ed Mathews	55.00	28.00	16.50
42	Sam Calderone	10.00	5.00	3.00
47	Joey Jay	10.00	5.00	3.00
48	Andy Pafko	12.00	6.00	3.50
---	Dr. Charles Lacks (trainer)	10.00	5.00	3.00
---	Joseph F. Taylor (asst. trainer)	10.00	5.00	3.00

1955 Johnston Cookies Braves

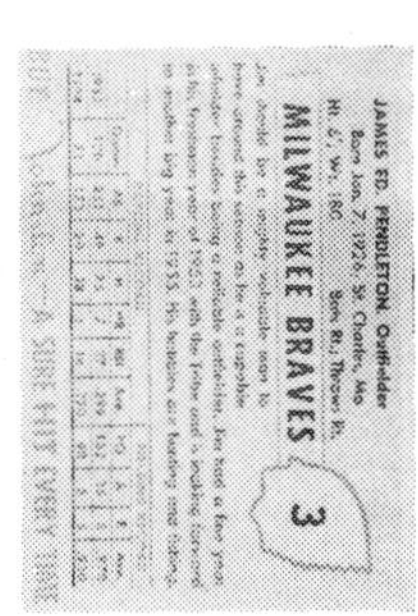

A third change in size and format was undertaken in the third and final year of Braves sets produced by Johnston's. The 35 cards in the 1955 set were issued in six fold-out panels of six cards each (Andy Pafko was double-printed). As in 1954, cards are numbered by uniform number, except those of the team equipment manager, trainer and road secretary (former Boston star Duffy Lewis). Single cards measure 2-7/8" by 4". Besides including panels in boxes of cookies, the '55 Johnston's could be ordered for 5¢ per panel by mail. The scarcest of the Johnston's issues, the 1955 set can be found today still in complete panels, or as single cards.

	NR MT	EX	VG
Complete Folder Set:	1200.	600.00	350.00
Complete Singles Set:	750.00	375.00	225.00
Common Player:	15.00	7.50	4.50
Common Folder:	110.00	55.00	33.00

		NR MT	EX	VG
1	Del Crandall	20.00	10.00	6.00
3	Jim Pendleton	15.00	7.50	4.50
4	Danny O'Connell	15.00	7.50	4.50
6	Jack Dittmer	15.00	7.50	4.50
9	Joe Adcock	20.00	10.00	6.00
10	Bob Buhl	18.00	9.00	5.50
11	Phil Paine	15.00	7.50	4.50
12	Ray Crone	15.00	7.50	4.50
15	Charlie Gorin	15.00	7.50	4.50
16	Dave Jolly	15.00	7.50	4.50
17	Chet Nichols	15.00	7.50	4.50
18	Chuck Tanner	20.00	10.00	6.00
19	Jim Wilson	15.00	7.50	4.50
20	Dave Koslo	15.00	7.50	4.50
21	Warren Spahn	65.00	33.00	20.00
22	Gene Conley	18.00	9.00	5.50
23	John Logan	18.00	9.00	5.50
24	Charlie White	15.00	7.50	4.50
28	Johnny Cooney	15.00	7.50	4.50
30	Roy Smalley	15.00	7.50	4.50
31	Bucky Walters	15.00	7.50	4.50
32	Ernie Johnson	15.00	7.50	4.50
33	Lew Burdette	25.00	12.50	7.50
34	Bobby Thomson	20.00	10.00	6.00
35	Bob Keely	15.00	7.50	4.50
38	Billy Bruton	18.00	9.00	5.50
39	George Crowe	15.00	7.50	4.50
40	Charlie Grimm	18.00	9.00	5.50
41	Eddie Mathews	65.00	33.00	20.00
44	Hank Aaron	350.00	175.00	105.00
47	Joe Jay	15.00	7.50	4.50
48	Andy Pafko	18.00	9.00	5.50
---	Dr. Charles K. Lacks	15.00	7.50	4.50
---	Duffy Lewis	15.00	7.50	4.50
---	Joe Taylor	15.00	7.50	4.50
---	Series 1 Folder (Hank Aaron, Lew Burdette, Del Crandall, Charlie Gorin, Bob Keely, Danny O'Connell)	375.00	187.00	112.00

		NR MT	EX	VG
---	Series 2 Folder (Joe Adcock, Joe Jay, Dr. Charles K. Lacks, Chet Nichols, Andy Pafko, Charlie White)	125.00	62.00	37.00
---	Series 3 Folder (Gene Conley, George Crowe, Jim Pendleton, Roy Smalley, Warren Spahn, Joe Taylor)	175.00	87.00	52.00
---	Series 4 Folder (Billy Bruton, John Cooney, Dave Jolly, Dave Koslo, Johnny Logan, Andy Pafko)	125.00	62.00	37.00
---	Series 5 Folder (Ray Crone, Ernie Johnson, Duffy Lewis, Eddie Mathews, Phil Paine, Chuck Tanner)	200.00	100.00	60.00
---	Series 6 Folder (Bob Buhl, Jack Dittmer, Charlie Grimm, Bobby Thomson, Bucky Walters, Jim Wilson)	125.00	62.00	37.00

1888 Joseph Hall Cabinets

These fourteen cabinet-size (6-1/2" by 4-1/2") cards feature team photos taken by Joseph Hall, a well-known photographer of the day. The cards, which are extremely rare, all have Hall's name beneath the photo and some include his Brooklyn address. The team is identified in large capital letters with the individual players identified in smaller type on both sides. Fourteen teams are known to date, but others may also exist, and Hall may have produced similar team cabinets in other years as well.

		NR MT	EX	VG
Complete Set:		1220.	61000.	40000.
Common Team:		6500.	3250.	2000.
(1)	Athletic Ball Club, 1888	7500.	3750.	2300.
(2)	Boston Ball Club, 1888	18000.	9000.	550.00
(3)	Brooklyn Ball Club, 1888	6500.	3250.	2000.
(4)	Chicago Ball Club, 1888	10000.	5000.	3000.
(5)	Cincinnati Ball Club, 1888	6500.	3250.	2000.
(6)	Cleveland Ball Club, 1888	6500.	3250.	2000.
(7)	Detroit Ball Club, 1888	8000.	4000.	2500.
(8)	Indianapolis Ball Club, 1888	6500.	3250.	2000.
(9)	Kansas City Ball Club, 1888	6500.	3250.	2000.
(10)	Louisville Ball Club, 1888	6500.	3250.	2000.
(11)	New York Ball Club, 1888 (wearing baseball uniforms)	10000.	5000.	3000.
(12)	New York Ball Club, 1888 (wearing tuxedos)	10000.	5000.	3000.
(13)	St. Louis Baseball Club, 1888	7500.	3750.	2300.
(14)	Washington Baseball Club, 1888	12500.	6250.	4000.

1893 Just So Tobacco

This set, issued by the Just So tobacco brand in 1893, is so rare that only seven examples are known, although more undoubtedly exist. The set apparently features only members of the Cleveland club, known then as the "Spiders". Measuring 2-1/2" by 3-7/8", these sepia-colored cards were printed on heavy paper. The player appears in a portrait photo with his name beneath and an ad for Just So Tobacco along the bottom. The existence of this set wasn't even established until the 1960s, and for 15 years only two subjects were known. In 1981, several more cards were discovered. To date only one copy of each of the known cards has turned up in collectors' hands, making it among the rarest of all baseball card issues.

		NR MT	EX	VG
Complete Set:		8200.	4100.	2460.
Common Player:		1200.	600.00	350.00
(1)	F.W. Boyd	1200.	600.00	350.00
(2)	Burkette	2500.	12500.	750.00
(3)	C.L. Childs	1200.	600.00	350.00
(4)	John Clarkson	3000.	1500.	900.00
(5)	C.M. Hastings	1200.	600.00	350.00
(6)	E.J. McKean	1200.	600.00	350.00
(7)	J.K. Virtue	1200.	600.00	350.00
(8)	T.C. Williams	1200.	600.00	350.00
9	Young	3500.	1750.	1050.

K

1982 K-Mart

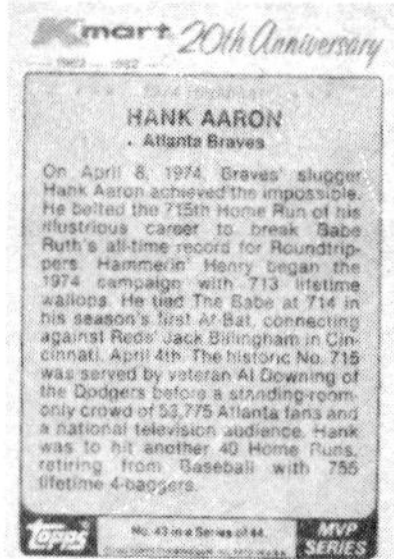

The first of what became dozens of boxed sets specially produced for retail chain stores by the major card producers, the 1982 K-Mart set has not enjoyed any collector popularity. The theme of the set is Most Valuable Players and selected record- breaking performances of the 1962-1981 seasons. The design used miniature reproductions of Topps cards of the era, except in a few cases where designs had to be created because original cards were never issued (1962 Maury Wills, 1975 Fred Lynn.) Originally sold for about $2 per boxed set of 44, large quantities were bought up by speculators who got burned when over-production and lack of demand caused the set to drop as low as 10¢. The 2-1/2" by 3-1/2" cards were printed by Topps.

		MT	NR MT	EX
Complete Set:		1.25	.90	.50
Common Player:		.03	.02	.01
1	Mickey Mantle	.40	.30	.15
2	Maury Wills	.05	.04	.02
3	Elston Howard	.03	.02	.01
4	Sandy Koufax	.10	.08	.04
5	Brooks Robinson	.05	.04	.02
6	Ken Boyer	.03	.02	.01
7	Zoilo Versalles	.03	.02	.01
8	Willie Mays	.10	.08	.04
9	Frank Robinson	.05	.04	.02
10	Bob Clemente	.10	.08	.04
11	Carl Yastrzemski	.10	.08	.04
12	Orlando Cepeda	.03	.02	.01
13	Denny McLain	.03	.02	.01
14	Bob Gibson	.05	.04	.02
15	Harmon Killebrew	.05	.04	.02
16	Willie McCovey	.05	.04	.02
17	Boog Powell	.03	.02	.01
18	Johnny Bench	.07	.05	.03
19	Vida Blue	.03	.02	.01
20	Joe Torre	.03	.02	.01
21	Rich Allen	.03	.02	.01
22	Johnny Bench	.07	.05	.03
23	Reggie Jackson	.07	.05	.03
24	Pete Rose	.12	.09	.05
25	Jeff Burroughs	.03	.02	.01
26	Steve Garvey	.07	.05	.03
27	Fred Lynn	.03	.02	.01
28	Joe Morgan	.05	.04	.02
29	Thurman Munson	.05	.04	.02
30	Joe Morgan	.05	.04	.02
31	Rod Carew	.07	.05	.03
32	George Foster	.03	.02	.01
33	Jim Rice	.05	.04	.02
34	Dave Parker	.05	.04	.02
35	Don Baylor	.03	.02	.01
36	Keith Hernandez	.03	.02	.01
37	Willie Stargell	.05	.04	.02
38	George Brett	.07	.05	.03
39	Mike Schmidt	.07	.05	.03
40	Rollie Fingers	.05	.04	.02
41	Mike Schmidt	.07	.05	.03
42	Don Drysdale	.05	.04	.02
43	Hank Aaron	.10	.08	.04
44	Pete Rose	.12	.09	.05

1987 K-Mart

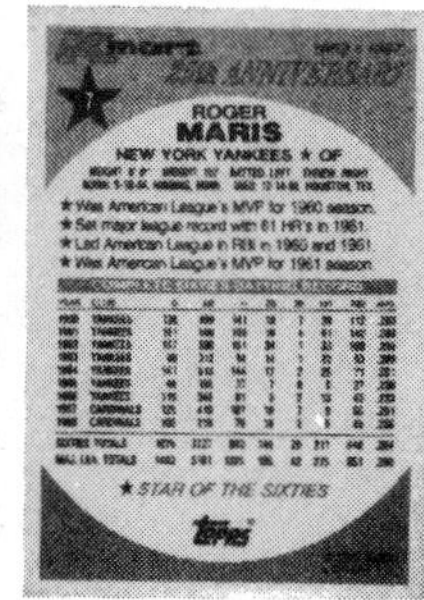

Produced by Topps for K-Mart, the 1987 K-Mart set was distributed by the department stores to celebrate their 25th anniversary. Entitled "Baseball's Stars of the Decades," the 33-card set was issued in a special cardboard box with one stick of bubblegum. The card fronts feature a full-color photo set diagonally against a red background. The backs contain career highlights plus pitching or batting statistics for the decade in which the player enjoyed his greatest success. Cards are the standard 2-1/2" by 3-1/2" size.

		MT	NR MT	EX
Complete Set:		5.00	3.75	2.00
Common Player:		.10	.08	.04
1	Hank Aaron	.50	.40	.20
2	Roberto Clemente	.40	.30	.15
3	Bob Gibson	.10	.08	.04
4	Harmon Killebrew	.10	.08	.04
5	Mickey Mantle	1.00	.70	.40
6	Juan Marichal	.10	.08	.04
7	Roger Maris	.30	.25	.12
8	Willie Mays	.50	.40	.20
9	Brooks Robinson	.30	.25	.12
10	Frank Robinson	.20	.15	.08
11	Carl Yastrzemski	.50	.40	.20
12	Johnny Bench	.30	.25	.12
13	Lou Brock	.20	.15	.08
14	Rod Carew	.30	.25	.12
15	Steve Carlton	.20	.15	.08
16	Reggie Jackson	.30	.25	.12
17	Jim Palmer	.10	.08	.04
18	Jim Rice	.10	.08	.04
19	Pete Rose	.60	.45	.25
20	Nolan Ryan	.20	.15	.08
21	Tom Seaver	.20	.15	.08
22	Willie Stargell	.10	.08	.04
23	Wade Boggs	.60	.45	.25
24	George Brett	.40	.30	.15
25	Gary Carter	.20	.15	.08
26	Dwight Gooden	.50	.40	.20
27	Rickey Henderson	.20	.15	.08
28	Don Mattingly	1.00	.70	.40
29	Dale Murphy	.40	.30	.15
30	Eddie Murray	.20	.15	.08
31	Mike Schmidt	.30	.25	.12
32	Darryl Strawberry	.40	.30	.15
33	Fernando Valenzuela	.10	.08	.04

1988 K-Mart

This 33-card boxed set, titled "Memorable Moments," was produced by Topps for distribution via K-Mart. Two previous Topps K-Mart sets were issued: a 44-card set in 1982 in honor of K-Mart's 20th anniversary and a 33-card set in 1987 for the company's 25th anniversary. The 1988 cards are standard-size with red, white and blue borders and a super glossy coating. Numbered card backs are printed in red and blue on white and highlight special events in the featured players' careers. The set was marketed in a bright yellow and green checklist box (gum included).

	MT	NR MT	EX
Complete Set:	5.00	3.75	2.00
Common Player:	.10	.08	.04

		NR MT	EX	VG
1	George Bell	.20	.15	.08
2	Wade Boggs	.80	.60	.30
3	George Brett	.30	.25	.12
4	Jose Canseco	.50	.40	.20
5	Jack Clark	.15	.11	.06
6	Will Clark	.25	.20	.10
7	Roger Clemens	.40	.30	.15
8	Vince Coleman	.15	.11	.06
9	Andre Dawson	.15	.11	.06
10	Dwight Gooden	.40	.30	.15
11	Pedro Guerrero	.15	.11	.06
12	Tony Gwynn	.25	.20	.10
13	Rickey Henderson	.25	.20	.10
14	Keith Hernandez	.15	.11	.06
15	Don Mattingly	1.50	1.25	.60
16	Mark McGwire	1.00	.70	.40
17	Paul Molitor	.12	.09	.05
18	Dale Murphy	.30	.25	.12
19	Tim Raines	.20	.15	.08
20	Dave Righetti	.12	.09	.05
21	Cap Ripken	.25	.20	.10
22	Pete Rose	.50	.40	.20
23	Nolan Ryan	.15	.11	.06
24	Benny Santiago	.25	.20	.10
25	Mike Schmidt	.30	.25	.12
26	Mike Scott	.10	.08	.04
27	Kevin Seitzer	.60	.45	.25
28	Ozzie Smith	.15	.11	.06
29	Darryl Strawberry	.30	.25	.12
30	Rick Sutcliffe	.10	.08	.04
31	Fernando Valenzuela	.15	.11	.06
32	Todd Worrell	.10	.08	.04
33	Robin Yount	.15	.11	.06

1955 Kahn's Wieners Reds

Compliments of Kahn's Wieners
"THE WIENER THE WORLD AWAITED"

The first of what would become 15 successive years of baseball card issues by the Kahn's meat company of Cincinnati is also the rarest. The set consists of six Cincinnati Redlegs player cards, 3-1/4" by 4". Printed in black and white, with blank backs, the '55 Kahn's cards were distributed at a one-day promotional event at a Cincinnati amuse- ment park, where the featured players were on hand to sign autographs. Like the other Kahn's issues through 1963, the '55 cards have a 1/2" white panel containing an advertising message below the player photo. These cards are sometimes found with this portion cut off, greatly reducing the value of the card.

		NR MT	EX	VG
Complete Set:		2750.	1375.	800.00
Common Player:		400.00	200.00	120.00
(1)	Gus Bell	750.00	375.00	230.00
(2)	Ted Kluszewski	650.00	325.00	200.00
(3)	Roy McMillan	400.00	200.00	120.00
(4)	Joe Nuxhall	400.00	200.00	120.00
(5)	Wally Post	400.00	200.00	120.00
(6)	Johnny Temple	400.00	200.00	120.00

1956 Kahn's Wieners Reds

Compliments of Kahn's Wieners
"THE WIENER THE WORLD AWAITED"

In 1956, Kahn's expanded its baseball card program to include 15 Redlegs players, and began issuing the cards one per pack in packages of hot dogs. Because the cards were packaged in direct contact with the meat, they are often found today in stained condition. In 3-1/4" by 4" format, black and white with blank backs, the '56 Kahn's cards can be distinguished from later issues by the presence of full stadium photographic back- grounds behind the player photos. Like all Kahn's issues, the 1956 set is unnumbered; the checklists are arranged alphabe- tically for convenience. The set features the first-ever baseball card of Hall of Famer Frank Robinson.

		NR MT	EX	VG
Complete Set:		1500.	750.00	450.00
Common Player:		75.00	37.00	22.00
(1)	Ed Bailey	75.00	37.00	22.00
(2)	Gus Bell	100.00	50.00	30.00
(3)	Joe Black	100.00	50.00	30.00
(4)	"Smokey" Burgess	100.00	50.00	30.00
(5)	Art Fowler	75.00	37.00	22.00
(6)	Hershell Freeman	75.00	37.00	22.00
(7)	Ray Jablonski	75.00	37.00	22.00
(8)	John Klippstein	75.00	37.00	22.00
(9)	Ted Kluszewski	125.00	62.00	37.00
(10)	Brooks Lawrence	75.00	37.00	22.00
(11)	Roy McMillan	75.00	37.00	22.00
(12)	Joe Nuxhall	100.00	50.00	30.00
(13)	Wally Post	75.00	37.00	22.00
(14)	Frank Robinson	300.00	150.00	90.00
(15)	Johnny Temple	100.00	50.00	30.00

1957 Kahn's Wieners

Compliments of Kahn's Wieners
"THE WIENER THE WORLD AWAITED"

In its third season of baseball card issue, Kahn's kept the basic 3-1/4" by 4" format, with black and white photos and blank backs. The issue was expanded to 28 players, all Pirates or Reds. The last of the blank-backed Kahn's sets, the 1957 Reds players can be distinguished from the 1956 issue by the general lack of background photo detail, in favor of a neutral light gray background. The Dick Groat card appears with two name variations, a facsimile autograph, "Richard Groat," and a printed "Dick Groat." Both Groat varieties are included in the complete set price.

		NR MT	EX	VG
Complete Set		2250.	1125.	700.00
Common Player		50.00	25.00	15.00
(1)	Tom Acker	50.00	25.00	15.00
(2)	Ed Bailey	50.00	25.00	15.00
(3)	Gus Bell	70.00	35.00	21.00
(4)	Smokey Burgess	70.00	35.00	21.00
(5)	Roberto Clemente	450.00	225.00	135.00
(6)	George Crowe	50.00	25.00	15.00
(7)	Elroy Face	70.00	35.00	21.00
(8)	Hershell Freeman	50.00	25.00	15.00
(9)	Robert Friend	50.00	25.00	15.00
(10)	Don Gross	50.00	25.00	15.00
(11a)	Dick Groat	70.00	35.00	21.00
(11b)	Richard Groat	175.00	87.00	52.00
(12)	Warren Hacker	50.00	25.00	15.00
(13)	Don Hoak	70.00	35.00	21.00
(14)	Hal Jeffcoat	50.00	25.00	15.00
(15)	Ron Kline	50.00	25.00	15.00
(16)	John Klippstein	50.00	25.00	15.00
(17)	Ted Kluszewski	100.00	50.00	30.00
(18)	Brooks Lawrence	50.00	25.00	15.00
(19)	Dale Long	50.00	25.00	15.00
(20)	Wm. Mazeroski	100.00	50.00	30.00
(21)	Roy McMillan	50.00	25.00	15.00
(22)	Joe Nuxhall	50.00	25.00	15.00
(23)	Wally Post	50.00	25.00	15.00
(24)	Frank Robinson	200.00	100.00	60.00
(25)	Johnny Temple	50.00	25.00	15.00
(26)	Frank Thomas	50.00	25.00	15.00
(27)	Bob Thurman	50.00	25.00	15.00
(28)	Lee Walls	50.00	25.00	15.00

1958 Kahn's Wieners

Long-time Cincinnati favorite Wally Post became the only Philadelphia Phillies ballplayer to appear in the 15-year run of Kahn's issues when he was traded in 1958, but included as part of the otherwise exclusively Pirates-Reds set. Like previous years, the '58 Kahn's were 3-1/4" by 4", with black and white player photos. Unlike previous years, however, the cards had printing on the back, a story by the pictured player, titled "My Greatest Thrill in Baseball." Quite similar to the 1959 issue, the '58 Kahn's can be distinguished by the fact that the top line of the advertising panel at bottom has the word "Wieners" in 1958, but not in 1959.

Compliments of Kahn's Wieners
"THE WIENER THE WORLD AWAITED"

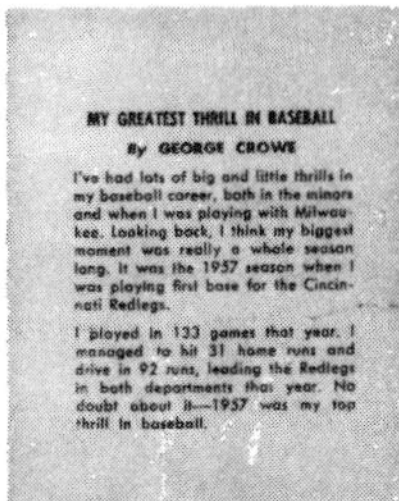

MY GREATEST THRILL IN BASEBALL

By GEORGE CROWE

I've had lots of big and little thrills in my baseball career, both in the minors and when I was playing with Milwaukee. Looking back, I think my biggest moment was really a whole season long. It was the 1957 season when I was playing first base for the Cincinnati Redlegs.

I played in 133 games that year. I managed to hit 31 home runs and drive in 92 runs, leading the Redlegs in both departments that year. No doubt about it—1957 was my top thrill in baseball.

		NR MT	EX	VG
Complete Set:		2500.	1250.	750.00
Common Player:		50.00	25.00	15.00
(1)	Ed Bailey	50.00	25.00	15.00
(2)	Gene Baker	50.00	25.00	15.00
(3)	Gus Bell	60.00	30.00	18.00
(4)	Smokey Burgess	60.00	30.00	18.00
(5)	Roberto Clemente	400.00	200.00	120.00
(6)	George Crowe	50.00	25.00	15.00
(7)	Elroy Face	60.00	30.00	18.00
(8)	Henry Foiles	50.00	25.00	15.00
(9)	Dee Fondy	50.00	25.00	15.00
(10)	Robert Friend	60.00	30.00	18.00
(11)	Richard Groat	60.00	30.00	18.00
(12)	Harvey Haddix	60.00	30.00	18.00
(13)	Don Hoak	60.00	30.00	18.00
(14)	Hal Jeffcoat	60.00	30.00	18.00
(15)	Ronald L. Kline	60.00	30.00	18.00
(16)	Ted Kluszewski	100.00	50.00	30.00
(17)	Vernon Law	60.00	30.00	18.00
(18)	Brooks Lawrence	50.00	25.00	15.00
(19)	William Mazeroski	100.00	50.00	30.00
(20)	Roy McMillan	50.00	25.00	15.00
(21)	Joe Nuxhall	60.00	30.00	18.00
(22)	Wally Post	275.00	137.00	80.00
(23)	John Powers	50.00	25.00	15.00
(24)	Robert T. Purkey	50.00	25.00	15.00
(25)	Charles Rabe	275.00	137.00	80.00
(26)	Frank Robinson	275.00	137.00	80.00
(27)	Robert Skinner	50.00	25.00	15.00
(28)	Johnny Temple	50.00	25.00	15.00
(29)	Frank Thomas	275.00	137.00	80.00

1959 Kahn's Wieners

Compliments of Kahn's
"THE WIENER THE WORLD AWAITED"

THE MOST DIFFICULT PLAY I HAVE TO MAKE

by GARY BELL

"I think the most difficult play for me to make as a pitcher is a bunt down the third base line. It is difficult because you must charge off the mound toward the line, field the ball, turn completely around and throw the ball hard to first base to get the hitter. I try to make this play by going over and fielding the ball with both feet planted firmly so I stay well balanced. That way, I don't have to throw off balance."

A third team was added to the Kahn's lineup in 1959, the Cleveland Indians joining the Pirates and Reds, bringing the number of cards in the set to 38. Again printed in black and white in the 3-1/4" by 4" size, the 1959 Kahn's cards can be differentiated from the previous issue by the lack of the word "Wieners" on the top line of the advertising panel at bottom. Backs again featured a story written by the pictured player, titled "The Toughest Play I Had to Make," "My Most Difficult Moment in Baseball," or "The Toughest Batters I Have to Face."

		NR MT	EX	VG
Complete Set:		3750.	1875.	1150.
Common Player:		40.00	20.00	12.00
(1)	Ed Bailey	40.00	20.00	12.00
(2)	Gary Bell	40.00	20.00	12.00
(3)	Gus Bell	50.00	25.00	15.00
(4)	Richard Brodowski	450.00	225.00	135.00
(5)	Forrest Burgess	50.00	25.00	15.00
(6)	Roberto Clemente	400.00	200.00	120.00
(7)	Rocky Colavito	75.00	37.00	22.00
(8)	ElRoy Face	50.00	25.00	15.00
(9)	Robert Friend	50.00	25.00	15.00
(10)	Joe Gordon	50.00	25.00	15.00
(11)	Jim Grant	40.00	20.00	12.00
(12)	Richard M. Groat	60.00	30.00	18.00
(13)	Harvey Haddix	350.00	175.00	105.00
(14)	Woodie Held	350.00	175.00	105.00
(15)	Don Hoak	45.00	22.00	13.50

		NR MT	EX	VG
(16)	Ronald Kline	40.00	20.00	12.00
(17)	Ted Kluszewski	75.00	37.00	22.00
(18)	Vernon Law	50.00	25.00	15.00
(19)	Jerry Lynch	40.00	20.00	12.00
(20)	Billy Martin	75.00	37.00	22.00
(21)	William Mazeroski	50.00	25.00	15.00
(22)	Cal McLish	350.00	175.00	105.00
(23)	Roy McMillan	40.00	20.00	12.00
(24)	Minnie Minoso	60.00	30.00	18.00
(25)	Russell Nixon	40.00	20.00	12.00
(26)	Joe Nuxhall	50.00	25.00	15.00
(27)	Jim Perry	50.00	25.00	15.00
(28)	Vada Pinson	60.00	30.00	18.00
(29)	Vic Power	40.00	20.00	12.00
(30)	Robert Purkey	40.00	20.00	12.00
(31)	Frank Robinson	175.00	87.00	52.00
(32)	Herb Score	50.00	25.00	15.00
(33)	Robert Skinner	40.00	20.00	12.00
(34)	George Strickland	40.00	20.00	12.00
(35)	Richard L. Stuart	45.00	22.00	13.50
(36)	John Temple	40.00	20.00	12.00
(37)	Frank Thomas	45.00	22.00	13.50
(38)	George A. Witt	40.00	20.00	12.00

1960 Kahn's Wieners

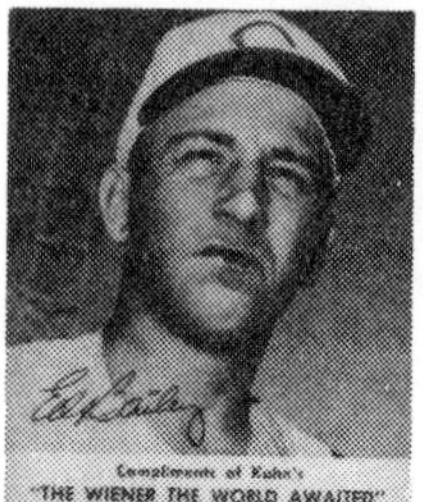
Compliments of Kahn's
"THE WIENER THE WORLD AWAITED"

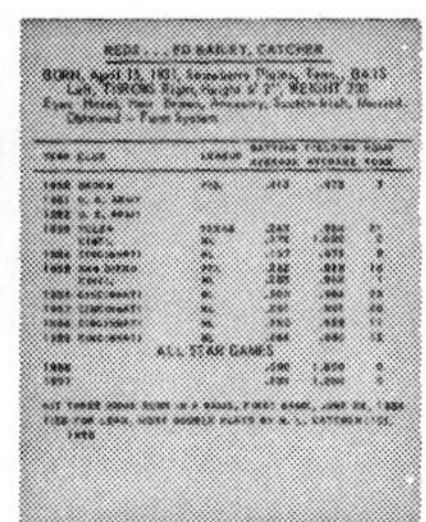

Three more teams joined the Kahn's roster in 1960, the Chicago Cubs, Chicago White Sox and St. Louis Cardinals. A total of 42 different players are represented in the set. Again 3-1/4" by 4" with black and white photos, the 1960 Kahn's cards featured for the first time player stats and personal data on the back, except Harvey Kuenn, which was issued with blank back, probably because of the lateness of his trade to the Indians.

		NR MT	EX	VG
Complete Set:		1900.	950.00	570.00
Common Player:		30.00	15.00	9.00
(1)	Ed Bailey	30.00	15.00	9.00
(2)	Gary Bell	30.00	15.00	9.00
(3)	Gus Bell	35.00	17.50	10.50
(4)	Forrest Burgess	35.00	17.50	10.50
(5)	Gino N. Cimoli	30.00	15.00	9.00
(6)	Roberto Clemente	250.00	125.00	75.00
(7)	ElRoy Face	35.00	17.50	10.50
(8)	Tito Francona	35.00	17.50	10.50
(9)	Robert Friend	35.00	17.50	10.50
(10)	Jim Grant	30.00	15.00	9.00
(11)	Richard Groat	40.00	20.00	12.00
(12)	Harvey Haddix	35.00	17.50	10.50
(13)	Woodie Held	30.00	15.00	9.00
(14)	Bill Henry	30.00	15.00	9.00
(15)	Don Hoak	35.00	17.50	10.50
(16)	Jay Hook	30.00	15.00	9.00
(17)	Eddie Kasko	30.00	15.00	9.00
(18)	Ronnie Kline	40.00	20.00	12.00
(19)	Ted Kluszewski	50.00	25.00	15.00
(20)	Harvey Kuenn	250.00	125.00	75.00
(21)	Vernon S. Law	35.00	17.50	10.50
(22)	Brooks Lawrence	30.00	15.00	9.00
(23)	Jerry Lynch	30.00	15.00	9.00
(24)	Billy Martin	60.00	30.00	18.00
(25)	William Mazeroski	40.00	20.00	12.00
(26)	Cal McLish	30.00	15.00	9.00
(27)	Roy McMillan	30.00	15.00	9.00
(28)	Don Newcombe	35.00	17.50	10.50
(29)	Russ Nixon	30.00	15.00	9.00
(30)	Joe Nuxhall	35.00	17.50	10.50
(31)	James J. O'Toole	30.00	15.00	9.00
(32)	Jim Perry	35.00	17.50	10.50
(33)	Vada Pinson	40.00	20.00	12.00
(34)	Vic Power	30.00	15.00	9.00
(35)	Robert T. Purkey	30.00	15.00	9.00
(36)	Frank Robinson	125.00	62.00	37.00
(37)	Herb Score	35.00	17.50	10.50
(38)	Robert R. Skinner	30.00	15.00	9.00
(39)	Richard L. Stuart	35.00	17.50	10.50
(40)	John Temple	30.00	15.00	9.00
(41)	Frank Thomas	40.00	20.00	12.00
(42)	Lee Walls	35.00	17.50	10.50

1961 Kahn's Wieners

PIRATES
Compliments of Kahn's
"THE WIENER THE WORLD AWAITED"

After a single season, the Chicago and St. Louis teams dropped out of the Kahn's program, but the 1961 set was larger than ever, at 43 cards. The same basic format - 3-1/4" by 4" size, black and white photos and statistical information on the back - was retained. For the first time in '61, the meat company made complete sets of the Kahn's cards available to collectors via a mail-in offer. This makes the 1961 and later Kahn's cards considerably easier to obtain than the earlier issues.

		NR MT	EX	VG
Complete Set:		1200.	600.00	360.00
Common Player:		18.00	9.00	5.50
(1)	John A. Antonelli	20.00	10.00	6.00
(2)	Ed Bailey	18.00	9.00	5.50
(3)	Gary Bell	18.00	9.00	5.50
(4)	Gus Bell	20.00	10.00	6.00
(5)	James P. Brosnan	18.00	9.00	5.50
(6)	Forrest Burgess	20.00	10.00	6.00
(7)	Gino Cimoli	18.00	9.00	5.50
(8)	Roberto Clemente	175.00	87.00	52.00
(9)	Gordon Coleman	18.00	9.00	5.50
(10)	Jimmie Dykes	20.00	10.00	6.00
(11)	ElRoy Face	25.00	12.50	7.50
(12)	Tito Francona	20.00	10.00	6.00
(13)	Robert Friend	20.00	10.00	6.00
(14)	Gene L. Freese	18.00	9.00	5.50
(15)	Jim Grant	18.00	9.00	5.50
(16)	Richard M. Groat	30.00	15.00	9.00
(17)	Harvey Haddix	20.00	10.00	6.00
(18)	Woodie Held	18.00	9.00	5.50
(19)	Don Hoak	20.00	10.00	6.00
(20)	Jay Hook	18.00	9.00	5.50
(21)	Joe Jay	18.00	9.00	5.50
(22)	Eddie Kasko	18.00	9.00	5.50
(23)	Willie Kirkland	18.00	9.00	5.50
(24)	Vernon S. Law	25.00	12.50	7.50
(25)	Jerry Lynch	18.00	9.00	5.50
(26)	Jim Maloney	25.00	12.50	7.50
(27)	William Mazeroski	30.00	15.00	9.00
(28)	Wilmer D. Mizell	20.00	10.00	6.00
(29)	Glenn R. Nelson	18.00	9.00	5.50
(30)	James J. O'Toole	18.00	9.00	5.50
(31)	Jim Perry	20.00	10.00	6.00
(32)	John M. Phillips	18.00	9.00	5.50
(33)	Vada E. Pinson Jr.	30.00	15.00	9.00
(34)	Wally Post	18.00	9.00	5.50
(35)	Vic Power	18.00	9.00	5.50
(36)	Robert T. Purkey	18.00	9.00	5.50
(37)	Frank Robinson	125.00	62.00	37.00
(38)	John A. Romano Jr.	18.00	9.00	5.50
(39)	Dick Schofield	18.00	9.00	5.50
(40)	Robert Skinner	18.00	9.00	5.50
(41)	Hal Smith	18.00	9.00	5.50
(42)	Richard Stuart	20.00	10.00	6.00
(43)	John E. Temple	18.00	9.00	5.50

1962 Kahn's Wieners

Compliments of Kahn's
"THE WIENER THE WORLD AWAITED"

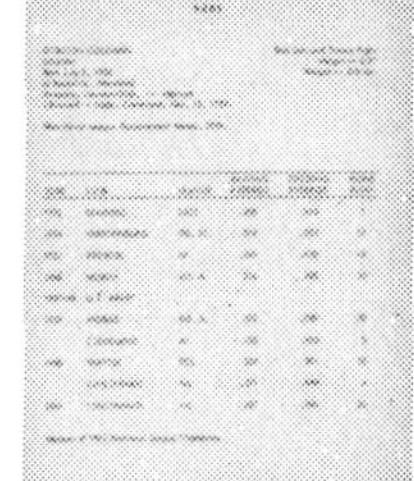

Besides the familiar Reds, Pirates and Indians players in the 1962 Kahn's set, a fourth team was added, the Minnesota Twins, though the overall size of the set was decreased from the previous year, to 38 players in 1962. The cards retained the 3-1/4" by 4" black and white format of previous years. The '62 Kahn's set is awash in variations. Besides the photo and front design variations on the Bell, Purkey and Power cards, each Cleveland player can be found with two back variations, listing the team either as "Cleveland" or "Cleveland Indians." The complete set values listed below include all variations.

		NR MT	EX	VG
Complete Set:		2400.	1200.	720.00
Common Player:		15.00	7.50	4.50
(1a)	Gary Bell (fat man in background)	150.00	75.00	45.00
(1b)	Gary Bell (no fat man)	40.00	20.00	12.00
(2)	James P. Brosnan	15.00	7.50	4.50
(3)	Forrest Burgess	20.00	10.00	6.00
(4)	Leonardo Cardenas	15.00	7.50	4.50
(5)	Roberto Clemente	125.00	62.00	37.00
(6a)	Ty Cline (Cleveland Indians back)	75.00	37.00	22.00
(6b)	Ty Cline (Cleveland back)	30.00	15.00	9.00
(7)	Gordon Coleman	15.00	7.50	4.50
(8)	Dick Donovan	30.00	15.00	9.00
(9)	John Edwards	15.00	7.50	4.50
(10a)	Tito Francona (Cleveland Indians back)	75.00	37.00	22.00
(10b)	Tito Francona (Cleveland back)	30.00	15.00	9.00
(11)	Gene Freese	15.00	7.50	4.50
(12)	Robert B. Friend	20.00	10.00	6.00
(13)	Joe Gibbon	90.00	45.00	27.00
(14a)	Jim Grant (Cleveland Indians back)	75.00	37.00	22.00
(14b)	Jim Grant (Cleveland back)	30.00	15.00	9.00
(15)	Richard M. Groat	25.00	12.50	7.50
(16)	Harvey Haddix	20.00	10.00	6.00
(17a)	Woodie Held (Cleveland Indians back)	90.00	45.00	27.00
(17b)	Woodie Held (Cleveland back)	30.00	15.00	9.00
(18)	Bill Henry	15.00	7.50	4.50
(19)	Don Hoak	20.00	10.00	6.00
(20)	Ken Hunt	15.00	7.50	4.50
(21)	Joseph R. Jay	15.00	7.50	4.50
(22)	Eddie Kasko	15.00	7.50	4.50
(23a)	Willie Kirkland (Cleveland Indians back)	75.00	37.00	22.00
(23b)	Willie Kirkland (Cleveland back)	30.00	15.00	9.00
(24a)	Barry Latman (Cleveland Indians back)	75.00	37.00	22.00
(24b)	Barry Latman (Cleveland back)	30.00	15.00	9.00
(25)	Jerry Lynch	15.00	7.50	4.50
(26)	Jim Maloney	20.00	10.00	6.00
(27)	William Mazeroski	25.00	12.50	7.50
(28)	Jim O'Toole	15.00	7.50	4.50
(29a)	Jim Perry (Cleveland Indians back)	90.00	45.00	27.00
(29b)	Jim Perry (Cleveland back)	30.00	15.00	9.00
(30a)	John M. Phillips (Cleveland Indians back)	75.00	37.00	22.00
(30b)	John M. Phillips (Cleveland back)	30.00	15.00	9.00
(31)	Vada E. Pinson	25.00	12.50	7.50
(32)	Wally Post	15.00	7.50	4.50
(33a)	Vic Power (Cleveland Indians back)	75.00	37.00	22.00
(33b)	Vic Power (Cleveland back)	30.00	15.00	9.00
(33c)	Vic Power (Minnesota Twins back)	150.00	75.00	45.00
(34a)	Robert T. Purkey (no autograph)	150.00	75.00	45.00
(34b)	Robert T. Purkey (with autograph)	40.00	20.00	12.00
(35)	Frank Robinson	80.00	40.00	24.00
(36a)	John Romano (Cleveland Indians back)	75.00	37.00	22.00
(36b)	John Romano (Cleveland back)	30.00	15.00	9.00
(37)	Dick Stuart	20.00	10.00	6.00
(38)	Bill Virdon	20.00	10.00	6.00

1962 Kahn's Wieners Atlanta Crackers

Compliments of Kahn's
"THE WIENER THE WORLD AWAITED"

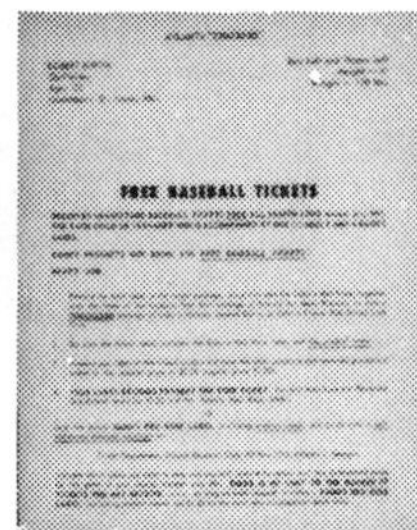
FREE BASEBALL TICKETS

Kahn's made a single foray into the minor league market in 1962 with a separate 24-card set of Atlanta Crackers. The cards feature the same basic format, 3-1/4" by 4", borderless black and white photos with a Kahn's ad message in a white panel below the picture, as the major league issue. The backs are slightly different, having a free ticket offer in place of the player stats. Atlanta was the top farm club of the St. Louis Cardinals in 1962. The most famous alumnus in the set is Tim McCarver.

		NR MT	EX	VG
Complete Set:		400.00	200.00	120.00
Common Player:		15.00	7.50	4.50
(1)	James (Jimmy) Edward Beauchamp	15.00	7.50	4.50
(2)	Gerald Peter Buchek	15.00	7.50	4.50
(3)	Robert Burda	15.00	7.50	4.50
(4)	Hal Deitz	15.00	7.50	4.50
(5)	Robert John Duliba	15.00	7.50	4.50
(6)	Harry Michael Fanok	15.00	7.50	4.50
(7)	Phil Gagliano	15.00	7.50	4.50
(8)	John Glenn	15.00	7.50	4.50
(9)	Leroy Gregory	15.00	7.50	4.50
(10)	Richard (Dick) Henry Hughes	15.00	7.50	4.50
(11)	John Charles Kucks, Jr.	15.00	7.50	4.50
(12)	Johnny Joe Lewis	15.00	7.50	4.50
(13)	James (Mac - Timmie) Timothy McCarver	35.00	17.50	10.50
(14)	Robert F. Milliken	15.00	7.50	4.50
(15)	Joe Morgan	15.00	7.50	4.50

		NR MT	EX	VG
(16)	Ronald Charles Plaza	15.00	7.50	4.50
(17)	Bob Sadowski	15.00	7.50	4.50
(18)	Jim Saul	15.00	7.50	4.50
(19)	Willard Schmidt	15.00	7.50	4.50
(20)	Joe Schultz	15.00	7.50	4.50
(21)	Thomas Michael (Mike) Shannon	20.00	10.00	6.00
(22)	Paul Louis Toth	15.00	7.50	4.50
(23)	Andrew Lou Vickery	15.00	7.50	4.50
(24)	Fred Dwight Whitfield	15.00	7.50	4.50

1963 Kahn's Wieners

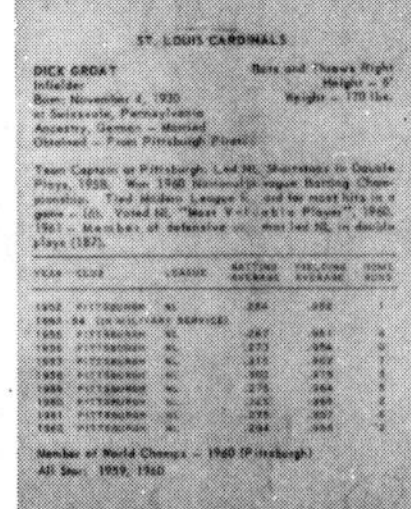

ST. LOUIS CARDINALS

DICK GROAT

Compliments of Kahn's
"THE WIENER THE WORLD AWAITED"

In 1963, for the first time since Kahn's began issuing baseball cards in 1955, the design underwent a significant change, white borders were added to the top and sides of player photo. Also, the card size was changed to 3-3/16" by 4-1/4". Statistical and personal data continued to be printed on the card backs. Joining traditional Reds, Pirates and Indians personnel in the 30-card 1963 set were a handful of New York Yankees and Dick Groat, in his new identity as a St. Louis Cardinal.

		NR MT	EX	VG
Complete Set:		800.00	400.00	240.00
Common Player:		15.00	7.50	4.50
(1)	Robert Bailey	15.00	7.50	4.50
(2)	Don Blasingame	15.00	7.50	4.50
(3)	Clete Boyer	25.00	12.50	7.50
(4)	Forrest Burgess	20.00	10.00	6.00
(5)	Leonardo Cardenas	15.00	7.50	4.50
(6)	Roberto Clemente	125.00	62.00	37.00
(7)	Don Clendennon (Donn Clendendon)	15.00	7.50	4.50
(8)	Gordon Coleman	15.00	7.50	4.50
(9)	John A. Edwards	15.00	7.50	4.50
(10)	Gene Freese	15.00	7.50	4.50
(11)	Robert B. Friend	20.00	10.00	6.00
(12)	Joe Gibbon	15.00	7.50	4.50
(13)	Dick Groat	25.00	12.50	7.50
(14)	Harvey Haddix	20.00	10.00	6.00
(15)	Elston Howard	30.00	15.00	9.00
(16)	Joey Jay	15.00	7.50	4.50
(17)	Eddie Kasko	15.00	7.50	4.50
(18)	Tony Kubek	30.00	15.00	9.00
(19)	Jerry Lynch	15.00	7.50	4.50
(20)	Jim Maloney	20.00	10.00	6.00
(21)	William Mazeroski	25.00	12.50	7.50
(22)	Joe Nuxhall	20.00	10.00	6.00
(23)	Jim O'Toole	15.00	7.50	4.50
(24)	Vada E. Pinson	25.00	12.50	7.50
(25)	Robert T. Purkey	15.00	7.50	4.50
(26)	Bob Richardson	30.00	15.00	9.00
(27)	Frank Robinson	70.00	35.00	21.00
(28)	Bill Stafford	20.00	10.00	6.00
(29)	Ralph W. Terry	25.00	12.50	7.50
(30)	Bill Virdon	20.00	10.00	6.00

1964 Kahn's Wieners

After nearly a decade of virtually identical card issues, the 1964 Kahn's issue was an abrupt change. In a new size, 3" by 3-1/2", the nearly square cards featured a borderless color photo. The only other design element on the front of the card was a facsimile autograph. The advertising slogan which had traditionally appeared on the front of the card was moved to the back, where it joined the player's stats and personal data. The teams in the 1964 issue once again reverted to the Reds, Pirates and Indians, for a total of 31 cards.

		NR MT	EX	VG
Complete Set:		925.00	462.00	277.00
Common Player:		9.00	4.50	2.75
(1)	Max Alvis	9.00	4.50	2.75
(2)	Bob Bailey	9.00	4.50	2.75
(3)	Leonardo Cardenas	9.00	4.50	2.75
(4)	Roberto Clemente	125.00	62.00	37.00
(5)	Donn A. Clendenon	9.00	4.50	2.75
(6)	Victor Davalillo	9.00	4.50	2.75
(7)	Dick Donovan	9.00	4.50	2.75
(8)	John A. Edwards	9.00	4.50	2.75
(9)	Robert Friend	15.00	7.50	4.50
(10)	Jim Grant	9.00	4.50	2.75
(11)	Tommy Harper	9.00	4.50	2.75
(12)	Woodie Held	9.00	4.50	2.75
(13)	Joey Jay	9.00	4.50	2.75
(14)	Jack Kralick	9.00	4.50	2.75
(15)	Jerry Lynch	9.00	4.50	2.75
(16)	Jim Maloney	15.00	7.50	4.50
(17)	William S. Mazeroski	20.00	10.00	6.00
(18)	Alvin McBean	9.00	4.50	2.75
(19)	Joe Nuxhall	15.00	7.50	4.50
(20)	Jim Pagliaroni	9.00	4.50	2.75
(21)	Vada E. Pinson Jr.	20.00	10.00	6.00
(22)	Robert T. Purkey	9.00	4.50	2.75
(23)	Pedro Ramos	9.00	4.50	2.75
(24)	Frank Robinson	70.00	35.00	21.00
(25)	John Romano	9.00	4.50	2.75
(26)	Pete Rose	400.00	200.00	120.00
(27)	John Tsitouris	9.00	4.50	2.75
(28)	Robert A. Veale Jr.	9.00	4.50	2.75
(29)	Bill Virdon	15.00	7.50	4.50
(30)	Leon Wagner	9.00	4.50	2.75
(31)	Fred Whitfield	9.00	4.50	2.75

1965 Kahn's Wieners

Compliments of Kahn's
"THE WIENER THE WORLD AWAITED"

There was little change for the Kahn's issue in 1965 beyond the addition of Milwaukee Braves players to the Reds, Pirates and Indians traditionally included in the set. At 45 players, the 1965 issue was the largest of the Kahn's sets. Once again in 3" by 3-1/2" size, the 1965s retained the borderless color photo design of the previous season. A look at the stats on the back will confirm the year of issue, however, since the last year of statistics is the year prior to the card's issue.

		NR MT	EX	VG
Complete Set:		1100.	550.00	330.00
Common Player:		12.00	6.00	3.50
(1)	Hank Aaron	125.00	62.00	37.00
(2)	Max Alvis	12.00	6.00	3.50
(3)	Jose Azcue	12.00	6.00	3.50
(4)	Bob Bailey	12.00	6.00	3.50
(5)	Frank Bolling	12.00	6.00	3.50
(6)	Leonardo Cardenas	12.00	6.00	3.50
(7)	Rico Ricardo Carty	15.00	7.50	4.50
(8)	Donn A. Clendenon	12.00	6.00	3.50
(9)	Tony Cloninger	12.00	6.00	3.50
(10)	Gordon Coleman	12.00	6.00	3.50
(11)	Victor Davalillo	12.00	6.00	3.50
(12)	John A. Edwards	12.00	6.00	3.50
(13)	Sam Ellis	12.00	6.00	3.50
(14)	Robert Friend	15.00	7.50	4.50
(15)	Tommy Harper	12.00	6.00	3.50
(16)	Chuck Hinton	12.00	6.00	3.50
(17)	Dick Howser	15.00	7.50	4.50
(18)	Joey Jay	12.00	6.00	3.50
(19)	Deron Johnson	12.00	6.00	3.50
(20)	Jack Kralick	12.00	6.00	3.50
(21)	Denny Lemaster	12.00	6.00	3.50
(22)	Jerry Lynch	12.00	6.00	3.50
(23)	Jim Maloney	15.00	7.50	4.50
(24)	Lee Maye	12.00	6.00	3.50
(25)	William S. Mazeroski	20.00	10.00	6.00
(26)	Alvin McBean	12.00	6.00	3.50
(27)	Bill McCool	12.00	6.00	3.50
(28)	Sam McDowell	15.00	7.50	4.50
(29)	Donald McMahon	12.00	6.00	3.50
(30)	Denis Menke	12.00	6.00	3.50
(31)	Joe Nuxhall	15.00	7.50	4.50
(32)	Gene Oliver	12.00	6.00	3.50
(33)	Jim O'Toole	12.00	6.00	3.50
(34)	Jim Pagliaroni	12.00	6.00	3.50
(35)	Vada E. Pinson Jr.	20.00	10.00	6.00
(36)	Frank Robinson	70.00	35.00	21.00
(37)	Pete Rose	250.00	125.00	75.00
(38)	Willie Stargell	70.00	35.00	21.00
(39)	Ralph W. Terry	12.00	6.00	3.50
(40)	Luis Tiant	20.00	10.00	6.00
(41)	Joe Torre	25.00	12.50	7.50
(42)	John Tsitouris	12.00	6.00	3.50
(43)	Robert A. Veale Jr.	12.00	6.00	3.50
(44)	Bill Virdon	15.00	7.50	4.50
(45)	Leon Wagner	12.00	6.00	3.50

1966 Kahn's Wieners

The fourth new format in five years greeted collector's with the introduction of Kahn's 1966 issue of 32 cards. The design consisted of a color photo bordered by white and yellow vertical stripes. The player's name was printed above the photo, and a facsimile autograph appeared across the photo. As printed, the cards were 2-13/16" by 4" in size. However, the top portion consisted of a 2-13/16" by 1-3/8" advertising panel with a red rose logo and the word "Kahn's," separated from the player portion of the card by a black dotted line. Naturally, many of the cards are found today with the top portion cut off. Values listed here are for cards with the top portion intact. Players from the Cincinnati Reds, Pittsburgh Pirates, Cleveland Indians and Atlanta Braves were included in the set. Since the cards are blank-backed, collectors must learn to differentiate player poses to determine year of issue for some cards.

		NR MT	EX	VG
Complete Set:		1200.	600.00	360.00
Common Player:		18.00	9.00	5.50
(1)	Henry Aaron	125.00	62.00	37.00
(2)	Felipe Alou	24.00	12.00	7.25
(3)	Max Alvis	18.00	9.00	5.50
(4)	Robert Bailey	18.00	9.00	5.50
(5)	Wade Blasingame	18.00	9.00	5.50
(6)	Frank Bolling	18.00	9.00	5.50
(7)	Leo Cardenas	18.00	9.00	5.50
(8)	Roberto Clemente	125.00	62.00	37.00
(9)	Tony Cloninger	18.00	9.00	5.50
(10)	Vic Davalillo	18.00	9.00	5.50
(11)	John Edwards	18.00	9.00	5.50
(12)	Sam Ellis	18.00	9.00	5.50
(13)	Pedro Gonzalez	18.00	9.00	5.50
(14)	Tommy Harper	18.00	9.00	5.50
(15)	Deron Johnson	18.00	9.00	5.50
(16)	Mack Jones	18.00	9.00	5.50
(17)	Denny Lemaster	18.00	9.00	5.50
(18)	Jim Maloney	24.00	12.00	7.25
(19)	William Mazeroski	28.00	14.00	8.50
(20)	Bill McCool	18.00	9.00	5.50
(21)	Sam McDowell	24.00	12.00	7.25
(22)	Denis Menke	18.00	9.00	5.50
(23)	Joe Nuxhall	24.00	12.00	7.25
(24)	Jim Pagliaroni	18.00	9.00	5.50
(25)	Milt Pappas	24.00	12.00	7.25
(26)	Vada Pinson	28.00	14.00	8.50
(27)	Pete Rose	250.00	125.00	75.00
(28)	Sonny Siebert	18.00	9.00	5.50
(29)	Willie Stargell	80.00	40.00	24.00
(30)	Joe Torre	28.00	14.00	8.50
(31)	Bob Veale	18.00	9.00	5.50
(32)	Fred Whitfield	18.00	9.00	5.50

1967 Kahn's Wieners

Retaining the basic format of the 1966 set (see listing for description), the '67 Kahn's set was expanded to 41 players through the addition of several New York Mets players to the previous season's lineup of Reds, Pirates, Indians and Braves. Making the 1967 set especially challenging for collectors is the fact that some cards are found in a smaller size and/or with different colored stripes bordering the color player photo. On the majority of cards, the size remained 2-13/16" by 4" (with ad at top; 2-13/16" by 2-5/8"without ad at top). However, because of packing in different products, the Ellis, Helms and Torre cards can be found in 2-13/16" by 3-1/4" size (with ad; 2-13/16" by 2-1/8" without ad). The handful of known border stripe variations are listed below. Values quoted are for cards with the top ad panel intact. All variation cards are included in the valuations given below for complete sets.

		NR MT	EX	VG
Complete Set:		1400.	700.00	420.00
Common Player:		18.00	9.00	5.50
(1)	Henry Aaron	125.00	62.00	37.00
(2)	Gene Alley	18.00	9.00	5.50
(3)	Felipe Alou	24.00	12.00	7.25
(4a)	Matty Alou (yellow & white striped border)	24.00	12.00	7.25
(4b)	Matty Alou (red & white striped border)	28.00	14.00	8.50
(5)	Max Alvis	18.00	9.00	5.50
(6a)	Ken Boyer (yellow & white striped border)	30.00	15.00	9.00
(6b)	Ken Boyer (red & white striped border)	35.00	17.50	10.50
(7)	Leo Cardenas	18.00	9.00	5.50
(8)	Rico Carty	24.00	12.00	7.25
(9)	Tony Cloninger	18.00	9.00	5.50
(10)	Tommy Davis	24.00	12.00	7.25
(11)	John Edwards	18.00	9.00	5.50
(12a)	Sam Ellis (large size)	18.00	9.00	5.50
(12b)	Sam Ellis (small size)	28.00	14.00	8.50
(13)	Jack Fisher	18.00	9.00	5.50
(14)	Steve Hargan	18.00	9.00	5.50
(15)	Tom Harper	18.00	9.00	5.50
(16a)	Tom Helms (large size)	18.00	9.00	5.50
(16b)	Tom Helms (small size)	28.00	14.00	8.50
(17)	Deron Johnson	18.00	9.00	5.50
(18)	Ken Johnson	18.00	9.00	5.50
(19)	Cleon Jones	18.00	9.00	5.50
(20a)	Ed Kranepool (yellow & white striped border)	18.00	9.00	5.50
(20b)	Ed Kranepool (red & white striped border)	25.00	12.50	7.50
(21a)	James Maloney (yellow & white striped border)	24.00	12.00	7.25
(21b)	James Maloney (red & white striped border)	28.00	14.00	8.50
(22)	Lee May	24.00	12.00	7.25
(23)	Wm. Mazeroski	28.00	14.00	8.50
(24)	Wm. McCool	18.00	9.00	5.50
(25)	Sam McDowell	24.00	12.00	7.25
(26)	Dennis Menke (Denis)	18.00	9.00	5.50
(27)	Jim Pagliaroni	18.00	9.00	5.50
(28)	Don Pavletich	18.00	9.00	5.50
(29)	Tony Perez	35.00	17.50	10.50
(30)	Vada Pinson	28.00	14.00	8.50
(31)	Dennis Ribant	18.00	9.00	5.50
(32)	Pete Rose	200.00	100.00	60.00
(33)	Art Shamsky	18.00	9.00	5.50
(34)	Bob Shaw	18.00	9.00	5.50
(35)	Sonny Siebert	18.00	9.00	5.50
(36)	Wm. Stargell (first name actually Wilver)	80.00	40.00	24.00
(37a)	Joe Torre (large size)	28.00	14.00	8.50
(37b)	Joe Torre (small size)	32.00	16.00	9.50
(38)	Bob Veale	18.00	9.00	5.50
(39)	Leon Wagner	18.00	9.00	5.50
(40)	Fred Whitfield	18.00	9.00	5.50
(41)	Woody Woodward	18.00	9.00	5.50

1968 Kahn's Wieners

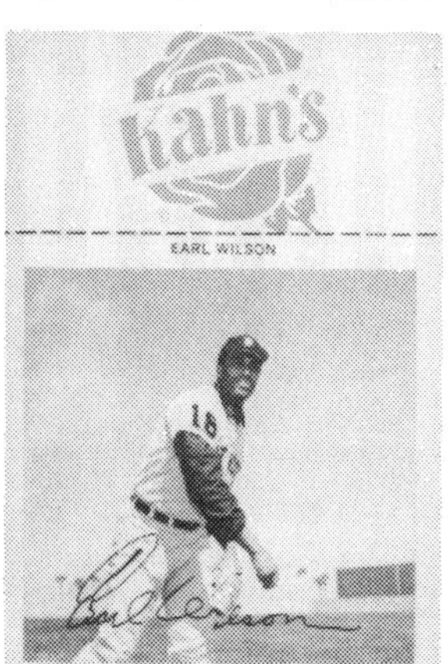

The number of card size and stripe color variations increased with the 1968 Kahn's issue (see 1967 listing), though the basic card design was retained from the previous two seasons: 2-13/16" by 4" size (with ad panel at top; 2-13/16" by 2-5/8" with ad panel cut off), color photo bordered by yellow and white vertical stripes. In addition to the basic issue, a number of the cards appear in a smaller, 2-13/16" by 3-1/4", size, while some of them, and others, appear with variations in the color of border stripes. One card, Maloney, can be found with a top portion advertising Blue Mountain brand meats, as well as Kahn's. All in all, quite a challenge for the specialist. The 1968 set featured the largest number of teams represented in any Kahn's issue: Atlanta Braves, Chicago Cubs and White Sox, Cincinnati Reds, Cleveland Indians, Detroit Tigers, New York Mets and Pittsburgh Pirates. Values quoted below are for cards with the ad panel at top; complete set prices include all variations.

		NR MT	EX	VG
Complete Set:		2000.	1000.	600.00
Common Player:		18.00	9.00	5.50
(1a)	Hank Aaron (large size)	125.00	62.00	37.00
(1b)	Hank Aaron (small size)	150.00	75.00	45.00
(2)	Tommy Agee	18.00	9.00	5.50
(3a)	Gene Alley (large size)	18.00	9.00	5.50
(3b)	Gene Alley (small size)	24.00	12.00	7.25
(4)	Felipe Alou	24.00	12.00	7.25
(5a)	Matty Alou (yellow striped border)	24.00	12.00	7.25
(5b)	Matty Alou (red striped border)	28.00	14.00	8.50
(6a)	Max Alvis (large size)	18.00	9.00	5.50
(6b)	Max Alvis (small size)	24.00	12.00	7.25
(7)	Gerry Arrigo	18.00	9.00	5.50
(8)	John Bench	450.00	225.00	135.00
(9a)	Clete Boyer (large size)	18.00	9.00	5.50
(9b)	Clete Boyer (small size)	24.00	12.00	7.25
(10)	Larry Brown	18.00	9.00	5.50
(11a)	Leo Cardenas (large size)	18.00	9.00	5.50
(11b)	Leo Cardenas (small size)	24.00	12.00	7.25
(12a)	Bill Freehan (large size)	24.00	12.00	7.25
(12b)	Bill Freehan (small size)	28.00	14.00	8.50
(13)	Steve Hargan	18.00	9.00	5.50
(14)	Joel Horlen	18.00	9.00	5.50
(15)	Tony Horton	24.00	12.00	7.25
(16)	Willie Horton	24.00	12.00	7.25
(17)	Ferguson Jenkins	32.00	16.00	9.50
(18)	Deron Johnson	18.00	9.00	5.50
(19)	Mack Jones	18.00	9.00	5.50
(20)	Bob Lee	18.00	9.00	5.50
(21a)	Jim Maloney (large size, rose logo)	24.00	12.00	7.25
(21b)	Jim Maloney (large size, blue mountain logo)	28.00	14.00	8.50
(21c)	Jim Maloney (small size, yellow & white striped border)	28.00	14.00	8.50
(21d)	Jim Maloney (small size, yellow, white & green striped border)	28.00	14.00	8.50
(22a)	Lee May (large size)	24.00	12.00	7.25
(22b)	Lee May (small size)	28.00	14.00	8.50
(23a)	Wm. Mazeroski (large size)	24.00	12.00	7.25
(23b)	Wm. Mazeroski (small size)	28.00	14.00	8.50
(24)	Dick McAuliffe	18.00	9.00	5.50
(25)	Bill McCool	18.00	9.00	5.50
(26a)	Sam McDowell (yellow striped border)	24.00	12.00	7.25
(26b)	Sam McDowell (red striped border)	28.00	14.00	8.50
(27a)	Tony Perez (yellow striped border)	35.00	17.50	10.50
(27b)	Tony Perez (red striped border)	40.00	20.00	12.00
(28)	Gary Peters	18.00	9.00	5.50
(29a)	Vada Pinson (large size)	24.00	12.00	7.25
(29b)	Vada Pinson (small size)	28.00	14.00	8.50
(30)	Chico Ruiz	18.00	9.00	5.50
(31a)	Ron Santo (yellow striped border)	24.00	12.00	7.25
(31b)	Ron Santo (red striped border)	28.00	14.00	8.50
(32)	Art Shamsky	18.00	9.00	5.50
(33)	Luis Tiant	24.00	12.00	7.25
(34a)	Joe Torre (large size)	28.00	14.00	8.50
(34b)	Joe Torre (small size)	32.00	16.00	9.50
(35a)	Bob Veale (large size)	18.00	9.00	5.50
(35b)	Bob Veale (small size)	24.00	12.00	7.25
(36)	Leon Wagner	18.00	9.00	5.50
(37)	Billy Williams	50.00	25.00	15.00
(38)	Earl Wilson	18.00	9.00	5.50

1969 Kahn's Wieners

In its 15th consecutive year of baseball card issuing, Kahn's continued the basic format adopted in 1966. The basic card issue of 22 players was printed in 2-13/16" by 4" size (with ad panel at top; 2-13/16" by 2-5/8" without panel) and are blanked-backed. Teams represented in the set included the Braves, Cubs, White Sox, Reds, Cardinals, Indians and Pirates. The cards featured a color photo and facsimile autograph bordered by yellow and white vertical stripes. At top was an ad panel consisting of the Kahn's red rose logo. However, because some cards were produced for inclusion in packages other than the standard hot dogs, a number of variations in card size and stripe color were created, as noted in the listings below. The smaller size cards, 2-13/16" by 3-1/4" with ad, 2-13/16" by 2-1/8" without ad, were created by

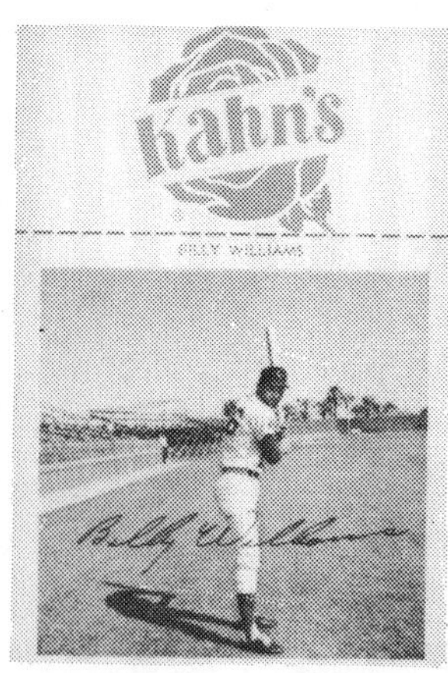

more closely cropping the player photo at top and bottom. Values quoted below are for cards with the top logo panel intact. Complete set values include all the variations.

		NR MT	EX	VG
Complete Set:		1000.	500.00	300.00
Common Player:		18.00	9.00	5.50
(1a)	Hank Aaron (large size)	125.00	62.00	37.00
(1b)	Hank Aaron (small size)	150.00	75.00	45.00
(2)	Matty Alou	24.00	12.00	7.25
(3)	Max Alvis	18.00	9.00	5.50
(4)	Gerry Arrigo	18.00	9.00	5.50
(5)	Steve Blass	18.00	9.00	5.50
(6)	Clay Carroll	18.00	9.00	5.50
(7)	Tony Cloninger	18.00	9.00	5.50
(8)	George Culver	18.00	9.00	5.50
(9)	Joel Horlen	18.00	9.00	5.50
(10)	Tony Horton	24.00	12.00	7.25
(11)	Alex Johnson	18.00	9.00	5.50
(12a)	Jim Maloney (large size)	24.00	12.00	7.25
(12b)	Jim Maloney (small size)	28.00	14.00	8.50
(13a)	Lee May (yellow striped border)	24.00	12.00	7.25
(13b)	Lee May (red striped border)	28.00	14.00	8.50
(14a)	Wm. Mazeroski (yellow striped border)	24.00	12.00	7.25
(14b)	Wm. Mazeroski (red striped border)	28.00	14.00	8.50
(15a)	Sam McDowell (yellow striped border)	24.00	12.00	7.25
(15b)	Sam McDowell (red striped border)	28.00	14.00	8.50
(16a)	Tony Perez (large size)	35.00	17.50	10.50
(16b)	Tony Perez (small size)	40.00	20.00	12.00
(17)	Gary Peters	18.00	9.00	5.50
(18a)	Ron Santo (yellow striped border)	24.00	12.00	7.25
(18b)	Ron Santo (red striped border)	28.00	14.00	8.50
(19)	Luis Tiant	24.00	12.00	7.25
(20)	Joe Torre	28.00	14.00	8.50
(21)	Bob Veale	18.00	9.00	5.50
(22)	Billy Williams	50.00	25.00	15.00

1987 Kahn's Wieners Reds

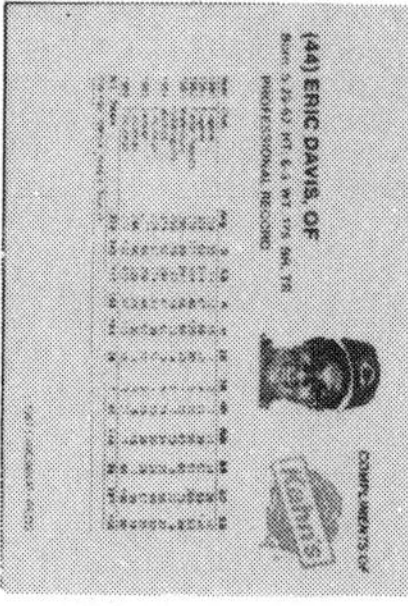

After a nearly 20-year layoff, Kahn's Wieners produced a baseball card set. Kahn's, who produced card sets between 1955 and 1968, sponsored a 28-card 9set that was distributed to fans attending the August 2nd game at Riverfront Stadium. The cards are the standard 2-1/2" by 3-1/2" size. The fronts offer a full-color player photo bordered in red and white. The backs carry the Kahn's logo and a head shot of the player.

		MT	NR MT	EX
Complete Set:		20.00	15.00	8.00
Common Player:		.20	.15	.08
6	Bo Diaz	.25	.20	.10
10	Terry Francona	.20	.15	.08
11	Kurt Stillwell	.70	.50	.30
12	Nick Esasky	.70	.50	.30
13	Dave Concepcion	.70	.50	.30
15	Barry Larkin	2.00	1.50	.80
16	Ron Oester	.20	.15	.08

		MT	NR MT	EX
21	Paul O'Neill	1.00	.70	.40
23	Lloyd McClendon	.40	.30	.15
25	Buddy Bell	.35	.25	.14
28	Kal Daniels	1.50	1.25	.60
29	Tracy Jones	.70	.50	.30
30	Guy Hoffman	.20	.15	.08
31	John Franco	.80	.60	.30
32	Tom Browning	.80	.60	.30
33	Ron Robinson	.25	.20	.10
34	Bill Gullickson	.20	.15	.08
35	Pat Pacillo	.30	.25	.12
39	Dave Parker	.80	.60	.30
43	Bill Landrum	.50	.40	.20
44	Eric Davis	4.00	3.00	1.50
46	Rob Murphy	.40	.30	.15
47	Frank Williams	.25	.20	.10
48	Ted Power	.20	.15	.08

1988 Kahn's Wieners Mets

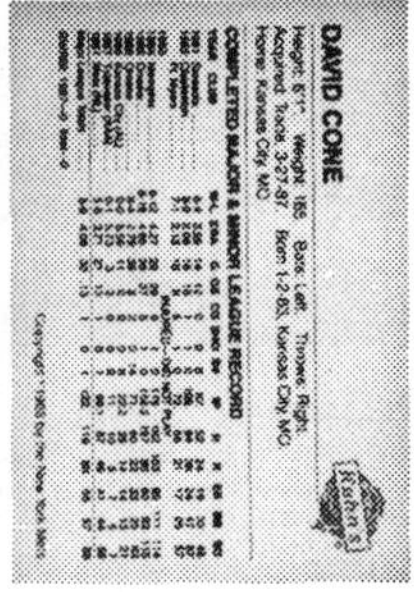

Approximately 50,000 Mets fans received this complimentary card set during a ballpark promotion sponsored by Kahn's Wieners. Twenty-five players are featured in the set, along with manager Davey Johnson, four coaches and a team photo. Card fronts have a dark blue border with an orange rectangle framing the full-color player photo. Card numbers reflecting the players' uniform numbers, are printed in white in the upper right corner of the card face, beside the team logo. The player name appears upper left and the player position is centered in the bottom margin. The card backs are black and white with red line accents. In addition to player acquisition date, birthday and residence, a paragraph-style career summary is included. The cards measure 2-1/2" by 3-1/2".

		MT	NR MT	EX
Complete Set:		14.00	10.50	5.50
Common Player:		.20	.15	.08
1	Mookie Wilson	.35	.25	.14
2	Mackey Sasser	.30	.25	.12
3	Bud Harrelson	.20	.15	.08
4	Lenny Dykstra	.40	.30	.15
5	Davey Johnson	.30	.25	.12
6	Wally Backman	.20	.15	.08
8	Gary Carter	.80	.60	.30
11	Tim Teufel	.20	.15	.08
12	Ron Darling	.60	.45	.25
13	Lee Mazzilli	.20	.15	.08
15	Rick Aguilera	.20	.15	.08
16	Dwight Gooden	2.00	1.50	.80
17	Keith Hernandez	.80	.60	.30
18	Darryl Strawberry	1.50	1.25	.60
19	Bob Ojeda	.35	.25	.14
20	Howard Johnson	.80	.60	.30
21	Kevin Elster	.50	.40	.20
22	Kevin McReynolds	.60	.45	.25
26	Terry Leach	.20	.15	.08
28	Bill Robinson	.20	.15	.08
29	Dave Magadan	.40	.30	.15
30	Mel Stottlemyre	.20	.15	.08
31	Gene Walter	.20	.15	.08
33	Barry Lyons	.20	.15	.08
34	Sam Perlozzo	.20	.15	.08
42	Roger McDowell	.30	.25	.12
44	David Cone	.70	.50	.30
48	Randy Myers	.50	.40	.20
50	Sid Fernandez	.35	.25	.14
52	Greg Pavlick	.20	.15	.08
---	Team Photo	.20	.15	.08

The values quoted are intended to reflect the market price.

1988 Kahn's Wieners Reds

This 26-card set was a one-time giveaway during the August 14th, 1988 Cincinnati Reds game. The glossy cards (2-1/2" by 3-1/2") feature full-color action photos inside red and white borders. The Reds logo, player uniform number, name and position are printed below the photo. The backs are black and white, with small player close-ups and career stats. A promotional 25-cent coupon for Kahn's Wieners was included with each set.

		MT	NR MT	EX
Complete Set:		12.00	9.00	4.75
Common Player:		.20	.15	.08
6	Bo Diaz	.25	.20	.10
8	Terry McGriff	.20	.15	.08
9	Eddie Milner	.20	.15	.08
10	Leon Durham	.30	.25	.12
11	Barry Larkin	.70	.50	.30
12	Nick Esasky	.30	.25	.12
13	Dave Concepcion	.40	.30	.15
14	Pete Rose	1.25	.90	.50
15	Jeff Treadway	.50	.40	.20
17	Chris Sabo	1.50	1.25	.60
20	Danny Jackson	.60	.45	.25
21	Paul O'Neill	.30	.25	.12
22	Dave Collins	.20	.15	.08
27	Jose Rijo	.35	.25	.14
28	Kal Daniels	.70	.50	.30
29	Tracy Jones	.50	.40	.20
30	Lloyd McClendon	.20	.15	.08
31	John Franco	.50	.40	.20
32	Tom Browning	.50	.40	.20
33	Ron Robinson	.25	.20	.10
40	Jack Armstrong	.25	.20	.10
44	Eric Davis	2.00	1.50	.80
46	Rob Murphy	.25	.20	.10
47	Frank Williams	.20	.15	.08
48	Tim Birtsas	.20	.15	.08
---	Coaches (Scott Breeden, Tommy Helms, Bruce Kimm, Jim Lett, Lee May, Tony Perez)	.20	.15	.08

1989 Kahn's Wieners Mets

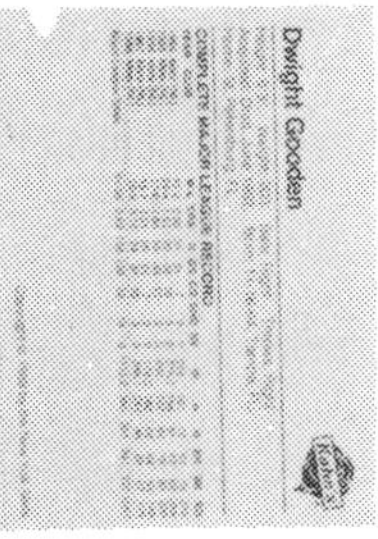

This 30-card New York Mets team set was sponsored by Kahn's Wieners and was given to fans attending the July 6, 1989 Mets game at Shea Stadium. The standard-size cards feature a full-color photo surrounded by a blue and orange border with the player's name and uniform number across the top. The backs include the Kahn's logo, along with player information and complete Major League stats. Four update cards were later added to the set.

		MT	NR MT	EX
Complete Set:		18.00	13.50	7.25
Common Player:		.20	.15	.08
1	Mookie Wilson	.35	.25	.14
2	Mackey Sasser	.25	.20	.10
3	Bud Harrelson	.20	.15	.08
5	Davey Johnson	.25	.20	.10
7	Juan Samuel	.40	.30	.15
8	Gary Carter	.50	.40	.20
9	Gregg Jefferies	2.00	1.50	.80
12	Ron Darling	.50	.40	.20
13	Lee Mazzilli	.20	.15	.08
16	Dwight Gooden	1.75	1.50	.70
17	Keith Hernandez	.60	.45	.25
18	Darryl Strawberry	1.25	.90	.50
19	Bob Ojeda	.25	.20	.10
20	Howard Johnson	.70	.50	.30
21	Kevin Elster	.35	.25	.14
22	Kevin McReynolds	.50	.40	.20
28	Bill Robinson	.20	.15	.08
29	Dave Magadan	.30	.25	.12
30	Mel Stottlemyre	.20	.15	.08
32	Mark Carreon	.40	.30	.15
33	Barry Lyons	.20	.15	.08
34	Sam Perlozzo	.20	.15	.08
38	Rick Aguilera	.20	.15	.08
44	David Cone	.50	.40	.20
46	Dave West	.60	.45	.25
48	Randy Myers	.35	.25	.14
50	Sid Fernandez	.35	.25	.14
51	Don Aase	.20	.15	.08
52	Greg Pavlick	.20	.15	.08
---	Team Card	.20	.15	.08
U)	Jeff Innis, Keith Miller, Jeff Musselman, Frank Viola	1.50	1.25	.60

1989 Kahn's Wieners Reds

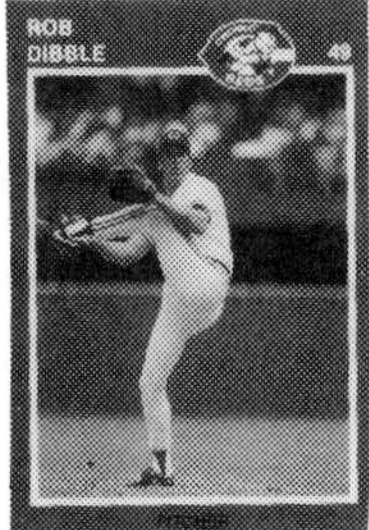

This 26-card Cincinnati Reds team set, sponsored by Kahn's Wieners, was distributed to fans attending the Aug. 6 Reds game at Riverfront Stadium. The standard-size, red-bordered cards feature action photos with the player's name in the upper left corner, his uniform number in the upper right and the Reds logo in the middle. The backs include a black-and-white head shot, player data and complete major and minor league stats. The Kahn's logo appears in the upper right corner of the back.

		MT	NR MT	EX
Complete Set:		10.00	7.50	4.00
Common Player:		.20	.15	.08
6	Bo Diaz	.20	.15	.08
7	Lenny Harris	.40	.30	.15
11	Barry Larkin	.50	.40	.20
12	Joel Youngblood	.20	.15	.08
14	Pete Rose	1.00	.70	.40
16	Ron Oester	.25	.20	.10
17	Chris Sabo	.40	.30	.15
20	Danny Jackson	.25	.20	.15
21	Paul O'Neill	.25	.20	.15
25	Todd Benzinger	.40	.30	.15
27	Jose Rijo	.25	.20	.10
28	Kal Daniels	.40	.30	.15
29	Herm Winningham	.20	.15	.08
30	Ken Griffey	.30	.25	.12
31	John Franco	.30	.25	.12
32	Tom Browning	.35	.25	.14
33	Ron Robinson	.20	.15	.08
34	Jeff Reed	.20	.15	.08
36	Rolando Roomes	.70	.50	.30
37	Norm Charlton	.50	.40	.20
42	Rick Mahler	.25	.20	.10
43	Kent Tekulve	.20	.15	.08
44	Eric Davis	2.00	1.50	.80
48	Tim Birtsas	.20	.15	.08
49	Rob Dibble	.60	.45	.25
---	Coaches Card	.20	.15	.08

1986 Kas Potato Chips

One of a handful of 2-7/8" round baseball card "discs" created by Mike Schecter Associates for inclusion in boxes of potato chips, the 20-card Kas set features players of the defending National League Champion St. Louis Cardinals. Fronts feature color photo on which the team logos have been removed from the caps by airbrushing the photos, indicating Kas did not license with the Cardinals for use of its uniform logos. Card backs have minimal personal data and 1985 stats.

	MT	NR MT	EX
Complete Set:	18.00	13.50	7.25
Common Player:	.70	.50	.30

		MT	NR MT	EX
1	Vince Coleman	2.25	1.75	.90
2	Ken Dayley	.70	.50	.30
3	Tito Landrum	.70	.50	.30
4	Steve Braun	.70	.50	.30
5	Danny Cox	1.25	.90	.50
6	Bob Forsch	.80	.60	.30
7	Ozzie Smith	1.50	1.25	.60
8	Brian Harper	.70	.50	.30
9	Jack Clark	1.50	1.25	.60
10	Todd Worrell	2.25	1.75	.90
11	Joaquin Andujar	.70	.50	.30
12	Tom Nieto	.70	.50	.30
13	Kurt Kepshire	.70	.50	.30
14	Terry Pendleton	1.00	.70	.40
15	Tom Herr	1.00	.70	.40
16	Darrell Porter	.70	.50	.30
17	John Tudor	1.00	.70	.40
18	Jeff Lahti	.70	.50	.30
19	Andy Van Slyke	1.25	.90	.50
20	Willie McGee	1.50	1.25	.60

1986 Kay Bee

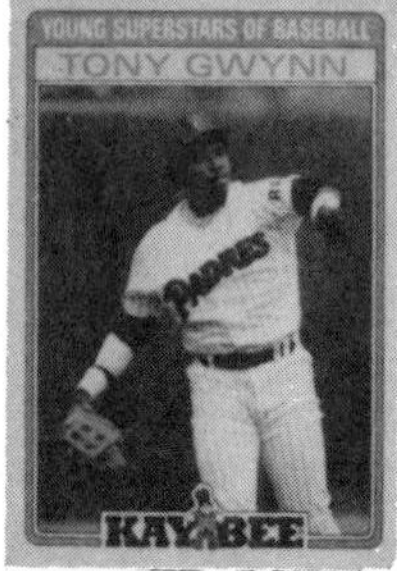

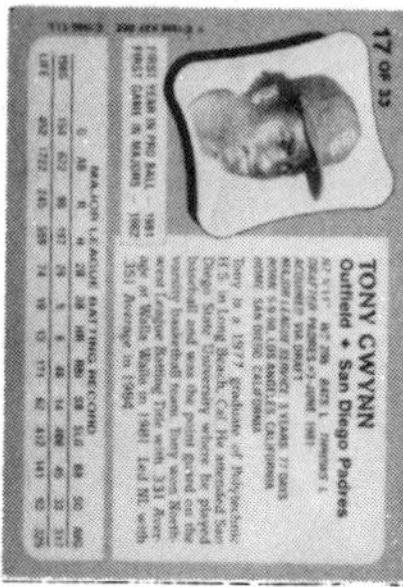

One of the most-widely distributed of the specialty boxed sets of 1986, the Kay Bee toy store chain sets of "Young Superstars of Baseball" was produced by Topps. The 2-1/2" by 3-1/2" cards are printed on white stock with a glossy surface finish. Backs, printed in red and black, are strongly reminiscent of the 1971 Topps cards. While the set concentrated on "young" stars of the game, few of the year's top rookies were included.

		MT	NR MT	EX
	Complete Set:	5.00	3.75	2.00
	Common Player:	.05	.04	.02
1	Rick Aguilera	.12	.09	.05
2	Chris Brown	.15	.11	.06
3	Tom Browning	.07	.05	.03
4	Tom Brunansky	.07	.05	.03
5	Vince Coleman	.50	.40	.20
6	Ron Darling	.10	.08	.04
7	Alvin Davis	.10	.08	.04
8	Mariano Duncan	.07	.05	.03
9	Shawon Dunston	.07	.05	.03
10	Sid Fernandez	.10	.08	.04
11	Tony Fernandez	.10	.08	.04
12	Brian Fisher	.10	.08	.04
13	John Franco	.07	.05	.03
14	Julio Franco	.10	.08	.04
15	Dwight Gooden	.50	.40	.20
16	Ozzie Guillen	.15	.11	.06
17	Tony Gwynn	.30	.25	.12
18	Jimmy Key	.10	.08	.04
19	Don Mattingly	1.75	1.25	.70
20	Oddibe McDowell	.15	.11	.06
21	Roger McDowell	.15	.11	.06
22	Dan Pasqua	.10	.08	.04
23	Terry Pendleton	.07	.05	.03
24	Jim Presley	.10	.08	.04
25	Kirby Puckett	.25	.20	.10
26	Earnie Riles	.07	.05	.03
27	Bret Saberhagen	.15	.11	.06
28	Mark Salas	.05	.04	.02
29	Juan Samuel	.12	.09	.05
30	Jeff Stone	.05	.04	.02
31	Darryl Strawberry	.40	.30	.15
32	Andy Van Slyke	.10	.08	.04
33	Frank Viola	.12	.09	.05

1987 Kay Bee

For a second straight year, Topps produced a 33- card set for the Kay Bee toy store chain. Called "Superstars of Baseball," the cards in the set measure the standard 2-1/2" by 3-1/2" size. The glossy-coated card fronts carry a full-color player photo plus the Kay Bee logo. The card backs, reminiscent of those found in the 1971 Topps set, offer a black and white head shot of the player along with his name, position, personal information, playing record and a brief biography. The set was packaged in a specially designed box.

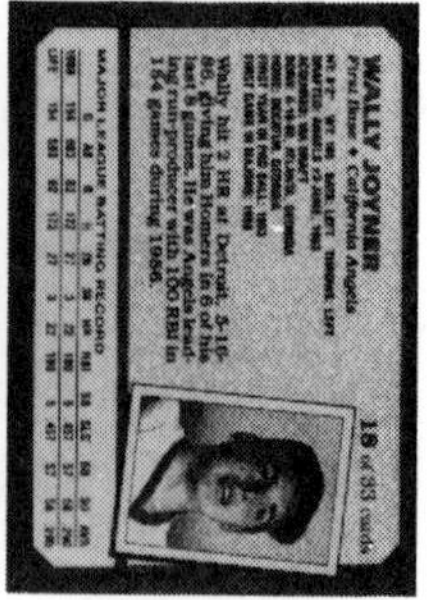

		MT	NR MT	EX
	Complete Set:	5.00	3.75	2.00
	Common Player:	.05	.04	.02
1	Harold Baines	.10	.08	.04
2	Jesse Barfield	.12	.09	.05
3	Don Baylor	.10	.08	.04
4	Wade Boggs	1.00	.70	.40
5	George Brett	.40	.30	.15
6	Hubie Brooks	.07	.05	.03
7	Jose Canseco	1.00	.70	.40
8	Gary Carter	.20	.15	.08
9	Joe Carter	.12	.09	.05
10	Roger Clemens	.40	.30	.15
11	Vince Coleman	.15	.11	.06
12	Glenn Davis	.15	.11	.06
13	Dwight Gooden	.40	.30	.15
14	Pedro Guerrero	.15	.11	.06
15	Tony Gwynn	.25	.20	.10
16	Rickey Henderson	.25	.20	.10
17	Keith Hernandez	.20	.15	.08
18	Wally Joyner	.50	.40	.20
19	Don Mattingly	1.75	1.25	.70
20	Jack Morris	.15	.11	.06
21	Dale Murphy	.30	.25	.12
22	Eddie Murray	.25	.20	.10
23	Dave Parker	.15	.11	.06
24	Kirby Puckett	.25	.20	.10
25	Tim Raines	.25	.20	.10
26	Jim Rice	.25	.20	.10
27	Dave Righetti	.12	.09	.05
28	Ryne Sandberg	.20	.15	.08
29	Mike Schmidt	.30	.25	.12
30	Mike Scott	.12	.09	.05
31	Darryl Strawberry	.40	.30	.15
32	Fernando Valenzuela	.20	.15	.08
33	Dave Winfield	.20	.15	.08

1988 Kay Bee

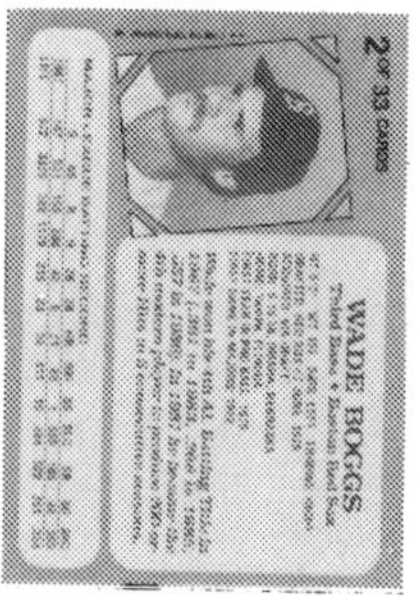

This 33-card boxed set was produced by Topps for exclusive distribution via Kay Bee toy stores nationwide. Card fronts are super glossy and feature full-color player action photos below a bright red and yellow player name banner. Photos are framed in green above a large, cartoon-style Kay Bee logo. Card backs feature player closeups in a horizontal layout in blue ink on a green and white background. Card backs are numbered and carry a player name section that includes biographical information, career data and major league batting stats.

		MT	NR MT	EX
	Complete Set:	5.00	3.75	2.00
	Common Player:	.10	.08	.04
1	George Bell	.20	.15	.08
2	Wade Boggs	1.00	.70	.40
3	Jose Canseco	1.00	.70	.40
4	Joe Carter	.12	.09	.05
5	Jack Clark	.15	.11	.06
6	Alvin Davis	.10	.08	.04
7	Eric Davis	.80	.60	.30
8	Andre Dawson	.15	.11	.06
9	Darrell Evans	.10	.08	.04
10	Dwight Evans	.10	.08	.04
11	Gary Gaetti	.12	.09	.05
12	Pedro Guerrero	.15	.11	.06
13	Tony Gwynn	.25	.20	.10
14	Howard Johnson	.12	.09	.05
15	Wally Joyner	.30	.25	.12
16	Don Mattingly	1.75	1.25	.70
17	Willie McGee	.10	.08	.04
18	Mark McGwire	1.00	.70	.40
19	Paul Molitor	.12	.09	.05
20	Dale Murphy	.30	.25	.12
21	Dave Parker	.15	.11	.06
22	Lance Parrish	.15	.11	.06
23	Kirby Puckett	.25	.20	.10
24	Tim Raines	.25	.20	.10
25	Cal Ripken	.30	.25	.12
26	Juan Samuel	.12	.09	.05
27	Mike Schmidt	.30	.25	.12
28	Ruben Sierra	.12	.09	.05
29	Darryl Strawberry	.40	.30	.15
30	Danny Tartabull	.12	.09	.05
31	Alan Trammell	.15	.11	.06
32	Tim Wallach	.10	.08	.04
33	Dave Winfield	.20	.15	.08

1988 Kay Bee

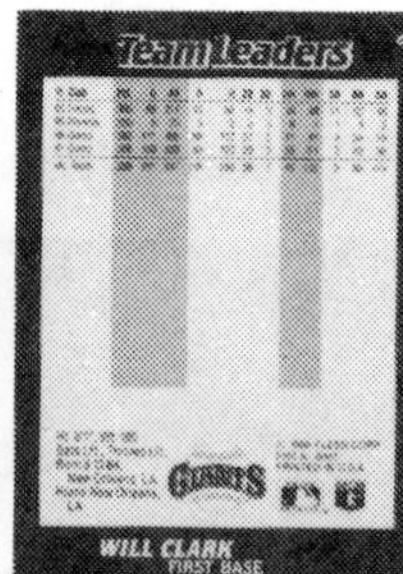

This first-year boxed edition of 44 player and 6 team logo cards was produced by Fleer for distribution by Kay Bee toy stores nationwide. Full-color player photos are framed in black against a bright red border. Lettering is blue, yellow and black. The "Fleer Team Leaders 1988" logo is printed vertically along the left side of the card front; the Kay Bee logo appears in the lower right corner of the photo; player's name, team and position are centered in the bottom margin. Card backs (red, white and pink) repeat the Team Leaders logo, followed by stats, personal data, team and major league baseball logos. The player's name, card number and position are listed on the lower border. The set includes six team logo sticker cards that feature black and white stadium photos on the backs.

		MT	NR MT	EX
	Complete Set:	5.00	3.75	2.00
	Common Player:	.05	.04	.02
1	George Bell	.20	.15	.08
2	Wade Boggs	1.00	.70	.40
3	Jose Canseco	1.00	.70	.40
4	Will Clark	.25	.20	.10
5	Roger Clemens	.40	.30	.15
6	Eric Davis	.80	.60	.30
7	Andre Dawson	.15	.11	.06
8	Julio Franco	.07	.05	.03
9	Andres Galarraga	.15	.11	.06
10	Dwight Gooden	.40	.30	.15
11	Tony Gwynn	.25	.20	.10
12	Tom Henke	.05	.04	.02
13	Orel Hershiser	.10	.08	.04
14	Kent Hrbek	.15	.11	.06
15	Ted Higuera	.10	.08	.04
16	Wally Joyner	.30	.25	.12
17	Jimmy Key	.07	.05	.03
18	Mark Langston	.10	.08	.04
19	Don Mattingly	1.75	1.25	.70
20	Willie McGee	.10	.08	.04
21	Mark McGwire	1.00	.70	.40
22	Paul Molitor	.12	.09	.05
23	Jack Morris	.12	.09	.05
24	Dale Murphy	.30	.25	.12
25	Larry Parrish	.05	.04	.02
26	Kirby Puckett	.20	.15	.08
27	Tim Raines	.20	.15	.08
28	Jeff Reardon	.07	.05	.03
29	Dave Righetti	.12	.09	.05
30	Cal Ripken, Jr.	.30	.25	.12
31	Don Robinson	.05	.04	.02
32	Bret Saberhagen	.15	.11	.06
33	Juan Samuel	.12	.09	.05
34	Mike Schmidt	.30	.25	.12
35	Mike Scott	.12	.09	.05
36	Kevin Seitzer	.60	.45	.25
37	Dave Smith	.05	.04	.02
38	Ozzie Smith	.15	.11	.06
39	Zane Smith	.05	.04	.02
40	Darryl Strawberry	.40	.30	.15
41	Rick Sutcliffe	.10	.08	.04
42	Bobby Thigpen	.07	.05	.03
43	Alan Trammell	.15	.11	.06
44	Andy Van Slyke	.10	.08	.04

1989 Kay-Bee Superstars

The top stars of baseball were featured in this 33-card boxed set produced by Topps for the Kay-Bee Toy store chain. The glossy, standard-size cards display the Kee-Bee logo below the player photo on the front. The top of the card is headlined "Superstars of Baseball," with the player's name underneath. The backs of the cards include a small black-and-white player photo and personal data.

		MT	NR MT	EX
Complete Set:		5.00	3.75	2.00
Common Player:		.10	.08	.04
1	Wade Boggs	1.00	.70	.40
2	George Brett	.15	.11	.08
3	Jose Canseco	1.00	.70	.40
4	Gary Carter	.10	.08	.04
5	Jack Clark	.10	.08	.04
6	Will Clark	1.00	.70	.40
7	Roger Clemens	.25	.20	.10
8	Eric Davis	.60	.45	.25
9	Andre Dawson	.15	.11	.06
10	Dwight Evans	.10	.08	.04
11	Carlton Fisk	.10	.08	.04
12	Andres Galarraga	.10	.08	.04
13	Kirk Gibson	.10	.08	.04
14	Doc Gooden	.30	.25	.12
15	Mike Greenwell	.30	.25	.12
16	Pedro Guerrero	.15	.11	.08
17	Tony Gwynn	.25	.20	.10
18	Rickey Henderson	.25	.20	.10
19	Orel Hershiser	.15	.11	.06
20	Don Mattingly	1.25	.90	.50
21	Mark McGwire	.90	.70	.35
22	Dale Murphy	.20	.15	.08
23	Eddie Murray	.15	.11	.06
24	Kirby Puckett	.25	.20	.10
25	Rock Raines	.15	.11	.06
26	Ryne Sanberg	.15	.11	.06
27	Mike Schmidt	.30	.25	.12
28	Ozzie Smith	.10	.08	.04
29	Darryl Strawberry	.30	.25	.12
30	Alan Trammell	.12	.09	.05
31	Frank Viola	.12	.09	.05
32	Dave Winfield	.12	.09	.05
33	Robin Yount			

The values quoted are intended to reflect the market price.

1986 Keller's Butter Phillies

It's a good thing the Keller's Butter set of six Philadelphia Phillies players is downright unattractive or their value would be sky high. One card was printed on each one pound package of butter. The 2-1/2" by 2-3/4" cards feature crude drawings of the players. The backs are blank.

		MT	NR MT	EX
Complete Set:		18.00	9.00	5.50
Common Player:		1.00	.70	.40
(1)	Steve Carlton	4.00	2.00	1.25
(2)	Von Hayes	3.00	1.50	.90
(3)	Gary Redus	1.00	.70	.40
(4)	Juan Samuel	3.00	1.50	.90
(5)	Mike Schmidt	8.00	4.00	2.50
(6)	Glenn Wilson	1.50	1.25	.60

1970 Kellogg's

For 14 years in the 1970s and early 1980s, the Kellogg's cereal company provided Topps with virtually the only meaningful national competition in the baseball card market. Kellogg's kicked off its baseball card program in 1970 with a 75-player set of simulated 3-D cards. Single cards were available in selected brands of the company's cereal, while a mail-in program offered complete sets. The 3-D effect was achieved by the sandwiching of a clear color player photo between

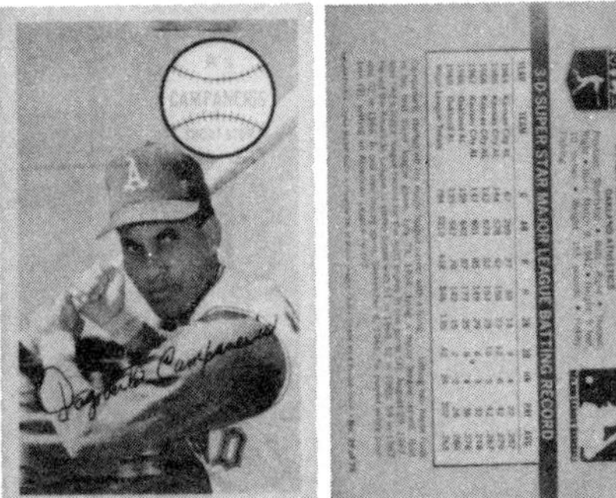

a purposely blurred stadium background scene and a layer of ribbed plastic. The relatively narrow dimension of the card, 2-1/4" by 3-1/2" and the nature of the plastic overlay seem to conspire to cause the cards to curl, often cracking the plastic layer, if not stored properly. Cards with major cracks in the plastic can be considered in Fair condition, at best.

		NR MT	EX	VG
Complete Set:		150.00	75.00	45.00
Common Player: 1-15		.80	.40	.25
Common Player: 16-30		.90	.45	.25
Common Player: 31-75		.80	.40	.25
1	Ed Kranepool	1.50	.70	.45
2	Pete Rose	20.00	10.00	6.00
3	Cleon Jones	.80	.40	.25
4	Willie McCovey	3.50	1.75	1.00
5	Mel Stottlemyre	1.00	.50	.30
6	Frank Howard	1.25	.60	.40
7	Tom Seaver	5.00	2.50	1.50
8	Don Sutton	2.50	1.25	.70
9	Jim Wynn	.80	.40	.25
10	Jim Maloney	.80	.40	.25
11	Tommie Agee	.80	.40	.25
12	Willie Mays	8.00	4.00	2.50
13	Juan Marichal	3.00	1.50	.90
14	Dave McNally	.90	.45	.25
15	Frank Robinson	3.50	1.75	1.00
16	Carlos May	1.00	.50	.30
17	Bill Singer	1.00	.50	.30
18	Rick Reichardt	1.00	.50	.30
19	Boog Powell	1.50	.70	.45
20	Gaylord Perry	3.50	1.75	1.00
21	Brooks Robinson	6.00	3.00	1.75
22	Luis Aparicio	3.50	1.75	1.00
23	Joel Horlen	1.00	.50	.30
24	Mike Epstein	1.00	.50	.30
25	Tom Haller	1.00	.50	.30
26	Willie Crawford	1.00	.50	.30
27	Roberto Clemente	10.00	5.00	3.00
28	Matty Alou	1.25	.60	.40
29	Willie Stargell	4.00	2.00	1.25
30	Tim Cullen	1.00	.50	.30
31	Randy Hundley	.80	.40	.25
32	Reggie Jackson	6.50	3.25	2.00
33	Rich Allen	1.25	.60	.40
34	Tim McCarver	1.00	.50	.30
35	Ray Culp	.80	.40	.25
36	Jim Fregosi	.90	.45	.25
37	Billy Williams	3.00	1.50	.90
38	Johnny Odom	.80	.40	.25
39	Bert Campaneris	.90	.45	.25
40	Ernie Banks	3.50	1.75	1.00
41	Chris Short	.80	.40	.25
42	Ron Santo	.90	.45	.25
43	Glenn Beckert	.80	.40	.25
44	Lou Brock	3.50	1.75	1.00
45	Larry Hisle	.80	.40	.25
46	Reggie Smith	.90	.45	.25
47	Rod Carew	4.00	2.00	1.25
48	Curt Flood	.90	.45	.25
49	Jim Lonborg	.80	.40	.25
50	Sam McDowell	.90	.45	.25
51	Sal Bando	.90	.45	.25
52	Al Kaline	4.00	2.00	1.25
53	Gary Nolan	.80	.40	.25
54	Rico Petrocelli	.80	.40	.25
55	Ollie Brown	.80	.40	.25
56	Luis Tiant	1.25	.60	.40
57	Bill Freehan	.90	.45	.25
58	Johnny Bench	5.00	2.50	1.50
59	Joe Pepitone	.90	.45	.25
60	Bobby Murcer	1.00	.50	.30
61	Harmon Killebrew	3.50	1.75	1.00
62	Don Wilson	.80	.40	.25
63	Tony Oliva	1.25	.60	.40
64	Jim Perry	.90	.45	.25
65	Mickey Lolich	1.25	.60	.40
66	Coco Laboy	.80	.40	.25
67	Dean Chance	.80	.40	.25
68	Ken Harrelson	.90	.45	.25
69	Willie Horton	.90	.45	.25
70	Wally Bunker	.80	.40	.25
71a	Bob Gibson (1959 IP blank)	5.00	2.50	1.50
71b	Bob Gibson (1959 IP 76)	3.00	1.50	.90
72	Joe Morgan	3.00	1.50	.90
73	Denny McLain	1.25	.60	.40
74	Tommy Harper	.80	.40	.25
75	Don Mincher	1.25	.60	.40

1971 Kellogg's

The scarcest and most valuable of the Kellogg's editions, the 75-card 1971 set was the only one not offered by the company on a mail-in basis; the

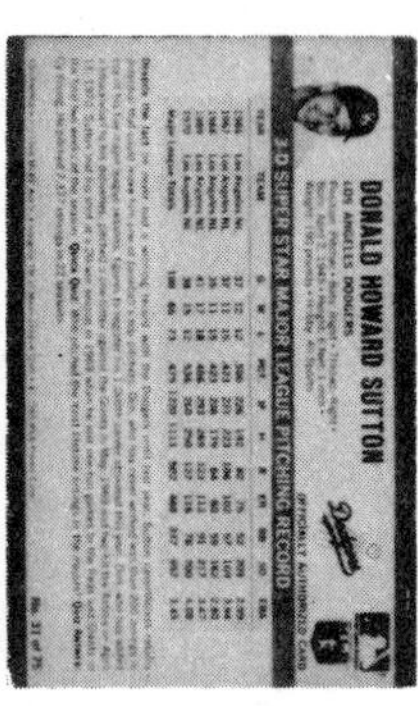

only way to complete it was to buy ... and buy and buy ... boxes of cereal. Kellogg's again used the simulated 3-D effect in the cards' design, with the same result being many of the 2-1/4" by 3-1/2" cards are found today with cracks resulting from the cards' curling. A number of scarcer back variations are checklisted below. In addition, all 75 cards can be found with and without the 1970 date before the "Xograph" copyright line on the back; though there is no difference in value.

		NR MT	EX	VG
Complete Set:		800.00	400.00	240.00
Common Player:		8.00	4.00	2.50
1a	Wayne Simpson (SO 120)	12.00	6.00	3.50
1b	Wayne Simpson (SO 119)	15.00	7.50	4.50
2	Tom Seaver	30.00	15.00	9.00
3a	Jim Perry (IP 2238)	10.00	5.00	3.00
3b	Jim Perry (IP 2239)	15.00	7.50	4.50
4a	Bob Robertson (RBI 94)	8.00	4.00	2.50
4b	Bob Robertson (RBI 95)	12.00	6.00	3.50
5	Roberto Clemente	35.00	17.50	10.50
6a	Gaylord Perry (IP 2014)	15.00	7.50	4.50
6b	Gaylord Perry (IP 2015)	20.00	10.00	6.00
7a	Felipe Alou (1970 Oakland NL)	15.00	7.50	4.50
7b	Felipe Alou (1970 Oakland AL)	10.00	5.00	3.00
8	Denis Menke	8.00	4.00	2.50
9a	Don Kessinger (Hits 849)	10.00	5.00	3.00
9b	Don Kessinger (Hits 850)	15.00	7.50	4.50
10	Willie Mays	35.00	17.50	10.50
11	Jim Hickman	8.00	4.00	2.50
12	Tony Oliva	12.00	6.00	3.50
13	Manny Sanguillen	8.00	4.00	2.50
14a	Frank Howard (1968 Washington NL)	18.00	9.00	5.50
14b	Frank Howard (1968 Washington AL)	12.00	6.00	3.50
15	Frank Robinson	25.00	12.50	7.50
16	Willie Davis	10.00	5.00	3.00
17	Lou Brock	20.00	10.00	6.00
18	Cesar Tovar	8.00	4.00	2.50
19	Luis Aparicio	15.00	7.50	4.50
20	Boog Powell	12.00	6.00	3.50
21a	Dick Selma (SO 584)	8.00	4.00	2.50
21b	Dick Selma (SO 587)	12.00	6.00	3.50
22	Danny Walton	8.00	4.00	2.50
23	Carl Morton	8.00	4.00	2.50
24a	Sonny Siebert (SO 1054)	8.00	4.00	2.50
24b	Sonny Siebert (SO 1055)	12.00	6.00	3.50
25	Jim Merritt	8.00	4.00	2.50
26a	Jose Cardenal (Hits 828)	8.00	4.00	2.50
26b	Jose Cardenal (Hits 829)	12.00	6.00	3.50
27	Don Mincher	8.00	4.00	2.50
28a	Clyde Wright (California state logo)	8.00	4.00	2.50
28b	Clyde Wright (Angels crest logo)	12.00	6.00	3.50
29	Les Cain	8.00	4.00	2.50
30	Danny Cater	8.00	4.00	2.50
31	Don Sutton	15.00	7.50	4.50
32	Chuck Dobson	8.00	4.00	2.50
33	Willie McCovey	20.00	10.00	6.00
34	Mike Epstein	8.00	4.00	2.50
35a	Paul Blair (Runs 386)	8.00	4.00	2.50
35b	Paul Blair (Runs 385)	12.00	6.00	3.50
36a	Gary Nolan (SO 577)	8.00	4.00	2.50
36b	Gary Nolan (SO 581)	12.00	6.00	3.50
37	Sam McDowell	10.00	5.00	3.00
38	Amos Otis	10.00	5.00	3.00
39a	Ray Fosse (RBI 69)	8.00	4.00	2.50
39b	Ray Fosse (RBI 70)	12.00	6.00	3.50
40	Mel Stottlemyre	10.00	5.00	3.00
41	Cito Gaston	8.00	4.00	2.50
42	Dick Dietz	8.00	4.00	2.50
43	Roy White	10.00	5.00	3.00
44	Al Kaline	25.00	12.50	7.50
45	Carlos May	8.00	4.00	2.50
46a	Tommie Agee (RBI 313)	8.00	4.00	2.50
46b	Tommie Agee (RBI 314)	12.00	6.00	3.50
47	Tommy Harper	8.00	4.00	2.50
48	Larry Dierker	8.00	4.00	2.50
49	Mike Cuellar	10.00	5.00	3.00
50	Ernie Banks	25.00	12.50	7.50
51	Bob Gibson	20.00	10.00	6.00
52	Reggie Smith	10.00	5.00	3.00
53a	Matty Alou (RBI 273)	10.00	5.00	3.00
53b	Matty Alou (RBI 274)	15.00	7.50	4.50
54a	Alex Johnson (California state logo)	8.00	4.00	2.50
54b	Alex Johnson (Angels crest logo)	12.00	6.00	3.50
55	Harmon Killebrew	20.00	10.00	6.00
56	Billy Grabarkewitz	8.00	4.00	2.50
57	Rich Allen	12.00	6.00	3.50
58	Tony Perez	15.00	7.50	4.50
59a	Dave McNally (SO 1065)	10.00	5.00	3.00
59b	Dave McNally (SO 1067)	15.00	7.50	4.50
60a	Jim Palmer (SO 564)	15.00	7.50	4.50
60b	Jim Palmer (SO 567)	20.00	10.00	6.00
61	Billy Williams	15.00	7.50	4.50

		NR MT	EX	VG
62	Joe Torre	12.00	6.00	3.50
63a	Jim Northrup (AB 2773)	8.00	4.00	2.50
63b	Jim Northrup (AB 2772)	12.00	6.00	3.50
64a	Jim Fregosi (Calif. state logo - Hits 1326)	8.00	4.00	2.50
64b	Jim Fregosi (Calif. state logo - Hits 1327)	12.00	6.00	3.50
64c	Jim Fregosi (Angels crest logo)	12.00	6.00	3.50
65	Pete Rose	75.00	37.00	22.00
66a	Bud Harrelson (RBI 112)	8.00	4.00	2.50
66b	Bud Harrelson (RBI 113)	12.00	6.00	3.50
67	Tony Taylor	8.00	4.00	2.50
68	Willie Stargell	20.00	10.00	6.00
69	Tony Horton	8.50	4.25	2.50
70a	Claude Osteen (no number)	20.00	10.00	6.00
70b	Claude Osteen (#70 on back)	8.00	4.00	2.50
71	Glenn Beckert	10.00	5.00	3.00
72	Nate Colbert	8.00	4.00	2.50
73a	Rick Monday (AB 1705)	10.00	5.00	3.00
73b	Rick Monday (AB 1704)	15.00	7.50	4.50
74a	Tommy John (BB 444)	15.00	7.50	4.50
74b	Tommy John (BB 443)	20.00	10.00	6.00
75	Chris Short	12.00	6.00	3.50

1972 Kellogg's

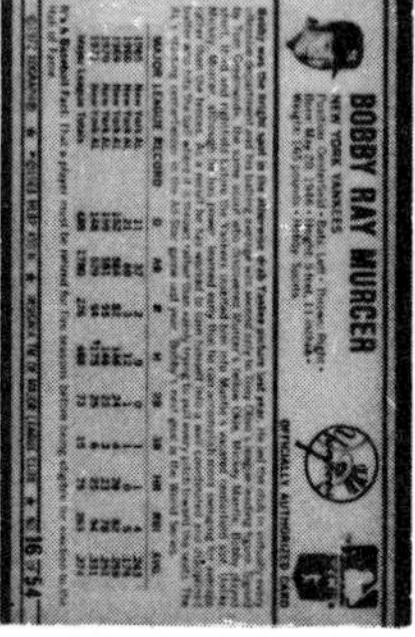

For 1972, Kellogg's reduced both the number of cards in its set and the dimensions of each card, moving to a 2-1/8" by 3-1/4" size and fixing the set at 54 cards. Once again, the cards were produced to simulate a 3-D effect (see description for 1970 Kellogg's). The set was available via a mail-in offer. The checklist includes variations which resulted from the correction of erroneous statistics on the backs of some cards. The complete set values quoted do not include the scarcer variations.

	NR MT	EX	VG
Complete Set:	55.00	27.00	16.50
Common Player:	.70	.35	.20

		NR MT	EX	VG
1a	Tom Seaver (1970 ERA 2.85)	9.00	4.50	2.75
1b	Tom Seaver (1970 ERA 2.81)	6.50	3.25	2.00
2	Amos Otis	.80	.40	.25
3a	Willie Davis (Runs 842)	1.25	.60	.40
3b	Willie Davis (Runs 841)	.80	.40	.25
4	Wilbur Wood	.80	.40	.25
5	Bill Parsons	.70	.35	.20
6	Pete Rose	20.00	10.00	6.00
7a	Willie McCovey (HR 360)	5.00	2.50	1.50
7b	Willie McCovey (HR 370)	3.50	1.75	1.00
8	Fergie Jenkins	1.25	.60	.40
9a	Vida Blue (ERA 2.35)	1.50	.70	.45
9b	Vida Blue (ERA 2.31)	.90	.45	.25
10	Joe Torre	.90	.45	.25
11	Merv Rettenmund	.70	.35	.20
12	Bill Melton	.70	.35	.20
13a	Jim Palmer (Games 170)	4.75	2.50	1.50
13b	Jim Palmer (Games 168)	3.00	1.50	.90
14	Doug Rader	.70	.35	.20
15a	Dave Roberts (...Seaver, the NL leader...)	1.25	.60	.40
15b	Dave Roberts (...Seaver, the league leader...)	.70	.35	.20
16	Bobby Murcer	.80	.40	.25
17	Wes Parker	.70	.35	.20
18a	Joe Coleman (BB 394)	1.25	.60	.40
18b	Joe Coleman (BB 393)	.70	.35	.20
19	Manny Sanguillen	.70	.35	.20
20	Reggie Jackson	4.50	2.25	1.25
21	Ralph Garr	.70	.35	.20
22	Jim "Catfish" Hunter	2.50	1.25	.70
23	Rick Wise	.70	.35	.20
24	Glenn Beckert	.70	.35	.20
25	Tony Oliva	.90	.45	.25
26a	Bob Gibson (SO 2577)	4.75	2.50	1.50
26b	Bob Gibson (SO 2578)	3.00	1.50	.90
27a	Mike Cuellar (1971 ERA 3.80)	1.25	.60	.40
27b	Mike Cuellar (1971 ERA 3.08)	.80	.40	.25
28	Chris Speier	.70	.35	.20
29a	Dave McNally (ERA 3.18)	1.25	.60	.40
29b	Dave McNally (ERA 3.15)	.80	.40	.25
30	Chico Cardenas	.70	.35	.20
31a	Bill Freehan (AVG. .263)	1.25	.60	.40
31b	Bill Freehan (AVG. .262)	.80	.40	.25
32a	Bud Harrelson (Hits 634)	1.25	.60	.40
32b	Bud Harrelson (Hits 624)	.70	.35	.20
33a	Sam McDowell (...less than 200 innings...)	1.25	.60	.40
33b	Sam McDowell (...less than 225 innings...)	.80	.40	.25
34a	Claude Osteen (1971 ERA 3.25)	1.25	.60	.40
34b	Claude Osteen (1971 ERA 3.51)	.70	.35	.20
35	Reggie Smith	.80	.40	.25
36	Sonny Siebert	.70	.35	.20
37	Lee May	.80	.40	.25
38	Mickey Lolich	.90	.45	.25
39a	Cookie Rojas (2B 149)	1.25	.60	.40
39b	Cookie Rojas (2B 150)	.70	.35	.20
40	Dick Drago	.70	.35	.20
41	Nate Colbert	.70	.35	.20
42	Andy Messersmith	.70	.35	.20
43a	Dave Johnson (AVG. .262)	1.50	.70	.45
43b	Dave Johnson (AVG. .264)	.90	.45	.25
44	Steve Blass	.70	.35	.20
45	Bob Robertson	.70	.35	.20
46a	Billy Williams (...missed only one last season...)	5.00	2.50	1.50
46b	Billy Williams (phrase omitted)	3.00	1.50	.90
47	Juan Marichal	3.00	1.50	.90
48	Lou Brock	3.50	1.75	1.00
49	Roberto Clemente	7.00	3.50	2.00
50	Mel Stottlemyre	.80	.40	.25
51	Don Wilson	.70	.35	.20
52a	Sal Bando (RBI 355)	1.25	.60	.40
52b	Sal Bando (RBI 356)	.80	.40	.25
53a	Willie Stargell (2B 197)	5.00	2.50	1.50
53b	Willie Stargell (2B 196)	3.00	1.50	.90
54a	Willie Mays (RBI 1855)	12.00	6.00	3.50
54b	Willie Mays (RBI 1856)	8.50	4.25	2.50

1972 Kellogg's

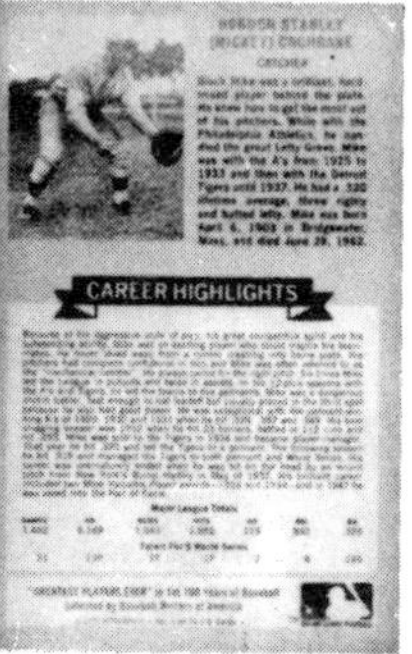

Kellogg's issued a second baseball card set in 1972, inserted into packages of breakfast rolls. The 2-1/4" by 3-1/2" cards also featured a simulated 3-D effect, but the 15 players in the set were "All-Time Baseball Greats", rather than current players. The set is virtually identical to a Rold Gold pretzel issue of 1970; the only difference being the 1972 copyright date on the back of the Kellog's cards, while the pretzel issue bears a 1970 date. The pretzel cards are considerably scarcer than the Kellogg's.

	NR MT	EX	VG
Complete Set:	15.00	7.50	4.50
Common Player:	.50	.25	.15

		NR MT	EX	VG
1	Walter Johnson	1.25	.60	.40
2	Rogers Hornsby	.80	.40	.25
3	John McGraw	.50	.25	.15
4	Mickey Cochrane	.50	.25	.15
5	George Sisler	.50	.25	.15
6	Babe Ruth	3.50	1.75	1.00
7	Robert "Lefty" Grove	.70	.35	.20
8	Harold "Pie" Traynor	.50	.25	.15
9	Honus Wagner	1.00	.50	.30
10	Eddie Collins	.50	.25	.15
11	Tris Speaker	.70	.35	.20
12	Cy Young	.80	.40	.25
13	Lou Gehrig	2.00	1.00	.60
14	Babe Ruth	3.50	1.75	1.00
15	Ty Cobb	2.00	1.00	.60

1973 Kellogg's

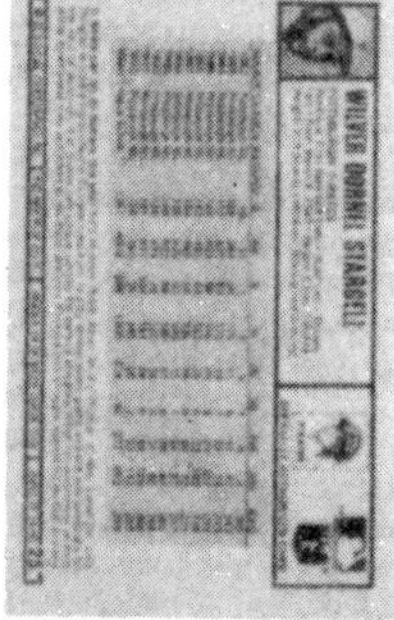

The lone exception to Kellogg's long run of simulated 3-D effect cards came in 1973, when the cereal company's 54-card set was produced by "normal" printing methods. In 2'1/4" by 3-1/2" size, the design was otherwise quite compatible with the issues which preceded and succeeded it. Because it was available via a mail-in offer, it is not as scarce as some other Kellogg's issues.

	NR MT	EX	VG
Complete Set:	55.00	28.00	16.50
Common Player:	.50	.25	.15

		NR MT	EX	VG
1	Amos Otis	.60	.30	.20
2	Ellie Rodriguez	.50	.25	.15
3	Mickey Lolich	.80	.40	.25
4	Tony Oliva	.80	.40	.25
5	Don Sutton	1.25	.60	.40
6	Pete Rose	11.00	5.50	3.25
7	Steve Carlton	4.00	2.00	1.25
8	Bobby Bonds	.70	.35	.20
9	Wilbur Wood	.60	.30	.20
10	Billy Williams	2.50	1.25	.70
11	Steve Blass	.50	.25	.15
12	Jon Matlack	.50	.25	.15
13	Cesar Cedeno	.70	.35	.20
14	Bob Gibson	2.50	1.25	.70
15	Sparky Lyle	.60	.30	.20
16	Nolan Ryan	3.50	1.75	1.00
17	Jim Palmer	2.50	1.25	.70
18	Ray Fosse	.50	.25	.15
19	Bobby Murcer	.60	.30	.20
20	Jim "Catfish" Hunter	2.50	1.25	.70
21	Tug McGraw	.80	.40	.25
22	Reggie Jackson	4.50	2.25	1.25
23	Bill Stoneman	.50	.25	.15
24	Lou Piniella	.80	.40	.25
25	Willie Stargell	2.50	1.25	.70
26	Dick Allen	.90	.45	.25
27	Carlton Fisk	1.25	.60	.40
28	Fergie Jenkins	.90	.45	.25
29	Phil Niekro	1.50	.70	.45
30	Gary Nolan	.50	.25	.15
31	Joe Torre	.80	.40	.25
32	Bobby Tolan	.50	.25	.15
33	Nate Colbert	.50	.25	.15
34	Joe Morgan	2.50	1.25	.70
35	Bert Blyleven	.90	.45	.25
36	Joe Rudi	.60	.30	.20
37	Ralph Garr	.50	.25	.15
38	Gaylord Perry	2.00	1.00	.60
39	Bobby Grich	.60	.30	.20
40	Lou Brock	2.50	1.25	.70
41	Pete Broberg	.50	.25	.15
42	Manny Sanguillen	.50	.25	.15
43	Willie Davis	.60	.30	.20
44	Dave Kingman	.90	.45	.25
45	Carlos May	.50	.25	.15
46	Tom Seaver	4.00	2.00	1.25
47	Mike Cuellar	.60	.30	.20
48	Joe Coleman	.50	.25	.15
49	Claude Osteen	.50	.25	.15
50	Steve Kline	.50	.25	.15
51	Rod Carew	4.00	2.00	1.25
52	Al Kaline	3.50	1.75	1.00
53	Larry Dierker	.50	.25	.15
54	Ron Santo	.70	.35	.20

1974 Kellogg's

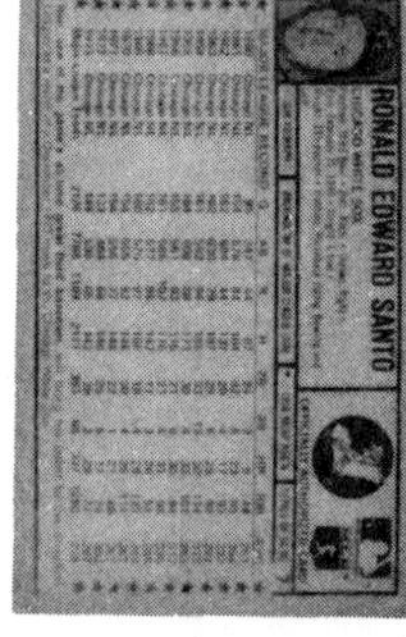

For 1974, Kellogg's returned to the use of simulated 3-D for its 54-player baseball card issue (see 1970 Kellogg's listing for description). In 2-1/8" by 3-1/4" size, the cards were available as a complete set via a mail-in offer.

	NR MT	EX	VG
Complete Set:	55.00	28.00	16.50
Common Player:	.50	.25	.15

		NR MT	EX	VG
1	Bob Gibson	3.50	1.75	1.00
2	Rick Monday	.70	.35	.20
3	Joe Coleman	.50	.25	.15
4	Bert Campaneris	.70	.35	.20
5	Carlton Fisk	1.25	.60	.40
6	Jim Palmer	2.50	1.25	.70
7a	Ron Santo (Chicago Cubs)	1.50	.70	.45
7b	Ron Santo (Chicago White Sox)	.80	.40	.25
8	Nolan Ryan	3.50	1.75	1.00
9	Greg Luzinski	.80	.40	.25
10a	Buddy Bell (Runs 134)	1.50	.70	.45
10b	Buddy Bell (Runs 135)	.80	.40	.25
11	Bob Watson	.50	.25	.15
12	Bill Singer	.50	.25	.15
13	Dave May	.50	.25	.15
14	Jim Brewer	.50	.25	.15

		NR MT	EX	VG
15	Manny Sanguillen	.50	.25	.15
16	Jeff Burroughs	.50	.25	.15
17	Amos Otis	.50	.25	.15
18	Ed Goodson	.50	.25	.15
19	Nate Colbert	.50	.25	.15
20	Reggie Jackson	4.00	2.00	1.25
21	Ted Simmons	.90	.45	.25
22	Bobby Murcer	.60	.30	.20
23	Willie Horton	.60	.30	.20
24	Orlando Cepeda	1.25	.60	.40
25	Ron Hunt	.50	.25	.15
26	Wayne Twitchell	.50	.25	.15
27	Ron Fairly	.50	.25	.15
28	Johnny Bench	3.50	1.75	1.00
29	John Mayberry	.50	.25	.15
30	Rod Carew	3.50	1.75	1.00
31	Ken Holtzman	.50	.25	.15
32	Billy Williams	2.50	1.25	.70
33	Dick Allen	.80	.40	.25
34a	Wilbur Wood (SO 959)	1.25	.60	.40
34b	Wilbur Wood (SO 960)	.70	.35	.20
35	Danny Thompson	.50	.25	.15
36	Joe Morgan	2.50	1.25	.70
37	Willie Stargell	3.00	1.50	.90
38	Pete Rose	13.00	6.50	4.00
39	Bobby Bonds	.70	.35	.20
40	Chris Speier	.50	.25	.15
41	Sparky Lyle	.60	.30	.20
42	Cookie Rojas	.50	.25	.15
43	Tommy Davis	.60	.30	.20
44	Jim "Catfish" Hunter	2.50	1.25	.70
45	Willie Davis	.60	.30	.20
46	Bert Blyleven	.90	.45	.25
47	Pat Kelly	.50	.25	.15
48	Ken Singleton	.60	.30	.20
49	Manny Mota	.60	.30	.20
50	Dave Johnson	.90	.45	.25
51	Sal Bando	.60	.30	.20
52	Tom Seaver	3.50	1.75	1.00
53	Felix Millan	.50	.25	.15
54	Ron Blomberg	.80	.40	.25

1975 Kellogg's

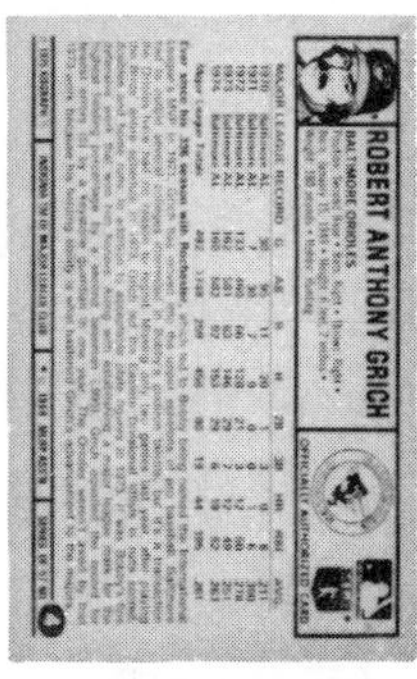

While the card size remained the same at 2-1/8" by 3-1/4", the size of the 1975 Kellogg's "3-D" set was increased by three, to 57 cards. Despite the fact cards could be obtained by a mail-in offer, as well as in cereal boxes, the '75 Kellogg's are noticeably scarcer than the company's other issues, with the exception of the 1971 set. Also helping to raise the value of the cards is the presence of an unusually large number of current and future Hall of Famers.

		NR MT	EX	VG
	Complete Set:	150.00	75.00	45.00
	Common Player:	2.00	1.00	.60
1	Roy White	3.50	1.75	1.00
2	Ross Grimsley	2.00	1.00	.60
3	Reggie Smith	2.50	1.25	.70
4a	Bob Grich ("...1973 work..." in last line)	4.00	2.00	1.25
4b	Bob Grich (no "...1973 work...")	2.50	1.25	.70
5	Greg Gross	2.00	1.00	.60
6	Bob Watson	2.00	1.00	.60
7	Johnny Bench	11.00	5.50	3.25
8	Jeff Burroughs	2.00	1.00	.60
9	Elliott Maddox	2.00	1.00	.60
10	Jon Matlack	2.00	1.00	.60
11	Pete Rose	24.00	12.00	7.25
12	Leroy Stanton	2.00	1.00	.60
13	Bake McBride	2.00	1.00	.60
14	Jorge Orta	2.00	1.00	.60
15	Al Oliver	2.50	1.25	.70
16	John Briggs	2.00	1.00	.60
17	Steve Garvey	9.00	4.50	2.75
18	Brooks Robinson	10.00	5.00	3.00
19	John Hiller	2.00	1.00	.60
20	Lynn McGlothen	2.00	1.00	.60
21	Cleon Jones	2.00	1.00	.60
22	Fergie Jenkins	2.50	1.25	.70
23	Bill North	2.00	1.00	.60
24	Steve Busby	2.00	1.00	.60
25	Richie Zisk	2.00	1.00	.60
26	Nolan Ryan	10.00	5.00	3.00
27	Joe Morgan	6.50	3.25	2.00
28	Joe Rudi	2.50	1.25	.70
29	Jose Cardenal	2.00	1.00	.60
30	Andy Messersmith	2.00	1.00	.60
31	Willie Montanez	2.00	1.00	.60
32	Bill Buckner	2.50	1.25	.70
33	Rod Carew	10.00	5.00	3.00
34	Lou Piniella	2.50	1.25	.70
35	Ralph Garr	2.00	1.00	.60
36	Mike Marshall	2.00	1.00	.60
37	Garry Maddox	2.00	1.00	.60
38	Dwight Evans	3.00	1.50	.90
39	Lou Brock	9.00	4.50	2.75
40	Ken Singleton	2.50	1.25	.70
41	Steve Braun	2.00	1.00	.60
42	Dick Allen	2.50	1.25	.70
43	Johnny Grubb	2.00	1.00	.60
44a	Jim Hunter (Oakland)	12.00	6.00	3.50
44b	Jim Hunter (New York)	8.00	4.00	2.50
45	Gaylord Perry	6.50	3.25	2.00
46	George Hendrick	2.00	1.00	.60
47	Sparky Lyle	2.50	1.25	.70
48	Dave Cash	2.00	1.00	.60
49	Luis Tiant	2.50	1.25	.70
50	Cesar Geronimo	2.00	1.00	.60
51	Carl Yastrzemski	16.00	8.00	4.75
52	Ken Brett	2.00	1.00	.60
53	Hal McRae	2.50	1.25	.70
54	Reggie Jackson	12.00	6.00	3.50
55	Rollie Fingers	3.50	1.75	1.00
56	Mike Schmidt	14.00	7.00	4.25
57	Richie Hebner	2.50	1.25	.70

1976 Kellogg's

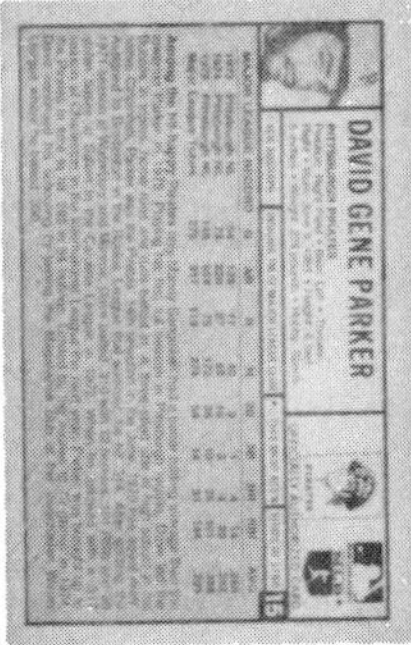

A sizeable list of corrected errors and other variation cards dots the checklist for the 57-card 1976 Kellogg's 3-D set. Again containing 57 cards, the first three cards in the set are found far less often than cards #4-57, indicating they were short-printed in relation to the rest of the set. The complete set values quoted below do not include the scarcer variation cards. Card size remained at 2-1/8" by 3-1/4".

		NR MT	EX	VG
	Complete Set:	70.00	35.00	21.00
	Common Player:	1.25	.60	.40
1	Steve Hargan	10.00	5.00	3.00
2	Claudell Washington	10.00	5.00	3.00
3	Don Gullett	10.00	5.00	3.00
4	Randy Jones	1.25	.60	.40
5	Jim "Catfish" Hunter	6.50	3.25	2.00
6a	Clay Carroll (Cincinnati)	3.00	1.50	.90
6b	Clay Carroll (Chicago)	1.50	.70	.45
7	Joe Rudi	1.50	.70	.45
8	Reggie Jackson	10.00	5.00	3.00
9	Felix Millan	1.25	.60	.40
10	Jim Rice	8.00	4.00	2.50
11	Bert Blyleven	2.50	1.25	.70
12	Ken Singleton	1.50	.70	.45
13	Don Sutton	2.50	1.25	.70
14	Joe Morgan	5.00	2.50	1.50
15	Dave Parker	4.00	2.00	1.25
16	Dave Cash	1.25	.60	.40
17	Ron LeFlore	1.25	.60	.40
18	Greg Luzinski	2.00	1.00	.60
19	Dennis Eckersley	2.25	1.25	.70
20	Bill Madlock	2.25	1.25	.70
21	George Scott	1.25	.60	.40
22	Willie Stargell	6.50	3.25	2.00
23	Al Hrabosky	1.25	.60	.40
24	Carl Yastrzemski	13.00	6.50	4.00
25	Jim Kaat	2.50	1.25	.70
26	Marty Perez	1.25	.60	.40
27	Bob Watson	1.25	.60	.40
28	Eric Soderholm	1.25	.60	.40
29	Bill Lee	1.25	.60	.40
30a	Frank Tanana (1975 ERA 2.63)	2.50	1.25	.70
30b	Frank Tanana (1975 ERA 2.62)	1.50	.70	.45
31	Fred Lynn	3.50	1.75	1.00
32a	Tom Seaver (1967 PCT. 552)	10.00	5.00	3.00
32b	Tom Seaver (1967 Pct. .552)	8.00	4.00	2.50
33	Steve Busby	1.25	.60	.40
34	Gary Carter	10.00	5.00	3.00
35	Rick Wise	1.25	.60	.40
36	Johnny Bench	10.00	5.00	3.00
37	Jim Palmer	8.00	4.00	2.50
38	Bobby Murcer	2.00	1.00	.60
39	Von Joshua	1.25	.60	.40
40	Lou Brock	8.00	4.00	2.50
41a	Mickey Rivers (last line begins "In three...")	2.75	1.50	.80
41b	Mickey Rivers (last line begins "The Yankees...")	1.25	.60	.40
42	Manny Sanguillen	1.25	.60	.40
43	Jerry Reuss	1.50	.70	.45
44	Ken Griffey	1.50	.70	.45
45a	Jorge Orta (AB 1616)	2.25	1.25	.70
45b	Jorge Orta (AB 1615)	1.25	.60	.40
46	John Mayberry	1.25	.60	.40
47a	Vida Blue (2nd line reads "...pitched more innings...")	3.00	1.50	.90
47b	Vida Blue (2nd line reads "...struck out more...")	2.00	1.00	.60
48	Rod Carew	10.00	5.00	3.00
49a	Jon Matlack (1975 ER 87)	2.25	1.25	.70
49b	Jon Matlack (1975 ER 86)	1.25	.60	.40
50	Boog Powell	2.50	1.25	.70
51a	Mike Hargrove (AB 935)	2.25	1.25	.70
51b	Mike Hargrove (AB 934)	1.25	.60	.40
52a	Paul Lindblad (1975 ERA 2.72)	2.25	1.25	.70
52b	Paul Lindblad (1975 ERA 2.73)	1.25	.60	.40
53	Thurman Munson	6.50	3.25	2.00
54	Steve Garvey	8.00	4.00	2.50
55	Pete Rose	18.00	9.00	5.50
56a	Greg Gross (Games 302)	2.25	1.25	.70
56b	Greg Gross (Games 334)	1.25	.60	.40
57	Ted Simmons	2.50	1.25	.70

1977 Kellogg's

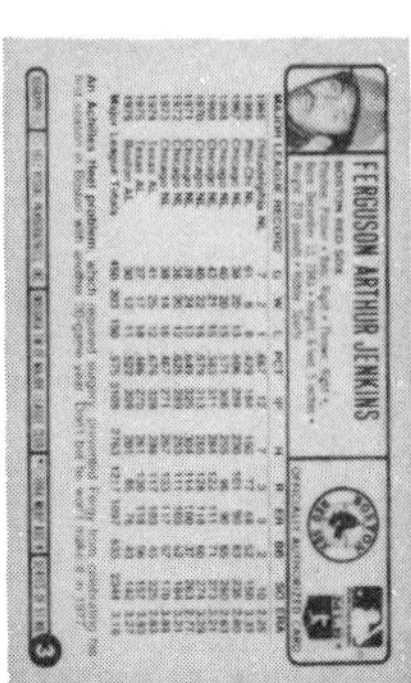

Other than another innovative card design to complement the simulated 3-D effect, there was little change in the 1977 Kellogg's issue. Set size remained at 57 cards, the set remained in the 2-1/8" by 3-1/4" format, and the cards were available either individually in boxes of cereal, or as a complete set via a mail-in box top offer. The 1977 set is the last in which Kellogg's used a player portrait photo on the back of the card.

		NR MT	EX	VG
	Complete Set:	55.00	28.00	16.50
	Common Player:	.40	.20	.12
1	George Foster	.90	.45	.25
2	Bert Campaneris	.60	.30	.20
3	Fergie Jenkins	.90	.45	.25
4	Dock Ellis	.40	.20	.12
5	John Montefusco	.40	.20	.12
6	George Brett	8.50	4.25	2.50
7	John Candelaria	.50	.25	.15
8	Fred Norman	.40	.20	.12
9	Bill Travers	.40	.20	.12
10	Hal McRae	.60	.30	.20
11	Doug Rau	.40	.20	.12
12	Greg Luzinski	.70	.35	.20
13	Ralph Garr	.40	.20	.12
14	Steve Garvey	4.50	2.25	1.25
15	Rick Manning	.40	.20	.12
16	Lyman Bostock	.50	.25	.15
17	Randy Jones	.40	.20	.12
18a	Ron Cey (58 homers in first sentence)	1.00	.50	.30
18b	Ron Cey (48 homers in first sentence)	.60	.30	.20
19	Dave Parker	1.25	.60	.40
20	Pete Rose	11.00	5.50	3.25
21a	Wayne Garland (last line begins "Prior to...")	.90	.45	.25
21b	Wayne Garland (last line begins "There he...")	.40	.20	.12
22	Bill North	.40	.20	.12
23	Thurman Munson	2.50	1.25	.70
24	Tom Poquette	.40	.20	.12
25	Ron LeFlore	.50	.25	.15
26	Mark Fidrych	.50	.25	.15
27	Sixto Lezcano	.40	.20	.12
28	Dave Winfield	4.00	2.00	1.25
29	Jerry Koosman	.50	.25	.15
30	Mike Hargrove	.40	.20	.12
31	Willie Montanez	.40	.20	.12
32	Don Stanhouse	.40	.20	.12
33	Jay Johnstone	.50	.25	.15
34	Bake McBride	.40	.20	.12
35	Dave Kingman	.70	.35	.20
36	Freddie Patek	.40	.20	.12
37	Garry Maddox	.50	.25	.15
38a	Ken Reitz (last line begins "The previous...")	.90	.45	.25
38b	Ken Reitz (last line begins "In late...")	.40	.20	.12
39	Bobby Grich	.60	.30	.20
40	Cesar Geronimo	.40	.20	.12
41	Jim Lonborg	.40	.20	.12
42	Ed Figueroa	.40	.20	.12
43	Bill Madlock	.80	.40	.25
44	Jerry Remy	.40	.20	.12
45	Frank Tanana	.50	.25	.15
46	Al Oliver	.90	.45	.25
47	Charlie Hough	.50	.25	.15
48	Lou Piniella	.70	.35	.20

		NR MT	EX	VG
49	Ken Griffey	.60	.30	.20
50	Jose Cruz	.60	.30	.20
51	Rollie Fingers	1.25	.60	.40
52	Chris Chambliss	.50	.25	.15
53	Rod Carew	4.00	2.00	1.25
54	Andy Messersmith	.40	.20	.12
55	Mickey Rivers	.40	.20	.12
56	Butch Wynegar	.40	.20	.12
57	Steve Carlton	5.00	2.50	1.50

1978 Kellogg's

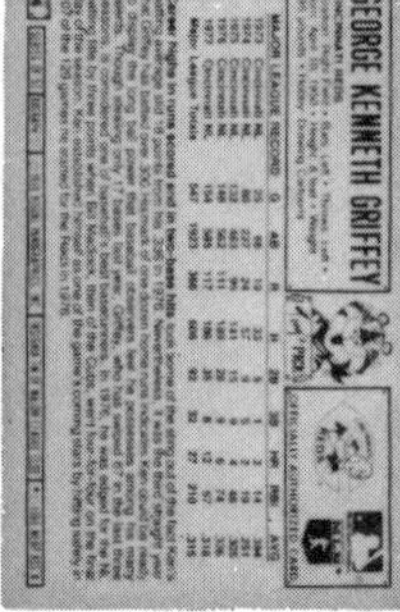

Besides the substitution of a Tony the Tiger drawing for a player portrait photo on the back of the card, the 1978 Kellogg's set offered no major changes from the previous few years issues. Cards were once again in the 2-1/8" by 3-1/4" format, with 57 cards comprising a complete set. Single cards were available in selected brands of the company's cereal, while complete sets could be obtained by a mail-in offer.

		NR MT	EX	VG
Complete Set:		40.00	20.00	12.00
Common Player:		.40	.20	.12
1	Steve Carlton	4.00	2.00	1.25
2	Bucky Dent	.50	.25	.15
3	Mike Schmidt	4.00	2.00	1.25
4	Ken Griffey	.50	.25	.15
5	Al Cowens	.40	.20	.12
6	George Brett	5.00	2.50	1.50
7	Lou Brock	3.00	1.50	.90
8	Rich Gossage	1.25	.60	.40
9	Tom Johnson	.40	.20	.12
10	George Foster	.70	.35	.20
11	Dave Winfield	3.50	1.75	1.00
12	Dan Meyer	.40	.20	.12
13	Chris Chambliss	.50	.25	.15
14	Paul Dade	.40	.20	.12
15	Jeff Burroughs	.40	.20	.12
16	Jose Cruz	.60	.30	.20
17	Mickey Rivers	.40	.20	.12
18	John Candelaria	.50	.25	.15
19	Ellis Valentine	.40	.20	.12
20	Hal McRae	.50	.25	.15
21	Dave Rozema	.40	.20	.12
22	Lenny Randle	.40	.20	.12
23	Willie McCovey	3.00	1.50	.90
24	Ron Cey	.70	.35	.20
25	Eddie Murray	10.00	5.00	3.00
26	Larry Bowa	.60	.30	.20
27	Tom Seaver	3.50	1.75	1.00
28	Garry Maddox	.50	.25	.15
29	Rod Carew	4.00	2.00	1.25
30	Thurman Munson	2.50	1.25	.70
31	Garry Templeton	.60	.30	.20
32	Eric Soderholm	.40	.20	.12
33	Greg Luzinski	.70	.35	.20
34	Reggie Smith	.50	.25	.15
35	Dave Goltz	.40	.20	.12
36	Tommy John	1.25	.60	.40
37	Ralph Garr	.40	.20	.12
38	Alan Bannister	.40	.20	.12
39	Bob Bailor	.40	.20	.12
40	Reggie Jackson	4.00	2.00	1.25
41	Cecil Cooper	.80	.40	.25
42	Burt Hooton	.40	.20	.12
43	Sparky Lyle	.50	.25	.15
44	Steve Ontiveros	.40	.20	.12
45	Rick Reuschel	.60	.30	.20
46	Lyman Bostock	.50	.25	.15
47	Mitchell Page	.40	.20	.12
48	Bruce Sutter	.70	.35	.20
49	Jim Rice	3.50	1.75	1.00
50	Bob Forsch	.40	.20	.12
51	Nolan Ryan	3.50	1.75	1.00
52	Dave Parker	1.25	.60	.40
53	Bert Blyleven	.90	.45	.25
54	Frank Tanana	.50	.25	.15
55	Ken Singleton	.50	.25	.15
56	Mike Hargrove	.40	.20	.12
57	Don Sutton	2.50	1.25	.70

1979 Kellogg's

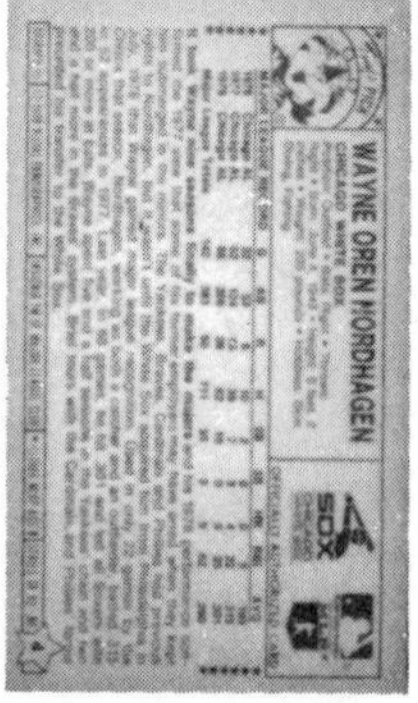

For its 1979 3-D issue, Kellogg's increased the size of the set to 60 cards, but reduced the width of the cards to 1-15/16". Depth stayed the same as in previous years, 3-1/4". The narrower card format seems to have compounded the problem of curling and subsequent cracking of the ribbed plastic surface which helps give the card a 3-D effect. Cards with major cracks can be graded no higher than VG. The complete set price in the checklist that follows does not include the scarcer variations. Numerous minor variations featuring copyright and trademark logos can be found in the set.

		NR MT	EX	VG
Complete Set:		30.00	15.00	9.00
Common Player:		.30	.15	.09
1	Bruce Sutter	.80	.40	.25
2	Ted Simmons	.70	.35	.20
3	Ross Grimsley	.30	.15	.09
4	Wayne Nordhagen	.30	.15	.09
5a	Jim Palmer (PCT. .649)	2.25	1.25	.70
5b	Jim Palmer (PCT. .650)	1.50	.70	.45
6	John Henry Johnson	.30	.15	.09
7	Jason Thompson	.30	.15	.09
8	Pat Zachry	.30	.15	.09
9	Dennis Eckersley	.60	.30	.20
10a	Paul Splittorff (IP 1665)	.60	.30	.20
10b	Paul Splittorff (IP 1666)	.30	.15	.09
11a	Ron Guidry (Hits 397)	2.00	1.00	.60
11b	Ron Guidry (Hits 396)	1.25	.60	.40
12	Jeff Burroughs	.30	.15	.09
13	Rod Carew	2.50	1.25	.70
14a	Buddy Bell (no trade line in bio)	1.25	.60	.40
14b	Buddy Bell (trade line in bio)	.60	.30	.20
15	Jim Rice	2.50	1.25	.70
16	Garry Maddox	.50	.25	.15
17	Willie McCovey	2.50	1.25	.70
18	Steve Carlton	2.50	1.25	.70
19a	J. R. Richard (stats begin with 1972)	.60	.30	.20
19b	J. R. Richard (stats begin with 1971)	.30	.15	.09
20	Paul Molitor	.90	.45	.25
21a	Dave Parker (AVG. .281)	2.00	1.00	.60
21b	Dave Parker (AVG. .318)	1.00	.50	.30
22a	Pete Rose (1978 3B 3)	12.00	6.00	3.50
22b	Pete Rose (1978 3B 33)	8.00	4.00	2.50
23a	Vida Blue (Runs 819)	1.25	.60	.40
23b	Vida Blue (Runs 818)	.60	.30	.20
24	Richie Zisk	.30	.15	.09
25a	Darrell Porter (2B 101)	.80	.40	.25
25b	Darrell Porter (2B 111)	.40	.20	.12
26a	Dan Driessen (Games 642)	.80	.40	.25
26b	Dan Driessen (Games 742)	.40	.20	.12
27a	Geoff Zahn (1978 Minnesota)	.60	.30	.20
27b	Geoff Zahn (1978 Minnesota)	.30	.15	.09
28	Phil Niekro	1.25	.60	.40
29	Tom Seaver	2.50	1.25	.70
30	Fred Lynn	1.00	.50	.30
31	Bill Bonham	.30	.15	.09
32	George Foster	.70	.35	.20
33a	Terry Puhl (last line of bio begins "Terry...")	.60	.30	.20
33b	Terry Puhl (last line of bio begins "His...")	.30	.15	.09
34a	John Candelaria (age is 24)	.90	.45	.25
34b	John Candelaria (age is 25)	.50	.25	.15
35	Bob Knepper	.40	.20	.12
36	Freddie Patek	.30	.15	.09
37	Chris Chambliss	.40	.20	.12
38a	Bob Forsch (1977 Games 86)	.80	.40	.25
38b	Bob Forsch (1977 Games 35)	.40	.20	.12
39a	Ken Griffey (1978 AB 674)	.90	.45	.25
39b	Ken Griffey (1978 AB 614)	.50	.25	.15
40	Jack Clark	.90	.45	.25
41a	Dwight Evans (1978 Hits 13)	1.50	.70	.45
41b	Dwight Evans (1978 Hits 123)	.90	.45	.25
42	Lee Mazzilli	.40	.20	.12
43	Mario Guerrero	.30	.15	.09
44	Larry Bowa	.50	.25	.15
45a	Carl Yastrzemski (Games 9930)	6.00	3.00	1.75
45b	Carl Yastrzemski (Games 9929)	4.00	2.00	1.25
46a	Reggie Jackson (1978 Games 162)	5.00	2.50	1.50
46b	Reggie Jackson (1978 Games 139)	3.00	1.50	.90
47	Rick Reuschel	.60	.30	.20
48a	Mike Flanagan (1976 SO 57)	.90	.45	.25
48b	Mike Flanagan (1976 SO 56)	.50	.25	.15
49a	Gaylord Perry (1973 Hits 325)	2.00	1.00	.60
49b	Gaylord Perry (1973 Hits 315)	1.25	.60	.40
50	George Brett	3.50	1.75	1.00
51a	Craig Reynolds (last line of bio begins "He spent...")	.60	.30	.20
51b	Craig Reynolds (last line of bio begins "In those...")	.30	.15	.09
52	Davey Lopes	.40	.20	.12
53a	Bill Almon (2B 31)	.60	.30	.20
53b	Bill Almon (2B 41)	.30	.15	.09
54	Roy Howell	.30	.15	.09
55	Frank Tanana	.50	.25	.15
56a	Doug Rau (1978 PCT. .577)	.60	.30	.20
56b	Doug Rau (1978 PCT. .625)	.30	.15	.09
57a	Rick Monday (1976 Runs 197)	.90	.45	.25
57b	Rick Monday (1976 Runs 107)	.50	.25	.15
58	Jon Matlack	.30	.15	.09
59a	Ron Jackson (last line of bio begins "His best...")	.60	.30	.20
59b	Ron Jackson (last line of bio begins "The Twins...")	.30	.15	.09
60	Jim Sundberg	.50	.25	.15

1980 Kellogg's

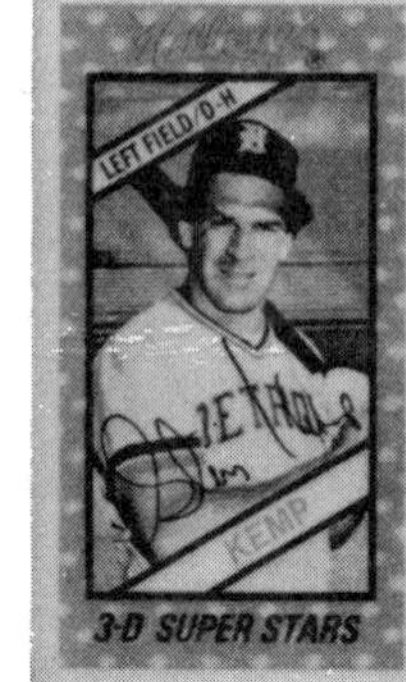

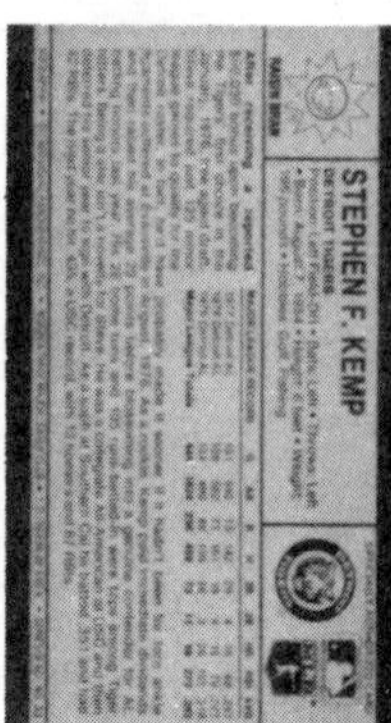

The 1980 cereal company issue featured the narrowest format of any Kellogg's card, 1-7/8" by 3-1/4". For the second straight year, set size remained at 60 cards, available either singly in boxes of cereal, or as complete sets by a mail-in offer.

		NR MT	EX	VG
Complete Set:		20.00	10.00	6.00
Common Player:		.30	.15	.09
1	Ross Grimsley	.30	.15	.09
2	Mike Schmidt	3.00	1.50	.90
3	Mike Flanagan	.40	.20	.12
4	Ron Guidry	.90	.45	.25
5	Bert Blyleven	.80	.40	.25
6	Dave Kingman	.70	.35	.20
7	Jeff Newman	.30	.15	.09
8	Steve Rogers	.30	.15	.09
9	George Brett	3.00	1.50	.90
10	Bruce Sutter	.70	.35	.20
11	Gorman Thomas	.40	.20	.12
12	Darrell Porter	.30	.15	.09
13	Roy Smalley	.30	.15	.09
14	Steve Carlton	1.75	.90	.50
15	Jim Palmer	1.50	.70	.45
16	Bob Bailor	.30	.15	.09
17	Jason Thompson	.30	.15	.09
18	Graig Nettles	.80	.40	.25
19	Ron Cey	.50	.25	.15
20	Nolan Ryan	1.75	.90	.50
21	Ellis Valentine	.30	.15	.09
22	Larry Hisle	.30	.15	.09
23	Dave Parker	.90	.45	.25
24	Eddie Murray	2.50	1.25	.70
25	Willie Stargell	1.75	.90	.50
26	Reggie Jackson	2.50	1.25	.70
27	Carl Yastrzemski	3.50	1.75	1.00
28	Andre Thornton	.40	.20	.12
29	Davey Lopes	.40	.20	.12
30	Ken Singleton	.40	.20	.12
31	Steve Garvey	2.50	1.25	.70
32	Dave Winfield	2.50	1.25	.70
33	Steve Kemp	.40	.20	.12
34	Claudell Washington	.40	.20	.12
35	Pete Rose	6.50	3.25	2.00
36	Cesar Cedeno	.40	.20	.12
37	John Stearns	.30	.15	.09
38	Lee Mazzilli	.30	.15	.09
39	Larry Bowa	.40	.20	.12
40	Fred Lynn	.80	.40	.25
41	Carlton Fisk	.90	.45	.25
42	Vida Blue	.50	.25	.15
43	Keith Hernandez	1.25	.60	.40
44	Jim Rice	1.75	.90	.50
45	Ted Simmons	.80	.40	.25
46	Chet Lemon	.30	.15	.09
47	Fergie Jenkins	.50	.25	.15
48	Gary Matthews	.40	.20	.12
49	Tom Seaver	2.50	1.25	.70
50	George Foster	.70	.35	.20
51	Phil Niekro	1.25	.60	.40
52	Johnny Bench	2.50	1.25	.70
53	Buddy Bell	.50	.25	.15
54	Lance Parrish	.90	.45	.25
55	Joaquin Andujar	.30	.15	.09
56	Don Baylor	.50	.25	.15
57	Jack Clark	.80	.40	.25
58	J.R. Richard	.30	.15	.09
59	Bruce Bochte	.30	.15	.09
60	Rod Carew	2.50	1.25	.70

1981 Kellogg's

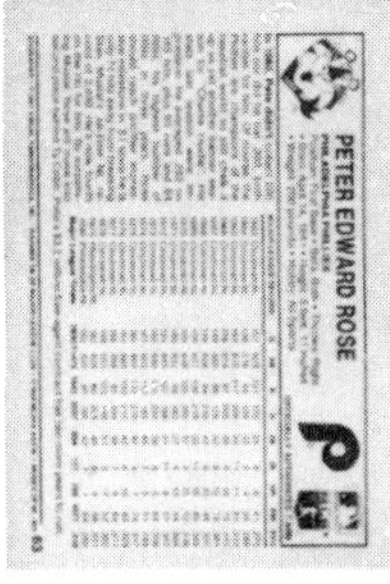

"Bigger" is the word to best describe Kellogg's 1981 card set. Not only were the cards themselves larger than ever before (or since) at 2-1/2" by 3-1/2", but the size of the set was increased to 66, the largest since the 75-card issues of 1970-1971. The '81 Kellogg's set was available only as complete sets by mail. It is thought that the wider format of the 1981s may help prevent the problems of curling and cracking from which other years of Kellogg's issues suffer.

		MT	NR MT	EX
Complete Set:		8.00	4.00	2.00
Common Player:		.08	.04	.02
1	George Foster	.15	.08	.04
2	Jim Palmer	.30	.15	.08
3	Reggie Jackson	.60	.30	.15
4	Al Oliver	.15	.08	.04
5	Mike Schmidt	.70	.35	.20
6	Nolan Ryan	.40	.20	.10
7	Bucky Dent	.10	.05	.03
8	George Brett	.70	.35	.20
9	Jim Rice	.35	.20	.09
10	Steve Garvey	.40	.20	.10
11	Willie Stargell	.30	.15	.08
12	Phil Niekro	.25	.13	.06
13	Dave Parker	.20	.10	.05
14	Cesar Cedeno	.10	.05	.03
15	Don Baylor	.10	.05	.03
16	J.R. Richard	.08	.04	.02
17	Tony Perez	.15	.08	.04
18	Eddie Murray	.60	.30	.15
19	Chet Lemon	.08	.04	.02
20	Ben Oglivie	.08	.04	.02
21	Dave Winfield	.50	.25	.13
22	Joe Morgan	.20	.10	.05
23	Vida Blue	.10	.05	.03
24	Willie Wilson	.15	.08	.04
25	Steve Henderson	.08	.04	.02
26	Rod Carew	.50	.25	.13
27	Garry Templeton	.08	.04	.02
28	Dave Concepcion	.10	.05	.03
29	Davey Lopes	.08	.04	.02
30	Ken Landreaux	.08	.04	.02
31	Keith Hernandez	.40	.20	.10
32	Cecil Cooper	.10	.05	.03
33	Rickey Henderson	.60	.30	.15
34	Frank White	.10	.05	.03
35	George Hendrick	.08	.04	.02
36	Reggie Smith	.10	.05	.03
37	Tug McGraw	.10	.05	.03
38	Tom Seaver	.50	.25	.13
39	Ken Singleton	.10	.05	.03
40	Fred Lynn	.20	.10	.05
41	Rich "Goose" Gossage	.20	.10	.05
42	Terry Puhl	.08	.04	.02
43	Larry Bowa	.10	.05	.03
44	Phil Garner	.08	.04	.02
45	Ron Guidry	.20	.10	.05
46	Lee Mazzilli	.08	.04	.02
47	Dave Kingman	.15	.08	.04
48	Carl Yastrzemski	.80	.40	.20
49	Rick Burleson	.08	.04	.02
50	Steve Carlton	.40	.20	.10
51	Alan Trammell	.30	.15	.08
52	Tommy John	.20	.10	.05
53	Paul Molitor	.20	.10	.05
54	Joe Charboneau	.08	.04	.02
55	Rick Langford	.08	.04	.02
56	Bruce Sutter	.10	.05	.03
57	Robin Yount	.35	.20	.09
58	Steve Stone	.08	.04	.02
59	Larry Gura	.08	.04	.02
60	Mike Flanagan	.10	.05	.03
61	Bob Horner	.15	.08	.04
62	Bruce Bochte	.08	.04	.02
63	Pete Rose	1.00	.50	.25
64	Buddy Bell	.15	.08	.04
65	Johnny Bench	.60	.30	.15
66	Mike Hargrove	.08	.04	.02

1982 Kellogg's

For the second straight year in 1982, Kellogg's cards were not inserted into cereal boxes, but had to be obtained by sending cash and box tops to the company for complete sets. The '82 cards were downsized both in number of cards in the set - 64 - and in physical dimensions, 2-1/8" by 3-1/4".

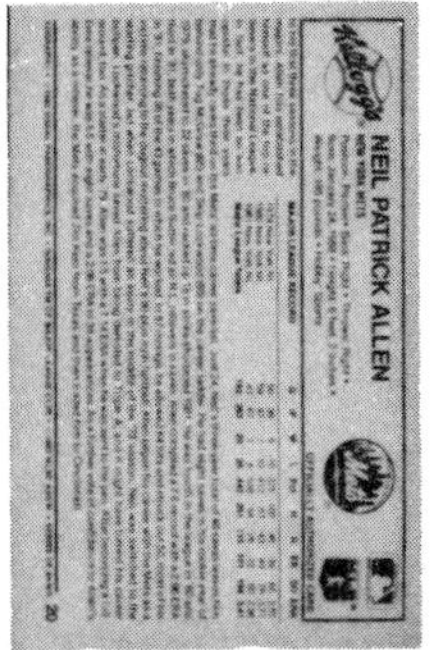

		MT	NR MT	EX
Complete Set:		12.00	6.00	3.00
Common Player:		.12	.06	.03
1	Richie Zisk	.12	.06	.03
2	Bill Buckner	.12	.06	.03
3	George Brett	.90	.45	.25
4	Rickey Henderson	.80	.40	.20
5	Jack Morris	.30	.15	.08
6	Ozzie Smith	.25	.13	.06
7	Rollie Fingers	.25	.13	.06
8	Tom Seaver	.50	.25	.13
9	Fernando Valenzuela	.60	.30	.15
10	Hubie Brooks	.12	.06	.03
11	Nolan Ryan	.50	.25	.13
12	Dave Winfield	.60	.30	.15
13	Bob Horner	.20	.10	.05
14	Reggie Jackson	.90	.45	.25
15	Burt Hooton	.12	.06	.03
16	Mike Schmidt	.90	.45	.25
17	Bruce Sutter	.20	.10	.05
18	Pete Rose	1.50	.70	.40
19	Dave Kingman	.20	.10	.05
20	Neil Allen	.12	.06	.03
21	Don Sutton	.25	.13	.06
22	Dave Concepcion	.20	.10	.05
23	Keith Hernandez	.50	.25	.13
24	Gary Carter	.70	.35	.20
25	Carlton Fisk	.30	.15	.08
26	Ron Guidry	.25	.13	.06
27	Steve Carlton	.50	.25	.13
28	Robin Yount	.40	.20	.10
29	John Castino	.12	.06	.03
30	Johnny Bench	.80	.40	.20
31	Bob Knepper	.12	.06	.03
32	Rich "Goose" Gossage	.20	.10	.05
33	Buddy Bell	.20	.10	.05
34	Art Howe	.12	.06	.03
35	Tony Armas	.12	.06	.03
36	Phil Niekro	.30	.15	.08
37	Len Barker	.12	.06	.03
38	Bobby Grich	.20	.10	.05
39	Steve Kemp	.12	.06	.03
40	Kirk Gibson	.35	.20	.09
41	Carney Lansford	.20	.10	.05
42	Jim Palmer	.40	.20	.10
43	Carl Yastrzemski	1.00	.50	.25
44	Rick Burleson	.12	.06	.03
45	Dwight Evans	.25	.13	.06
46	Ron Cey	.20	.10	.05
47	Steve Garvey	.70	.35	.20
48	Dave Parker	.30	.15	.08
49	Mike Easler	.12	.06	.03
50	Dusty Baker	.12	.06	.03
51	Rod Carew	.70	.35	.20
52	Chris Chambliss	.12	.06	.03
53	Tim Raines	.70	.35	.20
54	Chet Lemon	.12	.06	.03
55	Bill Madlock	.20	.10	.05
56	George Foster	.20	.10	.05
57	Dwayne Murphy	.12	.06	.03
58	Ken Singleton	.20	.10	.05
59	Mike Norris	.12	.06	.03
60	Cecil Cooper	.20	.10	.05
61	Al Oliver	.20	.10	.05
62	Willie Wilson	.25	.13	.06
63	Vida Blue	.20	.10	.05
64	Eddie Murray	.80	.40	.20

1983 Kellogg's

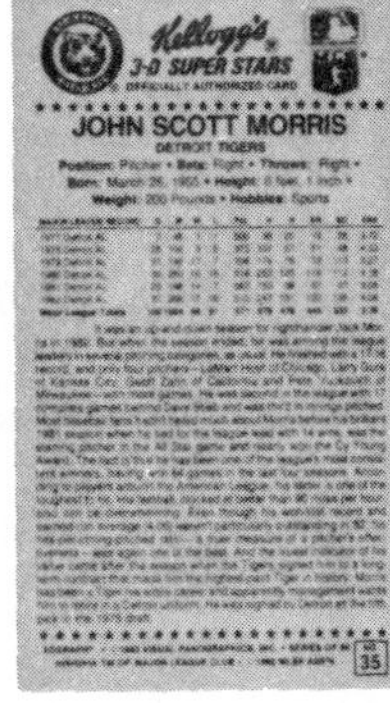

In its 14th and final year of baseball card issue, Kellogg's returned to the policy of inserting single cards into cereal boxes, as well as offering complete sets by a mail-in box top redemption offer. The 3-D cards themselves returned to a narrow - 1-7/8" by 3-1/4" format, while the set size was reduced to 60 cards.

		MT	NR MT	EX
Complete Set:		12.00	9.00	4.75
Common Player:		.10	.08	.04
1	Rod Carew	.50	.40	.20
2	Rollie Fingers	.20	.15	.08
3	Reggie Jackson	.50	.40	.20
4	George Brett	.70	.50	.30
5	Hal McRae	.15	.11	.06
6	Pete Rose	1.25	.90	.50
7	Fernando Valenzuela	.35	.25	.14
8	Rickey Henderson	.60	.45	.25
9	Carl Yastrzemski	.70	.50	.30
10	Rich "Goose" Gossage	.20	.15	.08
11	Eddie Murray	.50	.40	.20
12	Buddy Bell	.15	.11	.06
13	Jim Rice	.40	.30	.15
14	Robin Yount	.35	.25	.14
15	Dave Winfield	.50	.40	.20
16	Harold Baines	.20	.15	.08
17	Garry Templeton	.15	.11	.06
18	Bill Madlock	.25	.20	.10
19	Pete Vuckovich	.10	.08	.04
20	Pedro Guerrero	.25	.20	.10
21	Ozzie Smith	.20	.15	.08
22	George Foster	.20	.15	.08
23	Willie Wilson	.20	.15	.08
24	Johnny Ray	.15	.11	.06
25	George Hendrick	.10	.08	.04
26	Andre Thornton	.10	.08	.04
27	Leon Durham	.10	.08	.04
28	Cecil Cooper	.15	.11	.06
29	Don Baylor	.15	.11	.06
30	Lonnie Smith	.10	.08	.04
31	Nolan Ryan	.40	.30	.15
32	Dan Quiesenberry (Quisenberry)	.15	.11	.06
33	Len Barker	.10	.08	.04
34	Neil Allen	.10	.08	.04
35	Jack Morris	.30	.25	.12
36	Dave Stieb	.15	.11	.06
37	Bruce Sutter	.15	.11	.06
38	Jim Sundberg	.10	.08	.04
39	Jim Palmer	.35	.25	.14
40	Lance Parrish	.30	.25	.12
41	Floyd Bannister	.15	.11	.06
42	Larry Gura	.10	.08	.04
43	Britt Burns	.10	.08	.04
44	Toby Harrah	.10	.08	.04
45	Steve Carlton	.40	.30	.15
46	Greg Minton	.10	.08	.04
47	Gorman Thomas	.15	.11	.06
48	Jack Clark	.25	.20	.10
49	Keith Hernandez	.40	.30	.15
50	Greg Luzinski	.15	.11	.06
51	Fred Lynn	.25	.20	.10
52	Dale Murphy	.70	.50	.30
53	Kent Hrbek	.35	.25	.14
54	Bob Horner	.15	.11	.06
55	Gary Carter	.50	.40	.20
56	Carlton Fisk	.25	.20	.10
57	Dave Concepcion	.15	.11	.06
58	Mike Schmidt	.70	.50	.30
59	Bill Buckner	.15	.11	.06
60	Bobby Grich	.15	.11	.06

1969 Kelly's Potato Chips Pins

Consisting of 20 pins, each measuring approximately 1-3/16" in diameter, this set was issued by Kelly's Potato Chips in 1969 and has a heavy emphasis on St. Louis Cardinals. The pin has a black and white player photo in the center surrounded by either a red border (for A.L. players) or a blue border (for N.L. players) that displays the player's team and name at the top and bottom. "Kelly's" appears to the left while the word "Zip!" is printed to the right. The pins are unnumbered.

		NR MT	EX	VG
Complete Set:		150.00	75.00	45.00
Common Player:		1.50	.70	.45
(1)	Luis Aparicio	7.00	3.50	2.00
(2)	Ernie Banks	12.00	6.00	3.50
(3)	Glenn Beckert	1.50	.70	.45
(4)	Lou Brock	10.00	5.00	3.00
(5)	Curt Flood	2.00	1.00	.60
(6)	Bob Gibson	10.00	5.00	3.00
(7)	Joel Horlen	1.50	.70	.45
(8)	Al Kaline	10.00	5.00	3.00

		NR MT	EX	VG
(9)	Don Kessinger	1.50	.70	.45
(10)	Mickey Lolich	2.50	1.25	.70
(11)	Juan Marichal	8.00	4.00	2.50
(12)	Willie Mays	18.00	9.00	5.50
(13)	Tim McCarver	2.50	1.25	.70
(14)	Denny McLain	2.50	1.25	.70
(15)	Pete Rose	25.00	12.50	7.50
(16)	Ron Santo	2.50	1.25	.70
(17)	Joe Torre	2.50	1.25	.70
(18)	Pete Ward	1.50	.70	.45
(19)	Billy Williams	7.00	3.50	2.00
(20)	Carl Yastrzemski	20.00	10.00	6.00

1988 Kenner

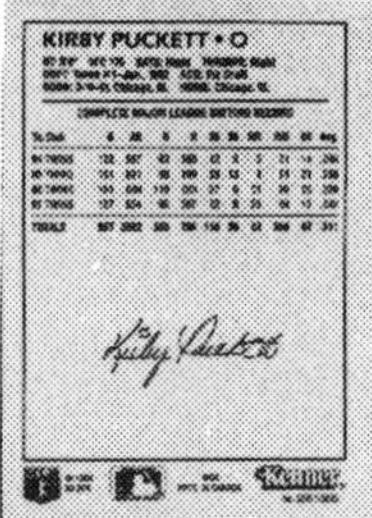

This massive three-sport set was distributed in conjuntion with Kenner's Starting Lineup sports figurines, one card per statue. Cards were not sold separately. Baseball, football and basketball stars are included in the lineup of full-color figurines, with 123 cards devoted to baseball. Individual major league team assortments include one to seven players per team. The figurines are mildly reminiscent of the 1950s Hartland Statues, but Kenner's version features smaller (4" to 6") figures and a more extensive catalog which includes athletes other than baseball players. The Starting Lineup cards feature action photos framed in red and white, with the "Starting Lineup" logo in the upper left corner and the player's name printed along the bottom border. Colorful team logos are superimposed in the lower right corner of the player photos. As an added incentive to collectors, five UPC codes from the sport statue packages could be redeemed for an autographed baseball. The values in the checklist that follows include both the statue and card for the 123 baseball players in the set. Several players which were included in the package's checklist were pulled before production.

		MT	NR MT	EX
Complete Set:		1300.	975.00	520.00
Common Player:		7.00	5.25	2.75
(1)	Alan Ashby	11.00	8.25	4.50
(2)	Harold Baines	8.00	6.00	3.25
(3)	Kevin Bass	11.00	8.25	4.50
(4)	Steve Bedrosian	8.00	6.00	3.25
(5)	Buddy Bell	8.00	6.00	3.25
(6)	George Bell	10.00	7.50	4.00
(7)	Mike Boddicker	8.00	6.00	3.25
(8)	Wade Boggs	11.00	8.25	4.50
(9)	Barry Bonds	11.00	8.25	4.50
(10)	Bobby Bonilla	11.00	8.25	4.50
(11)	Sid Bream	16.00	12.00	6.50
(12)	George Brett	10.00	7.50	4.00
(13)	Chris Brown	11.00	8.25	4.50
(14)	Tom Brunansky	10.00	7.50	4.00
(15)	Ellis Burks	25.00	18.50	10.00
(16)	Jose Canseco	40.00	30.00	16.00
(17)	Gary Carter	7.00	5.25	2.75
(18)	Joe Carter	10.00	7.50	4.00
(19)	Jack Clark	16.00	12.00	6.50
(20)	Will Clark	11.00	8.25	4.50
(21)	Roger Clemens	10.00	7.50	4.00
(22)	Vince Coleman	8.00	6.00	3.25
(23)	Kal Daniels	10.00	7.50	4.00
(24)	Alvin Davis	8.00	6.00	3.25
(25)	Eric Davis	10.00	7.50	4.00
(26)	Glenn Davis	11.00	8.25	4.50
(27)	Jody Davis	10.00	7.50	4.00
(28)	Andre Dawson	8.00	6.00	3.25
(29)	Rob Deer	8.00	6.00	3.25
(30)	Brian Downing	8.00	6.00	3.25
(31)	Mike Dunne	8.00	6.00	3.25
(32)	Shawon Dunston	16.00	12.00	6.50
(33)	Leon Durham	7.00	5.25	2.75
(34)	Len Dykstra	10.00	7.50	4.00
(35)	Dwight Evans	10.00	7.50	4.00
(36)	Carlton Fisk	10.00	7.50	4.00
(37)	John Franco	10.00	7.50	4.00
(38)	Julio Franco	10.00	7.50	4.00
(39)	Gary Gaetti	8.00	6.00	3.25
(40)	Dwight Gooden	10.00	7.50	4.00
(41)	Ken Griffey	10.00	7.50	4.00
(42)	Pedro Guerrero	8.00	6.00	3.25
(43)	Ozzie Guillen	10.00	7.50	4.00
(44)	Tony Gwynn	8.00	6.00	3.25
(45)	Mel Hall	10.00	7.50	4.00
(46)	Billy Hatcher	10.00	7.50	4.00
(47)	Von Hayes	11.00	8.25	4.50
(48)	Rickey Henderson	8.00	6.00	3.25
(49)	Keith Hernandez	10.00	7.50	4.00
(50)	Willie Hernandez	11.00	8.25	4.50
(51)	Tom Herr	10.00	7.50	4.00
(52)	Ted Higuera	11.00	8.25	4.50
(53)	Charlie Hough	10.00	7.50	4.00
(54)	Kent Hrbek	8.00	6.00	3.25
(55)	Pete Incaviglia	8.00	6.00	3.25
(56)	Howard Johnson	11.00	8.25	4.50
(57)	Wally Joyner	10.00	7.50	4.00
(58)	Terry Kennedy	10.00	7.50	4.00
(59)	John Kruk	11.00	8.25	4.50
(60)	Mark Langston	11.00	8.25	4.50
(61)	Carney Lansford	16.00	12.00	6.50
(62)	Jeffrey Leonard	7.00	5.25	2.75
(63)	Fred Lynn	8.00	6.00	3.25
(64)	Candy Maldonado	11.00	8.25	4.50
(65)	Mike Marshall	16.00	12.00	6.50
(66)	Don Mattingly	11.00	8.25	4.50
(67)	Willie McGee	8.00	6.00	3.25
(68)	Mark McGwire	20.00	15.00	8.00
(69)	Kevin McReynolds	11.00	8.25	4.50
(70)	Paul Molitor	8.00	6.00	3.25
(71)	Donnie Moore	11.00	8.25	4.50
(72)	Jack Morris	10.00	7.50	4.00
(73)	Dale Murphy	8.00	6.00	3.25
(74)	Eddie Murray	8.00	6.00	3.25
(75)	Matt Nokes	10.00	7.50	4.00
(76)	Pete O'Brien	10.00	7.50	4.00
(77)	Ken Oberkfell	10.00	7.50	4.00
(78)	Dave Parker	16.00	12.00	6.50
(79)	Larry Parrish	8.00	6.00	3.25
(80)	Ken Phelps	16.00	12.00	6.50
(81)	Jim Presley	8.00	6.00	3.25
(82)	Kirby Puckett	10.00	7.50	4.00
(83)	Dan Quisenberry	8.00	6.00	3.25
(84)	Tim Raines	10.00	7.50	4.00
(85)	Willie Randolph	8.00	6.00	3.25
(86)	Shane Rawley	10.00	7.50	4.00
(87)	Jeff Reardon	10.00	7.50	4.00
(88)	Gary Redus	11.00	8.25	4.50
(89)	Rick Reuschel	10.00	7.50	4.00
(90)	Jim Rice	8.00	6.00	3.25
(91)	Dave Righetti	8.00	6.00	3.25
(92)	Cal Ripken	10.00	7.50	4.00
(93)	Pete Rose	16.00	12.00	6.50
(94)	Nolan Ryan	20.00	15.00	8.00
(95)	Bret Saberhagen	8.00	6.00	3.25
(96)	Juan Samuel	8.00	6.00	3.25
(97)	Ryne Sandberg	8.00	6.00	3.25
(98)	Benito Santiago	10.00	7.50	4.00
(99)	Steve Sax	8.00	6.00	3.25
(100)	Mike Schmidt	10.00	7.50	4.00
(101)	Mike Scott	8.00	6.00	3.25
(102)	Kevin Seitzer	16.00	12.00	6.50
(103)	Ruben Sierra	11.00	8.25	4.50
(104)	Ozzie Smith	8.00	6.00	3.25
(105)	Zane Smith	10.00	7.50	4.00
(106)	Cory Snyder	10.00	7.50	4.00
(107)	Darryl Strawberry	8.00	6.00	3.25
(108)	Franklin Stubbs	16.00	12.00	6.50
(109)	B.J. Surhoff	10.00	7.50	4.00
(110)	Rick Sutcliffe	10.00	7.50	4.00
(111)	Pat Tabler	10.00	7.50	4.00
(112)	Danny Tartabull	10.00	7.50	4.00
(113)	Alan Trammell	10.00	7.50	4.00
(114)	Fernando Valenzuela	8.00	6.00	3.25
(115)	Andy Van Slyke	18.00	13.50	7.25
(116)	Frank Viola	10.00	7.50	4.00
(117)	Ozzie Virgil	8.00	6.00	3.25
(118)	Greg Walker	8.00	6.00	3.25
(119)	Lou Whitaker	8.00	6.00	3.25
(120)	Devon White	10.00	7.50	4.00
(121)	Dave Winfield	8.00	6.00	3.25
(122)	Mike Witt	8.00	6.00	3.25
(123)	Todd Worrell	11.00	8.25	4.50
(124)	Robin Yount	8.00	6.00	3.25

1989 Kenner

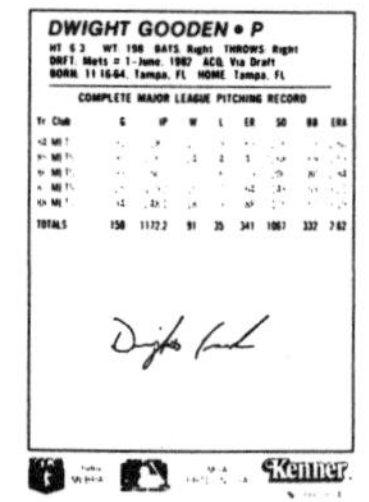

Kenner returned in 1989 with another set of sports figurines and accompanying trading cards. As in the previous year, the figurines were sold individually with one card packaged with each figure. No cards were sold separately. The cards have the "Starting Lineup" logo in the upper left, while the words "1989 Edition" appear in the lower right corner. The values listed below include both the figure and the card. The values are based on relative scarcity, resulting in some minor stars and common players being priced higher than superstars, whose cards and figures were produced in much greater numbers.

		MT	NR MT	EX
Complete Set:		1100.	825.00	450.00
Common Player:		4.00	3.00	1.50
(1)	Ozzie Smith	6.00	4.50	2.50
(2)	Tom Brunansky	7.00	5.25	2.75
(3)	Vince Coleman	6.00	4.50	2.50
(4)	Willie McGee	6.00	4.50	2.50
(5)	Todd Worrell	5.00	3.75	2.00
(6)	Tony Pena	7.00	5.25	2.75
(7)	Terry Pendleton	7.00	5.25	2.75
(8)	Pedro Guerrero	8.00	6.00	3.25
(9)	Mike Schmidt	8.00	6.00	3.25
(10)	Von Hayes	4.00	3.00	1.50
(11)	Juan Samuel	5.00	3.75	2.00
(12)	Steve Bedrosian	5.00	3.75	2.00
(13)	Milt Thompson	5.00	3.75	2.00
(14)	Phil Bradley	5.00	3.75	2.00
(15)	Chris James	6.00	4.50	2.50
(16)	Dale Murphy	8.00	6.00	3.25
(17)	Zane Smith	4.00	3.00	1.50
(18)	Gerald Perry	6.00	4.50	2.50
(19)	Dion James	6.00	4.50	2.50
(20)	Albert Hall	4.00	3.00	1.50
(21)	Bruce Sutter	5.00	3.75	2.00
(22)	Ron Gant	6.00	4.50	2.50
(23)	Tony Gwynn	7.00	5.25	2.75
(24)	Benito Santiago	6.00	4.50	2.50
(25)	John Kruk	5.00	3.75	2.00
(26)	Marvell Wynne	5.00	3.75	2.00
(27)	Roberto Alomar	7.00	5.25	2.75
(28)	Mark Davis	6.00	4.50	2.50
(29)	Ryne Sandberg	6.00	4.50	2.50
(30)	Andre Dawson	6.00	4.50	2.50
(31)	Greg Maddux	7.00	5.25	2.75
(32)	Rick Sutcliffe	5.00	3.75	2.00
(33)	Mark Grace	8.00	6.00	3.25
(34)	Shawon Dunston	4.00	3.00	1.50
(35)	Damon Berryhill	5.00	3.75	2.00
(36)	Barry Bonds	6.00	4.50	2.50
(37)	Andy Van Slyke	5.00	3.75	2.00
(38)	Bob Walk	5.00	3.75	2.00
(39)	Bobby Bonilla	5.00	3.75	2.00
(40)	Mike LaValliere	5.00	3.75	2.00
(41)	Doug Drabek	6.00	4.50	2.50
(42)	Jose Lind	6.00	4.50	2.50
(43)	Fernando Valenzuela	5.00	3.75	2.00
(44)	Mike Marshall	4.00	3.00	1.50
(45)	Orel Hershiser	8.00	6.00	3.25
(46)	John Shelby	4.00	3.00	1.50
(47)	Kirk Gibson	6.00	4.50	2.50
(48)	Mike Scioscia	5.00	3.75	2.00
(49)	Eric Davis	8.00	6.00	3.25
(50)	Kal Daniels	6.00	4.50	2.50
(51)	John Franco	6.00	4.50	2.50
(52)	Danny Jackson	5.00	3.75	2.00
(53)	Bo Diaz	5.00	3.75	2.00
(54)	Barry Larkin	7.00	5.25	2.75
(55)	Jeff Treadway	6.00	4.50	2.50
(56)	Chris Sabo	7.00	5.25	2.75
(57)	Darryl Strawberry	8.00	6.00	3.25
(58)	Keith Hernandez	6.00	4.50	2.50
(59)	Gary Carter	6.00	4.50	2.50
(60)	Dwight Gooden	9.00	6.75	3.50
(61)	Len Dykstra	4.00	3.00	1.50
(62)	David Cone	7.00	5.25	2.75
(63)	Kevin Elster	6.00	4.50	2.50
(64)	Kevin McReynolds	6.00	4.50	2.50
(65)	Randy Myers	6.00	4.50	2.50
(66)	Gregg Jefferies	15.00	11.00	6.00
(67)	Mike Scott	5.00	3.75	2.00
(68)	Glenn Davis	6.00	4.50	2.50
(69)	Kevin Bass	4.00	3.00	1.50
(70)	Dave Smith	4.00	3.00	1.50
(71)	Bill Doran	6.00	4.50	2.50
(72)	Gerald Young	4.00	3.00	1.50
(73)	Billy Hatcher	4.00	3.00	1.50
(74)	Will Clark	10.00	7.50	4.00
(75)	Candy Maldonado	4.00	3.00	1.50
(76)	Brett Butler	6.00	4.50	2.50
(77)	Kevin Mitchell	9.00	6.75	3.50
(78)	Jose Uribe	5.00	3.75	2.00
(79)	Robby Thompson	6.00	4.50	2.50
(80)	Tim Raines	7.00	5.25	2.75
(81)	Joe Carter	6.00	4.50	2.50
(82)	Mel Hall	5.00	3.75	2.00
(83)	Cory Snyder	6.00	4.50	2.50
(84)	Brook Jacoby	6.00	4.50	2.50
(85)	Greg Swindell	8.00	6.00	3.25
(86)	Doug Jones	6.00	4.50	2.50
(87)	Jack Morris	6.00	4.50	2.50
(88)	Alan Trammell	7.00	5.25	2.75
(89)	Matt Nokes	7.00	5.25	2.75
90	Luis Salazar	4.00	3.00	1.50
(91)	Chet Lemon	4.00	3.00	1.50
(92)	Lou Whitaker	6.00	4.50	2.50
(93)	Tom Brookens	4.00	3.00	1.50
(94)	Mike Henneman	6.00	4.50	2.50
(95)	Jose Canseco	15.00	11.00	6.00
(96)	Mark McGwire	10.00	7.50	4.00
(97)	Dave Parker	6.00	4.50	2.50
(98)	Dave Stewart	7.00	5.25	2.75
(99)	Bob Welch	6.00	4.50	2.50
(100)	Terry Steinbach	8.00	6.00	3.25
(101)	Carney Lansford	5.00	3.75	2.00
(102)	Dennis Eckersley	6.00	4.50	2.50
(103)	Walt Weiss	7.00	5.25	2.75
(104)	George Brett	8.00	6.00	3.25
105	Bret Saberhagen	8.00	6.00	3.25
(106)	Danny Tartabull	6.00	4.50	2.50
(107)	Kevin Seitzer	10.00	7.50	4.00
(108)	Bo Jackson	12.00	9.00	4.75
(109)	Kurt Stillwell	6.00	4.50	2.50
(110)	Pat Tabler	6.00	4.50	2.50
(111)	Mark Gubicza	7.00	5.25	2.75
(112)	Robin Yount	7.00	5.25	2.75
(113)	Rob Deer	5.00	3.75	2.00
(114)	Paul Molitor	6.00	4.50	2.50
(115)	Ted Higuera	6.00	4.50	2.50
(116)	B.J. Surhoff	6.00	4.50	2.50
(117)	Dan Plesac	6.00	4.50	2.50
(118)	Glenn Braggs	6.00	4.50	2.50
(119)	Wade Boggs	10.00	7.50	4.00
(120)	Roger Clemens	10.00	7.50	4.00
(121)	Jim Rice	6.00	4.50	2.50
(122)	Ellis Burks	8.00	6.00	3.25
(123)	Mike Greenwell	8.00	6.00	3.25
124	Lee Smith	5.00	3.75	2.00

	MT	NR MT	EX
(125) Marty Barrett	5.00	3.75	2.00
(126) Wally Joyner	8.00	6.00	3.25
(127) Mike Witt	4.00	3.00	1.50
(128) Devon White	6.00	4.50	2.50
(129) Johnny Ray	5.00	3.75	2.00
(130) Chili Davis	5.00	3.75	2.00
(131) Jack Howell	5.00	3.75	2.00
(132) Dick Schofield	5.00	3.75	2.00
(133) Rickey Henderson	8.00	6.00	3.25
(134) Don Mattingly	13.00	9.75	5.25
(135) Dave Winfield	7.00	5.25	2.75
(136) Dave Righetti	7.00	5.25	2.75
(137) Mike Pagliarulo	5.00	3.75	2.00
(138) Don Slaught	4.00	3.00	1.50
(139) Al Leiter	4.00	3.00	1.50
(140) George Bell	7.00	5.25	2.75
(141) Brady Anderson	6.00	4.50	2.50
(142) Cal Ripken	7.00	5.25	2.75
(143) Larry Sheets	4.00	3.00	1.50
(144) Pete Stanicek	4.00	3.00	1.50
(145) Kirby Puckett	8.00	6.00	3.25
(146) Kent Hrbek	6.00	4.50	2.50
(147) Gary Gaetti	6.00	4.50	2.50
(148) Jeff Reardon	5.00	3.75	2.00
(149) Dan Gladden	5.00	3.75	2.00
(150) Frank Viola	5.00	3.75	2.00
(151) Tim Laudner	4.00	3.00	1.50
(152) Alvin Davis	6.00	4.50	2.50
(153) Mark Langston	6.00	4.50	2.50
(154) Harold Reynolds	6.00	4.50	2.50
(155) Rey Quinones	4.00	3.00	1.50
(156) Harold Baines	6.00	4.50	2.50
(157) Ozzie Guillen	4.00	3.00	1.50
(158) Greg Walker	4.00	3.00	1.50
(159) Ivan Calderon	5.00	3.75	2.00
(160) Melido Perez	5.00	3.75	2.00
(161) Bobby Thigpen	7.00	5.25	2.75
(162) Dan Pasqua	6.00	4.50	2.50
(163) Pete Incaviglia	6.00	4.50	2.50
(164) Ruben Sierra	9.00	6.75	3.50
(165) Scott Fletcher	4.00	3.00	1.50
(166) Steve Buechele	4.00	3.00	1.50
(167) Jeff Russell	5.00	3.75	2.00

1989 Kenner Starting

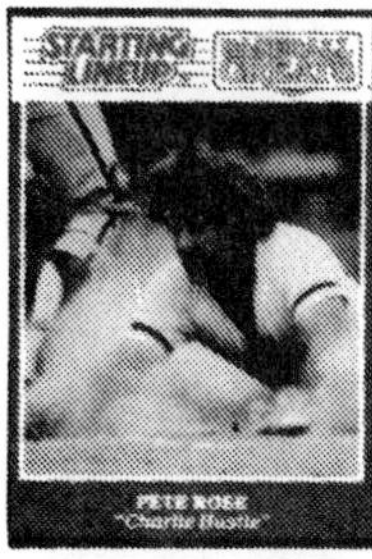

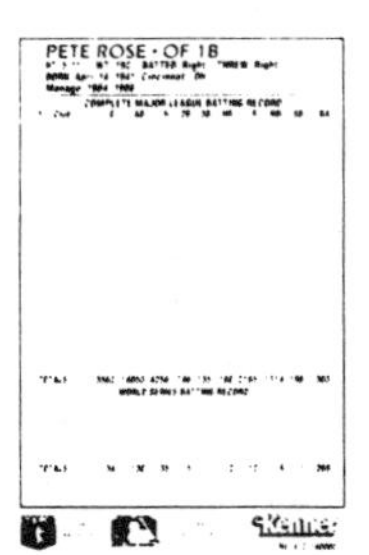

The "Baseball Greats" series of figurines and trading cards was an addition to the Kenner "Starting Lineup" series for 1989. The series features baseball greats of the past, and were packaged two figurines and two collector cards per package. The collector cards that accompany the figures feature an original action photo of the player done in a sepia-tone to enhance the historic nature of the set. The Starting Lineup logo and "Baseball Greats' heading appear at the top of the card. The player's name and a descriptive nickname, such as "Sultan of Swat" appear below the photo. The backs of the cards carry a blue-and- white color scheme and include career stats. The values listed below include both the figure and the card.

		MT	NR MT	EX
Complete Set:		150.00	110.00	60.00
Common Player:		10.00	7.50	4.00
(1)	Willie Mays/ Willie McCovey	12.00	9.00	4.75
(2)	Johnny Bench/ Pete Rose	10.00	7.50	4.00
(3)	Ernie Banks/ Billy Williams	12.00	9.00	4.75
(4)	Stan Musial/ Bob Gibson	12.00	9.00	4.75
(5)	Roberto Clemente/ Willie Stargell	10.00	7.00	4.00
(6)	Babe Ruth/ Lou Gehrig	15.00	11.00	6.00
(7)	Hank Aaron/ Eddie Mathews	25.00	20.00	10.00
(8)	Mickey Mantle/ Joe DiMaggio	15.00	11.00	6.00
(9)	Don Drysdale/ Reggie Jackson	15.00	11.00	6.00
(10)	Carl Yastrzemski/ Hank Aaron	18.00	13.50	7.25

1988 King-B

Created by Mike Schechter Associates, the 1988 King-B set consists of 24 numbered discs that measure 2-3/4" in size. The cards were inserted in specially marked 7/16 ounce tubs of Jerky Stuff (shredded beef jerky). The card fronts feature full-color photos surrounded by a blue border. The King-B logo appears in the upper left

portion of the disc. The disc backs are printed in blue on white stock and carry player personal and playing information. Team insignias have been airbrushed from the players' caps and jerseys.

		MT	NR MT	EX
Complete Set:		35.00	27.00	15.00
Common Player:		.75	.60	.30
1	Mike Schmidt	1.75	1.25	.70
2	Dale Murphy	1.75	1.25	.70
3	Kirby Puckett	1.50	1.25	.60
4	Ozzie Smith	1.00	.70	.40
5	Tony Gwynn	1.50	1.25	.60
6	Mark McGwire	2.50	2.00	1.00
7	George Brett	1.75	1.25	.70
8	Darryl Strawberry	1.75	1.25	.70
9	Wally Joyner	1.50	1.25	.60
10	Cory Snyder	1.00	.70	.40
11	Barry Bonds	1.00	.70	.40
12	Darrell Evans	.75	.60	.30
13	Mike Scott	.75	.60	.30
14	Andre Dawson	1.25	.90	.50
15	Don Mattingly	5.00	3.75	2.00
16	Candy Maldonado	.75	.60	.30
17	Alvin Davis	1.00	.70	.40
18	Carlton Fisk	1.00	.70	.40
19	Fernando Valenzuela	1.00	.70	.40
20	Roger Clemens	2.00	1.50	.80
21	Larry Parrish	.75	.60	.30
22	Eric Davis	2.00	1.50	.80
23	Paul Molitor	1.00	.70	.40
24	Cal Ripken, Jr.	1.75	1.25	.70

1989 King-B

The second King-B baseball card set created by Mike Schechter Associates also consists of 24 circular baseball cards measuring 2-3/4" across. The cards were inserted into specially-marked tubs of "Jerky Stuff." The card fronts feature full-color photos bordered in red. The King-B logo appears in the upper left portion of the disc. Like the 1988 set, the team insignias have airbrushed from uniforms and caps. The backs are printed in red and display personal information and stats.

		MT	NR MT	EX
Complete Set:		30.00	22.00	12.00
Common Player:		.75	.60	.30
1	Kirk Gibson	1.00	.70	.40
2	Eddie Murray	1.00	.70	.40
3	Wade Boggs	2.25	1.75	.90
4	Mark McGwire	2.25	1.75	.90
5	Ryne Sandberg	1.75	1.25	.70
6	Ozzie Guillen	.75	.60	.30
7	Chris Sabo	1.25	.90	.50
8	Joe Carter	1.00	.70	.40
9	Alan Trammell	1.00	.70	.40
10	Nolan Ryan	2.50	2.00	1.00
11	Bo Jackson	2.50	2.00	1.00
12	Orel Hershiser	1.00	.70	.40
13	Robin Yount	1.50	1.25	.60
14	Frank Viola	1.00	.70	.40
15	Darryl Strawberry	1.50	1.25	.60
16	Dave Winfield	1.00	.70	.40
17	Jose Canseco	3.50	2.75	1.50
18	Von Hayes	.75	.60	.30
19	Andy Van Slyke	.75	.60	.30
20	Pedro Guerrero	1.00	.70	.40
21	Tony Gwynn	1.75	1.25	.70
22	Will Clark	2.50	2.00	1.00
23	Danny Jackson	.75	.60	.30
24	Pete Incaviglia	.75	.60	.30

1986 Kitty Clover

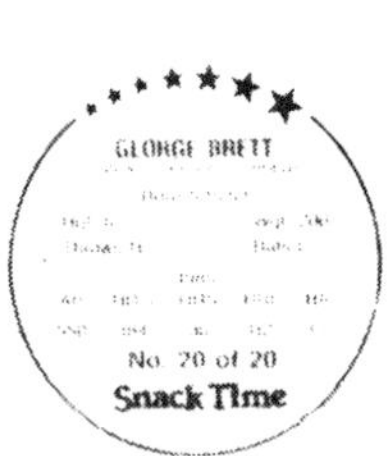

Twenty players of the 1985 World's Champion Kansas City Royals were featured in a round card set inserted into packages of potato chips in the K.C. area. The 2-7/8" discs were similar to a handful of snack issues produced by Mike Schecter Associates in that team logos have been airbrushed off the players' caps, and the photos of some of the players can be found on other regional issues of 1986.

		MT	NR MT	EX
Complete Set:		20.00	15.00	8.00
Common Player:		.70	.50	.30
1	Lonnie Smith	.70	.50	.30
2	Buddy Biancalana	.70	.50	.30
3	Bret Saberhagen	1.75	1.25	.70
4	Hal McRae	.90	.70	.35
5	Onix Concepcion	.70	.50	.30
6	Jorge Orta	.70	.50	.30
7	Bud Black	.70	.50	.30
8	Dan Quisenberry	1.00	.70	.40
9	Dane Iorg	.70	.50	.30
10	Charlie Leibrandt	.80	.60	.30
11	Pat Sheridan	.70	.50	.30
12	John Wathan	.80	.60	.30
13	Frank White	1.00	.70	.40
14	Darryl Motley	.70	.50	.30
15	Willie Wilson	1.25	.90	.50
16	Danny Jackson	1.25	.90	.50
17	Steve Balboni	.80	.60	.30
18	Jim Sundberg	.70	.50	.30
19	Mark Gubicza	1.25	.90	.50
20	George Brett	3.25	2.50	1.25

1987 Kraft

Kraft Foods, Inc. issued a 48-card set on specially marked packages of their Macaroni & Cheese Dinners. Titled "Home Plate Heroes," 24 two-card panels measuring 3-1/2" by 7-1/8" make up the set. Individual cards measure 2-1/4" by 3-1/2" and are numbered 1 through 48. The blank-backed cards feature fronts with full-color photos, although all team insignias have been erased. In conjunction with the card set, Kraft offered a contest to "Win A Day With A Major Leaguer." Mike Schecter Associates produced the set for Kraft. 120 different panel combinatons can be found.

		MT	NR MT	EX
Complete Set:		35.00	27.50	15.00
Common Player:		.20	.15	.08
1	Eddie Murray	.75	.60	.30
2	Dale Murphy	1.00	.70	.40
3	Cal Ripken	.75	.60	.30
4	Mike Scott	.35	.25	.14
5	Jim Rice	.50	.40	.20
6	Jody Davis	.20	.15	.08
7	Wade Boggs	1.50	1.25	.60
8	Ryne Sandberg	.50	.40	.20
9	Wally Joyner	1.50	1.25	.60
10	Eric Davis	1.25	.90	.50

		MT	NR MT	EX
11	Ozzie Guillen	.20	.15	.08
12	Tony Pena	.20	.15	.08
13	Harold Baines	.35	.25	.14
14	Johnny Ray	.20	.15	.08
15	Joe Carter	.35	.25	.14
16	Ozzie Smith	.35	.25	.14
17	Cory Snyder	.60	.45	.25
18	Vince Coleman	.35	.25	.14
19	Kirk Gibson	.50	.40	.20
20	Steve Garvey	.75	.60	.30
21	George Brett	1.00	.70	.40
22	John Tudor	.20	.15	.08
23	Robin Yount	.70	.50	.30
24	Von Hayes	.35	.25	.14
25	Kent Hrbek	.50	.40	.20
26	Darryl Strawberry	1.00	.70	.40
27	Kirby Puckett	.75	.60	.30
28	Ron Darling	.35	.25	.14
29	Don Mattingly	2.50	2.00	1.00
30	Mike Schmidt	1.00	.70	.40
31	Rickey Henderson	.75	.60	.30
32	Fernando Valenzuela	.50	.40	.20
33	Dave Winfield	.60	.45	.25
34	Pete Rose	1.25	.90	.50
35	Jose Canseco	2.00	1.50	.80
36	Glenn Davis	.35	.25	.14
37	Alvin Davis	.35	.25	.14
38	Steve Sax	.35	.25	.14
39	Pete Incaviglia	.70	.50	.30
40	Jeff Reardon	.35	.25	.14
41	Jesse Barfield	.35	.25	.14
42	Hubie Brooks	.20	.15	.08
43	George Bell	.50	.40	.20
44	Tony Gwynn	.75	.60	.30
45	Roger Clemens	1.00	.70	.40
46	Chili Davis	.20	.15	.08
47	Mike Witt	.20	.15	.08
48	Nolan Ryan	1.00	.70	.40

L

1912 L1 Leathers

One of the more unusual baseball collectibles of the tobacco era, the L1 "Leathers" were issued by Helmar Tobacco Co. in 1912 as a premium with its "Turkish Trophies" brand of ciarettes. The set featured 25 of the top baseball players and shared a checklist with the closely-related S81 "Silks," which were another part of the same promotion. The "Leathers," advertised as being 10" by 12", featured drawings of baseball players on horsehide-shaped pieces of leather. The drawings were based on the pictures used for the popular T-3 Turkey Red series issued a year earlier. Twenty of the 25 players in the "Leathers" set are from the T3 set. Five pitchers (Rube Marquard, Rube Benton, Marty O'Toole, Grover Alexander and Russ Ford) not pictured in T3 were added to the "Leathers" set, and the Frank Baker error was corrected. According to the promotion, each "Leather" was available in exchange for 50 Helmar coupons. In addition to the 25 baseball stars, the "Leathers" set also included more than one hundred other subjects, including female athletes and bathing beauties, famous generals, Indian chiefs, actresses, national flags, college mascots and others.

		NR MT	EX	VG
Complete Set:		1350.	58000.	29000.
Common Player:		2500.	1250.	750.00
86	Rube Marquard	5000.	2000.	800.00
87	Marty O'Toole	2500.	1250.	750.00
88	Rube Benton	2500.	1250.	750.00
89	Grover Alexander	6000.	3000.	1750.
90	Russ Ford	2500.	1250.	750.00
91	John McGraw	5250.	2100.	825.00
92	Nap Rucker	2500.	1250.	750.00
93	Mike Mitchell	2500.	1250.	750.00
94	Chief Bender	4500.	1800.	700.00
95	Home Run Baker	4500.	1800.	700.00
96	Nap Lajoie	7500.	3000.	1000.
97	Joe Tinker	4750.	1900.	775.00
98	Sherry Magee	2500.	1250.	750.00
99	Howie Camnitz	2500.	1250.	750.00
100	Eddie Collins	4900.	2000.	800.00
101	Red Dooin	2500.	1250.	750.00
102	Ty Cobb	15000.	6000.	2400.
103	Hugh Jennings	4500.	1800.	700.00
104	Roger Bresnahan	4500.	1800.	700.00
105	Jake Stahl	2500.	1250.	750.00
106	Tris Speaker	7500.	3000.	1200.
107	Ed Walsh	5500.	2100.	800.00
108	Christy Mathewson	9000.	4000.	1800.
109	Johnny Evers	5000.	2000.	800.00
110	Walter Johnson	10000.	4000.	1800.

1960 Lake to Lake Dairy Braves

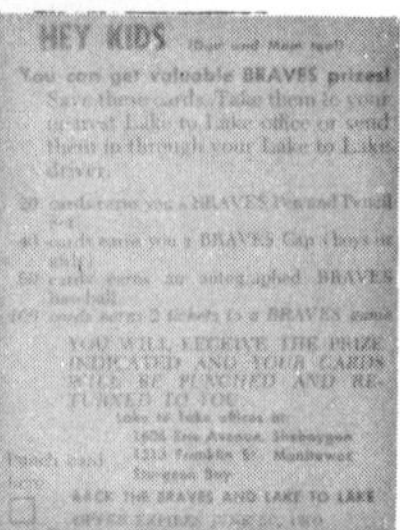

This 28-card set of unnumbered 2-1/2" by 3-1/4" cards offers a special challenge for the condition- conscious collector. Originally issued by being stapled to milk cartons, the cards were redeemable for prizes ranging from pen and pencil sets to Braves tickets. When sent in for redemption, the cards had a hole punched in the corner. Naturally, collectors most desire cards without the staple or punch holes. Cards are printed in blue ink on front, red ink on back. Because he was traded in May, and his card withdrawn, the Ray Boone card is scarce; the Billy Bruton card is unaccountably scarcer still.

		NR MT	EX	VG
Complete Set:		950.00	475.00	285.00
Common Player:		12.00	6.00	3.50
(1)	Henry Aaron	200.00	100.00	60.00
(2)	Joe Adcock	17.50	8.75	5.25
(3)	Ray Boone	125.00	62.00	37.00
(4)	Bill Bruton	200.00	100.00	60.00
(5)	Bob Buhl	17.50	8.75	5.25
(6)	Lou Burdette	20.00	10.00	6.00
(7)	Chuck Cottier	12.00	6.00	3.50
(8)	Wes Covington	15.00	7.50	4.50
(9)	Del Crandall	17.50	8.75	5.25
(10)	Charlie Dressen	15.00	7.50	4.50
(11)	Bob Giggie	12.00	6.00	3.50
(12)	Joey Jay	12.00	6.00	3.50
(13)	Johnny Logan	15.00	7.50	4.50
(14)	Felix Mantilla	12.00	6.00	3.50
(15)	Lee Maye	12.00	6.00	3.50
(16)	Don McMahon	12.00	6.00	3.50
(17)	George Myatt	12.00	6.00	3.50
(18)	Andy Pafko	15.00	7.50	4.50
(19)	Juan Pizarro	12.00	6.00	3.50
(20)	Mel Roach	12.00	6.00	3.50
(21)	Bob Rush	12.00	6.00	3.50
(22)	Bob Scheffing	12.00	6.00	3.50
(23)	Red Schoendienst	20.00	10.00	6.00
(24)	Warren Spahn	50.00	25.00	15.00
(25)	Al Spangler	12.00	6.00	3.50
(26)	Frank Torre	12.00	6.00	3.50
(27)	Carl Willey	12.00	6.00	3.50
(28)	Whitlow Wyatt	12.00	6.00	3.50

1948-49 Leaf

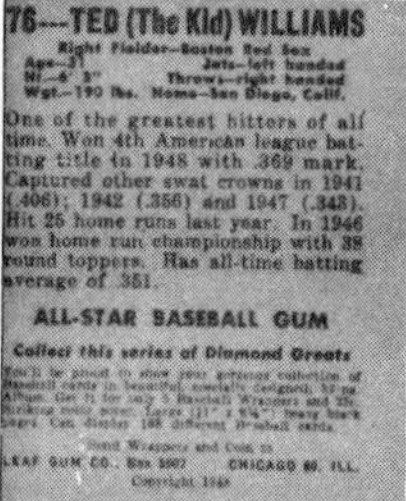

The first color baseball cards of the post-World War II era were the 98-card, 2-3/8" by 2-7/8", set produced by Chicago's Leaf Gum Company in 1948-1949. The color was crude, probably helping to make the set less popular than the Bowman issues of the same era. One of the toughest post-war sets to complete, exactly half of the Leaf issue - 49 of the cards - are significantly harder to find than the other 49. Probably intended to confound bubble gum buyers of the day, the set is skip-numbered between 1-168. Card backs contain offers of felt pennants, an album for the cards or 5-1/2" by 7-1/2" premium photos of Hall of Famers.

		NR MT	EX	VG
Complete Set:		30000.	15000.	9000.
Common Player:		20.00	10.00	6.00
Common Scarce Player:		300.00	150.00	90.00
1	Joe DiMaggio	1200.	600.00	350.00
3	Babe Ruth	1500.	750.00	450.00
4	Stan Musial	450.00	225.00	135.00
5	Virgil Trucks	300.00	150.00	90.00
8	Leroy Paige	2000.	1000.	600.00
10	Paul Trout	20.00	10.00	6.00
11	Phil Rizzuto	75.00	37.00	22.00
13	Casimer Michaels	300.00	150.00	90.00
14	Billy Johnson	18.00	9.00	5.50
17	Frank Overmire	20.00	10.00	6.00
19	John Wyrostek	300.00	150.00	90.00
20	Hank Sauer	300.00	150.00	90.00
22	Al Evans	20.00	10.00	6.00
26	Sam Chapman	20.00	10.00	6.00
27	Mickey Harris	20.00	10.00	6.00
28	Jim Hegan	20.00	10.00	6.00
29	Elmer Valo	20.00	10.00	6.00
30	Bill Goodman	300.00	150.00	90.00
31	Lou Brissie	20.00	10.00	6.00
32	Warren Spahn	200.00	100.00	60.00
33	Harry Lowrey	300.00	150.00	90.00
36	Al Zarilla	300.00	150.00	90.00
38	Ted Kluszewski	40.00	20.00	12.00
39	Ewell Blackwell	35.00	17.50	10.50
42	Kent Peterson	20.00	10.00	6.00
43	Eddie Stevens	300.00	150.00	90.00
45	Ken Keltner	300.00	150.00	90.00
46	Johnny Mize	90.00	45.00	27.00
47	George Vico	20.00	10.00	6.00
48	Johnny Schmitz	300.00	150.00	90.00
49	Del Ennis	20.00	10.00	6.00
50	Dick Wakefield	20.00	10.00	6.00
51	Alvin Dark	350.00	175.00	105.00
53	John Vandermeer (Vander Meer)	18.00	9.00	5.50
54	Bobby Adams	300.00	150.00	90.00
55	Tommy Henrich	350.00	175.00	105.00
56	Larry Jensen (Jansen)	20.00	10.00	6.00
57	Bob McCall	20.00	10.00	6.00
59	Lucius Appling	50.00	25.00	15.00
61	Jake Early	20.00	10.00	6.00
62	Eddie Joost	300.00	150.00	90.00
63	Barney McCosky	300.00	150.00	90.00
65	Bob Elliot (Elliott)	20.00	10.00	6.00
66	Orval Grove	300.00	150.00	90.00
68	Ed Miller	300.00	150.00	90.00
70	John Wagner	250.00	125.00	75.00
72	Hank Edwards	20.00	10.00	6.00
73	Pat Seerey	20.00	10.00	6.00
75	Dom DiMaggio	400.00	200.00	120.00
76	Ted Williams	900.00	450.00	275.00
77	Roy Smalley	20.00	10.00	6.00
78	Walter Evers	300.00	150.00	90.00
79	Jackie Robinson	550.00	225.00	165.00
81	George Kurowski	300.00	150.00	90.00
82	Johnny Lindell	20.00	10.00	6.00
83	Bobby Doerr	90.00	45.00	27.00
84	Sid Hudson	20.00	10.00	6.00
85	Dave Philley	300.00	150.00	90.00
86	Ralph Weigel	20.00	10.00	6.00
88	Frank Gustine	300.00	150.00	90.00
91	Ralph Kiner	90.00	45.00	27.00
93	Bob Feller	1200.	600.00	350.00
95	George Stirnweiss	20.00	10.00	6.00
97	Martin Marion	20.00	10.00	6.00
98	Hal Newhouser	400.00	200.00	125.00
102a	Gene Hermansk (incorrect spelling)	300.00	150.00	90.00
102b	Gene Hermanski (correct spelling)	20.00	10.00	6.00
104	Edward Stewart	300.00	150.00	90.00
106	Lou Boudreau	80.00	40.00	25.00
108	Matthew Batts	300.00	150.00	90.00
111	Gerald Priddy	20.00	10.00	6.00
113	Emil Leonard	300.00	150.00	90.00
117	Joe Gordon	20.00	10.00	6.00
120	George Kell	550.00	275.00	165.00
121	John Pesky	300.00	150.00	90.00
123	Clifford Fannin	300.00	150.00	90.00
125	Andy Pafko	20.00	10.00	6.00
127	Enos Slaughter	600.00	300.00	180.00
128	Warren Rosar	20.00	10.00	6.00
129	Kirby Higbe	300.00	150.00	90.00
131	Sid Gordon	300.00	150.00	90.00
133	Tommy Holmes	300.00	150.00	90.00
136a	Cliff Aberson (full sleeve)	20.00	10.00	6.00
136b	Cliff Aberson (short sleeve)	175.00	87.00	52.00
137	Harry Walker	300.00	150.00	90.00
138	Larry Doby	400.00	200.00	120.00
139	Johnny Hopp	20.00	10.00	6.00
142	Danny Murtaugh	300.00	150.00	90.00
143	Dick Sisler	300.00	150.00	90.00
144	Bob Dillinger	300.00	150.00	90.00
146	Harold Reiser	400.00	200.00	120.00
149	Henry Majeski	300.00	150.00	90.00
153	Floyd Baker	300.00	150.00	90.00
158	Harry Brecheen	300.00	150.00	90.00
159	Mizell Platt	20.00	10.00	6.00
160	Bob Scheffing	300.00	150.00	90.00
161	Vernon Stephens	400.00	200.00	120.00
163	Freddy Hutchinson	400.00	200.00	120.00
165	Dale Mitchell	300.00	150.00	90.00
168	Phil Cavaretta (Cavarretta)	300.00	150.00	90.00

A player's name in *italic* type indicates a rookie card. An (FC) indicates a player's first card for that particular card company.

1960 Leaf

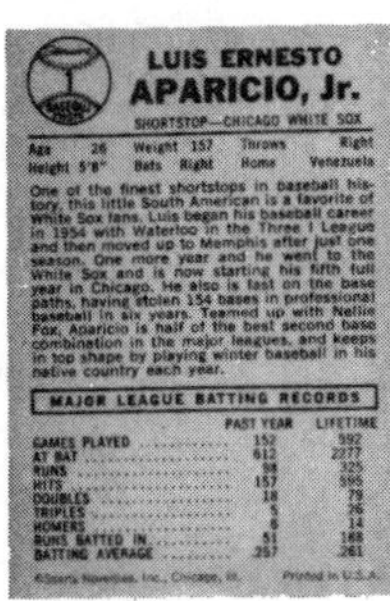

While known to the hobby as "Leaf" cards, this set of 144 cards carries the copyright of Sports Novelties Inc., Chicago. The 2-1/2" by 3-1/2" cards feature black and white player portrait photos, with background airbrushed away. Cards were sold in 5¢ wax packs with a marble, rather than a piece of bubble gum. The second half of the set, cards #73-144, are very scarce and make the set a real challenge for the collector. Card #25, Jim Grant, is found in two versions, with his own picture (black cap) and with a photo of Brooks Lawrence (white cap). Eight cards (#'s 1, 12, 17, 23, 35, 58, 61 and 72) exist with close-up photos that are much rarer than the normal cap to chest photos. It is believed the scarce "face only" cards are proof cards prepared by Leaf as only a handful are known to exist.

		NR MT	EX	VG
Complete Set:		1800.	900.00	550.00
Common Player: 1-72		4.00	2.00	1.25
Common Player: 73-144		15.00	7.50	4.50
1	Luis Aparicio	25.00	12.50	7.50
2	Woody Held	4.00	2.00	1.25
3	Frank Lary	3.00	1.50	.90
4	Camilo Pascual	3.00	1.50	.90
5	Frank Herrera	4.00	2.00	1.25
6	Felipe Alou	3.00	1.50	.90
7	Bennie Daniels	4.00	2.00	1.25
8	Roger Craig	3.00	1.50	.90
9	Eddie Kasko	4.00	2.00	1.25
10	Bob Grim	4.00	2.00	1.25
11	Jim Busby	4.00	2.00	1.25
12	Ken Boyer	4.00	2.00	1.25
13	Bob Boyd	4.00	2.00	1.25
14	Sam Jones	4.00	2.00	1.25
15	Larry Jackson	4.00	2.00	1.25
16	Roy Face	4.00	2.00	1.25
17	Walt Moryn	4.00	2.00	1.25
18	Jim Gilliam	4.00	2.00	1.25
19	Don Newcombe	3.00	1.50	.90
20	Glen Hobbie	4.00	2.00	1.25
21	Pedro Ramos	4.00	2.00	1.25
22	Ryne Duren	4.00	2.00	1.25
23	Joe Jay	4.00	2.00	1.25
24	Lou Berberet	4.00	2.00	1.25
25a	Jim Grant (white cap, photo actually Brooks Lawrence)	25.00	12.50	7.50
25b	Jim Grant (dark cap, correct photo)	50.00	25.00	15.00
26	Tom Borland	4.00	2.00	1.25
27	Brooks Robinson	50.00	25.00	15.00
28	Jerry Adair	3.00	1.50	.90
29	Ron Jackson	4.00	2.00	1.25
30	George Strickland	4.00	2.00	1.25
31	Rocky Bridges	4.00	2.00	1.25
32	Bill Tuttle	4.00	2.00	1.25
33	Ken Hunt	3.00	1.50	.90
34	Hal Griggs	4.00	2.00	1.25
35	Jim Coates	3.00	1.50	.90
36	Brooks Lawrence	4.00	2.00	1.25
37	Duke Snider	50.00	25.00	15.00
38	Al Spangler	4.00	2.00	1.25
39	Jim Owens	4.00	2.00	1.25
40	Bill Virdon	4.00	2.00	1.25
41	Ernie Broglio	4.00	2.00	1.25
42	Andre Rodgers	4.00	2.00	1.25
43	Julio Becquer	4.00	2.00	1.25
44	Tony Taylor	4.00	2.00	1.25
45	Jerry Lynch	3.00	1.50	.90
46	Cletis Boyer	4.00	2.00	1.25
47	Jerry Lumpe	3.00	1.50	.90
48	Charlie Maxwell	4.00	2.00	1.25
49	Jim Perry	3.00	1.50	.90
50	Danny McDevitt	4.00	2.00	1.25
51	Juan Pizarro	4.00	2.00	1.25
52	Dallas Green	4.00	2.00	1.25
53	Bob Friend	3.00	1.50	.90
54	Jack Sanford	3.00	1.50	.90
55	Jim Rivera	4.00	2.00	1.25
56	Ted Wills	4.00	2.00	1.25
57	Milt Pappas	3.00	1.50	.90
58a	Hal Smith (team & position on back)	4.00	2.00	1.25
58b	Hal Smith (team blackened out on back)	50.00	25.00	15.00
58c	Hal Smith (team missing on back)	50.00	25.00	15.00
59	Bob Avila	4.00	2.00	1.25
60	Clem Labine	3.00	1.50	.90
61	Vic Rehm	3.00	1.50	.90
62	John Gabler	3.00	1.50	.90
63	John Tsitouris	4.00	2.00	1.25
64	Dave Sisler	4.00	2.00	1.25
65	Vic Power	3.00	1.50	.90
66	Earl Battey	3.00	1.50	.90
67	Bob Purkey	3.00	1.50	.90
68	Moe Drabowsky	4.00	2.00	1.25
69	Hoyt Wilhelm	6.00	3.00	1.75
70	Humberto Robinson	4.00	2.00	1.25
71	Whitey Herzog	4.00	2.00	1.25
72	Dick Donovan	3.00	1.50	.90
73	Gordon Jones	15.00	7.50	4.50
74	Joe Hicks	15.00	7.50	4.50
75	Ray Culp	18.00	9.00	5.50
76	Dick Drott	15.00	7.50	4.50
77	Bob Duliba	15.00	7.50	4.50
78	Art Ditmar	18.00	9.00	5.50
79	Steve Korcheck	15.00	7.50	4.50
80	Henry Mason	15.00	7.50	4.50
81	Harry Simpson	15.00	7.50	4.50
82	Gene Green	15.00	7.50	4.50
83	Bob Shaw	15.00	7.50	4.50
84	Howard Reed	15.00	7.50	4.50
85	Dick Stigman	15.00	7.50	4.50
86	Rip Repulski	15.00	7.50	4.50
87	Seth Morehead	15.00	7.50	4.50
88	Camilo Carreon	15.00	7.50	4.50
89	John Blanchard	18.00	9.00	5.50
90	Billy Hoeft	15.00	7.50	4.50
91	Fred Hopke	18.00	9.00	5.50
92	Joe Martin	15.00	7.50	4.50
93	Wally Shannon	18.00	9.00	5.50
94	Baseball's Two Hal Smiths (Harold Raymond Smith, Harold Wayne Smith)	20.00	10.00	6.00
95	Al Schroll	15.00	7.50	4.50
96	John Kucks	15.00	7.50	4.50
97	Tom Morgan	15.00	7.50	4.50
98	Willie Jones	15.00	7.50	4.50
99	Marshall Renfroe	18.00	9.00	5.50
100	Willie Tasby	15.00	7.50	4.50
101	Irv Noren	15.00	7.50	4.50
102	Russ Snyder	15.00	7.50	4.50
103	Bob Turley	30.00	15.00	9.00
104	Jim Woods	15.00	7.50	4.50
105	Ronnie Kline	15.00	7.50	4.50
106	Steve Bilko	15.00	7.50	4.50
107	Elmer Valo	18.00	9.00	5.50
108	Tom McAvoy	18.00	9.00	5.50
109	Stan Williams	15.00	7.50	4.50
110	Earl Averill	15.00	7.50	4.50
111	Lee Walls	15.00	7.50	4.50
112	Paul Richards	18.00	9.00	5.50
113	Ed Sadowski	15.00	7.50	4.50
114	Stover McIlwain	18.00	9.00	5.50
115	Chuck Tanner (photo actually Ken Kuhn)	20.00	10.00	6.00
116	Lou Klimchock	15.00	7.50	4.50
117	Neil Chrisley	15.00	7.50	4.50
118	John Callison	20.00	10.00	6.00
119	Hal Smith	15.00	7.50	4.50
120	Carl Sawatski	15.00	7.50	4.50
121	Frank Leja	18.00	9.00	5.50
122	Earl Torgeson	15.00	7.50	4.50
123	Art Schult	15.00	7.50	4.50
124	Jim Brosnan	18.00	9.00	5.50
125	George Anderson	40.00	20.00	12.00
126	Joe Pignatano	15.00	7.50	4.50
127	Rocky Nelson	15.00	7.50	4.50
128	Orlando Cepeda	50.00	25.00	15.00
129	Daryl Spencer	15.00	7.50	4.50
130	Ralph Lumenti	15.00	7.50	4.50
131	Sam Taylor	15.00	7.50	4.50
132	Harry Brecheen	18.00	9.00	5.50
133	Johnny Groth	15.00	7.50	4.50
134	Wayne Terwilliger	15.00	7.50	4.50
135	Kent Hadley	18.00	9.00	5.50
136	Faye Throneberry	15.00	7.50	4.50
137	Jack Meyer	15.00	7.50	4.50
138	Chuck Cottier	15.00	7.50	4.50
139	Joe DeMaestri	18.00	9.00	5.50
140	Gene Freese	15.00	7.50	4.50
141	Curt Flood	40.00	20.00	12.00
142	Gino Cimoli	15.00	7.50	4.50
143	Clay Dalrymple	15.00	7.50	4.50
144	Jim Bunning	75.00	38.00	23.00

1985 Leaf-Donruss

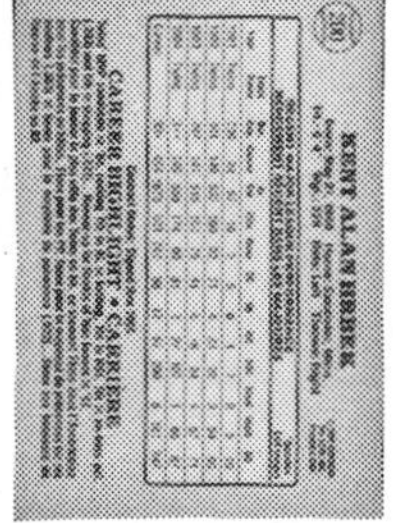

In an attempt to share in the Canadian baseball card market, Donruss, in 1985, issued a 264-card version of its regular set to be sold in Canada. Fronts of the 2-1/2" by 3-1/2" cards are virtually identical to the regular '85 Donruss cards of the same players, except that a green stylized leaf has been added to the logo in the upper-left. On back, player biographies have been re-written to accomodate both English and French versions, and new card numbers have been assigned. The 264 cards in this shortened set concentrate on star-caliber players, as well as those of Canada's two major league teams. A special two-card subset, "Canadian Greats," featured paintings of Dave Stieb and Tim Raines. The Leaf-Donruss cards were widely distributed in the U.S. through hobby dealers.

		MT	NR MT	EX
Complete Set:		27.00	20.00	11.00
Common Player:		.07	.05	.03
1	Ryne Sandberg (DK)	.30	.25	.12
2	Doug DeCinces (DK)	.07	.05	.03
3	Rich Dotson (DK)	.20	.15	.08
4	Bert Blyleven (DK)	.12	.09	.05
5	Lou Whitaker (DK)	.20	.15	.08
6	Dan Quisenberry (DK)	.20	.15	.08
7	Don Mattingly (DK)	5.00	3.75	2.00
8	Carney Lansford (DK)	.07	.05	.03
9	Frank Tanana (DK)	.07	.05	.03
10	Willie Upshaw (DK)	.07	.05	.03
11	Claudell Washington (DK)	.07	.05	.03
12	Mike Marshall (DK)	.15	.11	.06
13	Joaquin Andujar (DK)	.07	.05	.03
14	Cal Ripken, Jr. (DK)	.40	.30	.15
15	Jim Rice (DK)	.30	.25	.12
16	Don Sutton (DK)	.20	.15	.08
17	Frank Viola (DK)	.20	.15	.08
18	Alvin Davis (DK)	.25	.20	.10
19	Mario Soto (DK)	.07	.05	.03
20	Jose Cruz (DK)	.07	.05	.03
21	Charlie Lea (DK)	.07	.05	.03
22	Jesse Orosco (DK)	.07	.05	.03
23	Juan Samuel (DK)	.25	.20	.10
24	Tony Pena (DK)	.07	.05	.03
25	Tony Gwynn (DK)	.35	.25	.14
26	Bob Brenly (DK)	.07	.05	.03
27	Steve Kiefer (RR)	.07	.05	.03
28	Joe Morgan	.20	.15	.08
29	Luis Leal	.07	.05	.03
30	Dan Gladden	.15	.11	.06
31	Shane Rawley	.07	.05	.03
32	Mark Clear	.07	.05	.03
33	Terry Kennedy	.07	.05	.03
34	Hal McRae	.07	.05	.03
35	Mickey Rivers	.07	.05	.03
36	Tom Brunansky	.20	.15	.08
37	LaMarr Hoyt	.07	.05	.03
38	Orel Hershiser	6.00	4.50	2.50
39	Chris Bando	.07	.05	.03
40	Lee Lacy	.07	.05	.03
41	Lance Parrish	.25	.20	.10
42	George Foster	.12	.09	.05
43	Kevin McReynolds	.50	.40	.20
44	Robin Yount	.30	.25	.12
45	Craig McMurtry	.07	.05	.03
46	Mike Witt	.20	.15	.08
47	Gary Redus	.07	.05	.03
48	Dennis Rasmussen	.20	.15	.08
49	Gary Woods	.07	.05	.03
50	Phil Bradley	.60	.45	.25
51	Steve Bedrosian	.20	.15	.08
52	Duane Walker	.07	.05	.03
53	Geoff Zahn	.07	.05	.03
54	Dave Stieb	.20	.15	.08
55	Pascual Perez	.07	.05	.03
56	Mark Langston	.70	.50	.30
57	Bob Dernier	.07	.05	.03
58	Joe Cowley	.07	.05	.03
59	Dan Schatzeder	.07	.05	.03
60	Ozzie Smith	.15	.11	.06
61	Bob Knepper	.07	.05	.03
62	Keith Hernandez	.30	.25	.12
63	Rick Rhoden	.07	.05	.03
64	Alejandro Pena	.07	.05	.03
65	Damaso Garcia	.07	.05	.03
66	Chili Davis	.07	.05	.03
67	Al Oliver	.20	.15	.08
68	Alan Wiggins	.07	.05	.03
69	Darryl Motley	.07	.05	.03
70	Gary Ward	.07	.05	.03
71	John Butcher	.07	.05	.03
72	Scott McGregor	.07	.05	.03
73	Bruce Hurst	.20	.15	.08
74	Dwayne Murphy	.07	.05	.03
75	Greg Luzinski	.20	.15	.08
76	Pat Tabler	.07	.05	.03
77	Chet Lemon	.07	.05	.03
78	Jim Sundberg	.07	.05	.03
79	Wally Backman	.07	.05	.03
80	Terry Puhl	.07	.05	.03
81	Storm Davis	.07	.05	.03
82	Jim Wohlford	.07	.05	.03
83	Willie Randolph	.07	.05	.03
84	Ron Cey	.07	.05	.03
85	Jim Beattie	.07	.05	.03
86	Rafael Ramirez	.07	.05	.03
87	Cesar Cedeno	.07	.05	.03
88	Bobby Grich	.07	.05	.03
89	Jason Thompson	.07	.05	.03
90	Steve Sax	.15	.11	.06
91	Tony Fernandez	.15	.11	.06
92	Jeff Leonard	.07	.05	.03
93	Von Hayes	.07	.05	.03
94	Steve Garvey	.30	.25	.12
95	Steve Balboni	.07	.05	.03
96	Larry Parrish	.07	.05	.03
97	Tim Teufel	.07	.05	.03
98	Sammy Stewart	.07	.05	.03
99	Roger Clemens	6.00	4.50	2.50
100	Steve Kemp	.07	.05	.03
101	Tom Seaver	.35	.25	.14
102	Andre Thornton	.07	.05	.03
103	Kirk Gibson	.20	.15	.08
104	Ted Simmons	.20	.15	.08
105	David Palmer	.07	.05	.03
106	Roy Lee Jackson	.07	.05	.03
107	Kirby Puckett	6.00	4.50	2.50
108	Charlie Hough	.07	.05	.03
109	Mike Boddicker	.07	.05	.03
110	Willie Wilson	.20	.15	.08
111	Tim Lollar	.07	.05	.03
112	Tony Armas	.07	.05	.03
113	Steve Carlton	.30	.25	.12

		MT	NR MT	EX
114	Gary Lavelle	.07	.05	.03
115	Cliff Johnson	.07	.05	.03
116	Ray Burris	.07	.05	.03
117	Rudy Law	.07	.05	.03
118	Mike Scioscia	.07	.05	.03
119	Kent Tekulve	.07	.05	.03
120	George Vukovich	.07	.05	.03
121	Barbaro Garbey	.07	.05	.03
122	Mookie Wilson	.07	.05	.03
123	Ben Oglivie	.07	.05	.03
124	Jerry Mumphrey	.07	.05	.03
125	Willie McGee	.15	.11	.06
126	Jeff Reardon	.20	.15	.08
127	Dave Winfield	.30	.25	.12
128	Lee Smith	.07	.05	.03
129	Ken Phelps	.07	.05	.03
130	Rick Camp	.07	.05	.03
131	Dave Concepcion	.07	.05	.03
132	Rod Carew	.35	.25	.14
133	Andre Dawson	.25	.20	.10
134	Doyle Alexander	.07	.05	.03
135	Miguel Dilone	.07	.05	.03
136	Jim Gott	.07	.05	.03
137	Eric Show	.07	.05	.03
138	Phil Niekro	.20	.15	.08
139	Rick Sutcliffe	.20	.15	.08
140	Two For The Title (Don Mattingly, Dave Winfield)	2.00	1.50	.80
141	Ken Oberkfell	.07	.05	.03
142	Jack Morris	.15	.11	.06
143	Lloyd Moseby	.20	.15	.08
144	Pete Rose	.80	.60	.30
145	Gary Gaetti	.20	.15	.08
146	Don Baylor	.20	.15	.08
147	Bobby Meacham	.07	.05	.03
148	Frank White	.07	.05	.03
149	Mark Thurmond	.07	.05	.03
150	Dwight Evans	.20	.15	.08
151	Al Holland	.07	.05	.03
152	Joel Youngblood	.07	.05	.03
153	Rance Mulliniks	.07	.05	.03
154	Bill Caudill	.07	.05	.03
155	Carlton Fisk	.15	.11	.06
156	Rick Honeycutt	.07	.05	.03
157	John Candelaria	.07	.05	.03
158	Alan Trammell	.25	.20	.10
159	Darryl Strawberry	1.75	1.25	.70
160	Aurelio Lopez	.07	.05	.03
161	Enos Cabell	.07	.05	.03
162	Dion James	.07	.05	.03
163	Bruce Sutter	.20	.15	.08
164	Razor Shines	.07	.05	.03
165	Butch Wynegar	.07	.05	.03
166	Rich Bordi	.07	.05	.03
167	Spike Owen	.07	.05	.03
168	Chris Chambliss	.07	.05	.03
169	Dave Parker	.20	.15	.08
170	Reggie Jackson	.35	.25	.14
171	Bryn Smith	.07	.05	.03
172	Dave Collins	.07	.05	.03
173	Dave Engle	.07	.05	.03
174	Buddy Bell	.07	.05	.03
175	Mike Flanagan	.07	.05	.03
176	George Brett	.40	.30	.15
177	Graig Nettles	.20	.15	.08
178	Jerry Koosman	.07	.05	.03
179	Wade Boggs	3.00	2.25	1.25
180	Jody Davis	.07	.05	.03
181	Ernie Whitt	.07	.05	.03
182	Dave Kingman	.20	.15	.08
183	Vance Law	.07	.05	.03
184	Fernando Valenzuela	.20	.15	.08
185	Bill Madlock	.07	.05	.03
186	Brett Butler	.07	.05	.03
187	Doug Sisk	.07	.05	.03
188	Dan Petry	.07	.05	.03
189	Joe Niekro	.07	.05	.03
190	Rollie Fingers	.12	.09	.05
191	David Green	.07	.05	.03
192	Steve Rogers	.07	.05	.03
193	Ken Griffey	.07	.05	.03
194	Scott Sanderson	.07	.05	.03
195	Barry Bonnell	.07	.05	.03
196	Bruce Benedict	.07	.05	.03
197	Keith Moreland	.07	.05	.03
198	Fred Lynn	.20	.15	.08
199	Tim Wallach	.20	.15	.08
200	Kent Hrbek	.20	.15	.08
201	Pete O'Brien	.07	.05	.03
202	Bud Black	.07	.05	.03
203	Eddie Murray	.35	.25	.14
204	Goose Gossage	.15	.11	.06
205	Mike Schmidt	.40	.30	.15
206	Mike Easler	.07	.05	.03
207	Jack Clark	.15	.11	.06
208	Rickey Henderson	.35	.25	.14
209	Jesse Barfield	.12	.09	.05
210	Ron Kittle	.07	.05	.03
211	Pedro Guerrero	.15	.11	.06
212	Johnny Ray	.07	.05	.03
213	Julio Franco	.20	.15	.08
214	Hubie Brooks	.07	.05	.03
215	Darrell Evans	.20	.15	.08
216	Nolan Ryan	.30	.25	.12
217	Jim Gantner	.07	.05	.03
218	Tim Raines	.35	.25	.14
219	Dave Righetti	.15	.11	.06
220	Gary Matthews	.07	.05	.03
221	Jack Perconte	.07	.05	.03
222	Dale Murphy	.40	.30	.15
223	Brian Downing	.07	.05	.03
224	Mickey Hatcher	.07	.05	.03
225	Lonnie Smith	.07	.05	.03
226	Jorge Orta	.07	.05	.03
227	Milt Wilcox	.07	.05	.03
228	John Denny	.07	.05	.03
229	Marty Barrett	.07	.05	.03
230	Alfredo Griffin	.07	.05	.03
231	Harold Baines	.12	.09	.05
232	Bill Russell	.07	.05	.03
233	Marvell Wynne	.07	.05	.03
234	Dwight Gooden	6.00	4.50	2.50
235	Willie Hernandez	.07	.05	.03
236	Bill Gullickson	.07	.05	.03
237	Ron Guidry	.15	.11	.06
238	Leon Durham	.07	.05	.03
239	Al Cowens	.07	.05	.03
240	Bob Horner	.20	.15	.08
241	Gary Carter	.30	.25	.12
242	Glenn Hubbard	.07	.05	.03
243	Steve Trout	.07	.05	.03
244	Jay Howell	.07	.05	.03
245	Terry Francona	.07	.05	.03
246	Cecil Cooper	.07	.05	.03
247	Larry McWilliams	.07	.05	.03
248	George Bell	.25	.20	.10
249	Larry Herndon	.07	.05	.03
250	Ozzie Virgil	.07	.05	.03
251	Canadian Great (Dave Stieb)	.50	.40	.20
252	Canadian Great (Tim Raines)	.80	.60	.30
253	Ricky Horton	.12	.09	.05
254	Bill Buckner	.20	.15	.08
255	Dan Driessen	.07	.05	.03
256	Ron Darling	.15	.11	.06
257	Doug Flynn	.07	.05	.03
258	Darrell Porter	.07	.05	.03
259	George Hendrick	.07	.05	.03
653	Lou Gehrig Puzzle Card	.07	.05	.03
---	Checklist 1-26 DK	.07	.05	.03
---	Checklist 27-102	.07	.05	.03
---	Checklist 103-178	.07	.05	.03
---	Checklist 179-259	.07	.05	.03

1986 Leaf

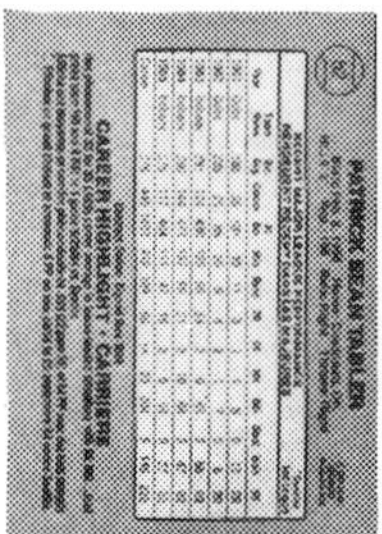

For its second Canadian card set, in 1986, the Donruss name was removed from the front of the company's 264-card issue, identifying the cards as "Leaf '86." Again concentrating on big-name stars and players from the Expos and Blue Jays, the 2-1/2" by 3-1/2" cards feature a design virtually identical to the 1986 Donruss cards. Backs were altered to allow the publication of career highlights in both English and French, and card numbers were changed. The "Canadian Greats" cards in the 1986 Leaf set, painted portraits rather than photos, were Jesse Barfield and Jeff Reardon. Besides being sold in its intended market in Canada, the set was widely distributed in the U.S. through hobby vendors.

		MT	NR MT	EX
	Complete Set:	30.00	22.00	12.00
	Common Player:	.07	.05	.03
1	Kirk Gibson (DK)	.20	.15	.08
2	Goose Gossage (DK)	.12	.09	.05
3	Willie McGee (DK)	.12	.09	.05
4	George Bell (DK)	.30	.25	.12
5	Tony Armas (DK)	.07	.05	.03
6	Chili Davis (DK)	.07	.05	.03
7	Cecil Cooper (DK)	.07	.05	.03
8	Mike Boddicker (DK)	.07	.05	.03
9	Davey Lopes (DK)	.07	.05	.03
10	Bill Doran (DK)	.07	.05	.03
11	Bret Saberhagen (DK)	.20	.15	.08
12	Brett Butler (DK)	.07	.05	.03
13	Harold Baines (DK)	.10	.08	.04
14	Mike Davis	.07	.05	.03
15	Tony Perez (DK)	.10	.08	.04
16	Willie Randolph (DK)	.07	.05	.03
17	Bob Boone (DK)	.07	.05	.03
18	Orel Hershiser (DK)	.60	.45	.25
19	Johnny Ray (DK)	.07	.05	.03
20	Gary Ward (DK)	.07	.05	.03
21	Rick Mahler (DK)	.07	.05	.03
22	Phil Bradley (DK)	.12	.09	.05
23	Jerry Koosman (DK)	.07	.05	.03
24	Tom Brunansky (DK)	.10	.08	.04
25	Andre Dawson (DK)	.25	.20	.10
26	Dwight Gooden (DK)	.80	.60	.30
27	Andres Galarraga (RR)	2.50	2.00	1.00
28	Fred McGriff (RR)	3.00	2.25	1.25
29	Dave Shipanoff (RR)	.07	.05	.03
30	Danny Jackson	.20	.15	.08
31	Robin Yount	.25	.20	.10
32	Mike Fitzgerald	.07	.05	.03
33	Lou Whitaker	.15	.11	.06
34	Alfredo Griffin	.07	.05	.03
35	"Oil Can" Boyd	.07	.05	.03
36	Ron Guidry	.15	.11	.06
37	Rickey Henderson	.30	.25	.12
38	Jack Morris	.15	.11	.06
39	Brian Downing	.07	.05	.03
40	Mike Marshall	.12	.09	.05
41	Tony Gwynn	.35	.25	.14
42	George Brett	.40	.30	.15
43	Jim Gantner	.07	.05	.03
44	Hubie Brooks	.07	.05	.03
45	Tony Fernandez	.15	.11	.06
46	Oddibe McDowell	.20	.15	.08
47	Ozzie Smith	.15	.11	.06
48	Ken Griffey	.07	.05	.03
49	Jose Cruz	.07	.05	.03
50	Mariano Duncan	.07	.05	.03
51	Mike Schmidt	.40	.30	.15
52	Pat Tabler	.07	.05	.03
53	Pete Rose	.80	.60	.30
54	Frank White	.07	.05	.03
55	Carney Lansford	.07	.05	.03
56	Steve Garvey	.30	.25	.12
57	Vance Law	.07	.05	.03
58	Tony Pena	.07	.05	.03
59	Wayne Tolleson	.07	.05	.03
60	Dale Murphy	.40	.30	.15
61	LaMarr Hoyt	.07	.05	.03
62	Ryne Sandberg	.25	.20	.10
63	Gary Carter	.30	.25	.12
64	Lee Smith	.07	.05	.03
65	Alvin Davis	.15	.11	.06
66	Edwin Nunez	.07	.05	.03
67	Kent Hrbek	.20	.15	.08
68	Dave Stieb	.10	.08	.04
69	Kirby Puckett	1.00	.70	.40
70	Paul Molitor	.12	.09	.05
71	Glenn Hubbard	.07	.05	.03
72	Lloyd Moseby	.07	.05	.03
73	Mike Smithson	.07	.05	.03
74	Jeff Leonard	.07	.05	.03
75	Danny Darwin	.07	.05	.03
76	Kevin McReynolds	.15	.11	.06
77	Bill Buckner	.07	.05	.03
78	Ron Oester	.07	.05	.03
79	Tommy Herr	.07	.05	.03
80	Mike Pagliarulo	.20	.15	.08
81	Ron Romanick	.07	.05	.03
82	Brook Jacoby	.10	.08	.04
83	Eddie Murray	.30	.25	.12
84	Gary Pettis	.07	.05	.03
85	Chet Lemon	.07	.05	.03
86	Toby Harrah	.07	.05	.03
87	Mike Scioscia	.07	.05	.03
88	Bert Blyleven	.12	.09	.05
89	Dave Righetti	.15	.11	.06
90	Bob Knepper	.07	.05	.03
91	Fernando Valenzuela	.20	.15	.08
92	Dave Dravecky	.07	.05	.03
93	Julio Franco	.10	.08	.04
94	Keith Moreland	.07	.05	.03
95	Darryl Motley	.07	.05	.03
96	Jack Clark	.15	.11	.06
97	Tim Wallach	.12	.09	.05
98	Steve Balboni	.07	.05	.03
99	Storm Davis	.07	.05	.03
100	Jay Howell	.07	.05	.03
101	Alan Trammell	.25	.20	.10
102	Willie Hernandez	.07	.05	.03
103	Don Mattingly	3.00	2.25	1.25
104	Lee Lacy	.07	.05	.03
105	Pedro Guerrero	.15	.11	.06
106	Willie Wilson	.10	.08	.04
107	Craig Reynolds	.07	.05	.03
108	Tim Raines	.30	.25	.12
109	Shane Rawley	.07	.05	.03
110	Larry Parrish	.07	.05	.03
111	Eric Show	.07	.05	.03
112	Mike Witt	.07	.05	.03
113	Dennis Eckersley	.10	.08	.04
114	Mike Moore	.07	.05	.03
115	Vince Coleman	1.00	.70	.40
116	Damaso Garcia	.07	.05	.03
117	Steve Carlton	.30	.25	.12
118	Floyd Bannister	.07	.05	.03
119	Mario Soto	.07	.05	.03
120	Fred Lynn	.10	.08	.04
121	Bob Horner	.10	.08	.04
122	Rick Sutcliffe	.10	.08	.04
123	Walt Terrell	.07	.05	.03
124	Keith Hernandez	.25	.20	.10
125	Dave Winfield	.30	.25	.12
126	Frank Viola	.20	.15	.08
127	Dwight Evans	.10	.08	.04
128	Willie Upshaw	.07	.05	.03
129	Andre Thornton	.07	.05	.03
130	Donnie Moore	.07	.05	.03
131	Darryl Strawberry	.70	.50	.30
132	Nolan Ryan	.30	.25	.12
133	Garry Templeton	.07	.05	.03
134	John Tudor	.07	.05	.03
135	Dave Parker	.15	.11	.06
136	Larry McWilliams	.07	.05	.03
137	Terry Pendleton	.07	.05	.03
138	Terry Puhl	.07	.05	.03
139	Bob Dernier	.07	.05	.03
140	Ozzie Guillen	.20	.15	.08
141	Jim Clancy	.07	.05	.03
142	Cal Ripken, Jr.	.35	.25	.14
143	Mickey Hatcher	.07	.05	.03
144	Dan Petry	.07	.05	.03
145	Rich Gedman	.07	.05	.03
146	Jim Rice	.30	.25	.12
147	Butch Wynegar	.07	.05	.03
148	Donnie Hill	.07	.05	.03
149	Jim Sundberg	.07	.05	.03
150	Joe Hesketh	.07	.05	.03
151	Chris Codiroli	.07	.05	.03
152	Charlie Hough	.07	.05	.03
153	Herman Winningham	.07	.05	.03
154	Dave Rozema	.07	.05	.03
155	Don Slaught	.07	.05	.03
156	Juan Beniquez	.07	.05	.03
157	Ted Higuera	.60	.45	.25
158	Andy Hawkins	.07	.05	.03
159	Don Robinson	.07	.05	.03
160	Glenn Wilson	.07	.05	.03
161	Earnest Riles	.07	.05	.03
162	Nick Esasky	.07	.05	.03
163	Carlton Fisk	.15	.11	.06
164	Claudell Washington	.07	.05	.03
165	Scott McGregor	.07	.05	.03
166	Nate Snell	.07	.05	.03
167	Ted Simmons	.10	.08	.04
168	Wade Boggs	1.50	1.25	.60
169	Marty Barrett	.07	.05	.03

		MT	NR MT	EX
170	Bud Black	.07	.05	.03
171	Charlie Leibrandt	.07	.05	.03
172	Charlie Lea	.07	.05	.03
173	Reggie Jackson	.30	.25	.12
174	Bryn Smith	.07	.05	.03
175	Glenn Davis	.60	.45	.25
176	Von Hayes	.07	.05	.03
177	Danny Cox	.07	.05	.03
178	Sam Khalifa	.07	.05	.03
179	Tom Browning	.12	.09	.05
180	Scott Garrelts	.07	.05	.03
181	Shawon Dunston	.10	.08	.04
182	Doyle Alexander	.07	.05	.03
183	Jim Presley	.10	.08	.04
184	Al Cowens	.07	.05	.03
185	Mark Salas	.07	.05	.03
186	Tom Niedenfuer	.07	.05	.03
187	Dave Henderson	.07	.05	.03
188	Lonnie Smith	.07	.05	.03
189	Bruce Bochte	.07	.05	.03
190	Leon Durham	.07	.05	.03
191	Terry Francona	.07	.05	.03
192	Bruce Sutter	.10	.08	.04
193	Steve Crawford	.07	.05	.03
194	Bob Brenly	.07	.05	.03
195	Dan Pasqua	.10	.08	.04
196	Juan Samuel	.12	.09	.05
197	Floyd Rayford	.07	.05	.03
198	Tim Burke	.12	.09	.05
199	Ben Oglivie	.07	.05	.03
200	Don Carman	.12	.09	.05
201	Lance Parrish	.20	.15	.08
202	Terry Forster	.07	.05	.03
203	Neal Heaton	.07	.05	.03
204	Ivan Calderon	.25	.20	.10
205	Jorge Orta	.07	.05	.03
206	Tom Henke	.10	.08	.04
207	Rick Reuschel	.10	.08	.04
208	Dan Quisenberry	.10	.08	.04
209	Ty-Breaking Hit (Pete Rose)	.30	.25	.12
210	Floyd Youmans	.15	.11	.06
211	Tom Filer	.07	.05	.03
212	R.J. Reynolds	.07	.05	.03
213	Gorman Thomas	.07	.05	.03
214	Canadian Great (Jeff Reardon)	.40	.30	.15
215	Chris Brown	.25	.20	.10
216	Rick Aguilera	.12	.09	.05
217	Ernie Whitt	.07	.05	.03
218	Joe Orsulak	.07	.05	.03
219	Jimmy Key	.10	.08	.04
220	Atlee Hammaker	.07	.05	.03
221	Ron Darling	.12	.09	.05
222	Zane Smith	.07	.05	.03
223	Bob Welch	.07	.05	.03
224	Reid Nichols	.07	.05	.03
225	Fleet Feet (Vince Coleman, Willie McGee)	.15	.11	.06
226	Mark Gubicza	.12	.09	.05
227	Tim Birtsas	.07	.05	.03
228	Mike Hargrove	.07	.05	.03
229	Randy St. Claire	.07	.05	.03
230	Larry Herndon	.07	.05	.03
231	Dusty Baker	.07	.05	.03
232	Mookie Wilson	.07	.05	.03
233	Jeff Lahti	.07	.05	.03
234	Tom Seaver	.30	.25	.12
235	Mike Scott	.15	.11	.06
236	Don Sutton	.20	.15	.08
237	Roy Smalley	.07	.05	.03
238	Bill Madlock	.07	.05	.03
239	Charles Hudson	.07	.05	.03
240	John Franco	.10	.08	.04
241	Frank Tanana	.07	.05	.03
242	Sid Fernandez	.10	.08	.04
243	Knuckle Brothers (Joe Niekro, Phil Niekro)	.10	.08	.04
244	Dennis Lamp	.07	.05	.03
245	Gene Nelson	.07	.05	.03
246	Terry Harper	.07	.05	.03
247	Vida Blue	.07	.05	.03
248	Roger McDowell	.20	.15	.08
249	Tony Bernazard	.07	.05	.03
250	Cliff Johnson	.07	.05	.03
251	Hal McRae	.07	.05	.03
252	Garth Iorg	.07	.05	.03
253	Mitch Webster	.20	.15	.08
254	Canadian Great (Jesse Barfield)	.60	.45	.25
255	Dan Driessen	.07	.05	.03
256	Mike Brown	.07	.05	.03
257	Ron Kittle	.07	.05	.03
258	Bo Diaz	.07	.05	.03
259	Hank Aaron Puzzle Card	.07	.05	.03
260	King of Kings (Pete Rose)	.50	.40	.20
---	Checklist 1-26 DK	.07	.05	.03
---	Checklist 27-106	.07	.05	.03
---	Checklist 107-186	.07	.05	.03
---	Checklist 187-260	.07	.05	.03

1987 Leaf

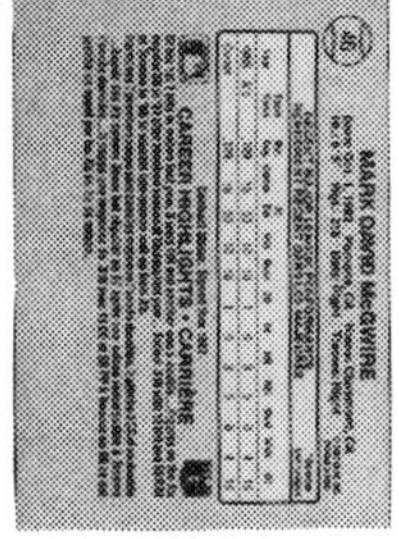

For the third consecutive season, Leaf-Donruss issued a Canadian baseball card set. The Canadian cards are nearly identical to the American set except for the name "Leaf" which appears on the front in place of "Donruss." The set contains 264 cards, each measuring the standard 2-1/2" by 3-1/2", with a special emphasis being placed on players from the Montreal and Toronto teams. The card backs feature career highlights written in both English and French. As in the previous years, two "Canadian Greats" cards appear in the set. These painted portraits feature Mark Eichhorn and Floyd Youmans.

	MT	NR MT	EX
Complete Set:	16.00	12.00	6.50
Common Player:	.06	.05	.02

		MT	NR MT	EX
1	Wally Joyner (DK)	.80	.60	.30
2	Roger Clemens (DK)	.50	.40	.20
3	Dale Murphy (DK)	.30	.25	.12
4	Darryl Strawberry (DK)	.30	.25	.12
5	Ozzie Smith (DK)	.10	.08	.04
6	Jose Canseco (DK)	5.00	3.75	2.00
7	Charlie Hough (DK)	.06	.05	.02
8	Brook Jacoby (DK)	.06	.05	.02
9	Fred Lynn (DK)	.10	.08	.04
10	Rick Rhoden (DK)	.06	.05	.02
11	Chris Brown (DK)	.08	.06	.03
12	Von Hayes (DK)	.08	.06	.03
13	Jack Morris (DK)	.15	.11	.06
14	Kevin McReynolds (DK)	.12	.09	.05
15	George Brett (DK)	.30	.25	.12
16	Ted Higuera (DK)	.12	.09	.05
17	Hubie Brooks (DK)	.06	.05	.02
18	Mike Scott (DK)	.10	.08	.04
19	Kirby Puckett (DK)	.20	.15	.08
20	Dave Winfield (DK)	.20	.15	.08
21	Lloyd Moseby (DK)	.06	.05	.02
22	Eric Davis (DK)	.50	.40	.20
23	Jim Presley (DK)	.08	.06	.03
24	Keith Moreland (DK)	.06	.05	.02
25	Greg Walker (DK)	.06	.05	.02
26	Steve Sax (DK)	.10	.08	.04
27	Checklist 1-27	.06	.05	.02
28	B.J. Surhoff (RR)	.35	.25	.14
29	Randy Myers (RR)	.20	.15	.08
30	Ken Gerhart (RR)	.12	.09	.05
31	Benito Santiago (RR)	.70	.50	.30
32	Greg Swindell (RR)	.40	.30	.15
33	Mike Birkbeck (RR)	.10	.08	.04
34	Terry Steinbach (RR)	.25	.20	.10
35	Bo Jackson (RR)	.90	.70	.35
36	Greg Maddux (RR)	.50	.40	.20
37	Jim Lindeman (RR)	.10	.08	.04
38	Devon White (RR)	.70	.50	.30
39	Eric Bell (RR)	.06	.05	.02
40	Will Fraser (RR)	.10	.08	.04
41	Jerry Browne (RR)	.10	.08	.04
42	Chris James (RR)	.35	.25	.14
43	Rafael Palmeiro (RR)	.60	.45	.25
44	Pat Dodson (RR)	.06	.05	.02
45	Duane Ward (RR)	.08	.06	.03
46	Mark McGwire (RR)	3.00	2.25	1.25
47	Bruce Fields (RR) (photo actually Darnell Coles)	.06	.05	.02
48	Jody Davis	.06	.05	.02
49	Roger McDowell	.10	.08	.04
50	Jose Guzman	.08	.06	.03
51	Oddibe McDowell	.06	.05	.02
52	Harold Baines	.10	.08	.04
53	Dave Righetti	.12	.09	.05
54	Moose Haas	.06	.05	.02
55	Mark Langston	.10	.08	.04
56	Kirby Puckett	.25	.20	.10
57	Dwight Evans	.08	.06	.03
58	Willie Randolph	.06	.05	.02
59	Wally Backman	.06	.05	.02
60	Bryn Smith	.06	.05	.02
61	Tim Wallach	.10	.08	.04
62	Joe Hesketh	.06	.05	.02
63	Garry Templeton	.06	.05	.02
64	Rob Thompson	.10	.08	.04
65	Canadian Greats (Floyd Youmans)	.25	.20	.10
66	Ernest Riles	.06	.05	.02
67	Robin Yount	.20	.15	.08
68	Darryl Strawberry	.35	.25	.14
69	Ernie Whitt	.05	.04	.02
70	Dave Winfield	.20	.15	.08
71	Paul Molitor	.12	.09	.05
72	Dave Stieb	.10	.08	.04
73	Tom Henke	.08	.06	.03
74	Frank Viola	.15	.11	.06
75	Scott Garrelts	.06	.05	.02
76	Mike Boddicker	.06	.05	.02
77	Keith Moreland	.06	.05	.02
78	Lou Whitaker	.15	.11	.06
79	Dave Parker	.15	.11	.06
80	Lee Smith	.08	.06	.03
81	Tom Candiotti	.06	.05	.02
82	Greg Harris	.06	.05	.02
83	Fred Lynn	.10	.08	.04
84	Dwight Gooden	.40	.30	.15
85	Ron Darling	.10	.08	.04
86	Mike Krukow	.06	.05	.02
87	Spike Owen	.06	.05	.02
88	Len Dykstra	.10	.08	.04
89	Rick Aguilera	.06	.05	.02
90	Jim Clancy	.06	.05	.02
91	Joe Johnson	.06	.05	.02
92	Damaso Garcia	.06	.05	.02
93	Sid Fernandez	.08	.06	.03
94	Bob Ojeda	.06	.05	.02
95	Ted Higuera	.10	.08	.04
96	George Brett	.30	.25	.12
97	Willie Wilson	.08	.06	.03
98	Cal Ripken	.25	.20	.10
99	Kent Hrbek	.15	.11	.06
100	Bert Blyleven	.10	.08	.04
101	Ron Guidry	.12	.09	.05
102	Andy Allanson	.08	.06	.03

		MT	NR MT	EX
103	Dave Henderson	.08	.06	.03
104	Kirk Gibson	.20	.15	.08
105	Lloyd Moseby	.06	.05	.02
106	Tony Fernandez	.10	.08	.04
107	Lance Parrish	.15	.11	.06
108	Ozzie Smith	.15	.11	.06
109	Gary Carter	.20	.15	.08
110	Eddie Murray	.25	.20	.10
111	Mike Witt	.06	.05	.02
112	Bobby Witt	.15	.11	.06
113	Willie McGee	.10	.08	.04
114	Steve Garvey	.20	.15	.08
115	Glenn Davis	.15	.11	.06
116	Jose Cruz	.06	.05	.02
117	Ozzie Guillen	.06	.05	.02
118	Alvin Davis	.10	.08	.04
119	Jose Rijo	.06	.05	.02
120	Bill Madlock	.06	.05	.02
121	Tommy Herr	.06	.05	.02
122	Mike Schmidt	.35	.25	.14
123	Mike Scioscia	.06	.05	.02
124	Terry Pendleton	.06	.05	.02
125	Leon Durham	.06	.05	.02
126	Alan Trammell	.20	.15	.08
127	Jesse Barfield	.10	.08	.04
128	Shawon Dunston	.08	.06	.03
129	Pete Rose	.50	.40	.20
130	Von Hayes	.06	.05	.02
131	Julio Franco	.08	.06	.03
132	Juan Samuel	.12	.09	.05
133	Joe Carter	.12	.09	.05
134	Brook Jacoby	.08	.06	.03
135	Jack Morris	.15	.11	.06
136	Bob Horner	.08	.06	.03
137	Calvin Schiraldi	.06	.05	.02
138	Tom Browning	.08	.06	.03
139	Shane Rawley	.06	.05	.02
140	Mario Soto	.06	.05	.02
141	Dale Murphy	.30	.25	.12
142	Hubie Brooks	.06	.05	.02
143	Jeff Reardon	.08	.06	.03
144	Will Clark	5.00	3.75	2.00
145	Ed Correa	.06	.05	.02
146	Glenn Wilson	.06	.05	.02
147	Johnny Ray	.06	.05	.02
148	Fernando Valenzuela	.15	.11	.06
149	Tim Raines	.25	.20	.10
150	Don Mattingly	1.75	1.25	.70
151	Jose Canseco	3.00	2.25	1.25
152	Gary Pettis	.06	.05	.02
153	Don Sutton	.15	.11	.06
154	Jim Presley	.08	.06	.03
155	Checklist 28-105	.06	.05	.02
156	Dale Sveum	.10	.08	.04
157	Cory Snyder	.50	.40	.20
158	Jeff Sellers	.08	.06	.03
159	Denny Walling	.06	.05	.02
160	Danny Cox	.06	.05	.02
161	Bob Forsch	.06	.05	.02
162	Joaquin Andujar	.06	.05	.02
163	Roberto Clemente Puzzle Card	.06	.05	.02
164	Paul Assenmacher	.08	.06	.03
165	Marty Barrett	.06	.05	.02
166	Ray Knight	.06	.05	.02
167	Rafael Santana	.06	.05	.02
168	Bruce Ruffin	.10	.08	.04
169	Buddy Bell	.06	.05	.02
170	Kevin Mitchell	.15	.11	.06
171	Ken Oberkfell	.06	.05	.02
172	Gene Garber	.06	.05	.02
173	Canadian Greats (Mark Eichhorn)	.25	.20	.10
174	Don Carman	.06	.05	.02
175	Jesse Orosco	.06	.05	.02
176	Mookie Wilson	.06	.05	.02
177	Gary Ward	.06	.05	.02
178	John Franco	.08	.06	.03
179	Eric Davis	.80	.60	.30
180	Walt Terrell	.06	.05	.02
181	Phil Niekro	.15	.11	.06
182	Pat Tabler	.06	.05	.02
183	Brett Butler	.06	.05	.02
184	George Bell	.20	.15	.08
185	Pete Incaviglia	.30	.25	.12
186	Pete O'Brien	.06	.05	.02
187	Jimmy Key	.08	.06	.03
188	Frank White	.06	.05	.02
189	Mike Pagliarulo	.08	.06	.03
190	Roger Clemens	.60	.45	.25
191	Rickey Henderson	.25	.20	.10
192	Mike Easler	.06	.05	.02
193	Wade Boggs	.80	.60	.30
194	Vince Coleman	.15	.11	.06
195	Charlie Kerfeld	.06	.05	.02
196	Dickie Thon	.06	.05	.02
197	Bill Doran	.06	.05	.02
198	Alfredo Griffin	.06	.05	.02
199	Carlton Fisk	.12	.09	.05
200	Phil Bradley	.08	.06	.03
201	Reggie Jackson	.25	.20	.10
202	Bob Boone	.07	.05	.03
203	Steve Sax	.10	.08	.04
204	Tom Niedenfuer	.06	.05	.02
205	Tim Burke	.06	.05	.02
206	Floyd Youmans	.06	.05	.02
207	Jay Tibbs	.06	.05	.02
208	Chili Davis	.06	.05	.02
209	Larry Parrish	.06	.05	.02
210	John Cerutti	.10	.08	.04
211	Kevin Bass	.06	.05	.02
212	Andre Dawson	.15	.11	.06
213	Bob Sebra	.06	.05	.02
214	Kevin McReynolds	.12	.09	.05
215	Jim Morrison	.06	.05	.02
216	Candy Maldonado	.06	.05	.02
217	John Kruk	.30	.25	.12
218	Todd Worrell	.10	.08	.04
219	Barry Bonds	.30	.25	.12
220	Andy McGaffigan	.06	.05	.02
221	Andres Galarraga	.12	.09	.05
222	Mike Fitzgerald	.06	.05	.02
223	Kirk McCaskill	.06	.05	.02
224	Dave Smith	.06	.05	.02
225	Ruben Sierra	.70	.50	.30

		MT	NR MT	EX
226	Scott Fletcher	.06	.05	.02
227	Chet Lemon	.06	.05	.02
228	Dan Petry	.06	.05	.02
229	Mark Eichhorn	.10	.08	.04
230	Cecil Cooper	.06	.05	.02
231	Willie Upshaw	.06	.05	.02
232	Don Baylor	.08	.06	.03
233	Keith Hernandez	.20	.15	.08
234	Ryne Sandberg	.20	.15	.08
235	Tony Gwynn	.25	.20	.10
236	Chris Brown	.06	.05	.02
237	Pedro Guerrero	.12	.09	.05
238	Mark Gubicza	.08	.06	.03
239	Sid Bream	.06	.05	.02
240	Joe Cowley	.06	.05	.02
241	Bill Buckner	.08	.06	.03
242	John Candelaria	.06	.05	.02
243	Scott McGregor	.06	.05	.02
244	Tom Brunansky	.10	.08	.04
245	Gary Gaetti	.12	.09	.05
246	Orel Hershiser	.20	.15	.08
247	Jim Rice	.20	.15	.08
248	Oil Can Boyd	.06	.05	.02
249	Bob Knepper	.06	.05	.02
250	Danny Tartabull	.20	.15	.08
251	John Cangelosi	.06	.05	.02
252	Wally Joyner	4.00	3.00	1.50
253	Bruce Hurst	.08	.06	.03
254	Rich Gedman	.06	.05	.02
255	Jim Deshaies	.10	.08	.04
256	Tony Pena	.06	.05	.02
257	Nolan Ryan	.20	.15	.08
258	Mike Scott	.10	.08	.04
259	Checklist 106-183	.06	.05	.02
260	Dennis Rasmussen	.08	.06	.03
261	Bret Saberhagen	.15	.11	.06
262	Steve Balboni	.06	.05	.02
263	Tom Seaver	.20	.15	.08
264	Checklist 184-264	.06	.05	.02

1987 Leaf Candy City Team

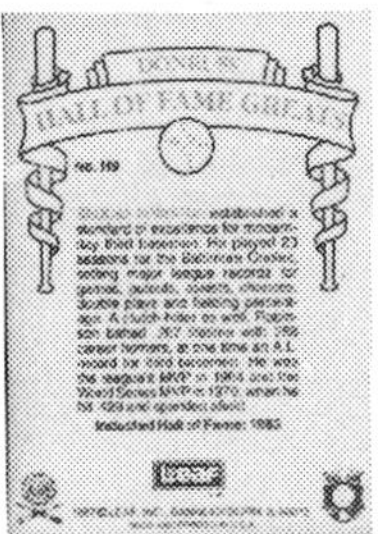

As part of their endorsement for the Seventh International Special Olympics Summer Games, Leaf produced an 18-card set of trading cards. Twelve of the 18 cards feature Baseball Hall of Fame greats. These cards measure 2-1/2" by 3-1/2" and are numbered H1 through H12. The remaining six cards in the set are numbered S1-S6 and feature unnamed Special Olympics champions. All cards feature the artwork of Dick Perez. The cards were available through a mail-in offer advertised at special store displays. Only the baseball-related subjects are listed in the checklist that follows.

		MT	NR MT	EX
Complete Set:		4.00	3.00	1.50
Common Player:		.15	.11	.06
1	Mickey Mantle	1.00	.70	.40
2	Yogi Berra	.40	.30	.15
3	Roy Campanella	.40	.30	.15
4	Stan Musial	.50	.40	.20
5	Ted Williams	.50	.40	.20
6	Duke Snider	.40	.30	.15
7	Hank Aaron	.50	.40	.20
8	Pee Wee Reese	.30	.25	.12
9	Brooks Robinson	.30	.25	.12
10	Al Kaline	.30	.25	.12
11	Willie McCovey	.25	.20	.10
12	Cool Papa Bell	.15	.11	.06

1988 Leaf

This 264-card set features full-color player photos from the 1988 Donruss 660-card standard issue, with emphasis on players from Montreal and Toronto. A graphic arts style border of red, blue and black stripes duplicates the design of the Donruss set, with the exception of a "Leaf '88" logo in the upper left corner that replaces the Donruss logo. Two special Canadian Greats cards are included in this set: Perez-Steele portraits of Tim Wallach and George Bell. The set also includes the portrait-style Diamond Kings cards (the set's first 26 cards, one for each individual team). The DK's carry the Donruss logo above the gold DK banner. All card backs in the 1988 Leaf set are bilingual (French/English), numbered, and

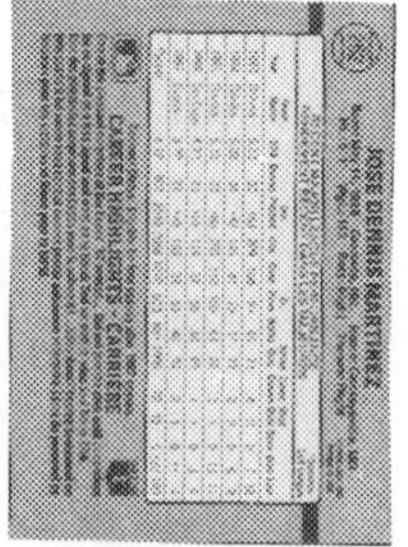

printed in black on white stock with a light blue border. Regular player card backs have a horizontal format containing personal data, stats and career summary. This set was sold in 10-card wax packs with one triple-piece puzzle card per pack and was distributed via larger hobby and retail shops in the U.S. and Canada.

		MT	NR MT	EX
Complete Set:		25.00	18.50	10.00
Common Player:		.06	.05	.02
1	Mark McGwire (DK)	.70	.50	.30
2	Tim Raines (DK)	.20	.15	.08
3	Benito Santiago (DK)	.15	.11	.06
4	Alan Trammell (DK)	.20	.15	.08
5	Danny Tartabull (DK)	.15	.11	.06
6	Ron Darling (DK)	.10	.08	.04
7	Paul Molitor (DK)	.10	.08	.04
8	Devon White (DK)	.15	.11	.06
9	Andre Dawson (DK)	.15	.11	.06
10	Julio Franco (DK)	.08	.06	.03
11	Scott Fletcher (DK)	.06	.05	.02
12	Tony Fernandez (DK)	.10	.08	.04
13	Shane Rawley (DK)	.06	.05	.02
14	Kal Daniels (DK)	.15	.11	.06
15	Jack Clark (DK)	.12	.09	.05
16	Dwight Evans (DK)	.08	.06	.03
17	Tommy John (DK)	.08	.06	.03
18	Andy Van Slyke (DK)	.10	.08	.04
19	Gary Gaetti (DK)	.10	.08	.04
20	Mark Langston (DK)	.08	.06	.03
21	Will Clark (DK)	.40	.30	.15
22	Glenn Hubbard (DK)	.06	.05	.02
23	Billy Hatcher (DK)	.06	.05	.02
24	Bob Welch (DK)	.08	.06	.03
25	Ivan Calderon (DK)	.08	.06	.03
26	Cal Ripken, Jr. (DK)	.25	.20	.10
27	Checklist 1-27	.06	.05	.02
28	Mackey Sasser (RR)	.12	.09	.05
29	Jeff Treadway (RR)	.25	.20	.10
30	Mike Campbell (RR)	.12	.09	.05
31	Lance Johnson (RR)	.10	.08	.04
32	Nelson Liriano (RR)	.10	.08	.04
33	Shawn Abner (RR)	.15	.11	.06
34	Roberto Alomar (RR)	.60	.45	.25
35	Shawn Hillegas (RR)	.15	.11	.06
36	Joey Meyer (RR)	.10	.08	.04
37	Kevin Elster (RR)	.15	.11	.06
38	Jose Lind (RR)	.20	.15	.08
39	Kirt Manwaring (RR)	.20	.15	.08
40	Mark Grace (RR)	6.00	4.50	2.50
41	Jody Reed (RR)	.25	.20	.10
42	John Farrell (RR)	.20	.15	.08
43	Al Leiter (RR)	.70	.50	.30
44	Gary Thurman (RR)	.25	.20	.10
45	Vincente Palacios (RR)	.10	.08	.04
46	Eddie Williams (RR)	.10	.08	.04
47	Jack McDowell (RR)	.25	.20	.10
48	Dwight Gooden	.40	.30	.15
49	Mike Witt	.06	.05	.02
50	Wally Joyner	.60	.45	.25
51	Brook Jacoby	.08	.06	.03
52	Bert Blyleven	.10	.08	.04
53	Ted Higuera	.10	.08	.04
54	Mike Scott	.10	.08	.04
55	Jose Guzman	.06	.05	.02
56	Roger Clemens	.40	.30	.15
57	Dave Righetti	.12	.09	.05
58	Benito Santiago	.20	.15	.08
59	Ozzie Guillen	.06	.05	.02
60	Matt Nokes	.35	.25	.14
61	Fernando Valenzuela	.15	.11	.06
62	Orel Hershiser	.20	.15	.08
63	Sid Fernandez	.08	.06	.03
64	Ozzie Virgil	.06	.05	.02
65	Wade Boggs	.70	.50	.30
66	Floyd Youmans	.06	.05	.02
67	Jimmy Key	.08	.06	.03
68	Bret Saberhagen	.15	.11	.06
69	Jody Davis	.06	.05	.02
70	Shawon Dunston	.06	.05	.02
71	Julio Franco	.08	.06	.03
72	Danny Cox	.06	.05	.02
73	Jim Clancy	.06	.05	.02
74	Mark Eichhorn	.06	.05	.02
75	Scott Bradley	.06	.05	.02
76	Charlie Liebrandt	.06	.05	.02
77	Nolan Ryan	.20	.15	.08
78	Ron Darling	.10	.08	.04
79	John Franco	.06	.05	.02
80	Dave Stieb	.08	.06	.03
81	Mike Fitzgerald	.06	.05	.02
82	Steve Bedrosian	.08	.06	.03
83	Dale Murphy	.30	.25	.12
84	Tim Burke	.06	.05	.02
85	Jack Morris	.12	.09	.05
86	Greg Walker	.06	.05	.02
87	Kevin Mitchell	.08	.06	.03
88	Doug Drabek	.06	.05	.02
89	Charlie Hough	.06	.05	.02
90	Tony Gwynn	.25	.20	.10
91	Rick Sutcliffe	.10	.08	.04
92	Shane Rawley	.06	.05	.02
93	George Brett	.30	.25	.12
94	Frank Viola	.12	.09	.05
95	Tony Pena	.06	.05	.02
96	Jim Deshaies	.06	.05	.02
97	Mike Scioscia	.06	.05	.02
98	Rick Rhoden	.06	.05	.02
99	Terry Kennedy	.06	.05	.02
100	Cal Ripken	.25	.20	.10
101	Pedro Guerrero	.12	.09	.05
102	Andy Van Slyke	.10	.08	.04
103	Willie McGee	.08	.06	.03
104	Mike Kingery	.06	.05	.02
105	Kevin Seitzer	.60	.45	.25
106	Robin Yount	.20	.15	.08
107	Tracy Jones	.08	.06	.03
108	Dave Magadan	.08	.06	.03
109	Mel Hall	.06	.05	.02
110	Billy Hatcher	.06	.05	.02
111	Todd Benzinger	.25	.20	.10
112	Mike LaValliere	.06	.05	.02
113	Barry Bonds	.12	.09	.05
114	Tim Raines	.20	.15	.08
115	Ozzie Smith	.12	.09	.05
116	Dave Winfield	.25	.20	.10
117	Keith Hernandez	.15	.11	.06
118	Jeffrey Leonard	.06	.05	.02
119	Larry Parrish	.06	.05	.02
120	Rob Thompson	.06	.05	.02
121	Andres Galarraga	.15	.11	.06
122	Mickey Hatcher	.06	.05	.02
123	Mark Langston	.10	.08	.04
124	Mike Schmidt	.30	.25	.12
125	Cory Snyder	.12	.09	.05
126	Andre Dawson	.15	.11	.06
127	Devon White	.10	.08	.04
128	Vince Coleman	.12	.09	.05
129	Bryn Smith	.06	.05	.02
130	Lance Parrish	.12	.09	.05
131	Willie Upshaw	.06	.05	.02
132	Pete O'Brien	.06	.05	.02
133	Tony Fernandez	.10	.08	.04
134	Billy Ripken	.12	.09	.05
135	Len Dykstra	.06	.05	.02
136	Kirk Gibson	.20	.15	.08
137	Kevin Bass	.06	.05	.02
138	Jose Canseco	3.00	2.25	1.25
139	Kent Hrbek	.15	.11	.06
140	Lloyd Moseby	.06	.05	.02
141	Marty Barrett	.06	.05	.02
142	Carmelo Martinez	.06	.05	.02
143	Tom Foley	.06	.05	.02
144	Kirby Puckett	.20	.15	.08
145	Rickey Henderson	.25	.20	.10
146	Juan Samuel	.10	.08	.04
147	Pete Incaviglia	.10	.08	.04
148	Greg Brock	.06	.05	.02
149	Eric Davis	.50	.40	.20
150	Kal Daniels	.12	.09	.05
151	Bob Boone	.06	.05	.02
152	John Cerutti	.06	.05	.02
153	Mike Greenwell	3.00	2.25	1.25
154	Oddibe McDowell	.06	.05	.02
155	Scott Fletcher	.06	.05	.02
156	Gary Carter	.20	.15	.08
157	Harold Baines	.12	.09	.05
158	Greg Swindell	.15	.11	.06
159	Mark McLemore	.06	.05	.02
160	Keith Moreland	.06	.05	.02
161	Jim Gantner	.06	.05	.02
162	Willie Randolph	.06	.05	.02
163	Fred Lynn	.10	.08	.04
164	B.J. Surhoff	.08	.06	.03
165	Ken Griffey	.06	.05	.02
166	Chet Lemon	.06	.05	.02
167	Alan Trammell	.15	.11	.06
168	Paul Molitor	.12	.09	.05
169	Lou Whitaker	.12	.09	.05
170	Will Clark	.50	.40	.20
171	Dwight Evans	.10	.08	.04
172	Eddie Murray	.25	.20	.10
173	Darrell Evans	.08	.06	.03
174	Ellis Burks	3.00	2.25	1.25
175	Ivan Calderon	.08	.06	.03
176	John Kruk	.08	.06	.03
177	Don Mattingly	3.00	2.25	1.25
178	Dick Schofield	.06	.05	.02
179	Bruce Hurst	.08	.06	.03
180	Ron Guidry	.10	.08	.04
181	Jack Clark	.12	.09	.05
182	Franklin Stubbs	.06	.05	.02
183	Bill Doran	.06	.05	.02
184	Joe Carter	.10	.08	.04
185	Steve Sax	.12	.09	.05
186	Glenn Davis	.12	.09	.05
187	Bo Jackson	.30	.25	.12
188	Bobby Bonilla	.12	.09	.05
189	Willie Wilson	.06	.05	.02
190	Danny Tartabull	.10	.08	.04
191	Bo Diaz	.06	.05	.02
192	Buddy Bell	.06	.05	.02
193	Tim Wallach	.10	.08	.04
194	Mark McGwire	.80	.60	.30
195	Carney Lansford	.06	.05	.02
196	Alvin Davis	.10	.08	.04
197	Von Hayes	.06	.05	.02
198	Mitch Webster	.06	.05	.02
199	Casey Candaele	.06	.05	.02
200	Gary Gaetti	.10	.08	.04
201	Tommy Herr	.06	.05	.02
202	Wally Backman	.06	.05	.02
203	Brian Downing	.06	.05	.02
204	Rance Mulliniks	.06	.05	.02
205	Craig Reynolds	.06	.05	.02
206	Ruben Sierra	.15	.11	.06
207	Ryne Sandberg	.20	.15	.08
208	Carlton Fisk	.12	.09	.05
209	Checklist 28-107	.06	.05	.02
210	Gerald Young	.20	.15	.08
211	MVP (Tim Raines)	.50	.40	.20
212	John Tudor	.06	.05	.02
213	Canadian Greats (George Bell)	.70	.50	.30
214	MVP (George Bell)	.40	.30	.15

		MT	NR MT	EX
215	Jim Rice	.20	.15	.08
216	Gerald Perry	.08	.06	.03
217	Dave Stewart	.06	.05	.02
218	Jose Uribe	.06	.05	.02
219	Rick Rueschel	.06	.05	.02
220	Darryl Strawberry	.30	.25	.12
221	Chris Brown	.06	.05	.02
223	Lee Mazzilli	.06	.05	.02
224	Denny Walling	.06	.05	.02
225	Jesse Barfield	.10	.08	.04
226	Barry Larkin	.10	.08	.04
227	Harold Reynolds	.06	.05	.02
228	Kevin McReynolds	.08	.06	.03
229	Todd Worrell	.08	.06	.03
230	Tommy John	.08	.06	.03
231	Rick Aguilera	.06	.05	.02
232	Bill Madlock	.06	.05	.02
233	Roy Smalley	.06	.05	.02
234	Jeff Musselman	.06	.05	.02
235	Mike Dunne	.08	.06	.03
236	Jerry Browne	.06	.05	.02
237	Sam Horn	.20	.15	.08
238	Howard Johnson	.08	.06	.03
239	Candy Maldonado	.06	.05	.02
240	Nick Esasky	.06	.05	.02
241	Geno Petralli	.06	.05	.02
242	Herm Winningham	.06	.05	.02
243	Roger McDowell	.06	.05	.02
244	Brian Fisher	.06	.05	.02
245	John Marzano	.12	.09	.05
246	Terry Pendleton	.06	.05	.02
247	Rick Leach	.06	.05	.02
248	Pascual Perez	.06	.05	.02
249	Mookie Wilson	.06	.05	.02
250	Ernie Whitt	.06	.05	.02
251	Ron Kittle	.06	.05	.02
252	Oil Can Boyd	.06	.05	.02
253	Jim Gott	.06	.05	.02
254	George Bell	.20	.15	.08
255	Canadian Greats (Tim Wallach)	.60	.45	.25
256	Luis Polonia	.10	.08	.04
257	Hubie Brooks	.06	.05	.02
258	Mickey Brantley	.06	.05	.02
259	Gregg Jefferies	4.50	3.50	1.75
260	Johnny Ray	.06	.05	.02
261	Checklist 108-187	.06	.05	.02
262	Dennis Martinez	.06	.05	.02
263	Stan Musial Puzzle Card	.06	.05	.02
264	Checklist 188-264	.06	.05	.02

1986 Lite Beer Astros

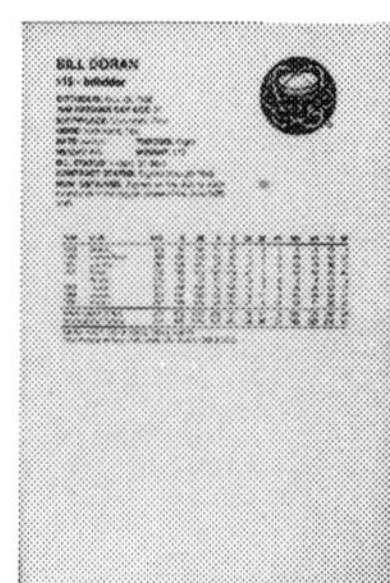

This 22-card regional set of the Houston Astros was sponsored by Lite Beer and given away in a special stadium promotion. The large (4-1/2" by 6-3/4") cards featured full-color photos surrounded by a wide, white border. Diagonal color bands of yellow, orange, red and purple extend throught the upper right and lower left corners of the card, which also displays the Astros' 25th Anniversary logo and the Lite Beer logo in opposite corners. The backs include player information and statistics.

		MT	NR MT	EX
Complete Set:		60.00	45.00	24.00
Common Player:		1.50	1.25	.60
3	Phil Garner	1.50	1.25	.60
6	Mark Bailey	1.50	1.25	.60
10	Dickie Thon	2.00	1.50	.80
11	Frank DiPino	1.50	1.25	.60
12	Craig Reynolds	1.50	1.25	.60
14	Alan Ashby	1.50	1.25	.60
17	Kevin Bass	3.00	2.25	1.25
19	Bill Doran	3.00	2.25	1.25
20	Jim Pankovits	1.50	1.25	.60
21	Terry Puhl	1.50	1.25	.60
22	Hal Lanier	1.50	1.25	.60
25	Jose Cruz	3.00	2.25	1.25
27	Glenn Davis	7.00	5.25	2.75
28	Billy Hatcher	2.50	2.00	1.00
29	Denny Walling	1.50	1.25	.60
33	Mike Scott	4.00	3.00	1.50
34	Nolan Ryan	7.00	5.25	2.75
37	Charlie Kerfeld	2.00	1.50	.80
39	Bob Knepper	2.00	1.50	.80
43	Jim Deshaies	3.00	2.25	1.25
45	Dave Smith	2.00	1.50	.80
53	Mike Madden	1.50	1.25	.60

1986 Lite Beer Rangers

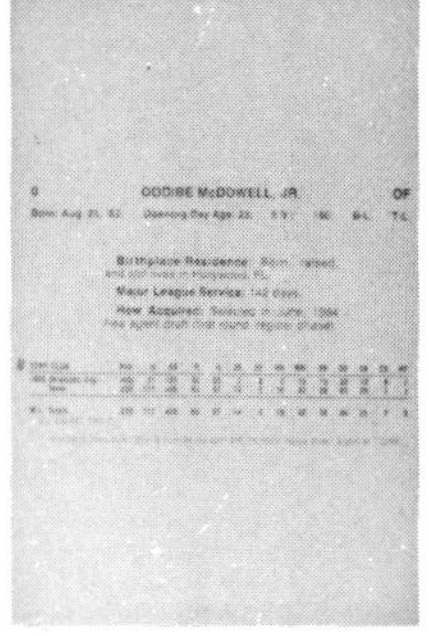

This postcard-size (approximately 4" by 6") regional set of 28 Texas Rangers cards was sponsored by Lite Beer and was available by mail directly from the Rangers. The fronts featured full-color photos surrounded by a wide, white border with the player's name, uniform number and postion appearing below. The Rangers logo is displayed in the lower left corner, while the Lite Beer logo is in the lower right.

		MT	NR MT	EX
Complete Set:		60.00	45.00	24.00
Common Player:		1.50	1.25	.60
0	Oddibe McDowell	3.00	2.25	1.25
1	Scott Fletcher	2.00	1.50	.80
2	Bobby Valentine	2.00	1.50	.80
4	Don Slaught	1.50	1.25	.60
5	Pete Incaviglia	6.00	4.50	2.50
9	Pete O'Brien	3.00	2.25	1.25
10	Art Howe	1.50	1.25	.60
11	Toby Harrah	2.00	1.50	.80
12	Geno Petralli	1.50	1.25	.60
13	Joe Ferguson	1.50	1.25	.60
14	Tim Foli	1.50	1.25	.60
15	Larry Parrish	2.50	2.00	1.00
16	Mike Mason	1.50	1.25	.60
17	Darrell Porter	2.00	1.50	.80
18	Ed Correa	3.00	2.25	1.25
19	Curtis Wilkerson	1.50	1.25	.60
22	Steve Buechele	3.00	2.25	1.25
23	Jose Guzman	4.00	3.00	1.50
24	Ricky Wright	1.50	1.25	.60
27	Greg Harris	1.50	1.25	.60
31	Tom Robson	1.50	1.25	.60
32	Gary Ward	2.00	1.50	.80
35	Tom House	1.50	1.25	.60
44	Tom Paciorek	1.50	1.25	.60
45	Dwayne Henry	2.00	1.50	.80
48	Bobby Witt	5.00	3.75	2.00
49	Charlie Hough	3.00	2.25	1.25
---	Arlington Stadium	1.50	1.25	.60

1886 Lorillard Team Card

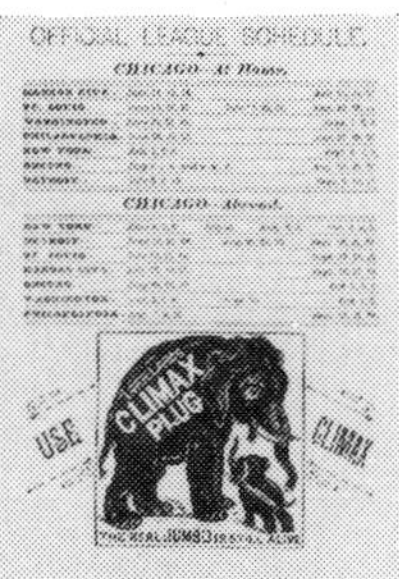

Issued in 1886 by Lorillard Tobacco Co., these 4" by 5-1/2" cards were issued for the Chicago, Detroit and New York baseball clubs. Each card carries the team's schedule (starting with June) on one side and features 11 player portraits enclosed in circles on the other. Both sides have advertising for Lorillard's Climax Plug tobacco.

		NR MT	EX	VG
Complete Set:		25500.	12500.	7000.
Common Team:		5000.	2500.	1500.
(1)	Chicago League Base Ball Club	6500.	3250.	2000.
(2)	Detroit League Base Ball Club	5500.	2750.	1650.
(3)	New York League Base Ball Club	8500.	425.00	2500.
(4)	Philadelphia League Base Ball Club	5000.	2500.	1500.

NOTE: A card number in parentheses () indicates the card set is unnumbered.

1988 Louisville Slugger

Two more cards were added to the Hillerich & Bradsby hangtag collection in 1988. Hillerich & Bradsby, makers of Louisville Slugger bats and gloves, produced the cards to be attached to the company's baseball gloves. The 1988 Eric Davis and Mike Pagliarulo cards bring the total number of Hillerich & Bradsby hangtags issued since the first ones in 1981 (Graig Nettles and Steve Garvey) to 13. A small round hole is punched in the upper left corner of each standard-size card to enable them to be attached to the gloves, making it hard to find undamaged cards. The 1988 cards are numbered and follow the same basic design as previous issues - bright blue and green borders, player name and position above the full-color photo (with autograph overprint), yellow Louisville Slugger logo across the bottom border. Beneath the logo are the words "Member Louisville Slugger Bat & Glove Advisory Staff." The card backs are blue and green and include the player name, short biography and a list of personal records and information.

		MT	NR MT	EX
Complete Set:		160.00	120.00	64.00
Common Player:		5.00	3.75	2.00
(1)	Eric Davis (1988)	10.00	7.50	4.00
(2)	Steve Garvey (Dodgers - 1981)	25.00	18.50	10.00
(3)	Steve Garvey (Padres - 1985)	12.00	9.00	4.75
(4)	Pedro Guerrero (1982)	12.00	9.00	4.75
(5)	Orel Hershiser (1986)	20.00	15.00	8.00
(6)	Ray Knight (Astros - 1984)	15.00	11.00	6.00
(7)	Ray Knight (Mets - 1984)	10.00	7.50	4.00
(8)	Fred Lynn (1982)	5.00	3.75	2.00
(9)	Gary Matthews (1985)	15.00	11.00	6.00
(10)	Graig Nettles (Yankees - 1981)	12.00	9.00	4.75
(11)	Graig Nettles (Padres - 1984)	10.00	7.50	4.00
(12)	Mike Pagliarulo (1988)	5.00	3.75	2.00
(13)	Rick Rhoden (1985)	10.00	7.50	4.00

1949 Lummis Peanut Butter Phillies

This 12-card regional set featuring the Phillies was issued in the Philadelphia area by Lummis Peanut Butter in 1949. The cards measure 3-1/4" by 4-1/4" and are unnumbered. The fronts feature an action photo with a facsimile autograph, while the backs advertise a game ticket promotion by Lummis Peanut Butter. The same photos and checklist were also used for a regional sticker card set issued by Sealtest Dairy the same year.

		NR MT	EX	VG
Complete Set:		900.00	450.00	275.00
Common Player:		70.00	35.00	20.00
(1)	Rich Ashburn	150.00	75.00	45.00
(2)	Hank Borowy	70.00	35.00	20.00
(3)	Del Ennis	90.00	45.00	27.00
(4)	Granny Hamner	70.00	35.00	20.00
(5)	Puddinhead Jones	70.00	35.00	20.00
(6)	Russ Meyer	70.00	35.00	20.00
(7)	Bill Nicholson	70.00	35.00	20.00
(8)	Robin Roberts	200.00	100.00	60.00
(9)	"Schoolboy" Rowe	70.00	35.00	20.00
(10)	Andy Seminick	70.00	35.00	20.00
(11)	Curt Simmons	90.00	45.00	27.00
(12)	Eddie Waitkus	70.00	35.00	20.00

Regional interest may affect the value of a card.

1916 M101-4 The Sporting News

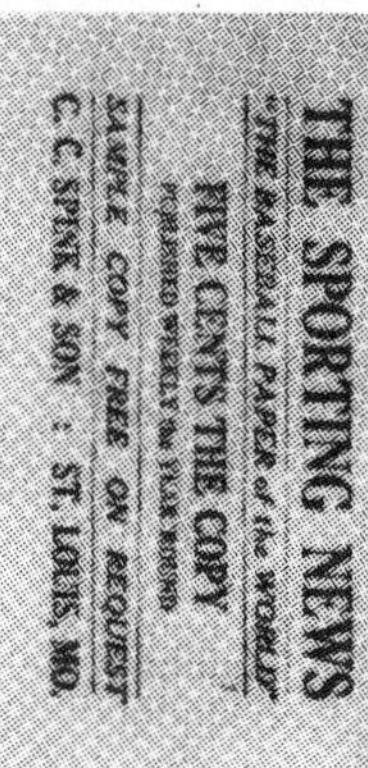

This 200-card set was issued as a premium by The Sporting News and was also used by Weil Baking, the Globe Stores, and several other regional advertisers. The 1-5/8" by 3" cards contain bordered black and white photos on the fronts, with the player name, position and team, as well as a card number. Card backs are in a horizontal format and show an advertisement for the sponsoring sports weekly. Most of the day's top players and many Hall of Famers are included in the set, with the Ty Cobb and Babe Ruth cards carrying the highest values. The complete set price includes all variations.

		NR MT	EX	VG
Complete Set:		10000.	5000.	3000.
Common Player:		25.00	12.50	7.50
1	Babe Adams	40.00	15.00	7.50
2	Sam Agnew	30.00	12.50	7.50
3	Eddie Ainsmith	25.00	12.50	7.50
4	Grover Alexander	75.00	37.00	22.00
5	Leon Ames	25.00	12.50	7.50
6	Jimmy Archer	25.00	12.50	7.50
7	Jimmy Austin	25.00	12.50	7.50
8	H.D. Baird	40.00	20.00	12.00
9	J. Franklin Baker	55.00	27.00	16.50
10	Dave Bancroft	55.00	27.00	16.50
11	Jack Barry	25.00	12.50	7.50
12	Zinn Beck	25.00	12.50	7.50
13	"Chief" Bender	55.00	27.00	16.50
14	Joe Benz	25.00	12.50	7.50
15	Bob Bescher	25.00	12.50	7.50
16	Al Betzel	25.00	12.50	7.50
17	Mordecai Brown	55.00	27.00	16.50
18	Eddie Burns	25.00	12.50	7.50
19	George Burns	40.00	20.00	12.00
20	Geo. J. Burns	25.00	12.50	7.50
21	Joe Bush	30.00	15.00	9.00
22	"Donie" Bush	35.00	17.50	10.50
23	Art Butler	25.00	12.50	7.50
24	Bobbie Byrne	25.00	12.50	7.50
25	Forrest Cady	40.00	20.00	12.00
26	Jimmy Callahan	25.00	12.50	7.50
27	Ray Caldwell	25.00	12.50	7.50
28	Max Carey	55.00	27.00	16.50
29	George Chalmers	25.00	12.50	7.50
30	Ray Chapman	30.00	15.00	9.00
31	Larry Cheney	25.00	12.50	7.50
32	Eddie Cicotte	35.00	17.50	10.50
33	Tom Clarke	25.00	12.50	7.50
34	Eddie Collins	65.00	32.00	19.50
35	"Shauno" Collins	25.00	12.50	7.50
36	Charles Comiskey	60.00	30.00	18.00
37	Joe Connolly	25.00	12.50	7.50
38	Ty Cobb	625.00	312.00	187.00
39	Harry Coveleskie (Coveleski)	25.00	12.50	7.50
40	Gavvy Cravath	30.00	15.00	9.00
41	Sam Crawford	55.00	27.00	16.50
42	Jean Dale	25.00	12.50	7.50
43	Jake Daubert	30.00	15.00	9.00
44	Charles Deal	25.00	12.50	7.50
45	Al Demaree	25.00	12.50	7.50
46	Josh Devore	40.00	20.00	12.00
47	William Doak	25.00	12.50	7.50
48	Bill Donovan	25.00	12.50	7.50
49	Charles Dooin	25.00	12.50	7.50
50	Mike Doolan	25.00	12.50	7.50
51	Larry Doyle	30.00	15.00	9.00
52	Jean Dubuc	25.00	12.50	7.50
53	Oscar Dugey	25.00	12.50	7.50
54	Johnny Evers	55.00	27.00	16.50
55	Urban Faber	55.00	27.00	16.50
56	"Hap" Felsch	35.00	17.50	10.50
57	Bill Fischer	25.00	12.50	7.50
58	Ray Fisher	25.00	12.50	7.50
59	Max Flack	25.00	12.50	7.50
60	Art Fletcher	25.00	12.50	7.50
61	Eddie Foster	25.00	12.50	7.50
62	Jacques Fournier	25.00	12.50	7.50
63	Del Gainer (Gainor)	25.00	12.50	7.50
64	"Chic" Gandil	50.00	25.00	15.00
65	Larry Gardner	25.00	12.50	7.50
66	Joe Gedeon	25.00	12.50	7.50
67	Gus Getz	25.00	12.50	7.50
68	Geo. Gibson	25.00	12.50	7.50
69	Wilbur Good	25.00	12.50	7.50
70	Hank Gowdy	25.00	12.50	7.50
71	John Graney	25.00	12.50	7.50
72	Clark Griffith	65.00	32.00	19.50
73	Tom Griffith	25.00	12.50	7.50
74	Heinie Groh	30.00	15.00	9.00
75	Earl Hamilton	25.00	12.50	7.50
76	Bob Harmon	25.00	12.50	7.50
77	Roy Hartzell	25.00	12.50	7.50
78	Claude Hendrix	25.00	12.50	7.50
79	Olaf Henriksen	25.00	12.50	7.50
80	John Henry	25.00	12.50	7.50
81	"Buck" Herzog	25.00	12.50	7.50
82	Hugh High	25.00	12.50	7.50
83	Dick Hoblitzell	25.00	12.50	7.50
84	Harry Hooper	55.00	27.00	16.50
85	Ivan Howard	25.00	12.50	7.50
86	Miller Huggins	55.00	27.00	16.50
87	Joe Jackson	725.00	362.00	217.00
88	William James	25.00	12.50	7.50
89	Harold Janvrin	25.00	12.50	7.50
90	Hugh Jennings	55.00	27.00	16.50
91	Walter Johnson	250.00	125.00	75.00
92	Fielder Jones	25.00	12.50	7.50
93	Joe Judge	40.00	20.00	12.00
94	Bennie Kauff	25.00	12.50	7.50
95	Wm. Killefer Jr.	25.00	12.50	7.50
96	Ed. Konetchy	25.00	12.50	7.50
97	Napoleon Lajoie	150.00	75.00	45.00
98	Jack Lapp	25.00	12.50	7.50
99	John Lavan	25.00	12.50	7.50
100	Jimmy Lavender	25.00	12.50	7.50
101	"Nemo" Leibold	25.00	12.50	7.50
102	H.B. Leonard	25.00	12.50	7.50
103	Duffy Lewis	30.00	15.00	9.00
104	Hans Lobert	25.00	12.50	7.50
105	Tom Long	25.00	12.50	7.50
106	Fred Luderus	25.00	12.50	7.50
107	Connie Mack	90.00	45.00	27.00
108	Lee Magee	25.00	12.50	7.50
109	Sherwood Magee	45.00	22.00	13.50
110	Al. Mamaux	25.00	12.50	7.50
111	Leslie Mann	25.00	12.50	7.50
112	"Rabbit" Maranville	55.00	27.00	16.50
113	Rube Marquard	55.00	27.00	16.50
114	J. Erskine Mayer	25.00	12.50	7.50
115	George McBride	25.00	12.50	7.50
116	John J. McGraw	70.00	35.00	21.00
117	Jack McInnis	25.00	12.50	7.50
118	Fred Merkle	30.00	15.00	9.00
119	Chief Meyers	25.00	12.50	7.50
120	Clyde Milan	25.00	12.50	7.50
121	John Miller	40.00	20.00	12.00
122	Otto Miller	25.00	12.50	7.50
123	Willie Mitchell	25.00	12.50	7.50
124	Fred Mollwitz	25.00	12.50	7.50
125	Pat Moran	25.00	12.50	7.50
126	Ray Morgan	25.00	12.50	7.50
127	Geo. Moriarty	25.00	12.50	7.50
128	Guy Morton	25.00	12.50	7.50
129	Mike Mowrey	40.00	20.00	12.00
130	Ed. Murphy	40.00	20.00	12.00
131	"Hy" Myers	25.00	12.50	7.50
132	J.A. Niehoff	25.00	12.50	7.50
133	Rube Oldring	25.00	12.50	7.50
134	Oliver O'Mara	25.00	12.50	7.50
135	Steve O'Neill	25.00	12.50	7.50
136	"Dode" Paskert	25.00	12.50	7.50
137	Roger Peckinpaugh	40.00	20.00	12.00
138	Walter Pipp	35.00	17.50	10.50
139	Derril Pratt (Derrill)	25.00	12.50	7.50
140	Pat Ragan	40.00	20.00	12.00
141	Bill Rariden	25.00	12.50	7.50
142	Eppa Rixey	55.00	27.00	16.50
143	Davey Robertson	25.00	12.50	7.50
144	Wilbert Robinson	55.00	27.00	16.50
145	Bob Roth	25.00	12.50	7.50
146	Ed. Roush	55.00	27.00	16.50
147	Clarence Rowland	25.00	12.50	7.50
148	"Nap" Rucker	25.00	12.50	7.50
149	Dick Rudolph	25.00	12.50	7.50
150	Reb Russell	25.00	12.50	7.50
151	Babe Ruth	1000.	500.00	300.00
152	Vic Saier	25.00	12.50	7.50
153	"Slim" Sallee	25.00	12.50	7.50
154	Ray Schalk	55.00	27.00	16.50
155	Walter Schang	25.00	12.50	7.50
156	Frank Schulte	25.00	12.50	7.50
157	Everett Scott	25.00	12.50	7.50
158	Jim Scott	25.00	12.50	7.50
159	Tom Seaton	25.00	12.50	7.50
160	Howard Shanks	25.00	12.50	7.50
161	Bob Shawkey	40.00	20.00	12.00
162	Ernie Shore	20.00	10.00	6.00
163	Burt Shotton	20.00	10.00	6.00
164	Geo. Sisler	65.00	32.00	19.50
165	J. Carlisle Smith	25.00	12.50	7.50
166	Fred Snodgrass	25.00	12.50	7.50
167	Geo. Stallings	25.00	12.50	7.50
168a	Oscar Stanage (catching)	40.00	20.00	12.00
168b	Oscar Stanage (portrait to waist)	40.00	20.00	12.00
169	Charles Stengel	225.00	112.00	67.00
170	Milton Stock	25.00	12.50	7.50
171	Amos Strunk	40.00	20.00	12.00
172	Billy Sullivan	25.00	12.50	7.50
173	"Jeff" Tesreau	25.00	12.50	7.50
174	Joe Tinker	55.00	27.00	16.50
175	Fred Toney	25.00	12.50	7.50
176	Terry Turner	25.00	12.50	7.50
177	George Tyler	40.00	20.00	12.00
178	Jim Vaughn	25.00	12.50	7.50
179	Bob Veach	25.00	12.50	7.50
180	James Viox	25.00	12.50	7.50
181	Oscar Vitt	25.00	12.50	7.50
182	Hans Wagner	250.00	125.00	75.00
183	Clarence Walker	40.00	20.00	12.00
184	Ed. Walsh	55.00	27.00	16.50
185	W. Wambsganss (photo actually Fritz Coumbe)	40.00	20.00	12.00
186	Buck Weaver	35.00	17.50	10.50
187	Carl Weilman	25.00	12.50	7.50
188	Zach Wheat	55.00	27.00	16.50
189	Geo. Whitted	25.00	12.50	7.50
190	Fred Williams	30.00	15.00	9.00
191	Art Wilson	25.00	12.50	7.50
192	J. Owen Wilson	25.00	12.50	7.50
193	Ivy Wingo	25.00	12.50	7.50
194	"Mel" Wolfgang	25.00	12.50	7.50
195	Joe Wood	35.00	17.50	10.50
196	Steve Yerkes	25.00	12.50	7.50
197	"Pep" Young	40.00	20.00	12.00
198	Rollie Zeider	25.00	12.50	7.50
199	Heiny Zimmerman	30.00	12.50	7.50
200	Ed. Zwilling	40.00	15.00	7.50

1915 M101-5 The Sporting News

This set, which is quite similar to the M101-5 The Sporting News issue, was also issued as a promotional premium by The Sporting News. The 200 black and white cards once again are printed with player photo, name, position, team and card number on the fronts and advertising on the backs. The set checklist is the same as for sets issued by Morehouse Baking and Standard Baking. Most of the players included in the 1-5/8" by 3" set also appear in the prior The Sporting News edition. The complete set price includes all variations.

		NR MT	EX	VG
Complete Set:		10000.	5000.	3000.
Common Player:		25.00	12.50	7.50
1	Babe Adams	40.00	15.00	7.50
2	Sam Agnew	30.00	12.50	7.50
3	Eddie Ainsmith	25.00	12.50	7.50
4	Grover Alexander	75.00	37.00	22.00
5	Leon Ames	25.00	12.50	7.50
6	Jimmy Archer	25.00	12.50	7.50
7	Jimmy Austin	25.00	12.50	7.50
8	J. Franklin Baker	55.00	27.00	16.50
9	Dave Bancroft	55.00	27.00	16.50
10	Jack Barry	25.00	12.50	7.50
11	Zinn Beck	25.00	12.50	7.50
12	Lute Boone	40.00	20.00	12.00
13	Joe Benz	25.00	12.50	7.50
14	Bob Bescher	25.00	12.50	7.50
15	Al Betzel	25.00	12.50	7.50
16	Roger Bresnahan	65.00	32.00	19.50
17	Eddie Burns	25.00	12.50	7.50
18	Geo. J. Burns	25.00	12.50	7.50
19	Joe Bush	30.00	15.00	9.00
20	Owen Bush	35.00	17.50	10.50
21	Art Butler	25.00	12.50	7.50
22	Bobbie Byrne	25.00	12.50	7.50
23a	Forrest Cady	75.00	37.00	22.00
23b	Mordecai Brown	65.00	32.00	19.50
24	Jimmy Callahan	25.00	12.50	7.50
25	Ray Caldwell	25.00	12.50	7.50
26	Max Carey	55.00	27.00	16.50
27	George Chalmers	25.00	12.50	7.50
28	Frank Chance	75.00	37.00	22.00
29	Ray Chapman	30.00	15.00	9.00
30	Larry Cheney	25.00	12.50	7.50
31	Eddie Cicotte	35.00	17.50	10.50
32	Tom Clarke	25.00	12.50	7.50
33	Eddie Collins	65.00	32.00	19.50
34	"Shauno" Collins	25.00	12.50	7.50
35	Charles Comisky (Comiskey)	60.00	30.00	18.00
36	Joe Connolly	25.00	12.50	7.50
37	Luther Cook	40.00	20.00	12.00
38	Jack Coombs	40.00	20.00	12.00
39	Dan Costello	40.00	20.00	12.00
40	Harry Coveleskie (Coveleski)	25.00	12.50	7.50
41	Gavvy Cravath	30.00	15.00	9.00
42	Sam Crawford	55.00	27.00	16.50
43	Jean Dale	25.00	12.50	7.50
44	Jake Daubert	30.00	15.00	9.00
45	Geo. A. Davis Jr.	40.00	20.00	12.00
46	Charles Deal	25.00	12.50	7.50
47	Al Demaree	25.00	12.50	7.50
48	William Doak	25.00	12.50	7.50
49	Bill Donovan	25.00	12.50	7.50
50	Charles Dooin	25.00	12.50	7.50
51	Mike Doolan	25.00	12.50	7.50
52	Larry Doyle	30.00	15.00	9.00
53	Jean Dubuc	25.00	12.50	7.50
54	Oscar Dugey	25.00	12.50	7.50
55	Johnny Evers	55.00	27.00	16.50
56	Urban Faber	55.00	27.00	16.50
57	"Hap" Felsch	35.00	17.50	10.50
58	Bill Fischer	25.00	12.50	7.50
59	Ray Fisher	25.00	12.50	7.50

		NR MT	EX	VG
60	Max Flack	25.00	12.50	7.50
61	Art Fletcher	25.00	12.50	7.50
62	Eddie Foster	25.00	12.50	7.50
63	Jacques Fournier	25.00	12.50	7.50
64	Del Gainer (Gainor)	25.00	12.50	7.50
65	Larry Gardner	25.00	12.50	7.50
66	Joe Gedeon	25.00	12.50	7.50
67	Gus Getz	25.00	12.50	7.50
68	Geo. Gibson	25.00	12.50	7.50
69	Wilbur Good	25.00	12.50	7.50
70	Hank Gowdy	25.00	12.50	7.50
71	John Graney	25.00	12.50	7.50
72	Tom Griffith	25.00	12.50	7.50
73	Heinie Groh	30.00	15.00	9.00
74	Earl Hamilton	25.00	12.50	7.50
75	Bob Harmon	25.00	12.50	7.50
76	Roy Hartzell	25.00	12.50	7.50
77	Claude Hendrix	25.00	12.50	7.50
78	Olaf Henriksen	25.00	12.50	7.50
79	John Henry	25.00	12.50	7.50
80	"Buck" Herzog	25.00	12.50	7.50
81	Hugh High	25.00	12.50	7.50
82	Dick Hoblitzell	25.00	12.50	7.50
83	Harry Hooper	55.00	27.00	16.50
84	Ivan Howard	25.00	12.50	7.50
85	Miller Huggins	55.00	27.00	16.50
86	Joe Jackson	725.00	362.00	217.00
87	William James	25.00	12.50	7.50
88	Harold Janvrin	25.00	12.50	7.50
89	Hugh Jennings	55.00	27.00	16.50
90	Walter Johnson	250.00	125.00	75.00
91	Fielder Jones	25.00	12.50	7.50
92	Bennie Kauff	25.00	12.50	7.50
93	Wm. Killefer Jr.	25.00	12.50	7.50
94	Ed. Konetchy	25.00	12.50	7.50
95	Napoleon Lajoie	150.00	75.00	45.00
96	Jack Lapp	25.00	12.50	7.50
97a	John Lavan (correct spelling)	40.00	20.00	12.00
97b	John Lavin (incorrect spelling)	40.00	20.00	12.00
98	Jimmy Lavender	25.00	12.50	7.50
99	"Nemo" Leibold	25.00	12.50	7.50
100	H.B. Leonard	25.00	12.50	7.50
101	Duffy Lewis	30.00	15.00	9.00
102	Hans Lobert	25.00	12.50	7.50
103	Tom Long	25.00	12.50	7.50
104	Fred Luderus	25.00	12.50	7.50
105	Connie Mack	90.00	45.00	27.00
106	Lee Magee	25.00	12.50	7.50
107	Al. Mamaux	25.00	12.50	7.50
108	Leslie Mann	25.00	12.50	7.50
109	"Rabbit" Maranville	55.00	27.00	16.50
110	Rube Marquard	55.00	27.00	16.50
111	Armando Marsans	40.00	20.00	12.00
112	J. Erskine Mayer	25.00	12.50	7.50
113	George McBride	25.00	12.50	7.50
114	John J. McGraw	70.00	35.00	21.00
115	Jack McInnis	25.00	12.50	7.50
116	Fred Merkle	30.00	15.00	9.00
117	Chief Meyers	25.00	12.50	7.50
118	Clyde Milan	25.00	12.50	7.50
119	Otto Miller	25.00	12.50	7.50
120	Willie Mitchel (Mitchell)	25.00	12.50	7.50
121	Fred Mollwitz	25.00	12.50	7.50
122	J. Herbert Moran	40.00	20.00	12.00
123	Pat Moran	25.00	12.50	7.50
124	Ray Morgan	25.00	12.50	7.50
125	Geo. Moriarty	25.00	12.50	7.50
126	Guy Morton	25.00	12.50	7.50
127	Ed. Murphy (photo actually Danny Murphy)	40.00	20.00	12.00
128	John Murray	40.00	20.00	12.00
129	"Hy" Myers	25.00	12.50	7.50
130	J.A. Niehoff	25.00	12.50	7.50
131	Leslie Nunamaker	40.00	20.00	12.00
132	Rube Oldring	25.00	12.50	7.50
133	Oliver O'Mara	25.00	12.50	7.50
134	Steve O'Neill	25.00	12.50	7.50
135	"Dode" Paskert	25.00	12.50	7.50
136	Roger Peckinpaugh (photo actually Gavvy Cravath)	40.00	20.00	12.00
137	E.J. Pfeffer (photo actually Jeff Pfeffer)	40.00	20.00	12.00
138	Geo. Pierce (Pearce)	40.00	20.00	12.00
139	Walter Pipp	35.00	17.50	10.50
140	Derril Pratt (Derrill)	25.00	12.50	7.50
141	Bill Rariden	25.00	12.50	7.50
142	Eppa Rixey	55.00	27.00	16.50
143	Davey Robertson	25.00	12.50	7.50
144	Wilbert Robertson	55.00	27.00	16.50
145	Bob Roth	25.00	12.50	7.50
146	Ed. Roush	55.00	27.00	16.50
147	Clarence Rowland	25.00	12.50	7.50
148	"Nap" Rucker	25.00	12.50	7.50
149	Dick Rudolph	25.00	12.50	7.50
150	Reb Russell	25.00	12.50	7.50
151	Babe Ruth	1000.	500.00	300.00
152	Vic Saier	25.00	12.50	7.50
153	"Slim" Sallee	25.00	12.50	7.50
154	"Germany" Schaefer	40.00	20.00	12.00
155	Ray Schalk	55.00	27.00	16.50
156	Walter Schang	25.00	12.50	7.50
157	Chas. Schmidt	40.00	20.00	12.00
158	Frank Schulte	25.00	12.50	7.50
159	Jim Scott	25.00	12.50	7.50
160	Everett Scott	25.00	12.50	7.50
161	Tom Seaton	25.00	12.50	7.50
162	Howard Shanks	25.00	12.50	7.50
163	Bob Shawkey (photo actually Jack McInnis)	40.00	20.00	12.00
164	Ernie Shore	25.00	12.50	7.50
165	Burt Shotton	25.00	12.50	7.50
166	George Sisler	65.00	32.00	19.50
167	J. Carlisle Smith	25.00	12.50	7.50
168	Fred Snodgrass	25.00	12.50	7.50
169	Geo. Stallings	25.00	12.50	7.50
170	Oscar Stanage (photo actually Chas. Schmidt)	35.00	17.50	10.50
171	Charles Stengel	225.00	112.00	67.00
172	Milton Stock	25.00	12.50	7.50
173	Amos Strunk (photo actually Olaf Henriksen)	40.00	20.00	12.00
174	Billy Sullivan	25.00	12.50	7.50
175	Chas. Tesreau	40.00	20.00	12.00
176	Jim Thorpe	1000.	500.00	300.00
177	Joe Tinker	55.00	27.00	16.50
178	Fred Toney	25.00	12.50	7.50
179	Terry Turner	25.00	12.50	7.50
180	Jim Vaughn	25.00	12.50	7.50
181	Bob Veach	25.00	12.50	7.50
182	James Voix	25.00	12.50	7.50
183	Oscar Vitt	25.00	12.50	7.50
184	Hans Wagner	250.00	125.00	75.00
185	Clarence Walker (photo not Walker)	40.00	20.00	12.00
186	Zach Wheat	55.00	27.00	16.50
187	Ed. Walsh	55.00	27.00	16.50
188	Buck Weaver	35.00	17.50	10.50
189	Carl Weilman	25.00	12.50	7.50
190	Geo. Whitted	25.00	12.50	7.50
191	Fred Williams	30.00	15.00	9.00
192	Art Wilson	25.00	12.50	7.50
193	J. Owen Wilson	25.00	12.50	7.50
194	Ivy Wingo	25.00	12.50	7.50
195	"Mel" Wolfgang	25.00	12.50	7.50
196	Joe Wood	35.00	17.50	10.50
197	Steve Yerkes	25.00	12.50	7.50
198	Rollie Zeider	25.00	12.50	7.50
199	Heiny Zimmerman	30.00	12.50	7.50
200	Ed. Zwilling	40.00	15.00	7.50

1919 M101-6 Sporting News

This set of glossy black and white player photos was issued in 1919 by The Sporting News. The cards measure 4-1/2" by 6-1/2" and included action photos with the player's name and team listed at the bottom of the borderless cards. The unnumbered cards had blank backs. There are two cards of Babe Ruth in the set, one identifying him as a member of the Red Sox, the other as a Yankee. The card of Hugh High actually pictures Bob Shawkey.

		NR MT	EX	VG
Complete Set:		15000.	7500.	4500.
Common Player:		45.00	22.00	13.50
(1)	Grover C. Alexander (Philadelphia)	90.00	45.00	27.00
(2)	Grover C. Alexander (Chicago)	90.00	45.00	27.00
(3)	Jim Bagby	45.00	22.00	13.50
(4)	Franklin Baker	75.00	37.00	22.00
(5)	Dave Bancroft	75.00	37.00	22.00
(6)	Jack Barry	45.00	22.00	13.50
(7)	Johnny Bates	45.00	22.00	13.50
(8)	Carson Bigbee	45.00	22.00	13.50
(9)	Geo. Burns	45.00	22.00	13.50
(10)	Owen Bush	45.00	22.00	13.50
(11)	Max Carey	75.00	37.00	22.00
(12)	Ray Chapman	50.00	25.00	15.00
(13)	Hal Chase	55.00	27.00	16.50
(14)	Eddie Cicotte	50.00	25.00	15.00
(15)	Ty Cobb	1200.	600.00	350.00
(16)	Eddie Collins	75.00	37.00	22.00
(17)	"Gavvy" Cravath	50.00	25.00	15.00
(18)	Walton Cruise	45.00	22.00	13.50
(19)	George Cutshaw	45.00	22.00	13.50
(20)	George Dauss	45.00	22.00	13.50
(21)	Dave Davenport	45.00	22.00	13.50
(22)	Bill Doak	45.00	22.00	13.50
(23)	Larry Doyle	45.00	22.00	13.50
(24)	Howard Ehmke	45.00	22.00	13.50
(25)	Urban Faber	75.00	37.00	22.00
(26)	Happy Felsch	65.00	32.00	19.50
(27)	Del Gainer (Gainor)	45.00	22.00	13.50
(28)	Chick Gandil	55.00	27.00	16.50
(29)	Larry Gardner	45.00	22.00	13.50
(30)	Mike Gonzales	45.00	22.00	13.50
(31)	Jack Graney	45.00	22.00	13.50
(32)	Heinie Groh	45.00	22.00	13.50
(33)	Earl Hamilton	45.00	22.00	13.50
(34)	Harry Heilmann	75.00	37.00	22.00
(35)	Hugh High (New York, photo actually Bob Shawkey)	45.00	22.00	13.50
(36)	Hugh High (Detroit)	45.00	22.00	13.50
(37)	Bill Hinchman	45.00	22.00	13.50
(38)	Walter Holke (New York)	45.00	22.00	13.50
(39)	Walter Holke (Boston)	45.00	22.00	13.50
(40)	Harry Hooper	75.00	37.00	22.00
(41)	Rogers Hornsby	300.00	150.00	90.00
(42)	Joe Jackson	1000.	500.00	300.00
(43)	Bill Jacobson	45.00	22.00	13.50
(44)	Walter Johnson	400.00	200.00	120.00
(45)	Sam Jones	45.00	22.00	13.50
(46)	Joe Judge	45.00	22.00	13.50
(47)	Benny Kauff	45.00	22.00	13.50
(48)	Ed Konetchy (Boston)	45.00	22.00	13.50
(49)	Ed Konetchy (Brooklyn)	45.00	22.00	13.50
(50)	Nemo Leibold	45.00	22.00	13.50
(51)	Duffy Lewis	45.00	22.00	13.50
(52)	Fred Luderas (Luderus)	45.00	22.00	13.50
(53)	Les Mann	45.00	22.00	13.50
(54)	"Rabbit" Maranville	75.00	37.00	22.00
(55)	John McGraw	90.00	45.00	27.00
(56)	Fred Merkle	50.00	25.00	15.00
(57)	Clyde Milan	45.00	22.00	13.50
(58)	Otto Miller	45.00	22.00	13.50
(59)	Guy Morton	45.00	22.00	13.50
(60)	Hy Myers	45.00	22.00	13.50
(61)	Greasy Neale	55.00	27.00	16.50
(62)	Dode Paskert	45.00	22.00	13.50
(63)	Roger Peckinpaugh	50.00	25.00	15.00
(64)	Jeff Pfeffer	45.00	22.00	13.50
(65)	Walter Pipp	65.00	32.00	19.50
(66)	Johnny Rawlings	45.00	22.00	13.50
(67)	Sam Rice	75.00	37.00	22.00
(68)	Ed Roush	75.00	37.00	22.00
(69)	Dick Rudolph	45.00	22.00	13.50
(70)	Babe Ruth (Red Sox)	1500.	750.00	450.00
(71)	"Babe" Ruth (New York)	1500.	750.00	450.00
(72)	Ray Schalk	75.00	37.00	22.00
(73)	Hank Severeid	45.00	22.00	13.50
(74)	Burt Shotton	45.00	22.00	13.50
(75)	Geo. Sisler	75.00	37.00	22.00
(76)	Jack Smith	45.00	22.00	13.50
(77)	Frank Snyder	45.00	22.00	13.50
(78)	Tris Speaker	90.00	45.00	27.00
(79)	Oscar Stanage	45.00	22.00	13.50
(80)	Casey Stengel	400.00	200.00	125.00
(81)	Amos Strunk	45.00	22.00	13.50
(82)	Fred Toney	45.00	22.00	13.50
(83)	Jim Vaughn	45.00	22.00	13.50
(84)	Bobby Veach	45.00	22.00	13.50
(85)	Oscar Vitt	45.00	22.00	13.50
(86)	"Honus" Wagner	500.00	250.00	150.00
(87)	Tilly Walker	45.00	22.00	13.50
(88)	Bill Wambsganss	50.00	25.00	15.00
(89)	"Buck" Weaver	65.00	32.00	19.50
(90)	Zack Wheat	75.00	37.00	22.00
(91)	George Whitted	45.00	22.00	13.50
(92)	Cy Williams	50.00	25.00	15.00
(93)	Ivy Wingo	45.00	22.00	13.50
(94)	Pep ("Pep" Young)	45.00	22.00	13.50
(95)	Heinie Zimmerman	45.00	22.00	13.50

1926 M101-7
Sporting News Supplements

This set of 11 player photos was issued as a supplement by The Sporting News in 1926. The sepia-toned portrait photos were enclosed inside an oval on the 7" x 10" supplements. The player's name and team are printed at the bottom, while a line identifying The Sporting News and the date appear in the upper left corner. The unnumbered set includes a half-dozen Hall of Famers.

		NR MT	EX	VG
Complete Set:		1200.	600.00	350.00
Common Player:		30.00	15.00	9.00
(1)	Hazen "Kiki" Cuyler	100.00	50.00	30.00
(2)	Rogers Hornsby	125.00	62.00	37.00
(3)	Tony Lazzeri	60.00	30.00	18.00
(4)	Harry E. Manush	90.00	45.00	27.00
(5)	John Mostil	30.00	15.00	9.00
(6)	Harry Rice	30.00	15.00	9.00
(7)	George Herman "Babe" Ruth	400.00	200.00	125.00
(8)	Al Simmons	90.00	45.00	27.00
(9)	Harold "Pie" Traynor	90.00	45.00	27.00
(10)	George Uhle	30.00	15.00	9.00
(11)	Glenn Wright	30.00	15.00	9.00

1911 M116 Sporting Life

This set of 1-1/2" by 2-3/4" cards was offered to subscribers of Sporting Life, a major competitor of The Sporting News in the early part of the century. The cards were issued in 24 series of 12 cards each. Specialists consider the set complete at 310 different cards, including variations on which the background is in blue, rather than pastel colors. Each of the 16 major league teams are represented by 13 to 21 players, with nine minor leaguers also included. The card fronts are black and white photos that have been hand colored and carry the player's name and team. The card backs show various ads

Livingstone, Philadelphia Amer.

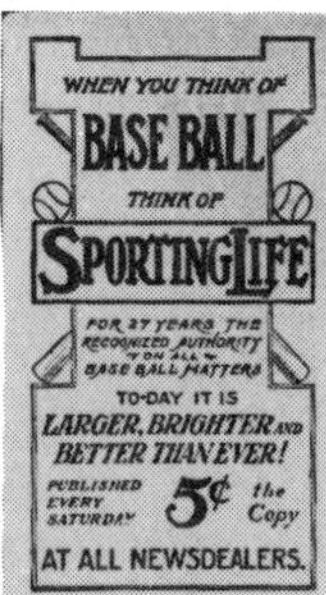
WHEN YOU THINK OF
BASE BALL
THINK OF
SPORTING LIFE
FOR 27 YEARS THE RECOGNIZED AUTHORITY ON ALL BASE BALL MATTERS
TO-DAY IT IS
LARGER, BRIGHTER AND BETTER THAN EVER!
PUBLISHED EVERY SATURDAY
5¢ the Copy
AT ALL NEWSDEALERS.

for the magazine. The last 72 cards issued are scarcer than the earlier series.

		NR MT	EX	VG
	Complete Set:	1200.	52000.	22500.
	Common Player:	150.00	75.00	45.00
(1)	Ed Abbaticchio	150.00	75.00	45.00
(2)	Babe Adams	400.00	175.00	75.00
(3)	Red Ames	400.00	175.00	75.00
(4)	Jimmy Archer	400.00	175.00	75.00
(5)	Frank Arrelanes (Arellanes)	150.00	75.00	45.00
(6)	Tommy Atkins	400.00	175.00	75.00
(7)	Jimmy Austin	400.00	175.00	75.00
(8)	Les Bachman (Backman)	150.00	75.00	45.00
(9)	Bill Bailey	150.00	75.00	45.00
(10)	Home Run Baker	500.00	250.00	100.00
(11)	Cy Barger	150.00	75.00	45.00
(12)	Jack Barry	150.00	75.00	45.00
(13)	Johnny Bates	150.00	75.00	45.00
(14)	Ginger Beaumont	150.00	75.00	45.00
(15)	Fred Beck	150.00	75.00	45.00
(16)	Heinie Beckendorf	150.00	75.00	45.00
(17)	Fred Beebe	150.00	75.00	45.00
(18)	George Bell	150.00	75.00	45.00
(19)	Harry Bemis	150.00	75.00	45.00
(20a)	Chief Bender (blue background)	900.00	450.00	200.00
(20b)	Chief Bender (pastel background)	500.00	250.00	100.00
(21)	Bill Bergen	150.00	75.00	45.00
(22)	Heinie Berger	150.00	75.00	45.00
(23)	Bob Bescher	150.00	75.00	45.00
(24)	Joe Birmingham	150.00	75.00	45.00
(25)	Lena Blackburn (Blackburne)	150.00	75.00	45.00
(26)	John Bliss	400.00	175.00	75.00
(27)	Bruno Block	400.00	175.00	75.00
(28)	Bill Bradley	150.00	75.00	45.00
(29)	Kitty Bransfield	150.00	75.00	45.00
(30)	Roger Bresnahan	700.00	350.00	200.00
(31)	Al Bridwell	150.00	75.00	45.00
(32)	Buster Brown (Boston N.L.)	150.00	75.00	45.00
(33a)	Mordecai Brown (blue background, Chicago N.L.)	900.00	450.00	200.00
(33b)	Mordecai Brown (pastel background, Chicago N.L.)	500.00	250.00	100.00
(34)	Al Burch	150.00	75.00	45.00
(35)	Donie Bush	150.00	75.00	45.00
(36)	Bobby Byrne	150.00	75.00	45.00
(37)	Howie Camnitz	150.00	75.00	45.00
(38)	Vin Campbell	400.00	175.00	75.00
(39)	Bill Carrigan	150.00	75.00	45.00
(40a)	Frank Chance (blue background)	900.00	450.00	200.00
(40b)	Frank Chance (pastel background)	500.00	250.00	100.00
(41)	Chappy Charles	150.00	75.00	45.00
(42a)	Hal Chase (blue background)	700.00	350.00	200.00
(42b)	Hal Chase (pastel background)	350.00	175.00	75.00
(43)	Ed Cicotte	200.00	90.00	40.00
(44)	Fred Clarke (Pittsburgh)	550.00	275.00	125.00
(45)	Nig Clarke (Cleveland)	150.00	75.00	45.00
(46)	Tommy Clarke (Cincinnati)	400.00	175.00	75.00
(47a)	Ty Cobb (blue background)	4500.	2000.	950.00
(47b)	Ty Cobb (pastel background)	2500.	1000.	475.00
(48a)	Eddie Collins (blue background)	1000.	500.00	225.00
(48b)	Eddie Collins (pastel background)	600.00	300.00	140.00
(49)	Ray Collins	400.00	175.00	75.00
(50)	Wid Conroy	150.00	75.00	45.00
(51)	Jack Coombs	175.00	65.00	25.00
(52)	Frank Corridon	150.00	75.00	45.00
(53)	Harry Coveleskie (Coveleski)	500.00	250.00	100.00
(54)	Doc Crandall	150.00	75.00	45.00
(55a)	Sam Crawford (blue background)	900.00	450.00	200.00
(55b)	Sam Crawford (pastel background)	500.00	250.00	100.00
(56)	Birdie Cree	150.00	75.00	45.00
(57)	Lou Criger	150.00	75.00	45.00
(58)	Dode Criss	400.00	175.00	75.00
(59)	Cliff Curtis	400.00	175.00	75.00
(60)	Bill Dahlen	150.00	75.00	45.00
(61)	Bill Davidson	400.00	175.00	75.00
(62a)	Harry Davis (blue background)	400.00	175.00	75.00
(62b)	Harry Davis (pastel background)	150.00	75.00	45.00
(63)	Jim Delehanty (Delahanty)	150.00	75.00	45.00
(64)	Ray Demmitt	400.00	175.00	75.00
(65)	Rube Dessau	400.00	175.00	75.00
(66)	Art Devlin	150.00	75.00	45.00
(67)	Josh Devore	400.00	175.00	75.00
(68)	Pat Donahue	150.00	75.00	45.00
(69)	Patsy Donovan	400.00	175.00	75.00
(70)	Wild Bill Donovan	150.00	75.00	45.00
(71a)	Red Dooin (blue background)	400.00	175.00	75.00
(71b)	Red Dooin (pastel background)	150.00	75.00	45.00

		NR MT	EX	VG
(72)	Mickey Doolan	150.00	75.00	45.00
(73)	Patsy Dougherty	150.00	75.00	45.00
(74)	Tom Downey	150.00	75.00	45.00
(75)	Jim Doyle	150.00	75.00	45.00
(76a)	Larry Doyle (blue background)	400.00	175.00	75.00
(76b)	Larry Doyle (pastel background)	30.00	15.00	9.00
(77)	Hugh Duffy	600.00	300.00	125.00
(78)	Jimmy Dygert	150.00	75.00	45.00
(79)	Dick Eagan (Egan)	150.00	75.00	45.00
(80)	Kid Elberfeld	150.00	75.00	45.00
(81)	Rube Ellis	150.00	75.00	45.00
(82)	Clyde Engle	150.00	75.00	45.00
(83)	Tex Erwin	400.00	175.00	75.00
(84)	Steve Evans	400.00	175.00	75.00
(85)	Johnny Evers	500.00	250.00	100.00
(86)	Bob Ewing	150.00	75.00	45.00
(87)	Cy Falkenberg	150.00	75.00	45.00
(88)	George Ferguson	150.00	75.00	45.00
(89)	Art Fletcher	400.00	175.00	75.00
(90)	Elmer Flick	500.00	250.00	100.00
(91)	John Flynn	400.00	175.00	75.00
(92)	Russ Ford	400.00	175.00	75.00
(93)	Eddie Foster	500.00	250.00	100.00
(94)	Bill Foxen	150.00	75.00	45.00
(95)	John Frill	500.00	250.00	100.00
(96)	Sam Frock	400.00	175.00	75.00
(97)	Art Fromme	150.00	75.00	45.00
(98)	Earl Gardner (New York A.L.)	400.00	175.00	75.00
(99)	Larry Gardner (Boston A.L.)	400.00	175.00	75.00
(100)	Harry Gaspar	400.00	175.00	75.00
(101)	Doc Gessler	150.00	75.00	45.00
(102a)	George Gibson (blue background)	400.00	175.00	75.00
(102b)	George Gibson (pastel background)	150.00	75.00	45.00
(103)	Bill Graham (St. Louis A.L.)	150.00	75.00	45.00
(104)	Peaches Graham (Boston N.L.)	150.00	75.00	45.00
(105)	Eddie Grant	150.00	75.00	45.00
(106)	Clark Griffith	500.00	250.00	100.00
(107)	Ed Hahn	150.00	75.00	45.00
(108)	Charley Hall	150.00	75.00	45.00
(109)	Bob Harmon	400.00	175.00	75.00
(110)	Topsy Hartsel	150.00	75.00	45.00
(111)	Roy Hartzell	150.00	75.00	45.00
(112)	Heinie Heitmuller	150.00	75.00	45.00
(113)	Buck Herzog	150.00	75.00	45.00
(114)	Dick Hoblitzel (Hoblitzell)	150.00	75.00	45.00
(115)	Danny Hoffman	150.00	75.00	45.00
(116)	Solly Hofman	150.00	75.00	45.00
(117)	Harry Hooper	700.00	350.00	150.00
(118)	Harry Howell	150.00	75.00	45.00
(119)	Miller Huggins	600.00	300.00	125.00
(120)	Long Tom Hughes	500.00	200.00	90.00
(121)	Rudy Hulswitt	150.00	75.00	45.00
(122)	John Hummel	150.00	75.00	45.00
(123)	George Hunter	150.00	75.00	45.00
(124)	Ham Hyatt	150.00	75.00	45.00
(125)	Fred Jacklitsch	150.00	75.00	45.00
(126a)	Hughie Jennings (blue background)	1000.	500.00	225.00
(126b)	Hughie Jennings (pastel background)	600.00	300.00	125.00
(127)	Walter Johnson	1500.	750.00	300.00
(128)	Davy Jones	150.00	75.00	45.00
(129)	Tom Jones	150.00	75.00	45.00
(130a)	Tim Jordan (blue background)	400.00	200.00	90.00
(130b)	Tim Jordan (pastel background)	150.00	75.00	45.00
(131)	Addie Joss	650.00	300.00	125.00
(132)	Johnny Kane	150.00	75.00	45.00
(133)	Ed Karger	150.00	75.00	45.00
(134)	Red Killifer (Killefer)	400.00	175.00	75.00
(135)	Johnny Kling	150.00	75.00	45.00
(136)	Otto Knabe	150.00	75.00	45.00
(137)	John Knight	400.00	175.00	75.00
(138)	Ed Konetchy	150.00	75.00	45.00
(139)	Harry Krause	150.00	75.00	45.00
(140)	Rube Kroh	150.00	75.00	45.00
(141)	Art Krueger	500.00	200.00	90.00
(142a)	Nap Lajoie (blue background)	1400.	700.00	315.00
(142b)	Nap Lajoie (pastel background)	850.00	400.00	190.00
(143)	Fred Lake (Boston N.L.)	150.00	75.00	45.00
(144)	Joe Lake (St. Louis A.L.)	400.00	175.00	75.00
(145)	Frank LaPorte	150.00	75.00	45.00
(146)	Jack Lapp	400.00	175.00	75.00
(147)	Chick Lathers	400.00	175.00	75.00
(148a)	Tommy Leach (blue background)	400.00	175.00	75.00
(148b)	Tommy Leach (pastel background)	150.00	75.00	45.00
(149)	Sam Leever	150.00	75.00	45.00
(150)	Lefty Leifield	150.00	75.00	45.00
(151)	Ed Lennox	150.00	75.00	45.00
(152)	Fred Linke (Link)	400.00	175.00	75.00
(153)	Paddy Livingstone (Livingston)	150.00	75.00	45.00
(154)	Hans Lobert	150.00	75.00	45.00
(155)	Bris Lord (Cleveland)	150.00	75.00	45.00
(156a)	Harry Lord (blue background, Boston A.L.)	400.00	200.00	90.00
(156b)	Harry Lord (pastel background, Boston A.L.)	150.00	75.00	45.00
(157)	Johnny Lush	150.00	75.00	45.00
(158)	Connie Mack	900.00	450.00	200.00
(159)	Tom Madden	400.00	175.00	75.00
(160)	Nick Maddox	150.00	75.00	45.00
(161)	Sherry Magee	175.00	65.00	25.00
(162a)	Christy Mathewson (Blue Background)	2500.	1000.	475.00
162b	Christy Mathewson (pastel background)	1500.	700.00	350.00
(163)	Al Mattern	150.00	75.00	45.00
(164)	Jimmy McAleer	150.00	75.00	45.00
(165)	George McBride	400.00	175.00	75.00
(166a)	Amby McConnell (Boston A.L.)	150.00	75.00	45.00
(166b)	Amby McConnell (Chicago A.L.)	4500.	2000.	800.00
(167)	Pryor McElveen	150.00	75.00	45.00
(168)	John McGraw	700.00	350.00	150.00
(169)	Deacon McGuire	150.00	75.00	45.00
(170)	Stuffy McInnes (McInnis)	400.00	175.00	75.00
(171)	Harry McIntire (McIntyre)	150.00	75.00	45.00
(172)	Matty McIntyre	150.00	75.00	45.00
(173)	Larry McLean	150.00	75.00	45.00
(174)	Tommy McMillan	150.00	75.00	45.00

		NR MT	EX	VG
(175a)	George McQuillan (blue background, Philadelphia N.L.)	400.00	200.00	90.00
(175b)	George McQuillan (pastel background, Philadelphia N.L.)	150.00	75.00	45.00
(175c)	George McQuillan (Cincinnati)	4500.	2000.	800.00
(176)	Paul Meloan	400.00	175.00	75.00
(177)	Fred Merkle	150.00	75.00	45.00
(178)	Clyde Milan	150.00	75.00	45.00
(179)	Dots Miller (Pittsburgh)	150.00	75.00	45.00
(180)	Warren Miller (Washington)	400.00	175.00	75.00
(181)	Fred Mitchell	500.00	200.00	90.00
(182)	Mike Mitchell	150.00	75.00	45.00
(183)	Earl Moore	150.00	75.00	45.00
(184)	Pat Moran	150.00	75.00	45.00
(185)	Lew Moren	150.00	75.00	45.00
(186)	Cy Morgan	150.00	75.00	45.00
(187)	George Moriarty	150.00	75.00	45.00
(188)	Mike Mowrey	400.00	175.00	75.00
(189)	George Mullin	150.00	75.00	45.00
(190)	Danny Murphy	150.00	75.00	45.00
(191)	Red Murray	150.00	75.00	45.00
(192)	Chief Myers (Meyers)	400.00	175.00	75.00
(193)	Tom Needham	150.00	75.00	45.00
(194)	Harry Niles	150.00	75.00	45.00
(195)	Rebel Oakes	400.00	175.00	75.00
(196)	Jack O'Connor	150.00	75.00	45.00
(197)	Paddy O'Connor	150.00	75.00	45.00
(198)	Bill O'Hara	500.00	200.00	90.00
(199)	Rube Oldring	150.00	75.00	45.00
(200)	Charley O'Leary	150.00	75.00	45.00
(201)	Orval Overall	150.00	75.00	45.00
(202)	Freddy Parent	150.00	75.00	45.00
(203)	Dode Paskert	400.00	175.00	75.00
(204)	Fred Payne	400.00	175.00	75.00
(205)	Barney Pelty	150.00	75.00	45.00
(206)	Hub Pernoll	400.00	175.00	75.00
(207)	George Perring	500.00	200.00	90.00
(208)	Big Jeff Pfeffer	400.00	175.00	75.00
(209)	Jack Pfiester	150.00	75.00	45.00
(210)	Art Phelan	400.00	175.00	75.00
(211)	Ed Phelps	150.00	75.00	45.00
(212)	Deacon Phillippe	150.00	75.00	45.00
(213)	Eddie Plank	900.00	450.00	200.00
(214)	Jack Powell	150.00	75.00	45.00
(215)	Billy Purtell	150.00	75.00	45.00
(216)	Farmer Ray	500.00	200.00	90.00
(217)	Bugs Raymond	150.00	75.00	45.00
(218)	Doc Reisling	150.00	75.00	45.00
(219)	Ed Reulbach	150.00	75.00	45.00
(220)	Lew Richie	150.00	75.00	45.00
(221)	Jack Rowan	150.00	75.00	45.00
(222)	Nap Rucker	150.00	75.00	45.00
(223)	Slim Sallee	150.00	75.00	45.00
(224)	Doc Scanlon	150.00	75.00	45.00
(225)	Germany Schaefer	150.00	75.00	45.00
(226)	Lou Schettler	400.00	175.00	75.00
(227)	Admiral Schlei	150.00	75.00	45.00
(228)	Boss Schmidt	150.00	75.00	45.00
(229)	Wildfire Schulte	150.00	75.00	45.00
(230)	Al Schweitzer	150.00	75.00	45.00
(231)	Jim Scott	400.00	175.00	75.00
(232)	Cy Seymour	150.00	75.00	45.00
(233)	Tillie Shafer	150.00	75.00	45.00
(234)	Bud Sharpe	400.00	175.00	75.00
(235)	Dave Shean	400.00	175.00	75.00
(236)	Jimmy Sheckard	150.00	75.00	45.00
(237)	Mike Simon	400.00	175.00	75.00
(238)	Charlie Smith (Boston N.L.)	400.00	175.00	75.00
(239)	Frank Smith (Chicago A.L.)	150.00	75.00	45.00
(240)	Harry Smith (Boston N.L.)	150.00	75.00	45.00
(241)	Fred Snodgrass	150.00	75.00	45.00
(242)	Bob Spade	150.00	75.00	45.00
(243)	Tully Sparks	150.00	75.00	45.00
(244)	Tris Speaker	1500.	750.00	300.00
(245)	Jake Stahl	150.00	75.00	45.00
(246)	George Stallings	150.00	75.00	45.00
(247)	Oscar Stanage	150.00	75.00	45.00
(248)	Harry Steinfeldt	175.00	75.00	30.00
(249)	Jim Stephens	150.00	75.00	45.00
(250)	George Stone	150.00	75.00	45.00
(251)	George Stovall	150.00	75.00	45.00
(252)	Gabby Street	150.00	75.00	45.00
(253)	Sailor Stroud	400.00	175.00	75.00
(254)	Amos Strunk	400.00	175.00	75.00
(255)	George Suggs	150.00	75.00	45.00
(256)	Billy Sullivan	150.00	75.00	45.00
(257)	Ed Summers	150.00	75.00	45.00
(258)	Bill Sweeney (Boston N.L.)	150.00	75.00	45.00
(259)	Jeff Sweeney (New York A.L.)	400.00	175.00	75.00
(260)	Lee Tannehill	150.00	75.00	45.00
(261a)	Fred Tenney (blue background)	400.00	175.00	75.00
(261b)	Fred Tenney (pastel background)	150.00	75.00	45.00
(262a)	Ira Thomas (blue background)	400.00	175.00	75.00
(262b)	Ira Thomas (pastel background)	150.00	75.00	45.00
(263)	Jack Thoney	150.00	75.00	45.00
(264)	Joe Tinker	500.00	250.00	100.00
(265)	John Titus	400.00	175.00	75.00
(266)	Terry Turner	150.00	75.00	45.00
(267)	Bob Unglaub	150.00	75.00	45.00
(268)	Rube Waddell	650.00	300.00	125.00
(269a)	Hans Wagner (blue background, Pittsburgh)	3000.	1500.	650.00
(269b)	Hans Wagner (pastel background, Pittsburgh)	1200.	600.00	250.00
(270)	Heinie Wagner (Boston A.L.)	150.00	75.00	45.00
(271)	Bobby Wallace	550.00	250.00	100.00
(272)	Ed Walsh (Chicago A.L.)	700.00	350.00	150.00
(273a)	Jimmy Walsh (grey background)	600.00	250.00	100.00
(273b)	Jimmy Walsh (white background)	600.00	250.00	100.00
(274)	Doc White	150.00	75.00	45.00
(275)	Kaiser Wilhelm	150.00	75.00	45.00
(276)	Ed Willett	150.00	75.00	45.00
(277)	Vic Willis	150.00	75.00	45.00
(278)	Art Wilson (New York N.L.)	150.00	75.00	45.00
(279)	Owen Wilson (Pittsburgh)	150.00	75.00	45.00
(280)	Hooks Wiltse	150.00	75.00	45.00
(281)	Harry Wolter	150.00	75.00	45.00
(282)	Smoky Joe Wood	400.00	175.00	75.00
(283)	Ralph Works	150.00	75.00	45.00

	NR MT	EX	VG
(284) Cy Young (Cleveland)	950.00	425.00	200.00
(285) Irv Young (Chicago A.L.)	150.00	75.00	45.00
(286) Heinie Zimmerman	400.00	175.00	75.00
(287) Dutch Zwilling	400.00	175.00	75.00

1888 M117 Sporting Times

Examples of these cards, issued in 1888 and 1889 by the Sporting Times weekly newspaper, are very rare. The complete set price includes all variations. The cabinet-size cards (7-1/4" by 4-1/2") feature line drawings of players in action poses on soft cardboard stock. The cards came in a variety of pastel colors surrounded by a 1/4" white border. The player's last name is printed on each drawing, as are the words "Courtesy Sporting Times New York." A pair of crossed bats and a baseball appear along the bottom of the card. Twenty-seven different players are known to exist. The drawing of Cap Anson is the same one used in the N28 Allen & Ginter series, and some of the other drawings are based on photos used in the popular Old Judge series. The Sporting Times set has an American Card Catalog number of M117.

		NR MT	EX	VG
Complete Set:		20000.	10000.	6000.
Common Player:		500.00	250.00	150.00
(1)	Cap Anson	2000.	1000.	600.00
(2)	Jersey Bakely	500.00	250.00	150.00
(3)	Dan Brouthers	1000.	500.00	300.00
(4)	Doc Bushong	500.00	250.00	150.00
(5)	Jack Clements	500.00	250.00	150.00
(6)	Commy Comiskey	1000.	500.00	300.00
(7)	Jerry Denny	500.00	250.00	150.00
(8)	Buck Ewing	1000.	500.00	300.00
(9)	Dude Esterbrook	500.00	250.00	150.00
(10)	Jay Faatz	500.00	250.00	150.00
(11)	Pud Galvin	1000.	500.00	300.00
(12)	Pebbly Jack Glasscock	500.00	250.00	150.00
(13)	Tim Keefe	1000.	500.00	300.00
(14)	King Kelly	1000.	500.00	300.00
(15)	Matt Kilroy	500.00	250.00	150.00
(16)	Arlie Latham	500.00	250.00	150.00
(17)	Doggie Miller	500.00	250.00	150.00
(18)	Hank O'Day	500.00	250.00	150.00
(19)	Fred Pfeffer	500.00	250.00	150.00
(20)	Henry Porter	500.00	250.00	150.00
(21)	Toad Ramsey	500.00	250.00	150.00
(22)	Long John Reilly	500.00	250.00	150.00
(23)	Mike Smith	500.00	250.00	150.00
(24)	Harry Stovey	500.00	250.00	150.00
(25)	Big Sam Thompson	1000.	500.00	300.00
(26)	Monte Ward	1000.	500.00	300.00
(27)	Mickey Welch	1000.	500.00	300.00

1987 M & M's

The M&M's "Star Lineup" set consists of 12 two card panels inserted in specially marked packages of large M&M's candy. The two-card panels measure 5" by 3-1/2" with individual cards measuring 2-1/2" by 3-1/2" in size. The full-color photos are enclosed by a wavy blue frame and a white border. Card backs are printed in red ink on white stock and carry the player's career statistics and highlights. All team insignias have been airbrushed away. The set was designed and produced by Mike Schechter and Associates.

NOTE: A card number in parentheses ( ) indicates the set is unnumbered.

		MT	NR MT	EX
Complete Panel Set:		18.00	13.50	7.25
Complete Singles Set:		8.00	6.00	3.25
Common Panel:		1.00	.70	.40
Common Single Player:		.10	.08	.04
Panel		1.50	1.25	.60
1	Wally Joyner	.50	.40	.20
2	Tony Pena	.10	.08	.04
Panel		1.50	1.25	.60
3	Mike Schmidt	.30	.25	.12
4	Ryne Sandberg	.20	.15	.08
Panel		2.25	1.75	.90
5	Wade Boggs	.70	.50	.30
6	Jack Morris	.20	.15	.08
Panel		1.25	.90	.50
7	Roger Clemens	.30	.25	.12
8	Harold Baines	.15	.11	.06
Panel		2.75	2.00	1.00
9	Dale Murphy	.30	.25	.12
10	Jose Canseco	1.00	.70	.40
Panel		3.25	2.50	1.25
11	Don Mattingly	1.25	.90	.50
12	Gary Carter	.20	.15	.08
Panel		1.50	1.25	.60
13	Cal Ripken, Jr.	.25	.20	.10
14	George Brett	.30	.25	.12
Panel		1.00	.70	.40
15	Kirby Puckett	.20	.15	.08
16	Joe Carter	.15	.11	.06
Panel		1.00	.70	.40
17	Mike Witt	.15	.11	.06
18	Mike Scott	.15	.11	.06
Panel		1.25	.90	.50
19	Fernando Valenzuela	.20	.15	.08
20	Steve Garvey	.20	.15	.08
Panel		1.00	.70	.40
21	Steve Sax	.15	.11	.06
22	Nolan Ryan	.20	.15	.08
Panel		1.25	.90	.50
23	Tony Gwynn	.25	.20	.10
24	Ozzie Smith	.15	.11	.06

1969 MLB Baseball Stars Photostamps

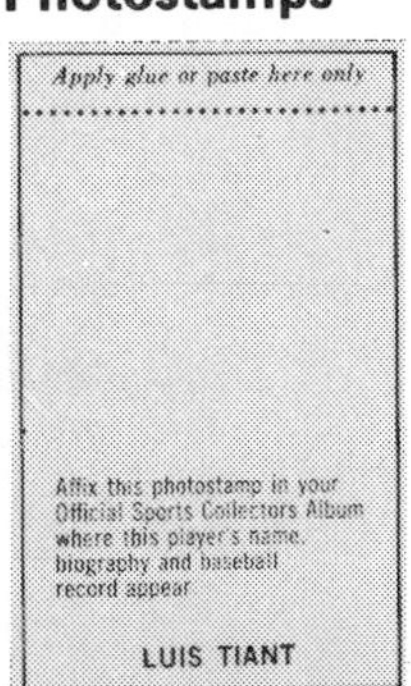

This set of 216 player stamps, sponsored by Major League Baseball, was issued in professional baseball's centennial year of 1969 and was sold in 18 different uncut sheets, with 12 stamps on each sheet. Each individual stamp measured 2" by 3-1/4". There were nine sheets picturing National League players and nine picturing American Leaguers. The full-color stamps displayed facsimilie autographs on the fronts. The backs carried instructions to moisten the stamps and place them in a special album that was also available. Many sheets of these stamps were uncovered by a dealer in the early 1980's and they were available at inexpensive prices.

		NR MT	EX	VG
Complete Sheet Set:		15.00	7.50	4.50
Complete Singles Set:		7.00	3.50	2.00
Common Sheet:		.75	.40	.25
Common Player:		.05	.03	.02
Sheet A.L. 1		1.00	.50	.30
(1)	Don Buford	.05	.03	.02
(2)	Mike Andrews	.05	.03	.02
(3)	Max Alvis	.05	.03	.02
(4)	Bill Freehan	.05	.03	.02
(5)	Horace Clarke	.05	.03	.02
(6)	Bernie Allen	.05	.03	.02
(7)	Jim Fregosi	.05	.03	.02
(8)	Joe Horlen	.05	.03	.02
(9)	Jerry Adair	.05	.03	.02
(10)	Harmon Killebrew	.25	.13	.08
(11)	Johnny Odom	.05	.03	.02
(12)	Steve Barber	.05	.03	.02
Sheet A.L. 2		1.00	.50	.30
(13)	Tom Harper	.05	.03	.02
(14)	John Powell	.10	.05	.03
(15)	Jose Santiago	.05	.03	.02
(16)	Sonny Siebert	.05	.03	.02
(17)	Mickey Lolich	.10	.05	.03
(18)	Tom Tresh	.05	.03	.02
(19)	Camilo Pascual	.05	.03	.02
(20)	Bob Rodgers	.05	.03	.02
(21)	Pete Ward	.05	.03	.02
(22)	Dave Morehead	.05	.03	.02
(23)	John Roseboro	.05	.03	.02
(24)	Campy Campaneris	.10	.05	.03
Sheet A.L. 3		1.00	.50	.30
(25)	Danny Cater	.05	.03	.02
(26)	Rich Rollins	.05	.03	.02
(27)	Brooks Robinson	.35	.20	.11
(28)	Rico Petrocelli	.05	.03	.02
(29)	Larry Brown	.05	.03	.02
(30)	Norm Cash	.05	.03	.02
(31)	Jake Gibbs	.05	.03	.02
(32)	Mike Epstein	.05	.03	.02
(33)	George Brunet	.05	.03	.02
(34)	Tom McCraw	.05	.03	.02
(35)	Steve Whitaker	.05	.03	.02
(36)	Bob Allison	.05	.03	.02
Sheet A.L. 4		1.00	.50	.30
(37)	Jim Kaat	.10	.05	.03
(38)	Sal Bando	.05	.03	.02
(39)	Ray Oyler	.05	.03	.02
(40)	Dave McNally	.05	.03	.02
(41)	George Scott	.05	.03	.02
(42)	Joe Azcue	.05	.03	.02
(43)	Jim Northrup	.05	.03	.02
(44)	Fritz Peterson	.05	.03	.02
(45)	Paul Casanova	.05	.03	.02
(46)	Roger Repoz	.05	.03	.02
(47)	Tommy John	.12	.06	.04
(48)	Moe Drabowsky	.05	.03	.02
Sheet A.L. 5		.75	.40	.25
(49)	Ed Kirkpatrick	.05	.03	.02
(50)	Dean Chance	.05	.03	.02
(51)	Mike Hershberger	.05	.03	.02
(52)	Jack Aker	.05	.03	.02
(53)	Andy Etchebarren	.05	.03	.02
(54)	Ray Culp	.05	.03	.02
(55)	Luis Tiant	.05	.03	.02
(56)	Willie Horton	.05	.03	.02
(57)	Roy White	.05	.03	.02
(58)	Ken McMullen	.05	.03	.02
(59)	Rick Reichardt	.05	.03	.02
(60)	Luis Aparicio	.20	.10	.06
Sheet A.L. 6		.75	.40	.25
(61)	Ken Berry	.05	.03	.02
(62)	Wally Bunker	.05	.03	.02
(63)	Tony Oliva	.10	.05	.03
(64)	Rick Monday	.05	.03	.02
(65)	Chico Salmon	.05	.03	.02
(66)	Paul Blair	.05	.03	.02
(67)	Jim Lonborg	.05	.03	.02
(68)	Zoilo Versalles	.05	.03	.02
(69)	Denny McLain	.10	.05	.03
(70)	Mel Stottlemyre	.05	.03	.02
(71)	Joe Coleman	.05	.03	.02
(72)	Bob Knoop	.05	.03	.02
Sheet A.L. 7		1.00	.50	.30
(73)	Chuck Hinton	.05	.03	.02
(74)	Duane Josephson	.05	.03	.02
(75)	Roger Nelson	.05	.03	.02
(76)	Ted Uhlaender	.05	.03	.02
(77)	John Donaldson	.05	.03	.02
(78)	Tommy Davis	.05	.03	.02
(79)	Frank Robinson	.25	.13	.08
(80)	Dick Ellsworth	.05	.03	.02
(81)	Sam McDowell	.05	.03	.02
(82)	Dick McAuliffe	.05	.03	.02
(83)	Bill Robinson	.05	.03	.02
(84)	Frank Howard	.10	.05	.03
Sheet A.L. 8		1.25	.60	.40
(85)	Ed Brinkman	.05	.03	.02
(86)	Vic Davalillo	.05	.03	.02
(87)	Gary Peters	.05	.03	.02
(88)	Joe Foy	.05	.03	.02
(89)	Rodney Carew	.35	.20	.11
(90)	Jim "Catfish" Hunter	.20	.10	.06
(91)	Gary Bell	.05	.03	.02
(92)	Dave Johnson	.10	.05	.03
(93)	Ken Harrelson	.05	.03	.02
(94)	Tony Horton	.05	.03	.02
(95)	Al Kaline	.25	.13	.08
(96)	Steve Hamilton	.05	.03	.02
Sheet A.L. 9		.50	.25	.15
(97)	Joseph Pepitone	.05	.03	.02
(98)	Ed Stroud	.05	.03	.02
(99)	Jim McGlothlin	.05	.03	.02
(100)	Wilbur Wood	.05	.03	.02
(101)	Paul Schaal	.05	.03	.02
(102)	Cesar Tovar	.05	.03	.02
(103)	Jim Nash	.05	.03	.02
(104)	Don Mincher	.05	.03	.02
(105)	Thomas Phoebus	.05	.03	.02
(106)	Reggie Smith	.05	.03	.02
(107)	Jose Cardenal	.05	.03	.02
(108)	Mickey Stanley	.05	.03	.02
Sheet N.L. 1		1.25	.60	.40
(109)	Billy Williams	.20	.10	.06
(110)	Mack Jones	.05	.03	.02
(111)	Tom Seaver	.35	.20	.11
(112)	Rich Allen	.10	.05	.03
(113)	Bob Veale	.05	.03	.02
(114)	Curt Flood	.05	.03	.02
(115)	Pat Jarvis	.05	.03	.02
(116)	Jim Merritt	.05	.03	.02
(117)	Joe Morgan	.20	.10	.06
(118)	Tom Haller	.05	.03	.02
(119)	Larry Stahl	.05	.03	.02
(120)	Willie McCovey	.25	.13	.08

	NR MT	EX	VG
Sheet N.L. 2	1.00	.50	.30
(121) Ron Hunt	.05	.03	.02
(122) Ernie Banks	.25	.13	.08
(123) Jim Fairey	.05	.03	.02
(124) Tommy Agee	.05	.03	.02
(125) Cookie Rojas	.05	.03	.02
(126) Mateo Alou	.05	.03	.02
(127) Mike Shannon	.05	.03	.02
(128) Milt Pappas	.05	.03	.02
(129) Johnny Bench	.35	.20	.11
(130) Larry Dierker	.05	.03	.02
(131) Willie Davis	.05	.03	.02
(132) Tony Gonzalez	.05	.03	.02
Sheet N.L. 3	1.00	.50	.30
(133) Dick Selma	.05	.03	.02
(134) Jim Ray Hart	.05	.03	.02
(135) Phil Regan	.05	.03	.02
(136) Manny Mota	.05	.03	.02
(137) Cleon Jones	.05	.03	.02
(138) Rick Wise	.05	.03	.02
(139) Willie Stargell	.25	.13	.08
(140) Robert Gibson	.25	.13	.08
(141) Rico Carty	.05	.03	.02
(142) Gary Nolan	.05	.03	.02
(143) Doug Rader	.05	.03	.02
(144) Wes Parker	.05	.03	.02
Sheet N.L. 4	.75	.40	.25
(145) Bill Singer	.05	.03	.02
(146) Bill McCool	.05	.03	.02
(147) Juan Marichal	.20	.10	.06
(148) Randy Hundley	.05	.03	.02
(149) "Mudcat" Grant	.05	.03	.02
(150) Ed Kranepool	.05	.03	.02
(151) Tony Taylor	.05	.03	.02
(152) Gene Alley	.05	.03	.02
(153) Dal Maxvill	.05	.03	.02
(154) Felipe Alou	.05	.03	.02
(155) Jim Maloney	.05	.03	.02
(156) Jesus Alou	.05	.03	.02
Sheet N.L. 5	2.25	1.25	.70
(157) Curt Blefary	.05	.03	.02
(158) Ron Fairly	.05	.03	.02
(159) Dick Kelley	.05	.03	.02
(160) Frank Linzy	.05	.03	.02
(161) Fergie Jenkins	.15	.08	.05
(162) Maury Wills	.10	.05	.03
(163) Jerry Grote	.05	.03	.02
(164) Chris Short	.05	.03	.02
(165) Jim Bunning	.12	.06	.04
(166) Nelson Briles	.05	.03	.02
(167) Orlando Cepeda	.10	.05	.03
(168) Pete Rose	.90	.45	.25
Sheet N.L. 6	.75	.40	.25
(169) Tony Cloninger	.05	.03	.02
(170) Jim Wynn	.05	.03	.02
(171) Jim Lefebvre	.05	.03	.02
(172) Ron Davis	.05	.03	.02
(173) Mike McCormick	.05	.03	.02
(174) Ron Santo	.05	.03	.02
(175) Ty Cline	.05	.03	.02
(176) Jerry Koosman	.05	.03	.02
(177) Mike Ryan	.05	.03	.02
(178) Jerry May	.05	.03	.02
(179) Tim McCarver	.05	.03	.02
(180) Phil Niekro	.12	.06	.04
Sheet N.L. 7	2.25	1.25	.70
(181) Hank Aaron	.50	.25	.15
(182) Tommy Helms	.05	.03	.02
(183) Denis Menke	.05	.03	.02
(184) Don Sutton	.12	.06	.04
(185) Al Ferrera	.05	.03	.02
(186) Willie Mays	.50	.25	.15
(187) Bill Hands	.05	.03	.02
(188) Rusty Staub	.05	.03	.02
(189) Bud Harrelson	.05	.03	.02
(190) Johnny Callison	.05	.03	.02
(191) Roberto Clemente	.50	.25	.15
(192) Julian Javier	.05	.03	.02
Sheet N.L. 8	.50	.25	.15
(193) Joe Torre	.05	.03	.02
(194) Bob Aspromonte	.05	.03	.02
(195) Lee May	.05	.03	.02
(196) Don Wilson	.05	.03	.02
(197) Claude Osteen	.05	.03	.02
(198) Ed Spiezio	.05	.03	.02
(199) Hal Lanier	.05	.03	.02
(200) Glenn Beckert	.05	.03	.02
(201) Bob Bailey	.05	.03	.02
(202) Ron Swoboda	.05	.03	.02
(203) John Briggs	.05	.03	.02
(204) Bill Mazeroski	.05	.03	.02
Sheet N.L. 9	.75	.40	.25
(205) Tommie Sisk	.05	.03	.02
(206) Louis Brock	.25	.13	.08
(207) Felix Millan	.05	.03	.02
(208) Tony Perez	.12	.06	.04
(209) John Edwards	.05	.03	.02
(210) Len Gabrielson	.05	.03	.02
(211) Ollie Brown	.05	.03	.02
(212) Gay Perry	.15	.08	.05
(213) Don Kessinger	.05	.03	.02
(214) John Bateman	.05	.03	.02
(215) Ed Charles	.05	.03	.02
(216) Woodie Fryman	.05	.03	.02

1969 MLBPA Pins

Issued by the Major League Baseball Players Association in 1969, this unnumbered set consists of 60 pins - 30 players from the N.L. and 30 from the A.L. Each pin measures approximately 7/8" in diameter and features a black and white player photo. A.L. players are surrounded by a red border, while N.L. players are framed in blue. The player's name and team appear at the top and bottom. Also along the bottom is a line reading" "1969 MLBPA MFG. R.R. Winona, MINN."

		NR MT	EX	VG
Complete Set:		150.00	75.00	45.00
Common Player:		.50	.25	.15
(1)	Hank Aaron	10.00	5.00	3.00
(2)	Richie Allen	2.75	1.50	.80
(3)	Felipe Alou	.75	.40	.25
(4)	Max Alvis	.50	.25	.15
(5)	Luis Aparicio	4.00	2.00	1.25
(6)	Ernie Banks	6.00	3.00	1.75
(7)	Johnny Bench	8.00	4.00	2.50
(8)	Lou Brock	5.00	2.50	1.50
(9)	George Brunet	.50	.25	.15
(10)	Johnny Callison	.75	.40	.25
(11)	Rod Carew	7.00	3.50	2.00
(12)	Orlando Cepeda	3.00	1.50	.90
(13)	Dean Chance	.50	.25	.15
(14)	Roberto Clemente	10.00	5.00	3.00
(15)	Willie Davis	.75	.40	.25
(16)	Don Drysdale	5.00	2.50	1.50
(17)	Ron Fairly	.75	.40	.25
(18)	Curt Flood	2.50	1.25	.70
(19)	Bill Freehan	.75	.40	.25
(20)	Jim Fregosi	.75	.40	.25
(21)	Bob Gibson	5.00	2.50	1.50
(22)	Ken Harrelson	.75	.40	.25
(23)	Bud Harrelson	.50	.25	.15
(24)	Jim Ray Hart	.50	.25	.15
(25)	Tommy Helms	.50	.25	.15
(26)	Joe Horlen	.50	.25	.15
(27)	Willie Horton	.75	.40	.25
(28)	Frank Howard	2.75	1.50	.80
(29)	Tony Horton	.75	.40	.25
(30)	Al Kaline	6.00	3.00	1.75
(31)	Don Kessinger	.75	.40	.25
(32)	Harmon Killebrew	6.00	3.00	1.75
(33)	Jerry Koosman	.75	.40	.25
(34)	Mickey Lolich	2.50	1.25	.70
(35)	Jim Lonborg	.75	.40	.25
(36)	Jim Maloney	.50	.25	.15
(37)	Juan Marichal	5.00	2.50	1.50
(38)	Willie Mays	10.00	5.00	3.00
(39)	Tim McCarver	2.50	1.25	.70
(40)	Willie McCovey	5.00	2.50	1.50
(41)	Sam McDowell	.75	.40	.25
(42)	Denny McLain	2.75	1.50	.80
(43)	Rick Monday	.75	.40	.25
(44)	Tony Oliva	2.75	1.50	.80
(45)	Joe Pepitone	.75	.40	.25
(46)	Boog Powell	2.75	1.50	.80
(47)	Rick Reichardt	.50	.25	.15
(48)	Pete Richert	.50	.25	.15
(49)	Brooks Robinson	7.00	3.50	2.00
(50)	Frank Robinson	6.00	3.00	1.75
(51)	Pete Rose	25.00	12.50	7.50
(52)	Ron Santo	2.50	1.25	.70
(53)	Mel Stottlemyre	.75	.40	.25
(54)	Ron Swoboda	.50	.25	.15
(55)	Luis Tiant	.75	.40	.25
(56)	Joe Torre	2.50	1.25	.70
(57)	Pete Ward	.50	.25	.15
(58)	Billy Williams	5.00	2.50	1.50
(59)	Jim Wynn	.75	.40	.25
(60)	Carl Yastrzemski	10.00	5.00	3.00

1989 Marathon Cubs

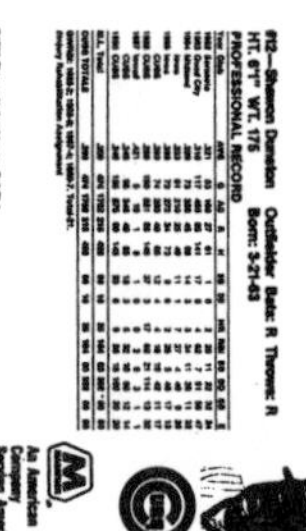

This colorful 25-card Cubs team set was sponsored by Marathon and was distributed as a stadium promotion to fans attending the August 10, 1989, game at Chicago's Wrigley Field. The oversize (2-3/4" by 4-1/4") feature an action photo inside a diagonal box on the card front, with the Chicago Cubs logo at the top and the player's uniform number, name and position along the bottom. The backs include a small black-and-white photo, player data and the Cubs and Marathon logos.

		MT	NR MT	EX
Complete Set:		10.00	7.50	4.00
Common Player:		.10	.08	.04
Coaches Card		.10	.08	.04
2	Vance Law	.10	.08	.04
4	Don Zimmer	.15	.11	.06
7	Joe Girardi	.50	.40	.20
8	Andre Dawson	.70	.50	.30
9	Damon Berryhill	.40	.30	.15
10	Lloyd McClendon	.50	.40	.20
12	Shawon Dunston	.50	.40	.20
15	Domingo Ramos	.10	.08	.04
17	Mark Grace	2.25	1.75	.90
18	Dwight Smith	2.75	2.00	1.00
19	Curt Wilkerson	.10	.08	.04
20	Jerome Walton	3.50	2.75	1.50
21	Scott Sanderson	.10	.08	.04
23	Ryne Sandberg	2.00	1.50	.80
28	Mitch Williams	1.00	.70	.40
31	Greg Maddux	.70	.50	.30
32	Calvin Schiraldi	.10	.08	.04
33	Mitch Webster	.10	.08	.04
36	Mike Bielecki	.40	.30	.15
39	Paul Kilgus	.10	.08	.04
40	Rick Sutcliffe	.40	.30	.15
41	Jeff Pico	.25	.20	.10
44	Steve Wilson	.50	.40	.20
50	Les Lancaster	.15	.11	.06

1988 Master Bread Twins

This set of 12 cardboard discs (2-3/4" diameter) features full-color photos of Minnesota Twins team members. Disc fronts have a bright blue background with red, yellow and black printing. A thin white line frames the player photo which is centered beneath a "Master Is Good Bread" headliner and a vivid yellow player/team name banner. Disc backs are black and white with five stars printed above the player's name, team, personal data, disc number, stats and "1988 Collector's Edition" banner. The discs were printed in Canada and marketed exclusively in Minnesota in packages of Master Bread, one disc per loaf.

		MT	NR MT	EX
Complete Set:		15.00	11.00	6.00
Common Player:		.50	.40	.20
1	Bert Blyleven	1.00	.70	.40
2	Frank Viola	2.25	1.75	.90
3	Juan Berenguer	.50	.40	.20
4	Jeff Reardon	.80	.60	.30
5	Tim Laudner	.50	.40	.20
6	Steve Lombardozzi	.50	.40	.20
7	Randy Bush	.50	.40	.20
8	Kirby Puckett	4.00	3.00	1.50
9	Gary Gaetti	1.75	1.25	.70
10	Kent Hrbek	1.75	1.25	.70
11	Greg Gagne	.50	.40	.20
12	Tom Brunansky	1.25	.90	.50

1970 McDonald's Brewers

Milwaukee in 1970 by issuing a set of six baseball card panels. Five of the panels picture five players and a team logo, while the sixth panel contains six players, resulting in 31 different players. The panels measure 9" by 9-1/2" and feature full-color paintings of the players. Each sheet displays the heading, "The original Milwaukee Brewers, 1970". The cards are unnumbered and the backs are blank. Although distributed by McDonald's, their name does not appear on the cards.

		NR MT	EX	VG
Complete Sheet:		7.00	3.50	2.00
Complete Singles Set:		4.00	2.00	1.25
Common Player:		.10	.05	.03
1	Ted Kubiak	.10	.05	.03
2	Ted Savage	.10	.05	.03
4	Dave Bristol	.10	.05	.03
5	Phil Roof	.10	.05	.03
6	Mike Hershberger	.10	.05	.03
7	Russ Snyder	.10	.05	.03
8	Mike Hegan	.10	.05	.03
9	Rich Rollins	.10	.05	.03
10	Max Alvis	.10	.05	.03
11	John Kennedy	.10	.05	.03
12	Dan Walton	.10	.05	.03
15	Jerry McNertney	.10	.05	.03
18	Wes Stock	.10	.05	.03
20	Wayne Comer	.10	.05	.03
21	Tommy Harper	.20	.15	.08
23	Bob Locker	.10	.05	.03
24	Lew Krausse	.10	.05	.03
25	John Gelnar	.10	.05	.03
26	Roy McMillan	.10	.05	.03
27	Cal Ermer	.10	.05	.03
28	Sandy Valdespino	.10	.05	.03
30	Jackie Moore	.10	.05	.03
32	Gene Brabender	.10	.05	.03
33	Marty Pattin	.10	.05	.03
34	Greg Goossen	.10	.05	.03
35	John Morris	.10	.05	.03
36	Steve Hovley	.10	.05	.03
38	Bob Meyer	.10	.05	.03
39	Bob Bolin	.10	.05	.03
43	John O'Donoghue	.10	.05	.03
49	George Lauzerique	.10	.05	.03
---)	Logo Card	.10	.05	.03

1986 Meadow Gold

This was the second set to be distributed by Meadow Gold Dairy (Beatrice Foods) in 1986. It was issued on Double Play ice cream cartons, one card per package. Full-color player photos have team logos and insignias airbrushed away. This 16-card set is very similar to the Meadow Gold popsicle set, but the photos are different in some instances. The cards measure 2-3/8" by 3-1/2". The Willie McGee card is reportedly tougher to find than other cards in the set.

		MT	NR MT	EX
Complete Set:		100.00	75.00	40.00
Common Player:		4.00	3.00	1.50
(1)	George Brett	7.00	5.25	2.75
(2)	Wade Boggs	10.00	7.50	4.00
(3)	Carlton Fisk	4.00	3.00	1.50
(4)	Steve Garvey	6.00	4.50	2.50
(5)	Dwight Gooden	7.50	5.75	3.00
(6)	Pedro Guerrero	4.00	3.00	1.50
(7)	Reggie Jackson	6.50	5.00	2.50
(8)	Don Mattingly	15.00	11.00	6.00
(9)	Willie McGee	4.00	3.00	1.50
(10)	Dale Murphy	7.00	5.25	2.75
(11)	Cal Ripken	6.50	5.00	2.50
(12)	Pete Rose	8.00	6.00	3.25
(13)	Ryne Sandberg	6.00	4.50	2.50
(14)	Mike Schmidt	7.00	5.25	2.75
(15)	Fernando Valenzuela	5.00	3.75	2.00
(16)	Dave Winfield	6.50	5.00	2.50

1986 Meadow Gold

Beatrice Foods produced this set of 20 cards on specially marked boxes of Meadow Gold Double Play popsicles, fudgesicles and bubble gum coolers. They came in two-card panels and have full-color player pictures with player name, team and position printed below the photo. Card backs are printed in red ink and feature player career highlights. The cards measure 2-3/8" by 3-1/2" and were distributed in the West and Midwest. It is considered one of the toughest 1986 regional sets to complete.

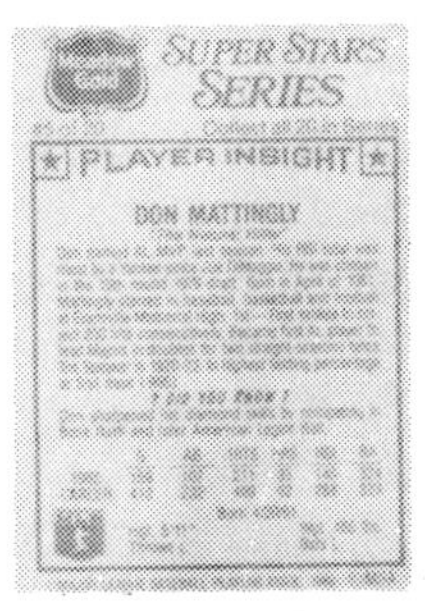

		MT	NR MT	EX
Complete Panel Set:		40.00	30.00	15.00
Complete Singles Set:		20.00	15.00	8.00
Common Panel:		2.00	1.50	.80
Common Single Player:		.30	.25	.12
Panel 1		5.00	3.75	2.00
1	George Brett	1.50	1.25	.60
2	Fernando Valenzuela	.70	.50	.30
Panel 2		6.50	5.00	2.50
3	Dwight Gooden	2.00	1.50	.80
4	Dale Murphy	1.50	1.25	.60
Panel 3		10.00	7.50	4.00
5	Don Mattingly	5.00	3.75	2.00
6	Reggie Jackson	2.00	1.50	.80
Panel 4		6.50	5.00	2.50
7	Dave Winfield	1.00	.70	.40
8	Pete Rose	2.00	1.50	.80
Panel 5		6.00	4.50	2.50
9	Wade Boggs	3.00	2.25	1.25
10	Willie McGee	.50	.40	.20
Panel 6		5.50	4.25	2.25
11	Cal Ripkin (Ripken)	1.25	.90	.50
12	Ryne Sandberg	2.00	1.50	.80
Panel 7		5.00	3.75	2.00
13	Carlton Fisk	.50	.40	.20
14	Jim Rice	1.00	.70	.40
Panel 8		7.00	5.25	2.75
15	Steve Garvey	1.00	.70	.40
16	Mike Schmidt	2.00	1.50	.80
Panel 9		4.00	3.00	1.50
17	Bruce Sutter	.60	.45	.25
18	Pedro Guerrero	.60	.45	.25
Panel 10		4.00	3.00	1.50
19	Rick Sutcliff (Sutcliffe)	.60	.45	.25
20	Rich Gossage	.60	.45	.25

1986 Meadow Gold Milk

The third set from Meadow Gold from 1986 came on milk cartons; on pint, quart and half-gallon size containers. The cards measure 2-1/2" by 3-1/2" and feature drawings instead of photographs. Different dairies distributed the cards in various colors of ink. The cards can be found printed in red, brown or black ink. The crude drawings have prevented this rare set from being higher in price. It was believed that Don Mattingly and Fernando Valenzuela were part of the original set, but it has since been proven they were not.

		MT	NR MT	EX
Complete Set:		50.00	37.00	20.00
Common Player:		2.00	1.50	.80
(1)	Wade Boggs	10.00	7.50	4.00
(2)	George Brett	5.00	3.75	2.00
(3)	Steve Carlton	3.00	2.25	1.25
(4)	Dwight Gooden	10.00	7.50	4.00
(5)	Willie McGee	2.00	1.50	.80
(6)	Dale Murphy	5.00	3.75	2.00
(7)	Cal Ripken, Jr.	4.00	3.00	1.50
(8)	Pete Rose	10.00	7.50	4.00
(9)	Ryne Sandberg	3.00	2.25	1.25
(10)	Mike Schmidt	5.00	3.75	2.00

1971 Milk Duds

These cards were issued on the backs of five-cent packages of Milk Duds candy. Most

collectors prefer to collect complete boxes, rather than cut-out cards, which measure approximately 1-13/16" by 2-5/8" when trimmed tightly. Values quoted below are for complete boxes. The set includes 37 National League and 32 American League players. Card numbers appear on the box flap, with each number from 1 through 24 being shared by three different players. A suffix (a, b and c) has been added for the collector's convenience. Harmon Killebrew, Brooks Robinson and Pete Rose were double-printed.

		NR MT	EX	VG
Complete Set:		1100.	550.00	330.00
Common Player:		7.00	3.50	2.00
1a	Frank Howard	11.00	5.50	3.25
1b	Fritz Peterson	7.00	3.50	2.00
1c	Pete Rose	80.00	40.00	24.00
2a	Johnny Bench	30.00	15.00	9.00
2b	Rico Carty	9.00	4.50	2.75
2c	Pete Rose	80.00	40.00	24.00
3a	Ken Holtzman	8.00	4.00	2.50
3b	Willie Mays	40.00	20.00	12.00
3c	Cesar Tovar	7.00	3.50	2.00
4a	Willie Davis	9.00	4.50	2.75
4b	Harmon Killebrew	20.00	10.00	6.00
4c	Felix Millan	7.00	3.50	2.00
5a	Billy Grabarkewitz	7.00	3.50	2.00
5b	Andy Messersmith	8.00	4.00	2.50
5c	Thurman Munson	20.00	10.00	6.00
6a	Luis Aparicio	18.00	9.00	5.50
6b	Lou Brock	25.00	12.50	7.50
6c	Bill Melton	7.00	3.50	2.00
7a	Ray Culp	7.00	3.50	2.00
7b	Willie McCovey	25.00	12.50	7.50
7c	Luke Walker	7.00	3.50	2.00
8a	Roberto Clemente	40.00	20.00	12.00
8b	Jim Merritt	7.00	3.50	2.00
8c	Claud Osteen (Claude)	8.00	4.00	2.50
9a	Stan Bahnsen	7.00	3.50	2.00
9b	Sam McDowell	9.00	4.50	2.75
9c	Billy Williams	18.00	9.00	5.50
10a	Jim Hickman	7.00	3.50	2.00
10b	Dave McNally	9.00	4.50	2.75
10c	Tony Perez	13.00	6.50	4.00
11a	Hank Aaron	40.00	20.00	12.00
11b	Glen Beckert (Glenn)	8.00	4.00	2.50
11c	Ray Fosse	7.00	3.50	2.00
12a	Alex Johnson	7.00	3.50	2.00
12b	Gaylord Perry	18.00	9.00	5.50
12c	Wayne Simpson	7.00	3.50	2.00
13a	Dave Johnson	9.00	4.50	2.75
13b	George Scott	8.00	4.00	2.50
13c	Tom Seaver	30.00	15.00	9.00
14a	Bill Freehan	9.00	4.50	2.75
14b	Bud Harrelson	8.00	4.00	2.50
14c	Manny Sanguillen	7.00	3.50	2.00
15a	Bob Gibson	25.00	12.50	7.50
15b	Rusty Staub	11.00	5.50	3.25
15c	Roy White	8.00	4.00	2.50
16a	Jim Fregosi	9.00	4.50	2.75
16b	Jim Hunter	18.00	9.00	5.50
16c	Mel Stottlemyer (Stottlemyre)	8.00	4.00	2.50
17a	Tommy Harper	7.00	3.50	2.00
17b	Frank Robinson	25.00	12.50	7.50
17c	Reggie Smith	9.00	4.50	2.75
18a	Orlando Cepeda	13.00	6.50	4.00
18b	Rico Petrocelli	8.00	4.00	2.50
18c	Brooks Robinson	25.00	12.50	7.50
19a	Tony Oliva	11.00	5.50	3.25
19b	Milt Pappas	8.00	4.00	2.50
19c	Bobby Tolan	7.00	3.50	2.00
20a	Ernie Banks	25.00	12.50	7.50
20b	Don Kessinger	8.00	4.00	2.50
20c	Joe Torre	9.00	4.50	2.75
21a	Fergie Jenkins	13.00	6.50	4.00
21b	Jim Palmer	18.00	9.00	5.50
21c	Ron Santo	9.00	4.50	2.75
22a	Randy Hundley	7.00	3.50	2.00
22b	Dennis Menke (Denis)	7.00	3.50	2.00
22c	Boog Powell	11.00	5.50	3.25
23a	Dick Dietz	7.00	3.50	2.00
23b	Tommy John	13.00	6.50	4.00
23c	Brooks Robinson	25.00	12.50	7.50
24a	Danny Cater	7.00	3.50	2.00
24b	Harmon Killebrew	18.00	9.00	5.50
24c	Jim Perry	8.00	4.00	2.50

1969 Milton Bradley

TOMMY JOHN P
5/22/43 6-3 TL BR
2 GROUND OUT RA1
3 BUNT OUT RA1
4 FLY OUT RH
5 BUNT-SINGLE RA1
6 BUNT OUT RA1
7 BUNT OUT OR FC-FRO
8 INFIELD FLY RH
9 SINGLE RA1
10 FLY OUT RH
11 GROUND OUT DP-H BR
12 HOME RUN

The first of three sets issued by Milton Bradley over a four-year period, the 1969 set contains 296 cards that were part of a baseball board game. The unnumbered cards measure 2" by 3" and have a white border surrounding the black-and-white player photo. The player's name appears above the photo in upper case letters. There are no team designations and the photos are airbrushed to eliminate all team insignias. The back of the card displays the player's name, position, birthdate, height and batting and throwing preferences along the top followed by a list of various game situations used in playing the board game. The cards have square corners.

	NR MT	EX	VG
Complete Set:	500.00	250.00	150.00
Common Player:	.40	.20	.12

#	Player	NR MT	EX	VG
(1)	Hank Aaron	25.00	12.50	7.50
(2)	Ted Abernathy	.40	.20	.12
(3)	Jerry Adair	.40	.20	.12
(4)	Tommy Agee	.40	.20	.12
(5)	Bernie Allen	.40	.20	.12
(6)	Hank Allen	.40	.20	.12
(7)	Richie Allen	2.25	1.25	.70
(8)	Gene Alley	.40	.20	.12
(9)	Bob Allison	.70	.35	.20
(10)	Felipe Alou	.80	.40	.25
(11)	Jesus Alou	.40	.20	.12
(12)	Matty Alou	.80	.40	.25
(13)	Max Alvis	.40	.20	.12
(14)	Mike Andrews	.40	.20	.12
(15)	Luis Aparicio	4.00	2.00	1.25
(16)	Jose Arcia	.40	.20	.12
(17)	Bob Aspromonte	.40	.20	.12
(18)	Joe Azcue	.40	.20	.12
(19)	Ernie Banks	10.00	5.00	3.00
(20)	Steve Barber	.40	.20	.12
(21)	John Bateman	.40	.20	.12
(22)	Glen Beckert (Glenn)	.70	.35	.20
(23)	Gary Bell	1.00	.50	.30
(24)	John Bench	20.00	10.00	6.00
(25)	Ken Berry	.40	.20	.12
(26)	Frank Bertaina	.40	.20	.12
(27)	Paul Blair	.70	.35	.20
(28)	Wade Blasingame	1.00	.50	.30
(29)	Curt Blefary	.40	.20	.12
(30)	John Boccabella	1.00	.50	.30
(31)	Bobby Lee Bonds	1.00	.50	.30
(32)	Sam Bowens	1.00	.50	.30
(33)	Ken Boyer	2.25	1.25	.70
(34)	Charles Bradford	.40	.20	.12
(35)	Darrell Brandon	1.00	.50	.30
(36)	Jim Brewer	.40	.20	.12
(37)	John Briggs	.40	.20	.12
(38)	Nelson Briles	.40	.20	.12
(39)	Ed Brinkman	.40	.20	.12
(40)	Lou Brock	8.00	4.00	2.50
(41)	Gates Brown	.40	.20	.12
(42)	Larry Brown	.40	.20	.12
(43)	George Brunet	.40	.20	.12
(44)	Jerry Buchek	1.00	.50	.30
(45)	Don Buford	.40	.20	.12
(46)	Jim Bunning	2.75	1.50	.80
(47)	Johnny Callison	.80	.40	.25
(48)	Campy Campaneris	1.00	.50	.30
(49)	Jose Cardenal	.40	.20	.12
(50)	Leo Cardenas	.40	.20	.12
(51)	Don Cardwell	.40	.20	.12
(52)	Rod Carew	12.00	6.00	3.50
(53)	Paul Casanova	.40	.20	.12
(54)	Norm Cash	1.00	.50	.30
(55)	Danny Cater	.40	.20	.12
(56)	Orlando Cepeda	2.75	1.50	.80
(57)	Dean Chance	.40	.20	.12
(58)	Ed Charles	1.00	.50	.30
(59)	Horace Clarke	.40	.20	.12
(60)	Roberto Clemente	25.00	12.50	7.50
(61)	Donn Clendenon	.40	.20	.12
(62)	Ty Cline	.40	.20	.12
(63)	Nate Colbert	.40	.20	.12
(64)	Joe Coleman	.40	.20	.12
(65)	Bob Cox	1.00	.50	.30
(66)	Mike Cuellar	.70	.35	.20
(67)	Ray Culp	.40	.20	.12
(68)	Clay Dalrymple	1.00	.50	.30
(69)	Vic Davalillo	.40	.20	.12
(70)	Jim Davenport	.40	.20	.12
(71)	Ron Davis	1.00	.50	.30
(72)	Tommy Davis	.80	.40	.25
(73)	Willie Davis	.80	.40	.25
(74)	Chuck Dobson	.40	.20	.12
(75)	John Donaldson	.40	.20	.12
(76)	Al Downing	.70	.35	.20
(77)	Moe Drabowsky	.40	.20	.12
(78)	Dick Ellsworth	.40	.20	.12
(79)	Mike Epstein	.40	.20	.12
(80)	Andy Etchebarren	.40	.20	.12
(81)	Ron Fairly	.70	.35	.20
(82)	Dick Farrell	1.00	.50	.30
(83)	Curt Flood	1.50	.70	.45
(84)	Joe Foy	.40	.20	.12
(85)	Tito Francona	.40	.20	.12
(86)	Bill Freehan	1.00	.50	.30
(87)	Jim Fregosi	.80	.40	.25
(88)	Woodie Fryman	.40	.20	.12
(89)	Len Gabrielson	.40	.20	.12
(90)	Clarence Gaston	.40	.20	.12
(91)	Jake Gibbs	.40	.20	.12
(92)	Russ Gibson	.40	.20	.12
(93)	Dave Giusti	.40	.20	.12
(94)	Tony Gonzalez	.40	.20	.12
(95)	Jim Gosger	.40	.20	.12
(96)	Julio Gotay	1.00	.50	.30
(97)	Dick Green	.40	.20	.12
(98)	Jerry Grote	.70	.35	.20
(99)	Jimmie Hall	1.00	.50	.30
(100)	Tom Haller	.40	.20	.12
(101)	Steve Hamilton	.40	.20	.12
(102)	Ron Hansen	.40	.20	.12
(103)	Jim Hardin	.40	.20	.12
(104)	Tommy Harper	.40	.20	.12
(105)	Bud Harrelson	.70	.35	.20
(106)	Ken Harrelson	1.00	.50	.30
(107)	Jim Hart	.40	.20	.12
(108)	Woodie Held	1.00	.50	.30
(109)	Tommy Helms	.40	.20	.12
(110)	Elrod Hendricks	.40	.20	.12
(111)	Mike Hershberger	.40	.20	.12
(112)	Jack Hiatt	.40	.20	.12
(113)	Jim Hickman	.40	.20	.12
(114)	John Hiller	.40	.20	.12
(115)	Chuck Hinton	.40	.20	.12
(116)	Ken Holtzman	.80	.40	.25
(117)	Joel Horlen	.40	.20	.12
(118)	Tony Horton	1.00	.50	.30
(119)	Willie Horton	.80	.40	.25
(120)	Frank Howard	1.25	.60	.40
(121)	Dick Howser	1.00	.50	.30
(122)	Randy Hundley	.40	.20	.12
(123)	Ron Hunt	.40	.20	.12
(124)	Jim Hunter	4.00	2.00	1.25
(125)	Al Jackson	1.00	.50	.30
(126)	Larry Jackson	1.00	.50	.30
(127)	Reggie Jackson	60.00	30.00	18.00
(128)	Sonny Jackson	.40	.20	.12
(129)	Pat Jarvis	.40	.20	.12
(130)	Julian Javier	.40	.20	.12
(131)	Ferguson Jenkins	2.50	1.25	.70
(132)	Manny Jimenez	1.00	.50	.30
(133)	Tommy John	2.75	1.50	.80
(134)	Bob Johnson	.40	.20	.12
(135)	Dave Johnson	1.25	.60	.40
(136)	Deron Johnson	.40	.20	.12
(137)	Lou Johnson	1.00	.50	.30
(138)	Jay Johnstone	.70	.35	.20
(139)	Cleon Jones	.40	.20	.12
(140)	Dalton Jones	.40	.20	.12
(141)	Duane Josephson	.40	.20	.12
(142)	Jim Kaat	2.75	1.50	.80
(143)	Al Kaline	10.00	5.00	3.00
(144)	Don Kessinger	.70	.35	.20
(145)	Harmon Killebrew	8.00	4.00	2.50
(146)	Harold King	1.00	.50	.30
(147)	Ed Kirkpatrick	.40	.20	.12
(148)	Fred Klages	1.00	.50	.30
(149)	Ron Kline	1.00	.50	.30
(150)	Bobby Knoop	.40	.20	.12
(151)	Gary Kolb	1.00	.50	.30
(152)	Andy Kosco	.40	.20	.12
(153)	Ed Kranepool	.70	.35	.20
(154)	Lew Krausse	1.00	.50	.30
(155)	Harold Lanier	.70	.35	.20
(156)	Jim Lefebvre	.70	.35	.20
(157)	Denny Lemaster	.40	.20	.12
(158)	Dave Leonhard	.40	.20	.12
(159)	Don Lock	1.00	.50	.30
(160)	Mickey Lolich	2.50	1.25	.70
(161)	Jim Lonborg	.70	.35	.20
(162)	Mike Lum	1.00	.50	.30
(163)	Al Lyle	1.00	.50	.30
(164)	Jim Maloney	.70	.35	.20
(165)	Juan Marichal	6.00	3.00	1.75
(166)	J.C. Martin	.40	.20	.12
(167)	Marty Martinez	.40	.20	.12
(168)	Tom Matchick	.40	.20	.12
(169)	Ed Mathews	12.00	6.00	3.50
(170)	Dal Maxvill	.40	.20	.12
(171)	Jerry May	.40	.20	.12
(172)	Lee May	.80	.40	.25
(173)	Lee Maye	.40	.20	.12
(174)	Willie Mays	25.00	12.50	7.50
(175)	Bill Mazeroski	1.25	.60	.40
(176)	Richard McAuliffe	.40	.20	.12
(177)	Al McBean	.40	.20	.12
(178)	Tim McCarver	1.00	.50	.30
(179)	Bill McCool	.40	.20	.12
(180)	Mike McCormick	.40	.20	.12
(181)	Willie McCovey	8.00	4.00	2.50
(182)	Tom McCraw	.40	.20	.12
(183)	Lindy McDaniel	.40	.20	.12
(184)	Sam McDowell	.80	.40	.25
(185)	Orlando McFarlane	1.00	.50	.30
(186)	Jim McGlothlin	.40	.20	.12
(187)	Denny McLain	1.25	.60	.40
(188)	Ken McMullen	.40	.20	.12
(189)	Dave McNally	.80	.40	.25
(190)	Gerry McNertney	.40	.20	.12
(191)	Dennis Menke (Denis)	.40	.20	.12
(192)	Felix Millan	.40	.20	.12
(193)	Don Mincher	.40	.20	.12
(194)	Rick Monday	.80	.40	.25
(195)	Joe Morgan	6.00	3.00	1.75
(196)	Bubba Morton	1.00	.50	.30
(197)	Manny Mota	.80	.40	.25
(198)	Jim Nash	.40	.20	.12
(199)	Dave Nelson	1.00	.50	.30
(200)	Dick Nen	1.00	.50	.30
(201)	Phil Niekro	4.00	2.00	1.25
(202)	Jim Northrup	.40	.20	.12
(203)	Richard Nye	.40	.20	.12
(204)	Johnny Odom	.40	.20	.12
(205)	Tony Oliva	2.50	1.25	.70
(206)	Gene Oliver	1.00	.50	.30
(207)	Phil Ortega	1.00	.50	.30
(208)	Claude Osteen	.40	.20	.12
(209)	Ray Oyler	.40	.20	.12
(210)	Jose Pagan	.40	.20	.12
(211)	Jim Pagliaroni	1.00	.50	.30
(212)	Milt Pappas	.80	.40	.25
(213)	Wes Parker	.70	.35	.20
(214)	Camilo Pascual	1.50	.70	.45
(215)	Don Pavletich	1.00	.50	.30
(216)	Joe Pepitone	1.00	.50	.30
(217)	Tony Perez	2.75	1.50	.80
(218)	Gaylord Perry	3.25	1.75	1.00
(219)	Jim Perry	.70	.35	.20
(220)	Gary Peters	.40	.20	.12
(221)	Rico Petrocelli	.70	.35	.20
(222)	Adolfo Phillips	1.00	.50	.30
(223)	Tom Phoebus	.40	.20	.12
(224)	Vada Pinson	1.50	.70	.45
(225)	Boog Powell	2.25	1.25	.70
(226)	Frank Quilici	.40	.20	.12
(227)	Doug Rader	.40	.20	.12
(228)	Rich Reese	.40	.20	.12
(229)	Phil Regan	.40	.20	.12
(230)	Rick Reichardt	.40	.20	.12
(231)	Rick Renick	.40	.20	.12
(232)	Roger Repoz	.40	.20	.12
(233)	Dave Ricketts	.40	.20	.12
(234)	Bill Robinson	.40	.20	.12
(235)	Brooks Robinson	10.00	5.00	3.00
(236)	Frank Robinson	8.00	4.00	2.50
(237)	Bob Rodgers	1.50	.70	.45
(238)	Cookie Rojas	.40	.20	.12
(239)	Rich Rollins	.40	.20	.12
(240)	Phil Roof	.40	.20	.12
(241)	Pete Rose	60.00	30.00	18.00
(242)	John Roseboro	.70	.35	.20
(243)	Chico Ruiz	.40	.20	.12
(244)	Ray Sadecki	.40	.20	.12
(245)	Chico Salmon	.40	.20	.12
(246)	Jose Santiago	1.00	.50	.30
(247)	Ron Santo	2.25	1.25	.70
(248)	Tom Satriano	.40	.20	.12
(249)	Paul Schaal	.40	.20	.12
(250)	Tom Seaver	18.00	9.00	5.50
(251)	Art Shamsky	.40	.20	.12
(252)	Mike Shannon	.40	.20	.12
(253)	Chris Short	.40	.20	.12
(254)	Dick Simpson	1.00	.50	.30
(255)	Duke Sims	.40	.20	.12
(256)	Reggie Smith	1.00	.50	.30
(257)	Willie Smith	.40	.20	.12
(258)	Russ Snyder	.40	.20	.12
(259)	Al Spangler	.40	.20	.12
(260)	Larry Stahl	.40	.20	.12
(261)	Lee Stange	.40	.20	.12
(262)	Mickey Stanley	.40	.20	.12
(263)	Willie Stargell	8.00	4.00	2.50
(264)	Rusty Staub	1.25	.60	.40
(265)	Mel Stottlemyre	1.00	.50	.30
(266)	Ed Stroud	.40	.20	.12
(267)	Don Sutton	4.00	2.00	1.25
(268)	Ron Swoboda	.40	.20	.12
(269)	Jose Tartabull	.40	.20	.12
(270)	Tony Taylor	.40	.20	.12
(271)	Luis Tiant	2.50	1.25	.70
(272)	Bob Tillman	.40	.20	.12
(273)	Bobby Tolan	.70	.35	.20
(274)	Jeff Torborg	.40	.20	.12
(275)	Joe Torre	2.25	1.25	.70
(276)	Cesar Tovar	.40	.20	.12
(277)	Dick Tracewski	1.00	.50	.30
(278)	Tom Tresh	.70	.35	.20
(279)	Ted Uhlaender	.40	.20	.12
(280)	Del Unser	.40	.20	.12
(281)	Hilario Valdespino	1.00	.50	.30
(282)	Fred Valentine	1.00	.50	.30
(283)	Bob Veale	.40	.20	.12
(284)	Zoilo Versalles	.40	.20	.12
(285)	Pete Ward	.40	.20	.12
(286)	Al Weis	.40	.20	.12
(287)	Don Wert	.40	.20	.12
(288)	Bill White	.80	.40	.25
(289)	Roy White	.70	.35	.20
(290)	Fred Whitfield	1.00	.50	.30
(291)	Hoyt Wilhelm	4.00	2.00	1.25
(292)	Billy Williams	6.00	3.00	1.75
(293)	Maury Wills	2.50	1.25	.70
(294)	Earl Wilson	.40	.20	.12
(295)	Wilbur Wood	.70	.35	.20
(296)	Jerry Zimmerman	.40	.20	.12

1970 Milton Bradley

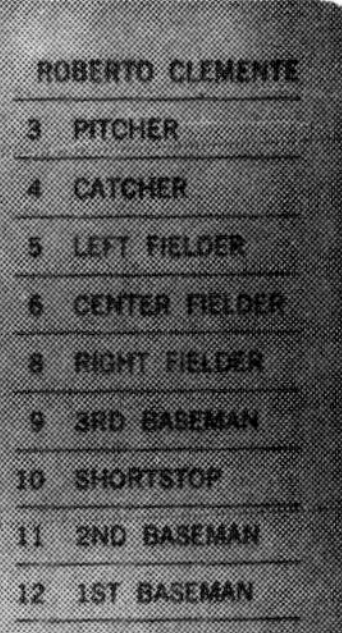

Except for the slightly larger (2-3/8" by 3-1/2") size, the format of the 1970 Milton Bradley set is similar to the 1969 Milton Bradley issue. Again designed for use with a baseball board game, the unnumbered black and white cards have rounded corners and wide white borders. The player's name appears in capital letters beneath the photo with his position, birthdate, height and batting and throwing preference on a line below. The back of the card shows the player's name along the top followed by a list of possible game situations used in playing the board game. There are no team designations on the cards and all team insignias have been airbrushed from the photos.

		NR MT	EX	VG
Complete Set:		300.00	150.00	90.00
Common Player:		2.00	1.00	.60
(1)	Hank Aaron	25.00	12.50	7.50
(2)	Ernie Banks	15.00	7.50	4.50
(3)	Lou Brock	15.00	7.50	4.50
(4)	Rod Carew	20.00	10.00	6.00
(5)	Roberto Clemente	25.00	12.50	7.50
(6)	Tommy Davis	2.00	1.00	.60
(7)	Bill Freehan	2.00	1.00	.60
(8)	Jim Fregosi	2.00	1.00	.60
(9)	Tom Haller	2.00	1.00	.60
(10)	Frank Howard	2.00	1.00	.60
(11)	Reggie Jackson	25.00	12.50	7.50
(12)	Harmon Killebrew	15.00	7.50	4.50
(13)	Mickey S. Lolich	3.50	1.75	1.00
(14)	Juan Marichal	15.00	7.50	4.50
(15)	Willie Mays	25.00	12.50	7.50
(16)	Willie McCovey	15.00	7.50	4.50
(17)	Sam McDowell	2.00	1.00	.60
(18)	Dennis Menke (Denis)	2.00	1.00	.60
(19)	Don Mincher	2.00	1.00	.60
(20)	Phil Niekro	15.00	7.50	4.50
(21)	Rico Petrocelli	2.00	1.00	.60
(22)	Boog Powell	3.50	1.75	1.00
(23)	Frank Robinson	15.00	7.50	4.50
(24)	Pete Rose	35.00	17.50	10.50
(25)	Ron Santo	3.50	1.75	1.00
(26)	Tom Seaver	20.00	10.00	6.00
(27)	Mel Stottlemyre	3.50	1.75	1.00
(28)	Tony Taylor	2.00	1.00	.60

1972 Milton Bradley

The 1972 Milton Bradley set, complete at 372 cards, was again designed for use with a baseball table game. The cards in the 1972 set are identical to the 1969 issue with square corners. The unnumbered black and white cards measure 2" by 3" and display the player's name along the top of the card. Again, all team insignias have been eliminated by airbrushing, and there are no team designations indicated. The back of the cards carry the player's name along with his position, birthdate, height and batting and throwing preferences followed by a list of possible game situations used in playing the baseball board game.

		NR MT	EX	VG
Complete Set:		600.00	300.00	180.00
Common Player:		.40	.20	.12
(1)	Hank Aaron	25.00	12.50	7.50
(2)	Tommie Aaron	1.00	.50	.30
(3)	Ted Abernathy	.40	.20	.12
(4)	Jerry Adair	.40	.20	.12
(5)	Tommy Agee	.40	.20	.12
(6)	Bernie Allen	.40	.20	.12
(7)	Hank Allen	.40	.20	.12
(8)	Richie Allen	2.25	1.25	.70
(9)	Gene Alley	.40	.20	.12
(10)	Bob Allison	.70	.35	.20
(11)	Sandy Alomar	1.00	.50	.30
(12)	Felipe Alou	.80	.40	.25
(13)	Jesus Alou	.40	.20	.12
(14)	Matty Alou	.80	.40	.25
(15)	Max Alvis	.40	.20	.12
(16)	Brant Alyea	1.00	.50	.30
(17)	Mike Andrews	.40	.20	.12
(18)	Luis Aparicio	4.00	2.00	1.25
(19)	Jose Arcia	.40	.20	.12
(20)	Gerald Arrigo	1.00	.50	.30
(21)	Bob Aspromonte	.40	.20	.12
(22)	Joe Azcue	.40	.20	.12
(23)	Robert Bailey	1.00	.50	.30
(24)	Sal Bando	1.50	.70	.45
(25)	Ernie Banks	10.00	5.00	3.00
(26)	Steve Barber	.40	.20	.12
(27)	Robert Barton	1.00	.50	.30
(28)	John Bateman	.40	.20	.12
(29)	Glen Beckert (Glenn)	.70	.35	.20
(30)	John Bench	8.50	4.25	2.50
(31)	Ken Berry	.40	.20	.12
(32)	Frank Bertaina	.40	.20	.12
(33)	Paul Blair	.70	.35	.20
(34)	Stephen Blass	1.00	.50	.30
(35)	Curt Blefary	.40	.20	.12
(36)	Bobby Bolin	1.00	.50	.30
(37)	Bobby Lee Bonds	1.00	.50	.30
(38)	Donald Bosch	1.00	.50	.30
(39)	Richard Bosman	1.00	.50	.30
(40)	Dave Boswell	1.00	.50	.30
(41)	Kenneth Boswell	1.00	.50	.30
(42)	Ken Boyer	2.25	1.25	.70
(43)	Charles Bradford	.40	.20	.12
(44)	Ronald Brand	1.00	.50	.30
(45)	Ken Brett	1.00	.50	.30
(46)	Jim Brewer	.40	.20	.12
(47)	John Briggs	.40	.20	.12
(48)	Nelson Briles	.40	.20	.12
(49)	Ed Brinkman	.40	.20	.12
(50)	James Britton	1.00	.50	.30
(51)	Lou Brock	8.00	4.00	2.50
(52)	Gates Brown	.40	.20	.12
(53)	Larry Brown	.40	.20	.12
(54)	George Brunet	.40	.20	.12
(55)	Don Buford	.40	.20	.12
(56)	Wallace Bunker	1.00	.50	.30
(57)	Jim Bunning	2.75	1.50	.80
(58)	William Butler	1.00	.50	.30
(59)	Johnny Callison	.80	.40	.25
(60)	Campy Campaneris	1.00	.50	.30
(61)	Jose Cardenal	.40	.20	.12
(62)	Leo Cardenas	.40	.20	.12
(63)	Don Cardwell	.40	.20	.12
(64)	Rod Carew	12.00	6.00	3.50
(65)	Cisco Carlos	1.00	.50	.30
(66)	Steve Carlton	25.00	12.50	7.50
(67)	Clay Carroll	1.50	.70	.45
(68)	Paul Casanova	.40	.20	.12
(69)	Norm Cash	1.00	.50	.30
(70)	Danny Cater	.40	.20	.12
(71)	Orlando Cepeda	2.75	1.50	.80
(72)	Dean Chance	.40	.20	.12
(73)	Horace Clarke	.40	.20	.12
(74)	Roberto Clemente	25.00	12.50	7.50
(75)	Donn Clendenon	.40	.20	.12
(76)	Ty Cline	.40	.20	.12
(77)	Nate Colbert	.40	.20	.12
(78)	Joe Coleman	.40	.20	.12
(79)	William Conigliaro	1.00	.50	.30
(80)	Casey Cox	1.00	.50	.30
(81)	Mike Cuellar	.70	.35	.20
(82)	Ray Culp	.40	.20	.12
(83)	George Culver	1.00	.50	.30
(84)	Vic Davalillo	.40	.20	.12
(85)	Jim Davenport	.40	.20	.12
(86)	Tommy Davis	.80	.40	.25
(87)	Willie Davis	.80	.40	.25
(88)	Larry Dierker	1.00	.50	.30
(89)	Richard Dietz	1.00	.50	.30
(90)	Chuck Dobson	.40	.20	.12
(91)	Pat Dobson	1.00	.50	.30
(92)	John Donaldson	.40	.20	.12
(93)	Al Downing	.70	.35	.20
(94)	Moe Drabowsky	.40	.20	.12
(95)	John Edwards	1.00	.50	.30
(96)	Thomas Egan	1.00	.50	.30
(97)	Dick Ellsworth	.40	.20	.12
(98)	Mike Epstein	.40	.20	.12
(99)	Andy Etchebarren	.40	.20	.12
(100)	Ron Fairly	.70	.35	.20
(101)	Frank Fernandez	1.00	.50	.30
(102)	Alfred Ferrara	1.00	.50	.30
(103)	Michael Fiore	1.00	.50	.30
(104)	Curt Flood	1.50	.70	.45
(105)	Vern Fuller	1.00	.50	.30
(106)	Joe Foy	.40	.20	.12
(107)	Tito Francona	.40	.20	.12
(108)	Bill Freehan	1.00	.50	.30
(109)	Jim Fregosi	.80	.40	.25
(110)	Woodie Fryman	.40	.20	.12
(111)	Len Gabrielson	.40	.20	.12
(112)	Philip Gagliano	1.00	.50	.30
(113)	Clarence Gaston	.40	.20	.12
(114)	Jake Gibbs	.40	.20	.12
(115)	Russ Gibson	.40	.20	.12
(116)	Dave Giusti	.40	.20	.12
(117)	Fred Gladding	1.00	.50	.30
(118)	Tony Gonzalez	.40	.20	.12
(119)	Jim Gosger	.40	.20	.12
(120)	James Grant	1.00	.50	.30
(121)	Thomas Griffin	1.00	.50	.30
(122)	Dick Green	.40	.20	.12
(123)	Jerry Grote	.70	.35	.20
(124)	Tom Hall	1.00	.50	.30
(125)	Tom Haller	.40	.20	.12
(126)	Steve Hamilton	.40	.20	.12
(127)	William Hands	1.00	.50	.30
(128)	James Hannan	1.00	.50	.30
(129)	Ron Hansen	.40	.20	.12
(130)	Jim Hardin	.40	.20	.12
(131)	Steve Hargan	1.00	.50	.30
(132)	Tommy Harper	.70	.35	.20
(133)	Bud Harrelson	.70	.35	.20
(134)	Ken Harrelson	1.00	.50	.30
(135)	Jim Hart	.40	.20	.12
(136)	Rich Hebner	1.00	.50	.30
(137)	Michael Hedlund	1.00	.50	.30
(138)	Tommy Helms	.40	.20	.12
(139)	Elrod Hendricks	.40	.20	.12
(140)	Ronald Herbel	1.00	.50	.30
(141)	Jack Hernandez	1.00	.50	.30
(142)	Mike Hershberger	.40	.20	.12
(143)	Jack Hiatt	.40	.20	.12
(144)	Jim Hickman	.40	.20	.12
(145)	Dennis Higgins	1.00	.50	.30
(146)	John Hiller	.40	.20	.12
(147)	Chuck Hinton	.40	.20	.12
(148)	Larry Hisle	1.50	.70	.45
(149)	Ken Holtzman	.80	.40	.25
(150)	Joel Horlen	.40	.20	.12
(151)	Tony Horton	1.00	.50	.30
(152)	Willie Horton	.80	.40	.25
(153)	Frank Howard	1.25	.60	.40
(154)	Robert Humphreys	1.00	.50	.30
(155)	Randy Hundley	.40	.20	.12
(156)	Ron Hunt	.40	.20	.12
(157)	Jim Hunter	4.00	2.00	1.25
(158)	Grant Jackson	1.00	.50	.30
(159)	Reggie Jackson	45.00	23.00	13.50
(160)	Sonny Jackson	.40	.20	.12
(161)	Pat Jarvis	.40	.20	.12
(162)	Larry Jaster	1.00	.50	.30
(163)	Julian Javier	.40	.20	.12
(164)	Ferguson Jenkins	2.50	1.25	.70
(165)	Tommy John	2.75	1.50	.80
(166)	Alexander Johnson	1.00	.50	.30
(167)	Bob Johnson	.40	.20	.12
(168)	Dave Johnson	1.25	.60	.40
(169)	Deron Johnson	.40	.20	.12
(170)	Jay Johnstone	.70	.35	.20
(171)	Cleon Jones	.40	.20	.12
(172)	Dalton Jones	.40	.20	.12
(173)	Mack Jones	1.00	.50	.30
(174)	Richard Joseph	1.00	.50	.30
(175)	Duane Josephson	.40	.20	.12
(176)	Jim Kaat	2.75	1.50	.80
(177)	Al Kaline	10.00	5.00	3.00
(178)	Richard Kelley	1.00	.50	.30
(179)	Harold Kelly	1.00	.50	.30
(180)	Gerald Kenney	1.00	.50	.30
(181)	Don Kessinger	.70	.35	.20
(182)	Harmon Killebrew	8.00	4.00	2.50
(183)	Ed Kirkpatrick	.40	.20	.12
(184)	Bobby Knoop	.40	.20	.12
(185)	Calvin Koonce	1.00	.50	.30
(186)	Jerry Koosman	2.50	1.25	.70
(187)	Andy Kosco	.40	.20	.12
(188)	Ed Kranepool	.70	.35	.20
(189)	Ted Kubiak	1.00	.50	.30
(190)	Jose Laboy	1.00	.50	.30
(191)	Joseph Lahoud	1.00	.50	.30
(192)	William Landis	1.00	.50	.30
(193)	Harold Lanier	.70	.35	.20
(194)	Fred Lasher	1.00	.50	.30
(195)	John Lazar	1.00	.50	.30
(196)	Jim Lefebvre	.70	.35	.20
(197)	Denny Lemaster	.40	.20	.12
(198)	Dave Leonhard	.40	.20	.12
(199)	Frank Linzy	1.00	.50	.30
(200)	Mickey Lolich	2.50	1.25	.70
(201)	Jim Lonborg	.70	.35	.20
(202)	Al Lyle	1.00	.50	.30
(203)	Jim Maloney	.70	.35	.20
(204)	Juan Marichal	6.00	3.00	1.75
(205)	David Marshall	1.00	.50	.30
(206)	J.C. Martin	.40	.20	.12
(207)	Marty Martinez	.40	.20	.12
(208)	Tom Matchick	.40	.20	.12
(209)	Dal Maxvill	.40	.20	.12
(210)	Carlos May	1.00	.50	.30
(211)	Jerry May	.40	.20	.12
(212)	Lee May	.80	.40	.25
(213)	Lee Maye	.40	.20	.12
(214)	Willie Mays	25.00	12.50	7.50
(215)	Bill Mazeroski	1.25	.60	.40
(216)	Richard McAuliffe	.40	.20	.12
(217)	Al McBean	.40	.20	.12
(218)	Tim McCarver	1.00	.50	.30
(219)	Bill McCool	.40	.20	.12
(220)	Mike McCormick	.40	.20	.12
(221)	Willie McCovey	8.00	4.00	2.50
(222)	Tom McCraw	.40	.20	.12
(223)	Lindy McDaniel	.40	.20	.12
(224)	Sam McDowell	.80	.40	.25
(225)	Leon McFadden	1.00	.50	.30
(226)	Daniel McGinn	1.00	.50	.30
(227)	Jim McGlothlin	.40	.20	.12
(228)	Fred McGraw	2.25	1.25	.70
(229)	Denny McLain	1.25	.60	.40
(230)	Ken McMullen	.40	.20	.12
(231)	Dave McNally	.80	.40	.25
(232)	Gerry McNertney	.40	.20	.12
(233)	William Melton	1.00	.50	.30
(234)	Dennis Menke (Denis)	.40	.20	.12
(235)	John Messersmith	1.50	.70	.45
(236)	Felix Millan	.40	.20	.12
(237)	Norman Miller	1.00	.50	.30
(238)	Don Mincher	.40	.20	.12
(239)	Rick Monday	.80	.40	.25
(240)	Donald Money	1.00	.50	.30
(241)	Barry Moore	1.00	.50	.30
(242)	Bob Moose	1.00	.50	.30
(243)	David Morehead	1.00	.50	.30
(244)	Joe Morgan	6.00	3.00	1.75
(245)	Curt Motton	1.00	.50	.30
(246)	Manny Mota	.80	.40	.25
(247)	Bob Murcer	2.25	1.25	.70
(248)	Thomas Murphy	1.00	.50	.30
(249)	Ivan Murrell	1.00	.50	.30
(250)	Jim Nash	.40	.20	.12
(251)	Joe Niekro	2.25	1.25	.70
(252)	Phil Niekro	4.00	2.00	1.25
(253)	Gary Nolan	1.00	.50	.30
(254)	Jim Northrup	.40	.20	.12
(255)	Richard Nye	.40	.20	.12
(256)	Johnny Odom	.40	.20	.12
(257)	John O'Donaghue	1.00	.50	.30
(258)	Tony Oliva	.40	.20	.12
(259)	Robert Oliver	1.00	.50	.30
(260)	Claude Osteen	.40	.20	.12
(261)	Ray Oyler	.40	.20	.12
(262)	Jose Pagan	.40	.20	.12
(263)	James Palmer	25.00	12.50	7.50
(264)	Milt Pappas	.80	.40	.25
(265)	Wes Parker	.70	.35	.20
(266)	Fred Patek	.40	.20	.12
(267)	Mike Paul	1.00	.50	.30
(268)	Joe Pepitone	1.00	.50	.30
(269)	Tony Perez	2.75	1.50	.80
(270)	Gaylord Perry	3.25	1.75	1.00

	NR MT	EX	VG
(271) Jim Perry	.70	.35	.20
(272) Gary Peters	.40	.20	.12
(273) Rico Petrocelli	.70	.35	.20
(274) Tom Phoebus	.40	.20	.12
(275) Lou Piniella	2.50	1.25	.70
(276) Vada Pinson	1.50	.70	.45
(277) Boog Powell	2.25	1.25	.70
(278) Jim Price	1.00	.50	.30
(279) Frank Quilici	.40	.20	.12
(280) Doug Rader	.40	.20	.12
(281) Ron Reed	1.00	.50	.30
(282) Rich Reese	.40	.20	.12
(283) Phil Regan	.40	.20	.12
(284) Rick Reichardt	.40	.20	.12
(285) Rick Renick	.40	.20	.12
(286) Roger Repoz	.40	.20	.12
(287) Dave Ricketts	.40	.20	.12
(288) Juan Rios	1.00	.50	.30
(289) Bill Robinson	.40	.20	.12
(290) Brooks Robinson	10.00	5.00	3.00
(291) Frank Robinson	8.00	4.00	2.50
(292) Aurelio Rodriguez	1.00	.50	.30
(293) Ellie Rodriguez	1.00	.50	.30
(294) Cookie Rojas	.40	.20	.12
(295) Rich Rollins	.40	.20	.12
(296) Vicente Romo	1.00	.50	.30
(297) Phil Roof	.40	.20	.12
(298) Pete Rose	45.00	23.00	13.50
(299) John Roseboro	.70	.35	.20
(300) Chico Ruiz	.40	.20	.12
(301) Mike Ryan	1.00	.50	.30
(302) Ray Sadecki	.40	.20	.12
(303) Chico Salmon	.40	.20	.12
(304) Manuel Sanguillen	1.00	.50	.30
(305) Ron Santo	2.25	1.25	.70
(306) Tom Satriano	.40	.20	.12
(307) Theodore Savage	1.00	.50	.30
(308) Paul Schaal	.40	.20	.12
(309) Dick Schofield	1.00	.50	.30
(310) George Scott	1.50	.70	.45
(311) Tom Seaver	18.00	9.00	5.50
(312) Art Shamsky	.40	.20	.12
(313) Mike Shannon	.40	.20	.12
(314) Chris Short	.40	.20	.12
(315) Duke Sims	.40	.20	.12
(316) William Singer	1.00	.50	.30
(317) Reggie Smith	1.00	.50	.30
(318) Willie Smith	.40	.20	.12
(319) Russ Snyder	.40	.20	.12
(320) Al Spangler	.40	.20	.12
(321) James Spencer	1.00	.50	.30
(322) Ed Spiezio	1.00	.50	.30
(323) Larry Stahl	.40	.20	.12
(324) Lee Stange	.40	.20	.12
(325) Mickey Stanley	.40	.20	.12
(326) Willie Stargell	8.00	4.00	2.50
(327) Rusty Staub	1.25	.60	.40
(328) James Stewart	1.00	.50	.30
(329) George Stone	1.00	.50	.30
(330) William Stoneman	1.00	.50	.30
(331) Mel Stottlemyre	1.00	.50	.30
(332) Ed Stroud	.40	.20	.12
(333) Ken Suarez	1.00	.50	.30
(334) Gary Sutherland	1.00	.50	.30
(335) Don Sutton	4.00	2.00	1.25
(336) Ron Swoboda	.40	.20	.12
(337) Fred Talbot	1.00	.50	.30
(338) Jose Tartabull	.40	.20	.12
(339) Kenneth Tatum	1.00	.50	.30
(340) Tony Taylor	.40	.20	.12
(341) Luis Tiant	2.50	1.25	.70
(342) Bob Tillman	.40	.20	.12
(343) Bobby Tolan	.70	.35	.20
(344) Jeff Torborg	.40	.20	.12
(345) Joe Torre	2.25	1.25	.70
(346) Cesar Tovar	.40	.20	.12
(347) Tom Tresh	.70	.35	.20
(348) Ted Uhlaender	.40	.20	.12
(349) Del Unser	.40	.20	.12
(350) Bob Veale	.40	.20	.12
(351) Zoilo Versalles	.40	.20	.12
(352) Luke Walker	1.00	.50	.30
(353) Pete Ward	.40	.20	.12
(354) Eddie Watt	1.00	.50	.30
(355) Ramon Webster	1.00	.50	.30
(356) Al Weis	.40	.20	.12
(357) Don Wert	.40	.20	.12
(358) Bill White	.80	.40	.25
(359) Roy White	.70	.35	.20
(360) Hoyt Wilhelm	4.00	2.00	1.25
(361) Billy Williams	6.00	3.00	1.75
(362) Walter Williams	1.00	.50	.30
(363) Maury Wills	2.50	1.25	.70
(364) Don Wilson	1.00	.50	.30
(365) Earl Wilson	.40	.20	.12
(366) Robert Wine	1.00	.50	.30
(367) Richard Wise	.40	.20	.12
(368) Wilbur Wood	.70	.35	.20
(369) William Woodward	1.00	.50	.30
(370) Clyde Wright	1.00	.50	.30
(371) James Wynn	1.50	.70	.45
(372) Jerry Zimmerman	.40	.20	.12

1984 Milton Bradley

In 1984 Milton Bradley printed their baseball game cards in full-color and adopted the standard baseball card size of 2-1/2" by 3-1/2". A total of 30 cards were in the set. The card fronts show the player photos with the team insignias and logos airbrushed away. The game is called Championship Baseball. Card backs varied in style; some had player statistics plus game information, and others only game information.

	MT	NR MT	EX
Complete Set:	10.00	7.50	4.00
Common Player:	.25	.20	.10

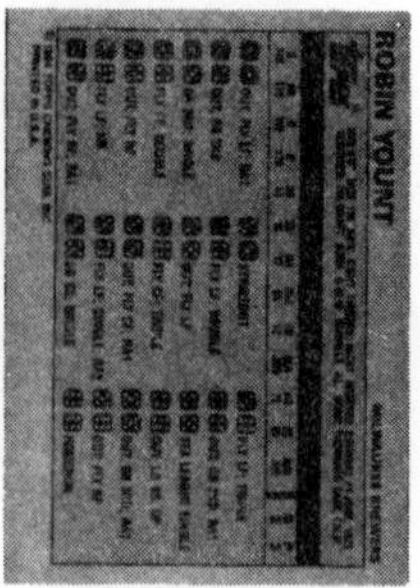

(1) Wade Boggs	1.50	1.25	.60
(2) George Brett	.80	.60	.30
(3) Rod Carew	.50	.40	.20
(4) Steve Carlton	.40	.30	.15
(5) Gary Carter	.50	.40	.20
(6) Dave Concepcion	.25	.20	.10
(7) Cecil Cooper	.25	.20	.10
(8) Andre Dawson	.35	.25	.14
(9) Carlton Fisk	.35	.25	.14
(10) Steve Garvey	.50	.40	.20
(11) Pedro Guerrero	.35	.25	.14
(12) Ron Guidry	.25	.20	.10
(13) Rickey Henderson	.60	.45	.25
(14) Reggie Jackson	.50	.40	.20
(15) Ron Kittle	.25	.20	.10
(16) Bill Madlock	.25	.20	.10
(17) Dale Murphy	.80	.60	.30
(18) Al Oliver	.25	.20	.10
(19) Darrell Porter	.25	.20	.10
(20) Cal Ripken	.60	.45	.25
(21) Pete Rose	1.25	.90	.50
(22) Steve Sax	.35	.25	.14
(23) Mike Schmidt	.80	.60	.30
(24) Ted Simmons	.25	.20	.10
(25) Ozzie Smith	.35	.25	.14
(26) Dave Stieb	.25	.20	.10
(27) Fernando Valenzuela	.35	.25	.14
(28) Lou Whitaker	.35	.25	.14
(29) Dave Winfield	.50	.40	.20
(30) Robin Yount	.40	.30	.15

1933 Minneapolis Star/ Worch Tobacco

This set of unnumbered postcard-size cards, apparently produced by the Minneapolis Star newspaper, was used as a promotion by Worch Cigar Co. of St. Paul, Minn. Although there is no advertising for Worch Cigars on the cards themselves, the cards were mailed in envelopes bearing the Worch name. The borderless cards featured action photos with the player's name and team appearing in hand-lettered type near the bottom.

	NR MT	EX	VG
Complete Set:	7000.	3500.	2100.
Common Player:	18.00	9.00	5.50
(1) Adams	18.00	9.00	5.50
(2) Dale Alexander	18.00	9.00	5.50
(3) Ivy Paul Andrews	18.00	9.00	5.50
(4a) Earl Averill (Cleveland)	40.00	20.00	12.00
(4b) Earl Averill (no team designation)	40.00	20.00	12.00
(5) Richard Bartell	18.00	9.00	5.50
(6) Herman Bell	18.00	9.00	5.50
(7) Walter Berger	18.00	9.00	5.50
(8) Huck Betts	18.00	9.00	5.50
(9) Max Bishop	18.00	9.00	5.50
(10) Jim Bottomley	40.00	20.00	12.00
(11a) Tom Bridges (name and team in box)	18.00	9.00	5.50
(11b) Tom Bridges (no box)	18.00	9.00	5.50
(12) Clint Brown	18.00	9.00	5.50
(13) May Carey	40.00	20.00	12.00
(14) Tex Carlton	18.00	9.00	5.50
(15) Chalmer Cissell	18.00	9.00	5.50
(16) Cochrane	40.00	20.00	12.00
(17) Collins	40.00	20.00	12.00
(18) Earle Combs	40.00	20.00	12.00
(19) Comorosky	18.00	9.00	5.50
(20) Crabtree	18.00	9.00	5.50
(21) Rodger Cramer (Roger)	18.00	9.00	5.50
(22) Pat Crawford	18.00	9.00	5.50
(23) Hugh Critz	18.00	9.00	5.50
(24) Frank Crosetti	25.00	12.50	7.50
(25a) Joe Cronin (name and team in box)	40.00	20.00	12.00
(25b) Joe Cronin (no box)	40.00	20.00	12.00
(26) Alvin Crowder	18.00	9.00	5.50
(27) Cuccinello	18.00	9.00	5.50
(28) Cuyler	40.00	20.00	12.00
(29) Geo. Davis	18.00	9.00	5.50
(30) Dizzy Dean	100.00	50.00	30.00
(31) Wm. Dickey	75.00	37.00	22.00
(32) Leo Durocher	60.00	30.00	18.00
(33) James Dykes	25.00	12.50	7.50
(34) George Earnshaw	18.00	9.00	5.50
(35) English	18.00	9.00	5.50
(36a) Richard Ferrell (name and team in box)	40.00	20.00	12.00
(36b) Richard Ferrell (no box)	40.00	20.00	12.00
(37a) Wesley Ferrell (name and team in box)	18.00	9.00	5.50
(37b) Wesley Ferrell (no box)	18.00	9.00	5.50
(38) Fred Fitzsimmons	18.00	9.00	5.50
(39) Lew Fonseca	25.00	12.50	7.50
(40) James Foxx	100.00	50.00	30.00
(41) Fred Frankhouse	18.00	9.00	5.50
(42) Frank Frisch	40.00	20.00	12.00
(43a) Leon Gaslin (name incorrect)	40.00	20.00	12.00
(43b) Leon Goslin (name correct)	40.00	20.00	12.00
(44) Lou Gehrig	350.00	175.00	105.00
(45) Charles Gehringer	40.00	20.00	12.00
(46) Vernon Gomez	40.00	20.00	12.00
(47) George Grantham	18.00	9.00	5.50
(48) Grimes The Lord Of Burleigh (Burleigh Grimes)	40.00	20.00	12.00
(49) Grimm	25.00	12.50	7.50
(50) Robert Grove	60.00	30.00	18.00
(51) Chic Hafey (Chick)	40.00	20.00	12.00
(52) Jess Haines	40.00	20.00	12.00
(53) Bill Hallahan	18.00	9.00	5.50
(54) Mel Harder	18.00	9.00	5.50
(55) Dave Harris	18.00	9.00	5.50
(56) Hartnett	40.00	20.00	12.00
(57) George Hass	18.00	9.00	5.50
(58) Ray Hayworth	18.00	9.00	5.50
(59) Hendrick	18.00	9.00	5.50
(60) Dutch Henry	18.00	9.00	5.50
(61) "Babe" Herman	25.00	12.50	7.50
(62) Bill Herman	40.00	20.00	12.00
(63) Frank Higgins	18.00	9.00	5.50
(64) O. Hildebrand	18.00	9.00	5.50
(65) Roger Hornsby (Rogers)	150.00	75.00	45.00
(66) Carl Hubbell	55.00	27.00	16.50
(67) Travis Jackson	40.00	20.00	12.00
(68) Smead Jolley	18.00	9.00	5.50
(69) Wm. Kamm	18.00	9.00	5.50
(70) Charles Klein	40.00	20.00	12.00
(71) Jos. Kuhel	18.00	9.00	5.50
(72) Tony Lazzeri	25.00	12.50	7.50
(73) Sam Leslie	18.00	9.00	5.50
(74) Al Lopez	40.00	20.00	12.00
(75) Red Lucas	18.00	9.00	5.50
(76) Adolfo Luque	18.00	9.00	5.50
(77) Connie Mack	75.00	37.00	22.00
(78) Gus Mancuso	18.00	9.00	5.50
(79) Henry Manush	40.00	20.00	12.00
(80) Fred Marberry	18.00	9.00	5.50
(81) Pepper Martin	25.00	12.50	7.50
(82) Wm. McKechnie	40.00	20.00	12.00
(83) Joe Medwick	40.00	20.00	12.00
(84) Jim Mooney	18.00	9.00	5.50
(85) Joe Moore	18.00	9.00	5.50
(86) Joe Mowry	18.00	9.00	5.50
(87) Van Mungo	18.00	9.00	5.50
(88) Buddy Myer	18.00	9.00	5.50
(89) "Lefty" O'Doul	25.00	12.50	7.50
(90) O'Farrell	18.00	9.00	5.50
(91) Orsatti	18.00	9.00	5.50
(92) Melvin Ott	65.00	32.00	19.50
(93) Parmelee	18.00	9.00	5.50
(94) Homer Peel	18.00	9.00	5.50
(95) George Pipgras	18.00	9.00	5.50
(96) Harry Rice	18.00	9.00	5.50
(97) Paul Richards	25.00	12.50	7.50
(98) Eppa Rixey	40.00	20.00	12.00
(99) Charles Ruffing	40.00	20.00	12.00
(100) Jack Russell	18.00	9.00	5.50
(101) Babe Ruth	700.00	350.00	210.00
(102) "Blondy" Ryan	18.00	9.00	5.50
(103) Wilfred Ryan	18.00	9.00	5.50
(104) Fred Schulte	18.00	9.00	5.50
(105) Schumacher	18.00	9.00	5.50
(106) Luke Sewel (Sewell)	18.00	9.00	5.50
(107) Al Simmons	40.00	20.00	12.00
(108) Ray Spencer	18.00	9.00	5.50
(109) Casey Stengel	250.00	125.00	75.00
(110) Stephenson	25.00	12.50	7.50
(111) Walter Stewart	18.00	9.00	5.50
(112) John T. Stone	18.00	9.00	5.50
(113) Suhr	18.00	9.00	5.50
(114) Dan Taylor	18.00	9.00	5.50
(115) Bill Terry	65.00	32.00	19.50
(116) Traynor	40.00	20.00	12.00
(117) William Urbanski	18.00	9.00	5.50
(118) Lloyd Vaughan	40.00	20.00	12.00
(119) Johnny Vergez	18.00	9.00	5.50
(120) George Walberg	18.00	9.00	5.50
(121) Bill Walker	18.00	9.00	5.50
(122) Gerald Walker	18.00	9.00	5.50
(123a) Lloyd Waner (background blanked out)	40.00	20.00	12.00
(123b) Lloyd Waner (with background)	40.00	20.00	12.00
(124a) Paul Waner (background blanked out)	40.00	20.00	12.00
(124b) Paul Waner (with background)	40.00	20.00	12.00
(125) Lon Warneke	18.00	9.00	5.50
(126) George Watkins	18.00	9.00	5.50
(127) Monte Weaver	18.00	9.00	5.50
(128) Sam West	18.00	9.00	5.50
(129) Earl Whitehill	18.00	9.00	5.50
(130) Hack Wilson	40.00	20.00	12.00
(131) Jimmy Wilson	18.00	9.00	5.50

1983 Minnesota Twins Team Issue

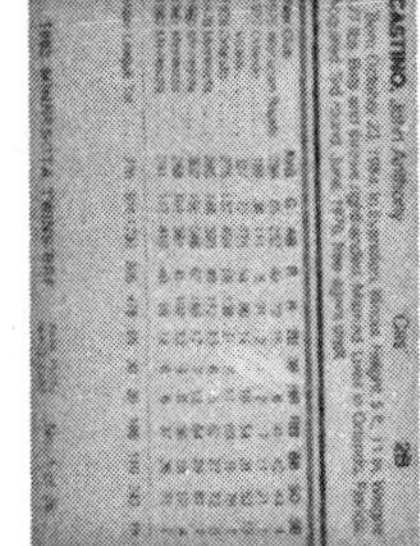

The Minnesota Twins produced a 36-card set in 1983 to be sold at concession stands and through the mail. The full-color, borderless cards measure the standard 2-1/2" by 3-1/2" and displayed the player's uniform number on a white Twins jersey at the bottom of the card. The backs, printed in red and blue on white stock, contain full career statistics.

		MT	NR MT	EX
	Complete Set:	9.00	6.75	3.50
	Common Player:	.10	.08	.04
1	John Anthony Castino	.10	.08	.04
2	James Michael Eisenreich	.20	.15	.08
3	Raymond Edward Smith	.10	.08	.04
4	Scott Matthew Ullger	.10	.08	.04
5	Gary Joseph Gaetti	.50	.40	.20
6	Michael Vaughn Hatcher	.10	.08	.04
7	Robert Van Mitchell	.10	.08	.04
8	Leonardo Lago Faedo, Jr.	.10	.08	.04
9	Kent Alan Hrbek	.75	.60	.30
10	Timothy Jon Laudner	.15	.11	.06
11	Frank John Viola, Jr.	.50	.40	.20
12	Bryan Alois Oelkers	.10	.08	.04
13	Richard Eugene Lysander	.10	.08	.04
14	Ralph David Engle	.10	.08	.04
15	Leonard Joseph Whitehouse, Jr.	.10	.08	.04
16	William Peter Filson	.10	.08	.04
17	Thomas Andrew Brunansky	.50	.40	.20
18	Robert Randall Bush	.10	.08	.04
19	Bradley David Havens	.10	.08	.04
20	Albert Hamilton Williams	.10	.08	.04
21	Gary Lamell Ward	.10	.08	.04
22	Jack William O'Connor	.10	.08	.04
23	Robert Ernie Castillo, Jr.	.10	.08	.04
24	Ronald Washington	.10	.08	.04
25	Ronald Gene Davis	.10	.08	.04
26	Jay Thomas Kelly	.15	.11	.06
27	William Frederick Gardner	.10	.08	.04
28	Richard Francis Stelmaszek	.10	.08	.04
29	James Robert Lemon	.10	.08	.04
30	John Joseph Podres	.15	.11	.06
31	Minnesota's Native Sons (Jim Eisenreich, Kent Hrbek, Tim Laudner)	.25	.20	.10
32	Twins' Catchers (Dave Engle, Tim Laudner)	.10	.08	.04
33	The Lumber Company (Tom Brunansky, Gary Gaetti, Kent Hrbek, Gary Ward)	.35	.25	.14
34	Twins' Coaches (Billy Gardner, Tom Kelly, Jim Lemon, Johnny Podres, Rick Stelmaszek)	.10	.08	.04
35	Team Photo	.10	.08	.04
36	Metrodome/Checklist	.10	.08	.04

1984 Minnesota Twins Team Issue

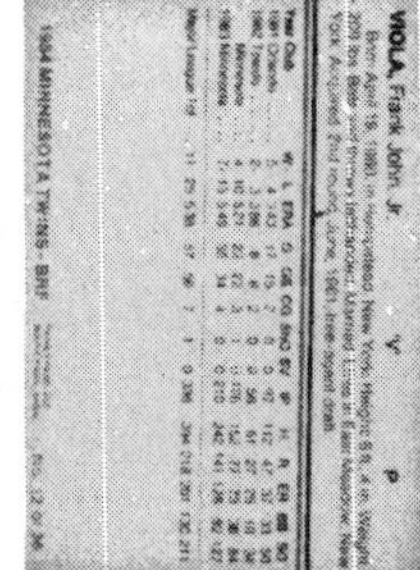

This team-issued set from the Minnesota Twins consists of 36 full-color, borderless cards, each measuring 2-1/2" by 3-1/2". As in the previous year, the player's uniform number appears on a white Twins jersey at the bottom of the card. The backs are again printed in red and blue on white card stock and include the player's complete career stats. The set features several special cards, including one of Harmon Killebrew. The set was sold at the ballpark and through the team's gift catalog.

		MT	NR MT	EX
	Complete Set:	6.00	4.50	2.50
	Common Player:	.08	.06	.03
1	John Anthony Castino	.08	.06	.03
2	James Michael Eisenreich	.10	.08	.04
3	Alfonso Jimenez	.08	.06	.03
4	David Keith Meier	.08	.06	.03
5	Gary Joseph Gaetti	.35	.25	.14
6	Michael Vaughn Hatcher	.08	.06	.03
7	Jeffrey Scott Reed	.08	.06	.03
8	Timothy Shawn Teufel	.10	.08	.04
9	Leonardo Lago Faedo, Jr.	.08	.06	.03
10	Kent Alan Hrbek	.50	.40	.20
11	Timothy Jon Laudner	.15	.11	.06
12	Frank John Viola, Jr.	.35	.25	.14
13	Kenneth Marvin Schrom	.08	.06	.03
14	Larry John Pashnick	.08	.06	.03
15	Ralph David Engle	.08	.06	.03
16	Keith Martin Comstock	.10	.08	.04
17	William Peter Filson	.08	.06	.03
18	Thomas Andrew Brunansky	.35	.25	.14
19	Robert Randall Bush	.08	.06	.03
20	Darrell Wayne Brown	.08	.06	.03
21	Albert Hamilton Williams	.08	.06	.03
22	Michael Charles Walters	.08	.06	.03
23	John David Butcher	.08	.06	.03
24	Robert Ernie Castillo, Jr.	.08	.06	.03
25	Ronald Washington	.08	.06	.03
26	Ronald Gene Davis	.08	.06	.03
27	Jay Thomas Kelly	.15	.11	.06
28	William Frederick Gardner	.08	.06	.03
29	Richard Francis Stelmaszek	.08	.06	.03
30	James Robert Lemon	.08	.06	.03
31	John Joseph Podres	.10	.08	.04
32	Billy Mike Smithson	.08	.06	.03
33	Harmon Killebrew	.50	.40	.20
34	Team Photo	.08	.06	.03
35	Logo Card	.08	.06	.03
36	Metrodome/Checklist	.08	.06	.03

1985 Minnesota Twins Team Issue

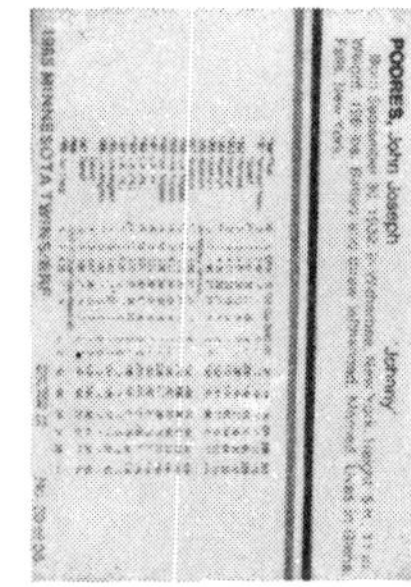

Similar in format to the previous two yers, this 36-card team-issued set features full-color, borderless cards of the Minnesota Twins. The player's uniform number is again displayed on a white Twins jersey in the lower right corner, and the 1985 All-Star Game logo is shown in the lower left, in recognition of the Twins' hosting the summer classic. The All-Star Game logo also appears on a special card in the set that lists on the back all Twins who have been selected for previous All-Star Games. The set was sold at ballpark concession stands and through the mail.

		MT	NR MT	EX
	Complete Set:	6.00	4.50	2.50
	Common Player:	.08	.06	.03
1	Alvaro Alberto Espinoza	.08	.06	.03
2	Roy Frederick Smalley, III	.10	.08	.04
3	Pedro Oliva, Jr.	.15	.11	.06
4	David Keith Meier	.08	.06	.03
5	Gary Joseph Gaetti	.35	.25	.14
6	Michael Vaughn Hatcher	.08	.06	.03
7	Jeffrey Scott Reed	.08	.06	.03
8	Timothy Shawn Teufel	.10	.08	.04
9	Mark Bruce Salas	.08	.06	.03
10	Kent Alan Hrbek	.50	.40	.20
11	Timothy Jon Laudner	.15	.11	.06
12	Frank John Viola, Jr.	.35	.25	.14
13	Kenneth Marvin Schrom	.08	.06	.03
14	Richard Eugene Lysander	.08	.06	.03
15	Ralph David Engle	.08	.06	.03
16	Andre Anter David	.08	.06	.03
17	Leonard Joseph Whitehouse, Jr.	.08	.06	.03
18	William Peter Filson	.08	.06	.03
19	Thomas Andrew Brunansky	.35	.25	.14
20	Robert Randall Bush	.08	.06	.03
21	Gregory Carpenter Gagne	.08	.06	.03
22	John Daniel Butcher	.08	.06	.03
23	Michael Steven Stenhouse	.08	.06	.03
24	Kirby Puckett	.80	.60	.30
25	Thomas Carl Klawitter	.08	.06	.03
26	Curtis Ray Wardle	.08	.06	.03
27	Richard Martin Yett	.15	.11	.06
28	Ronald Washington	.08	.06	.03
29	Ronald Gene Davis	.08	.06	.03
30	Jay Thomas Kelly	.15	.11	.06
31	William Frederick Gardner	.08	.06	.03
32	Richard Francis Stelmaszek	.08	.06	.03
33	John Joseph Podres	.10	.08	.04
34	Billy Mike Smithson	.08	.06	.03
35	1985 All-Star Game Logo Card	.08	.06	.03
36	Twins Logo/Checklist	.08	.06	.03

1986 Minnesota Twins Team Issue

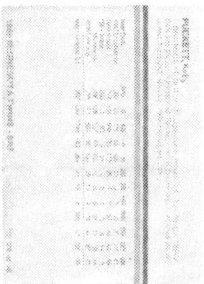

This team-issued set contains 36 2-9/16" by 3-1/2" full-color cards. Fronts feature the Twins 25th anniversary logo and a jersey at the bottom of each card with the player's uniform number. All cards, except an action shot of Bert Blyleven, are posed photos, with a facsimile autograph on each. The set also includes a checklist and a team photo.

		MT	NR MT	EX
	Complete Set:	6.00	4.50	2.50
	Common Player:	.08	.06	.03
1	Christopher Francis Pittaro	.08	.06	.03
2	Stephen Paul Lombardozzi	.15	.11	.06
3	Roy Frederick Smalley, III	.10	.08	.04
4	Pedro Oliva, Jr.	.15	.11	.06
5	Gary Joseph Gaetti	.50	.40	.20
6	Michael Vaughn Hatcher	.08	.06	.03
7	Jeffrey Scott Reed	.08	.06	.03
8	Mark Bruce Salas	.08	.06	.03
9	Kent Alan Hrbek	.60	.45	.25
10	Timothy Jon Laudner	.15	.11	.06
11	Frank John Viola, Jr.	.50	.40	.20
12	Dennis Allen Burtt	.08	.06	.03
13	Alejandro Sanchez	.08	.06	.03
14	LeRoy Purdy Smith, III	.08	.06	.03
15	William Lamar Beane, III	.08	.06	.03
16	William Peter Filson	.08	.06	.03
17	Thomas Andrew Brunansky	.35	.25	.14
18	Robert Randall Bush	.08	.06	.03
19	Frank Anthony Eufemia, III	.08	.06	.03
20	John Mark Davidson	.15	.11	.06
21	Rik Aalbert Blyleven	.25	.20	.10
22	Gregory Carpenter Gagne	.15	.11	.06
23	John Daniel Butcher	.08	.06	.03
24	Kirby Puckett	.80	.60	.30
25	William Carol Latham, Jr.	.08	.06	.03
26	Ronald Washington	.08	.06	.03
27	Ronald Gene Davis	.08	.06	.03
28	Jay Thomas Kelly	.15	.11	.06
29	Richard Stanley Such	.08	.06	.03
30	Richard Francis Stelmaszek	.08	.06	.03
31	Raymond Robert Miller	.08	.06	.03
32	Willard Wayne Terwilliger	.08	.06	.03
33	Billy Mike Smithson	.08	.06	.03
34	Alvis Woods	.08	.06	.03
35	Team Photo	.08	.06	.03
36	Twins Logo/Checklist	.08	.06	.03

1987 Minnesota Twins Team Issue

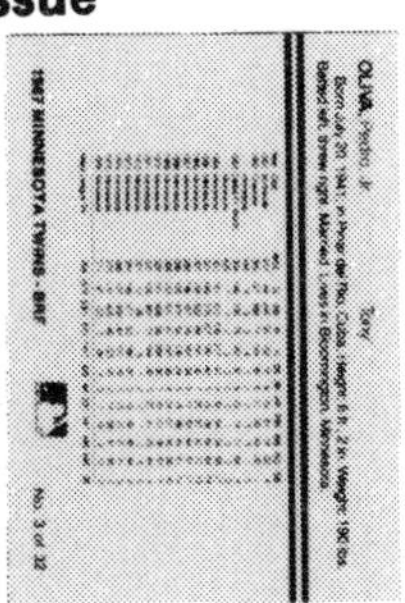

The Minnesota Twins produced a 32-card set of 2-1/2" by 3-1/2" full-color baseball cards to be sold at the ballpark and through their souvenir catalog. The card fronts are borderless, containing only the player photo. The backs are printed in blue and red on white card stock and carry the player's personal data and career record. The Twins also produced a post card set which was similar in design to the standard-size card set, but utilized different photos.

		MT	NR MT	EX
Complete Set:		6.00	4.50	2.50
Common Player:		.08	.06	.03
1	Stephen Paul Lombardozzi	.15	.11	.06
2	Roy Frederick Smalley III	.10	.08	.04
3	Pedro Oliva, Jr.	.15	.11	.06
4	Gregory Carpenter Gagne	.15	.11	.06
5	Gary Joseph Gaetti	.50	.40	.20
6	Jay Thomas Kelly	.15	.11	.06
7	Thomas Andrew Nieto	.08	.06	.03
8	Mark Bruce Salas	.08	.06	.03
9	Kent Alan Hrbek	.60	.45	.25
10	Timothy Jon Laudner	.15	.11	.06
11	Frank John Viola, Jr.	.50	.40	.20
12	Lester Paul Straker	.25	.20	.10
13	George Allen Frazier	.08	.06	.03
14	Keith Rowe Atherton	.08	.06	.03
15	Thomas Andrew Brunansky	.35	.25	.14
16	Robert Randall Bush	.08	.06	.03
17	Albert Dwayne Newman	.08	.06	.03
18	John Mark Davidson	.08	.06	.03
19	Rik Aalbert Blyleven	.25	.20	.10
20	Clinton Daniel Gladden III	.15	.11	.06
21	Kirby Puckett	.80	.60	.30
22	Mark Steven Portugal	.08	.06	.03
23	Juan Bautista Berenguer	.08	.06	.03
24	Jeffrey James Reardon	.30	.25	.12
25	Richard Stanley Such	.08	.06	.03
26	Richard Francis Stelmaszek	.08	.06	.03
27	Warren Richard Renick	.08	.06	.03
28	Willard Wayne Terwilliger	.08	.06	.03
29	Joseph Charles Klink	.08	.06	.03
30	Billy Mike Smithson	.08	.06	.03
31	Team Photo	.08	.06	.03
32	Twins Logo/Checklist	.08	.06	.03

1988 Minnesota Twins Team Issue

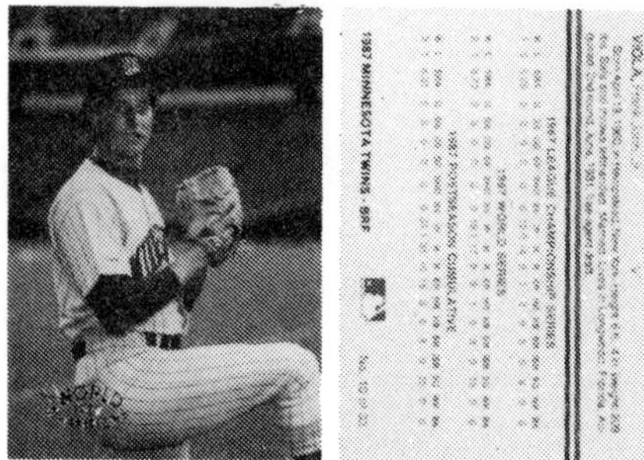

The Twins issued this 33-card set (including checklist) to commemorate the team's 1987 Series victory. The slightly oversized cards (2-5/8" x 3-7/16") feature deluxe player photos printed on heavy stock with a gold-embossed "1987 World Champions" logo in the lower left corner. Many photos are duplicates of the regular season set but several new photos, including a group team shot, are included. Numbered card backs are red, white and blue and contain a player name, personal info and stats. A limited edition of 5000 sets were printed but only a few hundred were sold before the cards were taken off the market due to Major League Baseball licensing restrictions.

		MT	NR MT	EX
Complete Set:		150.00	110.00	60.00
Common Player:		1.25	.90	.50
1	Stephen Paul Lombardozzi	1.25	.90	.50
2	Roy Frederick Smalley, III	1.25	.90	.50
3	Pedro Oliva, Jr.	1.25	.90	.50
4	Gregory Carpenter Gagne	3.00	2.25	1.25
5	Gary Joseph Gaetti	12.00	9.00	4.75
6	Eugene Thomas Larkin	3.00	2.25	1.25
7	Jay Thomas Kelly	2.00	1.50	.80
8	Kent Alan Hrbek	12.00	9.00	4.75
9	Timothy Jon Laudner	2.00	1.50	.80
10	Frank John Viola, Jr.	15.00	11.00	6.00
11	Lester Paul Straker	1.25	.90	.50
12	Donald Edward Baylor	2.00	1.50	.80
13	George Allen Frazier	1.25	.90	.50
14	Keith Rowe Atherton	1.25	.90	.50
15	Thomas Andrew Brunansky	10.00	7.50	4.00
16	Robert Randall Bush	2.00	1.50	.80
17	Albert Dwayne Newman	1.25	.90	.50
18	John Mark Davidson	1.25	.90	.50
19	Rik Aalbert Blyleven	10.00	7.50	4.00
20	Daniel Ernest Schatzeder	1.25	.90	.50
21	Clinton Daniel Gladden III	3.00	2.25	1.25
22	Salvatore Philip Butera	1.25	.90	.50
23	Kirby Puckett	25.00	20.00	10.00
24	Joseph Franklin Niekro	2.00	1.50	.80
25	Juan Bautista Berenguer	1.25	.90	.50
26	Jeffrey James Reardon	4.00	3.00	1.50
27	Richard Stanley Such	1.25	.90	.50
28	Richard Francis Stelmaszek	1.25	.90	.50
29	Warren Richard Renick	1.25	.90	.50
30	Willard Wayne Terwilliger	1.25	.90	.50
31	Team Photo	1.25	.90	.50
32	World Champions Team Logo Card	1.25	.90	.50
33	Team Logo Card/Checklist	1.25	.90	.50

1959 Morrell Meats Dodgers

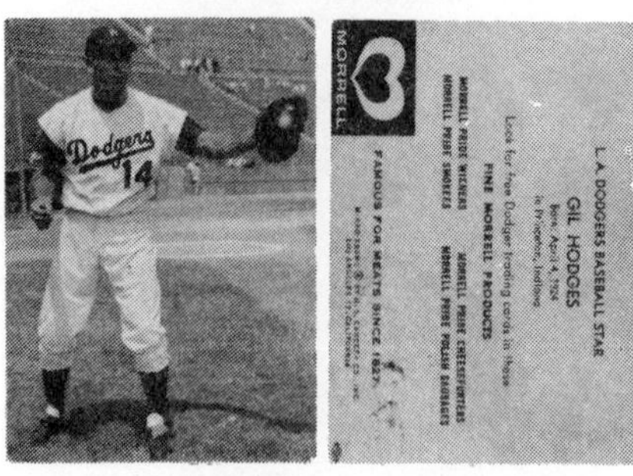

This popular set of Los Angeles Dodgers player cards was the first issue of a three-year run for the Southern California meat company. The 12 cards in this 2-1/2" by 3-1/2" set are unnumbered and feature fullframe, unbordered color photos. Card backs feature a company ad and list only the player's name, birthdate and birthplace. Two interesting errors exist in the set, as the cards for Clem Labine and Norm Larker show photos of Stan Williams and Joe Pignatano, respectively. Dodger greats Sandy Koufax and Duke Snider are key cards in the set.

		NR MT	EX	VG
Complete Set:		1200.	600.00	350.00
Common Player:		50.00	25.00	15.00
(1)	Don Drysdale	100.00	50.00	30.00
(2)	Carl Furillo	65.00	32.00	19.50
(3)	Jim Gilliam	65.00	32.00	19.50
(4)	Gil Hodges	100.00	50.00	30.00
(5)	Sandy Koufax	225.00	112.00	70.00
(6)	Clem Labine (photo actually Stan Williams)	50.00	25.00	15.00
(7)	Norm Larker (photo actually Joe Pignatano)	50.00	25.00	15.00
(8)	Charlie Neal	50.00	25.00	15.00
(9)	Johnny Podres	65.00	32.00	19.50
(10)	John Roseboro	50.00	25.00	15.00
(11)	Duke Snider	225.00	112.00	70.00
(12)	Don Zimmer	80.00	40.00	25.00

1960 Morrell Meats Dodgers

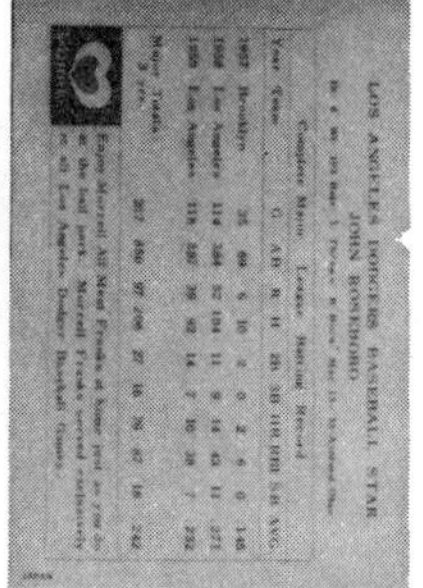

This 12-card set is the same 2-1/2" by 3-1/2" size as the 1959 set, and again features unbordered color card fronts. Five of the players included are new to the Morrell's sets. Card backs in 1960 list player statistics and brief personal data on each player. Cards for Gil Hodges, Carl Furillo and Duke Snider are apparently more scarce than others in the set. The 1960 set is again unnumbered.

		NR MT	EX	VG
Complete Set:		800.00	400.00	250.00
Common Player:		15.00	7.50	4.50
(1)	Walt Alston	25.00	12.50	7.50
(2)	Roger Craig	15.00	7.50	4.50
(3)	Don Drysdale	40.00	20.00	12.00
(4)	Carl Furillo	90.00	45.00	27.00
(5)	Gil Hodges	125.00	62.00	37.00
(6)	Sandy Koufax	125.00	62.00	37.00
(7)	Wally Moon	15.00	7.50	4.50
(8)	Charlie Neal	15.00	7.50	4.50
(9)	Johnny Podres	20.00	10.00	6.00
(10)	John Roseboro	15.00	7.50	4.50
(11)	Larry Sherry	15.00	7.50	4.50
(12)	Duke Snider	225.00	112.00	70.00

1961 Morrell Meats Dodgers

The Morrell set shrunk to just six cards in 1961, with a format almost identical to the 1960 cards.

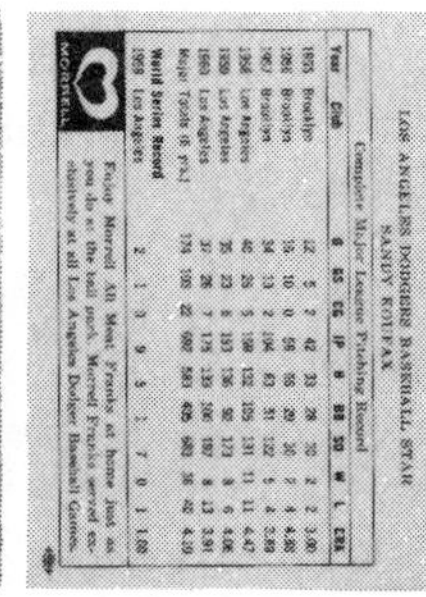

Card fronts are again full-color, unbordered photos, with player statistics on the backs. The unnumbered cards measure a slightly smaller 2-1/4" by 3-1/4", and comparison of statistical information can also distinguish the cards from the 1960 version. Top cards in the set are Don Drysdale and Sandy Koufax, who are also the only two players to appear in all three years of the Morrell Meats sets.

		NR MT	EX	VG
Complete Set:		200.00	100.00	60.00
Common Player:		15.00	7.50	4.50
(1)	Tommy Davis	20.00	10.00	6.00
(2)	Don Drysdale	40.00	20.00	12.00
(3)	Frank Howard	20.00	10.00	6.00
(4)	Sandy Koufax	80.00	40.00	24.00
(5)	Norm Larker	15.00	7.50	4.50
(6)	Maury Wills	25.00	12.50	7.50

1952 Mother's Cookies

This is one of the most popular regional minor league sets ever issued. Cards of Pacific Coast League players were included in packages of cookies. Distribution was limited to the West Coast. The 64 cards feature full color photos on a colored background, with player name and team. The cards measure 2- 13/16" by 3-1/2", though the cards' rounded corners cause some variation in listed size. Card backs feature a very brief player statistic, card numbers and an offer for purchasing postage stamps. Five cards (11, 16, 29, 37 and 43) are considered scarce, while card #4 (Chuck Connors) is the most popular.

		NR MT	EX	VG
Complete Set:		1500.	750.00	450.00
Common Player:		12.00	6.00	3.50
1	Johnny Lindell	18.00	9.00	5.50
2	Jim Davis	12.00	6.00	3.50
3	Al Gettle (Gettel)	12.00	6.00	3.50
4	Chuck Connors	200.00	100.00	60.00
5	Joe Grace	12.00	6.00	3.50
6	Eddie Basinski	12.00	6.00	3.50
7	Gene Handley	12.00	6.00	3.50
8	Walt Judnich	12.00	6.00	3.50
9	Jim Marshall	12.00	6.00	3.50
10	Max West	12.00	6.00	3.50
11	Bill MacCawley	50.00	25.00	15.00
12	Moreno Peiretti	12.00	6.00	3.50
13	Fred Haney	18.00	9.00	5.50
14	Earl Johnson	12.00	6.00	3.50
15	Dave Dahle	12.00	6.00	3.50
16	Bob Talbot	50.00	25.00	15.00
17	Smokey Singleton	12.00	6.00	3.50
18	Frank Austin	12.00	6.00	3.50
19	Joe Gordon	18.00	9.00	5.50
20	Joe Marty	12.00	6.00	3.50
21	Bob Gillespie	12.00	6.00	3.50
22	Red Embree	12.00	6.00	3.50
23	Lefty Olsen	12.00	6.00	3.50
24	Whitey Wietelmann	12.00	6.00	3.50
25	Frank O'Doul	18.00	9.00	5.50
26	Memo Luna	12.00	6.00	3.50
27	John Davis	12.00	6.00	3.50
28	Dick Faber	12.00	6.00	3.50
29	Buddy Peterson	125.00	62.00	37.00

		NR MT	EX	VG
30	Hank Schenz	12.00	6.00	3.50
31	Tookie Gilbert	12.00	6.00	3.50
32	Mel Ott	60.00	30.00	18.00
33	Sam Chapman	12.00	6.00	3.50
34	Dick Cole	12.00	6.00	3.50
35	John Ragni	12.00	6.00	3.50
36	Tom Saffell	12.00	6.00	3.50
37	Roy Welmaker	50.00	25.00	15.00
38	Lou Stringer	12.00	6.00	3.50
39	Artie Wilson	12.00	6.00	3.50
40	Chuck Stevens	12.00	6.00	3.50
41	Charlie Schanz	12.00	6.00	3.50
42	Al Lyons	12.00	6.00	3.50
43	Joe Erautt	125.00	62.00	37.00
44	Clarence Maddern	12.00	6.00	3.50
45	Gene Baker	12.00	6.00	3.50
46	Tom Heath	12.00	6.00	3.50
47	Al Lien	12.00	6.00	3.50
48	Bill Reeder	12.00	6.00	3.50
49	Bob Thurman	12.00	6.00	3.50
50	Ray Orteig	12.00	6.00	3.50
51	Joe Brovia	12.00	6.00	3.50
52	Jim Russell	12.00	6.00	3.50
53	Fred Sanford	12.00	6.00	3.50
54	Jim Gladd	12.00	6.00	3.50
55	Clay Hopper	12.00	6.00	3.50
56	Bill Glynn	12.00	6.00	3.50
57	Mike McCormick	12.00	6.00	3.50
58	Richie Myers	12.00	6.00	3.50
59	Vinnie Smith	12.00	6.00	3.50
60	Stan Hack	18.00	9.00	5.50
61	Bob Spicer	12.00	6.00	3.50
62	Jack Hollis	12.00	6.00	3.50
63	Ed Chandler	12.00	6.00	3.50
64	Bill Moisan	18.00	9.00	5.50

1953 Mother's Cookies

The 1953 Mother's Cookies cards are again 2-3/16" by 3-1/2", with rounded corners. There are 63 players from Pacific Coast League teams included. The full-color fronts have facsimile autographs rather than printed player names, and card backs offer a trading card album. Cards are generally more plentiful than in the 1952 set, with 11 of the cards apparently double printed.

		NR MT	EX	VG
Complete Set:		425.00	213.00	128.00
Common Player:		6.00	3.00	1.75
1	Lee Winter	9.00	4.50	2.75
2	Joe Ostrowski	6.00	3.00	1.75
3	Will Ramsdell	6.00	3.00	1.75
4	Bobby Bragan	9.00	4.50	2.75
5	Fletcher Robbe	6.00	3.00	1.75
6	Aaron Robinson	6.00	3.00	1.75
7	Augie Galan	6.00	3.00	1.75
8	Buddy Peterson	6.00	3.00	1.75
9	Frank Lefty O'Doul	18.00	9.00	5.50
10	Walt Pocekay	6.00	3.00	1.75
11	Nini Tornay	6.00	3.00	1.75
12	Jim Moran	6.00	3.00	1.75
13	George Schmees	6.00	3.00	1.75
14	Al Widmar	6.00	3.00	1.75
15	Ritchie Myers	6.00	3.00	1.75
16	Bill Howerton	6.00	3.00	1.75
17	Chuck Stevens	6.00	3.00	1.75
18	Joe Brovia	6.00	3.00	1.75
19	Max West	6.00	3.00	1.75
20	Eddie Malone	6.00	3.00	1.75
21	Gene Handley	6.00	3.00	1.75
22	William D. McCawley	6.00	3.00	1.75
23	Bill Sweeney	6.00	3.00	1.75
24	Tom Alston	6.00	3.00	1.75
25	George Vico	6.00	3.00	1.75
26	Hank Arft	6.00	3.00	1.75
27	Al Benton	6.00	3.00	1.75
28	"Pete" Milne	6.00	3.00	1.75
29	Jim Gladd	6.00	3.00	1.75
30	Earl Rapp	6.00	3.00	1.75
31	Ray Orteig	6.00	3.00	1.75
32	Eddie Basinski	6.00	3.00	1.75
33	Reno Cheso	6.00	3.00	1.75
34	Clarence Maddern	6.00	3.00	1.75
35	Marino Pieretti	6.00	3.00	1.75
36	Bill Raimondi	6.00	3.00	1.75
37	Frank Kelleher	6.00	3.00	1.75
38	George Bamberger	18.00	9.00	5.50
39	Dick Smith	6.00	3.00	1.75
40	Charley Schanz	6.00	3.00	1.75
41	John Van Cuyk	6.00	3.00	1.75
42	Lloyd Hittle	6.00	3.00	1.75
43	Tommy Heath	6.00	3.00	1.75
44	Frank Kalin	6.00	3.00	1.75
45	Jack Tobin	6.00	3.00	1.75
46	Jim Davis	6.00	3.00	1.75
47	Claude Christie	6.00	3.00	1.75
48	Elvin Tappe	6.00	3.00	1.75
49	Stan Hack	9.00	4.50	2.75
50	Fred Richards	6.00	3.00	1.75
51	Clay Hopper	6.00	3.00	1.75
52	Roy Welmaker	6.00	3.00	1.75
53	Red Adams	6.00	3.00	1.75
54	Piper Davis	6.00	3.00	1.75
55	Spider Jorgensen	6.00	3.00	1.75
56	Lee Walls	6.00	3.00	1.75
57	Jack Phillips	6.00	3.00	1.75
58	Red Lynn	6.00	3.00	1.75
59	Eddie Beckman	6.00	3.00	1.75
60	Gene Desautels	6.00	3.00	1.75
61	Bob Dillinger	6.00	3.00	1.75
62	Al Federoff	6.00	3.00	1.75
63	Bill Boemler	6.00	3.00	1.75

1983 Mother's Cookies Giants

After putting out Pacific Coast League sets in 1952 and 1953 Mother's Cookies distributed this full-color set of 20 San Francisco Giants cards three decades later. The 2-1/2" by 3-1/2" cards were produced by Barry Colla and included the Giants logo and player's name on the attractive card fronts. Card backs are numbered and contain biographical information, the Mother's Cookies logo, and a space for the player's autograph. Fifteen cards were given to every fan at the August 7, 1983 Giants game, with each fan also receiving a coupon good for five additional cards.

		MT	NR MT	EX
Complete Set:		18.00	13.50	7.25
Common Player:		.50	.40	.20
1	Frank Robinson	1.50	1.25	.60
2	Jack Clark	2.50	2.00	1.00
3	Chili Davis	1.50	1.25	.60
4	Johnnie LeMaster	.50	.40	.20
5	Greg Minton	.50	.40	.20
6	Bob Brenly	.70	.50	.30
7	Fred Breining	.50	.40	.20
8	Jeff Leonard	1.00	.70	.40
9	Darrell Evans	1.50	1.25	.60
10	Tom O'Malley	.50	.40	.20
11	Duane Kuiper	.50	.40	.20
12	Mike Krukow	.70	.50	.30
13	Atlee Hammaker	.70	.50	.30
14	Gary Lavelle	.50	.40	.20
15	Bill Laskey	.50	.40	.20
16	Max Venable	.50	.40	.20
17	Joel Youngblood	.50	.40	.20
18	Dave Bergman	.50	.40	.20
19	Mike Vail	.50	.40	.20
20	Andy McGaffigan	.50	.40	.20

1984 Mother's Cookies A's

Following the success of their one set in 1983, Mother's Cookies issued five more team sets of cards in 1984. The A's set measures 2-1/2" by 3-1/2", and card fronts feature unbordered color photos with rounded corners. Card backs are quite similar in format to the 1983 Mother's Cookies Giants, with brief biographical information, card numbers, Mother's Cookies logo and space for player autograph. There are 28 cards in the A's set, with 20 of the cards distributed during a stadium promotion. Fans also received a coupon redeemable for eight additional cards. Since these additional cards do not necessarily complete collectors' sets, Mother's Cookies cards become very popular among card traders. The A's set includes cards for the manager, coaches and a checklist.

		MT	NR MT	EX
Complete Set:		15.00	11.00	6.00
Common Player:		.50	.40	.20
1	Steve Boros	.50	.40	.20
2	Rickey Henderson	3.00	2.25	1.25
3	Joe Morgan	1.50	1.25	.60
4	Dwayne Murphy	.70	.50	.30
5	Mike Davis	.70	.50	.30
6	Bruce Bochte	.50	.40	.20
7	Carney Lansford	.80	.60	.30
8	Steve McCatty	.50	.40	.20
9	Mike Heath	.50	.40	.20
10	Chris Codiroli	.50	.40	.20
11	Bill Almon	.50	.40	.20
12	Bill Caudill	.50	.40	.20
13	Donnie Hill	.50	.40	.20
14	Lary Sorenson	.50	.40	.20
15	Dave Kingman	.80	.60	.30
16	Garry Hancock	.50	.40	.20
17	Jeff Burroughs	.60	.45	.25
18	Tom Burgmeier	.50	.40	.20
19	Jim Essian	.50	.40	.20
20	Mike Warren	.50	.40	.20
21	Davey Lopes	.60	.45	.25
22	Ray Burris	.50	.40	.20
23	Tony Phillips	.50	.40	.20
24	Tim Conroy	.50	.40	.20
25	Jeff Bettendorf	.50	.40	.20
26	Keith Atherton	.60	.45	.25
27	A's Coaches (Clete Boyer, Bob Didier, Jackie Moore, Ron Schueler, Billy Williams)	.50	.40	.20
28	Oakland Coliseum/Checklist	.50	.40	.20

1984 Mother's Cookies Astros

Mother's Cookies also issued a full-color team set for the Houston Astros in 1984. The Astros set measures 2-1/2" by 3-1/2", and card fronts feature unbordered color photos with rounded corners. Card backs are quite similar in format to the 1983 Mother's Cookies Giants, with brief biographical information, card numbers, Mother's Cookies logo and space for player autograph. There are 28 cards in the Astros set, with 20 of the cards distributed during a stadium promotion. Fans also received a coupon redeemable for eight additional cards. Since these additional cards do not necessarily complete collectors' sets, Mother's Cookies cards became very popular among card traders. The Astros set includes one card for the coaches and a checklist.

		MT	NR MT	EX
Complete Set:		15.00	11.00	6.00
Common Player:		.50	.40	.20
1	Nolan Ryan	2.50	2.00	1.00
2	Joe Niekro	.60	.45	.25
3	Alan Ashby	.50	.40	.20
4	Bill Doran	1.00	.70	.40
5	Phil Garner	.60	.45	.25
6	Ray Knight	.60	.45	.25
7	Dickie Thon	.60	.45	.25
8	Jose Cruz	.70	.50	.30
9	Jerry Mumphrey	.50	.40	.20
10	Terry Puhl	.50	.40	.20
11	Enos Cabell	.50	.40	.20
12	Harry Spilman	.50	.40	.20
13	Dave Smith	.60	.45	.25
14	Mike Scott	1.25	.90	.50
15	Bob Lillis	.50	.40	.20
16	Bob Knepper	.60	.45	.25
17	Frank DiPino	.50	.40	.20
18	Tom Wieghaus	.50	.40	.20
19	Denny Walling	.50	.40	.20
20	Tony Scott	.50	.40	.20
21	Alan Bannister	.50	.40	.20
22	Bill Dawley	.50	.40	.20
23	Vern Ruhle	.50	.40	.20
24	Mike LaCoss	.50	.40	.20

		MT	NR MT	EX
25	Mike Madden	.50	.40	.20
26	Craig Reynolds	.50	.40	.20
27	Astros Coaches (Cot Deal, Don Leppert, Denis Menke, Les Moss, Jerry Walker)	.50	.40	.20
28	Astros Logo/Checklist	.50	.40	.20

1984 Mother's Cookies Giants

Mother's Cookies issued a second annual full-color card set for the San Francisco Giants in 1984. The Giants set measures 2-1/2" by 3-1/2", and the round-cornered cards feature drawings of former Giant All-Star team selections. Card backs are quite similar in format to the 1983 Mother's Cookies Giants, with brief biographical information, card numbers and Mother's Cookies logo. No autograph space is included. There are 28 cards in the Giants set, with 20 of the cards distributed during a stadium promotion. Fans also received a coupon redeemable for eight additional cards. Since these additional cards do not necessarily complete collectors' sets, Mother's Cookies cards became very popular among card traders. Card number 28 is a checklist chart.

		MT	NR MT	EX
	Complete Set:	18.00	13.50	7.25
	Common Player:	.50	.40	.20
1	Willie Mays	2.50	2.00	1.00
2	Willie McCovey	2.00	1.50	.80
3	Juan Marichal	2.00	1.50	.80
4	Gaylord Perry	2.00	1.50	.80
5	Tom Haller	.60	.45	.25
6	Jim Davenport	.50	.40	.20
7	Jack Clark	1.25	.90	.50
8	Greg Minton	.50	.40	.20
9	Atlee Hammaker	.50	.40	.20
10	Gary Lavelle	.50	.40	.20
11	Orlando Cepeda	1.00	.70	.40
12	Bobby Bonds	.80	.60	.30
13	John Antonelli	.60	.45	.25
14	Bob Schmidt (photo actually Wes Westrum)	.50	.40	.20
15	Sam Jones	.50	.40	.20
16	Mike McCormick	.60	.45	.25
17	Ed Bailey	.50	.40	.20
18	Stu Miller	.50	.40	.20
19	Felipe Alou	.70	.50	.30
20	Jim Hart	.60	.45	.25
21	Dick Dietz	.50	.40	.20
22	Chris Speier	.50	.40	.20
23	Bobby Murcer	.70	.50	.30
24	John Montefusco	.50	.40	.20
25	Vida Blue	.70	.50	.30
26	Ed Whitson	.50	.40	.20
27	Darrell Evans	.70	.50	.30
28	All-Star Game Logo/Checklist	.50	.40	.20

1984 Mother's Cookies Mariners

Mother's Cookies also issued a full-color set for the Seattle Mariners in 1984. The Mariners set measures 2-1/2" by 3-1/2", and card fronts feature unbordered color photos with rounded corners. Card backs are quite similar in format to the 1983 Mother's Cookies Giants, with brief biographical information, card numbers, Mother's Cookies logo and space for player autograph. There are 28 cards in the Mariners set, with 20 of the cards distributed during a stadium promotion. Fans also received a coupon redeemable for eight additional cards. Since these additional cards do not necessarily complete collectors' sets, Mother's Cookies cards became very popular among card traders. The Mariners set includes one card each for the manager, coaches and a checklist.

		MT	NR MT	EX
	Complete Set:	15.00	11.00	6.00
	Common Player:	.50	.40	.20
1	Del Crandall	.60	.45	.25
2	Barry Bonnell	.50	.40	.20
3	Dave Henderson	.70	.50	.30
4	Bob Kearney	.50	.40	.20
5	Mike Moore	.50	.40	.20
6	Spike Owen	.70	.50	.30
7	Gorman Thomas	.70	.50	.30
8	Ed Vande Berg	.50	.40	.20
9	Matt Young	.60	.45	.25
10	Larry Milbourne	.50	.40	.20
11	Dave Beard	.50	.40	.20
12	Jim Beattie	.50	.40	.20
13	Mark Langston	1.50	1.25	.60
14	Orlando Mercado	.50	.40	.20
15	Jack Perconte	.50	.40	.20
16	Pat Putnam	.50	.40	.20
17	Paul Mirabella	.50	.40	.20
18	Domingo Ramos	.50	.40	.20
19	Al Cowens	.50	.40	.20
20	Mike Stanton	.50	.40	.20
21	Steve Henderson	.50	.40	.20
22	Bob Stoddard	.50	.40	.20
23	Alvin Davis	1.75	1.25	.70
24	Phil Bradley	1.50	1.25	.60
25	Roy Thomas	.50	.40	.20
26	Darnell Coles	.80	.60	.30
27	Mariners Coaches (Chuck Cottier, Frank Funk, Ben Hines, Phil Roof, Rick Sweet)	.50	.40	.20
28	Seattle Kingdome/Checklist	.50	.40	.20

1984 Mother's Cookies Padres

Mother's Cookies also issued a full-color set for the San Diego Padres in 1984. The Padres set measures 2-1/2" by 3-1/2", and card fronts feature unbordered color photos with rounded corners. Card backs are quite similar in format to the 1983 Mother's Cookies Giants, with brief biographical information, card numbers, Mother's Cookies logo and space for player autograph. There are 28 cards in the Padres set, with 20 of the cards distributed during a stadium promotion. Fans also received a coupon redeemable for eight additional cards. Since these additional cards do not necessarily complete collector's sets, Mother's Cookies cards became very popular among card traders. The Padres set includes one card each for the manager, coaches and a checklist.

		MT	NR MT	EX
	Complete Set:	18.00	13.50	7.25
	Common Player:	.50	.40	.20
1	Dick Williams	.50	.40	.20
2	Rich Gossage	1.00	.70	.40
3	Tim Lollar	.50	.40	.20
4	Eric Show	.70	.50	.30
5	Terry Kennedy	.60	.45	.25
6	Kurt Bevacqua	.50	.40	.20
7	Steve Garvey	2.00	1.50	.80
8	Garry Templeton	.70	.50	.30
9	Tony Gwynn	3.50	2.75	1.50
10	Alan Wiggins	.50	.40	.20
11	Dave Dravecky	.60	.45	.25
12	Tim Flannery	.50	.40	.20
13	Kevin McReynolds	2.25	1.75	.90
14	Bobby Brown	.50	.40	.20
15	Ed Whitson	.50	.40	.20
16	Doug Gwosdz	.50	.40	.20
17	Luis DeLeon	.50	.40	.20
18	Andy Hawkins	.60	.45	.25
19	Craig Lefferts	.50	.40	.20
20	Carmelo Martinez	.60	.45	.25
21	Sid Monge	.50	.40	.20
22	Graig Nettles	.80	.60	.30
23	Mario Ramirez	.50	.40	.20
24	Luis Salazar	.50	.40	.20
25	Champ Summers	.50	.40	.20
26	Mark Thurmond	.50	.40	.20
27	Padres Coaches (Harry Dunlop, Deacon Jones, Jack Krol, Norm Sherry, Ozzie Virgil)	.50	.40	.20
28	Jack Murphy Stadium/Checklist	.50	.40	.20

1985 Mother's Cookies A's

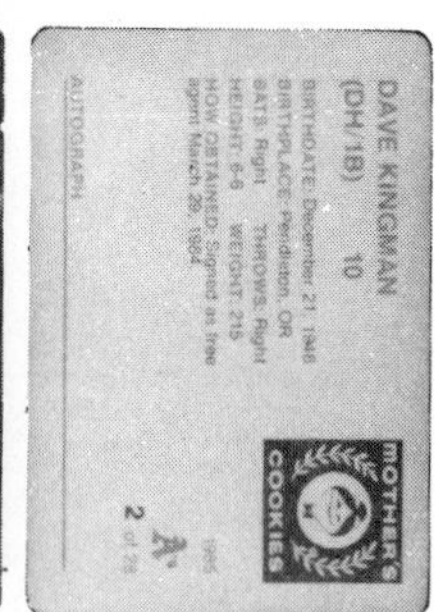

Mother's Cookies again issued five full-color sets for major league teams in 1985. The A's set measures 2-1/2" by 3-1/2", and card fronts feature unbordered color photos with rounded corners. Card backs are quite similar in format to the 1984 Mother's Cookies A's, with brief biographical information card numbers, Mother's Cookies logo and space for player autograph. Card backs are dated 1985. There are 28 cards in the A's set, which was distributed in its entirety during a stadium promotion. The A's set includes one card each for the manager, coaches and a checklist.

		MT	NR MT	EX
	Complete Set:	12.00	9.00	4.75
	Common Player:	.40	.30	.15
1	Jackie Moore	.40	.30	.15
2	Dave Kingman	.70	.50	.30
3	Don Sutton	1.00	.70	.40
4	Mike Heath	.40	.30	.15
5	Alfredo Griffin	.60	.45	.25
6	Dwayne Murphy	.60	.45	.25
7	Mike Davis	.60	.45	.25
8	Carney Lansford	.70	.50	.30
9	Chris Codiroli	.40	.30	.15
10	Bruce Bochte	.40	.30	.15
11	Mickey Tettleton	.50	.40	.20
12	Donnie Hill	.40	.30	.15
13	Rob Picciolo	.40	.30	.15
14	Dave Collins	.50	.40	.20
15	Dusty Baker	.60	.45	.25
16	Tim Conroy	.40	.30	.15
17	Keith Atherton	.40	.30	.15
18	Jay Howell	.60	.45	.25
19	Mike Warren	.40	.30	.15
20	Steve McCatty	.40	.30	.15
21	Bill Krueger	.40	.30	.15
22	Curt Young	.70	.50	.30
23	Dan Meyer	.40	.30	.15
24	Mike Gallego	.50	.40	.20
25	Jeff Kaiser	.40	.30	.15
26	Steve Henderson	.40	.30	.15
27	A's Coaches (Clete Boyer, Bob Didier, Dave McKay, Wes Stock, Billy Williams)	.40	.30	.15
28	Oakland Coliseum/Checklist	.40	.30	.15

1985 Mother's Cookies Astros

Mother's Cookies issued a second annual full-color set for the Houston Astros in 1985. The Astros set measures 2-1/2" by 3-1/2", and card fronts feature unbordered color photos with rounded corners. Card backs are quite similar in format to the 1984 Mother's Cookies Astros, with brief biographical information, card number, Mother's Cookies logo and space for player autograph. Card backs are dated 1985. There are 28 cards in the Astros set, which was distributed in its entirety during a stadium promotion. The Astros set includes one card each for the manager, coaches and a checklist.

		MT	NR MT	EX
Complete Set:		12.00	9.00	4.75
Complete Player:		.40	.30	.15
1	Bob Lillis	.40	.30	.15
2	Nolan Ryan	2.00	1.50	.80
3	Phil Garner	.50	.40	.20
4	Jose Cruz	.60	.45	.25
5	Denny Walling	.40	.30	.15
6	Joe Niekro	.60	.45	.25
7	Terry Puhl	.40	.30	.15
8	Bill Doran	.60	.45	.25
9	Dickie Thon	.40	.30	.15
10	Enos Cabell	.40	.30	.15
11	Frank Dipino (DiPino)	.40	.30	.15
12	Julio Solano	.40	.30	.15
13	Alan Ashby	.40	.30	.15
14	Craig Reynolds	.40	.30	.15
15	Jerry Mumphrey	.40	.30	.15
16	Bill Dawley	.40	.30	.15
17	Mark Bailey	.40	.30	.15
18	Mike Scott	1.00	.70	.40
19	Harry Spilman	.40	.30	.15
20	Bob Knepper	.50	.40	.20
21	Dave Smith	.50	.40	.20
22	Kevin Bass	.60	.45	.25
23	Tim Tolman	.40	.30	.15
24	Jeff Calhoun	.40	.30	.15
25	Jim Pankovits	.40	.30	.15
26	Ron Mathis	.40	.30	.15
27	Astros Coaches (Cot Deal, Matt Galante, Don Leppert, Denis Menke, Jerry Walker)	.40	.30	.15
28	Astros Logo/Checklist	.40	.30	.15

1985 Mother's Cookies Giants

Mother's Cookies issued a third annual full-color set for the San Francisco Giants in 1985. The Giants set measures 2-1/2" by 3-1/2", and card fronts feature unbordered color photos of current players with rounded corners. Card backs are quite similar in format to the 1983 Mother's Cookies Giants, with brief biographical information, card numbers, Mother's Cookies logo and space for player autograph. Card backs are dated 1985. There are 28 cards in the Giants set, which was distributed in its entirety during a stadium promotion. The Giants set includes one card each for the manager, coaches and a checklist.

		MT	NR MT	EX
Complete Set:		12.00	9.00	4.75
Common Player:		.40	.30	.15
1	Jim Davenport	.40	.30	.15
2	Chili Davis	.60	.45	.25
3	Dan Gladden	.60	.45	.25
4	Jeff Leonard	.60	.45	.25
5	Manny Trillo	.50	.40	.20
6	Atlee Hammaker	.50	.40	.20
7	Bob Brenly	.50	.40	.20
8	Greg Minton	.40	.30	.15
9	Bill Laskey	.40	.30	.15
10	Vida Blue	.60	.45	.25
11	Mike Krukow	.50	.40	.20
12	Frank Williams	.60	.45	.25
13	Jose Uribe	.50	.40	.20
14	Johnnie LeMaster	.40	.30	.15
15	Scot Thompson	.40	.30	.15
16	Dave LaPoint	.50	.40	.20
17	David Green	.40	.30	.15
18	Chris Brown	1.00	.70	.40
19	Joel Youngblood	.40	.30	.15
20	Mark Davis	.40	.30	.15
21	Jim Gott	.40	.30	.15
22	Doug Gwosdz	.40	.30	.15
23	Scott Garrelts	.50	.40	.20
24	Gary Rajsich	.40	.30	.15
25	Rob Deer	1.00	.70	.40
26	Brad Wellman	.40	.30	.15
27	Coaches (Rocky Bridges, Chuck Hiller, Tom McCraw, Bob Miller, Jack Mull)	.40	.30	.15
28	Candlestick Park/Checklist	.40	.30	.15

1985 Mother's Cookies Mariners

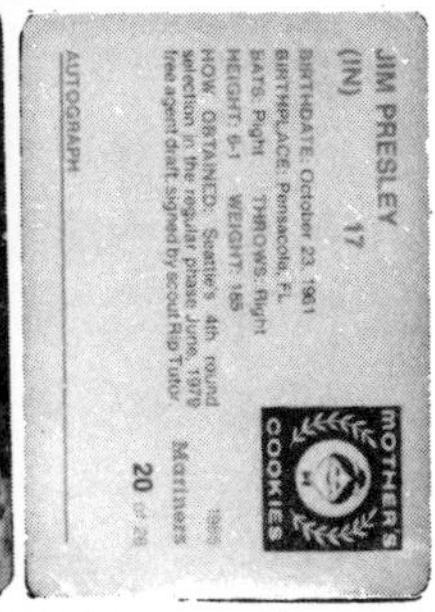

Mother's Cookies issued a second annual full-color set for the Seattle Mariners in 1985. The Mariners set measures 2-1/2" by 3-1/2", and card fronts feature unbordered color photos with rounded corners. Card backs are quite similar in format to the 1984 Mother's Cookies Mariners, with brief biographical information, card numbers, Mother's Cookies logo and space for player autograph. Card backs are dated 1985. There are 28 cards in the Mariners set, which was distributed in its entirety during a stadium promotion. The Mariners set includes one card each for the coaches and a checklist.

		MT	NR MT	EX
Complete Set:		13.00	9.75	5.25
Common Player:		.40	.30	.15
1	Chuck Cottier	.40	.30	.15
2	Alvin Davis	1.25	.90	.50
3	Mark Langston	1.00	.70	.40
4	Dave Henderson	.40	.30	.15
5	Ed Vande Berg	.40	.30	.15
6	Al Cowens	.40	.30	.15
7	Spike Owen	.40	.30	.15
8	Mike Moore	.40	.30	.15
9	Gorman Thomas	.60	.45	.25
10	Barry Bonnell	.40	.30	.15
11	Jack Perconte	.40	.30	.15
12	Domingo Ramos	.40	.30	.15
13	Bob Kearney	.40	.30	.15
14	Matt Young	.40	.30	.15
15	Jim Beattie	.40	.30	.15
16	Mike Stanton	.40	.30	.15
17	David Valle	.50	.40	.20
18	Ken Phelps	.60	.45	.25
19	Salome Barojas	.40	.30	.15
20	Jim Presley	1.50	1.25	.60
21	Phil Bradley	1.00	.70	.40
22	Dave Geisel	.40	.30	.15
23	Harold Reynolds	.80	.60	.30
24	Edwin Nunez	.50	.40	.20
25	Mike Morgan	.40	.30	.15
26	Ivan Calderon	.80	.60	.30
27	Mariners Coaches (Deron Johnson, Jim Mahoney, Marty Martinez, Phil Regan, Phil Roof)	.40	.30	.15
28	Seattle Kingdome/Checklist	.40	.30	.15

1985 Mother's Cookies Padres

Mother's Cookies issued a second annual full-color set for the San Diego Padres in 1985. The Padres set measures 2-1/2" by 3-1/2", and card fronts feature unbordered color photos with rounded corners. Card backs are quite similar in format to the 1984 Mother's Cookies Padres, with brief biographical information, card numbers, Mother's Cookies logo and space for player autograph. Card backs are dated 1985. There are 28 cards in the Padres set, which was distributed in its entirety during a stadium promotion. The Padres set includes one card each for the manager, coaches and a checklist.

		MT	NR MT	EX
Complete Set:		12.00	9.00	4.75
Common Player:		.40	.30	.15
1	Dick Williams	.40	.30	.15
2	Tony Gwynn	3.00	2.25	1.25
3	Kevin McReynolds	1.50	1.25	.60
4	Graig Nettles	.70	.50	.30
5	Rich Gossage	.90	.70	.35
6	Steve Garvey	1.75	1.25	.70
7	Garry Templeton	.50	.40	.20
8	Dave Dravecky	.50	.40	.20
9	Eric Show	.60	.45	.25
10	Terry Kennedy	.50	.40	.20
11	Luis DeLeon	.40	.30	.15
12	Bruce Bochy	.40	.30	.15
13	Andy Hawkins	.50	.40	.20
14	Kurt Bevacqua	.40	.30	.15
15	Craig Lefferts	.40	.30	.15
16	Mario Ramirez	.40	.30	.15
17	LaMarr Hoyt	.40	.30	.15
18	Jerry Royster	.40	.30	.15
19	Tim Stoddard	.40	.30	.15
20	Tim Flannery	.40	.30	.15
21	Mark Thurmond	.40	.30	.15
22	Greg Booker	.50	.40	.20
23	Bobby Brown	.40	.30	.15
24	Carmelo Martinez	.50	.40	.20
25	Al Bumbry	.40	.30	.15
26	Jerry Davis	.40	.30	.15
27	Padres Coaches (Galen Cisco, Harry Dunlop, Deacon Jones, Jack Krol, Ozzie Virgil)	.40	.30	.15
28	Jack Murphy Stadium/Checklist	.40	.30	.15

1986 Mother's Cookies A's

Mother's Cookies produced four more full-color team card sets in 1986, with only the San Diego Padres not repeating from the 1985 group. The third annual set for the Oakland A's measures 2-1/2" by 3-1/2", and card fronts feature unbordered color photos with rounded corners. Card backs are quite similar in format to previous years, with brief biographical information, card numbers and the Mother's Cookies logo. Card backs are dated 1986. There are 28 cards in the A's set, with 20 of the cards distributed during a stadium promotion. Each fan also received a coupon redeemable for eight additional cards. The A's set includes one card each for the manager, coaches and a checklist.

		MT	NR MT	EX
Complete Set:		22.00	16.50	8.75
Common Player:		.30	.25	.12
1	Jackie Moore	.30	.25	.12
2	Dave Kingman	.60	.45	.25
3	Dusty Baker	.40	.30	.15
4	Joaquin Andujar	.40	.30	.15
5	Alfredo Griffin	.40	.30	.15
6	Dwayne Murphy	.40	.30	.15
7	Mike Davis	.40	.30	.15
8	Carney Lansford	.50	.40	.20
9	Jose Canseco	15.00	11.00	6.00
10	Bruce Bochte	.30	.25	.12
11	Mickey Tettleton	.30	.25	.12
12	Donnie Hill	.30	.25	.12
13	Jose Rijo	.60	.45	.25
14	Rick Langford	.30	.25	.12
15	Chris Codiroli	.30	.25	.12
16	Moose Haas	.30	.25	.12
17	Keith Atherton	.30	.25	.12
18	Jay Howell	.40	.30	.15
19	Tony Phillips	.30	.25	.12
20	Steve Henderson	.30	.25	.12
21	Bill Krueger	.30	.25	.12
22	Steve Ontiveros	.40	.30	.15
23	Bill Bathe	.30	.25	.12
24	Rickey Peters	.30	.25	.12
25	Tim Birtsas	.30	.25	.12
26	Trainers Card (Frank Ciensczyk, Larry Davis, Steve Vucinich, Barry Weinberg)	.30	.25	.12
27	Coaches Card (Bob Didier, Dave McKay, Jeff Newman, Ron Plaza, Wes Stock, Bob Watson)	.30	.25	.12
28	Oakland Coliseum/Checklist	.30	.25	.12

1986 Mother's Cookies Astros

Mother's Cookies produced a third annual set for the Houston Astros in 1985. The set measure

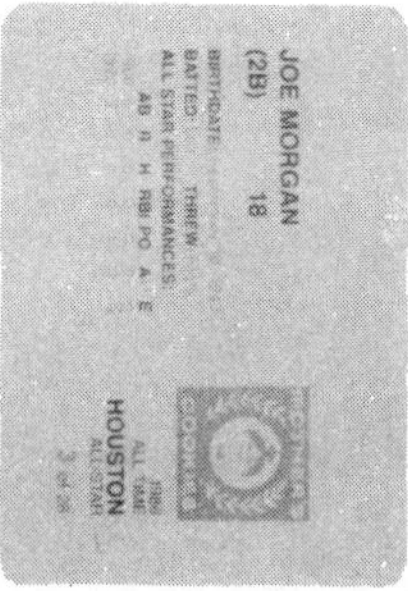

2-1/2" by 3-1/2", and card fronts feature unbordered color paintings of Houston's past All-Star Game per- formers. The round-cornered cards have backs quite similar in format to previous years, with brief biographical information, card numbers and the Mother's Cookies logo. Card backs are dated 1986. There are 28 cards in the Astros set, with 20 of the cards distributed during a stadium promotion. Each fan also received a coupon redeemable for eight additional cards. The Astros set also includes a checklist card.

		MT	NR MT	EX
Complete Set:		10.00	7.50	4.00
Common Player:		.30	.25	.12
1	Dick Farrell	.30	.25	.12
2	Hal Woodeschick (Woodeshick)	.30	.25	.12
3	Joe Morgan	1.00	.70	.40
4	Claude Raymond	.30	.25	.12
5	Mike Cuellar	.40	.30	.15
6	Rusty Staub	.60	.45	.25
7	Jimmy Wynn	.40	.30	.15
8	Larry Dierker	.40	.30	.15
9	Denis Menke	.30	.25	.12
10	Don Wilson	.30	.25	.12
11	Cesar Cedeno	.50	.40	.20
12	Lee May	.40	.30	.15
13	Bob Watson	.40	.30	.15
14	Ken Forsch	.40	.30	.15
15	Joaquin Andujar	.40	.30	.15
16	Terry Puhl	.30	.25	.12
17	Joe Niekro	.40	.30	.15
18	Craig Reynolds	.30	.25	.12
19	Joe Sambito	.30	.25	.12
20	Jose Cruz	.60	.45	.25
21	J.R. Richard	.40	.30	.15
22	Bob Knepper	.40	.30	.15
23	Nolan Ryan	1.50	1.25	.60
24	Ray Knight	.40	.30	.15
25	Bill Dawley	.30	.25	.12
26	Dickie Thon	.40	.30	.15
27	Jerry Mumphrey	.30	.25	.12
28	Astros Logo/Checklist	.30	.25	.12

1986 Mother's Cookies Giants

Mother's Cookies produced a fourth annual set for the San Francisco Giants in 1985. Cards in the set measure 2-1/2" by 3-1/2", and the fronts feature unbordered color photos with rounded corners. Card backs are quite similar in format to previous years, with brief biographical information, card numbers, and the Mother's Cookies logo. Card backs are dated 1986. There are 28 cards in the Giants set, with 20 of the cards distributed during a stadium promotion. Each fan also received a coupon redeemable for eight additional cards. The Giants set also includes a card for the manager and a checklist.

		MT	NR MT	EX
Complete Set:		18.00	13.50	7.25
Common Player:		.30	.25	.12
1	Roger Craig	.40	.30	.15
2	Chili Davis	.60	.45	.25
3	Dan Gladden	.40	.30	.15
4	Jeff Leonard	.60	.45	.25
5	Bob Brenly	.40	.30	.15
6	Atlee Hammaker	.40	.30	.15
7	Will Clark	10.00	7.50	4.00
8	Greg Minton	.30	.25	.12
9	Candy Maldonado	.40	.30	.15
10	Vida Blue	.50	.40	.20
11	Mike Krukow	.40	.30	.15
12	Bob Melvin	.40	.30	.15
13	Jose Uribe	.40	.30	.15
14	Dan Driessen	.40	.30	.15
15	Jeff Robinson	.50	.40	.20
16	Rob Thompson	.80	.60	.30
17	Mike LaCoss	.30	.25	.12
18	Chris Brown	.35	.25	.14
19	Scott Garrelts	.50	.40	.20
20	Mark Davis	.50	.40	.20
21	Jim Gott	.30	.25	.12
22	Brad Wellman	.30	.25	.12
23	Roger Mason	.30	.25	.12
24	Bill Laskey	.30	.25	.12
25	Brad Gulden	.30	.25	.12
26	Joel Youngblood	.30	.25	.12
27	Juan Berenguer	.30	.25	.12
28	Coaches/Checklist (Bill Fahey, Bob Lillis, Gordy MacKenzie, Jose Morales, Norm Sherry)	.30	.25	.12

1986 Mother's Cookies Mariners

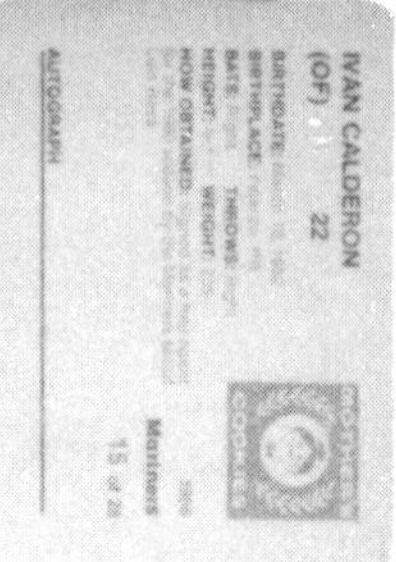

Mother's Cookies produced a third annual set for the Seattle Mariners in 1985. The set measures 2-1/2" by 3-1/2", and card fronts feature unbordered color photos with rounded corners. Card backs are quite similar in format to previous years, with brief biographical information, card numbers and the Mother's Cookies logo. Card backs are dated 1986. There are 28 cards in the Mariners set, with 20 of the cards distributed during a stadium promotion. Each fan also received a coupon redeemable for eight additional cards. The Mariners set also includes a card for the manager and a checklist.

		MT	NR MT	EX
Complete Set:		12.00	9.00	4.75
Common Player:		.30	.25	.12
1	Dick Williams	.30	.25	.12
2	Alvin Davis	1.00	.70	.40
3	Mark Langston	.80	.60	.30
4	Dave Henderson	.50	.40	.20
5	Steve Yeager	.30	.25	.12
6	Al Cowens	.30	.25	.12
7	Jim Presley	.70	.50	.30
8	Phil Bradley	.70	.50	.30
9	Gorman Thomas	.50	.40	.20
10	Barry Bonnell	.30	.25	.12
11	Milt Wilcox	.30	.25	.12
12	Domingo Ramos	.30	.25	.12
13	Paul Mirabella	.30	.25	.12
14	Matt Young	.30	.25	.12
15	Ivan Calderon	.60	.45	.25
16	Bill Swift	.40	.30	.15
17	Pete Ladd	.30	.25	.12
18	Ken Phelps	.40	.30	.15
19	Karl Best	.30	.25	.12
20	Spike Owen	.40	.30	.15
21	Mike Moore	.30	.25	.12
22	Danny Tartabull	1.75	1.25	.70
23	Bob Kearney	.30	.25	.12
24	Edwin Nunez	.30	.25	.12
25	Mike Morgan	.30	.25	.12
26	Roy Thomas	.30	.25	.12
27	Jim Beattie	.30	.25	.12
28	Coaches/Checklist (Deron Johnson, Marty Martinez, Phil Regan, Phil Roof, Ozzie Virgil)	.30	.25	.12

1987 Mother's Cookies A's

Continuing with a tradition of producing beautiful baseball cards, Mother's Cookies of Oakland, Calif. issued a 28-card set featuring every Oakland A's player to have been elected to the All-Star Game since 1968. The full-color photos came from the private collection of nationally known photographer Doug McWilliams. Twenty of the 28 cards were given out to fans attending the A's game of July 5th. An additional eight cards were available by redeeming a mail-in certificate. The cards, which measure 2-1/2" by 3-1/2", feature rounded corners. The card backs carry the player's All-Star Game statistics.

		MT	NR MT	EX
Complete Set:		16.00	12.00	6.50
Common Player:		.30	.25	.12
1	Bert Campaneris	.40	.30	.15
2	Rick Monday	.40	.30	.15
3	John Odom	.30	.25	.12
4	Sal Bando	.40	.30	.15
5	Reggie Jackson	1.50	1.25	.60
6	Jim Hunter	1.00	.70	.40
7	Vida Blue	.50	.40	.20
8	Dave Duncan	.30	.25	.12
9	Joe Rudi	.40	.30	.15
10	Rollie Fingers	.70	.50	.30
11	Ken Holtzman	.40	.30	.15
12	Dick Williams	.40	.30	.15
13	Alvin Dark	.30	.25	.12
14	Gene Tenace	.40	.30	.15
15	Claudell Washington	.40	.30	.15
16	Phil Garner	.30	.25	.12
17	Wayne Gross	.30	.25	.12
18	Matt Keough	.30	.25	.12
19	Jeff Newman	.30	.25	.12
20	Rickey Henderson	1.50	1.25	.60
21	Tony Armas	.40	.30	.15
22	Mike Norris	.30	.25	.12
23	Billy Martin	.50	.40	.20
24	Bill Caudill	.30	.25	.12
25	Jay Howell	.40	.30	.15
26	Jose Canseco	3.00	2.25	1.25
27	Jose and Reggie (Jose Canseco, Reggie Jackson)	2.00	1.50	.80
28	A's Logo/Checklist	.30	.25	.12

1987 Mother's Cookies Astros

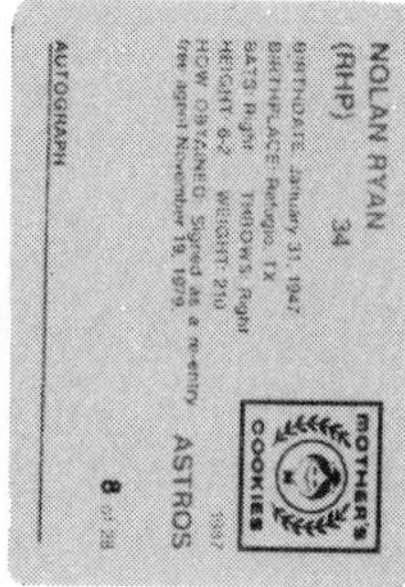

Twenty of 28 cards featuring Astros players were given out to the first 25,000 fans attending the July 17th game at the Astrodome. An additional eight cards (though not necessarily the exact eight needed to complete a set) were available from the card producer, Mother's Cookies, by redeeming a mail-in certificate. The cards have rounded corners and measure the standard 2-1/2" by 3-1/2". The backs are printed in purple and orange and contain personal player information, the Mother's Cookies logo, the card number and a spot for the player's autograph.

		MT	NR MT	EX
Complete Set:		10.00	7.50	4.00
Common Player:		.30	.25	.12
1	Hal Lanier	.30	.25	.12
2	Mike Scott	1.00	.70	.40
3	Jose Cruz	.50	.40	.20
4	Bill Doran	.50	.40	.20
5	Bob Knepper	.40	.30	.15
6	Phil Garner	.40	.30	.15
7	Terry Puhl	.30	.25	.12
8	Nolan Ryan	2.00	1.50	.80
9	Kevin Bass	.50	.40	.20
10	Glenn Davis	1.00	.70	.40
11	Alan Ashby	.30	.25	.12
12	Charlie Kerfeld	.30	.25	.12
13	Denny Walling	.30	.25	.12
14	Danny Darwin	.30	.25	.12
15	Mark Bailey	.30	.25	.12
16	Davey Lopes	.40	.30	.15
17	Dave Meads	.40	.30	.15
18	Aurelio Lopez	.30	.25	.12
19	Craig Reynolds	.30	.25	.12
20	Dave Smith	.40	.30	.15
21	Larry Anderson (Andersen)	.30	.25	.12

		MT	NR MT	EX
22	Jim Pankovits	.30	.25	.12
23	Jim Deshaies	.50	.40	.20
24	Bert Pena	.30	.25	.12
25	Dickie Thon	.30	.25	.12
26	Billy Hatcher	.50	.40	.20
27	Astros Coaches (Yogi Berra, Matt Galante, Denis Menke, Les Moss, Gene Tenace)	.30	.25	.12
28	Houston Astrodome/Checklist	.30	.25	.12

1987 Mother's Cookies Dodgers

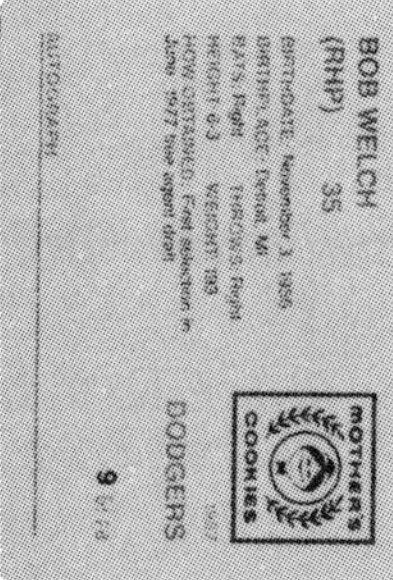

Mother's Cookies produced for the first time in 1987 a baseball card set featuring the Los Angeles Dodgers. Twenty of the 28 cards in the set were given out to youngsters 14 and under at Dodger Stadium on August 9th. An additional eight cards were available from Mother's Cookies via a mail-in coupon card. The borderless, full-color cards measure 2-1/2" by 3-1/2" and have rounded corners. A special album designed to house the set was available for $3.95 through a mail-in offer.

		MT	NR MT	EX
	Complete Set:	10.00	7.50	4.00
	Common Player:	.30	.25	.12
1	Tom Lasorda	.40	.30	.15
2	Pedro Guerrero	.80	.60	.30
3	Steve Sax	.80	.60	.30
4	Fernando Valenzuela	1.00	.70	.40
5	Mike Marshall	.70	.50	.30
6	Orel Hershiser	1.00	.70	.40
7	Mariano Duncan	.30	.25	.12
8	Bill Madlock	.40	.30	.15
9	Bob Welch	.40	.30	.15
10	Mike Scioscia	.40	.30	.15
11	Mike Ramsey	.30	.25	.12
12	Matt Young	.30	.25	.12
13	Franklin Stubbs	.40	.30	.15
14	Tom Niedenfuer	.40	.30	.15
15	Reggie Williams	.40	.30	.15
16	Rick Honeycutt	.30	.25	.12
17	Dave Anderson	.30	.25	.12
18	Alejandro Pena	.40	.30	.15
19	Ken Howell	.30	.25	.12
20	Len Matuszek	.30	.25	.12
21	Tim Leary	.40	.30	.15
22	Tracy Woodson	.40	.30	.15
23	Alex Trevino	.30	.25	.12
24	Ken Landreaux	.30	.25	.12
25	Mickey Hatcher	.30	.25	.12
26	Brian Holton	.40	.30	.15
27	Dodgers' Coaches (Joey Amalfitano, Mark Cresse, Don McMahon, Manny Mota, Ron Perranoski, Bill Russell)	.30	.25	.12
28	Dodger Stadium/Checklist	.30	.25	.12

1987 Mother's Cookies Giants

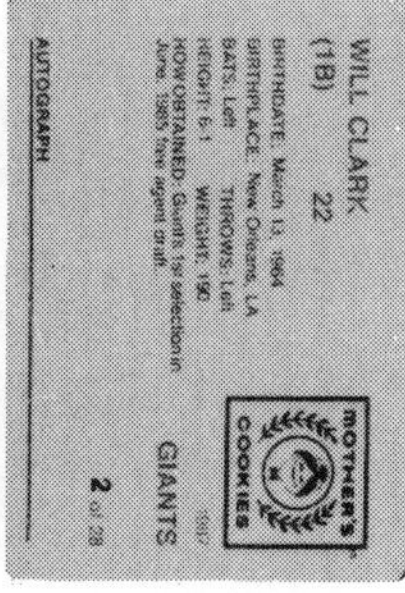

Distribution of the 1987 Mother's Cookies Giants, cards took place at Candlestick Park for the Giants' June 27th game. Twenty of the 28 cards in the set were given to the first 25,000 fans entering the park. The starter packet of 20 cards contained a mail-in coupon card which was good for an additional eight cards. The cards, which measure 2-1/2" by 3-1/2" in size have rounded corners. The card backs are printed in red and purple and contain personal and statistical information along with the Mother's Cookies logo.

		MT	NR MT	EX
	Complete Set:	12.00	9.00	4.75
	Common Player:	.30	.25	.12
1	Roger Craig	.40	.30	.15
2	Will Clark	4.50	3.50	1.75
3	Chili Davis	.40	.30	.15
4	Bob Brenly	.30	.25	.12
5	Chris Brown	.30	.25	.12
6	Mike Krukow	.40	.30	.15
7	Candy Maldonado	.40	.30	.15
8	Jeffrey Leonard	.50	.40	.20
9	Greg Minton	.30	.25	.12
10	Robby Thompson	.40	.30	.15
11	Scott Garrelts	.30	.25	.12
12	Bob Melvin	.30	.25	.12
13	Jose Uribe	.30	.25	.12
14	Mark Davis	.30	.25	.12
15	Eddie Milner	.30	.25	.12
16	Harry Spilman	.30	.25	.12
17	Kelly Downs	.60	.45	.25
18	Chris Speier	.30	.25	.12
19	Jim Gott	.30	.25	.12
20	Joel Youngblood	.30	.25	.12
21	Mike LaCoss	.30	.25	.12
22	Matt Williams	1.75	1.25	.70
23	Roger Mason	.30	.25	.12
24	Mike Aldrete	.60	.45	.25
25	Jeff Robinson	.40	.30	.15
26	Mark Grant	.30	.25	.12
27	Coaches (Bill Fahey, Bob Lillis, Gordon MacKenzie, Jose Morales, Norm Sherry, Don Zimmer)	.30	.25	.12
28	Candlestick Park/Checklist	.30	.25	.12

1987 Mother's Cookies Mariners

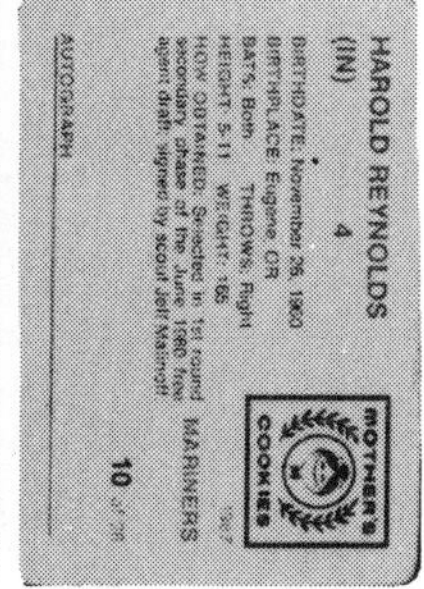

For the fourth consecutive year, Mother's Cookies issued a baseball card set featuring the Seattle Mariners. Twenty of the 28 cards in the set were distributed to the first 20,000 fans entering the Kingdome on August 9th. An additional eight cards (though not necessarily the eight cards needed to complete the set) were available by redeeming a mail-in certificate. Collectors were encouraged to trade to complete a set. The 2-1/2" by 3-1/2" full-color cards feature glossy finishes and rounded corners. A specially designed album to house the set was available.

		MT	NR MT	EX
	Complete Set:	8.00	6.00	3.25
	Common Player:	.30	.25	.12
1	Dick Williams	.30	.25	.12
2	Alvin Davis	.80	.60	.30
3	Mike Moore	.30	.25	.12
4	Jim Presley	.60	.45	.25
5	Mark Langston	.70	.50	.30
6	Phil Bradley	.60	.45	.25
7	Ken Phelps	.40	.30	.15
8	Mike Morgan	.30	.25	.12
9	David Valle	.30	.25	.12
10	Harold Reynolds	.40	.30	.15
11	Edwin Nunez	.30	.25	.12
12	Bob Kearney	.30	.25	.12
13	Scott Bankhead	.40	.30	.15
14	Scott Bradley	.30	.25	.12
15	Mickey Brantley	.40	.30	.15
16	Mark Huismann	.30	.25	.12
17	Mike Kingery	.40	.30	.15
18	John Moses	.30	.25	.12
19	Donell Nixon	.40	.30	.15
20	Rey Quinones	.40	.30	.15
21	Domingo Ramos	.30	.25	.12
22	Jerry Reed	.30	.25	.12
23	Rich Renteria	.40	.30	.15
24	Rich Monteleone	.40	.30	.15
25	Mike Trujillo	.30	.25	.12
26	Bill Wilkinson	.40	.30	.15
27	John Christensen	.30	.25	.12
28	Coaches/Checklist (Billy Connors, Frank Howard, Phil Roof, Bobby Tolan, Ozzie Virgil)	.30	.25	.12

1987 Mother's Cookies Rangers

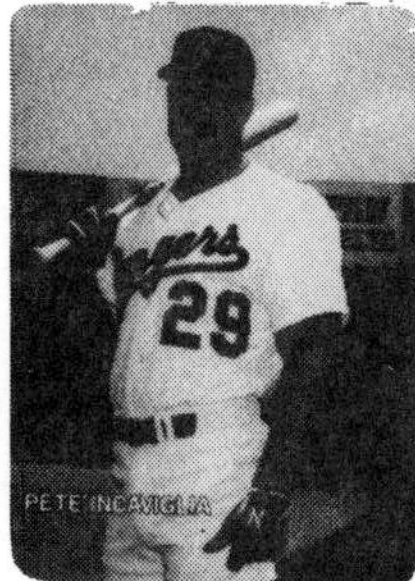

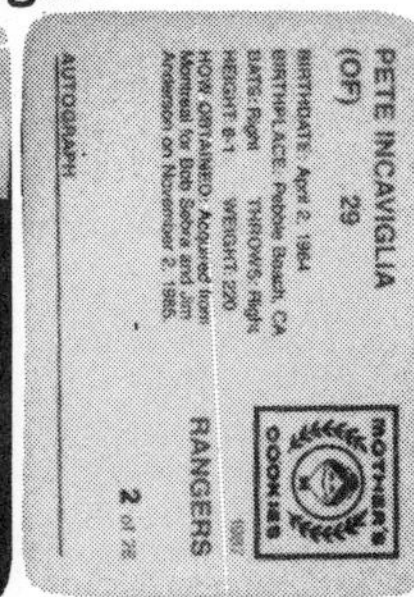

While Mother's Cookies of Oakland, Calif., had been producing high-quality baseball card sets of various teams, the Texas Rangers were highlighted for the first time in 1987. Twenty cards from the 28-card set were handed out to the first 25,000 fans entering Arlington Stadium on July 17th. An additional eight cards (though not necessarily the eight needed to complete a set) were available by redeeming a mail-in certificate. The cards, which measure 2-1/2" by 3-1/2", have rounded corners and glossy finishes like all Mother's Cookies issued in 1987.

		MT	NR MT	EX
	Complete Set:	10.00	7.50	4.00
	Complete Set:	.30	.25	.12
1	Bobby Valentine	.40	.30	.15
2	Pete Incaviglia	1.00	.70	.40
3	Charlie Hough	.40	.30	.15
4	Oddibe McDowell	.50	.40	.20
5	Larry Parrish	.50	.40	.20
6	Scott Fletcher	.40	.30	.15
7	Steve Buechele	.30	.25	.12
8	Tom Paciorek	.30	.25	.12
9	Pete O'Brien	.60	.45	.25
10	Darrell Porter	.30	.25	.12
11	Greg Harris	.30	.25	.12
12	Don Slaught	.30	.25	.12
13	Ruben Sierra	1.75	1.25	.70
14	Curtis Wilkerson	.30	.25	.12
15	Dale Mohorcic	.40	.30	.15
16	Ron Meredith	.30	.25	.12
17	Mitch Williams	.40	.30	.15
18	Bob Brower	.40	.30	.15
19	Edwin Correa	.30	.25	.12
20	Geno Petralli	.30	.25	.12
21	Mike Loynd	.40	.30	.15
22	Jerry Browne	.40	.30	.15
23	Jose Guzman	.50	.40	.20
24	Jeff Kunkel	.30	.25	.12
25	Bobby Witt	.60	.45	.25
26	Jeff Russell	.30	.25	.12
27	Trainers (Danny Wheat, Bill Zeigler)	.30	.25	.12
28	Rangers' Coaches/Checklist (Joe Ferguson, Tim Foli, Tom House, Art Howe, Dave Oliver, Tom Robson)	.30	.25	.12

1987 Mother's Cookies Mark McGwire

A four-card set featuring outstanding rookie Mark McGwire of the Oakland Athletics was produced by Mother's Cookies of Oakland, Calif. Cards are 2-1/2" by 3-1/2" and have rounded corners and glossy finishes like other Mother's issues. The four-card set was obtainable by two methods. A complete set could be received by sending in eight proof-of-purchase seals. Also, sets could be secured at the National Sports Collectors Convention held July 9-12 in San Francisco. Convention goers received one card as a bonus for each Mother's Cookies baseball card album purchased.

	MT	NR MT	EX
Complete Set:	20.00	15.00	8.00
Common Player:	4.00	3.00	1.50

		MT	NR MT	EX
1	Mark McGwire (portrait)	4.00	3.00	1.50
2	Mark McGwire (leaning on bat rack)	4.00	3.00	1.50
3	Mark McGwire (beginning batting swing)	4.00	3.00	1.50
4	Mark McGwire (batting follow-through)	4.00	3.00	1.50

1988 Mother's Cookies A's

Complete at 28 cards (including checklist), the 1988 Mother's Cookies A's set features full-color, borderless cards with rounded corners in the standard 2-1/2" by 3-1/2" size. The backs are printed in red and purple on white and include biographical information, the Mother's Cookies logo and card number. Starter sets of 20 cards were distributed at the stadium along with a promotional card redeemable for another eights cards (not necessarily those needed to complete the set). An album to house the cards was also available.

		MT	NR MT	EX
	Complete Set:	16.00	12.00	6.50
	Common Player:	.30	.25	.12
1	Tony LaRussa	.30	.25	.12
2	Mark McGwire	3.00	2.25	1.25
3	Dave Stewart	.50	.40	.20
4	Mickey Tettleton	.30	.25	.12
5	Dave Parker	.70	.50	.30
6	Carney Lansford	.50	.40	.20
7	Jose Canseco	3.00	2.25	1.25
8	Don Baylor	.50	.40	.20
9	Bob Welch	.40	.30	.15
10	Dennis Eckersley	.40	.30	.15
11	Walt Weiss	1.50	1.25	.60
12	Tony Phillips	.30	.25	.12
13	Steve Ontiveros	.30	.25	.12
14	Dave Henderson	.30	.25	.12
15	Stan Javier	.30	.25	.12
16	Ron Hassey	.30	.25	.12
17	Curt Young	.40	.30	.15
18	Glenn Hubbard	.30	.25	.12
19	Storm Davis	.30	.25	.12
20	Eric Plunk	.30	.25	.12
21	Matt Young	.30	.25	.12
22	Mike Gallego	.30	.25	.12
23	Rick Honeycutt	.30	.25	.12
24	Doug Jennings	.50	.40	.20
25	Gene Nelson	.30	.25	.12
26	Greg Cadaret	.40	.30	.15
27	A's Coaches (Dave Duncan, Rene Lachemann, Jim Lefebvre, Dave McKay, Mike Paul, Bob Watson)	.30	.25	.12
28	Jose Canseco, Mark McGwire	3.00	2.25	1.25

1988 Mother's Cookies Astros

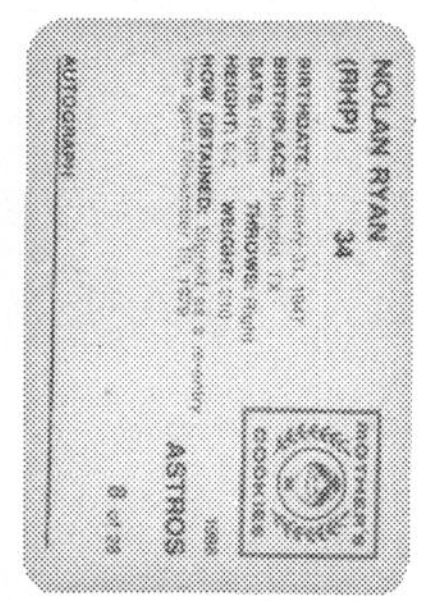

One of six team sets issued by Mother's Cookies in 1988, the 28-card Houston Astros set is similar in design to other Mother's Cookies sets. The cards are the standard 2-1/2" by 3-1/2" size with rounded corners and feature full-color, borderless photos on the fronts with the player's name in an upper or lower corner. The backs feature red and purple printing on white and include brief biographical information, the Mother's logo and card number. Twenty of the cards were distributed in a stadium promotion, along with a redemption card that could be exchanged for an additional eight cards (but not necessarily the eight needed to complete the set.) An album was also available to house the set.

		MT	NR MT	EX
	Complete Set:	10.00	7.50	4.00
	Common Player:	.30	.25	.12
1	Hal Lanier	.30	.25	.12
2	Mike Scott	.90	.70	.35
3	Gerald Young	.70	.50	.30
4	Bill Doran	.50	.40	.20
5	Bob Knepper	.40	.30	.15
6	Billy Hatcher	.50	.40	.20
7	Terry Puhl	.30	.25	.12
8	Nolan Ryan	1.50	1.25	.60
9	Kevin Bass	.50	.40	.20
10	Glenn Davis	.90	.70	.35
11	Alan Ashby	.30	.25	.12
12	Steve Henderson	.30	.25	.12
13	Denny Walling	.30	.25	.12
14	Danny Darwin	.30	.25	.12
15	Mark Bailey	.30	.25	.12
16	Ernie Camacho	.30	.25	.12
17	Rafael Ramirez	.30	.25	.12
18	Jeff Heathcock	.30	.25	.12
19	Craig Reynolds	.30	.25	.12
20	Dave Smith	.40	.30	.15
21	Larry Andersen	.30	.25	.12
22	Jim Pankovits	.30	.25	.12
23	Jim Deshaies	.40	.30	.15
24	Juan Agosto	.30	.25	.12
25	Chuck Jackson	.40	.30	.15
26	Joaquin Andujar	.40	.30	.15
27	Astros Coaches (Yogi Berra, Gene Clines, Matt Galante, Marc Hill, Denis Menke, Les Moss)	.30	.25	.12
28	Trainers Card/Checklist (Doc Ewell, Dave Labossiere, Dennis Liborio)	.30	.25	.12

1988 Mother's Cookies Dodgers

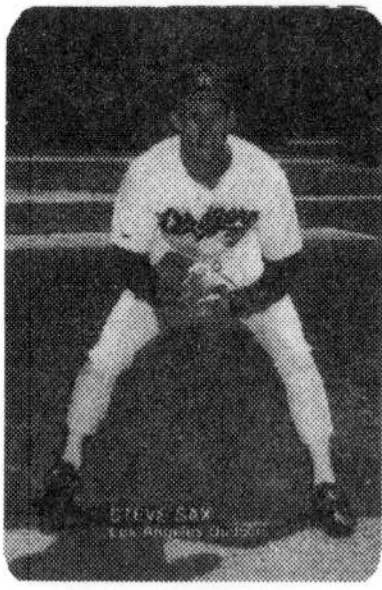

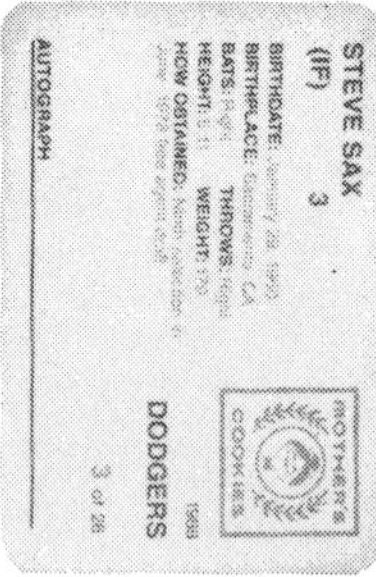

Similar in design to other Mother's Cookies sets, the 1988 Dodgers issue featured full-color, borderless photos with backs printed in red and purple. The 28 cards in the set measure the standard 2-1/2" by 3-1/2" with rounded corners. Starter packs of 20 cards were distributed at a ballpark promotion along with a coupon card that could be exchanged for an additional eight cards at a local card show or through the mail. The backs of the cards include brief player information, the Mother's Cookies logo and card number. The promotion also included a special album to house the set.

		MT	NR MT	EX
	Complete Set:	10.00	7.50	4.00
	Common Player:	.30	.25	.12
1	Tom Lasorda	.40	.30	.15
2	Pedro Guerrero	.80	.60	.30
3	Steve Sax	.80	.60	.30
4	Fernando Valenzuela	1.00	.70	.40
5	Mike Marshall	.70	.50	.30
6	Orel Hershiser	1.00	.70	.40
7	Alfredo Griffin	.30	.25	.12
8	Kirk Gibson	1.00	.70	.40
9	Don Sutton	.50	.40	.20
10	Mike Scioscia	.40	.30	.15
11	Franklin Stubbs	.40	.30	.15
12	Mike Davis	.40	.30	.15
13	Jesse Orosco	.40	.30	.15
14	John Shelby	.30	.25	.12
15	Rick Dempsey	.40	.30	.15
16	Jay Howell	.40	.30	.15
17	Dave Anderson	.30	.25	.12
18	Alejandro Pena	.40	.30	.15
19	Jeff Hamilton	.40	.30	.15
20	Danny Heep	.30	.25	.12
21	Tim Leary	.40	.30	.15
22	Brad Havens	.30	.25	.12
23	Tim Belcher	.60	.45	.25
24	Ken Howell	.30	.25	.12
25	Mickey Hatcher	.30	.25	.12
26	Brian Holton	.30	.25	.12
27	Mike Devereaux	.60	.45	.25
28	Dodgers Coaches/Checklist (Joe Amalfitano, Mark Cresse, Joe Ferguson, Ben Hines, Manny Mota, Ron Perranoski, Bill Russell)	.30	.25	.12

1988 Mother's Cookies Giants

One of six team sets issued in 1988 by Mother's Cookies, this 28-card Giants set featured full-color borderless photos on a standard-size card with rounded corners. The backs, printed in red and purple, include brief player information, the Mother's Cookies logo and card number. Twenty different cards were distributed as a starter set at a stadium promotion along with a coupon card that could be redeemed for an additional eight cards (not necessarily those needed to complete the set). The redemption cards could be exchanged through the mail or redeemed at a local card show.

		MT	NR MT	EX
	Complete Set:	12.00	9.00	4.75
	Common Player:	.30	.25	.12
1	Roger Craig	.40	.30	.15
2	Will Clark	3.50	2.75	1.50
3	Kevin Mitchell	1.50	1.25	.60
4	Bob Brenly	.40	.30	.15
5	Mike Aldrete	.40	.30	.15
6	Mike Krukow	.40	.30	.15
7	Candy Maldonado	.40	.30	.15
8	Jeffrey Leonard	.40	.30	.15
9	Dave Dravecky	.40	.30	.15
10	Robby Thompson	.40	.30	.15
11	Scott Garrelts	.30	.25	.12
12	Bob Melvin	.30	.25	.12
13	Jose Uribe	.30	.25	.12
14	Brett Butler	.40	.30	.15
15	Rick Reuschel	.50	.40	.20
16	Harry Spilman	.30	.25	.12
17	Kelly Downs	.50	.40	.20
18	Chris Speier	.30	.25	.12
19	Atlee Hammaker	.30	.25	.12
20	Joel Youngblood	.30	.25	.12
21	Mike LaCoss	.30	.25	.12
22	Don Robinson	.30	.25	.12
23	Mark Wasinger	.40	.30	.15
24	Craig Lefferts	.30	.25	.12
25	Phil Garner	.30	.25	.12
26	Joe Price	.30	.25	.12
27	Giants Coaches (Dusty Baker, Bill Fahey, Bob Lillis, Gordie MacKenzie, Jose Morales, Norm Sherry)	.30	.25	.12
28	Logo Card/Checklist	.30	.25	.12

1988 Mother's Cookies Mariners

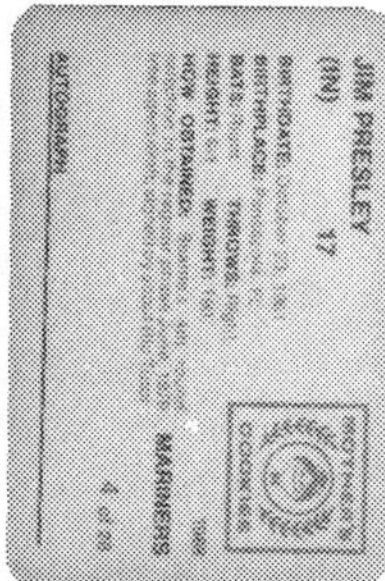

Similar in design to other Mother's Cookies sets, the 28-card Mariners issue featured full-color, borderless photos on a standard-size card with rounded corners. The backs, printed in red and purple, included brief biographical information, the Mother's Cookies logo and card number. Twenty-card starter packs were distributed at a stadium promotion, where fans also received a coupon card that could be exchanged for an additional eight cards (not necessarily those needed to complete the set). The coupon card could be redeemed through the mail or exchanged at a local baseball card show. As with the rest of the 1988 Mother's Cookies sets, an album was also available to house the cards.

		MT	NR MT	EX
Complete Set:		8.00	6.00	3.25
Common Player:		.30	.25	.12
1	Dick Williams	.30	.25	.12
2	Alvin Davis	.70	.50	.30
3	Mike Moore	.30	.25	.12
4	Jim Presley	.50	.40	.20
5	Mark Langston	.60	.45	.25
6	Henry Cotto	.30	.25	.12
7	Ken Phelps	.40	.30	.15
8	Steve Trout	.30	.25	.12
9	David Valle	.30	.25	.12
10	Harold Reynolds	.40	.30	.15
11	Edwin Nunez	.30	.25	.12
12	Glenn Wilson	.30	.25	.12
13	Scott Bankhead	.30	.25	.12
14	Scott Bradley	.30	.25	.12
15	Mickey Brantley	.30	.25	.12
16	Bruce Fields	.30	.25	.12
17	Mike Kingery	.30	.25	.12
18	Mike Campbell	.50	.40	.20
19	Mike Jackson	.40	.30	.15
20	Rey Quinones	.30	.25	.12
21	Mario Diaz	.30	.25	.12
22	Jerry Reed	.30	.25	.12
23	Rich Renteria	.30	.25	.12
24	Julio Solano	.30	.25	.12
25	Bill Swift	.30	.25	.12
26	Bill Wilkinson	.30	.25	.12
27	Mariners Coaches (Billy Connors, Frank Howard, Phil Roof, Jim Snyder, Ozzie Virgil)	.30	.25	.12
28	Trainers Card/Checklist (Henry Genzale, Rick Griffin)	.30	.25	.12

1988 Mother's Cookies Rangers

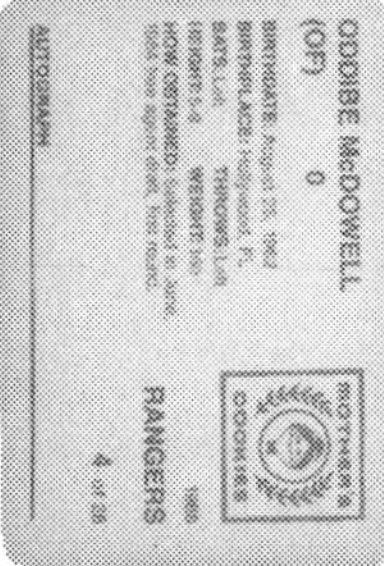

This 28-card set featuring the Texas Rangers was one of six team sets issued in 1988 by Mother's Cookies. Similar to other Mother's Cookies sets, the Rangers issue features full-color, borderless cards printed in the standard 2-1/2" by 3-1/2" format with rounded corners. The backs were printed in red and purple on white and included player information, the Mother's Cookies logo and card number. Twenty-card starter packs were distributed at a stadium promotion that included a redemption card good for another eight cards (not necessarily those needed to complete the set) either through the mail or at a local card show.

		MT	NR MT	EX
Complete Set:		8.00	6.00	3.25
Common Player:		.30	.25	.12
1	Bobby Valentine	.40	.30	.15
2	Pete Incaviglia	.70	.50	.30
3	Charlie Hough	.40	.30	.15
4	Oddibe McDowell	.50	.40	.20
5	Larry Parrish	.50	.40	.20
6	Scott Fletcher	.40	.30	.15
7	Steve Buechele	.40	.30	.15
8	Steve Kemp	.40	.30	.15
9	Pete O'Brien	.60	.45	.25
10	Ruben Sierra	.90	.70	.35
11	Mike Stanley	.50	.40	.20
12	Jose Cecena	.40	.30	.15
13	Cecil Espy	.40	.30	.15
14	Curtis Wilkerson	.30	.25	.12
15	Dale Mohorcic	.30	.25	.12
16	Ray Hayward	.30	.25	.12
17	Mitch Williams	.40	.30	.15
18	Bob Brower	.30	.25	.12
19	Paul Kilgus	.40	.30	.15
20	Geno Petralli	.30	.25	.12
21	James Steels	.30	.25	.12
22	Jerry Browne	.30	.25	.12
23	Jose Guzman	.40	.30	.15
24	DeWayne Vaughn	.40	.30	.15
25	Bobby Witt	.50	.40	.20
26	Jeff Russell	.30	.25	.12
27	Rangers Coaches (Richard Egan, Tom House, Art Howe, Davey Lopes, David Oliver, Tom Robson)	.30	.25	.12
28	Trainers Card/Checklist (Danny Wheat, Bill Zeigler)	.30	.25	.12

1988 Mother's Cookies Will Clark

In a baseball spring training-related promotion, Mother's Cookies of Oakland, Calif. produced a full-color four-card set featuring San Francisco Giants first baseman Will Clark. The cards, which have glossy finishes and rounded corners, came cellophane- wrapped in specially marked 18-ounce packages of Mother's Cookies products. The cards are identical in style to the regular Mother's Cookies issues.

		MT	NR MT	EX
Complete Set:		16.00	12.00	6.50
Common Player:		4.00	3.00	1.50
1	Will Clark (bat on shoulder)	4.00	3.00	1.50
2	Will Clark (kneeling)	4.00	3.00	1.50
3	Will Clark (batting follow-thru)	4.00	3.00	1.50
4	Will Clark (heading for first base)	4.00	3.00	1.50

1988 Mother's Cookies Mark McGwire

For the second consecutive year, Mother's Cookies devoted a four-card set to Oakland A's slugger Mark McGwire. The full-color cards have rounded corners and measure 2-1/2" by 3-1/2" in size. The cards were issued in specially marked 18-ounce packages of Mother's Cookies products in the northern California area. The cards are identical in design to the regular team issues produced by Mother's.

		MT	NR MT	EX
Complete Set:		15.00	11.00	6.00
Common Player:		3.00	2.25	1.25
1	Mark McGwire (holding oversized bat)	3.00	2.25	1.25
2	Mark McGwire (fielding)	3.00	2.25	1.25
3	Mark McGwire (kneeling)	3.00	2.25	1.25
4	Mark McGwire (bat in air)	3.00	2.25	1.25

1989 Mother's Cookies A's

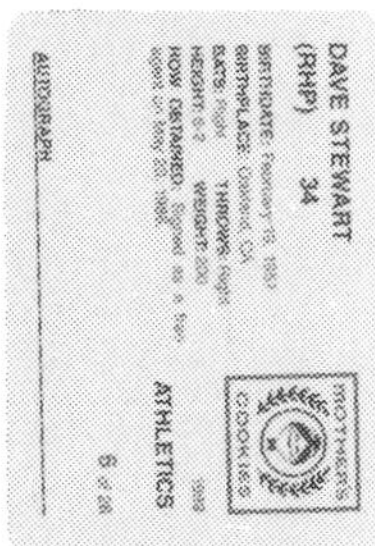

The 1989 Mother's Cookies A's set consists of 28 cards designed in the traditional style: a glossy card with a borderless photo and rounded corners. A starter set of the cards was used as a stadium promotion and distributed to fans attending the July 30 Oakland game.

		MT	NR MT	EX
Complete Set:		12.00	9.00	4.75
Common Player:		.30	.25	.12
1	Tony LaRussa	.30	.25	.12
2	Mark McGwire	2.75	2.00	1.00
3	Terry Steinbach	.60	.45	.25
4	Dave Parker	.60	.45	.25
5	Carney Lansford	.50	.40	.20
6	Dave Stewart	.50	.40	.20
7	Jose Canseco	3.00	2.25	1.25
8	Walt Weiss	.50	.40	.20
9	Bob Welch	.40	.30	.15
10	Dennis Eckersley	.40	.30	.15
11	Tony Phillips	.30	.25	.12
12	Mike Moore	.50	.40	.20
13	Dave Henderson	.30	.25	.12
14	Curt Young	.30	.25	.12
15	Ron Hassey	.30	.25	.12
16	Eric Plunk	.30	.25	.12
17	Luis Polonia	.30	.25	.12
18	Storm Davis	.30	.25	.12
19	Glenn Hubbard	.30	.25	.12
20	Greg Cadaret	.30	.25	.12
21	Stan Javier	.30	.25	.12
22	Felix Jose	.40	.30	.15
23	Mike Gallego	.30	.25	.12
24	Todd Burns	.30	.25	.12
25	Rick Honeycutt	.30	.25	.12
26	Gene Nelson	.30	.25	.12
27	A's Coaches (Dave Duncan, Rene Lachemann, Art Kusnyer, Tommie Reynolds, Merv Rettenmund)	.30	.25	.12
28	Walt Wiess, Mark McGwire & Jose Canseco	.70	.50	.30

1989 Mother's Cookies A's Rookies

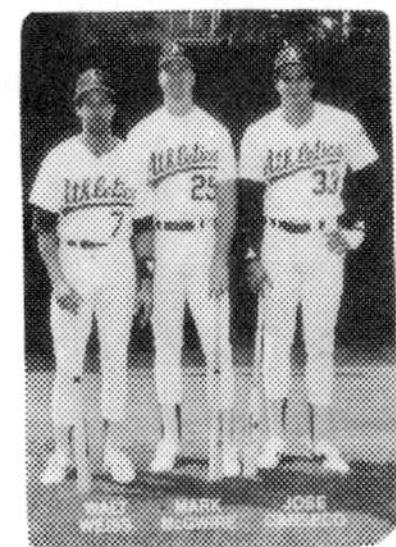

This four-card set features the American League Rookies of the Year for 1986, 1987 and 1988, all members of the Oakland A's. The 2-1/2" by 3-1/2" cards feature full color photos in the traditional Mother's Cookies style. One card was devoted to each player along with a special card showcasing all three players, Weiss, McGwire and Canseco, together. The cards were distributed one per box in Mother's Cookies.

		MT	NR MT	EX
Complete Set:		10.00	7.50	4.00
Common Player:		2.00	1.50	.80
1	Jose Canseco	3.50	2.75	1.50
2	Mark McGwire	3.00	2.25	1.25
3	Walt Weiss	2.00	1.50	.80
4	Walt Weiss, Mark McGwire, & Jose Canseco	3.00	2.25	1.25

1989 Mother's Cookies Astros

The 1989 Houston Astros team set issued by Mother's Cookies consisted of 28 cards designed in the traditional style of borderless photos and rounded corners. Partial sets were distributed to fans attending the July 22 Astros game at the Houston Astrodome. The cards feature the photography of Barry Colla and display the Mother's Cookies logo on the back.

		MT	NR MT	EX
Complete Set:		10.00	7.50	4.00
Common Player:		.30	.25	.12
1	Art Howe	.30	.25	.12
2	Mike Scott	.90	.70	.25
3	Gerald Young	.50	.40	.20
4	Bill Doran	.50	.40	.20
5	Billy Hatcher	.50	.40	.20
6	Terry Puhl	.30	.25	.12
7	Bob Knepper	.30	.25	.12
8	Kevin Bass	.50	.40	.20
9	Glenn Davis	.90	.70	.35
10	Alann Ashby	.30	.25	.12
11	Bob Forsch	.30	.25	.12
12	Greg Gross	.30	.25	.12
13	Danny Darwin	.30	.25	.12
14	Craig Biggio	1.00	.70	.40

		MT	NR MT	EX
15	Jim Clancy	.30	.25	.12
16	Rafael Ramirez	.30	.25	.12
17	Alex Trevino	.30	.25	.12
18	Craig Reynolds	.30	.25	.12
19	Dave Smith	.40	.30	.15
20	Larry Andersen	.30	.25	.12
21	Eric Yelding	.60	.45	.25
22	Jim Deshaies	.40	.30	.15
23	Juan Agosto	.30	.25	.12
24	Rick Rhoden	.30	.25	.12
25	Ken Caminiti	.60	.45	.25
26	Dave Meads	.30	.25	.12
27	Astro Coaches (Yogi Berra, Matt Galante, Phil Garner, Les Moss, Ed Napoleon, Ed Ott)	.30	.25	.12
28	Trainers Card/Checklist (Dave Labossiere, Doc Ewell Equip. Mgr.- Dennis Liborio)	.30	.25	.12

The values quoted are intended to reflect the market price.

1989 Mother's Cookies Dodgers

This 28-card set features the players and coaching staff of the Los Angeles Dodgers. The cards follow the traditional Mother's Cookies style featuring rounded corners, borderless color photos, horizontal backs and are 2-1/2" by 3-1/2" in size. Initially twenty cards were given away as starter sets at Dodger Stadium.

		MT	NR MT	EX
	Complete Set:	8.00	6.00	3.25
	Common Player:	.30	.15	.03
1	Tom Lasorda	.40	.30	.15
2	Eddie Murray	.60	.45	.25
3	Mike Scioscia	.40	.30	.15
4	Fernando Valenzuela	.60	.45	.25
5	Mike Marshall	.50	.40	.20
6	Orel Hershiser	.80	.60	.30
7	Alfredo Griffin	.35	.25	.14
8	Kirk Gibson	.70	.50	.30
9	John Tudor	.40	.30	.15
10	Willie Randolph	.40	.30	.15
11	Franklin Stubbs	.30	.25	.12
12	Mike Davis	.30	.25	.12
13	Mike Morgan	.30	.25	.12
14	John Shelby	.30	.25	.12
15	Rick Dempsey	.30	.25	.12
16	Jay Howell	.40	.30	.15
17	Dave Anderson	.30	.25	.12
18	Alejandro Pena	.35	.25	.14
19	Jeff Hamilton	.35	.25	.14
20	Ricky Horton	.30	.25	.12
21	Tim Leary	.40	.30	.15
22	Ray Searage	.30	.25	.12
23	Tim Belcher	.70	.50	.30
24	Tim Crews	.30	.25	.12
25	Mickey Hatcher	.30	.25	.12
26	Mariano Duncan	.35	.25	.14
27	Coaches Card	.30	.25	.12
28	Checklist	.30	.25	.12

1989 Mother's Cookies Giants

The 1989 Mother's Cookies Giants set consists of 28 cards, all featuring borderless, color photos with rounded corners. Starter sets of the cards were distributed as a stadium promotion to fans attending the Aug. 6, 1989, Giants game at Candlestick Park.

		MT	NR MT	EX
	Complete Set:	12.00	9.00	4.75
	Common Player:	.30	.25	.12
1	Roger Craig	.40	.30	.15
2	Will Clark	1.25	.90	.50
3	Kevin Mitchell	1.00	.70	.40
4	Kelly Downs	.35	.25	.14
5	Brett Butler	.40	.30	.15
6	Mike Krukow	.30	.25	.12
7	Candy Maldonado	.30	.25	.12
8	Terry Kennedy	.30	.25	.12
9	Dave Dravecky	.40	.30	.15
10	Robby Thompson	.40	.30	.15
11	Scott Garrelts	.40	.30	.15
12	Matt Williams	.70	.50	.30
13	Jose Uribe	.30	.25	.12
14	Tracy Jones	.30	.25	.12
15	Rick Reuschel	.40	.30	.15
16	Ernest Riles	.30	.25	.12
17	Jeff Brantley	.50	.40	.20
18	Chris Speier	.30	.25	.12
19	Atlee Hammaker	.30	.25	.12
20	Ed Jurak	.30	.25	.12
21	Mike LaCoss	.30	.25	.12
22	Don Robinson	.30	.25	.12
23	Kirt Manwaring	.50	.40	.20
24	Craig Lefferts	.30	.25	.12
25	Donnell Nixon	.30	.25	.12
26	Joe Price	.30	.25	.12
27	Rich Gossage	.30	.25	.12
28	Coaches/Checklist (Bill Fahey, Dusty Baker, Bob Lillis, Wendell Kim, Norm Sherry)	.30	.25	.12

Regional interest may affect the value of a card.

1989 Mother's Cookies Mariners

For the sixth straight season Mother's Cookies released a set of the Seattle Mariners. The 1989 issue features 28 cards. Starter sets featuring 20 cards were distribted at a Mariner home game. The cards are 2-1/2" by 3-1/2" in size and feature borderless full color photos. The card backs are printed horizontally. Rookie sensation Ken Griffey Jr. was included in the 1989 issue.

		MT	NR MT	EX
	Complete Set:	10.00	7.50	4.00
	Common Player:	.30	.25	.12
1	Jim Lefebvre	.30	.25	.12
2	Alvin Davis	.50	.40	.20
3	Ken Griffey, Jr.	5.00	3.75	2.00
4	Jim Presley	.50	.40	.20
5	Mark Langston	.70	.50	.30
6	Henry Cotto	.30	.25	.12
7	Mickey Brantley	.30	.25	.12
8	Jeffrey Leonard	.70	.50	.30
9	Dave Valle	.35	.25	.14
10	Harold Reynolds	.70	.50	.30
11	Edgar Martinez	.40	.30	.15
12	Tom Niedenfuer	.30	.25	.12
13	Scott Bankhead	.50	.40	.20
14	Scott Bradley	.35	.25	.14
15	Omar Vizquel	.40	.30	.15
16	Erik Hanson,			
17	Bill Swift	.40	.30	.15
18	Mike Campbell	.30	.25	.12
19	Mike Jackson	.35	.25	.14
20	Rich Renteria	.30	.25	.12
21	Mario Diaz	.30	.25	.12
22	Jerry Reed	.30	.25	.12
23	Darnell Coles	.35	.25	.14
24	Steve Trout	.30	.25	.12
25	Mike Schooler	.60	.45	.25
26	Julio Solano	.30	.25	.12
27	Coaches Card	.30	.25	.12
28	Checklist	.30	.25	.12

1989 Mother's Cookies Rangers

The 1989 Mother's Cookies Rangers team set featured the traditional borderless photos and rounded corners. The standard-size set consisted of 28 cards featuring the photography of Barry Colla. Partial sets were distributed to fans attending the July 30, 1989 game at Arlington Stadium.

		MT	NR MT	EX
	Complete Set:	9.00	6.75	3.50
	Common Player:	.30	.25	.12
1	Bobby Valentine	.40	.30	.15
2	Nolan Ryan	1.50	1.25	.60
3	Julio Franco	.70	.50	.30
4	Charlie Hough	.40	.30	.15
5	Rafael Palmeiro	.70	.50	.30
6	Jeff Russell	.30	.25	.12
7	Ruben Sierra	.90	.70	.35
8	Steve Buechele	.30	.25	.12
9	Buddy Bell	.40	.30	.15
10	Pete Incaviglia	.40	.30	.15
11	Geno Petralli	.30	.25	.12
12	Cecil Espy	.40	.30	.15
13	Scott Fletcher	.30	.25	.12
14	Bobby Witt	.30	.25	.12
15	Brad Arnsberg	.40	.30	.15
16	Rick Leach	.30	.25	.12
17	Jamie Moyer	.40	.30	.15
18	Kevin Brown	.50	.40	.20
19	Jeff Kunkel	.30	.25	.12
20	Craig McMurtry	.30	.25	.12
21	Kenny Rogers	.50	.40	.20
22	Mike Stanley	.30	.25	.12
23	Cecilio Guante	.50	.40	.20
24	Jim Sundberg	.50	.40	.20
25	Jose Guzman	.50	.40	.20
26	Jeff Stone	.50	.40	.20
27	Rangers Coaches (Dick Egan, Tom Robson, Toby Harrah, Dave Oliver, Tom House, Dave Lopes)	.30	.25	.12
28	Trainers Card/checklist (Bill Ziegler, Danny Wheat)	.30	.25	.12

1989 Mother's Cookies Jose Canseco

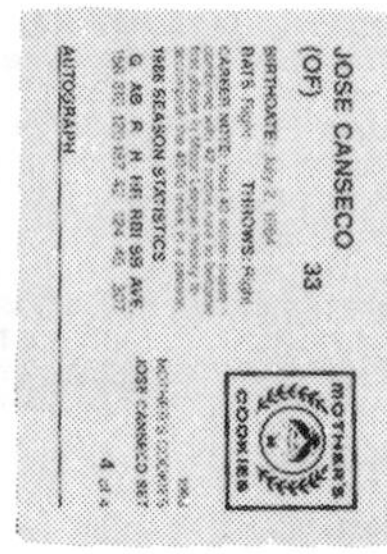

This special insert 4-card glossy set features Canseco in two posed (one standing, one kneeling) and two action (one batting, one running) shots. Full-color card fronts have rounded corners. Flip sides are numbered, printed in red and purple, and carry 1988 stats and career notes. Cards are individually cello-wrapped and inserted in Mother's Fudge 'N Chips, Oatmeal Raisin and Cocadas cookie bags.

		MT	NR MT	EX
	Complete Set:	15.00	11.00	6.00
	Common Player:	3.00	2.25	1.25
1	Jose Canseco (ball in hand)	3.00	2.25	1.25
2	Jose Canseco (on one knee grasping bat)	3.00	2.25	1.25
3	Jose Canseco (swinging-in act.	3.00	2.25	1.25
4	Jose Canseco (baserunning)	3.00	2.25	1.25

1989 Mother's Cookies Will Clark

Will Clark is featured on a special-edition glossy 4-card set inserted in Mother's big bag chocolate chip cookies. The standard-size (2-1/2" by 3-1/2") cards feature Clark in two posed (batting and catching) and two action (batting and running) shots. Purple and red backs (numbered) list 1986-88 stats.

		MT	NR MT	EX
Complete Set:		10.00	7.50	4.00
Common Player:		2.00	1.50	.80
1	Will Clark (displaying ball in glove)	2.00	1.50	.80
2	Will Clark (batting stance)	2.00	1.50	.80
3	Will Clark (in action-after swing)	2.00	1.50	.80
4	Will Clark (heading towards first)	2.00	1.50	.80

1989 Mother's Cookies Ken Griffey Jr.

KEN GRIFFEY, JR.
(OF)
24
MOTHER'S COOKIES
AUTOGRAPH

This four-card set featuring Ken Griffey, Jr. was issued by Mother's Cookies and was available only in cookie packages in the states of Washington and Oregon. The cards were also available at a Seattle Mariners Kingdome Baseball Card Show on Aug. 20, 1989, where the set was introduced. The cards were then packed inside specially-marked bags of cookies, one card per bag. The cards display the traditional Mother's Cookie's design: glossy, borderless cards with rounded corners.

		MT	NR MT	EX
Complete Set:		16.00	12.00	6.50
Common Player:		3.50	2.75	1.50
1	Ken Griffey, Jr. (arms folded)	3.50	2.75	1.50
2	Ken Griffey, Jr. (ball in hand)	3.50	2.75	1.50
3	Ken Griffey, Jr. (bat over left shoulder)	3.50	2.75	1.50
4	Ken Griffey, Jr. (back of jersey showing)	3.50	2.75	1.50

1989 Mother's Cookies Mark McGwire

This special edition 4-card set features full-color glossy player photos by Barry Colla on standard-size (2-1/2" by 3-1/2") cards with rounded corners. Photos feature four different batting poses. Numbered flip sides, printed in purple and red, carry 1987 and 1988 statistics. Cards are individually cello-wrapped and inserted in Mother's Cookie Parade variety cookie bags.

		MT	NR MT	EX
Complete Set:		15.00	11.00	6.00
Common Player:		3.00	2.25	1.25
1	Mark McGwire (bat on shoulder)	3.00	2.25	1.25
2	Mark McGwire (batting stance)	3.00	2.25	1.25
3	Mark McGwire (bat in front)	3.00	2.25	1.25
4	Mark McGwire (batting follow through)	3.00	2.25	1.25

1887 N28 Allen & Ginter

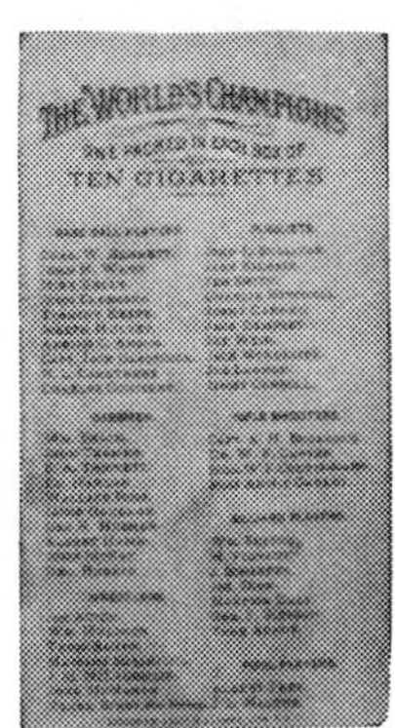

Generally considered the first of the tobacco card issues, this 50-card set was titled "The World Champions" and included 10 baseball players and 40 other sports personalities such as John L. Sullivan and Buffalo Bill Cody. The 1-1/2" by 2-3/4" cards were inserted in boxes of Allen & Ginter cigarettes. The card fronts are color lithographs on white card stock, and are considered among the most attractive cards ever produced. All card backs have a complete checklist for this unnumbered set, which includes six eventual Hall of Famers (Cap Anson, John Clarkson, Charles Comiskey, Timothy Keefe, Mike Kelly and John Ward). Eight of the 10 players shown are from the National League and the other two from the American Association, then also considered a major league.

		NR MT	EX	VG
Complete Set:		16475.	6500.	3500.
Common Player:		450.00	200.00	90.00
(1)	Adrian C. Anson	3000.	1250.	500.00
(2)	Chas. W. Bennett	450.00	200.00	90.00
(3)	R.L. Caruthers	600.00	250.00	95.00
(4)	John Clarkson	1500.	600.00	250.00
(5)	Charles Comiskey	2000.	800.00	350.00
(6)	Capt. John Glasscock	450.00	200.00	90.00
(7)	Timothy Keefe	1750.	625.00	260.00
(8)	Mike Kelly	2500.	1050.	400.00
(9)	Joseph Mulvey	500.00	225.00	90.00
(10)	John M. Ward	1700.	775.00	300.00

1888 N29 Allen & Ginter

After their 1887 first series of tobacco cards proved a success, Allen & Ginter issued a second series of "World Champions" in 1888. Once again, 50 of these 1-1/2" by 2-3/4" color cards were produced, in virtually the same style as the year before. Only six baseball players are included in this set, with New York Giants catcher Buck Ewing the only player of note. The most obvious difference from the 1887 cards is the absence of the Allen & Ginter name on the card fronts. All six baseball players are from National League teams.

		NR MT	EX	VG
Complete Set:		17000.	7500.	3300.
Common Player:		1500.	700.00	275.00
(1)	Wm. Ewing	7500.	3000.	1500.
(2)	Jas. H. Fogarty (middle initial actually G.)	1500.	700.00	275.00
(3)	Charles H. Getzin (Getzein)	1500.	700.00	275.00
(4)	Geo. F. Miller	1500.	700.00	275.00
(5)	John Morrell (Morrill)	1500.	700.00	275.00
(6)	James Ryan	1500.	700.00	275.00

1888 N135 Talk of the Diamond

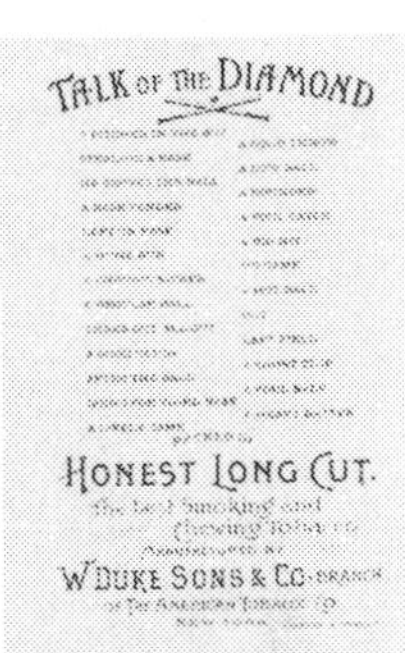

One of the more obscure 19th Century tobacco issues is a 25-card set issued by Honest Long Cut Tobacco in the late 1880's. Titled "Talk of the Diamond," the set features full-color cards measuring 4-1/8" by 2-1/2". Each card features a cartoon-like drawing illustrating a popular baseball term or expression. The left portion of the card pictures an unspecified player in a fielding position, and some of the artwork for that part of the set was borrowed from the more popular Buchner Gold Coin set (N284) issued about the same time. Because the "Talk of the Diamond" set does not feature individual players it has never really captured the attention of baseball card collectors. It does, however, hold interest as a novelty item of the period. It carries an N135 American Card Catalog designation.

		NR MT	EX	VG
Complete Set:		875.00	437.00	262.00
Common Player:		35.00	17.50	10.50
(1)	A Base Tender	35.00	17.50	10.50
(2)	A Big Hit	35.00	17.50	10.50
(3)	A Chronic Kicker	35.00	17.50	10.50
(4)	A Foul Balk	35.00	17.50	10.50
(5)	A Foul Catch	35.00	17.50	10.50
(6)	A Good Catch	35.00	17.50	10.50
(7)	A Good Throw	35.00	17.50	10.50
(8)	A Heavy Batter	35.00	17.50	10.50
(9)	A Home Run	35.00	17.50	10.50
(10)	A Hot Ball	35.00	17.50	10.50
(11)	A Low Ball	35.00	17.50	10.50
(12)	A Pitcher in the Box	35.00	17.50	10.50
(13)	A Regular Ball	35.00	17.50	10.50
(14)	A Rounder	35.00	17.50	10.50
(15)	A Short Stop	35.00	17.50	10.50
(16)	After the Ball	35.00	17.50	10.50
(17)	Going for Third Base	35.00	17.50	10.50
(18)	He Serves the Ball	35.00	17.50	10.50
(19)	Left Field	35.00	17.50	10.50
(20)	Left on Base	35.00	17.50	10.50
(21)	Lively Game	35.00	17.50	10.50
(22)	No Game	35.00	17.50	10.50
(23)	Out	35.00	17.50	10.50
(24)	Stealing a Base	35.00	17.50	10.50
(25)	Three out-All out	35.00	17.50	10.50

1893 N142 Duke Cabinets

These color cabinet cards, which measure 6" x 9-1/2", were produced by W.H. Duke sometime between 1893 and 1895. The player name is centered at the bottom of the card front. The brand name "Honest" is located in the lower left corner with the words "New York" in the lower right corner. Three cyclists are also part of the set.

		NR MT	EX	VG
Complete Set:		14500.	7250.	4250.
Common Player:		3000.	1500.	900.00
(1)	G.S. Davis	3000.	1500.	900.00
(2)	E.J. Delehanty	4000.	2000.	1250.
(3)	W.M. Nash	3000.	1500.	900.00
(4)	W. Robinson	4500.	2250.	1350.

1888 N162 Goodwin Champions

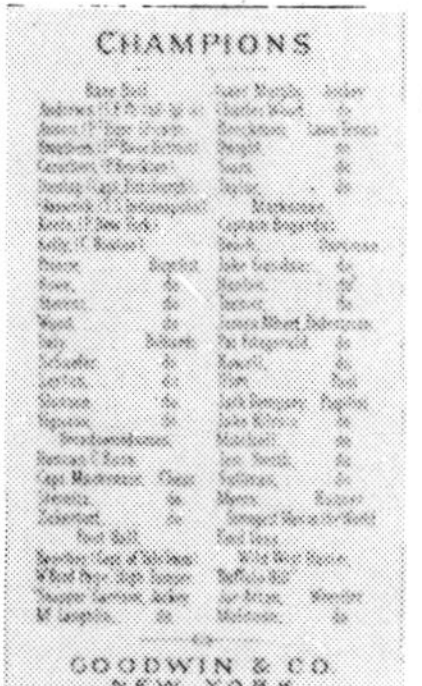

Issued in 1888 by New York's Goodwin & Co., the 50-card "Champions" set includes eight baseball players - seven from the National League and one from the American Association. The full-color cards, which measure 1-1/2" by 2-5/8", were inserted in packages of Old Judge and Gypsy Queen Cigarettes. A small ad for the cards lists all 50 subjects of the "Champions" set, which also included popular billiards players, bicyclists, marksmen, pugilists, runners, wrestlers, college football stars, weightlifters, and Wild West star Buffalo Bill Cody. Four of the eight baseball players in the set (Anson, Kelly, Keefe and Brouthers) are Hall of Famers. The cards feature very attractive player portraits, making the "Champions" set among the most beautiful of all the 19th Century tobacco inserts.

		NR MT	EX	VG
Complete Set:		25000.	11700.	6000.
Common Player:		1000.	500.00	200.00
(1)	Ed Andrews	1000.	500.00	200.00
(2)	Cap Anson	7000.	3000.	1350.
(3)	Dan Brouthers	2800.	1250.	525.00
(4)	Parisian Bob Caruthers	1200.	550.00	225.00
(5)	Sure Shot Dunlap	1000.	500.00	200.00
(6)	Pebbly Jack Glasscock	1400.	600.00	250.00
(7)	Tim Keefe	3200.	1400.	600.00
(8)	King Kelly	5000.	2500.	1150.

1886 N167 Old Judge

Produced in 1886, the rare N167 Old Judge tobacco cards were the first to be issued by New York's Goodwin & Co., the parent firm of Old Judge Cigarettes. The 1-1/2" by 2-1/2" sepia-toned cards were printed on thin paper and featured only members of the New York National League club. Twelve subjects are known to exist, five of whom are Hall of Famers. The front of each card lists the player's name, position and team and has the words "Old Judge" at the top. The backs contain another ad for the Old Judge brand and also include a line noting that the player poses were "copied from by J. Wood, 208, N.Y."

		NR MT	EX	VG
Complete Set:		22500.	11225.	7000.
Common Player:		1200.	600.00	350.00
(1)	Roger Connor	2500.	1250.	750.00
(2)	Larry Corcoran	1200.	600.00	350.00
(3)	Mike Dorgan	1200.	600.00	350.00
(4)	Dude Esterbrook	1200.	600.00	350.00
(5)	Buck Ewing	2500.	1250.	750.00
(6)	Joe Gerhardt	1200.	600.00	350.00
(7)	Pete Gillespie	1200.	600.00	350.00
(8)	Tim Keefe	2500.	1250.	750.00
(9)	Orator Jim O'Rourke	2500.	1250.	750.00
(10)	Danny Richardson	1200.	600.00	350.00
(11)	Monte Ward	2500.	1250.	750.00
(12)	Mickey Welsh (Welch)	2500.	1250.	750.00

1887-1890 N172 Old Judge

One of the most fascinating of all card sets, these cards were issued by the Goodwin & Co. tobacco firm in their Old Judge and, to a lesser extent, Gypsy Queen cigarettes. Players from more than 40 major and minor league teams are pictured on the 1-1/2" by 2-1/2" cards, with some 518 different players known to exist. Up to 17 different pose and team variations exist for some players, and the cards were issued both with and without dates on the card fronts, numbered and unnumbered, and with both handwritten and machine-printed names. Known variations number in the thousands. The cards themselves are blank-backed, sepia-toned photographs pasted onto thick cardboard. The listings are based on the recordings in the The Cartophilic Society's World Index, Part IV, compiled by E.C. Wharton-Tigar with the help of many collectors, especially Donald J. McPherson and Lew Lipset. Because of the set's vastness, no complete set price is given. The list below does not include variations, however, a complete checklist of the N172 set, including all known variations, appears as a separate appendix in the back of this catalog.

		NR MT	EX	VG
Common Player:		100.00	50.00	30.00
Brown's Champions		175.00	87.00	52.00
Dotted Ties		300.00	150.00	90.00
1	Gus Albert (Alberts)	100.00	50.00	30.00
2	Alcott	100.00	50.00	30.00
3	Alexander	100.00	50.00	30.00
4	Myron Allen (Kansas City - fielding, 32)	100.00	50.00	30.00
5	Bob Allen (Pittsburgh, Philadelphia)	100.00	50.00	30.00
6	Uncle Bill Alvord	100.00	50.00	30.00
7	Varney Anderson	100.00	50.00	30.00
8	Wally Andrews (Omaha)	100.00	50.00	30.00
9	Ed Andrews (Philadelphia)	100.00	50.00	30.00
9-6	Ed Andrews, Buster Hoover	150.00	75.00	45.00
10	Bill Annis	100.00	50.00	30.00
11	Cap Anson	1500.	750.00	450.00
12	Old Hoss Ardner	100.00	50.00	30.00
13	Tug Arundel	100.00	50.00	30.00
14	Jersey Bakley (Bakely)	100.00	50.00	30.00
15	Fido Baldwin (Chicago, Columbus)	100.00	50.00	30.00
16	Kid Baldwin (Cincinnati)	100.00	50.00	30.00
17	Lady Baldwin (Detroit, Cincinnati)	100.00	50.00	30.00
18	James Banning	100.00	50.00	30.00
19	Samuel Barkley	100.00	50.00	30.00
20	John Barnes	100.00	50.00	30.00
21	Bald Billy Barnie	90.00	45.00	27.00
22	Charles Bassett	100.00	50.00	30.00
23	Charles Bastian	100.00	50.00	30.00
23-6	Charles Bastian, Schriver	150.00	75.00	45.00
24	Ed Beatin	100.00	50.00	30.00
25	Jake Beckley	600.00	300.00	175.00
26	Stephen Behel (dotted tie)	350.00	175.00	105.00
27	Charles Bennett	100.00	50.00	30.00
28	Louis Bierbauer	100.00	50.00	30.00
28-5	Louis Bierbauer, Gamble	150.00	75.00	45.00
29	Bill Bishop	100.00	50.00	30.00
30	Bill Blair	100.00	50.00	30.00
31	Ned Bligh	100.00	50.00	30.00
32	Bogart	100.00	50.00	30.00
33	Boyce	100.00	50.00	30.00
34	Boyd	100.00	50.00	30.00
35	Honest John Boyle (St. Louis, Chicago)	100.00	50.00	30.00
36	Handsome Boyle (Indianapolis, New York)	100.00	50.00	30.00
37	Nick Bradley (Kansas City, Worcester)	100.00	50.00	30.00
38	Grin Bradley (Sioux City)	100.00	50.00	30.00
39	Stephen Brady (dotted tie)	350.00	175.00	105.00
40	Breckenridge	300.00	150.00	90.00
41	Timothy Brosnam	100.00	50.00	30.00
42	Cal Broughton	100.00	50.00	30.00
43	Dan Brouthers	550.00	275.00	165.00
44	Thomas Brown (Pittsburgh, Boston)	100.00	50.00	30.00
45	California Brown (New York)	100.00	50.00	30.00
46	Pete Browning	150.00	75.00	45.00
47	Charles Brynan	100.00	50.00	30.00
48	Al Buckenberger	150.00	75.00	45.00
49	Dick Buckley	100.00	50.00	30.00
50	Charles Buffinton	100.00	50.00	30.00
51	Ernest Burch	100.00	50.00	30.00
52	Bill Burdick	100.00	50.00	30.00
53	Black Jack Burdock	100.00	50.00	30.00
54	Robert Burks (Burk)	80.00	40.00	24.00
55	Watch Burnham	150.00	75.00	45.00
56	James Burns (Kansas City, Omaha)	100.00	50.00	30.00
57	No World Index listing			
58	Oyster Burns (Baltimore, Brooklyn)	100.00	50.00	30.00
59	Thomas Burns (Chicago)	100.00	50.00	30.00
60	Doc Bushong (Brooklyn)	100.00	50.00	30.00
60-1	Doc Bushong (Brown's Champions)	175.00	87.00	52.00
61	Patsy Cahill	100.00	50.00	30.00
62	Count Campau	100.00	50.00	30.00
63	Jimmy Canavan	100.00	50.00	30.00
64	Bart Cantz	100.00	50.00	30.00
65	Handsome Jack Carney	100.00	50.00	30.00
66	Hick Carpenter	100.00	50.00	30.00
67	Cliff Carroll (Washington)	80.00	40.00	24.00
68	Scrappy Carroll (St. Paul, Chicago)	100.00	50.00	30.00
69	Fred Carroll (Pittsburgh)	100.00	50.00	30.00
70	Jumbo Cartwright	100.00	50.00	30.00
71	Parisian Bob Caruthers (Brooklyn)	125.00	62.00	37.00
71-1	Parisian Bob Caruthers (Brown's Champions)	225.00	112.00	75.00
72	Dan Casey	100.00	50.00	30.00
73	Icebox Chamberlain	100.00	50.00	30.00
74	Cupid Childs	100.00	50.00	30.00
75	Spider Clark (Washington)	100.00	50.00	30.00
76	Bob Clark (Brooklyn)	100.00	50.00	30.00
76-6	Bob Clark, Mickey Hughes	150.00	75.00	45.00
77	Dad Clarke	100.00	50.00	30.00
78	John Clarkson	550.00	275.00	165.00
79	Jack Clements	100.00	50.00	30.00
80	Elmer Cleveland	100.00	50.00	30.00
81	Monk Cline	100.00	50.00	30.00
82	Cody	100.00	50.00	30.00
83	John Coleman	100.00	50.00	30.00
84	Bill Collins (NY, Newark)	100.00	50.00	30.00
85	Hub Collins (Louisville, Brooklyn)	100.00	50.00	30.00
86	Commy Comiskey (St. Louis, Chicago)	600.00	300.00	175.00
86-1	Commy Comiskey (Brown's Champions)	750.00	375.00	225.00
87	Pete Connell	100.00	50.00	30.00
88	Roger Connor	500.00	250.00	150.00
89	Dick Conway (Boston, Worcester)	100.00	50.00	30.00
90	Pete Conway (Detroit, Pittsburgh, Indianapolis)	100.00	50.00	30.00
91	Jim Conway (Kansas City)	100.00	50.00	30.00
92	Paul Cook	100.00	50.00	30.00
93	Jimmy Cooney	80.00	40.00	24.00
94	Larry Corcoran	100.00	50.00	30.00
95	Pop Corkhill	100.00	50.00	30.00
96	Cannonball Crane (NY)	100.00	50.00	30.00
97	Samuel Crane (Washington)	100.00	50.00	30.00
98	Jack Crogan (Croghan)	100.00	50.00	30.00
99	John Crooks	100.00	50.00	30.00
100	Lave Cross	100.00	50.00	30.00
101	N.C. Crossley	100.00	50.00	30.00
102	Joe Crotty (Sioux City)	100.00	50.00	30.00
102-1	Joe Crotty (dotted tie)	300.00	150.00	90.00
103	Billy Crowell	100.00	50.00	30.00
104	Jim Cudworth	100.00	50.00	30.00
105	Bert Cunningham	100.00	50.00	30.00

		NR MT	EX	VG
106	Tacks Curtis	100.00	50.00	30.00
107	Ed Cushman (dotted tie)	350.00	175.00	105.00
107-2	Ed Cushman (Toledo)	150.00	75.00	45.00
108	Tony Cusick	100.00	50.00	30.00
109	Dailey (Oakland)	300.00	150.00	90.00
110	Edward Dailey (Daily) (Philadelphia, Washington, Columbus)	100.00	50.00	30.00
111	Bill Daley (Boston)	100.00	50.00	30.00
112	Con Daley (Daily) (Boston, Indianapolis)	100.00	50.00	30.00
113	Abner Dalrymple	100.00	50.00	30.00
114	Tido Daly (Chicago, Washington)	100.00	50.00	30.00
115	Sun Daly (Minneapolis)	100.00	50.00	30.00
116	Law Daniels	100.00	50.00	30.00
117	Dell Darling	100.00	50.00	30.00
118	William Darnbrough	100.00	50.00	30.00
118-1	Davin	300.00	150.00	90.00
119	Jumbo Davis	100.00	50.00	30.00
120	Pat Dealey	100.00	50.00	30.00
121	Tom Deasley	100.00	50.00	30.00
122	Harry Decker	100.00	50.00	30.00
123	Ed Delahanty	650.00	325.00	200.00
124	Jerry Denny	100.00	50.00	30.00
125	Jim Devlin	100.00	50.00	30.00
126	Tom Dolan	100.00	50.00	30.00
127	Jack Donahue (San Fran)	300.00	150.00	90.00
128	Jim Donahue (Kansas City)	100.00	50.00	30.00
128-1	Jim Donohue (Donahue) (dotted tie)	300.00	150.00	90.00
129	Jim Donnelly	100.00	50.00	30.00
130	Dooley	300.00	150.00	90.00
131	Doran	100.00	50.00	30.00
132	Mike Dorgan	100.00	50.00	30.00
133	Doyle	300.00	150.00	90.00
134	Home Run Duffe (Duffee)	100.00	50.00	30.00
135	Hugh Duffy	550.00	275.00	165.00
136	Dan Dugdale	100.00	50.00	30.00
137	Duck Duke	100.00	50.00	30.00
138	Sure Shot Dunlap	100.00	50.00	30.00
139	Dunn	100.00	50.00	30.00
140	Jesse Duryea	100.00	50.00	30.00
141	Frank Dwyer	100.00	50.00	30.00
142	Billy Earle	100.00	50.00	30.00
143	Buck Ebright	100.00	50.00	30.00
144	Red Ehret	100.00	50.00	30.00
145	R. Emmerke	100.00	50.00	30.00
146	Dude Esterbrook	100.00	50.00	30.00
147	Henry Esterday	100.00	50.00	30.00
148	Long John Ewing (Louisville)	100.00	50.00	30.00
149	Buck Ewing (New York)	500.00	250.00	150.00
149-11	Willie Breslin - mascot, Buck Ewing	500.00	250.00	150.00
150	Jay Faatz	100.00	50.00	30.00
151	Bill Fagan	100.00	50.00	30.00
152	Bill Farmer	100.00	50.00	30.00
153	Sid Farrar	100.00	50.00	30.00
154	Jack Farrell (Washington, Baltimore)	100.00	50.00	30.00
155	Duke Farrell (Chicago)	100.00	50.00	30.00
156	Frank Fennelly	100.00	50.00	30.00
157	Charlie Ferguson	100.00	50.00	30.00
158	Alex Ferson	100.00	50.00	30.00
159	Wallace Fessenden (umpire)	175.00	87.00	52.00
160	Jocko Fields	100.00	50.00	30.00
161	Fischer	100.00	50.00	30.00
162	Thomas Flanigan (Flanagan)	100.00	50.00	30.00
163	Silver Flint	100.00	50.00	30.00
164	Thomas Flood	100.00	50.00	30.00
164-1	Jocko Flynn	300.00	150.00	90.00
165	Jim Fogarty	100.00	50.00	30.00
166	Frank Foreman	100.00	50.00	30.00
167	Tom Forster (Hartford)	150.00	75.00	45.00
167-2	Tom Forster (dotted tie, incorrect name (F.W. Foster) on front)	350.00	175.00	105.00
168	Elmer Foster (New York, Minneapolis)	100.00	50.00	30.00
168-1	Elmer Foster (dotted tie)	300.00	150.00	90.00
169	No World Index listing			
170	Dave Foutz (Brooklyn)	100.00	50.00	30.00
170-1	Dave Foutz (Brown's Champions)	175.00	87.00	52.00
171	Julie Freeman	100.00	50.00	30.00
172	Will Fry	100.00	50.00	30.00
172-1	Fudger	300.00	150.00	90.00
173	William Fuller (Milwaukee)	100.00	50.00	30.00
174	Shorty Fuller (St. Louis)	100.00	50.00	30.00
175	Chris Fulmer	100.00	50.00	30.00
175-6	Chris Fulmer, Foghorn Tucker	150.00	75.00	45.00
176	Honest John Gaffney	100.00	50.00	30.00
177	Pud Galvin	500.00	250.00	150.00
178	Bob Gamble	80.00	40.00	24.00
179	Charlie Ganzel	100.00	50.00	30.00
180	Gid Gardner	100.00	50.00	30.00
180-5	Gid Gardner, Miah Murray	100.00	50.00	30.00
181	Hank Gastreich	100.00	50.00	30.00
182	Emil Geiss	100.00	50.00	30.00
183	Frenchy Genins	100.00	50.00	30.00
184	Bill George	100.00	50.00	30.00
185	Joe Gerhardt	100.00	50.00	30.00
186	Charlie Getzein	100.00	50.00	30.00
187	Bobby Gilks	100.00	50.00	30.00
188	Pete Gillespie	65.00	32.00	19.50
189	Barney Gilligan	100.00	50.00	30.00
190	Frank Gilmore	100.00	50.00	30.00
191	Pebbly Jack Glasscock	125.00	62.00	37.00
192	Kid Gleason (Philadelphia)	110.00	55.00	30.00
193	Will Gleason (Athletics)	100.00	50.00	30.00
193-1	Will Gleason (Brown's Champions)	175.00	87.00	52.00
194	Mouse Glenn	100.00	50.00	30.00
195	Mike Goodfellow	100.00	50.00	30.00

		NR MT	EX	VG
196	Piano Legs Gore	100.00	50.00	30.00
197	Frank Graves	100.00	50.00	30.00
198	Bill Greenwood	100.00	50.00	30.00
199	Ed Greer	100.00	50.00	30.00
200	Mike Griffin	100.00	50.00	30.00
201	Clark Griffith	650.00	325.00	200.00
202	Henry Gruber	100.00	50.00	30.00
203	Ad Gumbert	100.00	50.00	30.00
204	Tom Gunning	100.00	50.00	30.00
205	Joe Gunson	100.00	50.00	30.00
206	Gentleman George Haddock	100.00	50.00	30.00
207	Bill Hafner (Hoffner)	100.00	50.00	30.00
208	Willie Hahm (mascot)	200.00	100.00	60.00
209	Bill Hallman	100.00	50.00	30.00
210	Sliding Billy Hamilton	550.00	275.00	165.00
211	Frank Hankinson (dotted tie)	275.00	137.00	82.00
212	Ned Hanlon	110.00	55.00	30.00
213	William Hanrahan	100.00	50.00	30.00
213-1	Hapeman	300.00	150.00	90.00
214	Pa Harkins	100.00	50.00	30.00
215	Bill Hart	100.00	50.00	30.00
216	Bill Hasamdear	80.00	40.00	24.00
217	Gill Hatfield	100.00	50.00	30.00
218	Egyptian Healey (Healy)	100.00	50.00	30.00
219	Healy	100.00	50.00	30.00
220	Guy Hecker	100.00	50.00	30.00
221	Tony Hellman	100.00	50.00	30.00
222	Hardie Henderson	100.00	50.00	30.00
222-10	Ed Greer, Henderson	150.00	75.00	45.00
223	Moxie Hengle	100.00	50.00	30.00
224	John Henry	100.00	50.00	30.00
225	Ed Herr	100.00	50.00	30.00
226	Hunkey Hines (St. Louis Whites)	100.00	50.00	30.00
227	Paul Hines (Washington, Indianapolis)	100.00	50.00	30.00
228	Texas Wonder Hoffman	100.00	50.00	30.00
229	Eddie Hogan	100.00	50.00	30.00
230	Bill Holbert	100.00	50.00	30.00
230-1	Bill Holbert (dotted tie)	300.00	150.00	90.00
231	Bug Holliday	100.00	50.00	30.00
232	Charles Hoover (Chicago, Kansas City)	100.00	50.00	30.00
233	Buster Hoover (Philadelphia)	100.00	50.00	30.00
234	Jack Horner	100.00	50.00	30.00
234-3	Jack Horner, E.H. Warner	150.00	75.00	45.00
235	Joe Hornung	100.00	50.00	30.00
236	Pete Hotaling	100.00	50.00	30.00
237	Bill Howes (Hawes)	100.00	50.00	30.00
238	Dummy Hoy	200.00	100.00	60.00
239	Nat Hudson (St. Louis)	100.00	50.00	30.00
239-1	Nat Hudson (Brown's Champions)	175.00	87.00	52.00
240	Mickey Hughes	100.00	50.00	30.00
241	Hungler	100.00	50.00	30.00
242	Wild Bill Hutchinson	100.00	50.00	30.00
243	John Irwin (Washington)	100.00	50.00	30.00
244	Cutrate Irwin (Philadelphia)	100.00	50.00	30.00
245	A.C. Jantzen	100.00	50.00	30.00
246	Frederick Jevne	100.00	50.00	30.00
247	Spud Johnson	100.00	50.00	30.00
248	Dick Johnston	100.00	50.00	30.00
249	Jordan	100.00	50.00	30.00
250	Heinie Kappell (Kappel)	100.00	50.00	30.00
251	Tim Keefe (New York)	500.00	250.00	150.00
251-8	Keefe, Danny Richardson	500.00	250.00	150.00
252	George Keefe (Washington)	100.00	50.00	30.00
253	Jim Keenan	100.00	50.00	30.00
254	King Kelly (Boston)	650.00	325.00	200.00
255	John Kelly (Louisville)	100.00	50.00	30.00
255-3	Honest John Kelly (umpire)	100.00	50.00	30.00
255-4	Kelly, Jim Powell	125.00	62.00	37.00
256	No World Index listing			
257	Charles Kelly (Philadelphia)	100.00	50.00	30.00
258	Rudy Kemmler (St. Paul)	100.00	50.00	30.00
258-1	Rudy Kemler (Kemmler) (Brown's Champions)	175.00	87.00	52.00
259	Theodore Kennedy	100.00	50.00	30.00
260	J.J. Kenyon	100.00	50.00	30.00
261	John Kerins	100.00	50.00	30.00
262	Matt Kilroy	100.00	50.00	30.00
263	Silver King	100.00	50.00	30.00
264	August Kloff (Klopf)	100.00	50.00	30.00
265	William Klusman	100.00	50.00	30.00
266	Philip Knell	100.00	50.00	30.00
267	Fred Knouff	100.00	50.00	30.00
268	Charles Kremmeyer (Krehmeyer)	300.00	150.00	90.00
269	Bill Krieg	100.00	50.00	30.00
269-10	August Kloff, Bill Krieg	150.00	75.00	45.00
270	Gus Krock	100.00	50.00	30.00
271	Willie Kuehne	100.00	50.00	30.00
272	Fred Lange	100.00	50.00	30.00
273	Ted Larkin	100.00	50.00	30.00
274	Arlie Latham (St. Louis)	110.00	55.00	30.00
274-1	Arlie Latham (Brown's Champions)	200.00	100.00	60.00
275	Chuck Lauer (Laver)	100.00	50.00	30.00
276	John Leighton	100.00	50.00	30.00
276-5	Levy	300.00	150.00	90.00
277	Tom Loftus	150.00	75.00	45.00
278	Germany Long (Kansas City, Chicago Maroons)	80.00	40.00	24.00
279	Danny Long (Oakland)	300.00	150.00	90.00
280	Tom Lovett	100.00	50.00	30.00
281	Bobby Lowe	150.00	75.00	45.00
282	Jack Lynch	100.00	50.00	30.00
282-1	Jack Lynch (dotted tie)	350.00	175.00	105.00
283	Denny Lyons (Athletics)	100.00	50.00	30.00
284	Harry Lyons (St. Louis)	100.00	50.00	30.00

		NR MT	EX	VG
285	Connie Mack (Washington)	1200.	600.00	350.00
286	Reddie Mack (Louisville, Baltimore)	100.00	50.00	30.00
287	Little Mac Macullar	100.00	50.00	30.00
288	Kid Madden	100.00	50.00	30.00
289	Danny Mahoney	100.00	50.00	30.00
290	Grasshopper Maines (Mains)	100.00	50.00	30.00
291	Fred Mann	100.00	50.00	30.00
292	Jimmy Manning	100.00	50.00	30.00
293	Lefty Marr	100.00	50.00	30.00
294	Willie Breslin (mascot)	150.00	75.00	45.00
295	Leech Maskrey	100.00	50.00	30.00
296	Bobby Mathews	80.00	40.00	24.00
297	Mike Mattimore	100.00	50.00	30.00
298	Smiling Al Maul	100.00	50.00	30.00
299	Al Mays (Columbus)	100.00	50.00	30.00
299-1	Al Mays (dotted tie)	300.00	150.00	90.00
300	Jimmy McAleer	80.00	40.00	24.00
301	Tommy McCarthy (Philadelphia, St. Louis)	500.00	250.00	150.00
302	John McCarthy (McCarty) (Kansas City)	80.00	40.00	24.00
303	Jim McCauley	100.00	50.00	30.00
304	Bill McClellan	100.00	50.00	30.00
305	Jerry McCormack (McCormick)	100.00	50.00	30.00
306	Jim McCormick	80.00	40.00	24.00
307	McCreachery (photo actually Deacon White)	100.00	50.00	30.00
308	McCullum (McCallum)	100.00	50.00	30.00
308-1	McDonald	300.00	150.00	90.00
309	Chippy McGarr	100.00	50.00	30.00
310	Jack McGeachy	100.00	50.00	30.00
311	John McGlone	100.00	50.00	30.00
312	Deacon McGuire	80.00	40.00	24.00
313	Bill McGunnigle	150.00	75.00	45.00
314	Ed McKean	100.00	50.00	30.00
315	Alex McKinnon	100.00	50.00	30.00
316	Tom McLaughlin (dotted tie)	300.00	150.00	90.00
317	Bid McPhee	100.00	50.00	30.00
318	James McQuaid (Denver)	100.00	50.00	30.00
319	John McQuaid (umpire)	150.00	75.00	45.00
320	Jim McTamany	100.00	50.00	30.00
321	George McVey	100.00	50.00	30.00
321-1	Steady Pete Meegan	300.00	150.00	90.00
322	John Messitt	100.00	50.00	30.00
323	Doggie Miller (Pittsburgh)	100.00	50.00	30.00
324	Joseph Miller (Omaha, Minneapolis)	100.00	50.00	30.00
325	Jocko Milligan	100.00	50.00	30.00
326	E.L. Mills	100.00	50.00	30.00
327	Daniel Minnehan (Minahan)	100.00	50.00	30.00
328	Sam Moffet	100.00	50.00	30.00
329	Honest John Morrill	100.00	50.00	30.00
330	Ed Morris	100.00	50.00	30.00
331	Count Mullane	110.00	55.00	30.00
332	Joseph Mulvey	80.00	40.00	24.00
333	P.L. Murphy (St. Paul)	100.00	50.00	30.00
334	Pat Murphy (New York)	100.00	50.00	30.00
335	Miah Murray	100.00	50.00	30.00
336	Truthful Jim Mutrie	200.00	100.00	60.00
337	George Myers (Indianapolis)	100.00	50.00	30.00
338	Al Myers (Washington, Philadelphia)	100.00	50.00	30.00
339	Tom Nagle	100.00	50.00	30.00
340	Billy Nash	100.00	50.00	30.00
341	Candy Nelson (dotted tie)	300.00	150.00	90.00
342	Kid Nichols (Omaha)	650.00	325.00	200.00
343	Samuel Nichols (Nichol) (Pittsburgh)	100.00	50.00	30.00
344	J.W. Nicholson (Chicago Maroons)	100.00	50.00	30.00
345	Parson Nicholson (St. Louis, Cleveland)	100.00	50.00	30.00
346	Little Nick Nicol (Cincinnati)	100.00	50.00	30.00
346-1	Little Nick Nicoll (Nicol) (Brown's Champions)	175.00	87.00	52.00
346-8	Little Nick Nicol, Big John Reilly	150.00	75.00	45.00
347	Frederick Nyce	100.00	50.00	30.00
348	Doc Oberlander	100.00	50.00	30.00
349	Jack O'Brien (Brooklyn, Baltimore)	100.00	50.00	30.00
350	Billy O'Brien (Washington)	100.00	50.00	30.00
351	Darby O'Brien (Brooklyn)	100.00	50.00	30.00
352	John O'Brien (Cleveland)	100.00	50.00	30.00
353	P.J. O'Connell	100.00	50.00	30.00
354	Rowdy Jack O'Connor	100.00	50.00	30.00
355	Hank O'Day	80.00	40.00	24.00
356	Tip O'Neil (O'Neill) (St. Louis)	80.00	40.00	24.00
356-6	Tip O'Neil (O'Neill) (Brown's Champions)	175.00	87.00	52.00
357	Tip O'Neill (photo actually Deacon White, St. Louis)	80.00	40.00	24.00
357-1	O'Neill (Oakland)	300.00	150.00	90.00
358	Orator Jim O'Rourke (New York)	500.00	250.00	150.00
359	Tom O'Rourke (Boston)	100.00	50.00	30.00
360	Dave Orr	100.00	50.00	30.00
360-1	Dave Orr (dotted tie)	300.00	150.00	90.00
361	Charles Parsons	100.00	50.00	30.00
362	Owen Patton	100.00	50.00	30.00
363	Jimmy Peeples (Peoples)	100.00	50.00	30.00
363-3	Hardie Henderson, Jimmy Peeples	150.00	75.00	45.00
364	Hip Perrier	300.00	150.00	90.00
365	Patrick Pettee	100.00	50.00	30.00
365-5	Bobby Lowe, Patrick Pettee	150.00	75.00	45.00
366	Fred Pfeffer	100.00	50.00	30.00

		NR MT	EX	VG
367	Dick Phelan	100.00	50.00	30.00
368	Bill Phillips	100.00	50.00	30.00
369	Jack Pickett	100.00	50.00	30.00
370	George Pinkney	100.00	50.00	30.00
371	Tom Poorman	100.00	50.00	30.00
372	Henry Porter	100.00	50.00	30.00
373	Jim Powell	100.00	50.00	30.00
373-1	Thomas Powers	300.00	150.00	90.00
374	Blondie Purcell	100.00	50.00	30.00
375	Tom Quinn (Baltimore)	100.00	50.00	30.00
376	Joe Quinn (Boston, Des Moines)	100.00	50.00	30.00
377	Old Hoss Radbourn	500.00	250.00	150.00
378	Shorty Radford	100.00	50.00	30.00
379	Toad Ramsey	100.00	50.00	30.00
380	Rehse	100.00	50.00	30.00
381	Long John Reilly (Cincinnati)	100.00	50.00	30.00
382	Princeton Charlie Reilly (St. Paul)	100.00	50.00	30.00
383	Charlie Reynolds	100.00	50.00	30.00
384	Hardy Richardson (Detroit, Boston)	100.00	50.00	30.00
385	Danny Richardson (NY)	100.00	50.00	30.00
386	Charles Ripslager (dot tie)	300.00	150.00	90.00
387	John Roach	100.00	50.00	30.00
388	Uncle Robbie Robinson (Athletics)	550.00	275.00	165.00
389	M.C. Robinson (Minneapolis)	100.00	50.00	30.00
390	Yank Robinson (St. Louis)	100.00	50.00	30.00
390-6	Yank Robinson (Brown's Champions)	175.00	87.00	52.00
391	George Rooks	100.00	50.00	30.00
392	Chief Roseman (dotted tie)	300.00	150.00	90.00
393	Dave Rowe (Kansas City)	100.00	50.00	30.00
394	Jack Rowe (Detroit)	100.00	50.00	30.00
395	Amos Rusie	650.00	325.00	200.00
396	Jimmy Ryan	100.00	50.00	30.00
397	Doc Sage	100.00	50.00	30.00
397-4	Doc Sage, Bill Van Dyke	100.00	50.00	30.00
398	Ben Sanders	100.00	50.00	30.00
399	Frank Scheibeck	100.00	50.00	30.00
400	Al Schellhase (Schellhasse)	100.00	50.00	30.00
401	William Schenkel	100.00	50.00	30.00
402	Schildknecht	100.00	50.00	30.00
403	Gus Schmelz	100.00	50.00	30.00
404	Jumbo Schoeneck	100.00	50.00	30.00
405	Pop Schriver	100.00	50.00	30.00
406	Emmett Seery	100.00	50.00	30.00
407	Billy Serad	100.00	50.00	30.00
408	Ed Seward	100.00	50.00	30.00
409	Orator Shafer (Shaffer) (Des Moines)	100.00	50.00	30.00
410	Taylor Shafer (Shaffer) (St. Paul)	100.00	50.00	30.00
411	Daniel Shannon	100.00	50.00	30.00
412	William Sharsig	100.00	50.00	30.00
413	Samuel Shaw (Baltimore, Newark)	100.00	50.00	30.00
414	John Shaw (Minneapolis)	100.00	50.00	30.00
415	Bill Shindle	100.00	50.00	30.00
416	George Shoch	100.00	50.00	30.00
417	Otto Shomberg (Schomberg)	100.00	50.00	30.00
418	Lev Shreve	100.00	50.00	30.00
419	Ed Silch	100.00	50.00	30.00
420	Mike Slattery	100.00	50.00	30.00
421	Skyrocket Smith (Louisville)	100.00	50.00	30.00
422	Phenomenal Smith (Baltimore, Athletics)	300.00	150.00	90.00
423	Mike Smith (Cincinnati)	100.00	50.00	30.00
424	Sam Smith (Des Moines)	100.00	50.00	30.00
425	Germany Smith (Brooklyn)	100.00	50.00	30.00
426	Pap Smith (Pittsburgh, Boston)	100.00	50.00	30.00
427	Nick Smith (St. Joseph)	100.00	50.00	30.00
428	P.T. Somers	100.00	50.00	30.00
429	Joe Sommer	100.00	50.00	30.00
430	Pete Sommers	100.00	50.00	30.00
431	Little Bill Sowders (Boston)	100.00	50.00	30.00
432	John Sowders (St. Paul, Kansas City)	100.00	50.00	30.00
433	Charlie Sprague	100.00	50.00	30.00
434	Ed Sproat	100.00	50.00	30.00
435	Harry Staley	100.00	50.00	30.00
436	Dan Stearns	100.00	50.00	30.00
437	Cannonball Stemmyer (Stemmeyer)	100.00	50.00	30.00
438	B.F. Stephens	80.00	40.00	24.00
439	John Sterling	100.00	50.00	30.00
439-1	Stockwell	300.00	150.00	90.00
440	Harry Stovey	150.00	75.00	45.00
441	Scott Stratton	100.00	50.00	30.00
442	Joe Straus (Strauss)	100.00	50.00	30.00
443	Cub Stricker	100.00	50.00	30.00
444	Marty Sullivan (Chicago, Indianapolis)	100.00	50.00	30.00
445	Mike Sullivan (Athletics)	80.00	40.00	24.00
446	Billy Sunday	500.00	250.00	150.00
447	Sy Sutcliffe	100.00	50.00	30.00
448	Ezra Sutton	100.00	50.00	30.00
449	Ed Swartwood	100.00	50.00	30.00
450	Park Swartzel	100.00	50.00	30.00
451	Pete Sweeney	100.00	50.00	30.00
451-1	Louis Sylvester	300.00	150.00	90.00
452	Pop Tate	100.00	50.00	30.00
453	Patsy Tebeau	100.00	50.00	30.00
454	John Tener	200.00	100.00	60.00
455	Adonis Terry	80.00	40.00	24.00
456	Big Sam Thompson	500.00	250.00	150.00
457	Silent Mike Tiernan	100.00	50.00	30.00
458	Cannonball Titcomb	100.00	50.00	30.00
459	Buster Tomney	100.00	50.00	30.00
460	Stephen Toole	100.00	50.00	30.00
461	Sleepy Townsend	100.00	50.00	30.00
462	Bill Traffley	100.00	50.00	30.00
463	George Treadway	100.00	50.00	30.00
464	Sam Trott	100.00	50.00	30.00
464-6	Oyster Burns, Sam Trott	150.00	75.00	45.00
465	Foghorn Tucker	100.00	50.00	30.00
466	A.M. Tuckerman	100.00	50.00	30.00
467	George Turner	100.00	50.00	30.00
468	Larry Twitchell	100.00	50.00	30.00
469	Jim Tyng	100.00	50.00	30.00
470	Bill Van Dyke	80.00	40.00	24.00
471	Rip Van Haltren	80.00	40.00	24.00
472	Farmer Vaughn	100.00	50.00	30.00
472-1	Veach	300.00	150.00	90.00
473	Lee Viau	100.00	50.00	30.00
474	Bill Vinton	100.00	50.00	30.00
475	Joe Visner	100.00	50.00	30.00
476	Christian Von Der Ahe (Brown's Champions)	300.00	150.00	90.00
477	Reddy Walsh	100.00	50.00	30.00
478	Monte Ward	500.00	250.00	150.00
479	E.H. Warner	100.00	50.00	30.00
480	Bill Watkins	100.00	50.00	30.00
481	Farmer Weaver	100.00	50.00	30.00
482	Count Weber	100.00	50.00	30.00
483	Stump Weidman	100.00	50.00	30.00
484	Wild Bill Weidner (Widner)	100.00	50.00	30.00
485	Curt Welch (Athletics)	100.00	50.00	30.00
485-1	Curt Welch (Brown's Champions)	175.00	87.00	52.00
485-7	Will Gleason, Curt Welch	150.00	75.00	45.00
486	Smiling Mickey Welch (New York)	550.00	275.00	165.00
487	Jake Wells (Kansas City)	100.00	50.00	30.00
488	Frank Wells (Milwaukee)	100.00	50.00	30.00
489	Joe Werrick	100.00	50.00	30.00
490	Buck West	100.00	50.00	30.00
491	A.C. "Cannonball" Weyhing	100.00	50.00	30.00
492	John Weyhing	100.00	50.00	30.00
493	Bobby Wheelock	100.00	50.00	30.00
494	Pat Whitacre (Whitaker)	80.00	40.00	24.00
495	Pat Whitaker	100.00	50.00	30.00
496	Deacon White (Detroit, Pittsburgh)	80.00	40.00	24.00
497	Bill White (Louisville)	100.00	50.00	30.00
498	Grasshopper Whitney (Washington, Indianapolis)	100.00	50.00	30.00
499	Art Whitney (Pittsburgh, New York)	100.00	50.00	30.00
500	G. Whitney (St. Joseph)	100.00	50.00	30.00
501	James Williams	100.00	50.00	30.00
502	Ned Williamson	100.00	50.00	30.00
502-7	Willie Hahm - mascot, Ned Williamson	160.00	80.00	48.00
503	C.H. Willis	100.00	50.00	30.00
504	Watt Wilmot	100.00	50.00	30.00
505	George Winkleman (Winkelman)	100.00	50.00	30.00
506	Medoc Wise	100.00	50.00	30.00
507	Chicken Wolf	100.00	50.00	30.00
508	George "Dandy" Wood (L.F.)	100.00	50.00	30.00
509	Pete Wood (P.)	100.00	50.00	30.00
510	Harry Wright	1200.	600.00	350.00
511	Chief Zimmer	100.00	50.00	30.00
512	Frank Zinn	100.00	50.00	30.00

1888-89 N173
Old Judge Cabinets

These large cabinet cards were issued by Goodwin & Co. in 1888 and 1889. They were a popular premium available by exchanging coupons found in Old Judge or Dogs Head brand cigarettes. The cabinet cards consist of 3-3/4" by 5-3/4" photographs affixed to a cardboard backing that measures approximately 4-1/4" by 6-1/2". The mounting is usually a yellow color, but backings have also been found in pink, blue or black. An ad for Old Judge Cigarettes appears along the bottom of the cabinet. (Cabinets obtained by exchanging coupons from Dogs Head cigarettes include an ad for both Old Judge and Dogs Head, and are considered scarcer.) According to an advertising sheet, cabinets were available of "every prominent player in the National League, Western League and American Association." There are additions to the following checklist that will be included in subsequent editions of this catalog. The poses used for the cabinet photos are enlarged versions of the popular N172 Old Judge cards.

		NR MT	EX	VG
	Complete Set:			
	Common Player:	350.00	175.00	105.00
(1)	Bob Allen	350.00	175.00	105.00
(2)	Ed Andrews (both hands at shoulder level)	350.00	175.00	105.00
(3)	Ed Andrews (one hand above head)	350.00	175.00	105.00
(4)	Ed Andrews, Buster Hoover	700.00	350.00	210.00
(5)	Cap Anson (Dogs Head)	5000.	2500.	1500.
(6)	Fido Baldwin (Chicago, pitching)	350.00	175.00	105.00
(7)	Fido Baldwin (Chicago, with bat)	350.00	175.00	105.00
(8)	Kid Baldwin (Detroit)	350.00	175.00	105.00
(9)	John Barnes	350.00	175.00	105.00
(10)	Bald Billy Barnie	350.00	175.00	105.00
(11)	Charles Bassett	350.00	175.00	105.00
(12)	Charles Bastian (Chicago)	350.00	175.00	105.00
(13)	Charles Bastian (Philly)	350.00	175.00	105.00
(14)	Bastian, Pop Schriver	350.00	175.00	105.00
(15)	Ed Beatin	350.00	175.00	105.00
(16)	Charles Bennett (Dogs H)	350.00	175.00	105.00
(17)	Louis Bierbauer	350.00	175.00	105.00
(18)	Ned Bligh	350.00	175.00	105.00
(19)	Bogart	350.00	175.00	105.00
(20)	Handsome Boyle (Indy)	350.00	175.00	105.00
(21)	Honest John Boyle (St. Louis, bat at side)	350.00	175.00	105.00
(22)	Honest John Boyle (St. Louis, bat in air)	350.00	175.00	105.00
(23)	Grin Bradley	350.00	175.00	105.00
(24)	Dan Brouthers (catching)	1600.	800.00	475.00
(25)	Dan Brouthers (with bat, Dogs Head)	1500.	750.00	450.00
(26)	California Brown (Boston, catching)	350.00	175.00	105.00
(27)	California Brown (Boston, with bat)	350.00	175.00	105.00
(28)	Thomas Brown (New York, throwing)	350.00	175.00	105.00
(29)	Thomas Brown (New York, with bat)	350.00	175.00	105.00
(30)	Charles Brynan (Chicago)	350.00	175.00	105.00
(31)	Charles Brynan (Des Moines)	350.00	175.00	105.00
(32)	Al Buckenberger	350.00	175.00	105.00
(33)	Dick Buckley	350.00	175.00	105.00
(34)	Charles Buffinton (hands chest high)	350.00	175.00	105.00
(35)	Charles Buffinton (right hand above head, Dogs Head)	350.00	175.00	105.00
(36)	Black Jack Burdock	350.00	175.00	105.00
(37)	James Burns (Kansas City)	350.00	175.00	105.00
(38)	Oyster Burns (Brooklyn)	350.00	175.00	105.00
(39)	Thomas Burns (Chicago, bat at side)	350.00	175.00	105.00
(40)	Thomas Burns (Chicago, bat in air)	350.00	175.00	105.00
(41)	Thomas Burns (catching)	350.00	175.00	105.00
(42)	Doc Bushong	350.00	175.00	105.00
(43)	Hick Carpenter	350.00	175.00	105.00
(44)	Jumbo Cartwright	350.00	175.00	105.00
(45)	Parisian Bob Caruthers (holding ball)	350.00	175.00	105.00
(46)	Parisian Bob Caruthers (with bat)	350.00	175.00	105.00
(47)	Daniel Casey	350.00	175.00	105.00
(48)	Icebox Chamberlain (boths hands at chest level)	350.00	175.00	105.00
(49)	Icebox Chamberlain (right hand extended)	350.00	175.00	105.00
(50)	Chamberlain (with bat)	350.00	175.00	105.00
(51)	Cupid Childs	350.00	175.00	105.00
(52)	Clark (Brooklyn, catching)	350.00	175.00	105.00
(53)	Bob Clark (Brooklyn, right hand shoulder high)	350.00	175.00	105.00
(54)	Bob Clark, Mickey Hughes (Dogs Head)	350.00	175.00	105.00
(55)	Dad Clark (Clarke) (Chicago)	350.00	175.00	105.00
(56)	John Clarkson (Dogs Head)	2250.	1125.	700.00
(57)	John Clarkson (right arm extended)	1600.	800.00	475.00
(58)	John Clarkson (with bat)	1600.	800.00	475.00
(59)	Jack Clements (hands on knees)	350.00	175.00	105.00
(60)	Jack Clements (hands outstreched at neck level)	350.00	175.00	105.00
(61)	Jack Clements (with bat)	350.00	175.00	105.00
(62)	Monk Cline	350.00	175.00	105.00
(63)	John Coleman (holding ball)	350.00	175.00	105.00
(64)	John Coleman (with bat)	350.00	175.00	105.00
(65)	Hub Collins	350.00	175.00	105.00
(66)	Commy Comiskey (arms folded)	1600.	800.00	475.00
(67)	Commy Comiskey (Dogs Head)	1500.	750.00	450.00
(68)	Roger Connor (catching)	1600.	800.00	475.00
(69)	Roger Connor (hands on knees)	1600.	800.00	475.00

		NR MT	EX	VG
(70)	Roger Connor (with bat)	1600.	800.00	475.00
(71)	Jim Conway (Kansas City)	350.00	175.00	105.00
(72)	Pete Conway (Detroit)	350.00	175.00	105.00
(73)	Paul Cook (fielding)	350.00	175.00	105.00
(74)	Paul Cook (wearing mask)	350.00	175.00	105.00
(75)	Pop Corkhill	350.00	175.00	105.00
(76)	Samuel Crane	350.00	175.00	105.00
(77)	Lave Cross	350.00	175.00	105.00
(78)	Edward Daily	350.00	175.00	105.00
(79)	Bill Daley (Boston)	350.00	175.00	105.00
(80)	Con Daley (Daily) (Indianapolis)	350.00	175.00	105.00
(81)	Abner Dalrymple	350.00	175.00	105.00
(82)	Sun Daly (Minneapolis)	350.00	175.00	105.00
(83)	Tido Daly (Washington)	350.00	175.00	105.00
(84)	Tido Daly (Chicago)	350.00	175.00	105.00
(85)	Dell Darling	350.00	175.00	105.00
(86)	William Darnbrough	350.00	175.00	105.00
(87)	Big Ed Delehanty (bat held at right shoulder)	1850.	925.00	575.00
(88)	Big Ed Delehanty (bat held at horizontal level)	1850.	925.00	575.00
(89)	Jerry Denny	350.00	175.00	105.00
(90)	Jim Devlin (pitching)	350.00	175.00	105.00
(91)	Jim Devlin (sliding)	350.00	175.00	105.00
(92)	Jim Donnelly	350.00	175.00	105.00
(93)	Home Run Duffe (Duffee) (bending)	350.00	175.00	105.00
(94)	Home Run Duffe (Duffee) (catching, standing upright)	350.00	175.00	105.00
(95)	Home Run Duffe (Duffee) (with bat)	350.00	175.00	105.00
(96)	Hugh Duffy (catching)	1600.	800.00	475.00
(97)	Hugh Duffy (fielding)	1600.	800.00	475.00
(98)	Hugh Duffy (with bat)	1600.	800.00	475.00
(99)	Duck Duke	350.00	175.00	105.00
(100)	Sure Shot Dunlap (arms at side)	350.00	175.00	105.00
(101)	Sure Shot Dunlap (Dogs H)	350.00	175.00	105.00
(102)	Jesse Duryea	350.00	175.00	105.00
(103)	Frank Dwyer (bat at side)	350.00	175.00	105.00
(104)	Frank Dwyer (bat in air)	350.00	175.00	105.00
(105)	Frank Dwyer (ball in hands)	350.00	175.00	105.00
(106)	Frank Dwyer (hands cupped at chest)	350.00	175.00	105.00
(107)	Billy Earle	350.00	175.00	105.00
(108)	Red Ehret	350.00	175.00	105.00
(109)	Dude Esterbrook	350.00	175.00	105.00
(110)	Buck Ewing (New York, bat at side)	1600.	800.00	475.00
(111)	Buck Ewing (New York, bat in air)	1600.	800.00	475.00
(112)	Buck Ewing (New York, hands at head level)	1600.	800.00	475.00
(113)	Buck Ewing (New York, hands on knees)	1600.	800.00	475.00
(114)	Willie Breslin-mascot, Buck Ewing	350.00	175.00	105.00
(115)	Long John Ewing (Louisville)	350.00	175.00	105.00
(116)	Jay Faatz	350.00	175.00	105.00
(117)	Bill Farmer	350.00	175.00	105.00
(118)	Sid Farrar (hands outstreched at head level)	350.00	175.00	105.00
(119)	Sid Farrar (stooping)	350.00	175.00	105.00
(120)	Duke Farrell (fielding)	350.00	175.00	105.00
(121)	Duke Farrell (hands on knees)	350.00	175.00	105.00
(122)	Frank Fennelly	350.00	175.00	105.00
(123)	Charlie Ferguson	350.00	175.00	105.00
(124)	Alex Ferson	350.00	175.00	105.00
(125)	Jocko Fields	350.00	175.00	105.00
(126)	Silver Flint (with bat)	350.00	175.00	105.00
(127)	Silver Flint (with mask)	350.00	175.00	105.00
(128)	Jim Fogarty (catching, hands at neck level)	350.00	175.00	105.00
(129)	Jim Fogarty (running to left, hands at head level)	350.00	175.00	105.00
(130)	Jim Fogarty (sliding)	350.00	175.00	105.00
(131)	Jim Fogarty (with bat)	350.00	175.00	105.00
(132)	Elmer Foster (Minneapolis)	350.00	175.00	105.00
(133)	Elmer Foster (New York)	350.00	175.00	105.00
(134)	Dave Foutz	350.00	175.00	105.00
(135)	Shorty Fuller (catching)	350.00	175.00	105.00
(136)	Shorty Fuller (hands on knees)	350.00	175.00	105.00
(137)	Shorty Fuller (swinging bat)	350.00	175.00	105.00
(138)	Chris Fulmer, Foghorn Tucker (Dogs Head)	1000.	500.00	300.00
(139)	Pud Galvin	350.00	175.00	105.00
(140)	Charlie Ganzel (catching, hands at shoulder level)	350.00	175.00	105.00
(141)	Charlie Ganzel (catching, hands at thigh level)	350.00	175.00	105.00
(142)	Charlie Ganzel (with bat)	350.00	175.00	105.00
(143)	Gid Gardner	350.00	175.00	105.00
(144)	Hank Gastreich	350.00	175.00	105.00
(145)	Frenchy Genins (bat in air, looking at camera)	350.00	175.00	105.00
(146)	Frenchy Genins (swinging at ball)	350.00	175.00	105.00
(147)	Bill George	350.00	175.00	105.00
(148)	Charlie Getzein	350.00	175.00	105.00
(149)	Bobby Gilks	350.00	175.00	105.00
(150)	Barney Gilligan	350.00	175.00	105.00
(151)	Frank Gilmore	350.00	175.00	105.00
(152)	Pebbly Jack Glasscock (Dogs Head)	350.00	175.00	105.00
(153)	Pebbly Jack Glasscock (hands on knees)	350.00	175.00	105.00
(154)	Pebbly Jack Glasscock (throwing)	350.00	175.00	105.00
(155)	Kid Gleason (Philadelphia, fielding)	350.00	175.00	105.00
(156)	Kid Gleason (Philadelphia, pitching)	350.00	175.00	105.00
(157)	Will Gleason (Louisville)	350.00	175.00	105.00
(158)	Mouse Glenn	350.00	175.00	105.00
(159)	Piano Legs Gore (fielding)	350.00	175.00	105.00
(160)	Piano Legs Gore (with bat)	350.00	175.00	105.00
(161)	Henry Gruber	350.00	175.00	105.00
(162)	Ad Gumbert (right hand at eye level)	350.00	175.00	105.00
(163)	Ad Gumbert (right hand at waist level)	350.00	175.00	105.00
(164)	Tom Gunning	350.00	175.00	105.00
(165)	Joe Gunson	350.00	175.00	105.00
(166)	Bill Hallman	350.00	175.00	105.00
(167)	Billy Hamilton (fielding)	1600.	800.00	475.00
(168)	Billy Hamilton (with bat)	1600.	800.00	475.00
(169)	Ned Hanlon	350.00	175.00	105.00
(170)	William Hanrahan	350.00	175.00	105.00
(171)	Gill Hatfield (bat at waist)	350.00	175.00	105.00
(172)	Hatfield (bat over shoulder)	350.00	175.00	105.00
(173)	Gill Hatfield (catching)	350.00	175.00	105.00
(174)	Egyptian Healey	350.00	175.00	105.00
(175)	Hardie Henderson	350.00	175.00	105.00
(176)	Moxie Hengle	350.00	175.00	105.00
(177)	John Henry	350.00	175.00	105.00
(178)	Paul Hines	350.00	175.00	105.00
(179)	Texas Wonder Hoffman	350.00	175.00	105.00
(180)	Bug Holliday	350.00	175.00	105.00
(181)	Buster Hoover (Philadelphia)	350.00	175.00	105.00
(182)	Charles Hoover (Chicago or Kansas City)	350.00	175.00	105.00
(183)	Joe Hornung	350.00	175.00	105.00
(184)	Dummy Hoy	350.00	175.00	105.00
(185)	Nat Hudson	350.00	175.00	105.00
(186)	Mickey Hughes (holding ball at chest)	350.00	175.00	105.00
(187)	Mickey Hughes (holding ball at side)	350.00	175.00	105.00
(188)	Mickey Hughes (right hand extended)	350.00	175.00	105.00
(189)	Wild Bill Hutchinson (ball in hand, right heel hidden)	350.00	175.00	105.00
(190)	Wild Bill Hutchinson (ball in hand, right heel visible)	350.00	175.00	105.00
(191)	Bill Hutchinson (with bat)	350.00	175.00	105.00
(192)	Cutrate Irwin (Philadelphia, catching)	350.00	175.00	105.00
(193)	Cutrate Irwin (Philadelphia, throwing)	350.00	175.00	105.00
(194)	John Irwin (Washington)	350.00	175.00	105.00
(195)	A.C. Jantzen	350.00	175.00	105.00
(196)	Spud Johnson	350.00	175.00	105.00
(197)	Johnston (hands on hip)	350.00	175.00	105.00
(198)	Dick Johnston (with bat)	350.00	175.00	105.00
(199)	Tim Keefe (Dogs Head)	2000.	1000.	600.00
(200)	Tim Keefe (hands at chest)	1600.	800.00	475.00
(201)	Tim Keefe (pitching, right hand at head level)	1600.	800.00	475.00
(202)	Tim Keefe (pitching, right hand at waist level)	1600.	800.00	475.00
(203)	Charles Kelly (Philadelphia)	350.00	175.00	105.00
(204)	King Kelly (Boston, Dogs H)	1750.	875.00	525.00
(205)	John Kerins	350.00	175.00	105.00
(206)	Silver King (hands at chest level)	350.00	175.00	105.00
(207)	Silver King (hands at chin)	350.00	175.00	105.00
(208)	William Klusman	350.00	175.00	105.00
(209)	Gus Krock (right hand extended)	350.00	175.00	105.00
(210)	Gus Krock (with bat)	350.00	175.00	105.00
(211)	Willie Kuehne	350.00	175.00	105.00
(212)	Ted Larkin	350.00	175.00	105.00
(213)	Arlie Latham (throwing)	350.00	175.00	105.00
(214)	Arlie Latham (with bat)	350.00	175.00	105.00
(215)	Germany Long	350.00	175.00	105.00
(216)	Tom Lovett (right hand extended)	350.00	175.00	105.00
(217)	Tom Lovett (with bat)	350.00	175.00	105.00
(218)	Denny Lyons (left hand above head)	350.00	175.00	105.00
(219)	Denny Lyons (with bat)	350.00	175.00	105.00
(220)	Connie Mack	5000.	2500.	1500.
(221)	Little Mac Macullar	350.00	175.00	105.00
(222)	Kid Madden (ball in left hand at eye level)	350.00	175.00	105.00
(223)	Kid Madden (ball in hand above head)	350.00	175.00	105.00
(224)	Kid Madden (ball in hands at neck level)	350.00	175.00	105.00
(225)	Jimmy Manning (fielding)	350.00	175.00	105.00
(226)	Jimmy Manning (with bat)	350.00	175.00	105.00
(227)	Lefty Marr	350.00	175.00	105.00
(228)	Leech Maskrey	350.00	175.00	105.00
(229)	Mike Mattimore	350.00	175.00	105.00
(230)	Smiling Al Maul	350.00	175.00	105.00
(231)	Al Mays	350.00	175.00	105.00
(232)	Jimmy McAleer	350.00	175.00	105.00
(233)	Tommy McCarthy (right hand at head level)	1500.	750.00	450.00
(234)	Tommy McCarthy (with bat)	1500.	750.00	450.00
(235)	Deacon McGuire	350.00	175.00	105.00
(236)	Bill McGunnigle	350.00	175.00	105.00
(237)	Ed McKean (hands above head)	350.00	175.00	105.00
(238)	Ed McKean (with bat)	350.00	175.00	105.00
(239)	James McQuaid	350.00	175.00	105.00
(240)	Doggie Miller (Pittsburgh, ball in hands)	350.00	175.00	105.00
(241)	Doggie Miller (Pittsburgh, Dogs Head)	350.00	175.00	105.00
(242)	Joseph Miller (Minneapolis, hands outstretched)	350.00	175.00	105.00
(243)	Joseph Miller (Minneapolis, with bat)	350.00	175.00	105.00
(244)	Jocko Milligan (bat at side)	350.00	175.00	105.00
(245)	Jocko Milligan (bat in air)	350.00	175.00	105.00
(246)	Jocko Milligan (stooping)	350.00	175.00	105.00
(247)	Daniel Minnehan (Minahan)	350.00	175.00	105.00
(248)	Sam Moffet	350.00	175.00	105.00
(249)	Honest John Morrill	350.00	175.00	105.00
(250)	Joseph Mulvey (catching)	350.00	175.00	105.00
(251)	Joseph Mulvey (with bat)	350.00	175.00	105.00
(252)	Pat Murphy	350.00	175.00	105.00
(253)	Miah Murray	350.00	175.00	105.00
(254)	Truthful Jim Mutrie	350.00	175.00	105.00
(255)	Al Myers (Washington)	350.00	175.00	105.00
(256)	George Myers (Indianapolis)	350.00	175.00	105.00
(257)	Tom Nagle	350.00	175.00	105.00
(258)	Billy Nash (hands on knees)	350.00	175.00	105.00
(259)	Billy Nash (throwing)	350.00	175.00	105.00
(260)	Kid Nichols	1800.	900.00	550.00
(261)	Little Nick Nicol, Big John Reilly	350.00	175.00	105.00
(262)	Darby O'Brien (Brooklyn)	350.00	175.00	105.00
(263)	John O'Brien (Cleveland)	350.00	175.00	105.00
(264)	Rowdy Jack O'Connor	350.00	175.00	105.00
(265)	Hank O'Day	350.00	175.00	105.00
(266)	Tip O'Neill (bat held horizontally)	350.00	175.00	105.00
(267)	O'Neill (bat over shoulder)	350.00	175.00	105.00
(268)	Tip O'Neill (fielding)	350.00	175.00	105.00
(269)	Tip O'Neill (throwing)	350.00	175.00	105.00
(270)	Orator Jim O'Rourke (New York, right hand in air)	1600.	800.00	475.00
(271)	Orator Jim O'Rourke (New York, with bat)	1600.	800.00	475.00
(272)	Tom O'Rourke (Boston)	350.00	175.00	105.00
(273)	Dave Orr	350.00	175.00	105.00
(274)	Fred Pfeffer (right hand at neck level)	350.00	175.00	105.00
(275)	Fred Pfeffer (with bat)	350.00	175.00	105.00
(276)	Dick Phelan	350.00	175.00	105.00
(277)	Jack Pickett (right hand at head level)	350.00	175.00	105.00
(278)	Jack Pickett (stooping)	350.00	175.00	105.00
(279)	Jack Pickett (with bat)	350.00	175.00	105.00
(280)	George Pinkney (bat in air, nearly vertical)	350.00	175.00	105.00
(281)	George Pinkney (bat over right shoulder)	350.00	175.00	105.00
(282)	Jim Powell	350.00	175.00	105.00
(283)	Blondie Purcell	350.00	175.00	105.00
(284)	Joe Quinn (ball in hands)	350.00	175.00	105.00
(285)	Joe Quinn (ready to run)	350.00	175.00	105.00
(286)	Old Hoss Radbourn (Dogs Head)	2000.	1000.	600.00
(287)	Old Hoss Radbourn (hands on hips with bat)	1600.	800.00	475.00
(288)	Toad Ramsey	350.00	175.00	105.00
(289)	Princeton Charlie Reilly (St. Paul)	350.00	175.00	105.00
(290)	Long John Reilly (Cincinnati)	350.00	175.00	105.00
(291)	Danny Richardson (New York, arms at side)	350.00	175.00	105.00
(292)	Danny Richardson (New York, right hand at head level)	350.00	175.00	105.00
(293)	Hardy Richardson (Boston, hands at head level)	350.00	175.00	105.00
(294)	Hardy Richardson (Boston or Detroit, with bat)	350.00	175.00	105.00
(295)	Uncle Robbie Robinson (Athletics, catching)	1700.	850.00	475.00
(296)	Uncle Robbie Robinson (Athletics, with bat)	1700.	850.00	475.00
(297)	Yank Robinson (St. Louis, fielding)	350.00	175.00	105.00
(298)	Yank Robinson (St. Louis, with bat)	350.00	175.00	105.00
(299)	Dave Rowe (Kansas City, Dogs Head)	350.00	175.00	105.00
(300)	Jack Rowe (Detroit)	350.00	175.00	105.00
(301)	Jimmy Ryan (fielding)	350.00	175.00	105.00
(302)	Jimmy Ryan (with bat)	350.00	175.00	105.00
(303)	Ben Sanders (hands at neck level)	350.00	175.00	105.00
(304)	Ben Sanders (right hand at head level)	350.00	175.00	105.00
(305)	Frank Scheibeck	350.00	175.00	105.00
(306)	Gus Schmelz	350.00	175.00	105.00
(307)	Jumbo Schoeneck	350.00	175.00	105.00
(308)	Pop Schriver (hands at ankle level)	350.00	175.00	105.00
(309)	Pop Schriver (hands cupped at chest level)	350.00	175.00	105.00
(310)	Emmett Seery	350.00	175.00	105.00
(311)	Ed Seward	350.00	175.00	105.00
(312)	Daniel Shannon	350.00	175.00	105.00
(313)	William Sharsig	350.00	175.00	105.00
(314)	George Shoch	350.00	175.00	105.00
(315)	Otto Shomberg (Schomberg)	350.00	175.00	105.00
(316)	Lev Shreve	350.00	175.00	105.00
(317)	Mike Slattery	350.00	175.00	105.00
(318)	Germany Smith (Brooklyn, hands on knees)	350.00	175.00	105.00

	NR MT	EX	VG
(319) Germany Smith (Brooklyn, right hand at head level)	350.00	175.00	105.00
(320) Germany Smith (Brooklyn, with bat)	350.00	175.00	105.00
(321) Pap Smith (Pittsburg, hands on knees)	350.00	175.00	105.00
(322) Pap Smith (Pittsburg or Boston, with bat)	350.00	175.00	105.00
(323) Little Bill Sowders	350.00	175.00	105.00
(324) Charlie Sprague	350.00	175.00	105.00
(325) Harry Staley	350.00	175.00	105.00
(326) Dan Stearns	350.00	175.00	105.00
(327) Stovey (hands on knees)	350.00	175.00	105.00
(328) Harry Stovey (with bat)	350.00	175.00	105.00
(329) Joe Straus (Strauss)	350.00	175.00	105.00
(330) Cub Stricker	350.00	175.00	105.00
(331) Marty Sullivan (Indianapolis)	350.00	175.00	105.00
(332) Marty Sullivan (Chicago)	350.00	175.00	105.00
(333) Billy Sunday (bending to left)	1000.	500.00	300.00
(334) Billy Sunday (with bat)	1000.	500.00	300.00
(335) Ezra Sutton (hands at shoulder level)	350.00	175.00	105.00
(336) Ezra Sutton (with bat)	350.00	175.00	105.00
(337) Park Swartzel	350.00	175.00	105.00
(338) Pop Tate	350.00	175.00	105.00
(339) Patsy Tebeau	350.00	175.00	105.00
(340) John Tener	350.00	175.00	105.00
(341) Adonis Terry (arms extended)	350.00	175.00	105.00
(342) Adonis Terry (with bat)	350.00	175.00	105.00
(343) Big Sam Thompson (Detroit)	1600.	800.00	475.00
(344) Big Sam Thompson (Philadelphia)	1600.	800.00	475.00
(345) Silent Mike Tiernan	350.00	175.00	105.00
(346) Cannonball Titcomb	350.00	175.00	105.00
(347) Buster Tomney	350.00	175.00	105.00
(348) Sleepy Townsend (hands at head level)	350.00	175.00	105.00
(349) Sleepy Townsend (with bat)	350.00	175.00	105.00
(350) Bill Traffley	350.00	175.00	105.00
(351) Foghorn Tucker	350.00	175.00	105.00
(352) George Turner	350.00	175.00	105.00
(353) Larry Twitchell	350.00	175.00	105.00
(354) Jim Tyng	350.00	175.00	105.00
(355) Rip Van Haltren (hands above waist)	350.00	175.00	105.00
(356) Rip Van Haltren (right hand at right thigh)	350.00	175.00	105.00
(357) Rip Van Haltren (with bat)	350.00	175.00	105.00
(358) Farmer Vaughn	350.00	175.00	105.00
(359) Joe Visner (arms at side)	350.00	175.00	105.00
(360) Joe Visner (with bat)	350.00	175.00	105.00
(361) Monte Ward (Dogs Head)	2000.	1000.	600.00
(362) Monte Ward (hands on hips)	1600.	800.00	475.00
(363) Monte Ward (throwing)	1600.	800.00	475.00
(364) Bill Watkins	350.00	175.00	105.00
(365) Farmer Weaver	350.00	175.00	105.00
(366) Stump Weidman	350.00	175.00	105.00
(367) Wild Bill Weidner	350.00	175.00	105.00
(368) Curt Welch (Athletics)	350.00	175.00	105.00
(369) Will Gleason, Curt Welch	1000.	500.00	300.00
(370) Mickey Welch (New York)	350.00	175.00	105.00
(371) A.C. "Cannonball" Weyhing	350.00	175.00	105.00
(372) John Weyhing	350.00	175.00	105.00
(373) Deacon White (hands above head)	350.00	175.00	105.00
(374) Deacon White (looking down at ball)	350.00	175.00	105.00
(375) Art Whitney (Pittsburg)	350.00	175.00	105.00
(376) Grasshopper Whitney (Washington)	350.00	175.00	105.00
(377) Ned Williamson (arm folded)	350.00	175.00	105.00
(378) Ned Williamson (with bat)	350.00	175.00	105.00
(379) Watt Wilmot	350.00	175.00	105.00
(380) Medoc Wise	350.00	175.00	105.00
(381) Chicken Wolf	350.00	175.00	105.00
(382) George "Dandy" Wood (L.F., both hands at neck level)	350.00	175.00	105.00
(383) George "Dandy" Wood (L.F., right hand at head level)	350.00	175.00	105.00
(384) Pete Wood (P., with bat)	350.00	175.00	105.00
(385) Harry Wright	4000.	2000.	1200.

1887 N184 Kimball Champions

Similar to sets issued by Allen & Ginter and Goodwin, the Kimball tobacco company of Rochester, N.Y., issued its own 50-card set of "Champions of Games and Sport" in 1888, and included four baseball players among the "billiardists, girl riders, tight-rope walkers" and other popular celebrities featured in the series. Measuring 1-1/2" by 2-3/4", the color lithographs were inserted in packages of Kimball Cigarettes. The artwork on the card features a posed portrait, which occupies the top three-fourths, and a drawing of the player in action at the bottom. The back of the card contains an ad for Kimball Cigarettes along with a list of the various sports and activities depicted in the set. James O'Neill, whose name is misspelled on the

card, is the best known of the four baseball players. His .435 batting average in 1887 is the highest ever recorded. The Kimball promotion also included an album to house the card set.

	NR MT	EX	VG
Complete Set:	2300.	1150.	700.00
Common Player:	550.00	275.00	165.00
(1) E.A. Burch	550.00	275.00	165.00
(2) Dell Darling	550.00	275.00	165.00
(3) Hardie Henderson	550.00	275.00	165.00
(4) James O'Neil (O'Neill)	650.00	325.00	200.00

1887 N284 Buchner Gold Coin

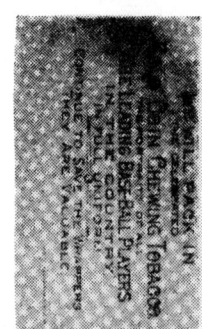

Issued circa 1887, the N284 issue was produced by D. Buchner & Company for its Gold Coin brand of chewing tobacco. Actually, the series was not comprised only of baseball players - actors, jockeys, firemen and policemen were also included. The cards, which measure 1-3/4" by 3", are color drawings. The set is not a popular one among collectors as the drawings do not represent the players designated on the cards. In most instances, players at a given position share the same drawing depicted on the card front. Three different card backs are found, all advising collectors to save the valuable chewing tobacco wrappers. Wrappers could be redeemed for various prizes. Although not picturing actual baseball players, this 44-card set issued by S.F. Hess & Co. has a baseball theme. The cards measured 2-7/8" by 1-1/2" and featured pictures of newspaper boys from eight different papers in eight different cities (Rochester, Cleveland, Philadelphia, Boston, Albany, Detroit, New York and Syracuse). The boys are pictured in a portrait photo wearing a baseball-style shirt bearing the name of their newspaper. The boy's name, position and newspaper are printed below, while the words "Newsboys League" appears in capital letters at the top of the card. No identification is provided for the four Philadelphia newsboys, so a photo description is provided in the checklist that follows.

	NR MT	EX	VG
Complete Set:	20000.	10000.	6000.
Common Player:	90.00	45.00	27.00
(1) Ed Andrews (hands at neck)	90.00	45.00	27.00
(2) Andrews (hands waist high)	110.00	55.00	33.00
(3) Cap Anson (hands outstretched)	500.00	250.00	150.00
(4) Cap Anson (left hand on hip)	550.00	275.00	165.00
(5) Tug Arundel	90.00	45.00	27.00
(6) Sam Barkley (Pittsburgh)	90.00	45.00	27.00
(7) Sam Barkley (St. Louis)	125.00	62.00	37.00
(8) Charley Bassett	90.00	45.00	27.00
(9) Charlie Bastian	90.00	45.00	27.00
(10) Ed Beecher	90.00	45.00	27.00
(11) Charlie Bennett	90.00	45.00	27.00
(12) Handsome Henry Boyle	110.00	55.00	33.00
(13) Dan Brouthers (hands outstretched)	225.00	112.00	67.00
(14) Dan Brouthers (with bat)	250.00	125.00	75.00
(15) Tom Brown	90.00	45.00	27.00
(16) Jack Burdock	90.00	45.00	27.00
(17) Oyster Burns (Baltimore)	110.00	55.00	33.00
(18) Tom Burns (Chicago)	90.00	45.00	27.00
(19) Doc Bushong	125.00	62.00	37.00
(20) John Cahill	110.00	55.00	33.00
(21) Cliff Carroll (Washington)	90.00	45.00	27.00
(22) Fred Carroll (Pittsburgh)	90.00	45.00	27.00
(23) Parisian Bob Carruthers (Caruthers)	150.00	75.00	45.00
(24) Dan Casey	125.00	62.00	37.00
(25) John Clarkson (ball at chest)	225.00	112.00	67.00
(26) John Clarkson (arm oustretched)	250.00	125.00	75.00
(27) Jack Clements	90.00	45.00	27.00
(28) John Coleman	90.00	45.00	27.00
(29) Charles Comiskey	500.00	250.00	150.00
(30) Roger Connor (hands outstretched)	225.00	112.00	67.00
(31) Roger Connor (hands oustreteched, face level)	250.00	125.00	75.00
(32) Corbett	110.00	55.00	33.00
(33) Sam Craig (Crane)	110.00	55.00	33.00
(34) Sam Crane	110.00	55.00	33.00
(35) Crowley	110.00	55.00	33.00
(36) Ed Cushmann (Cushman)	110.00	55.00	33.00
(37) Ed Dailey (Daily)	90.00	45.00	27.00
(38) Con Daley (Daily)	90.00	45.00	27.00
(39) Pat Deasley	110.00	55.00	33.00
(40) Jerry Denny (hands on knees)	90.00	45.00	27.00
(41) Jerry Denny (hands on thighs)	110.00	55.00	33.00
(42) Jim Donnelly	90.00	45.00	27.00
(43) Jim Donohue (Donahue)	110.00	55.00	33.00
(44) Mike Dorgan (right field)	90.00	45.00	27.00
(45) Mike Dorgan (batter)	110.00	55.00	33.00
(46) Sure Shot Dunlap	90.00	45.00	27.00
(47) Dude Esterbrook	110.00	55.00	33.00
(48) Buck Ewing (ready to tag)	225.00	112.00	67.00
(49) Buck Ewing (hands at neck)	250.00	125.00	75.00
(50) Sid Farrar	90.00	45.00	27.00
(51) Jack Farrell (ready to tag)	90.00	45.00	27.00
(52) Jack Farrell (hands at knees)	110.00	55.00	33.00
(53) Charlie Ferguson	90.00	45.00	27.00
(54) Silver Flint	90.00	45.00	27.00
(55) Jim Fogerty (Fogarty)	90.00	45.00	27.00
(56) Tom Forster	110.00	55.00	33.00
(57) Dave Foutz	150.00	75.00	45.00
(58) Chris Fulmer	110.00	55.00	33.00
(59) Joe Gerhardt	110.00	55.00	33.00
(60) Charlie Getzein	90.00	45.00	27.00
(61) Pete Gillespie (left field)	90.00	45.00	27.00
(62) Pete Gillespie (batter)	110.00	55.00	33.00
(63) Barney Gilligan	90.00	45.00	27.00
(64) Pebbly Jack Glasscock (fielding grounder)	110.00	55.00	33.00
(65) Pebbly Jack Glasscock (hands on knees)	125.00	62.00	37.00
(66) Will Gleason	125.00	62.00	37.00
(67) Piano Legs Gore	90.00	45.00	27.00
(68) Frank Hankinson	110.00	55.00	33.00
(69) Ned Hanlon	90.00	45.00	27.00
(70) Hart	110.00	55.00	33.00
(71) Egyptian Healy	90.00	45.00	27.00
(72) Paul Hines (centre field)	90.00	45.00	27.00
(73) Paul Hines (batter)	110.00	55.00	33.00
(74) Joe Hornung	90.00	45.00	27.00
(75) Cutrate Irwin	90.00	45.00	27.00
(76) Dick Johnston	90.00	45.00	27.00
(77) Tim Keefe (right arm outstretched)	225.00	112.00	67.00
(78) Keefe (arm outstretched)	250.00	125.00	75.00
(79) King Kelly (right field)	250.00	125.00	75.00
(80) King Kelly (catcher)	275.00	137.00	82.00
(81) Kennedy	110.00	55.00	33.00
(82) Matt Kilroy	110.00	55.00	33.00
(83) Arlie Latham	150.00	75.00	45.00
(84) Jimmy Manning	90.00	45.00	27.00
(85) Bill McClellan (existence not confirmed)			
(86) Jim McCormick	110.00	55.00	33.00
(87) Jack McGeachy	90.00	45.00	27.00
(88) Jumbo McGinnis	125.00	62.00	37.00
(89) George Meyers (Myers)	110.00	55.00	33.00
(90) Doggie Miller	90.00	45.00	27.00
(91) Honest John Morrill (hands outstretched)	90.00	45.00	27.00
(92) Honest John Morrill (hands at neck)	110.00	55.00	33.00
(93) Tom Morrissy (Morrissey)	110.00	55.00	33.00
(94) Joe Mulvey (hands on knees)	90.00	45.00	27.00
(95) Joe Mulvey (hands above head)	110.00	55.00	33.00
(96) Al Myers	90.00	45.00	27.00
(97) Candy Nelson	110.00	55.00	33.00
(98) Little Nick Nichol	125.00	62.00	37.00
(99) Billy O'Brien	90.00	45.00	27.00
(100) Tip O'Neil (O'Neill)	150.00	75.00	45.00
(101) Orator Jim O'Rourke (hands cupped)	225.00	112.00	67.00
(102) Orator Jim O'Rourke (hands on thighs)	250.00	125.00	75.00
(103) Dave Orr	110.00	55.00	33.00
(104) Jimmy Peoples	90.00	45.00	27.00

	NR MT	EX	VG
(105) Fred Pfeffer	90.00	45.00	27.00
(106) Bill Phillips	90.00	45.00	27.00
(107) Mark Polhemus	90.00	45.00	27.00
(108) Henry Porter	90.00	45.00	27.00
(109) Blondie Purcell	110.00	55.00	33.00
(110) Old Hoss Radbourn (hands at chest)	225.00	112.00	67.00
(111) Old Hoss Radbourn (hands above waist)	250.00	125.00	75.00
(112) Danny Richardson (New York, hands at knees)	90.00	45.00	27.00
(113) Danny Richardson (New York, foot on base)	110.00	55.00	33.00
(114) Hardy Richardson (Detroit, hands at right shoulder)	90.00	45.00	27.00
(115) Hardy Richardson (Detroit, hands above head)	110.00	55.00	33.00
(116) Yank Robinson	125.00	62.00	37.00
(117) George Rooks	110.00	55.00	33.00
(118) Chief Rosemann (Roseman)	110.00	55.00	33.00
(119) Jimmy Ryan	110.00	55.00	33.00
(120) Emmett Seery (hands at right shoulder)	90.00	45.00	27.00
(121) Emmett Seery (hands outstretched)	110.00	55.00	33.00
(122) Otto Shomberg (Schomberg)	90.00	45.00	27.00
(123) Pap Smith	90.00	45.00	27.00
(124) Joe Strauss	110.00	55.00	33.00
(125) Danny Sullivan	125.00	62.00	37.00
(126) Marty Sullivan	90.00	45.00	27.00
(127) Billy Sunday	125.00	62.00	37.00
(128) Ezra Sutton	90.00	45.00	27.00
(129) Big Sam Thompson (hand at belt)	225.00	112.00	67.00
(130) Big Sam Thompson (hands chest high)	250.00	125.00	75.00
(131) Chris Von Der Ahe	500.00	250.00	150.00
(132) Ward (fielding grounder)	225.00	112.00	67.00
(133) Monte Ward (hands by knee)	250.00	125.00	75.00
(134) Ward (hands on knees)	250.00	125.00	75.00
(135) Curt Welch	125.00	62.00	37.00
(136) Deacon White	110.00	55.00	33.00
(137) Art Whitney (Pittsburgh)	90.00	45.00	27.00
(138) Grasshopper Whitney (Washington)	90.00	45.00	27.00
(139) Ned Williamson (fielding grounder)	125.00	62.00	37.00
(140) Ned Williamson (hands at chest)	150.00	75.00	45.00
(141) Medoc Wise	90.00	45.00	27.00
(142) Dandy Wood (hands at right shoulder)	90.00	45.00	27.00
(143) Dandy Wood (stealing base)	110.00	55.00	33.00

1895 N300 Mayo's Cut Plug

These 1-5/8" by 2-7/8" cards were issued by the Mayo Tobacco Works of Richmond, Virginia. There are 48 cards in the set, with 40 different players pictured. Twenty-eight of the players are pictured in uniform and 12 are shown in street clothes. Eight players appear both ways. Eight of the uniformed players also appear in two variations, creating the 48-card total. Card fronts are black and white or sepia portraits on black cardboard, with a Mayo's Cut Plug ad at the bottom of each card. Cards are unnumbered.

	NR MT	EX	VG
Complete Set:	25000.	12500.	7500.
Common Player:	300.00	150.00	90.00
(1) Charlie Abbey	300.00	150.00	90.00
(2) Cap Anson	2000.	1000.	600.00
(3) Jimmy Bannon	300.00	150.00	90.00
(4a) Dan Brouthers (Baltimore on shirt)	800.00	400.00	250.00
(4b) Dan Brouthers (Louisville on shirt)	900.00	450.00	275.00
(5) Ed Cartwright	300.00	150.00	90.00
(6) John Clarkson	800.00	400.00	250.00
(7) Tommy Corcoran	300.00	150.00	90.00
(8) Lave Cross	300.00	150.00	90.00
(9) Bill Dahlen	300.00	150.00	90.00
(10) Tom Daly	300.00	150.00	90.00
(11) Ed Delehanty (Delahanty)	900.00	450.00	275.00
(12) Hugh Duffy	800.00	400.00	250.00
(13a) Buck Ewing (Cleveland on shirt)	800.00	400.00	250.00
(13b) Buck Ewing (Cincinnati on shirt)	900.00	450.00	275.00
(14) Dave Foutz	300.00	150.00	90.00
(15) Charlie Ganzel	300.00	150.00	90.00
(16a) Jack Glasscock (Pittsburg on shirt)	325.00	162.00	100.00
(16b) Jack Glasscock (Louisville on shirt)	350.00	175.00	105.00
(17) Mike Griffin	300.00	150.00	90.00
(18a) George Haddock (no team on shirt)	350.00	175.00	105.00
(18b) George Haddock (Philadelphia on shirt)	300.00	150.00	90.00
(19) Bill Hallman	300.00	150.00	90.00
(20) Billy Hamilton	800.00	400.00	250.00
(21) Bill Joyce	300.00	150.00	90.00
(22) Brickyard Kennedy	300.00	150.00	90.00
(23a) Tom Kinslow (no team on shirt)	350.00	175.00	105.00
(23b) Tom Kinslow (Pittsburg on shirt)	300.00	150.00	90.00
(24) Arlie Latham	325.00	162.00	100.00
(25) Herman Long	325.00	162.00	100.00
(26) Tom Lovett	300.00	150.00	90.00
(27) Bobby Lowe	350.00	175.00	105.00
(28) Tommy McCarthy	700.00	350.00	210.00
(29) Yale Murphy	300.00	150.00	90.00
(30) Billy Nash	325.00	162.00	100.00
(31) Kid Nichols	850.00	425.00	260.00
(32a) Fred Pfeffer (2nd Base)	300.00	150.00	90.00
(32b) Fred Pfeffer (Retired)	350.00	175.00	105.00
(33) Wilbert Robinson	875.00	437.00	265.00
(34a) Amos Russie (incorrect spelling)	875.00	437.00	265.00
(34b) Amos Rusie (correct spell)	800.00	400.00	250.00
(35) Jimmy Ryan	325.00	162.00	100.00
(36) Bill Shindle	300.00	150.00	90.00
(37) Germany Smith	300.00	150.00	90.00
(38) Otis Stocksdale (Stockdale)	300.00	150.00	90.00
(39) Tommy Tucker	300.00	150.00	90.00
(40a) Monte Ward (2nd Base)	800.00	400.00	250.00
(40b) Monte Ward (Retired)	900.00	450.00	275.00

1896 N301 Mayo Die-Cuts

Mayo Tobacco Works of Richmond, Va., issued an innovative, if not very popular, series of die-cut baseball player figures in 1896. These tiny (1 1/2" long by just 3/16" wide) cardboard figures were inserted in packages of Mayo's Cut Plug Tobacco and wre designed to be used as part of a baseball board game. A "grandstand, base and teetotum" were available free by mail to complete the game pieces. Twenty-eight different die-cut figures were available, representing 26 unspecified New York and Boston players along with two umpires. The players are shown in various action poses--either running, batting, pitching or fielding. The backs carry an ad for Mayo's Tobacco. The players shown do not relate to any actual members of the New York or Boston clubs, diminishing the popularity of this issue, which has an American Card Catalog designation of N301.

	NR MT	EX	VG
Complete Set:	1000.	500.00	300.00
Common Player:	35.00	17.50	10.50
(1a) Pitcher (Boston)	35.00	17.50	10.50
(1b) Pitcher (New York)	35.00	17.50	10.50
(2a) 1st Baseman (Boston)	35.00	17.50	10.50
(2b) 1st Baseman (New York)	35.00	17.50	10.50
(3a) 2nd Baseman (Boston)	35.00	17.50	10.50
(3b) 2nd Baseman (New York)	35.00	17.50	10.50
(4a) 3rd Baseman (Boston)	35.00	17.50	10.50
(4b) 3rd Baseman (New York)	35.00	17.50	10.50
(5a) Right Fielder (Boston)	35.00	17.50	10.50
(5b) Right Fielder (New York)	35.00	17.50	10.50
(6a) Center Fielder (Boston)	35.00	17.50	10.50
(6b) Center Fielder (New York)	35.00	17.50	10.50
(7a) Left Fielder (Boston)	35.00	17.50	10.50
(7b) Left Fielder (New York)	35.00	17.50	10.50
(8a) Short Stop (Boston)	35.00	17.50	10.50
(8b) Short Stop (New York)	35.00	17.50	10.50
(9a) Catcher (Boston)	35.00	17.50	10.50
(9b) Catcher (New York)	35.00	17.50	10.50
(10a) Batman (Boston)	35.00	17.50	10.50
(10b) Batman (New York)	35.00	17.50	10.50
(11a) Runner (Boston, standing upright)	35.00	17.50	10.50
(11b) Runner (New York, standing upright)	35.00	17.50	10.50
(12a) Runner (Boston, bent slightly forward)	35.00	17.50	10.50
(12b) Runner (New York, bent slightly forward)	35.00	17.50	10.50
(13a) Runner (Boston, bent well forward)	35.00	17.50	10.50
(13b) Runner (New York, bent well forward)	35.00	17.50	10.50
(14) Umpire (facing front)	35.00	17.50	10.50
(15) Field Umpire (rear view)	35.00	17.50	10.50

1888 N321 S.F. Hess

One of several tobacco card sets produced by S.F. Hess & Co. of Rochester, the N321 set is a rare 40-card issue featuring players from the California League. The cards measure 2-7/8" by 1-1/2" and feature color drawings of players. The player's name and team are printed along the top margin of the card, while the words "S.F. Hess and Co.'s/Creole Cigarettes" appear at the bottom. "California League" is also printed in large capital letters above the player drawing, while the 1888 copyright date appears below. There are 35 players (including one umpire) in the set, and five players are pictured on two cards each, resulting in 40 different cards.

	NR MT	EX	VG
Complete Set:	20000.	10000.	6000.
Common Player:	500.00	250.00	150.00
(1) Bennett	500.00	250.00	150.00
(2) Borchers	500.00	250.00	150.00
(3) Buckley	500.00	250.00	150.00
(4) Burke (batting)	500.00	250.00	150.00
(5) Burke (ready to pitch)	500.00	250.00	150.00
(6) Burnett	500.00	250.00	150.00
(7) Carroll	500.00	250.00	150.00
(8) Donohue	500.00	250.00	150.00
(9) Donovan	500.00	250.00	150.00
(10) Finn	500.00	250.00	150.00
(11) Gagus	500.00	250.00	150.00
(12) Hanley	500.00	250.00	150.00
(13) Hardie (C., wearing mask)	500.00	250.00	150.00
(14) Hardie (C.F., with bat)	500.00	250.00	150.00
(15) Hayes	500.00	250.00	150.00
(16) Lawton	500.00	250.00	150.00
(17) Levy	500.00	250.00	150.00
(18) Long	500.00	250.00	150.00
(19) McCord	500.00	250.00	150.00
(20) Meegan	500.00	250.00	150.00
(21) Moore	500.00	250.00	150.00
(22) Mullee	500.00	250.00	150.00
(23) Newhert	500.00	250.00	150.00
(24) Noonan	500.00	250.00	150.00
(25) O'Day	500.00	250.00	150.00
(26) Perrier	500.00	250.00	150.00
(27) Powers (1st B., catching)	500.00	250.00	150.00
(28) Powers (1st B. & Capt., with bat)	500.00	250.00	150.00
(29) Ryan	500.00	250.00	150.00
(30) Selna	500.00	250.00	150.00
(31) Shea	500.00	250.00	150.00
(32) J. Sheridan (umpire)	500.00	250.00	150.00
(33) "Big" Smith	500.00	250.00	150.00
(34) H. Smith	500.00	250.00	150.00
(35) J. Smith	500.00	250.00	150.00
(36) Smett	500.00	250.00	150.00
(37) Stockwell (throwing)	500.00	250.00	150.00
(38) Stockwell (with bat)	500.00	250.00	150.00
(39) Sweeney	500.00	250.00	150.00
(40) Whitehead	500.00	250.00	150.00

1888 N333 S.F. Hess Newsboys League

Issued circa 1887, the N284 issue was produced by D. Buchner & Company for its Gold Coin brand of chewing tobacco. Actually, the series was not comprised only of baseball players - actors, jockeys, firemen and policemen were also included. The cards, which measure 1-3/4" by 3", are color drawings. The set is not a popular one among collectors as the drawings do not

represent the players designated on the cards. In most instances, players at a given position share the same drawing depicted on the card front. Three different card backs are found, all advising collectors to save the valuable chewing tobacco wrappers. Wrappers could be redeemed for various prizes. Although not picturing actual baseball players, this 44-card set issued by S.F. Hess & Co. has a baseball theme. The cards measured 2-7/8" by 1-1/2" and featured pictures of newspaper boys from eight different papers in eight different cities (Rochester, Cleveland, Philadelphia, Boston, Albany, Detroit, New York and Syracuse). The boys are pictured in a portrait photo wearing a baseball-style shirt bearing the name of their newspaper. The boy's name, position and newspaper are printed below, while the words "Newsboys League" appears in capital letters at the top of the card. No identification is provided for the four Philadelphia newsboys, so a photo description is provided in the checklist that follows.

		NR MT	EX	VG
	Complete Set:	3100.	1550.	930.00
	Common Player:	70.00	35.00	21.00
(1)	R.J. Bell	70.00	35.00	21.00
(2)	Binden	70.00	35.00	21.00
(3)	Bowen	70.00	35.00	21.00
(4)	Boyle	70.00	35.00	21.00
(5)	Britcher	70.00	35.00	21.00
(6)	Caine	70.00	35.00	21.00
(7)	I. Cohen	70.00	35.00	21.00
(8)	R. Cohen	70.00	35.00	21.00
(9)	Cross	70.00	35.00	21.00
(10)	F. Cuddy	70.00	35.00	21.00
(11)	E. Daisey	70.00	35.00	21.00
(12)	Davis	70.00	35.00	21.00
(13)	B. Dinsmore	70.00	35.00	21.00
(14)	Donovan	70.00	35.00	21.00
(15)	A. Downer	70.00	35.00	21.00
(16)	Fanelly	70.00	35.00	21.00
(17)	J. Flood	70.00	35.00	21.00
(18)	C. Gallagher	70.00	35.00	21.00
(19)	M.H. Gallagher	70.00	35.00	21.00
(20)	D. Galligher	70.00	35.00	21.00
(21)	J. Galligher	70.00	35.00	21.00
(22)	Haskins	70.00	35.00	21.00
(23)	Herze	70.00	35.00	21.00
(24)	F. Horan	70.00	35.00	21.00
(25)	Hosler	70.00	35.00	21.00
(26)	Hyde	70.00	35.00	21.00
(27)	Keilty	70.00	35.00	21.00
(28)	C. Kellogg	70.00	35.00	21.00
(29)	Mahoney	70.00	35.00	21.00
(30)	Mayer	70.00	35.00	21.00
(31)	I. McDonald	70.00	35.00	21.00
(32)	McGrady	70.00	35.00	21.00
(33)	O'Brien	70.00	35.00	21.00
(34)	E.C. Murphy	70.00	35.00	21.00
(35)	Sabin	70.00	35.00	21.00
(36)	Shedd	70.00	35.00	21.00
(37)	R. Sheehan	70.00	35.00	21.00
(38)	Smith	70.00	35.00	21.00
(39)	Talbot	70.00	35.00	21.00
(40)	Walsh	70.00	35.00	21.00
(41)	Philadelphia newsboy (hair parted on right side)	70.00	35.00	21.00
(42)	Philadelphia newsboy (hair parted on left side)	70.00	35.00	21.00
(43)	Philadelphia newsboy (no part in hair)	70.00	35.00	21.00
(44)	Philadelphia newsboy (head shaved)	70.00	35.00	21.00

Definitions for grading conditions are located in the Introduction section at the front of this book.

1889 N338-1 S.F. Hess California League

This tobacco card set picturing players from the California League is one of the rarest of all 19th century issues. Issued in the late 1880s by S.F. Hess & Co. of Rochester, these 2-7/8" by 1-1/2" cards are so rare that only several examples are known to exist. Some of the photos in the N338-1 set are identical to the drawings in the N321 set, issued by S.F. Hess in 1888. The N338-1 cards are found with the words "California League" printed in an arc either above or below the player photo. The player's name appears below the photo. At the bottom of the card the words "S.F. Hess & Co.'s Creole Cigarettes" are printed in a rolling style.

		NR MT	EX	VG
	Complete Set:	16000.	8000.	4800.
	Common Player:	1000.	500.00	300.00
(1)	Borsher	1000.	500.00	300.00
(2)	Carroll	1000.	500.00	300.00
(3)	C. Ebright	1000.	500.00	300.00
(4)	P. Incell	1000.	500.00	300.00
(5)	C.F. Lawton	1000.	500.00	300.00
(6)	C.F. Levy (throwing)	1000.	500.00	300.00
(7)	C.F. Levy (with bat)	1000.	500.00	300.00
(8)	C. McDonald	1000.	500.00	300.00
(9)	P Meegan	1000.	500.00	300.00
(10)	S.S. Newhert	1000.	500.00	300.00
(11)	P. Noonan	1000.	500.00	300.00
(12)	R.F. Perrier	1000.	500.00	300.00
(13)	Perrier, H. Smith	1000.	500.00	300.00
(14)	Ryan	1000.	500.00	300.00
(15)	J. Smith, N. Smith	1000.	500.00	300.00
(16)	P. Sweeney	1000.	500.00	300.00

1889 N338-2 S.F. Hess

The most popular of the S.F. Hess & Co. issues, this 21-card set was issued in 1889 and pictures 16 players from the New York Giants, two New York Mets players, two from St. Louis and one from Detroit. The cards measure 2-3/4" by 1-1/2" and feature sepia-toned photographs, most of which are enclosed in ovals with a dark background. The player's name is printed in capital letters just beneath the photo, and the S.F. Hess & Co. logo appears at the bottom (without using the Creole Cigarette brand name).

		NR MT	EX	VG
	Complete Set:	21000.	10500.	6300.
	Common Player:	750.00	375.00	225.00
(1)	Bill Brown	750.00	375.00	225.00
(2)	Roger Conner (Connor)	1800.	900.00	550.00
(3)	Ed Crane	750.00	375.00	225.00
(4)	Buck Ewing	1800.	900.00	550.00
(5)	Elmer Foster	750.00	375.00	225.00
(6)	Wm. George	750.00	375.00	225.00
(7)	Joe Gerhardt	750.00	375.00	225.00
(8)	Chas. Getzein	750.00	375.00	225.00
(9)	Geo. Gore	750.00	375.00	225.00
(10)	Gil Hatfield	750.00	375.00	225.00
(11)	Tim Keefe	1800.	900.00	550.00
(12)	Arlie Latham	750.00	375.00	225.00
(13)	Pat Murphy	750.00	375.00	225.00
(14)	Jim Mutrie	750.00	375.00	225.00
(15)	Dave Orr	750.00	375.00	225.00
(16)	Danny Richardson	750.00	375.00	225.00
(17)	Mike Slattery	750.00	375.00	225.00
(18)	Silent Mike Tiernan	750.00	375.00	225.00
(19)	Lidell Titcomb	750.00	375.00	225.00
(20)	Johnny Ward	1800.	900.00	550.00
(21)	Curt Welch	750.00	375.00	225.00
(22)	Mickey Welch	1800.	900.00	550.00
(23)	Arthur Whitney	750.00	375.00	225.00

1886 N370 Lone Jack

The 1886 Lone Jack set is among the rarest of all 19th Century tobacco issues. Issued by the Lone Jack Cigarette Co. of Lynchburg, Va., the set consists of 13 subjects, all members of the champion St. Louis Browns. Photos for the set are enlarged versions of those used in the more popular N172 Old Judge series. Cards in the set measure 2-1/2" by 1-1/2" and carry an ad for Lone Jack Cigarettes along the bottom of the front. The set features the Browns' starting lineup for 1886 along with their two top pitchers, backup catcher and owner, Chris Von Der Ahe.

		NR MT	EX	VG
	Complete Set:	10000.	5000.	3000.
	Common Player:	600.00	300.00	180.00
(1)	Doc Bushong	600.00	300.00	180.00
(2)	Parisian Bob Caruthers	600.00	300.00	180.00
(3)	Commy Commiskey (Comiskey)	2500.	1250.	750.00
(4)	Dave Foutz	600.00	300.00	180.00
(5)	Will Gleason	600.00	300.00	180.00
(6)	Nat Hudson	600.00	300.00	180.00
(7)	Rudy Kimler (Kemmler)	600.00	300.00	180.00
(8)	Arlie Latham	600.00	300.00	180.00
(9)	Little Nick Nicol	600.00	300.00	180.00
(10)	Tip O'Neil (O'Neill)	600.00	300.00	180.00
(11)	Yank Robinson	600.00	300.00	180.00
(12)	Chris Von Der Ahe	1250.	625.00	400.00
(13)	Curt Welsh (Welch)	600.00	300.00	180.00

1888 N403 Yum Yum Tobacco

An extremely rare series of tobacco cards, this set was issued in 1888 by August Beck & Co. of Chicago. The cards, which vary slightly in size but average 1-3/8" by 2-3/4", were distributed in packages of the company's Yum Yum smoking and chewing tobacco. Yum Yum cards carry the American Card Catalog designation N403 and arefound in two distinct types: photographic portraits and full-length action drawings that appear to be copied from photos used in the Old Judge sets of the same period. In both types, the player's name and position appear in capital letters below the photo, while the very bottom of the card states: 'Smoke and Chew "Yum Yum" Tobacco. A. Beck & Co. Chicago, Ill." Players from all eight National League clubs, plus Brooklyn of the American Association, are included in the set.

		NR MT	EX	VG
Complete Set:		35000.	17500.	10500.
Common Line Drawing:		500.00	250.00	150.00
Common Portrait:		750.00	375.00	230.00
(1)	Cap Anson	5000.	2500.	1500.
(2)	Lady Baldwin	500.00	250.00	150.00
(3)	Dan Brouthers	1000.	500.00	300.00
(4)	Bill "California" Brown	500.00	250.00	150.00
(5)	Buffington (Buffinton)	600.00	300.00	180.00
(6)	Thomas Burns (portrait)	750.00	375.00	230.00
(7)	Thomas Burns (with bat)	500.00	250.00	150.00
(8)	John Clarkson (portrait)	1800.	900.00	550.00
(9)	John Clarkson (throwing)	1000.	500.00	300.00
(10)	John Coleman	750.00	375.00	230.00
(11)	Larry Corcoran	750.00	375.00	230.00
(12)	Tido Daily (Daly) (photo actually Billy Sunday)	750.00	375.00	230.00
(13)	Tom Deasley	750.00	375.00	230.00
(14)	Mike Dorgan	750.00	375.00	230.00
(15)	Buck Ewing (portrait)	1800.	900.00	550.00
(16)	Buck Ewing (with bat)	1000.	500.00	300.00
(17)	Silver Flint	750.00	375.00	230.00
(18)	Pud Galvin	1000.	500.00	300.00
(19)	Joe Gerhardt	750.00	375.00	230.00
(20)	Pete Gillespie	750.00	375.00	230.00
(21)	Pebbly Jack Glasscock	500.00	250.00	150.00
(22)	Ed Greer	750.00	375.00	230.00
(23)	Tim Keefe (pitching)	1000.	500.00	300.00
(24)	Tim Keefe (portrait)	1800.	900.00	550.00
(25)	King Kelly	1200.	600.00	350.00
26	King Kelly (photo)	5000.	2500.	1500.
(27)	Gus Krock	750.00	375.00	230.00
(28)	Connie Mack	1400.	700.00	425.00
(29)	Kid Madden	500.00	250.00	150.00
(30)	Doggie Miller	500.00	250.00	150.00
(31)	Billy Nash	500.00	250.00	150.00
(32)	O'Rourke (portrait)	1800.	900.00	550.00
(33)	O'Rourke (with bat)	1000.	500.00	300.00
(34)	Danny Richardson	750.00	375.00	230.00
(35)	Chief Roseman	750.00	375.00	230.00
(36)	Jimmy Ryan (portrait)	750.00	375.00	230.00
(37)	Jimmy Ryan (throwing)	500.00	250.00	150.00
(38)	Little Bill Sowders	500.00	250.00	150.00
(39)	Marty Sullivan	750.00	375.00	230.00
(40)	Billy Sunday (line drawing)	900.00	450.00	275.00
(41)	Billy Sunday (portrait)	1500.	750.00	450.00
(42)	Ezra Sutton	500.00	250.00	150.00
(43)	Tiernan (portrait)	750.00	375.00	230.00
(44)	Tiernan (with bat)	500.00	250.00	150.00
(45)	Rip Van Haltren (photo not Van Haltren)	750.00	375.00	230.00
(46)	Mickey Welch (hands clasped at chest)	1000.	500.00	300.00
(47)	Mickey Welch (portrait)	1800.	900.00	550.00
(48)	Mickey Welch (right arm extended)	1000.	500.00	300.00
(49)	Grasshopper Whitney	500.00	250.00	150.00
(50)	George "Dandy" Wood	500.00	250.00	150.00

1889 N526 No. 7/ Diamond Cigars

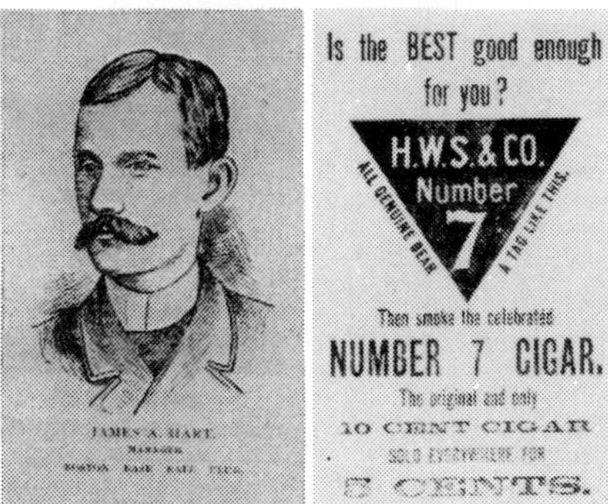

Two versions of this set picturing Boston players were issued in 1889 by Number 7 Cigars and Diamond S Cigars. The cards measure approximately 3-1/8" by 4-1/2" and feature black and white line portrait drawings of the players with their name printed below in capital letters along with the team name ("Boston Base Ball Club"). The backs carry an ad for either Number 7 Cigars, a product of H.W.S. & Co., or Diamond S Cigars, advertised as the "Best 10 cent Cigar in America." Except for the backs, the two sets are identical.

		NR MT	EX	VG
Complete Set:		9500.	4750.	3000.
Common Player:		400.00	200.00	120.00
(1)	C.W. Bennett	400.00	200.00	120.00
(2)	Dennis Brouthers	1000.	500.00	300.00
(3)	T.T. Brown	400.00	200.00	120.00
(4)	John G. Clarkson	1000.	500.00	300.00
(5)	C.W. Ganzel	400.00	200.00	120.00
(6)	James A. Hart	400.00	200.00	120.00
(7)	R.F. Johnston	400.00	200.00	120.00
(8)	M.J. Kelly	1200.	600.00	350.00
(9)	M.J. Madden	400.00	200.00	120.00
(10)	Wm. Nash	400.00	200.00	120.00
(11)	Jos. Quinn	400.00	200.00	120.00
(12)	Chas. Radbourn	1000.	500.00	300.00
(13)	J.B. Ray (should be I.B.)	400.00	200.00	120.00
(14)	Hardie Richardson	400.00	200.00	120.00
(15)	Wm. Sowders	400.00	200.00	120.00

1895 N566 Newsboy

Issued in the 1890s by the National Tobacco Works, this massive cabinet card set was distributed as a premium with the Newsboy tobacco brand. Although the set contained over 500 popular actresses, athletes, politicians and other celebrities of the day, only a dozen cards of baseball players have been found. The cards measure 4-1/4" by 6-1/2" and feature sepia-toned photographs mounted on a backing that has "Newsboy" written in script in the lower left corner. Each photograph is numbered. The baseball players included in the set are all members of the 1894 New York Giants, except Dave Foutz, who was Brooklyn's playing manager. There are two known poses of John Ward.

		NR MT	EX	VG
Complete Set:		15500.	7750.	5000.
Common Player:		750.00	375.00	225.00
174	W.H. Murphy	750.00	375.00	225.00
175	Amos Rusie	3500.	1750.	1050.
176	Michael Tiernan	750.00	375.00	225.00
177	E.D. Burke	750.00	375.00	225.00
178	J.J. Doyle	750.00	375.00	225.00
179	W.B. Fuller	750.00	375.00	225.00
180	Geo. Van Haltren	850.00	425.00	255.00
181	Dave Foutz	750.00	375.00	225.00
182	Jouett Meekin	850.00	425.00	255.00
201	W.H. Clark (Clarke)	750.00	375.00	225.00
202	Parke Wilson	750.00	375.00	225.00
586	John M. Ward (portrait, arms folded)	2500.	1250.	750.00
587	John M. Ward (standing, with bat)	1800.	900.00	550.00

1887 N690 Kalamazoo Bats

This set, issued circa 1887 by Charles Gross & Co. of Philadelphia, is one of the most popular and most difficult of all 19th century tobacco issues. The cards measure a rather large 2-1/4" by 4" and feature a sepia-toned photograph on heavy cardboard. The player's name and team appear inside a white rectangle at the bottom of the photo, while a small ad for Kalamazoo Bats cigarettes is included at the very bottom of the card. Some cards carry an 1887 copyright line, but there are indications that some of the cards date from 1886 or even 1888. The unnumbered set pictures players from four teams - two from New York (Giants and Mets) and two from Philadelphia (Athletics and Phillies). A few of the cards picture more than one player, and some cards have been found with an ad on the back

offering various prizes in exchange for saving the cards. The set has been assigned the American Card Catalog number N690. Because of the rareness of the N690 Kalamazoo Bats issue, no complete set is given.

Complete Set:				
Common Player:		650.00	325.00	200.00
(1)	Ed Andrews	650.00	325.00	200.00
(2)	Charles Bastian, Lyons	800.00	400.00	250.00
(3)	Louis Bierbauer	650.00	325.00	200.00
(4)	Louis Bierbauer, Gallagher	800.00	400.00	250.00
(5)	Buffington (Buffinton)	650.00	325.00	200.00
(6)	Daniel Casey	650.00	325.00	195.00
(7)	Jack Clements	650.00	325.00	200.00
(8)	Roger Connor	3000.	1500.	900.00
(9)	Larry Corcoran	1200.	600.00	350.00
(10)	Ed Cushman	1200.	600.00	350.00
(11)	Pat Deasley	1200.	600.00	350.00
(12)	Jim Devlin	650.00	325.00	200.00
(13)	Jim Donahue	1200.	600.00	350.00
(14)	Mike Dorgan	1200.	600.00	350.00
(15)	Dude Esterbrooke (Esterbrook)	1200.	600.00	350.00
(16)	Buck Ewing	3000.	1500.	900.00
(17)	Sid Farrar	650.00	325.00	200.00
(18)	Charlie Ferguson	650.00	325.00	200.00
(19)	Jim Fogarty	650.00	325.00	200.00
(20)	Fogarty, Deacon McGuire	800.00	400.00	250.00
(21)	Elmer Foster	1200.	600.00	350.00
(22)	Whitey Gibson	650.00	325.00	200.00
(23)	Pete Gillespie	600.00	300.00	180.00
(24)	Tom Gunning	650.00	325.00	200.00
(25)	Cutrate Irwin	650.00	325.00	200.00
(26)	Irwin, Smiling Al Maul	800.00	400.00	250.00
(27)	Tim Keefe	1800.	900.00	540.00
(28)	Ted Larkin	650.00	325.00	200.00
(29)	Ted Larkins, Jocko Milligan	800.00	400.00	250.00
(30)	Jack Lynch	1200.	600.00	350.00
(31)	Denny Lyons	650.00	325.00	200.00
(32)	Denny Lyons, Taylor	650.00	325.00	200.00
(33)	Fred Mann	600.00	300.00	180.00
(34)	Fred Mann, Uncle Robbie Robinson	1800.	900.00	550.00
(35)	Charlie Mason	650.00	325.00	200.00
(36)	Bobby Mathews	650.00	325.00	200.00
(37)	Smiling Al Maul	650.00	325.00	200.00
(38)	Al Mays	1200.	600.00	350.00
(39)	Jim McGan (McGarr)	650.00	325.00	200.00
(40)	Deacon McGuire (catching)	650.00	325.00	200.00
(41)	Deacon McGuire (throwing)	650.00	325.00	200.00
(42)	Jocko Milligan, Harry Stowe (Stovey)	800.00	400.00	250.00
(43)	Joseph Mulvey	650.00	325.00	200.00
(44)	Candy Nelson	1200.	600.00	350.00
(45)	Orator Jim O'Rourke	3000.	1500.	900.00
(46)	Dave Orr	1200.	600.00	350.00
(47)	Tom Poorman	650.00	325.00	200.00
(48)	Danny Richardson	1200.	600.00	350.00
(49)	Uncle Robbie Robinson	2000.	1000.	600.00
(50)	Chief Roseman	1200.	600.00	350.00
(51)	Harry Stowe (Stovey) (hands on hips)	750.00	375.00	230.00
(52)	Harry Stowe (Stovey) (hands outstretched)	750.00	375.00	230.00
(53)	Sleepy Townsend	650.00	325.00	200.00
(54)	Jocko Milligan, Sleepy Townsend	800.00	400.00	250.00
(55)	Monte Ward	3000.	1500.	900.00
(56)	Gus Weyhing	650.00	325.00	200.00
(57)	George "Dandy" Wood	650.00	325.00	200.00
(58)	Harry Wright	2500.	1250.	750.00

1887 N690 Kalamazoo Bats Cabinets

Another extremely rare issue, this series of cabinet cards was issued either as a proof or a premium by Charles Gross & Co. of Philadelphia, makers of the Kalamazoo Bats brand of cigarettes. Two distinct types have been found, both measuring 4-1/4" by 6-1/2". One variety displays the photo on a black mount with the words "Smoke Kalamazoo Bats" embossed in gold to the left. The other contains no advertising, although there is an oval embossment on the card, along with the words "Chas. Gross & Co." and an 1887 copyright line. These cards also have a distinctive pink color on the back of the cardboard mount. Because of the rareness of the N690 Kalamazoo Bats Cabinets, no complete set price is given.

Complete Set:				
Common Player:		1200.	600.00	350.00
Common Team:		10000.	5000.	3000.
(1)	Ed Andrews	1200.	600.00	350.00
(2)	Charles Bastian, Daniel Casey, Taylor	1200.	600.00	350.00
(3)	Charles Bastian, Denny Lyons	1200.	600.00	350.00
(4)	Louis Bierbauer, Gallagher	1200.	600.00	350.00
(5)	Charles Buffington (Buffinton)	1200.	600.00	350.00
(6)	Daniel Casey	1200.	600.00	350.00
(7)	Jack Clements	1200.	600.00	350.00
(8)	Jim Devlin	1200.	600.00	350.00
(9)	Sid Farrar	1200.	600.00	350.00
(10)	Charlie Ferguson	1200.	600.00	350.00
(11)	Jim Fogarty	1200.	600.00	350.00
(12)	Whitey Gibson	1200.	600.00	350.00
(13)	Tom Gunning	1200.	600.00	350.00
(14)	Cutrate Irwin	1200.	600.00	350.00
(15)	Cutrate Irwin, Smiling Al Maul	1200.	600.00	350.00
(16)	Ted Larkins (Larkin), Jocko Milligan	1200.	600.00	350.00
(17)	Denny Lyons	1200.	600.00	350.00
(18)	Denny Lyons, Taylor	1200.	600.00	350.00
(19)	Fred Mann	1200.	600.00	350.00
(20)	Bobby Mathews	1200.	600.00	350.00
(21)	Smiling Al Maul	1200.	600.00	350.00
(22)	Chippy McCan (McGarr)	1200.	600.00	350.00
(23)	Deacon McGuire	1200.	600.00	350.00
(24)	Jocko Milligan, Harry Stowe (Stovey)	1200.	600.00	350.00
(25)	Joseph Mulvey	1200.	600.00	350.00
(26)	Tim Poorman	1200.	600.00	350.00
(27)	Ed Seward	1200.	600.00	350.00
(28)	Harry Stowe (Stovey)	1200.	600.00	350.00
(29)	Sleepy Townsend	1200.	600.00	350.00
(30)	George "Dandy" Wood	1200.	600.00	350.00
(31)	Athletic Club	10000.	5000.	3000.
(32)	Boston B.B.C.	20000.	10000.	6000.
(33)	Philadelphia B.B.C.	10000.	5000.	3000.
(34)	Pittsburg B.B.C.	10000.	5000.	3000.

1887 N690-1 Kalamazoo Bats Team Cards

The six team photos in this set were issued by Charles Gross & Co. of Philadelphia as a promotion for its Kalamazoo Bats brand of cigarettes. The cards, which are similar in design to the related N690 series, are extremely rare. They feature a team photo with the caption in a white box at the bottom of the photo and an ad for Kalamazoo Bats to the left.

		NR MT	EX	VG
Complete Set:		25000.	12500.	7500.
Common Team:		4000.	2000.	1250.
(1)	Athletic Club	4000.	2000.	1250.
(2)	Baltimore B.B.C.	4000.	2000.	1250.
(3)	Boston B.B.C.	5000.	2500.	1500.
(4)	Detroit B.B.C.	4000.	2000.	1250.
(5)	Philadelphia B.B.C.	4000.	2000.	1250.
(6)	Pittsburg B.B.C.	4000.	2000.	1250.

1969 Nabisco Team Flakes

This set of cards is seen in two different sizes: 1- 15/16" by 3" and 1-3/4" by 2-15/16". This is explained by the varying widths of the card borders on the backs of Nabisco cereal packages. Cards are action color photos bordered in yellow. Twenty-four of the top players in the game are included in the set, which was issued in three series of eight cards each. No team insignias are visible on any of the cards. Packages described the cards as "Mini Posters."

		NR MT	EX	VG
Complete Set:		600.00	300.00	180.00
Common Player:		4.00	2.00	1.25
(1)	Hank Aaron	60.00	30.00	18.00
(2)	Richie Allen	7.00	3.50	2.00
(3)	Lou Brock	40.00	20.00	12.00
(4)	Paul Casanova	4.00	2.00	1.25
(5)	Roberto Clemente	60.00	30.00	18.00
(6)	Al Ferrara	4.00	2.00	1.25
(7)	Bill Freehan	5.00	2.50	1.50
(8)	Jim Fregosi	5.00	2.50	1.50
(9)	Bob Gibson	20.00	10.00	6.00
(10)	Tony Horton	5.00	2.50	1.50
(11)	Tommy John	10.00	5.00	3.00
(12)	Al Kaline	40.00	20.00	12.00
(13)	Jim Lonborg	4.00	2.00	1.25
(14)	Juan Marichal	20.00	10.00	6.00
(15)	Willie Mays	60.00	30.00	18.00
(16)	Rick Monday	5.00	2.50	1.50
(17)	Tony Oliva	6.00	3.00	1.75
(18)	Brooks Robinson	45.00	22.00	13.50
(19)	Frank Robinson	40.00	20.00	12.00
(20)	Pete Rose	65.00	32.00	19.50
(21)	Ron Santo	6.00	3.00	1.75
(22)	Tom Seaver	50.00	25.00	15.00
(23)	Rusty Staub	6.00	3.00	1.75
(24)	Mel Stottlemyre	5.00	2.50	1.50

Regional interest may affect the value of a card.

1983 Nalley Potato Chips Mariners

These large (8-11/16" by 10-11/16") photo cards were issued only in the area of Washington state by Nalley Potato Chips. The six Seattle Mariners are pictured in full color on the entire back panel of each box. On the side panels, detailed player stats and biographies are listed on one side, with a Mariners schedule and ticket discount offer on the other side.

		MT	NR MT	EX
Complete Set:		25.00	18.50	10.00
Common Player:		2.50	2.00	1.00
8	Rick Sweet	6.00	4.50	2.50
16	Al Cowens	2.50	2.00	1.00
21	Todd Cruz	2.50	2.00	1.00
22	Richie Zisk	3.50	2.75	1.50
36	Gaylord Perry	10.00	7.50	4.00
37	Bill Caudill	2.50	2.00	1.00

1986 National Photo Royals

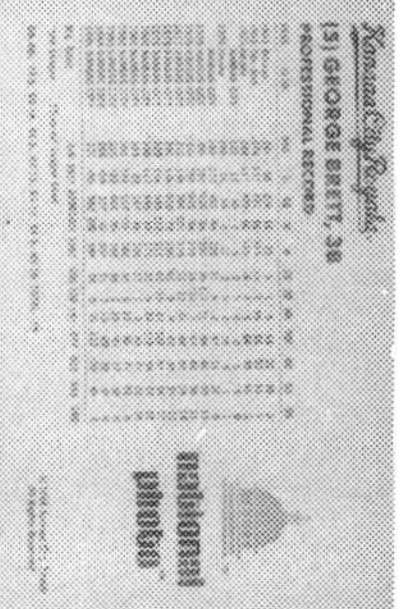

These 2-7/8" by 4-1/4" cards were a team issue produced in conjunction with National Photo. The 24- card set includes 21 players, manager Dick Howser, a card commemorating the Royals' 1985 World Championship and a discount offer card from National Photo. Card fronts feature full-color action photos with a blue "Kansas City Royals" at the top of each card. Each player's name, number and position are also included. Card backs list complete professional career statistics, along with the National Photo logo.

		MT	NR MT	EX
Complete Set:		10.00	7.50	4.00
Common Player:		.25	.20	.10
1	Buddy Biancalana	.25	.20	.10
3	Jorge Orta	.25	.20	.10
4	Greg Pryor	.25	.20	.10
5	George Brett	2.00	1.50	.80
6	Willie Wilson	.70	.50	.30
8	Jim Sundberg	.25	.20	.10
10	Dick Howser	.35	.25	.14
11	Hal McRae	.50	.40	.20
20	Frank White	.50	.40	.20
21	Lonnie Smith	.35	.25	.14
22	Dennis Leonard	.35	.25	.14
23	Mark Gubicza	.70	.50	.30
24	Darryl Motley	.25	.20	.10
25	Danny Jackson	.70	.50	.30
26	Steve Farr	.25	.20	.10
29	Dan Quisenberry	.50	.40	.20
31	Bret Saberhagen	1.00	.70	.40
35	Lynn Jones	.25	.20	.10
37	Charlie Leibrandt	.35	.25	.14
38	Mark Huismann	.25	.20	.10
40	Buddy Black	.35	.25	.14
45	Steve Balboni	.35	.25	.14
---	Header Card	.25	.20	.10
---	Discount Card	.25	.20	.10

1952 National Tea Labels

Another set of bread end-labels, this issue consists of 42 players, although there is speculation that six more labels may exist. The unnumbered labels measure approximately 2-3/4" by 2-11/16" and are sometimes referred to as "Red Borders" because of their wide, red borders. The player's name and team are printed alongside his photo, and the slogan "Eat More Bread for Health" also appears.

		NR MT	EX	VG
Complete Set:		2000.	1000.	600.00
Common Player:		100.00	50.00	30.00
(1)	Gene Bearden	100.00	50.00	30.00
(2)	Yogi Berra	300.00	150.00	90.00
(3)	Lou Brissie	100.00	50.00	30.00
(4)	Sam Chapman	100.00	50.00	30.00
(5)	Chuck Diering	100.00	50.00	30.00
(6)	Dom DiMaggio	125.00	62.00	37.00
(7)	Bruce Edwards	100.00	50.00	30.00
(8)	Del Ennis	100.00	50.00	30.00
(9)	Ferris Fain	100.00	50.00	30.00
(10)	Howie Fox	100.00	50.00	30.00
(11)	Sid Gordon	100.00	50.00	30.00
(12)	John Groth	100.00	50.00	30.00
(13)	Granny Hamner	100.00	50.00	30.00
(14)	Sheldon Jones	100.00	50.00	30.00
(15)	Howie Judson	100.00	50.00	30.00
(16)	Sherman Lollar	100.00	50.00	30.00
(17)	Clarence Marshall	100.00	50.00	30.00
(18)	Don Mueller	100.00	50.00	30.00
(19)	Danny Murtaugh	100.00	50.00	30.00
(20)	Dave Philley	100.00	50.00	30.00
(21)	Jerry Priddy	100.00	50.00	30.00
(22)	Robin Roberts	175.00	87.00	52.00
(23)	Eddie Robinson	100.00	50.00	30.00
(24)	Preacher Roe	125.00	62.00	37.00
(25)	Stan Rojek	100.00	50.00	30.00
(26)	Al Rosen	125.00	62.00	37.00
(27)	Bob Rush	100.00	50.00	30.00
(28)	Hank Sauer	100.00	50.00	30.00
(29)	Enos Slaughter	175.00	87.00	52.00
(30)	Duke Snider	300.00	150.00	90.00
(31)	Warren Spahn	200.00	100.00	60.00
(32)	Gerry Staley	100.00	50.00	30.00
(33)	Virgil Stallcup	100.00	50.00	30.00
(34)	George Stirnweiss	100.00	50.00	30.00
(35)	Earl Torgeson	100.00	50.00	30.00
(36)	Dizzy Trout	100.00	50.00	30.00
(37)	Mickey Vernon	100.00	50.00	30.00
(38)	Wally Westlake	100.00	50.00	30.00
(39)	Johnny Wyrostek	100.00	50.00	30.00
(40)	Eddie Yost	100.00	50.00	30.00

1984 Nestle

The 792 cards in the 1984 Nestle set are identical to those in the 1984 Topps regular issue set except for the Nestle logo which replaces the Topps logo in the upper right corner of the card front. The set was issued by Nestle as six sheets (24" by 48" each) of 132 cards. A few enterprising dealers bought up the major portion of the 5,000 sheet sets that were sup- posedly issued and had them professionally cut into individual cards. Due to the ease in handling single cards, sets of individual cards have a greater value than complete sheet sets.

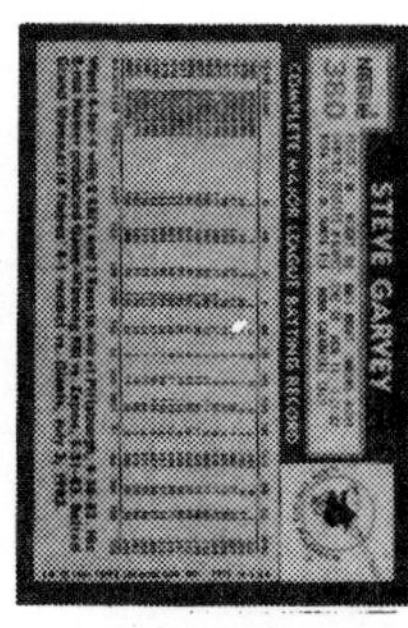

	MT	NR MT	EX
Complete Singles Set:	475.00	350.00	190.00
Common Single Player:	.20	.15	.08
Complete Sheet Set:	350.00	262.00	140.00
Sheet A:	200.00	150.00	80.00
Sheet B:	20.00	15.00	8.00
Sheet C:	20.00	15.00	8.00
Sheet D:	20.00	15.00	8.00
Sheet E:	20.00	15.00	8.00
Sheet F:	20.00	15.00	8.00

#	Player	MT	NR MT	EX
1	1983 Highlight (Steve Carlton)	1.75	1.25	.70
2	1983 Highlight (Rickey Henderson)	1.75	1.25	.70
3	1983 Highlight (Dan Quisenberry)	.30	.25	.12
4	1983 Highlight (Steve Carlton, Gaylord Perry, Nolan Ryan)	2.00	1.50	.80
5	1983 Highlight (Bob Forsch, Dave Righetti, Mike Warren)	.70	.50	.30
6	1983 Highlight (Johnny Bench, Gaylord Perry, Carl Yastrzemski)	2.00	1.50	.80
7	Gary Lucas	.20	.15	.08
8	Don Mattingly	275.00	200.00	100.00
9	Jim Gott	.20	.15	.08
10	Robin Yount	5.00	3.75	2.00
11	Twins Batting & Pitching Leaders (Kent Hrbek, Ken Schrom)	.70	.50	.30
12	Billy Sample	.20	.15	.08
13	Scott Holman	.20	.15	.08
14	Tom Brookens	.20	.15	.08
15	Burt Hooton	.30	.25	.12
16	Omar Moreno	.20	.15	.08
17	John Denny	.20	.15	.08
18	Dale Berra	.20	.15	.08
19	Ray Fontenot	.30	.25	.12
20	Greg Luzinski	.60	.45	.25
21	Joe Altobelli	.20	.15	.08
22	Bryan Clark	.20	.15	.08
23	Keith Moreland	.30	.25	.12
24	John Martin	.20	.15	.08
25	Glenn Hubbard	.30	.25	.12
26	Bud Black	.30	.25	.12
27	Daryl Sconiers	.20	.15	.08
28	Frank Viola	5.00	3.75	2.00
29	Danny Heep	.20	.15	.08
30	Wade Boggs	50.00	37.00	20.00
31	Andy McGaffigan	.20	.15	.08
32	Bobby Ramos	.20	.15	.08
33	Tom Burgmeier	.20	.15	.08
34	Eddie Milner	.20	.15	.08
35	Don Sutton	2.00	1.50	.80
36	Denny Walling	.20	.15	.08
37	Rangers Batting & Pitching Leaders (Buddy Bell, Rick Honeycutt)	.40	.30	.15
38	Luis DeLeon	.20	.15	.08
39	Garth Iorg	.20	.15	.08
40	Dusty Baker	.40	.30	.15
41	Tony Bernazard	.20	.15	.08
42	Johnny Grubb	.20	.15	.08
43	Ron Reed	.20	.15	.08
44	Jim Morrison	.20	.15	.08
45	Jerry Mumphrey	.20	.15	.08
46	Ray Smith	.20	.15	.08
47	Rudy Law	.20	.15	.08
48	Julio Franco	1.50	1.25	.60
49	John Stuper	.20	.15	.08
50	Chris Chambliss	.30	.25	.12
51	Jim Frey	.20	.15	.08
52	Paul Splittorff	.30	.25	.12
53	Juan Beniquez	.20	.15	.08
54	Jesse Orosco	.30	.25	.12
55	Dave Concepcion	.50	.40	.20
56	Gary Allenson	.20	.15	.08
57	Dan Schatzeder	.20	.15	.08
58	Max Venable	.20	.15	.08
59	Sammy Stewart	.20	.15	.08
60	Paul Molitor	1.25	.90	.50
61	Chris Codiroli	.30	.25	.12
62	Dave Hostetler	.20	.15	.08
63	Ed Vande Berg	.20	.15	.08
64	Mike Scioscia	.30	.25	.12
65	Kirk Gibson	4.00	3.00	1.50
66	Astros Batting & Pitching Leaders (Jose Cruz, Nolan Ryan)	1.00	.70	.40
67	Gary Ward	.30	.25	.12
68	Luis Salazar	.20	.15	.08
69	Rod Scurry	.20	.15	.08
70	Gary Matthews	.30	.25	.12
71	Leo Hernandez	.20	.15	.08
72	Mike Squires	.20	.15	.08
73	Jody Davis	.30	.25	.12
74	Jerry Martin	.20	.15	.08
75	Bob Forsch	.30	.25	.12
76	Alfredo Griffin	.30	.25	.12
77	Brett Butler	.30	.25	.12
78	Mike Torrez	.30	.25	.12
79	Rob Wilfong	.20	.15	.08
80	Steve Rogers	.30	.25	.12
81	Billy Martin	.50	.40	.20
82	Doug Bird	.20	.15	.08
83	Richie Zisk	.30	.25	.12
84	Lenny Faedo	.20	.15	.08
85	Atlee Hammaker	.20	.15	.08
86	John Shelby	1.00	.70	.40

#	Player	MT	NR MT	EX
87	Frank Pastore	.20	.15	.08
88	Rob Picciolo	.20	.15	.08
89	Mike Smithson	.20	.15	.08
90	Pedro Guerrero	3.50	2.75	1.50
91	Dan Spillner	.20	.15	.08
92	Lloyd Moseby	.40	.30	.15
93	Bob Knepper	.30	.25	.12
94	Mario Ramirez	.20	.15	.08
95	Aurelio Lopez	.20	.15	.08
96	Royals Batting & Pitching Leaders (Larry Gura, Hal McRae)	.40	.30	.15
97	LaMarr Hoyt	.20	.15	.08
98	Steve Nicosia	.20	.15	.08
99	Craig Lefferts	.70	.50	.30
100	Reggie Jackson	10.00	7.50	4.00
101	Porfirio Altamirano	.20	.15	.08
102	Ken Oberkfell	.20	.15	.08
103	Dwayne Murphy	.30	.25	.12
104	Ken Dayley	.30	.25	.12
105	Tony Armas	.30	.25	.12
106	Tim Stoddard	.20	.15	.08
107	Ned Yost	.20	.15	.08
108	Randy Moffitt	.20	.15	.08
109	Brad Wellman	.20	.15	.08
110	Ron Guidry	2.75	2.00	1.00
111	Bill Virdon	.30	.25	.12
112	Tom Niedenfuer	.30	.25	.12
113	Kelly Paris	.20	.15	.08
114	Checklist 1-132	.20	.15	.08
115	Andre Thornton	.30	.25	.12
116	George Bjorkman	.20	.15	.08
117	Tom Veryzer	.20	.15	.08
118	Charlie Hough	.30	.25	.12
119	Johnny Wockenfuss	.20	.15	.08
120	Keith Hernandez	5.00	3.75	2.00
121	Pat Sheridan	.70	.50	.30
122	Cecilio Guante	.30	.25	.12
123	Butch Wynegar	.30	.25	.12
124	Damaso Garcia	.20	.15	.08
125	Britt Burns	.20	.15	.08
126	Braves Batting & Pitching Leaders (Craig McMurtry, Dale Murphy)	1.25	.90	.50
127	Mike Madden	.20	.15	.08
128	Rick Manning	.20	.15	.08
129	Bill Laskey	.20	.15	.08
130	Ozzie Smith	2.00	1.50	.80
131	Batting Leaders (Wade Boggs, Bill Madlock)	2.50	2.00	1.00
132	Home Run Leaders (Jim Rice, Mike Schmidt)	2.00	1.50	.80
133	Runs Batted in Leaders (Cecil Cooper, Dale Murphy, Jim Rice)	2.00	1.50	.80
134	Stolen Base Leaders (Rickey Henderson, Tim Raines)	1.75	1.25	.70
135	Victory Leaders (John Denny, LaMarr Hoyt)	.30	.25	.12
136	Strikeout Leaders (Steve Carlton, Jack Morris)	1.00	.70	.40
137	Earned Run Average Leaders (Atlee Hammaker, Rick Honeycutt)	.30	.25	.12
138	Leading Firemen (Al Holland, Dan Quisenberry)	.30	.25	.12
139	Bert Campaneris	.40	.30	.15
140	Storm Davis	.50	.40	.20
141	Pat Corrales	.20	.15	.08
142	Rich Gale	.20	.15	.08
143	Jose Morales	.20	.15	.08
144	Brian Harper	.20	.15	.08
145	Gary Lavelle	.20	.15	.08
146	Ed Romero	.20	.15	.08
147	Dan Petry	.30	.25	.12
148	Joe Lefebvre	.20	.15	.08
149	Jon Matlack	.30	.25	.12
150	Dale Murphy	15.00	11.00	6.00
151	Steve Trout	.20	.15	.08
152	Glenn Brummer	.20	.15	.08
153	Dick Tidrow	.20	.15	.08
154	Dave Henderson	.40	.30	.15
155	Frank White	.40	.30	.15
156	Athletics Batting & Pitching Leaders (Tim Conroy, Rickey Henderson)	1.00	.70	.40
157	Gary Gaetti	2.50	2.00	1.00
158	John Curtis	.20	.15	.08
159	Darryl Cias	.20	.15	.08
160	Mario Soto	.30	.25	.12
161	Junior Ortiz	.20	.15	.08
162	Bob Ojeda	.40	.30	.15
163	Lorenzo Gray	.20	.15	.08
164	Scott Sanderson	.20	.15	.08
165	Ken Singleton	.40	.30	.15
166	Jamie Nelson	.20	.15	.08
167	Marshall Edwards	.20	.15	.08
168	Juan Bonilla	.20	.15	.08
169	Larry Parrish	.40	.30	.15
170	Jerry Reuss	.30	.25	.12
171	Frank Robinson	.40	.30	.15
172	Frank DiPino	.20	.15	.08
173	Marvell Wynne	.80	.60	.30
174	Juan Berenguer	.20	.15	.08
175	Graig Nettles	.80	.60	.30
176	Lee Smith	.60	.45	.25
177	Jerry Hairston	.20	.15	.08
178	Bill Krueger	.20	.15	.08
179	Buck Martinez	.20	.15	.08
180	Manny Trillo	.30	.25	.12
181	Roy Thomas	.20	.15	.08
182	Darryl Strawberry	60.00	45.00	24.00
183	Al Williams	.20	.15	.08
184	Mike O'Berry	.20	.15	.08
185	Sixto Lezcano	.20	.15	.08
186	Cardinals Batting & Pitching Leaders (Lonnie Smith, John Stuper)	.20	.15	.08
187	Luis Aponte	.20	.15	.08
188	Bryan Little	.20	.15	.08
189	Tim Conroy	.30	.25	.12
190	Ben Oglivie	.30	.25	.12
191	Mike Boddicker	.30	.25	.12
192	Nick Esasky	1.25	.90	.50
193	Darrell Brown	.20	.15	.08
194	Domingo Ramos	.20	.15	.08
195	Jack Morris	3.50	2.75	1.50
196	Don Slaught	.40	.30	.15
197	Gary Hancock	.20	.15	.08
198	Bill Doran	1.50	1.25	.60

#	Player	MT	NR MT	EX
199	Willie Hernandez	.30	.25	.12
200	Andre Dawson	4.50	3.50	1.75
201	Bruce Kison	.20	.15	.08
202	Bobby Cox	.20	.15	.08
203	Matt Keough	.20	.15	.08
204	Bobby Meacham	.40	.30	.15
205	Greg Minton	.20	.15	.08
206	Andy Van Slyke	5.00	3.75	2.00
207	Donnie Moore	.20	.15	.08
208	Jose Oquendo	.20	.15	.08
209	Manny Sarmiento	.20	.15	.08
210	Joe Morgan	3.00	2.25	1.25
211	Rick Sweet	.20	.15	.08
212	Broderick Perkins	.20	.15	.08
213	Bruce Hurst	.60	.45	.25
214	Paul Householder	.20	.15	.08
215	Tippy Martinez	.20	.15	.08
216	White Sox Batting & Pitching Leaders (Richard Dotson, Carlton Fisk)	.40	.30	.15
217	Alan Ashby	.20	.15	.08
218	Rick Waits	.20	.15	.08
219	Joe Simpson	.20	.15	.08
220	Fernando Valenzuela	5.00	3.75	2.00
221	Cliff Johnson	.20	.15	.08
222	Rick Honeycutt	.20	.15	.08
223	Wayne Krenchicki	.20	.15	.08
224	Sid Monge	.20	.15	.08
225	Lee Mazzilli	.30	.25	.12
226	Juan Eichelberger	.20	.15	.08
227	Steve Braun	.20	.15	.08
228	John Rabb	.20	.15	.08
229	Paul Owens	.20	.15	.08
230	Rickey Henderson	10.00	7.50	4.00
231	Gary Woods	.20	.15	.08
232	Tim Wallach	.70	.50	.30
233	Checklist 133-264	.20	.15	.08
234	Rafael Ramirez	.20	.15	.08
235	Matt Young	.40	.30	.15
236	Ellis Valentine	.20	.15	.08
237	John Castino	.20	.15	.08
238	Reid Nichols	.20	.15	.08
239	Jay Howell	.30	.25	.12
240	Eddie Murray	8.00	6.00	3.25
241	Billy Almon	.20	.15	.08
242	Alex Trevino	.20	.15	.08
243	Pete Ladd	.20	.15	.08
244	Candy Maldonado	.60	.45	.25
245	Rick Sutcliffe	.70	.50	.30
246	Mets Batting & Pitching Leaders (Tom Seaver, Mookie Wilson)	.70	.50	.30
247	Onix Concepcion	.20	.15	.08
248	Bill Dawley	.20	.15	.08
249	Jay Johnstone	.30	.25	.12
250	Bill Madlock	.60	.45	.25
251	Tony Gwynn	12.00	9.00	4.75
252	Larry Christenson	.20	.15	.08
253	Jim Wohlford	.20	.15	.08
254	Shane Rawley	.30	.25	.12
255	Bruce Benedict	.20	.15	.08
256	Dave Geisel	.20	.15	.08
257	Julio Cruz	.20	.15	.08
258	Luis Sanchez	.20	.15	.08
259	Sparky Anderson	.30	.25	.12
260	Scott McGregor	.30	.25	.12
261	Bobby Brown	.20	.15	.08
262	Tom Candiotti	.80	.60	.30
263	Jack Fimple	.20	.15	.08
264	Doug Frobel	.20	.15	.08
265	Donnie Hill	.20	.15	.08
266	Steve Lubratich	.20	.15	.08
267	Carmelo Martinez	.60	.45	.25
268	Jack O'Connor	.20	.15	.08
269	Aurelio Rodriguez	.30	.25	.12
270	Jeff Russell	.40	.30	.15
271	Moose Haas	.20	.15	.08
272	Rick Dempsey	.30	.25	.12
273	Charlie Puleo	.20	.15	.08
274	Rick Monday	.30	.25	.12
275	Len Matuszek	.20	.15	.08
276	Angels Batting & Pitching Leaders (Rod Carew, Geoff Zahn)	.70	.50	.30
277	Eddie Whitson	.20	.15	.08
278	Jorge Bell	6.00	4.50	2.50
279	Ivan DeJesus	.20	.15	.08
280	Floyd Bannister	.30	.25	.12
281	Larry Milbourne	.20	.15	.08
282	Jim Barr	.20	.15	.08
283	Larry Biittner	.20	.15	.08
284	Howard Bailey	.20	.15	.08
285	Darrell Porter	.30	.25	.12
286	Lary Sorensen	.20	.15	.08
287	Warren Cromartie	.20	.15	.08
288	Jim Beattie	.20	.15	.08
289	Randy Johnson	.20	.15	.08
290	Dave Dravecky	.30	.25	.12
291	Chuck Tanner	.30	.25	.12
292	Tony Scott	.20	.15	.08
293	Ed Lynch	.20	.15	.08
294	U.L. Washington	.20	.15	.08
295	Mike Flanagan	.30	.25	.12
296	Jeff Newman	.20	.15	.08
297	Bruce Berenyi	.20	.15	.08
298	Jim Gantner	.30	.25	.12
299	John Butcher	.20	.15	.08
300	Pete Rose	25.00	18.50	10.00
301	Frank LaCorte	.20	.15	.08
302	Barry Bonnell	.20	.15	.08
303	Marty Castillo	.20	.15	.08
304	Warren Brusstar	.20	.15	.08
305	Roy Smalley	.20	.15	.08
306	Dodgers Batting & Pitching Leaders (Pedro Guerrero, Bob Welch)	.60	.45	.25
307	Bobby Mitchell	.20	.15	.08
308	Ron Hassey	.20	.15	.08
309	Tony Phillips	.30	.25	.12
310	Willie McGee	3.00	2.25	1.25
311	Jerry Koosman	.40	.30	.15
312	Jorge Orta	.20	.15	.08
313	Mike Jorgensen	.20	.15	.08
314	Orlando Mercado	.20	.15	.08
315	Bob Grich	.30	.25	.12
316	Mark Bradley	.20	.15	.08
317	Greg Pryor	.20	.15	.08
318	Bill Gullickson	.20	.15	.08

No.	Player	MT	NR MT	EX
319	Al Bumbry	.20	.15	.08
320	Bob Stanley	.20	.15	.08
321	Harvey Kuenn	.20	.15	.08
322	Ken Schrom	.20	.15	.08
323	Alan Knicely	.20	.15	.08
324	Alejandro Pena	.80	.60	.30
325	Darrell Evans	.40	.30	.15
326	Bob Kearney	.20	.15	.08
327	Ruppert Jones	.20	.15	.08
328	Vern Ruhle	.20	.15	.08
329	Pat Tabler	.50	.40	.20
330	John Candelaria	.40	.30	.15
331	Bucky Dent	.30	.25	.12
332	Kevin Gross	1.00	.70	.40
333	Larry Herndon	.20	.15	.08
334	Chuck Rainey	.20	.15	.08
335	Don Baylor	.50	.40	.20
336	Mariners Batting & Pitching Leaders (Pat Putnam, Matt Young)	.20	.15	.08
337	Kevin Hagen	.20	.15	.08
338	Mike Warren	.20	.15	.08
339	Roy Lee Jackson	.20	.15	.08
340	Hal McRae	.40	.30	.15
341	Dave Tobik	.20	.15	.08
342	Tim Foli	.20	.15	.08
343	Mark Davis	.20	.15	.08
344	Rick Miller	.20	.15	.08
345	Kent Hrbek	4.00	3.00	1.50
346	Kurt Bevacqua	.20	.15	.08
347	Allan Ramirez	.20	.15	.08
348	Toby Harrah	.30	.25	.12
349	Bob Gibson	.20	.15	.08
350	George Foster	.80	.60	.30
351	Russ Nixon	.20	.15	.08
352	Dave Stewart	.60	.45	.25
353	Jim Anderson	.20	.15	.08
354	Jeff Burroughs	.20	.15	.08
355	Jason Thompson	.20	.15	.08
356	Glenn Abbott	.20	.15	.08
357	Ron Cey	.40	.30	.15
358	Bob Dernier	.20	.15	.08
359	Jim Acker	.30	.25	.12
360	Willie Randolph	.50	.40	.20
361	Dave Smith	.30	.25	.12
362	David Green	.20	.15	.08
363	Tim Laudner	.20	.15	.08
364	Scott Fletcher	.40	.30	.15
365	Steve Bedrosian	.40	.30	.15
366	Padres Batting & Pitching Leaders (Dave Dravecky, Terry Kennedy)	.20	.15	.08
367	Jamie Easterly	.20	.15	.08
368	Hubie Brooks	.30	.25	.12
369	Steve McCatty	.20	.15	.08
370	Tim Raines	5.00	3.75	2.00
371	Dave Gumpert	.20	.15	.08
372	Gary Roenicke	.20	.15	.08
373	Bill Scherrer	.20	.15	.08
374	Don Money	.20	.15	.08
375	Dennis Leonard	.30	.25	.12
376	Dave Anderson	.30	.25	.12
377	Danny Darwin	.30	.25	.12
378	Bob Brenly	.20	.15	.08
379	Checklist 265-396	.20	.15	.08
380	Steve Garvey	8.00	6.00	3.25
381	Ralph Houk	.20	.15	.08
382	Chris Nyman	.20	.15	.08
383	Terry Puhl	.20	.15	.08
384	Lee Tunnell	.20	.15	.08
385	Tony Perez	1.00	.70	.40
386	George Hendrick AS	.30	.25	.12
387	Johnny Ray AS	.30	.25	.12
388	Mike Schmidt AS	3.00	2.25	1.25
389	Ozzie Smith AS	1.25	.90	.50
390	Tim Raines AS	2.00	1.50	.80
391	Dale Murphy AS	3.00	2.25	1.25
392	Andre Dawson AS	1.75	1.25	.70
393	Gary Carter AS	2.00	1.50	.80
394	Steve Rogers AS	.30	.25	.12
395	Steve Carlton AS	2.00	1.50	.80
396	Jesse Orosco AS	.30	.25	.12
397	Eddie Murray AS	2.50	2.00	1.00
398	Lou Whitaker AS	1.25	.90	.50
399	George Brett AS	3.00	2.25	1.25
400	Cal Ripken AS	2.75	2.00	1.00
401	Jim Rice AS	2.00	1.50	.80
402	Dave Winfield AS	2.50	2.00	1.00
403	Lloyd Moseby AS	.30	.25	.12
404	Ted Simmons AS	.40	.30	.15
405	LaMarr Hoyt AS	.30	.25	.12
406	Ron Guidry AS	1.25	.90	.50
407	Dan Quisenberry AS	.30	.25	.12
408	Lou Piniella	.80	.60	.30
409	Juan Agosto	.40	.30	.15
410	Claudell Washington	.30	.25	.12
411	Houston Jimenez	.20	.15	.08
412	Doug Rader	.20	.15	.08
413	Spike Owen	.30	.25	.12
414	Mitchell Page	.20	.15	.08
415	Tommy John	1.25	.90	.50
416	Dane Iorg	.20	.15	.08
417	Mike Armstrong	.20	.15	.08
418	Ron Hodges	.20	.15	.08
419	John Henry Johnson	.20	.15	.08
420	Cecil Cooper	.60	.45	.25
421	Charlie Lea	.20	.15	.08
422	Jose Cruz	.30	.25	.12
423	Mike Morgan	.20	.15	.08
424	Dann Bilardello	.20	.15	.08
425	Steve Howe	.30	.25	.12
426	Orioles Batting & Pitching Leaders (Mike Boddicker, Cal Ripken)	.90	.70	.35
427	Rick Leach	.20	.15	.08
428	Fred Breining	.20	.15	.08
429	Randy Bush	.20	.15	.08
430	Rusty Staub	.50	.40	.20
431	Chris Bando	.20	.15	.08
432	Charlie Hudson	.80	.60	.30
433	Rich Hebner	.20	.15	.08
434	Harold Baines	1.75	1.25	.70
435	Neil Allen	.20	.15	.08
436	Rick Peters	.20	.15	.08
437	Mike Proly	.20	.15	.08
438	Biff Pocoroba	.20	.15	.08
439	Bob Stoddard	.20	.15	.08

No.	Player	MT	NR MT	EX
440	Steve Kemp	.30	.25	.12
441	Bob Lillis	.20	.15	.08
442	Byron McLaughlin	.20	.15	.08
443	Benny Ayala	.20	.15	.08
444	Steve Renko	.20	.15	.08
445	Jerry Remy	.20	.15	.08
446	Luis Pujols	.20	.15	.08
447	Tom Brunansky	1.25	.90	.50
448	Ben Hayes	.20	.15	.08
449	Joe Pettini	.20	.15	.08
450	Gary Carter	6.00	4.50	2.50
451	Bob Jones	.20	.15	.08
452	Chuck Porter	.20	.15	.08
453	Willie Upshaw	.30	.25	.12
454	Joe Beckwith	.20	.15	.08
455	Terry Kennedy	.30	.25	.12
456	Cubs Batting & Pitching Leaders (Keith Moreland, Fergie Jenkins)	.50	.40	.20
457	Dave Rozema	.20	.15	.08
458	Kiko Garcia	.20	.15	.08
459	Kevin Hickey	.20	.15	.08
460	Dave Winfield	6.00	4.50	2.50
461	Jim Maler	.20	.15	.08
462	Lee Lacy	.20	.15	.08
463	Dave Engle	.20	.15	.08
464	Jeff Jones	.20	.15	.08
465	Mookie Wilson	.30	.25	.12
466	Gene Garber	.20	.15	.08
467	Mike Ramsey	.20	.15	.08
468	Geoff Zahn	.20	.15	.08
469	Tom O'Malley	.20	.15	.08
470	Nolan Ryan	6.00	4.50	2.50
471	Dick Howser	.30	.25	.12
472	Mike Brown	.20	.15	.08
473	Jim Dwyer	.20	.15	.08
474	Greg Bargar	.20	.15	.08
475	Gary Redus	.80	.60	.30
476	Tom Tellmann	.20	.15	.08
477	Rafael Landestoy	.20	.15	.08
478	Alan Bannister	.20	.15	.08
479	Frank Tanana	.30	.25	.12
480	Ron Kittle	.80	.60	.30
481	Mark Thurmond	.30	.25	.12
482	Enos Cabell	.20	.15	.08
483	Fergie Jenkins	1.75	1.25	.70
484	Ozzie Virgil	.20	.15	.08
485	Rick Rhoden	.40	.30	.15
486	Yankees Batting & Pitching Leaders (Don Baylor, Ron Guidry)	.60	.45	.25
487	Ricky Adams	.20	.15	.08
488	Jesse Barfield	1.50	1.25	.60
489	Dave Von Ohlen	.20	.15	.08
490	Cal Ripken	9.00	6.75	3.50
491	Bobby Castillo	.20	.15	.08
492	Tucker Ashford	.20	.15	.08
493	Mike Norris	.20	.15	.08
494	Chili Davis	.30	.25	.12
495	Rollie Fingers	2.50	2.00	1.00
496	Terry Francona	.20	.15	.08
497	Bud Anderson	.20	.15	.08
498	Rich Gedman	.30	.25	.12
499	Mike Witt	.70	.50	.30
500	George Brett	15.00	11.00	6.00
501	Steve Henderson	.20	.15	.08
502	Joe Torre	.30	.25	.12
503	Elias Sosa	.20	.15	.08
504	Mickey Rivers	.20	.15	.08
505	Pete Vuckovich	.20	.15	.08
506	Ernie Whitt	.20	.15	.08
507	Mike LaCoss	.20	.15	.08
508	Mel Hall	.30	.25	.12
509	Brad Havens	.20	.15	.08
510	Alan Trammell	5.00	3.75	2.00
511	Marty Bystrom	.20	.15	.08
512	Oscar Gamble	.20	.15	.08
513	Dave Beard	.20	.15	.08
514	Floyd Rayford	.20	.15	.08
515	Gorman Thomas	.30	.25	.12
516	Expos Batting & Pitching Leaders (Charlie Lea, Al Oliver)	.20	.15	.08
517	John Moses	.20	.15	.08
518	Greg Walker	1.25	.90	.50
519	Ron Davis	.20	.15	.08
520	Bob Boone	.30	.25	.12
521	Pete Falcone	.20	.15	.08
522	Dave Bergman	.20	.15	.08
523	Glenn Hoffman	.20	.15	.08
524	Carlos Diaz	.20	.15	.08
525	Willie Wilson	.60	.45	.25
526	Ron Oester	.20	.15	.08
527	Checklist 397-528	.20	.15	.08
528	Mark Brouhard	.20	.15	.08
529	Keith Atherton	.60	.45	.25
530	Dan Ford	.20	.15	.08
531	Steve Boros	.20	.15	.08
532	Eric Show	.40	.30	.15
533	Ken Landreaux	.20	.15	.08
534	Pete O'Brien	1.50	1.25	.60
535	Bo Diaz	.30	.25	.12
536	Doug Bair	.20	.15	.08
537	Johnny Ray	.40	.30	.15
538	Kevin Bass	.40	.30	.15
539	George Frazier	.20	.15	.08
540	George Hendrick	.30	.25	.12
541	Dennis Lamp	.20	.15	.08
542	Duane Kuiper	.20	.15	.08
543	Craig McMurtry	.40	.30	.15
544	Cesar Geronimo	.20	.15	.08
545	Bill Buckner	.60	.45	.25
546	Indians Batting & Pitching Leaders (Mike Hargrove, Lary Sorensen)	.20	.15	.08
547	Mike Moore	.20	.15	.08
548	Ron Jackson	.20	.15	.08
549	Walt Terrell	1.00	.70	.40
550	Jim Rice	6.00	4.50	2.50
551	Scott Ullger	.20	.15	.08
552	Ray Burris	.20	.15	.08
553	Joe Nolan	.20	.15	.08
554	Ted Power	.30	.25	.12
555	Greg Brock	.50	.40	.20
556	Joey McLaughlin	.20	.15	.08
557	Wayne Tolleson	.20	.15	.08
558	Mike Davis	.30	.25	.12
559	Mike Scott	1.50	1.25	.60

No.	Player	MT	NR MT	EX
560	Carlton Fisk	2.00	1.50	.80
561	Whitey Herzog	.30	.25	.12
562	Manny Castillo	.20	.15	.08
563	Glenn Wilson	.30	.25	.12
564	Al Holland	.20	.15	.08
565	Leon Durham	.30	.25	.12
566	Jim Bibby	.20	.15	.08
567	Mike Heath	.20	.15	.08
568	Pete Filson	.20	.15	.08
569	Bake McBride	.20	.15	.08
570	Dan Quisenberry	.40	.30	.15
571	Bruce Bochy	.20	.15	.08
572	Jerry Royster	.20	.15	.08
573	Dave Kingman	.80	.60	.30
574	Brian Downing	.30	.25	.12
575	Jim Clancy	.30	.25	.12
576	Giants Batting & Pitching Leaders (Atlee Hammaker, Jeff Leonard)	.20	.15	.08
577	Mark Clear	.20	.15	.08
578	Lenn Sakata	.20	.15	.08
579	Bob James	.20	.15	.08
580	Lonnie Smith	.30	.25	.12
581	Jose DeLeon	1.00	.70	.40
582	Bob McClure	.20	.15	.08
583	Derrel Thomas	.20	.15	.08
584	Dave Schmidt	.20	.15	.08
585	Dan Driessen	.30	.25	.12
586	Joe Niekro	.40	.30	.15
587	Von Hayes	.40	.30	.15
588	Milt Wilcox	.20	.15	.08
589	Mike Easler	.30	.25	.12
590	Dave Stieb	.50	.40	.20
591	Tony LaRussa	.30	.25	.12
592	Andre Robertson	.20	.15	.08
593	Jeff Lahti	.20	.15	.08
594	Gene Richards	.20	.15	.08
595	Jeff Reardon	.50	.40	.20
596	Ryne Sandberg	15.00	11.00	6.00
597	Rick Camp	.20	.15	.08
598	Rusty Kuntz	.20	.15	.08
599	Doug Sisk	.20	.15	.08
600	Rod Carew	7.00	5.25	2.75
601	John Tudor	.60	.45	.25
602	John Wathan	.30	.25	.12
603	Renie Martin	.20	.15	.08
604	John Lowenstein	.20	.15	.08
605	Mike Caldwell	.20	.15	.08
606	Blue Jays Batting & Pitching Leaders (Lloyd Moseby, Dave Stieb)	.40	.30	.15
607	Tom Hume	.20	.15	.08
608	Bobby Johnson	.20	.15	.08
609	Dan Meyer	.20	.15	.08
610	Steve Sax	2.50	2.00	1.00
611	Chet Lemon	.30	.25	.12
612	Harry Spilman	.20	.15	.08
613	Greg Gross	.20	.15	.08
614	Len Barker	.20	.15	.08
615	Garry Templeton	.30	.25	.12
616	Don Robinson	.20	.15	.08
617	Rick Cerone	.20	.15	.08
618	Dickie Noles	.20	.15	.08
619	Jerry Dybzinski	.20	.15	.08
620	Al Oliver	.70	.50	.30
621	Frank Howard	.30	.25	.12
622	Al Cowens	.20	.15	.08
623	Ron Washington	.20	.15	.08
624	Terry Harper	.20	.15	.08
625	Larry Gura	.20	.15	.08
626	Bob Clark	.20	.15	.08
627	Dave LaPoint	.40	.30	.15
628	Ed Jurak	.20	.15	.08
629	Rick Langford	.20	.15	.08
630	Ted Simmons	.80	.60	.30
631	Denny Martinez	.30	.25	.12
632	Tom Foley	.20	.15	.08
633	Mike Krukow	.30	.25	.12
634	Mike Marshall	1.50	1.25	.60
635	Dave Righetti	2.75	2.00	1.00
636	Pat Putnam	.20	.15	.08
637	Phillies Batting & Pitching Leaders (John Denny, Gary Matthews)	.20	.15	.08
638	George Vukovich	.20	.15	.08
639	Rick Lysander	.20	.15	.08
640	Lance Parrish	3.00	2.25	1.25
641	Mike Richardt	.20	.15	.08
642	Tom Underwood	.20	.15	.08
643	Mike Brown	.20	.15	.08
644	Tim Lollar	.20	.15	.08
645	Tony Pena	.40	.30	.15
646	Checklist 529-660	.20	.15	.08
647	Ron Roenicke	.20	.15	.08
648	Len Whitehouse	.20	.15	.08
649	Tom Herr	.40	.30	.15
650	Phil Niekro	2.75	2.00	1.00
651	John McNamara	.20	.15	.08
652	Rudy May	.20	.15	.08
653	Dave Stapleton	.20	.15	.08
654	Bob Bailor	.20	.15	.08
655	Amos Otis	.30	.25	.12
656	Bryn Smith	.20	.15	.08
657	Thad Bosley	.20	.15	.08
658	Jerry Augustine	.20	.15	.08
659	Duane Walker	.20	.15	.08
660	Ray Knight	.30	.25	.12
661	Steve Yeager	.20	.15	.08
662	Tom Brennan	.20	.15	.08
663	Johnnie LeMaster	.20	.15	.08
664	Dave Stegman	.20	.15	.08
665	Buddy Bell	.40	.30	.15
666	Tigers Batting & Pitching Leaders (Jack Morris, Lou Whitaker)	.70	.50	.30
667	Vance Law	.30	.25	.12
668	Larry McWilliams	.20	.15	.08
669	Dave Lopes	.20	.15	.08
670	Rich Gossage	2.00	1.50	.80
671	Jamie Quirk	20	.15	.08
672	Ricky Nelson	.20	.15	.08
673	Mike Walters	.20	.15	.08
674	Tim Flannery	.20	.15	.08
675	Pascual Perez	.30	.25	.12
676	Brian Giles	.20	.15	.08
677	Doyle Alexander	.30	.25	.12
678	Chris Speier	.20	.15	.08
679	Art Howe	.20	.15	.08

#	Player	MT	NR MT	EX
680	Fred Lynn	2.25	1.75	.90
681	Tom Lasorda	.40	.30	.15
682	Dan Morogiello	.20	.15	.08
683	Marty Barrett	2.00	1.50	.80
684	Bob Shirley	.20	.15	.08
685	Willie Aikens	.20	.15	.08
686	Joe Price	.20	.15	.08
687	Roy Howell	.20	.15	.08
688	George Wright	.20	.15	.08
689	Mike Fischlin	.20	.15	.08
690	Jack Clark	3.50	2.75	1.50
691	Steve Lake	.20	.15	.08
692	Dickie Thon	.30	.25	.12
693	Alan Wiggins	.20	.15	.08
694	Mike Stanton	.20	.15	.08
695	Lou Whitaker	3.00	2.25	1.25
696	Pirates Batting & Pitching Leaders (Bill Madlock, Rick Rhoden)	.50	.40	.20
697	Dale Murray	.20	.15	.08
698	Marc Hill	.20	.15	.08
699	Dave Rucker	.20	.15	.08
700	Mike Schmidt	18.00	13.50	7.25
701	NL Active Career Batting Leaders (Bill Madlock, Dave Parker, Pete Rose)	2.00	1.50	.80
702	NL Active Career Hit Leaders (Tony Perez, Pete Rose, Rusty Staub)	2.00	1.50	.80
703	NL Active Career Home Run Leaders (Dave Kingman, Tony Perez, Mike Schmidt)	2.00	1.50	.80
704	NL Active Career RBI Leaders (Al Oliver, Tony Perez, Rusty Staub)	.60	.45	.25
705	NL Active Career Stolen Bases Leaders (Larry Bowa, Cesar Cedeno, Joe Morgan)	.70	.50	.30
706	NL Active Career Victory Leaders (Steve Carlton, Fergie Jenkins, Tom Seaver)	1.75	1.25	.70
707	NL Active Career Strikeout Leaders (Steve Carlton, Nolan Ryan, Tom Seaver)	2.00	1.50	.80
708	NL Active Career ERA Leaders (Steve Carlton, Steve Rogers, Tom Seaver)	1.75	1.25	.70
709	NL Active Career Save Leaders (Gene Garber, Tug McGraw, Bruce Sutter)	.50	.40	.20
710	AL Active Career Batting Leaders (George Brett, Rod Carew, Cecil Cooper)	2.00	1.50	.80
711	AL Active Career Hit Leaders (Bert Campaneris, Rod Carew, Reggie Jackson)	1.75	1.25	.70
712	AL Active Career Home Run Leaders (Reggie Jackson, Greg Luzinski, Graig Nettles)	1.50	1.25	.60
713	AL Active Career RBI Leaders (Reggie Jackson, Graig Nettles, Ted Simmons)	1.50	1.25	.60
714	AL Active Career Stolen Bases Leaders (Bert Campaneris, Dave Lopes, Omar Moreno)	.40	.30	.15
715	AL Active Career Victory Leaders (Tommy John, Jim Palmer, Don Sutton)	1.25	.90	.50
716	AL Active Strikeout Leaders (Bert Blyleven, Jerry Koosman, Don Sutton)	.70	.50	.30
717	AL Active Career ERA Leaders (Rollie Fingers, Ron Guidry, Jim Palmer)	1.25	.90	.50
718	AL Active Career Save Leaders (Rollie Fingers, Rich Gossage, Dan Quisenberry)	.90	.70	.35
719	Andy Hassler	.20	.15	.08
720	Dwight Evans	.80	.60	.30
721	Del Crandall	.20	.15	.08
722	Bob Welch	.40	.30	.15
723	Rich Dauer	.20	.15	.08
724	Eric Rasmussen	.20	.15	.08
725	Cesar Cedeno	.30	.25	.12
726	Brewers Batting & Pitching Leaders (Moose Haas, Ted Simmons)	.30	.25	.12
727	Joel Youngblood	.20	.15	.08
728	Tug McGraw	.30	.25	.12
729	Gene Tenace	.30	.25	.12
730	Bruce Sutter	1.25	.90	.50
731	Lynn Jones	.20	.15	.08
732	Terry Crowley	.20	.15	.08
733	Dave Collins	.30	.25	.12
734	Odell Jones	.20	.15	.08
735	Rick Burleson	.30	.25	.12
736	Dick Ruthven	.20	.15	.08
737	Jim Essian	.20	.15	.08
738	Bill Schroeder	.60	.45	.25
739	Bob Watson	.30	.25	.12
740	Tom Seaver	7.00	5.25	2.75
741	Wayne Gross	.20	.15	.08
742	Dick Williams	.20	.15	.08
743	Don Hood	.20	.15	.08
744	Jamie Allen	.20	.15	.08
745	Dennis Eckersley	.50	.40	.20
746	Mickey Hatcher	.20	.15	.08
747	Pat Zachry	.20	.15	.08
748	Jeff Leonard	.30	.25	.12
749	Doug Flynn	.20	.15	.08
750	Jim Palmer	5.00	3.75	2.00
751	Charlie Moore	.20	.15	.08
752	Phil Garner	.30	.25	.12
753	Doug Gwosdz	.20	.15	.08
754	Kent Tekulve	.30	.25	.12
755	Garry Maddox	.30	.25	.12
756	Reds Batting & Pitching Leaders (Ron Oester, Mario Soto)	.20	.15	.08
757	Larry Bowa	.40	.30	.15
758	Bill Stein	.20	.15	.08
759	Richard Dotson	.40	.30	.15
760	Bob Horner	.80	.60	.30
761	John Montefusco	.20	.15	.08
762	Rance Mulliniks	.20	.15	.08
763	Craig Swan	.20	.15	.08
764	Mike Hargrove	.20	.15	.08
765	Ken Forsch	.20	.15	.08
766	Mike Vail	.20	.15	.08
767	Carney Lansford	.40	.30	.15
768	Champ Summers	.20	.15	.08
769	Bill Caudill	.20	.15	.08
770	Ken Griffey	.30	.25	.12
771	Billy Gardner	.20	.15	.08
772	Jim Slaton	.20	.15	.08
773	Todd Cruz	.20	.15	.08
774	Tom Gorman	.20	.15	.08
775	Dave Parker	1.75	1.25	.70
776	Craig Reynolds	.20	.15	.08
777	Tom Paciorek	.20	.15	.08
778	Andy Hawkins	.80	.60	.30
779	Jim Sundberg	.20	.15	.08
780	Steve Carlton	6.00	4.50	2.50
781	Checklist 661-792	.20	.15	.08
782	Steve Balboni	.30	.25	.12
783	Luis Leal	.20	.15	.08
784	Leon Roberts	.20	.15	.08
785	Joaquin Andujar	.30	.25	.12
786	Red Sox Batting & Pitching Leaders (Wade Boggs, Bob Ojeda)	1.25	.90	.50
787	Bill Campbell	.20	.15	.08
788	Milt May	.20	.15	.08
789	Bert Blyleven	1.25	.90	.50
790	Doug DeCinces	.30	.25	.12
791	Terry Forster	.30	.25	.12
792	Bill Russell	.30	.25	.12

1984 Nestle Dream Team

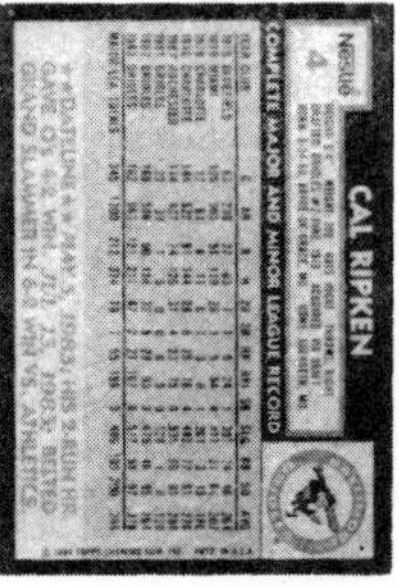

This set was issued by the Nestle candy company in conjunction with Topps. Cards are in standard 2-1/2" by 3-1/2" size and feature the top 22 players of 1984, 11 from each league. This full-color "Dream Team" includes one player at each position, plus right- and left-handed starting pitchers and one reliever. Card fronts have a Nestle logo in the upper-right corner and card backs have the candy company logo in the upper left. An unnumbered checklist was included with the set.

#	Player	MT	NR MT	EX
	Complete Set:	20.00	15.00	8.00
	Common Player:	.60	.45	.25
1	Eddie Murray	1.75	1.25	.70
2	Lou Whitaker	1.00	.70	.40
3	George Brett	2.25	1.75	.90
4	Cal Ripken	2.00	1.50	.80
5	Jim Rice	1.25	.90	.50
6	Dave Winfield	1.50	1.25	.60
7	Lloyd Moseby	.60	.45	.25
8	Lance Parrish	1.00	.70	.40
9	LaMarr Hoyt	.60	.45	.25
10	Ron Guidry	.80	.60	.30
11	Dan Quisenberry	.60	.45	.25
12	Steve Garvey	1.50	1.25	.60
13	Johnny Ray	.60	.45	.25
14	Mike Schmidt	2.25	1.75	.90
15	Ozzie Smith	.80	.60	.30
16	Andre Dawson	1.00	.70	.40
17	Tim Raines	1.50	1.25	.60
18	Dale Murphy	2.25	1.75	.90
19	Tony Pena	.60	.45	.25
20	John Denny	.60	.45	.25
21	Steve Carlton	1.25	.90	.50
22	Al Holland	.60	.45	.25
---	Checklist	.30	.25	.12

1987 Nestle

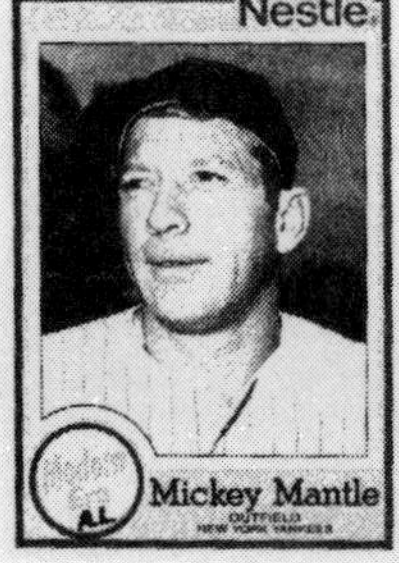

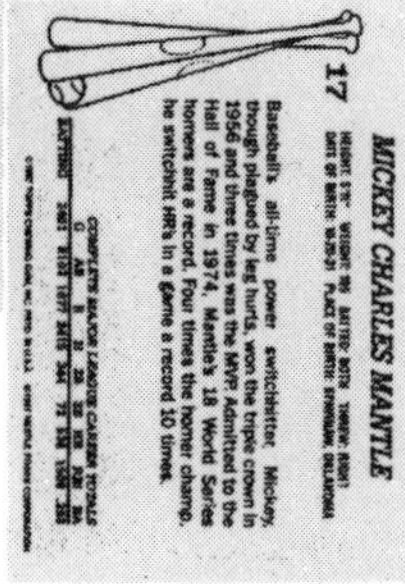

Nestle, in conjunction with Topps, issued a 33-card set in 1987. Card #'s 1-11 feature black and white photos of players from the "Golden Era." Card #'s 12-33 feature full-color photos of American (12-22.00) and National League (23-33.00) players from the "Modern Era" of baseball. Interestingly, the Feller card is not a photo but rather a color rendering of his 1953 Topps card. The cards measure 2-1/2" by 3-1/2" and have all team emblems airbrushed away. Three cards were inserted in specially marked six-packs of various Nestle candy bars. Two complete sets were available through a mail-in offer for $1.50 and three proof of purchase seals.

#	Player	MT	NR MT	EX
	Complete Set:	8.00	6.00	3.25
	Common Player:	.12	.09	.05
1	Lou Gehrig	.50	.40	.20
2	Rogers Hornsby	.25	.20	.10
3	Pie Traynor	.12	.09	.05
4	Honus Wagner	.30	.25	.12
5	Babe Ruth	.80	.60	.30
6	Tris Speaker	.20	.15	.08
7	Ty Cobb	.60	.45	.25
8	Mickey Cochrane	.12	.09	.05
9	Walter Johnson	.30	.25	.12
10	Carl Hubbell	.12	.09	.05
11	Jimmie Foxx	.25	.20	.10
12	Rod Carew	.30	.25	.12
13	Nellie Fox	.12	.09	.05
14	Brooks Robinson	.30	.25	.12
15	Luis Aparicio	.12	.09	.05
16	Frank Robinson	.20	.15	.08
17	Mickey Mantle	1.00	.70	.40
18	Ted Williams	.50	.40	.20
19	Yogi Berra	.30	.25	.12
20	Bob Feller	.25	.20	.10
21	Whitey Ford	.25	.20	.10
22	Harmon Killebrew	.20	.15	.08
23	Stan Musial	.50	.40	.20
24	Jackie Robinson	.40	.30	.15
25	Eddie Mathews	.20	.15	.08
26	Ernie Banks	.20	.15	.08
27	Roberto Clemente	.40	.30	.15
28	Willie Mays	.50	.40	.20
29	Hank Aaron	.50	.40	.20
30	Johnny Bench	.30	.25	.12
31	Bob Gibson	.20	.15	.08
32	Warren Spahn	.20	.15	.08
33	Duke Snider	.25	.20	.10

1988 Nestle

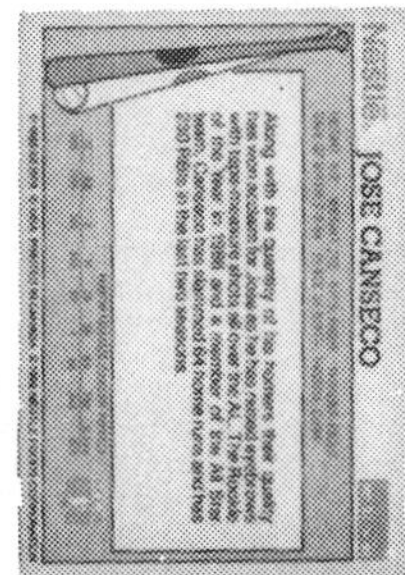

This 44-card set was produced by Mike Schechter Associates for Nestle. "Dream Team" packets of 3 player cards and one checklist card were inserted in 6-packs of Nestle's chocolate candy bars. The 1988 issue, similar to the 33-card Nestle set produced by Topps, features current players divided into four Dream Teams (East and West teams for each league). The "1988 Nestle" header appears at the top of the red and yellow-bordered cards. Below the player closeup (in a plain airbrushed cap) is a blue oval player name banner. Card backs are red, white and blue with card numbers printed upper right above personal stats, career highlights and major league totals. The bright red, blue and yellow checklist card outlines two special offers; one for an uncut sheet of all 44 player cards and one for a 1988 replica autographed baseball.

#	Player	MT	NR MT	EX
	Complete Set:	18.00	13.50	7.25
	Common Player:	.25	.20	.10
1	Roger Clemens	.75	.60	.30
2	Dale Murphy	.60	.45	.25
3	Eric Davis	.60	.45	.25
4	Gary Gaetti	.30	.25	.12
5	Ozzie Smith	.35	.25	.14
6	Mike Schmidt	.60	.45	.25
7	Ozzie Guillen	.25	.20	.10
8	John Franco	.25	.20	.10
9	Andre Dawson	.40	.30	.15
10	Mark McGwire	1.00	.70	.40
11	Bret Saberhagen	.35	.25	.14
12	Benny Santiago	.35	.25	.14
13	Jose Uribe	.25	.20	.10
14	Will Clark	.50	.40	.20
15	Don Mattingly	1.75	1.25	.70

		MT	NR MT	EX
16	Juan Samuel	.30	.25	.12
17	Jack Clark	.35	.25	.14
18	Darryl Strawberry	.75	.60	.30
19	Bill Doran	.25	.20	.10
20	Pete Incaviglia	.30	.25	.12
21	Dwight Gooden	.75	.60	.30
22	Willie Randolph	.25	.20	.10
23	Tim Wallach	.25	.20	.10
24	Pedro Guerrero	.35	.25	.14
25	Steve Bedrosian	.25	.20	.10
26	Gary Carter	.50	.40	.20
27	Jeff Reardon	.25	.20	.10
28	Dave Righetti	.35	.25	.14
29	Frank White	.25	.20	.10
30	Buddy Bell	.25	.20	.10
31	Tim Raines	.50	.40	.20
32	Wade Boggs	1.00	.70	.40
33	Dave Winfield	.50	.40	.20
34	George Bell	.40	.30	.15
35	Alan Trammell	.40	.30	.15
36	Joe Carter	.30	.25	.12
37	Jose Canseco	1.50	1.25	.60
38	Carlton Fisk	.40	.30	.15
39	Kirby Puckett	.50	.40	.20
40	Tony Gwynn	.50	.40	.20
41	Matt Nokes	.40	.30	.15
42	Keith Hernandez	.40	.30	.15
43	Nolan Ryan	.40	.30	.15
44	Wally Joyner	.50	.40	.20

1954 N.Y. Journal-American

Issued during the Golden Age of baseball in New York City, this 59-card set features only players from the three New York teams of the day - the Giants, Yankees and Dodgers. The 2" by 4" cards were issued at newsstands with the purchase of the now-extinct newspaper. Card fronts have promotional copy and a contest serial number in addition to the player's name and photo. Cards are black and white and unnumbered. Many of the game's top stars are included, such as Mickey Mantle, Willie Mays, Gil Hodges, Duke Snider, Jackie Robinson and Yogi Berra. Card backs featured team schedules. It has been theorized that a 60th Dodgers card should exist. Don Hoak and Bob Milliken have been suggested as the missing card, but the existence of either card has never been confirmed.

		NR MT	EX	VG
Complete Set:		2000.	1000.	600.00
Common Player:		10.00	5.00	3.00
(1)	Johnny Antonelli	12.00	6.00	3.50
(2)	Hank Bauer	20.00	10.00	6.00
(3)	Yogi Berra	75.00	37.00	22.00
(4)	Joe Black	12.00	6.00	3.50
(5)	Harry Byrd	10.00	5.00	3.00
(6)	Roy Campanella	65.00	32.00	19.50
(7)	Andy Carey	10.00	5.00	3.00
(8)	Jerry Coleman	10.00	5.00	3.00
(9)	Joe Collins	10.00	5.00	3.00
(10)	Billy Cox	10.00	5.00	3.00
(11)	Al Dark	12.00	6.00	3.50
(12)	Carl Erskine	20.00	10.00	6.00
(13)	Whitey Ford	40.00	20.00	12.00
(14)	Carl Furillo	20.00	10.00	6.00
(15)	Junior Gilliam	20.00	10.00	6.00
(16)	Ruben Gomez	10.00	5.00	3.00
(17)	Marv Grissom	10.00	5.00	3.00
(18)	Jim Hearn	10.00	5.00	3.00
(19)	Gil Hodges	35.00	17.50	10.50
(20)	Bobby Hofman	10.00	5.00	3.00
(21)	Jim Hughes	10.00	5.00	3.00
(22)	Monte Irvin	25.00	12.50	7.50
(23)	Larry Jansen	10.00	5.00	3.00
(24)	Ray Katt	10.00	5.00	3.00
(25)	Steve Kraly	10.00	5.00	3.00
(26)	Bob Kuzava	10.00	5.00	3.00
(27)	Clem Labine	12.00	6.00	3.50
(28)	Frank Leja	10.00	5.00	3.00
(29)	Don Liddle	10.00	5.00	3.00
(30)	Whitey Lockman	10.00	5.00	3.00
(31)	Billy Loes	10.00	5.00	3.00
(32)	Eddie Lopat	20.00	10.00	6.00
		MT	NR MT	EX
(33)	Gil McDougald	20.00	10.00	6.00
(34)	Sal Maglie	12.00	6.00	3.50
(35)	Mickey Mantle	450.00	225.00	135.00
(36)	Willie Mays	175.00	87.00	52.00
(37)	Russ Meyer	10.00	5.00	3.00
(38)	Bill Miller	10.00	5.00	3.00
(39)	Tom Morgan	10.00	5.00	3.00
(40)	Don Mueller	10.00	5.00	3.00
(41)	Don Newcombe	20.00	10.00	6.00
(42)	Irv Noren	10.00	5.00	3.00
(43)	Erv Palica	10.00	5.00	3.00
(44)	PeeWee Reese	55.00	27.00	16.50
(45)	Allie Reynolds	20.00	10.00	6.00
(46)	Dusty Rhodes	10.00	5.00	3.00
(47)	Phil Rizzuto	35.00	17.50	10.50
(48)	Ed Robinson	10.00	5.00	3.00
(49)	Jackie Robinson	225.00	112.00	67.00
(50)	Preacher Roe	20.00	10.00	6.00
(51)	George Shuba	10.00	5.00	3.00
(52)	Duke Snider	150.00	75.00	45.00
(53)	Hank Thompson	10.00	5.00	3.00
(54)	Wes Westrum	10.00	5.00	3.00
(55)	Hoyt Wilhelm	30.00	15.00	9.00
(56)	Davey Williams	10.00	5.00	3.00
(57)	Dick Williams	12.00	6.00	3.50
(58)	Gene Woodling	12.00	6.00	3.50
(59)	Al Worthington	10.00	5.00	3.00

1984 N.Y. Mets M.V.P. Club

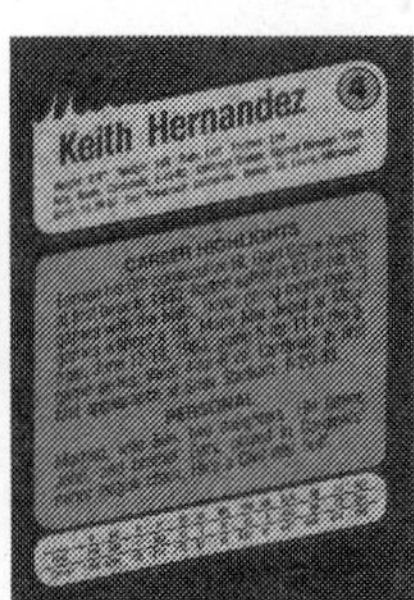

This nine-card, uncut panel was issued - along with other souvenir items - as a promotion by the New York Mets M.V.P. (Most Valuable Person) Club. Available from the club by mail, the perforated panel features eight full-color player cards, plus a special promotional card in the center. The full panel measures 7-1/2" by 10-1/2", with individual cards measuring the standard 2-1/2" by 3-1/2". Card backs are numbered in the upper right corner and include player stats and career highlights.

		MT	NR MT	EX
Complete Panel Set:		12.00	9.00	4.75
Complete Singles Set:		4.00	3.00	1.50
Common Single Player:		.15	.11	.06
Panel		12.00	9.00	4.75
1	Dave Johnson	.30	.25	.12
2	Ron Darling	.40	.30	.15
3	George Foster	.40	.30	.15
4	Keith Hernandez	.60	.45	.25
5	Jesse Orosco	.15	.11	.06
6	Rusty Staub	.30	.25	.12
7	Darryl Strawberry	2.00	1.50	.80
8	Mookie Wilson	.30	.25	.12
---	Membership Card	.05	.04	.02

1985 N.Y. Mets Super Fan Club

This specially-produced nine-card panel was issued as part of a souvenir package by the New York Mets Super Fan Club. The full-color, perforated panel measures 7-1/2" by 10-1/2" and features eight standard-size player cards, plus a special promotional card in the center. The uncut sheet was available by mail directly from the club. The backs are numbered in the upper right corner and include player statistics and career highlights.

		MT	NR MT	EX
Complete Panel Set:		15.00	11.00	6.00
Complete Singles Set:		4.00	3.00	1.50
Common Single Player:		.15	.11	.06
Panel		15.00	11.00	6.00
1	Wally Backman	.15	.11	.06
2	Bruce Berenyi	.15	.11	.06
3	Gary Carter	.60	.45	.25
4	George Foster	.40	.30	.15
5	Dwight Gooden	2.00	1.50	.80
6	Keith Hernandez	.60	.45	.25
7	Doug Sisk	.15	.11	.06
8	Darryl Strawberry	1.75	1.25	.70
---	Membership Card	.05	.04	.02

1986 N.Y. Mets

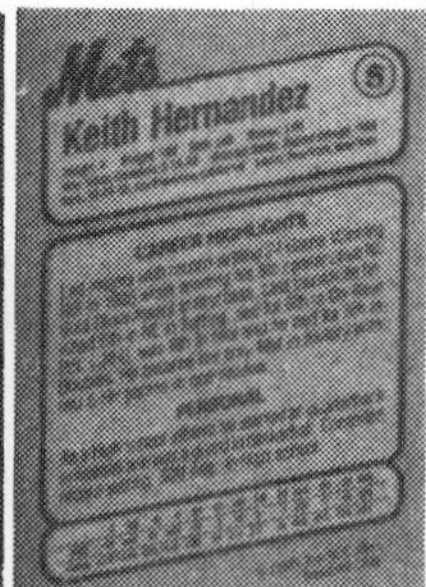

This special nine-card panel was issued by the fan club of the 1986 World Champion New York Mets, along with other souvenir items gained with membership in the club. Included in the full-color set are eight top Mets players, with a promotional card in the center of the panel. Individual cards measure 2-1/2" by 3-1/2", and are perforated at the edges to facilitate separation. The full panel measures 70-1/2" by 10-1/2". Card fronts feature posed photos of each player, along with name, position and team logo. Backs feature career and personal data, and are printed in the team's blue and orange colors.

		MT	NR MT	EX
Complete Panel Set:		12.00	9.00	4.75
Complete Singles Set:		4.00	3.00	1.50
Common Single Player:		.15	.11	.06
Panel		12.00	9.00	4.75
1	Wally Backman	.15	.11	.06
2	Gary Carter	.70	.50	.30
3	Ron Darling	.40	.30	.15
4	Dwight Gooden	1.25	.90	.50
5	Keith Hernandez	.60	.45	.25
6	Howard Johnson	.70	.50	.30
7	Roger McDowell	.40	.30	.15
8	Darryl Strawberry	1.25	.90	.50
---	Membership Card	.05	.04	.02

1985 Nike

Nike, the athletic shoe company, has produced posters and counter display cards of its posters for several years, but in 1985 issued a five-card set. The cards are borderless, color miniature versions (3-1/16" by 5-1/16") of the Nike posters. Backs feature personal data and career highlights, along with the warning, "Promotional Use Only/Not For Resale." The five-card set includes two baseball players.

	MT	NR MT	EX
Complete Set:	70.00	50.00	27.00
Common Player:	4.00	3.00	1.50

		MT	NR MT	EX
(1)	Dwight Gooden (baseball)	12.00	9.00	4.75
(2)	Michael Jordan (basketball)	40.00	30.00	15.00
(3)	James Lofton (football)	4.00	3.00	1.50
(4)	John McEnroe (tennis)	10.00	7.50	4.00
(5)	Lance Parrish (baseball)	4.00	3.00	1.50

1953 Northland Bread Labels

This bread end-label set consists of 32 players - two from each major league team. The unnumbered black and white labels measure approximately 2-11/16" square and include the slogan "Bread for Energy" along the top. An album to house the labels was also part of the promotion.

		NR MT	EX	VG
Complete Set:		2000.	1000.	600.00
Common Player:		50.00	25.00	15.00
(1)	Cal Abrams	50.00	25.00	15.00
(2)	Richie Ashburn	60.00	30.00	18.00
(3)	Gus Bell	50.00	25.00	15.00
(4)	Jim Busby	50.00	25.00	15.00
(5)	Clint Courtney	50.00	25.00	15.00
(6)	Billy Cox	50.00	25.00	15.00
(7)	Jim Dyck	50.00	25.00	15.00
(8)	Nellie Fox	60.00	30.00	18.00
(9)	Sid Gordon	50.00	25.00	15.00
(10)	Warren Hacker	50.00	25.00	15.00
(11)	Jim Hearn	50.00	25.00	15.00
(12)	Fred Hutchinson	55.00	27.00	16.50
(13)	Monte Irvin	90.00	45.00	27.00
(14)	Jackie Jensen	60.00	30.00	18.00
(15)	Ted Kluszewski	60.00	30.00	18.00
(16)	Bob Lemon	90.00	45.00	27.00
(17)	Maury McDermott	50.00	25.00	15.00
(18)	Minny Minoso	60.00	30.00	18.00
(19)	Johnny Mize	90.00	45.00	27.00
(20)	Mel Parnell	50.00	25.00	15.00
(21)	Howie Pollet	50.00	25.00	15.00
(22)	Jerry Priddy	50.00	25.00	15.00
(23)	Allie Reynolds	60.00	30.00	18.00
(24)	Preacher Roe	60.00	30.00	18.00
(25)	Al Rosen	60.00	30.00	18.00
(26)	Connie Ryan	50.00	25.00	15.00
(27)	Hank Sauer	50.00	25.00	15.00
(28)	Red Schoendienst	60.00	30.00	18.00
(29)	Bobby Shantz	55.00	27.00	16.50
(30)	Enos Slaughter	90.00	45.00	27.00
(31)	Warren Spahn	100.00	50.00	30.00
(32)	Gus Zernial	50.00	25.00	15.00

1960 Nu-Card

These large, 3-1/4" by 5-3/8" cards are printed in a mock newspaper format, with a headline, picture and story describing one of baseball's greatest events. There are 72 events featured in the set, which is printed in red and black. Each card is numbered in the upper left corner. The card backs offer a quiz question and answer. Certain cards in the set can be found with the fronts printed entirely in black. These cards may command a slight premium.

		NR MT	EX	VG
Complete Set:		175.00	87.00	52.00
Common Player:		1.00	.50	.30
1	Babe Hits 3 Homers In A Series Game	10.00	5.00	3.00
2	Podres Pitching Wins Series	.75	.40	.25
3	Bevans Pitches No Hitter, Almost	.75	.40	.25
4	Box Score Devised By Reporter	1.00	.50	.30
5	VanderMeer Pitches 2 No Hitters	1.00	.50	.30
6	Indians Take Bums	1.00	.50	.30
7	DiMag Comes Thru	10.00	5.00	3.00
8	Mathewson Pitches 3 W.S. Shutouts	1.75	.90	.50
9	Haddix Pitches 12 Perfect Innings	.75	.40	.25
10	Thomson's Homer Sinks Dodgers	1.75	.90	.50
11	Hubbell Strikes Out 5 A.L. Stars	1.50	.70	.45
12	Pickoff Ends Series (Marty Marion)	.75	.40	.25
13	Cards Take Series From Yanks (Grover Cleveland Alexander)	1.50	.70	.45
14	Dizzy And Daffy Win Series	3.50	1.75	1.00
15	Owen Drops 3rd Strike	.75	.40	.25
16	Ruth Calls His Shot	8.00	4.00	2.50
17	Merkle Pulls Boner	.75	.40	.25
18	Larsen Hurls Perfect World Series Game	1.50	.70	.45
19	Bean Ball Ends Career Of Mickey Cochrane	1.25	.60	.40
20	Banks Belts 47 Homers, Earns MVP Honors	2.00	1.00	.60
21	Stan Musial Hits 5 Homers In 1 Day	3.50	1.75	1.00
22	Mickey Mantle Hits Longest Homer	12.00	6.00	3.50
23	Sievers Captures Home Run Title	.75	.40	.25
24	Gehrig Consecutive Game Record Ends	10.00	5.00	3.00
25	Red Schoendienst Key Player In Victory	.75	.40	.25
26	Midget Pinch-Hits For St. Louis Browns (Eddie Gaedel)	1.25	.60	.40
27	Willie Mays Makes Greatest Catch	4.00	2.00	1.25
28	Homer By Berra Puts Yanks In 1st Place	3.00	1.50	.90
29	Campy National League's MVP	3.00	1.50	.90
30	Bob Turley Hurls Yanks To Championship	.75	.40	.25
31	Dodgers Take Series From Sox In Six	.75	.40	.25
32	Furillo Hero As Dodgers Beat Chicago	.75	.40	.25
33	Adcock Gets Four Homers And A Double	.75	.40	.25
34	Dickey Chosen All Star Catcher	1.25	.60	.40
35	Burdette Beats Yanks In 3 Series Games	1.00	.50	.30
36	Umpires Clear White Sox Bench	1.00	.50	.30
37	Reese Honored As Greatest Dodger S.S.	2.50	1.25	.70
38	Joe DiMaggio Hits In 56 Straight Games	10.00	5.00	3.00
39	Ted Williams Hits .406 For Season	5.00	2.50	1.50
40	Johnson Pitches 56 Scoreless Innings	2.25	1.25	.70
41	Hodges Hits 4 Home Runs In Nite Game	1.75	.90	.50
42	Greenberg Returns To Tigers From Army	1.25	.60	.40
43	Ty Cobb Named Best Player Of All Time	10.00	5.00	3.00
44	Robin Roberts Wins 28 Games	1.25	.60	.40
45	Rizzuto's 2 Runs Save 1st Place	1.50	.70	.45
46	Tigers Beat Out Senators For Pennant (Hal Newhouser)	.75	.40	.25
47	Babe Ruth Hits 60th Home Run	9.00	4.50	2.75
48	Cy Young Honored	1.75	.90	.50
49	Killebrew Starts Spring Training	1.75	.90	.50
50	Mantle Hits Longest Homer At Stadium	12.00	6.00	3.50
51	Braves Take Pennant (Hank Aaron)	3.50	1.75	1.00
52	Ted Williams Hero Of All Star Game	5.00	2.50	1.50
53	Robinson Saves Dodgers For Playoffs (Jackie Robinson)	3.50	1.75	1.00
54	Snodgrass Muffs A Fly Ball	.75	.40	.25
55	Snider Belts 2 Homers	2.25	1.25	.70
56	New York Giants Win 26 Straight Games (Christy Mathewson)	1.75	.90	.50
57	Ted Kluszewski Stars In 1st Game Win	.75	.40	.25
58	Ott Walks 5 Times In A Single Game (Mel Ott)	1.25	.60	.40
59	Harvey Kuenn Takes Batting Title	.75	.40	.25
60	Bob Feller Hurls 3rd No-Hitter Of Career	2.25	1.25	.70
61	Yanks Champs Again! (Casey Stengel)	1.50	.70	.45
62	Aaron's Bat Beats Yankees In Series	4.00	2.00	1.25
63	Warren Spahn Beats Yanks in World Series	1.50	.70	.45
64	Ump's Wrong Call Helps Dodgers	.75	.40	.25
65	Kaline Hits 3 Homers, 2 In Same Inning	2.00	1.00	.60
66	Bob Allison Named A.L. Rookie of Year	.75	.40	.25
67	McCovey Blasts Way Into Giant Lineup	1.75	.90	.50
68	Colavito Hits Four Homers In One Game	1.00	.50	.30
69	Erskine Sets Strike Out Record In W.S.	.75	.40	.25
70	Sal Maglie Pitches No-Hit Game	.75	.40	.25
71	Early Wynn Victory Crushes Yanks	1.25	.60	.40
72	Nellie Fox American League's M.V.P.	3.00	1.50	.90

1961 Nu-Card

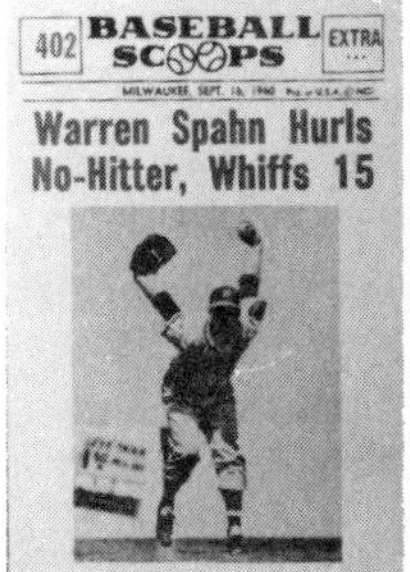

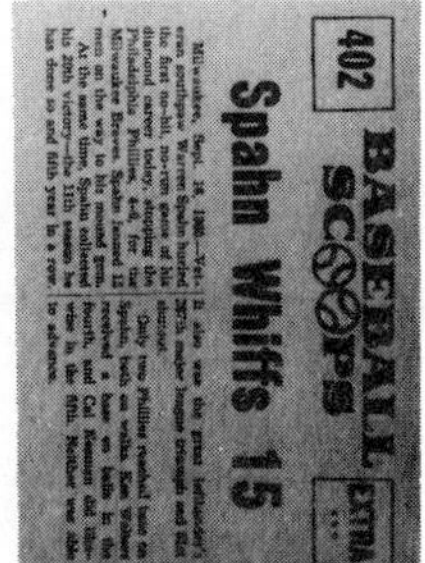

Very similar in style to their set of the year before, the Nu-Card Baseball Scoops were issued in a smaller 2-1/2" by 3-1/2" size, but still featured the mock newspaper card front. This 80-card set is numbered from 401 to 480, with numbers shown on both the card front and back. These cards, which commemor- ate great moments in individual players' careers, included only the headline and black and white photo on the fronts, with the descriptive story on the card backs. Cards are again printed in red and black. It appears the set may have been counterfeited, though when is not known. These cards can be determined by examining the card photo for unusual blurring and fuzziness.

		NR MT	EX	VG
Complete Set:		80.00	40.00	24.00
Common Player:		.30	.15	.09
401	Gentile Powers Birds Into 1st	1.00	.50	.30
402	Warren Spahn Hurls No-Hitter, Whiffs 15	1.00	.50	.30
403	Mazeroski's Homer Wins Series For Bucs	.75	.40	.25
404	Willie Mays' 3 Triples Paces Giants	2.50	1.25	.70
405	Woodie Held Slugs 2 Homers, 6 RBIs	.30	.15	.09
406	Vern Law Winner Of Cy Young Award	.40	.20	.12
407	Runnels Makes 9 Hits in Twin-Bill	.30	.15	.09
408	Braves' Lew Burdette Wins No-Hitter, 1 0	.70	.35	.20
409	Dick Stuart Hits 3 Homers, Single	.30	.15	.09
410	Don Cardwell Of Cubs Pitches No-Hit Game	.30	.15	.09
411	Camilo Pascual Strikes Out 15 Bosox	.30	.15	.09
412	Eddie Mathews Blasts 300th Big League HR	1.00	.50	.30
413	Groat, NL Bat King, Named Loop's MVP	.70	.35	.20
414	AL Votes To Expand To 10 Teams (Gene Autry)	1.25	.60	.40
415	Bobby Richardson Sets Series Mark	.75	.40	.25
416	Maris Nips Mantle For AL MVP Award	2.50	1.25	.70
417	Merkle Pulls Boner	.30	.15	.09
418	Larsen Hurls Perefect World Series Game	.75	.40	.25
419	Bean Ball Ends Career Of Mickey Cochrane	.70	.35	.20
420	Banks Belts 47 Homers, Earns MVP Award	1.50	.70	.45
421	Stan Musial Hits 5 Homers In 1 Day	2.50	1.25	.70
422	Mickey Mantle Hits Longest Homer	10.00	5.00	3.00
423	Sievers Captures Home Run Title	.30	.15	.09
424	Gehrig Consecutive Game Record Ends	5.00	2.50	1.50
425	Red Schoendienst Key Player In Victory	.70	.35	.20
426	Midget Pinch-Hits For St. Louis Browns (Eddie Gaedel)	.75	.40	.25
427	Willie Mays Makes Greatest Catch	2.50	1.25	.70
428	Robinson Saves Dodgers For Playoffs	2.50	1.25	.70
429	Campy Most Valuable Player	2.50	1.25	.70
430	Turley Hurls Yanks To Championship	.40	.20	.12
431	Dodgers Take Series From Sox In Six (Larry Sherry)	.30	.15	.09
432	Furillo Hero In 3rd World Series Game	.70	.35	.20

		NR MT	EX	VG
433	Adcock Gets Four Homers, Double	.70	.35	.20
434	Dickey Chosen All Star Catcher	1.00	.50	.30
435	Burdette Beats Yanks In 3 Series Games	.75	.40	.25
436	Umpires Clear White Sox Bench	.30	.15	.09
437	Reese Honored As Greatest Dodgers S.S.	1.50	.70	.45
438	Joe DiMaggio Hits In 56 Straight Games	5.00	2.50	1.50
439	Ted Williams Hits .406 For Season	4.00	2.00	1.25
440	Johnson Pitches 56 Scoreless Innings	2.50	1.25	.70
441	Hodges Hits 4 Home Runs In Nite Game	1.50	.70	.45
442	Greenberg Returns To Tigers From Army	1.00	.50	.30
443	Ty Cobb Named Best Player Of All Time	4.00	2.00	1.25
444	Robin Roberts Wins 28 Games	1.00	.50	.30
445	Rizzuto's 2 Runs Save 1st Place	1.25	.60	.40
446	Tigers Beat Out Senators For Pennant (Hal Newhouser)	.30	.15	.09
447	Babe Ruth Hits 60th Home Run	6.00	3.00	1.75
448	Cy Young Honored	1.50	.70	.45
449	Killebrew Starts Spring Training	1.25	.60	.40
450	Mantle Hits Longest Homer At Stadium	9.00	4.50	2.75
451	Braves Take Pennant	.30	.15	.09
452	Ted Williams Hero Of All Star Game	2.50	1.25	.70
453	Homer By Berra Puts Yanks In 1st Place	2.50	1.25	.70
454	Snodgrass Muffs A Fly Ball	.30	.15	.09
455	Babe Hits 3 Homers In A Series Game	5.00	2.50	1.50
456	New York Wins 26 Straight Games	.30	.15	.09
457	Ted Kluszewski Stars In 1st Series Win	.40	.20	.12
458	Ott Walks 5 Times In A Single Game	1.00	.50	.30
459	Harvey Kuenn Takes Batting Title	.40	.20	.12
460	Bob Feller Hurls 3rd No-Hitter Of Career	2.50	1.25	.70
461	Yanks Champs Again! (Casey Stengel)	1.50	.70	.45
462	Aaron's Bat Beats Yankees In Series	2.50	1.25	.70
463	Warren Spahn Beats Yanks In World Series	1.00	.50	.30
464	Ump's Wrong Call Helps Dodgers	.30	.15	.09
465	Kaline Hits 3 Homers, 2 In Same Inning	1.50	.70	.45
466	Bob Allison Named A.L. Rookie Of Year	.40	.20	.12
467	DiMag Comes Thru	5.00	2.50	1.50
468	Colavito Hits Four Homers In One Game	.70	.35	.20
469	Erskine Sets Strike Out Record In W.S.	.70	.35	.20
470	Sal Maglie Pitches No-Hit Game	.70	.35	.20
471	Early Wynn Victory Crushes Yanks	1.00	.50	.30
472	Nellie Fox American League's MVP	.75	.40	.25
473	Pickoff Ends Series (Marty Marion)	.40	.20	.12
474	Podres Pitching Wins Series	.80	.40	.25
475	Owen Drops 3rd Strike	.30	.15	.09
476	Dizzy And Daffy Win Series	2.50	1.25	.70
477	Mathewson Pitches 3 W.S. Shutouts	1.50	.70	.45
478	Haddix Pitches 12 Perfect Innings	.40	.20	.12
479	Hubbell Strike Out 5 A.L. Stars	1.00	.50	.30
480	Homer Sinks Dodgers (Bobby Thomson)	1.25	.60	.40

1965 O-Pee-Chee

Identical in design to the 1965 Topps set, the Canadian-issued 1965 O-Pee-Chee set was printed on gray stock and consists of 283 cards, each measuring the standard 2-1/2" by 3-1/2". The words "Printed in Canada" appear along the bottom of the back of the cards.

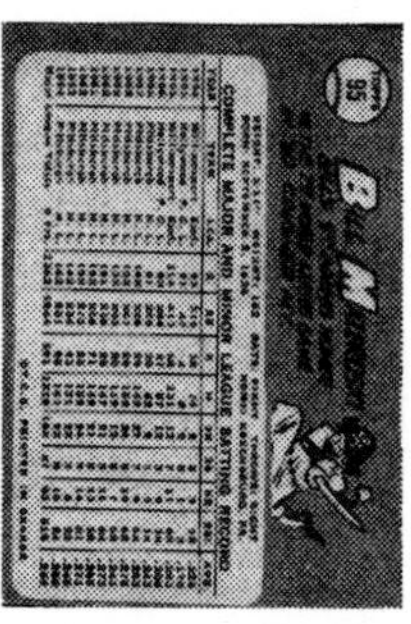

	NR MT	EX	VG
Complete Set:	1500.	750.00	450.00
Common Player:	1.75	.90	.50

		NR MT	EX	VG
1	A.L. Batting Leaders (Elston Howard, Tony Oliva, Brooks Robinson)	5.00	2.00	1.25
2	N.L. Batting Leaders (Hank Aaron, Rico Carty, Bob Clemente)	4.00	2.00	1.25
3	A.L. Home Run Leaders (Harmon Killebrew, Mickey Mantle, Boog Powell)	9.00	4.50	2.75
4	N.L. Home Run Leaders (Johnny Callison, Orlando Cepeda, Jim Ray Hart, Willie Mays, Billy Williams)	3.50	1.75	1.00
5	A.L. RBI Leaders (Harmon Killebrew, Mickey Mantle, Brooks Robinson, Dick Stuart)	9.00	4.50	2.75
6	N.L. RBI Leaders (Ken Boyer, Willie Mays, Ron Santo)	3.50	1.75	1.00
7	A.L. ERA Leaders (Dean Chance, Joel Horlen)	2.00	1.00	.60
8	N.L. ERA Leaders (Don Drysdale, Sandy Koufax)	3.50	1.75	1.00
9	A.L. Pitching Leaders (Wally Bunker, Dean Chance, Gary Peters, Juan Pizarro, Dave Wickersham)	2.00	1.00	.60
10	N.L. Pitching Leaders (Larry Jackson, Juan Marichal, Ray Sadecki)	2.75	1.50	.80
11	A.L. Strikeout Leaders (Dean Chance, Al Downing, Camilo Pascual)	2.00	1.00	.60
12	N.L. Strikeout Leaders (Don Drysdale, Bob Gibson, Bob Veale)	2.75	1.50	.80
13	Pedro Ramos	1.75	.90	.50
14	Len Gabrielson	1.75	.90	.50
15	Robin Roberts	5.00	2.50	1.50
16	Astros Rookies (Sonny Jackson, Joe Morgan)	100.00	50.00	30.00
17	Johnny Romano	1.75	.90	.50
18	Bill McCool	1.75	.90	.50
19	Gates Brown	1.75	.90	.50
20	Jim Bunning	3.00	1.50	.90
21	Don Blasingame	1.75	.90	.50
22	Charlie Smith	1.75	.90	.50
23	Bob Tiefenauer	1.75	.90	.50
24	Twins Team	3.00	1.50	.90
25	Al McBean	1.75	.90	.50
26	Bobby Knoop	1.75	.90	.50
27	Dick Bertell	1.75	.90	.50
28	Barney Schultz	1.75	.90	.50
29	Felix Mantilla	1.75	.90	.50
30	Jim Bouton	2.25	1.25	.70
31	Mike White	1.75	.90	.50
32	Herman Franks	1.75	.90	.50
33	Jackie Brandt	1.75	.90	.50
34	Cal Koonce	1.75	.90	.50
35	Ed Charles	1.75	.90	.50
36	Bobby Wine	1.75	.90	.50
37	Fred Gladding	1.75	.90	.50
38	Jim King	1.75	.90	.50
39	Gerry Arrigo	1.75	.90	.50
40	Frank Howard	2.25	1.25	.70
41	White Sox Rookies (Bruce Howard, Marv Staehle)	1.75	.90	.50
42	Earl Wilson	1.75	.90	.50
43	Mike Shannon	2.00	1.00	.60
44	Wade Blasingame	1.75	.90	.50
45	Roy McMillan	1.75	.90	.50
46	Bob Lee	1.75	.90	.50
47	Tommy Harper	1.75	.90	.50
48	Claude Raymond	1.75	.90	.50
49	Orioles Rookies (Curt Blefary, John Miller)	2.25	1.25	.70
50	Juan Marichal	7.00	3.50	2.00
51	Billy Bryan	1.75	.90	.50
52	Ed Roebuck	1.75	.90	.50
53	Dick McAuliffe	2.00	1.00	.60
54	Joe Gibbon	1.75	.90	.50
55	Tony Conigliaro	2.25	1.25	.70
56	Ron Kline	1.75	.90	.50
57	Cards Team	2.00	1.00	.60
58	Fred Talbot	1.75	.90	.50
59	Nate Oliver	1.75	.90	.50
60	Jim O'Toole	1.75	.90	.50
61	Chris Cannizzaro	1.75	.90	.50
62	Jim Katt (Kaat)	3.00	1.50	.90
63	Ty Cline	1.75	.90	.50
64	Lou Burdette	2.00	1.00	.60
65	Tony Kubek	3.00	1.50	.90
66	Bill Rigney	1.75	.90	.50
67	Harvey Haddix	2.00	1.00	.60
68	Del Crandall	2.00	1.00	.60
69	Bill Virdon	2.00	1.00	.60
70	Bill Skowron	2.00	1.00	.60
71	John O'Donoghue	1.75	.90	.50
72	Tony Gonzalez	1.75	.90	.50
73	Dennis Ribant	1.75	.90	.50
74	Red Sox Rookies (Rico Petrocelli, Jerry Stephenson)	2.25	1.25	.70
75	Deron Johnson	1.75	.90	.50
76	Sam McDowell	2.00	1.00	.60
77	Doug Camilli	1.75	.90	.50
78	Dal Maxvill	1.75	.90	.50
79	Checklist 1	2.75	1.50	.80
80	Turk Farrell	1.75	.90	.50
81	Don Buford	1.75	.90	.50
82	Brave Rookies (Santos Alomar, John Braun)	1.75	.90	.50
83	George Thomas	1.75	.90	.50
84	Ron Herbel	1.75	.90	.50
85	Willie Smith	1.75	.90	.50
86	Les Narum	1.75	.90	.50
87	Nelson Mathews	1.75	.90	.50
88	Jack Lamabe	1.75	.90	.50
89	Mike Hershberger	1.75	.90	.50
90	Rich Rollins	1.75	.90	.50
91	Cubs Team	2.00	1.00	.60
92	Dick Howser	2.25	1.25	.70
93	Jack Fisher	1.75	.90	.50
94	Charlie Lau	1.75	.90	.50
95	Bill Mazeroski	2.50	1.25	.70
96	Sonny Siebert	1.75	.90	.50
97	Pedro Gonzalez	1.75	.90	.50
98	Bob Miller	1.75	.90	.50
99	Gil Hodges	4.00	2.00	1.25
100	Ken Boyer	2.50	1.25	.70
101	Fred Newman	1.75	.90	.50
102	Steve Boros	1.75	.90	.50
103	Harvey Kuenn	2.00	1.00	.60
104	Checklist 2	2.75	1.50	.80
105	Chico Salmon	1.75	.90	.50
106	Gene Oliver	1.75	.90	.50
107	Phillies Rookies (Pat Corrales, Costen Shockley)	2.00	1.00	.60
108	Don Mincher	1.75	.90	.50
109	Walt Bond	1.75	.90	.50
110	Ron Santo	2.25	1.25	.70
111	Lee Thomas	1.75	.90	.50
112	Derrell Griffith	1.75	.90	.50
113	Steve Barber	1.75	.90	.50
114	Jim Hickman	1.75	.90	.50
115	Bobby Richardson	2.75	1.50	.80
116	Cardinals Rookies (Dave Dowling, Bob Tolan)	2.00	1.00	.60
117	Wes Stock	1.75	.90	.50
118	Hal Lanier	2.00	1.00	.60
119	John Kennedy	1.75	.90	.50
120	Frank Robinson	9.00	4.50	2.75
121	Gene Alley	1.75	.90	.50
122	Bill Pleis	1.75	.90	.50
123	Frank Thomas	1.75	.90	.50
124	Tom Satriano	1.75	.90	.50
125	Juan Pizarro	1.75	.90	.50
126	Dodgers Team	3.00	1.50	.90
127	Frank Lary	1.75	.90	.50
128	Vic Davalillo	1.75	.90	.50
129	Bennie Daniels	1.75	.90	.50
130	Al Kaline	9.00	4.50	2.75
131	Johnny Keane	2.00	1.00	.60
132	World Series Game 1 (Cards Take Opener)	2.25	1.25	.70
133	World Series Game 2 (Stottlemyre Wins)	2.75	1.50	.80
134	World Series Game 3 (Mantle's Clutch HR)	15.00	7.50	4.50
135	World Series Game 4 (Boyer's Grand Slam)	2.25	1.25	.70
136	World Series Game 5 (10th Inning Triumph)	2.25	1.25	.70
137	World Series Game 6 (Bouton Wins Again)	2.75	1.50	.80
138	World Series Game 7 (Gibson Wins Finale)	2.75	1.50	.80
139	World Series Summary (The Cards Celebrate)	2.25	1.25	.70
140	Dean Chance	1.75	.90	.50
141	Charlie James	1.75	.90	.50
142	Bill Monbouquette	1.75	.90	.50
143	Pirates Rookies (John Gelnar, Jerry May)	1.75	.90	.50
144	Ed Kranepool	2.00	1.00	.60
145	Luis Tiant	4.00	2.00	1.25
146	Ron Hansen	1.75	.90	.50
147	Dennis Bennett	1.75	.90	.50
148	Willie Kirkland	1.75	.90	.50
149	Wayne Schurr	1.75	.90	.50
150	Brooks Robinson	11.50	5.75	3.50
151	Athletics Team	2.00	1.00	.60
152	Phil Ortega	1.75	.90	.50
153	Norm Cash	2.00	1.00	.60
154	Bob Humphreys	1.75	.90	.50
155	Roger Maris	30.00	15.00	9.00
156	Bob Sadowski	1.75	.90	.50
157	Zolio Versalles	2.00	1.00	.60
158	Dick Sisler	1.75	.90	.50
159	Jim Duffalo	1.75	.90	.50
160	Bob Clemente	50.00	25.00	15.00
161	Frank Baumann	1.75	.90	.50
162	Russ Nixon	1.75	.90	.50
163	John Briggs	1.75	.90	.50
164	Al Spangler	1.75	.90	.50
165	Dick Ellsworth	1.75	.90	.50
166	Indians Rookies (Tommie Agee, George Culver)	2.00	1.00	.60
167	Bill Wakefield	1.75	.90	.50
168	Dick Green	1.75	.90	.50
169	Dave Vineyard	1.75	.90	.50
170	Hank Aaron	30.00	15.00	9.00
171	Jim Roland	1.75	.90	.50
172	Jim Piersall	2.00	1.00	.60
173	Tigers Team	2.25	1.25	.70
174	Joe Jay	1.75	.90	.50
175	Bob Aspromonte	1.75	.90	.50
176	Willie McCovey	9.00	4.50	2.75
177	Pete Mikkelsen	1.75	.90	.50
178	Dalton Jones	1.75	.90	.50
179	Hal Woodeshick	1.75	.90	.50
180	Bob Allison	2.00	1.00	.60
181	Senators Rookies (Don Loun, Joe McCabe)	1.75	.90	.50
182	Mike de la Hoz	1.75	.90	.50
183	Dave Nicholson	1.75	.90	.50
184	John Boozer	1.75	.90	.50
185	Max Alvis	1.75	.90	.50
186	Billy Cowan	1.75	.90	.50
187	Casey Stengel	9.00	4.50	2.75
188	Sam Bowens	1.75	.90	.50

		NR MT	EX	VG
189	Checklist 3	2.75	1.50	.80
190	Bill White	2.00	1.00	.60
191	Phil Regan	1.75	.90	.50
192	Jim Coker	1.75	.90	.50
193	Gaylord Perry	9.00	4.50	2.75
194	Rookie Stars (Bill Kelso, Rick Reichardt)	1.75	.90	.50
195	Bob Veale	1.75	.90	.50
196	Ron Fairly	2.00	1.00	.60
197	Diego Segui	1.75	.90	.50
198	Smoky Burgess	2.00	1.00	.60
199	Bob Heffner	1.75	.90	.50
200	Joe Torre	2.50	1.25	.70
201	Twins Rookies (Cesar Tovar, Sandy Valdespino)	2.00	1.00	.60
202	Leo Burke	1.75	.90	.50
203	Dallas Green	2.00	1.00	.60
204	Russ Snyder	1.75	.90	.50
205	Warren Spahn	9.00	4.50	2.75
206	Willie Horton	2.00	1.00	.60
207	Pete Rose	200.00	100.00	60.00
208	Tommy John	7.00	3.50	2.00
209	Pirates Team	2.00	1.00	.60
210	Jim Fregosi	2.00	1.00	.60
211	Steve Ridzik	1.75	.90	.50
212	Ron Brand	1.75	.90	.50
213	Jim Davenport	1.75	.90	.50
214	Bob Purkey	1.75	.90	.50
215	Pete Ward	1.75	.90	.50
216	Al Worthington	1.75	.90	.50
217	Walt Alston	2.75	1.50	.80
218	Dick Schofield	1.75	.90	.50
219	Bob Meyer	1.75	.90	.50
220	Bill Williams	6.00	3.00	1.75
221	John Tsitouris	1.75	.90	.50
222	Bob Tillman	1.75	.90	.50
223	Dan Osinski	1.75	.90	.50
224	Bob Chance	1.75	.90	.50
225	Bo Belinsky	2.00	1.00	.60
226	Yankees Rookies (Jake Gibbs, Elvio Jimenez)	2.00	1.00	.60
227	Bobby Klaus	1.75	.90	.50
228	Jack Sanford	1.75	.90	.50
229	Lou Clinton	1.75	.90	.50
230	Ray Sadecki	1.75	.90	.50
231	Jerry Adair	1.75	.90	.50
232	Steve Blass	2.00	1.00	.60
233	Don Zimmer	2.00	1.00	.60
234	White Sox Team	2.00	1.00	.60
235	Chuck Hinton	1.75	.90	.50
236	Dennis McLain	5.00	2.50	1.50
237	Bernie Allen	1.75	.90	.50
238	Joe Moeller	1.75	.90	.50
239	Doc Edwards	1.75	.90	.50
240	Bob Bruce	1.75	.90	.50
241	Mack Jones	1.75	.90	.50
242	George Brunet	1.75	.90	.50
243	Reds Rookies (Ted Davidson, Tommy Helms)	2.00	1.00	.60
244	Lindy McDaniel	1.75	.90	.50
245	Joe Pepitone	2.25	1.25	.70
246	Tom Butters	1.75	.90	.50
247	Wally Moon	2.00	1.00	.60
248	Gus Triandos	1.75	.90	.50
249	Dave McNally	2.00	1.00	.60
250	Willie Mays	60.00	30.00	17.50
251	Billy Herman	2.25	1.25	.70
252	Pete Richert	1.75	.90	.50
253	Danny Cater	1.75	.90	.50
254	Roland Sheldon	1.75	.90	.50
255	Camilo Pascual	2.00	1.00	.60
256	Tito Francona	1.75	.90	.50
257	Jim Wynn	2.00	1.00	.60
258	Larry Bearnarth	1.75	.90	.50
259	Tigers Rookies (Jim Northrup, Ray Oyler)	2.00	1.00	.60
260	Don Drysdale	12.00	6.00	3.50
261	Duke Carmel	1.75	.90	.50
262	Bud Daley	1.75	.90	.50
263	Marty Keough	1.75	.90	.50
264	Bob Buhl	1.75	.90	.50
265	Jim Pagliaroni	1.75	.90	.50
266	Bert Campaneris	2.75	1.50	.80
267	Senators Team	2.00	1.00	.60
268	Ken McBride	1.75	.90	.50
269	Frank Bolling	1.75	.90	.50
270	Milt Pappas	2.00	1.00	.60
271	Don Wert	1.75	.90	.50
272	Chuck Schilling	1.75	.90	.50
273	Checklist 4	2.75	1.50	.80
274	Lum Harris	1.75	.90	.50
275	Dick Groat	2.25	1.25	.70
276	Hoyt Wilhelm	5.00	2.50	1.50
277	Johnny Lewis	1.75	.90	.50
278	Ken Retzer	1.75	.90	.50
279	Dick Tracewski	1.75	.90	.50
280	Dick Stuart	2.00	1.00	.60
281	Bill Stafford	1.75	.90	.50
282	Giants Rookies (Dick Estelle, Masanori Murakami)	2.25	1.25	.70
283	Fred Whitfield	2.25	1.25	.70

1966 O-Pee-Chee

Utilizing the same design as the 1966 Topps set, the 1966 O-Pee-Chee set consists of 196 cards, measuring 2-1/2" by 3-1/2". The words "Ptd. in Canada" appear along the bottom on the back of the cards.

	NR MT	EX	VG
Complete Set:	1200.	600.00	350.00
Common Player:	1.75	.90	.50

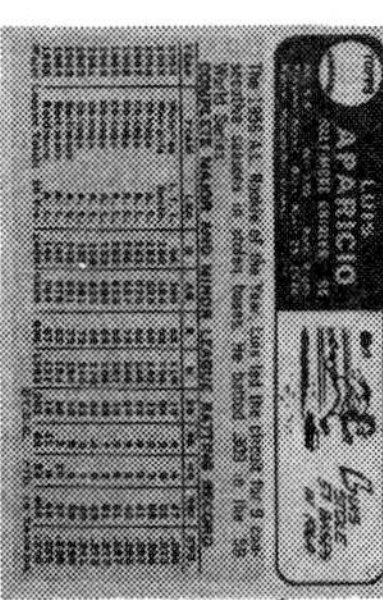

		NR MT	EX	VG
1	Willie Mays	150.00	75.00	45.00
2	Ted Abernathy	1.75	.90	.50
3	Sam Mele	1.75	.90	.50
4	Ray Culp	1.75	.90	.50
5	Jim Fregosi	2.00	1.00	.60
6	Chuck Schilling	1.75	.90	.50
7	Tracy Stallard	1.75	.90	.50
8	Floyd Robinson	1.75	.90	.50
9	Clete Boyer	2.00	1.00	.60
10	Tony Cloninger	1.75	.90	.50
11	Senators Rookies (Brant Alyea, Pete Craig)	1.75	.90	.50
12	John Tsitouris	1.75	.90	.50
13	Lou Johnson	1.75	.90	.50
14	Norm Siebern	1.75	.90	.50
15	Vern Law	2.00	1.00	.60
16	Larry Brown	1.75	.90	.50
17	Johnny Stephenson	1.75	.90	.50
18	Roland Sheldon	1.75	.90	.50
19	Giants Team	2.00	1.00	.60
20	Willie Horton	2.00	1.00	.60
21	Don Nottebart	1.75	.90	.50
22	Joe Nossek	1.75	.90	.50
23	Jack Sanford	1.75	.90	.50
24	Don Kessinger	2.00	1.00	.60
25	Pete Ward	1.75	.90	.50
26	Ray Sadecki	1.75	.90	.50
27	Orioles Rookies (Andy Etchebarren, Darold Knowles)	1.75	.90	.50
28	Phil Niekro	9.00	4.50	2.75
29	Mike Brumley	1.75	.90	.50
30	Pete Rose	90.00	45.00	27.00
31	Jack Cullen	1.75	.90	.50
32	Adolfo Phillips	1.75	.90	.50
33	Jim Pagliaroni	1.75	.90	.50
34	Checklist 1	2.75	1.50	.80
35	Ron Swoboda	2.00	1.00	.60
36	Jim Hunter	20.00	10.00	6.00
37	Billy Herman	2.25	1.25	.70
38	Ron Nischwitz	1.75	.90	.50
39	Ken Henderson	1.75	.90	.50
40	Jim Grant	1.75	.90	.50
41	Don LeJohn	1.75	.90	.50
42	Aubrey Gatewood	1.75	.90	.50
43	Don Landrum	1.75	.90	.50
44	Indians Rookies (Bill Davis, Tom Kelley)	1.75	.90	.50
45	Jim Gentile	1.75	.90	.50
46	Howie Koplitz	1.75	.90	.50
47	J.C. Martin	1.75	.90	.50
48	Paul Blair	2.00	1.00	.60
49	Woody Woodward	1.75	.90	.50
50	Mickey Mantle	200.00	100.00	60.00
51	Gordon Richardson	1.75	.90	.50
52	Power Plus (Johnny Callison, Wes Covington)	2.00	1.00	.60
53	Bob Duliba	1.75	.90	.50
54	Jose Pagan	1.75	.90	.50
55	Ken Harrelson	2.25	1.25	.70
56	Sandy Valdespino	1.75	.90	.50
57	Jim Lefebvre	1.75	.90	.50
58	Dave Wickersham	1.75	.90	.50
59	Reds Team	2.00	1.00	.60
60	Curt Flood	2.25	1.25	.70
61	Bob Bolin	1.75	.90	.50
62	Merritt Ranew	1.75	.90	.50
63	Jim Stewart	1.75	.90	.50
64	Bob Bruce	1.75	.90	.50
65	Leon Wagner	1.75	.90	.50
66	Al Weis	1.75	.90	.50
67	Mets Rookies (Cleon Jones, Dick Selma)	2.00	1.00	.60
68	Hal Reniff	1.75	.90	.50
69	Ken Hamlin	1.75	.90	.50
70	Carl Yastrzemski	50.00	25.00	15.00
71	Frank Carpin	1.75	.90	.50
72	Tony Perez	7.00	3.50	2.00
73	Jerry Zimmerman	1.75	.90	.50
74	Don Mossi	1.75	.90	.50
75	Tommy Davis	2.25	1.25	.70
76	Red Schoendienst	2.00	1.00	.60
77	Johnny Orsino	1.75	.90	.50
78	Frank Linzy	1.75	.90	.50
79	Joe Pepitone	2.25	1.25	.70
80	Richie Allen	2.50	1.25	.70
81	Ray Oyler	1.75	.90	.50
82	Bob Hendley	1.75	.90	.50
83	Albie Pearson	1.75	.90	.50
84	Braves Rookies (Jim Beauchamp, Dick Kelley)	1.75	.90	.50
85	Eddie Fisher	1.75	.90	.50
86	John Bateman	1.75	.90	.50
87	Dan Napoleon	1.75	.90	.50
88	Fred Whitfield	1.75	.90	.50
89	Ted Davidson	1.75	.90	.50
90	Luis Aparicio	5.00	2.50	1.50
91	Bob Uecker	25.00	12.50	7.50
92	Yankees Team	3.00	1.50	.90
93	Jim Lonborg	2.00	1.00	.60
94	Matty Alou	2.00	1.00	.60
95	Pete Richert	1.75	.90	.50
96	Felipe Alou	2.00	1.00	.60
97	Jim Merritt	1.75	.90	.50
98	Don Demeter	1.75	.90	.50
99	Buc Belters (Donn Clendenon, Willie Stargell)	2.75	1.50	.80
100	Sandy Koufax	45.00	23.00	13.50
101	Checklist 2	2.75	1.50	.80
102	Ed Kirkpatrick	1.75	.90	.50
103	Dick Groat	2.25	1.25	.70
104	Alex Johnson	1.75	.90	.50
105	Milt Pappas	2.00	1.00	.60
106	Rusty Staub	2.25	1.25	.70
107	A's Rookies (Larry Stahl, Ron Tompkins)	1.75	.90	.50
108	Bobby Klaus	1.75	.90	.50
109	Ralph Terry	1.75	.90	.50
110	Ernie Banks	12.00	6.00	3.50
111	Gary Peters	1.75	.90	.50
112	Manny Mota	2.00	1.00	.60
113	Hank Aguirre	1.75	.90	.50
114	Jim Gosger	1.75	.90	.50
115	Bill Henry	1.75	.90	.50
116	Walt Alston	2.75	1.50	.80
117	Jake Gibbs	1.75	.90	.50
118	Mike McCormick	1.75	.90	.50
119	Art Shamsky	1.75	.90	.50
120	Harmon Killebrew	9.00	4.50	2.75
121	Ray Herbert	1.75	.90	.50
122	Joe Gaines	1.75	.90	.50
123	Pirates Rookies (Frank Bork, Jerry May)	1.75	.90	.50
124	Tug McGraw	2.50	1.25	.70
125	Lou Brock	9.00	4.50	2.75
126	Jim Palmer	125.00	62.00	37.00
127	Ken Berry	1.75	.90	.50
128	Jim Landis	1.75	.90	.50
129	Jack Kralick	1.75	.90	.50
130	Joe Torre	2.50	1.25	.70
131	Angels Team	2.00	1.00	.60
132	Orlando Cepeda	2.75	1.50	.80
133	Don McMahon	1.75	.90	.50
134	Wes Parker	2.00	1.00	.60
135	Dave Morehead	1.75	.90	.50
136	Woody Held	1.75	.90	.50
137	Pat Corrales	2.00	1.00	.60
138	Roger Repoz	1.75	.90	.50
139	Cubs Rookies (Byron Browne, Don Young)	1.75	.90	.50
140	Jim Maloney	2.00	1.00	.60
141	Tom McCraw	1.75	.90	.50
142	Don Dennis	1.75	.90	.50
143	Jose Tartabull	1.75	.90	.50
144	Don Schwall	1.75	.90	.50
145	Bill Freehan	2.00	1.00	.60
146	George Altman	1.75	.90	.50
147	Lum Harris	1.75	.90	.50
148	Bob Johnson	1.75	.90	.50
149	Dick Nen	1.75	.90	.50
150	Rocky Colavito	2.50	1.25	.70
151	Gary Wagner	1.75	.90	.50
152	Frank Malzone	1.75	.90	.50
153	Rico Carty	2.25	1.25	.70
154	Chuck Hiller	1.75	.90	.50
155	Marcelino Lopez	1.75	.90	.50
156	Double Play Combo (Hal Lanier, Dick Schofield)	2.00	1.00	.60
157	Rene Lachemann	1.75	.90	.50
158	Jim Brewer	1.75	.90	.50
159	Chico Ruiz	1.75	.90	.50
160	Whitey Ford	9.00	4.50	2.75
161	Jerry Lumpe	1.75	.90	.50
162	Lee Maye	1.75	.90	.50
163	Tito Francona	1.75	.90	.50
164	White Sox Rookies (Tommie Agee, Marv Staehle)	2.00	1.00	.60
165	Don Lock	1.75	.90	.50
166	Chris Krug	1.75	.90	.50
167	Boog Powell	2.50	1.25	.70
168	Dan Osinski	1.75	.90	.50
169	Duke Sims	1.75	.90	.50
170	Cookie Rojas	1.75	.90	.50
171	Nick Willhite	1.75	.90	.50
172	Mets Team	2.75	1.50	.80
173	Al Spangler	1.75	.90	.50
174	Ron Taylor	1.75	.90	.50
175	Bert Campaneris	2.25	1.25	.70
176	Jim Davenport	1.75	.90	.50
177	Hector Lopez	2.00	1.00	.60
178	Bob Tillman	1.75	.90	.50
179	Cards Rookies (Dennis Aust, Bob Tolan)	2.00	1.00	.60
180	Vada Pinson	2.25	1.25	.70
181	Al Worthington	1.75	.90	.50
182	Jerry Lynch	1.75	.90	.50
183	Checklist 3	2.75	1.50	.80
184	Denis Menke	1.75	.90	.50
185	Bob Buhl	1.75	.90	.50
186	Ruben Amaro	1.75	.90	.50
187	Chuck Dressen	1.75	.90	.50
188	Al Luplow	1.75	.90	.50
189	John Roseboro	1.75	.90	.50
190	Jimmie Hall	1.75	.90	.50
191	Darrell Sutherland	1.75	.90	.50
192	Vic Power	1.75	.90	.50
193	Dave McNally	2.00	1.00	.60
194	Senators Team	2.00	1.00	.60
195	Joe Morgan	9.00	4.50	2.75
196	Don Pavletich	2.00	1.00	.60

1967 O-Pee-Chee

Cards in the 196-card Canadian set are nearly identical in design to the 1967 Topps set, except the words "Printed in Canada" are found on the back in the lower right corner. Cards measure 2-1/2" by 3-1/2".

	NR MT	EX	VG
Complete Set:	800.00	400.00	250.00
Common Player:	1.50	.70	.45

		NR MT	EX	VG
1	The Champs (Hank Bauer, Brooks Robinson, Frank Robinson)	7.00	2.00	1.25
2	Jack Hamilton	1.50	.70	.45
3	Duke Sims	1.50	.70	.45

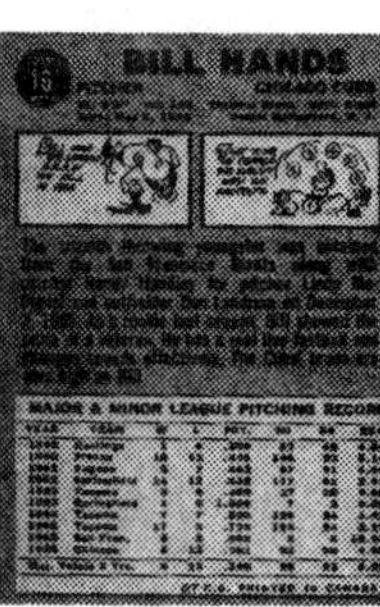

		NR MT	EX	VG
4	Hal Lanier	1.50	.70	.45
5	Whitey Ford	7.00	3.50	2.00
6	Dick Simpson	1.50	.70	.45
7	Don McMahon	1.50	.70	.45
8	Chuck Harrison	1.50	.70	.45
9	Ron Hansen	1.50	.70	.45
10	Matty Alou	1.50	.70	.45
11	Barry Moore	1.50	.70	.45
12	Dodgers Rookies (Jim Campanis, Bill Singer)	1.50	.70	.45
13	Joe Sparma	1.50	.70	.45
14	Phil Linz	1.50	.70	.45
15	Earl Battey	1.50	.70	.45
16	Bill Hands	1.50	.70	.45
17	Jim Gosger	1.50	.70	.45
18	Gene Oliver	1.50	.70	.45
19	Jim McGlothlin	1.50	.70	.45
20	Orlando Cepeda	3.00	1.50	.90
21	Dave Bristol	1.50	.70	.45
22	Gene Brabender	1.50	.70	.45
23	Larry Elliot	1.50	.70	.45
24	Bob Allen	1.50	.70	.45
25	Elston Howard	2.00	1.00	.60
26	Bob Priddy	1.50	.70	.45
27	Bob Saverine	1.50	.70	.45
28	Barry Latman	1.50	.70	.45
29	Tom McCraw	1.50	.70	.45
30	Al Kaline	6.00	3.00	1.75
31	Jim Brewer	1.50	.70	.45
32	Bob Bailey	1.50	.70	.45
33	Athletic Rookies (Sal Bando, Randy Schwartz)	1.75	.90	.50
34	Pete Cimino	1.50	.70	.45
35	Rico Carty	1.50	.70	.45
36	Bob Tillman	1.50	.70	.45
37	Rick Wise	1.50	.70	.45
38	Bob Johnson	1.50	.70	.45
39	Curt Simmons	1.50	.70	.45
40	Rick Reichardt	1.50	.70	.45
41	Joe Hoerner	1.50	.70	.45
42	Mets Team	2.00	1.00	.60
43	Chico Salmon	1.50	.70	.45
44	Joe Nuxhall	1.50	.70	.45
45	Roger Maris	25.00	12.50	7.50
46	Lindy McDaniel	1.50	.70	.45
47	Ken McMullen	1.50	.70	.45
48	Bill Freehan	1.50	.70	.45
49	Roy Face	1.50	.70	.45
50	Tony Oliva	2.00	1.00	.60
51	Astros Rookies (Dave Adlesh, Wes Bales)	1.50	.70	.45
52	Dennis Higgins	1.50	.70	.45
53	Clay Dalrymple	1.50	.70	.45
54	Dick Green	1.50	.70	.45
55	Don Drysdale	6.00	3.00	1.75
56	Jose Tartabull	1.50	.70	.45
57	Pat Jarvis	1.50	.70	.45
58	Paul Schaal	1.50	.70	.45
59	Ralph Terry	1.50	.70	.45
60	Luis Aparicio	4.00	2.00	1.25
61	Gordy Coleman	1.50	.70	.45
62	Checklist 1 (Frank Robinson)	2.50	1.25	.70
63	Cards' Clubbers (Lou Brock, Curt Flood)	3.50	1.75	1.00
64	Fred Valentine	1.50	.70	.45
65	Tom Haller	1.50	.70	.45
66	Manny Mota	1.50	.70	.45
67	Ken Berry	1.50	.70	.45
68	Bob Buhl	1.50	.70	.45
69	Vic Davalillo	1.50	.70	.45
70	Ron Santo	1.75	.90	.50
71	Camilo Pascual	1.50	.70	.45
72	Tigers Rookies (George Korince, John Matchick)	1.50	.70	.45
73	Rusty Staub	2.00	1.00	.60
74	Wes Stock	1.50	.70	.45
75	George Scott	1.50	.70	.45
76	Jim Barbieri	1.50	.70	.45
77	Dooley Womack	1.50	.70	.45
78	Pat Corrales	1.50	.70	.45
79	Bubba Morton	1.50	.70	.45
80	Jim Maloney	1.50	.70	.45
81	Eddie Stanky	1.50	.70	.45
82	Steve Barber	1.50	.70	.45
83	Ollie Brown	1.50	.70	.45
84	Tommie Sisk	1.50	.70	.45
85	Johnny Callison	1.50	.70	.45
86	Mike McCormick	1.50	.70	.45
87	George Altman	1.50	.70	.45
88	Mickey Lolich	2.00	1.00	.60
89	Felix Millan	1.50	.70	.45
90	Jim Nash	1.50	.70	.45
91	Johnny Lewis	1.50	.70	.45
92	Ray Washburn	1.50	.70	.45
93	Yankees Rookies (Stan Bahnsen, Bobby Murcer)	2.00	1.00	.60
94	Ron Fairly	1.50	.70	.45
95	Sonny Siebert	1.50	.70	.45
96	Art Shamsky	1.50	.70	.45
97	Mike Cuellar	1.50	.70	.45
98	Rich Rollins	1.50	.70	.45
99	Lee Stange	1.50	.70	.45

		NR MT	EX	VG
100	Frank Robinson	10.00	5.00	3.00
101	Ken Johnson	1.50	.70	.45
102	Phillies Team	1.50	.70	.45
103	Checklist 2 (Mickey Mantle)	15.00	7.50	4.50
104	Minnie Rojas	1.50	.70	.45
105	Ken Boyer	2.00	1.00	.60
106	Randy Hundley	1.50	.70	.45
107	Joel Horlen	1.50	.70	.45
108	Alex Johnson	1.50	.70	.45
109	Tribe Thumpers (Rocky Colavito, Leon Wagner)	1.50	.70	.45
110	Jack Aker	1.50	.70	.45
111	John Kennedy	1.50	.70	.45
112	Dave Wickersham	1.50	.70	.45
113	Dave Nicholson	1.50	.70	.45
114	Jack Balschun	1.50	.70	.45
115	Paul Casanova	1.50	.70	.45
116	Herman Franks	1.50	.70	.45
117	Darrell Brandon	1.50	.70	.45
118	Bernie Allen	1.50	.70	.45
119	Wade Blasingame	1.50	.70	.45
120	Floyd Robinson	1.50	.70	.45
121	Ed Bressoud	1.50	.70	.45
122	George Brunet	1.50	.70	.45
123	Pirates Rookies (Jim Price, Luke Walker)	1.50	.70	.45
124	Jim Stewart	1.50	.70	.45
125	Moe Drabowsky	1.50	.70	.45
126	Tony Taylor	1.50	.70	.45
127	John O'Donoghue	1.50	.70	.45
128	Ed Spiezio	1.50	.70	.45
129	Phil Roof	1.50	.70	.45
130	Phil Regan	1.50	.70	.45
131	Yankees Team	3.00	1.50	.90
132	Ozzie Virgil	1.50	.70	.45
133	Ron Kline	1.50	.70	.45
134	Gates Brown	1.50	.70	.45
135	Deron Johnson	1.50	.70	.45
136	Carroll Sembera	1.50	.70	.45
137	Twins Rookies (Ron Clark, Jim Ollum)	1.50	.70	.45
138	Dick Kelley	1.50	.70	.45
139	Dalton Jones	1.50	.70	.45
140	Willie Stargell	7.00	3.50	2.00
141	John Miller	1.50	.70	.45
142	Jackie Brandt	1.50	.70	.45
143	Sox Sockers (Don Buford, Pete Ward)	1.50	.70	.45
144	Bill Hepler	1.50	.70	.45
145	Larry Brown	1.50	.70	.45
146	Steve Carlton	30.00	15.00	9.00
147	Tom Egan	1.50	.70	.45
148	Adolfo Phillips	1.50	.70	.45
149	Joe Moeller	1.50	.70	.45
150	Mickey Mantle	200.00	100.00	60.00
151	World Series Game 1 (Moe Mows Down 11)	1.75	.90	.50
152	World Series Game 2 (Palmer Blanks Dodgers)	2.50	1.25	.70
153	World Series Game 3 (Blair's Homer Defeats L.A.)	1.75	.90	.50
154	World Series Game 4 (Orioles Win 4th Straight)	1.75	.90	.50
155	World Series Summary (The Winners Celebrate)	1.75	.90	.50
156	Ron Herbel	1.50	.70	.45
157	Danny Cater	1.50	.70	.45
158	Jimmy Coker	1.50	.70	.45
159	Bruce Howard	1.50	.70	.45
160	Willie Davis	1.75	.90	.50
161	Dick Williams	1.50	.70	.45
162	Billy O'Dell	1.50	.70	.45
163	Vic Roznovsky	1.50	.70	.45
164	Dwight Siebler	1.50	.70	.45
165	Cleon Jones	1.50	.70	.45
166	Ed Mathews	6.00	3.00	1.75
167	Senators Rookies (Joe Coleman, Tim Cullen)	1.50	.70	.45
168	Ray Culp	1.50	.70	.45
169	Horace Clarke	1.50	.70	.45
170	Dick McAuliffe	1.50	.70	.45
171	Calvin Koonce	1.50	.70	.45
172	Bill Heath	1.50	.70	.45
173	Cards Team	1.50	.70	.45
174	Dick Radatz	1.50	.70	.45
175	Bobby Knoop	1.50	.70	.45
176	Sammy Ellis	1.50	.70	.45
177	Tito Fuentes	1.50	.70	.45
178	John Buzhardt	1.50	.70	.45
179	Braves Rookies (Cecil Upshaw, Charles Vaughan)	1.50	.70	.45
180	Curt Blefary	1.50	.70	.45
181	Terry Fox	1.50	.70	.45
182	Ed Charles	1.50	.70	.45
183	Jim Pagliaroni	1.50	.70	.45
184	George Thomas	1.50	.70	.45
185	Ken Holtzman	1.50	.70	.45
186	Mets Maulers (Ed Kranepool, Ron Swoboda)	1.50	.70	.45
187	Pedro Ramos	1.50	.70	.45
188	Ken Harrelson	1.50	.70	.45
189	Chuck Hinton	1.50	.70	.45
190	Turk Farrell	1.50	.70	.45
191	Checklist 3 (Willie Mays)	3.25	1.75	1.00
192	Fred Gladding	1.50	.70	.45
193	Jose Cardenal	1.50	.70	.45
194	Bob Allison	1.50	.70	.45
195	Al Jackson	1.50	.70	.45
196	Johnny Romano	1.50	.60	.40

1968 O-Pee-Chee

The O-Pee-Chee set for 1968 again consisted of 196 cards, each measuring the standard 2-1/2" by 3-1/2". The card design is identical to the 1968 Topps set, except the color of the backs is slightly different and the words "Ptd. in Canada" appear in the lower right corner of the back.

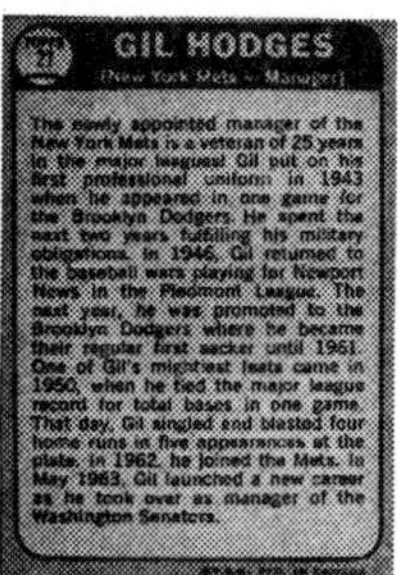

		NR MT	EX	VG
	Complete Set:	1500.	750.00	450.00
	Common Player:	1.00	.50	.30
1	N.L. Batting Leaders (Matty Alou, Bob Clemente, Tony Gonzales)	4.00	1.50	.90
2	A.L. Batting Leaders (Al Kaline, Frank Robinson, Carl Yastrzemski)	3.00	1.50	.90
3	N.L. RBI Leaders (Hank Aaron, Orlando Cepeda, Bob Clemente)	3.00	1.50	.90
4	A.L. RBI Leaders (Harmon Killebrew, Frank Robinson, Carl Yastrzemski)	3.00	1.50	.90
5	N.L. Home Run Leaders (Hank Aaron, Willie McCovey, Ron Santo, Jim Wynn)	3.00	1.50	.90
6	N.L. Home Run Leaders (Frank Howard, Harmon Killebrew, Carl Yastrzemski)	3.00	1.50	.90
7	N.L. ERA Leaders (Jim Bunning, Phil Niekro, Chris Short)	1.75	.90	.50
8	A.L. ERA Leaders (Joe Horlen, Gary Peters, Sonny Siebert)	1.25	.60	.40
9	N.L. Pitching Leaders (Jim Bunning, Ferguson Jenkins, Mike McCormick, Claude Osteen)	1.75	.90	.50
10	A.L. Pitching Leaders (Dean Chance, Jim Lonborg, Earl Wilson)	1.25	.60	.40
11	N.L. Strikeout Leaders (Jim Bunning, Ferguson Jenkins, Gaylord Perry)	2.00	1.00	.60
12	A.L. Strikeout Leaders (Dean Chance, Jim Lonborg, Sam McDowell)	1.25	.60	.40
13	Chuck Hartenstein	1.00	.50	.30
14	Jerry McNertney	1.00	.50	.30
15	Ron Hunt	1.00	.50	.30
16	Indians Rookies (Lou Piniella, Richie Scheinblum)	1.75	.90	.50
17	Dick Hall	1.00	.50	.30
18	Mike Hershberger	1.00	.50	.30
19	Juan Pizarro	1.00	.50	.30
20	Brooks Robinson	9.00	4.50	2.75
21	Ron Davis	1.00	.50	.30
22	Pat Dobson	1.00	.50	.30
23	Chico Cardenas	1.00	.50	.30
24	Bobby Locke	1.00	.50	.30
25	Julian Javier	1.00	.50	.30
26	Darrell Brandon	1.00	.50	.30
27	Gil Hodges	3.00	1.50	.90
28	Ted Uhlaender	1.00	.50	.30
29	Joe Verbanic	1.00	.50	.30
30	Joe Torre	1.75	.90	.50
31	Ed Stroud	1.00	.50	.30
32	Joe Gibbon	1.00	.50	.30
33	Pete Ward	1.00	.50	.30
34	Al Ferrara	1.00	.50	.30
35	Steve Hargan	1.00	.50	.30
36	Pirates Rookies (Bob Moose, Bob Robertson)	1.25	.60	.40
37	Billy Williams	4.00	2.00	1.25
38	Tony Pierce	1.00	.50	.30
39	Cookie Rojas	1.00	.50	.30
40	Denny McLain	2.50	1.25	.70
41	Julio Gotay	1.00	.50	.30
42	Larry Haney	1.00	.50	.30
43	Gary Bell	1.00	.50	.30
44	Frank Kostro	1.00	.50	.30
45	Tom Seaver	70.00	35.00	20.00
46	Dave Ricketts	1.00	.50	.30
47	Ralph Houk	1.25	.60	.40
48	Ted Davidson	1.00	.50	.30
49	Ed Brinkman	1.00	.50	.30
50	Willie Mays	40.00	20.00	12.50
51	Bob Locker	1.00	.50	.30
52	Hawk Taylor	1.00	.50	.30
53	Gene Alley	1.00	.50	.30
54	Stan Williams	1.00	.50	.30
55	Felipe Alou	1.00	.50	.30
56	Orioles Rookies (Dave Leonhard, Dave May)	1.00	.50	.30
57	Dan Schneider	1.00	.50	.30
58	Ed Mathews	5.00	2.50	1.50
59	Don Lock	1.00	.50	.30
60	Ken Holtzman	1.25	.60	.40
61	Reggie Smith	1.50	.70	.45
62	Chuck Dobson	1.00	.50	.30
63	Dick Kenworthy	1.00	.50	.30
64	Jim Merritt	1.00	.50	.30
65	John Roseboro	1.00	.50	.30
66	Casey Cox	1.00	.50	.30
67	Checklist 1 (Jim Kaat)	2.00	1.00	.60
68	Ron Willis	1.00	.50	.30
69	Tom Tresh	1.25	.60	.40
70	Bob Veale	1.00	.50	.30
71	Vern Fuller	1.00	.50	.30
72	Tommy John	2.50	1.25	.70
73	Jim Hart	1.00	.50	.30
74	Milt Pappas	1.25	.60	.40
75	Don Mincher	1.00	.50	.30
76	Braves Rookies (Jim Britton, Ron Reed)	1.25	.60	.40
77	Don Wilson	1.25	.60	.40
78	Jim Northrup	1.00	.50	.30
79	Ted Kubiak	1.00	.50	.30

		NR MT	EX	VG
80	Rod Carew	50.00	25.00	15.00
81	Larry Jackson	1.00	.50	.30
82	Sam Bowens	1.00	.50	.30
83	John Stephenson	1.00	.50	.30
84	Bob Tolan	1.00	.50	.30
85	Gaylord Perry	4.00	2.00	1.25
86	Willie Stargell	6.00	3.00	1.75
87	Dick Williams	1.25	.60	.40
88	Phil Regan	1.00	.50	.30
89	Jake Gibbs	1.00	.50	.30
90	Vada Pinson	1.50	.70	.45
91	Jim Ollom	1.00	.50	.30
92	Ed Kranepool	1.25	.60	.40
93	Tony Cloninger	1.00	.50	.30
94	Lee Maye	1.00	.50	.30
95	Bob Aspromonte	1.00	.50	.30
96	Senators Rookies (Frank Coggins, Dick Nold)	1.00	.50	.30
97	Tom Phoebus	1.00	.50	.30
98	Gary Sutherland	1.00	.50	.30
99	Rocky Colavito	1.75	.90	.50
100	Bob Gibson	15.00	7.50	4.50
101	Glenn Beckert	1.25	.60	.40
102	Jose Cardenal	1.00	.50	.30
103	Don Sutton	3.00	1.50	.90
104	Dick Dietz	1.00	.50	.30
105	Al.Downing	1.25	.60	.40
106	Dalton Jones	1.00	.50	.30
107	Checklist 2 (Juan Marichal)	2.50	1.25	.70
108	Don Pavletich	1.00	.50	.30
109	Bert Campaneris	1.25	.60	.40
110	Hank Aaron	40.00	20.00	12.00
111	Rich Reese	1.00	.50	.30
112	Woody Fryman	1.00	.50	.30
113	Tigers Rookies (Tom Matchick, Daryl Patterson)	1.00	.50	.30
114	Ron Swoboda	1.00	.50	.30
115	Sam McDowell	1.25	.60	.40
116	Ken McMullen	1.00	.50	.30
117	Larry Jaster	1.00	.50	.30
118	Mark Belanger	1.25	.60	.40
119	Ted Savage	1.00	.50	.30
120	Mel Stottlemyre	1.25	.60	.40
121	Jimmie Hall	1.00	.50	.30
122	Gene Mauch	1.25	.60	.40
123	Jose Santiago	1.00	.50	.30
124	Nate Oliver	1.00	.50	.30
125	Joe Horlen	1.00	.50	.30
126	Bob Etheridge	1.00	.50	.30
127	Paul Lindblad	1.00	.50	.30
128	Astros Rookies (Tom Dukes, Alonzo Harris)	1.00	.50	.30
129	Mickey Stanley	1.00	.50	.30
130	Tony Perez	3.00	1.50	.90
131	Frank Bertaina	1.00	.50	.30
132	Bud Harrelson	1.25	.60	.40
133	Fred Whitfield	1.00	.50	.30
134	Pat Jarvis	1.00	.50	.30
135	Paul Blair	1.25	.60	.40
136	Randy Hundley	1.00	.50	.30
137	Twins Team	1.25	.60	.40
138	Ruben Amaro	1.00	.50	.30
139	Chris Short	1.00	.50	.30
140	Tony Conigliaro	1.50	.70	.45
141	Dal Maxvill	1.00	.50	.30
142	White Sox Rookies (Buddy Bradford, Bill Voss)	1.00	.50	.30
143	Pete Cimino	1.00	.50	.30
144	Joe Morgan	3.00	1.50	.90
145	Don Drysdale	6.00	3.00	1.75
146	Sal Bando	1.25	.60	.40
147	Frank Linzy	1.00	.50	.30
148	Dave Bristol	1.00	.50	.30
149	Bob Saverine	1.00	.50	.30
150	Bob Clemente	40.00	20.00	12.00
151	World Series Game 1 (Brock Socks 4 Hits)	2.75	1.50	.80
152	World Series Game 2 (Yaz Smashes Two Homers)	4.00	2.00	1.25
153	World Series Game 3 (Briles Cools Off Boston)	1.75	.90	.50
154	World Series Game 4 (Gibson Hurls Shutout)	2.75	1.50	.80
155	World Series Game 5 (Lonborg Wins Again)	1.75	.90	.50
156	World Series Game 6 (Petrocelli Socks Two Homers)	1.75	.90	.50
157	World Series Game 7 (St. Louis Wins It)	1.75	.90	.50
158	World Series Summary (The Cardinals Celebrate)	1.75	.90	.50
159	Don Kessinger	1.25	.60	.40
160	Earl Wilson	1.00	.50	.30
161	Norm Miller	1.00	.50	.30
162	Cards Rookies (Hal Gilson, Mike Torrez)	1.25	.60	.40
163	Gene Brabender	1.00	.50	.30
164	Ramon Webster	1.00	.50	.30
165	Tony Oliva	1.75	.90	.50
166	Claude Raymond	1.00	.50	.30
167	Elston Howard	1.75	.90	.50
168	Dodgers Team	1.75	.90	.50
169	Bob Bolin	1.00	.50	.30
170	Jim Fregosi	1.25	.60	.40
171	Don Nottebart	1.00	.50	.30
172	Walt Williams	1.00	.50	.30
173	John Boozer	1.00	.50	.30
174	Bob Tillman	1.00	.50	.30
175	Maury Wills	2.50	1.25	.70
176	Bob Allen	1.00	.50	.30
177	Mets Rookies (Jerry Koosman, Nolan Ryan)	700.00	350.00	210.00
178	Don Wert	1.00	.50	.30
179	Bill Stoneman	1.00	.50	.30
180	Curt Flood	1.50	.70	.45
181	Jerry Zimmerman	1.00	.50	.30
182	Dave Gusti	1.00	.50	.30
183	Bob Kennedy	1.00	.50	.30
184	Lou Johnson	1.00	.50	.30
185	Tom Haller	1.00	.50	.30
186	Eddie Watt	1.00	.50	.30
187	Sonny Jackson	1.00	.50	.30
188	Cap Peterson	1.00	.50	.30
189	Bill Landis	1.00	.50	.30
190	Bill White	1.25	.60	.40
191	Dan Frisella	1.00	.50	.30
192	Checklist 3 (Carl Yastrzemski)	3.50	1.75	1.00
193	Jack Hamilton	1.00	.50	.30
194	Don Buford	1.00	.50	.30
195	Joe Pepitone	1.25	.60	.40
196	Gary Nolan	1.25	.50	.30

1969 O-Pee-Chee

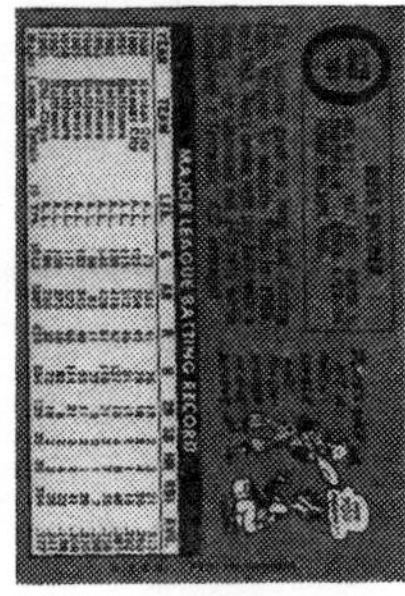

O-Pee-Chee increased the number of cards in its 1969 O-Pee-Chee set to 218, maintaining the standard 2-1/2" by 3-1/2" size. The card design is identical to the 1969 Topps set, except for a slightly different color on the back of the cards and the words "Ptd. in Canada," which appear along the bottom.

		NR MT	EX	VG
	Complete Set:	500.00	250.00	150.00
	Common Player:	1.00	.50	.30
1	A.L. Batting Leaders (Danny Cater, Tony Oliva, Carl Yastrzemski)	4.00	1.50	.90
2	N.L. Batting Leaders (Felipe Alou, Matty Alou, Pete Rose)	3.00	1.50	.90
3	A.L. RBI Leaders (Ken Harrelson, Frank Howard, Jim Northrup)	1.25	.60	.40
4	N.L. RBI Leaders (Willie McCovey, Ron Santo, Billy Williams)	2.50	1.25	.70
5	A.L. Home Run Leaders (Ken Harrelson, Willie Horton, Frank Howard)	1.25	.60	.40
6	N.L. Home Run Leaders (Richie Allen, Ernie Banks, Willie McCovey)	2.50	1.25	.70
7	A.L. ERA Leaders (Sam McDowell, Dave McNally, Luis Tiant)	1.25	.60	.40
8	N.L. ERA Leaders (Bobby Bolin, Bob Gibson, Bob Veale)	2.00	1.00	.60
9	A.L. Pitching Leaders (Denny McLain, Dave McNally, Mel Stottlemyre, Luis Tiant)	1.25	.60	.40
10	N.L. Pitching Leaders (Bob Gibson, Fergie Jenkins, Juan Marichal)	2.50	1.25	.70
11	A.L. Strikeout Leaders (Sam McDowell, Denny McLain, Luis Tiant)	1.25	.60	.40
12	N.L. Strikeout Leaders (Bob Gibson, Fergie Jenkins, Bill Singer)	2.00	1.00	.60
13	Mickey Stanley	1.00	.50	.30
14	Al McBean	1.00	.50	.30
15	Boog Powell	1.75	.90	.50
16	Giants Rookies (Cesar Gutierrez, Rich Robertson)	1.00	.50	.30
17	Mike Marshall	1.50	.70	.45
18	Dick Schofield	1.00	.50	.30
19	Ken Suarez	1.00	.50	.30
20	Ernie Banks	6.00	3.00	1.75
21	Jose Santiago	1.00	.50	.30
22	Jesus Alou	1.00	.50	.30
23	Lew Krausse	1.00	.50	.30
24	Walt Alston	1.75	.90	.50
25	Roy White	1.25	.60	.40
26	Clay Carroll	1.00	.50	.30
27	Bernie Allen	1.00	.50	.30
28	Mike Ryan	1.00	.50	.30
29	Dave Morehead	1.00	.50	.30
30	Bob Allison	1.25	.60	.40
31	Mets Rookies (Gary Gentry, Amos Otis)	1.25	.60	.40
32	Sammy Ellis	1.00	.50	.30
33	Wayne Causey	1.00	.50	.30
34	Gary Peters	1.00	.50	.30
35	Joe Morgan	3.00	1.50	.90
36	Luke Walker	1.00	.50	.30
37	Curt Motton	1.00	.50	.30
38	Zoilo Versalles	1.00	.50	.30
39	Dick Hughes	1.00	.50	.30
40	Mayo Smith	1.00	.50	.30
41	Bob Barton	1.00	.50	.30
42	Tommy Harper	1.25	.60	.40
43	Joe Niekro	1.50	.70	.45
44	Danny Cater	1.00	.50	.30
45	Maury Wills	1.75	.90	.50
46	Fritz Peterson	1.00	.50	.30
47	Paul Popovich	1.00	.50	.30
48	Brant Alyea	1.00	.50	.30
49	Royals Rookies (Steve Jones, Eliseo Rodriguez)	1.00	.50	.30
50	Bob Clemente	25.00	12.50	7.50
51	Woody Fryman	1.00	.50	.30
52	Mike Andrews	1.00	.50	.30
53	Sonny Jackson	1.00	.50	.30
54	Cisco Carlos	1.00	.50	.30
55	Jerry Grote	1.25	.60	.40
56	Rich Reese	1.00	.50	.30
57	Checklist 1 (Denny McLain)	2.00	1.00	.60
58	Fred Gladding	1.00	.50	.30
59	Jay Johnstone	1.25	.60	.40
60	Nelson Briles	1.00	.50	.30
61	Jimmie Hall	1.00	.50	.30
62	Chico Salmon	1.00	.50	.30
63	Jim Hickman	1.00	.50	.30
64	Bill Monbouquette	1.00	.50	.30
65	Willie Davis	1.50	.70	.45
66	Orioles Rookies (Mike Adamson, Merv Rettenmund)	1.25	.60	.40
67	Bill Stoneman	1.00	.50	.30
68	Dave Duncan	1.00	.50	.30
69	Steve Hamilton	1.00	.50	.30
70	Tommy Helms	1.00	.50	.30
71	Steve Whitaker	1.00	.50	.30
72	Ron Taylor	1.00	.50	.30
73	Johnny Briggs	1.00	.50	.30
74	Preston Gomez	1.00	.50	.30
75	Luis Aparicio	4.00	2.00	1.25
76	Norm Miller	1.00	.50	.30
77	Ron Perranoski	1.00	.50	.30
78	Tom Satriano	1.00	.50	.30
79	Milt Pappas	1.25	.60	.40
80	Norm Cash	1.25	.60	.40
81	Mel Queen	1.00	.50	.30
82	Pirates Rookies (Rich Hebner, Al Oliver)	6.00	3.00	1.75
83	Mike Ferraro	1.00	.50	.30
84	Bob Humphreys	1.00	.50	.30
85	Lou Brock	7.00	3.50	2.00
86	Pete Richert	1.00	.50	.30
87	Horace Clarke	1.00	.50	.30
88	Rich Nye	1.00	.50	.30
89	Russ Gibson	1.00	.50	.30
90	Jerry Koosman	1.75	.90	.50
91	Al Dark	1.25	.60	.40
92	Jack Billingham	1.00	.50	.30
93	Joe Foy	1.00	.50	.30
94	Hank Aguirre	1.00	.50	.30
95	Johnny Bench	50.00	25.00	15.00
96	Denver Lemaster	1.00	.50	.30
97	Buddy Bradford	1.00	.50	.30
98	Dave Giusti	1.00	.50	.30
99	Twins Rookies (Danny Morris, Graig Nettles)	8.00	4.00	2.50
100	Hank Aaron	40.00	20.00	12.00
101	Daryl Patterson	1.00	.50	.30
102	Jim Davenport	1.00	.50	.30
103	Roger Repoz	1.00	.50	.30
104	Steve Blass	1.00	.50	.30
105	Rick Monday	1.25	.60	.40
106	Jim Hannan	1.00	.50	.30
107	Checklist 2 (Bob Gibson)	2.00	1.00	.60
108	Tony Taylor	1.00	.50	.30
109	Jim Lonborg	1.25	.60	.40
110	Mike Shannon	1.00	.50	.30
111	Johnny Morris	1.00	.50	.30
112	J.C. Martin	1.00	.50	.30
113	Dave May	1.00	.50	.30
114	Yankees Rookies (Alan Closter, John Cumberland)	1.00	.50	.30
115	Bill Hands	1.00	.50	.30
116	Chuck Harrison	1.00	.50	.30
117	Jim Fairey	1.00	.50	.30
118	Stan Williams	1.00	.50	.30
119	Doug Rader	1.00	.50	.30
120	Pete Rose	50.00	25.00	15.00
121	Joe Grzenda	1.00	.50	.30
122	Ron Fairly	1.25	.60	.40
123	Wilbur Wood	1.25	.60	.40
124	Hank Bauer	1.25	.60	.40
125	Ray Sadecki	1.00	.50	.30
126	Dick Tracewski	1.00	.50	.30
127	Kevin Collins	1.00	.50	.30
128	Tommie Aaron	1.25	.60	.40
129	Bill McCool	1.00	.50	.30
130	Carl Yastrzemski	25.00	12.50	7.50
131	Chris Cannizzaro	1.00	.50	.30
132	Dave Baldwin	1.00	.50	.30
133	Johnny Callison	1.25	.60	.40
134	Jim Weaver	1.00	.50	.30
135	Tommy Davis	1.50	.70	.45
136	Cards Rookies (Steve Huntz, Mike Torrez)	1.25	.60	.40
137	Wally Bunker	1.00	.50	.30
138	John Bateman	1.00	.50	.30
139	Andy Kosco	1.00	.50	.30
140	Jim Lefebvre	1.00	.50	.30
141	Bill Dillman	1.00	.50	.30
142	Woody Woodward	1.00	.50	.30
143	Joe Nossek	1.00	.50	.30
144	Bob Hendley	1.00	.50	.30
145	Max Alvis	1.00	.50	.30
146	Jim Perry	1.25	.60	.40
147	Leo Durocher	1.50	.70	.45
148	Lee Stange	1.00	.50	.30
149	Ollie Brown	1.00	.50	.30
150	Denny McLain	2.00	1.00	.60
151	Clay Dalrymple	1.50	.70	.45
152	Tommie Sisk	1.00	.50	.30
153	Ed Brinkman	1.00	.50	.30
154	Jim Britton	1.00	.50	.30
155	Pete Ward	1.00	.50	.30
156	Astros Rookies (Hal Gilson, Leon McFadden)	1.00	.50	.30
157	Bob Rodgers	1.25	.60	.40
158	Joe Gibbon	1.00	.50	.30
159	Jerry Adair	1.00	.50	.30
160	Vada Pinson	1.50	.70	.45
161	John Purdin	1.00	.50	.30
162	World Series Game 1 (Gibson Fans 17; Sets New Record)	2.50	1.25	.70
163	World Series Game 2 (Tiger Homers Deck The Cards)	1.75	.90	.50
164	World Series Game 3 (McCarver's Homer Puts St. Louis Ahead)	1.75	.90	.50
165	World Series Game 4 (Brock's Lead Off Homer Starts Cards' Romp)	2.50	1.25	.70

		NR MT	EX	VG
166	World Series Game 5 (Kaline's Key Hit Sparks Tiger Rally)	2.50	1.25	.70
167	World Series Game 6 (Tiger 10-Run Inning Ties Mark)	1.75	.90	.50
168	World Series Game 7 (Lolich Series Hero, Outduels Gibson)	2.50	1.25	.70
169	World Series Summary (Tigers Celebrate Their Victory)	1.75	.90	.50
170	Frank Howard	1.50	.70	.45
171	Glenn Beckert	1.25	.60	.40
172	Jerry Stephenson	1.00	.50	.30
173	White Sox Rookies (Bob Christian, Gerry Nyman)	1.00	.50	.30
174	Grant Jackson	1.00	.50	.30
175	Jim Bunning	2.50	1.25	.70
176	Joe Azcue	1.00	.50	.30
177	Ron Reed	1.00	.50	.30
178	Ray Oyler	1.00	.50	.30
179	Don Pavletich	1.00	.50	.30
180	Willie Horton	1.25	.60	.40
181	Mel Nelson	1.00	.50	.30
182	Bill Rigney	1.00	.50	.30
183	Don Shaw	1.00	.50	.30
184	Roberto Pena	1.00	.50	.30
185	Tom Phoebus	1.00	.50	.30
186	John Edwards	1.00	.50	.30
187	Leon Wagner	1.00	.50	.30
188	Rick Wise	1.00	.50	.30
189	Red Sox Rookies (Joe Lahoud, John Thibdeau)	1.00	.50	.30
190	Willie Mays	40.00	20.00	12.00
191	Lindy McDaniel	1.00	.50	.30
192	Jose Pagan	1.00	.50	.30
193	Don Cardwell	1.00	.50	.30
194	Ted Uhlaender	1.00	.50	.30
195	John Odom	1.00	.50	.30
196	Lum Harris	1.00	.50	.30
197	Dick Selma	1.00	.50	.30
198	Willie Smith	1.00	.50	.30
199	Jim French	1.00	.50	.30
200	Bob Gibson	6.00	3.00	1.75
201	Russ Snyder	1.00	.50	.30
202	Don Wilson	1.00	.50	.30
203	Dave Johnson	1.50	.70	.45
204	Jack Hiatt	1.00	.50	.30
205	Rick Reichardt	1.00	.50	.30
206	Phillies Rookies (Larry Hisle, Barry Lersch)	1.25	.60	.40
207	Roy Face	1.25	.60	.40
208	Donn Clendenon	1.50	.70	.45
209	Larry Haney	1.00	.50	.30
210	Felix Millan	1.00	.50	.30
211	Galen Cisco	1.00	.50	.30
212	Tom Tresh	1.25	.60	.40
213	Gerry Arrigo	1.00	.50	.30
214	Checklist 3	1.75	.90	.50
215	Rico Petrocelli	1.25	.60	.40
216	Don Sutton	3.00	1.50	.90
217	John Donaldson	1.00	.50	.30
218	John Roseboro	1.25	.50	.30

1969 O-Pee-Chee Deckle

Very similar in design to the Topps Deckle Edge set of the same year, the 1969 O-Pee-Chee Deckle-Edge set consists of 24 unnumbered black and white cards. The Canadian-issued O-Pee-Chee cards, measuring 2-1/8" by 3-1/8", are slightly smaller than the corresponding Topps set, but feature the same "deckle cut" borders. The O-Pee-Chee set is blank-backed and has the facsimile autographs in black ink, rather than blue.

		NR MT	EX	VG
Complete Set:		125.00	62.00	37.00
Common Player:		1.50	.70	.45
(1)	Rich Allen	3.00	1.50	.90
(2)	Luis Aparicio	4.50	2.25	1.25
(3)	Rodney Carew	8.00	4.00	2.50
(4)	Roberto Clemente	25.00	12.50	7.50
(5)	Curt Flood	2.00	1.00	.60
(6)	Bill Freehan	2.00	1.00	.60
(7)	Robert Gibson	5.00	2.50	1.50
(8)	Ken Harrelson	1.75	.90	.50
(9)	Tommy Helms	1.50	.70	.45
(10)	Tom Haller	1.75	.90	.50
(11)	Willie Horton	1.50	.70	.45
(12)	Frank Howard	2.50	1.25	.70
(13)	Willie McCovey	6.00	3.00	1.75
(14)	Denny McLain	2.50	1.25	.70
(15)	Juan Marichal	5.00	2.50	1.50
(16)	Willie Mays	25.00	12.50	7.50
(17)	John "Boog" Powell	2.50	1.25	.70
(18)	Brooks Robinson	10.00	5.00	3.00
(19)	Ronald Santo	2.25	1.25	.70
(20)	Rusty Staub	2.00	1.00	.60
(21)	Mel Stottlemyre	1.50	.70	.45
(22)	Luis Tiant	1.50	.70	.45
(23)	Maurie Wills	2.25	1.25	.70
(24)	Carl Yastrzemski	20.00	10.00	6.00

1970 O-Pee-Chee

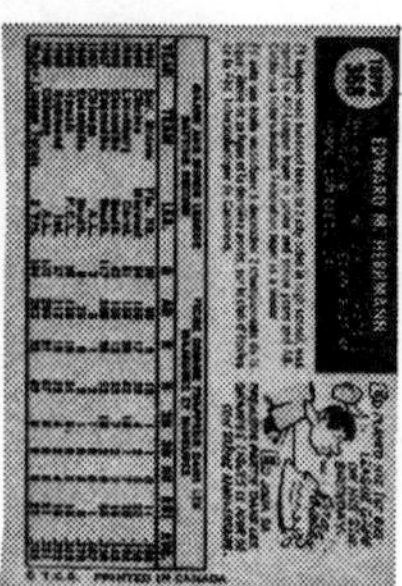

The 1970 O-Pee-Chee set, identical in design to the 1970 Topps set, expanded to 546 cards, measuring 2-1/2" by 3-1/2". The Canadian-issued O-Pee-Chee set is easy to distinguish because the backs are printed in both French and English and include the words "Printed in Canada."

		NR MT	EX	VG
Complete Set:		1000.	500.00	300.00
Common Player:		.75	.40	.25
1	World Champions (Mets Team)	3.50	1.50	.90
2	Diego Segui	.75	.40	.25
3	Darrel Chaney	.75	.40	.25
4	Tom Egan	.75	.40	.25
5	Wes Parker	1.00	.50	.30
6	Grant Jackson	.75	.40	.25
7	Indians Rookies (Gary Boyd, Russ Nagelson)	.75	.40	.25
8	Jose Martinez	.75	.40	.25
9	Checklist 1	1.50	.70	.45
10	Carl Yastrzemski	25.00	12.50	7.50
11	Nate Colbert	.75	.40	.25
12	John Hiller	.75	.40	.25
13	Jack Hiatt	.75	.40	.25
14	Hank Allen	.75	.40	.25
15	Larry Dierker	.75	.40	.25
16	Charlie Metro	.75	.40	.25
17	Hoyt Wilhelm	2.50	1.25	.70
18	Carlos May	.75	.40	.25
19	John Boccabella	.75	.40	.25
20	Dave McNally	1.00	.50	.30
21	Athletics Rookies (Vida Blue, Gene Tenace)	2.00	1.00	.60
22	Ray Washburn	.75	.40	.25
23	Bill Robinson	.75	.40	.25
24	Dick Selma	.75	.40	.25
25	Cesar Tovar	.75	.40	.25
26	Tug McGraw	1.25	.60	.40
27	Chuck Hinton	.75	.40	.25
28	Billy Wilson	.75	.40	.25
29	Sandy Alomar	.75	.40	.25
30	Matty Alou	1.00	.50	.30
31	Marty Pattin	.75	.40	.25
32	Harry Walker	.75	.40	.25
33	Don Wert	.75	.40	.25
34	Willie Crawford	.75	.40	.25
35	Joe Horlen	.75	.40	.25
36	Red Rookies (Danny Breeden, Bernie Carbo)	.75	.40	.25
37	Dick Drago	.75	.40	.25
38	Mack Jones	.75	.40	.25
39	Mike Nagy	.75	.40	.25
40	Rich Allen	1.50	.70	.45
41	George Lauzerique	.75	.40	.25
42	Tito Fuentes	.75	.40	.25
43	Jack Aker	.75	.40	.25
44	Roberto Pena	.75	.40	.25
45	Dave Johnson	1.25	.60	.40
46	Ken Rudolph	.75	.40	.25
47	Bob Miller	.75	.40	.25
48	Gil Garrido	.75	.40	.25
49	Tim Cullen	.75	.40	.25
50	Tommie Agee	1.00	.50	.30
51	Bob Christian	.75	.40	.25
52	Bruce Dal Canton	.75	.40	.25
53	John Kennedy	.75	.40	.25
54	Jeff Torborg	.75	.40	.25
55	John Odom	.75	.40	.25
56	Phillies Rookies (Joe Lis, Scott Reid)	.75	.40	.25
57	Pat Kelly	.75	.40	.25
58	Dave Marshall	.75	.40	.25
59	Dick Ellsworth	.75	.40	.25
60	Jim Wynn	1.00	.50	.30
61	N.L. Batting Leaders (Bob Clemente, Cleon Jones, Pete Rose)	2.50	1.25	.70
62	A.L. Batting Leaders (Rod Carew, Tony Oliva, Reggie Smith)	1.75	.90	.50
63	N.L. RBI Leaders (Willie McCovey, Tony Perez, Ron Santo)	1.75	.90	.50
64	A.L. RBI Leaders (Reggie Jackson, Harmon Killebrew, Boog Powell)	2.00	1.00	.60
65	N.L. Home Run Leaders (Hank Aaron, Lee May, Willie McCovey)	2.25	1.25	.70
66	A.L. Home Run Leaders (Frank Howard, Reggie Jackson, Harmon Killebrew)	2.00	1.00	.60
67	N.L. ERA Leaders (Steve Carlton, Bob Gibson, Juan Marichal)	2.25	1.25	.70
68	A.L. ERA Leaders (Dick Bosman, Mike Cuellar, Jim Palmer)	1.50	.70	.45
69	N.L. Pitching Leaders (Fergie Jenkins, Juan Marichal, Phil Niekro, Tom Seaver)	1.75	.90	.50
70	A.L. Pitching Leaders (Dave Boswell, Mike Cuellar, Dennis McLain, Dave McNally, Jim Perry, Mel Stottlemyre)	1.25	.60	.40
71	N.L. Strikeout Leaders (Bob Gibson, Fergie Jenkins, Bill Singer)	1.75	.90	.50
72	A.L. Strikeout Leaders (Mickey Lolich, Sam McDowell, Andy Messersmith)	1.25	.60	.40
73	Wayne Granger	.75	.40	.25
74	Angels Rookies (Greg Washburn, Wally Wolf)	.75	.40	.25
75	Jim Kaat	1.50	.70	.45
76	Carl Taylor	.75	.40	.25
77	Frank Linzy	.75	.40	.25
78	Joe Lahoud	.75	.40	.25
79	Clay Kirby	.75	.40	.25
80	Don Kessinger	1.00	.50	.30
81	Dave May	.75	.40	.25
82	Frank Fernandez	.75	.40	.25
83	Don Cardwell	.75	.40	.25
84	Paul Casanova	.75	.40	.25
85	Max Alvis	.75	.40	.25
86	Lum Harris	.75	.40	.25
87	Steve Renko	.75	.40	.25
88	Pilots Rookies (Dick Baney, Miguel Fuentes)	.75	.40	.25
89	Juan Rios	.75	.40	.25
90	Tim McCarver	1.25	.60	.40
91	Rich Morales	.75	.40	.25
92	George Culver	.75	.40	.25
93	Rick Renick	.75	.40	.25
94	Fred Patek	.75	.40	.25
95	Earl Wilson	.75	.40	.25
96	Cards Rookies (Leron Lee, Jerry Reuss)	1.50	.70	.45
97	Joe Moeller	.75	.40	.25
98	Gates Brown	.75	.40	.25
99	Bobby Pfeil	.75	.40	.25
100	Mel Stottlemyre	1.00	.50	.30
101	Bobby Floyd	.75	.40	.25
102	Joe Rudi	1.00	.50	.30
103	Frank Reberger	.75	.40	.25
104	Gerry Moses	.75	.40	.25
105	Tony Gonzalez	.75	.40	.25
106	Darold Knowles	.75	.40	.25
107	Bobby Etheridge	.75	.40	.25
108	Tom Burgmeier	.75	.40	.25
109	Expos Rookies (Garry Jestadt, Carl Morton)	.75	.40	.25
110	Bob Moose	.75	.40	.25
111	Mike Hegan	.75	.40	.25
112	Dave Nelson	.75	.40	.25
113	Jim Ray	.75	.40	.25
114	Gene Michael	1.00	.50	.30
115	Alex Johnson	.75	.40	.25
116	Sparky Lyle	1.25	.60	.40
117	Don Young	.75	.40	.25
118	George Mitterwald	.75	.40	.25
119	Chuck Taylor	.75	.40	.25
120	Sal Bando	1.00	.50	.30
121	Orioles Rookies (Fred Beene, Terry Crowley)	.75	.40	.25
122	George Stone	.75	.40	.25
123	Don Gutteridge	.75	.40	.25
124	Larry Jaster	.75	.40	.25
125	Deron Johnson	.75	.40	.25
126	Marty Martinez	.75	.40	.25
127	Joe Coleman	.75	.40	.25
128	Checklist 2	1.50	.70	.45
129	Jimmie Price	.75	.40	.25
130	Ollie Brown	.75	.40	.25
131	Dodgers Rookies (Ray Lamb, Bob Stinson)	.75	.40	.25
132	Jim McGlothlin	.75	.40	.25
133	Clay Carroll	.75	.40	.25
134	Danny Walton	.75	.40	.25
135	Dick Dietz	.75	.40	.25
136	Steve Hargan	.75	.40	.25
137	Art Shamsky	.75	.40	.25
138	Joe Foy	.75	.40	.25
139	Rich Nye	.75	.40	.25
140	Reggie Jackson	55.00	28.00	16.50
141	Pirates Rookies (Dave Cash, Johnny Jeter)	.75	.40	.25
142	Fritz Peterson	.75	.40	.25
143	Phil Gagliano	.75	.40	.25
144	Ray Culp	.75	.40	.25
145	Rico Carty	1.00	.50	.30
146	Danny Murphy	.75	.40	.25
147	Angel Hermoso	.75	.40	.25
148	Earl Weaver	1.25	.60	.40
149	Billy Champion	.75	.40	.25
150	Harmon Killebrew	4.00	2.00	1.25
151	Dave Roberts	.75	.40	.25
152	Ike Brown	.75	.40	.25
153	Gary Gentry	.75	.40	.25
154	Senators Rookies (Jan Dukes, Jim Miles)	.75	.40	.25
155	Denis Menke	.75	.40	.25
156	Eddie Fisher	.75	.40	.25
157	Manny Mota	1.00	.50	.30
158	Jerry McNertney	.75	.40	.25
159	Tommy Helms	.75	.40	.25
160	Phil Niekro	2.50	1.25	.70
161	Richie Scheinblum	.75	.40	.25
162	Jerry Johnson	.75	.40	.25
163	Syd O'Brien	.75	.40	.25
164	Ty Cline	.75	.40	.25
165	Ed kirkpatrick	.75	.40	.25
166	Al Oliver	2.50	1.25	.70
167	Bill Burbach	.75	.40	.25

No.	Card	NR MT	EX	VG
168	Dave Watkins	.75	.40	.25
169	Tom Hall	.75	.40	.25
170	Billy Williams	3.00	1.50	.90
171	Jim Nash	.75	.40	.25
172	Braves Rookies (Ralph Garr, Garry Hill)	1.00	.50	.30
173	Jim Hicks	.75	.40	.25
174	Ted Sizemore	.75	.40	.25
175	Dick Bosman	.75	.40	.25
176	Jim Hart	.75	.40	.25
177	Jim Northrup	.75	.40	.25
178	Denny Lemaster	.75	.40	.25
179	Ivan Murrell	.75	.40	.25
180	Tommy John	1.75	.90	.50
181	Sparky Anderson	1.25	.60	.40
182	Dick Hall	.75	.40	.25
183	Jerry Grote	.75	.40	.25
184	Ray Fosse	.75	.40	.25
185	Don Mincher	.75	.40	.25
186	Rick Joseph	.75	.40	.25
187	Mike Hedlund	.75	.40	.25
188	Manny Sanguillen	.75	.40	.25
189	Yankees Rookies (Dave McDonald, Thurman Munson)	55.00	28.00	16.50
190	Joe Torre	1.25	.60	.40
191	Vicente Romo	.75	.40	.25
192	Jim Qualls	.75	.40	.25
193	Mike Wegener	.75	.40	.25
194	Chuck Manuel	.75	.40	.25
195	N.L. Playoff Game 1 (Seaver Wins Opener!)	2.00	1.00	.60
196	N.L. Playoff Game 2 (Mets Show Muscle!)	1.00	.50	.30
197	N.L. Playoff Game 3 (Ryan Saves The Day!)	2.00	1.00	.60
198	N.L. Playoff Summary (We're Number One!)	1.00	.50	.30
199	A.L. Playoff Game 1 (Orioles Win A Squeaker!)	1.00	.50	.30
200	A.L. Playoff Game 2 (Powell Scores Winning Run!)	1.25	.60	.40
201	A.L. Playoff Game 3 (Birds Wrap It Up!)	1.00	.50	.30
202	A.L. Playoffs Summary (Sweep Twins In Three!)	1.00	.50	.30
203	Rudy May	.75	.40	.25
204	Len Gabrielson	.75	.40	.25
205	Bert Campaneris	1.00	.50	.30
206	Clete Boyer	.75	.40	.25
207	Tigers Rookies (Norman McRae, Bob Reed)	.75	.40	.25
208	Fred Gladding	.75	.40	.25
209	Ken Suarez	.75	.40	.25
210	Juan Marichal	3.50	1.75	1.00
211	Ted Williams	8.00	4.00	2.50
212	Al Santorini	.75	.40	.25
213	Andy Etchebarren	.75	.40	.25
214	Ken Boswell	.75	.40	.25
215	Reggie Smith	1.00	.50	.30
216	Chuck Hartenstein	.75	.40	.25
217	Ron Hansen	.75	.40	.25
218	Ron Stone	.75	.40	.25
219	Jerry Kenney	.75	.40	.25
220	Steve Carlton	20.00	10.00	6.00
221	Ron Brand	.75	.40	.25
222	Jim Rooker	.75	.40	.25
223	Nate Oliver	.75	.40	.25
224	Steve Barber	.75	.40	.25
225	Lee May	1.00	.50	.30
226	Ron Perranoski	.75	.40	.25
227	Astros Rookies (John Mayberry, Bob Watkins)	1.00	.50	.30
228	Aurelio Rodriguez	.75	.40	.25
229	Rich Robertson	.75	.40	.25
230	Brooks Robinson	10.00	5.00	3.00
231	Luis Tiant	1.25	.60	.40
232	Bob Didier	.75	.40	.25
233	Lew Krausse	.75	.40	.25
234	Tommy Dean	.75	.40	.25
235	Mike Epstein	.75	.40	.25
236	Bob Veale	.75	.40	.25
237	Russ Gibson	.75	.40	.25
238	Jose Laboy	.75	.40	.25
239	Ken Berry	.75	.40	.25
240	Fergie Jenkins	1.50	.70	.45
241	Royals Rookies (Al Fitzmorris, Scott Northey)	.75	.40	.25
242	Walter Alston	1.25	.60	.40
243	Joe Sparma	.75	.40	.25
244	Checklist 3	1.50	.70	.45
245	Leo Cardenas	.75	.40	.25
246	Jim McAndrew	.75	.40	.25
247	Lou Klimchock	.75	.40	.25
248	Jesus Alou	.75	.40	.25
249	Bob Locker	.75	.40	.25
250	Willie McCovey	4.50	2.25	1.25
251	Dick Schofield	.75	.40	.25
252	Lowell Palmer	.75	.40	.25
253	Ron Woods	.75	.40	.25
254	Camilo Pascual	1.00	.50	.30
255	Jim Spencer	.75	.40	.25
256	Vic Davalillo	.75	.40	.25
257	Dennis Higgins	.75	.40	.25
258	Paul Popovich	.75	.40	.25
259	Tommie Reynolds	.75	.40	.25
260	Claude Osteen	.75	.40	.25
261	Curt Motton	.75	.40	.25
262	Padres Rookies (Jerry Morales, Jim Williams)	.75	.40	.25
263	Duane Josephson	.75	.40	.25
264	Rich Hebner	.75	.40	.25
265	Randy Hundley	.75	.40	.25
266	Wally Bunker	.75	.40	.25
267	Twins Rookies (Herman Hill, Paul Ratliff)	.75	.40	.25
268	Claude Raymond	.75	.40	.25
269	Cesar Gutierrez	.75	.40	.25
270	Chris Short	.75	.40	.25
271	Greg Goossen	.75	.40	.25
272	Hector Torres	.75	.40	.25
273	Ralph Houk	1.00	.50	.30
274	Gerry Arrigo	.75	.40	.25
275	Duke Sims	.75	.40	.25
276	Ron Hunt	.75	.40	.25
277	Paul Doyle	.75	.40	.25
278	Tommie Aaron	.75	.40	.25
279	Bill Lee	1.00	.50	.30
280	Donn Clendenon	.75	.40	.25
281	Casey Cox	.75	.40	.25
282	Steve Huntz	.75	.40	.25
283	Angel Bravo	.75	.40	.25
284	Jack Baldschun	.75	.40	.25
285	Paul Blair	1.00	.50	.30
286	Dodgers Rookies (Bill Buckner, Jack Jenkins)	4.00	2.00	1.25
287	Fred Talbot	.75	.40	.25
288	Larry Hisle	1.00	.50	.30
289	Gene Brabender	.75	.40	.25
290	Rod Carew	11.00	5.50	3.25
291	Leo Durocher	1.25	.60	.40
292	Eddie Leon	.75	.40	.25
293	Bob Bailey	.75	.40	.25
294	Jose Azcue	.75	.40	.25
295	Cecil Upshaw	.75	.40	.25
296	Woody Woodward	.75	.40	.25
297	Curt Blefary	.75	.40	.25
298	Ken Henderson	.75	.40	.25
299	Buddy Bradford	.75	.40	.25
300	Tom Seaver	30.00	15.00	9.00
301	Chico Salmon	.75	.40	.25
302	Jeff James	.75	.40	.25
303	Brant Alyea	.75	.40	.25
304	Bill Russell	1.25	.60	.40
305	World Series Game 1 (Buford Belts Leadoff Homer!)	1.00	.50	.30
306	World Series Game 2 (Clendenon's Homer Breaks Ice!)	1.00	.50	.30
307	World Series Game 3 (Agee's Catch Saves The Day!)	1.00	.50	.30
308	World Series Game 4 (Martin's Bunt Ends Deadlock!)	1.00	.50	.30
309	World Series Game 5 (Koosman Shuts The Door!)	1.00	.50	.30
310	World Series Summary (Mets Whoop It Up!)	1.00	.50	.30
311	Dick Green	.75	.40	.25
312	Mike Torrez	.75	.40	.25
313	Mayo Smith	.75	.40	.25
314	Bill McCool	.75	.40	.25
315	Luis Aparicio	3.50	1.75	1.00
316	Skip Guinn	.75	.40	.25
317	Red Sox Rookies (Luis Alvarado, Billy Conigliaro)	.75	.40	.25
318	Willie Smith	.75	.40	.25
319	Clayton Dalrymple	.75	.40	.25
320	Jim Maloney	.75	.40	.25
321	Lou Piniella	1.25	.60	.40
322	Luke Walker	.75	.40	.25
323	Wayne Comer	.75	.40	.25
324	Tony Taylor	.75	.40	.25
325	Dave Boswell	.75	.40	.25
326	Bill Voss	.75	.40	.25
327	Hal King	.75	.40	.25
328	George Brunet	.75	.40	.25
329	Chris Cannizzaro	.75	.40	.25
330	Lou Brock	4.50	2.25	1.25
331	Chuck Dobson	.75	.40	.25
332	Bobby Wine	.75	.40	.25
333	Bobby Murcer	1.25	.60	.40
334	Phil Regan	.75	.40	.25
335	Bill Freehan	1.00	.50	.30
336	Del Unser	.75	.40	.25
337	Mike McCormick	.75	.40	.25
338	Paul Schaal	.75	.40	.25
339	Johnny Edwards	.75	.40	.25
340	Tony Conigliaro	1.00	.50	.30
341	Bill Sudakis	.75	.40	.25
342	Wilbur Wood	1.00	.50	.30
343	Checklist 4	2.00	1.00	.60
344	Marcelino Lopez	.75	.40	.25
345	Al Ferrara	.75	.40	.25
346	Red Schoendienst	1.00	.50	.30
347	Russ Snyder	.75	.40	.25
348	Mets Rookies (Jesse Hudson, Mike Jorgensen)	.75	.40	.25
349	Steve Hamilton	.75	.40	.25
350	Roberto Clemente	30.00	15.00	9.00
351	Tom Murphy	.75	.40	.25
352	Bob Barton	.75	.40	.25
353	Stan Williams	.75	.40	.25
354	Amos Otis	1.00	.50	.30
355	Doug Rader	.75	.40	.25
356	Fred Lasher	.75	.40	.25
357	Bob Burda	.75	.40	.25
358	Pedro Borbon	.75	.40	.25
359	Phil Roof	.75	.40	.25
360	Curt Flood	1.25	.60	.40
361	Ray Jarvis	.75	.40	.25
362	Joe Hague	.75	.40	.25
363	Tom Shopay	.75	.40	.25
364	Dan McGinn	.75	.40	.25
365	Zoilo Versalles	.75	.40	.25
366	Barry Moore	.75	.40	.25
367	Mike Lum	.75	.40	.25
368	Ed Herrmann	.75	.40	.25
369	Alan Foster	.75	.40	.25
370	Tommy Harper	.75	.40	.25
371	Rod Gaspar	.75	.40	.25
372	Dave Giusti	.75	.40	.25
373	Roy White	.75	.40	.25
374	Tommie Sisk	.75	.40	.25
375	Johnny Callison	.75	.40	.25
376	Lefty Phillips	.75	.40	.25
377	Bill Butler	.75	.40	.25
378	Jim Davenport	.75	.40	.25
379	Tom Tischinski	.75	.40	.25
380	Tony Perez	2.00	1.00	.60
381	Athletics Rookies (Bobby Brooks, Mike Olivo)	.75	.40	.25
382	Jack DiLauro	.75	.40	.25
383	Mickey Stanley	.75	.40	.25
384	Gary Neibauer	.75	.40	.25
385	George Scott	.75	.40	.25
386	Bill Dillman	.75	.40	.25
387	Orioles Team	1.00	.50	.30
388	Byron Browne	.75	.40	.25
389	Jim Shellenback	.75	.40	.25
390	Willie Davis	1.00	.50	.30
391	Larry Brown	.75	.40	.25
392	Walt Hriniak	.75	.40	.25
393	John Gelnar	.75	.40	.25
394	Gil Hodges	2.50	1.25	.70
395	Walt Williams	.75	.40	.25
396	Steve Blass	.75	.40	.25
397	Roger Repoz	.75	.40	.25
398	Bill Stoneman	.75	.40	.25
399	Yankees Team	2.00	1.00	.60
400	Denny McLain	1.50	.70	.45
401	Giants Rookies (John Harrell, Bernie Williams)	.75	.40	.25
402	Ellie Rodriguez	.75	.40	.25
403	Jim Bunning	2.00	1.00	.60
404	Rich Reese	.75	.40	.25
405	Bill Hands	.75	.40	.25
406	Mike Andrews	.75	.40	.25
407	Bob Watson	.75	.40	.25
408	Paul Lindblad	.75	.40	.25
409	Bob Tolan	.75	.40	.25
410	Boog Powell	1.50	.70	.45
411	Dodgers Team	1.00	.50	.30
412	Larry Burchart	.75	.40	.25
413	Sonny Jackson	.75	.40	.25
414	Paul Edmondson	.75	.40	.25
415	Julian Javier	.75	.40	.25
416	Joe Verbanic	.75	.40	.25
417	John Bateman	.75	.40	.25
418	John Donaldson	.75	.40	.25
419	Ron Taylor	.75	.40	.25
420	Ken McMullen	.75	.40	.25
421	Pat Dobson	.75	.40	.25
422	Royals Team	1.00	.50	.30
423	Jerry May	.75	.40	.25
424	Mike Kilkenny	.75	.40	.25
425	Bobby Bonds	1.25	.60	.40
426	Bill Rigney	.75	.40	.25
427	Fred Norman	.75	.40	.25
428	Don Buford	.75	.40	.25
429	Cubs Rookies (Randy Bobb, Jim Cosman)	.75	.40	.25
430	Andy Messersmith	1.00	.50	.30
431	Ron Swoboda	.75	.40	.25
432	Checklist 5	1.50	.70	.45
433	Ron Bryant	.75	.40	.25
434	Felipe Alou	1.00	.50	.30
435	Nelson Briles	.75	.40	.25
436	Phillies Team	1.00	.50	.30
437	Danny Cater	.75	.40	.25
438	Pat Jarvis	.75	.40	.25
439	Lee Maye	.75	.40	.25
440	Bill Mazeroski	1.25	.60	.40
441	John O'Donoghue	.75	.40	.25
442	Gene Mauch	1.00	.50	.30
443	Al Jackson	.75	.40	.25
444	White Sox Rookies (Billy Farmer, John Matias)	.75	.40	.25
445	Vada Pinson	1.25	.60	.40
446	Billy Grabarkewitz	.75	.40	.25
447	Lee Stange	.75	.40	.25
448	Astros Team	1.00	.50	.30
449	Jim Palmer	6.50	3.25	2.00
450	Willie McCovey AS	2.50	1.25	.70
451	Boog Powell AS	1.00	.50	.30
452	Felix Millan AS	.75	.40	.25
453	Rod Carew AS	3.00	1.50	.90
454	Ron Santo AS	1.00	.50	.30
455	Brooks Robinson AS	2.50	1.25	.70
456	Don Kessinger AS	.75	.40	.25
457	Rico Petrocelli AS	.75	.40	.25
458	Pete Rose AS	15.00	7.50	4.50
459	Reggie Jackson AS	10.00	5.00	3.00
460	Matty Alou AS	.75	.40	.25
461	Carl Yastrzemski AS	4.00	2.00	1.25
462	Hank Aaron As	4.50	2.25	1.25
463	Frank Robinson AS	2.50	1.25	.70
464	Johnny Bench AS	3.50	1.75	1.00
465	Bill Freehan AS	.75	.40	.25
466	Juan Marichal AS	1.75	.90	.50
467	Denny McLain AS	1.00	.50	.30
468	Jerry Koosman AS	.75	.40	.25
469	Sam McDowell AS	.75	.40	.25
470	Willie Stargell	5.00	2.50	1.50
471	Chris Zachary	.75	.40	.25
472	Braves Team	1.00	.50	.30
473	Don Bryant	.75	.40	.25
474	Dick Kelley	.75	.40	.25
475	Dick McAuliffe	.75	.40	.25
476	Don Shaw	.75	.40	.25
477	Orioles Rookies (Roger Freed, Al Severinsen)	.75	.40	.25
478	Bob Heise	.75	.40	.25
479	Dick Woodson	.75	.40	.25
480	Glenn Beckert	.75	.40	.25
481	Jose Tartabull	.75	.40	.25
482	Tom Hilgendorf	.75	.40	.25
483	Gail Hopkins	.75	.40	.25
484	Gary Nolan	.75	.40	.25
485	Jay Johnstone	1.00	.50	.30
486	Terry Harmon	.75	.40	.25
487	Cisco Carlos	.75	.40	.25
488	J.C. Martin	.75	.40	.25
489	Eddie Kasko	.75	.40	.25
490	Bill Singer	.75	.40	.25
491	Graig Nettles	3.00	1.50	.90
492	Astros Rookies (Keith Lampard, Scipio Spinks)	.75	.40	.25
493	Lindy McDaniel	.75	.40	.25
494	Larry Stahl	.75	.40	.25
495	Dave Morehead	.75	.40	.25
496	Steve Whitaker	.75	.40	.25
497	Eddie Watt	.75	.40	.25
498	Al Weis	.75	.40	.25
499	Skip Lockwood	.75	.40	.25
500	Hank Aaron	30.00	15.00	9.00
501	White Sox Team	1.00	.50	.30
502	Rollie Fingers	2.50	1.25	.70
503	Dal Maxvill	.75	.40	.25
504	Don Pavletich	.75	.40	.25
505	Ken Holtzman	1.00	.50	.30
506	Ed Stroud	.75	.40	.25
507	Pat Corrales	.75	.40	.25
508	Joe Niekro	1.00	.50	.30
509	Expos Team	1.00	.50	.30

		NR MT	EX	VG
510	Tony Oliva	1.50	.70	.45
511	Joe Hoerner	.75	.40	.25
512	Billy Harris	.75	.40	.25
513	Preston Gomez	.75	.40	.25
514	Steve Hovley	.75	.40	.25
515	Don Wilson	.75	.40	.25
516	Yankees Rookies (John Ellis, Jim Lyttle)	.75	.40	.25
517	Joe Gibbon	.75	.40	.25
518	Bill Melton	.75	.40	.25
519	Don McMahon	.75	.40	.25
520	Willie Horton	1.00	.50	.30
521	Cal Koonce	.75	.40	.25
522	Angels Team	1.00	.50	.30
523	Jose Pena	.75	.40	.25
524	Alvin Dark	1.00	.50	.30
525	Jerry Adair	.75	.40	.25
526	Ron Herbel	.75	.40	.25
527	Don Bosch	.75	.40	.25
528	Elrod Hendricks	.75	.40	.25
529	Bob Aspromonte	.75	.40	.25
530	Bob Gibson	10.00	5.00	3.00
531	Ron Clark	.75	.40	.25
532	Danny Murtaugh	.75	.40	.25
533	Buzz Stephen	.75	.40	.25
534	Twins Team	1.00	.50	.30
535	Andy Kosco	.75	.40	.25
536	Mike Kekich	.75	.40	.25
537	Joe Morgan	3.00	1.50	.90
538	Bob Humphreys	.75	.40	.25
539	Phillies Rookies (Larry Bowa, Dennis Doyle)	2.00	1.00	.60
540	Gary Peters	.75	.40	.25
541	Bill Heath	.75	.40	.25
542	Checklist 6	1.50	.70	.45
543	Clyde Wright	.75	.40	.25
544	Reds Team	1.00	.50	.30
545	Ken Harrelson	1.00	.50	.30
546	Ron Reed	1.00	.40	.25

1971 O-Pee-Chee

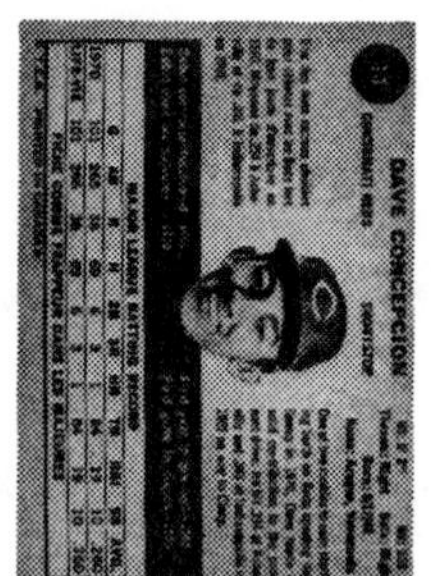

For 1971 O-Pee-Chee increased the number of cards in its set to 752, the same as the 1971 Topps set, which shares the same black-bordered design. The backs of the Canadian-issued O-Pee-Chee cards are yellow, rather than green, and the backs (except card numbers 524-752) are printed in both French and English. The words "Printed in Canada" appear on the back. Fourteen of the O-Pee-Chee cards have different photos from their corresponding Topps' cards or list the player with a different team. The cards measure the standard 2-1/2" by 3-1/2".

	NR MT	EX	VG
Complete Set:	1200.	600.00	350.00
Common Player: 1-523	.60	.30	.20
Common Player: 524-643	.75	.40	.25
Common Player: 644-752	2.00	1.00	.60

		NR MT	EX	VG
1	World Champions (Orioles Team)	3.00	1.25	.75
2	Dock Ellis	.60	.30	.20
3	Dick McAuliffe	.60	.30	.20
4	Vic Davalillo	.60	.30	.20
5	Thurman Munson	15.00	7.50	4.50
6	Ed Spiezio	.60	.30	.20
7	Jim Holt	.60	.30	.20
8	Mike McQueen	.60	.30	.20
9	George Scott	.60	.30	.20
10	Claude Osteen	.50	.25	.15
11	Elliott Maddox	.60	.30	.20
12	Johnny Callison	.75	.40	.25
13	White Sox Rookies (Charlie Brinkman, Dick Moloney)	.60	.30	.20
14	Dave Concepcion	3.00	1.50	.90
15	Andy Messersmith	.75	.40	.25
16	Ken Singleton	1.25	.60	.40
17	Billy Sorrell	.60	.30	.20
18	Norm Miller	.60	.30	.20
19	Skip Pitlock	.60	.30	.20
20	Reggie Jackson	40.00	20.00	12.00
21	Dan McGinn	.60	.30	.20
22	Phil Roof	.60	.30	.20
23	Oscar Gamble	.75	.40	.25
24	Rich Hand	.60	.30	.20
25	Clarence Gaston	.60	.30	.20
26	Bert Blyleven	15.00	7.50	4.50
27	Pirates Rookies (Fred Cambria, Gene Clines)	.60	.30	.20
28	Ron Klimkowski	.60	.30	.20
29	Don Buford	.60	.30	.20
30	Phil Niekro	2.25	1.25	.70
31	John Bateman	1.00	.50	.30
32	Jerry DaVanon	1.00	.50	.30
33	Del Unser	.60	.30	.20
34	Sandy Vance	.60	.30	.20
35	Lou Piniella	1.00	.50	.30
36	Dean Chance	.50	.25	.15
37	Rich McKinney	.60	.30	.20
38	Jim Colborn	.60	.30	.20
39	Tigers Rookies (Gene Lamont, Lerrin LaGrow)	.60	.30	.20
40	Lee May	.75	.40	.25
41	Rick Austin	.60	.30	.20
42	Boots Day	.60	.30	.20
43	Steve Kealey	.60	.30	.20
44	Johnny Edwards	.60	.30	.20
45	Jim Hunter	2.50	1.25	.70
46	Dave Campbell	.60	.30	.20
47	Johnny Jeter	.60	.30	.20
48	Dave Baldwin	.60	.30	.20
49	Don Money	.60	.30	.20
50	Willie McCovey	4.00	2.00	1.25
51	Steve Kline	.60	.30	.20
52	Braves Rookies (Oscar Brown, Earl Williams)	.50	.25	.15
53	Paul Blair	.75	.40	.25
54	Checklist 1	1.50	.70	.45
55	Steve Carlton	15.00	7.50	4.50
56	Duane Josephson	.60	.30	.20
57	Von Joshua	.60	.30	.20
58	Bill Lee	.75	.40	.25
59	Gene Mauch	.75	.40	.25
60	Dick Bosman	.60	.30	.20
61	A.L. Batting Leaders (Alex Johnson, Tony Oliva, Carl Yastrzemski)	1.25	.60	.40
62	N.L. Batting Leaders (Rico Carty, Manny Sanguillen, Joe Torre)	.75	.40	.25
63	A.L. RBI Leaders (Tony Conigliaro, Frank Howard, Boog Powell)	.75	.40	.25
64	N.L. RBI Leaders (Johnny Bench, Tony Perez, Billy Williams)	1.25	.60	.40
65	A.L. HR Leaders (Frank Howard, Harmon Killebrew, Carl Yastrzemski)	1.00	.50	.30
66	N.L. HR Leaders (Johnny Bench, Tony Perez, Billy Williams)	1.00	.50	.30
67	A.L. ERA Leaders (Jim Palmer, Diego Segui, Clyde Wright)	.75	.40	.25
68	N.L. ERA Leader (Tom Seaver, Wayne Simpson, Luke Walker)	1.00	.50	.30
69	A.L. Pitching Leaders (Mike Cuellar, Dave McNally, Jim Perry)	.75	.40	.25
70	N.L. Pitching Leaders (Bob Gibson, Fergie Jenkins, Gaylord Perry)	1.00	.50	.30
71	A.L. Strikeout Leaders (Bob Johnson, Mickey Lolich, Sam McDowell)	.75	.40	.25
72	N.L. Strikeout Leaders (Bob Gibson, Fergie Jenkins, Tom Seaver)	1.25	.60	.40
73	George Brunet	1.00	.50	.30
74	Twins Rookies (Pete Hamm, Jim Nettles)	.60	.30	.20
75	Gary Nolan	.60	.30	.20
76	Ted Savage	.60	.30	.20
77	Mike Compton	.60	.30	.20
78	Jim Spencer	.60	.30	.20
79	Wade Blasingame	.60	.30	.20
80	Bill Melton	.60	.30	.20
81	Felix Millan	.60	.30	.20
82	Casey Cox	.60	.30	.20
83	Met Rookies (Randy Bobb, Tim Foli)	.50	.25	.15
84	Marcel Lachemann	.60	.30	.20
85	Billy Grabarkewitz	.60	.30	.20
86	Mike Kilkenny	.60	.30	.20
87	Jack Heidemann	.60	.30	.20
88	Hal King	.60	.30	.20
89	Ken Brett	.60	.30	.20
90	Joe Pepitone	.50	.25	.15
91	Bob Lemon	1.00	.50	.30
92	Fred Wenz	.60	.30	.20
93	Senators Rookies (Norm McRae, Denny Riddleberger)	.60	.30	.20
94	Don Hahn	.60	.30	.20
95	Luis Tiant	1.00	.50	.30
96	Joe Hague	.60	.30	.20
97	Floyd Wicker	.60	.30	.20
98	Joe Decker	.60	.30	.20
99	Mark Belanger	.75	.40	.25
100	Pete Rose	40.00	20.00	12.00
101	Les Cain	.60	.30	.20
102	Astros Rookies (Ken Forsch, Larry Howard)	.75	.40	.25
103	Rich Severson	.60	.30	.20
104	Dan Frisella	.60	.30	.20
105	Tony Conigliaro	.75	.40	.25
106	Tom Dukes	.60	.30	.20
107	Roy Foster	.60	.30	.20
108	John Cumberland	.60	.30	.20
109	Steve Hovley	.60	.30	.20
110	Bill Mazeroski	1.00	.50	.30
111	Yankees Rookies (Loyd Colson, Bobby Mitchell)	.60	.30	.20
112	Manny Mota	.75	.40	.25
113	Jerry Crider	.60	.30	.20
114	Billy Conigliaro	.60	.30	.20
115	Donn Clendenon	.60	.30	.20
116	Ken Sanders	.60	.30	.20
117	Ted Simmons	4.00	2.00	1.25
118	Cookie Rojas	.60	.30	.20
119	Frank Lucchesi	.60	.30	.20
120	Willie Horton	.75	.40	.25
121	Cubs Rookies (Jim Dunegan, Roe Skidmore)	.60	.30	.20
122	Eddie Watt	.60	.30	.20
123	Checklist 2	1.50	.70	.45
124	Don Gullett	.75	.40	.25
125	Ray Fosse	.60	.30	.20
126	Danny Coombs	.60	.30	.20
127	Danny Thompson	.60	.30	.20
128	Frank Johnson	.60	.30	.20
129	Aurelio Monteagudo	.60	.30	.20
130	Denis Menke	.60	.30	.20
131	Curt Blefary	.60	.30	.20
132	Jose Laboy	.60	.30	.20
133	Mickey Lolich	1.00	.50	.30
134	Jose Arcia	.60	.30	.20
135	Rick Monday	.75	.40	.25
136	Duffy Dyer	.60	.30	.20
137	Marcelino Lopez	.60	.30	.20
138	Phillies Rookies (Joe Lis, Willie Montanez)	.75	.40	.25
139	Paul Casanova	.60	.30	.20
140	Gaylord Perry	3.00	1.50	.90
141	Frank Quilici	.60	.30	.20
142	Mack Jones	.60	.30	.20
143	Steve Blass	.60	.30	.20
144	Jackie Hernandez	1.00	.50	.30
145	Bill Singer	.60	.30	.20
146	Ralph Houk	.75	.40	.25
147	Bob Priddy	.60	.30	.20
148	John Mayberry	.60	.30	.20
149	Mike Hershberger	.60	.30	.20
150	Sam McDowell	.75	.40	.25
151	Tommy Davis	1.25	.60	.40
152	Angels Rookies (Lloyd Allen, Winston Llenas)	.60	.30	.20
153	Gary Ross	.60	.30	.20
154	Cesar Gutierrez	.60	.30	.20
155	Ken Henderson	.60	.30	.20
156	Bart Johnson	.60	.30	.20
157	Bob Bailey	.60	.30	.20
158	Jerry Reuss	.75	.40	.25
159	Jarvis Tatum	.60	.30	.20
160	Tom Seaver	20.00	10.00	6.00
161	Ron Hunt	1.00	.50	.30
162	Jack Billingham	.60	.30	.20
163	Buck Martinez	.60	.30	.20
164	Reds Rookies (Frank Duffy, Milt Wilcox)	.75	.40	.25
165	Cesar Tovar	.60	.30	.20
166	Joe Hoerner	.60	.30	.20
167	Tom Grieve	.60	.30	.20
168	Bruce Dal Canton	.60	.30	.20
169	Ed Herrmann	.60	.30	.20
170	Mike Cuellar	.75	.40	.25
171	Bobby Wine	.60	.30	.20
172	Duke Sims	1.00	.50	.30
173	Gil Garrido	.60	.30	.20
174	Dave LaRoche	.60	.30	.20
175	Jim Hickman	.60	.30	.20
176	Red Sox Rookies (Doug Griffin, Bob Montgomery)	.60	.30	.20
177	Hal McRae	.75	.40	.25
178	Dave Duncan	.60	.30	.20
179	Mike Corkins	.60	.30	.20
180	Al Kaline	10.00	5.00	3.00
181	Hal Lanier	.75	.40	.25
182	Al Downing	1.00	.50	.30
183	Gil Hodges	2.50	1.25	.70
184	Stan Bahnsen	.60	.30	.20
185	Julian Javier	.60	.30	.20
186	Bob Spence	.60	.30	.20
187	Ted Abernathy	.60	.30	.20
188	Dodgers Rookies (Mike Strahler, Bob Valentine)	1.00	.50	.30
189	George Mitterwald	.60	.30	.20
190	Bob Tolan	.60	.30	.20
191	Mike Andrews	1.00	.50	.30
192	Billy Wilson	.60	.30	.20
193	Bob Grich	1.25	.60	.40
194	Mike Lum	.60	.30	.20
195	A.L. Playoff Game 1 (Powell Muscles Twins!)	1.00	.50	.30
196	A.L. Playoff Game 2 (McNally Makes It Two Straight!)	1.00	.50	.30
197	A.L. Playoff Game 3 (Palmer Mows 'Em Down!)	1.25	.60	.40
198	A.L. Playoffs Summary (A Team Effort!)	1.00	.50	.30
199	N.L. Playoff Game 1 (Cline Pinch Triple Decides It!)	1.00	.50	.30
200	N.L. Playoff Game 2 (Tolan Scores For Third Time!)	1.00	.50	.30
201	N.L. Playoff Game 3 (Cline Scores Winning Run!)	1.00	.50	.30
202	Claude Raymond	1.00	.50	.30
203	Larry Gura	.75	.40	.25
204	Brewers Rookies (George Kopacz, Bernie Smith)	.60	.30	.20
205	Gerry Moses	.60	.30	.20
206	Checklist 3	1.50	.70	.45
207	Alan Foster	1.00	.50	.30
208	Billy Martin	1.25	.60	.40
209	Steve Renko	.60	.30	.20
210	Rod Carew	18.00	9.00	5.50
211	Phil Hennigan	.60	.30	.20
212	Rich Hebner	.60	.30	.20
213	Frank Baker	.60	.30	.20
214	Al Ferrara	.60	.30	.20
215	Diego Segui	.60	.30	.20
216	Cardinals Rookies (Reggie Cleveland, Luis Melendez)	.60	.30	.20
217	Ed Stroud	.60	.30	.20
218	Tony Cloninger	.60	.30	.20
219	Elrod Hendricks	.60	.30	.20
220	Ron Santo	1.00	.50	.30
221	Dave Morehead	.60	.30	.20
222	Bob Watson	.60	.30	.20
223	Cecil Upshaw	.60	.30	.20
224	Alan Gallagher	.60	.30	.20
225	Gary Peters	.60	.30	.20
226	Bill Russell	.75	.40	.25
227	Floyd Weaver	.60	.30	.20
228	Wayne Garrett	.60	.30	.20
229	Jim Hannan	.60	.30	.20
230	Willie Stargell	4.00	2.00	1.25
231	Indians Rookies (Vince Colbert, John Lowenstein)	.60	.30	.20
232	John Strohmayer	.60	.30	.20
233	Larry Bowa	1.00	.50	.30
234	Jim Lyttle	.60	.30	.20
235	Nate Colbert	.60	.30	.20
236	Bob Humphreys	.60	.30	.20
237	Cesar Cedeno	1.25	.60	.40
238	Chuck Dobson	.60	.30	.20
239	Red Schoendienst	.75	.40	.25
240	Clyde Wright	.60	.30	.20
241	Dave Nelson	.60	.30	.20
242	Jim Ray	.60	.30	.20
243	Carlos May	.60	.30	.20

		NR MT	EX	VG
244	Bob Tillman	.60	.30	.20
245	Jim Kaat	1.50	.70	.45
246	Tony Taylor	.60	.30	.20
247	Royals Rookies (Jerry Cram, Paul Splittorff)	.75	.40	.25
248	Hoyt Wilhelm	3.50	1.75	1.00
249	Chico Salmon	.60	.30	.20
250	Johnny Bench	15.00	7.50	4.50
251	Frank Reberger	.60	.30	.20
252	Eddie Leon	.60	.30	.20
253	Bill Sudakis	.60	.30	.20
254	Cal Koonce	.60	.30	.20
255	Bob Robertson	.60	.30	.20
256	Tony Gonzalez	.60	.30	.20
257	Nelson Briles	.60	.30	.20
258	Dick Green	.60	.30	.20
259	Dave Marshall	.60	.30	.20
260	Tommy Harper	.60	.30	.20
261	Darold Knowles	.60	.30	.20
262	Padres Rookies (Dave Robinson, Jim Williams)	.60	.30	.20
263	John Ellis	.60	.30	.20
264	Joe Morgan	2.50	1.25	.70
265	Jim Northrup	.60	.30	.20
266	Bill Stoneman	.60	.30	.20
267	Rich Morales	.60	.30	.20
268	Phillies Team	.75	.40	.25
269	Gail Hopkins	.60	.30	.20
270	Rico Carty	.75	.40	.25
271	Bill Zepp	.60	.30	.20
272	Tommy Helms	.60	.30	.20
273	Pete Richert	.60	.30	.20
274	Ron Slocum	.60	.30	.20
275	Vada Pinson	.75	.40	.25
276	Giants Rookies (Mike Davison, George Foster)	3.00	1.50	.90
277	Gary Waslewski	.60	.30	.20
278	Jerry Grote	.60	.30	.20
279	Lefty Phillips	.60	.30	.20
280	Fergie Jenkins	2.00	1.00	.60
281	Danny Walton	.60	.30	.20
282	Jose Pagan	.60	.30	.20
283	Dick Such	.60	.30	.20
284	Jim Gosger	.60	.30	.20
285	Sal Bando	.75	.40	.25
286	Jerry McNertney	.60	.30	.20
287	Mike Fiore	.60	.30	.20
288	Joe Moeller	.60	.30	.20
290	Tony Oliva	1.25	.60	.40
291	George Culver	.60	.30	.20
292	Jay Johnstone	.75	.40	.25
293	Pat Corrales	.60	.30	.20
294	Steve Dunning	.60	.30	.20
295	Bobby Bonds	1.00	.50	.30
296	Tom Timmermann	.60	.30	.20
297	Johnny Briggs	.60	.30	.20
298	Jim Nelson	.60	.30	.20
299	Ed Kirkpatrick	.60	.30	.20
300	Brooks Robinson	3.00	1.50	.90
301	Earl Wilson	.60	.30	.20
302	Phil Gagliano	.60	.30	.20
303	Lindy McDaniel	.60	.30	.20
304	Ron Brand	.60	.30	.20
305	Reggie Smith	.75	.40	.25
306	Jim Nash	.60	.30	.20
307	Don Wert	.60	.30	.20
308	Cards Team	.75	.40	.25
309	Dick Ellsworth	.60	.30	.20
310	Tommie Agee	.60	.30	.20
311	Lee Stange	.60	.30	.20
312	Harry Walker	.60	.30	.20
313	Tom Hall	.60	.30	.20
314	Jeff Torborg	.60	.30	.20
315	Ron Fairly	.75	.40	.25
316	Fred Scherman	.60	.30	.20
317	Athletics Rookies (Jim Driscoll, Angel Mangual)	.60	.30	.20
318	Rudy May	.60	.30	.20
319	Ty Cline	.60	.30	.20
320	Dave McNally	.75	.40	.25
321	Tom Matchick	.60	.30	.20
322	Jim Beauchamp	.60	.30	.20
323	Billy Champion	.60	.30	.20
324	Graig Nettles	1.75	.90	.50
325	Juan Marichal	4.00	2.00	1.25
326	Richie Scheinblum	.60	.30	.20
327	World Series Game 1 (Powell Homers To Opposite Field!)	1.00	.50	.30
328	World Series Game 2 (Buford Goes 2 For 4!)	1.00	.50	.30
329	World Series Game 3 (F. Robinson Shows Muscle!)	1.50	.70	.45
330	World Series Game 4 (Reds Stay Alive!)	1.00	.50	.30
331	World Series Game 5 (B. Robinson Commits Robbery!)	1.50	.70	.45
332	World Series Summary (Clinching Performance!)	1.00	.50	.30
333	Clay Kirby	.60	.30	.20
334	Roberto Pena	.60	.30	.20
335	Jerry Koosman	.75	.40	.25
336	Tigers Team	.75	.40	.25
337	Jesus Alou	.60	.30	.20
338	Gene Tenace	.60	.30	.20
339	Wayne Simpson	.60	.30	.20
340	Rico Petrocelli	.75	.40	.25
341	Steve Garvey	60.00	30.00	18.00
342	Frank Tepedino	.60	.30	.20
343	Pirates Rookies (Ed Acosta, Milt May)	.60	.30	.20
344	Ellie Rodriguez	.60	.30	.20
345	Joe Horlen	.60	.30	.20
346	Lum Harris	.60	.30	.20
347	Ted Uhlaender	.60	.30	.20
348	Fred Norman	.60	.30	.20
349	Rich Reese	.60	.30	.20
350	Billy Williams	3.00	1.50	.90
351	Jim Shellenback	.60	.30	.20
352	Denny Doyle	.60	.30	.20
353	Carl Taylor	.60	.30	.20
354	Don McMahon	.60	.30	.20
355	Bud Harrelson	.60	.30	.20
356	Bob Locker	.60	.30	.20
357	Reds Team	1.00	.50	.30
358	Danny Cater	.60	.30	.20
359	Ron Reed	.60	.30	.20
360	Jim Fregosi	.75	.40	.25
361	Don Sutton	2.50	1.25	.70
362	Orioles Rookies (Mike Adamson, Roger Freed)	.60	.30	.20
363	Mike Nagy	.60	.30	.20
364	Tommy Dean	.60	.30	.20
365	Bob Johnson	.60	.30	.20
366	Ron Stone	.60	.30	.20
367	Dalton Jones	.60	.30	.20
368	Bob Veale	.60	.30	.20
369	Checklist 4	1.50	.70	.45
370	Joe Torre	1.50	.70	.45
371	Jack Hiatt	.60	.30	.20
372	Lew Krausse	.60	.30	.20
373	Tom McCraw	.60	.30	.20
374	Clete Boyer	.75	.40	.25
375	Steve Hargan	.60	.30	.20
376	Expos Rookies (Clyde Mashore, Ernie McAnally)	.60	.30	.20
377	Greg Garrett	.60	.30	.20
378	Tito Fuentes	.60	.30	.20
379	Wayne Granger	.60	.30	.20
380	Ted Williams	3.00	1.50	.90
381	Fred Gladding	.60	.30	.20
382	Jake Gibbs	.60	.30	.20
383	Rod Gaspar	.60	.30	.20
384	Rollie Fingers	2.00	1.00	.60
385	Maury Wills	1.00	.50	.30
386	Red Sox Team	.75	.40	.25
387	Ron Herbel	.60	.30	.20
388	Al Oliver	1.25	.60	.40
389	Ed Brinkman	.60	.30	.20
390	Glenn Beckert	.75	.40	.25
391	Twins Rookies (Steve Brye, Cotton Nash)	.60	.30	.20
392	Grant Jackson	.60	.30	.20
393	Merv Rettenmund	.60	.30	.20
394	Clay Carroll	.60	.30	.20
395	Roy White	.75	.40	.25
396	Dick Schofield	.60	.30	.20
397	Alvin Dark	.75	.40	.25
398	Howie Reed	.60	.30	.20
399	Jim French	.60	.30	.20
400	Hank Aaron	10.00	5.00	3.00
401	Tom Murphy	.60	.30	.20
402	Dodgers Team	1.00	.50	.30
403	Joe Coleman	.60	.30	.20
404	Astros Rookies (Buddy Harris, Roger Metzger)	.60	.30	.20
405	Leo Cardenas	.60	.30	.20
406	Ray Sadecki	.60	.30	.20
407	Joe Rudi	.75	.40	.25
408	Rafael Robles	.60	.30	.20
409	Don Pavletich	.60	.30	.20
410	Ken Holtzman	.75	.40	.25
411	George Spriggs	.60	.30	.20
412	Jerry Johnson	.60	.30	.20
413	Pat Kelly	.60	.30	.20
414	Woodie Fryman	.60	.30	.20
415	Mike Hegan	.60	.30	.20
416	Gene Alley	.60	.30	.20
417	Dick Hall	.60	.30	.20
418	Adolfo Phillips	.60	.30	.20
419	Ron Hansen	.60	.30	.20
420	Jim Merritt	.60	.30	.20
421	John Stephenson	.60	.30	.20
422	Frank Bertaina	.60	.30	.20
423	Tigers Rookies (Tim Marting, Dennis Saunders)	.60	.30	.20
424	Roberto Rodriguez	.60	.30	.20
425	Doug Rader	.60	.30	.20
426	Chris Cannizzaro	.60	.30	.20
427	Bernie Allen	.60	.30	.20
428	Jim McAndrew	.60	.30	.20
429	Chuck Hinton	.60	.30	.20
430	Wes Parker	.75	.40	.25
431	Tom Burgmeier	.60	.30	.20
432	Bob Didier	.60	.30	.20
433	Skip Lockwood	.60	.30	.20
434	Gary Sutherland	.60	.30	.20
435	Jose Cardenal	.60	.30	.20
436	Wilbur Wood	.75	.40	.25
437	Danny Murtaugh	.60	.30	.20
438	Mike McCormick	.60	.30	.20
439	Phillie Rookies (Greg Luzinski, Scott Reid)	1.50	.70	.45
440	Bert Campaneris	.50	.25	.15
441	Milt Pappas	.50	.25	.15
442	Angels Team	.75	.40	.25
443	Rich Robertson	.60	.30	.20
444	Jimmie Price	.60	.30	.20
445	Art Shamsky	.60	.30	.20
446	Bobby Bolin	.60	.30	.20
447	Cesar Geronimo	.60	.30	.20
448	Dave Roberts	.60	.30	.20
449	Brant Alyea	.60	.30	.20
450	Bob Gibson	8.00	4.00	2.50
451	Joe Keough	.60	.30	.20
452	John Boccabella	.60	.30	.20
453	Terry Crowley	.60	.30	.20
454	Mike Paul	.60	.30	.20
455	Don Kessinger	.75	.40	.25
456	Bob Meyer	.60	.30	.20
457	Willie Smith	.60	.30	.20
458	White Sox Rookies (Dave Lemonds, Ron Lolich)	.60	.30	.20
459	Jim LeFebvre	.60	.30	.20
460	Fritz Peterson	.60	.30	.20
461	Jim Hart	.60	.30	.20
462	Senators Team	.75	.40	.25
463	Tom Kelley	.60	.30	.20
464	Aurelio Rodriguez	.60	.30	.20
465	Tim McCarver	1.00	.50	.30
466	Ken Berry	.60	.30	.20
467	Al Santorini	.60	.30	.20
468	Frank Fernandez	.60	.30	.20
469	Bob Aspromonte	.60	.30	.20
470	Bob Oliver	.60	.30	.20
471	Tom Griffin	.60	.30	.20
472	Ken Rudolph	.60	.30	.20
473	Gary Wagner	.60	.30	.20
474	Jim Fairey	.60	.30	.20
475	Ron Perranoski	.60	.30	.20
476	Dal Maxvill	.60	.30	.20
477	Earl Weaver	1.00	.50	.30
478	Bernie Carbo	.60	.30	.20
479	Dennis Higgins	.60	.30	.20
480	Manny Sanguillen	.60	.30	.20
481	Daryl Patterson	.60	.30	.20
482	Padres Team	.75	.40	.25
483	Gene Michael	.75	.40	.25
484	Don Wilson	.60	.30	.20
485	Ken McMullen	.60	.30	.20
486	Steve Huntz	.60	.30	.20
487	Paul Schaal	.60	.30	.20
488	Jerry Stephenson	.60	.30	.20
489	Luis Alvarado	.60	.30	.20
490	Deron Johnson	.60	.30	.20
491	Jim Hardin	.60	.30	.20
492	Ken Boswell	.60	.30	.20
493	Dave May	.60	.30	.20
494	Braves Rookies (Ralph Garr, Rick Kester)	.75	.40	.25
495	Felipe Alou	.50	.25	.15
496	Woody Woodward	.60	.30	.20
497	Horacio Pina	.60	.30	.20
498	John Kennedy	.60	.30	.20
499	Checklist 5	1.50	.70	.45
500	Jim Perry	.75	.40	.25
501	Andy Etchebarren	.60	.30	.20
502	Cubs Team	.75	.40	.25
503	Gates Brown	.60	.30	.20
504	Ken Wright	.60	.30	.20
505	Ollie Brown	.60	.30	.20
506	Bobby Knoop	.60	.30	.20
507	George Stone	.60	.30	.20
508	Roger Repoz	.60	.30	.20
509	Jim Grant	.60	.30	.20
510	Ken Harrelson	.75	.40	.25
511	Chris Short	.60	.30	.20
512	Red Sox Rookies (Mike Garman, Dick Mills)	.60	.30	.20
513	Nolan Ryan	30.00	15.00	9.00
514	Ron Woods	.60	.30	.20
515	Carl Morton	.60	.30	.20
516	Ted Kubiak	.60	.30	.20
517	Charlie Fox	.60	.30	.20
518	Joe Grzenda	.60	.30	.20
519	Willie Crawford	.60	.30	.20
520	Tommy John	2.00	1.00	.60
521	Leron Lee	.60	.30	.20
522	Twins Team	.75	.40	.25
523	John Odom	.60	.30	.20
524	Mickey Stanley	.75	.40	.25
525	Ernie Banks	12.00	6.00	3.50
526	Ray Jarvis	.75	.40	.25
527	Cleon Jones	.75	.40	.25
528	Wally Bunker	.75	.40	.25
529	N.L. Rookies (Bill Buckner, Enzo Hernandez, Marty Perez)	1.50	.70	.45
530	Carl Yastrzemski	25.00	12.50	7.50
531	Mike Torrez	1.00	.50	.30
532	Bill Rigney	.75	.40	.25
533	Mike Ryan	.75	.40	.25
534	Luke Walker	.75	.40	.25
535	Curt Flood	1.25	.60	.40
536	Claude Raymond	.75	.40	.25
537	Tom Egan	.75	.40	.25
538	Angel Bravo	.75	.40	.25
539	Larry Brown	.75	.40	.25
540	Larry Dierker	.75	.40	.25
541	Bob Burda	.75	.40	.25
542	Bob Miller	.75	.40	.25
543	Yankees Team	1.75	.90	.50
544	Vida Blue	1.50	.70	.45
545	Dick Dietz	.75	.40	.25
546	John Matias	.75	.40	.25
547	Pat Dobson	.75	.40	.25
548	Don Mason	.75	.40	.25
549	Jim Brewer	.75	.40	.25
550	Harmon Killebrew	15.00	7.50	4.50
551	Frank Linzy	.75	.40	.25
552	Buddy Bradford	.75	.40	.25
553	Kevin Collins	.75	.40	.25
554	Lowell Palmer	.75	.40	.25
555	Walt Williams	.75	.40	.25
556	Jim McGlothlin	.75	.40	.25
557	Tom Satriano	.75	.40	.25
558	Hector Torres	.75	.40	.25
559	A.L. Rookies (Terry Cox, Bill Gogolewski, Gary Jones)	1.50	.70	.45
560	Rusty Staub	1.25	.60	.40
561	Syd O'Brien	.75	.40	.25
562	Dave Giusti	.75	.40	.25
563	Giants Team	1.00	.50	.30
564	Al Fitzmorris	.75	.40	.25
565	Jim Wynn	1.00	.50	.30
566	Tim Cullen	.75	.40	.25
567	Walt Alston	1.50	.70	.45
568	Sal Campisi	.75	.40	.25
569	Ivan Murrell	.75	.40	.25
570	Jim Palmer	15.00	7.50	4.50
571	Ted Sizemore	.75	.40	.25
572	Jerry Kenney	.75	.40	.25
573	Ed Kranepool	1.00	.50	.30
574	Jim Bunning	2.50	1.25	.70
575	Bill Freehan	1.00	.50	.30
576	Cubs Rookies (Brock Davis, Adrian Garrett, Garry Jestadt)	.75	.40	.25
577	Jim Lonborg	1.00	.50	.30
578	Eddie Kasko	1.00	.50	.30
579	Marty Pattin	.75	.40	.25
580	Tony Perez	3.00	1.50	.90
581	Roger Nelson	.75	.40	.25
582	Dave Cash	.75	.40	.25
583	Ron Cook	.75	.40	.25
584	Indians Team	1.00	.50	.30
585	Willie Davis	1.00	.50	.30
586	Dick Woodson	.75	.40	.25
587	Sonny Jackson	.75	.40	.25
588	Tom Bradley	.75	.40	.25
589	Bob Barton	.75	.40	.25
590	Alex Johnson	.75	.40	.25
591	Jackie Brown	.75	.40	.25
592	Randy Hundley	.75	.40	.25
593	Jack Aker	.75	.40	.25

		NR MT	EX	VG
594	Cards Rookies (Bob Chlupsa, Al Hrabosky, Bob Stinson)	1.00	.50	.30
595	Dave Johnson	1.25	.60	.40
596	Mike Jorgensen	.75	.40	.25
597	Ken Suarez	.75	.40	.25
598	Rick Wise	.75	.40	.25
599	Norm Cash	1.25	.60	.40
600	Willie Mays	30.00	15.00	9.00
601	Ken Tatum	.75	.40	.25
602	Marty Martinez	.75	.40	.25
603	Pirates Team	1.00	.50	.30
604	John Gelnar	.75	.40	.25
605	Orlando Cepeda	2.00	1.00	.60
606	Chuck Taylor	.75	.40	.25
607	Paul Ratliff	.75	.40	.25
608	Mike Wegener	.75	.40	.25
609	Leo Durocher	1.25	.60	.40
610	Amos Otis	1.00	.50	.30
611	Tom Phoebus	.75	.40	.25
612	Indians Rookies (Lou Camilli, Ted Ford, Steve Mingori)	.75	.40	.25
613	Pedro Borbon	.75	.40	.25
614	Billy Cowan	.75	.40	.25
615	Mel Stottlemyre	1.00	.50	.30
616	Larry Hisle	1.00	.50	.30
617	Clay Dalrymple	.75	.40	.25
618	Tug McGraw	1.25	.60	.40
619	Checklist 6	2.00	1.00	.60
620	Frank Howard	1.50	.70	.45
621	Ron Bryant	.75	.40	.25
622	Joe LaHoud	.75	.40	.25
623	Pat Jarvis	.75	.40	.25
624	Athletics Team	1.00	.50	.30
625	Lou Brock	9.00	4.50	2.75
626	Freddie Patek	.75	.40	.25
627	Steve Hamilton	.75	.40	.25
628	John Bateman	.75	.40	.25
629	John Hiller	.75	.40	.25
630	Roberto Clemente	15.00	7.50	4.50
631	Eddie Fisher	.75	.40	.25
632	Darrel Chaney	.75	.40	.25
633	A.L. Rookies (Bobby Brooks, Pete Koegel, Scott Northey)	.75	.40	.25
634	Phil Regan	.75	.40	.25
635	Bob Murcer	1.25	.60	.40
636	Denny Lemaster	.75	.40	.25
637	Dave Bristol	.75	.40	.25
638	Stan Williams	.75	.40	.25
639	Tom Haller	.75	.40	.25
640	Frank Robinson	15.00	7.50	4.50
641	Mets Team	1.50	.70	.45
642	Jim Roland	.75	.40	.25
643	Rick Reichardt	.75	.40	.25
644	Jim Stewart	2.00	1.00	.60
645	Jim Maloney	2.00	1.00	.60
646	Bobby Floyd	2.00	1.00	.60
647	Juan Pizarro	2.00	1.00	.60
648	Mets Rookies (Rich Folkers, Ted Martinez, Jon Matlack)	2.50	1.25	.70
649	Sparky Lyle	2.50	1.25	.70
650	Rich Allen	5.00	2.50	1.50
651	Jerry Robertson	2.00	1.00	.60
652	Braves Team	2.50	1.25	.70
653	Russ Snyder	2.00	1.00	.60
654	Don Shaw	2.00	1.00	.60
655	Mike Epstein	2.00	1.00	.60
656	Gerry Nyman	2.00	1.00	.60
657	Jose Azcue	2.00	1.00	.60
658	Paul Lindblad	2.00	1.00	.60
659	Byron Browne	2.00	1.00	.60
660	Ray Culp	2.00	1.00	.60
661	Chuck Tanner	2.50	1.25	.70
662	Mike Hedlund	2.00	1.00	.60
663	Marv Staehle	2.00	1.00	.60
664	Major League Rookies (Archie Reynolds, Bob Reynolds, Ken Reynolds)	2.00	1.00	.60
665	Ron Swoboda	2.00	1.00	.60
666	Gene Brabender	2.00	1.00	.60
667	Pete Ward	2.00	1.00	.60
668	Gary Neibauer	2.00	1.00	.60
669	Ike Brown	2.00	1.00	.60
670	Bill Hands	2.00	1.00	.60
671	Bill Voss	2.00	1.00	.60
672	Ed Crosby	2.00	1.00	.60
673	Gerry Janeski	2.00	1.00	.60
674	Expos Team	2.50	1.25	.70
675	Dave Boswell	2.00	1.00	.60
676	Tommie Reynolds	2.00	1.00	.60
677	Jack DiLauro	2.00	1.00	.60
678	George Thomas	2.00	1.00	.60
679	Don O'Riley	2.00	1.00	.60
680	Don Mincher	2.00	1.00	.60
681	Bill Butler	2.00	1.00	.60
682	Terry Harmon	2.00	1.00	.60
683	Bill Burbach	2.00	1.00	.60
684	Curt Motton	2.00	1.00	.60
685	Moe Drabowsky	2.00	1.00	.60
686	Chico Ruiz	2.00	1.00	.60
687	Ron Taylor	2.00	1.00	.60
688	Sparky Anderson	2.50	1.25	.70
689	Frank Baker	2.00	1.00	.60
690	Bob Moose	2.00	1.00	.60
691	Bob Heise	2.00	1.00	.60
692	A.L. Rookies (Hal Haydel, Rogelio Moret, Wayne Twitchell)	2.00	1.00	.60
693	Jose Pena	2.00	1.00	.60
694	Rick Renick	2.00	1.00	.60
695	Joe Niekro	2.50	1.25	.70
696	Jerry Morales	2.00	1.00	.60
697	Rickey Clark	2.00	1.00	.60
698	Brewers Team	3.00	1.50	.90
699	Jim Britton	2.00	1.00	.60
700	Boog Powell	3.00	1.50	.90
701	Bob Garibaldi	2.00	1.00	.60
702	Milt Ramirez	2.00	1.00	.60
703	Mike Kekich	2.00	1.00	.60
704	J.C. Martin	2.00	1.00	.60
705	Dick Selma	2.00	1.00	.60
706	Joe Foy	2.00	1.00	.60
707	Fred Lasher	2.00	1.00	.60
708	Russ Nagelson	2.00	1.00	.60
709	Major League Rookies (Dusty Baker, Don Baylor, Tom Paciorek)	12.00	6.00	3.50
710	Sonny Siebert	2.00	1.00	.60
711	Larry Stahl	2.00	1.00	.60
712	Jose Martinez	2.00	1.00	.60
713	Mike Marshall	2.50	1.25	.70
714	Dick Williams	2.50	1.25	.70
715	Horace Clarke	2.00	1.00	.60
716	Dave Leonhard	2.00	1.00	.60
717	Tommie Aaron	2.00	1.00	.60
718	Billy Wynne	2.00	1.00	.60
719	Jerry May	2.00	1.00	.60
720	Matty Alou	2.50	1.25	.70
721	John Morris	2.00	1.00	.60
722	Astros Team	2.50	1.25	.70
723	Vicente Romo	2.00	1.00	.60
724	Tom Tischinski	2.00	1.00	.60
725	Gary Gentry	2.00	1.00	.60
726	Paul Popovich	2.00	1.00	.60
727	Ray Lamb	2.00	1.00	.60
728	N.L. Rookies (Keith Lampard, Wayne Redmond, Bernie Williams)	2.00	1.00	.60
729	Dick Billings	2.00	1.00	.60
730	Jim Rooker	2.00	1.00	.60
731	Jim Qualls	2.00	1.00	.60
732	Bob Reed	2.00	1.00	.60
733	Lee Maye	2.00	1.00	.60
734	Rob Gardner	2.00	1.00	.60
735	Mike Shannon	2.50	1.25	.70
736	Mel Queen	2.00	1.00	.60
737	Preston Gomez	2.00	1.00	.60
738	Russ Gibson	2.00	1.00	.60
739	Barry Lersch	2.00	1.00	.60
740	Luis Aparicio	8.00	4.00	2.50
741	Skip Guinn	2.00	1.00	.60
742	Royals Team	2.50	1.25	.70
743	John O'Donoghue	2.00	1.00	.60
744	Chuck Manuel	2.00	1.00	.60
745	Sandy Alomar	2.00	1.00	.60
746	Andy Kosco	2.00	1.00	.60
747	N.L. Rookies (Balor Moore, Al Severinsen, Scipio Spinks)	2.00	1.00	.60
748	John Purdin	2.00	1.00	.60
749	Ken Sztokkiewicz	2.00	1.00	.60
750	Denny McLain	3.00	1.50	.90
751	Al Weis	2.00	1.00	.60
752	Dick Drago	2.50	1.00	.60

1972 O-Pee-Chee

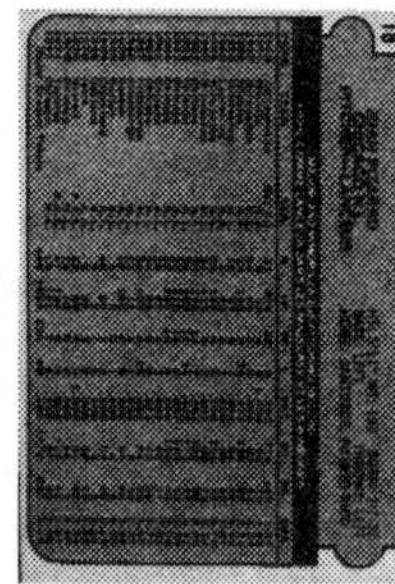

Identical in design to the Topps cards of the same year, the Canadian-issued 1972 O-Pee-Chee set numbers 525 cards, measuring 2-1/2" by 3-1/2". The backs state "Printed in Canada" and are written in both French and English. Unlike the 1972 Topps set, the O-Pee-Chee card of Gil Hodges notes the Mets' manager's death.

		NR MT	EX	VG
	Complete Set:	750.00	375.00	225.00
	Common Player:	.70	.35	.20
1	World Champions (Pirates Team)	2.50	1.00	.60
2	Ray Culp	.70	.35	.20
3	Bob Tolan	.70	.35	.20
4	Checklist 1	1.25	.60	.40
5	John Bateman	.70	.35	.20
6	Fred Scherman	.70	.35	.20
7	Enzo Hernandez	.70	.35	.20
8	Ron Swoboda	.70	.35	.20
9	Stan Williams	.70	.35	.20
10	Amos Otis	.75	.40	.25
11	Bobby Valentine	.75	.40	.25
12	Jose Cardenal	.70	.35	.20
13	Joe Grzenda	.70	.35	.20
14	Phillies Rookies (Mike Anderson, Pete Koegel, Wayne Twitchell)	.70	.35	.20
15	Walt Williams	.70	.35	.20
16	Mike Jorgensen	.70	.35	.20
17	Dave Duncan	.70	.35	.20
18	Juan Pizarro	.70	.35	.20
19	Billy Cowan	.70	.35	.20
20	Don Wilson	.70	.35	.20
21	Braves Team	.75	.40	.25
22	Rob Gardner	.70	.35	.20
23	Ted Kubiak	.70	.35	.20
24	Ted Ford	.70	.35	.20
25	Bill Singer	.70	.35	.20
26	Andy Etchebarren	.70	.35	.20
27	Bob Johnson	.70	.35	.20
28	Twins Rookies (Steve Brye, Bob Gebhard, Hal Haydel)	.70	.35	.20
29	Bill Bonham	.70	.35	.20
30	Rico Petrocelli	.75	.40	.25
31	Cleon Jones	.70	.35	.20
32	Cleon Jones IA	.70	.35	.20
33	Billy Martin	1.25	.60	.40
34	Billy Martin IA	.75	.40	.25
35	Jerry Johnson	.70	.35	.20
36	Jerry Johnson IA	.70	.35	.20
37	Carl Yastrzemski	15.00	7.50	4.50
38	Carl Yastrzemski IA	9.00	4.50	2.75
39	Bob Barton	.70	.35	.20
40	Bob Barton IA	.70	.35	.20
41	Tommy Davis	.75	.40	.25
42	Tommy Davis IA	.70	.35	.20
43	Rick Wise	.70	.35	.20
44	Rick Wise IA	.70	.35	.20
45	Glenn Beckert	.75	.40	.25
46	Glenn Beckert IA	.70	.35	.20
47	John Ellis	.70	.35	.20
48	John Ellis IA	.70	.35	.20
49	Willie Mays	15.00	7.50	4.50
50	Willie Mays IA	9.00	4.50	2.75
51	Harmon Killebrew	3.00	1.50	.90
52	Harmon Killebrew IA	1.50	.70	.45
53	Bud Harrelson	.75	.40	.25
54	Bud Harrelson IA	.70	.35	.20
55	Clyde Wright	.70	.35	.20
56	Rich Chiles	.70	.35	.20
57	Bob Oliver	.70	.35	.20
58	Ernie McAnally	.70	.35	.20
59	Fred Stanley	.70	.35	.20
60	Manny Sanguillen	.70	.35	.20
61	Cubs Rookies (Gene Hiser, Burt Hooton, Earl Stephenson)	.75	.40	.25
62	Angel Mangual	.70	.35	.20
63	Duke Sims	.70	.35	.20
64	Pete Broberg	.70	.35	.20
65	Cesar Cedeno	.75	.40	.25
66	Ray Corbin	.70	.35	.20
67	Red Schoendienst	.75	.40	.25
68	Jim York	.70	.35	.20
69	Roger Freed	.70	.35	.20
70	Mike Cuellar	.75	.40	.25
71	Angels Team	.75	.40	.25
72	Bruce Kison	.70	.35	.20
73	Steve Huntz	.70	.35	.20
74	Cecil Upshaw	.70	.35	.20
75	Bert Campaneris	.75	.40	.25
76	Don Carrithers	.70	.35	.20
77	Ron Theobald	.70	.35	.20
78	Steve Arlin	.70	.35	.20
79	Red Sox Rookies (Cecil Cooper, Carlton Fisk, Mike Garman)	45.00	23.00	13.50
80	Tony Perez	1.25	.60	.40
81	Mike Hedlund	.70	.35	.20
82	Ron Woods	.70	.35	.20
83	Dalton Jones	.70	.35	.20
84	Vince Colbert	.70	.35	.20
85	N.L. Batting Leaders (Glenn Beckert, Ralph Garr, Joe Torre)	.75	.40	.25
86	A.L. Batting Leaders (Bobby Murcer, Tony Oliva, Merv Rettenmund)	.75	.40	.25
87	N.L. RBI Leaders (Hank Aaron, Willie Stargell, Joe Torre)	1.25	.60	.40
88	A.L. RBI Leaders (Harmon Killebrew, Frank Robinson, Reggie Smith)	1.25	.60	.40
89	N.L. Home Run Leaders (Hank Aaron, Lee May, Willie Stargell)	1.25	.60	.40
90	A.L. Home Run Leaders (Norm Cash, Reggie Jackson, Bill Melton)	1.00	.50	.30
91	N.L. ERA Leaders (Dave Roberts, Tom Seaver, Don Wilson)	1.00	.50	.30
92	A.L ERA Leaders (Vida Blue, Jim Palmer, Wilbur Wood)	1.00	.50	.30
93	N.L. Pitching Leaders (Steve Carlton, Al Downing, Fergie Jenkins, Tom Seaver)	1.25	.60	.40
94	A.L. Pitching Leaders (Vida Blue, Mickey Lolich, Wilbur Wood)	.75	.40	.25
95	N.L. Strikeout Leaders (Fergie Jenkins, Tom Seaver, Bill Stoneman)	1.00	.50	.30
96	A.L. Strikeout Leaders (Vida Blue, Joe Coleman, Mickey Lolich)	.75	.40	.25
97	Tom Kelley	.70	.35	.20
98	Chuck Tanner	.75	.40	.25
99	Ross Grimsley	.70	.35	.20
100	Frank Robinson	3.00	1.50	.90
101	Astros Rookies (Ray Busse, Bill Greif, J.R. Richard)	.75	.40	.25
102	Lloyd Allen	.70	.35	.20
103	Checklist 2	1.25	.60	.40
104	Toby Harrah	.75	.40	.25
105	Gary Gentry	.70	.35	.20
106	Brewers Team	.75	.40	.25
107	Jose Cruz	1.25	.60	.40
108	Gary Waslewski	.70	.35	.20
109	Jerry May	.70	.35	.20
110	Ron Hunt	.70	.35	.20
111	Jim Grant	.70	.35	.20
112	Greg Luzinski	.75	.40	.25
113	Rogelio Moret	.70	.35	.20
114	Bill Buckner	.75	.40	.25
115	Jim Fregosi	.75	.40	.25
116	Ed Farmer	.70	.35	.20
117	Cleo James	.70	.35	.20
118	Skip Lockwood	.70	.35	.20
119	Marty Perez	.70	.35	.20
120	Bill Freehan	.75	.40	.25
121	Ed Sprague	.70	.35	.20
122	Larry Biittner	.70	.35	.20
123	Ed Acosta	.70	.35	.20
124	Yankees Rookies (Alan Closter, Roger Hambright, Rusty Torres)	.70	.35	.20
125	Dave Cash	.70	.35	.20
126	Bart Johnson	.70	.35	.20
127	Duffy Dyer	.70	.35	.20
128	Eddie Watt	.70	.35	.20
129	Charlie Fox	.70	.35	.20
130	Bob Gibson	3.00	1.50	.90
131	Jim Nettles	.70	.35	.20
132	Joe Morgan	1.75	.90	.50
133	Joe Keough	.70	.35	.20
134	Carl Morton	.70	.35	.20
135	Vada Pinson	.75	.40	.25
136	Darrel Chaney	.70	.35	.20
137	Dick Williams	.75	.40	.25

#	Card	NR MT	EX	VG
138	Mike Kekich	.70	.35	.20
139	Tim McCarver	.75	.40	.25
140	Pat Dobson	.70	.35	.20
141	Mets Rookies (Buzz Capra, Jon Matlack, Leroy Stanton)	.75	.40	.25
142	Chris Chambliss	1.00	.50	.30
143	Garry Jestadt	.70	.35	.20
144	Marty Pattin	.70	.35	.20
145	Don Kessinger	.75	.40	.25
146	Steve Kealey	.70	.35	.20
147	Dave Kingman	2.50	1.25	.70
148	Dick Billings	.70	.35	.20
149	Gary Neibauer	.70	.35	.20
150	Norm Cash	.75	.40	.25
151	Jim Brewer	.70	.35	.20
152	Gene Clines	.70	.35	.20
153	Rick Auerbach	.70	.35	.20
154	Ted Simmons	1.25	.60	.40
155	Larry Dierker	.70	.35	.20
156	Twins Team	.75	.40	.25
157	Don Gullett	.75	.40	.25
158	Jerry Kenney	.70	.35	.20
159	John Boccabella	.70	.35	.20
160	Andy Messersmith	.75	.40	.25
161	Brock Davis	.70	.35	.20
162	Brewers Rookies (Jerry Bell, Darrell Porter, Bob Reynolds) (Porter and Bell photos transposed)	.75	.40	.25
163	Tug McGraw	1.00	.50	.30
164	Tug McGraw IA	.75	.40	.25
165	Chris Speier	.70	.35	.20
166	Chris Speier IA	.70	.35	.20
167	Deron Johnson	.70	.35	.20
168	Deron Johnson IA	.70	.35	.20
169	Vida Blue	1.00	.50	.30
170	Vida Blue IA	.75	.40	.25
171	Darrell Evans	1.00	.50	.30
172	Darrell Evans IA	.75	.40	.25
173	Clay Kirby	.70	.35	.20
174	clay Kirby IA	.70	.35	.20
175	Tom Haller	.70	.35	.20
176	Tom Haller IA	.70	.35	.20
177	Paul Schaal	.70	.35	.20
178	Paul Schaal IA	.70	.35	.20
179	Dock Ellis	.70	.35	.20
180	Dock Ellis IA	.70	.35	.20
181	Ed Kranepool	.75	.40	.25
182	Ed Kranepool IA	.70	.35	.20
183	Bill Melton	.70	.35	.20
184	Bill Melton IA	.70	.35	.20
185	Ron Bryant	.70	.35	.20
186	Ron Bryant IA	.70	.35	.20
187	Gates Brown	.70	.35	.20
188	Frank Lucchesi	.70	.35	.20
189	Gene Tenace	.70	.35	.20
190	Dave Giusti	.70	.35	.20
191	Jeff Burroughs	.75	.40	.25
192	Cubs Team	.75	.40	.25
193	Kurt Bevacqua	.70	.35	.20
194	Fred Norman	.70	.35	.20
195	Orlando Cepeda	1.25	.60	.40
196	Mel Queen	.70	.35	.20
197	Johnny Briggs	.70	.35	.20
198	Dodgers Rookies (Charlie Hough, Bob O'Brien, Mike Strahler)	1.00	.50	.30
199	Mike Fiore	.70	.35	.20
200	Lou Brock	3.00	1.50	.90
201	Phil Roof	.70	.35	.20
202	Scipio Spinks	.70	.35	.20
203	Ron Blomberg	.70	.35	.20
204	Tommy Helms	.70	.35	.20
205	Dick Drago	.70	.35	.20
206	Dal Maxvill	.70	.35	.20
207	Tom Egan	.70	.35	.20
208	Milt Pappas	.75	.40	.25
209	Joe Rudi	.75	.40	.25
210	Denny McLain	1.00	.50	.30
211	Gary Sutherland	.70	.35	.20
212	Grant Jackson	.70	.35	.20
213	Angels Rookies (Art Kusnyer, Billy Parker, Tom Silverio)	.70	.35	.20
214	Mike McQueen	.70	.35	.20
215	Alex Johnson	.70	.35	.20
216	Joe Niekro	.75	.40	.25
217	Roger Metzger	.70	.35	.20
218	Eddie Kasko	.70	.35	.20
219	Rennie Stennett	.70	.35	.20
220	Jim Perry	.75	.40	.25
221	N.L. Playoffs	.75	.40	.25
222	A.L. Playoffs	.75	.40	.25
223	World Series Game 1	.75	.40	.25
224	World Series Game 2	.75	.40	.25
225	World Series Game 3	.75	.40	.25
226	World Series Game 4	1.25	.60	.40
227	World Series Game 5	.75	.40	.25
228	World Series Game 6	.75	.40	.25
229	World Series Game 7	.75	.40	.25
230	World Series Summary	.75	.40	.25
231	Casey Cox	.70	.35	.20
232	Giants Rookies (Chris Arnold, Jim Barr, Dave Rader)	.70	.35	.20
233	Jay Johnstone	.75	.40	.25
234	Ron Taylor	.70	.35	.20
235	Merv Rettenmund	.70	.35	.20
236	Jim McGlothlin	.70	.35	.20
237	Yankees Team	1.00	.50	.30
238	Leron Lee	.70	.35	.20
239	Tom Timmermann	.70	.35	.20
240	Rich Allen	1.25	.60	.40
241	Rollie Fingers	1.75	.90	.50
242	Don Mincher	.70	.35	.20
243	Frank Linzy	.70	.35	.20
244	Steve Braun	.70	.35	.20
245	Tommie Agee	.70	.35	.20
246	Tom Burgmeier	.70	.35	.20
247	Milt May	.70	.35	.20
248	Tom Bradley	.70	.35	.20
249	Harry Walker	.70	.35	.20
250	Boog Powell	1.00	.50	.30
251	Checklist 3	1.25	.60	.40
252	Ken Reynolds	.70	.35	.20
253	Sandy Alomar	.70	.35	.20
254	Boots Day	.70	.35	.20
255	Jim Lonborg	.75	.40	.25
256	George Foster	1.25	.60	.40
257	Tigers Rookies (Jim Foor, Tim Hosley, Paul Jata)	.70	.35	.20
258	Randy Hundley	.70	.35	.20
259	Sparky Lyle	.75	.40	.25
260	Ralph Garr	.70	.35	.20
261	Steve Mingori	.70	.35	.20
262	Padres Team	.75	.40	.25
263	Felipe Alou	.75	.40	.25
264	Tommy John	1.50	.70	.45
265	Wes Parker	.75	.40	.25
266	Bobby Bolin	.70	.35	.20
267	Dave Concepcion	1.50	.70	.45
268	A's Rookies (Dwain Anderson, Chris Floethe)	.70	.35	.20
269	Don Hahn	.70	.35	.20
270	Jim Palmer	3.00	1.50	.90
271	Ken Rudolph	.70	.35	.20
272	Mickey Rivers	.75	.40	.25
273	Bobby Floyd	.70	.35	.20
274	Al Severinsen	.70	.35	.20
275	Cesar Tovar	.70	.35	.20
276	Gene Mauch	.75	.40	.25
277	Elliot Maddox	.70	.35	.20
278	Dennis Higgins	.70	.35	.20
279	Larry Brown	.70	.35	.20
280	Willie McCovey	3.00	1.50	.90
281	Bill Parsons	.70	.35	.20
282	Astros Team	.75	.40	.25
283	Darrell Brandon	.70	.35	.20
284	Ike Brown	.70	.35	.20
285	Gaylord Perry	3.00	1.50	.90
286	Gene Alley	.70	.35	.20
287	Jim Hardin	.70	.35	.20
288	Johnny Jeter	.70	.35	.20
289	Syd O'Brien	.70	.35	.20
290	Sonny Siebert	.70	.35	.20
291	Hal McRae	.75	.40	.25
292	Hal McRae IA	.50	.25	.15
293	Danny Frisella	.70	.35	.20
294	Dan Frisella IA	.70	.35	.20
295	Dick Dietz	.70	.35	.20
296	Dick Dietz IA	.70	.35	.20
297	Claude Osteen	.70	.35	.20
298	Claude Osteen IA	.70	.35	.20
299	Hank Aaron	15.00	7.50	4.50
300	Hank Aaron IA	9.00	4.50	2.75
301	George Mitterwald	.70	.35	.20
302	George Mitterwald IA	.70	.35	.20
303	Joe Pepitone	.75	.40	.25
304	Joe Pepitone IA	.70	.35	.20
305	Ken Boswell	.70	.35	.20
306	Ken Boswell IA	.70	.35	.20
307	Steve Renko	.70	.35	.20
308	Steve Renko IA	.70	.35	.20
309	Roberto Clemente	15.00	7.50	4.50
310	Roberto Clemente IA	9.00	4.50	2.75
311	Clay Carroll	.70	.35	.20
312	Clay Carroll IA	.70	.35	.20
313	Luis Aparicio	2.00	1.00	.60
314	Luis Aparicio IA	1.00	.50	.30
315	Paul Splittorff	.70	.35	.20
316	Cardinals Rookies (Jim Bibby, Santiago Guzman, Jorge Roque)	.75	.40	.25
317	Rich Hand	.70	.35	.20
318	Sonny Jackson	.70	.35	.20
319	Aurelio Rodriguez	.70	.35	.20
320	Steve Blass	.70	.35	.20
321	Joe Lahoud	.70	.35	.20
322	Jose Pena	.70	.35	.20
323	Earl Weaver	.75	.40	.25
324	Mike Ryan	.70	.35	.20
325	Mel Stottlemyre	.75	.40	.25
326	Pat Kelly	.70	.35	.20
327	Steve Stone	1.00	.50	.30
328	Red Sox Team	1.00	.50	.30
329	Roy Foster	.70	.35	.20
330	Jim Hunter	2.50	1.25	.70
331	Stan Swanson	.70	.35	.20
332	Buck Martinez	.70	.35	.20
333	Steve Barber	.70	.35	.20
334	Rangers Rookies (Bill Fahey, Jim Mason, Tom Ragland)	.70	.35	.20
335	Bill Hands	.70	.35	.20
336	Marty Martinez	.70	.35	.20
337	Mike Kilkenny	.70	.35	.20
338	Bob Grich	.75	.40	.25
339	Ron Cook	.70	.35	.20
340	Roy White	.75	.40	.25
341	Boyhood Photo (Joe Torre)	.75	.40	.25
342	Boyhood Photo (Wilbur Wood)	.70	.35	.20
343	Boyhood Photo (Willie Stargell)	1.25	.60	.40
344	Boyhood Photo (Dave McNally)	.75	.40	.25
345	Boyhood Photo (Rick Wise)	.70	.35	.20
346	Boyhood Photo (Jim Fregosi)	.75	.40	.25
347	Boyhood Photo (Tom Seaver)	1.50	.70	.45
348	Boyhood Photo (Sal Bando)	.75	.40	.25
349	Al Fitzmorris	.70	.35	.20
350	Frank Howard	1.25	.60	.40
351	Braves Rookies (Jimmy Britton, Tom House, Rick Kester)	.70	.35	.20
352	Dave LaRoche	.70	.35	.20
353	Art Shamsky	.70	.35	.20
354	Tom Murphy	.70	.35	.20
355	Bob Watson	.70	.35	.20
356	Gerry Moses	.70	.35	.20
357	Woodie Fryman	.70	.35	.20
358	Sparky Anderson	.75	.40	.25
359	Don Pavletich	.70	.35	.20
360	Dave Roberts	.70	.35	.20
361	Mike Andrews	.70	.35	.20
362	Mets Team	1.00	.50	.30
363	Ron Klimkowski	.70	.35	.20
364	Johnny Callison	.75	.40	.25
365	Dick Bosman	.70	.35	.20
366	Jimmy Rosario	.70	.35	.20
367	Ron Perranoski	.70	.35	.20
368	Danny Thompson	.70	.35	.20
369	Jim LeFebvre	.70	.35	.20
370	Don Buford	.70	.35	.20
371	Denny LeMaster	.70	.35	.20
372	Royals Rookies (Lance Clemons, Monty Montgomery)	.70	.35	.20
373	John Mayberry	.70	.35	.20
374	Jack Heidemann	.70	.35	.20
375	Reggie Cleveland	.70	.35	.20
376	Andy Kosco	.70	.35	.20
377	Terry Harmon	.70	.35	.20
378	Checklist 4	1.50	.70	.45
379	Ken Berry	.70	.35	.20
380	Earl Williams	.70	.35	.20
381	White Sox Team	.75	.40	.25
382	Joe Gibbon	.70	.35	.20
383	Brant Alyea	.70	.35	.20
384	Dave Campbell	.70	.35	.20
385	Mickey Stanley	.70	.35	.20
386	Jim Colborn	.70	.35	.20
387	Horace Clarke	.70	.35	.20
388	Charlie Williams	.70	.35	.20
389	Bill Rigney	.70	.35	.20
390	Willie Davis	.75	.40	.25
391	Ken Sanders	.70	.35	.20
392	Pirates Rookies (Fred Cambria, Richie Zisk)	.75	.40	.25
393	Curt Motton	.70	.35	.20
394	Ken Forsch	.70	.35	.20
395	Matty Alou	.75	.40	.25
396	Paul Lindblad	.70	.35	.20
397	Phillies Team	.75	.40	.25
398	Larry Hisle	.75	.40	.25
399	Milt Wilcox	.75	.40	.25
400	Tony Oliva	1.25	.60	.40
401	Jim Nash	.70	.35	.20
402	Bobby Heise	.70	.35	.20
403	John Cumberland	.70	.35	.20
404	Jeff Torborg	.70	.35	.20
405	Ron Fairly	.75	.40	.25
406	George Hendrick	1.00	.50	.30
407	Chuck Taylor	.70	.35	.20
408	Jim Northrup	.70	.35	.20
409	Frank Baker	.70	.35	.20
410	Fergie Jenkins	1.25	.60	.40
411	Bob Montgomery	.70	.35	.20
412	Dick Kelley	.70	.35	.20
413	White Sox Rookies (Don Eddy, Dave Lemonds)	.70	.35	.20
414	Bob Miller	.70	.35	.20
415	Cookie Rojas	.70	.35	.20
416	Johnny Edwards	.70	.35	.20
417	Tom Hall	.70	.35	.20
418	Tom Shopay	.70	.35	.20
419	Jim Spencer	.70	.35	.20
420	Steve Carlton	15.00	7.50	4.50
421	Ellie Rodriguez	.70	.35	.20
422	Ray Lamb	.70	.35	.20
423	Oscar Gamble	.75	.40	.25
424	Bill Gogolewski	.70	.35	.20
425	Ken Singleton	.75	.40	.25
426	Ken Singleton IA	.70	.35	.20
427	Tito Fuentes	.70	.35	.20
428	Tito Fuentes IA	.70	.35	.20
429	Bob Robertson	.70	.35	.20
430	Bob Robertson IA	.70	.35	.20
431	Clarence Gaston	.70	.35	.20
432	Clarence Gaston IA	.70	.35	.20
433	Johnny Bench	20.00	10.00	6.00
434	Johnny Bench IA	6.00	3.00	1.75
435	Reggie Jackson	20.00	10.00	6.00
436	Reggie Jackson IA	6.00	3.00	1.75
437	Maury Wills	1.00	.50	.30
438	Maury Wills IA	.75	.40	.25
439	Billy Williams	2.50	1.25	.70
440	Billy Williams IA	1.25	.60	.40
441	Thurman Munson	12.00	6.00	3.50
442	Thurman Munson IA	4.00	2.00	1.25
443	Ken Henderson	.70	.35	.20
444	Ken Henderson IA	.70	.35	.20
445	Tom Seaver	15.00	7.50	4.50
446	Tom Seaver IA	9.00	4.50	2.75
447	Willie Stargell	3.00	1.50	.90
448	Willie Stargell IA	1.50	.70	.45
449	Bob Lemon	1.25	.60	.40
450	Mickey Lolich	1.00	.50	.30
451	Tony LaRussa	.75	.40	.25
452	Ed Herrmann	.70	.35	.20
453	Barry Lersch	.70	.35	.20
454	A's Team	1.00	.50	.30
455	Tommy Harper	.75	.40	.25
456	Mark Belanger	.75	.40	.25
457	Padres Rookies (Darcy Fast, Mike Ivie, Derrel Thomas)	.70	.35	.20
458	Aurelio Monteagudo	.70	.35	.20
459	Rick Renick	.70	.35	.20
460	Al Downing	.70	.35	.20
461	Tim Cullen	.70	.35	.20
462	Rickey Clark	.70	.35	.20
463	Bernie Carbo	.70	.35	.20
464	Jim Roland	.70	.35	.20
465	Gil Hodges	2.50	1.25	.70
466	Norm Miller	.70	.35	.20
467	Steve Kline	.70	.35	.20
468	Richie Scheinblum	.70	.35	.20
469	Ron Herbel	.70	.35	.20
470	Ray Fosse	.70	.35	.20
471	Luke Walker	.70	.35	.20
472	Phil Gagliano	.70	.35	.20
473	Dan McGinn	.70	.35	.20
474	Orioles Rookies (Don Baylor, Roric Harrison, Johnny Oates)	1.50	.70	.45
475	Gary Nolan	.70	.35	.20
476	Lee Richard	.70	.35	.20
477	Tom Phoebus	.70	.35	.20
478	Checklist 5	1.50	.70	.45
479	Don Shaw	.70	.35	.20
480	Lee May	.75	.40	.25
481	Billy Conigliaro	.70	.35	.20
482	Joe Hoerner	.70	.35	.20
483	Ken Suarez	.70	.35	.20
484	Lum Harris	.70	.35	.20
485	Phil Regan	.70	.35	.20
486	John Lowenstein	.70	.35	.20
487	Tigers Team	1.00	.50	.30

#	Player	NR MT	EX	VG
488	Mike Nagy	.70	.35	.20
489	Expos Rookies (Terry Humphrey, Keith Lampard)	.70	.35	.20
490	Dave McNally	.75	.40	.25
491	Boyhood Photos (Lou Piniella)	.75	.40	.25
492	Boyhood Photos (Mel Stottlemyre)	.75	.40	.25
493	Boyhood Photos (Bob Bailey)	.70	.35	.20
494	Boyhood Photos (Willie Horton)	.70	.35	.20
495	Boyhood Photos (Bill Melton)	.70	.35	.20
496	Boyhood Photos (Bud Harrelson)	.70	.35	.20
497	Boyhood Photos (Jim Perry)	.70	.35	.20
498	Boyhood Photos (Brooks Robinson)	1.25	.60	.40
499	Vicente Romo	.70	.35	.20
500	Joe Torre	1.00	.50	.30
501	Pete Hamm	.70	.35	.20
502	Jackie Hernandez	.70	.35	.20
503	Gary Peters	.70	.35	.20
504	Ed Spiezio	.70	.35	.20
505	Mike Marshall	.75	.40	.25
506	Indians Rookies (Terry Ley, Jim Moyer, Dick Tidrow)	.70	.35	.20
507	Fred Gladding	.70	.35	.20
508	Ellie Hendricks	.70	.35	.20
509	Don McMahon	.70	.35	.20
510	Ted Williams	3.00	1.50	.90
511	Tony Taylor	.70	.35	.20
512	Paul Popovich	.70	.35	.20
513	Lindy McDaniel	.70	.35	.20
514	Ted Sizemore	.70	.35	.20
515	Bert Blyleven	2.25	1.25	.70
516	Oscar Brown	.70	.35	.20
517	Ken Brett	.70	.35	.20
518	Wayne Garrett	.70	.35	.20
519	Ted Abernathy	.70	.35	.20
520	Larry Bowa	1.00	.50	.30
521	Alan Foster	.70	.35	.20
522	Dodgers Team	1.00	.50	.30
523	Chuck Dobson	.70	.35	.20
524	Reds Rookies (Ed Armbrister, Mel Behney)	.70	.35	.20
525	Carlos May	.75	.30	.20

1973 O-Pee-Chee

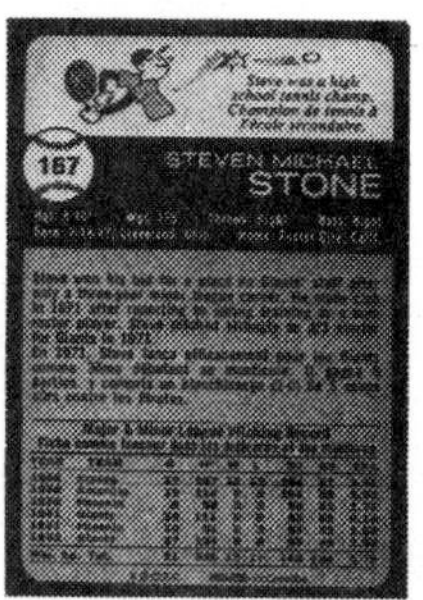

The 1973 Canadian-issued O-Pee-Chee set numbered 660 cards and is identical in design to the 1973 Topps set. The backs of the O-Pee-Chee cards are written in both French and English and contain the line "Printed in Canada" along the bottom. The cards measure 2-1/2" by 3-1/2"

	NR MT	EX	VG
Complete Set:	700.00	350.00	210.00
Common Player:	.40	.20	.12

#	Player	NR MT	EX	VG
1	All Time Home Run Leaders (Hank Aaron, Willie Mays, Babe Ruth)	7.50	2.50	1.50
2	Rich Hebner	.40	.20	.12
3	Jim Lonborg	.50	.25	.15
4	John Milner	.40	.20	.12
5	Ed Brinkman	.40	.20	.12
6	Mac Scarce	.40	.20	.12
7	Rangers Team	.75	.40	.25
8	Tom Hall	.40	.20	.12
9	Johnny Oates	.40	.20	.12
10	Don Sutton	1.20	.60	.35
11	Chris Chambliss	.60	.30	.20
12	Padres Mgr./Coaches (Dave Garcia, Johnny Podres, Bob Skinner, Whitey Wietelmann, Don Zimmer)	.40	.20	.12
13	George Hendrick	.60	.30	.20
14	Sonny Siebert	.40	.20	.12
15	Ralph Garr	.40	.20	.12
16	Steve Braun	.40	.20	.12
17	Fred Gladding	.40	.20	.12
18	Leroy Stanton	.40	.20	.12
19	Tim Foli	.40	.20	.12
20	Stan Bahnsen	.40	.20	.12
21	Randy Hundley	.40	.20	.12
22	Ted Abernathy	.40	.20	.12
23	Dave Kingman	1.00	.50	.30
24	Al Santorini	.40	.20	.12
25	Roy White	.50	.25	.15
26	Pirates Team	.75	.40	.25
27	Bill Gogolewski	.40	.20	.12
28	Hal McRae	.50	.25	.15
29	Tony Taylor	.40	.20	.12
30	Tug McGraw	.75	.40	.25
31	Buddy Bell	2.50	1.25	.70
32	Fred Norman	.40	.20	.12
33	Jim Breazeale	.40	.20	.12
34	Pat Dobson	.40	.20	.12
35	Willie Davis	.50	.25	.15
36	Steve Barber	.40	.20	.12
37	Bill Robinson	.40	.20	.12
38	Mike Epstein	.40	.20	.12
39	Dave Roberts	.40	.20	.12
40	Reggie Smith	.50	.25	.15
41	Tom Walker	.40	.20	.12
42	Mike Andrews	.40	.20	.12
43	Randy Moffitt	.40	.20	.12
44	Rick Monday	.50	.25	.15
45	Ellie Rodriguez	.40	.20	.12
46	Lindy McDaniel	.40	.20	.12
47	Luis Melendez	.40	.20	.12
48	Paul Splittorff	.40	.20	.12
49	Twins Mgr./Coaches (Vern Morgan, Frank Quilici, Bob Rodgers, Ralph Rowe, Al Worthington)	.40	.20	.12
50	Roberto Clemente	12.00	6.00	3.50
51	Chuck Seelbach	.40	.20	.12
52	Denis Menke	.40	.20	.12
53	Steve Dunning	.40	.20	.12
54	Checklist 1	1.00	.50	.30
55	Jon Matlack	.50	.25	.15
56	Merv Rettenmund	.40	.20	.12
57	Derrel Thomas	.40	.20	.12
58	Mike Paul	.40	.20	.12
59	Steve Yeager	.50	.25	.15
60	Ken Holtzman	.50	.25	.15
61	Batting Leaders (Rod Carew, Billy Williams)	1.25	.60	.40
62	Home Run Leaders (Dick Allen, Johnny Bench)	1.00	.50	.30
63	Runs Batted In Leaders (Dick Allen, Johnny Bench)	1.00	.50	.30
64	Stolen Base Leaders (Lou Brock, Bert Campaneris)	.75	.40	.25
65	Earned Run Average Leaders (Steve Carlton, Luis Tiant)	.75	.40	.25
66	Victory Leaders (Steve Carlton, Gaylord Perry, Wilbur Wood)	1.00	.50	.30
67	Strikeout Leaders (Steve Carlton, Nolan Ryan)	2.00	1.00	.60
68	Leading Firemen (Clay Carroll, Sparky Lyle)	.50	.25	.15
69	Phil Gagliano	.40	.20	.12
70	Milt Pappas	.50	.25	.15
71	Johnny Briggs	.40	.20	.12
72	Ron Reed	.40	.20	.12
73	Ed Herrmann	.40	.20	.12
74	Billy Champion	.40	.20	.12
75	Vada Pinson	.50	.25	.15
76	Doug Rader	.40	.20	.12
77	Mike Torrez	.50	.25	.15
78	Richie Scheinblum	.40	.20	.12
79	Jim Willoughby	.40	.20	.12
80	Tony Oliva	1.00	.50	.30
81	Cubs Mgr./Coaches (Hank Aguirre, Ernie Banks, Larry Jansen, Whitey Lockman, Pete Reiser)	.40	.20	.12
82	Fritz Peterson	.40	.20	.12
83	Leron Lee	.40	.20	.12
84	Rollie Fingers	1.25	.60	.40
85	Ted Simmons	1.00	.50	.30
86	Tom McCraw	.40	.20	.12
87	Ken Boswell	.40	.20	.12
88	Mickey Stanley	.40	.20	.12
89	Jack Billingham	.40	.20	.12
90	Brooks Robinson	3.00	1.50	.90
91	Dodgers Team	1.00	.50	.30
92	Jerry Bell	.40	.20	.12
93	Jesus Alou	.40	.20	.12
94	Dick Billings	.40	.20	.12
95	Steve Blass	.40	.20	.12
96	Doug Griffin	.40	.20	.12
97	Willie Montanez	.40	.20	.12
98	Dick Woodson	.40	.20	.12
99	Carl Taylor	.40	.20	.12
100	Hank Aaron	15.00	7.50	4.50
101	Ken Henderson	.40	.20	.12
102	Rudy May	.40	.20	.12
103	Celerino Sanchez	.40	.20	.12
104	Reggie Cleveland	.40	.20	.12
105	Carlos May	.40	.20	.12
106	Terry Humphrey	.40	.20	.12
107	Phil Hennigan	.40	.20	.12
108	Bill Russell	.50	.25	.15
109	Doyle Alexander	.75	.40	.25
110	Bob Watson	.40	.20	.12
111	Dave Nelson	.40	.20	.12
112	Gary Ross	.40	.20	.12
113	Jerry Grote	.40	.20	.12
114	Lynn McGlothen	.40	.20	.12
115	Ron Santo	.75	.40	.25
116	Yankees Mgr./Coaches (Jim Hegan, Ralph Houk, Elston Howard, Dick Howser, Jim Turner)	.50	.25	.15
117	Ramon Hernandez	.40	.20	.12
118	John Mayberry	.40	.20	.12
119	Larry Bowa	.75	.40	.25
120	Joe Coleman	.40	.20	.12
121	Dave Rader	.40	.20	.12
122	Jim Strickland	.40	.20	.12
123	Sandy Alomar	.40	.20	.12
124	Jim Hardin	.40	.20	.12
125	Ron Fairly	.50	.25	.15
126	Jim Brewer	.40	.20	.12
127	Brewers Team	.75	.40	.25
128	Ted Sizemore	.40	.20	.12
129	Terry Forster	.50	.25	.15
130	Pete Rose	15.00	7.50	4.50
131	Red Sox Mgr./Coaches (Doug Camilli, Eddie Kasko, Don Lenhardt, Eddie Popowski, Lee Stange)	.40	.20	.12
132	Matty Alou	.50	.25	.15
133	Dave Roberts	.40	.20	.12
134	Milt Wilcox	.40	.20	.12
135	Lee May	.50	.25	.15
136	Orioles Mgr./Coaches (George Bamberger, Jim Frey, Billy Hunter, George Staller, Earl Weaver)	.75	.40	.25
137	Jim Beauchamp	.40	.20	.12
138	Horacio Pina	.40	.20	.12
139	Carmen Fanzone	.40	.20	.12
140	Lou Piniella	.75	.40	.25
141	Bruce Kison	.40	.20	.12
142	Thurman Munson	4.00	2.00	1.25
143	John Curtis	.40	.20	.12
144	Marty Perez	.40	.20	.12
145	Bobby Bonds	.75	.40	.25
146	Woodie Fryman	.40	.20	.12
147	Mike Anderson	.40	.20	.12
148	Dave Goltz	.50	.25	.15
149	Ron Hunt	.40	.20	.12
150	Wilbur Wood	.50	.25	.15
151	Wes Parker	.50	.25	.15
152	Dave May	.40	.20	.12
153	Al Hrabosky	.50	.25	.15
154	Jeff Torborg	.40	.20	.12
155	Sal Bando	.50	.25	.15
156	Cesar Geronimo	.40	.20	.12
157	Denny Riddleberger	.40	.20	.12
158	Astros Team	.75	.40	.25
159	Clarence Gaston	.40	.20	.12
160	Jim Palmer	3.00	1.50	.90
161	Ted Martinez	.40	.20	.12
162	Pete Broberg	.40	.20	.12
163	Vic Davalillo	.40	.20	.12
164	Monty Montgomery	.40	.20	.12
165	Luis Aparicio	1.75	.90	.50
166	Terry Harmon	.40	.20	.12
167	Steve Stone	.50	.25	.15
168	Jim Northrup	.40	.20	.12
169	Ron Schueler	.40	.20	.12
170	Harmon Killebrew	2.50	1.25	.70
171	Bernie Carbo	.40	.20	.12
172	Steve Kline	.40	.20	.12
173	Hal Breeden	.40	.20	.12
174	Rich Gossage	4.00	2.00	1.25
175	Frank Robinson	2.50	1.25	.70
176	Chuck Taylor	.40	.20	.12
177	Bill Plummer	.40	.20	.12
178	Don Rose	.40	.20	.12
179	A's Mgr./Coaches (Jerry Adair, Vern Hoscheit, Irv Noren, Wes Stock, Dick Williams)	.50	.25	.15
180	Fergie Jenkins	1.25	.60	.40
181	Jack Brohamer	.40	.20	.12
182	Mike Caldwell	.50	.25	.15
183	Don Buford	.40	.20	.12
184	Jerry Koosman	.50	.25	.15
185	Jim Wynn	.50	.25	.15
186	Bill Fahey	.40	.20	.12
187	Luke Walker	.40	.20	.12
188	Cookie Rojas	.40	.20	.12
189	Grg Luzinski	.75	.40	.25
190	Bob Gibson	2.50	1.25	.70
191	Tigers Team	1.00	.50	.30
192	Pat Jarvis	.40	.20	.12
193	Carlton Fisk	2.50	1.25	.70
194	Jorge Orta	.40	.20	.12
195	Clay Carroll	.40	.20	.12
196	Ken McMullen	.40	.20	.12
197	Ed Goodson	.40	.20	.12
198	Horace Clarke	.40	.20	.12
199	Bert Blyleven	1.25	.60	.40
200	Billy Williams	1.75	.90	.50
201	A.L. Playoffs (Hendrick Scores Winning Run)	.75	.40	.25
202	N.L. Playoffs (Foster's Run Decides It)	.75	.40	.25
203	World Series Game 1 (Tenace The Menace)	.75	.40	.25
204	World Series Game 2 (A's Make It Two Straight)	.75	.40	.25
205	World Series Game 3 (Reds Win Squeeker)	.75	.40	.25
206	World Series Game 4 (Tenace Singles In Ninth)	.75	.40	.25
207	World Series Game 5 (Odom Out At Plate)	.75	.40	.25
208	World Series Game 6 (Reds' Slugging Ties Series)	.75	.40	.25
209	World Series Game 7 (Campy Starts Winning Rally)	.75	.40	.25
210	World Series Summary (World Champions)	.75	.40	.25
211	Balor Moore	.40	.20	.12
212	Joe Lahoud	.40	.20	.12
213	Steve Garvey	12.00	6.00	3.50
214	Dave Hamilton	.40	.20	.12
215	Dusty Baker	.50	.25	.15
216	Toby Harrah	.50	.25	.15
217	Don Wilson	.40	.20	.12
218	Aurelio Rodriguez	.40	.20	.12
219	Cardinals Team	.75	.40	.25
220	Nolan Ryan	18.00	9.00	5.50
221	Fred Kendall	.40	.20	.12
222	Rob Gardner	.40	.20	.12
223	Bud Harrelson	.50	.25	.15
224	Bill Lee	.40	.20	.12
225	Al Oliver	1.00	.50	.30
226	Ray Fosse	.40	.20	.12
227	Wayne Twitchell	.40	.20	.12
228	Bobby Darwin	.40	.20	.12
229	Roric Harrison	.40	.20	.12
230	Joe Morgan	2.00	1.00	.60
231	Bill Parsons	.40	.20	.12
232	Ken Singleton	.50	.25	.15
233	Ed Kirkpatrick	.40	.20	.12
234	Bill North	.40	.20	.12
235	Jim Hunter	2.00	1.00	.60
236	Tito Fuentes	.40	.20	.12
237	Braves Mgr./Coaches (Lew Burdette, Jim Busby, Roy Hartsfield, Eddie Mathews, Ken Silvestri)	1.00	.50	.30
238	Tony Muser	.40	.20	.12
239	Pete Richert	.40	.20	.12
240	Bobby Murcer	.50	.25	.15
241	Dwain Anderson	.40	.20	.12
242	George Culver	.40	.20	.12
243	Angels Team	.75	.40	.25
244	Ed Acosta	.40	.20	.12
245	Carl Yastrzemski	15.00	7.50	4.50
246	Ken Sanders	.40	.20	.12
247	Del Unser	.40	.20	.12

		NR MT	EX	VG
248	Jerry Johnson	.40	.20	.12
249	Larry Biittner	.40	.20	.12
250	Manny Sanguillen	.40	.20	.12
251	Roger Nelson	.40	.20	.12
252	Giants Mgr./Coaches (Joe Amalfitano, Charlie Fox, Andy Gilbert, Don McMahon, John McNamara)	.40	.20	.12
253	Mark Belanger	.50	.25	.15
254	Bill Stoneman	.40	.20	.12
255	Reggie Jackson	15.00	7.50	4.50
256	Chris Zachary	.40	.20	.12
257	Mets Mgr./Coaches (Yogi Berra, Roy McMillan, Joe Pignatano, Rube Walker, Eddie Yost)	1.00	.50	.30
258	Tommy John	1.25	.60	.40
259	Jim Holt	.40	.20	.12
260	Gary Nolan	.40	.20	.12
261	Pat Kelly	.40	.20	.12
262	Jack Aker	.40	.20	.12
263	George Scott	.40	.20	.12
264	Checklist 2	1.00	.50	.30
265	Gene Michael	.50	.25	.15
266	Mike Lum	.40	.20	.12
267	Lloyd Allen	.40	.20	.12
268	Jerry Morales	.40	.20	.12
269	Tim McCarver	.75	.40	.25
270	Luis Tiant	.75	.40	.25
271	Tom Hutton	.40	.20	.12
272	Ed Farmer	.40	.20	.12
273	Chris Speier	.40	.20	.12
274	Darold Knowles	.40	.20	.12
275	Tony Perez	1.25	.60	.40
276	Joe Lovitto	.40	.20	.12
277	Bob Miller	.40	.20	.12
278	Orioles Team	.75	.40	.25
279	Mike Strahler	.40	.20	.12
280	Al Kaline	3.00	1.50	.90
281	Mike Jorgensen	.40	.20	.12
282	Steve Hovley	.40	.20	.12
283	Ray Sadecki	.40	.20	.12
284	Glenn Borgmann	.40	.20	.12
285	Don Kessinger	.50	.25	.15
286	Frank Linzy	.40	.20	.12
287	Eddie Leon	.40	.20	.12
288	Gary Gentry	.40	.20	.12
289	Bob Oliver	.40	.20	.12
290	Cesar Cedeno	.50	.25	.15
291	Rogelio Moret	.40	.20	.12
292	Jose Cruz	.50	.25	.15
293	Bernie Allen	.40	.20	.12
294	Steve Arlin	.40	.20	.12
295	Bert Campaneris	.50	.25	.15
296	Reds Mgr./Coaches (Sparky Anderson, Alex Grammas, Ted Kluszewski, George Scherger, Larry Shepard)	.50	.25	.15
297	Walt Williams	.40	.20	.12
298	Ron Bryant	.40	.20	.12
299	Ted Ford	.40	.20	.12
300	Steve Carlton	12.00	6.00	3.50
301	Billy Grabarkewitz	.40	.20	.12
302	Terry Crowley	.40	.20	.12
303	Nelson Briles	.40	.20	.12
304	Duke Sims	.40	.20	.12
305	Willie Mays	15.00	7.50	4.50
306	Tom Burgmeier	.40	.20	.12
307	Boots Day	.40	.20	.12
308	Skip Lockwood	.40	.20	.12
309	Paul Popovich	.40	.20	.12
310	Dick Allen	.75	.40	.25
311	Joe Decker	.40	.20	.12
312	Oscar Brown	.40	.20	.12
313	Jim Ray	.40	.20	.12
314	Ron Swoboda	.40	.20	.12
315	John Odom	.40	.20	.12
316	Padres Team	.75	.40	.25
317	Danny Cater	.40	.20	.12
318	Jim McGlothlin	.40	.20	.12
319	Jim Spencer	.40	.20	.12
320	Lou Brock	2.75	1.50	.80
321	Rich Hinton	.40	.20	.12
322	Garry Maddox	.75	.40	.25
323	Tigers Mgr./Coaches (Art Fowler, Billy Martin, Charlie Silvera, Dick Tracewski)	1.00	.50	.30
324	Al Downing	.40	.20	.12
325	Boog Powell	.75	.40	.25
326	Darrell Brandon	.40	.20	.12
327	John Lowenstein	.40	.20	.12
328	Bill Bonham	.40	.20	.12
329	Ed Kranepool	.50	.25	.15
330	Rod Carew	18.00	9.00	5.50
331	Carl Morton	.40	.20	.12
332	John Felske	.40	.20	.12
333	Gene Clines	.40	.20	.12
334	Freddie Patek	.40	.20	.12
335	Bob Tolan	.40	.20	.12
336	Tom Bradley	.40	.20	.12
337	Dave Duncan	.40	.20	.12
338	Checklist 3	1.00	.50	.30
339	Dick Tidrow	.40	.20	.12
340	Nate Colbert	.40	.20	.12
341	Boyhood Photo (Jim Palmer)	1.00	.50	.30
342	Boyhood Photo (Sam McDowell)	.50	.25	.15
343	Boyhood Photo (Bobby Murcer)	.50	.25	.15
344	Boyhood Photo (Jim Hunter)	1.00	.50	.30
345	Boyhood Photo (Chris Speier)	.40	.20	.12
346	Boyhood Photo (Gaylord Perry)	1.00	.50	.30
347	Royals Team	.75	.40	.25
348	Rennie Stennett	.40	.20	.12
349	Dick McAuliffe	.40	.20	.12
350	Tom Seaver	12.00	6.00	3.50
351	Jimmy Stewart	.40	.20	.12
352	Don Stanhouse	.40	.20	.12
353	Steve Brye	.40	.20	.12
354	Billy Parker	.40	.20	.12
355	Mike Marshall	.50	.25	.15
356	White Sox Mgr./Coaches (Joe Lonnett, Jim Mahoney, Al Monchak, Johnny Sain, Chuck Tanner)	.50	.25	.15
357	Ross Grimsley	.40	.20	.12
358	Jim Nettles	.40	.20	.12
359	Cecil Upshaw	.40	.20	.12
360	Joe Rudi (photo actually Gene Tenace)	.50	.25	.15
361	Fran Healy	.40	.20	.12
362	Eddie Watt	.40	.20	.12
363	Jackie Hernandez	.40	.20	.12
364	Rick Wise	.40	.20	.12
365	Rico Petrocelli	.50	.25	.15
366	Brock Davis	.40	.20	.12
367	Burt Hooton	.50	.25	.15
368	Bill Buckner	.75	.40	.25
369	Lerrin laGrow	.40	.20	.12
370	Willie Stargell	2.50	1.25	.70
371	Mike Kekich	.40	.20	.12
372	Oscar Gamble	.40	.20	.12
373	Clyde Wright	.40	.20	.12
374	Darrell Evans	.75	.40	.25
375	Larry Dierker	.40	.20	.12
376	Frank Duffy	.40	.20	.12
377	Expos Mgr./Coaches (Dave Bristol, Larry Doby, Gene Mauch, Cal McLish, Jerry Zimmerman)	.50	.25	.15
378	Lenny Randle	.40	.20	.12
379	Cy Acosta	.40	.20	.12
380	Johnny Bench	12.00	6.00	3.50
381	Vicente Romo	.40	.20	.12
382	Mike Hegan	.40	.20	.12
383	Diego Segui	.40	.20	.12
384	Don Baylor	1.00	.50	.30
385	Jim Perry	.50	.25	.15
386	Don Money	.40	.20	.12
387	Jim Barr	.40	.20	.12
388	Ben Oglivie	.50	.25	.15
389	Mets Team	1.00	.50	.30
390	Mickey Lolich	.75	.40	.25
391	Lee Lacy	.50	.25	.15
392	Dick Drago	.40	.20	.12
393	Jose Cardenal	.40	.20	.12
394	Sparky Lyle	.50	.25	.15
395	Roger Metzger	.40	.20	.12
396	Grant Jackson	.40	.20	.12
397	Dave Cash	.40	.20	.12
398	Rich Hand	.40	.20	.12
399	George Foster	1.25	.60	.40
400	Gaylord Perry	2.00	1.00	.60
401	Clyde Mashore	.40	.20	.12
402	Jack Hiatt	.40	.20	.12
403	Sonny Jackson	.40	.20	.12
404	Chuck Brinkman	.40	.20	.12
405	Cesar Tovar	.40	.20	.12
406	Paul Lindblad	.40	.20	.12
407	Felix Millan	.40	.20	.12
408	Jim Colborn	.40	.20	.12
409	Ivan Murrell	.40	.20	.12
410	Willie McCovey	2.75	1.50	.80
411	Ray Corbin	.40	.20	.12
412	Manny Mota	.50	.25	.15
413	Tom Timmermann	.40	.20	.12
414	Ken Rudolph	.40	.20	.12
415	Marty Pattin	.40	.20	.12
416	Paul Schaal	.40	.20	.12
417	Scipio Spinks	.40	.20	.12
418	Bobby Grich	.50	.25	.15
419	Casey Cox	.40	.20	.12
420	Tommie Agee	.40	.20	.12
421	Angels Mgr./Coaches (Tom Morgan, Salty Parker, Jimmie Reese, John Roseboro, Bobby Winkles)	.40	.20	.12
422	Bob Robertson	.40	.20	.12
423	Johnny Jeter	.40	.20	.12
424	Denny Doyle	.40	.20	.12
425	Alex Johnson	.40	.20	.12
426	Dave Laroche	.40	.20	.12
427	Rick Auerbach	.40	.20	.12
428	Wayne Simpson	.40	.20	.12
429	Jim Fairey	.40	.20	.12
430	Vida Blue	.75	.40	.25
431	Gerry Moses	.40	.20	.12
432	Dan Frisella	.40	.20	.12
433	Willie Horton	.50	.25	.15
434	Giants Team	.75	.40	.25
435	Rico Carty	.50	.25	.15
436	Jim McAndrew	.40	.20	.12
437	John Kennedy	.40	.20	.12
438	Enzo Hernandez	.40	.20	.12
439	Eddie Fisher	.40	.20	.12
440	Glenn Beckert	.50	.25	.15
441	Gail Hopkins	.40	.20	.12
442	Dick Dietz	.40	.20	.12
443	Danny Thompson	.40	.20	.12
444	Ken Brett	.40	.20	.12
445	Ken Berry	.40	.20	.12
446	Jerry Reuss	.50	.25	.15
447	Joe Hague	.40	.20	.12
448	John Hiller	.35	.20	.11
449	Indians Mgr./Coaches (Ken Aspromonte, Rocky Colavito, Joe Lutz, Warren Spahn)	.40	.20	.12
450	Joe Torre	.75	.40	.25
451	John Vukovich	.40	.20	.12
452	Paul Casanova	.40	.20	.12
453	Checklist 4	1.00	.50	.30
454	Tom Haller	.40	.20	.12
455	Bill Melton	.40	.20	.12
456	Dick Green	.40	.20	.12
457	John Strohmayer	.40	.20	.12
458	Jim Mason	.40	.20	.12
459	Jimmy Howarth	.40	.20	.12
460	Bill Freehan	.50	.25	.15
461	Mike Corkins	.40	.20	.12
462	Ron Blomberg	.40	.20	.12
463	Ken Tatum	.40	.20	.12
464	Cubs Team	.75	.40	.25
465	Dave Giusti	.40	.20	.12
466	Jose Arcia	.40	.20	.12
467	Mike Ryan	.40	.20	.12
468	Tom Griffin	.40	.20	.12
469	Dan Monzon	.40	.20	.12
470	Mike Cuellar	.50	.25	.15
471	Hit Leader (Ty Cobb)	2.00	1.00	.60
472	Grand Slam Leader (Lou Gehrig)	2.00	1.00	.60
473	Total Bases Leader (Hank Aaron)	2.00	1.00	.60
474	R.B.I. Leader (Babe Ruth)	3.00	1.50	.90
475	Batting Leader (Ty Cobb)	2.00	1.00	.60
476	Shutout Leader (Walter Johnson)	1.00	.50	.30
477	Victory Leader (Cy Young)	1.00	.50	.30
478	Strikeout Leader (Walter Johnson)	1.00	.50	.30
479	Hal Lanier	.50	.25	.15
480	Juan Marichal	2.50	1.25	.70
481	White Sox Team	.75	.40	.25
482	Rick Reuschel	1.25	.60	.40
483	Dal Maxvill	.40	.20	.12
484	Ernie McAnally	.40	.20	.12
485	Norm Cash	.75	.40	.25
486	Phillies Mgr./Coaches (Carroll Beringer, Billy DeMars, Danny Ozark, Ray Rippelmeyer, Bobby Wine)	.40	.20	.12
487	Bruce Dal Canton	.40	.20	.12
488	Dave Campbell	.40	.20	.12
489	Jeff Burroughs	.50	.25	.15
490	Claude Osteen	.40	.20	.12
491	Bob Montgomery	.40	.20	.12
492	Pedro Borbon	.40	.20	.12
493	Duffy Dyer	.40	.20	.12
494	Rich Morales	.40	.20	.12
495	Tommy Helms	.40	.20	.12
496	Ray Lamb	.40	.20	.12
497	Cardinals Mgr./Coaches (Vern Benson, George Kissell, Red Schoendienst, Barney Schultz)	.50	.25	.15
498	Graig Nettles	1.50	.70	.45
499	Bob Moose	.40	.20	.12
500	A's Team	1.00	.50	.30
501	Larry Gura	.40	.20	.12
502	Bobby Valentine	.50	.25	.15
503	Phil Niekro	2.00	1.00	.60
504	Earl Williams	.40	.20	.12
505	Bob Bailey	.40	.20	.12
506	Bart Johnson	.40	.20	.12
507	Darrel Chaney	.40	.20	.12
508	Gates Brown	.40	.20	.12
509	Jim Nash	.40	.20	.12
510	Amos Otis	.40	.20	.12
511	Sam McDowell	.50	.25	.15
512	Dalton Jones	.40	.20	.12
513	Dave Marshall	.40	.20	.12
514	Jerry Kenney	.40	.20	.12
515	Andy Messersmith	.50	.25	.15
516	Danny Walton	.40	.20	.12
517	Pirates Mgr./Coaches (Don Leppert, Bill Mazeroski, Dave Ricketts, Bill Virdon, Mel Wright)	.50	.25	.15
518	Bob Veale	.40	.20	.12
519	John Edwards	.40	.20	.12
520	Mel Stottlemyre	.50	.25	.15
521	Braves Team	.75	.40	.25
522	Leo Cardenas	.40	.20	.12
523	Wayne Granger	.40	.20	.12
524	Gene Tenace	.40	.20	.12
525	Jim Fregosi	.50	.25	.15
526	Ollie Brown	.40	.20	.12
527	Dan McGinn	.40	.20	.12
528	Paul Blair	.50	.25	.15
529	Milt May	.40	.20	.12
530	Jim Kaat	2.00	1.00	.60
531	Ron Woods	.40	.20	.12
532	Steve Mingori	.40	.20	.12
533	Larry Stahl	.40	.20	.12
534	Dave Lemonds	.40	.20	.12
535	John Callison	.50	.25	.15
536	Phillies Team	.75	.40	.25
537	Bill Slayback	.40	.20	.12
538	Jim Hart	.40	.20	.12
539	Tom Murphy	.40	.20	.12
540	Cleon Jones	.40	.20	.12
541	Bob Bolin	.40	.20	.12
542	Pat Corrales	.40	.20	.12
543	Alan Foster	.40	.20	.12
544	Von Joshua	.40	.20	.12
545	Orlando Cepeda	2.00	1.00	.60
546	Jim York	.40	.20	.12
547	Bobby Heise	.40	.20	.12
548	Don Durham	.40	.20	.12
549	Rangers Mgr./Coaches (Chuck Estrada, Whitey Herzog, Chuck Hiller, Jackie Moore)	.50	.25	.15
550	Dave Johnson	.75	.40	.25
551	Mike Kilkenny	.40	.20	.12
552	J.C. Martin	.40	.20	.12
553	Mickey Scott	.40	.20	.12
554	Dave Concepcion	.75	.40	.25
555	Bill Hands	.40	.20	.12
556	Yankees Team	1.25	.60	.40
557	Bernie Williams	.40	.20	.12
558	Jerry May	.40	.20	.12
559	Barry Lersch	.40	.20	.12
560	Frank Howard	1.00	.50	.30
561	Jim Geddes	.40	.20	.12
562	Wayne Garrett	.40	.20	.12
563	Larry Haney	.40	.20	.12
564	Mike Thompson	.40	.20	.12
565	Jim Hickman	.40	.20	.12
566	Lew Krausse	.40	.20	.12
567	Bob Fenwick	.40	.20	.12
568	Ray Newman	.40	.20	.12
569	Dodgers Mgr./Coaches (Red Adams, Walt Alston, Monty Basgall, Jim Gilliam, Tom Lasorda)	1.25	.60	.40
570	Bill Singer	.40	.20	.12
571	Rusty Torres	.40	.20	.12
572	Gary Sutherland	.40	.20	.12
573	Fred Beene	.40	.20	.12
574	Bob Didier	.40	.20	.12
575	Dock Ellis	.40	.20	.12
576	Expos Team	.75	.40	.25
577	Eric Soderholm	.40	.20	.12
578	Ken Wright	.40	.20	.12
579	Tom Grieve	.40	.20	.12
580	Joe Pepitone	.50	.25	.15

		NR MT	EX	VG
581	Steve Kealey	.40	.20	.12
582	Darrell Porter	.50	.25	.15
583	Bill Grief	.40	.20	.12
584	Chris Arnold	.40	.20	.12
585	Joe Niekro	.50	.25	.15
586	Bill Sudakis	.40	.20	.12
587	Rich McKinney	.40	.20	.12
588	Checklist 5	5.00	2.50	1.50
589	Ken Forsch	.40	.20	.12
590	Deron Johnson	.40	.20	.12
591	Mike Hedlund	.40	.20	.12
592	John Boccabella	.40	.20	.12
593	Royals Mgr./Coaches (Galen Cisco, Harry Dunlop, Charlie Lau, Jack McKeon)	.40	.20	.12
594	Vic Harris	.40	.20	.12
595	Don Gullett	.40	.20	.12
596	Red Sox Team	1.00	.50	.30
597	Mickey Rivers	.50	.25	.15
598	Phil Roof	.40	.20	.12
599	Ed Crosby	.40	.20	.12
600	Dave McNally	.50	.25	.15
601	Rookie Catchers (George Pena, Sergio Robles, Rick Stelmaszek)	.40	.20	.12
602	Rookie Pitchers (Mel Behney, Ralph Garcia, Doug Rau)	.40	.20	.12
603	Rookie Third Basemen (Terry Hughes, Bill McNulty, Ken Reitz)	.40	.20	.12
604	Rookie Pitchers (Jesse Jefferson, Dennis O'Toole, Bob Strampe)	.40	.20	.12
605	Rookie First Basemen (Pat Bourque, Enos Cabell, Gonzalo Marquez)	.40	.20	.12
606	Rookie Outfielders (Gary Matthews, Tom Paciorek, Jorge Roque)	1.75	.90	.50
607	Rookie Shortstops (Ray Busse, Pepe Frias, Mario Guerrero)	.40	.20	.12
608	Rookie Pitchers (Steve Busby, Dick Colpaert, George Medich)	.50	.25	.15
609	Rookie Second Basemen (Larvell Blanks, Pedro Garcia, Dave Lopes)	1.75	.90	.50
610	Rookie Pitchers (Jimmy Freeman, Charlie Hough, Hank Webb)	.75	.40	.25
611	Rookie Outfielders (Rich Coggins, Jim Wohlford, Richie Zisk)	.75	.40	.25
612	Rookie Pitchers (Steve Lawson, Bob Reynolds, Brent Strom)	.40	.20	.12
613	Rookie Catchers (Bob Boone, Mike Ivie, Skip Jutze)	2.25	1.25	.70
614	Rookie Outfielders (Alonza Bumbry, Dwight Evans, Charlie Spikes)	30.00	15.00	9.00
615	Rookie Third Basemen (Ron Cey, John Hilton, Mike Schmidt)	300.00	150.00	90.00
616	Rookie Pitchers (Norm Angelini, Steve Blateric, Mike Garman)	.40	.20	.12
617	Rich Chiles	.40	.20	.12
618	Andy Etchebarren	.40	.20	.12
619	Billy Wilson	.40	.20	.12
620	Tommy Harper	.40	.20	.12
621	Joe Ferguson	.50	.25	.15
622	Larry Hisle	.50	.25	.15
623	Steve Renko	.40	.20	.12
624	Astros Mgr./Coaches (Leo Durocher, Preston Gomez, Grady Hatton, Hub Kittle, Jim Owens)	.75	.40	.25
625	Angel Mangual	.40	.20	.12
626	Bob Barton	.40	.20	.12
627	Luis Alvardo	.40	.20	.12
628	Jim Slaton	.35	.20	.11
629	Indians Team	.75	.40	.25
630	Denny McLain	1.00	.50	.30
631	Tom Matchick	.40	.20	.12
632	Dick Selma	.40	.20	.12
633	Ike Brown	.40	.20	.12
634	Alan Closter	.40	.20	.12
635	Gene Alley	.40	.20	.12
636	Rick Clark	.40	.20	.12
637	Norm Miller	.40	.20	.12
638	Ken Reynolds	.40	.20	.12
639	Willie Crawford	.40	.20	.12
640	Dick Bosman	.40	.20	.12
641	Reds Team	.75	.40	.25
642	Jose LaBoy	.40	.20	.12
643	Al Fitzmorris	.40	.20	.12
644	Jack Heidemann	.40	.20	.12
645	Bob Locker	.40	.20	.12
646	Brewers Mgr./Coaches (Del Crandall, Harvey Kuenn, Joe Nossek, Bob Shaw, Jim Walton)	.50	.25	.15
647	George Stone	.40	.20	.12
648	Tom Egan	.40	.20	.12
649	Rich Folkers	.40	.20	.12
650	Felipe Alou	.50	.25	.15
651	Don Carrithers	.40	.20	.12
652	Ted Kubiak	.40	.20	.12
653	Joe Hoerner	.40	.20	.12
654	Twins Team	.75	.40	.25
655	Clay Kirby	.40	.20	.12
656	John Ellis	.40	.20	.12
657	Bob Johnson	.40	.20	.12
658	Elliott Maddox	.40	.20	.12
659	Jose Pagan	.40	.20	.12
660	Fred Scherman	.50	.15	.09

1973 O-Pee-Chee Team Checklists

Similar to the 1973 Topps Team Checklists cards, this set was produced in Canada. The set consists of 24 unnumbered cards (2-1/2" x 3-1/2") with blue borders. The card fronts contain facsimile autographs of players from the same team. The backs contain team checklists of players found in the 1973 O-Pee-Chee regular issue set. The card backs contain the French translation for Team Checklist plus a copyright line "O.P.C. Printed in Canada."

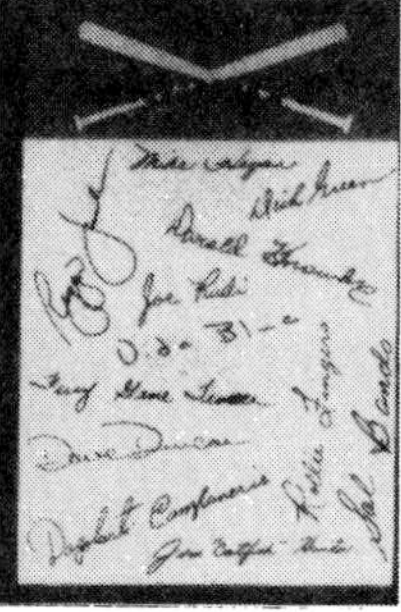

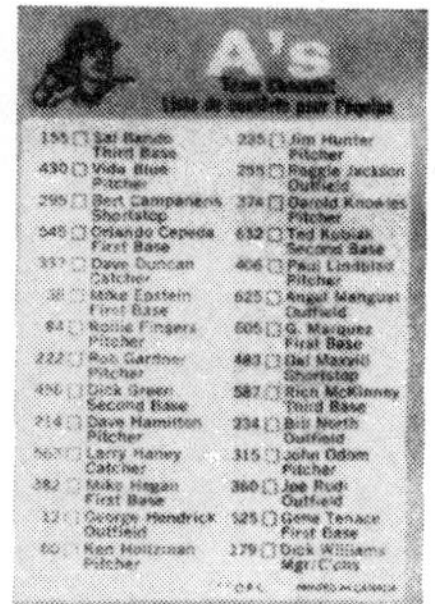

		NR MT	EX	VG
	Complete Set:	12.00	6.00	3.50
	Common Player:	.50	.25	.15
(1)	Atlanta Braves	.50	.25	.15
(2)	Baltimore Orioles	.50	.25	.15
(3)	Boston Red Sox	.50	.25	.15
(4)	California Angels	.50	.25	.15
(5)	Chicago Cubs	.50	.25	.15
(6)	Chicago White Sox	.50	.25	.15
(7)	Cincinnati Reds	.50	.25	.15
(8)	Cleveland Indians	.50	.25	.15
(9)	Detroit Tigers	.75	.40	.25
(10)	Houston Astros	.50	.25	.15
(11)	Kansas City Royals	.50	.25	.15
(12)	Los Angeles Dodgers	.50	.25	.15
(13)	Milwaukee Brewers	.50	.25	.15
(14)	Minnesota Twins	.50	.25	.15
(15)	Montreal Expos	.50	.25	.15
(16)	New York Mets	.75	.40	.25
(17)	New York Yankees	.50	.25	.15
(18)	Oakland A's	.75	.40	.25
(19)	Philadelphia Phillies	.50	.25	.15
(20)	Pittsburgh Pirates	.50	.25	.15
(21)	St. Louis Cardinals	.50	.25	.15
(22)	San Diego Padres	.50	.25	.15
(23)	San Francisco Giants	.50	.25	.15
(24)	Texas Rangers	.50	.25	.15

1974 O-Pee-Chee

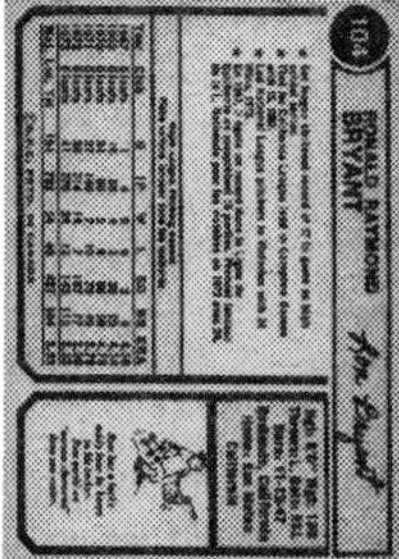

Again numbering 660 cards, the 1974 O-Pee-Chee set borrows its design from the Topps set of the same year. The cards measure the standard 2- 1/2" by 3-1/2" and the backs are printed in both French and English and state "Printed in Canada." Ten of the cards in the O-Pee-Chee set have fronts that differ from their corresponding Topps cards, including most of the Hank Aaron "specials" that lead off the set. And, because the O-Pee-Chee cards were printed later than the corresponding Topps cards, there are no "Washington, Nat'l. League" variations in the O-Pee-Chee set.

		NR MT	EX	VG
	Complete Set:	500.00	250.00	150.00
	Common Player:	.25	.13	.08
1	Hank Aaron	15.00	7.50	4.50
2	Aaron Special 1954-57	3.00	1.50	.90
3	Aaron Special 1958-59	9.00	4.50	2.75
4	Aaron Special 1960-61	9.00	4.50	2.75
5	Aaron Special 1962-63	9.00	4.50	2.75
6	Aaron Special 1964-65	9.00	4.50	2.75
7	Aaron Special 1966-67	9.00	4.50	2.75
8	Aaron Special 1968-69	9.00	4.50	2.75
9	Aaron Special 1970-73	3.00	1.50	.90
10	Johnny Bench	5.50	2.75	1.75
11	Jim Bibby	.30	.15	.09
12	Dave May	.25	.13	.08
13	Tom Hilgendorf	.25	.13	.08
14	Paul Popovich	.25	.13	.08
15	Joe Torre	.75	.40	.25
16	Orioles Team	.75	.40	.25
17	Doug Bird	.25	.13	.08
18	Gary Thomasson	.25	.13	.08
19	Gerry Moses	.25	.13	.08
20	Nolan Ryan	15.00	7.50	4.50
21	Bob Gallagher	.25	.13	.08
22	Cy Acosta	.25	.13	.08
23	Craig Robinson	.25	.13	.08
24	John Hiller	.30	.15	.09
25	Ken Singleton	.40	.20	.12
26	Bill Campbell	.25	.13	.08
27	George Scott	.30	.15	.09
28	Manny Sanguillen	.30	.15	.09
29	Phil Niekro	1.50	.70	.45
30	Bobby Bonds	.40	.20	.12
31	Astros Mgr./Coaches (Roger Craig, Preston Gomez, Grady Hatton, Hub Kittle, Bob Lillis)	.25	.13	.08
32	John Grubb	.25	.13	.08
33	Don Newhauser	.25	.13	.08
34	Andy Kosco	.25	.13	.08
35	Gaylord Perry	1.75	.90	.50
36	Cardinals Team	.75	.40	.25
37	Dave Sells	.25	.13	.08
38	Don Kessinger	.30	.15	.09
39	Ken Suarez	.25	.13	.08
40	Jim Palmer	2.75	1.50	.80
41	Bobby Floyd	.25	.13	.08
42	Claude Osteen	.30	.15	.09
43	Jim Wynn	.30	.15	.09
44	Mel Stottlemyre	.40	.20	.12
45	Dave Johnson	.50	.25	.15
46	Pat Kelly	.25	.13	.08
47	Dick Ruthven	.25	.13	.08
48	Dick Sharon	.25	.13	.08
49	Steve Renko	.25	.13	.08
50	Rod Carew	15.00	7.50	4.50
51	Bob Heise	.25	.13	.08
52	Al Oliver	1.00	.50	.30
53	Fred Kendall	.25	.13	.08
54	Elias Sosa	.25	.13	.08
55	Frank Robinson	2.50	1.25	.70
56	Mets Team	1.00	.50	.30
57	Darold Knowles	.25	.13	.08
58	Charlie Spikes	.25	.13	.08
59	Ross Grimsley	.30	.15	.09
60	Lou Brock	2.50	1.25	.70
61	Luis Aparicio	1.75	.90	.50
62	Bob Locker	.25	.13	.08
63	Bill Sudakis	.25	.13	.08
64	Doug Rau	.25	.13	.08
65	Amos Otis	.30	.15	.09
66	Sparky Lyle	.40	.20	.12
67	Tommy Helms	.25	.13	.08
68	Grant Jackson	.25	.13	.08
69	Del Unser	.25	.13	.08
70	Dick Allen	.75	.40	.25
71	Danny Frisella	.25	.13	.08
72	Aurelio Rodriguez	.25	.13	.08
73	Mike Marshall	.30	.15	.09
74	Twins Team	.75	.40	.25
75	Jim Colborn	.25	.13	.08
76	Mickey Rivers	.30	.15	.09
77	Rich Troedson	.25	.13	.08
78	Giants Mgr./Coaches (Joe Amalfitano, Charlie Fox, Andy Gilbert, Don McMahon, John McNamara)	.25	.13	.08
79	Gene Tenace	.30	.15	.09
80	Tom Seaver	9.00	4.50	2.75
81	Frank Duffy	.25	.13	.08
82	Dave Giusti	.25	.13	.08
83	Orlando Cepeda	1.00	.50	.30
84	Rick Wise	.30	.15	.09
85	Joe Morgan	1.75	.90	.50
86	Joe Ferguson	.25	.13	.08
87	Fergie Jenkins	1.00	.50	.30
88	Freddie Patek	.25	.13	.08
89	Jackie Brown	.25	.13	.08
90	Bobby Murcer	.50	.25	.15
91	Ken Forsch	.25	.13	.08
92	Paul Blair	.30	.15	.09
93	Rod Gilbreath	.25	.13	.08
94	Tigers Team	.75	.40	.25
95	Steve Carlton	9.00	4.50	2.75
96	Jerry Hairston	.25	.13	.08
97	Bob Bailey	.25	.13	.08
98	Bert Blyleven	1.00	.50	.30
99	George Theodore	1.00	.50	.30
100	Willie Stargell	2.00	1.00	.60
101	Bobby Valentine	.30	.15	.09
102	Bill Greif	.25	.13	.08
103	Sal Bando	.30	.15	.09
104	Ron Bryant	.25	.13	.08
105	Carlton Fisk	1.25	.60	.40
106	Harry Parker	.25	.13	.08
107	Alex Johnson	.25	.13	.08
108	Al Hrabosky	.30	.15	.09
109	Bob Grich	.40	.20	.12
110	Billy Williams	1.75	.90	.50
111	Clay Carroll	.30	.15	.09
112	Dave Lopes	.30	.15	.09
113	Dick Drago	.25	.13	.08
114	Angels Team	.75	.40	.25
115	Willie Horton	.30	.15	.09
116	Jerry Reuss	.30	.15	.09
117	Ron Blomberg	.25	.13	.08
118	Bill Lee	.30	.15	.09
119	Phillies Mgr./Coaches (Carroll Beringer, Billy DeMars, Danny Ozark, Ray Ripplemeyer, Bobby Wine)	.25	.13	.08
120	Wilbur Wood	.30	.15	.09
121	Larry Lintz	.25	.13	.08
122	Jim Holt	.25	.13	.08
123	Nelson Briles	.25	.13	.08
124	Bob Coluccio	.25	.13	.08
125	Nate Colbert	.25	.13	.08
126	Checklist 1	1.00	.50	.30
127	Tom Paciorek	.30	.15	.09
128	John Ellis	.25	.13	.08
129	Chris Speier	.30	.15	.09
130	Reggie Jackson	18.00	9.00	5.50
131	Bob Boone	.40	.20	.12
132	Felix Millan	.25	.13	.08
133	David Clyde	.30	.15	.09
134	Denis Menke	.25	.13	.08
135	Roy White	.30	.15	.09

#	Card	NR MT	EX	VG
136	Rick Reuschel	.75	.40	.25
137	Al Bumbry	.30	.15	.09
138	Ed Brinkman	.30	.15	.09
139	Aurelio Monteagudo	.25	.13	.08
140	Darrell Evans	.50	.25	.15
141	Pat Bourque	.25	.13	.08
142	Pedro Garcia	.25	.13	.08
143	Dick Woodson	.25	.13	.08
144	Dodgers Mgr./Coaches (Red Adams, Walter Alston, Monty Basgall, Jim Gilliam, Tom Lasorda)	1.25	.60	.40
145	Dock Ellis	.25	.13	.08
146	Ron Fairly	.30	.15	.09
147	Bart Johnson	.25	.13	.08
148	Dave Hilton	.25	.13	.08
149	Mac Scarce	.25	.13	.08
150	John Mayberry	.25	.13	.08
151	Diego Segui	.25	.13	.08
152	Oscar Gamble	.25	.13	.08
153	Jon Matlack	.30	.15	.09
154	Astros Team	.75	.40	.25
155	Bert Campaneris	.40	.20	.12
156	Randy Moffitt	.25	.13	.08
157	Vic Harris	.25	.13	.08
158	Jack Billingham	.25	.13	.08
159	Jim Ray Hart	.25	.13	.08
160	Brooks Robinson	2.50	1.25	.70
161	Ray Burris	.30	.15	.09
162	Bill Freehan	.40	.20	.12
163	Ken Berry	.25	.13	.08
164	Tom House	.30	.15	.09
165	Willie Davis	.40	.20	.12
166	Mickey Lolich	1.50	.70	.45
167	Luis Tiant	.50	.25	.15
168	Danny Thompson	.25	.13	.08
169	Steve Rogers	.50	.25	.15
170	Bill Melton	.25	.13	.08
171	Eduardo Rodriguez	.25	.13	.08
172	Gene Clines	.25	.13	.08
173	Randy Jones	.30	.15	.09
174	Bill Robinson	.25	.13	.08
175	Reggie Cleveland	.25	.13	.08
176	John Lowenstein	.25	.13	.08
177	Dave Roberts	.25	.13	.08
178	Garry Maddox	.30	.15	.09
179	Mets Mgr./Coaches (Yogi Berra, Roy McMillan, Joe Pignatano, Rube Walker, Eddie Yost)	1.00	.50	.30
180	Ken Holtzman	.30	.15	.09
181	Cesar Geronimo	.25	.13	.08
182	Lindy McDaniel	.25	.13	.08
183	Johnny Oates	.25	.13	.08
184	Rangers Team	.75	.40	.25
185	Jose Cardenal	.30	.15	.09
186	Fred Scherman	.25	.13	.08
187	Don Baylor	.75	.40	.25
188	Rudy Meoli	.25	.13	.08
189	Jim Brewer	.25	.13	.08
190	Tony Oliva	.75	.40	.25
191	Al Fitzmorris	.25	.13	.08
192	Mario Guerrero	.25	.13	.08
193	Tom Walker	.25	.13	.08
194	Darrell Porter	.30	.15	.09
195	Carlos May	.25	.13	.08
196	Jim Hunter	2.50	1.25	.70
197	Vicente Romo	.25	.13	.08
198	Dave Cash	.25	.13	.08
199	Mike Kekich	.25	.13	.08
200	Cesar Cedeno	.40	.20	.12
201	Batting Leaders (Rod Carew, Pete Rose)	2.50	1.25	.70
202	Home Run Leaders (Ken Boyer, Reggie Jackson, Willie Stargell)	1.75	.90	.50
203	Runs Batted In (Reggie Jackson, Willie Stargell)	1.75	.90	.50
204	Stolen Base Leaders (Lou Brock, Tommy Harper)	1.00	.50	.30
205	Victory Leaders (Ron Bryant, Wilbur Wood)	.40	.20	.12
206	Earned Run Average Leaders (Jim Palmer, Tom Seaver)	1.75	.90	.50
207	Strikeout Leaders (Nolan Ryan, Tom Seaver)	1.75	.90	.50
208	Leading Firemen (John Hiller, Mike Marshall)	.40	.20	.12
209	Ted Sizemore	.25	.13	.08
210	Bill Singer	.25	.13	.08
211	Cubs Team	.75	.40	.25
212	Rollie Fingers	1.25	.60	.40
213	Dave Rader	.25	.13	.08
214	Billy Grabarkewitz	.25	.13	.08
215	Al Kaline	2.50	1.25	.70
216	Ray Sadecki	.25	.13	.08
217	Tim Foli	.25	.13	.08
218	Johnny Briggs	.25	.13	.08
219	Doug Griffin	.25	.13	.08
220	Don Sutton	1.25	.60	.40
221	White Sox Mgr./Coaches (Joe Lonnett, Jim Mahoney, Alex Monchak, Johnny Sain, Chuck Tanner)	.30	.15	.09
222	Ramon Hernandez	.25	.13	.08
223	Jeff Burroughs	.30	.15	.09
224	Roger Metzger	.25	.13	.08
225	Paul Splittorff	.30	.15	.09
226	Padres Team	.75	.40	.25
227	Mike Lum	.25	.13	.08
228	Ted Kubiak	.25	.13	.08
229	Fritz Peterson	.25	.13	.08
230	Tony Perez	1.00	.50	.30
231	Dick Tidrow	.25	.13	.08
232	Steve Brye	.25	.13	.08
233	Jim Barr	.25	.13	.08
234	John Milner	.25	.13	.08
235	Dave McNally	.40	.20	.12
236	Cardinals Mgr./Coaches (Vern Benson, George Kissell, Johnny Lewis, Red Schoendienst, Barney Schultz)	.40	.20	.12
237	Ken Brett	.25	.13	.08
238	Fran Healy	.25	.13	.08
239	Bill Russell	.30	.15	.09
240	Joe Coleman	.25	.13	.08
241	Glenn Beckert	.30	.15	.09
242	Bill Gogolewski	.25	.13	.08
243	Bob Oliver	.25	.13	.08
244	Carl Morton	.25	.13	.08
245	Cleon Jones	.25	.13	.08
246	A's Team	1.00	.50	.30
247	Rick Miller	.25	.13	.08
248	Tom Hall	.25	.13	.08
249	George Mitterwald	.25	.13	.08
250	Willie McCovey	3.00	1.50	.90
251	Graig Nettles	1.25	.60	.40
252	Dave Parker	18.00	9.00	5.50
253	John Boccabella	.25	.13	.08
254	Stan Bahnsen	.25	.13	.08
255	Larry Bowa	.40	.20	.12
256	Tom Griffin	.25	.13	.08
257	Buddy Bell	.75	.40	.25
258	Jerry Morales	.25	.13	.08
259	Bob Reynolds	.25	.13	.08
260	Ted Simmons	.75	.40	.25
261	Jerry Bell	.25	.13	.08
262	Ed Kirkpatrick	.25	.13	.08
263	Checklist 2	1.00	.50	.30
264	Joe Rudi	.30	.15	.09
265	Tug McGraw	.40	.20	.12
266	Jim Northrup	.30	.15	.09
267	Andy Messersmith	.30	.15	.09
268	Tom Grieve	.25	.13	.08
269	Bob Johnson	.25	.13	.08
270	Ron Santo	.50	.25	.15
271	Bill Hands	.25	.13	.08
272	Paul Casanova	.25	.13	.08
273	Checklist 3	1.00	.50	.30
274	Fred Beene	.25	.13	.08
275	Ron Hunt	.25	.13	.08
276	Angels Mgr./Coaches (Tom Morgan, Salty Parker, Jimmie Reese, John Roseboro, Bobby Winkles)	.25	.13	.08
277	Gary Nolan	.25	.13	.08
278	Cookie Rojas	.30	.15	.09
279	Jim Crawford	.25	.13	.08
280	Carl Yastrzemski	18.00	9.00	5.50
281	Giants Team	.75	.40	.25
282	Doyle Alexander	.40	.20	.12
283	Mike Schmidt	60.00	30.00	18.00
284	Dave Duncan	.25	.13	.08
285	Reggie Smith	.40	.20	.12
286	Tony Muser	.25	.13	.08
287	Clay Kirby	.25	.13	.08
288	Gorman Thomas	1.00	.50	.30
289	Rick Auerbach	.25	.13	.08
290	Vida Blue	.40	.20	.12
291	Don Hahn	.25	.13	.08
292	Chuck Seelbach	.25	.13	.08
293	Milt May	.25	.13	.08
294	Steve Foucault	.25	.13	.08
295	Rick Monday	.30	.15	.09
296	Ray Corbin	.25	.13	.08
297	Hal Breeden	.25	.13	.08
298	Roric Harrison	.25	.13	.08
299	Gene Michael	.30	.15	.09
300	Pete Rose	18.00	9.00	5.50
301	Bob Montgomery	.25	.13	.08
302	Rudy May	.25	.13	.08
303	George Hendrick	.30	.15	.09
304	Don Wilson	.25	.13	.08
305	Tito Fuentes	.25	.13	.08
306	Orioles Mgr./Coaches (George Bamberger, Jim Frey, Billy Hunter, George Staller, Earl Weaver)	.50	.25	.15
307	Luis Melendez	.25	.13	.08
308	Bruce Dal Canton	.25	.13	.08
309	Dave Roberts	.25	.13	.08
310	Terry Forster	.30	.15	.09
311	Jerry Grote	.30	.15	.09
312	Deron Johnson	.25	.13	.08
313	Barry Lersch	.25	.13	.08
314	Brewers Team	.75	.40	.25
315	Ron Cey	.50	.25	.15
316	Jim Perry	.30	.15	.09
317	Richie Zisk	.30	.15	.09
318	Jim Merritt	.25	.13	.08
319	Randy Hundley	.25	.13	.08
320	Dusty Baker	.40	.20	.12
321	Steve Braun	.25	.13	.08
322	Ernie McAnally	.25	.13	.08
323	Richie Scheinblum	.25	.13	.08
324	Steve Kline	.25	.13	.08
325	Tommy Harper	.30	.15	.09
326	Reds Mgr./Coaches (Sparky Anderson, Alex Grammas, Ted Kluszewski, George Scherger, Larry Shepard)	.40	.20	.12
327	Tom Timmermann	.25	.13	.08
328	Skip Jutze	.25	.13	.08
329	Mark Belanger	.30	.15	.09
330	Juan Marichal	1.75	.90	.50
331	All-Star Catchers (Johnny Bench, Carlton Fisk)	1.50	.70	.45
332	All-Star First Basemen (Hank Aaron, Dick Allen)	1.50	.70	.45
333	All-Star Second Basemen (Rod Carew, Joe Morgan)	1.50	.70	.45
334	All-Star Third Baseman (Brooks Robinson, Ron Santo)	1.00	.50	.30
335	All-Star Shortstops (Bert Campaneris, Chris Speier)	.40	.20	.12
336	All-Star Left Fielders (Bobby Murcer, Pete Rose)	2.00	1.00	.60
337	All-Star Center Fielders (Cesar Cedeno, Amos Otis)	.40	.20	.12
338	All-Star Right Fielders (Reggie Jackson, Billy Williams)	1.50	.70	.45
339	All-Star Pitchers (Jim Hunter, Rick Wise)	.40	.20	.12
340	Thurman Munson	3.00	1.50	.90
341	Dan Driessen	.50	.25	.15
342	Jim Lonborg	.30	.15	.09
343	Royals Team	.75	.40	.25
344	Mike Caldwell	.25	.13	.08
345	Bill North	.25	.13	.08
346	Ron Reed	.25	.13	.08
347	Sandy Alomar	.25	.13	.08
348	Pete Richert	.25	.13	.08
349	John Vukovich	.25	.13	.08
350	Bob Gibson	1.75	.90	.50
351	Dwight Evans	2.50	1.25	.70
352	Bill Stoneman	.25	.13	.08
353	Rich Coggins	.25	.13	.08
354	Cubs Mgr./Coaches (Hank Aguirre, Whitey Lockman, Jim Marshall, J.C. Martin, Al Spangler)	.25	.13	.08
355	Dave Nelson	.25	.13	.08
356	Jerry Koosman	.40	.20	.12
357	Buddy Bradford	.25	.13	.08
358	Dal Maxvill	.25	.13	.08
359	Brent Strom	.25	.13	.08
360	Greg Luzinski	.75	.40	.25
361	Don Carrithers	.25	.13	.08
362	Hal King	.25	.13	.08
363	Yankees Team	1.00	.50	.30
364	Clarence Gaston	.25	.13	.08
365	Steve Busby	.30	.15	.09
366	Larry Hisle	.30	.15	.09
367	Norm Cash	.40	.20	.12
368	Manny Mota	.30	.15	.09
369	Paul Lindblad	.25	.13	.08
370	Bob Watson	.30	.15	.09
371	Jim Slaton	.25	.13	.08
372	Ken Reitz	.25	.13	.08
373	John Curtis	.25	.13	.08
374	Marty Perez	.25	.13	.08
375	Earl Williams	.25	.13	.08
376	Jorge Orta	.25	.13	.08
377	Ron Woods	.25	.13	.08
378	Burt Hooton	.30	.15	.09
379	Rangers Mgr./Coaches (Art Fowler, Frank Lucchesi, Billy Martin, Jackie Moore, Charlie Silvera)	.75	.40	.25
380	Bud Harrelson	.30	.15	.09
381	Charlie Sands	.25	.13	.08
382	Bob Moose	.25	.13	.08
383	Phillies Team	.75	.40	.25
384	Chris Chambliss	.40	.20	.12
385	Don Gullett	.30	.15	.09
386	Gary Matthews	.40	.20	.12
387	Rich Morales	.25	.13	.08
388	Phil Roof	.25	.13	.08
389	Gates Brown	.25	.13	.08
390	Lou Piniella	.50	.25	.15
391	Billy Champion	.25	.13	.08
392	Dick Green	.25	.13	.08
393	Orlando Pena	.25	.13	.08
394	Ken Henderson	.25	.13	.08
395	Doug Rader	.25	.13	.08
396	Tommy Davis	.40	.20	.12
397	George Stone	.25	.13	.08
398	Duke Sims	.25	.13	.08
399	Mike Paul	.25	.13	.08
400	Harmon Killebrew	2.00	1.00	.60
401	Elliot Maddox	.25	.13	.08
402	Jim Rooker	.25	.13	.08
403	Red Sox Mgr./Coaches (Don Bryant, Darrell Johnson, Eddie Popowski, Lee Stange, Don Zimmer)	.25	.13	.08
404	Jim Howarth	.25	.13	.08
405	Ellie Rodriguez	.25	.13	.08
406	Steve Arlin	.25	.13	.08
407	Jim Wohlford	.25	.13	.08
408	Charlie Hough	.40	.20	.12
409	Ike Brown	.25	.13	.08
410	Pedro Borbon	.25	.13	.08
411	Frank Baker	.25	.13	.08
412	Chuck Taylor	.25	.13	.08
413	Don Money	.25	.13	.08
414	Checklist 4	1.00	.50	.30
415	Gary Gentry	.25	.13	.08
416	White Sox Team	.75	.40	.25
417	Rich Folkers	.25	.13	.08
418	Walt Williams	.25	.13	.08
419	Wayne Twitchell	.25	.13	.08
420	Ray Fosse	.25	.13	.08
421	Dan Fife	.25	.13	.08
422	Gonzalo Marquez	.25	.13	.08
423	Fred Stanley	.25	.13	.08
424	Jim Beauchamp	.25	.13	.08
425	Pete Broberg	.25	.13	.08
426	Rennie Stennett	.25	.13	.08
427	Bobby Bolin	.25	.13	.08
428	Gary Sutherland	.25	.13	.08
429	Dick Lange	.25	.13	.08
430	Matty Alou	.40	.20	.12
431	Gene Garber	.40	.20	.12
432	Chris Arnold	.25	.13	.08
433	Lerrin LaGrow	.25	.13	.08
434	Ken McMullen	.25	.13	.08
435	Dave Concepcion	.50	.25	.15
436	Don Hood	.25	.13	.08
437	Jim Lyttle	.25	.13	.08
438	Ed Herrmann	.25	.13	.08
439	Norm Miller	.25	.13	.08
440	Jim Kaat	1.00	.50	.30
441	Tom Ragland	.25	.13	.08
442	Alan Foster	.25	.13	.08
443	Tom Hutton	.25	.13	.08
444	Vic Davalillo	.25	.13	.08
445	George Medich	.25	.13	.08
446	Len Randle	.25	.13	.08
447	Twins Mgr./Coaches (Vern Morgan, Frank Quilici, Bob Rodgers, Ralph Rowe)	.25	.13	.08
448	Ron Hodges	.25	.13	.08
449	Tom McCraw	.25	.13	.08
450	Rich Hebner	.25	.13	.08
451	Tommy John	1.25	.60	.40
452	Gene Hiser	.25	.13	.08
453	Balor Moore	.25	.13	.08
454	Kurt Bevacqua	.25	.13	.08
455	Tom Bradley	.25	.13	.08
456	Dave Winfield	35.00	17.50	10.50
457	Chuck Goggin	.25	.13	.08
458	Jim Ray	.25	.13	.08
459	Reds Team	.75	.40	.25
460	Boog Powell	.75	.40	.25
461	John Odom	.25	.13	.08
462	Luis Alvarado	.25	.13	.08
463	Pat Dobson	.25	.13	.08
464	Jose Cruz	.40	.20	.12
465	Dick Bosman	.25	.13	.08
466	Dick Billings	.25	.13	.08
467	Winston Llenas	.25	.13	.08
468	Pepe Frias	.25	.13	.08

No.	Card	NR MT	EX	VG
469	Joe Decker	.25	.13	.08
470	A.L. Playoffs	1.50	.70	.45
471	N.L. Playoffs	.75	.40	.25
472	World Series Game 1	.75	.40	.25
473	World Series Game 2	1.50	.70	.45
474	World Series Game 3	.75	.40	.25
475	World Series Game 4	.75	.40	.25
476	World Series Game 5	.75	.40	.25
477	World Series Game 6	1.50	.70	.45
478	World Series Game 7	.75	.40	.25
479	World Series Summary	.75	.40	.25
480	Willie Crawford	.25	.13	.08
481	Jerry Terrell	.25	.13	.08
482	Bob Didier	.25	.13	.08
483	Braves Team	.75	.40	.25
484	Carmen Fanzone	.25	.13	.08
485	Felipe Alou	.40	.20	.12
486	Steve Stone	.30	.15	.09
487	Ted Martinez	.25	.13	.08
488	Andy Etchebarren	.25	.13	.08
489	Pirates Mgr./Coaches (Don Leppert, Bill Mazeroski, Danny Murtaugh, Don Osborn, Bob Skinner)	.25	.13	.08
490	Vada Pinson	.40	.20	.12
491	Roger Nelson	.25	.13	.08
492	Mike Rogodzinski	.25	.13	.08
493	Joe Hoerner	.25	.13	.08
494	Ed Goodson	.25	.13	.08
495	Dick McAuliffe	.30	.15	.09
496	Tom Murphy	.25	.13	.08
497	Bobby Mitchell	.25	.13	.08
498	Pat Corrales	.30	.15	.09
499	Rusty Torres	.25	.13	.08
500	Lee May	.40	.20	.12
501	Eddie Leon	.25	.13	.08
502	Dave LaRoche	.25	.13	.08
503	Eric Soderholm	.25	.13	.08
504	Joe Niekro	.40	.20	.12
505	Bill Buckner	.50	.25	.15
506	Ed Farmer	.25	.13	.08
507	Larry Stahl	.25	.13	.08
508	Expos Team	.75	.40	.25
509	Jesse Jefferson	.25	.13	.08
510	Wayne Garrett	.25	.13	.08
511	Toby Harrah	.30	.15	.09
512	Joe Lahoud	.25	.13	.08
513	Jim Campanis	.25	.13	.08
514	Paul Schaal	.25	.13	.08
515	Willie Montanez	.30	.15	.09
516	Horacio Pina	.25	.13	.08
517	Mike Hegan	.25	.13	.08
518	Derrel Thomas	.25	.13	.08
519	Bill Sharp	.25	.13	.08
520	Tim McCarver	.50	.25	.15
521	Indians Mgr./Coaches (Ken Aspromonte, Clay Bryant, Tony Pacheco)	.25	.13	.08
522	J.R. Richard	.40	.20	.12
523	Cecil Cooper	1.25	.60	.40
524	Bill Plummer	.25	.13	.08
525	Clyde Wright	.25	.13	.08
526	Frank Tepedino	.25	.13	.08
527	Bobby Darwin	.25	.13	.08
528	Bill Bonham	.25	.13	.08
529	Horace Clarke	.25	.13	.08
530	Mickey Stanley	.25	.13	.08
531	Expos Mgr./Coaches (Dave Bristol, Larry Doby, Gene Mauch, Cal McLish, Jerry Zimmerman)	.25	.13	.08
532	Skip Lockwood	.25	.13	.08
533	Mike Phillips	.25	.13	.08
534	Eddie Watt	.25	.13	.08
535	Bob Tolan	.25	.13	.08
536	Duffy Dyer	.25	.13	.08
537	Steve Mingori	.25	.13	.08
538	Cesar Tovar	.25	.13	.08
539	Lloyd Allen	.25	.13	.08
540	Bob Robertson	.25	.13	.08
541	Indians Team	.75	.40	.25
542	Rich Gossage	1.50	.70	.45
543	Danny Cater	.25	.13	.08
544	Ron Schueler	.25	.13	.08
545	Billy Conigliaro	.25	.13	.08
546	Mike Corkins	.25	.13	.08
547	Glenn Borgmann	.25	.13	.08
548	Sonny Siebert	.25	.13	.08
549	Mike Jorgensen	.25	.13	.08
550	Sam McDowell	.30	.15	.09
551	Von Joshua	.25	.13	.08
552	Denny Doyle	.25	.13	.08
553	Jim Willoughby	.25	.13	.08
554	Tim Johnson	.25	.13	.08
555	Woodie Fryman	.25	.13	.08
556	Dave Campbell	.25	.13	.08
557	Jim McGlothlin	.25	.13	.08
558	Bill Fahey	.25	.13	.08
559	Darrel Chaney	.25	.13	.08
560	Mike Cuellar	.30	.15	.09
561	Ed Kranepool	.30	.15	.09
562	Jack Aker	.25	.13	.08
563	Hal McRae	.40	.20	.12
564	Mike Ryan	.25	.13	.08
565	Milt Wilcox	.30	.15	.09
566	Jackie Hernandez	.25	.13	.08
567	Red Sox Team	.75	.40	.25
568	Mike Torrez	.30	.15	.09
569	Rick Dempsey	.40	.20	.12
570	Ralph Garr	.30	.15	.09
571	Rich Hand	.25	.13	.08
572	Enzo Hernandez	.25	.13	.08
573	Mike Adams	.25	.13	.08
574	Bill Parsons	.25	.13	.08
575	Steve Garvey	18.00	9.00	5.50
576	Scipio Spinks	.25	.13	.08
577	Mike Sadek	.25	.13	.08
578	Ralph Houk	.30	.15	.09
579	Cecil Upshaw	.25	.13	.08
580	Jim Spencer	.25	.13	.08
581	Fred Norman	.25	.13	.08
582	Bucky Dent	.75	.40	.25
583	Marty Pattin	.25	.13	.08
584	Ken Rudolph	.25	.13	.08
585	Merv Rettenmund	.25	.13	.08
586	Jack Brohamer	.25	.13	.08
587	Larry Christenson	.25	.13	.08
588	Hal Lanier	.30	.15	.09
589	Boots Day	.25	.13	.08
590	Rogelio Moret	.25	.13	.08
591	Sonny Jackson	.25	.13	.08
592	Ed Bane	.25	.13	.08
593	Steve Yeager	.30	.15	.09
594	Lee Stanton	.25	.13	.08
595	Steve Blass	.25	.13	.08
596	Rookie Pitchers (Wayne Garland, Fred Holdsworth, Mark Littell, Dick Pole)	.40	.20	.12
597	Rookie Shortstops (Dave Chalk, John Gamble, Pete MacKanin, Manny Trillo)	.75	.40	.25
598	Rookie Outfielders (Dave Augustine, Ken Griffey, Steve Ontiveros, Jim Tyrone)	1.50	.70	.45
599	Rookie Pitchers (Ron Diorio, Dave Freisleben, Frank Riccelli, Greg Shanahan)	.25	.13	.08
600	Rookie Infielders (Ron Cash, Jim Cox, Bill Madlock, Reggie Sanders)	3.00	1.50	.90
601	Rookie Outfielders (Ed Armbrister, Rich Bladt, Brian Downing, Bake McBride)	1.00	.50	.30
602	Rookie Pitchers (Glenn Abbott, Rick Henninger, Craig Swan, Dan Vossler)	.40	.20	.12
603	Rookie Catchers (Barry Foote, Tom Lundstedt, Charlie Moore, Sergio Robles)	.30	.15	.09
604	Rookie Infielders (Terry Hughes, John Knox, Andy Thornton, Frank White)	1.50	.70	.45
605	Rookie Pitchers (Vic Albury, Ken Frailing, Kevin Kobel, Frank Tanana)	1.00	.50	.30
606	Rookie Outfielders (Jim Fuller, Wilbur Howard, Tommy Smith, Otto Velez)	.25	.13	.08
607	Rookie Shortstops (Leo Foster, Tom Heintzelman, Dave Rosello, Frank Taveras)	.25	.13	.08
608	Rookie Pitchers (Bob Apodaco, Dick Baney, John D'Acquisto, Mike Wallace)	.25	.13	.08
609	Rico Petrocelli	.30	.15	.09
610	Dave Kingman	.75	.40	.25
611	Rick Stelmaszek	.25	.13	.08
612	Luke Walker	.25	.13	.08
613	Dan Monzon	.25	.13	.08
614	Adrian Devine	.25	.13	.08
615	Rookie Pitchers (Johnny Jeter, Tom Underwood)			
616	Larry Gura	.25	.13	.08
617	Ted Ford	.25	.13	.08
618	Jim Mason	.25	.13	.08
619	Mike Anderson	.25	.13	.08
620	Al Downing	.30	.15	.09
621	Bernie Carbo	.25	.13	.08
622	Phil Gagliano	.25	.13	.08
623	Celerino Sanchez	.25	.13	.08
624	Bob Miller	.25	.13	.08
625	Ollie Brown	.25	.13	.08
626	Pirates Team	.75	.40	.25
627	Carl Taylor	.25	.13	.08
628	Ivan Murrell	.25	.13	.08
629	Rusty Staub	.50	.25	.15
630	Tommie Agee	.25	.13	.08
631	Steve Barber	.25	.13	.08
632	George Culver	.25	.13	.08
633	Dave Hamilton	.25	.13	.08
634	Braves Mgr./Coaches (Jim Busby, Eddie Mathews, Connie Ryan, Herm Starrette)	.75	.40	.25
635	John Edwards	.25	.13	.08
636	Dave Goltz	.25	.13	.08
637	Checklist 5	1.00	.50	.30
638	Ken Sanders	.25	.13	.08
639	Joe Lovitto	.25	.13	.08
640	Milt Pappas	.30	.15	.09
641	Chuck Brinkman	.25	.13	.08
642	Terry Harmon	.25	.13	.08
643	Dodgers Team	.75	.40	.25
644	Wayne Granger	.25	.13	.08
645	Ken Boswell	.25	.13	.08
646	George Foster	1.25	.60	.40
647	Juan Beniquez	.50	.25	.15
648	Terry Crowley	.25	.13	.08
649	Fernando Gonzalez	.25	.13	.08
650	Mike Epstein	.25	.13	.08
651	Leron Lee	.25	.13	.08
652	Gail Hopkins	.25	.13	.08
653	Bob Stinson	.25	.13	.08
654	Jesus Alou	.30	.15	.09
655	Mike Tyson	.25	.13	.08
656	Adrian Garrett	.25	.13	.08
657	Jim Shellenback	.25	.13	.08
658	Lee Lacy	.30	.15	.09
659	Joe Lis	.25	.13	.08
660	Larry Dierker	.40	.13	.08

1974 O-Pee-Chee Team Checklists

The 1974 O-Pee-Chee Team Checklists set is nearly identical to its Topps counterpart of the same year. Twenty-four unnumbered cards that measure 2-1/2" by 3-1/2" make up the set. The card fronts contain facsimile autographs while the backs carry a team checklist of players found in the regular issue O-Pee-Chee set of 1974. The cards have red borders and can be differentiated from the U.S. version by the "O.P.C. Printed in Canada" line on the back.

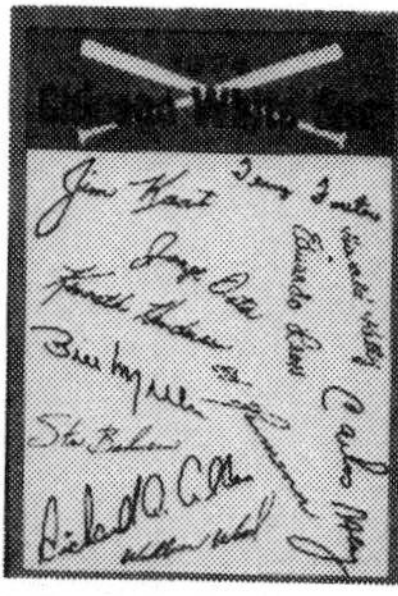

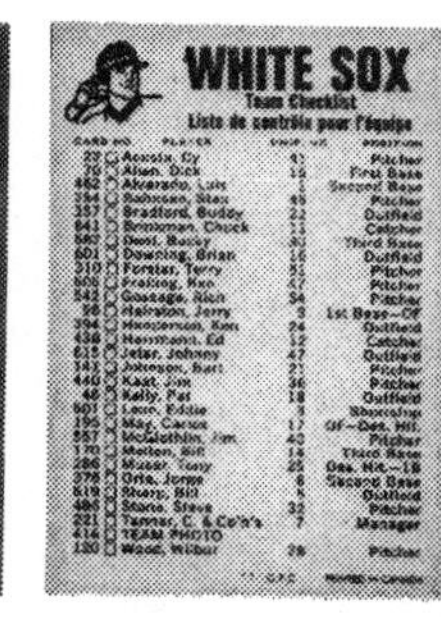

		NR MT	EX	VG
	Complete Set:	6.50	3.25	2.00
	Common Checklist:	.25	.13	.08
(1)	Atlanta Braves	.25	.13	.08
(2)	Baltimore Orioles	.25	.13	.08
(3)	Boston Red Sox	.25	.13	.08
(4)	California Angels	.25	.13	.08
(5)	Chicago Cubs	.25	.13	.08
(6)	Chicago White Sox	.25	.13	.08
(7)	Cincinnati Reds	.25	.13	.08
(8)	Cleveland Indians	.25	.13	.08
(9)	Detroit Tigers	.35	.20	.11
(10)	Houston Astros	.25	.13	.08
(11)	Kansas City Royals	.25	.13	.08
(12)	Los Anglees Dodgers	.35	.20	.11
(13)	Milwaukee Brewers	.25	.13	.08
(14)	Minnesota Twins	.25	.13	.08
(15)	Montreal Expos	.25	.13	.08
(16)	New York Mets	.35	.20	.11
(17)	New York Yankees	.35	.20	.11
(18)	Oakland A's	.35	.20	.11
(19)	Philadelphia Phillies	.25	.13	.08
(20)	Pittsburgh Pirates	.25	.13	.08
(21)	St. Louis Cardinals	.25	.13	.08
(22)	San Diego Padres	.25	.13	.08
(23)	San Francisco Giants	.25	.13	.08
(24)	Texas Rangers	.25	.13	.08

1975 O-Pee-Chee

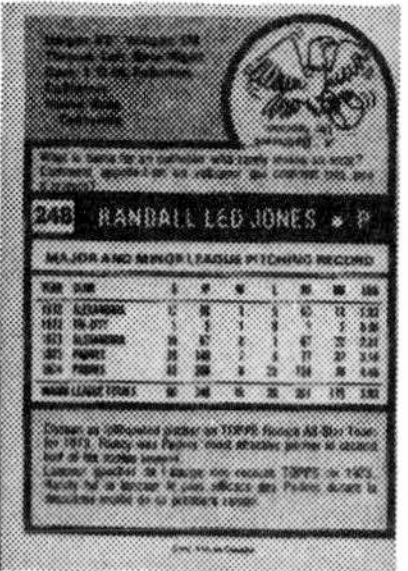

The 1975 O-Pee-Chee set was again complete at 660 cards, each measuring 2-1/2" by 3-1/2", and using the same design as the 1975 Topps set. The backs of the O-Pee-Chee cards are written in both French and English and state that the cards were printed in Canada.

		NR MT	EX	VG
	Complete Set:	750.00	375.00	225.00
	Common Player:	.20	.10	.06
1	'74 Highlights (Hank Aaron)	10.00	5.00	3.00
2	'74 Highlights (Lou Brock)	1.25	.60	.40
3	'74 Highlights (Bob Gibson)	1.25	.60	.40
4	'74 Highlights (Al Kaline)	1.25	.60	.40
5	'74 Highlights (Nolan Ryan)	1.75	.90	.50
6	'74 Highlights (Mike Marshall)	.30	.15	.09
7	'74 Highlights (Dick Bosman, Steve Busby, Nolan Ryan)	.75	.40	.25
8	Rogelio Moret	.20	.10	.06
9	Frank Tepedino	.20	.10	.06
10	Willie Davis	.30	.15	.09
11	Bill Melton	.20	.10	.06
12	David Clyde	.25	.13	.08
13	Gene Locklear	.20	.10	.06
14	Milt Wilcox	.25	.13	.08
15	Jose Cardenal	.25	.13	.08
16	Frank Tanana	.50	.25	.15
17	Dave Concepcion	.50	.25	.15
18	Tigers Team (Ralph Houk)	.75	.40	.25
19	Jerry Koosman	.40	.20	.12
20	Thurman Munson	3.50	1.75	1.00
21	Rollie Fingers	1.25	.60	.40
22	Dave Cash	.20	.10	.06
23	Bill Russell	.25	.13	.08
24	Al Fitzmorris	.20	.10	.06
25	Lee May	.30	.15	.09
26	Dave McNally	.30	.15	.09
27	Ken Reitz	.20	.10	.06
28	Tom Murphy	.20	.10	.06
29	Dave Parker	6.00	3.00	1.75
30	Bert Blyleven	.75	.40	.25

No.	Card	NR MT	EX	VG
31	Dave Rader	.20	.10	.06
32	Reggie Cleveland	.20	.10	.06
33	Dusty Baker	.30	.15	.09
34	Steve Renko	.20	.10	.06
35	Ron Santo	.40	.20	.12
36	Joe Lovitto	.20	.10	.06
37	Dave Freisleben	.20	.10	.06
38	Buddy Bell	.75	.40	.25
39	Andy Thornton	.60	.30	.20
40	Bill Singer	.20	.10	.06
41	Cesar Geronimo	.20	.10	.06
42	Joe Coleman	.20	.10	.06
43	Cleon Jones	.20	.10	.06
44	Pat Dobson	.25	.13	.08
45	Joe Rudi	.30	.15	.09
46	Phillies Team (Danny Ozark)	.60	.30	.20
47	Tommy John	1.00	.50	.30
48	Freddie Patek	.20	.10	.06
49	Larry Dierker	.20	.10	.06
50	Brooks Robinson	5.00	2.50	1.50
51	Bob Forsch	.75	.40	.25
52	Darrell Porter	.25	.13	.08
53	Dave Giusti	.20	.10	.06
54	Eric Soderholm	.20	.10	.06
55	Bobby Bonds	.40	.20	.12
56	Rick Wise	.25	.13	.08
57	Dave Johnson	.40	.20	.12
58	Chuck Taylor	.20	.10	.06
59	Ken Henderson	.20	.10	.06
60	Fergie Jenkins	1.00	.50	.30
61	Dave Winfield	8.00	4.00	2.50
62	Fritz Peterson	.20	.10	.06
63	Steve Swisher	.20	.10	.06
64	Dave Chalk	.20	.10	.06
65	Don Gullett	.25	.13	.08
66	Willie Horton	.20	.10	.06
67	Tug McGraw	.40	.20	.12
68	Ron Blomberg	.25	.13	.08
69	John Odom	.20	.10	.06
70	Mike Schmidt	25.00	12.50	7.50
71	Charlie Hough	.30	.15	.09
72	Royals Team (Jack McKeon)	.60	.30	.20
73	J.R. Richard	.30	.15	.09
74	Mark Belanger	.30	.15	.09
75	Ted Simmons	.60	.30	.20
76	Ed Sprague	.20	.10	.06
77	Richie Zisk	.25	.13	.08
78	Ray Corbin	.20	.10	.06
79	Gary Matthews	.30	.15	.09
80	Carlton Fisk	1.25	.60	.40
81	Ron Reed	.20	.10	.06
82	Pat Kelly	.20	.10	.06
83	Jim Merritt	.20	.10	.06
84	Enzo Hernandez	.20	.10	.06
85	Bill Bonham	.20	.10	.06
86	Joe Lis	.20	.10	.06
87	George Foster	1.00	.50	.30
88	Tom Egan	.20	.10	.06
89	Jim Ray	.20	.10	.06
90	Rusty Staub	.40	.20	.12
91	Dick Green	.20	.10	.06
92	Cecil Upshaw	.20	.10	.06
93	Dave Lopes	.30	.15	.09
94	Jim Lonborg	.25	.13	.08
95	John Mayberry	.25	.13	.08
96	Mike Cosgrove	.20	.10	.06
97	Earl Williams	.20	.10	.06
98	Rich Folkers	.20	.10	.06
99	Mike Hegan	.20	.10	.06
100	Willie Stargell	2.00	1.00	.60
101	Expos Team (Gene Mauch)	.60	.30	.20
102	Joe Decker	.20	.10	.06
103	Rick Miller	.20	.10	.06
104	Bill Madlock	1.25	.60	.40
105	Buzz Capra	.20	.10	.06
106	Mike Hargrove	.30	.15	.09
107	Jim Barr	.20	.10	.06
108	Tom Hall	.20	.10	.06
109	George Hendrick	.30	.15	.09
110	Wilbur Wood	.25	.13	.08
111	Wayne Garrett	.20	.10	.06
112	Larry Hardy	.20	.10	.06
113	Elliott Maddox	.20	.10	.06
114	Dick Lange	.20	.10	.06
115	Joe Ferguson	.20	.10	.06
116	Lerrin LaGrow	.20	.10	.06
117	Orioles Team (Earl Weaver)	.75	.40	.25
118	Mike Anderson	.20	.10	.06
119	Tommy Helms	.20	.10	.06
120	Steve Busby (photo actually Fran Healy)	.25	.13	.08
121	Bill North	.20	.10	.06
122	Al Hrabosky	.25	.13	.08
123	Johnny Briggs	.20	.10	.06
124	Jerry Reuss	.30	.15	.09
125	Ken Singleton	.30	.15	.09
126	Checklist 1-132	1.00	.50	.30
127	Glenn Borgmann	.20	.10	.06
128	Bill Lee	.25	.13	.08
129	Rick Monday	.30	.15	.09
130	Phil Niekro	1.50	.70	.45
131	Toby Harrah	.25	.13	.08
132	Randy Moffitt	.20	.10	.06
133	Dan Driessen	.30	.15	.09
134	Ron Hodges	.20	.10	.06
135	Charlie Spikes	.20	.10	.06
136	Jim Mason	.20	.10	.06
137	Terry Forster	.25	.13	.08
138	Del Unser	.20	.10	.06
139	Horacio Pina	.20	.10	.06
140	Steve Garvey	6.00	3.00	1.75
141	Mickey Stanley	.25	.13	.08
142	Bob Reynolds	.20	.10	.06
143	Cliff Johnson	.25	.13	.08
144	Jim Wohlford	.20	.10	.06
145	Ken Holtzman	.30	.15	.09
146	Padres Team (John McNamara)	.60	.30	.20
147	Pedro Garcia	.20	.10	.06
148	Jim Rooker	.20	.10	.06
149	Tim Foli	.20	.10	.06
150	Bob Gibson	2.00	1.00	.60
151	Steve Brye	.20	.10	.06
152	Mario Guerrero	.20	.10	.06
153	Rick Reuschel	.40	.20	.12
154	Mike Lum	.20	.10	.06
155	Jim Bibby	.25	.13	.08
156	Dave Kingman	1.00	.50	.30
157	Pedro Borbon	.20	.10	.06
158	Jerry Grote	.25	.13	.08
159	Steve Arlin	.20	.10	.06
160	Graig Nettles	1.25	.60	.40
161	Stan Bahnsen	.20	.10	.06
162	Willie Montanez	.20	.10	.06
163	Jim Brewer	.20	.10	.06
164	Mickey Rivers	.25	.13	.08
165	Doug Rader	.20	.10	.06
166	Woodie Fryman	.20	.10	.06
167	Rich Coggins	.20	.10	.06
168	Bill Greif	.20	.10	.06
169	Cookie Rojas	.25	.13	.08
170	Bert Campaneris	.40	.20	.12
171	Ed Kirkpatrick	.20	.10	.06
172	Red Sox Team (Darrell Johnson)	1.00	.50	.30
173	Steve Rogers	.30	.15	.09
174	Bake McBride	.25	.13	.08
175	Don Money	.25	.13	.08
176	Burt Hooton	.25	.13	.08
177	Vic Correll	.20	.10	.06
178	Cesar Tovar	.20	.10	.06
179	Tom Bradley	.20	.10	.06
180	Joe Morgan	2.00	1.00	.60
181	Fred Beene	.20	.10	.06
182	Don Hahn	.20	.10	.06
183	Mel Stottlemyre	.30	.15	.09
184	Jorge Orta	.20	.10	.06
185	Steve Carlton	6.00	3.00	1.75
186	Willie Crawford	.20	.10	.06
187	Denny Doyle	.20	.10	.06
188	Tom Griffin	.20	.10	.06
189	1951 - MVPs (Larry (Yogi) Berra, Roy Campanella)	1.25	.60	.40
190	1952 - MVPs (Hank Sauer, Bobby Shantz)	.40	.20	.12
191	1953 - MVPs (Roy Campanella, Al Rosen)	.75	.40	.25
192	1954 - MVPs (Yogi Berra, Willie Mays)	1.25	.60	.40
193	1955 - MVPs (Yogi Berra, Roy Campanella)	1.25	.60	.40
194	1956 - MVPs (Mickey Mantle, Don Newcombe)	2.50	1.25	.70
195	1957 - MVPs (Hank Aaron, Mickey Mantle)	5.00	2.50	1.50
196	1958 - MVPs (Ernie Banks, Jackie Jensen)	.75	.40	.25
197	1959 - MVPs (Ernie Banks, Nellie Fox)	.75	.40	.25
198	1960 - MVPs (Dick Groat, Roger Maris)	1.00	.50	.30
199	1961 - MVPs (Roger Maris, Frank Robinson)	1.25	.60	.40
200	1962- MVPs (Mickey Mantle, Maury Wills)	2.50	1.25	.70
201	1963 - MVPs (Elston Howard, Sandy Koufax)	1.25	.60	.40
202	1964 - MVPs (Ken Boyer, Brooks Robinson)	1.00	.50	.30
203	1965 - MVPs (Willie Mays, Zoilo Versalles)	1.00	.50	.30
204	1966 - MVPs (Bob Clemente, Frank Robinson)	1.25	.60	.40
205	1967 - MVPs (Orlando Cepeda, Carl Yastrzemski)	1.00	.50	.30
206	1968 - MVPs (Bob Gibson, Denny McLain)	1.00	.50	.30
207	1969 - MVPs (Harmon Killebrew, Willie McCovey)	1.25	.60	.40
208	1970 - MVPs (Johnny Bench, Boog Powell)	1.00	.50	.30
209	1971 - MVPs (Vida Blue, Joe Torre)	.40	.20	.12
210	1972 - MVPs (Rich Allen, Johnny Bench)	1.00	.50	.30
211	1973 - MVPs (Reggie Jackson, Pete Rose)	2.00	1.00	.60
212	1974 - MVPs (Jeff Burroughs, Steve Garvey)	.75	.40	.25
213	Oscar Gamble	.25	.13	.08
214	Harry Parker	.20	.10	.06
215	Bobby Valentine	.30	.15	.09
216	Giants Team (Wes Westrum)	.60	.30	.20
217	Lou Piniella	.50	.25	.15
218	Jerry Johnson	.20	.10	.06
219	Ed Herrmann	.20	.10	.06
220	Don Sutton	1.25	.60	.40
221	Aurelio Rodriquez (Rodriguez)	.25	.13	.08
222	Dan Spillner	.20	.10	.06
223	Robin Yount	100.00	50.00	30.00
224	Ramon Hernandez	.20	.10	.06
225	Bob Grich	.30	.15	.09
226	Bill Campbell	.20	.10	.06
227	Bob Watson	.25	.13	.08
228	George Brett	100.00	50.00	30.00
229	Barry Foote	.20	.10	.06
230	Jim Hunter	1.50	.70	.45
231	Mike Tyson	.20	.10	.06
232	Diego Segui	.20	.10	.06
233	Billy Grabarkewitz	.20	.10	.06
234	Tom Grieve	.20	.10	.06
235	Jack Billingham	.20	.10	.06
236	Angels Team (Dick Williams)	.60	.30	.20
237	Carl Morton	.20	.10	.06
238	Dave Duncan	.20	.10	.06
239	George Stone	.20	.10	.06
240	Garry Maddox	.30	.15	.09
241	Dick Tidrow	.20	.10	.06
242	Jay Johnstone	.30	.15	.09
243	Jim Kaat	1.00	.50	.30
244	Bill Buckner	.40	.20	.12
245	Mickey Lolich	.40	.20	.12
246	Cardinals Team (Red Schoendienst)	.60	.30	.20
247	Enos Cabell	.20	.10	.06
248	Randy Jones	.25	.13	.08
249	Danny Thompson	.20	.10	.06
250	Ken Brett	.20	.10	.06
251	Fran Healy	.20	.10	.06
252	Fred Scherman	.20	.10	.06
253	Jesus Alou	.25	.13	.08
254	Mike Torrez	.25	.13	.08
255	Dwight Evans	1.25	.60	.40
256	Billy Champion	.20	.10	.06
257	Checklist 133-264	1.00	.50	.30
258	Dave LaRoche	.20	.10	.06
259	Len Randle	.20	.10	.06
260	Johnny Bench	7.00	3.50	2.00
261	Andy Hassler	.20	.10	.06
262	Rowland Office	.20	.10	.06
263	Jim Perry	.25	.13	.08
264	John Milner	.20	.10	.06
265	Ron Bryant	.20	.10	.06
266	Sandy Alomar	.20	.10	.06
267	Dick Ruthven	.20	.10	.06
268	Hal McRae	.30	.15	.09
269	Doug Rau	.20	.10	.06
270	Ron Fairly	.25	.13	.08
271	Jerry Moses	.20	.10	.06
272	Lynn McGlothen	.20	.10	.06
273	Steve Braun	.20	.10	.06
274	Vicente Romo	.20	.10	.06
275	Paul Blair	.25	.13	.08
276	White Sox Team (Chuck Tanner)	.60	.30	.20
277	Frank Taveras	.20	.10	.06
278	Paul Lindblad	.20	.10	.06
279	Milt May	.20	.10	.06
280	Carl Yastrzemski	8.00	4.00	2.50
281	Jim Slaton	.20	.10	.06
282	Jerry Morales	.20	.10	.06
283	Steve Foucault	.20	.10	.06
284	Ken Griffey	.60	.30	.20
285	Ellie Rodriguez	.20	.10	.06
286	Mike Jorgensen	.20	.10	.06
287	Roric Harrison	.20	.10	.06
288	Bruce Ellingsen	.20	.10	.06
289	Ken Rudolph	.20	.10	.06
290	Jon Matlack	.25	.13	.08
291	Bill Sudakis	.20	.10	.06
292	Ron Schueler	.20	.10	.06
293	Dick Sharon	.20	.10	.06
294	Geoff Zahn	.30	.15	.09
295	Vada Pinson	.40	.20	.12
296	Alan Foster	.20	.10	.06
297	Craig Kusick	.20	.10	.06
298	Johnny Grubb	.25	.13	.08
299	Bucky Dent	.40	.20	.12
300	Reggie Jackson	10.00	5.00	3.00
301	Dave Roberts	.20	.10	.06
302	Rick Burleson	.40	.20	.12
303	Grant Jackson	.20	.10	.06
304	Pirates Team (Danny Murtaugh)	.60	.30	.20
305	Jim Colborn	.20	.10	.06
306	Batting Leaders (Rod Carew, Ralph Garr)	.55	.30	.15
307	Home Run Leaders (Dick Allen, Mike Schmidt)	.75	.40	.25
308	Runs Batted In (Johnny Bench, Jeff Burroughs)	.75	.40	.25
309	Stolen Base Leaders (Lou Brock, Bill North)	.75	.40	.25
310	Victory Leaders (Jim Hunter, Fergie Jenkins, Andy Messersmith, Phil Niekro)	.75	.40	.25
311	Earned Run Average Leaders (Buzz Capra, Jim Hunter)	.50	.25	.15
312	Strikeout Leaders (Steve Carlton, Nolan Ryan)	1.50	.70	.45
313	Leading Firemen (Terry Forster, Mike Marshall)	.40	.20	.12
314	Buck Martinez	.20	.10	.06
315	Don Kessinger	.25	.13	.08
316	Jackie Brown	.20	.10	.06
317	Joe Lahoud	.20	.10	.06
318	Ernie McAnally	.20	.10	.06
319	Johnny Oates	.20	.10	.06
320	Pete Rose	18.00	9.00	5.50
321	Rudy May	.20	.10	.06
322	Ed Goodson	.20	.10	.06
323	Fred Holdsworth	.20	.10	.06
324	Ed Kranepool	.30	.15	.09
325	Tony Oliva	.75	.40	.25
326	Wayne Twitchell	.20	.10	.06
327	Jerry Hairston	.20	.10	.06
328	Sonny Siebert	.20	.10	.06
329	Ted Kubiak	.20	.10	.06
330	Mike Marshall	.30	.15	.09
331	Indians Team (Frank Robinson)	.60	.30	.20
332	Fred Kendall	.20	.10	.06
333	Dick Drago	.20	.10	.06
334	Greg Gross	.20	.10	.06
335	Jim Palmer	5.00	2.50	1.50
336	Rennie Stennett	.20	.10	.06
337	Kevin Kobel	.20	.10	.06
338	Rick Stelmaszek	.20	.10	.06
339	Jim Fregosi	.30	.15	.09
340	Paul Splittorff	.25	.13	.08
341	Hal Breeden	.20	.10	.06
342	Leroy Stanton	.20	.10	.06
343	Danny Frisella	.20	.10	.06
344	Ben Oglivie	.30	.15	.09
345	Clay Carroll	.25	.13	.08
346	Bobby Darwin	.20	.10	.06
347	Mike Caldwell	.20	.10	.06
348	Tony Muser	.20	.10	.06
349	Ray Sadecki	.20	.10	.06
350	Bobby Murcer	.40	.20	.12
351	Bob Boone	.30	.15	.09
352	Darold Knowles	.20	.10	.06
353	Luis Melendez	.20	.10	.06
354	Dick Bosman	.20	.10	.06
355	Chris Cannizzaro	.20	.10	.06
356	Rico Petrocelli	.25	.13	.08
357	Ken Forsch	.20	.10	.06
358	Al Bumbry	.25	.13	.08

		NR MT	EX	VG
359	Paul Popovich	.20	.10	.06
360	George Scott	.30	.15	.09
361	Dodgers Team (Walter Alston)	.75	.40	.25
362	Steve Hargan	.20	.10	.06
363	Carmen Fanzone	.20	.10	.06
364	Doug Bird	.20	.10	.06
365	Bob Bailey	.20	.10	.06
366	Ken Sanders	.20	.10	.06
367	Craig Robinson	.20	.10	.06
368	Vic Albury	.20	.10	.06
369	Merv Rettenmund	.20	.10	.06
370	Tom Seaver	5.00	2.50	1.50
371	Gates Brown	.25	.13	.08
372	John D'Acquisto	.20	.10	.06
373	Bill Sharp	.20	.10	.06
374	Eddie Watt	.20	.10	.06
375	Roy White	.30	.15	.09
376	Steve Yeager	.20	.10	.06
377	Tom Hilgendorf	.20	.10	.06
378	Derrel Thomas	.20	.10	.06
379	Bernie Carbo	.20	.10	.06
380	Sal Bando	.30	.15	.09
381	John Curtis	.20	.10	.06
382	Don Baylor	.75	.40	.25
383	Jim York	.20	.10	.06
384	Brewers Team (Del Crandall)	.60	.30	.20
385	Dock Ellis	.20	.10	.06
386	Checklist 265-396	1.00	.50	.30
387	Jim Spencer	.20	.10	.06
388	Steve Stone	.25	.13	.08
389	Tony Solaita	.20	.10	.06
390	Ron Cey	.40	.20	.12
391	Don DeMola	.20	.10	.06
392	Bruce Bochte	.30	.15	.09
393	Gary Gentry	.20	.10	.06
394	Larvell Blanks	.20	.10	.06
395	Bud Harrelson	.25	.13	.08
396	Fred Norman	.20	.10	.06
397	Bill Freehan	.30	.15	.09
398	Elias Sosa	.20	.10	.06
399	Terry Harmon	.20	.10	.06
400	Dick Allen	.75	.40	.25
401	Mike Wallace	.20	.10	.06
402	Bob Tolan	.25	.13	.08
403	Tom Buskey	.20	.10	.06
404	Ted Sizemore	.20	.10	.06
405	John Montague	.20	.10	.06
406	Bob Gallagher	.20	.10	.06
407	Herb Washington	.30	.15	.09
408	Clyde Wright	.20	.10	.06
409	Bob Robertson	.20	.10	.06
410	Mike Cueller (Cuellar)	.30	.15	.09
411	George Mitterwald	.20	.10	.06
412	Bill Hands	.20	.10	.06
413	Marty Pattin	.20	.10	.06
414	Manny Mota	.30	.15	.09
415	John Hiller	.25	.13	.08
416	Larry Lintz	.20	.10	.06
417	Skip Lockwood	.20	.10	.06
418	Leo Foster	.20	.10	.06
419	Dave Goltz	.25	.13	.08
420	Larry Bowa	.40	.20	.12
421	Mets Team (Yogi Berra)	.75	.40	.25
422	Brian Downing	.30	.15	.09
423	Clay Kirby	.20	.10	.06
424	John Lowenstein	.20	.10	.06
425	Tito Fuentes	.20	.10	.06
426	George Medich	.25	.13	.08
427	Clarence Gaston	.20	.10	.06
428	Dave Hamilton	.20	.10	.06
429	Jim Dwyer	.20	.10	.06
430	Luis Tiant	.50	.25	.15
431	Rod Gilbreath	.20	.10	.06
432	Ken Berry	.20	.10	.06
433	Larry Demery	.20	.10	.06
434	Bob Locker	.20	.10	.06
435	Dave Nelson	.20	.10	.06
436	Ken Frailing	.20	.10	.06
437	Al Cowens	.30	.15	.09
438	Don Carrithers	.20	.10	.06
439	Ed Brinkman	.25	.13	.08
440	Andy Messersmith	.30	.15	.09
441	Bobby Heise	.20	.10	.06
442	Maximino Leon	.20	.10	.06
443	Twins Team (Frank Quillici)	.60	.30	.20
444	Gene Garber	.25	.13	.08
445	Felix Millan	.20	.10	.06
446	Bart Johnson	.20	.10	.06
447	Terry Crowley	.20	.10	.06
448	Frank Duffy	.20	.10	.06
449	Charlie Williams	.20	.10	.06
450	Willie McCovey	2.50	1.25	.70
451	Rick Dempsey	.30	.15	.09
452	Angel Mangual	.20	.10	.06
453	Claude Osteen	.25	.13	.08
454	Doug Griffin	.20	.10	.06
455	Don Wilson	.20	.10	.06
456	Bob Coluccio	.20	.10	.06
457	Mario Mendoza	.20	.10	.06
458	Ross Grimsley	.25	.13	.08
459	A.L. Championships	.75	.40	.25
460	N.L. Championships	.75	.40	.25
461	World Series Game 1	1.25	.60	.40
462	World Series Game 2	.75	.40	.25
463	World Series Game 3	1.00	.50	.30
464	World Series Game 4	.75	.40	.25
465	World Series Game 5	.75	.40	.25
466	World Series Summary	.75	.40	.25
467	Ed Halicki	.20	.10	.06
468	Bobby Mitchell	.20	.10	.06
469	Tom Dettore	.20	.10	.06
470	Jeff Burroughs	.30	.15	.09
471	Bob Stinson	.20	.10	.06
472	Bruce Dal Canton	.20	.10	.06
473	Ken McMullen	.20	.10	.06
474	Luke Walker	.20	.10	.06
475	Darrell Evans	.50	.25	.15
476	Ed Figueroa	.25	.13	.08
477	Tom Hutton	.20	.10	.06
478	Tom Burgmeier	.20	.10	.06
479	Ken Boswell	.20	.10	.06
480	Carlos May	.25	.13	.08
481	Will McEnaney	.25	.13	.08
482	Tom McCraw	.20	.10	.06
483	Steve Ontiveros	.20	.10	.06
484	Glenn Beckert	.30	.15	.09
485	Sparky Lyle	.30	.15	.09
486	Ray Fosse	.20	.10	.06
487	Astros Team (Preston Gomez)	.60	.30	.20
488	Bill Travers	.20	.10	.06
489	Cecil Cooper	.75	.40	.25
490	Reggie Smith	.30	.15	.09
491	Doyle Alexander	.30	.15	.09
492	Rich Hebner	.20	.10	.06
493	Don Stanhouse	.20	.10	.06
494	Pete LaCock	.20	.10	.06
495	Nelson Briles	.20	.10	.06
496	Pepe Frias	.20	.10	.06
497	Jim Nettles	.20	.10	.06
498	Al Downing	.25	.13	.08
499	Marty Perez	.20	.10	.06
500	Nolan Ryan	6.00	3.00	1.75
501	Bill Robinson	.20	.10	.06
502	Pat Bourque	.20	.10	.06
503	Fred Stanley	.20	.10	.06
504	Buddy Bradford	.20	.10	.06
505	Chris Speier	.20	.10	.06
506	Leron Lee	.20	.10	.06
507	Tom Carroll	.20	.10	.06
508	Bob Hansen	.20	.10	.06
509	Dave Hilton	.20	.10	.06
510	Vida Blue	.40	.20	.12
511	Rangers Team (Billy Martin)	.60	.30	.20
512	Larry Milbourne	.20	.10	.06
513	Dick Pole	.20	.10	.06
514	Jose Cruz	.40	.20	.12
515	Manny Sanguillen	.25	.13	.08
516	Don Hood	.20	.10	.06
517	Checklist 397-528	1.00	.50	.30
518	Leo Cardenas	.20	.10	.06
519	Jim Todd	.20	.10	.06
520	Amos Otis	.30	.15	.09
521	Dennis Blair	.20	.10	.06
522	Gary Sutherland	.20	.10	.06
523	Tom Paciorek	.25	.13	.08
524	John Doherty	.20	.10	.06
525	Tom House	.20	.10	.06
526	Larry Hisle	.30	.15	.09
527	Mac Scarce	.20	.10	.06
528	Eddie Leon	.20	.10	.06
529	Gary Thomasson	.20	.10	.06
530	Gaylord Perry	2.00	1.00	.60
531	Reds Team (Sparky Anderson)	.75	.40	.25
532	Gorman Thomas	.40	.20	.12
533	Rudy Meoli	.20	.10	.06
534	Alex Johnson	.20	.10	.06
535	Gene Tenace	.25	.13	.08
536	Bob Moose	.20	.10	.06
537	Tommy Harper	.25	.13	.08
538	Duffy Dyer	.20	.10	.06
539	Jesse Jefferson	.20	.10	.06
540	Lou Brock	2.50	1.25	.70
541	Roger Metzger	.20	.10	.06
542	Pete Broberg	.20	.10	.06
543	Larry Biittner	.20	.10	.06
544	Steve Mingori	.20	.10	.06
545	Billy Williams	2.00	1.00	.60
546	John Knox	.20	.10	.06
547	Von Joshua	.20	.10	.06
548	Charlie Sands	.20	.10	.06
549	Bill Butler	.20	.10	.06
550	Ralph Garr	.25	.13	.08
551	Larry Christenson	.20	.10	.06
552	Jack Brohamer	.20	.10	.06
553	John Boccabella	.20	.10	.06
554	Rich Gossage	1.00	.50	.30
555	Al Oliver	.75	.40	.25
556	Tim Johnson	.20	.10	.06
557	Larry Gura	.20	.10	.06
558	Dave Roberts	.20	.10	.06
559	Bob Montgomery	.20	.10	.06
560	Tony Perez	.75	.40	.25
561	A's Team (Alvin Dark)	.75	.40	.25
562	Gary Nolan	.20	.10	.06
563	Wilbur Howard	.20	.10	.06
564	Tommy Davis	.30	.15	.09
565	Joe Torre	.50	.25	.15
566	Ray Burris	.20	.10	.06
567	Jim Sundberg	.60	.30	.20
568	Dale Murray	.20	.10	.06
569	Frank White	.40	.20	.12
570	Jim Wynn	.30	.15	.09
571	Dave Lemanczyk	.20	.10	.06
572	Roger Nelson	.20	.10	.06
573	Orlando Pena	.20	.10	.06
574	Tony Taylor	.20	.10	.06
575	Gene Clines	.20	.10	.06
576	Phil Roof	.20	.10	.06
577	John Morris	.20	.10	.06
578	Dave Tomlin	.20	.10	.06
579	Skip Pitlock	.20	.10	.06
580	Frank Robinson	2.50	1.25	.70
581	Darrel Chaney	.20	.10	.06
582	Eduardo Rodriguez	.20	.10	.06
583	Andy Etchebarren	.20	.10	.06
584	Mike Garman	.20	.10	.06
585	Chris Chambliss	.30	.15	.09
586	Tim McCarver	.40	.20	.12
587	Chris Ward	.20	.10	.06
588	Rick Auerbach	.20	.10	.06
589	Braves Team (Clyde King)	.60	.30	.20
590	Cesar Cedeno	.40	.20	.12
591	Glenn Abbott	.20	.10	.06
592	Balor Moore	.20	.10	.06
593	Gene Lamont	.20	.10	.06
594	Jim Fuller	.20	.10	.06
595	Joe Niekro	.40	.20	.12
596	Ollie Brown	.20	.10	.06
597	Winston Llenas	.20	.10	.06
598	Bruce Kison	.20	.10	.06
599	Nate Colbert	.20	.10	.06
600	Rod Carew	7.00	3.50	2.00
601	Juan Beniquez	.30	.15	.09
602	John Vukovich	.20	.10	.06
603	Lew Kruasse	.20	.10	.06
604	Oscar Zamora	.20	.10	.06
605	John Ellis	.20	.10	.06
606	Bruce Miller	.20	.10	.06
607	Jim Holt	.20	.10	.06
608	Gene Michael	.25	.13	.08
609	Ellie Hendricks	.20	.10	.06
610	Ron Hunt	.20	.10	.06
611	Yankees Team (Bill Virdon)	1.00	.50	.30
612	Terry Hughes	.20	.10	.06
613	Bill Parsons	.20	.10	.06
614	Rookie Pitchers (Jack Kecek, Dyar Miller, Vern Ruhle, Paul Siebert)	.20	.10	.06
615	Rookie Pitchers (Pat Darcy, Dennis Leonard, Tom Underwood, Hank Webb)	.40	.20	.12
616	Rookie Outfielders (Dave Augustine, Pepe Mangual, Jim Rice, John Scott)	30.00	15.00	9.00
617	Mike Cubbage, Doug DeCinces, Reggie Sanders, Manny Trillo	1.00	.50	.30
618	Rookie Pitchers (Jamie Easterly, Tom Johnson, Scott McGregor, Rick Rhoden)	2.50	1.25	.70
619	Rookie Outfielders (Benny Ayala, Nyls Nyman, Tommy Smith, Jerry Turner)	.20	.10	.06
620	Catchers-Outfielders (Gary Carter, Marc Hill, Danny Meyer, Leon Roberts)	35.00	17.50	10.50
621	Rookie Pitchers (John Denny, Rawly Eastwick, Jim Kern, Juan Veintidos)			
622	Rookie Outfielders (Ed Armbrister, Fred Lynn, Tom Poquette, Terry Whitfield)	8.00	4.00	2.50
623	Rookie Infielders (Phil Garner, Keith Hernandez, Bob Sheldon, Tom Veryzer)	20.00	10.00	6.00
624	Rookie Pitchers (Doug Knoieczny, Gary Lavelle, Jim Otten, Eddie Solomon)	.30	.15	.09
625	Boog Powell	.60	.30	.20
626	Larry Haney	.20	.10	.06
627	Tom Walker	.20	.10	.06
628	Ron LeFlore	.60	.30	.20
629	Joe Hoerner	.20	.10	.06
630	Greg Luzinski	.60	.30	.20
631	Lee Lacy	.25	.13	.08
632	Morris Nettles	.20	.10	.06
633	Paul Casanova	.20	.10	.06
634	Cy Acosta	.20	.10	.06
635	Chuck Dobson	.20	.10	.06
636	Charlie Moore	.20	.10	.06
637	Ted Martinez	.20	.10	.06
638	Cubs Team (Jim Marshall)	.60	.30	.20
639	Steve Kline	.20	.10	.06
640	Harmon Killebrew	2.00	1.00	.60
641	Jim Northrup	.25	.13	.08
642	Mike Phillips	.20	.10	.06
643	Brent Strom	.20	.10	.06
644	Bill Fahey	.20	.10	.06
645	Danny Cater	.20	.10	.06
646	Checklist 529-660	1.00	.50	.30
647	Claudell Washington	1.00	.50	.30
648	Dave Pagan	.20	.10	.06
649	Jack Heidemann	.20	.10	.06
650	Dave May	.20	.10	.06
651	John Morlan	.20	.10	.06
652	Lindy McDaniel	.20	.10	.06
653	Lee Richards	.20	.10	.06
654	Jerry Terrell	.20	.10	.06
655	Rico Carty	.30	.15	.09
656	Bill Plummer	.20	.10	.06
657	Bob Oliver	.20	.10	.06
658	Vic Harris	.20	.10	.06
659	Bob Apodaca	.20	.10	.06
660	Hank Aaron	9.00	4.00	2.50

1976 O-Pee-Chee

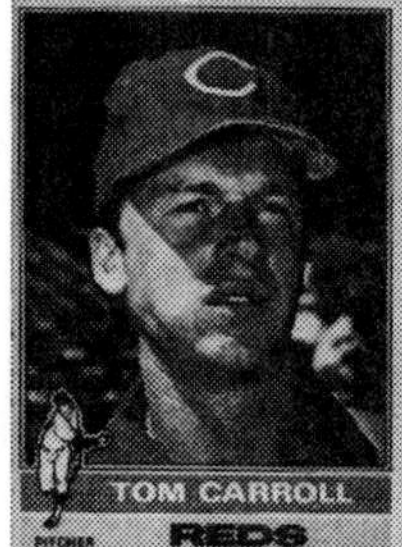

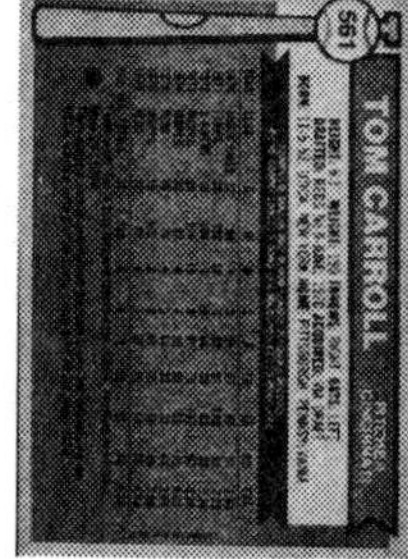

Identical in design to the 1976 Topps set, the Canadian-issued 1976 O-Pee-Chee set again contained 660 cards, each measuring 2-1/2" by 3 1/2". The backs are printed in both French and English and state "Ptd. in Canada."

		NR MT	EX	VG
Complete Set:		325.00	162.00	97.00
Common Player:		.20	.10	.06
1	'75 Record Breaker (Hank Aaron)	10.00	5.00	3.00
2	'75 Record Breaker (Bobby Bonds)	.40	.20	.12

No.	Card	NR MT	EX	VG
3	'75 Record Breaker (Mickey Lolich)	.30	.15	.09
4	'75 Record Breaker (Dave Lopes)	.30	.15	.09
5	'75 Record Breaker (Tom Seaver)	1.25	.60	.40
6	'75 Record Breaker (Rennie Stennett)	.25	.13	.08
7	Jim Umbarger	.20	.10	.06
8	Tito Fuentes	.20	.10	.06
9	Paul Lindblad	.20	.10	.06
10	Lou Brock	2.00	1.00	.60
11	Jim Hughes	.20	.10	.06
12	Richie Zisk	.25	.13	.08
13	Johnny Wockenfuss	.20	.10	.06
14	Gene Garber	.25	.13	.08
15	George Scott	.30	.15	.09
16	Bob Apodaca	.20	.10	.06
17	Yankees Team (Billy Martin)	1.00	.50	.30
18	Dale Murray	.20	.10	.06
19	George Brett	15.00	7.50	4.50
20	Bob Watson	.25	.13	.08
21	Dave LaRoche	.20	.10	.06
22	Bill Russell	.25	.13	.08
23	Brian Downing	.25	.13	.08
24	Cesar Geronimo	.20	.10	.06
25	Mike Torrez	.25	.13	.08
26	Andy Thornton	.30	.15	.09
27	Ed Figueroa	.20	.10	.06
28	Dusty Baker	.30	.15	.09
29	Rick Burleson	.30	.15	.09
30	John Montefusco	.30	.15	.09
31	Len Randle	.20	.10	.06
32	Danny Frisella	.20	.10	.06
33	Bill North	.20	.10	.06
34	Mike Garman	.20	.10	.06
35	Tony Oliva	.50	.25	.15
36	Frank Taveras	.20	.10	.06
37	John Hiller	.25	.13	.08
38	Garry Maddox	.25	.13	.08
39	Pete Broberg	.20	.10	.06
40	Dave Kingman	.75	.40	.25
41	Tippy Martinez	.40	.20	.12
42	Barry Foote	.20	.10	.06
43	Paul Splittorff	.25	.13	.08
44	Doug Rader	.20	.10	.06
45	Boog Powell	.40	.20	.12
46	Dodgers Team (Walter Alston)	1.00	.50	.30
47	Jesse Jefferson	.20	.10	.06
48	Dave Concepcion	.40	.20	.12
49	Dave Duncan	.20	.10	.06
50	Fred Lynn	1.75	.90	.50
51	Ray Burris	.20	.10	.06
52	Dave Chalk	.20	.10	.06
53	Mike Beard	.20	.10	.06
54	Dave Rader	.20	.10	.06
55	Gaylord Perry	1.75	.90	.50
56	Bob Tolan	.25	.13	.08
57	Phil Garner	.30	.15	.09
58	Ron Reed	.20	.10	.06
59	Larry Hisle	.25	.13	.08
60	Jerry Reuss	.30	.15	.09
61	Ron LeFlore	.30	.15	.09
62	Johnny Oates	.20	.10	.06
63	Bobby Darwin	.20	.10	.06
64	Jerry Koosman	.30	.15	.09
65	Chris Chambliss	.25	.13	.08
66	Father and Son (Buddy Bell, Gus Bell)	.40	.20	.12
67	Father and Son (Bob Boone, Ray Boone)	.25	.13	.08
68	Father and Son (Joe Coleman, Joe Coleman, Jr.)	.25	.13	.08
69	Father and Son (Jim Hegan, Mike Hegan)	.25	.13	.08
70	Father and Son (Roy Smalley, Roy Smalley, Jr.)	.25	.13	.08
71	Steve Rogers	.25	.13	.08
72	Hal McRae	.30	.15	.09
73	Orioles Team (Earl Weaver)	.75	.40	.25
74	Oscar Gamble	.25	.13	.08
75	Larry Dierker	.20	.10	.06
76	Willie Crawford	.20	.10	.06
77	Pedro Bobon	.20	.10	.06
78	Cecil Cooper	.75	.40	.25
79	Jerry Morales	.20	.10	.06
80	Jim Kaat	.75	.40	.25
81	Darrell Evans	.40	.20	.12
82	Von Joshua	.20	.10	.06
83	Jim Spencer	.20	.10	.06
84	Brent Strom	.20	.10	.06
85	Mickey Rivers	.25	.13	.08
86	Mike Tyson	.20	.10	.06
87	Tom Burgmeier	.20	.10	.06
88	Duffy Dyer	.20	.10	.06
89	Vern Ruhle	.20	.10	.06
90	Sal Bando	.30	.15	.09
91	Tom Hutton	.20	.10	.06
92	Eduardo Rodriguez	.20	.10	.06
93	Mike Phillips	.20	.10	.06
94	Jim Dwyer	.20	.10	.06
95	Brooks Robinson	2.00	1.00	.60
96	Doug Bird	.20	.10	.06
97	Wilbur Howard	.20	.10	.06
98	Dennis Eckersley	1.50	.70	.45
99	Lee Lacy	.25	.13	.08
100	Jim Hunter	1.75	.90	.50
101	Pete LaCock	.20	.10	.06
102	Jim Willoughby	.20	.10	.06
103	Biff Pocoroba	.20	.10	.06
104	Reds Team (Sparky Anderson)	.75	.40	.25
105	Gary Lavelle	.20	.10	.06
106	Tom Grieve	.20	.10	.06
107	Dave Roberts	.20	.10	.06
108	Don Kirkwood	.20	.10	.06
109	Larry Lintz	.20	.10	.06
110	Carlos May	.25	.13	.08
111	Danny Thompson	.20	.10	.06
112	Kent Tekulve	.75	.40	.25
113	Gary Sutherland	.20	.10	.06
114	Jay Johnstone	.30	.15	.09
115	Ken Holtzman	.30	.15	.09
116	Charlie Moore	.20	.10	.06
117	Mike Jorgensen	.20	.10	.06
118	Red Sox Team (Darrell Johnson)	.75	.40	.25
119	Checklist 1-132	1.00	.50	.30
120	Rusty Staub	.40	.20	.12
121	Tony Solaita	.20	.10	.06
122	Mike Cosgrove	.20	.10	.06
123	Walt Williams	.20	.10	.06
124	Doug Rau	.20	.10	.06
125	Don Baylor	.50	.25	.15
126	Tom Dettore	.20	.10	.06
127	Larvell Blanks	.20	.10	.06
128	Ken Griffey	.30	.15	.09
129	Andy Etchebarren	.20	.10	.06
130	Luis Tiant	.40	.20	.12
131	Bill Stein	.20	.10	.06
132	Don Hood	.20	.10	.06
133	Gary Matthews	.30	.15	.09
134	Mike Ivie	.20	.10	.06
135	Bake McBride	.25	.13	.08
136	Dave Goltz	.25	.13	.08
137	Bill Robinson	.20	.10	.06
138	Lerrin LaGrow	.20	.10	.06
139	Gorman Thomas	.30	.15	.09
140	Vida Blue	.40	.20	.12
141	Larry Parrish	1.50	.70	.45
142	Dick Drago	.20	.10	.06
143	Jerry Grote	.25	.13	.08
144	Al Fitzmorris	.20	.10	.06
145	Larry Bowa	.30	.15	.09
146	George Medich	.25	.13	.08
147	Astros Team (Bill Virdon)	.60	.30	.20
148	Stan Thomas	.20	.10	.06
149	Tommy Davis	.30	.15	.09
150	Steve Garvey	6.00	3.00	1.75
151	Bill Bonham	.20	.10	.06
152	Leroy Stanton	.20	.10	.06
153	Buzz Capra	.20	.10	.06
154	Bucky Dent	.30	.15	.09
155	Jack Billingham	.20	.10	.06
156	Rico Carty	.30	.15	.09
157	Mike Caldwell	.20	.10	.06
158	Ken Reitz	.20	.10	.06
159	Jerry Terrell	.20	.10	.06
160	Dave Winfield	6.00	3.00	1.75
161	Bruce Kison	.20	.10	.06
162	Jack Pierce	.20	.10	.06
163	Jim Slaton	.20	.10	.06
164	Pepe Mangual	.20	.10	.06
165	Gene Tenace	.25	.13	.08
166	Skip Lockwood	.20	.10	.06
167	Freddie Patek	.20	.10	.06
168	Tom Hilgendorf	.20	.10	.06
169	Graig Nettles	1.00	.50	.30
170	Rick Wise	.25	.13	.08
171	Greg Gross	.20	.10	.06
172	Rangers Team (Frank Lucchesi)	.60	.30	.20
173	Steve Swisher	.20	.10	.06
174	Charlie Hough	.30	.15	.09
175	Ken Singleton	.30	.15	.09
176	Dick Lange	.20	.10	.06
177	Marty Perez	.20	.10	.06
178	Tom Buskey	.20	.10	.06
179	George Foster	.75	.40	.25
180	Rich Gossage	1.00	.50	.30
181	Willie Montanez	.20	.10	.06
182	Harry Rasmussen	.20	.10	.06
183	Steve Braun	.20	.10	.06
184	Bill Greif	.20	.10	.06
185	Dave Parker	2.00	1.00	.60
186	Tom Walker	.20	.10	.06
187	Pedro Garcia	.20	.10	.06
188	Fred Scherman	.20	.10	.06
189	Claudell Washington	.40	.20	.12
190	Jon Matlack	.25	.13	.08
191	N.L. Batting Leaders (Bill Madlock, Manny Sanguillen, Ted Simmons)	.50	.25	.15
192	A.L. Batting Leaders (Rod Carew, Fred Lynn, Thurman Munson)	1.25	.60	.40
193	N.L. Home Run Leaders (Dave Kingman, Greg Luzinski, Mike Schmidt)	1.00	.50	.30
194	A.L. Home Run Leaders (Reggie Jackson, John Mayberry, George Scott)	1.00	.50	.30
195	N.L. Runs Batted In Ldrs. (Johnny Bench, Greg Luzinski, Tony Perez)	1.00	.50	.30
196	A.L. Runs Batted In Ldrs. (Fred Lynn, John Mayberry, George Scott)	.50	.25	.15
197	N.L. Stolen Base Leaders (Lou Brock, Dave Lopes, Joe Morgan)	.75	.40	.25
198	A.L. Stolen Base Leaders (Amos Otis, Mickey Rivers, Claudell Washington)	.40	.20	.12
199	N.L. Victory Leaders (Randy Jones, Andy Messersmith, Tom Seaver)	.60	.30	.20
200	A.L. Victory Leaders (Vida Blue, Jim Hunter, Jim Palmer)	.75	.40	.25
201	N.L. Earned Run Average Ldrs. (Randy Jones, Andy Messersmith, Tom Seaver)	.60	.30	.20
202	A.L. Earned Run Average Ldrs. (Dennis Eckersley, Jim Hunter, Jim Palmer, Jim Palmer)	.75	.40	.25
203	N.L. Strikeout Leaders (Andy Messersmith, John Montefusco, Tom Seaver)	.60	.30	.20
204	A.L. Strikeout Leaders (Bert Blyleven, Gaylord Perry, Frank Tanana)	.50	.25	.15
205	Major League Leading Firemen (Rich Gossage, Al Hrabosky)	.40	.20	.12
206	Manny Trillo	.25	.13	.08
207	Andy Hassler	.20	.10	.06
208	Mike Lum	.20	.10	.06
209	Alan Ashby	.30	.15	.09
210	Lee May	.30	.15	.09
211	Clay Carroll	.25	.13	.08
212	Pat Kelly	.20	.10	.06
213	Dave Heaverlo	.20	.10	.06
214	Eric Soderholm	.20	.10	.06
215	Reggie Smith	.30	.15	.09
216	Expos Team (Karl Kuehl)	.60	.30	.20
217	Dave Freisleben	.20	.10	.06
218	John Knox	.20	.10	.06
219	Tom Murphy	.20	.10	.06
220	Manny Sanguillen	.25	.13	.08
221	Jim Todd	.20	.10	.06
222	Wayne Garrett	.20	.10	.06
223	Ollie Brown	.20	.10	.06
224	Jim York	.20	.10	.06
225	Roy White	.30	.15	.09
226	Jim Sundberg	.25	.13	.08
227	Oscar Zamora	.20	.10	.06
228	John Hale	.20	.10	.06
229	Jerry Remy	.30	.15	.09
230	Carl Yastrzemski	8.00	4.00	2.50
231	Tom House	.20	.10	.06
232	Frank Duffy	.20	.10	.06
233	Grant Jackson	.20	.10	.06
234	Mike Sadek	.20	.10	.06
235	Bert Blyleven	1.00	.50	.30
236	Royals Team (Whitey Herzog)	.60	.30	.20
237	Dave Hamilton	.20	.10	.06
238	Larry Biittner	.20	.10	.06
239	John Curtis	.20	.10	.06
240	Pete Rose	15.00	7.50	4.50
241	Hector Torres	.20	.10	.06
242	Dan Meyer	.20	.10	.06
243	Jim Rooker	.20	.10	.06
244	Bill Sharp	.20	.10	.06
245	Felix Millan	.20	.10	.06
246	Cesar Tovar	.20	.10	.06
247	Terry Harmon	.20	.10	.06
248	Dick Tidrow	.20	.10	.06
249	Cliff Johnson	.25	.13	.08
250	Fergie Jenkins	.75	.40	.25
251	Rick Monday	.30	.15	.09
252	Tim Nordbrook	.20	.10	.06
253	Bill Buckner	.40	.20	.12
254	Rudy Meoli	.20	.10	.06
255	Fritz Peterson	.20	.10	.06
256	Rowland Office	.20	.10	.06
257	Ross Grimsley	.25	.13	.08
258	Nyls Nyman	.20	.10	.06
259	Darrel Chaney	.20	.10	.06
260	Steve Busby	.25	.13	.08
261	Gary Thomasson	.20	.10	.06
262	Checklist 133-264	1.00	.50	.30
263	Lyman Bostock	.75	.40	.25
264	Steve Renko	.20	.10	.06
265	Willie Davis	.30	.15	.09
266	Alan Foster	.20	.10	.06
267	Aurelio Rodriguez	.25	.13	.08
268	Del Unser	.20	.10	.06
269	Rick Austin	.20	.10	.06
270	Willie Stargell	2.25	1.25	.70
271	Jim Lonborg	.25	.13	.08
272	Rick Dempsey	.30	.15	.09
273	Joe Niekro	.30	.15	.09
274	Tommy Harper	.25	.13	.08
275	Rick Manning	.25	.13	.08
276	Mickey Scott	.20	.10	.06
277	Cubs Team (Jim Marshall)	.60	.30	.20
278	Bernie Carbo	.20	.10	.06
279	Roy Howell	.20	.10	.06
280	Burt Hooton	.25	.13	.08
281	Dave May	.20	.10	.06
282	Dan Osborn	.20	.10	.06
283	Merv Rettenmund	.20	.10	.06
284	Steve Ontiveros	.20	.10	.06
285	Mike Cuellar	.30	.15	.09
286	Jim Wohlford	.20	.10	.06
287	Pete Mackanin	.20	.10	.06
288	Bill Campbell	.20	.10	.06
289	Enzo Hernandez	.20	.10	.06
290	Ted Simmons	.60	.30	.20
291	Ken Sanders	.20	.10	.06
292	Leon Roberts	.20	.10	.06
293	Bill Castro	.20	.10	.06
294	Ed Kirkpatrick	.20	.10	.06
295	Dave Cash	.20	.10	.06
296	Pat Dobson	.25	.13	.08
297	Roger Metzger	.20	.10	.06
298	Dick Bosman	.20	.10	.06
299	Champ Summers	.20	.10	.06
300	Johnny Bench	6.00	3.00	1.75
301	Jackie Brown	.20	.10	.06
302	Rick Miller	.20	.10	.06
303	Steve Foucault	.20	.10	.06
304	Angels Team (Dick Williams)	.60	.30	.20
305	Andy Messersmith	.25	.13	.08
306	Rod Gilbreath	.20	.10	.06
307	Al Bumbry	.25	.13	.08
308	Jim Barr	.20	.10	.06
309	Bill Melton	.20	.10	.06
310	Randy Jones	.25	.13	.08
311	Cookie Rojas	.25	.13	.08
312	Don Carrithers	.20	.10	.06
313	Dan Ford	.25	.13	.08
314	Ed Kranepool	.25	.13	.08
315	Al Hrabosky	.25	.13	.08
316	Robin Yount	8.00	4.00	2.50
317	John Candelaria	1.75	.90	.50
318	Bob Boone	.30	.15	.09
319	Larry Gura	.20	.10	.06
320	Willie Horton	.30	.15	.09
321	Jose Cruz	.30	.15	.09
322	Glenn Abbott	.20	.10	.06
323	Rob Sperring	.20	.10	.06
324	Jim Bibby	.25	.13	.08
325	Tony Perez	.60	.30	.20
326	Dick Pole	.20	.10	.06
327	Dave Moates	.20	.10	.06
328	Carl Morton	.20	.10	.06
329	Joe Ferguson	.20	.10	.06
330	Nolan Ryan	5.00	2.50	1.50
331	Padres Team (John McNamara)	.60	.30	.20
332	Charlie Williams	.20	.10	.06
333	Bob Coluccio	.20	.10	.06
334	Dennis Leonard	.30	.15	.09

		NR MT	EX	VG
335	Bob Grich	.30	.15	.09
336	Vic Albury	.20	.10	.06
337	Bud Harrelson	.25	.13	.08
338	Bob Bailey	.20	.10	.06
339	John Denny	.50	.25	.15
340	Jim Rice	10.00	5.00	3.00
341	All Time All-Stars (Lou Gehrig)	2.00	1.00	.60
342	All Time All-Stars (Rogers Hornsby)	1.00	.50	.30
343	All Time All-Stars (Pie Traynor)	.75	.40	.25
344	All Time All-Stars (Honus Wagner)	1.00	.50	.30
345	All Time All-Stars (Babe Ruth)	3.00	1.50	.90
346	All Time All-Stars (Ty Cobb)	2.00	1.00	.60
347	All Time All-Stars (Ted Williams)	2.00	1.00	.60
348	All Time All-Stars (Mickey Cochrane)	.75	.40	.25
349	All Time All-Stars (Walter Johnson)	1.00	.50	.30
350	All Time All-Stars (Lefty Grove)	.75	.40	.25
351	Randy Hundley	.20	.10	.06
352	Dave Giusti	.20	.10	.06
353	Sixto Lezcano	.30	.15	.09
354	Ron Blomberg	.25	.13	.08
355	Steve Carlton	5.00	2.50	1.50
356	Ted Martinez	.20	.10	.06
357	Ken Forsch	.20	.10	.06
358	Buddy Bell	.40	.20	.12
359	Rick Reuschel	.30	.15	.09
360	Jeff Burroughs	.25	.13	.08
361	Tigers Team (Ralph Houk)	.75	.40	.25
362	Will McEnaney	.20	.10	.06
363	Dave Collins	.60	.30	.20
364	Elias Sosa	.20	.10	.06
365	Carlton Fisk	1.00	.50	.30
366	Bobby Valentine	.30	.15	.09
367	Bruce Miller	.20	.10	.06
368	Wilbur Wood	.25	.13	.08
369	Frank White	.30	.15	.09
370	Ron Cey	.30	.15	.09
371	Ellie Hendricks	.20	.10	.06
372	Rick Baldwin	.20	.10	.06
373	Johnny Briggs	.20	.10	.06
374	Dan Warthen	.20	.10	.06
375	Ron Fairly	.25	.13	.08
376	Rich Hebner	.20	.10	.06
377	Mike Hegan	.20	.10	.06
378	Steve Stone	.25	.13	.08
379	Ken Boswell	.20	.10	.06
380	Bobby Bonds	.30	.15	.09
381	Denny Doyle	.20	.10	.06
382	Matt Alexander	.20	.10	.06
383	John Ellis	.20	.10	.06
384	Phillies Team (Danny Ozark)	.60	.30	.20
385	Mickey Lolich	.40	.20	.12
386	Ed Goodson	.20	.10	.06
387	Mike Miley	.20	.10	.06
388	Stan Perzanowski	.20	.10	.06
389	Glenn Adams	.20	.10	.06
390	Don Gullett	.25	.13	.08
391	Jerry Hairston	.20	.10	.06
392	Checklist 265-396	1.00	.50	.30
393	Paul Mitchell	.20	.10	.06
394	Fran Healy	.20	.10	.06
395	Jim Wynn	.25	.13	.08
396	Bill Lee	.25	.13	.08
397	Tim Foli	.20	.10	.06
398	Dave Tomlin	.20	.10	.06
399	Luis Melendez	.20	.10	.06
400	Rod Carew	5.00	2.50	1.50
401	Ken Brett	.20	.10	.06
402	Don Money	.20	.10	.06
403	Geoff Zahn	.20	.10	.06
404	Enos Cabell	.20	.10	.06
405	Rollie Fingers	1.00	.50	.30
406	Ed Herrmann	.20	.10	.06
407	Tom Underwood	.20	.10	.06
408	Charlie Spikes	.20	.10	.06
409	Dave Lemanczyk	.20	.10	.06
410	Ralph Garr	.25	.13	.08
411	Bill Singer	.20	.10	.06
412	Toby Harrah	.25	.13	.08
413	Pete Varney	.20	.10	.06
414	Wayne Garland	.20	.10	.06
415	Vada Pinson	.40	.20	.12
416	Tommy John	1.00	.50	.30
417	Gene Clines	.20	.10	.06
418	Jose Morales	.20	.10	.06
419	Reggie Cleveland	.20	.10	.06
420	Joe Morgan	2.25	1.25	.70
421	A's Team	.60	.30	.20
422	Johnny Grubb	.20	.10	.06
423	Ed Halicki	.20	.10	.06
424	Phil Roof	.20	.10	.06
425	Rennie Stennett	.20	.10	.06
426	Bob Forsch	.25	.13	.08
427	Kurt Bevacqua	.20	.10	.06
428	Jim Crawford	.20	.10	.06
429	Fred Stanley	.20	.10	.06
430	Jose Cardenal	.25	.13	.08
431	Dick Ruthven	.20	.10	.06
432	Tom Veryzer	.20	.10	.06
433	Rick Waits	.20	.10	.06
434	Morris Nettles	.20	.10	.06
435	Phil Niekro	1.75	.90	.50
436	Bill Fahey	.20	.10	.06
437	Terry Forster	.25	.13	.08
438	Doug DeCinces	.40	.20	.12
439	Rick Rhoden	.50	.25	.15
440	John Mayberry	.25	.13	.08
441	Gary Carter	15.00	7.50	4.50
442	Hank Webb	.20	.10	.06
443	Giants Team	.60	.30	.20
444	Gary Nolan	.20	.10	.06
445	Rico Petrocelli	.25	.13	.08
446	Larry Haney	.20	.10	.06
447	Gene Locklear	.20	.10	.06

		NR MT	EX	VG
448	Tom Johnson	.20	.10	.06
449	Bob Robertson	.20	.10	.06
450	Jim Palmer	2.75	1.50	.80
451	Buddy Bradford	.20	.10	.06
452	Tom Hausman	.20	.10	.06
453	Lou Piniella	.50	.25	.15
454	Tom Griffin	.20	.10	.06
455	Dick Allen	.50	.25	.15
456	Joe Coleman	.20	.10	.06
457	Ed Crosby	.20	.10	.06
458	Earl Williams	.20	.10	.06
459	Jim Brewer	.20	.10	.06
460	Cesar Cedeno	.30	.15	.09
461	NL and AL Championships	.75	.40	.25
462	1975 World Series	.75	.40	.25
463	Steve Hargan	.20	.10	.06
464	Ken Henderson	.20	.10	.06
465	Mike Marshall	.25	.13	.08
466	Bob Stinson	.20	.10	.06
467	Woodie Fryman	.20	.10	.06
468	Jesus Alou	.25	.13	.08
469	Rawly Eastwick	.20	.10	.06
470	Bobby Murcer	.40	.20	.12
471	Jim Burton	.20	.10	.06
472	Bob Davis	.20	.10	.06
473	Paul Blair	.25	.13	.08
474	Ray Corbin	.20	.10	.06
475	Joe Rudi	.30	.15	.09
476	Bob Moose	.35	.20	.11
477	Indians Team (Frank Robinson)	.60	.30	.20
478	Lynn McGlothen	.20	.10	.06
479	Bobby Mitchell	.20	.10	.06
480	Mike Schmidt	15.00	7.50	4.50
481	Rudy May	.20	.10	.06
482	Tim Hosley	.20	.10	.06
483	Mickey Stanley	.25	.13	.08
484	Eric Raich	.20	.10	.06
485	Mike Hargrove	.25	.13	.08
486	Bruce Dal Canton	.20	.10	.06
487	Leron Lee	.20	.10	.06
488	Claude Osteen	.25	.13	.08
489	Skip Jutze	.20	.10	.06
490	Frank Tanana	.30	.15	.09
491	Terry Crowley	.20	.10	.06
492	Marty Pattin	.20	.10	.06
493	Derrel Thomas	.20	.10	.06
494	Craig Swan	.25	.13	.08
495	Nate Colbert	.20	.10	.06
496	Juan Beniquez	.25	.13	.08
497	Joe McIntosh	.20	.10	.06
498	Glenn Borgmann	.20	.10	.06
499	Mario Guerrero	.20	.10	.06
500	Reggie Jackson	9.00	4.50	2.75
501	Billy Champion	.20	.10	.06
502	Tim McCarver	.40	.20	.12
503	Elliott Maddox	.20	.10	.06
504	Pirates Team (Danny Murtaugh)	.60	.30	.20
505	Mark Belanger	.25	.13	.08
506	George Mitterwald	.20	.10	.06
507	Ray Bare	.20	.10	.06
508	Duane Kuiper	.20	.10	.06
509	Bill Hands	.20	.10	.06
510	Amos Otis	.30	.15	.09
511	Jamie Easterley	.20	.10	.06
512	Ellie Rodriguez	.20	.10	.06
513	Bart Johnson	.20	.10	.06
514	Dan Driessen	.30	.15	.09
515	Steve Yeager	.20	.10	.06
516	Wayne Granger	.20	.10	.06
517	John Milner	.20	.10	.06
518	Doug Flynn	.20	.10	.06
519	Steve Brye	.20	.10	.06
520	Willie McCovey	2.00	1.00	.60
521	Jim Colborn	.20	.10	.06
522	Ted Sizemore	.20	.10	.06
523	Bob Montgomery	.20	.10	.06
524	Pete Falcone	.20	.10	.06
525	Billy Williams	1.75	.90	.50
526	Checklist 397-528	1.00	.50	.30
527	Mike Anderson	.20	.10	.06
528	Dock Ellis	.20	.10	.06
529	Deron Johnson	.20	.10	.06
530	Don Sutton	1.25	.60	.40
531	Mets Team (Joe Frazier)	.75	.40	.25
532	Milt May	.20	.10	.06
533	Lee Richard	.20	.10	.06
534	Stan Bahnsen	.20	.10	.06
535	Dave Nelson	.20	.10	.06
536	Mike Thompson	.20	.10	.06
537	Tony Muser	.20	.10	.06
538	Pat Darcy	.20	.10	.06
539	John Balaz	.20	.10	.06
540	Bill Freehan	.30	.15	.09
541	Steve Mingori	.20	.10	.06
542	Keith Hernandez	8.00	4.00	2.50
543	Wayne Twitchell	.20	.10	.06
544	Pepe Frias	.20	.10	.06
545	Sparky Lyle	.30	.15	.09
546	Dave Rosello	.20	.10	.06
547	Roric Harrison	.20	.10	.06
548	Manny Mota	.25	.13	.08
549	Randy Tate	.20	.10	.06
550	Hank Aaron	9.00	4.50	2.75
551	Jerry DaVanon	.20	.10	.06
552	Terry Humphrey	.20	.10	.06
553	Randy Moffitt	.20	.10	.06
554	Ray Fosse	.20	.10	.06
555	Dyar Miller	.20	.10	.06
556	Twins Team (Gene Mauch)	.60	.30	.20
557	Dan Spillner	.20	.10	.06
558	Clarence Gaston	.20	.10	.06
559	Clyde Wright	.20	.10	.06
560	Jorge Orta	.20	.10	.06
561	Tom Carroll	.20	.10	.06
562	Adrian Garrett	.20	.10	.06
563	Larry Demery	.20	.10	.06
564	Bubble Gum Blowing Champ (Kurt Bevacqua)	.25	.13	.08
565	Tug McGraw	.30	.15	.09
566	Ken McMullen	.20	.10	.06
567	George Stone	.20	.10	.06

		NR MT	EX	VG
568	Rob Andrews	.20	.10	.06
569	Nelson Briles	.20	.10	.06
570	George Hendrick	.30	.15	.09
571	Don DeMola	.20	.10	.06
572	Rich Coggins	.20	.10	.06
573	Bill Travers	.20	.10	.06
574	Don Kessinger	.25	.13	.08
575	Dwight Evans	.75	.40	.25
576	Maximino Leon	.20	.10	.06
577	Marc Hill	.20	.10	.06
578	Ted Kubiak	.20	.10	.06
579	Clay Kirby	.20	.10	.06
580	Bert Campaneris	.30	.15	.09
581	Cardinals Team (Red Schoendienst)	.60	.30	.20
582	Mike Kekich	.20	.10	.06
583	Tommy Helms	.20	.10	.06
584	Stan Wall	.20	.10	.06
585	Joe Torre	.40	.20	.12
586	Ron Schueler	.20	.10	.06
587	Leo Cardenas	.20	.10	.06
588	Kevin Kobel	.20	.10	.06
589	Rookie Pitchers (Santo Alcala, Mike Flanagan, Joe Pactwa, Pablo Torrealba)	1.25	.60	.40
590	Rookie Outfielders (Henry Cruz, Chet Lemon, Ellis Valentine, Terry Whitfield)	.75	.40	.25
591	Rookie Pitchers (Steve Grilli, Craig Mitchell, Jose Sosa, George Throop)	.20	.10	.06
592	Rookie Infielders (Dave McKay, Willie Randolph, Jerry Royster, Roy Staiger)	2.25	1.25	.70
593	Rookie Pitchers (Larry Anderson, Ken Crosby, Mark Littell, Butch Metzger)	.20	.10	.06
594	Rookie Catchers & Outfielders (Andy Merchant, Ed Ott, Royle Stillman, Jerry White)	.20	.10	.06
595	Rookie Pitchers (Steve Barr, Art DeFilippis, Randy Lerch, Sid Monge)	.20	.10	.06
596	Rookie Infielders (Lamar Johnson, Johnnie LeMaster, Jerry Manuel, Craig Reynolds)	.30	.15	.09
597	Rookie Pitchers (Don Aase, Jack Kucek, Frank LaCorte, Mike Pazik)	.40	.20	.12
598	Rookie Outfielders (Hector Cruz, Jamie Quirk, Jerry Turner, Joe Wallis)	.20	.10	.06
599	Rookie Pitchers (Rob Dressler, Ron Guidry, Bob McClure, Pat Zachry)	15.00	7.50	4.50
600	Tom Seaver	5.00	2.50	1.50
601	Ken Rudolph	.20	.10	.06
602	Doug Konieczny	.20	.10	.06
603	Jim Holt	.20	.10	.06
604	Joe Lovitto	.20	.10	.06
605	Al Downing	.25	.13	.08
606	Brewers Team (Alex Grammas)	.60	.30	.20
607	Rich Hinton	.20	.10	.06
608	Vic Correll	.20	.10	.06
609	Fred Norman	.20	.10	.06
610	Greg Luzinski	.40	.20	.12
611	Rich Folkers	.20	.10	.06
612	Joe Lahoud	.20	.10	.06
613	Tim Johnson	.20	.10	.06
614	Fernando Arroyo	.20	.10	.06
615	Mike Cubbage	.20	.10	.06
616	Buck Martinez	.20	.10	.06
617	Darold Knowles	.20	.10	.06
618	Jack Brohamer	.20	.10	.06
619	Bill Butler	.20	.10	.06
620	Al Oliver	.60	.30	.20
621	Tom Hall	.20	.10	.06
622	Rick Auerbach	.20	.10	.06
623	Bob Allietta	.20	.10	.06
624	Tony Taylor	.20	.10	.06
625	J.R. Richard	.25	.13	.08
626	Bob Sheldon	.20	.10	.06
627	Bill Plummer	.20	.10	.06
628	John D'Acquisto	.20	.10	.06
629	Sandy Alomar	.20	.10	.06
630	Chris Speier	.25	.13	.08
631	Braves Team (Dave Bristol)	.60	.30	.20
632	Rogelio Moret	.20	.10	.06
633	John Stearns	.25	.13	.08
634	Larry Christenson	.20	.10	.06
635	Jim Fregosi	.25	.13	.08
636	Joe Decker	.20	.10	.06
637	Bruce Bochte	.25	.13	.08
638	Doyle Alexander	.30	.15	.09
639	Fred Kendall	.20	.10	.06
640	Bill Madlock	.75	.40	.25
641	Tom Paciorek	.25	.13	.08
642	Dennis Blair	.20	.10	.06
643	Checklist 529-660	1.00	.50	.30
644	Tom Bradley	.20	.10	.06
645	Darrell Porter	.25	.13	.08
646	John Lowenstein	.20	.10	.06
647	Ramon Hernandez	.20	.10	.06
648	Al Cowens	.25	.13	.08
649	Dave Roberts	.20	.10	.06
650	Thurman Munson	5.00	2.50	1.50
651	John Odom	.20	.10	.06
652	Ed Armbrister	.20	.10	.06
653	Mike Norris	.25	.13	.08
654	Doug Griffin	.20	.10	.06
655	Mike Vail	.20	.10	.06
656	White Sox Team (Chuck Tanner)	.60	.30	.20
657	Roy Smalley	.40	.20	.12
658	Jerry Johnson	.20	.10	.06
659	Ben Oglivie	.30	.15	.09
660	Dave Lopes	.60	.25	.15

A player's name in *italic* type indicates a rookie card. An (FC) indicates a player's first card for that particular card company.

1977 O-Pee-Chee

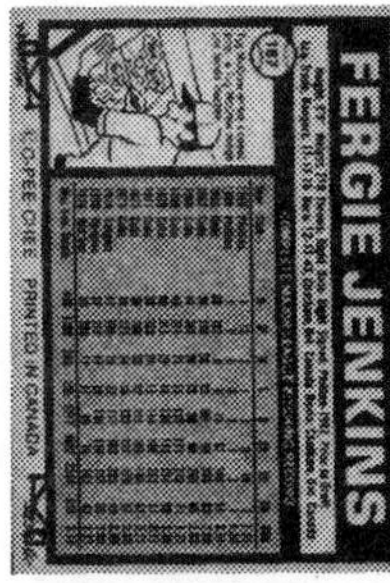

The 1977 O-Pee-Chee set represents a change in philosphy for the Canadian company. The design of the set is still identical to the Topps set of the same year, but the number of cards was reduced to 264 with more emphasis on players from the two Canadian teams. The backs are printed in English only but state "O-Pee-Chee Printed in Canada." Some of the photos in the O-Pee-Chee set differ from the 1977 Topps set. The cards measure the standard 2-1/2" by 3-1/2".

	NR MT	EX	VG
Complete Set:	150.00	75.00	45.00
Common Player:	.15	.08	.05

No.	Player	NR MT	EX	VG
1	Batting Leaders (George Brett, Bill Madlock)	3.00	1.50	.90
2	Home Run Leaders (Graig Nettles, Mike Schmidt)	1.00	.50	.30
3	Runs Batted In Leaders (George Foster, Lee May)	.40	.20	.12
4	Stolen Base Leaders (Dave Lopes, Bill North)	.25	.13	.08
5	Victory Leaders (Randy Jones, Jim Palmer)	.75	.40	.25
6	Strikeout Leaders (Nolan Ryan, Tom Seaver)	1.25	.60	.40
7	Earned Run Avg. Leaders (John Denny, Mark Fidrych)	.30	.15	.09
8	Leading Firemen (Bill Campbell, Rawly Eastwick)	.25	.13	.08
9	Mike Jorgensen	.15	.08	.05
10	Jim Hunter	1.50	.70	.45
11	Ken Griffey	.25	.13	.08
12	Bill Campbell	.15	.08	.05
13	Otto Velez	.15	.08	.05
14	Milt May	.15	.08	.05
15	Dennis Eckersley	.30	.15	.09
16	John Mayberry	.20	.10	.06
17	Larry Bowa	.25	.13	.08
18	Don Carrithers	.15	.08	.05
19	Ken Singleton	.25	.13	.08
20	Bill Stein	.15	.08	.05
21	Ken Brett	.12	.06	.04
22	Gary Woods	.15	.08	.05
23	Steve Swisher	.15	.08	.05
24	Don Sutton	1.25	.60	.40
25	Willie Stargell	2.25	1.25	.70
26	Jerry Koosman	.25	.13	.08
27	Del Unser	.15	.08	.05
28	Bob Grich	.25	.13	.08
29	Jim Slaton	.15	.08	.05
30	Thurman Munson	3.50	1.75	1.00
31	Dan Driessen	.20	.10	.06
32	Tom Bruno	.15	.08	.05
33	Larry Hisle	.20	.10	.06
34	Phil Garner	.20	.10	.06
35	Mike Hargrove	.20	.10	.06
36	Jackie Brown	.15	.08	.05
37	Carl Yastrzemski	4.50	2.25	1.25
38	Dave Roberts	.15	.08	.05
39	Ray Fosse	.15	.08	.05
40	Dave McKay	.15	.08	.05
41	Paul Splittorff	.20	.10	.06
42	Garry Maddox	.20	.10	.06
43	Phil Niekro	1.25	.60	.40
44	Roger Metzger	.15	.08	.05
45	Gary Carter	8.00	4.00	2.50
46	Jim Spencer	.15	.08	.05
47	Ross Grimsley	.20	.10	.06
48	Bob Bailor	.15	.08	.05
49	Chris Chambliss	.25	.13	.08
50	Will McEnaney	.15	.08	.05
51	Lou Brock	3.00	1.50	.90
52	Rollie Fingers	.75	.40	.25
53	Chris Speier	.15	.08	.05
54	Bombo Rivera	.15	.08	.05
55	Pete Broberg	.15	.08	.05
56	Bill Madlock	.50	.25	.15
57	Rick Rhoden	.25	.13	.08
58	Blue Jay Coaches (Don Leppert, Bob Miller, Jackie Moore, Harry Warner)	.50	.25	.15
59	John Candelaria	.40	.20	.12
60	Ed Kranepool	.20	.10	.06
61	Dave LaRoche	.15	.08	.05
62	Jim Rice	5.00	2.50	1.50
63	Don Stanhouse	.15	.08	.05
64	Jason Thompson	.50	.25	.15
65	Nolan Ryan	4.00	2.00	1.25
66	Tom Poquette	.15	.08	.05
67	Leon Hooten	.15	.08	.05
68	Bob Boone	.20	.10	.06
69	Mickey Rivers	.20	.10	.06
70	Gary Nolan	.15	.08	.05
71	Sixto Lezcano	.15	.08	.05
72	Larry Parrish	.30	.15	.09
73	Dave Goltz	.15	.08	.05
74	Bert Campaneris	.25	.13	.08
75	Vida Blue	.30	.15	.09
76	Rick Cerone	.25	.13	.08
77	Ralph Garr	.20	.10	.06
78	Ken Forsch	.15	.08	.05
79	Willie Montanez	.15	.08	.05
80	Jim Palmer	3.00	1.50	.90
81	Jerry White	.15	.08	.05
82	Gene Tenace	.20	.10	.06
83	Bobby Murcer	.30	.15	.09
84	Garry Templeton	.75	.40	.25
85	Bill Singer	.15	.08	.05
86	Buddy Bell	.30	.15	.09
87	Luis Tiant	.40	.20	.12
88	Rusty Staub	.30	.15	.09
89	Sparky Lyle	.25	.13	.08
90	Jose Morales	.15	.08	.05
91	Dennis Leonard	.20	.10	.06
92	Tommy Smith	.15	.08	.05
93	Steve Carlton	4.50	2.25	1.25
94	John Scott	.15	.08	.05
95	Bill Bonham	.15	.08	.05
96	Dave Lopes	.25	.13	.08
97	Jerry Reuss	.25	.13	.08
98	Dave Kingman	.50	.25	.15
99	Dan Warthen	.15	.08	.05
100	Johnny Bench	4.00	2.00	1.25
101	Bert Blyleven	.50	.25	.15
102	Cecil Cooper	.50	.25	.15
103	Mike Willis	.15	.08	.05
104	Dan Ford	.20	.10	.06
105	Frank Tanana	.25	.13	.08
106	Bill North	.15	.08	.05
107	Joe Ferguson	.15	.08	.05
108	Dick Williams	.20	.10	.06
109	John Denny	.20	.10	.06
110	Willie Randolph	.40	.20	.12
111	Reggie Cleveland	.15	.08	.05
112	Doug Howard	.15	.08	.05
113	Randy Jones	.20	.10	.06
114	Rico Carty	.25	.13	.08
115	Mark Fidrych	.40	.20	.12
116	Darrell Porter	.20	.10	.06
117	Wayne Garrett	.15	.08	.05
118	Greg Luzinski	.40	.20	.12
119	Jim Barr	.15	.08	.05
120	George Foster	.75	.40	.25
121	Phil Roof	.15	.08	.05
122	Bucky Dent	.25	.13	.08
123	Steve Braun	.15	.08	.05
124	Checklist 1-132	1.00	.50	.30
125	Lee May	.25	.13	.08
126	Woodie Fryman	.15	.08	.05
127	Jose Cardenal	.20	.10	.06
128	Doug Rau	.15	.08	.05
129	Rennie Stennett	.15	.08	.05
130	Pete Vuckovich	.40	.20	.12
131	Cesar Cedeno	.30	.15	.09
132	Jon Matlack	.20	.10	.06
133	Don Baylor	.50	.25	.15
134	Darrel Chaney	.15	.08	.05
135	Tony Perez	.75	.40	.25
136	Aurelio Rodriguez	.20	.10	.06
137	Carlton Fisk	.75	.40	.25
138	Wayne Garland	.15	.08	.05
139	Dave Hilton	.15	.08	.05
140	Rawly Eastwick	.15	.08	.05
141	Amos Otis	.20	.10	.06
142	Tug McGraw	.25	.13	.08
143	Rod Carew	4.00	2.00	1.25
144	Mike Torrez	.20	.10	.06
145	Sal Bando	.25	.13	.08
146	Dock Ellis	.15	.08	.05
147	Jose Cruz	.30	.15	.09
148	Alan Ashby	.15	.08	.05
149	Gaylord Perry	1.50	.70	.45
150	Keith Hernandez	2.50	1.25	.70
151	Dave Pagan	.15	.08	.05
152	Richie Zisk	.20	.10	.06
153	Steve Rogers	.20	.10	.06
154	Mark Belanger	.20	.10	.06
155	Andy Messersmith	.20	.10	.06
156	Dave Winfield	4.00	2.00	1.25
157	Chuck Hartenstein	.15	.08	.05
158	Manny Trillo	.20	.10	.06
159	Steve Yeager	.15	.08	.05
160	Cesar Geronimo	.15	.08	.05
161	Jim Rooker	.15	.08	.05
162	Tim Foli	.15	.08	.05
163	Fred Lynn	1.25	.60	.40
164	Ed Figueroa	.15	.08	.05
165	Johnny Grubb	.15	.08	.05
166	Pedro Garcia	.15	.08	.05
167	Ron LeFlore	.20	.10	.06
168	Rich Hebner	.15	.08	.05
169	Larry Herndon	.25	.13	.08
170	George Brett	9.00	4.50	2.75
171	Joe Kerrigan	.15	.08	.05
172	Bud Harrelson	.20	.10	.06
173	Bobby Bonds	.30	.15	.09
174	Bill Travers	.15	.08	.05
175	John Lowenstein	.15	.08	.05
176	Butch Wynegar	.40	.20	.12
177	Pete Falcone	.15	.08	.05
178	Claudell Washington	.25	.13	.08
179	Checklist 133-264	1.00	.50	.30
180	Dave Cash	.15	.08	.05
181	Fred Norman	.15	.08	.05
182	Roy White	.20	.10	.06
183	Marty Perez	.15	.08	.05
184	Jesse Jefferson	.15	.08	.05
185	Jim Sundberg	.20	.10	.06
186	Dan Meyer	.15	.08	.05
187	Fergie Jenkins	.75	.40	.25
188	Tom Veryzer	.15	.08	.05
189	Dennis Blair	.15	.08	.05
190	Rick Manning	.15	.08	.05
191	Doug Bird	.15	.08	.05
192	Al Bumbry	.20	.10	.06
193	Dave Roberts	.15	.08	.05
194	Larry Christenson	.15	.08	.05
195	Chet Lemon	.30	.15	.09
196	Ted Simmons	.50	.25	.15
197	Ray Burris	.15	.08	.05
198	Expos Coaches (Jim Brewer, Billy Gardner, Mickey Vernon, Ozzie Virgil)	.20	.10	.06
199	Ron Cey	.30	.15	.09
200	Reggie Jackson	6.00	3.00	1.75
201	Pat Zachry	.15	.08	.05
202	Doug Ault	.15	.08	.05
203	Al Oliver	.60	.30	.20
204	Robin Yount	4.00	2.00	1.25
205	Tom Seaver	4.00	2.00	1.25
206	Joe Rudi	.20	.10	.06
207	Barry Foote	.15	.08	.05
208	Toby Harrah	.20	.10	.06
209	Jeff Burroughs	.20	.10	.06
210	George Scott	.20	.10	.06
211	Jim Mason	.15	.08	.05
212	Vern Ruhle	.15	.08	.05
213	Fred Kendall	.15	.08	.05
214	Rick Reuschel	.30	.15	.09
215	Hal McRae	.25	.13	.08
216	Chip Lang	.15	.08	.05
217	Graig Nettles	.75	.40	.25
218	George Hendrick	.25	.13	.08
219	Glenn Abbott	.15	.08	.05
220	Joe Morgan	1.25	.60	.40
221	Sam Ewing	.15	.08	.05
222	George Medich	.15	.08	.05
223	Reggie Smith	.30	.15	.09
224	Dave Hamilton	.15	.08	.05
225	Pepe Frias	.15	.08	.05
226	Jay Johnstone	.25	.13	.08
227	J.R. Richard	.20	.10	.06
228	Doug DeCinces	.35	.20	.11
229	Dave Lemanczyk	.15	.08	.05
230	Rick Monday	.25	.13	.08
231	Manny Sanguillen	.20	.10	.06
232	John Montefusco	.20	.10	.06
233	Duane Kuiper	.15	.08	.05
234	Ellis Valentine	.20	.10	.06
235	Dick Tidrow	.15	.08	.05
236	Ben Oglivie	.20	.10	.06
237	Rick Burleson	.20	.10	.06
238	Roy Hartsfield	.30	.15	.09
239	Lyman Bostock	.30	.15	.09
240	Pete Rose	10.00	5.00	3.00
241	Mike Ivie	.15	.08	.05
242	Dave Parker	3.00	1.50	.90
243	Bill Greif	.15	.08	.05
244	Freddie Patek	.15	.08	.05
245	Mike Schmidt	10.00	5.00	3.00
246	Brian Downing	.20	.10	.06
247	Steve Hargan	.15	.08	.05
248	Dave Collins	.20	.10	.06
249	Felix Millan	.15	.08	.05
250	Don Gullett	.20	.10	.06
251	Jerry Royster	.15	.08	.05
252	Earl Williams	.15	.08	.05
253	Frank Duffy	.15	.08	.05
254	Tippy Martinez	.20	.10	.06
255	Steve Garvey	4.00	2.00	1.25
256	Alvis Woods	.15	.08	.05
257	John Hiller	.20	.10	.06
258	Dave Concepcion	.30	.15	.09
259	Dwight Evans	.75	.40	.25
260	Pete MacKanin	.15	.08	.05
261	Record Breaker (George Brett)	1.50	.70	.45
262	Record Breaker (Minnie Minoso)	.30	.15	.09
263	Record Breaker (Jose Morales)	.20	.10	.06
264	Record Breaker (Nolan Ryan)	1.25	.50	.30

1978 O-Pee-Chee

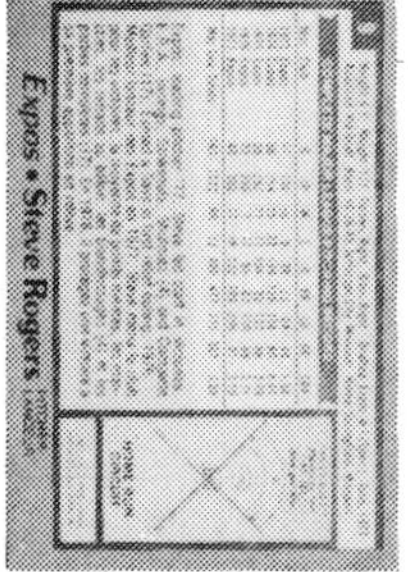

The 1978 O-Pee-Chee set was further reduced to 242 cards and again had heavy representation from the two Canadian teams. The cards measure the standard 2-1/2" by 3-1/2" and the backs are printed in both French and English. The cards use the same design as the 1978 Topps set. Some of the cards contain an extra line on the front indicating a team change.

	NR MT	EX	VG
Complete Set:	100.00	50.00	30.00
Common Player:	.10	.05	.03

No.	Player	NR MT	EX	VG
1	Batting Leaders (Rod Carew, Dave Parker)	.75	.30	.20
2	Home Run Leaders (George Foster, Jim Rice)	.25	.13	.08
3	Runs Batted In Ldrs. (George Foster, Larry Hisle)	.25	.13	.08

		NR MT	EX	VG
4	Stolen Base Leaders (Freddie Patek, Frank Taveras)	.10	.05	.03
5	Victory Leaders (Steve Carlton, Dave Goltz, Dennis Leonard, Jim Palmer)	.50	.25	.15
6	Strikeout Leaders (Phil Niekro, Nolan Ryan)	.30	.15	.09
7	Earned Run Avg. Ldrs. (John Candelaria, Frank Tanana)	.10	.05	.03
8	Leading Firemen (Bill Campbell, Rollie Fingers)	.30	.15	.09
9	Steve Rogers	.10	.05	.03
10	Graig Nettles	.25	.13	.08
11	Doug Capilla	.10	.05	.03
12	George Scott	.15	.08	.05
13	Gary Woods	.10	.05	.03
14	Tom Veryzer	.15	.08	.05
15	Wayne Garland	.10	.05	.03
16	Amos Otis	.15	.08	.05
17	Larry Christenson	.10	.05	.03
18	Dave Cash	.10	.05	.03
19	Jim Barr	.10	.05	.03
20	Ruppert Jones	.15	.08	.05
21	Eric Soderholm	.10	.05	.03
22	Jesse Jefferson	.10	.05	.03
23	Jerry Morales	.10	.05	.03
24	Doug Rau	.10	.05	.03
25	Rennie Stennett	.10	.05	.03
26	Lee Mazzilli	.20	.10	.06
27	Dick Williams	.15	.08	.05
28	Joe Rudi	.20	.10	.06
29	Robin Yount	1.75	.90	.50
30	Don Gullett	.10	.05	.03
31	Roy Howell	.07	.04	.02
32	Cesar Geronimo	.10	.05	.03
33	Rick Langford	.07	.04	.02
34	Dan Ford	.15	.08	.05
35	Gene Tenace	.15	.08	.05
36	Santo Alcala	.10	.05	.03
37	Rick Burleson	.15	.08	.05
38	Dave Rozema	.10	.05	.03
39	Duane Kuiper	.10	.05	.03
40	Ron Fairly	.20	.10	.06
41	Dennis Leonard	.15	.08	.05
42	Greg Luzinski	.30	.15	.09
43	Willie Montanez	.15	.08	.05
44	Enos Cabell	.10	.05	.03
45	Ellis Valentine	.15	.08	.05
46	Steve Stone	.15	.08	.05
47	Lee May	.15	.08	.05
48	Roy White	.15	.08	.05
49	Jerry Garvin	.10	.05	.03
50	Johnny Bench	3.00	1.50	.90
51	Garry Templeton	.25	.13	.08
52	Doyle Alexander	.20	.10	.06
53	Steve Henderson	.20	.10	.06
54	Stan Bahnsen	.10	.05	.03
55	Dan Meyer	.10	.05	.03
56	Rick Reuschel	.20	.10	.06
57	Reggie Smith	.20	.10	.06
58	Blue Jays Team	.15	.08	.05
59	John Montefusco	.15	.08	.05
60	Dave Parker	1.75	.90	.50
61	Jim Bibby	.10	.05	.03
62	Fred Lynn	.75	.40	.25
63	Jose Morales	.10	.05	.03
64	Aurelio Rodriguez	.15	.08	.05
65	Frank Tanana	.20	.10	.06
66	Darrell Porter	.15	.08	.05
67	Otto Velez	.10	.05	.03
68	Larry Bowa	.20	.10	.06
69	Jim Hunter	1.50	.70	.45
70	George Foster	.60	.30	.20
71	Cecil Cooper	.15	.08	.05
72	Gary Alexander	.07	.04	.02
73	Paul Thormodsgard	.10	.05	.03
74	Toby Harrah	.15	.08	.05
75	Mitchell Page	.10	.05	.03
76	Alan Ashby	.10	.05	.03
77	Jorge Orta	.10	.05	.03
78	Dave Winfield	3.00	1.50	.90
79	Andy Messersmith	.20	.10	.06
80	Ken Singleton	.20	.10	.06
81	Will McEnaney	.10	.05	.03
82	Lou Piniella	.30	.15	.09
83	Bob Forsch	.15	.08	.05
84	Dan Driessen	.15	.08	.05
85	Dave Lemanczyk	.10	.05	.03
86	Paul Dade	.10	.05	.03
87	Bill Campbell	.10	.05	.03
88	Ron LeFlore	.15	.08	.05
89	Bill Madlock	.40	.20	.12
90	Tony Perez	.25	.13	.08
91	Freddie Patek	.10	.05	.03
92	Glenn Abbott	.10	.05	.03
93	Garry Maddox	.15	.08	.05
94	Steve Staggs	.10	.05	.03
95	Bobby Murcer	.20	.10	.06
96	Don Sutton	1.00	.50	.30
97	Al Oliver	.75	.40	.25
98	Jon Matlack	.20	.10	.06
99	Sam Mejias	.10	.05	.03
100	Pete Rose	5.00	2.50	1.50
101	Randy Jones	.15	.08	.05
102	Sixto Lezcano	.10	.05	.03
103	Jim Clancy	.20	.10	.06
104	Butch Wynegar	.15	.08	.05
105	Nolan Ryan	3.00	1.50	.90
106	Wayne Gross	.10	.05	.03
107	Bob Watson	.15	.08	.05
108	Joe Kerrigan	.15	.08	.05
109	Keith Hernandez	3.00	1.50	.90
110	Reggie Jackson	5.00	2.50	1.50
111	Denny Doyle	.10	.05	.03
112	Sam Ewing	.10	.05	.03
113	Bert Blyleven	.75	.40	.25
114	Andre Thornton	.20	.10	.06
115	Milt May	.10	.05	.03
116	Jim Colborn	.10	.05	.03
117	Warren Cromartie	.15	.08	.05
118	Ted Sizemore	.10	.05	.03
119	Checklist 1-121	.75	.40	.25
120	Tom Seaver	3.00	1.50	.90
121	Luis Gomez	.10	.05	.03
122	Jim Spencer	.15	.08	.05
123	Leroy Stanton	.10	.05	.03
124	Luis Tiant	.30	.15	.09
125	Mark Belanger	.15	.08	.05
126	Jackie Brown	.10	.05	.03
127	Bill Buckner	.25	.13	.08
128	Bill Robinson	.10	.05	.03
129	Rick Cerone	.15	.08	.05
130	Ron Cey	.25	.13	.08
131	Jose Cruz	.25	.13	.08
132	Len Randle	.07	.04	.02
133	Bob Grich	.20	.10	.06
134	Jeff Burroughs	.15	.08	.05
135	Gary Carter	5.00	2.50	1.50
136	Milt Wilcox	.10	.05	.03
137	Carl Yastrzemski	2.75	1.50	.80
138	Dennis Eckersley	.25	.13	.08
139	Tim Nordbrook	.10	.05	.03
140	Ken Griffey	.25	.13	.08
141	Bob Boone	.20	.10	.06
142	Dave Goltz	.10	.05	.03
143	Al Cowens	.10	.05	.03
144	Bill Atkinson	.10	.05	.03
145	Chris Chambliss	.20	.10	.06
146	Jim Slaton	.15	.08	.05
147	Bill Stein	.10	.05	.03
148	Bob Bailor	.10	.05	.03
149	J.R. Richard	.15	.08	.05
150	Ted Simmons	.40	.20	.12
151	Rick Manning	.10	.05	.03
152	Lerrin LaGrow	.10	.05	.03
153	Larry Parrish	.20	.10	.06
154	Eddie Murray	30.00	15.00	9.00
155	Phil Niekro	1.00	.50	.30
156	Bake McBride	.10	.05	.03
157	Pete Vuckovich	.15	.08	.05
158	Ivan DeJesus	.10	.05	.03
159	Rick Rhoden	.20	.10	.06
160	Joe Morgan	1.25	.60	.40
161	Ed Ott	.10	.05	.03
162	Don Stanhouse	.10	.05	.03
163	Jim Rice	5.00	2.50	1.50
164	Bucky Dent	.20	.10	.06
165	Jim Kern	.10	.05	.03
166	Doug Rader	.10	.05	.03
167	Steve Kemp	.20	.10	.06
168	John Mayberry	.15	.08	.05
169	Tim Foli	.15	.08	.05
170	Steve Carlton	3.00	1.50	.90
171	Pepe Frias	.10	.05	.03
172	Pat Zachry	.10	.05	.03
173	Don Baylor	.40	.20	.12
174	Sal Bando	.15	.08	.05
175	Alvis Woods	.10	.05	.03
176	Mike Hargrove	.15	.08	.05
177	Vida Blue	.25	.13	.08
178	George Hendrick	.15	.08	.05
179	Jim Palmer	1.75	.90	.50
180	Andre Dawson	3.50	1.75	1.00
181	Paul Moskau	.10	.05	.03
182	Mickey Rivers	.15	.08	.05
183	Checklist 122-242	.75	.40	.25
184	Jerry Johnson	.10	.05	.03
185	Willie McCovey	1.75	.90	.50
186	Enrique Romo	.10	.05	.03
187	Butch Hobson	.15	.08	.05
188	Rusty Staub	.30	.15	.09
189	Wayne Twitchell	.10	.05	.03
190	Steve Garvey	3.50	1.75	1.00
191	Rick Waits	.10	.05	.03
192	Doug DeCinces	.20	.10	.06
193	Tom Murphy	.10	.05	.03
194	Rich Hebner	.10	.05	.03
195	Ralph Garr	.15	.08	.05
196	Bruce Sutter	.60	.30	.20
197	Tom Poquette	.10	.05	.03
198	Wayne Garrett	.10	.05	.03
199	Pedro Borbon	.10	.05	.03
200	Thurman Munson	3.00	1.50	.90
201	Rollie Fingers	.60	.30	.20
202	Doug Ault	.10	.05	.03
203	Phil Garner	.10	.05	.03
204	Lou Brock	1.75	.90	.50
205	Ed Kranepool	.15	.08	.05
206	Bobby Bonds	.30	.15	.09
207	Expos Team	.15	.08	.05
208	Bump Wills	.10	.05	.03
209	Gary Matthews	.20	.10	.06
210	Carlton Fisk	.75	.40	.25
211	Jeff Byrd	.10	.05	.03
212	Jason Thompson	.15	.08	.05
213	Larvell Blanks	.10	.05	.03
214	Sparky Lyle	.20	.10	.06
215	George Brett	3.50	1.75	1.00
216	Del Unser	.10	.05	.03
217	Manny Trillo	.15	.08	.05
218	Roy Hartsfield	.15	.08	.05
219	Carlos Lopez	.10	.05	.03
220	Dave Concepcion	.25	.13	.08
221	John Candelaria	.20	.10	.06
222	Dave Lopes	.20	.10	.06
223	Tim Blackwell	.15	.08	.05
224	Chet Lemon	.20	.10	.06
225	Mike Schmidt	6.00	3.00	1.75
226	Cesar Cedeno	.25	.13	.08
227	Mike Willis	.10	.05	.03
228	Willie Randolph	.20	.10	.06
229	Doug Bair	.10	.05	.03
230	Rod Carew	3.00	1.50	.90
231	Mike Flanagan	.20	.10	.06
232	Chris Speier	.10	.05	.03
233	Don Aase	.20	.10	.06
234	Buddy Bell	.25	.13	.08
235	Mark Fidrych	.20	.10	.06
236	Record Breaker (Lou Brock)	.60	.30	.20
237	Record Breaker (Sparky Lyle)	.15	.08	.05
238	Record Breaker (Willie McCovey)	.60	.30	.20
239	Record Breaker (Brooks Robinson)	.75	.40	.25
240	Record Breaker (Pete Rose)	1.75	.90	.50
241	Record Breaker (Nolan Ryan)	.75	.40	.25
242	Record Breaker (Reggie Jackson)	1.50	.50	.30

1979 O-Pee-Chee

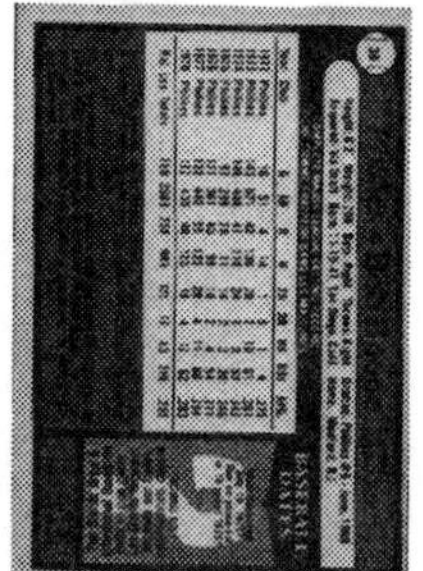

The 1979 O-Pee-Chee cards are nearly identical in design to the Topps set of the same year, but display the O-Pee-Chee logo inside the baseball in the lower left corner of the front. The number of cards in the set was increased to 374, each measuring 2-1/2" by 3-1/2".

		NR MT	EX	VG
Complete Set:		80.00	40.00	24.00
Common Player:		.10	.05	.03
1	Lee May	.30	.10	.06
2	Dick Drago	.10	.05	.03
3	Paul Dade	.10	.05	.03
4	Ross Grimsley	.15	.08	.05
5	Joe Morgan	.30	.15	.09
6	Kevin Kobel	.10	.05	.03
7	Terry Forster	.15	.08	.05
8	Paul Molitor	3.50	1.75	1.00
9	Steve Carlton	3.50	1.75	1.00
10	Dave Goltz	.15	.08	.05
11	Dave Winfield	3.50	1.75	1.00
12	Dave Rozema	.10	.05	.03
13	Ed Figueroa	.10	.05	.03
14	Alan Ashby	.10	.05	.03
15	Dale Murphy	7.00	3.50	2.00
16	Dennis Eckersley	.20	.10	.06
17	Ron Blomberg	.10	.05	.03
18	Wayne Twitchell	.10	.05	.03
19	Al Hrabosky	.15	.08	.05
20	Fred Norman	.10	.05	.03
21	Steve Garvey	1.75	.90	.50
22	Willie Stargell	1.75	.90	.50
23	John Hale	.10	.05	.03
24	Mickey Rivers	.15	.08	.05
25	Jack Brohamer	.10	.05	.03
26	Tom Underwood	.10	.05	.03
27	Mark Belanger	.15	.08	.05
28	Elliott Maddox	.10	.05	.03
29	John Candelaria	.20	.10	.06
30	Shane Rawley	.75	.40	.25
31	Steve Yeager	.10	.05	.03
32	Warren Cromartie	.10	.05	.03
33	Jason Thompson	.15	.08	.05
34	Roger Erickson	.10	.05	.03
35	Gary Matthews	.20	.10	.06
36	Pete Falcone	.10	.05	.03
37	Dick Tidrow	.10	.05	.03
38	Bob Boone	.15	.08	.05
39	Jim Bibby	.10	.05	.03
40	Len Barker	.15	.08	.05
41	Robin Yount	3.00	1.50	.90
42	Sam Mejias	.10	.05	.03
43	Ray Burris	.10	.05	.03
44	Tom Seaver	1.75	.90	.50
45	Roy Howell	.10	.05	.03
46	Jim Todd	.10	.05	.03
47	Frank Duffy	.10	.05	.03
48	Joel Youngblood	.10	.05	.03
49	Vida Blue	.20	.10	.06
50	Cliff Johnson	.15	.08	.05
51	Nolan Ryan	3.00	1.50	.90
52	Ozzie Smith	15.00	7.50	4.50
53	Jim Sundberg	.15	.08	.05
54	Mike Paxton	.10	.05	.03
55	Lou Whitaker	1.75	.90	.50
56	Dan Schatzeder	.10	.05	.03
57	Rick Burleson	.15	.08	.05
58	Doug Bair	.09	.05	.03
59	Ted Martinez	.10	.05	.03
60	Bob Watson	.15	.08	.05
61	Jim Clancy	.15	.08	.05
62	Rowland Office	.10	.05	.03
63	Bobby Murcer	.20	.10	.06
64	Don Gullett	.15	.08	.05
65	Tom Paciorek	.10	.05	.03
66	Rick Rhoden	.20	.10	.06
67	Duane Kuiper	.10	.05	.03
68	Bruce Boisclair	.10	.05	.03
69	Manny Sarmiento	.10	.05	.03
70	Wayne Cage	.10	.05	.03
71	John Hiller	.15	.08	.05
72	Rick Cerone	.15	.08	.05
73	Dwight Evans	.40	.20	.12
74	Buddy Solomon	.10	.05	.03
75	Roy White	.15	.08	.05
76	Mike Flanagan	.15	.08	.05
77	Tom Johnson	.10	.05	.03
78	Glenn Burke	.10	.05	.03

		NR MT	EX	VG
79	Frank Taveras	.10	.05	.03
80	Don Sutton	1.75	.90	.50
81	Leon Roberts	.10	.05	.03
82	George Hendrick	.15	.08	.05
83	Aurelio Rodriguez	.10	.05	.03
84	Ron Reed	.10	.05	.03
85	Alvis Woods	.10	.05	.03
86	Jim Beattie	.10	.05	.03
87	Larry Hisle	.15	.08	.05
88	Mike Garman	.10	.05	.03
89	Tim Johnson	.10	.05	.03
90	Paul Splittorff	.15	.08	.05
91	Darrel Chaney	.10	.05	.03
92	Mike Torrez	.15	.08	.05
93	Eric Soderholm	.10	.05	.03
94	Ron Cey	.20	.10	.06
95	Randy Jones	.15	.08	.05
96	Bill Madlock	.30	.15	.09
97	Steve Kemp	.15	.08	.05
98	Bob Apodaca	.10	.05	.03
99	Johnny Grubb	.10	.05	.03
100	Larry Milbourne	.10	.05	.03
101	Johnny Bench	1.75	.90	.50
102	Dave Lemanczyk	.10	.05	.03
103	Reggie Cleveland	.10	.05	.03
104	Larry Bowa	.20	.10	.06
105	Denny Martinez	.15	.08	.05
106	Bill Travers	.10	.05	.03
107	Willie McCovey	1.25	.60	.40
108	Wilbur Wood	.15	.08	.05
109	Dennis Leonard	.15	.08	.05
110	Roy Smalley	.15	.08	.05
111	Cesar Geronimo	.10	.05	.03
112	Jesse Jefferson	.10	.05	.03
113	Dave Revering	.10	.05	.03
114	Rich Gossage	.60	.30	.20
115	Steve Stone	.15	.08	.05
116	Doug Flynn	.10	.05	.03
117	Bob Forsch	.15	.08	.05
118	Paul Mitchell	.10	.05	.03
119	Toby Harrah	.15	.08	.05
120	Steve Rogers	.15	.08	.05
121	Checklist 1-125	.15	.08	.05
122	Balor Moore	.10	.05	.03
123	Rick Reuschel	.20	.10	.06
124	Jeff Burroughs	.15	.08	.05
125	Willie Randolph	.20	.10	.06
126	Bob Stinson	.10	.05	.03
127	Rick Wise	.15	.08	.05
128	Luis Gomez	.10	.05	.03
129	Tommy John	.75	.40	.25
130	Richie Zisk	.15	.08	.05
131	Mario Guerrero	.10	.05	.03
132	Oscar Gamble	.15	.08	.05
133	Don Money	.10	.05	.03
134	Joe Rudi	.15	.08	.05
135	Woodie Fryman	.10	.05	.03
136	Butch Hobson	.10	.05	.03
137	Jim Colborn	.10	.05	.03
138	Tom Grieve	.10	.05	.03
139	Andy Messersmith	.15	.08	.05
140	Andre Thornton	.15	.08	.05
141	Kevin Kravec	.10	.05	.03
142	Bobby Bonds	.25	.13	.08
143	Jose Cruz	.20	.10	.06
144	Dave Lopes	.20	.10	.06
145	Jerry Garvin	.10	.05	.03
146	Pepe Frias	.10	.05	.03
147	Mitchell Page	.10	.05	.03
148	Ted Sizemore	.10	.05	.03
149	Rich Gale	.10	.05	.03
150	Steve Ontiveros	.10	.05	.03
151	Rod Carew	3.00	1.50	.90
152	Lary Sorensen	.10	.05	.03
153	Willie Montanez	.10	.05	.03
154	Floyd Bannister	.25	.13	.08
155	Bert Blyleven	.30	.15	.09
156	Ralph Garr	.15	.08	.05
157	Thurman Munson	1.75	.90	.50
158	Bob Robertson	.10	.05	.03
159	Jon Matlack	.15	.08	.05
160	Carl Yastrzemski	3.50	1.75	1.00
161	Gaylord Perry	1.25	.60	.40
162	Mike Tyson	.10	.05	.03
163	Cecil Cooper	.30	.15	.09
164	Pedro Borbon	.10	.05	.03
165	Art Howe	.10	.05	.03
166	Joe Coleman	.10	.05	.03
167	George Brett	4.00	2.00	1.25
168	Gary Alexander	.10	.05	.03
169	Chet Lemon	.15	.08	.05
170	Craig Swan	.10	.05	.03
171	Chris Chambliss	.15	.08	.05
172	John Montague	.10	.05	.03
173	Ron Jackson	.10	.05	.03
174	Jim Palmer	1.25	.60	.40
175	Willie Upshaw	.75	.40	.25
176	Tug McGraw	.20	.10	.06
177	Bill Buckner	.25	.13	.08
178	Doug Rau	.10	.05	.03
179	Andre Dawson	3.50	1.75	1.00
180	Jim Wright	.10	.05	.03
181	Garry Templeton	.15	.08	.05
182	Bill Bonham	.10	.05	.03
183	Lee Mazzilli	.15	.08	.05
184	Alan Trammell	5.00	2.50	1.50
185	Amos Otis	.15	.08	.05
186	Tom Dixon	.10	.05	.03
187	Mike Cubbage	.10	.05	.03
188	Sparky Lyle	.20	.10	.06
189	Juan Bernhardt	.10	.05	.03
190	Bump Wills	.15	.08	.05
191	Dave Kingman	.30	.15	.09
192	Lamar Johnson	.10	.05	.03
193	Lance Rautzhan	.10	.05	.03
194	Ed Herrmann	.10	.05	.03
195	Bill Campbell	.10	.05	.03
196	Gorman Thomas	.15	.08	.05
197	Paul Moskau	.10	.05	.03
198	Dale Murray	.10	.05	.03
199	John Mayberry	.15	.08	.05
200	Phil Garner	.15	.08	.05
201	Dan Ford	.10	.05	.03
202	Gary Thomasson	.10	.05	.03
203	Rollie Fingers	.60	.30	.20
204	Al Oliver	.40	.20	.12
205	Doug Ault	.10	.05	.03
206	Scott McGregor	.15	.08	.05
207	Dave Cash	.10	.05	.03
208	Bill Plummer	.10	.05	.03
209	Ivan DeJesus	.10	.05	.03
210	Jim Rice	3.50	1.75	1.00
211	Ray Knight	.20	.10	.06
212	Paul Hartzell	.10	.05	.03
213	Tim Foli	.10	.05	.03
214	Butch Wynegar	.10	.05	.03
215	Darrell Evans	.25	.13	.08
216	Ken Griffey	.25	.13	.08
217	Doug DeCinces	.20	.10	.06
218	Ruppert Jones	.15	.08	.05
219	Bob Montgomery	.10	.05	.03
220	Rick Manning	.10	.05	.03
221	Chris Speier	.10	.05	.03
222	Bobby Valentine	.15	.08	.05
223	Dave Parker	1.75	.90	.50
224	Larry Biittner	.10	.05	.03
225	Ken Clay	.10	.05	.03
226	Gene Tenace	.15	.08	.05
227	Frank White	.20	.10	.06
228	Rusty Staub	.25	.13	.08
229	Lee Lacy	.15	.08	.05
230	Doyle Alexander	.20	.10	.06
231	Bruce Bochte	.15	.08	.05
232	Steve Henderson	.10	.05	.03
233	Jim Lonborg	.15	.08	.05
234	Dave Concepcion	.25	.13	.08
235	Jerry Morales	.10	.05	.03
236	Len Randle	.10	.05	.03
237	Bill Lee	.15	.08	.05
238	Bruce Sutter	.60	.30	.20
239	Jim Essian	.10	.05	.03
240	Graig Nettles	.40	.20	.12
241	Otto Velez	.09	.05	.03
242	Checklist 126-250	.15	.08	.05
243	Reggie Smith	.20	.10	.06
244	Stan Bahnsen	.10	.05	.03
245	Garry Maddox	.10	.05	.03
246	Joaquin Andujar	.20	.10	.06
247	Dan Driessen	.15	.08	.05
248	Bob Grich	.20	.10	.06
249	Fred Lynn	.60	.30	.20
250	Skip Lockwood	.10	.05	.03
251	Craig Reynolds	.09	.05	.03
252	Willie Horton	.15	.08	.05
253	Rick Waits	.10	.05	.03
254	Bucky Dent	.20	.10	.06
255	Bob Knepper	.20	.10	.06
256	Miguel Dilone	.10	.05	.03
257	Bob Owchinko	.10	.05	.03
258	Al Cowens	.10	.05	.03
259	Bob Bailor	.10	.05	.03
260	Larry Christenson	.10	.05	.03
261	Tony Perez	.50	.25	.15
262	Blue Jays Team	.20	.10	.06
263	Glenn Abbott	.10	.05	.03
264	Ron Guidry	.75	.40	.25
265	Ed Kranepool	.15	.08	.05
266	Charlie Hough	.15	.08	.05
267	Ted Simmons	.30	.15	.09
268	Jack Clark	1.25	.60	.40
269	Enos Cabell	.10	.05	.03
270	Gary Carter	4.00	2.00	1.25
271	Sam Ewing	.10	.05	.03
272	Tom Burgmeier	.10	.05	.03
273	Freddie Patek	.10	.05	.03
274	Frank Tanana	.15	.08	.05
275	Leroy Stanton	.10	.05	.03
276	Ken Forsch	.10	.05	.03
277	Ellis Valentine	.15	.08	.05
278	Greg Luzinski	.30	.15	.09
279	Rick Bosetti	.10	.05	.03
280	John Stearns	.15	.08	.05
281	Enrique Romo	.10	.05	.03
282	Bob Bailey	.10	.05	.03
283	Sal Bando	.15	.08	.05
284	Matt Keough	.10	.05	.03
285	Biff Pocoroba	.10	.05	.03
286	Mike Lum	.10	.05	.03
287	Jay Johnstone	.15	.08	.05
288	John Montefusco	.15	.08	.05
289	Ed Ott	.10	.05	.03
290	Dusty Baker	.20	.10	.06
291	Rico Carty	.15	.08	.05
292	Nino Espinosa	.10	.05	.03
293	Rich Hebner	.10	.05	.03
294	Cesar Cedeno	.25	.13	.08
295	Darrell Porter	.15	.08	.05
296	Rod Gilbreath	.10	.05	.03
297	Jim Kern	.10	.05	.03
298	Claudell Washington	.15	.08	.05
299	Luis Tiant	.30	.15	.09
300	Mike Parrott	.10	.05	.03
301	Pete Broberg	.10	.05	.03
302	Greg Gross	.10	.05	.03
303	Darold Knowles	.10	.05	.03
304	Paul Blair	.15	.08	.05
305	Julio Cruz	.15	.08	.05
306	Hal McRae	.20	.10	.06
307	Ken Reitz	.10	.05	.03
308	Tom Murphy	.10	.05	.03
309	Terry Whitfield	.10	.05	.03
310	J.R. Richard	.15	.08	.05
311	Mike Hargrove	.15	.08	.05
312	Rick Dempsey	.15	.08	.05
313	Phil Niekro	1.75	.90	.50
314	Bob Stanley	.20	.10	.06
315	Jim Spencer	.10	.05	.03
316	George Foster	.50	.25	.15
317	Dave LaRoche	.10	.05	.03
318	Rudy May	.10	.05	.03
319	Jeff Newman	.10	.05	.03
320	Rick Monday	.15	.08	.05
321	Omar Moreno	.15	.08	.05
322	Dave McKay	.10	.05	.03
323	Mike Schmidt	3.25	1.75	1.00
324	Ken Singleton	.20	.10	.06
325	Jerry Remy	.10	.05	.03
326	Bert Campaneris	.20	.10	.06
327	Pat Zachry	.10	.05	.03
328	Larry Herndon	.15	.08	.05
329	Mark Fidrych	.20	.10	.06
330	Del Unser	.10	.05	.03
331	Gene Garber	.10	.05	.03
332	Bake McBride	.10	.05	.03
333	Jorge Orta	.10	.05	.03
334	Don Kirkwood	.10	.05	.03
335	Don Baylor	.40	.20	.12
336	Bill Robinson	.10	.05	.03
337	Manny Trillo	.15	.08	.05
338	Eddie Murray	4.25	2.25	1.25
339	Tom Hausman	.10	.05	.03
340	George Scott	.10	.05	.03
341	Rick Sweet	.10	.05	.03
342	Lou Piniella	.25	.13	.08
343	Pete Rose	6.00	3.00	1.75
344	Stan Papi	.10	.05	.03
345	Jerry Koosman	.15	.08	.05
346	Hosken Powell	.10	.05	.03
347	George Medich	.10	.05	.03
348	Ron LeFlore	.10	.05	.03
349	Expos Team	.20	.10	.06
350	Lou Brock	1.25	.60	.40
351	Bill North	.10	.05	.03
352	Jim Hunter	.60	.30	.20
353	Checklist 251-374	.15	.08	.05
354	Ed Halicki	.10	.05	.03
355	Tom Hutton	.10	.05	.03
356	Mike Caldwell	.10	.05	.03
357	Larry Parrish	.15	.08	.05
358	Geoff Zahn	.10	.05	.03
359	Derrel Thomas	.10	.05	.03
360	Carlton Fisk	.75	.40	.25
361	John Henry Johnson	.10	.05	.03
362	Dave Chalk	.10	.05	.03
363	Dan Meyer	.10	.05	.03
364	Sixto Lezcano	.10	.05	.03
365	Rennie Stennett	.10	.05	.03
366	Mike Willis	.10	.05	.03
367	Buddy Bell	.15	.08	.05
368	Mickey Stanley	.15	.08	.05
369	Dave Rader	.10	.05	.03
370	Burt Hooton	.15	.08	.05
371	Keith Hernandez	1.50	.70	.45
372	Bill Stein	.10	.05	.03
373	Hal Dues	.10	.05	.03
374	Reggie Jackson	1.50	.60	.30

1980 O-Pee-Chee

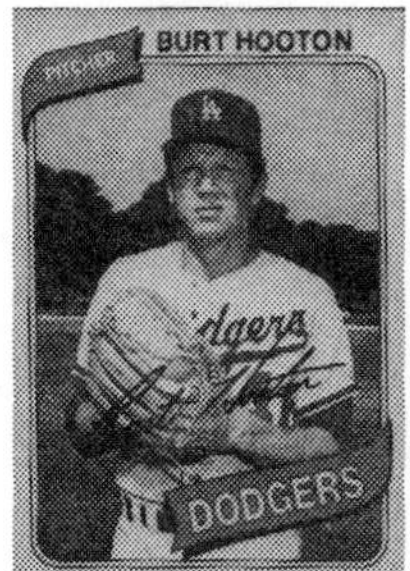

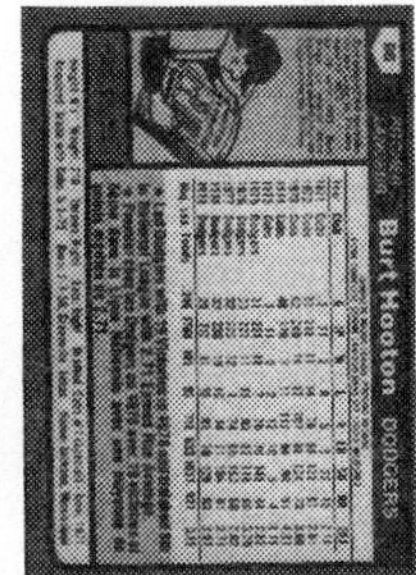

The 1980 Canadian-issued O-Pee-Chee set was again complete at 374 cards, which measure 2-1/2" by 3-1/2" and share the same design as the 1980 Topps set. The O-Pee-Chee cards are printed on a white stock, rather than the traditional gray stock used by Topps, and the backs of the Canadian-issued cards are written in both French and English. Some of the cards include an extra line on the front indicating a new team designation.

		NR MT	EX	VG
Complete Set:		50.00	25.00	15.00
Common Player:		.10	.05	.03
1	Craig Swan	.15	.05	.03
2	Denny Martinez	.15	.08	.05
3	Dave Cash	.10	.05	.03
4	Bruce Sutter	.50	.25	.15
5	Ron Jackson	.10	.05	.03
6	Balor Moore	.10	.05	.03
7	Dan Ford	.10	.05	.03
8	Pat Putnam	.10	.05	.03
9	Derrel Thomas	.10	.05	.03
10	Jim Slaton	.10	.05	.03
11	Lee Mazzilli	.15	.08	.05
12	Del Unser	.10	.05	.03
13	Mark Wagner	.10	.05	.03
14	Vida Blue	.20	.10	.06
15	Jay Johnstone	.15	.08	.05
16	Julio Cruz	.10	.05	.03
17	Tony Scott	.10	.05	.03
18	Jeff Newman	.10	.05	.03
19	Luis Tiant	.25	.13	.08
20	Carlton Fisk	.60	.30	.20
21	Dave Palmer	.30	.15	.09
22	Bombo Rivera	.10	.05	.03
23	Bill Fahey	.10	.05	.03
24	Frank White	.20	.10	.06
25	Rico Carty	.15	.08	.05
26	Bill Bonham	.10	.05	.03
27	Rick Miller	.10	.05	.03
28	J.R. Richard	.15	.08	.05
29	Joe Ferguson	.10	.05	.03
30	Bill Madlock	.30	.15	.09
31	Pete Vuckovich	.15	.08	.05

		NR MT	EX	VG
32	Doug Flynn	.10	.05	.03
33	Bucky Dent	.20	.10	.06
34	Mike Ivie	.10	.05	.03
35	Bob Stanley	.15	.08	.05
36	Al Bumbry	.15	.08	.05
37	Gary Carter	2.00	1.00	.60
38	John Milner	.10	.05	.03
39	Sid Monge	.10	.05	.03
40	Bill Russell	.15	.08	.05
41	John Stearns	.15	.08	.05
42	Dave Stieb	1.50	.70	.45
43	Ruppert Jones	.15	.08	.05
44	Bob Owchinko	.10	.05	.03
45	Ron LeFlore	.20	.10	.06
46	Ted Sizemore	.10	.05	.03
47	Ted Simmons	.30	.15	.09
48	Pepe Frias	.15	.08	.05
49	Ken Landreaux	.15	.08	.05
50	Manny Trillo	.15	.08	.05
51	Rick Dempsey	.15	.08	.05
52	Cecil Cooper	.30	.15	.09
53	Bill Lee	.15	.08	.05
54	Victor Cruz	.10	.05	.03
55	Johnny Bench	2.00	1.00	.60
56	Rich Dauer	.10	.05	.03
57	Frank Tanana	.15	.08	.05
58	Francisco Barrios	.10	.05	.03
59	Bob Horner	.90	.45	.25
60	Fred Lynn	.30	.15	.09
61	Bob Knepper	.15	.08	.05
62	Sparky Lyle	.15	.08	.05
63	Larry Cox	.10	.05	.03
64	Dock Ellis	.15	.08	.05
65	Phil Garner	.12	.06	.04
66	Greg Luzinski	.30	.15	.09
67	Checklist 1-125	.40	.20	.12
68	Dave Lemanczyk	.10	.05	.03
69	Tony Perez	.50	.25	.15
70	Gary Thomasson	.10	.05	.03
71	Craig Reynolds	.10	.05	.03
72	Amos Otis	.15	.08	.05
73	Biff Pocoroba	.10	.05	.03
74	Matt Keough	.10	.05	.03
75	Bill Buckner	.25	.13	.08
76	John Castino	.12	.06	.04
77	Rich Gossage	.50	.25	.15
78	Gary Alexander	.10	.05	.03
79	Phil Huffman	.10	.05	.03
80	Bruce Bochte	.15	.08	.05
81	Darrell Evans	.25	.13	.08
82	Terry Puhl	.15	.08	.05
83	Jason Thompson	.15	.08	.05
84	Lary Sorenson	.10	.05	.03
85	Jerry Remy	.10	.05	.03
86	Tony Brizzolara	.10	.05	.03
87	Willie Wilson	.25	.13	.08
88	Eddie Murray	3.00	1.50	.90
89	Larry Christenson	.10	.05	.03
90	Bob Randall	.10	.05	.03
91	Greg Pryor	.10	.05	.03
92	Glenn Abbott	.10	.05	.03
93	Jack Clark	1.00	.50	.30
94	Rick Waits	.10	.05	.03
95	Luis Gomez	.10	.05	.03
96	Burt Hooton	.15	.08	.05
97	John Henry Johnson	.10	.05	.03
98	Ray Knight	.15	.08	.05
99	Rick Reuschel	.20	.10	.06
100	Champ Summers	.10	.05	.03
101	Ron Davis	.20	.10	.06
102	Warren Cromartie	.10	.05	.03
103	Ken Reitz	.10	.05	.03
104	Hal McRae	.20	.10	.06
105	Alan Ashby	.10	.05	.03
106	Kevin Kobel	.10	.05	.03
107	Buddy Bell	.25	.13	.08
108	Dave Goltz	.20	.10	.06
109	John Montefusco	.10	.05	.03
110	Lance Parrish	1.25	.60	.40
111	Mike LaCoss	.10	.05	.03
112	Jim Rice	2.00	1.00	.60
113	Steve Carlton	2.00	1.00	.60
114	Sixto Lezcano	.10	.05	.03
115	Ed Halicki	.10	.05	.03
116	Jose Morales	.10	.05	.03
117	Dave Concepcion	.25	.13	.08
118	Joe Cannon	.10	.05	.03
119	Willie Montanez	.15	.08	.05
120	Lou Piniella	.25	.13	.08
121	Bill Stein	.10	.05	.03
122	Dave Winfield	1.50	.70	.45
123	Alan Trammell	1.25	.60	.40
124	Andre Dawson	1.25	.60	.40
125	Marc Hill	.10	.05	.03
126	Don Aase	.15	.08	.05
127	Dave Kingman	.40	.20	.12
128	Checklist 126-250	.40	.20	.12
129	Dennis Lamp	.10	.05	.03
130	Phil Niekro	.75	.40	.25
131	Tim Foli	.05	.03	.02
132	Jim Clancy	.15	.08	.05
133	Bill Atkinson	.15	.08	.05
134	Paul Dade	.05	.03	.02
135	Dusty Baker	.20	.10	.06
136	Al Oliver	.30	.15	.09
137	Dave Chalk	.10	.05	.03
138	Bill Robinson	.10	.05	.03
139	Robin Yount	1.50	.70	.45
140	Dan Schatzeder	.15	.08	.05
141	Mike Schmidt	3.00	1.50	.90
142	Ralph Garr	.15	.08	.05
143	Dale Murphy	4.50	2.25	1.25
144	Jerry Koosman	2.00	1.00	.60
145	Tom Veryzer	.10	.05	.03
146	Rick Bosetti	.10	.05	.03
147	Jim Spencer	.10	.05	.03
148	Gaylord Perry	.75	.40	.25
149	Paul Blair	.15	.08	.05
150	Don Baylor	.30	.15	.09
151	Dave Rozema	.10	.05	.03
152	Steve Garvey	1.75	.90	.50
153	Elias Sosa	.10	.05	.03
154	Larry Gura	.10	.05	.03
155	Tim Johnson	.10	.05	.03

		NR MT	EX	VG
156	Steve Henderson	.10	.05	.03
157	Ron Guidry	.75	.40	.25
158	Mike Edwards	.10	.05	.03
159	Butch Wynegar	.15	.08	.05
160	Randy Jones	.15	.08	.05
161	Denny Walling	.10	.05	.03
162	Mike Hargrove	.15	.08	.05
163	Dave Parker	.75	.40	.25
164	Roger Metzger	.10	.05	.03
165	Johnny Grubb	.10	.05	.03
166	Steve Kemp	.15	.08	.05
167	Bob Lacey	.10	.05	.03
168	Chris Speier	.10	.05	.03
169	Dennis Eckersley	.15	.08	.05
170	Keith Hernandez	1.25	.60	.40
171	Claudell Washington	.15	.08	.05
172	Tom Underwood	.10	.05	.03
173	Dan Driessen	.15	.08	.05
174	Al Cowens	.10	.05	.03
175	Rich Hebner	.10	.05	.03
176	Willie McCovey	1.25	.60	.40
177	Carney Lansford	.30	.15	.09
178	Ken Singleton	.20	.10	.06
179	Jim Essian	.10	.05	.03
180	Mike Vail	.10	.05	.03
181	Randy Lerch	.10	.05	.03
182	Larry Parrish	.20	.10	.06
183	Checklist 251-374	.40	.20	.12
184	George Hendrick	.15	.08	.05
185	Bob Davis	.10	.05	.03
186	Gary Matthews	.15	.08	.05
187	Lou Whitaker	.75	.40	.25
188	Darrell Porter	.10	.05	.03
189	Wayne Gross	.10	.05	.03
190	Bobby Murcer	.20	.10	.06
191	Willie Aikens	.15	.08	.05
192	Jim Kern	.10	.05	.03
193	Cesar Cedeno	.20	.10	.06
194	Joel Youngblood	.10	.05	.03
195	Ross Grimsley	.15	.08	.05
196	Jerry Mumphrey	.20	.10	.06
197	Kevin Bell	.10	.05	.03
198	Garry Maddox	.15	.08	.05
199	Dave Freisleben	.10	.05	.03
200	Ed Ott	.10	.05	.03
201	Enos Cabell	.10	.05	.03
202	Pete LaCock	.10	.05	.03
203	Fergie Jenkins	.40	.20	.12
204	Milt Wilcox	.15	.08	.05
205	Ozzie Smith	1.25	.60	.40
206	Ellis Valentine	.15	.08	.05
207	Dan Meyer	.10	.05	.03
208	Barry Foote	.10	.05	.03
209	George Foster	.40	.20	.12
210	Dwight Evans	.50	.25	.15
211	Paul Molitor	.75	.40	.25
212	Tony Solaita	.10	.05	.03
213	Bill North	.10	.05	.03
214	Paul Splittorff	.15	.08	.05
215	Bobby Bonds	.25	.13	.08
216	Butch Hobson	.10	.05	.03
217	Mark Belanger	.15	.08	.05
218	Grant Jackson	.10	.05	.03
219	Tom Hutton	.10	.05	.03
220	Pat Zachry	.10	.05	.03
221	Duane Kuiper	.10	.05	.03
222	Larry Hisle	.15	.08	.05
223	Mike Krukow	.15	.08	.05
224	Johnnie LeMaster	.10	.05	.03
225	Billy Almon	.15	.08	.05
226	Joe Niekro	.15	.08	.05
227	Dave Revering	.10	.05	.03
228	Don Sutton	.75	.40	.25
229	John Hiller	.15	.08	.05
230	Alvis Woods	.10	.05	.03
231	Mark Fidrych	.15	.08	.05
232	Duffy Dyer	.10	.05	.03
233	Nino Espinosa	.10	.05	.03
234	Doug Bair	.10	.05	.03
235	George Brett	3.25	1.75	1.00
236	Mike Torrez	.15	.08	.05
237	Frank Taveras	.10	.05	.03
238	Bert Blyleven	.30	.15	.09
239	Willie Randolph	.15	.08	.05
240	Mike Sadek	.10	.05	.03
241	Jerry Royster	.10	.05	.03
242	John Denny	.15	.08	.05
243	Rick Monday	.15	.08	.05
244	Jesse Jefferson	.10	.05	.03
245	Aurelio Rodriguez	.15	.08	.05
246	Bob Boone	.15	.08	.05
247	Cesar Geronimo	.10	.05	.03
248	Bob Shirley	.10	.05	.03
249	Expos Team	.20	.10	.06
250	Bob Watson	.15	.08	.05
251	Mickey Rivers	.15	.08	.05
252	Mke Tyson	.15	.08	.05
253	Wayne Nordhagen	.10	.05	.03
254	Roy Howell	.10	.05	.03
255	Lee May	.15	.08	.05
256	Jerry Martin	.10	.05	.03
257	Bake McBride	.10	.05	.03
258	Silvio Martinez	.10	.05	.03
259	Jim Mason	.10	.05	.03
260	Tom Seaver	1.50	.70	.45
261	Rick Wortham	.10	.05	.03
262	Mike Cubbage	.10	.05	.03
263	Gene Garber	.10	.05	.03
264	Bert Campaneris	.15	.08	.05
265	Tom Buskey	.10	.05	.03
266	Leon Roberts	.10	.05	.03
267	Ron Cey	.20	.10	.06
268	Steve Ontiveros	.10	.05	.03
269	Mike Caldwell	.10	.05	.03
270	Nelson Norman	.10	.05	.03
271	Steve Rogers	.15	.08	.05
272	Jim Morrison	.10	.05	.03
273	Clint Hurdle	.10	.05	.03
274	Dale Murray	.10	.05	.03
275	Jim Barr	.10	.05	.03
276	Jim Sundberg	.15	.08	.05
277	Willie Horton	.15	.08	.05
278	Andre Thornton	.20	.10	.06
279	Bob Forsch	.15	.08	.05

		NR MT	EX	VG
280	Joe Strain	.10	.05	.03
281	Rudy May	.15	.08	.05
282	Pete Rose	3.50	1.75	1.00
283	Jeff Burroughs	.15	.08	.05
284	Rick Langford	.10	.05	.03
285	Ken Griffey	.20	.10	.06
286	Bill Nahorodny	.15	.08	.05
287	Art Howe	.10	.05	.03
288	Ed Figueroa	.10	.05	.03
289	Joe Rudi	.15	.08	.05
290	Alfredo Griffin	.15	.08	.05
291	Dave Lopes	.15	.08	.05
292	Rick Manning	.10	.05	.03
293	Dennis Leonard	.15	.08	.05
294	Bud Harrelson	.10	.05	.03
295	Skip Lockwood	.15	.08	.05
296	Roy Smalley	.15	.08	.05
297	Kent Tekulve	.15	.08	.05
298	Scot Thompson	.10	.05	.03
299	Ken Kravec	.10	.05	.03
300	Blue Jays Team	.20	.10	.06
301	Scott Sanderson	.12	.06	.04
302	Charlie Moore	.10	.05	.03
303	Nolan Ryan	4.00	2.00	1.25
304	Bob Bailor	.10	.05	.03
305	Bob Stinson	.10	.05	.03
306	Al Hrabosky	.15	.08	.05
307	Mitchell Page	.10	.05	.03
308	Garry Templeton	.15	.08	.05
309	Chet Lemon	.15	.08	.05
310	Jim Palmer	1.00	.50	.30
311	Rick Cerone	.15	.08	.05
312	Jon Matlack	.15	.08	.05
313	Don Money	.10	.05	.03
314	Reggie Jackson	2.00	1.00	.60
315	Brian Downing	.15	.08	.05
316	Woodie Fryman	.10	.05	.03
317	Alan Bannister	.10	.05	.03
318	Ron Reed	.10	.05	.03
319	Willie Stargell	1.25	.60	.40
320	Jerry Garvin	.10	.05	.03
321	Cliff Johnson	.10	.05	.03
322	Doug DeCinces	.20	.10	.06
323	Gene Richards	.10	.05	.03
324	Joaquin Andujar	.15	.08	.05
325	Richie Zisk	.15	.08	.05
326	Bob Grich	.20	.10	.06
327	Gorman Thomas	.15	.08	.05
328	Chris Chambliss	.15	.08	.05
329	Blue Jays Future Stars (Butch Edge, Pat Kelly, Ted Wilborn)	.10	.05	.03
330	Larry Bowa	.20	.10	.06
331	Barry Bonnell	.15	.08	.05
332	John Candelaria	.15	.08	.05
333	Toby Harrah	.15	.08	.05
334	Larry Biittner	.10	.05	.03
335	Mike Flanagan	.15	.08	.05
336	Ed Kranepool	.15	.08	.05
337	Ken Forsch	.10	.05	.03
338	John Mayberry	.15	.08	.05
339	Rick Burleson	.15	.08	.05
340	Milt May	.15	.08	.05
341	Roy White	.15	.08	.05
342	Joe Morgan	.75	.40	.25
343	Rollie Fingers	.40	.20	.12
344	Mario Mendoza	.10	.05	.03
345	Stan Bahnsen	.10	.05	.03
346	Tug McGraw	.20	.10	.06
347	Rusty Staub	.25	.13	.08
348	Tommy John	.50	.25	.15
349	Ivan DeJesus	.10	.05	.03
350	Reggie Smith	.20	.10	.06
351	Expos Future Stars (Tony Bernazard, Randy Miller, John Tamargo)	.25	.13	.08
352	Floyd Bannister	.15	.08	.05
353	Rod Carew	.75	.40	.25
354	Otto Velez	.10	.05	.03
355	Gene Tenace	.15	.08	.05
356	Freddie Patek	.15	.08	.05
357	Elliott Maddox	.10	.05	.03
358	Pat Underwood	.10	.05	.03
359	Graig Nettles	.30	.15	.09
360	Rodney Scott	.10	.05	.03
361	Terry Whitfield	.10	.05	.03
362	Fred Norman	.10	.05	.03
363	Sal Bando	.15	.08	.05
364	Greg Gross	.60	.30	.20
365	Carl Yastrzemski	1.00	.50	.30
366	Paul Hartzell	.10	.05	.03
367	Jose Cruz	.20	.10	.06
368	Shane Rawley	.15	.08	.05
369	Jerry White	.10	.05	.03
370	Rick Wise	.15	.08	.05
371	Steve Yeager	.10	.05	.03
372	Omar Moreno	.10	.05	.03
373	Bump Wills	.10	.05	.03
374	Craig Kusick	.15	.05	.03

1981 O-Pee-Chee

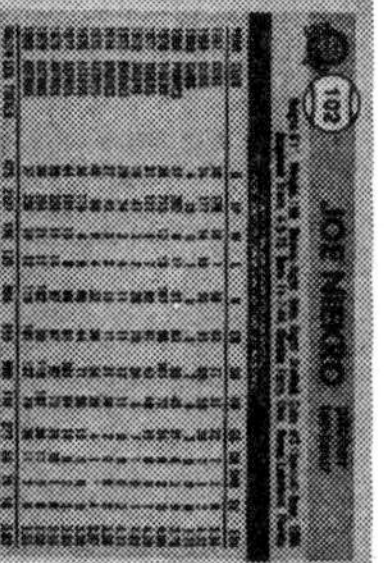

The Canadian version of the 1981 Topps set consists of 374 cards. This O-Pee-Chee set features many cards which note a player team change. These notations could be accomplished as the O-Pee-Chee cards were printed after the Topps. The cards measure 2-1/2" by 3-1/2" and have texts that are written in both English and French. The cards were printed on both white and grey stock. Cards with grey stock are valued three times greater than those with white stock.

		MT	NR MT	EX
	Complete Set:	40.00	30.00	15.00
	Common Player:	.08	.06	.03
1	Frank Pastore	.08	.06	.03
2	Phil Huffman	.08	.06	.03
3	Len Barker	.10	.08	.04
4	Robin Yount	.75	.60	.30
5	Dave Stieb	.40	.30	.15
6	Gary Carter	1.00	.70	.40
7	Butch Hobson	.08	.06	.03
8	Lance Parrish	.60	.45	.25
9	Bruce Sutter	.25	.20	.10
10	Mike Flanagan	.10	.08	.04
11	Paul Mirabella	.08	.06	.03
12	Craig Reynolds	.08	.06	.03
13	Joe Charboneau	.10	.08	.04
14	Dan Driessen	.10	.08	.04
15	Larry Parrish	.10	.08	.04
16	Ron Davis	.08	.06	.03
17	Cliff Johnson	.08	.06	.03
18	Bruce Bochte	.08	.06	.03
19	Jim Clancy	.10	.08	.04
20	Bill Russell	.10	.08	.04
21	Ron Oester	.08	.06	.03
22	Danny Darwin	.10	.08	.04
23	Willie Aikens	.08	.06	.03
24	Don Stanhouse	.08	.06	.03
25	Sixto Lezcano	.08	.06	.03
26	U.L. Washington	.08	.06	.03
27	Champ Summers	.08	.06	.03
28	Enrique Romo	.08	.06	.03
29	Gene Tenace	.10	.08	.04
30	Jack Clark	.40	.30	.15
31	Checklist 1-125	.08	.06	.03
32	Ken Oberkfell	.08	.06	.03
33	Rick Honeycutt	.10	.08	.04
34	Al Bumbry	.10	.08	.04
35	John Tamargo	.08	.06	.03
36	Ed Farmer	.08	.06	.03
37	Gary Roenicke	.08	.06	.03
38	Tim Foli	.03	.02	.01
39	Eddie Murray	1.25	.90	.50
40	Roy Howell	.08	.06	.03
41	Bill Gullickson	.25	.20	.10
42	Jerry White	.08	.06	.03
43	Tim Blackwell	.08	.06	.03
44	Steve Henderson	.08	.06	.03
45	Enos Cabell	.08	.06	.03
46	Rick Bossetti	.08	.06	.03
47	Bill North	.08	.06	.03
48	Rich Gossage	.30	.25	.12
49	Bob Shirley	.08	.06	.03
50	Dave Lopes	.10	.08	.04
51	Shane Rawley	.10	.08	.04
52	Lloyd Moseby	1.50	1.25	.60
53	Burt Hooton	.10	.08	.04
54	Ivan DeJesus	.08	.06	.03
55	Mike Norris	.08	.06	.03
56	Del Unser	.08	.06	.03
57	Dave Revering	.08	.06	.03
58	Joel Youngblood	.08	.06	.03
59	Steve McCatty	.08	.06	.03
60	Willie Randolph	.10	.08	.04
61	Butch Wynegar	.10	.08	.04
62	Gary Lavelle	.08	.06	.03
63	Willie Montanez	.08	.06	.03
64	Terry Puhl	.08	.06	.03
65	Scott McGregor	.10	.08	.04
66	Buddy Bell	.15	.11	.06
67	Toby Harrah	.10	.08	.04
68	Jim Rice	.75	.60	.30
69	Darrell Evans	.15	.11	.06
70	Al Oliver	.10	.08	.04
71	Hal Dues	.08	.06	.03
72	Barry Evans	.08	.06	.03
73	Doug Bair	.08	.06	.03
74	Mike Hargrove	.10	.08	.04
75	Reggie Smith	.12	.09	.05
76	Mario Mendoza	.08	.06	.03
77	Mike Barlow	.08	.06	.03
78	Garth Iorg	.08	.06	.03
79	Jeff Reardon	1.00	.70	.40
80	Roger Erickson	.08	.06	.03
81	Dave Stapleton	.08	.06	.03
82	Barry Bonnell	.08	.06	.03
83	Dave Concepcion	.15	.11	.06
84	Johnnie LeMaster	.08	.06	.03
85	Mike Caldwell	.08	.06	.03
86	Wayne Gross	.08	.06	.03
87	Rick Camp	.08	.06	.03
88	Joe Lefebvre	.08	.06	.03
89	Darrell Jackson	.08	.06	.03
90	Bake McBride	.08	.06	.03
91	Tim Stoddard	.08	.06	.03
92	Mike Easler	.12	.09	.05
93	Jim Bibby	.08	.06	.03
94	Kent Tekulve	.10	.08	.04
95	Jim Sundberg	.10	.08	.04
96	Tommy John	.40	.30	.15
97	Chris Speier	.08	.06	.03
98	Clint Hurdle	.08	.06	.03
99	Phil Garner	.10	.08	.04
100	Rod Carew	1.00	.70	.40
101	Steve Stone	.10	.08	.04
102	Joe Niekro	.12	.09	.05
103	Jerry Martin	.08	.06	.03
104	Ron LeFlore	.08	.06	.03
105	Jose Cruz	.12	.09	.05
106	Don Money	.08	.06	.03
107	Bobby Brown	.08	.06	.03
108	Larry Herndon	.08	.06	.03
109	Dennis Eckersley	.12	.09	.05
110	Carl Yastrzemski	1.25	.90	.50
111	Greg Minton	.08	.06	.03
112	Dan Schatzeder	.08	.06	.03
113	George Brett	2.00	1.50	.80
114	Tom Underwood	.08	.06	.03
115	Roy Smalley	.08	.06	.03
116	Carlton Fisk	.30	.25	.12
117	Pete Falcone	.08	.06	.03
118	Dale Murphy	2.25	1.75	.90
119	Tippy Martinez	.08	.06	.03
120	Larry Bowa	.12	.09	.05
121	Julio Cruz	.08	.06	.03
122	Jim Gantner	.10	.08	.04
123	Al Cowens	.08	.06	.03
124	Jerry Garvin	.08	.06	.03
125	Andre Dawson	.60	.45	.25
126	Charlie Leibrandt	.40	.30	.15
127	Willie Stargell	.75	.60	.30
128	Andre Thornton	.12	.09	.05
129	Art Howe	.08	.06	.03
130	Larry Gura	.08	.06	.03
131	Jerry Remy	.08	.06	.03
132	Rick Dempsey	.10	.08	.04
133	Alan Trammell	.25	.20	.10
134	Mike LaCoss	.08	.06	.03
135	Gorman Thomas	.10	.08	.04
136	Expos Future Stars (Bobby Pate, Tim Raines, Roberto Ramos)	10.00	7.50	4.00
137	Bill Madlock	.20	.15	.08
138	Rich Dotson	.15	.11	.06
139	Oscar Gamble	.08	.06	.03
140	Bob Forsch	.10	.08	.04
141	Miguel Dilone	.08	.06	.03
142	Jackson Todd	.08	.06	.03
143	Dan Meyer	.08	.06	.03
144	Garry Templeton	.10	.08	.04
145	Mickey Rivers	.10	.08	.04
146	Alan Ashby	.08	.06	.03
147	Dale Berra	.10	.08	.04
148	Randy Jones	.10	.08	.04
149	Joe Nolan	.08	.06	.03
150	Mark Fidrych	.12	.09	.05
151	Tony Armas	.12	.09	.05
152	Steve Kemp	.10	.08	.04
153	Jerry Reuss	.10	.08	.04
154	Rick Langford	.08	.06	.03
155	Chris Chambliss	.12	.09	.05
156	Bob McClure	.08	.06	.03
157	John Wathan	.10	.08	.04
158	John Curtis	.08	.06	.03
159	Steve Howe	.15	.11	.06
160	Garry Maddox	.10	.08	.04
161	Dan Graham	.08	.06	.03
162	Doug Corbett	.08	.06	.03
163	Rob Dressler	.08	.06	.03
164	Bucky Dent	.10	.08	.04
165	Alvis Woods	.08	.06	.03
166	Floyd Bannister	.12	.09	.05
167	Lee Mazzilli	.10	.08	.04
168	Don Robinson	.08	.06	.03
169	John Mayberry	.08	.06	.03
170	Woodie Fryman	.08	.06	.03
171	Gene Richards	.08	.06	.03
172	Rick Burleson	.10	.08	.04
173	Bump Wills	.08	.06	.03
174	Glenn Abbott	.08	.06	.03
175	Dave Collins	.10	.08	.04
176	Mike Krukow	.10	.08	.04
177	Rick Monday	.10	.08	.04
178	Dave Parker	.50	.40	.20
179	Rudy May	.08	.06	.03
180	Pete Rose	3.00	2.25	1.25
181	Elias Sosa	.08	.06	.03
182	Bob Grich	.12	.09	.05
183	Fred Norman	.08	.06	.03
184	Jim Dwyer	.08	.06	.03
185	Dennis Leonard	.10	.08	.04
186	Gary Matthews	.12	.09	.05
187	Ron Hassey	.08	.06	.03
188	Doug DeCinces	.12	.09	.05
189	Craig Swan	.08	.06	.03
190	Cesar Cedeno	.12	.09	.05
191	Rick Sutcliffe	.40	.30	.15
192	Kiko Garcia	.08	.06	.03
193	Pete Vuckovich	.10	.08	.04
194	Tony Bernazard	.10	.08	.04
195	Keith Hernandez	.60	.45	.25
196	Jerry Mumphrey	.08	.06	.03
197	Jim Kern	.08	.06	.03
198	Jerry Dybzinski	.08	.06	.03
199	John Lowenstein	.08	.06	.03
200	George Foster	.20	.15	.08
201	Phil Niekro	.60	.45	.25
202	Bill Buckner	.15	.11	.06
203	Steve Carlton	1.00	.70	.40
204	John D'Acquisto	.08	.06	.03
205	Rick Reuschel	.12	.09	.05
206	Dan Quisenberry	.20	.15	.08
207	Mike Schmidt	.75	.60	.30
208	Bob Watson	.08	.06	.03
209	Jim Spencer	.08	.06	.03
210	Jim Palmer	.60	.45	.25
211	Derrel Thomas	.08	.06	.03
212	Steve Nicosia	.08	.06	.03
213	Omar Moreno	.08	.06	.03
214	Richie Zisk	.10	.08	.04
215	Larry Hisle	.10	.08	.04
216	Mike Torrez	.10	.08	.04
217	Rich Hebner	.08	.06	.03
218	Britt Burns	.15	.11	.06
219	Ken Landreaux	.08	.06	.03
220	Tom Seaver	1.00	.70	.40
221	Bob Davis	.08	.06	.03
222	Jorge Orta	.08	.06	.03
223	Bobby Bonds	.12	.09	.05
224	Pat Zachry	.08	.06	.03
225	Ruppert Jones	.08	.06	.03
226	Duane Kuiper	.08	.06	.03
227	Rodney Scott	.08	.06	.03
228	Tom Paciorek	.08	.06	.03
229	Rollie Fingers	.50	.40	.20
230	George Hendrick	.10	.08	.04
231	Tony Perez	.25	.20	.10
232	Grant Jackson	.08	.06	.03
233	Damaso Garcia	.15	.11	.06
234	Lou Whitaker	.40	.30	.15
235	Scott Sanderson	.08	.06	.03
236	Mike Ivie	.08	.06	.03
237	Charlie Moore	.08	.06	.03
238	Blue Jays Future Stars (Luis Leal, Brian Milner, Ken Schrom)	.15	.11	.06
239	Rick Miller	.08	.06	.03
240	Nolan Ryan	1.00	.70	.40
241	Checklist 126-250	.08	.06	.03
242	Chet Lemon	.10	.08	.04
243	Dave Palmer	.10	.08	.04
244	Ellis Valentine	.08	.06	.03
245	Carney Lansford	.15	.11	.06
246	Ed Ott	.08	.06	.03
247	Glenn Hubbard	.08	.06	.03
248	Joey McLaughlin	.08	.06	.03
249	Jerry Narron	.08	.06	.03
250	Ron Guidry	.40	.30	.15
251	Steve Garvey	1.00	.70	.40
252	Victor Cruz	.08	.06	.03
253	Bobby Murcer	.12	.09	.05
254	Ozzie Smith	.50	.40	.20
255	John Stearns	.08	.06	.03
256	Bill Campbell	.08	.06	.03
257	Rennie Stennett	.08	.06	.03
258	Rick Waits	.08	.06	.03
259	Gary Lucas	.08	.06	.03
260	Ron Cey	.15	.11	.06
261	Rickey Henderson	3.00	2.25	1.25
262	Sammy Stewart	.08	.06	.03
263	Brian Downing	.10	.08	.04
264	Mark Bomback	.08	.06	.03
265	John Candelaria	.10	.08	.04
266	Renie Martin	.08	.06	.03
267	Stan Bahnsen	.08	.06	.03
268	Expos Team	.12	.09	.05
269	Ken Forsch	.08	.06	.03
270	Greg Luzinski	.20	.15	.08
271	Ron Jackson	.08	.06	.03
272	Wayne Garland	.08	.06	.03
273	Milt May	.08	.06	.03
274	Rick Wise	.08	.06	.03
275	Dwight Evans	.25	.20	.10
276	Sal Bando	.10	.08	.04
277	Alfredo Griffin	.12	.09	.05
278	Rick Sofield	.08	.06	.03
279	Bob Knepper	.10	.08	.04
280	Ken Griffey	.12	.09	.05
281	Ken Singleton	.10	.08	.04
282	Ernie Whitt	.08	.06	.03
283	Billy Sample	.08	.06	.03
284	Jack Morris	.50	.40	.20
285	Dick Ruthven	.08	.06	.03
286	Johnny Bench	1.00	.70	.40
287	Dave Smith	.30	.25	.12
288	Amos Otis	.10	.08	.04
289	Dave Goltz	.08	.06	.03
290	Bob Boone	.08	.06	.03
291	Aurelio Lopez	.08	.06	.03
292	Tom Hume	.08	.06	.03
293	Charlie Lea	.15	.11	.06
294	Bert Blyleven	.20	.15	.08
295	Hal McRae	.12	.09	.05
296	Bob Stanley	.10	.08	.04
297	Bob Bailor	.08	.06	.03
298	Jerry Koosman	.12	.09	.05
299	Eliott Maddox	.08	.06	.03
300	Paul Molitor	.25	.20	.10
301	Matt Keough	.08	.06	.03
302	Pat Putnam	.08	.06	.03
303	Dan Ford	.08	.06	.03
304	John Castino	.08	.06	.03
305	Barry Foote	.08	.06	.03
306	Lou Piniella	.12	.09	.05
307	Gene Garber	.08	.06	.03
308	Rick Manning	.08	.06	.03
309	Don Baylor	.15	.11	.06
310	Vida Blue	.10	.08	.04
311	Doug Flynn	.08	.06	.03
312	Rick Rhoden	.12	.09	.05
313	Fred Lynn	.25	.20	.10
314	Rich Dauer	.08	.06	.03
315	Kirk Gibson	3.00	2.25	1.25
316	Ken Reitz	.08	.06	.03
317	Lonnie Smith	.10	.08	.04
318	Steve Yeager	.08	.06	.03
319	Rowland Office	.08	.06	.03
320	Tom Burgmeier	.08	.06	.03
321	Leon Durham	.60	.45	.25
322	Neil Allen	.10	.08	.04
323	Ray Burris	.08	.06	.03
324	Mike Willis	.08	.06	.03
325	Ray Knight	.10	.08	.04
326	Rafael Landestoy	.08	.06	.03
327	Moose Haas	.08	.06	.03
328	Ross Baumgarten	.08	.06	.03
329	Joaquin Andujar	.10	.08	.04
330	Frank White	.12	.09	.05
331	Blue Jays Team	.12	.09	.05
332	Dick Drago	.08	.06	.03
333	Sid Monge	.08	.06	.03
334	Joe Sambito	.08	.06	.03
335	Rick Cerone	.08	.06	.03
336	Eddie Whitson	.08	.06	.03
337	Sparky Lyle	.10	.08	.04
338	Checklist 251-374	.08	.06	.03
339	Jon Matlack	.10	.08	.04
340	Ben Oglivie	.10	.08	.04
341	Dwayne Murphy	.10	.08	.04
342	Terry Crowley	.08	.06	.03
343	Frank Taveras	.08	.06	.03
344	Steve Rogers	.10	.08	.04
345	Warren Cromartie	.08	.06	.03
346	Bill Caudill	.08	.06	.03
347	Harold Baines	2.25	1.75	.90
348	Frank LaCorte	.08	.06	.03
349	Glenn Hoffman	.08	.06	.03
350	J.R. Richard	.10	.08	.04
351	Otto Velez	.08	.06	.03
352	Ted Simmons	.20	.15	.08
353	Terry Kennedy	.12	.09	.05

		MT	NR MT	EX
354	Al Hrabosky	.10	.08	.04
355	Bob Horner	.30	.25	.12
356	Cecil Cooper	.15	.11	.06
357	Bob Welch	.15	.11	.06
358	Paul Moskau	.08	.06	.03
359	Dave Rader	.08	.06	.03
360	Willie Wilson	.15	.11	.06
361	Dave Kingman	.10	.08	.04
362	Joe Rudi	.10	.08	.04
363	Rich Gale	.08	.06	.03
364	Steve Trout	.10	.08	.04
365	Graig Nettles	.10	.08	.04
366	Lamar Johnson	.08	.06	.03
367	Denny Martinez	.10	.08	.04
368	Manny Trillo	.10	.08	.04
369	Frank Tanana	.10	.08	.04
370	Reggie Jackson	1.25	.90	.50
371	Bill Lee	.10	.08	.04
372	Jay Johnstone	.10	.08	.04
373	Jason Thompson	.08	.06	.03
374	Tom Hutton	.08	.06	.03

1981 O-Pee-Chee Posters

Inserted inside the regular 1981 O-Pee-Chee wax packs, these full-color posters measure approximately 4-7/8" by 6-7/8". The set is complete at 24 posters and includes 12 players from the Blue Jays and 12 from the Expos. The blank-backed posters are numbered in the border below the photo where the caption is written in both French and English. The photos are surrounded by a blue border for Blue Jays players or a red border for Expos. Because they were inserted in wax packs, the posters generally contain folds.

		MT	NR MT	EX
Complete Set:		3.50	2.75	1.50
Common Player:		.10	.08	.04
1	Willie Montanez	.10	.08	.04
2	Rodney Scott	.10	.08	.04
3	Chris Speier	.10	.08	.04
4	Larry Parrish	.25	.20	.10
5	Warren Cromartie	.10	.08	.04
6	Andre Dawson	.75	.60	.30
7	Ellis Valentine	.15	.11	.06
8	Gary Carter	.75	.60	.30
9	Steve Rogers	.15	.11	.06
10	Woodie Fryman	.10	.08	.04
11	Jerry White	.10	.08	.04
12	Scott Sanderson	.10	.08	.04
13	John Mayberry	.15	.11	.06
14	Damasa Garcia (Damaso)	.20	.15	.08
15	Alfredo Griffin	.25	.20	.10
16	Garth Iorg	.10	.08	.04
17	Alvis Woods	.10	.08	.04
18	Rick Bosetti	.10	.08	.04
19	Barry Bonnell	.10	.08	.04
20	Ernie Whitt	.20	.15	.08
21	Jim Clancy	.20	.15	.08
22	Dave Stieb	.40	.30	.15
23	Otto Velez	.10	.08	.04
24	Lloyd Moseby	.30	.25	.12

1982 O-Pee-Chee

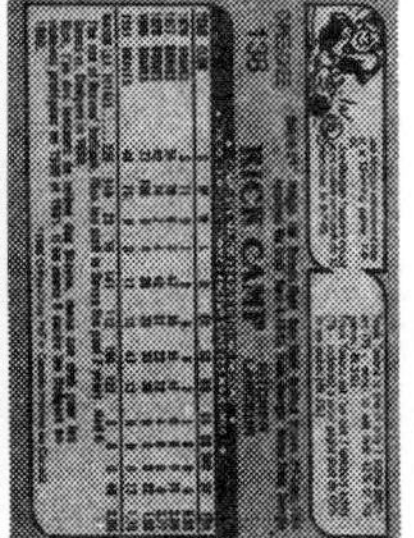

1982 O-Pee-Chee

The 1982 O-Pee-Chee set, complete at 396 cards, is nearly identical in design to the 1982 Topps set, except the Canadian-issued cards display the O-Pee-Chee logo on the front of the card and list the player's position in both French and English. The backs of the cards, which measure the standard 2-1/2" by 3-1/2", are also bilingual. Some of the cards carry an extra line on the front indicating an off-season trade.

		MT	NR MT	EX
Complete Set:		35.00	26.00	14.00
Common Player:		.08	.06	.03
1	Dan Spillner	.08	.06	.03
2	Ken Singleton AS	.10	.08	.04
3	John Candelaria	.10	.08	.04
4	Frank Tanana	.10	.08	.04
5	Reggie Smith	.12	.09	.05
6	Rick Monday	.10	.08	.04
7	Scott Sanderson	.08	.06	.03
8	Rich Dauer	.08	.06	.03
9	Ron Guidry	.30	.25	.12
10	Ron Guidry IA	.15	.11	.06
11	Tom Brookens	.08	.06	.03
12	Moose Haas	.08	.06	.03
13	Chet Lemon	.10	.08	.04
14	Steve Howe	.10	.08	.04
15	Ellis Valentine	.08	.06	.03
16	Toby Harrah	.10	.08	.04
17	Darrell Evans	.12	.09	.05
18	Johnny Bench	.75	.60	.30
19	Ernie Whitt	.08	.06	.03
20	Garry Maddox	.10	.08	.04
21	Graig Nettles IA	.12	.09	.05
22	Al Oliver IA	.12	.09	.05
23	Bob Boone	.10	.08	.04
24	Pete Rose IA	1.00	.70	.40
25	Jerry Remy	.08	.06	.03
26	Jorge Orta	.08	.06	.03
27	Bobby Bonds	.12	.09	.05
28	Jim Clancy	.10	.08	.04
29	Dwayne Murphy	.10	.08	.04
30	Tom Seaver	.50	.40	.20
31	Tom Seaver IA	.25	.20	.10
32	Claudell Washington	.10	.08	.04
33	Bob Shirley	.08	.06	.03
34	Bob Forsch	.10	.08	.04
35	Willie Aikens	.08	.06	.03
36	Rod Carew AS	.30	.25	.12
37	Willie Randolph	.10	.08	.04
38	Charlie Lea	.08	.06	.03
39	Lou Whitaker	.25	.20	.10
40	Dave Parker	.25	.20	.10
41	Dave Parker IA	.12	.09	.05
42	Mark Belanger	.10	.08	.04
43	Rick Langford	.08	.06	.03
44	Rollie Fingers IA	.10	.08	.04
45	Rick Cerone	.08	.06	.03
46	Johnny Wockenfuss	.08	.06	.03
47	Jack Morris AS	.20	.15	.08
48	Cesar Cedeno	.12	.09	.05
49	Alvis Woods	.08	.06	.03
50	Buddy Bell	.12	.09	.05
51	Mickey Rivers IA	.08	.06	.03
52	Steve Rogers	.10	.08	.04
53	Blue Jays Team	.12	.09	.05
54	Ron Hassey	.08	.06	.03
55	Rick Burleson	.10	.08	.04
56	Harold Baines	.60	.45	.25
57	Craig Reynolds	.08	.06	.03
58	Carlton Fisk AS	.12	.09	.05
59	Jim Kern	.08	.06	.03
60	Tony Armas	.10	.08	.04
61	Warren Cromartie	.08	.06	.03
62	Graig Nettles	.15	.11	.06
63	Jerry Koosman	.10	.08	.04
64	Pat Zachry	.08	.06	.03
65	Terry Kennedy	.10	.08	.04
66	Richie Zisk	.10	.08	.04
67	Rich Gale	.08	.06	.03
68	Steve Carlton	.75	.60	.30
69	Greg Luzinski IA	.10	.08	.04
70	Tim Raines	1.50	1.25	.60
71	Roy Lee Jackson	.08	.06	.03
72	Carl Yastrzemski	1.00	.70	.40
73	John Castino	.08	.06	.03
74	Joe Niekro	.12	.09	.05
75	Tommy John	.20	.15	.08
76	Dave Winfield AS	.20	.15	.08
77	Miguel Dilone	.08	.06	.03
78	Gary Gray	.08	.06	.03
79	Tom Hume	.08	.06	.03
80	Jim Palmer	.50	.40	.20
81	Jim Palmer IA	.25	.20	.10
82	Vida Blue IA	.10	.08	.04
83	Garth Iorg	.08	.06	.03
84	Rennie Stennett	.08	.06	.03
85	Dave Lopes IA	.10	.08	.04
86	Dave Concepcion	.15	.11	.06
87	Matt Keough	.08	.06	.03
88	Jim Spencer	.08	.06	.03
89	Steve Henderson	.08	.06	.03
90	Nolan Ryan	.60	.45	.25
91	Carney Lansford	.12	.09	.05
92	Bake McBride	.08	.06	.03
93	Dave Stapleton	.08	.06	.03
94	Expos Team	.12	.09	.05
95	Ozzie Smith	.25	.20	.10
96	Rich Hebner	.08	.06	.03
97	Tim Foli	.08	.06	.03
98	Darrell Porter	.10	.08	.04
99	Barry Bonnell	.08	.06	.03
100	Mike Schmidt	1.00	.70	.40
101	Mike Schmidt IA	.50	.40	.20
102	Dan Briggs	.08	.06	.03
103	Al Cowens	.08	.06	.03
104	Grant Jackson	.08	.06	.03
105	Kirk Gibson	.60	.45	.25
106	Dan Schatzeder	.08	.06	.03
107	Juan Berenguer	.08	.06	.03
108	Jack Morris	.40	.30	.15
109	Dave Revering	.08	.06	.03
110	Carlton Fisk	.25	.20	.10
111	Carlton Fisk IA	.12	.09	.05
112	Billy Sample	.08	.06	.03
113	Steve McCatty	.08	.06	.03
114	Ken Landreaux	.08	.06	.03
115	Gaylord Perry	.30	.25	.12
116	Elias Sosa	.08	.06	.03
117	Rich Gossage IA	.12	.09	.05
118	Expos Future Stars (Terry Francona, Brad Mills, Bryn Smith)	.25	.20	.10
119	Billy Almon	.08	.06	.03
120	Gary Lucas	.08	.06	.03
121	Ken Oberkfell	.08	.06	.03
122	Steve Carlton IA	.30	.25	.12
123	Jeff Reardon	.20	.15	.08
124	Bill Buckner	.15	.11	.06
125	Danny Ainge	.15	.11	.06
126	Paul Splittorff	.10	.08	.04
127	Lonnie Smith	.10	.08	.04
128	Rudy May	.08	.06	.03
129	Checklist 1-132	.08	.06	.03
130	Julio Cruz	.08	.06	.03
131	Stan Bahnsen	.08	.06	.03
132	Pete Vuckovich	.10	.08	.04
133	Luis Salazar	.08	.06	.03
134	Dan Ford	.08	.06	.03
135	Denny Martinez	.10	.08	.04
136	Lary Sorensen	.08	.06	.03
137	Fergie Jenkins	.20	.15	.08
138	Rick Camp	.08	.06	.03
139	Wayne Nordhagen	.08	.06	.03
140	Ron LeFlore	.10	.08	.04
141	Rick Sutcliffe	.20	.15	.08
142	Rick Waits	.08	.06	.03
143	Mookie Wilson	.12	.09	.05
144	Greg Minton	.08	.06	.03
145	Bob Horner	.30	.25	.12
146	Joe Morgan IA	.15	.11	.06
147	Larry Gura	.08	.06	.03
148	Alfredo Griffin	.10	.08	.04
149	Pat Putnam	.08	.06	.03
150	Ted Simmons	.20	.15	.08
151	Gary Matthews	.10	.08	.04
152	Greg Luzinski	.15	.11	.06
153	Mike Flanagan	.10	.08	.04
154	Jim Morrison	.08	.06	.03
155	Otto Velez	.08	.06	.03
156	Frank White	.10	.08	.04
157	Doug Corbett	.08	.06	.03
158	Brian Downing	.10	.08	.04
159	Willie Randolph IA	.10	.08	.04
160	Luis Tiant	.15	.11	.06
161	Andre Thornton	.12	.09	.05
162	Amos Otis	.10	.08	.04
163	Paul Mirabella	.08	.06	.03
164	Bert Blyleven	.20	.15	.08
165	Rowland Office	.08	.06	.03
166	Gene Tenace	.10	.08	.04
167	Cecil Cooper	.15	.11	.06
168	Bruce Benedict	.08	.06	.03
169	Mark Clear	.08	.06	.03
170	Jim Bibby	.08	.06	.03
171	Ken Griffey IA	.10	.08	.04
172	Bill Gullickson	.10	.08	.04
173	Mike Scioscia	.08	.06	.03
174	Doug DeCinces	.12	.09	.05
175	Jerry Mumphrey	.08	.06	.03
176	Rollie Fingers	.20	.15	.08
177	George Foster IA	.12	.09	.05
178	Mitchell Page	.08	.06	.03
179	Steve Garvey	.75	.60	.30
180	Steve Garvey IA	.30	.25	.12
181	Woodie Fryman	.08	.06	.03
182	Larry Herndon	.08	.06	.03
183	Frank White IA	.10	.08	.04
184	Alan Ashby	.08	.06	.03
185	Phil Niekro	.40	.30	.15
186	Leon Roberts	.08	.06	.03
187	Rod Carew	.75	.60	.30
188	Willie Stargell IA	.30	.25	.12
189	Joel Youngblood	.08	.06	.03
190	J.R. Richard	.10	.08	.04
191	Tim Wallach	1.75	1.25	.70
192	Broderick Perkins	.08	.06	.03
193	Johnny Grubb	.08	.06	.03
194	Larry Bowa	.12	.09	.05
195	Paul Molitor	.20	.15	.08
196	Willie Upshaw	.10	.08	.04
197	Roy Smalley	.08	.06	.03
198	Chris Speier	.08	.06	.03
199	Don Aase	.08	.06	.03
200	George Brett	1.25	.90	.50
201	George Brett IA	.60	.45	.25
202	Rick Manning	.08	.06	.03
203	Blue Jays Future Stars (Jesse Barfield, Brian Milner, Boomer Wells)	3.00	2.25	1.25
204	Rick Reuschel	.12	.09	.05
205	Neil Allen	.08	.06	.03
206	Leon Durham	.12	.09	.05
207	Jim Gantner	.08	.06	.03
208	Joe Morgan	.30	.25	.12
209	Gary Lavelle	.08	.06	.03
210	Keith Hernandez	.50	.40	.20
211	Joe Charboneau	.08	.06	.03
212	Mario Mendoza	.08	.06	.03
213	Willie Randolph AS	.10	.08	.04
214	Lance Parrish	.40	.30	.15
215	Mike Krukow	.10	.08	.04
216	Ron Cey	.12	.09	.05
217	Ruppert Jones	.08	.06	.03
218	Dave Lopes	.10	.08	.04
219	Steve Yeager	.08	.06	.03
220	Manny Trillo	.10	.08	.04
221	Dave Concepcion IA	.10	.08	.04
222	Butch Wynegar	.10	.08	.04
223	Lloyd Moseby	.20	.15	.08
224	Bruce Bochte	.08	.06	.03
225	Ed Ott	.08	.06	.03
226	Checklist 133-264	.08	.06	.03
227	Ray Burris	.08	.06	.03

228	Reggie Smith IA	.10	.08	.04
229	Oscar Gamble	.08	.06	.03
230	Willie Wilson	.15	.11	.06
231	Brian Kingman	.08	.06	.03
232	John Stearns	.08	.06	.03
233	Duane Kuiper	.08	.06	.03
234	Don Baylor	.15	.11	.06
235	Mike Easler	.10	.08	.04
236	Lou Piniella	.12	.09	.05
237	Robin Yount	.60	.45	.25
238	Kevin Saucier	.08	.06	.03
239	Jon Matlack	.10	.08	.04
240	Bucky Dent	.12	.09	.05
241	Bucky Dent IA	.10	.08	.04
242	Milt May	.08	.06	.03
243	Lee Mazzilli	.10	.08	.04
244	Gary Carter	.75	.60	.30
245	Ken Reitz	.08	.06	.03
246	Scott McGregor AS	.10	.08	.04
247	Pedro Guerrero	.60	.45	.25
248	Art Howe	.08	.06	.03
249	Dick Tidrow	.08	.06	.03
250	Tug McGraw	.12	.09	.05
251	Fred Lynn	.25	.20	.10
252	Fred Lynn IA	.12	.09	.05
253	Gene Richards	.08	.06	.03
254	Jorge Bell	10.00	7.50	4.00
255	Tony Perez	.25	.20	.10
256	Tony Perez IA	.12	.09	.05
257	Rich Dotson	.10	.08	.04
258	Bo Diaz	.10	.08	.04
259	Rodney Scott	.08	.06	.03
260	Bruce Sutter	.15	.11	.06
261	George Brett AS	.60	.45	.25
262	Rick Dempsey	.10	.08	.04
263	Mike Phillips	.08	.06	.03
264	Jerry Garvin	.08	.06	.03
265	Al Bumbry	.08	.06	.03
266	Hubie Brooks	.15	.11	.06
267	Vida Blue	.12	.09	.05
268	Rickey Henderson	1.25	.90	.50
269	Rick Peters	.08	.06	.03
270	Rusty Staub	.15	.11	.06
271	Sixto Lezcano	.08	.06	.03
272	Bump Wills	.08	.06	.03
273	Gary Allenson	.08	.06	.03
274	Randy Jones	.10	.08	.04
275	Bob Watson	.10	.08	.04
276	Dave Kingman	.15	.11	.06
277	Terry Puhl	.08	.06	.03
278	Jerry Reuss	.10	.08	.04
279	Sammy Stewart	.08	.06	.03
280	Ben Oglivie	.10	.08	.04
281	Kent Tekulve	.10	.08	.04
282	Ken Macha	.08	.06	.03
283	Ron Davis	.08	.06	.03
284	Bob Grich	.12	.09	.05
285	Sparky Lyle	.12	.09	.05
286	Rich Gossage AS	.12	.09	.05
287	Dennis Eckersley	.12	.09	.05
288	Garry Templeton	.10	.08	.04
289	Bob Stanley	.10	.08	.04
290	Ken Singleton	.12	.09	.05
291	Mickey Hatcher	.08	.06	.03
292	Dave Palmer	.08	.06	.03
293	Damaso Garcia	.10	.08	.04
294	Don Money	.08	.06	.03
295	George Hendrick	.10	.08	.04
296	Steve Kemp	.10	.08	.04
297	Dave Smith	.12	.09	.05
298	Bucky Dent AS	.10	.08	.04
299	Steve Trout	.08	.06	.03
300	Reggie Jackson	.75	.60	.30
301	Reggie Jackson IA	.30	.25	.12
302	Doug Flynn	.08	.06	.03
303	Wayne Gross	.08	.06	.03
304	Johnny Bench IA	.40	.30	.15
305	Don Sutton	.40	.30	.15
306	Don Sutton IA	.20	.15	.08
307	Mark Bomback	.08	.06	.03
308	Charlie Moore	.08	.06	.03
309	Jeff Burroughs	.10	.08	.04
310	Mike Hargrove	.10	.08	.04
311	Enos Cabell	.08	.06	.03
312	Lenny Randle	.08	.06	.03
313	Ivan DeJesus	.08	.06	.03
314	Buck Martinez	.08	.06	.03
315	Burt Hooton	.10	.08	.04
316	Scott McGregor	.10	.08	.04
317	Dick Ruthven	.08	.06	.03
318	Mike Heath	.08	.06	.03
319	Ray Knight	.10	.08	.04
320	Chris Chambliss	.10	.08	.04
321	Chris Chambliss IA	.10	.08	.04
322	Ross Baumgarten	.08	.06	.03
323	Bill Lee	.10	.08	.04
324	Gorman Thomas	.10	.08	.04
325	Jose Cruz	.12	.09	.05
326	Al Oliver	.15	.11	.06
327	Jackson Todd	.08	.06	.03
328	Ed Farmer	.08	.06	.03
329	U.L. Washington	.08	.06	.03
330	Ken Griffey	.15	.11	.06
331	John Milner	.08	.06	.03
332	Don Robinson	.08	.06	.03
333	Cliff Johnson	.08	.06	.03
334	Fernando Valenzuela	1.25	.90	.50
335	Jim Sundberg	.10	.08	.04
336	George Foster	.15	.11	.06
337	Pete Rose AS	.75	.60	.30
338	Dave Lopes AS	.10	.08	.04
339	Mike Schmidt AS	.40	.30	.15
340	Dave Concepcion AS	.10	.08	.04
341	Andre Dawson AS	.20	.15	.08
342	George Foster AS	.12	.09	.05
343	Dave Parker AS	.15	.11	.06
344	Gary Carter AS	.30	.25	.12
345	Fernando Valenzuela AS	.30	.25	.12
346	Tom Seaver AS	.30	.25	.12
347	Bruce Sutter AS	.10	.08	.04
348	Darrell Porter IA	.08	.06	.03
349	Dave Collins	.08	.06	.03
350	Amos Otis IA	.08	.06	.03
351	Frank Taveras	.08	.06	.03
352	Dave Winfield	.40	.30	.15
353	Larry Parrish	.10	.08	.04
354	Roberto Ramos	.08	.06	.03
355	Dwight Evans	.20	.15	.08
356	Mickey Rivers	.10	.08	.04
357	Butch Hobson	.08	.06	.03
358	Carl Yastrzemski IA	.30	.25	.12
359	Ron Jackson	.08	.06	.03
360	Len Barker	.08	.06	.03
361	Pete Rose	2.00	1.50	.80
362	Kevin Hickey	.08	.06	.03
363	Rod Carew IA	.30	.25	.12
364	Hector Cruz	.08	.06	.03
365	Bill Madlock	.15	.11	.06
366	Jim Rice	.75	.60	.30
367	Ron Cey IA	.10	.08	.04
368	Luis Leal	.08	.06	.03
369	Dennis Leonard	.10	.08	.04
370	Mike Norris	.08	.06	.03
371	Tom Paciorek	.08	.06	.03
372	Willie Stargell	.60	.45	.25
373	Dan Driessen	.08	.06	.03
374	Larry Bowa IA	.10	.08	.04
375	Dusty Baker	.12	.09	.05
376	Joey McLaughlin	.08	.06	.03
377	Reggie Jackson AS	.40	.30	.15
378	Mike Caldwell	.08	.06	.03
379	Andre Dawson	.40	.30	.15
380	Dave Stieb	.15	.11	.06
381	Alan Trammell	.40	.30	.15
382	John Mayberry	.08	.06	.03
383	John Wathan	.10	.08	.04
384	Hal McRae	.12	.09	.05
385	Ken Forsch	.08	.06	.03
386	Jerry White	.08	.06	.03
387	Tom Veryzer	.08	.06	.03
388	Joe Rudi	.10	.08	.04
389	Bob Knepper	.10	.08	.04
390	Eddie Murray	1.00	.70	.40
391	Dale Murphy	1.75	1.25	.70
392	Bob Boone IA	.08	.06	.03
393	Al Hrabosky	.10	.08	.04
394	Checklist 265-396	.08	.06	.03
395	Omar Moreno	.08	.06	.03
396	Rich Gossage	.25	.20	.10

1982 O-Pee-Chee Posters

The 24 posters in this Canadian set, which features 12 players from the Expos and 12 from the Blue Jays, were inserted in regular 1982 O-Pee-Chee wax packs. The posters measure approximately 4-7/8" by 6-7/8" and are usually found with fold marks. The blank-backed posters are numbered in the bottom border where the captions appear in both French and English. Red borders surround the photos of Blue Jays players, while blue borders are used for the Expos.

		MT	NR MT	EX
	Complete Set:	3.50	2.75	1.50
	Common Player:	.10	.08	.04
1	John Mayberry	.15	.11	.06
2	Damaso Garcia	.20	.15	.08
3	Ernie Whitt	.20	.15	.08
4	Lloyd Moseby	.30	.25	.12
5	Alvis Woods	.10	.08	.04
6	Dave Stieb	.40	.30	.15
7	Roy Lee Jackson	.10	.08	.04
8	Joey McLaughlin	.10	.08	.04
9	Luis Leal	.10	.08	.04
10	Aurelio Rodriguez	.15	.11	.06
11	Otto Velez	.10	.08	.04
12	Juan Berenger (Berenguer)	.15	.11	.06
13	Warren Cromartie	.10	.08	.04
14	Rodney Scott	.10	.08	.04
15	Larry Parrish	.25	.20	.10
16	Gary Carter	.75	.60	.30
17	Tim Raines	.75	.60	.30
18	Andre Dawson	.75	.60	.30
19	Terry Francona	.10	.08	.04
20	Steve Rogers	.15	.11	.06
21	Bill Gullickson	.15	.11	.06
22	Scott Sanderson	.10	.08	.04
23	Jeff Reardon	.30	.25	.12
24	Jerry White			

GRADING GUIDE

Mint (MT): A perfect card. Well-centered with all corners sharp and square. No creases, stains, edge nicks, surface marks, yellowing or fading.

Near Mint (NR MT): A nearly perfect card. At first glance, a NR MT card appears to be perfect. May have one corner not perfectly sharp. May be slightly off-center. No surface marks, creases, or loss of gloss.

Excellent (EX): Corners are still fairly sharp with only moderate wear. Borders may be off center. No creases or stains on fronts or backs, but may show slight loss of surface luster.

Very Good (VG): Shows obvious handling. May have rounded corners, minor creases, major gum or wax stains. No major creases, tape marks, writing, etc.

Good (G): A well-worn card, but exhibits no intentional damage. May have major or multiple creases. Corners may be rounded well beyond card border.

1983 O-Pee-Chee

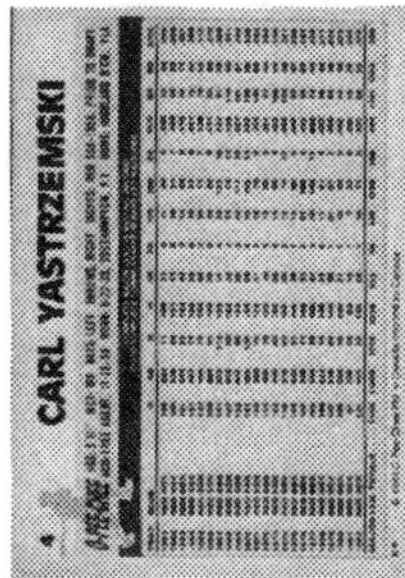

Again complete at 396 cards, the 1983 O-Pee-Chee set borrows its design from the 1983 Topps set, except the Canadian-issued cards display the O-Pee-Chee logo on the front of the card and show the player's position in both French and English. The backs of the cards are also printed in both languages. The cards measure the standard 2-1/2" by 3-1/2". Some cards carry the extra line on the front indicating an off-season trade.

		MT	NR MT	EX
	Complete Set:	50.00	37.50	20.00
	Common Player:	.08	.06	.03
1	Rusty Staub	.15	.11	.06
2	Larry Parrish	.10	.08	.04
3	George Brett	.75	.60	.30
4	Carl Yastrzemski	.75	.60	.30
5	Super Veteran (Al Oliver)	.10	.08	.04
6	Bill Virdon	.08	.06	.03
7	Gene Richards	.08	.06	.03
8	Steve Balboni	.12	.09	.05
9	Joey McLaughlin	.08	.06	.03
10	Gorman Thomas	.10	.08	.04
11	Chris Chambliss	.10	.08	.04
12	Ray Burris	.08	.06	.03
13	Larry Herndon	.08	.06	.03
14	Ozzie Smith	.20	.15	.08
15	Ron Cey	.12	.09	.05
16	Willie Wilson	.15	.11	.06
17	Kent Tekulve	.10	.08	.04
18	Super Veteran (Kent Tekulve)	.10	.08	.04
19	Oscar Gamble	.08	.06	.03
20	Carlton Fisk	.20	.15	.08
21	Dale Murphy AS	.60	.45	.25
22	Randy Lerch	.08	.06	.03
23	Dale Murphy	1.25	.90	.50
24	Steve Mura	.08	.06	.03
25	Hal McRae	.12	.09	.05
26	Dennis Lamp	.08	.06	.03
27	Ron Washington	.08	.06	.03
28	Bruce Bochte	.08	.06	.03
29	Randy Jones	.10	.08	.04
30	Jim Rice	.60	.45	.25
31	Bill Gullickson	.10	.08	.04
32	Dave Concepcion AS	.10	.08	.04
33	Super Veteran (Ted Simmons)	.12	.09	.05
34	Bobby Cox	.08	.06	.03
35	Rollie Fingers	.25	.20	.10
36	Super Veteran (Rollie Fingers)	.15	.11	.06
37	Mike Hargrove	.10	.08	.04
38	Roy Smalley	.08	.06	.03
39	Terry Puhl	.08	.06	.03
40	Fernando Valenzuela	.25	.20	.10
41	Garry Maddox	.10	.08	.04
42	Dale Murray	.08	.06	.03
43	Bob Dernier	.10	.08	.04
44	Don Robinson	.08	.06	.03
45	John Mayberry	.10	.08	.04
46	Richard Dotson	.10	.08	.04
47	Wayne Nordhagen	.08	.06	.03
48	Lary Sorenson	.08	.06	.03
49	Willie McGee	2.25	1.75	.90
50	Bob Horner	.20	.15	.08
51	Super Veteran (Rusty Staub)	.12	.09	.05
52	Tom Seaver	.50	.40	.20
53	Chet Lemon	.10	.08	.04
54	Scott Sanderson	.08	.06	.03
55	Mookie Wilson	.10	.08	.04
56	Reggie Jackson	.60	.45	.25
57	Tim Blackwell	.08	.06	.03
58	Keith Moreland	.10	.08	.04
59	Alvis Woods	.08	.06	.03
60	Johnny Bench	.50	.40	.20

#	Card	MT	NR MT	EX
61	Super Veteran (Johnny Bench)	.20	.15	.08
62	Jim Gott	.12	.09	.05
63	Rick Monday	.10	.08	.04
64	Gary Matthews	.10	.08	.04
65	Jack Morris	.30	.25	.12
66	Lou Whitaker	.30	.25	.12
67	U.L. Washington	.08	.06	.03
68	Eric Show	.20	.15	.08
69	Lee Lacy	.08	.06	.03
70	Steve Carlton	.50	.40	.20
71	Super Veteran (Steve Carlton)	.25	.20	.10
72	Tom Paciorek	.08	.06	.03
73	Manny Trillo	.10	.08	.04
74	Super Veteran (Tony Perez)	.12	.09	.05
75	Amos Otis	.10	.08	.04
76	Rick Mahler	.10	.08	.04
77	Hosken Powell	.08	.06	.03
78	Bill Caudill	.08	.06	.03
79	Dan Petry	.10	.08	.04
80	George Foster	.15	.11	.06
81	Joe Morgan	.30	.25	.12
82	Burt Hooton	.10	.08	.04
83	Ryne Sandberg	10.00	7.50	4.00
84	Alan Ashby	.08	.06	.03
85	Ken Singleton	.10	.08	.04
86	Tom Hume	.08	.06	.03
87	Dennis Leonard	.10	.08	.04
88	Jim Gantner	.08	.06	.03
89	Leon Roberts	.08	.06	.03
90	Jerry Reuss	.10	.08	.04
91	Ben Oglivie	.10	.08	.04
92	Super Veteran (Sparky Lyle)	.10	.08	.04
93	John Castino	.08	.06	.03
94	Phil Niekro	.30	.25	.12
95	Alan Trammell	.40	.30	.15
96	Gaylord Perry	.30	.25	.12
97	Tom Herr	.12	.09	.05
98	Vance Law	.08	.06	.03
99	Dickie Noles	.08	.06	.03
100	Pete Rose	1.50	1.25	.60
101	Super Veteran (Pete Rose)	.70	.50	.30
102	Dave Concepcion	.12	.09	.05
103	Darrell Porter	.10	.08	.04
104	Ron Guidry	.25	.20	.10
105	Don Baylor	.15	.11	.06
106	Steve Rogers AS	.10	.08	.04
107	Greg Minton	.08	.06	.03
108	Glenn Hoffman	.08	.06	.03
109	Luis Leal	.08	.06	.03
110	Ken Griffey	.12	.09	.05
111	Expos Team	.12	.09	.05
112	Luis Pujols	.08	.06	.03
113	Julio Cruz	.08	.06	.03
114	Jim Slaton	.08	.06	.03
115	Chili Davis	.15	.11	.06
116	Pedro Guerrero	.30	.25	.12
117	Mike Ivie	.08	.06	.03
118	Chris Welsh	.08	.06	.03
119	Frank Pastore	.08	.06	.03
120	Len Barker	.08	.06	.03
121	Chris Speier	.08	.06	.03
122	Bobby Murcer	.10	.08	.04
123	Bill Russell	.10	.08	.04
124	Lloyd Moseby	.12	.09	.05
125	Leon Durham	.12	.09	.05
126	Super Veteran (Carl Yastrzemski)	.30	.25	.12
127	John Candelaria	.10	.08	.04
128	Phil Garner	.10	.08	.04
129	Checklist 1-132	.08	.06	.03
130	Dave Stieb	.15	.11	.06
131	Geoff Zahn	.08	.06	.03
132	Todd Cruz	.08	.06	.03
133	Tony Pena	.10	.08	.04
134	Hubie Brooks	.12	.09	.05
135	Dwight Evans	.15	.11	.06
136	Willie Aikens	.08	.06	.03
137	Woodie Fryman	.08	.06	.03
138	Rick Dempsey	.10	.08	.04
139	Bruce Berenyi	.08	.06	.03
140	Willie Randolph	.10	.08	.04
141	Eddie Murray	.60	.45	.25
142	Mike Caldwell	.08	.06	.03
143	Tony Gwynn	15.00	11.00	6.00
144	Super Veteran (Tommy John)	.12	.09	.05
145	Don Sutton	.30	.25	.12
146	Super Veteran (Don Sutton)	.15	.11	.06
147	Rick Manning	.08	.06	.03
148	George Hendrick	.10	.08	.04
149	Johnny Ray	.15	.11	.06
150	Bruce Sutter	.15	.11	.06
151	Super Veteran (Bruce Sutter)	.10	.08	.04
152	Jay Johnstone	.10	.08	.04
153	Jerry Koosman	.10	.08	.04
154	Johnnie LeMaster	.08	.06	.03
155	Dan Quisenberry	.15	.11	.06
156	Luis Salazar	.08	.06	.03
157	Steve Bedrosian	.15	.11	.06
158	Jim Sundberg	.10	.08	.04
159	Super Veteran (Gaylord Perry)	.15	.11	.06
160	Dave Kingman	.15	.11	.06
161	Super Veteran (Dave Kingman)	.10	.08	.04
162	Mark Clear	.08	.06	.03
163	Cal Ripken	1.75	1.25	.70
164	Dave Palmer	.08	.06	.03
165	Dan Driessen	.10	.08	.04
166	Tug McGraw	.12	.09	.05
167	Denny Martinez	.10	.08	.04
168	Juan Eichelberger	.08	.06	.03
169	Doug Flynn	.08	.06	.03
170	Steve Howe	.10	.08	.04
171	Frank White	.12	.09	.05
172	Mike Flanagan	.10	.08	.04
173	Andre Dawson AS	.15	.11	.06
174	Manny Trillo AS	.10	.08	.04
175	Bo Diaz	.10	.08	.04
176	Dave Righetti	.30	.25	.12
177	Harold Baines	.25	.20	.10
178	Vida Blue	.12	.09	.05
179	Super Veteran (Luis Tiant)	.10	.08	.04
180	Rickey Henderson	.75	.60	.30
181	Rick Rhoden	.12	.09	.05
182	Fred Lynn	.20	.15	.08
183	Ed Vande Berg	.10	.08	.04
184	Dwayne Murphy	.10	.08	.04
185	Tim Lollar	.08	.06	.03
186	Dave Tobik	.08	.06	.03
187	Super Veteran (Tug McGraw)	.10	.08	.04
188	Rick Miller	.08	.06	.03
189	Dan Schatzeder	.08	.06	.03
190.	Cecil Cooper	.12	.09	.05
191	Jim Beattie	.08	.06	.03
192	Rich Dauer	.08	.06	.03
193	Al Cowens	.08	.06	.03
194	Roy Lee Jackson	.08	.06	.03
195	Mike Gates	.08	.06	.03
196	Tommy John	.20	.15	.08
197	Bob Forsch	.10	.08	.04
198	Steve Garvey	.60	.45	.25
199	Brad Mills	.08	.06	.03
200	Rod Carew	.60	.45	.25
201	Super Veteran (Rod Carew)	.30	.25	.12
202	Blue Jays Team	.12	.09	.05
203	Floyd Bannister	.10	.08	.04
204	Bruce Benedict	.08	.06	.03
205	Dave Parker	.30	.25	.12
206	Ken Oberkfell	.08	.06	.03
207	Super Veteran (Graig Nettles)	.10	.08	.04
208	Sparky Lyle	.10	.08	.04
209	Jason Thompson	.08	.06	.03
210	Jack Clark	.20	.15	.08
211	Jim Kaat	.15	.11	.06
212	John Stearns	.08	.06	.03
213	Tom Burgmeier	.08	.06	.03
214	Jerry White	.08	.06	.03
215	Mario Soto	.10	.08	.04
216	Scott McGregor	.10	.08	.04
217	Tim Stoddard	.08	.06	.03
218	Bill Laskey	.08	.06	.03
219	Super Veteran (Reggie Jackson)	.30	.25	.12
220	Dusty Baker	.10	.08	.04
221	Joe Niekro	.10	.08	.04
222	Damaso Garcia	.10	.08	.04
223	John Montefusco	.08	.06	.03
224	Mickey Rivers	.10	.08	.04
225	Enos Cabell	.08	.06	.03
226	LaMarr Hoyt	.10	.08	.04
227	Tim Raines	.40	.30	.15
228	Joaquin Andujar	.10	.08	.04
229	Tim Wallach	.25	.20	.10
230	Fergie Jenkins	.15	.11	.06
231	Super Veteran (Fergie Jenkins)	.10	.08	.04
232	Tom Brunansky	.25	.20	.10
233	Ivan DeJesus	.08	.06	.03
234	Bryn Smith	.10	.08	.04
235	Claudell Washington	.10	.08	.04
236	Steve Renko	.08	.06	.03
237	Dan Norman	.08	.06	.03
238	Cesar Cedeno	.12	.09	.05
239	Dave Stapleton	.08	.06	.03
240	Rich Gossage	.25	.20	.10
241	Super Veteran (Rich Gossage)	.12	.09	.05
242	Bob Stanley	.10	.08	.04
243	Rich Gale	.08	.06	.03
244	Sixto Lezcano	.08	.06	.03
245	Steve Sax	.25	.20	.10
246	Jerry Mumphrey	.08	.06	.03
247	Dave Smith	.10	.08	.04
248	Bake McBride	.08	.06	.03
249	Checklist 133-264	.08	.06	.03
250	Bill Buckner	.15	.11	.06
251	Kent Hrbek	.50	.40	.20
252	Gene Tenace	.10	.08	.04
253	Charlie Lea	.08	.06	.03
254	Rick Cerone	.08	.06	.03
255	Gene Garber	.08	.06	.03
256	Super Veteran (Gene Garber)	.08	.06	.03
257	Jesse Barfield	.75	.60	.30
258	Dave Winfield	.40	.30	.15
259	Don Money	.08	.06	.03
260	Steve Kemp	.10	.08	.04
261	Steve Yeager	.08	.06	.03
262	Keith Hernandez	.40	.30	.15
263	Tippy Martinez	.08	.06	.03
264	Super Veteran (Joe Morgan)	.12	.09	.05
265	Joel Youngblood	.08	.06	.03
266	Bruce Sutter AS	.10	.08	.04
267	Terry Francona	.08	.06	.03
268	Neil Allen	.08	.06	.03
269	Ron Oester	.08	.06	.03
270	Dennis Eckersley	.12	.09	.05
271	Dale Berra	.08	.06	.03
272	Al Bumbry	.08	.06	.03
273	Lonnie Smith	.10	.08	.04
274	Terry Kennedy	.10	.08	.04
275	Ray Knight	.10	.08	.04
276	Mike Norris	.08	.06	.03
277	Rance Mulliniks	.08	.06	.03
278	Dan Spillner	.08	.06	.03
279	Bucky Dent	.10	.08	.04
280	Bert Blyleven	.15	.11	.06
281	Barry Bonnell	.08	.06	.03
282	Reggie Smith	.10	.08	.04
283	Super Veteran (Reggie Smith)	.10	.08	.04
284	Ted Simmons	.15	.11	.06
285	Lance Parrish	.30	.25	.12
286	Larry Christenson	.08	.06	.03
287	Ruppert Jones	.08	.06	.03
288	Bob Welch	.10	.08	.04
289	John Wathan	.10	.08	.04
290	Jeff Reardon	.12	.09	.05
291	Dave Revering	.08	.06	.03
292	Craig Swan	.08	.06	.03
293	Graig Nettles	.15	.11	.06
294	Alfredo Griffin	.10	.08	.04
295	Jerry Remy	.08	.06	.03
296	Joe Sambito	.08	.06	.03
297	Ron LeFlore	.10	.08	.04
298	Brian Downing	.10	.08	.04
299	Jim Palmer	.40	.30	.15
300	Mike Schmidt	1.50	1.25	.60
301	Super Veteran (Mike Schmidt)	1.00	.70	.40
302	Ernie Whitt	.08	.06	.03
303	Andre Dawson	.30	.25	.12
304	Super Veteran (Bobby Murcer)	.10	.08	.04
305	Larry Bowa	.12	.09	.05
306	Lee Mazzilli	.10	.08	.04
307	Lou Piniella	.12	.09	.05
308	Buck Martinez	.08	.06	.03
309	Jerry Martin	.08	.06	.03
310	Greg Luzinski	.15	.11	.06
311	Al Oliver	.15	.11	.06
312	Mike Torrez	.10	.08	.04
313	Dick Ruthven	.08	.06	.03
314	Gary Carter AS	.30	.25	.12
315	Rick Burleson	.10	.08	.04
316	Super Veteran (Phil Niekro)	.15	.11	.06
317	Moose Haas	.08	.06	.03
318	Carney Lansford	.12	.09	.05
319	Tim Foli	.08	.06	.03
320	Steve Rogers	.10	.08	.04
321	Kirk Gibson	.30	.25	.12
322	Glenn Hubbard	.08	.06	.03
323	Luis DeLeon	.08	.06	.03
324	Mike Marshall	.20	.15	.08
325	Von Hayes	.20	.15	.08
326	Garth Iorg	.08	.06	.03
327	Jose Cruz	.12	.09	.05
328	Super Veteran (Jim Palmer)	.15	.11	.06
329	Darrell Evans	.12	.09	.05
330	Buddy Bell	.12	.09	.05
331	Mike Krukow	.10	.08	.04
332	Omar Moreno	.08	.06	.03
333	Dave LaRoche	.08	.06	.03
334	Super Veteran (Dave LaRoche)	.08	.06	.03
335	Bill Madlock	.15	.11	.06
336	Garry Templeton	.10	.08	.04
337	John Lowenstein	.08	.06	.03
338	Willie Upshaw	.10	.08	.04
339	Dave Hostetler	.08	.06	.03
340	Larry Gura	.08	.06	.03
341	Doug DeCinces	.12	.09	.05
342	Mike Schmidt AS	.40	.30	.15
343	Charlie Hough	.10	.08	.04
344	Andre Thornton	.10	.08	.04
345	Jim Clancy	.10	.08	.04
346	Ken Forsch	.08	.06	.03
347	Sammy Stewart	.08	.06	.03
348	Alan Bannister	.08	.06	.03
349	Checklist 265-396	.08	.06	.03
350	Robin Yount	.40	.30	.15
351	Warren Cromartie	.08	.06	.03
352	Tim Raines AS	.30	.25	.12
353	Tony Armas	.10	.08	.04
354	Super Veteran (Tom Seaver)	.25	.20	.10
355	Tony Perez	.20	.15	.08
356	Toby Harrah	.10	.08	.04
357	Dan Ford	.08	.06	.03
358	Charlie Puleo	.08	.06	.03
359	Dave Collins	.08	.06	.03
360	Nolan Ryan	1.00	.70	.40
361	Super Veteran (Nolan Ryan)	.25	.20	.10
362	Bill Almon	.08	.06	.03
363	Eddie Milner	.08	.06	.03
364	Gary Lucas	.08	.06	.03
365	Dave Lopes	.10	.08	.04
366	Bob Boone	.10	.08	.04
367	Biff Pocoroba	.08	.06	.03
368	Richie Zisk	.10	.08	.04
369	Tony Bernazard	.08	.06	.03
370	Gary Carter	.50	.40	.20
371	Paul Molitor	.20	.15	.08
372	Art Howe	.08	.06	.03
373	Pete Rose AS	.60	.45	.25
374	Glenn Adams	.08	.06	.03
375	Pete Vukovich	.10	.08	.04
376	Gary Lavelle	.08	.06	.03
377	Lee May	.10	.08	.04
378	Super Veteran (Lee May)	.10	.08	.04
379	Butch Wynegar	.10	.08	.04
380	Ron Davis	.08	.06	.03
381	Bob Grich	.12	.09	.05
382	Gary Roenicke	.08	.06	.03
383	Jim Kaat	.15	.11	.06
384	Steve Carlton AS	.30	.25	.12
385	Mike Easler	.10	.08	.04
386	Rod Carew AS	.30	.25	.12
387	Bobby Grich AS	.10	.08	.04
388	George Brett AS	.40	.30	.15
389	Robin Yount AS	.20	.15	.08
390	Reggie Jackson AS	.30	.25	.12
391	Rickey Henderson AS	.30	.25	.12
392	Fred Lynn AS	.12	.09	.05
393	Carlton Fisk AS	.12	.09	.05
394	Pete Vukovich AS	.10	.08	.04
395	Larry Gura AS	.10	.08	.04
396	Dan Quisenberry AS	.10	.08	.04

1984 O-Pee-Chee

Almost identical in design to the 1984 Topps set, the 1984 O-Pee-Chee set contains 396 cards. The O-Pee-Chee cards display the Canadian company's logo in the upper right corner and the backs of the cards are printed in both English and French. The cards measure 2-1/2" by 3-1/2", and some include the extra line on the front of the card to indicate a trade.

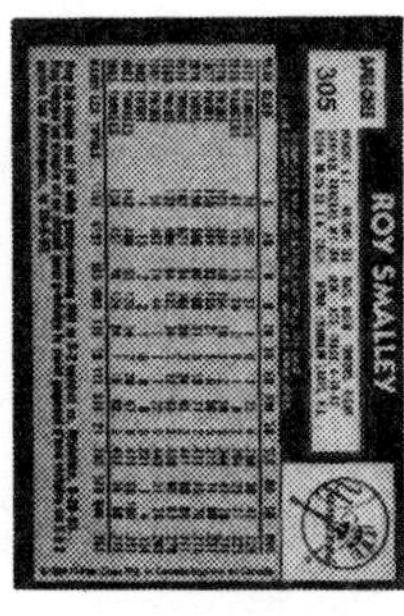

		MT	NR MT	EX
Complete Set:		35.00	26.00	14.00
Common Player:		.08	.06	.03
1	Pascual Perez	.10	.08	.04
2	Cal Ripken	.50	.40	.20
3	Lloyd Moseby	.10	.08	.04
4	Mel Hall	.12	.09	.05
5	Willie Wilson	.15	.11	.06
6	Mike Morgan	.08	.06	.03
7	Gary Lucas	.08	.06	.03
8	Don Mattingly	20.00	15.00	8.00
9	Jim Gott	.08	.06	.03
10	Robin Yount	.30	.25	.12
11	Joey McLaughlin	.08	.06	.03
12	Billy Sample	.08	.06	.03
13	Oscar Gamble	.08	.06	.03
14	Bill Russell	.10	.08	.04
15	Burt Hooton	.10	.08	.04
16	Omar Moreno	.08	.06	.03
17	Dave Lopes	.10	.08	.04
18	Dale Berra	.08	.06	.03
19	Rance Mulliniks	.08	.06	.03
20	Greg Luzinski	.10	.08	.04
21	Doug Sisk	.10	.08	.04
22	Don Robinson	.08	.06	.03
23	Keith Moreland	.10	.08	.04
24	Richard Dotson	.10	.08	.04
25	Glenn Hubbard	.08	.06	.03
26	Rod Carew	.40	.30	.15
27	Alan Wiggins	.08	.06	.03
28	Frank Viola	.25	.20	.10
29	Phil Niekro	.25	.20	.10
30	Wade Boggs	6.00	4.50	2.50
31	Dave Parker	.25	.20	.10
32	Bobby Ramos	.08	.06	.03
33	Tom Burgmeier	.08	.06	.03
34	Eddie Milner	.08	.06	.03
35	Don Sutton	.25	.20	.10
36	Glenn Wilson	.12	.09	.05
37	Mike Krukow	.10	.08	.04
38	Dave Collins	.08	.06	.03
39	Garth Iorg	.08	.06	.03
40	Dusty Baker	.10	.08	.04
41	Tony Bernazard	.08	.06	.03
42	Claudell Washington	.10	.08	.04
43	Cecil Cooper	.12	.09	.05
44	Dan Driessen	.10	.08	.04
45	Jerry Mumphrey	.08	.06	.03
46	Rick Rhoden	.10	.08	.04
47	Rudy Law	.08	.06	.03
48	Julio Franco	.30	.25	.12
49	Mike Norris	.08	.06	.03
50	Chris Chambliss	.10	.08	.04
51	Pete Falcone	.08	.06	.03
52	Mike Marshall	.15	.11	.06
53	Amos Otis	.10	.08	.04
54	Jesse Orosco	.10	.08	.04
55	Dave Concepcion	.12	.09	.05
56	Gary Allenson	.08	.06	.03
57	Dan Schatzeder	.08	.06	.03
58	Jerry Remy	.08	.06	.03
59	Carney Lansford	.12	.09	.05
60	Paul Molitor	.20	.15	.08
61	Chris Codiroli	.08	.06	.03
62	Dave Hostetler	.08	.06	.03
63	Ed Vande Berg	.08	.06	.03
64	Ryne Sandberg	1.00	.70	.40
65	Kirk Gibson	.30	.25	.12
66	Nolan Ryan	.30	.25	.12
67	Gary Ward	.08	.06	.03
68	Luis Salazar	.08	.06	.03
69	Dan Quisenberry	.15	.11	.06
70	Gary Matthews	.10	.08	.04
71	Pete O'Brien	.75	.60	.30
72	John Wathan	.10	.08	.04
73	Jody Davis	.12	.09	.05
74	Kent Tekulve	.10	.08	.04
75	Bob Forsch	.10	.08	.04
76	Alfredo Griffin	.10	.08	.04
77	Bryn Smith	.10	.08	.04
78	Mike Torrez	.10	.08	.04
79	Mike Hargrove	.10	.08	.04
80	Steve Rogers	.10	.08	.04
81	Bake McBride	.08	.06	.03
82	Doug DeCinces	.12	.09	.05
83	Richie Zisk	.10	.08	.04
84	Randy Bush	.08	.06	.03
85	Atlee Hammaker	.10	.08	.04
86	Chet Lemon	.10	.08	.04
87	Frank Pastore	.08	.06	.03
88	Alan Trammell	.30	.25	.12
89	Terry Francona	.08	.06	.03
90	Pedro Guerrero	.30	.25	.12
91	Dan Spillner	.08	.06	.03
92	Lloyd Moseby	.10	.08	.04
93	Bob Knepper	.10	.08	.04
94	Ted Simmons	.15	.11	.06
95	Aurelio Lopez	.08	.06	.03
96	Bill Buckner	.15	.11	.06
97	LaMarr Hoyt	.08	.06	.03
98	Tom Brunansky	.15	.11	.06
99	Ron Oester	.08	.06	.03
100	Reggie Jackson	.50	.40	.20

		MT	NR MT	EX
101	Ron Davis	.08	.06	.03
102	Ken Oberkfell	.08	.06	.03
103	Dwayne Murphy	.10	.08	.04
104	Jim Slaton	.08	.06	.03
105	Tony Armas	.10	.08	.04
106	Ernie Whitt	.08	.06	.03
107	Johnnie LeMaster	.08	.06	.03
108	Randy Moffitt	.08	.06	.03
109	Terry Forster	.10	.08	.04
110	Ron Guidry	.25	.20	.10
111	Bill Virdon	.08	.06	.03
112	Doyle Alexander	.12	.09	.05
113	Lonnie Smith	.10	.08	.04
114	Checklist	.08	.06	.03
115	Andre Thornton	.10	.08	.04
116	Jeff Reardon	.15	.11	.06
117	Tom Herr	.12	.09	.05
118	Charlie Hough	.10	.08	.04
119	Phil Garner	.10	.08	.04
120	Keith Hernandez	.30	.25	.12
121	Rich Gossage	.20	.15	.08
122	Ted Simmons	.15	.11	.06
123	Butch Wynegar	.10	.08	.04
124	Damaso Garcia	.10	.08	.04
125	Britt Burns	.08	.06	.03
126	Bert Blyleven	.15	.11	.06
127	Carlton Fisk	.20	.15	.08
128	Rick Manning	.08	.06	.03
129	Bill Laskey	.08	.06	.03
130	Ozzie Smith	.15	.11	.06
131	Bo Diaz	.08	.06	.03
132	Tom Paciorek	.08	.06	.03
133	Dave Rozema	.08	.06	.03
134	Dave Stieb	.15	.11	.06
135	Brian Downing	.10	.08	.04
136	Rick Camp	.08	.06	.03
137	Willie Aikens	.08	.06	.03
138	Charlie Moore	.08	.06	.03
139	George Frazier	.08	.06	.03
140	Storm Davis	.10	.08	.04
141	Glenn Hoffman	.08	.06	.03
142	Charlie Lea	.08	.06	.03
143	Mike Vail	.08	.06	.03
144	Steve Sax	.15	.11	.06
145	Gary Lavelle	.08	.06	.03
146	Gorman Thomas	.10	.08	.04
147	Dan Petry	.10	.08	.04
148	Mark Clear	.08	.06	.03
149	Dave Beard	.08	.06	.03
150	Dale Murphy	.75	.60	.30
151	Steve Trout	.08	.06	.03
152	Tony Pena	.10	.08	.04
153	Geoff Zahn	.08	.06	.03
154	Dave Henderson	.10	.08	.04
155	Frank White	.12	.09	.05
156	Dick Ruthven	.08	.06	.03
157	Gary Gaetti	.40	.30	.15
158	Lance Parrish	.30	.25	.12
159	Joe Price	.08	.06	.03
160	Mario Soto	.10	.08	.04
161	Tug McGraw	.12	.09	.05
162	Bob Ojeda	.10	.08	.04
163	George Hendrick	.10	.08	.04
164	Scott Sanderson	.08	.06	.03
165	Ken Singleton	.10	.08	.04
166	Terry Kennedy	.10	.08	.04
167	Gene Garber	.08	.06	.03
168	Juan Bonilla	.08	.06	.03
169	Larry Parrish	.10	.08	.04
170	Jerry Reuss	.10	.08	.04
171	John Tudor	.12	.09	.05
172	Dave Kingman	.15	.11	.06
173	Garry Templeton	.10	.08	.04
174	Bob Boone	.10	.08	.04
175	Graig Nettles	.12	.09	.05
176	Lee Smith	.10	.08	.04
177	LaMarr Hoyt	.08	.06	.03
178	Bill Krueger	.08	.06	.03
179	Buck Martinez	.08	.06	.03
180	Manny Trillo	.10	.08	.04
181	Lou Whitaker	.25	.20	.10
182	Darryl Strawberry	7.50	5.75	3.00
183	Neil Allen	.08	.06	.03
184	Jim Rice	.30	.25	.12
185	Sixto Lezcano	.08	.06	.03
186	Tom Hume	.08	.06	.03
187	Garry Maddox	.10	.08	.04
188	Bryan Little	.08	.06	.03
189	Jose Cruz	.12	.09	.05
190	Ben Oglivie	.10	.08	.04
191	Cesar Cedeno	.12	.09	.05
192	Nick Esasky	.30	.25	.12
193	Ken Forsch	.08	.06	.03
194	Jim Palmer	.30	.25	.12
195	Jack Morris	.25	.20	.10
196	Steve Howe	.10	.08	.04
197	Harold Baines	.15	.11	.06
198	Bill Doran	.60	.45	.25
199	Willie Hernandez	.12	.09	.05
200	Andre Dawson	.30	.25	.12
201	Bruce Kison	.08	.06	.03
202	Bobby Cox	.08	.06	.03
203	Matt Keough	.08	.06	.03
204	Ron Guidry	.25	.20	.10
205	Greg Minton	.08	.06	.03
206	Al Holland	.08	.06	.03
207	Luis Leal	.08	.06	.03
208	Jose Oquendo	.08	.06	.03
209	Leon Durham	.12	.09	.05
210	Joe Morgan	.25	.20	.10
211	Lou Whitaker AS	.12	.09	.05
212	George Brett AS	.20	.15	.08
213	Bruce Hurst	.10	.08	.04
214	Steve Carlton	.40	.30	.15
215	Tippy Martinez	.08	.06	.03
216	Ken Landreaux	.08	.06	.03
217	Alan Ashby	.08	.06	.03
218	Dennis Eckersley	.12	.09	.05
219	Craig McMurtry	.08	.06	.03
220	Fernando Valenzuela	.30	.25	.12
221	Cliff Johnson	.08	.06	.03
222	Rick Honeycutt	.08	.06	.03
223	George Brett	.60	.45	.25
224	Rusty Staub	.12	.09	.05

		MT	NR MT	EX
225	Lee Mazzilli	.10	.08	.04
226	Pat Putnam	.08	.06	.03
227	Bob Welch	.10	.08	.04
228	Rick Cerone	.08	.06	.03
229	Lee Lacy	.08	.06	.03
230	Rickey Henderson	.50	.40	.20
231	Gary Redus	.25	.20	.10
232	Tim Wallach	.15	.11	.06
233	Checklist	.08	.06	.03
234	Rafael Ramirez	.08	.06	.03
235	Matt Young	.12	.09	.05
236	Ellis Valentine	.08	.06	.03
237	John Castino	.08	.06	.03
238	Eric Show	.10	.08	.04
239	Bob Horner	.15	.11	.06
240	Eddie Murray	.50	.40	.20
241	Billy Almon	.08	.06	.03
242	Greg Brock	.10	.08	.04
243	Bruce Sutter	.15	.11	.06
244	Dwight Evans	.15	.11	.06
245	Rick Sutcliffe	.12	.09	.05
246	Terry Crowley	.08	.06	.03
247	Fred Lynn	.20	.15	.08
248	Bill Dawley	.08	.06	.03
249	Dave Stapleton	.08	.06	.03
250	Bill Madlock	.15	.11	.06
251	Jim Sundberg	.10	.08	.04
252	Steve Yeager	.08	.06	.03
253	Jim Wohlford	.08	.06	.03
254	Shane Rawley	.10	.08	.04
255	Bruce Benedict	.08	.06	.03
256	Dave Geisel	.08	.06	.03
257	Julio Cruz	.08	.06	.03
258	Luis Sanchez	.08	.06	.03
259	Von Hayes	.12	.09	.05
260	Scott McGregor	.10	.08	.04
261	Tom Seaver	.30	.25	.12
262	Doug Flynn	.08	.06	.03
263	Wayne Gross	.08	.06	.03
264	Larry Gura	.08	.06	.03
265	John Montefusco	.08	.06	.03
266	Dave Winfield	.30	.25	.12
267	Tim Lollar	.08	.06	.03
268	Ron Washington	.08	.06	.03
269	Mickey Rivers	.10	.08	.04
270	Mookie Wilson	.10	.08	.04
271	Moose Haas	.08	.06	.03
272	Rick Dempsey	.10	.08	.04
273	Dan Quisenberry	.15	.11	.06
274	Steve Henderson	.08	.06	.03
275	Len Matuszek	.08	.06	.03
276	Frank Tanana	.10	.08	.04
277	Dave Righetti	.20	.15	.08
278	Jorge Bell	1.25	.90	.50
279	Ivan DeJesus	.08	.06	.03
280	Floyd Bannister	.10	.08	.04
281	Dale Murray	.08	.06	.03
282	Andre Robertson	.08	.06	.03
283	Rollie Fingers	.20	.15	.08
284	Tommy John	.20	.15	.08
285	Darrell Porter	.10	.08	.04
286	Lary Sorensen	.08	.06	.03
287	Warren Cromartie	.08	.06	.03
288	Jim Beattie	.08	.06	.03
289	Blue Jays Team	.12	.09	.05
290	Dave Dravecky	.10	.08	.04
291	Eddie Murray AS	.25	.20	.10
292	Greg Bargar	.08	.06	.03
293	Tom Underwood	.08	.06	.03
294	U.L. Washington	.08	.06	.03
295	Mike Flanagan	.10	.08	.04
296	Rich Gedman	.10	.08	.04
297	Bruce Berenyi	.08	.06	.03
298	Jim Gantner	.08	.06	.03
299	Bill Caudill	.08	.06	.03
300	Pete Rose	1.25	.90	.50
301	Steve Kemp	.10	.08	.04
302	Barry Bonnell	.08	.06	.03
303	Joel Youngblood	.08	.06	.03
304	Rick Langford	.08	.06	.03
305	Roy Smalley	.08	.06	.03
306	Ken Griffey	.12	.09	.05
307	Al Oliver	.12	.09	.05
308	Ron Hassey	.08	.06	.03
309	Len Barker	.08	.06	.03
310	Willie McGee	.30	.25	.12
311	Jerry Koosman	.10	.08	.04
312	Jorge Orta	.08	.06	.03
313	Pete Vuckovich	.10	.08	.04
314	George Wright	.08	.06	.03
315	Bob Grich	.12	.09	.05
316	Jesse Barfield	.25	.20	.10
317	Willie Upshaw	.10	.08	.04
318	Bill Gullickson	.10	.08	.04
319	Ray Burris	.08	.06	.03
320	Bob Stanley	.10	.08	.04
321	Ray Knight	.10	.08	.04
322	Ken Schrom	.08	.06	.03
323	Johnny Ray	.10	.08	.04
324	Brian Giles	.08	.06	.03
325	Darrell Evans	.12	.09	.05
326	Mike Caldwell	.08	.06	.03
327	Ruppert Jones	.08	.06	.03
328	Chris Speier	.08	.06	.03
329	Bobby Castillo	.08	.06	.03
330	John Candelaria	.10	.08	.04
331	Bucky Dent	.10	.08	.04
332	Expos Team	.12	.09	.05
333	Larry Herndon	.08	.06	.03
334	Chuck Rainey	.08	.06	.03
335	Don Baylor	.15	.11	.06
336	Bob James	.12	.09	.05
337	Jim Clancy	.10	.08	.04
338	Duane Kuiper	.08	.06	.03
339	Roy Lee Jackson	.08	.06	.03
340	Hal McRae	.12	.09	.05
341	Larry McWilliams	.08	.06	.03
342	Tim Foli	.08	.06	.03
343	Fergie Jenkins	.15	.11	.06
344	Dickie Thon	.10	.08	.04
345	Kent Hrbek	.30	.25	.12
346	Larry Bowa	.12	.09	.05
347	Buddy Bell	.12	.09	.05
348	Toby Harrah	.10	.08	.04

		MT	NR MT	EX
349	Dan Ford	.08	.06	.03
350	George Foster	.15	.11	.06
351	Lou Piniella	.12	.09	.05
352	Dave Stewart	.12	.09	.05
353	Mike Easler	.10	.08	.04
354	Jeff Burroughs	.10	.08	.04
355	Jason Thompson	.08	.06	.03
356	Glenn Abbott	.08	.06	.03
357	Ron Cey	.12	.09	.05
358	Bob Dernier	.08	.06	.03
359	Jim Acker	.08	.06	.03
360	Willie Randolph	.10	.08	.04
361	Mike Schmidt	.60	.45	.25
362	David Green	.08	.06	.03
363	Cal Ripken AS	.30	.25	.12
364	Jim Rice AS	.25	.20	.10
365	Steve Bedrosian	.10	.08	.04
366	Gary Carter	.40	.30	.15
367	Chili Davis	.12	.09	.05
368	Hubie Brooks	.12	.09	.05
369	Steve McCatty	.08	.06	.03
370	Tim Raines	.30	.25	.12
371	Joaquin Andujar	.10	.08	.04
372	Gary Roenicke	.08	.06	.03
373	Ron Kittle	.12	.09	.05
374	Rich Dauer	.08	.06	.03
375	Dennis Leonard	.10	.08	.04
376	Rick Burleson	.10	.08	.04
377	Eric Rasmussen	.08	.06	.03
378	Dave Winfield	.30	.25	.12
379	Checklist	.08	.06	.03
380	Steve Garvey	.40	.30	.15
381	Jack Clark	.20	.15	.08
382	Odell Jones	.08	.06	.03
383	Terry Puhl	.08	.06	.03
384	Joe Niekro	.10	.08	.04
385	Tony Perez	.15	.11	.06
386	George Hendrick AS	.10	.08	.04
387	Johnny Ray AS	.10	.08	.04
388	Mike Schmidt AS	.30	.25	.12
389	Ozzie Smith AS	.10	.08	.04
390	Tim Raines AS	.20	.15	.08
391	Dale Murphy AS	.30	.25	.12
392	Andre Dawson AS	.15	.11	.06
393	Gary Carter AS	.20	.15	.08
394	Steve Rogers AS	.10	.08	.04
395	Steve Carlton AS	.20	.15	.08
396	Jesse Orosco AS	.10	.08	.04

1985 O-Pee-Chee

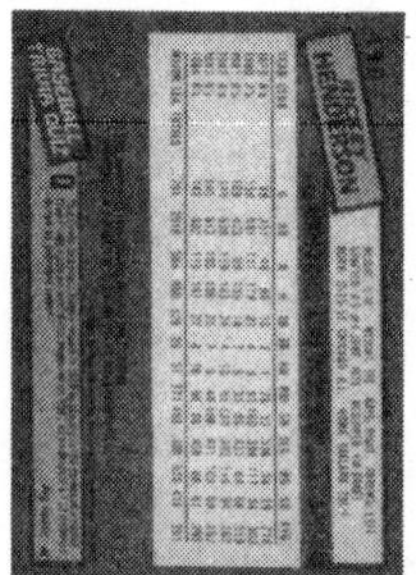

This 396-card set is almost identical in design to the 1985 Topps set. Measuring 2-1/2" by 3-1/2", the fronts of the Canadian-issued cards display the O-Pee-Chee logo in the upper left corner, and the backs of the cards are printed in both French and English. A "traded" line appears on the front of some of the cards to indicate a change in teams.

	MT	NR MT	EX
Complete Set:	40.00	30.00	15.00
Common Player:	.06	.05	.02

		MT	NR MT	EX
1	Tom Seaver	.25	.20	.10
2	Gary Lavelle	.06	.05	.02
3	Tim Wallach	.12	.09	.05
4	Jim Wohlford	.06	.05	.02
5	Jeff Robinson	.10	.08	.04
6	Willie Wilson	.15	.11	.06
7	Cliff Johnson	.06	.05	.02
8	Willie Randolph	.08	.06	.03
9	Larry Herndon	.06	.05	.02
10	Kirby Puckett	10.00	7.50	4.00
11	Mookie Wilson	.08	.06	.03
12	Dave Lopes	.08	.06	.03
13	Tim Lollar	.06	.05	.02
14	Chris Bando	.06	.05	.02
15	Jerry Koosman	.08	.06	.03
16	Bobby Meacham	.06	.05	.02
17	Mike Scott	.15	.11	.06
18	Rich Gedman	.08	.06	.03
19	George Frazier	.06	.05	.02
20	Chet Lemon	.08	.06	.03
21	Dave Concepcion	.10	.08	.04
22	Jason Thompson	.06	.05	.02
23	Bret Saberhagen	2.75	2.00	1.00
24	Jesse Barfield	.15	.11	.06
25	Steve Bedrosian	.10	.08	.04
26	Roy Smalley	.06	.05	.02
27	Bruce Berenyi	.06	.05	.02
28	Butch Wynegar	.08	.06	.03
29	Alan Ashby	.06	.05	.02
30	Cal Ripken	.40	.30	.15
31	Luis Leal	.06	.05	.02
32	Dave Dravecky	.08	.06	.03
33	Tito Landrum	.06	.05	.02
34	Pedro Guerrero	.20	.15	.08
35	Graig Nettles	.12	.09	.05
36	Fred Breining	.06	.05	.02
37	Roy Lee Jackson	.06	.05	.02
38	Steve Henderson	.06	.05	.02
39	Gary Pettis	.10	.08	.04
40	Phil Niekro	.20	.15	.08
41	Dwight Gooden	10.00	7.50	4.00
42	Luis Sanchez	.06	.05	.02
43	Lee Smith	.10	.08	.04
44	Dickie Thon	.10	.08	.04
45	Greg Minton	.06	.05	.02
46	Mike Flanagan	.10	.08	.04
47	Bud Black	.10	.08	.04
48	Tony Fernandez	.75	.60	.30
49	Carlton Fisk	.15	.11	.06
50	John Candelaria	.08	.06	.03
51	Bob Watson	.06	.05	.02
52	Rick Leach	.06	.05	.02
53	Rick Rhoden	.08	.06	.03
54	Cesar Cedeno	.10	.08	.04
55	Frank Tanana	.08	.06	.03
56	Larry Bowa	.10	.08	.04
57	Willie McGee	.20	.15	.08
58	Rich Dauer	.06	.05	.02
59	Jorge Bell	.50	.40	.20
60	George Hendrick	.08	.06	.03
61	Donnie Moore	.06	.05	.02
62	Mike Ramsey	.06	.05	.02
63	Nolan Ryan	.30	.25	.12
64	Mark Bailey	.06	.05	.02
65	Bill Buckner	.10	.08	.04
66	Jerry Reuss	.08	.06	.03
67	Mike Schmidt	.40	.30	.15
68	Von Hayes	.12	.09	.05
69	Phil Bradley	.70	.50	.30
70	Don Baylor	.12	.09	.05
71	Julio Cruz	.06	.05	.02
72	Rick Sutcliffe	.10	.08	.04
73	Storm Davis	.08	.06	.03
74	Mike Krukow	.08	.06	.03
75	Willie Upshaw	.08	.06	.03
76	Craig Lefferts	.06	.05	.02
77	Lloyd Moseby	.10	.08	.04
78	Ron Davis	.06	.05	.02
79	Rick Mahler	.08	.06	.03
80	Keith Hernandez	.25	.20	.10
81	Vance Law	.06	.05	.02
82	Joe Price	.06	.05	.02
83	Dennis Lamp	.06	.05	.02
84	Gary Ward	.08	.06	.03
85	Mike Marshall	.12	.09	.05
86	Marvell Wynne	.06	.05	.02
87	David Green	.06	.05	.02
88	Bryn Smith	.08	.06	.03
89	Sixto Lezcano	.06	.05	.02
90	Rich Gossage	.15	.11	.06
91	Jeff Burroughs	.08	.06	.03
92	Bobby Brown	.06	.05	.02
93	Oscar Gamble	.06	.05	.02
94	Rick Dempsey	.08	.06	.03
95	Jose Cruz	.10	.08	.04
96	Johnny Ray	.10	.08	.04
97	Joel Youngblood	.06	.05	.02
98	Eddie Whitson	.06	.05	.02
99	Milt Wilcox	.06	.05	.02
100	George Brett	.40	.30	.15
101	Jim Acker	.06	.05	.02
102	Jim Sundberg	.08	.06	.03
103	Ozzie Virgil	.08	.06	.03
104	Mike Fitzgerald	.08	.06	.03
105	Ron Kittle	.10	.08	.04
106	Pascual Perez	.08	.06	.03
107	Barry Bonnell	.06	.05	.02
108	Lou Whitaker	.20	.15	.08
109	Gary Roenicke	.06	.05	.02
110	Alejandro Pena	.08	.06	.03
111	Doug DeCinces	.10	.08	.04
112	Doug Flynn	.06	.05	.02
113	Tom Herr	.10	.08	.04
114	Bob James	.06	.05	.02
115	Rickey Henderson	.30	.25	.12
116	Pete Rose	.75	.60	.30
117	Greg Gross	.06	.05	.02
118	Eric Show	.08	.06	.03
119	Buck Martinez	.06	.05	.02
120	Steve Kemp	.08	.06	.03
121	Checklist 1-132	.06	.05	.02
122	Tom Brunansky	.12	.09	.05
123	Dave Kingman	.12	.09	.05
124	Garry Templeton	.08	.06	.03
125	Kent Tekulve	.08	.06	.03
126	Darryl Strawberry	3.00	2.25	1.25
127	Mark Gubicza	.25	.20	.10
128	Ernie Whitt	.06	.05	.02
129	Don Robinson	.06	.05	.02
130	Al Oliver	.10	.08	.04
131	Mario Soto	.08	.06	.03
132	Jeff Leonard	.08	.06	.03
133	Andre Dawson	.25	.20	.10
134	Bruce Hurst	.08	.06	.03
135	Bobby Cox	.06	.05	.02
136	Matt Young	.06	.05	.02
137	Bob Forsch	.08	.06	.03
138	Ron Darling	.70	.50	.30
139	Steve Trout	.06	.05	.02
140	Geoff Zahn	.06	.05	.02
141	Ken Forsch	.06	.05	.02
142	Jerry Willard	.06	.05	.02
143	Bill Gullickson	.08	.06	.03
144	Mike Mason	.06	.05	.02
145	Alvin Davis	1.25	.90	.50
146	Gary Redus	.08	.06	.03
147	Willie Aikens	.06	.05	.02
148	Steve Yeager	.06	.05	.02
149	Dickie Noles	.06	.05	.02
150	Jim Rice	.30	.25	.12
151	Moose Haas	.06	.05	.02
152	Steve Balboni	.08	.06	.03
153	Frank LaCorte	.06	.05	.02
154	Argenis Salazar	.06	.05	.02
155	Bob Grich	.10	.08	.04
156	Craig Reynolds	.06	.05	.02
157	Bill Madlock	.10	.08	.04
158	Pat Tabler	.10	.08	.04
159	Don Slaught	.06	.05	.02
160	Lance Parrish	.20	.15	.08
161	Ken Schrom	.06	.05	.02
162	Wally Backman	.08	.06	.03
163	Dennis Eckersley	.10	.08	.04
164	Dave Collins	.06	.05	.02
165	Dusty Baker	.08	.06	.03
166	Claudell Washington	.08	.06	.03
167	Rick Camp	.06	.05	.02
168	Garth Iorg	.06	.05	.02
169	Shane Rawley	.08	.06	.03
170	George Foster	.12	.09	.05
171	Tony Bernazard	.06	.05	.02
172	Don Sutton	.20	.15	.08
173	Jerry Remy	.06	.05	.02
174	Rick Honeycutt	.06	.05	.02
175	Dave Parker	.20	.15	.08
176	Buddy Bell	.10	.08	.04
177	Steve Garvey	.30	.25	.12
178	Miguel Dilone	.06	.05	.02
179	Tommy John	.15	.11	.06
180	Dave Winfield	.30	.25	.12
181	Alan Trammell	.30	.25	.12
182	Rollie Fingers	.15	.11	.06
183	Larry McWilliams	.06	.05	.02
184	Carmen Castillo	.06	.05	.02
185	Al Holland	.06	.05	.02
186	Jerry Mumphrey	.06	.05	.02
187	Chris Chambliss	.08	.06	.03
188	Jim Clancy	.08	.06	.03
189	Glenn Wilson	.10	.08	.04
190	Rusty Staub	.10	.08	.04
191	Ozzie Smith	.12	.09	.05
192	Howard Johnson	.60	.45	.25
193	Jimmy Key	.60	.45	.25
194	Terry Kennedy	.08	.06	.03
195	Glenn Hubbard	.06	.05	.02
196	Pete O'Brien	.10	.08	.04
197	Keith Moreland	.08	.06	.03
198	Eddie Milner	.06	.05	.02
199	Dave Engle	.06	.05	.02
200	Reggie Jackson	.30	.25	.12
201	Burt Hooton	.08	.06	.03
202	Gorman Thomas	.08	.06	.03
203	Larry Parrish	.08	.06	.03
204	Bob Stanley	.08	.06	.03
205	Steve Rogers	.08	.06	.03
206	Phil Garner	.08	.06	.03
207	Ed Vande Berg	.06	.05	.02
208	Jack Clark	.15	.11	.06
209	Bill Campbell	.06	.05	.02
210	Gary Matthews	.08	.06	.03
211	Dave Palmer	.06	.05	.02
212	Tony Perez	.15	.11	.06
213	Sammy Stewart	.06	.05	.02
214	John Tudor	.10	.08	.04
215	Bob Brenly	.06	.05	.02
216	Jim Gantner	.06	.05	.02
217	Bryan Clark	.06	.05	.02
218	Doyle Alexander	.10	.08	.04
219	Bo Diaz	.08	.06	.03
220	Fred Lynn	.15	.11	.06
221	Eddie Murray	.40	.30	.15
222	Hubie Brooks	.10	.08	.04
223	Tom Hume	.06	.05	.02
224	Al Cowens	.06	.05	.02
225	Mike Boddicker	.10	.08	.04
226	Len Matuszek	.06	.05	.02
227	Danny Darwin	.06	.05	.02
228	Scott McGregor	.08	.06	.03
229	Dave LaPoint	.06	.05	.02
230	Gary Carter	.30	.25	.12
231	Joaquin Andujar	.08	.06	.03
232	Rafael Ramirez	.06	.05	.02
233	Wayne Gross	.06	.05	.02
234	Neil Allen	.06	.05	.02
235	Gary Maddox	.08	.06	.03
236	Mark Thurmond	.06	.05	.02
237	Julio Franco	.12	.09	.05
238	Ray Burris	.06	.05	.02
239	Tim Teufel	.08	.06	.03
240	Dave Stieb	.12	.09	.05
241	Brett Butler	.08	.06	.03
242	Greg Brock	.08	.06	.03
243	Barbaro Garbey	.06	.05	.02
244	Greg Walker	.10	.08	.04
245	Chili Davis	.10	.08	.04
246	Darrell Porter	.08	.06	.03
247	Tippy Martinez	.06	.05	.02
248	Terry Forster	.08	.06	.03
249	Harold Baines	.15	.11	.06
250	Jesse Orosco	.08	.06	.03
251	Brad Gulden	.06	.05	.02
252	Mike Hargrove	.08	.06	.03
253	Nick Esasky	.08	.06	.03
254	Frank Williams	.06	.05	.02
255	Lonnie Smith	.08	.06	.03
256	Daryl Sconiers	.06	.05	.02
257	Bryan Little	.06	.05	.02
258	Terry Francona	.06	.05	.02
259	Mark Langston	.60	.45	.25
260	Dave Righetti	.15	.11	.06
261	Checklist 133-264	.06	.05	.02
262	Bob Horner	.15	.11	.06
263	Mel Hall	.08	.06	.03
264	John Shelby	.08	.06	.03
265	Juan Samuel	.15	.11	.06
266	Frank Viola	.12	.09	.05
267	Jim Fanning	.06	.05	.02
268	Dick Ruthven	.06	.05	.02
269	Bobby Ramos	.06	.05	.02
270	Dan Quisenberry	.12	.09	.05
271	Dwight Evans	.15	.11	.06
272	Andre Thornton	.08	.06	.03
273	Orel Hershiser	1.50	1.25	.60
274	Ray Knight	.08	.06	.03
275	Bill Caudill	.06	.05	.02
276	Charlie Hough	.08	.06	.03
277	Tim Raines	.30	.25	.12
278	Mike Squires	.06	.05	.02
279	Alex Trevino	.06	.05	.02
280	Ron Romanick	.15	.11	.06
281	Tom Niedenfuer	.08	.06	.03

		MT	NR MT	EX
282	Mike Stenhouse	.06	.05	.02
283	Terry Puhl	.06	.05	.02
284	Hal McRae	.10	.08	.04
285	Dan Driessen	.08	.06	.03
286	Rudy Law	.06	.05	.02
287	Walt Terrell	.08	.06	.03
288	Jeff Kunkel	.08	.06	.03
289	Bob Knepper	.08	.06	.03
290	Cecil Cooper	.12	.09	.05
291	Bob Welch	.10	.08	.04
292	Frank Pastore	.06	.05	.02
293	Dan Schatzeder	.06	.05	.02
294	Tom Nieto	.06	.05	.02
295	Joe Niekro	.10	.08	.04
296	Ryne Sandberg	.30	.25	.12
297	Gary Lucas	.06	.05	.02
298	John Castino	.06	.05	.02
299	Bill Doran	.08	.06	.03
300	Rod Carew	.30	.25	.12
301	John Montefusco	.06	.05	.02
302	Johnnie LeMaster	.06	.05	.02
303	Jim Beattie	.06	.05	.02
304	Gary Gaetti	.12	.09	.05
305	Dale Berra	.06	.05	.02
306	Rick Reuschel	.10	.08	.04
307	Ken Oberkfell	.06	.05	.02
308	Kent Hrbek	.20	.15	.08
309	Mike Witt	.10	.08	.04
310	Manny Trillo	.08	.06	.03
311	Jim Gott	.06	.05	.02
312	LaMarr Hoyt	.06	.05	.02
313	Dave Schmidt	.06	.05	.02
314	Ron Oester	.06	.05	.02
315	Doug Sisk	.06	.05	.02
316	John Lowenstein	.06	.05	.02
317	Derrel Thomas	.06	.05	.02
318	Ted Simmons	.12	.09	.05
319	Darrell Evans	.10	.08	.04
320	Dale Murphy	.50	.40	.20
321	Ricky Horton	.20	.15	.08
322	Ken Phelps	.08	.06	.03
323	Lee Mazzilli	.08	.06	.03
324	Don Mattingly	8.00	6.00	3.25
325	John Denny	.06	.05	.02
326	Ken Singleton	.08	.06	.03
327	Brook Jacoby	.15	.11	.06
328	Greg Luzinski	.12	.09	.05
329	Bob Ojeda	.08	.06	.03
330	Leon Durham	.08	.06	.03
331	Bill Laskey	.06	.05	.02
332	Ben Oglivie	.08	.06	.03
333	Willie Hernandez	.08	.06	.03
334	Bob Dernier	.06	.05	.02
335	Bruce Benedict	.06	.05	.02
336	Rance Mulliniks	.06	.05	.02
337	Rick Cerone	.06	.05	.02
338	Britt Burns	.06	.05	.02
339	Danny Heep	.06	.05	.02
340	Robin Yount	.30	.25	.12
341	Andy Van Slyke	.10	.08	.04
342	Curt Wilkerson	.06	.05	.02
343	Bill Russell	.08	.06	.03
344	Dave Henderson	.08	.06	.03
345	Charlie Lea	.06	.05	.02
346	Terry Pendleton	.60	.45	.25
347	Carney Lansford	.10	.08	.04
348	Bob Boone	.08	.06	.03
349	Mike Easler	.08	.06	.03
350	Wade Boggs	3.00	2.25	1.25
351	Atlee Hammaker	.08	.06	.03
352	Joe Morgan	.15	.11	.06
353	Damaso Garcia	.08	.06	.03
354	Floyd Bannister	.08	.06	.03
355	Bert Blyleven	.15	.11	.06
356	John Butcher	.06	.05	.02
357	Fernando Valenzuela	.30	.25	.12
358	Tony Pena	.08	.06	.03
359	Mike Smithson	.06	.05	.02
360	Steve Carlton	.30	.25	.12
361	Alfredo Griffin	.08	.06	.03
362	Craig McMurtry	.06	.05	.02
363	Bill Dawley	.06	.05	.02
364	Richard Dotson	.08	.06	.03
365	Carmelo Martinez	.08	.06	.03
366	Ron Cey	.10	.08	.04
367	Tony Scott	.06	.05	.02
368	Dave Bergman	.06	.05	.02
369	Steve Sax	.15	.11	.06
370	Bruce Sutter	.12	.09	.05
371	Mickey Rivers	.08	.06	.03
372	Kirk Gibson	.25	.20	.10
373	Scott Sanderson	.06	.05	.02
374	Brian Downing	.08	.06	.03
375	Jeff Reardon	.12	.09	.05
376	Frank DiPino	.06	.05	.02
377	Checklist 265-396	.06	.05	.02
378	Alan Wiggins	.06	.05	.02
379	Charles Hudson	.08	.06	.03
380	Ken Griffey	.10	.08	.04
381	Tom Paciorek	.06	.05	.02
382	Jack Morris	.20	.15	.08
383	Tony Gwynn	.50	.40	.20
384	Jody Davis	.08	.06	.03
385	Jose DeLeon	.08	.06	.03
386	Bob Kearney	.06	.05	.02
387	George Wright	.06	.05	.02
388	Ron Guidry	.20	.15	.08
389	Rick Manning	.06	.05	.02
390	Sid Fernandez	.75	.60	.30
391	Bruce Bochte	.06	.05	.02
392	Dan Petry	.08	.06	.03
393	Tim Stoddard	.06	.05	.02
394	Tony Armas	.08	.06	.03
395	Paul Molitor	.15	.11	.06
396	Mike Heath	.06	.05	.02

1985 O-Pee-Chee Posters

The 1985 O-Pee-Chee Poster set consists of 24 players, 12 from the Expos and 12 from the Blue Jays. The blank-backed posters measure approximately 4-7/8" by 6-7/8" and generally have fold marks because they were inserted in the regular 1985 O-Pee-Chee wax packs. The card number, written inboth French and English, appears in the bottom border. The full-color player photos are surrounded by a red border for Expos and a blue border for Blue Jays.

		MT	NR MT	EX
Complete Set:		4.00	3.00	1.50
Common Player:		.10	.08	.04
1	Mike Fitzgerald	.10	.08	.04
2	Dan Driessen	.15	.11	.06
3	Dave Palmer	.15	.11	.06
4	U.L. Washington	.10	.08	.04
5	Hubie Brooks	.25	.20	.10
6	Tim Wallach	.40	.30	.15
7	Tim Raines	.75	.60	.30
8	Herm Winningham	.15	.11	.06
9	Andre Dawson	.75	.60	.30
10	Charlie Lea	.10	.08	.04
11	Steve Rogers	.15	.11	.06
12	Jeff Reardon	.30	.25	.12
13	Buck Martinez	.10	.08	.04
14	Willie Upshaw	.25	.20	.10
15	Damaso Garcia	.20	.15	.08
16	Tony Fernandez	.40	.30	.15
17	Rance Mulliniks	.10	.08	.04
18	George Bell	.75	.60	.30
19	Lloyd Moseby	.30	.25	.12
20	Jesse Barfield	.50	.40	.20
21	Doyle Alexander	.25	.20	.10
22	Dave Stieb	.40	.30	.15
23	Bill Caudill	.10	.08	.04
24	Gary Lavelle	.10	.08	.04

1986 O-Pee-Chee

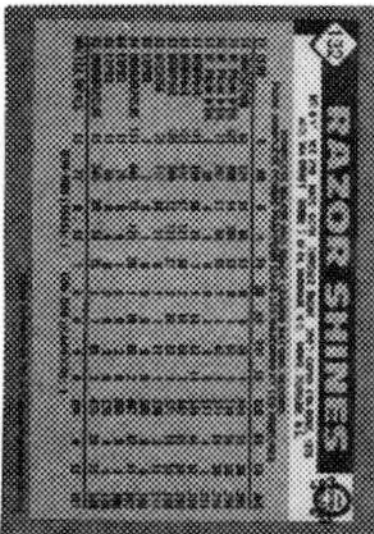

As usual, the 1986 O-Pee-Chee set was issued in close simulation of the Topps cards for the same year. The 396 cards in the set are 2-1/2" by 3-1/2" and use almost all of the same pictures as the Topps set. The O-Pee-Chee cards, being a Canadian issue, list player information in both English and French. There is an abundance of players from the two Canadian teams - Toronto and Montreal. As the O-Pee-Chee set was issued later in the year than the Topps regular issue, players who changed teams after the printing date are noted with a traded line at the bottom of the player photo. O-Pee-Chee's logo appears in the upper right of each card front.

		MT	NR MT	EX
Complete Set:		18.00	13.50	7.25
Common Player:		.05	.04	.02
1	Pete Rose	.70	.50	.30
2	Ken Landreaux	.05	.04	.02
3	Rob Picciolo	.05	.04	.02
4	Steve Garvey	.25	.20	.10
5	Andy Hawkins	.05	.04	.02
6	Rudy Law	.05	.04	.02
7	Lonnie Smith	.07	.05	.03
8	Dwayne Murphy	.07	.05	.03
9	Moose Haas	.05	.04	.02
10	Tony Gwynn	.35	.25	.14
11	Bob Ojeda	.07	.05	.03
12	Jose Uribe	.12	.09	.05
13	Bob Kearney	.05	.04	.02
14	Julio Cruz	.05	.04	.02
15	Eddie Whitson	.05	.04	.02
16	Rick Schu	.05	.04	.02
17	Mike Stenhouse	.05	.04	.02
18	Lou Thornton	.05	.04	.02
19	Ryne Sandberg	.25	.20	.10
20	Lou Whitaker	.15	.11	.06
21	Mark Brouhard	.05	.04	.02
22	Gary Lavelle	.05	.04	.02
23	Manny Lee	.10	.08	.04
24	Don Slaught	.05	.04	.02
25	Willie Wilson	.10	.08	.04
26	Mike Marshall	.10	.08	.04
27	Ray Knight	.07	.05	.03
28	Mario Soto	.07	.05	.03
29	Dave Anderson	.05	.04	.02
30	Eddie Murray	.35	.25	.14
31	Dusty Baker	.07	.05	.03
32	Steve Yeager	.05	.04	.02
33	Andy Van Slyke	.12	.09	.05
34	Dave Righetti	.15	.11	.06
35	Jeff Reardon	.10	.08	.04
36	Burt Hooton	.05	.04	.02
37	Johnny Ray	.07	.05	.03
38	Glenn Hoffman	.05	.04	.02
39	Rick Mahler	.05	.04	.02
40	Ken Griffey	.07	.05	.03
41	Brad Wellman	.05	.04	.02
42	Joe Hesketh	.05	.04	.02
43	Mark Salas	.05	.04	.02
44	Jorge Orta	.05	.04	.02
45	Damaso Garcia	.05	.04	.02
46	Jim Acker	.05	.04	.02
47	Bill Madlock	.10	.08	.04
48	Bill Almon	.05	.04	.02
49	Rick Manning	.05	.04	.02
50	Dan Quisenberry	.07	.05	.03
51	Jim Gantner	.05	.04	.02
52	Kevin Bass	.07	.05	.03
53	Len Dykstra	.40	.30	.15
54	John Franco	.10	.08	.04
55	Fred Lynn	.12	.09	.05
56	Jim Morrison	.05	.04	.02
57	Bill Doran	.07	.05	.03
58	Leon Durham	.07	.05	.03
59	Andre Thornton	.07	.05	.03
60	Dwight Evans	.10	.08	.04
61	Larry Herndon	.05	.04	.02
62	Bob Boone	.07	.05	.03
63	Kent Hrbek	.15	.11	.06
64	Floyd Bannister	.07	.05	.03
65	Harold Baines	.10	.08	.04
66	Pat Tabler	.07	.05	.03
67	Carmelo Martinez	.05	.04	.02
68	Ed Lynch	.05	.04	.02
69	George Foster	.10	.08	.04
70	Dave Winfield	.25	.20	.10
71	Ken Schrom	.05	.04	.02
72	Toby Harrah	.05	.04	.02
73	Jackie Gutierrez	.05	.04	.02
74	Rance Mulliniks	.05	.04	.02
75	Jose DeLeon	.05	.04	.02
76	Ron Romanick	.05	.04	.02
77	Charlie Leibrandt	.07	.05	.03
78	Bruce Benedict	.05	.04	.02
79	Dave Schmidt	.05	.04	.02
80	Darryl Strawberry	.40	.30	.15
81	Wayne Krenchicki	.05	.04	.02
82	Tippy Martinez	.05	.04	.02
83	Phil Garner	.05	.04	.02
84	Darrell Porter	.05	.04	.02
85	Tony Perez	.10	.08	.04
86	Tom Waddell	.05	.04	.02
87	Tim Hulett	.05	.04	.02
88	Barbaro Garbey	.05	.04	.02
89	Randy St. Claire	.05	.04	.02
90	Garry Templeton	.07	.05	.03
91	Tim Teufel	.05	.04	.02
92	Al Cowens	.05	.04	.02
93	Scot Thompson	.05	.04	.02
94	Tom Herr	.07	.05	.03
95	Ozzie Virgil	.05	.04	.02
96	Jose Cruz	.07	.05	.03
97	Gary Gaetti	.12	.09	.05
98	Roger Clemens	2.50	2.00	1.00
99	Vance Law	.07	.05	.03
100	Nolan Ryan	.25	.20	.10
101	Mike Smithson	.05	.04	.02
102	Rafael Santana	.05	.04	.02
103	Darrell Evans	.10	.08	.04
104	Rich Gossage	.12	.09	.05
105	Gary Ward	.07	.05	.03
106	Jim Gott	.05	.04	.02
107	Rafael Ramirez	.05	.04	.02
108	Ted Power	.05	.04	.02
109	Ron Guidry	.15	.11	.06
110	Scott McGregor	.07	.05	.03
111	Mike Scioscia	.07	.05	.03
112	Glenn Hubbard	.05	.04	.02
113	U.L. Washington	.05	.04	.02
114	Al Oliver	.10	.08	.04
115	Jay Howell	.07	.05	.03
116	Brook Jacoby	.10	.08	.04
117	Willie McGee	.12	.09	.05
118	Jerry Royster	.05	.04	.02
119	Barry Bonnell	.05	.04	.02
120	Steve Carlton	.25	.20	.10
121	Alfredo Griffin	.07	.05	.03
122	David Green	.05	.04	.02
123	Greg Walker	.07	.05	.03
124	Frank Tanana	.07	.05	.03
125	Dave Lopes	.07	.05	.03
126	Mike Krukow	.07	.05	.03
127	Jack Howell	.20	.15	.08
128	Greg Harris	.05	.04	.02
129	Herm Winningham	.10	.08	.04
130	Alan Trammell	.25	.20	.10
131	Checklist 1-132	.05	.04	.02
132	Razor Shines	.05	.04	.02
133	Bruce Sutter	.10	.08	.04
134	Carney Lansford	.07	.05	.03
135	Joe Niekro	.07	.05	.03
136	Ernie Whitt	.07	.05	.03
137	Charlie Moore	.05	.04	.02
138	Mel Hall	.07	.05	.03

		MT	NR MT	EX
139	Roger McDowell	.30	.25	.12
140	John Candelaria	.07	.05	.03
141	Bob Rodgers	.05	.04	.02
142	Manny Trillo	.05	.04	.02
143	Dave Palmer	.05	.04	.02
144	Robin Yount	.25	.20	.10
145	Pedro Guerrero	.15	.11	.06
146	Von Hayes	.07	.05	.03
147	Lance Parrish	.15	.11	.06
148	Mike Heath	.05	.04	.02
149	Brett Butler	.07	.05	.03
150	Joaquin Andujar	.07	.05	.03
151	Graig Nettles	.10	.08	.04
152	Pete Vuckovich	.05	.04	.02
153	Jason Thompson	.05	.04	.02
154	Bert Roberge	.05	.04	.02
155	Bob Grich	.07	.05	.03
156	Roy Smalley	.05	.04	.02
157	Ron Hassey	.05	.04	.02
158	Bob Stanley	.05	.04	.02
159	Orel Hershiser	.70	.50	.30
160	Chet Lemon	.07	.05	.03
161	Terry Puhl	.05	.04	.02
162	Dave LaPoint	.07	.05	.03
163	Onix Concepcion	.05	.04	.02
164	Steve Balboni	.05	.04	.02
165	Mike Davis	.07	.05	.03
166	Dickie Thon	.05	.04	.02
167	Zane Smith	.07	.05	.03
168	Jeff Burroughs	.05	.04	.02
169	Alex Trevino	.05	.04	.02
170	Gary Carter	.25	.20	.10
171	Tito Landrum	.05	.04	.02
172	Sammy Stewart	.05	.04	.02
173	Wayne Gross	.05	.04	.02
174	Britt Burns	.05	.04	.02
175	Steve Sax	.12	.09	.05
176	Jody Davis	.07	.05	.03
177	Joel Youngblood	.05	.04	.02
178	Fernando Valenzuela	.20	.15	.08
179	Storm Davis	.05	.04	.02
180	Don Mattingly	2.50	2.00	1.00
181	Steve Bedrosian	.10	.08	.04
182	Jesse Orosco	.07	.05	.03
183	Gary Roenicke	.05	.04	.02
184	Don Baylor	.10	.08	.04
185	Rollie Fingers	.15	.11	.06
186	Ruppert Jones	.05	.04	.02
187	Scott Fletcher	.05	.04	.02
188	Bob Dernier	.05	.04	.02
189	Mike Mason	.05	.04	.02
190	George Hendrick	.05	.04	.02
191	Wally Backman	.07	.05	.03
192	Oddibe McDowell	.20	.15	.08
193	Bruce Hurst	.10	.08	.04
194	Ron Cey	.07	.05	.03
195	Dave Concepcion	.07	.05	.03
196	Doyle Alexander	.07	.05	.03
197	Dale Murray	.05	.04	.02
198	Mark Langston	.12	.09	.05
199	Dennis Eckersley	.10	.08	.04
200	Mike Schmidt	.35	.25	.14
201	Nick Esasky	.05	.04	.02
202	Ken Dayley	.05	.04	.02
203	Rick Cerone	.05	.04	.02
204	Larry McWilliams	.05	.04	.02
205	Brian Downing	.07	.05	.03
206	Danny Darwin	.05	.04	.02
207	Bill Caudill	.05	.04	.02
208	Dave Rozema	.05	.04	.02
209	Eric Show	.07	.05	.03
210	Brad Komminsk	.05	.04	.02
211	Chris Bando	.05	.04	.02
212	Chris Speier	.05	.04	.02
213	Jim Clancy	.07	.05	.03
214	Randy Bush	.05	.04	.02
215	Frank White	.07	.05	.03
216	Dan Petry	.07	.05	.03
217	Tim Wallach	.10	.08	.04
218	Mitch Webster	.20	.15	.08
219	Dennis Lamp	.05	.04	.02
220	Bob Horner	.10	.08	.04
221	Dave Henderson	.07	.05	.03
222	Dave Smith	.07	.05	.03
223	Willie Upshaw	.07	.05	.03
224	Cesar Cedeno	.07	.05	.03
225	Ron Darling	.12	.09	.05
226	Lee Lacy	.05	.04	.02
227	John Tudor	.07	.05	.03
228	Jim Presley	.12	.09	.05
229	Bill Gullickson	.05	.04	.02
230	Terry Kennedy	.07	.05	.03
231	Bob Knepper	.07	.05	.03
232	Rick Rhoden	.07	.05	.03
233	Richard Dotson	.07	.05	.03
234	Jesse Barfield	.12	.09	.05
235	Butch Wynegar	.05	.04	.02
236	Jerry Reuss	.07	.05	.03
237	Juan Samuel	.12	.09	.05
238	Larry Parrish	.07	.05	.03
239	Bill Buckner	.07	.05	.03
240	Pat Sheridan	.05	.04	.02
241	Tony Fernandez	.10	.08	.04
242	Rich Thompson	.05	.04	.02
243	Rickey Henderson	.35	.25	.14
244	Craig Lefferts	.05	.04	.02
245	Jim Sundberg	.05	.04	.02
246	Phil Niekro	.20	.15	.08
247	Terry Harper	.05	.04	.02
248	Spike Owen	.05	.04	.02
249	Bret Saberhagen	.25	.20	.10
250	Dwight Gooden	1.25	.90	.50
251	Rich Dauer	.05	.04	.02
252	Keith Hernandez	.25	.20	.10
253	Bo Diaz	.05	.04	.02
254	Ozzie Guillen	.25	.20	.10
255	Tony Armas	.07	.05	.03
256	Andre Dawson	.15	.11	.06
257	Doug DeCinces	.07	.05	.03
258	Tim Burke	.15	.11	.06
259	Dennis Boyd	.07	.05	.03
260	Tony Pena	.07	.05	.03
261	Sal Butera	.05	.04	.02
262	Wade Boggs	1.50	1.25	.60
263	Checklist 133-254	.05	.04	.02
264	Ron Oester	.05	.04	.02
265	Ron Davis	.05	.04	.02
266	Keith Moreland	.07	.05	.03
267	Paul Molitor	.12	.09	.05
268	John Denny	.05	.04	.02
269	Frank Viola	.12	.09	.05
270	Jack Morris	.15	.11	.06
271	Dave Collins	.05	.04	.02
272	Bert Blyleven	.10	.08	.04
273	Jerry Willard	.05	.04	.02
274	Matt Young	.05	.04	.02
275	Charlie Hough	.07	.05	.03
276	Dave Dravecky	.07	.05	.03
277	Garth Iorg	.05	.04	.02
278	Hal McRae	.07	.05	.03
279	Curt Wilkerson	.05	.04	.02
280	Tim Raines	.25	.20	.10
281	Bill Laskey	.05	.04	.02
282	Jerry Mumphrey	.05	.04	.02
283	Pat Clements	.05	.04	.02
284	Bob James	.05	.04	.02
285	Buddy Bell	.07	.05	.03
286	Tom Brookens	.05	.04	.02
287	Dave Parker	.12	.09	.05
288	Ron Kittle	.07	.05	.03
289	Johnnie LeMaster	.05	.04	.02
290	Carlton Fisk	.15	.11	.06
291	Jimmy Key	.10	.08	.04
292	Gary Matthews	.07	.05	.03
293	Marvell Wynne	.05	.04	.02
294	Danny Cox	.07	.05	.03
295	Kirk Gibson	.20	.15	.08
296	Mariano Duncan	.07	.05	.03
297	Ozzie Smith	.12	.09	.05
298	Craig Reynolds	.05	.04	.02
299	Bryn Smith	.05	.04	.02
300	George Brett	.35	.25	.14
301	Walt Terrell	.07	.05	.03
302	Greg Gross	.05	.04	.02
303	Claudell Washington	.07	.05	.03
304	Howard Johnson	.07	.05	.03
305	Phil Bradley	.10	.08	.04
306	R.J. Reynolds	.05	.04	.02
307	Bob Brenly	.05	.04	.02
308	Hubie Brooks	.07	.05	.03
309	Alvin Davis	.12	.09	.05
310	Donnie Hill	.05	.04	.02
311	Dick Schofield	.05	.04	.02
312	Tom Filer	.05	.04	.02
313	Mike Fitzgerald	.05	.04	.02
314	Marty Barrett	.07	.05	.03
315	Mookie Wilson	.07	.05	.03
316	Alan Knicely	.05	.04	.02
317	Ed Romero	.05	.04	.02
318	Glenn Wilson	.05	.04	.02
319	Bud Black	.05	.04	.02
320	Jim Rice	.25	.20	.10
321	Terry Pendleton	.07	.05	.03
322	Dave Kingman	.10	.08	.04
323	Gary Pettis	.05	.04	.02
324	Dan Schatzeder	.05	.04	.02
325	Juan Beniquez	.05	.04	.02
326	Kent Tekulve	.07	.05	.03
327	Mike Pagliarulo	.10	.08	.04
328	Pete O'Brien	.07	.05	.03
329	Kirby Puckett	.60	.45	.25
330	Rick Sutcliffe	.10	.08	.04
331	Alan Ashby	.05	.04	.02
332	Willie Randolph	.07	.05	.03
333	Tom Henke	.07	.05	.03
334	Ken Oberkfell	.05	.04	.02
335	Don Sutton	.20	.15	.08
336	Dan Gladden	.05	.04	.02
337	George Vuckovich	.05	.04	.02
338	Jorge Bell	.25	.20	.10
339	Jim Dwyer	.05	.04	.02
340	Cal Ripken	.35	.25	.14
341	Willie Hernandez	.05	.04	.02
342	Gary Redus	.05	.04	.02
343	Jerry Koosman	.07	.05	.03
344	Jim Wohlford	.05	.04	.02
345	Donnie Moore	.05	.04	.02
346	Floyd Youmans	.20	.15	.08
347	Gorman Thomas	.07	.05	.03
348	Cliff Johnson	.05	.04	.02
349	Ken Howell	.05	.04	.02
350	Jack Clark	.12	.09	.05
351	Gary Lucas	.05	.04	.02
352	Bob Clark	.05	.04	.02
353	Dave Stieb	.10	.08	.04
354	Tony Bernazard	.05	.04	.02
355	Lee Smith	.07	.05	.03
356	Mickey Hatcher	.05	.04	.02
357	Ed Vande Berg	.05	.04	.02
358	Rick Dempsey	.05	.04	.02
359	Bobby Cox	.05	.04	.02
360	Lloyd Moseby	.07	.05	.03
361	Shane Rawley	.07	.05	.03
362	Garry Maddox	.07	.05	.03
363	Buck Martinez	.05	.04	.02
364	Ed Nunez	.05	.04	.02
365	Luis Leal	.05	.04	.02
366	Dale Berra	.05	.04	.02
367	Mike Boddicker	.07	.05	.03
368	Greg Brock	.07	.05	.03
369	Al Holland	.05	.04	.02
370	Vince Coleman	1.00	.70	.40
371	Rod Carew	.25	.20	.10
372	Ben Oglivie	.05	.04	.02
373	Lee Mazzilli	.07	.05	.03
374	Terry Francona	.05	.04	.02
375	Rich Gedman	.07	.05	.03
376	Charlie Lea	.05	.04	.02
377	Joe Carter	.10	.08	.04
378	Bruce Bochte	.05	.04	.02
379	Bobby Meacham	.05	.04	.02
380	LaMarr Hoyt	.05	.04	.02
381	Jeff Leonard	.07	.05	.03
382	Ivan Calderon	.30	.25	.12
383	Chris Brown	.20	.15	.08
384	Steve Trout	.07	.05	.03
385	Cecil Cooper	.07	.05	.03
386	Cecil Fielder	.05	.04	.02
387	Tim Flannery	.05	.04	.02
388	Chris Codiroli	.05	.04	.02
389	Glenn Davis	.50	.40	.20
390	Tom Seaver	.25	.20	.10
391	Julio Franco	.10	.08	.04
392	Tom Brunansky	.10	.08	.04
393	Rob Wilfong	.05	.04	.02
394	Reggie Jackson	.30	.25	.12
395	Scott Garrelts	.05	.04	.02
396	Checklist 255-396	.05	.04	.02

1986 O-Pee-Chee Box Panels

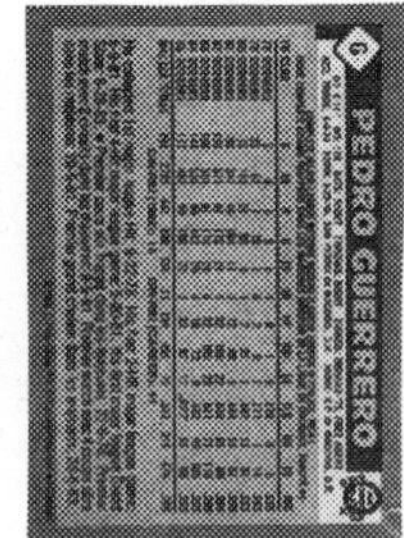

The Canadian card company licensed by Topps to distribute cards in Canada is O-Pee-Chee. In 1986, O-Pee-Chee issued wax pack boxes with baseball cards printed on the box bottoms. Four cards appear on four different boxes making a complete set of 16. The cards are identical to the 1986 Topps wax box issue with the exception of the O-Pee-Chee logo replacing Topps and the addition of French on the card backs. These bilingual cards were issued in Canada but are readily available in the USA. The cards are the standard 2-1/2" by 3-1/2" size, printed in full-color with black and red card backs. The panel cards are not numbered but instead are lettered from A through P.

		MT	NR MT	EX
Complete Set:		10.00	7.50	4.00
Complete Singles Set:		6.00	4.50	2.50
Common Panel:		3.00	2.25	1.25
Common Single Player:		.15	.11	.06
Panel		3.25	2.50	1.25
A	Jorge Bell	.30	.25	.12
B	Wade Boggs	.70	.50	.30
C	George Brett	.50	.40	.20
D	Vince Coleman	.50	.40	.20
Panel		2.75	2.00	1.00
E	Carlton Fisk	.20	.15	.08
F	Dwight Gooden	.70	.50	.30
G	Pedro Guerrero	.20	.15	.08
H	Ron Guidry	.20	.15	.08
Panel		3.50	2.75	1.50
I	Reggie Jackson	.40	.30	.15
J	Don Mattingly	.90	.70	.35
K	Oddibe McDowell	.15	.11	.06
L	Willie McGee	.20	.15	.08
Panel		3.25	2.50	1.25
M	Dale Murphy	.50	.40	.20
N	Pete Rose	.70	.50	.30
O	Bret Saberhagen	.20	.15	.08
P	Fernando Valenzuela	.25	.20	.10

1987 O-Pee-Chee

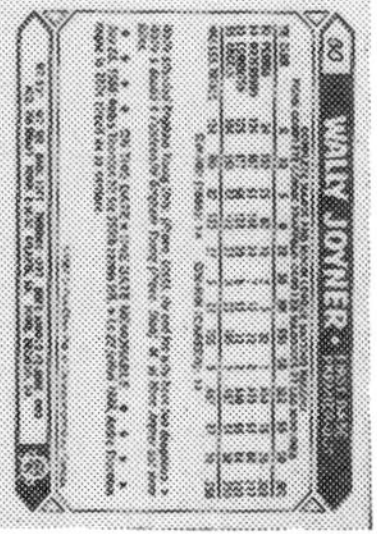

O-Pee-Chee of London, Ont., under license from the Topps Chewing Gum Co., continued a practice started in 1965 by issuing a baseball card set for 1987. The 396-card set is identical in design to the regular Topps set, save the name "O-Pee-Chee" replacing "Topps" in the lower right corner. Because the set is issued after its American counterpart, several cards appear with trade notations and corrected logos on the fronts. The cards, which are printed on white stock and are the standard 2-1/2" by 3-1/2", feature backs written in both English and French.

		MT	NR MT	EX
Complete Set:		16.00	12.00	6.50
Common Player:		.04	.03	.02
1	Ken Oberkfell	.04	.03	.02
2	Jack Howell	.07	.05	.03
3	Hubie Brooks	.07	.05	.03
4	Bob Grich	.07	.05	.03
5	Rick Leach	.04	.03	.02
6	Phil Niekro	.15	.11	.06
7	Rickey Henderson	.25	.20	.10
8	Terry Pendleton	.07	.05	.03
9	Jay Tibbs	.04	.03	.02
10	Cecil Cooper	.10	.08	.04
11	Mario Soto	.07	.05	.03
12	George Bell	.20	.15	.08
13	Nick Esasky	.04	.03	.02
14	Larry McWilliams	.04	.03	.02
15	Dan Quisenberry	.07	.05	.03
16	Ed Lynch	.04	.03	.02
17	Pete O'Brien	.07	.05	.03
18	Luis Aguayo	.04	.03	.02
19	Matt Young	.04	.03	.02
20	Gary Carter	.20	.15	.08
21	Tom Paciorek	.04	.03	.02
22	Doug DeCinces	.07	.05	.03
23	Lee Smith	.07	.05	.03
24	Jesse Barfield	.10	.08	.04
25	Bert Blyleven	.10	.08	.04
26	Greg Brock	.07	.05	.03
27	Dan Petry	.07	.05	.03
28	Rick Dempsey	.04	.03	.02
29	Jimmy Key	.10	.08	.04
30	Tim Raines	.20	.15	.08
31	Bruce Hurst	.07	.05	.03
32	Manny Trillo	.04	.03	.02
33	Andy Van Slyke	.10	.08	.04
34	Ed Vande Berg	.04	.03	.02
35	Sid Bream	.07	.05	.03
36	Dave Winfield	.20	.15	.08
37	Scott Garrelts	.04	.03	.02
38	Dennis Leonard	.04	.03	.02
39	Marty Barrett	.07	.05	.03
40	Dave Righetti	.12	.09	.05
41	Bo Diaz	.04	.03	.02
42	Gary Redus	.04	.03	.02
43	Tom Niedenfuer	.04	.03	.02
44	Greg Harris	.04	.03	.02
45	Jim Presley	.07	.05	.03
46	Danny Gladden	.07	.05	.03
47	Ron Smalley	.04	.03	.02
48	Wally Backman	.07	.05	.03
49	Tom Seaver	.20	.15	.08
50	Dave Smith	.07	.05	.03
51	Mel Hall	.07	.05	.03
52	Tim Flannery	.04	.03	.02
53	Julio Cruz	.04	.03	.02
54	Dick Schofield	.04	.03	.02
55	Tim Wallach	.10	.08	.04
56	Glenn Davis	.12	.09	.05
57	Darren Daulton	.04	.03	.02
58	Chico Walker	.04	.03	.02
59	Garth Iorg	.04	.03	.02
60	Tony Pena	.07	.05	.03
61	Ron Hassey	.04	.03	.02
62	Dave Dravecky	.07	.05	.03
63	Jorge Orta	.04	.03	.02
64	Al Nipper	.04	.03	.02
65	Tom Browning	.10	.08	.04
66	Marc Sullivan	.04	.03	.02
67	Todd Worrell	.15	.11	.06
68	Glenn Hubbard	.04	.03	.02
69	Carney Lansford	.07	.05	.03
70	Charlie Hough	.07	.05	.03
71	Lance McCullers	.07	.05	.03
72	Walt Terrell	.07	.05	.03
73	Bob Kearney	.04	.03	.02
74	Dan Pasqua	.07	.05	.03
75	Ron Darling	.10	.08	.04
76	Robin Yount	.20	.15	.08
77	Pat Tabler	.07	.05	.03
78	Tom Foley	.04	.03	.02
79	Juan Nieves	.10	.08	.04
80	Wally Joyner	1.50	1.25	.60
81	Wayne Krenchicki	.04	.03	.02
82	Kirby Puckett	.25	.20	.10
83	Bob Ojeda	.07	.05	.03
84	Mookie Wilson	.07	.05	.03
85	Kevin Bass	.07	.05	.03
86	Kent Tekulve	.07	.05	.03
87	Mark Salas	.04	.03	.02
88	Brian Downing	.07	.05	.03
89	Ozzie Guillen	.07	.05	.03
90	Dave Stieb	.10	.08	.04
91	Rance Mulliniks	.04	.03	.02
92	Mike Witt	.07	.05	.03
93	Charlie Moore	.04	.03	.02
94	Jose Uribe	.04	.03	.02
95	Oddibe McDowell	.07	.05	.03
96	Ray Soff	.04	.03	.02
97	Glenn Wilson	.04	.03	.02
98	Brook Jacoby	.07	.05	.03
99	Darryl Motley	.04	.03	.02
100	Steve Garvey	.20	.15	.08
101	Frank White	.07	.05	.03
102	Mike Moore	.04	.03	.02
103	Rick Aguilera	.07	.05	.03
104	Buddy Bell	.07	.05	.03
105	Floyd Youmans	.07	.05	.03
106	Lou Whitaker	.15	.11	.06
107	Ozzie Smith	.12	.09	.05
108	Jim Gantner	.04	.03	.02
109	R.J. Reynolds	.04	.03	.02
110	Jonn Tudor	.07	.05	.03
111	Alfredo Griffin	.07	.05	.03
112	Mike Flanagan	.07	.05	.03
113	Neil Allen	.04	.03	.02
114	Ken Griffey	.07	.05	.03
115	Donnie Moore	.04	.03	.02
116	Bob Horner	.10	.08	.04
117	Ron Shepherd	.04	.03	.02
118	Cliff Johnson	.04	.03	.02
119	Vince Coleman	.15	.11	.06
120	Eddie Murray	.25	.20	.10
121	Dwayne Murphy	.04	.03	.02

		MT	NR MT	EX
122	Jim Clancy	.07	.05	.03
123	Ken Landreaux	.04	.03	.02
124	Tom Nieto	.04	.03	.02
125	Bob Brenly	.04	.03	.02
126	George Brett	.30	.25	.12
127	Vance Law	.04	.03	.02
128	Checklist 1-132	.04	.03	.02
129	Bob Knepper	.07	.05	.03
130	Dwight Gooden	.50	.40	.20
131	Juan Bonilla	.04	.03	.02
132	Tim Burke	.04	.03	.02
133	Bob McClure	.04	.03	.02
134	Scott Bailes	.10	.08	.04
135	Mike Easler	.07	.05	.03
136	Ron Romanick	.04	.03	.02
137	Rich Gedman	.07	.05	.03
138	Bob Dernier	.04	.03	.02
139	John Denny	.04	.03	.02
140	Bret Saberhagen	.15	.11	.06
141	Herm Winningham	.04	.03	.02
142	Rick Sutcliffe	.10	.08	.04
143	Ryne Sandberg	.20	.15	.08
144	Mike Scioscia	.07	.05	.03
145	Charlie Kerfeld	.04	.03	.02
146	Jim Rice	.20	.15	.08
147	Steve Trout	.04	.03	.02
148	Jesse Orosco	.07	.05	.03
149	Mike Boddicker	.07	.05	.03
150	Wade Boggs	.80	.60	.30
151	Dane Iorg	.04	.03	.02
152	Rick Burleson	.07	.05	.03
153	Duane Ward	.04	.03	.02
154	Rick Reuschel	.07	.05	.03
155	Nolan Ryan	.20	.15	.08
156	Bill Caudill	.04	.03	.02
157	Danny Darwin	.04	.03	.02
158	Ed Romero	.04	.03	.02
159	Bill Almon	.04	.03	.02
160	Julio Franco	.10	.08	.04
161	Kent Hrbek	.15	.11	.06
162	Chill Davis	.07	.05	.03
163	Kevin Gross	.07	.05	.03
164	Carlton Fisk	.12	.09	.05
165	Jeff Reardon	.10	.08	.04
166	Bob Boone	.07	.05	.03
167	Rick Honeycutt	.04	.03	.02
168	Dan Schatzeder	.04	.03	.02
169	Jim Wohlford	.04	.03	.02
170	Phil Bradley	.10	.08	.04
171	Ken Schrom	.04	.03	.02
172	Ron Oester	.04	.03	.02
173	Juan Beniquez	.04	.03	.02
174	Tony Armas	.07	.05	.03
175	Bob Stanley	.04	.03	.02
176	Steve Buechele	.04	.03	.02
177	Keith Moreland	.07	.05	.03
178	Cecil Fielder	.04	.03	.02
179	Gary Gaetti	.12	.09	.05
180	Chris Brown	.07	.05	.03
181	Tom Herr	.07	.05	.03
182	Lee Lacy	.04	.03	.02
183	Ozzie Virgil	.04	.03	.02
184	Paul Molitor	.10	.08	.04
185	Roger McDowell	.07	.05	.03
186	Mike Marshall	.10	.08	.04
187	Ken Howell	.04	.03	.02
188	Rob Deer	.07	.05	.03
189	Joe Hesketh	.04	.03	.02
190	Jim Sundberg	.04	.03	.02
191	Kelly Gruber	.04	.03	.02
192	Cory Snyder	.40	.30	.15
193	Dave Concepcion	.07	.05	.03
194	Kirk McCaskill	.04	.03	.02
195	Mike Pagliarulo	.07	.05	.03
196	Rick Manning	.04	.03	.02
197	Brett Butler	.07	.05	.03
198	Tony Gwynn	.30	.25	.12
199	Mariano Duncan	.04	.03	.02
200	Pete Rose	.50	.40	.20
201	John Cangelosi	.07	.05	.03
202	Danny Cox	.07	.05	.03
203	Butch Wynegar	.04	.03	.02
204	Chris Chambliss	.07	.05	.03
205	Graig Nettles	.07	.05	.03
206	Chet Lemon	.07	.05	.03
207	Don Aase	.04	.03	.02
208	Mike Mason	.04	.03	.02
209	Alan Trammell	.20	.15	.08
210	Lloyd Moseby	.07	.05	.03
211	Richard Dotson	.07	.05	.03
212	Mike Fitzgerald	.04	.03	.02
213	Darrell Porter	.04	.03	.02
214	Checklist 133-264	.04	.03	.02
215	Mark Langston	.10	.08	.04
216	Steve Farr	.04	.03	.02
217	Dann Bilardello	.04	.03	.02
218	Gary Ward	.04	.03	.02
219	Cecilio Guante	.04	.03	.02
220	Joe Carter	.10	.08	.04
221	Ernie Whitt	.07	.05	.03
222	Denny Walling	.04	.03	.02
223	Charlie Leibrandt	.07	.05	.03
224	Wayne Tolleson	.04	.03	.02
225	Mike Smithson	.04	.03	.02
226	Zane Smith	.07	.05	.03
227	Terry Puhl	.04	.03	.02
228	Eric Davis	.80	.60	.30
229	Don Mattingly	1.50	1.25	.60
230	Don Baylor	.07	.05	.03
231	Frank Tanana	.07	.05	.03
232	Tom Brookens	.04	.03	.02
233	Steve Bedrosian	.10	.08	.04
234	Wallace Johnson	.04	.03	.02
235	Alvin Davis	.10	.08	.04
236	Tommy John	.12	.09	.05
237	Jim Morrison	.04	.03	.02
238	Ricky Horton	.07	.05	.03
239	Shane Rawley	.07	.05	.03
240	Steve Balboni	.04	.03	.02
241	Mike Krukow	.04	.03	.02
242	Rick Mahler	.04	.03	.02
243	Bill Doran	.07	.05	.03
244	Mark Clear	.04	.03	.02
245	Willie Upshaw	.07	.05	.03

		MT	NR MT	EX
246	Hal McRae	.07	.05	.03
247	Jose Canseco	2.75	2.00	1.00
248	George Hendrick	.04	.03	.02
249	Doyle Alexander	.07	.05	.03
250	Teddy Higuera	.10	.08	.04
251	Tom Hume	.04	.03	.02
252	Denny Martinez	.07	.05	.03
253	Eddie Milner	.04	.03	.02
254	Steve Sax	.12	.09	.05
255	Juan Samuel	.10	.08	.04
256	Dave Bergman	.04	.03	.02
257	Bob Forsch	.04	.03	.02
258	Steve Yeager	.04	.03	.02
259	Don Sutton	.12	.09	.05
260	Vida Blue	.07	.05	.03
261	Tom Brunansky	.10	.08	.04
262	Joe Sambito	.04	.03	.02
263	Mitch Webster	.07	.05	.03
264	Checklist 265-396	.04	.03	.02
265	Darrell Evans	.10	.08	.04
266	Dave Kingman	.12	.09	.05
267	Howard Johnson	.07	.05	.03
268	Greg Pryor	.04	.03	.02
269	Tippy Martinez	.04	.03	.02
270	Jody Davis	.07	.05	.03
271	Steve Carlton	.20	.15	.08
272	Andres Galarraga	.60	.45	.25
273	Fernando Valenzuela	.20	.15	.08
274	Jeff Hearron	.04	.03	.02
275	Ray Knight	.07	.05	.03
276	Bill Madlock	.07	.05	.03
277	Tom Henke	.07	.05	.03
278	Gary Pettis	.04	.03	.02
279	Jimy Williams	.04	.03	.02
280	Jeffrey Leonard	.07	.05	.03
281	Bryn Smith	.07	.05	.03
282	John Cerutti	.10	.08	.04
283	Gary Roenicke	.04	.03	.02
284	Joaquin Andujar	.07	.05	.03
285	Dennis Boyd	.07	.05	.03
286	Tim Hulett	.04	.03	.02
287	Craig Lefferts	.04	.03	.02
288	Tito Landrum	.04	.03	.02
289	Manny Lee	.04	.03	.02
290	Leon Durham	.07	.05	.03
291	Johnny Ray	.07	.05	.03
292	Franklin Stubbs	.07	.05	.03
293	Bob Rodgers	.04	.03	.02
294	Terry Francona	.04	.03	.02
295	Len Dykstra	.10	.08	.04
296	Tom Candiotti	.04	.03	.02
297	Frank DiPino	.04	.03	.02
298	Craig Reynolds	.04	.03	.02
299	Jerry Hairston	.04	.03	.02
300	Reggie Jackson	.25	.20	.10
301	Luis Aquino	.07	.05	.03
302	Greg Walker	.07	.05	.03
303	Terry Kennedy	.07	.05	.03
304	Phil Garner	.04	.03	.02
305	John Franco	.10	.08	.04
306	Bill Buckner	.07	.05	.03
307	Kevin Mitchell	.25	.20	.10
308	Don Slaught	.04	.03	.02
309	Harold Baines	.10	.08	.04
310	Frank Viola	.12	.09	.05
311	Dave Lopes	.07	.05	.03
312	Cal Ripken	.25	.20	.10
313	John Candelaria	.07	.05	.03
314	Bob Sebra	.04	.03	.02
315	Bud Black	.04	.03	.02
316	Brian Fisher	.07	.05	.03
317	Clint Hurdle	.04	.03	.02
318	Ernie Riles	.07	.05	.03
319	Dave LaPoint	.07	.05	.03
320	Barry Bonds	.60	.45	.25
321	Tim Stoddard	.04	.03	.02
322	Ron Cey	.07	.05	.03
323	Al Newman	.04	.03	.02
324	Jerry Royster	.04	.03	.02
325	Garry Templeton	.07	.05	.03
326	Mark Gubicza	.10	.08	.04
327	Andre Thornton	.07	.05	.03
328	Bob Welch	.07	.05	.03
329	Tony Fernandez	.10	.08	.04
330	Mike Scott	.10	.08	.04
331	Jack Clark	.12	.09	.05
332	Danny Tartabull	.60	.45	.25
333	Greg Minton	.04	.03	.02
334	Ed Correa	.07	.05	.03
335	Candy Maldonado	.07	.05	.03
336	Dennis Lamp	.04	.03	.02
337	Sid Fernandez	.07	.05	.03
338	Greg Gross	.04	.03	.02
339	Willie Hernandez	.04	.03	.02
340	Roger Clemens	.60	.45	.25
341	Mickey Hatcher	.04	.03	.02
342	Bob James	.04	.03	.02
343	Jose Cruz	.07	.05	.03
344	Bruce Sutter	.10	.08	.04
345	Andre Dawson	.15	.11	.06
346	Shawon Dunston	.07	.05	.03
347	Scott McGregor	.04	.03	.02
348	Carmelo Martinez	.04	.03	.02
349	Storm Davis	.07	.05	.03
350	Keith Hernandez	.20	.15	.08
351	Andy McGaffigan	.04	.03	.02
352	Dave Parker	.12	.09	.05
353	Ernie Camacho	.04	.03	.02
354	Eric Show	.07	.05	.03
355	Don Carman	.15	.11	.06
356	Floyd Bannister	.07	.05	.03
357	Willie McGee	.10	.08	.04
358	Atlee Hammaker	.04	.03	.02
359	Dale Murphy	.35	.25	.14
360	Pedro Guerrero	.12	.09	.05
361	Will Clark	.90	.70	.35
362	Bill Campbell	.04	.03	.02
363	Alejandro Pena	.07	.05	.03
364	Dennis Rasmussen	.07	.05	.03
365	Rick Rhoden	.07	.05	.03
366	Randy St. Claire	.04	.03	.02
367	Willie Wilson	.10	.08	.04
368	Dwight Evans	.10	.08	.04
369	Moose Haas	.04	.03	.02

		MT	NR MT	EX
370	Fred Lynn	.10	.08	.04
371	Mark Eichhorn	.07	.05	.03
372	Dave Schmidt	.04	.03	.02
373	Jerry Reuss	.07	.05	.03
374	Lance Parrish	.15	.11	.06
375	Ron Guidry	.12	.09	.05
376	Jack Morris	.15	.11	.06
377	Willie Randolph	.07	.05	.03
378	Joel Youngblood	.04	.03	.02
379	Darryl Strawberry	.40	.30	.15
380	Rich Gossage	.10	.08	.04
381	Dennis Eckersley	.10	.08	.04
382	Gary Lucas	.04	.03	.02
383	Ron Davis	.04	.03	.02
384	Pete Incaviglia	.35	.25	.14
385	Orel Hershiser	.20	.15	.08
386	Kirk Gibson	.20	.15	.08
387	Don Robinson	.04	.03	.02
388	Darnell Coles	.07	.05	.03
389	Von Hayes	.07	.05	.03
390	Gary Matthews	.07	.05	.03
391	Jay Howell	.07	.05	.03
392	Tim Laudner	.04	.03	.02
393	Rod Scurry	.04	.03	.02
394	Tony Bernazard	.04	.03	.02
395	Damasco Garcia	.04	.03	.02
396	Mike Schmidt	.35	.25	.14

1987 O-Pee-Chee Box Panels

For the second consecutive year, O-Pee-Chee placed baseball cards on the bottoms of their retail wax pack boxes. The 2-1/8" by 3" cards were issued in panels of four and are slightly smaller in size than the regular issue O-Pee-Chee cards. The card fronts are identical in design to the regular issue, while the backs contain a newspaper-type commentary written in both French and English. Collectors may note the 1987 Topps wax box cards were issued on side panels as opposed to box bottoms. Because the O-Pee-Chee wax boxes are smaller in size than their U.S. counterparts, printing cards on side panels could not be accomplished.

		MT	NR MT	EX
Complete Panel Set:		6.00	4.50	2.50
Complete Singles Set:		2.50	2.00	1.00
Common Single Player:		.15	.11	.06
Panel		1.75	1.25	.70
A	Don Baylor	.15	.11	.06
B	Steve Carlton	.30	.25	.12
C	Ron Cey	.15	.11	.06
D	Cecil Cooper	.15	.11	.06
Panel		2.75	2.00	1.00
E	Rickey Henderson	.40	.30	.15
F	Jim Rice	.30	.25	.12
G	Don Sutton	.20	.15	.08
H	Dave Winfield	.35	.25	.14

1988 O-Pee-Chee

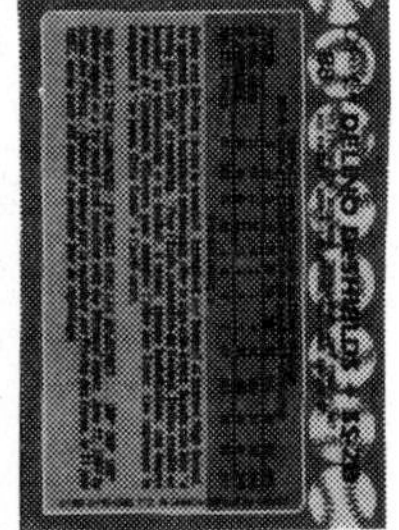

Under license from Topps, O-Pee-Chee uses the same player photos as the Toppps issue, but the Canadian edition includes only 396 cards (one-half the number in the Topps set). The OPC set was printed after the U.S. press run, so several cards carry overprints on the fronts, indicating changes in players' teams. New teams are named in the overprints; card headers bear the former team names. This set follows the same basic design as the 1988 Topps cards. The team name appears in large bright letters above the player photo and the player name is printed on a colorful diagonal strip across the lower right corner. The O-Pee-Chee logo appears in place of the Topps logo, both front and back. A four-card subset consists of #1 and #2 draft choices for the Expos (Nathan Minchey and Delino DeShields) and Blue Jays (Alex Sanchez and Derek Bell). Top draft subset cards are distinguished by a yellow or orange triangle in the lower right corner bearing the player's name above the words "Choisi au repecharge." Card backs are bilingual (English-French) and printed in black on orange. This series was marketed primarily in Canada in four separate display boxes, with four cards printed one each box bottom. Individual card packs contain seven cards and one stick of gum.

		MT	NR MT	EX
Complete Set:		20.00	15.00	8.00
Common Player:		.03	.02	.01
1	Chris James	.05	.04	.02
2	Steve Buechele	.03	.02	.01
3	Mike Henneman	.12	.09	.05
4	Eddie Murray	.20	.15	.08
5	Bret Saberhagen	.12	.09	.05
6	Nathan Minchey	.20	.15	.08
7	Harold Reynolds	.05	.04	.02
8	Bo Jackson	.20	.15	.08
9	Mike Easler	.05	.04	.02
10	Ryne Sandberg	.15	.11	.06
11	Mike Young	.05	.04	.02
12	Tony Phillips	.03	.02	.01
13	Andres Thomas	.05	.04	.02
14	Tim Burke	.03	.02	.01
15	Chili Davis	.05	.04	.02
16	Jim Lindeman	.05	.04	.02
17	Ron Oester	.03	.02	.01
18	Craig Reynolds	.03	.02	.01
19	Juan Samuel	.09	.07	.04
20	Kevin Gross	.05	.04	.02
21	Cecil Fielder	.03	.02	.01
22	Greg Swindell	.09	.07	.04
23	Jose DeLeon	.03	.02	.01
24	Jim Deshaies	.05	.04	.02
25	Andres Galarraga	.10	.08	.04
26	Mitch Williams	.05	.04	.02
27	R.J. Reynolds	.03	.02	.01
28	Jose Nunez	.12	.09	.05
29	Angel Salazar	.03	.02	.01
30	Sid Fernandez	.07	.05	.03
31	Keith Moreland	.05	.04	.02
32	John Kruk	.09	.07	.04
33	Rob Deer	.05	.04	.02
34	Ricky Horton	.05	.04	.02
35	Harold Baines	.09	.07	.04
36	Jamie Moyer	.03	.02	.01
37	Kevin McReynolds	.07	.05	.03
38	Ozzie Smith	.09	.07	.04
39	Ron Darling	.09	.07	.04
40	Orel Hershiser	.15	.11	.06
41	Bob Melvin	.03	.02	.01
42	Alfredo Griffin	.05	.04	.02
43	Dick Schofield	.03	.02	.01
44	Terry Steinbach	.09	.07	.04
45	Kent Hrbek	.12	.09	.05
46	Darnell Coles	.05	.04	.02
47	Jimmy Key	.05	.04	.02
48	Alan Ashby	.03	.02	.01
49	Julio Franco	.07	.05	.03
50	Hubie Brooks	.05	.04	.02
51	Chris Bando	.03	.02	.01
52	Fernando Valenzuela	.12	.09	.05
53	Kal Daniels	.12	.09	.05
54	Jim Clancy	.05	.04	.02
55	Phil Bradley	.07	.05	.03
56	Andy McGaffigan	.03	.02	.01
57	Mike LaVaillere	.05	.04	.02
58	Dave Magadan	.07	.05	.03
59	Danny Cox	.05	.04	.02
60	Rickey Henderson	.20	.15	.08
61	Jim Rice	.15	.11	.06
62	Calvin Schiraldi	.03	.02	.01
63	Jerry Mumphrey	.03	.02	.01
64	Ken Caminiti	.09	.07	.04
65	Leon Durham	.05	.04	.02
66	Shane Rawley	.05	.04	.02
67	Ken Oberkfell	.03	.02	.01
68	Keith Hernandez	.12	.09	.05
69	Bob Brenly	.03	.02	.01
70	Roger Clemens	.40	.30	.15
71	Gary Pettis	.03	.02	.01
72	Dennis Eckersley	.07	.05	.03
73	Dave Smith	.05	.04	.02
74	Cal Ripken	.20	.15	.08
75	Joe Carter	.09	.07	.04
76	Denny Martinez	.05	.04	.02
77	Juan Beniquez	.03	.02	.01
78	Tim Laudner	.03	.02	.01
79	Ernie Whitt	.05	.04	.02
80	Mark Langston	.09	.07	.04
81	Dale Sveum	.05	.04	.02
82	Dion James	.03	.02	.01
83	Dave Valle	.03	.02	.01
84	Bill Wegman	.03	.02	.01
85	Howard Johnson	.07	.05	.03
86	Benito Santiago	.35	.25	.14
87	Casey Candaele	.03	.02	.01
88	Delino DeShields	7.00	5.25	2.75
89	Dave Winfield	.15	.11	.06
90	Dale Murphy	.25	.20	.10
91	Jay Howell	.05	.04	.02
92	Ken Williams	.12	.09	.05
93	Bob Sebra	.03	.02	.01
94	Tim Wallach	.07	.05	.03
95	Lance Parrish	.09	.07	.04
96	Todd Benzinger	.20	.15	.08
97	Scott Garrelts	.03	.02	.01
98	Jose Guzman	.05	.04	.02
99	Jeff Reardon	.07	.05	.03

		MT	NR MT	EX
100	Jack Clark	.09	.07	.04
101	Tracy Jones	.09	.07	.04
102	Barry Larkin	.09	.07	.04
103	Curt Young	.05	.04	.02
104	Juan Nieves	.05	.04	.02
105	Terry Pendleton	.05	.04	.02
106	Rod Ducey	.09	.07	.04
107	Scott Bailes	.05	.04	.02
108	Eric King	.05	.04	.02
109	Mike Pagliarulo	.07	.05	.03
110	Teddy Higuera	.07	.05	.03
111	Pedro Guerrero	.09	.07	.04
112	Chris Brown	.05	.04	.02
113	Kelly Gruber	.03	.02	.01
114	Jack Howell	.05	.04	.02
115	Johnny Ray	.05	.04	.02
116	Mark Eichhorn	.05	.04	.02
117	Tony Pena	.05	.04	.02
118	Bob Welch	.05	.04	.02
119	Mike Kingery	.03	.02	.01
120	Kirby Puckett	.20	.15	.08
121	Charlie Hough	.05	.04	.02
122	Tony Bernazard	.03	.02	.01
123	Tom Candiotti	.03	.02	.01
124	Ray Knight	.05	.04	.02
125	Bruce Hurst	.07	.05	.03
126	Steve Jeltz	.03	.02	.01
127	Ron Guidry	.09	.07	.04
128	Duane Ward	.03	.02	.01
129	Greg Minton	.03	.02	.01
130	Buddy Bell	.05	.04	.02
131	Denny Walling	.03	.02	.01
132	Donnie Hill	.03	.02	.01
133	Wayne Tolleson	.03	.02	.01
134	Bob Rodgers	.03	.02	.01
135	Todd Worrell	.07	.05	.03
136	Brian Dayett	.03	.02	.01
137	Chris Bosio	.03	.02	.01
138	Mitch Webster	.05	.04	.02
139	Jerry Browne	.03	.02	.01
140	Jesse Barfield	.09	.07	.04
141	Doug DeCinces	.05	.04	.02
142	Andy Van Slyke	.07	.05	.03
143	Doug Drabek	.05	.04	.02
144	Jeff Parrett	.12	.09	.05
145	Bill Madlock	.07	.05	.03
146	Larry Herndon	.03	.02	.01
147	Bill Buckner	.07	.05	.03
148	Carmelo Martinez	.05	.04	.02
149	Ken Howell	.03	.02	.01
150	Eric Davis	.40	.30	.15
151	Randy Ready	.03	.02	.01
152	Jeffrey Leonard	.05	.04	.02
153	Dave Steib	.07	.05	.03
154	Jeff Stone	.03	.02	.01
155	Dave Righetti	.09	.07	.04
156	Gary Matthews	.05	.04	.02
157	Gary Carter	.15	.11	.06
158	Bob Boone	.05	.04	.02
159	Glenn Davis	.09	.07	.04
160	Willie McGee	.07	.05	.03
161	Bryn Smith	.03	.02	.01
162	Mark McLemore	.03	.02	.01
163	Dale Mohorcic	.03	.02	.01
164	Mike Flanagan	.05	.04	.02
165	Robin Yount	.15	.11	.06
166	Bill Doran	.05	.04	.02
167	Rance Mulliniks	.03	.02	.01
168	Wally Joyner	.40	.30	.15
169	Cory Snyder	.12	.09	.05
170	Rich Gossage	.07	.05	.03
171	Rick Mahler	.03	.02	.01
172	Henry Cotto	.03	.02	.01
173	George Bell	.15	.11	.06
174	B.J. Surhoff	.09	.07	.04
175	Kevin Bass	.05	.04	.02
176	Jeff Reed	.03	.02	.01
177	Frank Tanana	.05	.04	.02
178	Darryl Strawberry	.30	.25	.12
179	Lou Whitaker	.09	.07	.04
180	Terry Kennedy	.05	.04	.02
181	Mariano Duncan	.03	.02	.01
182	Ken Phelps	.03	.02	.01
183	Bob Dernier	.03	.02	.01
184	Ivan Calderon	.05	.04	.02
185	Rick Rhoden	.05	.04	.02
186	Rafael Palmeiro	.40	.30	.15
187	Kelly Downs	.07	.05	.03
188	Spike Owen	.03	.02	.01
189	Bobby Bonilla	.09	.07	.04
190	Candy Maldonado	.05	.04	.02
191	John Cerutti	.05	.04	.02
192	Devon White	.12	.09	.05
193	Brian Fisher	.05	.04	.02
194	Alex Sanchez	.20	.15	.08
195	Dan Quisenberry	.05	.04	.02
196	Dave Engle	.03	.02	.01
197	Lance McCullers	.05	.04	.02
198	Franklin Stubbs	.03	.02	.01
199	Scott Bradley	.03	.02	.01
200	Wade Boggs	.70	.50	.30
201	Kirk Gibson	.12	.09	.05
202	Brett Butler	.05	.04	.02
203	Dave Anderson	.03	.02	.01
204	Donnie Moore	.03	.02	.01
205	Nelson Liriano	.09	.07	.04
206	Danny Gladden	.03	.02	.01
207	Dan Pasqua	.05	.04	.02
208	Robbie Thompson	.05	.04	.02
209	Richard Dotson	.05	.04	.02
210	Willie Randolph	.05	.04	.02
211	Danny Tartabull	.12	.09	.05
212	Greg Brock	.05	.04	.02
213	Albert Hall	.03	.02	.01
214	Dave Schmidt	.03	.02	.01
215	Von Hayes	.05	.04	.02
216	Herm Winningham	.03	.02	.01
217	Mike Davis	.03	.02	.01
218	Charlie Leibrandt	.03	.02	.01
219	Mike Stanley	.03	.02	.01
220	Tom Henke	.05	.04	.02
221	Dwight Evans	.07	.05	.03
222	Willie Wilson	.07	.05	.03
223	Stan Jefferson	.03	.02	.01

		MT	NR MT	EX
224	Mike Dunne	.09	.07	.04
225	Mike Scioscia	.05	.04	.02
226	Larry Parrish	.05	.04	.02
227	Mike Scott	.09	.07	.04
228	Wallace Johnson	.03	.02	.01
229	Jeff Musselman	.05	.04	.02
230	Pat Tabler	.05	.04	.02
231	Paul Molitor	.09	.07	.04
232	Bob James	.03	.02	.01
233	Joe Niekro	.05	.04	.02
234	Oddibe McDowell	.05	.04	.02
235	Gary Ward	.03	.02	.01
236	Ted Power	.03	.02	.01
237	Pascual Perez	.05	.04	.02
238	Luis Polonia	.09	.07	.04
239	Mike Diaz	.05	.04	.02
240	Lee Smith	.05	.04	.02
241	Willie Upshaw	.05	.04	.02
242	Tim Neidenfuer	.03	.02	.01
243	Tim Raines	.20	.15	.08
244	Jeff Robinson	.12	.09	.05
245	Rich Gedman	.05	.04	.02
246	Scott Bankhead	.03	.02	.01
247	Andre Dawson	.12	.09	.05
248	Brook Jacoby	.07	.05	.03
249	Mike Marshall	.07	.05	.03
250	Nolan Ryan	.15	.11	.06
251	Tom Foley	.03	.02	.01
252	Bob Brower	.03	.02	.01
254	Scott McGregor	.03	.02	.01
255	Ken Griffey	.05	.04	.02
256	Ken Schrom	.03	.02	.01
257	Gary Gaetti	.09	.07	.04
258	Ed Nunez	.03	.02	.01
259	Frank Viola	.09	.07	.04
260	Vince Coleman	.09	.07	.04
261	Reid Nichols	.03	.02	.01
262	Tim Flannery	.03	.02	.01
263	Glenn Braggs	.05	.04	.02
264	Garry Templeton	.05	.04	.02
265	Bo Diaz	.03	.02	.01
266	Matt Nokes	.30	.25	.12
267	Barry Bonds	.09	.07	.04
268	Bruce Ruffin	.03	.02	.01
269	Ellis Burks	.80	.60	.30
270	Mike Witt	.05	.04	.02
271	Ken Gerhart	.05	.04	.02
272	Lloyd Moseby	.05	.04	.02
273	Garth Iorg	.03	.02	.01
274	Mike Greenwell	.80	.60	.30
275	Kevin Seitzer	.60	.45	.25
276	Luis Salazar	.03	.02	.01
277	Shawon Dunston	.05	.04	.02
278	Rick Reuschel	.05	.04	.02
279	Randy St. Claire	.03	.02	.01
280	Pete Incaviglia	.07	.05	.03
281	Mike Boddicker	.05	.04	.02
282	Jay Tibbs	.03	.02	.01
283	Shane Mack	.09	.07	.04
284	Walt Terrell	.03	.02	.01
285	Jim Presley	.07	.05	.03
286	Greg Walker	.05	.04	.02
287	Dwight Gooden	.30	.25	.12
288	Jim Morrison	.03	.02	.01
289	Gene Garber	.03	.02	.01
290	Tony Fernandez	.07	.05	.03
291	Ozzie Virgil	.03	.02	.01
292	Carney Lansford	.05	.04	.02
293	Jim Acker	.03	.02	.01
294	Tommy Hinzo	.05	.04	.02
295	Bert Blyleven	.09	.07	.04
296	Ozzie Guillen	.05	.04	.02
297	Zane Smith	.05	.04	.02
298	Milt Thompson	.03	.02	.01
299	Len Dykstra	.05	.04	.02
300	Don Mattingly	1.25	.90	.50
301	Bud Black	.03	.02	.01
302	Jose Uribe	.03	.02	.01
303	Manny Lee	.03	.02	.01
304	Sid Bream	.05	.04	.02
305	Steve Sax	.09	.07	.04
306	Billy Hatcher	.05	.04	.02
307	John Shelby	.05	.04	.02
308	Lee Mazzilli	.05	.04	.02
309	Bill Long	.09	.07	.04
310	Tom Herr	.05	.04	.02
311	Derek Bell	.20	.15	.08
312	George Brett	.25	.20	.10
313	Bob McClure	.03	.02	.01
314	Jimy Williams	.03	.02	.01
315	Dave Parker	.09	.07	.04
316	Doyle Alexander	.05	.04	.02
317	Dan Plesac	.07	.05	.03
318	Mel Hall	.05	.04	.02
319	Ruben Sierra	.12	.09	.05
320	Alan Trammell	.12	.09	.05
321	Mike Schmidt	.25	.20	.10
322	Wally Ritchie	.05	.04	.02
324	Danny Jackson	.07	.05	.03
325	Glenn Hubbard	.03	.02	.01
326	Frank White	.05	.04	.02
327	Larry Sheets	.05	.04	.02
328	John Cangelosi	.03	.02	.01
329	Bill Gullickson	.03	.02	.01
330	Eddie Whitson	.03	.02	.01
331	Brian Downing	.05	.04	.02
332	Gary Redus	.03	.02	.01
333	Wally Backman	.03	.02	.01
334	Dwayne Murphy	.03	.02	.01
335	Claudell Washington	.05	.04	.02
336	Dave Concepcion	.05	.04	.02
337	Jim Gantner	.03	.02	.01
338	Marty Barrett	.05	.04	.02
339	Mickey Hatcher	.03	.02	.01
340	Jack Morris	.12	.09	.05
341	John Franco	.07	.05	.03
342	Ron Robinson	.03	.02	.01
343	Greg Gagne	.03	.02	.01
344	Steve Bedrosian	.07	.05	.03
345	Scott Fletcher	.03	.02	.01
346	Vance Law	.05	.04	.02
347	Joe Johnson	.03	.02	.01
348	Jim Eisenreich	.03	.02	.01
349	Alvin Davis	.09	.07	.04
350	Will Clark	.35	.25	.14
351	Mike Aldrete	.05	.04	.02
352	Billy Ripken	.12	.09	.05
353	Dave Stewart	.05	.04	.02
354	Neal Heaton	.03	.02	.01
355	Roger McDowell	.05	.04	.02
356	John Tudor	.05	.04	.02
357	Floyd Bannister	.05	.04	.02
358	Rey Quinones	.03	.02	.01
359	Glenn Wilson	.03	.02	.01
360	Tony Gwynn	.20	.15	.08
361	Greg Maddux	.50	.40	.20
362	Juan Castillo	.03	.02	.01
363	Willie Fraser	.03	.02	.01
364	Nick Esasky	.03	.02	.01
365	Floyd Youmans	.03	.02	.01
366	Chet Lemon	.05	.04	.02
367	Matt Young	.03	.02	.01
368	Gerald Young	.20	.15	.08
369	Bob Stanley	.03	.02	.01
370	Jose Canseco	.90	.70	.35
371	Joe Hesketh	.03	.02	.01
372	Rick Sutcliffe	.07	.05	.03
375	Tom Brunansky	.07	.05	.03
376	Jody Davis	.05	.04	.02
377	Sam Horn	.15	.11	.06
378	Mark Gubicza	.07	.05	.03
379	Rafael Ramirez	.03	.02	.01
380	Joe Magrane	.15	.11	.06
381	Pete O'Brien	.05	.04	.02
382	Lee Guetterman	.03	.02	.01
383	Eric Bell	.03	.02	.01
384	Gene Larkin	.12	.09	.05
385	Carlton Fisk	.09	.07	.04
386	Mike Fitzgerald	.03	.02	.01
387	Kevin Mitchell	.07	.05	.03
388	Jim Winn	.03	.02	.01
389	Mike Smithson	.03	.02	.01
390	Darrell Evans	.07	.05	.03
391	Terry Leach	.03	.02	.01
392	Charlie Kerfeld	.03	.02	.01
393	Mike Krukow	.03	.02	.01
394	Mark McGwire	.80	.60	.30
395	Fred McGriff	.25	.20	.10
396	DeWayne Buice	.05	.04	.02

A player's name in italic type indicates a rookie card.

1988 O-Pee-Chee Box Panels

A Topps licensee, O-Pee-Chee of Canada issued this 16-card set on retail display box bottoms. Cards feature popular current players and are identified by alphabet (A-P) rather than numbers. Player photos are the same ones used on the 1988 Topps U.S. issue and cards follow the same design as Topps' regular issue set - team name in large, brightly colored letters at the top of the player photo, player name in a diagonal strip across the lower right corner of the card. The O-Pee-Chee logo replaces the Topps logo on both front and back. O-Pee-Chee horizontal orange and black card backs are bilingual (French/English) and include complete major and minor league career stats.

		MT	NR MT	EX
Complete Panel Set:		8.00	6.00	3.25
Complete Singles Set:		3.50	2.75	1.50
Common Single Player:		.08	.06	.03
Panel		1.00	.70	.40
A	Don Baylor	.15	.11	.06
B	Steve Bedrosian	.15	.11	.06
C	Juan Beniquez	.08	.06	.03
D	Bob Boone	.08	.06	.03
Panel		1.75	1.25	.70
E	Darrell Evans	.10	.08	.04
F	Tony Gwynn	.40	.30	.15
G	John Kruk	.20	.15	.08
H	Marvell Wynne	.08	.06	.03
Panel		2.50	2.00	1.00
I	Joe Carter	.15	.11	.06
J	Eric Davis	.40	.30	.15
K	Howard Johnson	.10	.08	.04
L	Darryl Strawberry	.40	.30	.15
Panel		2.50	2.00	1.00
M	Rickey Henderson	.40	.30	.15
N	Nolan Ryan	.30	.25	.12
O	Mike Schmidt	.40	.30	.15
P	Kent Tekulve	.08	.06	.03

1986 Oh Henry Indians

This 30-card set of Cleveland Indians players was distributed by the team at a special

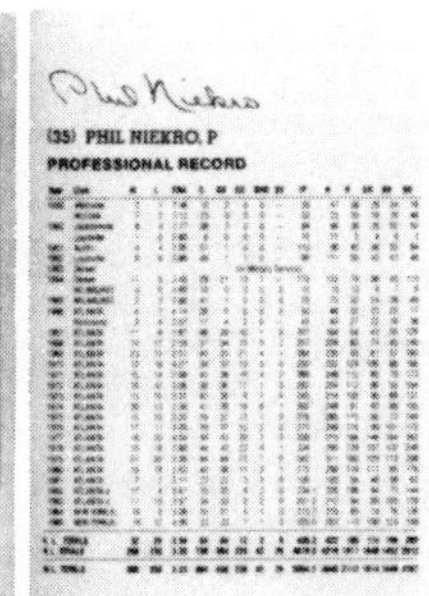

Photo/Baseball Card Day at Municipal Stadium. The cards were printed within a special three-panel, perforated fold-out piece which featured four action shots of the Indians on the cover. Unfolded, there are two panels containing the baseball cards and a third which contains a team photo. Cards measure 2-1/4" by 3-1/8" and are full-color studio portraits. Photos are framed in blue with a white border and list player name, number and position. Card fronts also include a picture of the sponsoring candy bar. Card backs include facsimile autograph and professional records. Each card is perforated for separation.

		MT	NR MT	EX
Complete Set:		11.00	8.25	4.50
Common Player:		.15	.11	.06
2	Brett Butler	.50	.40	.20
4	Tony Bernazard	.15	.11	.06
6	Andy Allanson	.25	.20	.10
7	Pat Corrales	.15	.11	.06
8	Carmen Castillo	.15	.11	.06
10	Pat Tabler	.30	.25	.12
13	Ernie Camacho	.15	.11	.06
14	Julio Franco	1.00	.70	.40
15	Dan Rohn	.15	.11	.06
18	Ken Schrom	.15	.11	.06
20	Otis Nixon	.20	.15	.08
22	Fran Mullins	.15	.11	.06
23	Chris Bando	.15	.11	.06
24	Ed Williams	.35	.25	.14
26	Brook Jacoby	.80	.60	.30
27	Mel Hall	.30	.25	.12
29	Andre Thornton	.30	.25	.12
30	Joe Carter	1.00	.70	.40
35	Phil Niekro	.80	.60	.30
36	Jamie Easterly	.15	.11	.06
37	Don Schulze	.15	.11	.06
42	Rich Yett	.20	.15	.08
43	Scott Bailes	.35	.25	.14
44	Neal Heaton	.15	.11	.06
46	Jim Kern	.15	.11	.06
48	Dickie Noles	.15	.11	.06
49	Tom Candiotti	.25	.20	.10
53	Reggie Ritter	.15	.11	.06
54	Tom Waddell	.15	.11	.06
---	Coaching Staff (Jack Aker, Bobby Bonds, Doc Edwards, Johnny Goryl)	.15	.11	.06

Regional interest may affect the value of a card.

1965 Old London Coins

These 1-1/2" diameter metal coins were included in Old London snack food packages. The 40 coins in this set feature two players from each of the major leagues' 20 teams, with the exception of St. Louis (3) and the New York Mets (1). Coin fronts have color photos and player names, while the silver-colored coin backs give brief biographies of each player. An Old London logo is also displayed on each coin back. Space Magic, Ltd. produced the coins. This is the same company which produced similar sets for Topps in 1964 and 1971.

		NR MT	EX	VG
Complete Set:		500.00	250.00	150.00
Common Player:		2.50	1.25	.70
(1)	Henry Aaron	50.00	25.00	15.00
(2)	Richie Allen	5.00	2.50	1.50
(3)	Bob Allison	3.00	1.50	.90
(4)	Ernie Banks	25.00	12.50	7.50
(5)	Ken Boyer	5.00	2.50	1.50
(6)	Jim Bunning	8.00	4.00	2.50

		MT	NR MT	EX
(7)	Orlando Cepeda	8.00	4.00	2.50
(8)	Dean Chance	2.50	1.25	.70
(9)	Rocky Colavito	5.00	2.50	1.50
(10)	Vic Davalillo	2.50	1.25	.70
(11)	Tommy Davis	5.00	2.50	1.50
(12)	Ron Fairly	3.00	1.50	.90
(13)	Dick Farrell	2.50	1.25	.70
(14)	Jim Fregosi	4.00	2.00	1.25
(15)	Bob Friend	4.00	2.00	1.25
(16)	Dick Groat	5.00	2.50	1.50
(17)	Ron Hunt	2.50	1.25	.70
(18)	Chuck Hinton	2.50	1.25	.70
(19)	Ken Johnson	2.50	1.25	.70
(20)	Al Kaline	25.00	12.50	7.50
(21)	Harmon Killebrew	20.00	10.00	6.00
(22)	Don Lock	2.50	1.25	.70
(23)	Mickey Mantle	100.00	50.00	30.00
(24)	Roger Maris	25.00	12.50	7.50
(25)	Willie Mays	50.00	25.00	15.00
(26)	Bill Mazeroski	6.50	3.25	2.00
(27)	Gary Peters	2.50	1.25	.70
(28)	Vada Pinson	5.00	2.50	1.50
(29)	John Powell	5.00	2.50	1.50
(30)	Dick Radatz	2.50	1.25	.70
(31)	Brooks Robinson	25.00	12.50	7.50
(32)	Frank Robinson	25.00	12.50	7.50
(33)	Tracy Stallard	2.50	1.25	.70
(34)	Joe Torre	6.50	3.25	2.00
(35)	Leon Wagner	2.50	1.25	.70
(36)	Pete Ward	2.50	1.25	.70
(37)	Dave Wickersham	2.50	1.25	.70
(38)	Billy Williams	18.00	9.00	5.50
(39)	John Wyatt	2.50	1.25	.70
(40)	Carl Yastrzemski	50.00	25.00	15.00

1910 Orange Borders

Known in the hobby as "Orange Borders", these 1-5/8" by 2-5/8" cards were issued in 1910 and were printed on candy boxes that displayed the words "American Sports and Candy and Jewelry." The end flaps indicate the producers as the "Geo. Davis Co., Inc." and the "P.R. Warren Co., Warrenville Lowell, Mass." According to the box, the complete set includes "144 leading ball-players," but to date only 25 different subjects are known. When found today, these black and white photos are usually surrounded by orange borders which, in reality, were part of the candy box.

		NR MT	EX	VG
Complete Set:		3500.	1750.	1050
Common Player:		60.00	30.00	18.00
(1)	Bill Bergen	60.00	30.00	18.00
(2)	Bill Carrigan	60.00	30.00	18.00
(3)	Hal Chase	70.00	35.00	21.00
(4)	Fred Clark (Clarke)	125.00	62.00	37.00
(5)	Ty Cobb	525.00	262.00	157.00
(6)	Sam Crawford	125.00	62.00	37.00
(7)	Lou Criger	60.00	30.00	18.00
(8)	Art Devlin	60.00	30.00	18.00
(9)	Mickey Doolan	60.00	30.00	18.00
(10)	George Gibson	60.00	30.00	18.00
(11)	Nap Lajoie	200.00	100.00	60.00
(12)	Frank LaPorte	60.00	30.00	18.00
(13)	Harry Lord	60.00	30.00	18.00
(14)	Christy Mathewson	200.00	100.00	60.00
(15)	John McGraw	150.00	75.00	45.00
(16)	Dots Miller	60.00	30.00	18.00
(17)	George Mullin	60.00	30.00	18.00
(18)	Eddie Plank	125.00	62.00	37.00
(19)	Tris Speaker	60.00	30.00	18.00
(20)	Jake Stahl	60.00	30.00	18.00
(21)	Honus Wagner (batting)	325.00	162.00	97.00
(22)	Honus Wagner (portrait)	325.00	162.00	97.00
(23)	Jack Warhop	60.00	30.00	18.00
(24)	American League Champions, 1909	60.00	30.00	18.00
(25)	National League Champions, 1909	60.00	30.00	18.00

The values quoted are intended to reflect the market price.

1910-12 P2 Sweet Caporal Pins

Expanding their premiums to include more than just trading cards, the American Tobacco Company issued a series of baseball pins between 1910 and 1912. The sepia-colored pins, each measuring 7/8" in diameter, were distributed under the Sweet Caporal brand name. The set includes 152 different major league players, but because of numerous "large letter" variations, collectors generally consider the set complete at 204 different pins. Fifty of the players are pictured on a second pin that usually displays the same photo but has the player's name and team designation printed in larger letters. Two players (Roger Bresnahan and Bobby Wallace) have three pins each. It is now generally accepted that there are 153 pins with "small letters" and another 51 "large letter" variations in a complete set. Research among advanced collectors has shown that 19 of the pins, including six of the "large letter" variations, are considered more difficult to find. The back of each pin has either a black or a red paper insert advertising Sweet Caporal Cigarettes. The red backings, issued only with the "large letter" pins are generally less common. The Sweet Caporal pins are closely related to the popular T205 Gold Border tobacco cards, also issued by the American Tobacco Company about the same time. All but nine of the players featured in the pin set were also pictured on T205 cards, and in nearly all cases the photos are identical. The Sweet Caporal pins are designated as P2 in the American Card Catalog. The complete set price includes all variations.

		NR MT	EX	VG
Complete Set:		5000.	2500.	1500.
Common Player:		10.00	5.00	3.00
(1)	Ed Abbaticchio	10.00	5.00	3.00
(2)	Red Ames	10.00	5.00	3.00
(3a)	Jimmy Archer (small letters)	10.00	5.00	3.00
(3b)	Jimmy Archer (large letters)	20.00	10.00	6.00
(4a)	Jimmy Austin (small letters)	10.00	5.00	3.00
(4b)	Jimmy Austin (large letters)	20.00	10.00	6.00
(5)	Home Run Baker	30.00	15.00	9.00
(6)	Neal Ball	10.00	5.00	3.00
(7)	Cy Barger	10.00	5.00	3.00
(8)	Jack Barry	10.00	5.00	3.00
(9)	Johnny Bates	10.00	5.00	3.00
(10)	Beals Becker	10.00	5.00	3.00
(11)	Fred Beebe	10.00	5.00	3.00
(12a)	George Bell (small letters)	10.00	5.00	3.00
(12b)	George Bell (large letters)	20.00	10.00	6.00
(13a)	Chief Bender (small letters)	30.00	15.00	9.00
(13b)	Chief Bender (large letters)	50.00	25.00	15.00
(14)	Bill Bergen	10.00	5.00	3.00
(15)	Bob Bescher	10.00	5.00	3.00
(16)	Joe Birmingham	10.00	5.00	3.00
(17)	Kitty Bransfield	35.00	17.50	10.50
(18a)	Roger Bresnahan (mouth closed, small letters)	30.00	15.00	9.00
(18b)	Roger Bresnahan (mouth closed, large letters)	90.00	45.00	27.00
(19)	Roger Bresnahan (mouth open)	30.00	15.00	9.00
(20)	Al Bridwell	10.00	5.00	3.00
(21a)	Mordecai Brown (small letters)	30.00	15.00	9.00
(21b)	Mordecai Brown (large letters)	50.00	25.00	15.00
(22)	Bobby Byrne	10.00	5.00	3.00
(23)	Nixey Callahan	10.00	5.00	3.00
(24a)	Howie Camnitz (small letters)	10.00	5.00	3.00
(24b)	Howie Camnitz (large letters)	20.00	10.00	6.00
(25a)	Bill Carrigan (small letters)	10.00	5.00	3.00
(25b)	Bill Carrigan (large letters)	20.00	10.00	6.00
(26a)	Frank Chance (small letters)	35.00	17.50	10.50
(26b)	Frank Chance (large letters)	50.00	25.00	15.00
(27)	Hal Chase (different photo, small letters)	15.00	7.50	4.50
(28)	Hal Chase (different photo, large letters)	25.00	12.50	7.50
(29)	Ed Cicotte	15.00	7.50	4.50
(30a)	Fred Clarke (small letters)	30.00	15.00	9.00
(30b)	Fred Clarke (large letters)	50.00	25.00	15.00
(31a)	Ty Cobb (small letters)	200.00	100.00	60.00
(31b)	Ty Cobb (large letters)	325.00	162.00	97.00
(32a)	Eddie Collins (small letters)	30.00	15.00	9.00
(32b)	Eddie Collins (large letters)	70.00	35.00	21.00
(33)	Doc Crandall	10.00	5.00	3.00
(34)	Birdie Cree	35.00	17.50	10.50
(35)	Bill Dahlen	10.00	5.00	3.00
(36)	Jim Delahanty	10.00	5.00	3.00
(37)	Art Devlin	10.00	5.00	3.00
(38)	Josh Devore	10.00	5.00	3.00
(39)	Wild Bill Donovan	35.00	17.50	10.50
(40a)	Red Dooin (small letters)	10.00	5.00	3.00
(40b)	Red Dooin (large letters)	20.00	10.00	6.00
(41a)	Mickey Doolan (small letters)	10.00	5.00	3.00
(41b)	Mickey Doolan (large letters)	20.00	10.00	6.00
(42)	Patsy Dougherty	10.00	5.00	3.00
(43a)	Tom Downey (small letters)	10.00	5.00	3.00
(43b)	Tom Downey (large letters)	20.00	10.00	6.00
(44a)	Larry Doyle (small letters)	10.00	5.00	3.00
(44b)	Larry Doyle (large letters)	20.00	10.00	6.00
(45)	Louis Drucke	10.00	5.00	3.00
(46a)	Hugh Duffy (small letters)	30.00	15.00	9.00
(46b)	Hugh Duffy (large letters)	50.00	25.00	15.00
(47)	Jimmy Dygert	10.00	5.00	3.00
(48a)	Kid Elberfeld (small letters)	10.00	5.00	3.00
(48b)	Kid Elberfeld (large letters)	20.00	10.00	6.00
(49a)	Clyde Engle (small letters)	10.00	5.00	3.00
(49b)	Clyde Engle (large letters)	20.00	10.00	6.00
(50)	Tex Erwin	10.00	5.00	3.00
(51)	Steve Evans	10.00	5.00	3.00
(52)	Johnny Evers	30.00	15.00	9.00
(53)	Cecil Ferguson	10.00	5.00	3.00
(54)	John Flynn	10.00	5.00	3.00
(55a)	Russ Ford (small letters)	10.00	5.00	3.00
(55b)	Russ Ford (large letters)	20.00	10.00	6.00
(56)	Art Fromme	10.00	5.00	3.00
(57)	Harry Gaspar	10.00	5.00	3.00
(58a)	George Gibson (small letters)	10.00	5.00	3.00
(58b)	George Gibson (large letters)	20.00	10.00	6.00
(59)	Eddie Grant	35.00	17.50	10.50
(60)	Dolly Gray	10.00	5.00	3.00
(61a)	Clark Griffith (small letters)	30.00	15.00	9.00
(61b)	Clark Griffith (large letters)	50.00	25.00	15.00
(62)	Bob Groom	10.00	5.00	3.00
(63)	Bob Harmon	10.00	5.00	3.00
(64)	Topsy Hartsel	10.00	5.00	3.00
(65)	Arnold Hauser	35.00	17.50	10.50
(66)	Ira Hemphill	10.00	5.00	3.00
(67a)	Buck Herzog (small letters)	10.00	5.00	3.00
(67b)	Buck Herzog (large letters)	20.00	10.00	6.00
(68)	Dick Hoblitzell	10.00	5.00	3.00
(69)	Danny Hoffman	10.00	5.00	3.00
(70)	Harry Hooper	10.00	5.00	3.00
(71a)	Miller Huggins (small letters)	30.00	15.00	9.00
(71b)	Miller Huggins (large letters)	50.00	25.00	15.00
(72)	John Hummel	10.00	5.00	3.00
(73)	Hugh Jennings (different photo, small letters)	30.00	15.00	9.00
(74)	Hugh Jennings (different photo, large letters)	50.00	25.00	15.00
(75a)	Walter Johnson (small letters)	90.00	45.00	27.00
(75b)	Walter Johnson (large letters)	125.00	62.00	37.00
(76)	Tom Jones	35.00	17.50	10.50
(77)	Ed Karger	10.00	5.00	3.00
(78)	Ed Killian	35.00	17.50	10.50
(79a)	Jack Knight (small letters)	10.00	5.00	3.00
(79b)	Jack Knight (large letters)	20.00	10.00	6.00
(80)	Ed Konetchy	10.00	5.00	3.00
(81)	Harry Krause	10.00	5.00	3.00
(82)	Rube Kroh	10.00	5.00	3.00
(83)	Nap Lajoie	60.00	30.00	18.00
(84a)	Frank LaPorte (small letters)	10.00	5.00	3.00
(84b)	Frank LaPorte (large letters)	20.00	10.00	6.00
(85)	Arlie Latham	10.00	5.00	3.00
(86a)	Tommy Leach (small letters)	10.00	5.00	3.00
(86b)	Tommy Leach (large letters)	20.00	10.00	6.00
(87)	Sam Leever	10.00	5.00	3.00
(88)	Lefty Leifield	10.00	5.00	3.00
(89)	Hans Lobert	10.00	5.00	3.00
(90a)	Harry Lord (small letters)	10.00	5.00	3.00

	NR MT	EX	VG
(90b) Harry Lord (large letters)	20.00	10.00	6.00
(91) Paddy Livingston	10.00	5.00	3.00
(92) Nick Maddox	10.00	5.00	3.00
(93) Sherry Magee	12.00	6.00	3.50
(94) Rube Marquard	30.00	15.00	9.00
(95a) Christy Mathewson (small letters)	90.00	45.00	27.00
(95b) Christy Mathewson (large letters)	110.00	55.00	33.00
(96a) Al Mattern (small letters)	10.00	5.00	3.00
(96b) Al Mattern (large letters)	20.00	10.00	6.00
(97) George McBride	10.00	5.00	3.00
(98a) John McGraw (small letters)	40.00	20.00	12.00
(98b) John McGraw (large letters)	60.00	30.00	18.00
(99a) Larry McLean (small letters)	10.00	5.00	3.00
(99b) Larry McLean (large letters)	20.00	10.00	6.00
(100) Harry McIntyre (Cubs)	10.00	5.00	3.00
(101a) Matty McIntyre (White Sox, small letters)	10.00	5.00	3.00
(101b) Matty McIntyre (White Sox, large letters)	20.00	10.00	6.00
(102) Fred Merkle	12.00	6.00	3.50
(103) Chief Meyers	10.00	5.00	3.00
(104) Clyde Milan	10.00	5.00	3.00
(105) Dots Miller	10.00	5.00	3.00
(106) Mike Mitchell	10.00	5.00	3.00
(107) Pat Moran	10.00	5.00	3.00
(108a) George Mullen (Mullin) (small letters)	10.00	5.00	3.00
(108b) George Mullen (Mullin) (large letters)	20.00	10.00	6.00
(109) Danny Murphy	10.00	5.00	3.00
(110a) Red Murray (small letters)	20.00	10.00	6.00
(110b) Red Murray (large letters)	10.00	5.00	3.00
(111) Tom Needham	35.00	17.50	10.50
(112a) Rebel Oakes (small letters)	10.00	5.00	3.00
(112b) Rebel Oakes (large letters)	20.00	10.00	6.00
(113) Rube Oldring	10.00	5.00	3.00
(114) Charley O'Leary	10.00	5.00	3.00
(115) Orval Overall	35.00	17.50	10.50
(116) Fred Parent	10.00	5.00	3.00
(117a) Dode Paskert (small letters)	10.00	5.00	3.00
(117b) Dode Paskert (large letters)	20.00	10.00	6.00
(118) Barney Pelty	10.00	5.00	3.00
(119) Jake Pfeister	10.00	5.00	3.00
(120) Eddie Phelps	10.00	5.00	3.00
(121) Deacon Phillippe	10.00	5.00	3.00
(122) Jack Quinn	10.00	5.00	3.00
(123) Ed Reulbach	10.00	5.00	3.00
124 Lew Richie	10.00	5.00	3.00
(125) Jack Rowan	10.00	5.00	3.00
(126a) Nap Rucker (small letters)	10.00	5.00	3.00
(126b) Nap Rucker (large letters)	20.00	10.00	6.00
(127) Doc Scanlon (Scanlan)	35.00	17.50	10.50
(128) Germany Schaefer	10.00	5.00	3.00
(129) Jimmy Scheckard (Sheckard)	10.00	5.00	3.00
(130a) Boss Schmidt (small letters)	10.00	5.00	3.00
(130b) Boss Schmidt (large letters)	20.00	10.00	6.00
(131) Wildfire Schulte	10.00	5.00	3.00
(132) Hap Smith	10.00	5.00	3.00
(133a) Tris Speaker (small letters)	50.00	25.00	15.00
(133b) Tris Speaker (large letters)	70.00	35.00	21.00
(134) Oscar Stanage	10.00	5.00	3.00
(135) Harry Steinfeldt	15.00	7.50	4.50
(136) George Stone	10.00	5.00	3.00
(137a) George Stoval (Stovall) (small letters)	10.00	5.00	3.00
(137b) George Stoval (Stovall) (large letters)	20.00	10.00	6.00
(138a) Gabby Street (small letters)	10.00	5.00	3.00
(138b) Gabby Street (large letters)	20.00	10.00	6.00
(139) George Suggs	10.00	5.00	3.00
(140a) Ira Thomas (small letters)	10.00	5.00	3.00
(140b) Ira Thomas (large letters)	20.00	10.00	6.00
(141a) Joe Tinker (small letters)	30.00	15.00	9.00
(141b) Joe Tinker (large letters)	50.00	25.00	15.00
(142a) John Titus (small letters)	10.00	5.00	3.00
(142b) John Titus (large letters)	20.00	10.00	6.00
(143) Terry Turner	20.00	10.00	6.00
(144) Heinie Wagner	10.00	5.00	3.00
(145a) Bobby Wallace (with cap, small letters)	30.00	15.00	9.00
(145b) Bobby Wallace (with cap, large letters)	50.00	25.00	15.00
(146) Bobby Wallace (without cap)	30.00	15.00	9.00
(147) Ed Walsh	30.00	15.00	9.00
(148) Jack Warhop	35.00	17.50	10.50
(149a) Zach Wheat (small letters)	30.00	15.00	9.00
(149b) Zach Wheat (large letters)	50.00	25.00	15.00
(150) Doc White	10.00	5.00	3.00
(151) Art Wilson (Giants)	35.00	17.50	10.50
(152) Owen Wilson (Pirates)	10.00	5.00	3.00
(153) Hooks Wiltse	10.00	5.00	3.00
(154) Harry Wolter	10.00	5.00	3.00
(155a) Cy Young (small letters)	55.00	27.00	16.50
(155b) Cy Young (large letters)	75.00	37.00	22.00

1930 PM8
Our National Game Pins

This unnumbered 30-pin set issued in the 1930s carries the American Card Catalog designation PM8 and is known as "Our National Game." The pins, which measure 7/8" in diamter, have a "tab" rather than a pin back. The black and white player photo is tinted blue, and the player's name and team are printed in a band near the bottom.

	NR MT	EX	VG
Complete Set:	450.00	225.00	135.00
Common Player:	6.00	3.00	1.75
(1) Wally Berger	6.00	3.00	1.75
(2) Lou Chiozza	6.00	3.00	1.75
(3) Joe Cronin	12.00	6.00	3.50
(4) Frank Crosetti	8.00	4.00	2.50
(5) Jerome (Dizzy) Dean	25.00	12.50	7.50
(6) Frank DeMaree	6.00	3.00	1.75
(7) Joe DiMaggio	70.00	35.00	21.00
(8) Bob Feller	20.00	10.00	6.00
(9) Jimmy Foxx	20.00	10.00	6.00
(10) Charles Gehringer	12.00	6.00	3.50
(11) Lou Gehrig	70.00	35.00	21.00
(12) Lefty Gomez	12.00	6.00	3.50
(13) Hank Greenberg	12.00	6.00	3.50
(14) Irving (Bump) Hadley	6.00	3.00	1.75
(15) Leo Hartnett	12.00	6.00	3.50
(16) Carl Hubbell	12.00	6.00	3.50
(17) John (Buddy) Lewis	6.00	3.00	1.75
(18) Gus Mancuso	6.00	3.00	1.75
(19) Joe McCarthy	12.00	6.00	3.50
(20) Joe Medwick	12.00	6.00	3.50
(21) Joe Moore	6.00	3.00	1.75
(22) Mel Ott	12.00	6.00	3.50
(23) Jake Powell	6.00	3.00	1.75
(24) Jimmy Ripple	6.00	3.00	1.75
(25) Red Ruffing	12.00	6.00	3.50
(26) Hal Schumacher	6.00	3.00	1.75
(27) George Selkirk	6.00	3.00	1.75
(28) "Al" Simmons	12.00	6.00	3.50
(29) Bill Terry	12.00	6.00	3.50
(30) Harold Trosky	6.00	3.00	1.75

1956 PM15
Yellow Basepath Pins

Issued circa 1956, the sponsor of this 32-pin set is not indicated. The set, which has been assigned the American Carc Catalog designation PM15, is commonly called "Yellow Basepaths" because of the design of the pin, which features a black and white player photo set inside a green infield with yellow basepaths. The unnumbered pins measure 7/8" in diameter. The names of Kluszewski and Mathews are misspelled.

	NR MT	EX	VG
Complete Set:	1800.	900.00	540.00
Common Player:	25.00	12.50	7.50
(1) Hank Aaron	125.00	62.00	37.00
(2) Joe Adcock	30.00	15.00	9.00
(3) Luis Aparicio	50.00	25.00	15.00
(4) Richie Ashburn	40.00	20.00	12.00
(5) Gene Baker	25.00	12.50	7.50
(6) Ernie Banks	60.00	30.00	18.00
(7) Yogi Berra	70.00	35.00	21.00
(8) Bill Bruton	25.00	12.50	7.50
(9) Larry Doby	30.00	15.00	9.00
(10) Bob Friend	25.00	12.50	7.50
(11) Nellie Fox	40.00	20.00	12.00
(12) Jim Greengrass	25.00	12.50	7.50
(13) Steve Gromek	25.00	12.50	7.50
(14) Johnny Groth	25.00	12.50	7.50
(15) Gil Hodges	60.00	30.00	18.00
(16) Al Kaline	60.00	30.00	18.00
(17) Ted Kluzewski (Kluszewski)	35.00	17.50	10.50
(18) Johnny Logan	25.00	12.50	7.50
(19) Dale Long	25.00	12.50	7.50
(20) Mickey Mantle	400.00	200.00	120.00
(21) Ed Mathews	60.00	30.00	18.00
(22) Orestes Minoso	30.00	15.00	9.00
(23) Stan Musial	125.00	62.00	37.00
(24) Don Newcombe	30.00	15.00	9.00
(25) Bob Porterfield	25.00	12.50	7.50
(26) Pee Wee Reese	70.00	35.00	21.00
(27) Robin Roberts	50.00	25.00	15.00
(28) Red Schoendienst	35.00	17.50	10.50
(29) Duke Snider	70.00	35.00	21.00
(30) Vern Stephens	25.00	12.50	7.50
(31) Gene Woodling	25.00	12.50	7.50
(32) Gus Zernial	25.00	12.50	7.50

1932 PR2
Orbit Gum Pins - Numbered

Issued circa 1933, this skip-numbered set of small (13/16" in diameter) pins was produced by Orbit Gum and carries the American Card Catalog designation of PR2. A player lithograph is set against a green background with the player's name and team printed on a strip of yellow below. The pin number is at the very bottom.

	NR MT	EX	VG
Complete Set:	1200.	600.00	360.00
Common Player:	15.00	7.50	4.50
1 Ivy Andrews	15.00	7.50	4.50
2 Carl Reynolds	15.00	7.50	4.50
3 Riggs Stephenson	18.00	9.00	5.50
4 Lon Warneke	15.00	7.50	4.50
5 Frank Grube	15.00	7.50	4.50
6 "Kiki" Cuyler	27.00	13.50	8.00
7 Marty McManus	15.00	7.50	4.50
8 "Lefty" Clark	15.00	7.50	4.50
9 George Blaeholder	15.00	7.50	4.50
10 Willie Kamm	15.00	7.50	4.50
11 Jimmy "Dykes"	18.00	9.00	5.50
12 Earl Averill	27.00	13.50	8.00
13 Pat Malone	15.00	7.50	4.50
14 "Dizzy" Dean	60.00	30.00	18.00
15 Dick Bartell	15.00	7.50	4.50
16 Guy Bush	15.00	7.50	4.50
17 Bud Tinning	15.00	7.50	4.50
18 Jimmy Foxx	45.00	22.00	13.50
19 "Mule" Haas	15.00	7.50	4.50
20 Lew Fonseca	15.00	7.50	4.50
21 "Pepper" Martin	20.00	10.00	6.00
22 Phil Collins	15.00	7.50	4.50
23 Bill Cissell	15.00	7.50	4.50
24 Bump Hadley	15.00	7.50	4.50
25 Smead Jolley	15.00	7.50	4.50
26 Burleigh Grimes	27.00	13.50	8.00
27 Dale Alexander	15.00	7.50	4.50
28 Mickey Cochrane	30.00	15.00	9.00
29 Mel Harder	15.00	7.50	4.50
30 Mark Koenig	15.00	7.50	4.50
31a "Lefty" O'Doul (Dodgers)	45.00	22.00	13.50
31b "Lefty" O'Doul (Giants)	20.00	10.00	6.00
32a Woody English (with bat)	15.00	7.50	4.50
32b Woody English (without bat)	45.00	22.00	13.50
33a Billy Jurges (with bat)	15.00	7.50	4.50
33b Billy Jurges (without bat)	45.00	22.00	13.50
34 Bruce Campbell	15.00	7.50	4.50
35 Joe Vosmik	15.00	7.50	4.50
36 Dick Porter	15.00	7.50	4.50
37 Charlie Grimm	18.00	9.00	5.50
38 Geo. Earnshaw	15.00	7.50	4.50
39 Al Simmons	27.00	13.50	8.00
40 "Red" Lucas	15.00	7.50	4.50
51 Wally Berger	15.00	7.50	4.50
52 Jim Levey	15.00	7.50	4.50
58 Ernie Lombardi	27.00	13.50	8.00
64 Jack Burns	15.00	7.50	4.50
67 Billy Herman	27.00	13.50	8.00
72 Bill Hallahan	15.00	7.50	4.50
92 Don Brennan	15.00	7.50	4.50
96 Sam Byrd	15.00	7.50	4.50
99 Ben Chapman	15.00	7.50	4.50
103 John Allen	15.00	7.50	4.50
107 Tony Lazzeri	24.00	12.00	7.25
111 Earl Combs (Earle)	27.00	13.50	8.00
116 Joe Sewell	27.00	13.50	8.00
120 Vernon Gomez	30.00	15.00	9.00

1932 PR3
Orbit Gum Pins - Unnumbered

This set, issued by Orbit Gum circa 1934, has the American Card Catalog designation PR3. The

pins are identical to the PR2 set, except they are unnumbered.

		NR MT	EX	VG
Complete Set:		2100.	1050.	630.00
Common Player:		25.00	12.50	7.50
(1)	Dale Alexander	25.00	12.50	7.50
(2)	Ivy Andrews	25.00	12.50	7.50
(3)	Earl Averill	40.00	20.00	12.00
(4)	Dick Bartell	25.00	12.50	7.50
(5)	Wally Berger	25.00	12.50	7.50
(6)	George Blaeholder	25.00	12.50	7.50
(7)	Jack Burns	25.00	12.50	7.50
(8)	Guy Bush	25.00	12.50	7.50
(9)	Bruce Campbell	25.00	12.50	7.50
(10)	Bill Cissell	25.00	12.50	7.50
(11)	"Lefty" Clark	25.00	12.50	7.50
(12)	Mickey Cochrane	45.00	22.00	13.50
(13)	Phil Collins	25.00	12.50	7.50
(14)	"Kiki" Cuyler	40.00	20.00	12.00
(15)	"Dizzy" Dean	75.00	37.00	22.00
(16)	Jimmy "Dykes"	27.00	13.50	8.00
(17)	Geo. Earnshaw	25.00	12.50	7.50
(18)	Woody English	25.00	12.50	7.50
(19)	Lew Fonseca	25.00	12.50	7.50
(20)	Jimmy Foxx	60.00	30.00	18.00
(21)	Burleigh Grimes	40.00	20.00	12.00
(22)	Charlie Grimm	27.00	13.50	8.00
(23)	"Lefty" Grove	65.00	32.00	19.50
(24)	Frank Grube	25.00	12.50	7.50
(25)	"Mule" Haas	25.00	12.50	7.50
(26)	Bump Hadley	25.00	12.50	7.50
(27)	"Chick" Hafey	50.00	25.00	15.00
(28)	Jesse Haines	50.00	25.00	15.00
(29)	Bill Hallahan	25.00	12.50	7.50
(30)	Mel Harder	25.00	12.50	7.50
(31)	"Gabby" Hartnett	50.00	25.00	15.00
(32)	"Babe" Herman	35.00	17.50	10.50
(33)	Billy Herman	40.00	20.00	12.00
(34)	Rogers Hornsby	75.00	37.00	22.00
(35)	Roy Johnson	30.00	15.00	9.00
(36)	Smead Jolley	25.00	12.50	7.50
(37)	Billy Jurges	25.00	12.50	7.50
(38)	Willie Kamm	25.00	12.50	7.50
(39)	Mark Koenig	25.00	12.50	7.50
(40)	Jim Levey	25.00	12.50	7.50
(41)	Ernie Lombardi	40.00	20.00	12.00
(42)	Red Lucas	25.00	12.50	7.50
(43)	Ted Lyons	50.00	25.00	15.00
(44)	Connie Mack	70.00	35.00	21.00
(45)	Pat Malone	25.00	12.50	7.50
(46)	"Pepper" Martin	27.00	13.50	8.00
(47)	Marty McManus	25.00	12.50	7.50
(48)	"Lefty" O'Doul	25.00	12.50	7.50
(49)	Dick Porter	25.00	12.50	7.50
(50)	Carl Reynolds	25.00	12.50	7.50
(51)	Charlie Root	30.00	15.00	9.00
(52)	Bob Seeds	30.00	15.00	9.00
(53)	Al Simmons	40.00	20.00	12.00
(54)	Riggs Stephenson	27.00	13.50	8.00
(55)	Bud Tinning	25.00	12.50	7.50
(56)	Joe Vosmik	25.00	12.50	7.50
(57)	Rube Walberg	30.00	15.00	9.00
(58)	Paul Waner	50.00	25.00	15.00
(59)	Lon Warneke	25.00	12.50	7.50
(60)	Pinky Whitney	30.00	15.00	9.00

1930 PR4 Cracker Jack Pins

Although no manufacturer is indicated on the pins themselves, this 25-player set was apparently issued by Cracker Jack in the early 1930's. Each pin measures 13/16" in diameter and features a line drawing of a player portrait. The unnumbered pins are printed in blue and gray with a background of yellow. The player's name appears below.

		NR MT	EX	VG
Complete Set:		600.00	300.00	180.00
Common Player:		12.00	6.00	3.50
(1)	Charles Berry	12.00	6.00	3.50
(2)	Bill Cissell	12.00	6.00	3.50
(3)	KiKi Cuyler	25.00	12.50	7.50
(4)	Dizzy Dean	40.00	20.00	12.00
(5)	Wesley Ferrell	12.00	6.00	3.50
(6)	Frank Frisch	25.00	12.50	7.50
(7)	Lou Gehrig	75.00	37.00	22.00
(8)	Vernon Gomez	25.00	12.50	7.50
(9)	Goose Goslin	25.00	12.50	7.50
(10)	George Grantham	12.00	6.00	3.50
(11)	Charley Grimm	15.00	7.50	4.50
(12)	Lefty Grove	30.00	15.00	9.00
(13)	Gabby Hartnett	25.00	12.50	7.50
(14)	Travis Jackson	25.00	12.50	7.50
(15)	Tony Lazzeri	20.00	10.00	6.00
(16)	Ted Lyons	25.00	12.50	7.50
(17)	Rabbit Maranville	25.00	12.50	7.50
(18)	Carl Reynolds	12.00	6.00	3.50
(19)	Charles Ruffing	25.00	12.50	7.50
(20)	Al Simmons	25.00	12.50	7.50
(21)	Gus Suhr	12.00	6.00	3.50
(22)	Bill Terry	25.00	12.50	7.50
(23)	Dazzy Vance	25.00	12.50	7.50
(24)	Paul Waner	25.00	12.50	7.50
(25)	Lon Warneke	12.00	6.00	3.50

1933 PX3 Double Header Pins

Issued by Gum, Inc. circa 1933, this unnumbered set consists of 43 metal discs approximately 1-1/4" in diameter. The front of the pin lists the player's name and team beneath his picture. The numbers "1" or "2" also appear inside a small circle at the bottom of the disc, and the wrapper advised collectors to "Put 1 and 2 together and make a double header." The set is designated as PX3 in the American Card Catalog.

		NR MT	EX	VG
Complete Set:		950.00	475.00	265.00
Common Player:		15.00	7.50	4.50
(1)	"Sparky" Adams	15.00	7.50	4.50
(2)	Dale Alexander	15.00	7.50	4.50
(3)	Earl Averill	30.00	15.00	9.00
(4)	Dick Bartell	15.00	7.50	4.50
(5)	Walter Berger	15.00	7.50	4.50
(6)	"Sunny" Jim Bottomley	30.00	15.00	9.00
(7)	"Lefty" Brandt	15.00	7.50	4.50
(8)	Owen T. Carroll	15.00	7.50	4.50
(9)	"Lefty" Clark	15.00	7.50	4.50
(10)	Mickey Cochrane	30.00	15.00	9.00
(11)	Joe Cronin	30.00	15.00	9.00
(12)	Jimmy Dykes	18.00	9.00	5.50
(13)	George Earnshaw	15.00	7.50	4.50
(14)	Wes Ferrell	15.00	7.50	4.50
(15)	Neal Finn	15.00	7.50	4.50
(16)	Lew Fonseca	15.00	7.50	4.50
(17)	Jimmy Foxx	45.00	22.00	13.50
(18)	Frankie Frisch	30.00	15.00	9.00
(19)	"Chick" Fullis	15.00	7.50	4.50
(20)	Charley Gehringer	30.00	15.00	9.00
(21)	"Goose" Goslin	30.00	15.00	9.00
(22)	Johnny Hodapp	15.00	7.50	4.50
(23)	Frank Hogan	15.00	7.50	4.50
(24)	Si Johnson	15.00	7.50	4.50
(25)	Joe Judge	15.00	7.50	4.50
(26)	"Chuck" Klein	30.00	15.00	9.00
(27)	Al Lopez	30.00	15.00	9.00
(28)	Ray Lucas	15.00	7.50	4.50
(29)	Red Lucas	15.00	7.50	4.50
(30)	Ted Lyons	30.00	15.00	9.00
(31)	"Firpo" Marberry	15.00	7.50	4.50
(32)	Oscar Melillo	15.00	7.50	4.50
(33)	Lefty O'Doul	18.00	9.00	5.50
(34)	George Pipgras	15.00	7.50	4.50
(35)	Flint Rhem	15.00	7.50	4.50
(36)	Sam Rice	30.00	15.00	9.00
(37)	"Muddy" Ruel	15.00	7.50	4.50
(38)	Harry Seibold	15.00	7.50	4.50
(39)	Al Simmons	30.00	15.00	9.00
(40)	Joe Vosmik	15.00	7.50	4.50
(41)	Gerald Walker	15.00	7.50	4.50
(42)	"Pinky" Whitney	15.00	7.50	4.50
(43)	Hack Wilson	30.00	15.00	9.00

1909-12 PX7 Domino Discs

Domino Discs, distributed by Sweet Caporal Cigarettes from 1909 to 1912, are among the more obscure 20th Century tobacco issues. Although the disc set contains many of the same players - some even pictured in the same poses - as the Sweet Caporal P2 pin set, the discs have always lagged behind the pins in collector appeal. The Domino Discs, so called because each disc has a large, white domino printed on the back,

measure approximately 1-1/8" in diameter amd are made of thin card cardboard surrounded by a metal rim. The fronts of the discs contain a player portrait photo set against a background of either red, green or blue. The words "Sweet Caporal Cigarettes" appear on the front along with the player's last name and team. There are 135 different major leaguers featured in the set, each pictured in two different poses for a total of 270 different subjects. Also known to exist as part of the set is a "game disc" which pictures a "generic" player and contains the words "Home Team" against a red background on one side and "Visiting Team" with a green background on the reverse. Because each of the 135 players in the set can theoretically be found with three different background colors and with varying numbers of dots on the dominoes, there is almost an impossible number of variations available. Collectors, however, generally collect the discs without regard to background color or domino arrangement. The Domino Disc set was assigned the designation PX7 in the American Card Catalog.

		NR MT	EX	VG
Complete Set:		4250.	2125.	1250.
Complete Set: (Including variations)		8500.	4250.	2650.
Common Player:		15.00	7.50	4.50
(1)	Red Ames	15.00	7.50	4.50
(2)	Jimmy Archer	15.00	7.50	4.50
(3)	Jimmy Austin	15.00	7.50	4.50
(4)	Home Run Baker	40.00	20.00	12.00
(5)	Neal Ball	15.00	7.50	4.50
(6)	Cy Barger	15.00	7.50	4.50
(7)	Jack Barry	15.00	7.50	4.50
(8)	Johnny Bates	15.00	7.50	4.50
(9)	Beals Becker	15.00	7.50	4.50
(10)	George Bell	15.00	7.50	4.50
(11)	Chief Bender	40.00	20.00	12.00
(12)	Bill Bergen	15.00	7.50	4.50
(13)	Bob Bescher	15.00	7.50	4.50
(14)	Joe Birmingham	15.00	7.50	4.50
(15)	Roger Bresnahan	40.00	20.00	12.00
(16)	Al Bridwell	15.00	7.50	4.50
(17)	Mordecai Brown	40.00	20.00	12.00
(18)	Bobby Byrne	15.00	7.50	4.50
(19)	Nixey Callahan	15.00	7.50	4.50
(20)	Howie Camnitz	15.00	7.50	4.50
(21)	Bill Carrigan	15.00	7.50	4.50
(22)	Frank Chance	35.00	17.50	10.50
(23)	Hal Chase	20.00	10.00	6.00
(24)	Ed Cicotte	20.00	10.00	6.00
(25)	Fred Clarke	35.00	17.50	10.50
(26)	Ty Cobb	450.00	225.00	135.00
(27)	Eddie Collins	40.00	20.00	12.00
(28)	Doc Crandall	15.00	7.50	4.50
(29)	Birdie Cree	15.00	7.50	4.50
(30)	Bill Dahlen	15.00	7.50	4.50
(31)	Jim Delahanty	15.00	7.50	4.50
(32)	Art Devlin	15.00	7.50	4.50
(33)	Josh Devore	15.00	7.50	4.50
(34)	Red Dooin	15.00	7.50	4.50
(35)	Mickey Doolan	15.00	7.50	4.50
(36)	Patsy Dougherty	15.00	7.50	4.50
(37)	Tom Downey	15.00	7.50	4.50
(38)	Larry Doyle	15.00	7.50	4.50
(39)	Louis Drucke	15.00	7.50	4.50
(40)	Clyde Engle	15.00	7.50	4.50
(41)	Tex Erwin	15.00	7.50	4.50
(42)	Steve Evans	15.00	7.50	4.50
(43)	Johnny Evers	40.00	20.00	12.00
(44)	Cecil Ferguson	15.00	7.50	4.50
(45)	Russ Ford	15.00	7.50	4.50
(46)	Art Fromme	15.00	7.50	4.50
(47)	Harry Gaspar	15.00	7.50	4.50
(48)	George Gibson	15.00	7.50	4.50
(49)	Eddie Grant	15.00	7.50	4.50
(50)	Clark Griffith	40.00	20.00	12.00
(51)	Bob Groom	15.00	7.50	4.50
(52)	Bob Harmon	15.00	7.50	4.50
(53)	Topsy Hartsel	15.00	7.50	4.50
(54)	Arnold Hauser	15.00	7.50	4.50
(55)	Dick Hoblitzell	15.00	7.50	4.50
(56)	Danny Hoffman	15.00	7.50	4.50
(57)	Miller Huggins	40.00	20.00	12.00
(58)	John Hummel	15.00	7.50	4.50
(59)	Hugh Jennings	40.00	20.00	12.00
(60)	Walter Johnson	200.00	100.00	60.00
(61)	Ed Karger	15.00	7.50	4.50
(62a)	Jack Knight (Yankees)	15.00	7.50	4.50
(62b)	Jack Knight (Senators)	15.00	7.50	4.50
(63)	Ed Konetchy	15.00	7.50	4.50
(64)	Harry Krause	15.00	7.50	4.50
(65)	Frank LaPorte	15.00	7.50	4.50
(66)	Nap Lajoie	125.00	62.00	37.00
(67)	Tommy Leach	15.00	7.50	4.50
(68)	Sam Leever	15.00	7.50	4.50
(69)	Lefty Leifield	15.00	7.50	4.50
(70)	Paddy Livingston	15.00	7.50	4.50
(71)	Hans Lobert	15.00	7.50	4.50
(72)	Harry Lord	15.00	7.50	4.50

		NR MT	EX	VG
(73)	Nick Maddox	15.00	7.50	4.50
(74)	Sherry Magee	15.00	7.50	4.50
(75)	Rube Marquard	40.00	20.00	12.00
(76)	Christy Mathewson	200.00	100.00	60.00
(77)	Al Mattern	15.00	7.50	4.50
(78)	George McBride	15.00	7.50	4.50
(79)	John McGraw	100.00	50.00	30.00
(80)	Harry McIntire (McIntyre)	15.00	7.50	4.50
(81)	Matty McIntyre	15.00	7.50	4.50
(82)	Larry McLean	15.00	7.50	4.50
(83)	Fred Merkle	15.00	7.50	4.50
(84)	Chief Meyers	15.00	7.50	4.50
(85)	Clyde Milan	15.00	7.50	4.50
(86)	Dots Miller	15.00	7.50	4.50
(87)	Mike Mitchell	15.00	7.50	4.50
(88a)	Pat Moran (Cubs)	15.00	7.50	4.50
(88b)	Pat Moran (Phillies)	15.00	7.50	4.50
(89)	George Mullen (Mullin)	15.00	7.50	4.50
(90)	Danny Murphy	15.00	7.50	4.50
(91)	Red Murray	15.00	7.50	4.50
(92)	Tom Needham	15.00	7.50	4.50
(93)	Rebel Oakes	15.00	7.50	4.50
(94)	Rube Oldring	15.00	7.50	4.50
(95)	Fred Parent	15.00	7.50	4.50
(96)	Dode Paskert	15.00	7.50	4.50
(97)	Barney Pelty	15.00	7.50	4.50
(98)	Eddie Phelps	15.00	7.50	4.50
(99)	Deacon Phillippe	15.00	7.50	4.50
(100)	Jack Quinn	15.00	7.50	4.50
(101)	Ed Reulbach	15.00	7.50	4.50
(102)	Lew Richie	15.00	7.50	4.50
(103)	Jack Rowan	15.00	7.50	4.50
(104)	Nap Rucker	15.00	7.50	4.50
(105a)	Doc Scanlon (Scanlan) (Superbas)	15.00	7.50	4.50
(105b)	Doc Scanlon (Scanlan) (Phillies)	15.00	7.50	4.50
(106)	Germany Schaefer	15.00	7.50	4.50
(107)	Boss Schmidt	15.00	7.50	4.50
(108)	Wildfire Schulte	15.00	7.50	4.50
(109)	Jimmy Sheckard	15.00	7.50	4.50
(110)	Hap Smith	15.00	7.50	4.50
(111)	Tris Speaker	125.00	62.00	37.00
(112)	Harry Stovall	15.00	7.50	4.50
(113a)	Gabby Street (Senators)	15.00	7.50	4.50
(113b)	Gabby Street (Yankees)	15.00	7.50	4.50
(114)	George Suggs	15.00	7.50	4.50
(115)	Ira Thomas	15.00	7.50	4.50
(116)	Joe Tinker	40.00	20.00	12.00
(117)	John Titus	15.00	7.50	4.50
(118)	Terry Turner	15.00	7.50	4.50
(119)	Heinie Wagner	15.00	7.50	4.50
(120)	Bobby Wallace	35.00	17.50	10.50
(121)	Ed Walsh	40.00	20.00	12.00
(122)	Jack Warhop	15.00	7.50	4.50
(123)	Zach Wheat	40.00	20.00	12.00
(124)	Doc White	15.00	7.50	4.50
(125a)	Art Wilson (dark cap, Pirates)	15.00	7.50	4.50
(125b)	Art Wilson (dark cap, Giants)	15.00	7.50	4.50
(126a)	Owen Wilson (white cap, Giants)	15.00	7.50	4.50
(126b)	Owen Wilson (white cap, Pirates)	15.00	7.50	4.50
(127)	Hooks Wiltse	15.00	7.50	4.50
(128)	Harry Wolter	15.00	7.50	4.50
(129)	Cy Young	150.00	75.00	45.00

1988 Pacific Trading Cards

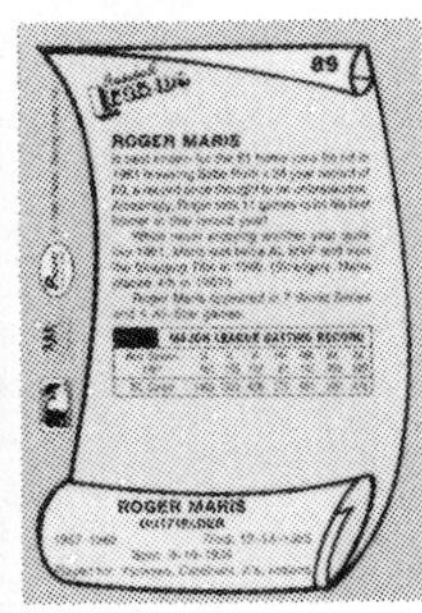

Pacific Trading Cards rounded up 110 photos of the greatest baseball players from the past 40 years for its 1988 "Baseball Legends" set. All players featured in the set are (or were) members of the Major League Baseball Alumni Association. Card fronts feature silver outer borders and large, clear full-color player photos outlined in black against colorful banner-style inner borders of red, blue, green, orange or gold. The player's name and position are printed in white letters on the lower portion of the banner. Card backs are numbered and carry the Baseball Legends logo, player biography, major league career stats, and personal information. The cards were sold in boxed sets via candy wholesalers, with emphasis on Midwest and New England states. Complete collector sets in clear plastic boxes were made available via dealers or directly from Pacific Trading Cards.

		MT	NR MT	EX
Complete Set:		12.00	9.00	4.75
Common Player:		.06	.05	.02
1	Hank Aaron	.50	.40	.20
2	Red Shoendienst (Schoendienst)	.10	.08	.04
3	Brooks Robinson	.30	.25	.12
4	Luke Appling	.15	.11	.06
5	Gene Woodling	.06	.05	.02
6	Stan Musial	.50	.40	.20
7	Mickey Mantle	1.00	.70	.40
8	Richie Ashburn	.10	.08	.04
9	Ralph Kiner	.20	.15	.08
10	Phil Rizzuto	.20	.15	.08
11	Harvey Haddix	.06	.05	.02
12	Ken Boyer	.10	.08	.04
13	Clete Boyer	.06	.05	.02
14	Ken Harrelson	.06	.05	.02
15	Robin Roberts	.20	.15	.08
16	Catfish Hunter	.20	.15	.08
17	Frank Howard	.10	.08	.04
18	Jim Perry	.06	.05	.02
19	Elston Howard	.10	.08	.04
20	Jim Bouton	.10	.08	.04
21	Pee Wee Reese	.25	.20	.10
22	Mel Stottlemyer (Stottlemyre)	.10	.08	.04
23	Hank Sauer	.06	.05	.02
24	Willie Mays	.50	.40	.20
25	Tom Tresh	.06	.05	.02
26	Roy Sievers	.06	.05	.02
27	Leo Durocher	.15	.11	.06
28	Al Dark	.10	.08	.04
29	Tony Kubek	.15	.11	.06
30	Johnny Vander Meer	.10	.08	.04
31	Joe Adcock	.10	.08	.04
32	Bob Lemon	.20	.15	.08
33	Don Newcombe	.15	.11	.06
34	Thurman Munson	.20	.15	.08
35	Earl Battey	.06	.05	.02
36	Ernie Banks	.30	.25	.12
37	Matty Alou	.06	.05	.02
38	Dave McNally	.06	.05	.02
39	Mickey Lolich	.10	.08	.04
40	Jackie Robinson	.50	.40	.20
41	Allie Reynolds	.15	.11	.06
42	Don Larson (Larsen)	.10	.08	.04
43	Fergie Jenkins	.15	.11	.06
44	Jim Gilliam	.10	.08	.04
45	Bobby Thomson	.10	.08	.04
46	Sparky Anderson	.10	.08	.04
47	Roy Campanella	.30	.25	.12
48	Marv Throneberry	.10	.08	.04
49	Bill Virdon	.06	.05	.02
50	Ted Williams	.50	.40	.20
51	Minnie Minoso	.10	.08	.04
52	Bob Turley	.10	.08	.04
53	Yogi Berra	.30	.25	.12
54	Juan Marichal	.20	.15	.08
55	Duke Snider	.30	.25	.12
56	Harvey Kuenn	.10	.08	.04
57	Nellie Fox	.15	.11	.06
58	Felipe Alou	.06	.05	.02
59	Tony Oliva	.10	.08	.04
60	Bill Mazeroski	.10	.08	.04
61	Bobby Shantz	.10	.08	.04
62	Mark Fidrych	.06	.05	.02
63	Johnny Mize	.15	.11	.06
64	Ralph Terry	.06	.05	.02
65	Gus Bell	.06	.05	.02
66	Jerry Koosman	.10	.08	.04
67	Mike McCormick	.06	.05	.02
68	Lou Burdette	.10	.08	.04
69	George Kell	.15	.11	.06
70	Vic Raschi	.10	.08	.04
71	Chuck Connors	.20	.15	.08
72	Ted Kluszewski	.10	.08	.04
73	Bobby Doerr	.15	.11	.06
74	Bobby Richardson	.15	.11	.06
75	Carl Erskine	.15	.11	.06
76	Hoyt Wilhelm	.20	.15	.08
77	Bob Purkey	.06	.05	.02
78	Bob Friend	.06	.05	.02
79	Monte Irvin	.15	.11	.06
80	Jim Longborg (Lonborg)	.06	.05	.02
81	Wally Moon	.06	.05	.02
82	Moose Skowron	.10	.08	.04
83	Tommy Davis	.10	.08	.04
84	Enos Slaughter	.20	.15	.08
85	Sal Maglie	.10	.08	.04
86	Harmon Killebrew	.25	.20	.10
87	Gil Hodges	.25	.20	.10
88	Jim Kaat	.10	.08	.04
89	Roger Maris	.30	.25	.12
90	Billy Williams	.20	.15	.08
91	Luis Aparicio	.15	.11	.06
92	Jim Bunning	.15	.11	.06
93	Bill Freehan	.06	.05	.02
94	Orlando Cepeda	.10	.08	.04
95	Early Wynn	.20	.15	.08
96	Tug McGraw	.10	.08	.04
97	Ron Santo	.10	.08	.04
98	Del Crandall	.06	.05	.02
99	Sal Bando	.06	.05	.02
100	Joe DiMaggio	.70	.50	.30
101	Bob Feller	.30	.25	.12
102	Larry Doby	.15	.11	.06
103	Rollie Fingers	.15	.11	.06
104	Al Kaline	.30	.25	.12
105	Johnny Podres	.10	.08	.04
106	Lou Boudreau	.15	.11	.06
107	Zoilo Versalles	.06	.05	.02
108	Dick Groat	.06	.05	.02
109	Warren Spahn	.25	.20	.10
110	Johnny Bench	.40	.30	.15

1989 Pacific Trading Cards

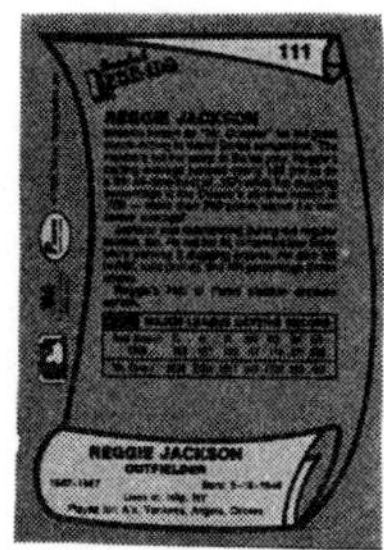

Pacific Trading Cards issued its Baseball Legends II set as a carry over of its initial set. The photos are printed on silver background and have colorful inner borders of red, blue, orange or gold. Players' names and positions are printed in white letters below the photos. The card backs once again present the "Baseball Legends" logo, player biography, major league career statistics, and personal information. The Baseball Legends II are numbered 110-220 and were available in wax packs at a limited number of retail chains. The complete set was also made available via dealers or could be ordered directly from Pacific Trading Cards.

		MT	NR MT	EX
Complete Set:		9.00	6.75	3.50
Common Player:		.06	.05	.02
111	Reggie Jackson	.30	.25	.12
112	Rich Reese	.06	.05	.02
113	Frankie Frisch	.15	.11	.06
114	Ed Kranepool	.06	.05	.02
115	Al Hrabosky	.06	.05	.02
116	Eddie Mathews	.25	.20	.10
117	Ty Cobb	.50	.40	.20
118	Jim Davenport	.06	.05	.02
119	Buddy Lewis	.06	.05	.02
120	Virgil Trucks	.10	.08	.04
121	Del Ennis	.06	.05	.02
122	Dick Radatz	.06	.05	.02
123	Andy Pafko	.12	.09	.05
124	Wilbur Wood	.10	.08	.04
125	Joe Sewell	.15	.11	.06
126	Herb Score	.06	.05	.02
127	Paul Waner	.06	.05	.02
128	Lloyd Waner	.06	.05	.02
129	Brooks Robinson	.30	.25	.12
130	Bo Belinsky	.10	.08	.04
131	Phil Cavaretta	.06	.05	.02
132	Claude Osteen	.06	.05	.02
133	Tito Francona	.06	.05	.02
134	Billy Pierce	.06	.05	.02
135	Roberto Clemente	.50	.40	.20
136	Spud Chandler	.06	.05	.02
137	Enos Slaughter	.25	.20	.10
138	Ken Holtzman	.06	.05	.02
139	John Hopp	.06	.05	.02
140	Tony LaRussa	.06	.05	.02
141	Ryne Duren	.06	.05	.02
142	Glenn Beckert	.06	.05	.02
143	Ken Keltner	.06	.05	.02
144	Hank Bauer	.15	.11	.06
145	Roger Craig	.10	.08	.04
146	Frank Baker	.10	.08	.04
147	Jim O'Toole	.06	.05	.02
148	Rogers Hornsby	.30	.25	.12
149	Jose Cardenal	.06	.05	.02
150	Bobby Doerr	.10	.08	.04
151	Mickey Cochrane	.10	.08	.04
152	Gaylord Perry	.10	.08	.04
153	Frank Thomas	.06	.05	.02
154	Ted Williams	.40	.30	.15
155	Sam McDowell	.10	.08	.04
156	Bob Feller	.20	.15	.08
157	Bert Campaneris	.06	.05	.02
158	Thornton Lee	.06	.05	.02
159	Gary Peters	.06	.05	.02
160	Joe Medwick	.10	.08	.04
161	Joe Nuxhall	.10	.08	.04
162	Joe Schultz	.06	.05	.02
163	Harmon Killebrew	.25	.20	.10
164	Bucky Walters	.06	.05	.02
165	Bobby Allison	.10	.08	.04
166	Lou Boudreau	.15	.11	.08
167	Joe Cronin	.10	.08	.04
168	Mike Torrez	.10	.08	.04
169	Rich Rollins	.06	.05	.02
170	Tony Cuccinello	.06	.05	.02
171	Hoyt Wilhelm	.20	.15	.08
172	Ernie Harwell	.10	.08	.04
173	George Foster	.06	.05	.02
174	Lou Gehrig	.80	.60	.30
175	Dave Kingman	.06	.05	.02
176	Babe Ruth	1.00	.70	.40
177	Joe Black	.10	.08	.04
178	Roy Face	.10	.08	.04
179	Earl Weaver	.06	.05	.02
180	Johnny Mize	.15	.11	.06
181	Roger Cramer	.06	.05	.02
182	Jim Piersall	.06	.05	.02
183	Ned Garver	.06	.05	.02
184	Billy Williams	.25	.20	.10
185	Lefty Grove	.15	.11	.06
186	Jim Grant	.06	.05	.02
187	Elmer Valo	.06	.05	.02
188	Ewell Blackwell	.10	.08	.04
189	Mel Ott	.20	.15	.08
190	Harry Walker	.06	.05	.02
191	Bill Campbell	.06	.05	.02
192	Walter Johnson	.30	.25	.12
193	Jim "Catfish" Hunter	.10	.08	.04
194	Charlie Keller	.10	.08	.04
195	Hank Greenberg	.15	.11	.06
196	Bobby Murcer	.06	.05	.02
197	Al Lopez	.06	.05	.02

		MT	NR MT	EX
198	Vida Blue	.10	.08	.04
199	Shag Crawford	.06	.05	.02
200	Arky Vaughan	.10	.08	.04
201	Smoky Burgess	.25	.20	.10
202	Rip Sewell	.06	.05	.02
203	Earl Averill	.10	.08	.04
204	Milt Pappas	.06	.05	.02
205	Mel Harder	.06	.05	.02
206	Sam Jethroe	.06	.05	.02
207	Randy Hundley	.06	.05	.02
208	Jessie Haines	.10	.08	.04
209	Jack Brickhouse	.10	.08	.04
210	Whitey Ford	.20	.15	.08
211	Honus Wagner	1.00	.70	.40
212	Phil Niekro	.10	.08	.04
213	Gary Bell	.06	.05	.02
214	Jon Matlack	.06	.05	.02
215	Moe Drabowsky	.06	.05	.02
216	Edd Roush	.10	.08	.04
217	Joel Horlen	.06	.05	.02
218	Casey Stengel	.30	.25	.12
219	Burt Hooton	.06	.05	.02
220	Joe Jackson	.80	.60	.30

Regional interest may affect the value of a card.

1988 Pacific Trading Cards "Eight Men Out"

Pacific Trading Cards produced this 110-card set featuring baseball players from the 1919 World Series and uniformed actors from Orion's movie "Eight Men Out." Card fronts feature a burgundy outer border and a thin silver inner border framing the player photos (actor photos are full-color, vintage photos are sepia-toned). A silver banner beneath the photo, outlined in black, bears a brief photo caption. The Eight Men Out logo appears lower right. The card backs are printed in burgundy and black on white, with a silver border, and include the actor/player's name and a paragraph-style biography. Pacific Trading Cards' "Eight Men Out" set was distributed by hobby stores nationwide in 10-card wax packs.

		MT	NR MT	EX
	Complete Set:	9.00	6.75	3.50
	Common Player:	.03	.02	.01
1	We're going to see the Sox!	.03	.02	.01
2	White Sox Win the Pennant!	.03	.02	.01
3	The Series	.03	.02	.01
4	1919 Chicago White Sox	.03	.02	.01
5	The Black Sox Scandal	.03	.02	.01
6	Eddie Cicotte - 29-7 in 1919	.03	.02	.01
7	"Buck's there faverit"	.03	.02	.01
8	Eddie Collins	.03	.02	.01
9	Michael Rooker as Arnold "Chick" Gandil	.03	.02	.01
10	Charlie Sheen as Oscar "Hap" Felsch	.03	.02	.01
11	James Read as Claude "Lefty" Williams	.03	.02	.01
12	John Cusack as George Buck Weaver	.03	.02	.01
13	D.B. Sweeney as "Shoeless" Joe Jackson	.03	.02	.01
14	David Strathairn as Eddie Cicotte	.03	.02	.01
15	Perry Lang as Fred McMullin	.03	.02	.01
16	Don Harvey as Charles "Swede" Risberg	.03	.02	.01
17	The Gamblers - Burns and Maharg	.03	.02	.01
18	Sleepy Bill Burns	.03	.02	.01
19	The Key is Cicotte	.03	.02	.01
20	C'moan, Betsy	.03	.02	.01
21	The Fix	.03	.02	.01
22	Chick approaches Cicotte	.03	.02	.01
23	"Kid" Gleason	.03	.02	.01
24	Charles Comiskey - Owner	.03	.02	.01
25	Arnold "Chick" Gandil - First Baseman	.03	.02	.01
26	Charles "Swede" Risberg	.03	.02	.01
27	Sport Sullivan	.03	.02	.01
28	Abe Attell/Arnold Rothstein	.03	.02	.01
29	Hugh Fullerton - Sports Writer	.03	.02	.01
30	Ring Lardner - Sports Writer	.03	.02	.01
31	"Shoeless"Joe working on his batting eye	.03	.02	.01
32	"Shoeless" Joe	.03	.02	.01
33	Buck can't sleep	.03	.02	.01
34	George "Buck" Weaver	.03	.02	.01
35	Hugh and Ring confront Kid	.03	.02	.01
36	Joe doesn't want to play.	.03	.02	.01
37	"Shoeless" Joe Jackson	.03	.02	.01
38	"Sore Arm, Cicotte", "Old Man Cicotte"	.03	.02	.01
39	The fix is on.	.03	.02	.01
40	Buck's playing to win.	.03	.02	.01
41	Hap makes a great catch.	.03	.02	.01
42	Hugh and Ring suspect!	.03	.02	.01
43	Ray gets things going.	.03	.02	.01
44	Lefty loses Game Two	.03	.02	.01
45	Lefty crosses up Ray Schalk's signals.	.03	.02	.01
46	Chick's RBI wins Game Three	.03	.02	.01
47	Dickie Kerr Wins Game Three	.03	.02	.01
48	Chick leaves Buck stranded at third.	.03	.02	.01
49	Williams loses Game Five	.03	.02	.01
50	Ray Schalk	.03	.02	.01
51	Schalk blocks the plate.	.03	.02	.01
52	Schalk is thrown out.	.03	.02	.01
53	Chicago stick ball game.	.03	.02	.01
54	I'm forever blowing ballgames.	.03	.02	.01
55	Felsch Scores Jackson	.03	.02	.01
56	Kerr wins Game Six.	.03	.02	.01
57	Where's the money?	.03	.02	.01
58	Cicotte wins Game Seven.	.03	.02	.01
59	Kid watches Eddie.	.03	.02	.01
60	Lefty is threatened	.03	.02	.01
61	James! Get your arm ready! Fast!	.03	.02	.01
62	"Shoeless" Joe's Home Run	.03	.02	.01
63	Buck played his best	.03	.02	.01
64	Hugh exposes the fix.	.03	.02	.01
65	Sign the petition	.03	.02	.01
66	Baseball owners hire a commissioner	.03	.02	.01
67	Judge Kenesaw Mountain Landis	.03	.02	.01
68	Grand jury summoned	.03	.02	.01
69	Say it ain't so, Joe!	.03	.02	.01
70	"The Swede's a Hard Guy"	.03	.02	.01
71	Buck loves the game.	.03	.02	.01
72	The trial.	.03	.02	.01
73	Kid Gleason take the stand.	.03	.02	.01
74	The Verdict	.03	.02	.01
75	Eight Men Out	.03	.02	.01
76	Oscar "Happy" Felsch	.03	.02	.01
77	Who's Joe Jackson?	.03	.02	.01
78	Ban Johnson - President	.03	.02	.01
79	Judge Landis - Commissioner of Baseball	.03	.02	.01
80	Charles A. Comiskey - Owner	.03	.02	.01
81	Heinie Groh - Third Baseman	.03	.02	.01
82	Slim Sallee - Pitcher	.03	.02	.01
83	Dutch Ruether - Pitcher	.03	.02	.01
84	Edd Roush - Outfielder	.03	.02	.01
85	Morrie Rath - Second Baseman	.03	.02	.01
86	Bill Rariden - Catcher	.03	.02	.01
87	Jimmy Ring - Pitcher	.03	.02	.01
88	Greasy Neale - Outfielder	.03	.02	.01
89	Pat Moran - Manager	.03	.02	.01
90	Adolfo Luque - Pitcher	.03	.02	.01
91	Larry Kopf - Shortstop	.03	.02	.01
92	Ray Fisher - Pitcher	.03	.02	.01
93	Hod Eller - Pitcher	.03	.02	.01
94	Pat Duncan - Outfielder	.03	.02	.01
95	Jake Daubert - First Baseman	.03	.02	.01
96	Red Faber - Pitcher	.03	.02	.01
97	Dickie Kerr - Pitcher	.03	.02	.01
98	Shano Collins - Outfielder	.03	.02	.01
99	Eddie Collins - Second Baseman	.03	.02	.01
100	Ray Schalk - Catcher	.03	.02	.01
101	Nemo Liebold - Outfielder	.03	.02	.01
102	Kid Gleason - Manager	.03	.02	.01
103	Swede Risberg - Shortstop	.03	.02	.01
104	Eddie Cicotte - Pitcher	.03	.02	.01
105	Fred McMullin - Infielder	.03	.02	.01
106	Chick Gandil - First Baseman	.03	.02	.01
107	Buck Weaver - Third Baseman	.03	.02	.01
108	Lefty Williams - Pitcher	.03	.02	.01
109	Happy Felsch - Outfielder	.03	.02	.01
110	Shoeless Joe Jackson - Outfielder	.03	.02	.01

1958 Packard-Bell

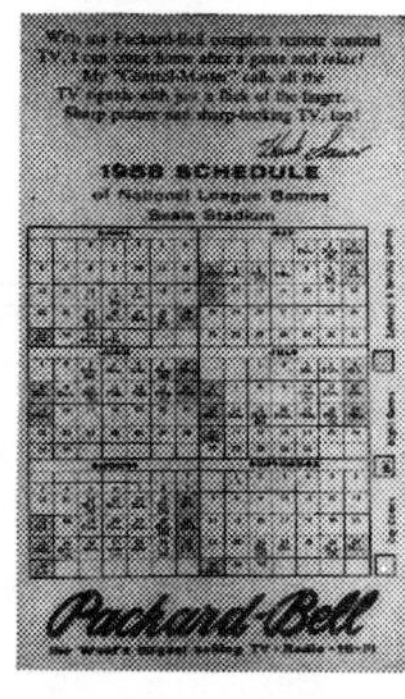

Issued in 1958 by Packard-Bell, the "world's largest seller of TVs, radios and hi-fis", this seven-card set was distributed in California and features members of the Los Angeles Dodgers and San Francisco Giants. The large (3-1/2" by 5-1/2") cards are unnumbered and carry an American Card Catalog designation of H801-5.

		NR MT	EX	VG
	Complete Set:	250.00	125.00	75.00
	Common Player:	12.00	6.00	3.50
(1)	Walter Alston	35.00	17.50	10.50
(2)	John A. Antonelli	12.00	6.00	3.50
(3)	Jim Gilliam	25.00	12.50	7.50
(4)	Gil Hodges	50.00	25.00	15.00
(5)	Willie Mays	100.00	50.00	30.00
(6)	Bill Rigney	12.00	6.00	3.50
(7)	Hank Sauer	12.00	6.00	3.50

1963 Pepsi-Cola Colt .45'S

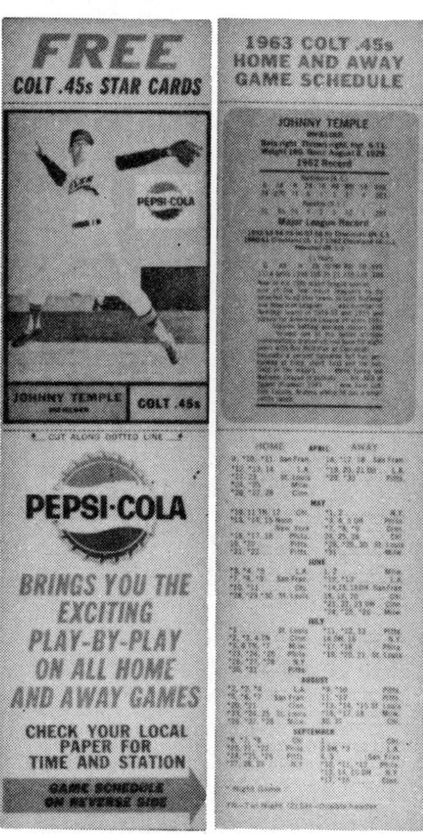

This 16-card set was distributed regionally in Texas in bottled six-packs of Pepsi. The cards were issued on panels 2-3/8" by 9-1/8", which were fit in between the bottles in each carton. Values quoted in the checklist below are for complete panels. A standard 2-3/8" by 3-3/4" card was printed on each panel, which also included promos for Pepsi and the Colt .45's, as well as a team schedule. Card fronts were black and white posed action photos with blue and red trim. Player name and position and Pepsi logo are also included. Card backs offer player statistics and career highlights. The John Bateman card, which was apparently never distributed publicly, is among the rarest collectible baseball cards of the 1960s. The complete set price does not include the Bateman card.

		NR MT	EX	VG
Complete Set:		200.00	100.00	60.00
Common Player:		7.00	3.50	2.00
1	Bob Aspromonte	7.00	3.50	2.00
2	John Bateman	500.00	250.00	150.00
3	Bob Bruce	7.00	3.50	2.00
4	Jim Campbell	7.00	3.50	2.00
5	Dick Farrell	7.00	3.50	2.00
6	Ernie Fazio	7.00	3.50	2.00
7	Carroll Hardy	7.00	3.50	2.00
8	J.C. Hartman	7.00	3.50	2.00
9	Ken Johnson	7.00	3.50	2.00
10	Bob Lillis	7.00	3.50	2.00
11	Don McMahon	7.00	3.50	2.00
12	Pete Runnels	10.00	5.00	3.00
13	Al Spangler	7.00	3.50	2.00
14	Rusty Staub	25.00	12.50	7.50
15	Johnny Temple	7.00	3.50	2.00
16	Carl Warwick	60.00	30.00	18.00

1988 Pepsi-Cola/Kroger

Approximately 38,000 sets of cards were given to fans at Tiger Stadium on July 30th, 1988. The set, sponsored by Pepsi-Cola and Kroger, includes 25 oversized (2-7/8" by 4-1/4") cards printed on glossy white stock with blue and orange borders. The card backs include small black and white close-up photos, the players' professional records and sponsor logos. The numbers in the following checklist refer to the players' uniform.

		MT	NR MT	EX
Complete Set:		9.00	6.75	3.50
Common Player:		.20	.15	.08
1	Lou Whitaker	.70	.50	.30
2	Alan Trammell	.90	.70	.35
8	Mike Heath	.20	.15	.08
11	Sparky Anderson	.40	.30	.15
12	Luis Salazar	.20	.15	.08
14	Dave Bergman	.20	.15	.08
15	Pat Sheridan	.20	.15	.08
16	Tom Brookens	.20	.15	.08
19	Doyle Alexander	.25	.20	.10
21	Guillermo Hernandez	.25	.20	.10
22	Ray Knight	.25	.20	.10
24	Gary Pettis	.20	.15	.08
25	Eric King	.30	.25	.12
26	Frank Tanana	.30	.25	.12
31	Larry Herndon	.20	.15	.08
32	Jim Walewander	.25	.20	.10
33	Matt Nokes	.90	.70	.35
34	Chet Lemon	.25	.20	.10
35	Walt Terrell	.25	.20	.10
39	Mike Henneman	.40	.30	.15
41	Darrell Evans	.40	.30	.15
44	Jeff Robinson	.50	.40	.20
47	Jack Morris	.70	.50	.30
48	Paul Gibson	.30	.25	.12
---	Coaches (Billy Consolo, Alex Grammas, Billy Muffett, Vada Pinson, Dick Tracewski)	.20	.15	.08

1985 Performance Printing Rangers

A local printing company sponsored this 28-card set of the Texas Rangers. The 2-3/8" by 3-1/2" cards are in full color and are numbered on the back by uniform number. Card fronts feature full-color, game-action photos. The 25 players on the Rangers' active roster at press time are included, along with manager Bobby Valentine and unnumbered coaches and trainer cards. The black and white card backs have a smaller portrait photo of each player, as well as biographical information and career statistics.

		MT	NR MT	EX
Complete Set:		6.00	4.50	2.50
Common Player:		.12	.09	.05

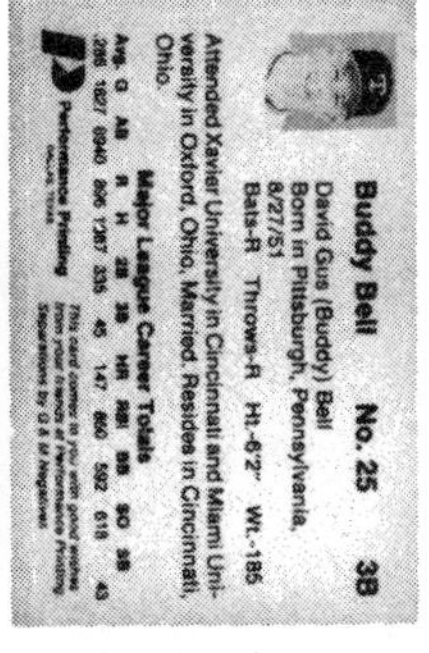

0	Oddibe McDowell	.50	.40	.20
1	Bill Stein	.12	.09	.05
2	Bobby Valentine	.15	.11	.06
3	Wayne Tolleson	.12	.09	.05
4	Don Slaught	.12	.09	.05
5	Alan Bannister	.12	.09	.05
6	Bobby Jones	.12	.09	.05
7	Glenn Brummer	.12	.09	.05
8	Luis Pujols	.12	.09	.05
9	Pete O'Brien	.50	.40	.20
11	Toby Harrah	.20	.15	.08
13	Tommy Dunbar	.12	.09	.05
15	Larry Parrish	.30	.25	.12
16	Mike Mason	.12	.09	.05
19	Curtis Wilkerson	.12	.09	.05
24	Dave Schmidt	.15	.11	.06
25	Buddy Bell	.50	.40	.20
27	Greg Harris	.15	.11	.06
30	Dave Rozema	.12	.09	.05
32	Gary Ward	.20	.15	.08
36	Dickie Noles	.12	.09	.05
41	Chris Welsh	.12	.09	.05
44	Cliff Johnson	.12	.09	.05
46	Burt Hooton	.20	.15	.08
48	Dave Stewart	.40	.30	.15
49	Charlie Hough	.30	.25	.12
---	Trainers (Danny Wheat, Bill Ziegler)	.12	.09	.05
---	Rangers Coaches (Rich Donnelly, Glenn Ezell, Tom House, Art Howe, Wayne Terwilliger)	.12	.09	.05

1986 Performance Printing Rangers

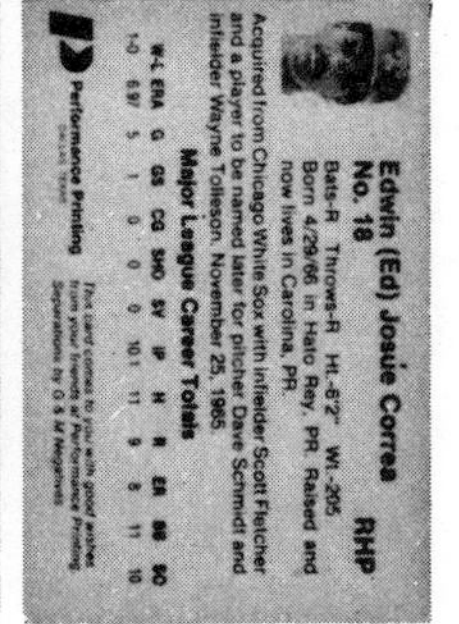

For the second time, the Texas Rangers issued a full-color card set in conjunction with this local printing company. Fronts of the 28-card set include player name, position and team logo beneath the color photo. Backs of the 2-3/8" by 3-1/2" cards are in black and white, with a small portrait photo of each player along with personal and professional statistics. Cards were distributed at the August 23 Rangers home game, and the set includes all of the Rangers' fine rookies such as Bobby Witt, Pete Incaviglia, Edwin Correa and Ruben Sierra.

		MT	NR MT	EX
Complete Set:		10.00	7.50	4.00
Common Player:		.10	.08	.04
0	Oddibe McDowell	.50	.40	.20
1	Scott Fletcher	.20	.15	.08
2	Bobby Valentine	.15	.11	.06
3	Ruben Sierra	5.00	3.75	2.00
4	Don Slaught	.10	.08	.04
9	Pete O'Brien	.40	.30	.15
11	Toby Harrah	.20	.15	.08
12	Geno Petralli	.10	.08	.04
15	Larry Parrish	.25	.20	.10
16	Mike Mason	.10	.08	.04
17	Darrell Porter	.15	.11	.06
18	Edwin Correa	.40	.30	.15
19	Curtis Wilkerson	.10	.08	.04
22	Steve Buechele	.30	.25	.12
23	Jose Guzman	.40	.30	.15
24	Ricky Wright	.10	.08	.04
27	Greg Harris	.15	.11	.06
28	Mitch Williams	.30	.25	.12
29	Pete Incaviglia	1.25	.90	.50
32	Gary Ward	.15	.11	.06
34	Dale Mohorcic	.30	.25	.12
40	Jeff Russell	.10	.08	.04

		MT	NR MT	EX
44	Tom Paciorek	.10	.08	.04
46	Mike Loynd	.30	.25	.12
48	Bobby Witt	.60	.45	.25
49	Charlie Hough	.25	.20	.10
---	Coaching Staff (Joe Ferguson, Tim Foli, Tom House, Art Howe, Tom Robson)	.10	.08	.04
---	Trainers (Danny Wheat, Bill Zeigler)	.10	.08	.04

1981 Perma-Graphics All-Star Credit Cards

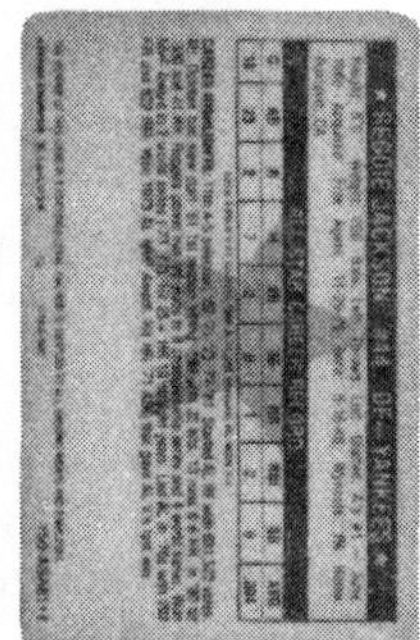

Using the same "credit card" style of its previous 1981 issue, Perma-Graphics issued an 18-card set in the fall of 1981 featuring the starting players from the 1981 All-Star Game. The front of the card contains a full-color photo, plus the player's name, position and team. The back includes personal data, career records, highlights and an "autograph panel."

		MT	NR MT	EX
Complete Set:		30.00	22.50	12.50
Common Player:		.70	.50	.30
1	Gary Carter	1.25	.90	.50
2	Dave Concepcion	.70	.50	.30
3	Andre Dawson	1.25	.90	.50
4	George Foster	.70	.50	.30
5	Davey Lopes	.70	.50	.30
6	Dave Parker	.90	.70	.35
7	Pete Rose	4.00	3.00	1.50
8	Mike Schmidt	3.00	2.25	1.25
9	Fernando Valenzuela	1.25	.90	.50
10	George Brett	2.00	1.50	.80
11	Rod Carew	3.00	2.25	1.25
12	Bucky Dent	.70	.50	.30
13	Carlton Fisk	1.25	.90	.50
14	Reggie Jackson	1.50	1.25	.60
15	Jack Morris	.90	.70	.35
16	Willie Randolph	.70	.50	.30
17	Ken Singleton	.70	.50	.30
18	Dave Winfield	1.25	.90	.50

1981 Perma-Graphics Super Star Credit Cards

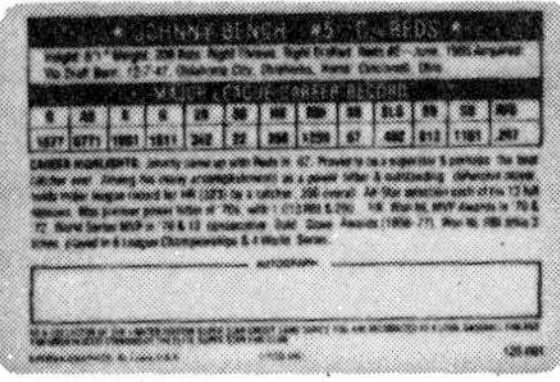

Issued in 1981 by Perma-Graphics of Maryland Heights, Mo., this innovative 32-card set was printed on high-impact, permanently laminated vinyl to give the appearance of a real credit card. The front of the wallet-sized cards includes career statistics and highlights, along with an "autograph panel" for obtaining the player's signature.

		MT	NR MT	EX
Complete Set:		40.00	30.00	15.00
Common Player:		.70	.50	.30

		MT	NR MT	EX
1	Johnny Bench	3.00	2.25	1.25
2	Mike Schmidt	3.00	2.25	1.25
3	George Brett	2.00	1.50	.80
4	Carl Yastrzemski	3.00	2.25	1.25
5	Pete Rose	4.00	3.00	1.50
6	Bob Horner	.70	.50	.30
7	Reggie Jackson	2.50	2.00	1.00
8	Keith Hernandez	1.00	.70	.40
9	George Foster	.70	.50	.30
10	Garry Templeton	.70	.50	.30
11	Tom Seaver	2.00	1.50	.80
12	Steve Garvey	1.25	.90	.50
13	Dave Parker	.75	.60	.30
14	Willie Stargell	1.00	.70	.40
15	Cecil Cooper	.70	.50	.30
16	Steve Carlton	2.00	1.50	.80
17	Ted Simmons	.70	.50	.30
18	Dave Kingman	.70	.50	.30
19	Rickey Henderson	1.50	1.25	.60
20	Fred Lynn	.75	.60	.30
21	Dave Winfield	1.25	.90	.50
22	Rod Carew	2.00	1.50	.80
23	Jim Rice	1.00	.70	.40
24	Bruce Sutter	.70	.50	.30
25	Cesar Cedeno	.70	.50	.30
26	Nolan Ryan	2.00	1.50	.80
27	Dusty Baker	.70	.50	.30
28	Jim Palmer	2.00	1.50	.80
29	Gorman Thomas	.70	.50	.30
30	Ben Oglivie	.70	.50	.30
31	Willie Wilson	.70	.50	.30
32	Gary Carter	1.25	.90	.50

1982 Perma-Graphics All-Star Credit Cards

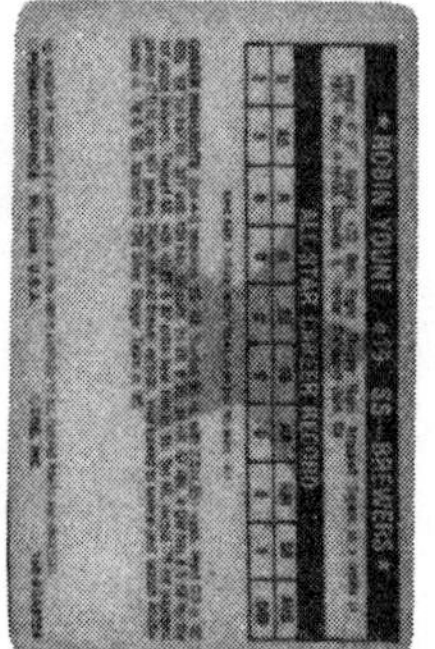

Perma-Graphics issued its second "All-Star Credit Card" set in the fall of 1982. Consisting of 18 cards, the set pictured the starters from both leagues in the 1982 All-Star Game. It was also available in a limited-edition "gold" version, which is generally two to three times the value of the regular edition.

		MT	NR MT	EX
Complete Set:		25.00	20.00	10.00
Common Player:		.50	.40	.20
1	Dennis Eckersley	1.00	.70	.40
2	Cecil Cooper	.60	.45	.25
3	Carlton Fisk	1.00	.70	.40
4	Robin Yount	2.00	1.50	.80
5	Bobby Grich	.60	.45	.25
6	Rickey Henderson	2.00	1.50	.80
7	Reggie Jackson	2.00	1.50	.80
8	Fred Lynn	.75	.60	.30
9	George Brett	2.00	1.50	.80
10	Gary Carter	1.25	.90	.50
11	Dave Concepcion	.60	.45	.25
12	Andre Dawson	1.25	.90	.50
13	Tim Raines	1.25	.90	.50
14	Dale Murphy	1.50	1.25	.60
15	Steve Rogers	.50	.40	.20
16	Pete Rose	3.00	2.25	1.25
17	Mike Schmidt	2.50	2.00	1.00
18	Manny Trillo	.50	.40	.20

1982 Perma Graphics Super Star Credit Cards

Perma-Graphics reduced its "Superstar Credit Card Set" to 24 players in 1982, maintaining the same basic credit card appearance. The player photos on the front of the cards are surrounded by a wood-tone border and the backs include the usual personal data, career statistics, highlights and autograph panel. The set was also issued in a limited-edition "gold" version. The special "gold" cards are generally worth two to three times the value of a regular-edition card.

		MT	NR MT	EX
Complete Set:		35.00	27.50	15.00
Common Player:		.50	.40	.20
1	Johnny Bench	2.00	1.50	.80
2	Tom Seaver	2.00	1.50	.80
3	Mike Schmidt	2.00	1.50	.80
4	Gary Carter	1.25	.90	.50
5	Willie Stargell	1.00	.70	.40
6	Tim Raines	1.25	.90	.50
7	Bill Madlock	.60	.45	.25
8	Keith Hernandez	1.00	.70	.40
9	Pete Rose	3.00	2.25	1.25
10	Steve Carlton	2.00	1.50	.80
11	Steve Garvey	1.25	.90	.50
12	Fernando Valenzuela	1.00	.70	.40
13	Carl Yastrzemski	2.00	1.50	.80
14	Dave Winfield	1.25	.90	.50
15	Carney Lansford	.60	.45	.25
16	Rollie Fingers	.75	.60	.30
17	Tony Armas	.50	.40	.20
18	Cecil Cooper	.60	.45	.25
19	George Brett	2.00	1.50	.80
20	Reggie Jackson	2.00	1.50	.80
21	Rod Carew	2.00	1.50	.80
22	Eddie Murray	1.25	.90	.50
23	Rickey Henderson	2.00	1.50	.80
24	Kirk Gibson	1.00	.70	.40

1983 Perma-Graphics All-Star Credit Cards

The final issue from Perma-Graphics, this 18-card set was produced in the fall of 1983 and features the 18 starting players from the 1983 All-Star Game. Similar to other Perma-Graphics sets, the cards were printed on wallet-size vinyl to give the appearance of a real credit card. The set was also available in a limited-edition "gold" version, which carries a value two to three times a regular set or card.

		MT	NR MT	EX
Complete Set:		25.00	20.00	10.00
Common Player:		.50	.40	.20
1	George Brett	2.00	1.50	.80
2	Rod Carew	2.00	1.50	.80
3	Fred Lynn	.75	.60	.30
4	Jim Rice	1.00	.70	.40
5	Ted Simmons	.60	.45	.25
6	Dave Stieb	.60	.45	.25
7	Manny Trillo	.50	.40	.20
8	Dave Winfield	1.25	.90	.50
9	Robin Yount	2.00	1.50	.80
10	Gary Carter	1.25	.90	.50
11	Andre Dawson	1.50	1.25	.60
12	Dale Murphy	1.50	1.25	.60
13	Al Oliver	.60	.45	.25
14	Tim Raines	1.25	.90	.50
15	Steve Sax	.75	.60	.30
16	Mike Schmidt	2.00	1.50	.80
17	Ozzie Smith	.75	.60	.30
18	Mario Soto	.50	.40	.20

1983 Perma-Graphics Super Star Credit Cards

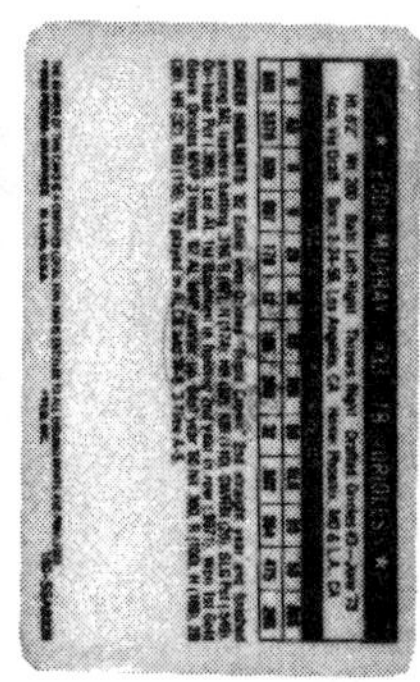

Similar in design to its previous sets, Perma-Graphics increased the number of cards in its 1983 "Superstar" set to 36, including 18 players from each league. The front of the vinyl card has a full-color photo with the player's name, team, league and position below. The backs contain career records, highlights and autograph panel. The cards were also issued in a special "gold" edition, which are valued at two to three times a regular edition card.

		MT	NR MT	EX
Complete Set:		40.00	30.00	15.00
Common Player:		.50	.40	.20
1	Bill Buckner	.60	.45	.25
2	Steve Carlton	2.00	1.50	.90
3	Gary Carter	1.25	.90	.50
4	Andre Dawson	1.50	1.25	.60
5	Pedro Guerrero	.75	.60	.30
6	George Hendrick	.50	.40	.20
7	Keith Hernandez	1.00	.70	.40
8	Bill Madlock	.60	.45	.25
9	Dale Murphy	1.50	1.25	.60
10	Al Oliver	.60	.45	.25
11	Dave Parker	.75	.60	.30
12	Darrell Porter	.50	.40	.20
13	Pete Rose	3.00	2.25	1.25
14	Mike Schmidt	2.00	1.50	.80
15	Lonnie Smith	.50	.40	.20
16	Ozzie Smith	.75	.60	.30
17	Bruce Sutter	.60	.45	.25
18	Fernando Valenzuela	1.00	.70	.40
19	George Brett	2.00	1.50	.80
20	Rod Carew	2.00	1.50	.80
21	Cecil Cooper	.60	.45	.25
22	Doug DeCinces	.50	.40	.20
23	Rollie Fingers	.75	.60	.30
24	Damaso Garcia	.50	.40	.20
25	Toby Harrah	.50	.40	.20
26	Rickey Henderson	2.00	1.50	.80
27	Reggie Jackson	2.00	1.50	.80
28	Hal McRae	.60	.45	.25
29	Eddie Murray	1.25	.90	.50
30	Lance Parrish	1.00	.70	.40
31	Jim Rice	1.00	.70	.40
32	Gorman Thomas	.50	.40	.20
33	Willie Wilson	.60	.45	.25
34	Dave Winfield	1.25	.90	.50
35	Carl Yastrzemski	2.00	1.50	.80
36	Robin Yount	2.00	1.50	.80

1961 Peters Meats Twins

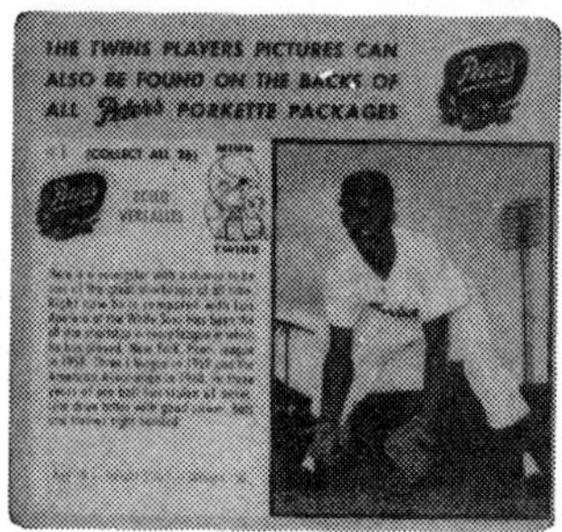

This set, featuring the first-year 1961 Minnesota Twins, is in a large, 4-5/8" by 3-1/2", format. Cards are on thick cardboard and heavily waxed, as they were used as partial packaging for the company's meat products. Card fronts feature full-color photos, team and Peters logos, and biographical information. The cards are blank-backed.

		NR MT	EX	VG
Complete Set:		600.00	300.00	175.00
Common Player:		12.00	6.00	3.50
1	Zoilo Versalles	20.00	10.00	6.00
2	Eddie Lopat	20.00	10.00	6.00
3	Pedro Ramos	12.00	6.00	3.50
4	Charles "Chuck" Stobbs	12.00	6.00	3.50
5	Don Mincher	20.00	10.00	6.00
6	Jack Kralick	12.00	6.00	3.50
7	Jim Kaat	50.00	25.00	15.00

		NR MT	EX	VG
8	Hal Naragon	12.00	6.00	3.50
9	Don Lee	12.00	6.00	3.50
10	Harry "Cookie" Lavagetto	15.00	7.50	4.50
11	Tom "Pete" Whisenant	12.00	6.00	3.50
12	Elmer Valo	12.00	6.00	3.50
13	Ray Moore	12.00	6.00	3.50
14	Billy Gardner	12.00	6.00	3.50
15	Lenny Green	12.00	6.00	3.50
16	Sam Mele	12.00	6.00	3.50
17	Jim Lemon	15.00	7.50	4.50
18	Harmon "Killer" Killebrew	150.00	75.00	45.00
19	Paul Giel	15.00	7.50	4.50
20	Reno Bertoia	12.00	6.00	3.50
21	Clyde McCullough	12.00	6.00	3.50
22	Earl Battey	20.00	10.00	6.00
23	Camilo Pascual	20.00	10.00	6.00
24	Dan Dobbek	12.00	6.00	3.50
25	Joe "Valvy" Valdivielso	12.00	6.00	3.50
26	Billy Consolo	12.00	6.00	3.50

1970 Pictures of Champions Orioles

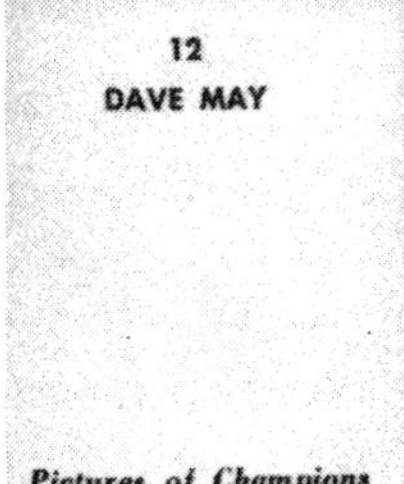

Issued in 1970 in the Baltimore area, this 16-card regional set pictures members of the Baltimore Orioles. The cards measure 2-1/8" by 2-3/4" and feature black and white player photos on orange card stock. Little is known about the method of distribution.

		NR MT	EX	VG
	Complete Set:	30.00	15.00	9.00
	Common Player:	.50	.25	.15
4	Earl Weaver	2.00	1.00	.60
5	Brooks Robinson	10.00	5.00	3.00
7	Mark Belanger	1.25	.60	.40
8	Andy Etchebarren	.50	.25	.15
9	Don Buford	.50	.25	.15
10	Ellie Hendricks	.50	.25	.15
12	Dave May	.50	.25	.15
15	Dave Johnson	2.00	1.00	.60
16	Dave McNally	1.00	.50	.30
20	Frank Robinson	8.00	4.00	2.50
22	Jim Palmer	8.00	4.00	2.50
24	Pete Richert	.50	.25	.15
29	Dick Hall	.50	.25	.15
35	Mike Cuellar	1.00	.50	.30
39	Eddie Watt	.50	.25	.15
40	Dave Leonhard	.50	.25	.15

1939 Play Ball

With the issuance of this card set by Gum Incorporated, a new era of baseball cards was born. Although the cards are black and white, the full-frame, actual photos on the card fronts are of better quality than previously seen, and the 2-1/2" by 3-1/4" size was larger and more popular than the smaller tobacco and caramel cards of the early 20th Century. Card backs featured player names and extensive biographies. There are 162 cards in the set, including superstars Joe DiMaggio and Ted Williams. Card number 126 was never issued. The complete set price does not include all back variations found in the low-numbered series.

		NR MT	EX	VG
	Complete Set:	13500.	6750.	4250.
	Common Player: 1-115	20.00	10.00	6.00
	Common Player: 116-162	115.00	57.00	34.00
1	Alvin Jacob Powell	150.00	40.00	25.00
2a	Lee Theo Grissom (name in upper case letters)	25.00	9.00	5.50
2b	Lee Theo Grissom (name in upper and lower case)	35.00	12.50	7.50
3a	Charles Herbert Ruffing (name in upper case letters)	125.00	62.00	37.00
3b	Charles Herbert Ruffing (name in upper and lower case)	135.00	67.00	40.00
4a	Eldon LeRoy Auker (name in upper case letters)	20.00	10.00	6.00
4b	Eldon LeRoy Auker (name in upper and lower case)	22.00	11.00	6.50
5a	James Luther Sewell (name in upper case letters)	22.00	11.00	6.50
5b	James Luther Sewell (name in upper and lower case)	24.00	12.00	7.25
6a	Leo Ernest Durocher (name in upper case letters)	100.00	50.00	30.00
6b	Leo Ernest Durocher (name in upper and lower case)	125.00	62.00	37.00
7a	Robert Pershing Doerr (name in upper case letters)	100.00	50.00	30.00
7b	Robert Pershing Doerr (name in upper and lower case)	100.00	50.00	30.00
8	Henry Pippen	20.00	10.00	6.00
9a	James Tobin (name in upper case letters)	20.00	10.00	6.00
9b	James Tobin (name in upper and lower case)	22.00	11.00	6.50
10	James Brooklyn DeShong	20.00	10.00	6.00
11	John Costa Rizzo	20.00	10.00	6.00
12	Hershel Ray Martin (Herschel)	20.00	10.00	6.00
13a	Luke Daniel Hamlin (name in upper case letters)	20.00	10.00	6.00
13b	Luke Daniel Hamlin (name in upper and lower case)	22.00	11.00	6.50
14a	James R. Tabor ("...Tabor batted .295,...")	20.00	10.00	6.00
14b	James R. Tabor ("...Tabor batted 295,...")	22.00	11.00	6.50
15a	Paul Derringer (name in upper case letters)	22.00	11.00	6.50
15b	Paul Derringer (name in upper and lower case)	24.00	12.00	7.25
16	John Peacock	20.00	10.00	6.00
17	Emerson Dickman	20.00	10.00	6.00
18a	Harry Danning (name in upper case letters)	20.00	10.00	6.00
18b	Harry Danning (name in upper and lower case)	22.00	11.00	6.50
19	Paul Dean	35.00	17.50	10.50
20	Joseph Heving	20.00	10.00	6.00
21a	Emil Leonard (name in upper case letters)	20.00	10.00	6.00
21b	Emil Leonard (name in upper and lower case)	22.00	11.00	6.50
22a	William Henry Walters (name in upper case letters)	22.00	11.00	6.50
22b	William Henry Walters (name in upper and lower case)	24.00	12.00	7.25
23	Burgess U. Whitehead	20.00	10.00	6.00
24a	Richard S. Coffman (S. Richard) ("...Senators the same year.")	20.00	10.00	6.00
24b	Richard S. Coffman (S. Richard) ("...Browns the same year.")	35.00	17.50	10.50
25a	George Alexander Selkirk (name in upper case letters)	35.00	17.50	10.50
25b	George Alexander Selkirk (name in upper and lower case)	40.00	20.00	12.00
26a	Joseph Paul DiMaggio ("...206 hits in 1938 games...")	1700.	850.00	475.00
26b	Joseph Paul DiMaggio ("...206 hits in 138 games...")	1800.	900.00	550.00
27a	Fred Ray Ostermueller (name in upper case letters)	20.00	10.00	6.00
27b	Fred Ray Ostermueller (name in upper and lower case)	22.00	11.00	6.50
28	Sylvester Johnson	20.00	10.00	6.00
29a	John Francis Wilson (name in upper case letters)	20.00	10.00	6.00
29b	John Francis Wilson (name in upper and lower case)	22.00	11.00	6.50
30a	William Malcolm Dickey (name in upper case letters)	200.00	100.00	60.00
30b	William Malcolm Dickey (name in upper and lower case)	225.00	125.00	70.00
31a	Samuel West (name in upper case letters)	20.00	10.00	6.00
31b	Samuel West (name in upper and lower case)	22.00	11.00	6.50
32	Robert I. Seeds	20.00	10.00	6.00
33	Del Howard Young (name actually Del Edward)	20.00	10.00	6.00
34a	Frank Joseph Demaree (Joseph Franklin) (name in upper case letters)	20.00	10.00	6.00
34b	Frank Joseph Demaree (Joseph Franklin) (name in upper and lower case)	22.00	11.00	6.50
35a	William Frederick Jurges (name in upper case letters)	22.00	11.00	6.50
35b	William Frederick Jurges (name in upper and lower case)	24.00	12.00	7.25
36a	Frank Andrew McCormick (name in upper case letters)	20.00	10.00	6.00
36b	Frank Andrew McCormick (name in upper and lower case)	22.00	11.00	6.50
37	Virgil Lawrence Davis	20.00	10.00	6.00
38a	William Harrison Myers (name in upper case letters)	20.00	10.00	6.00
38b	William Harrison Myers (name in upper and lower case)	22.00	11.00	6.50
39a	Richard Benjamin Ferrell (name in upper case letters)	100.00	50.00	30.00
39b	Richard Benjamin Ferrell (name in upper and lower case)	125.00	62.00	37.00
40	James Charles Bagby Jr.	20.00	10.00	6.00
41a	Lonnie Warneke ("...the earned run department...")	20.00	10.00	6.00
41b	Lonnie Warneke ("...the earned-run department...")	22.00	11.00	6.50
42	Arndt Jorgens	24.00	12.00	7.25
43	Melo Almada	20.00	10.00	6.00
44	Donald Henry Heffner	20.00	10.00	6.00
45a	Merrill May (name in upper case letters)	20.00	10.00	6.00
45b	Merrill May (name in upper and lower case)	22.00	11.00	6.50
46a	Morris Arnovich (name in upper case letters)	20.00	10.00	6.00
46b	Morris Arnovich (name in upper and lower case)	22.00	11.00	6.50
47a	John Kelly Lewis, Jr. (name in upper case letters)	20.00	10.00	6.00
47b	John Kelly Lewis, Jr. (name in upper and lower case)	22.00	11.00	6.50
48a	Vernon Gomez (name in upper case letters)	200.00	100.00	60.00
48b	Vernon Gomez (name in upper and lower case)	225.00	125.00	70.00
49	Edward Miller	20.00	10.00	6.00
50a	Charles Len Gehringer (name actually Charles Leonard) (name in upper case letters)	200.00	100.00	60.00
50b	Charles Len Gehringer (name actually Charles Leonard) (name in upper & lower case)	225.00	125.00	70.00
51a	Melvin Thomas Ott (name in upper case)	200.00	100.00	60.00
51b	Melvin Thomas Ott (name in upper and lower case)	225.00	125.00	70.00
52a	Thomas D. Henrich (name in upper case letters)	40.00	20.00	12.00
52b	Thomas D. Henrich (name in upper and lower case)	45.00	22.00	13.50
53a	Carl Owen Hubbell (name in upper case letters)	200.00	100.00	60.00
53b	Carl Owen Hubbell (name in upper and lower case)	225.00	125.00	70.00
54a	Harry Edward Gumbert (name in upper case letters)	20.00	10.00	6.00
54b	Harry Edward Gumbert (name in upper and lower case)	22.00	11.00	6.50
55a	Floyd E. Vaughan (Joseph Floyd) (name in upper case letters)	115.00	57.00	34.00
55b	Floyd E. Vaughan (Joseph Floyd) (name in upper and lower case)	125.00	62.00	37.00
56a	Henry Greenberg (name in upper case letters)	150.00	75.00	45.00
56b	Henry Greenberg (name in upper and lower case)	160.00	80.00	48.00
57a	John A. Hassett (name in upper case letters)	20.00	10.00	6.00
57b	John A. Hassett (name in upper and lower case)	22.00	11.00	6.50
58	Louis Peo Chiozza	20.00	10.00	6.00
59	Kendall Chase	20.00	10.00	6.00
60a	Lynwood Thomas Rowe (name in upper case letters)	22.00	11.00	6.50
60b	Lynwood Thomas Rowe (name in upper and lower case)	24.00	12.00	7.25
61a	Anthony F. Cuccinello (name in upper case letters)	20.00	10.00	6.00
61b	Anthony F. Cuccinello (name in upper and lower case)	22.00	11.00	6.50
62	Thomas Carey	20.00	10.00	6.00
63	Emmett Mueller	20.00	10.00	6.00
64a	Wallace Moses, Jr. (name in upper case letters)	20.00	10.00	6.00
64b	Wallace Moses, Jr. (name in upper and lower case)	22.00	11.00	6.50
65a	Harry Francis Craft (name in upper case letters)	20.00	10.00	6.00
65b	Harry Francis Craft (name in upper and lower case)	22.00	11.00	6.50
66	James A. Ripple	20.00	10.00	6.00
67	Edwin Joost	20.00	10.00	6.00
68	Fred Singleton	20.00	10.00	6.00
69	Elbert Preston Fletcher (Elburt)	20.00	10.00	6.00
70	Fred Maloy Frankhouse (Meloy)	20.00	10.00	6.00
71a	Marcellus Monte Pearson (name actually Montgomery Marcellus) (name in upper case)	24.00	12.00	7.25
71b	Marcellus Monte Pearson (name actually Montgomery Marcellus) (name in upper & lower)	35.00	17.50	10.50
72a	Debs Garms (Born: Bango, Tex.)	20.00	10.00	6.00
72b	Debs Garms (Born: Bangs, Tex.)	25.00	12.50	7.50
73a	Harold H. Schumacher (Born: Dolgville, N.Y.)	22.00	11.00	6.50
73b	Harold H. Schumacher (Born: Dolgeville, N.Y.)	40.00	20.00	12.00
74a	Harry A. Lavagetto (name in upper case letters)	24.00	12.00	7.25
74b	Harry A. Lavagetto (name in upper and lower case)	15.00	7.50	4.50
75a	Stanley Bordagaray (name in upper case letters)	20.00	10.00	6.00
75b	Stanley Bordagaray (name in upper and lower case)	22.00	11.00	6.50
76	Goodwin George Rosen	20.00	10.00	6.00
77	Lewis Sidney Riggs	20.00	10.00	6.00
78a	Julius Joseph Solters (name in upper case letters)	20.00	10.00	6.00
78b	Julius Joseph Solters (name in upper and lower case)	22.00	11.00	6.50
79a	Joseph Gregg Moore (given name is Joe) (Weight: 157 lbs.)	20.00	10.00	6.00
79b	Joseph Gregg Moore (given name is Joe) (Weight: 175 lbs.)	25.00	12.50	7.50
80a	Irwin Fox (Ervin) (Weight: 165 lbs.)	20.00	10.00	6.00
80b	Irwin Fox (Ervin) (Weight: 157 lbs.)	25.00	12.50	7.50
81a	Ellsworth Dahlgren (name in upper case letters)	24.00	12.00	7.25
81b	Ellsworth Dahlgren (name in upper and lower case)	35.00	17.50	10.50

		NR MT	EX	VG
82a	Charles Herbert Klein (name in upper case letters)	165.00	82.00	49.00
82b	Charles Herbert Klein (name in upper and lower case)	175.00	87.00	52.00
83a	August Richard Suhr (name in upper case letters)	20.00	10.00	6.00
83b	August Richard Suhr (name in upper and lower case)	22.00	11.00	6.50
84	Lamar Newsome	20.00	10.00	6.00
85	John Walter Cooney	20.00	10.00	6.00
86a	Adolph Camilli (Adolf) ("...start of the 1928 season,...")	22.00	11.00	6.50
86b	Adolph Camilli (Adolf) ("...start of the 1938 season,...")	35.00	17.50	10.50
87	Milburn G. Shoffner (middle initial actually J.)	20.00	10.00	6.00
88	Charles Keller	50.00	25.00	15.00
89a	Lloyd James Waner (name in upper case letters)	125.00	62.00	37.00
89b	Lloyd James Waner (name in upper and lower case)	135.00	67.00	40.00
90a	Robert H. Klinger (name in upper case letters)	20.00	10.00	6.00
90b	Robert H. Klinger (name in upper and lower case)	22.00	11.00	6.50
91a	John H. Knott (name in upper case letters)	20.00	10.00	6.00
91b	John H. Knott (name in upper and lower case)	22.00	11.00	6.50
92a	Ted Williams (name in upper case letters)	1500.	750.00	450.00
92b	Ted Williams (name in upper and lower case)	1800.	900.00	550.00
93	Charles M. Gelbert	20.00	10.00	6.00
94	Henry E. Manush	115.00	57.00	34.00
95a	Whitlow Wyatt (name in upper case letters)	22.00	11.00	6.50
95b	Whitlow Wyatt (name in upper and lower case)	24.00	12.00	7.25
96a	Ernest Gordon Phelps (name in upper case letters)	22.00	11.00	6.50
96b	Ernest Gordon Phelps (name in upper and lower case)	24.00	12.00	7.25
97a	Robert Lee Johnson (name in upper case letters)	20.00	10.00	6.00
97b	Robert Lee Johnson (name in upper and lower case)	22.00	11.00	6.50
98	Arthur Carter Whitney	20.00	10.00	6.00
99a	Walter Anton Berger (name in upper case letters)	22.00	11.00	6.50
99b	Walter Anton Berger (name in upper and lower case)	24.00	12.00	7.25
100a	Charles Solomon Myer (name in upper case letters)	20.00	10.00	6.00
100b	Charles Solomon Myer (name in upper and lower case)	22.00	11.00	6.50
101a	Roger M. Cramer ("...the Martinburg Club...")	20.00	10.00	6.00
101b	Roger M. Cramer ("...the Martinsburg Club...")	25.00	12.50	7.50
102a	Lemuel Floyd Young (name in upper case letters)	20.00	10.00	6.00
102b	Lemuel Floyd Young (name in upper and lower case)	22.00	11.00	6.50
103	Morris Berg	22.00	11.00	6.50
104a	Thomas Davis Bridges ("...280 games, winning 283,...")	22.00	11.00	6.50
104b	Thomas Davis Bridges ("...280 games, winning 133,...")	35.00	17.50	10.50
105a	Donald Eric McNair (name in upper case letters)	20.00	10.00	6.00
105b	Donald Eric McNair (name in upper and lower case)	22.00	11.00	6.50
106	Albert Stark	20.00	10.00	6.00
107	Joseph Franklin Vosmik	20.00	10.00	6.00
108a	Frank Witman Hayes (name in upper case letters)	20.00	10.00	6.00
108b	Frank Witman Hayes (name in upper and lower case)	22.00	11.00	6.50
109a	Myril Hoag (name in upper case letters)	20.00	10.00	6.00
109b	Myril Hoag (name in upper and lower case)	22.00	11.00	6.50
110	Fred L. Fitzsimmons	22.00	11.00	6.50
111a	Van Lingle Mungo (name in upper case letters)	35.00	17.50	10.50
111b	Van Lingle Mungo (name in upper and lower case)	40.00	20.00	12.00
112a	Paul Glee Waner ("...Waner, the older...")	125.00	62.00	37.00
112b	Paul Glee Waner ("...Waner, the elder...")	150.00	75.00	45.00
113	Al Schacht	25.00	12.50	7.50
114a	Cecil Travis (name in upper case letters)	20.00	10.00	6.00
114b	Cecil Travis (name in upper and lower case)	22.00	11.00	6.50
115a	Ralph Kress (name in upper case letters)	20.00	10.00	6.00
115b	Ralph Kress (name in upper and lower case)	22.00	11.00	6.50
116	Eugene A. Desautels	115.00	57.00	34.00
117	Wayne Ambler	115.00	57.00	34.00
118	Lynn Nelson	115.00	57.00	34.00
119	Willard McKee Hershberger	115.00	57.00	34.00
120	Harold Benton Warstler (middle name actually Burton)	115.00	57.00	34.00
121	William J. Posedel	115.00	57.00	34.00
122	George Hartley McQuinn	115.00	57.00	34.00
123	Ray T. Davis	115.00	57.00	34.00
124	Walter George Brown	115.00	57.00	34.00
125	Clifford George Melton	115.00	57.00	34.00
126	Not Issued			
127	Gilbert Herman Brack	115.00	57.00	34.00
128	Joseph Emil Bowman	115.00	57.00	34.00
129	William Swift	115.00	57.00	34.00
130	Wilbur Lee Brubaker	115.00	57.00	34.00
131	Morton Cecil Cooper	115.00	57.00	34.00
132	James Roberson Brown	115.00	57.00	34.00
133	Lynn Myers	115.00	57.00	34.00
134	Forrest Pressnell	115.00	57.00	34.00
135	Arnold Malcolm Owen	115.00	57.00	34.00
136	Roy Chester Bell	115.00	57.00	34.00
137	Peter William Appleton	115.00	57.00	34.00
138	George Washington Case Jr.	115.00	57.00	34.00
139	Vitautas C. Tamulis	115.00	57.00	34.00
140	Raymond Hall Hayworth	115.00	57.00	34.00
141	Peter Coscarart	115.00	57.00	34.00
142	Ira Kendall Hutchinson	115.00	57.00	34.00
143	Howard Earl Averill	275.00	140.00	85.00
144	Henry J. Bonura	115.00	57.00	34.00
145	Hugh Noyes Mulcahy	115.00	57.00	34.00
146	Thomas Sunkel	115.00	57.00	34.00
147	George D. Coffman	115.00	57.00	34.00
148	William Trotter	115.00	57.00	34.00
149	Max Edward West	115.00	57.00	34.00
150	James Elton Walkup	115.00	57.00	34.00
151	Hugh Thomas Casey	125.00	62.00	37.00
152	Roy Weatherly	115.00	57.00	34.00
153	Paul H. Trout	125.00	62.00	37.00
154	John W. Hudson	115.00	57.00	34.00
155	James Paul Outlaw (middle name actually Paulus)	115.00	57.00	34.00
156	Raymond Berres	115.00	57.00	34.00
157	Donald Willard Padgett (middle name actually Wilson)	115.00	57.00	34.00
158	Luther Baxter Thomas	115.00	57.00	34.00
159	Russell E. Evans	115.00	57.00	34.00
160	Eugene Moore Jr.	115.00	57.00	34.00
161	Linus Reinhard Frey	135.00	67.00	40.00
162	Lloyd Albert Moore	250.00	90.00	55.00

1940 Play Ball

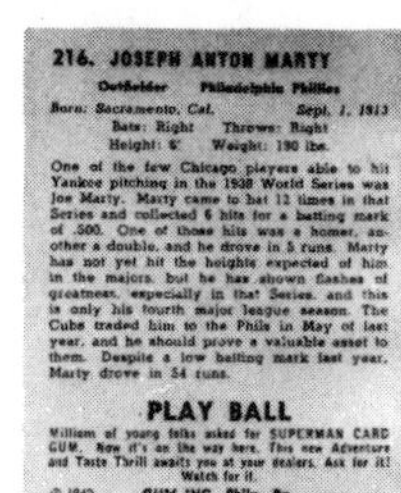

Following the success of their initial effort in 1939, Gum Incorporated issued a bigger and better set in 1940. The 240 black and white cards are once again in the 2-1/2" by 3-1/8" size, but the photos on the card fronts are enclosed by a frame which listed the player's name. Card backs again offer extensive biographies. Backs are also dated. A number of old-timers were issued along with the current day's players, and many Hall of Famers are included. The final 60 cards of the set are more difficult to obtain.

	NR MT	EX	VG
Complete Set:	20000.	10000.	6000.
Common Player: 1-120	22.00	11.00	6.50
Common Player: 121-180	25.00	12.50	7.50
Common Player: 181-240	80.00	40.00	24.00

		NR MT	EX	VG
1	Joe DiMaggio	2000.	1000.	600.00
2	"Art" Jorgens	25.00	12.50	7.50
3	"Babe" Dahlgren	25.00	12.50	7.50
4	"Tommy" Henrich	35.00	17.50	10.50
5	"Monte" Pearson	25.00	12.50	7.50
6	"Lefty" Gomez	200.00	100.00	60.00
7	"Bill" Dickey	200.00	100.00	60.00
8	"Twinkletoes" Selkirk	25.00	12.50	7.50
9	"Charley" Keller	35.00	17.50	10.50
10	"Red" Ruffing	75.00	37.00	22.00
11	"Jake" Powell	25.00	12.50	7.50
12	"Johnny" Schulte	25.00	12.50	7.50
13	"Jack" Knott	22.00	11.00	6.50
14	"Rabbit" McNair	22.00	11.00	6.50
15	George Case	22.00	11.00	6.50
16	Cecil Travis	22.00	11.00	6.50
17	"Buddy" Myer	22.00	11.00	6.50
18	"Charley" Gelbert	22.00	11.00	6.50
19	"Ken" Chase	22.00	11.00	6.50
20	"Buddy" Lewis	22.00	11.00	6.50
21	"Rick" Ferrell	65.00	32.00	19.50
22	"Sammy" West	22.00	11.00	6.50
23	"Dutch" Leonard	22.00	11.00	6.50
24	Frank "Blimp" Hayes	22.00	11.00	6.50
25	"Cherokee" Bob Johnson	22.00	11.00	6.50
26	"Wally" Moses	22.00	11.00	6.50
27	"Ted" Williams	1800.	900.00	550.00
28	"Gene" Desautels	22.00	11.00	6.50
29	"Doc" Cramer	22.00	11.00	6.50
30	"Moe" Berg	25.00	12.50	7.50
31	"Jack" Wilson	22.00	11.00	6.50
32	"Jim" Bagby	22.00	11.00	6.50
33	"Fritz" Ostermueller	22.00	11.00	6.50
34	John Peacock	22.00	11.00	6.50
35	"Joe" Heving	22.00	11.00	6.50
36	"Jim" Tabor	22.00	11.00	6.50
37	Emerson Dickman	22.00	11.00	6.50
38	"Bobby" Doerr	100.00	50.00	30.00
39	"Tom" Carey	22.00	11.00	6.50
40	"Hank" Greenberg	250.00	125.00	75.00
41	"Charley" Gehringer	150.00	75.00	45.00
42	"Bud" Thomas	22.00	11.00	6.50
43	Pete Fox	22.00	11.00	6.50
44	"Dizzy" Trout	25.00	12.50	7.50
45	"Red" Kress	22.00	11.00	6.50
46	Earl Averill	100.00	50.00	30.00
47	"Old Os" Vitt	22.00	11.00	6.50
48	"Luke" Sewell	25.00	12.50	7.50
49	"Stormy Weather" Weatherly	22.00	11.00	6.50
50	"Hal" Trosky	22.00	11.00	6.50
51	"Don" Heffner	22.00	11.00	6.50
52	Myril Hoag	22.00	11.00	6.50
53	"Mac" McQuinn	22.00	11.00	6.50
54	"Bill" Trotter	22.00	11.00	6.50
55	"Slick" Coffman	22.00	11.00	6.50
56	"Eddie" Miller	22.00	11.00	6.50
57	Max West	22.00	11.00	6.50
58	"Bill" Posedel	22.00	11.00	6.50
59	"Rabbit" Warstler	22.00	11.00	6.50
60	John Cooney	22.00	11.00	6.50
61	"Tony" Cuccinello	22.00	11.00	6.50
62	"Buddy" Hassett	22.00	11.00	6.50
63	"Pete" Cascarart	22.00	11.00	6.50
64	"Van" Mungo	30.00	15.00	9.00
65	"Fitz" Fitzsimmons	25.00	12.50	7.50
66	"Babe" Phelps	25.00	12.50	7.50
67	"Whit" Wyatt	25.00	12.50	7.50
68	"Dolph" Camilli	25.00	12.50	7.50
69	"Cookie" Lavagetto	25.00	12.50	7.50
70	"Hot Potato" Hamlin	22.00	11.00	6.50
71	"Mel" Almada	22.00	11.00	6.50
72	"Chuck" Dressen	25.00	12.50	7.50
73	"Bucky" Walters	25.00	12.50	7.50
74	"Duke" Derringer	25.00	12.50	7.50
75	"Buck" McCormick	22.00	11.00	6.50
76	"Lonny" Frey	22.00	11.00	6.50
77	"Bill" Hershberger	22.00	11.00	6.50
78	"Lew" Riggs	22.00	11.00	6.50
79	"Wildfire" Craft	22.00	11.00	6.50
80	"Bill" Myers	22.00	11.00	6.50
81	"Wally" Berger	25.00	12.50	7.50
82	"Hank" Gowdy	22.00	11.00	6.50
83	"Clif" Melton (Cliff)	22.00	11.00	6.50
84	"Jo-Jo" Moore	22.00	11.00	6.50
85	"Hal" Schumacher	25.00	12.50	7.50
86	Harry Gumbert	22.00	11.00	6.50
87	Carl Hubbell	200.00	100.00	60.00
88	"Mel" Ott	200.00	100.00	60.00
89	"Bill" Jurges	25.00	12.50	7.50
90	Frank Demaree	22.00	11.00	6.50
91	Bob "Suitcase" Seeds	22.00	11.00	6.50
92	"Whitey" Whitehead	22.00	11.00	6.50
93	Harry "The Horse" Danning	22.00	11.00	6.50
94	"Gus" Suhr	22.00	11.00	6.50
95	"Mul" Mulcahy	22.00	11.00	6.50
96	"Heinie" Mueller	22.00	11.00	6.50
97	"Morry" Arnovich	22.00	11.00	6.50
98	"Pinky" May	22.00	11.00	6.50
99	"Syl" Johnson	22.00	11.00	6.50
100	"Hersh" Martin	22.00	11.00	6.50
101	"Del" Young	22.00	11.00	6.50
102	"Chuck" Klein	150.00	75.00	45.00
103	"Elbie" Fletcher	22.00	11.00	6.50
104	"Big Poison" Waner	150.00	75.00	45.00
105	"Little Poison" Waner	150.00	75.00	45.00
106	"Pep" Young	22.00	11.00	6.50
107	"Arky" Vaughan	100.00	50.00	30.00
108	"Johnny" Rizzo	22.00	11.00	6.50
109	"Don" Padgett	22.00	11.00	6.50
110	"Tom" Sunkel	22.00	11.00	6.50
111	"Mickey" Owen	22.00	11.00	6.50
112	"Jimmy" Brown	22.00	11.00	6.50
113	"Mort" Cooper	22.00	11.00	6.50
114	"Lon" Warneke	22.00	11.00	6.50
115	"Mike" Gonzales (Gonzalez)	22.00	11.00	6.50
116	"Al" Schacht	25.00	12.50	7.50
117	"Dolly" Stark	22.00	11.00	6.50
118	"Schoolboy" Hoyt	100.00	50.00	30.00
119	"Ol Pete" Alexander	180.00	90.00	54.00
120	Walter "Big Train" Johnson	275.00	137.00	82.00
121	Atley Donald	25.00	12.50	7.50
122	"Sandy" Sundra	25.00	12.50	7.50
123	"Hildy" Hildebrand	25.00	12.50	7.50
124	"Colonel" Combs	135.00	67.00	40.00
125	"Art" Fletcher	25.00	12.50	7.50
126	"Jake" Solters	25.00	12.50	7.50
127	"Muddy" Ruel	25.00	12.50	7.50
128	"Pete" Appleton	25.00	12.50	7.50
129	"Bucky" Harris	100.00	50.00	30.00
130	"Deerfoot" Milan	25.00	12.50	7.50
131	"Zeke" Bonura	25.00	12.50	7.50
132	Connie Mack	225.00	112.00	67.00
133	"Jimmie" Foxx	275.00	137.00	82.00
134	"Joe" Cronin	150.00	75.00	45.00
135	"Line Drive" Nelson	25.00	12.50	7.50
136	"Cotton" Pippen	25.00	12.50	7.50
137	"Bing" Miller	25.00	12.50	7.50
138	"Beau" Bell	25.00	12.50	7.50
139	Elden Auker (Eldon)	25.00	12.50	7.50
140	"Dick" Coffman	25.00	12.50	7.50
141	"Casey" Stengel	200.00	100.00	60.00
142	"Highpockets" Kelly	100.00	50.00	30.00
143	"Gene" Moore	25.00	12.50	7.50
144	"Joe" Vosmik	25.00	12.50	7.50
145	"Vito" Tamulis	25.00	12.50	7.50
146	"Tot" Pressnell	25.00	12.50	7.50
147	"Johnny" Hudson	25.00	12.50	7.50
148	"Hugh" Casey	25.00	12.50	7.50
149	"Pinky" Shoffner	25.00	12.50	7.50
150	"Whitey" Moore	25.00	12.50	7.50
151	Edwin Joost	25.00	12.50	7.50
152	"Jimmy" Wilson	25.00	12.50	7.50
153	"Bill" McKechnie	100.00	50.00	30.00
154	"Jumbo" Brown	25.00	12.50	7.50
155	"Ray" Hayworth	25.00	12.50	7.50
156	"Daffy" Dean	30.00	15.00	9.00
157	"Lou" Chiozza	25.00	12.50	7.50
158	"Stonewall" Jackson	100.00	50.00	30.00
159	"Pancho" Snyder	25.00	12.50	7.50
160	"Hans" Lobert	25.00	12.50	7.50
161	"Debs" Garms	25.00	12.50	7.50
162	"Joe" Bowman	25.00	12.50	7.50
163	"Spud" Davis	25.00	12.50	7.50
164	"Ray" Berres	25.00	12.50	7.50
165	"Bob" Klinger	25.00	12.50	7.50
166	"Bill" Brubaker	25.00	12.50	7.50
167	"Frankie" Frisch	150.00	75.00	45.00

		NR MT	EX	VG
168	"Honus" Wagner	275.00	137.00	82.00
169	"Gabby" Street	25.00	12.50	7.50
170	"Tris" Speaker	250.00	125.00	75.00
171	Harry Heilmann	150.00	75.00	45.00
172	"Chief" Bender	150.00	75.00	45.00
173	"Larry" Lajoie	275.00	137.00	82.00
174	"Johnny" Evers	150.00	75.00	45.00
175	"Christy" Mathewson	275.00	137.00	82.00
176	"Heinie" Manush	150.00	75.00	45.00
177	Frank "Homerun" Baker	150.00	75.00	45.00
178	Max Carey	150.00	75.00	45.00
179	George Sisler	135.00	67.00	40.00
180	"Mickey" Cochrane	150.00	75.00	45.00
181	"Spud" Chandler	80.00	40.00	25.00
182	"Knick" Knickerbocker	80.00	40.00	25.00
183	Marvin Breuer	80.00	40.00	25.00
184	"Mule" Haas	80.00	40.00	24.00
185	"Joe" Kuhel	80.00	40.00	24.00
186	Taft Wright	80.00	40.00	24.00
187	"Jimmy" Dykes	60.00	30.00	18.00
188	"Joe" Krakauskas	80.00	40.00	24.00
189	"Jim" Bloodworth	80.00	40.00	24.00
190	"Charley" Berry	80.00	40.00	24.00
191	John Babich	80.00	40.00	24.00
192	"Dick" Siebert	80.00	40.00	24.00
193	"Chubby" Dean	80.00	40.00	24.00
194	"Sam" Chapman	80.00	40.00	24.00
195	"Dee" Miles	80.00	40.00	24.00
196	"Nonny" Nonnenkamp	80.00	40.00	24.00
197	"Lou" Finney	80.00	40.00	24.00
198	"Denny" Galehouse	80.00	40.00	24.00
199	"Pinky" Higgins	80.00	40.00	24.00
200	"Soupy" Campbell	80.00	40.00	24.00
201	Barney McCosky	80.00	40.00	24.00
202	"Al" Milnar	80.00	40.00	24.00
203	"Bad News" Hale	80.00	40.00	24.00
204	Harry Eisenstat	80.00	40.00	24.00
205	"Rollie" Hemsley	80.00	40.00	24.00
206	"Chet" Laabs	80.00	40.00	24.00
207	"Gus" Mancuso	80.00	40.00	24.00
208	Lee Gamble	80.00	40.00	24.00
209	"Hy" Vandenberg	80.00	40.00	24.00
210	"Bill" Lohrman	80.00	40.00	24.00
211	"Pop" Joiner	80.00	40.00	24.00
212	"Babe" Young	80.00	40.00	24.00
213	John Rucker	80.00	40.00	24.00
214	"Ken" O'Dea	80.00	40.00	24.00
215	"Johnnie" McCarthy	80.00	40.00	24.00
216	"Joe" Marty	80.00	40.00	24.00
217	Walter Beck	80.00	40.00	24.00
218	"Wally" Millies	80.00	40.00	24.00
219	"Russ" Bauers	80.00	40.00	24.00
220	Mace Brown	80.00	40.00	24.00
221	Lee Handley	80.00	40.00	24.00
222	"Max" Butcher	80.00	40.00	24.00
223	Hugh "Ee-Yah" Jennings	150.00	75.00	45.00
224	"Pie" Traynor	250.00	125.00	75.00
225	"Shoeless Joe" Jackson	1500.	750.00	450.00
226	Harry Hooper	150.00	75.00	45.00
227	"Pop" Haines	150.00	75.00	45.00
228	"Charley" Grimm	80.00	40.00	25.00
229	"Buck" Herzog	80.00	40.00	24.00
230	"Red" Faber	150.00	75.00	45.00
231	"Dolf" Luque	80.00	40.00	24.00
232	"Goose" Goslin	150.00	75.00	45.00
233	"Moose" Earnshaw	80.00	40.00	24.00
234	Frank "Husk" Chance	200.00	100.00	60.00
235	John J. McGraw	250.00	125.00	75.00
236	"Sunny Jim" Bottomley	150.00	75.00	45.00
237	"Wee Willie" Keeler	225.00	112.00	67.00
238	"Poosh 'Em Up Tony" Lazzeri	100.00	50.00	30.00
239	George Uhle	80.00	40.00	25.00
240	"Bill" Atwood	200.00	60.00	35.00

1941 Play Ball

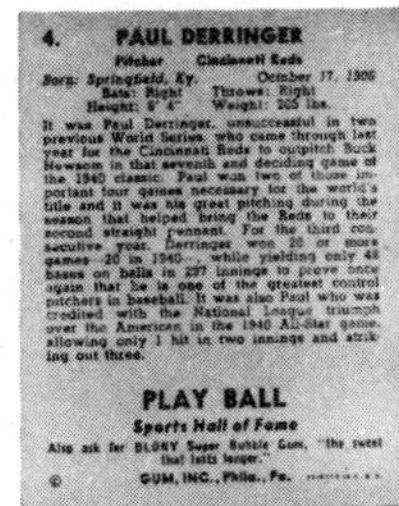
4. PAUL DERRINGER

Pitcher Cincinnati Reds

Born: Springfield, Ky. October 17, 1906

Bats: Right Throws: Right

It was Paul Derringer, unsuccessful in two previous World Series, who came through last year for the Cincinnati Reds to outpitch Buck Newsom in that seventh and deciding game of the 1940 classic. Paul won two of those important four games necessary for the world's title and it was his great pitching during the season that helped bring the Reds to their second straight pennant. For the third consecutive year, Derringer won 20 or more games—20 in 1940—, while yielding only 48 bases on balls in 297 innings to prove once again that he is one of the greatest control pitchers in baseball. It was also Paul who was credited with the National League triumph over the American in the 1940 All-Star game, allowing only 1 hit in two innings and striking out three.

PLAY BALL

Sports Hall of Fame

Also ask for BLONY Super Bubble Gum, "the sweet that lasts longer."

© GUM, INC., Phila., Pa.

While the card backs are quite similar to the black and white cards Gum Incorporated issued in 1940, the card fronts in the 1941 set are printed in color. Many of the card photos, however, are just color versions of the player's 1940 card. The cards are still in the 2-1/2" by 3-1/8" size, but only 72 cards are included in the set. Joe DiMaggio and Ted Williams continue to be the key players in the set, while card numbers 49-72 are rarer than the lower-numbered cards. The cards were printed in sheets, and can still be found that way, or in paper strips, lacking the cardboard backing.

		NR MT	EX	VG
Complete Set:		14500.	6500.	4000.
Common Player: 1-48		55.00	27.00	16.50
Common Player: 49-72		75.00	37.00	22.00
1	"Eddie" Miller	200.00	100.00	60.00
2	Max West	55.00	27.00	16.50
3	"Bucky" Walters	55.00	27.00	16.50
4	"Duke" Derringer	75.00	37.00	22.00
5	"Buck" McCormick	55.00	27.00	16.50
6	Carl Hubbell	250.00	125.00	75.00
7	"The Horse" Danning	55.00	27.00	16.50
8	"Mel" Ott	300.00	150.00	90.00
9	"Pinky" May	55.00	27.00	16.50
10	"Arky" Vaughan	75.00	37.00	22.00
11	Debs Garms	55.00	27.00	16.50
12	"Jimmy" Brown	55.00	27.00	16.50
13	"Jimmie" Foxx	375.00	187.00	110.00
14	"Ted" Williams	2000.	1000.	600.00
15	"Joe" Cronin	175.00	87.00	50.00
16	"Hal" Trosky	55.00	27.00	16.50
17	"Stormy" Weatherly	55.00	27.00	16.50
18	"Hank" Greenberg	350.00	175.00	105.00
19	"Charley" Gehringer	250.00	125.00	75.00
20	"Red" Ruffing	175.00	87.00	50.00
21	"Charlie" Keller	75.00	37.00	22.00
22	"Indian Bob" Johnson	55.00	27.00	16.50
23	"Mac" McQuinn	55.00	27.00	16.50
24	"Dutch" Leonard	55.00	27.00	16.50
25	"Gene" Moore	55.00	27.00	16.50
26	Harry "Gunboat" Gumbert	55.00	27.00	16.50
27	"Babe" Young	55.00	27.00	16.50
28	"Joe" Marty	55.00	27.00	16.50
29	"Jack" Wilson	55.00	27.00	16.50
30	"Lou" Finney	55.00	27.00	16.50
31	"Joe" Kuhel	55.00	27.00	16.50
32	Taft Wright	55.00	27.00	16.50
33	"Happy" Milnar	55.00	27.00	16.50
34	"Rollie" Hemsley	55.00	27.00	16.50
35	"Pinky" Higgins	55.00	27.00	16.50
36	Barney McCosky	55.00	27.00	16.50
37	"Soupy" Campbell	55.00	27.00	16.50
38	Atley Donald	75.00	37.00	22.00
39	"Tommy" Henrich	75.00	37.00	22.00
40	"Johnny" Babich	55.00	27.00	16.50
41	Frank "Blimp" Hayes	55.00	27.00	16.50
42	"Wally" Moses	55.00	27.00	16.50
43	Albert "Bronk" Brancato	55.00	27.00	16.50
44	"Sam" Chapman	55.00	27.00	16.50
45	Elden Auker (Eldon)	55.00	27.00	16.50
46	"Sid" Hudson	55.00	27.00	16.50
47	"Buddy" Lewis	55.00	27.00	16.50
48	Cecil Travis	55.00	27.00	16.50
49	"Babe" Dahlgren	75.00	37.00	22.00
50	"Johnny" Cooney	75.00	37.00	22.00
51	"Dolph" Camilli	55.00	27.00	16.50
52	Kirby Higbe	75.00	37.00	22.00
53	Luke "Hot Potato" Hamlin	75.00	37.00	22.00
54	"Pee Wee" Reese	600.00	300.00	175.00
55	"Whit" Wyatt	75.00	37.00	22.00
56	"Vandy" Vander Meer	75.00	37.00	22.00
57	"Moe" Arnovich	75.00	37.00	22.00
58	"Frank" Demaree	75.00	37.00	22.00
59	"Bill" Jurges	75.00	37.00	22.00
60	"Chuck" Klein	250.00	125.00	75.00
61	"Vince" DiMaggio	200.00	100.00	60.00
62	"Elbie" Fletcher	75.00	37.00	22.00
63	"Dom" DiMaggio	200.00	100.00	60.00
64	"Bobby" Doerr	225.00	112.00	70.00
65	"Tommy" Bridges	75.00	37.00	22.00
66	Harland Clift (Harlond)	75.00	37.00	22.00
67	"Walt" Judnich	75.00	37.00	22.00
68	"Jack" Knott	75.00	37.00	22.00
69	George Case	75.00	37.00	22.00
70	"Bill" Dickey	650.00	325.00	200.00
71	"Joe" DiMaggio	2500.	1250.	750.00
72	"Lefty" Gomez	700.00	300.00	175.00

1976 Playboy Press Who Was Harry Steinfeldt?

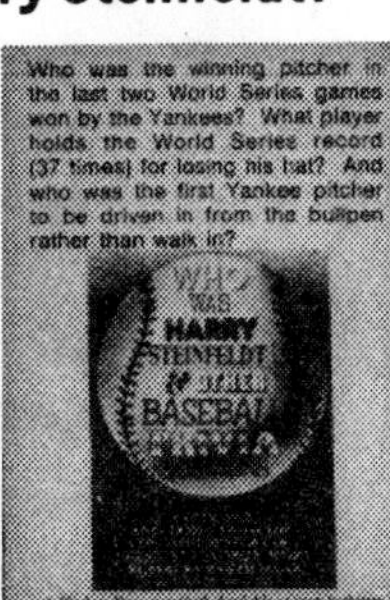
Who was the winning pitcher in the last two World Series games won by the Yankees? What player holds the World Series record (37 times) for losing his hat? And who was the first Yankee pitcher to be driven in from the bullpen rather than walk in?

This 12-card set was issued in 1976 by Playboy Press to promote author Bert Randolph Sugar's book "Who Was Harry Steinfeldt? & Other Baseball Trivia Questions." (Steinfeldt was the third baseman in the Cubs' famous infield that featured Hall of Famers Tinker, Evers and Chance). The black and white cards measure the standard 2-1/2" by 3-1/2" with a player photo on the front and a trivia question and ad for the book on the back.

		NR MT	EX	VG
Complete Set:		90.00	45.00	27.00
Common Player:		2.00	1.00	.60
(1)	Frankie Baumholtz	2.00	1.00	.60
(2)	Jim Bouton	3.00	1.50	.90
(3)	Tony Conigliaro	3.00	1.50	.90
(4)	Don Drysdale	7.00	3.50	2.00
(5)	Hank Greenberg	7.00	3.50	2.00
(6)	Walter Johnson	12.00	6.00	3.50
(7)	Billy Loes	2.00	1.00	.60
(8)	Johnny Mize	6.00	3.00	1.75
(9)	Frank "Lefty" O'Doul	2.00	1.00	.60
(10)	Babe Ruth	35.00	17.50	10.50
(11)	Johnny Sain	2.50	1.25	.70
(12)	Jim Thorpe	12.00	6.00	3.50

1910 Plow Boy Tobacco

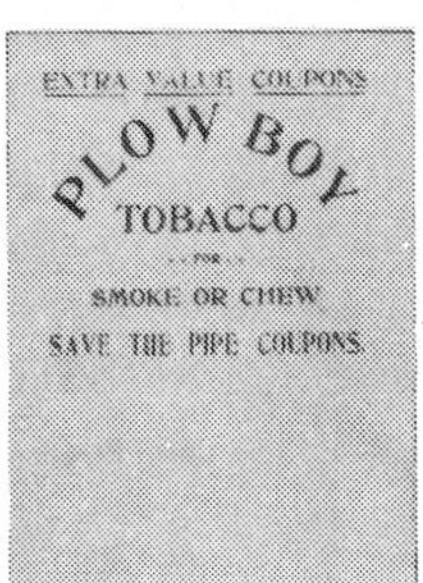

Plowboy Tobacco, a product of the Spaulding & Merrick Company, issued a set of cabinet-size cards in the Chicago area featuring members of the Cubs and the White Sox. From the checklist of the 50 known cards, it appears that the bulk of the set was originally issued in 1910 with a few additional cards appearing over the next several years. The set appears to be complete at 25 Cubs and 25 White Sox players, although there is some speculation that other cards may still be discovered. Measuring approximately 5-3/4" by 8", the Plowboys are one of the largest tobacco cards of the 20th Century. They feature very nice sepia-toned player photos in poses not found on other tobacco issues. The player's name appears in the lower left corner, while the team name appears in the lower right. Two different backs are known to exist. One consists of a simple advertisement for Plowboy Tobacco, while a second more difficult variety includes a list of premiums available in exchange for coupons. The set is among the rarest of all 20th Century tobacco issues.

		NR MT	EX	VG
Complete Set:		9000.	4500.	2750.
Common Player:		200.00	100.00	60.00
(1)	Jimmy Archer	200.00	100.00	60.00
(2)	Ginger Beaumont	200.00	100.00	60.00
(3)	Lena Blackburne	200.00	100.00	60.00
(4)	Bruno Block	200.00	100.00	60.00
(5)	Ping Bodie	200.00	100.00	60.00
(6)	Mordecai Brown	500.00	250.00	150.00
(7)	Al Carson	200.00	100.00	60.00
(8)	Frank Chance	550.00	275.00	165.00
(9)	Ed Cicotte	275.00	137.00	80.00
(10)	King Cole	200.00	100.00	60.00
(11)	Eddie Collins	500.00	250.00	150.00
(12)	George Davis	200.00	100.00	60.00
(13)	Patsy Dougherty	200.00	100.00	60.00
(14)	Johnny Evers	500.00	250.00	150.00
(15)	Chick Gandel (Gandil)	275.00	137.00	80.00
(16)	Ed Hahn	200.00	100.00	60.00
(17)	Solly Hoffman (Hofman)	200.00	100.00	60.00
(18)	Del Howard	200.00	100.00	60.00
(19)	Bill Jones	200.00	100.00	60.00
(20)	Johnny Kling	200.00	100.00	60.00
(21)	Rube Kroh	200.00	100.00	60.00
(22)	Frank Lange	200.00	100.00	60.00
(23)	Fred Luderus	200.00	100.00	60.00
(24)	Harry McIntyre	200.00	100.00	60.00
(25)	Ward Miller	200.00	100.00	60.00
(26)	Charlie Mullen	200.00	100.00	60.00
(27)	Tom Needham	200.00	100.00	60.00
(28)	Fred Olmstead	200.00	100.00	60.00
(29)	Orval Overall	200.00	100.00	60.00
(30)	Fred Parent	200.00	100.00	60.00
(31)	Fred Payne	200.00	100.00	60.00
(32)	Francis "Big Jeff" Pfeffer	200.00	100.00	60.00
(33)	Jake Pfeister	200.00	100.00	60.00
(34)	Billy Purtell	200.00	100.00	60.00
(35)	Ed Reulbach	200.00	100.00	60.00
(36)	Lew Richie	200.00	100.00	60.00
(37)	Jimmy Scheckard (Sheckard)	200.00	100.00	60.00
(38)	Wildfire Schulte	200.00	100.00	60.00
(39a)	Jim Scot (name incorrect)	200.00	100.00	60.00
(39b)	Jim Scott (name correct)	200.00	100.00	60.00
(40)	Frank Smith	200.00	100.00	60.00
(41)	Harry Steinfeldt	200.00	100.00	60.00
(42)	Billy Sullivan	200.00	100.00	60.00
(43)	Lee Tannehill	200.00	100.00	60.00
(44)	Joe Tinker	500.00	250.00	150.00
(45)	Ed Walsh	500.00	250.00	150.00
(46)	Doc White	200.00	100.00	60.00
(47)	Irv Young	200.00	100.00	60.00
(48)	Rollie Zeider	200.00	100.00	60.00
(49)	Heinie Zimmerman	200.00	100.00	60.00

1985 Polaroid/J.C. Penney Indians

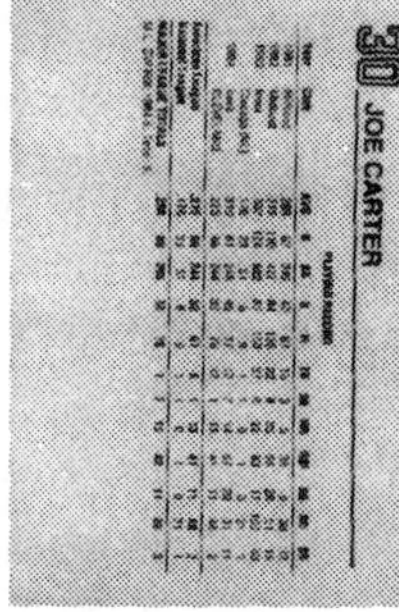

While the Cleveland Indians continued its four-year tradition of baseball card promotional game issues in 1985, the sponsor changed from Wheaties to Polaroid/J.C. Penney. The 32-card set features 30 player cards, a manager card and a group card of the coaching staff. Though produced in the "safety set" format - slightly oversize (2-13/16" by 4-1/8") with wide white borders - the Indians cards carry no safety message. Backs, once again numbered by uniform number, contain major and minor league stats.

		MT	NR MT	EX
Complete Set:		13.00	9.75	5.25
Common Player:		.25	.20	.10
2	Brett Butler	.70	.50	.30
4	Tony Bernazard	.40	.30	.15
8	Carmen Castillo	.25	.20	.10
10	Pat Tabler	.40	.30	.15
12	Benny Ayala	.25	.20	.10
13	Ernie Camacho	.25	.20	.10
14	Julio Franco	1.00	.70	.40
16	Jerry Willard	.25	.20	.10
18	Pat Corrales	.30	.25	.12
20	Otis Nixon	.30	.25	.12
21	Mike Hargrove	.30	.25	.12
22	Mike Fischlin	.25	.20	.10
23	Chris Bando	.25	.20	.10
24	George Vukovich	.25	.20	.10
26	Brook Jacoby	.70	.50	.30
27	Mel Hall	.50	.40	.20
28	Bert Blyleven	1.00	.70	.40
29	Andre Thornton	.50	.40	.20
30	Joe Carter	1.00	.70	.40
32	Rick Behenna	.25	.20	.10
33	Roy Smith	.25	.20	.10
35	Jerry Reed	.25	.20	.10
36	Jamie Easterly	.25	.20	.10
38	Dave Von Ohlen	.25	.20	.10
41	Rich Thompson	.25	.20	.10
43	Bryan Clark	.25	.20	.10
44	Neal Heaton	.50	.40	.20
48	Vern Ruhle	.25	.20	.10
49	Jeff Barkley	.25	.20	.10
50	Ramon Romero	.25	.20	.10
54	Tom Waddell	.25	.20	.10
---	Tribe Coaching Staff (Bobby Bonds, Johnny Goryl, Don McMahon, Ed Napolean, Dennis Sommers)	.25	.20	.10

1889 Police Gazette Cabinets

Issued in the late 1880s as a premium by Police Gazette, a popular newspaper of the day, these cabinet cards were only recently discovered and are very rare. The 4-1/2" by 6-1/2" cards consist of oval, sepia-toned photographs mounted on cardboard of various colors. Only eight players are known and, except for Keefe, their photographs correspond to those used in the better-known S.F. Hess card series. All of the cards display the name of the player next to his portrait, along with the signature of "Richard K. Fox" and a line identifying him as "Editor and Proprietor/Police Gazette/Franklin Square, New York."

		NR MT	EX	VG
Complete Set:		16000.	8000.	4800.
Common Player:		1500.	750.00	450.00
(1)	Roger Conner (Connor)	2500.	1250.	750.00
(2)	Jerry Denny	1500.	750.00	450.00
(3)	Buck Ewing	2500.	1250.	750.00
(4)	Elmer Foster	1500.	750.00	450.00
(5)	Pebbly Jack Glasscock	1500.	750.00	450.00
(6)	Tim Keefe	2500.	1250.	750.00
(7)	Tip O'Neil	2000.	1000.	600.00
(8)	Curt Welch	1500.	750.00	450.00

1970 Police/Fire Safety Senators

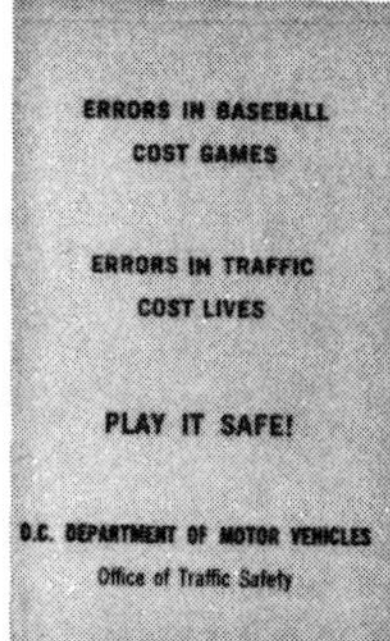

ERRORS IN BASEBALL
COST GAMES
ERRORS IN TRAFFIC
COST LIVES
PLAY IT SAFE!
D.C. DEPARTMENT OF MOTOR VEHICLES
Office of Traffic Safety

Distributed in 1970 by the Washington, D.C. Department of Motor Vehicles, this regional set, promoting traffic safety, was one of the first police sets ever issued. Featuring black and white player photos of the Washington Senators, the cards measure 2-1/2" by 3-7/8" and have large borders surrounding the pictures with the player's name and position below. The team name appears in smaller type at the bottom. The 1970 set can be found on either pink card stock, used for the original print run, or on bright yellow stock, used for two subsequent printings. The additional print runs resulted in a scarce card of Dave Nelson, who replaced the traded Aurelio Rodriguez for the final printing. The Nelson card is found only on yellow stock, while the other players in the set can be found on both yellow and pink. The pink varieties carry a higher value. The backs of the cards offer traffic safety tips and identify the manufacturer of the sets as the "D.C. Department of Motor Vehicles/Office of Traffic Safety."

		NR MT	EX	VG
Complete Set: (pink stock)		110.00	55.00	33.00
Common Player: (pink stock)		7.00	3.50	2.00
Complete Set: (yellow stock)		300.00	150.00	90.00
Common Player: (yellow stock)		2.00	1.00	.60
(1a)	Dick Bosman (pink stock)	7.00	3.50	2.00
(1b)	Dick Bosman (yellow stock)	2.00	1.00	.60
(2a)	Eddie Brinkman (pink stock)	7.00	3.50	2.00
(2b)	Eddie Brinkman (yellow stock)	2.00	1.00	.60
(3a)	Paul Casanova (pink stock)	7.00	3.50	2.00
(3b)	Paul Casanova (yellow stock)	2.00	1.00	.60
(4a)	Mike Epstein (pink stock)	7.00	3.50	2.00
(4b)	Mike Epstein (yellow stock)	2.00	1.00	.60
(5a)	Frank Howard (pink stock)	15.00	7.50	4.50
(5b)	Frank Howard (yellow stock)	7.00	3.50	2.00
(6a)	Darold Knowles (pink stock)	7.00	3.50	2.00
(6b)	Darold Knowles (yellow stock)	2.00	1.00	.60
(7a)	Lee Maye (pink stock)	7.00	3.50	2.00
(7b)	Lee Maye (yellow stock)	2.00	1.00	.60
(8)	Dave Nelson	250.00	125.00	75.00
(9a)	Aurelio Rodriguez (pink stock)	7.00	3.50	2.00
(9b)	Aurelio Rodriguez (yellow stock)	5.00	2.50	1.50
(10a)	John Roseboro (pink stock)	7.00	3.50	2.00
(10b)	John Roseboro (yellow stock)	2.00	1.00	.60
(11a)	Ed Stroud (pink stock)	7.00	3.50	2.00
(11b)	Ed Stroud (yellow stock)	2.00	1.00	.60

A player's name in *italic* type indicates a rookie card. An (FC) indicates a player's first card for that particular card company.

1971 Police/Fire Safety Senators

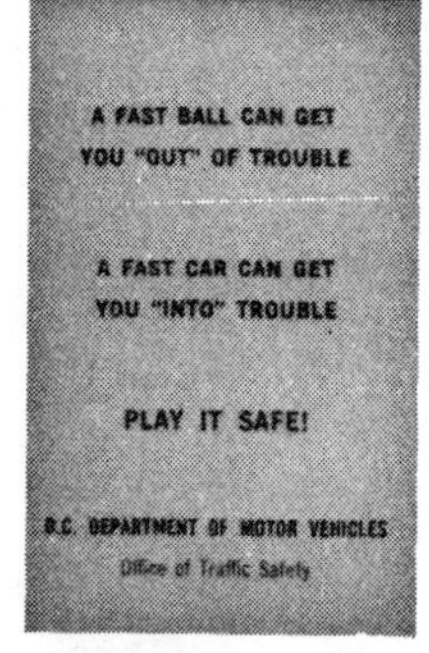

A FAST BALL CAN GET
YOU "OUT" OF TROUBLE
A FAST CAR CAN GET
YOU "INTO" TROUBLE
PLAY IT SAFE!
D.C. DEPARTMENT OF MOTOR VEHICLES
Office of Traffic Safety

The 1971 Senators safety set was again issued by the Washington, D.C., Department of Motor Vehicles and was similar in design and size (2-1/2" by 3-7/8") to the previous year, except that it was printed on a pale yellow stock. The set, which features several new players, including Denny McLain and Toby Harrah, contains no scarce cards. The backs contain traffic safety messages.

		NR MT	EX	VG
Complete Set:		10.00	5.00	3.00
Common Player:		1.00	.50	.30
(1)	Dick Bosman	1.00	.50	.30
(2)	Paul Casanova	1.00	.50	.30
(3)	Tim Cullen	1.00	.50	.30
(4)	Joe Foy	1.00	.50	.30
(5)	Toby Harrah	2.00	1.00	.60
(6)	Frank Howard	5.00	2.50	1.50
(7)	Elliott Maddox	1.00	.50	.30
(8)	Tom McCraw	1.00	.50	.30
(9)	Denny McLain	3.00	1.50	.90
(10)	Don Wert	1.00	.50	.30

1979 Police/Fire Safety Giants

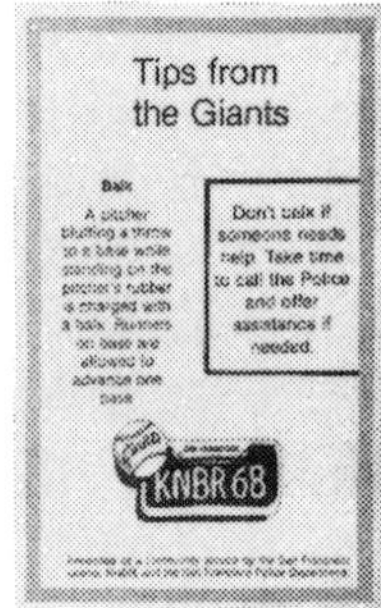

Each of the full-color cards measures 2-5/8" by 4-1/8" and is numbered by player uniform number. The set includes 20 Giants players and coaches. The player's name, position and facsimile autograph are on the card fronts, along with the Giants logo. Card backs have a "Tip from the Giants" and sponsor logos for the Giants and radio station KNBR, all printed the Giants' orange and black colors. Half of the set was distributed at a ballpark promotion during the 1979 season, while the other cards were available only from police agencies in several San Francisco Bay area counties.

		NR MT	EX	VG
Complete Set:		20.00	10.00	6.00
Common Player:		.40	.20	.12
1	Dave Bristol	.40	.20	.12
2	Marc Hill	.40	.20	.12
3	Mike Sadek	.50	.25	.15
5	Tom Haller	.40	.20	.12
6	Joe Altobelli	.50	.25	.15
8	Larry Shepard	.50	.25	.15
9	Heity Cruz	.40	.20	.12
10	Johnnie LeMaster	.40	.20	.12
12	Jim Davenport	.40	.20	.12
14	Vida Blue	.80	.40	.25
15	Mike Ivie	.40	.20	.12
16	Roger Metzger	.40	.20	.12
17	Randy Moffitt	.40	.20	.12
18	Bill Madlock	1.25	.60	.40
21	Rob Andrews	.50	.25	.15
22	Jack Clark	2.50	1.25	.70
25	Dave Roberts	.40	.20	.12
26	John Montefusco	.50	.25	.15
28	Ed Halicki	.50	.25	.15
30	John Tamargo	.40	.20	.12

		NR MT	EX	VG
31	Larry Herndon	.40	.20	.12
36	Bill North	.50	.25	.15
39	Bob Knepper	.70	.35	.20
40	John Curtis	.50	.25	.15
41	Darrell Evans	1.25	.60	.40
43	Tom Griffin	.50	.25	.15
44	Willie McCovey	3.00	1.50	.90
46	Gary Lavelle	.50	.25	.15
49	Max Venable	.50	.25	.15

1980 Police/Fire Safety Dodgers

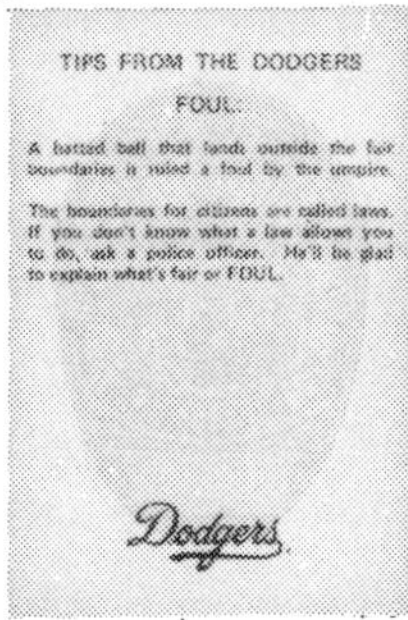

Producers of one of the most popular police and safety sets in baseball, the Los Angeles Dodgers began this successful promotion in 1980. The 2-13/16" by 4-1/8" cards feature attractive, full-color photos on the card fronts, along with brief personal statistics. Card backs include "Tips from the Dodgers" along with the team and Los Angeles Police Department logos. The 30 cards are numbered by player uniform number, with an unnumbered team card also included in the set.

		NR MT	EX	VG
	Complete Set:	8.00	4.00	2.50
	Common Player:	.30	.15	.09
5	Johnny Oates	.30	.15	.09
6	Steve Garvey	1.50	.70	.45
7	Steve Yeager	.30	.15	.09
8	Reggie Smith	.50	.25	.15
9	Gary Thomasson	.30	.15	.09
10	Ron Cey	.50	.25	.15
12	Dusty Baker	.40	.20	.12
13	Joe Ferguson	.30	.15	.09
15	Davey Lopes	.50	.25	.15
16	Rick Monday	.40	.20	.12
18	Bill Russell	.40	.20	.12
20	Don Sutton	.80	.40	.25
21	Jay Johnstone	.40	.20	.12
23	Teddy Martinez	.30	.15	.09
27	Joe Beckwith	.30	.15	.09
28	Pedro Guerrero	1.00	.50	.30
29	Don Stanhouse	.30	.15	.09
30	Derrel Thomas	.30	.15	.09
31	Doug Rau	.30	.15	.09
34	Ken Brett	.30	.15	.09
35	Bob Welch	.50	.25	.15
37	Robert Castillo	.30	.15	.09
38	Dave Goltz	.40	.20	.12
41	Jerry Reuss	.50	.25	.15
43	Rick Sutcliffe	.60	.30	.20
44	Mickey Hatcher	.40	.20	.12
46	Burt Hooton	.40	.20	.12
49	Charlie Hough	.40	.20	.12
51	Terry Forster	.40	.20	.12
---	Team Photo	.30	.15	.09

1980 Police/Fire Safety Giants

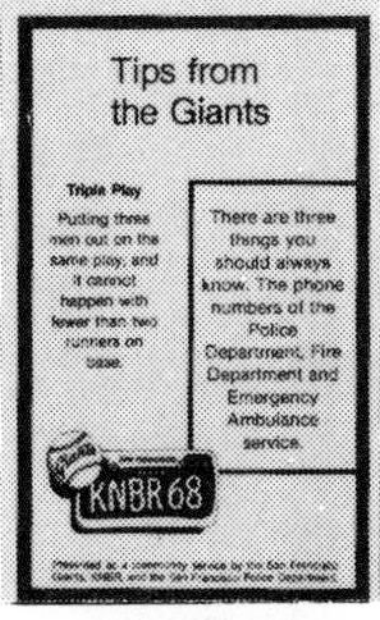

The 1980 Giants police set is virtually identical in format to its 1979 forerunner. Card design and colors are the same on both front and back, with radio station KNBR and the San Francisco Police Department once again co-sponsors. The 2-5/8" by 4-1/8" cards again feature fronts with full-color photos and facsimile autographs, while backs are in the team's orange and black colors. The set numbers 31 players and coaches, with each card numbered by uniform number. As in 1979, half the cards were distributed at a stadium promotion, with the remainder available only from police officers.

		NR MT	EX	VG
	Complete Set:	11.00	5.50	3.25
	Common Player:	.30	.15	.09
1	Dave Bristol	.30	.15	.09
2	Marc Hill	.30	.15	.09
3	Mike Sadek	.30	.15	.09
5	Jim Lefebvre	.30	.15	.09
6	Rennie Stennett	.30	.15	.09
7	Milt May	.30	.15	.09
8	Vern Benson	.30	.15	.09
9	Jim Wohlford	.30	.15	.09
10	Johnnie LeMaster	.30	.15	.09
12	Jim Davenport	.30	.15	.09
14	Vida Blue	.80	.40	.25
15	Mike Ivie	.30	.15	.09
16	Roger Metzger	.30	.15	.09
17	Randy Moffitt	.30	.15	.09
19	Al Holland	.30	.15	.09
20	Joe Strain	.30	.15	.09
22	Jack Clark	2.25	1.25	.70
26	John Montefusco	.40	.20	.12
28	Ed Halicki	.30	.15	.09
31	Larry Herndon	.40	.20	.12
32	Ed Whitson	.40	.20	.12
36	Bill North	.30	.15	.09
38	Greg Minton	.30	.15	.09
39	Bob Knepper	.50	.25	.15
41	Darrell Evans	.90	.45	.25
42	John Van Ornum	.30	.15	.09
43	Tom Griffin	.30	.15	.09
44	Willie McCovey	2.50	1.25	.70
45	Terry Whitfield	.30	.15	.09
46	Gary Lavelle	.30	.15	.09
47	Don McMahon	.30	.15	.09

1981 Police/Fire Safety Braves

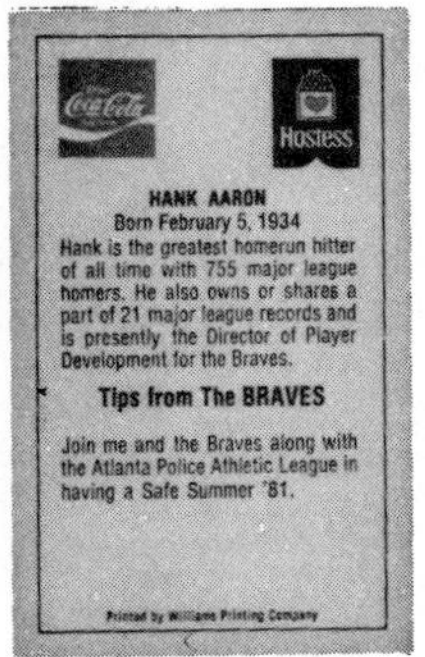

The first Atlanta Braves police set was a cooperative effort of the team, Hostess, Coca-Cola and the Atlanta Police Department. Card fronts feature full-color photos of 27 different Braves and manager Bobby Cox. Police and team logos are on the card backs. Card backs offer capsule biographies of the players, along with a tip for youngsters. The 2-5/8" by 4-1/8" cards are numbered by uniform number. Terry Harper (#19) appears to be somewhat scarcer than the other cards in the set. Reportedly, 33,000 sets were printed.

		MT	NR MT	EX
	Complete Set:	12.00	9.00	4.75
	Common Player:	.30	.25	.12
1	Jerry Royster	.30	.25	.12
3	Dale Murphy	2.50	2.00	1.00
4	Biff Pocoroba	.30	.25	.12
5	Bob Horner	1.00	.70	.40
6	Bob Cox	.30	.25	.12
9	Luis Gomez	.30	.25	.12
10	Chris Chambliss	.40	.30	.15
15	Bill Nahorodny	.30	.25	.12
16	Rafael Ramirez	.35	.25	.14
17	Glenn Hubbard	.35	.25	.14
18	Claudell Washington	.40	.30	.15
19	Terry Harper	.70	.50	.30
20	Bruce Benedict	.30	.25	.12
24	John Montefusco	.30	.25	.12
25	Rufino Linares	.30	.25	.12
26	Gene Garber	.30	.25	.12
30	Brian Asselstine	.30	.25	.12
34	Larry Bradford	.30	.25	.12
35	Phil Niekro	1.50	1.25	.60
37	Rick Camp	.30	.25	.12
39	Al Hrabosky	.35	.25	.14
40	Tommy Boggs	.30	.25	.12
42	Rick Mahler	.40	.30	.15
45	Ed Miller	.30	.25	.12
46	Gaylord Perry	1.50	1.25	.60
49	Preston Hanna	.30	.25	.12
---	Hank Aaron	2.50	2.00	1.00

1981 Police/Fire Safety Dodgers

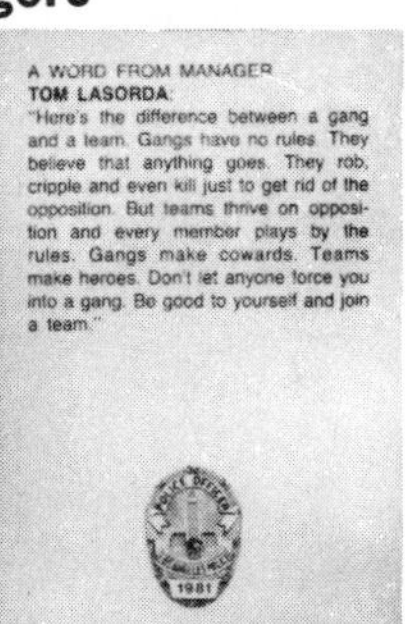

Very similar in format to their successful set of the year before, the Los Angeles Dodgers 1981 police set grew to 32 cards (from 30). This was due to the acquisitions of Ken Landreaux and Dave Stewart shortly before printing of the sets. These two cards may even have been added after the initial printing run, making them slightly more difficult to obtain. The full-color cards are again 2-13/16" by 4-1/8", with a safety tip on the card back. Each card front has the line "LAPD Salutes the 1981 Dodgers."

		MT	NR MT	EX
	Complete Set:	10.00	7.50	4.00
	Common Player:	.20	.15	.08
2	Tom Lasorda	.40	.30	.15
3	Rudy Law	.20	.15	.08
6	Steve Garvey	1.25	.90	.50
7	Steve Yeager	.20	.15	.08
8	Reggie Smith	.40	.30	.15
10	Ron Cey	.40	.30	.15
12	Dusty Baker	.30	.25	.12
13	Joe Ferguson	.20	.15	.08
14	Mike Scioscia	.30	.25	.12
15	Davey Lopes	.35	.25	.14
16	Rick Monday	.30	.25	.12
18	Bill Russell	.30	.25	.12
21	Jay Johnstone	.25	.20	.10
26	Don Stanhouse	.20	.15	.08
27	Joe Beckwith	.20	.15	.08
28	Pete Guerrero	.70	.50	.30
30	Derrel Thomas	.20	.15	.08
34	Fernando Valenzuela	2.00	1.50	.80
35	Bob Welch	.40	.30	.15
36	Pepe Frias	.20	.15	.08
37	Robert Castillo	.20	.15	.08
38	Dave Goltz	.25	.20	.10
41	Jerry Reuss	.35	.25	.14
43	Rick Sutcliffe	.50	.40	.20
44a	Mickey Hatcher	.25	.20	.10
44b	Ken Landreaux	.70	.50	.30
46	Burt Hooton	.25	.20	.10
48	Dave Stewart	1.50	1.25	.60
51	Terry Forster	.25	.20	.10
57	Steve Howe	.25	.20	.10
---	Coaching Staff (Monty Basgall, Mark Cresse, Tom Lasorda, Manny Mota, Danny Ozark, Ron Perranoski)	.20	.15	.08
---	Team Photo/Checklist	.20	.15	.08

1981 Police/Fire Safety Mariners

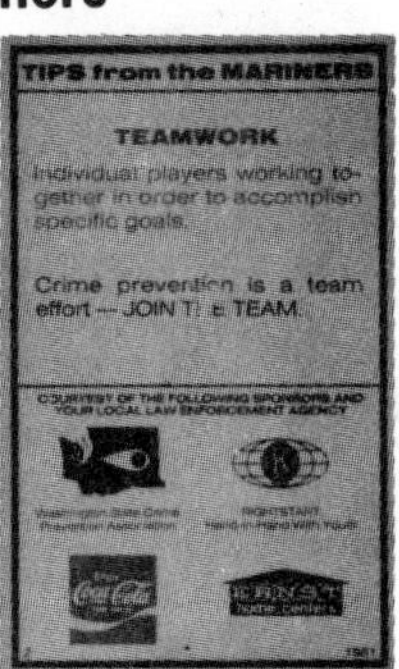

These 2-5/8" by 4-1/8" cards were co-sponsored by the Washington State Crime Prevention Assoc., Coca-Cola, Kiawanis and Ernst Home Centers. There are 16 players featured in this full-color set with each card numbered in the lower left of the card back. Card fronts list player name and position and have a team logo. Card backs are printed in blue and red and offer a "Tip from the Mariners" along with the four sponsor logos.

	MT	NR MT	EX
Complete Set:	5.00	3.75	2.00
Common Player:	.25	.20	.10

		MT	NR MT	EX
1	Jeff Burroughs	.35	.25	.14
2	Floyd Bannister	.60	.45	.25
3	Glenn Abbott	.25	.20	.10
4	Jim Anderson	.25	.20	.10
5	Danny Meyer	.25	.20	.10
6	Dave Edler	.25	.20	.10
7	Julio Cruz	.25	.20	.10
8	Kenny Clay	.25	.20	.10
9	Lenny Randle	.25	.20	.10
10	Mike Parrott	.25	.20	.10
11	Tom Paciorek	.25	.20	.10
12	Jerry Narron	.25	.20	.10
13	Richie Zisk	.35	.25	.14
14	Maury Wills	.50	.40	.20
15	Joe Simpson	.25	.20	.10
16	Shane Rawley	.60	.45	.25

1981 Police/Fire Safety Royals

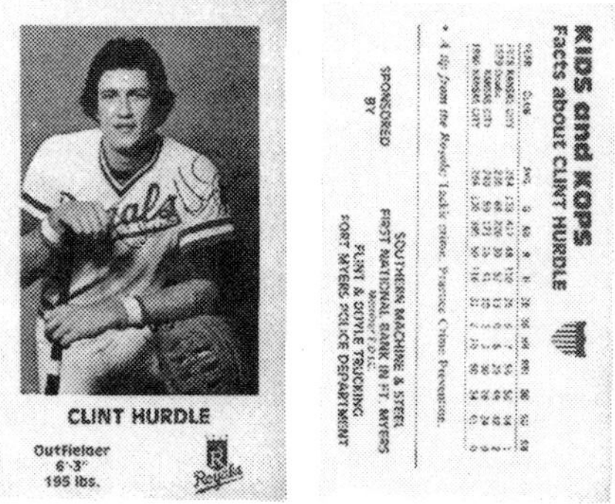

Ten of the most popular 1981 Kansas City players are featured in this 2-1/2" by 4-1/8" card set. Card fronts feature full-color photos with player name, position, facsimile autograph and team logo. Backs include player statistics, a tip from the Royals and list the four sponsoring organizations. Surprisingly, the set was issued by the Ft. Myers, Fla., police department near the Royals' spring training headquarters.

		MT	NR MT	EX
	Complete Set:	35.00	26.00	14.00
	Common Player:	1.50	1.25	.60
(1)	Willie Mays Aikens	1.50	1.25	.60
(2)	George Brett	18.00	13.50	7.25
(3)	Rich Gale	1.50	1.25	.60
(4)	Clint Hurdle	1.50	1.25	.60
(5)	Dennis Leonard	2.00	1.50	.80
(6)	Hal McRae	2.25	1.75	.90
(7)	Amos Otis	2.00	1.50	.80
(8)	U.L. Washington	1.50	1.25	.60
(9)	Frank White	3.50	2.75	1.50
(10)	Willie Wilson	4.00	3.00	1.50

1982 Police/Fire Safety Braves

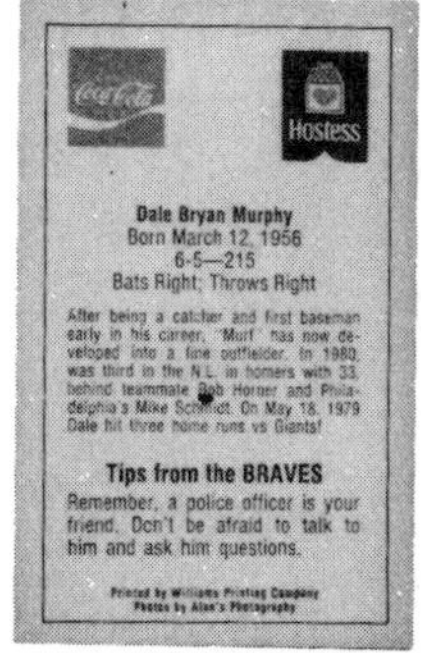

After their successful debut in 1981, the Atlanta Braves, the Atlanta Police Department, Coca-Cola and Hostess issued another card set in '82. This 30- card set is extremely close in format to the 1981 set and again measures 2-5/8" by 4-1/8". The full-color player photos are outstanding, and each card front also bears a statement marking the 1982 Braves' record-breaking 13-game win streak at the season's beginning. Card backs offer short biographies and "Tips from the Braves." Sponsors logos are also included. Reportedly, only 8,000 of these sets were printed.

		MT	NR MT	EX
	Complete Set:	20.00	15.00	8.00
	Common Player:	.30	.25	.12
1	Jerry Royster	.30	.25	.12
3	Dale Murphy	3.50	2.75	1.50
4	Biff Pocoroba	.30	.25	.12
5	Bob Horner	1.25	.90	.50
6	Randy Johnson	.30	.25	.12
8	Bob Watson	2.00	1.50	.80
9	Joe Torre	.40	.30	.15
10	Chris Chambliss	.40	.30	.15
15	C. Washington	.40	.30	.15
16	Rafael Ramirez	.35	.25	.14
17	Glenn Hubbard	.35	.25	.14
20	Bruce Benedict	.30	.25	.12
22	Brett Butler	.70	.50	.30
23	Tommie Aaron	.40	.30	.15
25	Rufino Linares	.30	.25	.12
26	Gene Garber	.30	.25	.12
27	Larry McWilliams	.30	.25	.12
28	Larry Whisenton	.30	.25	.12
32	Steve Bedrosian	1.00	.70	.40
35	Phil Niekro	2.00	1.50	.80
37	Rick Camp	.30	.25	.12
38	Joe Cowley	.30	.25	.12
39	Al Hrabosky	.35	.25	.14
42	Rick Mahler	.40	.30	.15
43	Bob Walk	.35	.25	.14
45	Bob Gibson	1.50	1.25	.60
49	Preston Hanna	.30	.25	.12
52	Joe Pignatano	.30	.25	.12
53	Dal Maxvill	.30	.25	.12
54	Rube Walker	.30	.25	.12

1982 Police/Fire Safety Brewers

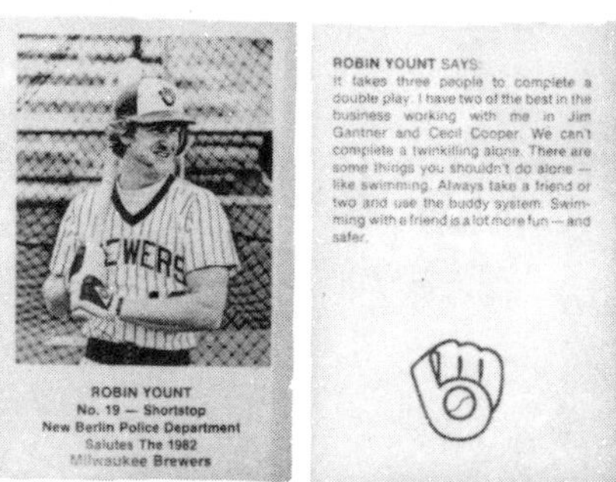

The inaugural Milwaukee Brewers police set contains 30 cards in a 2-13/16" by 4-1/8" format. There are 26 players included in the set, which is numbered by player uniform number. Unnumbered cards were also issued for general manager Harry Dalton, manager Buck Rodgers, the coaches and a team card with checklist. The full-color photos are especially attractive, printed on the cards' crisp white stock. A number of Wisconsin law enforcement agencies distributed the cards and credit lines on the card fronts were changed accordingly.

		MT	NR MT	EX
	Complete Set:	15.00	11.00	6.00
	Common Player:	.30	.25	.12
4	Paul Molitor	1.00	.70	.40
5	Ned Yost	.30	.25	.12
7	Don Money	.25	.20	.10
9	Larry Hisle	.25	.20	.10
10	Bob McClure	.30	.25	.12
11	Ed Romero	.30	.25	.12
13	Roy Howell	.30	.25	.12
15	Cecil Cooper	.50	.40	.20
17	Jim Gantner	.30	.25	.12
19	Robin Yount	1.50	1.25	.60
20	Gorman Thomas	.40	.30	.15
22	Charlie Moore	.30	.25	.12
23	Ted Simmons	.50	.40	.20
24	Ben Oglivie	.30	.25	.12
26	Kevin Bass	.60	.45	.25
28	Jamie Easterly	.30	.25	.12
29	Mark Brouhard	.30	.25	.12
30	Moose Haas	.30	.25	.12
34	Rollie Fingers	.70	.50	.30
35	Randy Lerch	.30	.25	.12
37	Buck Rodgers	.30	.25	.12
41	Jim Slaton	.30	.25	.12
45	Doug Jones	.30	.25	.12
46	Jerry Augustine	.30	.25	.12
47	Dwight Bernard	.30	.25	.12
48	Mike Caldwell	.25	.20	.10
50	Pete Vuckovich	.30	.25	.12
---	Team Photo/Checklist	.30	.25	.12
---	Harry Dalton (general mgr.)	.30	.25	.12
---	Coaches Card (Pat Dobson, Larry Haney, Ron Hansen, Cal McLish, Buck Rodgers, Harry Warner)	.30	.25	.12

1982 Police/Fire Safety Dodgers

Again issued in the same 2-13/16" by 4-1/8" size of the '80 and '81 sets, the 1982 Los Angeles set commemorates the team's 1981 World Champion- ship. In addition to the 26 cards

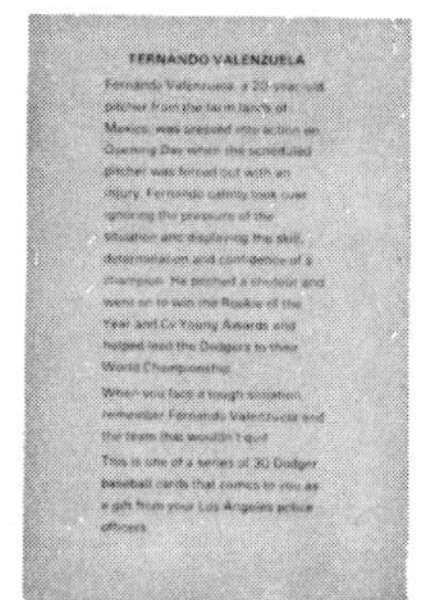

numbered by uniform for players and manager Tom Lasorda, there are four unnumbered cards which feature the team winning the division, league and World Series titles, plus one of the World Series trophy. The full-color card photos are once again vivid portraits on a clean white card stock. Card backs offer brief biographies and stadium information in addition to a safety tip.

		MT	NR MT	EX
	Complete Set:	6.00	4.50	2.50
	Common Player:	.15	.11	.06
2	Tom Lasorda	.30	.25	.12
6	Steve Garvey	1.00	.70	.40
7	Steve Yeager	.15	.11	.06
8	Mark Belanger	.20	.15	.08
10	Ron Cey	.30	.25	.12
12	Dusty Baker	.25	.20	.10
14	Mike Scioscia	.25	.20	.10
16	Rick Monday	.25	.20	.10
18	Bill Russell	.20	.15	.08
21	Jay Johnstone	.20	.15	.08
26	Alejandro Pena	.60	.45	.25
28	Pedro Guerrero	.80	.60	.30
30	Derrel Thomas	.15	.11	.06
31	Jorge Orta	.15	.11	.06
34	Fernando Valenzuela	1.00	.70	.40
35	Bob Welch	.35	.25	.14
38	Dave Goltz	.15	.11	.06
40	Ron Roenicke	.15	.11	.06
41	Jerry Reuss	.25	.20	.10
44	Ken Landreaux	.15	.11	.06
46	Burt Hooton	.20	.15	.08
48	Dave Stewart	.30	.25	.12
49	Tom Niedenfuer	.35	.25	.14
51	Terry Forster	.20	.15	.08
52	Steve Sax	.90	.70	.35
57	Steve Howe	.20	.15	.08
---	Division Championship	.15	.11	.06
---	League Championship	.15	.11	.06
---	World Series Championship	.15	.11	.06
---	Trophy Card/Checklist	.15	.11	.06

1983 Police/Fire Safety Braves

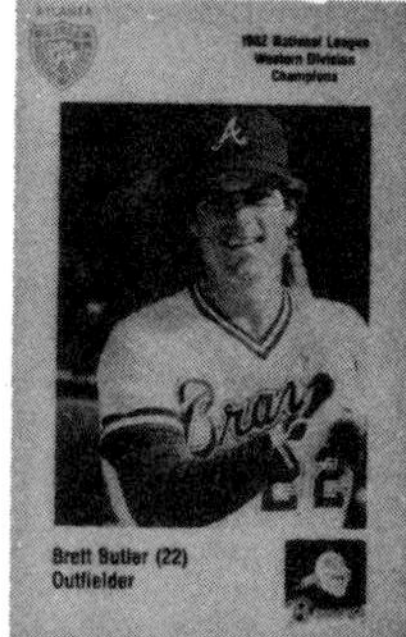

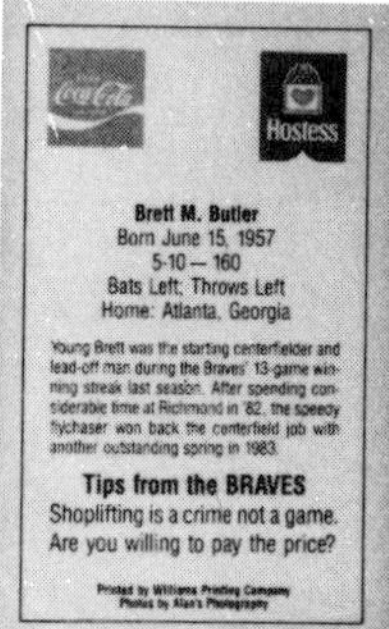

An almost exact replica of their 1982 set, the 1983 Atlanta Braves police set includes 30 cards numbered by uniform. Sponsors Hostess, Coca-Cola and the Atlanta Police Department returned for the third year. The cards are again 2-5/8" by 4-1/8", with full-color photos and police and team logos on the card fronts. A statement noting the team's 1982 National League Western Division title in the upper right corner is the key difference on the card fronts. As in 1982, 8,000 sets were reportedly printed.

		MT	NR MT	EX
	Complete Set:	15.00	11.00	6.00
	Common Player:	.30	.25	.12
1	Jerry Royster	.30	.25	.12
3	Dale Murphy	3.50	2.75	1.50
4	Biff Pocoroba	.30	.25	.12
5	Bob Horner	1.00	.70	.40
6	Randy Johnson	.30	.25	.12
8	Bob Watson	.35	.25	.14
9	Joe Torre	.40	.30	.15

		MT	NR MT	EX
10	Chris Chambliss	.40	.30	.15
11	Ken Smith	.30	.25	.12
15	Claudell Washington	.40	.30	.15
16	Rafael Ramirez	.35	.25	.14
17	Glenn Hubbard	.35	.25	.14
19	Terry Harper	.30	.25	.12
20	Bruce Benedict	.30	.25	.12
22	Brett Butler	.40	.30	.15
24	Larry Owen	.30	.25	.12
26	Gene Garber	.30	.25	.12
27	Pascual Perez	.35	.25	.14
29	Craig McMurtry	.35	.25	.14
32	Steve Bedrosian	.60	.45	.25
33	Pete Falcone	.30	.25	.12
35	Phil Niekro	1.50	1.25	.60
36	Sonny Jackson	.30	.25	.12
37	Rick Camp	.30	.25	.12
45	Bob Gibson	1.25	.90	.50
49	Rick Behenna	.30	.25	.12
51	Terry Forster	.35	.25	.14
52	Joe Pignatano	.30	.25	.12
53	Dal Maxvill	.30	.25	.12
54	Rube Walker	.30	.25	.12

1983 Police/Fire Safety Brewers

Similar to 1982, a number of issuer variations exist for the 1983 Brewers police set, as law enforcement agencies throughout the state distributed the set with their own credit lines on the cards. At least 28 variations are known to exist, with those issued by smaller agencies being scarcest. Prices quoted below are for the most common variations, generally the Milwaukee police department and a few small-town departments whose entire supply of police cards seem to have fallen into dealers' hands. Some specialists are willing to pay a premium for the scarcer departments' issues. The 30 2-13/16" by 4-1/8" cards include 29 players and coaches, along with a team card (with a checklist back). The team card and group coaches' card are unnumbered, while the others are numbered by uniform number.

		MT	NR MT	EX
Complete Set:		7.00	5.25	2.75
Common Player:		.20	.15	.08
4	Paul Molitor	.90	.70	.35
5	Ned Yost	.20	.15	.08
7	Don Money	.25	.20	.10
8	Rob Picciolo	.20	.15	.08
10	Bob McClure	.20	.15	.08
11	Ed Romero	.20	.15	.08
13	Roy Howell	.20	.15	.08
15	Cecil Cooper	.50	.40	.20
16	Marshall Edwards	.20	.15	.08
17	Jim Gantner	.30	.25	.12
19	Robin Yount	1.25	.90	.50
20	Gorman Thomas	.40	.30	.15
21	Don Sutton	.60	.45	.25
22	Charlie Moore	.20	.15	.08
23	Ted Simmons	.50	.40	.20
24	Ben Oglivie	.30	.25	.12
26	Bob Skube	.20	.15	.08
27	Pete Ladd	.20	.15	.08
28	Jamie Easterly	.20	.15	.08
30	Moose Haas	.20	.15	.08
32	Harvey Kuenn	.30	.25	.12
34	Rollie Fingers	.70	.50	.30
40	Bob Gibson	.20	.15	.08
41	Jim Slaton	.20	.15	.08
42	Tom Tellmann	.20	.15	.08
46	Jerry Augustine	.20	.15	.08
48	Mike Caldwell	.25	.20	.10
50	Pete Vuckovich	.30	.25	.12
---	Team Photo/Checklist	.20	.15	.08
---	Coaches Card (Pat Dobson, Dave Garcia, Larry Haney, Ron Hansen)	.20	.15	.08

1983 Police/Fire Safety Dodgers

While these full-color cards remained 2-13/16" by 4-1/8" and card fronts were similar to those of previous years, the card backs are quite different. Card backs are in a horizontal design for the first time, and include a small head portrait photo of the player in the upper left corner. Fairly complete player statistics are included but there is no safety tip. The 30 cards are numbered by uniform number, with an unnumbered coaches card also included. Fronts include the year, team logo, player name and number.

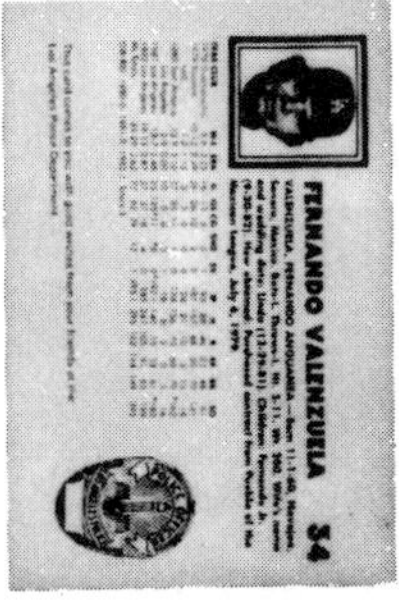

		MT	NR MT	EX
Complete Set:		6.00	4.50	2.50
Common Player:		.15	.11	.06
2	Tom Lasorda	.30	.25	.12
3	Steve Sax	.60	.45	.25
5	Mike Marshall	.60	.45	.25
7	Steve Yeager	.15	.11	.06
12	Dusty Baker	.25	.20	.10
14	Mike Scioscia	.25	.20	.10
16	Rick Monday	.25	.20	.10
17	Greg Brock	.40	.30	.15
18	Bill Russell	.20	.15	.08
20	Candy Maldonado	.40	.30	.15
21	Ricky Wright	.15	.11	.06
22	Mark Bradley	.15	.11	.06
23	Dave Sax	.15	.11	.06
26	Alejandro Pena	.25	.20	.10
27	Joe Beckwith	.15	.11	.06
28	Pedro Guerrero	.60	.45	.25
30	Derrel Thomas	.15	.11	.06
34	Fernando Valenzuela	.70	.50	.30
35	Bob Welch	.30	.25	.12
38	Pat Zachry	.15	.11	.06
40	Ron Roenicke	.15	.11	.06
41	Jerry Reuss	.25	.20	.10
43	Jose Morales	.15	.11	.06
44	Ken Landreaux	.15	.11	.06
46	Burt Hooton	.20	.15	.08
47	Larry White	.15	.11	.06
48	Dave Stewart	.25	.20	.10
49	Tom Niedenfuer	.20	.15	.08
57	Steve Howe	.20	.15	.08
---	Coaches Card (Joe Amalfitano, Monty Basgall, Mark Cresse, Manny Mota, Ron Perranoski)	.15	.11	.06

1983 Police/Fire Safety Royals

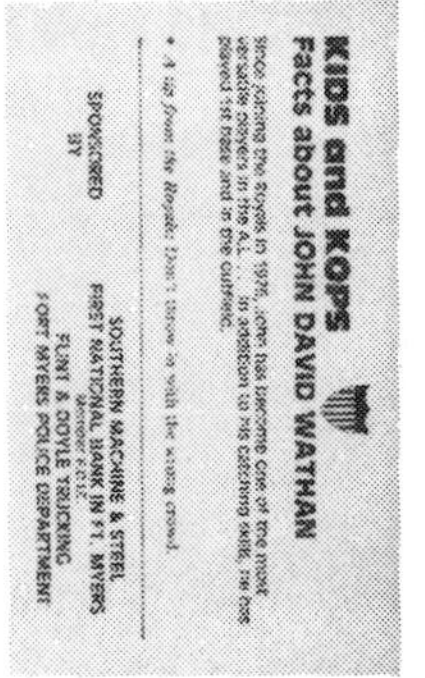

After skipping the 1982 season, the Ft. Myers, Fla., police department issued a Royals safety set in 1983 that is almost identical to their set of 1981. The set is again 2-1/2" by 4-1/8" and numbers just 10 players. Cards are unnumbered, with vertical fronts and horizontal backs. Card fronts have team logos, player name and position and facsimile autographs. Backs list the four sponsoring organizations, a "Tip from the Royals" and a "Kids and Cops Fact" about each player.

		MT	NR MT	EX
Complete Set:		30.00	23.00	12.00
Common Player:		1.00	.70	.40
(1)	Willie Mays Aikens	1.00	.70	.40
(2)	George Brett	18.00	13.50	7.25
(3)	Dennis Leonard	2.00	1.50	.80
(4)	Hal McRae	2.00	1.50	.80
(5)	Amos Otis	2.00	1.50	.80
(6)	Dan Quisenberry	3.00	2.25	1.25
(7)	U.L. Washington	1.00	.70	.40
(8)	John Wathan	2.00	1.50	.80
(9)	Frank White	3.50	2.75	1.50
(10)	Willie Wilson	3.75	2.75	1.50

1984 Police/Fire Safety Blue Jays

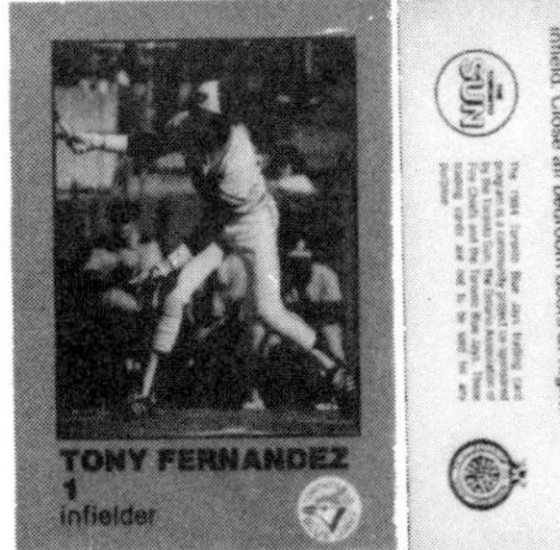

This 35-card set was issued in conjuction with the Toronto Sun newspaper and various Ontario area fire departments. The cards feature full-color action photos on the fronts, along with the player name, number and position. Rather than the customary wide white border on front, the Blue Jays fire safety set features bright blue borders. The card backs include brief player biographies and a fire safety tip. The 2-1/2" by 3-1/2" cards were distributed five at a time at two-week intervals during the summer of 1984.

		MT	NR MT	EX
Complete Set:		10.00	7.50	4.00
Common Player:		.20	.15	.08
1	Tony Fernandez	1.00	.70	.40
3	Jimy Williams	.20	.15	.08
4	Alfredo Griffin	.30	.25	.12
5	Rance Mulliniks	.20	.15	.08
6	Bobby Cox	.20	.15	.08
7	Damaso Garcia	.30	.25	.12
8	John Sullivan	.20	.15	.08
9	Rick Leach	.20	.15	.08
10	Dave Collins	.25	.20	.10
11	George Bell	1.50	1.25	.60
12	Ernie Whitt	.30	.25	.12
13	Buck Martinez	.20	.15	.08
15	Lloyd Moseby	.50	.40	.20
16	Garth Iorg	.20	.15	.08
17	Kelly Gruber	.25	.20	.10
18	Jim Clancy	.30	.25	.12
23	Mitch Webster	.50	.40	.20
24	Willie Aikens	.20	.15	.08
25	Roy Lee Jackson	.20	.15	.08
26	Willie Upshaw	.30	.25	.12
27	Jimmy Key	1.00	.70	.40
29	Jesse Barfield	.80	.60	.30
31	Jim Acker	.20	.15	.08
33	Doyle Alexander	.30	.25	.12
34	Stan Clarke	.20	.15	.08
35	Bryan Clark	.20	.15	.08
37	Dave Stieb	.60	.45	.25
38	Jim Gott	.20	.15	.08
41	Al Widmar	.20	.15	.08
42	Billy Smith	.20	.15	.08
43	Cito Gaston	.20	.15	.08
44	Cliff Johnson	.20	.15	.08
48	Luis Leal	.20	.15	.08
53	Dennis Lamp	.20	.15	.08
---	Team Logo/Checklist	.20	.15	.08

1984 Police/Fire Safety Braves

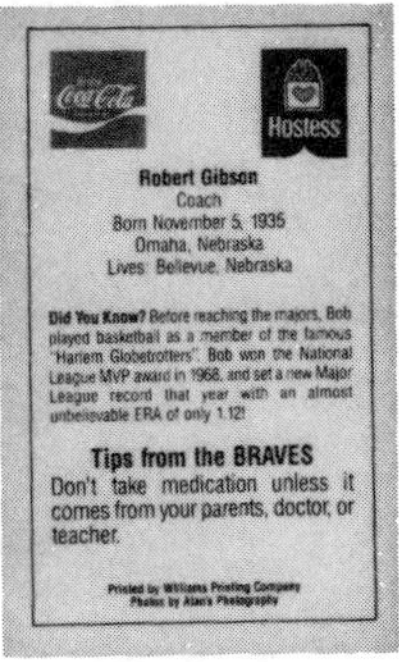

A fourth annual effort by the Braves, the Atlanta Police Department, Coca-Cola and Hostess. This 30- card set continued to be printed in a 2-5/8" by 4-1/8" format, with full-color photos plus team and police logos on the card fronts. For the first time, the cards also have a large logo and date in the upper right corner. Hostess and Coke logos again are on the card backs, with brief player information and a safety tip. Two cards in the set (Pascual Perez and Rafael Ramirez) were issued in Spanish. Cards were distributed two per week by Atlanta police officers. As in 1982 and 1983, a reported 8,000 sets were printed.

		MT	NR MT	EX
Complete Set:		12.00	9.00	4.75
Common Player:		.25	.20	.10
1	Jerry Royster	.25	.20	.10
3	Dale Murphy	3.50	2.75	1.50
5	Bob Horner	1.00	.70	.40
6	Randy Johnson	.25	.20	.10
8	Bob Watson	.30	.25	.12
9	Joe Torre	.40	.30	.15
10	Chris Chambliss	.40	.30	.15
11	Mike Jorgensen	.25	.20	.10
15	Claudell Washington	.40	.30	.15
16	Rafael Ramirez	.30	.25	.12
17	Glenn Hubbard	.30	.25	.12
19	Terry Harper	.25	.20	.10
20	Bruce Benedict	.25	.20	.10
25	Alex Trevino	.25	.20	.10
26	Gene Garber	.25	.20	.10
27	Pascual Perez	.30	.25	.12
28	Gerald Perry	1.50	1.25	.60
29	Craig McMurtry	.25	.20	.10
31	Donnie Moore	.25	.20	.10
32	Steve Bedrosian	.60	.45	.25
33	Pete Falcone	.25	.20	.10
37	Rick Camp	.25	.20	.10
39	Len Barker	.25	.20	.10
42	Rick Mahler	.40	.30	.15
45	Bob Gibson	1.25	.90	.50
51	Terry Forster	.30	.25	.12
52	Joe Pignatano	.25	.20	.10
53	Dal Maxvill	.25	.20	.10
54	Rube Walker	.25	.20	.10
55	Luke Appling	.60	.45	.25

1984 Police/Fire Safety Brewers

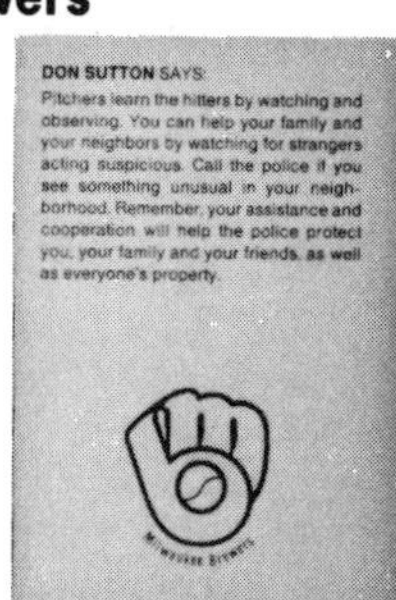

The king of the variations again in 1984, the Milwaukee Brewers set has been found with more than 50 different police agencies' credit lines on the front of the cards. Once again, law enforcement agencies statewide participated in distributing the sets. Some departments also include a badge of the participating agency on the card backs. The full-color cards measure 2-13/16" by 4-1/8". There are 28 numbered player and manager cards, along with an unnumbered coaches card and a team card. Player names, uniform numbers and positions are listed on each card front. Prices listed are for the most common variety (Milwaukee police department); sets issued by smaller departments may be worth a premium to specialists.

		MT	NR MT	EX
Complete Set:		6.00	4.50	2.50
Common Player:		.15	.11	.06
2	Randy Ready	.30	.25	.12
4	Paul Molitor	.80	.60	.30
8	Jim Sundberg	.15	.11	.06
9	Rene Lachemann	.15	.11	.06
10	Bob McClure	.15	.11	.06
11	Ed Romero	.15	.11	.06
13	Roy Howell	.15	.11	.06
14	Dion James	.50	.40	.20
15	Cecil Cooper	.40	.30	.15
17	Jim Gantner	.25	.20	.10
19	Robin Yount	1.25	.90	.50
20	Don Sutton	.50	.40	.20
21	Bill Schroeder	.30	.25	.12
22	Charlie Moore	.15	.11	.06
23	Ted Simmons	.40	.30	.15
24	Ben Oglivie	.25	.20	.10
25	Bobby Clark	.15	.11	.06
27	Pete Ladd	.15	.11	.06
28	Rick Manning	.15	.11	.06
29	Mark Brouhard	.15	.11	.06
30	Moose Haas	.15	.11	.06
34	Rollie Fingers	.60	.45	.25
42	Tom Tellmann	.15	.11	.06
43	Chuck Porter	.15	.11	.06
46	Jerry Augustine	.15	.11	.06
47	Jaime Cocanower	.15	.11	.06
48	Mike Caldwell	.20	.15	.08
50	Pete Vuckovich	.25	.20	.10
---	Team Photo/Checklist	.15	.11	.06
---	Coaches Card (Pat Dobson, Dave Garcia, Larry Haney, Tom Trebelhorn)	.15	.11	.06

1984 Police/Fire Safety Dodgers

This was the fifth yearly effort of the Dodgers and the Los Angeles Police Department. There are 30 cards in the set, which remains 2-13/16" by 4-1/8". Card fronts are designed somewhat differently than previous years, with more posed photos, bolder player names and numbers and a different team logo. Card backs again feature a small portrait photo in the upper left corner, along with brief biographical information and an anti-drug tip. Card backs are in Dodger blue. Cards are numbered by uniform number, with an unnumbered coaches card also included.

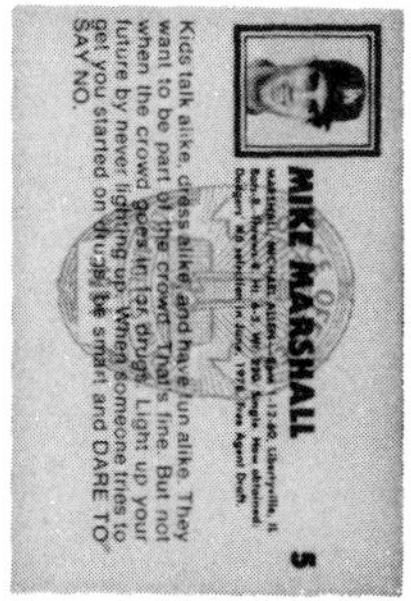

		MT	NR MT	EX
Complete Set:		8.00	6.00	3.25
Common Player:		.15	.11	.06
2	Tom Lasorda	.30	.25	.12
3	Steve Sax	.60	.45	.25
5	Mike Marshall	.50	.40	.20
7	Steve Yeager	.15	.11	.06
9	Greg Brock	.30	.25	.12
10	Dave Anderson	.20	.15	.08
14	Mike Scioscia	.25	.20	.10
16	Rick Monday	.25	.20	.10
17	Rafael Landestoy	.15	.11	.06
18	Bill Russell	.20	.15	.08
20	Candy Maldonado	.25	.20	.10
21	Bob Bailor	.15	.11	.06
25	German Rivera	.15	.11	.06
26	Alejandro Pena	.25	.20	.10
27	Carlos Diaz	.15	.11	.06
28	Pedro Guerrero	.70	.50	.30
31	Jack Fimple	.15	.11	.06
34	Fernando Valenzuela	.70	.50	.30
35	Bob Welch	.30	.25	.12
38	Pat Zachry	.15	.11	.06
40	Rick Honeycutt	.15	.11	.06
41	Jerry Reuss	.25	.20	.10
43	Jose Morales	.15	.11	.06
44	Ken Landreaux	.15	.11	.06
45	Terry Whitfield	.15	.11	.06
46	Burt Hooton	.20	.15	.08
49	Tom Niedenfuer	.20	.15	.08
55	Orel Hershiser	2.50	2.00	1.00
56	Richard Rodas	.15	.11	.06
---	Coaches Card (Joe Amalfitano, Monty Basgall, Mark Cresse, Manny Mota, Ron Perranoski)	.15	.11	.06

1985 Police/Fire Safety Blue Jays

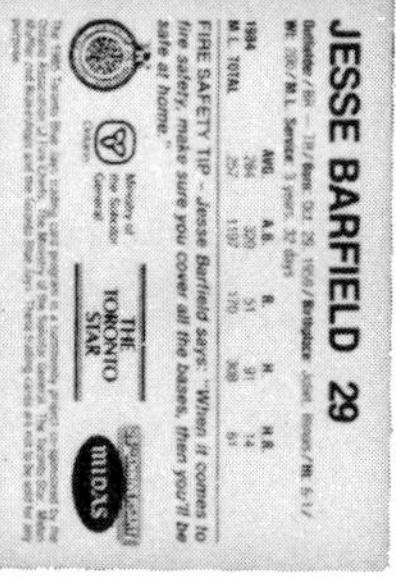

The Toronto Blue Jays issued a 35-card fire safety set for the second year in a row in 1985. Cards feature players, coaches, manager, checklist and team picture. The full-color photos are on the card fronts with a blue border. The backs feature player stats and a safety tip. The cards measure 2-1/2" by 3-1/2" and were distributed throughout the Province of Ontario, Canada.

		MT	NR MT	EX
Complete Set:		8.00	6.00	3.25
Common Player:		.20	.15	.08
1	Tony Fernandez	.70	.50	.30
3	Jimy Williams	.20	.15	.08
4	Manny Lee	.25	.20	.10
5	Rance Mulliniks	.20	.15	.08
6	Bobby Cox	.20	.15	.08
7	Damaso Garcia	.30	.25	.12
8	John Sullivan	.20	.15	.08
11	George Bell	1.25	.90	.50
12	Ernie Whitt	.30	.25	.12
13	Buck Martinez	.20	.15	.08
15	Lloyd Moseby	.40	.30	.15
16	Garth Iorg	.20	.15	.08
17	Kelly Gruber	.20	.15	.08
18	Jim Clancy	.30	.25	.12
22	Jimmy Key	.50	.40	.20
23	Mitch Webster	.25	.20	.10
24	Willie Aikens	.20	.15	.08
25	Len Matuszek	.20	.15	.08
26	Willie Upshaw	.30	.25	.12
28	Lou Thornton	.20	.15	.08
29	Jesse Barfield	.80	.60	.30
30	Ron Musselman	.20	.15	.08
31	Jim Acker	.20	.15	.08
33	Doyle Alexander	.30	.25	.12
36	Bill Caudill	.20	.15	.08
37	Dave Stieb	.50	.40	.20
41	Al Widmar	.20	.15	.08
42	Billy Smith	.20	.15	.08
43	Cito Gaston	.20	.15	.08
44	Jeff Burroughs	.20	.15	.08
46	Gary Lavelle	.20	.15	.08
48	Luis Leal	.20	.15	.08
50	Tom Henke	.40	.30	.15
53	Dennis Lamp	.20	.15	.08
---	Team Logo/Checklist	.20	.15	.08
---	Team Photo/Schedule	.20	.15	.08

1985 Police/Fire Safety Braves

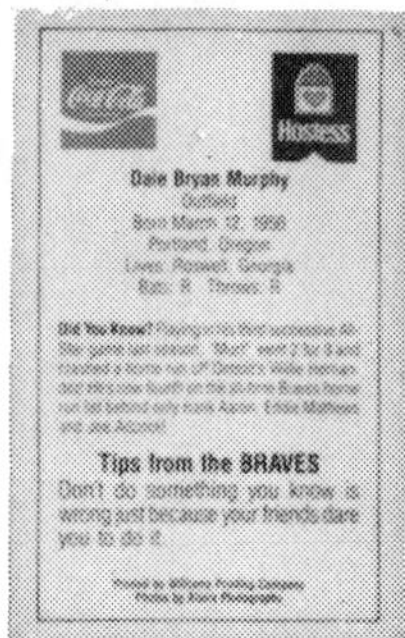

There are again 30 full-color cards in this fifth annual set. Hostess, Coca-Cola and the Atlanta Police Department joined the team as sponsors again for the 2-5/8" by 4-1/8" set. Card backs are similar to previous years, with the only difference on the fronts being a swap in position for the year and team logo. The cards are checklisted by uniform number.

		MT	NR MT	EX
Complete Set:		12.00	9.00	4.75
Common Player:		.25	.20	.10
2	Albert Hall	.40	.30	.15
3	Dale Murphy	3.25	2.50	1.25
5	Rick Cerone	.25	.20	.10
7	Bobby Wine	.25	.20	.10
10	Chris Chambliss	.35	.25	.14
11	Bob Horner	1.00	.70	.40
12	Paul Runge	.30	.25	.12
15	Claudell Washington	.35	.25	.14
16	Rafael Ramirez	.30	.25	.12
17	Glenn Hubbard	.30	.25	.12
18	Paul Zuvella	.30	.25	.12
19	Terry Harper	.25	.20	.10
20	Bruce Benedict	.25	.20	.10
22	Eddie Haas	.25	.20	.10
24	Ken Oberkfell	.30	.25	.12
26	Gene Garber	.25	.20	.10
27	Pascual Perez	.30	.25	.12
28	Gerald Perry	1.00	.70	.40
29	Craig McMurtry	.25	.20	.10
32	Steve Bedrosian	.50	.40	.20
33	Johnny Sain	.35	.25	.14
34	Zane Smith	.60	.45	.25
36	Brad Komminsk	.25	.20	.10
37	Rick Camp	.25	.20	.10
39	Len Barker	.25	.20	.10
40	Bruce Sutter	.70	.50	.30
42	Rick Mahler	.35	.25	.14
51	Terry Forster	.30	.25	.12
52	Leo Mazzone	.25	.20	.10
53	Bobby Dews	.25	.20	.10

1985 Police/Fire Safety Brewers

The Brewers changed the size of their annual police set in 1985, but almost imperceptibly. The full-color cards are 2-3/4" by 4-1/8", a slight 1/16" narrower than the four previous efforts. Player and team name on the card fronts are much bolder than in previous years. Once again, numerous area police groups distributed the sets, leading to nearly 60 variations, as each agency put their own credit line on the cards. Card backs include the Brewers logo, a safety tip and, in some cases, a badge of the participating law enforcement group. There are 27 numbered player cards (by uniform number) and three unnumbered cards - team roster, coaches and a

newspaper carrier card. Prices are for the most common departments.

		MT	NR MT	EX
Complete Set:		6.00	4.50	2.50
Common Player:		.15	.11	.06
2	Randy Ready	.15	.11	.06
4	Paul Molitor	.70	.50	.30
5	Doug Loman	.15	.11	.06
7	Paul Householder	.15	.11	.06
10	Bob McClure	.15	.11	.06
11	Ed Romero	.15	.11	.06
14	Dion James	.25	.20	.10
15	Cecil Cooper	.40	.30	.15
17	Jim Gantner	.25	.20	.10
18	Danny Darwin	.20	.15	.08
19	Robin Yount	1.00	.70	.40
21	Bill Schroeder	.20	.15	.08
22	Charlie Moore	.15	.11	.06
23	Ted Simmons	.40	.30	.15
24	Ben Oglivie	.25	.20	.10
26	Brian Giles	.15	.11	.06
27	Pete Ladd	.15	.11	.06
28	Rick Manning	.15	.11	.06
29	Mark Brouhard	.15	.11	.06
30	Moose Haas	.15	.11	.06
31	George Bamberger	.15	.11	.06
34	Rollie Fingers	.60	.45	.25
40	Bob Gibson	.15	.11	.06
41	Ray Searage	.15	.11	.06
47	Jaime Cocanower	.15	.11	.06
48	Ray Burris	.15	.11	.06
49	Ted Higuera	1.25	.90	.50
50	Pete Vuckovich	.25	.20	.10
---	Coaches Card (Andy Etchebarren, Larry Haney, Frank Howard, Tony Muser, Herm Starrette)	.15	.11	.06
---	Team Photo	.15	.11	.06

1985 Police/Fire Safety Phillies

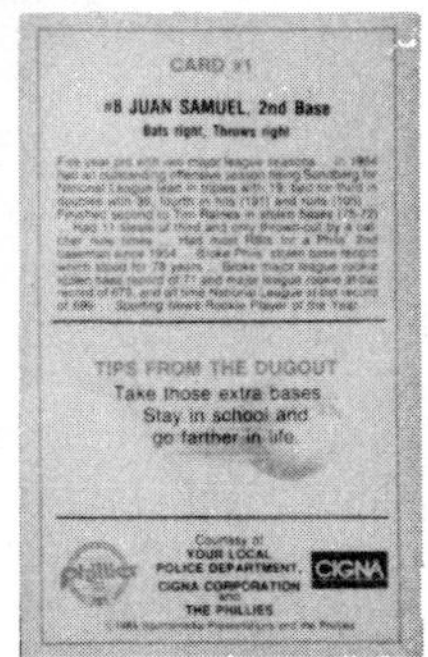

This is a brilliantly colored 2-5/8" by 4-1/8" set, co-sponsored by the Phillies and Cigna Corporation. Card fronts include the player name, number, position and team logo. The 16 cards are numbered on the back and include biographical information and a safety tip. The cards were distributed by several Philadelphia area police departments.

		MT	NR MT	EX
Complete Set:		7.00	5.25	2.75
Common Player:		.15	.11	.06
1	Juan Samuel	.50	.40	.20
2	Von Hayes	.35	.25	.14
3	Ozzie Virgil	.20	.15	.08
4	Mike Schmidt	1.25	.90	.50
5	Greg Gross	.15	.11	.06
6	Tim Corcoran	.15	.11	.06
7	Jerry Koosman	.25	.20	.10
8	Jeff Stone	.20	.15	.08
9	Glenn Wilson	.25	.20	.10
10	Steve Jeltz	.20	.15	.08
11	Garry Maddox	.20	.15	.08
12	Steve Carlton	.90	.70	.35
13	John Denny	.15	.11	.06
14	Kevin Gross	.30	.25	.12
15	Shane Rawley	.30	.25	.12
16	Charlie Hudson	.25	.20	.10

1986 Police/Fire Safety Astros

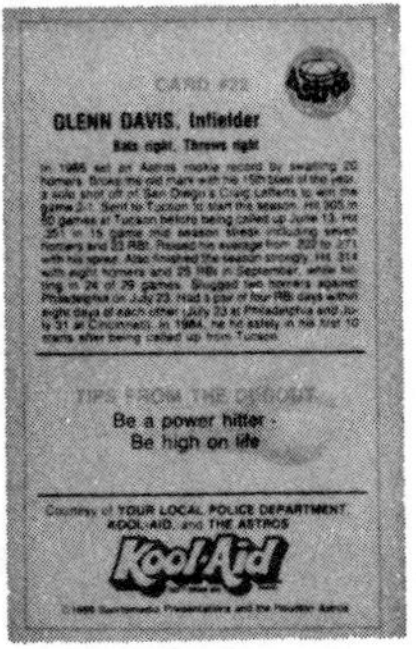

This full-color police safety set for the 1986 Houston Astros was issued by the Houston Police Department and sponsored by Kool-Aid. The 26-card set was distributed at the Astrodome on June 14, when 15,000 sets of the first 12 cards were given away. The balance of the set was distributed throughout the summer by the Houston police. The cards feature player photos on the fronts and a safety tip on the card backs. The cards measure 4-1/8" by 2-5/8".

		MT	NR MT	EX
Complete Set:		8.00	6.00	3.25
Common Player:		.20	.15	.08
1	Jim Pankovits	.20	.15	.08
2	Nolan Ryan	1.25	.90	.50
3	Mike Scott	.60	.45	.25
4	Kevin Bass	.40	.30	.15
5	Bill Doran	.40	.30	.15
6	Hal Lanier	.20	.15	.08
7	Denny Walling	.20	.15	.08
8	Alan Ashby	.20	.15	.08
9	Phil Garner	.25	.20	.10
10	Charlie Kerfeld	.25	.20	.10
11	Dave Smith	.30	.25	.12
12	Jose Cruz	.35	.25	.14
13	Craig Reynolds	.20	.15	.08
14	Mark Bailey	.20	.15	.08
15	Bob Knepper	.30	.25	.12
16	Julio Solano	.20	.15	.08
17	Dickie Thon	.25	.20	.10
18	Mike Madden	.20	.15	.08
19	Jeff Calhoun	.20	.15	.08
20	Tony Walker	.20	.15	.08
21	Terry Puhl	.20	.15	.08
22	Glenn Davis	1.00	.70	.40
23	Billy Hatcher	.40	.30	.15
24	Jim Deshaies	.40	.30	.15
25	Frank DiPino	.20	.15	.08
26	Coaching Staff (Yogi Berra, Matt Galante, Denis Menke, Les Moss, Gene Tenace)	.20	.15	.08

1986 Police/Fire Safety Blue Jays

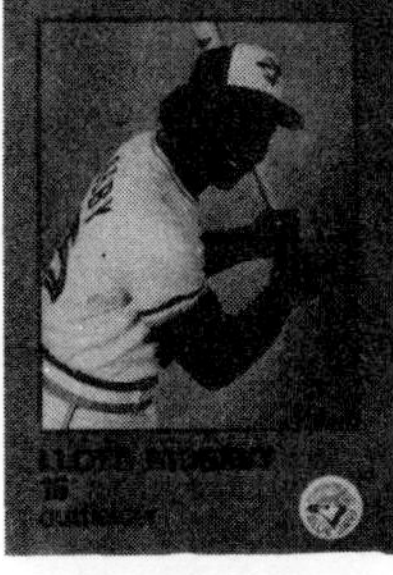

This was the third consecutive year the Toronto Blue Jays issued a fire safety set of 36 baseball cards. The cards were given out at many fire stations in Ontario, Canada. The cards are printed in full color and include players and other personnel. The set was co-sponsored by the local fire departments, Bubble Yum and the Toronto Star. The cards measure 2-1/2" by 3-1/2".

		MT	NR MT	EX
Complete Set:		8.00	6.00	3.25
Common Player:		.20	.15	.08
1	Tony Fernandez	.70	.50	.30
3	Jimy Williams	.20	.15	.08
5	Rance Mulliniks	.20	.15	.08
7	Damaso Garcia	.30	.25	.12
8	John Sullivan	.20	.15	.08
9	Rick Leach	.20	.15	.08
11	George Bell	1.25	.90	.50
12	Ernie Whitt	.30	.25	.12
13	Buck Martinez	.20	.15	.08
15	Lloyd Moseby	.40	.30	.15
16	Garth Iorg	.20	.15	.08
17	Kelly Gruber	.20	.15	.08
18	Jim Clancy	.30	.25	.12
22	Jimmy Key	.50	.40	.20
23	Cecil Fielder	.20	.15	.08
24	John McLaren	.20	.15	.08
25	Steve Davis	.20	.15	.08
26	Willie Upshaw	.30	.25	.12
29	Jesse Barfield	.80	.60	.30
31	Jim Acker	.20	.15	.08
33	Doyle Alexander	.30	.25	.12
36	Bill Caudill	.20	.15	.08
37	Dave Stieb	.50	.40	.20
38	Mark Eichhorn	.40	.30	.15
39	Don Gordon	.25	.20	.10
41	Al Widmar	.20	.15	.08
42	Billy Smith	.20	.15	.08
43	Cito Gaston	.20	.15	.08
44	Cliff Johnson	.20	.15	.08
46	Gary Lavelle	.20	.15	.08
49	Tom Filer	.20	.15	.08
50	Tom Henke	.40	.30	.15
53	Dennis Lamp	.20	.15	.08
54	Jeff Hearron	.20	.15	.08
---	Team Photo	.20	.15	.08
---	10th Anniversary Logo Card	.20	.15	.08

1986 Police/Fire Safety Braves

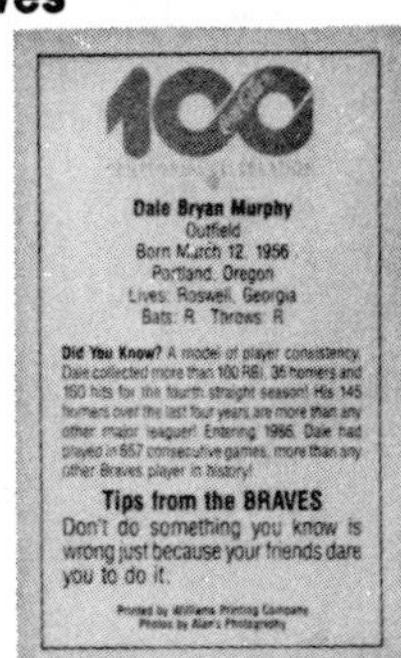

100
Dale Bryan Murphy
Outfield
Tips from the BRAVES
Don't do something you know is wrong just because your friends dare you to do it.

The Police Athletic League of Atlanta issued a 30- card full-color set featuring the Atlanta Braves players and personnel. The cards measure 2-5/8" by 4-1/8". Card fronts include player photos with name, uniform number and position below the photo. The cards backs offer the 100th Anniversary Coca-Cola logo, player information, statistics and a safety related tip. This was the sixth consecutive year that the Braves issued a safety set. The cards were available from police officers in Atlanta.

		MT	NR MT	EX
Complete Set:		11.00	8.25	4.50
Common Player:		.25	.20	.10
2	Russ Nixon	.25	.20	.10
3	Dale Murphy	2.75	2.00	1.00
4	Bob Skinner	.25	.20	.10
5	Billy Sample	.25	.20	.10
7	Chuck Tanner	.35	.25	.14
8	Willie Stargell	.80	.60	.30
9	Ozzie Virgil	.35	.25	.14
10	Chris Chambliss	.35	.25	.14
11	Bob Horner	.80	.60	.30
14	Andres Thomas	.50	.40	.20
15	Claudell Washington	.35	.25	.14
16	Rafael Ramirez	.30	.25	.12
17	Glenn Hubbard	.30	.25	.12
18	Omar Moreno	.25	.20	.10
19	Terry Harper	.25	.20	.10
20	Bruce Benedict	.25	.20	.10
23	Ted Simmons	.50	.40	.20
24	Ken Oberkfell	.30	.25	.12
26	Gene Garber	.25	.20	.10
29	Craig McMurtry	.25	.20	.10
30	Paul Assenmacher	.40	.30	.15
33	Johnny Sain	.30	.25	.12
34	Zane Smith	.40	.30	.15
38	Joe Johnson	.25	.20	.10
40	Bruce Sutter	.60	.45	.25
42	Rick Mahler	.35	.25	.14
46	David Palmer	.25	.20	.10
48	Duane Ward	.30	.25	.12
49	Jeff Dedmon	.25	.20	.10
52	Al Monchak	.25	.20	.10

1986 Police/Fire Safety Brewers

The Milwaukee Brewers, in conjunction with the Milwaukee Police Department, WTMJ Radio and Kinney Shoes, produced this attractive police safety set of 30 cards. The cards measure 2-13/16" by 4-1/2". A thin black border encloses a full-color Player photo on the front. The card backs give a safety tip and promos for the sponsor. The cards were distributed throughout

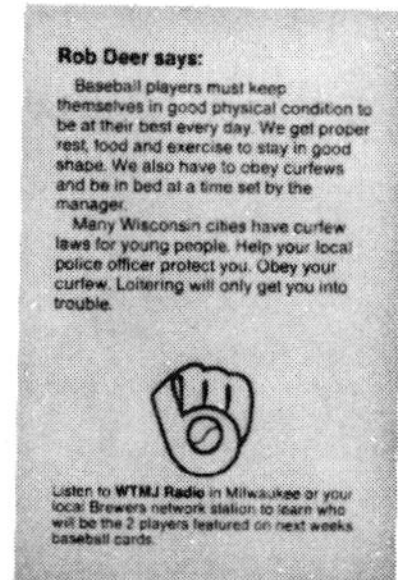

The Fond du Lac Police Dept, KFIZ Radio, and National Exchange Bank & Trust present the 1986

Rob Deer says:
Baseball players must keep themselves in good physical condition to be at their best every day. We get proper rest, food and exercise to stay in good shape. We also have to obey curfews and be in bed at a time set by the manager.
Many Wisconsin cities have curfew laws for young people. Help your local police officer protect you. Obey your curfew. Loitering will only get you into trouble.

the state of Wisconsin by numerous police departments; those of the smaller departments generally being scarcer than those issued in the big cities. Prices quoted below are for the most common departments' issues.

		MT	NR MT	EX
Complete Set:		6.00	4.50	2.50
Common Player:		.15	.11	.06
1	Ernest Riles	.30	.25	.12
2	Randy Ready	.15	.11	.06
3	Juan Castillo	.20	.15	.08
4	Paul Molitor	.70	.50	.30
7	Paul Householder	.15	.11	.06
10	Bob McClure	.15	.11	.06
11	Rick Cerone	.15	.11	.06
13	Billy Jo Robidoux	.30	.25	.12
15	Cecil Cooper	.40	.30	.15
16	Mike Felder	.30	.25	.12
17	Jim Gantner	.25	.20	.10
18	Danny Darwin	.20	.15	.08
19	Robin Yount	1.00	.70	.40
20	Juan Nieves	.40	.30	.15
21	Bill Schroeder	.15	.11	.06
22	Charlie Moore	.15	.11	.06
24	Ben Oglivie	.25	.20	.10
25	Mark Clear	.15	.11	.06
28	Rick Manning	.15	.11	.06
31	George Bamberger	.15	.11	.06
37	Dan Plesac	.60	.45	.25
39	Tim Leary	.15	.11	.06
41	Ray Searage	.15	.11	.06
43	Chuck Porter	.15	.11	.06
45	Rob Deer	.40	.30	.15
46	Bill Wegman	.30	.25	.12
47	Jamie Cocanower	.15	.11	.06
49	Ted Higuera	.50	.40	.20
---	Coaches Card (Andy Etchebarren, Larry Haney, Frank Howard, Tony Muser, Herm Starrette)	.15	.11	.06
---	Team Photo/Roster	.15	.11	.06

1986 Police/Fire Safety Dodgers

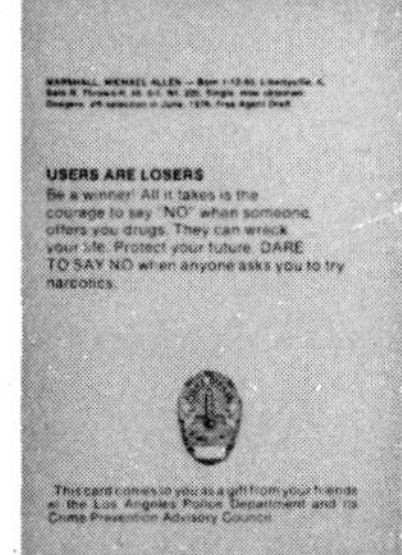

USERS ARE LOSERS
Be a winner! All it takes is the courage to say "NO" when someone offers you drugs. They can wreck your life. Protect your future. DARE TO SAY NO when anyone asks you to try narcotics.

After skipping the 1985 season, the Los Angeles Dodgers once again issued baseball cards related to police safety. The club had issued sets from 1980-84. The 1986 set features 30 full-color glossy cards measuring 2-1/4" by 4-1/8". The cards are numbered according to player uniforms. The backs feature brief player data and a safety tip from the Los Angeles Police Department. The sets were given away May 18 during Baseball Card Day at Dodger Stadium.

		MT	NR MT	EX
Complete Set:		6.50	5.00	2.50
Common Player:		.15	.11	.06
2	Tom Lasorda	.25	.20	.10
3	Steve Sax	.50	.40	.20
5	Mike Marshall	.40	.30	.15
9	Greg Brock	.25	.20	.10
10	Dave Anderson	.15	.11	.06
12	Bill Madlock	.30	.25	.12
14	Mike Scioscia	.25	.20	.10
17	Len Matuszek	.15	.11	.06
18	Bill Russell	.20	.15	.08
22	Franklin Stubbs	.25	.20	.10
23	Enos Cabell	.15	.11	.06
25	Mariano Duncan	.20	.15	.08
26	Alejandro Pena	.25	.20	.10
27	Carlos Diaz	.15	.11	.06
28	Pedro Guerrero	.60	.45	.25
29	Alex Trevino	.15	.11	.06
31	Ed Vande Berg	.15	.11	.06
34	Fernando Valenzuela	.60	.45	.25
35	Bob Welch	.30	.25	.12
40	Rick Honeycutt	.15	.11	.06
41	Jerry Reuss	.25	.20	.10
43	Ken Howell	.20	.15	.08
44	Ken Landreaux	.15	.11	.06
45	Terry Whitfield	.15	.11	.06
48	Dennis Powell	.20	.15	.08
49	Tom Niedenfuer	.20	.15	.08
51	Reggie Williams	.20	.15	.08
55	Orel Hershiser	1.00	.70	.40
---	Team Photo/Checklist	.15	.11	.06
---	Coaching Staff (Joe Amalfitano, Monty Basgall, Mark Cresse, Ben Hines, Don McMahon, Manny Mota, Ron Perranoski)	.15	.11	.06

1986 Police/Fire Safety Phillies

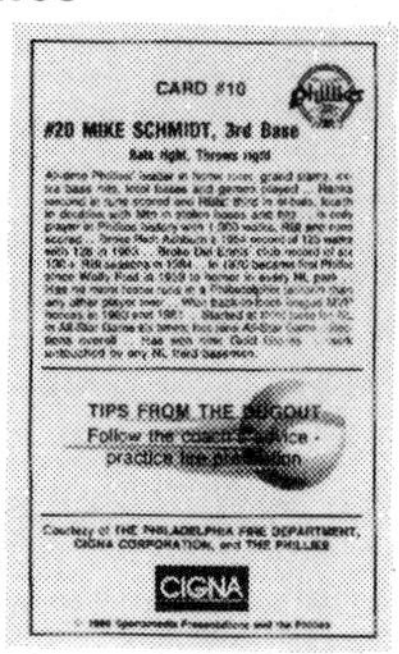

CARD #10
#20 MIKE SCHMIDT, 3rd Base
Bats right, Throws right
TIPS FROM THE DUGOUT
CIGNA

For the second straight year, the Philadelphia Phillies issued a 16-card safety set. However, in 1986 the set was issued in conjunction with the Philadelphia Fire Department rather than the police. Cigna Corporation remained a sponsor. The cards, which measure 2-5/8" by 4-1/8" in size, feature full color photos. Along with other pertinent information, the card backs contain a short player biography and a "Tips From The Dugout" fire safety hint.

		MT	NR MT	EX
Complete Set:		7.00	5.25	2.75
Common Player:		.15	.11	.06
1	Juan Samuel	.50	.40	.20
2	Don Carman	.35	.25	.14
3	Von Hayes	.30	.25	.12
4	Kent Tekulve	.20	.15	.08
5	Greg Gross	.15	.11	.06
6	Shane Rawley	.25	.20	.10
7	Darren Daulton	.20	.15	.08
8	Kevin Gross	.25	.20	.10
9	Steve Jeltz	.15	.11	.06
10	Mike Schmidt	1.25	.90	.50
11	Steve Bedrosian	.35	.25	.14
12	Gary Redus	.15	.11	.06
13	Charles Hudson	.15	.11	.06
14	John Russell	.20	.15	.08
15	Fred Toliver	.20	.15	.08
16	Glenn Wilson	.20	.15	.08

1987 Police/Fire Safety Astros

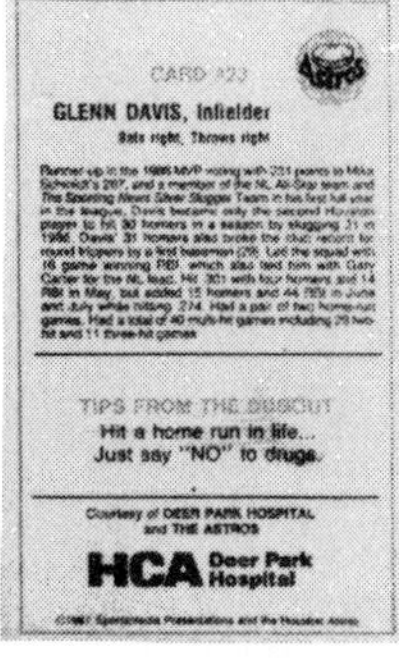

CARD #23
GLENN DAVIS, Infielder
Bats right, Throws right
TIPS FROM THE DUGOUT
Hit a home run in life...
Just say "NO" to drugs.
Courtesy of DEER PARK HOSPITAL and THE ASTROS
HCA Deer Park Hospital

The 1987 Houston Astros safety set was produced through the combined efforts of the Astros, Deer Park Hospital and Sportsmedia Presentations. #'s 1-12 were handed out to youngsters 14 and under at the Astrodome on July 14th. The balance of the distribution was handled by Deer Park Hospital. The cards, which measure 2-5/8" by 4-1/8", contain full-color photos. The backs offer a brief team/player history and a "Tips From The Dugout" anti-drug message.

		MT	NR MT	EX
Complete Set:		8.00	6.00	3.25
Common Player:		.20	.15	.08
1	Larry Andersen	.20	.15	.08
2	Mark Bailey	.20	.15	.08
3	Jose Cruz	.35	.25	.14
4	Danny Darwin	.25	.20	.10
5	Bill Doran	.40	.30	.15
6	Billy Hatcher	.40	.30	.15
7	Hal Lanier	.20	.15	.08
8	Davey Lopes	.30	.25	.12
9	Dave Meads	.30	.25	.12
10	Craig Reynolds	.20	.15	.08
11	Mike Scott	.60	.45	.25
12	Denny Walling	.20	.15	.08
13	Aurelio Lopez	.20	.15	.08
14	Dickie Thon	.25	.20	.10
15	Terry Puhl	.20	.15	.08
16	Nolan Ryan	1.25	.90	.50
17	Dave Smith	.30	.25	.12
18	Julio Solano	.20	.15	.08
19	Jim Deshaies	.30	.25	.12
20	Bob Knepper	.30	.25	.12
21	Alan Ashby	.20	.15	.08
22	Kevin Bass	.40	.30	.15
23	Glenn Davis	1.00	.70	.40
24	Phil Garner	.25	.20	.10
25	Jim Pankovits	.20	.15	.08
26	Coaching Staff (Yogi Berra, Matt Galante, Denis Menke, Les Moss, Gene Tenace)	.20	.15	.08

1987 Police/Fire Safety Blue Jays

For the fourth consecutive year, the Toronto Blue Jays issued a fire safety set of 36 cards. As in 1986, the set was sponsored by the local fire departments and governing agencies, Bubble Yum and the Toronto Star. The card fronts feature a full-color photo surrounded by a white border. The backs carry a fire safety tip and logos of all sponsors, plus player personal data and statistics. Produced on thin stock, cards in the set are the standard 2-1/2" by 3-1/2" size.

		MT	NR MT	EX
Complete Set:		9.00	6.75	3.50
Common Player:		.15	.11	.06
1	Tony Fernandez	.50	.40	.20
3	Jimy Williams	.15	.11	.06
5	Rance Mulliniks	.15	.11	.06
8	John Sullivan	.15	.11	.06
9	Rick Leach	.15	.11	.06
10	Mike Sharperson	.20	.15	.08
11	George Bell	1.00	.70	.40
12	Ernie Whitt	.25	.20	.10
15	Lloyd Moseby	.35	.25	.14
16	Garth Iorg	.15	.11	.06
17	Kelly Gruber	.15	.11	.06
18	Jim Clancy	.25	.20	.10
19	Fred McGriff	2.00	1.50	.80
22	Jimmy Key	.40	.30	.15
23	Cecil Fielder	.15	.11	.06
24	John McLaren	.15	.11	.06
26	Willie Upshaw	.25	.20	.10
29	Jesse Barfield	.60	.45	.25
31	Duane Ward	.15	.11	.06
33	Joe Johnson	.15	.11	.06
35	Jeff Musselman	.35	.25	.14
37	Dave Stieb	.40	.30	.15
38	Mark Eichhorn	.20	.15	.08
40	Rob Ducey	.20	.15	.08
41	Al Widmar	.15	.11	.06
42	Billy Smith	.15	.11	.06
43	Cito Gaston	.15	.11	.06
45	Jose Nunez	.35	.25	.14
46	Gary Lavelle	.15	.11	.06
47	Matt Stark	.15	.11	.06
48	Craig McMurtry	.15	.11	.06
50	Tom Henke	.30	.25	.12
54	Jeff Hearron	.15	.11	.06
55	John Cerutti	.20	.15	.08
---	Logo/Won-Loss Record	.15	.11	.06
---	Team Photo/Checklist	.15	.11	.06

1987 Police/Fire Safety Brewers

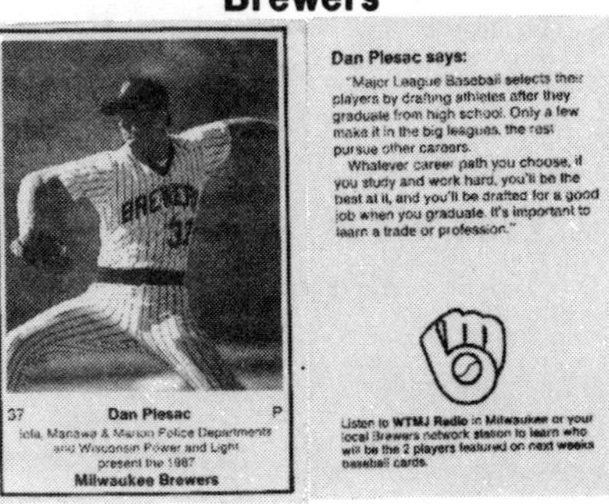

Dan Plesac says:
37 Dan Plesac P
Milwaukee Brewers

The Milwaukee Brewers issued a safety set in 1987 for the sixth consecutive year. As in the past, many local police departments throughout Wisconsin participated in the giveaway program. The Milwaukee version was sponsored by Kinney Shoe Stores and WTMJ Radio and was handed out to youngsters attending the Baseball Card Day at County Stadium on May 9th. The cards, which measure 2-1/4" by 4-1/8", feature full-color photos plus a safety tip on the backs. Chris Bosio can be found with a uniform number of 26 or 29. The card was corrected to #29 in later printings.

		MT	NR MT	EX
Complete Set:		6.00	4.50	2.50
Common Player:		.15	.11	.06
1	Ernest Riles	.15	.11	.06
2	Edgar Diaz	.20	.15	.08
3	Juan Castillo	.15	.11	.06
4	Paul Molitor	.60	.45	.25
5	B.J. Surhoff	.60	.45	.25
7	Dale Sveum	.35	.25	.14
9	Greg Brock	.25	.20	.10
13	Billy Jo Robidoux	.15	.11	.06
14	Jim Paciorek	.15	.11	.06
15	Cecil Cooper	.30	.25	.12
16	Mike Felder	.15	.11	.06
17	Jim Gantner	.20	.15	.08
19	Robin Yount	1.00	.70	.40
20	Juan Nieves	.30	.25	.12
21	Bill Schroeder	.15	.11	.06
25	Mark Clear	.15	.11	.06
26a	Glenn Braggs	.60	.45	.25
26b	Chris Bosio	1.00	.70	.40
28	Rick Manning	.15	.11	.06
29	Chris Bosio	.30	.25	.12
32	Chuck Crim	.25	.20	.10
34	Mark Ciardi	.20	.15	.08
37	Dan Plesac	.40	.30	.15
38	John Henry Johnson	.15	.11	.06
40	Mike Birbeck	.25	.20	.10
42	Tom Trebelhorn	.20	.15	.08
45	Rob Deer	.30	.25	.12
46	Bill Wegman	.20	.15	.08
49	Ted Higuera	.40	.30	.15
---	Coaches Card (Andy Etchebarren, Larry Haney, Chuck Hartenstein, Dave Hilton, Tony Muser)	.15	.11	.06
---	Team Photo/Roster	.15	.11	.06

1987 Police/Fire Safety Dodgers

Producing a police set for the seventh time in eight years, the 1987 edition contains 30 cards which measure 2-13/16" by 4-1/8". The set includes a special Dodger Stadium 25th Anniversary card. The card fronts contain a full-color photo plus the Dodger Stadium 25th Anniversay logo. The photos are a mix of action and posed shots. The backs contain personal player data plus a police safety tip. The cards were given out April 24th at Dodger Stadium and were distributed by the Los Angeles police department at a rate of two cards per week.

		MT	NR MT	EX
Complete Set:		6.00	4.50	2.50
Common Player:		.15	.11	.06
2	Tom Lasorda	.25	.20	.10
3	Steve Sax	.50	.40	.20
5	Mike Marshall	.40	.30	.15
10	Dave Anderson	.15	.11	.06
12	Bill Madlock	.30	.25	.12
14	Mike Scioscia	.25	.20	.10
15	Gilberto Reyes	.15	.11	.06
17	Len Matuszek	.15	.11	.06
21	Reggie Williams	.15	.11	.06
22	Franklin Stubbs	.25	.20	.10
23	Tim Leary	.15	.11	.06
25	Mariano Duncan	.15	.11	.06
26	Alejandro Pena	.25	.20	.10
28	Pedro Guerrero	.60	.45	.25
29	Alex Trevino	.15	.11	.06
33	Jeff Hamilton	.35	.25	.14
34	Fernando Valenzuela	.60	.45	.25
35	Bob Welch	.30	.25	.12
36	Matt Young	.15	.11	.06
40	Rick Honeycutt	.15	.11	.06
41	Jerry Reuss	.25	.20	.10
43	Ken Howell	.15	.11	.06
44	Ken Landreaux	.15	.11	.06
46	Ralph Bryant	.25	.20	.10
47	Jose Gonzalez	.30	.25	.12
49	Tom Niedenfuer	.20	.15	.08
51	Brian Holton	.30	.25	.12
55	Orel Hershiser	1.00	.70	.40
---	Coaching Staff (Joe Amalfitano, Mark Cresse, Tom Lasorda, Don McMahon, Manny Mota, Ron Perranoski, Bill Russell)	.15	.11	.06
---	Dodger Stadium/Checklist	.15	.11	.06

Regional interest may affect the value of a card.

1988 Police/Fire Safety Astros

This set of 26 full-color cards highlighting the Houston Astros was produced by the team, in conjunction with Deer Park Hospital and Sportsmedia Promotions for distribution to fans 14 years and younger at a ballpark giveaway. The 2-5/8" by 4-1/8" cards feature full-color player photos framed by a narrow blue border with an orange player/team name block below the photo. The blue and white card backs have orange borders and list card numbers, player information, career highlights and anti-drug tips.

		MT	NR MT	EX
Complete Set:		8.00	6.00	3.25
Common Player:		.20	.15	.08
1	Juan Agosto	.20	.15	.08
2	Larry Andersen	.20	.15	.08
3	Joaquin Andujar	.30	.25	.12
4	Alan Ashby	.20	.15	.08
5	Mark Bailey	.20	.15	.08
6	Kevin Bass	.40	.30	.15
7	Danny Darwin	.25	.20	.10
8	Glenn Davis	1.00	.70	.40
9	Jim Deshaies	.30	.25	.12
10	Bill Doran	.40	.30	.15
11	Billy Hatcher	.40	.30	.15
12	Jeff Heathcock	.20	.15	.08
13	Steve Henderson	.20	.15	.08
14	Chuck Jackson	.30	.25	.12
15	Bob Knepper	.30	.25	.12
16	Jim Pankovits	.20	.15	.08
17	Terry Puhl	.20	.15	.08
18	Rafael Ramirez	.20	.15	.08
19	Craig Reynolds	.20	.15	.08
20	Nolan Ryan	1.25	.90	.50
21	Mike Scott	.60	.45	.25
22	Dave Smith	.30	.25	.12
23	Denny Walling	.20	.15	.08
24	Gerald Young	.60	.45	.25
25	Hal Lanier	.20	.15	.08
26	Coaching Staff (Yogi Berra, Gene Clines, Matt Galante, Marc Hill, Denis Menke, Les Moss)	.20	.15	.08

1988 Police/Fire Safety Blue Jays

This 36-card set features full-color action photos on 3-1/2" by 5" cards with white borders

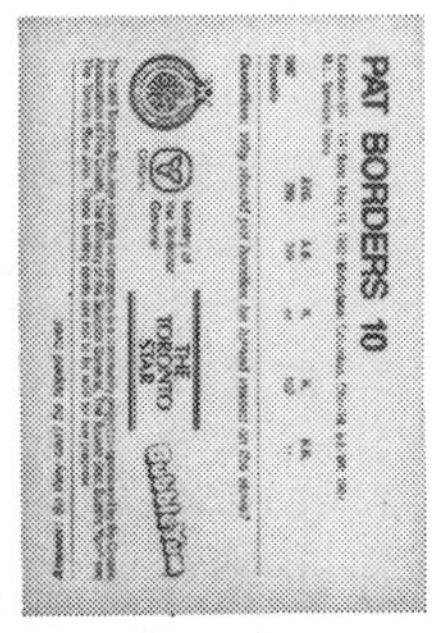

and a thin black line framing the photos. Card numbers (player's uniform #) appear lower left, team logo lower right; player's name and position are printed bottom center. Card backs are blue on white and include personal and career info, 1987 and career stats, sponsor logos and a fire safety tip. The set includes 34 player cards, a team photo checklist card and a team logo card with a year-by-year won/loss record. The set was sponsored by the Ontario Fire Chief Association, Ontario's Solicitor General, The Toronto Star and Bubble Yum and was distributed free as part of a community service project.

		MT	NR MT	EX
Complete Set:		7.00	5.25	2.75
Common Player:		.15	.11	.06
1	Tony Fernandez	.60	.45	.25
2	Nelson Liriano	.25	.20	.10
3	Jimy Williams	.15	.11	.06
4	Manny Lee	.15	.11	.06
5	Rance Mulliniks	.15	.11	.06
6	Silvestre Campusuano	.40	.30	.15
7	John McLaren	.15	.11	.06
8	John Sullivan	.15	.11	.06
9	Rick Leach	.15	.11	.06
10	Pat Borders	.40	.30	.15
11	George Bell	1.00	.70	.40
12	Ernie Whitt	.25	.20	.10
13	Jeff Musselman	.20	.15	.08
15	Lloyd Moseby	.30	.25	.12
16	Todd Stottlemyre	.60	.45	.25
17	Kelly Gruber	.15	.11	.06
18	Jim Clancy	.25	.20	.10
19	Fred McGriff	1.00	.70	.40
21	Juan Beniquez	.15	.11	.06
22	Jimmy Key	.40	.30	.15
23	Cecil Fielder	.15	.11	.06
29	Jesse Barfield	.60	.45	.25
31	Duane Ward	.15	.11	.06
36	David Wells	.25	.20	.10
37	Dave Stieb	.40	.30	.15
38	Mark Eichhorn	.20	.15	.08
40	Rob Ducey	.15	.11	.06
41	Al Widmar	.15	.11	.06
42	Billy Smith	.15	.11	.06
43	Cito Gaston	.15	.11	.06
46	Mike Flanagan	.25	.20	.10
50	Tom Henke	.25	.20	.10
55	John Cerutti	.20	.15	.08
57	Winston Llenas	.15	.11	.06
---	Team Photo	.15	.11	.06
---	Team Logo	.15	.11	.06

1988 Police/Fire Safety Brewers

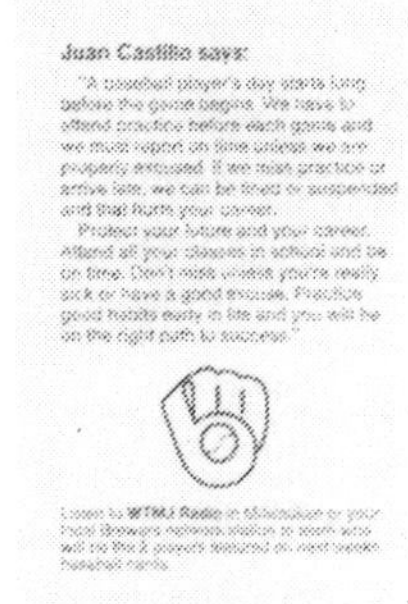

This 30-card set is the 7th annual issue sponsored by the Milwaukee Police Department for local distribution during a crime prevention promotion. The full-color card fronts (2-3/4" by 4-1/8") feature the same design as the 1987 set with white borders and a black frame outling the player photo and name. Sponsor credits and the team name are listed below the photo. The vertical card backs are blue on white with messages from the player and sponsors. Two group photos - one of the team's five coaches and one of the team (with a checklist back) - are unnumbered and printed horizontally. Card numbers refer to the players uniform numbers.

		MT	NR MT	EX
Complete Set:		6.00	4.50	2.50
Common Player:		.15	.11	.06
1	Ernest Riles	.15	.11	.06
3	Juan Castillo	.15	.11	.06
4	Paul Molitor	.60	.45	.25
5	B.J. Surhoff	.30	.25	.12
7	Dale Sveum	.20	.15	.08
9	Greg Brock	.20	.15	.08
11	Charlie O'Brien	.20	.15	.08
14	Jim Adduci	.15	.11	.06
16	Mike Felder	.15	.11	.06
17	Jim Gantner	.20	.15	.08
19	Robin Yount	1.00	.70	.40
20	Juan Nieves	.25	.20	.10
21	Bill Schroeder	.15	.11	.06
23	Joey Meyer	.35	.25	.14
25	Mark Clear	.15	.11	.06
26	Glenn Braggs	.30	.25	.12
28	Odell Jones	.15	.11	.06
29	Chris Bosio	.15	.11	.06
30	Steve Kiefer	.15	.11	.06
32	Chuck Crim	.15	.11	.06
33	Jay Aldrich	.15	.11	.06
37	Dan Plesac	.40	.30	.15
40	Mike Birkbeck	.20	.15	.08
42	Tom Trebelhorn	.15	.11	.06
43	Dave Stapleton	.25	.20	.10
45	Rob Deer	.30	.25	.12
46	Bill Wegman	.20	.15	.08
49	Ted Higuera	.40	.30	.15
---	Coaches Card (Andy Etchebarren, Larry Haney, Chuck Hartenstein, Dave Hilton, Tony Muser)	.15	.11	.06
---	Team Photo	.15	.11	.06

1988 Police/Fire Safety Dodgers

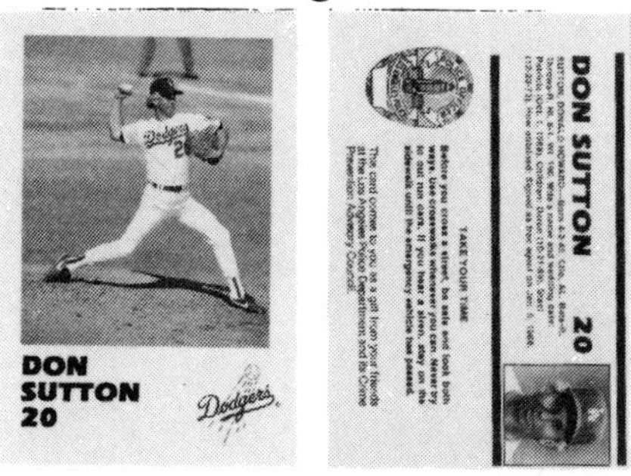

The Los Angeles police department sponsored this 30-card set (2-3/4" by 4-1/8") for use in a local crime prevention promotion. The sets include an unnumbered manager/coaches photo and three double-photo cards. The double cards feature posed closeups; the rest are action photos. The card fronts have white borders, with the team logo lower right and a bold black player name lower left. Card backs are black and white with a small closeup photo of the player, followed by personal and career info, a crime prevention tip and a LAPD badge logo. Card numbers refer to players' uniform numbers (the double-photo cards carry two numbers on both front and back).

		MT	NR MT	EX
Complete Set:		5.00	3.75	2.00
Common Player:		.15	.11	.06
2	Tom Lasorda	.25	.20	.10
3	Steve Sax	.50	.40	.20
5	Mike Marshall	.40	.30	.15
7	Alfredo Griffin	.20	.15	.08
9	Mickey Hatcher	.15	.11	.06
10	Dave Anderson	.15	.11	.06
12	Danny Heep	.15	.11	.06
14	Mike Scioscia	.20	.15	.08
17-21	Tito Landrum, Len Matuszek	.15	.11	.06
20	Don Sutton	.40	.30	.15
22	Franklin Stubbs	.20	.15	.08
23	Kirk Gibson	.60	.45	.25
25	Mariano Duncan	.15	.11	.06
26	Alejandro Pena	.20	.15	.08
27-52	Tim Crews, Mike Sharperson	.25	.20	.10
28	Pedro Guerrero	.50	.40	.20
29	Alex Trevino	.15	.11	.06
31	John Shelby	.15	.11	.06
33	Jeff Hamilton	.25	.20	.10
34	Fernando Valenzuela	.60	.45	.25
37	Mike Davis	.20	.15	.08
41	Brad Havens	.15	.11	.06
43	Ken Howell	.15	.11	.06
47	Jesse Orosco	.20	.15	.08
49-57	Tim Belcher, Shawn Hillegas	.30	.25	.12
50	Jay Howell	.20	.15	.08
51	Brian Holton	.20	.15	.08
54	Tim Leary	.25	.20	.10
55	Orel Hershiser	.80	.60	.30
---	Manager/Coaches (Joe Amalfitano, Steve Boros, Mark Cresse, Joe Ferguson, Tom Lasorda, Manny Mota, Ron Perranoski, Bill Russell)	.15	.11	.06

Regional interest may affect the value of a card.

1988 Police/Fire Safety Tigers

This unnumbered issue, sponsored by the Michigan State Police features 13 players and manager Sparky Anderson in full-color standard-size (2-1/2" by 3-1/2") cards. Player photos are framed by a blue border, with the Detroit logo upper left and a large name block that lists the player's name, position batting/throwing preference, height, weight and birthday beneath the photo. The backs carry an anti-drug or anti-crime message.

		MT	NR MT	EX
Complete Set:		35.00	25.00	14.00
Common Player:		.50	.40	.20
(1)	Doyle Alexander	.50	.40	.20
(2)	Sparky Anderson	.50	.40	.20
(3)	Dave Bergman	.50	.40	.20
(4)	Tom Brookens	.50	.40	.20
(5)	Darrell Evans	.60	.45	.25
(6)	Larry Herndon	.50	.40	.20
(7)	Chet Lemon	.50	.40	.20
(8)	Jack Morris	.80	.60	.30
(9)	Matt Nokes	.80	.60	.30
(10)	Jeff Robinson	.60	.45	.25
(11)	Frank Tanana	.40	.30	.15
(12)	Walt Terrell	.50	.40	.20
(13)	Alan Trammell	1.00	.70	.40
(14)	Lou Whitaker	.80	.60	.30

1989 Police/Fire Safety Blue Jays

The 1989 Toronto Blue Jays safety set consisted of 34 standard-size cards co-sponsored by the Ontario Association of Fire Chiefs, Oh Henry! candy bars and A&P supermarkets. The card fronts feature color photos with the player's uniform number in large type in the upper left corner. His name and position are to the right above the photo. The Blue Jays "On the Move" logo is centered at the bottom. The backs of the cards include fire safety messages.

		MT	NR MT	EX
Complete Set:		6.00	4.50	2.50
Common Player:		.15	.11	.06
1	Tony Fernandez	.50	.40	.20
2	Nelson Liriano	.15	.11	.06
3	Jimy Williams	.15	.11	.06
4	Manny Lee	.15	.11	.06
5	Rance Mulliniks	.15	.11	.06
6	Silvestre Campusano	.20	.15	.08
7	John McLaren	.15	.11	.06
8	John Sullivan	.15	.11	.06
9	Bob Brenly	.15	.11	.06
10	Pat Borders	.30	.25	.12
11	George Bell	.90	.70	.35
12	Ernie Whitt	.25	.20	.10
13	Jeff Musselman	.15	.11	.06
15	Lloyd Moseby	.25	.20	.10
16	Greg Myers	.40	.30	.15
17	Kelly Gruber	.30	.25	.12
18	Tom Lawless	.15	.11	.06
19	Fred McGriff	1.00	.70	.40
22	Jimmy Key	.25	.20	.10
25	Mike Squires	.15	.11	.06
26	Sal Butera	.15	.11	.06
29	Jesse Barfield	.40	.30	.15
30	Todd Stottlemyre	.40	.30	.15
31	Duane Ward	.15	.11	.06
36	David Wells	.20	.15	.08
37	Dave Steib	.40	.30	.20
40	Rob Ducey	.15	.11	.06
41	Al Widman	.15	.11	.06
43	Cito Gaston	.20	.15	.08
44	Frank Wills	.15	.11	.06
45	Jose Nunez	.20	.15	.08
46	Mike Flanagan	.20	.15	.08
50	Tom Henke	.20	.15	.08
55	John Cerutti	.20	.15	.08
---	Team Photo, Team Logo	.15	.11	.06

1989 Police/Fire Safety Brewers

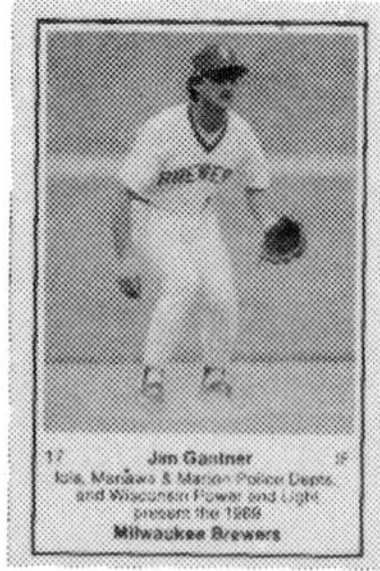

Jim Gantner says:

"Teamwork is very important in baseball. We know that we can't do it alone. Baseball players work together with their teammates and help each other. We develop strong friendships which last after our playing days are over.

Your teammates are your family, your teachers, and your local police officers. They want to be your friends. Take advantage of their friendship and ask them for advice when needed. They'll work with you, help you, and be the friends you need to succeed in life."

Listen to **WTMJ Radio** in Milwaukee or your local Brewers network station to learn who will be the 2 players featured on next weeks baseball cards.

The Milwaukee Brewers, in conjunction with various corporate and civic sponsors, issued a 30-card police set in 1989, the eighth consecutive police set issued by the club. Some 95 law enforcement agencies in Wisconsin participated in the program, each releasing their own version of the same set. The cards measure 2-13/16" by 4-1/8" and feature full-color action photos with the player's name, uniform number and position below, along with the sponsoring agencies. The backs include the traditional safety messages. The cards were distributed in complete sets at a stadium promotion and also handed out individually over the course of the summer by uniformed police officers in various Wisconsin cities and counties.

		MT	NR MT	EX
Complete Set:		7.00	5.25	2.75
Common Player:		.15	.11	.06
1	Gary Sheffield	1.00	.70	.40
4	Paul Molitor	.60	.45	.25
5	B.J. Surhoff	.30	.25	.12
6	Bill Spiers	.80	.60	.30
7	Dale Sveum	.20	.15	.08
9	Greg Brock	.20	.15	.08
14	Gus Polidor	.15	.11	.06
16	Mike Felder	.15	.11	.06
17	Jim Gantner	.20	.15	.08
19	Robin Yount	1.00	.70	.40
20	Juan Nieves	.20	.15	.08
22	Charlie O'Brien	.20	.15	.08
23	Joey Meyer	.15	.11	.06
25	Dave Engle	.15	.11	.06
26	Glenn Braggs	.25	.20	.10
27	Paul Mirabella	.15	.11	.06
29	Chris Bosio	.20	.15	.08
30	Terry Francona	.15	.11	.06
32	Chuck Crim	.15	.11	.06
37	Dan Plesac	.35	.25	.14
40	Mike Birkbeck	.15	.11	.06
41	Mark Knudson	.20	.15	.08
42	Tom Trebelhorn	.15	.11	.06
45	Rob Deer	.30	.25	.12
46	Bill Wegman	.15	.11	.06
48	Bryan Clutterbuck	.15	.11	.06
49	Teddy Higuera	.40	.30	.15
---	Team Photo, Coaching Staff	.15	.11	.06

1989 Police/Fire Safety Dodgers

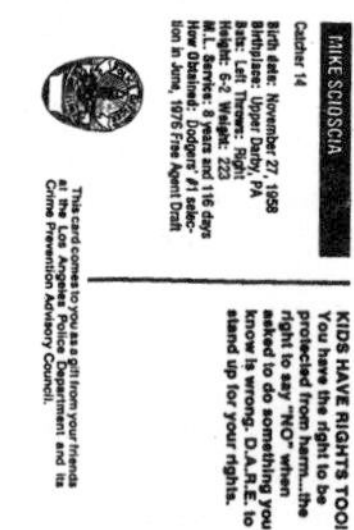

The Los Angeles Dodgers and the L.A. Police Department teamed up in 1989 to produce a 30-card police set. The cards, which measure

4-1/4" by 2-5/8", feature color action photos with the player's name and uniform number below. The Dodgers logo and "1989" appear in the upper left. The backs include player information plus a safety message.

		MT	NR MT	EX
Complete Set:		5.00	3.75	2.00
Common Player:		.15	.11	.06
2	Tom Lasorda	.25	.20	.10
3	Jeff Hamilton	.25	.20	.10
5	Mike Marshall	.30	.25	.12
7	Alfredo Griffin	.15	.11	.06
9	Mickey Hatcher	.15	.11	.06
10	Dave Anderson	.15	.11	.06
12	Willie Randolph	.25	.20	.10
14	Mike Scioscia	.20	.15	.08
17	Rick Dempsey	.15	.11	.06
20	Mike Davis	.15	.11	.06
21	Tracy Woodson	.25	.20	.10
22	Franklin Stubbs	.15	.11	.06
23	Kirk Gibson	.40	.30	.15
25	Mariano Duncan	.20	.15	.08
26	Alejandro Pena	.15	.11	.06
27	Mike Sharperson	.20	.15	.08
29	Ricky Horton	.15	.11	.06
30	John Tudor	.25	.20	.10
31	John Shelby	.15	.11	.06
33	Eddie Murray	.60	.45	.25
34	Fernando Valenzuela	.40	.30	.15
36	Mike Morgan	.15	.11	.06
48	Ramon Martinez	.60	.45	.25
50	Jay Howell	.20	.15	.08
52	Tim Crews	.15	.11	.06
54	Tim Leary	.20	.15	.08
55	Orel Hershiser	.80	.60	.30
57	Ray Searage	.15	.11	.06
---	Dodger Coaches	.15	.11	.06

1989 Police/Fire Safety Tigers

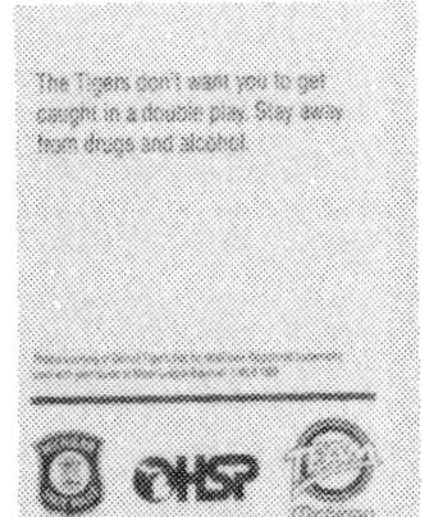

The Tigers don't want you to get caught in a double play. Stay away from drugs and alcohol.

This unnumbered issue, distributed and sponsored by the Michigan State Police Department features 14 full-color 2-1/2" by 3-1/2" cards. Player photos are framed by a blue and orange border, with the team logo in the upper left and biographical information below the photo. The card backs featue anti-drug or anti-crime messages.

		MT	NR MT	EX
Complete Set:		9.00	6.75	3.50
Common Player:		.25	.20	.10
(1)	Doyle Alexander	.35	.25	.14
(2)	Sparky Anderson	.50	.40	.20
(3)	Dave Bergman	.25	.20	.10
(4)	Mike Henneman	.50	.40	.20
(5)	Guillermo Hernandez	.35	.25	.14
(6)	Chet Lemon	.35	.25	.14
(7)	Fred Lynn	.40	.30	.15
(8)	Jack Morris	.50	.40	.20
(9)	Matt Nokes	.50	.40	.20
(10)	Jeff Robinson	.40	.30	.15
(11)	Pat Sheridan	.25	.20	.10
(12)	Frank Tanana	.40	.30	.15
(13)	Alan Trammell	.90	.70	.35
(14)	Lou Whitaker	.60	.45	.25

1960 Post Cereal

These cards were issued on the backs of Grape Nuts cereal and measure an oversized 7" by 8-3/4". The nine cards in the set include five baseball players (Al Kaline, Mickey Mantle, Don Drysdale, Harmon Killebrew and Ed Mathews) as well as two football and two basketball players. The full-color photos were placed on a color background and bordered by a wood frame design. The cards covered the entire back of the cereal box and were blank backed. Card fronts also include the player's name and team and a facsimile autograph. A panel on the side of the box contains player biographical information. A scarce set, the cards are very difficult to obtain in mint condition.

		NR MT	EX	VG
Complete Set:		4000.	2000.	1200.
Common Player:		300.00	150.00	90.00
(1)	Bob Cousy	300.00	150.00	90.00
(2)	Don Drysdale	400.00	200.00	120.00
(3)	Frank Gifford	400.00	200.00	120.00
(4)	Al Kaline	450.00	225.00	135.00
(5)	Harmon Killebrew	400.00	200.00	120.00
(6)	Ed Mathews	400.00	200.00	120.00
(7)	Mickey Mantle	1200.	600.00	360.00
(8)	Bob Pettit	300.00	150.00	90.00
(9)	John Unitas	300.00	150.00	90.00

1961 Post Cereal

Two hundred different players are included in this set, but with variations the number of different cards exceeds 350. This was the first large-scale card set by the cereal company and it proved very popular with fans. Cards were issued both singly and in various panel sizes on the thick cardboard stock of cereal boxes, as well on thinner stock, in team sheets issued directly by Post via a mail-in offer. About 10 cards in the set were issued in significantly smaller quantities, making their prices much higher than other comparable players in the set. Individual cards measure a 3-1/2" by 2-1/2", and all cards are numbered in the upper left corner. Card fronts have full-color portait photos of the player, along with biographical information and 1960 and career statistics. Card backs are blank. The complete set price includes does not include the scarcer variations.

		NR MT	EX	VG
Complete Set:		1400.	700.00	420.00
Common Player:		1.50	.70	.45
1a	Yogi Berra (box)	20.00	10.00	6.00
1b	Yogi Berra (company)	15.00	7.50	4.50
2a	Elston Howard (box)	5.00	2.50	1.50
2b	Elston Howard (company)	3.00	1.50	.90
3a	Bill Skowron (box)	2.50	1.25	.70
3b	Bill Skowron (company)	2.50	1.25	.70
4a	Mickey Mantle (box)	75.00	37.00	22.00
4b	Mickey Mantle (company)	75.00	37.00	22.00
5	Bob Turley (company)	12.00	6.00	3.50
6a	Whitey Ford (box)	8.00	4.00	2.50
6b	Whitey Ford (company)	8.00	4.00	2.50
7a	Roger Maris (box)	12.00	6.00	3.50
7b	Roger Maris (company)	12.00	6.00	3.50
8a	Bobby Richardson (box)	3.00	1.50	.90
8b	Bobby Richardson (company)	3.00	1.50	.90
9a	Tony Kubek (box)	3.00	1.50	.90
9b	Tony Kubek (company)	3.00	1.50	.90
10	Gil McDougald (box)	25.00	12.50	7.50
11	Cletis Boyer (box)	2.00	1.00	.60
12a	Hector Lopez (box)	2.00	1.00	.60
12b	Hector Lopez (company)	2.00	1.00	.60
13	Bob Cerv (box)	2.00	1.00	.60
14	Ryne Duren (box)	2.00	1.00	.60
15	Bobby Shantz (box)	2.00	1.00	.60
16	Art Ditmar (box)	2.00	1.00	.60
17	Jim Coates (box)	2.00	1.00	.60
18	John Blanchard (box)	2.00	1.00	.60
19a	Luis Aparicio (box)	5.00	2.50	1.50
19b	Luis Aparicio (company)	5.00	2.50	1.50
20a	Nelson Fox (box)	4.00	2.00	1.25
20b	Nelson Fox (company)	4.00	2.00	1.25
21a	Bill Pierce (box)	6.00	3.00	1.75
21b	Bill Pierce (company)	3.50	1.75	1.00
22a	Early Wynn (box)	7.00	3.50	2.00
22b	Early Wynn (company)	12.00	6.00	3.50
23	Bob Shaw (box)	75.00	37.00	22.00
24a	Al Smith (box)	3.00	1.50	.90
24b	Al Smith (company)	1.50	.70	.45
25a	Minnie Minoso (box)	2.50	1.25	.70
25b	Minnie Minoso (company)	2.50	1.25	.70
26a	Roy Sievers (box)	1.75	.90	.50
26b	Roy Sievers (company)	1.75	.90	.50
27a	Jim Landis (box)	2.00	1.00	.60
27b	Jim Landis (company)	1.50	.70	.45
28a	Sherman Lollar (box)	3.00	1.50	.90
28b	Sherman Lollar (company)	1.50	.70	.45
29	Gerry Staley (box)	1.50	.70	.45
30a	Gene Freese (box, White Sox)	1.50	.70	.45
30b	Gene Freese (company, Reds)	6.00	3.00	1.75
31	Ted Kluszewski (box)	3.00	1.50	.90
32	Turk Lown (box)	1.50	.70	.45
33a	Jim Rivera (box)	1.50	.70	.45
33b	Jim Rivera (company)	1.50	.70	.45
34	Frank Baumann (box)	1.50	.70	.45
35a	Al Kaline (box)	12.00	6.00	3.50
35b	Al Kaline (company)	10.00	5.00	3.00
36a	Rocky Colavito (box)	6.00	3.00	1.75
36b	Rocky Colavito (company)	3.50	1.75	1.00
37a	Charley Maxwell (box)	4.00	2.00	1.25
37b	Charley Maxwell (company)	1.50	.70	.45
38a	Frank Lary (box)	1.50	.70	.45
38b	Frank Lary (company)	1.50	.70	.45
39a	Jim Bunning (box)	4.00	2.00	1.25
39b	Jim Bunning (company)	4.00	2.00	1.25
40a	Norm Cash (box)	2.00	1.00	.60
40b	Norm Cash (company)	2.00	1.00	.60
41a	Frank Bolling (box, Tigers)	8.00	4.00	2.50
41b	Frank Bolling (company, Braves)	5.00	2.50	1.50
42a	Don Mossi (box)	1.50	.70	.45
42b	Don Mossi (company)	1.50	.70	.45
43a	Lou Berberet (box)	1.50	.70	.45
43b	Lou Berberet (company)	1.50	.70	.45
44	Dave Sisler (box)	1.50	.70	.45
45	Ed Yost (box)	1.50	.70	.45
46	Pete Burnside (box)	1.50	.70	.45
47a	Pete Runnels (box)	3.00	1.50	.90
47b	Pete Runnnels (company)	1.75	.90	.50
48a	Frank Malzone (box)	1.50	.70	.45
48b	Frank Malzone (company)	1.50	.70	.45
49a	Vic Wertz (box)	5.00	2.50	1.50
49b	Vic Wertz (company)	3.00	1.50	.90
50a	Tom Brewer (box)	2.50	1.25	.70
50b	Tom Brewer (company)	1.50	.70	.45
51a	Willie Tasby (box, no sold line)	8.00	4.00	2.50
51b	Willie Tasby (company, sold line)	1.50	.70	.45
52a	Russ Nixon (box)	1.50	.70	.45
52b	Russ Nixon (company)	1.50	.70	.45
53a	Don Buddin (box)	1.50	.70	.45
53b	Don Buddin (company)	1.50	.70	.45
54a	Bill Monbouquette (box)	1.50	.70	.45
54b	Bill Monbouquette (company)	1.50	.70	.45
55a	Frank Sullivan (box, Red Sox)	1.50	.70	.45
55b	Frank Sullivan (company, Phillies)	18.00	9.00	5.50
56a	Haywood Sullivan (box)	1.50	.70	.45
56b	Haywood Sullivan (company)	1.50	.70	.45
57a	Harvey Kuenn (box, Indians)	3.00	1.50	.90
57b	Harvey Kuenn (company, Giants)	6.00	3.00	1.75
58a	Gary Bell (box)	5.00	2.50	1.50
58b	Gary Bell (company)	1.75	.90	.50
59a	Jim Perry (box)	1.75	.90	.50
59b	Jim Perry (company)	1.75	.90	.50
60a	Jim Grant (box)	3.00	1.50	.90
60b	Jim Grant (company)	1.75	.90	.50
61a	Johnny Temple (box)	1.50	.70	.45
61b	Johnny Temple (company)	1.50	.70	.45
62a	Paul Foytack (box)	1.50	.70	.45
62b	Paul Foytack (company)	1.50	.70	.45
63a	Vic Power (box)	1.50	.70	.45
63b	Vic Power (company)	1.50	.70	.45
64a	Tito Francona (box)	1.50	.70	.45
64b	Tito Francona (company)	1.50	.70	.45
65a	Ken Aspromonte (box, no sold line)	6.00	3.00	1.75
65b	Ken Aspromonte (company, sold line)	6.00	3.00	1.75
66	Bob Wilson (box)	1.50	.70	.45
67a	John Romano (box)	1.50	.70	.45
67b	John Romano (company)	1.50	.70	.45
68a	Jim Gentile (box)	2.50	1.25	.70
68b	Jim Gentile (company)	1.50	.70	.45
69a	Gus Triandos (box)	3.00	1.50	.90
69b	Gus Triandos (company)	1.50	.70	.45
70	Gene Woodling (box)	15.00	7.50	4.50
71a	Milt Pappas (box)	3.00	1.50	.90
71b	Milt Pappas (company)	1.50	.70	.45
72a	Ron Hansen (box)	3.00	1.50	.90
72b	Ron Hansen (company)	1.50	.70	.45
73	Chuck Estrada (company)	75.00	37.00	22.00
74a	Steve Barber (box)	1.50	.70	.45
74b	Steve Barber (company)	1.50	.70	.45
75a	Brooks Robinson (box)	12.00	6.00	3.50
75b	Brooks Robinson (company)	10.00	5.00	3.00
76a	Jackie Brandt (box)	1.50	.70	.45
76b	Jackie Brandt (company)	1.50	.70	.45
77a	Marv Breeding (box)	1.50	.70	.45
77b	Marv Breedding (company)	1.50	.70	.45
78	Hal Brown (box)	1.50	.70	.45
79	Billy Klaus (box)	1.50	.70	.45
80a	Hoyt Wilhelm (box)	5.00	2.50	1.50
80b	Hoyt Wilhelm (company)	6.00	3.00	1.75
81a	Jerry Lumpe (box)	6.00	3.00	1.75
81b	Jerry Lumpe (company)	4.00	2.00	1.25
82a	Norm Siebern (box)	1.50	.70	.45
82b	Norm Siebern (company)	1.50	.70	.45
83a	Bud Daley (box)	1.75	.90	.50
83b	Bud Daley (company)	2.50	1.25	.70

		NR MT	EX	VG
84a	Bill Tuttle (box)	1.50	.70	.45
84b	Bill Tuttle (company)	1.50	.70	.45
85a	Marv Throneberry (box)	2.50	1.25	.70
85b	Marv Throneberry (company)	2.50	1.25	.70
86a	Dick Williams (box)	1.75	.90	.50
86b	Dick Williams (company)	2.00	1.00	.60
87a	Ray Herbert (box)	1.50	.70	.45
87b	Ray Herbert (company)	2.00	1.00	.60
88a	Whitey Herzog (box)	2.00	1.00	.60
88b	Whitey Herzog (company)	2.00	1.00	.60
89a	Ken Hamlin (box, no sold line)	1.50	.70	.45
89b	Ken Hamlin (company, sold line)	8.00	4.00	2.50
90a	Hank Bauer (box)	2.00	1.00	.60
90b	Hank Bauer (company)	2.00	1.00	.60
91a	Bob Allison (box, Minneapolis)	4.00	2.00	1.25
91b	Bob Allison (company, Minnesota)	5.00	2.50	1.50
92a	Harmon Killebrew (box, Minneapolis)	12.00	6.00	3.50
92b	Harmon Killebrew (company, Minnesota)	10.00	5.00	3.00
93a	Jim Lemon (box, Minneapolis)	40.00	20.00	12.00
93b	Jim Lemon (company, Minnesota)	5.00	2.50	1.50
94	Chuck Stobbs (company)	125.00	62.00	37.00
95a	Reno Bertoia (box, Minneapolis)	1.50	.70	.45
95b	Reno Bertoia (company, Minnesota)	4.00	2.00	1.25
96a	Billy Gardner (box, Minneapolis)	1.50	.70	.45
96b	Billy Gardner (company, Minnesota)	4.00	2.00	1.25
97a	Earl Battey (box, Minneapolis)	4.00	2.00	1.25
97b	Earl Battey (company, Minnesota)	4.00	2.00	1.25
98a	Pedro Ramos (box, Minneapolis)	1.50	.70	.45
98b	Pedro Ramos (company, Minnesota)	4.00	2.00	1.25
99a	Camilio Pascual (Camilo) (box, Minneapolis)	1.50	.70	.45
99b	Camilio Pascual (Camilo) (company, Minnesota)	4.00	2.00	1.25
100a	Billy Consolo (box, Minneapolis)	1.50	.70	.45
100b	Billy Consolo (company, Minnesota)	4.00	2.00	1.25
101a	Warren Spahn (box)	15.00	7.50	4.50
101b	Warren Spahn (company)	8.00	4.00	2.50
102a	Lew Burdette (box)	2.50	1.25	.70
102b	Lew Burdette (company)	2.50	1.25	.70
103a	Bob Buhl (box)	1.50	.70	.45
103b	Bob Buhl (company)	1.50	.70	.45
104a	Joe Adcock (box)	4.00	2.00	1.25
104b	Joe Adcock (company)	2.50	1.25	.70
105a	John Logan (box)	4.00	2.00	1.25
105b	John Logan (company)	1.75	.90	.50
106	Ed Mathews (company)	25.00	12.50	7.50
107a	Hank Aaron (box)	18.00	9.00	5.50
107b	Hank Aaron (company)	18.00	9.00	5.50
108a	Wes Covington (box)	1.50	.70	.45
108b	Wes Covington (company)	1.50	.70	.45
109a	Bill Bruton (box, Braves)	6.00	3.00	1.75
109b	Bill Bruton (company, Tigers)	8.00	4.00	2.50
110a	Del Crandall (box)	4.00	2.00	1.25
110b	Del Crandall (company)	1.75	.90	.50
111	Red Schoendienst (box)	5.00	2.50	1.50
112	Juan Pizarro (box)	1.50	.70	.45
113	Chuck Cottier (box)	8.00	4.00	2.50
114	Al Spangler (box)	1.50	.70	.45
115a	Dick Farrell (box)	6.00	3.00	1.75
115b	Dick Farrell (company)	4.00	2.00	1.25
116a	Jim Owens (box)	6.00	3.00	1.75
116b	Jim Owens (company)	4.00	2.00	1.25
117a	Robin Roberts (box)	6.00	3.00	1.75
117b	Robin Roberts (company)	6.00	3.00	1.75
118a	Tony Taylor (box)	1.50	.70	.45
118b	Tony Taylor (company)	1.50	.70	.45
119a	Lee Walls (box)	1.50	.70	.45
119b	Lee Walls (company)	1.50	.70	.45
120a	Tony Curry (box)	1.50	.70	.45
120b	Tony Curry (company)	1.50	.70	.45
121a	Pancho Herrera (box)	1.50	.70	.45
121b	Pancho Herrera (company)	1.50	.70	.45
122a	Ken Walters (box)	1.50	.70	.45
122b	Ken Walters (company)	1.50	.70	.45
123a	John Callison (box)	1.50	.70	.45
123b	John Callison (company)	1.50	.70	.45
124a	Gene Conley (box, Phillies)	1.50	.70	.45
124b	Gene Conley (company, Red Sox)	15.00	7.50	4.50
125a	Bob Friend (box)	4.00	2.00	1.25
125b	Bob Friend (company)	2.00	1.00	.60
126a	Vernon Law (box)	4.00	2.00	1.25
126b	Vernon Law (company)	2.00	1.00	.60
127a	Dick Stuart (box)	1.50	.70	.45
127b	Dick Stuart (company)	1.50	.70	.45
128a	Bill Mazeroski (box)	2.50	1.25	.70
128b	Bill Mazeroski (company)	2.50	1.25	.70
129a	Dick Groat (box)	3.00	1.50	.90
129b	Dick Groat (company)	2.00	1.00	.60
130a	Don Hoak (box)	1.50	.70	.45
130b	Don Hoak (company)	1.50	.70	.45
131a	Bob Skinner (box)	1.50	.70	.45
131b	Bob Skinner (company)	1.50	.70	.45
132a	Bob Clemente (box)	20.00	10.00	6.00
132b	Bob Clemente (company)	18.00	9.00	5.50
133	Roy Face (box)	3.00	1.50	.90
134	Harvey Haddix (box)	1.75	.90	.50
135	Bill Virdon (box)	25.00	12.50	7.50
136a	Gino Cimoli (box)	1.50	.70	.45
136b	Gino Cimoli (company)	1.50	.70	.45
137	Rocky Nelson (box)	1.50	.70	.45
138a	Smoky Burgess (box)	1.75	.90	.50
138b	Smoky Burgess (company)	1.75	.90	.50
139	Hal Smith (box)	1.50	.70	.45
140	Wilmer Mizell (box)	1.50	.70	.45
141a	Mike McCormick (box)	1.50	.70	.45
141b	Mike McCormick (company)	1.50	.70	.45
142a	John Antonelli (box, Giants)	3.00	1.50	.90
142b	John Antonelli (company, Indians)	4.00	2.00	1.25
143a	Sam Jones (box)	4.00	2.00	1.25
143b	Sam Jones (company)	2.00	1.00	.60
144a	Orlando Cepeda (box)	5.00	2.50	1.50
144b	Orlando Cepeda (company)	5.00	2.50	1.50
145a	Willie Mays (box)	18.00	9.00	5.50
145b	Willie Mays (company)	18.00	9.00	5.50
146a	Willie Kirkland (box, Giants)	5.00	2.50	1.50
146b	Willie Kirkland (company, Indians)	5.00	2.50	1.50
147a	Willie McCovey (box)	7.00	3.50	2.00
147b	Willie McCovey (company)	10.00	5.00	3.00
148a	Don Blasingame (box)	1.50	.70	.45
148b	Don Blasingame (company)	1.50	.70	.45
149a	Jim Davenport (box)	1.50	.70	.45
149b	Jim Davenport (company)	1.50	.70	.45
150a	Hobie Landrith (box)	1.50	.70	.45
150b	Hobie Landrith (company)	1.50	.70	.45
151	Bob Schmidt (box)	1.50	.70	.45
152a	Ed Bressoud (box)	1.50	.70	.45
152b	Ed Bressoud (company)	1.50	.70	.45
153a	Andre Rodgers (box, no traded line)	6.00	3.00	1.75
153b	Andre Rodgers (box, traded line)	1.50	.70	.45
154	Jack Sanford (box)	1.50	.70	.45
155	Billy O'Dell (box)	1.50	.70	.45
156a	Norm Larker (box)	2.50	1.25	.70
156b	Norm Larker (company)	2.50	1.25	.70
157a	Charlie Neal (box)	1.50	.70	.45
157b	Charlie Neal (company)	1.50	.70	.45
158a	Jim Gilliam (box)	4.00	2.00	1.25
158b	Jim Gilliam (company)	2.50	1.25	.70
159a	Wally Moon (box)	1.50	.70	.45
159b	Wally Moon (company)	1.50	.70	.45
160a	Don Drysdale (box)	7.00	3.50	2.00
160b	Don Drysdale (company)	8.00	4.00	2.50
161a	Larry Sherry (box)	1.50	.70	.45
161b	Larry Sherry (company)	1.50	.70	.45
162	Stan Williams (box)	5.00	2.50	1.50
163	Mel Roach (box)	40.00	20.00	12.00
164a	Maury Wills (box)	4.00	2.00	1.25
164b	Maury Wills (company)	4.00	2.00	1.25
165	Tom Davis (box)	2.00	1.00	.60
166a	John Roseboro (box)	1.50	.70	.45
166b	John Roseboro (company)	1.50	.70	.45
167a	Duke Snider (box)	8.00	4.00	2.50
167b	Duke Snider (company)	10.00	5.00	3.00
168a	Gil Hodges (box)	5.00	2.50	1.50
168b	Gil Hodges (company)	6.00	3.00	1.75
169	John Podres (box)	2.50	1.25	.70
170	Ed Roebuck (box)	1.50	.70	.45
171a	Ken Boyer (box)	6.00	3.00	1.75
171b	Ken Boyer (company)	4.00	2.00	1.25
172a	Joe Cunningham (box)	1.50	.70	.45
172b	Joe Cunningham (company)	1.50	.70	.45
173a	Daryl Spencer (box)	1.50	.70	.45
173b	Daryl Spencer (company)	1.50	.70	.45
174a	Larry Jackson (box)	1.50	.70	.45
174b	Larry Jackson (company)	1.50	.70	.45
175a	Lindy McDaniel (box)	1.50	.70	.45
175b	Lindy McDaniel (company)	1.50	.70	.45
176a	Bill White (box)	1.75	.90	.50
176b	Bill White (company)	1.75	.90	.50
177a	Alex Grammas (box)	1.50	.70	.45
177b	Alex Grammas (company)	1.50	.70	.45
178a	Curt Flood (box)	2.00	1.00	.60
178b	Curt Flood (company)	2.00	1.00	.60
179a	Ernie Broglio (box)	1.50	.70	.45
179b	Ernie Broglio (company)	1.50	.70	.45
180a	Hal Smith (box)	1.50	.70	.45
180b	Hal Smith (company)	1.50	.70	.45
181a	Vada Pinson (box)	2.50	1.25	.70
181b	Vada Pinson (company)	2.50	1.25	.70
182a	Frank Robinson (box)	12.00	6.00	3.50
182b	Frank Robinson (company)	18.00	9.00	5.50
183	Roy McMillan (box)	55.00	27.00	16.50
184a	Bob Purkey (box)	1.50	.70	.45
184b	Bob Purkey (company)	1.50	.70	.45
185a	Ed Kasko (box)	1.50	.70	.45
185b	Ed Kasko (company)	1.50	.70	.45
186a	Gus Bell (box)	1.50	.70	.45
186b	Gus Bell (company)	1.50	.70	.45
187a	Jerry Lynch (box)	1.50	.70	.45
187b	Jerry Lynch (company)	1.50	.70	.45
188a	Ed Bailey (box)	1.50	.70	.45
188b	Ed Bailey (company)	1.50	.70	.45
189a	Jim O'Toole (box)	1.50	.70	.45
189b	Jim O'Toole (company)	1.50	.70	.45
190a	Billy Martin (box, no sold line)	3.00	1.50	.90
190b	Billy Martin (company, sold line)	9.00	4.50	2.75
191a	Ernie Banks (box)	9.00	4.50	2.75
191b	Ernie Banks (company)	9.00	4.50	2.75
192a	Richie Ashburn (box)	3.00	1.50	.90
192b	Richie Ashburn (company)	3.00	1.50	.90
193a	Frank Thomas (box)	35.00	17.50	10.50
193b	Frank Thomas (company)	5.00	2.50	1.50
194a	Don Cardwell (box)	1.50	.70	.45
194b	Don Cardwell (company)	2.00	1.00	.60
195a	George Altman (box)	1.50	.70	.45
195b	George Altman (company)	2.00	1.00	.60
196a	Ron Santo (box)	3.00	1.50	.90
196b	Ron Santo (company)	3.00	1.50	.90
197a	Glen Hobbie (box)	1.50	.70	.45
197b	Glen Hobbie (company)	2.00	1.00	.60
198a	Sam Taylor (box)	1.50	.70	.45
198b	Sam Taylor (company)	2.00	1.00	.60
199a	Jerry Kindall (box)	1.50	.70	.45
199b	Jerry Kindall (company)	2.00	1.00	.60
200a	Don Elston (box)	3.00	1.50	.90
200b	Don Elston (company)	3.00	1.50	.90

1962 Post Cereal

Like the 1961 Post set, there are 200 players pictured in the set of 3-1/2" by 2-1/2" cards. Differences include a Post logo on the card fronts and the player's name in script lettering. Cards are again blank backed and were issued in panels of five to seven cards on cereal boxes. American League players are numbered 1-100 and National League players 101-200. With variations there are 210 of the full-color cards known. A handful of the '62 cards were also issued in smaller quantities. The cards of Mickey Mantle and Roger Maris were reproduced in a special two-card panel for a Life magazine insert. the card stock for this insert is slightly thinner, with white margins. The 1962 Post Canadian and Jell-O sets have virtually the same checklist as this set. The complete set price does not include the scarcer variations.

		NR MT	EX	VG
	Complete Set:	1100.	550.00	330.00
	Common Player:	1.50	.70	.45
1	Bill Skowron	4.00	2.00	1.25
2	Bobby Richardson	3.00	1.50	.90
3	Cletis Boyer	2.00	1.00	.60
4	Tony Kubek	3.00	1.50	.90
5a	Mickey Mantle (from box, no printing on back)	65.00	32.00	19.50
5b	Mickey Mantle (from ad, printing on back)	70.00	35.00	21.00
6a	Roger Maris (from box, no printing on back)	10.00	5.00	3.00
6b	Roger Maris (from ad, printing on back)	12.00	6.00	3.50
7	Yogi Berra	10.00	5.00	3.00
8	Elston Howard	3.00	1.50	.90
9	Whitey Ford	7.00	3.50	2.00
10	Ralph Terry	2.00	1.00	.60
11	John Blanchard	2.00	1.00	.60
12	Luis Arroyo	2.00	1.00	.60
13	Bill Stafford	2.00	1.00	.60
14a	Norm Cash (Throws: Right)	2.00	1.00	.60
14b	Norm Cash (Throws: Left)	5.00	2.50	1.50
15	Jake Wood	1.50	.70	.45
16	Steve Boros	1.50	.70	.45
17	Chico Fernandez	1.50	.70	.45
18	Bill Bruton	1.50	.70	.45
19	Rocky Colavito	3.00	1.50	.90
20	Al Kaline	8.00	4.00	2.50
21	Dick Brown	1.50	.70	.45
22	Frank Lary	1.50	.70	.45
23	Don Mossi	1.50	.70	.45
24	Phil Regan	1.50	.70	.45
25	Charley Maxwell	1.50	.70	.45
26	Jim Bunning	3.00	1.50	.90
27a	Jim Gentile (Home: Baltimore)	1.50	.70	.45
27b	Jim Gentile (Home: San Lorenzo)	5.00	2.50	1.50
28	Marv Breeding	1.50	.70	.45
29	Brooks Robinson	8.00	4.00	2.50
30	Ron Hansen	1.50	.70	.45
31	Jackie Brandt	1.50	.70	.45
32	Dick Williams	1.75	.90	.50
33	Gus Triandos	1.50	.70	.45
34	Milt Pappas	1.50	.70	.45
35	Hoyt Wilhelm	4.00	2.00	1.25
36	Chuck Estrada	5.00	2.50	1.50
37	Vic Power	1.50	.70	.45
38	Johnny Temple	1.50	.70	.45
39	Bubba Phillips	1.50	.70	.45
40	Tito Francona	1.50	.70	.45
41	Willie Kirkland	1.50	.70	.45
42	John Romano	1.50	.70	.45
43	Jim Perry	1.75	.90	.50
44	Woodie Held	1.50	.70	.45
45	Chuck Essegian	1.50	.70	.45
46	Roy Sievers	1.75	.90	.50
47	Nellie Fox	3.50	1.75	1.00
48	Al Smith	1.50	.70	.45
49	Luis Aparicio	4.00	2.00	1.25
50	Jim Landis	1.50	.70	.45
51	Minnie Minoso	2.00	1.00	.60
52	Andy Carey	1.50	.70	.45

		NR MT	EX	VG
53	Sherman Lollar	1.50	.70	.45
54	Bill Pierce	1.75	.90	.50
55	Early Wynn	25.00	12.50	7.50
56	Chuck Schilling	1.50	.70	.45
57	Pete Runnels	1.50	.70	.45
58	Frank Malzone	1.50	.70	.45
59	Don Buddin	1.50	.70	.45
60	Gary Geiger	1.50	.70	.45
61	Carl Yastrzemski	30.00	15.00	9.00
62	Jackie Jensen	2.00	1.00	.60
63	Jim Pagliaroni	1.50	.70	.45
64	Don Schwall	1.50	.70	.45
65	Dale Long	1.50	.70	.45
66	Chuck Cottier	1.50	.70	.45
67	Billy Klaus	1.50	.70	.45
68	Coot Veal	1.50	.70	.45
69	Marty Keough	25.00	12.50	7.50
70	Willie Tasby	1.50	.70	.45
71	Gene Woodling	1.50	.70	.45
72	Gene Green	1.50	.70	.45
73	Dick Donovan	1.50	.70	.45
74	Steve Bilko	1.50	.70	.45
75	Rocky Bridges	1.50	.70	.45
76	Eddie Yost	1.50	.70	.45
77	Leon Wagner	1.50	.70	.45
78	Albie Pearson	1.50	.70	.45
79	Ken Hunt	1.50	.70	.45
80	Earl Averill	1.50	.70	.45
81	Ryne Duren	1.50	.70	.45
82	Ted Kluszewski	2.50	1.25	.70
83	Bob Allison	20.00	10.00	6.00
84	Billy Martin	3.50	1.75	1.00
85	Harmon Killebrew	7.00	3.50	2.00
86	Zoilo Versalles	1.50	.70	.45
87	Lenny Green	1.50	.70	.45
88	Bill Tuttle	1.50	.70	.45
89	Jim Lemon	1.50	.70	.45
90	Earl Battey	1.50	.70	.45
91	Camilo Pascual	1.50	.70	.45
92	Norm Siebern	45.00	22.00	13.50
93	Jerry Lumpe	1.50	.70	.45
94	Dick Howser	2.00	1.00	.60
95a	Gene Stephens (Born: Jan. 5)	1.50	.70	.45
95b	Gene Stephens (Born: Jan. 20)	5.00	2.50	1.50
96	Leo Posada	1.50	.70	.45
97	Joe Pignatano	1.50	.70	.45
98	Jim Archer	1.50	.70	.45
99	Haywood Sullivan	1.50	.70	.45
100	Art Ditmar	1.50	.70	.45
101	Gil Hodges	50.00	25.00	15.00
102	Charlie Neal	1.50	.70	.45
103	Daryl Spencer	15.00	7.50	4.50
104	Maury Wills	4.00	2.00	1.25
105	Tommy Davis	2.00	1.00	.60
106	Willie Davis	1.75	.90	.50
107	John Roseboro	1.50	.70	.45
108	John Podres	2.50	1.25	.70
109a	Sandy Koufax (blue lines around stats)	25.00	12.50	7.50
109b	Sandy Koufax (red lines around stats)	15.00	7.50	4.50
110	Don Drysdale	7.00	3.50	2.00
111	Larry Sherry	1.50	.70	.45
112	Jim Gilliam	2.50	1.25	.70
113	Norm Larker	25.00	12.50	7.50
114	Duke Snider	8.00	4.00	2.50
115	Stan Williams	1.50	.70	.45
116	Gordy Coleman	60.00	30.00	18.00
117	Don Blasingame	1.50	.70	.45
118	Gene Freese	1.50	.70	.45
119	Ed Kasko	1.50	.70	.45
120	Gus Bell	1.50	.70	.45
121	Vada Pinson	2.50	1.25	.70
122	Frank Robinson	15.00	7.50	4.50
123	Bob Purkey	1.50	.70	.45
124a	Joey Jay (blue lines around stats)	8.00	4.00	2.50
124b	Joey Jay (red lines around stats)	1.50	.70	.45
125	Jim Brosnan	15.00	7.50	4.50
126	Jim O'Toole	1.50	.70	.45
127	Jerry Lynch	45.00	22.00	13.50
128	Wally Post	1.50	.70	.45
129	Ken Hunt	1.50	.70	.45
130	Jerry Zimmerman	1.50	.70	.45
131	Willie McCovey	60.00	30.00	18.00
132	Jose Pagan	1.50	.70	.45
133	Felipe Alou	1.75	.90	.50
134	Jim Davenport	1.50	.70	.45
135	Harvey Kuenn	2.00	1.00	.60
136	Orlando Cepeda	3.50	1.75	1.00
137	Ed Bailey	1.50	.70	.45
138	Sam Jones	1.50	.70	.45
139	Mike McCormick	1.50	.70	.45
140	Juan Marichal	60.00	30.00	18.00
141	Jack Sanford	1.50	.70	.45
142	Willie Mays	20.00	10.00	6.00
143	Stu Miller (photo actually Chuck Hiller)	6.00	3.00	1.75
144	Joe Amalfitano	10.00	5.00	3.00
145a	Joe Adock (name incorrect)	25.00	12.50	7.50
145b	Joe Adcock (name correct)	2.00	1.00	.60
146	Frank Bolling	1.50	.70	.45
147	Ed Mathews	7.00	3.50	2.00
148	Roy McMillan	1.50	.70	.45
149	Hank Aaron	20.00	10.00	6.00
150	Gino Cimoli	1.50	.70	.45
151	Frank Thomas	1.50	.70	.45
152	Joe Torre	3.00	1.50	.90
153	Lou Burdette	2.50	1.25	.70
154	Bob Buhl	1.50	.70	.45
155	Carlton Willey	1.50	.70	.45
156	Lee Maye	1.50	.70	.45
157	Al Spangler	1.50	.70	.45
158	Bill White	30.00	15.00	9.00
159	Ken Boyer	3.00	1.50	.90
160	Joe Cunningham	1.50	.70	.45
161	Carl Warwick	1.50	.70	.45
162	Carl Sawatski	1.50	.70	.45
163	Lindy McDaniel	1.50	.70	.45
164	Ernie Broglio	1.50	.70	.45
165	Larry Jackson	1.50	.70	.45
166	Curt Flood	2.00	1.00	.60
167	Curt Simmons	1.50	.70	.45
168	Alex Grammas	1.50	.70	.45
169	Dick Stuart	1.50	.70	.45
170	Bill Mazeroski	2.50	1.25	.70
171	Don Hoak	1.50	.70	.45
172	Dick Groat	2.00	1.00	.60
173a	Roberto Clemente (blue lines around stats)	25.00	12.50	7.50
173b	Roberto Clemente (red lines around stats)	15.00	7.50	4.50
174	Bob Skinner	1.50	.70	.45
175	Bill Virdon	1.75	.90	.50
176	Smoky Burgess	1.75	.90	.50
177	Elroy Face	1.75	.90	.50
178	Bob Friend	1.50	.70	.45
179	Vernon Law	1.50	.70	.45
180	Harvey Haddix	1.50	.70	.45
181	Hal Smith	1.50	.70	.45
182	Ed Bouchee	1.50	.70	.45
183	Don Zimmer	1.50	.70	.45
184	Ron Santo	2.50	1.25	.70
185	Andre Rodgers	1.50	.70	.45
186	Richie Ashburn	3.00	1.50	.90
187a	George Altman (last line is "...1955).)	1.50	.70	.45
187b	George Altman (last line is "...1955.")	3.00	1.50	.90
188	Ernie Banks	8.00	4.00	2.50
189	Sam Taylor	1.50	.70	.45
190	Don Elston	1.50	.70	.45
191	Jerry Kindall	1.50	.70	.45
192	Pancho Herrera	1.50	.70	.45
193	Tony Taylor	1.50	.70	.45
194	Ruben Amaro	1.50	.70	.45
195	Don Demeter	1.50	.70	.45
196	Bobby Gene Smith	1.50	.70	.45
197	Clay Dalrymple	1.50	.70	.45
198	Robin Roberts	5.00	2.50	1.50
199	Art Mahaffey	1.50	.70	.45
200	John Buzhardt	2.50	1.25	.70

1962 Post Cereal Canadian

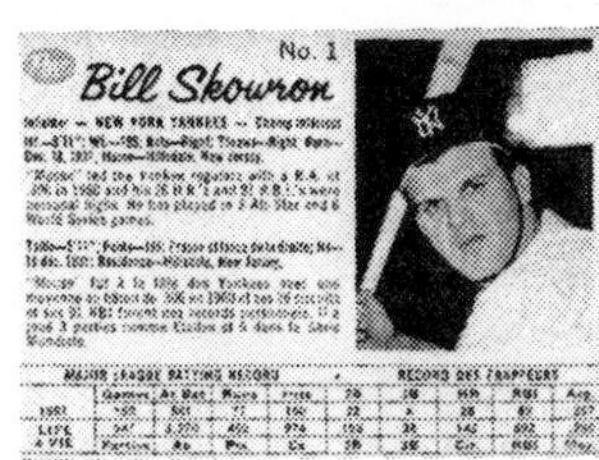

This Canadian set of cards is scarce due to the much more limited distribution in Canada. The cards were printed on the back of the cereal box itself and contains a full-color player photo with biography and statistics given in both French and English. The card backs are blank. Cards measure 3-1/2" by 2-1/2". This 200-card set is very similar to the Post Cereal cards printed in the United States. the Post logo appears at the upper left corner in the Canadian issue. Several cards are scarce because of limited distribution and there are two Whitey Ford cards, the corrected version being the most scarce. The complete set price does not include the scarcer variations.

		NR MT	EX	VG
Complete Set:		2000.	1000.	600.00
Common Player:		2.50	1.25	.70
1	Bill Skowron	8.00	4.00	2.50
2	Bobby Richardson	6.00	3.00	1.75
3	Cletis Boyer	3.50	1.75	1.00
4	Tony Kubek	6.00	3.00	1.75
5a	Mickey Mantle (script name large)	150.00	75.00	45.00
5b	Mickey Mantle (script name small)	90.00	45.00	27.00
6	Roger Maris	15.00	7.50	4.50
7	Yogi Berra	15.00	7.50	4.50
8	Elston Howard	4.00	2.00	1.25
9a	Whitey Ford (Dodgers)	20.00	10.00	6.00
9b	Whitey Ford (Yankees)	35.00	17.50	10.50
10	Ralph Terry	25.00	12.50	7.50
11	John Blanchard	3.00	1.50	.90
12	Luis Arroyo	3.00	1.50	.90
13	Bill Stafford	3.00	1.50	.90
14	Norm Cash	4.00	2.00	1.25
15	Jake Wood	2.50	1.25	.70
16	Steve Boros	2.50	1.25	.70
17	Chico Fernandez	2.50	1.25	.70
18	Bill Bruton	2.50	1.25	.70
19a	Rocky Colavito (script name large)	7.00	3.50	2.00
19b	Rocky Colavito (script name small)	7.00	3.50	2.00
20	Al Kaline	15.00	7.50	4.50
21	Dick Brown	7.00	3.50	2.00
22a	Frank Lary (French bio variation)	7.00	3.50	2.00
22b	Frank Lary (French bio variation)	7.00	3.50	2.00
23	Don Mossi	2.50	1.25	.70
24	Phil Regan	2.50	1.25	.70
25	Charley Maxwell	2.50	1.25	.70
26	Jim Bunning	6.00	3.00	1.75
27a	Jim Gentile (French bio variation)	5.00	2.50	1.50
27b	Jim Gentile (French bio variation)	5.00	2.50	1.50
28	Marv Breeding	2.50	1.25	.70
29	Brooks Robinson	25.00	12.50	7.50
30	Ron Hansen	2.50	1.25	.70
31	Jackie Brandt	2.50	1.25	.70
32	Dick Williams	25.00	12.50	7.50
33	Gus Triandos	2.50	1.25	.70
34	Milt Pappas	3.00	1.50	.90
35	Hoyt Wilhelm	15.00	7.50	4.50
36	Chuck Estrada	2.50	1.25	.70
37	Vic Power	2.50	1.25	.70
38	Johnny Temple	2.50	1.25	.70
39	Bubba Phillips	25.00	12.50	7.50
40	Tito Francona	2.50	1.25	.70
41	Willie Kirkland	7.00	3.50	2.00
42	John Romano	7.00	3.50	2.00
43	Jim Perry	4.00	2.00	1.25
44	Woodie Held	2.50	1.25	.70
45	Chuck Essegian	2.50	1.25	.70
46	Roy Sievers	3.50	1.75	1.00
47	Nellie Fox	6.00	3.00	1.75
48	Al Smith	2.50	1.25	.70
49	Luis Aparicio	15.00	7.50	4.50
50	Jim Landis	2.50	1.25	.70
51	Minnie Minoso	25.00	12.50	7.50
52	Andy Carey	7.00	3.50	2.00
53	Sherman Lollar	2.50	1.25	.70
54	Bill Pierce	3.50	1.75	1.00
55	Early Wynn	12.00	6.00	3.50
56	Chuck Schilling	2.50	1.25	.70
57	Pete Runnels	3.00	1.50	.90
58	Frank Malzone	2.50	1.25	.70
59	Don Buddin	7.00	3.50	2.00
60	Gary Geiger	2.50	1.25	.70
61	Carl Yastrzemski	40.00	20.00	12.00
62	Jackie Jensen	9.00	4.50	2.75
63	Jim Pagliaroni	2.50	1.25	.70
64	Don Schwall	2.50	1.25	.70
65	Dale Long	2.50	1.25	.70
66	Chuck Cottier	2.50	1.25	.70
67	Billy Klaus	2.50	1.25	.70
68	Coot Veal	2.50	1.25	.70
69	Marty Keough	2.50	1.25	.70
70	Willie Tasby	25.00	12.50	7.50
71	Gene Woodling (photo reversed)	3.00	1.50	.90
72	Gene Green	2.50	1.25	.70
73	Dick Donovan	2.50	1.25	.70
74	Steve Bilko	2.50	1.25	.70
75	Rocky Bridges	6.00	3.00	1.75
76	Eddie Yost	2.50	1.25	.70
77	Leon Wagner	25.00	12.50	7.50
78	Albie Pearson	7.00	3.50	2.00
79	Ken Hunt	2.50	1.25	.70
80	Earl Averill	2.50	1.25	.70
81	Ryne Duren	4.00	2.00	1.25
82	Ted Kluszewski	4.00	2.00	1.25
83	Bob Allison	3.00	1.50	.90
84	Billy Martin	6.00	3.00	1.75
85	Harmon Killebrew	12.00	6.00	3.50
86	Zoilo Versalles	2.50	1.25	.70
87	Lenny Green	2.50	1.25	.70
88	Bill Tuttle	2.50	1.25	.70
89	Jim Lemon	2.50	1.25	.70
90	Earl Battey	2.50	1.25	.70
91	Camilo Pascual	3.00	1.50	.90
92	Norm Siebern	2.50	1.25	.70
93	Jerry Lumpe	2.50	1.25	.70
94	Dick Howser	25.00	12.50	7.50
95	Gene Stephens	2.50	1.25	.70
96	Leo Posada	2.50	1.25	.70
97	Joe Pignatano	2.50	1.25	.70
98	Jim Archer	2.50	1.25	.70
99	Haywood Sullivan	25.00	12.50	7.50
100	Art Ditmar	25.00	12.50	7.50
101	Gil Hodges	12.00	6.00	3.50
102	Charlie Neal	2.50	1.25	.70
103	Daryl Spencer	2.50	1.25	.70
104	Maury Wills	5.00	2.50	1.50
105	Tommy Davis	9.00	4.50	2.75
106	Willie Davis	4.00	2.00	1.25
107	John Roseboro	3.00	1.50	.90
108	John Podres	4.00	2.00	1.25
109	Sandy Koufax	30.00	15.00	9.00
110	Don Drysdale	15.00	7.50	4.50
111	Larry Sherry	25.00	12.50	7.50
112	Jim Gilliam	25.00	12.50	7.50
113	Norm Larker	2.50	1.25	.70
114	Duke Snider	25.00	12.50	7.50
115	Stan Williams	2.50	1.25	.70
116	Gordy Coleman	2.50	1.25	.70
117	Don Blasingame	25.00	12.50	7.50
118	Gene Freese	7.00	3.50	2.00
119	Ed Kasko	2.50	1.25	.70
120	Gus Bell	2.50	1.25	.70
121	Vada Pinson	5.00	2.50	1.50
122	Frank Robinson	15.00	7.50	4.50
123	Bob Purkey	25.00	12.50	7.50
124	Joey Jay	2.50	1.25	.70
125	Jim Brosnan	3.00	1.50	.90
126	Jim O'Toole	2.50	1.25	.70
127	Jerry Lynch	2.50	1.25	.70
128	Wally Post	55.00	27.00	16.50
129	Ken Hunt	2.50	1.25	.70
130	Jerry Zimmerman	2.50	1.25	.70
131	Willie McCovey	15.00	7.50	4.50
132	Jose Pagan	2.50	1.25	.70
133	Felipe Alou	3.50	1.75	1.00
134	Jim Davenport	2.50	1.25	.70
135	Harvey Kuenn	4.00	2.00	1.25
136	Orlando Cepeda	6.00	3.00	1.75
137	Ed Bailey	25.00	12.50	7.50
138	Sam Jones	25.00	12.50	7.50
139	Mike McCormick	2.50	1.25	.70
140	Juan Marichal	15.00	7.50	4.50
141	Jack Sanford	2.50	1.25	.70
142a	Willie Mays (big head)	35.00	17.50	10.50
142b	Willie Mays (small head)	50.00	25.00	15.00
143	Stu Miller	2.50	1.25	.70
144	Joe Amalfitano	25.00	12.50	7.50
145	Joe Adcock	4.00	2.00	1.25

		NR MT	EX	VG
146	Frank Bolling	2.50	1.25	.70
147	Ed Mathews	12.00	6.00	3.50
148	Roy McMillan	2.50	1.25	.70
149a	Hank Aaron (script name large)	35.00	17.50	10.50
149b	Hank Aaron (script name small)	35.00	17.50	10.50
150	Gino Cimoli	2.50	1.25	.70
151	Frank Thomas	2.50	1.25	.70
152	Joe Torre	5.00	2.50	1.50
153	Lou Burdette	5.00	2.50	1.50
154	Bob Buhl	3.00	1.50	.90
155	Carlton Willey	2.50	1.25	.70
156	Lee Maye	2.50	1.25	.70
157	Al Spangler	2.50	1.25	.70
158	Bill White	3.50	1.75	1.00
159	Ken Boyer	30.00	15.00	9.00
160	Joe Cunningham	2.50	1.25	.70
161	Carl Warwick	7.00	3.50	2.00
162	Carl Sawatski	2.50	1.25	.70
163	Lindy McDaniel	2.50	1.25	.70
164	Ernie Broglio	2.50	1.25	.70
165	Larry Jackson	2.50	1.25	.70
166	Curt Flood	4.00	2.00	1.25
167	Curt Simmons	8.00	4.00	2.50
168	Alex Grammas	2.50	1.25	.70
169	Dick Stuart	3.00	1.50	.90
170	Bill Mazeroski	25.00	12.50	7.50
171	Don Hoak	2.50	1.25	.70
172	Dick Groat	9.00	4.50	2.75
173	Roberto Clemente	30.00	15.00	9.00
174	Bob Skinner	2.50	1.25	.70
175	Bill Virdon	4.00	2.00	1.25
176	Smoky Burgess	8.00	4.00	2.50
177	Elroy Face	8.00	4.00	2.50
178	Bob Friend	3.00	1.50	.90
179	Vernon Law	3.50	1.75	1.00
180	Harvey Haddix	3.00	1.50	.90
181	Hal Smith	25.00	12.50	7.50
182	Ed Bouchee	2.50	1.25	.70
183	Don Zimmer	4.00	2.00	1.25
184	Ron Santo	5.00	2.50	1.50
185	Andre Rodgers	2.50	1.25	.70
186	Richie Ashburn	6.00	3.00	1.75
187	George Altman	2.50	1.25	.70
188	Ernie Banks	25.00	12.50	7.50
189	Sam Taylor	2.50	1.25	.70
190	Don Elston	2.50	1.25	.70
191	Jerry Kindall	2.50	1.25	.70
192	Pancho Herrera	2.50	1.25	.70
193	Tony Taylor	2.50	1.25	.70
194	Ruben Amaro	2.50	1.25	.70
195	Don Demeter	25.00	12.50	7.50
196	Bobby Gene Smith	2.50	1.25	.70
197	Clay Dalrymple	2.50	1.25	.70
198	Robin Roberts	12.00	6.00	3.50
199	Art Mahaffey	2.50	1.25	.70
200	John Buzhardt	5.00	2.50	1.50

1963 Post Cereal

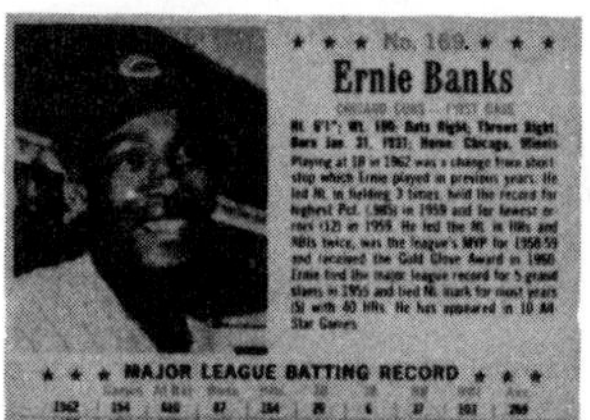

Another 200-player, 3-1/2" by 2-1/2" set that, with variations, totals more than 205 cards. Numerous color variations also exist due to the different cereal boxes on which the cards were printed. As many as 25 cards in the set are considered scarce, making it much more difficult to complete than the other major Post sets. Star cards also command higher prices than in the '61 or '62 Post cards. The 1963 Post cards are almost identical to the '63 Jell-O set, which is a slight 1/4" narrower. Cards are still blank backed, with a color player photo, biographies and statistics on the numbered card fronts. No Post logo appears on the '63 cards. The complete set price Joes not include the scarcer variations.

	NR MT	EX	VG
Complete Set:	3250.	1625.	975.00
Common Player:	1.50	.70	.45

		NR MT	EX	VG
1	Vic Power	3.50	1.75	1.00
2	Bernie Allen	1.50	.70	.45
3	Zoilo Versalles	1.50	.70	.45
4	Rich Rollins	1.50	.70	.45
5	Harmon Killebrew	12.00	6.00	3.50
6	Lenny Green	35.00	17.50	10.50
7	Bob Allison	1.75	.90	.50
8	Earl Battey	1.50	.70	.45
9	Camilo Pascual	1.50	.70	.45
10	Jim Kaat	3.00	1.50	.90
11	Jack Kralick	1.50	.70	.45
12	Bill Skowron	2.00	1.00	.60
13	Bobby Richardson	3.00	1.50	.90
14	Cletis Boyer	2.00	1.00	.60
15	Mickey Mantle	325.00	162.00	97.00
16	Roger Maris	150.00	75.00	45.00
17	Yogi Berra	15.00	7.50	4.50
18	Elston Howard	3.00	1.50	.90
19	Whitey Ford	8.00	4.00	2.50
20	Ralph Terry	2.00	1.00	.60

		NR MT	EX	VG
21	John Blanchard	2.00	1.00	.60
22	Bill Stafford	2.00	1.00	.60
23	Tom Tresh	2.00	1.00	.60
24	Steve Bilko	1.50	.70	.45
25	Bill Moran	1.50	.70	.45
26a	Joe Koppe (1962 Avg. is .277)	1.50	.70	.45
26b	Joe Koppe (1962 Avg. is .227)	12.00	6.00	3.50
27	Felix Torres	1.50	.70	.45
28a	Leon Wagner (lifetime Avg. is .278)	1.50	.70	.45
28b	Leon Wagner (lifetime Avg. is .272)	12.00	6.00	3.50
29	Albie Pearson	1.50	.70	.45
30	Lee Thomas (photo actually George Thomas)	70.00	35.00	21.00
31	Bob Rodgers	1.50	.70	.45
32	Dean Chance	1.50	.70	.45
33	Ken McBride	1.50	.70	.45
34	George Thomas (photo actually Lee Thomas)	1.50	.70	.45
35	Joe Cunningham	1.50	.70	.45
36a	Nelson Fox (no bat showing)	3.50	1.75	1.00
36b	Nelson Fox (part of bat showing)	10.00	5.00	3.00
37	Luis Aparicio	4.00	2.00	1.25
38	Al Smith	25.00	12.50	7.50
39	Floyd Robinson	80.00	40.00	24.00
40	Jim Landis	1.50	.70	.45
41	Charlie Maxwell	1.50	.70	.45
42	Sherman Lollar	1.50	.70	.45
43	Early Wynn	6.00	3.00	1.75
44	Juan Pizarro	1.50	.70	.45
45	Ray Herbert	1.50	.70	.45
46	Norm Cash	2.00	1.00	.60
47	Steve Boros	1.50	.70	.45
48	Dick McAuliffe	25.00	12.50	7.50
49	Bill Bruton	1.50	.70	.45
50	Rocky Colavito	3.00	1.50	.90
51	Al Kaline	10.00	5.00	3.00
52	Dick Brown	1.50	.70	.45
53	Jim Bunning	90.00	45.00	27.00
54	Hank Aguirre	1.50	.70	.45
55	Frank Lary	1.50	.70	.45
56	Don Mossi	1.50	.70	.45
57	Jim Gentile	1.50	.70	.45
58	Jackie Brandt	1.50	.70	.45
59	Brooks Robinson	10.00	5.00	3.00
60	Ron Hansen	1.50	.70	.45
61	Jerry Adair	150.00	75.00	45.00
62	John Powell	3.00	1.50	.90
63	Russ Snyder	1.50	.70	.45
64	Steve Barber	1.50	.70	.45
65	Milt Pappas	1.50	.70	.45
66	Robin Roberts	4.00	2.00	1.25
67	Tito Francona	1.50	.70	.45
68	Jerry Kindall	1.50	.70	.45
69	Woodie Held	1.50	.70	.45
70	Bubba Phillips	15.00	7.50	4.50
71	Chuck Essegian	1.50	.70	.45
72	Willie Kirkland	1.50	.70	.45
73	Al Luplow	1.50	.70	.45
74	Ty Cline	1.50	.70	.45
75	Dick Donovan	1.50	.70	.45
76	John Romano	1.50	.70	.45
77	Pete Runnels	1.50	.70	.45
78	Ed Bressoud	1.50	.70	.45
79	Frank Malzone	1.50	.70	.45
80	Carl Yastrzemski	275.00	137.00	82.00
81	Gary Geiger	1.50	.70	.45
82	Lou Clinton	1.50	.70	.45
83	Earl Wilson	1.50	.70	.45
84	Bill Monbouquette	1.50	.70	.45
85	Norm Siebern	1.50	.70	.45
86	Jerry Lumpe	80.00	40.00	24.00
87	Manny Jimenez	80.00	40.00	24.00
88	Gino Cimoli	1.50	.70	.45
89	Ed Charles	1.50	.70	.45
90	Ed Rakow	1.50	.70	.45
91	Bob Del Greco	1.50	.70	.45
92	Haywood Sullivan	1.50	.70	.45
93	Chuck Hinton	1.50	.70	.45
94	Ken Retzer	1.50	.70	.45
95	Harry Bright	1.50	.70	.45
96	Bob Johnson	1.50	.70	.45
97	Dave Stenhouse	15.00	7.50	4.50
98	Chuck Cottier	25.00	12.50	7.50
99	Tom Cheney	1.50	.70	.45
100	Claude Osteen	15.00	7.50	4.50
101	Orlando Cepeda	3.00	1.50	.90
102	Charley Hiller	1.50	.70	.45
103	Jose Pagan	1.50	.70	.45
104	Jim Davenport	1.50	.70	.45
105	Harvey Kuenn	2.00	1.00	.60
106	Willie Mays	25.00	12.50	7.50
107	Felipe Alou	1.75	.90	.50
108	Tom Haller	90.00	45.00	27.00
109	Juan Marichal	6.00	3.00	1.75
110	Jack Sanford	1.50	.70	.45
111	Bill O'Dell	1.50	.70	.45
112	Willie McCovey	7.00	3.50	2.00
113	Lee Walls	1.50	.70	.45
114	Jim Gilliam	3.00	1.50	.90
115	Maury Wills	3.00	1.50	.90
116	Ron Fairly	1.50	.70	.45
117	Tommy Davis	2.00	1.00	.60
118	Duke Snider	8.00	4.00	2.50
119	Willie Davis	150.00	75.00	45.00
120	John Roseboro	1.50	.70	.45
121	Sandy Koufax	15.00	7.50	4.50
122	Stan Williams	1.50	.70	.45
123	Don Drysdale	7.00	3.50	2.00
124a	Daryl Spencer (no arm showing)	1.50	.70	.45
124b	Daryl Spencer (part of arm showing)	10.00	5.00	3.00
125	Gordy Coleman	1.50	.70	.45
126	Don Blasingame	1.50	.70	.45
127	Leo Cardenas	1.50	.70	.45
128	Eddie Kasko	150.00	75.00	45.00
129	Jerry Lynch	15.00	7.50	4.50
130	Vada Pinson	2.00	1.00	.60

		NR MT	EX	VG
131a	Frank Robinson (no stripes on hat)	8.00	4.00	2.50
131b	Frank Robinson (stripes on hat)	15.00	7.50	4.50
132	John Edwards	1.50	.70	.45
133	Joey Jay	1.50	.70	.45
134	Bob Purkey	1.50	.70	.45
135	Marty Keough	15.00	7.50	4.50
136	Jim O'Toole	1.50	.70	.45
137	Dick Stuart	1.50	.70	.45
138	Bill Mazeroski	2.00	1.00	.60
139	Dick Groat	2.00	1.00	.60
140	Don Hoak	30.00	15.00	9.00
141	Bob Skinner	15.00	7.50	4.50
142	Bill Virdon	2.00	1.00	.60
143	Roberto Clemente	20.00	10.00	6.00
144	Smoky Burgess	1.75	.90	.50
145	Bob Friend	1.50	.70	.45
146	Al McBean	1.50	.70	.45
147	El Roy Face (Elroy)	2.00	1.00	.60
148	Joe Adcock	2.00	1.00	.60
149	Frank Bolling	1.50	.70	.45
150	Roy McMillan	1.50	.70	.45
151	Eddie Mathews	6.00	3.00	1.75
152	Hank Aaron	70.00	35.00	21.00
153	Del Crandall	30.00	15.00	9.00
154a	Bob Shaw (third sentence has "In 1959" twice)	10.00	5.00	3.00
154b	Bob Shaw (third sentence has "In 1959" once)	1.50	.70	.45
155	Lew Burdette	2.00	1.00	.60
156	Joe Torre	3.00	1.50	.90
157	Tony Cloninger	1.50	.70	.45
158	Bill White	2.00	1.00	.60
159	Julian Javier	1.50	.70	.45
160	Ken Boyer	3.00	1.50	.90
161	Julio Gotay	1.50	.70	.45
162	Curt Flood	90.00	45.00	27.00
163	Charlie James	1.50	.70	.45
164	Gene Oliver	1.50	.70	.45
165	Ernie Broglio	1.50	.70	.45
166	Bob Gibson	7.00	3.50	2.00
167a	Lindy McDaniel (asterisk before trade line)	1.50	.70	.45
167b	Lindy McDaniel (no asterisk before trade line)	5.00	2.50	1.50
168	Ray Washburn	1.50	.70	.45
169	Ernie Banks	8.00	4.00	2.50
170	Ron Santo	2.00	1.00	.60
171	George Altman	1.50	.70	.45
172	Billy Williams	90.00	45.00	27.00
173	Andre Rodgers	6.00	3.00	1.75
174	Ken Hubbs	20.00	10.00	6.00
175	Don Landrum	1.50	.70	.45
176	Dick Bertell	15.00	7.50	4.50
177	Roy Sievers	1.75	.90	.50
178	Tony Taylor	1.50	.70	.45
179	John Callison	1.75	.90	.50
180	Don Demeter	1.50	.70	.45
181	Tony Gonzalez	1.50	.70	.45
182	Wes Covington	20.00	10.00	6.00
183	Art Mahaffey	1.50	.70	.45
184	Clay Dalrymple	1.50	.70	.45
185	Al Spangler	1.50	.70	.45
186	Roman Mejias	1.50	.70	.45
187	Bob Aspromonte	275.00	137.00	82.00
188	Norm Larker	30.00	15.00	9.00
189	Johnny Temple	1.50	.70	.45
190	Carl Warwick	1.50	.70	.45
191	Bob Lillis	1.50	.70	.45
192	Dick Farrell	1.50	.70	.45
193	Gil Hodges	7.00	3.50	2.00
194	Marv Throneberry	3.00	1.50	.90
195	Charlie Neal	10.00	5.00	3.00
196	Frank Thomas	150.00	75.00	45.00
197	Richie Ashburn	20.00	10.00	6.00
198	Felix Mantilla	1.50	.70	.45
199	Rod Kanehl	20.00	10.00	6.00
200	Roger Craig	3.00	1.50	.90

1986 Provigo Expos

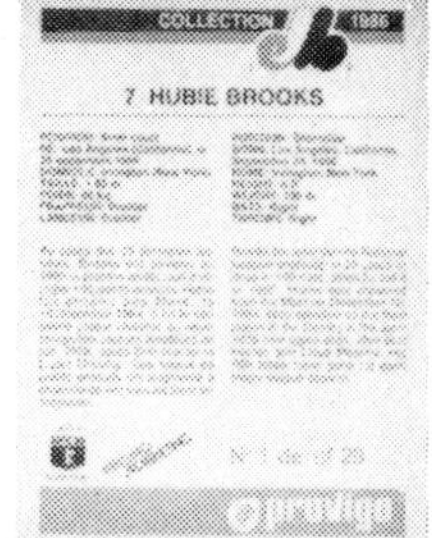

This 28-card set was issued in three-card panels of 7-1/2" by 3-3/8". Each card measures 2-1/2" by 3-3/8", and each panel includes two players and an advertising card. Panels are perforated to allow for separation, if desired. Card fronts have high quality game-action color photos with the player's name, uniform number and Expos and Provigo logos. Card backs include biographical information in both French and English and list the card's number within the set. There are 24 player, one manager and two coaches cards, along with a card of the Expos mascot, Youppi.

	MT	NR MT	EX
Complete Panel Set:	12.00	9.00	4.75
Complete Singles Set:	5.00	3.75	2.00

		MT	NR MT	EX
Common Panel:		.35	.25	.14
Common Single Player:		.06	.05	.02
Panel 1		.80	.60	.30
1	Hubie Brooks	.50	.40	.20
2	Dann Bilardello	.06	.05	.02
---	Checklist	.03	.02	.01
Panel 2		.35	.25	.14
3	Buck Rodgers	.12	.09	.05
4	Andy McGaffigan	.06	.05	.02
---	Album Offer	.03	.02	.01
Panel 3		.60	.45	.25
5	Mitch Webster	.15	.11	.06
6	Jim Wohlford	.06	.05	.02
---	Album Offer	.03	.02	.01
Panel 4		2.00	1.50	.80
7	Tim Raines	1.00	.70	.40
8	Jay Tibbs	.06	.05	.02
---	Album Offer	.03	.02	.01
Panel 5		3.50	2.75	1.50
9	Andre Dawson	1.50	1.25	.60
10	Andres Galarraga	1.50	1.25	.60
---	Album Offer	.03	.02	.01
Panel 6		.70	.50	.30
11	Tim Wallach	.40	.30	.15
12	Dan Schatzeder	.06	.05	.02
---	Checklist	.03	.02	.01
Panel 7		.50	.40	.20
13	Jeff Reardon	.30	.25	.12
14	Expos' Coaching Staff (Larry Bearnarth, Joe Kerrigan, Bobby Winkles)	.06	.05	.02
---	Album Offer	.03	.02	.01
Panel 8		.35	.25	.14
15	Jason Thompson	.06	.05	.02
16	Bert Roberge	.06	.05	.02
---	$1 Expos Ticket Coupon	.03	.02	.01
Panel 9		.35	.25	.14
17	Al Newman	.06	.05	.02
18	Tim Burke	.25	.20	.10
---	Album Offer	.03	.02	.01
Panel 10		.35	.25	.14
19	Bryn Smith	.15	.11	.06
20	Wayne Krenchicki	.06	.05	.02
---	Album Offer	.03	.02	.01
Panel 11		.35	.25	.14
21	Joe Hesketh	.08	.06	.03
22	Herman Winningham	.06	.05	.02
---	Album Offer	.03	.02	.01
Panel 12		.60	.45	.25
23	Vance Law	.08	.06	.03
24	Floyd Youmans	.15	.11	.06
---	Album Offer	.03	.02	.01
Panel 13		.50	.40	.20
25	Jeff Parrett	.12	.09	.05
26	Mike Fitzgerald	.06	.05	.02
---	Album Offer	.03	.02	.01
Panel 14		.35	.25	.14
27	Youppi (Team Mascot)	.06	.05	.02
28	Expos' Coaching Staff (Ron Hansen, Ken Macha, Rick Renick)	.06	.05	.02
---	Album Offer	.03	.02	.01

1986 Quaker Oats

The Quaker Company, in conjunction with Topps, produced this 33-card set of current baseball stars for packaging in groups of three in Chewy Granola Bars packages. The cards are noted as the "1st Annual Collectors Edition." They are numbered and measure 2-1/2" by 3-1/2". Card fronts feature full-color player photos with the product name at the top and the player name, team and position below the photo. The complete set was offered via mail order by the Quaker Company.

		MT	NR MT	EX
Complete Set:		8.00	6.00	3.25
Common Player:		.15	.11	.06
1	Willie McGee	.15	.11	.06
2	Dwight Gooden	.60	.45	.25
3	Vince Coleman	.30	.25	.12
4	Gary Carter	.25	.20	.10
5	Jack Clark	.15	.11	.06
6	Steve Garvey	.25	.20	.10
7	Tony Gwynn	.35	.25	.14
8	Dale Murphy	.40	.30	.15
9	Dave Parker	.15	.11	.06
10	Tim Raines	.25	.20	.10
11	Pete Rose	.60	.45	.25
12	Nolan Ryan	.25	.20	.10
13	Ryne Sandberg	.20	.15	.08
14	Mike Schmidt	.35	.25	.14
15	Ozzie Smith	.15	.11	.06
16	Darryl Strawberry	.40	.30	.15
17	Fernando Valenzuela	.20	.15	.08
18	Don Mattingly	1.50	1.25	.60
19	Bret Saberhagen	.20	.15	.08
20	Ozzie Guillen	.15	.11	.06
21	Bert Blyleven	.15	.11	.06
22	Wade Boggs	.80	.60	.30
23	George Brett	.40	.30	.15
24	Darrell Evans	.15	.11	.06
25	Rickey Henderson	.35	.25	.14
26	Reggie Jackson	.30	.25	.12
27	Eddie Murray	.30	.25	.12
28	Phil Niekro	.20	.15	.08
29	Dan Quisenberry	.15	.11	.06
30	Jim Rice	.25	.20	.10
31	Cal Ripken	.30	.25	.12
32	Tom Seaver	.25	.20	.10
33	Dave Winfield	.25	.20	.10
---	Offer Card	.03	.02	.01

1943 R302-1 M.P. & Co.

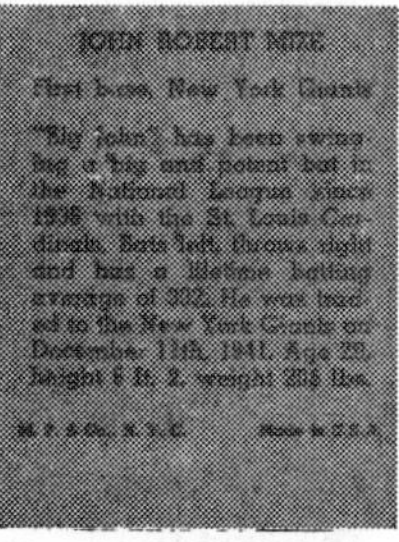

One of the few baseball card sets issued during the war years, this set of unnumbered cards, each measuring approximately 2-11/16" by 2-1/4", feature rather crude drawings that have little resemblance to the player named. The cards were originally produced in strips and sold inexpensively in candy stores. The backs contain brief player write-ups.

		NR MT	EX	VG
Complete Set:		400.00	200.00	120.00
Common Player:		6.00	3.00	1.75
(1)	Ernie Bonham	6.00	3.00	1.75
(2)	Lou Boudreau	12.00	6.00	3.50
(3)	Dolph Camilli	6.00	3.00	1.75
(4)	Mort Cooper	6.00	3.00	1.75
(5)	Walker Cooper	6.00	3.00	1.75
(6)	Joe Cronin	12.00	6.00	3.50
(7)	Hank Danning	6.00	3.00	1.75
(8)	Bill Dickey	18.00	9.00	5.50
(9)	Joe DiMaggio	75.00	37.00	22.00
(10)	Bobby Feller	20.00	10.00	6.00
(11)	Jimmy Foxx	20.00	10.00	6.00
(12)	Hank Greenberg	15.00	7.50	4.50
(13)	Stan Hack	6.00	3.00	1.75
(14)	Tom Henrich	7.00	3.50	2.00
(15)	Carl Hubbell	12.00	6.00	3.50
(16)	Joe Medwick	12.00	6.00	3.50
(17)	John Mize	12.00	6.00	3.50
(18)	Lou Novikoff	6.00	3.00	1.75
(19)	Mel Ott	15.00	7.50	4.50
(20)	Pee Wee Reese	20.00	10.00	6.00
(21)	Pete Reiser	6.00	3.00	1.75
(22)	Charlie Ruffing	12.00	6.00	3.50
(23)	Johnny Vander Meer	7.00	3.50	2.00
(24)	Ted Williams	50.00	25.00	15.00

1949 R302-2 M.P. & Co.

This set appears to be a re-issue of M.P. & Company's 1943 card set with different players and numbers added to the back. The cards, which measure 2-11/16" by 2-1/4", feature crude drawings of generic baseball players which have little resemblance to the player named. The backs include the card number and player information. The numbering sequence begins with card 100, and numbers 104, 118, and 120 are unknown, while two of the cards (Henrich and Kozar) are unnumbered. The set is assigned the American Card Catalog number R302-2.

		NR MT	EX	VG
Complete Set:		375.00	187.00	112.00
Common Player:		6.00	3.00	1.75
100	Lou Boudreau	12.00	6.00	3.50
101	Ted Williams	50.00	25.00	15.00
102	Buddy Kerr	6.00	3.00	1.75
103	Bobby Feller	20.00	10.00	6.00
104	Unknown			
105	Joe DiMaggio	75.00	37.00	22.00
106	Pee Wee Reese	20.00	10.00	6.00
107	Ferris Fain	6.00	3.00	1.75
108	Andy Pafko	6.00	3.00	1.75
109	Del Ennis	6.00	3.00	1.75
110	Ralph Kiner	12.00	6.00	3.50
111	Nippy Jones	6.00	3.00	1.75
112	Del Rice	6.00	3.00	1.75
113	Hank Sauer	6.00	3.00	1.75
114	Gil Coan	6.00	3.00	1.75
115	Eddie Joost	6.00	3.00	1.75
116	Alvin Dark	7.00	3.50	2.00
117	Larry Berra	20.00	10.00	6.00
118	Unknown			
119	Bob Lemon	12.00	6.00	3.50
120	Unknown			
121	Johnny Pesky	6.00	3.00	1.75
122	Johnny Sain	7.00	3.50	2.00
123	Hoot Evers	6.00	3.00	1.75
124	Larry Doby	7.00	3.50	2.00
---	Tom Henrich	7.00	3.50	2.00
---	Al Kozar	6.00	3.00	1.75

1939 R303-A Goudey Premiums

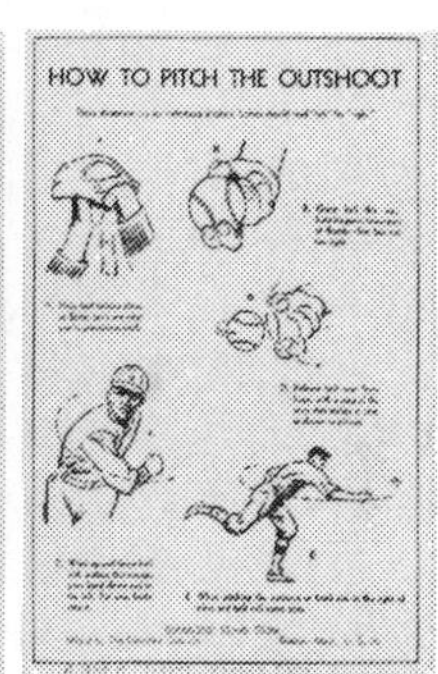

Although this unnumbered set of paper premiums has the name "Diamond Stars Gum" on the back, it is not related to National Chicle's Diamond Stars card sets. Rather, this 48-player set was a premium issued by the Goudey Gum Company. Each premium photo measures 6-3/16" by 4" and is printed in a brown-toned sepia. The front of the photo includes a facsimile autograph, while the back contains drawings that illustrate various baseball tips.

		NR MT	EX	VG
Complete Set:		2150.	1075.	625.00
Common Player:		25.00	12.50	7.50
(1)	Luke Appling	45.00	22.00	13.50
(2)	Earl Averill	45.00	22.00	13.50
(3)	Wally Berger	25.00	12.50	7.50
(4)	Darrell Blanton	25.00	12.50	7.50
(5)	Zeke Bonura	25.00	12.50	7.50
(6)	Mace Brown	25.00	12.50	7.50
(7)	George Case	25.00	12.50	7.50
(8)	Ben Chapman	25.00	12.50	7.50
(9)	Joe Cronin	45.00	22.00	13.50
(10)	Frank Crosetti	25.00	12.50	7.50
(11)	Paul Derringer	25.00	12.50	7.50
(12)	Bill Dickey	75.00	37.00	22.00
(13)	Joe DiMaggio	200.00	100.00	60.00
(14)	Bob Feller	80.00	40.00	24.00
(15)	Jimmy Foxx	80.00	40.00	24.00
(16)	Charles Gehringer	45.00	22.00	13.50
(17)	Lefty Gomez	45.00	22.00	13.50
(18)	Ival Goodman	25.00	12.50	7.50
(19)	Joe Gordon	25.00	12.50	7.50
(20)	Hank Greenberg	45.00	22.00	13.50
(21)	Buddy Hassett	25.00	12.50	7.50

		NR MT	EX	VG
(22)	Jeff Heath	25.00	12.50	7.50
(23)	Tom Henrich	25.00	12.50	7.50
(24)	Billy Herman	40.00	20.00	12.00
(25)	Frank Higgins	25.00	12.50	7.50
(26)	Fred Hutchinson	25.00	12.50	7.50
(27)	Bob Johnson	25.00	12.50	7.50
(28)	Ken Keltner	25.00	12.50	7.50
(29)	Mike Kreevich	25.00	12.50	7.50
(30)	Ernie Lombardi	45.00	22.00	13.50
(31)	Gus Mancuso	25.00	12.50	7.50
(32)	Eric McNair	25.00	12.50	7.50
(33)	Van Mungo	25.00	12.50	7.50
(34)	Buck Newsom	25.00	12.50	7.50
(35)	Mel Ott	35.00	17.50	10.50
(36)	Marvin Owen	25.00	12.50	7.50
(37)	Frank Pytlak	25.00	12.50	7.50
(38)	Woodrow Rich	25.00	12.50	7.50
(39)	Charley Root	25.00	12.50	7.50
(40)	Al Simmons	45.00	22.00	13.50
(41)	James Tabor	25.00	12.50	7.50
(42)	Cecil Travis	25.00	12.50	7.50
(43)	Hal Trosky	25.00	12.50	7.50
(44)	Arky Vaughan	45.00	22.00	13.50
(45)	Joe Vosmik	25.00	12.50	7.50
(46)	Lon Warneke	25.00	12.50	7.50
(47)	Ted Williams	300.00	150.00	90.00
(48)	Rudy York	25.00	12.50	7.50

1939 R303-B Goudey Premiums

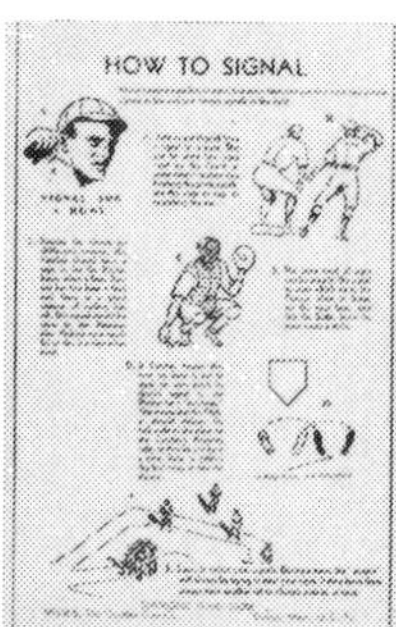

Although larger (7-5/16" by 4-3/4"), the photos in this 24- player set are identical to those in the R303-A set of the same year, and the format of the set is unchanged. The set, designated as R303-B, can be found in both black and white and sepia.

		NR MT	EX	VG
Complete Set:		1000.	500.00	300.00
Common Player:		20.00	10.00	6.00
(1)	Luke Appling	40.00	20.00	12.00
(2)	George Case	20.00	10.00	6.00
(3)	Ben Chapman	20.00	10.00	6.00
(4)	Joe Cronin	40.00	20.00	12.00
(5)	Bill Dickey	50.00	25.00	15.00
(6)	Joe DiMaggio	250.00	125.00	75.00
(7)	Bob Feller	60.00	30.00	18.00
(8)	Jimmy Foxx	60.00	30.00	18.00
(9)	Lefty Gomez	40.00	20.00	12.00
(10)	Ival Goodman	20.00	10.00	6.00
(11)	Joe Gordon	22.00	11.00	6.50
(12)	Hank Greenberg	40.00	20.00	12.00
(13)	Jeff Heath	20.00	10.00	6.00
(14)	Billy Herman	35.00	17.50	10.50
(15)	Frank Higgins	20.00	10.00	6.00
(16)	Ken Keltner	22.00	11.00	6.50
(17)	Mike Kreevich	20.00	10.00	6.00
(18)	Ernie Lombardi	35.00	17.50	10.50
(19)	Gus Mancuso	20.00	10.00	6.00
(20)	Mel Ott	40.00	20.00	12.00
(21)	Al Simmons	40.00	20.00	12.00
(22)	Arky Vaughan	40.00	20.00	12.00
(23)	Joe Vosmik	20.00	10.00	6.00
(24)	Rudy York	20.00	10.00	6.00

1933 R308 Tatoo Orbit

This obscure set of cards, issued by Tatoo Orbit, is numbered from 151 through 207, with a few of the numbers still unknown. The tiny cards measure just 1-7/8" by 1-1/4" and were considered more of a novelty item because the crude player drawings on the cards actually "developed" when moistened and exposed to light.

		NR MT	EX	VG
Complete Set:		1600.	800.00	480.00
Common Player:		20.00	10.00	6.00
151	Vernon Gomez	40.00	20.00	12.00
152	Kiki Cuyler	40.00	20.00	12.00
153	Jimmy Foxx	75.00	38.00	23.00
154	Al Simmons	40.00	20.00	12.00
155	Chas. J. Grimm	22.00	11.00	6.50
156	William Jurges	20.00	10.00	6.00
157	Chuck Klein	40.00	20.00	12.00
158	Richard Bartell	20.00	10.00	6.00

		NR MT	EX	VG
159	Pepper Martin	25.00	12.50	7.50
160	Earl Averill	40.00	20.00	12.00
161	William Dickey	50.00	25.00	15.00
162	Wesley Ferrell	20.00	10.00	6.00
163	Oral Hildebrand	20.00	10.00	6.00
164	Wm. Kamm	20.00	10.00	6.00
165	Earl Whitehill	20.00	10.00	6.00
166	Charles Fullis	20.00	10.00	6.00
167	Jimmy Dykes	22.00	11.00	6.50
168	Ben Cantwell	20.00	10.00	6.00
169	George Earnshaw	20.00	10.00	6.00
170	Jackson Stephenson	22.00	11.00	6.50
171	Randolph Moore	20.00	10.00	6.00
172	Ted Lyons	40.00	20.00	12.00
173	Goose Goslin	40.00	20.00	12.00
174	E. Swanson	20.00	10.00	6.00
175	Lee Roy Mahaffey	20.00	10.00	6.00
176	Joe Cronin	40.00	20.00	12.00
177	Tom Bridges	20.00	10.00	6.00
178	Henry Manush	40.00	20.00	12.00
179	Walter Stewart	20.00	10.00	6.00
180	Frank Pytlak	20.00	10.00	6.00
181	Dale Alexander	20.00	10.00	6.00
182	Robert Grove	50.00	25.00	15.00
183	Charles Gehringer	40.00	20.00	12.00
184	Lewis Fonseca	20.00	10.00	6.00
185	Alvin Crowder	20.00	10.00	6.00
186	Mickey Cochrane	40.00	20.00	12.00
187	Max Bishop	20.00	10.00	6.00
188	Connie Mack	50.00	25.00	15.00
189	Guy Bush	20.00	10.00	6.00
190	Charlie Root	20.00	10.00	6.00
191a	Burleigh Grimes	40.00	20.00	12.00
191b	Gabby Hartnett	40.00	20.00	12.00
192	Pat Malone	20.00	10.00	6.00
193	Woody English	20.00	10.00	6.00
194	Lonnie Warneke	20.00	10.00	6.00
195	Babe Herman	22.00	11.00	6.50
196	Unknown			
197	Unknown			
198	Unknown			
199	Unknown			
200	Gabby Hartnett	40.00	20.00	12.00
201	Paul Waner	40.00	20.00	12.00
202	Dizzy Dean	100.00	50.00	30.00
203	Unknown			
204	Unknown			
205	Jim Bottomley	40.00	20.00	12.00
206	Unknown			
207	Charles Hafey	40.00	20.00	12.00
208	Unknown			
209	Unknown			
210	Unknown			

1934 R309-1 Goudey Premiums

Consisting of just four unnumbered cards, this set of black and white photos was printed on heavy cardboard and issued as a premium by the Goudey Gum Co. in 1934. The cards measure 5-1/2" by 8-5/16" and were accented with a gold, picture-frame border and an easel stand on the back.

		NR MT	EX	VG
Complete Set:		4000.	2000.	1200.
Common Player:		800.00	400.00	240.00
(1)	American League All-Stars of 1933	800.00	400.00	240.00
(2)	National League All-Stars of 1933	800.00	400.00	240.00
(3)	"Worlds Champions 1933" (New York Giants)	1000.	500.00	300.00
(4)	George Herman (Babe) Ruth	1200.	600.00	360.00

1935 R309-2 Goudey Premiums

The 18 glossy, black-and-white photos in this set, issued as a premium by Goudey in 1935, measure 5-1/2" by 9", and were printed on thin paper. The unnumbered set includes three team photos and 15 players, whose names are written in script in the "wide pen" style used by Goudey in other issues.

		NR MT	EX	VG
Complete Set:		2500.	1250.	750.00
Common Player:		100.00	50.00	30.00
(1)	Elden Auker	100.00	50.00	30.00
(2)	Johnny Babich	100.00	50.00	30.00
(3)	Dick Bartell	100.00	50.00	30.00
(4)	Lester R. Bell	100.00	50.00	30.00
(5)	Wally Berger	100.00	50.00	30.00
(6)	Mickey Cochrane	200.00	100.00	60.00
(7)	Ervin Fox	100.00	50.00	30.00
(8)	Vernon Gomez	100.00	50.00	30.00
(9)	Leon "Goose" Goslin	200.00	100.00	60.00
(10)	Hank Greenberg	200.00	100.00	60.00
(11)	Oscar Melillo	100.00	50.00	30.00
(12)	Mel Ott	200.00	100.00	60.00
(13)	Schoolboy Rowe	100.00	50.00	30.00
(14)	Vito Tamulis	100.00	50.00	30.00
(15)	Gerald Walker	100.00	50.00	30.00
(16)	Boston Red Sox	150.00	75.00	45.00
(17)	Cleveland Indians	150.00	75.00	45.00
(18)	Washington Senators	150.00	75.00	45.00

1934 R310 Butterfinger

Cards in this 65-card set were available as a premium from Butterfinger and other candy products. The unnumbered cards measure approximately 7-3/4" by 9-3/4" and the heavy cardboard variety carry advertising for Butterfinger. The cards feature a player photo with facsimilie autograph surrounded by an off-white border. The cards are found on either paper or heavy cardboard stock, with the cardboard versions commanding a price about triple that listed here. The Foxx card is found spelled both "Fox" and "Foxx."

		NR MT	EX	VG
Complete Set:		1800.	900.00	540.00
Common Player:		15.00	7.50	4.50
1	Earl Averill	30.00	15.00	9.00
2	Richard Bartell	15.00	7.50	4.50
3	Larry Benton	15.00	7.50	4.50
4	Walter Berger	15.00	7.50	4.50
5	Jim Bottomley	30.00	15.00	9.00
6	Ralph Boyle	15.00	7.50	4.50
7	Tex Carleton	15.00	7.50	4.50
8	Owen T. Carroll	15.00	7.50	4.50
9	Ben Chapman	15.00	7.50	4.50
10	Gordon "Mickey" Cochrane	30.00	15.00	9.00
11	James Collins	15.00	7.50	4.50
12	Joe Cronin	30.00	15.00	9.00
13	Alvin Crowder	15.00	7.50	4.50
14	Dizzy Dean	60.00	30.00	18.00
15	Paul Derringer	15.00	7.50	4.50
16	William Dickey	45.00	22.00	13.50
17	Leo Durocher	30.00	15.00	9.00
18	George Earnshaw	15.00	7.50	4.50
19	Richard Farrell	30.00	15.00	9.00
20	Lew Fonseca	15.00	7.50	4.50
21a	Jimmy Fox (name incorrect)	50.00	25.00	15.00
21b	Jimmy Foxx (name correct)	50.00	25.00	15.00
22	Benny Frey	15.00	7.50	4.50
23	Frankie Frisch	30.00	15.00	9.00
24	Lou Gehrig	100.00	50.00	30.00
25	Charles Gehringer	30.00	15.00	9.00
26	Vernon Gomez	30.00	15.00	9.00
27	Ray Grabowski	15.00	7.50	4.50
28	Robert Grove	45.00	22.00	13.50
29	George "Mule" Haas	15.00	7.50	4.50

		NR MT	EX	VG
30	"Chick" Hafey	30.00	15.00	9.00
31	Stanley Harris	30.00	15.00	9.00
32	J. Francis Hogan	15.00	7.50	4.50
33	Ed Holley	15.00	7.50	4.50
34	Rogers Hornsby	50.00	25.00	15.00
35	Waite Hoyt	30.00	15.00	9.00
36	Walter Johnson	55.00	27.00	16.50
37	Jim Jordan	15.00	7.50	4.50
38	Joe Kuhel	15.00	7.50	4.50
39	Hal Lee	15.00	7.50	4.50
40	Gus Mancuso	15.00	7.50	4.50
41	Henry Manush	30.00	15.00	9.00
42	Fred Marberry	15.00	7.50	4.50
43	Pepper Martin	20.00	10.00	6.00
44	Oscar Melillo	15.00	7.50	4.50
45	Johnny Moore	15.00	7.50	4.50
46	Joe Morrissey	15.00	7.50	4.50
47	Joe Mowrey	15.00	7.50	4.50
48	Bob O'Farrell	15.00	7.50	4.50
49	Melvin Ott	40.00	20.00	12.00
50	Monte Pearson	15.00	7.50	4.50
51	Carl Reynolds	15.00	7.50	4.50
52	Charles Ruffing	30.00	15.00	9.00
53	Babe Ruth	150.00	75.00	45.00
54	John "Blondy" Ryan	15.00	7.50	4.50
55	Al Simmons	30.00	15.00	9.00
56	Al Spohrer	15.00	7.50	4.50
57	Gus Suhr	15.00	7.50	4.50
58	Steve Swetonic	15.00	7.50	4.50
59	Dazzy Vance	30.00	15.00	9.00
60	Joe Vosmik	15.00	7.50	4.50
61	Lloyd Waner	30.00	15.00	9.00
62	Paul Waner	30.00	15.00	9.00
63	Sam West	15.00	7.50	4.50
64	Earl Whitehill	15.00	7.50	4.50
65	Jimmy Wilson	15.00	7.50	4.50

1936 R311 Glossy Finish

The cards in this 28-card set, which was available as a premium in 1936, measure 6" by 8" and were printed on a glossy cardboard. The photos are either black and white or sepia-toned and include a facsimilie autograph. The unnumbered set includes individual players and team photos. The Boston Red Sox team card can be found in two varieties; one shows the sky above the building on the card's right side, while the other does not. Some of the cards are scarcer than others in the set and command a premium. Babe Ruth is featured on the Boston Braves team card.

		NR MT	EX	VG
	Complete Set:	900.00	450.00	275.00
	Common Player:	15.00	7.50	4.50
(1)	Earl Averill	30.00	15.00	9.00
(2)	James L. "Jim" Bottomley	30.00	15.00	9.00
(3)	Gordon S. "Mickey" Cochrane	30.00	15.00	9.00
(4)	Joe Cronin	30.00	15.00	9.00
(5)	Jerome "Dizzy" Dean	50.00	25.00	15.00
(6)	Jimmy Dykes	20.00	10.00	6.00
(7)	Jimmy Foxx	45.00	22.00	13.50
(8)	Frankie Frisch	30.00	15.00	9.00
(9)	Henry "Hank" Greenberg	30.00	15.00	9.00
(10)	Mel Harder	15.00	7.50	4.50
(11)	Ken Keltner	15.00	7.50	4.50
(12)	Pepper Martin	50.00	25.00	15.00
(13)	Lynwood "Schoolboy" Rowe	15.00	7.50	4.50
(14)	William "Bill" Terry	35.00	17.50	10.50
(15)	Harold "Pie" Traynor	30.00	15.00	9.00
(16)	American League All-Stars - 1935	50.00	25.00	15.00
(17)	American League Pennant Winners - 1934 (Detroit Tigers)	30.00	15.00	9.00
(18)	Boston Braves - 1935	150.00	75.00	45.00
(19)	Boston Red Sox	30.00	15.00	9.00
(20)	Brooklyn Dodgers - 1935	75.00	37.00	22.00
(21)	Chicago White Sox - 1935	30.00	15.00	9.00
(22)	Columbus Red Birds (1934 Pennant Winners of American Association)	20.00	10.00	6.00
(23)	National League All-Stars - 1934	50.00	25.00	15.00
(24)	National League Champions - 1935 (Chicago Cubs)	30.00	15.00	9.00
(25)	New York Yankees - 1935	100.00	50.00	30.00
(26)	Pittsburgh Pirates - 1935	30.00	15.00	9.00
(27)	St. Louis Browns - 1935	30.00	15.00	9.00
(28)	The World Champions, 1934 (St. Louis Cardinals)	30.00	15.00	9.00

1936 R311 Leather Finish

This set of 15 unnumbered cards, issued as a premium in 1936, is distinctive because of its uneven, leather-like surface. The cards measure 6" by 8" and display a facsimilie autograph on the black and white photo surrounded by a plain border. The cards are unnumbered and include individual player photos, multi-player photos and team photos of the 1935 pennant winners.

		NR MT	EX	VG
	Complete Set:	700.00	350.00	210.00
	Common Player:	20.00	10.00	6.00
(1)	Frank Crosetti, Joe DiMaggio, Tony Lazzeri	150.00	75.00	45.00
(2)	Paul Derringer	20.00	10.00	6.00
(3)	Wes Ferrell	20.00	10.00	6.00
(4)	Jimmy Foxx	65.00	32.00	19.50
(5)	Charlie Gehringer	40.00	20.00	12.00
(6)	Mel Harder	20.00	10.00	6.00
(7)	Gabby Hartnett	40.00	20.00	12.00
(8)	Rogers Hornsby	65.00	32.00	19.50
(9)	Connie Mack	55.00	27.00	16.50
(10)	Van Mungo	20.00	10.00	6.00
(11)	Steve O'Neill	20.00	10.00	6.00
(12)	Charles Ruffing	40.00	20.00	12.00
(13)	Arky Vaughan, Honus Wagner	65.00	32.00	19.50
(14)	American League Pennant Winners - 1935 (Detroit Tigers)	30.00	15.00	9.00
(15)	National League Pennant Winners - 1935 (Chicago Cubs)	30.00	15.00	9.00

1936 R312

The 50 cards in this set are black and white photos that have been tinted in soft pastel colors. The set includes 25 individual player portraits, 14 multi-player cards and 11 action photos. Six of the action photos include facsimilie autographs, while the other five have printed legends. The Allen card is more scarce than the others in the set.

		NR MT	EX	VG
	Complete Set:	1750.	875.00	525.00
	Common Player:	20.00	10.00	6.00
(1)	John Thomas Allen	30.00	15.00	9.00
(2)	Nick Altrock, Al Schact	20.00	10.00	6.00
(3)	Ollie Bejma, Rolly Hemsley	20.00	10.00	6.00
(4)	Les Bell, Zeke Bonura	20.00	10.00	6.00
(5)	Cy Blanton	20.00	10.00	6.00
(6)	Cliff Bolton, Earl Whitehill	20.00	10.00	6.00
(7)	Frenchy Bordagaray, George Earnshaw	20.00	10.00	6.00
(8)	Mace Brown	20.00	10.00	6.00
(9)	Dolph Camilli	20.00	10.00	6.00
(10)	Phil Cavaretta (Cavarretta), Frank Demaree, Augie Galan, Stan Hack, Gabby Hartnett, Billy Herman, Billy Jurges, Chuck Klein, Fred Lindstrom	40.00	20.00	12.00
(11)	Phil Cavaretta (Cavarretta), Stan Hack, Billy Herman, Billy Jurges	25.00	12.50	7.50
(12)	Gordon Cochrane	40.00	20.00	12.00
(13)	Jim Collins, Stan Hack	20.00	10.00	6.00
(14)	Rip Collins	20.00	10.00	6.00
(15)	Joe Cronin, Buckey Harris (Bucky)	40.00	20.00	12.00
(16)	Alvin Crowder	20.00	10.00	6.00
(17)	Kiki Cuyler	40.00	20.00	12.00
(18)	Kiki Cuyler, Tris Speaker, Danny Taylor	40.00	20.00	12.00
(19)	"Bill" Dickey	20.00	10.00	6.00
(20)	Joe DiMagio (DiMaggio)	250.00	125.00	75.00
(21)	"Chas." Dressen	20.00	10.00	6.00
(22)	Rick Ferrell, Russ Van Atta	20.00	10.00	6.00
(23)	Pete Fox, Goose Goslin, "Jo Jo" White	35.00	17.50	10.50
(24)	Jimmey Foxx (Jimmie), Luke Sewell	50.00	25.00	15.00
(25)	Benny Frey	20.00	10.00	6.00
(26)	Augie Galan, "Pie" Traynor	35.00	17.50	10.50
(27)	Lefty Gomez, Myril Hoag	35.00	17.50	10.50
(28)	"Hank" Greenberg	40.00	20.00	12.00
(29)	Lefty Grove, Connie Mack	60.00	30.00	18.00
(30)	Muel Haas (Mule), Mike Kreevich, Dixie Walker	20.00	10.00	6.00
(31)	Mel Harder	20.00	10.00	6.00
(32)	Gabby Hartnett (Mickey Cochrane, Frank Demaree, Ernie Quigley (ump) in photo)	35.00	17.50	10.50
(33)	Gabby Hartnett, Lonnie Warnecke (Warneke)	30.00	15.00	9.00
(34)	Roger Hornsby (Rogers)	60.00	30.00	18.00
(35)	Rogers Hornsby, Allen Sothoren	40.00	20.00	12.00
(36)	Ernie Lombardi	40.00	20.00	12.00
(37)	Al Lopez	40.00	20.00	12.00
(38)	Pepper Martin	25.00	12.50	7.50
(39)	"Johnny" Mize	40.00	20.00	12.00
(40)	Van L. Mungo	20.00	10.00	6.00
(41)	Bud Parmelee	20.00	10.00	6.00
(42)	Schoolboy Rowe	20.00	10.00	6.00
(43)	Chas. Ruffing	40.00	20.00	12.00
(44)	Eugene Schott	20.00	10.00	6.00
(45)	Casey Stengel	100.00	50.00	30.00
(46)	Bill Sullivan	20.00	10.00	6.00
(47)	Bill Swift	20.00	10.00	6.00
(48)	Floyd Vaughan, Hans Wagner	50.00	25.00	15.00
(49)	L. Waner, P. Waner, Big Jim Weaver	45.00	23.00	13.50
(50)	Ralph Winegarner	20.00	10.00	6.00

1936 R313

Issued in 1936 by the National Chicle Company, this set consists of 120 cards, each measuring 3-1/4" by 5-3/8". The black and white cards are blank-backed and unnumbered. Although issued by National Chicle, the name of the company does not appear on the cards. The set includes individual player portraits with facsimilie autographs, multi-player cards and action photos. The cards, known in the hobby as "Fine Pen" because of the thin style of writing used for the facsimilie autographs, were originally available as an in-store premium.

		NR MT	EX	VG
	Complete Set:	1500.	750.00	450.00
	Common Player:	8.00	4.00	2.50
(1)	Melo Almada	8.00	4.00	2.50
(2)	Nick Altrock, Al Schacht	8.00	4.00	2.50
(3)	Paul Andrews	8.00	4.00	2.50
(4)	Elden Auker (Eldon)	8.00	4.00	2.50
(5)	Earl Averill	16.00	8.00	4.75
(6)	John Babich, James Bucher	8.00	4.00	2.50
(7)	Jim Becher (Bucher)	8.00	4.00	2.50
(8)	Moe Berg	10.00	5.00	3.00
(9)	Walter Berger	8.00	4.00	2.50
(10)	Charles Berry	8.00	4.00	2.50
(11)	Ralph Birkhofer (Birkofer)	8.00	4.00	2.50
(12)	"Cy" Blanton	8.00	4.00	2.50
(13)	O. Bluege	8.00	4.00	2.50
(14)	Cliff Bolton	8.00	4.00	2.50
(15)	Zeke Bonura	8.00	4.00	2.50
(16)	Stan Bordagaray, George Earnshaw	8.00	4.00	2.50
(17)	Jim Bottomley, Charley Gelbert	14.00	7.00	4.25
(18)	Thos. Bridges	8.00	4.00	2.50
(19)	Sam Byrd	8.00	4.00	2.50
(20)	Dolph Camilli	8.00	4.00	2.50
(21)	Dolph Camilli, Billy Jurges	8.00	4.00	2.50
(22)	Bruce Campbell	8.00	4.00	2.50
(23)	Walter "Kit" Carson	8.00	4.00	2.50
(24)	Ben Chapman	8.00	4.00	2.50
(25)	Harlond Clift, Luke Sewell	8.00	4.00	2.50
(26)	Mickey Cochrane, Jimmy Fox (Foxx), Al Simmons	20.00	10.00	6.00
(27)	"Rip" Collins	8.00	4.00	2.50
(28)	Joe Cronin	16.00	8.00	4.75
(29)	Frank Crossetti (Crosetti)	10.00	5.00	3.00
(30)	Frank Crosetti, Jimmy Dykes	10.00	5.00	3.00
(31)	Kiki Cuyler, Gabby Hartnett	20.00	10.00	6.00

		NR MT	EX	VG
(32)	Paul Derringer	8.00	4.00	2.50
(33)	Bill Dickey, Hank Greenberg	25.00	12.50	7.50
(34)	Bill Dietrich	8.00	4.00	2.50
(35)	Joe DiMaggio, Hank Erickson	125.00	62.00	37.00
(36)	Carl Doyle	8.00	4.00	2.50
(37)	Charles Dressen, Bill Myers	8.00	4.00	2.50
(38)	Jimmie Dykes	10.00	5.00	3.00
(39)	Rick Ferrell, Wess Ferrell (Wes)	8.00	4.00	2.50
(40)	Pete Fox	8.00	4.00	2.50
(41)	Frankie Frisch	20.00	10.00	6.00
(42)	Milton Galatzer	8.00	4.00	2.50
(43)	Chas. Gehringer	20.00	10.00	6.00
(44)	Charley Gelbert	8.00	4.00	2.50
(45)	Joe Glenn	8.00	4.00	2.50
(46)	Jose Gomez	8.00	4.00	2.50
(47)	Lefty Gomez, Red Ruffing	20.00	10.00	6.00
(48)	Vernon Gomez	20.00	10.00	6.00
(49)	Leon Goslin	20.00	10.00	6.00
(50)	Hank Gowdy	8.00	4.00	2.50
(51)	"Hank" Greenberg	20.00	10.00	6.00
(52)	"Lefty" Grove	20.00	10.00	6.00
(53)	Stan Hack	8.00	4.00	2.50
(54)	Odell Hale	8.00	4.00	2.50
(55)	Wild Bill Hallahan	8.00	4.00	2.50
(56)	Mel Harder	8.00	4.00	2.50
(57)	Stanley Bucky Harriss (Harris)	16.00	8.00	4.75
(58)	Gabby Hartnett, Rip Radcliff	14.00	7.00	4.25
(59)	Gabby Hartnett, L. Waner	20.00	10.00	6.00
(60)	Gabby Hartnett, Lon Warnecke (Warneke)	14.00	7.00	4.25
(61)	Buddy Hassett	8.00	4.00	2.50
(62)	Babe Herman	10.00	5.00	3.00
(63)	Frank Higgins	8.00	4.00	2.50
(64)	Oral C. Hildebrand	8.00	4.00	2.50
(65)	Myril Hoag	8.00	4.00	2.50
(66)	Rogers Hornsby	25.00	12.50	7.50
(67)	Waite Hoyt	16.00	8.00	4.75
(68)	Willis G. Hudlin	8.00	4.00	2.50
(69)	"Woody" Jensen	8.00	4.00	2.50
(70)	Woody Jenson (Jensen)	8.00	4.00	2.50
(71)	William Knickerbocker	8.00	4.00	2.50
(72)	Joseph Kuhel	8.00	4.00	2.50
(73)	Cookie Lavagetto	10.00	5.00	3.00
(74)	Thornton Lee	8.00	4.00	2.50
(75)	Ernie Lombardi	16.00	8.00	4.75
(76)	Red Lucas	8.00	4.00	2.50
(77)	Connie Mack, John McGraw	30.00	15.00	9.00
(78)	Pepper Martin	12.00	6.00	3.50
(79)	George McQuinn	8.00	4.00	2.50
(80)	George McQuinn, Lee Stine	8.00	4.00	2.50
(81)	Joe Medwick	16.00	8.00	4.75
(82)	Oscar Melillo	8.00	4.00	2.50
(83)	"Buddy" Meyer	8.00	4.00	2.50
(84)	Randy Moore	8.00	4.00	2.50
(85)	T. Moore, Jimmie Wilson	8.00	4.00	2.50
(86)	Wallace Moses	8.00	4.00	2.50
(87)	V. Mungo	8.00	4.00	2.50
(88)	Lamar Newsom	8.00	4.00	2.50
(89)	Lewis "Buck" Newsom (Louis)	8.00	4.00	2.50
(90)	Steve O'Neill	8.00	4.00	2.50
(91)	Tommie Padden	8.00	4.00	2.50
(92)	E. Babe Philips (Phelps)	8.00	4.00	2.50
(93)	Bill Rogel (Rogell)	8.00	4.00	2.50
(94)	Lynn "Schoolboy" Rowe	8.00	4.00	2.50
(95)	Luke Sewell	8.00	4.00	2.50
(96)	Al Simmons	20.00	10.00	6.00
(97)	Casey Stengel	30.00	15.00	9.00
(98)	Bill Swift	8.00	4.00	2.50
(99)	Cecil Travis	8.00	4.00	2.50
(100)	"Pie" Traynor	20.00	10.00	6.00
(101)	William Urbansky (Urbanski)	8.00	4.00	2.50
(102)	Arky Vaughn (Vaughan)	20.00	10.00	6.00
(103)	Joe Vosmik	8.00	4.00	2.50
(104)	Honus Wagner	30.00	15.00	9.00
(105)	Rube Walberg	8.00	4.00	2.50
(106)	Bill Walker	8.00	4.00	2.50
(107)	Gerald Walker	8.00	4.00	2.50
(108)	L. Waner, P. Waner, Big Jim Weaver	20.00	10.00	6.00
(109)	George Washington	8.00	4.00	2.50
(110)	Bill Werber	8.00	4.00	2.50
(111)	Sam West	8.00	4.00	2.50
(112)	Pinkey Whitney	8.00	4.00	2.50
(113)	Vernon Wiltshere (Wilshere)	8.00	4.00	2.50
(114)	"Pep" Young	8.00	4.00	2.50
(115)	Chicago White Sox 1936	8.00	4.00	2.50
(116)	Fence Busters	8.00	4.00	2.50
(117)	Talking It Over (Leo Durocher)	10.00	5.00	3.00
(118)	There She Goes! Chicago City Series	8.00	4.00	2.50
(119)	Ump Says No - Cleveland vs. Detroit	8.00	4.00	2.50
(120)	World Series 1935 (Phil Cavarretta, Goose Goslin, Lon Warneke)	10.00	5.00	3.00

1936 R314

Issued in 1936 by the Goudey Gum Company, these cards are known in the hobby as "Wide Pens" because of the distinctive, thick style of writing used for the facsimilie autographs. The black and white, unnumbered cards measure 3-1/4" by 5-1/2" and are found in several

different types. Some cards have borders, while others do not, and cards are found both with and without a "Litho USA" line along the bottom. Some cards in the set are found on a creamy paper stock. The set includes both major leaguers and players from the Canadian minor league teams in Montreal and Toronto. The cards were originally available as an in-store premium.

		NR MT	EX	VG
	Complete Set:	1400.	700.00	425.00
	Common Player:	8.00	4.00	2.50
(1)	Ethan Allen	8.00	4.00	2.50
(2)	Earl Averill	16.00	8.00	4.75
(3)	Dick Bartell (portrait)	8.00	4.00	2.50
(4)	Dick Bartell (sliding)	8.00	4.00	2.50
(5)	Walter Berger	8.00	4.00	2.50
(6)	Geo. Blaeholder	8.00	4.00	2.50
(7)	"Cy" Blanton	8.00	4.00	2.50
(8)	"Cliff" Bolton	8.00	4.00	2.50
(9)	Stan Bordagaray	8.00	4.00	2.50
(10)	Tommy Bridges	8.00	4.00	2.50
(11)	Bill Brubaker	8.00	4.00	2.50
(12)	Sam Byrd	8.00	4.00	2.50
(13)	Dolph Camilli	8.00	4.00	2.50
(14)	Clydell Castleman (pitching)	8.00	4.00	2.50
(15)	Clydell Castleman (portrait)	8.00	4.00	2.50
(16)	"Phil" Cavaretta (Cavarretta)	8.00	4.00	2.50
(17)	Ben Chapman, Bill Werber	8.00	4.00	2.50
(18)	Mickey Cochrane	20.00	10.00	6.00
(19)	Earl Coombs (Earle Combs)	16.00	8.00	4.75
(20)	Joe Coscarart	8.00	4.00	2.50
(21)	Joe Cronin	16.00	8.00	4.75
(22)	Frank Crosetti	10.00	5.00	3.00
(23)	Tony Cuccinello	8.00	4.00	2.50
(24)	"Kiki" Cuyler	16.00	8.00	4.75
(25)	Curt Davis	8.00	4.00	2.50
(26)	Virgil Davis	8.00	4.00	2.50
(27)	Paul Derringer	8.00	4.00	2.50
(28)	Bill Dickey	20.00	10.00	6.00
(29)	Joe DiMaggio, Joe McCarthy	90.00	45.00	27.00
(30)	Jimmy Dykes	10.00	5.00	3.00
(31)	Rick Ferrell	16.00	8.00	4.75
(32)	Wes Ferrell	8.00	4.00	2.50
(33)	Rick Ferrell, Wes Ferrell	14.00	7.00	4.25
(34)	Lou Finney	8.00	4.00	2.50
(35)	Erwin "Pete" Fox	8.00	4.00	2.50
(36)	Tony Freitas	8.00	4.00	2.50
(37)	Lonnie Frey	8.00	4.00	2.50
(38)	Frankie Frisch	20.00	10.00	6.00
(39)	"Augie" Galan	8.00	4.00	2.50
(40)	Charles Gehringer	20.00	10.00	6.00
(41)	Charlie Gelbert	8.00	4.00	2.50
(42)	"Lefty" Gomez	20.00	10.00	6.00
(43)	"Goose" Goslin	20.00	10.00	6.00
(44)	Earl Grace	8.00	4.00	2.50
(45)	Hank Greenberg	20.00	10.00	6.00
(46)	"Mule" Haas	8.00	4.00	2.50
(47)	Odell Hale	8.00	4.00	2.50
(48)	Bill Hallahan	8.00	4.00	2.50
(49)	"Mel" Harder	8.00	4.00	2.50
(50)	"Bucky" Harris	16.00	8.00	4.75
(51)	"Gabby" Hartnett	20.00	10.00	6.00
(52)	Ray Hayworth	8.00	4.00	2.50
(53)	"Rollie" Hemsley	8.00	4.00	2.50
(54)	Babe Herman	10.00	5.00	3.00
(55)	Frank Higgins	8.00	4.00	2.50
(56)	Oral Hildebrand	8.00	4.00	2.50
(57)	Myril Hoag	8.00	4.00	2.50
(58)	Waite Hoyt	16.00	8.00	4.75
(59)	Woody Jensen	8.00	4.00	2.50
(60)	Bob Johnson	8.00	4.00	2.50
(61)	"Buck" Jordan	8.00	4.00	2.50
(62)	Alex Kampouris	8.00	4.00	2.50
(63)	"Chuck" Klein	20.00	10.00	6.00
(64)	Joe Kuhel	8.00	4.00	2.50
(65)	Lyn Lary	8.00	4.00	2.50
(66)	Harry Lavagetto	10.00	5.00	3.00
(67)	Sam Leslie	8.00	4.00	2.50
(68)	Freddie Lindstrom	16.00	8.00	4.75
(69)	Lombardi	16.00	8.00	4.75
(70)	"Al" Lopez	16.00	8.00	4.75
(71)	Dan MacFayden	8.00	4.00	2.50
(72)	John Marcum	8.00	4.00	2.50
(73)	"Pepper" Martin	12.00	6.00	3.50
(74)	Eric McNair	8.00	4.00	2.50
(75)	"Ducky" Medwick	16.00	8.00	4.75
(76)	Gene Moore	8.00	4.00	2.50
(77)	Randy Moore	8.00	4.00	2.50
(78)	Terry Moore	8.00	4.00	2.50
(79)	Edward Moriarty	8.00	4.00	2.50
(80)	"Wally" Moses	8.00	4.00	2.50
(81)	"Buddy" Myer	8.00	4.00	2.50
(82)	"Buck" Newsom	8.00	4.00	2.50
(83)	Steve O'Neill, Frank Pytlak	8.00	4.00	2.50
(84)	Fred Ostermueller	8.00	4.00	2.50
(85)	Marvin Owen	8.00	4.00	2.50
(86)	Tommy Padden	8.00	4.00	2.50
(87)	Ray Pepper	8.00	4.00	2.50
(88)	Tony Piet	8.00	4.00	2.50
(89)	"Rabbit" Pytlak	8.00	4.00	2.50
(90)	"Rip" Radcliff	8.00	4.00	2.50
(91)	Bobby Reis	8.00	4.00	2.50
(92)	"Lew" Riggs	8.00	4.00	2.50
(93)	Bill Rogell	8.00	4.00	2.50
(94)	"Red" Rolfe	10.00	5.00	3.00
(95)	"Schoolboy" Rowe	8.00	4.00	2.50
(96)	Al Schacht	8.00	4.00	2.50
(97)	"Luke" Sewell	8.00	4.00	2.50
(98)	Al Simmons	8.00	4.00	2.50
(99)	John Stone	8.00	4.00	2.50
(100)	Gus Suhr	8.00	4.00	2.50
(101)	Joe Sullivan	8.00	4.00	2.50
(102)	Bill Swift	8.00	4.00	2.50
(103)	Vito Tamulis	8.00	4.00	2.50
(104)	Dan Taylor	8.00	4.00	2.50
(105)	Cecil Travis	8.00	4.00	2.50
(106)	Hal Trosky	8.00	4.00	2.50
(107)	"Bill" Urbanski	8.00	4.00	2.50
(108)	Russ Van Atta	8.00	4.00	2.50
(109)	"Arky" Vaughan	20.00	10.00	6.00
(110)	Gerald Walker	8.00	4.00	2.50
(111)	"Buck" Walter (Bucky)	8.00	4.00	2.50
(112)	Lloyd Waner	20.00	10.00	6.00
(113)	Paul Waner	20.00	10.00	6.00
(114)	"Lon" Warneke	8.00	4.00	2.50
(115)	Warstler	8.00	4.00	2.50
(116)	Bill Werber	8.00	4.00	2.50
(117)	"Jo Jo" White	8.00	4.00	2.50
(118)	Burgess Whitehead	8.00	4.00	2.50
(119)	John Whitehead	8.00	4.00	2.50
(120)	Whitlow Wyatt	8.00	4.00	2.50

1930 R315

Issued in 1928, the 58 cards in this set can be found in either black and white or yellow and black. The unnumbered, blank-backed cards measure 3-1/4" by 5-1/4" and feature both portraits and action photos. The set includes several different types of cards, depending on the caption. Cards can be found with the player's name and team inside a white box in a lower corner; other cards add the position and team in small type in the bottom border; a third type has the player's name in hand lettering near the bottom; and the final type includes the position and team printed in small type along the bottom border.

		NR MT	EX	VG
	Complete Set:	500.00	250.00	150.00
	Common Player:	10.00	5.00	3.00
(1)	Earl Averill	20.00	10.00	6.00
(2)	"Benny" Bengough	10.00	5.00	3.00
(3)	Laurence Benton (Lawrence)	10.00	5.00	3.00
(4)	"Max" Bishop	10.00	5.00	3.00
(5)	"Sunny Jim" Bottomley	20.00	10.00	6.00
(6)	Bill Cissell	10.00	5.00	3.00
(7)	Bud Clancey (Clancy)	10.00	5.00	3.00
(8)	"Freddy" Fitzsimmons	10.00	5.00	3.00
(9)	"Jimmy" Foxx	30.00	15.00	9.00
(10)	"Johnny" Fredericks (Frederick)	10.00	5.00	3.00
(11)	Frank Frisch	25.00	12.50	7.50
(12)	"Lou" Gehrig	100.00	50.00	30.00
(13)	"Goose" Goslin	20.00	10.00	6.00
(14)	Burleigh Grimes	20.00	10.00	6.00
(15)	"Lefty" Grove	25.00	12.50	7.50
(16)	"Mule" Haas	10.00	5.00	3.00
(17)	Harvey Hendricks (Hendrick)	10.00	5.00	3.00
(18)	"Babe" Herman	12.00	6.00	3.50
(19)	"Roger" Hornsby (Rogers)	30.00	15.00	9.00
(20)	Karl Hubbell (Carl)	20.00	10.00	6.00
(21)	"Stonewall" Jackson	20.00	10.00	6.00
(22)	Smead Jolley	10.00	5.00	3.00
(23)	"Chuck" Klein	20.00	10.00	6.00
(24)	Mark Koenig	10.00	5.00	3.00
(25)	"Tony" Lazerri (Lazzeri)	15.00	7.50	4.50
(26)	Fred Leach	10.00	5.00	3.00

		NR MT	EX	VG
(27)	"Freddy" Lindstrom	20.00	10.00	6.00
(28)	Fred Marberry	10.00	5.00	3.00
(29)	"Bing" Miller	10.00	5.00	3.00
(30)	"Bob" O'Farrell	10.00	5.00	3.00
(31)	Frank O'Doul	12.00	6.00	3.50
(32)	"Herbie" Pennock	20.00	10.00	6.00
(33)	George Pipgras	10.00	5.00	3.00
(34)	Andrew Reese	10.00	5.00	3.00
(35)	Carl Reynolds	10.00	5.00	3.00
(36)	"Babe" Ruth	100.00	50.00	30.00
(37)	"Bob" Shawkey	12.00	6.00	3.50
(38)	Art Shires	10.00	5.00	3.00
(39)	"Al" Simmons	20.00	10.00	6.00
(40)	"Riggs" Stephenson	12.00	6.00	3.50
(41)	"Bill" Terry	25.00	12.50	7.50
(42)	"Pie" Traynor	20.00	10.00	6.00
(43)	"Dazzy" Vance	20.00	10.00	6.00
(44)	Paul Waner	20.00	10.00	6.00
(45)	"Hack" Wilson	20.00	10.00	6.00
(46)	"Tom" Zachary	10.00	5.00	3.00

1929 R316

This set of 101 unnumbered cards was issued in 1929 and measures 3-1/2" by 4-1/2". The cards feature black-and-white photos with the player's name printed in script near the bottom of the photo. The backs of the cards are blank. Four of the cards (Hadley, Haines, Siebold and Todt) are considered to be scarcer than the rest of the set.

		NR MT	EX	VG
	Complete Set:	2600.	1300.	780.00
	Common Player:	15.00	7.50	4.50
(1)	Dale Alexander	15.00	7.50	4.50
(2)	Ethan N. Allen	15.00	7.50	4.50
(3)	Larry Benton	15.00	7.50	4.50
(4)	Moe Berg	20.00	10.00	6.00
(5)	Max Bishop	15.00	7.50	4.50
(6)	Del Bissonette	15.00	7.50	4.50
(7)	Lucerne A. Blue	15.00	7.50	4.50
(8)	James Bottomley	30.00	15.00	9.00
(9)	Guy T. Bush	15.00	7.50	4.50
(10)	Harold G. Carlson	15.00	7.50	4.50
(11)	Owen Carroll	15.00	7.50	4.50
(12)	Chalmers W. Cissell (Chalmer)	15.00	7.50	4.50
(13)	Earl Combs	30.00	15.00	9.00
(14)	Hugh M. Critz	15.00	7.50	4.50
(15)	H.J. DeBerry	15.00	7.50	4.50
(16)	Pete Donohue	15.00	7.50	4.50
(17)	Taylor Douthit	15.00	7.50	4.50
(18)	Chas. W. Dressen	18.00	9.00	5.50
(19)	Jimmy Dykes	18.00	9.00	5.50
(20)	Howard Ehmke	15.00	7.50	4.50
(21)	Elwood English	15.00	7.50	4.50
(22)	Urban Faber	30.00	15.00	9.00
(23)	Fred Fitzsimmons	15.00	7.50	4.50
(24)	Lewis A. Fonseca	15.00	7.50	4.50
(25)	Horace H. Ford	15.00	7.50	4.50
(26)	Jimmy Foxx	40.00	20.00	12.00
(27)	Frank Frisch	30.00	15.00	9.00
(28)	Lou Gehrig	150.00	75.00	45.00
(29)	Charles Gehringer	30.00	15.00	9.00
(30)	Leon Goslin	30.00	15.00	9.00
(31)	George Grantham	15.00	7.50	4.50
(32)	Burleigh Grimes	30.00	15.00	9.00
(33)	Robert Grove	35.00	17.50	10.50
(34)	Bump Hadley	100.00	50.00	30.00
(35)	Charlie Hafey	30.00	15.00	9.00
(36)	Jesse J. Haines	100.00	50.00	30.00
(37)	Harvey Hendrick	15.00	7.50	4.50
(38)	Floyd C. Herman	18.00	9.00	5.50
(39)	Andy High	15.00	7.50	4.50
(40)	Urban J. Hodapp	15.00	7.50	4.50
(41)	Frank Hogan	15.00	7.50	4.50
(42)	Rogers Hornsby	40.00	20.00	12.00
(43)	Waite Hoyt	30.00	15.00	9.00
(44)	Willis Hudlin	15.00	7.50	4.50
(45)	Frank O. Hurst	15.00	7.50	4.50
(46)	Charlie Jamieson	15.00	7.50	4.50
(47)	Roy C. Johnson	15.00	7.50	4.50
(48)	Percy Jones	15.00	7.50	4.50
(49)	Sam Jones	15.00	7.50	4.50
(50)	Joseph Judge	15.00	7.50	4.50
(51)	Willie Kamm	15.00	7.50	4.50
(52)	Charles Klein	30.00	15.00	9.00
(53)	Mark Koenig	15.00	7.50	4.50
(54)	Ralph Kress	15.00	7.50	4.50
(55)	Fred M. Leach	15.00	7.50	4.50
(56)	Fred Lindstrom	30.00	15.00	9.00
(57)	Ad Liska	15.00	7.50	4.50
(58)	Fred Lucas (Red)	15.00	7.50	4.50
(59)	Fred Maguire	15.00	7.50	4.50
(60)	Perce L. Malone	15.00	7.50	4.50
(61)	Harry Manush (Henry)	30.00	15.00	9.00
(62)	Walter Maranville	30.00	15.00	9.00
(63)	Douglas McWeeney (McWeeny)	15.00	7.50	4.50
(64)	Oscar Melillo	15.00	7.50	4.50
(65)	Ed "Bing" Miller	15.00	7.50	4.50
(66)	Frank O'Doul	18.00	9.00	5.50
(67)	Melvin Ott	35.00	17.50	10.50
(68)	Herbert Pennock	30.00	15.00	9.00
(69)	William W. Regan	15.00	7.50	4.50
(70)	Harry F. Rice	15.00	7.50	4.50
(71)	Sam Rice	30.00	15.00	9.00
(72)	Lance Richbourgh (Richbourg)	15.00	7.50	4.50
(73)	Eddie Rommel	15.00	7.50	4.50
(74)	Chas. H. Root	15.00	7.50	4.50
(75)	Ed Roush	30.00	15.00	9.00
(76)	Harold Ruel (Herold)	15.00	7.50	4.50
(77)	Charles Ruffing	30.00	15.00	9.00
(78)	Jack Russell	15.00	7.50	4.50
(79)	Babe Ruth	125.00	62.00	37.00
(80)	Fred Schulte	15.00	7.50	4.50
(81)	Harry Seibold	100.00	50.00	30.00
(82)	Joe Sewell	30.00	15.00	9.00
(83)	Luke Sewell	15.00	7.50	4.50
(84)	Art Shires	15.00	7.50	4.50
(85)	Al Simmons	30.00	15.00	9.00
(86)	Bob Smith	15.00	7.50	4.50
(87)	Riggs Stephenson	18.00	9.00	5.50
(88)	Wm. H. Terry	35.00	17.50	10.50
(89)	Alphonse Thomas	15.00	7.50	4.50
(90)	Lafayette F. Thompson	15.00	7.50	4.50
(91)	Phil Todt	100.00	50.00	30.00
(92)	Harold J. Traynor	30.00	15.00	9.00
(93)	Dazzy Vance	30.00	15.00	9.00
(94)	Lloyd Waner	30.00	15.00	9.00
(95)	Paul Waner	30.00	15.00	9.00
(96)	Jimmy Welsh	15.00	7.50	4.50
(97)	Earl Whitehill	15.00	7.50	4.50
(98)	A.C. Whitney	15.00	7.50	4.50
(99)	Claude Willoughby	15.00	7.50	4.50
(100)	Hack Wilson	30.00	15.00	9.00
(101)	Tom Zachary	15.00	7.50	4.50

1937 R326 Goudey Big League Baseball Movies

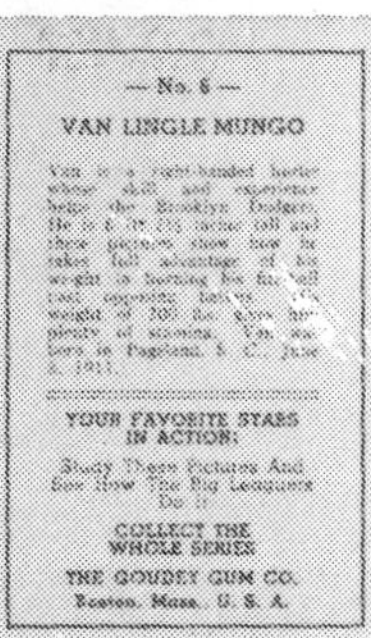

Issued circa 1937, this set of "flip movies" was comprised of small (2" by 3") booklets whose pages produced a movie effect when flipped rapidly, similar to a penny arcade novelty popular at the time. There are 13 players in the set, each movie having two clearly labeled parts. The cover of the booklets identify the set as "Big League Baseball Movies." Issued by Goudey, they carry the American Card Catalog designation R326.

		NR MT	EX	VG
	Complete Set:	1500.	750.00	450.00
	Common Player:	25.00	12.50	7.50
1a	John Irving Burns (Part 1)	25.00	12.50	7.50
1b	John Irving Burns (Part 2)	25.00	12.50	7.50
2a	Joe Vosmik (Part 1)	25.00	12.50	7.50
2b	Joe Vosmik (Part 2)	25.00	12.50	7.50
3a	Mel Ott (Part 1)	60.00	30.00	18.00
3b	Mel Ott (Part 2)	60.00	30.00	18.00
4a	Joe DiMaggio (Part 1)	250.00	125.00	75.00
4b	Joe DiMaggio (Part 2)	250.00	125.00	75.00
5a	Wally Moses (Part 1)	25.00	12.50	7.50
5b	Wally Moses (Part 2)	25.00	12.50	7.50
6a	Van Lingle Mungo (Part 1)	25.00	12.50	7.50
6b	Van Lingle Mungo (Part 2)	25.00	12.50	7.50
7a	Luke Appling (Part 1)	40.00	20.00	12.00
7b	Luke Appling (Part 2)	40.00	20.00	12.00
8a	Bob Feller (Part 1)	80.00	40.00	25.00
8b	Bob Feller (Part 2)	80.00	40.00	25.00
9a	Paul Derringer (Part 1)	25.00	12.50	7.50
9b	Paul Derringer (Part 2)	25.00	12.50	7.50
10a	Paul Waner (Part 1)	40.00	20.00	12.00
10b	Paul Waner (Part 2)	40.00	20.00	12.00
11a	Joe Medwick (Part 1)	40.00	20.00	12.00
11b	Joe Medwick (Part 2)	40.00	20.00	12.00
12a	James Emory Foxx (Part 1)	80.00	40.00	25.00
12b	James Emory Foxx (Part 2)	80.00	40.00	25.00
13a	Wally Berger (Part 1)	25.00	12.50	7.50
13b	Wally Berger (Part 2)	25.00	12.50	7.50

1935 R332 Schutter-Johnson

MAJOR LEAGUE SECRETS
No. 18. Sacrifice Bunting

Schutter-Johnson Candy Corp.
Chicago—Brooklyn

This 50-card set was issued by the Schutter-Johnson Candy Corp. of Chicago and Brooklyn circa 1930 and features drawings of major league players offering baseball playing tips. The cards measure 2-1/4" by 2-7/8". The drawings on the front are set against a red background, while the backs are titled "Major League Secrets" and give the player's advice on some aspect of the game. The Schutter-Johnson name appears at the bottom.

		NR MT	EX	VG
	Complete Set:	3200.	1600.	960.00
	Common Player:	35.00	17.50	10.50
1	Al Simmons	50.00	25.00	15.00
2	Lloyd Waner	50.00	25.00	15.00
3	Kiki Cuyler	50.00	25.00	15.00
4	Frank Frisch	60.00	30.00	18.00
5	Chick Hafey	50.00	25.00	15.00
6	Bill Klem (umpire)	50.00	25.00	15.00
7	Rogers Hornsby	90.00	45.00	27.00
8	Carl Mays	35.00	17.50	10.50
9	Chas. Wrigley (umpire)	35.00	17.50	10.50
10	Christy Mathewson	90.00	45.00	27.00
11	Bill Dickey	70.00	35.00	21.00
12	Walter Berger	35.00	17.50	10.50
13	George Earnshaw	35.00	17.50	10.50
14	"Hack" Wilson	50.00	25.00	15.00
15	Charley Grimm	35.00	17.50	10.50
16	Lloyd Waner, Paul Waner	50.00	25.00	15.00
17	Chuck Klein	50.00	25.00	15.00
18	Woody English	35.00	17.50	10.50
19	Grover Alexander	70.00	35.00	21.00
20	Lou Gehrig	200.00	100.00	60.00
21	Wes Ferrell	35.00	17.50	10.50
22	Carl Hubbell	60.00	30.00	18.00
23	Pie Traynor	50.00	25.00	15.00
24	Gus Mancuso	35.00	17.50	10.50
25	Ben Cantwell	35.00	17.50	10.50
26	Babe Ruth	350.00	175.00	105.00
27	"Goose" Goslin	50.00	25.00	15.00
28	Earle Combs	50.00	25.00	15.00
29	"Kiki" Cuyler	50.00	25.00	15.00
30	Jimmy Wilson	35.00	17.50	10.50
31	Dizzy Dean	100.00	50.00	30.00
32	Mickey Cochrane	60.00	30.00	18.00
33	Ted Lyons	50.00	25.00	15.00
34	Si Johnson	35.00	17.50	10.50
35	Dizzy Dean	100.00	50.00	30.00
36	Pepper Martin	40.00	20.00	12.00
37	Joe Cronin	50.00	25.00	15.00
38	Gabby Hartnett	50.00	25.00	15.00
39	Oscar Melillo	35.00	17.50	10.50
40	Ben Chapman	35.00	17.50	10.50
41	John McGraw	70.00	35.00	21.00
42	Babe Ruth	150.00	75.00	45.00
43	"Red" Lucas	35.00	17.50	10.50
44	Charley Root	35.00	17.50	10.50
45	Dazzy Vance	50.00	25.00	15.00
46	Hugh Critz	35.00	17.50	10.50
47	"Firpo" Marberry	35.00	17.50	10.50
48	Grover Alexander	70.00	35.00	21.00
49	Lefty Grove	70.00	35.00	21.00
50	Heinie Meine	35.00	17.50	10.50

1932 R337

No. 410
JIMMY DYKES
Chicago White Sox

He is one of the few players who can play every position in the field but catch. A timely batter and dependable fielder, he hit 265 in over 130 games and played three infield positions in 1932. Played with Philadelphia Athletics for over 12 years, finally traded to White Sox this year. Dykes is 36 years old, about five feet nine inches tall and weighs 175 lbs.

Issued circa 1932, little is known about the origin of this 24-card set, which is numbered from

401 through 424. The cards measure 2-5/16" by 2-13/16", and the design is similar to the M.P. & Co. sets with a crude drawing of the player on the front. The back of the card displays the card number at the top followed by the player's name, team and a brief write-up. Card numbers 403, 413, and 414 are missing and probably correspond to the three unnumbered cards in the set (Foxx, Johnson and Traynor).

		NR MT	EX	VG
Complete Set:		1400.	700.00	420.00
Common Player:		35.00	17.50	10.50
401	Johnny Vergez	35.00	17.50	10.50
402	Babe Ruth	350.00	175.00	105.00
403	Not Issued			
404	George Pipgras	35.00	17.50	10.50
405	Bill Terry	60.00	30.00	18.00
406	George Connally	35.00	17.50	10.50
407	Watson Clark	35.00	17.50	10.50
408	"Lefty" Grove	70.00	35.00	21.00
409	Henry Johnson	35.00	17.50	10.50
410	Jimmy Dykes	35.00	17.50	10.50
411	Henry Hine Schuble	35.00	17.50	10.50
412	Bucky Harris	50.00	25.00	15.00
413	Not Issued			
414	Not Issued			
415	Al Simmons	50.00	25.00	15.00
416	Henry "Heinie" Manush	50.00	25.00	15.00
417	Glen Myatt	35.00	17.50	10.50
418	Babe Herman	40.00	20.00	12.00
419	Frank Frisch	60.00	30.00	18.00
420	Tony Lazzeri	40.00	20.00	12.00
421	Paul Waner	50.00	25.00	15.00
422	Jimmy Wilson	35.00	17.50	10.50
423	Charles Grimm	35.00	17.50	10.50
424	Dick Bartell	35.00	17.50	10.50
---	Jimmy Fox (Foxx)	100.00	50.00	30.00
---	Roy Johnson	35.00	17.50	10.50
---	Pie Traynor	50.00	25.00	15.00

1934 R342 Goudey Baseball Thum Movies

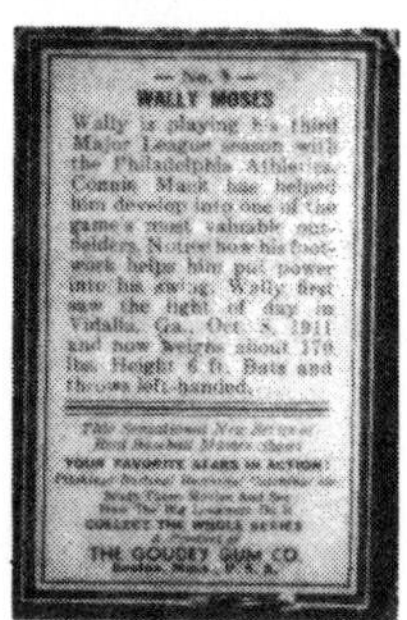

Assigned the American Card Catalog number R342, these 2" by 3" booklets are similar to the "Big League Baseball Movies" (R326) issued by Goudey circa 1937. The "Thum Movies" set consists of 13 players. The booklets are numbered on the top of the back page.

		NR MT	EX	VG
Complete Set:		900.00	450.00	275.00
Common Player:		35.00	17.50	10.50
1	John Irving Burns	35.00	17.50	10.50
2	Joe Vosmik	35.00	17.50	10.50
3	Mel Ott	80.00	40.00	24.00
4	Joe DiMaggio	250.00	125.00	75.00
5	Wally Moses	35.00	17.50	10.50
6	Van Lingle Mungo	35.00	17.50	10.50
7	Luke Appling	60.00	30.00	18.00
8	Bob Feller	90.00	45.00	27.00
9	Paul Derringer	35.00	17.50	10.50
10	Paul Waner	60.00	30.00	18.00
11	Joe Medwick	60.00	30.00	18.00
12	James Emory Foxx	90.00	45.00	27.00
13	Wally Berger	35.00	17.50	10.50

1936 R344 National Chicle

Issued by National Chicle in 1936, this 20-card set was a paper issue distributed with Batter-Up Gum. Unfolded, each paper measured 3-5/8" by 6". The numbered set featured a series of baseball tips from Rabbit Maranville and are illustrated with line drawings.

		NR MT	EX	VG
Complete Set:		400.00	200.00	120.00
Common Card:		20.00	10.00	6.00
1	How to Pitch the Out Shoot	20.00	10.00	6.00
2	How to Throw the In Shoot	20.00	10.00	6.00
3	How to Pitch the Drop	20.00	10.00	6.00
4	How to Pitch the Floater	20.00	10.00	6.00
5	How to Run Bases	20.00	10.00	6.00
6	How to Slide	20.00	10.00	6.00
7	How to Catch Flies	20.00	10.00	6.00
8	How to Field Grounders	20.00	10.00	6.00
9	How to Tag A Man Out	20.00	10.00	6.00
10	How to Cover A Base	20.00	10.00	6.00
11	How to Bat	20.00	10.00	6.00
12	How to Steal Bases	20.00	10.00	6.00
13	How to Bunt	20.00	10.00	6.00
14	How to Coach Base Runner	20.00	10.00	6.00
15	How to Catch Behind the Bat	20.00	10.00	6.00
16	How to Throw to Bases	20.00	10.00	6.00
17	How to Signal	20.00	10.00	6.00
18	How to Umpire Balls and Strikes	20.00	10.00	6.00
19	How to Umpire Bases	20.00	10.00	6.00
20	How to Lay Out a Ball Field	20.00	10.00	6.00

1947 R346 Blue Tint

Issued during 1948-49, the cards in this 48-card set derive their name from the distinctive blue coloring used to tint the black and white photos. The cards have blank backs and measure 2" by 2-5/8". The set, which has a high percentage of New York players, was originally issued in strips of six or eight cards each and therefore would be more appropriately cataloged as a "W" strip card set, although collectors still commonly refer to it by the R346 designation. The set includes two major variations: Leo Durocher can be found as both a Dodger and a Giant; and Mel Ott can be found as a Giant or with no team designation. The complete set price does not include the variations.

		NR MT	EX	VG
Complete Set:		1150.	575.00	345.00
Common Player:		12.00	6.00	3.50
1	Bill Johnson	12.00	6.00	3.50
2a	Leo Durocher (Brooklyn)	25.00	12.50	7.50
2b	Leo Durocher (New York)	25.00	12.50	7.50
3	Marty Marion	15.00	7.50	4.50
4	Ewell Blackwell	15.00	7.50	4.50
5	John Lindell	12.00	6.00	3.50
6	Larry Jansen	12.00	6.00	3.50
7	Ralph Kiner	25.00	12.50	7.50
8	Chuck Dressen	12.00	6.00	3.50
9	Bobby Brown	15.00	7.50	4.50
10	Luke Appling	25.00	12.50	7.50
11	Bill Nicholson	12.00	6.00	3.50
12	Phil Masi	12.00	6.00	3.50
13	Frank Shea	12.00	6.00	3.50
14	Bob Dillinger	12.00	6.00	3.50
15	Pete Suder	12.00	6.00	3.50
16	Joe DiMaggio	150.00	75.00	45.00
17	John Corriden	12.00	6.00	3.50
18a	Mel Ott (New York)	30.00	15.00	9.00
18b	Mel Ott (no team designation)	30.00	15.00	9.00
19	Warren Rosar	12.00	6.00	3.50
20	Warren Spahn	30.00	15.00	9.00
21	Allie Reynolds	18.00	9.00	5.50
22	Lou Boudreau	25.00	12.50	7.50
23	Harry Majeski	12.00	6.00	3.50
24	Frank Crosetti	15.00	7.50	4.50
25	Gus Niarhos	12.00	6.00	3.50
26	Bruce Edwards	12.00	6.00	3.50
27	Rudy York	12.00	6.00	3.50
28	Don Black	12.00	6.00	3.50
29	Lou Gehrig	150.00	75.00	45.00
30	Johnny Mize	25.00	12.50	7.50
31	Ed Stanky	15.00	7.50	4.50
32	Vic Raschi	15.00	7.50	4.50
33	Cliff Mapes	12.00	6.00	3.50
34	Enos Slaughter	25.00	12.50	7.50
35	Hank Greenberg	25.00	12.50	7.50
36	Jackie Robinson	90.00	45.00	27.00
37	Frank Hiller	12.00	6.00	3.50
38	Bob Elliot (Elliott)	12.00	6.00	3.50
39	Harry Walker	12.00	6.00	3.50
40	Ed Lopat	15.00	7.50	4.50
41	Bobby Thomson	15.00	7.50	4.50
42	Tommy Henrich	18.00	9.00	5.50
43	Bobby Feller	40.00	20.00	12.00
44	Ted Williams	90.00	45.00	27.00
45	Dixie Walker	12.00	6.00	3.50
46	Johnnie Vander Meer	15.00	7.50	4.50
47	Clint Hartung	12.00	6.00	3.50
48	Charlie Keller	18.00	9.00	5.50

1950 R423

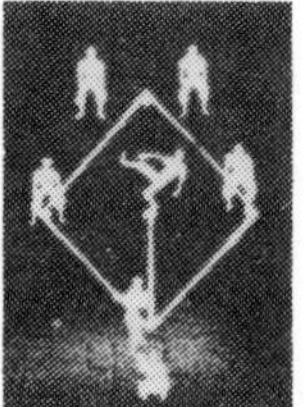

These tiny (3/4" by 5/8") cards are numbered from 1 through 120, although many numbers are still unknown or were never issued. The cards were available in long perforated strips from vending machines in the 1950s. The cards are printed on thin stock and include the player's name beneath his photo. The backs display a rough drawing of a baseball infield with tiny figures at the various positions. It appears the cards were intended to be used to play a game of baseball.

		NR MT	EX	VG
Complete Set:		110.00	55.00	28.00
Common Player:		.40	.20	.12
(1)	Richie Ashburn	.90	.45	.25
(2)	Unknown			
(3)	Frank Baumholtz	.40	.20	.12
(4)	Ralph Branca	.50	.25	.15
(5)	Unknown			
(6)	Unknown			
(7)	Unknown			
(8)	Harry Brecheen	.40	.20	.12
(9)	Chico Carrasquel	.40	.20	.12
(10)	Jerry Coleman	.40	.20	.12
(11)	Walker Cooper	.40	.20	.12
(12)	Unknown			
(13)	Phil Cavaretta (Cavarretta)	.40	.20	.12
(14)	Ty Cobb	7.00	3.50	2.00
(15)	Unknown			
(16)	Unknown			
(17)	Frank Crosetti	.50	.25	.15
(18)	Larry Doby	.90	.45	.25
(19)	Walter Dropo	.40	.20	.12
(20)	Unknown			
(21)	Dizzy Dean	3.00	1.50	.90
(22)	Bill Dickey	1.75	.90	.50
(23)	Murray Dickson (Murry)	.40	.20	.12
(24)	Dom DiMaggio	.90	.45	.25
(25)	Joe DiMaggio	7.00	3.50	2.00
(26)	Unknown			
(27)	Unknown			
(28)	Bob Elliott	.40	.20	.12
(29)	Unknown			
(30)	Unknown			
(31)	Bob Feller	2.50	1.25	.70
(32)	Frank Frisch	1.00	.50	.30
(33)	Unknown			
(34)	Unknown			
(35)	Lou Gehrig	7.00	3.50	2.00
(36)	Joe Gordon	.50	.25	.15
(37)	Unknown			
(38)	Hank Greenberg	1.25	.60	.40
(39)	Lefty Grove	1.25	.60	.40
(40)	Unknown			
(41)	Unknown			
(42)	Ken Heintzelman	.40	.20	.12
(43)	Unknown			
(44)	Jim Hearn	.40	.20	.12
(45)	Unknown			
(46)	Harry Heilman (Heilmann)	.90	.45	.25
(47)	Tommy Henrich	.50	.25	.15
(48)	Roger Hornsby (Rogers)	2.00	1.00	.60
(49)	Unknown			
(50)	Edwin Joost	.40	.20	.12
(51)	Unknown			
(52)	Unknown			
(53)	Nippy Jones	.40	.20	.12
(54)	Walter Johnson	3.00	1.50	.90
(55)	Ellis Kinder	.40	.20	.12
(56)	Jim Konstanty	.40	.20	.12
(57)	Unknown			
(58)	Ralph Kiner	1.00	.50	.30
(59)	Bob Lemon	.90	.45	.25
(60)	Unknown			
(61)	Unknown			

		NR MT	EX	VG
(62)	Unknown			
(63)	Cass Michaels	.40	.20	.12
(64)	Unknown			
(65)	Unknown			
(66)	Clyde McCullough	.40	.20	.12
(67)	Connie Mack	1.00	.50	.30
(68)	Christy Mathewson	2.50	1.25	.70
(69)	Joe Medwick	.90	.45	.25
(70)	Johnny Mize	1.00	.50	.30
(71)	Terry Moore	.40	.20	.12
(72)	Stan Musial	3.50	1.75	1.00
(73)	Hal Newhouser	.50	.25	.15
(74)	Don Newcombe	.50	.25	.15
(75)	Lefty O'Doul	.50	.25	.15
(76)	Unknown			
(77)	Mel Parnell	.40	.20	.12
(78)	Unknown			
(79)	Gerald Priddy	.40	.20	.12
(80)	Dave Philley	.40	.20	.12
(81)	Bob Porterfield	.40	.20	.12
(82)	Andy Pafko	.50	.25	.15
(83)	Howie Pollet	.40	.20	.12
(84)	Herb Pennock	.40	.20	.12
(85)	Al Rosen	.90	.45	.25
(86)	Peewee Reese	1.75	.90	.50
(87)	Del Rice	.40	.20	.12
(88)	Unknown			
(89)	Unknown			
(90)	Unknown			
(91)	Unknown			
(92)	Babe Ruth	15.00	7.50	4.50
(93)	Casey Stengel	2.25	1.25	.70
(94)	Vern Stephens	.40	.20	.12
(95)	Duke Snider	2.25	1.25	.70
(96)	Enos Slaughter	.90	.45	.25
(97)	Al Schoendienst	.50	.25	.15
(98)	Gerald Staley	.40	.20	.12
(99)	Clyde Shoun	.40	.20	.12
(100)	Unknown			
(101)	Unknown			
(102)	Al Simmons	.90	.45	.25
(103)	George Sisler	.90	.45	.25
(104)	Tris Speaker	1.25	.60	.40
(105)	Ed Stanky	.50	.25	.15
(106)	Virgil Trucks	.40	.20	.12
(107)	Henry Thompson	.40	.20	.12
(108)	Unknown			
(109)	Dazzy Vance	.90	.45	.25
(110)	Lloyd Waner	.90	.45	.25
(111)	Paul Waner	.90	.45	.25
(112)	Gene Woodling	.40	.20	.12
(113)	Ted Williams	5.00	2.50	1.50
(114)	Unknown			
(115)	Wes Westrum	.40	.20	.12
(116)	Johnny Wyrostek	.40	.20	.12
(117)	Eddie Yost	.40	.20	.12
(118)	Allen Zarilla	.40	.20	.12
(119)	Gus Zernial	.40	.20	.12
(120)	Sam Zoldack (Zoldak)	.40	.20	.12

1984 Ralston Purina

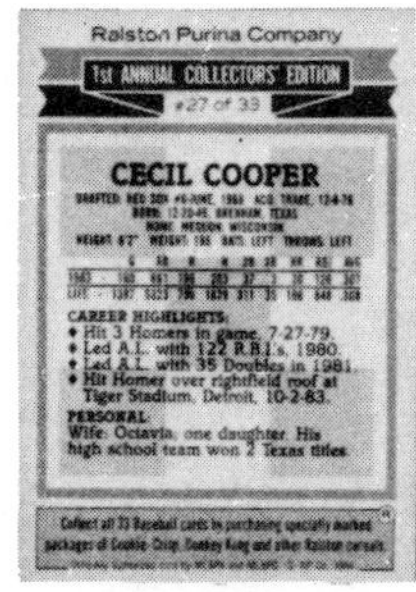

This set, produced in conjunction with Topps, has 33 of the game's top players, and is titled "1st Annual Collector's Edition." The full-color photos on the 2-1/2" by 3-1/2" cards are all close-up poses. Topps' logo appears only on the card fronts, and the backs are completely different from Topps' regular issue of 1984. Card backs feature a checkerboard look, coinciding with the well-known Ralston Purina logo. Cards are numbered 1-33, with odd numbers for American Leaguers and even numbered cards for National League players. Four cards were packed in boxes of Cookie Crisp and Donkey Kong Junior brand cereals, and the complete set was available via a mail-in offer.

		MT	NR MT	EX
Complete Set:		4.00	3.00	1.50
Common Player:		.10	.08	.04
1	Eddie Murray	.30	.25	.12
2	Ozzie Smith	.10	.08	.04
3	Ted Simmons	.10	.08	.04
4	Pete Rose	.50	.40	.20
5	Greg Luzinski	.10	.08	.04
6	Andre Dawson	.15	.11	.06
7	Dave Winfield	.25	.20	.10
8	Tom Seaver	.25	.20	.10
9	Jim Rice	.25	.20	.10
10	Fernando Valenzuela	.20	.15	.08
11	Wade Boggs	.60	.45	.25
12	Dale Murphy	.35	.25	.14
13	George Brett	.35	.25	.14
14	Nolan Ryan	.20	.15	.08
15	Rickey Henderson	.30	.25	.12
16	Steve Carlton	.25	.20	.10
17	Rod Carew	.25	.20	.10
18	Steve Garvey	.25	.20	.10
19	Reggie Jackson	.25	.20	.10
20	Dave Concepcion	.10	.08	.04
21	Robin Yount	.20	.15	.08
22	Mike Schmidt	.35	.25	.14
23	Jim Palmer	.20	.15	.08
24	Bruce Sutter	.10	.08	.04
25	Dan Quisenberry	.10	.08	.04
26	Bill Madlock	.10	.08	.04
27	Cecil Cooper	.10	.08	.04
28	Gary Carter	.25	.20	.10
29	Fred Lynn	.15	.11	.06
30	Pedro Guerrero	.15	.11	.06
31	Ron Guidry	.15	.11	.06
32	Keith Hernandez	.20	.15	.08
33	Carlton Fisk	.15	.11	.06

1987 Ralston Purina

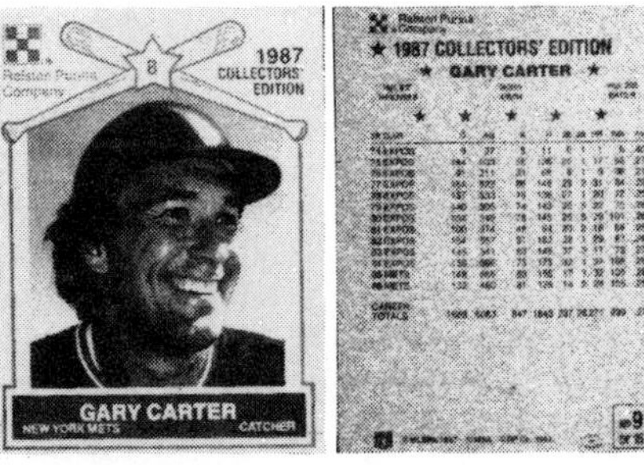

The Ralston Purina Company, in conjunction with Mike Schecter Associates, issued a 15-card set in specially marked boxes of Cookie Crisp and Honey Graham Chex brands of cereal. Three different cards, each measuring 2-1/2" by 3-1/2" and wrapped in cellophane, were inserted in each box. The card fronts contain a full-color photo with the team insignia airbrushed away. Above the photo are two yellow crossed bats and a star, with the player's uniform number inside the star. The card backs are grey with red printing and contain the set name, card number, player's name, personal information and career major league statistics. As part of the Ralston Purina promotion, the company advertised an uncut sheet of cards which was available by finding an "instant-winner" game card or sending $1 plus two non-winning cards. Cards on the uncut sheet are identical in design to the single cards, save the omission of the words "1987 Collectors Edition" in the upper right corner. A complete uncut sheet in mint condition is valued at $10.

		MT	NR MT	EX
Complete Set:		15.00	11.00	6.00
Common Player:		1.00	.70	.40
1	Nolan Ryan	1.25	.90	.50
2	Steve Garvey	1.25	.90	.50
3	Wade Boggs	2.00	1.50	.80
4	Dave Winfield	1.25	.90	.50
5	Don Mattingly	3.00	2.25	1.25
6	Don Sutton	1.00	.70	.40
7	Dave Parker	1.00	.70	.40
8	Eddie Murray	1.25	.90	.50
9	Gary Carter	1.25	.90	.50
10	Roger Clemens	1.50	1.25	.60
11	Fernando Valenzuela	1.25	.90	.50
12	Cal Ripken Jr.	1.25	.90	.50
13	Ozzie Smith	1.00	.70	.40
14	Mike Schmidt	1.50	1.25	.60
15	Ryne Sandberg	1.25	.90	.50

1989 Ralston Purina

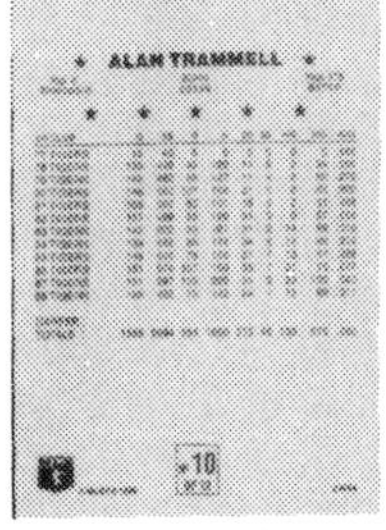

The Ralston Purina Co., in conjunction with Mike Schechter Associates, issued a 12-card "Superstars" set in 1989. As part of a late-spring and early-summer promotion, the standard-size cards were inserted, two per box, in specially-marked boxes of Crisp Crunch, Honey Nut O's, Fruit Rings and Frosted Flakes in most parts of the country. Ads on cereal boxes also offered complete sets through a mail-in offer. The fronts of the cards feature full-color player photos flanked by stars in all four corners. "Super Stars" appears at the top; the player's name and position are at the bottom. The backs include player stats and data, the card number and copyright line.

		MT	NR MT	EX
Complete Set:		10.00	7.50	4.00
Common Player:		.80	.60	.30
1	Ozzie Smith	.80	.60	.30
2	Andre Dawson	.80	.60	.30
3	Darryl Strawberry	1.00	.70	.40
4	Mike Schmidt	1.25	.90	.50
5	Orel Hershiser	.90	.70	.35
6	Tim Raines	.80	.60	.30
7	Roger Clemens	1.25	.90	.50
8	Kirby Puckett	1.25	.90	.50
9	George Brett	1.00	.70	.40
10	Alan Trammell	.80	.60	.30
11	Don Mattingly	2.25	1.75	.90
12	Jose Canseco	2.00	1.50	.80

1954 Red Heart Dog Food

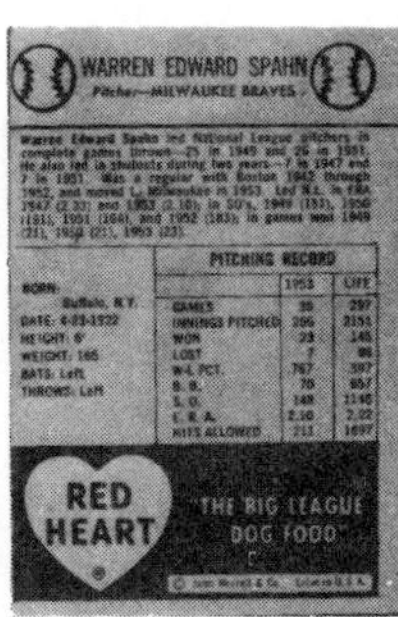

This set of 33 cards was issued in three color-coded series by the Red Heart Dog Food Co. Card fronts feature hand-colored photos on either a blue, green or red background. The 11 red-background cards are scarcer than the 11-card blue or green series. Backs of the 2-5/8" by 3-3/4" cards contain biographical and statistical information along with a Red Heart ad. Each 11-card series was available via a mail-in offer. As late as the early 1970s, the company was still sending cards to collectors who requested them.

		NR MT	EX	VG
Complete Set:		1600.	800.00	480.00
Common Player:		20.00	10.00	6.00
(1)	Richie Ashburn	35.00	17.50	10.50
(2)	Frankie Baumholtz	25.00	12.50	7.50
(3)	Gus Bell	20.00	10.00	6.00
(4)	Billy Cox	25.00	12.50	7.50
(5)	Alvin Dark	25.00	12.50	7.50
(6)	Carl Erskine	30.00	15.00	9.00
(7)	Ferris Fain	20.00	10.00	6.00
(8)	Dee Fondy	20.00	10.00	6.00
(9)	Nelson Fox	30.00	15.00	9.00
(10)	Jim Gilliam	30.00	15.00	9.00
(11)	Jim Hegan	25.00	12.50	7.50
(12)	George Kell	30.00	15.00	9.00
(13)	Ted Kluszewski	30.00	15.00	9.00
(14)	Ralph Kiner	40.00	20.00	12.00
(15)	Harvey Kuenn	25.00	12.50	7.50
(16)	Bob Lemon	40.00	20.00	12.00
(17)	Sherman Lollar	20.00	10.00	6.00
(18)	Mickey Mantle	400.00	200.00	120.00
(19)	Billy Martin	40.00	20.00	12.00
(20)	Gil McDougald	30.00	15.00	9.00
(21)	Roy McMillan	20.00	10.00	6.00
(22)	Minnie Minoso	25.00	12.50	7.50
(23)	Stan Musial	225.00	112.00	67.00
(24)	Billy Pierce	25.00	12.50	7.50
(25)	Al Rosen	30.00	15.00	9.00
(26)	Hank Sauer	20.00	10.00	6.00
(27)	Red Schoendienst	30.00	15.00	9.00
(28)	Enos Slaughter	30.00	15.00	9.00
(29)	Duke Snider	75.00	37.00	22.00
(30)	Warren Spahn	50.00	25.00	15.00
(31)	Sammy White	20.00	10.00	6.00
(32)	Eddie Yost	20.00	10.00	6.00
(33)	Gus Zernial	20.00	10.00	6.00

1982 Red Lobster Cubs

This 28-card set was co-sponsored by the team and a seafood restaurant chain for distribution at a 1982 Cubs promotional game. Card fronts are unbordered color photos, with player name,

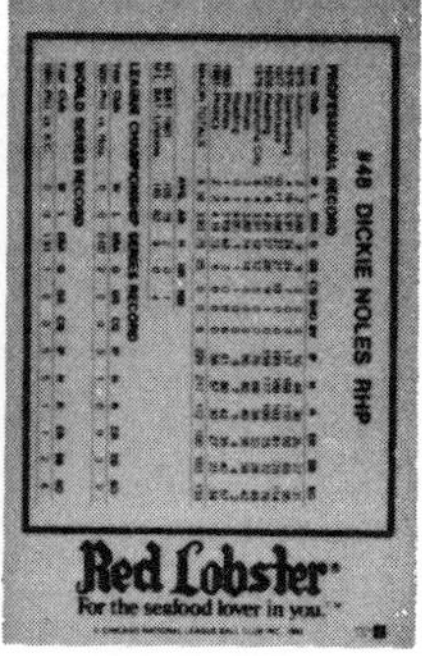

number, position and a superimposed facsimile autograph. The set includes 25 players on the 2-1/4" by 3-1/2" cards, along with a card for manager Lee Elia, an unnumbered card for the coaching staff and a team picture. Card backs have complete player statistics and a Red Lobster ad.

		MT	NR MT	EX
Complete Set:		12.00	9.00	4.75
Common Player:		.20	.15	.08
1	Larry Bowa	.40	.30	.15
4	Lee Elia	.20	.15	.08
6	Keith Moreland	.40	.30	.15
7	Jody Davis	.40	.30	.15
10	Leon Durham	.40	.30	.15
15	Junior Kennedy	.20	.15	.08
17	Bump Wills	.20	.15	.08
18	Scot Thompson	.20	.15	.08
21	Jay Johnstone	.25	.20	.10
22	Bill Buckner	.40	.30	.15
23	Ryne Sandberg	3.00	2.25	1.25
24	Jerry Morales	.20	.15	.08
25	Gary Woods	.20	.15	.08
28	Steve Henderson	.20	.15	.08
29	Bob Molinaro	.20	.15	.08
31	Fergie Jenkins	.70	.50	.30
33	Al Ripley	.20	.15	.08
34	Randy Martz	.20	.15	.08
36	Mike Proly	.20	.15	.08
37	Ken Kravec	.20	.15	.08
38	Willie Hernandez	.30	.25	.12
39	Bill Campbell	.20	.15	.08
41	Dick Tidrow	.20	.15	.08
46	Lee Smith	.50	.40	.20
47	Doug Bird	.20	.15	.08
48	Dickie Noles	.20	.15	.08
---	Team Photo	.20	.15	.08
---	Coaching Staff (Billy Connors, Tom Harmon, Gordy MacKenzie, John Vuckovich, Billy Williams)	.25	.20	.10

1952 Red Man Tobacco

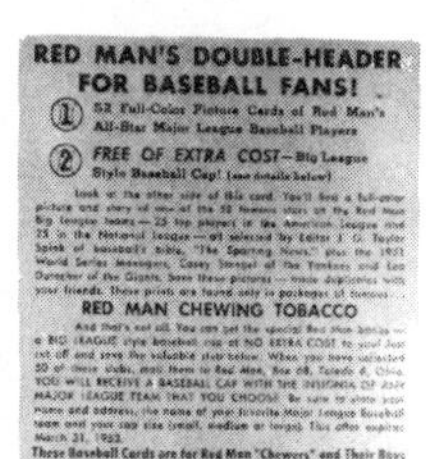

This was the first national set of tobacco cards produced since the golden days of tobacco sets in the early part of the century. There are 52 cards in the set, with 25 top players and one manager from each league. Player selection was made by editor J.G. Taylor Spink of The Sporting News. Cards measure 3-1/2"by 4", including a 1/2" tab at the bottom of each card. These tabs were redeemable for a free baseball cap from Red Man. Cards are harder to find with tabs intact, and thus more valuable in that form. Values quoted here are for cards with tabs. Cards with the tabs removed would be valued about 35-40 percent of the quoted figures. Card fronts are full color paintings of each player with biographical information inset in the portrait area. Card backs contain company advertising. Cards are numbered and dated only on the tabs.

		NR MT	EX	VG
Complete Set:		2100.	1050.	630.00
Common Player:		20.00	10.00	6.00
1A	Casey Stengel	55.00	27.00	16.50
1N	Leo Durocher	40.00	20.00	12.00
2A	Roberto Avila	20.00	10.00	6.00
2N	Richie Ashburn	35.00	17.50	10.50
3A	Larry "Yogi" Berra	80.00	40.00	24.00
3N	Ewell Blackwell	25.00	12.50	7.50
4A	Gil Coan	20.00	10.00	6.00
4N	Cliff Chambers	20.00	10.00	6.00
5A	Dom DiMaggio	30.00	15.00	9.00
5N	Murry Dickson	20.00	10.00	6.00
6A	Larry Doby	30.00	15.00	9.00
6N	Sid Gordon	20.00	10.00	6.00
7A	Ferris Fain	25.00	12.50	7.50
7N	Granny Hamner	20.00	10.00	6.00
8A	Bob Feller	80.00	40.00	24.00
8N	Jim Hearn	20.00	10.00	6.00
9A	Nelson Fox	35.00	17.50	10.50
9N	Monte Irvin	50.00	25.00	15.00
10A	Johnny Groth	20.00	10.00	6.00
10N	Larry Jansen	20.00	10.00	6.00
11A	Jim Hegan	20.00	10.00	6.00
11N	Willie Jones	20.00	10.00	6.00
12A	Eddie Joost	20.00	10.00	6.00
12N	Ralph Kiner	50.00	25.00	15.00
13A	George Kell	50.00	25.00	15.00
13N	Whitey Lockman	20.00	10.00	6.00
14A	Gil McDougald	30.00	15.00	9.00
14N	Sal Maglie	25.00	12.50	7.50
15A	Orestes Minoso	25.00	12.50	7.50
15N	Willie Mays	150.00	75.00	45.00
16A	Bill Pierce	25.00	12.50	7.50
16N	Stan Musial	150.00	75.00	45.00
17A	Bob Porterfield	20.00	10.00	6.00
17N	Pee Wee Reese	75.00	37.00	22.00
18A	Eddie Robinson	20.00	10.00	6.00
18N	Robin Roberts	50.00	25.00	15.00
19A	Saul Rogovin	20.00	10.00	6.00
19N	Al Schoendienst	30.00	15.00	9.00
20A	Bobby Shantz	25.00	12.50	7.50
20N	Enos Slaughter	50.00	25.00	15.00
21A	Vern Stephens	20.00	10.00	6.00
21N	Duke Snider	100.00	50.00	30.00
22A	Vic Wertz	20.00	10.00	6.00
22N	Warren Spahn	60.00	30.00	18.00
23A	Ted Williams	175.00	87.00	52.00
23N	Eddie Stanky	25.00	12.50	7.50
24A	Early Wynn	50.00	25.00	15.00
24N	Bobby Thomson	30.00	15.00	9.00
25A	Eddie Yost	20.00	10.00	6.00
25N	Earl Torgeson	20.00	10.00	6.00
26A	Gus Zernial	20.00	10.00	6.00
26N	Wes Westrum	20.00	10.00	6.00

1953 Red Man Tobacco

This was the chewing tobacco company's second annual set of 3-1/2" by 4" cards, including the tabs at the bottom of the cards. Formats for both the fronts and backs are similar to the '52 edition. The 1953 Red Man cards, however, include card numbers within the player biographical section, and the card backs are headlined "New for '53." Once again, cards with intact tabs (which were redeemable for a free cap) are more valuable. Prices below are for cards with tabs. Cards with tabs removed are worth about 35-40 percent of the stated values. Each league is represented by 25 players and a manager on the full-color cards, a total of 52.

		NR MT	EX	VG
Complete Set:		2350.	1175.	705.00
Common Player:		20.00	10.00	6.00
1A	Casey Stengel	55.00	27.00	16.50
1N	Charlie Dressen	25.00	12.50	7.50
2A	Hank Bauer	25.00	12.50	7.50
2N	Bobby Adams	20.00	10.00	6.00
3A	Larry "Yogi" Berra	80.00	40.00	24.00
3N	Richie Ashburn	35.00	17.50	10.50
4A	Walt Dropo	20.00	10.00	6.00
4N	Joe Black	25.00	12.50	7.50
5A	Nelson Fox	35.00	17.50	10.50
5N	Roy Campanella	80.00	40.00	24.00
6A	Jackie Jensen	25.00	12.50	7.50
6N	Ted Kluszewski	30.00	15.00	9.00
7A	Eddie Joost	20.00	10.00	6.00
7N	Whitey Lockman	20.00	10.00	6.00
8A	George Kell	50.00	25.00	15.00
8N	Sal Maglie	25.00	12.50	7.50
9A	Dale Mitchell	20.00	10.00	6.00
9N	Andy Pafko	25.00	12.50	7.50
10A	Phil Rizzuto	60.00	30.00	18.00
10N	Pee Wee Reese	75.00	37.00	22.00
11A	Eddie Robinson	20.00	10.00	6.00
11N	Robin Roberts	50.00	25.00	15.00
12A	Gene Woodling	25.00	12.50	7.50
12N	Al Schoendienst	30.00	15.00	9.00
13A	Gus Zernial	20.00	10.00	6.00
13N	Enos Slaughter	50.00	25.00	15.00
14A	Early Wynn	50.00	25.00	15.00
14N	Edwin "Duke" Snider	100.00	50.00	30.00
15A	Joe Dobson	20.00	10.00	6.00
15N	Ralph Kiner	50.00	25.00	15.00
16A	Billy Pierce	25.00	12.50	7.50
16N	Hank Sauer	20.00	10.00	6.00
17A	Bob Lemon	50.00	25.00	15.00
17N	Del Ennis	20.00	10.00	6.00
18A	Johnny Mize	50.00	25.00	15.00
18N	Granny Hamner	20.00	10.00	6.00
19A	Bob Porterfield	20.00	10.00	6.00
19N	Warren Spahn	60.00	30.00	18.00
20A	Bobby Shantz	25.00	12.50	7.50
20N	Wes Westrum	20.00	10.00	6.00
21A	"Mickey" Vernon	25.00	12.50	7.50
21N	Hoyt Wilhelm	50.00	25.00	15.00
22A	Dom DiMaggio	30.00	15.00	9.00
22N	Murry Dickson	20.00	10.00	6.00
23A	Gil McDougald	30.00	15.00	9.00
23N	Warren Hacker	20.00	10.00	6.00
24A	Al Rosen	30.00	15.00	9.00
24N	Gerry Staley	20.00	10.00	6.00
25A	Mel Parnell	20.00	10.00	6.00
25N	Bobby Thomson	25.00	12.50	7.50
26A	Roberto Avila	20.00	10.00	6.00
26N	Stan Musial	150.00	75.00	45.00

1954 Red Man Tobacco

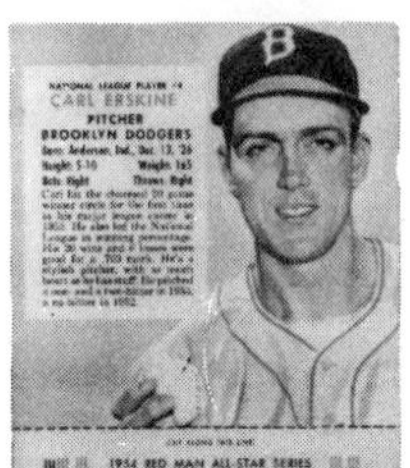

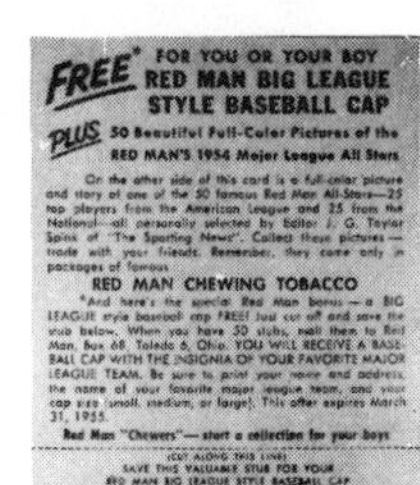

In 1954, the Red Man set eliminated managers from the set, and issued only 25 player cards for each league. There are, however, four variations which bring the total set size to 54 full-color cards. Two cards exist for Gus Bell and Enos Slaughter, while American Leaguers George Kell, Sam Mele and Dave Philley are each shown with two different teams. Complete set prices quoted below do not include the scarcer of the variation pairs. Cards still measure 3-1/2" by 4" with tabs intact. Cards without tabs are worth about 35-40 per cent of the values quoted below. Formats for the cards remain virtually unchanged, with card numbers included within the player information boxes as well as on the tabs.

		NR MT	EX	VG
Complete Set:		1950.	975.00	585.00
Common Player:		20.00	10.00	6.00
1A	Bobby Avila	20.00	10.00	6.00
1N	Richie Ashburn	35.00	17.50	10.50
2A	Jim Busby	20.00	10.00	6.00
2N	Billy Cox	25.00	12.50	7.50
3A	Nelson Fox	35.00	17.50	10.50
3N	Del Crandall	25.00	12.50	7.50
4Aa	George Kell (Boston)	65.00	32.00	19.50
4Ab	George Kell (Chicago)	75.00	37.00	22.00
4N	Carl Erskine	30.00	15.00	9.00
5A	Sherman Lollar	20.00	10.00	6.00
5N	Monte Irvin	50.00	25.00	15.00
6Aa	Sam Mele (Baltimore)	50.00	25.00	15.00
6Ab	Sam Mele (Chicago)	75.00	37.00	22.00
6N	Ted Kluszewski	30.00	15.00	9.00
7A	Orestes Minoso	25.00	12.50	7.50
7N	Don Mueller	20.00	10.00	6.00
8A	Mel Parnell	20.00	10.00	6.00
8N	Andy Pafko	25.00	12.50	7.50
9Aa	Dave Philley (Cleveland)	50.00	25.00	15.00
9Ab	Dave Philley (Philadelphia)	75.00	37.00	22.00
9N	Del Rice	20.00	10.00	6.00
10A	Billy Pierce	25.00	12.50	7.50
10N	Al Schoendienst	30.00	15.00	9.00
11A	Jim Piersall	25.00	12.50	7.50
11N	Warren Spahn	60.00	30.00	18.00
12A	Al Rosen	30.00	15.00	9.00
12N	Curt Simmons	25.00	12.50	7.50
13A	"Mickey" Vernon	25.00	12.50	7.50
13N	Roy Campanella	80.00	40.00	24.00
14A	Sammy White	20.00	10.00	6.00
14N	Jim Gilliam	30.00	15.00	9.00
15A	Gene Woodling	25.00	12.50	7.50
15N	"Pee Wee" Reese	75.00	37.00	22.00
16A	Ed "Whitey" Ford	65.00	32.00	19.50
16N	Edwin "Duke" Snider	100.00	50.00	30.00
17A	Phil Rizzuto	60.00	30.00	18.00
17N	Rip Repulski	20.00	10.00	6.00
18A	Bob Porterfield	20.00	10.00	6.00
18N	Robin Roberts	50.00	25.00	15.00
19A	Al "Chico" Carrasquel	20.00	10.00	6.00
19Na	Enos Slaughter	90.00	45.00	27.00
19Nb	Gus Bell	90.00	45.00	27.00
20A	Larry "Yogi" Berra	80.00	40.00	24.00
20N	Johnny Logan	20.00	10.00	6.00

		NR MT	EX	VG
21A	Bob Lemon	50.00	25.00	15.00
21N	Johnny Antonelli	25.00	12.50	7.50
22A	Ferris Fain	25.00	12.50	7.50
22N	Gil Hodges	55.00	27.00	16.50
23A	Hank Bauer	25.00	12.50	7.50
23N	Eddie Mathews	55.00	27.00	16.50
24A	Jim Delsing	20.00	10.00	6.00
24N	Lew Burdette	30.00	15.00	9.00
25A	Gil McDougald	30.00	15.00	9.00
25N	Willie Mays	150.00	75.00	45.00

1955 Red Man Tobacco

These 50 cards are quite similar to the 1954 edition, with card fronts virtually unchanged except for the data in the biographical box on the color picture area. This set of the 3-1/2" by 4" cards includes 25 players from each league, with no known variations. As with all Red Man sets, those cards complete with the redeemable tabs are more valuable. Values quoted below are for cards with tabs. Cards with the tabs removed are worth about 35-40 percent of those figures.

		NR MT	EX	VG
Complete Set:		1700.	850.00	510.00
Common Player:		20.00	10.00	6.00
1A	Ray Boone	20.00	10.00	6.00
1N	Richie Ashburn	35.00	17.50	10.50
2A	Jim Busby	20.00	10.00	6.00
2N	Del Crandall	25.00	12.50	7.50
3A	Ed "Whitey" Ford	55.00	27.00	16.50
3N	Gil Hodges	65.00	32.00	19.50
4A	Nelson Fox	35.00	17.50	10.50
4N	Brooks Lawrence	20.00	10.00	6.00
5A	Bob Grim	20.00	10.00	6.00
5N	Johnny Logan	20.00	10.00	6.00
6A	Jack Harshman	20.00	10.00	6.00
6N	Sal Maglie	25.00	12.50	7.50
7A	Jim Hegan	20.00	10.00	6.00
7N	Willie Mays	150.00	75.00	45.00
8A	Bob Lemon	50.00	25.00	15.00
8N	Don Mueller	20.00	10.00	6.00
9A	Irv Noren	20.00	10.00	6.00
9N	Bill Sarni	20.00	10.00	6.00
10A	Bob Porterfield	20.00	10.00	6.00
10N	Warren Spahn	60.00	30.00	18.00
11A	Al Rosen	30.00	15.00	9.00
11N	Henry Thompson	20.00	10.00	6.00
12A	"Mickey" Vernon	25.00	12.50	7.50
12N	Hoyt Wilhelm	50.00	25.00	15.00
13A	Vic Wertz	20.00	10.00	6.00
13N	Johnny Antonelli	25.00	12.50	7.50
14A	Early Wynn	50.00	25.00	15.00
14N	Carl Erskine	30.00	15.00	9.00
15A	Bobby Avila	20.00	10.00	6.00
15N	Granny Hamner	20.00	10.00	6.00
16A	Larry "Yogi" Berra	80.00	40.00	24.00
16N	Ted Kluszewski	30.00	15.00	9.00
17A	Joe Coleman	20.00	10.00	6.00
17N	Pee Wee Reese	75.00	37.00	22.00
18A	Larry Doby	30.00	15.00	9.00
18N	Al Schoendienst	30.00	15.00	9.00
19A	Jackie Jensen	25.00	12.50	7.50
19N	Duke Snider	100.00	50.00	30.00
20A	Pete Runnels	20.00	10.00	6.00
20N	Frank Thomas	20.00	10.00	6.00
21A	Jim Piersall	25.00	12.50	7.50
21N	Ray Jablonski	20.00	10.00	6.00
22A	Hank Bauer	25.00	12.50	7.50
22N	James "Dusty" Rhodes	20.00	10.00	6.00
23A	"Chico" Carrasquel	20.00	10.00	6.00
23N	Gus Bell	20.00	10.00	6.00
24A	Orestes Minoso	25.00	12.50	7.50
24N	Curt Simmons	25.00	12.50	7.50
25A	Sandy Consuegra	20.00	10.00	6.00
25N	Marvin Grissom	20.00	10.00	6.00

1886 Red Stocking Cigars

This set of Boston Red Stockings schedule cards was issued in 1886, and the three known cards measure 6-1/2" by 3-3/4". The cards were printed in black and red. One side carries the 1886 Boston schedule, while the other side features a full-length player drawing. Both sides include advertising for "Red Stocking" cigars. Only three different players are known.

		NR MT	EX	VG
Complete Set:		8500.	4250.	2650.
Common Player:		2500.	1250.	750.00
(1)	C.G. Buffington	2500.	1250.	750.00
(2)	Capt. John F. Morrill	2500.	1250.	750.00
(3)	Charles Radbourn	3500.	1750.	1050.

1977 Redpath Sugar Expos

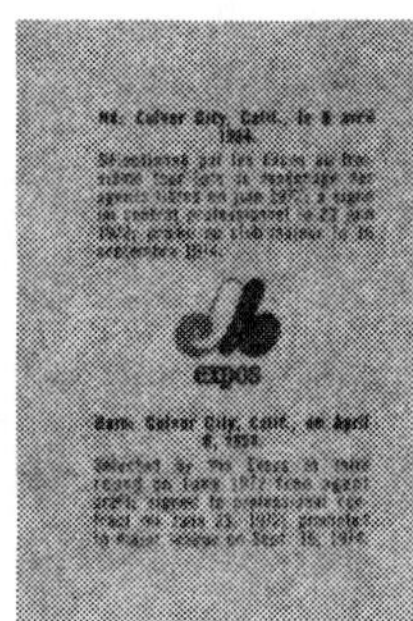

One of the more obscure regional Canadian issues, this 30-player set features members of the Expos and was printed on sugar packets distributed in the Montreal area in 1977. The front of the packet features a color photo of the player with his name, uniform number, position, height and weight listed in both English and French. A line identifying Redpath Sugar appears alongside the photo. The backs display the Expos logo and brief player highlights (again printed in both French and English). The set has been seen in uncut sheets, revealing that the packets of Steve Rogers and David Cash, Jr. were double printed.

		NR MT	EX	VG
Complete Set:		40.00	20.00	12.00
Common Player:		1.00	.50	.30
1	Osvaldo Jose Virgil	1.00	.50	.30
2	James Thomas Brewer	1.00	.50	.30
3	James Barton Vernon	1.00	.50	.30
4	Chris Edward Speier	1.00	.50	.30
5	Peter Mackanin Jr.	1.00	.50	.30
6	William Frederick Gardner	1.00	.50	.30
8	Gary Edmund Carter	5.00	2.50	1.50
9	Barry Clifton Foote	1.00	.50	.30
10	Andre Dawson	7.00	3.50	2.00
11	Ronald Wayne Garrett	1.00	.50	.30
14	Samuel Elias Mejias	1.00	.50	.30
15	Larry Alton Parrish	2.00	1.00	.60
16	Michael Jorgensen	1.00	.50	.30
17	Ellis Clarence Valentine	1.00	.50	.30
18	Joseph Thomas Kerrigan	1.00	.50	.30
20	William Henry McEnaney	1.00	.50	.30
23	Richard Hirshfield Williams	1.25	.60	.40
24	Atanasio Rigal Perez	3.00	1.50	.90
25	Delbert Bernard Unser	1.00	.50	.30
26	Donald Joseph Stanhouse	1.00	.50	.30
30	David Cash, Jr.	1.00	.50	.30
31	Jackie Gene Brown	1.00	.50	.30
34	Jose Manual Morales	1.00	.50	.30
35	Gerald Ellis Hannahs	1.00	.50	.30
38	Jesus Maria Frias (Andujar)	1.00	.50	.30
39	Daniel Dean Warthen	1.00	.50	.30
42	William Cecil Glenn Atkinson	1.00	.50	.30
45	Stephen Douglas Rogers	1.50	.70	.45
48	Jeffrey Michael Terpko	1.00	.50	.30
49	Warren Livingston Cromartie	1.00	.50	.30

A player's name in *italic* type indicates a rookie card. An (FC) indicates a player's first card for that particular card company.

1946 Remar Bread Oakland Oaks

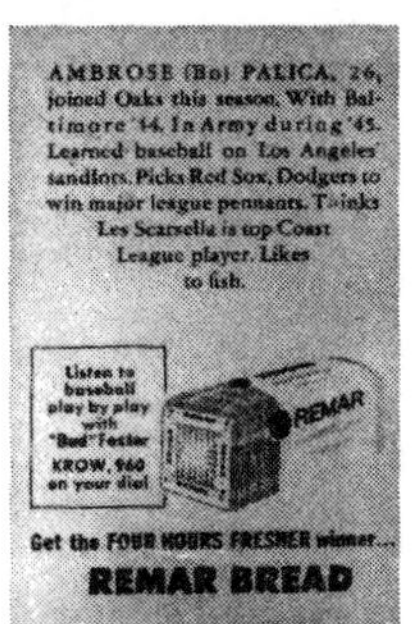

Remar Baking Company issued several baseball card sets in the northern California area from 1946-1950, all picturing members of the Oakland Oaks of the Pacific Coast League. The 1946 set consists of 23 cards (five unnumbered, 18 numbered). Measuring 2" by 3", the cards were printed on heavy paper and feature black and white photos with the player's name, team and position at the bottom. The backs contain a brief write-up plus an ad for Remar Bread printed in red. The cards were distributed one per week. The first five cards were unnumbered. The rest of the set is numbered on the front, but begins with number "5", rather than "6".

		NR MT	EX	VG
Complete Set:		400.00	200.00	120.00
Common Player:		12.00	6.00	3.50
5	Hershell Martin (Herschel)	12.00	6.00	3.50
6	Bill Hart	12.00	6.00	3.50
7	Charlie Gassaway	12.00	6.00	3.50
8	Wally Westlake	12.00	6.00	3.50
9	Mickey Burnett	12.00	6.00	3.50
10	Charles (Casey) Stengel	90.00	45.00	27.00
11	Charlie Metro	12.00	6.00	3.50
12	Tom Hafey	12.00	6.00	3.50
13	Tony Sabol	12.00	6.00	3.50
14	Ed Kearse	12.00	6.00	3.50
15	Bud Foster (announcer)	12.00	6.00	3.50
16	Johnny Price	12.00	6.00	3.50
17	Gene Bearden	12.00	6.00	3.50
18	Floyd Speer	12.00	6.00	3.50
19	Bryan Stephens	12.00	6.00	3.50
20	Rinaldo (Rugger) Ardizoia	12.00	6.00	3.50
21	Ralph Buxton	12.00	6.00	3.50
22	Ambrose (Bo) Palica	12.00	6.00	3.50
---	Brooks Holder	15.00	7.50	4.50
---	Henry (Cotton) Pippen	15.00	7.50	4.50
---	Billy Raimondi	70.00	35.00	21.00
---	Les Scarsella	15.00	7.50	4.50
---	Glen (Gabby) Stewart	15.00	7.50	4.50

1947 Remar Bread Oakland Oaks

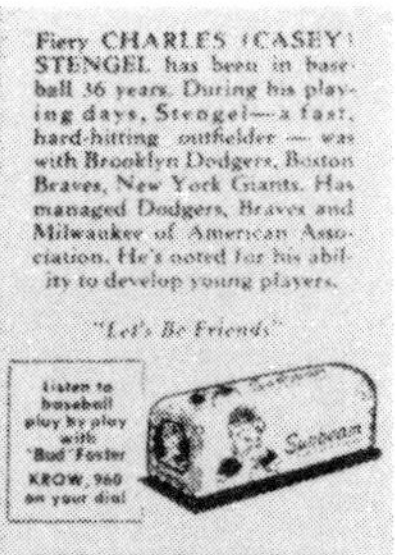

Remar's second set consisted of 25 numbered cards, again measuring 2" by 3". The cards are nearly identical to the previous year's set, except the loaf of bread on the back is printed in blue, rather than red.

		NR MT	EX	VG
Complete Set:		300.00	150.00	90.00
Common Player:		10.00	5.00	3.00
1	Billy Raimondi	10.00	5.00	3.00
2	Les Scarsella	10.00	5.00	3.00
3	Brooks Holder	10.00	5.00	3.00
4	Charlie Gassaway	10.00	5.00	3.00
5	Mickey Burnett	10.00	5.00	3.00
6	Ralph Buxton	10.00	5.00	3.00

		NR MT	EX	VG
7	Ed Kearse	10.00	5.00	3.00
8	Charles (Casey) Stengel	75.00	38.00	23.00
9	Bud Foster (announcer)	10.00	5.00	3.00
10	Ambrose (Bo) Palica	10.00	5.00	3.00
11	Tom Hafey	10.00	5.00	3.00
12	Hershel Martin (Herschel)	10.00	5.00	3.00
13	Henry (Cotton) Pippen	10.00	5.00	3.00
14	Floyd Speer	10.00	5.00	3.00
15	Tony Sabol	10.00	5.00	3.00
16	Will Hafey	10.00	5.00	3.00
17	Ray Hamrick	10.00	5.00	3.00
18	Maurice Van Robays	10.00	5.00	3.00
19	Dario Lodigiani	10.00	5.00	3.00
20	Mel (Dizz) Duezabou	10.00	5.00	3.00
21	Damon Hayes	10.00	5.00	3.00
22	Gene Lillard	10.00	5.00	3.00
23	Aldon Wilkie	10.00	5.00	3.00
24	Dewey Soriano	10.00	5.00	3.00
25	Glen Crawford	10.00	5.00	3.00

1949 Remar Bread Oakland Oaks

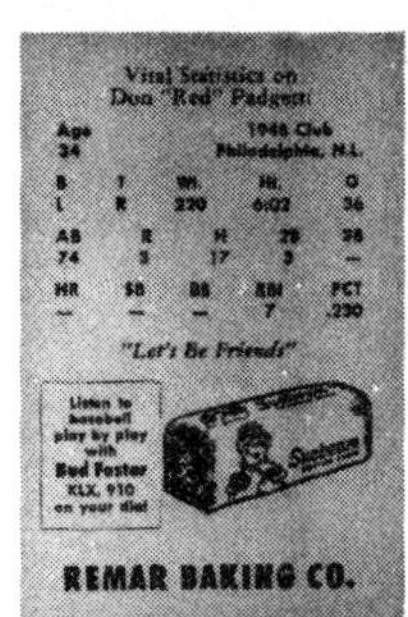

The 1949 Remar Bread issue was increased to 32 cards, again measuring 2" by 3". Unlike the two earlier sets, photos in the 1949 Remar set are surrounded by a thin, white border and are unnumbered. The player's name, team and position appear below the black and white photo. The backs are printed in blue and include the player's 1948 statistics and the distinctive loaf of bread.

		NR MT	EX	VG
	Complete Set:	325.00	162.00	97.00
	Common Player:	6.00	3.00	1.75
(1)	Ralph Buxton	6.00	3.00	1.75
(2)	Milo Candini	15.00	7.50	4.50
(3)	Rex Cecil	15.00	7.50	4.50
(4)	Loyd Christopher (Lloyd)	6.00	3.00	1.75
(5)	Charles Dressen	12.00	6.00	3.50
(6)	Mel Duezabou	6.00	3.00	1.75
(7)	Bud Foster (sportscaster)	6.00	3.00	1.75
(8)	Charlie Gassaway	6.00	3.00	1.75
(9)	Ray Hamrick	6.00	3.00	1.75
(10)	Jack Jensen	15.00	7.50	4.50
(11)	Earl Jones	6.00	3.00	1.75
(12)	George Kelly	18.00	9.00	5.50
(13)	Frank Kerr	15.00	7.50	4.50
(14)	Richard Kryhoski	6.00	3.00	1.75
(15)	Harry Lavagetto	12.00	6.00	3.50
(16)	Dario Lodigiani	6.00	3.00	1.75
(17)	Billy Martin	60.00	30.00	18.00
(18)	George Metkovich	6.00	3.00	1.75
(19)	Frank Nelson	6.00	3.00	1.75
(20)	Don Padgett	6.00	3.00	1.75
(21)	Alonzo Perry	15.00	7.50	4.50
(22)	Bill Raimondi	6.00	3.00	1.75
(23)	Earl Rapp	6.00	3.00	1.75
(24)	Eddie Samcoff	6.00	3.00	1.75
(25)	Les Scarsella	6.00	3.00	1.75
(26)	Forest Thompson (Forrest)	15.00	7.50	4.50
(27)	Earl Toolson	6.00	3.00	1.75
(28)	Lou Tost	15.00	7.50	4.50
(29)	Maurice Van Robays	6.00	3.00	1.75
(30)	Jim Wallace	6.00	3.00	1.75
(31)	Arthur Lee Wilson	6.00	3.00	1.75
(32)	Parnell Woods	15.00	7.50	4.50

1950 Remar Bread Oakland Oaks

The most common of the Remar Bread issues, the 1950 set contains 27 unnumbered cards, again measuring 2" by 3" and featuring members of the Oakland Oaks. The cards are nearly identical to the previous year's set but can be differentiated by the 1949 statistics on the back.

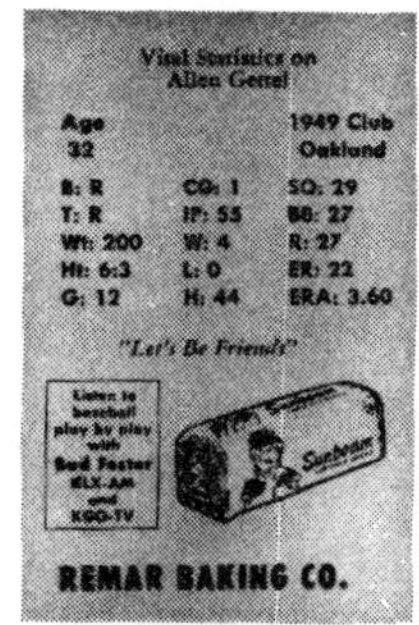

		NR MT	EX	VG
	Complete Set:	190.00	95.00	57.00
	Common Player:	6.00	3.00	1.75
(1)	George Bamberger	12.00	6.00	3.50
(2)	Hank Behrman	6.00	3.00	1.75
(3)	Loyd Christopher (Lloyd)	6.00	3.00	1.75
(4)	Chuck Dressen	12.00	6.00	3.50
(5)	Mel Duezabou	6.00	3.00	1.75
(6)	Augie Galan	6.00	3.00	1.75
(7)	Charlie Gassaway	6.00	3.00	1.75
(8)	Allen Gettel	6.00	3.00	1.75
(9)	Ernie W. Groth	6.00	3.00	1.75
(10)	Ray Hamrick	6.00	3.00	1.75
(11)	Earl Harrist	6.00	3.00	1.75
(12)	Billy Herman	18.00	9.00	5.50
(13)	Bob Hofman	6.00	3.00	1.75
(14)	George Kelly	18.00	9.00	5.50
(15)	Harry Lavagetto	12.00	6.00	3.50
(16)	Eddie Malone	6.00	3.00	1.75
(17)	George Metkovich	6.00	3.00	1.75
(18)	Frank Nelson	6.00	3.00	1.75
(19)	Rafael (Ray) Noble	6.00	3.00	1.75
(20)	Don Padgett	6.00	3.00	1.75
(21)	Earl Rapp	6.00	3.00	1.75
(22)	Clyde Shoun	6.00	3.00	1.75
(23)	Forrest Thompson	6.00	3.00	1.75
(24)	Louis Tost	6.00	3.00	1.75
(25)	Dick Wakefield	12.00	6.00	3.50
(26)	Artie Wilson	6.00	3.00	1.75
(27)	Roy Zimmerman	6.00	3.00	1.75

1988 Revco

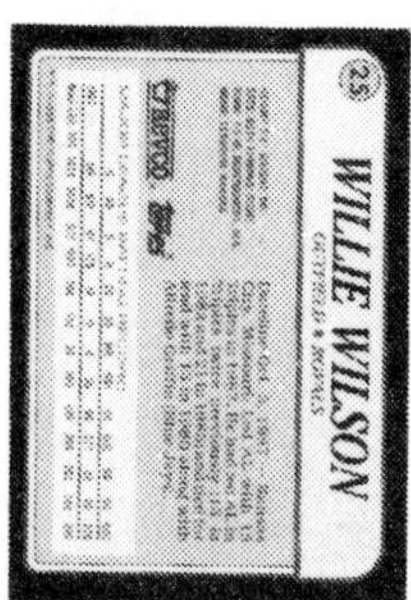

This super-glossy boxed set of 33 standard-size cards was produced by Topps for exclusive distribution by Revco stores east of the Mississippi River. Card fronts feature a large blue Revco logo in the upper left corner opposite a yellow and black boxed "Topps League Leader" label. Player photos are framed in black and orange with a diagonal player name banner in the lower right corner that lists the player's name, team and position on white, orange and gold stripes. The numbered card backs are horizontal, printed in red and black on white stock and include the player name, followed by personal biographical data, batting/pitching stats and a brief career summary.

		MT	NR MT	EX
	Complete Set:	5.00	3.75	2.00
	Common Player:	.05	.04	.02
1	Tony Gwynn	.25	.20	.10
2	Andre Dawson	.15	.11	.06
3	Vince Coleman	.15	.11	.06
4	Jack Clark	.15	.11	.06
5	Tim Raines	.25	.20	.10
6	Tim Wallach	.10	.08	.04
7	Juan Samuel	.10	.08	.04
8	Nolan Ryan	.15	.11	.06
9	Rick Sutcliffe	.10	.08	.04
10	Kent Tekulve	.05	.04	.02
11	Steve Bedrosian	.10	.08	.04
12	Orel Hershiser	.10	.08	.04
13	Rick Rueschel	.07	.05	.03
14	Fernando Valenzuela	.20	.15	.08
15	Bob Welch	.07	.05	.03
16	Wade Boggs	1.00	.70	.40
17	Mark McGwire	1.00	.70	.40
18	George Bell	.20	.15	.08
19	Harold Reynolds	.05	.04	.02
20	Paul Molitor	.12	.09	.05
21	Kirby Puckett	.25	.20	.10
22	Kevin Seitzer	.60	.45	.25
23	Brian Downing	.05	.04	.02
24	Dwight Evans	.10	.08	.04
25	Willie Wilson	.07	.05	.03
26	Danny Tartabull	.12	.09	.05
27	Jimmy Key	.07	.05	.03
28	Roger Clemens	.40	.30	.15
29	Dave Stewart	.10	.08	.04
30	Mark Eichhorn	.05	.04	.02
31	Tom Henke	.05	.04	.02
32	Charlie Hough	.05	.04	.02
33	Mark Langston	.10	.08	.04

1988 Rite Aid

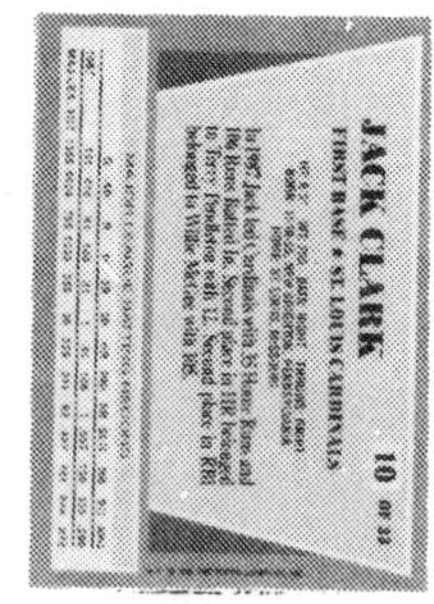

This premiere edition was produced by Topps for distribution by Rite Aid drug and discount stores in the Eastern United States. The boxed set includes 33 standard-size full-color cards with at least one card for each major league team. Four cards in the set highlight MVP's from the 1987 season. Card fronts have white borders and carry a yellow "Team MVP's" header above the player photo which is outlined in red and blue. A large Rite Aid logo appears upper left; the players name appears bottom center. The numbered card backs are black on blue and white card stock in a horizontal layout containing the player name, biography and statistics.

		MT	NR MT	EX
	Complete Set:	5.00	3.75	2.00
	Common Player:	.05	.04	.02
1	Dale Murphy	.30	.25	.12
2	Andre Dawson	.15	.11	.06
3	Eric Davis	.50	.40	.20
4	Mike Scott	.10	.08	.04
5	Pedro Guerrero	.15	.11	.06
6	Tim Raines	.25	.20	.10
7	Darryl Strawberry	.40	.30	.15
8	Mike Schmidt	.30	.25	.12
9	Mike Dunne	.10	.08	.04
10	Jack Clark	.15	.11	.06
11	Tony Gwynn	.25	.20	.10
12	Will Clark	.30	.25	.12
13	Cal Ripken	.30	.25	.12
14	Wade Boggs	1.00	.70	.40
15	Wally Joyner	.30	.25	.12
16	Harold Baines	.12	.09	.05
17	Joe Carter	.12	.09	.05
18	Alan Trammell	.15	.11	.06
19	Kevin Seitzer	.60	.45	.25
20	Paul Molitor	.12	.09	.05
21	Kirby Puckett	.25	.20	.10
22	Don Mattingly	1.75	1.25	.70
23	Mark McGwire	1.00	.70	.40
24	Alvin Davis	.10	.08	.04
25	Ruben Sierra	.12	.09	.05
26	George Bell	.20	.15	.08
27	Jack Morris	.12	.09	.05
28	Jeff Reardon	.07	.05	.03
29	John Tudor	.07	.05	.03
30	Rick Rueschel	.07	.05	.03
31	Gary Gaetti	.12	.09	.05
32	Jeffrey Leonard	.05	.04	.02
33	Frank Viola	.12	.09	.05

1955 Rodeo Meats Athletics

This set of 2-1/2" by 3-1/2" color cards was issued by a local meat company to commemorate the first year of the Athletics in Kansas City. There are 38 different players included in the set, with nine players known to apppear in two different variations for a total of 47 cards in the set. Most variations are in background colors, although Bobby Shantz is also listed incorrectly as "Schantz" on one variation. The cards are unnumbered, with the Rodeo logo and player name on the fronts, and an ad for a scrapbook album listed on the backs.

		NR MT	EX	VG
Complete Set:		4000.	2000.	1200.
Common Player:		70.00	35.00	21.00
(1)	Joe Astroth	70.00	35.00	21.00
(2)	Harold Bevan	100.00	50.00	30.00
(3)	Charles Bishop	100.00	50.00	30.00
(4)	Don Bollweg	100.00	50.00	30.00
(5)	Lou Boudreau	200.00	100.00	60.00
(6)	Cloyd Boyer (blue background)	100.00	50.00	30.00
(7)	Cloyd Boyer (pink background)	70.00	35.00	21.00
(8)	Ed Burtschy	100.00	50.00	30.00
(9)	Art Ceccarelli	70.00	35.00	21.00
(10)	Joe DeMaestri (pea green background)	100.00	50.00	30.00
(11)	Joe DeMaestri (light green background)	70.00	35.00	21.00
(12)	Art Ditmar	70.00	35.00	21.00
(13)	John Dixon	100.00	50.00	30.00
(14)	Jim Finigan	70.00	35.00	21.00
(15)	Marion Fricano	100.00	50.00	30.00
(16)	John Gray	100.00	50.00	30.00
(17)	Tom Gorman	70.00	35.00	21.00
(18)	Ray Herbert	70.00	35.00	21.00
(19)	Forest "Spook" Jacobs (Forrest)	100.00	50.00	30.00
(20)	Alex Kellner	100.00	50.00	30.00
(21)	Harry Kraft (Craft)	70.00	35.00	21.00
(22)	Jack Littrell	70.00	35.00	21.00
(23)	Hector Lopez	80.00	40.00	24.00
(24)	Oscar Melillo	70.00	35.00	21.00
(25)	Arnold Portocarrero (purple background)	100.00	50.00	30.00
(26)	Arnold Portocarrero (grey background)	70.00	35.00	21.00
(27)	Vic Power (pink background)	125.00	62.00	37.00
(28)	Vic Power (yellow background)	80.00	40.00	24.00
(29)	Vic Raschi	100.00	50.00	30.00
(30)	Bill Renna (dark pink background)	100.00	50.00	30.00
(31)	Bill Renna (light pink background)	70.00	35.00	21.00
(32)	Al Robertson	100.00	50.00	30.00
(33)	Johnny Sain	125.00	62.00	37.00
(34a)	Bobby Schantz (incorrect spelling)	200.00	100.00	60.00
(34b)	Bobby Shantz (correct spelling)	125.00	62.00	37.00
(35)	Wilmer Shantz (orange background)	100.00	50.00	30.00
(36)	Wilmer Shantz (purple background)	70.00	35.00	21.00
(37)	Harry Simpson	70.00	35.00	21.00
(38)	Enos Slaughter	300.00	150.00	90.00
(39)	Lou Sleater	70.00	35.00	21.00
(40)	George Susce	70.00	35.00	21.00
(41)	Bob Trice	100.00	50.00	30.00
(42)	Elmer Valo (yellow background)	100.00	50.00	30.00
(43)	Elmer Valo (green background)	70.00	35.00	21.00
(44)	Bill Wilson (yellow background)	100.00	50.00	30.00
(45)	Bill Wilson (purple background)	70.00	35.00	21.00
(46)	Gus Zernial	80.00	40.00	24.00

1956 Rodeo Meats Athletics

Rodeo Meats issued another Kansas City Athletics set in 1956, but this one was a much smaller 13-card set. The 2-1/2" by 3-1/2" cards are again unnumbered, with the player name and Rodeo logo on the fronts. Card backs feature some of the same graphics and copy as the 1955 cards, but the album offer is omitted. The full-color cards were only available in packages of Rodeo hot dogs.

		NR MT	EX	VG
Complete Set:		1000.	500.00	300.00
Common Player:		70.00	35.00	21.00
(1)	Joe Astroth	70.00	35.00	21.00
(2)	Lou Boudreau	200.00	100.00	60.00
(3)	Joe DeMaestri	70.00	35.00	21.00
(4)	Art Ditmar	70.00	35.00	21.00
(5)	Jim Finigan	70.00	35.00	21.00
(6)	Hector Lopez	80.00	40.00	24.00
(7)	Vic Power	80.00	40.00	24.00
(8)	Bobby Shantz	125.00	62.00	37.00
(9)	Harry Simpson	70.00	35.00	21.00
(10)	Enos Slaughter	200.00	100.00	60.00
(11)	Elmer Valo	70.00	35.00	21.00
(12)	Gus Zernial	80.00	40.00	24.00

1970 Rold Gold Pretzels

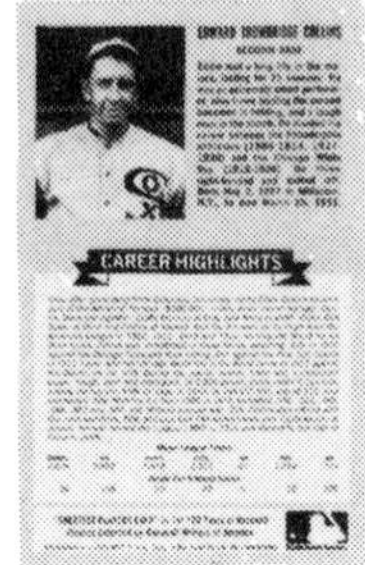

The 1970 Rold Gold Pretzels set of 15 cards honors the "Greatest Players Ever" in the first 100 years of baseball as chosen by the Baseball Writers of America. The cards, which measure 2-1/4" by 3-1/2" in size, feature a simulated 3-D effect. The set was re-released in 1972 by Kellogg's in packages of Danish-Go-Rounds. Rold Gold cards can be differen- tiated from the Kellogg's cards of 1972 by the 1970 copyright date found on the card reverse.

		NR MT	EX	VG
Complete Set:		40.00	20.00	12.00
Common Player:		1.00	.50	.30
1	Walter Johnson	2.50	1.25	.70
2	Rogers Hornsby	1.50	.70	.45
3	John McGraw	1.00	.50	.30
4	Mickey Cochrane	1.00	.50	.30
5	George Sisler	1.00	.50	.30
6	Babe Ruth	10.00	5.00	3.00
7	Robert "Lefty" Grove	1.50	.70	.45
8	Harold "Pie" Traynor	1.00	.50	.30
9	Honus Wagner	1.75	.90	.50
10	Eddie Collins	1.00	.50	.30
11	Tris Speaker	1.50	.70	.45
12	Cy Young	1.00	.50	.30
13	Lou Gehrig	6.00	3.00	1.75
14	Babe Ruth	10.00	5.00	3.00
15	Ty Cobb	6.00	3.00	1.75

1950 Royal Desserts

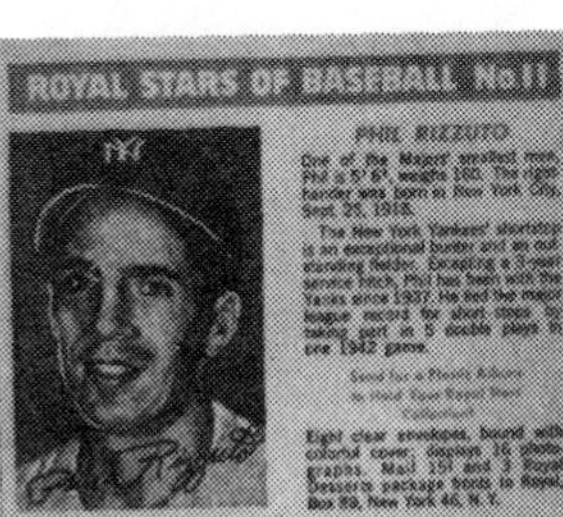

This set of 24 cards was issued one per box on the backs of various Royal Dessert products over a period of three years. The basic set contains 24 players, however a number of variations create the much higher total for the set. In 1950, Royal issued cards with two different tints - black and white with red, or blue and white with red. Over the next two years, various sentences of the cards' biographies were updated up to three times in some cases. Some players from the set left the majors after 1950 and others were apparently never updated, but the 23 biography updates that do exist, added to the original 24 cards issued in 1950, give the set a total of 47 cards. The 2-1/2" by 3-1/2" cards are blank-backed with personal and playing biographies alongside the card front photos.

		NR MT	EX	VG
Complete Set:		900.00	450.00	270.00
Common Player:		20.00	10.00	6.00
1a	Stan Musial (2nd paragraph begins "Musial's 207...")	125.00	62.00	37.00
1b	Stan Musial (2nd paragraph begins "Musial batted...")	125.00	62.00	37.00
2a	Pee Wee Reese (2nd paragraph begins "Pee Wee's...")	70.00	35.00	21.00
2b	Pee Wee Reese (2nd paragraph begins "Captain...")	70.00	35.00	21.00
3a	George Kell (2nd paragraph ends "...in 1945, '46.")	35.00	17.50	10.50
3b	George Kell (2nd paragraph ends "...two base hits, 56.")	35.00	17.50	10.50
4a	Dom DiMaggio (2nd paragraph ends "...during 1947.")	30.00	15.00	9.00
4b	Dom DiMaggio (2nd paragraph ends "...with 11.")	30.00	15.00	9.00
5a	Warren Spahn (2nd paragraph ends "...shutouts 7.")	50.00	25.00	15.00
5b	Warren Spahn (2nd paragraph ends "...with 191.")	50.00	25.00	15.00
6a	Andy Pafko (2nd paragraph ends "...7 games.")	25.00	12.50	7.50
6b	Andy Pafko (2nd paragraph ends "...National League.")	25.00	12.50	7.50
6c	Andy Pafko (2nd paragraph ends "...weighs 190.")	25.00	12.50	7.50
7a	Andy Seminick (2nd paragraph ends "...as outfield.")	20.00	10.00	6.00
7b	Andy Seminick (2nd paragraph ends "...since 1916.")	20.00	10.00	6.00
7c	Andy Seminick (2nd paragraph ends "...in the outfield.")	20.00	10.00	6.00
7d	Andy Seminick (2nd paragraph ends "...right handed.")	20.00	10.00	6.00
8a	Lou Brissie (2nd paragraph ends "...when pitching.")	20.00	10.00	6.00
8b	Lou Brissie (2nd paragraph ends "...weighs 215.")	20.00	10.00	6.00
9a	Ewell Blackwell (2nd paragraph begins "Despite recent illness...")	25.00	12.50	7.50
9b	Ewell Blackwell (2nd paragraph begins "Blackwell's...")	25.00	12.50	7.50
10a	Bobby Thomson (2nd paragraph begins "In 1949...")	25.00	12.50	7.50
10b	Bobby Thomson (2nd paragraph begins "Thomson is...")	25.00	12.50	7.50
11a	Phil Rizzuto (2nd paragraph ends "...one 1942 game.")	60.00	30.00	18.00
11b	Phil Rizzuto (2nd paragraph ends "...Most Valuable Player.")	60.00	30.00	18.00
12	Tommy Henrich	30.00	15.00	9.00
13	Joe Gordon	25.00	12.50	7.50
14a	Ray Scarborough (Senators)	20.00	10.00	6.00
14b	Ray Scarborough (White Sox, 2nd paragraph ends "...military service.")	20.00	10.00	6.00
14c	Ray Scarborough (White Sox, 2nd paragraph ends "...the season.")	20.00	10.00	6.00
14d	Ray Scarborough (Red Sox)	20.00	10.00	6.00
15a	Stan Rojek (Pirates)	20.00	10.00	6.00
15b	Stan Rojek (Browns)	20.00	10.00	6.00
16	Luke Appling	30.00	15.00	9.00
17	Willard Marshall	20.00	10.00	6.00
18	Alvin Dark	30.00	15.00	9.00
19a	Dick Sisler (2nd paragraph ends "...service record.")	20.00	10.00	6.00
19b	Dick Sisler (2nd paragraph ends "...National League flag.")	20.00	10.00	6.00
19c	Dick Sisler (2nd paragraph ends "...Nov. 2, 1920.")	20.00	10.00	6.00
19d	Dick Sisler (2nd paragraph ends "...from '46 to '48.")	20.00	10.00	6.00
20	Johnny Ostrowski	20.00	10.00	6.00
21a	Virgil Trucks (2nd paragraph ends "...in military service.")	25.00	12.50	7.50
21b	Virgil Trucks (2nd paragraph ends "...that year.")	25.00	12.50	7.50
21c	Virgil Trucks (2nd paragraph ends "...for military service.")	25.00	12.50	7.50
22	Eddie Robinson	20.00	10.00	6.00
23	Nanny Fernandez	20.00	10.00	6.00
24	Ferris Fain	25.00	12.50	7.50

1952 Royal Desserts

This set, issued as a premium by Royal Desserts in 1952, consists of 16 unnumbered black and white cards, each measuring 5" by 7". The cards include the inscription "To A Royal Fan" along with the player's facsimile autograph.

		NR MT	EX	VG
Complete Set:		400.00	200.00	120.00
Common Player:		15.00	7.50	4.50
(1)	Ewell Blackwell	18.00	9.00	5.50
(2)	Leland V. Brissie Jr.	15.00	7.50	4.50
(3)	Alvin Dark	18.00	9.00	5.50
(4)	Dom DiMaggio	25.00	12.50	7.50

		NR MT	EX	VG
(5)	Ferris Fain	15.00	7.50	4.50
(6)	George Kell	28.00	14.00	8.50
(7)	Stan Musial	75.00	37.00	22.00
(8)	Andy Pafko	18.00	9.00	5.50
(9)	Pee Wee Reese	35.00	17.50	10.50
(10)	Phil Rizzuto	35.00	17.50	10.50
(11)	Eddie Robinson	15.00	7.50	4.50
(12)	Ray Scarborough	15.00	7.50	4.50
(13)	Andy Seminick	15.00	7.50	4.50
(14)	Dick Sisler	15.00	7.50	4.50
(15)	Warren Spahn	35.00	17.50	10.50
(16)	Bobby Thomson	25.00	12.50	7.50

NOTE: A card number in parentheses ( ) indicates the set is unnumbered.

1989 Ryan Commemorative Trading Card

This special card was issued with a watch commemorating Nolan Ryan's historical achievement of 5000 strikeouts. The card was produced and distributed by All-Star Time, Inc. The front of the card features Ryan holding a 5000K ball and wearing a sponsor's cap. This is the only known card of Ryan where he is wearing a cap other than one from MLB. Along with the watch and trading card each collector received a handsome display box and a certificate of authenticity.

	MT	NR MT	EX
Nolan Ryan (Trading Card)	200.00	150.00	80.00

1909 S74 Silks - White

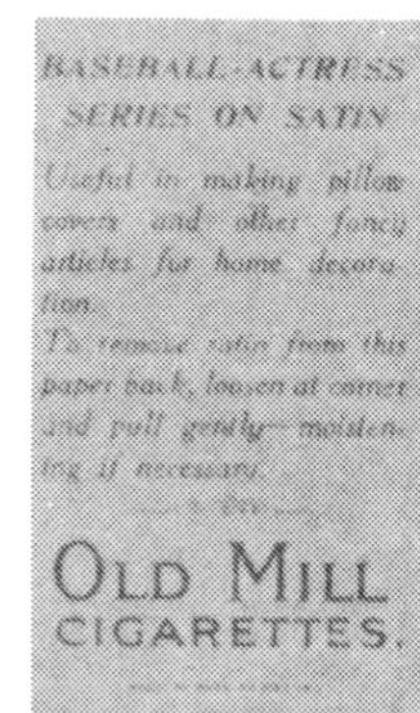

Designated as S74 in Jefferson Burdick's American Card Catalog, these small, delicate fabric collectibles are growing in popularity among advanced collectors. Another tobacco issue from the 1910-1911 period, the silks were issued as premiums with three different brands of cigarettes: Turkey Red, Old Mill and Helmar. The satin-like silks can be found in two different styles, either "white" or "colored." The white silks measure 1 7/8" by 3" and were originally issued with a brown paper backing that carried an advertisement for one of the three cigarette brands mentioned above. The backing also advised that the silks were "useful in making pillow covers and other fancy articles for home decoration." Many undoubtedly were used for such purposes, making silks with the paper backing still intact more difficult to find. White silks must, however, have the backing intact to command top value. Although similar, the S74 "colored" silks, as their name indicates were issued in a variety of colors. They are also slightly larger, measuring 1-7/8" by 3-1/2", and were issued without a paper backing. The colored silks, therefore, contained the cigarette brand name on the lower front of the fabric, either "Old Mill Cigarettes" or "Turkey Red Cigarettes." (No colored silks advertising the Helmar brand are known to exist.) There are 121 different players reported; six have been found in two poses, resulting in 127 different subjects. Ninety-two subjects are known in the "white" silk, while 120 have been found in the "colored." The silks feature the same players pictured in the popular T205 Gold Border tobacco card set.

		NR MT	EX	VG
Complete Set:		35000.	13500.	6000.
Common Player:		175.00	87.00	52.00
(1)	Home Run Baker	450.00	225.00	135.00
(2)	Cy Barger	175.00	87.00	52.00
(3)	Jack Barry	175.00	87.00	52.00
(4)	Johnny Bates	175.00	87.00	52.00
(5)	Fred Beck	175.00	87.00	52.00
(6)	Beals Becker	175.00	87.00	52.00
(7)	George Bell	175.00	87.00	52.00
(8)	Chief Bender	450.00	225.00	135.00
(9)	Roger Bresnahan	450.00	225.00	135.00
(10)	Al Bridwell	175.00	87.00	52.00
(11)	Mordecai Brown	450.00	225.00	135.00
(12)	Bobby Byrne	175.00	87.00	52.00
(13)	Howie Camnitz	175.00	87.00	52.00
(14)	Bill Carrigan	175.00	87.00	52.00
(15)	Frank Chance	500.00	250.00	150.00
(16)	Hal Chase	250.00	125.00	50.00
(17)	Fred Clarke	450.00	225.00	135.00
(18)	Ty Cobb	3000.	1500.	600.00
(19)	Eddie Collins	450.00	225.00	135.00
(20)	Doc Crandall	175.00	87.00	52.00
(21)	Lou Criger	175.00	87.00	52.00
(22)	Jim Delahanty	175.00	87.00	52.00
(23)	Art Devlin	175.00	87.00	52.00
(24)	Red Dooin	175.00	87.00	52.00
(25)	Mickey Doolan	175.00	87.00	52.00
(26)	Larry Doyle	175.00	87.00	52.00
(27)	Jimmy Dygert	175.00	87.00	52.00
(28)	Kid Elberfield (Elberfeld)	175.00	87.00	52.00
(29)	Steve Evans	175.00	87.00	52.00
(30)	Johnny Evers	450.00	225.00	135.00
(31)	Bob Ewing	175.00	87.00	52.00
(32)	Art Fletcher	175.00	87.00	52.00
(33)	John Flynn	175.00	87.00	52.00
(34)	Bill Foxen	175.00	87.00	52.00
(35)	George Gibson	175.00	87.00	52.00
(36)	Peaches Graham (Cubs)	175.00	87.00	52.00
(37)	Peaches Graham (Rustlers)	175.00	87.00	52.00
(38)	Clark Griffith	450.00	225.00	135.00
(39)	Topsy Hartsel	175.00	87.00	52.00
(40)	Arnold Hauser	175.00	87.00	52.00
(41)	Charlie Hemphill	175.00	87.00	52.00
(42)	Tom Jones	175.00	87.00	52.00
(43)	Jack Knight	175.00	87.00	52.00
(44)	Ed Konetchy	175.00	87.00	52.00
(45)	Harry Krause	175.00	87.00	52.00
(46)	Tommy Leach	175.00	87.00	52.00
(47)	Rube Marquard	450.00	225.00	135.00
(48)	Christy Mathewson	900.00	400.00	190.00
(49)	Al Mattern	175.00	87.00	52.00
(50)	Amby McConnell	175.00	87.00	52.00
(51)	John McGraw	500.00	250.00	150.00
(52)	Harry McIntire (McIntyre)	175.00	87.00	52.00
(53)	Fred Merkle	200.00	100.00	60.00
(54)	Chief Meyers	175.00	87.00	52.00
(55)	Dots Miller	175.00	87.00	52.00
(56)	Danny Murphy	175.00	87.00	52.00
(57)	Red Murray	175.00	87.00	52.00
(58)	Tom Needham	175.00	87.00	52.00
(59)	Rebel Oakes	175.00	87.00	52.00
(60)	Rube Oldring	175.00	87.00	52.00
(61)	Orval Overall	175.00	87.00	52.00
(62)	Fred Parent	175.00	87.00	52.00
(63)	Fred Payne	175.00	87.00	52.00
(64)	Barney Pelty	175.00	87.00	52.00
(65)	Deacon Phillippe	175.00	87.00	52.00
(66)	Jack Quinn	175.00	87.00	52.00
(67)	Bugs Raymond	175.00	87.00	52.00
(68)	Ed Reulbach	175.00	87.00	52.00
(69)	Doc Scanlon (Scanlan)	175.00	87.00	52.00
(70)	Germany Schaefer	175.00	87.00	52.00
(71)	Admiral Schlei	175.00	87.00	52.00
(72)	Wildfire Schulte	175.00	87.00	52.00
(73)	Dave Shean	175.00	87.00	52.00
(74)	Jimmy Sheckard	175.00	87.00	52.00
(75)	Hap Smith (Superbas)	175.00	87.00	52.00
(76)	Harry Smith (Rustlers)	700.00	350.00	190.00
(77)	Fred Snodgrass	175.00	87.00	52.00
(78)	Tris Speaker	600.00	300.00	100.00
(79)	Harry Steinfeldt (Cubs)	200.00	100.00	60.00
(80)	Harry Steinfeldt (Rustlers)	200.00	100.00	60.00
(81)	George Stone	175.00	87.00	52.00
(82)	Gabby Street	175.00	87.00	52.00
(83)	Ed Summers	175.00	87.00	52.00
(84)	Lee Tannehill	175.00	87.00	52.00
(85)	Joe Tinker	450.00	225.00	135.00
(86)	John Titus	175.00	87.00	52.00
(87)	Terry Turner	175.00	87.00	52.00
(88)	Bobby Wallace	450.00	225.00	135.00
(89)	Doc White	175.00	87.00	52.00
(90)	Ed Willett	175.00	87.00	52.00
(91)	Art Wilson	175.00	87.00	52.00
(92)	Harry Wolter	175.00	87.00	52.00

1910 S74 Silks - Colored

		NR MT	EX	VG
Complete Set:		32500.	14700.	6900.
Common Player:		150.00	75.00	45.00
(1)	Red Ames	150.00	75.00	45.00
(2)	Jimmy Archer	150.00	75.00	45.00
(3)	Home Run Baker	350.00	175.00	105.00
(4)	Cy Barger	150.00	75.00	45.00
(5)	Jack Barry	150.00	75.00	45.00
(6)	Johnny Bates	150.00	75.00	45.00
(7)	Beals Becker	150.00	75.00	45.00
(8)	George Bell	150.00	75.00	45.00
(9)	Chief Bender	350.00	175.00	105.00
(10)	Bill Bergen	150.00	75.00	45.00
(11)	Bob Bescher	150.00	75.00	45.00
(12)	Roger Bresnahan (mouth closed)	400.00	190.00	90.00
(13)	Roger Bresnahan (mouth open)	400.00	190.00	90.00
(14)	Al Bridwell	150.00	75.00	45.00
(15)	Mordecai Brown	350.00	175.00	105.00
(16)	Bobby Byrne	150.00	75.00	45.00
(17)	Howie Camnitz	150.00	75.00	45.00
(18)	Bill Carrigan	150.00	75.00	45.00
(19)	Frank Chance	400.00	200.00	120.00
(20)	Hal Chase	250.00	125.00	75.00
(21)	Ed Cicotte	200.00	100.00	60.00
(22)	Fred Clarke	350.00	175.00	105.00
(23)	Ty Cobb	2500.	1250.	750.00
(24)	Eddie Collins	350.00	175.00	105.00
(25)	Doc Crandall	150.00	75.00	45.00
(26)	Bill Dahlen	150.00	75.00	45.00
(27)	Jake Daubert	200.00	100.00	60.00
(28)	Jim Delahanty	150.00	75.00	45.00
(29)	Art Devlin	150.00	75.00	45.00
(30)	Josh Devore	150.00	75.00	45.00
(31)	Red Dooin	150.00	75.00	45.00
(32)	Mickey Doolan	150.00	75.00	45.00
(33)	Tom Downey	150.00	75.00	45.00
(34)	Larry Doyle	150.00	75.00	45.00
(35)	Hugh Duffy	350.00	175.00	105.00
(36)	Jimmy Dygert	150.00	75.00	45.00
(37)	Kid Elberfield (Elberfeld)	150.00	75.00	45.00
(38)	Steve Evans	150.00	75.00	45.00
(39)	Johnny Evers	350.00	175.00	105.00
(40)	Bob Ewing	150.00	75.00	45.00
(41)	Art Fletcher	150.00	75.00	45.00
(42)	John Flynn	150.00	75.00	45.00
(43)	Russ Ford	150.00	75.00	45.00
(44)	Bill Foxen	150.00	75.00	45.00
(45)	Art Fromme	150.00	75.00	45.00
(46)	George Gibson	150.00	75.00	45.00
(47)	Peaches Graham	150.00	75.00	45.00
(48)	Eddie Grant	150.00	75.00	45.00
(49)	Clark Griffith	350.00	175.00	105.00
(50)	Topsy Hartsel	150.00	75.00	45.00
(51)	Arnold Hauser	150.00	75.00	45.00
(52)	Charlie Hemphill	150.00	75.00	45.00
(53)	Dick Hoblitzell	150.00	75.00	45.00
(54)	Miller Huggins	350.00	175.00	105.00
(55)	John Hummel	150.00	75.00	45.00
(56)	Walter Johnson	900.00	450.00	270.00
(57)	Davy Jones	150.00	75.00	45.00
(58)	Johnny Kling	150.00	75.00	45.00
(59)	Jack Knight	150.00	75.00	45.00
(60)	Ed Konetchy	150.00	75.00	45.00
(61)	Harry Krause	150.00	75.00	45.00
(62)	Tommy Leach	150.00	75.00	45.00
(63)	Lefty Leifield	150.00	75.00	45.00
(64)	Hans Lobert	150.00	75.00	45.00
(65)	Rube Marquard	350.00	175.00	105.00
(66)	Christy Mathewson	900.00	450.00	270.00
(67)	Al Mattern	150.00	75.00	45.00
(68)	Amby McConnell	150.00	75.00	45.00
(69)	John McGraw	400.00	200.00	120.00
(70)	Harry McIntire (McIntyre)	150.00	75.00	45.00
(71)	Fred Merkle	200.00	100.00	60.00
(72)	Chief Meyers	150.00	75.00	45.00
(73)	Dots Miller	150.00	75.00	45.00
(74)	Mike Mitchell	150.00	75.00	45.00
(75)	Pat Moran	150.00	75.00	45.00
(76)	George Moriarty	150.00	75.00	45.00
(77)	George Mullin	150.00	75.00	45.00
(78)	Danny Murphy	150.00	75.00	45.00
(79)	Red Murray	150.00	75.00	45.00
(80)	Tom Needham	150.00	75.00	45.00
(81)	Rebel Oakes	150.00	75.00	45.00
(82)	Rube Oldring	150.00	75.00	45.00
(83)	Orval Overall	150.00	75.00	45.00
(84)	Fred Parent	150.00	75.00	45.00
(85)	Dode Paskert	150.00	75.00	45.00
(86)	Billy Payne	150.00	75.00	45.00

		NR MT	EX	VG
(87)	Barney Pelty	150.00	75.00	45.00
(88)	Deacon Phillippe	150.00	75.00	45.00
(89)	Jack Quinn	150.00	75.00	45.00
(90)	Bugs Raymond	150.00	75.00	45.00
(91)	Ed Reulbach	150.00	75.00	45.00
(92)	Jack Rowan	150.00	75.00	45.00
(93)	Nap Rucker	150.00	75.00	45.00
(94)	Doc Scanlon (Scanlan)	150.00	75.00	45.00
(95)	Germany Schaefer	150.00	75.00	45.00
(96)	Admiral Schlei	150.00	75.00	45.00
(97)	Wildfire Schulte	150.00	75.00	45.00
(98)	Dave Shean	150.00	75.00	45.00
(99)	Jimmy Sheckard	150.00	75.00	45.00
(100)	Happy Smith	150.00	75.00	45.00
(101)	Fred Snodgrass	150.00	75.00	45.00
(102)	Tris Speaker	600.00	300.00	180.00
(103)	Jake Stahl	150.00	75.00	45.00
(104)	Harry Steinfeldt	200.00	100.00	60.00
(105)	George Stone	150.00	75.00	45.00
(106)	Gabby Street	150.00	75.00	45.00
(107)	Ed Summers	150.00	75.00	45.00
(108)	Lee Tannehill	150.00	75.00	45.00
(109)	Joe Tinker	350.00	175.00	105.00
(110)	John Titus	150.00	75.00	45.00
(111)	Terry Turner	150.00	75.00	45.00
(112)	Bobby Wallace	350.00	175.00	105.00
(113)	Zack Wheat	350.00	175.00	105.00
(114)	Doc White (White Sox)	150.00	75.00	45.00
(115)	Kirby White (Pirates)	150.00	75.00	45.00
(116)	Ed Willett	150.00	75.00	45.00
(117)	Owen Wilson	150.00	75.00	45.00
(118)	Hooks Wiltse	150.00	75.00	45.00
(119)	Harry Wolter	150.00	75.00	45.00
(120)	Cy Young	750.00	375.00	225.00

1912 S81 Silks

The 1912 S81 "Silks," so-called because they featured pictures of baseball players on a satin-like fabric rather than paper or cardboard, are closely related to the better-known T3 Turkey Red cabinet cards of the same era. The silks, which featured 25 of the day's top baseball players among its other various subjects, were available as a premium with Helmar "Turkish Trophies" cigarettes. According to an advertising sheet, one silk could be obtained for 25 Helmar coupons. The silks measure 7" by 9" and, with a few exceptions, used the same pictures featured on the popular Turkey Red cards. Five players (pitchers Rube Marquard, Rube Benton, Marty O'Toole, Grover Alexander and Russ Ford) appear in the "Silks" set that were not included in the T3 set. In addition, an error involving the Frank Baker card was corrected for the "Silks" set. (In the T3 set, Baker's card actually pictured Jack Barry.) Several years ago a pair of New England collectors found a small stack of Christy Mathewson "Silks," making his, by far, the most common. Otherwise, the "Silks" are generally so rare that it is difficult to determine the relative scarcity of the others. Baseball enthusiasts are usually only attracted to the 25 baseball players in the "Silks" premium set, but it is interesting to note that the promotion also offered dozens of other subjects, including "beautiful women in bathing and athletic costumes, charming dancers in gorgeous attire, national flags and generals on horseback."

		NR MT	EX	VG
Complete Set:		90000.	45000.	27500.
Common Player:		1500.	750.00	450.00
111	Rube Marquard	4000.	2000.	1200.
112	Marty O'Toole	1500.	750.00	450.00
113	Rube Benton	1500.	750.00	450.00
114	Grover Alexander	4500.	2250.	1350.
115	Russ Ford	1700.	850.00	500.00
116	John McGraw	5000.	2500.	1500.
117	Nap Rucker	1500.	750.00	450.00
118	Mike Mitchell	1500.	750.00	450.00
119	Chief Bender	4000.	2000.	1200.
120	Home Run Baker	4000.	2000.	1200.
121	Nap Lajoie	5500.	2250.	1650.
122	Joe Tinker	4000.	2000.	1200.
123	Sherry Magee	1500.	750.00	450.00
124	Howie Camnitz	1500.	750.00	450.00
125	Eddie Collins	4000.	2000.	1200.
126	Red Dooin	1500.	750.00	450.00
127	Ty Cobb	10000.	5000.	3000.
128	Hugh Jennings	4000.	2000.	1200.
129	Roger Bresnahan	4000.	2000.	1200.
130	Jake Stahl	1700.	850.00	500.00
131	Tris Speaker	6500.	3250.	2000.
132	Ed Walsh	4000.	2000.	1200.
133	Christy Mathewson	2800.	1400.	800.00
134	Johnny Evers	4500.	2250.	1350.
135	Walter Johnson	7000.	3500.	2200.

1962 Salada Tea/ Junket Dessert Coins

These 1-3/8" diameter plastic coins were issued in packages of Salada Tea and Junket Pudding mix. There are 221 different players available, with variations bringing the total of different coins to 261. Each coin has a paper color photo inserted in the front which contains the player's name and position plus the coin number. The plastic rims come in six different colors, all color coded per team. (For example, the New York Yankees are found with light blue rims). Production began with 180 coins, but the addition of the New York Mets and Houston Colt .45's to the National League allowed the company to expand the set's size. Twenty expansion players were added along with 21 other players. Several players' coins were dropped after the initial "180" run, causing some scarcities. A Gary Geiger coin with a "BO," instead of a "B", on his cap is sometimes found on collectors' want lists. Most Salada experts do not consider this coin to be a legitimate variation. The mark, which somewhat resembles an "O", is merely a printing smear and not an intended cap emblem. It has also been determined by Salada experts that a Jim Lemon coin with red shirt buttons does not exist.

		NR MT	EX	VG
Complete Set: (without variations)		2500.	1250.	750.00
Complete Set: (with variations)		6000.	3000.	1750.
Common Player:		2.00	1.00	.60
1	Jim Gentile	4.00	2.00	1.25
2	Bill Pierce	110.00	55.00	33.00
3	Chico Fernandez	2.00	1.00	.60
4	Tom Brewer	35.00	17.50	10.50
5	Woody Held	2.50	1.25	.70
6	Ray Herbert	35.00	17.50	10.50
7a	Ken Aspromonte (Angels)	15.00	7.50	4.50
7b	Ken Aspromonte (Indians)	4.00	2.00	1.25
8	Whitey Ford	25.00	12.50	7.50
9	Jim Lemon	2.50	1.25	.70
10	Billy Klaus	2.00	1.00	.60
11	Steve Barber	35.00	17.50	10.50
12	Nellie Fox	10.00	5.00	3.00
13	Jim Bunning	8.00	4.00	2.50
14	Frank Malzone	2.50	1.25	.70
15	Tito Francona	2.50	1.25	.70
16	Bobby Del Greco	2.00	1.00	.60
17a	Steve Bilko (red shirt buttons)	7.00	3.50	2.00
17b	Steve Bilko (white shirt buttons)	4.00	2.00	1.25
18	Tony Kubek	55.00	27.00	16.50
19	Earl Battey	2.50	1.25	.70
20	Chuck Cottier	2.00	1.00	.60
21	Willie Tasby	2.00	1.00	.60
22	Bob Allison	3.00	1.50	.90
23	Roger Maris	30.00	15.00	9.00
24a	Earl Averill (red shirt buttons)	7.00	3.50	2.00
24b	Earl Averill (white shirt buttons)	4.00	2.00	1.25
25	Jerry Lumpe	2.50	1.25	.70
26	Jim Grant	35.00	17.50	10.50
27	Carl Yastrzemski	70.00	35.00	21.00
28	Rocky Colavito	5.00	2.50	1.50
29	Al Smith	2.00	1.00	.60
30	Jim Busby	35.00	17.50	10.50
31	Dick Howser	3.00	1.50	.90
32	Jim Perry	3.00	1.50	.90
33	Yogi Berra	30.00	15.00	9.00
34a	Ken Hamlin (red shirt buttons)	7.00	3.50	2.00
34b	Ken Hamlin (white shirt buttons)	4.00	2.00	1.25
35	Dale Long	2.50	1.25	.70
36	Harmon Killebrew	20.00	10.00	6.00
37	Dick Brown	2.00	1.00	.60
38	Gary Geiger	2.00	1.00	.60
39a	Minnie Minoso (White Sox)	35.00	17.50	10.50
39b	Minnie Minoso (Cardinals)	18.00	9.00	5.50
40	Brooks Robinson	35.00	17.50	10.50
41	Mickey Mantle	90.00	45.00	27.00
42	Bennie Daniels	2.00	1.00	.60
43	Billy Martin	7.00	3.50	2.00
44	Vic Power	2.50	1.25	.70
45	Joe Pignatano	2.00	1.00	.60
46a	Ryne Duren (red shirt buttons)	7.00	3.50	2.00
46b	Ryne Duren (white shirt buttons)	4.00	2.00	1.25
47a	Pete Runnels (2B)	10.00	5.00	3.00
47b	Pete Runnels (1B)	4.00	2.00	1.25
48a	Dick Williams (name on right)	1000.	500.00	300.00
48b	Dick Williams (name on left)	4.00	2.00	1.25
49	Jim Landis	2.00	1.00	.60
50	Steve Boros	2.00	1.00	.60
51a	Zoilo Versalles (red shirt buttons)	7.00	3.50	2.00
51b	Zoilo Versalles (white shirt buttons)	4.00	2.00	1.25
52a	Johnny Temple (Indians)	15.00	7.50	4.50
52b	Johnny Temple (Orioles)	4.00	2.00	1.25
53a	Jackie Brandt (Oriole)	3.50	1.75	1.00
53b	Jackie Brandt (Orioles)	800.00	400.00	240.00
54	Joe McClain	2.00	1.00	.60
55	Sherm Lollar	2.50	1.25	.70
56	Gene Stephens	2.00	1.00	.60
57a	Leon Wagner (red shirt buttons)	7.00	3.50	2.00
57b	Leon Wagner (white shirt buttons)	4.00	2.00	1.25
58	Frank Lary	2.50	1.25	.70
59	Bill Skowron	6.00	3.00	1.75
60	Vic Wertz	2.50	1.25	.70
61	Willie Kirkland	2.00	1.00	.60
62	Leo Posada	2.00	1.00	.60
63a	Albie Pearson (red shirt buttons)	7.00	3.50	2.00
63b	Albie Pearson (white shirt buttons)	4.00	2.00	1.25
64	Bobby Richardson	8.00	4.00	2.50
65a	Marv Breeding (SS)	15.00	7.50	4.50
65b	Marv Breeding (2B)	4.00	2.00	1.25
66	Roy Sievers	80.00	40.00	24.00
67	Al Kaline	30.00	15.00	9.00
68a	Don Buddin (Red Sox)	15.00	7.50	4.50
68b	Don Buddin (Colts)	4.00	2.00	1.25
69a	Lenny Green (red shirt buttons)	7.00	3.50	2.00
69B	Lenny Green (white shirt buttons)	4.00	2.00	1.25
70	Gene Green	35.00	17.50	10.50
71	Luis Aparicio	13.00	6.50	4.00
72	Norm Cash	6.00	3.00	1.75
73	Jackie Jensen	40.00	20.00	12.00
74	Bubba Phillips	2.00	1.00	.60
75	Jim Archer	2.00	1.00	.60
76a	Ken Hunt (red shirt buttons)	7.00	3.50	2.00
76b	Ken Hunt (white shirt buttons)	4.00	2.00	1.25
77	Ralph Terry	3.00	1.50	.90
78	Camilo Pascual	2.50	1.25	.70
79	Marty Keough	35.00	17.50	10.50
80	Cletis Boyer	3.50	1.75	1.00
81	Jim Pagliaroni	2.00	1.00	.60
82a	Gene Leek (red shirt buttons)	7.00	3.50	2.00
82b	Gene Leek (white shirt buttons)	4.00	2.00	1.25
83	Jake Wood	2.00	1.00	.60
84	Coot Veal	35.00	17.50	10.50
85	Norm Siebern	2.50	1.25	.70
86a	Andy Carey (White Sox)	40.00	20.00	12.00
86b	Andy Carey (Phillies)	4.00	2.00	1.25
87a	Bill Tuttle (red shirt buttons)	7.00	3.50	2.00
87b	Bill Tuttle (white shirt buttons)	4.00	2.00	1.25
88a	Jimmy Piersall (Indians)	15.00	7.50	4.50
88b	Jimmy Piersall (Senators)	4.00	2.00	1.25
89	Ron Hansen	35.00	17.50	10.50
90a	Chuck Stobbs (red shirt buttons)	7.00	3.50	2.00
90b	Chuck Stobbs (white shirt buttons)	4.00	2.00	1.25
91a	Ken McBride (red shirt buttons)	7.00	3.50	2.00
91b	Ken McBride (white shirt buttons)	4.00	2.00	1.25
92	Bill Bruton	2.50	1.25	.70
93	Gus Triandos	2.50	1.25	.70
94	John Romano	2.00	1.00	.60
95	Elston Howard	7.00	3.50	2.00
96	Gene Woodling	2.50	1.25	.70
97a	Early Wynn (pitching pose)	60.00	30.00	18.00
97b	Early Wynn (portrait)	25.00	12.50	7.50
98	Milt Pappas	2.50	1.25	.70
99	Bill Monbouquette	2.50	1.25	.70
100	Wayne Causey	2.00	1.00	.60
101	Don Elston	2.00	1.00	.60
102a	Charlie Neal (Dodgers)	15.00	7.50	4.50
102b	Charlie Neal (Mets)	4.00	2.00	1.25
103	Don Blasingame	2.00	1.00	.60
104	Frank Thomas	35.00	17.50	10.50
105	Wes Covington	2.50	1.25	.70
106	Chuck Hiller	2.00	1.00	.60
107	Don Hoak	2.50	1.25	.70
108a	Bob Lillis (Cardinals)	30.00	15.00	9.00
108b	Bob Lillis (Colts)	4.00	2.00	1.25
109	Sandy Koufax	40.00	20.00	12.00
110	Gordy Coleman	2.00	1.00	.60
111	Ed Matthews (Mathews)	20.00	10.00	6.00
112	Art Mahaffey	2.00	1.00	.60
113a	Ed Bailey (red period above "i" in Giants)	7.00	3.50	2.00
113b	Ed Bailey (white period)	4.00	2.00	1.25
114	Smoky Burgess	3.50	1.75	1.00
115	Bill White	3.50	1.75	1.00
116	Ed Bouchee	35.00	17.50	10.50
117	Bob Buhl	2.50	1.25	.70
118	Vada Pinson	4.00	2.00	1.25
119	Carl Sawatski	2.00	1.00	.60
120	Dick Stuart	2.50	1.25	.70
121	Harvey Kuenn	50.00	25.00	15.00

		NR MT	EX	VG
122	Pancho Herrera	2.00	1.00	.60
123a	Don Zimmer (Cubs)	15.00	7.50	4.50
123b	Don Zimmer (Mets)	5.00	2.50	1.50
124	Wally Moon	2.50	1.25	.70
125	Joe Adcock	3.50	1.75	1.00
126	Joey Jay	2.00	1.00	.60
127a	Maury Wills (blue "3" on shirt)	15.00	7.50	4.50
127b	Maury Wills (red "3" on shirt)	7.00	3.50	2.00
128	George Altman	2.00	1.00	.60
129a	John Buzhardt (Phillies)	15.00	7.50	4.50
129b	John Buzhardt (White Sox)	6.00	3.00	1.75
130	Felipe Alou	3.00	1.50	.90
131	Bill Mazeroski	4.00	2.00	1.25
132	Ernie Broglio	2.00	1.00	.60
133	John Roseboro	2.50	1.25	.70
134	Mike McCormick	2.50	1.25	.70
135a	Chuck Smith (Phillies)	15.00	7.50	4.50
135b	Chuck Smith (White Sox)	6.00	3.00	1.75
136	Ron Santo	4.00	2.00	1.25
137	Gene Freese	2.00	1.00	.60
138	Dick Groat	4.00	2.00	1.25
139	Curt Flood	4.00	2.00	1.25
140	Frank Bolling	2.00	1.00	.60
141	Clay Dalrymple	2.00	1.00	.60
142	Willie McCovey	35.00	17.50	10.50
143	Bob Skinner	2.50	1.25	.70
144	Lindy McDaniel	2.00	1.00	.60
145	Glen Hobbie	2.00	1.00	.60
146a	Gil Hodges (Dodgers)	50.00	25.00	15.00
146b	Gil Hodges (Mets)	25.00	12.50	7.50
147	Eddie Kasko	2.00	1.00	.60
148	Gino Cimoli	35.00	17.50	10.50
149	Willie Mays	65.00	32.00	19.50
150	Roberto Clemente	50.00	25.00	15.00
151	Red Schoendienst	6.00	3.00	1.75
152	Joe Torre	4.00	2.00	1.25
153	Bob Purkey	2.50	1.25	.70
154a	Tommy Davis (3B)	10.00	5.00	3.00
154b	Tommy Davis (OF)	5.00	2.50	1.50
155a	Andre Rogers (incorrect spelling)	8.00	4.00	2.50
155b	Andre Rodgers (correct spelling)	3.50	1.75	1.00
156	Tony Taylor	2.00	1.00	.60
157	Bob Friend	3.00	1.50	.90
158a	Gus Bell (Redlegs)	8.00	4.00	2.50
158b	Gus Bell (Mets)	4.50	2.25	1.25
159	Roy McMillan	2.50	1.25	.70
160	Carl Warwick	2.00	1.00	.60
161	Willie Davis	3.50	1.75	1.00
162	Sam Jones	55.00	27.00	16.50
163	Ruben Amaro	2.00	1.00	.60
164	Sam Taylor	2.00	1.00	.60
165	Frank Robinson	30.00	15.00	9.00
166	Lou Burdette	3.00	1.50	.90
167	Ken Boyer	5.00	2.50	1.50
168	Bill Virdon	3.50	1.75	1.00
169	Jim Davenport	2.00	1.00	.60
170	Don Demeter	2.00	1.00	.60
171	Richie Ashburn	45.00	22.00	13.50
172	John Podres	4.00	2.00	1.25
173a	Joe Cunningham (Cardinals)	55.00	27.00	16.50
173b	Joe Cunningham (White Sox)	25.00	12.50	7.50
174	ElRoy Face	3.50	1.75	1.00
175	Orlando Cepeda	7.00	3.50	2.00
176a	Bobby Gene Smith (Phillies)	15.00	7.50	4.50
176b	Bobby Gene Smith (Mets)	4.00	2.00	1.25
177a	Ernie Banks (OF)	40.00	20.00	12.00
177b	Ernie Banks (SS)	25.00	12.50	7.50
178a	Daryl Spencer (3B)	15.00	7.50	4.50
178b	Daryl Spencer (1B)	4.00	2.00	1.25
179	Bob Schmidt	35.00	17.50	10.50
180	Hank Aaron	60.00	30.00	18.00
181	Hobie Landrith	5.00	2.50	1.50
182a	Ed Broussard	400.00	200.00	120.00
182b	Ed Bressoud	25.00	12.50	7.50
183	Felix Mantilla	5.00	2.50	1.50
184	Dick Farrell	5.00	2.50	1.50
185	Bob Miller	5.00	2.50	1.50
186	Don Taussig	5.00	2.50	1.50
187	Pumpsie Green	5.00	2.50	1.50
188	Bobby Shantz	9.00	4.50	2.75
189	Roger Craig	9.00	4.50	2.75
190	Hal Smith	5.00	2.50	1.50
191	John Edwards	5.00	2.50	1.50
192	John DeMerit	5.00	2.50	1.50
193	Joe Amalfitano	5.00	2.50	1.50
194	Norm Larker	5.00	2.50	1.50
195	Al Heist	5.00	2.50	1.50
196	Al Spangler	5.00	2.50	1.50
197	Alex Grammas	5.00	2.50	1.50
198	Gerry Lynch	5.00	2.50	1.50
199	Jim McKnight	5.00	2.50	1.50
200	Jose Pagen (Pagan)	5.00	2.50	1.50
201	Junior Gilliam	18.00	9.00	5.50
202	Art Ditmar	5.00	2.50	1.50
203	Pete Daley	5.00	2.50	1.50
204	Johnny Callison	12.00	6.00	3.50
205	Stu Miller	5.00	2.50	1.50
206	Russ Snyder	5.00	2.50	1.50
207	Billy Williams	30.00	15.00	9.00
208	Walter Bond	5.00	2.50	1.50
209	Joe Koppe	5.00	2.50	1.50
210	Don Schwall	20.00	10.00	6.00
211	Billy Gardner	9.00	4.50	2.75
212	Chuck Estrada	5.00	2.50	1.50
213	Gary Bell	5.00	2.50	1.50
214	Floyd Robinson	5.00	2.50	1.50
215	Duke Snider	45.00	22.00	13.50
216	Lee Maye	5.00	2.50	1.50
217	Howie Bedell	5.00	2.50	1.50
218	Bob Will	5.00	2.50	1.50
219	Dallas Green	9.00	4.50	2.75
220	Carroll Hardy	12.00	6.00	3.50
221	Danny O'Connell	5.00	2.50	1.50

1963 Salada Tea/ Junket Dessert Coins

A much smaller set of baseball coins was issued by Salada/Junket in 1963. The 63 coins issued were called "All-Star Baseball Coins" and included most the top players of the day. Unlike 1962, the coins were made of metal and measured a slightly larger 1-1/2" diameter. American League players have blue rims on their coins, while National Leaguers are rimmed in red. Coin fronts contain no printing on the full-color player photos, while backs list coin number, player name, team and position, along with brief statistics and the sponsors' logos.

		NR MT	EX	VG
	Complete Set:	700.00	350.00	205.00
	Common Player:	3.00	1.50	.90
1	Don Drysdale	18.00	9.00	5.50
2	Dick Farrell	3.00	1.50	.90
3	Bob Gibson	18.00	9.00	5.50
4	Sandy Koufax	30.00	15.00	9.00
5	Juan Marichal	18.00	9.00	5.50
6	Bob Purkey	3.00	1.50	.90
7	Bob Shaw	3.00	1.50	.90
8	Warren Spahn	18.00	9.00	5.50
9	Johnny Podres	5.00	2.50	1.50
10	Art Mahaffey	3.00	1.50	.90
11	Del Crandall	4.00	2.00	1.25
12	John Roseboro	4.00	2.00	1.25
13	Orlando Cepeda	7.00	3.50	2.00
14	Bill Mazeroski	5.00	2.50	1.50
15	Ken Boyer	5.00	2.50	1.50
16	Dick Groat	5.00	2.50	1.50
17	Ernie Banks	20.00	10.00	6.00
18	Frank Bolling	3.00	1.50	.90
19	Jim Davenport	3.00	1.50	.90
20	Maury Wills	6.00	3.00	1.75
21	Tommy Davis	4.00	2.00	1.25
22	Willie Mays	40.00	20.00	12.00
23	Roberto Clemente	40.00	20.00	12.00
24	Henry Aaron	40.00	20.00	12.00
25	Felipe Alou	4.00	2.00	1.25
26	Johnny Callison	4.00	2.00	1.25
27	Richie Ashburn	8.00	4.00	2.50
28	Eddie Mathews	18.00	9.00	5.50
29	Frank Robinson	20.00	10.00	6.00
30	Billy Williams	18.00	9.00	5.50
31	George Altman	3.00	1.50	.90
32	Hank Aguirre	3.00	1.50	.90
33	Jim Bunning	8.00	4.00	2.50
34	Dick Donovan	3.00	1.50	.90
35	Bill Monbouquette	3.00	1.50	.90
36	Camilo Pascual	4.00	2.00	1.25
37	David Stenhouse	3.00	1.50	.90
38	Ralph Terry	4.00	2.00	1.25
39	Hoyt Wilhelm	12.00	6.00	3.50
40	Jim Kaat	8.00	4.00	2.50
41	Ken McBride	3.00	1.50	.90
42	Ray Herbert	3.00	1.50	.90
43	Milt Pappas	4.00	2.00	1.25
44	Earl Battey	3.00	1.50	.90
45	Elston Howard	6.00	3.00	1.75
46	John Romano	3.00	1.50	.90
47	Jim Gentile	3.00	1.50	.90
48	Billy Moran	3.00	1.50	.90
49	Rich Rollins	3.00	1.50	.90
50	Luis Aparicio	12.00	6.00	3.50
51	Norm Siebern	3.00	1.50	.90
52	Bobby Richardson	7.00	3.50	2.00
53	Brooks Robinson	25.00	12.50	7.50
54	Tom Tresh	4.00	2.00	1.25
55	Leon Wagner	3.00	1.50	.90
56	Mickey Mantle	90.00	45.00	27.00
57	Roger Maris	25.00	12.50	7.50
58	Rocky Colavito	5.00	2.50	1.50
59	Lee Thomas	3.00	1.50	.90
60	Jim Landis	3.00	1.50	.90
61	Pete Runnels	4.00	2.00	1.25
62	Yogi Berra	25.00	12.50	7.50
63	Al Kaline	25.00	12.50	7.50

1958 San Francisco Call-Bulletin Giants

These unnumbered cards, picturing members of the San Francisco Giants, were inserted in copies of the San Francisco Call-Bulletin newspaper as part of a promotional contest. The 25 cards in the set measure 2" by 4" and were printed on orange paper. The top of the card contains a black and white player photo, while the bottom contains a perforated stub with a serial number used to win prizes. (Cards without the stub intact are approximately 50 percent of the prices listed.) The contest name, "Giant Payoff", appears prominently on both sides of the stub. The back of the card contains a 1958 Giants schedule.

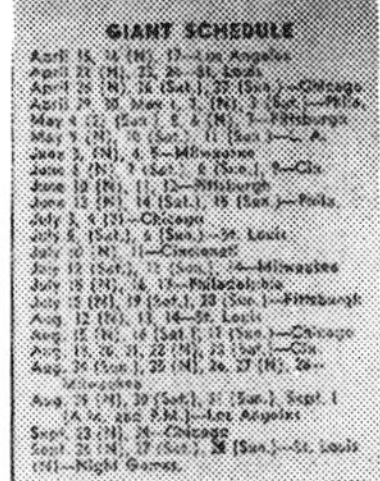

		NR MT	EX	VG
	Complete Set:	900.00	450.00	275.00
	Common Player:	10.00	5.00	3.00
(1)	Johnny Antonelli	15.00	7.50	4.50
(2)	Curt Barclay	10.00	5.00	3.00
(3)	Tom Bowers	350.00	175.00	105.00
(4)	Ed Bressoud	75.00	37.00	22.00
(5)	Orlando Cepeda	75.00	38.00	23.00
(6)	Ray Crone	10.00	5.00	3.00
(7)	Jim Davenport	15.00	7.50	4.50
(8)	Paul Giel	10.00	5.00	3.00
(9)	Ruben Gomez	10.00	5.00	3.00
(10)	Marv Grissom	10.00	5.00	3.00
(11)	Ray Jablonski	35.00	17.50	10.50
(12)	Willie Kirkland	100.00	50.00	30.00
(13)	Whitey Lockman	15.00	7.50	4.50
(14)	Willie Mays	300.00	150.00	90.00
(15)	Mike McCormick	15.00	7.50	4.50
(16)	Stu Miller	15.00	7.50	4.50
(17)	Ramon Monzant	10.00	5.00	3.00
(18)	Danny O'Connell	10.00	5.00	3.00
(19)	Bill Rigney	15.00	7.50	4.50
(20)	Hank Sauer	15.00	7.50	4.50
(21)	Bob Schmidt	10.00	5.00	3.00
(22)	Daryl Spencer	10.00	5.00	3.00
(23)	Valmy Thomas	10.00	5.00	3.00
(24)	Bobby Thomson	20.00	10.00	6.00
(25)	Allan Worthington	10.00	5.00	3.00

1986 Schnucks Milk Cardinals

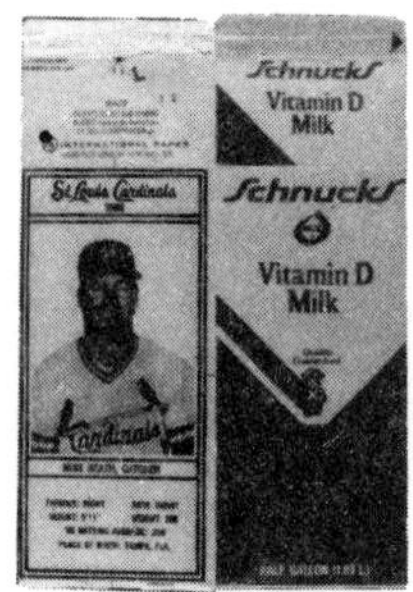

These milk carton panels were issued by Schnucks supermarkets in the St. Louis and southwestern Illinois areas. The 3-3/4" by 7-1/2" blank-backed panels feature black and white photos of 24 different St. Louis players along with personal information and 1985 playing statistics. A mascot and schedule card were also included in the set.

		MT	NR MT	EX
	Complete Set:	35.00	27.00	15.00
	Common Player:	.60	.45	.25
(1)	Jack Clark	2.50	2.00	1.00
(2)	Vince Coleman	3.50	2.75	1.50
(3)	Tim Conroy	.60	.45	.25
(4)	Danny Cox	1.25	.90	.50
(5)	Ken Dayley	.60	.45	.25
(6)	Bob Forsch	.60	.45	.25
(7)	Mike Heath	.60	.45	.25
(8)	Tom Herr	1.25	.90	.50
(9)	Rick Horton	.60	.45	.25
(10)	Clint Hurdle	.60	.45	.25
(11)	Kurt Kepshire	.60	.45	.25
(12)	Jeff Lahti	.60	.45	.25
(13)	Tito Landrum	.60	.45	.25
(14)	Mike Lavalliere	.90	.70	.35
(15)	Tom Lawless	.60	.45	.25
(16)	Willie McGee	2.50	2.00	1.00
(17)	Jose Oquendo	.90	.70	.35
(18)	Rick Ownbey	.60	.45	.25
(19)	Terry Pendleton	1.25	.90	.50
(20)	Pat Perry	.60	.45	.25
(21)	Ozzie Smith	3.00	2.25	1.25
(22)	John Tudor	1.50	1.25	.60
(23)	Andy Van Slyke	2.50	2.00	1.00
(24)	Todd Worrell	2.50	2.00	1.00
(25)	Fred Bird (mascot)	.60	.45	.25
(26)	1986 Cardinals Schedule	.60	.45	.25

1988 Score

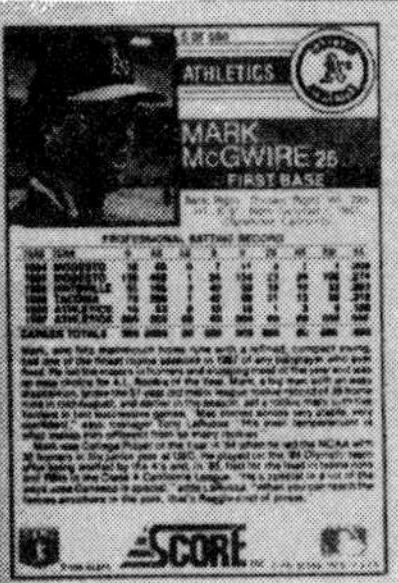

A fifth member joined the group of nationally distributed baseball cards in 1988. Titled "Score," the new cards are characterized by extremely sharp and excellent full-color photography and printing. Card backs are full-color also and carry a player head-shot, along with a brief biography and player personal and statistical information. The 660 cards in the set each measure 2-1/2" by 3-1/2" in size. The fronts come with one of six different border colors - blue, red, green, purple, orange and gold - which are equally divided at 110 cards per color. The Score set was produced by Major League Marketing, the same company that markets the "triple-action" Sportflics card sets.

		MT	NR MT	EX
Complete Set:		25.00	20.00	10.00
Common Player:		.04	.03	.02
1	Don Mattingly	1.50	1.25	.60
2	Wade Boggs	.80	.60	.30
3	Tim Raines	.20	.15	.08
4	Andre Dawson	.15	.11	.06
5	Mark McGwire	1.25	.90	.50
6	Kevin Seitzer	.60	.45	.25
7	Wally Joyner	.35	.25	.14
8	Jesse Barfield	.10	.08	.04
9	Pedro Guerrero	.15	.11	.06
10	Eric Davis	.60	.45	.25
11	George Brett	.30	.25	.12
12	Ozzie Smith	.12	.09	.05
13	Rickey Henderson	.25	.20	.10
14	Jim Rice	.20	.15	.08
15	*Matt Nokes*	.50	.40	.20
16	Mike Schmidt	.40	.30	.15
17	Dave Parker	.12	.09	.05
18	Eddie Murray	.25	.20	.10
19	Andres Galarraga	.12	.09	.05
20	Tony Fernandez	.10	.08	.04
21	Kevin McReynolds	.12	.09	.05
22	B.J. Surhoff	.10	.08	.04
23	Pat Tabler	.06	.05	.02
24	Kirby Puckett	.25	.20	.10
25	Benny Santiago	.35	.25	.14
26	Ryne Sandberg	.20	.15	.08
27	Kelly Downs	.08	.06	.03
28	Jose Cruz	.06	.05	.02
29	Pete O'Brien	.06	.05	.02
30	Mark Langston	.10	.08	.04
31	Lee Smith	.08	.06	.03
32	Juan Samuel	.10	.08	.04
33	Kevin Bass	.06	.05	.02
34	R.J. Reynolds	.04	.03	.02
35	Steve Sax	.12	.09	.05
36	John Kruk	.08	.06	.03
37	Alan Trammell	.15	.11	.06
38	Chris Bosio	.06	.05	.02
39	Brook Jacoby	.08	.06	.03
40	Willie McGee	.10	.08	.04
41	Dave Magadan	.10	.08	.04
42	Fred Lynn	.10	.08	.04
43	Kent Hrbek	.12	.09	.05
44	Brian Downing	.06	.05	.02
45	Jose Canseco	1.75	1.25	.70
46	Jim Presley	.08	.06	.03
47	Mike Stanley	.06	.05	.02
48	Tony Pena	.06	.05	.02
49	David Cone	.80	.60	.30
50	Rick Sutcliffe	.08	.06	.03
51	Doug Drabek	.06	.05	.02
52	Bill Doran	.06	.05	.02
53	Mike Scioscia	.06	.05	.02
54	Candy Maldonado	.06	.05	.02
55	Dave Winfield	.20	.15	.08
56	Lou Whitaker	.20	.15	.08
57	Tom Henke	.06	.05	.02
58	Ken Gerhart	.06	.05	.02
59	Glenn Braggs	.08	.06	.03
60	Julio Franco	.08	.06	.03
61	Charlie Leibrandt	.06	.05	.02
62	Gary Gaetti	.10	.08	.04
63	Bob Boone	.06	.05	.02
64	*Luis Polonia*	.20	.15	.08
65	Dwight Evans	.10	.08	.04
66	Phil Bradley	.08	.06	.03
67	Mike Boddicker	.06	.05	.02
68	Vince Coleman	.15	.11	.06
69	Howard Johnson	.08	.06	.03
70	Tim Wallach	.08	.06	.03
71	Keith Moreland	.06	.05	.02
72	Barry Larkin	.20	.15	.08
73	Alan Ashby	.04	.03	.02
74	Rick Rhoden	.06	.05	.02
75	Darrell Evans	.08	.06	.03
76	Dave Stieb	.08	.06	.03
77	Dan Plesac	.08	.06	.03
78	Will Clark	1.25	.90	.50
79	Frank White	.06	.05	.02
80	Joe Carter	.10	.08	.04
81	Mike Witt	.06	.05	.02
82	Terry Steinbach	.10	.08	.04
83	Alvin Davis	.10	.08	.04
84	Tom Herr	.06	.05	.02
85	Vance Law	.06	.05	.02
86	Kal Daniels	.15	.11	.06
87	Rick Honeycutt	.04	.03	.02
88	Alfredo Griffin	.06	.05	.02
89	Bret Saberhagen	.20	.15	.08
90	Bert Blyleven	.10	.08	.04
91	Jeff Reardon	.08	.06	.03
92	Cory Snyder	.15	.11	.06
93	Greg Walker	.06	.05	.02
94	*Joe Magrane*	.40	.30	.15
95	Rob Deer	.06	.05	.02
96	Ray Knight	.06	.05	.02
97	Casey Candaele	.04	.03	.02
98	John Cerutti	.06	.05	.02
99	Buddy Bell	.08	.06	.03
100	Jack Clark	.12	.09	.05
101	Eric Bell	.06	.05	.02
102	Willie Wilson	.08	.06	.03
103	Dave Schmidt	.04	.03	.02
104	Dennis Eckersley	.10	.08	.04
105	Don Sutton	.12	.09	.05
106	Danny Tartabull	.15	.11	.06
107	Fred McGriff	1.00	.70	.40
108	*Les Straker*	.15	.11	.06
109	Lloyd Moseby	.06	.05	.02
110	Roger Clemens	.50	.40	.20
111	Glenn Hubbard	.04	.03	.02
112	*Ken Williams*	.20	.15	.08
113	Ruben Sierra	.35	.25	.14
114	Stan Jefferson	.06	.05	.02
115	Milt Thompson	.04	.03	.02
116	Bobby Bonilla	.12	.09	.05
117	Wayne Tolleson	.04	.03	.02
118	*Matt Williams*	1.75	1.25	.70
119	Chet Lemon	.06	.05	.02
120	Dale Sveum	.06	.05	.02
121	Dennis Boyd	.06	.05	.02
122	Brett Butler	.06	.05	.02
123	Terry Kennedy	.06	.05	.02
124	Jack Howell	.06	.05	.02
125	Curt Young	.06	.05	.02
126a	Dale Valle (first name incorrect)	.25	.20	.10
126b	Dave Valle (correct spelling)	.06	.05	.02
127	Curt Wilkerson	.04	.03	.02
128	Tim Teufel	.04	.03	.02
129	Ozzie Virgil	.04	.03	.02
130	Brian Fisher	.06	.05	.02
131	Lance Parrish	.12	.09	.05
132	Tom Browning	.08	.06	.03
133a	Larry Anderson (incorrect spelling)	.25	.20	.10
133b	Larry Andersen (correct spelling)	.06	.05	.02
134a	Bob Brenley (incorrect spelling)	.25	.20	.10
134b	Bob Brenly (correct spelling)	.06	.05	.02
135	Mike Marshall	.10	.08	.04
136	Gerald Perry	.08	.06	.03
137	Bobby Meacham	.04	.03	.02
138	Larry Herndon	.04	.03	.02
139	*Fred Manrique*	.12	.09	.05
140	Charlie Hough	.06	.05	.02
141	Ron Darling	.10	.08	.04
142	Herm Winningham	.04	.03	.02
143	Mike Diaz	.06	.05	.02
144	*Mike Jackson*	.15	.11	.06
145	Denny Walling	.04	.03	.02
146	Rob Thompson	.06	.05	.02
147	Franklin Stubbs	.06	.05	.02
148	Albert Hall	.04	.03	.02
149	Bobby Witt	.08	.06	.03
150	Lance McCullers	.06	.05	.02
151	Scott Bradley	.04	.03	.02
152	Mark McLemore	.04	.03	.02
153	Tim Laudner	.04	.03	.02
154	Greg Swindell	.15	.11	.06
155	Marty Barrett	.06	.05	.02
156	Mike Heath	.04	.03	.02
157	Gary Ward	.06	.05	.02
158a	Lee Mazilli (incorrect spelling)	.25	.20	.10
158b	Lee Mazzilli (correct spelling)	.08	.06	.03
159	Tom Foley	.04	.03	.02
160	Robin Yount	.30	.25	.12
161	Steve Bedrosian	.10	.08	.04
162	Bob Walk	.04	.03	.02
163	Nick Esasky	.06	.05	.02
164	*Ken Caminiti*	.25	.20	.10
165	Jose Uribe	.04	.03	.02
166	Dave Anderson	.04	.03	.02
167	Ed Whitson	.04	.03	.02
168	Ernie Whitt	.06	.05	.02
169	Cecil Cooper	.08	.06	.03
170	Mike Pagliarulo	.08	.06	.03
171	Pat Sheridan	.04	.03	.02
172	Chris Bando	.04	.03	.02
173	Lee Lacy	.04	.03	.02
174	Steve Lombardozzi	.04	.03	.02
175	Mike Greenwell	1.25	.90	.50
176	Greg Minton	.04	.03	.02
177	Moose Haas	.04	.03	.02
178	Mike Kingery	.04	.03	.02
179	Greg Harris	.04	.03	.02
180	Bo Jackson	1.00	.70	.40
181	Carmelo Martinez	.06	.05	.02
182	Alex Trevino	.04	.03	.02
183	Ron Oester	.04	.03	.02
184	Danny Darwin	.04	.03	.02
185	Mike Krukow	.06	.05	.02
186	Rafael Palmeiro	.35	.25	.14
187	Tim Burke	.04	.03	.02
188	Roger McDowell	.08	.06	.03
189	Garry Templeton	.06	.05	.02
190	Terry Pendleton	.06	.05	.02
191	Larry Parrish	.06	.05	.02
192	Rey Quinones	.04	.03	.02
193	Joaquin Andujar	.06	.05	.02
194	Tom Brunansky	.08	.06	.03
195	Donnie Moore	.04	.03	.02
196	Dan Pasqua	.08	.06	.03
197	Jim Gantner	.04	.03	.02
198	Mark Eichhorn	.06	.05	.02
199	John Grubb	.04	.03	.02
200	*Bill Ripken*	.20	.15	.08
201	*Sam Horn*	.30	.25	.12
202	Todd Worrell	.08	.06	.03
203	Terry Leach	.04	.03	.02
204	Garth Iorg	.04	.03	.02
205	Brian Dayett	.04	.03	.02
206	Bo Diaz	.06	.05	.02
207	Craig Reynolds	.04	.03	.02
208	Brian Holton	.08	.06	.03
209	Marvelle Wynne (Marvell)	.04	.03	.02
210	Dave Concepcion	.06	.05	.02
211	Mike Davis	.06	.05	.02
212	Devon White	.15	.11	.06
213	Mickey Brantley	.04	.03	.02
214	Greg Gagne	.04	.03	.02
215	Oddibe McDowell	.06	.05	.02
216	Jimmy Key	.08	.06	.03
217	Dave Bergman	.04	.03	.02
218	Calvin Schiraldi	.04	.03	.02
219	Larry Sheets	.06	.05	.02
220	Mike Easler	.06	.05	.02
221	Kurt Stillwell	.08	.06	.03
222	*Chuck Jackson*	.15	.11	.06
223	Dave Martinez	.08	.06	.03
224	Tim Leary	.06	.05	.02
225	Steve Garvey	.20	.15	.08
226	Greg Mathews	.06	.05	.02
227	Doug Sisk	.04	.03	.02
228	Dave Henderson	.08	.06	.03
229	Jimmy Dwyer	.04	.03	.02
230	Larry Owen	.04	.03	.02
231	Andre Thornton	.06	.05	.02
232	Mark Salas	.04	.03	.02
233	Tom Brookens	.04	.03	.02
234	Greg Brock	.06	.05	.02
235	Rance Mulliniks	.04	.03	.02
236	Bob Brower	.06	.05	.02
237	Joe Niekro	.06	.05	.02
238	Scott Bankhead	.04	.03	.02
239	Doug DeCinces	.06	.05	.02
240	Tommy John	.12	.09	.05
241	Rich Gedman	.06	.05	.02
242	Ted Power	.04	.03	.02
243	*Dave Meads*	.12	.09	.05
244	Jim Sundberg	.06	.05	.02
245	Ken Oberkfell	.04	.03	.02
246	Jimmy Jones	.08	.06	.03
247	Ken Landreaux	.04	.03	.02
248	Jose Oquendo	.04	.03	.02
249	*John Mitchell*	.15	.11	.06
250	Don Baylor	.08	.06	.03
251	Scott Fletcher	.06	.05	.02
252	Al Newman	.04	.03	.02
253	Carney Lansford	.08	.06	.03
254	Johnny Ray	.06	.05	.02
255	Gary Pettis	.04	.03	.02
256	Ken Phelps	.06	.05	.02
257	Rick Leach	.04	.03	.02
258	Tim Stoddard	.04	.03	.02
259	Ed Romero	.04	.03	.02
260	Sid Bream	.06	.05	.02
261a	Tom Neidenfuer (incorrect spelling)	.25	.20	.10
261b	Tom Niedenfuer (correct spelling)	.06	.05	.02
262	Rick Dempsey	.06	.05	.02
263	Lonnie Smith	.06	.05	.02
264	Bob Forsch	.06	.05	.02
265	Barry Bonds	.10	.08	.04
266	Willie Randolph	.06	.05	.02
267	Mike Ramsey	.04	.03	.02
268	Don Slaught	.04	.03	.02
269	Mickey Tettleton	.04	.03	.02
270	Jerry Reuss	.06	.05	.02
271	Marc Sullivan	.04	.03	.02
272	Jim Morrison	.04	.03	.02
273	Steve Balboni	.06	.05	.02
274	Dick Schofield	.04	.03	.02
275	John Tudor	.08	.06	.03
276	*Gene Larkin*	.20	.15	.08
277	Harold Reynolds	.06	.05	.02
278	Jerry Browne	.06	.05	.02
279	Willie Upshaw	.06	.05	.02
280	Ted Higuera	.08	.06	.03
281	Terry McGriff	.04	.03	.02
282	Terry Puhl	.04	.03	.02
283	*Mark Wasinger*	.12	.09	.05
284	Luis Salazar	.04	.03	.02
285	Ted Simmons	.08	.06	.03
286	John Shelby	.04	.03	.02
287	*John Smiley*	.30	.25	.12
288	Curt Ford	.04	.03	.02
289	Steve Crawford	.04	.03	.02
290	Dan Quisenberry	.06	.05	.02
291	Alan Wiggins	.04	.03	.02
292	Randy Bush	.04	.03	.02
293	John Candelaria	.06	.05	.02
294	Tony Phillips	.04	.03	.02
295	Mike Morgan	.04	.03	.02
296	Bill Wegman	.04	.03	.02
297a	Terry Franconia (incorrect spelling)	.25	.20	.10
297b	Terry Francona (correct spelling)	.06	.05	.02
298	Mickey Hatcher	.04	.03	.02
299	Andres Thomas	.06	.05	.02
300	Bob Stanley	.04	.03	.02
301	*Alfredo Pedrique*	.12	.09	.05
302	Jim Lindeman	.06	.05	.02
303	Wally Backman	.06	.05	.02
304	Paul O'Neill	.06	.05	.02
305	Hubie Brooks	.08	.06	.03
306	Steve Buechele	.04	.03	.02
307	Bobby Thigpen	.08	.06	.03
308	George Hendrick	.06	.05	.02

		MT	NR MT	EX
309	John Moses	.04	.03	.02
310	Ron Guidry	.12	.09	.05
311	Bill Schroeder	.04	.03	.02
312	*Jose Nunez*	.20	.15	.08
313	Bud Black	.04	.03	.02
314	Joe Sambito	.04	.03	.02
315	Scott McGregor	.06	.05	.02
316	Rafael Santana	.04	.03	.02
317	Frank Williams	.04	.03	.02
318	Mike Fitzgerald	.04	.03	.02
319	Rick Mahler	.04	.03	.02
320	Jim Gott	.04	.03	.02
321	Mariano Duncan	.04	.03	.02
322	Jose Guzman	.06	.05	.02
323	Lee Guetterman	.04	.03	.02
324	Dan Gladden	.04	.03	.02
325	Gary Carter	.15	.11	.06
326	Tracy Jones	.10	.08	.04
327	Floyd Youmans	.04	.03	.02
328	Bill Dawley	.04	.03	.02
329	*Paul Noce*	.10	.08	.04
330	Angel Salazar	.04	.03	.02
331	Goose Gossage	.12	.09	.05
332	George Frazier	.04	.03	.02
333	Ruppert Jones	.04	.03	.02
334	Billy Jo Robidoux	.04	.03	.02
335	Mike Scott	.10	.08	.04
336	Randy Myers	.10	.08	.04
337	Bob Sebra	.04	.03	.02
338	Eric Show	.06	.05	.02
339	Mitch Williams	.06	.05	.02
340	Paul Molitor	.10	.08	.04
341	Gus Polidor	.04	.03	.02
342	Steve Trout	.04	.03	.02
343	Jerry Don Gleaton	.04	.03	.02
344	Bob Knepper	.06	.05	.02
345	Mitch Webster	.06	.05	.02
346	John Morris	.04	.03	.02
347	Andy Hawkins	.04	.03	.02
348	Dave Leiper	.04	.03	.02
349	Ernest Riles	.04	.03	.02
350	Dwight Gooden	.40	.30	.15
351	Dave Righetti	.12	.09	.05
352	Pat Dodson	.04	.03	.02
353	John Habyan	.04	.03	.02
354	Jim Deshaies	.06	.05	.02
355	Butch Wynegar	.04	.03	.02
356	Bryn Smith	.04	.03	.02
357	Matt Young	.04	.03	.02
358	*Tom Pagnozzi*	.12	.09	.05
359	Floyd Rayford	.04	.03	.02
360	Darryl Strawberry	.30	.25	.12
361	Sal Butera	.04	.03	.02
362	Domingo Ramos	.04	.03	.02
363	Chris Brown	.06	.05	.02
364	Jose Gonzalez	.04	.03	.02
365	Dave Smith	.06	.05	.02
366	Andy McGaffigan	.04	.03	.02
367	Stan Javier	.04	.03	.02
368	Henry Cotto	.04	.03	.02
369	Mike Birkbeck	.06	.05	.02
370	Len Dykstra	.08	.06	.03
371	Dave Collins	.06	.05	.02
372	Spike Owen	.04	.03	.02
373	Geno Petralli	.04	.03	.02
374	Ron Karkovice	.04	.03	.02
375	Shane Rawley	.06	.05	.02
376	*DeWayne Buice*	.15	.11	.06
377	*Bill Pecota*	.15	.11	.06
378	Leon Durham	.06	.05	.02
379	Ed Olwine	.04	.03	.02
380	Bruce Hurst	.08	.06	.03
381	Bob McClure	.04	.03	.02
382	Mark Thurmond	.04	.03	.02
383	Buddy Biancalana	.04	.03	.02
384	Tim Conroy	.04	.03	.02
385	Tony Gwynn	.25	.20	.10
386	Greg Gross	.04	.03	.02
387	*Barry Lyons*	.12	.09	.05
388	Mike Felder	.04	.03	.02
389	Pat Clements	.04	.03	.02
390	Ken Griffey	.06	.05	.02
391	Mark Davis	.04	.03	.02
392	Jose Rijo	.06	.05	.02
393	Mike Young	.04	.03	.02
394	Willie Fraser	.06	.05	.02
395	Dion James	.06	.05	.02
396	*Steve Shields*	.12	.09	.05
397	Randy St. Claire	.04	.03	.02
398	Danny Jackson	.12	.09	.05
399	Cecil Fielder	.60	.45	.25
400	Keith Hernandez	.15	.11	.06
401	Don Carman	.06	.05	.02
402	*Chuck Crim*	.12	.09	.05
403	Rob Woodward	.04	.03	.02
404	Junior Ortiz	.04	.03	.02
405	Glenn Wilson	.06	.05	.02
406	Ken Howell	.04	.03	.02
407	Jeff Kunkel	.04	.03	.02
408	Jeff Reed	.04	.03	.02
409	Chris James	.10	.08	.04
410	Zane Smith	.06	.05	.02
411	Ken Dixon	.04	.03	.02
412	Ricky Horton	.06	.05	.02
413	Frank DiPino	.04	.03	.02
414	*Shane Mack*	.15	.11	.06
415	Danny Cox	.06	.05	.02
416	Andy Van Slyke	.10	.08	.04
417	Danny Heep	.04	.03	.02
418	John Cangelosi	.04	.03	.02
419a	John Christiansen (incorrect spelling)	.25	.20	.10
419b	John Christensen (correct spelling)	.06	.05	.02
420	*Joey Cora*	.12	.09	.05
421	Mike LaValliere	.06	.05	.02
422	Kelly Gruber	.04	.03	.02
423	Bruce Benedict	.04	.03	.02
424	Len Matuszek	.04	.03	.02
425	Kent Tekulve	.06	.05	.02
426	Rafael Ramirez	.04	.03	.02
427	Mike Flanagan	.06	.05	.02
428	Mike Gallego	.04	.03	.02
429	Juan Castillo	.04	.03	.02
430	Neal Heaton	.04	.03	.02
431	Phil Garner	.04	.03	.02
432	*Mike Dunne*	.20	.15	.08
433	Wallace Johnson	.04	.03	.02
434	Jack O'Connor	.04	.03	.02
435	Steve Jeltz	.04	.03	.02
436	*Donnell Nixon*	.15	.11	.06
437	Jack Lazorko	.04	.03	.02
438	*Keith Comstock*	.12	.09	.05
439	Jeff Robinson	.04	.03	.02
440	Graig Nettles	.08	.06	.03
441	Mel Hall	.06	.05	.02
442	*Gerald Young*	.30	.25	.12
443	Gary Redus	.04	.03	.02
444	Charlie Moore	.04	.03	.02
445	Bill Madlock	.08	.06	.03
446	Mark Clear	.04	.03	.02
447	Greg Booker	.04	.03	.02
448	Rick Schu	.04	.03	.02
449	Ron Kittle	.06	.05	.02
450	Dale Murphy	.30	.25	.12
451	Bob Dernier	.04	.03	.02
452	Dale Mohorcic	.06	.05	.02
453	Rafael Belliard	.04	.03	.02
454	Charlie Puleo	.04	.03	.02
455	Dwayne Murphy	.06	.05	.02
456	Jim Eisenreich	.04	.03	.02
457	David Palmer	.04	.03	.02
458	Dave Stewart	.08	.06	.03
459	Pascual Perez	.06	.05	.02
460	Glenn Davis	.12	.09	.05
461	Dan Petry	.06	.05	.02
462	Jim Winn	.04	.03	.02
463	Darrell Miller	.04	.03	.02
464	Mike Moore	.04	.03	.02
465	Mike LaCoss	.04	.03	.02
466	Steve Farr	.04	.03	.02
467	Jerry Mumphrey	.04	.03	.02
468	Kevin Gross	.06	.05	.02
469	Bruce Bochy	.04	.03	.02
470	Orel Hershiser	.20	.15	.08
471	Eric King	.06	.05	.02
472	*Ellis Burks*	1.50	1.25	.60
473	Darren Daulton	.04	.03	.02
474	Mookie Wilson	.06	.05	.02
475	Frank Viola	.12	.09	.05
476	Ron Robinson	.04	.03	.02
477	Bob Melvin	.04	.03	.02
478	Jeff Musselman	.06	.05	.02
479	Charlie Kerfeld	.04	.03	.02
480	Richard Dotson	.06	.05	.02
481	Kevin Mitchell	.70	.50	.30
482	Gary Roenicke	.04	.03	.02
483	Tim Flannery	.04	.03	.02
484	Rich Yett	.04	.03	.02
485	Pete Incaviglia	.12	.09	.05
486	Rick Cerone	.04	.03	.02
487	Tony Armas	.06	.05	.02
488	Jerry Reed	.04	.03	.02
489	Davey Lopes	.06	.05	.02
490	Frank Tanana	.06	.05	.02
491	Mike Loynd	.04	.03	.02
492	Bruce Ruffin	.06	.05	.02
493	Chris Speier	.04	.03	.02
494	Tom Hume	.04	.03	.02
495	Jesse Orosco	.06	.05	.02
496	*Robby Wine, Jr.*	.12	.09	.05
497	*Jeff Montgomery*	.20	.15	.08
498	Jeff Dedmon	.04	.03	.02
499	Luis Aguayo	.04	.03	.02
500	Reggie Jackson (1968-75 Oakland Athletics)	.20	.15	.08
501	Reggie Jackson (1976 Baltimore Orioles)	.20	.15	.08
502	Reggie Jackson (1977-81 New York Yankees)	.20	.15	.08
503	Reggie Jackson (1982-86 California Angels)	.20	.15	.08
504	Reggie Jackson (1987 Oakland Athletics)	.20	.15	.08
505	Billy Hatcher	.06	.05	.02
506	Ed Lynch	.04	.03	.02
507	Willie Hernandez	.06	.05	.02
508	Jose DeLeon	.06	.05	.02
509	Joel Youngblood	.04	.03	.02
510	Bob Welch	.08	.06	.03
511	Steve Ontiveros	.04	.03	.02
512	Randy Ready	.04	.03	.02
513	Juan Nieves	.06	.05	.02
514	Jeff Russell	.04	.03	.02
515	Von Hayes	.06	.05	.02
516	Mark Gubicza	.10	.08	.04
517	Ken Dayley	.04	.03	.02
518	Don Aase	.04	.03	.02
519	Rick Reuschel	.08	.06	.03
520	*Mike Henneman*	.25	.20	.10
521	Rick Aguilera	.04	.03	.02
522	Jay Howell	.06	.05	.02
523	Ed Correa	.04	.03	.02
524	Manny Trillo	.06	.05	.02
525	Kirk Gibson	.15	.11	.06
526	*Wally Ritchie*	.12	.09	.05
527	Al Nipper	.04	.03	.02
528	Atlee Hammaker	.04	.03	.02
529	Shawon Dunston	.08	.06	.03
530	Jim Clancy	.06	.05	.02
531	Tom Paciorek	.04	.03	.02
532	Joel Skinner	.04	.03	.02
533	Scott Garrelts	.04	.03	.02
534	Tom O'Malley	.04	.03	.02
535	John Franco	.08	.06	.03
536	*Paul Kilgus*	.20	.15	.08
537	Darrell Porter	.06	.05	.02
538	Walt Terrell	.06	.05	.02
539	*Bill Long*	.15	.11	.06
540	George Bell	.20	.15	.08
541	Jeff Sellers	.06	.05	.02
542	*Joe Boever*	.12	.09	.05
543	Steve Howe	.06	.05	.02
544	Scott Sanderson	.04	.03	.02
545	Jack Morris	.15	.11	.06
546	*Todd Benzinger*	.30	.25	.12
547	Steve Henderson	.04	.03	.02
548	Eddie Milner	.04	.03	.02
549	*Jeff Robinson*	.35	.25	.14
550	Cal Ripken, Jr.	.25	.20	.10
551	Jody Davis	.06	.05	.02
552	Kirk McCaskill	.06	.05	.02
553	Craig Lefferts	.04	.03	.02
554	Darnell Coles	.06	.05	.02
555	Phil Niekro	.15	.11	.06
556	Mike Aldrete	.06	.05	.02
557	Pat Perry	.04	.03	.02
558	Juan Agosto	.04	.03	.02
559	Rob Murphy	.06	.05	.02
560	Dennis Rasmussen	.08	.06	.03
561	Manny Lee	.04	.03	.02
562	*Jeff Blauser*	.20	.15	.08
563	Bob Ojeda	.06	.05	.02
564	Dave Dravecky	.06	.05	.02
565	Gene Garber	.04	.03	.02
566	Ron Roenicke	.04	.03	.02
567	*Tommy Hinzo*	.12	.09	.05
568	*Eric Nolte*	.12	.09	.05
569	Ed Hearn	.04	.03	.02
570	*Mark Davidson*	.12	.09	.05
571	*Jim Walewander*	.12	.09	.05
572	Donnie Hill	.04	.03	.02
573	Jamie Moyer	.06	.05	.02
574	Ken Schrom	.04	.03	.02
575	Nolan Ryan	.40	.30	.15
576	Jim Acker	.04	.03	.02
577	Jamie Quirk	.04	.03	.02
578	*Jay Aldrich*	.10	.08	.04
579	Claudell Washington	.06	.05	.02
580	Jeff Leonard	.06	.05	.02
581	Carmen Castillo	.04	.03	.02
582	Daryl Boston	.04	.03	.02
583	*Jeff DeWillis*	.15	.11	.06
584	*John Marzano*	.20	.15	.08
585	Bill Gullickson	.06	.05	.02
586	Andy Allanson	.08	.06	.03
587	Lee Tunnell	.04	.03	.02
588	Gene Nelson	.04	.03	.02
589	Dave LaPoint	.06	.05	.02
590	Harold Baines	.10	.08	.04
591	Bill Buckner	.08	.06	.03
592	Carlton Fisk	.20	.15	.08
593	Rick Manning	.04	.03	.02
594	*Doug Jones*	.35	.25	.14
595	Tom Candiotti	.04	.03	.02
596	Steve Lake	.04	.03	.02
597	*Jose Lind*	.25	.20	.10
598	*Ross Jones*	.12	.09	.05
599	Gary Matthews	.06	.05	.02
600	Fernando Valezuela	.15	.11	.06
601	Dennis Martinez	.06	.05	.02
602	*Les Lancaster*	.15	.11	.06
603	Ozzie Guillen	.06	.05	.02
604	Tony Bernazard	.04	.03	.02
605	Chili Davis	.06	.05	.02
606	Roy Smalley	.04	.03	.02
607	Ivan Calderon	.08	.06	.03
608	Jay Tibbs	.04	.03	.02
609	Guy Hoffman	.04	.03	.02
610	Doyle Alexander	.06	.05	.02
611	Mike Bielecki	.04	.03	.02
612	*Shawn Hillegas*	.15	.11	.06
613	Keith Atherton	.04	.03	.02
614	Eric Plunk	.04	.03	.02
615	Sid Fernandez	.08	.06	.03
616	Dennis Lamp	.04	.03	.02
617	Dave Engle	.04	.03	.02
618	Harry Spilman	.04	.03	.02
619	Don Robinson	.06	.05	.02
620	*John Farrell*	.30	.25	.12
621	*Nelson Liriano*	.15	.11	.06
622	Floyd Bannister	.06	.05	.02
623	Rookie Prospect *(Randy Milligan)*	.50	.40	.20
624	Rookie Prospect (Kevin Elster)	.30	.25	.12
625	Rookie Prospect *(Jody Reed)*	.60	.45	.25
626	Rookie Prospect (Shawn Abner)	.20	.15	.08
627	Rookie Prospect *(Kirt Manwaring)*	.30	.25	.12
628	Rookie Prospect *(Pete Stanicek)*	.20	.15	.08
629	Rookie Prospect *(Rob Ducey)*	.12	.09	.05
630	Rookie Prospect (Steve Kiefer)	.04	.03	.02
631	Rookie Prospect *(Gary Thurman)*	.25	.20	.10
632	Rookie Prospect *(Darrel Akerfelds)*	.12	.09	.05
633	Rookie Prospect (Dave Clark)	.10	.08	.04
634	Rookie Prospect *(Roberto Kelly)*	1.00	.70	.40
635	Rookie Prospect *(Keith Hughes)*	.15	.11	.06
636	Rookie Prospect *(John Davis)*	.15	.11	.06
637	Rookie Prospect *(Mike Devereaux)*	.30	.25	.12
638	Rookie Prospect *(Tom Glavine)*	.35	.25	.14
639	Rookie Prospect *(Keith Miller)*	.25	.20	.10
640	Rookie Prospect *(Chris Gwynn)*	.20	.15	.08
641	Rookie Prospect *(Tim Crews)*	.15	.11	.06
642	Rookie Prospect *(Mackey Sasser)*	.20	.15	.08
643	Rookie Prospect *(Vicente Palacios)*	.15	.11	.06
644	Rookie Prospect (Kevin Romine)	.06	.05	.02
645	Rookie Prospect *(Gregg Jefferies)*	3.50	2.75	1.50
646	Rookie Prospect *(Jeff Treadway)*	.35	.25	.14
647	Rookie Prospect *(Ronnie Gant)*	.80	.60	.30

		MT	NR MT	EX
648	Rookie Sluggers (Mark McGwire, Matt Nokes)	.30	.25	.12
649	Speed and Power (Eric Davis, Tim Raines)	.25	.20	.10
650	Game Breakers (Jack Clark, Don Mattingly)	.60	.45	.25
651	Super Shortstops (Tony Fernandez, Cal Ripken, Jr., Alan Trammell)	.15	.11	.06
652	1987 Highlights (Vince Coleman)	.08	.06	.03
653	1987 Highlights (Kirby Puckett)	.12	.09	.05
654	1987 Highlights (Benito Santiago)	.10	.08	.04
655	1987 Highlights (Juan Nieves)	.06	.05	.02
656	1987 Highlights (Steve Bedrosian)	.06	.05	.02
657	1987 Highlights (Mike Schmidt)	.15	.11	.06
658	1987 Highlights (Don Mattingly)	.60	.45	.25
659	1987 Highlights (Mark McGwire)	.40	.30	.15
660	1987 Highlights (Paul Molitor)	.08	.06	.03

1988 Score Box Panels

This 18-card set, produced by Major League Marketing and manufactured by Optigraphics, is the premiere box-bottom set issued under the Score trademark. The set features 1987 major league All-star players in full-color action poses, framed by a white border. A "1987 All-Star" banner (red or purple) curves above an orange player name block beneath the player photo. Card backs are printed in red, blue, gold and black and carry the card number, player name and position and league logo. Six colorful "Great Moments in Baseball" trivia cards are also included in this set. Each trivia card highlights an historical event at a famous ballpark.

		MT	NR MT	EX
Complete Panel Set:		8.00	6.00	3.25
Complete Singles Set:		3.00	2.25	1.25
Common Panel:		1.50	1.25	.60
Common Single Player:		.15	.11	.06
Panel		1.50	1.25	.60
1	Terry Kennedy	.15	.11	.06
3	Willie Randolph	.15	.11	.06
15	Eric Davis	.50	.40	.20
Panel		2.25	1.75	.90
3	Don Mattingly	.90	.70	.35
5	Cal Ripken, Jr.	.35	.25	.14
11	Jack Clark	.25	.20	.10
Panel		1.75	1.25	.70
4	Wade Boggs	.60	.45	.25
9	Bret Saberhagen	.20	.15	.08
12	Ryne Sandberg	.30	.25	.12
Panel		1.50	1.25	.60
6	George Bell	.25	.20	.10
13	Mike Schmidt	.35	.25	.14
18	Mike Scott	.15	.11	.06
Panel		1.75	1.25	.70
7	Rickey Henderson	.35	.25	.14
16	Andre Dawson	.25	.20	.10
17	Darryl Strawberry	.40	.30	.15
Panel		1.50	1.25	.60
8	Dave Winfield	.25	.20	.10
10	Gary Carter	.20	.15	.08
14	Ozzie Smith	.15	.11	.06

NOTE: A card number in parentheses ( ) indicates the card set is unnumbered.

1988 Score Traded

This 110-card set featuring new rookies and traded veterans is similar in design to the 1988 Score set, except for a change in border color. Individual standard-size player cards (2-1/2" by 3-1/2") feature a bright orange border framing full-figure action photos highlighted by a thin white outline. The player name (in white) is centered in the bottom margin, flanked by three yellow stars lower left and a yellow Score logo lower right. The backs carry full-color player close-ups on a cream-colored background, followed by card number, team name and logo, player personal information and a purple stats chart that lists year-by-year and major league totals. A brief player profile follows the stats chart and, on some cards, information is included about the player's trade or acquisition. The update set also includes 10 Magic Motion 3-D trivia cards.

		MT	NR MT	EX
Complete Set:		80.00	60.00	30.00
Common Player:		.08	.06	.03
1T	Jack Clark	.20	.15	.08
2T	Danny Jackson	.20	.15	.08
3T	Brett Butler	.10	.08	.04
4T	Kurt Stillwell	.12	.09	.05
5T	Tom Brunansky	.15	.11	.06
6T	Dennis Lamp	.08	.06	.03
7T	Jose DeLeon	.10	.08	.04
8T	Tom Herr	.12	.09	.05
9T	Keith Moreland	.10	.08	.04
10T	Kirk Gibson	.20	.15	.08
11T	Bud Black	.08	.06	.03
12T	Rafael Ramirez	.08	.06	.03
13T	Luis Salazar	.08	.06	.03
14T	Goose Gossage	.15	.11	.06
15T	Bob Welch	.15	.11	.06
16T	Vance Law	.10	.08	.04
17T	Ray Knight	.10	.08	.04
18T	Dan Quisenberry	.10	.08	.04
19T	Don Slaught	.08	.06	.03
20T	Lee Smith	.12	.09	.05
21T	Rick Cerone	.08	.06	.03
22T	Pat Tabler	.10	.08	.04
23T	Larry McWilliams	.08	.06	.03
24T	Rick Horton	.10	.08	.04
25T	Graig Nettles	.12	.09	.05
26T	Dan Petry	.10	.08	.04
27T	Joe Rijo	.10	.08	.04
28T	Chili Davis	.10	.08	.04
29T	Dickie Thon	.10	.08	.04
30T	Mackey Sasser(FC)	.15	.11	.06
31T	Mickey Tettleton	.08	.06	.03
32T	Rick Dempsey	.08	.06	.03
33T	Ron Hassey	.08	.06	.03
34T	Phil Bradley	.12	.09	.05
35T	Jay Howell	.10	.08	.04
36T	Bill Buckner	.12	.09	.05
37T	Alfredo Griffin	.10	.08	.04
38T	Gary Pettis	.08	.06	.03
39T	Calvin Schiraldi	.08	.06	.03
40T	John Candelaria	.10	.08	.04
41T	Joe Orsulak	.08	.06	.03
42T	Willie Upshaw	.10	.08	.04
43T	Herm Winningham	.08	.06	.03
44T	Ron Kittle	.12	.09	.05
45T	Bob Dernier	.08	.06	.03
46T	Steve Balboni	.10	.08	.04
47T	Steve Shields	.08	.06	.03
48T	Henry Cotto	.08	.06	.03
49T	Dave Henderson	.10	.08	.04
50T	Dave Parker	.15	.11	.06
51T	Mike Young	.08	.06	.03
52T	Mark Salas	.08	.06	.03
53T	Mike Davis	.08	.06	.03
54T	Rafael Santana	.08	.06	.03
55T	Don Baylor	.15	.11	.06
56T	Dan Pasqua	.12	.09	.05
57T	Ernest Riles	.08	.06	.03
58T	Glenn Hubbard	.08	.06	.03
59T	Mike Smithson	.08	.06	.03
60T	Richard Dotson	.10	.08	.04
61T	Jerry Reuss	.10	.08	.04
62T	Mike Jackson	.10	.08	.04
63T	Floyd Bannister	.10	.08	.04
64T	Jesse Orosco	.10	.08	.04
65T	Larry Parrish	.10	.08	.04
66T	Jeff Bittiger(FC)	.20	.15	.08
67T	Ray Hayward(FC)	.10	.08	.04
68T	Ricky Jordan(FC)	5.00	3.75	2.00
69T	Tommy Gregg(FC)	.12	.09	.05
70T	Brady Anderson(FC)	.50	.40	.20
71T	Jeff Montgomery	.08	.06	.03
72T	Darryl Hamilton(FC)	.35	.25	.14
73T	Cecil Espy(FC)	.10	.08	.04
74T	Greg Briley(FC)	3.00	2.25	1.25
75T	Joey Meyer(FC)	.20	.15	.08
76T	Mike Macfarlane(FC)	.25	.20	.10
77T	Oswald Peraza(FC)	.20	.15	.08
78T	Jack Armstrong(FC)	6.00	4.50	2.50
79T	Don Heinkel(FC)	.20	.15	.08
80T	Mark Grace(FC)	30.00	22.50	12.50
81T	Steve Curry(FC)	.20	.15	.08
82T	Damon Berryhill(FC)	.70	.50	.30
83T	Steve Ellsworth(FC)	.20	.15	.08
84T	Pete Smith(FC)	.12	.09	.05
85T	Jack McDowell	.25	.20	.10
86T	Rob Dibble(FC)	1.50	1.25	.60
87T	Brian Harvey(FC)	.70	.50	.30
88T	John Dopson(FC)	.25	.20	.10
89T	Dave Gallagher(FC)	.25	.20	.10
90T	Todd Stottlemyre(FC)	.80	.60	.30
91T	Mike Schooler(FC)	1.00	.70	.40
92T	Don Gordon(FC)	.08	.06	.03
93T	Sil Campusano(FC)	.25	.20	.10
94T	Jeff Pico(FC)	.25	.20	.10
95T	Jay Buhner(FC)	.30	.25	.12
96T	Nelson Santovenia(FC)	.35	.25	.14
97T	Al Leiter(FC)	.30	.25	.12
98T	Luis Alicea(FC)	.20	.15	.08
99T	Pat Borders(FC)	.25	.20	.10
100T	Chris Sabo(FC)	5.00	3.75	2.00
101T	Tim Belcher(FC)	1.25	.90	.50
102T	Walt Weiss(FC)	2.75	2.00	1.00
103T	Craig Biggio(FC)	3.50	2.75	1.50
104T	Don August(FC)	.25	.20	.10
105T	Roberto Alomar(FC)	7.00	5.25	2.75
106T	Todd Burns(FC)	.30	.25	.12
107T	John Costello(FC)	.20	.15	.08
108T	Melido Perez(FC)	.80	.60	.30
109T	Darrin Jackson(FC)	.12	.09	.05
110T	Orestes Destrade(FC)	.15	.11	.06

1988 Score Young Superstar Series I

This 40-card standard-size set (2-1/2" by 3-1/2" cards) from Optigraphics was divided into five separate 8-card sets. Similar to the company's regular issue, these cards are distinguished by excellent full-color photography on both front and back. The glossy player photos, with team logo in the lower right corner, are centered on a white background and framed by a vivid blue and green border. A player name banner beneath the photo includes the name, position and uniform number. The card backs feature ful-color player closeups beneath a hot pink player name/Score logo banner. Hot pink also frames the personal stats (in green), career stats (in black) and career biography (in blue). The backs also include quotes from well-known baseball authorities discussing player performance. This set was distributed via a write-in offer printed on 1988 Score 17-card package wrappers.

		MT	NR MT	EX
Complete Set:		9.00	6.75	3.50
Common Player:		.10	.08	.04
1	Mark McGwire	1.25	.90	.50
2	Benito Santiago	.30	.25	.12
3	Sam Horn	.25	.20	.10
4	Chris Bosio	.10	.08	.04
5	Matt Nokes	.40	.30	.15
6	Ken Williams	.15	.11	.06
7	Dion James	.10	.08	.04
8	B.J. Surhoff	.25	.20	.10
9	Joe Margrane	.20	.15	.08
10	Kevin Seitzer	.90	.70	.35
11	Stanley Jefferson	.10	.08	.04
12	Devon White	.30	.25	.12
13	Nelson Liriano	.15	.11	.06
14	Chris James	.25	.20	.10
15	Mike Henneman	.15	.11	.06
16	Terry Steinbach	.20	.15	.08
17	John Kruk	.25	.20	.10
18	Matt Williams	.30	.25	.12
19	Kelly Downs	.25	.20	.10
20	Bill Ripken	.15	.11	.06
21	Ozzie Guillen	.10	.08	.04
22	Luis Polonia	.15	.11	.06
23	Dave Magadan	.20	.15	.08
24	Mike Greenwell	1.00	.70	.40
25	Will Clark	.50	.40	.20
26	Mike Dunne	.20	.15	.08
27	Wally Joyner	.50	.40	.20
28	Robby Thompson	.10	.08	.04
29	Ken Caminiti	.20	.15	.08
30	Jose Canseco	1.75	1.25	.70
31	Todd Benzinger	.30	.25	.12
32	Pete Incaviglia	.20	.15	.08
33	John Farrell	.20	.15	.08
34	Casey Candaele	.10	.08	.04
35	Mike Aldrete	.10	.08	.04
36	Ruben Sierra	.40	.30	.15
37	Ellis Burks	1.00	.70	.40
38	Tracy Jones	.20	.15	.08
39	Kal Daniels	.30	.25	.12
40	Cory Snyder	.30	.25	.12

1988 Score Young Superstar Series II

This set of 40 standard-size cards (2-1/2" by 3-1/2") and five Magic trivia cards is part of a double series issued by Score. Each series is divided into five smaller sets of eight baseball cards and one trivia card. The design on both series is similar, except for border color. Series I has blue and green borders. Series II has red and blue borders framing full-color player photos with the player name and team logo printed beneath the photo. The card backs carry full-color head shots and stats in a variety of colors. Young Superstar series were offered via a write-in offer on the backs of 1988 Score card package wrappers. For each 8-card subset, collectors were instructed to send two Score wrappers and $1. Complete sets were offered by a number of hobby dealers nationwide.

		MT	NR MT	EX
Complete Set:		9.00	6.75	3.50
Common Player:		.10	.08	.04
1	Don Mattingly	2.25	1.75	.90
2	Glenn Braggs	.15	.11	.06
3	Dwight Gooden	.70	.50	.30
4	Jose Lind	.25	.20	.10
5	Danny Tartabull	.30	.25	.12
6	Tony Fernandez	.15	.11	.06
7	Julio Franco	.15	.11	.06
8	Andres Galarraga	.30	.25	.12
9	Bobby Bonilla	.25	.20	.10
10	Eric Davis	.70	.50	.30
11	Gerald Young	.25	.20	.10
12	Barry Bonds	.25	.20	.10
13	Jerry Browne	.10	.08	.04
14	Jeff Blauser	.15	.11	.06
15	Mickey Brantley	.10	.08	.04
16	Floyd Youmans	.10	.08	.04
17	Bret Saberhagen	.25	.20	.10
18	Shawon Dunston	.15	.11	.06
19	Len Dykstra	.15	.11	.06
20	Darryl Strawberry	.70	.50	.30
21	Rick Aguilera	.10	.08	.04
22	Ivan Calderon	.10	.08	.04
23	Roger Clemens	.70	.50	.30
24	Vince Coleman	.30	.25	.12
25	Gary Thurman	.25	.20	.10
26	Jeff Treadway	.25	.20	.10
27	Oddibe McDowell	.10	.08	.04
28	Fred McGriff	.40	.30	.15
29	Mark McLemore	.10	.08	.04
30	Jeff Musselman	.10	.08	.04
31	Mitch Williams	.10	.08	.04
32	Dan Plesac	.15	.11	.06
33	Juan Nieves	.10	.08	.04
34	Barry Larkin	.30	.25	.12
35	Greg Mathews	.15	.11	.06
36	Shane Mack	.10	.08	.04
37	Scott Bankhead	.10	.08	.04
38	Eric Bell	.10	.08	.04
39	Greg Swindell	.25	.20	.10
40	Kevin Elster	.20	.15	.08

A player's name in italic type indicates a rookie card.

1989 Score

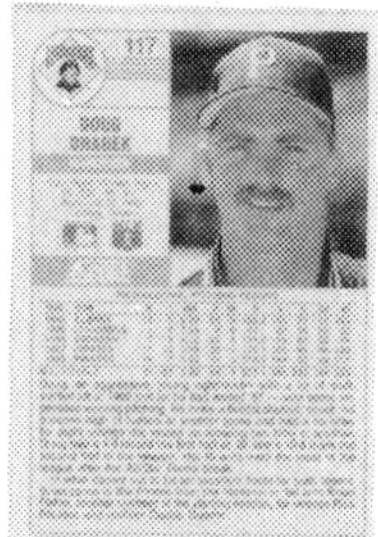

This set of 660 cards plus 56 Magic Motion trivia cards is the second annual basic issue from Score. Full-color player photos highlight 651 individual players and 9 season highlights, including the first Wrigley Field night game. Action photos are framed by thin brightly colored borders (green, cyan blue, purple, orange, red, royal blue) with a baseball diamond logo/player name beneath the photo. Full-color player close-ups (1-5/16" by 1-5/8") are printed on the pastel-colored backs, along with the card number, personal information, stats and career highlights. The cards measure 2-1/2" by 3-1/2" in size.

		MT	NR MT	EX
Complete Set:		25.00	20.00	10.00
Common Player:		.03	.02	.01
1	Jose Canseco	1.25	.90	.50
2	Andre Dawson	.15	.11	.06
3	Mark McGwire	.60	.45	.25
4	Benny Santiago	.12	.09	.05
5	Rick Reuschel	.08	.06	.03
6	Fred McGriff	.35	.25	.14
7	Kal Daniels	.12	.09	.05
8	Gary Gaetti	.12	.09	.05
9	Ellis Burks	.50	.40	.20
10	Darryl Strawberry	.35	.25	.14
11	Julio Franco	.08	.06	.03
12	Lloyd Moseby	.06	.05	.02
13	*Jeff Pico*	.20	.15	.08
14	Johnny Ray	.06	.05	.02
15	Cal Ripken, Jr.	.30	.25	.12
16	Dick Schofield	.03	.02	.01
17	Mel Hall	.06	.05	.02
18	Bill Ripken	.06	.05	.02
19	Brook Jacoby	.08	.06	.03
20	Kirby Puckett	.35	.25	.14
21	Bill Doran	.06	.05	.02
22	Pete O'Brien	.06	.05	.02
23	Matt Nokes	.15	.11	.06
24	Brian Fisher	.06	.05	.02
25	Jack Clark	.12	.09	.05
26	Gary Pettis	.03	.02	.01
27	Dave Valle	.03	.02	.01
28	Willie Wilson	.08	.06	.03
29	Curt Young	.06	.05	.02
30	Dale Murphy	.30	.25	.12
31	Barry Larkin	.10	.08	.04
32	Dave Stewart	.08	.06	.03
33	Mike LaValliere	.06	.05	.02
34	Glen Hubbard	.03	.02	.01
35	Ryne Sandberg	.20	.15	.08
36	Tony Pena	.06	.05	.02
37	Greg Walker	.06	.05	.02
38	Von Hayes	.08	.06	.03
39	Kevin Mitchell	.40	.30	.15
40	Tim Raines	.25	.20	.10
41	Keith Hernandez	.20	.15	.08
42	Keith Moreland	.06	.05	.02
43	Ruben Sierra	.30	.25	.12
44	Chet Lemon	.06	.05	.02
45	Willie Randolph	.06	.05	.02
46	Andy Allanson	.03	.02	.01
47	Candy Maldonado	.06	.05	.02
48	Sid Bream	.06	.05	.02
49	Denny Walling	.03	.02	.01
50	Dave Winfield	.25	.20	.10
51	Alvin Davis	.10	.08	.04
52	Cory Snyder	.15	.11	.06
53	Hubie Brooks	.08	.06	.03
54	Chili Davis	.06	.05	.02
55	Kevin Seitzer	.25	.20	.10
56	Jose Uribe	.03	.02	.01
57	Tony Fernandez	.10	.08	.04
58	Tim Teufel	.03	.02	.01
59	Oddibe McDowell	.06	.05	.02
60	Les Lancaster	.06	.05	.02
61	Billy Hatcher	.06	.05	.02
62	Dan Gladden	.03	.02	.01
63	Marty Barrett	.06	.05	.02
64	Nick Esasky	.06	.05	.02
65	Wally Joyner	.20	.15	.08
66	Mike Greenwell	.60	.45	.25
67	Ken Williams	.06	.05	.02
68	Bob Horner	.08	.06	.03
69	Steve Sax	.12	.09	.05
70	Rickey Henderson	.30	.25	.12
71	Mitch Webster	.06	.05	.02
72	Rob Deer	.06	.05	.02
73	Jim Presley	.06	.05	.02
74	Albert Hall	.03	.02	.01
75a	George Brett ("...game's top hitters at 33..." on back)	.70	.50	.25
75b	George Brett ("...game's top hitters at 35..." on back)	.30	.25	.12
76	Brian Downing	.06	.05	.02
77	Dave Martinez	.06	.05	.02
78	Scott Fletcher	.06	.05	.02
79	Phil Bradley	.08	.06	.03
80	Ozzie Smith	.12	.09	.05
81	Larry Sheets	.06	.05	.02
82	Mike Aldrete	.06	.05	.02
83	Darnell Coles	.06	.05	.02
84	Len Dykstra	.08	.06	.03
85	Jim Rice	.20	.15	.08
86	Jeff Treadway	.10	.08	.04
87	Jose Lind	.08	.06	.03
88	Willie McGee	.10	.08	.04
89	Mickey Brantley	.03	.02	.01
90	Tony Gwynn	.30	.25	.12
91	R.J. Reynolds	.03	.02	.01
92	Milt Thompson	.03	.02	.01
93	Kevin McReynolds	.12	.09	.05
94	Eddie Murray	.25	.20	.10
95	Lance Parrish	.12	.09	.05
96	Ron Kittle	.06	.05	.02
97	Gerald Young	.10	.08	.04
98	Ernie Whitt	.06	.05	.02
99	Jeff Reed	.03	.02	.01
100	Don Mattingly	1.25	.90	.50
101	Gerald Perry	.08	.06	.03
102	Vance Law	.06	.05	.02
103	John Shelby	.03	.02	.01
104	*Chris Sabo*	1.00	.70	.40
105	Danny Tartabull	.15	.11	.06
106	Glenn Wilson	.06	.05	.02
107	Mark Davidson	.06	.05	.02
108	Dave Parker	.10	.08	.04
109	Eric Davis	.35	.25	.14
110	Alan Trammell	.15	.11	.06
111	Ozzie Virgil	.03	.02	.01
112	Frank Tanana	.06	.05	.02
113	Rafael Ramirez	.03	.02	.01
114	Dennis Martinez	.06	.05	.02
115	Jose DeLeon	.06	.05	.02
116	Bob Ojeda	.06	.05	.02
117	Doug Drabek	.06	.05	.02
118	Andy Hawkins	.03	.02	.01
119	Greg Maddux(FC)	.10	.08	.04
120	Cecil Fielder (photo on back reversed)	.70	.50	.30
121	Mike Scioscia	.06	.05	.02
122	Dan Petry	.06	.05	.02
123	Terry Kennedy	.06	.05	.02
124	Kelly Downs	.08	.06	.03
125a	Greg Gross (first name incorrect on card back)	.20	.15	.08
125b	Greg Gross (first name correct on card back)	.08	.06	.03
126	Fred Lynn	.10	.08	.04
127	Barry Bonds	.10	.08	.04
128	Harold Baines	.10	.08	.04
129	Doyle Alexander	.06	.05	.02
130	Kevin Elster	.08	.06	.03
131	Mike Heath	.03	.02	.01
132	Teddy Higuera	.08	.06	.03
133	Charlie Leibrandt	.06	.05	.02
134	Tim Laudner	.03	.02	.01
135a	Ray Knight (photo reversed)	.60	.45	.25
135b	Ray Knight (correct photo)	.08	.06	.03
136	Howard Johnson	.08	.06	.03
137	Terry Pendleton	.08	.06	.03
138	Andy McGaffigan	.03	.02	.01
139	Ken Oberkfell	.03	.02	.01
140	Butch Wynegar	.03	.02	.01
141	Rob Murphy	.03	.02	.01
142	*Rich Renteria*(FC)	.12	.09	.05
143	Jose Guzman	.08	.06	.03
144	Andres Galarraga	.12	.09	.05
145	Rick Horton	.06	.05	.02
146	Frank DiPino	.03	.02	.01
147	Glenn Braggs	.06	.05	.02
148	John Kruk	.06	.05	.02
149	Mike Schmidt	.35	.25	.14
150	Lee Smith	.08	.06	.03
151	Robin Yount	.25	.20	.10
152	Mark Eichhorn	.06	.05	.02
153	DeWayne Buice	.04	.03	.02
154	B.J. Surhoff	.08	.06	.03
155	Vince Coleman	.12	.09	.05
156	Tony Phillips	.03	.02	.01
157	Willie Fraser	.03	.02	.01
158	Lance McCullers	.06	.05	.02
159	Greg Gagne	.03	.02	.01
160	Jesse Barfield	.08	.06	.03
161	Mark Langston	.08	.06	.03
162	Kurt Stillwell	.06	.05	.02
163	Dion James	.03	.02	.01
164	Glenn Davis	.12	.09	.05
165	Walt Weiss	.40	.30	.15
166	Dave Concepcion	.08	.06	.03
167	Alfredo Griffin	.06	.05	.02
168	*Don Heinkel*	.15	.11	.06
169	Luis Rivera(FC)	.03	.02	.01
170	Shane Rawley	.06	.05	.02
171	Darrell Evans	.08	.06	.03
172	Robby Thompson	.06	.05	.02
173	Jody Davis	.06	.05	.02
174	Andy Van Slyke	.12	.09	.05
175	Wade Boggs ("And his .364 career BA..." on back)	1.25	.90	.50
176	Garry Templeton	.06	.05	.02
177	Gary Redus	.03	.02	.01
178	Craig Lefferts	.03	.02	.01
179	Carney Lansford	.06	.05	.02
180	Ron Darling	.10	.08	.04
181	Kirk McCaskill	.06	.05	.02
182	Tony Armas	.06	.05	.02
183	Steve Farr	.03	.02	.01
184	Tom Brunansky	.10	.08	.04
185	*Bryan Harvey*	.20	.15	.08
186	Mike Marshall	.10	.08	.04
187	Bo Diaz	.06	.05	.02
188	Willie Upshaw	.06	.05	.02
189	Mike Pagliarulo	.08	.06	.03
190	Mike Krukow	.06	.05	.02
191	Tommy Herr	.06	.05	.02
192	Jim Pankovits	.03	.02	.01
193	Dwight Evans	.10	.08	.04
194	Kelly Gruber	.03	.02	.01
195	Bobby Bonilla	.10	.08	.04
196	Wallace Johnson	.03	.02	.01
197	Dave Stieb	.08	.06	.03
198	*Pat Borders*	.20	.15	.08
199	Rafael Palmeiro	.12	.09	.05
200	Doc Gooden	.40	.30	.15
201	Pete Incaviglia	.08	.06	.03
202	Chris James	.08	.06	.03
203	Marvell Wynne	.03	.02	.01
204	Pat Sheridan	.03	.02	.01
205	Don Baylor	.08	.06	.03
206	Paul O'Neill	.03	.02	.01
207	Pete Smith	.08	.06	.03
208	Mark McLemore	.03	.02	.01
209	Henry Cotto	.03	.02	.01
210	Kirk Gibson	.15	.11	.06
211	Claudell Washington	.06	.05	.02
212	Randy Bush	.03	.02	.01
213	Joe Carter	.10	.08	.04
214	Bill Buckner	.08	.06	.03
215	Bert Blyleven (year of birth is 1957)	.25	.20	.10
216	Brett Butler	.06	.05	.02
217	Lee Mazzilli	.06	.05	.02
218	Spike Owen	.03	.02	.01
219	Bill Swift	.03	.02	.01
220	Tim Wallach	.08	.06	.03
221	David Cone	.30	.25	.12
222	Don Carman	.06	.05	.02
223	Rich Gossage	.10	.08	.04
224	Bob Walk	.03	.02	.01
225	Dave Righetti	.10	.08	.04
226	Kevin Bass	.06	.05	.02
227	Kevin Gross	.06	.05	.02
228	Tim Burke	.03	.02	.01
229	Rick Mahler	.03	.02	.01
230	Lou Whitaker	.15	.11	.06
231	*Luis Alicea*	.15	.11	.06
232	Roberto Alomar	.40	.30	.15
233	Bob Boone	.06	.05	.02
234	Dickie Thon	.03	.02	.01

		MT	NR MT	EX
235	Shawon Dunston	.08	.06	.03
236	Pete Stanicek	.08	.06	.03
237	*Craig Biggio*	.60	.45	.25
238	Dennis Boyd	.06	.05	.02
239	Tom Candiotti	.03	.02	.01
240	Gary Carter	.15	.11	.06
241	Mike Stanley	.03	.02	.01
242	Ken Phelps	.06	.05	.02
243	Chris Bosio	.03	.02	.01
244	Les Straker	.06	.05	.02
245	Dave Smith	.06	.05	.02
246	John Candelaria	.06	.05	.02
247	Joe Orsulak	.03	.02	.01
248	Storm Davis	.08	.06	.03
249	Floyd Bannister	.06	.05	.02
250	Jack Morris	.12	.09	.05
251	Bret Saberhagen	.12	.09	.05
252	Tom Niedenfuer	.06	.05	.02
253	Neal Heaton	.03	.02	.01
254	Eric Show	.06	.05	.02
255	Juan Samuel	.10	.08	.04
256	Dale Sveum	.06	.05	.02
257	Jim Gott	.03	.02	.01
258	Scott Garrelts	.03	.02	.01
259	Larry McWilliams	.03	.02	.01
260	Steve Bedrosian	.08	.06	.03
261	Jack Howell	.06	.05	.02
262	Jay Tibbs	.03	.02	.01
263	Jamie Moyer	.03	.02	.01
264	Doug Sisk	.03	.02	.01
265	Todd Worrell	.08	.06	.03
266	John Farrell	.08	.06	.03
267	Dave Collins	.06	.05	.02
268	Sid Fernandez	.08	.06	.03
269	Tom Brookens	.03	.02	.01
270	Shane Mack	.06	.05	.02
271	Paul Kilgus	.08	.06	.03
272	Chuck Crim	.03	.02	.01
273	Bob Knepper	.06	.05	.02
274	Mike Moore	.03	.02	.01
275	Guillermo Hernandez	.06	.05	.02
276	Dennis Eckersley	.10	.08	.04
277	Graig Nettles	.10	.08	.04
278	Rich Dotson	.06	.05	.02
279	Larry Herndon	.03	.02	.01
280	Gene Larkin	.08	.06	.03
281	Roger McDowell	.08	.06	.03
282	Greg Swindell	.10	.08	.04
283	Juan Agosto	.03	.02	.01
284	Jeff Robinson	.06	.05	.02
285	Mike Dunne	.08	.06	.03
286	Greg Mathews	.06	.05	.02
287	Kent Tekulve	.06	.05	.02
288	Jerry Mumphrey	.03	.02	.01
289	Jack McDowell	.08	.06	.03
290	Frank Viola	.12	.09	.05
291	Mark Gubicza	.08	.06	.03
292	Dave Schmidt	.03	.02	.01
293	Mike Henneman	.08	.06	.03
294	Jimmy Jones	.03	.02	.01
295	Charlie Hough	.06	.05	.02
296	Rafael Santana	.03	.02	.01
297	Chris Speier	.03	.02	.01
298	Mike Witt	.06	.05	.02
299	Pascual Perez	.06	.05	.02
300	Nolan Ryan	.35	.25	.14
301	Mitch Williams	.06	.05	.02
302	Mookie Wilson	.06	.05	.02
303	Mackey Sasser	.06	.05	.02
304	John Cerutti	.06	.05	.02
305	Jeff Reardon	.08	.06	.03
306	Randy Myers	.08	.06	.03
307	Greg Brock	.06	.05	.02
308	Bob Welch	.08	.06	.03
309	Jeff Robinson	.12	.09	.05
310	Harold Reynolds	.06	.05	.02
311	Jim Walewander	.03	.02	.01
312	Dave Magadan	.08	.06	.03
313	Jim Gantner	.03	.02	.01
314	Walt Terrell	.06	.05	.02
315	Wally Backman	.06	.05	.02
316	Luis Salazar	.03	.02	.01
317	Rick Rhoden	.06	.05	.02
318	Tom Henke	.06	.05	.02
319	*Mike Macfarlane*	.20	.15	.08
320	Dan Plesac	.08	.06	.03
321	Calvin Schiraldi	.03	.02	.01
322	Stan Javier	.03	.02	.01
323	Devon White	.10	.08	.04
324	Scott Bradley	.03	.02	.01
325	Bruce Hurst	.08	.06	.03
326	Manny Lee	.03	.02	.01
327	Rick Aguilera	.03	.02	.01
328	Bruce Ruffin	.03	.02	.01
329	Ed Whitson	.03	.02	.01
330	Bo Jackson	.40	.30	.15
331	Ivan Calderon	.06	.05	.02
332	Mickey Hatcher	.03	.02	.01
333	Barry Jones(FC)	.03	.02	.01
334	Ron Hassey	.03	.02	.01
335	Bill Wegman	.03	.02	.01
336	Damon Berryhill	.15	.11	.06
337	Steve Ontiverso	.03	.02	.01
338	Dan Pasqua	.08	.06	.03
339	Bill Pecota	.06	.05	.02
340	Greg Cadaret	.06	.05	.02
341	Scott Bankhead	.03	.02	.01
342	Ron Guidry	.12	.09	.05
343	Danny Heep	.03	.02	.01
344	Bob Brower	.03	.02	.01
345	Rich Gedman	.06	.05	.02
346	*Nelson Santovenia*	.20	.15	.08
347	George Bell	.20	.15	.08
348	Ted Power	.03	.02	.01
349	Mark Grant	.03	.02	.01
350a	Roger Clemens (778 Wins)	1.00	.70	.40
350b	Roger Clemens (78 Wins)	.40	.30	.15
351	Bill Long	.06	.05	.02
352	Jay Bell(FC)	.06	.05	.02
353	Steve Balboni	.06	.05	.02
354	Bob Kipper	.03	.02	.01
355	Steve Jeltz	.03	.02	.01
356	Jesse Orosco	.06	.05	.02
357	Bob Dernier	.03	.02	.01
358	Mickey Tettleton	.03	.02	.01
359	Duane Ward(FC)	.03	.02	.01
360	Darrin Jackson(FC)	.08	.06	.03
361	Rey Quinones	.03	.02	.01
362	Mark Grace	1.75	1.25	.70
363	Steve Lake	.03	.02	.01
364	Pat Perry	.03	.02	.01
365	Terry Steinbach	.08	.06	.03
366	Alan Ashby	.03	.02	.01
367	Jeff Montgomery	.06	.05	.02
368	Steve Buechele	.03	.02	.01
369	Chris Brown	.06	.05	.02
370	Orel Hershiser	.20	.15	.08
371	Todd Benzinger	.10	.08	.04
372	Ron Gant	.15	.11	.06
373	Paul Assenmacher(FC)	.03	.02	.01
374	Joey Meyer	.08	.06	.03
375	Neil Allen	.03	.02	.01
376	Mike Davis	.06	.05	.02
377	Jeff Parrett(FC)	.08	.06	.03
378	Jay Howell	.06	.05	.02
379	Rafael Belliard	.03	.02	.01
380	Luis Polonia	.06	.05	.02
381	Keith Atherton	.03	.02	.01
382	Kent Hrbek	.15	.11	.06
383	Bob Stanley	.03	.02	.01
384	Dave LaPoint	.06	.05	.02
385	Rance Mulliniks	.03	.02	.01
386	Melido Perez	.08	.06	.03
387	Doug Jones	.10	.08	.04
388	Steve Lyons	.03	.02	.01
389	Alejandro Pena	.06	.05	.02
390	Frank White	.06	.05	.02
391	Pat Tabler	.06	.05	.02
392	Eric Plunk(FC)	.03	.02	.01
393	Mike Maddux(FC)	.03	.02	.01
394	Allan Anderson(FC)	.06	.05	.02
395	Bob Brenly	.03	.02	.01
396	Rick Cerone	.03	.02	.01
397	Scott Terry(FC)	.08	.06	.03
398	Mike Jackson	.06	.05	.02
399	Bobby Thigpen	.08	.06	.03
400	Don Sutton	.12	.09	.05
401	Cecil Espy	.06	.05	.02
402	Junior Ortiz	.03	.02	.01
403	Mike Smithson	.03	.02	.01
404	Bud Black	.03	.02	.01
405	Tom Foley	.03	.02	.01
406	Andres Thomas	.06	.05	.02
407	Rick Sutcliffe	.08	.06	.03
408	Brian Harper	.03	.02	.01
409	John Smiley	.10	.08	.04
410	Juan Nieves	.06	.05	.02
411	Shawn Abner	.08	.06	.03
412	Wes Gardner(FC)	.06	.05	.02
413	Darren Daulton	.03	.02	.01
414	Juan Berenguer	.03	.02	.01
415	Charles Hudson	.03	.02	.01
416	Rick Honeycutt	.03	.02	.01
417	Greg Booker	.03	.02	.01
418	Tim Belcher	.08	.06	.03
419	Don August	.08	.06	.03
420	Dale Mohorcic	.03	.02	.01
421	Steve Lombardozzi	.03	.02	.01
422	Atlee Hammaker	.03	.02	.01
423	Jerry Don Gleaton	.03	.02	.01
424	Scott Bailes(FC)	.03	.02	.01
425	Bruce Sutter	.08	.06	.03
426	Randy Ready	.03	.02	.01
427	Jerry Reed	.03	.02	.01
428	Bryn Smith	.03	.02	.01
429	Tim Leary	.06	.05	.02
430	Mark Clear	.03	.02	.01
431	Terry Leach	.03	.02	.01
432	John Moses	.03	.02	.01
433	Ozzie Guillen	.06	.05	.02
434	Gene Nelson	.03	.02	.01
435	Gary Ward	.06	.05	.02
436	Luis Aguayo	.03	.02	.01
437	Fernando Valenzuela	.15	.11	.06
438	Jeff Russell	.03	.02	.01
439	Cecilio Guante	.03	.02	.01
440	Don Robinson	.03	.02	.01
441	Rick Anderson(FC)	.03	.02	.01
442	Tom Glavine	.08	.06	.03
443	Daryl Boston	.03	.02	.01
444	Joe Price	.03	.02	.01
445	Stewart Cliburn	.03	.02	.01
446	Manny Trillo	.03	.02	.01
447	Joel Skinner	.03	.02	.01
448	Charlie Puleo	.03	.02	.01
449	Carlton Fisk	.12	.09	.05
450	Will Clark	.50	.40	.20
451	Otis Nixon	.03	.02	.01
452	Rick Schu	.03	.02	.01
453	Todd Stottlemyre	.15	.11	.06
454	Tim Birtsas	.03	.02	.01
455	*Dave Gallagher*	.20	.15	.08
456	Barry Lyons	.03	.02	.01
457	Fred Manrique	.06	.05	.02
458	Ernest Riles	.03	.02	.01
459	*Doug Jennings*(FC)	.20	.15	.08
460	Joe Magrane	.08	.06	.03
461	Jamie Quirk	.03	.02	.01
462	*Jack Armstrong*	.50	.40	.20
463	Bobby Witt	.08	.06	.03
464	Keith Miller	.06	.05	.02
465	*Todd Burns*	.30	.25	.12
466	*John Dopson*	.20	.15	.08
467	Rich Yett	.03	.02	.01
468	Craig Reynolds	.03	.02	.01
469	Dave Bergman	.03	.02	.01
470	Rex Hudler	.03	.02	.01
471	Eric King	.03	.02	.01
472	Joaquin Andujar	.06	.05	.02
473	*Sil Campusano*	.20	.15	.08
474	Terry Mulholland(FC)	.03	.02	.01
475	Mike Flanagan	.06	.05	.02
476	Greg Harris	.03	.02	.01
477	Tommy John	.10	.08	.04
478	Dave Anderson	.03	.02	.01
479	Fred Toliver	.03	.02	.01
480	Jimmy Key	.08	.06	.03
481	Donell Nixon	.03	.02	.01
482	Mark Portugal(FC)	.03	.02	.01
483	Tom Pagnozzi	.06	.05	.02
484	Jeff Kunkel	.03	.02	.01
485	Frank Williams	.03	.02	.01
486	Jody Reed	.10	.08	.04
487	Roberto Kelly	.25	.20	.10
488	Shawn Hillegas	.06	.05	.02
489	Jerry Reuss	.06	.05	.02
490	Mark Davis	.03	.02	.01
491	Jeff Sellers	.03	.02	.01
492	Zane Smith	.06	.05	.02
493	Al Newman(FC)	.03	.02	.01
494	Mike Young	.03	.02	.01
495	Larry Parrish	.06	.05	.02
496	Herm Winningham	.03	.02	.01
497	Carmen Castillo	.03	.02	.01
498	Joe Hesketh	.03	.02	.01
499	Darrell Miller	.03	.02	.01
500	Mike LaCoss	.03	.02	.01
501	Charlie Lea	.03	.02	.01
502	Bruce Benedict	.03	.02	.01
503	Chuck Finley(FC)	.03	.02	.01
504	Brad Wellman(FC)	.03	.02	.01
505	Tim Crews	.06	.05	.02
506	Ken Gerhart	.06	.05	.02
507	Brian Holton (Born: Jan. 25, 1965 Denver, CO)	.20	.15	.08
508	Dennis Lamp	.03	.02	.01
509	Bobby Meacham (1984 Games is 099)	.20	.15	.08
510	Tracy Jones	.08	.06	.03
511	Mike Fitzgerald	.03	.02	.01
512	*Jeff Bittiger*	.12	.09	.05
513	Tim Flannery	.03	.02	.01
514	Ray Hayward(FC)	.03	.02	.01
515	Dave Leiper	.03	.02	.01
516	Rod Scurry	.03	.02	.01
517	Carmelo Martinez	.03	.02	.01
518	Curtis Wilkerson	.03	.02	.01
519	Stan Jefferson	.03	.02	.01
520	Dan Quisenberry	.06	.05	.02
521	Lloyd McClendon(FC)	.03	.02	.01
522	Steve Trout	.03	.02	.01
523	Larry Andersen	.03	.02	.01
524	Don Aase	.03	.02	.01
525	Bob Forsch	.06	.05	.02
526	Geno Petralli	.03	.02	.01
527	Angel Salazar	.03	.02	.01
528	*Mike Schooler*	.20	.15	.08
529	Jose Oquendo	.03	.02	.01
530	Jay Buhner	.10	.08	.04
531	Tom Bolton(FC)	.06	.05	.02
532	Al Nipper	.03	.02	.01
533	Dave Henderson	.08	.06	.03
534	*John Costello*(FC)	.20	.15	.08
535	Donnie Moore	.03	.02	.01
536	Mike Laga	.03	.02	.01
537	Mike Gallego	.03	.02	.01
538	Jim Clancy	.06	.05	.02
539	Joel Youngblood	.03	.02	.01
540	Rick Leach	.03	.02	.01
541	Kevin Romine	.03	.02	.01
542	Mark Salas	.03	.02	.01
543	Greg Minton	.03	.02	.01
544	Dave Palmer	.03	.02	.01
545	Dwayne Murphy	.06	.05	.02
546	Jim Deshaies	.03	.02	.01
547	Don Gordon(FC)	.03	.02	.01
548	*Ricky Jordan*	1.25	.90	.50
549	Mike Boddicker	.06	.05	.02
550	Mike Scott	.10	.08	.04
551	Jeff Ballard(FC)	.08	.06	.03
552a	Jose Rijo (uniform number #24 on card back)	.20	.15	.08
552b	Jose Rijo (uniforn number #27 on card back)	.08	.06	.03
553	Danny Darwin	.03	.02	.01
554	Tom Browning	.08	.06	.03
555	Danny Jackson	.12	.09	.05
556	Rick Dempsey	.06	.05	.02
557	Jeffrey Leonard	.06	.05	.02
558	Jeff Musselman	.06	.05	.02
559	Ron Robinson	.03	.02	.01
560	John Tudor	.08	.06	.03
561	Don Slaught	.03	.02	.01
562	Dennis Rasmussen	.08	.06	.03
563	*Brady Anderson*	.30	.25	.12
564	Pedro Guerrero	.12	.09	.05
565	Paul Molitor	.12	.09	.05
566	*Terry Clark*(FC)	.15	.11	.06
567	Terry Puhl	.03	.02	.01
568	Mike Campbell(FC)	.08	.06	.03
569	Paul Mirabella	.03	.02	.01
570	Jeff Hamilton(FC)	.06	.05	.02
571	*Oswald Peraza*	.20	.15	.08
572	Bob McClure	.03	.02	.01
573	*Jose Bautista*(FC)	.15	.11	.06
574	Alex Trevino	.03	.02	.01
575	John Franco	.08	.06	.03
576	*Mark Parent*(FC)	.15	.11	.06
577	Nelson Liriano	.06	.05	.02
578	Steve Shields	.03	.02	.01
579	Odell Jones	.03	.02	.01
580	Al Leiter	.20	.15	.08
581	Dave Stapleton(FC)	.06	.05	.02
582	1988 World Series (Jose Canseco, Kirk Gibson, Orel Hershiser, Dave Stewart)	.20	.15	.08
583	Donnie Hill	.03	.02	.01
584	Chuck Jackson	.06	.05	.02
585	Rene Gonzales(FC)	.06	.05	.02
586	Tracy Woodson(FC)	.08	.06	.03
587	Jim Adduci(FC)	.03	.02	.01
588	Mario Soto	.06	.05	.02
589	Jeff Blauser	.08	.06	.03
590	Jim Traber	.06	.05	.02
591	Jon Perlman(FC)	.03	.02	.01
592	Mark Williamson(FC)	.06	.05	.02
593	Dave Meads	.03	.02	.01
594	Jim Eisenreich	.03	.02	.01
595	*Paul Gibson*(FC)	.15	.11	.06
596	Mike Birkbeck	.03	.02	.01
597	Terry Francona	.03	.02	.01

		MT	NR MT	EX
598	Paul Zuvella(FC)	.03	.02	.01
599	Franklin Stubbs	.03	.02	.01
600	Gregg Jefferies	1.50	1.25	.60
601	John Cangelosi	.03	.02	.01
602	Mike Sharperson(FC)	.03	.02	.01
603	Mike Diaz	.06	.05	.02
604	*Gary Varsho*(FC)	.20	.15	.08
605	*Terry Blocker*(FC)	.12	.09	.05
606	Charlie O'Brien(FC)	.03	.02	.01
607	Jim Eppard(FC)	.08	.06	.03
608	John Davis	.03	.02	.01
609	Ken Griffey, Sr.	.08	.06	.03
610	Buddy Bell	.06	.05	.02
611	Ted Simmons	.08	.06	.03
612	Matt Williams	.10	.08	.04
613	Danny Cox	.06	.05	.02
614	Al Pedrique	.03	.02	.01
615	Ron Oester	.03	.02	.01
616	*John Smoltz*(FC)	.50	.40	.20
617	Bob Melvin	.03	.02	.01
618	*Rob Dibble*	.25	.20	.10
619	Kirt Manwaring	.10	.08	.04
620	1989 Rookie (Felix Fermin)(FC)	.06	.05	.02
621	1989 Rookie *(Doug Dascenzo)*(FC)	.25	.20	.10
622	1989 Rookie *(Bill Brennan)*(FC)	.20	.15	.08
623	1989 Rookie *(Carlos Quintana)*(FC)	.40	.30	.15
624	1989 Rookie *(Mike Harkey)*(FC)	.40	.30	.15
625	1989 Rookie *(Gary Sheffield)*(FC)	1.50	1.25	.60
626	1989 Rookie (Tom Prince)(FC)	.08	.06	.03
627	1989 Rookie *(Steve Searcy)*(FC)	.25	.20	.10
628	1989 Rookie *(Charlie Hayes)*(FC)	.25	.20	.10
629	1989 Rookie *(Felix Jose)*(FC)	.35	.25	.14
630	1989 Rookie *(Sandy Alomar)*(FC)	1.50	1.25	.60
631	1989 Rookie *(Derek Lilliquist)*(FC)	.40	.30	.15
632	1989 Rookie (Geronimo Berroa)(FC)	.06	.05	.02
633	1989 Rookie *(Luis Medina)*(FC)	.35	.25	.14
634	1989 Rookie *(Tom Gordon)*(FC)	1.00	.70	.40
635	1989 Rookie *(Ramon Martinez)*(FC)	1.00	.70	.40
636	1989 Rookie *(Craig Worthington)*(FC)	.50	.40	.20
637	1989 Rookie (Edgar Martinez)(FC)	.35	.25	.14
638	1989 Rookie *(Chad Krueter)*(FC)	.20	.15	.08
639	1989 Rookie *(Ron Jones)*(FC)	.30	.25	.12
640	1989 Rookie *(Van Snider)*(FC)	.20	.15	.08
641	1989 Rookie *(Lance Blankenship)*(FC)	.25	.20	.10
642	1989 Rookie *(Dwight Smith)*(FC)	3.00	2.25	1.25
643	1989 Rookie *(Cameron Drew)*(FC)	.20	.15	.08
644	1989 Rookie *(Jerald Clark)*(FC)	.20	.15	.08
645	1989 Rookie *(Randy Johnson)*(FC)	.50	.40	.20
646	1989 Rookie *(Norm Charlton)*(FC)	.20	.15	.08
647	1989 Rookie (Todd Frohwirth)(FC)	.08	.06	.03
648	1989 Rookie *(Luis de los Santos)*(FC)	.20	.15	.08
649	1989 Rookie *(Tim Jones)*(FC)	.15	.11	.06
650	1989 Rookie *(Dave West)*(FC)	.40	.30	.15
651	1989 Rookie *(Bob Milacki)*(FC)	.25	.20	.10
652	1988 Highlight (Wrigley Field)	.06	.05	.02
653	1988 Highlight (Orel Hershiser)	.10	.08	.04
654a	1988 Highlight (Wade Boggs) ("...sixth consecutive seaason..." on back)	1.00	.70	.40
654b	1988 Highlight (Wade Boggs) ("...sixth consecutive season..." on back)	.30	.25	.12
655	1988 Highlight (Jose Canseco)	.60	.45	.25
656	1988 Highlight (Doug Jones)	.06	.05	.02
657	1988 Highlight (Rickey Henderson)	.12	.09	.05
658	1988 Highlight (Tom Browning)	.06	.05	.02
659	1988 Highlight (Mike Greenwell)	.30	.25	.12
660	1988 Highlight (A.L. Win Streak)	.06	.05	.02

1989 Score Rising Star

Similar in design to the Score Superstar set, this 100-card set showcased a host of rookies including Gary Sheffield and Gregg Jefferies. The full-color action photos are surrounded by a bright blue border with a green inner highlight line. The Score logo appears in the upper left in green and white. The player's name, position and team are found at the bottom. The flip sides display a full-color close-up of the player above his name and career highlights. The card number and player's rookie year are featured to the right. A "Rising Star" headline highlights the top border. Like the "Score Superstar" the Score "Rising Star" set was marketed as a combination with a related magazine. "1988-89 Baseball's 100 Hottest Rookies" accompanies the set which also includes six Magic Motion baseball trivia cards featuring "Rookies to Remember." The magazine/card sets were available at a select group of retailers.

		MT	NR MT	EX
Complete Set:		12.00	9.00	4.75
Common Player:		.07	.05	.03
1	Gregg Jefferies	.80	.60	.30
2	Vicente Palacios	.15	.11	.06
3	Cameron Drew	.25	.20	.10
4	Doug Dascenzo	.12	.09	.05
5	Luis Medina	.12	.09	.05
6	Craig Worthington	.20	.15	.08
7	Rob Ducey	.08	.06	.04
8	Hal Morris	.10	.08	.04
9	Bill Brennan	.07	.05	.03
10	Gary Sheffield	.80	.60	.30
11	Mike Devereaux	.10	.08	.04
12	Hensley Meulens	.40	.30	.15
13	Carlos Quintana	.20	.15	.08
14	Todd Frohwirth	.07	.05	.03
15	Scott Lusader	.09	.07	.04
16	Mark Carreon	.15	.11	.06
17	Torey Lovullo	.20	.15	.08
18	Randy Velarde	.12	.09	.05
19	Billy Bean	.09	.07	.04
20	Lance Blankenship	.15	.11	.06
21	Chris Gwynn	.15	.11	.06
22	Felix Jose	.20	.15	.08
23	Derek Lilliquist	.20	.15	.08
24	Gary Thurman	.07	.05	.03
25	Ron Jones	.20	.15	.08
26	Dave Justice	.40	.30	.15
27	Johnny Paredes	.08	.06	.03
28	Tim Jones	.10	.08	.04
29	Jose Gonzalez	.40	.30	.15
30	Geronimo Berroa	.15	.11	.06
31	Trevor Wilson	.12	.09	.05
32	Morris Madden	.30	.25	.12
33	Lance Johnson	.15	.11	.06
34	Marvin Freeman	.07	.05	.03
35	Jose Cecena	.07	.05	.03
36	Jim Corsi	.07	.05	.03
37	Rolando Roomes	.25	.20	.10
38	Scott Medvin	.07	.05	.03
39	Charlie Hayes	.20	.15	.08
40	Edgar Martinez	.15	.11	.06
41	Van Snider	.20	.15	.08
42	John Fishel	.07	.05	.02
43	Bruce Fields	.07	.05	.03
44	Darryl Hamilton	.09	.07	.04
45	Tom Prince	.09	.07	.03
46	Kirt Manwaring	.20	.15	.08
47	Steve Searcy	.12	.09	.05
48	Mike Harkey	.20	.15	.08
49	German Gonzalez	.07	.05	.03
50	Tony Perezchica	.07	.05	.03
51	Chad Kreuter	.15	.11	.06
52	Luis de los Santos	.10	.08	.04
53	Steve Curry	.07	.05	.03
54	Greg Bailey	.30	.25	.12
55	Ramon Martinez	.30	.25	.12
56	Ron Tingley	.07	.05	.03
57	Randy Kramer	.07	.05	.03
58	Alex Madrid	.07	.05	.03
59	Kevin Reimer	.15	.11	.06
60	Dave Otto	.07	.05	.03
61	Ken Patterson	.07	.05	.03
62	Keith Miller	.10	.08	.04
63	Randy Johnson	.10	.08	.04
64	Dwight Smith	1.00	.70	.40
65	Eric Yelding	.20	.15	.08
66	Bob Geren	.40	.30	.15
67	Shane Turner	.25	.20	.10
68	Tom Gordon	.70	.50	.30
69	Jeff Huson	.30	.25	.12
70	Marty Brown	.25	.20	.10
71	Nelson Santovenia	.20	.15	.08
72	Roberto Alomar	.20	.15	.08
73	Mike Schooler	.15	.11	.06
74	Pete Smith	.10	.08	.04
75	John Costello	.07	.05	.03
76	Chris Sabo	.20	.15	.08
77	Damon Berryhill	.09	.07	.04
78	Mark Grace	.60	.45	.25
79	Melido Perez	.07	.05	.03
80	Al Leiter	.07	.05	.03
81	Todd Stottlemyre	.20	.15	.08
82	Mackey Sasser	.07	.05	.03
83	Don August	.07	.05	.03
84	Jeff Treadway	.07	.05	.03
85	Jody Reed	.09	.07	.05
86	Mike Campbell	.07	.05	.03
87	Ron Gant	.09	.07	.04
88	Ricky Jordan	.30	.25	.12
89	Terry Clark	.07	.05	.03
90	Roberto Kelly	.20	.15	.08
91	Pat Borders	.20	.15	.08
92	Bryan Harvey	.20	.15	.08
93	Joey Meyer	.20	.15	.08
94	Tim Belcher	.25	.20	.10
95	Walt Weiss	.15	.11	.06
96	Dave Gallagher	.15	.11	.06
97	Mike Macfarlane	.07	.05	.03
98	Craig Biggio	.30	.25	.12
99	Jack Armstrong	.07	.05	.03
100	Todd Burns	.07	.05	.03

1989 Score Superstar

This 100-card set features full-color action photos of baseball's superstars, and also includes six Magic Motion "Rookies to Remember" baseball trivia cards. The card fronts contain a bright red border with a blue line inside highlighting the photo. The Score logo appears in the bottom left corner. The player ID is displayed in unique fashion using overlapping triangles in white, green, and yellow. The flip side features a full-color player close-up directly beneath a bright red "Superstar" headline. The set was marketed along with the magazine "1989 Baseball's 100 Hottest Players". The magazine/card set combo was available at select retailers.

		MT	NR MT	EX
Complete Set:		10.00	7.50	4.00
Common Player:		.06	.05	.02
1	Jose Canseco	1.00	.70	.40
2	David Cone	.15	.11	.06
3	Dave Winfield	.15	.11	.06
4	George Brett	.15	.11	.06
5	Frank Viola	.09	.07	.05
6	Cory Snyder	.06	.05	.02
7	Alan Trammell	.09	.07	.04
8	Dwight Evans	.09	.07	.04
9	Tim Leary	.06	.05	.03
10	Don Mattingly	1.25	.90	.50
11	Kirby Puckett	.30	.25	.12
12	Carney Lansford	.06	.05	.02
13	Dennis Martinez	.06	.05	.02
14	Kent Hrbek	.10	.08	.04
15	Doc Gooden	.30	.25	.12
16	Dennis Eckersley	.08	.06	.03
17	Kevin Seitzer	.08	.06	.03
18	Lee Smith	.06	.05	.02
19	Danny Tartabull	.15	.11	.06
20	Gerald Perry	.06	.05	.02
21	Gary Gaetti	.10	.08	.04
22	Rick Reuschel	.08	.06	.03
23	Keith Hernandez	.08	.06	.03
24	Jeff Reardon	.06	.05	.02
25	Mark McGwire	.80	.60	.30
26	Juan Samuel	.06	.05	.02
27	Jack Clark	.06	.05	.02
28	Robin Yount	.15	.11	.06
29	Steve Bedrosian	.06	.05	.02
30	Kirk Gibson	.08	.06	.03
31	Barry Bonds	.08	.06	.03
32	Dan Plesac	.06	.05	.02
33	Steve Sax	.06	.05	.02
34	Jeff Robinson	.06	.05	.02
35	Orel Hershiser	.10	.08	.04
36	Julio Franco	.08	.06	.03
37	Dave Righetti	.06	.05	.02
38	Bob Knepper	.06	.05	.02
39	Carlton Fisk	.08	.06	.03
41	Doug Jones	.06	.05	.02
42	Bobby Bonilla	.20	.15	.08
43	Ellis Burks	.30	.25	.12
44	Pedro Guerrero	.15	.11	.06
45	Rickey Henderson	.25	.20	.12
46	Glenn Davis	.10	.08	.04
47	Benny Santiago	.15	.11	.06
48	Greg Maddux	.20	.15	.08
49	Teddy Higuera	.06	.05	.02
50	Darryl Strawberry	.30	.25	.12
51	Mike Scott	.08	.06	.03
52	Mike Henneman	.06	.05	.02
53	Eric Davis	.35	.25	.12
54	Paul Molitor	.09	.07	.04
55	Rafael Palmeiro	.06	.05	.02
56	Joe Carter	.09	.07	.05
57	Ryne Sandberg	.15	.11	.06
58	Tony Fernandez	.08	.06	.03
59	Barry Larkin	.10	.08	.04
60	Ozzie Guillen	.06	.05	.02
61	Tom Browning	.06	.05	.02
62	Mark Davis	.08	.06	.03
63	Tom Henke	.06	.05	.02

		MT	NR MT	EX
64	Nolan Ryan	.60	.45	.25
65	Fred McGriff	.30	.25	.12
66	Dale Murphy	.10	.08	.06
67	Mark Langston	.10	.08	.06
68	Bobby Thigpen	.06	.05	.02
69	Mark Gubicza	.08	.06	.03
70	Mike Greenwell	.50	.40	.20
71	Ron Darling	.06	.05	.02
72	Gerald Young	.06	.05	.02
73	Wally Joyner	.10	.08	.04
74	Andres Galarraga	.10	.08	.04
75	Danny Jackson	.06	.05	.02
76	Mike Schmidt	.25	.20	.10
77	Cal Ripken, Jr.	.15	.11	.06
78	Alvin Davis	.08	.06	.03
79	Bruce Hurst	.06	.05	.02
80	Andre Dawson	.12	.09	.05
81	Bob Boone	.06	.05	.02
82	Harold Reynolds	.06	.05	.02
83	Eddie Murray	.06	.05	.02
84	Robby Thompson	.06	.05	.02
85	Will Clark	1.00	.70	.40
86	Vince Coleman	.09	.07	.04
87	Doug Drabek	.06	.05	.02
88	Ozzie Smith	.08	.06	.03
89	Bob Welch	.06	.05	.02
90	Roger Clemens	.25	.20	.10
91	George Bell	.08	.06	.03
92	Andy Van Slyke	.08	.06	.03
93	Willie McGee	.06	.05	.02
94	Todd Worrell	.06	.05	.02
95	Tim Raines	.06	.05	.02
96	Kevin McReynolds	.10	.08	.04
97	John Franco	.06	.05	.02
98	Jim Gott	.06	.05	.02
99	Johnny Ray	.06	.05	.02
100	Wade Boggs	.80	.60	.30

1989 Score Traded

Score issued its second consecutive traded set in 1989 to supplement and update its regular set. The 110-card traded set features the same basic card design as the regular 1989 Score set. The set consists of rookies and traded players pictured with correct teams. The set was sold by hobby dealers in a special box that included an assortment of "Magic Motion" trivia cards.

		MT	NR MT	EX
	Complete Set:	15.00	11.00	6.00
	Common Player:	.06	.05	.02
1T	Rafael Palmeiro	.10	.08	.04
2T	Nolan Ryan	1.50	1.25	.60
3T	Jack Clark	.10	.08	.04
4T	Dave LaPoint	.06	.05	.02
5T	Mike Moore	.08	.06	.03
6T	Pete O'Brien	.06	.05	.02
7T	Jeffrey Leonard	.06	.05	.02
8T	Rob Murphy	.06	.05	.02
9T	Tom Herr	.06	.05	.02
10T	Claudell Washington	.06	.05	.02
11T	Mike Pagliarulo	.06	.05	.02
12T	Steve Lake	.06	.05	.02
13T	Spike Owen	.06	.05	.02
14T	Andy Hawkins	.06	.05	.02
15T	Todd Benzinger	.06	.05	.02
16T	Mookie Wilson	.06	.05	.03
17T	Bert Blyleven	.08	.06	.03
18T	Jeff Treadway	.06	.05	.02
19T	Bruce Hurst	.08	.06	.03
20T	Steve Sax	.12	.09	.05
21T	Juan Samuel	.06	.05	.02
22T	Jesse Barfield	.06	.05	.02
23T	Carmelo Castillo	.06	.05	.02
24T	Terry Leach	.06	.05	.02
25T	Mark Langston	.12	.09	.05
26T	Eric King	.06	.05	.02
27T	Steve Balboni	.06	.05	.02
28T	Len Dykstra	.06	.05	.02
29T	Keith Moreland	.06	.05	.02
30T	Terry Kennedy	.06	.05	.02
31T	Eddie Murray	.12	.09	.05
32T	Mitch Williams	.10	.08	.04
33T	Jeff Parrett	.06	.05	.02
34T	Wally Backman	.06	.05	.02
35T	Julio Franco	.10	.08	.04
36T	Lance Parrish	.06	.05	.02
37T	Nick Esasky	.06	.05	.02
38T	Luis Polonia	.06	.05	.02
39T	Kevin Gross	.06	.05	.02
40T	John Dopson	.06	.05	.02
41T	Willie Randolph	.08	.06	.03
42T	Jim Clancy	.06	.05	.02
43T	Tracy Jones	.06	.05	.02
44T	Phil Bradley	.06	.05	.02
45T	Milt Thompson	.06	.05	.02
46T	Chris James	.06	.05	.02
47T	Scott Fletcher	.06	.05	.02
48T	Kal Daniels	.08	.06	.03
49T	Steve Bedrosian	.06	.05	.02
50T	Rickey Henderson	.40	.30	.15
51T	Dion James	.06	.05	.02
52T	Tim Leary	.06	.05	.02
53T	Roger McDowell	.06	.05	.02
54T	Mel Hall	.06	.05	.02
55T	Dickie Thon	.06	.05	.02
56T	Zane Smith	.06	.05	.02
57T	Danny Heep	.06	.05	.02
58T	Bob McClure	.06	.05	.02
59T	Brian Holton	.06	.05	.02
60T	Randy Ready	.06	.05	.02
61T	Bob Melvin	.06	.05	.02
62T	Harold Baines	.08	.06	.03
63T	Lance McCullers	.06	.05	.02
64T	Jody Davis	.06	.05	.02
65T	Darrell Evans	.06	.05	.02
66T	Joel Youngblood	.08	.06	.03
67T	Frank Viola	.08	.06	.03
68T	Mike Aldrete	.06	.05	.02
69T	Greg Cadaret	.06	.05	.02
70T	John Kruk	.06	.05	.02
71T	Pat Sheridan	.06	.05	.02
72T	Oddibe McDowell	.06	.05	.02
73T	Tom Brookens	.06	.05	.02
74T	Bob Boone	.08	.06	.03
75T	Walt Terrell	.06	.05	.02
76T	Joel Skinner	.06	.05	.02
77T	Randy Johnson	.10	.08	.04
78T	Felix Fermin	.06	.05	.03
79T	Rick Mahler	.06	.05	.03
80T	Rich Dotson	.06	.05	.03
81T	Cris Carpenter(FC)	.20	.15	.08
82T	Bill Spiers(FC)	.35	.25	.14
83T	Junior Felix(FC)	1.25	.90	.50
84T	Joe Girardi(FC)	.30	.25	.12
85T	Jerome Walton(FC)	2.50	2.00	1.00
86T	Greg Litton(FC)	.25	.20	.10
87T	Greg Harris(FC)	.20	.15	.08
88T	Jim Abbott(FC)	2.00	1.50	.80
89T	Kevin Brown(FC)	.30	.25	.12
90T	John Wetteland(FC)	.50	.40	.20
91T	Gary Wayne(FC)	.20	.15	.08
92T	Rich Monteleone(FC)	.25	.20	.10
93T	Bob Geren(FC)	.50	.40	.20
94T	Clay Parker(FC)	.20	.15	.08
95T	Steve Finley(FC)	.35	.25	.14
96T	Gregg Olson(FC)	1.25	.90	.50
97T	Ken Patterson(FC)	.15	.11	.06
98T	Ken Hill(FC)	.20	.15	.08
99T	Scott Scudder(FC)	.35	.25	.14
100T	Ken Griffey, Jr.(FC)	6.00	4.50	2.50
101T	Jeff Brantley(FC)	.25	.20	.10
102T	Donn Pall(FC)	.15	.11	.06
103T	Carlos Martinez(FC)	.30	.25	.12
104T	Joe Oliver(FC)	.40	.30	.15
105T	Omar Vizquel(FC)	.25	.20	.10
106T	Joey Belle(FC)	1.00	.70	.40
107T	Kenny Rogers(FC)	.20	.15	.08
108T	Mark Carreon(FC)	.15	.11	.06
109T	Rolando Roomes(FC)	.20	.15	.08
110T	Pete Harnsisch(FC)	.20	.15	.08

1989 Score Yankees

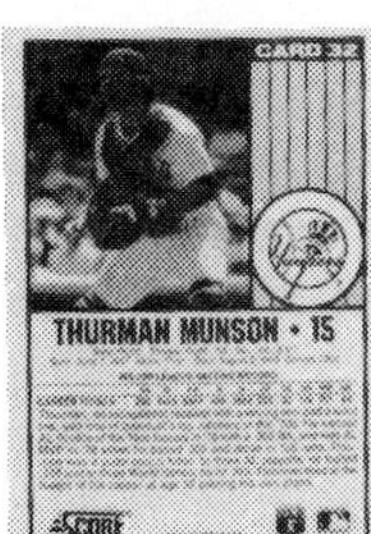

This 33-card New York Yankee team set was produced by Score as an in-stadium promotion in 1989 and was distributed to fans attending the July 29 game at Yankee Stadium. The standard-size cards include a full-color player photo with a line drawing of the famous Yankee Stadium facade running along the top of the card. The player's name, "New York Yankees" and position appear below the photo. A second full-color photo is included on the back of the card, along with stats, data and a brief player profile. The set includes a special Thurman Munson commemorative card.

		MT	NR MT	EX
	Complete Set:	8.00	6.00	3.25
	Common Player:	.15	.11	.06
1	Don Mattingly	1.75	1.25	.70
2	Steve Sax	.30	.25	.12
3	Alvaro Espinoza	.40	.30	.15
4	Luis Polonia	.20	.15	.08
5	Jesse Barfield	.25	.20	.10
6	Dave Righetti	.25	.20	.10
7	Dave Winfield	.25	.20	.10
8	John Candelaria	.15	.11	.06
9	Wayne Tolleson	.15	.11	.06
10	Ken Phelps	.15	.11	.06
11	Rafael Santana	.15	.11	.06
12	Don Slaught	.15	.11	.06
13	Mike Pagliarulo	.20	.15	.08
14	Lance McCullers	.20	.15	.08
15	Dave LaPoint	.20	.15	.08
16	Dale Mohorcic	.15	.11	.06
17	Steve Balboni	.15	.11	.06
18	Roberto Kelly	.50	.40	.20
19	Andy Hawkins	.25	.20	.10
20	Mel Hall	.20	.15	.08
21	Tom Brookens	.15	.11	.06
22	Deion Sanders	1.00	.70	.40
23	Richard Dotson	.15	.11	.06
24	Lee Guetterman	.15	.11	.06
25	Bob Geren	.50	.40	.20
26	Jimmy Jones	.20	.15	.08
27	Chuck Cary	.20	.15	.08
28	Ron Guidry	.25	.20	.10
29	Hal Morris	.25	.20	.10
30	Clay Parker	.25	.20	.10
31	Dallas Green	.20	.15	.08
32	Thurman Munson	.70	.50	.30
33	Sponsor Card	.15	.11	.06

1989 Score Young Superstar Series I

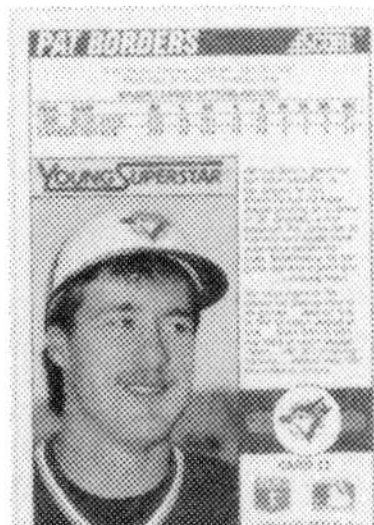

This standard-size card set (2-1/2" by 3-1/2") displays full-color action photos with a high gloss finish. The card fronts feature a red and blue border surrounding the photo with the team logo in the lower right. A red band beneath the photo provided the setting for the player ID including name, position, and team number. The flip side features a red "Young Superstar" headline above a close-up photo. Above the headline, appears the player's personal information and statistics in orange and black ink respectively. The top of the flip side highlights the player's name and the Score logo in white within a purple band. To the right of the close-up photo a condensed scouting report and career highlights are revealed. The card number and related logos appear on the bottom portion. Five trivia cards featuring "A Year to Remember" accompanied the series. Each trivia card relates to a highlight from the past 56 years. This set was distributed via a write-in offer with Score card wrappers.

		MT	NR MT	EX
	Complete Set:	8.00	6.00	3.25
	Common Player:	.10	.08	.04
1	Gregg Jefferies	1.00	.70	.40
2	Jody Reed	.10	.08	.04
3	Mark Grace	.40	.30	.15
4	Dave Gallagher	.15	.11	.06
5	Bo Jackson	1.00	.70	.40
6	Jay Buhner	.10	.08	.04
7	Melido Perez	.10	.08	.04
8	Bobby Witt	.10	.08	.04
9	David Cone	.15	.11	.06
10	Chris Sabo	.15	.11	.06
11	Pat Borders	.10	.08	.04
12	Mark Grant	.10	.08	.04
13	Mike Macfarlane	.10	.08	.04
14	Mike Jackson	.10	.08	.04
15	Ricky Jordan	.30	.25	.12
16	Ron Gant	.10	.08	.04
17	Al Leiter	.10	.08	.04
18	Jeff Parrett	.10	.08	.04
19	Pete Smith	.10	.08	.04
20	Walt Weiss	.15	.11	.06
21	Doug Drabek	.12	.09	.05
22	Kirt Manwaring	.15	.11	.06
23	Keith Miller	.10	.08	.04
24	Damon Berryhill	.12	.09	.05
25	Gary Sheffield	1.00	.70	.40
26	Brady Anderson	.20	.15	.08
27	Mitch Williams	.15	.11	.06
28	Roberto Alomar	.30	.25	.12
29	Bobby Thigpen	.12	.09	.05
30	Bryan Harvey	.10	.08	.04
31	Jose Rijo	.15	.11	.06
32	Dave West	.35	.25	.12
33	Joey Meyer	.10	.08	.04
34	Allan Anderson	.12	.09	.05
35	Rafael Palmeiro	.20	.15	.08
36	Tim Belcher	.30	.25	.12
37	John Smiley	.15	.11	.06
38	Mackey Sasser	.10	.08	.04
39	Greg Maddux	.30	.25	.12
40	Ramon Martinez	.60	.45	.25
41	Randy Myers	.12	.09	.05
42	Scott Bankhead	.15	.11	.06

A player's name in italic type indicates a rookie card.

1989 Score Young Superstar Series II

		MT	NR MT	EX
Complete Set:		7.00	5.25	2.75
Common Player:		.10	.08	.04
1	Sandy Alomar	.60	.45	.25
2	Tom Gordon	.60	.45	.25
3	Ron Jones	.30	.25	.12
4	Todd Burns	.10	.08	.04
5	Paul O'Neill	.10	.08	.04
6	Gene Larkin	.10	.08	.04
7	Eric King	.10	.08	.04
8	Jeff Robinson	.10	.08	.04
9	Bill Wegman	.10	.08	.04
10	Cecil Espy	.12	.09	.05
11	Jose Guzman	.10	.08	.04
12	Kelly Gruber	.20	.15	.08
13	Duane Ward	.10	.08	.04
14	Mark Gubicza	.25	.20	.10
15	Norm Charlton	.20	.15	.08
16	Jose Oquendo	.10	.08	.04
17	Geronimo Berroa	.15	.11	.06
18	Dwight Smith	1.00	.70	.40
19	Lance McCullers	.10	.08	.04
20	Jimmy Jones	.10	.08	.04
21	Craig Worthington	.25	.20	.10
22	Mike Devereaux	.12	.09	.05
23	Bob Milacki	.15	.11	.06
24	Dale Sveum	.10	.08	.04
25	Carlos Quintana	.20	.15	.08
26	Luis Medina	.15	.11	.06
27	Steve Searcy	.15	.11	.06
28	Don August	.10	.08	.04
29	Shawn Hillegas	.10	.08	.04
30	Mike Campbell	.10	.08	.04
31	Mike Harkey	.25	.20	.10
32	Randy Johnson	.20	.15	.08
33	Craig Biggio	.35	.25	.12
34	Mike Schooler	.12	.09	.05
35	Andres Thomas	.10	.08	.04
36	Van Snider	.20	.15	.08
37	Cameron Drew	.15	.11	.06
38	Kevin Mitchell	.70	.50	.30
39	Lance Johnson	.15	.11	.06
40	Chad Kreuter	.20	.15	.08
41	Danny Jackson	.10	.08	.04
42	Kurt Stillwell	.10	.08	.04

1990 Score

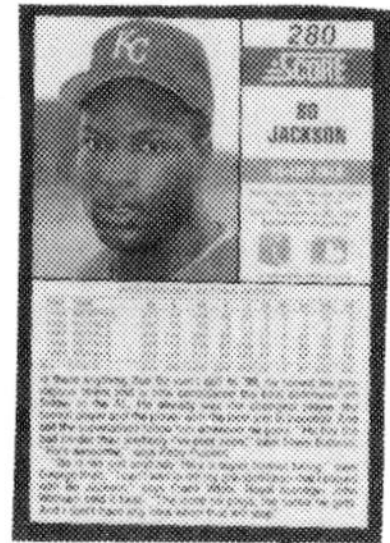

The regular Score set increased to 704 cards in 1990. Included were a series of cards picturing first-round draft picks, a ~xpanded subset of rookie cards, four World Series specials, five Highlight cards, and a 13-card "Dream Team" series featuring the game's top players pictured on old tobacco-style cards. For the first time in a Score set, team logos are displayed on the card fronts in the lower right corner. Card backs again include a full-color portrait photo with player data. A one-paragraph write-up of each player was again provided by former Sports Illustrated editor Les Woodcock. The Score set was again distributed with "Magic Motion" triva cards, this year using "Baseball's Most Valuable Players" as its theme.

		MT	NR MT	EX
Complete Set:		40.00	30.00	15.00
Common Player:		.04	.03	.02
1	Don Mattingly	.80	.60	.30
2	Cal Ripken, Jr.	.25	.20	.10
3	Dwight Evans	.08	.06	.03
4	Barry Bonds	.12	.09	.05
5	Kevin McReynolds	.12	.09	.05
6	Ozzie Guillen	.05	.04	.02
7	Terry Kennedy	.04	.03	.02
8	Bryan Harvey	.06	.05	.02
9	Alan Trammell	.09	.07	.04
10	Cory Snyder	.09	.07	.04
11	Jody Reed	.05	.04	.02
12	Roberto Alomar	.20	.15	.08
13	Pedro Guerrero	.09	.07	.04
14	Gary Redus	.04	.03	.02
15	Marty Barrett	.05	.04	.02
16	Ricky Jordan	.35	.25	.12
17	Joe Magrane	.07	.05	.03
18	Sid Fernandez	.07	.05	.03
19	Rich Dotson	.04	.03	.02
20	Jack Clark	.09	.07	.04
21	Bob Walk	.05	.04	.02
22	Ron Karkovice	.04	.03	.02
23	Lenny Harris(FC)	.10	.07	.04
24	Phil Bradley	.06	.05	.02
25	Andres Galarraga	.15	.11	.06
26	Brian Downing	.06	.05	.02
27	Dave Martinez	.06	.05	.02
28	Eric King	.04	.03	.02
29	Barry Lyons	.04	.03	.02
30	Dave Schmidt	.04	.03	.02
31	Mike Boddicker	.06	.05	.04
32	Tom Foley	.04	.03	.02
33	Brady Anderson	.07	.05	.03
34	Jim Presley	.05	.04	.02
35	Lance Parrish	.06	.05	.02
36	Von Hayes	.09	.07	.03
37	Lee Smith	.06	.05	.02
38	Herm Winningham	.04	.03	.02
39	Alejandro Pena	.04	.03	.02
40	Mike Scott	.09	.07	.04
41	Joe Orsulak	.04	.03	.02
42	Rafael Ramirez	.05	.04	.02
43	Gerald Young	.05	.04	.02
44	Dick Schofield	.05	.04	.02
45	Dave Smith	.06	.05	.02
46	Dave Magadan	.07	.05	.03
47	Dennis Martinez	.06	.05	.02
48	Greg Minton	.04	.03	.02
49	Milt Thompson	.04	.03	.02
50	Orel Hershiser	.12	.09	.05
51	Bip Roberts(FC)	.09	.07	.04
52	Jerry Browne	.09	.07	.04
53	Bob Ojeda	.05	.04	.02
54	Fernando Valenzuela	.09	.07	.04
55	Matt Nokes	.09	.07	.04
56	Brook Jacoby	.08	.06	.03
57	Frank Tanana	.05	.04	.02
58	Scott Fletcher	.05	.04	.02
59	Ron Oester	.05	.04	.02
60	Bob Boone	.08	.06	.03
61	Dan Gladden	.08	.06	.03
62	Darnell Coles	.04	.03	.02
63	Gregg Olson	.60	.45	.25
64	Todd Burns	.05	.04	.02
65	Todd Benzinger	.07	.05	.03
66	Dale Murphy	.12	.09	.05
67	Mike Flanagan	.06	.05	.02
68	Jose Oquendo	.06	.05	.02
69	Cecil Espy	.08	.06	.03
70	Chris Sabo	.10	.07	.04
71	Shane Rawley	.05	.04	.02
72	Tom Brunansky	.08	.06	.03
73	Vance Law	.05	.04	.02
74	B.J. Surhoff	.08	.06	.03
75	Lou Whitaker	.09	.07	.04
76	Ken Caminiti	.09	.07	.04
77	Nelson Liriano	.04	.03	.02
78	Tommy Gregg	.09	.07	.04
79	Don Slaught	.05	.04	.02
80	Eddie Murray	.12	.09	.05
81	Joe Boever	.08	.06	.02
82	Charlie Leibrandt	.06	.05	.02
83	Jose Lind	.06	.05	.02
84	Tony Phillips	.05	.04	.02
85	Mitch Webster	.04	.03	.02
86	Dan Plesac	.07	.05	.02
87	Rick Mahler	.05	.04	.02
88	Steve Lyons	.05	.04	.02
89	Tony Fernandez	.09	.07	.04
90	Ryne Sandberg	.20	.15	.08
91	Nick Esasky	.09	.07	.04
92	Luis Salazar	.04	.03	.02
93	Pete Incaviglia	.08	.06	.03
94	Ivan Calderon	.06	.05	.02
95	Jeff Treadway	.06	.05	.02
96	Kurt Stillwell	.06	.05	.02
97	Gary Sheffield	.50	.40	.20
98	Jeffrey Leonard	.07	.05	.03
99	Andres Thomas	.05	.04	.02
100	Roberto Kelly	.15	.11	.06
101	Alvaro Espinoza(FC)	.15	.11	.06
102	Greg Gagne	.05	.04	.02
103	John Farrell	.05	.04	.02
104	Willie Wilson	.05	.04	.02
105	Glenn Braggs	.08	.06	.03
106	Chet Lemon	.06	.05	.02
107	Jamie Moyer	.06	.05	.02
108	Chuck Crim	.04	.03	.02
109	Dave Valle	.04	.03	.02
110	Walt Weiss	.10	.07	.04
111	Larry Sheets	.04	.03	.02
112	Don Robinson	.05	.04	.02
113	Danny Heep	.04	.03	.02
114	Carmelo Martinez	.06	.05	.02
115	Dave Gallagher	.08	.06	.03
116	Mike LaValliere	.05	.04	.02
117	Bob McClure	.04	.03	.02
118	Rene Gonzales	.04	.03	.02
119	Mark Parent	.05	.04	.02
120	Wally Joyner	.15	.11	.06
121	Mark Gubicza	.09	.07	.04
122	Tony Pena	.08	.06	.03
123	Carmen Castillo	.04	.03	.02
124	Howard Johnson	.20	.15	.08
125	Steve Sax	.10	.08	.04
126	Tim Belcher	.10	.08	.04
127	Tim Burke	.06	.05	.02
128	Al Newman	.04	.03	.02
129	Dennis Rasmussen	.05	.04	.02
130	Doug Jones	.06	.05	.02
131	Fred Lynn	.09	.07	.04
132	Jeff Hamilton	.06	.05	.02
133	German Gonzalez	.05	.04	.02
134	John Morris	.05	.04	.02
135	Dave Parker	.10	.08	.04
136	Gary Pettis	.05	.04	.02
137	Dennis Boyd	.07	.05	.02
138	Candy Maldonado	.06	.05	.02
139	Rick Cerone	.04	.03	.02
140	George Brett	.15	.11	.06
141	Dave Clark	.05	.04	.02
142	Dickie Thon	.05	.04	.02
143	Junior Ortiz	.04	.03	.02
144	Don August	.06	.05	.02
145	Gary Gaetti	.10	.08	.04
146	Kirt Manwaring	.12	.09	.05
147	Jeff Reed	.04	.03	.02
148	Jose Alvarez(FC)	.08	.06	.03
149	Mike Schooler	.08	.06	.03
150	Mark Grace	.50	.40	.20
151	Geronimo Berroa	.08	.06	.03
152	Barry Jones	.04	.03	.02
153	Geno Petralli	.05	.04	.02
154	Jim Deshaies	.08	.06	.03
155	Barry Larkin	.15	.11	.06
156	Alfredo Griffin	.05	.04	.02
157	Tom Henke	.06	.05	.02
158	Mike Jeffcoat(FC)	.05	.04	.02
159	Bob Welch	.09	.07	.04
160	Julio Franco	.10	.08	.04
161	Henry Cotto	.04	.03	.02
162	Terry Steinbach	.10	.08	.04
163	Damon Berryhill	.08	.06	.03
164	Tim Crews	.04	.03	.02
165	Tom Browning	.09	.07	.04
166	Frd Manrique	.04	.03	.02
167	Harold Reynolds	.09	.07	.04
168	Ron Hassey	.05	.04	.02
169	Shawon Dunston	.08	.06	.03
170	Bobby Bonilla	.15	.11	.06
171	Tom Herr	.07	.05	.03
172	Mike Heath	.04	.03	.02
173	Rich Gedman	.05	.04	.02
174	Bill Ripken	.05	.04	.02
175	Pete O'Brien	.07	.05	.03
176a	Lloyd McClendon (uniform number 1 on back)	5.00	3.75	2.00
176b	Lloyd McClendon (uniform number 10 on back)	.20	.15	.08
177	Brian Holton	.05	.04	.02
178	Jeff Blauser	.05	.04	.02
179	Jim Eisenreich	.05	.04	.02
180	Bert Blyleven	.09	.07	.04
181	Rob Murphy	.05	.04	.02
182	Bill Doran	.07	.05	.03
183	Curt Ford	.04	.03	.02
184	Mike Henneman	.06	.05	.02
185	Eric Davis	.30	.25	.12
186	Lance McCullers	.06	.05	.03
187	*Steve Davis*(FC)	.25	.20	.10
188	Bill Wegman	.05	.04	.02
189	Brian Harper	.06	.05	.02
190	Mike Moore	.09	.07	.04
191	Dale Mohorcic	.04	.03	.02
192	Tim Wallach	.09	.07	.04
193	Keith Hernandez	.09	.07	.04
194	Dave Righetti	.07	.05	.03
195	Bret Saberhagen	.15	.11	.06
196	Paul Kilgus	.04	.03	.02
197	Bud Black	.05	.04	.02
198	Juan Samuel	.09	.07	.04
199	Kevin Seitzer	.15	.11	.06
200	Darryl Strawberry	.30	.25	.12
201	Dave Steib	.09	.07	.04
202	Charlie Hough	.06	.05	.02
203	Jack Morris	.08	.06	.03
204	Rance Mulliniks	.04	.03	.02
205	Alvin Davis	.10	.08	.04
206	Jack Howell	.06	.05	.02
207	Ken Patterson(FC)	.06	.05	.02
208	Terry Pendleton	.09	.07	.03
209	Craig Lefferts	.06	.05	.02
210	Kevin Brown(FC)	.10	.08	.04
211	Dan Petry	.04	.03	.02
212	Dave Leiper	.06	.05	.02
213	Daryl Boston	.04	.03	.02
214	Kevin Hickey(FC)	.08	.06	.03
215	Mike Krukow	.06	.05	.02
216	Terry Francona	.04	.03	.02
217	Kirk McCaskill	.08	.06	.03
218	Scott Bailes	.05	.04	.02
219	Bob Forsch	.04	.03	.02
220	Mike Aldrete	.05	.04	.02
221	Steve Buechele	.06	.05	.02
222	Jesse Barfield	.09	.07	.05
223	Juan Berenguer	.06	.05	.02
224	Andy McGaffigan	.06	.05	.02
225	Pete Smith	.09	.07	.04
226	Mike Witt	.06	.05	.02
227	Jay Howell	.08	.06	.03
228	Scott Bradley	.05	.04	.02
229	*Jerome Walton*	1.25	.90	.50
230	Greg Swindell	.15	.11	.06
231	Atlee Hammaker	.04	.03	.02
232	Mike Devereaux	.09	.07	.04
233	Ken Hill	.09	.07	.04
234	Craig Worthington	.15	.11	.06
235	Scott Terry	.08	.06	.03
236	Brett Butler	.09	.07	.04
237	Doyle Alexander	.07	.05	.03
238	Dave Anderson	.04	.03	.02
239	Bob Milacki	.10	.08	.04
240	Dwight Smith	.50	.40	.20
241	Otis Nixon	.04	.03	.02
242	Pat Tabler	.06	.05	.02
243	Derek Lilliquist	.12	.09	.05
244	Danny Tartabull	.15	.11	.06
245	Wade Boggs	.30	.25	.12
246	Scott Garrelts	.08	.06	.03
247	Spike Owen	.04	.03	.02

No.	Player	MT	NR MT	EX
248	Norm Charlton	.12	.09	.05
249	Gerald Perry	.06	.05	.02
250	Nolan Ryan	.50	.40	.20
251	Kevin Gross	.07	.05	.03
252	Randy Milligan	.07	.05	.03
253	Mike LaCoss	.05	.04	.02
254	Dave Bergman	.04	.03	.02
255	Tony Gwynn	.35	.25	.12
256	Felix Fermin	.04	.03	.02
257	Greg Harris	.10	.08	.04
258	*Junior Felix*	.40	.30	.15
259	Mark Davis	.09	.07	.04
260	Vince Coleman	.15	.11	.06
261	Paul Gibson	.10	.08	.04
262	Mitch Williams	.10	.08	.04
263	Jeff Russell	.08	.06	.03
264	*Omar Vizquel*	.10	.07	.04
265	Andre Dawson	.12	.09	.05
266	Storm Davis	.08	.06	.03
267	Guillermo Hernandez	.04	.03	.02
268	Mike Felder	.05	.04	.02
269	Tom Candiotti	.05	.04	.02
270	Bruce Hurst	.09	.07	.04
271	Fred McGriff	.30	.25	.12
272	Glenn Davis	.15	.11	.60
273	John Franco	.09	.07	.04
274	Rich Yett	.04	.03	.02
275	Craig Biggio	.15	.11	.06
276	Gene Larkin	.05	.04	.02
277	Rob Dibble	.15	.11	.06
278	Randy Bush	.05	.04	.02
279	Kevin Bass	.08	.06	.03
280	Bo Jackson	.50	.40	.20
281	Wally Backman	.06	.05	.02
282	Larry Andersen	.04	.03	.02
283	Chris Bosio	.09	.07	.04
284	Juan Agosto	.04	.03	.02
285	Ozzie Smith	.10	.08	.04
286	George Bell	.10	.08	.04
287	Rex Hudler	.05	.04	.02
288	Pat Borders	.10	.08	.04
289	Danny Jackson	.07	.05	.03
290	Carlton Fisk	.09	.07	.04
291	Tracy Jones	.05	.04	.02
292	Allan Anderson	.07	.05	.03
293	Johnny Ray	.07	.05	.03
294	Lee Guetterman	.04	.03	.02
295	Paul O'Neill	.09	.07	.05
296	Carney Lansford	.08	.06	.03
297	Tom Brookens	.04	.03	.02
298	Claudell Washington	.08	.06	.03
299	Hubie Brooks	.08	.06	.03
300	Will Clark	.80	.60	.30
301	*Kenny Rogers*	.20	.15	.08
302	Darrell Evans	.07	.05	.03
303	Greg Briley	.25	.20	.10
304	Donn Pall	.09	.07	.04
305	Teddy Higuera	.09	.07	.04
306	Dan Pasqua	.07	.05	.02
307	Dave Winfield	.15	.11	.06
308	Dennis Powell	.04	.03	.02
309	Jose DeLeon	.08	.06	.03
310	Roger Clemens	.25	.20	.10
311	Melido Perez	.09	.07	.04
312	Devon White	.09	.07	.04
313	Doc Gooden	.25	.20	.10
314	*Carlos Martinez*	.20	.15	.08
315	Dennis Eckersley	.10	.08	.04
316	Clay Parker	.12	.09	.05
317	Rick Honeycutt	.05	.04	.02
318	Tim Laudner	.05	.04	.02
319	Joe Carter	.10	.08	.04
320	Robin Yount	.20	.15	.08
321	Felix Jose	.15	.11	.06
322	Mickey Tettleton	.09	.07	.04
323	Mike Gallego	.04	.03	.02
324	Edgar Martinez	.09	.07	.04
325	Dave Henderson	.09	.07	.04
326	Chili Davis	.09	.07	.04
327	Steve Balboni	.05	.04	.02
328	Jody Davis	.04	.03	.02
329	Shawn Hillegas	.04	.03	.02
330	Jim Abbott	.70	.50	.30
331	John Dopson	.10	.08	.04
332	Mark Williamson	.04	.03	.02
333	Jeff Robinson	.08	.06	.03
334	John Smiley	.09	.07	.04
335	Bobby Thigpen	.07	.05	.03
336	Garry Templeton	.05	.04	.02
337	Marvell Wynne	.05	.04	.02
338a	Ken Griffey, Sr. (uniform number 25 on card back)	.80	.60	.30
338b	Ken Griffey, Jr. (unifrom number 30 on card back)	1.00	.70	.40
339	*Steve Finley*	.25	.20	.10
340	Ellis Burks	.25	.20	.10
341	Frank Williams	.04	.03	.02
342	Mike Morgan	.05	.04	.02
343	Kevin Mitchell	.35	.25	.12
344	Joel Youngblood	.04	.03	.02
345	Mike Greenwell	.50	.40	.20
346	Glenn Wilson	.05	.04	.02
347	John Costello	.05	.04	.02
348	Wes Gardner	.04	.03	.02
349	Jeff Ballard	.09	.07	.04
350	Mark Thurmond	.04	.03	.02
351	Randy Myers	.07	.05	.03
352	Shawn Abner	.07	.05	.03
353	Jesse Orosco	.04	.03	.02
354	Greg Walker	.05	.04	.02
355	Pete Harnisch	.15	.11	.06
356	Steve Farr	.05	.04	.02
357	Dave LaPoint	.05	.04	.02
358	Willie Fraser	.05	.04	.02
359	Mickey Hatcher	.04	.03	.02
360	Rickey Henderson	.30	.25	.12
361	Mike Fitzgerald	.04	.03	.02
362	Bill Schroeder	.04	.03	.02
363	Mark Carreon	.10	.08	.04
364	Ron Jones	.10	.08	.04
365	Jeff Montgomery	.06	.05	.02
366	Bill Krueger(FC)	.04	.03	.02
367	John Cangelosi	.04	.03	.02
368	Jose Gonzalez	.10	.08	.04
369	*Greg Hibbard*(FC)	.30	.25	.12
370	John Smoltz	.15	.11	.06
371	*Jeff Brantley*	.15	.11	.06
372	Frank White	.08	.06	.03
373	Ed Whitson	.06	.05	.02
374	Willie McGee	.09	.07	.04
375	Jose Canseco	.70	.50	.30
376	Randy Ready	.04	.03	.02
377	Don Aase	.04	.03	.02
378	Tony Armas	.05	.04	.02
379	Steve Bedrosian	.07	.05	.03
380	Chuck Finley	.07	.05	.03
381	Kent Hrbek	.12	.09	.05
382	Jim Gantner	.06	.05	.02
383	Mel Hall	.06	.05	.02
384	Mike Marshall	.07	.05	.03
385	Mark McGwire	.70	.50	.30
386	Wayne Tolleson	.04	.03	.02
387	Brian Holton	.05	.04	.02
388	*John Wetteland*	.30	.25	.12
389	Darren Daulton	.04	.03	.02
390	Rob Deer	.07	.05	.03
391	John Moses	.04	.03	.02
392	Todd Worrell	.07	.05	.03
393	Chuck Cary(FC)	.10	.08	.04
394	Stan Javier	.05	.04	.02
395	Willie Randolph	.09	.07	.04
396	Bill Buckner	.06	.05	.02
397	Robby Thompson	.07	.05	.02
398	Mike Scioscia	.07	.05	.03
399	Lonnie Smith	.09	.07	.04
400	Kirby Puckett	.40	.30	.15
401	Mark Langston	.15	.11	.06
402	Danny Darwin	.04	.03	.02
403	Greg Maddux	.15	.11	.06
404	Lloyd Moseby	.07	.05	.02
405	Rafael Palmeiro	.09	.07	.04
406	Chad Kreuter	.10	.08	.04
407	Jimmy Key	.09	.07	.05
408	Tim Birtsas	.04	.03	.02
409	Tim Raines	.10	.08	.04
410	Dave Stewart	.09	.07	.04
411	*Eric Yelding*(FC)	.30	.25	.12
412	*Kent Anderson*(FC)	.20	.15	.08
413	Les Lancaster	.05	.04	.02
414	Rick Dempsey	.04	.03	.02
415	Randy Johnson	.10	.08	.04
416	Gary Carter	.07	.05	.03
417	Rolando Roomes	.15	.11	.06
418	Dan Schatzeder	.04	.03	.02
419	Bryn Smith	.07	.05	.03
420	Ruben Sierra	.20	.15	.08
421	Steve Jeltz	.04	.03	.02
422	Ken Oberkfell	.04	.03	.02
423	Sid Bream	.04	.03	.02
424	Jim Clancy	.04	.03	.02
425	Kelly Gruber	.09	.07	.04
426	Rick Leach	.04	.03	.02
427	Lenny Dykstra	.07	.05	.03
428	Jeff Pico	.06	.05	.02
429	John Cerutti	.06	.05	.02
430	David Cone	.15	.11	.06
431	Jeff Kunkel	.04	.03	.02
432	Luis Aquino	.05	.04	.02
433	Ernie Whitt	.05	.04	.02
434	Bo Diaz	.05	.04	.02
435	Steve Lake	.04	.03	.02
436	Pat Perry	.04	.03	.02
437	Mike Davis	.05	.04	.02
438	Cecilio Guante	.04	.03	.02
439	Duane Ward	.04	.03	.02
440	Andy Van Slyke	.10	.08	.04
441	Gene Nelson	.04	.03	.02
442	Luis Polonia	.06	.05	.02
443	Kevin Elster	.06	.05	.02
444	Keith Moreland	.06	.05	.02
445	Roger McDowell	.06	.05	.02
446	Ron Darling	.08	.06	.03
447	Ernest Riles	.04	.03	.02
448	Mookie Wilson	.08	.06	.03
449a	*Bill Spiers* (66 missing for year of birth)	2.25	1.75	.90
449b	*Bill Spiers* (1966 for birth year)	.25	.20	.10
450	Rick Sutcliffe	.07	.05	.03
451	Nelson Santovenia	.10	.08	.04
452	Andy Allanson	.04	.03	.02
453	Bob Melvin	.04	.03	.02
454	Benny Santiago	.12	.09	.05
455	Jose Uribe	.05	.04	.02
456	Bill Landrum(FC)	.08	.06	.03
457	Bobby Witt	.07	.05	.03
458	Kevin Romine	.07	.05	.03
459	Lee Mazzilli	.04	.03	.02
460	Paul Molitor	.10	.08	.04
461	Ramon Martinez(FC)	.40	.30	.15
462	Frank DiPino	.04	.03	.02
463	Walt Terrell	.06	.05	.02
464	*Bob Geren*	.30	.25	.12
465	Rick Reuchel	.09	.07	.04
466	Mark Grant	.06	.05	.02
467	John Kruk	.07	.05	.03
468	Gregg Jefferies	.80	.60	.30
469	R.J. Reynolds	.04	.03	.02
470	Harold Baines	.09	.07	.04
471	Dennis Lamp	.04	.03	.02
472	Tom Gordon	.60	.45	.25
473	Terry Puhl	.04	.03	.02
474	Curtis Wilkerson	.04	.03	.02
475	Dan Quisenberry	.05	.04	.02
476	Oddibe McDowell	.07	.05	.03
477	Zane Smith	.04	.03	.02
478	Franklin Stubbs	.04	.03	.02
479	Wallace Johnson	.04	.03	.02
480	Jay Tibbs	.04	.03	.02
481	Tom Glavine	.09	.07	.03
482	Manny Lee	.05	.04	.02
483	Joe Hesketh	.04	.03	.02
484	Mike Bielecki	.07	.05	.03
485	Greg Brock	.06	.05	.02
486	Pascual Perez	.06	.05	.02
487	Kirk Gibson	.09	.07	.04
488	Scott Sanderson	.05	.04	.02
489	Domingo Ramos	.04	.03	.02
490	Kal Daniels	.10	.08	.04
491a	David Wells (Reverse negative on back photo)	7.00	5.25	2.75
491b	David Wells (Corrected)	.05	.04	.02
492	Jerry Reed	.04	.03	.02
493	Eric Show	.06	.05	.02
494	Mike Pagliarulo	.06	.05	.02
495	Ron Robinson	.05	.04	.02
496	Brad Komminsk	.04	.03	.02
497	*Greg Litton*	.25	.20	.10
498	Chris James	.07	.05	.02
499	Luis Quinones(FC)	.05	.04	.02
500	Frank Viola	.10	.08	.04
501	Tim Teufel	.05	.04	.02
502	Terry Leach	.04	.03	.02
503	Matt Williams	.20	.15	.08
504	Tim Leary	.06	.05	.02
505	Doug Drabek	.06	.05	.02
506	Mariano Duncan	.06	.05	.02
507	Charlie Hayes	.10	.08	.04
508	*Joey Belle*	1.00	.70	.40
509	Pat Sheridan	.05	.04	.02
510	Mackey Sasser	.05	.04	.02
511	Jose Rijo	.09	.07	.04
512	Mike Smithson	.04	.03	.02
513	Gary Ward	.04	.03	.02
514	Dion James	.06	.05	.02
515	Jim Gott	.06	.05	.02
516	Drew Hall(FC)	.07	.05	.03
517	Doug Bair	.04	.03	.02
518	*Scott Scudder*	.20	.15	.08
519	Rick Aguilera	.06	.05	.02
520	Rafael Belliard	.05	.04	.02
521	Jay Buhner	.10	.08	.04
522	Jeff Reardon	.06	.05	.02
523	Steve Rosenberg(FC)	.09	.07	.04
524	Randy Velarde(FC)	.09	.07	.04
525	Jeff Musselman	.09	.07	.04
526	Bill Long	.06	.05	.02
527	*Gary Wayne*	.10	.08	.04
528	*Dave Johnson*(FC)	.15	.11	.06
529	Ron Kittle	.08	.06	.03
530	Erik Hanson(FC)	.20	.15	.08
531	Steve Wilson(FC)	.20	.15	.08
532	Joey Meyer	.04	.03	.02
533	Curt Young	.04	.03	.02
534	Kelly Downs	.06	.05	.02
535	Joe Girardi	.20	.15	.08
536	Lance Blankenship	.09	.07	.04
537	Greg Mathews	.05	.04	.02
538	Donell Nixon	.04	.03	.02
539	Mark Knudson(FC)	.09	.07	.04
540	*Jeff Wetherby*(FC)	.30	.25	.12
541	Darrin Jackson	.04	.03	.02
542	Terry Mulholland	.09	.07	.03
543	Eric Hetzel(FC)	.15	.11	.06
544	*Rick Reed*(FC)	.25	.20	.10
545	Dennis Cook(FC)	.20	.15	.08
546	Mike Jackson	.05	.04	.02
547	Brian Fisher	.06	.05	.02
548	*Gene Harris*(FC)	.20	.15	.08
549	Jeff King(FC)	.20	.15	.08
550	Dave Dravecky (Salute)	.10	.08	.04
551	Randy Kutcher(FC)	.08	.06	.03
552	Mark Portugal	.06	.05	.02
553	*Jim Corsi*(FC)	.12	.09	.05
554	Todd Stottlemyre	.12	.09	.05
555	Scott Bankhead	.09	.07	.04
556	Ken Dayley	.05	.04	.02
557	*Rick Wrona*(FC)	.25	.20	.10
558	*Sammy Sosa*(FC)	.35	.25	.14
559	Keith Miller	.08	.06	.03
560	Ken Griffey Jr.	3.00	2.25	1.25
561a	Ryne Sandberg (No Errors- 3B Position designation)	20.00	15.00	8.00
561b	Ryne Sandberg (No Errors- No position designation)	.70	.50	.30
562	Billy Hatcher	.06	.05	.02
563	Jay Bell(FC)	.09	.07	.04
564	*Jack Daugherty*(FC)	.30	.25	.12
565	*Rich Monteleone*	.20	.15	.08
566	Bo Jackson (All-Star MVP)	.60	.45	.25
567	*Tony Fossas*(FC)	.10	.08	.04
568	*Roy Smith*(FC)	.15	.11	.06
569	*Jaime Navarro*(FC)	.35	.25	.14
570	Lance Johnson(FC)	.15	.11	.06
571	*Mike Dyer*(FC)	.25	.20	.10
572	*Kevin Ritz*(FC)	.20	.15	.08
573	Dave West	.15	.11	.06
574	*Gary Mielke*(FC)	.25	.20	.10
575	Scott Lusader(FC)	.09	.07	.04
576	*Joe Oliver*	.30	.25	.12
577	Sandy Alomar, Jr.	.60	.45	.25
578	Andy Benes(FC)	.80	.60	.30
579	Tim Jones	.07	.05	.03
580	*Randy McCament*(FC)	.25	.20	10.00
581	Curt Schilling(FC)	.15	.11	.06
582	*John Orton*(FC)	.25	.20	.10
583a	*Milt Cuyler* (played in 998 games)(FC)	2.00	1.50	.80
583b	*Milt Cuyler* (played in 98 games)(FC)	.40	.30	.15
584	*Eric Anthony*(FC)	2.00	1.50	.80
585	*Greg Vaughn*(FC)	1.75	1.25	.70
586	*Deion Sanders*(FC)	.50	.40	.20
587	Jose DeJesus(FC)	.15	.11	.06
588	*Chip Hale*(FC)	.30	.25	.12
589	*John Olerud*(FC)	2.50	2.00	1.00
590	*Steve Olin*(FC)	.35	.25	.12
591	*Marquis Grissom*(FC)	1.25	.90	.50
592	*Moises Alou*(FC)	.50	.40	.20
593	Mark Lemke(FC)	.10	.08	.04
594	*Dean Palmer*(FC)	.30	.25	.12
595	Robin Ventura(FC)	.70	.50	.30
596	*Tino Martinez*(FC)	.60	.45	.25
597	*Mike Huff*(FC)	.25	.20	.10
598	*Scott Hemond*(FC)	.25	.20	.10
599	*Wally Whitehurst*(FC)	.20	.15	.08
600	*Todd Zeile*(FC)	2.00	1.50	.80
601	Glenallen Hill(FC)	.35	.25	.14
602	Hal Morris(FC)	.15	.11	.06
603	Juan Bell(FC)	.15	.11	.06
604	*Bobby Rose*(FC)	.25	.20	.10
605	*Matt Merullo*(FC)	.20	.15	.08

		MT	NR MT	EX
606	*Kevin Maas*(FC)	.20	.15	.08
607	*Randy Nosek*(FC)	.25	.20	.10
608	*Billy Bates*(FC)	.20	.15	.08
609	*Mike Stanton*(FC)	.25	.20	.10
610	*Goose Gozzo*(FC)	.30	.25	.12
611	*Charles Nagy*(FC)	.25	.20	.10
612	*Scott Coolbaugh*(FC)	.30	.25	.12
613	*Jose Vizcaino*(FC)	.35	.25	.12
614	*Greg Smith*(FC)	.20	.15	.08
615	*Jeff Huson*(FC)	.25	.20	.10
616	*Mickey Weston*(FC)	.20	.15	.08
617	*John Pawlowski*(FC)	.20	.15	.08
618	*Joe Skalski*(FC)	.20	.15	.08
619	*Bernie Williams*(FC)	.90	.70	.35
620	*Shawn Holman*(FC)	.25	.20	.10
621	*Gary Eave*(FC)	.25	.20	.10
622	*Darrin Fletcher*(FC)	.25	.20	.10
623	*Pat Combs*(FC)	.90	.70	.35
624	*Mike Blowers*(FC)	.30	.25	.12
625	*Kevin Appier*(FC)	.30	.25	.12
626	*Pat Austin*(FC)	.30	.25	.12
627	*Kelly Mann*(FC)	.40	.30	.15
628	*Matt Kinzer*(FC)	.25	.20	.10
629	*Chris Hammond*(FC)	.25	.20	.10
630	*Dean Wilkins*(FC)	.25	.20	.10
631	*Larry Walker*(FC)	.25	.20	.10
632	*Blaine Beatty*(FC)	.40	.30	.15
633	Tom Barrett(FC)	.12	.09	.05
634	*Stan Belinda*(FC)	.35	.25	.14
635	*Tex Smith*(FC)	.25	.20	.10
636	Hensley Meulens(FC)	.40	.30	.15
637	*Juan Gonzalez*(FC)	.60	.45	.25
638	*Lenny Webster*(FC)	.25	.20	.10
639	*Mark Gardner*(FC)	.35	.25	.14
640	*Tommy Greene*(FC)	.25	.20	.10
641	*Mike Hartley*(FC)	.25	.20	.10
642	*Phil Stephenson*(FC)	.15	.11	.06
643	*Kevin Mmahat*(FC)	.15	.11	.06
644	*Ed Whited*(FC)	.15	.11	.06
645	*Delino DeShields*(FC)	1.00	.70	.40
646	Kevin Blankenship(FC)	.15	.11	.06
647	*Paul Sorrento*(FC)	.40	.30	.15
648	*Mike Roesler*(FC)	.25	.20	.12
649	*Jason Grimsley*(FC)	.25	.20	.10
650	*Dave Justice*(FC)	.50	.40	.20
651	*Scott Cooper*(FC)	.25	.20	.10
652	Dave Eiland(FC)	.15	.11	.06
653	*Mike Munoz*(FC)	.25	.20	.10
654	*Jeff Fischer*(FC)	.25	.20	.10
655	*Terry Jorgenson*(FC)	.20	.15	.08
656	*George Canale*(FC)	.40	.30	.15
657	*Brian DuBois*(FC)	.40	.30	.15
658	Carlos Quintana	.10	.08	.04
659	Luis De los santos	.10	.08	.04
660	Jerald Clark	.10	.08	.04
661	#1 Draft Pick *(Donald Harris)*(FC)	.30	.25	.12
662	#1 Draft Pick *(Paul Coleman)*(FC)	.40	.30	.15
663	#1 Draft Pick *(Frank Thomas)*(FC)	.60	.45	.25
664	#1 Draft Pick *(Brent Mayne)*(FC)	.20	.15	.08
665	#1 Draft Pick *(Eddie Zosky)*(FC)	.20	.15	.08
666	#1 Draft Pick *(Steve Hosey)*(FC)	.20	.15	.08
667	#1 Draft Pick *(Scott Bryant)*(FC)	.20	.15	.08
668	#1 Draft Pick *(Tom Goodwin)*(FC)	.40	.30	.15
669	#1 Draft Pick *(Cal Eldred)*(FC)	.20	.15	.08
670	#1 Draft Pick *(Earl Cunningham)*(FC)	.50	.40	.20
671	#1 Draft Pick *(Alan Zinter)*(FC)	.25	.20	.10
672	#1 Draft Pick *(Chuck Knoblauch)*(FC)	.25	.20	.10
673	#1 Draft Pick *(Kyle Abbott)*(FC)	.25	.20	.10
674	#1 Draft Pick *(Roger Salkeld)*(FC)	.30	.25	.12
675	#1 Draft Pick *(Maurice Vaughn)*(FC)	.30	.25	.12
676	#1 Draft Pick *(Kiki Jones)*(FC)	.25	.20	.10
677	#1 Draft Pick *(Tyler Houston)*(FC)	.40	.30	.15
678	#1 Draft Pick *(Jeff Jackson)*(FC)	.40	.30	.15
679	#1 Draft Pick *(Greg Gohr)* (#1 Draft Pick)(FC)	.25	.20	.10
680	#1 Draft Pick *(Ben McDonald)* (#1 Draft Pick)(FC)	2.50	2.00	1.00
681	#1 Draft Pick *(Greg Blosser)* (#1 Draft Pick)(FC)	.30	.25	.12
682	#1 Draft Pick *(Willie Green)* (#1 Draft Pick)(FC)	.25	.20	.10
683	Dream Team (Wade Boggs)	.20	.15	.08
684	Dream Team (Will Clark)	.20	.15	.08
685	Dream Team (Tony Gwynn)	.20	.15	.08
686	Dream Team (Rickey Henderson)	.20	.15	.08
687	Dream Team (Bo Jackson)	.60	.45	.25
688	Dream Team (Mark Langston)	.20	.15	.11
689	Dream Team (Barry Larkin)	.20	.15	.11
690	Dream Team (Kirby Puckett)	.20	.15	.11
691	Dream Team (Ryne Sanberg)	.20	.15	.11
692	Dream Team (Mike Scott)	.20	.15	.11
693	Dream Team (Terry Steinbach)	.20	.15	.11
694	Dream Team (Bobby Thigpen)	.20	.15	.11
695	Dream Team (Mitch Williams)	.20	.15	.11
696	5000 K (Nolan Ryan)	.50	.40	.20
697	FB/BB NIKE (Bo Jackson)	15.00	11.00	6.00
698	ALCS MVP (Rickey Henderson)	.25	.20	.10
699	NLCS MVP (Will Clark)	.35	.25	.14
700	World Series 1,2	.30	.25	.12
701	Candlestick	.30	.25	.12
702	World Series Game 3	.30	.25	.12
703	World Series Wrap-up	.30	.25	.12
704	200 Hit (Wade Boggs)	.25	.20	.10

1989 Scoremasters

This unique 42-card boxed set from Score was reproduced from original artwork done by sports artist Jeffrey Rubin. The paintings are reproduced on a standard-size, white, glossy stock, and the set includes the top stars of the game, including four key rookies (Walton, Gordon, Jefferies and Griffey Jr.).

		MT	NR MT	EX
Complete Set:		13.00	9.75	5.25
Common Player:		.20	.15	.08
1	Bo Jackson	.70	.50	.30
2	Jerome Walton	1.50	1.25	.60
3	Cal Ripken, Jr.	.35	.25	.12
4	Mike Scott	.20	.15	.08
5	Nolan Ryan	.80	.60	.30
6	Don Mattingly	1.25	.90	.50
7	Tom Gordon	1.00	.70	.40
8	Jack Morris	.20	.15	.08
9	Carlton Fisk	.30	.25	.12
10	Will Clark	1.00	.70	.40
11	George Brett	.40	.30	.15
12	Kevin Mitchell	.40	.30	.15
13	Mark Langston	.30	.25	.12
14	Dave Stewart	.20	.15	.08
15	Dale Murphy	.25	.20	.10
16	Gary Gaetti	.20	.15	.08
17	Wade Boggs	.50	.40	.20
18	Eric Davis	.70	.50	.30
19	Kirby Puckett	.70	.50	.30
20	Roger Clemens	.50	.40	.20
21	Orel Hershiser	.30	.25	.12
22	Mark Grace	.50	.40	.20
23	Ryne Sandberg	.35	.25	.12
24	Barry Larkin	.20	.15	.08
25	Ellis Burks	.40	.30	.15
26	Doc Gooden	.40	.30	.15
27	Ozzie Smith	.25	.20	.10
28	Andre Dawson	.20	.15	.08
29	Julio Franco	.20	.15	.08
30	Ken Griffey, Jr.	1.50	1.25	.60
31	Ruben Sierra	.30	.25	.12
32	Mark McGwire	.80	.60	.30
33	Andres Galarraga	.20	.15	.08
34	Joe Carter	.30	.25	.12
35	Vince Coleman	.20	.15	.08
36	Mike Greenwell	.50	.40	.20
37	Tony Gwynn	.40	.30	.15
38	Andy Van Slyke	.20	.15	.08
39	Gregg Jefferies	1.00	.70	.40
40	Jose Canseco	1.00	.70	.40
41	Dave Winfield	.20	.15	.08
42	Darryl Strawberry	.40	.30	.15

1888 Scrapps

The origin of these die-cut, embossed player busts is not known, but they were apparently part of a book of "punch-outs" issued in the late 1880s. When out of their original album, they apparently resembled scraps of paper, presumably leading to their unusual name. An earlier theory that they were issued by "Scrapps Tobacco" has since been discounted after research indicated there never was such a company. The die-cuts include 18 different players - nine members of the American Association St. Louis Browns and nine from the National League Detroit Wolverines. Although they vary slightly in size, the player busts are generally about 2" wide and 3" high. The drawings for the St. Louis player busts were taken from the Old Judge "Brown's Champions" set. The player's name appears along the bottom.

		NR MT	EX	VG
Complete Set:		6000.	3000.	1750.
Common Player:		250.00	125.00	75.00
(1)	C.W. Bennett	250.00	125.00	75.00
(2)	D. Brouthers	500.00	250.00	150.00
(3)	A.J. Bushong	250.00	125.00	75.00
(4)	Robert L. Caruthers	250.00	125.00	75.00
(5)	Charles Comiskey	500.00	250.00	150.00
(6)	F. Dunlap	300.00	150.00	90.00
(7)	David L. Foutz	250.00	125.00	75.00
(8)	C.H. Getzen (Geitzen)	300.00	150.00	90.00
(9)	Wm. Gleason	250.00	125.00	75.00
(10)	E. Hanlon	300.00	150.00	90.00
(11)	Walter A. Latham	250.00	125.00	75.00
(12)	James O'Neill	250.00	125.00	75.00
(13)	H. Richardson	300.00	150.00	90.00
(14)	Wm. Robinson	500.00	250.00	150.00
(15)	J.C. Rowe	300.00	150.00	90.00
(16)	S. Thompson	500.00	250.00	150.00
(17)	Curtis Welch	250.00	125.00	75.00
(18)	J.L. White	300.00	150.00	90.00

1949 Sealtest Phillies

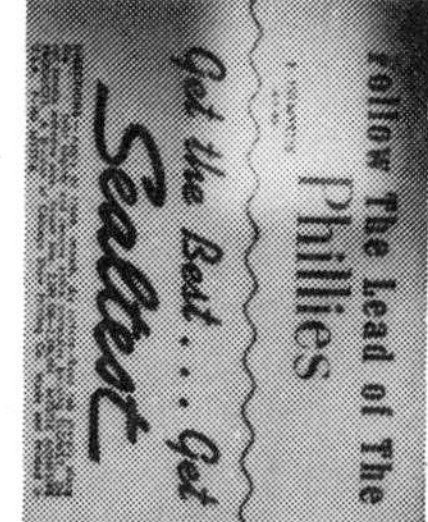

This regional Phillies set was issued in the Philadelphia area in 1949 by Sealtest Dairy. It consisted of 12 large (3-1/4" by 4-1/4") sticker cards with peel-off backs. The front of the unnumbered cards featured an action photo with facsimile autograph, while the back was an advertisement for Sealtest products. The same photos and checklist were also used for the Lummis Peanut Butter card set issued in Philadelphia the same year.

		NR MT	EX	VG
Complete Set:		700.00	350.00	200.00
Common Player:		40.00	20.00	12.00
(1)	Rich Ashburn	110.00	55.00	35.00
(2)	Hank Borowy	40.00	20.00	12.00
(3)	Del Ennis	60.00	30.00	17.50
(4)	Granny Hamner	40.00	20.00	12.00
(5)	Puddinhead Jones	40.00	20.00	12.00
(6)	Russ Meyer	40.00	20.00	12.00
(7)	Bill Nicholson	40.00	20.00	12.00
(8)	Robin Roberts	150.00	75.00	45.00
(9)	"Schoolboy" Rowe	40.00	20.00	12.00
(10)	Andy Seminick	40.00	20.00	12.00
(11)	Curt Simmons	60.00	30.00	18.00
(12)	Eddie Waitkus	40.00	20.00	12.00

1983 7-11 Slurpee Coins

This first production of player coins by 7-Eleven stores was distributed only in the Los Angeles area. The test promotion, which awarded a coin to every purchaser of a large Slurpee drink, must have proved successful, as it was expanded nationally in subsequent years. Six California Angels and six Los Angeles Dodgers are included in the full-color set, with Angels players in red backgrounds and the Dodgers in blue. The 1-3/4" diameter plastic coins feature both an action and a portrait photo of the player, which can be alternately seen by moving the coin slightly from side to side. The 12 coin backs are numbered and include brief statistics and the company logo.

		MT	NR MT	EX
Complete Set:		18.00	13.50	7.25
Common Player:		.70	.50	.30
1	Rod Carew	2.50	2.00	1.00
2	Steve Sax	2.00	1.50	.80
3	Fred Lynn	1.00	.70	.40
4	Pedro Guerrero	2.00	1.50	.80
5	Reggie Jackson	3.50	2.75	1.50
6	Dusty Baker	.70	.50	.30
7	Doug DeCinces	.70	.50	.30
8	Fernando Valenzuela	2.50	2.00	1.00
9	Tommy John	1.00	.70	.40
10	Rick Monday	.70	.50	.30
11	Bobby Grich	.70	.50	.30
12	Greg Brock	.70	.50	.30

1984 7-11 Slurpee Coins Eastern Region

The 7-Eleven coins were distributed nationally in 1984, with different players displayed on 72 total coins. The coins, called "Slurpee Discs," were issued in three different regional sets of 24 coins each. East, West, and Central regional series were distributed, with players on teams in those areas of the country dominating the region's set. George Brett, Andre Dawson, Dale Murphy, Eddie Murray, Mike Schmidt and Robin Yount appear in all three of the full-color sets. At least one player appears from every major league team. The formats are very similar to the 1983 coins, with double-image photos on the fronts and statistics and coin numbers on the backs.

		MT	NR MT	EX
Complete Set:		75.00	55.00	30.00
Common Player:		.70	.50	.30
1	Andre Dawson	1.50	1.25	.35
2	Robin Yount	2.00	1.50	.80
3	Dale Murphy	1.25	.90	.50
4	Mike Schmidt	2.00	1.50	.80
5	George Brett	1.25	.90	.50
6	Eddie Murray	1.25	.90	.50
7	Dave Winfield	1.00	.70	.40
8	Tom Seaver	2.00	1.50	.80
9	Mike Boddicker	.60	.45	.25
10	Wade Boggs	2.00	1.50	.80
11	Bill Madlock	.70	.50	.30
12	Steve Carlton	2.00	1.50	.80
13	Dave Stieb	.60	.45	.25
14	Cal Ripken, Jr.	1.25	.90	.50
15	Jim Rice	1.00	.70	.40
16	Ron Guidry	.80	.60	.30
17	Darryl Strawberry	2.00	1.50	.80
18	Tony Pena	.60	.45	.25
19	John Denny	.60	.45	.25
20	Tim Raines	1.00	.70	.40
21	Rick Dempsey	.60	.45	.25
22	Rich Gossage	.80	.60	.30
23	Gary Matthews	.60	.45	.25
24	Keith Hernandez	1.00	.70	.40

1984 7-11 Slurpee Coins Central Region

		MT	NR MT	EX
1	Andre Dawson	1.50	1.25	.60
2	Robin Yount	2.00	1.50	.80
3	Dale Murphy	1.25	.90	.50
4	Mike Schmidt	2.00	1.50	.80
5	George Brett	1.25	.90	.50
6	Eddie Murray	1.25	.90	.50
7	Bruce Sutter	.70	.50	.30
8	Cecil Cooper	.70	.50	.30
9	Willie McGee	.80	.60	.30
10	Mike Hargrove	.60	.45	.25
11	Kent Hrbek	1.00	.70	.40
12	Carlton Fisk	1.00	.70	.50
13	Mario Soto	.60	.45	.25
14	Lonnie Smith	.60	.45	.25
15	Gary Carter	1.00	.70	.40
16	Lou Whitaker	.90	.70	.35
17	Ron Kittle	.60	.45	.25
18	Paul Molitor	.80	.60	.30
19	Ozzie Smith	1.00	.70	.50
20	Fergie Jenkins	.70	.50	.30
21	Ted Simmons	.70	.50	.30
22	Pete Rose	2.00	1.50	.80
23	LaMarr Hoyt	.60	.45	.25
24	Dan Quisenberry	.70	.50	.30

1984 7-11 Slurpee Coins Western Region

		MT	NR MT	EX
1	Andre Dawson	1.50	1.25	.60
2	Robin Yount	2.00	1.50	.80
3	Dale Murphy	1.25	.90	.50
4	Mike Schmidt	2.00	1.50	.80
5	George Brett	1.25	.90	.50
6	Eddie Murray	1.25	.90	.50
7	Steve Garvey	1.00	.70	.40
8	Rod Carew	2.00	1.50	.80
9	Fernando Valenzuela	1.00	.70	.40
10	Bob Horner	.70	.50	.30
11	Buddy Bell	.60	.45	.25
12	Reggie Jackson	2.00	1.50	.80
13	Nolan Ryan	2.00	1.50	.80
14	Pedro Guerrero	.80	.60	.30
15	Atlee Hammaker	.60	.45	.25
16	Fred Lynn	.80	.60	.30
17	Terry Kennedy	.60	.45	.25
18	Dusty Baker	.60	.45	.25
19	Jose Cruz	.60	.45	.25
20	Steve Rogers	.60	.45	.25
21	Rickey Henderson	2.00	1.50	.80
22	Steve Sax	.80	.60	.30
23	Dickie Thon	.60	.45	.25
24	Matt Young	.60	.45	.25

1985 7-11 Slurpee Coins Eastern Region

In 1985, the "Slurpee Disc" promotion was further expanded to a total of 94 full-color coins. The formats were very similar to the previous two years, but there were six different regional sets. Five of these regional series contain 16 coins, with a Detroit series totaling 14. The other five regions are: East, West, Great Lakes, Central and Southeast. The coins are again 1-1/4" in diameter, printed on plastic with double-image photos. All coins are numbered. No player appears in all regions. although several are in two or more.

		MT	NR MT	EX
Complete Set:		90.00	67.00	35.00
Common Player:		.60	.45	.25
1	Eddie Murray	1.00	.70	.40
2	George Brett	1.25	.90	.50
3	Steve Carlton	2.00	1.50	.80
4	Jim Rice	1.00	.70	.40
5	Dave Winfield	1.00	.70	.40
6	Mike Boddicker	.60	.45	.25
7	Wade Boggs	1.75	1.25	.70
8	Dwight Evans	.90	.70	.35
9	Dwight Gooden	2.00	1.50	.80
10	Keith Hernandez	.90	.70	.35
11	Bill Madlock	.60	.45	.25
12	Don Mattingly	2.50	2.00	1.00
13	Dave Righetti	.70	.50	.30
14	Cal Ripken, Jr.	1.00	.70	.40
15	Juan Samuel	.70	.50	.30
16	Mike Schmidt	2.00	1.50	.80

M.L. TEAM ADDRESSES

Collectors often request the addresses of M.L. teams so they may direct autograph requests to players. Here they are:

American League

Baltimore Orioles: Memorial Stadium, Baltimore, MD 21218.

Boston Red Sox: Fenway Park, 24 Yawkey Way, Boston, MA 02215.

California Angels: Anaheim Stadium, 2000 State College Blvd., Anaheim, CA 92806.

Chicago White Sox: Comiskey Park, 324 W. 35th St., Chicago, IL 60616.

Cleveland Indians: Boudreau Blvd., Cleveland, OH 44114.

Detroit Tigers: Tiger Stadium, Detroit, MI 48216.

Kansas City Royals: P.O. Box 419969, Kansas City, MO 64141.

Milwaukee Brewers: Milw. County Stadium, Milwaukee, WI 53214.

Minnesota Twins: 501 Chicago Ave. S., Minneapolis, MN 55415.

New York Yankees: Yankee Stadium, Bronx, NY 10451.

Oakland A's: Oakland Alameda Co. Coliseum, P.O. Box 2220, Oakland, CA 94621.

Seattle Mariners: P.O. Box 4100, Seattle, WA 98104.

Texas Rangers: P.O. Box 1111, Arlington, TX 76010.

Toronto Blue Jays: Skydome, 300 The Esplanade West, Suite #3200, Toronto, Ont., Canada M5V 3B3.

National League

Atlanta Braves: P.O. Box 4064, Atlanta, GA 30302.

Chicago Cubs: Wrigley Field, 1060 W. Addison St., Chicago, IL 60613.

Cincinnati Reds: Riverfront Stadium, Cincinnati, OH 45202.

Houston Astros: P.O. Box 288, Houston, TX 77001.

Los Angeles Dodgers: Dodger Stadium, 1000 Elysian Park Ave., L.A., CA 90012.

Montreal Expos: P.O. Box 500, Station M, Montreal, Quebec, Canada H1V 3P2.

New York Mets: Shea Stadium, Flushing, NY 11368.

Philadelphia Phillies: P.O. Box 7575, Philadelphia, PA 19101

Pittsburgh Pirates: Three Rivers Stadium, 600 Stadium Circle, Pittsburgh, PA 15212

St. Louis Cardinals: 250 Stadium Plaza, St. Louis, MO 63102.

San Diego Padres: P.O. Box 2000, San Diego, CA 92120.

San Francisco Giants: Candlestick Park, San Francisco, CA 94124.

1985 7-11 Slurpee Coins Southwest/Central Region

		MT	NR MT	EX
1	Nolan Ryan	2.00	1.50	.80
2	George Brett	1.25	.90	.50
3	Dave Winfield	1.00	.70	.40
4	Mike Schmidt	2.00	1.50	.80
5	Bruce Sutter	.60	.45	.25
6	Joaquin Andujar	.60	.45	.25
7	Willie Hernandez	.60	.45	.25
8	Wade Boggs	1.75	1.25	.70
9	Gary Carter	1.00	.70	.40
10	Jose Cruz	.60	.45	.25
11	Kent Hrbek	.70	.50	.30
12	Reggie Jackson	2.00	1.50	.80
13	Lance Parrish	.70	.50	.30
14	Terry Puhl	.60	.45	.25
15	Dan Quisenberry	.60	.45	.25
16	Ozzie Smith	.80	.60	.30

1985 7-11 Slurpee Coins Western Region

		MT	NR MT	EX
1	Mike Schmidt	2.00	1.50	.80
2	Jim Rice	1.00	.70	.40
3	Dale Murphy	1.25	.90	.50
4	Eddie Murray	1.00	.70	.40
5	Dave Winfield	1.00	.70	.40
6	Rod Carew	2.00	1.50	.80
7	Alvin Davis	.70	.50	.30
8	Steve Garvey	1.00	.70	.40
9	Rich Gossage	.60	.45	.25
10	Pedro Guerrero	.70	.50	.30
11	Tony Gwynn	1.00	.70	.40
12	Rickey Henderson	2.00	1.50	.80
13	Reggie Jackson	2.00	1.50	.80
14	Jeff Leonard	.60	.45	.25
15	Alejandro Pena	.60	.45	.25
16	Fernando Valenzuela	.90	.70	.35

1985 7-11 Slurpee Coins Tigers

		MT	NR MT	EX
1	Sparky Anderson	.60	.45	.25
2	Darrell Evans	.80	.60	.30
3	Kirk Gibson	1.25	.90	.50
4	Willie Hernandez	.60	.45	.25
5	Larry Herndon	.60	.45	.25
6	Chet Lemon	.60	.45	.25
7	Aurelio Lopez	.60	.45	.25
8	Jack Morris	1.00	.70	.40
9	Lance Parrish	1.00	.70	.40
10	Dan Petry	.60	.45	.25
11	Dave Rozema	.60	.45	.25
12	Alan Trammell	1.75	1.25	.70
13	Lou Whitaker	1.50	1.25	.60
14	Milt Wilcox	.60	.45	.25

1985 7-11 Slurpee Coins Southeastern Region

		MT	NR MT	EX
1	Dale Murphy	1.25	.90	.50
2	Steve Carlton	2.00	1.50	.80
3	Nolan Ryan	2.00	1.50	.80
4	Bruce Sutter	.60	.45	.25
5	Dave Winfield	1.00	.70	.40
6	Steve Bedrosian	.60	.45	.25
7	Andre Dawson	1.25	.90	.50
8	Kirk Gibson	.80	.60	.30
9	Fred Lynn	.60	.45	.25
10	Gary Matthews	.60	.45	.25
11	Phil Niekro	.70	.50	.30
12	Tim Raines	1.00	.70	.40
13	Darryl Strawberry	2.00	1.50	.80
14	Dave Stieb	.60	.45	.25
15	Willie Upshaw	.60	.45	.25
16	Lou Whitaker	.70	.50	.30

1985 7-11 Slurpee Coins Great Lakes Region

		MT	NR MT	EX
1	Willie Hernandez	.60	.45	.25
2	George Brett	1.25	.90	.50
3	Dave Winfield	1.00	.70	.40
4	Eddie Murray	1.00	.70	.40
5	Bruce Sutter	.60	.45	.25
6	Harold Baines	.60	.45	.25
7	Bert Blyleven	.60	.45	.25
8	Leon Durham	.60	.45	.25
9	Chet Lemon	.60	.45	.25
10	Pete Rose	2.00	1.50	.80
11	Ryne Sandberg	2.00	1.50	.80
12	Tom Seaver	2.00	1.50	.80
13	Mario Soto	.60	.45	.25
14	Rick Sutcliffe	.60	.45	.25
15	Alan Trammell	.90	.70	.35
16	Robin Yount	2.00	1.50	.80

1986 7-11 Slurpee Coins Eastern Region

This marked the fourth year of production for these coins, issued with the purchase of a large Slurpee drink at 7-Eleven stores. Once again, there are different regional issues, with 16 coins issued for four different regions in 1986. The 1-3/4" diameter plastic coins each feature three different players' pictures, which can be seen alternately by tilting from side to side. Eight of the coins are the same in every region. Each coin is numbered on the back, along with brief player information.

		MT	NR MT	EX
	Complete Set:	70.00	52.00	27.00
	Common Player:	.40	.30	.15
1	Dwight Gooden	1.50	1.25	.60
2	Batting Champs (Wade Boggs, George Brett, Pete Rose)	2.00	1.50	.80
3	MVP's (Keith Hernandez, Don Mattingly, Cal Ripken, Jr.)	1.75	1.25	.70
4	Slugging Champs (Harold Baines, Pedro Guerrero, Dave Parker)	.60	.45	.25
5	Home Run Champs (Dale Murphy, Jim Rice, Mike Schmidt)	2.00	1.50	.80
6	Cy Young Winners (Ron Guidry, Bret Saberhagen, Fernando Valenzuela)	.70	.50	.30
7	Bullpen Aces (Rich Gossage, Dan Quisenberry, Bruce Sutter)	.50	.40	.20
8	Strikeout Kings (Steve Carlton, Nolan Ryan, Tom Seaver)	3.00	2.25	1.25
9	1985 Rookies (Steve Lyons, Rick Schu, Larry Sheets)	.50	.40	.20
10	Bullpen Aces (Jeff Reardon, Dave Righetti, Bob Stanley)	.50	.40	.20
11	Power Hitters (George Bell, Darryl Strawberry, Dave Winfield)	1.75	1.25	.70
12	Base Stealers (Rickey Henderson, Tim Raines, Juan Samuel)	1.75	1.25	.70
13	Home Run Hitters (Andre Dawson, Dwight Evans, Eddie Murray)	1.25	.90	.50
14	Ace Pitchers (Mike Boddicker, Ron Darling, Dave Stieb)	.40	.30	.15
15	1985 Bullpen Rookies (Tim Burke, Brian Fisher, Roger McDowell)	.50	.40	.20
16	Sluggers (Jesse Barfield, Gary Carter, Fred Lynn)	.70	.50	.30

1986 7-11 Slurpee Coins Mideastern Region

		MT	NR MT	EX
1	Dwight Gooden	1.50	1.25	.60
2	Batting Champs (Wade Boggs, George Brett, Pete Rose)	2.00	1.50	.80
3	MVP's (Keith Hernandez, Don Mattingly, Cal Ripken)	1.75	1.25	.70
4	Slugging Champs (Harold Baines, Pedro Guerrero, Dave Parker)	.60	.45	.25
5	Home Run Champs (Dale Murphy, Jim Rice, Mike Schmidt)	2.00	1.50	.80
6	Cy Young Winners (Ron Guidry, Bret Saberhagen, Fernando Valenzuela)	.70	.50	.30
7	Bullpen Aces (Rich Gossage, Dan Quisenberry, Bruce Sutter)	.50	.40	.20
8	Strikeout Kings (Steve Carlton, Nolan Ryan, Tom Seaver)	3.00	2.25	1.25
9	MVP's (Willie Hernandez, Ryne Sandberg, Robin Yount)	1.00	.70	.40
10	Ace Pitchers (Bert Blyleven, Jack Morris, Rick Sutcliffe)	.50	.40	.20
11	Bullpen Aces (Rollie Fingers, Bob James, Lee Smith)	.40	.30	.15
12	All-Star Catchers (Carlton Fisk, Lance Parrish, Tony Pena)	.60	.45	.25
13	1985 Rookies (Shawon Dunston, Ozzie Guillen, Ernest Riles)	.80	.60	.30
14	Star Outfielders (Brett Butler, Chet Lemon, Willie Wilson)	.40	.30	.15
15	Home Run Hitters (Tom Brunansky, Cecil Cooper, Darrell Evans)	.40	.30	.15
16	Big Hitters (Kirk Gibson, Paul Molitor, Greg Walker)	.60	.45	.25

Wrong backs, blank backs

Collectors occasionally find recent (1980s) cards which have wrong backs (player on front doesn't match bio/stats on back) or blank backs. Such cards result from mistakes in the printing process. They aren't very popular with collectors, so they have little, if any, premium value. Most collectors feel they are merely damaged cards and value them lower than correctly printed specimens. The only exception seems to be currently hot superstars or rookie cards, for which a few collectors are willing to pay premiums.

Errors/variations

Collectors often wonder about errors found on cards, usually in the statistics or personal data on the card's back.

Such errors *add nothing* to the value of the card. The only time an error like this is likely to increase a card's value is if the manufacturer corrects the error in a later printing, thus creating two distinct variations. If enough collectors feel the variations are a desirable part of that issue, the value may increase. Whether the error version or the corrected card will have the greater value usually depends on relative scarcity. The more common version will almost always be worth less. So quite often, the error card can be worth less than the corrected version.

Collector-only issues

Collectors may find some recent issues not included in this volume. In most cases these are illegal, unauthorized "collector-only" issues. Such cards often show nothing but the player's photo and his name on the front, and his name and perhaps a line or two of statistics on the back. The sets usually lack a manufacturer's name. They are often sold at shows and in shops, and frequently carry high price tags.

The cards *are not* legitimate issues. They can be printed and reprinted at will, so they lack any scarcity value.

Card company addresses

Collectors frequently want to know the addresses of the major baseball-card manufacturing companies. They are:

Topps Chewing Gum Co.
254 36th St.
Brooklyn, N.Y. 11232
Fleer Corp.
10th & Somerville
Philadelphia, Pa. 19141
Leaf-Donruss Co.
P.O. Box 2038
Memphis, Tenn. 38101
Sportflics/Score
Major League Marketing, Inc.
55 Ford Rd.
Westport, Ct. 06880
Upper Deck Co.
23705 Via Del Rio
Yorba Linda, CA 92686

1986 7-11 Slurpee Coins Midwest Region

#	Player	MT	NR MT	EX
1	Dwight Gooden	1.50	1.25	.60
2	Batting Champs (Wade Boggs, George Brett, Pete Rose)	2.00	1.50	.80
3	MVP's (Keith Hernandez, Don Mattingly, Cal Ripken, Jr.)	1.75	1.25	.70
4	Slugging Champs (Harold Baines, Pedro Guerrero, Dave Parker)	.60	.45	.25
5	Home Run Champs (Dale Murphy, Jim Rice, Mike Schmidt)	2.00	1.50	.80
6	Cy Young Winners (Ron Guidry, Bret Saberhagen, Fernando Valenzuela)	.70	.50	.30
7	Bullpen Aces (Rich Gossage, Dan Quisenberry, Bruce Sutter)	.50	.40	.20
8	Stikeout Kings (Steve Carlton, Nolan Ryan, Tom Seaver)	3.00	2.25	1.25
9	1985 Rookies (Vince Coleman, Glenn Davis, Oddibe McDowell)	2.00	1.50	.80
10	Gold Glovers (Buddy Bell, Ozzie Smith, Lou Whitaker)	.60	.45	.25
11	Ace Pitchers (Mike Scott, Mario Soto, John Tudor)	.40	.30	.15
12	Bullpen Aces (Jeff Lahti, Ted Power, Dave Smith)	.40	.30	.15
13	Big Hitters (Jack Clark, Jose Cruz, Bob Horner)	.60	.45	.25
14	Star Second Basemen (Bill Doran, Tommy Herr, Ron Oester)	.40	.30	.15
15	1985 Rookie Pitchers (Tom Browning, Joe Hesketh, Todd Worrell)	.60	.45	.25
16	Top Switch-Hitters (Willie McGee, Jerry Mumphrey, Pete Rose)	1.00	.70	.40

1986 7-11 Slurpee Coins Western Region

#	Player	MT	NR MT	EX
1	Dwight Gooden	1.50	1.25	.60
2	Batting Champs (Wade Boggs, George Brett, Pete Rose)	2.00	1.50	.80
3	MVP's (Keith Hernandez, Don Mattingly, Cal Ripken, Jr.)	1.75	1.25	.70
4	Slugging Champs (Harold Baines, Pedro Guerrero, Dave Parker)	.60	.45	.25
5	Home Run Champs (Dale Murphy, Jim Rice, Mike Schmidt)	2.00	1.50	.80
6	Cy Young Winners (Ron Guidry, Bret Saberhagen, Fernando Valenzuela)	.70	.50	.30
7	Bullpen Aces (Rich Gossage, Dan Quisenberry, Bruce Sutter)	.50	.40	.20
8	Strikeout Kings (Steve Carlton, Nolan Ryan, Tom Seaver)	3.00	2.25	1.25
9	Home Run Champs (Reggie Jackson, Dave Kingman, Gorman Thomas)	1.25	.90	.50
10	Batting Champs (Rod Carew, Tony Gwynn, Carney Lansford)	1.25	.90	.50
11	Sluggers (Phil Bradley, Mike Marshall, Graig Nettles)	.50	.40	.20
12	Ace Pitchers (Andy Hawkins, Orel Hershiser, Mike Witt)	.50	.40	.20
13	1985 Rookies (Chris Brown, Ivan Calderon, Mariano Duncan)	.70	.50	.30
14	Big Hitters (Steve Garvey, Bill Madlock, Jim Presley)	.70	.50	.30
15	Bullpen Aces (Jay Howell, Donnie Moore, Ed Nunez)	.40	.30	.15
16	1985 Bullpen Rookies (Karl Best, Stewart Cliburn, Steve Ontiveros)	.40	.30	.15

1987 7-11 Slurpee Coins Eastern Region

Continuing with a tradition started in 1983, 7-Eleven stores offered a free "Super Star Sports Coin" with the purchase of a Slurpee drink. Five different regional sets of Slurpee coins were issued for 1987, a total of 75 coins. Each coin measures 1-3/4" in diameter and features a multiple image effect which allows three different pictures to be seen, depending on how the coin is tilted. The coin reverses contain career records and personal player information.

#	Player	MT	NR MT	EX
	Complete Set:	45.00	33.00	18.00
	Common Player:	.40	.30	.15
1	Gary Carter	1.00	.70	.40
2	Don Baylor	.50	.40	.20
3	Rickey Henderson	1.00	.70	.40
4	Lenny Dykstra	.70	.50	.30
5	Wade Boggs	1.75	1.25	.70
6	Mike Pagliarulo	.60	.45	.25
7	Dwight Gooden	1.25	.90	.50
8	Roger Clemens	1.25	.90	.50
9	Dave Righetti	.70	.50	.30
10	Keith Hernandez	.90	.70	.35
11	Pat Dodson	.50	.40	.20
12	Don Mattingly	2.25	1.75	.90
13	Darryl Strawberry	1.25	.90	.50
14	Jim Rice	1.00	.70	.40
15	Dave Winfield	1.00	.70	.40

1987 7-11 Slurpee Coins Mideastern Region

#	Player	MT	NR MT	EX
1	Gary Carter	1.00	.70	.40
2	Marty Barrett	.50	.40	.20
3	Jody Davis	.50	.40	.20
4	Don Aase	.40	.30	.15
5	Lenny Dykstra	.70	.50	.30
6	Wade Boggs	1.75	1.25	.70
7	Keith Moreland	.50	.40	.20
8	Mike Boddicker	.40	.30	.15
9	Dwight Gooden	1.25	.90	.50
10	Roger Clemens	1.25	.90	.50
11	Ryne Sandberg	1.00	.70	.40
12	Eddie Murray	1.00	.70	.40
13	Keith Hernandez	.90	.70	.35
14	Jim Rice	1.00	.70	.40
15	Lee Smith	.50	.40	.20
16	Cal Ripken, Jr.	1.00	.70	.40

1987 7-11 Slurpee Coins Great Lakes Region

#	Player	MT	NR MT	EX
1	Harold Baines	.60	.45	.25
2	Jody Davis	.50	.40	.20
3	John Cangelosi	.50	.40	.20
4	Shawon Dunston	.70	.50	.30
5	Dave Cochrane	.40	.30	.15
6	Leon Durham	.50	.40	.20
7	Carlton Fisk	.70	.50	.30
8	Dennis Eckersley	.40	.30	.15
9	Ozzie Guillen	.50	.40	.20
10	Gary Matthews	.50	.40	.20
11	Ron Karkovice	.50	.40	.20
12	Keith Moreland	.50	.40	.20
13	Bobby Thigpen	.50	.40	.20
14	Ryne Sandberg	1.00	.70	.40
15	Greg Walker	.50	.40	.20
16	Lee Smith	.50	.40	.20

1987 7-11 Slurpee Coins Western Region

#	Player	MT	NR MT	EX
1	Doug DeCinces	.50	.40	.20
2	Mariano Duncan	.40	.30	.15
3	Wally Joyner	1.75	1.25	.70
4	Pedro Guerrero	.70	.50	.30
5	Kirk McCaskill	.40	.30	.15
6	Orel Hershiser	.60	.45	.25
7	Gary Pettis	.40	.30	.15
8	Mike Marshall	.60	.45	.25
9	Dick Schofield	.40	.30	.15
10	Steve Sax	.80	.60	.30
11	Don Sutton	.80	.60	.30
12	Mike Scioscia	.40	.30	.15
13	Devon White	.90	.70	.35
14	Franklin Stubbs	.50	.40	.20
15	Mike Witt	.50	.40	.20
16	Fernando Valenzuela	1.00	.70	.40

1987 7-11 Slurpee Coins Tigers

#	Player	MT	NR MT	EX
1	Darnell Coles	.40	.30	.15
2	Darrell Evans	.60	.45	.25
3	Kirk Gibson	1.00	.70	.40
4	Willie Hernandez	.50	.40	.20
5	Larry Herndon	.50	.40	.20
6	Chet Lemon	.50	.40	.20
7	Dwight Lowry	.40	.30	.15
8	Jack Morris	.90	.70	.35
9	Dan Petry	.50	.40	.20
10	Frank Tanana	.40	.30	.15
11	Alan Trammell	1.00	.70	.40
12	Lou Whitaker	.90	.70	.35

1985 7-11 Twins

The Minnesota Twins, in co-operation with 7-Eleven and the Fire Marshall's Association, issued this set of 13 baseball fire safety cards. The card fronts feature full-color pictures of Twins players. A fire safety tip and short player history appear on the back. The cards were given out at all 7-Eleven stores in the state and at the Twins June 3 baseball game. Each fan received one baseball card with a poster which told how to collect the other cards in the set. Twelve cards feature players and the 13th card has an artist's rendering of Twins players on the front and a checklist of the set on the back. A group of 50,000 cards was distributed to fifth graders throughout the state by the fire departments.

#	Player	MT	NR MT	EX
	Complete Set:	6.00	4.50	2.50
	Common Player:	.20	.15	.08
1	Kirby Puckett	2.00	1.50	.80
2	Frank Viola	1.00	.70	.40
3	Mickey Hatcher	.20	.15	.08
4	Kent Hrbek	1.25	.90	.50
5	John Butcher	.20	.15	.08
6	Roy Smalley	.20	.15	.08
7	Tom Brunansky	.80	.60	.30
8	Ron Davis	.20	.15	.08
9	Gary Gaetti	1.00	.70	.40
10	Tim Teufel	.30	.25	.12
11	Mike Smithson	.20	.15	.08
12	Tim Laudner	.30	.25	.12
---	Checklist	.10	.08	.04

1984 7-Up Cubs

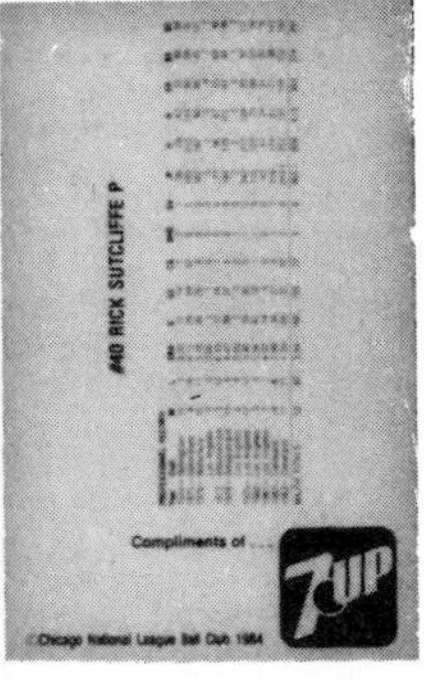

The Chicago Cubs and 7-Up issued this 28-card set featuring full-color game-action photos on a 2-1/4" by 3-1/2" borderless front. The backs have the player's stats and personal information. This was the third consecutive year the Cubs issued this type of set as a giveaway at a "Baseball Card Day" promotional game.

#	Player	MT	NR MT	EX
	Complete Set:	12.00	9.00	4.75
	Common Player:	.20	.15	.08
1	Larry Bowa	.40	.30	.15
6	Keith Moreland	.40	.30	.15
7	Jody Davis	.40	.30	.15
10	Leon Durham	.40	.30	.15
11	Ron Cey	.40	.30	.15
15	Ron Hassey	.20	.15	.08

		MT	NR MT	EX
18	Richie Hebner	.20	.15	.08
19	Dave Owen	.20	.15	.08
20	Bob Dernier	.20	.15	.08
21	Jay Johnstone	.25	.20	.10
23	Ryne Sandberg	3.00	2.25	1.25
24	Scott Sanderson	.25	.20	.10
25	Gary Woods	.20	.15	.08
27	Thad Bosley	.20	.15	.08
28	Henry Cotto	.30	.25	.12
34	Steve Trout	.25	.20	.10
36	Gary Matthews	.40	.30	.15
39	George Frazier	.20	.15	.08
40	Rick Sutcliffe	.80	.60	.30
41	Warren Brusstar	.20	.15	.08
42	Rich Bordi	.20	.15	.08
43	Dennis Eckersley	.50	.40	.20
44	Dick Ruthven	.20	.15	.08
46	Lee Smith	.50	.40	.20
47	Rick Reuschel	.50	.40	.20
49	Tim Stoddard	.20	.15	.08
---	Jim Frey	.20	.15	.08
---	Cubs Coaches (Ruben Amaro, Billy Connors, Johnny Oates, John Vukovich, Don Zimmer)	.20	.15	.08

1985 7-Up Cubs

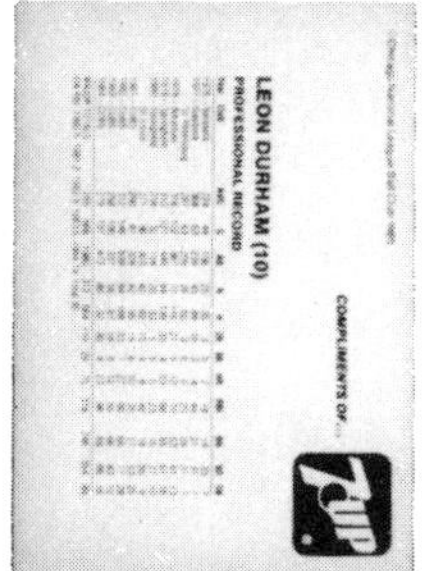

This was the second year a Chicago Cubs card set was released with 7-Up as the sponsor. The set has 28 unnumbered cards in the standard 2-1/2" by 3-1/2" size. They were distributed to fans attending the Cubs game on August 14 at Wrigley Field. They feature full-color game-action photos of the players. Card backs contain the player's professional stats.

		MT	NR MT	EX
	Complete Set:	7.00	5.25	2.75
	Common Player:	.10	.08	.04
1	Larry Bowa	.25	.20	.10
6	Keith Moreland	.30	.25	.12
7	Jody Davis	.30	.25	.12
10	Leon Durham	.30	.25	.12
11	Ron Cey	.30	.25	.12
15	Davey Lopes	.25	.20	.10
16	Steve Lake	.10	.08	.04
18	Richie Hebner	.10	.08	.04
20	Bob Dernier	10	.08	.04
21	Scott Sanderson	15	.11	.06
22	Billy Hatcher	.30	.25	.12
23	Ryne Sandberg	2.00	1.50	.80
24	Brian Dayett	.10	.08	.04
25	Gary Woods	.10	.08	.04
27	Thad Bosley	.10	.08	.04
28	Chris Speier	.10	.08	.04
31	Ray Fontenot	.10	.08	.04
34	Steve Trout	.20	.15	.08
36	Gary Matthews	.30	.25	.12
39	George Frazier	.10	.08	.04
40	Rick Sutcliffe	.70	.50	.30
41	Warren Brusstar	.10	.08	.04
42	Lary Sorensen	.10	.08	.04
43	Dennis Eckersley	.40	.30	.15
44	Dick Ruthven	.10	.08	.04
46	Lee Smith	.35	.25	.14
---	Jim Frey	.10	.08	.04
---	Coaching Staff (Ruben Amaro, Billy Connors, Johnny Oates, John Vukovich, Don Zimmer)	.10	.08	.04

1948 Signal Gasoline Oakland Oaks

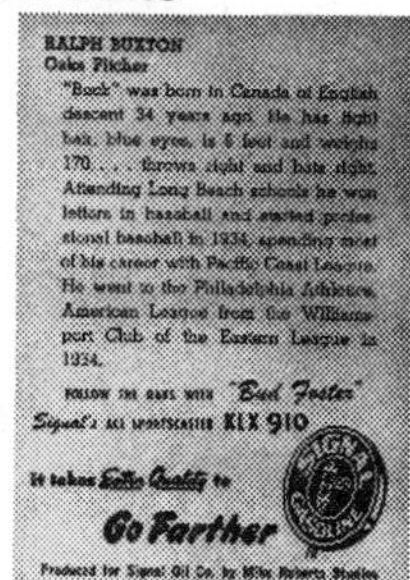

Issued by Signal Oil in the Oakland area in 1948, this 24-card set features members of the Oakland Oaks of the Pacific Coast League. The unnumbered cards, measuring 2-3/8" by 3-1/2", were given away at gas stations. The front consists of a color photo, while the backs (printed in either blue or black) contain a brief player write-up along with a Signal Oil ad and logo.

		NR MT	EX	VG
	Complete Set:	425.00	212.00	135.00
	Common Player:	12.00	6.00	3.50
(1)	John C. Babich	12.00	6.00	3.50
(2)	Ralph Buxton	12.00	6.00	3.50
(3)	Loyd E. Christopher (Lloyd)	12.00	6.00	3.50
(4)	Merrill Russell Combs	12.00	6.00	3.50
(5)	Melvin E. Deuzabou	12.00	6.00	3.50
(6)	Nicholas ("Nick") Etten	20.00	10.00	6.00
(7)	Bud Foster (announcer)	12.00	6.00	3.50
(8)	Charles Gassaway	12.00	6.00	3.50
(9)	Will Hafey	12.00	6.00	3.50
(10)	Ray Hamrick	12.00	6.00	3.50
(11)	Brooks Richard Holder	20.00	10.00	6.00
(12)	Earl Jones	12.00	6.00	3.50
(13)	Harry "Cookie" Lavagetto	15.00	7.50	4.50
(14)	Robert E. Lillard	12.00	6.00	3.50
(15)	Dario Lodigiani	12.00	6.00	3.50
(16)	Ernie Lombardi	30.00	15.00	9.00
(17)	Alfred Manuel Martin	75.00	38.00	23.00
(18)	George Michael Metkovich	12.00	6.00	3.50
(19)	William L. Raimondi	12.00	6.00	3.50
(20)	Les George Scarsella	12.00	6.00	3.50
(21)	Floyd Vernie Speer	12.00	6.00	3.50
(22)	Charles "Casey" Stengel	75.00	38.00	23.00
(23)	Maurice Van Robays	12.00	6.00	3.50
(24)	Aldon Jay Wilkie	12.00	6.00	3.50

1947 Smith's Oakland Oaks

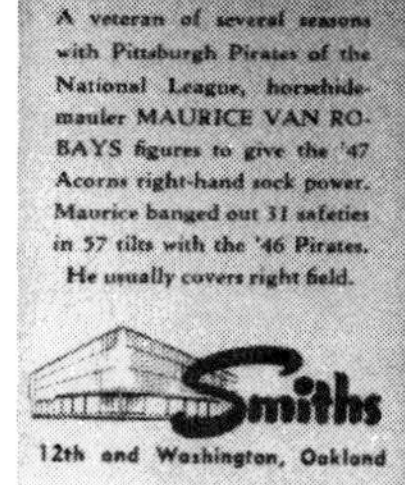

This regional set of Oakland Oaks (Pacific Coast League) cards was issued in 1947 by Smith's Clothing stores and is numbered in the lower right corner. The card fronts include a black and white photo with the player's name, team and position below. The backs carry a brief player write-up and an advertisement for Smith's Clothing. The cards measure 2" by 3". The Max Marshall card was apparently short-printed and is much scarcer than the rest of the set.

		NR MT	EX	VG
	Complete Set:	500.00	6.00	3.50
	Common Player:	12.00	6.00	3.50
1	Charles (Casey) Stengel	75.00	6.00	3.50
2	Billy Raimondi	12.00	6.00	3.50
3	Les Scarsella	12.00	6.00	3.50
4	Brooks Holder	12.00	6.00	3.50
5	Ray Hamrick	12.00	6.00	3.50
6	Gene Lillard	12.00	6.00	3.50
7	Maurice Van Robays	12.00	6.00	3.50
8	Charlie (Sheriff) Gassaway	12.00	6.00	3.50
9	Henry (Cotton) Pippen	12.00	6.00	3.50
10	James Arnold	12.00	6.00	3.50
11	Ralph (Buck) Buxton	12.00	6.00	3.50
12	Ambrose (Bo) Palica	12.00	6.00	3.50
13	Tony Sabol	12.00	6.00	3.50
14	Ed Kearse	12.00	6.00	3.50
15	Bill Hart	12.00	6.00	3.50
16	Donald (Snuffy) Smith	12.00	6.00	3.50
17	Oral (Mickey) Burnett	12.00	6.00	3.50
18	Tom Hafey	12.00	6.00	3.50
19	Will Hafey	12.00	6.00	3.50
20	Paul Gillespie	25.00	6.00	3.50
21	Damon Hayes	25.00	6.00	3.50
22	Max Marshall	125.00	6.00	3.50
23	Mel (Dizz) Duezabou	12.00	6.00	3.50
24	Mel Reeves	12.00	6.00	3.50
25	Joe Faria	25.00	6.00	3.50

1948 Smith's Oakland Oaks

The 1948 Smith's Clothing issue was another 25-card regional set featuring members of the Oakland Oaks of the Pacific Coast League. Almost

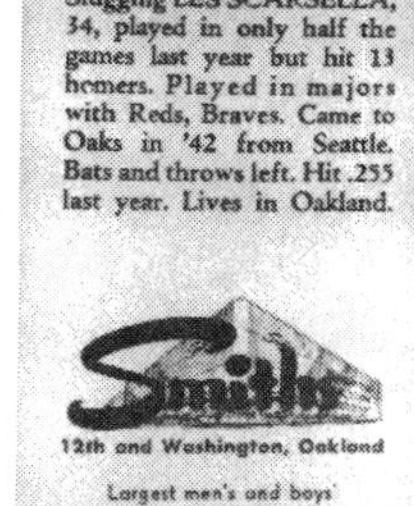

identical to the 1947 Smith's issue, the black and white cards again measure 2" by 3" but were printed on heavier, glossy stock. The player's name, team and position appear below the photo with the card number in the lower right corner. The back has a brief player write-up and an ad for Smith's Clothing. Among the scarcest of all the 20th Century tobacco issues, the T4 Obak Premiums were cabinet-sized cards distributed in conjunction with the more popular and better-known Obak T212 card set. Both sets were issued in 1911 by Obak "mouthpiece" cigarettes and featured players from the Pacific Coast League. The Obak Premiums measured a large 5" by 7" and wre printed on a cardboard-like paper. The attractive cards featured a greyish monochome player photo inside a 3-1/2" by 5" oval. There was no printing on the front of the card to identify the player or indicate the Manufacturer, and the backs of the cards were blank. In most cases the photos used for the premiums were identical to the T212 photos, except for some cropping differences. Under the Obak mail-in promotion, 50 coupons from cigarette packages were required to obtain just one premium card, which may explain their extreme scarcity today. According to the coupon, all 175 players pictured in the regular T212 set were available as premium cards, but todate 30 different players have been found in the larger cabinet size. Most of the Obak premiums that exist in original condition contain a number, written in pencil on the back of the card, that corresponds to the checklist printed on the coupon. Because of their extreme scarcity, these cards are quite expensive and generally appeal only to the very advanced Pacific Coast League collectors.

		NR MT	EX	VG
	Complete Set:	400.00	6.00	3.50
	Common Player:	12.00	6.00	3.50
1	Billy Raimondi	12.00	6.00	3.50
2	Brooks Holder	12.00	6.00	3.50
3	Will Hafey	20.00	6.00	3.50
4	Nick Etten	12.00	6.00	3.50
5	Lloyd Christopher	12.00	6.00	3.50
6	Les Scarsella	12.00	6.00	3.50
7	Ray Hamrick	12.00	6.00	3.50
8	Gene Lillard	12.00	6.00	3.50
9	Maurice Van Robays	12.00	6.00	3.50
10	Charlie Gassaway	12.00	6.00	3.50
11	Ralph (Buck) Buxton	12.00	6.00	3.50
12	Tom Hafey	12.00	6.00	3.50
13	Damon Hayes	12.00	6.00	3.50
14	Mel (Dizz) Duezabou	12.00	6.00	3.50
15	Dario Lodigiani	12.00	6.00	3.50
16	Vic Buccola	12.00	6.00	3.50
17	Billy Martin	75.00	6.00	3.50
18	Floyd Speer	12.00	6.00	3.50
19	Eddie Samcoff	12.00	6.00	3.50
20	Charles (Casey) Stengel	75.00	6.00	3.50
21	Lloyd Hittle	12.00	6.00	3.50
22	Johnny Babich	12.00	6.00	3.50
23	Merrill Combs	12.00	6.00	3.50
24	Eddie Murphy	12.00	6.00	3.50
25	Bob Klinger	12.00	6.00	3.50

1984 Smokey Bear Angels

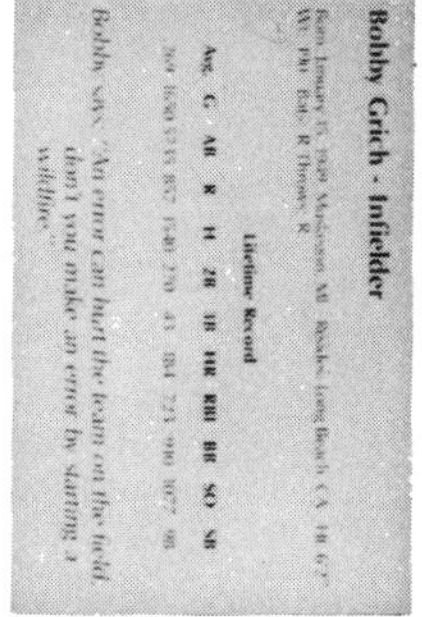

This 32-card set was distributed at a June home game to fans 14 and under. Cards measure 2-1/2" by 3-1/2". The full-color card fronts list the player name along with the team logo and Forestry service logos commemorating the 40th birthday of Smokey the the Bear. The black and white card backs list tips for preventing forest fires.

		MT	NR MT	EX
Complete Set:		8.00	6.00	3.25
Common Player:		.20	.15	.08
(1)	Don Aase	.20	.15	.08
(2)	Juan Beniquez	.20	.15	.08
(3)	Bob Boone	.30	.25	.12
(4)	Rick Burleson	.30	.25	.12
(5)	Rod Carew	1.00	.70	.40
(6)	John Curtis	.20	.15	.08
(7)	Doug DeCinces	.30	.25	.12
(8)	Brian Downing	.30	.25	.12
(9)	Ken Forsch	.20	.15	.08
(10)	Bobby Grich	.30	.25	.12
(11)	Reggie Jackson	1.25	.90	.50
(12)	Ron Jackson	.20	.15	.08
(13)	Tommy John	.60	.45	.25
(14)	Curt Kaufman	.20	.15	.08
(15)	Bruce Kison	.20	.15	.08
(16)	Frank LaCorte	.20	.15	.08
(17)	Fred Lynn	.60	.45	.25
(18)	John McNamara	.20	.15	.08
(19)	Jerry Narron	.20	.15	.08
(20)	Gary Pettis	.40	.30	.15
(21)	Robert Picciolo	.20	.15	.08
(22)	Ron Romanick	.20	.15	.08
(23)	Luis Sanchez	.20	.15	.08
(24)	Dick Schofield	.30	.25	.12
(25)	Daryl Sconiers	.20	.15	.08
(26)	Jim Slaton	.20	.15	.08
(27)	Ellis Valentine	.20	.15	.08
(28)	Robert Wilfong	.20	.15	.08
(29)	Mike Witt	.50	.40	.20
(30)	Geoff Zahn	.20	.15	.08
---	Forestry Dept. Logo Card	.10	.08	.04
---	Smokey Logo Card	.10	.08	.04

1984 Smokey Bear Dodgers

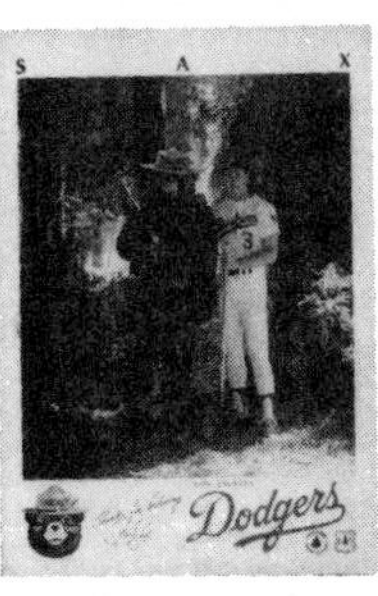

Unlike the California Angels and San Diego Padres sets issued in conjunction with the Forestry Service in 1984, the Los Angeles Dodgers set contains only three players, pictured on much larger 5" by 7" cards. Ken Landreaux, Tom Niedenfuer and Steve Sax (plus a Smokey the Bear card) are pictured on the cards. Each player is pictured in a forest scene on the full-color fronts. Backs of the unnumbered cards have brief biographical information and lifetime statistics. The cards were distributed at a Dodgers home game.

		MT	NR MT	EX
Complete Set:		10.00	7.50	4.00
Common Player:		2.50	2.00	1.00
(1)	Ken Landreaux	2.50	2.00	1.00
(2)	Tom Niedenfuer	2.50	2.00	1.00
(3)	Steve Sax	5.00	3.75	2.00
(4)	Smokey Bear	.50	.40	.20

1984 Smokey Bear Jackson Mets In Majors

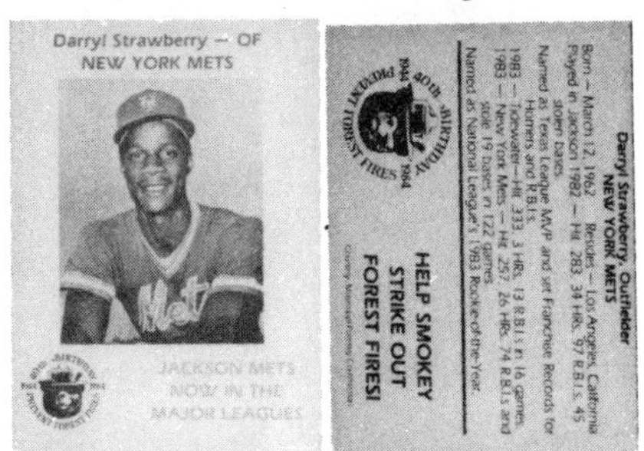

This set, issued in conjunction with the Mississippi Forestry Commission, features big leaguers who played for the Mets' Double-A farm club. The fifteen 3" by 4" cards have a black and white portrait photo on the front with the name, position and major league team shown in blue. A Smokey the Bear logo is also included. Card backs feature player information and career highlights.

		MT	NR MT	EX
Complete Set:		60.00	45.00	25.00
Common Player:		1.00	.70	.40
(1)	Neil Allen	1.00	.70	.40
(2)	Wally Backman	2.00	1.50	.80
(3)	Hubie Brooks	3.00	2.25	1.25
(4)	Jody Davis	2.00	1.50	.80
(5)	Brian Giles	1.00	.70	.40
(6)	Dave Johnson	2.00	1.50	.80
(7)	Tim Leary	2.00	1.50	.80
(8)	Lee Mazzilli	2.00	1.50	.80
(9)	Jesse Orosco	2.00	1.50	.80
(10)	Jeff Reardon	3.00	2.25	1.25
(11)	Doug Sisk	1.00	.70	.40
(12)	Darryl Strawberry	20.00	15.00	8.00
(13)	Mookie Wilson	4.00	3.00	1.50
(14)	Marvel Wynne (Marvell)	2.00	1.50	.80
(15)	Ned Yost	1.00	.70	.40

1984 Smokey Bear Padres

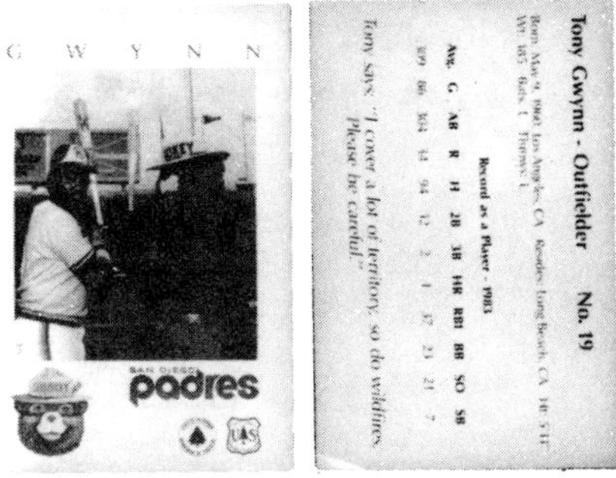

This set of 28 full-color cards is very similar in format to the Angels set of the same year. San Diego Padres players are posed in photos with Smokey the Bear. Forestry Department and team logos are also pictured on the card fronts. The Padres cards feature players, coaches, broadcasters and the Famous Chicken, all posing with Smokey. The backs of the cards which were distributed at a Padres home game, offer brief player information and a fire prevention tip.

		MT	NR MT	EX
Complete Set:		10.00	7.50	4.00
Common Player:		.25	.20	.10
1	Garry Templeton	.40	.30	.15
2	Alan Wiggins	.25	.20	.10
4	Luis Salazar	.25	.20	.10
6	Steve Garvey	1.25	.90	.50
7	Kurt Bevacqua	.25	.20	.10
10	Doug Gwosdz	.25	.20	.10
11	Tim Flannery	.25	.20	.10
16	Terry Kennedy	.40	.30	.15
18	Kevin McReynolds	1.25	.90	.50
19	Tony Gwynn	1.50	1.25	.60
20	Bobby Brown	.25	.20	.10
30	Eric Show	.50	.40	.20
31	Ed Whitson	.25	.20	.10
35	Luis DeLeon	.25	.20	.10
38	Mark Thurmond	.25	.20	.10
42	Sid Monge	.25	.20	.10
43	Dave Dravecky	.40	.30	.15
48	Tim Lollar	.25	.20	.10
---	Smokey Logo Card	.25	.20	.10
---	The Chicken (mascot)	.40	.30	.15
---	Dave Campbell (broadcaster)	.25	.20	.10
---	Jerry Coleman (broadcaster)	.25	.20	.10
---	Harry Dunlop (coach)	.25	.20	.10
---	Harold (Doug) Harvey (umpire)	.25	.20	.10
---	Jack Krol (coach)	.25	.20	.10
---	Jack McKeon (vice-president)	.25	.20	.10
---	Norm Sherry (coach)	.25	.20	.10
---	Ozzie Virgil (coach)	.25	.20	.10
---	Dick Williams (manager)	.25	.20	.10

1985 Smokey Bear Angels

The California Forestry Service and the California Angels gave this full-color set of oversized baseball cards to fans attending the July 14 game at Anaheim Stadium. The 24 cards feature player photos on the fronts with their last name at the top of the cards above the picture. On the card bottoms are the logos for Smokey Bear, the Angels, the State Forestry Service and

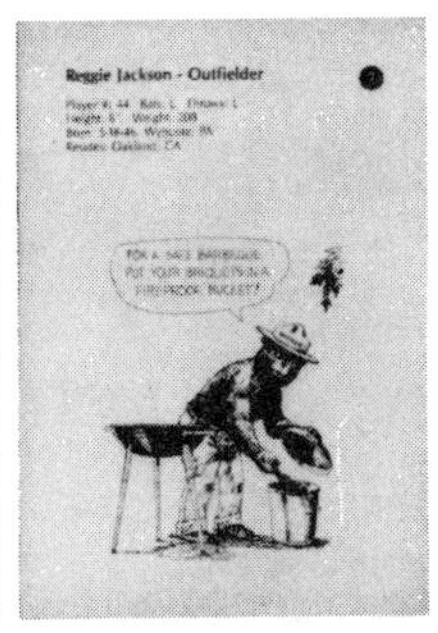

the U.S. Forestry Service. The cards measure 4-1/4" by 6". On the card backs, printed in black and white, are personal data, limited playing stats and a wildfire safety tip from Smokey the Bear.

		MT	NR MT	EX
Complete Set:		7.00	5.25	2.75
Complete Set:		.20	.15	.08
1	Mike Witt	.50	.40	.20
2	Reggie Jackson	1.25	.90	.50
3	Bob Boone	.30	.25	.12
4	Mike Brown	.20	.15	.08
5	Rod Carew	1.00	.70	.40
6	Doug DeCinces	.30	.25	.12
7	Brian Downing	.30	.25	.12
8	Ken Forsch	.20	.15	.08
9	Gary Pettis	.20	.15	.08
10	Jerry Narron	.20	.15	.08
11	Ron Romanick	.20	.15	.08
12	Bobby Grich	.30	.25	.12
13	Dick Schofield	.30	.25	.12
14	Juan Beniquez	.20	.15	.08
15	Geoff Zahn	.20	.15	.08
16	Luis Sanchez	.20	.15	.08
17	Jim Slaton	.20	.15	.08
18	Doug Corbett	.20	.15	.08
19	Ruppert Jones	.20	.15	.08
20	Rob Wilfong	.20	.15	.08
21	Donnie Moore	.20	.15	.08
22	Pat Clements	.20	.15	.08
23	Tommy John	.60	.45	.25
24	Gene Mauch	.30	.25	.12

1986 Smokey Bear Angels

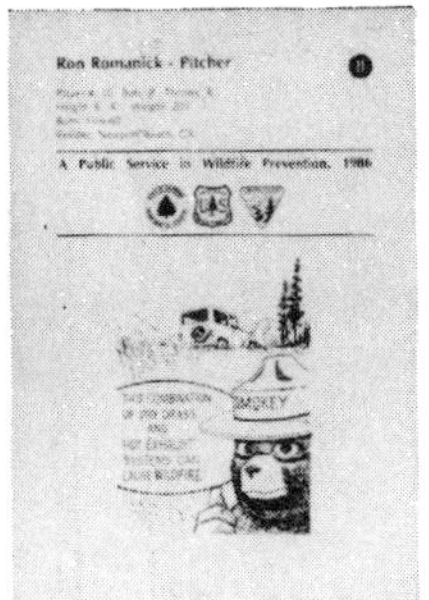

The California Angels, in conjuction with the Forestry Service, issued this 24-card set of Wildfire Prevention baseball cards. The cards measure 4-1/4" by 6" and offer a full-color front with the player's picture placed in an oval frame. The card backs have player stats with a drawing and slogan for fire prevention. The sets were given out on August 9th at the Angels game in Anaheim Stadium.

		MT	NR MT	EX
Complete Set:		8.00	6.00	3.25
Common Player:		.20	.15	.08
1	Mike Witt	.50	.40	.20
2	Reggie Jackson	1.25	.90	.50
3	Bob Boone	.30	.25	.12
4	Don Sutton	.60	.45	.25
5	Kirk McCaskill	.50	.40	.20
6	Doug DeCinces	.30	.25	.12
7	Brian Downing	.30	.25	.12
8	Doug Corbett	.20	.15	.08
9	Gary Pettis	.20	.15	.08
10	Jerry Narron	.20	.15	.08
11	Ron Romanick	.20	.15	.08
12	Bobby Grich	.30	.25	.12
13	Dick Schofield	.30	.25	.12
14	George Hendrick	.30	.25	.12
15	Rick Burleson	.30	.25	.12
16	John Candelaria	.30	.25	.12
17	Jim Slaton	.20	.15	.08
18	Darrell Miller	.30	.25	.12
19	Ruppert Jones	.20	.15	.08
20	Rob Wilfong	.20	.15	.08
21	Donnie Moore	.20	.15	.08
22	Wally Joyner	2.50	2.00	1.00
23	Terry Forster	.30	.25	.12
24	Gene Mauch	.30	.25	.12

1987 Smokey Bear

The U.S. Forestry Service and Major League Baseball united in an effort to promote National Smokey the Bear Day. Two perforated sheets of baseball cards, one each for the American and National Leagues, were produced by the Forestry Service. The sheet of American Leaguers measures 18" by 24" and contains 16 full-color cards. The National League sheet measures 20" by 18" and contains 15 cards. Each individual card is 4" by 6" and contains a fire prevention tip on the back. An average number of 25,000 sets was sent to all teams.

		MT	NR MT	EX
Complete Set:		8.00	6.00	3.25
Common Player:		.20	.15	.08
1A	Jose Canseco	1.50	1.25	.60
1N	Steve Sax	.40	.30	.15
2A	Dennis "Oil Can" Boyd	.20	.15	.08
2Na	Dale Murphy (shirttail out)	5.00	3.75	2.00
2Nb	Dale Murphy (shirttail in)	.80	.60	.30
3A	John Candelaria	.20	.15	.08
3Na	Jody Davis (standing)	3.50	2.75	1.50
3Nb	Jody Davis (kneeling)	.25	.20	.10
4A	Harold Baines	.30	.25	.12
4N	Bill Gullickson	.20	.15	.08
5A	Joe Carter	.30	.25	.12
5N	Mike Scott	.30	.25	.12
6A	Jack Morris	.40	.30	.15
6N	Roger McDowell	.25	.20	.10
7A	Buddy Biancalana	.20	.15	.08
7N	Steve Bedrosian	.30	.25	.12
8A	Kirby Puckett	.70	.50	.30
8N	Johnny Ray	.25	.20	.10
9A	Mike Pagliarulo	.25	.20	.10
9N	Ozzie Smith	.30	.25	.12
10A	Larry Sheets	.25	.20	.10
10N	Steve Garvey	.60	.45	.25
11A	Mike Moore	.20	.15	.08
11N	Smokey Bear Logo Card	.05	.04	.02
12A	Charlie Hough	.20	.15	.08
12N	Mike Krukow	.20	.15	.08
13A	Smokey Bear Logo Card	.05	.04	.02
13N	Smokey Bear	.05	.04	.02
14A	Tom Henke	.20	.15	.08
14N	Mike Fitzgerald	.20	.15	.08
15A	Jim Gantner	.20	.15	.08
15N	National League Logo Card	.05	.04	.02
16A	American League Logo Card	.05	.04	.02

1987 Smokey Bear A's

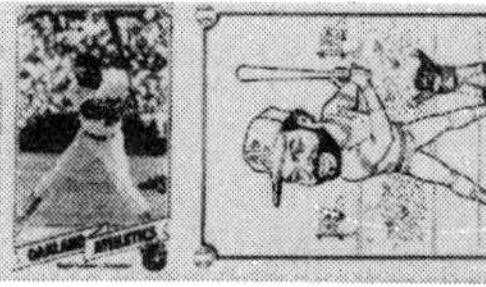
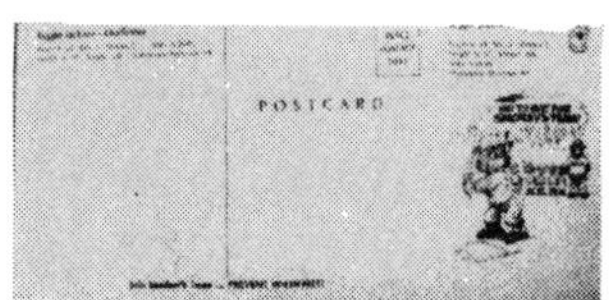

The 1987 Smokey Bear A's set is not comparable to any other Smokey Bear issue produced in 1987 or before. The 12 cards in the set are bound together in a book titled "Smokey Bear's Fire Prevention Color-Grams." The Color-Gram cards feature two cards in one. A near-standard size (2-1/2" by 3-3/4") black and white card is attached to a large perforated (3-3/4" by 6") card, also black and white. The large card, which has a postcard back, features a caricature photo of the player and is intended to be colored and then mailed. The card backs contain personal and statistical information and carry a Smokey the Bear cartoon message. The books were distributed at an Oakland A's game during the 1987 season.

		MT	NR MT	EX
Complete Book:		6.00	4.50	2.50
Complete Singles Set:		3.00	2.25	1.25
Common Single Player:		.15	.11	.06
(1)	Joaquin Andujar	.20	.15	.08
(2)	Jose Canseco	1.50	1.25	.60
(3)	Mike Davis	.25	.20	.10
(4)	Alfredo Griffin	.25	.20	.10
(5)	Moose Haas	.15	.11	.06
(6)	Jay Howell	.25	.20	.10
(7)	Reggie Jackson	.80	.60	.30
(8)	Carney Lansford	.30	.25	.12
(9)	Dwayne Murphy	.25	.20	.10
(10)	Tony Phillips	.15	.11	.06
(11)	Dave Stewart	.40	.30	.15
(12)	Curt Young	.30	.25	.12

1987 Smokey Bear Angels

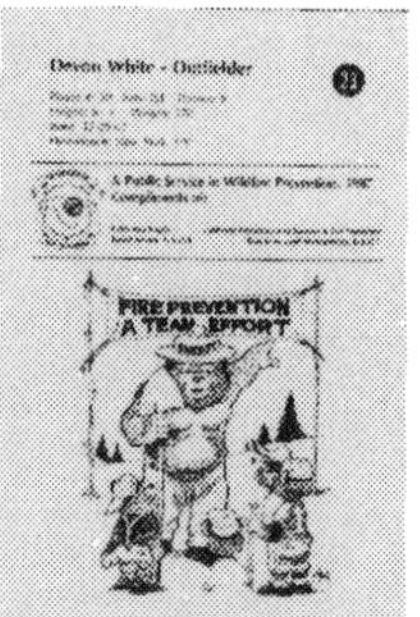

A 24-card set featuring the California Angels and produced by the U.S. Forestry Service was distributed to 25,000 fans in attendance at Anaheim Stadium on August 1st. The full-color cards measure 4" x 6". The card fronts carry a unique design with baseballs and bats framing the player photo. Only the player's last name is given on the card fronts. The backs contain the player's name, position and personal statistics along with a Smokey Bear cartoon and a fire prevention tip.

		MT	NR MT	EX
Complete Set:		8.00	6.00	3.25
Common Player:		.20	.15	.08
1	John Candelaria	.30	.25	.12
2	Don Sutton	.60	.45	.25
3	Mike Witt	.50	.40	.20
4	Gary Lucas	.20	.15	.08
5	Kirk McCaskill	.30	.25	.12
6	Chuck Finley	.30	.25	.12
7	Willie Fraser	.30	.25	.12
8	Donnie Moore	.20	.15	.08
9	Urbano Lugo	.20	.15	.08
10	Butch Wynegar	.25	.20	.10
11	Darrell Miller	.20	.15	.08
12	Wally Joyner	2.00	1.50	.80
13	Mark McLemore	.20	.15	.08
14	Mark Ryal	.20	.15	.08
15	Dick Schofield	.25	.20	.10
16	Jack Howell	.30	.25	.12
17	Doug DeCinces	.30	.25	.12
18	Gus Polidor	.20	.15	.08
19	Brian Downing	.30	.25	.12
20	Gary Pettis	.20	.15	.08
21	Ruppert Jones	.20	.15	.08
22	George Hendrick	.25	.20	.10
23	Devon White	1.25	.90	.50
---	Smokey Bear Logo Card/Checklist	.10	.08	.04

1987 Smokey Bear Braves

Cards from the 1987 Smokey Bear Atlanta Braves set were given out at several different Braves games, with about 25,000 sets in all being distributed. The 4" by 6" cards feature Atlanta players in an oval frame, bordered in red, white and blue. Only the player's last name is listed on the card fronts. Card backs contain the player's name, position and personal data plus a Smokey Bear cartoon with a fire safety message.

		MT	NR MT	EX
Complete Set:		12.00	9.00	4.75
Common Player:		.20	.15	.08
1	Zane Smith	.40	.30	.15
2	Charlie Puleo	.20	.15	.08
3	Randy O'Neal	.20	.15	.08
4	David Palmer	.20	.15	.08
5	Rick Mahler	.30	.25	.12
6	Ed Olwine	.20	.15	.08
7	Jeff Dedmon	.20	.15	.08
8	Paul Assenmacher	.30	.25	.12
9	Gene Garber	.20	.15	.08
10	Jim Acker	.20	.15	.08
11	Bruce Benedict	.20	.15	.08
12	Ozzie Virgil	.20	.15	.08
13	Ted Simmons	.40	.30	.15
14	Dale Murphy	1.75	1.25	.70
15	Graig Nettles	.40	.30	.15
16	Ken Oberkfell	.20	.15	.08
17	Gerald Perry	.60	.45	.25
18	Rafael Ramirez	.20	.15	.08
19	Ken Griffey	.30	.25	.12
20	Andres Thomas	.30	.25	.12
21	Glenn Hubbard	.20	.15	.08
22	Damaso Garcia	.20	.15	.08
23	Gary Roenicke	.20	.15	.08
24	Dion James	.30	.25	.12
25	Albert Hall	.20	.15	.08
26	Chuck Tanner	.20	.15	.08
---	Smokey Bear Logo Card/Checklist	.10	.08	.04

1987 Smokey Bear Cardinals

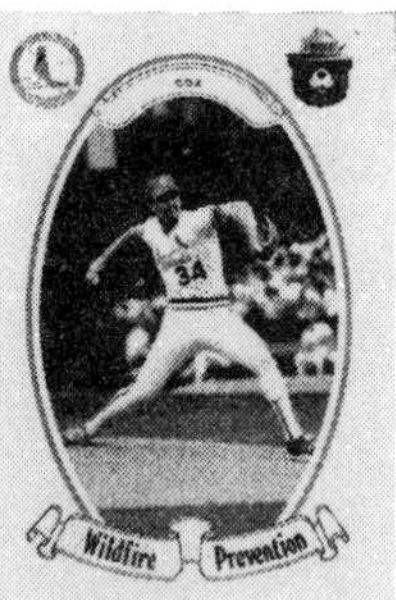

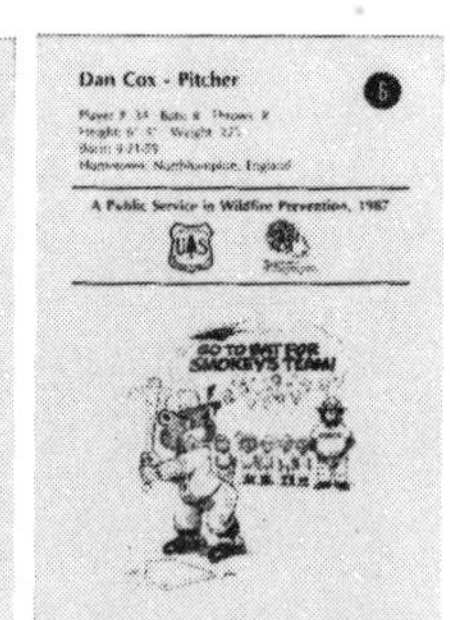

Approximately 25,000 fans in attendance at Busch Stadium on August 24th received a 25-card set featuring the St. Louis Cardinals. Produced by the U.S. Forestry Service, the cards measure 4" by 6". The card fronts feature a full-color photo set inside an oval frame. Only the player's last name appears on the front. The card reverse carries the player's name, position and personal data plus a Smokey Bear cartoon with a fire prevention message.

		MT	NR MT	EX
Complete Set:		8.00	6.00	3.25
Common Player:		.20	.15	.08
1	Ray Soff	.20	.15	.08
2	Todd Worrell	.50	.40	.20
3	John Tudor	.35	.25	.14
4	Pat Perry	.20	.15	.08
5	Rick Horton	.20	.15	.08
6	Dan Cox	.30	.25	.12
7	Bob Forsch	.30	.25	.12
8	Greg Mathews	.40	.30	.15
9	Bill Dawley	.20	.15	.08
10	Steve Lake	.20	.15	.08
11	Tony Pena	.30	.25	.12
12	Tom Pagnozzi	.30	.25	.12
13	Jack Clark	.80	.60	.30
14	Jim Lindeman	.35	.25	.14
15	Mike Laga	.20	.15	.08
16	Terry Pendleton	.40	.30	.15
17	Ozzie Smith	.80	.60	.30
18	Jose Oquendo	.20	.15	.08
19	Tom Lawless	.20	.15	.08
20	Tom Herr	.30	.25	.12
21	Curt Ford	.20	.15	.08
22	Willie McGee	.70	.50	.30
23	Tito Landrum	.20	.15	.08
24	Vince Coleman	.80	.60	.30
25	Whitey Herzog	.30	.25	.12

1987 Smokey Bear Dodgers

The 40-card Smokey Bear Dodgers set features "25 Years of Dodger All-Stars." The cards, which measure 2-1/2" by 3-3/4", were given out to

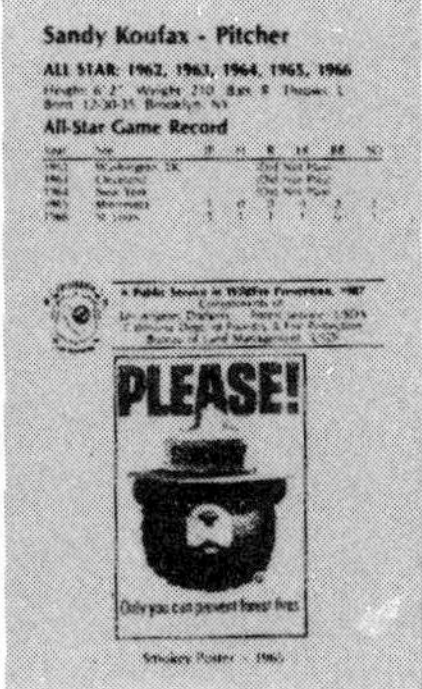

fans 14 years of age and younger at the September 18th game at Dodgers Stadium. The card fronts contain full-color photos set in the shape of Dodger Stadium and have attractive silver borders. The backs carry the player's All-Star Game record plus a fire prevention message. Many of the photos used in the set were from team-issued picture packs sold by the Dodgers in the past.

		MT	NR MT	EX
Complete Set:		10.00	7.50	4.00
Common Player:		.20	.15	.08
(1)	Walt Alston	.40	.30	.15
(2)	Dusty Baker	.25	.20	.10
(3)	Jim Brewer	.20	.15	.08
(4)	Ron Cey	.30	.25	.12
(5)	Tommy Davis	.25	.20	.10
(6)	Willie Davis	.25	.20	.10
(7)	Don Drysdale	.80	.60	.30
(8)	Steve Garvey	.80	.60	.30
(9)	Bill Grabarkewitz	.20	.15	.08
(10)	Pedro Guerrero	.50	.40	.20
(11)	Tom Haller	.20	.15	.08
(12)	Orel Hershiser	.60	.45	.25
(13)	Burt Hooton	.20	.15	.08
(14)	Steve Howe	.20	.15	.08
(15)	Tommy John	.50	.40	.20
(16)	Sandy Koufax	1.25	.90	.50
(17)	Tom Lasorda	.30	.25	.12
(18)	Jim Lefebvre	.20	.15	.08
(19)	Davey Lopes	.25	.20	.10
(20)	Mike Marshall (outfielder)	.40	.30	.15
(21)	Mike Marshall (pitcher)	.25	.20	.10
(22)	Andy Messersmith	.20	.15	.08
(23)	Rick Monday	.25	.20	.10
(24)	Manny Mota	.25	.20	.10
(25)	Claude Osteen	.20	.15	.08
(26)	Johnny Podres	.30	.25	.12
(27)	Phil Regan	.20	.15	.08
(28)	Jerry Reuss	.25	.20	.10
(29)	Rick Rhoden	.25	.20	.10
(30)	John Roseboro	.25	.20	.10
(31)	Bill Russell	.25	.20	.10
(32)	Steve Sax	.40	.30	.15
(33)	Bill Singer	.20	.15	.08
(34)	Reggie Smith	.25	.20	.10
(35)	Don Sutton	.60	.45	.25
(36)	Fernando Valenzuela	.70	.50	.30
(37)	Bob Welch	.30	.25	.12
(38)	Maury Wills	.40	.30	.15
(39)	Jim Wynn	.20	.15	.08
(40)	Logo Card/Checklist	.10	.08	.04

1987 Smokey Bear Rangers

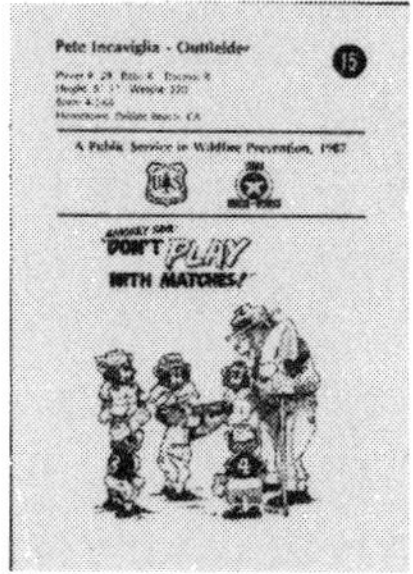

The 1987 Smokey Bear Rangers set is made up of 32 full-color cards. Co-sponsored by the Texas Rangers, U.S. Forest Service and Texas Forest Service, the set was given out to fans at special promotions at Arlington Stadium. The cards measure 4-1/4" by 6" and feature full-color photos on the fronts. The backs contain brief player personal information, along with the card number and a Smokey the Bear message. Cards of Mike Mason and Tom Paciorek were withdrawn from the sets given out by the Rangers and are quite scarce.

		MT	NR MT	EX
Complete Set:		70.00	52.00	27.00
Common Player:		.30	.25	.12
1	Charlie Hough	.60	.45	.25
2	Greg Harris	.30	.25	.12
3	Jose Guzman	.60	.45	.25
4	Mike Mason	25.00	20.00	10.00
5	Dale Mohorcic	.50	.40	.20
6	Bobby Witt	.80	.60	.30
7	Mitch Williams	.50	.40	.20
8	Geno Petralli	.30	.25	.12
9	Don Slaught	.30	.25	.12
10	Darrell Porter	.30	.25	.12
11	Steve Beuchele	.40	.30	.15
12	Pete O'Brien	.60	.45	.25
13	Scott Fletcher	.40	.30	.15
14	Tom Paciorek	25.00	20.00	10.00
15	Pete Incaviglia	1.00	.70	.40
16	Oddibe McDowell	.60	.45	.25
17	Ruben Sierra	1.50	1.25	.60
18	Larry Parrish	.50	.40	.20
19	Bobby Valentine	.40	.30	.15
20	Tom House	.30	.25	.12
21	Tom Robson	.30	.25	.12
22	Edwin Correa	.40	.30	.15
23	Mike Stanley	.60	.45	.25
24	Joe Ferguson	.30	.25	.12
25	Art Howe	.30	.25	.12
26	Bob Brower	.50	.40	.20
27	Mike Loynd	.50	.40	.20
28	Curtis Wilkerson	.30	.25	.12
29	Tim Foli	.30	.25	.12
30	Dave Oliver	.30	.25	.12
31	Jerry Browne	.50	.40	.20
32	Jeff Russell	.30	.25	.12

1988 Smokey Bear Angels

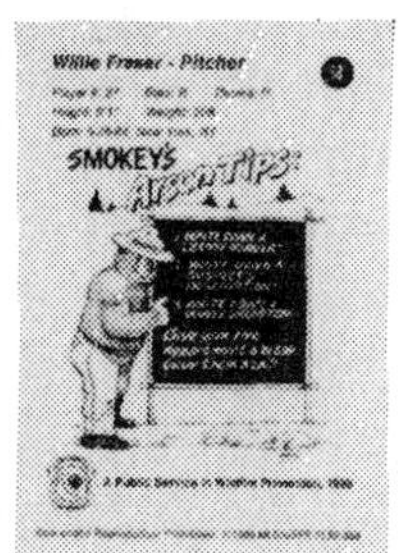

This set includes 25 borderless full-color cards (2-1/2" by 3-1/2") that are highlighted by a thin white inset outline on the card fronts. The player name, team logo and a Smokey Bear picture logo appear in the lower right corner. The backs are black and white and include personal information and a large cartoon-style fire prevention logo. The set also includes a team logo checklist card. Part of the U.S. Forest Service fire prevention campaign, the cards were distributed in three separate in-stadium giveaways during August and September, 1988 games.

		MT	NR MT	EX
Complete Set:		10.00	7.50	4.00
Common Player:		.30	.25	.12
1	Cookie Rojas	.30	.25	.12
2	Johnny Ray	.40	.30	.15
3	Jack Howell	.40	.30	.15
4	Mike Witt	.50	.40	.20
5	Tony Armas	.40	.30	.15
6	Gus Polidor	.30	.25	.12
7	DeWayne Buice	.40	.30	.15
8	Dan Petry	.40	.30	.15
9	Bob Boone	.40	.30	.15
10	Chili Davis	.40	.30	.15
11	Greg Minton	.30	.25	.12
12	Kirk McCaskill	.40	.30	.15
13	Devon White	.80	.60	.30
14	Willie Fraser	.30	.25	.12
15	Chuck Finley	.30	.25	.12
16	Dick Schofield	.30	.25	.12
17	Wally Joyner	1.50	1.25	.60
18	Brian Downing	.40	.30	.15
19	Stewart Cliburn	.30	.25	.12
20	Donnie Moore	.30	.25	.12
21	Bryan Harvey	.40	.30	.15
22	Mark McLemore	.30	.25	.12
23	Butch Wynegar	.30	.25	.12
24	George Hendrick	.40	.30	.15
---	Team Logo/Checklist	.30	.25	.12

Regional interest may affect the value of a card.

1988 Smokey Bear Cardinals

This set of 25 oversized (3" by 5") cards features full-color action photos that fill the entire card fronts. A thin white line frames the player photo. The player name, team logo and Smokey Bear picture logo are printed in the lower right corner. The black and white cards backs contain player information and a Smokey Bear fire prevention cartoon. The card sets were distributed to young St. Louis fans as part of a Forest Service fire prevention campaign. The National Association of State Foresters co-sponsored this set.

		MT	NR MT	EX
Complete Set:		10.00	7.50	4.00
Common Player:		.20	.15	.08
1	Whitey Herzog	.30	.25	.12
2	Danny Cox	.30	.25	.12
3	Ken Dayley	.20	.15	.08
4	Jose DeLeon	.30	.25	.12
5	Bob Forsch	.30	.25	.12
6	Joe Magrane	.50	.40	.20
7	Greg Mathews	.30	.25	.12
8	Scott Terry	.20	.15	.08
9	John Tudor	.35	.25	.14
10	Todd Worrell	.50	.40	.20
11	Steve Lake	.20	.15	.08
12	Tom Pagnozzi	.20	.15	.08
13	Tony Pena	.30	.25	.12
14	Bob Horner	.35	.25	.14
15	Tom Lawless	.20	.15	.08
16	Jose Oquendo	.20	.15	.08
17	Terry Pendleton	.40	.30	.15
18	Ozzie Smith	.80	.60	.30
19	Vince Coleman	.80	.60	.30
20	Curt Ford	.20	.15	.08
21	Willie McGee	.70	.50	.30
22	Larry McWilliams	.20	.15	.08
23	Steve Peters	.30	.25	.12
24	Luis Alicea	.30	.25	.12
25	Tom Brunansky	.50	.40	.20

The values quoted are intended to reflect the market price.

1988 Smokey Bear Dodgers

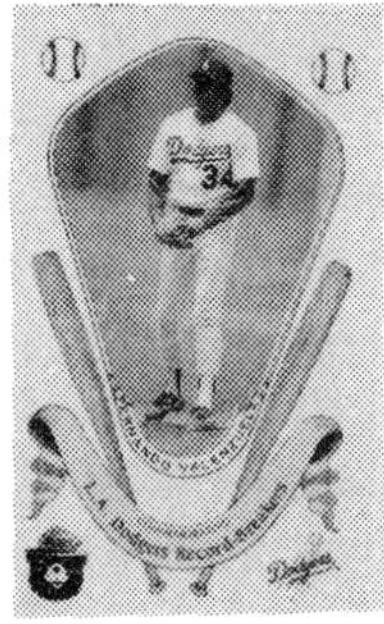

Record-breaking Dodgers from the past three decades are featured on this 32-card perforated sheet. Individual cards measure 2-1/2" by 4" and are printed on a light blue background in a design similar to the 1987 Smokey Bear Dodgers All-Star set. The black and white card backs contain the player name, a brief summary of the player's record-breaking performance and a reproduction of one of a number of Smokey Bear fire prevention posters printed during the 1950s through the 1980s. The sheets were distributed to fans in Dodger Stadium. Sponsors the Piedmont brand of the Liggert & Meyers Tobacco Co., the stamps include the Forest Service, California Dept. of Forestry and the Bureau of Land Management.

		MT	NR MT	EX
Complete Set:		10.00	7.50	4.00
Common Player:		.20	.15	.08
1	Walter Alston	.40	.30	.15
2	John Roseboro	.25	.20	.10
3	Frank Howard	.40	.30	.15
4	Sandy Koufax	1.25	.90	.50
5	Manny Mota	.25	.20	.10

		MT	NR MT	EX
6	Record Pitchers (Sandy Koufax, Jerry Reuss, Bill Singer)	.70	.50	.30
7	Maury Wills	.40	.30	.15
8	Tommy Davis	.25	.20	.10
9	Phil Regan	.20	.15	.08
10	Wes Parker	.20	.15	.08
11	Don Drysdale	.80	.60	.30
12	Willie Davis	.25	.20	.10
13	Bill Russell	.25	.20	.10
14	Jim Brewer	.20	.15	.08
15	Record Fielders (Ron Cey, Steve Garvey, Davey Lopes, Bill Russell)	.50	.40	.20
16	Mike Marshall (pitcher)	.25	.20	.10
17	Steve Garvey	.80	.60	.30
18	Davey Lopes	.25	.20	.10
19	Burt Hooton	.20	.15	.08
20	Jim Wynn	.20	.15	.08
21	Record Hitters (Dusty Baker, Ron Cey, Steve Garvey, Reggie Smith)	.50	.40	.20
22	Dusty Baker	.25	.20	.10
23	Tom Lasorda	.30	.25	.12
24	Fernando Valenzuela	.70	.50	.30
25	Steve Sax	.40	.30	.15
26	Dodger Stadium	.20	.15	.08
27	Ron Cey	.30	.25	.12
28	Pedro Guerrero	.50	.40	.20
29	Mike Marshall (outfielder)	.40	.30	.15
30	Don Sutton	.60	.45	.25
---	Logo Card/Checklist	.20	.15	.08
---	Smokey Bear	.20	.15	.08

1988 Smokey Bear Padres

This 33-card oversized (3" by 5") set was produced in conjunction with the U.S. Forest Service as a fire prevention campaign promotion. A full-color player photo, framed by a thin white line, fills the card face. The player number and position and Smokey Bear logo appear lower right. The black and white card backs are printed in horizontal postcard format, with player info and a Smokey Bear cartoon on the left half of the card back. The set was available for purchase at the Padres Gift Shop. Cards of Candy Sierra and Larry Bowa were not released by the Padres and are quite rare. The complete set price does not include the two rare cards.

		MT	NR MT	EX
Complete Set:		12.00	9.00	4.75
Common Player:		.30	.25	.12
(1)	Shawn Abner	.50	.40	.20
(2)	Roberto Alomar	1.25	.90	.50
(3)	Sandy Alomar	.30	.25	.12
(4)	Greg Booker	.30	.25	.12
(5)	Larry Bowa	10.00	7.50	4.00
(6)	Chris Brown	.40	.30	.15
(7)	Mark Davis	.30	.25	.12
(8)	Pat Dobson	.30	.25	.12
(9)	Tim Flannery	.30	.25	.12
(10)	Mark Grant	.30	.25	.12
(11)	Tony Gwynn	1.50	1.25	.60
(12)	Andy Hawkins	.50	.40	.20
(13)	Stan Jefferson	.30	.25	.12
(14)	Jimmy Jones	.30	.25	.12
(15)	John Kruk	.80	.60	.30
(16)	Dave Leiper	.30	.25	.12
(17)	Shane Mack	.40	.30	.15
(18)	Carmelo Martinez	.40	.30	.15
(19)	Lance McCullers	.40	.30	.15
(20)	Keith Moreland	.40	.30	.15
(21)	Eric Nolte	.40	.30	.15
(22)	Amos Otis	.30	.25	.12
(23)	Mark Parent	.40	.30	.15
(24)	Randy Ready	.30	.25	.12
(25)	Greg Riddoch	.30	.25	.12
(26)	Benito Santiago	.80	.60	.30
(27)	Eric Show	.50	.40	.20
(28)	Candy Sierra	10.00	7.50	4.00
(29)	Denny Sommers	.30	.25	.12
(30)	Garry Templeton	.40	.30	.15
(31)	Dickie Thon	.40	.30	.15
(32)	Ed Whitson	.30	.25	.12
(33)	Marvell Wynne	.30	.25	.12

1988 Smokey Bear Rangers

This 21-card oversized (3-1/2" by 5") set was distributed to Rangers' fans at Smokey Bear Game Day on August 7th. The card fronts feature full-color action photos framed in an oval blue and red border on a white background. A nameplate above the photo identifies the player and a "Wildfire Prevention" logo is printed beneath the photo. Rangers (left) and Smokey (right) logos fill the upper corners of the card face. The card backs are black and white and include player info., U.S. and Texas Forest Service logos, and fire prevention tips.

		MT	NR MT	EX
Complete Set:		9.00	6.75	3.50
Common Player:		.30	.25	.12
1	Tom O'Malley	.30	.25	.12
2	Pete O'Brien	.50	.40	.20
3	Geno Petralli	.30	.25	.12
4	Pete Incaviglia	.70	.50	.30
5	Oddibe McDowell	.50	.40	.20
6	Dale Mohorcic	.30	.25	.12
7	Bobby Witt	.60	.45	.25
8	Bobby Valentine	.40	.30	.15
9	Ruben Sierra	1.00	.70	.40
10	Scott Fletcher	.40	.30	.15
11	Mike Stanley	.40	.30	.15
12	Steve Buechele	.40	.30	.15
13	Charlie Hough	.50	.40	.20
14	Larry Parrish	.40	.30	.15
15	Jerry Browne	.30	.25	.12
16	Bob Brower	.30	.25	.12
17	Jeff Russell	.30	.25	.12
18	Edwin Correa	.30	.25	.12
19	Mitch Williams	.40	.30	.15
20	Jose Guzman	.40	.30	.15
21	Curtis Wilkerson	.30	.25	.12

1988 Smokey Bear Royals

This 28-card set featuring full-color player caricatures by K.K. Goodale was produced for an in-stadium promotion on August 14, 1988. The 3" by 5" cards depict players, manager and coaches in action poses against a white background with a Royals logo upper left, opposite the Smokey Bear logo. The backs are black and white and contain brief player data and a Smokey cartoon.

		MT	NR MT	EX
Complete Set:		12.00	9.00	4.75
Common Player:		.20	.15	.08
1	John Wathan	.30	.25	.12
2	Royals Coaches (Frank Funk, Adrian Garrett, Mike Lum, Ed Napolean, Bob Schaefer, Jim Schaefer)	.20	.15	.08
3	Willie Wilson	.40	.30	.15
4	Danny Tartabull	.70	.50	.30
5	Bo Jackson	1.50	1.25	.60
6	Gary Thurman	.40	.30	.15
7	Jerry Don Gleaton	.20	.15	.08
8	Floyd Bannister	.30	.25	.12
9	Buddy Black	.20	.15	.08
10	Steve Farr	.20	.15	.08
11	Gene Garber	.20	.15	.08
12	Mark Gubicza	.50	.40	.20
13	Charlie Liebrandt	.30	.25	.12
14	Ted Power	.20	.15	.08
15	Dan Quisenberry	.30	.25	.12
16	Bret Saberhagen	.70	.50	.30
17	Mike Macfarlane	.30	.25	.12
18	Scotti Madison	.30	.25	.12
19	Jamie Quirk	.20	.15	.08
20	George Brett	1.25	.90	.50
21	Kevin Seitzer	.80	.60	.30
22	Bill Pecota	.20	.15	.08
23	Kurt Stillwell	.35	.25	.14
24	Brad Wellman	.20	.15	.08
25	Frank White	.30	.25	.12
26	Jim Eisenreich	.20	.15	.08
27	Smokey Bear	.20	.15	.08
---	Checklist	.20	.15	.08

1988 Smokey Bear Twins

This 8-1/4" by 3-3/4" booklet contains a dozen postcards called Color-Grams featuring caricatures (suitable for coloring) of star players from the Minnesota Twins. Postcards are attached along a perforated edge to a baseball card-size stub with a black and white photo of the featured player. The backs of the postcards include the player name and personal information. The card stubs include the same information, along with a fire prevention tip. Twins Color-Grams were produced as a public service by the U.S. Forest Service and Dept. of Agriculture and were distributed to fans at the Metrodome.

		MT	NR MT	EX
Complete Set:		12.00	.50	.30
Common Player:		.70	.50	.30
(1)	Bert Blyleven	1.00	.50	.30
(2)	Randy Bush	.70	.50	.30
(3)	Gary Gaetti	1.50	.50	.30
(4)	Greg Gagne	.70	.50	.30
(5)	Dan Gladden	.70	.50	.30
(6)	Kent Hrbek	1.75	.50	.30
(7)	Gene Larkin	.70	.50	.30
(8)	Tim Laudner	.70	.50	.30
(9)	Al Newman	.70	.50	.30
(10)	Kirby Puckett	2.00	.50	.30
(11)	Jeff Reardon	1.00	.50	.30
(12)	Frank Viola	1.75	.50	.30

Regional interest may affect the value of a card.

Mint (Mt.): A perfect card. Well-centered, with equal borders. Four sharp, square corners. No creases, edge dents, surface scratches, paper flaws, loss of luster, yellowing or fading, regardless of age. No imperfectly printed card — out of register, badly cut or ink-flawed — or card stained by contact with gum, wax or other substances can truly be considered Mint, even if new out of the pack.

Near Mint (Nr. Mt.): A nearly perfect card. At first glance, a Near Mint card appears perfect; under closer examination, however, a minor flaw will be discovered. On well-centered cards, three of the four corners must be perfectly sharp. A slightly off-center card would also fit this grade.

Excellent (Ex.): Corners more sharp than rounded. Card borders may be off center. No creases. No gum, wax or product stains, front or back. Surfaces may show some loss of luster.

1989 Smokey Bear Angels

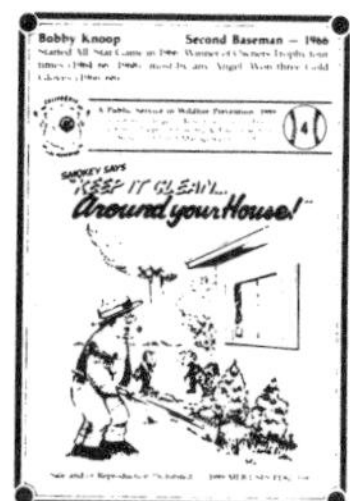

The U.S. Forest Service, in conjunction with the California Angels, issued a 20-card set of "Angels All-Stars" in 1989. The standard-size cards are printed on a silver background and the player photos are bordered in red. Beneath the photo a banner stretches across homeplate, reading "Angels All-Stars," along with the player's name and position, which are flanked by Smokey Bear on the left and the Angels 1989 All-Star Game logo on the right. Card backs highlight the player's career with the Angels and include an illustrated fire prevention tip.

		MT	NR MT	EX
Complete Set:		6.00	4.50	2.50
Common Player:		.20	.15	.08
1	Bill Rigney	.20	.15	.08
2	Dean Chance	.20	.15	.08
3	Jim Fregosi	.40	.30	.15
4	Bobby Knoop	.40	.30	.15

		MT	NR MT	EX
5	Don Mincher	.20	.15	.08
6	Clyde Wright	.20	.15	.08
7	Nolan Ryan	1.00	.70	.40
8	Frank Robinson	.80	.60	.30
9	Frank Tanana	.20	.15	.08
10	Rod Carew	.50	.40	.20
11	Bobby Grich	.20	.15	.08
12	Brian Downing	.20	.15	.08
13	Don Baylor	.35	.25	.14
14	Fred Lynn	.20	.15	.08
15	Reggie Jackson	.70	.50	.30
16	Doug DeCinces	.20	.15	.08
17	Bob Boone	.20	.15	.08
18	Wally Joyner	.60	.45	.25
19	Mike Witt	.20	.15	.08
20	Johnny Ray	.20	.15	.08

1989 Smokey Bear Cardinals

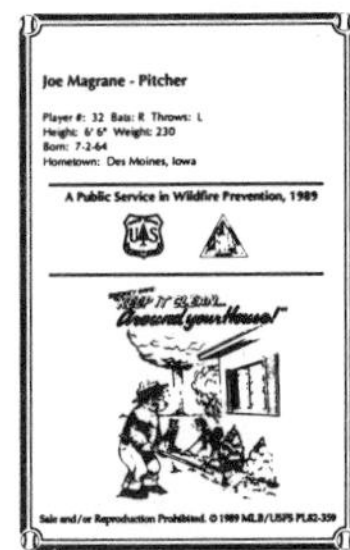

This 25-card set featuring action player photos was issued by the U.S. Forest Service to promote fire safety. The cards measure 4" by 6" and include the player's name, team logo and a small picture of Smokey Bear beneath the player photo.

		MT	NR MT	EX
Complete Set:		10.00	7.50	4.00
Common Player:		.20	.15	.08
(1)	Tom Brunansky	.50	.40	.20
(2)	Cris Carpenter	.50	.40	.20
(3)	Vince Coleman	.80	.60	.30
(4)	John Costello	.30	.25	.12
(5)	Ken Dayley	.20	.15	.08
(6)	Jose DeLeon	.35	.25	.14
(7)	Frank DiPino	.20	.15	.08
(8)	Whitey Herzog	.30	.25	.12
(9)	Ken Hill	.80	.60	.30
(10)	Pedro Guerrero	.80	.60	.30
(11)	Tim Jones	.30	.25	.12
(12)	Jim Lindeman	.20	.15	.08
(13)	Joe Magrane	.50	.40	.20
(14)	Willie McGee	.50	.40	.20
(15)	John Morris	.30	.25	.12
(16)	Jose Oquendo	.30	.25	.12
(17)	Tom Pagnozzi	.20	.15	.08
(18)	Tony Pena	.30	.25	.12
(19)	Terry Pendleton	.30	.25	.12
(20)	Dan Quisenberry	.20	.15	.08
(21)	Ozzie Smith	.80	.60	.30
(22)	Scott Terry	.30	.25	.12
(23)	Milt Thompson	.30	.25	.12
(24)	Denny Walling	.20	.15	.11
(25)	Todd Worrell	.50	.40	.20

1953 Spic and Span Braves

The first of several regional issues from a Milwaukee dry cleaner, the 1953-54 Spic and Span Braves set consists of 27 cards, each measuring 3-1/4" by 5-1/2". The fronts of the card have a facsimile autograph beneath the player photo. Cards are found with blank backs or with a Spic and Span advertising message on the back.

		NR MT	EX	VG
Complete Set:		550.00	275.00	165.00
Common Player:		18.00	9.00	5.50
(1)	Joe Adcock	30.00	15.00	9.00
(2)	John Antonelli	25.00	12.50	7.50
(3)	Vern Bickford	18.00	9.00	5.50
(4)	Bill Bruton	25.00	12.50	7.50
(5)	Bob Buhl	25.00	12.50	7.50
(6)	Lew Burdette	30.00	15.00	9.00
(7)	Dick Cole	18.00	9.00	5.50
(8)	Walker Cooper	18.00	9.00	5.50
(9)	Del Crandall	30.00	15.00	9.00
(10)	George Crowe	18.00	9.00	5.50
(11)	Jack Dittmer	18.00	9.00	5.50
(12)	Sid Gordon	18.00	9.00	5.50
(13)	Ernie Johnson	18.00	9.00	5.50
(14)	Dave Jolly	18.00	9.00	5.50
(15)	Don Liddle	18.00	9.00	5.50
(16)	John Logan	25.00	12.50	7.50
(17)	Ed Mathews	50.00	25.00	15.00
(18)	Dan O'Connell	18.00	9.00	5.50
(19)	Andy Pafko	25.00	12.50	7.50
(20)	Jim Pendleton	18.00	9.00	5.50
(21)	Ebba St. Claire	18.00	9.00	5.50
(22)	Warren Spahn	50.00	25.00	15.00
(23)	Max Surkont	18.00	9.00	5.50
(24)	Bob Thomson	25.00	12.50	7.50
(25)	Bob Thorpe	18.00	9.00	5.50
(26)	Roberto Vargas	18.00	9.00	5.50
(27)	Jim Wilson	18.00	9.00	5.50

1953 Spic and Span Braves 7x10 Photos

This regional set was issued by Spic and Span Dry Cleaners of Milwaukee over a four-year period and consists of 13 large (7" by 10") photos of Braves players. Of all the various Spic and Span sets, this one seems to be the easiest to find. The fronts feature a player photo with a facsimile autograph below. The Spic and Span logo also appears on the fronts, while the backs are blank. A photo of Milwaukee County Stadium also exists but is not generally considered to be part of the set.

		NR MT	EX	VG
Complete Set:		250.00	125.00	75.00
Common Player:		10.00	5.00	3.00
(1)	Joe Adcock	18.00	9.00	5.50
(2)	Bill Bruton	12.00	6.00	3.50
(3)	Bob Buhl	12.00	6.00	3.50
(4)	Lew Burdette	18.00	9.00	5.50
(5)	Del Crandall	18.00	9.00	5.50
(6)	Jack Dittmer	10.00	5.00	3.00
(7)	John Logan	12.00	6.00	3.50
(8)	Ed Mathews	50.00	25.00	15.00
(9)	Chet Nichols	10.00	5.00	3.00
(10)	Dan O'Connell	10.00	5.00	3.00
(11)	Andy Pafko	12.00	6.00	3.50
(12)	Warren Spahn	50.00	25.00	15.00
(13)	Bob Thomson	12.00	6.00	3.50

1954 Spic and Span Braves

Issued during the three-year period from 1954-1956, this Spic and Span set consists of 18 postcard-size (4" by 6") cards. The front of the cards include a facsimile autograph printed in white and the Spic and Span logo.

		NR MT	EX	VG
Complete Set:		400.00	200.00	120.00
Common Player:		12.00	6.00	3.50
(1)	Hank Aaron	125.00	62.00	37.00
(2)	Joe Adcock	25.00	12.50	7.50
(3)	Bill Bruton	18.00	9.00	5.50
(4)	Bob Buhl	18.00	9.00	5.50
(5)	Lew Burdette	25.00	12.50	7.50
(6)	Gene Conley	18.00	9.00	5.50
(7)	Del Crandall	25.00	12.50	7.50
(8)	Ray Crone	12.00	6.00	3.50
(9)	Jack Dittmer	12.00	6.00	3.50
(10)	Ernie Johnson	12.00	6.00	3.50
(11)	Dave Jolly	12.00	6.00	3.50
(12)	John Logan	18.00	9.00	5.50
(13)	Ed Mathews	50.00	25.00	15.00
(14)	Chet Nichols	12.00	6.00	3.50
(15)	Dan O'Connell	12.00	6.00	3.50
(16)	Andy Pafko	18.00	9.00	5.50
(17)	Warren Spahn	50.00	25.00	15.00
(18)	Bob Thomson	18.00	9.00	5.50

1955 Spic an Span Braves Die-Cuts

This 17-card, die-cut set is the rarest of all the Spic and Span issues. The stand-ups, which measure approximately 7-1/2" by 7", picture the players in action poses and were designed to be punched out, allowing them to stand up. Most cards were used in this fashion, making better-condition cards very rare today. The front of the card includes a facsimile autograph and the Spic and Span logo.

		NR MT	EX	VG
Complete Set:		3000.	1500.	900.00
Common Player:		110.00	55.00	33.00
(1)	Hank Aaron	500.00	250.00	150.00
(2)	Joe Adcock	175.00	87.00	52.00
(3)	Bill Bruton	150.00	75.00	45.00
(4)	Bob Buhl	150.00	75.00	45.00
(5)	Lew Burdette	175.00	87.00	52.00
(6)	Gene Conley	150.00	75.00	45.00
(7)	Del Crandall	175.00	87.00	52.00
(8)	Jack Dittmer	110.00	55.00	33.00
(9)	Ernie Johnson	110.00	55.00	33.00
(10)	Dave Jolly	110.00	55.00	33.00
(11)	John Logan	150.00	75.00	45.00
(12)	Ed Mathews	350.00	175.00	105.00
(13)	Chet Nichols	110.00	55.00	33.00
(14)	Dan O'Connell	110.00	55.00	33.00
(15)	Andy Pafko	150.00	75.00	45.00
(16)	Warren Spahn	350.00	175.00	105.00
(17)	Bob Thomson	150.00	75.00	45.00
(18)	Jim Wilson	110.00	55.00	33.00

1957 Spic and Span Braves

This 20-card set was issued in 1957, the year the Braves were World Champions, and is a highly desirable set. The cards measure 4" by 5" and have a wide, white border surrounding the player photo. A blue Spic and Span logo appears in the extreme lower right corner, and the card includes a salutation and facsimile autograph, also in blue.

		NR MT	EX	VG
Complete Set:		400.00	200.00	120.00
Common Player:		12.00	6.00	3.50
(1)	Hank Aaron	125.00	62.00	37.00
(2)	Joe Adcock	25.00	12.50	7.50
(3)	Bill Bruton	18.00	9.00	5.50
(4)	Bob Buhl	18.00	9.00	5.50
(5)	Lew Burdette	25.00	12.50	7.50
(6)	Gene Conley	18.00	9.00	5.50
(7)	Wes Covington	18.00	9.00	5.50
(8)	Del Crandall	25.00	12.50	7.50
(9)	Ray Crone	12.00	6.00	3.50
(10)	Fred Haney	18.00	9.00	5.50
(11)	Ernie Johnson	12.00	6.00	3.50
(12)	Felix Mantilla	25.00	12.50	7.50
(13)	Ed Mathews	60.00	30.00	18.00
(14)	John Logan	18.00	9.00	5.50
(15)	Dan O'Connell	12.00	6.00	3.50
(16)	Andy Pafko	18.00	9.00	5.50
(17)	Red Schoendienst	40.00	20.00	12.00
(18)	Warren Spahn	60.00	30.00	18.00
(19)	Bob Thomson	18.00	9.00	5.50
(20)	Bob Trowbridge	25.00	12.50	7.50

1960 Spic and Span Braves

Spic and Span's final Milwaukee Braves issue consisted of 26 cards, each mesauring 2-3/4" by 3-1/8". The fronts contain a white-bordered photo with no printing, while the backs include a facsimile autograph and the words "Photographed and Autographed Exclusively for Spic and Span." The 1960 set includes the only known variation in the Spic and Span sets. A "flopped" negative error showing catcher Del Crandall batting left-handed was later corrected.

		NR MT	EX	VG
Complete Set:		600.00	300.00	180.00
Common Player:		12.00	6.00	3.50
(1)	Hank Aaron	125.00	62.00	37.00
(2)	Joe Adcock	25.00	12.50	7.50
(3)	Bill Bruton	18.00	9.00	5.50
(4)	Bob Buhl	18.00	9.00	5.50
(5)	Lew Burdette	25.00	12.50	7.50
(6)	Chuck Cottier	12.00	6.00	3.50
(7a)	Del Crandall (photo reversed)	35.00	17.50	10.50
(7b)	Del Crandall (correct photo)	35.00	17.50	10.50
(8)	Chuck Dressen	12.00	6.00	3.50
(9)	Joey Jay	12.00	6.00	3.50
(10)	John Logan	18.00	9.00	5.50
(11)	Felix Mantilla	12.00	6.00	3.50
(12)	Ed Mathews	60.00	30.00	18.00
(13)	Lee Maye	12.00	6.00	3.50
(14)	Don McMahon	12.00	6.00	3.50
(15)	George Myatt	12.00	6.00	3.50
(16)	Andy Pafko	18.00	9.00	5.50
(17)	Juan Pizarro	12.00	6.00	3.50
(18)	Mel Roach	12.00	6.00	3.50
(19)	Bob Rush	12.00	6.00	3.50
(20)	Bob Scheffing	12.00	6.00	3.50
(21)	Red Schoendienst	35.00	17.50	10.50
(22)	Warren Spahn	60.00	30.00	18.00
(23)	Al Spangler	12.00	6.00	3.50
(24)	Frank Torre	12.00	6.00	3.50
(25)	Carl Willey	12.00	6.00	3.50
(26)	Whit Wyatt	12.00	6.00	3.50

1933 Sport Kings

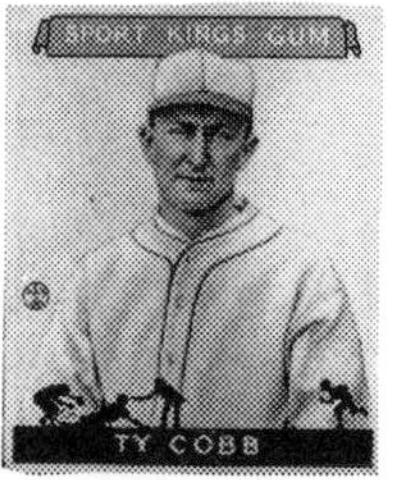

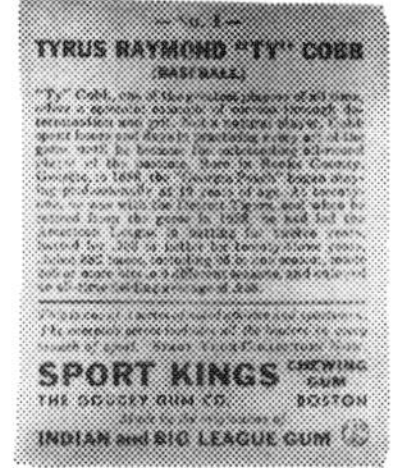

This 48-card set was issued by the Goudey Gum Company. Participants in 18 different sports are included in the set, which honors the top sports figures of the era. Three baseball players are pictured on the 2-3/8" by 2-7/8" cards. The card fronts are color portraits and include the player's name and silhouette representations of the respective sport. The card backs are numbered and list biographical information and a company ad.

		NR MT	EX	VG
Complete Set:		6000.	3000.	1750.
Common Player: 1-24		22.00	11.00	6.50
Common Player: 25-48		55.00	27.50	16.50
1	Ty Cobb	750.00	375.00	225.00
2	Babe Ruth	1200.	600.00	360.00
3	Nat Holman	45.00	22.50	13.50
4	Red Grange	200.00	100.00	60.00
5	Ed Wachter	40.00	20.00	12.00
6	Jim Thorpe	400.00	200.00	120.00
7	Bobby Walthour, Sr.	22.00	11.00	6.50
8	Walter Hagen	30.00	15.00	9.00
9	Ed Blood	22.00	11.00	6.50
10	Anston Lekang	22.00	11.00	6.50
11	Charles Jewtraw	22.00	11.00	6.50
12	Bobby McLean	22.00	11.00	6.50
13	Laverne Fator	22.00	11.00	6.50
14	Jim Londos	22.00	11.00	6.50
15	Reggie McNamara	22.00	11.00	6.50
16	Bill Tilden	30.00	15.00	9.00
17	Jack Dempsey	115.00	57.50	34.50
18	Gene Tunney	95.00	47.50	28.50
19	Eddie Shore	75.00	37.50	22.50
20	Duke Kahanamoku	40.00	20.00	12.00
21	Johnny Weissmuller	130.00	65.00	39.00
22	Gene Sarazen	30.00	15.00	9.00
23	Vincent Richards	22.00	11.00	6.50
24	Howie Morenz	100.00	50.00	30.00
25	Ralph Snoddy	55.00	27.50	16.50
26	James Wedell	55.00	27.50	16.50
27	Roscoe Turner	65.00	32.50	19.50
28	James Doolittle	85.00	42.50	25.50
29	Ace Bailey	175.00	87.50	52.50
30	Irvin Johnson	125.00	62.50	37.50
31	Bobby Walthour, Jr.	65.00	32.50	19.50
32	Joe Lopchick	125.00	62.50	37.50
33	Eddie Burke	75.00	37.50	22.50
34	Irving Jaffee	55.00	27.50	16.50
35	Knute Rockne	500.00	250.00	150.00
36	Willie Hoppe	55.00	27.50	16.50
37	Helene Madison	55.00	27.50	16.50
38	Bobby Jones	95.00	47.50	28.50
39	Jack Westrope	55.00	27.50	16.50
40	Don George	55.00	27.50	16.50
41	Jim Browning	55.00	27.50	16.50
42	Carl Hubbell	250.00	125.00	75.00
43	Primo Carnera	70.00	35.00	21.00
44	Max Baer	90.00	45.00	27.00
45	Babe Didrickson	275.00	137.50	82.50
46	Ellsworth Vines	55.00	27.50	16.50
47	J.H. Stevens	55.00	27.50	16.50
48	Leonard Seppala	70.00	35.00	21.00

1975 Sspc

This set, issued by the Sport Star Publishing Company in 1976 as a collectors' issue, was withdrawn from the market because of legal entanglements. Because SSPC agreed never to reprint the issue, some collectors feel it has an air of legitimacy. The complete set contains 630 full-color cards, each 2-1/2" by 3-1/2" in size. The cards look similar to 1953 Bowmans, with only the player picture (no identification) on the fronts. Card backs are in a vertical format, with personal stats, brief biographies and card numbers.

		NR MT	EX	VG
Complete Set:		50.00	25.00	15.00
Common Player:		.06	.03	.02
1	Lee William (Buzz) Capra	.10	.05	.03
2	Thomas Ross House	.06	.03	.02
3	Maximino Leon	.06	.03	.02
4	Carl Wendle Morton	.06	.03	.02
5	Philip Henry Niekro	.70	.35	.20
6	Michael Wayne Thompson	.06	.03	.02
7	Elias Sosa (Martinez)	.06	.03	.02
8	Larvell Blanks	.06	.03	.02
9	Darrell Wayne Evans	.20	.10	.06
10	Rodney Joe Gilbreath	.06	.03	.02
11	Michael Ken-Wai Lum	.06	.03	.02
12	Craig George Robinson	.06	.03	.02
13	Earl Craig Williams, Jr.	.06	.03	.02
14	Victor Crosby Correll	.06	.03	.02
15	Biff Pocoroba	.06	.03	.02
16	Johnny B. (Dusty) Baker, Jr.	.10	.05	.03
17	Ralph Allen Garr	.07	.04	.02
18	Clarence Edward (Cito) Gaston	.06	.03	.02
19	David LaFrance May	.06	.03	.02
20	Rowland Johnnie Office	.06	.03	.02
21	Robert Brooks Beall	.06	.03	.02
22	George Lee (Sparky) Anderson	.10	.05	.03
23	John Eugene Billingham	.06	.03	.02
24	Pedro Rodriguez Borbon	.06	.03	.02
25	Clay Palmer Carroll	.07	.04	.02
26	Patrick Leonard Darcy	.06	.03	.02
27	Donald Edward Gullett	.07	.04	.02
28	Clayton Laws Kirby	.06	.03	.02
29	Gary Lynn Nolan	.06	.03	.02
30	Fredie Hubert Norman	.06	.03	.02
31	Johnny Lee Bench	5.00	2.50	1.50
32	William Francis Plummer	.06	.03	.02
33	Darrel Lee Chaney	.06	.03	.02
34	David Ismael Concepcion	.15	.08	.05
35	Terrence Michael Crowley	.06	.03	.02
36	Daniel Driessen	.07	.04	.02
37	Robert Douglas Flynn, Jr.	.06	.03	.02
38	Joe Leonard Morgan	.70	.35	.20
39	Atanasio Rigal (Tony) Perez	.40	.20	.12
40	George Kenneth (Ken) Griffey	.15	.08	.05
41	Peter Edward Rose	8.00	4.00	2.50
42	Edison Rosanda Armbrister	.06	.03	.02
43	John Christopher Vukovich	.06	.03	.02
44	George Arthur Foster	.20	.10	.06
45	Cesar Francisco Geronimo	.06	.03	.02
46	Mervin Weldon Rettenmund	.06	.03	.02
47	James Frederick Crawford	.06	.03	.02
48	Kenneth Roth Forsch	.06	.03	.02
49	Douglas James Konieczny	.06	.03	.02
50	Joseph Franklin Niekro	.12	.06	.04
51	Clifford Johnson	.06	.03	.02
52	Alfred Henry (Skip) Jutze	.06	.03	.02
53	Milton Scott May	.06	.03	.02
54	Robert Patrick Andrews	.06	.03	.02
55	Kenneth George Boswell	.06	.03	.02
56	Tommy Vann Helms	.06	.03	.02
57	Roger Henry Metzger	.06	.03	.02
58	Lawrence William Milbourne	.06	.03	.02
59	Douglas Lee Rader	.06	.03	.02
60	Robert Jose Watson	.07	.04	.02
61	Enos Milton Cabell, Jr.	.06	.03	.02
62	Jose Delan Cruz	.15	.08	.05
63	Cesar Cedeno	.15	.08	.05
64	Gregory Eugene Gross	.06	.03	.02
65	Wilbur Leon Howard	.06	.03	.02
66	Alphonso Erwin Downing	.06	.03	.02
67	Burt Carlton Hooton	.07	.04	.02
68	Charles Oliver Hough	.10	.05	.03
69	Thomas Edward John	.40	.20	.12
70	John Alexander Messersmith	.07	.04	.02
71	Douglas James Rau	.06	.03	.02
72	Richard Alan Rhoden	.12	.06	.04
73	Donald Howard Sutton	.60	.30	.20
74	Frederick Steven Auerbach	.06	.03	.02
75	Ronald Charles Cey	.12	.06	.04
76	Ivan De Jesus	.06	.03	.02
77	Steven Patrick Garvey	4.00	2.00	1.25
78	Leonadus Lacy	.07	.04	.02
79	David Earl Lopes	.10	.05	.03
80	Kenneth Lee McMullen	.06	.03	.02
81	Joseph Vance Ferguson	.06	.03	.02
82	Paul Ray Powell	.06	.03	.02
83	Stephen Wayne Yeager	.06	.03	.02
84	Willie Murphy Crawford	.06	.03	.02
85	Henry Cruz	.06	.03	.02
86	Charles Fuqua Manuel	.06	.03	.02
87	Manuel Mota	.10	.05	.03
88	Thomas Marian Paciorek	.06	.03	.02
89	James Sherman Wynn	.10	.05	.03
90	Walter Emmons Alston	.30	.15	.09
91	William Joseph Buckner	.15	.08	.05
92	James Leland Barr	.06	.03	.02
93	Ralph Michael (Mike) Caldwell	.06	.03	.02
94	John Francis D'Acquisto	.06	.03	.02
95	David Wallace Heaverlo	.06	.03	.02
96	Gary Robert Lavelle	.06	.03	.02
97	John Joseph Montefusco, Jr.	.06	.03	.02
98	Charles Prosek Williams	.06	.03	.02
99	Christopher Paul Arnold	.06	.03	.02
100	Mark Kevin Hill (Marc)	.06	.03	.02
101	David Martin Rader	.06	.03	.02
102	Charles Bruce Miller	.06	.03	.02
103	Guillermo Naranjo (Willie) Montanez	.07	.04	.02
104	Steven Robert Ontiveros	.06	.03	.02
105	Chris Edward Speier	.07	.04	.02
106	Derrel Osbon Thomas	.06	.03	.02
107	Gary Leah Thomasson	.06	.03	.02
108	Glenn Charles Adams	.06	.03	.02
109	Von Everett Joshua	.06	.03	.02
110	Gary Nathaniel Matthews	.10	.05	.03
111	Bobby Ray Murcer	.12	.06	.04
112	Horace Arthur Speed III	.06	.03	.02
113	Wesley Noreen Westrum	.06	.03	.02
114	Richard Nevin Folkers	.06	.03	.02
115	Alan Benton Foster	.06	.03	.02
116	David James Freisleben	.06	.03	.02
117	Daniel Vincent Frisella	.06	.03	.02
118	Randall Leo Jones	.07	.04	.02
119	Daniel Ray Spillner	.06	.03	.02
120	Howard Lawrence (Larry) Hardy	.06	.03	.02
121	Cecil Randolph (Randy) Hundley	.06	.03	.02
122	Fred Lyn Kendall	.06	.03	.02
123	John Francis McNamara	.06	.03	.02
124	Rigoberto (Tito) Fuentes	.06	.03	.02
125	Enzo Octavio Hernandez	.06	.03	.02
126	Stephen Michael Huntz	.06	.03	.02
127	Michael Wilson Ivie	.06	.03	.02
128	Hector Epitacio Torres	.06	.03	.02
129	Theodore Rodger Kubiak	.06	.03	.02
130	John Maywood Grubb, Jr.	.06	.03	.02
131	John Henry Scott	.06	.03	.02
132	Robert Tolan	.07	.04	.02

		NR MT	EX	VG
133	David Mark Winfield	5.00	2.50	1.50
134	William Joseph Gogolewski	.06	.03	.02
135	Danny L. Osborn	.06	.03	.02
136	James Lee Kaat	.25	.13	.08
137	Claude Wilson Osteen	.07	.04	.02
138	Cecil Lee Upshaw, Jr.	.06	.03	.02
139	Wilbur Forrester Wood, Jr.	.07	.04	.02
140	Lloyd Cecil Allen	.06	.03	.02
141	Brian Jay Downing	.10	.05	.03
142	James Sarkis Essian, Jr.	.06	.03	.02
143	Russell Earl (Bucky) Dent	.12	.06	.04
144	Jorge Orta	.06	.03	.02
145	Lee Edward Richard	.06	.03	.02
146	William Allen Stein	.06	.03	.02
147	Kenneth Joseph Henderson	.06	.03	.02
148	Carlos May	.07	.04	.02
149	Nyls Wallace Rex Nyman	.06	.03	.02
150	Robert Pasquali Coluccio, Jr.	.06	.03	.02
151	Charles William Tanner, Jr.	.10	.05	.03
152	Harold Patrick (Pat) Kelly	.06	.03	.02
153	Jerry Wayne Hairston	.06	.03	.02
154	Richard Fred (Pete) Varney, Jr.	.06	.03	.02
155	William Edwin Melton	.07	.04	.02
156	Richard Michael Gossage	.50	.25	.15
157	Terry Jay Forster	.07	.04	.02
158	Richard Michael Hinton	.06	.03	.02
159	Nelson Kelley Briles	.06	.03	.02
160	Alan James Fitzmorris	.06	.03	.02
161	Stephen Bernard Mingori	.06	.03	.02
162	Martin William Pattin	.06	.03	.02
163	Paul William Splittorff, Jr.	.07	.04	.02
164	Dennis Patrick Leonard	.07	.04	.02
165	John Albert (Buck) Martinez	.06	.03	.02
166	Gorrell Robert (Bob) Stinson III	.06	.03	.02
167	George Howard Brett	6.00	3.00	1.75
168	Harmon Clayton Killebrew, Jr.	4.00	2.00	1.25
169	John Claiborn Mayberry	.07	.04	.02
170	Freddie Joe Patek	.06	.03	.02
171	Octavio (Cookie) Rojas	.06	.03	.02
172	Rodney Darrell Scott	.06	.03	.02
173	Tolia (Tony) Solaita	.06	.03	.02
174	Frank White, Jr.	.10	.05	.03
175	Alfred Edward Cowens, Jr.	.06	.03	.02
176	Harold Abraham McRae	.12	.06	.04
177	Amos Joseph Otis	.07	.04	.02
178	Vada Edward Pinson, Jr.	.20	.10	.06
179	James Eugene Wohlford	.06	.03	.02
180	James Douglas Bird	.06	.03	.02
181	Mark Alan Littell	.06	.03	.02
182	Robert McClure	.06	.03	.02
183	Steven Lee Busby	.07	.04	.02
184	Francis Xavier Healy	.06	.03	.02
185	Dorrel Norman Elvert (Whitey) Herzog	.10	.05	.03
186	Andrew Earl Hassler	.06	.03	.02
187	Lynn Nolan Ryan, Jr.	5.00	2.50	1.50
188	William Robert Singer	.06	.03	.02
189	Frank Daryl Tanana	.10	.05	.03
190	Eduardo Figueroa	.06	.03	.02
191	David S. Collins	.07	.04	.02
192	Richard Hirshfeld Williams	.07	.04	.02
193	Eliseo Rodriguez	.06	.03	.02
194	David Lee Chalk	.06	.03	.02
195	Winston Enriquillo Llenas	.06	.03	.02
196	Rudolph Bart Meoli	.06	.03	.02
197	Orlando Ramirez	.06	.03	.02
198	Gerald Peter Remy	.06	.03	.02
199	Billy Edward Smith	.06	.03	.02
200	Bruce Anton Bochte	.06	.03	.02
201	Joseph Michael Lahoud, Jr.	.06	.03	.02
202	Morris Nettles, Jr.	.06	.03	.02
203	John Milton (Mickey) Rivers	.07	.04	.02
204	Leroy Bobby Stanton	.06	.03	.02
205	Victor Albury	.06	.03	.02
206	Thomas Henry Burgmeier	.06	.03	.02
207	William Franklin Butler	.06	.03	.02
208	William Richard Campbell	.06	.03	.02
209	Alton Ray Corbin	.06	.03	.02
210	George Henry (Joe) Decker, Jr.	.06	.03	.02
211	James Michael Hughes	.06	.03	.02
212	Edward Norman Bane (photo actually Mike Pazik)	.06	.03	.02
213	Glenn Dennis Borgmann	.06	.03	.02
214	Rodney Cline Carew	5.00	2.50	1.50
215	Stephen Robert Brye	.06	.03	.02
216	Darnell Glenn (Dan) Ford	.06	.03	.02
217	Antonio Oliva	.25	.13	.08
218	David Allan Goltz	.07	.04	.02
219	Rikalbert Blyleven	.30	.15	.09
220	Larry Eugene Hisle	.07	.04	.02
221	Stephen Russell Braun, III	.06	.03	.02
222	Jerry Wayne Terrell	.06	.03	.02
223	Eric Thane Soderholm	.06	.03	.02
224	Philip Anthony Roof	.06	.03	.02
225	Danny Leon Thompson	.06	.03	.02
226	James William Colborn	.06	.03	.02
227	Thomas Andrew Murphy	.06	.03	.02
228	Eduardo Rodriguez	.06	.03	.02
229	James Michael Slaton	.06	.03	.02
230	Edward Nelson Sprague	.06	.03	.02
231	Charles William Moore, Jr.	.06	.03	.02
232	Darrell Ray Porter	.07	.04	.02
233	Kurt Anthony Bevacqua	.06	.03	.02
234	Pedro Garcia	.06	.03	.02
235	James Michael (Mike) Hegan	.06	.03	.02
236	Donald Wayne Money	.07	.04	.02
237	George C. Scott, Jr.	.07	.04	.02
238	Robin R. Yount	4.00	2.00	1.25
239	Henry Louis Aaron	6.00	3.00	1.75
240	Robert Walker Ellis	.06	.03	.02
241	Sixto Lezcano	.06	.03	.02
242	Robert Vance Mitchell	.06	.03	.02
243	James Gorman Thomas, III	.10	.05	.03
244	William Edward Travers	.06	.03	.02
245	Peter Sven Broberg	.06	.03	.02
246	William Howard Sharp	.06	.03	.02
247	Arthur Bobby Lee Darwin	.06	.03	.02
248	Rick Gerald Austin (photo actually Larry Anderson)	.06	.03	.02
249	Lawrence Dennis Anderson (photo actually Rick Austin)	.06	.03	.02
250	Thomas Antony Bianco	.06	.03	.02
251	DeLancy LaFayette Currence	.06	.03	.02
252	Steven Raymond Foucault	.06	.03	.02
253	William Alfred Hands, Jr.	.06	.03	.02
254	Steven Lowell Hargan	.06	.03	.02
255	Ferguson Arthur Jenkins	.30	.15	.09
256	Bob Mitchell Sheldon	.06	.03	.02
257	James Umbarger	.06	.03	.02
258	Clyde Wright	.06	.03	.02
259	William Roger Fahey	.06	.03	.02
260	James Howard Sundberg	.07	.04	.02
261	Leonardo Alfonso Cardenas	.06	.03	.02
262	James Louis Fregosi	.10	.05	.03
263	Dudley Michael (Mike) Hargrove	.07	.04	.02
264	Colbert Dale (Toby) Harrah	.10	.05	.03
265	Roy Lee Howell	.06	.03	.02
266	Leonard Shenoff Randle	.06	.03	.02
267	Roy Frederick Smalley III	.07	.04	.02
268	James Lloyd Spencer	.06	.03	.02
269	Jeffrey Alan Burroughs	.07	.04	.02
270	Thomas Alan Grieve	.06	.03	.02
271	Joseph Lovitto, Jr.	.06	.03	.02
272	Frank Joseph Lucchesi	.06	.03	.02
273	David Earl Nelson	.06	.03	.02
274	Ted Lyle Simmons	.20	.10	.06
275	Louis Clark Brock	4.00	2.00	1.25
276	Ronald Ray Fairly	.07	.04	.02
277	Arnold Ray (Bake) McBride	.06	.03	.02
278	Carl Reginald (Reggie) Smith	.12	.06	.04
279	William Henry Davis	.10	.05	.03
280	Kenneth John Reitz	.06	.03	.02
281	Charles William (Buddy) Bradford	.06	.03	.02
282	Luis Antonio Melendez	.06	.03	.02
283	Michael Ray Tyson	.06	.03	.02
284	Ted Crawford Sizemore	.06	.03	.02
285	Mario Miguel Guerrero	.06	.03	.02
286	Larry Lintz	.06	.03	.02
287	Kenneth Victor Rudolph	.06	.03	.02
288	Richard Arlin Billings	.06	.03	.02
289	Jerry Wayne Mumphrey	.10	.05	.03
290	Michael Sherman Wallace	.06	.03	.02
291	Alan Thomas Hrabosky	.07	.04	.02
292	Kenneth Lee Reynolds	.06	.03	.02
293	Michael Douglas Garman	.06	.03	.02
294	Robert Herbert Forsch	.10	.05	.03
295	John Allen Denny	.07	.04	.02
296	Harold R. Rasmussen	.06	.03	.02
297	Lynn Everratt McGlothen (Everett)	.06	.03	.02
298	Michael Roswell Barlow	.06	.03	.02
299	Gregory John Terlecky	.06	.03	.02
300	Albert Fred (Red) Schoendienst	.10	.05	.03
301	Ricky Eugene Reuschel	.12	.06	.04
302	Steven Michael Stone	.07	.04	.02
303	William Gordon Bonham	.06	.03	.02
304	Oscar Joseph Zamora	.06	.03	.02
305	Kenneth Douglas Frailing	.06	.03	.02
306	Milton Edward Wilcox	.07	.04	.02
307	Darold Duane Knowles	.06	.03	.02
308	Rufus James (Jim) Marshall	.06	.03	.02
309	Bill Madlock, Jr.	.25	.13	.08
310	Jose Domec Cardenal	.07	.04	.02
311	Robert James (Rick) Monday, Jr.	.10	.05	.03
312	Julio Ruben (Jerry) Morales	.06	.03	.02
313	Timothy Kenneth Hosley	.06	.03	.02
314	Gene Taylor Hiser	.06	.03	.02
315	Donald Eulon Kessinger	.07	.04	.02
316	Jesus Manuel (Manny) Trillo	.10	.05	.03
317	Ralph Pierre (Pete) LaCock, Jr.	.06	.03	.02
318	George Eugene Mitterwald	.06	.03	.02
319	Steven Eugene Swisher	.06	.03	.02
320	Robert Walter Sperring	.06	.03	.02
321	Victor Lanier Harris	.06	.03	.02
322	Ronald Ray Dunn	.06	.03	.02
323	Jose Manuel Morales	.06	.03	.02
324	Peter MacKanin, Jr.	.06	.03	.02
325	James Charles Cox	.06	.03	.02
326	Larry Alton Parrish	.12	.06	.04
327	Michael Jorgensen	.06	.03	.02
328	Timothy John Foli	.06	.03	.02
329	Harold Noel Breeden	.06	.03	.02
330	Nathan Colbert, Jr.	.06	.03	.02
331	Jesus Maria (Pepe) Frias	.06	.03	.02
332	James Patrick (Pat) Scanlon	.06	.03	.02
333	Robert Sherwood Bailey	.06	.03	.02
334	Gary Edmund Carter	4.00	2.00	1.25
335	Jose Mauel (Pepe) Mangual	.06	.03	.02
336	Lawrence David Biittner	.06	.03	.02
337	James Lawrence Lyttle, Jr.	.06	.03	.02
338	Gary Roenicke	.07	.04	.02
339	Anthony Scott	.06	.03	.02
340	Jerome Cardell White	.06	.03	.02
341	James Edward Dwyer	.06	.03	.02
342	Ellis Clarence Valentine	.06	.03	.02
343	Frederick John Scherman, Jr.	.06	.03	.02
344	Dennis Herman Blair	.06	.03	.02
345	Woodrow Thompson Fryman	.07	.04	.02
346	Charles Gilbert Taylor	.06	.03	.02
347	Daniel Dean Warthen	.06	.03	.02
348	Donald George Carrithers	.06	.03	.02
349	Stephen Douglas Rogers	.07	.04	.02
350	Dale Albert Murray	.06	.03	.02
351	Edwin Donald (Duke) Snider	3.00	1.50	.90
352	Ralph George Houk	.07	.04	.02
353	John Frederick Hiller	.07	.04	.02
354	Michael Stephen Lolich	.20	.10	.06
355	David Lawrence Lemancyzk	.06	.03	.02
356	Lerrin Harris LaGrow	.06	.03	.02
357	Fred Arroyo	.06	.03	.02
358	Joseph Howard Coleman	.06	.03	.02
359	Benjamin A. Oglivie	.07	.04	.02
360	Willie Wattison Horton	.10	.05	.03
361	John Clinton Knox	.06	.03	.02
362	Leon Kauffman Roberts	.06	.03	.02
363	Ronald LeFlore	.10	.05	.03
364	Gary Lynn Sutherland	.06	.03	.02
365	Daniel Thomas Meyer	.06	.03	.02
366	Aurelio Rodriguez	.07	.04	.02
367	Thomas Martin Veryzer	.06	.03	.02
368	Lavern Jack Pierce	.06	.03	.02
369	Eugene Richard Michael	.06	.03	.02
370	Robert (Billy) Baldwin	.06	.03	.02
371	William James Gates Brown	.06	.03	.02
372	Mitchell Jack (Mickey) Stanley	.07	.04	.02
373	Terryal Gene Humphrey	.06	.03	.02
374	Doyle Lafayette Alexander	.12	.06	.04
375	Miguel Angel (Mike) Cuellar	.10	.05	.03
376	Marcus Wayne Garland	.06	.03	.02
377	Ross Albert Grimsley III	.07	.04	.02
378	Grant Dwight Jackson	.06	.03	.02
379	Dyar K. Miller	.06	.03	.02
380	James Alvin Palmer	4.00	2.00	1.25
381	Michael Augustine Torrez	.07	.04	.02
382	Michael Henry Willis	.06	.03	.02
383	David Edwin Duncan	.06	.03	.02
384	Elrod Jerome Hendricks	.06	.03	.02
385	James Neamon Hutto Jr.	.06	.03	.02
386	Robert Michael Bailor	.06	.03	.02
387	Douglas Vernon DeCinces	.10	.05	.03
388	Robert Anthony Grich	.10	.05	.03
389	Lee Andrew May	.07	.04	.02
390	Anthony Joseph Muser	.06	.03	.02
391	Timothy C. Nordbrook	.06	.03	.02
392	Brooks Calbert Robinson, Jr.	5.00	2.50	1.50
393	Royle Stillman	.06	.03	.02
394	Don Edward Baylor	.15	.08	.05
395	Paul L.D. Blair	.07	.04	.02
396	Alonza Benjamin Bumbry	.07	.04	.02
397	Larry Duane Harlow	.06	.03	.02
398	Herman Thomas (Tommy) Davis, Jr.	.10	.05	.03
399	James Thomas Northrup	.07	.04	.02
400	Kenneth Wayne Singleton	.12	.06	.04
401	Thomas Michael Shopay	.06	.03	.02
402	Fredrick Michael Lynn	.40	.20	.12
403	Carlton Ernest Fisk	.50	.25	.15
404	Cecil Celester Cooper	.20	.10	.06
405	James Edward Rice	4.00	2.00	1.25
406	Juan Jose Beniquez	.06	.03	.02
407	Robert Dennis Doyle	.06	.03	.02
408	Dwight Michael Evans	.20	.10	.06
409	Carl Michael Yastrzemski	6.00	3.00	1.75
410	Richard Paul Burleson	.07	.04	.02
411	Bernardo Carbo	.06	.03	.02
412	Douglas Lee Griffin, Jr.	.06	.03	.02
413	Americo P. Petrocelli	.07	.04	.02
414	Robert Edward Montgomery	.06	.03	.02
415	Timothy P. Blackwell	.06	.03	.02
416	Richard Alan Miller	.06	.03	.02
417	Darrell Dean Johnson	.06	.03	.02
418	Jim Scott Burton	.06	.03	.02
419	James Arthur Willoughby	.06	.03	.02
420	Rogelio (Roger) Moret	.06	.03	.02
421	William Francis Lee, III	.07	.04	.02
422	Richard Anthony Drago	.06	.03	.02
423	Diego Pablo Segui	.06	.03	.02
424	Luis Clemente Tiant	.15	.08	.05
425	James Augustus (Catfish) Hunter	3.00	1.50	.90
426	Richard Clyde Sawyer	.06	.03	.02
427	Rudolph May Jr.	.07	.04	.02
428	Richard William Tidrow	.06	.03	.02
429	Albert Walter (Sparky) Lyle	.12	.06	.04
430	George Francis (Doc) Medich	.06	.03	.02
431	Patrick Edward Dobson, Jr.	.07	.04	.02
432	David Percy Pagan	.06	.03	.02
433	Thurman Lee Munson	4.00	2.00	1.25
434	Carroll Christopher Chambliss	.10	.05	.03
435	Roy Hilton White	.12	.06	.04
436	Walter Allen Williams	.06	.03	.02
437	Graig Nettles	.30	.15	.09
438	John Rikard (Rick) Dempsey	.07	.04	.02
439	Bobby Lee Bonds	.12	.06	.04
440	Edward Martin Hermann (Herrmann)	.06	.03	.02
441	Santos Alomar	.06	.03	.02
442	Frederick Blair Stanley	.06	.03	.02
443	Terry Bertland Whitfield	.06	.03	.02
444	Richard Alan Bladt	.06	.03	.02
445	Louis Victor Piniella	.12	.06	.04
446	Richard Allen Coggins	.06	.03	.02
447	Edwin Albert Brinkman	.07	.04	.02
448	James Percy Mason	.06	.03	.02
449	Larry Murray	.06	.03	.02
450	Ronald Mark Blomberg	.07	.04	.02
451	Elliott Maddox	.06	.03	.02
452	Kerry Dineen	.06	.03	.02
453	Alfred Manuel (Billy) Martin	.15	.08	.05
454	Dave Bergman	.06	.03	.02
455	Otoniel Velez	.06	.03	.02
456	Joseph Walter Hoerner	.06	.03	.02
457	Frank Edwin (Tug) McGraw, Jr.	.12	.06	.04
458	Henry Eugene (Gene) Garber	.06	.03	.02
459	Steven Norman Carlton	4.00	2.00	1.25
460	Larry Richard Christenson	.06	.03	.02
461	Thomas Gerald Underwood	.06	.03	.02
462	James Reynold Lonborg	.07	.04	.02
463	John William (Jay) Johnstone, Jr.	.07	.04	.02
464	Lawrence Robert Bowa	.12	.06	.04
465	David Cash, Jr.	.06	.03	.02
466	Ollie Lee Brown	.06	.03	.02
467	Gregory Michael Luzinski	.12	.06	.04
468	Johnny Lane Oates	.06	.03	.02
469	Michael Allen Anderson	.06	.03	.02

		NR MT	EX	VG
470	Michael Jack Schmidt	6.00	3.00	1.75
471	Robert Raymond Boone	.07	.04	.02
472	Thomas George Hutton	.06	.03	.02
473	Richard Anthony Allen	.15	.08	.05
474	Antonio Taylor	.06	.03	.02
475	Jerry Lindsey Martin	.06	.03	.02
476	Daniel Leonard Ozark	.06	.03	.02
477	Richard David Ruthven	.06	.03	.02
478	James Richard Todd, Jr.	.06	.03	.02
479	Paul Aaron Lindblad	.06	.03	.02
480	Roland Glen Fingers	.50	.25	.15
481	Vida Blue, Jr.	.15	.08	.05
482	Kenneth Dale Holtzman	.07	.04	.02
483	Richard Allen Bosman	.06	.03	.02
484	Wilfred Charles (Sonny) Siebert	.06	.03	.02
485	William Glenn Abbott	.06	.03	.02
486	Stanley Raymond Bahnsen	.06	.03	.02
487	Michael Norris	.06	.03	.02
488	Alvin Ralph Dark	.07	.04	.02
489	Claudell Washington	.10	.05	.03
490	Joseph Oden Rudi	.10	.05	.03
491	William Alex North	.06	.03	.02
492	Dagoberto Blanco (Bert) Campaneris	.12	.06	.04
493	Fury Gene Tenace	.07	.04	.02
494	Reginald Martinez Jackson	2.50	1.25	.70
495	Philip Mason Garner	.07	.04	.02
496	Billy Leo Williams	3.00	1.50	.90
497	Salvatore Leonard Bando	.10	.05	.03
498	James William Holt	.06	.03	.02
499	Teodoro Noel Martinez	.06	.03	.02
500	Raymond Earl Fosse	.06	.03	.02
501	Matthew Alexander	.06	.03	.02
502	Wallace Larry Haney	.06	.03	.02
503	Angel Luis Mangual	.06	.03	.02
504	Fred Ray Beene	.06	.03	.02
505	Thomas William Buskey	.06	.03	.02
506	Dennis Lee Eckersley	.10	.05	.03
507	Roric Edward Harrison	.06	.03	.02
508	Donald Harris Hood	.06	.03	.02
509	James Lester Kern	.06	.03	.02
510	David Eugene LaRoche	.06	.03	.02
511	Fred Ingels (Fritz) Peterson	.06	.03	.02
512	James Michael Strickland	.06	.03	.02
513	Michael Richard (Rick) Waits	.06	.03	.02
514	Alan Dean Ashby	.06	.03	.02
515	John Charles Ellis	.06	.03	.02
516	Rick Cerone	.07	.04	.02
517	David Gus (Buddy) Bell	.15	.08	.05
518	John Anthony Brohamer, Jr.	.06	.03	.02
519	Ricardo Adolfo Jacobo Carty	.10	.05	.03
520	Edward Carlton Crosby	.06	.03	.02
521	Frank Thomas Duffy	.06	.03	.02
522	Duane Eugene Kuiper (photo actually Rick Manning)	.06	.03	.02
523	Joseph Anthony Lis	.06	.03	.02
524	John Wesley (Boog) Powell	.25	.13	.08
525	Frank Robinson	4.00	2.00	1.25
526	Oscar Charles Gamble	.07	.04	.02
527	George Andrew Hendrick	.07	.04	.02
528	John Lee Lowenstein	.06	.03	.02
529	Richard Eugene Manning (photo actually Duane Kuiper)	.06	.03	.02
530	Tommy Alexander Smith	.06	.03	.02
531	Leslie Charles (Charlie) Spikes	.06	.03	.02
532	Steve Jack Kline	.06	.03	.02
533	Edward Emil Kranepool	.07	.04	.02
534	Michael Vail	.06	.03	.02
535	Delbert Bernard Unser	.06	.03	.02
536	Felix Bernardo Martinez Millan	.06	.03	.02
537	Daniel Joseph (Rusty) Staub	.20	.10	.06
538	Jesus Maria Rojas Alou	.07	.04	.02
539	Ronald Wayne Garrett	.06	.03	.02
540	Michael Dwaine Phillips	.06	.03	.02
541	Joseph Paul Torre	.20	.10	.06
542	David Arthur Kingman	.30	.15	.09
543	Eugene Anthony Clines	.06	.03	.02
544	Jack Seale Heidemann	.06	.03	.02
545	Derrel McKinley (Bud) Harrelson	.07	.04	.02
546	John Hardin Stearns	.06	.03	.02
547	John David Milner	.06	.03	.02
548	Robert John Apodaca	.06	.03	.02
549	Claude Edward (Skip) Lockwood Jr.	.06	.03	.02
550	Kenneth George Sanders	.06	.03	.02
551	George Thomas (Tom) Seaver	5.00	2.50	1.50
552	Ricky Alan Baldwin	.06	.03	.02
553	Jonathan Trumpbour Matlack	.07	.04	.02
554	Henry Gaylon Webb	.06	.03	.02
555	Randall Lee Tate	.06	.03	.02
556	Tom Edward Hall	.06	.03	.02
557	George Heard Stone Jr.	.06	.03	.02
558	Craig Steven Swan	.06	.03	.02
559	Gerald Allen Cram	.06	.03	.02
560	Roy J. Staiger	.06	.03	.02
561	Kenton C. Tekulve	.10	.05	.03
562	Jerry Reuss	.10	.05	.03
563	John R. Candelaria	.12	.06	.04
564	Lawrence C. Demery	.06	.03	.02
565	David John Giusti Jr.	.06	.03	.02
566	James Phillip Rooker	.06	.03	.02
567	Ramon Gonzalez Hernandez	.06	.03	.02
568	Bruce Eugene Kison	.06	.03	.02
569	Kenneth Alven Brett (Alvin)	.07	.04	.02
570	Robert Ralph Moose Jr.	.06	.03	.02
571	Manuel Jesus Sanguillen	.07	.04	.02
572	David Gene Parker	3.00	1.50	.90
573	Wilver Dornel Stargell	4.00	2.00	1.25
574	Richard Walter Zisk	.07	.04	.02
575	Renaldo Antonio Stennett	.06	.03	.02
576	Albert Oliver Jr.	.30	.15	.09
577	William Henry Robinson Jr.	.06	.03	.02
578	Robert Eugene Robertson	.06	.03	.02
579	Richard Joseph Hebner	.06	.03	.02
580	Edgar Leon Kirkpatrick	.06	.03	.02
581	Don Robert (Duffy) Dyer	.06	.03	.02
582	Craig Reynolds	.06	.03	.02
583	Franklin Fabian Taveras	.06	.03	.02
584	William Larry Randolph	.20	.10	.06
585	Arthur H. Howe	.06	.03	.02
586	Daniel Edward Murtaugh	.07	.04	.02
587	Charles Richard (Rich) McKinney	.06	.03	.02
588	James Edward Goodson	.06	.03	.02
589	George Brett, Al Cowans/Checklist	.80	.40	.25
590	Keith Hernandez, Lou Brock Checklist	.80	.40	.25
591	Jerry Koosman, Duke Snider Checklist	.30	.15	.09
592	John Knox, Maury Wills/Checklist	.10	.05	.03
593a	Catfish Hunter, Noland Ryan Checklist	25.00	12.50	7.50
593b	Catfish Hunter, Nolan Ryan Checklist	.50	.25	.15
594	Ralph Branca, Carl Erskine, Pee Wee Reese/Checklist	.25	.13	.08
595	Willie Mays, Herb Score/Checklist	.70	.35	.20
596	Larry Eugene Cox	.06	.03	.02
597	Eugene William Mauch	.07	.04	.02
598	William Frederick (Whitey) Wietelmann	.06	.03	.02
599	Wayne Kirby Simpson	.06	.03	.02
600	Melvin Erskine Thomason	.06	.03	.02
601	Issac Bernard (Ike) Hampton	.06	.03	.02
602	Kenneth S. Crosby	.06	.03	.02
603	Ralph Emanuel Rowe	.06	.03	.02
604	James Vernon Tyrone	.06	.03	.02
605	Michael Dennis Kelleher	.06	.03	.02
606	Mario Mendoza	.06	.03	.02
607	Michael George Rogodzinski	.06	.03	.02
608	Robert Collins Gallagher	.06	.03	.02
609	Jerry Martin Koosman	.12	.06	.04
610	Joseph Filmore Frazier	.06	.03	.02
611	Karl Kuehl	.06	.03	.02
612	Frank J. LaCorte	.06	.03	.02
613	Raymond Douglas Bare	.06	.03	.02
614	Billy Arnold Muffett	.06	.03	.02
615	William Harry Laxton	.06	.03	.02
616	Willie Howard Mays	6.00	3.00	1.75
617	Philip Joseph Cavaretta (Cavarretta)	.07	.04	.02
618	Theodore Bernard Kluszewski	.15	.08	.05
619	Elston Gene Howard	.15	.08	.05
620	Alexander Peter Grammas	.06	.03	.02
621	James Barton (Mickey) Vernon	.07	.04	.02
622	Richard Allan Sisler	.06	.03	.02
623	Harvey Haddix, Jr.	.07	.04	.02
624	Bobby Brooks Winkles	.06	.03	.02
625	John Michael Pesky	.07	.04	.02
626	James Houston Davenport	.06	.03	.02
627	David Allen Tomlin	.06	.03	.02
628	Roger Lee Craig	.07	.04	.02
629	John Joseph Amalfitano	.06	.03	.02
630	James Harrison Reese	.06	.03	.02

1948 Sport Thrills

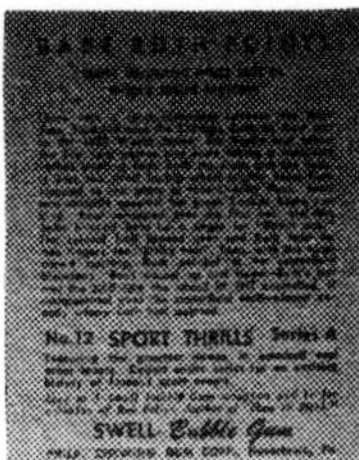

This is a set of black and white cards which depict memorable events in baseball history. The cards measure 2-1/2" by 3" and have a picture frame border and event title on the card fronts. The card backs describe the event in detail. Twenty cards were produced in this set by the Swell Gum Company of Philadelphia. Each card is numbered, and card numbers 9, 11, 16 and 20 are considered more difficult to obtain.

		NR MT	EX	VG
	Complete Set:	900.00	450.00	270.00
	Common Player:	15.00	7.50	4.50
1	Greatest Single Inning (Mickey Cochrane, Jimmy Foxx, George Haas, Bing Miller, Al Simmons)	40.00	20.00	12.00
2	Amazing Record (Pete Reiser)	15.00	7.50	4.50
3	Dramatic Debut (Jackie Robinson)	90.00	45.00	27.00
4	Greatest Pitcher (Walter Johnson)	50.00	25.00	15.00
5	Three Strikes Not Out! (Tommy Henrich, Mickey Owen)	15.00	7.50	4.50
6	Home Run Wins Series (Bill Dickey)	20.00	10.00	6.00
7	Never Say Die Pitcher (Hal Schumacher)	15.00	7.50	4.50
8	Five Strikeouts! (Carl Hubbell)	20.00	10.00	6.00
9	Greatest Catch! (Al Gionfriddo)	40.00	20.00	12.00
10	No Hits! No Runs! (Johnny Vander Meer)	15.00	7.50	4.50
11	Bases Loaded! (Tony Lazzeri, Bob O'Farrell)	40.00	20.00	12.00
12	Most Dramatic Home Run (Lou Gehrig, Babe Ruth)	100.00	50.00	30.00
13	Winning Run (Tommy Bridges, Mickey Cochrane, Goose Goslin)	15.00	7.50	4.50
14	Great Slugging (Lou Gehrig)	100.00	50.00	30.00
15	Four Men to Stop Him! (Jim Bagby, Al Smith)	15.00	7.50	4.50
16	Three Run Homer in Ninth! (Joe DiMaggio, Joe Gordon, Ted Williams)	125.00	62.00	37.00
17	Football Block! (Whitey Kurowski, Johnny Lindell)	15.00	7.50	4.50
18	Home Run to Fame (Pee Wee Reese)	40.00	20.00	12.00
19	Strikout Record! (Bob Feller)	50.00	25.00	15.00
20	Rifle Arm! (Carl Furillo)	50.00	25.00	15.00

1986 Sportflics

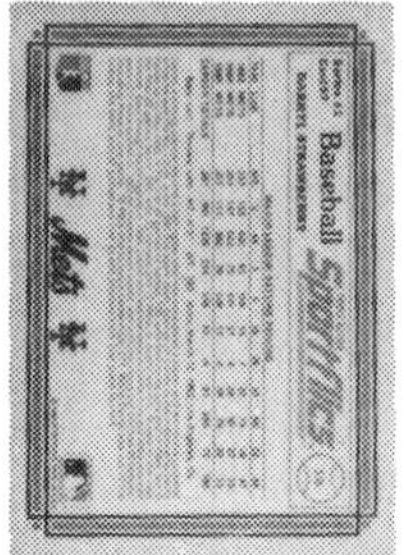

The premiere issue from Sportflics was distributed nationally by Amurol Division of Wrigley Gum Company. These high quality, three-phase "Magic Motion" cards depict three different photos per card, with each visible separately as the card is tilted. The 1986 issue features 200 full-color baseball cards plus 133 trivia cards. The cards come in the standard 2-1/2" by 3-1/2" size with the backs containing player stats and personal information. There are three different types of picture cards: 1) Tri-Star cards - 50 cards feature three players on one card; 2) Big Six cards - 10 cards which have six players in special categories; and 3) the Big Twelve card of 12 World Series players from the Kansas City Royals. The trivia cards are 1-3/4" by 2" and do not have player photos.

		MT	NR MT	EX
	Complete Set:	40.00	30.00	16.00
	Common Player:	.10	.08	.04
1	George Brett	1.00	.70	.40
2	Don Mattingly	4.00	3.00	1.50
3	Wade Boggs	2.00	1.50	.80
4	Eddie Murray	.60	.45	.25
5	Dale Murphy	1.00	.70	.40
6	Rickey Henderson	.70	.50	.30
7	Harold Baines	.20	.15	.08
8	Cal Ripken, Jr.	.60	.45	.25
9	Orel Hershiser	.40	.30	.15
10	Bret Saberhagen	.30	.25	.12
11	Tim Raines	.40	.30	.15
12	Fernando Valenzuela	.30	.25	.12
13	Tony Gwynn	.60	.45	.25
14	Pedro Guerrero	.25	.20	.10
15	Keith Hernandez	.35	.25	.14
16	Ernest Riles	.20	.15	.08
17	Jim Rice	.40	.30	.15
18	Ron Guidry	.25	.20	.10
19	Willie McGee	.25	.20	.10
20	Ryne Sandberg	.40	.30	.15
21	Kirk Gibson	.35	.25	.14
22	Ozzie Guillen	.30	.25	.12
23	Dave Parker	.25	.20	.10
24	Vince Coleman	2.00	1.50	.80
25	Tom Seaver	.40	.30	.15
26	Brett Butler	.10	.08	.04
27	Steve Carlton	.40	.30	.15
28	Gary Carter	.35	.25	.14
29	Cecil Cooper	.15	.11	.06
30	Jose Cruz	.10	.08	.04
31	Alvin Davis	.20	.15	.08
32	Dwight Evans	.15	.11	.06
33	Julio Franco	.15	.11	.06
34	Damaso Garcia	.10	.08	.04
35	Steve Garvey	.40	.30	.15
36	Kent Hrbek	.25	.20	.10
37	Reggie Jackson	.50	.40	.20
38	Fred Lynn	.20	.15	.08
39	Paul Molitor	.15	.11	.06
40	Jim Presley	.15	.11	.06
41	Dave Righetti	.20	.15	.08
42a	Robin Yount (Yankees logo on back)	2.00	1.50	.80
42b	Robin Yount (Brewers logo on back)	.60	.45	.25

#	Player	MT	NR MT	EX
43	Nolan Ryan	.60	.45	.25
44	Mike Schmidt	1.00	.70	.40
45	Lee Smith	.10	.08	.04
46	Rick Sutcliffe	.15	.11	.06
47	Bruce Sutter	.15	.11	.06
48	Lou Whitaker	.20	.15	.08
49	Dave Winfield	.50	.40	.20
50	Pete Rose	1.50	1.25	.60
51	National League MVPs (Steve Garvey, Pete Rose, Ryne Sandberg)	.70	.50	.30
52	Slugging Stars (Harold Baines, George Brett, Jim Rice)	.35	.25	.14
53	No-Hitters (Phil Niekro, Jerry Reuss, Mike Witt)	.15	.11	.06
54	Big Hitters (Don Mattingly, Cal Ripken, Jr., Robin Yount)	1.25	.90	.50
55	Bullpen Aces (Goose Gossage, Dan Quisenberry, Lee Smith)	.10	.08	.04
56	Rookies of the Year (Pete Rose, Steve Sax, Darryl Strawberry)	.80	.60	.30
57	American League MVPs (Don Baylor, Reggie Jackson, Cal Ripken, Jr.)	.35	.25	.14
58	Repeat Batting Champs (Bill Madlock, Dave Parker, Pete Rose)	.60	.45	.25
59	Cy Young Winners (Mike Flanagan, Ron Guidry, LaMarr Hoyt)	.10	.08	.04
60	Double Award Winners (Tom Seaver, Rick Sutcliffe, Fernando Valenzuela)	.20	.15	.08
61	Home Run Champs (Tony Armas, Reggie Jackson, Jim Rice)	.25	.20	.10
62	National League MVPs (Keith Hernandez, Dale Murphy, Mike Schmidt)	.50	.40	.20
63	American League MVPs (George Brett, Fred Lynn, Robin Yount)	.30	.25	.12
64	Comeback Players (Bert Blyleven, John Denny, Jerry Koosman)	.10	.08	.04
65	Cy Young Relievers (Rollie Fingers, Willie Hernandez, Bruce Sutter)	.15	.11	.06
66	Rookies Of The Year (Andre Dawson, Bob Horner, Gary Matthews)	.15	.11	.06
67	Rookies Of The Year (Carlton Fisk, Ron Kittle, Tom Seaver)	.15	.11	.06
68	Home Run Champs (George Foster, Dave Kingman, Mike Schmidt)	.30	.25	.12
69	Double Award Winners (Rod Carew, Cal Ripken, Jr., Pete Rose)	.70	.50	.30
70	Cy Young Winners (Steve Carlton, Tom Seaver, Rick Sutcliffe)	.25	.20	.10
71	Top Sluggers (Reggie Jackson, Fred Lynn, Robin Yount)	.30	.25	.12
72	Rookies of the Year (Dave Righetti, Rick Sutcliffe, Fernando Valenzuela)	.15	.11	.06
73	Rookies Of The Year (Fred Lynn, Eddie Murray, Cal Ripken, Jr.)	.25	.20	.10
74	Rookies Of The Year (Rod Carew, Alvin Davis, Lou Whitaker)	.20	.15	.08
75	Batting Champs (Wade Boggs, Carney Lansford, Don Mattingly)	1.50	1.25	.60
76	Jesse Barfield	.20	.15	.08
77	Phil Bradley	.15	.11	.06
78	Chris Brown	.25	.20	.10
79	Tom Browning	.30	.25	.12
80	Tom Brunansky	.15	.11	.06
81	Bill Buckner	.10	.08	.04
82	Chili Davis	.10	.08	.04
83	Mike Davis	.10	.08	.04
84	Rich Gedman	.10	.08	.04
85	Willie Hernandez	.10	.08	.04
86	Ron Kittle	.10	.08	.04
87	Lee Lacy	.10	.08	.04
88	Bill Madlock	.15	.11	.06
89	Mike Marshall	.15	.11	.06
90	Keith Moreland	.10	.08	.04
91	Graig Nettles	.15	.11	.06
92	Lance Parrish	.20	.15	.08
93	Kirby Puckett	.40	.30	.15
94	Juan Samuel	.20	.15	.08
95	Steve Sax	.20	.15	.08
96	Dave Stieb	.10	.08	.04
97	Darryl Strawberry	.80	.60	.30
98	Willie Upshaw	.10	.08	.04
99	Frank Viola	.20	.15	.08
100	Dwight Gooden	1.50	1.25	.60
101	Joaquin Andujar	.10	.08	.04
102	George Bell	.40	.30	.15
103	Bert Blyleven	.15	.11	.06
104	Mike Boddicker	.10	.08	.04
105	Britt Burns	.10	.08	.04
106	Rod Carew	.40	.30	.15
107	Jack Clark	.25	.20	.10
108	Danny Cox	.10	.08	.04
109	Ron Darling	.15	.11	.06
110	Andre Dawson	.25	.20	.10
111	Leon Durham	.10	.08	.04
112	Tony Fernandez	.15	.11	.06
113	Tom Herr	.10	.08	.04
114	Teddy Higuera	.80	.60	.30
115	Bob Horner	.15	.11	.06
116	Dave Kingman	.15	.11	.06
117	Jack Morris	.20	.15	.08
118	Dan Quisenberry	.10	.08	.04
119	Jeff Reardon	.15	.11	.06
120	Bryn Smith	.10	.08	.04
121	Ozzie Smith	.25	.20	.10
122	John Tudor	.15	.11	.06
123	Tim Wallach	.15	.11	.06
124	Willie Wilson	.15	.11	.06
125	Carlton Fisk	.25	.20	.10
126	RBI Sluggers (Gary Carter, George Foster, Al Oliver)	.15	.11	.06
127	Run Scorers (Keith Hernandez, Tim Raines, Ryne Sandberg)	.25	.20	.10
128	Run Scorers (Paul Molitor, Cal Ripken, Jr., Willie Wilson)	.20	.15	.08
129	No-Hitters (John Candelaria, Dennis Eckersley, Bob Forsch)	.10	.08	.04
130	World Series MVPs (Ron Cey, Rollie Fingers, Pete Rose)	.50	.40	.20
131	All-Star Game MVPs (Dave Concepcion, George Foster, Bill Madlock)	.10	.08	.04

#	Player	MT	NR MT	EX
132	Cy Young Winners (Vida Blue, John Denny, Fernando Valenzuela)	.15	.11	.06
133	Comeback Players (Doyle Alexander, Joaquin Andujar, Richard Dotson)	.10	.08	.04
134	Big Winners (John Denny, Tom Seaver, Rick Sutcliffe)	.15	.11	.06
135	Veteran Pitchers (Phil Niekro, Tom Seaver, Don Sutton)	.25	.20	.10
136	Rookies Of The Year (Vince Coleman, Dwight Gooden, Alfredo Griffin)	.80	.60	.30
137	All-Star Game MVPs (Gary Carter, Steve Garvey, Fred Lynn)	.20	.15	.08
138	Veteran Hitters (Tony Perez, Pete Rose, Rusty Staub)	.50	.40	.20
139	Power Hitters (George Foster, Jim Rice, Mike Schmidt)	.30	.25	.12
140	Batting Champs (Bill Buckner, Tony Gwynn, Al Oliver)	.20	.15	.08
141	No-Hitters (Jack Morris, Dave Righetti, Nolan Ryan)	.20	.15	.08
142	No-Hitters (Vida Blue, Bert Blyleven, Tom Seaver)	.15	.11	.06
143	Strikeout Kings (Dwight Gooden, Nolan Ryan, Fernando Valenzuela)	1.25	.90	.50
144	Base Stealers (Dave Lopes, Tim Raines, Willie Wilson)	.15	.11	.06
145	RBI Sluggers (Tony Armas, Cecil Cooper, Eddie Murray)	.15	.11	.06
146	American League MVPs (Rod Carew, Rollie Fingers, Jim Rice)	.25	.20	.10
147	World Series MVPs (Rick Dempsey, Reggie Jackson, Alan Trammell)	.25	.20	.10
148	World Series MVPs (Pedro Guerrero, Darrell Porter, Mike Schmidt)	.20	.15	.08
149	ERA Leaders (Mike Boddicker, Ron Guidry, Rick Sutcliffe)	.10	.08	.04
150	Comeback Players (Reggie Jackson, Dave Kingman, Fred Lynn)	.20	.15	.08
151	Buddy Bell	.15	.11	.06
152	Dennis Boyd	.10	.08	.04
153	Dave Concepcion	.15	.11	.06
154	Brian Downing	.10	.08	.04
155	Shawon Dunston	.15	.11	.06
156	John Franco	.15	.11	.06
157	Scott Garrelts	.10	.08	.04
158	Bob James	.10	.08	.04
159	Charlie Leibrandt	.10	.08	.04
160	Oddibe McDowell	.30	.25	.12
161	Roger McDowell	.50	.40	.20
162	Mike Moore	.10	.08	.04
163	Phil Niekro	.25	.20	.10
164	Al Oliver	.15	.11	.06
165	Tony Pena	.10	.08	.04
166	Ted Power	.10	.08	.04
167	Mike Scioscia	.10	.08	.04
168	Mario Soto	.10	.08	.04
169	Bob Stanley	.10	.08	.04
170	Garry Templeton	.10	.08	.04
171	Andre Thornton	.10	.08	.04
172	Alan Trammell	.30	.25	.12
173	Doug DeCinces	.10	.08	.04
174	Greg Walker	.10	.08	.04
175	Don Sutton	.25	.20	.10
176	1985 Award Winners (Vince Coleman, Dwight Gooden, Ozzie Guillen, Don Mattingly, Wille McGee, Bret Saberhagen)	1.25	.90	.50
177	1985 Hot Rookies (Stewart Cliburn, Brian Fisher, Joe Hesketh, Joe Orsulak, Mark Salas, Larry Sheets)	.40	.30	.15
178	Future Stars (Jose Canseco, Mark Funderburk, Mike Greenwell, Steve Lombardozzi, Billy Joe Robidoux, Dan Tartabull)	20.00	15.00	8.00
179	1985 Gold Glovers (George Brett, Ron Guidry, Keith Hernandez, Don Mattingly, Willie McGee, Dale Murphy)	1.25	.90	.50
180	Active .300 Hitters (Wade Boggs, George Brett, Rod Carew, Cecil Cooper, Don Mattingly, Willie Wilson)	1.25	.90	.50
181	Active .300 Hitters (Pedro Guerrero, Tony Gwynn, Keith Hernandez, Bill Madlock, Dave Parker, Pete Rose)	.70	.50	.30
182	1985 Milestones (Rod Carew, Phil Niekro, Pete Rose, Nolan Ryan, Tom Seaver, Matt Tallman)	1.50	1.25	.60
183	1985 Triple Crown (Wade Boggs, Darrell Evans, Don Mattingly, Willie McGee, Dale Murphy, Dave Parker)	1.25	.90	.50
184	1985 Highlights (Wade Boggs, Dwight Gooden, Rickey Henderson, Don Mattingly, Willie McGee, John Tudor)	1.50	1.25	.60
185	1985 20-Game Winners (Joaquin Andujar, Tom Browning, Dwight Gooden, Ron Guidry, Bret Saberhagen, John Tudor)	.60	.45	.25
186	Kansas City Royals (Steve Balboni, George Brett, Dane Iorg, Danny Jackson, Charlie Leibrandt, Darryl Motley, Dan Quisenberry, Bret Saberhagen, Lonnie Smith, Jim Sundberg, Frank White, Willie Wilson)	.40	.30	.15
187	Hubie Brooks	.10	.08	.04
188	Glenn Davis	.60	.45	.25
189	Darrell Evans	.10	.08	.04
190	Rich Gossage	.15	.11	.06
191	Andy Hawkins	.10	.08	.04
192	Jay Howell	.10	.08	.04
193	LaMarr Hoyt	.10	.08	.04
194	Davey Lopes	.10	.08	.04
195	Mike Scott	.20	.15	.08
196	Ted Simmons	.15	.11	.06
197	Gary Ward	.10	.08	.04
198	Bob Welch	.15	.11	.06
199	Mike Young	.10	.08	.04
200	Buddy Biancalana	.10	.08	.04

1986 Sportflics Decade Greats

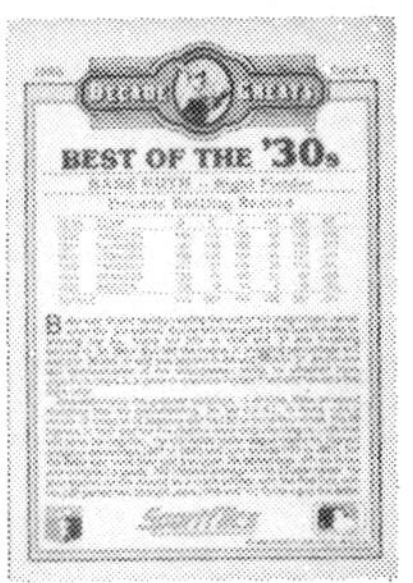

This set, produced by Sportflics, features outstand- ing players, by position, from the 1930s to the 1980s by decades. The card fronts are printed in sepia-toned photos or full-color with the Sportflics three-phase "Magic Motion" animation. The complete set contains 75 cards with 59 single player cards and 16 multi-player cards. Biographies appear on the card backs which are printed in full-color and color-coded by decade. The set was distributed only through hobby dealers and is in the popular 2-1/2" by 3-1/2" size.

#	Player	MT	NR MT	EX
	Complete Set:	14.00	10.50	5.50
	Common Player:	.15	.11	.06
1	Babe Ruth	2.50	2.00	1.00
2	Jimmie Foxx	.40	.30	.15
3	Lefty Grove	.30	.25	.12
4	Hank Greenberg	.30	.25	.12
5	Al Simmons	.15	.11	.06
6	Carl Hubbell	.30	.25	.12
7	Joe Cronin	.25	.20	.10
8	Mel Ott	.30	.25	.12
9	Lefty Gomez	.30	.25	.12
10	Lou Gehrig	1.50	1.25	.60
11	Pie Traynor	.15	.11	.06
12	Charlie Gehringer	.30	.25	.12
13	Catchers (Mickey Cochrane, Bill Dickey, Gabby Hartnett)	.30	.25	.12
14	Pitchers (Dizzy Dean, Paul Derringer, Red Ruffing)	.30	.25	.12
15	Outfielders (Earl Averill, Joe Medwick, Paul Waner)	.15	.11	.06
16	Bob Feller	.60	.45	.25
17	Lou Boudreau	.15	.11	.06
18	Enos Slaughter	.25	.20	.10
19	Hal Newhouser	.15	.11	.06
20	Joe DiMaggio	1.50	1.25	.60
21	Pee Wee Reese	.40	.30	.15
22	Phil Rizzuto	.30	.25	.12
23	Ernie Lombardi	.15	.11	.06
24	Infielders (Joe Cronin, George Kell, Johnny Mize)	.15	.11	.06
25	Ted Williams	1.25	.90	.50
26	Mickey Mantle	3.00	2.25	1.25
27	Warren Spahn	.30	.25	.12
28	Jackie Robinson	1.00	.70	.40
29	Ernie Banks	.30	.25	.12
30	Stan Musial	1.00	.70	.40
31	Yogi Berra	.60	.45	.25
32	Duke Snider	.70	.50	.30
33	Roy Campanella	.70	.50	.30
34	Eddie Mathews	.30	.25	.12
35	Ralph Kiner	.30	.25	.12
36	Early Wynn	.25	.20	.10
37	Double Play Duo (Luis Aparicio, Nellie Fox)	.25	.20	.10
38	First Basemen (Gil Hodges, Ted Kluszewski, Mickey Vernon)	.25	.20	.10
40	Henry Aaron	1.00	.70	.40
41	Frank Robinson	.30	.25	.12
42	Bob Gibson	.30	.25	.12
43	Roberto Clemente	1.00	.70	.40
44	Whitey Ford	.40	.30	.15
45	Brooks Robinson	.50	.40	.20
46	Juan Marichal	.25	.20	.10
47	Carl Yastrzemski	1.00	.70	.40
48	First Basemen (Orlando Cepeda, Harmon Killebrew, Willie McCovey)	.30	.25	.12
49	Catchers (Bill Freehan, Elston Howard, Joe Torre)	.15	.11	.06
50	Willie Mays	1.00	.70	.40
51	Outfielders (Al Kaline, Tony Oliva, Billy Williams)	.30	.25	.12
52	Tom Seaver	.60	.45	.25
53	Reggie Jackson	.70	.50	.30
54	Steve Carlton	.40	.30	.15
55	Mike Schmidt	.70	.50	.30
56	Joe Morgan	.25	.20	.10
57	Jim Rice	.40	.30	.15
58	Jim Palmer	.30	.25	.12
59	Lou Brock	.30	.25	.12
60	Pete Rose	1.25	.90	.50
61	Steve Garvey	.40	.30	.15
62	Catchers (Carlton Fisk, Thurman Munson, Ted Simmons)	.25	.20	.10
63	Pitchers (Vida Blue, Catfish Hunter, Nolan Ryan)	.30	.25	.12
64	George Brett	.80	.60	.30
65	Don Mattingly	2.25	1.75	.90
66	Fernando Valenzuela	.30	.25	.12
67	Dale Murphy	.80	.60	.30
68	Wade Boggs	1.50	1.25	.60
69	Rickey Henderson	.60	.45	.25
70	Eddie Murray	.60	.45	.25
71	Ron Guidry	.25	.20	.10

		MT	NR MT	EX
72	Catchers (Gary Carter, Lance Parrish, Tony Pena)	.30	.25	.12
73	Infielders (Cal Ripken, Jr., Lou Whitaker, Robin Yount)	.30	.25	.12
74	Outfielders (Pedro Guerrero, Tim Raines, Dave Winfield)	.30	.25	.12
75	Dwight Gooden	1.00	.70	.40

1986 Sportflics Rookies

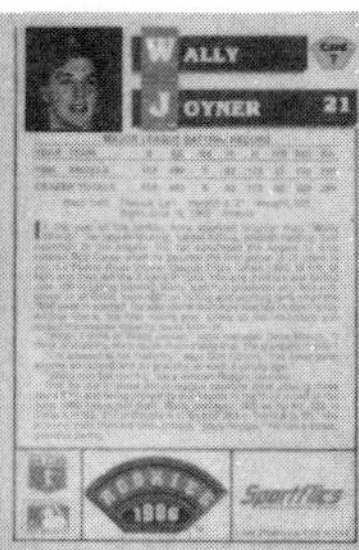

The 1986 Rookies set issued by Sportflics offers 50 cards and features 47 individual rookie players. In addition, there are two Tri-Star cards; one highlights former Rookies of the Year and the other features three prominent players. There is one "Big Six" card featuring six superstars. The full-color photos on the 2-1/2" by 3-1/2" cards use Sportflics three-phase "Magic Motion" animation. The set was packaged in an attractive collector box which also contained 34 trivia cards that measure 1-3/4" by 2". The set was distributed only by hobby dealers.

		MT	NR MT	EX
	Complete Set:	20.00	15.00	8.00
	Common Player:	.20	.15	.08
1	John Kruk	.80	.60	.30
2	Edwin Correa	.20	.15	.08
3	Pete Incaviglia	.50	.40	.20
4	Dale Sveum	.30	.25	.12
5	Juan Nieves	.30	.25	.12
6	Will Clark	3.50	2.75	1.50
7	Wally Joyner	2.50	2.00	1.00
8	Lance McCullers	.20	.15	.08
9	Scott Bailes	.20	.15	.08
10	Dan Plesac	.40	.30	.15
11	Jose Canseco	4.00	3.00	1.50
12	Bobby Witt	.40	.30	.15
13	Barry Bonds	.70	.50	.30
14	Andres Thomas	.20	.15	.08
15	Jim Deshaies	.30	.25	.12
16	Ruben Sierra	2.00	1.50	.80
17	Steve Lombardozzi	.20	.15	.08
18	Cory Snyder	.50	.40	.20
19	Reggie Williams	.20	.15	.08
20	Mitch Williams	.20	.15	.08
21	Glenn Braggs	.30	.25	.12
22	Danny Tartabull	.80	.60	.30
23	Charlie Kerfeld	.20	.15	.08
24	Paul Assenmacher	.20	.15	.08
25	Robby Thompson	.30	.25	.12
26	Bobby Bonilla	.70	.50	.30
27	Andres Galarraga	.70	.50	.30
28	Billy Jo Robidoux	.20	.15	.08
29	Bruce Ruffin	.30	.25	.12
30	Greg Swindell	.60	.45	.25
31	John Cangelosi	.20	.15	.08
32	Jim Traber	.20	.15	.08
33	Russ Morman	.20	.15	.08
34	Barry Larkin	.60	.45	.25
35	Todd Worrell	.50	.40	.20
36	John Cerutti	.20	.15	.08
37	Mike Kingery	.20	.15	.08
38	Mark Eichhorn	.20	.15	.08
39	Scott Bankhead	.20	.15	.08
40	Bo Jackson	2.00	1.50	.80
41	Greg Mathews	.30	.25	.12
42	Eric King	.20	.15	.08
43	Kal Daniels	.80	.60	.30
44	Calvin Schiraldi	.20	.15	.08
45	Mickey Brantley	.20	.15	.08
46	Outstanding Rookie Seasons (Fred Lynn, Willie Mays, Pete Rose)	.80	.60	.30
47	Outstanding Rookie Seasons (Dwight Gooden, Tom Seaver, Fernando Valenzuela)	.80	.60	.30
48	Outstanding Rookie Seasons (Eddie Murray, Dave Righetti, Cal Ripken, Jr., Steve Sax, Darryl Strawberry, Lou Whitaker)	.60	.45	.25
49	Kevin Mitchell	2.00	1.50	.80
50	Mike Diaz	.20	.15	.08

1987 Sportflics

For its second season in the national baseball card market, Sportflics' basic issue was again a 200-card set of 2-1/2" by 3-1/2" "Magic Motion" cards, which offer three different photos on the same card, each visible in turn as the card is moved from top to bottom or side to side. Besides single-player cards, the '87 Sportflics set

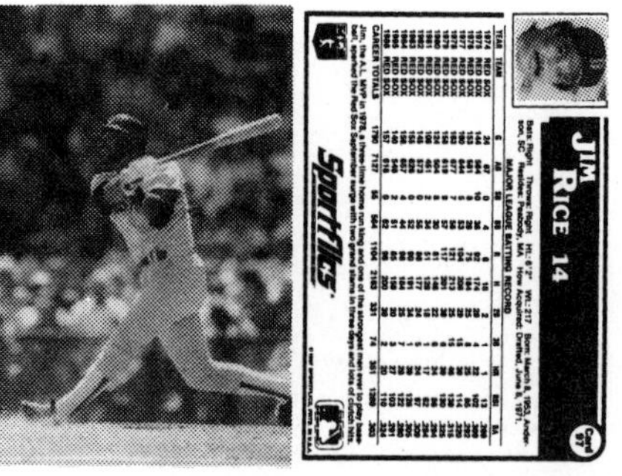

includes several three- and six-player cards, though not as many as in the 1986 set. The card backs feature a small player portrait photo on the single-player cards, an innovation for 1987.

		MT	NR MT	EX
	Complete Set:	35.00	27.50	15.00
	Common Player:	.10	.08	.04
1	Don Mattingly	3.00	2.25	1.25
2	Wade Boggs	1.75	1.25	.70
3	Dale Murphy	.50	.40	.20
4	Rickey Henderson	.90	.70	.35
5	George Brett	.70	.50	.30
6	Eddie Murray	.50	.40	.20
7	Kirby Puckett	.90	.70	.35
8	Ryne Sandberg	.80	.60	.30
9	Cal Ripken Jr.	.50	.40	.20
10	Roger Clemens	1.00	.70	.40
11	Ted Higuera	.15	.11	.06
12	Steve Sax	.20	.15	.08
13	Chris Brown	.10	.08	.04
14	Jesse Barfield	.15	.11	.06
15	Kent Hrbek	.20	.15	.08
16	Robin Yount	.30	.25	.12
17	Glenn Davis	.25	.20	.10
18	Hubie Brooks	.10	.08	.04
19	Mike Scott	.15	.11	.06
20	Darryl Strawberry	.70	.50	.30
21	Alvin Davis	.15	.11	.06
22	Eric Davis	1.00	.70	.40
23	Danny Tartabull	.30	.25	.12
24a	Cory Snyder (Pat Tabler photo on back (facing front), 3/4 swing on front)	1.50	1.25	.60
24b	Cory Snyder (Pat Tabler photo on back (facing front), 1/4 swing on front)	1.50	1.25	.60
24c	Cory Snyder (Snyder photo on back (facing to side))	1.00	.70	.40
25	Pete Rose	1.25	.90	.50
26	Wally Joyner	1.50	1.25	.60
27	Pedro Guerrero	.20	.15	.08
28	Tom Seaver	.30	.25	.12
29	Bob Knepper	.10	.08	.04
30	Mike Schmidt	.80	.60	.30
31	Tony Gwynn	.50	.40	.20
32	Don Slaught	.10	.08	.04
33	Todd Worrell	.30	.25	.12
34	Tim Raines	.40	.30	.15
35	Dave Parker	.20	.15	.08
36	Bob Ojeda	.10	.08	.04
37	Pete Incaviglia	.50	.40	.20
38	Bruce Hurst	.15	.11	.06
39	Bobby Witt	.40	.30	.15
40	Steve Garvey	.40	.30	.15
41	Dave Winfield	.40	.30	.15
42	Jose Cruz	.10	.08	.04
43	Orel Hershiser	.40	.30	.15
44	Reggie Jackson	.50	.40	.20
45	Chili Davis	.10	.08	.04
46	Robby Thompson	.30	.25	.12
47	Dennis Boyd	.10	.08	.04
48	Kirk Gibson	.30	.25	.12
49	Fred Lynn	.20	.15	.08
50	Gary Carter	.30	.25	.12
51	George Bell	.40	.30	.15
52	Pete O'Brien	.10	.08	.04
53	Ron Darling	.15	.11	.06
54	Paul Molitor	.15	.11	.06
55	Mike Pagliarulo	.15	.11	.06
56	Mike Boddicker	.10	.08	.04
57	Dave Righetti	.20	.15	.08
58	Len Dykstra(FC)	.15	.11	.06
59	Mike Witt	.10	.08	.04
60	Tony Bernazard	.10	.08	.04
61	John Kruk	.30	.25	.12
62	Mike Krukow	.10	.08	.04
63	Sid Fernandez	.15	.11	.06
64	Gary Gaetti	.20	.15	.08
65	Vince Coleman	.30	.25	.12
66	Pat Tabler	.10	.08	.04
67	Mike Scioscia	.10	.08	.04
68	Scott Garrelts	.10	.08	.04
69	Brett Butler	.10	.08	.04
70	Bill Buckner	.10	.08	.04
71a	Dennis Rasmussen (John Montefusco photo on back)	.25	.20	.10
71b	Dennis Rasmussen (Rasmussen photo on back)	.15	.11	.06
72	Tim Wallach	.15	.11	.06
73	Bob Horner	.15	.11	.06
74	Willie McGee	.15	.11	.06
75	American League First Basemen (Wally Joyner, Don Mattingly, Eddie Murray)	1.50	1.25	.60
76	Jesse Orosco	.10	.08	.04
77	National League Relief Pitchers (Jeff Reardon, Dave Smith, Todd Worrell)	.15	.11	.06
78	Candy Maldonado	.10	.08	.04
79	National League Shortstops (Hubie Brooks, Shawon Dunston, Ozzie Smith)	.15	.11	.06
80	American League Left Fielders (George Bell, Jose Canseco, Jim Rice)	1.50	1.25	.60
81	Bert Blyleven	.15	.11	.06
82	Mike Marshall	.15	.11	.06
83	Ron Guidry	.20	.15	.08
84	Julio Franco	.15	.11	.06
85	Willie Wilson	.15	.11	.06
86	Lee Lacy	.10	.08	.04
87	Jack Morris	.20	.15	.08
88	Ray Knight	.10	.08	.04
89	Phil Bradley	.15	.11	.06
90	Jose Canseco	3.00	2.25	1.25
91	Gary Ward	.10	.08	.04
92	Mike Easler	.10	.08	.04
93	Tony Pena	.10	.08	.04
94	Dave Smith	.10	.08	.04
95	Will Clark	3.50	2.75	1.50
96	Lloyd Moseby	.10	.08	.04
97	Jim Rice	.40	.30	.15
98	Shawon Dunston	.15	.11	.06
99	Don Sutton	.25	.20	.10
100	Dwight Gooden	1.00	.70	.40
101	Lance Parrish	.20	.15	.08
102	Mark Langston	.15	.11	.06
103	Floyd Youmans	.10	.08	.04
104	Lee Smith	.10	.08	.04
105	Willie Hernandez	.10	.08	.04
106	Doug DeCinces	.10	.08	.04
107	Ken Schrom	.10	.08	.04
108	Don Carman	.10	.08	.04
109	Brook Jacoby	.15	.11	.06
110	Steve Bedrosian	.15	.11	.06
111	American League Pitchers (Roger Clemens, Teddy Higuera, Jack Morris)	.50	.40	.20
112	American League Second Basemen (Marty Barrett, Tony Bernazard, Lou Whitaker)	.10	.08	.04
113	American League Shortstops (Tony Fernandez, Scott Fletcher, Cal Ripken)	.25	.20	.10
114	American League Third Basemen (Wade Boggs, George Brett, Gary Gaetti)	.80	.60	.30
115	National League Third Basemen (Chris Brown, Mike Schmidt, Tim Wallach)	.35	.25	.14
116	National League Second Basemen (Bill Doran, Johnny Ray, Ryne Sandberg)	.15	.11	.06
117	National League Right Fielders (Kevin Bass, Tony Gwynn, Dave Parker)	.25	.20	.10
118	Hot Rookie Prospects (David Clark, Pat Dodson, Ty Gainey, Phil Lombardi, Benito Santiago, Terry Steinbach)	1.75	1.25	.70
119	1986 Season Highlights (Dave Righetti, Mike Scott, Fernando Valenzuela)	.15	.11	.06
120	National League Pitchers (Dwight Gooden, Mike Scott, Fernando Valenzuela)	.40	.30	.15
121	Johnny Ray	.10	.08	.04
122	Keith Moreland	.10	.08	.04
123	Juan Samuel	.15	.11	.06
124	Wally Backman	.10	.08	.04
125	Nolan Ryan	2.00	1.50	.80
126	Greg Harris	.10	.08	.04
127	Kirk McCaskill	.10	.08	.04
128	Dwight Evans	.15	.11	.06
129	Rick Rhoden	.10	.08	.04
130	Bill Madlock	.15	.11	.06
131	Oddibe McDowell	.10	.08	.04
132	Darrell Evans	.10	.08	.04
133	Keith Hernandez	.30	.25	.12
134	Tom Brunansky	.15	.11	.06
135	Kevin McReynolds	.20	.15	.08
136	Scott Fletcher	.10	.08	.04
137	Lou Whitaker	.20	.15	.08
138	Carney Lansford	.10	.08	.04
139	Andre Dawson	.25	.20	.10
140	Carlton Fisk	.20	.15	.08
141	Buddy Bell	.15	.11	.06
142	Ozzie Smith	.20	.15	.08
143	Dan Pasqua	.15	.11	.06
144	Kevin Mitchell	1.50	1.25	.60
145	Bret Saberhagen	.25	.20	.10
146	Charlie Kerfeld	.10	.08	.04
147	Phil Niekro	.25	.20	.10
148	John Candelaria	.10	.08	.04
149	Rich Gedman	.10	.08	.04
150	Fernando Valenzuela	.30	.25	.12
151	National League Catchers (Gary Carter, Tony Pena, Mike Scioscia)	.15	.11	.06
152	National League Left Fielders (Vince Coleman, Jose Cruz, Tim Raines)	.20	.15	.08
153	American League Right Fielders (Harold Baines, Jesse Barfield, Dave Winfield)	.25	.20	.10
154	American League Catchers (Rich Gedman, Lance Parrish, Don Slaught)	.10	.08	.04
155	National League Center Fielders (Eric Davis, Kevin McReynolds, Dale Murphy)	.70	.50	.30
156	1986 Season Highlights (Jim Deshaies, Mike Schmidt, Don Sutton)	.30	.25	.12
157	American League Speedburners (John Cangelosi, Rickey Henderson, Gary Pettis)	.25	.20	.10
158	Hot Rookie Prospects (Randy Asadoor, Casey Candaele, Dave Cochrane, Rafael Palmeiro, Tim Pyznarski, Kevin Seitzer)	2.25	1.75	.90
159	The Best of the Best (Roger Clemens, Dwight Gooden, Rickey Henderson, Don Mattingly, Dale Murphy, Eddie Murray)	1.25	.90	.50
160	Roger McDowell	.15	.11	.06

		MT	NR MT	EX
161	Brian Downing	.10	.08	.04
162	Bill Doran	.10	.08	.04
163	Don Baylor	.15	.11	.06
164	Alfredo Griffin	.10	.08	.04
165	Don Aase	.10	.08	.04
166	Glenn Wilson	.10	.08	.04
167	Dan Quisenberry	.10	.08	.04
168	Frank White	.10	.08	.04
169	Cecil Cooper	.15	.11	.06
170	Jody Davis	.10	.08	.04
171	Harold Baines	.20	.15	.08
172	Rob Deer	.10	.08	.04
173	John Tudor	.15	.11	.06
174	Larry Parrish	.10	.08	.04
175	Kevin Bass	.10	.08	.04
176	Joe Carter	.15	.11	.06
177	Mitch Webster	.10	.08	.04
178	Dave Kingman	.15	.11	.06
179	Jim Presley	.15	.11	.06
180	Mel Hall	.10	.08	.04
181	Shane Rawley	.10	.08	.04
182	Marty Barrett	.10	.08	.04
183	Damaso Garcia	.10	.08	.04
184	Bobby Grich	.10	.08	.04
185	Leon Durham	.10	.08	.04
186	Ozzie Guillen	.10	.08	.04
187	Tony Fernandez	.15	.11	.06
188	Alan Trammell	.30	.25	.12
189	Jim Clancy	.10	.08	.04
190	Bo Jackson	4.00	3.00	1.50
191	Bob Forsch	.10	.08	.04
192	John Franco	.10	.08	.04
193	Von Hayes	.10	.08	.04
194	American League Relief Pitchers (Don Aase, Mark Eichhorn, Dave Righetti)	.10	.08	.04
195	National League First Basemen (Will Clark, Glenn Davis, Keith Hernandez)	1.00	.70	.40
196	1986 Season Highlights (Roger Clemens, Joe Cowley, Bob Horner)	.35	.25	.14
197	The Best of the Best (Wade Boggs, George Brett, Hubie Brooks, Tony Gwynn, Tim Raines, Ryne Sandberg)	.80	.60	.30
198	American League Center Fielders (Rickey Henderson, Fred Lynn, Kirby Puckett)	.25	.20	.10
199	National League Speedburners (Vince			

26330

1987 Sportflics Rookie Discs

The 1987 Sportflics Rookie Discs set consists of seven discs which measure 4" in diameter. The front of the discs offer three "Magic Motion" photos in full color, encompassed by a blue border. The disc backs are printed in red, blue, yellow and green and include the team logo, player statistics, player biography and the disc number. The set was issued with Cooperstown Timeless Trivia Cards.

		MT	NR MT	EX
Complete Set:		20.00	15.00	8.00
Common Player:		1.00	.70	.40
1	Casey Candaele	1.00	.70	.40
2	Mark McGwire	4.00	3.00	1.50
3	Kevin Seitzer	3.00	2.25	1.25
4	Joe Magrane	2.00	1.50	.80
5	Benito Santiago	2.50	2.00	1.00
6	Dave Magadan	2.00	1.50	.80
7	Devon White	2.50	2.00	1.00

1987 Sportflics Rookie Prospects

The 1987 Sportflics Rookie Prospects set consists of 10 cards that are the standard 2-1/2" by 3-1/2" size. The card fronts feature Sportflics' "Magic Motion" process. Card backs contain a player photo plus a short biography and player personal and statistical information. The set was offered in two separately wrapped mylar packs of five cards to hobby dealers purchasing cases of Sportflics' Team Preview set. Twenty-four packs of "Rookie Prospects" cards were included with each case.

		MT	NR MT	EX
Complete Set:		10.00	7.50	4.00
Common Player:		.50	.40	.20
1	Terry Steinbach	1.00	.70	.40
2	Rafael Palmeiro	1.50	1.25	.60
3	Dave Magadan	1.00	.70	.40
4	Marvin Freeman	.50	.40	.20
5	Brick Smith	.50	.40	.20
6	B.J. Surhoff	1.25	.90	.50
7	John Smiley	.50	.40	.20
8	Alonzo Powell	.50	.40	.20
9	Benny Santiago	1.50	1.25	.60
10	Devon White	1.50	1.25	.60

1987 Sportflics Rookies

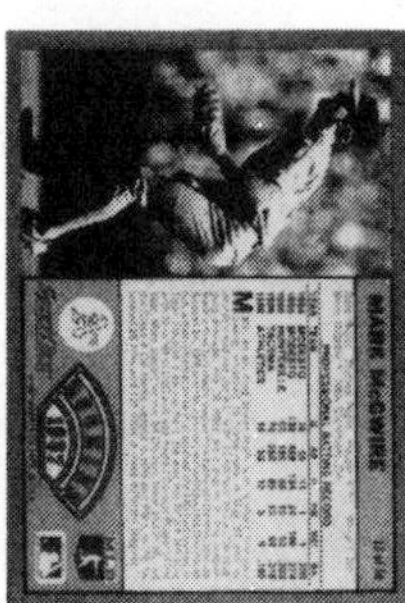

The 1987 Sportflics Rookies set was issued in two series of 25 cards. The first was released in July with the second series following in October. The cards, which are the standard 2-1/2" by 3-1/2", feature Sportflics' special "Magic Motion" process. The card fronts contain a full-color photo and present three different pictures, depending on how the card is held. The backs also contain a full-color photo along with player statistics and a biography.

		MT	NR MT	EX
Complete Set:		15.00	11.00	6.00
Common Player:		.20	.15	.08
1	Eric Bell	.20	.15	.08
2	Chris Bosio	.20	.15	.08
3	Bob Brower	.20	.15	.08
4	Jerry Browne	.20	.15	.08
5	Ellis Burks	1.50	1.25	.60
6	Casey Candaele	.20	.15	.08
7	Joey Cora	.20	.15	.08
8	Ken Gerhart	.30	.25	.12
9	Mike Greenwell	2.00	1.50	.80
10	Stan Jefferson	.20	.15	.08
11	Dave Magadan	.40	.30	.15
12	Joe Magrane	.40	.30	.15
13	Fred McGriff	.80	.60	.30
14	Mark McGwire	2.00	1.50	.80
15	Mark McLemore	.20	.15	.08
16	Jeff Musselman	.20	.15	.08
17	Matt Nokes	.70	.50	.30
18	Paul O'Neill	.20	.15	.08
19	Luis Polonia	.20	.15	.08
20	Benny Santiago	.80	.60	.30
21	Kevin Seitzer	1.00	.70	.40
22	Terry Steinbach	.30	.25	.12
23	B.J. Surhoff	.70	.50	.30
24	Devon White	1.00	.70	.40
25	Matt Williams	.40	.30	.15
26	DeWayne Buice	.20	.15	.08
27	Willie Fraser	.20	.15	.08
28	Bill Ripken	.30	.25	.12
29	Mike Henneman	.30	.25	.12
30	Shawn Hillegas	.20	.15	.08
31	Shane Mack	.20	.15	.08
32	Rafael Palmeiro	.70	.50	.30
33	Mike Jackson	.20	.15	.08
34	Gene Larkin	.20	.15	.08
35	Jimmy Jones	.20	.15	.08
36	Gerald Young	.40	.30	.15
37	Ken Caminiti	.20	.15	.08
38	Sam Horn	.60	.45	.25
39	David Cone	1.00	.70	.40
40	Mike Dunne	.50	.40	.20
41	Ken Williams	.30	.25	.12
42	John Morris	.20	.15	.08
43	Jim Lindeman	.30	.25	.12
44	Todd Benzinger	.70	.50	.30
45	Mike Stanley	.30	.25	.12
46	Les Straker	.20	.15	.08
47	Jeff Robinson	.50	.40	.20
48	Jeff Blauser	.30	.25	.12
49	John Marzano	.30	.25	.12
50	Keith Miller	.30	.25	.12

1987 Sportflics Superstar Discs

Released in three series of six discs and numbered 1 through 18, the 1987 Sportflics Superstar Disc set features the special "Magic Motion" process. Each disc, which measures 4-1/2" in diameter, contains three different player photos, depending which way it is tilted. A red border, containing eleven stars, the player's name and uniform number, surrounds the photo. The backs have a turquoise border which carries the words "Superstar Disc Collector Series." The backs also include the team logo, player statistics, player biography and the disc number. The discs were issued with eighteen 1-3/4" by 2-1/2" Cooperstown Timeless Trivia Cards.

		MT	NR MT	EX
Complete Set:		65.00	49.00	26.00
Common Player:		2.00	1.50	.80
1	Jose Canseco	6.00	4.50	2.50
2	Mike Scott	2.00	1.50	.80
3	Ryne Sandberg	2.50	2.00	1.00
4	Mike Schmidt	3.75	2.75	1.50
5	Dale Murphy	3.75	2.75	1.50
6	Fernando Valenzuela	2.50	2.00	1.00
7	Tony Gwynn	3.50	2.75	1.50
8	Cal Ripken	3.50	2.75	1.50
9	Gary Carter	2.75	2.00	1.00
10	Cory Snyder	2.75	2.00	1.00
11	Kirby Puckett	3.00	2.25	1.25
12	George Brett	3.75	2.75	1.50
13	Keith Hernandez	2.50	2.00	1.00
14	Rickey Henderson	3.50	2.75	1.50
15	Tim Raines	2.75	2.00	1.00
16	Bo Jackson	3.50	2.75	1.50
17	Pete Rose	4.00	3.00	1.50
18	Eric Davis	3.75	2.75	1.50

1987 Sportflics Team Preview

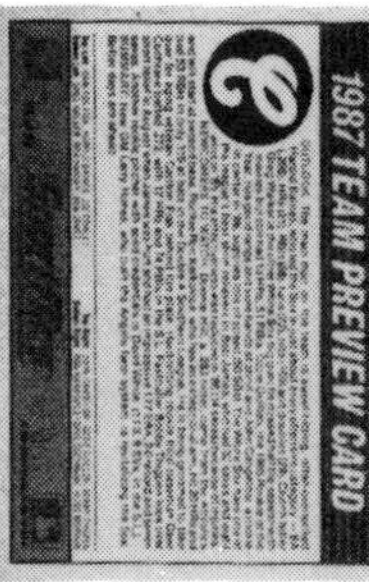

The 1987 Sportflics Team Preview set appeared to be a good idea, but never caught on with collectors. The intent of the set is to provide a pre-season look at each of the 26 major league clubs. The card backs contain three categories of the team preview Outlook, Newcomers to Watch and Summary. Using the "Magic Motion" process, 12 different players are featured on the card fronts. Four of the different player photos can be made visible at once. The cards, which measure 2-1/2" by 3-1/2", were issued with team logo/trivia cards in a specially designed box.

		MT	NR MT	EX
Complete Set:		10.00	7.50	4.00
Common Team:		.40	.30	.15
1	Texas Rangers (Scott Fletcher, Greg Harris, Charlie Hough, Pete Incaviglia, Mike			

		MT	NR MT	EX
	Loynd, Oddibe McDowell, Pete O'Brien, Larry Parrish, Ruben Sierra, Don Slaught, Mitch Williams, Bobby Witt)	.50	.40	.20
2	New York Mets (Wally Backman, Gary Carter, Ron Darling, Lenny Dykstra, Sid Fernandez, Dwight Gooden, Keith Hernandez, Dave Magadan, Kevin McReynolds, Randy Myers, Bob Ojeda, Darryl Strawberry)	.70	.50	.30
3	Cleveland Indians (Tony Bernazard, Brett Butler, Tom Candiotti, Joe Carter, Julio Franco, Mel Hall, Brook Jacoby, Phil Niekro, Ken Schrom, Cory Snyder, Greg Swindell, Pat Tabler)	.50	.40	.20
4	Cincinnati Reds (Buddy Bell, Tom Browning, Kal Daniels, Eric Davis, John Franco, Bill Gullickson, Tracy Jones, Barry Larkin, Rob Murphy, Paul O'Neill, Dave Parker, Pete Rose)	.60	.45	.25
5	Toronto Blue Jays (Jesse Barfield, George Bell, John Cerutti, Mark Eichhorn, Tony Fernandez, Tom Henke, Glenallen Hill, Jimmy Key, Fred McGriff, Lloyd Moseby, Dave Stieb, Willie Upshaw)	.50	.40	.20
6	Philadelphia Phillies (Steve Bedrosian, Don Carman, Marvin Freeman, Kevin Gross, Von Hayes, Shane Rawley, Bruce Ruffin, Juan Samuel, Mike Schmidt, Kent Tekulve, Milt Thompson, Glenn Wilson)	.50	.40	.20
7	New York Yankees (Rickey Henderson, Phil Lombardi, Don Mattingly, Mike Pagliarulo, Dan Pasqua, Willie Randolph, Dennis Rasmussen, Rick Rhoden, Dave Righetti, Joel Skinner, Bob Tewksbury, Dave Winfield)	.80	.60	.30
8	Houston Astros (Kevin Bass, Jose Cruz, Glenn Davis, Jim Deshaies, Bill Doran, Ty Gainey, Charlie Kerfeld, Bob Knepper, Nolan Ryan, Mike Scott, Dave Smith, Robby Wine)	.40	.30	.15
9	Boston Red Sox (Marty Barrett, Don Baylor, Wade Boggs, Dennis Boyd, Roger Clemens, Pat Dodson, Dwight Evans, Mike Greenwell, Dave Henderson, Bruce Hurst, Jim Rice, Calvin Schiraldi)	.60	.45	.25
10	San Francisco Giants (Bob Brenly, Chris Brown, Will Clark, Chili Davis, Kelly Downs, Scott Garrelts, Mark Grant, Mike Krukow, Jeff Leonard, Candy Maldonado, Terry Mulholland, Robby Thompson)	.50	.40	.20
11	California Angels (John Candelaria, Doug DeCinces, Brian Downing, Ruppert Jones, Wally Joyner, Kirk McCaskill, Darrell Miller, Donnie Moore, Gary Pettis, Don Sutton, Devon White, Mike Witt)	.50	.40	.20
12	St. Louis Cardinals (Jack Clark, Vince Coleman, Danny Cox, Bob Forsch, Tom Herr, Joe Magrane, Willie McGee, Terry Pendleton, Ozzie Smith, John Tudor, Andy Van Slyke, Todd Worrell)	.60	.45	.25
13	Kansas City Royals (George Brett, Mark Gubicza, Bo Jackson, Charlie Leibrandt, Hal McRae, Dan Quisenberry, Bret Saberhagen, Kevin Seitzer, Lonnie Smith, Danny Tartabull, Frank White, Willie Wilson)	.50	.40	.20
14	Los Angeles Dodgers (Ralph Bryant, Mariano Duncan, Jose Gonzalez, Pedro Guerrero, Orel Hershiser, Mike Marshall, Steve Sax, Mike Scioscia, Franklin Stubbs, Fernando Valenzuela, Reggie Williams, Matt Young)	.50	.40	.20
15	Detroit Tigers (Darnell Coles, Darrell Evans, Kirk Gibson, Willie Hernandez, Eric King, Chet Lemon, Dwight Lowry, Jack Morris, Dan Petry, Frank Tanana, Alan Trammell, Lou Whitaker)	.60	.45	.25
16	San Diego Padres (Randy Asadoor, Steve Garvey, Tony Gwynn, Andy Hawkins, Jim Jones, John Kruk, Craig Lefferts, Shane Mack, Lance McCullers, Kevin Mitchell, Benny Santiago, Ed Wojna)	.50	.40	.20
17	Minnesota Twins (Bert Blyleven, Tom Brunansky, Gary Gaetti, Greg Gagne, Kent Hrbek, Joe Klink, Steve Lombardozzi, Kirby Puckett, Jeff Reardon, Mark Salas, Roy Smalley, Frank Viola)	.60	.45	.25
18	Pittsburgh Pirates (Barry Bonds, Bobby Bonilla, Sid Bream, Mike Diaz, Brian Fisher, Jim Morrison, Joe Orsulak, Bob Patterson, Tony Pena, Johnny Ray, R.J. Reynolds, John Smiley)	.50	.40	.20
19	Milwaukee Brewers (Glenn Braggs, Rob Deer, Teddy Higuera, Paul Molitor, Juan Nieves, Dan Plesac, Tim Pyznarski, Ernest Riles, Billy Jo Robidoux, B.J. Surhoff, Dale Sveum, Robin Yount)	.50	.40	.20
20	Montreal Expos (Hubie Brooks, Tim Burke, Casey Candaele, Dave Collins, Mike Fitzgerald, Andres Galarraga, Billy Moore, Alonzo Powell, Randy St. Claire, Tim Wallach, Mitch Webster, Floyd Youmans)	.50	.40	.20
21	Baltimore Orioles (Don Aase, Eric Bell, Mike Boddicker, Ken Gerhardt, Terry Kennedy, Ray Knight, Lee Lacy, Fred Lynn, Eddie Murray, Cal Ripken, Jr., Larry Sheets, Jim Traber)	.50	.40	.20
22	Chicago Cubs (Jody Davis, Shawon Dunston, Leon Durham, Dennis Eckersley, Greg Maddux, Dave Martinez, Keith Moreland, Jerry Mumphrey, Rafael Palmeiro, Ryne Sandberg, Scott Sanderson, Lee Smith)	.40	.30	.15
23	Oakland Athletics (Jose Canseco, Mike Davis, Alfredo Griffin, Reggie Jackson, Carney Lansford, Mark McGwire, Dwayne Murphy, Rob Nelson, Tony Phillips, Jose Rijo, Terry Steinbach, Curt Young)	.70	.50	.30
24	Atlanta Braves (Paul Assenmacher, Gene Garber, Tom Glavine, Ken Griffey, Glenn Hubbard, Dion James, Rick Mahler, Dale Murphy, Ken Oberkfell, David Palmer, Zane Smith, Andres Thomas)	.50	.40	.20
25	Seattle Mariners (Scott Bankhead, Phil Bradley, Scott Bradley, Mickey Brantley, Alvin Davis, Steve Fireovid, Mark Langston, Mike Moore, Donell Nixon, Ken Phelps, Jim Presley, Dave Valle)	.40	.30	.15
26	Chicago White Sox (Harold Baines, John Cangelosi, Dave Cochrane, Joe Cowley, Carlton Fisk, Ozzie Guillen, Ron Hassey, Bob James, Ron Karkovice, Russ Mormon, Bobby Thigpen, Greg Walker)	.40	.30	.15

1988 Sportflics

The design of the 1988 Sportflics set differs greatly from the previous two years. Besides increasing the number of cards in the set to 225, Sportflics included the player name, team and uniform number on the card front. The triple-action color photos are surrounded by a red border. The backs are re-designed, also. Full-color action photos, plus extensive statistics and informative biographies are utilized. Three highlights cards and three rookie prospects card are included in the set. The cards are the standard 2-1/2" by 3-1/2".

		MT	NR MT	EX
Complete Set:		35.00	27.50	15.00
Common Player:		.10	.08	.04
1	Don Mattingly	2.50	2.00	1.00
2	Tim Raines	.35	.25	.14
3	Andre Dawson	.25	.20	.10
4	George Bell	.30	.25	.12
5	Joe Carter	.15	.11	.06
6	Matt Nokes	.50	.40	.20
7	Dave Winfield	.35	.25	.14
8	Kirby Puckett	.50	.40	.20
9	Will Clark	2.00	1.50	.80
10	Eric Davis	.70	.50	.30
11	Rickey Henderson	.50	.40	.20
12	Ryne Sandberg	.25	.20	.10
13	Jesse Barfield	.15	.11	.06
14	Ozzie Guillen	.10	.08	.04
15	Bret Saberhagen	.20	.15	.08
16	Tony Gwynn	.40	.30	.15
17	Kevin Seitzer	.50	.40	.20
18	Jack Clark	.20	.15	.08
19	Danny Tartabull	.30	.25	.12
20	Ted Higuera	.15	.11	.06
21	Charlie Leibrandt, Jr.	.10	.08	.04
22	Benny Santiago	.50	.40	.20
23	Fred Lynn	.15	.11	.06
24	Rob Thompson	.10	.08	.04
25	Alan Trammell	.25	.20	.10
26	Tony Fernandez	.15	.11	.06
27	Rick Sutcliffe	.15	.11	.06
28	Gary Carter	.25	.20	.10
29	Cory Snyder	.30	.25	.12
30	Lou Whitaker	.20	.15	.08
31	Keith Hernandez	.25	.20	.10
32	Mike Witt	.10	.08	.04
33	Harold Baines	.15	.11	.06
34	Robin Yount	.25	.20	.10
35	Mike Schmidt	.80	.60	.30
36	Dion James	.10	.08	.04
37	Tom Candiotti	.10	.08	.04
38	Tracy Jones	.15	.11	.06
39	Nolan Ryan	.80	.60	.30
40	Fernando Valenzuela	.25	.20	.10
41	Vance Law	.10	.08	.04
42	Roger McDowell	.10	.08	.04
43	Carlton Fisk	.15	.11	.06
44	Scott Garrelts	.10	.08	.04
45	Lee Guetterman	.10	.08	.04
46	Mark Langston	.15	.11	.06
47	Willie Randolph	.10	.08	.04
48	Bill Doran	.10	.08	.04
49	Larry Parrish	.10	.08	.04
50	Wade Boggs	1.25	.90	.50
51	Shane Rawley	.10	.08	.04
52	Alvin Davis	.15	.11	.06
53	Jeff Reardon	.15	.11	.06
54	Jim Presley	.10	.08	.04
55	Kevin Bass	.10	.08	.04
56	Kevin McReynolds	.20	.15	.08
57	B.J. Surhoff	.15	.11	.06
58	Julio Franco	.15	.11	.06
59	Eddie Murray	.40	.30	.15
60	Jody Davis	.10	.08	.04
61	Todd Worrell	.15	.11	.06
62	Von Hayes	.10	.08	.04
63	Billy Hatcher	.10	.08	.04
64	John Kruk	.15	.11	.06
65	Tom Henke	.10	.08	.04
66	Mike Scott	.15	.11	.06
67	Vince Coleman	.20	.15	.08
68	Ozzie Smith	.20	.15	.08
69	Ken Williams	.20	.15	.08
70	Steve Bedrosian	.15	.11	.06
71	Luis Polonia	.20	.15	.08
72	Brook Jacoby	.15	.11	.06
73	Ron Darling	.15	.11	.06
74	Lloyd Moseby	.10	.08	.04
75	Wally Joyner	.40	.30	.15
76	Dan Quisenberry	.10	.08	.04
77	Scott Fletcher	.10	.08	.04
78	Kirk McCaskill	.10	.08	.04
79	Paul Molitor	.15	.11	.06
80	Mike Aldrete	.10	.08	.04
81	Neal Heaton	.10	.08	.04
82	Jeffrey Leonard	.10	.08	.04
83	Dave Magadan	.15	.11	.06
84	Danny Cox	.10	.08	.04
85	Lance McCullers	.10	.08	.04
86	Jay Howell	.10	.08	.04
87	Charlie Hough	.10	.08	.04
88	Gene Garber	.10	.08	.04
89	Jesse Orosco	.10	.08	.04
90	Don Robinson	.10	.08	.04
91	Willie McGee	.15	.11	.06
92	Bert Blyleven	.15	.11	.06
93	Phil Bradley	.15	.11	.06
94	Terry Kennedy	.10	.08	.04
95	Kent Hrbek	.20	.15	.08
96	Juan Samuel	.15	.11	.06
97	Pedro Guerrero	.20	.15	.08
98	Sid Bream	.10	.08	.04
99	Devon White	.30	.25	.12
100	Mark McGwire	1.25	.90	.50
101	Dave Parker	.15	.11	.06
102	Glenn Davis	.20	.15	.08
103	Greg Walker	.10	.08	.04
104	Rick Rhoden	.10	.08	.04
105	Mitch Webster	.10	.08	.04
106	Lenny Dykstra	.10	.08	.04
107	Gene Larkin	.15	.11	.06
108	Floyd Youmans	.10	.08	.04
109	Andy Van Slyke	.15	.11	.06
110	Mike Scioscia	.10	.08	.04
111	Kirk Gibson	.25	.20	.10
112	Kal Daniels	.30	.25	.12
113	Ruben Sierra	.50	.40	.20
114	Sam Horn	.30	.25	.12
115	Ray Knight	.10	.08	.04
116	Jimmy Key	.10	.08	.04
117	Bo Diaz	.10	.08	.04
118	Mike Greenwell	1.00	.70	.40
119	Barry Bonds	.20	.15	.08
120	Reggie Jackson	.40	.30	.15
121	Mike Pagliarulo	.15	.11	.06
122	Tommy John	.20	.15	.08
123	Bill Madlock	.15	.11	.06
124	Ken Caminiti	.30	.25	.12
125	Gary Ward	.10	.08	.04
126	Candy Maldonado	.10	.08	.04
127	Harold Reynolds	.10	.08	.04
128	Joe Magrane	.30	.25	.12
129	Mike Henneman	.25	.20	.10
130	Jim Gantner	.10	.08	.04
131	Bobby Bonilla	.15	.11	.06
132	John Farrell	.30	.25	.12
133	Frank Tanana	.10	.08	.04
134	Zane Smith	.10	.08	.04
135	Dave Righetti	.20	.15	.08
136	Rick Reuschel	.10	.08	.04
137	Dwight Evans	.15	.11	.06
138	Howard Johnson	.10	.08	.04
139	Terry Leach	.10	.08	.04
140	Casey Candaele	.10	.08	.04
141	Tom Herr	.10	.08	.04
142	Tony Pena	.10	.08	.04
143	Lance Parrish	.20	.15	.08
144	Ellis Burks	1.25	.90	.50
145	Pete O'Brien	.10	.08	.04
146	Mike Boddicker	.10	.08	.04
147	Buddy Bell	.10	.08	.04
148	Bo Jackson	.80	.60	.30
149	Frank White	.10	.08	.04
150	George Brett	.60	.45	.25
151	Tim Wallach	.10	.08	.04
152	Cal Ripken, Jr.	.40	.30	.15
153	Brett Butler	.10	.08	.04
154	Gary Gaetti	.15	.11	.06
155	Darryl Strawberry	.60	.45	.25
156	Alfredo Griffin	.10	.08	.04
157	Marty Barrett	.10	.08	.04
158	Jim Rice	.30	.25	.12
159	Terry Pendleton	.10	.08	.04
160	Orel Hershiser	.35	.25	.14
161	Larry Sheets	.10	.08	.04
162	Dave Stewart	.10	.08	.04
163	Shawon Dunston	.15	.11	.06
164	Keith Moreland	.10	.08	.04
165	Ken Oberkfell	.10	.08	.04
166	Ivan Calderon	.10	.08	.04
167	Bob Welch	.15	.11	.06
168	Fred McGriff	.40	.30	.15
169	Pete Incaviglia	.15	.11	.06
170	Dale Murphy	.60	.45	.25
171	Mike Dunne	.25	.20	.10
172	Chili Davis	.10	.08	.04
173	Milt Thompson	.10	.08	.04
174	Terry Steinbach	.15	.11	.06
175	Oddibe McDowell	.10	.08	.04
176	Jack Morris	.20	.15	.08
177	Sid Fernandez	.15	.11	.06
178	Ken Griffey	.10	.08	.04
179	Lee Smith	.10	.08	.04
180	1987 Highlights (Juan Nieves, Kirby Puckett, Mike Schmidt)	.25	.20	.10
181	Brian Downing	.10	.08	.04
182	Andres Galarraga	.20	.15	.08
183	Rob Deer	.10	.08	.04

		MT	NR MT	EX
184	Greg Brock	.10	.08	.04
185	Doug DeCinces	.10	.08	.04
186	Johnny Ray	.10	.08	.04
187	Hubie Brooks	.10	.08	.04
188	Darrell Evans	.10	.08	.04
189	Mel Hall	.10	.08	.04
190	Jim Deshaies	.10	.08	.04
191	Dan Plesac	.15	.11	.06
192	Willie Wilson	.15	.11	.06
193	Mike LaValliere	.10	.08	.04
194	Tom Brunansky	.15	.11	.06
195	John Franco	.15	.11	.06
196	Frank Viola	.20	.15	.08
197	Bruce Hurst	.10	.08	.04
198	John Tudor	.10	.08	.04
199	Bob Forsch	.10	.08	.04
200	Dwight Gooden	.60	.45	.25
201	Jose Canseco	2.00	1.50	.80
202	Carney Lansford	.10	.08	.04
203	Kelly Downs	.10	.08	.04
204	Glenn Wilson	.10	.08	.04
205	Pat Tabler	.10	.08	.04
206	Mike Davis	.10	.08	.04
207	Roger Clemens	.60	.45	.25
208	Dave Smith	.10	.08	.04
209	Curt Young	.10	.08	.04
210	Mark Eichhorn	.10	.08	.04
211	Juan Nieves	.10	.08	.04
212	Bob Boone	.10	.08	.04
213	Don Sutton	.20	.15	.08
214	Willie Upshaw	.10	.08	.04
215	Jim Clancy	.10	.08	.04
216	Bill Ripken	.25	.20	.10
217	Ozzie Virgil	.10	.08	.04
218	Dave Concepcion	.10	.08	.04
219	Alan Ashby	.10	.08	.04
220	Mike Marshall	.15	.11	.06
221	1987 Highlights (Vince Coleman, Mark McGwire, Paul Molitor)	.50	.40	.20
222	1987 Highlights (Steve Bedrosian, Don Mattingly, Benito Santiago)	.80	.60	.30
223	Hot Rookie Prospects (Shawn Abner, Jay Buhner, Gary Thurman)	.40	.30	.15
224	Hot Rookie Prospects (Tim Crews, John Davis, Vincente Palacios)	.30	.25	.12
225	Hot Rookie Prospects (Keith Miller, Jody Reed, Jeff Treadway)	.50	.40	.20

1988 Sportflics Gamewinners

This set of 25 standard-size cards (2-1/2" by 3-1/2"), featuring star players in the Sportflics patented 3-D Magic Motion design, was issued by Weiser Card Co. of Plainsboro, N.J., for use as a youth organizational fundraiser. (Weiser's president is former Yankees outfielder Bobby Murcer.) A limited number of sets was produced for test marketing in the Northwestern U.S., with plans for a 1989 set to be marketed nationwide. A green- and-yellow Gamewinners logo banner spans the upper border of the cards face, with a matching player name (with uniform number and position) below the full-color triple photo. The card backs carry large full-color player photos (1-3/4" by 1-3/4"), along with stats, personal information and career high- lights.

		MT	NR MT	EX
Complete Set:		10.00	7.50	4.00
Common Player:		.20	.15	.08
1	Don Mattingly	2.50	2.00	1.00
2	Mark McGwire	1.00	.70	.40
3	Wade Boggs	1.50	1.25	.60
4	Will Clark	.60	.45	.25
5	Eric Davis	.80	.60	.30
6	Willie Randolph	.20	.15	.08
7	Dave Winfield	.50	.40	.20
8	Rickey Henderson	.60	.45	.25
9	Dwight Gooden	.80	.60	.30
10	Benny Santiago	.40	.30	.15
11	Keith Hernandez	.40	.30	.15
12	Juan Samuel	.30	.25	.12
13	Kevin Seitzer	.60	.45	.25
14	Gary Carter	.50	.40	.20
15	Darryl Strawberry	.80	.60	.30
16	Rick Rhoden	.20	.15	.08
17	Howard Johnson	.20	.15	.08
18	Matt Nokes	.50	.40	.20
19	Dave Righetti	.30	.25	.12
20	Roger Clemens	.80	.60	.30
21	Mike Schmidt	.70	.50	.30
22	Kevin McReynolds	.30	.25	.12
23	Mike Pagliarulo	.20	.15	.08
24	Kevin Elster	.20	.15	.08
25	Jack Clark	.30	.25	.12

1989 Sportflics

This basic issue includes 225 standard-size player cards (2-1/2" by 3-1/2") and 153 trivia cards, all featuring the patented Magic Motion design. A 5-card sub-set of triple photo cards called "Tri-Star" features a mix of veterans and rookies. The card fronts feature a white outer border and double color inner border in one of six color schemes (i.e. red, blue, purple). The inner border color changes when the card is tilted and the bottom border carries a double stripe of colors. The player name appears in the top border, player postition and uniform number appear, alternately, in the bottom border. The card backs contain crisp 1-7/8" by 1-3/4" player action shots, along with personal information, stats and career highlights. "The Unforgettables" trivia cards in this set salute members of the Hall of Fame.

		MT	NR MT	EX
Complete Set:		40.00	30.00	15.00
Common Player:		.10	.08	.04
1	Jose Canseco	1.75	1.25	.70
2	Wally Joyner	.40	.30	.15
3	Roger Clemens	.60	.45	.25
4	Greg Swindell	.15	.11	.06
5	Jack Morris	.20	.15	.08
6	Mickey Brantley	.10	.08	.04
7	Jim Presley	.15	.11	.06
8	Pete O'Brien	.10	.08	.04
9	Jesse Barfield	.15	.11	.06
10	Frank Viola	.20	.15	.08
11	Kevin Bass	.10	.08	.04
12	Glenn Wilson	.10	.08	.04
13	Chris Sabo	1.00	.70	.40
14	Fred McGriff	.50	.40	.20
15	Mark Grace	1.25	.90	.50
16	Devon White	.20	.15	.08
17	Juan Samuel	.15	.11	.06
18	Lou Whitaker	.25	.20	.10
19	Greg Walker	.10	.08	.04
20	Roberto Alomar	.50	.40	.20
21	Mike Schmidt	.60	.45	.25
22	Benny Santiago	.25	.20	.10
23	Dave Stewart	.10	.08	.04
24	Dave Winfield	.35	.25	.14
25	George Bell	.30	.25	.12
26	Jack Clark	.20	.15	.08
27	Doug Drabek	.10	.08	.04
28	Ron Gant	.15	.11	.06
29	Glenn Braggs	.10	.08	.04
30	Rafael Palmeiro	.20	.15	.08
31	Brett Butler	.10	.08	.04
32	Ron Darling	.15	.11	.06
33	Alvin Davis	.15	.11	.06
34	Bob Walk	.10	.08	.04
35	Dave Stieb	.15	.11	.06
36	Orel Hershiser	.40	.30	.15
37	John Farrell	.15	.11	.06
38	Doug Jones	.10	.08	.04
39	Kelly Downs	.10	.08	.04
40	Bob Boone	.10	.08	.04
41	Gary Sheffield	2.25	1.75	.90
42	Doug Dascenzo	.30	.25	.12
43	Chad Krueter	.20	.15	.08
44	Ricky Jordan	1.75	1.25	.70
45	Dave West	.70	.50	.30
46	Danny Tartabull	.30	.25	.12
47	Teddy Higuera	.15	.11	.06
48	Gary Gaetti	.15	.11	.06
49	Dave Parker	.15	.11	.06
50	Don Mattingly	3.00	2.25	1.25
51	David Cone	.25	.20	.10
52	Kal Daniels	.25	.20	.10
53	Carney Lansford	.10	.08	.04
54	Mike Marshall	.15	.11	.06
55	Kevin Seitzer	.30	.25	.12
56	Mike Henneman	.10	.08	.04
57	Bill Doran	.10	.08	.04
58	Steve Sax	.20	.15	.08
59	Lance Parrish	.15	.11	.06
60	Keith Hernandez	.25	.20	.10
61	Jose Uribe	.10	.08	.04
62	Jose Lind	.15	.11	.06
63	Steve Bedrosian	.15	.11	.06
64	George Brett	.60	.45	.25
65	Kirk Gibson	.25	.20	.10
66	Cal Ripken, Jr.	.50	.40	.20
67	Mitch Webster	.10	.08	.04
68	Fred Lynn	.15	.11	.06
69	Eric Davis	.60	.45	.25
70	Bo Jackson	.70	.50	.30
71	Kevin Elster	.15	.11	.06
72	Rick Reuschel	.10	.08	.04
73	Tim Burke	.10	.08	.04
74	Mark Davis	.10	.08	.04
75	Claudell Washington	.10	.08	.04
76	Lance McCullers	.10	.08	.04
77	Mike Moore	.10	.08	.04
78	Robby Thompson	.10	.08	.04
79	Roger McDowell	.10	.08	.04
80	Danny Jackson	.15	.11	.06
81	Tim Leary	.10	.08	.04
82	Bobby Witt	.15	.11	.06
83	Jim Gott	.10	.08	.04
84	Andy Hawkins	.10	.08	.04
85	Ozzie Guillen	.10	.08	.04
86	John Tudor	.15	.11	.06
87	Todd Burns	.25	.20	.10
88	Dave Gallagher	.25	.20	.10
89	Jay Buhner	.15	.11	.06
90	Gregg Jefferies	2.00	1.50	.80
91	Bob Welch	.15	.11	.06
92	Charlie Hough	.10	.08	.04
93	Tony Fernandez	.15	.11	.06
94	Ozzie Virgil	.10	.08	.04
95	Andre Dawson	.25	.20	.10
96	Hubie Brooks	.10	.08	.04
97	Kevin McReynolds	.20	.15	.08
98	Mike LaValliere	.10	.08	.04
99	Terry Pendleton	.10	.08	.04
100	Wade Boggs	1.75	1.25	.70
101	Dennis Eckersley	.15	.11	.06
102	Mark Gubicza	.15	.11	.06
103	Frank Tanana	.10	.08	.04
104	Joe Carter	.15	.11	.06
105	Ozzie Smith	.20	.15	.08
106	Dennis Martinez	.10	.08	.04
107	Jeff Treadway	.15	.11	.06
108	Greg Maddux	.15	.11	.06
109	Bret Saberhagen	.20	.15	.08
110	Dale Murphy	.60	.45	.25
111	Rob Deer	.10	.08	.04
112	Pete Incaviglia	.15	.11	.06
113	Vince Coleman	.20	.15	.08
114	Tim Wallach	.15	.11	.06
115	Nolan Ryan	.60	.45	.25
116	Walt Weiss	.35	.25	.14
117	Brian Downing	.10	.08	.04
118	Melido Perez	.15	.11	.06
119	Terry Steinbach	.15	.11	.06
120	Mike Scott	.15	.11	.06
121	Tim Belcher	.15	.11	.06
122	Mike Boddicker	.10	.08	.04
123	Len Dykstra	.10	.08	.04
124	Fernando Valenzuela	.25	.20	.10
125	Gerald Young	.15	.11	.06
126	Tom Henke	.10	.08	.04
127	Dave Henderson	.10	.08	.04
128	Dan Plesac	.15	.11	.06
129	Chili Davis	.10	.08	.04
130	Bryan Harvey	.25	.20	.10
131	Don August	.15	.11	.06
132	Mike Harkey	.50	.40	.20
133	Luis Polonia	.10	.08	.04
134	Craig Worthington	.35	.25	.14
135	Joey Meyer	.15	.11	.06
136	Barry Larkin	.25	.20	.10
137	Glenn Davis	.20	.15	.08
138	Mike Scioscia	.10	.08	.04
139	Andres Galarraga	.20	.15	.08
140	Doc Gooden	.60	.45	.25
141	Keith Moreland	.10	.08	.04
142	Kevin Mitchell	.10	.08	.04
143	Mike Greenwell	.80	.60	.30
144	Mel Hall	.10	.08	.04
145	Rickey Henderson	.50	.40	.20
146	Barry Bonds	.20	.15	.08
147	Eddie Murray	.40	.30	.15
148	Lee Smith	.10	.08	.04
149	Julio Franco	.15	.11	.06
150	Tim Raines	.35	.25	.14
151	Mitch Williams	.10	.08	.04
152	Tim Laudner	.10	.08	.04
153	Mike Pagliarulo	.15	.11	.06
154	Floyd Bannister	.10	.08	.04
155	Gary Carter	.25	.20	.10
156	Kirby Puckett	.40	.30	.15
157	Harold Baines	.20	.15	.08
158	Dave Righetti	.20	.15	.08
159	Mark Langston	.15	.11	.06
160	Tony Gwynn	.50	.40	.20
161	Tom Brunansky	.15	.11	.06
162	Vance Law	.10	.08	.04
163	Kelly Gruber	.10	.08	.04
164	Gerald Perry	.15	.11	.06
165	Harold Reynolds	.10	.08	.04
166	Andy Van Slyke	.15	.11	.06
167	Jimmy Key	.15	.11	.06
168	Jeff Reardon	.15	.11	.06
169	Milt Thompson	.10	.08	.04
170	Will Clark	.80	.60	.30
171	Chet Lemon	.10	.08	.04
172	Pat Tabler	.10	.08	.04
173	Jim Rice	.30	.25	.12
174	Billy Hatcher	.10	.08	.04
175	Bruce Hurst	.15	.11	.06
176	John Franco	.15	.11	.06
177	Van Snider	.25	.20	.10
178	Ron Jones	.35	.25	.14
179	Jerald Clark	.30	.25	.12
180	Tom Browning	.15	.11	.06
181	Von Hayes	.10	.08	.04
182	Bobby Bonilla	.15	.11	.06
183	Todd Worrell	.15	.11	.06
184	John Kruk	.15	.11	.06
185	Scott Fletcher	.10	.08	.04
186	Willie Wilson	.15	.11	.06
187	Jody Davis	.10	.08	.04
188	Kent Hrbek	.20	.15	.08
189	Ruben Sierra	.35	.25	.14
190	Shawon Dunston	.15	.11	.06
191	Ellis Burks	.70	.50	.30
192	Brook Jacoby	.15	.11	.06
193	Jeff Robinson	.15	.11	.06
194	Rich Dotson	.10	.08	.04
195	Johnny Ray	.10	.08	.04
196	Cory Snyder	.25	.20	.10

		MT	NR MT	EX
197	Mike Witt	.10	.08	.04
198	Marty Barrett	.10	.08	.04
199	Robin Yount	.30	.25	.12
200	Mark McGwire	1.00	.70	.40
201	Ryne Sandberg	.30	.25	.12
202	John Candelaria	.10	.08	.04
203	Matt Nokes	.20	.15	.08
204	Dwight Evans	.15	.11	.06
205	Darryl Strawberry	.60	.45	.25
206	Willie McGee	.15	.11	.06
207	Bobby Thigpen	.15	.11	.06
208	B.J. Surhoff	.15	.11	.06
209	Paul Molitor	.15	.11	.06
210	Jody Reed	.15	.11	.06
211	Doyle Alexander	.10	.08	.04
212	Dennis Rasmussen	.15	.11	.06
213	Kevin Gross	.10	.08	.04
214	Kirk McCaskill	.10	.08	.04
215	Alan Trammell	.30	.25	.12
216	Damon Berryhill	.15	.11	.06
217	Rick Sutcliffe	.15	.11	.06
218	Don Slaught	.10	.08	.04
219	Carlton Fisk	.30	.25	.12
220	Allan Anderson	.10	.08	.04
221	1988 Highlights (Wade Boggs, Jose Canseco, Mike Greenwell)	1.50	1.25	.60
222	1988 Highlights (Tom Browning, Dennis Eckersley, Orel Hershiser)	.25	.20	.10
223	Hot Rookie Prospects (Sandy Alomar, Gregg Jefferies, Gary Sheffield)	2.00	1.50	.80
224	Hot Rookie Prospects (Randy Johnson, Ramon Martinez, Bob Milacki)	.60	.45	.25
225	Hot Rookie Prospects (Geronimo Berroa, Cameron Drew, Ron Jones)	.35	.25	.14

1990 Sportflics

The Sportflics set for 1990 again contained 225 cards. The cards feature the unique "Magic Motion" effect which displays either of two different photos depending on how the card is tilted. (Previous years' sets had used three photos per card.) The two-photo "Magic Motion" sequence is designed to depict sequential game-action, showing a batter following through on his swing, a pitcher completing his motion, etc. Sportflics also added a moving red and yellow "marquee" border on the cards to compliment the animation effect. The player's name, which appears below the animation, remains stationary. The set includes 19 special rookie cards. The backs contain a color player photo, team logo, player information and stats. The cards were distributed in non-transparent mylar packs with small MVP trivia cards.

		MT	NR MT	EX
Complete Set:		35.00	25.00	14.00
Common Player:		.10	.08	.04
1	Kevin Mitchell	.40	.30	.15
2	Wade Boggs	1.00	.70	.40
3	Cory Snyder	.10	.08	.04
4	Paul O'Neill	.10	.08	.04
5	Will Clark	1.00	.70	.40
6	Tony Fernandez	.10	.08	.04
7	Ken Griffey, Jr.	1.75	1.25	.70
8	Nolan Ryan	.60	.45	.25
9	Rafael Palmeiro	.10	.08	.04
10	Jesse Barfield	.10	.08	.04
11	Kirby Puckett	.40	.30	.15
12	Steve Sax	.10	.08	.04
13	Fred McGriff	.40	.30	.15
14	Gregg Jefferies	1.50	1.25	.06
15	Mark Grace	.90	.70	.35
16	Devon White	.10	.08	.04
17	Juan Samuel	.15	.11	.06
18	Robin Yount	.25	.20	.10
19	Glenn Davis	.10	.08	.04
20	Jeffrey Leonard	.10	.08	.04
21	Chili Davis	.10	.08	.04
22	Craig Biggio	.70	.50	.30
23	Jose Canseco	1.50	1.25	.70
24	Derek Lilliquist	.30	.25	.12
25	Chris Bosio	.10	.08	.04
26	Dave Steib	.10	.08	.04
27	Bobby Thigpen	.10	.08	.04
28	Jack Clark	.10	.08	.04
29	Kevin Ritz	.30	.25	.12
30	Tom Gordon	.80	.60	.30
31	Bryan Harvey	.10	.08	.04
32	Jim Deshaies	.10	.08	.04
33	Terry Steinbach	.15	.11	.06
34	Tom Glavine	.15	.11	.06
35	Bob Welch	.10	.08	.04
36	Charlie Hayes	.20	.15	.08
37	Jeff Reardon	.10	.08	.04
38	Joe Orsulak	.10	.08	.04
39	Scott Garrelts	.10	.08	.04
40	Bob Boone	.10	.08	.04
41	Scott Bankhead	.10	.08	.04
42	Tom Henke	.10	.08	.04
43	Greg Briley	.40	.30	.15
44	Teddy Higuera	.10	.08	.04
45	Pat Borders	.10	.08	.04
46	Kevin Seitzer	.15	.11	.06
47	Bruce Hurst	.15	.11	.06
48	Ozzie Guillen	.10	.08	.04
49	Wally Joyner	.50	.40	.20
50	Mike Greenwell	.40	.30	.15
51	Gary Gaetti	.12	.09	.05
52	Gary Sheffield	1.25	.90	.50
53	Dennis Martinez	.10	.08	.04
54	Ryne Sanberg	.20	.15	.08
55	Mike Scott	.12	.09	.05
56	Todd Benzinger	.10	.08	.04
57	Kelly Gruber	.15	.11	.06
58	Jose Lind	.10	.08	.04
59	Allan Anderson	.10	.08	.04
60	Robby Thompson	.10	.08	.04
61	John Smoltz	.30	.25	.12
62	Mark Davis	.12	.09	.05
63	Tom Herr	.10	.08	.06
64	Randy Johnson	.20	.15	.08
65	Lonnie Smith	.10	.08	.04
66	Pedro Guerrero	.15	.11	.06
67	Jerome Walton	1.50	1.25	.60
68	Ramon Martinez	.40	.30	.15
69	Tim Raines	.12	.09	.05
70	Matt Williams	.20	.15	.08
71	Joe Oliver	.35	.25	.12
72	Nick Esasky	.12	.09	.05
73	Kevin Brown	.25	.20	.10
74	Walt Weiss	.12	.09	.05
75	Roger McDowell	.10	.08	.04
76	Jose DeLeon	.10	.08	.04
77	Brian Downing	.10	.08	.04
78	Jay Howell	.10	.08	.04
79	Jose Uribe	.10	.08	.04
80	Ellis Burks	.50	.40	.20
81	Sammy Sosa	.50	.40	.20
82	Johnny Ray	.50	.40	.20
83	Danny Darwin	.10	.08	.04
84	Carney Lansford	.12	.09	.05
85	Jose Oquendo	.10	.08	.04
86	John Cerutti	.10	.08	.04
87	Dave Winfield	.15	.11	.08
88	Dave Righetti	.10	.08	.04
89	Danny Jackson	.10	.08	.04
90	Andy Benes	.70	.50	.30
91	Tom Browning	.10	.08	.04
92	Pete O'Brien	.10	.08	.04
93	Roberto Alomar	.15	.11	.06
94	Bret Saberhagen	.15	.11	.06
95	Phil Bradley	.10	.08	.04
96	Doug Jones	.10	.08	.04
97	Eric Davis	.80	.60	.30
98	Tony Gwynn	.40	.30	.15
99	Jim Abbott	.70	.50	.30
100	Cal Ripken, Jr.	.15	.11	.06
101	Andy Van Slyke	.12	.09	.05
102	Dan Plesac	.10	.08	.04
103	Lou Whitaker	.10	.08	.04
104	Steve Bedrosian	.10	.08	.04
105	Dave Gallagher	.10	.08	.04
106	Keith Hernandez	.10	.08	.04
107	Duane Ward	.10	.08	.04
108	Andre Dawson	.15	.11	.08
109	Howard Johnson	.20	.15	.08
110	Mark Langston	.12	.09	.05
111	Jerry Browne	.10	.08	.04
112	Alvin Davis	.10	.08	.04
113	Sid Fernandez	.10	.08	.04
114	Mike Devereaux	.10	.08	.04
115	Benny Santiago	.12	.09	.05
116	Bip Roberts	.10	.08	.04
117	Craig Worthington	.15	.11	.06
118	Kevin Elster	.10	.08	.04
119	Harold Reynolds	.10	.08	.04
120	Joe Carter	.15	.11	.06
121	Brian Harper	.10	.08	.04
122	Frank Viola	.15	.11	.06
123	Jeff Ballard	.10	.08	.04
124	John Kruk	.10	.08	.04
125	Harold Baines	.10	.08	.04
126	Tom Candiotti	.10	.08	.04
127	Kevin McReynolds	.15	.11	.06
128	Mookie Wilson	.10	.08	.04
129	Danny Tartabull	.12	.09	.05
130	Craig Lefferts	.10	.08	.04
131	Jose DeJesus	.15	.11	.06
132	John Orton	.30	.20	.10
133	Curt Schilling	.20	.15	.08
134	Marquis Grissom	1.25	.90	.50
135	Greg Vaughn	1.25	.90	.50
136	Brett Butler	.10	.08	.04
137	Rob Deer	.10	.08	.04
138	John Franco	.10	.08	.04
139	Keith Moreland	.10	.08	.04
140	Dave Smith	.10	.08	.04
141	Mark McGwire	1.00	.70	.40
142	Vince Coleman	.15	.11	.06
143	Barry Bonds	.15	.11	.06
144	Mike Henneman	.10	.08	.04
145	Doc Gooden	.30	.25	.12
146	Darryl Strawberry	.30	.25	.12
147	Von Hayes	.10	.08	.04
148	Andres Galarraga	.12	.09	.05
149	Roger Clemens	.25	.20	.10
150	Don Mattingly	1.50	1.25	.60
151	Joe Magrane	.10	.08	.04
152	Dwight Smith	.60	.45	.25
153	Ricky Jordan	.30	.25	.12
154	Alan Trammell	.10	.08	.04
155	Brook Jacoby	.10	.08	.04
156	Lenny Dykstra	.10	.08	.04
157	Mike LaValliere	.10	.08	.04
158	Julio Franco	.12	.09	.05
159	Joey Belle	.80	.60	.30
160	Barry Larkin	.15	.11	.06
161	Rick Reuschel	.10	.08	.04
162	Nelson Santovenia	.10	.08	.04
163	Mike Scioscia	.10	.08	.04
164	Damon Berryhill	.10	.08	.04
165	Todd Worrell	.10	.08	.04
166	Jim Eisenreich	.10	.08	.04
167	Ivan Calderon	.10	.08	.04
168	Goose Gozzo	.25	.20	.10
169	Kirk McCaskill	.10	.08	.04
170	Dennis Eckersley	.10	.08	.04
171	Mickey Tettleton	.12	.09	.05
172	Chuck Finley	.10	.08	.04
173	Dave Magadan	.10	.08	.04
174	Terry Pendleton	.10	.08	.04
175	Willie Randolph	.10	.08	.04
176	Jeff Huson	.25	.20	.10
177	Todd Zeile	2.00	1.50	.80
178	Steve Olin	.40	.30	.15
179	Eric Anthony	1.50	1.25	.60
180	Scott Coolbaugh	.50	.40	.20
181	Rick Sutcliffe	.10	.08	.04
182	Tim Wallach	.10	.08	.04
183	Paul Molitor	.12	.09	.05
184	Roberto Kelly	.12	.09	.05
185	Mike Moore	.10	.08	.04
186	Junior Felix	.70	.50	.30
187	Mike Schooler	.10	.08	.04
188	Ruben Sierra	.30	.25	.12
189	Dale Murphy	.12	.09	.05
190	Dan Gladden	.10	.08	.04
191	John Smiley	.10	.08	.04
192	Jeff Russell	.10	.08	.04
193	Bert Blyleven	.10	.08	.04
194	Dave Stewart	.12	.09	.05
195	Bobby Bonilla	.12	.09	.05
196	Mitch Williams	.10	.08	.04
197	Orel Hershiser	.20	.15	.08
198	Kevin Bass	.10	.08	.04
199	Tim Burke	.10	.08	.04
200	Bo Jackson	1.25	.90	.50
201	David Cone	.12	.09	.05
202	Gary Pettis	.10	.08	.04
203	Kent Hrbek	.10	.08	.04
204	Carlton Fisk	.10	.08	.04
205	Bob Geren	.30	.25	.12
206	Bill Spiers	.40	.30	.15
207	Oddibe McDowell	.10	.08	.04
208	Rickey Henderson	.30	.25	.12
209	Ken Caminiti	.10	.08	.04
210	Devon White	.10	.08	.04
211	Greg Maddux	.15	.11	.06
212	Ed Whitson	.10	.08	.04
213	Carlos Martinez	.25	.20	.10
214	George Brett	.25	.20	.10
215	Gregg Olson	.50	.40	.20
216	Kenny Rogers	.20	.15	.08
217	Dwight Evans	.10	.08	.04
218	Pat Tabler	.10	.08	.04
219	Jeff Treadway	.10	.08	.04
220	Scott Fletcher	.10	.08	.04
221	Deion Sanders	.70	.50	.30
222	Robin Ventura	.70	.50	.30
223	Chip Hale	.50	.40	.20
224	Tommy Greene	.40	.30	.15
225	Dean Palmer	.40	.30	.15

1977 Sportscaster

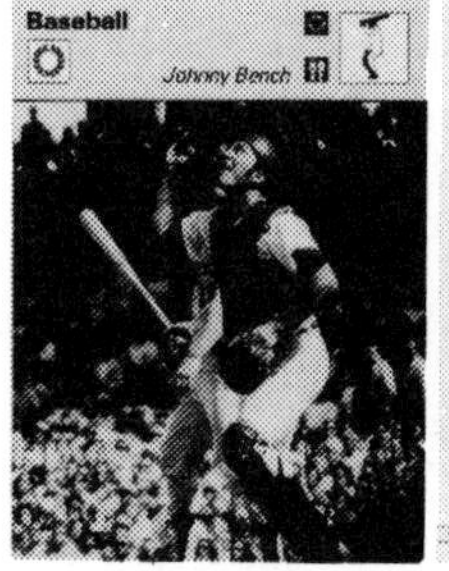

This massive set of full-color cards, which includes players from dozens of different sports - some of them very obscure - contains more than 2,000 different subjects, making it one of the biggest sets of trading cards ever issued. Available by mail subscription from 1977 through 1979, the Sportscaster cards are large, measuring 6-1/4" by 4-3/4". Subscribers were mailed one series of 24 cards each for $1.89 plus postage every month or so. The cards are not numbered, making it very difficult to assemble a complete set. The set has an international flavor to it, including such sports as rugby, soccer, lawn bowling, fencing, karate, bicycling, curling, skiing, bullfighting, auto racing, mountain climbing, hang gliding, yachting, sailing, badminton, bobsledding, etc. Each card has a series of legends in the upper right corner to assist collectors in the various methods of sorting. Most popular among American collectors are the baseball and football stars in the set, which includes the 140 baseball subjects listed here. The checklist includes many

Hall of Famers and future Hall of Famers. The card backs contain detailed write-ups of the player featured.

	NR MT	EX	VG
Complete Set:	250.00	125.00	75.00
Common Player:	.40	.20	.12
(1) Henry Aaron	8.00	4.00	2.50
(2) Danny Ainge	.75	.40	.25
(3) Emmett Ashford (umpire)	.40	.20	.12
(4) Ernie Banks	4.50	2.25	1.25
(5) Johnny Bench	5.00	2.50	1.50
(6) Vida Blue	.75	.40	.25
(7) Bert Blyleven	1.25	.60	.40
(8) Bobby Bonds	.75	.40	.25
(9) Lyman Bostock	.75	.40	.25
(10) George Brett	5.00	2.50	1.50
(11) Lou Brock	3.50	1.75	1.00
(12) Jeff Burroughs	.40	.20	.12
(13) Roy Campanella	4.50	2.25	1.25
(14) John Candelaria	.30	.15	.09
(15) Rod Carew	5.00	2.50	1.50
(16) Steve Carlton	5.00	2.50	1.50
(17) Ron Cey	.75	.40	.25
(18) Roberto Clemente	8.00	4.00	2.50
(19) Steve Dembowski	.40	.20	.12
(20) Joe DiMaggio	8.00	4.00	2.50
(21) Dennis Eckersley	.75	.40	.25
(22) Mark Fidrych	.75	.40	.25
(23) Carlton Fisk	1.50	.70	.45
(24) Mike Flanagan	.75	.40	.25
(25) Steve Garvey	5.00	2.50	1.50
(26) Ron Guidry	2.00	1.00	.60
(27) Gil Hodges	2.00	1.00	.60
(28) Jim Hunter	3.00	1.50	.90
(29) Tommy John	2.00	1.00	.60
(30) Randy Jones	.40	.20	.12
(31) Dave Kingman	1.25	.60	.40
(32) Sandy Koufax	5.00	2.50	1.50
(33) Tommy Lasorda	.75	.40	.25
(34) Ron LeFlore	.40	.20	.12
(35) Greg Luzinski	.75	.40	.25
(36) Billy Martin	1.25	.60	.40
(37) Willie Mays	8.00	4.00	2.50
(38) Lee Mazzilli	.75	.40	.25
(39) Willie McCovey	3.50	1.75	1.00
(40) Joe Morgan	4.50	2.25	1.25
(41) Thurman Munson	3.00	1.50	.90
(42) Stan Musial	8.00	4.00	2.50
(43) Phil Niekro	2.50	1.25	.70
(44) Jim Palmer	3.00	1.50	.90
(45) Dave Parker	1.50	.70	.45
(46) Freddie Patek	.40	.20	.12
(47) Gaylord Perry	3.00	1.50	.90
(48) Jim Piersall	.75	.40	.25
(49) Vada Pinson	.75	.40	.25
(50) Rick Reuschel	.75	.40	.25
(51) Jim Rice	4.50	2.25	1.25
(52) J.R. Richard	.75	.40	.25
(53) Brooks Robinson	5.00	2.50	1.50
(54) Frank Robinson	4.50	2.25	1.25
(55) Jackie Robinson	5.00	2.50	1.50
(56) Pete Rose	10.00	5.00	3.00
(57) Joe Rudi	.75	.40	.25
(58) Babe Ruth	15.00	7.50	4.50
(59) Nolan Ryan	3.50	1.75	1.00
(60) Tom Seaver	5.00	2.50	1.50
(61) Warren Spahn	4.50	2.25	1.25
(62) Monty Stratton	.40	.20	.12
(63) Craig Swan	.40	.20	.12
(64) Frank Tanana	.75	.40	.25
(65) Ron Taylor	.40	.20	.12
(66) Garry Templeton	.75	.40	.25
(67) Gene Tenace	.40	.20	.12
(68) Bobby Thomson	1.25	.60	.40
(69) Andre Thornton	.75	.40	.25
(70) Johnny VanderMeer	.75	.40	.25
(71) Ted Williams	8.00	4.00	2.50
(72) Maury Wills	1.25	.60	.40
(73) Hack Wilson	2.00	1.00	.60
(74) Dave Winfield (hitting)	4.50	2.25	1.25
(75) Dave Winfield (portrait)	4.50	2.25	1.25
(76) Cy Young	3.00	1.50	.90
(77) The 1927 Yankees	1.25	.60	.40
(78) 1969 Mets	1.25	.60	.40
(79) All-Star Game (Steve Garvey, Joe Morgan)	3.00	1.50	.90
(80) Amateur Draft (Rick Monday)	.40	.20	.12
(81) At-A-Glance Reference (Tom Seaver)	3.00	1.50	.90
(82) Babe Ruth Baseball (Ed Figueroa)	.40	.20	.12
(83) Baltimore Memorial Stadium	.40	.20	.12
(84) Boston's Fenway Park	.40	.20	.12
(85) Brother vs. Brother (Joe Niekro)	.75	.40	.25
(86) Busch Memorial Stadium	.40	.20	.12
(87) Candlestick Park	.40	.20	.12
(88) Cape Cod League (Jim Beattie)	.40	.20	.12
(89) A Century and a Half of Baseball (Johnny Bench)	3.50	1.75	1.00
(90) Cy Young Award (Tom Seaver)	3.00	1.50	.90
(91) The Dean Brothers (Dizzy Dean, Paul Dean)	3.00	1.50	.90
(92) Designated Hitter (Rusty Staub)	.75	.40	.25
(93) Dodger Stadium	.40	.20	.12
(94) Don Larsen's Perfect Game (Don Larsen)	1.25	.60	.40
(95) The Double Steal (Davey Lopes)	.40	.20	.12
(96) Fenway Park	.40	.20	.12
(97) The Firemen (Goose Gossage)	1.50	.70	.45
(98) Forever Blowing Bubbles (Davey Lopes)	.75	.40	.25
(99) The Forsch Brothers (Bob Forsch, Ken Forsch)	.40	.20	.12
(100) Four Home Runs In A Game (Mike Schmidt)	4.50	2.25	1.25
(101) 400-Homer Club (Duke Snider)	4.50	2.25	1.25
(102) Great Moments (Bob Gibson)	3.00	1.50	.90
(103) Great Moments (Ferguson Jenkins)	1.50	.70	.45
(104) Great Moments (Mickey Lolich)	1.50	.70	.45
(105) Great Moments (Carl Yastrzemski)	4.50	2.25	1.25
(106) Hidden Ball	.40	.20	.12
(107) Hit And Run (George Foster)	1.25	.60	.40
(108) Hitting The Cutoff Man	.40	.20	.12
(109) Hitting Pitchers (Don Drysdale)	3.00	1.50	.90
(110) Infield Fly Rule (Bobby Grich)	.75	.40	.25
(111) Instruction (Rod Carew)	4.50	2.25	1.25
(112) Interference (Johnny Bench)	4.50	2.25	1.25
(113) Iron Mike (Pitching Machine)	.40	.20	.12
(114) Keeping Score	.40	.20	.12
(115) Like Father, Like Son (Roy Smalley)	.40	.20	.12
(116) Lingo I	.40	.20	.12
(117) Lingo II (Earl Weaver)	.40	.20	.12
(118) Little Leagues To Big Leagues (Hector Torres)	.40	.20	.12
(119) Maris and Mantle (Mickey Mantle, Roger Maris)	9.00	4.50	2.75
(120) Measurements (Memorial Stadium)	.40	.20	.12
(121) The Money Game (Dennis Eckersley)	.75	.40	.25
(122) NCAA Tournament	.40	.20	.12
(123) The Oakland A's, 1971-75	1.25	.60	.40
(124) The Perfect Game (Sandy Koufax)	4.50	2.25	1.25
(125) Pickoff (Luis Tiant)	.75	.40	.25
(126) The Presidential Ball (William Howard Taft)	.40	.20	.12
(127) Relief Pitching (Mike Marshall)	.75	.40	.25
(128) The Rules (Hank Aaron)	4.50	2.25	1.25
(129) Rundown	.40	.20	.12
(130) 7th Game of the World Series (Bert Campaneris)	.75	.40	.25
(131) Shea Stadium	.40	.20	.12
(132) The 3000 Hit Club (Roberto Clemente)	4.50	2.25	1.25
(133) Training Camps	.40	.20	.12
(134) Triple Crown (Carl Yastrzemski)	4.50	2.25	1.25
(135) Triple Play (Rick Burleson)	.75	.40	.25
(136) Triple Play (Bill Wambsganss)	.75	.40	.25
(137) Umpires Strike	.40	.20	.12
(138) Veterans Stadium	.40	.20	.12
(139) Wrigley Marathon (Mike Schmidt)	4.50	2.25	1.25
(140) Yankee Stadium	.40	.20	.12

1981 Squirt

These cards, issued in conjunction with Topps, were issued as two-card panels in eight-pack cartons of the soft drink. Individual cards measure the standard 2-1/2" by 3-1/2", while the vertical panels measure 2-1/2" by 10-1/2", with a promotional card reading "Free Topps 1981 Baseball Cards" attached. The promotional card is blank-backed, while the player card backs are similar to Topps' regular issue, though re-numbered for inclusion in this 33-card set. Most of the game's top players are included. There are only 22 different two-card panels, as card numbers 1-11 appear in two different bottom panel combinations. Card fronts feature a color player portrait photo within a baseball design, team and position designation, and the Squirt logo.

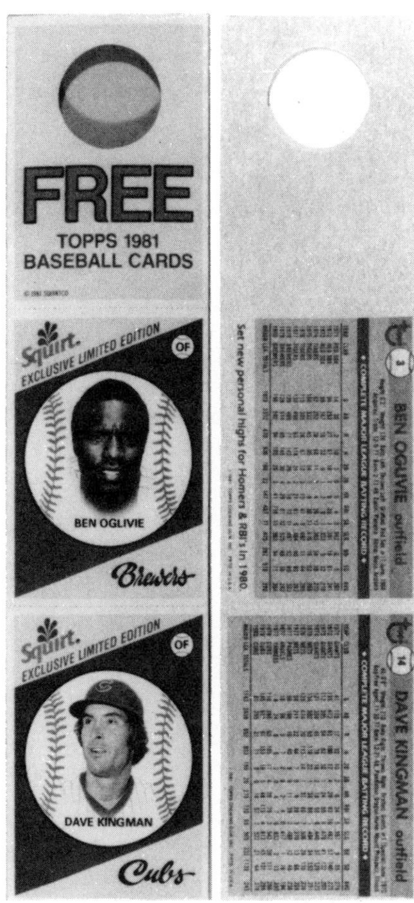

	MT	NR MT	EX
Complete Panel Set:	25.00	20.00	10.00
Complete Singles Set:	15.00	11.00	6.00
Common Panel:	.50	.40	.20
Common Single Player:	.15	.11	.06
Panel 1	.80	.60	.30
1 George Brett	.30	.25	.12
12 Garry Templeton	.25	.20	.10
Panel 2	.80	.60	.30
1 George Brett	.30	.25	.12
23 Jerry Mumphrey	.25	.20	.10
Panel 3	.50	.40	.20
2 George Foster	.25	.20	.10
13 Rick Burleson	.25	.20	.10
Panel 4	.50	.40	.20
2 George Foster	.25	.20	.10
24 Tony Armas	.25	.20	.10
Panel 5	.50	.40	.20
3 Ben Oglivie	.15	.11	.06
14 Dave Kingman	.15	.11	.06
Panel 6	.50	.40	.20
3 Ben Oglivie	.15	.11	.06
25 Fred Lynn	.15	.11	.06
Panel 7	2.50	2.00	1.00
4 Steve Garvey	1.00	.70	.40
15 Eddie Murray	1.50	1.25	.60
Panel 8	1.50	1.25	.60
4 Steve Garvey	1.00	.70	.40
26 Ron LeFlore	.25	.20	.10
Panel 9	2.00	1.50	.80
5 Reggie Jackson	1.00	.70	.40
16 Don Sutton	1.00	.70	.40
Panel 10	1.25	.90	.50
5 Reggie Jackson	1.00	.70	.40
27 Steve Kemp	.15	.11	.06
Panel 11	.50	.40	.20
6 Bill Buckner	.15	.11	.06
17 Dusty Baker	.25	.20	.10
Panel 12	7.00	5.25	2.75
6 Bill Buckner	.15	.11	.06
28 Rickey Henderson	6.00	4.50	2.50
Panel 13	.60	.45	.25
7 Jim Rice	.15	.11	.06
18 Jack Clark	.15	.11	.06
Panel 14	.50	.40	.20
7 Jim Rice	.15	.11	.06
29 John Castino	.25	.20	.10
Panel 15	3.00	2.25	1.25
8 Mike Schmidt	1.00	.70	.40
19 Dave Winfield	1.00	.70	.40
Panel 16	1.25	.90	.50
8 Mike Schmidt	1.00	.70	.40
30 Cecil Cooper	.20	.15	.08
Panel 17	3.00	2.25	1.25
9 Rod Carew	1.00	.70	.40
20 Johnny Bench	1.00	.70	.40
Panel 18	1.25	.90	.50
9 Rod Carew	1.00	.70	.40
31 Bruce Bochte	.25	.20	.10
Panel 19	.50	.40	.20
10 Dave Parker	.25	.20	.10
21 Lee Mazzilli	.25	.20	.10
Panel 20	.50	.40	.20
10 Dave Parker	.25	.20	.10
32 Joe Charboneau	.25	.20	.10
Panel 21	2.00	1.50	.80
11 Pete Rose	1.25	.90	.50
22 Al Oliver	.50	.40	.20
Panel 22	2.00	1.50	.80
11 Pete Rose	1.25	.90	.50
33 Chet Lemon	.25	.20	.10

1982 Squirt

This set was again prepared in conjunction with Topps, but the 1982 Squirt cards are completely different from Topps' regular issue. Only 22 players are included in the full-color set, with the 2-1/2" by 3-1/2" player cards available on one- or two-player panels. Card panels come in four variations, with free grocery contest and scratch-off game cards taking one or two of the positins on the three-card panels. Card backs are numbered and list player statistics.

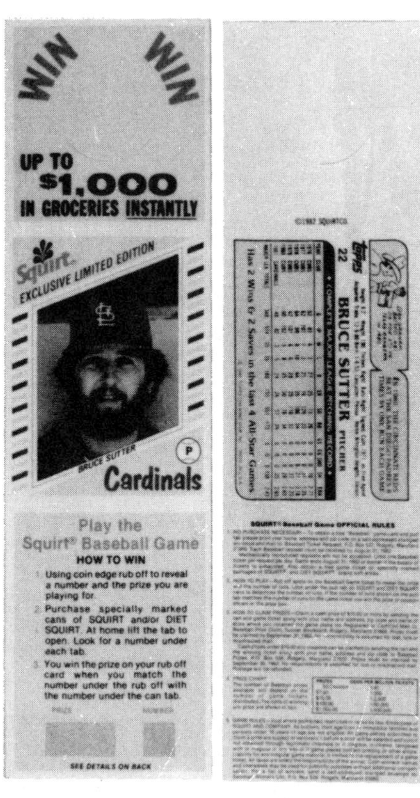

		MT	NR MT	EX
Complete Set:		7.00	5.25	2.75
Common Player:		.15	.11	.06
1	Cecil Cooper	.25	.20	.10
2	Jerry Remy	.15	.11	.06
3	George Brett	.80	.60	.30
4	Alan Trammell	.35	.25	.14
5	Reggie Jackson	.80	.60	.30
6	Kirk Gibson	.35	.25	.14
7	Dave Winfield	.50	.40	.20
8	Carlton Fisk	.30	.25	.12
9	Ron Guidry	.30	.25	.12
10	Dennis Leonard	.15	.11	.06
11	Rollie Fingers	.30	.25	.12
12	Pete Rose	1.00	.70	.40
13	Phil Garner	.15	.11	.06
14	Mike Schmidt	.80	.60	.30
15	Dave Concepcion	.20	.15	.08
16	George Hendrick	.15	.11	.06
17	Andre Dawson	.35	.25	.14
18	George Foster	.20	.15	.08
19	Gary Carter	.50	.40	.20
20	Fernando Valenzuela	.40	.30	.15
21	Tom Seaver	.50	.40	.20
22	Bruce Sutter	.25	.20	.10

1953 Stahl-Meyer Franks

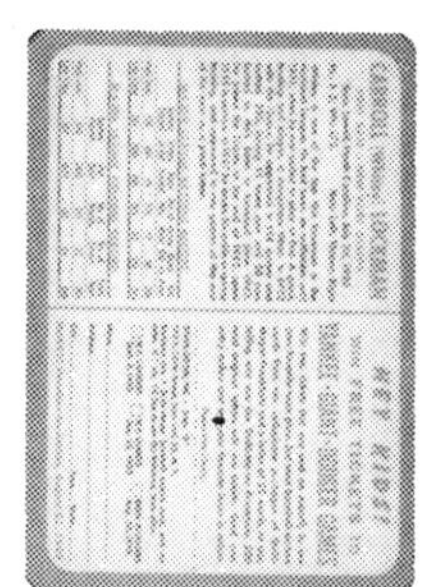

These nine cards, issued in packages of hot dogs by a New York area meat company, feature three players from each of the New York teams of the day - Dodgers Giants and Yankees. Cards in the set measure 3-1/4" by 4-1/2". The card fronts in this unnumbered set feature color photos with player name and facsimile autograph. The backs list both biographical and statistical information on half the card and a ticket offer promotion on the other half. The card corners are cut diagonally, although some cards (apparently cut from sheets) with square corners have been seen. Cards are white-bordered.

		NR MT	EX	VG
Complete Set:		4000.	2000.	1200.
Common Player:		125.00	62.00	37.00
(1)	Hank Bauer	150.00	75.00	45.00
(2)	Roy Campanella	500.00	250.00	150.00
(3)	Gil Hodges	275.00	137.00	82.00
(4)	Monte Irvin	200.00	100.00	60.00
(5)	Whitey Lockman	125.00	62.00	37.00
(6)	Mickey Mantle	1800.	900.00	540.00
(7)	Phil Rizzuto	275.00	137.00	82.00
(8)	Duke Snider	500.00	250.00	150.00
(9)	Bobby Thompson	150.00	75.00	45.00

1954 Stahl-Meyer Franks

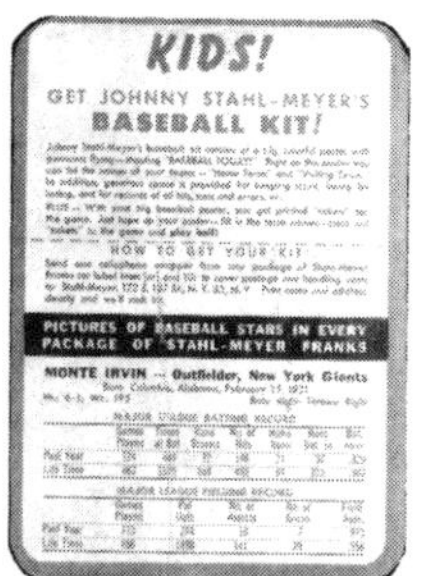

The 1954 set of Stahl-Meyer Franks was increased to 12 cards which retained the 3-1/4" by 4-1/2" size. The most prominent addition to the '54 set was New York Giants slugger Willie Mays. The card fronts are identical in format to the previous year's set. However, the backs are different as they are designed on a vertical format. The backs also contain an advertisement for a "Johnny Stahl-Meyer Baseball Kit." The cards in the set are unnumbered.

		NR MT	EX	VG
Complete Set:		5200.	2600.	1560.
Common Player:		125.00	62.00	37.00
(1)	Hank Bauer	150.00	75.00	45.00
(2)	Carl Erskine	150.00	75.00	45.00
(3)	Gil Hodges	300.00	150.00	90.00
(4)	Monte Irvin	225.00	112.00	67.00
(5)	Whitey Lockman	125.00	62.00	37.00
(6)	Gil McDougald	150.00	75.00	45.00
(7)	Mickey Mantle	2000.	1000.	600.00
(8)	Willie Mays	1000.	500.00	300.00
(9)	Don Mueller	125.00	62.00	37.00
(10)	Don Newcombe	150.00	75.00	45.00
(11)	Phil Rizzuto	300.00	150.00	90.00
(12)	Duke Snider	525.00	262.00	157.00

1955 Stahl-Meyer Franks

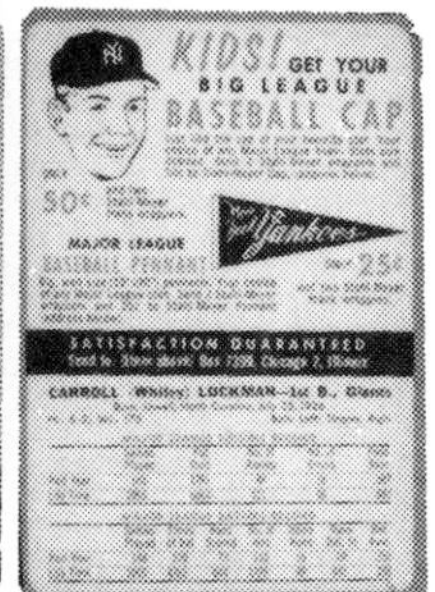

Eleven of the 12 players in the 1955 set are the same as those featured in 1954. The exception is the New York Giants Dusty Rhodes, who replaced Willie Mays on the 3-1/4" by 4-1/2" cards. The card fronts are again full-color photos bordered in yellow with diagonal corners, and four players from each of the three New York teams are featured. The backs offer a new promotion, with a drawing of Mickey Mantle and advertisements selling pennants and caps. Player statistics are still included on the vertical card backs. The cards in the set are unnumbered.

		NR MT	EX	VG
Complete Set:		4300.	2150.	1290.
Common Player:		125.00	62.00	37.00
(1)	Hank Bauer	150.00	75.00	45.00
(2)	Carl Erskine	150.00	75.00	45.00
(3)	Gil Hodges	300.00	150.00	90.00
(4)	Monte Irvin	200.00	100.00	60.00
(5)	Whitey Lockman	125.00	62.00	37.00
(6)	Mickey Mantle	2000.	1000.	600.00
(7)	Gil McDougald	150.00	75.00	45.00
(8)	Don Mueller	125.00	62.00	37.00
(9)	Don Newcombe	150.00	75.00	45.00
(10)	Jim Rhodes	125.00	62.00	37.00
(11)	Phil Rizzuto	300.00	150.00	90.00
(12)	Duke Snider	525.00	262.00	157.00

1983 Star Co. Mike Schmidt

The first issue offered by the Star Company, this 15-card set was produced in 1983 and spotlights Mike Schmidt. Subtitled "Ten Years of Excellence", the cards measure the standard 2-1/2" by 3-1/2" and feature full-color photos showing Schmidt in various action and portrait poses surrounded by a bright red border. The backs contain statistics and biographical information. The set was available only through hobby dealers. (Star Co. cards are generally collected only as complete sets, and cards are rarely bought or sold individually.)

	MT	NR MT	EX
Complete Set:	60.00	45.00	25.00

1984 Star Co. George Brett

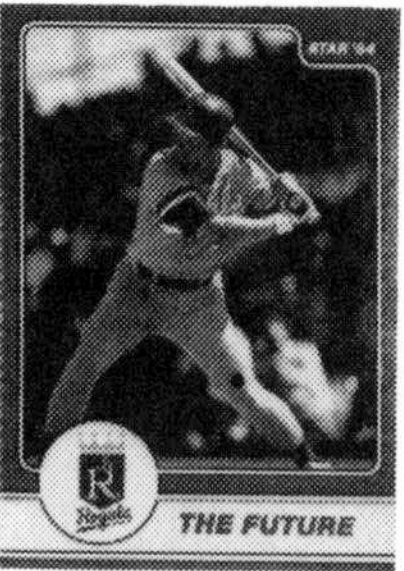

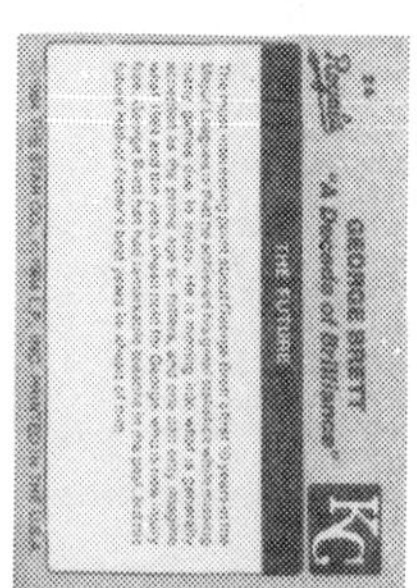

Issued by the Star Co. in 1984, this 24-card set features Royals star George Brett and was subtitled "A Decade of Brilliance". Bordered in blue, the cards are standard size and were issued in eight three-card, perforated panels. The Royals' logo appears in the lower left corner.

	MT	NR MT	EX
Complete Set:	18.00	13.50	7.25

1984 Star Co. Steve Carlton

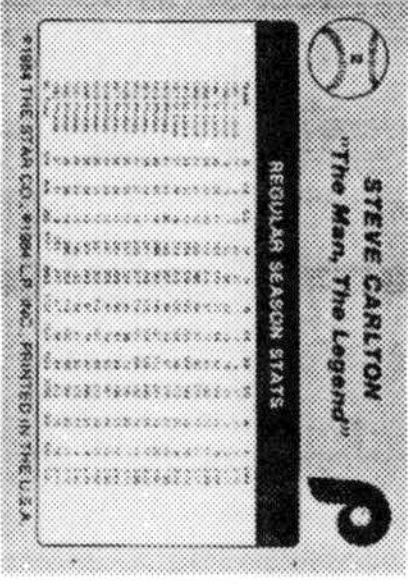

This 24-card set featuring Steve Carlton was issued by the Star Co. in 1984. Like all Star Co. issues, the set was available only from hobby dealers. It was issued in eight perforated panels of three cards each. The photos picture Carlton in various stages of his career, both as a Phillie and as a Cardinal, and the cards display the corresponding team logo in the lower left corner. The backs contain statistics and career highlights.

	MT	NR MT	EX
Complete Set:	50.00	37.00	20.00

1984 Star Co. Steve Garvey

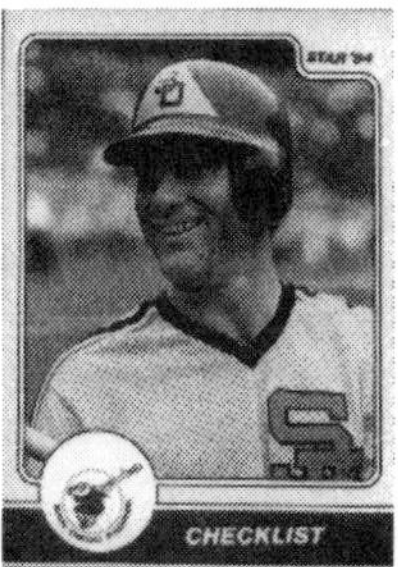

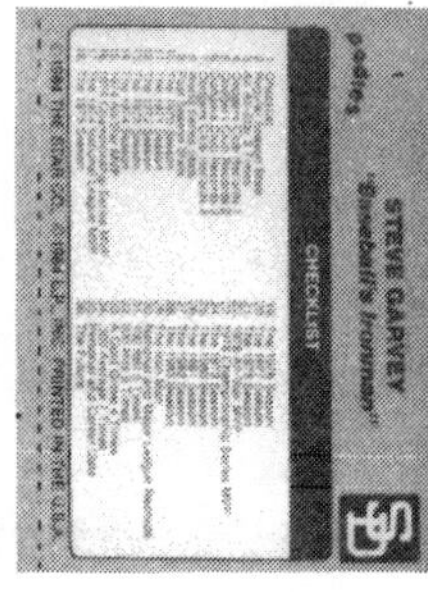

The 36-card Steve Garvey set consists of 12 three-card panels. The full-color photos, surrounded by either a blue or a yellow border, show Garvey as a member of both the Dodgers and the Padres, and the cards display the appropriate team logo in the lower left corner. The backs contain highlights and statistics.

	MT	NR MT	EX
Complete Set:	18.00	13.50	7.25

1984 Star Co. Darryl Strawberry

The Star Co. honored Darryl Strawberry with a 36-card set in 1984. Issued in 12 perforated panels of three cards each, the blue-bordered cards display the Mets logo in the lower left corner. Some of the backs contain biographical and statistical information, while others are puzzle backs.

	MT	NR MT	EX
Complete Set:	40.00	30.00	15.00

1984 Star Co. Carl Yastrzemski

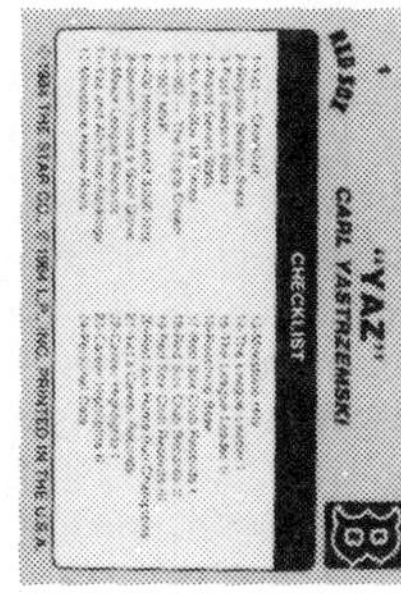

Red Sox star Carl Yastrzemski was featured in a 24-card set issued by the Star Co. in 1984. Following the same style as the 1984 Star Co. sets, the cards were issued in three-card panels and feature the team logo in the lower left corner. (Star Co. cards are generally collected as complete sets, and cards are rarely bought or sold individually.)

	MT	NR MT	EX
Complete Set:	20.00	15.00	7.50

1985 Star Co. Reggie Jackson

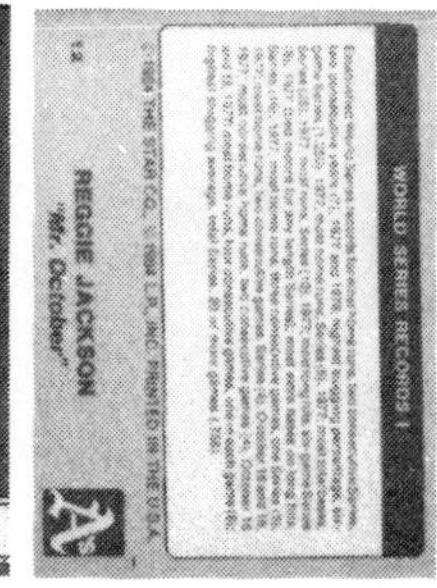

This 36-card set featuring Reggie Jackson was issued by the Star Co. in 1985 and pictures the slugger as a member of the A's, Orioles, Yankees and Angels. It was issued in 12 panels of three cards each.

	MT	NR MT	EX
Complete Set:	20.00	15.00	7.50

1986 Star Co. Wade Boggs

This 24-card set, produced by the Star Co. in 1986, features photos of Wade Boggs, whose name appears inside a circle in the lower left corner of the red-bordered cards. The set was issued in three-card panels and was also available in a special, limited-edition glossy format which commands a value about three times that of the regular set.

	MT	NR MT	EX
Complete Set:	12.00	9.00	4.75

1986 Star Co. Jose Canseco

Oakland slugger Jose Canseco was featured in a 15-card set issued by the Star Co. in 1986. The yellow-bordered cards display the name "Jose" in the lower left corner. Eight of the card backs form a puzzle. The set was also issued in a limited-edition glossy format which is valued about three times the price of the regular set.

	MT	NR MT	EX
Complete Set:	30.00	22.00	12.00

1986 Star Co. Rod Carew

Subtitled "Baseball's Hit Man", this 24-card set of Rod Carew was issued by the Star Co. in 1986 and pictures Carew as both a Twin and an Angel.

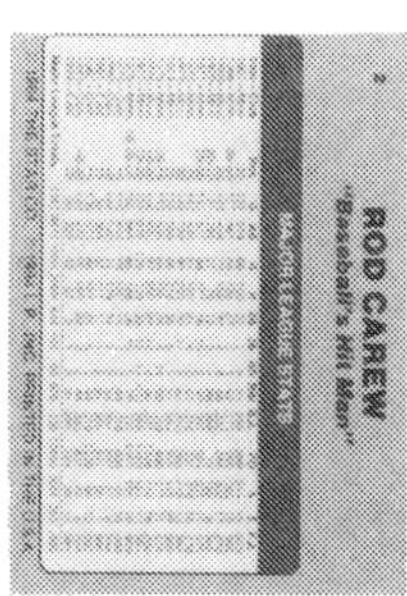

It was issued in eight perforated panels of three cards each.

	MT	NR MT	EX
Complete Set:	15.00	11.00	6.00

1986 Star Co. Wally Joyner

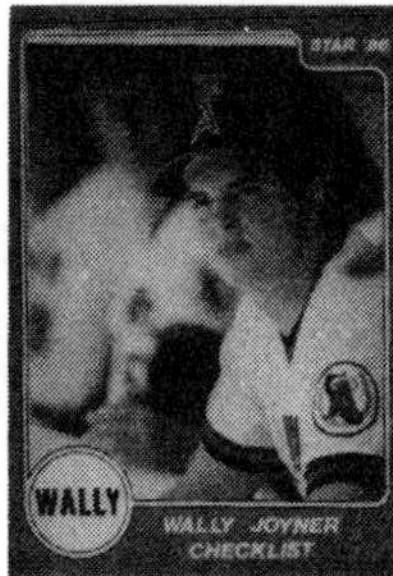

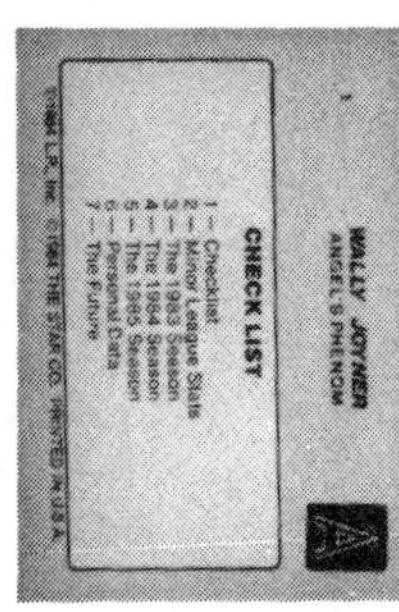

This 15-card set, issued by the Star Co. in 1986, features Wally Joyner and follows the same format as other Star Co. issues. It was also available in a limited-edition glossy version which is valued about four times the price of a regular set.

	MT	NR MT	EX
Complete Set:	10.00	7.50	4.00

1986 Star Co. Don Mattingly

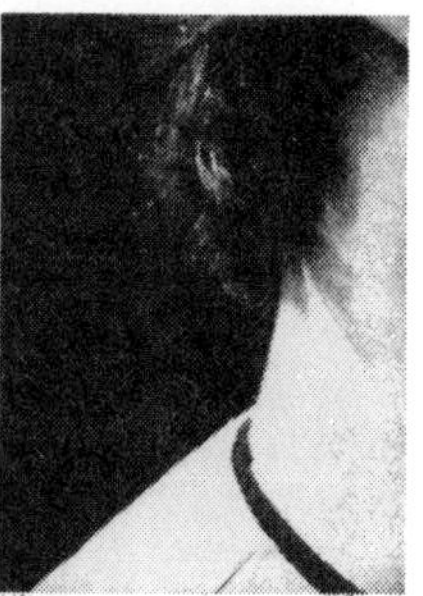

Yankees superstar Don Mattingly was featured in a 24-card set by the Star Co. in 1986. The set, which follows the same format as other Star Co. issues, was also available in a limited-edition glossy version valued about three times the price of the regular set. (Star Co. cards are generally collected only as complete sets, and cards are rarely bought or sold individually.)

	MT	NR MT	EX
Complete Set:	16.00	12.00	6.50

1986 Star Co. Dale Murphy

Issued by the Star Co. in 1986, this 24-card set of Braves star Dale Murphy was issued in eight three-card panels. The backs contain statistics and career highlights.

	MT	NR MT	EX
Complete Set:	12.00	9.00	4.75

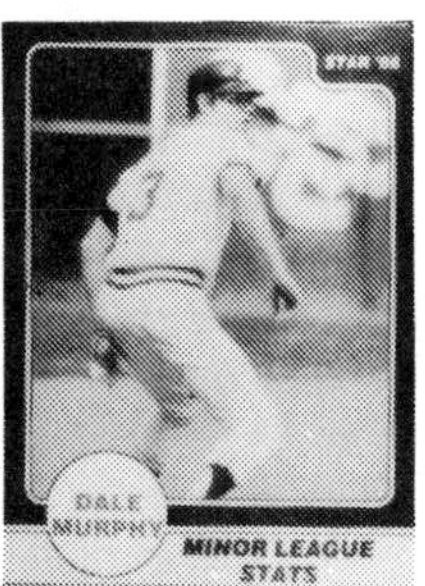

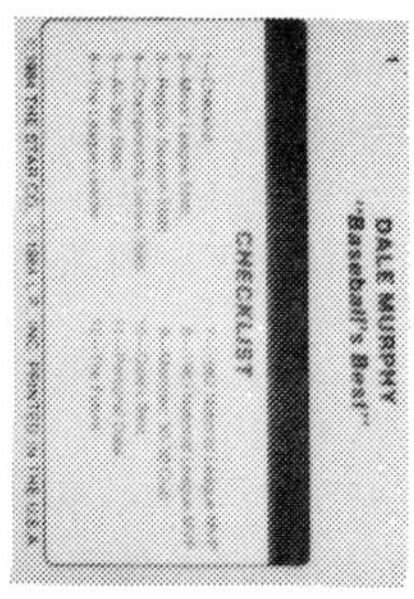

1986 Star Co. Jim Rice

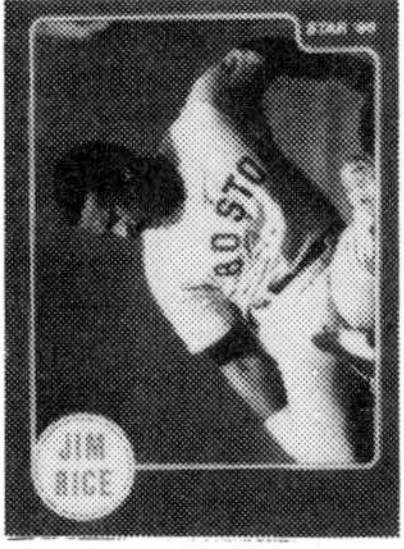

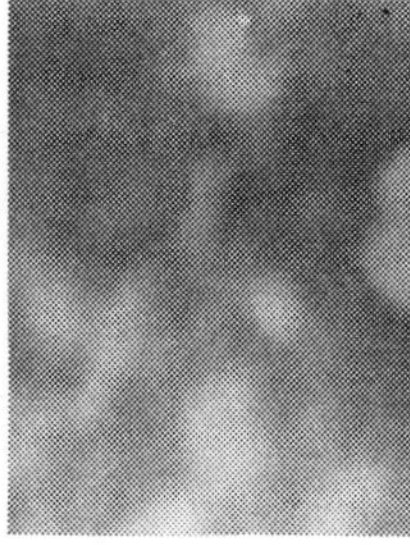

This 24-card set featuring Jim Rice was issued in three-card panels by the Star Co. in 1986. A limited-edition glossy version generally sells for about four times the price of a regular set.

	MT	NR MT	EX
Complete Set:	7.00	5.25	2.75

1986 Star Co. Nolan Ryan

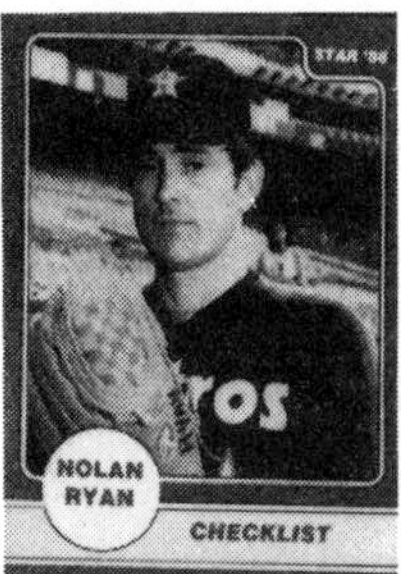

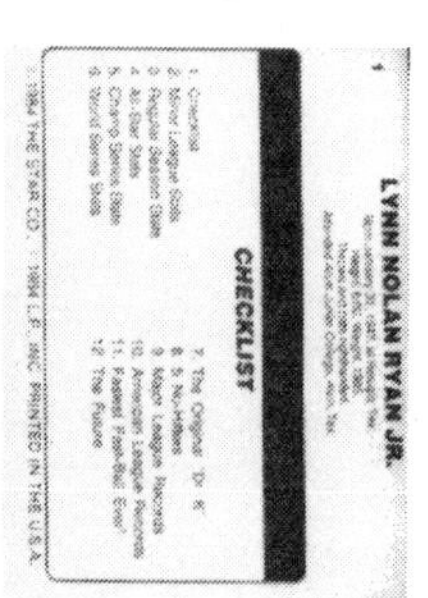

This 1986 set from the Star Co. pictures Noln Ryan as a member of the Angels and Astros. The 24-card set was issued in eight three-card panels with bright green borders. Twelve of the card backs form a puzzle.

	MT	NR MT	EX
Complete Set:	30.00	22.00	12.00

1986 Star Co. Tom Seaver

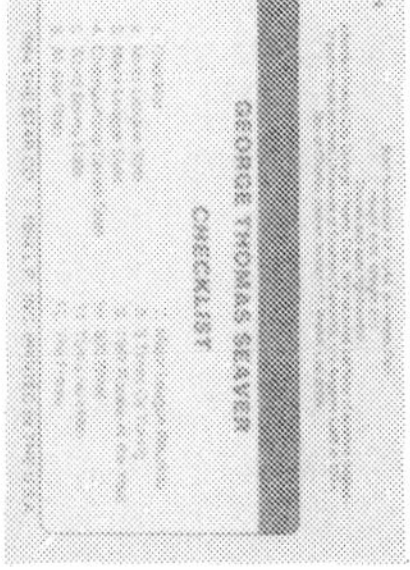

Issued in 1986, this 24-card set was also issued in eight panels of three cards each and pictures Seaver as a member of the Reds, Mets and White Sox. The cards have light blue borders and twelve of the backs form a puzzle.

	MT	NR MT	EX
Complete Set:	18.00	13.50	7.25

1987 Star Co. Gary Carter

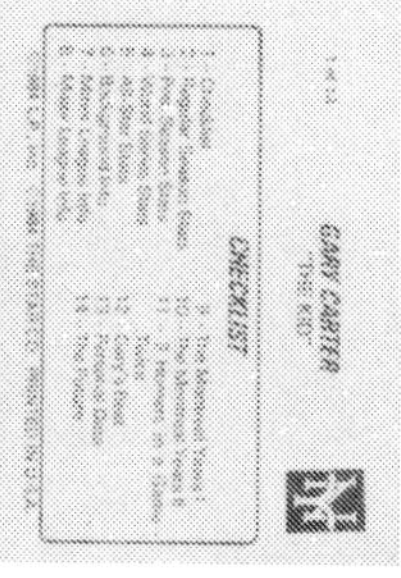

Subtitled "The Kid", this 14-card set features Gary Carter and displays the name "Gary" in the lower left corner of the bluebordered cards. A limited-edition glossy version of the set was also printed and commands a value about twice that of the regular edition. (Star Co. cards are generally collected only as complete sets, and cards are rarely bought or sold individually.)

	MT	NR MT	EX
Complete Set:	7.00	5.25	2.75

1987 Star Co. Roger Clemens

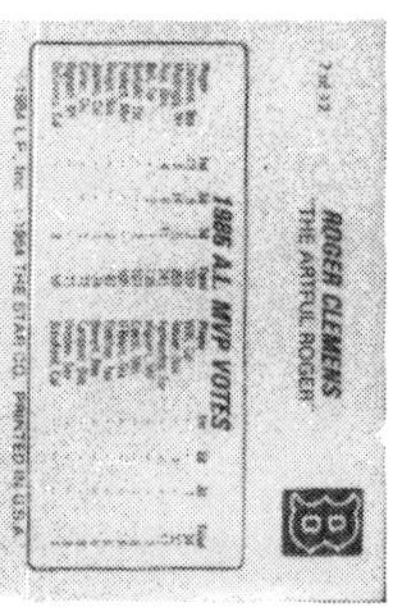

This 12-card set featuring Red Sox pitcher Roger Clemens, issued by the Star Co. in 1987, was subtitled "The Artful Roger" and featured bright red borders. A limited number of sets were also produced in a special glossy format, which command a value about two to three times the price of a regular set.

	MT	NR MT	EX
Complete Set:	15.00	11.00	6.00

1987 Star Co. Roger Clemens Update

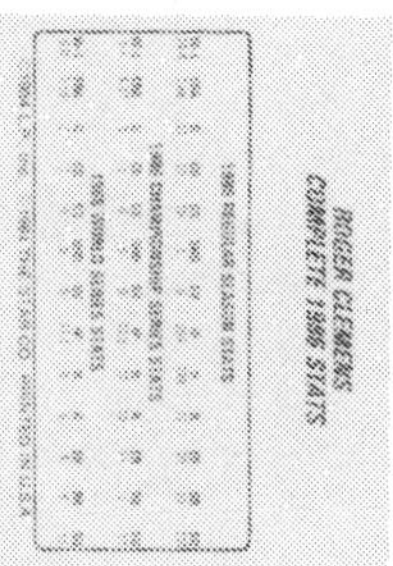

Late in 1987, the Star Co. issued a second set featuring Roger Clemens to update its earlier set devoted to the Boston hurler. Consisting of just five cards, the set had pinkish-colored borders and followed the same design as other Star Co. sets. A special limited-edition glossy version was available and is worth about twice the value of a regular set.

	MT	NR MT	EX
Complete Set:	9.00	6.75	3.50

1987 Star Co. Keith Hernandez

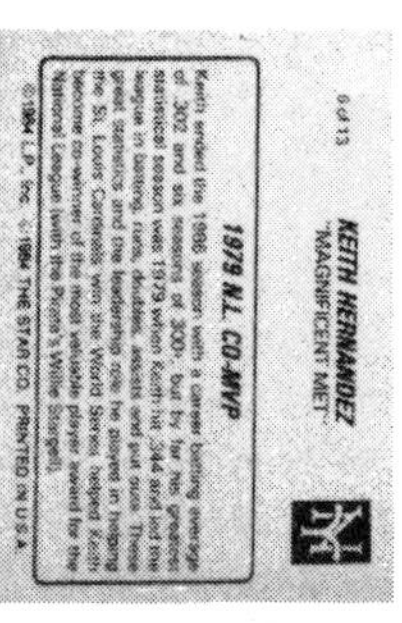

This 13-card set featuring Keith Hernandez was issued by the Star Co. in 1987. The orange-bordered cards are subtitled "Magnificient Met" and display the name "Keith" in the lower left corner. It was also printed in a limited-edition glossy version which is valued at between two and three times the price of a regular set.

	MT	NR MT	EX
Complete Set:	6.00	4.50	2.50

1987 Star Co. Tim Raines

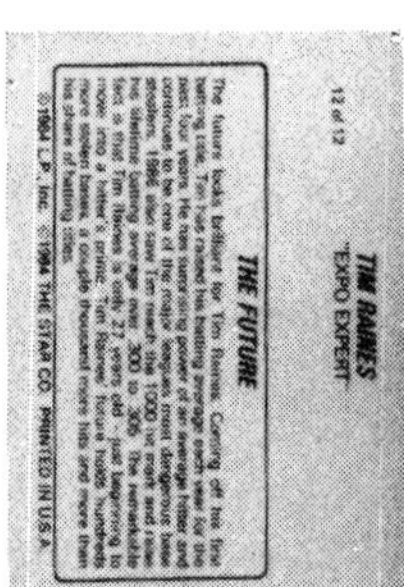

Subtitled "Expo Expert", this 12-card set of Tim Raines was issued by the Star Co. in 1987 and has bright blue borders. A limited number of glossy sets were also available and are generally worth about two to three times the value of a regular set.

	MT	NR MT	EX
Complete Set:	8.00	6.00	3.25

1987 Star Co. Fernando Valenzuela

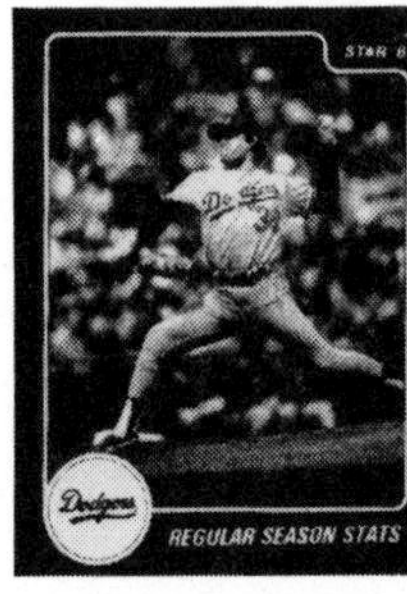

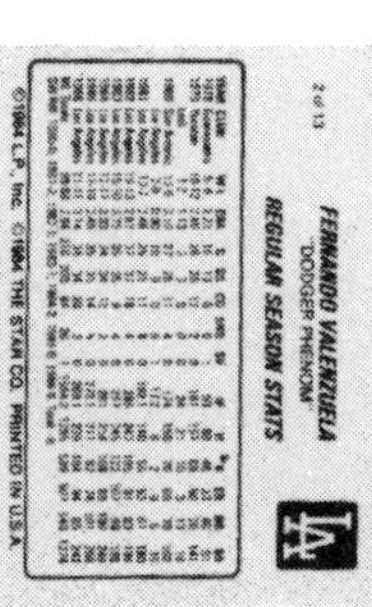

Complete at 13 cards, this 1987 Star Co. set features Fernando Valenzuela. The blue-bordered cards display the Dodgers logo in the lower left corner. Similar in design to other Star Co. issues, the set was also available in a limited-edition glossy version worth about two to three times the value of a regular set. (Star Co. cards are generally collected only as complete sets, and cards are rarely bought or sold individually.)

	MT	NR MT	EX
Complete Set:	6.00	4.50	2.50

1988 Star Co. "Baseball's Best"

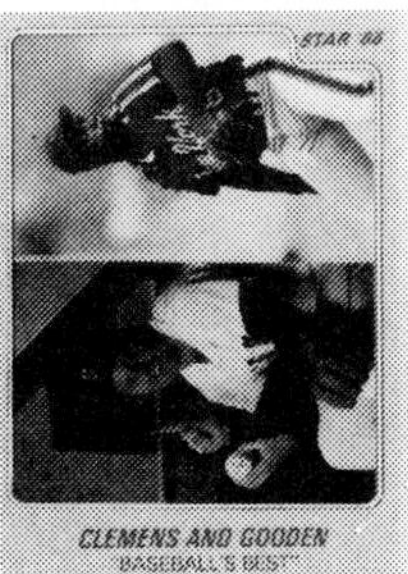

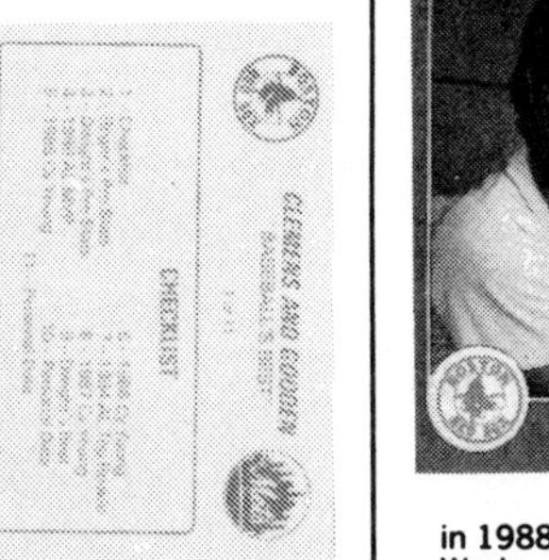

This 11-card Star Co. set is titled "Baseball's Best" and features both Roger Clemens and Dwight Gooden. There are five cards of each hurler, plus one combination card picturing both. A limited-edition glossy version of the set was available and sells for about twice the value of a regular set.

	MT	NR MT	EX
Complete Set:	10.00	7.50	4.50

1988 Star Co. "Baseball's Best"

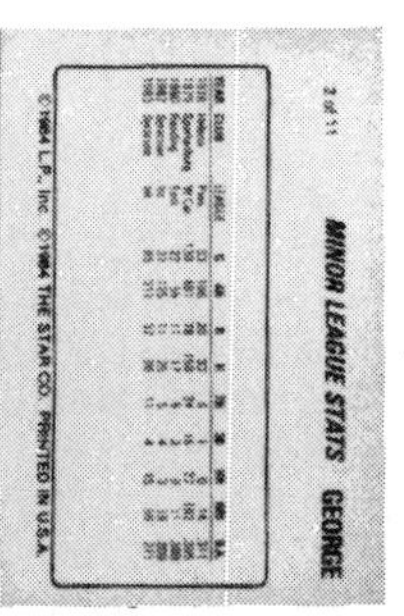

Issued in both a regular edition and a limited-edition glossy format, this 11-card set pictures Blue Jays' star George Bell and was issued by the Star Co. in 1988. The glossy edition is worth about two to three times the value of a regular set.

	MT	NR MT	EX
Complete Set:	7.00	5.25	2.75

1988 Star Co. "Best Of '87"

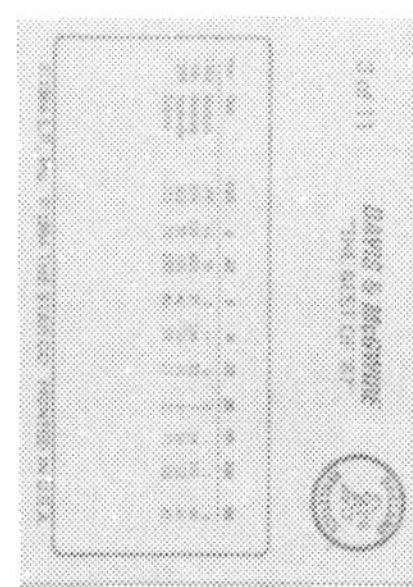

This 11-card set, issued by the Star Co. in 1988, features cards of both Eric Davis and Mark McGwire. There are five cards of each player, plus one combination card picturing both sluggers. The set was also issued in a limited-edition glossy format worth about twice the value of a regular set.

	MT	NR MT	EX
Complete Set:	8.00	6.00	3.25

1988 Star Co. Wade Boggs

An 11-card issue subtitled "Boston Hit Man" this aqua-bordered set was issued by the Star Co.

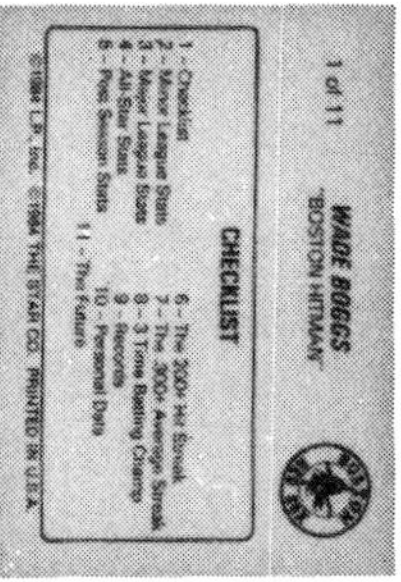

in 1988 and was the second Star Co. set featuring Wade Boggs. It was also available in a limited-edition glossy format, which is generally valued at about two times the price of a regular set.

	MT	NR MT	EX
Complete Set:	7.00	5.25	2.75

1988 Star Co. Gary Carter

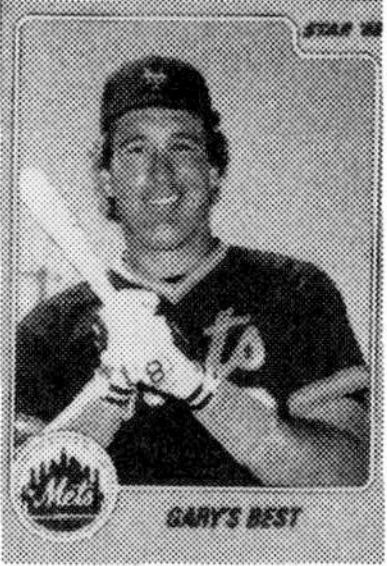

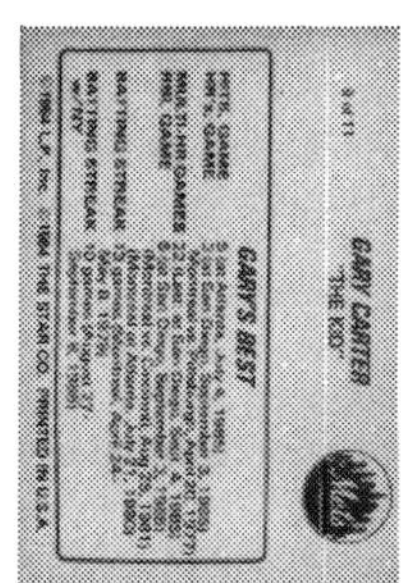

The Star Co. issued a second set featuring Gary Carter in 1988. Again titled "The Kid", the 11-card set has orange borders and displays the Mets logo in the lower left corner. A limited-edition glossy version of the set was available and is generally worth about twice the value of the regular set. (Star Co. cards are generally collected only as complete sets, and cards are rarely bought or sold individually.)

	MT	NR MT	EX
Complete Set:	6.00	4.50	2.50

1988 Star Co. Will Clark

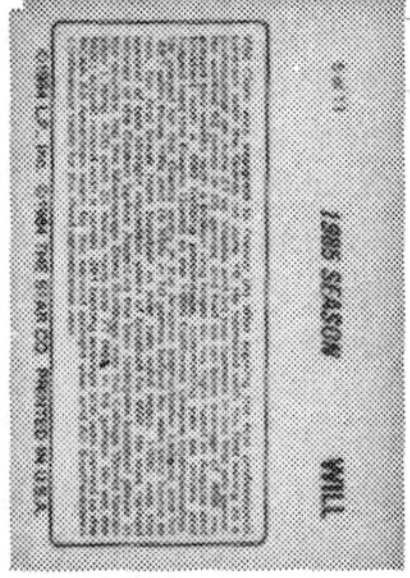

A 1988 issue from the Star Co., the yellow-bordered Will Clark set contains 11 cards. It was also available in a limited-edition glossy format that generally sells for about two to three times the value of a regular set.

	MT	NR MT	EX
Complete Set:	10.00	7.50	4.00

1988 Star Co. Andre Dawson

After the winning the N.L. Most Valuable Player Award in 1987, Andre Dawson was honored by the Star Co. with an 11-card set in 1988. Subtitled "The Hawk", the cards have pinkish-colored borders and display the Cubs logo in the lower left corner. A limited-edition glossy version of the set was available and generally is worth about twice the value of a regular set.

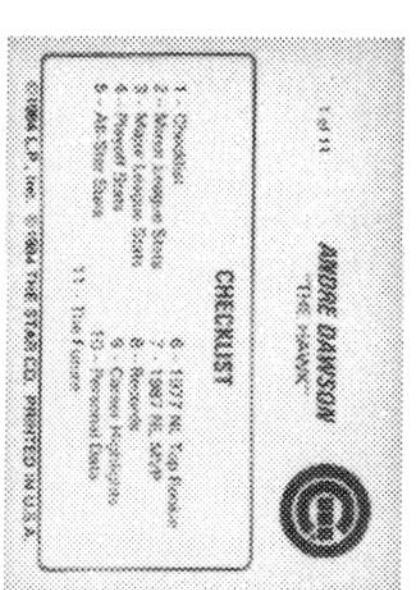

	MT	NR MT	EX
Complete Set:	7.00	5.25	2.75

1988 Star Co. Eric Davis

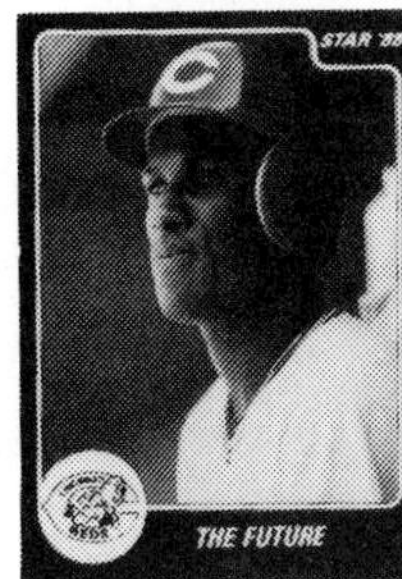

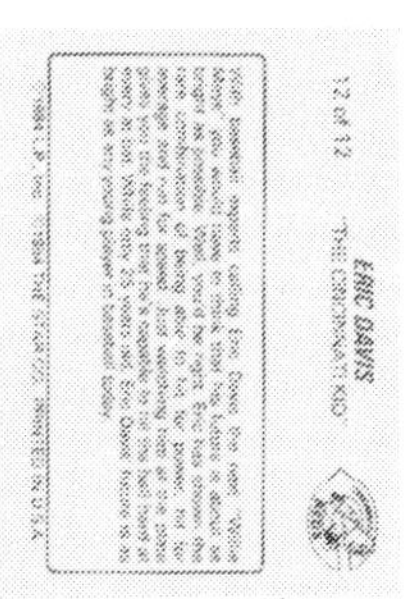

Subtitled "The Cincinnati Kid", this 12-card set featuring Eric Davis was issued by the Star Co. in 1988. The red-bordered set was also issued in a limited-edition glossy version, which commands a value about twice that of a regular set.

	MT	NR MT	EX
Complete Set:	9.00	6.75	3.50

1988 Star Co. Dwight Gooden

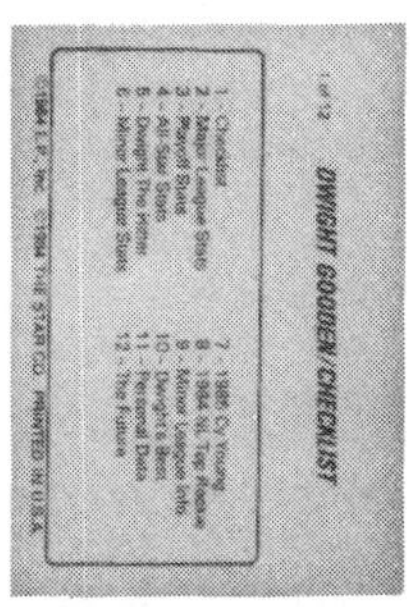

Mets pitching ace Dwight Gooden was featured in an 11-card Star Co. set in 1988. The blue-bordered cards display the name "Dwight" in the lower left corner. The set was also printed in a limited-edition glossy version which commands a value about twice that of a regular set.

	MT	NR MT	EX
Complete Set:	9.00	6.75	3.50

1988 Star Co. Tony Gwynn

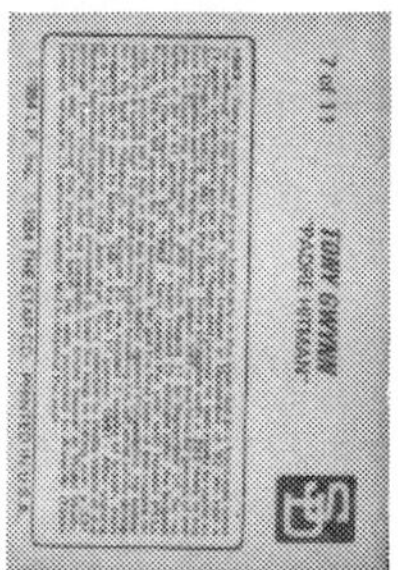

Padres star Tony Gwynn was featured in an 11-card set issued by the Star Co. in 1988. The cards have light brown borders and display the Padres logo in the lower left corner. Similar in design to other Star Co. issues, the set was also available in a limited-edition glossy format which commands a value about twice that of a regular set. (Star Co. cards are generally collected only as complete sets, and cards are rarely bought and sold individually.)

	MT	NR MT	EX
Complete Set:	8.00	6.00	3.25

1988 Star Co. "Hits 'R Us"

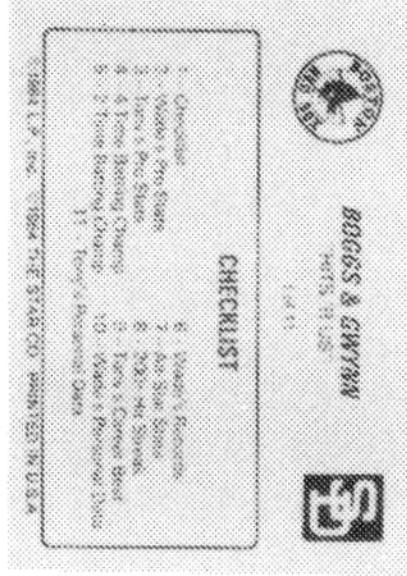

This 11-card set, issued by the Star Co. in 1988, features batting leaders Wade Boggs and Tony Gwynn. There are five cards of each player, plus one combination card picturing both superstars. Their respective team logos are displayed in the lower left corner. The set was also printed in a limited-edition glossy version which is worth about twice the value of a regular set.

	MT	NR MT	EX
Complete Set:	8.00	6.00	3.25

1988 Star Co. Bo Jackson

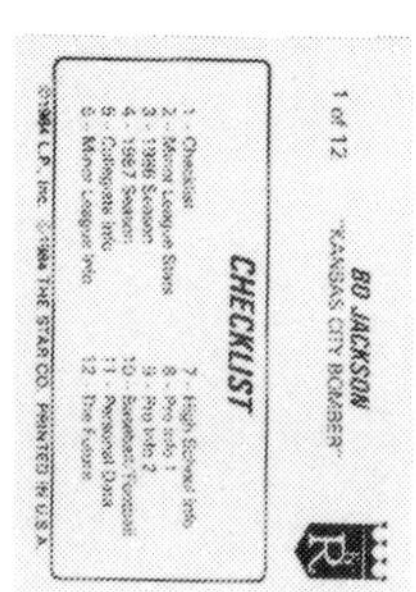

Royals star Bo Jackson was featured in a 12-card set issued by the Star Co. in 1988. The blue-bordered cards display the Royals logo in the lower left corner and are subtitled "Kansas City Bomber". In addition to the 12 regular cards picturing Jackson with the Royals, the Star Co. also released four additional unnumbered, blank-backed cards highlighting Jackson's collegiate football career at Auburn. The set was also issued in a limited-edition glossy format which is worth about twice the value of a regular set.

	MT	NR MT	EX
Complete Set:	15.00	11.00	6.00

1988 Star Co. Don Mattingly

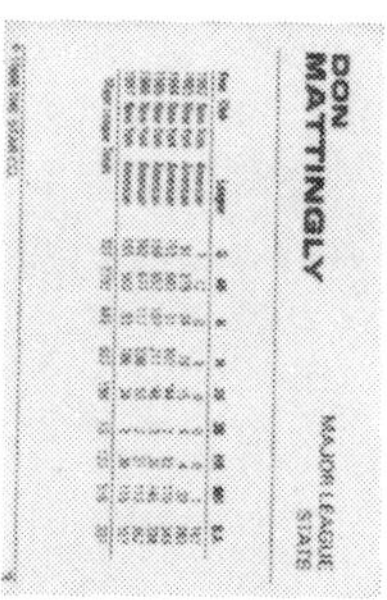

Yankees' star Don Mattingly was featured in his second Star Co. issue in 1988 with an 11-card set. The gray-bordered set, subtitled "Yankee Hit Man", was also available in a glossy format which is valued at about two times the price of a regular set.

	MT	NR MT	EX
Complete Set:	9.00	6.75	3.50

1988 Star Co. Mark McGwire

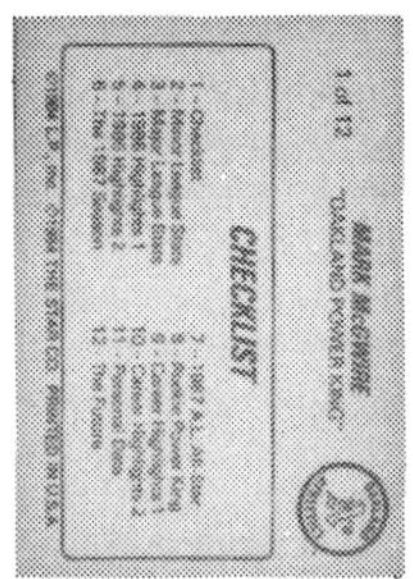

This 12-card set, issued by the Star Co. in 1988, features photos of A's slugger Mark McGwire and is subtitled "Oakland Power King". The yellow-bordered cards were also available in a limited-edition glossy version worth about twice the value of a regular set.

	MT	NR MT	EX
Complete Set:	8.00	6.00	3.25

1988 Star Co. Mark McGwire #2

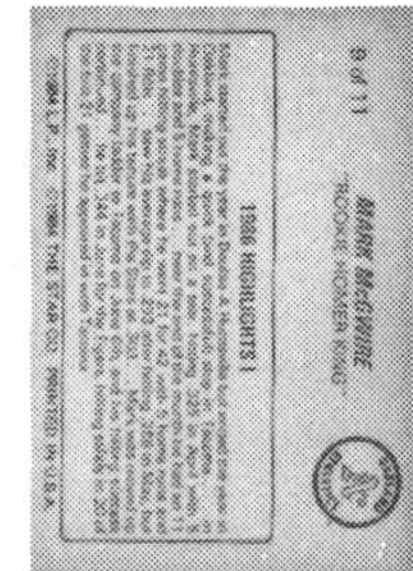

Oakland slugger Mark McGwire was featured in a second 11-card set by the Star Co. in 1988. Subtitled "Rookie Homer King", the cards feature aqua-colored borders. The set follows the same basic format as other Star Co. issues and was also available in a limited-edition glossy version which is valued at about twice the price of the regular set.

	MT	NR MT	EX
Complete Set:	8.00	6.00	3.25

1988 Star Co. Mark McGwire #3

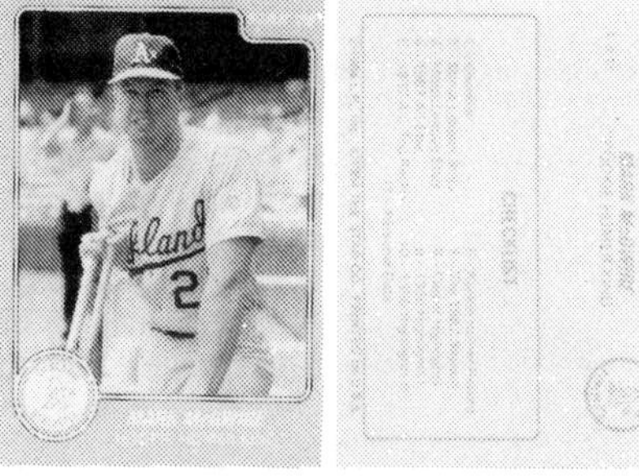

Capitalizing on the popularity of Mark McGwire, the Star Co. issued a third set featuring the A's slugger in 1988. Again titled "Rookie Homer King", the 11-card set has green borders and was also available in a limited-edition glossy version which commands a value about twice that of a regular set. (Star Co. cards are generally collected only as complete sets, and cards are rarely bought or sold individually.)

	MT	NR MT	EX
Complete Set:	7.00	5.25	2.75

1988 Star Co. Mike Scott

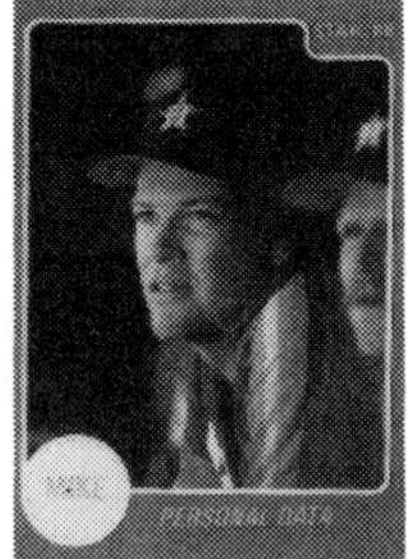

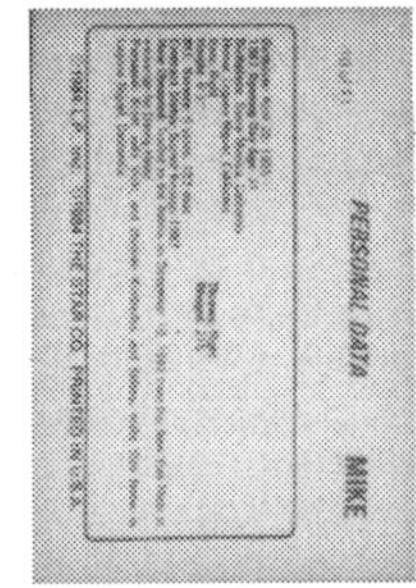

Mike Scott was featured in an 11-card Star Co. set in 1988. The green-bordered cards display the name "Mike" in the lower left corner and were also issued in a limited-edition glossy version, which are worth twice as much as a regular set.

	MT	NR MT	EX
Complete Set:	6.00	4.50	2.50

1988 Star Co. Kevin Seitzer

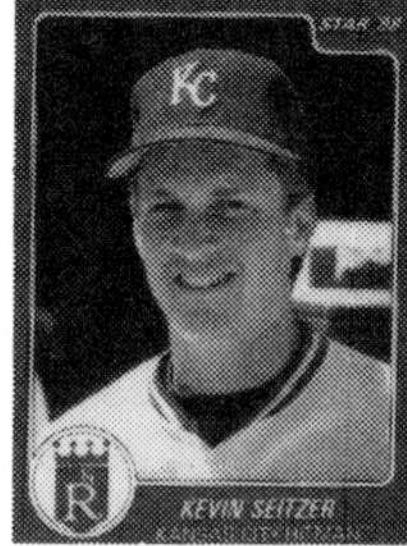

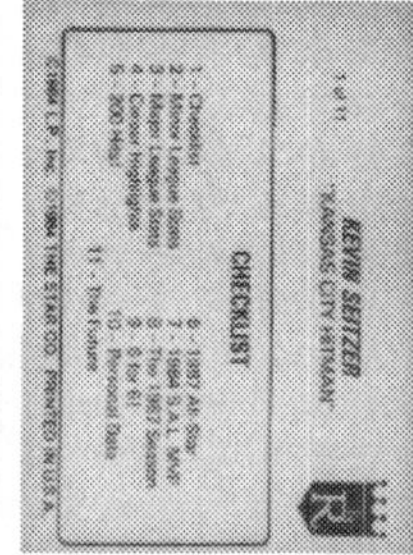

Subtitled "Kansas City Hitman", this 11-card set features Kevin Seitzer. The cards have blue borders with yellow accents and display the Royals logo in the lower left corner. The set was also issued in a limited-edition glossy version which generally sells for about twice the value of the regular set.

	MT	NR MT	EX
Complete Set:	6.00	4.50	2.50

1988 Star Co. Cory Snyder

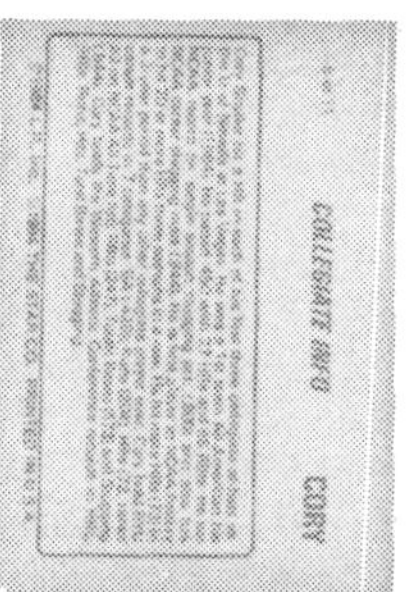

The Star Co. honored Cory Snyder with an 11-card set in 1988. The red-bordered set was issued in a regular edition, a glossy edition and a special "sticker" back version. The special editions are generally worth about two to three times the value of a regular set.

	MT	NR MT	EX
Complete Set:	6.00	4.50	2.50

1988 Star Co. Dave Winfield

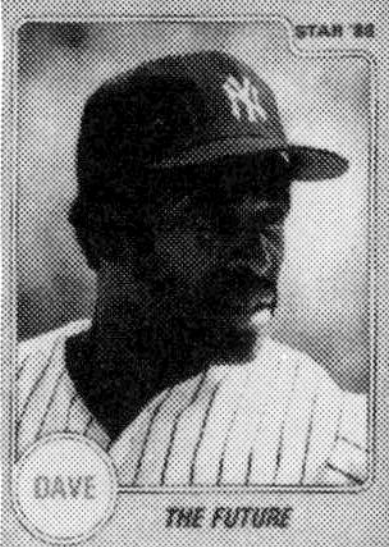

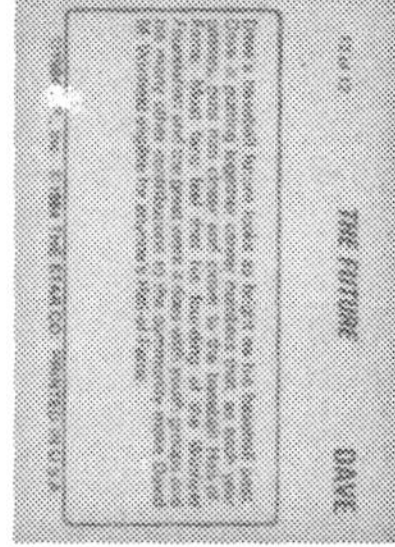

The Star Co. honored Dave Winfield with a 12-card set in 1988. The gray-bordered cards display the name "Dave" in the lower left corner. The set was also issued in a limited-edition glossy version which is generally worth about two times the value of a regular set. (Star Co. cards are generally collected only as complete sets, and cards are rarely bought or sold individually.)

	MT	NR MT	EX
Complete Set:	6.00	4.50	2.50

1988 Star Co. Platinum

Twelve single-player subsets make up the 1988 Star Platinum set. Ten cards were devoted to each player. The card numbers are displayed in the price list below. 1,000 total sets were issued.

	MT	NR MT	EX
Complete Set:	700.00	525.00	275.00
Don Mattingly (1-10)	200.00	150.00	80.00
Dwight Gooden (11-20)	50.00	37.00	20.00
Roger Clemens (21-30)	40.00	30.00	15.00
Mike Schmidt (31-40)	70.00	52.00	27.00
Wade Boggs (41-50)	50.00	37.00	20.00
Mark McGwire (51-60)	50.00	37.00	20.00
Jose Canseco (61-70)	100.00	75.00	40.00
Andre Dawson (71-80)	30.00	22.00	12.00
Eric Davis (81-90)	40.00	30.00	15.00
George Brett (91-100)	40.00	30.00	15.00
Darryl Strawberry (101-110)	50.00	37.00	20.00
Dale Murphy (111-120)	40.00	30.00	15.00

1989 Star Co. Gold Edition

This 180-card set was actually released at the end of 1988 and into 1989. Twenty single-player subsets are included. The high quality photographs feature a special gold embossing. The cards devoted to each player are noted by number in the corresponding price list.

	MT	NR MT	EX
Complete Set:	900.00	675.00	350.00
Gregg Jefferies (1-10)	100.00	75.00	40.00
Sam Horn (11-20)	20.00	15.00	8.00
Don Mattingly (21-30)	225.00	175.00	90.00
Matt Nokes (31-40)	20.00	15.00	8.00
Darryl Strawberry (41-50)	40.00	30.00	15.00
Will Clark (51-60)	30.00	22.00	12.00
Wade Boggs (61-70)	30.00	22.00	12.00
Mark Grace (71-80)	40.00	30.00	15.00
Bo Jackson (81-90)	200.00	150.00	80.00
Jose Canseco (91-100)	100.00	75.00	40.00
Eric Davis (101-110)	30.00	22.00	12.00
Orel Hershiser (111-120)	30.00	22.00	12.00
Mike Greenwell (121-130)	30.00	22.00	12.00
Dave Winfield (131-140)	25.00	18.00	10.00
Alan Trammell (141-150)	20.00	15.00	8.00
Kirby Puckett (161-170)	40.00	30.00	15.00
Roger Clemens (171-180)	30.00	22.00	12.00
Kevin Seitzer (151-160)	30.00	22.00	12.00

1989 Star Co. Platinum

14 of baseball's top players are featured in this 140-card set. Cards 21-30 were devoted to Gregg Jefferies, but a cuontract dispute prevented its release. The corresponding card numbers are provided for each player.

	MT	NR MT	EX
Complete Set:	450.00	325.00	175.00
Jose Canseco (1-10)	50.00	37.00	20.00
Mike Greenwell (11-20)	35.00	27.00	15.00
Wade Boggs (31-40)	30.00	22.00	12.00
Don Mattingly (41-50)	80.00	60.00	33.00
Kirby Puckett (51-60)	40.00	30.00	15.00
Dwight Gooden (61-70)	30.00	22.00	12.00
Alan Trammell (71-80)	25.00	18.00	10.00
Darryl Strawberry (81-90)	30.00	22.00	12.00
Orel Hershiser (91-100)	30.00	22.00	12.00
Will Clark (101-110)	50.00	37.00	20.00
Roger Clemens (111-120)	25.00	18.00	10.00
Eric Davis (121-130)	30.00	22.00	12.00
George Brett (131-140)	30.00	22.00	12.00
Frank Viola (141-150)	30.00	22.00	12.00

1989 Star Co. Silver Series

Thius 90-card set features ten player subsets including young superstar Ken Griffey, Jr. Only 2,000 sets were printed and each is serial numbered. The card subsets were released in pairs, one established player and one future star. The corresponding card numbers are provided in the price list for the respective player.

	MT	NR MT	EX
Complete Set:	300.00	225.00	125.00
Ken Griffey, Jr. (1-9)	80.00	60.00	33.00
Wade Boggs (10-18)	20.00	15.00	8.00
Ricky Jordan (19-27)	25.00	18.00	10.00
Mike Greenwell (28-36)	20.00	15.00	8.00
Sandy Alomar, Jr. (37-45)	40.00	30.00	15.00
Mike Schmidt (46-54)	50.00	37.00	20.00
Gary Sheffield (55-63)	30.00	22.00	12.00
Will Clark (64-72)	40.00	30.00	15.00
Ron Jones (73-81)	20.00	15.00	8.00
Kirby Puckett (82-90)	30.00	22.00	12.00

1928 Star Player Candy

This somewhat confusing issue can be dated to 1928, although little is known about its origin. The producer of the set is not identified, but experienced collectors generally refer to it as the Star Player Candy set, apparently because it was distributed with a product of that name. The cards measure 1-7/8" by 2-7/8", are sepia-toned and blank-backed. The player's name (but no team designation) appears in the border below the photo in brown capital letters. To date the checklist of baseball players numbers 72, but more may exist, and cards of football players have also been found.

		NR MT	EX	VG
Complete Set:		9000.	4500.	2700.
Common Player:		60.00	30.00	18.00
(1)	Dave Bancroft	125.00	62.00	37.00
(2)	Emile Barnes	60.00	30.00	18.00
(3)	L.A. Blue	60.00	30.00	18.00
(4)	Garland Buckeye	60.00	30.00	18.00
(5)	George Burns	60.00	30.00	18.00
(6)	Guy T. Bush	60.00	30.00	18.00
(7)	Owen T. Carroll	60.00	30.00	18.00
(8)	Chalmer Cissell	60.00	30.00	18.00
(9)	Ty Cobb	1200.	600.00	360.00
(10)	Gordon Cochrane	125.00	62.00	37.00
(11)	Richard Coffman	60.00	30.00	18.00
(12)	Eddie Collins	125.00	62.00	37.00
(13)	Stanley Coveleskie (Coveleski)	125.00	62.00	37.00
(14)	Hugh Critz	60.00	30.00	18.00
(15)	Hazen Cuyler	125.00	62.00	37.00
(16)	Charles Dressen	75.00	37.00	22.00
(17)	Joe Dugan	75.00	37.00	22.00
(18)	Elwood English	60.00	30.00	18.00
(19)	Bib Falk (Bibb)	60.00	30.00	18.00
(20)	Ira Flagstead	60.00	30.00	18.00
(21)	Bob Fothergill	60.00	30.00	18.00
(22)	Frank T. Frisch	125.00	62.00	37.00
(23)	Foster Ganzel	60.00	30.00	18.00
(24)	Lou Gehrig	1200.	600.00	360.00
(25)	Chas. Gihringer (Gehringer)	125.00	62.00	37.00
(26)	George Gerken	60.00	30.00	18.00
(27)	Grant Gillis	60.00	30.00	18.00
(28)	Miguel Gonzales	60.00	30.00	18.00
(29)	Sam Gray	60.00	30.00	18.00
(30)	Chas. J. Grimm	75.00	37.00	22.00
(31)	Robert M. Grove	200.00	100.00	60.00
(32)	Chas. J. Hafey	125.00	62.00	37.00
(33)	Jesse Haines	125.00	62.00	37.00
(34)	Chas. L. Hartnett	125.00	62.00	37.00
(35)	Clifton HHeathcote	60.00	30.00	18.00
(36)	Harry Heilmann	125.00	62.00	37.00
(37)	John Heving	60.00	30.00	18.00
(38)	Waite Hoyt	125.00	62.00	37.00
(39)	Chas. Jamieson	60.00	30.00	18.00
(40)	Joe Judge	60.00	30.00	18.00
(41)	Willie Kamm	60.00	30.00	18.00
(42)	George Kelly	125.00	62.00	37.00
(43)	Tony Lazzeri	100.00	50.00	30.00
(44)	Adolfo Luque	60.00	30.00	18.00
(45)	Ted Lyons	125.00	62.00	37.00
(46)	Hugh McMullen	60.00	30.00	18.00
(47)	Bob Meusel	75.00	37.00	22.00
(48)	Wilcey Moore (Wilcy)	60.00	30.00	18.00
(49)	Ed C. Morgan	60.00	30.00	18.00
(50)	Herb Pennock	125.00	62.00	37.00
(51)	Everett Purdy	60.00	30.00	18.00
(52)	William Regan	60.00	30.00	18.00
(53)	Eppa Rixey	125.00	62.00	37.00
(54)	Charles Root	75.00	37.00	22.00
(55)	Jack Rothrock	60.00	30.00	18.00
(56)	Harold Ruel (Herold)	60.00	30.00	18.00
(57)	Babe Ruth	1500.	750.00	450.00
(58)	Wally Schang	60.00	30.00	18.00
(59)	Joe Sewell	125.00	62.00	37.00
(60)	Luke Sewell	60.00	30.00	18.00
(61)	Joe Shaute	60.00	30.00	18.00
(62)	George Sisler	125.00	62.00	37.00
(63)	Tris Speaker	200.00	100.00	60.00
(64)	Riggs Stephenson	75.00	37.00	22.00
(65)	Jack Tavener	60.00	30.00	18.00
(66)	Al Thomas	60.00	30.00	18.00
(67)	Harold J. Traynor	125.00	62.00	37.00
(68)	George Uhle	60.00	30.00	18.00
(69)	Dazzy Vance	125.00	62.00	37.00
(70)	Cy Williams	75.00	37.00	22.00
(71)	Ken Williams	75.00	37.00	22.00
(72)	Lewis R. Wilson	125.00	62.00	37.00

1952 Star-Cal Decals - Type 1

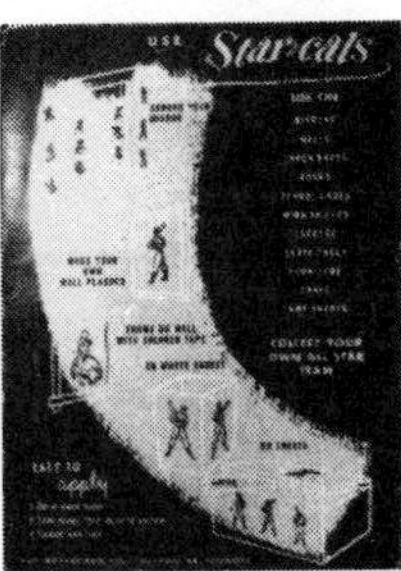

The Meyercord Company of Chicago issued two sets of baseball pla decals in 1952. The Type I Star-cal Decal set consists of 68 different major leaguers, each pictured on a large (4-1/8" by 6-1/8") decal. The player's name and facsimile autograph appear on the decal, along with the decal number listed on the checklist follows.

		NR MT	EX	VG
Complete Set:		2500.	1250.	750.00
Common Player:		12.00	6.00	3.50
70A	Allie Reynolds	18.00	9.00	5.50
70B	Ed Lopat	18.00	9.00	5.50
70C	Yogi Berra	50.00	25.00	15.00
70D	Vic Raschi	18.00	9.00	5.50
70E	Jerry Coleman	15.00	7.50	4.50
70F	Phil Rizzuto	35.00	17.50	10.50
70G	Mickey Mantle	650.00	325.00	195.00
71A	Mel Parnell	12.00	6.00	3.50
71B	Ted Williams	125.00	62.00	37.00
71C	Ted Williams	125.00	62.00	37.00
71D	Vern Stephens	12.00	6.00	3.50
71E	Billy Goodman	12.00	6.00	3.50
71F	Dom DiMaggio	15.00	7.50	4.50
71G	Dick Gernert	12.00	6.00	3.50
71H	Hoot Evers	12.00	6.00	3.50
72A	George Kell	25.00	12.50	7.50
72B	Hal Newhouser	15.00	7.50	4.50
72C	Hoot Evers	12.00	6.00	3.50
72D	Vic Wertz	15.00	7.50	4.50
72E	Fred Hutchinson	15.00	7.50	4.50
72F	Bill Groth	12.00	6.00	3.50
73A	Al Zarilla	12.00	6.00	3.50
73B	Billy Pierce	15.00	7.50	4.50
73C	Eddie Robinson	12.00	6.00	3.50
73D	Chico Carrasquel	12.00	6.00	3.50
73E	Minnie Minoso	15.00	7.50	4.50
73F	Jim Busby	12.00	6.00	3.50
73G	Nellie Fox	18.00	9.00	5.50
73H	Sam Mele	12.00	6.00	3.50
74A	Larry Doby	18.00	9.00	5.50
74B	Al Rosen	15.00	7.50	4.50
74C	Bob Lemon	25.00	12.50	7.50
74D	Jim Hegan	12.00	6.00	3.50
74E	Bob Feller	50.00	25.00	15.00
74F	Dale Mitchell	12.00	6.00	3.50
75A	Ned Garver	12.00	6.00	3.50
76A	Gus Zernial	12.00	6.00	3.50
76B	Ferris Fain	12.00	6.00	3.50
76C	Bobby Shantz	15.00	7.50	4.50
77A	Richie Ashburn	18.00	9.00	5.50
77B	Ralph Kiner	25.00	12.50	7.50
77C	Curt Simmons	15.00	7.50	4.50
78A	Bobby Thomson	15.00	7.50	4.50
78B	Alvin Dark	15.00	7.50	4.50
78C	Sal Maglie	15.00	7.50	4.50
78D	Larry Jansen	12.00	6.00	3.50
78E	Willie Mays	225.00	112.00	67.00

		NR MT	EX	VG
78F	Monte Irvin	20.00	10.00	6.00
78G	Whitey Lockman	12.00	6.00	3.50
79A	Gil Hodges	30.00	15.00	9.00
79B	Pee Wee Reese	40.00	20.00	12.00
79C	Roy Campanella	50.00	25.00	15.00
79D	Don Newcombe	18.00	9.00	5.50
79E	Duke Snider	70.00	35.00	21.00
79F	Preacher Roe	15.00	7.50	4.50
79G	Jackie Robinson	100.00	50.00	30.00
80A	Eddie Miksis	12.00	6.00	3.50
80B	Dutch Leonard	12.00	6.00	3.50
80C	Randy Jackson	12.00	6.00	3.50
80D	Bob Rush	12.00	6.00	3.50
80E	Hank Sauer	12.00	6.00	3.50
80F	Phil Cavarretta	12.00	6.00	3.50
80G	Warren Hacker	12.00	6.00	3.50
81A	Red Schoendienst	18.00	9.00	5.50
81B	Wally Westlake	12.00	6.00	3.50
81C	Cliff Chambers	12.00	6.00	3.50
81D	Enos Slaughter	25.00	12.50	7.50
81E	Stan Musial	110.00	55.00	33.00
81F	Stan Musial	110.00	55.00	33.00
81G	Jerry Staley	12.00	6.00	3.50

1952 Star-Cal Decals - Type 2

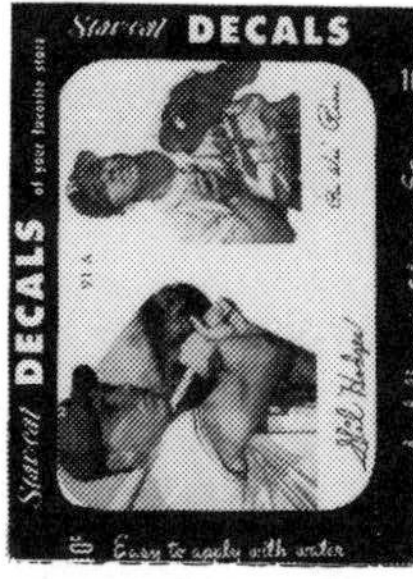

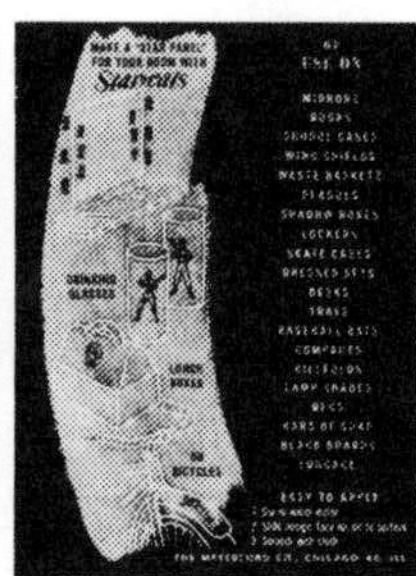

Also produced by Chicago's Meyercord Company in 1952, these Star-cal decals are similar to the Type I variety, except the decal sheets are smaller, measuring 4-1/8" by 3-1/16", and each sheet features two players instead of one.

		NR MT	EX	VG
Complete Set:		1200.	600.00	360.00
Common Player:		12.00	6.00	3.50
84A	Vic Raschi, Allie Reynolds	18.00	9.00	5.50
84B	Yogi Berra, Ed Lopat	60.00	30.00	18.00
84C	Jerry Coleman, Phil Rizzuto	30.00	15.00	9.00
85A	Ted Williams, Ted Williams	150.00	75.00	45.00
85B	Dom DiMaggio, Mel Parnell	15.00	7.50	4.50
85C	Billy Goodman, Vern Stephens	12.00	6.00	3.50
86A	George Kell, Hal Newhouser	20.00	10.00	6.00
86B	Hoot Evers, Vic Wertz	12.00	6.00	3.50
86C	Bill Groth, Fred Hutchinson	12.00	6.00	3.50
87A	Eddie Robinson, Eddie Robinson	12.00	6.00	3.50
87B	Chico Carrasquel, Minnie Minoso	15.00	7.50	4.50
87C	Nellie Fox, Billy Pierce	18.00	9.00	5.50
87D	Jim Busby, Al Zarilla	12.00	6.00	3.50
88A	Jim Hegan, Bob Lemon	20.00	10.00	6.00
88B	Larry Doby, Bob Feller	50.00	25.00	15.00
88C	Dale Mitchell, Al Rosen	15.00	7.50	4.50
89A	Ned Garver, Ned Garver	12.00	6.00	3.50
89B	Ferris Fain, Gus Zernial	12.00	6.00	3.50
89C	Richie Ashburn, Richie Ashburn	18.00	9.00	5.50
89D	Ralph Kiner, Ralph Kiner	25.00	12.50	7.50
90A	Monty Irvin, Willie Mays	200.00	100.00	60.00
90B	Larry Jansen, Sal Maglie	12.00	6.00	3.50
90C	Al Dark, Bobby Thomson	15.00	7.50	4.50
91A	Gil Hodges, Pee Wee Reese	50.00	25.00	15.00
91B	Roy Campanella, Jackie Robinson	125.00	62.00	37.00
91C	Preacher Roe, Duke Snider	75.00	37.00	22.00
92A	Phil Cavarretta, Dutch Leonard	12.00	6.00	3.50
92B	Randy Jackson, Eddie Miksis	12.00	6.00	3.50
92C	Bob Rush, Hank Sauer	12.00	6.00	3.50
93A	Stan Musial, Stan Musial	125.00	62.00	37.00
93B	Red Schoendienst, Enos Slaughter	20.00	10.00	6.00
93C	Cliff Chambers, Wally Westlake	12.00	6.00	3.50

1983 Stuart Expos

This set of Montreal Expos players and coaches was issued by a Montreal area baking company for inclusion in packages of snack cakes. The 30 cards feature full-color player photos, with the

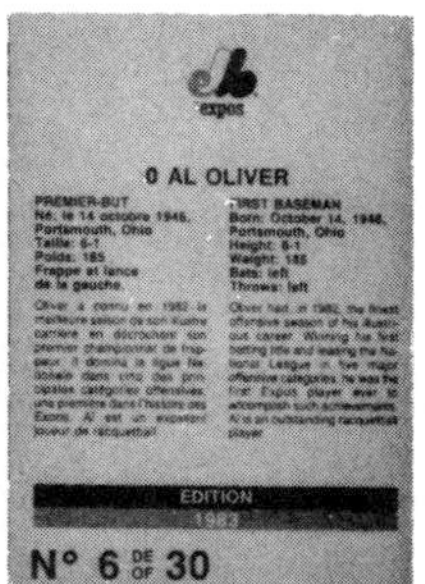

player name, number and team logo also on the card fronts. The backs list brief player biographies in both English and French. Twenty-five players are pictured on the 2-1/2" by 3-1/2" cards.

		MT	NR MT	EX
Complete Set:		12.00	9.00	4.75
Common Player:		.25	.20	.10
1	Bill Virdon	.25	.20	.10
2	Woodie Fryman	.25	.20	.10
3	Vern Rapp	.25	.20	.10
4	Andre Dawson	2.00	1.50	.80
5	Jeff Reardon	.70	.50	.30
6	Al Oliver	.50	.40	.20
7	Doug Flynn	.25	.20	.10
8	Gary Carter	1.00	.70	.40
9	Tim Raines	1.50	1.25	.60
10	Steve Rogers	.30	.25	.12
11	Billy DeMars	.25	.20	.10
12	Tim Wallach	1.00	.70	.40
13	Galen Cisco	.25	.20	.10
14	Terry Francona	.25	.20	.10
15	Bill Gullickson	.25	.20	.10
16	Ray Burris	.25	.20	.10
17	Scott Sanderson	.35	.25	.14
18	Warren Cromartie	.25	.20	.10
19	Jerry White	.25	.20	.10
20	Bobby Ramos	.25	.20	.10
21	Jim Wohlford	.25	.20	.10
22	Dan Schatzeder	.25	.20	.10
23	Charlie Lea	.25	.20	.10
24	Bryan Little	.25	.20	.10
25	Mel Wright	.25	.20	.10
26	Tim Blackwell	.25	.20	.10
27	Chris Speier	.25	.20	.10
28	Randy Lerch	.25	.20	.10
29	Bryn Smith	.35	.25	.14
30	Brad Mills	.25	.20	.10

1984 Stuart Expos

For the second year in a row, Stuart Cakes issued a full-color card set of the Montreal Expos. The 2-1/2" by 3-1/2" cards again list the player name and number along with the team and company logos on the card fronts. The backs are bilingual with biographical information in both English and French. The 40-card set was issued in two series. Card numbers 21-40, issued late in the summer, are more difficult to find than the first 20 cards. The 40 cards include players, the manager, coaches and team mascot.

		MT	NR MT	EX
Complete Set:		40.00	30.00	15.00
Common Player: 1-20		.25	.20	.10
Common Player: 21-40		.50	.40	.20
1	Youppi! (mascot)	.25	.20	.10
2	Bill Virdon	.25	.20	.10
3	Billy DeMars	.25	.20	.10
4	Galen Cisco	.25	.20	.10
5	Russ Nixon	.25	.20	.10
6	Felipe Alou	.25	.20	.10
7	Dan Schatzeder	.25	.20	.10
8	Charlie Lea	.25	.20	.10
9	Bobby Ramos	.25	.20	.10
10	Bob James	.25	.20	.10
11	Andre Dawson	1.25	.90	.50
12	Gary Lucas	.25	.20	.10
13	Jeff Reardon	.50	.40	.20
14	Tim Wallach	1.00	.70	.40
15	Gary Carter	1.25	.90	.50
16	Bill Gullickson	.25	.20	.10
17	Pete Rose	4.00	3.00	1.50
18	Terry Francona	.25	.20	.10
19	Steve Rogers	.30	.25	.12
20	Tim Raines	1.50	1.25	.60
21	Bryn Smith	.50	.40	.20
22	Greg Harris	.50	.40	.20
23	David Palmer	.50	.40	.20
24	Jim Wohlford	.50	.40	.20
25	Miguel Dilone	.50	.40	.20
26	Mike Stenhouse	.50	.40	.20
27	Chris Speier	.50	.40	.20
28	Derrel Thomas	.50	.40	.20
29	Doug Flynn	.50	.40	.20
30	Bryan Little	.50	.40	.20
31	Argenis Salazar	.50	.40	.20
32	Mike Fuentes	.50	.40	.20
33	Joe Kerrigan	.50	.40	.20
34	Andy McGaffigan	.45	.35	.20
35	Fred Breining	.50	.40	.20
36	Expos 1983 All-Stars (Gary Carter, Andre Dawson, Tim Raines, Steve Rogers)	1.50	1.25	.60
37	Co-Players Of The Year (Andre Dawson, Tim Raines)	1.50	1.25	.60
38	Expos' Coaching Staff (Felipe Alou, Galen Cisco, Billy DeMars, Joe Kerrigan, Russ Nixon, Bill Virdon)	.50	.40	.20
39	Team Photo	.50	.40	.20
40	Checklist	.50	.40	.20

1987 Stuart

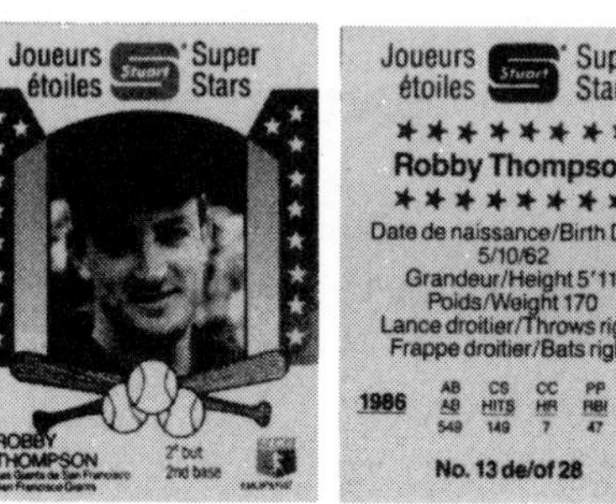

Twenty-eight four-part folding panels make up the 1987 Stuart Super Stars set, which was issued only in Canada. Three player cards and a sweepstakes entry form card comprise each panel. All 26 major league teams are included with the Montreal Expos and Toronto Blue Jays being represented twice. The cards, which are full color and measure 2-1/2" by 3-1/2", are written in both English and French. The card backs contain the player's previous year's statistics. All team insignias have been airbrushed away.

		MT	NR MT	EX
Complete Panel Set:		50.00	37.00	20.00
Complete Singles Set:		20.00	15.00	8.00
Common Panel:		.80	.60	.30
Common Single Player:		.10	.08	.04
Panel (New York Mets)		4.00	3.00	1.50
1a	Gary Carter	.50	.40	.20
1b	Keith Hernandez	.40	.30	.15
1c	Darryl Strawberry	.60	.45	.25
Panel (Atlanta Braves)		2.25	1.75	.90
2a	Bruce Benedict	.10	.08	.04
2b	Ken Griffey	.15	.11	.06
2c	Dale Murphy	.60	.45	.25
Panel (Chicago Cubs)		1.50	1.25	.60
3a	Jody Davis	.15	.11	.06
3b	Andre Dawson	.30	.25	.12
3c	Leon Durham	.15	.11	.06
Panel (Cincinnati Reds)		2.50	2.00	1.00
4a	Buddy Bell	.15	.11	.06
4b	Eric Davis	.60	.45	.25
4c	Dave Parker	.25	.20	.10
Panel (Houston Astros)		2.25	1.75	.90
5a	Glenn Davis	.25	.20	.10
5b	Nolan Ryan	.70	.50	.30
5c	Mike Scott	.25	.20	.10
Panel (Los Angeles Dodgers)		2.25	1.75	.90
6a	Pedro Guerrero	.25	.20	.10
6b	Mike Marshall	.20	.15	.08
6c	Fernando Valenzuela	.40	.30	.15
Panel (Montreal Expos)		1.75	1.25	.70
7a	Tim Raines	.40	.30	.15
7b	Tim Wallach	.20	.15	.08
7c	Mitch Webster	.10	.08	.04
Panel (Montreal Expos)		.80	.60	.30
8a	Hubie Brooks	.15	.11	.06
8b	Bryn Smith	.10	.08	.04
8c	Floyd Youmans	.10	.08	.04
Panel (Philadelphia Phillies)		2.25	1.75	.90
9a	Shane Rawley	.10	.08	.04
9b	Juan Samuel	.20	.15	.08
9c	Mike Schmidt	.80	.60	.30
Panel (Pittsburgh Pirates)		.80	.60	.30
10a	Jim Morrison	.10	.08	.04
10b	Johnny Ray	.15	.11	.06
10c	R.J. Reynolds	.10	.08	.04
Panel (St. Louis Cardinals)		2.00	1.50	.80
11a	Jack Clark	.25	.20	.10
11b	Vince Coleman	.30	.25	.12
11c	Ozzie Smith	.25	.20	.10
Panel (San Diego Padres)		3.00	2.25	1.25

		MT	NR MT	EX
12a	Steve Garvey	.50	.40	.20
12b	Tony Gwynn	.50	.40	.20
12c	John Kruk	.20	.15	.08
Panel	(San Francisco Giants)	.80	.60	.30
13a	Chili Davis	.10	.08	.04
13b	Jeffrey Leonard	.10	.08	.04
13c	Robbie Thompson	.10	.08	.04
Panel	(Baltimore Orioles)	3.00	2.25	1.25
14a	Fred Lynn	.25	.20	.10
14b	Eddie Murray	.50	.40	.20
14c	Cal Ripken	.50	.40	.20
Panel	(Boston Red Sox)	4.00	3.00	1.50
15a	Don Baylor	.15	.11	.06
15b	Wade Boggs	.80	.60	.30
15c	Roger Clemens	.60	.45	.25
Panel		2.50	2.00	1.00
16a	Doug DeCinces	.10	.08	.04
16b	Wally Joyner	.80	.60	.30
16c	Mike Witt	.10	.08	.04
Panel	(Chicago White Sox)	1.50	1.25	.60
17a	Harold Baines	.20	.15	.08
17b	Carlton Fisk	.25	.20	.10
17c	Ozzie Guillen	.15	.11	.06
Panel	(Cleveland Indians)	1.00	.70	.40
18a	Joe Carter	.20	.15	.08
18b	Julio Franco	.15	.11	.06
18c	Pat Tabler	.10	.08	.04
Panel	(Detroit Tigers)	2.50	2.00	1.00
19a	Kirk Gibson	.40	.30	.15
19b	Jack Morris	.25	.20	.10
19c	Alan Trammell	.40	.30	.15
Panel	(Kansas City Royals)	2.50	2.00	1.00
20a	George Brett	.60	.45	.25
20b	Bret Saberhagen	.30	.25	.12
20c	Willie Wilson	.15	.11	.06
Panel	(Milwaukee Brewers)	2.00	1.50	.80
21a	Cecil Cooper	.15	.11	.06
21b	Paul Molitor	.20	.15	.08
21c	Robin Yount	.40	.30	.15
Panel	(Minnesota Twins)	2.50	2.00	1.00
22a	Tom Brunansky	.20	.15	.08
22b	Kent Hrbek	.30	.25	.12
22c	Kirby Puckett	.50	.40	.20
Panel	(New York Yankees)	5.00	3.75	2.00
23a	Rickey Henderson	.50	.40	.20
23b	Don Mattingly	1.00	.70	.40
23c	Dave Winfield	.50	.40	.20
Panel	(Oakland A's)	2.75	2.00	1.00
24a	Jose Canseco	.90	.70	.35
24b	Alfredo Griffin	.10	.08	.04
24c	Carney Lansford	.10	.08	.04
Panel	25 (Seattle Mariners)	1.50	1.25	.60
25a	Phil Bradley	.15	.11	.06
25b	Alvin Davis	.20	.15	.08
25c	Mark Langston	.20	.15	.08
Panel	(Texas Rangers)	1.50	1.25	.60
26a	Pete Incaviglia	.30	.25	.12
26b	Pete O'Brien	.10	.08	.04
26c	Larry Parrish	.10	.08	.04
Panel	(Toronto Blue Jays)	2.25	1.75	.90
27a	Jesse Barfield	.20	.15	.08
27b	George Bell	.40	.30	.15
27c	Tony Fernandez	.20	.15	.08
Panel	(Toronto Blue Jays)	.80	.60	.30
28a	Lloyd Moseby	.10	.08	.04
28b	Dave Stieb	.15	.11	.06
28c	Ernie Whitt	.10	.08	.04

1962 Sugardale Weiners

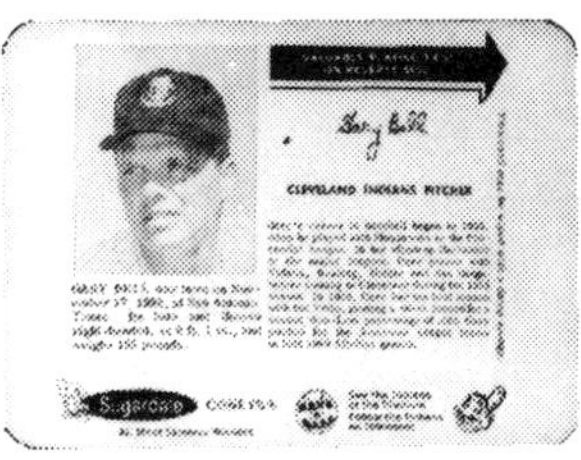

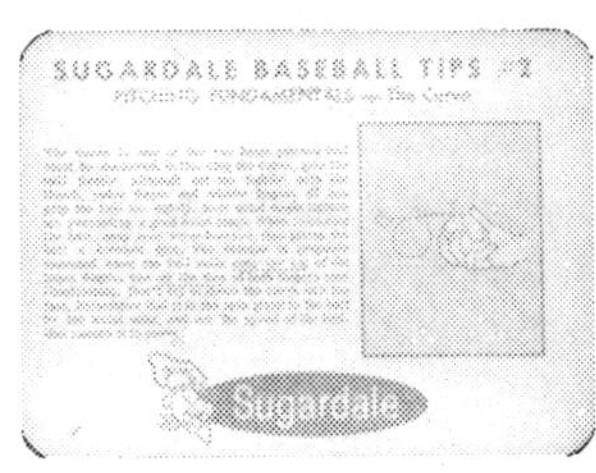

The Sugardale Meats set of black and white cards measure 5-1/8" by 3-3/4". The 22-card set includes 18 Cleveland Indians and four Pittsburgh Pirates players. The Indians cards are numbered from 1-19 with card number 6 not issued. The Pirates cards are lettered from A to D. The card fronts contain a relatively small player photo, with biographical information and Sugardale logo. The backs are printed in red and offer playing tips and another company logo. Card number 10 (Bob Nieman) is considerably more scarce than other cards in the set.

		NR MT	EX	VG
Complete Set:		2000.	1000.	600.00
Common Player:		40.00	20.00	12.00
A	Dick Groat	70.00	35.00	21.00
B	Roberto Clemente	500.00	300.00	150.00
C	Don Hoak	55.00	27.00	16.50
D	Dick Stuart	55.00	27.00	16.50
1	Barry Latman	40.00	20.00	12.00
2	Gary Bell	45.00	22.00	13.50
3	Dick Donovan	40.00	20.00	12.00
4	Frank Funk	40.00	20.00	12.00
5	Jim Perry	60.00	30.00	18.00
6	Not issued			
7	Johnny Romano	40.00	20.00	12.00
8	Ty Cline	40.00	20.00	12.00
9	Tito Francona	45.00	22.00	13.50
10	Bob Nieman	300.00	150.00	90.00
11	Willie Kirkland	40.00	20.00	12.00
12	Woodie Held	45.00	22.00	13.50
13	Jerry Kindall	40.00	20.00	12.00
14	Bubba Phillips	40.00	20.00	12.00
15	Mel Harder	45.00	22.00	13.50
16	Salty Parker	40.00	20.00	12.00
17	Ray Katt	40.00	20.00	12.00
18	Mel McGaha	40.00	20.00	12.00
19	Pedro Ramos	40.00	20.00	12.00

1963 Sugardale Weiners

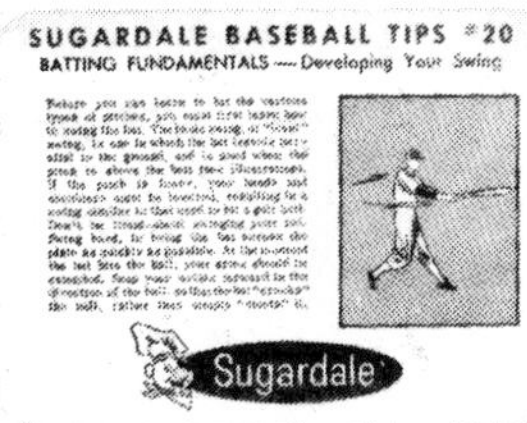

Sugardale Meats again featured Cleveland and Pittsburgh players in its 1963 set, which grew to 31 cards. The black and white cards again measure 5-1/8" by 3-3/4", and consist of 28 Indians and five Pirates players. Card formats are virtually identical to the 1962 cards, with the only real difference being the information included in the player biographies. The cards are numbered 1-38, with numbers 6, 21, 22 and 29-32 not issued. Cards for Bob Skinner (#35) and Jim Perry (#5) are scarce as these two players were traded during the season and their cards withdrawn from distribution. The red card backs again offer playing tips.

		NR MT	EX	VG
Complete Set:		2000.	1000.	600.00
A	Don Cardwell	40.00	20.00	12.00
B	Robert R. Skinner	125.00	62.00	37.00
C	Donald B. Schwall	40.00	20.00	12.00
D	Jim Pagliaroni	40.00	20.00	12.00
E	Dick Schofield	45.00	22.00	13.50
1	Barry Latman	40.00	20.00	12.00
2	Gary Bell	45.00	22.00	13.50
3	Dick Donovan	40.00	20.00	12.00
4	Joe Adcock	60.00	30.00	18.00
5	Jim Perry	150.00	75.00	45.00
6	Not issued			
7	Johnny Romano	40.00	20.00	12.00
8	Mike De La Hoz	40.00	20.00	12.00
9	Tito Francona	45.00	22.00	13.50
10	Gene Green	40.00	20.00	12.00
11	Willie Kirkland	40.00	20.00	12.00
12	Woodie Held	45.00	22.00	13.50
13	Jerry Kindall	40.00	20.00	12.00
14	Max Alvis	45.00	22.00	13.50
15	Mel Harder	45.00	22.00	13.50
16	George Strickland	40.00	20.00	12.00
17	Elmer Valo	40.00	20.00	12.00
18	Birdie Tebbetts	45.00	22.00	13.50
19	Pedro Ramos	40.00	20.00	12.00
20	Al Luplow	40.00	20.00	12.00
21	Not issued			
22	Not issued			
23	Jim Grant	45.00	22.00	13.50
24	Victor Davalillo	45.00	22.00	13.50
25	Jerry Walker	40.00	20.00	12.00
26	Sam McDowell	60.00	30.00	18.00
27	Fred Whitfield	40.00	20.00	12.00
28	Jack Kralick	40.00	20.00	12.00
29	Not issued			
30	Not issued			
31	Not issued			
32	Not issued			
33	Bob Allen	40.00	20.00	12.00

1911 T3 Turkey Reds

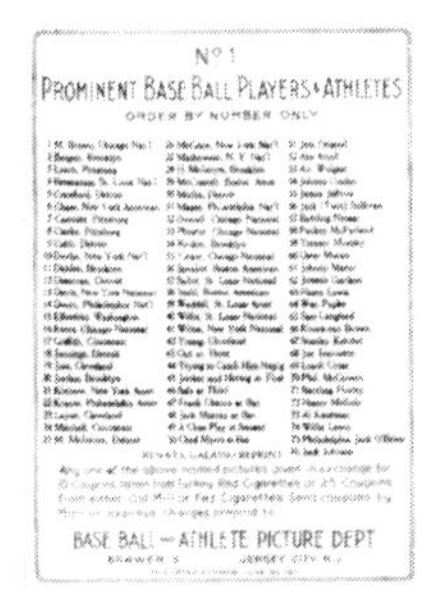

Turkey Reds are the only cabinet cards the average collector can have a realistic chance to complete. Obtained by mailing in coupons found in Turkey Red, Fez and Old Mill brand cigarettes, the Turkey Reds measure 5 3/4" by 8", a size known to collectors as "cabinet cards." Turkey Reds feature full color lithograph fronts with wide gray frames. Backs carried either a numbered ordering list or an ad for Turkey Red cigarettes. The Turkey Red series consists of 25 boxers and 100 baseball players. Despite their cost, Turkey Reds remain very popular today as the most attractive of the cabinet sets.

		NR MT	EX	VG
Complete Set:		52000.	26000.	10600.
Common Player: 1-50		250.00	125.00	75.00
Common Player: 77-126		275.00	137.00	82.00
1	Mordecai Brown	850.00	425.00	265.00
2	Bill Bergen	250.00	125.00	75.00
3	Tommy Leach	250.00	125.00	75.00
4	Roger Bresnahan	800.00	400.00	250.00
5	Sam Crawford	800.00	400.00	250.00
6	Hal Chase	400.00	200.00	125.00
7	Howie Camnitz	250.00	125.00	75.00
8	Fred Clarke	700.00	350.00	200.00
9	Ty Cobb	6500.	3250.	2000.
10	Art Devlin	250.00	125.00	75.00
11	Bill Dahlen	250.00	125.00	75.00
12	Wil Bill Donovan	250.00	125.00	75.00
13	Larry Doyle	250.00	125.00	75.00
14	Red Dooin	250.00	125.00	75.00
15	Kid Elberfeld	250.00	125.00	75.00
16	Johnny Evers	800.00	400.00	250.00
17	Clark Griffith	800.00	400.00	250.00
18	Hughie Jennings	800.00	400.00	250.00
19	Addie Joss	800.00	400.00	250.00
20	Tim Jordan	250.00	125.00	75.00
21	Red Kleinow	250.00	125.00	75.00
22	Harry Krause	250.00	125.00	75.00
23	Nap Lajoie	1500.	750.00	450.00
24	Mike Mitchell	250.00	125.00	75.00
25	Matty McIntyre	250.00	125.00	75.00
26	John McGraw	1350.	775.00	375.00
27	Christy Mathewson	2500.	1250.	750.00
28a	Harry McIntyre (Brooklyn)	250.00	125.00	75.00
28b	Harry McIntyre (Brooklyn and Chicago)	350.00	175.00	105.00
29	Amby McConnell	250.00	125.00	75.00
30	George Mullin	250.00	125.00	75.00
31	Sherry Magee	250.00	125.00	75.00
32	Orval Overall	250.00	125.00	75.00
33	Jake Pfeister	250.00	125.00	75.00
34	Nap Rucker	250.00	125.00	75.00
35	Joe Tinker	800.00	400.00	250.00
36	Tris Speaker	1500.	750.00	450.00
37	Slim Sallee	250.00	125.00	75.00
38	Jake Stahl	250.00	125.00	75.00
39	Rube Waddell	800.00	400.00	250.00
40a	Vic Willis (Pittsburg)	250.00	125.00	82.00
40b	Vic Willis (Pittsburg and St. Louis)	350.00	175.00	105.00
41	Hooks Wiltse	250.00	125.00	82.00
42	Cy Young	1800.	900.00	550.00
43	Out At Third	200.00	100.00	60.00
44	Trying To Catch Him Napping	200.00	100.00	60.00
45	Jordan & Herzog At First	250.00	125.00	75.00
46	Safe At Third	200.00	100.00	60.00
47	Frank Chance At Bat	850.00	425.00	265.00
48	Jack Murray At Bat	150.00	75.00	45.00
49	A Close Play At Second	150.00	75.00	45.00
50	Chief Myers At Bat	150.00	75.00	45.00
77	Red Ames	275.00	150.00	80.00
78	Home Run Baker	800.00	400.00	250.00
79	George Bell	275.00	150.00	80.00
80	Chief Bender	850.00	425.00	265.00
81	Bob Bescher	275.00	150.00	80.00
82	Kitty Bransfield	275.00	150.00	80.00

		NR MT	EX	VG
83	Al Bridwell	275.00	150.00	80.00
84	George Browne	275.00	150.00	80.00
85	Bill Burns	275.00	150.00	80.00
86	Bill Carrigan	275.00	150.00	80.00
87	Eddie Collins	850.00	425.00	265.00
88	Harry Coveleski	275.00	150.00	80.00
89	Lou Criger	275.00	150.00	80.00
90a	Mickey Doolin (name incorrect)	375.00	187.00	112.00
90b	Mickey Doolan (name correct)	275.00	150.00	80.00
91	Tom Downey	275.00	150.00	80.00
92	Jimmy Dygert	275.00	150.00	80.00
93	Art Fromme	275.00	150.00	80.00
94	George Gibson	275.00	150.00	80.00
95	Peaches Graham	275.00	150.00	80.00
96	Bob Groom	275.00	150.00	80.00
97	Dick Hoblitzell	275.00	150.00	80.00
98	Solly Hofman	275.00	150.00	80.00
99	Walter Johnson	2800.	1400.	875.00
100	Davy Jones	275.00	150.00	80.00
101	Wee Willie Keeler	450.00	225.00	135.00
102	Johnny Kling	275.00	150.00	80.00
103	Ed Konetchy	275.00	150.00	80.00
104	Ed Lennox	275.00	150.00	80.00
105	Hans Lobert	275.00	150.00	80.00
106	Harry Lord	275.00	150.00	80.00
107	Rube Manning	275.00	150.00	80.00
108	Fred Merkle	275.00	150.00	80.00
109	Pat Moran	275.00	150.00	80.00
110	George McBride	275.00	150.00	80.00
111	Harry Niles	275.00	150.00	80.00
112a	Dode Paskert (Cincinnati)	350.00	175.00	105.00
112b	Dode Paskert (Cincinnati and Philadelphia)	275.00	150.00	80.00
113	Bugs Raymond	275.00	150.00	80.00
114	Bob Rhoades (Rhoads)	350.00	175.00	105.00
115	Admiral Schlei	275.00	150.00	80.00
116	Boss Schmidt	275.00	150.00	80.00
117	Wildfire Schulte	275.00	150.00	80.00
118	Frank Smith	275.00	150.00	80.00
119	George Stone	275.00	150.00	80.00
120	Gabby Street	275.00	150.00	80.00
121	Billy Sullivan	275.00	150.00	80.00
122a	Fred Tenney (New York)	350.00	175.00	105.00
122b	Fred Tenney (New York and Boston)	275.00	150.00	80.00
123	Ira Thomas	275.00	150.00	80.00
124	Bobby Wallace	700.00	350.00	200.00
125	Ed Walsh	800.00	400.00	250.00
126	Owen Wilson	275.00	150.00	80.00

1911 T4 Obak Premiums

The 1948 Smith's Clothing issue was another 25-card regional set featuring members of the Oakland Oaks of the Pacific Coast League. Almost identical to the 1947 Smith's issue, the black and white cards again measure 2" by 3" but were printed on heavier, glossy stock. The player's name, team and position appear below the photo with the card number in the lower right corner. The back has a brief player write-up and an ad for Smith's Clothing. Among the scarcest of all the 20th Century tobacco issues, the T4 Obak Premiums were cabinet-sized cards distributed in conjunction with the more popular and better-known Obak T212 card set. Both sets were issued in 1911 by Obak "mouthpiece" cigarettes and featured players from the Pacific Coast League. The Obak Premiums measured a large 5" by 7" and wre printed on a cardboard-like paper. The attractive cards featured a greyish monochome player photo inside a 3-1/2" by 5" oval. There was no printing on the front of the card to identify the player or indicate the Manufacturer, and the backs of the cards were blank. In most cases the photos used for the premiums were identical to the T212 photos, except for some cropping differences. Under the Obak mail-in promotion, 50 coupons from cigarette packages were required to obtain just one premium card, which may explain their extreme scarcity today. According to the coupon, all 175 players pictured in the regular T212 set were available as premium cards, but todate 30 different players have been found in the larger cabinet size. Most of the Obak premiums that exist in original condition contain a number, written in pencil on the back of the card, that corresponds to the checklist printed on the coupon. Because of their extreme scarcity, these cards are quite expensive and generally appeal only to the very advanced Pacific Coast League collectors.

		NR MT	EX	VG
Complete Set:		9500.	4750.	2850.
Common Player:		300.00	150.00	90.00
3	Howard	300.00	150.00	90.00
22	Christian	300.00	150.00	90.00
24	Maggert	300.00	150.00	90.00
33	Flater	300.00	150.00	90.00
34	Zacher	300.00	150.00	90.00
37	Ryan	300.00	150.00	90.00
49	Kuhn	300.00	150.00	90.00
59	Baum	300.00	150.00	90.00
71	Melchoir	300.00	150.00	90.00
72	Vitt	300.00	150.00	90.00
74	Berry	300.00	150.00	90.00
75	Miller	300.00	150.00	90.00
76	Tennant	300.00	150.00	90.00
77	Mohler	300.00	150.00	90.00
79	Sutor	300.00	150.00	90.00
80	Browning	300.00	150.00	90.00
81	Ryan	300.00	150.00	90.00
82	Powell	300.00	150.00	90.00
83	Schmidt	300.00	150.00	90.00
84	Meikle	300.00	150.00	90.00
85	Madden	300.00	150.00	90.00
87	Moskiman	300.00	150.00	90.00
88	Zamlock	300.00	150.00	90.00
92	Carlisle	300.00	150.00	90.00
97	Stewart	300.00	150.00	90.00
111	Mundorff	300.00	150.00	90.00
140	Annis	300.00	150.00	90.00
159	Dashwood	300.00	150.00	90.00
167	Spencer	300.00	150.00	90.00

1911 T5 Pinkerton

Because they were photographs affixed to a cardboard backing, the cards in the 1911 T5 Pinkerton set are considered by today's advanced collectors to be "true" cabinet cards. The Pinkerton cabinets are a rather obscure issue, and because of their original method of distribution, it would be virtually impossible to assemble a complete set today. It has never actually been determined how many subjects in the set even exist. Pinkerton, the parent of Red Man and other tobacco products, offered the cabinets in exchange for coupons found in cigarette packages. According to an original advertising sheet, some 376 different photos were available. A consumer could exchange ten coupons for the cabinet card of his choice. The photos available included players from the 16 major league teams plus five teams from the American Association (Indianapolis, Columbus, Toledo, Kansas City and Minneapolis.) Pinkerton cabinet cards have been found to vary in both size and type of mount. The most desirable combination is a 3-3/8" by 5-1/2" photograph afffixed to a thick, cardboard mount measuring approximately 4-3/4" by 7- 3/4". But original Pinkerton cabinets have also been found in slightly different sizes with less substantial backings. The most attractive mounts are embossed around the picture, but some Pinkertons have been found with a white border surrounding the photograph. Prices listed are for cards with cardboard mounts. Cards with paper mounts are worth about 75 of listed prices. Collectors should be aware that some of the Pinkerton photos were reproduced in postcard size issues in later years. Because of the rareness of the T5s, no complete set price is given.

		NR MT	EX	VG
Complete Set:				
Common Player:		150.00	75.00	45.00
101	Jim Stephens	150.00	75.00	45.00
102	Bobby Wallace	300.00	150.00	90.00
103	Joe Lake	150.00	75.00	45.00
104	George Stone	150.00	75.00	45.00
105	Jack O'Connor	150.00	75.00	45.00
106	Bill Abstein	150.00	75.00	45.00
107	Rube Waddell	300.00	150.00	90.00
108	Roy Hartzell	150.00	75.00	45.00
109	Danny Hoffman	150.00	75.00	45.00
110	Dode Cris	150.00	75.00	45.00
111	Al Schweitzer	150.00	75.00	45.00
112	Art Griggs	150.00	75.00	45.00
113	Bill Bailey	150.00	75.00	45.00
114	Pat Newman	150.00	75.00	45.00
115	Harry Howell	150.00	75.00	45.00
117	Hobe Ferris	150.00	75.00	45.00
118	John McAleese	150.00	75.00	45.00
119	Ray Demmitt	150.00	75.00	45.00
120	Red Fisher	150.00	75.00	45.00
121	Frank Truesdale	150.00	75.00	45.00
122	Barney Pelty	150.00	75.00	45.00
123	Ed Killifer (Killefer)	150.00	75.00	45.00
151	Matty McIntyre	150.00	75.00	45.00
152	Jim Delahanty	150.00	75.00	45.00
153	Hughey Jennings	300.00	150.00	90.00
154	Ralph Works	150.00	75.00	45.00
155	George Moriarity (Moriarty)	150.00	75.00	45.00
156	Sam Crawford	300.00	150.00	90.00
157	Boss Schmidt	150.00	75.00	45.00
158	Owen Bush	150.00	75.00	45.00
159	Ty Cobb	1500.	750.00	450.00
160	Bill Donovan	150.00	75.00	45.00
161	Oscar Stanage	150.00	75.00	45.00
162	George Mullin	150.00	75.00	45.00
163	Davy Jones	150.00	75.00	45.00
164	Charley O'Leary	150.00	75.00	45.00
165	Tom Jones	150.00	75.00	45.00
166	Joe Casey	150.00	75.00	45.00
167	Ed Willetts (Willett)	150.00	75.00	45.00
168	Ed Lafeite (Lafitte)	150.00	75.00	45.00
169	Ty Cobb	1500.	750.00	450.00
170	Ty Cobb	1500.	750.00	450.00
201	John Evers	300.00	150.00	90.00
202	Mordecai Brown	300.00	150.00	90.00
203	King Cole	150.00	75.00	45.00
204	Johnny Cane	150.00	75.00	45.00
205	Heinie Zimmerman	150.00	75.00	45.00
206	Wildfire Schulte	150.00	75.00	45.00
207	Frank Chance	300.00	150.00	90.00
208	Joe Tinker	300.00	150.00	90.00
209	Orvall Overall	150.00	75.00	45.00
210	Jimmy Archer	150.00	75.00	45.00
211	Johnny Kling	150.00	75.00	45.00
212	Jimmy Sheckard	150.00	75.00	45.00
213	Harry McIntyre	150.00	75.00	45.00
214	Lew Richie	150.00	75.00	45.00
215	Ed Ruelbach	150.00	75.00	45.00
216	Artie Hoffman (Hofman)	150.00	75.00	45.00
217	Jake Pfeister	150.00	75.00	45.00
218	Harry Steinfeldt	150.00	75.00	45.00
219	Tom Needham	150.00	75.00	45.00
220	Ginger Beaumont	150.00	75.00	45.00
251	Christy Mathewson	700.00	350.00	200.00
252	Fred Merkle	150.00	75.00	45.00
253	Hooks Wiltsie	150.00	75.00	45.00
254	Art Devlin	150.00	75.00	45.00
255	Fred Snodgrass	150.00	75.00	45.00
256	Josh Devore	150.00	75.00	45.00
257	Red Murray	150.00	75.00	45.00
258	Cy Seymour	150.00	75.00	45.00
259	Al Bridwell	150.00	75.00	45.00
260	Larry Doyle	150.00	75.00	45.00
261	Bugs Raymond	150.00	75.00	45.00
262	Doc Crandall	150.00	75.00	45.00
263	Admiral Schlei	150.00	75.00	45.00
264	Chief Myers (Meyers)	150.00	75.00	45.00
265	Bill Dahlen	150.00	75.00	45.00
266	Beals Becker	150.00	75.00	45.00
267	Louis Drucke	150.00	75.00	45.00
301	Fred Luderus	150.00	75.00	45.00
302	John Titus	150.00	75.00	45.00
303	Red Dooin	150.00	75.00	45.00
304	Eddie Stack	150.00	75.00	45.00
305	Kitty Bransfield	150.00	75.00	45.00
306	Sherry Magee	150.00	75.00	45.00
307	Otto Knabe	150.00	75.00	45.00
308	Jimmy "Runt" Walsh	150.00	75.00	45.00
309	Earl Moore	150.00	75.00	45.00
310	Mickey Doolan	150.00	75.00	45.00
311	Ad Brennan	150.00	75.00	45.00
312	Bob Ewing	150.00	75.00	45.00
313	Lou Schettler	150.00	75.00	45.00
351	Joe Willis	150.00	75.00	45.00
352	Rube Ellis	150.00	75.00	45.00
353	Steve Evans	150.00	75.00	45.00
354	Miller Huggins	300.00	150.00	90.00
355	Arnold Hauser	150.00	75.00	45.00
356	Frank Corridon	150.00	75.00	45.00
357	Roger Bresnahan	300.00	150.00	90.00
358	Slim Sallee	150.00	75.00	45.00
359	Mike Mowrey	150.00	75.00	45.00
360	Ed Konetchy	150.00	75.00	45.00
361	Beckman	150.00	75.00	45.00
362	Rebel Oakes	150.00	75.00	45.00
363	Johnny Lush	150.00	75.00	45.00
364	Eddie Phelps	150.00	75.00	45.00
365	Robert Harmon	150.00	75.00	45.00
401	Lew Moren	150.00	75.00	45.00
402	George McQuillian (McQuillan)	150.00	75.00	45.00
403	Johnny Bates	150.00	75.00	45.00
404	Eddie Grant	150.00	75.00	45.00
405	Tommy McMillan	150.00	75.00	45.00
406	Tommy Clark (Clarke)	150.00	75.00	45.00
407	Jack Rowan	150.00	75.00	45.00
408	Bob Bescher	150.00	75.00	45.00
409	Fred Beebe	150.00	75.00	45.00
410	Tom Downey	150.00	75.00	45.00
411	George Suggs	150.00	75.00	45.00
412	Hans Lobert	150.00	75.00	45.00
413	Jimmy Phelan	150.00	75.00	45.00
414	Dode Paskert	150.00	75.00	45.00
415	Ward Miller	150.00	75.00	45.00
416	Dick Egan	150.00	75.00	45.00
417	Art Fromme	150.00	75.00	45.00
418	Bill Burns	150.00	75.00	45.00
419	Clark Griffith	300.00	150.00	90.00
420	Dick Hoblitzell	150.00	75.00	45.00

Card company addresses

Collectors frequently want to know the addresses of the major baseball-card manufacturing companies. They are:

Topps Chewing Gum Co.
254 36th St.
Brooklyn, N.Y. 11232
Fleer Corp.
10th & Somerville
Philadelphia, Pa. 19141
Leaf-Donruss Co.
P.O. Box 2038
Memphis, Tenn. 38101
Sportflics/Score
Major League Marketing, Inc.
55 Ford Rd.
Westport, Ct. 06880
Upper Deck Co.
23705 Via Del Rio
Yorba Linda, CA 92686

Wrong backs, blank backs

Collectors occasionally find recent (1980s) cards which have wrong backs (player on front doesn't match bio/stats on back) or blank backs. Such cards result from mistakes in the printing process. They aren't very popular with collectors, so they have little, if any, premium value. Most collectors feel they are merely damaged cards and value them lower than correctly printed specimens. The only exception seems to be currently hot superstars or rookie cards, for which a few collectors are willing to pay premiums.

Errors/variations

Collectors often wonder about errors found on cards, usually in the statistics or personal data on the card's back.

Such errors *add nothing* to the value of the card. The only time an error like this is likely to increase a card's value is if the manufacturer corrects the error in a later printing, thus creating two distinct variations. If enough collectors feel the variations are a desirable part of that issue, the value may increase. Whether the error version or the corrected card will have the greater value usually depends on relative scarcity. The more common version will almost always be worth less. So quite often, the error card can be worth less than the corrected version.

Collector-only issues

Collectors may find some recent issues not included in this volume. In most cases these are illegal, unauthorized "collector-only" issues. Such cards often show nothing but the player's photo and his name on the front, and his name and perhaps a line or two of statistics on the back. The sets usually lack a manufacturer's name. They are often sold at shows and in shops, and frequently carry high price tags.

The cards *are not* legitimate issues. They can be printed and reprinted at will, so they lack any scarcity value.

NOTE: A card number in parentheses ( ) indicates the card set is unnumbered.

No.	Player	NR MT	EX	VG
421	Harry Gasper	150.00	75.00	45.00
422	Dave Altizer	150.00	75.00	45.00
423	Larry McLean	150.00	75.00	45.00
424	Mike Mitchell	150.00	75.00	45.00
451	John Hummel	150.00	75.00	45.00
452	Tony Smith	150.00	75.00	45.00
453	Bill Davidson	150.00	75.00	45.00
454	Ed Lennox	150.00	75.00	45.00
455	Zach Wheat	300.00	150.00	90.00
457	Elmer Knetzer	150.00	75.00	45.00
458	Rube Dessau	150.00	75.00	45.00
459	George Bell	150.00	75.00	45.00
460	Jake Daubert	150.00	75.00	45.00
461	Doc Scanlan	150.00	75.00	45.00
462	Nap Rucker	150.00	75.00	45.00
463	Cy Barger	150.00	75.00	45.00
464	Kaiser Wilhelm	150.00	75.00	45.00
465	Bill Bergen	150.00	75.00	45.00
466	Tex Erwin	150.00	75.00	45.00
501	Chief Bender	300.00	150.00	90.00
502	John Coombs	150.00	75.00	45.00
503	Eddie Plank	300.00	150.00	90.00
504	Amos Strunk	150.00	75.00	45.00
505	Connie Mack	450.00	225.00	135.00
506	Ira Thomas	150.00	75.00	45.00
507	Biscoe Lord (Briscoe)	150.00	75.00	45.00
508	Stuffy McInnis	150.00	75.00	45.00
509	Jimmy Dygert	150.00	75.00	45.00
510	Rube Oldring	150.00	75.00	45.00
511	Eddie Collins	300.00	150.00	90.00
512	Home Run Baker	300.00	150.00	90.00
513	Harry Krause	150.00	75.00	45.00
514	Harry Davis	150.00	75.00	45.00
515	Jack Barry	150.00	75.00	45.00
516	Jack Lapp	150.00	75.00	45.00
517	Cy Morgan	150.00	75.00	45.00
518	Danny Murphy	150.00	75.00	45.00
519	Topsy Hartsell	150.00	75.00	45.00
520	Paddy Livingston	150.00	75.00	45.00
521	P. Adkins	150.00	75.00	45.00
522	Eddie Collins	300.00	150.00	90.00
523	Paddy Livingston	150.00	75.00	45.00
551	Doc Gessler	150.00	75.00	45.00
552	Bill Cunningham	150.00	75.00	45.00
554	John Henry	150.00	75.00	45.00
555	Jack Lelivelt	150.00	75.00	45.00
556	Bobby Groome	150.00	75.00	45.00
557	Doc Ralston	150.00	75.00	45.00
558	Kid Elberfelt (Elberfeld)	150.00	75.00	45.00
559	Doc Reisling	150.00	75.00	45.00
560	Herman Schaefer	150.00	75.00	45.00
561	Walter Johnson	700.00	350.00	200.00
562	Dolly Gray	150.00	75.00	45.00
563	Wid Conroy	150.00	75.00	45.00
564	Charley Street	150.00	75.00	45.00
565	Bob Unglaub	150.00	75.00	45.00
566	Clyde Milan	150.00	75.00	45.00
567	George Browne	150.00	75.00	45.00
568	George McBride	150.00	75.00	45.00
569	Red Killifer (Killefer)	150.00	75.00	45.00
601	Addie Joss	300.00	150.00	90.00
602	Addie Joss	300.00	150.00	90.00
603	Napoleon Lajoie	375.00	187.00	112.00
604	Nig Clark (Clarke)	150.00	75.00	45.00
605	Cy Falkenberg	150.00	75.00	45.00
606	Harry Bemis	150.00	75.00	45.00
607	George Stovall	150.00	75.00	45.00
608	Fred Blanding	150.00	75.00	45.00
609	Elmer Koestner	150.00	75.00	45.00
610	Ted Easterly	150.00	75.00	45.00
611	Willie Mitchell	150.00	75.00	45.00
612	Hornhorst	150.00	75.00	45.00
613	Elmer Flick	300.00	150.00	90.00
614	Speck Harkness	150.00	75.00	45.00
615	Tuck Turner	150.00	75.00	45.00
616	Joe Jackson	1500.	750.00	450.00
617	Grover Land	150.00	75.00	45.00
618	Gladstone Graney	150.00	75.00	45.00
619	Dave Callahan	150.00	75.00	45.00
620	Ben DeMott	150.00	75.00	45.00
621	Neill Ball (Neal)	150.00	75.00	45.00
622	Dode Birmingham	150.00	75.00	45.00
623	George Kaler (Kahler)	150.00	75.00	45.00
624	Sid Smith	150.00	75.00	45.00
625	Bert Adams	150.00	75.00	45.00
626	Bill Bradley	150.00	75.00	45.00
627	Napoleon Lajoie	450.00	225.00	135.00
651	Bill Corrigan (Carrigan)	150.00	75.00	45.00
652	Joe Wood	150.00	75.00	45.00
653	Heinie Wagner	150.00	75.00	45.00
654	Billy Purtell	150.00	75.00	45.00
655	Frank Smith	150.00	75.00	45.00
656	Harry Lord	150.00	75.00	45.00
657	Patsy Donovan	150.00	75.00	45.00
658	Duffy Lewis	150.00	75.00	45.00
659	Jack Kleinow	150.00	75.00	45.00
660	Ed Karger	150.00	75.00	45.00
661	Clyde Engle	150.00	75.00	45.00
662	Ben Hunt	150.00	75.00	45.00
663	Charlie Smith	150.00	75.00	45.00
664	Tris Speaker	400.00	200.00	120.00
665	Tom Madden	150.00	75.00	45.00
666	Larry Gardner	150.00	75.00	45.00
667	Harry Hooper	300.00	150.00	90.00
668	Marty McHale	150.00	75.00	45.00
669	Ray Collins	150.00	75.00	45.00
670	Jake Stahl	150.00	75.00	45.00
701	Dave Shean	150.00	75.00	45.00
702	Roy Miller	150.00	75.00	45.00
703	Fred Beck	150.00	75.00	45.00
704	Bill Collings (Collins)	150.00	75.00	45.00
705	Bill Sweeney	150.00	75.00	45.00
706	Buck Herzog	150.00	75.00	45.00
707	Bud Sharp (Sharpe)	150.00	75.00	45.00
708	Cliff Curtis	150.00	75.00	45.00
709	Al Mattern	150.00	75.00	45.00
710	Buster Brown	150.00	75.00	45.00
711	Bill Rariden	150.00	75.00	45.00
712	Grant	150.00	75.00	45.00
713	Ed Abbaticchio	150.00	75.00	45.00
714	Cecil Ferguson	150.00	75.00	45.00
715	Billy Burke	150.00	75.00	45.00
716	Sam Frock	150.00	75.00	45.00
717	Wilbur Goode (Good)	150.00	75.00	45.00
751	Charlie French	150.00	75.00	45.00
752	Patsy Dougherty	150.00	75.00	45.00
753	Shano Collins	150.00	75.00	45.00
754	Fred Parent	150.00	75.00	45.00
755	Willis Cole	150.00	75.00	45.00
756	Billy Sullivan	150.00	75.00	45.00
757	Rube Sutor (Suter)	150.00	75.00	45.00
758	Chick Gandil	150.00	75.00	45.00
759	Jim Scott	150.00	75.00	45.00
760	Ed Walsh	300.00	150.00	90.00
761	Gavvy Cravath	150.00	75.00	45.00
762	Bobby Messenger	150.00	75.00	45.00
763	Doc White	150.00	75.00	45.00
764	Rollie Zeider	150.00	75.00	45.00
765	Fred Payne	150.00	75.00	45.00
766	Lee Tannehill	150.00	75.00	45.00
767	Eddie Hahn	150.00	75.00	45.00
768	Hugh Duffy	300.00	150.00	90.00
769	Fred Olmstead	150.00	75.00	45.00
770	Lena Blackbourne (Blackburne)	150.00	75.00	45.00
771	Young "Cy" Young	150.00	75.00	45.00
801	Lew Brockett	150.00	75.00	45.00
802	Frank Laporte (LaPorte)	150.00	75.00	45.00
803	Bert Daniels	150.00	75.00	45.00
804	Walter Blair	150.00	75.00	45.00
805	Jack Knight	150.00	75.00	45.00
806	Jimmy Austin	150.00	75.00	45.00
807	Hal Chase	175.00	87.00	52.00
808	Birdie Cree	150.00	75.00	45.00
809	Jack Quinn	150.00	75.00	45.00
810	Walter Manning	150.00	75.00	45.00
811	Jack Warhop	150.00	75.00	45.00
812	Jeff Sweeney	150.00	75.00	45.00
813	Charley Hemphill	150.00	75.00	45.00
814	Harry Wolters	150.00	75.00	45.00
815	Tom Hughes	150.00	75.00	45.00
816	Earl Gardiner (Gardner)	150.00	75.00	45.00
851	John Flynn	150.00	75.00	45.00
852	Bill Powell	150.00	75.00	45.00
853	Honus Wagner	1000.	500.00	300.00
854	Bill Powell	150.00	75.00	45.00
855	Fred Clarke	300.00	150.00	90.00
856	Owen Wilson	150.00	75.00	45.00
857	George Gibson	150.00	75.00	45.00
858	Mike Simon	150.00	75.00	45.00
859	Tommy Leach	150.00	75.00	45.00
860	Lefty Leifeld (Leifield)	150.00	75.00	45.00
861	Nick Maddox	150.00	75.00	45.00
862	Dots Miller	150.00	75.00	45.00
863	Howard Camnitz	150.00	75.00	45.00
864	Deacon Phillippi (Phillippe)	150.00	75.00	45.00
865	Babe Adams	150.00	75.00	45.00
866	Ed Abbaticchio	150.00	75.00	45.00
867	Paddy O'Connor	150.00	75.00	45.00
868	Bobby Byrne	150.00	75.00	45.00
869	Vin Campbell	150.00	75.00	45.00
870	Ham Hyatt	150.00	75.00	45.00
871	Sam Leever	150.00	75.00	45.00
872	Hans Wagner	1000.	500.00	300.00
873	Hans Wagner	1000.	500.00	300.00
874	Bill McKecknie (McKechnie)	300.00	150.00	90.00
875	Kirby White	150.00	75.00	45.00
901	Jimmie Burke	150.00	75.00	45.00
902	Charlie Carr	150.00	75.00	45.00
903	Larry Cheney	150.00	75.00	45.00
904	Chet Chadbourne	150.00	75.00	45.00
905	Dan Howley	150.00	75.00	45.00
906	Jimmie Burke	150.00	75.00	45.00
907	Ray Mowe	150.00	75.00	45.00
908	Billy Milligan	150.00	75.00	45.00
909	Frank Oberlin	150.00	75.00	45.00
910	Ralph Glaze	150.00	75.00	45.00
911	O'Day	150.00	75.00	45.00
912	Kerns	150.00	75.00	45.00
913	Jim Duggan	150.00	75.00	45.00
914	Simmy Murch	150.00	75.00	45.00
915	Frank Delehanty	150.00	75.00	45.00
916	Craig	150.00	75.00	45.00
917	Jack Coffee (Coffey)	150.00	75.00	45.00
918	Lefty George	150.00	75.00	45.00
919	Otto Williams	150.00	75.00	45.00
920	M. Hayden	150.00	75.00	45.00
951	Joe Cantillion	150.00	75.00	45.00
952	Smith	150.00	75.00	45.00
953	Claud Rossman (Claude)	150.00	75.00	45.00
1001	Tony James	150.00	75.00	45.00
1002	Jack Powell	150.00	75.00	45.00
1003	Wm. J. Harbeau	150.00	75.00	45.00
1004	Homer Smoot	150.00	75.00	45.00
1051	Bill Friel	150.00	75.00	45.00
1052	Bill Friel	150.00	75.00	45.00
1053	Fred Odwell	150.00	75.00	45.00
1054	Alex Reilley	150.00	75.00	45.00
1055	Eugene Packard	150.00	75.00	45.00
1056	Irve Wrattan	150.00	75.00	45.00
1057	"Red" Nelson	150.00	75.00	45.00
1058	George Perring	150.00	75.00	45.00
1059	Glen Liebhardt	150.00	75.00	45.00
1060	Jimmie O'Rourke	150.00	75.00	45.00
1061	Fred Cook	150.00	75.00	45.00
1062	Charles Arbogast	150.00	75.00	45.00
1063	Jerry Downs	150.00	75.00	45.00
1064	"Bunk" Congalton	150.00	75.00	45.00

	NR MT	EX	VG
1065 Fred Carisch	150.00	75.00	45.00
1066 "Red" Sitton	150.00	75.00	45.00
1067 George Kaler (Kahler)	150.00	75.00	45.00
1068 Arthur Kruger	150.00	75.00	45.00
1102 Earl Yingling	150.00	75.00	45.00
1103 Jerry Freeman	150.00	75.00	45.00
1104 Harry Hinchman	150.00	75.00	45.00
1105 Jim Baskette	150.00	75.00	45.00
1106 Denny Sullivan	150.00	75.00	45.00
1107 Carl Robinson	150.00	75.00	45.00
1108 Bill Rodgers	150.00	75.00	45.00
1109 Hi West	150.00	75.00	45.00
1110 Billy Hallman	150.00	75.00	45.00
1111 Wm. Elwert	150.00	75.00	45.00
1112 Piano Legs Hickman	150.00	75.00	45.00
1113 Joe McCarthy	350.00	175.00	105.00
1114 Fred Abbott	150.00	75.00	45.00
1115 Jack Gilligan	150.00	75.00	45.00

1913 T200 Fatima Team Cards

Issued by the Ligget & Myers Tobacco Co. in 1913 with Fatima brand cigarettes, the T200 set consists of eight National and eight American League team cards. The cards measure 2-5/8" by 4-3/4" and are glossy photographs on paper stock. Although it is unknown why, several of the cards are more difficult to obtain than others. The team cards feature 369 different players, managers and mascots. The card backs contain an offer for an enlarged copy (13" by 21") of a team card, minus the advertising on front, in exchange for 40 Fatima cigarette coupons. These large T200 premiums are very rare and have a value of 12-15 times greater than a common T200 card.

	NR MT	EX	VG
Complete Set:	7500.	3750.	1650.
Common Team:	250.00	125.00	75.00
(1) Boston Nationals	475.00	237.00	142.00
(2) Brooklyn Nationals	250.00	125.00	75.00
(3) Chicago Nationals	250.00	125.00	75.00
(4) Cincinnati Nationals	250.00	125.00	75.00
(5) New York Nationals	350.00	175.00	105.00
(6) Philadelphia Nationals	250.00	125.00	75.00
(7) Pittsburgh Nationals	250.00	125.00	75.00
(8) St. Louis Nationals	475.00	237.00	142.00
(9) Boston Americans	275.00	137.00	83.00
(10) Chicago Americans	300.00	150.00	90.00
(11) Cleveland Americans	500.00	250.00	150.00
(12) Detroit Americans	700.00	350.00	150.00
(13) New York Americans	1200.	600.00	350.00
(14) Philadelphia Americans	250.00	125.00	75.00
(15) St. Louis Americans	1000.	500.00	300.00
(16) Washington Americans	400.00	200.00	80.00

1911 T201 Mecca Double Folders

These cards found in packages of Mecca cigarettes feature one player when the card is open, and another when the card is folded; two players sharing the same pair of legs. Mecca Double Folders measure 2-1/4" by 4-11/16." The fronts are color lithographs with the player's name appearing in black script in the upper left. The backs are printed in red and contain an innovation in the form of player statistics. The 50-card set contains 100 different players including a number of Hall of Famers. The Mecca Double Folders, with two players (Topps "borrowed" the idea in 1955) and statistics, were one of the most innovative series of the tobacco card era.

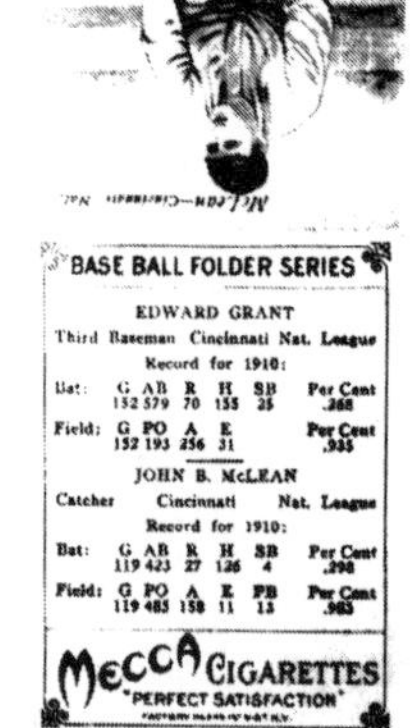

	NR MT	EX	VG
Complete Set:	10000.	5000.	3000.
Common Player:	75.00	37.00	22.00
(1) Abstein, Butler	75.00	37.00	22.00
(2) Baker, Collins	400.00	200.00	125.00
(3) Baker, Downie (Downey)	75.00	37.00	22.00
(4) Barrett, McGlynn	75.00	37.00	22.00
(5) Barry, Lapp	75.00	37.00	22.00
(6) Bender, Oldring	250.00	125.00	75.00
(7) Bergen, Wheat	250.00	125.00	75.00
(8) Blair, Hartzell	75.00	37.00	22.00
(9) Bresnahan, Huggins	500.00	250.00	150.00
(10) Bridwell, Matthewson (Mathewson)	750.00	375.00	230.00
(11) Brown, Hofman	250.00	125.00	75.00
(12) Byrne, Clarke	200.00	100.00	60.00
(13) Chance, Evers	450.00	225.00	135.00
(14) Chase, Sweeney	125.00	62.00	37.00
(15) Cicotte, Thoney	100.00	50.00	30.00
(16) Clarke, Gaspar	75.00	37.00	22.00
(17) Cobb, Crawford	2500.	1250.	750.00
(18) Cole, Kling	75.00	37.00	22.00
(19) Coombs, Thomas	75.00	37.00	22.00
(20) Daubert, Rucker	100.00	50.00	30.00
(21) Donovan, Stroud	75.00	37.00	22.00
(22) Dooin, Titus	75.00	37.00	22.00
(23) Dougherty, Lord	400.00	200.00	125.00
(24) Downs, Odwell	75.00	37.00	22.00
(25) Doyle, Meyers	75.00	37.00	22.00
(26) Dygert, Seymour	75.00	37.00	22.00
(27) Elberfeld, McBride	75.00	37.00	22.00
(28) Falkenberg, Lajoie	500.00	250.00	150.00
(29) Fitzpatrick, Killian	75.00	37.00	22.00
(30) Ford, Johnson	75.00	37.00	22.00
(31) Foster, Ward	75.00	37.00	22.00
(32) Gardner, Speaker	150.00	75.00	45.00
(33) Gibson, Leach	75.00	37.00	22.00
(34) Graham, Mattern	75.00	37.00	22.00
(35) Grant, McLean	75.00	37.00	22.00
(36) Hauser, Lush	75.00	37.00	22.00
(37) Herzog, Miller	75.00	37.00	22.00
(38) Hickman, Hinchman	75.00	37.00	22.00
(39) Jennings, Summers	250.00	125.00	75.00
(40) Johnson, Street	750.00	375.00	230.00
(41) LaPorte, Stephens	75.00	37.00	22.00
(42) Lake, Wallace	200.00	100.00	60.00
(43) Leifield, Simon	75.00	37.00	22.00
(44) Lobert, Moore	75.00	37.00	22.00
(45) McCabe, Starr	75.00	37.00	22.00
(46) McCarty, McGinnity	200.00	100.00	60.00
(47) Merkle, Wiltse	100.00	50.00	30.00
(48) Payne, Walsh	250.00	125.00	75.00
(49) Stovall, Turner	75.00	37.00	22.00
(50) Williams, Woodruff	75.00	37.00	22.00

1912 T202 Hassan Triple Folders

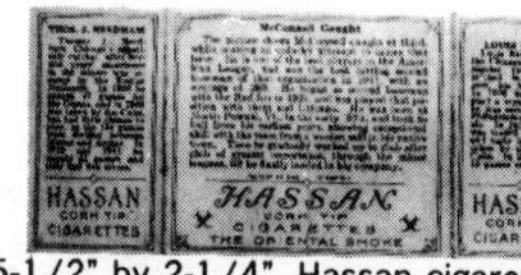

Measuring 5-1/2" by 2-1/4", Hassan cigarette cards carried the concept of multiple-player cards even further than the innovative Mecca set of the previous year. Scored so that the two end cards - which are full-color and very close to exact duplicates of T205 "Gold Borders" - can fold over the black and white center panel, the Hassan Triple Folder appears like a booklet when closed. The two end cards are individual player cards, while the larger center panel contains an action scene. Usually the two player cards are not related to the action scene. The unique Hassan Triple Folders feature player biographies on the back of the two individual cards with a description of the action on the back of the center panel. Values depend on the player featured in the center panel, as well as the players featured on the end cards.

	NR MT	EX	VG
Complete Set of 132:	50000.	25000.	15000.
Common Player:	175.00	87.00	52.00
(1a) A Close Play At The Home Plate (LaPorte, Wallace)	250.00	125.00	75.00
(1b) A Close Play At The Home Plate (Pelty, Wallace)	250.00	125.00	75.00
(2) A Desperate Slide For Third (Ty Cobb, O'Leary)	2500.	1250.	750.00
(3a) A Great Batsman (Barger, Bergen)	175.00	87.00	52.00
(3b) A Great Batsman (Bergen, Rucker)	175.00	87.00	52.00
(4) Ambrose McConnell At Bat (Blair, Quinn)	175.00	87.00	52.00
(5) A Wide Throw Saves Crawford (Mullin, Stanage)	175.00	87.00	52.00
(6) Baker Gets His Man (Baker, Collins)	500.00	250.00	150.00
(7) Birmingham Gets To Third (Johnson, Street)	750.00	375.00	225.00
(8) Birmingham's Home Run (Birmingham, Turner)	800.00	400.00	250.00
(9) Bush Just Misses Austin (Magee, Moran)	175.00	87.00	52.00
(10a) Carrigan Blocks His Man (Gaspar, McLean)	175.00	87.00	52.00
(10b) Carrigan Blocks His Man (Carrigan, Wagner)	175.00	87.00	52.00
(11) Catching Him Napping (Bresnahan, Oakes)	400.00	200.00	120.00
(12) Caught Asleep Off First (Bresnahan, Harmon)	400.00	200.00	120.00
(13a) Chance Beats Out A Hit (Chance, Foxen)	400.00	200.00	120.00
(13b) Chance Beats Out A Hit (Archer, McIntyre)	175.00	87.00	52.00
(13c) Chance Beats Out A Hit (Archer, Overall)	175.00	87.00	52.00
(13d) Chance Beats Out A Hit (Archer, Rowan)	175.00	87.00	52.00
(13e) Chance Beats Out A Hit (Chance, Shean)	400.00	200.00	120.00
(14a) Chase Dives Into Third (Chase, Wolter)	175.00	87.00	52.00
(14b) Chase Dives Into Third (Clarke, Gibson)	250.00	125.00	75.00
(14c) Chase Dives Into Third (Gibson, Phillippe)	175.00	87.00	52.00
(15a) Chase Gets Ball Too Late (Egan, Mitchell)	175.00	87.00	52.00
(15b) Chase Gets Ball Too Late (Chase, Wolter)	175.00	87.00	52.00
(16a) Chase Guarding First (Chase, Wolter)	175.00	87.00	52.00
(16b) Chase Guarding First (Clarke, Gibson)	250.00	125.00	75.00
(16c) Chase Guarding First (Gibson, Leifield)	175.00	87.00	52.00
(17) Chase Ready For The Squeeze Play (Magee, Paskert)	175.00	87.00	52.00
(18) Chase Safe At Third (Baker, Barry)	400.00	200.00	120.00
(19) Chief Bender Waiting For A Good One (Bender, Thomas)	400.00	200.00	120.00
(20) Clarke Hikes For Home (Bridwell, Kling)	175.00	87.00	52.00
(21) Close At First (Ball, Stovall)	175.00	87.00	52.00
(22a) Close At The Plate (Payne, Walsh)	400.00	200.00	120.00
(22b) Close At The Plate (Payne, White)	175.00	87.00	52.00
(23) Close At Third - Speaker (Speaker, Wood)	500.00	250.00	150.00
(24) Close At Third - Wagner (Carrigan, Wagner)	175.00	87.00	52.00
(25a) Collins Easily Safe (Byrne, Clarke)	300.00	150.00	90.00
(25b) Collins Easily Safe (Baker, Collins)	500.00	250.00	150.00
(25c) Collins Easily Safe (Collins, Murphy)	400.00	200.00	120.00
(26) Crawford About To Smash One (Stanage, Summers)	175.00	87.00	52.00
(27) Cree Rolls Home (Daubert, Hummel)	175.00	87.00	52.00
(28) Davy Jones' Great Slide (Delahanty, Jones)	175.00	87.00	52.00
(29a) Devlin Gets His Man (Devlin (Giants), Mathewson)	1000.	500.00	300.00
(29b) Devlin Gets His Man (Devlin (Rustlers), Mathewson)	650.00	325.00	200.00
(29c) Devlin Gets His Man (Fletcher, Mathewson)	650.00	325.00	200.00
(29d) Devlin Gets His Man (Mathewson, Meyers)	650.00	325.00	200.00
(30a) Donlin Out At First (Camnitz, Gibson)	175.00	87.00	52.00
(30b) Donlin Out At First (Doyle, Merlke)	175.00	87.00	52.00
(30c) Donlin Out At First (Leach, Wilson)	175.00	87.00	52.00
(30d) Donlin Out At First (Dooin, Magee)	175.00	87.00	52.00
(30e) Donlin Out At First (Gibson, Phillippe)	175.00	87.00	52.00
(31a) Dooin Gets His Man (Dooin, Doolan)	175.00	87.00	52.00
(31b) Dooin Gets His Man (Dooin, Lobert)	175.00	87.00	52.00
(31c) Dooin Gets His Man (Dooin, Titus)	175.00	87.00	52.00
(32) Easy For Larry (Doyle, Merlke)	175.00	87.00	52.00
(33) Elberfeld Beats The Throw (Elberfeld, Milan)	175.00	87.00	52.00

		NR MT	EX	VG
(34)	Elberfeld Gets His Man (Elberfeld, Milan)	175.00	87.00	52.00
(35)	Engle In A Close Play (Engle, Speaker)	450.00	225.00	135.00
(36a)	Evers Makes A Safe Slide (Archer, Evers)	400.00	200.00	120.00
(36b)	Evers Makes A Safe Slide (Chance, Evers)	500.00	250.00	150.00
(36c)	Evers Makes A Safe Slide (Archer, Overall)	175.00	87.00	52.00
(36d)	Evers Makes A Safe Slide (Archer, Reulbach)	175.00	87.00	52.00
(36e)	Evers Makes A Safe Slide (Chance, Tinker)	550.00	275.00	165.00
(37)	Fast Work At Third (Cobb, O'Leary)	2500.	1250.	750.00
(38a)	Ford Putting Over A Spitter (Ford, Vaughn)	175.00	87.00	52.00
(38b)	Ford Putting Over A Spitter (Sweeney, Ford)	175.00	87.00	52.00
(39)	Good Play At Third (Cobb, Moriarity)	2500.	1250.	750.00
(40)	Grant Gets His Man (Grant, Hoblitzell)	175.00	87.00	52.00
(41a)	Hal Chase Too Late (McConnell, McIntyre)	175.00	87.00	52.00
(41b)	Hal Chase Too Late (McLean, Suggs)	175.00	87.00	52.00
(42)	Harry Lord At Third (Lennox, Tinker)	150.00	75.00	45.00
(43)	Hartzell Covering Third (Dahlen, Scanlan)	175.00	87.00	52.00
(44)	Hartsel Strikes Out (Gray, Groom)	175.00	87.00	52.00
(45)	Held At Third (Lord, Tannehill)	175.00	87.00	52.00
(46)	Jake Stahl Guarding First (Cicotte, Stahl)	175.00	87.00	52.00
(47)	Jim Delahanty At Bat (Delahanty, Jones)	175.00	87.00	52.00
(48a)	Just Before The Battle (Ames, Meyers)	175.00	87.00	52.00
(48b)	Just Before The Battle (Bresnahan, McGraw)	500.00	250.00	150.00
(48c)	Just Before The Battle (Crandall, Meyers)	175.00	87.00	52.00
(48d)	Just Before The Battle (Becker, Devore)	175.00	87.00	52.00
(48e)	Just Before The Battle (Fletcher, Mathewson)	650.00	325.00	200.00
(48f)	Just Before The Battle (Marquard, Meyers)	400.00	200.00	120.00
(48g)	Just Before The Battle (Jennings, McGraw)	550.00	275.00	165.00
(48h)	Just Before The Battle (Mathewson, Meyers)	650.00	325.00	200.00
(48i)	Just Before The Battle (Murray, Snodgrass)	175.00	87.00	52.00
(48j)	Just Before The Battle (Meyers, Wiltse)	175.00	87.00	52.00
(49)	Knight Catches A Runner (Johnson, Knight)	750.00	375.00	225.00
(50a)	Lobert Almost Caught (Bridwell, Kling)	175.00	87.00	52.00
(50b)	Lobert Almost Caught (Kling, Young)	550.00	275.00	165.00
(50c)	Lobert Almost Caught (Kling, Mattern)	175.00	87.00	52.00
(50d)	Lobert Almost Caught (Kling, Steinfeldt)	175.00	87.00	52.00
(51)	Lobert Gets Tenney (Dooin, Lobert)	175.00	87.00	52.00
(52)	Lord Catches His Man (Lord, Tannehil)	175.00	87.00	52.00
(53)	McConnell Caught (Needham, Richie)	175.00	87.00	52.00
(54)	McIntyre At Bat (McConnell, McIntyre)	175.00	87.00	52.00
(55)	Moriarty Spiked (Stanage, Willett)	175.00	87.00	52.00
(56)	Nearly Caught (Bates, Bescher)	175.00	87.00	52.00
(57)	Oldring Almost Home (Lord, Oldring)	175.00	87.00	52.00
(58)	Schaefer On First (McBride, Milan)	175.00	87.00	52.00
(59)	Schaefer Steals Second (Clark Griffith, McBride)	400.00	200.00	120.00
(60)	Scoring From Second (Lord, Oldring)	175.00	87.00	52.00
(61a)	Scrambling Back To First (Barger, Bergen)	175.00	87.00	52.00
(61b)	Scrambling Back To First (Chase, Wolter)	175.00	87.00	52.00
(62)	Speaker Almost Caught (Clarke, Miller)	300.00	150.00	90.00
(63)	Speaker Rounding Third (Speaker, Wood)	500.00	250.00	150.00
(64)	Speaker Scores (Engle, Speaker)	500.00	250.00	150.00
(65)	Stahl Safe (Austin, Stovall)	175.00	87.00	52.00
(66)	Stone About To Swing (Schulte, Sheckard)	175.00	87.00	52.00
(67a)	Sullivan Puts Up A High One (Evans, Huggins)	400.00	200.00	125.00
(67b)	Sullivan Puts Up A High One (Gray, Groom)	175.00	87.00	52.00
(68a)	Sweeney Gets Stahl (Ford, Vaughn)	175.00	87.00	52.00
(68b)	Sweeney Gets Stahl (Ford, Sweeney)	175.00	87.00	52.00
(69)	Tenney Lands Safely (Latham, Raymond)	175.00	87.00	52.00
(70a)	The Athletic Infield (Baker, Barry)	400.00	200.00	125.00
(70b)	The Athletic Infield (Brown, Graham)	400.00	200.00	125.00
(70c)	The Athletic Infield (Hauser, Konetchy)	150.00	75.00	45.00
(70d)	The Athletic Infield (Krause, Thomas)	175.00	87.00	52.00
(71)	The Pinch Hitter (Egan, Hoblitzell)	175.00	87.00	52.00
(72)	The Scissors Slide (Birmingham, Turner)	175.00	87.00	52.00
(73a)	Tom Jones At Bat (Fromme, McLean)	175.00	87.00	52.00
(73b)	Tom Jones At Bat (Gaspar, McLean)	175.00	87.00	52.00
(74a)	Too Late For Devlin (Ames, Meyers)	175.00	87.00	52.00
(74b)	Too Late For Devlin (Crandall, Meyers)	175.00	87.00	52.00
(74c)	Too Late For Devlin (Devlin (Giants), Mathewson)	850.00	425.00	265.00
(74d)	Too Late For Devlin (Devlin (Rustlers), Mathewson)	650.00	325.00	200.00
(74e)	Too Late For Devlin (Marquard, Meyers)	400.00	200.00	120.00
(74f)	Too Late For Devlin (Meyers, Wiltse)	175.00	87.00	52.00
(75a)	Ty Cobb Steals Third (Cobb, Jennings)	3000.	1500.	900.00
(75b)	Ty Cobb Steals Third (Cobb, Moriarty)	2500.	1250.	750.00
(75c)	Ty Cobb Steals Third (Austin, Stovall)	1200.	600.00	350.00
(76)	Wheat Strikes Out (Dahlen, Wheat)	450.00	225.00	135.00

1900 T203 Baseball Comics

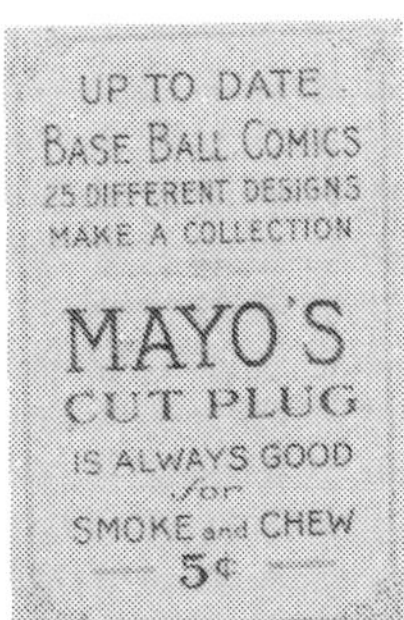

As their name implies, the T203 Baseball Comics feature cartoon-like drawings that illustrate various baseball phrases and terminology. Issued with Winner Cut Plug and Mayo Cut Plug tobacco products, the complete setconsists of 25 different comics, each measuring approximately 2-1/16" by 3 1/8". Because they do not picture individual players, these cards have never attracted much of a following among serious baseball card collectors. They do, however, hold some interest as a novelty item of the period.

		NR MT	EX	VG
	Complete Set:	900.00	450.00	270.00
	Common Player:	25.00	12.50	7.50
(1)	"A Crack Outfielder"	25.00	12.50	7.50
(2)	"A Fancy Twirler"	25.00	12.50	7.50
(3)	"A Fine Slide"	25.00	12.50	7.50
(4)	"A Fowl Bawl"	25.00	12.50	7.50
(5)	"A Great Game"	25.00	12.50	7.50
(6)	"A Home Run"	25.00	12.50	7.50
(7)	"An All Star Battery"	25.00	12.50	7.50
(8)	"A Short Stop"	25.00	12.50	7.50
(9)	"A Star Catcher"	25.00	12.50	7.50
(10)	"A White Wash"	25.00	12.50	7.50
(11)	"A Tie Game"	25.00	12.50	7.50
(12)	"A Two Bagger"	25.00	12.50	7.50
(13)	"A Wild Pitch"	25.00	12.50	7.50
(14)	"Caught Napping"	25.00	12.50	7.50
(15)	"On To The Curves"	25.00	12.50	7.50
(16)	"Out"	25.00	12.50	7.50
(17)	"Put Out On 1st"	25.00	12.50	7.50
(18)	"Right Over The Plate"	25.00	12.50	7.50
(19)	"Rooting For The Home Team"	25.00	12.50	7.50
(20)	"Stealing A Base"	25.00	12.50	7.50
(21)	"Stealing Home"	25.00	12.50	7.50
(22)	"Strike One"	25.00	12.50	7.50
(23)	"The Bleacher"	25.00	12.50	7.50
(24)	"The Naps"	25.00	12.50	7.50
(25)	"The Red Sox"	25.00	12.50	7.50

The values quoted are intended to reflect the market price.

1909 T204 Ramly

While issued with both Ramly and T.T.T. brand Turkish tobacco cigarettes, the 121 cards in this set take their name from the more common of the two brands. By any name, the set is one of the more interesting and attractive of the early 20th Century. The 2-1/2" by 2-1/2" cards carry black and white oval photographic portraits with impressive gold embossed frames and borders on the front. Toward the bottom appears the player's last name, position, team and league. The backs carry only the most basic information on the cigarette company. Due to their scarcity, the Ramly set is not widely collected. The complete set price does not include the scarce variations.

		NR MT	EX	VG
	Complete Set:	60000.	30000.	18000.
	Common Player:	300.00	150.00	90.00
(1)	Whitey Alperman	300.00	150.00	90.00
(2)	John Anderson	300.00	150.00	90.00
(3)	Jimmy Archer	300.00	150.00	90.00
(4)	Frank Arrelanes (Arellanes)	300.00	150.00	90.00
(5)	Jim Ball	300.00	150.00	90.00
(6)	Neal Ball	300.00	150.00	90.00
(7a)	Frank C. Bancroft (photo inside oval frame)	300.00	150.00	90.00
(7b)	Frank C. Bancroft (photo inside square frame)	1200.	600.00	350.00
(8)	Johnny Bates	300.00	150.00	90.00
(9)	Fred Beebe	300.00	150.00	90.00
(10)	George Bell	300.00	150.00	90.00
(11)	Chief Bender	1400.	700.00	375.00
(12)	Walter Blair	300.00	150.00	90.00
(13)	Cliff Blankenship	300.00	150.00	90.00
(14)	Frank Bowerman	300.00	150.00	90.00
(15a)	Wm. Bransfield (photo inside oval frame)	300.00	150.00	90.00
(15b)	Wm. Bransfield (photo inside square frame)	1750.	875.00	525.00
(16)	Roger Bresnahan	600.00	300.00	180.00
(17)	Al Bridwell	300.00	150.00	90.00
(18)	Mordecai Brown	1400.	700.00	400.00
(19)	Fred Burchell	300.00	150.00	90.00
(20a)	Jesse C. Burkett (photo inside oval frame)	1200.	600.00	350.00
(20b)	Jesse C. Burkett (photo inside square frame)	2000.	1000.	600.00
(21)	Bobby Byrnes (Byrne)	300.00	150.00	90.00
(22)	Bill Carrigan	300.00	150.00	90.00
(23)	Frank Chance	1500.	750.00	450.00
(24)	Charlie Chech	300.00	150.00	90.00
(25)	Ed Cicolte (Cicotte)	400.00	200.00	125.00
(26)	Bill Clymer	300.00	150.00	90.00
(27)	Andy Coakley	300.00	150.00	90.00
(28)	Jimmy Collins	1300.	650.00	375.00
(29)	Ed. Collins	2000.	1000.	600.00
(30)	Wid Conroy	300.00	150.00	90.00
(31)	Jack Coombs	300.00	150.00	90.00
(32)	Doc Crandall	300.00	150.00	90.00
(33)	Lou Criger	300.00	150.00	90.00
(34)	Harry Davis	300.00	150.00	90.00
(35)	Art Devlin	300.00	150.00	90.00
(36a)	Wm. H. Dineen (Dinneen) (photo inside oval frame)	300.00	150.00	90.00
(36b)	Wm. H. Dineen (Dinneen) (photo inside square frame)	1000.	500.00	300.00
(37)	Jiggs Donahue	300.00	150.00	90.00
(38)	Mike Donlin	300.00	150.00	90.00
(39)	Wild Bill Donovan	300.00	150.00	90.00
(40)	Gus Dorner	300.00	150.00	90.00
(41)	Joe Dunn	300.00	150.00	90.00
(42)	Kid Elberfield (Elberfeld)	300.00	150.00	90.00
(43)	Johnny Evers	1400.	700.00	400.00
(44)	Bob Ewing	300.00	150.00	90.00
(45)	Cecil Ferguson	300.00	150.00	90.00
(46)	Hobe Ferris	300.00	150.00	90.00
(47)	Jerry Freeman	300.00	150.00	90.00
(48)	Art Fromme	300.00	150.00	90.00
(49)	Bob Ganley	300.00	150.00	90.00
(50)	Doc Gessler	300.00	150.00	90.00
(51)	Peaches Graham	300.00	150.00	90.00
(52)	Clark Griffith	1200.	600.00	350.00
(53)	Roy Hartzell	300.00	150.00	90.00
(54)	Charlie Hemphill	300.00	150.00	90.00
(55)	Dick Hoblitzel (Hoblitzell)	300.00	150.00	90.00
(56)	Geo. Howard	300.00	150.00	90.00
(57)	Harry Howell	300.00	150.00	90.00
(58)	Miller Huggins	1400.	700.00	400.00
(59)	John Hummell (Hummel)	300.00	150.00	90.00
(60)	Walter Johnson	3500.	1750.	850.00
(61)	Thos. Jones	300.00	150.00	90.00
(62)	Mike Kahoe	300.00	150.00	90.00
(63)	Ed Kargar	300.00	150.00	90.00
(64)	Wee Willie Keeler	2000.	1000.	600.00
(65)	Red Kleinon (Kleinow)	300.00	150.00	90.00
(66)	Jack Knight	300.00	150.00	90.00
(67)	Ed Konetchey (Konetchy)	300.00	150.00	90.00
(68)	Vive Lindaman	300.00	150.00	90.00
(69)	Hans Loebert (Lobert)	300.00	150.00	90.00
(70)	Harry Lord	300.00	150.00	90.00
(71)	Harry Lumley	300.00	150.00	90.00
(72)	Johnny Lush	300.00	150.00	90.00
(73)	Rube Manning	300.00	150.00	90.00
(74)	Jimmy McAleer	300.00	150.00	90.00
(75)	Amby McConnell	300.00	150.00	90.00
(76)	Moose McCormick	300.00	150.00	90.00
(77)	Harry McIntyre	300.00	150.00	90.00
(78)	Larry McLean	300.00	150.00	90.00
(79)	Fred Merkle	300.00	150.00	90.00

	NR MT	EX	VG
(80) Clyde Milan	300.00	150.00	90.00
(81) Mike Mitchell	300.00	150.00	90.00
(82a) Pat Moran (photo inside oval frame)	300.00	150.00	90.00
(82b) Pat Moran (photo inside square frame)	500.00	250.00	150.00
(83) Cy Morgan	300.00	150.00	90.00
(84) Tim Murname (Murnane)	300.00	150.00	90.00
(85) Danny Murphy	300.00	150.00	90.00
(86) Red Murray	300.00	150.00	90.00
(87) Doc Newton	300.00	150.00	90.00
(88) Simon Nichols (Nicholls)	300.00	150.00	90.00
(89) Harry Niles	300.00	150.00	90.00
(90) Bill O'Hare (O'Hara)	300.00	150.00	90.00
(91) Charley O'Leary	300.00	150.00	90.00
(92) Dode Paskert	300.00	150.00	90.00
(93) Barney Pelty	300.00	150.00	90.00
(94) Jake Pfeister	300.00	150.00	90.00
(95) Ed Plank	2250.	1125.	675.00
(96) Jack Powell	300.00	150.00	90.00
(97) Bugs Raymond	300.00	150.00	90.00
(98) Tom Reilly	300.00	150.00	90.00
(99) Claude Ritchey	300.00	150.00	90.00
(100) Nap Rucker	300.00	150.00	90.00
(101) Ed Ruelbach (Reulbach)	300.00	150.00	90.00
(102) Slim Sallee	300.00	150.00	90.00
(103) Germany Schaefer	300.00	150.00	90.00
(104) Jimmy Schekard (Sheckard)	300.00	150.00	90.00
(105) Admiral Schlei	300.00	150.00	90.00
(106) Wildfire Schulte	300.00	150.00	90.00
(107) Jimmy Sebring	300.00	150.00	90.00
(108) Bill Shipke	300.00	150.00	90.00
(109) Charlie Smith	300.00	150.00	90.00
(110) Tubby Spencer	300.00	150.00	90.00
(111) Jake Stahl	300.00	150.00	90.00
(112) Jim Stephens	300.00	150.00	90.00
(113) Harry Stienfeldt (Steinfeldt)	300.00	150.00	90.00
(114) Gabby Street	300.00	150.00	90.00
(115) Bill Sweeney	300.00	150.00	90.00
(116) Fred Tenney	300.00	150.00	90.00
(117) Ira Thomas	300.00	150.00	90.00
(118) Joe Tinker	1500.	750.00	450.00
(119) Bob Unclane (Unglaub)	300.00	150.00	90.00
(120) Heinie Wagner	300.00	150.00	90.00
(121) Bobby Wallace	1200.	600.00	350.00

1911 T205 Gold Border

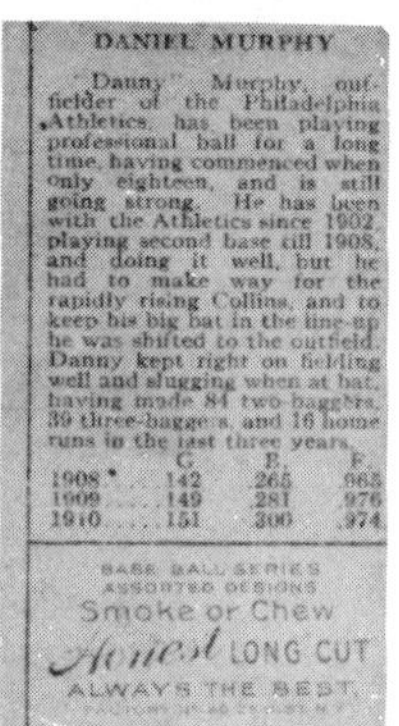

Taking their hobby nickname from their border color, these cards were issued in a number of different cigarette brands. The cards measure 1-1/2" by 2-5/8". American League cards feature a color lithograph of the player inside a stylized baseball diamond. National League cards have head- and-shoulders portraits and a plain background, plus the first ever use of a facsimile autograph in a major card set. The 12 minor league players in the set feature three-quarter length portraits or action pictures in an elaborate frame of columns and other devices. Card backs of the major leaguers carry the player's full name (a first) and statistics. Card backs of the minor leaguers lack the statistics. The complete set price does not include the scarcer variations.

	NR MT	EX	VG
Complete Set:	65000.	32500.	20000.
Common Player:	100.00	50.00	30.00
(1) Edward J. Abbaticchio	100.00	50.00	30.00
(2) Doc Adkins	375.00	150.00	90.00
(3) Leon K. Ames	100.00	50.00	30.00
(4) Jas. P. Archer	100.00	50.00	30.00
(5) Jimmy Austin	100.00	50.00	30.00
(6) Bill Bailey	100.00	50.00	30.00
(7) Home Run Baker	500.00	250.00	150.00
(8) Neal Ball	600.00	50.00	30.00
(9) E.B. Barger (full "B" on cap)	100.00	50.00	30.00
(10) E.B. Barger (partial "B" on cap)	500.00	175.00	105.00
(11) Jack Barry	100.00	50.00	30.00
(12) Emil Batch	375.00	150.00	90.00
(13) John W. Bates	100.00	50.00	30.00
(14) Fred Beck	100.00	50.00	30.00
(15) B. Becker	100.00	50.00	30.00
(16) George G. Bell	100.00	50.00	30.00
(17) Chas. Bender	600.00	250.00	150.00
(18) William Bergen	100.00	50.00	30.00
(19) Bob Bescher	100.00	50.00	30.00
(20) Joe Birmingham	100.00	50.00	30.00
(21) Lena Blackburne	100.00	50.00	30.00
(22) William E. Bransfield	100.00	50.00	30.00
(23) Roger P. Bresnahan (mouth closed)	600.00	250.00	150.00
(24) Roger P. Bresnahan (mouth open)	750.00	300.00	180.00
(25) A.H. Bridwell	100.00	50.00	30.00
(26) Mordecai Brown	600.00	250.00	150.00
(27) Robert Byrne	100.00	50.00	30.00
(28) Hick Cady	375.00	150.00	90.00
(29) H. Camnitz	100.00	50.00	30.00
(30) Bill Carrigan	100.00	50.00	30.00
(31) Frank J. Chance	600.00	250.00	150.00
(32a) Hal Chase (both ears show, gold diamond frame extends below shoulders)	200.00	100.00	60.00
(32b) Hal Chase (both ears show, gold diamond frame ends at shoulders)	200.00	100.00	60.00
(33) Hal Chase (only left ear shows)	650.00	275.00	165.00
(34) Ed Cicotte	150.00	75.00	45.00
(35) Fred C. Clarke	350.00	137.00	82.00
(36) Ty Cobb	4000.	1725.	625.00
(37) Eddie Collins (mouth closed)	600.00	175.00	105.00
(38) Eddie Collins (mouth open)	750.00	250.00	150.00
(39) Jimmy Collins	600.00	250.00	150.00
(40) Frank J. Corridon	100.00	50.00	30.00
(41a) Otis Crandall ("t" not crossed in name)	100.00	50.00	30.00
(41b) Otis Crandall ("t" crossed in name)	100.00	50.00	30.00
(42) Lou Criger	100.00	50.00	30.00
(43) W.F. Dahlen	325.00	137.00	82.00
(44) Jake Daubert	125.00	55.00	33.00
(45) Jim Delahanty	100.00	50.00	30.00
(46) Arthur Devlin	100.00	50.00	30.00
(47) Josh Devore	100.00	50.00	30.00
(48) W.R. Dickson	100.00	50.00	30.00
(49) Jiggs Donohue (Donahue)	500.00	250.00	150.00
(50) Chas. S. Dooin	100.00	50.00	30.00
(51) Michael J. Doolan	100.00	50.00	30.00
(52a) Patsy Dougherty (red sock for team emblem)	100.00	50.00	30.00
(52b) Patsy Dougherty (white sock for team emblem)	350.00	175.00	105.00
(53) Thomas Downey	100.00	50.00	30.00
(54) Larry Doyle	100.00	50.00	30.00
(55) Hugh Duffy	600.00	250.00	150.00
(56) Jack Dunn	375.00	150.00	90.00
(57) Jimmy Dygert	100.00	50.00	30.00
(58) R. Egan	100.00	50.00	30.00
(59) Kid Elberfeld	100.00	50.00	30.00
(60) Clyde Engle	100.00	50.00	30.00
(61) Louis Evans	100.00	50.00	30.00
(62) John J. Evers	500.00	200.00	120.00
(63) Robert Ewing	100.00	50.00	30.00
(64) G.C. Ferguson	100.00	50.00	30.00
(65) Ray Fisher	450.00	175.00	105.00
(66) Arthur Fletcher	100.00	50.00	30.00
(67) John A. Flynn	100.00	50.00	30.00
(68) Russ Ford (black cap)	100.00	50.00	30.00
(69) Russ Ford (white cap)	450.00	175.00	105.00
(70) Wm. A. Foxen	100.00	50.00	30.00
(71) Jimmy Frick	375.00	150.00	90.00
(72) Arthur Fromme	100.00	50.00	30.00
(73) Earl Gardner	100.00	50.00	30.00
(74) H.L. Gaspar	100.00	50.00	30.00
(75) George Gibson	100.00	50.00	30.00
(76) Wilbur Goode	100.00	50.00	30.00
(77) George F. Graham (Rustlers)	100.00	50.00	30.00
(78) George F. Graham (Cubs)	500.00	250.00	150.00
(79) Edward L. Grant	450.00	200.00	120.00
(80a) Dolly Gray (no stats on back)	100.00	50.00	30.00
(80b) Dolly Gray (stats on back)	275.00	137.00	82.00
(81) Clark Griffith	500.00	250.00	150.00
(82) Bob Groom	100.00	50.00	30.00
(83) Charlie Hanford	375.00	150.00	90.00
(84) Bob Harmon (both ears show)	100.00	50.00	30.00
(85) Bob Harmon (only left ear shows)	500.00	250.00	150.00
(86) Topsy Hartsel	100.00	50.00	30.00
(87) Arnold J. Hauser	100.00	50.00	30.00
(88) Charlie Hemphill	100.00	50.00	30.00
(89) C.L. Herzog	100.00	50.00	30.00
(90a) R. Hoblitzell (no stats on back)	600.00	300.00	180.00
(90b) R. Hoblitzell ("Cin." after 2nd 1908 in stats)	300.00	150.00	90.00
(90c) R. Hoblitzel (name incorrect, no "Cin." after 1908 in stats)	100.00	50.00	30.00
(90d) R. Hoblitzell (name correct, no "Cin." after 1908 in stats)	300.00	150.00	90.00
(91) Danny Hoffman	100.00	50.00	30.00
(92) Miller J. Huggins	450.00	225.00	135.00
(93) John E. Hummel	100.00	50.00	30.00
(94) Fred Jacklitsch	100.00	50.00	30.00
(95) Hughie Jennings	600.00	250.00	150.00
(96) Walter Johnson	2000.	900.00	400.00
(97) D. Jones	100.00	50.00	30.00
(98) Tom Jones	100.00	50.00	30.00
(99) Addie Joss	800.00	300.00	180.00
(100) Ed Karger	375.00	137.00	82.00
(101) Ed Killian	100.00	50.00	30.00
(102) Red Kleinow	375.00	137.00	82.00
(103) John G. Kling	100.00	50.00	30.00
(104) Jack Knight	100.00	50.00	30.00
(105) Ed Konetchy	100.00	50.00	30.00
(106) Harry Krause	100.00	50.00	30.00
(107) Floyd M. Kroh	100.00	50.00	30.00
(108) Frank LaPorte	100.00	50.00	30.00
(109) Frank Lang (Lange)	100.00	50.00	30.00
(110a) A. Latham (A. Latham on back)	100.00	50.00	30.00
(110b) A. Latham (W.A. Latham on back)	100.00	50.00	30.00
(111) Thomas W. Leach	100.00	50.00	30.00
(112) Watty Lee	375.00	150.00	90.00
(113) Sam Leever	100.00	50.00	30.00
(114a) A. Leifield (initial "A." on front)	100.00	50.00	30.00
(114b) A.P. Leifield (initials "A.P." on front)	100.00	50.00	30.00
(115) Edgar Lennox	100.00	50.00	30.00
(116) Paddy Livingston	100.00	50.00	30.00
(117) John B. Lobert	100.00	50.00	30.00
(118) Bris Lord (Athletics)	100.00	50.00	30.00
(119) Harry Lord (White Sox)	100.00	50.00	30.00
(120) Jno. C. Lush	100.00	50.00	30.00
(121) Nick Maddox	100.00	50.00	30.00
(122) Sherwood R. Magee	110.00	55.00	33.00
(123) R.W. Marquard	550.00	200.00	120.00
(124) C. Mathewson	1050.	400.00	137.00
(125) A.A. Mattern	100.00	50.00	30.00
(126) Sport McAllister	375.00	150.00	90.00
(127) George McBride	100.00	50.00	30.00
(128) Amby McConnell	100.00	50.00	30.00
(129) P.M. McElveen	100.00	50.00	30.00
(130) J.J. McGraw	600.00	250.00	150.00
(131) Harry McIntyre (Cubs)	100.00	50.00	30.00
(132) Matty McIntyre (White Sox)	100.00	50.00	30.00
(133) M.A. McLean (initials actually J.B.)	100.00	50.00	30.00
(134) Fred Merkle	125.00	55.00	33.00
(135) George Merritt	375.00	150.00	90.00
(136) J.T. Meyers	100.00	50.00	30.00
(137) Clyde Milan	100.00	50.00	30.00
(138) J.D. Miller	100.00	50.00	30.00
(139) M.F. Mitchell	100.00	50.00	30.00
(140a) P.J. Moran (stray line of type below stats)	100.00	50.00	30.00
(140b) P.J. Moran (no stray line)	100.00	50.00	30.00
(141) George Moriarty	100.00	50.00	30.00
(142) George Mullin	100.00	50.00	30.00
(143) Danny Murphy	100.00	50.00	30.00
(144) Jack Murray	100.00	50.00	30.00
(145) John Nee	375.00	150.00	90.00
(146) Thomas J. Needham	100.00	50.00	30.00
(147) Rebel Oakes	100.00	50.00	30.00
(148) Rube Oldring	100.00	50.00	30.00
(149) Charley O'Leary	100.00	50.00	30.00
(150) Fred Olmstead	100.00	50.00	30.00
(151) Orval Overall	100.00	50.00	30.00
(152) Freddy Parent	100.00	50.00	30.00
(153) George Paskert	100.00	50.00	30.00
(154) Billy Payne	100.00	50.00	30.00
(155) Barney Pelty	100.00	50.00	30.00
(156) John Pfeister	100.00	50.00	30.00
(157) Jimmy Phelan	375.00	150.00	90.00
(158) E.J. Phelps	100.00	50.00	30.00
(159) C. Phillippe	100.00	50.00	30.00
(160) Jack Quinn	100.00	50.00	30.00
(161) A.L. Raymond	500.00	250.00	150.00
(162) E.M. Reulbach	100.00	50.00	30.00
(163) Lewis Richie	100.00	50.00	30.00
(164) John A. Rowan	400.00	200.00	120.00
(165) George N. Rucker	100.00	50.00	30.00
(166) W.D. Scanlan	375.00	175.00	105.00
(167) Germany Schaefer	100.00	50.00	30.00
(168) George Schlei	100.00	50.00	30.00
(169) Boss Schmidt	100.00	50.00	30.00
(170) F.M. Schulte	100.00	50.00	30.00
(171) Jim Scott	100.00	50.00	30.00
(172) B.H. Sharpe	100.00	50.00	30.00
(173) David Shean (Rustlers)	100.00	50.00	30.00
(174) David Shean (Cubs)	500.00	250.00	150.00
(175) Jas. T. Sheckard	100.00	50.00	30.00
(176) Hack Simmons	100.00	50.00	30.00
(177) Tony Smith	100.00	50.00	30.00
(178) Fred C. Snodgrass	100.00	50.00	30.00
(179) Tris Speaker	725.00	300.00	180.00
(180) Jake Stahl	100.00	50.00	30.00
(181) Oscar Stanage	100.00	50.00	30.00
(182) Harry Steinfeldt	125.00	55.00	33.00
(183) George Stone	100.00	50.00	30.00
(184) George Stovall	100.00	50.00	30.00
(185) Gabby Street	100.00	50.00	30.00
(186) George F. Suggs	500.00	250.00	150.00
(187) Ed Summers	100.00	50.00	30.00
(188) Jeff Sweeney	400.00	175.00	105.00
(189) Lee Tannehill	100.00	50.00	30.00
(190) Ira Thomas	100.00	50.00	30.00
(191) Joe Tinker	600.00	250.00	150.00
(192) John Titus	100.00	50.00	30.00
(193) Terry Turner	500.00	250.00	150.00
(194) James Vaughn	100.00	50.00	30.00
(195) Heinie Wagner	400.00	175.00	105.00
(196) Bobby Wallace (with cap)	375.00	175.00	105.00
(197a) Bobby Wallace (no cap, one line of 1910 stats)	600.00	250.00	150.00
(197b) Bobby Wallace (no cap, two lines of 1910 stats)	625.00	275.00	165.00
(198) Ed Walsh	650.00	250.00	150.00
(199) Z.D. Wheat	500.00	200.00	120.00
(200) Doc White (White Sox)	100.00	50.00	30.00
(201) Kirb. White (Pirates)	400.00	200.00	120.00
(202) Irvin K. Wilhelm	500.00	250.00	150.00
(203) Ed Willett	100.00	50.00	30.00
(204) J. Owen Wilson	100.00	50.00	30.00
(205) George R. Wiltse (both ears show)	100.00	50.00	30.00
(206) George R. Wiltse (only right ear shows)	500.00	250.00	150.00
(207) Harry Wolter	100.00	50.00	30.00
(208) Cy Young	1000.	270.00	112.00

1909-1911 T206 White Border

The nearly 525 cards which make up the T206 set are the most popular of the early tobacco card issues. Players are depicted in a color

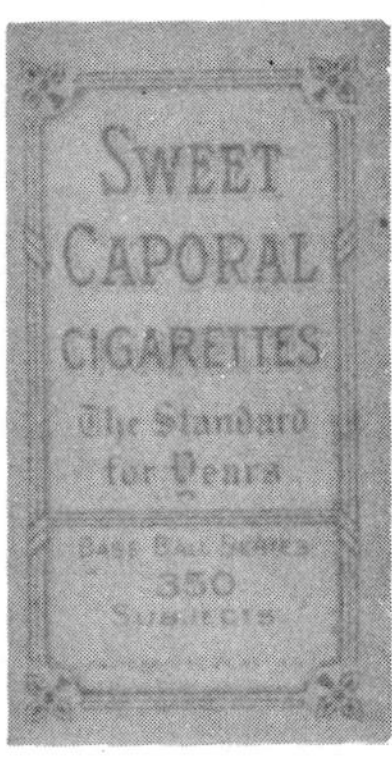

lithograph against a variety of colorful backgrounds, surrounded by a white border. The player names on the 1-1/2" by 2-5/8" cards appear at the bottom with the city and league, when a city had more than one team. Backs contain an ad for one of 16 brands of cigarettes. There are 389 major leaguer cards and 134 minor leaguer cards in the set, but with front/back varieties the number of potentially different cards runs into the thousands. The set features many expensive cards including a number of pose and/or team variations, along with the very scarce Eddie Plank card and the "King of Baseball Cards," the T206 Honus Wagner, the most avidly sought of all baseball cards. The complete set price does not include the Doyle (N.Y. Natl.), Magie, Plank and Wagner cards.

	NR MT	EX	VG
Complete Set:	1250.	55000.	32500.
Common Player:	90.00	45.00	27.00
Common Minor Leaguer:	95.00	47.00	28.00
Common Southern Leaguer:	225.00	112.00	67.00

		NR MT	EX	VG
(1)	Ed Abbaticchio (blue sleeves)	150.00	75.00	45.00
(2)	Ed Abbaticchio (brown sleeves)	90.00	45.00	27.00
(3)	Fred Abbott	95.00	47.00	28.00
(4)	Bill Abstein	90.00	45.00	27.00
(5)	Doc Adkins	95.00	47.00	28.00
(6)	Whitey Alperman	125.00	62.00	37.00
(7)	Red Ames (hands at chest)	125.00	62.00	37.00
(8)	Red Ames (hands above head)	125.00	62.00	37.00
(9)	Red Ames (portrait)	90.00	45.00	27.00
(10)	John Anderson	95.00	47.00	28.00
(11)	Frank Arellanes	90.00	45.00	27.00
(12)	Herman Armbruster	95.00	47.00	28.00
(13)	Harry Arndt	95.00	47.00	28.00
(14)	Jake Atz	90.00	45.00	27.00
(15)	Home Run Baker	450.00	225.00	135.00
(16)	Neal Ball (New York)	125.00	62.00	37.00
(17)	Neal Ball (Cleveland)	90.00	45.00	27.00
(18)	Jap Barbeau	125.00	62.00	37.00
(19)	Cy Barger	95.00	47.00	28.00
(20)	Jack Barry (Philadelphia)	90.00	45.00	27.00
(21)	Shad Barry (Milwaukee)	95.00	47.00	28.00
(22)	Jack Bastian	225.00	112.00	67.00
(23)	Emil Batch	95.00	47.00	28.00
(24)	Johnny Bates	125.00	62.00	37.00
(25)	Harry Bay	300.00	150.00	90.00
(26)	Ginger Beaumont	125.00	62.00	37.00
(27)	Fred Beck	90.00	45.00	27.00
(28)	Beals Becker	90.00	45.00	27.00
(29)	Jake Beckley	300.00	150.00	90.00
(30)	George Bell (hands above head)	125.00	62.00	37.00
(31)	George Bell (pitching follow thru)	90.00	45.00	27.00
(32)	Chief Bender (pitching, no trees in background)	400.00	200.00	120.00
(33)	Chief Bender (pitching, trees in background)	400.00	200.00	120.00
(34)	Chief Bender (portrait)	500.00	250.00	150.00
(35)	Bill Bergen (batting)	125.00	62.00	37.00
(36)	Bill Bergen (catching)	95.00	47.00	28.00
(37)	Heinie Berger	90.00	45.00	27.00
(38)	Bill Bernhard	225.00	112.00	67.00
(39)	Bob Bescher (hands in air)	90.00	45.00	27.00
(40)	Bob Bescher (portrait)	90.00	45.00	27.00
(41)	Joe Birmingham	135.00	67.00	40.00
(42)	Lena Blackburne	95.00	47.00	28.00
(43)	Jack Bliss	90.00	45.00	27.00
(44)	Frank Bowerman	125.00	62.00	37.00
(45)	Bill Bradley (portrait)	125.00	62.00	37.00
(46)	Bill Bradley (with bat)	90.00	45.00	27.00
(47)	Dave Brain	95.00	47.00	28.00
(48)	Kitty Bransfield	125.00	62.00	37.00
(49)	Roy Brashear	95.00	47.00	28.00
(50)	Ted Breitenstein	225.00	112.00	67.00
(51)	Roger Bresnahan (portrait)	550.00	275.00	165.00
(52)	Roger Bresnahan (with bat)	400.00	200.00	120.00
(53)	Al Bridwell (portrait, no cap)	90.00	45.00	27.00
(54)	Al Bridwell (portrait, with cap)	125.00	62.00	37.00
(55a)	George Brown (Browne) (Chicago)	125.00	62.00	37.00
(55b)	George Brown (Browne) (Washington)	1000.	500.00	300.00
(56)	Mordecai Brown (Chicago on shirt)	400.00	200.00	120.00
(57)	Mordecai Brown (Cubs on shirt)	550.00	275.00	165.00
(58)	Mordecai Brown (portrait)	450.00	225.00	135.00
(59)	Al Burch (batting)	275.00	137.00	80.00
(60)	Al Burch (fielding)	90.00	45.00	27.00
(61)	Fred Burchell	95.00	47.00	28.00
(62)	Jimmy Burke	95.00	47.00	28.00
(63)	Bill Burns	90.00	45.00	27.00
(64)	Donie Bush	90.00	45.00	27.00
(65)	John Butler	95.00	47.00	28.00
(66)	Bobby Byrne	90.00	45.00	27.00
(67)	Howie Camnitz (arm at side)	90.00	45.00	27.00
(68)	Howie Camnitz (arms folded)	125.00	62.00	37.00
(69)	Howie Camnitz (hands above head)	90.00	45.00	27.00
(70)	Billy Campbell	90.00	45.00	27.00
(71)	Scoops Carey	225.00	112.00	67.00
(72)	Charley Carr	95.00	47.00	28.00
(73)	Bill Carrigan	90.00	45.00	27.00
(74)	Doc Casey	95.00	47.00	28.00
(75)	Peter Cassidy	95.00	47.00	28.00
(76)	Frank Chance (batting)	400.00	200.00	120.00
(77)	Frank Chance (portrait, red background)	550.00	275.00	165.00
(78)	Frank Chance (portrait, yellow background)	450.00	225.00	135.00
(79)	Bill Chappelle	95.00	47.00	28.00
(80)	Chappie Charles	90.00	45.00	27.00
(81)	Hal Chase (holding trophy)	225.00	112.00	67.00
(82)	Hal Chase (portrait, blue background)	250.00	125.00	75.00
(83)	Hal Chase (portrait, pink background)	350.00	175.00	105.00
(84)	Hal Chase (throwing, dark cap)	200.00	100.00	60.00
(85)	Hal Chase (throwing, white cap)	475.00	237.00	145.00
(86)	Jack Chesbro	600.00	300.00	180.00
(87)	Ed Cicotte	175.00	87.00	52.00
(88)	Bill Clancy (Clancey)	95.00	47.00	28.00
(89)	Josh Clark (Clarke) (Columbus)	95.00	47.00	28.00
(90)	Fred Clarke (Pittsburg, holding bat)	400.00	200.00	120.00
(91)	Fred Clarke (Pittsburg, portrait)	450.00	225.00	135.00
(92)	Nig Clarke (Cleveland)	125.00	62.00	37.00
(93)	Bill Clymer	95.00	47.00	28.00
(94)	Ty Cobb (portrait, green background)	3000.	1500.	900.00
(95)	Ty Cobb (portrait, red background)	2250.	1125.	700.00
(96)	Ty Cobb (with bat off shoulder)	2000.	1000.	600.00
(97)	Ty Cobb (with bat on shoulder)	2500.	1250.	750.00
(98)	Cad Coles	225.00	112.00	67.00
(99)	Eddie Collins (Philadelphia)	500.00	250.00	150.00
(100)	Jimmy Collins (Minneapolis)	375.00	187.00	110.00
(101)	Bunk Congalton	95.00	47.00	28.00
(102)	Wid Conroy (fielding)	125.00	62.00	37.00
(103)	Wid Conroy (with bat)	90.00	45.00	27.00
(104)	Harry Covaleski (Coveleski)	125.00	62.00	37.00
(105)	Doc Crandall (portrait, no cap)	125.00	62.00	37.00
(106)	Doc Crandall (portrait, with cap)	90.00	45.00	27.00
(107)	Bill Cranston	250.00	125.00	75.00
(108)	Gavvy Cravath	175.00	87.00	52.00
(109)	Sam Crawford (throwing)	500.00	250.00	150.00
(110)	Sam Crawford (with bat)	450.00	225.00	135.00
(111)	Birdie Cree	90.00	45.00	27.00
(112)	Lou Criger	125.00	62.00	37.00
(113)	Dode Criss	125.00	62.00	37.00
(114)	Monte Cross	95.00	47.00	28.00
(115a)	Bill Dahlen (Boston)	150.00	75.00	45.00
(115b)	Bill Dahlen (Brooklyn)	600.00	300.00	175.00
(116)	Paul Davidson	95.00	47.00	28.00
(117)	George Davis (Chicago)	125.00	62.00	37.00
(118)	Harry Davis (Philadelphia, Davis on front)	90.00	45.00	27.00
(119)	Harry Davis (Philadelphia, H. Davis on front)	125.00	62.00	37.00
(120)	Frank Delehanty (Delahanty) (Louisville)	95.00	47.00	28.00
(121)	Jim Delehanty (Delahanty) (Washington)	125.00	62.00	37.00
(122a)	Ray Demmitt (New York)	90.00	45.00	27.00
(122b)	Ray Demmitt (St. Louis)	7500.	3750.	2300.
(123)	Rube Dessau	95.00	47.00	28.00
(124)	Art Devlin	125.00	62.00	37.00
(125)	Josh Devore	90.00	45.00	27.00
(126)	Bill Dineen (Dinneen)	90.00	45.00	27.00
(127)	Mike Donlin (fielding)	350.00	175.00	105.00
(128)	Mike Donlin (seated)	125.00	62.00	37.00
(129)	Mike Donlin (with bat)	90.00	45.00	27.00
(130)	Jiggs Donohue (Donahue)	125.00	62.00	37.00
(131)	Wild Bill Donovan (portrait)	125.00	62.00	37.00
(132)	Wild Bill Donovan (throwing)	90.00	45.00	27.00
(133)	Red Dooin	125.00	62.00	37.00
(134)	Mickey Doolan (batting)	90.00	45.00	27.00
(135)	Mickey Doolan (fielding)	90.00	45.00	27.00
(136)	Mickey Doolin (Doolan)	125.00	62.00	37.00
(137)	Gus Dorner	95.00	47.00	28.00
(138)	Patsy Dougherty (arm in air)	90.00	45.00	27.00
(139)	Patsy Dougherty (portrait)	125.00	62.00	37.00
(140)	Tom Downey (batting)	90.00	45.00	27.00
(141)	Tom Downey (fielding)	90.00	45.00	27.00
(142)	Jerry Downs	95.00	47.00	28.00
(143a)	Joe Doyle (N.Y. Natl., hands above head)	30000.	15000.	9000.
(143b)	Joe Doyle (N.Y., hands above head)	100.00	50.00	30.00
(144)	Larry Doyle (N.Y. Nat'l., portrait)	125.00	62.00	37.00
(145)	Larry Doyle (N.Y. Nat'l., throwing)	175.00	87.00	52.00
(146)	Larry Doyle (N.Y. Nat'l., with bat)	125.00	62.00	37.00
(147)	Jean Dubuc	90.00	45.00	27.00
(148)	Hugh Duffy	400.00	200.00	120.00
(149)	Jack Dunn (Baltimore)	95.00	47.00	28.00
(150)	Joe Dunn (Brooklyn)	100.00	50.00	30.00
(151)	Bull Durham	135.00	67.00	40.00
(152)	Jimmy Dygert	90.00	45.00	27.00
(153)	Ted Easterly	90.00	45.00	27.00
(154)	Dick Egan	90.00	45.00	27.00
(155a)	Kid Elberfeld (New York)	125.00	62.00	37.00
(155b)	Kid Elberfeld (Washington, portrait)	2000.	1000.	600.00
(156)	Kid Elberfeld (Washington, fielding)	90.00	45.00	27.00
(157)	Roy Ellam	250.00	125.00	75.00
(158)	Clyde Engle	90.00	45.00	27.00
(159)	Steve Evans	90.00	45.00	27.00
(160)	Johnny Evers (portrait)	650.00	325.00	200.00
(161)	Johnny Evers (with bat, Chicago on shirt)	400.00	200.00	120.00
(162)	Johnny Evers (with bat, Cubs on shirt)	500.00	250.00	150.00
(163)	Bob Ewing	125.00	62.00	37.00
(164)	Cecil Ferguson	90.00	45.00	27.00
(165)	Hobe Ferris	125.00	62.00	37.00
(166)	Lou Fiene (portrait)	90.00	45.00	27.00
(167)	Lou Fiene (throwing)	90.00	45.00	27.00
(168)	Steamer Flanagan	95.00	47.00	28.00
(169)	Art Fletcher	90.00	45.00	27.00
(170)	Elmer Flick	450.00	225.00	135.00
(171)	Russ Ford	90.00	45.00	27.00
(172)	Ed Foster	225.00	112.00	67.00
(173)	Jerry Freeman	95.00	47.00	28.00
(174)	John Frill	90.00	45.00	27.00
(175)	Charlie Fritz	225.00	112.00	67.00
(176)	Art Fromme	90.00	45.00	27.00
(177)	Chick Gandil	125.00	62.00	37.00
(178)	Bob Ganley	125.00	62.00	37.00
(179)	John Ganzel	95.00	47.00	28.00
(180)	Harry Gasper	90.00	45.00	27.00
(181)	Rube Geyer	90.00	45.00	27.00
(182)	George Gibson	125.00	62.00	37.00
(183)	Billy Gilbert	125.00	62.00	37.00
(184)	Wilbur Goode (Good)	125.00	62.00	37.00
(185)	Bill Graham (St. Louis)	90.00	45.00	27.00
(186)	Peaches Graham (Boston)	90.00	45.00	27.00
(187)	Dolly Gray	90.00	45.00	27.00
(188)	Ed Greminger	225.00	112.00	67.00
(189)	Clark Griffith (batting)	450.00	225.00	135.00
(190)	Clark Griffith (portrait)	500.00	250.00	150.00
(191)	Moose Grimshaw	95.00	47.00	28.00
(192)	Bob Groom	90.00	45.00	27.00
(193)	Guiheen	250.00	125.00	75.00
(194)	Ed Hahn	125.00	62.00	37.00
(195)	Bob Hall	95.00	47.00	28.00
(196)	Bill Hallman	95.00	47.00	28.00
(197)	Jack Hannifan (Hannifin)	95.00	47.00	28.00
(198)	Bill Hart (Little Rock)	300.00	150.00	90.00
(199)	Jimmy Hart (Montgomery)	250.00	125.00	75.00
(200)	Topsy Hartsel	90.00	45.00	27.00
(201)	Jack Hayden	95.00	47.00	28.00
(202)	J. Ross Helm	225.00	112.00	67.00
(203)	Charlie Hemphill	125.00	62.00	37.00
(204)	Buck Herzog (Boston)	90.00	45.00	27.00
(205)	Buck Herzog (New York)	125.00	62.00	37.00
(206)	Gordon Hickman	225.00	112.00	67.00
(207)	Bill Hinchman (Cleveland)	125.00	62.00	37.00
(208)	Harry Hinchman (Toledo)	95.00	47.00	28.00
(209)	Dick Hoblitzell	90.00	45.00	27.00
(210)	Danny Hoffman (St. Louis)	90.00	45.00	27.00
(211)	Izzy Hoffman (Providence)	95.00	47.00	28.00
(212)	Solly Hofman	90.00	45.00	27.00
(213)	Bock Hooker	225.00	112.00	67.00
(214)	Del Howard (Chicago)	90.00	45.00	27.00
(215)	Ernie Howard (Savannah)	225.00	112.00	67.00
(216)	Harry Howell (hand at waist)	90.00	45.00	27.00
(217)	Harry Howell (portrait)	90.00	45.00	27.00
(218)	Miller Huggins (hands at mouth)	400.00	200.00	120.00
(219)	Miller Huggins (portrait)	450.00	225.00	135.00
(220)	Rudy Hulswitt	90.00	45.00	27.00
(221)	John Hummel	90.00	45.00	27.00
(222)	George Hunter	90.00	45.00	27.00
(223)	Frank Isbell	135.00	67.00	40.00
(224)	Fred Jacklitsch	135.00	67.00	40.00
(225)	Jimmy Jackson	95.00	47.00	28.00
(226)	Hughie Jennings (one hand showing)	400.00	200.00	120.00
(227)	Hughie Jennings (both hands showing)	400.00	200.00	120.00
(228)	Hughie Jennings (portrait)	450.00	225.00	135.00
(229)	Walter Johnson (hands at chest)	900.00	450.00	275.00
(230)	Walter Johnson (portrait)	1400.	700.00	400.00
(231)	Fielder Jones (Chicago, hands at hips)	125.00	62.00	37.00
(232)	Fielder Jones (Chicago, portrait)	125.00	62.00	37.00
(233)	Davy Jones (Detroit)	90.00	45.00	27.00

	NR MT	EX	VG
(234) Tom Jones (St. Louis)	125.00	62.00	37.00
(235) Dutch Jordan (Atlanta)	225.00	112.00	67.00
(236) Tim Jordan (Brooklyn, batting)	90.00	45.00	27.00
(237) Tim Jordan (Brooklyn, portrait)	125.00	62.00	37.00
(238) Addie Joss (hands at chest)	450.00	225.00	135.00
(239) Addie Joss (portrait)	550.00	275.00	165.00
(240) Ed Karger	125.00	62.00	37.00
(241) Willie Keeler (portrait)	750.00	375.00	225.00
(242) Willie Keeler (with bat)	700.00	350.00	210.00
(243) Joe Kelley	300.00	150.00	90.00
(244) J.F. Kiernan	225.00	112.00	67.00
(245) Ed Killian (hands at chest)	90.00	45.00	27.00
(246) Ed Killian (portrait)	125.00	62.00	37.00
(247) Frank King	225.00	112.00	67.00
(248) Rube Kisinger (Kissinger)	95.00	47.00	28.00
(249a) Red Kleinow (Boston)	900.00	450.00	275.00
(249b) Red Kleinow (New York, catching)	90.00	45.00	27.00
(250) Red Kleinow (New York, with bat)	125.00	62.00	37.00
(251) Johnny Kling	125.00	62.00	37.00
(252) Otto Knabe	90.00	45.00	27.00
(253) Jack Knight (portrait)	90.00	45.00	27.00
(254) Jack Knight (with bat)	90.00	45.00	27.00
(255) Ed Konetchy (glove above head)	125.00	62.00	37.00
(256) Ed Konetchy (glove near ground)	90.00	45.00	27.00
(257) Harry Krause (pitching)	90.00	45.00	27.00
(258) Harry Krause (portrait)	90.00	45.00	27.00
(259) Rube Kroh	90.00	45.00	27.00
(260) Otto Kruger (Krueger)	95.00	47.00	28.00
(261) James Lafitte	225.00	112.00	67.00
(262) Nap Lajoie (portrait)	900.00	450.00	275.00
(263) Nap Lajoie (throwing)	700.00	350.00	200.00
(264) Nap Lajoie (with bat)	700.00	350.00	200.00
(265) Joe Lake (New York)	125.00	62.00	37.00
(266) Joe Lake (St. Louis, ball in hand)	90.00	45.00	27.00
(267) Joe Lake (St. Louis, no ball in hand)	90.00	45.00	27.00
(268) Frank LaPorte	90.00	45.00	27.00
(269) Arlie Latham	90.00	45.00	27.00
(270) Bill Lattimore	95.00	47.00	28.00
(271) Jimmy Lavender	95.00	47.00	28.00
(272) Tommy Leach (bending over)	90.00	45.00	27.00
(273) Tommy Leach (portrait)	125.00	62.00	37.00
(274) Lefty Leifield (batting)	90.00	45.00	27.00
(275) Lefty Leifield (pitching)	125.00	62.00	37.00
(276) Ed Lennox	90.00	45.00	27.00
(277) Harry Lentz (Sentz)	225.00	112.00	67.00
(278) Glenn Liebhardt	125.00	62.00	37.00
(279) Vive Lindaman	125.00	62.00	37.00
(280) Perry Lipe	225.00	112.00	67.00
(281) Paddy Livingstone (Livingston)	90.00	45.00	27.00
(282) Hans Lobert	125.00	62.00	37.00
(283) Harry Lord	90.00	45.00	27.00
(284) Harry Lumley	125.00	62.00	37.00
(285a) Carl Lundgren (Chicago)	700.00	350.00	200.00
(285b) Carl Lundgren (Kansas City)	95.00	47.00	28.00
(286) Nick Maddox	90.00	45.00	27.00
(287a) Sherry Magie (Magee)	15000.	7500.	4500.
(287b) Sherry Magee (portrait)	175.00	87.00	52.00
(288) Sherry Magee (with bat)	125.00	62.00	37.00
(289) Bill Malarkey	95.00	47.00	28.00
(290) Billy Maloney	95.00	47.00	28.00
(291) George Manion	225.00	112.00	67.00
(292) Rube Manning (batting)	125.00	62.00	37.00
(293) Rube Manning (pitching)	90.00	45.00	27.00
(294) Rube Marquard (hands at thighs)	500.00	250.00	150.00
(295) Rube Marquard (pitching follow thru)	450.00	225.00	135.00
(296) Rube Marquard (portrait)	475.00	237.00	140.00
(297) Doc Marshall	90.00	45.00	27.00
(298) Christy Mathewson (dark cap)	800.00	400.00	250.00
(299) Christy Mathewson (portrait)	1400.	700.00	400.00
(300) Christy Mathewson (white cap)	1200.	600.00	350.00
(301) Al Mattern	90.00	45.00	27.00
(302) John McAleese	90.00	45.00	27.00
(303) George McBride	90.00	45.00	27.00
(304) Pat McCauley	225.00	112.00	67.00
(305) Moose McCormick	90.00	45.00	27.00
(306) Pryor McElveen	90.00	45.00	27.00
(307) Dan McGann	95.00	47.00	28.00
(308) Jim McGinley	95.00	47.00	28.00
(309) Iron Man McGinnity	350.00	175.00	105.00
(310) Stoney McGlynn	95.00	47.00	28.00
(311) John McGraw (finger in air)	500.00	250.00	150.00
(312) John McGraw (glove at hip)	475.00	237.00	140.00
(313) John McGraw (portrait, no cap)	600.00	300.00	175.00
(314) John McGraw (portrait, with cap)	400.00	200.00	120.00
(315) Harry McIntyre (Brooklyn)	125.00	62.00	37.00
(316) Harry McIntyre (Brooklyn & Chicago)	90.00	45.00	27.00
(317) Matty McIntyre (Detroit)	90.00	45.00	27.00
(318) Larry McLean	90.00	45.00	27.00
(319) George McQuillan (ball in hand)	125.00	62.00	37.00
(320) George McQuillan (with bat)	90.00	45.00	27.00
(321) Fred Merkle (portrait)	150.00	75.00	45.00
(322) Fred Merkle (throwing)	125.00	62.00	37.00
(323) George Merritt	95.00	47.00	28.00
(324) Chief Meyers	90.00	45.00	27.00
(325) Clyde Milan	90.00	45.00	27.00
(326) Dots Miller (Pittsburg)	90.00	45.00	27.00
(327) Molly Miller (Dallas)	225.00	112.00	67.00
(328) Bill Milligan	95.00	47.00	28.00
(329) Fred Mitchell (Toronto)	95.00	47.00	28.00
(330) Mike Mitchell (Cincinnati)	90.00	45.00	27.00
(331) Dan Moeller	95.00	47.00	28.00
(332) Carlton Molesworth	225.00	112.00	67.00
(333) Herbie Moran (Providence)	95.00	47.00	28.00
(334) Pat Moran (Chicago)	90.00	45.00	27.00
(335) George Moriarty	90.00	45.00	27.00
(336) Mike Mowrey	90.00	45.00	27.00
(337) Dom Mullaney	225.00	112.00	67.00
(338) George Mullen (Mullin)	90.00	45.00	27.00
(339) George Mullin (throwing)	125.00	62.00	37.00
(340) George Mullin (with bat)	90.00	45.00	27.00
(341) Danny Murphy (batting)	90.00	45.00	27.00
(342) Danny Murphy (throwing)	125.00	62.00	37.00
(343) Red Murray (batting)	90.00	45.00	27.00
(344) Red Murray (portrait)	90.00	45.00	27.00
(345) Chief Myers (Meyers) (batting)	90.00	45.00	27.00
(346) Chief Myers (Meyers) (fielding)	90.00	45.00	27.00
(347) Billy Nattress	95.00	47.00	28.00
(348) Tom Needham	90.00	45.00	27.00
(349) Simon Nicholls (hands on knees)	125.00	62.00	37.00
(350) Simon Nichols (Nicholls) (batting)	90.00	45.00	27.00
(351) Harry Niles	125.00	62.00	37.00
(352) Rebel Oakes	90.00	45.00	27.00
(353) Frank Oberlin	95.00	47.00	28.00
(354) Peter O'Brien	95.00	47.00	28.00
(355a) Bill O'Hara (New York)	90.00	45.00	27.00
(355b) Bill O'Hara (St. Louis)	7500.	3750.	2250.
(356) Rube Oldring (batting)	90.00	45.00	27.00
(357) Rube Oldring (fielding)	125.00	62.00	37.00
(358) Charley O'Leary (hands on knees)	90.00	45.00	27.00
(359) Charley O'Leary (portrait)	125.00	62.00	37.00
(360) William J. O'Neil	95.00	47.00	28.00
(361) Al Orth	225.00	112.00	67.00
(362) William Otey	225.00	112.00	67.00
(363) Orval Overall (hand face level)	90.00	45.00	27.00
(364) Orval Overall (hands waist level)	90.00	45.00	27.00
(365) Orval Overall (portrait)	125.00	62.00	37.00
(366) Frank Owen	125.00	62.00	37.00
(367) George Paige	225.00	112.00	67.00
(368) Fred Parent	125.00	62.00	37.00
(369) Dode Paskert	90.00	45.00	27.00
(370) Jim Pastorius	125.00	62.00	37.00
(371) Harry Pattee	550.00	275.00	165.00
(372) Billy Payne	90.00	45.00	27.00
(373) Barney Pelty (horizontal photo)	350.00	175.00	105.00
(374) Barney Pelty (vertical photo)	90.00	45.00	27.00
(375) Hub Perdue	225.00	112.00	67.00
(376) George Perring	90.00	45.00	27.00
(377) Arch Persons	225.00	112.00	67.00
(378) Francis (Big Jeff) Pfeffer	90.00	45.00	27.00
(379) Jake Pfeister (Pfiester) (seated)	90.00	45.00	27.00
(380) Jake Pfeister (Pfiester) (throwing)	90.00	45.00	27.00
(381) Jimmy Phelan	95.00	47.00	28.00
(382) Eddie Phelps	90.00	45.00	27.00
(383) Deacon Phillippe	90.00	45.00	27.00
(384) Ollie Pickering	95.00	47.00	28.00
(385) Eddie Plank	25000.	12500.	7500.
(386) Phil Poland	95.00	47.00	28.00
(387) Jack Powell	125.00	62.00	37.00
(388) Mike Powers	350.00	175.00	105.00
(389) Billy Purtell	90.00	45.00	27.00
(390) Ambrose Puttman (Puttmann)	95.00	47.00	28.00
(391) Lee Quillen (Quillin)	95.00	47.00	28.00
(392) Jack Quinn	90.00	45.00	27.00
(393) Newt Randall	95.00	47.00	28.00
(394) Bugs Raymond	90.00	45.00	27.00
(395) Ed Reagan	225.00	112.00	67.00
(396) Ed Reulbach (glove showing)	275.00	137.00	80.00
(397) Ed Reulbach (no glove showing)	90.00	45.00	27.00
(398) Dutch Revelle	225.00	112.00	67.00
(399) Bob Rhoades (Rhoads) (hands at chest)	90.00	45.00	27.00
(400) Bob Rhoades (Rhoads) (right arm extended)	90.00	45.00	27.00
(401) Charlie Rhodes	90.00	45.00	27.00
(402) Claude Ritchey	125.00	62.00	37.00
(403) Lou Ritter	95.00	47.00	28.00
(404) Ike Rockenfeld	225.00	112.00	67.00
(405) Claude Rossman	90.00	45.00	27.00
(406) Nap Rucker (portrait)	125.00	62.00	37.00
(407) Nap Rucker (throwing)	90.00	45.00	27.00
(408) Dick Rudolph	95.00	47.00	28.00
(409) Ray Ryan	225.00	112.00	67.00
(410) Germany Schaefer (Detroit)	125.00	62.00	37.00
(411) Germany Schaefer (Washington)	90.00	45.00	27.00
(412) George Schirm	95.00	47.00	28.00
(413) Larry Schlafly	95.00	47.00	28.00
(414) Admiral Schlei (batting)	90.00	45.00	27.00
(415) Admiral Schlei (catching)	125.00	62.00	37.00
(416) Admiral Schlei (portrait)	90.00	45.00	27.00
(417) Boss Schmidt (portrait)	90.00	45.00	27.00
(418) Boss Schmidt (throwing)	125.00	62.00	37.00
(419) Ossee Schreck (Schreckengost)	95.00	47.00	28.00
(420) Wildfire Schulte (front view)	125.00	62.00	37.00
(421) Wildfire Schulte (back view)	90.00	45.00	27.00
(422) Jim Scott	90.00	45.00	27.00
(423) Charles Seitz	225.00	112.00	67.00
(424) Cy Seymour (batting)	125.00	62.00	37.00
(425) Cy Seymour (portrait)	90.00	45.00	27.00
(426) Cy Seymour (throwing)	90.00	45.00	27.00
(427) Spike Shannon	95.00	47.00	28.00
(428) Bud Sharpe	95.00	47.00	28.00
(429) Shag Shaughnessy	225.00	112.00	67.00
(430) Al Shaw (St. Louis)	125.00	62.00	37.00
(431) Hunky Shaw (Providence)	95.00	47.00	28.00
(432) Jimmy Sheckard (glove showing)	90.00	45.00	27.00
(433) Jimmy Sheckard (no glove showing)	125.00	62.00	37.00
(434) Bill Shipke	125.00	62.00	37.00
(435) Jimmy Slagle	95.00	47.00	28.00
(436) Carlos Smith (Shreveport)	225.00	112.00	67.00
(437) Frank Smith (Chicago, F. Smith on front)	250.00	125.00	75.00
(438a) Frank Smith (Chicago, white cap)	90.00	45.00	27.00
(438b) Frank Smith (Chicago & Boston)	900.00	450.00	275.00
(439) "Happy" Smith (Brooklyn)	90.00	45.00	27.00
(440) Heinie Smith (Buffalo)	95.00	47.00	28.00
(441) Sid Smith (Atlanta)	225.00	112.00	67.00
(442) Fred Snodgrass (batting)	125.00	62.00	37.00
(443) Fred Snodgrass (catching)	125.00	62.00	37.00
(444) Bob Spade	90.00	45.00	27.00
(445) Tris Speaker	900.00	450.00	275.00
(446) Tubby Spencer	125.00	62.00	37.00
(447) Jake Stahl (glove shows)	90.00	45.00	27.00
(448) Jake Stahl (no glove shows)	125.00	62.00	37.00
(449) Oscar Stanage	90.00	45.00	27.00
(450) Dolly Stark	225.00	112.00	67.00
(451) Charlie Starr	90.00	45.00	27.00
(452) Harry Steinfeldt (portrait)	150.00	75.00	45.00
(453) Harry Steinfeldt (with bat)	125.00	62.00	37.00
(454) Jim Stephens	90.00	45.00	27.00
(455) George Stone	125.00	62.00	37.00
(456) George Stovall (batting)	90.00	45.00	27.00
(457) George Stovall (portrait)	125.00	62.00	37.00
(458) Sam Strang	95.00	47.00	28.00
(459) Gabby Street (catching)	90.00	45.00	27.00
(460) Gabby Street (portrait)	90.00	45.00	27.00
(461) Billy Sullivan	125.00	62.00	37.00
(462) Ed Summers	90.00	45.00	27.00
(463) Bill Sweeney (Boston)	90.00	45.00	27.00
(464) Jeff Sweeney (New York)	90.00	45.00	27.00
(465) Jesse Tannehill (Washington)	90.00	45.00	27.00
(466) Lee Tannehill (Chicago, L. Tannehill on front)	125.00	62.00	37.00
(467) Lee Tannehill (Chicago, Tannehill on front)	90.00	45.00	27.00
(468) Dummy Taylor	95.00	47.00	28.00
(469) Fred Tenney	125.00	62.00	37.00
(470) Tony Thebo	225.00	112.00	67.00
(471) Jake Thielman	95.00	47.00	28.00
(472) Ira Thomas	90.00	45.00	27.00
(473) Woodie Thornton	225.00	112.00	67.00
(474) Joe Tinker (bat off shoulder)	450.00	225.00	135.00
(475) Joe Tinker (bat on shoulder)	450.00	225.00	135.00
(476) Joe Tinker (hands on knees)	500.00	250.00	150.00
(477) Joe Tinker (portrait)	550.00	275.00	165.00
(478) John Titus	90.00	45.00	27.00
(479) Terry Turner	125.00	62.00	37.00
(480) Bob Unglaub	90.00	45.00	27.00
(481) Juan Violat (Viola)	225.00	112.00	67.00
(482) Rube Waddell (portrait)	500.00	250.00	150.00
(483) Rube Waddell (throwing)	500.00	250.00	150.00
(484) Heinie Wagner (bat on left shoulder)	125.00	67.00	40.00
(485) Heinie Wagner (bat on right shoulder)	90.00	45.00	27.00
(486) Honus Wagner	200000	100000.	35000.
(487) Bobby Wallace	400.00	200.00	120.00
(488) Ed Walsh	550.00	275.00	165.00
(489) Jack Warhop	90.00	45.00	27.00
(490) Jake Weimer	125.00	62.00	37.00
(491) James Westlake	225.00	112.00	67.00
(492) Zack Wheat	550.00	275.00	165.00
(493) Doc White (Chicago, pitching)	90.00	45.00	27.00
(494) Doc White (Chicago, portrait)	125.00	62.00	37.00
(495) Foley White (Houston)	225.00	112.00	67.00
(496) Jack White (Buffalo)	95.00	47.00	28.00
(497) Kaiser Wilhelm (hands at chest)	125.00	62.00	37.00
(498) Kaiser Wilhelm (with bat)	90.00	45.00	27.00
(499) Ed Willett	90.00	45.00	27.00
(500) Ed Willetts (Willett)	90.00	45.00	27.00
(501) Jimmy Williams	125.00	62.00	37.00
(502) Vic Willis (Pittsburg)	90.00	45.00	27.00
(503) Vic Willis (St. Louis, throwing)	90.00	45.00	27.00
(504) Vic Willis (St. Louis, with bat)	90.00	45.00	27.00
(505) Owen Wilson	90.00	45.00	27.00
(506) Hooks Wiltse (pitching)	95.00	47.00	28.00
(507) Hooks Wiltse (portrait, no cap)	125.00	62.00	37.00
(508) Hooks Wiltse (portrait, with cap)	90.00	45.00	27.00
(509) Lucky Wright	95.00	47.00	28.00

		NR MT	EX	VG
(510)	Cy Young (Cleveland, glove shows)	750.00	375.00	225.00
(511)	Cy Young (Cleveland, bare hand shows)	750.00	375.00	225.00
(512)	Cy Young (Cleveland, portrait)	1400.	700.00	400.00
(513)	Irv Young (Minneapolis)	95.00	47.00	28.00
(514)	Heinie Zimmerman	90.00	45.00	27.00

1912 T207 Brown Background

Harry Lord

Harry Lord, the brilliant White Sox third baseman, came to Chicago in one of the queerest baseball deals ever recorded. Lord first achieved success in the New England League, where, in 1908, he was lifted to the Boston Americans. Although rated as a wonderful ball player, he fell out with the club management and was traded to Comiskey, who secured a star. Lord played wonderful ball in 1911 and is rated by many as the greatest third baseman now playing—a worthy successor to Bradley and Collins. Last season he batted .321, fielded .941 and led his club with stolen bases.

RECRUIT
LITTLE CIGARS

These 1-1/2" by 2-5/8" cards take their name from the background color which frames the rather drab sepia and white player drawings. They have tan borders making them less colorful than the more popular issues of their era. Player pictures are also on the dull side, with a white strip containing the player's last name, team and league. The card backs have the player's full name, a baseball biography and an ad for one of several brands of cigarettes. The set features 200 players including stars and three classic rarities: Irving Lewis (Boston-Nat.), Ward Miller (Chicago-Nat.) and Louis Lowdermilk (St. Louis-Nat.). There are a number of other scarce cards in the set, including a higher than usual number of obscure players.

		NR MT	EX	VG
	Complete Set:	80000.	32500.	14200.
	Common Player:	125.00	62.00	37.00
(1)	John B. Adams	250.00	125.00	75.00
(2)	Edward Ainsmith	125.00	62.00	37.00
(3)	Rafael Almeida	250.00	125.00	75.00
(4a)	James Austin (insignia on shirt)	175.00	87.00	52.00
(4b)	James Austin (no insignia on shirt)	250.00	125.00	75.00
(5)	Neal Ball	125.00	62.00	37.00
(6)	Eros Barger	125.00	62.00	37.00
(7)	Jack Barry	125.00	62.00	37.00
(8)	Charles Bauman	250.00	125.00	75.00
(9)	Beals Becker	125.00	62.00	37.00
(10)	Chief (Albert) Bender	550.00	275.00	165.00
(11)	Joseph Benz	250.00	125.00	75.00
(12)	Robert Bescher	125.00	62.00	37.00
(13)	Joe Birmingham	250.00	125.00	75.00
(14)	Russell Blackburne	250.00	125.00	75.00
(15)	Fred Blanding	250.00	125.00	75.00
(16)	Jimmy Block	125.00	62.00	37.00
(17)	Ping Bodie	125.00	62.00	37.00
(18)	Hugh Bradley	125.00	62.00	37.00
(19)	Roger Bresnahan	550.00	275.00	165.00
(20)	J.F. Bushelman	250.00	125.00	75.00
(21)	Henry (Hank) Butcher	250.00	125.00	75.00
(22)	Robert M. Byrne	125.00	62.00	37.00
(23)	John James Callahan	125.00	62.00	37.00
(24)	Howard Camnitz	125.00	62.00	37.00
(25)	Max Carey	375.00	187.00	112.00
(26)	William Carrigan	125.00	62.00	37.00
(27)	George Chalmers	125.00	62.00	37.00
(28)	Frank Leroy Chance	550.00	275.00	165.00
(29)	Edward Cicotte	150.00	75.00	45.00
(30)	Tom Clarke	125.00	62.00	37.00
(31)	Leonard Cole	125.00	62.00	37.00
(32)	John Collins	200.00	100.00	60.00
(33)	Robert Coulson	125.00	62.00	37.00
(34)	Tex Covington	125.00	62.00	37.00
(35)	Otis Crandall	125.00	62.00	37.00
(36)	William Cunningham	250.00	125.00	75.00
(37)	Dave Danforth	125.00	62.00	37.00
(38)	Bert Daniels	125.00	62.00	37.00
(39)	John Daubert	150.00	75.00	45.00
(40a)	Harry Davis (brown "C" on cap)	175.00	87.00	52.00
(40b)	Harry Davis (blue "C" on cap)	175.00	87.00	52.00
(41)	Jim Delehanty	125.00	62.00	37.00
(42)	Claude Derrick	125.00	62.00	37.00
(43)	Arthur Devlin	125.00	62.00	37.00
(44)	Joshua Devore	125.00	62.00	37.00
(45)	Mike Donlin	250.00	125.00	75.00
(46)	Edward Donnelly	250.00	125.00	75.00
(47)	Charles Dooin	125.00	62.00	37.00
(48)	Tom Downey	250.00	125.00	75.00
(49)	Lawrence Doyle	125.00	62.00	37.00
(50)	Del Drake	125.00	62.00	37.00
(51)	Ted Easterly	125.00	62.00	37.00
(52)	George Ellis	125.00	62.00	37.00
(53)	Clyde Engle	125.00	62.00	37.00
(54)	R.E. Erwin	125.00	62.00	37.00
(55)	Louis Evans	125.00	62.00	37.00
(56)	John Ferry	125.00	62.00	37.00
(57a)	Ray Fisher (blue cap)	175.00	87.00	52.00
(57b)	Ray Fisher (white cap)	175.00	87.00	52.00
(58)	Arthur Fletcher	125.00	62.00	37.00
(59)	Jacques Fournier	250.00	125.00	75.00
(60)	Arthur Fromme	125.00	62.00	37.00
(61)	Del Gainor	125.00	62.00	37.00
(62)	William Lawrence Gardner	125.00	62.00	37.00
(63)	Lefty George	125.00	62.00	37.00
(64)	Roy Golden	125.00	62.00	37.00
(65)	Harry Gowdy	125.00	62.00	37.00
(66)	George Graham	200.00	100.00	60.00
(67)	J.G. Graney	125.00	62.00	37.00
(68)	Vean Gregg	250.00	125.00	75.00
(69)	Casey Hageman	125.00	62.00	37.00
(70)	Charlie Hall	125.00	62.00	37.00
(71)	E.S. Hallinan	125.00	62.00	37.00
(72)	Earl Hamilton	125.00	62.00	37.00
(73)	Robert Harmon	125.00	62.00	37.00
(74)	Grover Hartley	250.00	125.00	75.00
(75)	Olaf Henriksen	125.00	62.00	37.00
(76)	John Henry	200.00	100.00	60.00
(77)	Charles Herzog	250.00	125.00	75.00
(78)	Robert Higgins	125.00	62.00	37.00
(79)	Chester Hoff	250.00	125.00	75.00
(80)	William Hogan	125.00	62.00	37.00
(81)	Harry Hooper	650.00	325.00	200.00
(82)	Ben Houser	250.00	125.00	75.00
(83)	Hamilton Hyatt	250.00	125.00	75.00
(84)	Walter Johnson	2000.	1000.	600.00
(85)	George Kaler	125.00	62.00	37.00
(86)	William Kelly	250.00	125.00	75.00
(87)	Jay Kirke	250.00	125.00	75.00
(88)	John Kling	125.00	62.00	37.00
(89)	Otto Knabe	125.00	62.00	37.00
(90)	Elmer Knetzer	125.00	62.00	37.00
(91)	Edward Konetchy	125.00	62.00	37.00
(92)	Harry Krause	125.00	62.00	37.00
(93)	"Red" Kuhn	250.00	125.00	75.00
(94)	Joseph Kutina	250.00	125.00	75.00
(95)	F.H. (Bill) Lange	250.00	125.00	75.00
(96)	Jack Lapp	125.00	62.00	37.00
(97)	W. Arlington Latham	125.00	62.00	37.00
(98)	Thomas W. Leach	125.00	62.00	37.00
(99)	Albert Leifield	125.00	62.00	37.00
(100)	Edgar Lennox	125.00	62.00	37.00
(101)	Duffy Lewis	125.00	62.00	37.00
(102a)	Irving Lewis (no emblem on sleeve)	7500.	3750.	2250.
(102b)	Irving Lewis (emblem on sleeve)	7000.	3500.	2000.
(103)	Jack Lively	125.00	62.00	37.00
(104a)	Paddy Livingston ("A" on shirt)	550.00	275.00	165.00
(104b)	Paddy Livingston (big "C" on shirt)	550.00	275.00	165.00
(104c)	Paddy Livingston (little "C" on shirt)	175.00	87.00	52.00
(105)	Briscoe Lord (Philadelphia)	125.00	62.00	37.00
(106)	Harry Lord (Chicago)	125.00	62.00	37.00
(107)	Louis Lowdermilk	5500.	2750.	1650.
(108)	Richard Marquard	550.00	275.00	165.00
(109)	Armando Marsans	125.00	62.00	37.00
(110)	George McBride	125.00	62.00	37.00
(111)	Alexander McCarthy	300.00	150.00	90.00
(112)	Edward McDonald	125.00	62.00	37.00
(113)	John J. McGraw	750.00	375.00	225.00
(114)	Harry McIntire (McIntyre)	125.00	62.00	37.00
(115)	Matthew McIntyre	125.00	62.00	37.00
(116)	William McKechnie	600.00	300.00	175.00
(117)	Larry McLean	125.00	62.00	37.00
(118)	Clyde Milan	125.00	62.00	37.00
(119)	John B. Miller (Pittsburg)	125.00	62.00	37.00
(120)	Otto Miller (Brooklyn)	250.00	125.00	75.00
(121)	Roy Miller (Boston)	250.00	125.00	75.00
(122)	Ward Miller (Chicago)	1000.	500.00	300.00
(123)	Mike Mitchell (Cleveland, front depicts Willie Mitchell)	200.00	100.00	60.00
(124)	Mike Mitchell (Cincinnati)	125.00	62.00	37.00
(125)	Geo. Mogridge	250.00	125.00	75.00
(126)	Earl Moore	250.00	125.00	75.00
(127)	Patrick J. Moran	125.00	62.00	37.00
(128)	Cy Morgan (Philadelphia)	125.00	62.00	37.00
(129)	Ray Morgan (Washington)	125.00	62.00	37.00
(130)	George Moriarty	250.00	125.00	75.00
(131a)	George Mullin ("D" on cap)	175.00	87.00	52.00
(131b)	George Mullin (no "D" on cap)	175.00	87.00	52.00
(132)	Thomas Needham	125.00	62.00	37.00
(133)	Red Nelson	250.00	125.00	75.00
(134)	Herbert Northen	125.00	62.00	37.00
(135)	Leslie Nunamaker	125.00	62.00	37.00
(136)	Rebel Oakes	125.00	62.00	37.00
(137)	Buck O'Brien	125.00	62.00	37.00
(138)	Rube Oldring	125.00	62.00	37.00
(139)	Ivan Olson	125.00	62.00	37.00
(140)	Martin J. O'Toole	125.00	62.00	37.00
(141)	George Paskart (Paskert)	125.00	62.00	37.00
(142)	Barney Pelty	250.00	125.00	75.00
(143)	Herbert Perdue	125.00	62.00	37.00
(144)	O.C. Peters	250.00	125.00	75.00
(145)	Arthur Phelan	250.00	125.00	75.00
(146)	Jack Quinn	125.00	62.00	37.00
(147)	Don Carlos Ragan	1100.	550.00	325.00
(148)	Arthur Rasmussen	1200.	600.00	350.00
(149)	Morris Rath	250.00	125.00	75.00
(150)	Edward Reulbach	125.00	62.00	37.00
(151)	Napoleon Rucker	125.00	62.00	37.00
(152)	J.B. Ryan	250.00	125.00	75.00
(153)	Victor Saier	2000.	1000.	600.00
(154)	William Scanlon	125.00	62.00	37.00
(155)	Germany Schaefer	125.00	62.00	37.00
(156)	Wilbur Schardt	125.00	62.00	37.00
(157)	Frank Schulte	125.00	62.00	37.00
(158)	Jim Scott	125.00	62.00	37.00
(159)	Henry Severoid (Severeid)	125.00	62.00	37.00
(160)	Mike Simon	125.00	62.00	37.00
(161)	Frank E. Smith (Cincinnati)	125.00	62.00	37.00
(162)	Wallace Smith (St. Louis)	125.00	62.00	37.00
(163)	Fred Snodgrass	125.00	62.00	37.00
(164)	Tristam Speaker	2500.	1250.	750.00
(165)	Harry Lee Spratt	125.00	62.00	37.00
(166)	Edward Stack	125.00	62.00	37.00
(167)	Oscar Stanage	125.00	62.00	37.00
(168)	William Steele	125.00	62.00	37.00
(169)	Harry Steinfeldt	125.00	62.00	37.00
(170)	George Stovall	125.00	62.00	37.00
(171)	Charles (Gabby) Street	125.00	62.00	37.00
(172)	Amos Strunk	125.00	62.00	37.00
(173)	William Sullivan	125.00	62.00	37.00
(174)	William J. Sweeney	250.00	125.00	75.00
(175)	Leeford Tannehill	125.00	62.00	37.00
(176)	C.D. Thomas	125.00	62.00	37.00
(177)	Joseph Tinker	550.00	275.00	165.00
(178)	Bert Tooley	125.00	62.00	37.00
(179)	Terence Turner (Terrence)	125.00	62.00	37.00
(180)	George Tyler	1300.	650.00	375.00
(181)	Jim Vaughn	125.00	62.00	37.00
(182)	Chas. (Heinie) Wagner	125.00	62.00	37.00
(183)	Ed (Dixie) Walker	125.00	62.00	37.00
(184)	Robert Wallace	375.00	187.00	112.00
(185)	John Warhop	125.00	62.00	37.00
(186)	George Weaver	250.00	125.00	75.00
(187)	Zach Wheat	450.00	225.00	135.00
(188)	G. Harris White	250.00	125.00	75.00
(189)	Ernest Wilie	250.00	125.00	75.00
(190)	Bob Williams	125.00	62.00	37.00
(191)	Arthur Wilson (New York)	250.00	125.00	75.00
(192)	Owen Wilson (Pittsburg)	125.00	62.00	37.00
(193)	George Wiltse	125.00	62.00	37.00
(194)	Ivey Wingo	125.00	62.00	37.00
(195)	Harry Wolverton	125.00	62.00	37.00
(196)	Joe Wood	200.00	100.00	60.00
(197)	Eugene Woodburn	250.00	125.00	75.00
(198)	Ralph Works	1000.	500.00	300.00
(199)	Stanley Yerkes	125.00	62.00	37.00
(200)	Rollie Zeider	200.00	100.00	60.00

1911 T208 Fireside

ATHLETICS SERIES
ONE IN EACH PACKAGE
OF
Cullivan's
Fireside...
PLAIN SCRAP
THOS. CULLIVAN
610 TURTLE STREET
SYRACUSE, N. Y.

The 1911 T208 Fireside set, an 18-card Philadelphia Athletics set issued by the Thomas Cullivan Tobacco Company of Syracuse, N.Y., is among the rarest and most valuable of all 20th Century tobacco issues. Cullivan issued the set to commemorate the Athletics' 1910 Championship season, and, except for pitcher Jack Coombs, the checklist includes nearly all key members of the club, including manager Connie Mack. The cards are the standard size for tobacco issues, 1-1/2" by 2-5/8". The front of each card features a player portrait set against a colored background. The player's name and the word "Athletics" appear at the bottom, while "World's Champions 1910" is printed along the top. The backs of the cards advertise the set as the "Athletics Series" and advise that one card is included in each package of "Cullivan's Fireside Plain Scrap" tobacco. Collectors should be aware that the same checklist was used for a similar Athletics set issued by Rochester Baking/Williams Baking (D359) and also that blank-backed versions are also known to exist, but these are classified as E104 cards in the American Card Catalog.

		NR MT	EX	VG
	Complete Set:	8500.	4250.	2550.
	Common Player:	300.00	150.00	90.00
(1)	Home Run Baker	750.00	375.00	225.00
(2)	Jack Barry	300.00	150.00	90.00
(3)	Chief Bender	750.00	375.00	225.00

		NR MT	EX	VG
(4)	Eddie Collins	750.00	375.00	225.00
(5)	Harry Davis	300.00	150.00	90.00
(6)	Jimmy Dygert	300.00	150.00	90.00
(7)	Topsy Hartsel	300.00	150.00	90.00
(8)	Harry Krause	300.00	150.00	90.00
(9)	Jack Lapp	300.00	150.00	90.00
(10)	Paddy Livingstone (Livingston)	300.00	150.00	90.00
(11)	Bris Lord	300.00	150.00	90.00
(12)	Connie Mack	1000.	500.00	300.00
(13)	Cy Morgan	300.00	150.00	90.00
(14)	Danny Murphy	300.00	150.00	90.00
(15)	Rube Oldring	300.00	150.00	90.00
(16)	Eddie Plank	1000.	500.00	300.00
(17)	Amos Strunk	300.00	150.00	90.00
(18)	Ira Thomas	300.00	150.00	90.00

1910 T209 Contentnea Series I

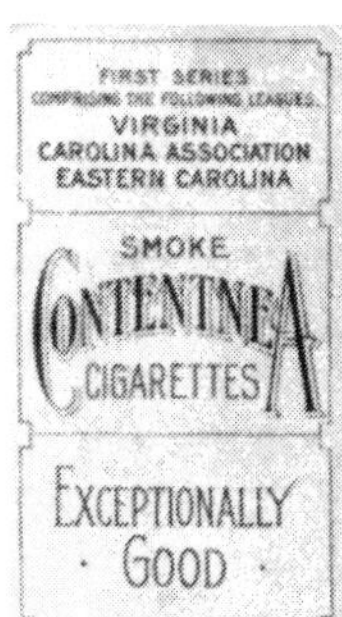

The 1910 Contentnea minor league set actually consists of two distinctively different series, both featuring players from the Virginia League, Carolina Association and Eastern Carolina League. The cards were distributed in packages of Contentnea Cigarettes. The first series, featuring color photographs, consists of just 16 cards, each measuring 1-9/16" by 2-11/16". The front of the card has the player's last name and team printed at the bottom, while the back identifies the card as "First Series" and carries an advertisement for Contentnea Cigarettes. The second series, believed to be issued later in 1910, is a massive 221-card set consisting of black and white player photos. The cards in this series are slightly larger, measuring 1-5/8" by 2-3/4". They carry the words "Photo Series" on the back, along with the cigarette advertisement. Only a handful of players in the Contentnea set ever advanced to the major leagues and the set contains no major stars. Subsequently, it generally holds interest only to collectors who specialize in the old Southern minor leagues.

		NR MT	EX	VG
Complete Set:		2000.	1000.	600.00
Common Player:		125.00	62.00	37.00
(1)	Armstrong	125.00	62.00	37.00
(2)	Booles	125.00	62.00	37.00
(3)	Bourquise (Bourquoise)	125.00	62.00	37.00
(4)	Cooper	125.00	62.00	37.00
(5)	Cowell	125.00	62.00	37.00
(6)	Crockett	125.00	62.00	37.00
(7)	Fullenwider	125.00	62.00	37.00
(8)	Gilmore	125.00	62.00	37.00
(9)	Hoffman	125.00	62.00	37.00
(10)	Lane	125.00	62.00	37.00
(11)	Martin	125.00	62.00	37.00
(12)	McGeehan	125.00	62.00	37.00
(13)	Pope	125.00	62.00	37.00
(14)	Sisson	125.00	62.00	37.00
(15)	Stubbe	125.00	62.00	37.00
(16)	Walsh	125.00	62.00	37.00

1910 T209 Contentnea Series II

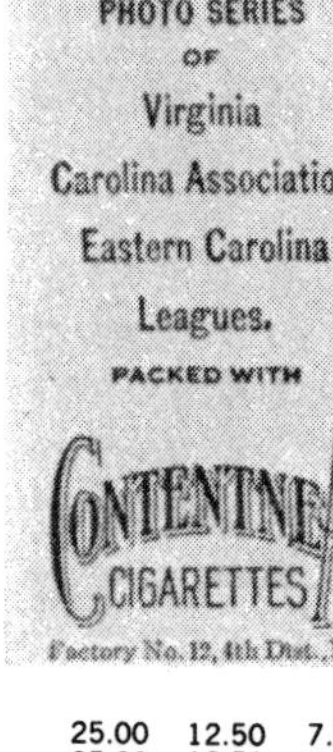

		NR MT	EX	VG
Complete Set:		5500.	2750.	1650.
Common Player:		25.00	12.50	7.50
(1)	Abercrombie	25.00	12.50	7.50
(2)	Andrada	25.00	12.50	7.50
(3)	Armstrong	25.00	12.50	7.50
(4)	Averett	25.00	12.50	7.50
(5)	Baker	25.00	12.50	7.50
(6)	Banner (Bonner)	25.00	12.50	7.50
(7)	Bausewein (Bansewein)	25.00	12.50	7.50
(8)	Beatty	25.00	12.50	7.50
(9)	Bentley	25.00	12.50	7.50
(10)	Beusse	25.00	12.50	7.50
(11)	Biel	25.00	12.50	7.50
(12)	Bigbie (Raleigh)	25.00	12.50	7.50
(13)	Bigbie (Richmond)	25.00	12.50	7.50
(14)	Blackstone	25.00	12.50	7.50
(15)	Bonner	25.00	12.50	7.50
(16)	Bourquin	25.00	12.50	7.50
(17)	Bowen	25.00	12.50	7.50
(18)	Boyle	25.00	12.50	7.50
(19)	Brandon	25.00	12.50	7.50
(20)	Brazelle (Brazell)	25.00	12.50	7.50
(21)	Brent	25.00	12.50	7.50
(22)	Brown	25.00	12.50	7.50
(23)	Busch	25.00	12.50	7.50
(24)	Bussey	25.00	12.50	7.50
(25)	Byrd	25.00	12.50	7.50
(26)	Cafalu (Cefalu)	25.00	12.50	7.50
(27)	Callahan	25.00	12.50	7.50
(28)	Chandler	25.00	12.50	7.50
(29)	Clapp	25.00	12.50	7.50
(30)	Clark (Clarke)	25.00	12.50	7.50
(31)	Clemens	25.00	12.50	7.50
(32)	Clunk	25.00	12.50	7.50
(33)	Cooper	25.00	12.50	7.50
(34)	Corbett	25.00	12.50	7.50
(35)	Cote	25.00	12.50	7.50
(36)	Coutts	25.00	12.50	7.50
(37)	Cowan (Cowen)	25.00	12.50	7.50
(38)	Cowells (Cowell)	25.00	12.50	7.50
(39)	Creagan (Cregan)	25.00	12.50	7.50
(40)	Crockett	25.00	12.50	7.50
(41)	Cross	25.00	12.50	7.50
(42)	Dailey	25.00	12.50	7.50
(43)	C. Derrck (Derrick)	25.00	12.50	7.50
(44)	F. Derrick	25.00	12.50	7.50
(45)	Doak (Greensboro)	25.00	12.50	7.50
(46)	Doak (Wilmington)	25.00	12.50	7.50
(47)	Dobard	25.00	12.50	7.50
(48)	Dobson	25.00	12.50	7.50
(49)	Doyle	25.00	12.50	7.50
(50)	Drumm	25.00	12.50	7.50
(51)	Duvie	25.00	12.50	7.50
(52)	Ebinger	25.00	12.50	7.50
(53)	Eldridge	25.00	12.50	7.50
(54)	Evvans	25.00	12.50	7.50
(55)	Fairbanks	25.00	12.50	7.50
(56)	Farmer	25.00	12.50	7.50
(57)	Ferrell	25.00	12.50	7.50
(58)	Fisher	25.00	12.50	7.50
(59)	Flowers	25.00	12.50	7.50
(60)	Fogarty	25.00	12.50	7.50
(61)	Foltz	25.00	12.50	7.50
(62)	Foreman	25.00	12.50	7.50
(63)	Forque	25.00	12.50	7.50
(64)	Francis	25.00	12.50	7.50
(65)	Fulton	25.00	12.50	7.50
(66)	Galvin	25.00	12.50	7.50
(67)	Gardin	25.00	12.50	7.50
(68)	Garman	25.00	12.50	7.50
(69)	Gastmeyer	25.00	12.50	7.50
(70)	Gaston	25.00	12.50	7.50
(71)	Gates	25.00	12.50	7.50
(72)	Gehring	25.00	12.50	7.50
(73)	Gillespie	25.00	12.50	7.50
(74)	Gorham	25.00	12.50	7.50
(75)	Griffin (Danville)	25.00	12.50	7.50
(76)	Griffin (Lynchburg)	25.00	12.50	7.50
(77)	Guiheen	25.00	12.50	7.50
(78)	Gunderson	25.00	12.50	7.50
(79)	Hale	25.00	12.50	7.50
(80)	Halland (Holland)	25.00	12.50	7.50
(81)	Hamilton	25.00	12.50	7.50
(82)	Hammersley	25.00	12.50	7.50
(83)	Handiboe	25.00	12.50	7.50
(84)	Hannifen (Hannifan)	25.00	12.50	7.50
(85)	Hargrave	25.00	12.50	7.50
(86)	Harrington	25.00	12.50	7.50
(87)	Harris	25.00	12.50	7.50
(88)	Hart	25.00	12.50	7.50
(89)	Hartley	25.00	12.50	7.50
(90)	Hawkins	25.00	12.50	7.50
(91)	Hearne (Hearn)	25.00	12.50	7.50
(92)	Hicks	25.00	12.50	7.50
(93)	Hobbs	25.00	12.50	7.50
(94)	Hoffman	25.00	12.50	7.50
(95)	Hooker	25.00	12.50	7.50
(96)	Howard	25.00	12.50	7.50
(97)	Howedel (Howedell)	25.00	12.50	7.50
(98)	Hudson	25.00	12.50	7.50
(99)	Humphrey	25.00	12.50	7.50
(100)	Hyames	25.00	12.50	7.50
(101)	Irvine	25.00	12.50	7.50
(102)	Irving	25.00	12.50	7.50
(103)	Jackson (Greensboro)	25.00	12.50	7.50
(104)	Jackson (Spartanburg)	25.00	12.50	7.50
(105)	Jenkins (Greenville)	25.00	12.50	7.50
(106)	Jenkins (Roanoke)	25.00	12.50	7.50
(107)	Jobson	25.00	12.50	7.50
(108)	Johnson	25.00	12.50	7.50
(109)	Keating	25.00	12.50	7.50
(110)	Kelley	25.00	12.50	7.50
(111)	Kelly (Anderson)	25.00	12.50	7.50
(112)	Kelly (Goldsboro)	25.00	12.50	7.50
(113)	"King" Kelly	25.00	12.50	7.50
(114)	King	25.00	12.50	7.50
(115)	Kite	25.00	12.50	7.50
(116)	Kunkle	25.00	12.50	7.50
(117)	Landgraff	25.00	12.50	7.50
(118)	Lane	25.00	12.50	7.50
(119)	Lathrop	25.00	12.50	7.50
(120)	Lavoia	25.00	12.50	7.50
(121)	Levy	25.00	12.50	7.50
(122)	Lloyd	25.00	12.50	7.50
(123)	Loval	25.00	12.50	7.50
(124)	Lucia	25.00	12.50	7.50
(125)	Luyster	25.00	12.50	7.50
(126)	MacConachie	25.00	12.50	7.50
(127)	Malcolm	25.00	12.50	7.50
(128)	Martin	25.00	12.50	7.50
(129)	Mayberry	25.00	12.50	7.50
(130)	A. McCarthy	25.00	12.50	7.50
(131)	J. McCarthy	25.00	12.50	7.50
(132)	McCormick	25.00	12.50	7.50
(133)	McFarland	25.00	12.50	7.50
(134)	McFarlin	25.00	12.50	7.50
(135)	C. McGeehan	25.00	12.50	7.50
(136)	Dan McGeehan	25.00	12.50	7.50
(137)	McHugh	25.00	12.50	7.50
(138)	McKeavitt (McKevitt)	25.00	12.50	7.50
(139)	Merchant	25.00	12.50	7.50
(140)	Midkiff	25.00	12.50	7.50
(141)	Miller	25.00	12.50	7.50
(142)	Missitt	25.00	12.50	7.50
(143)	Morgan	25.00	12.50	7.50
(144)	Morrissey (Morrisey)	25.00	12.50	7.50
(145)	Mullany (Mullaney)	25.00	12.50	7.50
(146)	Mullinix	25.00	12.50	7.50
(147)	Mundell	25.00	12.50	7.50
(148)	Munsen (Munson)	25.00	12.50	7.50
(149)	Murdock (Murdoch)	25.00	12.50	7.50
(150)	Newton	25.00	12.50	7.50
(151)	Noojin	25.00	12.50	7.50
(152)	Novak	25.00	12.50	7.50
(153)	Ochs	25.00	12.50	7.50
(154)	Painter	25.00	12.50	7.50
(155)	Peloguin	25.00	12.50	7.50
(156)	Phealean (Phelan)	25.00	12.50	7.50
(157)	Phoenix	25.00	12.50	7.50
(158)	Powell	25.00	12.50	7.50
(159)	Presley (Pressley), Pritchard	25.00	12.50	7.50
(160)	Priest	25.00	12.50	7.50
(161)	Prim	25.00	12.50	7.50
(162)	Pritchard	25.00	12.50	7.50
(163)	Rawe (Rowe)	25.00	12.50	7.50
(164)	Redfern (Redfearn)	25.00	12.50	7.50
(165)	Reggy	25.00	12.50	7.50
(166)	Richardson	25.00	12.50	7.50
(167)	Rickard	25.00	12.50	7.50
(168)	Rickert	25.00	12.50	7.50
(169)	Ridgeway (Ridgway)	25.00	12.50	7.50
(170)	Roth	25.00	12.50	7.50
(171)	Salve	25.00	12.50	7.50
(172)	Schmidt	25.00	12.50	7.50
(173)	Schrader	25.00	12.50	7.50
(174)	Schumaker	25.00	12.50	7.50
(175)	Sexton	25.00	12.50	7.50
(176)	Shanghnessy (Shaughnessy)	25.00	12.50	7.50
(177)	Sharp	25.00	12.50	7.50
(178)	Shaw	25.00	12.50	7.50
(179)	Simmons	25.00	12.50	7.50
(180)	A. Smith	25.00	12.50	7.50
(181)	D. Smith	25.00	12.50	7.50
(182)	Spratt	25.00	12.50	7.50
(183)	Springs	25.00	12.50	7.50
(184)	Stewart	25.00	12.50	7.50
(185)	Stoehr	25.00	12.50	7.50
(186)	Stouch	25.00	12.50	7.50
(187)	Sullivan	25.00	12.50	7.50
(188)	Swindell	25.00	12.50	7.50
(189)	Taxis	25.00	12.50	7.50
(190)	Templin	25.00	12.50	7.50
(191)	Thompson	25.00	12.50	7.50
(192)	B.E. Thompson	25.00	12.50	7.50
(193)	Tiedeman	25.00	12.50	7.50
(194)	Titman	25.00	12.50	7.50
(195)	Toner	25.00	12.50	7.50
(196)	Turner	25.00	12.50	7.50
(197)	Tydeman	25.00	12.50	7.50
(198)	Vail	25.00	12.50	7.50
(199)	Verbout	25.00	12.50	7.50
(200)	Vickery	25.00	12.50	7.50
(201)	Walker (Norfolk)	25.00	12.50	7.50
(202)	Walker (Spartanburg)	25.00	12.50	7.50
(203)	Wallace	25.00	12.50	7.50
(204)	Walsh	25.00	12.50	7.50
(205)	Walters	25.00	12.50	7.50
(206)	Watters	25.00	12.50	7.50
(207)	Waymack	25.00	12.50	7.50
(208)	Webb	25.00	12.50	7.50
(209)	Wehrell	25.00	12.50	7.50
(210)	Weldon	25.00	12.50	7.50
(211)	Welsher	25.00	12.50	7.50
(212)	Westlake	25.00	12.50	7.50
(213)	Williams	25.00	12.50	7.50
(214)	Willis	25.00	12.50	7.50
(215)	Wingo	25.00	12.50	7.50
(216)	Wolf	25.00	12.50	7.50
(217)	Wood	25.00	12.50	7.50
(218)	Woolums	25.00	12.50	7.50
(219)	Workman	25.00	12.50	7.50
(220)	Wright	25.00	12.50	7.50
(221)	Wynne	25.00	12.50	7.50

1910 T210 Old Mill Series I

Because of their distinctive red borders, this 1910 minor league tobacco issue is often called the Red Border set by collectors. A massive set, it consists of eight different series and totals some

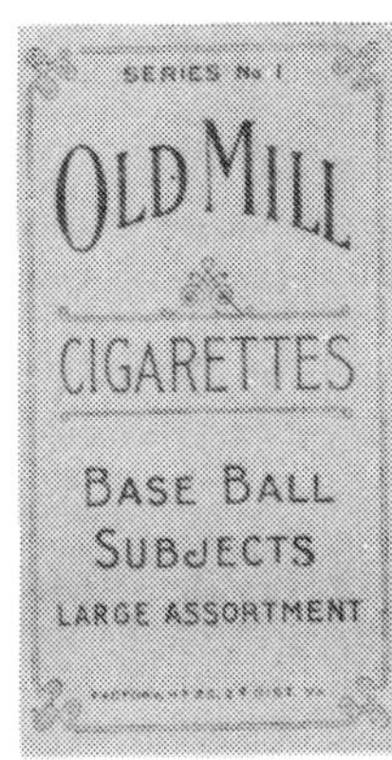

640 cards, each measuring 1-1/2" by 2-5/8". The fronts of the cards feature a glossy black and white photo, while the backs carry an ad for Old Mill Cigarettes. Each of the eight series is devoted to a different minor league. Series 1 features players from the South Atlantic League; Series 2 pictures players from the Virginia League; Series 3 is devoted to the Texas League; Series 4 features the Virginia Valley League; Series 5 pictures players from the Carolina Associations; Series 6 spotlights the Blue Grass League; Series 7 is devoted to the Eastern Carolina League; and Series 8 show players from the the Southern Association. The various series are identified by number along the top on the back of the cards. Collectors generally agree that Series 7 cards (Eastern Carolina League players) are the most difficult to find, while Series 2 cards (Virginia League) are the most common. The relative scarcity of the various series is reflected in the prices listed. Collectors should be aware that some Series 3 cards (Texas League) can be found with orange, rather than red, borders - apparently because not enough red ink was used during part of the print run.

		NR MT	EX	VG
Complete Set:		600.00	300.00	180.00
Common Player:		10.00	5.00	3.00
(1)	Bagwell	10.00	5.00	3.00
(2)	Balenti	10.00	5.00	3.00
(3)	Becker	10.00	5.00	3.00
(4)	Bensen	10.00	5.00	3.00
(5)	Benton	10.00	5.00	3.00
(6)	Bierkortte	10.00	5.00	3.00
(7)	Bierman	10.00	5.00	3.00
(8)	Breitenstein	10.00	5.00	3.00
(9)	Bremmerhof	10.00	5.00	3.00
(10)	Carter	10.00	5.00	3.00
(11)	Cavender	10.00	5.00	3.00
(12)	Collins	10.00	5.00	3.00
(13)	DeFraites	10.00	5.00	3.00
(14)	Dudley	10.00	5.00	3.00
(15)	Dwyer	10.00	5.00	3.00
(16)	Edwards	10.00	5.00	3.00
(17)	Enbanks	10.00	5.00	3.00
(18)	Eubank	10.00	5.00	3.00
(19)	Fox	10.00	5.00	3.00
(20)	Hannifan	10.00	5.00	3.00
(21)	Hartley	10.00	5.00	3.00
(22)	Hauser	10.00	5.00	3.00
(23)	Hille	10.00	5.00	3.00
(24)	Howard	10.00	5.00	3.00
(25)	Hoyt	10.00	5.00	3.00
(27)	Ison	10.00	5.00	3.00
(28)	Jones	10.00	5.00	3.00
(29)	Kalkhoff	10.00	5.00	3.00
(30)	Krebs	10.00	5.00	3.00
(31)	Lawrence	10.00	5.00	3.00
(32)	Lee (Jacksonville)	10.00	5.00	3.00
(33)	Lee (Macon)	10.00	5.00	3.00
(34)	Lewis (Columbia)	10.00	5.00	3.00
(35)	Lewis (Columbus)	10.00	5.00	3.00
(36)	Lipe (batting)	10.00	5.00	3.00
(37)	Lipe (portrait)	10.00	5.00	3.00
(38)	Long	10.00	5.00	3.00
(39)	Magoon	10.00	5.00	3.00
(40)	Manion	10.00	5.00	3.00
(41)	Marshall	10.00	5.00	3.00
(42)	Martin	10.00	5.00	3.00
(43)	Martina	10.00	5.00	3.00
(44)	Massing	10.00	5.00	3.00
(45)	McLeod	10.00	5.00	3.00
(46)	McMahon	10.00	5.00	3.00
(47)	Morse	10.00	5.00	3.00
(48)	Mullane	10.00	5.00	3.00
(49)	Mulldowney	10.00	5.00	3.00
(50)	Murch	10.00	5.00	3.00
(51)	Norcum	10.00	5.00	3.00
(52)	Pelkey	10.00	5.00	3.00
(53)	Petit	10.00	5.00	3.00
(54)	Pierce	10.00	5.00	3.00
(55)	Pope	10.00	5.00	3.00
(56)	Radebaugh	10.00	5.00	3.00
(57)	Raynolds	10.00	5.00	3.00
(58)	Reagan	10.00	5.00	3.00
(59)	Redfern (Redfearn)	10.00	5.00	3.00
(60)	Reynolds	10.00	5.00	3.00
(61)	Schulz	10.00	5.00	3.00
(62)	Schulze	10.00	5.00	3.00
(63)	Schwietzka	10.00	5.00	3.00
(64)	Shields	10.00	5.00	3.00
(65)	Sisson	10.00	5.00	3.00
(66)	Smith	10.00	5.00	3.00
(67)	Sweeney	10.00	5.00	3.00
(68)	Taffee	10.00	5.00	3.00
(69)	Toren	10.00	5.00	3.00
(70)	Viola	10.00	5.00	3.00
(71)	Wagner	10.00	5.00	3.00
(72)	Wahl	10.00	5.00	3.00
(73)	Weems	10.00	5.00	3.00
(74)	Wells	10.00	5.00	3.00
(75)	Wohlleben	10.00	5.00	3.00

1910 T210 Old Mill Series II

		NR MT	EX	VG
Complete Set:		625.00	312.00	187.00
Common Player:		9.00	4.50	2.75
(1)	Andrada	9.00	4.50	2.75
(2)	Archer	9.00	4.50	2.75
(3)	Baker	9.00	4.50	2.75
(4)	Beham	9.00	4.50	2.75
(5)	Bonner	9.00	4.50	2.75
(6)	Bowen	9.00	4.50	2.75
(7)	Brandon	9.00	4.50	2.75
(8)	Breivogel	9.00	4.50	2.75
(9)	Brooks	9.00	4.50	2.75
(10)	Brown	9.00	4.50	2.75
(11)	Busch	9.00	4.50	2.75
(12)	Bussey	9.00	4.50	2.75
(13)	Cefalu	9.00	4.50	2.75
(14)	Chandler	9.00	4.50	2.75
(15)	Clarke	9.00	4.50	2.75
(16)	Clunk	9.00	4.50	2.75
(17)	Cote	9.00	4.50	2.75
(18)	Cowan	9.00	4.50	2.75
(19)	Decker	9.00	4.50	2.75
(20)	Doyle	9.00	4.50	2.75
(21)	Eddowes	9.00	4.50	2.75
(22)	Fisher	9.00	4.50	2.75
(23)	Fox	9.00	4.50	2.75
(24)	Foxen	9.00	4.50	2.75
(25)	Gaston	9.00	4.50	2.75
(26)	Gehring	9.00	4.50	2.75
(27)	Griffin (Danville)	9.00	4.50	2.75
(28)	Griffin (Lynchburg)	9.00	4.50	2.75
(29)	Hale	9.00	4.50	2.75
(30)	Hamilton	9.00	4.50	2.75
(31)	Hanks	9.00	4.50	2.75
(32)	Hannafin	9.00	4.50	2.75
(33)	Hoffman	9.00	4.50	2.75
(34)	Holland	9.00	4.50	2.75
(35)	Hooker	9.00	4.50	2.75
(36)	Irving	9.00	4.50	2.75
(37)	Jackson (Lynchburg)	9.00	4.50	2.75
(38)	Jackson (Norfolk)	9.00	4.50	2.75
(39)	Jackson (Portsmouth)	9.00	4.50	2.75
(40)	Jackson (Richmond)	9.00	4.50	2.75
(41)	Jenkins	9.00	4.50	2.75
(42)	Keifel	9.00	4.50	2.75
(43)	Kirkpatrick	9.00	4.50	2.75
(44)	Kunkel	9.00	4.50	2.75
(45)	Landgraff	9.00	4.50	2.75
(46)	Larkins	9.00	4.50	2.75
(47)	Laughlin	9.00	4.50	2.75
(48)	Lawlor	9.00	4.50	2.75
(49)	Levy	9.00	4.50	2.75
(50)	Lloyd	9.00	4.50	2.75
(51)	Loos	9.00	4.50	2.75
(52)	Lovell	9.00	4.50	2.75
(53)	Lucia	9.00	4.50	2.75
(54)	MacConachie	9.00	4.50	2.75
(55)	Mayberry	9.00	4.50	2.75
(56)	McFarland	9.00	4.50	2.75
(57)	Messitt	9.00	4.50	2.75
(58)	Michel	9.00	4.50	2.75
(59)	Mullaney	9.00	4.50	2.75
(60)	Munson	9.00	4.50	2.75
(61)	Neuton	9.00	4.50	2.75
(62)	Nimmo	9.00	4.50	2.75
(63)	Norris	9.00	4.50	2.75
(64)	Peterson	9.00	4.50	2.75
(65)	Powell	9.00	4.50	2.75
(66)	Pressly (Pressley)	9.00	4.50	2.75
(67)	Pritchard	9.00	4.50	2.75
(68)	Revelle	9.00	4.50	2.75
(69)	Rowe	9.00	4.50	2.75
(70)	Schmidt	9.00	4.50	2.75
(71)	Schrader	9.00	4.50	2.75
(72)	Sharp	9.00	4.50	2.75
(73)	Shaw	9.00	4.50	2.75
(74)	Smith (Lynchburg, batting)	9.00	4.50	2.75
(75)	Smith (Lynchburg, catching)	9.00	4.50	2.75
(76)	Smith (Portsmouth)	9.00	4.50	2.75
(77)	Spicer	9.00	4.50	2.75
(78)	Titman	9.00	4.50	2.75
(79)	Toner	9.00	4.50	2.75
(80)	Tydeman	9.00	4.50	2.75
(81)	Vail	9.00	4.50	2.75
(82)	Verbout	9.00	4.50	2.75
(83)	Walker	9.00	4.50	2.75
(84)	Wallace	9.00	4.50	2.75
(85)	Waymack	9.00	4.50	2.75
(86)	Woolums	9.00	4.50	2.75
(87)	Zimmerman	9.00	4.50	2.75

1910 T210 Old Mill Series III

		NR MT	EX	VG
Complete Set:		775.00	387.00	232.00
Common Player:		10.00	5.00	3.00
(1)	Alexander	10.00	5.00	3.00
(2)	Ash	10.00	5.00	3.00
(3)	Bandy	10.00	5.00	3.00
(4)	Barenkemp	10.00	5.00	3.00
(5)	Belew	10.00	5.00	3.00
(6)	Bell	10.00	5.00	3.00
(7)	Bennett	10.00	5.00	3.00
(8)	Berlck	10.00	5.00	3.00
(9)	Billiard	10.00	5.00	3.00
(10)	Blanding	10.00	5.00	3.00
(11)	Blue	10.00	5.00	3.00
(12)	Burch	10.00	5.00	3.00
(13)	Burk	10.00	5.00	3.00
(14)	Carlin	10.00	5.00	3.00
(15)	Conaway	10.00	5.00	3.00
(16)	Corkhill	10.00	5.00	3.00
(17)	Cowan	10.00	5.00	3.00
(18)	Coyle	10.00	5.00	3.00
(19)	Crable	10.00	5.00	3.00
(20)	Curry	10.00	5.00	3.00
(21)	Dale	10.00	5.00	3.00
(22)	Davis	10.00	5.00	3.00
(23)	Deardorff	10.00	5.00	3.00
(24)	Donnelley	10.00	5.00	3.00
(25)	Doyle	10.00	5.00	3.00
(26)	Druke	10.00	5.00	3.00
(27)	Dugey	10.00	5.00	3.00
(28)	Ens	10.00	5.00	3.00
(29)	Evans	10.00	5.00	3.00
(30)	Fillman	10.00	5.00	3.00
(31)	Firestine	10.00	5.00	3.00
(32)	Francis	10.00	5.00	3.00
(33)	Galloway	10.00	5.00	3.00
(34)	Gardner	10.00	5.00	3.00
(35)	Gear	10.00	5.00	3.00
(36)	Glawe	10.00	5.00	3.00
(37)	Gordon	10.00	5.00	3.00
(38)	Gowdy	10.00	5.00	3.00
(39)	Harbison	10.00	5.00	3.00
(40)	Harper	10.00	5.00	3.00
(41)	Hicks	10.00	5.00	3.00
(42)	Hill	10.00	5.00	3.00
(43)	Hinninger	10.00	5.00	3.00
(44)	Hirsch	10.00	5.00	3.00
(45)	Hise	10.00	5.00	3.00
(46)	Hooks	10.00	5.00	3.00
(47)	Hornsby	10.00	5.00	3.00
(48)	Howell	10.00	5.00	3.00
(49)	Johnston	10.00	5.00	3.00
(50)	Jolley	10.00	5.00	3.00
(51)	Jones	10.00	5.00	3.00
(52)	Kaphan	10.00	5.00	3.00
(53)	Kipp	10.00	5.00	3.00
(54)	Leidy	10.00	5.00	3.00
(55)	Malloy	10.00	5.00	3.00
(56)	Maloney	10.00	5.00	3.00
(57)	Meagher	10.00	5.00	3.00
(58)	Merritt	10.00	5.00	3.00
(59)	McKay	10.00	5.00	3.00
(60)	Mills	10.00	5.00	3.00
(61)	Morris	10.00	5.00	3.00
(63)	Munsell	10.00	5.00	3.00
(64)	Nagel	10.00	5.00	3.00
(65)	Northen	10.00	5.00	3.00
(66)	Ogle	10.00	5.00	3.00
(67)	Onslow	10.00	5.00	3.00
(68)	Pendleton	10.00	5.00	3.00
(69)	Powell	10.00	5.00	3.00
(70)	Riley	10.00	5.00	3.00
(71)	Robertson	10.00	5.00	3.00
(72)	Rose	10.00	5.00	3.00
(73)	Salazor	10.00	5.00	3.00
(74)	Shindel	10.00	5.00	3.00
(75)	Shontz	10.00	5.00	3.00
(76)	Slaven	10.00	5.00	3.00
(77)	Smith (bat over shoulder)	10.00	5.00	3.00
(78)	Smith (bat at hip level)	10.00	5.00	3.00
(79)	Spangler	10.00	5.00	3.00
(80)	Stadeli	10.00	5.00	3.00
(81)	Stinson	10.00	5.00	3.00
(82)	Storch	10.00	5.00	3.00
(83)	Stringer	10.00	5.00	3.00
(84)	Tesreau	10.00	5.00	3.00
(85)	Thebo	10.00	5.00	3.00
(86)	Tullas	10.00	5.00	3.00
(87)	Walsh	10.00	5.00	3.00
(88)	Watson	10.00	5.00	3.00
(89)	Weber	10.00	5.00	3.00
(90)	Weeks	10.00	5.00	3.00
(91)	Wertherford	10.00	5.00	3.00
(92)	Wickenhofer	10.00	5.00	3.00
(93)	Williams	10.00	5.00	3.00
(94)	Woodburn	10.00	5.00	3.00
(95)	Yantz	10.00	5.00	3.00

1910 T210 Old Mill Series IV

		NR MT	EX	VG
Complete Set:		400.00	200.00	120.00
Common Player:		10.00	5.00	3.00
(1)	Aylor	10.00	5.00	3.00
(2)	Benney	10.00	5.00	3.00
(3)	Best	10.00	5.00	3.00
(4)	Bonno	10.00	5.00	3.00
(5)	Brown	10.00	5.00	3.00
(6)	Brumfield	10.00	5.00	3.00
(7)	Campbell	10.00	5.00	3.00
(8)	Canepa	10.00	5.00	3.00
(9)	Carney	10.00	5.00	3.00
(10)	Carter	10.00	5.00	3.00
(11)	Cochrane	10.00	5.00	3.00
(12)	Coller	10.00	5.00	3.00
(13)	Connolly	10.00	5.00	3.00
(14)	Davis	10.00	5.00	3.00
(15)	Connell	10.00	5.00	3.00
(16)	Doshmer	10.00	5.00	3.00
(17)	Dougherty	10.00	5.00	3.00

	NR MT	EX	VG
(18) Erlewein	10.00	5.00	3.00
(19) Farrell	10.00	5.00	3.00
(20) Geary	10.00	5.00	3.00
(21) Halterman	10.00	5.00	3.00
(22) Headly	10.00	5.00	3.00
(23) Hollis	10.00	5.00	3.00
(24) Hunter	10.00	5.00	3.00
(25) Johnson	10.00	5.00	3.00
(26) Kane	10.00	5.00	3.00
(27) Kuehn	10.00	5.00	3.00
(28) Leonard	10.00	5.00	3.00
(29) Lux	10.00	5.00	3.00
(30) McClain	10.00	5.00	3.00
(31) Mollenkamp	10.00	5.00	3.00
(32) Moore	10.00	5.00	3.00
(33) Moye	10.00	5.00	3.00
(34) O'Connor	10.00	5.00	3.00
(36) Pick	10.00	5.00	3.00
(37) Pickels	10.00	5.00	3.00
(38) Schafer	10.00	5.00	3.00
(39) Seaman	10.00	5.00	3.00
(40) Spicer	10.00	5.00	3.00
(41) Stanley	10.00	5.00	3.00
(42) Stockum	10.00	5.00	3.00
(43) Titlow	10.00	5.00	3.00
(44) Waldron	10.00	5.00	3.00
(45) Wills	10.00	5.00	3.00
(46) Witter	10.00	5.00	3.00
(47) Womach	10.00	5.00	3.00
(48) Young	10.00	5.00	3.00
(49) Zurlage	10.00	5.00	3.00

1910 T210 Old Mill Series V

	NR MT	EX	VG
Complete Set:	725.00	362.00	217.00
Common Player:	10.00	5.00	3.00
(1) Abercrombie	10.00	5.00	3.00
(2) Averett	10.00	5.00	3.00
(3) Bansewein	10.00	5.00	3.00
(4) Bentley	10.00	5.00	3.00
(5) C.G. Beusse	10.00	5.00	3.00
(6) Fred Beusse	10.00	5.00	3.00
(7) Bigbie	10.00	5.00	3.00
(8) Eivens	10.00	5.00	3.00
(9) Blackstone	10.00	5.00	3.00
(10) Brannon	10.00	5.00	3.00
(11) Brazell	10.00	5.00	3.00
(12) Brent	10.00	5.00	3.00
(13) Bullock	10.00	5.00	3.00
(14) Cashion	10.00	5.00	3.00
(15) Corbett	10.00	5.00	3.00
(16) Corbett	10.00	5.00	3.00
(17) Coutts	10.00	5.00	3.00
(18) Lave Cross	10.00	5.00	3.00
(19) Crouch	10.00	5.00	3.00
(20) C.L. Derrick	10.00	5.00	3.00
(21) F.B. Derrick	10.00	5.00	3.00
(22) Dobard	10.00	5.00	3.00
(23) Drumm	10.00	5.00	3.00
(24) Duvie	10.00	5.00	3.00
(25) Ehrhardt	10.00	5.00	3.00
(26) Eldridge	10.00	5.00	3.00
(27) Fairbanks	10.00	5.00	3.00
(28) Farmer	10.00	5.00	3.00
(29) Ferrell	10.00	5.00	3.00
(30) Finn	10.00	5.00	3.00
(31) Flowers	10.00	5.00	3.00
(32) Fogarty	10.00	5.00	3.00
(33) Francisco	10.00	5.00	3.00
(34) Gardin	10.00	5.00	3.00
(35) Gilmore	10.00	5.00	3.00
(36) Gorham	10.00	5.00	3.00
(37) Gorman	10.00	5.00	3.00
(38) Guss	10.00	5.00	3.00
(39) Hammersley	10.00	5.00	3.00
(40) Hargrave	10.00	5.00	3.00
(41) Harrington	10.00	5.00	3.00
(42) Harris	10.00	5.00	3.00
(43) Hartley	10.00	5.00	3.00
(44) Hayes	10.00	5.00	3.00
(45) Hicks	10.00	5.00	3.00
(46) Humphrey	10.00	5.00	3.00
(47) Jackson	10.00	5.00	3.00
(48) James	10.00	5.00	3.00
(49) Jenkins	10.00	5.00	3.00
(50) Johnston	10.00	5.00	3.00
(51) Kelly	10.00	5.00	3.00
(52) Laval	10.00	5.00	3.00
(53) Lothrop	10.00	5.00	3.00
(54) MacConachie	10.00	5.00	3.00
(55) Mangum	10.00	5.00	3.00
(56) A. McCarthy	10.00	5.00	3.00
(57) J. McCarthy	10.00	5.00	3.00
(58) McEnroe	10.00	5.00	3.00
(59) McFarlin	10.00	5.00	3.00
(60) McHugh	10.00	5.00	3.00
(61) McKevitt	10.00	5.00	3.00
(62) Midkiff	10.00	5.00	3.00
(63) Moore	10.00	5.00	3.00
(64) Noojin	10.00	5.00	3.00
(65) Ochs	10.00	5.00	3.00
(66) Painter	10.00	5.00	3.00
(67) Redfern (Redfearn)	10.00	5.00	3.00
(68) Reis	10.00	5.00	3.00
(69) Rickard	10.00	5.00	3.00
(70) Roth (batting)	10.00	5.00	3.00
(71) Roth (fielding)	10.00	5.00	3.00
(72) Smith	10.00	5.00	3.00
(73) Springs	10.00	5.00	3.00
(74) Stouch	10.00	5.00	3.00
(75) Taxis	10.00	5.00	3.00
(76) Templin	10.00	5.00	3.00
(77) Thrasher	10.00	5.00	3.00
(78) Trammell	10.00	5.00	3.00
(79) Walker	10.00	5.00	3.00
(80) Walters	10.00	5.00	3.00
(81) Wehrell	10.00	5.00	3.00
(82) Weldon	10.00	5.00	3.00
(83) Williams	10.00	5.00	3.00
(84) Wingo	10.00	5.00	3.00
(85) Workman	10.00	5.00	3.00
(86) Wynne	10.00	5.00	3.00
(87) Wysong	10.00	5.00	3.00

1910 T210 Old Mill Series VI

	NR MT	EX	VG
Complete Set:	1100.	550.00	330.00
Common Player:	12.00	6.00	3.50
(1) Angermeier (fielding)	12.00	6.00	3.50
(2) Angermeir (portrait)	12.00	6.00	3.50
(3) Atwell	12.00	6.00	3.50
(4) Badger	12.00	6.00	3.50
(5) Barnett	12.00	6.00	3.50
(6) Barney	12.00	6.00	3.50
(7) Beard	12.00	6.00	3.50
(8) Bohannon	12.00	6.00	3.50
(9) Callahan	12.00	6.00	3.50
(10) Chapman	12.00	6.00	3.50
(11) Chase	12.00	6.00	3.50
(12) Coleman	12.00	6.00	3.50
(13) Cornell (Frankfort)	12.00	6.00	3.50
(14) Cornell (Winchester)	12.00	6.00	3.50
(15) Creager	12.00	6.00	3.50
(16) Dailey	12.00	6.00	3.50
(17) Edington	12.00	6.00	3.50
(18) Elgin	12.00	6.00	3.50
(19) Ellis	12.00	6.00	3.50
(20) Everden	12.00	6.00	3.50
(21) Gisler	12.00	6.00	3.50
(22) Goodman	12.00	6.00	3.50
(23) Goostree (hands behind back)	12.00	6.00	3.50
(24) Goostree (leaning on bat)	12.00	6.00	3.50
(25) Haines	12.00	6.00	3.50
(26) Harold	12.00	6.00	3.50
(27) Heveron	12.00	6.00	3.50
(28) Hicks	12.00	6.00	3.50
(29) Hoffmann	12.00	6.00	3.50
(30) Horn	12.00	6.00	3.50
(31) Kaiser	12.00	6.00	3.50
(32) Keifel	12.00	6.00	3.50
(33) Kimbrough	12.00	6.00	3.50
(34) Kirchen	12.00	6.00	3.50
(35) Kircher	12.00	6.00	3.50
(36) Kuhlman	12.00	6.00	3.50
(37) Kuhlmann	12.00	6.00	3.50
(38) L'Heureux	12.00	6.00	3.50
(39) Mulvain	12.00	6.00	3.50
(40) McKernan	12.00	6.00	3.50
(41) Meyers	12.00	6.00	3.50
(42) Moloney	12.00	6.00	3.50
(43) Mullin	12.00	6.00	3.50
(44) Olson	12.00	6.00	3.50
(45) Oyler	12.00	6.00	3.50
(46) Reed	12.00	6.00	3.50
(47) Ross	12.00	6.00	3.50
(48) Scheneberg (fielding)	12.00	6.00	3.50
(49) Scheneberg (portrait)	12.00	6.00	3.50
(50) Schultz	12.00	6.00	3.50
(51) Scott	12.00	6.00	3.50
(52) Sinex	12.00	6.00	3.50
(53) Stengel	1000.	500.00	300.00
(54) Thoss	12.00	6.00	3.50
(55) Tilford	12.00	6.00	3.50
(56) Toney	12.00	6.00	3.50
(57) Van Landingham (Valladingham) (Lexington)	12.00	6.00	3.50
(58) Van Landingham (Valladingham) (Shelbyville)	12.00	6.00	3.50
(59) Viox	12.00	6.00	3.50
(60) Walden	12.00	6.00	3.50
(61) Whitaker	12.00	6.00	3.50
(62) Wills	12.00	6.00	3.50
(63) Womble	12.00	6.00	3.50
(64) Wright	12.00	6.00	3.50
(65) Yaeger	12.00	6.00	3.50
(66) Yancey	12.00	6.00	3.50

1910 T210 Old Mill Series VII

	NR MT	EX	VG
Complete Set:	1100.	550.00	330.00
Common Player:	15.00	7.50	4.50
(1) Armstrong	15.00	7.50	4.50
(2) Beatty	15.00	7.50	4.50
(3) Biel	15.00	7.50	4.50
(4) Bonner	15.00	7.50	4.50
(5) Brandt	15.00	7.50	4.50
(6) Brown	15.00	7.50	4.50
(7) Cantwell	15.00	7.50	4.50
(8) Carrol	15.00	7.50	4.50
(9) Cooney	15.00	7.50	4.50
(10) Cooper	15.00	7.50	4.50
(11) Cowell	15.00	7.50	4.50
(12) Creager (Cregan)	15.00	7.50	4.50
(13) Crockett	15.00	7.50	4.50
(14) Dailey	15.00	7.50	4.50
(15) Dobbs	15.00	7.50	4.50
(16) Dussault	15.00	7.50	4.50
(17) Dwyer	15.00	7.50	4.50
(18) Evans	15.00	7.50	4.50
(19) Forgue	15.00	7.50	4.50
(20) Fulton	15.00	7.50	4.50
(21) Galvin	15.00	7.50	4.50
(22) Gastmeyer (batting)	15.00	7.50	4.50
(23) Gastmeyer (fielding)	15.00	7.50	4.50
(24) Gates	15.00	7.50	4.50
(25) Gillespie	15.00	7.50	4.50
(26) Griffin	15.00	7.50	4.50
(27) Gunderson	15.00	7.50	4.50
(28) Ham	15.00	7.50	4.50
(29) Handibe (Handiboe)	15.00	7.50	4.50
(30) Hart	15.00	7.50	4.50
(31) Hartley	15.00	7.50	4.50
(32) Hobbs	15.00	7.50	4.50
(33) Hyames	15.00	7.50	4.50
(34) Irving	15.00	7.50	4.50
(35) Kaiser	15.00	7.50	4.50
(36) Kelley	15.00	7.50	4.50
(37) Kelly	15.00	7.50	4.50
(38) Kelly (mascot)	15.00	7.50	4.50
(39) Luyster	15.00	7.50	4.50
(40) MacDonald	15.00	7.50	4.50
(41) Malcolm	15.00	7.50	4.50
(42) Mayer	15.00	7.50	4.50
(43) McCormac (McCormick)	15.00	7.50	4.50
(44) McGeeham (McGeehan)	15.00	7.50	4.50
(45) Merchant	15.00	7.50	4.50
(46) Mills	15.00	7.50	4.50
(47) Morgan	15.00	7.50	4.50
(48) Morris	15.00	7.50	4.50
(49) Munson	15.00	7.50	4.50
(50) Newman	15.00	7.50	4.50
(51) Noval (Novak)	15.00	7.50	4.50
(52) O'Halloran	15.00	7.50	4.50
(53) Phelan	15.00	7.50	4.50
(54) Prim	15.00	7.50	4.50
(55) Reeves	15.00	7.50	4.50
(56) Richardson	15.00	7.50	4.50
(57) Schumaker	15.00	7.50	4.50
(58) Sharp	15.00	7.50	4.50
(59) Sherrill	15.00	7.50	4.50
(60) Simmons	15.00	7.50	4.50
(61) Steinbach	15.00	7.50	4.50
(62) Stohr	15.00	7.50	4.50
(63) Taylor	15.00	7.50	4.50
(64) Webb	15.00	7.50	4.50
(65) Whelan	15.00	7.50	4.50
(66) Wolf	15.00	7.50	4.50
(67) Wright	15.00	7.50	4.50

1910 T210 Old Mill Series VIII

	NR MT	EX	VG
Complete Set:	2000.	1000.	600.00
Common Player:	12.00	6.00	3.50
(1) Allen (Memphis)	12.00	6.00	3.50
(2) Allen (Mobile)	12.00	6.00	3.50
(3) Anderson	12.00	6.00	3.50
(4) Babb	12.00	6.00	3.50
(5) Bartley	12.00	6.00	3.50
(6) Bauer	12.00	6.00	3.50
(7) Bay	12.00	6.00	3.50
(8) Bayliss	12.00	6.00	3.50
(9) Berger	12.00	6.00	3.50
(10) Bernhard	12.00	6.00	3.50
(11) Bitroff	12.00	6.00	3.50
(12) Breitenstein	12.00	6.00	3.50
(13) Bronkie	12.00	6.00	3.50
(14) Brooks	12.00	6.00	3.50
(15) Burnett	12.00	6.00	3.50
(16) Cafalu	12.00	6.00	3.50
(17) Carson	12.00	6.00	3.50
(18) Case	12.00	6.00	3.50
(19) Chappelle	12.00	6.00	3.50
(20) Cohen	12.00	6.00	3.50
(21) Collins	12.00	6.00	3.50
(22) Crandall	12.00	6.00	3.50
(23) Cross	12.00	6.00	3.50
(24) Jud. Daly	12.00	6.00	3.50
(25) Davis	12.00	6.00	3.50
(26) Demaree	12.00	6.00	3.50
(27) DeMontreville	12.00	6.00	3.50
(28) E. DeMontreville	12.00	6.00	3.50
(29) Dick	12.00	6.00	3.50
(30) Dobbs	12.00	6.00	3.50
(31) Dudley	12.00	6.00	3.50
(32) Dunn	12.00	6.00	3.50
(33) Elliot	12.00	6.00	3.50
(34) Emery	12.00	6.00	3.50
(35) Erloff	12.00	6.00	3.50
(36) Farrell	12.00	6.00	3.50
(37) Fisher	12.00	6.00	3.50
(38) Fleharty	12.00	6.00	3.50
(39) Flood	12.00	6.00	3.50
(40) Foster	12.00	6.00	3.50
(41) Fritz	12.00	6.00	3.50
(42) Greminger	12.00	6.00	3.50
(43) Gribbon	12.00	6.00	3.50
(44) Griffin	12.00	6.00	3.50
(45) Gygli	12.00	6.00	3.50
(46) Hanks	12.00	6.00	3.50
(47) Hart	12.00	6.00	3.50
(48) Hess	12.00	6.00	3.50
(49) Hickman	12.00	6.00	3.50
(50) Hohnhorst	12.00	6.00	3.50
(51) Huelsman	12.00	6.00	3.50
(52) Jackson	1200.	600.00	350.00
(53) Jordan	12.00	6.00	3.50
(54) Kane	12.00	6.00	3.50
(55) Kelly	12.00	6.00	3.50
(56) Kerwin	12.00	6.00	3.50
(57) Keupper	12.00	6.00	3.50
(58) LaFitte	12.00	6.00	3.50
(59) Larsen	12.00	6.00	3.50
(60) Lindsay	12.00	6.00	3.50
(61) Lynch	12.00	6.00	3.50
(62) Manuel	12.00	6.00	3.50
(63) Manush	12.00	6.00	3.50
(64) Marcan	12.00	6.00	3.50
(65) Maxwell	12.00	6.00	3.50
(66) McBride	12.00	6.00	3.50
(67) McCreery	12.00	6.00	3.50
(68) McGilvray	12.00	6.00	3.50
(69) McLaurin	12.00	6.00	3.50

	NR MT	EX	VG
(70) McTigue	12.00	6.00	3.50
(71) Miller (Chattanooga)	12.00	6.00	3.50
(72) Miller (Montgomery)	12.00	6.00	3.50
(73) Molesworth	12.00	6.00	3.50
(74) Moran	12.00	6.00	3.50
(75) Newton	12.00	6.00	3.50
(76) Nolley	12.00	6.00	3.50
(77) Osteen	12.00	6.00	3.50
(78) Owen	12.00	6.00	3.50
(79) Paige	12.00	6.00	3.50
(80) Patterson	12.00	6.00	3.50
(81) Pepe	12.00	6.00	3.50
(82) Perdue	12.00	6.00	3.50
(83) Peters	12.00	6.00	3.50
(84) Phillips	12.00	6.00	3.50
(85) Pratt	12.00	6.00	3.50
(86) Rementer	12.00	6.00	3.50
(87) Rhodes	12.00	6.00	3.50
(88) Rhoton	12.00	6.00	3.50
(89) Robertson	12.00	6.00	3.50
(90) Rogers	12.00	6.00	3.50
(91) Rohe	12.00	6.00	3.50
(92) Seabough (Seabaugh)	12.00	6.00	3.50
(93) Seitz	12.00	6.00	3.50
(94) Schlitzer	12.00	6.00	3.50
(95) Schopp	12.00	6.00	3.50
(96) Siegle	12.00	6.00	3.50
(97) Smith	12.00	6.00	3.50
(98) Sid. Smith	12.00	6.00	3.50
(99) Steele	12.00	6.00	3.50
(100) Swacina	12.00	6.00	3.50
(101) Sweeney	12.00	6.00	3.50
(102) Thomas (fielding)	12.00	6.00	3.50
(103) Thomas (portrait)	12.00	6.00	3.50
(104) Vinson	12.00	6.00	3.50
(105) Wagner (Birmingham)	12.00	6.00	3.50
(106) Wagner (Mobile)	12.00	6.00	3.50
(107) Walker	12.00	6.00	3.50
(108) Wanner	12.00	6.00	3.50
(109) Welf	12.00	6.00	3.50
(110) Whiteman	12.00	6.00	3.50
(111) Whitney	12.00	6.00	3.50
(112) Wilder	12.00	6.00	3.50
(113) Wiseman	12.00	6.00	3.50
(114) Yerkes	12.00	6.00	3.50

1910 T211 Red Sun

The 1910 minor league tobacco set issued by Red Sun Cigarettes features 75 players from the Southern Association. Known by the American Card Catalog designation T211, the Red Sun issue is similar in size and style to the massive 640-card Old Mill set (T210) issued the same year. Cards in both sets measure 1-1/2" by 2-5/8" and feature glossy black and white player photos. Unlike the Old Mill set, however, the Red Sun cards have a green border surrounding the photograph and a bright red and white advertisement for Red Sun Cigarettes on the back. A line at the bottom promotes the cards as "First Series 1 to 75," implying that additional series would follow, but apparently none ever did. Each of the 75 subjects in the Red Sun set was also pictured in Series Eight of the Old Mill set. Because of the "glossy" nature of the photographs, cards in both the Old Mill and the Red Sun sets were susceptible to cracking, making condition and proper grading of these cards especially important to collectors.

	NR MT	EX	VG
Complete Set:	2700.	1350.	810.00
Common Player:	35.00	17.50	10.50
(1) Allen	35.00	17.50	10.50
(2) Anderson	35.00	17.50	10.50
(3) Babb	35.00	17.50	10.50
(4) Bartley	35.00	17.50	10.50
(5) Bay	35.00	17.50	10.50
(6) Bayliss	35.00	17.50	10.50
(7) Berger	35.00	17.50	10.50
(8) Bernard	35.00	17.50	10.50
(9) Bitroff	35.00	17.50	10.50
(10) Breitenstein	35.00	17.50	10.50
(11) Bronkie	35.00	17.50	10.50
(12) Brooks	35.00	17.50	10.50
(13) Cafalu	35.00	17.50	10.50
(14) Case	35.00	17.50	10.50
(15) Chappelle	35.00	17.50	10.50
(16) Cohen	35.00	17.50	10.50
(17) Cross	35.00	17.50	10.50
(18) Jud. Daly	35.00	17.50	10.50
(19) Davis	35.00	17.50	10.50
(20) DeMontreville	35.00	17.50	10.50
(21) E. DeMontreville	35.00	17.50	10.50
(22) Dick	35.00	17.50	10.50
(23) Dunn	35.00	17.50	10.50
(24) Erloff	35.00	17.50	10.50
(25) Fisher	35.00	17.50	10.50
(26) Flood	35.00	17.50	10.50
(27) Foster	35.00	17.50	10.50
(28) Fritz	35.00	17.50	10.50
(29) Greminger	35.00	17.50	10.50
(30) Gribbon	35.00	17.50	10.50
(31) Griffin	35.00	17.50	10.50
(32) Gygli	35.00	17.50	10.50
(33) Hanks	35.00	17.50	10.50
(34) Hart	35.00	17.50	10.50
(35) Hess	35.00	17.50	10.50
(36) Hickman	35.00	17.50	10.50
(37) Hohnhorst	35.00	17.50	10.50
(38) Huelsman	35.00	17.50	10.50
(39) Jordan	35.00	17.50	10.50
(40) Kane	35.00	17.50	10.50
(41) Kelly	35.00	17.50	10.50
(42) Kerwin	35.00	17.50	10.50
(43) Keupper	35.00	17.50	10.50
(44) LaFitte	35.00	17.50	10.50
(45) Lindsay	35.00	17.50	10.50
(46) Lynch	35.00	17.50	10.50
(47) Manush	35.00	17.50	10.50
(48) McCreery	35.00	17.50	10.50
(49) Miller	35.00	17.50	10.50
(50) Molesworth	35.00	17.50	10.50
(51) Moran	35.00	17.50	10.50
(52) Nolley	35.00	17.50	10.50
(53) Paige	35.00	17.50	10.50
(54) Pepe	35.00	17.50	10.50
(55) Perdue	35.00	17.50	10.50
(56) Pratt	35.00	17.50	10.50
(57) Rhoton	35.00	17.50	10.50
(58) Robertson	35.00	17.50	10.50
(59) Rogers	35.00	17.50	10.50
(60) Rohe	35.00	17.50	10.50
(61) Seabaugh	35.00	17.50	10.50
(62) Seitz	35.00	17.50	10.50
(63) Siegle	35.00	17.50	10.50
(64) Smith	35.00	17.50	10.50
(65) Sid. Smith	35.00	17.50	10.50
(66) Steele	35.00	17.50	10.50
(67) Swacina	35.00	17.50	10.50
(68) Sweeney	35.00	17.50	10.50
(69) Thomas	35.00	17.50	10.50
(70) Vinson	35.00	17.50	10.50
(71) Wagner	35.00	17.50	10.50
(72) Walker	35.00	17.50	10.50
(73) Welf	35.00	17.50	10.50
(74) Wilder	35.00	17.50	10.50
(75) Wiseman	35.00	17.50	10.50

1909 T212 Obak

OLSON, Portland

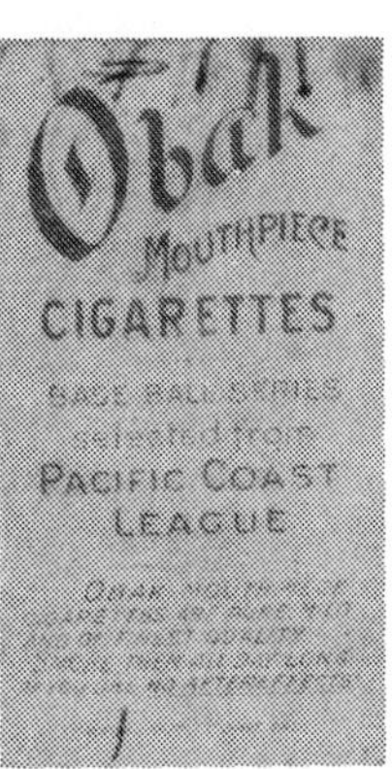

Collectors of early Pacific Coast League memorabilia consider the Obak Cigarette cards to be among the most signifiacant of all the 20th Century minor league tobacco issues. Produced annually from 1909 to 1911, the Obak cards were actually three separate and distinct sets, but because they were all grouped together under a single T212 designation in the American Card Catalog, they are generally collected that way today. The Obak sets are closely related in style to the more popular T206 "White Border" set issued over the same three-year period, and, in fact, were produced by the California branch of the same American Tobacco Company conglomerate. The Obaks are the standard tobacco card size, 1-1/2" by 2-5/8" and feature a colored lithograph, along with the player's name and team, on the front of the card. The year of issue can easily be determined by examing the back. The 1909 issue has blue printing with the name "Obak" appearing in an "Old English" type style; for 1910 the type face was changed to straight block letters; and in 1911 the backs were printed in red and included a brief biography and player statistics. There are 269 different players in the three issues, but, because many of the subjects appeared in more than one year, Obak collectors generally consider the set complete at 426 different cards. The 1909 edition featured only teams from the Pacific Coast League, while the 1910 and 1911 sets were expanded to also include players from the Northwestern League. The Obak sets offer advanced collectors a challenging number of variations, and they have additional appeal because about 40 percent of the checklisted players had major league experience.

	NR MT	EX	VG
Complete Set:	2300.	1150.	690.00
Common Player:	30.00	15.00	9.00
(1) Baum	30.00	15.00	9.00
(2) Bernard	30.00	15.00	9.00
(3) Berry	30.00	15.00	9.00
(4) Bodie	30.00	15.00	9.00
(5) Boyce	30.00	15.00	9.00
(6) Brackenridge	30.00	15.00	9.00
(7) N. Brashear	30.00	15.00	9.00
(8) Breen	30.00	15.00	9.00
(9) Brown	30.00	15.00	9.00
(10) D. Brown	30.00	15.00	9.00
(11) Browning	30.00	15.00	9.00
(12) Byrd	30.00	15.00	9.00
(13) Byrnes	30.00	15.00	9.00
(14) Cameron	30.00	15.00	9.00
(15) Carroll	30.00	15.00	9.00
(16) Carson	30.00	15.00	9.00
(17) Christian	30.00	15.00	9.00
(18) Coy	30.00	15.00	9.00
(19) Delmas	30.00	15.00	9.00
(20) Dillon	30.00	15.00	9.00
(21) Eagan	30.00	15.00	9.00
(22) Easterly (Eastley)	30.00	15.00	9.00
(23) Flannagan	30.00	15.00	9.00
(24) Fisher	30.00	15.00	9.00
(25) Fitzgerald	30.00	15.00	9.00
(26) Gandil	45.00	22.00	13.50
(27) Garrett	30.00	15.00	9.00
(28) Graham	30.00	15.00	9.00
(29) Graney	30.00	15.00	9.00
(30) Griffin	30.00	15.00	9.00
(31) Guyn	30.00	15.00	9.00
(32) Haley	30.00	15.00	9.00
(33) Harkins	30.00	15.00	9.00
(34) Henley	30.00	15.00	9.00
(35) Hitt	30.00	15.00	9.00
(36) Hogan	30.00	15.00	9.00
(37) W. Hogan	30.00	15.00	9.00
(38) Howard	30.00	15.00	9.00
(39) Howse	30.00	15.00	9.00
(40) Jansing	30.00	15.00	9.00
(41) LaLonge	30.00	15.00	9.00
(42) C. Lewis	30.00	15.00	9.00
(43) D. Lewis	35.00	17.50	10.50
(44) J. Lewis	30.00	15.00	9.00
(45) Martinez	30.00	15.00	9.00
(46) McArdle	30.00	15.00	9.00
(47) McCredie	30.00	15.00	9.00
(48) McKune	30.00	15.00	9.00
(49) Melchoir	30.00	15.00	9.00
(50) Mohler	30.00	15.00	9.00
(51) Mott	30.00	15.00	9.00
(52) Mundorff	30.00	15.00	9.00
(53) Murphy	30.00	15.00	9.00
(54) Nagle	30.00	15.00	9.00
(55) Nelson	30.00	15.00	9.00
(56) Olson	30.00	15.00	9.00
(57) Ornsdorff	30.00	15.00	9.00
(58) Ort	30.00	15.00	9.00
(59) Ragan	30.00	15.00	9.00
(60) Raymer	30.00	15.00	9.00
(61) Raymond	30.00	15.00	9.00
(62) Reidy	30.00	15.00	9.00
(63) Ryan	30.00	15.00	9.00
(64) Shinn	30.00	15.00	9.00
(65) Smith	30.00	15.00	9.00
(66) Speas	30.00	15.00	9.00
(67) Stoval (Stovall)	30.00	15.00	9.00
(68) Tennant	30.00	15.00	9.00
(69) Whalen	30.00	15.00	9.00
(70) Wheeler	30.00	15.00	9.00
(71) Wiggs	30.00	15.00	9.00
(72) Willett	30.00	15.00	9.00
(73) J. Williams	30.00	15.00	9.00
(74) R. Williams	30.00	15.00	9.00
(75) Willis	30.00	15.00	9.00
(76) Zeider	30.00	15.00	9.00

1910 T212 Obak

	NR MT	EX	VG
Complete Set:	2400.	1200.	720.00
Common Player:	10.00	5.00	3.00
(1) Agnew	10.00	5.00	3.00
(2) Akin	10.00	5.00	3.00
(3) Ames	10.00	5.00	3.00
(4) Annis	10.00	5.00	3.00
(5a) Armbuster (Armbruster) ("150 subjects" back)	15.00	7.50	4.50
(5b) Armbuster (Armbruster) ("175 subjects" back)	10.00	5.00	3.00
(6) Baker	10.00	5.00	3.00
(7) Bassey	10.00	5.00	3.00
(8) Baum	10.00	5.00	3.00
(9) Beall	10.00	5.00	3.00
(10) Bennett	10.00	5.00	3.00
(11) Bernard	10.00	5.00	3.00
(12a) Berry ("150 subjects" back)	15.00	7.50	4.50
(12b) Berry ("175 subjects" back)	10.00	5.00	3.00
(13) Blankenship	10.00	5.00	3.00

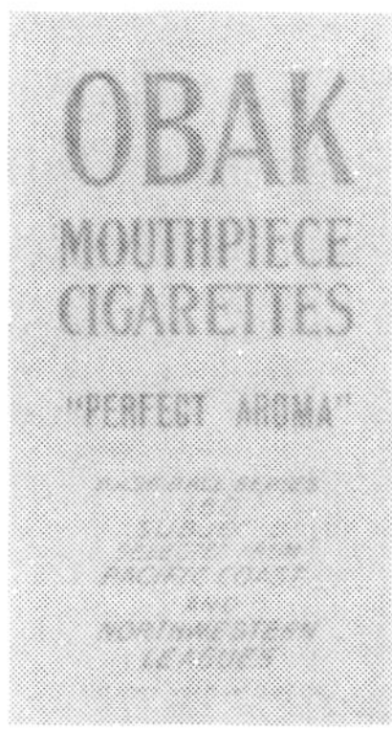

	NR MT	EX	VG
(14) Boardman	10.00	5.00	3.00
(15) Bodie	15.00	7.50	4.50
(16) Bonner	10.00	5.00	3.00
(17a) Brackenridge ("150 subjects" back)	15.00	7.50	4.50
(17b) Brackenridge ("175 subjects" back)	10.00	5.00	3.00
(18a) N. Brashear ("150 subjects" back)	15.00	7.50	4.50
(18b) N. Brashear ("175 subjects" back)	10.00	5.00	3.00
(19) R. Brashear	10.00	5.00	3.00
(20) Breen	10.00	5.00	3.00
(21a) Briggs ("150 subjects" back)	15.00	7.50	4.50
(21b) Briggs ("175 subjects" back)	10.00	5.00	3.00
(22) Brinker	10.00	5.00	3.00
(23) Briswalter	10.00	5.00	3.00
(24) Brooks	10.00	5.00	3.00
(25) Brown (Sacramento)	10.00	5.00	3.00
(26) Brown (Vancouver)	10.00	5.00	3.00
(27) D. Brown	10.00	5.00	3.00
(28) Browning	10.00	5.00	3.00
(29) Burrell	10.00	5.00	3.00
(30) Byrnes	10.00	5.00	3.00
(31a) Cameron ("150 subjects" back)	15.00	7.50	4.50
(31b) Cameron ("175 subjects" back)	10.00	5.00	3.00
(32) Capren (Capron)	10.00	5.00	3.00
(33) Carlisle	10.00	5.00	3.00
(34) Carroll	10.00	5.00	3.00
(35) Cartwright	10.00	5.00	3.00
(36) Casey	10.00	5.00	3.00
(37) Caslleton (Castleton)	10.00	5.00	3.00
(38) Chenault	10.00	5.00	3.00
(39) Christian	10.00	5.00	3.00
(40) Coleman	10.00	5.00	3.00
(41) Cooney	10.00	5.00	3.00
(42a) Coy ("150 subjects" back)	15.00	7.50	4.50
(42b) Coy ("175 subjects" back)	10.00	5.00	3.00
(43a) Criger ("150 subjects" back)	15.00	7.50	4.50
(43b) Criger ("175 subjects" back)	10.00	5.00	3.00
(44) Custer	10.00	5.00	3.00
(45) Cutshaw	10.00	5.00	3.00
(46) Daley	10.00	5.00	3.00
(47a) Danzig ("150 subjects" back)	15.00	7.50	4.50
(47b) Danzig ("175 subjects" back)	10.00	5.00	3.00
(48) Daringer	10.00	5.00	3.00
(49) Davis	10.00	5.00	3.00
(50) Delhi	10.00	5.00	3.00
(51) Delmas	10.00	5.00	3.00
(52a) Dillon ("150 subjects" back)	15.00	7.50	4.50
(52b) Dillon ("175 subjects" back)	10.00	5.00	3.00
(53) Dretchko	10.00	5.00	3.00
(54) Eastley	10.00	5.00	3.00
(55) Erickson	10.00	5.00	3.00
(56) Flannagan	10.00	5.00	3.00
(57) Fisher (Portland)	10.00	5.00	3.00
(58a) Fisher (Vernon, "150 subjects" back)	15.00	7.50	4.50
(58b) Fisher (Vernon, "175 subjects" back)	10.00	5.00	3.00
(59) Fitzgerald	10.00	5.00	3.00
(60) Flood	10.00	5.00	3.00
(61) Fournier	10.00	5.00	3.00
(62) Frisk	10.00	5.00	3.00
(63) Gaddy	10.00	5.00	3.00
(64) Gardner	10.00	5.00	3.00
(65) Garrett	10.00	5.00	3.00
(66) Greggs (Gregg)	10.00	5.00	3.00
(67a) Griffin ("150 subjects" back)	15.00	7.50	4.50
(67b) Griffin ("175 subjects" back)	10.00	5.00	3.00
(68) Gurney	10.00	5.00	3.00
(69) Hall (Seattle)	10.00	5.00	3.00
(70) Hall (Tacoma)	10.00	5.00	3.00
(71) Harkins	10.00	5.00	3.00
(72) Hartman	10.00	5.00	3.00
(73) Hendrix	10.00	5.00	3.00
(74a) Henley ("150 subjects" back)	15.00	7.50	4.50
(74b) Henley ("175 subjects" back)	10.00	5.00	3.00
(75) Hensling	10.00	5.00	3.00
(76) Hetling	10.00	5.00	3.00
(77) Hickey	10.00	5.00	3.00
(78a) Hiester ("150 subjects" back)	15.00	7.50	4.50
(78b) Hiester ("175 subjects" back)	10.00	5.00	3.00
(79) Hitt	10.00	5.00	3.00
(80) Hogan (Oakland)	10.00	5.00	3.00
(81a) Hogan (Vernon, "150 subjects" back)	15.00	7.50	4.50
(81b) Hogan (Vernon, "175 subjects" back)	10.00	5.00	3.00
(82) Hollis	10.00	5.00	3.00
(83) Holm	10.00	5.00	3.00
(84a) Howard ("150 subjects" back)	15.00	7.50	4.50
(84b) Howard ("175 subjects" back)	10.00	5.00	3.00
(85) Hunt	10.00	5.00	3.00
(86) James	10.00	5.00	3.00
(87) Jansing	10.00	5.00	3.00
(88) Jensen	10.00	5.00	3.00
(89) Johnston	10.00	5.00	3.00
(90) Keener	10.00	5.00	3.00
(91) Killilay	10.00	5.00	3.00
(92) Kippert	10.00	5.00	3.00
(93) Klein	10.00	5.00	3.00
(94a) Krapp ("150 subjects" back)	15.00	7.50	4.50
(94b) Krapp ("175 subjects" back)	10.00	5.00	3.00
(95) Kusel	10.00	5.00	3.00
(96a) LaLonge ("150 subjects" back)	15.00	7.50	4.50
(96b) LaLonge ("175 subjects" back)	10.00	5.00	3.00
(97) Lewis	10.00	5.00	3.00
(98) J. Lewis	10.00	5.00	3.00
(99) Lindsay	10.00	5.00	3.00
(100) Lively	10.00	5.00	3.00
(101) Lynch	10.00	5.00	3.00
(102a) Manush ("150 subjects" back)	15.00	7.50	4.50
(102b) Manush ("175 subjects" back)	10.00	5.00	3.00
(103) Martinke	10.00	5.00	3.00
(104a) McArdle ("150 subjects" back)	15.00	7.50	4.50
(104b) McArdle ("175 subjects" back)	10.00	5.00	3.00
(105a) McCredie ("150 subjects" back)	15.00	7.50	4.50
(105b) McCredie ("175 subjects" back)	10.00	5.00	3.00
(106a) Melchoir ("150 subjects" back)	15.00	7.50	4.50
(106b) Melchoir ("175 subjects" back)	10.00	5.00	3.00
(107) Miller (San Francisco)	10.00	5.00	3.00
(108) Miller (Seattle)	10.00	5.00	3.00
(109) Mitze	10.00	5.00	3.00
(110a) Mohler ("150 subjects" back)	15.00	7.50	4.50
(110b) Mohler ("175 subjects" back)	10.00	5.00	3.00
(111a) Moser ("150 subjects" back)	15.00	7.50	4.50
(111b) Moser ("175 subjects" back)	10.00	5.00	3.00
(112) Mott	10.00	5.00	3.00
(113a) Mundorf (name incorrect, "150 subjects" back)	50.00	25.00	15.00
(113b) Mundorff (name correct, "175 subjects" back)	10.00	5.00	3.00
(114a) Murphy ("150 subjects" back)	15.00	7.50	4.50
(114b) Murphy ("175 subjects" back)	10.00	5.00	3.00
(115) Nagle	10.00	5.00	3.00
(116) Nelson	10.00	5.00	3.00
(117) Netzel	10.00	5.00	3.00
(118) Nourse	10.00	5.00	3.00
(119) Nordyke	10.00	5.00	3.00
(120) Olson	10.00	5.00	3.00
(121) Orendorff (Orsnsdorff)	10.00	5.00	3.00
(122a) Ort ("150 subjects" back)	15.00	7.50	4.50
(122b) Ort ("175 subjects" back)	10.00	5.00	3.00
(123) Ostdiek	10.00	5.00	3.00
(124) Pennington	10.00	5.00	3.00
(125) Perrine	10.00	5.00	3.00
(126a) Perry ("150 subjects" back)	15.00	7.50	4.50
(126b) Perry ("175 subjects" back)	10.00	5.00	3.00
(127) Persons	10.00	5.00	3.00
(128a) Rapps ("150 subjects" back)	15.00	7.50	4.50
(128b) Rapps ("175 subjects" back)	10.00	5.00	3.00
(129) Raymer	10.00	5.00	3.00
(130) Raymond	10.00	5.00	3.00
(131) Rockenfield	10.00	5.00	3.00
(132) Roth	10.00	5.00	3.00
(133) D. Ryan	10.00	5.00	3.00
(134) J. Ryan	10.00	5.00	3.00
(135) Scharnweber	10.00	5.00	3.00
(136) Schmutz	10.00	5.00	3.00
(137) Seaton (Portland)	10.00	5.00	3.00
(138) Seaton (Seattle)	10.00	5.00	3.00
(139) Shafer	10.00	5.00	3.00
(140) Shaw	10.00	5.00	3.00
(141) Shea	10.00	5.00	3.00
(142) Shinn	10.00	5.00	3.00
(143) Smith	10.00	5.00	3.00
(144a) H. Smith ("150 subjects" back)	15.00	7.50	4.50
(144b) H. Smith ("175 subjects" back)	10.00	5.00	3.00
(145a) J. Smith ("150 subjects" back)	15.00	7.50	4.50
(145b) J. Smith ("175 subjects" back)	10.00	5.00	3.00
(146) Speas	10.00	5.00	3.00
(147) Spiesman	10.00	5.00	3.00
(148) Starkell	10.00	5.00	3.00
(149a) Steen ("150 subjects" back)	15.00	7.50	4.50
(149b) Steen ("175 subjects" back)	10.00	5.00	3.00
(150) Stevens	10.00	5.00	3.00
(151a) Stewart ("150 subjects" back)	15.00	7.50	4.50
(151b) Stewart ("175 subjects" back)	10.00	5.00	3.00
(152) Stovell (Stovall)	10.00	5.00	3.00
(153) Streib	10.00	5.00	3.00
(154) Sugden	10.00	5.00	3.00
(155) Sutor	10.00	5.00	3.00
(156) Swain	10.00	5.00	3.00
(157a) Swander ("150 subjects" back)	15.00	7.50	4.50
(157b) Swander ("175 subjects" back)	10.00	5.00	3.00
(158) Tennant	10.00	5.00	3.00
(159) Thomas	10.00	5.00	3.00
(160) Thompson	10.00	5.00	3.00
(161) Thorsen	10.00	5.00	3.00
(162a) Tonnesen ("150 subjects" back)	15.00	7.50	4.50
(162b) Tonnesen ("175 subjects" back)	10.00	5.00	3.00
(163) Tozer	10.00	5.00	3.00
(164) Van Buren	10.00	5.00	3.00
(165) Vitt	10.00	5.00	3.00
(166) Wares	10.00	5.00	3.00
(167) Waring	10.00	5.00	3.00
(168) Warren	10.00	5.00	3.00
(169) Weed	10.00	5.00	3.00
(170a) Whalen ("150 subjects" back)	15.00	7.50	4.50
(170b) Whalen ("175 subjects" back)	10.00	5.00	3.00
(171a) Willett ("150 subjects" back)	15.00	7.50	4.50
(171b) Willett ("175 subjects" back)	10.00	5.00	3.00
(172a) Williams ("150 subjects" back)	15.00	7.50	4.50
(172b) Williams ("175 subjects" back)	10.00	5.00	3.00
(173a) Willis ("150 subjects" back)	15.00	7.50	4.50
(173b) Willis ("175 subjects" back)	10.00	5.00	3.00
(174a) Wolverton ("150 subjects" back)	15.00	7.50	4.50
(174b) Wolverton ("175 subjects" back)	10.00	5.00	3.00
(175) Zackert	10.00	5.00	3.00

1911 T212 Obak

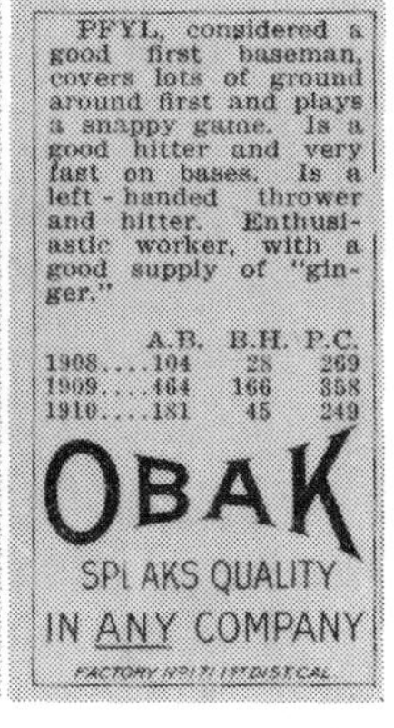

	NR MT	EX	VG
Complete Set:	1800.	900.00	540.00
Common Player:	10.00	5.00	3.00
(1) Abbott	10.00	5.00	3.00
(2) Ables	10.00	5.00	3.00
(3) Adams	10.00	5.00	3.00
(4) Agnew	10.00	5.00	3.00
(5) Akin	10.00	5.00	3.00
(6) Annis	10.00	5.00	3.00
(7) Arrelanes (Arellanes)	10.00	5.00	3.00
(8) Barry	10.00	5.00	3.00
(9) Bassey	10.00	5.00	3.00
(10) Baum	10.00	5.00	3.00
(11) Bennett	10.00	5.00	3.00
(12) Bernard	10.00	5.00	3.00
(13) Berry	10.00	5.00	3.00
(14) Bloomfield	10.00	5.00	3.00
(15) Bonner	10.00	5.00	3.00
(16) Brackenridge	10.00	5.00	3.00
(17) Brashear	10.00	5.00	3.00
(18) R. Brashear	10.00	5.00	3.00
(19) Brinker	10.00	5.00	3.00
(20) Brown	10.00	5.00	3.00
(21) Browning	10.00	5.00	3.00
(22) Bues	10.00	5.00	3.00
(23) Burrell	10.00	5.00	3.00
(24) Burns	10.00	5.00	3.00
(25) Butler	10.00	5.00	3.00
(26) Byram	10.00	5.00	3.00
(27) Carlisle	10.00	5.00	3.00

		NR MT	EX	VG
(28)	Carson	10.00	5.00	3.00
(29)	Cartwright	10.00	5.00	3.00
(30)	Casey	10.00	5.00	3.00
(31)	Castleton	10.00	5.00	3.00
(32)	Chadbourne	10.00	5.00	3.00
(33)	Christian	10.00	5.00	3.00
(34)	Coleman	10.00	5.00	3.00
(35)	Cooney	10.00	5.00	3.00
(36)	Coy	10.00	5.00	3.00
(37)	Criger	10.00	5.00	3.00
(38)	Crukshank	10.00	5.00	3.00
(39)	Cutshaw	10.00	5.00	3.00
(40)	Daley	10.00	5.00	3.00
(41)	Danzig	10.00	5.00	3.00
(42)	Dashwood	10.00	5.00	3.00
(43)	Davis	10.00	5.00	3.00
(44)	Delhi	10.00	5.00	3.00
(45)	Delmas	10.00	5.00	3.00
(46)	Dillon	10.00	5.00	3.00
(47)	Engel	10.00	5.00	3.00
(48)	Erickson	10.00	5.00	3.00
(49)	Fitzgerald	10.00	5.00	3.00
(50)	Flater	10.00	5.00	3.00
(51)	Frisk	10.00	5.00	3.00
(52)	Fullerton	10.00	5.00	3.00
(53)	Garrett	10.00	5.00	3.00
(54)	Goodman	10.00	5.00	3.00
(55)	Gordon	10.00	5.00	3.00
(56)	Grindle	10.00	5.00	3.00
(57)	Hall	10.00	5.00	3.00
(58)	Harris	10.00	5.00	3.00
(59)	Hasty	10.00	5.00	3.00
(60)	Henderson	10.00	5.00	3.00
(61)	Henley	10.00	5.00	3.00
(62)	Hetling	10.00	5.00	3.00
(63)	Hiester	10.00	5.00	3.00
(64)	Higgins	10.00	5.00	3.00
(65)	Hitt	10.00	5.00	3.00
(66)	Hoffman	10.00	5.00	3.00
(67)	Hogan	10.00	5.00	3.00
(68)	Holm	10.00	5.00	3.00
(69)	Householder	10.00	5.00	3.00
(70)	Hosp	10.00	5.00	3.00
(71)	Howard	10.00	5.00	3.00
(72)	Hunt	10.00	5.00	3.00
(73)	James	10.00	5.00	3.00
(74)	Jensen	10.00	5.00	3.00
(75)	Kading	10.00	5.00	3.00
(76)	Kane	10.00	5.00	3.00
(77)	Kippert	10.00	5.00	3.00
(78)	Knight	10.00	5.00	3.00
(79)	Koestner	10.00	5.00	3.00
(80)	Krueger	10.00	5.00	3.00
(81)	Kuhn	10.00	5.00	3.00
(82)	LaLonge	10.00	5.00	3.00
(83)	Lamline	10.00	5.00	3.00
(84)	Leard	10.00	5.00	3.00
(85)	Lerchen	10.00	5.00	3.00
(86)	Lewis	10.00	5.00	3.00
(87)	Madden	10.00	5.00	3.00
(88)	Maggert	10.00	5.00	3.00
(89)	Mahoney	10.00	5.00	3.00
(90)	McArdle	10.00	5.00	3.00
(91)	McCredie	10.00	5.00	3.00
(92)	McDonnell	10.00	5.00	3.00
(93)	Meikle	10.00	5.00	3.00
(94)	Melchoir	10.00	5.00	3.00
(95)	Mensor	10.00	5.00	3.00
(96)	Metzger	10.00	5.00	3.00
(97)	Miller (Oakland)	10.00	5.00	3.00
(98)	Miller (San Francisco)	10.00	5.00	3.00
(99)	Ten Million	10.00	5.00	3.00
(100)	Mitze	10.00	5.00	3.00
(101)	Mohler	10.00	5.00	3.00
(102)	Moore	10.00	5.00	3.00
(103)	Morse	10.00	5.00	3.00
(104)	Moskiman	10.00	5.00	3.00
(105)	Mundorff	10.00	5.00	3.00
(106)	Murray	10.00	5.00	3.00
(107)	Netzel	10.00	5.00	3.00
(108)	Nordyke	10.00	5.00	3.00
(109)	Nourse	10.00	5.00	3.00
(110)	O'Rourke	10.00	5.00	3.00
(111)	Ostdiek	10.00	5.00	3.00
(112)	Patterson	10.00	5.00	3.00
(113)	Pearce	10.00	5.00	3.00
(114)	Peckinpaugh	15.00	7.50	4.50
(115)	Pernoll	10.00	5.00	3.00
(116)	Pfyl	10.00	5.00	3.00
(117)	Powell	10.00	5.00	3.00
(118)	Raleigh	10.00	5.00	3.00
(119)	Rapps	10.00	5.00	3.00
(120)	Raymer	10.00	5.00	3.00
(121)	Raymond	10.00	5.00	3.00
(122)	Reddick	10.00	5.00	3.00
(123)	Roche	10.00	5.00	3.00
(124)	Rockenfield	10.00	5.00	3.00
(125)	Rogers	10.00	5.00	3.00
(126)	Ross	10.00	5.00	3.00
(127)	Ryan	10.00	5.00	3.00
(128)	J. Ryan	10.00	5.00	3.00
(129)	Scharnweber	10.00	5.00	3.00
(130)	Schmidt	10.00	5.00	3.00
(131)	Schmutz	10.00	5.00	3.00
(132)	Seaton (Portland)	10.00	5.00	3.00
(133)	Seaton (Seattle)	10.00	5.00	3.00
(134)	Shaw	10.00	5.00	3.00
(135)	Shea	10.00	5.00	3.00
(136)	Sheehan (Portland)	10.00	5.00	3.00
(137)	Sheehan (Vernon)	10.00	5.00	3.00
(138)	Shinn	10.00	5.00	3.00
(139)	Skeels	10.00	5.00	3.00
(140)	H. Smith	10.00	5.00	3.00
(141)	Speas	10.00	5.00	3.00
(142)	Spencer	10.00	5.00	3.00
(143)	Spiesman	10.00	5.00	3.00
(144)	Starkel	10.00	5.00	3.00
(145)	Steen	10.00	5.00	3.00
(146)	Stewart	10.00	5.00	3.00
(147)	Stinson	10.00	5.00	3.00
(148)	Stovall	10.00	5.00	3.00
(149)	Strand	10.00	5.00	3.00
(150)	Sutor	10.00	5.00	3.00
(151)	Swain	10.00	5.00	3.00
(152)	Tennant	10.00	5.00	3.00
(153)	Thomas (Sacramento)	10.00	5.00	3.00
(154)	Thomas (Victoria)	10.00	5.00	3.00
(155)	Thompson	10.00	5.00	3.00
(156)	Thornton	10.00	5.00	3.00
(157)	Thorsen	10.00	5.00	3.00
(158)	Tiedeman	10.00	5.00	3.00
(159)	Tozer	10.00	5.00	3.00
(160)	Van Buren	10.00	5.00	3.00
(161)	Vitt	10.00	5.00	3.00
(162)	Ward	10.00	5.00	3.00
(163)	Wares	10.00	5.00	3.00
(164)	Warren	10.00	5.00	3.00
(165)	Weaver	20.00	10.00	6.00
(166)	Weed	10.00	5.00	3.00
(167)	Wheeler	10.00	5.00	3.00
(168)	Wiggs	10.00	5.00	3.00
(169)	Willett	10.00	5.00	3.00
(170)	Williams	10.00	5.00	3.00
(171)	Wolverton	10.00	5.00	3.00
(172)	Zacher	10.00	5.00	3.00
(173)	Zackert	10.00	5.00	3.00
(174)	Zamlock	10.00	5.00	3.00
(175)	Zimmerman	10.00	5.00	3.00

1910 T213 Coupon - Type 1

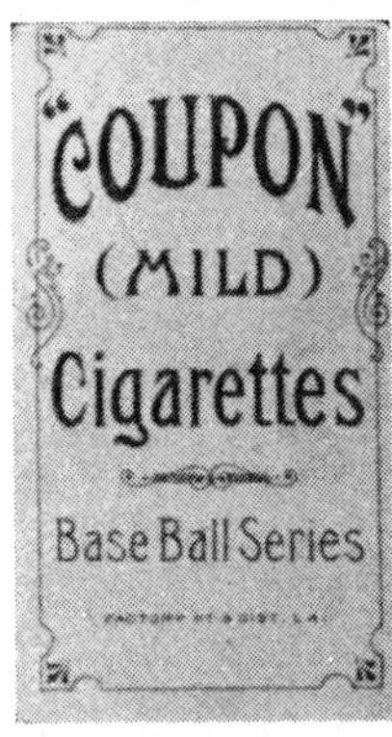

Because they feature the same photos used in the classic T206 tobacco set, some collectors fail to recognize the T213 Coupon set as a separate issue. Actually, the Coupon Cigarette cards make up three separate issues, produced from 1910 to 1919 and featuring a mix of players from the major leagues, the Federal League and the Southern League. While the fronts of the Coupon cards appear to be identical to the more popular T206 series, the backs clearly identify the cards as being a product of Coupon Cigarettes and allow the collector to easily differentiate between the three types. The Type I cards, produced in 1910, carry a general advertisement for Coupon "Mild" Cigarettes, while the Type II cards, issued from 1914 to 1916, contain the words "20 for 5 cents," and the Type III cards, issued in 1919, advertise "16 for 10 cts." Distribution of the Coupon cards was limited to the Louisiana area, making the set very obscure and difficult to checklist. Numerous variations further complicate the situation. To date, 68 different Type I cards have been found, 188 different Type II, and 69 Type III. Advanced collectors, however, speculate that more may exist. Type I cards are considered the rarest of the Coupon issues, and, because they were printed on a thinner stock, they are especially difficult to find in top condition. Although Type II cards are the most common, they were printed with a "glossy" coating, making them susceptible to cracking and creasing.

		NR MT	EX	VG
Complete Set:		7000.	3500.	2100.
Common Player:		65.00	32.00	19.50
(1)	Harry Bay	65.00	32.00	19.50
(2)	Beals Becker	65.00	32.00	19.50
(3)	Chief Bender	125.00	62.00	37.00
(4)	Bernhard	65.00	32.00	19.50
(5)	Ted Breitenstein	65.00	32.00	19.50
(6)	Bobby Byrne	65.00	32.00	19.50
(7)	Billy Campbell	65.00	32.00	19.50
(8)	Scoops Carey	125.00	62.00	37.00
(9)	Frank Chance	200.00	100.00	60.00
(10)	Chappy Charles	65.00	32.00	19.50
(11)	Hal Chase (portrait)	80.00	40.00	24.00
(12)	Hal Chase (throwing)	80.00	40.00	24.00
(13)	Ty Cobb	1000.	500.00	300.00
(14)	Bill Cranston	65.00	32.00	19.50
(15)	Birdie Cree	65.00	32.00	19.50
(16)	Wild Bill Donovan	65.00	32.00	19.50
(17)	Mickey Doolan	65.00	32.00	19.50
(18)	Jean Dubuc	65.00	32.00	19.50
(19)	Joe Dunn	65.00	32.00	19.50
(20)	Roy Ellam	65.00	32.00	19.50
(21)	Clyde Engle	65.00	32.00	19.50
(22)	Johnny Evers	125.00	62.00	37.00
(23)	Art Fletcher	65.00	32.00	19.50
(24)	Charlie Fritz	65.00	32.00	19.50
(25)	Ed Greminger	65.00	32.00	19.50
(26)	Bill Hart (Little Rock)	65.00	32.00	19.50
(27)	Jimmy Hart (Montgomery)	65.00	32.00	19.50
(28)	Topsy Hartsel	65.00	32.00	19.50
(29)	Gordon Hickman	65.00	32.00	19.50
(30)	Danny Hoffman	65.00	32.00	19.50
(31)	Harry Howell	65.00	32.00	19.50
(32)	Miller Huggins (hands at mouth)	125.00	62.00	37.00
(33)	Miller Huggins (portrait)	125.00	62.00	37.00
(34)	George Hunter	65.00	32.00	19.50
(35)	A.O. "Dutch" Jordan	65.00	32.00	19.50
(36)	Ed Killian	65.00	32.00	19.50
(37)	Otto Knabe	65.00	32.00	19.50
(38)	Frank LaPorte	65.00	32.00	19.50
(39)	Ed Lennox	65.00	32.00	19.50
(40)	Harry Lentz (Sentz)	65.00	32.00	19.50
(41)	Rube Marquard	125.00	62.00	37.00
(42)	Doc Marshall	65.00	32.00	19.50
(43)	Christy Mathewson	400.00	200.00	120.00
(44)	George McBride	65.00	32.00	19.50
(45)	Pryor McElveen	65.00	32.00	19.50
(46)	Matty McIntyre	65.00	32.00	19.50
(47)	Mike Mitchell	65.00	32.00	19.50
(48)	Carlton Molesworth	65.00	32.00	19.50
(49)	Mike Mowrey	65.00	32.00	19.50
(50)	Chief Myers (Meyers) (batting)	65.00	32.00	19.50
(51)	Chief Myers (Meyers) (fielding)	65.00	32.00	19.50
(52)	Dode Paskert	65.00	32.00	19.50
(53)	Hub Perdue	65.00	32.00	19.50
(54)	Arch Persons	65.00	32.00	19.50
(55)	Ed Reagan	65.00	32.00	19.50
(56)	Bob Rhoades (Rhoads)	65.00	32.00	19.50
(57)	Ike Rockenfeld	65.00	32.00	19.50
(58)	Claude Rossman	65.00	32.00	19.50
(59)	Boss Schmidt	65.00	32.00	19.50
(60)	Sid Smith	65.00	32.00	19.50
(61)	Charlie Starr	65.00	32.00	19.50
(62)	Gabby Street	65.00	32.00	19.50
(63)	Ed Summers	65.00	32.00	19.50
(64)	Jeff Sweeney	65.00	32.00	19.50
(65)	Ira Thomas	65.00	32.00	19.50
(66)	Woodie Thornton	65.00	32.00	19.50
(67)	Ed Willett	65.00	32.00	19.50
(68)	Owen Wilson	65.00	32.00	19.50

1914 T213 Coupon - Type 2

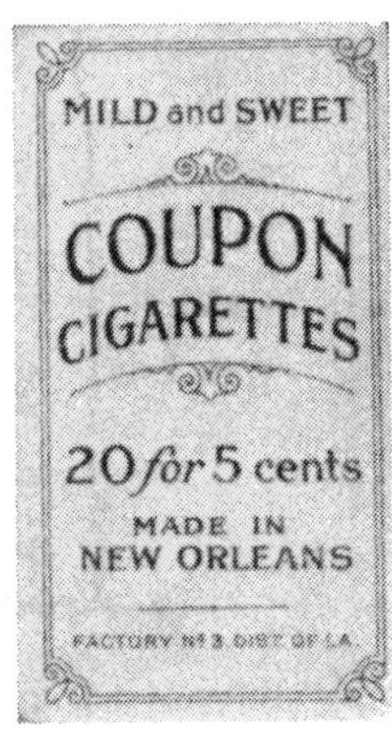

		NR MT	EX	VG
Complete Set:		8500.	4250.	2550.
Common Player:		30.00	15.00	9.00
(1a)	Red Ames (Cincinnati)	30.00	15.00	9.00
(1b)	Red Ames (St. Louis)	30.00	15.00	9.00
(2a)	Home Run Baker (Phila. Amer.)	70.00	35.00	21.00
(2b)	Home Run Baker (Philadelphia Amer.)	70.00	35.00	21.00
(2c)	Home Run Baker (New York)	70.00	35.00	21.00
(3)	Cy Barger	30.00	15.00	9.00
(4a)	Chief Bender (trees in background, Philadelphia Amer.)	70.00	35.00	21.00
(4b)	Chief Bender (trees in background, Baltimore)	70.00	35.00	21.00
(4c)	Chief Bender (trees in background, Philadelphia Nat.)	70.00	35.00	21.00
(5a)	Chief Bender (no trees in background, Philadelphia Amer.)	70.00	35.00	21.00
(5b)	Chief Bender (no trees in background, Baltimore)	70.00	35.00	21.00
(5c)	Chief Bender (no trees in background, Philadelphia Nat.)	70.00	35.00	21.00
(6)	Bill Bradley	30.00	15.00	9.00
(7a)	Roger Bresnahan (Chicago)	70.00	35.00	21.00
(7b)	Roger Bresnahan (Toledo)	70.00	35.00	21.00
(8a)	Al Bridwell (St. Louis)	30.00	15.00	9.00
(8b)	Al Bridwell (Nashville)	30.00	15.00	9.00
(9a)	Mordecai Brown (Chicago)	70.00	35.00	21.00
(9b)	Mordecai Brown (St. Louis)	70.00	35.00	21.00
(10)	Bobby Byrne	30.00	15.00	9.00
(11)	Howie Camnitz (arm at side)	30.00	15.00	9.00
(12a)	Howie Camnitz (Pittsburgh, hands above head)	30.00	15.00	9.00

No.	Player	NR MT	EX	VG
(12b)	Howie Camnitz (Savannah, hands above head)	30.00	15.00	9.00
(13)	Billy Campbell	30.00	15.00	9.00
(14a)	Frank Chance (batting, New York)	85.00	42.00	25.00
(14b)	Frank Chance (Los Angeles, batting)	85.00	42.00	25.00
(15a)	Frank Chance (New York, portrait)	85.00	42.00	25.00
(15b)	Frank Chance (Los Angeles, portrait)	85.00	42.00	25.00
(16a)	Bill Chapelle (Brooklyn, "R" on shirt)	30.00	15.00	9.00
(16b)	Larry Chapelle (Chappel) (Cleveland, no "R" on shirt, photo actually Bill Chapelle)	30.00	15.00	9.00
(17a)	Hal Chase (Chicago, holding trophy)	50.00	25.00	15.00
(17b)	Hal Chase (Buffalo, holding trophy)	50.00	25.00	15.00
(18a)	Hal Chase (Chicago, portrait, blue background)	50.00	25.00	15.00
(18b)	Hal Chase (Buffalo, portrait, blue background)	50.00	25.00	15.00
(19a)	Hal Chase (Chicago, throwing)	50.00	25.00	15.00
(19b)	Hal Chase (Buffalo, throwing)	50.00	25.00	15.00
(20)	Ty Cobb (portrait)	350.00	175.00	105.00
(21)	Ty Cobb (with bat off shoulder)	350.00	175.00	105.00
(22a)	Eddie Collins (Philadelphia, "A" on shirt)	70.00	35.00	21.00
(22b)	Eddie Collins (Chicago, "A" on shirt)	70.00	35.00	21.00
(22c)	Eddie Collins (Chicago, no "A" on shirt)	70.00	35.00	21.00
(23a)	Doc Crandall (St. Louis Nat.)	30.00	15.00	9.00
(23b)	Doc Crandall (St. Louis Fed.)	30.00	15.00	9.00
(24)	Sam Crawford	70.00	35.00	21.00
(25)	Birdie Cree	30.00	15.00	9.00
(26a)	Harry Davis (Phila. Amer.)	30.00	15.00	9.00
(26b)	Harry Davis (Philadelphia Amer.)	30.00	15.00	9.00
(27a)	Ray Demmitt (New York)	30.00	15.00	9.00
27b	Ray Demmitt (Chicago)	30.00	15.00	9.00
(28a)	Josh Devore (Philadelphia)	30.00	15.00	9.00
(28b)	Josh Devore (Chillicothe)	30.00	15.00	9.00
(29a)	Mike Donlin (New York)	30.00	15.00	9.00
(29b)	Mike Donlin (.300 batter 7 years)	30.00	15.00	9.00
(30)	Wild Bill Donovan	30.00	15.00	9.00
(31a)	Mickey Doolan (Baltimore, batting)	30.00	15.00	9.00
(31b)	Mickey Doolan (Chicago, batting)	30.00	15.00	9.00
(32a)	Mickey Doolan (Baltimore, fielding)	30.00	15.00	9.00
(32b)	Mickey Doolan (Chicago, fielding)	30.00	15.00	9.00
(33)	Tom Downey	30.00	15.00	9.00
(34)	Larry Doyle (batting)	30.00	15.00	9.00
(35)	Larry Doyle (portrait)	30.00	15.00	9.00
(36)	Jean Dubuc	30.00	15.00	9.00
(37)	Jack Dunn	30.00	15.00	9.00
(38a)	Kid Elberfield (Elberfeld) (Brooklyn)	30.00	15.00	9.00
(38b)	Kid Elberfield (Elberfeld) (Chatanooga)	30.00	15.00	9.00
(39)	Steve Evans	30.00	15.00	9.00
(40)	Johnny Evers	70.00	35.00	21.00
(41)	Russ Ford	30.00	15.00	9.00
(42)	Art Fromme	30.00	15.00	9.00
(43a)	Chick Gandil (Washington)	40.00	20.00	12.00
(43b)	Chick Gandil (Cleveland)	40.00	20.00	12.00
(44)	Rube Geyer	30.00	15.00	9.00
(45)	Clark Griffith	30.00	15.00	9.00
(46)	Bob Groom	30.00	15.00	9.00
(47a)	Buck Herzog ("B" on shirt)	30.00	15.00	9.00
(47b)	Buck Herzog (no "B" on shirt)	30.00	15.00	9.00
(48a)	Dick Hoblitzell (Cincinnati)	30.00	15.00	9.00
(48b)	Dick Hoblitzell (Boston Nat.)	30.00	15.00	9.00
(48c)	Dick Hoblitzell (Boston Amer.)	30.00	15.00	9.00
(49a)	Solly Hofman	30.00	15.00	9.00
(49b)	Solly Hofmann (Hofman)	30.00	15.00	9.00
(50)	Miller Huggins (hands at mouth)	70.00	35.00	21.00
(51)	Miller Huggins (portrait)	70.00	35.00	21.00
(52a)	John Hummel (Brooklyn Nat.)	30.00	15.00	9.00
(52b)	John Hummel (Brooklyn)	30.00	15.00	9.00
(53)	Hughie Jennings (both hands showing)	70.00	35.00	21.00
(54)	Hughie Jennings (one hand showing)	70.00	35.00	21.00
(55)	Walter Johnson	350.00	175.00	105.00
(56a)	Tim Jordan (Toronto)	30.00	15.00	9.00
(56b)	Tim Jordan (Ft. Worth)	30.00	15.00	9.00
(57a)	Joe Kelley (New York)	70.00	35.00	21.00
(57b)	Joe Kelley (Toronto)	70.00	35.00	21.00
(58)	Otto Knabe	30.00	15.00	9.00
(59a)	Ed Konetchy (Pittsburgh Nat.)	30.00	15.00	9.00
(59b)	Ed Konetchy (Pittsburgh Fed.)	30.00	15.00	9.00
(59c)	Ed Konetchy (Boston)	30.00	15.00	9.00
(60)	Harry Krause	30.00	15.00	9.00
(61a)	Nap Lajoie (Phila. Amer.)	110.00	55.00	33.00
(61b)	Nap Lajoie (Philadelphia Amer.)	110.00	55.00	33.00
(61c)	Nap Lajoie (Cleveland)	110.00	55.00	33.00
(62a)	Tommy Leach (Chicago)	30.00	15.00	9.00
(62b)	Tommy Leach (Cincinnati)	30.00	15.00	9.00
(62c)	Tommy Leach (Rochester)	30.00	15.00	9.00
(63)	Ed Lennox	30.00	15.00	9.00
(64a)	Sherry Magee (Phila. Nat.)	40.00	20.00	12.00
(64b)	Sherry Magee (Philadelphia Nat.)	40.00	20.00	12.00
(64c)	Sherry Magee (Boston)	40.00	20.00	12.00
(65a)	Rube Marquard (New York, pitching, "NY" on shirt)	70.00	35.00	21.00
(65b)	Rube Marquard (Brooklyn, pitching, no "NY" on shirt)	70.00	35.00	21.00
(66a)	Rube Marquard (New York, portrait, "NY" on shirt)	70.00	35.00	21.00
(66b)	Rube Marquard (Brooklyn, portrait, no "NY" on shirt)	70.00	35.00	21.00
(67)	Christy Mathewson	350.00	175.00	105.00
(68)	John McGraw (glove at side)	90.00	45.00	27.00
(69)	John McGraw (portrait)	90.00	45.00	27.00
(70)	Larry McLean	30.00	15.00	9.00
(71a)	George McQuillan (Pittsburgh)	30.00	15.00	9.00
(71b)	George McQuillan (Phila. Nat.)	30.00	15.00	9.00
(72c)	George McQuillan (Philadelphia Nat.)	30.00	15.00	9.00
(73)	Fred Merkle	40.00	20.00	12.00
(74a)	Chief Meyers (New York, fielding)	30.00	15.00	9.00
(74b)	Chief Meyers (Brooklyn, fielding)	30.00	15.00	9.00
(75a)	Chief Meyers (New York, portrait)	30.00	15.00	9.00
(75b)	Chief Meyers (Brooklyn, portrait)	30.00	15.00	9.00
(76)	Dots Miller	30.00	15.00	9.00
(77)	Mike Mitchell	30.00	15.00	9.00
(78a)	Mike Mowrey (Pittsburgh Nat.)	30.00	15.00	9.00
(78b)	Mike Mowrey (Pittsburgh Fed.)	30.00	15.00	9.00
(78c)	Mike Mowrey (Brooklyn)	30.00	15.00	9.00
(79a)	George Mullin (Indianapolis)	30.00	15.00	9.00
(79b)	George Mullin (Newark)	30.00	15.00	9.00
(80)	Danny Murphy	30.00	15.00	9.00
(81a)	Red Murray (New York)	30.00	15.00	9.00
(81b)	Red Murray (Chicago)	30.00	15.00	9.00
(81c)	Red Murray (Kansas City)	30.00	15.00	9.00
(82)	Tom Needham	30.00	15.00	9.00
(83)	Rebel Oakes	30.00	15.00	9.00
(84a)	Rube Oldring (Phila. Amer.)	30.00	15.00	9.00
(84b)	Rube Oldring (Philadelphia Amer.)	30.00	15.00	9.00
(85a)	Dode Paskert (Phila. Nat.)	30.00	15.00	9.00
(85b)	Dode Paskert (Philadelphia Nat.)	30.00	15.00	9.00
(86)	Billy Purtell	30.00	15.00	9.00
(87a)	Jack Quinn (Baltimore)	30.00	15.00	9.00
(87b)	Jack Quinn (Vernon)	30.00	15.00	9.00
(88a)	Ed Reulbach (Brooklyn Nat.)	30.00	15.00	9.00
(88b)	Ed Reulbach (Brooklyn Fed.)	30.00	15.00	9.00
(88c)	Ed Reulbach (Pittsburgh)	30.00	15.00	9.00
(89a)	Nap Rucker (Brooklyn)	30.00	15.00	9.00
(89b)	Nap Rucker (Brooklyn Nat.)	30.00	15.00	9.00
(90)	Dick Rudolph	30.00	15.00	9.00
(91a)	Germany Schaefer (Washington, "W" on shirt)	30.00	15.00	9.00
(91b)	Germany Schaefer (K.C. Fed., "W" on shirt)	30.00	15.00	9.00
(91c)	Germany Schaefer (New York, no "W" on shirt)	30.00	15.00	9.00
(92)	Admiral Schlei (batting)	30.00	15.00	9.00
(93)	Admiral Schlei (portrait)	30.00	15.00	9.00
(94)	Boss Schmidt	30.00	15.00	9.00
(95)	Wildfire Schulte	30.00	15.00	9.00
(96)	Frank Smith	30.00	15.00	9.00
(97)	Tris Speaker	100.00	50.00	30.00
(98)	George Stovall	30.00	15.00	9.00
(99)	Gabby Street (catching)	30.00	15.00	9.00
(100)	Gabby Street (portrait)	30.00	15.00	9.00
(101)	Ed Summers	30.00	15.00	9.00
(102a)	Bill Sweeney (Boston)	30.00	15.00	9.00
(102b)	Bill Sweeney (Chicago)	30.00	15.00	9.00
(103a)	Jeff Sweeney (New York)	30.00	15.00	9.00
(103b)	Jeff Sweeney (Richmond)	30.00	15.00	9.00
(104a)	Ira Thomas (Phila. Amer.)	30.00	15.00	9.00
(104b)	Ira Thomas (Philadelphia Amer.)	30.00	15.00	9.00
(105a)	Joe Tinker (Chicago Fed., bat off shoulder)	70.00	35.00	21.00
(105b)	Joe Tinker (Chicago Nat., bat on shoulder)	70.00	35.00	21.00
(106a)	Joe Tinker (Chicago Fed., bat off shoulder)	70.00	35.00	21.00
(106b)	Joe Tinker (Chicago Nat., bat off shoulder)	70.00	35.00	21.00
(107)	Heinie Wagner	30.00	15.00	9.00
(108a)	Jack Warhop (New York, "NY" on shirt)	30.00	15.00	9.00
(108b)	Jack Warhop (St. Louis, no "NY" om shirt)	30.00	15.00	9.00
(109a)	Zach Wheat (Brooklyn)	70.00	35.00	21.00
(109b)	Zach Wheat (Brooklyn Nat.)	70.00	35.00	21.00
(110)	Kaiser Wilhelm	30.00	15.00	9.00
(111a)	Ed Willett (St. Louis)	30.00	15.00	9.00
(111b)	Ed Willett (Memphis)	30.00	15.00	9.00
(112)	Owen Wilson	30.00	15.00	9.00
(113a)	Hooks Wiltse (New York, pitching)	30.00	15.00	9.00
(113b)	Hooks Wiltse (Brooklyn, pitching)	30.00	15.00	9.00
(113c)	Hooks Wiltse (Jersey City, pitching)	30.00	15.00	9.00
(114a)	Hooks Wiltse (New York, portrait)	30.00	15.00	9.00
(114b)	Hooks Wiltse (Brooklyn, portrait)	30.00	15.00	9.00
(114c)	Hooks Wiltse (Jersey City, portrait)	30.00	15.00	9.00
(115)	Heinie Zimmerman	30.00	15.00	9.00

1919 T213 Coupon - Type 3

	NR MT	EX	VG
Complete Set:	7500.	3750.	2250.
Common Player:	50.00	25.00	15.00

No.	Player	NR MT	EX	VG
(1)	Red Ames	50.00	25.00	15.00
(2)	Home Run Baker	100.00	50.00	30.00
(3)	Chief Bender (no trees in background)	100.00	50.00	30.00
(4)	Chief Bender (trees in background)	100.00	50.00	30.00
(5)	Roger Bresnahan	100.00	50.00	30.00
(6)	Al Bridwell	50.00	25.00	15.00
(7)	Miner Brown	50.00	25.00	15.00
(8)	Bobby Byrne	50.00	25.00	15.00
(9)	Frank Chance (batting)	110.00	55.00	33.00
(10)	Frank Chance (portrait)	110.00	55.00	33.00
(11)	Hal Chase (holding trophy)	65.00	32.00	19.50
(12)	Hal Chase (portrait)	65.00	32.00	19.50
(13)	Hal Chase (throwing)	65.00	32.00	19.50
(14)	Ty Cobb (batting)	1000.	500.00	300.00
(15)	Ty Cobb (portrait)	1000.	500.00	300.00
(16)	Eddie Collins	100.00	50.00	30.00
(17)	Sam Crawford	100.00	50.00	30.00
(18)	Harry Davis	50.00	25.00	15.00
(19)	Mike Donlin	50.00	25.00	15.00
(20)	Wild Bill Donovan	50.00	25.00	15.00
(21)	Mickey Doolan (batting)	50.00	25.00	15.00
(22)	Mickey Doolan (fielding)	50.00	25.00	15.00
(23)	Larry Doyle (batting)	50.00	25.00	15.00
(24)	Larry Doyle (portrait)	50.00	25.00	15.00
(25)	Jean Dubuc	50.00	25.00	15.00
(26)	Jack Dunn	50.00	25.00	15.00
(27)	Kid Elberfeld	50.00	25.00	15.00
(28)	Johnny Evers	100.00	50.00	30.00
(29)	Chick Gandil	55.00	27.00	16.50
(30)	Clark Griffith	50.00	25.00	15.00
(31)	Buck Herzog	50.00	25.00	15.00
(32)	Dick Hoblitzell	50.00	25.00	15.00
(33)	Miller Huggins (hands at mouth)	100.00	50.00	30.00
(34)	Miller Huggins (portrait)	100.00	50.00	30.00
(35)	John Hummel	50.00	25.00	15.00
(36)	Hughie Jennings (both hands showing)	100.00	50.00	30.00
(37)	Hughie Jennings (one hand showing)	100.00	50.00	30.00
(38)	Walter Johnson	450.00	225.00	135.00
(39)	Tim Jordan	50.00	25.00	15.00
(40)	Joe Kelley	100.00	50.00	30.00
(41)	Ed Konetchy	50.00	25.00	15.00
(42)	Larry Lajoie	100.00	50.00	30.00
(43)	Sherry Magee	55.00	27.00	16.50
(44)	Rube Marquard	100.00	50.00	30.00
(45)	Christy Mathewson	450.00	225.00	135.00
(47)	John McGraw (glove at side)	125.00	62.00	37.00
(48)	John McGraw (portrait)	125.00	62.00	37.00
(49)	George McQuillan	50.00	25.00	15.00
(50)	Fred Merkle	55.00	27.00	16.50
(51)	Dots Miller	50.00	25.00	15.00
(52)	Mike Mowrey	50.00	25.00	15.00
(53)	Chief Myers (Meyers) (Brooklyn)	50.00	25.00	15.00
(54)	Chief Myers (Meyers) (New Haven)	50.00	25.00	15.00
(55)	Dode Paskert	50.00	25.00	15.00
(56)	Jack Quinn	50.00	25.00	15.00
(57)	Ed Reulbach	50.00	25.00	15.00
(58)	Nap Rucker	50.00	25.00	15.00
(59)	Dick Rudolph	50.00	25.00	15.00
(60)	Herman Schaeffer (Schaefer)	50.00	25.00	15.00
(61)	Wildfire Schulte	50.00	25.00	15.00
(62)	Tris Speaker	200.00	100.00	60.00
(63)	Gabby Street (catching)	50.00	25.00	15.00
(64)	Gabby Street (portrait)	50.00	25.00	15.00
(65)	Jeff Sweeney	50.00	25.00	15.00
(66)	Ira Thomas	50.00	25.00	15.00
(67)	Joe Tinker	100.00	50.00	30.00
(68)	Zach Wheat	100.00	50.00	30.00
(69)	Geo. Wiltse	50.00	25.00	15.00
(70)	Heinie Zimmerman	50.00	25.00	15.00

1915 T214 Victory

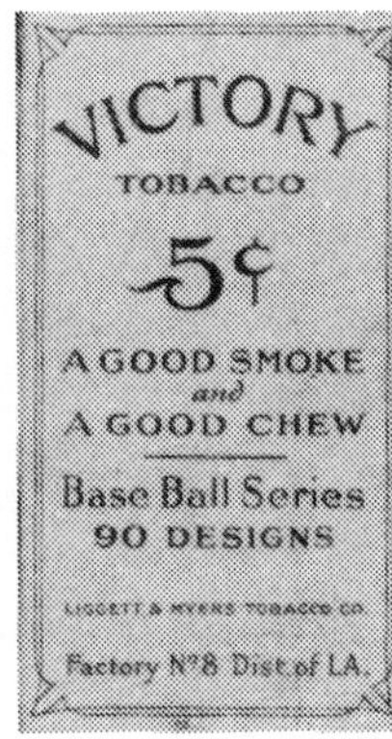

The T214 Victory set of 1915 is another obscure series of tobacco cards that is sometimes mistaken for the better-known T206 "White Border" set. The confusion is understandable because identical player poses were used for both sets. The Victory Tobacco set can be easily identified, however, by the advertising for the Victory brand on the back of the cards. The set features players from both the Federal League and the major leagues, and although the card backs advertise "90 Designs," only 30 different subjects have surfaced to date. The set had such limited distribution - apparently restricted to just the Louisiana area - and the cards are so rare that it may be virtually impossible to ever checklist the set completely. Except for the advertising on the backs, the Victory cards are almost identical to the "Type II" Coupon cards (T213), another obscure Louisiana tobacco set issued during the same period. Of the several tobacco sets issued in Louisiana in the early part of the 20th Century, the T214 Victory cards are considered the most difficult to find.

		NR MT	EX	VG
Complete Set:		9000.	4500.	2700.
Common Player:		275.00	137.00	82.00
(1)	Chief Bender	500.00	250.00	150.00
(2)	Roger Bresnahan	500.00	250.00	150.00
(3)	Howie Camnitz	275.00	137.00	82.00
(4)	Ty Cobb	2000.	1000.	600.00
(5)	Birdie Cree	275.00	137.00	82.00
(6)	Ray Demmitt	275.00	137.00	82.00
(7)	Mickey Doolan	275.00	137.00	82.00
(8)	Tom Downey	275.00	137.00	82.00
(9)	Kid Elberfeld	275.00	137.00	82.00
(10)	Russ Ford	275.00	137.00	82.00
(11)	Art Fromme	275.00	137.00	82.00
(12)	Rube Geyer	275.00	137.00	82.00
(13)	Clark Griffith	500.00	250.00	150.00
(14)	Bob Groom	275.00	137.00	82.00
(15)	Walter Johnson	900.00	450.00	275.00
(16)	Ed Konetchy	275.00	137.00	82.00
(17)	Nap Lajoie	750.00	375.00	225.00
(18)	Ed Lennox	275.00	137.00	82.00
(19)	Sherry Magee	275.00	137.00	82.00
(20)	Chief Meyers	275.00	137.00	82.00
(21)	George Mullin	275.00	137.00	82.00
(22)	Tom Needham	275.00	137.00	82.00
(23)	Rebel Oakes	275.00	137.00	82.00
(24)	Jack Quinn	275.00	137.00	82.00
(25)	Wildfire Schulte	275.00	137.00	82.00
(26)	Jeff Sweeney	275.00	137.00	82.00
(27)	Joe Tinker	500.00	250.00	150.00
(28)	Heinie Wagner	275.00	137.00	82.00
(29)	Zack Wheat	500.00	250.00	150.00
(30)	Hooks Wiltse	275.00	137.00	82.00

1910 T215 Red Cross - Type 1

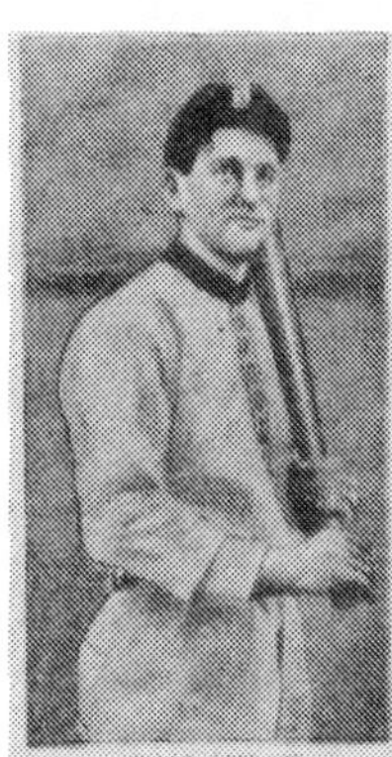

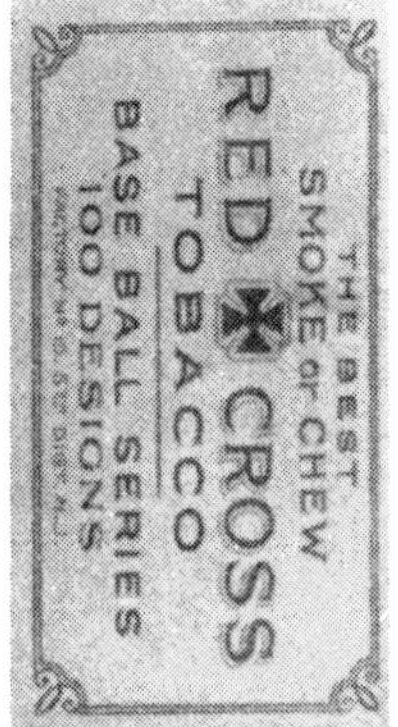

The T215 set issued by Red Cross Tobacco is another of the Louisiana area sets closely related to the popular T206 "White Border" tobacco cards. Very similar to the T213 Coupon cards, the Red Cross Tobacco cards are found in two distinct types, both featuring color player lithographs and measuring approximately 1-1/2" by 2-5/8", the standard tobacco card size. Type I Red Cross cards, issued from 1910 to 1912, have brown captions; while Type II cards, most of which appear to be from 1912, have blue printing. The backs of both types are identical, displaying the Red Cross name and emblem which can be used to positively identify the set and differentiate it from the other Louisiana sets of the same period. Numerous variations have been found, most of them involving minor caption changes.

		NR MT	EX	VG
Complete Set:		5500.	2750.	1650.
Common Player:		50.00	25.00	15.00
(1)	Red Ames	50.00	25.00	15.00
(2)	Home Run Baker	300.00	150.00	90.00
(3)	Neal Ball	50.00	25.00	15.00
(4)	Chief Bender (no trees in background)	300.00	150.00	90.00
(5)	Chief Bender (trees in background)	300.00	150.00	90.00
(6)	Al Bridwell	50.00	25.00	15.00
(7)	Bobby Byrne	50.00	25.00	15.00
(8)	Howie Camnitz	50.00	25.00	15.00
(9)	Frank Chance	300.00	150.00	90.00
(10)	Hal Chase	50.00	25.00	15.00
(11)	Ty Cobb	1000.	500.00	300.00
(12)	Eddie Collins	300.00	150.00	90.00
(13)	Wid Conroy	50.00	25.00	15.00
(14)	Doc Crandall	50.00	25.00	15.00
(15)	Sam Crawford	300.00	150.00	90.00
(16)	Birdie Cree	50.00	25.00	15.00
(17)	Harry Davis	50.00	25.00	15.00
(18)	Josh Devore	50.00	25.00	15.00
(19)	Mike Donlin	50.00	25.00	15.00
(20)	Mickey Doolan	50.00	25.00	15.00
(21)	Patsy Dougherty	50.00	25.00	15.00
(22)	Larry Doyle (batting)	50.00	25.00	15.00
(23)	Larry Doyle (portrait)	50.00	25.00	15.00
(24)	Kid Elberfeld	50.00	25.00	15.00
(25)	Russ Ford	50.00	25.00	15.00
(26)	Art Fromme	50.00	25.00	15.00
(27)	Clark Griffith	300.00	150.00	90.00
(28)	Topsy Hartsel	50.00	25.00	15.00
(29)	Dick Hoblitzell	50.00	25.00	15.00
(30)	Solly Hofman	50.00	25.00	15.00
(31)	Del Howard	50.00	25.00	15.00
(32)	Miller Huggins	300.00	150.00	90.00
(33)	John Hummel	50.00	25.00	15.00
(34)	Hughie Jennings (both hands showing)	300.00	150.00	90.00
(35)	Hughie Jennings (one hand showing)	300.00	150.00	90.00
(36)	Walter Johnson	450.00	225.00	135.00
(37)	Ed Konetchy	50.00	25.00	15.00
(38)	Harry Krause	50.00	25.00	15.00
(39)	Nap Lajoie	300.00	150.00	90.00
(40)	Arlie Latham	50.00	25.00	15.00
(41)	Tommy Leach	50.00	25.00	15.00
(42)	Lefty Leifield	50.00	25.00	15.00
(43)	Harry Lord	50.00	25.00	15.00
(44)	Sherry Magee	45.00	22.00	13.50
(45)	Rube Marquard (pitching)	300.00	150.00	90.00
(46)	Rube Marquard (portrait)	300.00	150.00	90.00
(47)	Christy Mathewson (dark cap)	450.00	225.00	135.00
(48)	Christy Mathewson (white cap)	450.00	225.00	135.00
(49)	Joe McGinnity	300.00	150.00	90.00
(50)	John McGraw (glove at hip)	175.00	87.00	52.00
(51)	John McGraw (portrait)	175.00	87.00	52.00
(52)	Harry McIntyre	50.00	25.00	15.00
(53)	Fred Merkle	45.00	22.00	13.50
(54)	Chief Meyers	50.00	25.00	15.00
(55)	Dots Miller	50.00	25.00	15.00
(56)	Danny Murphy	50.00	25.00	15.00
(57)	Red Murray	50.00	25.00	15.00
(58)	Rebel Oakes	50.00	25.00	15.00
(59)	Charley O'Leary	50.00	25.00	15.00
(60)	Dode Paskert	50.00	25.00	15.00
(61)	Barney Pelty	50.00	25.00	15.00
(62)	Jack Quinn	50.00	25.00	15.00
(63)	Ed Reulbach	50.00	25.00	15.00
(64)	Nap Rucker	50.00	25.00	15.00
(65)	Germany Schaefer	50.00	25.00	15.00
(66)	Wildfire Schulte	50.00	25.00	15.00
(67)	Jimmy Sheckard	50.00	25.00	15.00
(68a)	Frank Smith	50.00	25.00	15.00
(68b)	Frank Smither (Smith)	50.00	25.00	15.00
(69)	Tris Speaker	250.00	125.00	75.00
(70)	Jake Stahl	50.00	25.00	15.00
(71)	Harry Steinfeldt	45.00	22.00	13.50
(72)	Gabby Street (catching)	50.00	25.00	15.00
(73)	Gabby Street (portrait)	50.00	25.00	15.00
(74)	Jeff Sweeney	50.00	25.00	15.00
(75)	Lee Tannehill	50.00	25.00	15.00
(76)	Joe Tinker (bat off shoulder)	300.00	150.00	90.00
(77)	Joe Tinker (bat on shoulder)	300.00	150.00	90.00
(78)	Heinie Wagner	50.00	25.00	15.00
(79)	Jack Warhop	50.00	25.00	15.00
(80)	Zach Wheat	300.00	150.00	90.00
(81)	Doc White	50.00	25.00	15.00
(82)	Ed Willetts (Willett)	50.00	25.00	15.00
(83)	Owen Wilson	50.00	25.00	15.00
(84)	Hooks Wiltse (pitching)	50.00	25.00	15.00
(85)	Hooks Wiltse (portrait)	50.00	25.00	15.00
(86)	Cy Young	300.00	150.00	90.00

1912 T215 Red Cross - Type 2

		NR MT	EX	VG
Complete Set:		7000.	3500.	2100.
Common Player:		40.00	20.00	12.00
(1)	Red Ames	40.00	20.00	12.00
(2)	Chief Bender (no trees in background)	70.00	35.00	21.00
(3)	Chief Bender (trees in background)	70.00	35.00	21.00
(4)	Roger Bresnahan	70.00	35.00	21.00
(5)	Mordecai Brown	70.00	35.00	21.00
(6)	Bobby Byrne	40.00	20.00	12.00
(7)	Howie Camnitz	40.00	20.00	12.00
(8)	Frank Chance	70.00	35.00	21.00
(9)	Ty Cobb	900.00	450.00	270.00
(10)	Eddie Collins	70.00	35.00	21.00
(11)	Doc Crandall	40.00	20.00	12.00
(12)	Birdie Cree	40.00	20.00	12.00
(13)	Harry Davis	40.00	20.00	12.00
(14)	Josh Devore	40.00	20.00	12.00
(15)	Mike Donlin	40.00	20.00	12.00
(16)	Mickey Doolan (batting)	40.00	20.00	12.00
(17)	Mickey Doolan (fielding)	40.00	20.00	12.00
(18)	Patsy Dougherty	40.00	20.00	12.00
(19)	Larry Doyle (batting)	40.00	20.00	12.00
(20)	Larry Doyle (portrait)	40.00	20.00	12.00
(21)	Jean Dubuc	40.00	20.00	12.00
(22)	Kid Elberfeld	40.00	20.00	12.00
(23)	Johnny Evers	70.00	35.00	21.00
(24)	Russ Ford	40.00	20.00	12.00
(25)	Art Fromme	40.00	20.00	12.00
(26)	Clark Griffith	70.00	35.00	21.00
(27)	Bob Groom	40.00	20.00	12.00
(28)	Topsy Hartsel	40.00	20.00	12.00
(29)	Buck Herzog	40.00	20.00	12.00
(30)	Dick Hoblitzell	40.00	20.00	12.00
(31)	Solly Hofman	40.00	20.00	12.00
(32)	Miller Huggins (hands at mouth)	70.00	35.00	21.00
(33)	Miller Huggins (portrait)	70.00	35.00	21.00
(34)	John Hummel	40.00	20.00	12.00
(35)	Hughie Jennings	70.00	35.00	21.00
(36)	Walter Johnson	400.00	200.00	120.00
(37)	Joe Kelley	70.00	35.00	21.00
(38)	Ed Konetchy	40.00	20.00	12.00
(39)	Harry Krause	40.00	20.00	12.00
(40)	Nap Lajoie	225.00	112.00	67.00
(41)	Joe Lake	40.00	20.00	12.00
(42)	Tommy Leach	40.00	20.00	12.00
(43)	Lefty Leifield	40.00	20.00	12.00
(44)	Harry Lord	40.00	20.00	12.00
(45)	Rube Marquard	70.00	35.00	21.00
(46)	Christy Mathewson	400.00	200.00	120.00
(47)	John McGraw (glove at side)	80.00	40.00	24.00
(48)	John McGraw (portrait)	80.00	40.00	24.00
(49)	Larry McLean	40.00	20.00	12.00
(50)	Dots Miller	40.00	20.00	12.00
(51)	Mike Mitchell	40.00	20.00	12.00
(52)	Mike Mowrey	40.00	20.00	12.00
(53)	George Mullin	40.00	20.00	12.00
(54)	Danny Murphy	40.00	20.00	12.00
(55)	Red Murray	40.00	20.00	12.00
(56)	Rebel Oakes	40.00	20.00	12.00
(57)	Rube Oldring	40.00	20.00	12.00
(58)	Charley O'Leary	40.00	20.00	12.00
(59)	Dode Paskert	40.00	20.00	12.00
(60)	Barney Pelty	40.00	20.00	12.00
(61)	Billy Purtell	40.00	20.00	12.00
(62)	Ed Reulbach	40.00	20.00	12.00
(63)	Nap Rucker	40.00	20.00	12.00
(64a)	Germany Schaefer (Chicago)	40.00	20.00	12.00
(64b)	Germany Schaefer (Washington)	40.00	20.00	12.00
(65)	Wildfire Schulte	40.00	20.00	12.00
(66a)	Frank Smith	40.00	20.00	12.00
(66b)	Frank Smither (Smith)	40.00	20.00	12.00
(67)	Tris Speaker	200.00	100.00	60.00
(68)	Jake Stahl	40.00	20.00	12.00
(69)	Harry Steinfeldt	50.00	25.00	15.00
(70)	Ed Summers	40.00	20.00	12.00
(71)	Jeff Sweeney	40.00	20.00	12.00
(72)	Joe Tinker	70.00	35.00	21.00
(73)	Heinie Wagner	40.00	20.00	12.00
(74)	Jack Warhop	40.00	20.00	12.00
(75)	Doc White	40.00	20.00	12.00
(76)	Hooks Wiltse (pitching)	40.00	20.00	12.00
(77)	Hooks Wiltse (portrait)	40.00	20.00	12.00

NOTE: A card number in parentheses ( ) indicates the set is unnumbered.

1912 T215 Pirate

This set can be considerd a British version of the Red Cross set. Distributed by Pirate brand cigarettes of Bristol and London, England, the fronts of the cards are identical to the Type I Red Cross cards, but the green backs carry advertising for Pirate Cigarettes. It is believed that the Pirate cards were printed for distribution to U.S. servicemen in the South Seas. They are very rare in both England and the United States.

		NR MT	EX	VG
Complete Set:		12000.	6000.	3600.
Common Player:		100.00	50.00	30.00
(1)	Red Ames	100.00	50.00	30.00
(2)	Home Run Baker	225.00	112.00	67.00
(3)	Neal Ball	100.00	50.00	30.00
(4)	Chief Bender	225.00	112.00	67.00
(5)	Al Bridwell	100.00	50.00	30.00
(6)	Bobby Byrne	100.00	50.00	30.00
(7)	Howie Camnitz	100.00	50.00	30.00
(8)	Frank Chance	250.00	125.00	75.00
(9)	Hal Chase	100.00	50.00	30.00
(10)	Eddie Collins	250.00	125.00	75.00
(11)	Doc Crandall	100.00	50.00	30.00
(12)	Sam Crawford	225.00	112.00	67.00
(13)	Birdie Cree	100.00	50.00	30.00
(14)	Harry Davis	100.00	50.00	30.00
(15)	Josh Devore	100.00	50.00	30.00
(16)	Mike Donlin	100.00	50.00	30.00
(17)	Mickey Doolan (batting)	100.00	50.00	30.00
(18)	Mickey Doolan (fielding)	100.00	50.00	30.00
(19)	Patsy Dougherty	100.00	50.00	30.00
(20)	Larry Doyle (batting)	100.00	50.00	30.00
(21)	Larry Doyle (portrait)	100.00	50.00	30.00
(22)	Jean Dubuc	100.00	50.00	30.00
(23)	Kid Elberfeld	100.00	50.00	30.00
(24)	Steve Evans	100.00	50.00	30.00
(25)	Johnny Evers	225.00	112.00	67.00
(26)	Russ Ford	100.00	50.00	30.00
(27)	Art Fromme	100.00	50.00	30.00
(28)	Clark Griffith	225.00	112.00	67.00
(29)	Bob Groom	100.00	50.00	30.00
(30)	Topsy Hartsel	100.00	50.00	30.00
(31)	Buck Herzog	100.00	50.00	30.00
(32)	Dick Hoblitzell	100.00	50.00	30.00
(33)	Solly Hofman	100.00	50.00	30.00
(34)	Del Howard	100.00	50.00	30.00
(35)	Miller Huggins (hands at mouth)	225.00	112.00	67.00
(36)	Miller Huggins (portrait)	225.00	112.00	67.00
(37)	John Hummel	100.00	50.00	30.00
(38)	Hughie Jennings (both hands showing)	225.00	112.00	67.00
(39)	Hughie Jennings (one hand showing)	225.00	112.00	67.00
(40)	Walter Johnson	500.00	250.00	150.00
(41)	Joe Kelley	225.00	112.00	67.00
(42)	Ed Konetchy	100.00	50.00	30.00
(43)	Harry Krause	100.00	50.00	30.00
(44)	Nap Lajoie	400.00	200.00	120.00
(45)	Joe Lake	100.00	50.00	30.00
(46)	Lefty Leifield	100.00	50.00	30.00
(47)	Harry Lord	100.00	50.00	30.00
(48)	Sherry Magee	90.00	45.00	27.00
(49)	Rube Marquard (pitching)	225.00	112.00	67.00
(50)	Rube Marquard (portrait)	225.00	112.00	67.00
(51)	Joe McGinnity	225.00	112.00	67.00
(52)	John McGraw (glove at side)	300.00	150.00	90.00
(53)	John McGraw (portrait)	300.00	150.00	90.00
(54)	Harry McIntyre (Chicago)	100.00	50.00	30.00
(55)	Harry McIntyre (Brooklyn & Chicago)	100.00	50.00	30.00
(56)	Larry McLean	100.00	50.00	30.00
(57)	Fred Merkle	90.00	45.00	27.00
(58)	Chief Meyers	100.00	50.00	30.00
(59)	Mike Mitchell	100.00	50.00	30.00
(60)	Mike Mowrey	100.00	50.00	30.00
(61)	George Mullin	100.00	50.00	30.00
(62)	Danny Murphy	100.00	50.00	30.00
(63)	Red Murray	100.00	50.00	30.00
(64)	Rebel Oakes	100.00	50.00	30.00
(65)	Rube Oldring	100.00	50.00	30.00
(66)	Charley O'Leary	100.00	50.00	30.00
(67)	Dode Paskert	100.00	50.00	30.00
(68)	Barney Pelty	100.00	50.00	30.00
(69)	Billy Purtell	100.00	50.00	30.00
(70)	Jack Quinn	100.00	50.00	30.00
(71)	Ed Reulbach	100.00	50.00	30.00
(72)	Nap Rucker	100.00	50.00	30.00
(73)	Germany Schaefer	100.00	50.00	30.00
(74)	Wildfire Schulte	100.00	50.00	30.00
(75)	Jimmy Sheckard	100.00	50.00	30.00
(76)	Frank Smith	100.00	50.00	30.00
(77)	Tris Speaker	375.00	187.00	112.00
(78)	Jake Stahl	100.00	50.00	30.00
(79)	Harry Steinfeldt	100.00	50.00	30.00
(80)	Gabby Street	100.00	50.00	30.00
(81)	Ed Summers	100.00	50.00	30.00
(82)	Jeff Sweeney	100.00	50.00	30.00
(83)	Lee Tannehill	100.00	50.00	30.00
(84)	Ira Thomas	100.00	50.00	30.00
(85)	Joe Tinker	225.00	112.00	67.00
(86)	Heinie Wagner	100.00	50.00	30.00
(87)	Jack Warhop	100.00	50.00	30.00
(88)	Zack Wheat (Brooklyn)	225.00	112.00	67.00
(89)	Ed Willetts (Willett)	100.00	50.00	30.00
(90)	Owen Wilson	100.00	50.00	30.00
(91)	Hooks Wiltse (pitching)	100.00	50.00	30.00
(92)	Hooks Wiltse (portrait)	100.00	50.00	30.00

1914 T216 Kotton

The T216 baseball card set, issued by several brands of the Peoples Tobacco Co., is the last of the Louisiana area tobacco sets and the most confusing. Apparently issued over a period of several years between 1911 and 1916, the set employs the same pictures used in the E90-1 and E92 caramel card sets and is also closely related to the E106 American Caramel and D303 General Baking sets. Exact identification of cards from this era is often complicated by the fact that it was common for the same picture to be used in several different sets. Positive identification can usually be determined by the back of the cards. The Peoples Tobacco cards carry advertising for one of three brands of cigarettes: Kotton, Mino or Virginia Extra. The Kotton brand are the most common, while the Virginia Extra and Mino backs command a 50-100 premium. T216 card are found in two types; one has a glossy card stock, while a second scarcer type is printed on a thin paper. The thin paper cards command an additional 15 premium. There are 73 poses known to exist plus 29 variations, mostly involving caption changes. The cards represent players from both major leagues and the Federal League. Of the 73 poses identified, 23 were taken from the E90-1 set, 38 originated in the E92 set and a dozen appeared in both of the earlier caramel sets.

		NR MT	EX	VG
Complete Set:		11500.	5750.	3450.
Common Player:		50.00	25.00	15.00
(1)	Jack Barry (batting)	50.00	25.00	15.00
(2)	Jack Barry (fielding)	50.00	25.00	15.00
(3)	Harry Bemis	50.00	25.00	15.00
(4a)	Chief Bender (Philadelphia, striped cap)	100.00	50.00	30.00
(4b)	Chief Bender (Baltimore, striped cap)	100.00	50.00	30.00
(5a)	Chief Bender (Philadelphia, white cap)	100.00	50.00	30.00
(5b)	Chief Bender (Baltimore, white cap)	100.00	50.00	30.00
(6)	Bill Bergen	50.00	25.00	15.00
(7a)	Bob Bescher (Cincinnati)	50.00	25.00	15.00
(7b)	Bob Bescher (St. Louis)	50.00	25.00	15.00
(8)	Roger Bresnahan	100.00	50.00	30.00
(9)	Al Bridwell (batting)	50.00	25.00	15.00
(10a)	Al Bridwell (New York, sliding)	50.00	25.00	15.00
(10b)	Al Bridwell (St. Louis, sliding)	50.00	25.00	15.00
(11)	Donie Bush	50.00	25.00	15.00
(12)	Doc Casey	50.00	25.00	15.00
(13)	Frank Chance	110.00	55.00	33.00
(14a)	Hal Chase (New York, fielding)	65.00	32.00	19.50
(14b)	Hal Chase (Buffalo, fielding)	65.00	32.00	19.50
(15)	Hal Chase (portrait)	65.00	32.00	19.50
(16a)	Ty Cobb (Detroit Am., standing)	900.00	450.00	270.00
(16b)	Ty Cobb (Detroit Americans, standing)	900.00	450.00	270.00
(17)	"Ty" Cobb (batting)	900.00	450.00	270.00
(18a)	Eddie Collins (Phila. Am.)	100.00	50.00	30.00
(18b)	Eddie Collins (Phila. Amer.)	100.00	50.00	30.00
(19)	Eddie Collins (Chicago)	100.00	50.00	30.00
(20)	Sam Crawford	100.00	50.00	30.00
(21)	Harry Davis	50.00	25.00	15.00
(22)	Ray Demmitt	50.00	25.00	15.00
(23a)	Wild Bill Donovan (Detroit)	50.00	25.00	15.00
(23b)	Wild Bill Donovan (New York)	50.00	25.00	15.00
(24a)	Red Dooin (Philadelphia)	50.00	25.00	15.00
(24b)	Red Dooin (Cincinnati)	50.00	25.00	15.00
(25a)	Mickey Doolan (Philadelphia)	50.00	25.00	15.00
(25b)	Mickey Doolan (Baltimore)	50.00	25.00	15.00
(26)	Patsy Dougherty	50.00	25.00	15.00
(27a)	Larry Doyle, Larry Doyle (New York Nat'l, batting)	50.00	25.00	15.00
(28)	Larry Doyle (throwing)	50.00	25.00	15.00
(29)	Clyde Engle	50.00	25.00	15.00
(30a)	Johnny Evers (Chicago)	100.00	50.00	30.00
(30b)	Johnny Evers (Boston)	100.00	50.00	30.00
(31)	Art Fromme	50.00	25.00	15.00
(32a)	George Gibson (Pittsburg Nat'l, back view)	50.00	25.00	15.00
(32b)	George Gibson (Pittsburgh Nat'l., back view)	50.00	25.00	15.00
(33a)	George Gibson (Pittsburg Nat'l, front view)	50.00	25.00	15.00
(33b)	George Gibson (Pittsburgh Nat'l., front view)	50.00	25.00	15.00
(34a)	Topsy Hartsel (Phila. Am.)	50.00	25.00	15.00
(34b)	Topsy Hartsel (Phila. Amer.)	50.00	25.00	15.00
(35)	Roy Hartzell (batting)	50.00	25.00	15.00
(36)	Roy Hartzell (catching)	50.00	25.00	15.00
(37a)	Fred Jacklitsch (Philadelphia)	50.00	25.00	15.00
(37b)	Fred Jacklitsch (Baltimore)	50.00	25.00	15.00
(38a)	Hughie Jennings (orange background)	100.00	50.00	30.00
(38b)	Hughie Jennings (red background)	100.00	50.00	30.00
(39)	Red Kleinow	50.00	25.00	15.00
(40a)	Otto Knabe (Philadelphia)	50.00	25.00	15.00
(40b)	Otto Knabe (Baltimore)	50.00	25.00	15.00
(41)	Jack Knight	50.00	25.00	15.00
(42a)	Nap Lajoie (Philadelphia, fielding)	250.00	125.00	75.00
(42b)	Nap Lajoie (Cleveland, fielding)	250.00	125.00	75.00
(43)	Nap Lajoie (portrait)	250.00	125.00	75.00
(44a)	Hans Lobert (Cincinnati)	50.00	25.00	15.00
(44b)	Hans Lobert (New York)	50.00	25.00	15.00
(45)	Sherry Magee	55.00	27.00	16.50
(46)	Rube Marquard	100.00	50.00	30.00
(47a)	Christy Matthewson (Mathewson) (large print)	325.00	162.00	97.00
(47b)	Christy Matthewson (Mathewson) (small print)	325.00	162.00	97.00
(48a)	John McGraw (large print)	90.00	45.00	27.00
(48b)	John McGraw (small print)	90.00	45.00	27.00
(49)	Larry McLean	50.00	25.00	15.00
(50)	George McQuillan	50.00	25.00	15.00
(51)	Dots Miller (batting)	50.00	25.00	15.00
(52a)	Dots Miller (Pittsburg, fielding)	50.00	25.00	15.00
(52b)	Dots Miller (St. Louis, fielding)	50.00	25.00	15.00
(53a)	Danny Murphy (Philadelphia)	50.00	25.00	15.00
(53b)	Danny Murphy (Brooklyn)	50.00	25.00	15.00
(54)	Rebel Oakes	50.00	25.00	15.00
(55)	Bill O'Hara	50.00	25.00	15.00
(56)	Eddie Plank	110.00	55.00	33.00
(57a)	Germany Schaefer (Washington)	50.00	25.00	15.00
(57b)	Germany Schaefer (Newark)	50.00	25.00	15.00
(58)	Admiral Schlei	50.00	25.00	15.00
(59)	Boss Schmidt	50.00	25.00	15.00
(60)	Johnny Seigle	50.00	25.00	15.00
(61)	Dave Shean	50.00	25.00	15.00
(62)	Boss Smith (Schmidt)	50.00	25.00	15.00
(63)	Tris Speaker	200.00	100.00	60.00
(64)	Oscar Stanage	50.00	25.00	15.00
(65)	George Stovall	50.00	25.00	15.00
(66)	Jeff Sweeney	50.00	25.00	15.00
(67a)	Joe Tinker (Chicago Nat'l, batting)	100.00	50.00	30.00
(67b)	Joe Tinker (Chicago Feds, batting)	100.00	50.00	30.00
(68)	Joe Tinker (portrait)	100.00	50.00	30.00
(69a)	Honus Wagner (batting, S.S.)	400.00	200.00	120.00
(69b)	Honus Wagner (batting, 2b.)	400.00	200.00	120.00
(70a)	Honus Wagner (throwing, S.S.)	400.00	200.00	120.00

NOTE: A card number in parentheses ( ) indicates the card set is unnumbered.

	NR MT	EX	VG
(70b) Honus Wagner (throwing, 2b.)	400.00	200.00	120.00
(71) Hooks Wiltse	50.00	25.00	15.00
(72) Cy Young	225.00	112.00	67.00
(73a) Heinie Zimmerman (2b.)	50.00	25.00	15.00
(73b) Heinie Zimmerman (3b.)	50.00	25.00	15.00

1911 T217 Mono

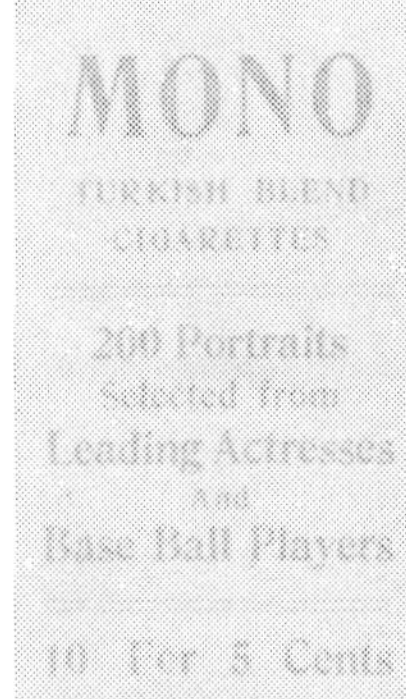

As was common with many tobacco issues of the period, the T217 set - distributed on the West Coast by Mono Cigarettes - feature both baseball players and "Leading Actresses." The 23 baseball players in the Mono set are all from the Pacific Coast League. Two of the players (Delhi and Hughie Smith) are shown in two poses, resulting in a total of 25 different cards. The players are pictured in black and white photos on a card that measures approximately 1-1/2" by 2-5/8", the standard size of a tobacco card. The player's name and team appear at the bottom, while the back of the card carries an advertisement for Mono Cigarettes. The Mono set, which can be dated to the 1909-1911 period, is among the rarest of all tobacco cards.

	NR MT	EX	VG
Complete Set:	6250.	3125.	1875.
Common Player:	225.00	112.00	67.00
(1) Aiken	225.00	112.00	67.00
(2) Curtis Bernard	225.00	112.00	67.00
(3) L. Burrell	225.00	112.00	67.00
(4) Chadbourn	225.00	112.00	67.00
(5) R. Couchman	225.00	112.00	67.00
(6) Elmer Criger	225.00	112.00	67.00
(7) Pete Daley	225.00	112.00	67.00
(8) W. Delhi (glove at chest level)	225.00	112.00	67.00
(9) W. Delhi (glove at shoulder level)	225.00	112.00	67.00
(10) Bert Delmas	225.00	112.00	67.00
(11) Ivan Howard	225.00	112.00	67.00
(12) Kitty Knight	225.00	112.00	67.00
(13) Gene Knapp (Krapp)	225.00	112.00	67.00
(14) Metzger	225.00	112.00	67.00
(15) Carl Mitze	225.00	112.00	67.00
(16) J. O'Rourke	225.00	112.00	67.00
(17) R. Peckinpaugh	250.00	125.00	75.00
(18) Walter Schmidt	225.00	112.00	67.00
(19) Hughie Smith (batting)	225.00	112.00	67.00
(20) Hughie Smith (fielding)	225.00	112.00	67.00
(21) Wm. Stein	225.00	112.00	67.00
(22) Elmer Thorsen	225.00	112.00	67.00
(23) Oscar Vitt	225.00	112.00	67.00
(24) Clyde Wares	225.00	112.00	67.00
(25) Geo. Wheeler	225.00	112.00	67.00

1914 T222 Fatima

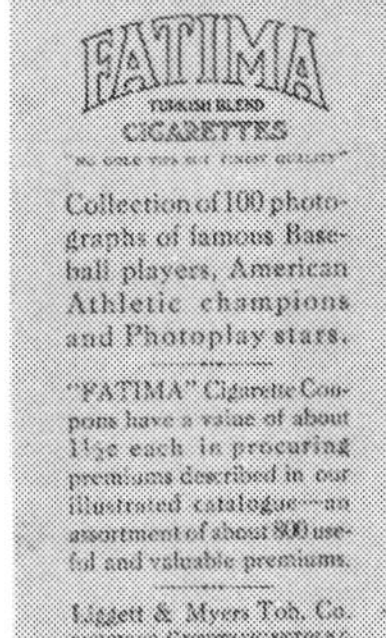

Unlike the typical 20th Century tobacco card issues, the T222 Fatima cards were glossy photographs on a thin paper stock and measure a larger 2-1/2" by 4-1/2". According to the back of the card, the set includes "100 photographs of famous Baseball Players, American Athletic Champions and Photoplay stars," but apparently not all were issued. The baseball portion of the set appears to be complete at 52, while only four other athletes and four "photoplay" stars have been found. The set, issued in 1913, includes players from 13 of the 16 major league teams (all except the Red Sox, White Sox and Pirates.) The set features a mix of stars and lesser-known players.

	NR MT	EX	VG
Complete Set:	15000.	7500.	4500.
Common Player:	150.00	75.00	45.00
(1) Grover Alexander	600.00	300.00	175.00
(2) Jimmy Archer	150.00	75.00	45.00
(3) Jimmy Austin	200.00	100.00	60.00
(4) Jack Barry	150.00	75.00	45.00
(5) George Baumgardner	150.00	75.00	45.00
(6) Rube Benton	150.00	75.00	45.00
(7) Roger Bresnahan	400.00	200.00	120.00
(8) Boardwalk Brown	150.00	75.00	45.00
(9) George Burns	150.00	75.00	45.00
(10) Bullet Joe Bush	160.00	80.00	48.00
(11) George Chalmers	150.00	75.00	45.00
(12) Frank Chance	450.00	225.00	135.00
(13) Al Demaree	150.00	75.00	45.00
(14) Art Fletcher	150.00	75.00	45.00
(15) Earl Hamilton	150.00	75.00	45.00
(16) John Henry	150.00	75.00	45.00
(17) Byron Houck	150.00	75.00	45.00
(18) Miller Huggins	400.00	200.00	120.00
(19) Hughie Jennings	400.00	200.00	120.00
(20) Walter Johnson	1500.	750.00	450.00
(21) Ray Keating	150.00	75.00	45.00
(22) Jack Lapp	150.00	75.00	45.00
(23) Tommy Leach	150.00	75.00	45.00
(24) Nemo Leibold	150.00	75.00	45.00
(25) Jack Lelivelt	200.00	100.00	60.00
(26) Hans Lobert	150.00	75.00	45.00
(27) Lee Magee	150.00	75.00	45.00
(28) Sherry Magee	160.00	80.00	48.00
(29) Fritz Maisel	150.00	75.00	45.00
(30) Rube Marquard	400.00	200.00	120.00
(31) George McBride	150.00	75.00	45.00
(32) Larry McLean	150.00	75.00	45.00
(33) Stuffy McInnis	150.00	75.00	45.00
(34) Ray Morgan	150.00	75.00	45.00
(35) Eddie Murphy	150.00	75.00	45.00
(36) Red Murray	150.00	75.00	45.00
(37) Rube Oldring	150.00	75.00	45.00
(38) Bill Orr	150.00	75.00	45.00
(39) Hub Perdue	150.00	75.00	45.00
(40) Art Phelan	150.00	75.00	45.00
(41) Ed Reulbach	150.00	75.00	45.00
(42) Vic Saier	150.00	75.00	45.00
(43) Slim Sallee	150.00	75.00	45.00
(44) Wally Schang	150.00	75.00	45.00
(45) Wildfire Schulte	150.00	75.00	45.00
(46) J.C. "Red" Smith	150.00	75.00	45.00
(47) Amos Strunk	150.00	75.00	45.00
(48) Bill Sweeney	150.00	75.00	45.00
(49) Lefty Tyler	150.00	75.00	45.00
(50) Ossie Vitt	150.00	75.00	45.00
(51) Ivy Wingo	150.00	75.00	45.00
(52) Heinie Zimmerman	150.00	75.00	45.00

1912 T227 Series of Champions

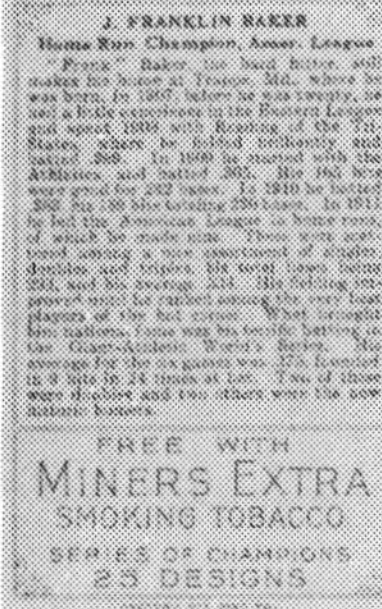

The 1912 "Series of Champions" card set issued by the "Honest Long Cut" and "Miners Extra" tobacco brands features several baseball stars among its 25 famous athletes of the day. Larger than a standard-size tobacco issue, each card in the "Champions" series measures 3-3/8" by 2-5/16". The back includes a relatively lengthy player biography, while the front features a lithograph of the player in action. Although the set includes only four baseball players, these attractive cards are popular among collectors because of the stature of the four players selected. The "Champions" series holds additional significance because it includes the only known baseball cards issued under the "Miners Extra" brand name. The set carries the American Card Catalog designation of T227.

	NR MT	EX	VG
Complete Set:	5200.	2600.	1560.
Common Player:	650.00	325.00	195.00
(1) "Home Run" Baker	650.00	325.00	195.00
(2) "Chief" Bender	650.00	325.00	195.00
(3) Ty Cobb	2500.	1250.	750.00
(4) R. Marquard	650.00	325.00	195.00

1922 T231 Fans

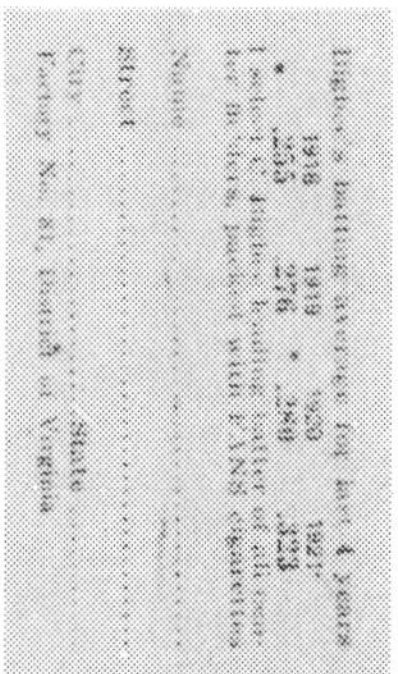

More mystery surrounds this obscure set, issued in 1922 by Fans Cigarettes, than any other tobacco issue. In fact, the only evidence of its existence is a photocopy of the front and back of a single card of Pittsburgh Pirates outfielder Carson Bigbee. Even the owner of the card is unknown. Assuming the photocopy is actual size, the card measures approximately 2-1/2" by 1-1/2" and is believed to be sepia-toned. Adding to the mystery is the number "85" which appears in the lower right corner on the front of the card, apparently indicating there were at least that many cards in the set - even though no other subjects have ever been found. The back of the card displays Bigbee's batting averages for each season from 1918 through 1921 and includes the line: "I select C. Bigbee leading batter of all center fielders, packed with FANS cigarettes." The statement is followed by blanks for a person to fill in his name and address, as if the card were some sort of "ballot." Although it has not received much publicity, this card - if it even exists - may be the rarest baseball card in the hobby. As such, no value will be placed on the card in this catalog until it is proven the card exists. The Card Catalog designation of T231. American Card Catalog designation is T231.

Complete Set:

85 Carson Bigbee

1914 T330-2 Piedmont Art Stamps

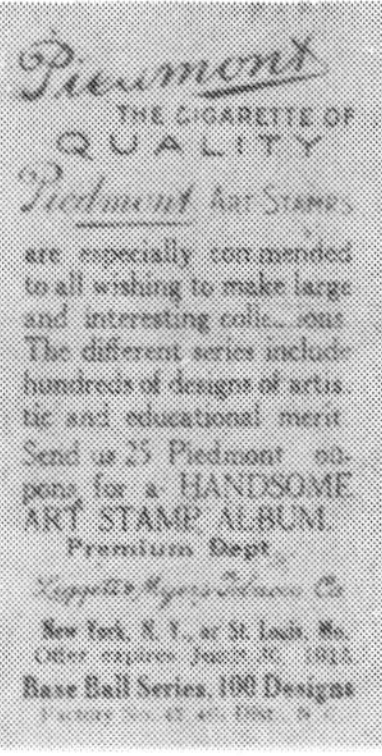

The 1914 series of "Piedmont Art Stamps" look like a fragile "stamp" version of the more popular T205 Gold Border tobacco cards. Issued by employed the same basic design as the T205 set produced three years earlier. The stamps in the Piedmont series measure 1-1/2" by 2-5/8". Even though the backs of the stamps advertise "100 designs," at least 102 different players are known.

And, because four of the players (Hal Chase, Eddie Collins, Russ Ford and Bobby Wallace) are pictured in two separate poses, there are actually 106 different stamps in a complete set. All but three of the subjects in the Piedmont set were taken from the T205 set, with the exceptions being Joe Wood, Walt Blair and Bill Killifer. Because of their fragile composition, and since they are "stamps" that were frequently stuck to album pages, examples of Piedmont Art Stamps in Mint or Near Mint condition are very scarce. The back of the stamps offered a "handsome" album in exchange for 25 Piedmont coupons. The set has an American Card Catalog designation of T330-2.

		NR MT	EX	VG
Complete Set:		7500.	3750.	2250.
Common Player:		50.00	25.00	15.00
(1)	Jimmy Archer	50.00	25.00	15.00
(2)	Jimmy Austin	50.00	25.00	15.00
(3)	Home Run Baker	100.00	50.00	30.00
(4)	Cy Barger	50.00	25.00	15.00
(5)	Jack Barry	50.00	25.00	15.00
(6)	Johnny Bates	50.00	25.00	15.00
(7)	Beals Becker	50.00	25.00	15.00
(8)	Chief Bender	100.00	50.00	30.00
(9)	Bob Bescher	50.00	25.00	15.00
(10)	Joe Birmingham	50.00	25.00	15.00
(11)	Walt Blair	50.00	25.00	15.00
(12)	Roger Bresnahan	100.00	50.00	30.00
(13)	Al Bridwell	50.00	25.00	15.00
(14)	Mordecai Brown	100.00	50.00	30.00
(15)	Bobby Byrne	50.00	25.00	15.00
(16)	Howie Camnitz	50.00	25.00	15.00
(17)	Bill Carrigan	50.00	25.00	15.00
(18)	Frank Chance	110.00	55.00	33.00
(19)	Hal Chase ("Chase" on front)	65.00	32.00	19.50
(20)	Hal Chase ("Hal Chase" on front)	65.00	32.00	19.50
(21)	Ed Cicotte	65.00	32.00	19.50
(22)	Fred Clarke	100.00	50.00	30.00
(23)	Ty Cobb	900.00	450.00	275.00
(24)	Eddie Collins (mouth closed)	100.00	50.00	30.00
(25)	Eddie Collins (mouth open)	100.00	50.00	30.00
(26)	Otis "Doc" Crandall	50.00	25.00	15.00
(27)	Bill Dahlen	50.00	25.00	15.00
(28)	Jake Daubert	60.00	30.00	18.00
(29)	Jim Delanhanty	50.00	25.00	15.00
(30)	Josh Devore	50.00	25.00	15.00
(31)	Red Dooin	50.00	25.00	15.00
(32)	Mickey Doolan	50.00	25.00	15.00
(33)	Tom Downey	50.00	25.00	15.00
(34)	Larry Doyle	50.00	25.00	15.00
(35)	Dick Egan	50.00	25.00	15.00
(36)	Kid Elberfield (Elberfeld)	50.00	25.00	15.00
(37)	Clyde Engle	50.00	25.00	15.00
(38)	Johnny Evers	100.00	50.00	30.00
(39)	Art Fletcher	50.00	25.00	15.00
(40)	Russ Ford (dark cap)	50.00	25.00	15.00
(41)	Russ Ford (white cap)	50.00	25.00	15.00
(42)	Art Fromme	50.00	25.00	15.00
(43)	George Gibson	50.00	25.00	15.00
(44)	William Goode (Wilbur Good)	50.00	25.00	15.00
(45)	Clark Griiffith	100.00	50.00	30.00
(46)	Bob Groom	50.00	25.00	15.00
(47)	Bob Harmon	50.00	25.00	15.00
(48)	Arnold Hauser	50.00	25.00	15.00
(49)	Buck Herzog	50.00	25.00	15.00
(50)	Dick Hoblitzell	50.00	25.00	15.00
(51)	Miller Huggins	100.00	50.00	30.00
(52)	John Hummel	50.00	25.00	15.00
(53)	Hughie Jennings	100.00	50.00	30.00
(54)	Walter Johnson	350.00	175.00	105.00
(55)	Davy Jones	50.00	25.00	15.00
(56)	Bill Killifer (Killefer)	75.00	37.00	22.00
(57)	Ed Konetchy	50.00	25.00	15.00
(58)	Frank LaPorte	50.00	25.00	15.00
(59)	Hans Lobert	50.00	25.00	15.00
(60)	Harry Lord	50.00	25.00	15.00
(61)	Sherry Magee	60.00	30.00	18.00
(62)	Rube Marquard	100.00	50.00	30.00
(63)	Christy Mathewson	350.00	175.00	105.00
(64)	George McBride	50.00	25.00	15.00
(65)	Larry McLean	50.00	25.00	15.00
(66)	Fred Merkle	60.00	30.00	18.00
(67)	Chief Meyers	50.00	25.00	15.00
(68)	Clyde Milan	50.00	25.00	15.00
(69)	Dots Miller	50.00	25.00	15.00
(70)	Mike Mitchell	50.00	25.00	15.00
(71)	Pat Moran	50.00	25.00	15.00
(72)	George Moriarity (Moriarty)	50.00	25.00	15.00
(73)	George Mullin	50.00	25.00	15.00
(74)	Danny Murphy	50.00	25.00	15.00
(75)	Jack "Red" Murray	50.00	25.00	15.00
(76)	Tom Needham	50.00	25.00	15.00
(77)	Rebel Oakes	50.00	25.00	15.00
(78)	Rube Oldring	50.00	25.00	15.00
(79)	Fred Parent	50.00	25.00	15.00
(80)	Dode Paskert	50.00	25.00	15.00
(81)	Jack Quinn	50.00	25.00	15.00
(82)	Ed Reulbach	50.00	25.00	15.00
(83)	Lewis Ritchie	50.00	25.00	15.00
(84)	Jack Rowan	50.00	25.00	15.00
(85)	Nap Rucker	50.00	25.00	15.00
(86)	Germany Schaefer	50.00	25.00	15.00
(87)	Wildfire Schulte	50.00	25.00	15.00
(88)	Jim Scott	50.00	25.00	15.00
(89)	Fred Snodgrass	50.00	25.00	15.00
(90)	Tris Speaker	300.00	150.00	90.00
(91)	Oscar Stamage (Stanage)	50.00	25.00	15.00
(92)	Jeff Sweeney	50.00	25.00	15.00
(93)	Ira Thomas	50.00	25.00	15.00
(94)	Joe Tinker	100.00	50.00	30.00
(95)	Terry Turner	50.00	25.00	15.00
(96)	Hippo Vaughn	50.00	25.00	15.00
(97)	Heinie Wagner	50.00	25.00	15.00
(98)	Bobby Wallace (no cap)	100.00	50.00	30.00
(99)	Bobby Wallace (with cap)	100.00	50.00	30.00
(100)	Ed Walsh	110.00	55.00	33.00
(101)	Zach Wheat	100.00	50.00	30.00
(102)	Irwin "Kaiser" Wilhelm	50.00	25.00	15.00
(103)	Ed Willett	50.00	25.00	15.00
(104)	Owen Wilson	50.00	25.00	15.00
(105)	Hooks Wiltse	50.00	25.00	15.00
(106)	Joe Wood	65.00	32.00	19.50

1911 T332 Helmar Stamps

In an interesting departure from the traditional tobacco cards of the period, Helmar Cigarettes in 1911 issued a series of small major league baseball player "stamps." The stamps, each measuring approximately 1-1/8" by 1-3/8", feature a black and white player portrait surrounded by a colorful, ornate frame. The stamps were originally issued in a 2" by 2 1/2" glassine envelope which advertised the Helmar brand and promoted "Philately - the Popular European Rage." To date, 181 different player stamps have been found. The set includes as many as 50 different frame designs are also known to exist. The Helmar stamp set has been assigned a T332 designation by the American Card Catalog.

		NR MT	EX	VG
Complete Set:		7000.	3500.	2100.
Common Player:		25.00	12.50	7.50
(1)	Babe Adams	25.00	12.50	7.50
(2)	Red Ames	25.00	12.50	7.50
(3)	Jimmy Archer	25.00	12.50	7.50
(4)	Jimmy Austin	25.00	12.50	7.50
(5)	Home Run Baker	75.00	37.00	22.00
(6)	Neal Ball	25.00	12.50	7.50
(7)	Cy Barger	25.00	12.50	7.50
(8)	Jack Barry	25.00	12.50	7.50
(9)	Johnny Bates	25.00	12.50	7.50
(10)	Fred Beck	25.00	12.50	7.50
(11)	Beals Becker	25.00	12.50	7.50
(12)	George Bell	25.00	12.50	7.50
(13)	Chief Bender	75.00	37.00	22.00
(14)	Bob Bescher	25.00	12.50	7.50
(15)	Joe Birmingham	25.00	12.50	7.50
(16)	John Bliss	25.00	12.50	7.50
(17)	Bruno Block	25.00	12.50	7.50
(18)	Ping Bodie	25.00	12.50	7.50
(19)	Roger Bresnahan	75.00	37.00	22.00
(20)	Al Bridwell	25.00	12.50	7.50
(21)	Lew Brockett	25.00	12.50	7.50
(22)	Mordecai Brown	75.00	37.00	22.00
(23)	Bill Burns	25.00	12.50	7.50
(24)	Donie Bush	25.00	12.50	7.50
(25)	Bobby Byrne	25.00	12.50	7.50
(26)	Nixey Callahan	25.00	12.50	7.50
(27)	Howie Camnitz	25.00	12.50	7.50
(28)	Max Carey	75.00	37.00	22.00
(29)	Bill Carrigan	25.00	12.50	7.50
(30)	Frank Chance	35.00	17.50	10.50
(31)	Hal Chase	20.00	10.00	6.00
(32)	Ed Cicotte	20.00	10.00	6.00
(33)	Fred Clarke	75.00	37.00	22.00
(34)	Tommy Clarke	25.00	12.50	7.50
(35)	Ty Cobb	750.00	375.00	225.00
(36)	King Cole	25.00	12.50	7.50
(37)	Eddie Collins (Philadelphia)	75.00	37.00	22.00
(38)	Shano Collins (Chicago)	75.00	37.00	22.00
(39)	Wid Conroy	25.00	12.50	7.50
(40)	Doc Crandall	25.00	12.50	7.50
(41)	Sam Crawford	75.00	37.00	22.00
(42)	Birdie Cree	25.00	12.50	7.50
(43)	Bill Dahlen	25.00	12.50	7.50
(44)	Jake Daubert	35.00	17.50	10.50
(45)	Harry Davis	25.00	12.50	7.50
(46)	Jim Delahanty	25.00	12.50	7.50
(47)	Art Devlin	25.00	12.50	7.50
(48)	Josh Devore	25.00	12.50	7.50
(49)	Mike Donlin	25.00	12.50	7.50
(50)	Wild Bill Donovan	25.00	12.50	7.50
(51)	Red Dooin	25.00	12.50	7.50
(52)	Mickey Doolan	25.00	12.50	7.50
(53)	Patsy Dougherty	25.00	12.50	7.50
(54)	Tom Downey	25.00	12.50	7.50
(55)	Larry Doyle	25.00	12.50	7.50
(56)	Louis Drucke	25.00	12.50	7.50
(57)	Clyde Engle	25.00	12.50	7.50
(58)	Tex Erwin	25.00	12.50	7.50
(59)	Steve Evans	25.00	12.50	7.50
(60)	Johnny Evers	75.00	37.00	22.00
(61)	Jack Ferry	25.00	12.50	7.50
(62)	Ray Fisher	25.00	12.50	7.50
(63)	Art Fletcher	25.00	12.50	7.50
(64)	Russ Ford	25.00	12.50	7.50
(65)	Art Fromme	25.00	12.50	7.50
(66)	Earl Gardner	25.00	12.50	7.50
(67)	Harry Gaspar	25.00	12.50	7.50
(68)	George Gibson	25.00	12.50	7.50
(69)	Roy Golden	25.00	12.50	7.50
(70)	Hank Gowdy	25.00	12.50	7.50
(71)	Peaches Graham	25.00	12.50	7.50
(72)	Eddie Grant	25.00	12.50	7.50
(73)	Dolly Gray	25.00	12.50	7.50
(74)	Clark Griffith	75.00	37.00	22.00
(75)	Bob Groom	25.00	12.50	7.50
(76)	Bob Harmon	25.00	12.50	7.50
(77)	Grover Hartley	25.00	12.50	7.50
(78)	Arnold Hauser	25.00	12.50	7.50
(79)	Buck Herzog	25.00	12.50	7.50
(80)	Dick Hoblitzell	25.00	12.50	7.50
(81)	Solly Hoffman (Hofman)	25.00	12.50	7.50
(82)	Miller Huggins	75.00	37.00	22.00
(83)	Long Tom Hughes	25.00	12.50	7.50
(84)	John Hummel	25.00	12.50	7.50
(85)	Hughie Jennings	75.00	37.00	22.00
(86)	Walter Johnson	300.00	150.00	90.00
(87)	Davy Jones	25.00	12.50	7.50
(88)	Johnny Kling	25.00	12.50	7.50
(89)	Otto Knabe	25.00	12.50	7.50
(90)	Jack Knight	25.00	12.50	7.50
(91)	Ed Konetchy	25.00	12.50	7.50
(92)	Harry Krause	25.00	12.50	7.50
(93)	Nap Lajoie	200.00	100.00	60.00
(94)	Joe Lake	25.00	12.50	7.50
(95)	Frank LaPorte	25.00	12.50	7.50
(96)	Tommy Leach	25.00	12.50	7.50
(97)	Lefty Leifield	25.00	12.50	7.50
(98)	Ed Lennox	25.00	12.50	7.50
(99)	Paddy Livingston	25.00	12.50	7.50
(100)	Hans Lobert	25.00	12.50	7.50
(101)	Harry Lord	25.00	12.50	7.50
(102)	Fred Luderas (Luderus)	25.00	12.50	7.50
(103)	Sherry Magee	35.00	17.50	10.50
(104)	Rube Marquard	75.00	37.00	22.00
(105)	Christy Mathewson	300.00	150.00	90.00
(106)	Al Mattern	25.00	12.50	7.50
(107)	George McBride	25.00	12.50	7.50
(108)	Amby McConnell	25.00	12.50	7.50
(109)	John McGraw	100.00	50.00	30.00
(110)	Harry McIntire (McIntyre)	25.00	12.50	7.50
(111)	Matty McIntyre	25.00	12.50	7.50
(112)	Larry McLean	25.00	12.50	7.50
(113)	Fred Merkle	35.00	17.50	10.50
(114)	Chief Meyers	25.00	12.50	7.50
(115)	Clyde Milan	25.00	12.50	7.50
(116)	Dots Miller	25.00	12.50	7.50
(117)	Mike Mitchell	25.00	12.50	7.50
(118)	Earl Moore	25.00	12.50	7.50
(119)	Pat Moran	25.00	12.50	7.50
(120)	George Moriarty	25.00	12.50	7.50
(121)	Mike Mowrey	25.00	12.50	7.50
(122)	George Mullin	25.00	12.50	7.50
(123)	Danny Murphy	25.00	12.50	7.50
(124)	Red Murray	25.00	12.50	7.50
(125)	Tom Needham	25.00	12.50	7.50
(126)	Rebel Oakes	25.00	12.50	7.50
(127)	Rube Oldring	25.00	12.50	7.50
(128)	Marty O'Toole	25.00	12.50	7.50
(129)	Fred Parent	25.00	12.50	7.50
(130)	Dode Paskert	25.00	12.50	7.50
(131)	Barney Pelty	25.00	12.50	7.50
(132)	Eddie Phelps	25.00	12.50	7.50
(133)	Jack Powell	25.00	12.50	7.50
(134)	Jack Quinn	25.00	12.50	7.50
(135)	Ed Reulbach	25.00	12.50	7.50
(136)	Lew Richie	25.00	12.50	7.50
(137)	Reggie Richter	25.00	12.50	7.50
(138)	Jack Rowan	25.00	12.50	7.50
(139)	Nap Rucker	25.00	12.50	7.50
(140)	Slim Sallee	25.00	12.50	7.50
(141)	Doc Scanlan	25.00	12.50	7.50
(142)	Germany Schaefer	25.00	12.50	7.50
(143)	Boss Schmidt	25.00	12.50	7.50
(144)	Wildfire Schulte	25.00	12.50	7.50
(145)	Jim Scott	25.00	12.50	7.50
(146)	Tillie Shafer	25.00	12.50	7.50
(147)	Dave Shean	25.00	12.50	7.50
(148)	Jimmy Sheckard	25.00	12.50	7.50
(149)	Mike Simon	25.00	12.50	7.50
(150)	Fred Snodgrass	25.00	12.50	7.50
(151)	Tris Speaker	250.00	125.00	75.00
(152)	Oscar Stanage	25.00	12.50	7.50
(153)	Bill Steele	25.00	12.50	7.50
(154)	Harry Stovall	25.00	12.50	7.50
(155)	Gabby Street	25.00	12.50	7.50
(156)	George Suggs	25.00	12.50	7.50
(157)	Billy Sullivan	25.00	12.50	7.50
(158)	Bill Sweeney	25.00	12.50	7.50
(159)	Jeff Sweeney	25.00	12.50	7.50
(160)	Lee Tannehill	25.00	12.50	7.50
(161)	Ira Thomas	25.00	12.50	7.50
(162)	Joe Tinker	75.00	37.00	22.00
(163)	John Titus	25.00	12.50	7.50
(164)	Fred Toney	25.00	12.50	7.50
(165)	Terry Turner	25.00	12.50	7.50
(166)	Hippo Vaughn	25.00	12.50	7.50
(167)	Heinie Wagner	25.00	12.50	7.50
(168)	Bobby Wallace	75.00	37.00	22.00
(169)	Ed Walsh	100.00	50.00	30.00
(170)	Jack Warhop	25.00	12.50	7.50
(171)	Zach Wheat	75.00	37.00	22.00
(172)	Doc White	25.00	12.50	7.50

NOTE: A card number in parentheses ( ) indicates the set is unnumbered.

	NR MT	EX	VG
(173) Ed Willett	25.00	12.50	7.50
(174) Art Wilson (New York)	25.00	12.50	7.50
(175) Owen Wilson (Pittsburgh)	25.00	12.50	7.50
(176) Hooks Wiltse	25.00	12.50	7.50
(177) Harry Wolter	25.00	12.50	7.50
(178) Harry Wolverton	25.00	12.50	7.50
(179) Cy Young	350.00	175.00	105.00
(180) Irv Young	25.00	12.50	7.50

1984 Tastykake Phillies

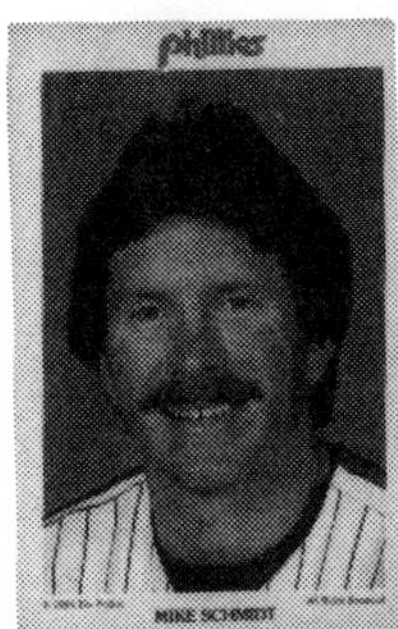

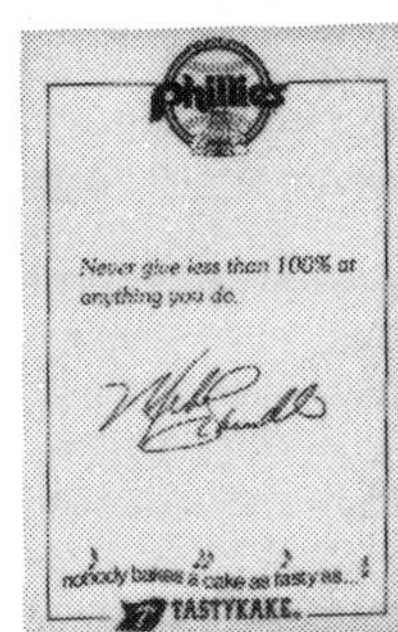

This 40-card regional set featuring the Philadelphia Phillies was issued as a promotion by Tastykake in 1984 and was distributed as a complete set to fans attending the April 21st game at Philadelphia's Veterans Stadium. The large (3-1/2" by 5-1/4") full-color cards have a white border surrounding the photo with "Phillies" at the top and the player's name at the bottom. A 1984 Phillies copyright line appears in the lower left corner. The backs display facsimile autographs, a brief inspirational message and the Tastykake and Phillies logos. The set includes special cards featuring the club's broadcasters, manager and coaches, a team photo, logo/checklist card and two action photos of Mike Schmidt and Steve Carlton, labeled "Future Hall of Famers".

	MT	NR MT	EX
Complete Set:	10.00	7.50	4.00
Common Player:	.20	.15	.08
(1) Luis Aguayo	.20	.15	.08
(2) Larry Andersen	.20	.15	.08
(3) Dave Bristol	.20	.15	.08
(4) Marty Bystrom	.20	.15	.08
(5) Bill Campbell	.20	.15	.08
(6) Steve Carlton	2.00	1.50	.80
(7) Future Hall of Famer (Steve Carlton)	1.50	1.25	.60
(8) Don Carman	.60	.45	.25
(9) Tim Corcoran	.20	.15	.08
(10) Ivan DeJesus	.20	.15	.08
(11) John Denny	.25	.20	.10
(12) Bo Diaz	.25	.20	.10
(13) John Felske	.20	.15	.08
(14) Kiko Garcia	.20	.15	.08
(15) Tony Ghelfi	.20	.15	.08
(16) Greg Gross	.20	.15	.08
(17) Kevin Gross	.50	.40	.20
(18) Von Hayes	.70	.50	.30
(19) Al Holland	.20	.15	.08
(20) Charles Hudson	.35	.25	.14
(21) Deron Johnson	.20	.15	.08
(22) Jerry Koosman	.25	.20	.10
(23) Joe Lefebvre	.20	.15	.08
(24) Sixto Lezcano	.20	.15	.08
(25) Garry Maddox	.25	.20	.10
(26) Len Matuszek	.20	.15	.08
(27) Tug McGraw	.40	.30	.15
(28) Claude Osteen	.20	.15	.08
(29) Paul Owens	.20	.15	.08
(30) John Russell	.30	.25	.12
(31) Mike Ryan	.20	.15	.08
(32) Juan Samuel	.60	.45	.25
(33) Mike Schmidt	3.00	2.25	1.25
(34) Future Hall of Famer (Mike Schmidt)	2.00	1.00	.60
(35) Jeff Stone	.25	.20	.10
(36) Ozzie Virgil	.25	.20	.10
(37) Dave Wehrmeister	.20	.15	.08
(38) Glenn Wilson	.25	.20	.10
(39) John Wockenfuss	.20	.15	.08
(40) Phillie Phanatic	.20	.15	.08
(41) Phillies Broadcasters (Richie Ashburn, Harry Kalas, Andy Musser, Chris Wheeler)	.25	.20	.10
(42) Veterans Stadium	.20	.15	.08
(43) Team Photo	.20	.15	.08
(44) Checklist	.20	.15	.08

1985 Tastykake Phillies

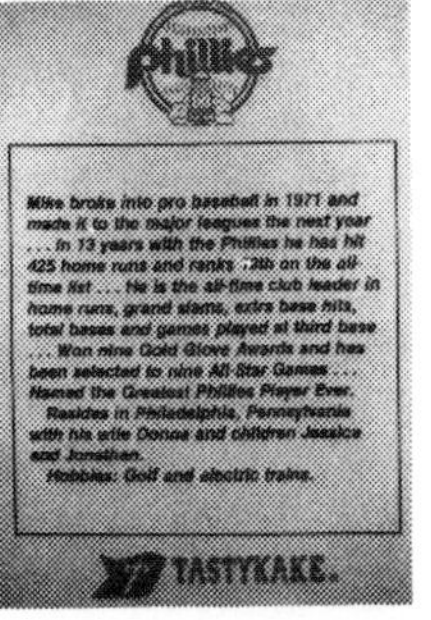

This regional set of Phillies cards, sponsored by Tastykake, was given away at a stadium promotion on April 21st at Philadelphia's Veterans Stadium. The 47 full-color cards measure a large 3" by 5" and are numbered according to the player's uniform number. In addition to player's from the 1985 Phillies roster, the set includes the manager, coaches, group photos, and cards of 14 promising minor leaguers in the club's farm system. The full-color cards are printed on a white, glossy stock and surrrounded by a white border. The player's uniform number, name and position appear below, with a 1985 Phillies copyright in the lower right corner. The backs of the cards display the Phillies and Tastykake logos at the top and bottom respectively, with player information in the center.

	MT	NR MT	EX
Complete Set:	12.00	9.00	4.75
Common Player:	.20	.15	.08
1 Checklist	.20	.15	.08
2 John Felske	.20	.15	.08
3 Dave Bristol	.20	.15	.08
4 Lee Elia	.20	.15	.08
5 Claude Osteen	.20	.15	.08
6 Mike Ryan	.20	.15	.08
7 Del Unser	.20	.15	.08
8 Phillies Coaching Staff (Dave Bristol, Lee Elia, John Felske, Hank King, Claude Osteen, Mike Ryan, Del Unser)	.20	.15	.08
9 Phillies Pitchers (Larry Andersen, Bill Campbell, Steve Carlton, Don Carman, John Denny, Kevin Gross, Al Holland, Charles Hudson, Jerry Koosman, Shane Rawley, Pat Zachry)	.30	.25	.12
10 Phillies Catchers (Darren Daulton, Bo Diaz, Ozzie Virgil)	.20	.15	.08
11 Phillies Infielders (Luis Aguayo, Ivan De Jesus, Steve Jeltz, John Russell, Juan Samuel, Mike Schmidt)	.50	.40	.20
12 Phillies Outfielders (Tim Corcoran, Greg Gross, Von Hayes, Jeff Stone, Glenn Wilson)	.25	.20	.10
13 Larry Andersen	.20	.15	.08
14 Steve Carlton	2.00	1.50	.80
15 Don Carman	.60	.45	.25
16 John Denny	.20	.15	.08
17 Tony Ghelfi	.20	.15	.08
18 Kevin Gross	.30	.25	.12
19 Al Holland	.20	.15	.08
20 Charles Hudson	.25	.20	.10
21 Jerry Koosman	.25	.20	.10
22 Shane Rawley	.30	.25	.12
23 Pat Zachry	.20	.15	.08
24 Darren Daulton	.20	.15	.08
25 Bo Diaz	.25	.20	.10
26 Ozzie Virgil	.25	.20	.10
27 John Wockenfuss	.20	.15	.08
28 Luis Aguayo	.20	.15	.08
29 Kiko Garcia	.20	.15	.08
30 Steve Jeltz	.20	.15	.08
31 John Russell	.30	.25	.12
32 Juan Samuel	.60	.45	.25
33 Mike Schmidt	3.00	2.25	1.25
34 Tim Corcoran	.20	.15	.08
35 Greg Gross	.20	.15	.08
36 Von Hayes	.60	.45	.25
37 Joe Lefebvre	.20	.15	.08
38 Garry Maddox	.25	.20	.10
40 Glenn Wilson	.25	.20	.10
41 Future Phillies (Ramon Caraballo, Mike Diaz)	.50	.40	.20
42 Future Phillies (Rodger Cole, Mike Maddux)	.50	.40	.20
43 Future Phillies (Chris James, Rick Schu)	1.00	.70	.40
44 Future Phillies (Ken Jackson, Francisco Melendez)	.25	.20	.10
45 Future Phillies (Rocky Childress, Randy Salava)	.25	.20	.10
46 Future Phillies (Ralph Citarella, Rich Surhoff)	.25	.20	.10
47 Team Photo	.20	.15	.08

1986 Tastykake Phillies

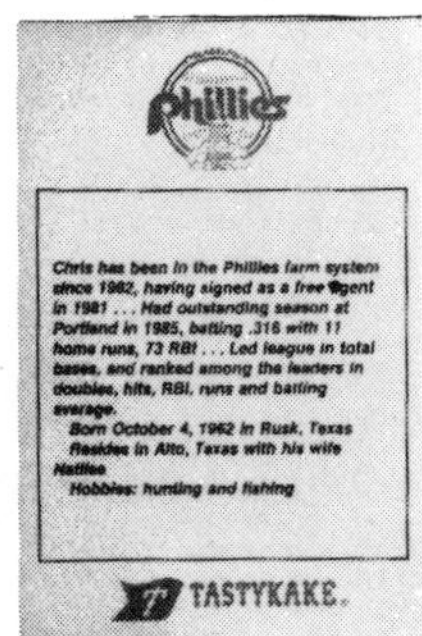

The 1986 Tastykake Phillies set consists of 49 cards that measure 3-1/2" by 5-1/4" in size. The cards were given away at the Phillies' annual baseball card day promotion. The card fronts feature a full-color photo along with the player's name, uniform number and position. The card backs are printed in red and black and carry a brief player biography. Five cards commemorating past Phillies' pennants were included in the set.

	MT	NR MT	EX
Complete Set:	12.00	9.00	4.75
Common Player:	.15	.11	.06
2 Jim Davenport	.15	.11	.06
3 Claude Osteen	.15	.11	.06
4 Lee Elia	.15	.11	.06
5 Mike Ryan	.15	.11	.06
6 John Russell	.20	.15	.08
7 John Felske	.15	.11	.06
8 Juan Samuel	.50	.40	.20
9 Von Hayes	.50	.40	.20
10 Darren Daulton	.15	.11	.06
11 Tom Foley	.15	.11	.06
12 Glenn Wilson	.20	.15	.08
14 Jeff Stone	.15	.11	.06
15 Rick Schu	.20	.15	.08
16 Luis Aguayo	.15	.11	.06
20 Mike Schmidt	2.00	1.50	.80
21 Greg Gross	.15	.11	.06
22 Gary Redus	.15	.11	.06
23 Joe Lefebvre	.15	.11	.06
24 Milt Thompson	.30	.25	.12
25 Del Unser	.15	.11	.06
26 Chris James	1.00	.70	.40
27 Kent Tekulve	.20	.15	.08
28 Shane Rawley	.25	.20	.10
29 Ronn Reynolds	.15	.11	.06
30 Steve Jeltz	.15	.11	.06
31 Garry Maddox	.25	.20	.10
32 Steve Carlton	1.50	1.25	.60
33 Dave Shipanoff	.15	.11	.06
35 Randy Lerch	.15	.11	.06
36 Robin Roberts	.60	.45	.25
39 Dave Rucker	.15	.11	.06
40 Steve Bedrosian	.40	.30	.15
41 Tom Hume	.15	.11	.06
42 Don Carman	.50	.40	.20
43 Fred Toliver	.20	.15	.08
46 Kevin Gross	.30	.25	.12
47 Larry Andersen	.15	.11	.06
48 Dave Stewart	.50	.40	.20
49 Charles Hudson	.20	.15	.08
50 Rocky Childress	.20	.15	.08
--- Future Phillies (Ramon Caraballo, Joe Cipolloni)	.20	.15	.08
--- Future Phillies (Arturo Gonzalez, Mike Maddux)	.40	.30	.15
--- Future Phillies (Ricky Jordan, Francisco Melendez)	3.00	2.25	1.25
--- Future Phillies (Randy Day, Kevin Ward)	.20	.15	.08
--- The 1915 Phillies	.15	.11	.06
--- The 1950 Phillies	.15	.11	.06
--- The 1980 Phillies	.15	.11	.06
--- The 1983 Phillies	.15	.11	.06
--- June 11, 1985 - A Night To Remember	.15	.11	.06

1987 Tastykake Phillies

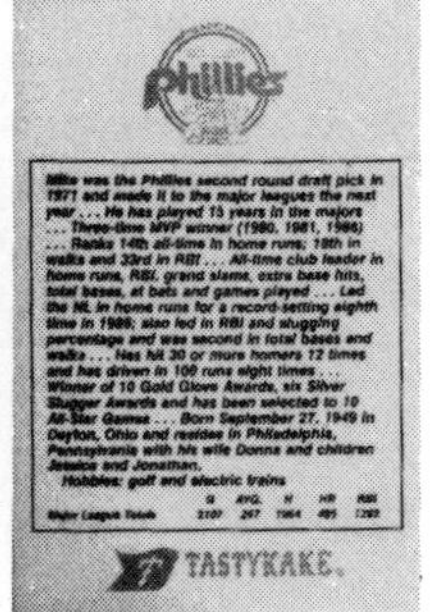

A 46-card set featuring the Philadelphia Phillies and sponsored by Tastykake was given out to fans present at Veterans Stadium for the Phillies' April 12th baseball card day promotion. The cards measure 3-1/2" by 5-1/4" with fronts that feature a full-color player photo framed with a white border. The player's number, name and position appear below the photo. Card backs are printed in red and black and contain a brief biography. The set was available for $4 via a mail-in offer to the Phillies ball club.

		MT	NR MT	EX
Complete Set:		10.00	7.50	4.00
Common Player:		.15	.11	.06
6	John Russell	.15	.11	.06
7	John Felske	.15	.11	.06
8	Juan Samuel	.50	.40	.20
10	Darren Daulton	.15	.11	.06
11	Greg Legg	.20	.15	.08
12	Glenn Wilson	.20	.15	.08
13	Lance Parrish	.50	.40	.20
14	Jeff Stone	.15	.11	.06
15	Rick Schu	.15	.11	.06
16	Luis Aguayo	.15	.11	.06
17	Ron Roenicke	.15	.11	.06
18	Chris James	1.00	.70	.40
20	Mike Schmidt	2.00	1.50	.80
21	Greg Gross	.15	.11	.06
23	Joe Cipolloni	.20	.15	.08
24	Milt Thompson	.20	.15	.08
27	Kent Tekulve	.20	.15	.08
28	Shane Rawley	.25	.20	.10
29	Ronn Reynolds	.15	.11	.06
30	Steve Jeltz	.15	.11	.06
33	Mike Jackson	.40	.30	.15
34	Mike Easler	.20	.15	.08
35	Dan Schatzeder	.15	.11	.06
37	Ken Dowell	.20	.15	.08
38	Jim Olander	.20	.15	.08
39a	Joe Cowley	.15	.11	.06
39b	Bob Scanlan	.20	.15	.08
40	Steve Bedrosian	.40	.30	.15
41	Tom Hume	.15	.11	.06
42	Don Carman	.30	.25	.12
43	Freddie Toliver	.15	.11	.06
44	Mike Maddux	.30	.25	.12
45	Greg Jelks	.40	.30	.15
46	Kevin Gross	.25	.20	.10
47	Bruce Ruffin	.40	.30	.15
48	Marvin Freeman	.30	.25	.12
49	Len Watts	.20	.15	.08
50	Tom Newell	.20	.15	.08
51	Ken Jackson	.30	.25	.12
52	Todd Frohwirth	.30	.25	.12
58	Doug Bair	.15	.11	.06
---	Shawn Burton, Rick Lundblade	.20	.15	.08
---	Jeff Kaye, Darren Loy	.20	.15	.08
---	Phillies Coaches (Jim Davenport, Lee Elia, Claude Osteen, Mike Ryan, Del Unser)	.15	.11	.06
---	Phillie Phanatic	.15	.11	.06
---	Team Photo	.15	.11	.06

1988 Tastykake Phillies

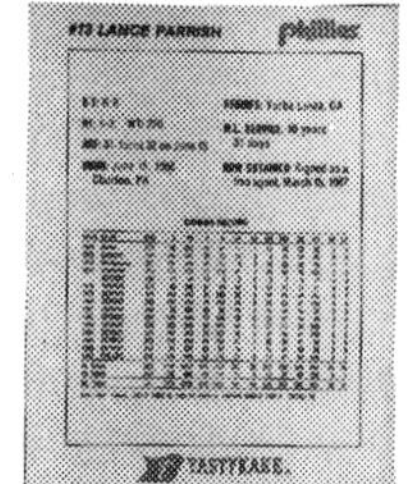

This 39-card set was co-produced by Tastykake and the Phillies. The semi-glossy oversize cards, 4-7/8" by 6-1/4", feature full-color action photos with white borders. The coaching staff, young player prospects, the team mascot and a full team photo are included in the set. The card backs carry personal data and career stats in black letters, with the Phillies and Tastykake logos in red. Card numbers correspond to player uniform numbers. The cards were available upon request from individual players and were not made available as a set. Nine cards (#'s 4, 6, 7, 11, 15 Gutierrez, 16 Bowa, 17, 33 and Broadcasters) were added later in the year. These cards have blank backs.

		MT	NR MT	EX
Complete Set:		12.00	9.00	4.75
Common Player:		.15	.11	.06
4a	Lee Elia (vertical format)	.15	.11	.06
4b	Lee Elia (horizontal format)	.15	.11	.06
6	John Russell	.15	.11	.06
7	John Vukovich	.15	.11	.06
8	Juan Samuel	.50	.40	.20
9	Von Hayes	.35	.25	.14
10	Darren Daulton	.15	.11	.06
11	Keith Miller	.40	.30	.15
13	Lance Parrish	.50	.40	.20
15a	Bill Almon	.15	.11	.06
15b	Jackie Gutierrez	.15	.11	.06
16a	Luis Aguayo	.15	.11	.06
16b	Larry Bowa	.20	.15	.08
17	Ricky Jordan	2.00	1.50	.80
18	Chris James	.40	.30	.15
19	Mike Young	.15	.11	.06
20	Mike Schmidt	2.00	1.50	.80
21	Greg Gross	.15	.11	.06
22	Bob Dernier	.15	.11	.06
24	Milt Thompson	.20	.15	.08
27	Kent Tekulve	.25	.20	.10
28	Shane Rawley	.25	.20	.10
29	Phil Bradley	.50	.40	.20
30	Steve Jeltz	.15	.11	.06
31	Jeff Calhoun	.15	.11	.06
33	Greg Harris	.15	.11	.06
38	Wally Ritchie	.25	.20	.10
40	Steve Bedrosian	.35	.25	.14
42	Don Carman	.25	.20	.10
44	Mike Maddux	.25	.20	.10
45	David Palmer	.15	.11	.06
46	Kevin Gross	.25	.20	.10
47	Bruce Ruffin	.20	.15	.08
52	Todd Frohwirth	.20	.15	.08
---	Coaching Staff (Dave Bristol, Claude Osteen, Mike Ryan, Tony Taylor, Del Unser, John Vukovich)	.15	.11	.06
---	Phillies Prospects (Tom Barrett, Brad Brink, Steve DeAngelis, Ron Jones, Keith Miller, Brad Moore, Howard Nichols, Shane Turner)	.40	.30	.15
---	Phillie Phanatic	.15	.11	.06
---	Team Photo	.15	.11	.06
---	Broadcasters (Richie Ashburn, Harry Kalas, Garry Maddox, Andy Musser, Chris Wheeler)	.15	.11	.06

1989 Tastykake Phillies

These oversize (approximately 4" by 6") cards feature very nice borderless action photos of the Philadelphia Phillies. The 36-card set was sponsored by Tastykake (whose logo appears on the bottom of the card backs) and was given to fans attending the May 13 Phillies game as a stadium promotion. The backs include player information and complete stats.

		MT	NR MT	EX
Complete Set:		15.00	11.00	6.00
Common Player:		.15	.11	.06
2	Larry Bowa	.15	.11	.06
3	Darold Knowles	.15	.11	.06
4a	Lenny Dykstra	.25	.20	.10
4b	Denis Menke	.15	.11	.06
5	Mike Ryan	.15	.11	.06
6	Dwayne Murphy	.15	.11	.06
7	John Vuckovich	.15	.11	.06
8a	Juan Samuel	.50	.40	.20
8b	Charlie Hayes	.25	.20	.10
9	Von Hayes	.35	.25	.12
10	Darren Daulton	.15	.11	.06
11	John Kruk	.25	.20	.10
12	Tony Taylor	.15	.11	.06
13	Roger McDowell	.25	.20	.10
15	Floyd Youmans	.15	.11	.06
16	Nick Leyva	.20	.15	.08
17	Ricky Jordan	1.00	.70	.40
18	Jim Adduci (Update Card)	.25	.20	.10
19	Tom Nieto	.15	.11	.06
20	Mike Schmidt	1.00	.70	.40
21	Dickie Thon	.15	.11	.06
22	Bob Dernier	.15	.11	.06
23	Randy Ready (Update Card)	.25	.20	.10
24	Curt Ford	.15	.11	.06
25	Steve Lake	.15	.11	.06
26	Chris James	.80	.60	.30
27	Randy O'Neal	.15	.11	.06
28	Tom Herr	.30	.25	.12
30	Steve Jeltz	.15	.11	.06
31	Mark Ryal	.25	.20	.15
33	Greg Harris	.15	.11	.06
34	Alex Madrid	.20	.15	.08
35	Eric Bullock (Update Card)	.25	.20	.10
39	Dennis Cook (Update Card)	.25	.20	.10
40	Steve Bedrosian	.35	.25	.12
41	Steve Ontiveros	.20	.15	.08
42	Don Carman	.20	.15	.08
43	Ken Howell	.15	.11	.06
44	Mike Maddux	.25	.20	.10
45	Terry Mulholland (Update Card)	.25	.20	.10
46	Larry McWilliams	.15	.11	.06
47	Bruce Ruffin	.30	.25	.12
49	Jeff Parrett	.30	.25	.12
52	Todd Frohwirth	.20	.15	.08
---	Sponsor Card	.15	.11	.06

1933 Tattoo Orbit

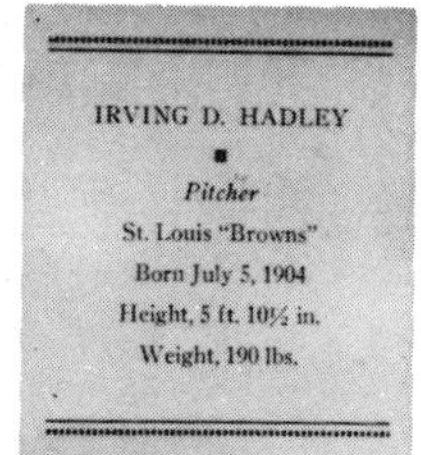

Found in 1¢ packages of Tattoo gum, these 2" by 2-1/4" cards were produced by the Orbit Gum Company of Chicago, Illinois. The fronts feature a photograph which is tinted to give skin some color. Stylized baseball park backgrounds are separated from the photograph by a black line. The rest of the background is printed in vivid red, yellow and green. Card backs have the player's name, team, position, birth date, height and weight. The 60-card set is not common, but their interesting format does not seem to have struck a responsive chord in today's of Bump Hadley and George Blaeholder are the most elusive, followed by those of Ivy Andrews and Rogers Hornsby.

		NR MT	EX	VG
Complete Set:		3000.	1500.	900.00
Common Player:		35.00	17.50	10.50
(1)	Dale Alexander	70.00	35.00	21.00
(2)	Ivy Paul Andrews	150.00	75.00	45.00
(3)	Earl Averill	70.00	35.00	21.00
(4)	Richard Bartell	35.00	17.50	10.50
(5)	Walter Berger	35.00	17.50	10.50
(6)	George F. Blaeholder	100.00	50.00	30.00
(7)	Irving J. Burns	35.00	17.50	10.50
(8)	Guy T. Bush	35.00	17.50	10.50
(9)	Bruce D. Campbell	35.00	17.50	10.50
(10)	William Cissell	35.00	17.50	10.50
(11)	Lefty Clark	35.00	17.50	10.50
(12)	Mickey Cochrane	65.00	32.00	19.50
(13)	Phil Collins	35.00	17.50	10.50
(14)	Hazen Kiki Cuyler	70.00	35.00	21.00
(15)	Dizzy Dean	150.00	75.00	45.00
(16)	Jimmy Dykes	40.00	20.00	12.00
(17)	George L. Earnshaw	35.00	17.50	10.50
(18)	Woody English	35.00	17.50	10.50
(19)	Lewis A. Fonseca	40.00	20.00	12.00
(20)	Jimmy Foxx	125.00	62.00	37.00
(21)	Burleigh A. Grimes	70.00	35.00	21.00
(22)	Charles John Grimm	40.00	20.00	12.00
(23)	Robert M. Grove	65.00	32.00	19.50
(24)	Frank Grube	35.00	17.50	10.50
(25)	George W. Haas	35.00	17.50	10.50
(26)	Irving D. Hadley	100.00	50.00	30.00
(27)	Chick Hafey	70.00	35.00	21.00
(28)	Jesse Joseph Haines	70.00	35.00	21.00
(29)	William Hallahan	35.00	17.50	10.50
(30)	Melvin Harder	35.00	17.50	10.50
(31)	Gabby Hartnett	70.00	35.00	21.00
(32)	Babe Herman	40.00	20.00	12.00
(33)	William Herman	70.00	35.00	21.00
(34)	Rogers Hornsby	200.00	100.00	60.00
(35)	Roy C. Johnson	35.00	17.50	10.50
(36)	J. Smead Jolley	35.00	17.50	10.50
(37)	William Jurges	35.00	17.50	10.50
(38)	William Kamm	35.00	17.50	10.50
(39)	Mark A. Koenig	35.00	17.50	10.50
(40)	James J. Levey	35.00	17.50	10.50
(41)	Ernie Lombardi	70.00	35.00	21.00
(42)	Red Lucas	35.00	17.50	10.50
(43)	Ted Lyons	70.00	35.00	21.00
(44)	Connie Mack	125.00	62.00	37.00
(45)	Pat Malone	35.00	17.50	10.50
(46)	Pepper Martin	40.00	20.00	12.00
(47)	Marty McManus	35.00	17.50	10.50
(48)	Frank J. O'Doul	40.00	20.00	12.00
(49)	Richard Porter	35.00	17.50	10.50
(50)	Carl N. Reynolds	35.00	17.50	10.50
(51)	Charles Henry Root	35.00	17.50	10.50
(52)	Robert Seeds	35.00	17.50	10.50
(53)	Al H. Simmons	70.00	35.00	21.00
(54)	Jackson Riggs Stepheson	40.00	20.00	12.00
(55)	Bud Tinning	35.00	17.50	10.50
(56)	Joe Vosmik	35.00	17.50	10.50
(57)	Rube Walberg	35.00	17.50	10.50
(58)	Paul Waner	70.00	35.00	21.00
(59)	Lonnie Warneke	35.00	17.50	10.50
(60)	Arthur C. Whitney	35.00	17.50	10.50

1986 Texas Gold Ice Cream Reds

One of the last regional baseball card sets produced during the 1986 season was a 28-card team set sponsored by a Cincinnati-area ice cream company and given to fans attending a

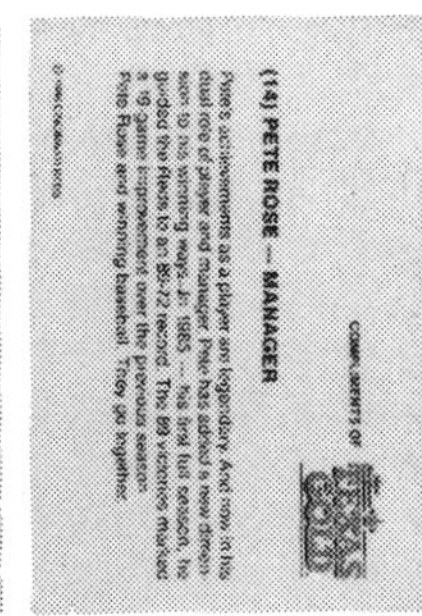

September 19th game. Photos on the 2-1/2" by 3-1/2" cards are game-action shots, and include three different cards of playing manager Pete Rose. The set is also notable for the inclusion of first cards of some of the Reds' young stars.

		MT	NR MT	EX
Complete Set:		25.00	20.00	10.00
Common Player:		.25	.20	.10
6	Bo Diaz	.35	.25	.14
9	Max Venable	.25	.20	.10
11	Kurt Stillwell	.80	.60	.30
12	Nick Esasky	.60	.45	.25
13	Dave Concepcion	.50	.40	.20
14a	Pete Rose (commemorative)	2.00	1.50	.80
14b	Pete Rose (infield)	2.00	1.50	.80
14c	Pete Rose (manager)	2.00	1.50	.80
16	Ron Oester	.25	.20	.10
20	Eddie Milner	.25	.20	.10
22	Sal Butera	.25	.20	.10
24	Tony Perez	.70	.50	.30
25	Buddy Bell	.35	.25	.14
28	Kal Daniels	1.50	1.25	.60
29	Tracy Jones	.80	.60	.30
31	John Franco	.80	.60	.30
32	Tom Browning	.60	.45	.25
33	Ron Robinson	.35	.25	.14
34	Bill Gullickson	.25	.20	.10
36	Mario Soto	.35	.25	.14
39	Dave Parker	1.00	.70	.40
40	John Denny	.25	.20	.10
44	Eric Davis	3.00	2.25	1.25
45	Chris Welsh	.25	.20	.10
48	Ted Power	.25	.20	.10
49	Joe Price	.25	.20	.10
---	Coaches Card (Scott Breeden, Billy DeMars, Tommy Helms, Bruce Kimm, Jim Lett, George Scherger)	.25	.20	.10
---	Logo/Coupon Card	.10	.08	.04

1985 Thom McAn Discs

One of the more obscure 1985 issues, this 47-card set of "Pro Player Discs" was issued by Thom McAn as a promotion for its "Jox" tennis shoes, which are advertised on the back of the cards. The discs, which measure 2-3/4" in diameter, feature black and white player photos against a background of either gold, yellow, red, pink, green or blue. Although not included in the "official" checklist released by the company, cards of George Brett have also been reported. The discs are unnumbered.

		MT	NR MT	EX
Complete Set:		70.00	52.00	27.00
Common Player:		1.00	.70	.40
(1)	Benny Ayala	1.00	.70	.40
(2)	Buddy Bell	1.25	.90	.50
(3)	Juan Beniquez	1.00	.70	.40
(4)	Tony Bernazard	1.00	.70	.40
(5)	Mike Boddicker	2.00	1.50	.80
(6)	George Brett	6.00	4.50	2.50
(7)	Bill Buckner	1.25	.90	.50
(8)	Rod Carew	4.00	3.00	1.50
(9)	Steve Carlton	4.00	3.00	1.50
(10)	Caesar Cedeno (Cesar)	1.25	.90	.50
(11)	Onix Concepcion	1.00	.70	.40
(12)	Cecil Cooper	1.25	.90	.50
(13)	Al Cowens	1.00	.70	.40
(14)	Jose Cruz	1.25	.90	.50
(15)	Ivan DeJesus	1.00	.70	.40
(16)	Luis DeLeon	1.00	.70	.40
(17)	Rich Gossage	1.25	.90	.50
(18)	Pedro Guerrero	2.50	2.00	1.00
(19)	Ron Guidry	1.50	1.25	.60
(20)	Tony Gwynn	3.00	2.25	1.25
(21)	Mike Hargrove	1.00	.70	.40
(22)	Keith Hernandez	1.75	1.25	.70
(23)	Bob Horner	1.25	.90	.50
(24)	Kent Hrbek	2.25	1.75	.90
(25)	Rick Langford	1.00	.70	.40
(26)	Jeff Leonard	1.50	1.25	.60
(27)	Willie McGee	1.50	1.25	.60
(28)	Jack Morris	1.75	1.25	.70
(29)	Jesse Orosco	1.00	.70	.40
(30)	Junior Ortiz	1.00	.70	.40
(31)	Terry Puhl	1.00	.70	.40
(32)	Dan Quisenberry	1.25	.90	.50
(33)	Johnny Ray	1.25	.90	.50
(34)	Cal Ripken	3.50	2.75	1.50
(35)	Ed Romero	1.00	.70	.40
(36)	Ryne Sandberg	5.00	3.75	2.00
(37)	Mike Schmidt	5.00	3.75	2.00
(38)	Tom Seaver	3.75	2.75	1.50
(39)	Rick Sutcliffe	1.25	.90	.50
(40)	Bruce Sutter	1.25	.90	.50
(41)	Alan Trammell	1.75	1.25	.70
(42)	Fernando Valenzuela	1.75	1.25	.70
(43)	Ozzie Virgil	1.00	.70	.40
(44)	Greg Walker	1.25	.90	.50
(45)	Willie Wilson	1.25	.90	.50
(46)	Dave Winfield	2.25	1.75	.90
(47)	Geoff Zahn	1.00	.70	.40

1983 Thorn Apple Valley Cubs

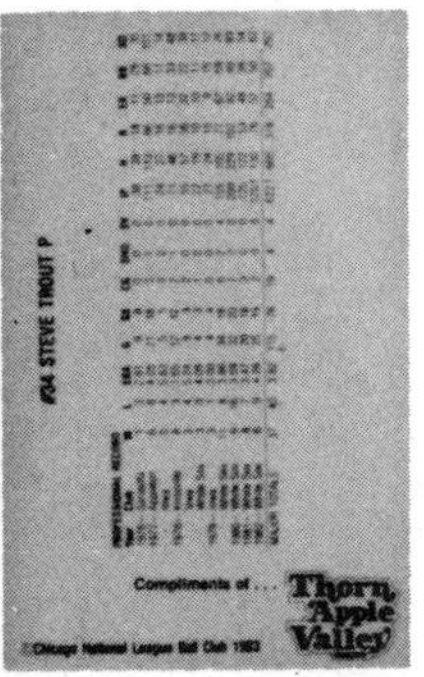

This set of 27 cards was issued in conjuction with a "Baseball Card Day" promotion at Wrigley Field in 1983. Thorn Apple Valley was the meat company which produced the hot dogs sold at the ballpark. The cards feature borderless color photos with the player's name, uniform number (also the card's number in the checklist) and an abbreviation for their position. Card backs feature annual statistics. Of the 27 cards, which measure 2-1/4" by 3-1/2", 25 feature players, one is a team card, and one features the manager and coaches.

		MT	NR MT	EX
Complete Set:		12.00	9.00	4.75
Common Player:		.20	.15	.08
1	Larry Bowa	.40	.30	.15
6	Keith Moreland	.40	.30	.15
7	Jody Davis	.40	.30	.15
10	Leon Durham	.40	.30	.15
11	Ron Cey	.40	.30	.15
16	Steve Lake	.20	.15	.08
20	Thad Bosley	.20	.15	.08
21	Jay Johnstone	.25	.20	.10
22	Bill Buckner	.40	.30	.15
23	Ryne Sandberg	3.00	2.25	1.25
24	Jerry Morales	.20	.15	.08
25	Gary Woods	.20	.15	.08
27	Mel Hall	.30	.25	.12
29	Tom Veryzer	.20	.15	.08
30	Chuck Rainey	.20	.15	.08
31	Fergie Jenkins	.70	.50	.30
32	Craig Lefferts	.30	.25	.12
33	Joe Carter	2.50	2.00	1.00
34	Steve Trout	.25	.20	.10
36	Mike Proly	.20	.15	.08
39	Bill Campbell	.20	.15	.08
41	Warren Brusstar	.20	.15	.08
44	Dick Ruthven	.20	.15	.08
46	Lee Smith	.50	.40	.20
48	Dickie Noles	.20	.15	.08
---	Coaching Staff (Ruben Amaro, Billy Connors, Duffy Dyer, Lee Elia, Fred Koenig, John Vukovich)	.20	.15	.08
---	Team Photo	.20	.15	.08

1947 Tip Top Bread

This 163-card set actually consists of a group of regional issues, some of which are more scarce then others. The 2-1/4" by 3" cards are borderless with a black and white player photo below which is a white strip containing the player's name, position, city name and league. Backs carry an advertisement. The set is known for a quantity of obscure players, many of whom played during the talent-lean World War II seasons. Overall it is a scarce set, with a number of interesting cards including first-issues of Yogi Berra and Joe Garagiola.

		NR MT	EX	VG
Complete Set:		12000.	6000.	3500.
Common Player:		35.00	17.50	10.50
(1)	Bill Ayers	35.00	17.50	10.50
(2)	Floyd Baker	50.00	25.00	15.00
(3)	Charles Barrett	50.00	25.00	15.00
(4)	Eddie Basinski	35.00	17.50	10.50
(5)	John Berardino	50.00	25.00	15.00
(6)	Larry Berra	325.00	162.00	97.00
(7)	Bill Bevens	50.00	25.00	15.00
(8)	Robert Blattner	35.00	17.50	10.50
(9)	Ernie Bonham	35.00	17.50	10.50
(10)	Bob Bragan	45.00	22.00	13.50
(11)	Ralph Branca	70.00	35.00	21.00
(12)	Alpha Brazle	35.00	17.50	10.50
(13)	Bobbie Brown	60.00	30.00	18.00
(14)	Mike Budnick	35.00	17.50	10.50
(15)	Ken Burkhart	35.00	17.50	10.50
(16)	Thomas Byrne	50.00	25.00	15.00
(17)	Earl Caldwell	50.00	25.00	15.00
(18)	"Hank" Camelli	50.00	25.00	15.00
(19)	Hugh Casey	45.00	22.00	13.50
(20)	Phil Cavarretta	65.00	32.00	19.50
(21)	Bob Chipman	50.00	25.00	15.00
(22)	Lloyd Christopher	50.00	25.00	15.00
(23)	Bill Cox	35.00	17.50	10.50
(24)	Bernard Creger	35.00	17.50	10.50
(25)	Frank Crosetti	65.00	32.00	19.50
(26)	Joffre Cross	35.00	17.50	10.50
(27)	Leon Culberson	50.00	25.00	15.00
(28)	Dick Culler	50.00	25.00	15.00
(29)	Dom DiMaggio	200.00	100.00	60.00
(30)	George Dickey	60.00	30.00	18.00
(31)	Chas. E. Diering	35.00	17.50	10.50
(32)	Joseph Dobson	50.00	25.00	15.00
(33)	Bob Doerr	275.00	137.00	82.00
(34)	Ervin Dusak	35.00	17.50	10.50
(35)	Bruce Edwards	40.00	20.00	12.00
(36)	Walter "Hoot" Evers	50.00	25.00	15.00
(37)	Clifford Fannin	35.00	17.50	10.50
(38)	"Nanny" Fernandez	50.00	25.00	15.00
(39)	Dave "Boo" Ferriss	50.00	25.00	15.00
(40)	Elbie Fletcher	35.00	17.50	10.50
(41)	Dennis Galehouse	35.00	17.50	10.50
(42)	Joe Garagiola	200.00	100.00	60.00
(43)	Sid Gordon	35.00	17.50	10.50
(44)	John Gorsica	50.00	25.00	15.00
(45)	Hal Gregg	40.00	20.00	12.00
(46)	Frank Gustine	35.00	17.50	10.50
(47)	Stanley Hack	65.00	32.00	19.50
(48)	Mickey Harris	50.00	25.00	15.00
(49)	Clinton Hartung	35.00	17.50	10.50
(50)	Joe Hatten	40.00	20.00	12.00
(51)	Frank Hayes	50.00	25.00	15.00
(52)	"Jeff" Heath	35.00	17.50	10.50
(53)	Tom Henrich	70.00	35.00	21.00
(54)	Gene Hermanski	40.00	20.00	12.00
(55)	Kirby Higbe	35.00	17.50	10.50
(56)	Ralph Hodgin	50.00	25.00	15.00
(57)	Tex Hughson	50.00	25.00	15.00
(58)	Fred Hutchinson	70.00	35.00	21.00
(59)	LeRoy Jarvis	35.00	17.50	10.50
(60)	"Si" Johnson	50.00	25.00	15.00
(61)	Don Johnson	50.00	25.00	15.00
(62)	Earl Johnson	50.00	25.00	15.00
(63)	John Jorgensen	40.00	20.00	12.00
(64)	Walter Judnick (Judnich)	35.00	17.50	10.50
(65)	Tony Kaufmann	35.00	17.50	10.50
(66)	George Kell	325.00	162.00	97.00
(67)	Charlie Keller	65.00	32.00	19.50
(68)	Bob Kennedy	50.00	25.00	15.00
(69)	Montia Kennedy	35.00	17.50	10.50
(70)	Ralph Kiner	80.00	40.00	24.00
(71)	Dave Koslo	35.00	17.50	10.50
(72)	Jack Kramer	35.00	17.50	10.50
(73)	Joe Kuhel	50.00	25.00	15.00
(74)	George Kurowski	35.00	17.50	10.50
(75)	Emil Kush	50.00	25.00	15.00
(76)	"Eddie" Lake	50.00	25.00	15.00
(77)	Harry Lavagetto	45.00	22.00	13.50
(78)	Bill Lee	50.00	25.00	15.00
(79)	Thornton Lee	50.00	25.00	15.00
(80)	Paul Lehner	35.00	17.50	10.50
(81)	John Lindell	50.00	25.00	15.00
(82)	Danny Litwhiler	50.00	25.00	15.00
(83)	"Mickey" Livingston	50.00	25.00	15.00
(84)	Carroll Lockman	35.00	17.50	10.50
(85)	Jack Lohrke	35.00	17.50	10.50
(86)	Ernie Lombardi	80.00	40.00	24.00
(87)	Vic Lombardi	40.00	20.00	12.00
(88)	Edmund Lopat	65.00	32.00	19.50
(89)	Harry Lowrey	50.00	25.00	15.00
(90)	Marty Marion	50.00	25.00	15.00

		NR MT	EX	VG
(91)	Willard Marshall	35.00	17.50	10.50
(92)	Phil Masi	50.00	25.00	15.00
(93)	Edward J. Mayo	50.00	25.00	15.00
(94)	Clyde McCullough	50.00	25.00	15.00
(95)	Frank Melton	40.00	20.00	12.00
(96)	Cass Michaels	50.00	25.00	15.00
(97)	Ed Miksis	40.00	20.00	12.00
(98)	Arthur Mills	50.00	25.00	15.00
(99)	Johnny Mize	80.00	40.00	24.00
(100)	Lester Moss	35.00	17.50	10.50
(101)	"Pat" Mullin	50.00	25.00	15.00
(102)	"Bob" Muncrief	35.00	17.50	10.50
(103)	George Munger	35.00	17.50	10.50
(104)	Fritz Ostermueller	35.00	17.50	10.50
(105)	James P. Outlaw	50.00	25.00	15.00
(106)	Frank "Stub" Overmire	50.00	25.00	15.00
(107)	Andy Pafko	60.00	30.00	18.00
(108)	Joe Page	50.00	25.00	15.00
(109)	Roy Partee	50.00	25.00	15.00
(110)	Johnny Pesky	60.00	30.00	18.00
(111)	Nelson Potter	35.00	17.50	10.50
(112)	Mel Queen	50.00	25.00	15.00
(113)	Marion Rackley	40.00	20.00	12.00
(114)	Al Reynolds	70.00	35.00	21.00
(115)	Del Rice	35.00	17.50	10.50
(116)	Marv Rickert	50.00	25.00	15.00
(117)	John Rigney	50.00	25.00	15.00
(118)	Aaron Robinson	50.00	25.00	15.00
(119)	"Preacher" Roe	45.00	22.00	13.50
(120)	Carvel Rowell	50.00	25.00	15.00
(121)	Jim Russell	35.00	17.50	10.50
(122)	Rip Russell	50.00	25.00	15.00
(123)	Phil Rizzuto	200.00	100.00	60.00
(124)	Connie Ryan	50.00	25.00	15.00
(125)	John Sain	90.00	45.00	27.00
(126)	Ray Sanders	50.00	25.00	15.00
(127)	Fred Sanford	35.00	17.50	10.50
(128)	Johnny Schmitz	50.00	25.00	15.00
(129)	Joe Schultz	35.00	17.50	10.50
(130)	"Rip" Sewell	35.00	17.50	10.50
(131)	Dick Sisler	35.00	17.50	10.50
(132)	"Sibby" Sisti	50.00	25.00	15.00
(133)	Enos Slaughter	80.00	40.00	24.00
(134)	"Billy" Southworth	50.00	25.00	15.00
(135)	Warren Spahn	325.00	162.00	97.00
(136)	Verne Stephens (Vern)	35.00	17.50	10.50
(137)	George Sternweiss (Stirnweiss)	50.00	25.00	15.00
(138)	Ed Stevens	40.00	20.00	12.00
(139)	Nick Strincevich	35.00	17.50	10.50
(140)	"Bobby" Sturgeon	50.00	25.00	15.00
(141)	Robt. "Bob" Swift	50.00	25.00	15.00
(142)	Geo. "Birdie" Tibbetts (Tebbetts)	55.00	27.00	16.50
(143)	"Mike" Tresh	55.00	27.00	16.50
(144)	Ken Trinkle	35.00	17.50	10.50
(145)	Paul "Diz" Trout	55.00	27.00	16.50
(146)	Virgil "Fire" Trucks	55.00	27.00	16.50
(147)	Thurman Tucker	50.00	25.00	15.00
(148)	Bill Voiselle	35.00	17.50	10.50
(149)	Hal Wagner	50.00	25.00	15.00
(150)	Honus Wagner	200.00	100.00	60.00
(151)	Eddy Waitkus	50.00	25.00	15.00
(152)	Richard "Dick" Wakefield	50.00	25.00	15.00
(153)	Jack Wallaesa	50.00	25.00	15.00
(154)	Charles Wensloff	50.00	25.00	15.00
(155)	Ted Wilks	35.00	17.50	10.50
(156)	Mickey Witek	35.00	17.50	10.50
(157)	"Jerry" Witte	35.00	17.50	10.50
(158)	Ed Wright	50.00	25.00	15.00
(159)	Taft Wright	50.00	25.00	15.00
(160)	Henry Wyse	50.00	25.00	15.00
(161)	"Rudy" York	55.00	27.00	16.50
(162)	Al Zarilla	35.00	17.50	10.50
(163)	Bill Zuber	50.00	25.00	15.00

1952 Tip Top Bread Labels

This unnumbered set of bread end-labels consists of 48 different labels, including two of Phil Rizzuto. The player's photo, name and team appear inside a star, with the words "Tip Top" printed above. The labels measure approximately 2-1/2" by 2-3/4".

		NR MT	EX	VG
Complete Set:		5100.	2550.	1530.
Common Player:		65.00	32.00	19.50
(1)	Hank Bauer	80.00	40.00	24.00
(2)	Yogi Berra	200.00	100.00	60.00
(3)	Ralph Branca	55.00	27.00	16.50
(4)	Lou Brissie	65.00	32.00	19.50
(5)	Roy Campanella	250.00	125.00	75.00
(6)	Phil Cavarreta (Cavarretta)	65.00	32.00	19.50
(7)	Murray Dickson (Murry)	65.00	32.00	19.50
(8)	Ferris Fain	65.00	32.00	19.50
(9)	Carl Furillo	80.00	40.00	24.00
(10)	Ned Garver	65.00	32.00	19.50
(11)	Sid Gordon	65.00	32.00	19.50
(12)	John Groth	65.00	32.00	19.50
(13)	Gran Hamner	65.00	32.00	19.50
(14)	Jim Hearn	65.00	32.00	19.50
(15)	Gene Hermanski	65.00	32.00	19.50
(16)	Gil Hodges	110.00	55.00	33.00
(17)	Larry Jansen	65.00	32.00	19.50
(18)	Eddie Joost	65.00	32.00	19.50
(19)	George Kell	100.00	50.00	30.00
(20)	Dutch Leonard	65.00	32.00	19.50
(21)	Whitey Lockman	65.00	32.00	19.50
(22)	Ed Lopat	80.00	40.00	24.00
(23)	Sal Maglie	55.00	27.00	16.50
(24)	Mickey Mantle	1200.	600.00	360.00
(25)	Gil McDougald	80.00	40.00	24.00
(26)	Dale Mitchell	65.00	32.00	19.50
(27)	Don Mueller	65.00	32.00	19.50
(28)	Andy Pafko	55.00	27.00	16.50
(29)	Bob Porterfield	65.00	32.00	19.50
(30)	Ken Raffensberger	65.00	32.00	19.50
(31)	Allie Reynolds	80.00	40.00	24.00
(32a)	Phil Rizutto (Rizzuto) ("NY" shows on shirt)	110.00	55.00	33.00
(32b)	Phil Rizutto (Rizzuto) (no "NY" visible on shirt)	110.00	55.00	33.00
(33)	Robin Roberts	100.00	50.00	30.00
(34)	Saul Rogovin	65.00	32.00	19.50
(35)	Ray Scarborough	65.00	32.00	19.50
(36)	Red Schoendienst	80.00	40.00	24.00
(37)	Dick Sisler	65.00	32.00	19.50
(38)	Enos Slaughter	100.00	50.00	30.00
(39)	Duke Snider	200.00	100.00	60.00
(40)	Warren Spahn	110.00	55.00	33.00
(41)	Vern Stephens	65.00	32.00	19.50
(42)	Earl Torgeson	65.00	32.00	19.50
(43)	Mickey Vernon	65.00	32.00	19.50
(44)	Ed Waitkus	65.00	32.00	19.50
(45)	Wes Westrum	65.00	32.00	19.50
(46)	Eddie Yost	65.00	32.00	19.50
(47)	Al Zarilla	65.00	32.00	19.50

1948 Topps Magic Photos

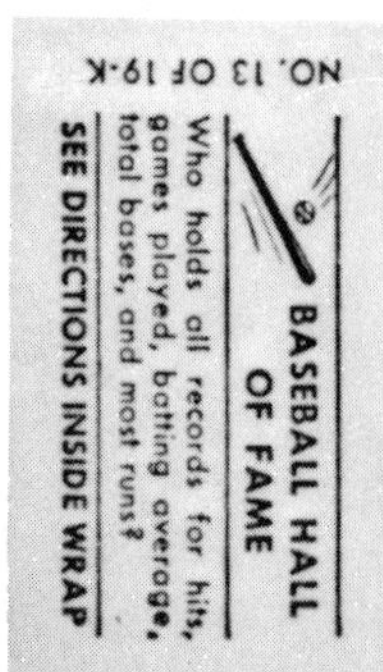

The first Topps baseball cards appeared as a subset of 19 cards from an issue of 252 "Magic Photos." The set takes its name from the self-developing nature of the cards. The cards were blank on the front when first taken from the wrapper. By spitting on the wrapper and holding it to the card while exposing it to light the black and white photo appeared. Measuring 7/8" by 1-1/2," the cards are very similar to Topps 1956 "Hocus Focus" issue.

		NR MT	EX	VG
Complete Set:		700.00	350.00	210.00
Common Player:		10.00	5.00	3.00
1	Lou Boudreau	20.00	10.00	6.00
2	Cleveland Indians	10.00	5.00	3.00
3	Bob Eliott	15.00	7.50	4.50
4	Cleveland Indians 4-3	10.00	5.00	3.00
5	Cleveland Indians 4-1 (Lou Boudreau Scoring)	20.00	10.00	6.00
6	"Babe" Ruth 714	150.00	75.00	45.00
7	Tris Speaker 793	25.00	12.50	7.50
8	Rogers Hornsby	35.00	17.50	10.50
9	Connie Mack	30.00	15.00	9.00
10	Christy Mathewson	40.00	20.00	12.00
11	Hans Wagner	40.00	20.00	12.00
12	Grover Alexander	30.00	15.00	9.00
13	Ty Cobb	100.00	50.00	30.00
14	Lou Gehrig	100.00	50.00	30.00
15	Walter Johnson	40.00	20.00	12.00
16	Cy Young	30.00	15.00	9.00
17	George Sisler 257	20.00	10.00	6.00
18	Tinker and Evers	20.00	10.00	6.00
19	Third Base Cleveland Indians	10.00	5.00	3.00

1951 Topps Blue Backs

Sold two cards in a package with a piece of candy for 1¢, the Topps Blue Backs are more scarce then their Red Back counterparts. The 2" by 2-5/8" cards carry a black and white player photograph on a red, white, yellow and green background along with the player's name and other information including their 1950 record on the front. The back is printed in blue on a white background. The 52-card set has varied baseball situations on them, making the playing of a rather elementary game of baseball possible. Although scarce, Blue Backs were printed on thick cardboard and have survived quite well over the years. There are, however, few stars (Johnny Mize and Enos Slaughter are two) in the set. Despite being a Topps product, Blue Backs do not currently enjoy great popularity.

		NR MT	EX	VG
Complete Set:		1900.	950.00	575.00
Common Player:		30.00	15.00	9.00
1	Eddie Yost	30.00	15.00	9.00
2	Henry (Hank) Majeski	30.00	15.00	9.00
3	Richie Ashburn	50.00	25.00	15.00
4	Del Ennis	30.00	15.00	9.00
5	Johnny Pesky	25.00	12.50	7.50
6	Albert (Red) Schoendienst	35.00	17.50	10.50
7	Gerald Staley	30.00	15.00	9.00
8	Dick Sisler	30.00	15.00	9.00
9	Johnny Sain	35.00	17.50	10.50
10	Joe Page	30.00	15.00	9.00
11	Johnny Groth	30.00	15.00	9.00
12	Sam Jethroe	30.00	15.00	9.00
13	James (Mickey) Vernon	25.00	12.50	7.50
14	George Munger	30.00	15.00	9.00
15	Eddie Joost	30.00	15.00	9.00
16	Murry Dickson	30.00	15.00	9.00
17	Roy Smalley	30.00	15.00	9.00
18	Ned Garver	30.00	15.00	9.00
19	Phil Masi	30.00	15.00	9.00
20	Ralph Branca	30.00	15.00	9.00
21	Billy Johnson	30.00	15.00	9.00
22	Bob Kuzava	30.00	15.00	9.00
23	Paul (Dizzy) Trout	30.00	15.00	9.00
24	Sherman Lollar	30.00	15.00	9.00
25	Sam Mele	30.00	15.00	9.00
26	Chico Carresquel (Carrasquel)	30.00	15.00	9.00
27	Andy Pafko	25.00	12.50	7.50
28	Harry (The Cat) Brecheen	30.00	15.00	9.00
29	Granville Hamner	30.00	15.00	9.00
30	Enos (Country) Slaughter	60.00	30.00	18.00
31	Lou Brissie	30.00	15.00	9.00
32	Bob Elliott	30.00	15.00	9.00
33	Don Lenhardt	30.00	15.00	9.00
34	Earl Torgeson	30.00	15.00	9.00
35	Tommy Byrne	30.00	15.00	9.00
36	Cliff Fannin	30.00	15.00	9.00
37	Bobby Doerr	55.00	27.00	16.50
38	Irv Noren	30.00	15.00	9.00
39	Ed Lopat	30.00	15.00	9.00
40	Vic Wertz	25.00	12.50	7.50
41	Johnny Schmitz	30.00	15.00	9.00
42	Bruce Edwards	30.00	15.00	9.00
43	Willie (Puddin' Head) Jones	30.00	15.00	9.00
44	Johnny Wyrostek	30.00	15.00	9.00
45	Bill Pierce	25.00	12.50	7.50
46	Gerry Priddy	30.00	15.00	9.00
47	Herman Wehmeier	30.00	15.00	9.00
48	Billy Cox	30.00	15.00	9.00
49	Henry (Hank) Sauer	30.00	15.00	9.00
50	Johnny Mize	60.00	30.00	18.00
51	Eddie Waitkus	30.00	15.00	9.00
52	Sam Chapman	30.00	15.00	9.00

1951 Topps Red Backs

Like the Blue Backs, the Topps Red Backs which were sold at the same time, came two to a package for 1¢. Their black and white photographs appear on a red, white, blue and yellow background. The back printing is red on white. Their 2" by 2-5/8" size is the same as Blue Backs. Also identical is the set size (52 cards) and the game situations to be found on the fronts of the cards, for use in playing a card game of baseball. Red Backs are more common than the Blue Backs by virtue of a recent discovery of a large hoard of unopened boxes.

		NR MT	EX	VG
Complete Set:		750.00	375.00	230.00
Common Player:		9.00	4.50	2.75
1	Larry (Yogi) Berra	75.00	38.00	23.50

		NR MT	EX	VG
2	Sid Gordon	5.00	2.50	1.50
3	Ferris Fain	9.00	4.50	2.75
4	Verne Stephens (Vern)	9.00	4.50	2.75
5	Phil Rizzuto	25.00	12.50	7.50
6	Allie Reynolds	10.00	5.00	3.00
7	Howie Pollet	5.00	2.50	1.50
8	Early Wynn	25.00	12.50	7.50
9	Roy Sievers	9.00	4.50	2.75
10	Mel Parnell	9.00	4.50	2.75
11	Gene Hermanski	5.00	2.50	1.50
12	Jim Hegan	5.00	2.50	1.50
13	Dale Mitchell	5.00	2.50	1.50
14	Wayne Terwilliger	5.00	2.50	1.50
15	Ralph Kiner	25.00	12.50	7.50
16	Preacher Roe	8.00	4.00	2.50
17	Dave Bell	8.00	4.00	2.50
18	Gerry Coleman	8.00	4.00	2.50
19	Dick Kokos	5.00	2.50	1.50
20	Dominick DiMaggio (Dominic)	10.00	5.00	3.00
21	Larry Jansen	5.00	2.50	1.50
22	Bob Feller	25.00	12.50	7.50
23	Ray Boone	9.00	4.50	2.75
24	Hank Bauer	10.00	5.00	3.00
25	Cliff Chambers	5.00	2.50	1.50
26	Luke Easter	9.00	4.50	2.75
27	Wally Westlake	5.00	2.50	1.50
28	Elmer Valo	5.00	2.50	1.50
29	Bob Kennedy	5.00	2.50	1.50
30	Warren Spahn	25.00	12.50	7.50
31	Gil Hodges	25.00	12.50	7.50
32	Henry Thompson	5.00	2.50	1.50
33	William Werle	5.00	2.50	1.50
34	Grady Hatton	5.00	2.50	1.50
35	Al Rosen	10.00	5.00	3.00
36a	Gus Zernial (Chicago in bio)	20.00	10.00	6.00
36b	Gus Zernial (Philadelphia in bio)	12.00	6.00	3.50
37	Wes Westrum	9.00	4.50	2.75
38	Ed (Duke) Snider	60.00	30.00	17.50
39	Ted Kluszewski	10.00	5.00	3.00
40	Mike Garcia	9.00	4.50	2.75
41	Whitey Lockman	5.00	2.50	1.50
42	Ray Scarborough	5.00	2.50	1.50
43	Maurice McDermott	5.00	2.50	1.50
44	Sid Hudson	5.00	2.50	1.50
45	Andy Seminick	5.00	2.50	1.50
46	Billy Goodman	5.00	2.50	1.50
47	Tommy Glaviano	5.00	2.50	1.50
48	Eddie Stanky	9.00	4.50	2.75
49	Al Zarilla	5.00	2.50	1.50
50	Monte Irvin	25.00	12.50	7.50
51	Eddie Robinson	5.00	2.50	1.50
52a	Tommy Holmes (Boston in bio)	20.00	10.00	6.00
52b	Tommy Holmes (Hartford in bio)	20.00	10.00	6.00

1951 Topps Connie Mack All-Stars

A set of die-cut, 2-1/16" by 5-1/4" cards, all eleven players are Hall of Famers. The cards feature a black and white photograph of the player printed on a red background with a red, white, blue, yellow and black plaque underneath. Like the "Current All-Stars," with which they were issued, the background could be removed making it possible for the card to stand up. This practice, however, resulted in the card's mutilation and lowers its condition in the eyes of today's collectors. Connie Mack All-Stars are scarce today and, despite being relatively expensive, retain a certain popularity as one of Topps first issues.

		NR MT	EX	VG
Complete Set:		9500.	4500.	1950.
Common Player:		350.00	150.00	60.00
(1)	Grover Cleveland Alexander	550.00	275.00	100.00
(2)	Gordon Stanley Cochrane	400.00	175.00	75.00
(3)	Edward Trowbridge Collins	350.00	150.00	60.00
(4)	James J. Collins	350.00	150.00	60.00
(5)	Henry Louis Gehrig	2000.	1000.	350.00
(6)	Walter Johnson	750.00	325.00	150.00
(7)	Connie Mack	400.00	175.00	75.00
(8)	Christopher Mathewson	750.00	325.00	135.00
(9)	George Herman Ruth	2250.	1150.	450.00
(10)	Tristram Speaker	575.00	275.00	100.00
(11)	John Peter Wagner	500.00	225.00	100.00

1951 Topps Current All-Stars

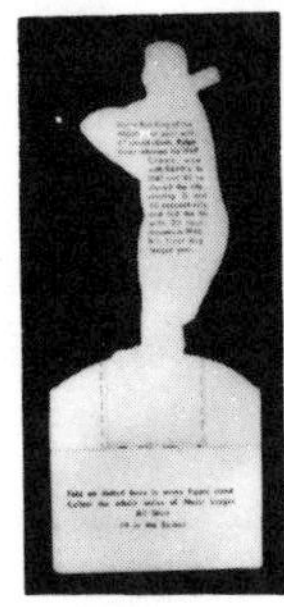

The Topps Current All-Stars are very similar to the Connie Mack All-Stars of the same year. The 2-1/16 by 5-1/4" cards have a black and white photograph on a red die-cut background. Most of the background could be folded over or removed so that the card would stand up. A plaque at the base carries brief biographical information. The set was to contain 11 cards, but only eight were actually issued in gum packs. Those of Jim Konstanty, Robin Roberts and Eddie Stanky were not released and are very rare. A big problem with the set is that if the card was used as it was intended it was folded and, thus, damaged from a collector's viewpoint. That makes top quality examples of any players difficult to find and quite expensive.

		NR MT	EX	VG
Complete Set:		40000.	20000.	8500.
Common Player:		500.00	250.00	100.00
(1)	Lawrence (Yogi) Berra	1500.	750.00	450.00
(2)	Lawrence Eugene Doby	750.00	375.00	150.00
(3)	Walter Dropo	750.00	375.00	150.00
(4)	Walter (Hoot) Evers	500.00	250.00	100.00
(5)	George Clyde Kell	1000.	500.00	200.00
(6)	Ralph McPherran Kiner	1075.	525.00	200.00
(7)	James Casimir Konstanty	8500.	4250.	2000.
(8)	Robert G. Lemon	1075.	525.00	200.00
(9)	Phillip Rizzuto	1200.	600.00	225.00
(10)	Robin Evan Roberts	9500.	4750.	2250.
(11)	Edward Raymond Stanky	8500.	4250.	2000.

1951 Topps Teams

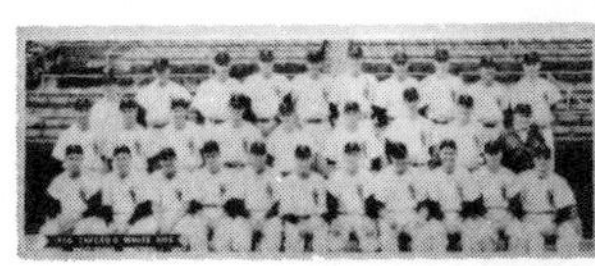

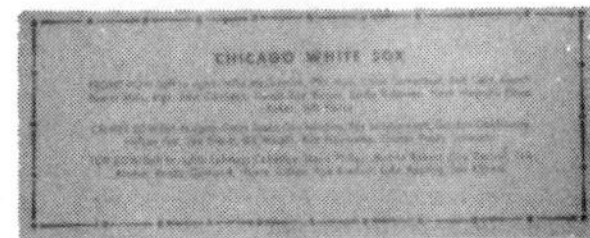

An innovative issue for 1951, the Topps team cards were a nine-card set, 5-1/4" by 2-1/16," which carried a black and white picture of a major league team surrounded by a yellow border on the front. The back identifies team members with red printing on white cardboard. There are two versions of each card, with and without the date "1950" in the banner that carries the team name. Undated versions are valued slightly higher than the cards with dates. Strangely only nine teams were issued. Scarcity varies, with the Cardinals and Red Sox being the most difficult to obtain. The complete set price does not include the scarcer variations.

		NR MT	EX	VG
Complete Set:		4500.	2200.	975.00
Common Team:		150.00	70.00	30.00
(1a)	Boston Red Sox (1950)	250.00	100.00	50.00
(1b)	Boston Red Sox (without 1950)	300.00	125.00	60.00
(2a)	Brooklyn Dodgers (1950)	300.00	125.00	60.00
(2b)	Brooklyn Dodgers (without 1950)	350.00	150.00	70.00
(3a)	Chicago White Sox (1950)	150.00	75.00	45.00
(3b)	Chicago White Sox (without 1950)	200.00	85.00	40.00
(4a)	Cincinnati Reds (1950)	150.00	70.00	30.00
(4b)	Cincinnati Reds (without 1950)	200.00	85.00	40.00
(5a)	New York Giants (1950)	250.00	100.00	50.00
(5b)	New York Giants (without 1950)	300.00	125.00	60.00
(6a)	Philadelphia Athletics (1950)	150.00	70.00	30.00
(6b)	Philadelphia Athletics (without 1950)	200.00	85.00	40.00
(7a)	Philadelphia Phillies (1950)	150.00	70.00	30.00
(7b)	Philadelphia Phillies (without 1950)	200.00	85.00	40.00
(8a)	St. Louis Cardinals (1950)	150.00	70.00	30.00
(8b)	St. Louis Cardinals (without 1950)	200.00	85.00	40.00
(9a)	Washington Senators (1950)	150.00	70.00	30.00
(9b)	Washington Senators (without 1950)	200.00	85.00	40.00

1952 Topps

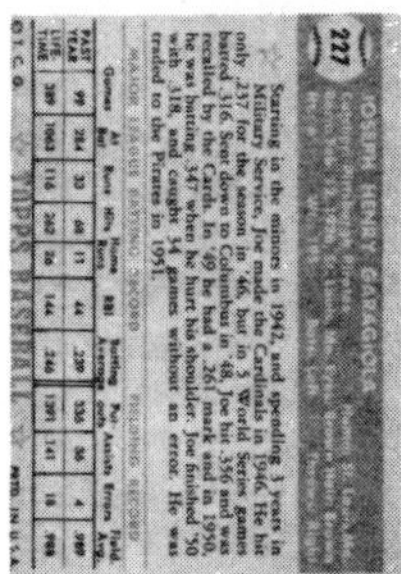

At 407 cards, the 1952 Topps set was the largest set of its day, both in number of cards and physical dimensions of the cards. Cards are 2-5/8" by 3-3/4" with a hand-colored black and white photo on front. Major baseball card innovations presented in the set include the first-ever use of color team logos as part of the design, and the inclusion of stats for the previous season and overall career on the backs. A major variety in the set is that first 80 cards can be found with backs printed entirely in black or black and red. Backs entirely in black command a $10-15 premium. Card numbers 311-407 were printed in limited supplies and are extremely rare.

		NR MT	EX	VG
Complete Set:		40000.	16000.	8000.
Common Player: 1-80		50.00	30.00	15.00
Common Player: 81-250		20.00	7.50	3.00
Common Player: 251-280		40.00	16.00	6.00
Common Player: 281-300		45.00	23.00	13.50
Common Player: 301-310		40.00	12.00	6.00
Common Player: 311-407		150.00	75.00	45.00
1	Andy Pafko	1200.	150.00	25.00
2	*James E. Runnels*	80.00	20.00	6.00
3	Hank Thompson	55.00	15.00	5.50
4	Don Lenhardt	55.00	15.00	5.50
5	Larry Jansen	55.00	15.00	5.50
6	Grady Hatton	55.00	15.00	5.50
7	Wayne Terwilliger	60.00	16.00	6.00
8	Fred Marsh	55.00	15.00	5.50
9	Bobby Hogue	65.00	18.00	6.50
10	Al Rosen	80.00	24.00	8.00
11	Phil Rizzuto	175.00	45.00	15.00
12	Monty Basgall	55.00	15.00	5.50
13	Johnny Wyrostek	55.00	15.00	5.50
14	Bob Elliott	55.00	15.00	5.50
15	Johnny Pesky	60.00	16.00	6.00
16	Gene Hermanski	55.00	15.00	5.50
17	Jim Hegan	55.00	15.00	5.50
18	Merrill Combs	55.00	15.00	5.50
19	Johnny Bucha	55.00	15.00	5.50
20	*Billy Loes*	125.00	56.00	35.00
21	Ferris Fain	60.00	16.00	6.00
22	Dom DiMaggio	80.00	20.00	8.00
23	Billy Goodman	55.00	15.00	5.50
24	Luke Easter	60.00	16.00	6.00
25	Johnny Groth	55.00	15.00	5.50
26	Monty Irvin	90.00	27.00	9.00
27	Sam Jethroe	55.00	15.00	5.50
28	Jerry Priddy	55.00	15.00	5.50
29	Ted Kluszewski	80.00	24.00	8.00
30	Mel Parnell	60.00	16.00	6.00
31	Gus Zernial	60.00	16.00	6.00
32	Eddie Robinson	55.00	15.00	5.50
33	Warren Spahn	200.00	80.00	50.00
34	Elmer Valo	55.00	15.00	5.50
35	Hank Sauer	60.00	16.00	6.00
36	Gil Hodges	150.00	75.00	45.00
37	Duke Snider	250.00	100.00	63.00
38	Wally Westlake	55.00	15.00	5.50
39	"Dizzy" Trout	60.00	16.00	6.00
40	Irv Noren	55.00	15.00	5.50
41	Bob Wellman	55.00	15.00	5.50
42	Lou Kretlow	55.00	15.00	5.50
43	Ray Scarborough	55.00	15.00	5.50
44	Con Dempsey	55.00	15.00	5.50
45	Eddie Joost	55.00	15.00	5.50
46	Gordon Goldsberry	55.00	15.00	5.50
47	Willie Jones	55.00	15.00	5.50
48a	Joe Page (Johnny Sain bio)			

		NR MT	EX	VG
		225.00	68.00	23.00
48b	Joe Page (correct bio)	80.00	24.00	8.00
49a	Johnny Sain (Joe Page bio)	225.00	68.00	23.00
49b	Johnny Sain (correct bio)	80.00	24.00	8.00
50	Marv Rickert	55.00	15.00	5.50
51	Jim Russell	60.00	16.00	6.00
52	Don Mueller	55.00	15.00	5.50
53	Chris Van Cuyk	60.00	16.00	6.00
54	Leo Kiely	55.00	15.00	5.50
55	Ray Boone	60.00	16.00	6.00
56	Tommy Glaviano	55.00	15.00	5.50
57	Ed Lopat	80.00	24.00	8.00
58	Bob Mahoney	55.00	15.00	5.50
59	Robin Roberts	125.00	38.00	12.50
60	Sid Hudson	55.00	15.00	5.50
61	"Tookie" Gilbert	55.00	15.00	5.50
62	Chuck Stobbs	55.00	15.00	5.50
63	Howie Pollet	55.00	15.00	5.50
64	Roy Sievers	65.00	18.00	6.50
65	Enos Slaughter	125.00	56.00	35.00
66	"Preacher" Roe	100.00	50.00	30.00
67	Allie Reynolds	80.00	24.00	8.00
68	Cliff Chambers	55.00	15.00	5.50
69	Virgil Stallcup	55.00	15.00	5.50
70	Al Zarilla	55.00	15.00	5.50
71	Tom Upton	55.00	15.00	5.50
72	Karl Olson	55.00	15.00	5.50
73	William Werle	55.00	15.00	5.50
74	Andy Hansen	55.00	15.00	5.50
75	Wes Westrum	60.00	16.00	6.00
76	Eddie Stanky	65.00	18.00	6.50
77	Bob Kennedy	55.00	15.00	5.50
78	Ellis Kinder	55.00	15.00	5.50
79	Gerald Staley	55.00	15.00	5.50
80	Herman Wehmeier	55.00	15.00	5.50
81	Vernon Law	25.00	11.00	6.25
82	Duane Pillette	20.00	9.00	5.00
83	Billy Johnson	20.00	9.00	5.00
84	Vern Stephens	20.00	9.00	5.00
85	Bob Kuzava	30.00	13.50	7.50
86	Ted Gray	20.00	9.00	5.00
87	Dale Coogan	20.00	9.00	5.00
88	Bob Feller	125.00	56.00	35.00
89	Johnny Lipon	20.00	9.00	5.00
90	Mickey Grasso	20.00	9.00	5.00
91	Al Schoendienst	75.00	38.00	23.00
92	Dale Mitchell	20.00	9.00	5.00
93	Al Sima	20.00	9.00	5.00
94	Sam Mele	20.00	9.00	5.00
95	Ken Holcombe	20.00	9.00	5.00
96	Willard Marshall	20.00	9.00	5.00
97	Earl Torgeson	20.00	9.00	5.00
98	Bill Pierce	25.00	11.00	6.25
99	Gene Woodling	40.00	18.00	10.00
100	Del Rice	20.00	9.00	5.00
101	Max Lanier	20.00	9.00	5.00
102	Bill Kennedy	20.00	9.00	5.00
103	Cliff Mapes	20.00	9.00	5.00
104	Don Kolloway	20.00	9.00	5.00
105	John Pramesa	20.00	9.00	5.00
106	Mickey Vernon	25.00	11.00	6.25
107	Connie Ryan	20.00	9.00	5.00
108	Jim Konstanty	25.00	11.00	6.25
109	Ted Wilks	20.00	9.00	5.00
110	Dutch Leonard	20.00	9.00	5.00
111	Harry Lowrey	20.00	9.00	5.00
112	Henry Majeski	20.00	9.00	5.00
113	Dick Sisler	20.00	9.00	5.00
114	Willard Ramsdell	20.00	9.00	5.00
115	George Munger	20.00	9.00	5.00
116	Carl Scheib	20.00	9.00	5.00
117	Sherman Lollar	25.00	11.00	6.25
118	Ken Raffensberger	20.00	9.00	5.00
119	Maurice McDermott	20.00	9.00	5.00
120	Bob Chakales	20.00	9.00	5.00
121	Gus Niarhos	20.00	9.00	5.00
122	Jack Jensen	70.00	35.00	21.00
123	Eddie Yost	25.00	11.00	6.25
124	Monte Kennedy	20.00	9.00	5.00
125	Bill Rigney	25.00	11.00	6.25
126	Fred Hutchinson	25.00	11.00	6.25
127	Paul Minner	20.00	9.00	5.00
128	Don Bollweg	30.00	13.50	7.50
129	Johnny Mize	70.00	35.00	21.00
130	Sheldon Jones	20.00	9.00	5.00
131	Morrie Martin	20.00	9.00	5.00
132	Clyde Kluttz	20.00	9.00	5.00
133	Al Widmar	20.00	9.00	5.00
134	Joe Tipton	20.00	9.00	5.00
135	Dixie Howell	20.00	9.00	5.00
136	Johnny Schmitz	25.00	11.00	6.25
137	*Roy McMillan*	25.00	11.00	6.25
138	Bill MacDonald	20.00	9.00	5.00
139	Ken Wood	20.00	9.00	5.00
140	John Antonelli	25.00	11.00	6.25
141	Clint Hartung	20.00	9.00	5.00
142	Harry Perkowski	20.00	9.00	5.00
143	Les Moss	20.00	9.00	5.00
144	Ed Blake	20.00	9.00	5.00
145	Joe Haynes	20.00	9.00	5.00
146	Frank House	20.00	9.00	5.00
147	Bob Young	20.00	9.00	5.00
148	Johnny Klippstein	20.00	9.00	5.00
149	Dick Kryhoski	20.00	9.00	5.00
150	Ted Beard	20.00	9.00	5.00
151	Wally Post	20.00	9.00	5.00
152	Al Evans	20.00	9.00	5.00
153	Bob Rush	20.00	9.00	5.00
154	Joe Muir	20.00	9.00	5.00
155	Frank Overmire	30.00	13.50	7.50
156	Frank Hiller	20.00	9.00	5.00
157	Bob Usher	20.00	9.00	5.00
158	Eddie Waitkus	20.00	9.00	5.00
159	Saul Rogovin	20.00	9.00	5.00
160	Owen Friend	20.00	9.00	5.00
161	Bud Byerly	20.00	9.00	5.00
162	Del Crandall	25.00	11.00	6.25
163	Stan Rojek	20.00	9.00	5.00
164	Walt Dubiel	20.00	9.00	5.00
165	Eddie Kazak	20.00	9.00	5.00
166	Paul LaPalme	20.00	9.00	5.00
167	Bill Howerton	20.00	9.00	5.00
168	Charlie Silvera	30.00	13.50	7.50
169	Howie Judson	20.00	9.00	5.00
170	Gus Bell	25.00	11.00	6.25
171	Ed Erautt	20.00	9.00	5.00
172	Eddie Miksis	20.00	9.00	5.00
173	Roy Smalley	20.00	9.00	5.00
174	Clarence Marshall	20.00	9.00	5.00
175	*Billy Martin*	300.00	150.00	90.00
176	Hank Edwards	20.00	9.00	5.00
177	Bill Wight	20.00	9.00	5.00
178	Cass Michaels	20.00	9.00	5.00
179	Frank Smith	20.00	9.00	5.00
180	*Charley Maxwell*	25.00	11.00	6.25
181	Bob Swift	20.00	9.00	5.00
182	Billy Hitchcock	20.00	9.00	5.00
183	Erv Dusak	20.00	9.00	5.00
184	Bob Ramazzotti	20.00	9.00	5.00
185	Bill Nicholson	20.00	9.00	5.00
186	Walt Masterson	20.00	9.00	5.00
187	Bob Miller	20.00	9.00	5.00
188	Clarence Podbielan	25.00	11.00	6.25
189	Pete Reiser	25.00	11.00	6.25
190	Don Johnson	20.00	9.00	5.00
191	Yogi Berra	375.00	187.00	112.00
192	Myron Ginsberg	20.00	9.00	5.00
193	Harry Simpson	20.00	9.00	5.00
194	Joe Hatten	20.00	9.00	5.00
195	*Orestes Minoso*	60.00	30.00	18.00
196	Solly Hemus	20.00	9.00	5.00
197	George Strickland	20.00	9.00	5.00
198	Phil Haugstad	25.00	11.00	6.25
199	George Zuverink	20.00	9.00	5.00
200	Ralph Houk	50.00	23.00	12.50
201	Alex Kellner	20.00	9.00	5.00
202	Joe Collins	30.00	13.50	7.50
203	Curt Simmons	25.00	11.00	6.25
204	Ron Northey	20.00	9.00	5.00
205	Clyde King	25.00	11.00	6.25
206	Joe Ostrowski	30.00	13.50	7.50
207	Mickey Harris	20.00	9.00	5.00
208	Marlin Stuart	20.00	9.00	5.00
209	Howie Fox	20.00	9.00	5.00
210	Dick Fowler	20.00	9.00	5.00
211	Ray Coleman	20.00	9.00	5.00
212	Ned Garver	20.00	9.00	5.00
213	Nippy Jones	20.00	9.00	5.00
214	Johnny Hopp	30.00	13.50	7.50
215	Hank Bauer	40.00	18.00	10.00
216	Richie Ashburn	60.00	30.00	18.00
217	George Stirnweiss	20.00	9.00	5.00
218	Clyde McCullough	20.00	9.00	5.00
219	Bobby Shantz	25.00	11.00	6.25
220	Joe Presko	20.00	9.00	5.00
221	Granny Hamner	20.00	9.00	5.00
222	"Hoot" Evers	20.00	9.00	5.00
223	Del Ennis	25.00	11.00	6.25
224	Bruce Edwards	20.00	9.00	5.00
225	Frank Baumholtz	20.00	9.00	5.00
226	Dave Philley	25.00	11.00	6.25
227	Joe Garagiola	100.00	50.00	30.00
228	Al Brazle	20.00	9.00	5.00
229	Gene Bearden	20.00	9.00	5.00
230	Matt Batts	20.00	9.00	5.00
231	Sam Zoldak	20.00	9.00	5.00
232	Billy Cox	30.00	13.50	7.50
233	*Bob Friend*	25.00	11.00	6.25
234	Steve Souchock	20.00	9.00	5.00
235	Walt Dropo	25.00	11.00	6.25
236	Ed Fitz Gerald	20.00	9.00	5.00
237	Jerry Coleman	30.00	13.50	7.50
238	Art Houtteman	20.00	9.00	5.00
239	Rocky Bridges	25.00	11.00	6.25
240	Jack Phillips	20.00	9.00	5.00
241	Tommy Byrne	20.00	9.00	5.00
242	Tom Poholsky	20.00	9.00	5.00
243	Larry Doby	40.00	16.00	9.00
244	Vic Wertz	25.00	11.00	6.25
245	Sherry Robertson	20.00	9.00	5.00
246	George Kell	50.00	23.00	12.50
247	Randy Gumpert	20.00	9.00	5.00
248	Frank Shea	20.00	9.00	5.00
249	Bobby Adams	20.00	9.00	5.00
250	Carl Erskine	50.00	30.00	15.00
251	Chico Carrasquel	40.00	16.00	6.00
252	Vern Bickford	40.00	16.00	6.00
253	Johnny Berardino	50.00	18.00	7.50
254	Joe Dobson	40.00	16.00	6.00
255	Clyde Vollmer	40.00	16.00	6.00
256	Pete Suder	40.00	16.00	6.00
257	Bobby Avila	40.00	16.00	6.00
258	Steve Gromek	40.00	16.00	6.00
259	Bob Addis	40.00	16.00	6.00
260	Pete Castiglione	40.00	16.00	6.00
261	Willie Mays	1000.	500.00	300.00
262	Virgil Trucks	45.00	18.00	6.75
263	Harry Brecheen	45.00	18.00	6.75
264	Roy Hartsfield	40.00	16.00	6.00
265	Chuck Diering	40.00	16.00	6.00
266	Murry Dickson	40.00	16.00	6.00
267	Sid Gordon	40.00	16.00	6.00
268	Bob Lemon	150.00	75.00	45.00
269	Willard Nixon	40.00	16.00	6.00
270	Lou Brissie	40.00	16.00	6.00
271	Jim Delsing	40.00	16.00	6.00
272	Mike Garcia	45.00	18.00	6.75
273	Erv Palica	45.00	18.00	6.75
274	Ralph Branca	60.00	25.00	9.00
275	Pat Mullin	40.00	16.00	6.00
276	Jim Wilson	40.00	16.00	6.00
277	Early Wynn	150.00	75.00	45.00
278	Al Clark	40.00	16.00	6.00
279	Ed Stewart	40.00	16.00	6.00
280	Cloyd Boyer	40.00	16.00	6.00
281	Tommy Brown	50.00	20.00	7.50
282	Birdie Tebbetts	50.00	20.00	7.50
283	Phil Masi	50.00	20.00	7.50
284	Hank Arft	50.00	20.00	7.50
285	Cliff Fannin	50.00	20.00	7.50
286	Joe DeMaestri	50.00	20.00	7.50
287	Steve Bilko	50.00	20.00	7.50
288	Chet Nichols	50.00	20.00	7.50
289	Tommy Holmes	55.00	25.00	8.25
290	Joe Astroth	50.00	20.00	7.50
291	Gil Coan	50.00	20.00	7.50
292	Floyd Baker	50.00	20.00	7.50
293	Sibby Sisti	50.00	20.00	7.50
294	Walker Cooper	50.00	20.00	7.50
295	Phil Cavarretta	55.00	22.00	8.25
296	"Red" Rolfe	50.00	20.00	7.50
297	Andy Seminick	50.00	20.00	7.50
298	Bob Ross	50.00	20.00	7.50
299	Ray Murray	50.00	20.00	7.50
300	Barney McCosky	50.00	20.00	7.50
301	Bob Porterfield	40.00	16.00	6.00
302	Max Surkont	40.00	16.00	6.00
303	Harry Dorish	40.00	16.00	6.00
304	Sam Dente	40.00	16.00	6.00
305	Paul Richards	45.00	18.00	6.75
306	Lou Sleator	40.00	16.00	6.00
307	Frank Campos	40.00	16.00	6.00
308	Luis Aloma	40.00	16.00	6.00
309	Jim Busby	40.00	16.00	6.00
310	George Metkovich	40.00	16.00	6.00
311	Mickey Mantle	8900.	4450.	2670.
312	Jackie Robinson	875.00	435.00	245.00
313	Bobby Thomson	175.00	90.00	48.00
314	Roy Campanella	1400.	700.00	375.00
315	Leo Durocher	250.00	100.00	63.00
316	Davey Williams	150.00	75.00	45.00
317	Connie Marrero	150.00	75.00	45.00
318	Hal Gregg	150.00	75.00	45.00
319	Al Walker	150.00	75.00	45.00
320	John Rutherford	150.00	75.00	45.00
321	*Joe Black*	225.00	90.00	56.00
322	Randy Jackson	150.00	75.00	45.00
323	Bubba Church	150.00	75.00	45.00
324	Warren Hacker	150.00	75.00	45.00
325	Bill Serena	150.00	75.00	45.00
326	George Shuba	150.00	75.00	45.00
327	Archie Wilson	150.00	75.00	45.00
328	Bob Borkowski	150.00	75.00	45.00
329	Ivan Delock	150.00	75.00	45.00
330	Turk Lown	150.00	75.00	45.00
331	Tom Morgan	160.00	80.00	48.00
332	Tony Bartirome	150.00	75.00	45.00
333	Pee Wee Reese	750.00	375.00	230.00
334	Wilmer Mizell	150.00	75.00	45.00
335	Ted Lepcio	150.00	75.00	45.00
336	Dave Koslo	150.00	75.00	45.00
337	Jim Hearn	150.00	75.00	45.00
338	Sal Yvars	150.00	75.00	45.00
339	Russ Meyer	150.00	75.00	45.00
340	Bob Hooper	150.00	75.00	45.00
341	Hal Jeffcoat	150.00	75.00	45.00
342	*Clem Labine*	200.00	90.00	52.00
343	Dick Gernert	150.00	75.00	45.00
344	Ewell Blackwell	160.00	80.00	48.00
345	Sam White	150.00	75.00	45.00
346	George Spencer	150.00	75.00	45.00
347	Joe Adcock	175.00	90.00	48.00
348	Bob Kelly	150.00	75.00	45.00
349	Bob Cain	150.00	75.00	45.00
350	Cal Abrams	150.00	75.00	45.00
351	Al Dark	200.00	90.00	52.00
352	Karl Drews	150.00	75.00	45.00
353	Bob Del Greco	150.00	75.00	45.00
354	Fred Hatfield	150.00	75.00	45.00
355	Bobby Morgan	150.00	75.00	45.00
356	Toby Atwell	150.00	75.00	45.00
357	Smoky Burgess	175.00	90.00	48.00
358	John Kucab	150.00	75.00	45.00
359	Dee Fondy	150.00	75.00	45.00
360	George Crowe	150.00	75.00	45.00
361	Bill Posedel	150.00	75.00	45.00
362	Ken Heintzelman	150.00	75.00	45.00
363	Dick Rozek	150.00	75.00	45.00
364	Clyde Sukeforth	150.00	75.00	45.00
365	"Cookie" Lavagetto	150.00	75.00	45.00
366	Dave Madison	150.00	75.00	45.00
367	Bob Thorpe	150.00	75.00	45.00
368	Ed Wright	150.00	75.00	45.00
369	*Dick Groat*	250.00	125.00	60.00
370	Billy Hoeft	150.00	75.00	45.00
371	Bob Hofman	150.00	75.00	45.00
372	*Gil McDougald*	250.00	120.00	67.00
373	Jim Turner	160.00	80.00	48.00
374	Al Benton	150.00	75.00	45.00
375	Jack Merson	150.00	75.00	45.00
376	Faye Throneberry	150.00	75.00	45.00
377	Chuck Dressen	175.00	90.00	52.00
378	Les Fusselman	150.00	75.00	45.00
379	Joe Rossi	150.00	75.00	45.00
380	Clem Koshorek	150.00	75.00	45.00
381	Milton Stock	150.00	75.00	45.00
382	Sam Jones	150.00	75.00	45.00
383	Del Wilber	150.00	75.00	45.00
384	Frank Crosetti	250.00	125.00	67.00
385	Herman Franks	150.00	75.00	45.00
386	Eddie Yuhas	150.00	75.00	45.00
387	Billy Meyer	150.00	75.00	45.00
388	Bob Chipman	150.00	75.00	45.00
389	Ben Wade	150.00	75.00	45.00
390	Glenn Nelson	150.00	75.00	45.00
391	Ben Chapman (photo actually Sam Chapman)	150.00	75.00	45.00
392	*Hoyt Wilhelm*	400.00	190.00	112.00
393	Ebba St. Claire	150.00	75.00	45.00
394	Billy Herman	200.00	90.00	52.00
395	Jake Pitler	150.00	75.00	45.00
396	*Dick Williams*	225.00	112.00	68.00
397	Forrest Main	150.00	75.00	45.00
398	Hal Rice	150.00	75.00	45.00
399	Jim Fridley	150.00	75.00	45.00
400	Bill Dickey	500.00	225.00	135.00
401	Bob Schultz	150.00	75.00	45.00
402	Earl Harrist	150.00	75.00	45.00
403	Bill Miller	160.00	80.00	48.00
404	Dick Brodowski	150.00	75.00	45.00
405	Eddie Pellagrini	150.00	75.00	45.00
406	*Joe Nuxhall*	175.00	87.00	52.00
407	*Ed Mathews*	2000.	1000.	600.00

NOTE: A card number in parentheses ( ) indicates the card set is unnumbered.

1953 Topps

The 1953 Topps set reflects the company's continuing legal battles with Bowman. The set, originally intended to consist of 280 cards, is lacking six numbers (#'s 253, 261, 267, 268, 271 and 275) which probably represent players whose contracts were lost to the competition. The 2-5/8" by 3-3/4" cards feature painted player pictures. A color team logo appears at a bottom panel (red for American Leauge and black for National.) Card backs contain the first baseball trivia questions along with brief statistics and player biographies. In the red panel at the top which lists the player's personal data, cards from the 2nd Series (#'s 86-165 plus 10, 44, 61, 72 and 81) can be found with that data printed in either black or white, black being the scarcer variety. Card numbers 221-280 are the scarce high numbers.

	NR MT	EX	VG
Complete Set:	12000.	6000.	3600.
Common Player Singleprint: 1-165	25.00	12.50	7.50
Common Player: 1-165	20.00	10.00	6.00
Common Player: 166-220	18.00	9.00	5.50
Common Player Singleprint: 221-280	90.00	45.00	27.00
Common Player: 221-280	45.00	23.00	13.50

#	Player	NR MT	EX	VG
1	Jackie Robinson	600.00	240.00	150.00
2	Luke Easter	25.00	12.50	7.50
3	George Crowe	25.00	12.50	7.50
4	Ben Wade	25.00	12.50	7.50
5	Joe Dobson	25.00	12.50	7.50
6	Sam Jones	25.00	12.50	7.50
7	Bob Borkowski	20.00	10.00	6.00
8	Clem Koshorek	20.00	10.00	6.00
9	Joe Collins	30.00	15.00	9.00
10	Smoky Burgess	30.00	15.00	9.00
11	Sal Yvars	25.00	12.50	7.50
12	Howie Judson	20.00	10.00	6.00
13	Connie Marrero	20.00	10.00	6.00
14	Clem Labine	25.00	12.50	7.50
15	Bobo Newsom	25.00	12.50	7.50
16	Harry Lowrey	20.00	10.00	6.00
17	Billy Hitchcock	25.00	12.50	7.50
18	Ted Lepcio	20.00	10.00	6.00
19	Mel Parnell	20.00	10.00	6.00
20	Hank Thompson	25.00	12.50	7.50
21	Billy Johnson	25.00	12.50	7.50
22	Howie Fox	25.00	12.50	7.50
23	Toby Atwell	20.00	10.00	6.00
24	Ferris Fain	25.00	12.50	7.50
25	Ray Boone	25.00	12.50	7.50
26	Dale Mitchell	20.00	10.00	6.00
27	Roy Campanella	200.00	80.00	50.00
28	Eddie Pellagrini	25.00	12.50	7.50
29	Hal Jeffcoat	25.00	12.50	7.50
30	Willard Nixon	25.00	12.50	7.50
31	Ewell Blackwell	40.00	20.00	12.00
32	Clyde Vollmer	25.00	12.50	7.50
33	Bob Kennedy	20.00	10.00	6.00
34	George Shuba	25.00	12.50	7.50
35	Irv Noren	25.00	12.50	7.50
36	Johnny Groth	20.00	10.00	6.00
37	Ed Mathews	100.00	50.00	30.00
38	Jim Hearn	20.00	10.00	6.00
39	Eddie Miksis	25.00	12.50	7.50
40	John Lipon	25.00	12.50	7.50
41	Enos Slaughter	90.00	45.00	27.00
42	Gus Zernial	20.00	10.00	6.00
43	Gil McDougald	50.00	25.00	15.00
44	Ellis Kinder	30.00	15.00	9.00
45	Grady Hatton	20.00	10.00	6.00
46	Johnny Klippstein	20.00	10.00	6.00
47	Bubba Church	20.00	10.00	6.00
48	Bob Del Greco	20.00	10.00	6.00
49	Faye Throneberry	20.00	10.00	6.00
50	Chuck Dressen	25.00	12.50	7.50
51	Frank Campos	20.00	10.00	6.00
52	Ted Gray	20.00	10.00	6.00
53	Sherman Lollar	20.00	10.00	6.00
54	Bob Feller	100.00	50.00	30.00
55	Maurice McDermott	20.00	10.00	6.00
56	Gerald Staley	20.00	10.00	6.00
57	Carl Scheib	25.00	12.50	7.50
58	George Metkovich	25.00	12.50	7.50
59	Karl Drews	20.00	10.00	6.00
60	Cloyd Boyer	20.00	10.00	6.00
61	Early Wynn	85.00	42.00	25.00
62	Monte Irvin	40.00	20.00	12.00
63	Gus Niarhos	20.00	10.00	6.00
64	Dave Philley	25.00	12.50	7.50
65	Earl Harrist	25.00	12.50	7.50
66	Orestes Minoso	30.00	15.00	9.00
67	Roy Sievers	25.00	12.50	7.50
68	Del Rice	25.00	12.50	7.50
69	Dick Brodowski	25.00	12.50	7.50
70	Ed Yuhas	25.00	12.50	7.50
71	Tony Bartirome	25.00	12.50	7.50
72	Fred Hutchinson	25.00	12.50	7.50
73	Eddie Robinson	25.00	12.50	7.50
74	Joe Rossi	25.00	12.50	7.50
75	Mike Garcia	25.00	12.50	7.50
76	Pee Wee Reese	150.00	75.00	45.00
77	John Mize	75.00	37.00	22.00
78	Al Schoendienst	75.00	38.00	23.00
79	Johnny Wyrostek	25.00	12.50	7.50
80	Jim Hegan	25.00	12.50	7.50
81	Joe Black	40.00	20.00	12.00
82	Mickey Mantle	2000.	1000.	600.00
83	Howie Pollet	25.00	12.50	7.50
84	Bob Hooper	20.00	10.00	6.00
85	Bobby Morgan	25.00	12.50	7.50
86	Billy Martin	90.00	45.00	27.50
87	Ed Lopat	35.00	17.50	10.50
88	Willie Jones	20.00	10.00	6.00
89	Chuck Stobbs	20.00	10.00	6.00
90	Hank Edwards	20.00	10.00	6.00
91	Ebba St. Claire	20.00	10.00	6.00
92	Paul Minner	20.00	10.00	6.00
93	Hal Rice	20.00	10.00	6.00
94	William Kennedy	20.00	10.00	6.00
95	Willard Marshall	20.00	10.00	6.00
96	Virgil Trucks	25.00	12.50	7.50
97	Don Kolloway	20.00	10.00	6.00
98	Cal Abrams	20.00	10.00	6.00
99	Dave Madison	20.00	10.00	6.00
100	Bill Miller	25.00	12.50	7.50
101	Ted Wilks	20.00	10.00	6.00
102	Connie Ryan	20.00	10.00	6.00
103	Joe Astroth	20.00	10.00	6.00
104	Yogi Berra	200.00	100.00	60.00
105	Joe Nuxhall	25.00	12.50	7.50
106	Johnny Antonelli	25.00	12.50	7.50
107	Danny O'Connell	20.00	10.00	6.00
108	Bob Porterfield	20.00	10.00	6.00
109	Alvin Dark	30.00	15.00	9.00
110	Herman Wehmeier	20.00	10.00	6.00
111	Hank Sauer	16.00	8.00	4.75
112	Ned Garver	20.00	10.00	6.00
113	Jerry Priddy	20.00	10.00	6.00
114	Phil Rizzuto	90.00	45.00	27.00
115	George Spencer	20.00	10.00	6.00
116	Frank Smith	20.00	10.00	6.00
117	Sid Gordon	20.00	10.00	6.00
118	Gus Bell	16.00	8.00	4.75
119	John Sain	40.00	20.00	12.00
120	Davey Williams	20.00	10.00	6.00
121	Walt Dropo	20.00	10.00	6.00
122	Elmer Valo	20.00	10.00	6.00
123	Tommy Byrne	20.00	10.00	6.00
124	Sibby Sisti	20.00	10.00	6.00
125	Dick Williams	25.00	12.50	7.50
126	Bill Connelly	20.00	10.00	6.00
127	Clint Courtney	20.00	10.00	6.00
128	Wilmer Mizell	20.00	10.00	6.00
129	Keith Thomas	20.00	10.00	6.00
130	Turk Lown	20.00	10.00	6.00
131	Harry Byrd	20.00	10.00	6.00
132	Tom Morgan	25.00	12.50	7.50
133	Gil Coan	20.00	10.00	6.00
134	Rube Walker	25.00	12.50	7.50
135	Al Rosen	35.00	17.50	10.50
136	Ken Heintzelman	20.00	10.00	6.00
137	John Rutherford	25.00	12.50	7.50
138	George Kell	60.00	30.00	18.00
139	Sammy White	20.00	10.00	6.00
140	Tommy Glaviano	20.00	10.00	6.00
141	Allie Reynolds	35.00	17.50	10.50
142	Vic Wertz	25.00	12.50	7.50
143	Billy Pierce	25.00	12.50	7.50
144	Bob Schultz	20.00	10.00	6.00
145	Harry Dorish	20.00	10.00	6.00
146	Granville Hamner	20.00	10.00	6.00
147	Warren Spahn	110.00	50.00	28.00
148	Mickey Grasso	20.00	10.00	6.00
149	Dom DiMaggio	25.00	12.50	7.50
150	Harry Simpson	20.00	10.00	6.00
151	Hoyt Wilhelm	50.00	30.00	15.00
152	Bob Adams	20.00	10.00	6.00
153	Andy Seminick	20.00	10.00	6.00
154	Dick Groat	25.00	12.50	7.50
155	Dutch Leonard	20.00	10.00	6.00
156	Jim Rivera	20.00	10.00	6.00
157	Bob Addis	20.00	10.00	6.00
158	*John Logan*	25.00	12.50	7.50
159	Wayne Terwilliger	20.00	10.00	6.00
160	Bob Young	20.00	10.00	6.00
161	Vern Bickford	20.00	10.00	6.00
162	Ted Kluszewski	35.00	17.50	10.50
163	Fred Hatfield	20.00	10.00	6.00
164	Frank Shea	20.00	10.00	6.00
165	Billy Hoeft	20.00	10.00	6.00
166	Bill Hunter	18.00	9.00	5.50
167	Art Schult	20.00	10.00	6.00
168	Willard Schmidt	18.00	9.00	5.50
169	Dizzy Trout	20.00	10.00	6.00
170	Bill Werle	18.00	9.00	5.50
171	Bill Glynn	18.00	9.00	5.50
172	Rip Repulski	18.00	9.00	5.50
173	Preston Ward	18.00	9.00	5.50
174	Billy Loes	20.00	10.00	6.00
175	Ron Kline	18.00	9.00	5.50
176	*Don Hoak*	20.00	10.00	6.00
177	Jim Dyck	18.00	9.00	5.50
178	Jim Waugh	18.00	9.00	5.50
179	Gene Hermanski	18.00	9.00	5.50
180	Virgil Stallcup	18.00	9.00	5.50
181	Al Zarilla	18.00	9.00	5.50
182	Bob Hofman	18.00	9.00	5.50
183	*Stu Miller*	20.00	10.00	6.00
184	*Hal Brown*	20.00	10.00	6.00
185	Jim Pendleton	18.00	9.00	5.50
186	Charlie Bishop	18.00	9.00	5.50
187	Jim Fridley	18.00	9.00	5.50
188	*Andy Carey*	20.00	10.00	6.00
189	Ray Jablonski	18.00	9.00	5.50
190	Dixie Walker	20.00	10.00	6.00
191	Ralph Kiner	50.00	25.00	15.00
192	Wally Westlake	18.00	9.00	5.50
193	Mike Clark	18.00	9.00	5.50
194	Eddie Kazak	18.00	9.00	5.50
195	Ed McGhee	18.00	9.00	5.50
196	Bob Keegan	18.00	9.00	5.50
197	Del Crandall	20.00	10.00	6.00
198	Forrest Main	18.00	9.00	5.50
199	Marion Fricano	18.00	9.00	5.50
200	Gordon Goldsberry	18.00	9.00	5.50
201	Paul LaPalme	18.00	9.00	5.50
202	Carl Sawatski	18.00	9.00	5.50
203	Cliff Fannin	18.00	9.00	5.50
204	Dick Bokelmann	18.00	9.00	5.50
205	Vern Benson	18.00	9.00	5.50
206	*Ed Bailey*	20.00	10.00	6.00
207	Whitey Ford	125.00	62.00	37.00
208	Jim Wilson	18.00	9.00	5.50
209	Jim Greengrass	18.00	9.00	5.50
210	*Bob Cerv*	20.00	10.00	6.00
211	J.W. Porter	18.00	9.00	5.50
212	Jack Dittmer	18.00	9.00	5.50
213	Ray Scarborough	20.00	10.00	6.00
214	*Bill Bruton*	20.00	10.00	6.00
215	*Gene Conley*	20.00	10.00	6.00
216	Jim Hughes	20.00	10.00	6.00
217	Murray Wall	18.00	9.00	5.50
218	Les Fusselman	18.00	9.00	5.50
219	Pete Runnels (photo actually Don Johnson)	20.00	10.00	6.00
220	Satchell Paige	400.00	200.00	120.00
221	Bob Milliken	90.00	45.00	27.00
222	Vic Janowicz	45.00	23.00	13.50
223	John O'Brien	45.00	23.00	13.50
224	Lou Sleater	45.00	23.00	13.50
225	Bobby Shantz	60.00	30.00	18.00
226	Ed Erautt	90.00	45.00	27.00
227	Morris Martin	45.00	23.00	13.50
228	Hal Newhouser	100.00	45.00	27.00
229	Rocky Krsnich	90.00	45.00	27.00
230	Johnny Lindell	45.00	23.00	13.50
231	Solly Hemus	45.00	23.00	13.50
232	Dick Kokos	90.00	45.00	27.00
233	Al Aber	90.00	45.00	27.00
234	Ray Murray	45.00	23.00	13.50
235	John Hetki	45.00	23.00	13.50
236	Harry Perkowski	90.00	45.00	27.00
237	Clarence Podbielan	45.00	23.00	13.50
238	Cal Hogue	45.00	23.00	13.50
239	Jim Delsing	90.00	45.00	27.00
240	Freddie Marsh	45.00	23.00	13.50
241	Al Sima	45.00	23.00	13.50
242	Charlie Silvera	90.00	45.00	27.00
243	Carlos Bernier	45.00	23.00	13.50
244	Willie Mays	1400.	560.00	350.00
245	Bill Norman	90.00	45.00	27.00
246	*Roy Face*	90.00	45.00	27.00
247	Mike Sandlock	45.00	23.00	13.50
248	Gene Stephens	45.00	23.00	13.50
249	Ed O'Brien	45.00	23.00	13.50
250	Bob Wilson	90.00	45.00	27.00
251	Sid Hudson	90.00	45.00	27.00
252	Henry Foiles	90.00	45.00	27.00
253	Not Issued			
254	Preacher Roe	80.00	40.00	24.00
255	Dixie Howell	90.00	45.00	27.00
256	Les Peden	90.00	45.00	27.00
257	Bob Boyd	90.00	45.00	27.00
258	*Jim Gilliam*	350.00	175.00	105.00
259	Roy McMillan	90.00	45.00	27.00
260	Sam Calderone	90.00	45.00	27.00
261	Not Issued			
262	Bob Oldis	90.00	45.00	27.00
263	*John Podres*	350.00	175.00	105.00
264	Gene Woodling	60.00	30.00	18.00
265	Jackie Jensen	150.00	75.00	45.00
266	Bob Cain	90.00	45.00	27.00
267	Not Issued			
268	Not Issued			
269	Duane Pillette	90.00	45.00	27.00
270	Vern Stephens	90.00	45.00	27.00
271	Not Issued			
272	Bill Antonello	90.00	45.00	27.00
273	*Harvey Haddix*	150.00	75.00	45.00
274	John Riddle	90.00	45.00	27.00
275	Not Issued			
276	Ken Raffensberger	45.00	23.00	13.50
277	Don Lund	90.00	45.00	27.00
278	Willie Miranda	90.00	45.00	27.00
279	Joe Coleman	45.00	23.00	13.50
280	Milt Bolling	400.00	100.00	50.00

1954 Topps

The first issue to use two player pictures on the front, the 1954 Topps set is very popular today. Solid color backgrounds frame both color head-and-shoulders and black and white action pictures of the player. The player's name, position, team and team logo appear at the top. Backs include an "Inside Baseball" cartoon regarding the player as well as statistics and biography. The 250-card, 2-5/8" by 3-3/4", set includes manager and coaches cards, and the first use of two players together on a modern card; the players were, appropriately, the O'Brien twins.

		NR MT	EX	VG
Complete Set:		7500.	3750.	2250.
Common Player: 1-50		15.00	7.50	4.50
Common Player: 51-75		35.00	17.50	10.50
Common Player: 76-250		15.00	7.50	4.50
1	Ted Williams	600.00	150.00	55.00
2	Gus Zernial	15.00	7.50	4.50
3	Monte Irvin	35.00	17.50	10.50
4	Hank Sauer	25.00	12.50	7.50
5	Ed Lopat	25.00	12.50	7.50
6	Pete Runnels	11.00	5.50	3.25
7	Ted Kluszewski	25.00	12.50	7.50
8	Bobby Young	15.00	7.50	4.50
9	Harvey Haddix	11.00	5.50	3.25
10	Jackie Robinson	250.00	125.00	70.00
11	Paul Smith	15.00	7.50	4.50
12	Del Crandall	11.00	5.50	3.25
13	Billy Martin	70.00	35.00	20.00
14	Preacher Roe	20.00	10.00	6.00
15	Al Rosen	20.00	10.00	6.00
16	Vic Janowicz	15.00	7.50	4.50
17	Phil Rizzuto	70.00	35.00	21.00
18	Walt Dropo	15.00	7.50	4.50
19	Johnny Lipon	15.00	7.50	4.50
20	Warren Spahn	100.00	50.00	30.00
21	Bobby Shantz	15.00	7.50	4.50
22	Jim Greengrass	15.00	7.50	4.50
23	Luke Easter	11.00	5.50	3.25
24	Granny Hamner	15.00	7.50	4.50
25	*Harvey Kuenn*	30.00	15.00	9.00
26	Ray Jablonski	15.00	7.50	4.50
27	Ferris Fain	11.00	5.50	3.25
28	Paul Minner	15.00	7.50	4.50
29	Jim Hegan	15.00	7.50	4.50
30	Ed Mathews	80.00	40.00	25.00
31	Johnny Klippstein	15.00	7.50	4.50
32	Duke Snider	125.00	56.00	35.00
33	Johnny Schmitz	15.00	7.50	4.50
34	Jim Rivera	15.00	7.50	4.50
35	Junior Gilliam	35.00	17.50	10.50
36	Hoyt Wilhelm	45.00	23.00	13.50
37	Whitey Ford	100.00	50.00	30.00
38	Eddie Stanky	11.00	5.50	3.25
39	Sherm Lollar	11.00	5.50	3.25
40	Mel Parnell	11.00	5.50	3.25
41	Willie Jones	15.00	7.50	4.50
42	Don Mueller	15.00	7.50	4.50
43	Dick Groat	15.00	7.50	4.50
44	Ned Garver	15.00	7.50	4.50
45	Richie Ashburn	30.00	15.00	9.00
46	Ken Raffensberger	15.00	7.50	4.50
47	Ellis Kinder	15.00	7.50	4.50
48	Billy Hunter	15.00	7.50	4.50
49	Ray Murray	15.00	7.50	4.50
50	Yogi Berra	250.00	125.00	75.00
51	Johnny Lindell	35.00	17.50	10.50
52	Vic Power	35.00	17.50	10.50
53	Jack Dittmer	35.00	17.50	10.50
54	Vern Stephens	35.00	17.50	10.50
55	Phil Cavarretta	22.00	11.00	6.50
56	Willie Miranda	25.00	12.50	7.50
57	Luis Aloma	35.00	17.50	10.50
58	Bob Wilson	35.00	17.50	10.50
59	Gene Conley	22.00	11.00	6.50
60	Frank Baumholtz	35.00	17.50	10.50
61	Bob Cain	35.00	17.50	10.50
62	Eddie Robinson	25.00	12.50	7.50
63	Johnny Pesky	22.00	11.00	6.50
64	Hank Thompson	35.00	17.50	10.50
65	Bob Swift	35.00	17.50	10.50
66	Ted Lepcio	35.00	17.50	10.50
67	Jim Willis	35.00	17.50	10.50
68	Sammy Calderone	35.00	17.50	10.50
69	Bud Podbielan	35.00	17.50	10.50
70	Larry Doby	45.00	23.00	13.50
71	Frank Smith	35.00	17.50	10.50
72	Preston Ward	35.00	17.50	10.50
73	Wayne Terwilliger	35.00	17.50	10.50
74	Bill Taylor	35.00	17.50	10.50
75	Fred Haney	35.00	17.50	10.50
76	Bob Scheffing	15.00	7.50	4.50
77	Ray Boone	13.00	6.50	4.00
78	Ted Kazanski	15.00	7.50	4.50
79	Andy Pafko	13.00	6.50	4.00
80	Jackie Jensen	15.00	7.50	4.50
81	Dave Hoskins	15.00	7.50	4.50
82	Milt Bolling	15.00	7.50	4.50
83	Joe Collins	15.00	7.50	4.50
84	Dick Cole	15.00	7.50	4.50
85	*Bob Turley*	15.00	7.50	4.50
86	Billy Herman	35.00	17.50	10.50
87	Roy Face	15.00	7.50	4.50
88	Matt Batts	15.00	7.50	4.50
89	Howie Pollet	15.00	7.50	4.50
90	Willie Mays	325.00	130.00	81.00
91	Bob Oldis	15.00	7.50	4.50
92	Wally Westlake	15.00	7.50	4.50
93	Sid Hudson	15.00	7.50	4.50
94	*Ernie Banks*	650.00	325.00	200.00
95	Hal Rice	15.00	7.50	4.50
96	Charlie Silvera	15.00	7.50	4.50
97	Jerry Lane	15.00	7.50	4.50
98	Joe Black	15.00	7.50	4.50
99	Bob Hofman	15.00	7.50	4.50
100	Bob Keegan	15.00	7.50	4.50
101	Gene Woodling	35.00	17.50	10.50
102	Gil Hodges	70.00	35.00	21.00
103	*Jim Lemon*	13.00	6.50	4.00
104	Mike Sandlock	15.00	7.50	4.50
105	Andy Carey	15.00	7.50	4.50
106	Dick Kokos	15.00	7.50	4.50
107	Duane Pillette	15.00	7.50	4.50
108	Thornton Kipper	15.00	7.50	4.50
109	Bill Bruton	13.00	6.50	4.00
110	Harry Dorish	15.00	7.50	4.50
111	Jim Delsing	15.00	7.50	4.50
112	Bill Renna	15.00	7.50	4.50
113	Bob Boyd	15.00	7.50	4.50
114	Dean Stone	15.00	7.50	4.50
115	"Rip" Repulski	15.00	7.50	4.50
116	Steve Bilko	15.00	7.50	4.50
117	Solly Hemus	15.00	7.50	4.50
118	Carl Scheib	15.00	7.50	4.50
119	Johnny Antonelli	13.00	6.50	4.00
120	Roy McMillan	15.00	7.50	4.50
121	Clem Labine	13.00	6.50	4.00
122	Johnny Logan	13.00	6.50	4.00
123	Bobby Adams	15.00	7.50	4.50
124	Marion Fricano	15.00	7.50	4.50
125	Harry Perkowski	15.00	7.50	4.50
126	Ben Wade	13.00	6.50	4.00
127	Steve O'Neill	15.00	7.50	4.50
128	*Henry Aaron*	1500.	750.00	450.00
129	Forrest Jacobs	15.00	7.50	4.50
130	Hank Bauer	35.00	17.50	10.50
131	Reno Bertoia	15.00	7.50	4.50
132	*Tom Lasorda*	175.00	87.00	50.00
133	Del Baker	15.00	7.50	4.50
134	Cal Hogue	15.00	7.50	4.50
135	Joe Presko	15.00	7.50	4.50
136	Connie Ryan	15.00	7.50	4.50
137	*Wally Moon*	15.00	7.50	4.50
138	Bob Borkowski	15.00	7.50	4.50
139	Ed & Johnny O'Brien	25.00	12.50	7.50
140	Tom Wright	15.00	7.50	4.50
141	*Joe Jay*	13.00	6.50	4.00
142	Tom Poholsky	15.00	7.50	4.50
143	Rollie Hemsley	15.00	7.50	4.50
144	Bill Werle	15.00	7.50	4.50
145	Elmer Valo	15.00	7.50	4.50
146	Don Johnson	15.00	7.50	4.50
147	John Riddle	15.00	7.50	4.50
148	Bob Trice	15.00	7.50	4.50
149	Jim Robertson	15.00	7.50	4.50
150	Dick Kryhoski	15.00	7.50	4.50
151	Alex Grammas	15.00	7.50	4.50
152	Mike Blyzka	15.00	7.50	4.50
153	"Rube" Walker	13.00	6.50	4.00
154	Mike Fornieles	15.00	7.50	4.50
155	Bob Kennedy	15.00	7.50	4.50
156	Joe Coleman	15.00	7.50	4.50
157	Don Lenhardt	15.00	7.50	4.50
158	"Peanuts" Lowrey	15.00	7.50	4.50
159	Dave Philley	15.00	7.50	4.50
160	"Red" Kress	15.00	7.50	4.50
161	John Hetki	15.00	7.50	4.50
162	Herman Wehmeier	15.00	7.50	4.50
163	Frank House	15.00	7.50	4.50
164	Stu Miller	15.00	7.50	4.50
165	Jim Pendleton	15.00	7.50	4.50
166	Johnny Podres	25.00	12.50	7.50
167	Don Lund	15.00	7.50	4.50
168	Morrie Martin	15.00	7.50	4.50
169	Jim Hughes	13.00	6.50	4.00
170	*Jim Rhodes*	13.00	6.50	4.00
171	Leo Kiely	15.00	7.50	4.50
172	Hal Brown	15.00	7.50	4.50
173	Jack Harshman	15.00	7.50	4.50
174	Tom Qualters	15.00	7.50	4.50
175	Frank Leja	15.00	7.50	4.50
176	Bob Keely	15.00	7.50	4.50
177	Bob Milliken	13.00	6.50	4.00
178	Bill Gylnn (Glynn)	15.00	7.50	4.50
179	Gair Allie	15.00	7.50	4.50
180	Wes Westrum	13.00	6.50	4.00
181	Mel Roach	15.00	7.50	4.50
182	Chuck Harmon	15.00	7.50	4.50
183	Earle Combs	35.00	17.50	10.50
184	Ed Bailey	15.00	7.50	4.50
185	Chuck Stobbs	15.00	7.50	4.50
186	Karl Olson	15.00	7.50	4.50
187	"Heinie" Manush	35.00	17.50	10.50
188	Dave Jolly	15.00	7.50	4.50
189	Bob Ross	15.00	7.50	4.50
190	Ray Herbert	15.00	7.50	4.50
191	*Dick Schofield*	13.00	6.50	4.00
192	"Cot" Deal	15.00	7.50	4.50
193	Johnny Hopp	15.00	7.50	4.50
194	Bill Sarni	15.00	7.50	4.50
195	Bill Consolo	15.00	7.50	4.50
196	Stan Jok	15.00	7.50	4.50
197	"Schoolboy" Rowe	13.00	6.50	4.00
198	Carl Sawatski	15.00	7.50	4.50
199	"Rocky" Nelson	15.00	7.50	4.50
200	Larry Jansen	15.00	7.50	4.50
201	*Al Kaline*	650.00	330.00	200.00
202	*Bob Purkey*	13.00	6.50	4.00
203	Harry Brecheen	13.00	6.50	4.00
204	Angel Scull	15.00	7.50	4.50
205	Johnny Sain	35.00	17.50	10.50
206	Ray Crone	15.00	7.50	4.50
207	Tom Oliver	15.00	7.50	4.50
208	Grady Hatton	15.00	7.50	4.50
209	Charlie Thompson	13.00	6.50	4.00
210	*Bob Buhl*	13.00	6.50	4.00
211	Don Hoak	13.00	6.50	4.00
212	Mickey Micelotta	15.00	7.50	4.50
213	John Fitzpatrick	15.00	7.50	4.50
214	Arnold Portocarrero	15.00	7.50	4.50
215	Ed McGhee	15.00	7.50	4.50
216	Al Sima	15.00	7.50	4.50
217	Paul Schreiber	15.00	7.50	4.50
218	Fred Marsh	15.00	7.50	4.50
219	Charlie Kress	15.00	7.50	4.50
220	Ruben Gomez	15.00	7.50	4.50
221	Dick Brodowski	15.00	7.50	4.50
222	Bill Wilson	15.00	7.50	4.50
223	Joe Haynes	15.00	7.50	4.50
224	Dick Weik	15.00	7.50	4.50
225	Don Liddle	15.00	7.50	4.50
226	Jehosie Heard	15.00	7.50	4.50
227	Buster Mills	15.00	7.50	4.50
228	Gene Hermanski	15.00	7.50	4.50
229	Bob Talbot	15.00	7.50	4.50
230	Bob Kuzava	15.00	7.50	4.50
231	Roy Smalley	15.00	7.50	4.50
232	Lou Limmer	15.00	7.50	4.50
233	Augie Galan	15.00	7.50	4.50
234	*Jerry Lynch*	13.00	6.50	4.00
235	Vern Law	13.00	6.50	4.00
236	Paul Penson	15.00	7.50	4.50
237	Mike Ryba	15.00	7.50	4.50
238	Al Aber	15.00	7.50	4.50
239	*Bill Skowron*	45.00	23.00	13.50
240	Sam Mele	15.00	7.50	4.50
241	Bob Miller	15.00	7.50	4.50
242	Curt Roberts	15.00	7.50	4.50
243	Ray Blades	15.00	7.50	4.50
244	Leroy Wheat	15.00	7.50	4.50
245	Roy Sievers	13.00	6.50	4.00
246	Howie Fox	15.00	7.50	4.50
247	Eddie Mayo	15.00	7.50	4.50
248	*Al Smith*	13.00	6.50	4.00
249	Wilmer Mizell	15.00	7.50	4.50
250	Ted Williams	625.00	125.00	55.00

1955 Topps

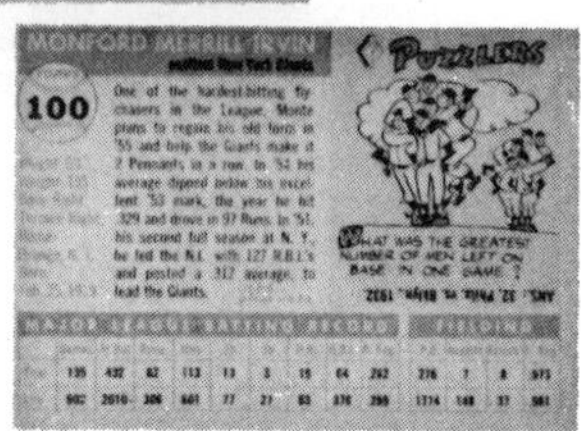

The 1955 Topps set is numerically the smallest of the regular issue Topps sets. The 3-3/4" by 2-5/8" cards mark the first time that Topps used a horizontal format. While that format was new, the design was not; they are very similar to the 1954 cards to the point many pictures appeared in both years. Although it was slated for a 210-card set, the 1955 Topps set turned out to be only 206 cards with numbers 175, 186, 203 and 209 never being released. The scarce high numbers in this set begin with #161.

		NR MT	EX	VG
Complete Set:		5500.	2800.	1650.
Common Player: 1-150		6.00	3.00	1.75
Common Player: 151-160		7.00	3.50	2.00
Common Player: 161-210		20.00	10.00	6.00
1	"Dusty" Rhodes	50.00	15.00	9.00
2	Ted Williams	400.00	160.00	100.00
3	Art Fowler	6.00	3.00	1.75
4	Al Kaline	175.00	87.00	50.00
5	Jim Gilliam	10.00	5.00	3.00
6	Stan Hack	6.00	3.00	1.75
7	Jim Hegan	6.00	3.00	1.75
8	Hal Smith	6.00	3.00	1.75
9	Bob Miller	6.00	3.00	1.75
10	Bob Keegan	6.00	3.00	1.75
11	Ferris Fain	6.00	3.00	1.75
12	"Jake" Thies	6.00	3.00	1.75
13	Fred Marsh	6.00	3.00	1.75
14	Jim Finigan	6.00	3.00	1.75
15	Jim Pendleton	6.00	3.00	1.75
16	Roy Sievers	7.00	3.50	2.00
17	Bobby Hofman	6.00	3.00	1.75
18	Russ Kemmerer	6.00	3.00	1.75
19	Billy Herman	15.00	7.50	4.50
20	Andy Carey	9.00	4.50	2.75
21	Alex Grammas	6.00	3.00	1.75
22	Bill Skowron	12.00	6.00	3.50
23	Jack Parks	6.00	3.00	1.75
24	Hal Newhouser	6.00	3.00	1.75
25	Johnny Podres	20.00	10.00	6.00
26	Dick Groat	7.00	3.50	2.00
27	Billy Gardner	6.00	3.00	1.75
28	Ernie Banks	150.00	75.00	45.00
29	Herman Wehmeier	6.00	3.00	1.75
30	Vic Power	6.00	3.00	1.75
31	Warren Spahn	60.00	30.00	18.00
32	Ed McGhee	6.00	3.00	1.75
33	Tom Qualters	6.00	3.00	1.75
34	Wayne Terwilliger	6.00	3.00	1.75
35	Dave Jolly	6.00	3.00	1.75
36	Leo Kiely	6.00	3.00	1.75
37	*Joe Cunningham*	7.00	3.50	2.00
38	Bob Turley	12.00	6.00	3.50
39	Bill Glynn	6.00	3.00	1.75
40	Don Hoak	7.00	3.50	2.00
41	Chuck Stobbs	6.00	3.00	1.75
42	"Windy" McCall	6.00	3.00	1.75
43	Harvey Haddix	6.00	3.00	1.75
44	"Corky" Valentine	6.00	3.00	1.75
45	Hank Sauer	6.00	3.00	1.75
46	Ted Kazanski	6.00	3.00	1.75

		NR MT	EX	VG
47	Hank Aaron	350.00	175.00	105.00
48	Bob Kennedy	6.00	3.00	1.75
49	J.W. Porter	6.00	3.00	1.75
50	Jackie Robinson	225.00	100.00	60.00
51	Jim Hughes	6.00	3.00	1.75
52	Bill Tremel	6.00	3.00	1.75
53	Bill Taylor	6.00	3.00	1.75
54	Lou Limmer	6.00	3.00	1.75
55	"Rip" Repulski	6.00	3.00	1.75
56	Ray Jablonski	6.00	3.00	1.75
57	*Billy O'Dell*	6.00	3.00	1.75
58	Jim Rivera	6.00	3.00	1.75
59	Gair Allie	6.00	3.00	1.75
60	Dean Stone	6.00	3.00	1.75
61	"Spook" Jacobs	6.00	3.00	1.75
62	Thornton Kipper	6.00	3.00	1.75
63	Joe Collins	9.00	4.50	2.75
64	*Gus Triandos*	7.00	3.50	2.00
65	Ray Boone	6.00	3.00	1.75
66	Ron Jackson	6.00	3.00	1.75
67	Wally Moon	6.00	3.00	1.75
68	Jim Davis	6.00	3.00	1.75
69	Ed Bailey	6.00	3.00	1.75
70	Al Rosen	12.00	6.00	3.50
71	Ruben Gomez	6.00	3.00	1.75
72	Karl Olson	6.00	3.00	1.75
73	Jack Shepard	6.00	3.00	1.75
74	Bob Borkowski	6.00	3.00	1.75
75	Sandy Amoros	6.00	3.00	1.75
76	Howie Pollet	6.00	3.00	1.75
77	Arnold Portocarrero	6.00	3.00	1.75
78	Gordon Jones	6.00	3.00	1.75
79	Danny Schell	6.00	3.00	1.75
80	Bob Grim	9.00	4.50	2.75
81	Gene Conley	6.00	3.00	1.75
82	Chuck Harmon	6.00	3.00	1.75
83	Tom Brewer	6.00	3.00	1.75
84	*Camilo Pascual*	7.00	3.50	2.00
85	*Don Mossi*	7.00	3.50	2.00
86	Bill Wilson	6.00	3.00	1.75
87	Frank House	6.00	3.00	1.75
88	*Bob Skinner*	7.00	3.50	2.00
89	Joe Frazier	6.00	3.00	1.75
90	Karl Spooner	9.00	4.50	2.75
91	Milt Bolling	6.00	3.00	1.75
92	*Don Zimmer*	25.00	12.50	7.50
93	Steve Bilko	6.00	3.00	1.75
94	Reno Bertoia	6.00	3.00	1.75
95	Preston Ward	6.00	3.00	1.75
96	Charlie Bishop	6.00	3.00	1.75
97	Carlos Paula	6.00	3.00	1.75
98	Johnny Riddle	6.00	3.00	1.75
99	Frank Leja	9.00	4.50	2.75
100	Monte Irvin	25.00	12.50	7.50
101	Johnny Gray	6.00	3.00	1.75
102	Wally Westlake	6.00	3.00	1.75
103	Charlie White	6.00	3.00	1.75
104	Jack Harshman	6.00	3.00	1.75
105	Chuck Diering	6.00	3.00	1.75
106	*Frank Sullivan*	6.00	3.00	1.75
107	Curt Roberts	6.00	3.00	1.75
108	"Rube" Walker	6.00	3.00	1.75
109	Ed Lopat	12.00	6.00	3.50
110	Gus Zernial	6.00	3.00	1.75
111	Bob Milliken	6.00	3.00	1.75
112	Nelson King	6.00	3.00	1.75
113	Harry Brecheen	6.00	3.00	1.75
114	Lou Ortiz	6.00	3.00	1.75
115	Ellis Kinder	6.00	3.00	1.75
116	Tom Hurd	6.00	3.00	1.75
117	Mel Roach	6.00	3.00	1.75
118	Bob Purkey	6.00	3.00	1.75
119	Bob Lennon	6.00	3.00	1.75
120	Ted Kluszewski	20.00	10.00	6.00
121	Bill Renna	6.00	3.00	1.75
122	Carl Sawatski	6.00	3.00	1.75
123	*Sandy Koufax*	800.00	400.00	250.00
124	*Harmon Killebrew*	250.00	100.00	63.00
125	*Ken Boyer*	40.00	20.00	12.00
126	*Dick Hall*	6.00	3.00	1.75
127	*Dale Long*	6.00	3.00	1.75
128	Ted Lepcio	6.00	3.00	1.75
129	Elvin Tappe	6.00	3.00	1.75
130	Mayo Smith	6.00	3.00	1.75
131	Grady Hatton	6.00	3.00	1.75
132	Bob Trice	6.00	3.00	1.75
133	Dave Hoskins	6.00	3.00	1.75
134	Joe Jay	6.00	3.00	1.75
135	Johnny O'Brien	6.00	3.00	1.75
136	"Bunky" Stewart	6.00	3.00	1.75
137	Harry Elliott	6.00	3.00	1.75
138	Ray Herbert	6.00	3.00	1.75
139	Steve Kraly	9.00	4.50	2.75
140	Mel Parnell	6.00	3.00	1.75
141	Tom Wright	6.00	3.00	1.75
142	Jerry Lynch	6.00	3.00	1.75
143	Dick Schofield	6.00	3.00	1.75
144	Joe Amalfitano	6.00	3.00	1.75
145	Elmer Valo	6.00	3.00	1.75
146	*Dick Donovan*	6.00	3.00	1.75
147	Laurin Pepper	6.00	3.00	1.75
148	Hal Brown	6.00	3.00	1.75
149	Ray Crone	6.00	3.00	1.75
150	Mike Higgins	6.00	3.00	1.75
151	"Red" Kress	7.00	3.50	2.00
152	*Harry Agganis*	75.00	38.00	23.00
153	"Bud" Podbielan	7.00	3.50	2.00
154	Willie Miranda	7.00	3.50	2.00
155	Ed Mathews	80.00	40.00	24.00
156	Joe Black	20.00	10.00	6.00
157	Bob Miller	7.00	3.50	2.00
158	Tom Carroll	20.00	10.00	6.00
159	Johnny Schmitz	7.00	3.50	2.00
160	Ray Narleski	7.00	3.50	2.00
161	*Chuck Tanner*	25.00	12.50	7.50
162	Joe Coleman	20.00	10.00	6.00
163	Faye Throneberry	20.00	10.00	6.00
164	*Roberto Clemente*	1000.	500.00	300.00
165	Don Johnson	20.00	10.00	6.00
166	Hank Bauer	30.00	15.00	9.00
167	Tom Casagrande	20.00	10.00	6.00
168	Duane Pillette	20.00	10.00	6.00
169	Bob Oldis	20.00	10.00	6.00
170	Jim Pearce	20.00	10.00	6.00
171	Dick Brodowski	20.00	10.00	6.00
172	Frank Baumholtz	20.00	10.00	6.00
173	Bob Kline	20.00	10.00	6.00
174	Rudy Minarcin	20.00	10.00	6.00
175	Not Issued			
176	Norm Zauchin	20.00	10.00	6.00
177	Jim Robertson	20.00	10.00	6.00
178	Bobby Adams	20.00	10.00	6.00
179	Jim Bolger	20.00	10.00	6.00
180	Clem Labine	18.00	9.00	5.50
181	Roy McMillan	20.00	10.00	6.00
182	Humberto Robinson	20.00	10.00	6.00
183	Tony Jacobs	20.00	10.00	6.00
184	Harry Perkowski	20.00	10.00	6.00
185	Don Ferrarese	20.00	10.00	6.00
186	Not Issued			
187	Gil Hodges	125.00	62.00	40.00
188	Charlie Silvera	18.00	9.00	5.50
189	Phil Rizzuto	125.00	56.00	35.00
190	Gene Woodling	20.00	10.00	6.00
191	Ed Stanky	18.00	9.00	5.50
192	Jim Delsing	20.00	10.00	6.00
193	Johnny Sain	35.00	17.50	10.50
194	Willie Mays	400.00	160.00	100.00
195	Ed Roebuck	18.00	9.00	5.50
196	Gale Wade	20.00	10.00	6.00
197	Al Smith	20.00	10.00	6.00
198	Yogi Berra	225.00	100.00	60.00
199	Bert Hamric	18.00	9.00	5.50
200	Jack Jensen	50.00	25.00	15.00
201	Sherm Lollar	18.00	9.00	5.50
202	Jim Owens	20.00	10.00	6.00
203	Not Issued			
204	Frank Smith	20.00	10.00	6.00
205	Gene Freese	20.00	10.00	6.00
206	Pete Daley	20.00	10.00	6.00
207	Bill Consolo	20.00	10.00	6.00
208	Ray Moore	20.00	10.00	6.00
209	Not Issued			
210	Duke Snider	400.00	95.00	50.00

1955 Topps Doubleheaders

This set is a throwback to the 1911 T201 Mecca Double Folders. The cards were perforated allowing them to be folded. Open, there is a color painting of a player set against a ballpark background. When folded , a different stadium and player appears, although both share the same lower legs and feet. Back gives abbreviated career histories. Placed side by side in reverse numerical order, the backgrounds form a continuous stadium scene. When open, the cards measure 2-1/16" by 4-7/8." The 66 cards in the set mean 132 total players, all of whom also appeared in the lower number regular 1955 Topps set.

		NR MT	EX	VG
Complete Set:		3500.	1750.	1050.
Common Player:		25.00	12.50	7.50
1	Al Rosen			
2	Chuck Diering	25.00	12.50	7.50
3	Monte Irvin			
4	Russ Kemmerer	25.00	12.50	7.50
5	Ted Kazanski			
6	Gordon Jones	25.00	12.50	7.50
7	Bill Taylor			
8	Billy O'Dell	25.00	12.50	7.50
9	J.W. Porter			
10	Thornton Kipper	25.00	12.50	7.50
11	Curt Roberts			
12	Arnie Portocarrero	25.00	12.50	7.50
13	Wally Westlake			
14	Frank House	25.00	12.50	7.50
15	"Rube" Walker			
16	Lou Limmer	25.00	12.50	7.50
17	Dean Stone			
18	Charlie White	25.00	12.50	7.50
19	Karl Spooner			
20	Jim Hughes	25.00	12.50	7.50
21	Bill Skowron			
22	Frank Sullivan	25.00	12.50	7.50
23	Jack Shepard			
24	Stan Hack	25.00	12.50	7.50
25	Jackie Robinson			
26	Don Hoak	275.00	137.00	80.00
27	"Dusty" Rhodes			
28	Jim Davis	25.00	12.50	7.50
29	Vic Power			
30	Ed Bailey	25.00	12.50	7.50
31	Howie Pollet			
32	Ernie Banks	150.00	75.00	45.00
33	Jim Pendleton			
34	Gene Conley	25.00	12.50	7.50
35	Karl Olson	25.00	12.50	7.50
36	Andy Carey	25.00	12.50	7.50
37	Wally Moon	25.00	12.50	7.50
38	Joe Cunningham	25.00	12.50	7.50
39	Fred Marsh			
40	"Jake" Thies	25.00	12.50	7.50
41	Ed Lopat			
42	Harvey Haddix	25.00	12.50	7.50
43	Leo Kiely			
44	Chuck Stobbs	25.00	12.50	7.50
45	Al Kaline			
46	"Corky" Valentine	300.00	150.00	90.00
47	"Spook" Jacobs			
48	Johnny Gray	25.00	12.50	7.50
49	Ron Jackson			
50	Jim Finigan	25.00	12.50	7.50
51	Ray Jablonski			
52	Bob Keegan	25.00	12.50	7.50
53	Billy Herman			
54	Sandy Amoros	25.00	12.50	7.50
55	Chuck Harmon			
56	Bob Skinner	25.00	12.50	7.50
57	Dick Hall			
58	Bob Grim	25.00	12.50	7.50
59	Billy Glynn			
60	Bob Miller	25.00	12.50	7.50
61	Billy Gardner			
62	John Hetki	25.00	12.50	7.50
63	Bob Borkowski			
64	Bob Turley	25.00	12.50	7.50
65	Joe Collins			
66	Jack Harshman	25.00	12.50	7.50
67	Jim Hegan			
68	Jack Parks	25.00	12.50	7.50
69	Ted Williams			
70	Hal Smith	300.00	150.00	90.00
71	Gair Allie			
72	Grady Hatton	25.00	12.50	7.50
73	Jerry Lynch			
74	Harry Brecheen	25.00	12.50	7.50
75	Tom Wright			
76	"Bunky" Stewart	25.00	12.50	7.50
77	Dave Hoskins			
78	Ed McGhee	25.00	12.50	7.50
79	Roy Sievers			
80	Art Fowler	25.00	12.50	7.50
81	Danny Schell			
82	Gus Triandos	25.00	12.50	7.50
83	Joe Frazier			
84	Don Mossi	25.00	12.50	7.50
85	Elmer Valo			
86	Hal Brown	25.00	12.50	7.50
87	Bob Kennedy			
88	"Windy" McCall	25.00	12.50	7.50
89	Ruben Gomez			
90	Jim Rivera	25.00	12.50	7.50
91	Lou Ortiz			
92	Milt Bolling	25.00	12.50	7.50
93	Carl Sawatski			
94	Elvin Tappe	25.00	12.50	7.50
95	Dave Jolly			
96	Bobby Hofman	25.00	12.50	7.50
97	Preston Ward			
98	Don Zimmer	25.00	12.50	7.50
99	Bill Renna			
100	Dick Groat	25.00	12.50	7.50
101	Bill Wilson			
102	Bill Tremel	25.00	12.50	7.50
103	Hank Sauer			
104	Camilo Pascual	25.00	12.50	7.50
105	Hank Aaron			
106	Ray Herbert	450.00	225.00	135.00
107	Alex Grammas			
108	Tom Qualters	25.00	12.50	7.50
109	Hal Newhouser			
110	Charlie Bishop	25.00	12.50	7.50
111	Harmon Killebrew			
112	John Podres	250.00	125.00	75.00
113	Ray Boone			
114	Bob Purkey	25.00	12.50	7.50
115	Dale Long			
116	Ferris Fain	25.00	12.50	7.50
117	Steve Bilko			
118	Bob Milliken	25.00	12.50	7.50
119	Mel Parnell			
120	Tom Hurd	25.00	12.50	7.50
121	Ted Kluszewski			
122	Jim Owens	25.00	12.50	7.50
123	Gus Zernial			
124	Bob Trice	25.00	12.50	7.50
125	"Rip" Repulski			
126	Ted Lepcio	25.00	12.50	7.50
127	Warren Spahn			
128	Tom Brewer	200.00	100.00	60.00
129	Jim Gilliam			
130	Ellis Kinder	25.00	12.50	7.50
131	Herm Wehmeier			
132	Wayne Terwilliger	25.00	12.50	7.50

1956 Topps

This 340-card set is quite similar in design to the 1955 Topps set, again using both a portrait

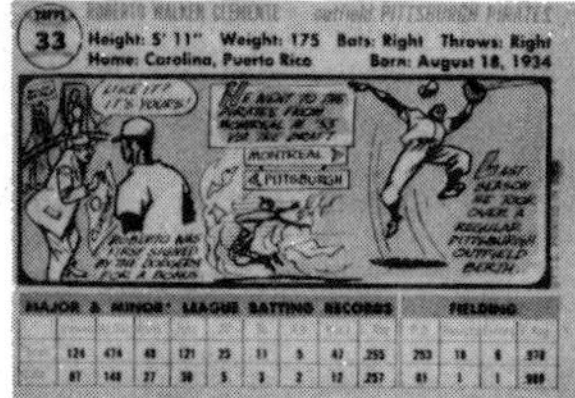

and an "action" picture. Some portraits are the same as those used in 1955 (and even 1954). Innovations found in the 1956 Topps set of 2-5/8" by 3-3/4" cards include team cards introduced as part of a regular set. Additionally, there are two unnumbered checklist cards (the complete set price quoted below does not include the checklist cards). Finally, there are cards of the two league presidents, William Harridge and Warren Giles. On the backs, a three-panel cartoon depicts big moments from the player's career while biographical information appears above the cartoon and the statistics below. Card backs for numbers 1-180 can be found with either white or grey cardboard. Some dealers charge a premium for grey backs (#'s 1-100) and white backs (#'s 101-180).

	NR MT	EX	VG
Complete Set:	6000.	3000.	1750.
Common Player: 1-100	7.00	3.50	2.00
Common Player: 101-180	10.00	5.00	3.00
Common Player: 181-260	15.00	7.50	4.50
Common Player: 261-340	10.00	5.00	3.00

		NR MT	EX	VG
1	William Harridge	150.00	25.00	3.75
2	Warren Giles	9.00	3.00	1.75
3	Elmer Valo	7.00	3.50	2.00
4	Carlos Paula	7.00	3.50	2.00
5	Ted Williams	250.00	100.00	63.00
6	Ray Boone	6.00	3.00	1.75
7	Ron Negray	7.00	3.50	2.00
8	Walter Alston	30.00	15.00	9.00
9	Ruben Gomez	7.00	3.50	2.00
10	Warren Spahn	35.00	17.50	10.50
11a	Cubs Team (with date)	40.00	20.00	12.00
11b	Cubs Team (no date, name centered)	9.00	4.50	2.75
11c	Cubs Team (no date, name at left)	12.00	6.00	3.50
12	Andy Carey	10.00	5.00	3.00
13	Roy Face	10.00	5.00	3.00
14	Ken Boyer	12.00	6.00	3.50
15	Ernie Banks	75.00	38.00	23.00
16	*Hector Lopez*	10.00	5.00	3.00
17	Gene Conley	6.00	3.00	1.75
18	Dick Donovan	7.00	3.50	2.00
19	Chuck Diering	7.00	3.50	2.00
20	Al Kaline	80.00	40.00	24.00
21	Joe Collins	10.00	5.00	3.00
22	Jim Finigan	7.00	3.50	2.00
23	Freddie Marsh	7.00	3.50	2.00
24	Dick Groat	10.00	5.00	3.00
25	Ted Kluszewski	15.00	7.50	4.50
26	Grady Hatton	7.00	3.50	2.00
27	Nelson Burbrink	7.00	3.50	2.00
28	Bobby Hofman	7.00	3.50	2.00
29	Jack Harshman	7.00	3.50	2.00
30	Jackie Robinson	150.00	60.00	38.00
31	Hank Aaron	200.00	100.00	60.00
32	Frank House	7.00	3.50	2.00
33	Roberto Clemente	250.00	100.00	63.00
34	Tom Brewer	7.00	3.50	2.00
35	Al Rosen	9.00	4.50	2.75
36	Rudy Minarcin	7.00	3.50	2.00
37	Alex Grammas	7.00	3.50	2.00
38	Bob Kennedy	7.00	3.50	2.00
39	Don Mossi	6.00	3.00	1.75
40	Bob Turley	9.00	4.50	2.75
41	Hank Sauer	7.00	3.50	2.00
42	Sandy Amoros	6.00	3.00	1.75
43	Ray Moore	7.00	3.50	2.00
44	"Windy" McCall	7.00	3.50	2.00
45	Gus Zernial	6.00	3.00	1.75
46	Gene Freese	7.00	3.50	2.00
47	Art Fowler	7.00	3.50	2.00
48	Jim Hegan	7.00	3.50	2.00
49	*Pedro Ramos*	6.00	3.00	1.75
50	"Dusty" Rhodes	6.00	3.00	1.75
51	Ernie Oravetz	7.00	3.50	2.00
52	Bob Grim	10.00	5.00	3.00
53	Arnold Portocarrero	7.00	3.50	2.00
54	Bob Keegan	7.00	3.50	2.00
55	Wally Moon	6.00	3.00	1.75
56	Dale Long	6.00	3.00	1.75
57	"Duke" Maas	7.00	3.50	2.00
58	Ed Roebuck	6.00	3.00	1.75
59	Jose Santiago	7.00	3.50	2.00
60	Mayo Smith	7.00	3.50	2.00
61	Bill Skowron	9.00	4.50	2.75
62	Hal Smith	7.00	3.50	2.00
63	*Roger Craig*	20.00	10.00	6.00
64	Luis Arroyo	7.00	3.50	2.00
65	Johnny O'Brien	7.00	3.50	2.00
66	Bob Speake	7.00	3.50	2.00
67	Vic Power	7.00	3.50	2.00
68	Chuck Stobbs	7.00	3.50	2.00
69	Chuck Tanner	10.00	5.00	3.00
70	Jim Rivera	7.00	3.50	2.00
71	Frank Sullivan	7.00	3.50	2.00
72a	Phillies Team (with date)	40.00	20.00	12.00
72b	Phillies Team (no date, name centered)	9.00	4.50	2.75
72c	Philadelphia Phillies (no date, name at left)	12.00	6.00	3.50
73	Wayne Terwilliger	7.00	3.50	2.00
74	Jim King	7.00	3.50	2.00
75	Roy Sievers	6.00	3.00	1.75
76	Ray Crone	7.00	3.50	2.00
77	Harvey Haddix	6.00	3.00	1.75
78	Herman Wehmeier	7.00	3.50	2.00
79	Sandy Koufax	300.00	150.00	90.00
80	Gus Triandos	6.00	3.00	1.75
81	Wally Westlake	7.00	3.50	2.00
82	Bill Renna	7.00	3.50	2.00
83	Karl Spooner	6.00	3.00	1.75
84	"Babe" Birrer	7.00	3.50	2.00
85a	Indians Team (with date)	40.00	20.00	12.00
85b	Indians Team (no date, name centered)	9.00	4.50	2.75
85c	Indians Team (no date, name at left)	12.00	6.00	3.50
86	Ray Jablonski	7.00	3.50	2.00
87	Dean Stone	7.00	3.50	2.00
88	Johnny Kucks	10.00	5.00	3.00
89	Norm Zauchin	7.00	3.50	2.00
90a	Redlegs Team (with date)	40.00	20.00	12.00
90b	Redlegs Team (no date, name centered)	9.00	4.50	2.75
90c	Redlegs Team (no date, name at left)	12.00	6.00	3.50
91	Gail Harris	7.00	3.50	2.00
92	"Red" Wilson	7.00	3.50	2.00
93	George Susce, Jr.	7.00	3.50	2.00
94	Ronnie Kline	7.00	3.50	2.00
95a	Braves Team (with date)	40.00	20.00	12.00
95b	Braves Team (no date, name centered)	9.00	4.50	2.75
95c	Braves Team (no date, name at left)	12.00	6.00	3.50
96	Bill Tremel	7.00	3.50	2.00
97	Jerry Lynch	7.00	3.50	2.00
98	Camilo Pascual	6.00	3.00	1.75
99	Don Zimmer	9.00	4.50	2.75
100a	Orioles Team (with date)	40.00	20.00	12.00
100b	Orioles Team (no date, name centered)	9.00	4.50	2.75
100c	Orioles Team (no date, name at left)	12.00	6.00	3.50
101	Roy Campanella	100.00	45.00	27.00
102	Jim Davis	10.00	5.00	3.00
103	Willie Miranda	10.00	5.00	3.00
104	Bob Lennon	10.00	5.00	3.00
105	Al Smith	10.00	5.00	3.00
106	Joe Astroth	10.00	5.00	3.00
107	Ed Mathews	35.00	17.50	10.50
108	Laurin Pepper	10.00	5.00	3.00
109	Enos Slaughter	25.00	12.50	7.50
110	Yogi Berra	125.00	56.00	35.00
111	Red Sox Team	10.00	5.00	3.00
112	Dee Fondy	10.00	5.00	3.00
113	Phil Rizzuto	50.00	25.00	15.00
114	Jim Owens	10.00	5.00	3.00
115	Jackie Jensen	10.00	5.00	3.00
116	Eddie O'Brien	10.00	5.00	3.00
117	Virgil Trucks	8.00	4.00	2.50
118	"Nellie" Fox	20.00	10.00	6.00
119	*Larry Jackson*	8.00	4.00	2.50
120	Richie Ashburn	30.00	15.00	9.00
121	Pirates Team	9.00	4.50	2.75
122	Willard Nixon	10.00	5.00	3.00
123	Roy McMillan	10.00	5.00	3.00
124	Don Kaiser	10.00	5.00	3.00
125	"Minnie" Minoso	15.00	7.50	4.50
126	Jim Brady	10.00	5.00	3.00
127	Willie Jones	10.00	5.00	3.00
128	Eddie Yost	10.00	5.00	3.00
129	"Jake" Martin	10.00	5.00	3.00
130	Willie Mays	225.00	90.00	56.00
131	Bob Roselli	10.00	5.00	3.00
132	Bobby Avila	10.00	5.00	3.00
133	Ray Narleski	10.00	5.00	3.00
134	Cardinals Team	9.00	4.50	2.75
135	Mickey Mantle	750.00	375.00	225.00
136	Johnny Logan	8.00	4.00	2.50
137	Al Silvera	10.00	5.00	3.00
138	Johnny Antonelli	8.00	4.00	2.50
139	Tommy Carroll	10.00	5.00	3.00
140	*Herb Score*	20.00	10.00	6.00
141	Joe Frazier	10.00	5.00	3.00
142	Gene Baker	10.00	5.00	3.00
143	Jim Piersall	10.00	5.00	3.00
144	Leroy Powell	10.00	5.00	3.00
145	Gil Hodges	45.00	23.00	13.50
146	Senators Team	9.00	4.50	2.75
147	Earl Torgeson	10.00	5.00	3.00
148	Alvin Dark	10.00	5.00	3.00
149	"Dixie" Howell	10.00	5.00	3.00
150	"Duke" Snider	100.00	45.00	27.00
151	"Spook" Jacobs	10.00	5.00	3.00
152	Billy Hoeft	10.00	5.00	3.00
153	Frank Thomas	10.00	5.00	3.00
154	Dave Pope	10.00	5.00	3.00
155	Harvey Kuenn	9.00	4.50	2.75
156	Wes Westrum	8.00	4.00	2.50
157	Dick Brodowski	10.00	5.00	3.00
158	Wally Post	10.00	5.00	3.00
159	Clint Courtney	10.00	5.00	3.00
160	Billy Pierce	9.00	4.50	2.75
161	Joe DeMaestri	10.00	5.00	3.00
162	"Gus" Bell	8.00	4.00	2.50
163	Gene Woodling	8.00	4.00	2.50
164	Harmon Killebrew	100.00	50.00	30.00
165	"Red" Schoendienst	25.00	12.50	7.50
166	Dodgers Team	200.00	100.00	60.00
167	Harry Dorish	10.00	5.00	3.00
168	Sammy White	10.00	5.00	3.00
169	Bob Nelson	10.00	5.00	3.00
170	Bill Virdon	9.00	4.50	2.75
171	Jim Wilson	10.00	5.00	3.00
172	*Frank Torre*	8.00	4.00	2.50
173	Johnny Podres	15.00	7.50	4.50
174	Glen Gorbous	10.00	5.00	3.00
175	Del Crandall	9.00	4.50	2.75
176	Alex Kellner	10.00	5.00	3.00
177	Hank Bauer	15.00	7.50	4.50
178	Joe Black	8.00	4.00	2.50
179	Harry Chiti	10.00	5.00	3.00
180	Robin Roberts	25.00	12.50	7.50
181	Billy Martin	70.00	35.00	21.00
182	Paul Minner	15.00	7.50	4.50
183	Stan Lopata	15.00	7.50	4.50
184	Don Bessent	15.00	7.50	4.50
185	Bill Bruton	15.00	7.50	4.50
186	Ron Jackson	15.00	7.50	4.50
187	Early Wynn	30.00	15.00	9.00
188	White Sox Team	15.00	7.50	4.50
189	Ned Garver	15.00	7.50	4.50
190	Carl Furillo	18.00	9.00	5.50
191	Frank Lary	15.00	7.50	4.50
192	"Smoky" Burgess	15.00	7.50	4.50
193	Wilmer Mizell	15.00	7.50	4.50
194	Monte Irvin	30.00	15.00	9.00
195	George Kell	30.00	15.00	9.00
196	Tom Poholsky	15.00	7.50	4.50
197	Granny Hamner	15.00	7.50	4.50
198	Ed Fitzgerald (Fitz Gerald)	15.00	7.50	4.50
199	Hank Thompson	15.00	7.50	4.50
200	Bob Feller	90.00	45.00	27.00
201	"Rip" Repulski	15.00	7.50	4.50
202	Jim Hearn	15.00	7.50	4.50
203	Bill Tuttle	15.00	7.50	4.50
204	Art Swanson	15.00	7.50	4.50
205	"Whitey" Lockman	15.00	7.50	4.50
206	Erv Palica	15.00	7.50	4.50
207	Jim Small	15.00	7.50	4.50
208	Elston Howard	25.00	12.50	7.50
209	Max Surkont	15.00	7.50	4.50
210	Mike Garcia	15.00	7.50	4.50
211	Murry Dickson	15.00	7.50	4.50
212	Johnny Temple	15.00	7.50	4.50
213	Tigers Team	18.00	9.00	5.00
214	Bob Rush	15.00	7.50	4.50
215	Tommy Byrne	15.00	7.50	4.50
216	Jerry Schoonmaker	15.00	7.50	4.50
217	Billy Klaus	15.00	7.50	4.50
218	Joe Nuxall (Nuxhall)	15.00	7.50	4.50
219	Lew Burdette	15.00	7.50	4.50
220	Del Ennis	15.00	7.50	4.50
221	Bob Friend	15.00	7.50	4.50
222	Dave Philley	15.00	7.50	4.50
223	Randy Jackson	15.00	7.50	4.50
224	"Bud" Podbielan	15.00	7.50	4.50
225	Gil McDougald	20.00	10.00	6.00
226	Giants Team	50.00	30.00	15.00
227	Russ Meyer	15.00	7.50	4.50
228	"Mickey" Vernon	15.00	7.50	4.50
229	Harry Brecheen	15.00	7.50	4.50
230	"Chico" Carrasquel	15.00	7.50	4.50
231	Bob Hale	15.00	7.50	4.50
232	"Toby" Atwell	15.00	7.50	4.50
233	Carl Erskine	20.00	10.00	6.00
234	"Pete" Runnels	15.00	7.50	4.50
235	Don Newcombe	18.00	9.00	5.50
236	Athletics Team	15.00	7.50	4.50
237	Jose Valdivielso	15.00	7.50	4.50
238	Walt Dropo	15.00	7.50	4.50
239	Harry Simpson	15.00	7.50	4.50
240	"Whitey" Ford	90.00	45.00	27.00
241	Don Mueller	15.00	7.50	4.50
242	Hershell Freeman	15.00	7.50	4.50
243	Sherm Lollar	15.00	7.50	4.50
244	Bob Buhl	15.00	7.50	4.50
245	Billy Goodman	15.00	7.50	4.50
246	Tom Gorman	15.00	7.50	4.50
247	Bill Sarni	15.00	7.50	4.50
248	Bob Porterfield	15.00	7.50	4.50
249	Johnny Klippstein	15.00	7.50	4.50
250	Larry Doby	15.00	7.50	4.50
251	Yankees Team	225.00	112.00	67.00
252	Vernon Law	15.00	7.50	4.50
253	Irv Noren	15.00	7.50	4.50
254	George Crowe	15.00	7.50	4.50
255	Bob Lemon	25.00	12.50	7.50
256	Tom Hurd	15.00	7.50	4.50
257	Bobby Thomson	15.00	7.50	4.50
258	Art Ditmar	15.00	7.50	4.50
259	Sam Jones	15.00	7.50	4.50
260	"Pee Wee" Reese	90.00	45.00	27.00
261	Bobby Shantz	8.00	4.00	2.50
262	Howie Pollet	6.00	3.00	1.75
263	Bob Miller	6.00	3.00	1.75
264	Ray Monzant	6.00	3.00	1.75
265	Sandy Consuegra	6.00	3.00	1.75
266	Don Ferrarese	6.00	3.00	1.75
267	Bob Nieman	10.00	5.00	3.00
268	Dale Mitchell	6.00	3.00	1.75
269	Jack Meyer	6.00	3.00	1.75
270	Billy Loes	8.00	4.00	2.50
271	Foster Castleman	6.00	3.00	1.75
272	Danny O'Connell	6.00	3.00	1.75
273	Walker Cooper	6.00	3.00	1.75
274	Frank Baumholtz	6.00	3.00	1.75
275	Jim Greengrass	6.00	3.00	1.75
276	George Zuverink	6.00	3.00	1.75
277	Daryl Spencer	6.00	3.00	1.75
278	Chet Nichols	6.00	3.00	1.75
279	Johnny Groth	6.00	3.00	1.75
280	Jim Gilliam	10.00	5.00	3.00
281	Art Houtteman	6.00	3.00	1.75
282	Warren Hacker	6.00	3.00	1.75
283	Hal Smith	6.00	3.00	1.75
284	Ike Delock	6.00	3.00	1.75
285	Eddie Miksis	6.00	3.00	1.75
286	Bill Wight	6.00	3.00	1.75

		NR MT	EX	VG
287	Bobby Adams	6.00	3.00	1.75
288	Bob Cerv	30.00	15.00	9.00
289	Hal Jeffcoat	6.00	3.00	1.75
290	Curt Simmons	10.00	5.00	3.00
291	Frank Kellert	6.00	3.00	1.75
292	*Luis Aparicio*	125.00	62.00	37.00
293	Stu Miller	6.00	3.00	1.75
294	Ernie Johnson	6.00	3.00	1.75
295	Clem Labine	8.00	4.00	2.50
296	Andy Seminick	6.00	3.00	1.75
297	Bob Skinner	10.00	5.00	3.00
298	Johnny Schmitz	6.00	3.00	1.75
299	Charley Neal	15.00	7.50	4.50
300	Vic Wertz	10.00	5.00	3.00
301	Marv Grissom	6.00	3.00	1.75
302	Eddie Robinson	9.00	4.50	2.75
303	Jim Dyck	6.00	3.00	1.75
304	Frank Malzone	10.00	5.00	3.00
305	Brooks Lawrence	6.00	3.00	1.75
306	Curt Roberts	6.00	3.00	1.75
307	Hoyt Wilhelm	35.00	17.50	10.50
308	"Chuck" Harmon	6.00	3.00	1.75
309	*Don Blasingame*	10.00	5.00	3.00
310	Steve Gromek	6.00	3.00	1.75
311	Hal Naragon	6.00	3.00	1.75
312	Andy Pafko	8.00	4.00	2.50
313	Gene Stephens	6.00	3.00	1.75
314	Hobie Landrith	6.00	3.00	1.75
315	Milt Bolling	6.00	3.00	1.75
316	Jerry Coleman	10.00	5.00	3.00
317	Al Aber	6.00	3.00	1.75
318	Fred Hatfield	6.00	3.00	1.75
319	Jack Crimian	6.00	3.00	1.75
320	Joe Adcock	8.00	4.00	2.50
321	Jim Konstanty	9.00	4.50	2.75
322	Karl Olson	6.00	3.00	1.75
323	Willard Schmidt	6.00	3.00	1.75
324	"Rocky" Bridges	6.00	3.00	1.75
325	Don Liddle	6.00	3.00	1.75
326	Connie Johnson	6.00	3.00	1.75
327	Bob Wiesler	6.00	3.00	1.75
328	Preston Ward	6.00	3.00	1.75
329	Lou Berberet	6.00	3.00	1.75
330	Jim Busby	6.00	3.00	1.75
331	Dick Hall	6.00	3.00	1.75
332	Don Larsen	25.00	12.50	7.50
333	Rube Walker	10.00	5.00	3.00
334	Bob Miller	6.00	3.00	1.75
335	Don Hoak	10.00	5.00	3.00
336	Ellis Kinder	6.00	3.00	1.75
337	Bobby Morgan	6.00	3.00	1.75
338	Jim Delsing	6.00	3.00	1.75
339	Rance Pless	6.00	3.00	1.75
340	Mickey McDermott	30.00	15.00	9.00
---	Checklist 1/3	225.00	90.00	56.00
---	Checklist 2/4	225.00	90.00	56.00

1956 Topps Hocus Focus Large

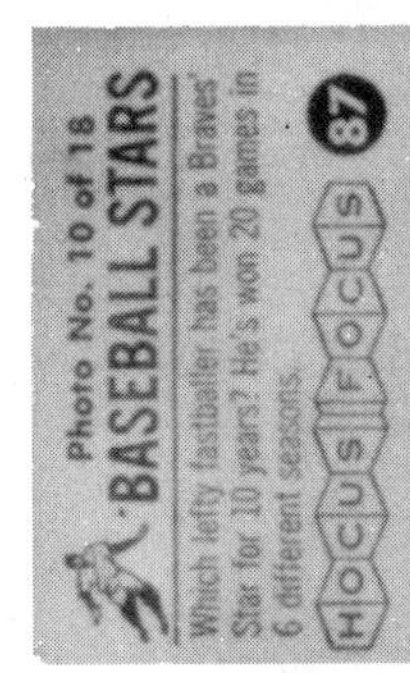

These sets are a direct descendant of the 1948 Topps Magic Photo" issue. Again, the baseball players were part of a larger overall series covering several topical areas. There are two distinct issues of Hocus Focus cards in 1956. The "large" cards, measuring 1" by 1-5/8," consists of 18 players. The "small" cards, 7/8 by 1-3/8," state on the back that they are a series of 23, though only 13 are known. Besides players on the cards themselves, the easiest way to distinguish Hocus Focus cards of 1956 from the Magic Photos series of 1948 is to remember that the 1956 cards actually have the words "Hocus Focus" on the back. The photos on these cards were developed by wetting the cards surface and exposing to light. Prices below are for cards with well- developed pictures. Cards with poorly developed photos are worth significantly less.

		NR MT	EX	VG
Complete Set:		525.00	262.00	157.00
Common Player:		10.00	5.00	3.00
1	Dick Groat	25.00	12.50	7.50
2	Ed Lopat	25.00	12.50	7.50
3	Hank Sauer	10.00	5.00	3.00
4	"Dusty" Rhodes	10.00	5.00	3.00
5	Ted Williams	125.00	62.00	37.00
6	Harvey Haddix	10.00	5.00	3.00
7	Ray Boone	10.00	5.00	3.00
8	Al Rosen	25.00	12.50	7.50
9	Mayo Smith	10.00	5.00	3.00
10	Warren Spahn	70.00	35.00	21.00
11	Jim Rivera	10.00	5.00	3.00
12	Ted Kluszewski	25.00	12.50	7.50
13	Gus Zernial	10.00	5.00	3.00
14	Jackie Robinson	100.00	50.00	30.00
15	Hal Smith	10.00	5.00	3.00
16	Johnny Schmitz	10.00	5.00	3.00
17	"Spook" Jacobs	10.00	5.00	3.00
18	Mel Parnell	10.00	5.00	3.00

1956 Topps Hocus Focus Small

		NR MT	EX	VG
Complete Set:		575.00	287.00	172.00
Common Player: 1-23		10.00	5.00	3.00
1	Babe Ruth	175.00	87.00	52.00
2	Unknown			
3	Dick Groat	15.00	7.50	4.50
4	Unknown			
5	Unknown			
6	"Dusty" Rhodes	10.00	5.00	3.00
7	Ted Williams	125.00	62.00	37.00
8	Harvey Haddix	10.00	5.00	3.00
9	Ray Boone	10.00	5.00	3.00
10	Unknown			
11	Unknown			
12	Warren Spahn	70.00	35.00	21.00
13	Jim Rivera	10.00	5.00	3.00
14	Ted Kluszewski	25.00	12.50	7.50
15	Gus Zernial	10.00	5.00	3.00
16	Unknown			
17	Unknown			
18	Johnny Schmitz	10.00	5.00	3.00
19	Unknown			
20	Karl Spooner	15.00	7.50	4.50
21	Ed Mathews	70.00	35.00	21.00
22	Unknown			
23	Unknown			

1956 Topps Pins

One of Topps first specialty issues, the 60-pin set of ballplayers issued in 1956 contains a high percentage of big-name stars which, combined with the scarcity of the pins, makes collecting a complete set extremely challenging. Compounding the situation is the fact that some pins are seen far less often than others, though the reason is unknown. Chuck Stobbs, Hector Lopez and Chuck Diering are unaccountably scarce. Measuring 1-1/8" in diameter, the pins utilize the same portraits found on 1956 Topps baseball cards. The photos are set against a solid color background.

		NR MT	EX	VG
Complete Set:		2500.	1250.	750.00
Common Player:		15.00	7.50	4.50
(1)	Hank Aaron	90.00	45.00	27.00
(2)	Sandy Amoros	15.00	7.50	4.50
(3)	Luis Arroyo	15.00	7.50	4.50
(4)	Ernie Banks	50.00	25.00	15.00
(5)	Yogi Berra	70.00	35.00	21.00
(6)	Joe Black	15.00	7.50	4.50
(7)	Ray Boone	15.00	7.50	4.50
(8)	Ken Boyer	20.00	10.00	6.00
(9)	Joe Collins	15.00	7.50	4.50
(10)	Gene Conley	15.00	7.50	4.50
(11)	Chuck Diering	225.00	112.00	67.00
(12)	Dick Donovan	15.00	7.50	4.50
(13)	Jim Finigan	15.00	7.50	4.50
(14)	Art Fowler	15.00	7.50	4.50
(15)	Ruben Gomez	15.00	7.50	4.50
(16)	Dick Groat	20.00	10.00	6.00
(17)	Harvey Haddix	15.00	7.50	4.50
(18)	Jack Harshman	15.00	7.50	4.50
(19)	Grady Hatton	15.00	7.50	4.50
(20)	Jim Hegan	15.00	7.50	4.50
(21)	Gil Hodges	40.00	20.00	12.00
(22)	Bobby Hofman	15.00	7.50	4.50
(23)	Frank House	15.00	7.50	4.50
(24)	Jackie Jensen	20.00	10.00	6.00
(25)	Al Kaline	60.00	30.00	18.00
(26)	Bob Kennedy	15.00	7.50	4.50
(27)	Ted Kluszewski	25.00	12.50	7.50
(28)	Dale Long	15.00	7.50	4.50
(29)	Hector Lopez	200.00	100.00	60.00
(30)	Ed Mathews	40.00	20.00	12.00
(31)	Willie Mays	90.00	45.00	27.00
(32)	Roy McMillan	15.00	7.50	4.50
(33)	Willie Miranda	15.00	7.50	4.50
(34)	Wally Moon	15.00	7.50	4.50
(35)	Don Mossi	15.00	7.50	4.50
(36)	Ron Negray	15.00	7.50	4.50
(37)	Johnny O'Brien	15.00	7.50	4.50
(38)	Carlos Paula	15.00	7.50	4.50
(39)	Vic Power	15.00	7.50	4.50
(40)	Jim Rivera	15.00	7.50	4.50
(41)	Phil Rizzuto	40.00	20.00	12.00
(42)	Jackie Robinson	90.00	45.00	27.00
(43)	Al Rosen	25.00	12.50	7.50
(44)	Hank Sauer	15.00	7.50	4.50
(45)	Roy Sievers	15.00	7.50	4.50
(46)	Bill Skowron	20.00	10.00	6.00
(47)	Al Smith	15.00	7.50	4.50
(48)	Hal Smith	15.00	7.50	4.50
(49)	Mayo Smith	15.00	7.50	4.50
(50)	Duke Snider	70.00	35.00	21.00
(51)	Warren Spahn	50.00	25.00	15.00
(52)	Karl Spooner	15.00	7.50	4.50
(53)	Chuck Stobbs	175.00	87.00	52.00
(54)	Frank Sullivan	15.00	7.50	4.50
(55)	Bill Tremel	15.00	7.50	4.50
(56)	Gus Triandos	15.00	7.50	4.50
(57)	Bob Turley	20.00	10.00	6.00
(58)	Herman Wehmeier	15.00	7.50	4.50
(59)	Ted Williams	110.00	55.00	33.00
(60)	Gus Zernial	15.00	7.50	4.50

1957 Topps

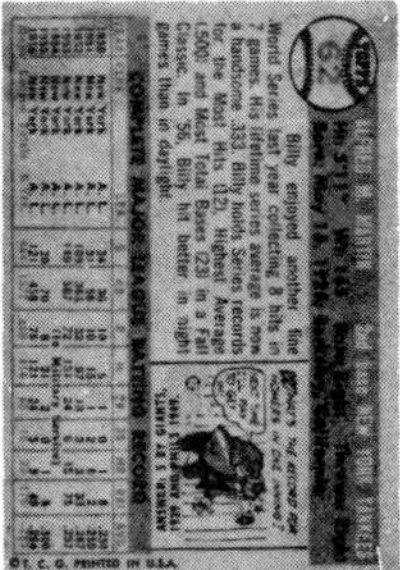

For 1957, Topps reduced the size of its cards to the now-standard 2-1/2" by 3-1/2." Set size was increased to 407 cards. Another change came in the form of the use of real color photographs as opposed to the hand-colored black and whites of previous years. For the first time since 1954, there were also cards with more than one player. The two, "Dodger Sluggers" and "Yankees' Power Hitters" began a trend toward the increased use of mulitple-player cards. Another first-time innovation, found on the backs, is complete players statistics. The scarce cards in the set are not the highest numbers, but rather numbers 265-352. Four unnumbered checklist cards were issued along with the set. They are quite expensive and are not included in the complete set prices quoted below.

		NR MT	EX	VG
Complete Set:		7000.	3500.	2000.
Common Player: 1-264		5.00	2.50	1.50
Common Player: 265-352		15.00	7.50	4.50
Common Player: 353-407		5.00	2.50	1.50
1	Ted Williams	425.00	100.00	38.00
2	Yogi Berra	150.00	70.00	45.00
3	Dale Long	5.00	2.50	1.50
4	Johnny Logan	5.00	2.50	1.50
5	Sal Maglie	8.00	4.00	2.50
6	Hector Lopez	5.00	2.50	1.50
7	Luis Aparicio	30.00	15.00	9.00
8	Don Mossi	5.00	2.50	1.50
9	Johnny Temple	5.00	2.50	1.50
10	Willie Mays	200.00	80.00	50.00
11	George Zuverink	5.00	2.50	1.50
12	Dick Groat	6.00	3.00	1.75
13	Wally Burnette	5.00	2.50	1.50
14	Bob Nieman	5.00	2.50	1.50
15	Robin Roberts	20.00	10.00	6.00
16	Walt Moryn	5.00	2.50	1.50
17	Billy Gardner	5.00	2.50	1.50
18	*Don Drysdale*	200.00	80.00	50.00
19	Bob Wilson	5.00	2.50	1.50
20	Hank Aaron (photo reversed)	225.00	125.00	70.00
21	Frank Sullivan	5.00	2.50	1.50
22	Jerry Snyder (photo actually Ed Fitz Gerald)	5.00	2.50	1.50
23	Sherm Lollar	5.00	2.50	1.50
24	*Bill Mazeroski*	30.00	15.00	9.00
25	Whitey Ford	45.00	22.00	13.50
26	Bob Boyd	5.00	2.50	1.50
27	Ted Kazanski	5.00	2.50	1.50
28	Gene Conley	5.00	2.50	1.50
29	*Whitey Herzog*	25.00	12.50	7.50
30	Pee Wee Reese	50.00	30.00	15.00
31	Ron Northey	5.00	2.50	1.50
32	Hersh Freeman	5.00	2.50	1.50
33	Jim Small	5.00	2.50	1.50
34	Tom Sturdivant	6.00	3.00	1.75
35	*Frank Robinson*	300.00	150.00	90.00
36	Bob Grim	6.00	3.00	1.75
37	Frank Torre	5.00	2.50	1.50
38	Nellie Fox	12.00	6.00	3.50

		NR MT	EX	VG
39	Al Worthington	5.00	2.50	1.50
40	Early Wynn	18.00	9.00	5.50
41	Hal Smith	5.00	2.50	1.50
42	Dee Fondy	5.00	2.50	1.50
43	Connie Johnson	5.00	2.50	1.50
44	Joe DeMaestri	5.00	2.50	1.50
45	Carl Furillo	9.00	4.50	2.75
46	Bob Miller	5.00	2.50	1.50
47	Don Blasingame	5.00	2.50	1.50
48	Bill Bruton	5.00	2.50	1.50
49	Daryl Spencer	5.00	2.50	1.50
50	Herb Score	6.00	3.00	1.75
51	Clint Courtney	5.00	2.50	1.50
52	Lee Walls	5.00	2.50	1.50
53	Clem Labine	6.00	3.00	1.75
54	Elmer Valo	5.00	2.50	1.50
55	Ernie Banks	70.00	35.00	21.00
56	Dave Sisler	5.00	2.50	1.50
57	Jim Lemon	5.00	2.50	1.50
58	Ruben Gomez	5.00	2.50	1.50
59	Dick Williams	6.00	3.00	1.75
60	Billy Hoeft	5.00	2.50	1.50
61	Dusty Rhodes	5.00	2.50	1.50
62	Billy Martin	40.00	20.00	12.00
63	Ike Delock	5.00	2.50	1.50
64	Pete Runnels	6.00	3.00	1.75
65	Wally Moon	5.00	2.50	1.50
66	Brooks Lawrence	5.00	2.50	1.50
67	Chico Carrasquel	5.00	2.50	1.50
68	Ray Crone	5.00	2.50	1.50
69	Roy McMillan	5.00	2.50	1.50
70	Richie Ashburn	15.00	7.50	4.50
71	Murry Dickson	5.00	2.50	1.50
72	Bill Tuttle	5.00	2.50	1.50
73	George Crowe	5.00	2.50	1.50
74	Vito Valentinetti	5.00	2.50	1.50
75	Jim Piersall	6.00	3.00	1.75
76	Bob Clemente	200.00	80.00	50.00
77	Paul Foytack	5.00	2.50	1.50
78	Vic Wertz	6.00	3.00	1.75
79	*Lindy McDaniel*	6.00	3.00	1.75
80	Gil Hodges	50.00	30.00	15.00
81	Herm Wehmeier	5.00	2.50	1.50
82	Elston Howard	10.00	5.00	3.00
83	Lou Skizas	5.00	2.50	1.50
84	Moe Drabowsky	5.00	2.50	1.50
85	Larry Doby	8.00	4.00	2.50
86	Bill Sarni	5.00	2.50	1.50
87	Tom Gorman	5.00	2.50	1.50
88	Harvey Kuenn	6.00	3.00	1.75
89	Roy Sievers	5.00	2.50	1.50
90	Warren Spahn	50.00	30.00	15.00
91	Mack Burk	5.00	2.50	1.50
92	Mickey Vernon	6.00	3.00	1.75
93	Hal Jeffcoat	5.00	2.50	1.50
94	Bobby Del Greco	5.00	2.50	1.50
95	Mickey Mantle	650.00	250.00	175.00
96	*Hank Aguirre*	6.00	3.00	1.75
97	Yankees Team	30.00	15.00	9.00
98	Al Dark	8.00	4.00	2.50
99	Bob Keegan	5.00	2.50	1.50
100	League Presidents (Warren Giles, William Harridge)	6.00	3.00	1.75
101	Chuck Stobbs	5.00	2.50	1.50
102	Ray Boone	5.00	2.50	1.50
103	Joe Nuxhall	6.00	3.00	1.75
104	Hank Foiles	5.00	2.50	1.50
105	Johnny Antonelli	5.00	2.50	1.50
106	Ray Moore	5.00	2.50	1.50
107	Jim Rivera	5.00	2.50	1.50
108	Tommy Byrne	6.00	3.00	1.75
109	Hank Thompson	5.00	2.50	1.50
110	Bill Virdon	6.00	3.00	1.75
111	Hal Smith	5.00	2.50	1.50
112	Tom Brewer	5.00	2.50	1.50
113	Wilmer Mizell	5.00	2.50	1.50
114	Braves Team	10.00	5.00	3.00
115	Jim Gilliam	8.00	4.00	2.50
116	Mike Fornieles	5.00	2.50	1.50
117	Joe Adcock	6.00	3.00	1.75
118	Bob Porterfield	5.00	2.50	1.50
119	Stan Lopata	5.00	2.50	1.50
120	Bob Lemon	18.00	9.00	5.50
121	*Cletis Boyer*	10.00	5.00	3.00
122	Ken Boyer	8.00	4.00	2.50
123	Steve Ridzik	5.00	2.50	1.50
124	Dave Philley	5.00	2.50	1.50
125	Al Kaline	60.00	30.00	18.00
126	Bob Wiesler	5.00	2.50	1.50
127	Bob Buhl	5.00	2.50	1.50
128	Ed Bailey	5.00	2.50	1.50
129	Saul Rogovin	5.00	2.50	1.50
130	Don Newcombe	10.00	5.00	3.00
131	Milt Bolling	5.00	2.50	1.50
132	Art Ditmar	6.00	3.00	1.75
133	Del Crandall	6.00	3.00	1.75
134	Don Kaiser	5.00	2.50	1.50
135	Bill Skowron	12.00	6.00	3.50
136	Jim Hegan	5.00	2.50	1.50
137	Bob Rush	5.00	2.50	1.50
138	Minnie Minoso	8.00	4.00	2.50
139	Lou Kretlow	5.00	2.50	1.50
140	Frank Thomas	5.00	2.50	1.50
141	Al Aber	5.00	2.50	1.50
142	Charley Thompson	5.00	2.50	1.50
143	Andy Pafko	6.00	3.00	1.75
144	Ray Narleski	5.00	2.50	1.50
145	Al Smith	5.00	2.50	1.50
146	Don Ferrarese	5.00	2.50	1.50
147	Al Walker	6.00	3.00	1.75
148	Don Mueller	5.00	2.50	1.50
149	Bob Kennedy	5.00	2.50	1.50
150	Bob Friend	6.00	3.00	1.75
151	Willie Miranda	5.00	2.50	1.50
152	Jack Harshman	5.00	2.50	1.50
153	Karl Olson	5.00	2.50	1.50
154	Red Schoendienst	20.00	10.00	6.00
155	Jim Brosnan	5.00	2.50	1.50
156	Gus Triandos	5.00	2.50	1.50
157	Wally Post	5.00	2.50	1.50
158	Curt Simmons	6.00	3.00	1.75
159	Solly Drake	5.00	2.50	1.50
160	Billy Pierce	6.00	3.00	1.75
161	Pirates Team	8.00	4.00	2.50
162	Jack Meyer	5.00	2.50	1.50
163	Sammy White	5.00	2.50	1.50
164	Tommy Carroll	6.00	3.00	1.75
165	Ted Kluszewski	18.00	9.00	5.50
166	Roy Face	6.00	3.00	1.75
167	Vic Power	5.00	2.50	1.50
168	Frank Lary	6.00	3.00	1.75
169	Herb Plews	5.00	2.50	1.50
170	Duke Snider	85.00	42.00	25.00
171	Red Sox Team	9.00	4.50	2.75
172	Gene Woodling	6.00	3.00	1.75
173	Roger Craig	8.00	4.00	2.50
174	Willie Jones	5.00	2.50	1.50
175	Don Larsen	8.00	4.00	2.50
176	Gene Baker	5.00	2.50	1.50
177	Eddie Yost	5.00	2.50	1.50
178	Don Bessent	5.00	2.50	1.50
179	Ernie Oravetz	5.00	2.50	1.50
180	Gus Bell	5.00	2.50	1.50
181	Dick Donovan	5.00	2.50	1.50
182	Hobie Landrith	5.00	2.50	1.50
183	Cubs Team	8.00	4.00	2.50
184	*Tito Francona*	6.00	3.00	1.75
185	Johnny Kucks	6.00	3.00	1.75
186	Jim King	5.00	2.50	1.50
187	Virgil Trucks	5.00	2.50	1.50
188	Felix Mantilla	5.00	2.50	1.50
189	Willard Nixon	5.00	2.50	1.50
190	Randy Jackson	5.00	2.50	1.50
191	Joe Margoneri	5.00	2.50	1.50
192	Jerry Coleman	6.00	3.00	1.75
193	Del Rice	5.00	2.50	1.50
194	Hal Brown	5.00	2.50	1.50
195	Bobby Avila	5.00	2.50	1.50
196	Larry Jackson	5.00	2.50	1.50
197	Hank Sauer	5.00	2.50	1.50
198	Tigers Team	9.00	4.50	2.75
199	Vernon Law	6.00	3.00	1.75
200	Gil McDougald	12.00	6.00	3.50
201	Sandy Amoros	5.00	2.50	1.50
202	Dick Gernert	5.00	2.50	1.50
203	Hoyt Wilhelm	18.00	9.00	5.50
204	Athletics Team	8.00	4.00	2.50
205	Charley Maxwell	5.00	2.50	1.50
206	Willard Schmidt	5.00	2.50	1.50
207	Billy Hunter	5.00	2.50	1.50
208	Lew Burdette	6.00	3.00	1.75
209	Bob Skinner	5.00	2.50	1.50
210	Roy Campanella	80.00	40.00	24.00
211	Camilo Pascual	5.00	2.50	1.50
212	*Rocco Colavito*	50.00	25.00	15.00
213	Les Moss	5.00	2.50	1.50
214	Phillies Team	8.00	4.00	2.50
215	Enos Slaughter	20.00	10.00	6.00
216	Marv Grissom	5.00	2.50	1.50
217	Gene Stephens	5.00	2.50	1.50
218	Ray Jablonski	5.00	2.50	1.50
219	Tom Acker	5.00	2.50	1.50
220	Jackie Jensen	6.00	3.00	1.75
221	Dixie Howell	5.00	2.50	1.50
222	Alex Grammas	5.00	2.50	1.50
223	Frank House	5.00	2.50	1.50
224	Marv Blaylock	5.00	2.50	1.50
225	Harry Simpson	5.00	2.50	1.50
226	Preston Ward	5.00	2.50	1.50
227	Jerry Staley	5.00	2.50	1.50
228	Smoky Burgess	6.00	3.00	1.75
229	George Susce	5.00	2.50	1.50
230	George Kell	18.00	9.00	5.50
231	Solly Hemus	5.00	2.50	1.50
232	Whitey Lockman	5.00	2.50	1.50
233	Art Fowler	5.00	2.50	1.50
234	Dick Cole	5.00	2.50	1.50
235	Tom Poholsky	5.00	2.50	1.50
236	Joe Ginsberg	5.00	2.50	1.50
237	Foster Castleman	5.00	2.50	1.50
238	Eddie Robinson	5.00	2.50	1.50
239	Tom Morgan	5.00	2.50	1.50
240	Hank Bauer	10.00	5.00	3.00
241	Joe Lonnett	5.00	2.50	1.50
242	Charley Neal	5.00	2.50	1.50
243	Cardinals Team	8.00	4.00	2.50
244	Billy Loes	5.00	2.50	1.50
245	Rip Repulski	5.00	2.50	1.50
246	Jose Valdivielso	5.00	2.50	1.50
247	Turk Lown	5.00	2.50	1.50
248	Jim Finigan	5.00	2.50	1.50
249	Dave Pope	5.00	2.50	1.50
250	Ed Mathews	30.00	15.00	9.00
251	Orioles Team	8.00	4.00	2.50
252	Carl Erskine	10.00	5.00	3.00
253	Gus Zernial	5.00	2.50	1.50
254	Ron Negray	5.00	2.50	1.50
255	Charlie Silvera	5.00	2.50	1.50
256	Ronnie Kline	5.00	2.50	1.50
257	Walt Dropo	5.00	2.50	1.50
258	Steve Gromek	5.00	2.50	1.50
259	Eddie O'Brien	5.00	2.50	1.50
260	Del Ennis	5.00	2.50	1.50
261	Bob Chakales	5.00	2.50	1.50
262	Bobby Thomson	6.00	3.00	1.75
263	George Strickland	5.00	2.50	1.50
264	Bob Turley	8.00	4.00	2.50
265	Harvey Haddix	20.00	10.00	6.00
266	Ken Kuhn	15.00	7.50	4.50
267	Danny Kravitz	15.00	7.50	4.50
268	Jackie Collum	15.00	7.50	4.50
269	Bob Cerv	15.00	7.50	4.50
270	Senators Team	25.00	12.50	7.50
271	Danny O'Connell	15.00	7.50	4.50
272	Bobby Shantz	25.00	12.50	7.50
273	Jim Davis	15.00	7.50	4.50
274	Don Hoak	18.00	9.00	5.50
275	Indians Team	25.00	12.50	7.50
276	Jim Pyburn	15.00	7.50	4.50
277	Johnny Podres	60.00	30.00	18.00
278	Fred Hatfield	15.00	7.50	4.50
279	Bob Thurman	15.00	7.50	4.50
280	Alex Kellner	15.00	7.50	4.50
281	Gail Harris	15.00	7.50	4.50
282	Jack Dittmer	15.00	7.50	4.50
283	*Wes Covington*	18.00	9.00	5.50
284	Don Zimmer	20.00	10.00	6.00
285	Ned Garver	15.00	7.50	4.50
286	*Bobby Richardson*	100.00	50.00	30.00
287	Sam Jones	15.00	7.50	4.50
288	Ted Lepcio	15.00	7.50	4.50
289	Jim Bolger	15.00	7.50	4.50
290	Andy Carey	18.00	9.00	5.50
291	Windy McCall	15.00	7.50	4.50
292	Billy Klaus	15.00	7.50	4.50
293	Ted Abernathy	15.00	7.50	4.50
294	Rocky Bridges	15.00	7.50	4.50
295	Joe Collins	18.00	9.00	5.50
296	Johnny Klippstein	15.00	7.50	4.50
297	Jack Crimian	15.00	7.50	4.50
298	Irv Noren	15.00	7.50	4.50
299	Chuck Harmon	15.00	7.50	4.50
300	Mike Garcia	18.00	9.00	5.50
301	Sam Esposito	15.00	7.50	4.50
302	Sandy Koufax	400.00	200.00	120.00
303	Billy Goodman	15.00	7.50	4.50
304	Joe Cunningham	18.00	9.00	5.50
305	Chico Fernandez	15.00	7.50	4.50
306	Darrell Johnson	18.00	9.00	5.50
307	Jack Phillips	15.00	7.50	4.50
308	Dick Hall	15.00	7.50	4.50
309	Jim Busby	15.00	7.50	4.50
310	Max Surkont	15.00	7.50	4.50
311	Al Pilarcik	15.00	7.50	4.50
312	*Tony Kubek*	125.00	62.00	37.00
313	Mel Parnell	18.00	9.00	5.50
314	Ed Bouchee	15.00	7.50	4.50
315	Lou Berberet	15.00	7.50	4.50
316	Billy O'Dell	15.00	7.50	4.50
317	Giants Team	40.00	20.00	12.00
318	Mickey McDermott	15.00	7.50	4.50
319	Gino Cimoli	18.00	9.00	5.50
320	Neil Chrisley	15.00	7.50	4.50
321	Red Murff	15.00	7.50	4.50
322	Redlegs Team	40.00	20.00	12.00
323	Wes Westrum	18.00	9.00	5.50
324	Dodgers Team	90.00	45.00	27.00
325	Frank Bolling	15.00	7.50	4.50
326	Pedro Ramos	15.00	7.50	4.50
327	Jim Pendleton	15.00	7.50	4.50
328	*Brooks Robinson*	350.00	175.00	105.00
329	White Sox Team	25.00	12.50	7.50
330	Jim Wilson	15.00	7.50	4.50
331	Ray Katt	15.00	7.50	4.50
332	Bob Bowman	15.00	7.50	4.50
333	Ernie Johnson	15.00	7.50	4.50
334	Jerry Schoonmaker	15.00	7.50	4.50
335	Granny Hamner	15.00	7.50	4.50
336	*Haywood Sullivan*	18.00	9.00	5.50
337	Rene Valdes	18.00	9.00	5.50
338	*Jim Bunning*	90.00	45.00	27.00
339	Bob Speake	15.00	7.50	4.50
340	Bill Wight	15.00	7.50	4.50
341	Don Gross	15.00	7.50	4.50
342	Gene Mauch	20.00	10.00	6.00
343	Taylor Phillips	15.00	7.50	4.50
344	Paul LaPalme	15.00	7.50	4.50
345	Paul Smith	15.00	7.50	4.50
346	Dick Littlefield	15.00	7.50	4.50
347	Hal Naragon	15.00	7.50	4.50
348	Jim Hearn	15.00	7.50	4.50
349	Nelson King	15.00	7.50	4.50
350	Eddie Miksis	15.00	7.50	4.50
351	Dave Hillman	15.00	7.50	4.50
352	Ellis Kinder	15.00	7.50	4.50
353	Cal Neeman	5.00	2.50	1.50
354	Rip Coleman	5.00	2.50	1.50
355	Frank Malzone	5.00	2.50	1.50
356	Faye Throneberry	5.00	2.50	1.50
357	Earl Torgeson	5.00	2.50	1.50
358	Jerry Lynch	5.00	2.50	1.50
359	Tom Cheney	5.00	2.50	1.50
360	Johnny Groth	5.00	2.50	1.50
361	Curt Barclay	5.00	2.50	1.50
362	Roman Mejias	5.00	2.50	1.50
363	Eddie Kasko	5.00	2.50	1.50
364	Cal McLish	5.00	2.50	1.50
365	Ossie Virgil	5.00	2.50	1.50
366	Ken Lehman	5.00	2.50	1.50
367	Ed Fitz Gerald	5.00	2.50	1.50
368	Bob Purkey	5.00	2.50	1.50
369	Milt Graff	5.00	2.50	1.50
370	Warren Hacker	5.00	2.50	1.50
371	Bob Lennon	5.00	2.50	1.50
372	Norm Zauchin	5.00	2.50	1.50
373	Pete Whisenant	5.00	2.50	1.50
374	Don Cardwell	5.00	2.50	1.50
375	*Jim Landis*	6.00	3.00	1.75
376	Don Elston	5.00	2.50	1.50
377	Andre Rodgers	5.00	2.50	1.50
378	Elmer Singleton	5.00	2.50	1.50
379	Don Lee	5.00	2.50	1.50
380	Walker Cooper	5.00	2.50	1.50
381	Dean Stone	5.00	2.50	1.50
382	Jim Brideweser	5.00	2.50	1.50
383	*Juan Pizarro*	6.00	3.00	1.75
384	Bobby Gene Smith	5.00	2.50	1.50
385	Art Houtteman	5.00	2.50	1.50
386	Lyle Luttrell	5.00	2.50	1.50
387	*Jack Sanford*	6.00	3.00	1.75
388	Pete Daley	5.00	2.50	1.50
389	Dave Jolly	5.00	2.50	1.50
390	Reno Bertoia	5.00	2.50	1.50
391	*Ralph Terry*	8.00	4.00	2.50
392	Chuck Tanner	6.00	3.00	1.75
393	Raul Sanchez	5.00	2.50	1.50
394	Luis Arroyo	5.00	2.50	1.50
395	Bubba Phillips	5.00	2.50	1.50
396	Casey Wise	5.00	2.50	1.50
397	Roy Smalley	5.00	2.50	1.50
398	Al Cicotte	6.00	3.00	1.75
399	Billy Consolo	5.00	2.50	1.50
400	Dodgers' Sluggers (Roy Campanella, Carl Furillo, Gil Hodges, Duke Snider)	150.00	60.00	38.00
401	*Earl Battey*	6.00	3.00	1.75
402	Jim Pisoni	5.00	2.50	1.50
403	Dick Hyde	5.00	2.50	1.50
404	Harry Anderson	5.00	2.50	1.50

		NR MT	EX	VG
405	Duke Maas	5.00	2.50	1.50
406	Bob Hale	5.00	2.50	1.50
407	Yankees' Power Hitters (Yogi Berra, Mickey Mantle)	350.00	140.00	88.00
---a	Checklist Series 1-2 (Big Blony ad on back)	125.00	56.00	35.00
---b	Checklist Series 1-2 (Bazooka ad on back)	125.00	56.00	35.00
---a	Checklist Series 2-3 (Big Blony ad on back)	175.00	70.00	44.00
---b	Checklist Series 2-3 (Bazooka ad on back)	175.00	70.00	44.00
---a	Checklist Series 3-4 (Big Blony ad on back)	350.00	140.00	88.00
---b	Checklist Series 3-4 (Bazooka ad on back)	350.00	140.00	88.00
---a	Checklist Series 4-5 (Big Blony ad on back)	450.00	225.00	135.00
---b	Checklist Series 4-5 (Bazooka ad on back)	450.00	225.00	135.00
---	Contest Card (Saturday, May 4th)	15.00	7.50	4.50
---	Contest Card (Saturday, May 25th)	15.00	7.50	4.50
---	Contest Card (Saturday, June 22nd)	15.00	7.50	4.50
---	Contest Card (Friday, July 19)	15.00	7.50	4.50
---	Lucky Penny Insert Card	15.00	7.50	4.50

1958 Topps

Topps continued to expand its set size in 1958 with the release of a 494-card set. One card (#145) was not issued after Ed Bouchee was suspended from baseball. Cards retained the 2-1/2" by 3-1/2" size. There are a number of variations, including yellow or white lettering on 33 cards between numbers 2-108 (higher priced yellow letter variations checklisted below are not included in the complete set prices). The number of multiple-player cards was increased. A major innovation is the addition of 20 "All-Star" cards. For the first time, checklists were incorporated into the numbered series, as the backs of team cards.

	NR MT	EX	VG
Complete Set:	4000.	2000.	1200.
Common Player: 1-110	5.00	2.50	1.50
Common Player: 111-440	2.50	1.25	.70
Common Player: 441-495	2.00	1.00	.60

		NR MT	EX	VG
1	Ted Williams	375.00	80.00	35.00
2a	Bob Lemon (yellow team letters)	35.00	17.50	10.50
2b	Bob Lemon (white team letters)	15.00	7.50	4.50
3	Alex Kellner	5.00	2.50	1.50
4	Hank Foiles	5.00	2.50	1.50
5	Willie Mays	150.00	75.00	45.00
6	George Zuverink	5.00	2.50	1.50
7	Dale Long	5.00	2.50	1.50
8a	Eddie Kasko (yellow name letters)	20.00	10.00	6.00
8b	Eddie Kasko (white name letters)	5.00	2.50	1.50
9	Hank Bauer	9.00	4.50	2.75
10	Lou Burdette	8.00	4.00	2.50
11a	Jim Rivera (yellow team letters)	20.00	10.00	6.00
11b	Jim Rivera (white team letters)	5.00	2.50	1.50
12	George Crowe	5.00	2.50	1.50
13a	Billy Hoeft (yellow name letters)	20.00	10.00	6.00
13b	Billy Hoeft (white name, orange triangle by foot)	6.00	3.00	1.75
13c	Billy Hoeft (white name, red triangle by foot)	5.00	2.50	1.50
14	Rip Repulski	5.00	2.50	1.50
15	Jim Lemon	5.00	2.50	1.50
16	Charley Neal	5.00	2.50	1.50
17	Felix Mantilla	5.00	2.50	1.50
18	Frank Sullivan	5.00	2.50	1.50
19	Giants Team/Checklist 1-88	10.00	5.00	3.00
20a	Gil McDougald (yellow name letters)	25.00	12.50	7.50
20b	Gil McDougald (white name letters)	9.00	4.50	2.75
21	Curt Barclay	5.00	2.50	1.50
22	Hal Naragon	5.00	2.50	1.50

		NR MT	EX	VG
23a	Bill Tuttle (yellow name letters)	20.00	10.00	6.00
23b	Bill Tuttle (white name letters)	5.00	2.50	1.50
24a	Hobie Landrith (yellow name letters)	20.00	10.00	6.00
24b	Hobie Landrith (white name letters)	5.00	2.50	1.50
25	Don Drysdale	40.00	20.00	12.00
26	Ron Jackson	5.00	2.50	1.50
27	Bud Freeman	5.00	2.50	1.50
28	Jim Busby	5.00	2.50	1.50
29	Ted Lepcio	5.00	2.50	1.50
30a	Hank Aaron (yellow name letters)	350.00	140.00	88.00
30b	Hank Aaron (white name letters)	150.00	60.00	38.00
31	Tex Clevenger	5.00	2.50	1.50
32a	J.W. Porter (yellow name letters)	20.00	10.00	6.00
32b	J.W. Porter (white name letters)	5.00	2.50	1.50
33a	Cal Neeman (yellow team letters)	20.00	10.00	6.00
33b	Cal Neeman (white team letters)	5.00	2.50	1.50
34	Bob Thurman	5.00	2.50	1.50
35a	Don Mossi (yellow team letters)	20.00	10.00	6.00
35b	Don Mossi (white team letters)	5.00	2.50	1.50
36	Ted Kazanski	5.00	2.50	1.50
37	*Mike McCormick* (photo actually Ray Monzant)	6.00	3.00	1.75
38	Dick Gernert	5.00	2.50	1.50
39	Bob Martyn	5.00	2.50	1.50
40	George Kell	12.00	6.00	3.50
41	Dave Hillman	5.00	2.50	1.50
42	*John Roseboro*	6.00	3.00	1.75
43	Sal Maglie	8.00	4.00	2.50
44	Senators Team/Checklist 1-88	10.00	5.00	3.00
45	Dick Groat	6.00	3.00	1.75
46a	Lou Sleater (yellow name letters)	20.00	10.00	6.00
46b	Lou Sleater (white name letters)	5.00	2.50	1.50
47	*Roger Maris*	300.00	110.00	70.00
48	Chuck Harmon	5.00	2.50	1.50
49	Smoky Burgess	6.00	3.00	1.75
50a	Billy Pierce (yellow team letters)	20.00	10.00	6.00
50b	Billy Pierce (white team letters)	6.00	3.00	1.75
51	Del Rice	5.00	2.50	1.50
52a	Bob Clemente (yellow team letters)	250.00	100.00	63.00
52b	Bob Clemente (white team letters)	125.00	62.00	37.00
53a	Morrie Martin (yellow name letters)	20.00	10.00	6.00
53b	Morrie Martin (white name letters)	5.00	2.50	1.50
54	*Norm Siebern*	7.00	3.50	2.00
55	Chico Carrasquel	5.00	2.50	1.50
56	Bill Fischer	5.00	2.50	1.50
57a	Tim Thompson (yellow name letters)	20.00	10.00	6.00
57b	Tim Thompson (white name letters)	5.00	2.50	1.50
58a	Art Schult (yellow team letters)	20.00	10.00	6.00
58b	Art Schult (white team letters)	5.00	2.50	1.50
59	Dave Sisler	5.00	2.50	1.50
60a	Del Ennis (yellow name letters)	20.00	10.00	6.00
60b	Del Ennis (white name letters)	5.00	2.50	1.50
61a	Darrell Johnson (yellow name letters)	20.00	10.00	6.00
61b	Darrell Johnson (white name letters)	6.00	3.00	1.75
62	Joe DeMaestri	5.00	2.50	1.50
63	Joe Nuxhall	6.00	3.00	1.75
64	Joe Lonnett	5.00	2.50	1.50
65a	Von McDaniel (yellow name letters)	20.00	10.00	6.00
65b	Von McDaniel (white name letters)	5.00	2.50	1.50
66	Lee Walls	5.00	2.50	1.50
67	Joe Ginsberg	5.00	2.50	1.50
68	Daryl Spencer	5.00	2.50	1.50
69	Wally Burnette	5.00	2.50	1.50
70a	Al Kaline (yellow name letters)	200.00	80.00	50.00
70b	Al Kaline (white name letters)	75.00	38.00	23.00
71	Dodgers Team/Checklist 1-88	18.00	9.00	5.50
72	Bud Byerly	5.00	2.50	1.50
73	Pete Daley	5.00	2.50	1.50
74	Roy Face	6.00	3.00	1.75
75	Gus Bell	5.00	2.50	1.50
76a	Dick Farrell (yellow team letters)	20.00	10.00	6.00
76b	Dick Farrell (white team letters)	5.00	2.50	1.50
77a	Don Zimmer (yellow team letters)	20.00	10.00	6.00
77b	Don Zimmer (white team letters)	6.00	3.00	1.75
78a	Ernie Johnson (yellow name letters)	20.00	10.00	6.00
78b	Ernie Johnson (white name letters)	5.00	2.50	1.50
79a	Dick Williams (yellow team letters)	20.00	10.00	6.00
79b	Dick Williams (white team letters)	6.00	3.00	1.75
80	Dick Drott	5.00	2.50	1.50
81a	*Steve Boros* (yellow team letters)	20.00	10.00	6.00

		NR MT	EX	VG
81b	*Steve Boros* (white team letters)	5.00	2.50	1.50
82	Ronnie Kline	5.00	2.50	1.50
83	Bob Hazle	5.00	2.50	1.50
84	Billy O'Dell	5.00	2.50	1.50
85a	Luis Aparicio (yellow team letters)	50.00	25.00	15.00
85b	Luis Aparicio (white team letters)	20.00	10.00	6.00
86	Valmy Thomas	5.00	2.50	1.50
87	Johnny Kucks	6.00	3.00	1.75
88	Duke Snider	60.00	30.00	18.00
89	Billy Klaus	5.00	2.50	1.50
90	Robin Roberts	15.00	7.50	4.50
91	Chuck Tanner	6.00	3.00	1.75
92a	Clint Courtney (yellow name letters)	20.00	10.00	6.00
92b	Clint Courtney (white name letters)	5.00	2.50	1.50
93	Sandy Amoros	5.00	2.50	1.50
94	Bob Skinner	5.00	2.50	1.50
95	Frank Bolling	5.00	2.50	1.50
96	Joe Durham	5.00	2.50	1.50
97a	Larry Jackson (yellow name letters)	20.00	10.00	6.00
97b	Larry Jackson (white name letters)	5.00	2.50	1.50
98a	Billy Hunter (yellow name letters)	20.00	10.00	6.00
98b	Billy Hunter (white name letters)	5.00	2.50	1.50
99	Bobby Adams	5.00	2.50	1.50
100a	Early Wynn (yellow team letters)	30.00	15.00	9.00
100b	Early Wynn (white team letters)	15.00	7.50	4.50
101a	Bobby Richardson (yellow name letters)	30.00	15.00	9.00
101b	Bobby Richardson (white name letters)	10.00	5.00	3.00
102	George Strickland	5.00	2.50	1.50
103	Jerry Lynch	5.00	2.50	1.50
104	Jim Pendleton	5.00	2.50	1.50
105	Billy Gardner	5.00	2.50	1.50
106	Dick Schofield	5.00	2.50	1.50
107	Ossie Virgil	5.00	2.50	1.50
108a	Jim Landis (yellow team letters)	20.00	10.00	6.00
108b	Jim Landis (white team letters)	5.00	2.50	1.50
109	Herb Plews	5.00	2.50	1.50
110	Johnny Logan	5.00	2.50	1.50
111	Stu Miller	2.50	1.25	.70
112	Gus Zernial	2.75	1.50	.80
113	Jerry Walker	2.50	1.25	.70
114	Irv Noren	2.50	1.25	.70
115	Jim Bunning	10.00	5.00	3.00
116	Dave Philley	2.75	1.50	.80
117	Frank Torre	2.50	1.25	.70
118	Harvey Haddix	2.50	1.25	.70
119	Harry Chiti	2.50	1.25	.70
120	Johnny Podres	5.00	2.50	1.50
121	Eddie Miksis	2.50	1.25	.70
122	Walt Moryn	2.50	1.25	.70
123	Dick Tomanek	2.50	1.25	.70
124	Bobby Usher	2.50	1.25	.70
125	Al Dark	3.75	2.00	1.25
126	Stan Palys	2.50	1.25	.70
127	Tom Sturdivant	3.75	2.00	1.25
128	*Willie Kirkland*	2.75	1.50	.80
129	Jim Derrington	2.50	1.25	.70
130	Jackie Jensen	3.75	2.00	1.25
131	Bob Henrich	2.50	1.25	.70
132	Vernon Law	3.25	1.75	1.00
133	Russ Nixon	2.50	1.25	.70
134	Phillies Team/Checklist 89-176	8.00	4.00	2.50
135	Mike Drabowsky	2.50	1.25	.70
136	Jim Finingan	2.50	1.25	.70
137	Russ Kemmerer	2.50	1.25	.70
138	Earl Torgeson	2.50	1.25	.70
139	George Brunet	2.50	1.25	.70
140	Wes Covington	2.75	1.50	.80
141	Ken Lehman	2.50	1.25	.70
142	Enos Slaughter	18.00	9.00	5.50
143	Billy Muffett	2.50	1.25	.70
144	Bobby Morgan	2.50	1.25	.70
145	Not Issued			
146	Dick Gray	2.50	1.25	.70
147	*Don McMahon*	3.25	1.75	1.00
148	Billy Consolo	2.50	1.25	.70
149	Tom Acker	2.50	1.25	.70
150	Mickey Mantle	500.00	225.00	140.00
151	Buddy Pritchard	2.50	1.25	.70
152	Johnny Antonelli	3.25	1.75	1.00
153	Les Moss	2.50	1.25	.70
154	Harry Byrd	2.50	1.25	.70
155	Hector Lopez	2.50	1.25	.70
156	Dick Hyde	2.50	1.25	.70
157	Dee Fondy	2.50	1.25	.70
158	Indians Team/Checklist 177-264	7.00	3.50	2.00
159	Taylor Phillips	2.50	1.25	.70
160	Don Hoak	2.75	1.50	.80
161	Don Larsen	6.00	3.00	1.75
162	Gil Hodges	18.00	9.00	5.50
163	Jim Wilson	2.50	1.25	.70
164	Bob Taylor	2.50	1.25	.70
165	Bob Nieman	2.50	1.25	.70
166	Danny O'Connell	2.50	1.25	.70
167	Frank Baumann	2.50	1.25	.70
168	Joe Cunningham	2.75	1.50	.80
169	Ralph Terry	2.75	1.50	.80
170	Vic Wertz	3.25	1.75	1.00
171	Harry Anderson	2.50	1.25	.70
172	Don Gross	2.50	1.25	.70
173	Eddie Yost	2.75	1.50	.80
174	A's Team/Checklist 89-176	8.00	4.00	2.50
175	*Marv Throneberry*	8.00	4.00	2.50
176	Bob Buhl	2.75	1.50	.80
177	Al Smith	2.50	1.25	.70
178	Ted Kluszewski	5.00	2.50	1.50

#	Player	NR MT	EX	VG
179	Willy Miranda	2.50	1.25	.70
180	Lindy McDaniel	2.50	1.25	.70
181	Willie Jones	2.50	1.25	.70
182	Joe Caffie	2.50	1.25	.70
183	Dave Jolly	2.50	1.25	.70
184	Elvin Tappe	2.50	1.25	.70
185	Ray Boone	2.75	1.50	.80
186	Jack Meyer	2.50	1.25	.70
187	Sandy Koufax	125.00	62.00	40.00
188	Milt Bolling (photo actually Lou Berberet)	2.50	1.25	.70
189	George Susce	2.50	1.25	.70
190	Red Schoendienst	15.00	7.50	4.50
191	Art Ceccarelli	2.50	1.25	.70
192	Milt Graff	2.50	1.25	.70
193	*Jerry Lumpe*	5.00	2.50	1.50
194	Roger Craig	3.25	1.75	1.00
195	Whitey Lockman	2.50	1.25	.70
196	Mike Garcia	2.75	1.50	.80
197	Haywood Sullivan	2.75	1.50	.80
198	Bill Virdon	3.25	1.75	1.00
199	Don Blasingame	2.50	1.25	.70
200	Bob Keegan	2.50	1.25	.70
201	Jim Bolger	2.50	1.25	.70
202	*Woody Held*	3.25	1.75	1.00
203	Al Walker	2.50	1.25	.70
204	Leo Kiely	2.50	1.25	.70
205	Johnny Temple	2.50	1.25	.70
206	Bob Shaw	3.25	1.75	1.00
207	Solly Hemus	2.50	1.25	.70
208	Cal McLish	2.50	1.25	.70
209	Bob Anderson	2.50	1.25	.70
210	Wally Moon	2.75	1.50	.80
211	Pete Burnside	2.50	1.25	.70
212	Bubba Phillips	2.50	1.25	.70
213	Red Wilson	2.50	1.25	.70
214	Willard Schmidt	2.50	1.25	.70
215	Jim Gilliam	5.00	2.50	1.50
216	Cards Team/Checklist 177-264	7.00	3.50	2.00
217	Jack Harshman	2.50	1.25	.70
218	Dick Rand	2.50	1.25	.70
219	Camilo Pascual	2.75	1.50	.80
220	Tom Brewer	2.50	1.25	.70
221	Jerry Kindall	2.50	1.25	.70
222	Bud Daley	2.50	1.25	.70
223	Andy Pafko	3.25	1.75	1.00
224	Bob Grim	3.75	2.00	1.25
225	Billy Goodman	2.50	1.25	.70
226	Bob Smith (photo actually Bobby Gene Smith)	2.50	1.25	.70
227	Gene Stephens	2.50	1.25	.70
228	Duke Maas	2.50	1.25	.70
229	Frank Zupo	2.50	1.25	.70
230	Richie Ashburn	8.00	4.00	2.50
231	Lloyd Merritt	2.50	1.25	.70
232	Reno Bertoia	2.50	1.25	.70
233	Mickey Vernon	2.75	1.50	.80
234	Carl Sawatski	2.50	1.25	.70
235	Tom Gorman	2.50	1.25	.70
236	Ed Fitz Gerald	2.50	1.25	.70
237	Bill Wight	2.50	1.25	.70
238	Bill Mazeroski	7.00	3.50	2.00
239	Chuck Stobbs	2.50	1.25	.70
240	Moose Skowron	7.00	3.50	2.00
241	Dick Littlefield	2.50	1.25	.70
242	Johnny Klippstein	2.50	1.25	.70
243	Larry Raines	2.50	1.25	.70
244	*Don Demeter*	2.75	1.50	.80
245	*Frank Lary*	2.75	1.50	.80
246	Yankees Team/Checklist 177-264	30.00	15.00	9.00
247	Casey Wise	2.50	1.25	.70
248	Herm Wehmeier	2.50	1.25	.70
249	Ray Moore	2.50	1.25	.70
250	Roy Sievers	3.25	1.75	1.00
251	Warren Hacker	2.50	1.25	.70
252	Bob Trowbridge	2.50	1.25	.70
253	Don Mueller	2.50	1.25	.70
254	Alex Grammas	2.50	1.25	.70
255	Bob Turley	5.00	2.50	1.50
256	White Sox Team/Checklist 265-352	8.00	4.00	2.50
257	Hal Smith	2.50	1.25	.70
258	Carl Erskine	5.00	2.50	1.50
259	Al Pilarcik	2.50	1.25	.70
260	Frank Malzone	2.75	1.50	.80
261	Turk Lown	2.50	1.25	.70
262	Johnny Groth	2.50	1.25	.70
263	Eddie Bressoud	2.75	1.50	.80
264	Jack Sanford	2.75	1.50	.80
265	Pete Runnels	2.75	1.50	.80
266	Connie Johnson	2.50	1.25	.70
267	Sherm Lollar	2.75	1.50	.80
268	Granny Hamner	2.50	1.25	.70
269	Paul Smith	2.50	1.25	.70
270	Warren Spahn	35.00	17.50	10.50
271	Billy Martin	10.00	5.00	3.00
272	Ray Crone	2.50	1.25	.70
273	Hal Smith	2.50	1.25	.70
274	Rocky Bridges	2.50	1.25	.70
275	Elston Howard	8.00	4.00	2.50
276	Bobby Avila	2.50	1.25	.70
277	Virgil Trucks	2.75	1.50	.80
278	Mack Burk	2.50	1.25	.70
279	Bob Boyd	2.50	1.25	.70
280	Jim Piersall	3.25	1.75	1.00
281	Sam Taylor	2.50	1.25	.70
282	Paul Foytack	2.50	1.25	.70
283	Ray Shearer	2.50	1.25	.70
284	Ray Katt	2.50	1.25	.70
285	Frank Robinson	65.00	33.00	20.00
286	Gino Cimoli	2.50	1.25	.70
287	Sam Jones	2.50	1.25	.70
288	Harmon Killebrew	50.00	30.00	15.00
289	Series Hurling Rivals (Lou Burdette, Bobby Shantz)	4.00	2.00	1.25
290	Dick Donovan	2.50	1.25	.70
291	Don Landrum	2.50	1.25	.70
292	Ned Garver	2.50	1.25	.70
293	Gene Freese	2.50	1.25	.70
294	Hal Jeffcoat	2.50	1.25	.70
295	Minnie Minoso	4.00	2.00	1.25
296	*Ryne Duren*	8.00	4.00	2.50
297	Don Buddin	2.50	1.25	.70
298	Jim Hearn	2.50	1.25	.70
299	Harry Simpson	3.75	2.00	1.25
300	League Presidents (Warren Giles, William Harridge)	3.75	2.00	1.25
301	Randy Jackson	2.50	1.25	.70
302	Mike Baxes	2.50	1.25	.70
303	Neil Chrisley	2.50	1.25	.70
304	Tigers' Big Bats (Al Kaline, Harvey Kuenn)	8.00	4.00	2.50
305	Clem Labine	2.75	1.50	.80
306	Whammy Douglas	2.50	1.25	.70
307	Brooks Robinson	70.00	35.00	20.00
308	Paul Giel	2.50	1.25	.70
309	Gail Harris	2.50	1.25	.70
310	Ernie Banks	50.00	25.00	15.00
311	Bob Purkey	2.50	1.25	.70
312	Red Sox Team/Checklist 353-440	8.00	4.00	2.50
313	Bob Rush	2.50	1.25	.70
314	Dodgers' Boss & Power (Walter Alston, Duke Snider)	15.00	7.50	4.50
315	Bob Friend	3.25	1.75	1.00
316	Tito Francona	2.75	1.50	.80
317	*Albie Pearson*	3.25	1.75	1.00
318	Frank House	2.50	1.25	.70
319	Lou Skizas	2.50	1.25	.70
320	Whitey Ford	35.00	17.50	10.50
321	Sluggers Supreme (Ted Kluszewski, Ted Williams)	15.00	7.50	4.50
322	Harding Peterson	2.50	1.25	.70
323	Elmer Valo	2.50	1.25	.70
324	Hoyt Wilhelm	15.00	7.50	4.50
325	Joe Adcock	3.25	1.75	1.00
326	Bob Miller	2.50	1.25	.70
327	Cubs Team/Checklist 265-352	8.00	4.00	2.50
328	Ike Delock	2.50	1.25	.70
329	Bob Cerv	2.50	1.25	.70
330	Ed Bailey	2.50	1.25	.70
331	Pedro Ramos	2.50	1.25	.70
332	Jim King	2.50	1.25	.70
333	Andy Carey	3.75	2.00	1.25
334	Mound Aces (Bob Friend, Billy Pierce)	3.25	1.75	1.00
335	Ruben Gomez	2.50	1.25	.70
336	Bert Hamric	2.50	1.25	.70
337	Hank Aguirre	2.50	1.25	.70
338	Walt Dropo	2.75	1.50	.80
339	Fred Hatfield	2.50	1.25	.70
340	Don Newcombe	6.00	3.00	1.75
341	Pirates Team/Checklist 265-352	8.00	4.00	2.50
342	Jim Brosnan	2.75	1.50	.80
343	*Orlando Cepeda*	50.00	25.00	15.00
344	Bob Porterfield	2.50	1.25	.70
345	Jim Hegan	2.50	1.25	.70
346	Steve Bilko	2.50	1.25	.70
347	Don Rudolph	2.50	1.25	.70
348	Chico Fernandez	2.50	1.25	.70
349	Murry Dickson	2.50	1.25	.70
350	Ken Boyer	5.00	2.50	1.50
351	Braves' Fence Busters (Hank Aaron, Joe Adcock, Del Crandall, Ed Mathews)	20.00	10.00	6.00
352	Herb Score	3.75	2.00	1.25
353	Stan Lopata	2.50	1.25	.70
354	Art Ditmar	3.75	2.00	1.25
355	Bill Bruton	2.75	1.50	.80
356	Bob Malkmus	2.50	1.25	.70
357	Danny McDevitt	2.50	1.25	.70
358	Gene Baker	2.50	1.25	.70
359	Billy Loes	2.50	1.25	.70
360	Roy McMillan	2.50	1.25	.70
361	Mike Fornieles	2.50	1.25	.70
362	Ray Jablonski	2.50	1.25	.70
363	Don Elston	2.50	1.25	.70
364	Earl Battey	2.75	1.50	.80
365	Tom Morgan	2.50	1.25	.70
366	Gene Green	2.50	1.25	.70
367	Jack Urban	2.50	1.25	.70
368	Rocky Colavito	10.00	5.00	3.00
369	Ralph Lumenti	2.50	1.25	.70
370	Yogi Berra	80.00	40.00	25.00
371	Marty Keough	2.50	1.25	.70
372	Don Cardwell	2.50	1.25	.70
373	Joe Pignatano	2.50	1.25	.70
374	Brooks Lawrence	2.50	1.25	.70
375	Pee Wee Reese	50.00	30.00	15.00
376	Charley Rabe	2.50	1.25	.70
377a	Braves Team (alphabetical checklist on back)	9.00	4.50	2.75
377b	Braves Team (numerical checklist on back)	60.00	30.00	18.00
378	Hank Sauer	2.75	1.50	.80
379	Ray Herbert	2.50	1.25	.70
380	Charley Maxwell	2.50	1.25	.70
381	Hal Brown	2.50	1.25	.70
382	Al Cicotte	3.75	2.00	1.25
383	Lou Berberet	2.50	1.25	.70
384	John Goryl	2.50	1.25	.70
385	Wilmer Mizell	2.50	1.25	.70
386	Birdie's Young Sluggers (Ed Bailey, Frank Robinson, Birdie Tebbetts)	7.00	3.50	2.00
387	Wally Post	2.50	1.25	.70
388	Billy Moran	2.50	1.25	.70
389	Bill Taylor	2.50	1.25	.70
390	Del Crandall	3.25	1.75	1.00
391	Dave Melton	2.50	1.25	.70
392	Bennie Daniels	2.50	1.25	.70
393	Tony Kubek	12.00	6.00	3.50
394	*Jim Grant*	3.25	1.75	1.00
395	Willard Nixon	2.50	1.25	.70
396	Dutch Dotterer	2.50	1.25	.70
397a	Tigers Team (alphabetical checklist on back)	9.00	4.50	2.75
397b	Tigers Team (numerical checklist on back)	60.00	30.00	18.00
398	Gene Woodling	2.75	1.50	.80
399	Marv Grissom	2.50	1.25	.70
400	Nellie Fox	8.00	4.00	2.50
401	Don Bessent	2.50	1.25	.70
402	Bobby Gene Smith	2.50	1.25	.70
403	Steve Korcheck	2.50	1.25	.70
404	Curt Simmons	3.25	1.75	1.00
405	Ken Aspromonte	2.50	1.25	.70
406	Vic Power	2.50	1.25	.70
407	Carlton Willey	2.50	1.25	.70
408a	Orioles Team (alphabetical checklist on back)	8.00	4.00	2.50
408b	Orioles Team (numerical checklist on back)	60.00	30.00	18.00
409	Frank Thomas	2.50	1.25	.70
410	Murray Wall	2.50	1.25	.70
411	*Tony Taylor*	2.75	1.50	.80
412	Jerry Staley	2.50	1.25	.70
413	*Jim Davenport*	2.75	1.50	.80
414	Sammy White	2.50	1.25	.70
415	Bob Bowman	2.50	1.25	.70
416	Foster Castleman	2.50	1.25	.70
417	Carl Furillo	6.00	3.00	1.75
418	World Series Batting Foes (Hank Aaron, Mickey Mantle)	100.00	45.00	27.00
419	Bobby Shantz	4.50	2.25	1.25
420	*Vada Pinson*	15.00	7.50	4.50
421	Dixie Howell	2.50	1.25	.70
422	Norm Zauchin	2.50	1.25	.70
423	Phil Clark	2.50	1.25	.70
424	Larry Doby	4.00	2.00	1.25
425	Sam Esposito	2.50	1.25	.70
426	Johnny O'Brien	2.50	1.25	.70
427	Al Worthington	2.50	1.25	.70
428a	Redlegs Team (alphabetical checklist on back)	8.00	4.00	2.50
428b	Redlegs Team (numerical checklist on back)	50.00	25.00	15.00
429	Gus Triandos	2.75	1.50	.80
430	Bobby Thomson	3.25	1.75	1.00
431	Gene Conley	2.75	1.50	.80
432	John Powers	2.50	1.25	.70
433	Pancho Herrera	2.50	1.25	.70
434	Harvey Kuenn	3.25	1.75	1.00
435	Ed Roebuck	2.50	1.25	.70
436	Rival Fence Busters (Willie Mays, Duke Snider)	35.00	17.50	10.50
437	Bob Speake	2.50	1.25	.70
438	Whitey Herzog	3.75	2.00	1.25
439	Ray Narleski	2.50	1.25	.70
440	Ed Mathews	30.00	15.00	9.00
441	Jim Marshall	2.00	1.00	.60
442	Phil Paine	2.00	1.00	.60
443	Billy Harrell	4.50	2.25	1.25
444	Danny Kravitz	2.00	1.00	.60
445	Bob Smith	2.00	1.00	.60
446	Carroll Hardy	4.50	2.25	1.25
447	Ray Monzant	2.00	1.00	.60
448	*Charlie Lau*	2.75	1.50	.80
449	Gene Fodge	2.00	1.00	.60
450	Preston Ward	4.50	2.25	1.25
451	Joe Taylor	2.00	1.00	.60
452	Roman Mejias	2.00	1.00	.60
453	Tom Qualters	2.00	1.00	.60
454	Harry Hanebrink	2.00	1.00	.60
455	Hal Griggs	2.00	1.00	.60
456	Dick Brown	2.00	1.00	.60
457	*Milt Pappas*	2.75	1.50	.80
458	Julio Becquer	2.00	1.00	.60
459	Ron Blackburn	2.00	1.00	.60
460	Chuck Essegian	2.00	1.00	.60
461	Ed Mayer	2.00	1.00	.60
462	Gary Geiger	4.50	2.25	1.25
463	Vito Valentinetti	2.00	1.00	.60
464	*Curt Flood*	12.00	6.00	3.50
465	Arnie Portocarrero	2.00	1.00	.60
466	Pete Whisenant	2.00	1.00	.60
467	Glen Hobbie	2.00	1.00	.60
468	Bob Schmidt	2.00	1.00	.60
469	Don Ferrarese	2.00	1.00	.60
470	R.C. Stevens	2.00	1.00	.60
471	Lenny Green	2.00	1.00	.60
472	Joe Jay	2.00	1.00	.60
473	Bill Renna	2.00	1.00	.60
474	Roman Semproch	2.00	1.00	.60
475	All-Star Managers (Fred Haney, Casey Stengel)	15.00	7.50	4.50
476	Stan Musial AS	25.00	12.50	7.50
477	Bill Skowron AS	4.00	2.00	1.25
478	Johnny Temple AS	2.50	1.25	.70
479	Nellie Fox AS	5.00	2.50	1.50
480	Eddie Mathews AS	10.00	5.00	3.00
481	Frank Malzone AS	2.50	1.25	.70
482	Ernie Banks AS	15.00	7.50	4.50
483	Luis Aparicio AS	8.00	4.00	2.50
484	Frank Robinson AS	12.00	6.00	3.50
485	Ted Williams AS	40.00	20.00	12.00
486	Willie Mays AS	30.00	15.00	9.00
487	Mickey Mantle AS	60.00	30.00	18.00
488	Hank Aaron AS	25.00	12.50	7.50
489	Jackie Jensen AS	3.25	1.75	1.00
490	Ed Bailey AS	2.50	1.25	.70
491	Sherm Lollar AS	2.50	1.25	.70
492	Bob Friend AS	3.25	1.75	1.00
493	Bob Turley AS	3.75	2.00	1.25
494	Warren Spahn AS	15.00	7.50	4.50
495	Herb Score AS	6.00	2.00	1.00
---	Contest Card (All-Star Game, July 8)	15.00	7.50	4.50
---	Felt Emblems Insert Card	15.00	7.50	4.50

1959 Topps

These 2-1/2" by 3-1/2" cards have a round photograph at the center of the front with a solid-color background and white border. A facsimile autograph is found across the photo. The 572-card set marks the largest set issued to that time. Card numbers below 507 have red and green printing with the card number in white in a green box. On high number cards beginning with #507, the printing is black and red and the card

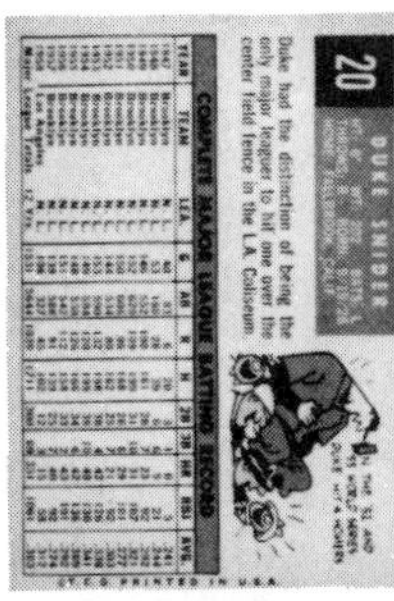

number is in a black box. Specialty cards include multiple-player cards, team cards with checklists, "All-Star" cards, highlights from previous season, and 31 "Rookie Stars." There is also a card of the commissioner, Ford Frick, and one Roy Campanella in a wheelchair. A handful of cards can be found with and without lines added to the biographies on back indicating trades or demotions; those without the added lines are considerably more rare and valuable and are not included in the complete set price. Card numbers 199-286 can be found with either white or grey backs, with the grey stock being the less common.

	NR MT	EX	VG
Complete Set:	4000.	2000.	1200.
Common Player: 1-110	4.00	2.00	1.25
Common Player: 111-506	2.50	1.25	.70
Common Player: 507-572	10.00	5.00	3.00

No.	Player	NR MT	EX	VG
1	Ford Frick	75.00	3.75	1.50
2	Eddie Yost	5.00	2.00	1.25
3	Don McMahon	4.00	2.00	1.25
4	Albie Pearson	4.00	2.00	1.25
5	Dick Donovan	4.00	2.00	1.25
6	Alex Grammas	4.00	2.00	1.25
7	Al Pilarcik	4.00	2.00	1.25
8	Phillies Team/Checklist 1-88	12.00	6.00	3.50
9	Paul Giel	4.00	2.00	1.25
10	Mickey Mantle	350.00	140.00	88.00
11	Billy Hunter	4.00	2.00	1.25
12	Vern Law	5.00	2.50	1.50
13	Dick Gernert	4.00	2.00	1.25
14	Pete Whisenant	4.00	2.00	1.25
15	Dick Drott	4.00	2.00	1.25
16	Joe Pignatano	4.00	2.00	1.25
17	Danny's All-Stars (Ted Kluszewski, Danny Murtaugh, Frank Thomas)	5.00	2.50	1.50
18	Jack Urban	4.00	2.00	1.25
19	Ed Bressoud	4.00	2.00	1.25
20	Duke Snider	50.00	25.00	15.00
21	Connie Johnson	4.00	2.00	1.25
22	Al Smith	4.00	2.00	1.25
23	Murry Dickson	5.00	2.50	1.50
24	Red Wilson	4.00	2.00	1.25
25	Don Hoak	4.50	2.25	1.25
26	Chuck Stobbs	4.00	2.00	1.25
27	Andy Pafko	4.50	2.25	1.25
28	Red Worthington	4.00	2.00	1.25
29	Jim Bolger	4.00	2.00	1.25
30	Nellie Fox	10.00	5.00	3.00
31	Ken Lehman	4.00	2.00	1.25
32	Don Buddin	4.00	2.00	1.25
33	Ed Fitz Gerald	4.00	2.00	1.25
34	Pitchers Beware (Al Kaline, Charlie Maxwell)	9.00	4.50	2.75
35	Ted Kluszewski	7.00	3.50	2.00
36	Hank Aguirre	4.00	2.00	1.25
37	Gene Green	4.00	2.00	1.25
38	Morrie Martin	4.00	2.00	1.25
39	Ed Bouchee	4.00	2.00	1.25
40	Warren Spahn	40.00	20.00	12.00
41	Bob Martyn	4.00	2.00	1.25
42	Murray Wall	4.00	2.00	1.25
43	Steve Bilko	4.00	2.00	1.25
44	Vito Valentinetti	4.00	2.00	1.25
45	Andy Carey	5.00	2.50	1.50
46	Bill Henry	4.00	2.00	1.25
47	Jim Finigan	4.00	2.00	1.25
48	Orioles Team/Checklist 1-88	10.00	5.00	3.00
49	Bill Hall	4.00	2.00	1.25
50	Willie Mays	125.00	56.00	35.00
51	Rip Coleman	4.00	2.00	1.25
52	Coot Veal	4.00	2.00	1.25
53	Stan Williams	4.00	2.00	1.25
54	Mel Roach	4.00	2.00	1.25
55	Tom Brewer	4.00	2.00	1.25
56	Carl Sawatski	4.00	2.00	1.25
57	Al Cicotte	4.00	2.00	1.25
58	Eddie Miksis	4.00	2.00	1.25
59	Irv Noren	4.00	2.00	1.25
60	Bob Turley	6.00	3.00	1.75
61	Dick Brown	4.00	2.00	1.25
62	Tony Taylor	4.00	2.00	1.25
63	Jim Hearn	4.00	2.00	1.25
64	Joe DeMaestri	4.00	2.00	1.25
65	Frank Torre	4.00	2.00	1.25
66	Joe Ginsberg	4.00	2.00	1.25
67	Brooks Lawrence	4.00	2.00	1.25
68	Dick Schofield	4.00	2.00	1.25
69	Giants Team/Checklist 89-176	12.00	6.00	3.50
70	Harvey Kuenn	5.00	2.50	1.50
71	Don Bessent	4.00	2.00	1.25
72	Bill Renna	4.00	2.00	1.25
73	Ron Jackson	4.00	2.00	1.25
74	Directing the Power (Cookie Lavagetto, Jim Lemon, Roy Sievers)	4.50	2.25	1.25
75	Sam Jones	4.00	2.00	1.25
76	Bobby Richardson	9.00	4.50	2.75
77	John Goryl	4.00	2.00	1.25
78	Pedro Ramos	4.00	2.00	1.25
79	Harry Chiti	4.00	2.00	1.25
80	Minnie Minoso	5.00	2.50	1.50
81	Hal Jeffcoat	4.00	2.00	1.25
82	Bob Boyd	4.00	2.00	1.25
83	Bob Smith	4.00	2.00	1.25
84	Reno Bertoia	4.00	2.00	1.25
85	Harry Anderson	4.00	2.00	1.25
86	Bob Keegan	4.00	2.00	1.25
87	Danny O'Connell	4.00	2.00	1.25
88	Herb Score	4.50	2.25	1.25
89	Billy Gardner	4.00	2.00	1.25
90	Bill Skowron	8.00	4.00	2.50
91	Herb Moford	4.00	2.00	1.25
92	Dave Philley	4.00	2.00	1.25
93	Julio Becquer	4.00	2.00	1.25
94	W. Sox Team/Checklist 89-176	15.00	7.50	4.50
95	Carl Willey	4.00	2.00	1.25
96	Lou Berberet	4.00	2.00	1.25
97	Jerry Lynch	4.00	2.00	1.25
98	Arnie Portocarrero	4.00	2.00	1.25
99	Ted Kazanski	4.00	2.00	1.25
100	Bob Cerv	4.00	2.00	1.25
101	Alex Kellner	4.00	2.00	1.25
102	*Felipe Alou*	6.00	3.00	1.75
103	Billy Goodman	4.00	2.00	1.25
104	Del Rice	4.00	2.00	1.25
105	Lee Walls	4.00	2.00	1.25
106	Hal Woodeshick	4.00	2.00	1.25
107	Norm Larker	4.00	2.00	1.25
108	Zack Monroe	5.00	2.50	1.50
109	Bob Schmidt	4.00	2.00	1.25
110	George Witt	4.00	2.00	1.25
111	Redlegs Team/Checklist 89-176	8.00	4.00	2.50
112	Billy Consolo	2.50	1.25	.70
113	Taylor Phillips	2.50	1.25	.70
114	Earl Battey	2.75	1.50	.80
115	Mickey Vernon	2.75	1.50	.80
116	*Bob Allison*	4.00	2.00	1.25
117	*John Blanchard*	3.25	1.75	1.00
118	John Buzhardt	2.50	1.25	.70
119	*John Callison*	4.00	2.00	1.25
120	Chuck Coles	2.50	1.25	.70
121	Bob Conley	2.50	1.25	.70
122	Bennie Daniels	2.50	1.25	.70
123	Don Dillard	2.50	1.25	.70
124	Dan Dobbek	2.50	1.25	.70
125	*Ron Fairly*	3.50	1.75	1.00
126	Eddie Haas	2.50	1.25	.70
127	Kent Hadley	2.50	1.25	.70
128	Bob Hartman	2.50	1.25	.70
129	Frank Herrera	2.50	1.25	.70
130	Lou Jackson	2.50	1.25	.70
131	*Deron Johnson*	3.25	1.75	1.00
132	Don Lee	2.50	1.25	.70
133	*Bob Lillis*	2.75	1.50	.80
134	Jim McDaniel	2.50	1.25	.70
135	Gene Oliver	2.50	1.25	.70
136	*Jim O'Toole*	2.75	1.50	.80
137	Dick Ricketts	2.50	1.25	.70
138	John Romano	2.50	1.25	.70
139	Ed Sadowski	2.50	1.25	.70
140	Charlie Secrest	2.50	1.25	.70
141	Joe Shipley	2.50	1.25	.70
142	Dick Stigman	2.50	1.25	.70
143	Willie Tasby	2.50	1.25	.70
144	Jerry Walker	2.50	1.25	.70
145	Dom Zanni	2.50	1.25	.70
146	Jerry Zimmerman	2.50	1.25	.70
147	Cub's Clubbers (Ernie Banks, Dale Long, Walt Moryn)	9.00	4.50	2.75
148	Mike McCormick	2.75	1.50	.80
149	Jim Bunning	8.00	4.00	2.50
150	Stan Musial	125.00	62.00	37.00
151	Bob Malkmus	2.50	1.25	.70
152	Johnny Klippstein	2.50	1.25	.70
153	Jim Marshall	2.50	1.25	.70
154	Ray Herbert	2.50	1.25	.70
155	Enos Slaughter	15.00	7.50	4.50
156	Ace Hurlers (Billy Pierce, Robin Roberts)	3.50	1.75	1.00
157	Felix Mantilla	2.50	1.25	.70
158	Walt Dropo	2.75	1.50	.80
159	Bob Shaw	2.50	1.25	.70
160	Dick Groat	3.00	1.50	.90
161	Frank Baumann	2.50	1.25	.70
162	Bobby G. Smith	2.50	1.25	.70
163	Sandy Koufax	125.00	56.00	35.00
164	Johnny Groth	2.50	1.25	.70
165	Bill Bruton	2.75	1.50	.80
166	Destruction Crew (Rocky Colavito, Larry Doby, Minnie Minoso)	3.25	1.75	1.00
167	Duke Maas	3.00	1.50	.90
168	Carroll Hardy	2.50	1.25	.70
169	Ted Abernathy	2.50	1.25	.70
170	Gene Woodling	2.75	1.50	.80
171	Willard Schmidt	2.50	1.25	.70
172	A's Team/Checklist 177-242	7.00	3.50	2.00
173	*Bill Monbouquette*	2.75	1.50	.80
174	Jim Pendleton	2.50	1.25	.70
175	Dick Farrell	2.50	1.25	.70
176	Preston Ward	2.50	1.25	.70
177	Johnny Briggs	2.50	1.25	.70
178	Ruben Amaro	2.50	1.25	.70
179	Don Rudolph	2.50	1.25	.70
180	Yogi Berra	60.00	30.00	18.00
181	Bob Porterfield	2.50	1.25	.70
182	Milt Graff	2.50	1.25	.70
183	Stu Miller	2.50	1.25	.70
184	Harvey Haddix	2.75	1.50	.80
185	Jim Busby	2.50	1.25	.70
186	Mudcat Grant	2.75	1.50	.80
187	Bubba Phillips	2.50	1.25	.70
188	Juan Pizarro	2.50	1.25	.70
189	Neil Chrisley	2.50	1.25	.70
190	Bill Virdon	2.75	1.50	.80
191	Russ Kemmerer	2.50	1.25	.70
192	Charley Beamon	2.50	1.25	.70
193	Sammy Taylor	2.50	1.25	.70
194	Jim Brosnan	2.75	1.50	.80
195	Rip Repulski	2.50	1.25	.70
196	Billy Moran	2.50	1.25	.70
197	Ray Semproch	2.50	1.25	.70
198	Jim Davenport	2.50	1.25	.70
199	Leo Kiely	2.50	1.25	.70
200	Warren Giles	2.75	1.50	.80
201	Tom Acker	2.50	1.25	.70
202	Roger Maris	125.00	56.00	35.00
203	Ozzie Virgil	2.50	1.25	.70
204	Casey Wise	2.50	1.25	.70
205	Don Larsen	7.00	3.50	2.00
206	Carl Furillo	5.00	2.50	1.50
207	George Strickland	2.50	1.25	.70
208	Willie Jones	2.50	1.25	.70
209	Lenny Green	2.50	1.25	.70
210	Ed Bailey	2.50	1.25	.70
211	Bob Blaylock	2.50	1.25	.70
212	Fence Busters (Hank Aaron, Eddie Mathews)	25.00	12.50	7.50
213	Jim Rivera	2.50	1.25	.70
214	Marcelino Solis	2.50	1.25	.70
215	Jim Lemon	2.50	1.25	.70
216	Andre Rodgers	2.50	1.25	.70
217	Carl Erskine	4.00	2.00	1.25
218	Roman Mejias	2.50	1.25	.70
219	George Zuverink	2.50	1.25	.70
220	Frank Malzone	2.75	1.50	.80
221	Bob Bowman	2.50	1.25	.70
222	Bobby Shantz	3.50	1.75	1.00
223	Cards Team/Checklist 265-352	7.00	3.50	2.00
224	*Claude Osteen*	3.00	1.50	.90
225	Johnny Logan	2.75	1.50	.80
226	Art Ceccarelli	2.50	1.25	.70
227	Hal Smith	2.50	1.25	.70
228	Don Gross	2.50	1.25	.70
229	Vic Power	2.50	1.25	.70
230	Bill Fischer	2.50	1.25	.70
231	Ellis Burton	2.50	1.25	.70
232	Eddie Kasko	2.50	1.25	.70
233	Paul Foytack	2.50	1.25	.70
234	Chuck Tanner	3.00	1.50	.90
235	Valmy Thomas	2.50	1.25	.70
236	Ted Bowsfield	2.50	1.25	.70
237	Run Preventers (Gil McDougald, Bobby Richardson, Bob Turley)	4.00	2.00	1.25
238	Gene Baker	2.50	1.25	.70
239	Bob Trowbridge	2.50	1.25	.70
240	Hank Bauer	7.00	3.50	2.00
241	Billy Muffett	2.50	1.25	.70
242	Ron Samford	2.50	1.25	.70
243	Marv Grissom	2.50	1.25	.70
244	Dick Gray	2.50	1.25	.70
245	Ned Garver	2.50	1.25	.70
246	J.W. Porter	2.50	1.25	.70
247	Don Ferrarese	2.50	1.25	.70
248	Red Sox Team/Checklist 177-264	8.00	4.00	2.50
249	Bobby Adams	2.50	1.25	.70
250	Billy O'Dell	2.50	1.25	.70
251	Cletis Boyer	4.50	2.25	1.25
252	Ray Boone	2.75	1.50	.80
253	Seth Morehead	2.50	1.25	.70
254	Zeke Bella	2.50	1.25	.70
255	Del Ennis	2.75	1.50	.80
256	Jerry Davie	2.50	1.25	.70
257	*Leon Wagner*	3.00	1.50	.90
258	Fred Kipp	2.50	1.25	.70
259	Jim Pisoni	2.50	1.25	.70
260	Early Wynn	15.00	7.50	4.50
261	Gene Stephens	2.50	1.25	.70
262	Hitters' Foes (Don Drysdale, Clem Labine, Johnny Podres)	8.00	4.00	2.50
263	Buddy Daley	2.50	1.25	.70
264	Chico Carrasquel	2.50	1.25	.70
265	Ron Kline	2.50	1.25	.70
266	Woody Held	2.75	1.50	.80
267	John Romonosky	2.50	1.25	.70
268	Tito Francona	2.75	1.50	.80
269	Jack Meyer	2.50	1.25	.70
270	Gil Hodges	18.00	9.00	5.50
271	*Orlando Pena*	2.75	1.50	.80
272	Jerry Lumpe	3.25	1.75	1.00
273	Joe Jay	2.50	1.25	.70
274	Jerry Kindall	2.50	1.25	.70
275	Jack Sanford	2.50	1.25	.70
276	Pete Daley	2.50	1.25	.70
277	Turk Lown	2.50	1.25	.70
278	Chuck Essegian	2.50	1.25	.70
279	Ernie Johnson	2.50	1.25	.70
280	Frank Bolling	2.50	1.25	.70
281	Walt Craddock	2.50	1.25	.70
282	R.C. Stevens	2.50	1.25	.70
283	Russ Heman	2.50	1.25	.70
284	Steve Korcheck	2.50	1.25	.70
285	Joe Cunningham	2.75	1.50	.80
286	Dean Stone	2.50	1.25	.70
287	Don Zimmer	2.75	1.50	.80
288	Dutch Dotterer	2.50	1.25	.70
289	Johnny Kucks	3.00	1.50	.90
290	Wes Covington	2.75	1.50	.80
291	Pitching Partners (Camilo Pascual, Pedro Ramos)	2.75	1.50	.80
292	Dick Williams	2.75	1.50	.80
293	Ray Moore	2.50	1.25	.70
294	Hank Foiles	2.50	1.25	.70
295	Billy Martin	15.00	7.50	4.50
296	*Ernie Broglio*	2.75	1.50	.80
297	*Jackie Brandt*	2.75	1.50	.80
298	Tex Clevenger	2.50	1.25	.70
299	Billy Klaus	2.50	1.25	.70
300	Richie Ashburn	12.00	6.00	3.50
301	Earl Averill	2.50	1.25	.70
302	Don Mossi	2.75	1.50	.80
303	Marty Keough	2.50	1.25	.70
304	Cubs Team/Checklist 265-352	7.00	3.50	2.00
305	Curt Raydon	2.50	1.25	.70
306	Jim Gilliam	5.00	2.50	1.50
307	Curt Barclay	2.50	1.25	.70
308	Norm Siebern	3.50	1.75	1.00

		NR MT	EX	VG
309	Sal Maglie	3.00	1.50	.90
310	Luis Aparicio	15.00	7.50	4.50
311	Norm Zauchin	2.50	1.25	.70
312	Don Newcombe	4.50	2.25	1.25
313	Frank House	2.50	1.25	.70
314	Don Cardwell	2.50	1.25	.70
315	Joe Adcock	3.00	1.50	.90
316a	Ralph Lumenti (without option statement)	80.00	40.00	24.00
316b	Ralph Lumenti (with option statement)	2.50	1.25	.70
317	N.L. Hitting Kings (Richie Ashburn, Willie Mays)	15.00	7.50	4.50
318	Rocky Bridges	2.50	1.25	.70
319	Dave Hillman	2.50	1.25	.70
320	Bob Skinner	2.75	1.50	.80
321a	Bob Giallombardo (without option statement)	80.00	40.00	24.00
321b	Bob Giallombardo (with option statement)	2.50	1.25	.70
322a	Harry Hanebrink (without trade statement)	65.00	33.00	18.00
322b	Harry Hanebrink (with trade statement)	2.50	1.25	.70
323	Frank Sullivan	2.50	1.25	.70
324	Don Demeter	2.50	1.25	.70
325	Ken Boyer	5.00	2.50	1.50
326	Marv Throneberry	4.00	2.00	1.25
327	*Gary Bell*	2.75	1.50	.80
328	Lou Skizas	2.50	1.25	.70
329	Tigers Team/Checklist 353-429	8.00	4.00	2.50
330	Gus Triandos	2.75	1.50	.80
331	Steve Boros	2.75	1.50	.80
332	Ray Monzant	2.50	1.25	.70
333	Harry Simpson	2.50	1.25	.70
334	Glen Hobbie	2.50	1.25	.70
335	Johnny Temple	2.50	1.25	.70
336a	Billy Loes (without trade statement)	65.00	33.00	18.00
336b	Billy Loes (with trade statement)	2.50	1.25	.70
337	George Crowe	2.50	1.25	.70
338	*George Anderson*	20.00	10.00	6.00
339	Roy Face	3.00	1.50	.90
340	Roy Sievers	2.75	1.50	.80
341	Tom Qualters	2.50	1.25	.70
342	Ray Jablonski	2.50	1.25	.70
343	Billy Hoeft	2.50	1.25	.70
344	Russ Nixon	2.50	1.25	.70
345	Gil McDougald	8.00	4.00	2.50
346	Batter Bafflers (Tom Brewer, Dave Sisler)	2.75	1.50	.80
347	Bob Buhl	2.75	1.50	.80
348	Ted Lepcio	2.50	1.25	.70
349	Hoyt Wilhelm	15.00	7.50	4.50
350	Ernie Banks	60.00	30.00	18.00
351	Earl Torgeson	2.50	1.25	.70
352	Robin Roberts	15.00	7.50	4.50
353	Curt Flood	3.00	1.50	.90
354	Pete Burnside	2.50	1.25	.70
355	Jim Piersall	3.00	1.50	.90
356	Bob Mabe	2.50	1.25	.70
357	*Dick Stuart*	4.50	2.25	1.25
358	Ralph Terry	2.75	1.50	.80
359	*Bill White*	15.00	7.50	4.50
360	Al Kaline	50.00	25.00	15.00
361	Willard Nixon	2.50	1.25	.70
362a	Dolan Nichols (without option statement)	80.00	40.00	24.00
362b	Dolan Nichols (with option statement)	2.50	1.25	.70
363	Bobby Avila	2.50	1.25	.70
364	Danny McDevitt	2.50	1.25	.70
365	Gus Bell	2.75	1.50	.80
366	Humberto Robinson	2.50	1.25	.70
367	Cal Neeman	2.50	1.25	.70
368	Don Mueller	2.50	1.25	.70
369	Dick Tomanek	2.50	1.25	.70
370	Pete Runnels	2.75	1.50	.80
371	Dick Brodowski	2.50	1.25	.70
372	Jim Hegan	2.50	1.25	.70
373	Herb Plews	2.50	1.25	.70
374	Art Ditmar	3.00	1.50	.90
375	Bob Nieman	2.50	1.25	.70
376	Hal Naragon	2.50	1.25	.70
377	Johnny Antonelli	2.75	1.50	.80
378	Gail Harris	2.50	1.25	.70
379	Bob Miller	2.50	1.25	.70
380	Hank Aaron	125.00	56.00	35.00
381	Mike Baxes	2.50	1.25	.70
382	Curt Simmons	2.75	1.50	.80
383	Words of Wisdom (Don Larsen, Casey Stengel)	5.00	2.50	1.50
384	Dave Sisler	2.50	1.25	.70
385	Sherm Lollar	2.75	1.50	.80
386	Jim Delsing	2.50	1.25	.70
387	Don Drysdale	25.00	12.50	7.00
388	Bob Will	2.50	1.25	.70
389	Joe Nuxhall	2.75	1.50	.80
390	Orlando Cepeda	9.00	4.50	2.75
391	Milt Pappas	2.75	1.50	.80
392	Whitey Herzog	4.50	2.25	1.25
393	Frank Lary	2.75	1.50	.80
394	Randy Jackson	2.50	1.25	.70
395	Elston Howard	7.00	3.50	2.00
396	Bob Rush	2.50	1.25	.70
397	Senators Team/Checklist 430-495	7.00	3.50	2.00
398	Wally Post	2.50	1.25	.70
399	Larry Jackson	2.50	1.25	.70
400	Jackie Jensen	4.00	2.00	1.25
401	Ron Blackburn	2.50	1.25	.70
402	Hector Lopez	2.50	1.25	.70
403	Clem Labine	2.75	1.50	.80
404	Hank Sauer	2.75	1.50	.80
405	Roy McMillan	2.50	1.25	.70
406	Solly Drake	2.50	1.25	.70
407	Moe Drabowsky	2.50	1.25	.70
408	Keystone Combo (Luis Aparicio, Nellie Fox)	7.00	3.50	2.00
409	Gus Zernial	2.75	1.50	.80
410	Billy Pierce	2.75	1.50	.80
411	Whitey Lockman	2.50	1.25	.70
412	Stan Lopata	2.50	1.25	.70
413	Camillo Pascual (Camilo)	2.75	1.50	.80
414	Dale Long	2.75	1.50	.80
415	Bill Mazeroski	3.50	1.75	1.00
416	Haywood Sullivan	2.50	1.25	.70
417	Virgil Trucks	3.00	1.50	.90
418	Gino Cimoli	2.50	1.25	.70
419	Braves Team/Checklist 353-429	8.00	4.00	2.50
420	Rocco Colavito	5.00	2.50	1.75
421	Herm Wehmeier	2.50	1.25	.70
422	Hobie Landrith	2.50	1.25	.70
423	Bob Grim	2.50	1.25	.70
424	Ken Aspromonte	2.50	1.25	.70
425	Del Crandall	2.75	1.50	.80
426	Jerry Staley	2.50	1.25	.70
427	Charlie Neal	2.50	1.25	.70
428	Buc Hill Aces (Roy Face, Bob Friend, Ron Kline, Vern Law)	3.25	1.75	1.00
429	Bobby Thomson	2.75	1.50	.80
430	Whitey Ford	25.00	12.50	7.50
431	Whammy Douglas	2.50	1.25	.70
432	Smoky Burgess	3.00	1.50	.90
433	Billy Harrell	2.50	1.25	.70
434	Hal Griggs	2.50	1.25	.70
435	Frank Robinson	40.00	20.00	12.00
436	Granny Hamner	2.50	1.25	.70
437	Ike Delock	2.50	1.25	.70
438	Sam Esposito	2.50	1.25	.70
439	Brooks Robinson	35.00	17.50	10.50
440	Lou Burdette	8.00	4.00	2.50
441	John Roseboro	2.75	1.50	.80
442	Ray Narleski	2.50	1.25	.70
443	Daryl Spencer	2.50	1.25	.70
444	*Ronnie Hansen*	2.75	1.50	.80
445	Cal McLish	2.50	1.25	.70
446	Rocky Nelson	2.50	1.25	.70
447	Bob Anderson	2.50	1.25	.70
448	Vada Pinson	4.00	2.00	1.25
449	Tom Gorman	2.50	1.25	.70
450	Ed Mathews	20.00	10.00	6.00
451	Jimmy Constable	2.50	1.25	.70
452	Chico Fernandez	2.50	1.25	.70
453	Les Moss	2.50	1.25	.70
454	Phil Clark	2.50	1.25	.70
455	Larry Doby	3.25	1.75	1.00
456	Jerry Casale	2.50	1.25	.70
457	Dodgers Team/Checklist 430-495	12.00	6.00	3.50
458	Gordon Jones	2.50	1.25	.70
459	Bill Tuttle	2.50	1.25	.70
460	Bob Friend	2.75	1.50	.80
461	Mantle Hits 42nd Homer For Crown	25.00	12.50	7.50
462	Colavito's Great Catch Saves Game	3.00	1.50	.90
463	Kaline Becomes Youngest Bat Champ	8.00	4.00	2.50
464	Mays' Catch Makes Series History	15.00	7.50	4.50
465	Sievers Sets Homer Mark	2.75	1.50	.80
466	Pierce All Star Starter	2.75	1.50	.80
467	Aaron Clubs World Series Homer	15.00	7.50	4.50
468	Snider's Play Brings L.A. Victory	9.00	4.50	2.75
469	Hustler Banks Wins M.V.P. Award	8.00	4.00	2.50
470	Musial Raps Out 3,000th Hit	12.00	6.00	3.50
471	Tom Sturdivant	3.00	1.50	.90
472	Gene Freese	2.50	1.25	.70
473	Mike Fornieles	2.50	1.25	.70
474	Moe Thacker	2.50	1.25	.70
475	Jack Harshman	2.50	1.25	.70
476	Indians Team/Checklist 496-572	7.00	3.50	2.00
477	Barry Latman	2.50	1.25	.70
478	Bob Clemente	70.00	35.00	21.00
479	Lindy McDaniel	2.50	1.25	.70
480	Red Schoendienst	12.00	6.00	3.50
481	Charley Maxwell	2.50	1.25	.70
482	Russ Meyer	2.50	1.25	.70
483	Clint Courtney	2.50	1.25	.70
484	Willie Kirkland	2.50	1.25	.70
485	Ryne Duren	3.50	1.75	1.00
486	Sammy White	2.50	1.25	.70
487	Hal Brown	2.50	1.25	.70
488	Walt Moryn	2.50	1.25	.70
489	John C. Powers	2.50	1.25	.70
490	Frank Thomas	2.50	1.25	.70
491	Don Blasingame	2.50	1.25	.70
492	Gene Conley	2.75	1.50	.80
493	Jim Landis	2.50	1.25	.70
494	Don Pavletich	2.50	1.25	.70
495	Johnny Podres	4.00	2.00	1.25
496	Wayne Terwilliger	2.50	1.25	.70
497	Hal R. Smith	2.50	1.25	.70
498	Dick Hyde	2.50	1.25	.70
499	Johnny O'Brien	2.50	1.25	.70
500	Vic Wertz	2.75	1.50	.80
501	Bobby Tiefenauer	2.50	1.25	.70
502	Al Dark	3.25	1.75	1.00
503	Jim Owens	2.50	1.25	.70
504	Ossie Alvarez	2.50	1.25	.70
505	Tony Kubek	8.00	4.00	2.50
506	Bob Purkey	2.50	1.25	.70
507	Bob Hale	10.00	5.00	3.00
508	Art Fowler	10.00	5.00	3.00
509	*Norm Cash*	25.00	12.50	7.50
510	Yankees Team/Checklist 496-572	45.00	22.00	13.50
511	George Susce	10.00	5.00	3.00
512	George Altman	10.00	5.00	3.00
513	Tom Carroll	10.00	5.00	3.00
514	*Bob Gibson*	300.00	120.00	75.00
515	Harmon Killebrew	110.00	50.00	28.00
516	Mike Garcia	11.00	5.50	3.25
517	Joe Koppe	10.00	5.00	3.00
518	*Mike Cueller (Cuellar)*	15.00	7.50	4.50
519	Infield Power (Dick Gernert, Frank Malzone, Pete Runnels)	12.00	6.00	3.50
520	Don Elston	10.00	5.00	3.00
521	Gary Geiger	10.00	5.00	3.00
522	Gene Snyder	10.00	5.00	3.00
523	Harry Bright	10.00	5.00	3.00
524	Larry Osborne	10.00	5.00	3.00
525	Jim Coates	11.00	5.50	3.25
526	Bob Speake	10.00	5.00	3.00
527	Solly Hemus	10.00	5.00	3.00
528	Pirates Team/Checklist 496-572	25.00	12.50	7.50
529	*George Bamberger*	11.00	5.50	3.25
530	Wally Moon	11.00	5.50	3.25
531	Ray Webster	10.00	5.00	3.00
532	Mark Freeman	10.00	5.00	3.00
533	Darrell Johnson	11.00	5.50	3.25
534	Faye Throneberry	10.00	5.00	3.00
535	Ruben Gomez	10.00	5.00	3.00
536	Dan Kravitz	10.00	5.00	3.00
537	Rodolfo Arias	10.00	5.00	3.00
538	Chick King	10.00	5.00	3.00
539	Gary Blaylock	10.00	5.00	3.00
540	Willy Miranda	10.00	5.00	3.00
541	Bob Thurman	10.00	5.00	3.00
542	*Jim Perry*	15.00	7.50	4.50
543	Corsair Outfield Trio (Bob Clemente, Bob Skinner, Bill Virdon)	35.00	17.50	10.50
544	Lee Tate	10.00	5.00	3.00
545	Tom Morgan	10.00	5.00	3.00
546	Al Schroll	10.00	5.00	3.00
547	Jim Baxes	10.00	5.00	3.00
548	Elmer Singleton	10.00	5.00	3.00
549	Howie Nunn	10.00	5.00	3.00
550	Roy Campanella	125.00	62.00	37.00
551	Fred Haney AS	11.00	5.50	3.25
552	Casey Stengel AS	30.00	15.00	9.00
553	Orlando Cepeda AS	12.00	6.00	3.50
554	Bill Skowron AS	12.00	6.00	3.50
555	Bill Mazeroski AS	12.00	6.00	3.50
556	Nellie Fox AS	15.00	7.50	4.50
557	Ken Boyer AS	12.00	6.00	3.50
558	Frank Malzone AS	11.00	5.50	3.25
559	Ernie Banks AS	30.00	15.00	9.00
560	Luis Aparicio AS	20.00	10.00	6.00
561	Hank Aaron AS	100.00	50.00	30.00
562	Al Kaline AS	35.00	17.50	10.50
563	Willie Mays AS	100.00	50.00	30.00
564	Mickey Mantle AS	200.00	100.00	60.00
565	Wes Covington AS	11.00	5.50	3.25
566	Roy Sievers AS	11.00	5.50	3.25
567	Del Crandall AS	11.00	5.50	3.25
568	Gus Triandos AS	11.00	5.50	3.25
569	Bob Friend AS	11.00	5.50	3.25
570	Bob Turley AS	11.00	5.50	3.25
571	Warren Spahn AS	35.00	17.50	10.50
572	Billy Pierce AS	15.00	6.00	3.25
---	Elect Your Favorite Rookie Insert (paper stock, September 29 date on back)	15.00	7.50	4.50
---	Felt Pennants Insert (paper stock)	15.00	7.50	4.50

1960 Topps

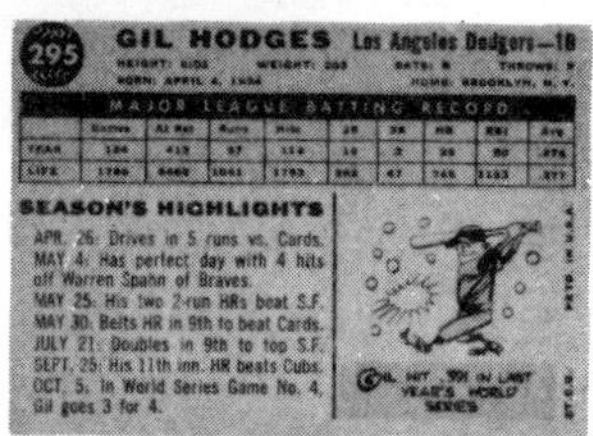

In 1960, Topps returned to a horizontal format (3-1/2" by 2-1/2") with a color portrait and a black and white "action" photograph on the front. The backs returned to the use of just the previous year and lifetime statistics along with a cartoon and short career summary or previous season highlights. Specialty cards in the 572-card set are multi-player cards, managers and coaches cards, and highlights of the 1959 World Series. Two groups of rookie cards are included. The first are numbers 117-148, which are the Sport Magazine rookies. The second group is called "Topps All-Star Rookies." Finally, there is a continuation of the All-Star cards to close out the set in the scarcer high numbers. Card #'s 375-440 can be found with backs printed on either white or grey cardboard, with the white stock being the less common.

		NR MT	EX	VG
	Complete Set:	3400.	1700.	1020.
	Common Player: 1-286	1.50	.70	.45
	Common Player: 287-440	1.75	.90	.50
	Common Player: 441-506	3.50	1.75	1.00
	Common Player: 507-572	8.00	4.00	2.50
1	Early Wynn	35.00	10.00	5.00
2	Roman Mejias	2.25	.70	.45
3	Joe Adcock	2.25	1.25	.70
4	Bob Purkey	1.50	.70	.45
5	Wally Moon	1.75	.90	.50
6	Lou Berberet	1.50	.70	.45
7	Master & Mentor (Willie Mays, Bill Rigney)	8.00	4.00	2.50
8	Bud Daley	1.50	.70	.45
9	Faye Throneberry	1.50	.70	.45
10	Ernie Banks	35.00	17.50	10.50
11	Norm Siebern	1.75	.90	.50
12	Milt Pappas	1.75	.90	.50
13	Wally Post	1.50	.70	.45
14	Jim Grant	1.50	.70	.45
15	Pete Runnels	1.75	.90	.50
16	Ernie Broglio	1.50	.70	.45
17	Johnny Callison	1.75	.90	.50
18	Dodgers Team/Checklist 1-88	10.00	5.00	3.00
19	Felix Mantilla	1.50	.70	.45
20	Roy Face	2.00	1.00	.60
21	Dutch Dotterer	1.50	.70	.45
22	Rocky Bridges	1.50	.70	.45
23	Eddie Fisher	1.50	.70	.45
24	Dick Gray	1.50	.70	.45
25	Roy Sievers	3.50	1.75	1.00
26	Wayne Terwilliger	1.50	.70	.45
27	Dick Drott	1.50	.70	.45
28	Brooks Robinson	35.00	17.50	10.50
29	Clem Labine	1.75	.90	.50
30	Tito Francona	1.75	.90	.50
31	Sammy Esposito	1.50	.70	.45
32	Sophomore Stalwarts (Jim O'Toole, Vada Pinson)	3.50	1.75	1.00
33	Tom Morgan	1.50	.70	.45
34	George Anderson	2.50	1.25	.70
35	Whitey Ford	25.00	12.50	7.50
36	Russ Nixon	1.50	.70	.45
37	Bill Bruton	1.75	.90	.50
38	Jerry Casale	1.50	.70	.45
39	Earl Averill	1.50	.70	.45
40	Joe Cunningham	1.75	.90	.50
41	Barry Latman	1.50	.70	.45
42	Hobie Landrith	1.50	.70	.45
43	Senators Team/Checklist 1-88	6.00	3.00	1.75
44	Bobby Locke	1.50	.70	.45
45	Roy McMillan	1.50	.70	.45
46	Jack Fisher	1.50	.70	.45
47	Don Zimmer	2.25	1.25	.70
48	Hal Smith	1.50	.70	.45
49	Curt Raydon	1.50	.70	.45
50	Al Kaline	25.00	12.50	7.50
51	Jim Coates	2.00	1.00	.60
52	Dave Philley	1.50	.70	.45
53	Jackie Brandt	1.50	.70	.45
54	Mike Fornieles	1.50	.70	.45
55	Bill Mazeroski	3.00	1.50	.90
56	Steve Korcheck	1.50	.70	.45
57	Win - Savers (Turk Lown, Gerry Staley)	1.75	.90	.50
58	Gino Cimoli	1.50	.70	.45
59	Juan Pizarro	1.50	.70	.45
60	Gus Triandos	1.75	.90	.50
61	Eddie Kasko	1.50	.70	.45
62	Roger Craig	2.25	1.25	.70
63	George Strickland	1.50	.70	.45
64	Jack Meyer	1.50	.70	.45
65	Elston Howard	6.00	3.00	1.75
66	Bob Trowbridge	1.50	.70	.45
67	*Jose Pagan*	1.75	.90	.50
68	Dave Hillman	1.50	.70	.45
69	Billy Goodman	1.50	.70	.45
70	Lou Burdette	3.25	1.75	1.00
71	Marty Keough	1.50	.70	.45
72	Tigers Team/Checklist 89-176	8.00	4.00	2.50
73	Bob Gibson	40.00	20.00	12.00
74	Walt Moryn	1.50	.70	.45
75	Vic Power	1.50	.70	.45
76	Bill Fischer	1.50	.70	.45
77	Hank Foiles	1.50	.70	.45
78	Bob Grim	1.50	.70	.45
79	Walt Dropo	1.75	.90	.50
80	Johnny Antonelli	2.00	1.00	.60
81	Russ Snyder	1.50	.70	.45
82	Ruben Gomez	1.50	.70	.45
83	Tony Kubek	4.50	2.25	1.25
84	Hal Smith	1.50	.70	.45
85	Frank Lary	1.75	.90	.50
86	Dick Gernert	1.50	.70	.45
87	John Romonosky	1.50	.70	.45
88	John Roseboro	1.75	.90	.50
89	Hal Brown	1.50	.70	.45
90	Bobby Avila	1.50	.70	.45
91	Bennie Daniels	1.50	.70	.45
92	Whitey Herzog	3.25	1.75	1.00
93	Art Schult	1.50	.70	.45
94	Leo Kiely	1.50	.70	.45
95	Frank Thomas	1.50	.70	.45
96	Ralph Terry	2.50	1.25	.70
97	Ted Lepcio	1.50	.70	.45
98	Gordon Jones	1.50	.70	.45
99	Lenny Green	1.50	.70	.45
100	Nellie Fox	7.00	3.50	2.00
101	Bob Miller	1.50	.70	.45
102	Kent Hadley	2.00	1.00	.60
103	Dick Farrell	1.50	.70	.45
104	Dick Schofield	1.50	.70	.45
105	Larry Sherry	1.50	.70	.45
106	Billy Gardner	1.50	.70	.45
107	Carl Willey	1.50	.70	.45
108	Pete Daley	1.50	.70	.45
109	Cletis Boyer	3.00	1.50	.90
110	Cal McLish	1.50	.70	.45
111	Vic Wertz	1.75	.90	.50
112	Jack Harshman	1.50	.70	.45
113	Bob Skinner	1.50	.70	.45
114	Ken Aspromonte	1.50	.70	.45
115	Fork & Knuckler (Roy Face, Hoyt Wilhelm)	4.00	2.00	1.25
116	Jim Rivera	1.50	.70	.45
117	Tom Borland	1.50	.70	.45
118	Bob Bruce	1.50	.70	.45
119	*Chico Cardenas*	1.75	.90	.50
120	Duke Carmel	1.50	.70	.45
121	Camilo Carreon	1.50	.70	.45
122	Don Dillard	1.50	.70	.45
123	Dan Dobbek	1.50	.70	.45
124	Jim Donohue	1.50	.70	.45
125	*Dick Ellsworth*	1.75	.90	.50
126	*Chuck Estrada*	1.75	.90	.50
127	Ronnie Hansen	1.50	.70	.45
128	Bill Harris	1.50	.70	.45
129	Bob Hartman	1.50	.70	.45
130	Frank Herrera	1.50	.70	.45
131	Ed Hobaugh	1.50	.70	.45
132	*Frank Howard*	10.00	5.00	3.00
133	*Manuel Javier*	2.00	1.00	.60
134	Deron Johnson	2.00	1.00	.60
135	Ken Johnson	1.50	.70	.45
136	*Jim Kaat*	25.00	12.50	7.50
137	Lou Klimchock	1.50	.70	.45
138	*Art Mahaffey*	1.75	.90	.50
139	Carl Mathias	1.50	.70	.45
140	Julio Navarro	1.50	.70	.45
141	Jim Proctor	1.50	.70	.45
142	Bill Short	2.00	1.00	.60
143	Al Spangler	1.50	.70	.45
144	Al Stieglitz	1.50	.70	.45
145	Jim Umbricht	1.50	.70	.45
146	Ted Wieand	1.50	.70	.45
147	Bob Will	1.50	.70	.45
148	*Carl Yastrzemski*	350.00	140.00	88.00
149	Bob Nieman	1.50	.70	.45
150	Billy Pierce	2.25	1.25	.70
151	Giants Team/Checklist 177-264	6.00	3.00	1.75
152	Gail Harris	1.50	.70	.45
153	Bobby Thomson	2.00	1.00	.60
154	Jim Davenport	1.50	.70	.45
155	Charlie Neal	1.50	.70	.45
156	Art Ceccarelli	1.50	.70	.45
157	Rocky Nelson	1.50	.70	.45
158	Wes Covington	1.50	.70	.45
159	Jim Piersall	2.00	1.00	.60
160	Rival All Stars (Ken Boyer, Mickey Mantle)	30.00	15.00	9.00
161	Ray Narleski	1.50	.70	.45
162	Sammy Taylor	1.50	.70	.45
163	Hector Lopez	2.00	1.00	.60
164	Reds Team/Checklist 89-176	7.00	3.50	2.00
165	Jack Sanford	1.50	.70	.45
166	Chuck Essegian	1.50	.70	.45
167	Valmy Thomas	1.50	.70	.45
168	Alex Grammas	1.50	.70	.45
169	Jake Striker	1.50	.70	.45
170	Del Crandall	2.00	1.00	.60
171	Johnny Groth	1.50	.70	.45
172	Willie Kirkland	1.50	.70	.45
173	Billy Martin	7.00	3.50	2.00
174	Indians Team/Checklist 89-176	6.00	3.00	1.75
175	Pedro Ramos	1.50	.70	.45
176	Vada Pinson	3.25	1.75	1.00
177	Johnny Kucks	1.50	.70	.45
178	Woody Held	1.50	.70	.45
179	Rip Coleman	1.50	.70	.45
180	Harry Simpson	1.50	.70	.45
181	Billy Loes	1.50	.70	.45
182	Glen Hobbie	1.50	.70	.45
183	Eli Grba	2.00	1.00	.60
184	Gary Geiger	1.50	.70	.45
185	Jim Owens	1.50	.70	.45
186	Dave Sisler	1.50	.70	.45
187	Jay Hook	1.50	.70	.45
188	Dick Williams	2.00	1.00	.60
189	Don McMahon	1.50	.70	.45
190	Gene Woodling	1.75	.90	.50
191	Johnny Klippstein	1.50	.70	.45
192	Danny O'Connell	1.50	.70	.45
193	Dick Hyde	1.50	.70	.45
194	Bobby Gene Smith	1.50	.70	.45
195	Lindy McDaniel	1.50	.70	.45
196	Andy Carey	2.00	1.00	.60
197	Ron Kline	1.50	.70	.45
198	Jerry Lynch	1.50	.70	.45
199	Dick Donovan	1.50	.70	.45
200	Willie Mays	100.00	50.00	30.00
201	Larry Osborne	1.50	.70	.45
202	Fred Kipp	1.50	.70	.45
203	Sammy White	1.50	.70	.45
204	Ryne Duren	2.50	1.25	.70
205	Johnny Logan	1.75	.90	.50
206	Claude Osteen	1.75	.90	.50
207	Bob Boyd	1.50	.70	.45
208	White Sox Team/Checklist 177-264	6.00	3.00	1.75
209	Ron Blackburn	1.50	.70	.45
210	Harmon Killebrew	20.00	10.00	6.00
211	Taylor Phillips	1.50	.70	.45
212	Walt Alston	6.00	3.00	1.75
213	Chuck Dressen	1.75	.90	.50
214	Jimmie Dykes	1.50	.70	.45
215	Bob Elliott	1.50	.70	.45
216	Joe Gordon	1.75	.90	.50
217	Charley Grimm	1.75	.90	.50
218	Solly Hemus	1.50	.70	.45
219	Fred Hutchinson	1.75	.90	.50
220	Billy Jurges	1.50	.70	.45
221	Cookie Lavagetto	1.50	.70	.45
222	Al Lopez	5.00	2.50	1.50
223	Danny Murtaugh	1.75	.90	.50
224	Paul Richards	1.75	.90	.50
225	Bill Rigney	1.50	.70	.45
226	Eddie Sawyer	1.50	.70	.45
227	Casey Stengel	18.00	9.00	5.50
228	Ernie Johnson	1.50	.70	.45
229	Joe Morgan	1.50	.70	.45
230	Mound Magicians (Bob Buhl, Lou Burdette, Warren Spahn)	6.00	3.00	1.75
231	Hal Naragon	1.50	.70	.45
232	Jim Busby	1.50	.70	.45
233	Don Elston	1.50	.70	.45
234	Don Demeter	1.50	.70	.45
235	Gus Bell	1.75	.90	.50
236	Dick Ricketts	1.50	.70	.45
237	Elmer Valo	2.00	1.00	.60
238	Danny Kravitz	1.50	.70	.45
239	Joe Shipley	1.50	.70	.45
240	Luis Aparicio	10.00	5.00	3.00
241	Albie Pearson	1.50	.70	.45
242	Cards Team/Checklist 265-352	6.00	3.00	1.75
243	Bubba Phillips	1.50	.70	.45
244	Hal Griggs	1.50	.70	.45
245	Eddie Yost	1.75	.90	.50
246	Lee Maye	1.50	.70	.45
247	Gil McDougald	4.50	2.25	1.25
248	Del Rice	1.50	.70	.45
249	*Earl Wilson*	1.75	.90	.50
250	Stan Musial	100.00	50.00	30.00
251	Bobby Malkmus	1.50	.70	.45
252	Ray Herbert	1.50	.70	.45
253	Eddie Bressoud	1.50	.70	.45
254	Arnie Portocarrero	1.50	.70	.45
255	Jim Gilliam	3.25	1.75	1.00
256	Dick Brown	1.50	.70	.45
257	Gordy Coleman	1.50	.70	.45
258	Dick Groat	4.00	2.00	1.25
259	George Altman	1.50	.70	.45
260	Power Plus (Rocky Colavito, Tito Francona)	3.00	1.50	.90
261	Pete Burnside	1.50	.70	.45
262	Hank Bauer	2.00	1.00	.60
263	Darrell Johnson	1.50	.70	.45
264	Robin Roberts	15.00	7.50	4.50
265	Rip Repulski	1.50	.70	.45
266	Joe Jay	1.50	.70	.45
267	Jim Marshall	1.50	.70	.45
268	Al Worthington	1.50	.70	.45
269	Gene Green	1.50	.70	.45
270	Bob Turley	3.25	1.75	1.00
271	Julio Becquer	1.50	.70	.45
272	Fred Green	1.50	.70	.45
273	Neil Chrisley	1.50	.70	.45
274	Tom Acker	1.50	.70	.45
275	Curt Flood	3.00	1.50	.90
276	Ken McBride	1.50	.70	.45
277	Harry Bright	1.50	.70	.45
278	Stan Williams	1.50	.70	.45
279	Chuck Tanner	2.50	1.25	.70
280	Frank Sullivan	1.50	.70	.45
281	Ray Boone	1.75	.90	.50
282	Joe Nuxhall	2.00	1.00	.60
283	John Blanchard	2.75	1.50	.80
284	Don Gross	1.50	.70	.45
285	Harry Anderson	1.50	.70	.45
286	Ray Semproch	1.50	.70	.45
287	Felipe Alou	2.50	1.25	.70
288	Bob Mabe	1.75	.90	.50
289	Willie Jones	1.75	.90	.50
290	Jerry Lumpe	2.00	1.00	.60
291	Bob Keegan	1.75	.90	.50
292	Dodger Backstops (Joe Pignatano, John Roseboro)	2.00	1.00	.60
293	Gene Conley	2.00	1.00	.60
294	Tony Taylor	1.50	.70	.45
295	Gil Hodges	18.00	9.00	5.50
296	Nelson Chittum	1.75	.90	.50
297	Reno Bertoia	1.75	.90	.50
298	George Witt	1.75	.90	.50
299	Earl Torgeson	1.75	.90	.50
300	Hank Aaron	125.00	56.00	35.00
301	Jerry Davie	1.75	.90	.50
302	Phillies Team/Checklist 353-429	7.00	3.50	2.00
303	Billy O'Dell	1.75	.90	.50
304	Joe Ginsberg	1.75	.90	.50
305	Richie Ashburn	7.00	3.50	2.00
306	Frank Baumann	1.75	.90	.50
307	Gene Oliver	1.75	.90	.50
308	Dick Hall	1.75	.90	.50
309	Bob Hale	1.75	.90	.50
310	Frank Malzone	2.00	1.00	.60
311	Raul Sanchez	1.75	.90	.50
312	Charlie Lau	2.00	1.00	.60
313	Turk Lown	1.75	.90	.50
314	Chico Fernandez	1.75	.90	.50
315	Bobby Shantz	3.25	1.75	1.00
316	*Willie McCovey*	200.00	100.00	60.00
317	Pumpsie Green	1.75	.90	.50
318	Jim Baxes	1.75	.90	.50
319	Joe Koppe	1.75	.90	.50
320	Bob Allison	2.25	1.25	.70
321	Ron Fairly	2.00	1.00	.60
322	Willie Tasby	1.75	.90	.50
323	Johnny Romano	1.75	.90	.50
324	Jim Perry	2.50	1.25	.70
325	Jim O'Toole	2.00	1.00	.60
326	Bob Clemente	75.00	37.00	22.00
327	*Ray Sadecki*	2.25	1.25	.70
328	Earl Battey	2.00	1.00	.60
329	Zack Monroe	2.25	1.25	.70
330	Harvey Kuenn	3.00	1.50	.90
331	Henry Mason	1.75	.90	.50
332	Yankees Team/Checklist 265-352	20.00	10.00	6.00
333	Danny McDevitt	1.75	.90	.50
334	Ted Abernathy	1.75	.90	.50
335	Red Schoendienst	10.00	5.00	3.00
336	Ike Delock	1.75	.90	.50
337	Cal Neeman	1.75	.90	.50
338	Ray Monzant	1.75	.90	.50
339	Harry Chiti	1.75	.90	.50
340	Harvey Haddix	2.25	1.25	.70
341	Carroll Hardy	1.75	.90	.50
342	Casey Wise	1.75	.90	.50
343	Sandy Koufax	90.00	45.00	27.00
344	Clint Courtney	1.75	.90	.50
345	Don Newcombe	2.50	1.25	.70
346	J.C. Martin (photo actually Gary Peters)	1.75	.90	.50
347	Ed Bouchee	1.75	.90	.50

		NR MT	EX	VG
348	Barry Shetrone	1.75	.90	.50
349	Moe Drabowsky	1.75	.90	.50
350	Mickey Mantle	350.00	140.00	88.00
351	Don Nottebart	1.75	.90	.50
352	Cincy Clouters (Gus Bell, Jerry Lynch, Frank Robinson)	5.00	2.50	1.50
353	Don Larsen	2.25	1.25	.70
354	Bob Lillis	1.75	.90	.50
355	Bill White	3.00	1.50	.90
356	Joe Amalfitano	1.75	.90	.50
357	Al Schroll	1.75	.90	.50
358	Joe DeMaestri	2.25	1.25	.70
359	Buddy Gilbert	1.75	.90	.50
360	Herb Score	2.50	1.25	.70
361	Bob Oldis	1.75	.90	.50
362	Russ Kemmerer	1.75	.90	.50
363	Gene Stephens	1.75	.90	.50
364	Paul Foytack	1.75	.90	.50
365	Minnie Minoso	3.00	1.50	.90
366	*Dallas Green*	3.25	1.75	1.00
367	Bill Tuttle	1.75	.90	.50
368	Daryl Spencer	1.75	.90	.50
369	Billy Hoeft	1.75	.90	.50
370	Bill Skowron	6.00	3.00	1.75
371	Bud Byerly	1.75	.90	.50
372	Frank House	1.75	.90	.50
373	Don Hoak	2.00	1.00	.60
374	Bob Buhl	2.00	1.00	.60
375	Dale Long	2.00	1.00	.60
376	Johnny Briggs	1.75	.90	.50
377	Roger Maris	90.00	45.00	27.00
378	Stu Miller	1.75	.90	.50
379	Red Wilson	1.75	.90	.50
380	Bob Shaw	1.75	.90	.50
381	Braves Team/Checklist 353-429	7.00	3.50	2.00
382	Ted Bowsfield	1.75	.90	.50
383	Leon Wagner	1.75	.90	.50
384	Don Cardwell	1.75	.90	.50
385	World Series Game 1 (Neal Steals Second)	3.50	1.75	1.00
386	World Series Game 2 (Neal Belts 2nd Homer)	3.50	1.75	1.00
387	World Series Game 3 (Furillo Breaks Up Game)	3.50	1.75	1.00
388	World Series Game 4 (Hodges' Winning Homer)	3.75	2.00	1.25
389	World Series Game 5 (Luis Swipes Base)	3.75	2.00	1.25
390	World Series Game 6 (Scrambling After Ball)	3.50	1.75	1.00
391	World Series Summary (The Champs Celebrate)	3.50	1.75	1.00
392	Tex Clevenger	1.75	.90	.50
393	Smoky Burgess	2.50	1.25	.70
394	Norm Larker	1.75	.90	.50
395	Hoyt Wilhelm	15.00	7.50	4.50
396	Steve Bilko	1.75	.90	.50
397	Don Blasingame	1.75	.90	.50
398	Mike Cuellar	2.25	1.25	.70
399	Young Hill Stars (Jack Fisher, Milt Pappas, Jerry Walker)	2.25	1.25	.70
400	Rocky Colavito	5.00	2.50	1.50
401	Bob Duliba	1.75	.90	.50
402	Dick Stuart	2.00	1.00	.60
403	Ed Sadowski	1.75	.90	.50
404	Bob Rush	1.75	.90	.50
405	Bobby Richardson	6.00	3.00	1.75
406	Billy Klaus	1.75	.90	.50
407	*Gary Peters* (photo actually J.C. Martin)	2.25	1.25	.70
408	Carl Furillo	4.00	2.00	1.25
409	Ron Samford	1.75	.90	.50
410	Sam Jones	1.75	.90	.50
411	Ed Bailey	1.75	.90	.50
412	Bob Anderson	1.75	.90	.50
413	A's Team/Checklist 430-495	7.00	3.50	2.00
414	Don Williams	1.75	.90	.50
415	Bob Cerv	1.75	.90	.50
416	Humberto Robinson	1.75	.90	.50
417	Chuck Cottier	1.75	.90	.50
418	Don Mossi	2.00	1.00	.60
419	George Crowe	1.75	.90	.50
420	Ed Mathews	25.00	12.50	7.50
421	Duke Maas	2.25	1.25	.70
422	Johnny Powers	1.75	.90	.50
423	Ed Fitz Gerald	1.75	.90	.50
424	Pete Whisenant	1.75	.90	.50
425	Johnny Podres	3.00	1.50	.90
426	Ron Jackson	1.75	.90	.50
427	Al Grunwald	1.75	.90	.50
428	Al Smith	1.75	.90	.50
429	American League Kings (Nellie Fox, Harvey Kuenn)	2.25	1.25	.70
430	Art Ditmar	2.00	1.00	.60
431	Andre Rodgers	1.75	.90	.50
432	Chuck Stobbs	1.75	.90	.50
433	Irv Noren	1.75	.90	.50
434	Brooks Lawrence	1.75	.90	.50
435	Gene Freese	1.75	.90	.50
436	Marv Throneberry	2.25	1.25	.70
437	Bob Friend	2.50	1.25	.70
438	Jim Coker	1.75	.90	.50
439	Tom Brewer	1.75	.90	.50
440	Jim Lemon	2.00	1.00	.60
441	Gary Bell	3.50	1.75	1.00
442	Joe Pignatano	3.50	1.75	1.00
443	Charlie Maxwell	3.50	1.75	1.00
444	Jerry Kindall	3.50	1.75	1.00
445	Warren Spahn	35.00	17.50	10.50
446	Ellis Burton	3.50	1.75	1.00
447	Ray Moore	3.50	1.75	1.00
448	*Jim Gentile*	4.00	2.00	1.25
449	Jim Brosnan	3.75	2.00	1.25
450	Orlando Cepeda	8.00	4.00	2.50
451	Curt Simmons	4.00	2.00	1.25
452	Ray Webster	3.50	1.75	1.00
453	Vern Law	4.50	2.25	1.25
454	Hal Woodeshick	3.50	1.75	1.00
455	Orioles Coaches (Harry Brecheen, Lum Harris, Eddie Robinson)	3.75	2.00	1.25
456	Red Sox Coaches (Del Baker, Billy Herman, Sal Maglie, Rudy York)	4.00	2.00	1.25
457	Cubs Coaches (Lou Klein, Charlie Root, Elvin Tappe)	3.75	2.00	1.25
458	White Sox Coaches (Ray Berres, Johnny Cooney, Tony Cuccinello, Don Gutteridge)	3.75	2.00	1.25
459	Reds Coaches (Cot Deal, Wally Moses, Reggie Otero)	3.75	2.00	1.25
460	Indians Coaches (Mel Harder, Red Kress, Bob Lemon, Jo-Jo White)	4.00	2.00	1.25
461	Tigers Coaches (Luke Appling, Tom Ferrick, Billy Hitchcock)	4.00	2.00	1.25
462	A's Coaches (Walker Cooper, Fred Fitzsimmons, Don Heffner)	3.75	2.00	1.25
463	Dodgers Coaches (Joe Becker, Bobby Bragan, Greg Mulleavy, Pete Reiser)	4.00	2.00	1.25
464	Braves Coaches (George Myatt, Andy Pafko, Bob Scheffing, Whitlow Wyatt)	3.75	2.00	1.25
465	Yankees Coaches (Frank Crosetti, Bill Dickey, Ralph Houk, Ed Lopat)	7.00	3.50	2.00
466	Phillies Coaches (Dick Carter, Andy Cohen, Ken Silvestri)	3.75	2.00	1.25
467	Pirates Coaches (Bill Burwell, Sam Narron, Frank Oceak, Mickey Vernon)	4.00	2.00	1.25
468	Cardinals Coaches (Ray Katt, Johnny Keane, Howie Pollet, Harry Walker)	3.75	2.00	1.25
469	Giants Coaches (Salty Parker, Bill Posedel, Wes Westrum)	3.75	2.00	1.25
470	Senators Coaches (Ellis Clary, Sam Mele, Bob Swift)	3.75	2.00	1.25
471	Ned Garver	3.50	1.75	1.00
472	Al Dark	4.50	2.25	1.25
473	Al Cicotte	3.50	1.75	1.00
474	Haywood Sullivan	3.75	2.00	1.25
475	Don Drysdale	30.00	15.00	9.00
476	Lou Johnson	3.50	1.75	1.00
477	Don Ferrarese	3.50	1.75	1.00
478	Frank Torre	3.50	1.75	1.00
479	Georges Maranda	3.50	1.75	1.00
480	Yogi Berra	40.00	20.00	12.00
481	Wes Stock	3.50	1.75	1.00
482	Frank Bolling	3.50	1.75	1.00
483	Camilo Pascual	3.75	2.00	1.25
484	Pirates Team/Checklist 430-495	15.00	7.50	4.50
485	Ken Boyer	4.50	2.25	1.25
486	Bobby Del Greco	3.50	1.75	1.00
487	Tom Sturdivant	3.50	1.75	1.00
488	Norm Cash	5.00	2.50	1.50
489	Steve Ridzik	3.50	1.75	1.00
490	Frank Robinson	30.00	15.00	9.00
491	Mel Roach	3.50	1.75	1.00
492	Larry Jackson	3.50	1.75	1.00
493	Duke Snider	40.00	20.00	12.00
494	Orioles Team/Checklist 496-572	7.00	3.50	2.00
495	Sherm Lollar	2.00	1.00	.60
496	Bill Virdon	4.00	2.00	1.25
497	John Tsitouris	3.50	1.75	1.00
498	Al Pilarcik	3.50	1.75	1.00
499	Johnny James	4.00	2.00	1.25
500	Johnny Temple	3.50	1.75	1.00
501	Bob Schmidt	3.50	1.75	1.00
502	Jim Bunning	8.00	4.00	2.50
503	Don Lee	3.50	1.75	1.00
504	Seth Morehead	3.50	1.75	1.00
505	Ted Kluszewski	5.00	2.50	1.50
506	Lee Walls	3.50	1.75	1.00
507	Dick Stigman	8.00	4.00	2.50
508	Billy Consolo	8.00	4.00	2.50
509	*Tommy Davis*	18.00	9.00	5.50
510	Jerry Staley	8.00	4.00	2.50
511	Ken Walters	8.00	4.00	2.50
512	Joe Gibbon	8.00	4.00	2.50
513	Cubs Team/Checklist 496-572	25.00	12.50	7.50
514	*Steve Barber*	9.00	4.50	2.75
515	Stan Lopata	8.00	4.00	2.50
516	Marty Kutyna	8.00	4.00	2.50
517	Charley James	8.00	4.00	2.50
518	*Tony Gonzalez*	9.00	4.50	2.75
519	Ed Roebuck	8.00	4.00	2.50
520	Don Buddin	8.00	4.00	2.50
521	Mike Lee	8.00	4.00	2.50
522	Ken Hunt	9.00	4.50	2.75
523	*Clay Dalrymple*	9.00	4.50	2.75
524	Bill Henry	8.00	4.00	2.50
525	Marv Breeding	8.00	4.00	2.50
526	Paul Giel	8.00	4.00	2.50
527	Jose Valdivielso	8.00	4.00	2.50
528	Ben Johnson	8.00	4.00	2.50
529	Norm Sherry	8.00	4.00	2.50
530	Mike McCormick	9.00	4.50	2.75
531	Sandy Amoros	8.00	4.00	2.50
532	Mike Garcia	10.00	5.00	3.00
533	Lu Clinton	8.00	4.00	2.50
534	Ken MacKenzie	8.00	4.00	2.50
535	Whitey Lockman	8.00	4.00	2.50
536	Wynn Hawkins	8.00	4.00	2.50
537	Red Sox Team/Checklist 496-572	25.00	12.50	7.50
538	Frank Barnes	8.00	4.00	2.50
539	Gene Baker	8.00	4.00	2.50
540	Jerry Walker	8.00	4.00	2.50
541	Tony Curry	8.00	4.00	2.50
542	Ken Hamlin	8.00	4.00	2.50
543	Elio Chacon	8.00	4.00	2.50
544	Bill Monbouquette	9.00	4.50	2.75
545	Carl Sawatski	8.00	4.00	2.50
546	Hank Aguirre	8.00	4.00	2.50
547	*Bob Aspromonte*	9.00	4.50	2.75
548	*Don Mincher*	9.00	4.50	2.75
549	John Buzhardt	8.00	4.00	2.50
550	Jim Landis	8.00	4.00	2.50
551	Ed Rakow	8.00	4.00	2.50
552	Walt Bond	8.00	4.00	2.50
553	Bill Skowron AS	12.00	6.00	3.50
554	Willie McCovey AS	45.00	22.00	13.50
555	Nellie Fox AS	15.00	7.50	4.50
556	Charlie Neal AS	9.00	4.50	2.75
557	Frank Malzone AS	9.00	4.50	2.75
558	Eddie Mathews AS	25.00	12.50	7.50
559	Luis Aparicio AS	18.00	9.00	5.50
560	Ernie Banks AS	40.00	20.00	12.00
561	Al Kaline AS	40.00	20.00	12.00
562	Joe Cunningham AS	9.00	4.50	2.75
563	Mickey Mantle AS	175.00	87.00	50.00
564	Willie Mays AS	85.00	42.00	25.00
565	Roger Maris AS	100.00	45.00	27.00
566	Hank Aaron AS	100.00	45.00	27.00
567	Sherm Lollar AS	9.00	4.50	2.75
568	Del Crandall AS	9.00	4.50	2.75
569	Camilo Pascual AS	9.00	4.50	2.75
570	Don Drysdale AS	30.00	15.00	9.00
571	Billy Pierce AS	9.00	4.50	2.75
572	Johnny Antonelli AS	15.00	5.00	2.75
---	Elect Your Favorite Rookie Insert (paper stock, no date on back)	15.00	7.50	4.50
---	Hot Iron Transfer Insert (paper stock)	15.00	7.50	4.50

1960 Topps Baseball Tattoos

Probably the least popular of all Topps products among parents and teachers, the Topps Tattoos were delightful little items on the reverse of the wrappers of Topps "Tattoo Bubble Gum." The entire wrapper was 1-9/16" by 3-1/2." The happy owner simply moistened his skin and applied the back of the wrapper to the wet spot. Presto, out came a "tattoo" in color (although often blurred by running colors). The set offered 96 tattoo possibilities of which 55 were players, 16 teams, 15 action shots and 10 autographed balls. Surviving specimens are very rare today.

		NR MT	EX	VG
Complete Set:		625.00	312.00	187.00
Common Player:		2.50	1.25	.70
(1)	Hank Aaron	25.00	12.50	7.50
(2)	Bob Allison	5.00	2.50	1.50
(3)	John Antonelli	5.00	2.50	1.50
(4)	Richie Ashburn	7.00	3.50	2.00
(5)	Ernie Banks	15.00	7.50	4.50
(6)	Yogi Berra	18.00	9.00	5.50
(7)	Lew Burdette	6.00	3.00	1.75
(8)	Orlando Cepeda	7.00	3.50	2.00
(9)	Rocky Colavito	6.00	3.00	1.75
(10)	Joe Cunningham	2.50	1.25	.70
(11)	Buddy Daley	2.50	1.25	.70
(12)	Don Drysdale	12.00	6.00	3.50
(13)	Ryne Duren	5.00	2.50	1.50
(14)	Roy Face	5.00	2.50	1.50
(15)	Whitey Ford	15.00	7.50	4.50
(16)	Nellie Fox	7.00	3.50	2.00
(17)	Tito Francona	2.50	1.25	.70
(18)	Gene Freese	2.50	1.25	.70
(19)	Jim Gilliam	6.00	3.00	1.75
(20)	Dick Groat	6.00	3.00	1.75
(21)	Ray Herbert	2.50	1.25	.70
(22)	Glen Hobbie	2.50	1.25	.70
(23)	Jackie Jensen	6.00	3.00	1.75
(24)	Sam Jones	2.50	1.25	.70
(25)	Al Kaline	15.00	7.50	4.50
(26)	Harmon Killebrew	12.00	6.00	3.50
(27)	Harvy Kuenn (Harvey)	6.00	3.00	1.75
(28)	Frank Lary	2.50	1.25	.70
(29)	Vernon Law	5.00	2.50	1.50
(30)	Frank Malzone	2.50	1.25	.70
(31)	Mickey Mantle	75.00	37.00	22.00
(32)	Roger Maris	15.00	7.50	4.50
(33)	Ed Mathews	12.00	6.00	3.50
(34)	Willie Mays	25.00	12.50	7.50
(35)	Cal Mclish	2.50	1.25	.70
(36)	Wally Moon	5.00	2.50	1.50
(37)	Walt Moryn	2.50	1.25	.70
(38)	Don Mossi	2.50	1.25	.70
(39)	Stan Musial	25.00	12.50	7.50
(40)	Charlie Neal	2.50	1.25	.70

		NR MT	EX	VG
(41)	Don Newcombe	5.00	2.50	1.50
(42)	Milt Pappas	5.00	2.50	1.50
(43)	Camilo Pascual	5.00	2.50	1.50
(44)	Billie Pierce (Billy)	5.00	2.50	1.50
(45)	Robin Roberts	12.00	6.00	3.50
(46)	Frank Robinson	15.00	7.50	4.50
(47)	Pete Runnels	5.00	2.50	1.50
(48)	Herb Score	5.00	2.50	1.50
(49)	Warren Spahn	12.00	6.00	3.50
(50)	Johnny Temple	2.50	1.25	.70
(51)	Gus Triandos	2.50	1.25	.70
(52)	Jerry Walker	2.50	1.25	.70
(53)	Bill White	5.00	2.50	1.50
(54)	Gene Woodling	5.00	2.50	1.50
(55)	Early Wynn	12.00	6.00	3.50
(56)	Chicago Cubs Logo	2.50	1.25	.70
(57)	Cincinnati Reds Logo	2.50	1.25	.70
(58)	Los Angeles Dodgers Logo	2.50	1.25	.70
(59)	Milwaukee Braves Logo	2.50	1.25	.70
(60)	Philadelphia Phillies Logo	2.50	1.25	.70
(61)	Pittsburgh Pirates Logo	5.00	2.50	1.50
(62)	San Francisco Giants Logo	2.50	1.25	.70
(63)	St. Louis Cardinals Logo	2.50	1.25	.70
(64)	Baltimore Orioles Logo	2.50	1.25	.70
(65)	Boston Red Sox Logo	2.50	1.25	.70
(66)	Chicago White Sox Logo	2.50	1.25	.70
(67)	Cleveland Indians Logo	2.50	1.25	.70
(68)	Detroit Tigers Logo	2.50	1.25	.70
(69)	Kansas City Athletics Logo	2.50	1.25	.70
(70)	New York Yankees Logo	6.00	3.00	1.75
(71)	Washington Senators Logo	2.50	1.25	.70
(72)	Autograph (Richie Ashburn)	2.50	1.25	.70
(73)	Autograph (Rocky Colavito)	2.50	1.25	.70
(74)	Autograph (Roy Face)	2.50	1.25	.70
(75)	Autograph (Jackie Jensen)	2.50	1.25	.70
(76)	Autograph (Harmon Killebrew)	5.00	2.50	1.50
(77)	Autograph (Mickey Mantle)	25.00	12.50	7.50
(78)	Autograph (Willie Mays)	10.00	5.00	3.00
(79)	Autograph (Stan Musial)	10.00	5.00	3.00
(80)	Autograph (Billy Pierce)	2.50	1.25	.70
(81)	Autograph (Jerry Walker)	2.50	1.25	.70
(82)	Run-Down	2.50	1.25	.70
(83)	Out At First	2.50	1.25	.70
(84)	The Final Word	2.50	1.25	.70
(85)	Twisting Foul	2.50	1.25	.70
(86)	Out At Home	2.50	1.25	.70
(87)	Circus Catch	2.50	1.25	.70
(88)	Great Catch	2.50	1.25	.70
(89)	Stolen Base	2.50	1.25	.70
(90)	Grand Slam Homer	2.50	1.25	.70
(91)	Double Play	2.50	1.25	.70
(92)	Right-Handed Follow-Thru (no caption)	2.50	1.25	.70
(93)	Right-Handed High Leg Kick (no caption)	2.50	1.25	.70
(94)	Left-Handed Pitcher (no caption)	2.50	1.25	.70
(95)	Right-Handed Batter (no caption)	2.50	1.25	.70
(96)	Left-Handed Batter (no caption)	2.50	1.25	.70

1961 Topps

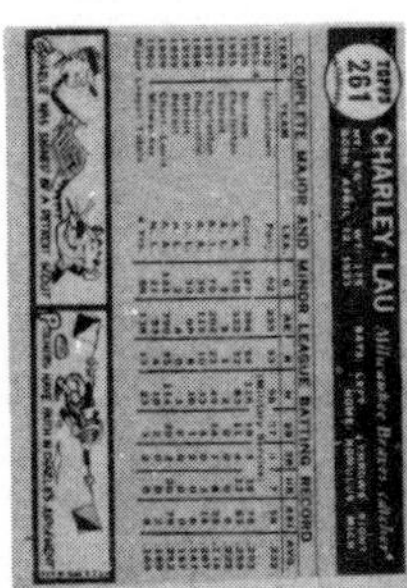

Except for some of the specialty cards, Topps returned to a vertical format with their 1961 cards. The set is numbered through 598, however only 587 cards were printed. No numbers 426, 587 and 588 were issued. Two cards numbered 463 exist (one a Braves team card and one a player card of Jack Fisher). Actually, the Braves team card is checklisted as #426. Designs for 1961 are basically large color portraits; the backs return to extensive statistics. A three-panel cartoon highlighting the player's career appears on the card backs. Innovations include numbered checklists, cards for statistical leaders, and 10 "Baseball Thrills" cards. The scarce high numbers are card numbers 523-589.

		NR MT	EX	VG
	Complete Set:	4800.	2400.	1450.
	Common Player: 1-370	1.00	.50	.30
	Common Player: 371-522	1.50	.70	.45
	Common Player: 523-589	20.00	10.00	6.00
1	Dick Groat	12.00	2.00	.70
2	Roger Maris	200.00	80.00	50.00
3	John Buzhardt	1.00	.50	.30
4	Lenny Green	1.00	.50	.30
5	Johnny Romano	1.00	.50	.30
6	Ed Roebuck	1.00	.50	.30
7	White Sox Team	2.50	1.25	.70
8	Dick Williams	1.50	.70	.45
9	Bob Purkey	1.00	.50	.30
10	Brooks Robinson	30.00	15.00	9.00
11	Curt Simmons	1.25	.60	.40
12	Moe Thacker	1.00	.50	.30
13	Chuck Cottier	1.00	.50	.30
14	Don Mossi	1.25	.60	.40
15	Willie Kirkland	1.00	.50	.30
16	Billy Muffett	1.00	.50	.30
17	Checklist 1-88	5.00	2.50	1.50
18	Jim Grant	1.00	.50	.30
19	Cletis Boyer	2.25	1.25	.70
20	Robin Roberts	10.00	5.00	3.00
21	*Zorro Versalles*	2.00	1.00	.60
22	Clem Labine	1.25	.60	.40
23	Don Demeter	1.00	.50	.30
24	Ken Johnson	1.00	.50	.30
25	Red's Heavy Artillery (Gus Bell, Vada Pinson, Frank Robinson)	6.00	3.00	1.75
26	Wes Stock	1.00	.50	.30
27	Jerry Kindall	1.00	.50	.30
28	Hector Lopez	1.50	.70	.45
29	Don Nottebart	1.00	.50	.30
30	Nellie Fox	6.00	3.00	1.75
31	Bob Schmidt	1.00	.50	.30
32	Ray Sadecki	1.00	.50	.30
33	Gary Geiger	1.00	.50	.30
34	Wynn Hawkins	1.00	.50	.30
35	*Ron Santo*	10.00	5.00	3.00
36	Jack Kralick	1.00	.50	.30
37	Charlie Maxwell	1.00	.50	.30
38	Bob Lillis	1.00	.50	.30
39	Leo Posada	1.00	.50	.30
40	Bob Turley	2.50	1.25	.70
41	N.L. Batting Leaders (Bob Clemente, Dick Groat, Norm Larker, Willie Mays)	4.00	2.00	1.25
42	A.L. Batting Leaders (Minnie Minoso, Pete Runnels, Bill Skowron, Al Smith)	2.50	1.25	.70
43	N.L. Home Run Leaders (Hank Aaron, Ernie Banks, Ken Boyer, Eddie Mathews)	4.00	2.00	1.25
44	A.L. Home Run Leaders (Rocky Colavito, Jim Lemon, Mickey Mantle, Roger Maris)	15.00	7.50	4.50
45	N.L. E.R.A. Leaders (Ernie Broglio, Don Drysdale, Bob Friend, Mike McCormick, Stan Williams)	3.25	1.75	1.00
46	A.L. E.R.A. Leaders (Frank Baumann, Hal Brown, Jim Bunning, Art Ditmar)	2.50	1.25	.70
47	N.L. Pitching Leaders (Ernie Broglio, Lou Burdette, Vern Law, Warren Spahn)	3.25	1.75	1.00
48	A.L. Pitching Leaders (Bud Daley, Art Ditmar, Chuck Estrada, Frank Lary, Milt Pappas, Jim Perry)	2.50	1.25	.70
49	N.L. Strikeout Leaders (Ernie Broglio, Don Drysdale, Sam Jones, Sandy Koufax)	4.00	2.00	1.25
50	A.L. Strikeout Leaders (Jim Bunning, Frank Lary, Pedro Ramos, Early Wynn)	3.00	1.50	.90
51	Tigers Team	3.50	1.75	1.00
52	George Crowe	1.00	.50	.30
53	Russ Nixon	1.00	.50	.30
54	Earl Francis	1.00	.50	.30
55	Jim Davenport	1.00	.50	.30
56	Russ Kemmerer	1.00	.50	.30
57	Marv Throneberry	1.75	.90	.50
58	Joe Schaffernoth	1.00	.50	.30
59	Jim Woods	1.00	.50	.30
60	Woodie Held	1.00	.50	.30
61	Ron Piche	1.00	.50	.30
62	Al Pilarcik	1.00	.50	.30
63	Jim Kaat	8.00	4.00	2.50
64	Alex Grammas	1.00	.50	.30
65	Ted Kluszewski	4.00	2.00	1.25
66	Bill Henry	1.00	.50	.30
67	Ossie Virgil	1.00	.50	.30
68	Deron Johnson	1.50	.70	.45
69	Earl Wilson	1.00	.50	.30
70	Bill Virdon	2.00	1.00	.60
71	Jerry Adair	1.25	.60	.40
72	Stu Miller	1.00	.50	.30
73	Al Spangler	1.00	.50	.30
74	Joe Pignatano	1.00	.50	.30
75	Lindy Shows Larry (Larry Jackson, Lindy McDaniel)	1.50	.70	.45
76	Harry Anderson	1.00	.50	.30
77	Dick Stigman	1.00	.50	.30
78	Lee Walls	1.00	.50	.30
79	Joe Ginsberg	1.00	.50	.30
80	Harmon Killebrew	18.00	9.00	5.50
81	Tracy Stallard	1.00	.50	.30
82	Joe Christopher	1.00	.50	.30
83	Bob Bruce	1.00	.50	.30
84	Lee Maye	1.00	.50	.30
85	Jerry Walker	1.00	.50	.30
86	Dodgers Team	3.50	1.75	1.00
87	Joe Amalfitano	1.00	.50	.30
88	Richie Ashburn	6.00	3.00	1.75
89	Billy Martin	6.00	3.00	1.75
90	Jerry Staley	1.00	.50	.30
91	Walt Moryn	1.00	.50	.30
92	Hal Naragon	1.00	.50	.30
93	Tony Gonzalez	1.00	.50	.30
94	Johnny Kucks	1.00	.50	.30
95	Norm Cash	3.50	1.75	1.00
96	Billy O'Dell	1.00	.50	.30
97	Jerry Lynch	1.00	.50	.30
98a	Checklist 89-176 (word "Checklist" in red on front)	7.00	3.50	2.00
98b	Checklist 89-176 ("Checklist" in yellow, 98 on back in black)	5.00	2.50	1.50
98c	Checklist 89-176 ("Checklist" in yellow, 98 on back in white)	7.00	3.50	2.00
99	Don Buddin	1.00	.50	.30
100	Harvey Haddix	1.50	.70	.45
101	Bubba Phillips	1.00	.50	.30
102	Gene Stephens	1.00	.50	.30
103	Ruben Amaro	1.00	.50	.30
104	John Blanchard	1.50	.70	.45
105	Carl Willey	1.00	.50	.30
106	Whitey Herzog	2.25	1.25	.70
107	Seth Morehead	1.00	.50	.30
108	Dan Dobbek	1.00	.50	.30
109	Johnny Podres	2.25	1.25	.70
110	Vada Pinson	3.00	1.50	.90
111	Jack Meyer	1.00	.50	.30
112	Chico Fernandez	1.00	.50	.30
113	Mike Fornieles	1.00	.50	.30
114	Hobie Landrith	1.00	.50	.30
115	Johnny Antonelli	1.25	.60	.40
116	Joe DeMaestri	1.50	.70	.45
117	Dale Long	1.25	.60	.40
118	Chris Cannizzaro	1.00	.50	.30
119	A's Big Armor (Hank Bauer, Jerry Lumpe, Norm Siebern)	1.50	.70	.45
120	Ed Mathews	15.00	7.50	4.50
121	Eli Grba	1.00	.50	.30
122	Cubs Team	2.50	1.25	.70
123	Billy Gardner	1.00	.50	.30
124	J.C. Martin	1.00	.50	.30
125	Steve Barber	1.00	.50	.30
126	Dick Stuart	1.25	.60	.40
127	Ron Kline	1.00	.50	.30
128	Rip Repulski	1.00	.50	.30
129	Ed Hobaugh	1.00	.50	.30
130	Norm Larker	1.00	.50	.30
131	Paul Richards	1.25	.60	.40
132	Al Lopez	3.00	1.50	.90
133	Ralph Houk	3.00	1.50	.90
134	Mickey Vernon	1.25	.60	.40
135	Fred Hutchinson	1.25	.60	.40
136	Walt Alston	4.00	2.00	1.25
137	Chuck Dressen	1.25	.60	.40
138	Danny Murtaugh	1.25	.60	.40
139	Solly Hemus	1.00	.50	.30
140	Gus Triandos	1.25	.60	.40
141	*Billy Williams*	90.00	45.00	27.00
142	Luis Arroyo	1.50	.70	.45
143	Russ Snyder	1.00	.50	.30
144	Jim Coker	1.00	.50	.30
145	Bob Buhl	1.25	.60	.40
146	Marty Keough	1.00	.50	.30
147	Ed Rakow	1.00	.50	.30
148	Julian Javier	1.25	.60	.40
149	Bob Oldis	1.00	.50	.30
150	Willie Mays	100.00	50.00	30.00
151	Jim Donohue	1.00	.50	.30
152	Earl Torgeson	1.00	.50	.30
153	Don Lee	1.00	.50	.30
154	Bobby Del Greco	1.00	.50	.30
155	Johnny Temple	1.00	.50	.30
156	Ken Hunt	1.00	.50	.30
157	Cal McLish	1.00	.50	.30
158	Pete Daley	1.00	.50	.30
159	Orioles Team	2.50	1.25	.70
160	Whitey Ford	25.00	12.50	7.50
161	Sherman Jones (photo actually Eddie Fisher)	1.00	.50	.30
162	Jay Hook	1.00	.50	.30
163	Ed Sadowski	1.00	.50	.30
164	Felix Mantilla	1.00	.50	.30
165	Gino Cimoli	1.00	.50	.30
166	Danny Kravitz	1.00	.50	.30
167	Giants Team	2.50	1.25	.70
168	Tommy Davis	3.00	1.50	.90
169	Don Elston	1.00	.50	.30
170	Al Smith	1.00	.50	.30
171	Paul Foytack	1.00	.50	.30
172	Don Dillard	1.00	.50	.30
173	Beantown Bombers (Jackie Jensen, Frank Malzone, Vic Wertz)	2.00	1.00	.60
174	Ray Semproch	1.00	.50	.30
175	Gene Freese	1.00	.50	.30
176	Ken Aspromonte	1.00	.50	.30
177	Don Larsen	1.50	.70	.45
178	Bob Nieman	1.00	.50	.30
179	Joe Koppe	1.00	.50	.30
180	Bobby Richardson	5.00	2.50	1.50
181	Fred Green	1.00	.50	.30
182	Dave Nicholson	1.00	.50	.30
183	Andre Rodgers	1.00	.50	.30
184	Steve Bilko	1.00	.50	.30
185	Herb Score	1.50	.70	.45
186	Elmer Valo	1.00	.50	.30
187	Billy Klaus	1.00	.50	.30
188	Jim Marshall	1.00	.50	.30
189	Checklist 177-264	5.00	2.50	1.50
190	Stan Williams	1.00	.50	.30
191	Mike de la Hoz	1.00	.50	.30
192	Dick Brown	1.00	.50	.30
193	Gene Conley	1.25	.60	.40
194	Gordy Coleman	1.00	.50	.30
195	Jerry Casale	1.00	.50	.30
196	Ed Bouchee	1.00	.50	.30
197	Dick Hall	1.00	.50	.30
198	Carl Sawatski	1.00	.50	.30
199	Bob Boyd	1.00	.50	.30
200	Warren Spahn	25.00	12.50	7.50
201	Pete Whisenant	1.00	.50	.30
202	Al Neiger	1.00	.50	.30
203	Eddie Bressoud	1.00	.50	.30
204	Bob Skinner	1.25	.60	.40
205	Bill Pierce	1.75	.90	.50
206	Gene Green	1.00	.50	.30
207	Dodger Southpaws (Sandy Koufax, Johnny Podres)	15.00	7.50	4.50
208	Larry Osborne	1.00	.50	.30
209	Ken McBride	1.00	.50	.30
210	Pete Runnels	1.25	.60	.40

No.	Card	NR MT	EX	VG
211	Bob Gibson	20.00	10.00	6.00
212	Haywood Sullivan	1.25	.60	.40
213	*Bill Stafford*	2.00	1.00	.60
214	Danny Murphy	1.00	.50	.30
215	Gus Bell	1.25	.60	.40
216	Ted Bowsfield	1.00	.50	.30
217	Mel Roach	1.00	.50	.30
218	Hal Brown	1.00	.50	.30
219	Gene Mauch	2.50	1.25	.70
220	Al Dark	1.25	.60	.40
221	Mike Higgins	1.00	.50	.30
222	Jimmie Dykes	1.00	.50	.30
223	Bob Scheffing	1.00	.50	.30
224	Joe Gordon	1.25	.60	.40
225	Bill Rigney	1.00	.50	.30
226	Harry Lavagetto	1.00	.50	.30
227	Juan Pizarro	1.00	.50	.30
228	Yankees Team	10.00	5.00	3.00
229	Rudy Hernandez	1.00	.50	.30
230	Don Hoak	1.25	.60	.40
231	Dick Drott	1.00	.50	.30
232	Bill White	1.50	.70	.45
233	Joe Jay	1.00	.50	.30
234	Ted Lepcio	1.00	.50	.30
235	Camilo Pascual	1.25	.60	.40
236	Don Gile	1.00	.50	.30
237	Billy Loes	1.00	.50	.30
238	Jim Gilliam	2.50	1.25	.70
239	Dave Sisler	1.00	.50	.30
240	Ron Hansen	1.00	.50	.30
241	Al Cicotte	1.00	.50	.30
242	Hal W. Smith	1.00	.50	.30
243	Frank Lary	1.25	.60	.40
244	Chico Cardenas	1.25	.60	.40
245	Joe Adcock	2.00	1.00	.60
246	Bob Davis	1.00	.50	.30
247	Billy Goodman	1.00	.50	.30
248	Ed Keegan	1.00	.50	.30
249	Reds Team	4.00	2.00	1.25
250	Buc Hill Aces (Roy Face, Vern Law)	2.00	1.00	.60
251	Bill Bruton	1.00	.50	.30
252	Bill Short	1.50	.70	.45
253	Sammy Taylor	1.00	.50	.30
254	Ted Sadowski	1.00	.50	.30
255	Vic Power	1.00	.50	.30
256	Billy Hoeft	1.00	.50	.30
257	Carroll Hardy	1.00	.50	.30
258	Jack Sanford	1.00	.50	.30
259	John Schaive	1.00	.50	.30
260	Don Drysdale	15.00	7.50	4.50
261	Charlie Lau	1.25	.60	.40
262	Tony Curry	1.00	.50	.30
263	Ken Hamlin	1.00	.50	.30
264	Glen Hobbie	1.00	.50	.30
265	Tony Kubek	5.00	2.50	1.50
266	Lindy McDaniel	1.00	.50	.30
267	Norm Siebern	1.25	.60	.40
268	Ike DeLock (Delock)	1.00	.50	.30
269	Harry Chiti	1.00	.50	.30
270	Bob Friend	1.50	.70	.45
271	Jim Landis	1.00	.50	.30
272	Tom Morgan	1.00	.50	.30
273	Checklist 265-352	5.00	2.50	1.50
274	Gary Bell	1.00	.50	.30
275	Gene Woodling	1.25	.60	.40
276	Ray Rippelmeyer	1.00	.50	.30
277	Hank Foiles	1.00	.50	.30
278	Don McMahon	1.00	.50	.30
279	Jose Pagan	1.00	.50	.30
280	Frank Howard	2.50	1.25	.70
281	Frank Sullivan	1.00	.50	.30
282	Faye Throneberry	1.00	.50	.30
283	Bob Anderson	1.00	.50	.30
284	Dick Gernert	1.00	.50	.30
285	Sherm Lollar	1.25	.60	.40
286	George Witt	1.00	.50	.30
287	Carl Yastrzemski	175.00	70.00	44.00
288	Albie Pearson	1.00	.50	.30
289	Ray Moore	1.00	.50	.30
290	Stan Musial	65.00	33.00	20.00
291	Tex Clevenger	1.00	.50	.30
292	Jim Baumer	1.00	.50	.30
293	Tom Sturdivant	1.00	.50	.30
294	Don Blasingame	1.00	.50	.30
295	Milt Pappas	1.25	.60	.40
296	Wes Covington	1.00	.50	.30
297	Athletics Team	2.50	1.25	.70
298	Jim Golden	1.00	.50	.30
299	Clay Dalrymple	1.00	.50	.30
300	Mickey Mantle	300.00	150.00	90.00
301	Chet Nichols	1.00	.50	.30
302	Al Heist	1.00	.50	.30
303	Gary Peters	1.25	.60	.40
304	Rocky Nelson	1.00	.50	.30
305	Mike McCormick	1.25	.60	.40
306	World Series Game 1 (Virdon Saves Game)	3.50	1.75	1.00
307	World Series Game 2 (Mantle Slams 2 Homers)	20.00	10.00	6.00
308	World Series Game 3 (Richardson Is Hero)	4.00	2.00	1.25
309	World Series Game 4 (Cimoli Is Safe In Crucial Play)	3.00	1.50	.90
310	World Series Game 5 (Face Saves the Day)	3.50	1.75	1.00
311	World Series Game 6 (Ford Pitches Second Shutout)	5.00	2.50	1.50
312	World Series Game 7 (Mazeroski's Homer Wins It!)	5.00	2.50	1.50
313	World Series Summary (The Winners Celebrate)	3.00	1.50	.90
314	Bob Miller	1.00	.50	.30
315	Earl Battey	1.25	.60	.40
316	Bobby Gene Smith	1.00	.50	.30
317	*Jim Brewer*	1.25	.60	.40
318	Danny O'Connell	1.00	.50	.30
319	Valmy Thomas	1.00	.50	.30
320	Lou Burdette	2.50	1.25	.70
321	Marv Breeding	1.00	.50	.30
322	Bill Kunkel	1.00	.50	.30
323	Sammy Esposito	1.00	.50	.30
324	Hank Aguirre	1.00	.50	.30
325	Wally Moon	1.25	.60	.40

No.	Card	NR MT	EX	VG
326	Dave Hillman	1.00	.50	.30
327	*Matty Alou*	4.00	2.00	1.25
328	Jim O'Toole	1.00	.50	.30
329	Julio Becquer	1.00	.50	.30
330	Rocky Colavito	3.00	1.50	.90
331	Ned Garver	1.00	.50	.30
332	Dutch Dotterer (photo actually Tommy Dotterer)	1.00	.50	.30
333	Fritz Brickell	1.50	.70	.45
334	Walt Bond	1.00	.50	.30
335	Frank Bolling	1.00	.50	.30
336	Don Mincher	1.25	.60	.40
337	Al's Aces (Al Lopez, Herb Score, Early Wynn)	3.50	1.75	1.00
338	Don Landrum	1.00	.50	.30
339	Gene Baker	1.00	.50	.30
340	Vic Wertz	1.25	.60	.40
341	Jim Owens	1.00	.50	.30
342	Clint Courtney	1.00	.50	.30
343	Earl Robinson	1.00	.50	.30
344	Sandy Koufax	80.00	40.00	24.00
345	Jim Piersall	2.00	1.00	.60
346	Howie Nunn	1.00	.50	.30
347	Cardinals Team	2.50	1.25	.70
348	Steve Boros	1.00	.50	.30
349	Danny McDevitt	1.50	.70	.45
350	Ernie Banks	30.00	15.00	9.00
351	Jim King	1.00	.50	.30
352	Bob Shaw	1.00	.50	.30
353	Howie Bedell	1.00	.50	.30
354	Billy Harrell	1.00	.50	.30
355	Bob Allison	1.25	.60	.40
356	Ryne Duren	2.25	1.25	.70
357	Daryl Spencer	1.00	.50	.30
358	Earl Averill	1.00	.50	.30
359	Dallas Green	1.25	.60	.40
360	Frank Robinson	20.00	10.00	6.00
361a	Checklist 353-429 ("Topps Baseball" in black on front)	5.00	2.50	1.50
361b	Checklist 353-429 ("Topps Baseball" in yellow)	6.00	3.00	1.75
362	Frank Funk	1.00	.50	.30
363	John Roseboro	1.25	.60	.40
364	Moe Drabowsky	1.00	.50	.30
365	Jerry Lumpe	1.25	.60	.40
366	Eddie Fisher	1.00	.50	.30
367	Jim Rivera	1.00	.50	.30
368	Bennie Daniels	1.00	.50	.30
369	Dave Philley	1.25	.60	.40
370	Roy Face	2.00	1.00	.60
371	Bill Skowron	5.00	2.50	1.50
372	Bob Hendley	1.50	.70	.45
373	Red Sox Team	5.00	2.50	1.50
374	Paul Giel	1.50	.70	.45
375	Ken Boyer	4.00	2.00	1.25
376	Mike Roarke	1.50	.70	.45
377	Ruben Gomez	1.50	.70	.45
378	Wally Post	1.50	.70	.45
379	Bobby Shantz	2.50	1.25	.70
380	Minnie Minoso	3.00	1.50	.90
381	Dave Wickersham	1.50	.70	.45
382	Frank Thomas	1.50	.70	.45
383	Frisco First Liners (Mike McCormick, Billy O'Dell, Jack Sanford)	2.00	1.00	.60
384	Chuck Essegian	1.50	.70	.45
385	Jim Perry	2.50	1.25	.70
386	Joe Hicks	1.50	.70	.45
387	Duke Maas	2.50	1.25	.70
388	Bob Clemente	80.00	40.00	25.00
389	Ralph Terry	3.00	1.50	.90
390	Del Crandall	2.50	1.25	.70
391	Winston Brown	1.50	.70	.45
392	Reno Bertoia	1.50	.70	.45
393	Batter Bafflers (Don Cardwell, Glen Hobbie)	1.75	.90	.50
394	Ken Walters	1.50	.70	.45
395	Chuck Estrada	1.50	.70	.45
396	Bob Aspromonte	1.50	.70	.45
397	Hal Woodeshick	1.50	.70	.45
398	Hank Bauer	2.50	1.25	.70
399	Cliff Cook	1.50	.70	.45
400	Vern Law	2.50	1.25	.70
401	Babe Ruth Hits 60th Homer	15.00	7.50	4.50
402	Larsen Pitches Perfect Game	10.00	5.00	3.00
403	Brooklyn-Boston Play 26-Inning Tie	2.00	1.00	.60
404	Hornsby Tops N.L. With .424 Average	3.50	1.75	1.00
405	Gehrig Benched After 2,130 Games	12.00	6.00	3.50
406	Mantle Blasts 565 ft. Home Run	30.00	15.00	9.00
407	Jack Chesbro Wins 41st Game	2.50	1.25	.70
408	Mathewson Strikes Out 267 Batters	3.50	1.75	1.00
409	Johnson Hurls 3rd Shutout in 4 Days	4.00	2.00	1.25
410	Haddix Pitches 12 Perfect Innings	2.50	1.25	.70
411	Tony Taylor	1.50	.70	.45
412	Larry Sherry	1.50	.70	.45
413	Eddie Yost	1.75	.90	.50
414	Dick Donovan	1.50	.70	.45
415	Hank Aaron	100.00	50.00	30.00
416	*Dick Howser*	8.00	4.00	2.50
417	*Juan Marichal*	100.00	50.00	30.00
418	Ed Bailey	1.50	.70	.45
419	Tom Borland	1.50	.70	.45
420	Ernie Broglio	1.50	.70	.45
421	Ty Cline	1.50	.70	.45
422	Bud Daley	1.50	.70	.45
423	Charlie Neal	1.50	.70	.45
424	Turk Lown	1.50	.70	.45
425	Yogi Berra	60.00	30.00	18.00
426	Not Issued			
427	Dick Ellsworth	1.50	.70	.45
428	Ray Barker	1.50	.70	.45
429	Al Kaline	35.00	17.50	10.50
430	Bill Mazeroski	3.50	1.75	1.00
431	Chuck Stobbs	1.50	.70	.45

No.	Card	NR MT	EX	VG
432	Coot Veal	1.50	.70	.45
433	Art Mahaffey	1.50	.70	.45
434	Tom Brewer	1.50	.70	.45
435	Orlando Cepeda	7.00	3.50	2.00
436	*Jim Maloney*	2.50	1.25	.70
437a	Checklist 430-506 (#440 is Louis Aparicio)	6.00	3.00	1.75
437b	Checklist 430-506 (#440 is Luis Aparicio)	6.50	3.25	2.00
438	Curt Flood	2.50	1.25	.70
439	*Phil Regan*	1.75	.90	.50
440	Luis Aparicio	12.00	6.00	3.50
441	Dick Bertell	1.50	.70	.45
442	Gordon Jones	1.50	.70	.45
443	Duke Snider	35.00	17.50	10.50
444	Joe Nuxhall	1.75	.90	.50
445	Frank Malzone	1.75	.90	.50
446	Bob "Hawk" Taylor	1.50	.70	.45
447	Harry Bright	1.50	.70	.45
448	Del Rice	1.50	.70	.45
449	*Bobby Bolin*	1.75	.90	.50
450	Jim Lemon	1.50	.70	.45
451	Power For Ernie (Ernie Broglio, Daryl Spencer, Bill White)	1.75	.90	.50
452	Bob Allen	1.50	.70	.45
453	Dick Schofield	1.50	.70	.45
454	Pumpsie Green	1.50	.70	.45
455	Early Wynn	15.00	7.50	4.50
456	Hal Bevan	1.50	.70	.45
457	Johnny James	1.50	.70	.45
458	Willie Tasby	1.50	.70	.45
459	Terry Fox	1.50	.70	.45
460	Gil Hodges	18.00	9.00	5.50
461	Smoky Burgess	2.50	1.25	.70
462	Lou Klimchock	1.50	.70	.45
463a	Braves Team (should be card #426)	4.00	2.00	1.25
463b	Jack Fisher	1.75	.90	.50
464	*Leroy Thomas*	1.50	.70	.45
465	Roy McMillan	1.50	.70	.45
466	Ron Moeller	1.50	.70	.45
467	Indians Team	3.50	1.75	1.00
468	Johnny Callison	1.75	.90	.50
469	Ralph Lumenti	1.50	.70	.45
470	Roy Sievers	1.75	.90	.50
471	Phil Rizzuto MVP	8.00	4.00	2.50
472	Yogi Berra MVP	25.00	12.50	7.50
473	Bobby Shantz MVP	3.50	1.75	1.00
474	Al Rosen MVP	3.50	1.75	1.00
475	Mickey Mantle MVP	90.00	45.00	27.00
476	Jackie Jensen MVP	3.50	1.75	1.00
477	Nellie Fox MVP	4.00	2.00	1.25
478	Roger Maris MVP	30.00	15.00	9.00
479	Jim Konstanty MVP	2.50	1.25	.70
480	Roy Campanella MVP	20.00	10.00	6.00
481	Hank Sauer MVP	2.50	1.25	.70
482	Willie Mays MVP	30.00	15.00	9.00
483	Don Newcombe MVP	3.50	1.75	1.00
484	Hank Aaron MVP	30.00	15.00	9.00
485	Ernie Banks MVP	20.00	10.00	6.00
486	Dick Groat MVP	3.50	1.75	1.00
487	Gene Oliver	1.50	.70	.45
488	Joe McClain	1.50	.70	.45
489	Walt Dropo	1.75	.90	.50
490	Jim Bunning	8.00	4.00	2.50
491	Phillies Team	3.50	1.75	1.00
492	Ron Fairly	1.75	.90	.50
493	Don Zimmer	2.00	1.00	.60
494	Tom Cheney	1.50	.70	.45
495	Elston Howard	6.00	3.00	1.75
496	Ken MacKenzie	1.50	.70	.45
497	Willie Jones	1.50	.70	.45
498	Ray Herbert	1.50	.70	.45
499	Chuck Schilling	1.50	.70	.45
500	Harvey Kuenn	3.00	1.50	.90
501	John DeMerit	1.50	.70	.45
502	Clarence Coleman	1.50	.70	.45
503	Tito Francona	1.75	.90	.50
504	Billy Consolo	1.50	.70	.45
505	Red Schoendienst	8.00	4.00	2.50
506	*Willie Davis*	7.00	3.50	2.00
507	Pete Burnside	1.50	.70	.45
508	Rocky Bridges	1.50	.70	.45
509	Camilo Carreon	1.50	.70	.45
510	Art Ditmar	2.50	1.25	.70
511	Joe Morgan	1.50	.70	.45
512	Bob Will	1.50	.70	.45
513	Jim Brosnan	1.75	.90	.50
514	Jake Wood	1.50	.70	.45
515	Jackie Brandt	1.50	.70	.45
516	Checklist 507-587	6.00	3.00	1.75
517	Willie McCovey	50.00	25.00	15.00
518	Andy Carey	1.50	.70	.45
519	Jim Pagliaroni	1.50	.70	.45
520	Joe Cunningham	1.75	.90	.50
521	Brother Battery (Larry Sherry, Norm Sherry)	2.00	1.00	.60
522	Dick Farrell	1.50	.70	.45
523	Joe Gibbon	20.00	10.00	6.00
524	Johnny Logan	22.00	11.00	6.50
525	*Ron Perranoski*	22.00	11.00	6.50
526	R.C. Stevens	20.00	10.00	6.00
527	Gene Leek	20.00	10.00	6.00
528	Pedro Ramos	20.00	10.00	6.00
529	Bob Roselli	20.00	10.00	6.00
530	Bobby Malkmus	20.00	10.00	6.00
531	Jim Coates	22.00	11.00	6.50
532	Bob Hale	20.00	10.00	6.00
533	Jack Curtis	20.00	10.00	6.00
534	Eddie Kasko	20.00	10.00	6.00
535	Larry Jackson	20.00	10.00	6.00
536	Bill Tuttle	20.00	10.00	6.00
537	Bobby Locke	20.00	10.00	6.00
538	Chuck Hiller	20.00	10.00	6.00
539	Johnny Klippstein	20.00	10.00	6.00
540	Jackie Jensen	30.00	15.00	9.00
541	Roland Sheldon	22.00	11.00	6.50
542	Twins Team	40.00	20.00	12.00
543	Roger Craig	35.00	17.50	10.50
544	George Thomas	20.00	10.00	6.00
545	Hoyt Wilhelm	55.00	28.00	16.50
546	Marty Kutyna	20.00	10.00	6.00
547	Leon Wagner	22.00	11.00	6.50

		NR MT	EX	VG
548	Ted Wills	20.00	10.00	6.00
549	Hal R. Smith	20.00	10.00	6.00
550	Frank Baumann	20.00	10.00	6.00
551	George Altman	20.00	10.00	6.00
552	Jim Archer	20.00	10.00	6.00
553	Bill Fischer	20.00	10.00	6.00
554	Pirates Team	35.00	17.50	10.50
555	Sam Jones	20.00	10.00	6.00
556	Ken R. Hunt	20.00	10.00	6.00
557	Jose Valdivielso	20.00	10.00	6.00
558	Don Ferrarese	20.00	10.00	6.00
559	Jim Gentile	22.00	11.00	6.50
560	Barry Latman	20.00	10.00	6.00
561	Charley James	20.00	10.00	6.00
562	Bill Monbouquette	22.00	11.00	6.50
563	Bob Cerv	22.00	11.00	6.50
564	Don Cardwell	20.00	10.00	6.00
565	Felipe Alou	25.00	12.50	7.50
566	Paul Richards AS	25.00	12.50	7.50
567	Danny Murtaugh AS	25.00	12.50	7.50
568	Bill Skowron AS	35.00	17.50	10.50
569	Frank Herrera AS	25.00	12.50	7.50
570	Nellie Fox AS	40.00	20.00	12.00
571	Bill Mazeroski AS	35.00	17.50	10.50
572	Brooks Robinson AS	80.00	40.00	24.00
573	Ken Boyer AS	35.00	17.50	10.50
574	Luis Aparicio AS	45.00	23.00	13.50
575	Ernie Banks AS	75.00	38.00	23.00
576	Roger Maris AS	90.00	45.00	27.00
577	Hank Aaron AS	150.00	75.00	45.00
578	Mickey Mantle AS	375.00	150.00	94.00
579	Willie Mays AS	150.00	75.00	45.00
580	Al Kaline AS	75.00	38.00	23.00
581	Frank Robinson AS	75.00	38.00	23.00
582	Earl Battey AS	25.00	12.50	7.50
583	Del Crandall AS	30.00	15.00	9.00
584	Jim Perry AS	30.00	15.00	9.00
585	Bob Friend AS	30.00	15.00	9.00
586	Whitey Ford AS	75.00	38.00	23.00
587	Not Issued			
588	Not Issued			
589	Warren Spahn AS	125.00	56.00	35.00

1961 Topps Dice Game

One of the more obscure Topps test issues that may have never actually been issued is the 1961 Topps Dice Game. Eighteen black and white cards, each measuring 2-1/2" by 3-1/2" in size, comprise the set. Interestingly, there are no identifying marks, such as copyrights or trademarks, to indicate the set was produced by Topps. The card backs contain various baseball plays that occur when a certain pitch is called and a specific number of the dice is rolled.

		NR MT	EX	VG
Complete Set:		7200.	3600.	2150.
Common Player:		100.00	50.00	30.00
(1)	Earl Battey	100.00	50.00	30.00
(2)	Del Crandall	100.00	50.00	30.00
(3)	Jim Davenport	100.00	50.00	30.00
(4)	Don Drysdale	300.00	150.00	90.00
(5)	Dick Groat	150.00	75.00	45.00
(6)	Al Kaline	600.00	300.00	175.00
(7)	Tony Kubek	150.00	75.00	45.00
(8)	Mickey Mantle	2500.	1250.	750.00
(9)	Willie Mays	1000.	500.00	300.00
(10)	Bill Mazeroski	150.00	75.00	45.00
(11)	Stan Musial	800.00	400.00	240.00
(12)	Camilo Pascual	100.00	50.00	30.00
(13)	Bobby Richardson	150.00	75.00	45.00
(14)	Brooks Robinson	400.00	200.00	120.00
(15)	Frank Robinson	300.00	150.00	90.00
(16)	Norm Siebern	100.00	50.00	30.00
(17)	Leon Wagner	100.00	50.00	30.00
(18)	Bill White	100.00	50.00	30.00

1961 Topps Magic Rub-Offs

Not too different in concept from the tattoos of the previous year, the Topps Magic Rub-Off was designed to leave impressions of team themes or individual players when properly applied. Measuring 2-1/16" by 3-1/16," the Magic Rub-Off was not designed specifically for application to the owner's skin. The set of 36 Rub-Offs seems to almost be a tongue-in-cheek product as the team

themes were a far cry from official logos, and the players seem to have been included for their nicknames. Among the players (one representing each team) the best known and most valuable are Yogi Berra and Ernie Banks.

		NR MT	EX	VG
Complete Set:		85.00	42.00	25.00
Common Player:		1.00	.50	.30
(1)	Baltimore Orioles Pennant	1.00	.50	.30
(2)	Ernie "Bingo" Banks	12.00	6.00	3.50
(3)	Yogi Berra	20.00	10.00	6.00
(4)	Boston Red Sox Pennant	1.00	.50	.30
(5)	Jackie "Ozark" Brandt	1.25	.60	.40
(6)	Jim "Professor" Brosnan	1.25	.60	.40
(7)	Chicago Cubs Pennant	1.00	.50	.30
(8)	Chicago White Sox Pennant	1.00	.50	.30
(9)	Cincinnati Red Legs Pennant	1.00	.50	.30
(10)	Cleveland Indians Pennant	1.00	.50	.30
(11)	Detroit Tigers Pennant	1.25	.60	.40
(12)	Henry "Dutch" Dotterer	1.25	.60	.40
(13)	Joe "Flash" Gordon	1.50	.70	.45
(14)	Harvey "The Kitten" Haddix	1.50	.70	.45
(15)	Frank "Pancho" Hererra	1.25	.60	.40
(16)	Frank "Tower" Howard	3.50	1.75	1.00
(17)	"Sad" Sam Jones	1.25	.60	.40
(18)	Kansas City Athletics Pennant	1.00	.50	.30
(19)	Los Angeles Angels Pennant	1.00	.50	.30
(20)	Los Angeles Dodgers Pennant	1.25	.60	.40
(21)	Omar "Turk" Lown	1.25	.60	.40
(22)	Billy "The Kid" Martin	6.00	3.00	1.75
(23)	Duane "Duke" Mass (Maas)	1.25	.60	.40
(24)	Charlie "Paw Paw" Maxwell	1.25	.60	.40
(25)	Milwaukee Braves Pennant	1.00	.50	.30
(26)	Minnesota Twins Pennant	1.00	.50	.30
(27)	"Farmer" Ray Moore	1.00	.50	.30
(28)	Walt "Moose" Moryn	1.00	.50	.30
(29)	New York Yankees Pennant	2.50	1.25	.70
(30)	Philadelphia Phillies Pennant	1.00	.50	.30
(31)	Pittsburgh Pirates Pennant	1.00	.50	.30
(32)	John "Honey" Romano	1.25	.60	.40
(33)	"Pistol Pete" Runnels	1.50	.70	.45
(34)	St. Louis Cardinals Pennant	1.00	.50	.30
(35)	San Francisco Giants Pennant	1.00	.50	.30
(36)	Washington Senators Pennant	1.00	.50	.30

1961 Topps Stamps

Issued as an added insert to 1961 Topps wax packs these 1-3/8" by 1-3/16" stamps were desigend to be collected and placed in an album which could be bought for an additional 10¢. Packs of cards contained two stamps. There are 208 stamps in a complete set which depict 207 different players (Al Kaline appears twice). There are 104 players on brown stamps and 104 on green. While there are many Hall of Famers on the stamps, prices remain low because there is relatively little interest in what is a non-card set.

		NR MT	EX	VG
Complete Set:		225.00	112.00	70.00
Stamp Album:		35.00	17.50	10.50
Common Player:		.40	.20	.12
(1)	Hank Aaron	10.00	5.00	3.00
(2)	Joe Adcock	.35	.20	.11
(3)	Hank Aguirre	.40	.20	.12
(4)	Bob Allison	.30	.15	.09
(5)	George Altman	.40	.20	.12
(6)	Bob Anderson	.40	.20	.12
(7)	Johnny Antonelli	.30	.15	.09
(8)	Luis Aparicio	1.50	.70	.45
(9)	Luis Arroyo	.35	.20	.11
(10)	Richie Ashburn	.80	.40	.25
(11)	Ken Aspromonte	.40	.20	.12
(12)	Ed Bailey	.40	.20	.12
(13)	Ernie Banks	6.00	3.00	1.75
(14)	Steve Barber	.40	.20	.12
(15)	Earl Battey	.30	.15	.09
(16)	Hank Bauer	.50	.25	.15
(17)	Gus Bell	.30	.15	.09
(18)	Yogi Berra	5.00	2.50	1.50
(19)	Reno Bertoia	.40	.20	.12
(20)	John Blanchard	.35	.20	.11
(21)	Don Blasingame	.40	.20	.12
(22)	Frank Bolling	.40	.20	.12
(23)	Steve Boros	.40	.20	.12
(24)	Ed Bouchee	.40	.20	.12
(25)	Bob Boyd	.40	.20	.12
(26)	Cletis Boyer	.35	.20	.11
(27)	Ken Boyer	.50	.25	.15
(28)	Jackie Brandt	.40	.20	.12
(29)	Marv Breeding	.40	.20	.12
(30)	Eddie Bressoud	.40	.20	.12
(31)	Jim Brewer	.40	.20	.12
(32)	Tom Brewer	.40	.20	.12
(33)	Jim Brosnan	.30	.15	.09
(34)	Bill Bruton	.40	.20	.12
(35)	Bob Buhl	.30	.15	.09
(36)	Jim Bunning	1.00	.50	.30
(37)	Smoky Burgess	.30	.15	.09
(38)	John Buzhardt	.40	.20	.12
(39)	Johnny Callison	.30	.15	.09
(40)	Chico Cardenas	.40	.20	.12
(41)	Andy Carey	.40	.20	.12
(42)	Jerry Casale	.40	.20	.12
(43)	Norm Cash	.50	.25	.15
(44)	Orlando Cepeda	1.25	.60	.40
(45)	Bob Cerv	.40	.20	.12
(46)	Harry Chiti	.40	.20	.12
(47)	Gene Conley	.30	.15	.09
(48)	Wes Covington	.40	.20	.12
(49)	Del Crandall	.35	.20	.11
(50)	Tony Curry	.40	.20	.12
(51)	Bud Daley	.40	.20	.12
(52)	Pete Daley	.40	.20	.12
(53)	Clay Dalrymple	.40	.20	.12
(54)	Jim Davenport	.40	.20	.12
(55)	Tommy Davis	.35	.20	.11
(56)	Bobby Del Greco	.40	.20	.12
(57)	Ike Delock	.40	.20	.12
(58)	Art Ditmar	.35	.20	.11
(59)	Dick Donovan	.40	.20	.12
(60)	Don Drysdale	6.00	3.00	1.75
(61)	Dick Ellsworth	.40	.20	.12
(62)	Don Elston	.40	.20	.12
(63)	Chuck Estrada	.40	.20	.12
(64)	Roy Face	.35	.20	.11
(65)	Dick Farrell	.40	.20	.12
(66)	Chico Fernandez	.40	.20	.12
(67)	Curt Flood	.35	.20	.11
(68)	Whitey Ford	4.00	2.00	1.25
(69)	Tito Francona	.40	.20	.12
(70)	Gene Freese	.40	.20	.12
(71)	Bob Friend	.35	.20	.11
(72)	Billy Gardner	.40	.20	.12
(73)	Ned Garver	.40	.20	.12
(74)	Gary Geiger	.40	.20	.12
(75)	Jim Gentile	.40	.20	.12
(76)	Dick Gernert	.40	.20	.12
(77)	Tony Gonzalez	.40	.20	.12
(78)	Alex Grammas	.40	.20	.12
(79)	Jim Grant	.40	.20	.12
(80)	Dick Groat	.35	.20	.11
(81)	Dick Hall	.40	.20	.12
(82)	Ron Hansen	.40	.20	.12
(83)	Bob Hartman	.40	.20	.12
(84)	Woodie Held	.40	.20	.12
(85)	Ray Herbert	.40	.20	.12
(86)	Frank Herrera	.40	.20	.12
(87)	Whitey Herzog	.50	.25	.15
(88)	Don Hoak	.30	.15	.09
(89)	Elston Howard	.80	.40	.25
(90)	Frank Howard	.50	.25	.15
(91)	Ken Hunt	.40	.20	.12
(92)	Larry Jackson	.40	.20	.12
(93)	Julian Javier	.40	.20	.12
(94)	Joe Jay	.40	.20	.12
(95)	Jackie Jensen	.50	.25	.15
(96)	Jim Kaat	1.00	.50	.30
(97a)	Al Kaline (green)	7.00	3.50	2.00
(97b)	Al Kaline (brown)	7.00	3.50	2.00
(98)	Eddie Kasko	.40	.20	.12
(99)	Russ Kemmerer	.40	.20	.12
(100)	Harmon Killebrew	5.00	2.50	1.50
(101)	Billy Klaus	.40	.20	.12
(102)	Ron Kline	.40	.20	.12
(103)	Johnny Klippstein	.40	.20	.12
(104)	Ted Kluszewski	.40	.20	.12
(105)	Tony Kubek	.80	.40	.25
(106)	Harvey Kuenn	.50	.25	.15
(107)	Jim Landis	.40	.20	.12
(108)	Hobie Landrith	.40	.20	.12
(109)	Norm Larker	.40	.20	.12

	NR MT	EX	VG
(110) Frank Lary	.40	.20	.12
(111) Barry Latman	.40	.20	.12
(112) Vern Law	.30	.15	.09
(113) Jim Lemon	.40	.20	.12
(114) Sherm Lollar	.30	.15	.09
(115) Dale Long	.30	.15	.09
(116) Jerry Lumpe	.40	.20	.12
(117) Jerry Lynch	.40	.20	.12
(118) Art Mahaffey	.40	.20	.12
(119) Frank Malzone	.40	.20	.12
(120) Felix Mantilla	.40	.20	.12
(121) Mickey Mantle	50.00	25.00	15.00
(122) Juan Marichal	5.00	2.50	1.50
(123) Roger Maris	12.00	6.00	3.50
(124) Billy Martin	1.00	.50	.30
(125) J.C. Martin	.40	.20	.12
(126) Ed Mathews	3.00	1.50	.90
(127) Charlie Maxwell	.40	.20	.12
(128) Willie Mays	7.00	3.50	2.00
(129) Bill Mazeroski	.50	.25	.15
(130) Mike McCormick	.40	.20	.12
(131) Willie McCovey	3.00	1.50	.90
(132) Lindy McDaniel	.40	.20	.12
(133) Roy McMillan	.40	.20	.12
(134) Minnie Minoso	.50	.25	.15
(135) Bill Monbouquette	.40	.20	.12
(136) Wally Moon	.30	.15	.09
(137) Stan Musial	7.00	3.50	2.00
(138) Charlie Neal	.40	.20	.12
(139) Rocky Nelson	.40	.20	.12
(140) Russ Nixon	.40	.20	.12
(141) Billy O'Dell	.40	.20	.12
(142) Jim O'Toole	.40	.20	.12
(143) Milt Pappas	.30	.15	.09
(144) Camilo Pascual	.30	.15	.09
(145) Jim Perry	.35	.20	.11
(146) Bubba Phillips	.40	.20	.12
(147) Bill Pierce	.35	.20	.11
(148) Jim Piersall	.35	.20	.11
(149) Vada Pinson	.50	.25	.15
(150) Johnny Podres	.35	.20	.11
(151) Wally Post	.40	.20	.12
(152) Vic Powers (Power)	.40	.20	.12
(153) Pedro Ramos	.40	.20	.12
(154) Robin Roberts	1.50	.70	.45
(155) Brooks Robinson	3.75	2.00	1.25
(156) Frank Robinson	3.50	1.75	1.00
(157) Ed Roebuck	.40	.20	.12
(158) John Romano	.40	.20	.12
(159) John Roseboro	.30	.15	.09
(160) Pete Runnels	.30	.15	.09
(161) Ed Sadowski	.40	.20	.12
(162) Jack Sanford	.40	.20	.12
(163) Ron Santo	.35	.20	.11
(164) Ray Semproch	.40	.20	.12
(165) Bobby Shantz	.50	.25	.15
(166) Bob Shaw	.40	.20	.12
(167) Larry Sherry	.40	.20	.12
(168) Norm Siebern	.40	.20	.12
(169) Roy Sievers	.35	.20	.11
(170) Curt Simmons	.30	.15	.09
(171) Dave Sisler	.40	.20	.12
(172) Bob Skinner	.40	.20	.12
(173) Al Smith	.40	.20	.12
(174) Hal Smith	.40	.20	.12
(175) Hal Smith	.40	.20	.12
(176) Duke Snider	3.75	2.00	1.25
(177) Warren Spahn	3.00	1.50	.90
(178) Daryl Spencer	.40	.20	.12
(179) Bill Stafford	.35	.20	.11
(180) Jerry Staley	.40	.20	.12
(181) Gene Stephens	.40	.20	.12
(182) Chuck Stobbs	.40	.20	.12
(183) Dick Stuart	.30	.15	.09
(184) Willie Tasby	.40	.20	.12
(185) Sammy Taylor	.40	.20	.12
(186) Tony Taylor	.40	.20	.12
(187) Johnny Temple	.40	.20	.12
(188) Marv Throneberry	.50	.25	.15
(189) Gus Triandos	.30	.15	.09
(190) Bob Turley	.35	.20	.11
(191) Bill Tuttle	.40	.20	.12
(192) Zorro Versalles	.40	.20	.12
(193) Bill Virdon	.35	.20	.11
(194) Lee Walls	.40	.20	.12
(195) Vic Wertz	.30	.15	.09
(196) Pete Whisenant	.40	.20	.12
(197) Bill White	.30	.15	.09
(198) Hoyt Wilhelm	1.50	.70	.45
(199) Bob Will	.40	.20	.12
(200) Carl Willey	.40	.20	.12
(201) Billy Williams	2.50	1.25	.70
(202) Dick Williams	.50	.25	.15
(203) Stan Williams	.40	.20	.12
(204) Gene Woodling	.35	.20	.11
(205) Early Wynn	2.00	1.00	.60
(206) Carl Yastrzemski	12.00	6.00	3.50
(207) Eddie Yost	.40	.20	.12

1962 Topps

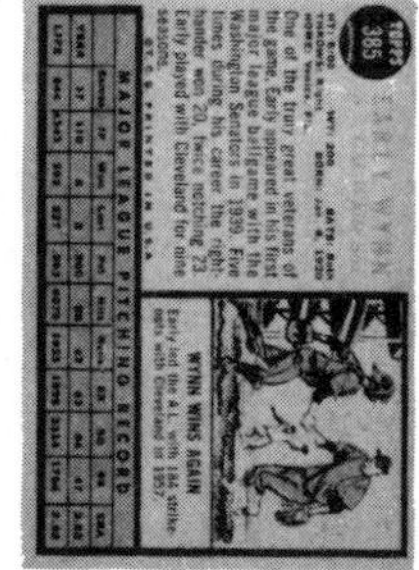

The 1962 Topps set established another plateau for set size with 598 cards. The 2-1/2" by 3-1/2" cards feature a photograph set against a woodgrain background. The lower righthand corner has been made to look like it is curling away. Many established specialty cards dot the set including statistical leaders, multi-player cards, team cards, checklists, World Series cards and All-Stars. Of note is that 1962 was the first year of the multi-player rookie card. There is a 9-card "In Action" subset and a 10-card run of special Babe Ruth cards. Photo variations of several cards in the 2nd Series (#'s 110-196) exist. All cards in the 2nd Series can be found with two distinct printing variations, an early printing with the cards containing a very noticeable greenish tint, having been corrected to clear photos in subsequent print runs. The complete set price in the checklist that follows does not include the higher-priced variations.

		NR MT	EX	VG
Complete Set:		4000.	1800.	1000.
Common Player: 1-370		1.50	.70	.40
Common Player: 371-522		2.50	1.25	.60
Common Player: 523-598		12.00	5.50	3.00
1	Roger Maris	250.00	45.00	27.00
2	Jim Brosnan	1.75	.60	.30
3	Pete Runnels	1.50	.70	.40
4	John DeMerit	2.00	.90	.50
5	Sandy Koufax	100.00	50.00	30.00
6	Marv Breeding	1.50	.70	.40
7	Frank Thomas	2.00	.90	.50
8	Ray Herbert	1.50	.70	.40
9	Jim Davenport	1.50	.70	.40
10	Bob Clemente	80.00	40.00	25.00
11	Tom Morgan	1.50	.70	.40
12	Harry Craft	1.50	.70	.40
13	Dick Howser	1.75	.80	.45
14	Bill White	1.50	.70	.40
15	Dick Donovan	1.50	.70	.40
16	Darrell Johnson	1.50	.70	.40
17	Johnny Callison	1.75	.80	.45
18	Managers' Dream (Mickey Mantle, Willie Mays)	100.00	50.00	30.00
19	*Ray Washburn*	1.50	.70	.40
20	Rocky Colavito	3.00	1.25	.70
21	Jim Kaat	4.00	1.75	1.00
22a	Checklist 1-88 (numbers 121 - 176 on back)	5.00	2.25	1.25
22b	Checklist 1-88 (numbers 33-88 on back)	4.00	1.75	1.00
23	Norm Larker	1.50	.70	.40
24	Tigers Team	3.50	1.50	.90
25	Ernie Banks	30.00	15.00	9.00
26	Chris Cannizzaro	2.00	.90	.50
27	Chuck Cottier	1.50	.70	.40
28	Minnie Minoso	2.50	1.25	.60
29	Casey Stengel	15.00	6.75	3.75
30	Ed Mathews	12.00	5.50	3.00
31	*Tom Tresh*	7.00	3.25	1.75
32	John Roseboro	1.75	.80	.45
33	Don Larsen	1.75	.80	.45
34	Johnny Temple	1.50	.70	.40
35	*Don Schwall*	1.75	.80	.45
36	Don Leppert	1.50	.70	.40
37	Tribe Hill Trio (Barry Latman, Jim Perry, Dick Stigman)	1.75	.80	.45
38	Gene Stephens	1.50	.70	.40
39	Joe Koppe	1.50	.70	.40
40	Orlando Cepeda	5.00	2.25	1.25
41	Cliff Cook	1.50	.70	.40
42	Jim King	1.50	.70	.40
43	Dodgers Team	3.50	1.50	.90
44	Don Taussig	1.50	.70	.40
45	Brooks Robinson	30.00	12.50	7.50
46	*Jack Baldschun*	1.50	.70	.40
47	Bob Will	1.50	.70	.40
48	Ralph Terry	2.50	1.25	.60
49	Hal Jones	1.50	.70	.40
50	Stan Musial	75.00	29.00	16.00
51	A.L. Batting Leaders (Norm Cash, Elston Howard, Al Kaline, Jim Piersall)	3.00	1.25	.70
52	N.L. Batting Leaders (Ken Boyer, Bob Clemente, Wally Moon, Vada Pinson)	3.50	1.50	.90
53	A.L. Home Run Leaders (Jim Gentile, Harmon Killebrew, Mickey Mantle, Roger Maris)	20.00	9.00	5.50
54	N.L. Home Run Leaders (Orlando Cepeda, Willie Mays, Frank Robinson)	3.50	1.50	.90
55	A.L. E.R.A. Leaders (Dick Donovan, Don Mossi, Milt Pappas, Bill Stafford)	2.50	1.25	.60
56	N.L. E.R.A. Leaders (Mike McCormick, Jim O'Toole, Curt Simmons, Warren Spahn)	3.00	1.25	.70
57	A.L. Win Leaders (Steve Barber, Jim Bunning, Whitey Ford, Frank Lary)	3.00	1.25	.70
58	N.L. Win Leaders (Joe Jay, Jim O'Toole, Warren Spahn)	3.00	1.25	.70
59	A.L. Strikeout Leaders (Jim Bunning, Whitey Ford, Camilo Pascual, Juan Pizzaro)	3.00	1.25	.70
60	N.L. Strikeout Leaders (Don Drysdale, Sandy Koufax, Jim O'Toole, Stan Williams)	3.50	1.50	.90
61	Cardinals Team	2.50	1.25	.60
62	Steve Boros	1.50	.70	.40
63	*Tony Cloninger*	2.00	.90	.50
64	Russ Snyder	1.50	.70	.40
65	Bobby Richardson	6.00	2.75	1.50
66	Cuno Barragon (Barragan)	1.50	.70	.40
67	Harvey Haddix	1.75	.80	.45
68	Ken L. Hunt	1.50	.70	.40
69	Phil Ortega	1.50	.70	.40

		NR MT	EX	VG
70	Harmon Killebrew	15.00	6.75	3.75
71	Dick LeMay	1.50	.70	.40
72	Bob's Pupils (Steve Boros, Bob Scheffing, Jake Wood)	1.75	.80	.45
73	Nellie Fox	7.00	3.25	1.75
74	Bob Lillis	1.50	.70	.40
75	Milt Pappas	1.75	.80	.45
76	Howie Bedell	1.50	.70	.40
77	Tony Taylor	1.50	.70	.40
78	Gene Green	1.50	.70	.40
79	Ed Hobaugh	1.50	.70	.40
80	Vada Pinson	2.50	1.25	.60
81	Jim Pagliaroni	1.50	.70	.40
82	Deron Johnson	1.50	.70	.40
83	Larry Jackson	1.50	.70	.40
84	Lenny Green	1.50	.70	.40
85	Gil Hodges	12.00	6.00	3.50
86	*Donn Clendenon*	1.75	.80	.45
87	Mike Roarke	1.50	.70	.40
88	Ralph Houk	2.50	1.25	.60
89	Barney Schultz	1.50	.70	.40
90	Jim Piersall	2.00	.90	.50
91	J.C. Martin	1.50	.70	.40
92	Sam Jones	1.50	.70	.40
93	John Blanchard	2.00	.90	.50
94	Jay Hook	2.00	.90	.50
95	Don Hoak	1.75	.80	.45
96	Eli Grba	1.50	.70	.40
97	Tito Francona	1.50	.70	.40
98	Checklist 89-176	4.00	1.75	1.00
99	*John Powell*	12.00	6.00	3.50
100	Warren Spahn	25.00	12.50	7.50
101	Carroll Hardy	1.50	.70	.40
102	Al Schroll	1.50	.70	.40
103	Don Blasingame	1.50	.70	.40
104	Ted Savage	1.50	.70	.40
105	Don Mossi	1.50	.70	.40
106	Carl Sawatski	1.50	.70	.40
107	Mike McCormick	1.50	.70	.40
108	Willie Davis	2.50	1.25	.60
109	Bob Shaw	1.50	.70	.40
110	Bill Skowron	5.00	2.25	1.25
111	Dallas Green	1.75	.80	.45
112	Hank Foiles	1.50	.70	.40
113	White Sox Team	2.50	1.25	.60
114	Howie Koplitz	1.50	.70	.40
115	Bob Skinner	1.50	.70	.40
116	Herb Score	2.00	.90	.50
117	Gary Geiger	1.50	.70	.40
118	Julian Javier	1.50	.70	.40
119	Danny Murphy	1.50	.70	.40
120	Bob Purkey	1.50	.70	.40
121	Billy Hitchcock	1.50	.70	.40
122	Norm Bass	1.50	.70	.40
123	Mike de la Hoz	1.50	.70	.40
124	Bill Pleis	1.50	.70	.40
125	Gene Woodling	1.75	.80	.45
126	Al Cicotte	1.50	.70	.40
127	Pride of the A's (Hank Bauer, Jerry Lumpe, Norm Siebern)	1.75	.80	.45
128	Art Fowler	1.50	.70	.40
129a	Lee Walls (facing left)	15.00	7.50	4.50
129b	Lee Walls (facing right)	1.50	.70	.40
130	Frank Bolling	1.50	.70	.40
131	*Pete Richert*	1.75	.80	.45
132a	Angels Team (with inset photos)	10.00	4.50	2.50
132b	Angels Team (without inset photos)	3.00	1.25	.70
133	Felipe Alou	1.75	.80	.45
134a	Billy Hoeft (green sky in background)	15.00	7.50	4.50
134b	Billy Hoeft (blue sky in background)	1.50	.70	.40
135	Babe As A Boy	7.00	3.25	1.75
136	Babe Joins Yanks	7.00	3.25	1.75
137	Babe and Mgr. Huggins	7.00	3.25	1.75
138	The Famous Slugger	7.00	3.25	1.75
139a	Hal Reniff (pitching)	40.00	20.00	12.00
139b	Hal Reniff (portrait)	18.00	9.00	5.50
139c	Babe Hits 60	7.00	3.25	1.75
140	Gehrig and Ruth	9.00	4.00	2.25
141	Twilight Years	7.00	3.25	1.75
142	Coaching for the Dodgers	7.00	3.25	1.75
143	Greatest Sports Hero	7.00	3.25	1.75
144	Farewell Speech	7.00	3.25	1.75
145	Barry Latman	1.50	.70	.40
146	Don Demeter	1.50	.70	.40
147a	Bill Kunkel (pitching)	15.00	7.50	4.50
147b	Bill Kunkel (portrait)	1.50	.70	.40
148	Wally Post	1.50	.70	.40
149	Bob Duliba	1.50	.70	.40
150	Al Kaline	25.00	12.50	7.50
151	Johnny Klippstein	1.50	.70	.40
152	Mickey Vernon	1.50	.70	.40
153	Pumpsie Green	1.50	.70	.40
154	Lee Thomas	1.50	.70	.40
155	Stu Miller	1.50	.70	.40
156	Merritt Ranew	1.50	.70	.40
157	Wes Covington	1.50	.70	.40
158	Braves Team	3.00	1.25	.70
159	Hal Reniff	2.00	.90	.50
160	Dick Stuart	1.50	.70	.40
161	Frank Baumann	1.50	.70	.40
162	Sammy Drake	2.00	.90	.50
163	Hot Corner Guardians (Cletis Boyer, Billy Gardner)	3.00	1.25	.70
164	Hal Naragon	1.50	.70	.40
165	Jackie Brandt	1.50	.70	.40
166	Don Lee	1.50	.70	.40
167	*Tim McCarver*	18.00	7.50	4.50
168	Leo Posada	1.50	.70	.40
169	Bob Cerv	2.00	.90	.50
170	Ron Santo	3.50	1.50	.90
171	Dave Sisler	1.50	.70	.40
172	Fred Hutchinson	1.50	.70	.40
173	Chico Fernandez	1.50	.70	.40
174a	Carl Willey (with cap)	15.00	7.50	4.50
174b	Carl Willey (no cap)	1.50	.70	.40
175	Frank Howard	3.00	1.25	.70
176a	Eddie Yost (batting)	15.00	7.50	4.50
176b	Eddie Yost (portrait)	1.50	.70	.40
177	Bobby Shantz	1.75	.80	.45

No.	Card	NR MT	EX	VG
178	Camilo Carreon	1.50	.70	.40
179	Tom Sturdivant	1.50	.70	.40
180	Bob Allison	1.75	.80	.45
181	Paul Brown	1.50	.70	.40
182	Bob Nieman	1.50	.70	.40
183	Roger Craig	3.00	1.25	.70
184	Haywood Sullivan	1.50	.70	.40
185	Roland Sheldon	2.00	.90	.50
186	*Mack Jones*	1.50	.70	.40
187	Gene Conley	1.50	.70	.40
188	Chuck Hiller	1.50	.70	.40
189	Dick Hall	1.50	.70	.40
190a	Wally Moon (with cap)	9.00	4.00	2.25
190b	Wally Moon (no cap)	1.75	.80	.45
191	Jim Brewer	1.50	.70	.40
192a	Checklist 177-264 (192 is Check List, 3)	6.00	2.75	1.50
192b	Checklist 177-264 (192 is Check List 3)	4.00	1.75	1.00
193	Eddie Kasko	1.50	.70	.40
194	*Dean Chance*	3.00	1.25	.70
195	Joe Cunningham	1.50	.70	.40
196	Terry Fox	1.50	.70	.40
197	Daryl Spencer	1.50	.70	.40
198	Johnny Keane	1.50	.70	.40
199	*Gaylord Perry*	150.00	60.00	38.50
200	Mickey Mantle	500.00	200.00	125.00
201	Ike Delock	1.50	.70	.40
202	Carl Warwick	1.50	.70	.40
203	Jack Fisher	1.50	.70	.40
204	Johnny Weekly	1.50	.70	.40
205	Gene Freese	1.50	.70	.40
206	Senators Team	2.50	1.25	.60
207	Pete Burnside	1.50	.70	.40
208	Billy Martin	6.00	2.75	1.50
209	*Jim Fregosi*	5.00	2.25	1.25
210	Roy Face	2.00	.90	.50
211	Midway Masters (Frank Bolling, Roy McMillan)	1.75	.80	.45
212	Jim Owens	1.50	.70	.40
213	Richie Ashburn	6.00	2.75	1.50
214	Dom Zanni	1.50	.70	.40
215	Woody Held	1.50	.70	.40
216	Ron Kline	1.50	.70	.40
217	Walt Alston	4.00	1.75	1.00
218	*Joe Torre*	10.00	4.50	2.50
219	*Al Downing*	4.00	1.75	1.00
220	Roy Sievers	1.75	.80	.45
221	Bill Short	1.50	.70	.40
222	Jerry Zimmerman	1.50	.70	.40
223	Alex Grammas	1.50	.70	.40
224	Don Rudolph	1.50	.70	.40
225	Frank Malzone	1.50	.70	.40
226	Giants Team	4.00	1.75	1.00
227	Bobby Tiefenauer	1.50	.70	.40
228	Dale Long	1.50	.70	.40
229	Jesus McFarlane	1.50	.70	.40
230	Camlio Pascual	1.75	.80	.45
231	Ernie Bowman	1.50	.70	.40
232	World Series Game 1 (Yanks Win Opener)	3.00	1.25	.70
233	World Series Game 2 (Jay Ties It Up)	3.00	1.25	.70
234	World Series Game 3 (Maris Wins It In The 9th)	8.00	3.50	2.00
235	World Series Game 4 (Ford Sets New Mark)	7.00	3.25	1.75
236	World Series Game 5 (Yanks Crush Reds In Finale)	3.00	1.25	.70
237	World Series Summary (The Winners Celebrate)	3.00	1.25	.70
238	Norm Sherry	1.50	.70	.40
239	Cecil Butler	1.50	.70	.40
240	George Altman	1.50	.70	.40
241	Johnny Kucks	1.50	.70	.40
242	Mel McGaha	1.50	.70	.40
243	Robin Roberts	12.00	5.50	3.00
244	Don Gile	1.50	.70	.40
245	Ron Hansen	1.50	.70	.40
246	Art Ditmar	1.50	.70	.40
247	Joe Pignatano	1.50	.70	.40
248	Bob Aspromonte	1.50	.70	.40
249	Ed Keegan	1.50	.70	.40
250	Norm Cash	3.00	1.25	.70
251	Yankees Team	8.00	3.50	2.00
252	Earl Francis	1.50	.70	.40
253	Harry Chiti	1.50	.70	.40
254	Gordon Windhorn	1.50	.70	.40
255	Juan Pizarro	1.50	.70	.40
256	Elio Chacon	2.00	.90	.50
257	Jack Spring	1.50	.70	.40
258	Marty Keough	1.50	.70	.40
259	Lou Klimchock	1.50	.70	.40
260	Bill Pierce	2.00	.90	.50
261	George Alusik	1.50	.70	.40
262	Bob Schmidt	1.50	.70	.40
263	The Right Pitch (Joe Jay, Bob Purkey, Jim Turner)	1.75	.80	.45
264	Dick Ellsworth	1.50	.70	.40
265	Joe Adcock	2.00	.90	.50
266	John Anderson	1.50	.70	.40
267	Dan Dobbek	1.50	.70	.40
268	Ken McBride	1.50	.70	.40
269	Bob Oldis	1.50	.70	.40
270	Dick Groat	2.00	.90	.50
271	Ray Rippelmeyer	1.50	.70	.40
272	Earl Robinson	1.50	.70	.40
273	Gary Bell	1.50	.70	.40
274	Sammy Taylor	1.50	.70	.40
275	Norm Siebern	1.50	.70	.40
276	Hal Kostad	1.50	.70	.40
277	Checklist 265-352	4.00	1.75	1.00
278	Ken Johnson	1.50	.70	.40
279	Hobie Landrith	2.00	.90	.50
280	Johnny Podres	2.50	1.25	.60
281	*Jake Gibbs*	2.25	1.00	.60
282	Dave Hillman	1.50	.70	.40
283	Charlie Smith	1.50	.70	.40
284	Ruben Amaro	1.50	.70	.40
285	Curt Simmons	2.00	.90	.50
286	Al Lopez	3.00	1.25	.70
287	George Witt	1.50	.70	.40
288	Billy Williams	25.00	12.50	7.50
289	Mike Krsnich	1.50	.70	.40
290	Jim Gentile	1.50	.70	.40
291	Hal Stowe	2.00	.90	.50
292	Jerry Kindall	1.50	.70	.40
293	Bob Miller	2.00	.90	.50
294	Phillies Team	2.50	1.25	.60
295	Vern Law	2.00	.90	.50
296	Ken Hamlin	1.50	.70	.40
297	Ron Perranoski	1.50	.70	.40
298	Bill Tuttle	1.50	.70	.40
299	*Don Wert*	1.50	.70	.40
300	Willie Mays	150.00	60.00	38.00
301	Galen Cisco	1.50	.70	.40
302	*John Edwards*	1.50	.70	.40
303	Frank Torre	1.50	.70	.40
304	Dick Farrell	1.50	.70	.40
305	Jerry Lumpe	1.50	.70	.40
306	Redbird Rippers (Larry Jackson, Lindy McDaniel)	1.75	.80	.45
307	Jim Grant	1.50	.70	.40
308	Neil Chrisley	2.00	.90	.50
309	Moe Morhardt	1.50	.70	.40
310	Whitey Ford	25.00	12.50	7.50
311	Kubek Makes The Double Play	3.50	1.50	.90
312	Spahn Shows No-Hit Form	7.00	3.50	2.00
313	Maris Blasts 61st	15.00	6.75	3.75
314	Colavito's Power	3.50	1.50	.90
315	Ford Tosses A Curve	6.00	2.75	1.50
316	Killebrew Sends One Into Orbit	5.00	2.25	1.25
317	Musial Plays 21st Season	12.00	5.50	3.00
318	The Switch Hitter Connects (Mickey Mantle)	30.00	13.50	7.50
319	McCormick Shows His Stuff	1.75	.80	.45
320	Hank Aaron	150.00	60.00	38.00
321	Lee Stange	1.50	.70	.40
322	Al Dark	1.75	.80	.45
323	Don Landrum	1.50	.70	.40
324	Joe McClain	1.50	.70	.40
325	Luis Aparicio	15.00	7.50	4.50
326	Tom Parsons	1.50	.70	.40
327	Ozzie Virgil	1.50	.70	.40
328	Ken Walters	1.50	.70	.40
329	Bob Bolin	1.50	.70	.40
330	Johnny Romano	1.50	.70	.40
331	Moe Drabowsky	1.50	.70	.40
332	Don Buddin	1.50	.70	.40
333	Frank Cipriani	1.50	.70	.40
334	Red Sox Team	3.50	1.50	.90
335	Bill Bruton	1.50	.70	.40
336	Billy Muffett	1.50	.70	.40
337	Jim Marshall	2.00	.90	.50
338	Billy Gardner	2.25	1.00	.60
339	Jose Valdivielso	1.50	.70	.40
340	Don Drysdale	30.00	15.00	9.00
341	Mike Hershberger	1.50	.70	.40
342	Ed Rakow	1.50	.70	.40
343	Albie Pearson	1.50	.70	.40
344	Ed Bauta	1.50	.70	.40
345	Chuck Schilling	1.50	.70	.40
346	Jack Kralick	1.50	.70	.40
347	Chuck Hinton	1.50	.70	.40
348	Larry Burright	1.50	.70	.40
349	Paul Foytack	1.50	.70	.40
350	Frank Robinson	30.00	12.50	7.50
351	Braves' Backstops (Del Crandall, Joe Torre)	3.00	1.25	.70
352	Frank Sullivan	1.50	.70	.40
353	Bill Mazeroski	3.50	1.50	.90
354	Roman Mejias	1.50	.70	.40
355	Steve Barber	1.50	.70	.40
356	Tom Haller	1.75	.80	.45
357	Jerry Walker	1.50	.70	.40
358	Tommy Davis	2.50	1.25	.60
359	Bobby Locke	1.50	.70	.40
360	Yogi Berra	60.00	30.00	18.00
361	Bob Hendley	1.50	.70	.40
362	Ty Cline	1.50	.70	.40
363	Bob Roselli	1.50	.70	.40
364	Ken Hunt	1.50	.70	.40
365	Charley Neal	2.00	.90	.50
366	Phil Regan	1.50	.70	.40
367	Checklist 353-429	4.00	1.75	1.00
368	Bob Tillman	1.50	.70	.40
369	Ted Bowsfield	1.50	.70	.40
370	Ken Boyer	4.00	1.75	1.00
371	Earl Battey	2.75	1.25	.70
372	Jack Curtis	2.50	1.25	.60
373	Al Heist	2.50	1.25	.60
374	Gene Mauch	2.75	1.25	.70
375	Ron Fairly	2.75	1.25	.70
376	Bud Daley	3.00	1.25	.70
377	Johnny Orsino	2.50	1.25	.60
378	Bennie Daniels	2.50	1.25	.60
379	Chuck Essegian	2.50	1.25	.60
380	Lou Burdette	4.00	1.75	1.00
381	Chico Cardenas	2.50	1.25	.60
382	Dick Williams	3.50	1.50	.90
383	Ray Sadecki	2.50	1.25	.60
384	Athletics Team	3.50	1.50	.90
385	Early Wynn	20.00	10.00	6.00
386	Don Mincher	2.50	1.25	.60
387	Lou Brock	125.00	56.00	35.00
388	Ryne Duren	2.75	1.25	.70
389	Smoky Burgess	3.00	1.25	.70
390	Orlando Cepeda AS	5.00	2.25	1.25
391	Bill Mazeroski AS	3.50	1.50	.90
392	Ken Boyer AS	3.50	1.50	.90
393	Roy McMillan AS	2.75	1.25	.70
394	Hank Aaron AS	30.00	15.00	9.00
395	Willie Mays AS	30.00	15.00	9.00
396	Frank Robinson AS	12.00	5.50	3.00
397	John Roseboro AS	2.75	1.25	.70
398	Don Drysdale AS	10.00	4.50	2.50
399	Warren Spahn AS	10.00	4.50	2.50
400	Elston Howard	7.00	3.25	1.75
401	AL & NL Homer Kings (Orlando Cepeda, Roger Maris)	20.00	9.00	5.00
402	Gino Cimoli	2.50	1.25	.60
403	Chet Nichols	2.50	1.25	.60
404	Tim Harkness	2.50	1.25	.60
405	Jim Perry	3.00	1.25	.70
406	Bob Taylor	2.50	1.25	.60
407	Hank Aguirre	2.50	1.25	.60
408	Gus Bell	3.00	1.25	.70
409	Pirates Team	3.50	1.50	.90
410	Al Smith	2.50	1.25	.60
411	Danny O'Connell	2.50	1.25	.60
412	Charlie James	2.50	1.25	.60
413	Matty Alou	3.50	1.50	.90
414	Joe Gaines	2.50	1.25	.60
415	Bill Virdon	3.50	1.50	.90
416	Bob Scheffing	2.50	1.25	.60
417	Joe Azcue	2.50	1.25	.60
418	Andy Carey	2.50	1.25	.60
419	Bob Bruce	2.50	1.25	.60
420	Gus Triandos	2.75	1.25	.70
421	Ken MacKenzie	3.00	1.25	.70
422	Steve Bilko	2.50	1.25	.60
423	Rival League Relief Aces (Roy Face, Hoyt Wilhelm)	5.00	2.25	1.25
424	Al McBean	2.50	1.25	.60
425	Carl Yastrzemski	200.00	80.00	50.00
426	Bob Farley	2.50	1.25	.60
427	Jake Wood	2.50	1.25	.60
428	Joe Hicks	2.50	1.25	.60
429	Bill O'Dell	2.50	1.25	.60
430	Tony Kubek	7.00	3.25	1.75
431	*Bob Rodgers*	3.00	1.25	.70
432	Jim Pendleton	2.50	1.25	.60
433	Jim Archer	2.50	1.25	.60
434	Clay Dalrymple	2.50	1.25	.60
435	Larry Sherry	2.50	1.25	.60
436	Felix Mantilla	3.00	1.25	.70
437	Ray Moore	2.50	1.25	.60
438	Dick Brown	2.50	1.25	.60
439	Jerry Buchek	2.50	1.25	.60
440	Joe Jay	2.50	1.25	.60
441	Checklist 430-506	5.00	2.25	1.25
442	Wes Stock	2.50	1.25	.60
443	Del Crandall	3.50	1.50	.90
444	Ted Wills	2.50	1.25	.60
445	Vic Power	2.50	1.25	.60
446	Don Elston	2.50	1.25	.60
447	Willie Kirkland	2.50	1.25	.60
448	Joe Gibbon	2.50	1.25	.60
449	Jerry Adair	2.50	1.25	.60
450	Jim O'Toole	2.50	1.25	.60
451	*Jose Tartabull*	2.75	1.25	.70
452	Earl Averill	2.50	1.25	.60
453	Cal McLish	2.50	1.25	.60
454	Floyd Robinson	2.50	1.25	.60
455	Luis Arroyo	3.00	1.25	.70
456	Joe Amalfitano	2.50	1.25	.60
457	Lou Clinton	2.50	1.25	.60
458a	Bob Buhl ("M" on cap)	2.75	1.25	.70
458b	Bob Buhl (plain cap)	60.00	30.00	18.00
459	Ed Bailey	2.50	1.25	.60
460	Jim Bunning	8.00	3.50	2.00
461	*Ken Hubbs*	8.00	3.50	2.00
462a	Willie Tasby ("W" on cap)	2.50	1.25	.60
462b	Willie Tasby (plain cap)	60.00	30.00	18.00
463	Hank Bauer	3.00	1.25	.70
464	*Al Jackson*	3.50	1.50	.90
465	Reds Team	4.00	1.75	1.00
466	Norm Cash AS	4.00	1.75	1.00
467	Chuck Schilling AS	3.00	1.25	.70
468	Brooks Robinson AS	12.00	5.50	3.00
469	Luis Aparicio AS	8.00	3.50	2.00
470	Al Kaline AS	10.00	4.50	2.50
471	Mickey Mantle AS	65.00	29.00	16.00
472	Rocky Colavito AS	5.00	2.25	1.25
473	Elston Howard AS	5.00	2.25	1.25
474	Frank Lary AS	3.00	1.25	.70
475	Whitey Ford AS	10.00	4.50	2.50
476	Orioles Team	3.50	1.50	.90
477	Andre Rodgers	2.50	1.25	.60
478	Don Zimmer	3.50	1.50	.90
479	*Joel Horlen*	2.75	1.25	.70
480	Harvey Kuenn	3.50	1.50	.90
481	Vic Wertz	2.75	1.25	.70
482	Sam Mele	2.50	1.25	.60
483	Don McMahon	2.50	1.25	.60
484	Dick Schofield	2.50	1.25	.60
485	Pedro Ramos	2.50	1.25	.60
486	Jim Gilliam	4.00	1.75	1.00
487	Jerry Lynch	2.50	1.25	.60
488	Hal Brown	2.50	1.25	.60
489	Julio Gotay	2.50	1.25	.60
490	Clete Boyer	4.00	1.75	1.00
491	Leon Wagner	2.50	1.25	.60
492	Hal Smith	2.50	1.25	.60
493	Danny McDevitt	2.50	1.25	.60
494	Sammy White	2.50	1.25	.60
495	Don Cardwell	2.50	1.25	.60
496	Wayne Causey	2.50	1.25	.60
497	Ed Bouchee	3.00	1.25	.70
498	Jim Donohue	2.50	1.25	.60
499	Zoilo Versalles	2.75	1.25	.70
500	Duke Snider	30.00	13.50	7.50
501	Claude Osteen	2.75	1.25	.70
502	Hector Lopez	3.00	1.25	.70
503	Danny Murtaugh	2.75	1.25	.70
504	Eddie Bressoud	2.50	1.25	.60
505	Juan Marichal	25.00	11.00	6.25
506	Charley Maxwell	2.50	1.25	.60
507	Ernie Broglio	2.50	1.25	.60
508	Gordy Coleman	2.50	1.25	.60
509	*Dave Giusti*	2.75	1.25	.70
510	Jim Lemon	2.50	1.25	.60
511	Bubba Phillips	2.50	1.25	.60
512	Mike Fornieles	2.50	1.25	.60
513	Whitey Herzog	4.00	1.75	1.00
514	Sherm Lollar	2.75	1.25	.70
515	Stan Williams	2.50	1.25	.60
516	Checklist 507-598	8.00	3.50	2.00
517	Dave Wickersham	2.50	1.25	.60
518	Lee Maye	2.50	1.25	.60
519	Bob Johnson	2.50	1.25	.60
520	Bob Friend	3.00	1.25	.70
521	Jacke Davis	2.50	1.25	.60
522	Lindy McDaniel	2.50	1.25	.60

		NR MT	EX	VG
523	Russ Nixon	12.00	5.50	3.00
524	Howie Nunn	12.00	5.50	3.00
525	George Thomas	12.00	5.50	3.00
526	Hal Woodeshick	12.00	5.50	3.00
527	*Dick McAuliffe*	15.00	5.00	2.75
528	Turk Lown	12.00	5.50	3.00
529	John Schaive	12.00	5.50	3.00
530	Bob Gibson	150.00	60.00	38.00
531	Bobby G. Smith	12.00	5.50	3.00
532	Dick Stigman	12.00	5.50	3.00
533	Charley Lau	13.00	5.75	3.25
534	Tony Gonzalez	12.00	5.50	3.00
535	Ed Roebuck	12.00	5.50	3.00
536	Dick Gernert	12.00	5.50	3.00
537	Indians Team	15.00	6.75	3.75
538	Jack Sanford	12.00	5.50	3.00
539	Billy Moran	12.00	5.50	3.00
540	Jim Landis	12.00	5.50	3.00
541	Don Nottebart	12.00	5.50	3.00
542	Dave Philley	12.00	5.50	3.00
543	Bob Allen	12.00	5.50	3.00
544	Willie McCovey	150.00	60.00	38.00
545	Hoyt Wilhelm	55.00	25.00	14.00
546	Moe Thacker	12.00	5.50	3.00
547	Don Ferrarese	12.00	5.50	3.00
548	Bobby Del Greco	12.00	5.50	3.00
549	Bill Rigney	12.00	5.50	3.00
550	Art Mahaffey	12.00	5.50	3.00
551	Harry Bright	12.00	5.50	3.00
552	Cubs Team	15.00	6.75	3.75
553	Jim Coates	15.00	6.75	3.75
554	Bubba Morton	12.00	5.50	3.00
555	John Buzhardt	12.00	5.50	3.00
556	Al Spangler	12.00	5.50	3.00
557	Bob Anderson	12.00	5.50	3.00
558	John Goryl	12.00	5.50	3.00
559	Mike Higgins	12.00	5.50	3.00
560	Chuck Estrada	12.00	5.50	3.00
561	Gene Oliver	12.00	5.50	3.00
562	Bill Henry	12.00	5.50	3.00
563	Ken Aspromonte	12.00	5.50	3.00
564	Bob Grim	12.00	5.50	3.00
565	Jose Pagan	12.00	5.50	3.00
566	Marty Kutyna	12.00	5.50	3.00
567	Tracy Stallard	12.00	5.50	3.00
568	Jim Golden	12.00	5.50	3.00
569	Ed Sadowski	12.00	5.50	3.00
570	Bill Stafford	15.00	6.75	3.75
571	Billy Klaus	12.00	5.50	3.00
572	Bob Miller	13.00	5.75	3.25
573	Johnny Logan	13.00	5.75	3.25
574	Dean Stone	12.00	5.50	3.00
575	Red Schoendienst	25.00	11.25	6.25
576	Russ Kemmerer	12.00	5.50	3.00
577	Dave Nicholson	12.00	5.50	3.00
578	Jim Duffalo	12.00	5.50	3.00
579	Jim Schaffer	12.00	5.50	3.00
580	Bill Monbouquette	13.00	5.75	3.25
581	Mel Roach	12.00	5.50	3.00
582	Ron Piche	12.00	5.50	3.00
583	Larry Osborne	12.00	5.50	3.00
584	Twins Team	15.00	6.75	3.75
585	Glen Hobbie	12.00	5.50	3.00
586	Sammy Esposito	12.00	5.50	3.00
587	Frank Funk	12.00	5.50	3.00
588	Birdie Tebbetts	12.00	5.50	3.00
589	Bob Turley	18.00	8.00	4.50
590	Curt Flood	18.00	8.00	4.50
591	Rookie Parade Pitchers *(Sam McDowell,* Ron Nischwitz, Art Quirk, *Dick Radatz, Ron Taylor)*	35.00	15.50	8.75
592	Rookie Parade Pitchers *(Bo Belinsky,* Joe Bonikowski, *Jim Bouton,* Dan Pfister, Dave Stenhouse)	45.00	20.00	11.25
593	Rookie Parade Pitchers (Craig Anderson, *Jack Hamilton,* Jack Lamabe, Bob Moorhead, *Bob Veale)*	25.00	11.25	6.25
594	Rookie Parade Catchers (Doug Camilli, *Doc Edwards,* Don Pavletich, Ken Retzer, *Bob Uecker)*	125.00	56.00	35.00
595	Rookie Parade Infielders *(Ed Charles,* Marlin Coughtry, Bob Sadowski, Felix Torres)	25.00	11.25	6.25
596	Rookie Parade Infielders *(Bernie Allen, Phil Linz, Joe Pepitone, Rich Rollins)*	80.00	40.00	24.00
597	Rookie Parade Infielders (Rod Kanehl, Jim McKnight, *Denis Menke,* Amado Samuel)	25.00	11.25	6.25
598	Rookie Parade Outfielders (Howie Goss, *Jim Hickman,* Manny Jimenez, Al Luplow, Ed Olivares)	90.00	45.00	27.00

1962 Topps Baseball Bucks

Issued in their own 1¢ package, the 1962 Topps "Baseball Bucks" were another in the growing list of specialty Topps items. The 96 Baseball Bucks in the set measure 4-1/8" by 1-3/4," and were designed to look vaguely like dollar bills. The center player portrait has a banner underneath with the player's name. His home park is shown on the right and there is some biographical information on the left. The back features a large denomination, with the player's league and team logo on either side.

		NR MT	EX	VG
Complete Set:		650.00	325.00	190.00
Common Player:		2.00	1.00	.60
(1)	Hank Aaron	30.00	15.00	9.00
(2)	Joe Adcock	3.00	1.50	.90
(3)	George Altman	2.00	1.00	.60
(4)	Jim Archer	2.00	1.00	.60
(5)	Richie Ashburn	5.00	2.50	1.50
(6)	Ernie Banks	20.00	10.00	8.00
(7)	Earl Battey	2.50	1.25	.70
(8)	Gus Bell	2.50	1.25	.70
(9)	Yogi Berra	18.00	9.00	5.50
(10)	Ken Boyer	3.00	1.50	.90
(11)	Jackie Brandt	2.00	1.00	.60
(12)	Jim Bunning	4.00	2.00	1.25
(13)	Lou Burdette	3.00	1.50	.90
(14)	Don Cardwell	2.00	1.00	.60
(15)	Norm Cash	3.00	1.50	.90
(16)	Orlando Cepeda	4.50	2.25	1.25
(17)	Bob Clemente	40.00	20.00	12.50
(18)	Rocky Colavito	3.00	1.50	.90
(19)	Chuck Cottier	2.00	1.00	.60
(20)	Roger Craig	2.50	1.25	.70
(21)	Bennie Daniels	2.00	1.00	.60
(22)	Don Demeter	2.00	1.00	.60
(23)	Don Drysdale	15.00	7.50	4.50
(24)	Chuck Estrada	2.00	1.00	.60
(25)	Dick Farrell	2.00	1.00	.60
(26)	Whitey Ford	12.00	6.00	3.50
(27)	Nellie Fox	4.00	2.00	1.25
(28)	Tito Francona	2.00	1.00	.60
(29)	Bob Friend	2.50	1.25	.70
(30)	Jim Gentile	2.00	1.00	.60
(31)	Dick Gernert	2.00	1.00	.60
(32)	Lenny Green	2.00	1.00	.60
(33)	Dick Groat	3.00	1.50	.90
(34)	Woody Held	2.00	1.00	.60
(35)	Don Hoak	2.50	1.25	.70
(36)	Gil Hodges	10.00	5.00	3.00
(37)	Frank Howard	3.00	1.50	.90
(38)	Elston Howard	4.00	2.00	1.25
(39)	Dick Howser	3.00	1.50	.90
(40)	Ken Hunt	2.00	1.00	.60
(41)	Larry Jackson	2.00	1.00	.60
(42)	Joe Jay	4.00	2.00	1.25
(43)	Al Kaline	12.00	6.00	3.50
(44)	Harmon Killebrew	12.00	6.00	3.50
(45)	Sandy Koufax	35.00	17.50	10.50
(46)	Harvey Kuenn	4.00	2.00	1.25
(47)	Jim Landis	2.00	1.00	.60
(48)	Norm Larker	2.00	1.00	.60
(49)	Frank Lary	2.00	1.00	.60
(50)	Jerry Lumpe	2.00	1.00	.60
(51)	Art Mahaffey	2.00	1.00	.60
(52)	Frank Malzone	2.00	1.00	.60
(53)	Felix Mantilla	2.50	1.25	.70
(54)	Mickey Mantle	125.00	62.00	37.00
(55)	Roger Maris	12.00	6.00	3.50
(56)	Ed Mathews	10.00	5.00	3.00
(57)	Willie Mays	35.00	17.50	10.50
(58)	Ken McBride	2.00	1.00	.60
(59)	Mike McCormick	2.00	1.00	.60
(60)	Minnie Minoso	4.00	2.00	1.25
(61)	Wally Moon	2.50	1.25	.70
(62)	Stu Miller	2.00	1.00	.60
(63)	Stan Musial	30.00	15.00	9.00
(64)	Danny O'Connell	2.00	1.00	.60
(65)	Jim O'Toole	4.00	2.00	1.25
(66)	Camilo Pascual	2.50	1.25	.70
(67)	Jim Perry	3.00	1.50	.90
(68)	Jimmy Piersall	4.00	2.00	1.25
(69)	Vada Pinson	6.00	3.00	1.75
(70)	Juan Pizarro	2.00	1.00	.60
(71)	Johnny Podres	3.00	1.50	.90
(72)	Vic Power	2.00	1.00	.60
(73)	Bob Purkey	12.00	6.00	3.50
(74)	Pedro Ramos	2.00	1.00	.60
(75)	Brooks Robinson	15.00	7.50	4.50
(76)	Floyd Robinson	2.00	1.00	.60
(77)	Frank Robinson	15.00	7.50	4.50
(78)	Johnny Romano	2.00	1.00	.60
(79)	Pete Runnels	2.50	1.25	.70
(80)	Don Schwall	2.00	1.00	.60
(81)	Bobby Shantz	3.00	1.50	.90
(82)	Norm Siebern	2.00	1.00	.60
(83)	Roy Sievers	2.50	1.25	.70
(84)	Hal (W.) Smith	2.00	1.00	.60
(85)	Warren Spahn	10.00	5.00	3.00
(86)	Dick Stuart	2.50	1.25	.70
(87)	Tony Taylor	2.00	1.00	.60
(88)	Lee Thomas	2.00	1.00	.60
(89)	Gus Triandos	2.50	1.25	.70
(90)	Leon Wagner	2.00	1.00	.60
(91)	Jerry Walker	2.00	1.00	.60
(92)	Bill White	2.50	1.25	.70
(93)	Billy Williams	9.00	4.50	2.75
(94)	Gene Woodling	2.50	1.25	.70
(95)	Early Wynn	9.00	4.50	2.75
(96)	Carl Yastrzemski	30.00	15.00	9.00

1962 Topps Stamps

An artistic improvement over the somewhat drab Topps stamps of the previous year, the 1962 stamps, 1-3/8" by 1-7/8," had color player photographs set on red or yellow backgrounds. As in 1961, they were issued in two-stamp panels as insert with Topps baseball cards. A change from 1961 was the inclusion of team emblems in the set. A complete set consists of 201 stamps; Roy Sievers was originally portrayed on the wrong team - Athletics - and was later corrected to the Phillies.

		NR MT	EX	VG
Complete Set:		220.00	110.00	67.00
Stamp Album:		35.00	17.50	10.50
Common Player:		.25	.13	.08
(1)	Hank Aaron	10.00	5.00	3.00
(2)	Jerry Adair	.25	.13	.08
(3)	Joe Adcock	.35	.20	.11
(4)	Bob Allison	.30	.15	.09
(5)	Felipe Alou	.35	.20	.11
(6)	George Altman	.25	.13	.08
(7)	Joe Amalfitano	.25	.13	.08
(8)	Ruben Amaro	.25	.13	.08
(9)	Luis Aparicio	1.50	.70	.45
(10)	Jim Archer	.25	.13	.08
(11)	Bob Aspromonte	.25	.13	.08
(12)	Ed Bailey	.25	.13	.08
(13)	Jack Baldschun	.25	.13	.08
(14)	Ernie Banks	6.00	3.00	1.75
(15)	Earl Battey	.30	.15	.09
(16)	Gus Bell	.35	.20	.11
(17)	Yogi Berra	5.00	2.50	1.50
(18)	Dick Bertell	.25	.13	.08
(19)	Steve Bilko	.25	.13	.08
(20)	Frank Bolling	.25	.13	.08
(21)	Steve Boros	.25	.13	.08
(22)	Ted Bowsfield	.25	.13	.08
(23)	Clete Boyer	.35	.20	.11
(24)	Ken Boyer	.50	.25	.15
(25)	Jackie Brandt	.25	.13	.08
(26)	Bill Bruton	.25	.13	.08
(27)	Jim Bunning	1.00	.50	.30
(28)	Lou Burdette	.35	.20	.11
(29)	Smoky Burgess	.30	.15	.09
(30)	Johnny Callizon (Callison)	.30	.15	.09
(31)	Don Cardwell	.25	.13	.08
(32)	Camilo Carreon	.25	.13	.08
(33)	Norm Cash	.50	.25	.15
(34)	Orlando Cepeda	1.00	.50	.30
(35)	Bob Clemente	15.00	7.50	4.50
(36)	Ty Cline	.25	.13	.08
(37)	Rocky Colavito	.80	.40	.25
(38)	Gordon Coleman	.25	.13	.08
(39)	Chuck Cottier	.25	.13	.08
(40)	Roger Craig	.35	.20	.11
(41)	Del Crandall	.35	.20	.11
(42)	Pete Daley	.25	.13	.08
(43)	Clay Dalrymple	.25	.13	.08
(44)	Bennie Daniels	.25	.13	.08
(45)	Jim Davenport	.25	.13	.08
(46)	Don Demeter	.25	.13	.08
(47)	Dick Donovan	.25	.13	.08
(48)	Don Drysdale	7.00	3.50	2.00
(49)	John Edwards	.25	.13	.08
(50)	Dick Ellsworth	.25	.13	.08
(51)	Chuck Estrada	.25	.13	.08
(52)	Roy Face	.35	.20	.11
(53)	Ron Fairly	.30	.15	.09
(54)	Dick Farrell	.25	.13	.08
(55)	Whitey Ford	5.00	2.50	1.50
(56)	Mike Fornieles	.25	.13	.08
(57)	Nellie Fox	.80	.40	.25
(58)	Tito Francona	.25	.13	.08
(59)	Gene Freese	.25	.13	.08
(60)	Bob Friend	.35	.20	.11
(61)	Gary Geiger	.25	.13	.08
(62)	Jim Gentile	.25	.13	.08
(63)	Tony Gonzalez	.25	.13	.08
(64)	Lenny Green	.25	.13	.08
(65)	Dick Groat	.35	.20	.11
(66)	Ron Hansen	.25	.13	.08
(67)	Al Heist	.25	.13	.08
(68)	Woody Held	.25	.13	.08
(69)	Ray Herbert	.25	.13	.08
(70)	Chuck Hinton	.25	.13	.08
(71)	Don Hoak	.30	.15	.09
(72)	Glen Hobbie	.25	.13	.08
(73)	Gil Hodges	5.00	2.50	1.50
(74)	Jay Hook	.35	.20	.11
(75)	Elston Howard	.80	.40	.25
(76)	Frank Howard	.50	.25	.15
(77)	Dick Howser	.35	.20	.11
(78)	Ken Hunt	.25	.13	.08
(79)	Larry Jackson	.25	.13	.08
(80)	Julian Javier	.25	.13	.08
(81)	Joe Jay	.25	.13	.08
(82)	Bob Johnson	.25	.13	.08
(83)	Sam Jones	.25	.13	.08
(84)	Al Kaline	7.00	3.50	2.00
(85)	Eddie Kasko	.25	.13	.08
(86)	Harmon Killebrew	5.00	2.50	1.50
(87)	Sandy Koufax	10.00	5.00	3.00
(88)	Jack Kralick	.25	.13	.08
(89)	Tony Kubek	.80	.40	.25
(90)	Harvey Kuenn	.50	.25	.15
(91)	Jim Landis	.25	.13	.08
(92)	Hobie Landrith	.35	.20	.11

	NR MT	EX	VG
(93) Frank Lary	.25	.13	.08
(94) Barry Latman	.25	.13	.08
(95) Jerry Lumpe	.25	.13	.08
(96) Art Mahaffey	.25	.13	.08
(97) Frank Malzone	.25	.13	.08
(98) Felix Mantilla	.35	.20	.11
(99) Mickey Mantle	45.00	22.00	13.50
(100) Juan Marichal	2.00	1.00	.60
(101) Roger Maris	5.00	2.50	1.50
(102) J.C. Martin	.25	.13	.08
(103) Ed Mathews	3.00	1.50	.90
(104) Willie Mays	7.00	3.50	2.00
(105) Bill Mazeroski	.50	.25	.15
(106) Ken McBride	.25	.13	.08
(107) Tim McCarver	.50	.25	.15
(108) Joe McClain	.25	.13	.08
(109) Mike McCormick	.25	.13	.08
(110) Lindy McDaniel	.25	.13	.08
(111) Roy McMillan	.25	.13	.08
(112) Bob L. Miller	.35	.20	.11
(113) Stu Miller	.25	.13	.08
(114) Minnie Minoso	.50	.25	.15
(115) Bill Monbouquette	.25	.13	.08
(116) Wally Moon	.30	.15	.09
(117) Don Mossi	.30	.15	.09
(118) Stan Musial	7.00	3.50	2.00
(119) Russ Nixon	.25	.13	.08
(120) Danny O'Connell	.25	.13	.08
(121) Jim O'Toole	.25	.13	.08
(122) Milt Pappas	.30	.15	.09
(123) Camilo Pascual	.30	.15	.09
(124) Albie Pearson	.25	.13	.08
(125) Jim Perry	.35	.20	.11
(126) Bubba Phillips	.25	.13	.08
(127) Jimmy Piersall	.35	.20	.11
(128) Vada Pinson	.50	.25	.15
(129) Juan Pizarro	.25	.13	.08
(130) Johnny Podres	.35	.20	.11
(131) Leo Posada	.25	.13	.08
(132) Vic Power	.25	.13	.08
(133) Bob Purkey	.25	.13	.08
(134) Pedro Ramos	.25	.13	.08
(135) Bobby Richardson	.80	.40	.25
(136) Brooks Robinson	3.75	2.00	1.25
(137) Floyd Robinson	.25	.13	.08
(138) Frank Robinson	3.50	1.75	1.00
(139) Bob Rodgers	.30	.15	.09
(140) Johnny Romano	.25	.13	.08
(141) John Roseboro	.30	.15	.09
(142) Pete Runnels	.30	.15	.09
(143) Ray Sadecki	.25	.13	.08
(144) Ron Santo	.35	.20	.11
(145) Chuck Schilling	.25	.13	.08
(146) Barney Schultz	.25	.13	.08
(147) Don Schwall	.25	.13	.08
(148) Bobby Shantz	.35	.20	.11
(149) Bob Shaw	.25	.13	.08
(150) Norm Siebern	.25	.13	.08
(151a) Roy Sievers (Kansas City)	1.00	.50	.30
(151b) Roy Sievers (Philadelphia)	.30	.15	.09
(152) Bill Skowron	.50	.25	.15
(153) Hal (W.) Smith	.25	.13	.08
(154) Duke Snider	3.75	2.00	1.25
(155) Warren Spahn	3.00	1.50	.90
(156) Al Spangler	.25	.13	.08
(157) Daryl Spencer	.25	.13	.08
(158) Gene Stephens	.25	.13	.08
(159) Dick Stuart	.30	.15	.09
(160) Haywood Sullivan	.25	.13	.08
(161) Tony Taylor	.25	.13	.08
(162) George Thomas	.25	.13	.08
(163) Lee Thomas	.25	.13	.08
(164) Bob Tiefenauer	.25	.13	.08
(165) Joe Torre	.50	.25	.15
(166) Gus Triandos	.30	.15	.09
(167) Bill Tuttle	.25	.13	.08
(168) Zoilo Versalles	.25	.13	.08
(169) Bill Virdon	.35	.20	.11
(170) Leon Wagner	.25	.13	.08
(171) Jerry Walker	.25	.13	.08
(172) Lee Walls	.25	.13	.08
(173) Bill White	.30	.15	.09
(174) Hoyt Wilhelm	1.50	.70	.45
(175) Billy Williams	2.00	1.00	.60
(176) Jake Wood	.25	.13	.08
(177) Gene Woodling	.35	.20	.11
(178) Early Wynn	2.00	1.00	.60
(179) Carl Yastrzemski	12.00	6.00	3.50
(180) Don Zimmer	.35	.20	.11
(181) Baltimore Orioles Logo	.25	.13	.08
(182) Boston Red Sox Logo	.25	.13	.08
(183) Chicago Cubs Logo	.25	.13	.08
(184) Chicago White Sox Logo	.25	.13	.08
(185) Cincinnati Reds Logo	.25	.13	.08
(186) Cleveland Indians Logo	.25	.13	.08
(187) Detroit Tigers Logo	.25	.13	.08
(188) Houston Colts Logo	.25	.13	.08
(189) Kansas City Athletics Logo	.25	.13	.08
(190) Los Angeles Angels Logo	.25	.13	.08
(191) Los Angeles Dodgers Logo	.25	.13	.08
(192) Milwaukee Braves Logo	.25	.13	.08
(193) Minnesota Twins Logo	.25	.13	.08
(194) New York Mets Logo	.35	.20	.11
(195) New York Yankees Logo	.35	.20	.11
(196) Philadelphia Phillies Logo	.25	.13	.08
(197) Pittsburgh Pirates Logo	.25	.13	.08
(198) St. Louis Cardinals Logo	.25	.13	.08
(199) San Francisco Giants Logo	.25	.13	.08
(200) Washington Senators Logo	.25	.13	.08

1963 Topps

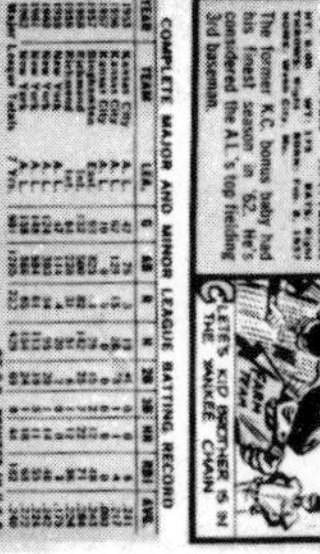

Although the number of cards dropped to 576, the 1963 Topps set is among the most popular of the 1960s. A color photo dominates the 2-1/2" by 3-1/2" card, but a colored circle at the bottom carries a black and white portrait as well. A colored band gives the player's name, team and position. The backs again feature career statistics and a cartoon, career summary and brief biographical details. The set is somewhat unlike those immediately preceding it in that there are fewer specialty cards. The major groupings are statistical leaders, World Series highlights and rookies. It is one rookie which makes the set special - Pete Rose. As one of most avidly sought cards in history and a high-numbered card at that, the Rose rookie card accounts for much of the value of a complete set.

	NR MT	EX	VG
Complete Set:	4000.	2000.	1250.
Common Player: 1-283	.70	.35	.20
Common Player: 284-446	2.00	1.00	.60
Common Player: 447-506	8.00	4.00	2.50
Common Player: 507-576	5.00	2.50	1.50

	NR MT	EX	VG
1 N.L. Batting Leaders (Hank Aaron, Tommy Davis, Stan Musial, Frank Robinson, Bill White)	40.00	6.00	3.50
2 A.L. Batting Leaders (Chuck Hinton, Mickey Mantle, Floyd Robinson, Pete Runnels, Norm Siebern)	15.00	7.50	4.50
3 N.L. Home Run Leaders (Hank Aaron, Ernie Banks, Orlando Cepeda, Willie Mays, Frank Robinson)	8.00	4.00	2.50
4 A.L. Home Run Leaders (Norm Cash, Rocky Colavito, Jim Gentile, Harmon Killebrew, Roger Maris, Leon Wagner)	4.00	2.00	1.25
5 N.L. E.R.A. Leaders (Don Drysdale, Bob Gibson, Sandy Koufax, Bob Purkey, Bob Shaw)	4.00	2.00	1.25
6 A.L. E.R.A. Leaders (Hank Aguirre, Dean Chance, Eddie Fisher, Whitey Ford, Robin Roberts)	3.50	1.75	1.00
7 N.L. Pitching Leaders (Don Drysdale, Joe Jay, Art Mahaffey, Billy O'Dell, Bob Purkey, Jack Sanford)	3.50	1.75	1.00
8 A.L. Pitching Leaders (Jim Bunning, Dick Donovan, Ray Herbert, Camilo Pascual, Ralph Terry)	3.00	1.50	.90
9 N.L. Strikeout Leaders (Don Drysdale, Dick Farrell, Bob Gibson, Sandy Koufax, Billy O'Dell)	4.00	2.00	1.25
10 A.L. Strikeout Leaders (Jim Bunning, Jim Kaat, Camilo Pascual, Juan Pizarro, Ralph Terry)	3.00	1.50	.90
11 Lee Walls	.70	.35	.20
12 Steve Barber	.70	.35	.20
13 Phillies Team	2.25	1.25	.70
14 Pedro Ramos	.70	.35	.20
15 Ken Hubbs	2.00	1.00	.60
16 Al Smith	.70	.35	.20
17 Ryne Duren	1.00	.50	.30
18 Buc Blasters (Smoky Burgess, Bob Clemente, Bob Skinner, Dick Stuart)	8.00	4.00	2.50
19 Pete Burnside	.70	.35	.20
20 Tony Kubek	5.00	2.50	1.50
21 Marty Keough	.70	.35	.20
22 Curt Simmons	1.00	.50	.30
23 Ed Lopat	1.25	.60	.40
24 Bob Bruce	.70	.35	.20
25 Al Kaline	25.00	12.50	7.50
26 Ray Moore	.70	.35	.20
27 Choo Choo Coleman	1.25	.60	.40
28 Mike Fornieles	.70	.35	.20
29a 1962 Rookie Stars (John Boozer, *Ray Culp, Sammy Ellis*, Jesse Gonder)	5.00	2.50	1.50
29b 1963 Rookie Stars (John Boozer, *Ray Culp, Sammy Ellis*, Jesse Gonder)	1.25	.60	.40
30 Harvey Kuenn	1.50	.70	.45
31 Cal Koonce	.70	.35	.20
32 Tony Gonzalez	.70	.35	.20
33 Bo Belinsky	2.00	1.00	.60
34 Dick Schofield	.70	.35	.20
35 John Buzhardt	.70	.35	.20
36 Jerry Kindall	.70	.35	.20
37 Jerry Lynch	.70	.35	.20
38 Bud Daley	1.25	.60	.40
39 Angels Team	2.25	1.25	.70
40 Vic Power	.70	.35	.20
41 Charlie Lau	1.00	.50	.30
42 Stan Williams	1.25	.60	.40
43 Veteran Masters (Casey Stengel, Gene Woodling)	4.00	2.00	1.25
44 Terry Fox	.70	.35	.20
45 Bob Aspromonte	.70	.35	.20
46 *Tommie Aaron*	1.25	.60	.40
47 Don Lock	.70	.35	.20
48 Birdie Tebbetts	.70	.35	.20
49 *Dal Maxvill*	1.25	.60	.40
50 Bill Pierce	1.25	.60	.40
51 George Alusik	.70	.35	.20
52 Chuck Schilling	.70	.35	.20
53 Joe Moeller	.70	.35	.20
54a 1962 Rookie Stars (Jack Cullen, *Dave DeBusschere*, Harry Fanok, Nelson Mathews)	6.50	3.25	2.00
54b 1963 Rookie Stars (Jack Cullen, *Dave DeBusschere*, Harry Fanok, Nelson Mathews)	3.00	1.50	.90
55 Bill Virdon	1.50	.70	.45
56 Dennis Bennett	.70	.35	.20
57 Billy Moran	.70	.35	.20
58 Bob Will	.70	.35	.20
59 Craig Anderson	1.00	.50	.30
60 Elston Howard	6.00	3.00	1.75
61 Ernie Bowman	.70	.35	.20
62 Bob Hendley	.70	.35	.20
63 Reds Team	2.50	1.25	.70
64 Dick McAuliffe	.90	.45	.25
65 Jackie Brandt	.70	.35	.20
66 Mike Joyce	.70	.35	.20
67 Ed Charles	.70	.35	.20
68 Friendly Foes (Gil Hodges, Duke Snider)	6.50	3.25	2.00
69 Bud Zipfel	.70	.35	.20
70 Jim O'Toole	.70	.35	.20
71 *Bobby Wine*	.90	.45	.25
72 Johnny Romano	.70	.35	.20
73 Bobby Bragan	.90	.45	.25
74 *Denver Lemaster*	.90	.45	.25
75 Bob Allison	1.25	.60	.40
76 Earl Wilson	.70	.35	.20
77 Al Spangler	.70	.35	.20
78 Marv Throneberry	3.50	1.75	1.00
79 Checklist 1-88	2.50	1.25	.70
80 Jim Gilliam	3.00	1.50	.90
81 Jimmie Schaffer	.70	.35	.20
82 Ed Rakow	.70	.35	.20
83 Charley James	.70	.35	.20
84 Ron Kline	.70	.35	.20
85 Tom Haller	.90	.45	.25
86 Charley Maxwell	.70	.35	.20
87 Bob Veale	.90	.45	.25
88 Ron Hansen	.70	.35	.20
89 Dick Stigman	.70	.35	.20
90 Gordy Coleman	.70	.35	.20
91 Dallas Green	.90	.45	.25
92 Hector Lopez	1.25	.60	.40
93 Galen Cisco	.90	.45	.25
94 Bob Schmidt	.70	.35	.20
95 Larry Jackson	.70	.35	.20
96 Lou Clinton	.70	.35	.20
97 Bob Duliba	.70	.35	.20
98 George Thomas	.70	.35	.20
99 Jim Umbricht	.70	.35	.20
100 Joe Cunningham	.90	.45	.25
101 Joe Gibbon	.70	.35	.20
102a Checklist 89-176 ("Checklist" in red on front)	3.00	1.50	.90
102b Checklist 89-176 ("Checklist" in white)	6.00	3.00	1.75
103 Chuck Essegian	.70	.35	.20
104 Lew Krausse	.70	.35	.20
105 Ron Fairly	.90	.45	.25
106 Bob Bolin	.70	.35	.20
107 Jim Hickman	1.00	.50	.30
108 Hoyt Wilhelm	9.00	4.50	2.75
109 Lee Maye	.70	.35	.20
110 Rich Rollins	.90	.45	.25
111 Al Jackson	1.00	.50	.30
112 Dick Brown	.70	.35	.20
113 Don Landrum (photo actally Ron Santo)	.90	.45	.25
114 Dan Osinski	.70	.35	.20
115 Carl Yastrzemski	80.00	40.00	25.00
116 Jim Brosnan	.90	.45	.25
117 Jacke Davis	.70	.35	.20
118 Sherm Lollar	.90	.45	.25
119 Bob Lillis	.70	.35	.20
120 Roger Maris	40.00	20.00	12.00
121 Jim Hannan	.70	.35	.20
122 Julio Gotay	.70	.35	.20
123 Frank Howard	2.50	1.25	.70
124 Dick Howser	1.50	.70	.45
125 Robin Roberts	6.00	3.00	1.75
126 Bob Uecker	30.00	15.00	9.00
127 Bill Tuttle	.70	.35	.20
128 Matty Alou	.90	.45	.25
129 Gary Bell	.70	.35	.20
130 Dick Groat	1.50	.70	.45
131 Senators Team	2.25	1.25	.70
132 Jack Hamilton	.70	.35	.20
133 Gene Freese	.70	.35	.20
134 Bob Scheffing	.70	.35	.20
135 Richie Ashburn	4.50	2.25	1.25
136 Ike Delock	.70	.35	.20
137 Mack Jones	.70	.35	.20
138 Pride of N.L. (Willie Mays, Stan Musial)	25.00	12.50	7.50
139 Earl Averill	.70	.35	.20
140 Frank Lary	.90	.45	.25
141 *Manny Mota*	4.00	2.00	1.25
142 World Series Game 1 (Yanks' Ford Wins Series Opener)	3.50	1.75	1.00
143 World Series Game 2 (Sanford Flashes Shutout Magic)	2.25	1.25	.70
144 World Series Game 3 (Maris Sparks Yankee Rally)	4.00	2.00	1.25
145 World Series Game 4 (Hiller Blasts Grand Slammer)	2.25	1.25	.70
146 World Series Game 5 (Tresh's Homer Defeats Giants)	3.00	1.50	.90
147 World Series Game 6 (Pierce Stars In 3 Hit Victory)	3.00	1.50	.90

		NR MT	EX	VG
148	World Series Game 7 (Yanks Celebrate As Terry Wins)	3.00	1.50	.90
149	Marv Breeding	.70	.35	.20
150	Johnny Podres	2.00	1.00	.60
151	Pirates Team	2.25	1.25	.70
152	Ron Nischwitz	.70	.35	.20
153	Hal Smith	.70	.35	.20
154	Walt Alston	3.00	1.50	.90
155	Bill Stafford	1.25	.60	.40
156	Roy McMillan	.70	.35	.20
157	*Diego Segui*	.90	.45	.25
158	1963 Rookie Stars (Rogelio Alvarez, *Tommy Harper*, Dave Roberts, Bob Saverine)	.90	.45	.25
159	Jim Pagliaroni	.70	.35	.20
160	Juan Pizarro	.70	.35	.20
161	Frank Torre	.70	.35	.20
162	Twins Team	2.25	1.25	.70
163	Don Larsen	1.25	.60	.40
164	Bubba Morton	.70	.35	.20
165	Jim Kaat	5.00	2.50	1.50
166	Johnny Keane	.70	.35	.20
167	Jim Fregosi	1.50	.70	.45
168	Russ Nixon	.70	.35	.20
169	1963 Rookie Stars (Dick Egan, Julio Navarro, Gaylord Perry, Tommie Sisk)	18.00	9.00	5.50
170	Joe Adcock	1.50	.70	.45
171	Steve Hamilton	.70	.35	.20
172	Gene Oliver	.70	.35	.20
173	Bomber's Best (Mickey Mantle, Bobby Richardson, Tom Tresh)	45.00	23.00	13.50
174	Larry Burright	1.00	.50	.30
175	Bob Buhl	.90	.45	.25
176	Jim King	.70	.35	.20
177	Bubba Phillips	.70	.35	.20
178	Johnny Edwards	.70	.35	.20
179	Ron Piche	.70	.35	.20
180	Bill Skowron	1.50	.70	.45
181	Sammy Esposito	.70	.35	.20
182	Albie Pearson	.70	.35	.20
183	Joe Pepitone	4.00	2.00	1.25
184	Vern Law	1.25	.60	.40
185	Chuck Hiller	.70	.35	.20
186	Jerry Zimmerman	.70	.35	.20
187	Willie Kirkland	.70	.35	.20
188	Eddie Bressoud	.70	.35	.20
189	Dave Giusti	.70	.35	.20
190	Minnie Minoso	1.50	.70	.45
191	Checklist 177-264	3.00	1.50	.90
192	Clay Dalrymple	.70	.35	.20
193	Andre Rodgers	.70	.35	.20
194	Joe Nuxhall	.90	.45	.25
195	Manny Jimenez	.70	.35	.20
196	Doug Camilli	.70	.35	.20
197	Roger Craig	2.00	1.00	.60
198	Lenny Green	.70	.35	.20
199	Joe Amalfitano	.70	.35	.20
200	Mickey Mantle	350.00	175.00	105.00
201	Cecil Butler	.70	.35	.20
202	Red Sox Team	2.50	1.25	.70
203	Chico Cardenas	.70	.35	.20
204	Don Nottebart	.70	.35	.20
205	Luis Aparicio	10.00	5.00	3.00
206	Ray Washburn	.70	.35	.20
207	Ken Hunt	.70	.35	.20
208	1963 Rookie Stars (Ron Herbel, John Miller, Ron Taylor, Wally Wolf)	.70	.35	.20
209	Hobie Landrith	.70	.35	.20
210	Sandy Koufax	125.00	56.00	35.00
211	Fred Whitfield	.70	.35	.20
212	Glen Hobbie	.70	.35	.20
213	Billy Hitchcock	.70	.35	.20
214	Orlando Pena	.70	.35	.20
215	Bob Skinner	.90	.45	.25
216	Gene Conley	.90	.45	.25
217	Joe Christopher	1.00	.50	.30
218	Tiger Twirlers (Jim Bunning, Frank Lary, Don Mossi)	2.00	1.00	.60
219	Chuck Cottier	.70	.35	.20
220	Camilo Pascual	.90	.45	.25
221	*Cookie Rojas*	.90	.45	.25
222	Cubs Team	2.25	1.25	.70
223	Eddie Fisher	.70	.35	.20
224	Mike Roarke	.70	.35	.20
225	Joe Jay	.70	.35	.20
226	Julian Javier	.90	.45	.25
227	Jim Grant	.70	.35	.20
228	1963 Rookie Stars (*Max Alvis, Bob Bailey, Ed Kranepool, Pedro Oliva)*	25.00	12.50	7.50
229	Willie Davis	1.50	.70	.45
230	Pete Runnels	.90	.45	.25
231	Eli Grba (photo actually Ryne Duren)	.90	.45	.25
232	Frank Malzone	.90	.45	.25
233	Casey Stengel	12.00	6.00	3.50
234	Dave Nicholson	.70	.35	.20
235	Billy O'Dell	.70	.35	.20
236	Bill Bryan	.70	.35	.20
237	Jim Coates	1.25	.60	.40
238	Lou Johnson	.70	.35	.20
239	Harvey Haddix	.90	.45	.25
240	Rocky Colavito	3.00	1.50	.90
241	Billy Smith	.70	.35	.20
242	Power Plus (Hank Aaron, Ernie Banks)	350.00	175.00	105.00
243	Don Leppert	.70	.35	.20
244	John Tsitouris	.70	.35	.20
245	Gil Hodges	12.00	6.00	3.50
246	Lee Stange	.70	.35	.20
247	Yankees Team	8.00	4.00	2.50
248	Tito Francona	.90	.45	.25
249	Leo Burke	.70	.35	.20
250	Stan Musial	100.00	45.00	27.00
251	Jack Lamabe	.70	.35	.20
252	Ron Santo	2.00	1.00	.60
253	1963 Rookie Stars (Len Gabrielson, Pete Jernigan, Deacon Jones, John Wojcik)	.70	.35	.20
254	Mike Hershberger	.70	.35	.20
255	Bob Shaw	.70	.35	.20
256	Jerry Lumpe	.90	.45	.25
257	Hank Aguirre	.70	.35	.20
258	Alvin Dark	.90	.45	.25
259	Johnny Logan	.90	.45	.25
260	Jim Gentile	.90	.45	.25
261	Bob Miller	.70	.35	.20
262	Ellis Burton	.70	.35	.20
263	Dave Stenhouse	.70	.35	.20
264	Phil Linz	1.50	.70	.45
265	Vada Pinson	2.50	1.25	.70
266	Bob Allen	.70	.35	.20
267	Carl Sawatski	.70	.35	.20
268	Don Demeter	.70	.35	.20
269	Don Mincher	.90	.45	.25
270	Felipe Alou	.90	.45	.25
271	Dean Stone	.70	.35	.20
272	Danny Murphy	.70	.35	.20
273	Sammy Taylor	1.00	.50	.30
274	Checklist 265-352	3.00	1.50	.90
275	Ed Mathews	12.00	6.00	3.50
276	Barry Shetrone	.70	.35	.20
277	Dick Farrell	.70	.35	.20
278	Chico Fernandez	.70	.35	.20
279	Wally Moon	.90	.45	.25
280	Bob Rodgers	.90	.45	.25
281	Tom Sturdivant	.70	.35	.20
282	Bob Del Greco	.70	.35	.20
283	Roy Sievers	.90	.45	.25
284	Dave Sisler	2.00	1.00	.60
285	Dick Stuart	2.25	1.25	.70
286	Stu Miller	2.00	1.00	.60
287	Dick Bertell	2.00	1.00	.60
288	White Sox Team	3.50	1.75	1.00
289	Hal Brown	2.75	1.50	.80
290	Bill White	2.25	1.25	.70
291	Don Rudolph	2.00	1.00	.60
292	Pumpsie Green	2.25	1.25	.70
293	Bill Pleis	2.00	1.00	.60
294	Bill Rigney	2.00	1.00	.60
295	Ed Roebuck	2.00	1.00	.60
296	Doc Edwards	2.25	1.25	.70
297	Jim Golden	2.00	1.00	.60
298	Don Dillard	2.00	1.00	.60
299	1963 Rookie Stars (Tom Butters, Bob Dustal, Dave Morehead, Dan Schneider)	2.00	1.00	.60
300	Willie Mays	125.00	56.00	35.00
301	Bill Fischer	2.00	1.00	.60
302	Whitey Herzog	3.50	1.75	1.00
303	Earl Francis	2.00	1.00	.60
304	Harry Bright	2.00	1.00	.60
305	Don Hoak	2.25	1.25	.70
306	Star Receivers (Earl Battey, Elston Howard)	3.50	1.75	1.00
307	Chet Nichols	2.00	1.00	.60
308	Camilo Carreon	2.00	1.00	.60
309	Jim Brewer	2.00	1.00	.60
310	Tommy Davis	3.00	1.50	.90
311	Joe McClain	2.00	1.00	.60
312	Colt .45s Team	9.00	4.50	2.75
313	Ernie Broglio	2.00	1.00	.60
314	John Goryl	2.00	1.00	.60
315	Ralph Terry	3.00	1.50	.90
316	Norm Sherry	1.25	.60	.40
317	Sam McDowell	3.00	1.50	.90
318	Gene Mauch	2.25	1.25	.70
319	Joe Gaines	2.00	1.00	.60
320	Warren Spahn	25.00	12.50	7.50
321	Gino Cimoli	2.00	1.00	.60
322	Bob Turley	2.25	1.25	.70
323	Bill Mazeroski	3.50	1.75	1.00
324	1963 Rookie Stars (*Vic Davalillo*, Phil Roof, *Pete Ward*, George Williams)	2.50	1.25	.70
325	Jack Sanford	2.00	1.00	.60
326	Hank Foiles	2.00	1.00	.60
327	Paul Foytack	2.00	1.00	.60
328	Dick Williams	2.75	1.50	.80
329	Lindy McDaniel	2.00	1.00	.60
330	Chuck Hinton	2.00	1.00	.60
331	Series Foes (Bill Pierce, Bill Stafford)	3.00	1.50	.90
332	Joel Horlen	2.00	1.00	.60
333	Carl Warwick	2.00	1.00	.60
334	Wynn Hawkins	2.25	1.25	.70
335	Leon Wagner	2.25	1.25	.70
336	Ed Bauta	2.00	1.00	.60
337	Dodgers Team	8.00	4.00	2.50
338	Russ Kemmerer	2.00	1.00	.60
339	Ted Bowsfield	2.00	1.00	.60
340	Yogi Berra	90.00	45.00	27.00
341	Jack Baldschun	2.00	1.00	.60
342	Gene Woodling	2.50	1.25	.70
343	Johnny Pesky	2.25	1.25	.70
344	Don Schwall	2.00	1.00	.60
345	Brooks Robinson	30.00	15.00	9.00
346	Billy Hoeft	2.00	1.00	.60
347	Joe Torre	4.50	2.25	1.25
348	Vic Wertz	2.25	1.25	.70
349	Zoilo Versalles	2.25	1.25	.70
350	Bob Purkey	2.00	1.00	.60
351	Al Luplow	2.00	1.00	.60
352	Ken Johnson	2.00	1.00	.60
353	Billy Williams	20.00	10.00	6.00
354	Dom Zanni	2.00	1.00	.60
355	Dean Chance	2.25	1.25	.70
356	John Schaive	2.00	1.00	.60
357	George Altman	2.00	1.00	.60
358	Milt Pappas	2.25	1.25	.70
359	Haywood Sullivan	2.25	1.25	.70
360	Don Drysdale	20.00	10.00	6.00
361	Clete Boyer	3.50	1.75	1.00
362	Checklist 353-429	4.00	2.00	1.25
363	Dick Radatz	2.25	1.25	.70
364	Howie Goss	2.00	1.00	.60
365	Jim Bunning	8.00	4.00	2.50
366	Tony Taylor	2.00	1.00	.60
367	Tony Cloninger	2.25	1.25	.70
368	Ed Bailey	2.00	1.00	.60
369	Jim Lemon	2.00	1.00	.60
370	Dick Donovan	2.00	1.00	.60
371	Rod Kanehl	2.25	1.25	.70
372	Don Lee	2.00	1.00	.60
373	Jim Campbell	2.00	1.00	.60
374	Claude Osteen	2.25	1.25	.70
375	Ken Boyer	4.00	2.00	1.25
376	Johnnie Wyatt	2.00	1.00	.60
377	Orioles Team	3.50	1.75	1.00
378	Bill Henry	2.00	1.00	.60
379	Bob Anderson	2.00	1.00	.60
380	Ernie Banks	40.00	20.00	12.00
381	Frank Baumann	2.00	1.00	.60
382	Ralph Houk	3.50	1.75	1.00
383	Pete Richert	2.00	1.00	.60
384	Bob Tillman	2.00	1.00	.60
385	Art Mahaffey	2.00	1.00	.60
386	1963 Rookie Stars (*John Bateman*, Larry Bearnarth, *Ed Kirkpatrick*, Garry Roggenburk)	2.25	1.25	.70
387	Al McBean	2.00	1.00	.60
388	Jim Davenport	2.00	1.00	.60
389	Frank Sullivan	2.00	1.00	.60
390	Hank Aaron	125.00	56.00	35.00
391	Bill Dailey	2.00	1.00	.60
392	Tribe Thumpers (Tito Francona, Johnny Romano)	2.25	1.25	.70
393	Ken MacKenzie	2.25	1.25	.70
394	Tim McCarver	4.00	2.00	1.25
395	Don McMahon	2.00	1.00	.60
396	Joe Koppe	2.00	1.00	.60
397	Athletics Team	3.50	1.75	1.00
398	Boog Powell	7.00	3.50	2.00
399	Dick Ellsworth	2.00	1.00	.60
400	Frank Robinson	45.00	23.00	13.50
401	Jim Bouton	8.00	4.00	2.50
402	Mickey Vernon	2.25	1.25	.70
403	Ron Perranoski	2.25	1.25	.70
404	Bob Oldis	2.00	1.00	.60
405	Floyd Robinson	2.00	1.00	.60
406	Howie Koplitz	2.00	1.00	.60
407	1963 Rookie Stars (Larry Elliot, Frank Kostro, Chico Ruiz, Dick Simpson)	2.00	1.00	.60
408	Billy Gardner	2.00	1.00	.60
409	Roy Face	2.75	1.50	.80
410	Earl Battey	2.25	1.25	.70
411	Jim Constable	2.00	1.00	.60
412	Dodgers' Big Three (Don Drysdale, Sandy Koufax, Johnny Podres)	25.00	12.50	7.50
413	Jerry Walker	2.00	1.00	.60
414	Ty Cline	2.00	1.00	.60
415	Bob Gibson	30.00	15.00	9.00
416	Alex Grammas	2.00	1.00	.60
417	Giants Team	3.50	1.75	1.00
418	Johnny Orsino	2.00	1.00	.60
419	Tracy Stallard	2.25	1.25	.70
420	Bobby Richardson	8.00	4.00	2.50
421	Tom Morgan	2.00	1.00	.60
422	Fred Hutchinson	2.25	1.25	.70
423	Ed Hobaugh	2.00	1.00	.60
424	Charley Smith	2.00	1.00	.60
425	Smoky Burgess	2.50	1.25	.70
426	Barry Latman	2.00	1.00	.60
427	Bernie Allen	2.00	1.00	.60
428	Carl Boles	2.00	1.00	.60
429	Lou Burdette	3.00	1.50	.90
430	Norm Siebern	2.25	1.25	.70
431a	Checklist 430-506 ("Checklist" in black on front)	4.50	2.25	1.25
431b	Checklist 430-506 ("Checklist" in white)	7.00	3.50	2.00
432	Roman Mejias	2.00	1.00	.60
433	Denis Menke	2.25	1.25	.70
434	Johnny Callison	2.50	1.25	.70
435	Woody Held	2.00	1.00	.60
436	Tim Harkness	2.25	1.25	.70
437	Bill Bruton	2.00	1.00	.60
438	Wes Stock	2.00	1.00	.60
439	Don Zimmer	2.75	1.50	.80
440	Juan Marichal	20.00	10.00	6.00
441	Lee Thomas	2.00	1.00	.60
442	J.C. Hartman	2.00	1.00	.60
443	Jim Piersall	2.75	1.50	.80
444	Jim Maloney	2.25	1.25	.70
445	Norm Cash	3.00	1.50	.90
446	Whitey Ford	30.00	15.00	9.00
447	Felix Mantilla	8.00	4.00	2.50
448	Jack Kralick	8.00	4.00	2.50
449	Jose Tartabull	8.00	4.00	2.50
450	Bob Friend	9.00	4.50	2.75
451	Indians Team	10.00	5.00	3.00
452	Barney Schultz	8.00	4.00	2.50
453	Jake Wood	8.00	4.00	2.50
454a	Art Fowler (card # on orange background)	10.00	5.00	3.00
454b	Art Fowler (card # on white background)	8.00	4.00	2.50
455	Ruben Amaro	8.00	4.00	2.50
456	Jim Coker	8.00	4.00	2.50
457	Tex Clevenger	9.00	4.50	2.75
458	Al Lopez	11.00	5.50	3.25
459	Dick LeMay	8.00	4.00	2.50
460	Del Crandall	9.00	4.50	2.75
461	Norm Bass	8.00	4.00	2.50
462	Wally Post	8.00	4.00	2.50
463	Joe Schaffernoth	8.00	4.00	2.50
464	Ken Aspromonte	8.00	4.00	2.50
465	Chuck Estrada	8.00	4.00	2.50
466	1963 Rookie Stars (*Bill Freehan*, Tony Martinez, Nate Oliver, Jerry Robinson)	25.00	12.50	7.50
467	Phil Ortega	8.00	4.00	2.50
468	Carroll Hardy	8.00	4.00	2.50
469	Jay Hook	9.00	4.50	2.75
470	Tom Tresh	20.00	10.00	6.00
471	Ken Retzer	8.00	4.00	2.50
472	Lou Brock	80.00	40.00	24.00
473	Mets Team	90.00	45.00	27.00
474	Jack Fisher	8.00	4.00	2.50
475	Gus Triandos	8.00	4.00	2.50
476	Frank Funk	8.00	4.00	2.50
477	Donn Clendenon	9.00	4.50	2.75
478	Paul Brown	8.00	4.00	2.50
479	*Ed Brinkman*	9.00	4.50	2.75
480	Bill Monbouquette	9.00	4.50	2.75
481	Bob Taylor	8.00	4.00	2.50
482	Felix Torres	8.00	4.00	2.50
483	Jim Owens	8.00	4.00	2.50
484	Dale Long	9.00	4.50	2.75
485	Jim Landis	8.00	4.00	2.50

		NR MT	EX	VG
486	Ray Sadecki	8.00	4.00	2.50
487	John Roseboro	9.00	4.50	2.75
488	Jerry Adair	8.00	4.00	2.50
489	Paul Toth	8.00	4.00	2.50
490	Willie McCovey	90.00	45.00	27.00
491	Harry Craft	8.00	4.00	2.50
492	Dave Wickersham	8.00	4.00	2.50
493	Walt Bond	8.00	4.00	2.50
494	Phil Regan	8.00	4.00	2.50
495	Frank Thomas	9.00	4.50	2.75
496	1963 Rookie Stars (Carl Bouldin, *Steve Dalkowski, Fred Newman*, Jack Smith)	9.00	4.50	2.75
497	Bennie Daniels	8.00	4.00	2.50
498	Eddie Kasko	8.00	4.00	2.50
499	J.C. Martin	8.00	4.00	2.50
500	Harmon Killebrew	90.00	45.00	27.00
501	Joe Azcue	8.00	4.00	2.50
502	Daryl Spencer	8.00	4.00	2.50
503	Braves Team	10.00	5.00	3.00
504	Bob Johnson	8.00	4.00	2.50
505	Curt Flood	12.00	6.00	3.50
506	Gene Green	9.00	4.50	2.75
507	Roland Sheldon	6.00	3.00	1.75
508	Ted Savage	5.00	2.50	1.50
509a	Checklist 507-576 (copyright centered)	15.00	7.50	4.50
509b	Checklist 509-576 (copyright to right)	12.00	6.00	3.50
510	Ken McBride	5.00	2.50	1.50
511	Charlie Neal	5.50	2.75	1.75
512	Cal McLish	5.00	2.50	1.50
513	Gary Geiger	5.00	2.50	1.50
514	Larry Osborne	5.00	2.50	1.50
515	Don Elston	5.00	2.50	1.50
516	Purnal Goldy	5.00	2.50	1.50
517	Hal Woodeshick	5.00	2.50	1.50
518	Don Blasingame	5.00	2.50	1.50
519	Claude Raymond	5.00	2.50	1.50
520	Orlando Cepeda	15.00	7.50	4.50
521	Dan Pfister	5.00	2.50	1.50
522	1963 Rookie Stars (Mel Nelson, Gary Peters, Art Quirk, Jim Roland)	5.50	2.75	1.75
523	Bill Kunkel	6.00	3.00	1.75
524	Cardinals Team	8.00	4.00	2.50
525	Nellie Fox	12.00	6.00	3.50
526	Dick Hall	5.00	2.50	1.50
527	Ed Sadowski	5.00	2.50	1.50
528	Carl Willey	5.50	2.75	1.75
529	Wes Covington	5.00	2.50	1.50
530	Don Mossi	5.50	2.75	1.75
531	Sam Mele	5.00	2.50	1.50
532	Steve Boros	5.00	2.50	1.50
533	Bobby Shantz	6.00	3.00	1.75
534	Ken Walters	5.00	2.50	1.50
535	Jim Perry	6.00	3.00	1.75
536	Norm Larker	5.00	2.50	1.50
537	1963 Rookie Stars (Pedro Gonzalez, *Ken McMullen, Pete Rose, Al Weis*)	600.00	240.00	150.00
538	George Brunet	5.00	2.50	1.50
539	Wayne Causey	5.00	2.50	1.50
540	Bob Clemente	150.00	75.00	45.00
541	Ron Moeller	5.00	2.50	1.50
542	Lou Klimchock	5.00	2.50	1.50
543	Russ Snyder	5.00	2.50	1.50
544	1963 Rookie Stars (Duke Carmel, Bill Haas, Dick Phillips, *Rusty Staub*)	25.00	12.50	7.50
545	Jose Pagan	5.00	2.50	1.50
546	Hal Reniff	6.00	3.00	1.75
547	Gus Bell	5.50	2.75	1.75
548	Tom Satriano	5.00	2.50	1.50
549	1963 Rookie Stars (*Marcelino Lopez*, Pete Lovrich, Elmo Plaskett, Paul Ratliff)	5.50	2.75	1.75
550	Duke Snider	70.00	35.00	20.00
551	Billy Klaus	5.00	2.50	1.50
552	Tigers Team	12.00	6.00	3.50
553	1963 Rookie Stars (Brock Davis, Jim Gosger, John Herrnstein, *Willie Stargell*)	225.00	90.00	56.00
554	Hank Fischer	5.00	2.50	1.50
555	John Blanchard	6.00	3.00	1.75
556	Al Worthington	5.00	2.50	1.50
557	Cuno Barragan	5.00	2.50	1.50
558	1963 Rookie Stars (Bill Faul, *Ron Hunt*, Bob Lipski, Al Moran)	6.00	3.00	1.75
559	Danny Murtaugh	5.50	2.75	1.75
560	Ray Herbert	5.00	2.50	1.50
561	Mike de la Hoz	5.00	2.50	1.50
562	1963 Rookie Stars (Randy Cardinal, *Dave McNally*, Don Rowe, Ken Rowe)	9.00	4.50	2.75
563	Mike McCormick	5.50	2.75	1.75
564	George Banks	5.00	2.50	1.50
565	Larry Sherry	5.00	2.50	1.50
566	Cliff Cook	5.50	2.75	1.75
567	Jim Duffalo	5.00	2.50	1.50
568	Bob Sadowski	5.00	2.50	1.50
569	Luis Arroyo	6.00	3.00	1.75
570	Frank Bolling	5.00	2.50	1.50
571	Johnny Klippstein	5.00	2.50	1.50
572	Jack Spring	5.00	2.50	1.50
573	Coot Veal	5.00	2.50	1.50
574	Hal Kolstad	5.00	2.50	1.50
575	Don Cardwell	5.50	2.50	1.50
576	Johnny Temple	8.00	2.50	1.25

1963 Topps Peel-Offs

Measuring 1-1/4" by 2-3/4," Topps Peel-Offs were an insert with 1963 Topps baseball cards. There are 46 players in the unnumbered set, each pictured in a color photo inside an oval with the player's name, team and position in a band below. The back of the Peel-Off is removable, leaving a sticky surface that made the Peel-Off a popular

decorative item among youngsters of the day. Naturally, that makes them quite scarce today, but as a non-card Topps issue, demand is not particularly strong.

		NR MT	EX	VG
	Complete Set:	175.00	87.00	52.00
	Common Player:	1.00	.50	.30
(1)	Hank Aaron	10.00	5.00	3.00
(2)	Luis Aparicio	3.00	1.50	.90
(3)	Richie Ashburn	2.00	1.00	.60
(4)	Bob Aspromonte	1.00	.50	.30
(5)	Ernie Banks	5.00	2.50	1.50
(6)	Ken Boyer	1.50	.70	.45
(7)	Jim Bunning	1.75	.90	.50
(8)	Johnny Callison	1.25	.60	.40
(9)	Orlando Cepeda	1.75	.90	.50
(10)	Bob Clemente	8.00	4.00	2.50
(11)	Rocky Colavito	1.75	.90	.50
(12)	Tommy Davis	1.50	.70	.45
(13)	Dick Donovan	1.00	.50	.30
(14)	Don Drysdale	4.00	2.00	1.25
(15)	Dick Farrell	1.00	.50	.30
(16)	Jim Gentile	1.00	.50	.30
(17)	Ray Herbert	1.00	.50	.30
(18)	Chuck Hinton	1.00	.50	.30
(19)	Ken Hubbs	1.50	.70	.45
(20)	Al Jackson	1.00	.50	.30
(21)	Al Kaline	5.00	2.50	1.50
(22)	Harmon Killebrew	5.00	2.50	1.50
(23)	Sandy Koufax	8.00	4.00	2.50
(24)	Jerry Lumpe	1.00	.50	.30
(25)	Art Mahaffey	1.00	.50	.30
(26)	Mickey Mantle	50.00	25.00	15.00
(27)	Willie Mays	10.00	5.00	3.00
(28)	Bill Mazeroski	1.50	.70	.45
(29)	Bill Monbouquette	1.00	.50	.30
(30)	Stan Musial	10.00	5.00	3.00
(31)	Camilo Pascual	1.25	.60	.40
(32)	Bob Purkey	1.00	.50	.30
(33)	Bobby Richardson	1.75	.90	.50
(34)	Brooks Robinson	6.00	3.00	1.75
(35)	Floyd Robinson	1.00	.50	.30
(36)	Frank Robinson	5.00	2.50	1.50
(37)	Bob Rodgers	1.00	.50	.30
(38)	Johnny Romano	1.00	.50	.30
(39)	Jack Sanford	1.00	.50	.30
(40)	Norm Siebern	1.00	.50	.30
(41)	Warren Spahn	5.00	2.50	1.50
(42)	Dave Stenhouse	1.00	.50	.30
(43)	Ralph Terry	1.25	.60	.40
(44)	Lee Thomas	1.00	.50	.30
(45)	Bill White	1.25	.60	.40
(46)	Carl Yastrzemski	12.00	6.00	3.50

1964 Topps

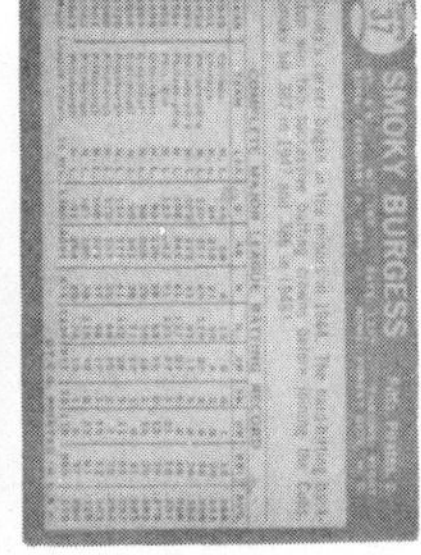

The 1964 Topps set is a 587-card issue of 2-1/2" by 3-1/2" cards which is considered by many as being among the company's best efforts. Card fronts feature a large color photo which blends into a top panel which contains the team name, while a panel below the picture carries the player's name and position. An interesting innovation on the back is a baseball quiz question which required the rubbing of a white panel to reveal the answer. As in 1963, specialty cards remained modest in number with a 12-card set of statistical leaders, a few multi-player cards, rookies and World Series highlights. An interesting card is an "In Memoriam" card for Ken Hubbs who was killed in an airplane crash.

		NR MT	EX	VG
	Complete Set:	2500.	1250.	750.00
	Common Player: 1-370	.70	.35	.20
	Common Player: 371-522	1.00	.50	.30
	Common Player: 523-587	4.00	2.00	1.25
1	N.L. E.R.A. Leaders (Dick Ellsworth, Bob Friend, Sandy Koufax)	10.00	3.00	1.50
2	A.L. E.R.A. Leaders (Camilo Pascual, Gary Peters, Juan Pizarro)	3.00	1.50	.90
3	N.L. Pitching Leaders (Sandy Koufax, Jim Maloney, Juan Marichal, Warren Spahn)	5.00	2.50	1.50
4a	A.L. Pitching Leaders (Jim Bouton, Whitey Ford, Camilo Pascual) (apostrophe after "Pitching" on back)	5.00	2.50	1.50
4b	A.L. Pitching Leaders (Jim Bouton, Whitey Ford, Camilo Pascual) (no apostrophe)	3.50	1.75	1.00
5	N.L. Strikeout Leaders (Don Drysdale, Sandy Koufax, Jim Maloney)	4.00	2.00	1.25
6	A.L. Strikeout Leaders (Jim Bunning, Camilo Pascual, Dick Stigman)	3.00	1.50	.90
7	N.L. Batting Leaders (Hank Aaron, Bob Clemente, Tommy Davis, Dick Groat)	5.00	2.50	1.50
8	A.L. Batting Leaders (Al Kaline, Rich Rollins, Carl Yastrzemski)	5.00	2.50	1.50
9	N.L. Home Run Leaders (Hank Aaron, Orlando Cepeda, Willie Mays, Willie McCovey)	5.00	2.50	1.50
10	A.L. Home Run Leaders (Bob Allison, Harmon Killebrew, Dick Stuart)	3.50	1.75	1.00
11	N.L. R.B.I. Leaders (Hank Aaron, Ken Boyer, Bill White)	4.50	2.25	1.25
12	A.L. R.B.I. Leaders (Al Kaline, Harmon Killebrew, Dick Stuart)	4.50	2.25	1.25
13	Hoyt Wilhelm	8.00	4.00	2.50
14	Dodgers Rookies (Dick Nen, Nick Willhite)	.70	.35	.20
15	Zoilo Versalles	.80	.40	.25
16	John Boozer	.70	.35	.20
17	Willie Kirkland	.70	.35	.20
18	Billy O'Dell	.70	.35	.20
19	Don Wert	.70	.35	.20
20	Bob Friend	1.25	.60	.40
21	Yogi Berra	30.00	15.00	9.00
22	Jerry Adair	.70	.35	.20
23	Chris Zachary	.70	.35	.20
24	Carl Sawatski	.70	.35	.20
25	Bill Monbouquette	.80	.40	.25
26	Gino Cimoli	.70	.35	.20
27	Mets Team	3.50	1.75	1.00
28	Claude Osteen	.80	.40	.25
29	Lou Brock	30.00	15.00	9.00
30	Ron Perranoski	.80	.40	.25
31	Dave Nicholson	.70	.35	.20
32	Dean Chance	1.25	.60	.40
33	Reds Rookies (Sammy Ellis, Mel Queen)	.80	.40	.25
34	Jim Perry	1.25	.60	.40
35	Ed Mathews	12.00	6.00	3.50
36	Hal Reniff	1.00	.50	.30
37	Smoky Burgess	1.25	.60	.40
38	*Jim Wynn*	1.50	.70	.45
39	Hank Aguirre	.70	.35	.20
40	Dick Groat	1.50	.70	.45
41	Friendly Foes (Willie McCovey, Leon Wagner)	3.00	1.50	.90
42	Moe Drabowsky	.70	.35	.20
43	Roy Sievers	.90	.45	.25
44	Duke Carmel	.80	.40	.25
45	Milt Pappas	.90	.45	.25
46	Ed Brinkman	.80	.40	.25
47	Giants Rookies (*Jesus Alou*, Ron Herbel)	1.25	.60	.40
48	Bob Perry	.70	.35	.20
49	Bill Henry	.70	.35	.20
50	Mickey Mantle	200.00	80.00	50.00
51	Pete Richert	.70	.35	.20
52	Chuck Hinton	.70	.35	.20
53	Denis Menke	.70	.35	.20
54	Sam Mele	.70	.35	.20
55	Ernie Banks	25.00	12.50	7.50
56	Hal Brown	.70	.35	.20
57	Tim Harkness	.80	.40	.25
58	Don Demeter	.70	.35	.20
59	Ernie Broglio	.70	.35	.20
60	Frank Malzone	.80	.40	.25
61	Angel Backstops (Bob Rodgers, Ed Sadowski)	.80	.40	.25
62	Ted Savage	.70	.35	.20
63	Johnny Orsino	.70	.35	.20
64	Ted Abernathy	.70	.35	.20
65	Felipe Alou	1.25	.60	.40
66	Eddie Fisher	.70	.35	.20
67	Tigers Team	3.50	1.75	1.00
68	Willie Davis	1.50	.70	.45
69	Clete Boyer	1.50	.70	.45
70	Joe Torre	2.50	1.25	.70
71	Jack Spring	.70	.35	.20
72	Chico Cardenas	.70	.35	.20
73	*Jimmie Hall*	.80	.40	.25
74	Pirates Rookies (Tom Butters, Bob Priddy)	.70	.35	.20
75	Wayne Causey	.70	.35	.20
76	Checklist 1-88	3.00	1.50	.90
77	Jerry Walker	.70	.35	.20
78	Merritt Ranew	.70	.35	.20
79	Bob Heffner	.70	.35	.20
80	Vada Pinson	2.50	1.25	.70
81	All-Star Vets (Nellie Fox, Harmon Killebrew)	4.00	2.00	1.25
82	Jim Davenport	.70	.35	.20
83	Gus Triandos	.80	.40	.25
84	Carl Willey	.80	.40	.25
85	Pete Ward	.80	.40	.25
86	Al Downing	1.50	.70	.45
87	Cardinals Team	4.00	2.00	1.25
88	John Roseboro	.80	.40	.25
89	Boog Powell	2.50	1.25	.70
90	Earl Battey	.80	.40	.25

No.	Card	NR MT	EX	VG
91	Bob Bailey	.80	.40	.25
92	Steve Ridzik	.70	.35	.20
93	Gary Geiger	.70	.35	.20
94	Braves Rookies (Jim Britton, Larry Maxie)	.70	.35	.20
95	George Altman	.80	.40	.25
96	Bob Buhl	.80	.40	.25
97	Jim Fregosi	1.25	.60	.40
98	Bill Bruton	.70	.35	.20
99	Al Stanek	.70	.35	.20
100	Elston Howard	5.00	2.50	1.50
101	Walt Alston	3.00	1.50	.90
102	Checklist 89-176	3.00	1.50	.90
103	Curt Flood	2.00	1.00	.60
104	Art Mahaffey	.70	.35	.20
105	Woody Held	.70	.35	.20
106	Joe Nuxhall	.80	.40	.25
107	White Sox Rookies (Bruce Howard, Frank Kreutzer)	.70	.35	.20
108	John Wyatt	.70	.35	.20
109	Rusty Staub	5.00	2.50	1.50
110	Albie Pearson	.70	.35	.20
111	Don Elston	.70	.35	.20
112	Bob Tillman	.70	.35	.20
113	Grover Powell	.80	.40	.25
114	Don Lock	.70	.35	.20
115	Frank Bolling	.70	.35	.20
116	Twins Rookies (Tony Oliva, Jay Ward)	4.00	2.00	1.25
117	Earl Francis	.70	.35	.20
118	John Blanchard	1.00	.50	.30
119	Gary Kolb	.70	.35	.20
120	Don Drysdale	15.00	7.50	4.50
121	Pete Runnels	.80	.40	.25
122	Don McMahon	.70	.35	.20
123	Jose Pagan	.70	.35	.20
124	Orlando Pena	.70	.35	.20
125	Pete Rose	125.00	56.00	35.00
126	Russ Snyder	.70	.35	.20
127	Angels Rookies (Aubrey Gatewood, Dick Simpson)	.70	.35	.20
128	*Mickey Lolich*	8.00	4.00	2.50
129	Amado Samuel	.80	.40	.25
130	Gary Peters	.80	.40	.25
131	Steve Boros	.80	.40	.25
132	Braves Team	2.25	1.25	.70
133	Jim Grant	.70	.35	.20
134	Don Zimmer	1.50	.70	.45
135	Johnny Callison	1.50	.70	.45
136	World Series Game 1 (Koufax Strikes Out 15)	5.00	2.50	1.50
137	World Series Game 2 (Davis Sparks Rally)	2.50	1.25	.70
138	World Series Game 3 (L.A. Takes 3rd Straight)	2.50	1.25	.70
139	World Series Game 4 (Sealing Yanks' Doom)	2.50	1.25	.70
140	World Series Summary (The Dodgers Celebrate)	2.50	1.25	.70
141	Danny Murtaugh	.80	.40	.25
142	John Bateman	.70	.35	.20
143	Bubba Phillips	.70	.35	.20
144	Al Worthington	.70	.35	.20
145	Norm Siebern	.80	.40	.25
146	Indians Rookies (Bob Chance, *Tommy John*)	60.00	30.00	18.00
147	Ray Sadecki	.70	.35	.20
148	J.C. Martin	.70	.35	.20
149	Paul Foytack	.70	.35	.20
150	Willie Mays	70.00	35.00	21.00
151	Athletics Team	2.25	1.25	.70
152	Denver Lemaster	.70	.35	.20
153	Dick Williams	1.50	.70	.45
154	Dick Tracewski	.70	.35	.20
155	Duke Snider	25.00	12.50	7.50
156	Bill Dailey	.70	.35	.20
157	Gene Mauch	.90	.45	.25
158	Ken Johnson	.70	.35	.20
159	Charlie Dees	.70	.35	.20
160	Ken Boyer	4.00	2.00	1.25
161	Dave McNally	1.25	.60	.40
162	Hitting Area (Vada Pinson, Dick Sisler)	.80	.40	.25
163	Donn Clendenon	1.00	.50	.30
164	Bud Daley	1.00	.50	.30
165	Jerry Lumpe	.80	.40	.25
166	Marty Keough	.70	.35	.20
167	Senators Rookies (Mike Brumley, *Lou Piniella*)	20.00	10.00	6.00
168	Al Weis	.70	.35	.20
169	Del Crandall	1.25	.60	.40
170	Dick Radatz	.80	.40	.25
171	Ty Cline	.70	.35	.20
172	Indians Team	2.25	1.25	.70
173	Ryne Duren	.90	.45	.25
174	Doc Edwards	.80	.40	.25
175	Billy Williams	8.00	4.00	2.50
176	Tracy Stallard	.80	.40	.25
177	Harmon Killebrew	12.00	6.00	3.50
178	Hank Bauer	.90	.45	.25
179	Carl Warwick	.70	.35	.20
180	Tommy Davis	1.50	.70	.45
181	Dave Wickersham	.70	.35	.20
182	Sox Sockers (Chuck Schilling, Carl Yastrzemski)	7.00	3.50	2.00
183	Ron Taylor	.70	.35	.20
184	Al Luplow	.70	.35	.20
185	Jim O'Toole	.70	.35	.20
186	Roman Mejias	.70	.35	.20
187	Ed Roebuck	.70	.35	.20
188	Checklist 177-264	3.00	1.50	.90
189	Bob Hendley	.70	.35	.20
190	Bobby Richardson	4.50	2.25	1.25
191	Clay Dalrymple	.70	.35	.20
192	Cubs Rookies (John Boccabella, Billy Cowan)	.70	.35	.20
193	Jerry Lynch	.70	.35	.20
194	John Goryl	.70	.35	.20
195	Floyd Robinson	.70	.35	.20
196	Jim Gentile	.80	.40	.25
197	Frank Lary	.80	.40	.25
198	Len Gabrielson	.70	.35	.20
199	Joe Azcue	.70	.35	.20
200	Sandy Koufax	80.00	40.00	25.00
201	Orioles Rookies (Sam Bowens, *Wally Bunker*)	.80	.40	.25
202	Galen Cisco	.80	.40	.25
203	John Kennedy	.70	.35	.20
204	Matty Alou	.90	.45	.25
205	Nellie Fox	4.00	2.00	1.25
206	Steve Hamilton	1.00	.50	.30
207	Fred Hutchinson	.80	.40	.25
208	Wes Covington	.70	.35	.20
209	Bob Allen	.70	.35	.20
210	Carl Yastrzemski	70.00	35.00	21.00
211	Jim Coker	.70	.35	.20
212	Pete Lovrich	.70	.35	.20
213	Angels Team	2.25	1.25	.70
214	Ken McMullen	.80	.40	.25
215	Ray Herbert	.70	.35	.20
216	Mike de la Hoz	.70	.35	.20
217	Jim King	.70	.35	.20
218	Hank Fischer	.70	.35	.20
219	Young Aces (Jim Bouton, Al Downing)	2.00	1.00	.60
220	Dick Ellsworth	.70	.35	.20
221	Bob Saverine	.70	.35	.20
222	Bill Pierce	.90	.45	.25
223	George Banks	.70	.35	.20
224	Tommie Sisk	.70	.35	.20
225	Roger Maris	45.00	23.00	13.50
226	Colts Rookies (*Gerald Grote*, Larry Yellen)	1.25	.60	.40
227	Barry Latman	.70	.35	.20
228	Felix Mantilla	.70	.35	.20
229	Charley Lau	.80	.40	.25
230	Brooks Robinson	20.00	10.00	6.00
231	Dick Calmus	.70	.35	.20
232	Al Lopez	3.00	1.50	.90
233	Hal Smith	.70	.35	.20
234	Gary Bell	.70	.35	.20
235	Ron Hunt	.80	.40	.25
236	Bill Faul	.70	.35	.20
237	Cubs Team	2.25	1.25	.70
238	Roy McMillan	.70	.35	.20
239	Herm Starrette	.70	.35	.20
240	Bill White	1.50	.70	.45
241	Jim Owens	.70	.35	.20
242	Harvey Kuenn	1.50	.70	.45
243	Phillies Rookies (*Richie Allen*, John Herrnstein)	8.00	4.00	2.50
244	*Tony LaRussa*	10.00	5.00	3.00
245	Dick Stigman	.70	.35	.20
246	Manny Mota	1.25	.60	.40
247	Dave DeBusschere	2.00	1.00	.60
248	Johnny Pesky	.80	.40	.25
249	Doug Camilli	.70	.35	.20
250	Al Kaline	18.00	9.00	5.50
251	Choo Choo Coleman	.80	.40	.25
252	Ken Aspromonte	.70	.35	.20
253	Wally Post	.70	.35	.20
254	Don Hoak	.80	.40	.25
255	Lee Thomas	.70	.35	.20
256	Johnny Weekly	.70	.35	.20
257	Giants Team	2.25	1.25	.70
258	Garry Roggenburk	.70	.35	.20
259	Harry Bright	1.00	.50	.30
260	Frank Robinson	18.00	9.00	5.50
261	Jim Hannan	.70	.35	.20
262	Cardinals Rookie Stars (Harry Fanok, *Mike Shannon*)	1.50	.70	.45
263	Chuck Estrada	.70	.35	.20
264	Jim Landis	.70	.35	.20
265	Jim Bunning	5.00	2.50	1.50
266	Gene Freese	.70	.35	.20
267	*Wilbur Wood*	1.50	.70	.45
268	Bill's Got It (Danny Murtaugh, Bill Virdon)	.90	.45	.25
269	Ellis Burton	.70	.35	.20
270	Rich Rollins	.70	.35	.20
271	Bob Sadowski	.70	.35	.20
272	Jake Wood	.70	.35	.20
273	Mel Nelson	.70	.35	.20
274	Checklist 265-352	3.00	1.50	.90
275	John Tsitouris	.70	.35	.20
276	Jose Tartabull	.70	.35	.20
277	Ken Retzer	.70	.35	.20
278	Bobby Shantz	1.50	.70	.45
279	Joe Koppe	.70	.35	.20
280	Juan Marichal	10.00	5.00	3.00
281	Yankees Rookies (Jake Gibbs, Tom Metcalf)	1.00	.50	.30
282	Bob Bruce	.70	.35	.20
283	*Tommy McCraw*	.80	.40	.25
284	Dick Schofield	.70	.35	.20
285	Robin Roberts	10.00	5.00	3.00
286	Don Landrum	.70	.35	.20
287	Red Sox Rookies (*Tony Conigliaro*, Bill Spanswick)	15.00	7.50	4.50
288	Al Moran	.80	.40	.25
289	Frank Funk	.70	.35	.20
290	Bob Allison	.90	.45	.25
291	Phil Ortega	.70	.35	.20
292	Mike Roarke	.70	.35	.20
293	Phillies Team	2.25	1.25	.70
294	Ken Hunt	.70	.35	.20
295	Roger Craig	1.50	.70	.45
296	Ed Kirkpatrick	.70	.35	.20
297	Ken MacKenzie	.70	.35	.20
298	Harry Craft	.70	.35	.20
299	Bill Stafford	1.00	.50	.30
300	Hank Aaron	65.00	33.00	20.00
301	Larry Brown	.70	.35	.20
302	Dan Pfister	.70	.35	.20
303	Jim Campbell	.70	.35	.20
304	Bob Johnson	.70	.35	.20
305	Jack Lamabe	.70	.35	.20
306	Giant Gunners (Orlando Cepeda, Willie Mays)	12.00	6.00	3.50
307	Joe Gibbon	.70	.35	.20
308	Gene Stephens	.70	.35	.20
309	Paul Toth	.70	.35	.20
310	Jim Gilliam	3.00	1.50	.90
311	Tom Brown	.70	.35	.20
312	Tigers Rookies (Fritz Fisher, Fred Gladding)	.70	.35	.20
313	Chuck Hiller	.70	.35	.20
314	Jerry Buchek	.70	.35	.20
315	Bo Belinsky	.90	.45	.25
316	Gene Oliver	.70	.35	.20
317	Al Smith	.70	.35	.20
318	Twins Team	2.25	1.25	.70
319	Paul Brown	.70	.35	.20
320	Rocky Colavito	3.00	1.50	.90
321	Bob Lillis	.70	.35	.20
322	George Brunet	.70	.35	.20
323	John Buzhardt	.70	.35	.20
324	Casey Stengel	12.00	6.00	3.50
325	Hector Lopez	1.00	.50	.30
326	Ron Brand	.70	.35	.20
327	Don Blasingame	.70	.35	.20
328	Bob Shaw	.70	.35	.20
329	Russ Nixon	.70	.35	.20
330	Tommy Harper	.80	.40	.25
331	A.L. Bombers (Norm Cash, Al Kaline, Mickey Mantle, Roger Maris)	55.00	27.00	16.50
332	Ray Washburn	.70	.35	.20
333	Billy Moran	.70	.35	.20
334	Lew Krausse	.70	.35	.20
335	Don Mossi	.80	.40	.25
336	Andre Rodgers	.70	.35	.20
337	Dodgers Rookies (*Al Ferrara, Jeff Torborg*)	.80	.40	.25
338	Jack Kralick	.70	.35	.20
339	Walt Bond	.70	.35	.20
340	Joe Cunningham	.80	.40	.25
341	Jim Roland	.70	.35	.20
342	Willie Stargell	25.00	12.50	7.50
343	Senators Team	2.25	1.25	.70
344	Phil Linz	1.00	.50	.30
345	Frank Thomas	.80	.40	.25
346	Joe Jay	.70	.35	.20
347	Bobby Wine	.80	.40	.25
348	Ed Lopat	.90	.45	.25
349	Art Fowler	.70	.35	.20
350	Willie McCovey	20.00	10.00	6.00
351	Dan Schneider	.70	.35	.20
352	Eddie Bressoud	.70	.35	.20
353	Wally Moon	.90	.45	.25
354	Dave Giusti	.70	.35	.20
355	Vic Power	.70	.35	.20
356	Reds Rookies (Bill McCool, Chico Ruiz)	.70	.35	.20
357	Charley James	.70	.35	.20
358	Ron Kline	.70	.35	.20
359	Jim Schaffer	.70	.35	.20
360	Joe Pepitone	2.50	1.25	.70
361	Jay Hook	.80	.40	.25
362	Checklist 353-429	3.00	1.50	.90
363	Dick McAuliffe	.80	.40	.25
364	Joe Gaines	.70	.35	.20
365	Cal McLish	.70	.35	.20
366	Nelson Mathews	.70	.35	.20
367	Fred Whitfield	.70	.35	.20
368	White Sox Rookies (Fritz Ackley, *Don Buford*)	.90	.45	.25
369	Jerry Zimmerman	.70	.35	.20
370	Hal Woodeshick	.70	.35	.20
371	Frank Howard	3.00	1.50	.90
372	Howie Koplitz	1.00	.50	.30
373	Pirates Team	3.00	1.50	.90
374	Bobby Bolin	1.00	.50	.30
375	Ron Santo	2.50	1.25	.70
376	Dave Morehead	1.00	.50	.30
377	Bob Skinner	1.00	.50	.30
378	Braves Rookies (Jack Smith, *Woody Woodward*)	1.25	.60	.40
379	Tony Gonzalez	1.00	.50	.30
380	Whitey Ford	25.00	12.50	7.50
381	Bob Taylor	1.25	.60	.40
382	Wes Stock	1.00	.50	.30
383	Bill Rigney	1.00	.50	.30
384	Ron Hansen	1.00	.50	.30
385	Curt Simmons	1.25	.60	.40
386	Lenny Green	1.00	.50	.30
387	Terry Fox	1.00	.50	.30
388	Athletics Rookies (John O'Donoghue, George Williams)	1.00	.50	.30
389	Jim Umbricht	1.00	.50	.30
390	Orlando Cepeda	4.50	2.25	1.25
391	Sam McDowell	1.25	.60	.40
392	Jim Pagliaroni	1.00	.50	.30
393	Casey Teaches (Ed Kranepool, Casey Stengel)	3.00	1.50	.90
394	Bob Miller	1.00	.50	.30
395	Tom Tresh	3.00	1.50	.90
396	Dennis Bennett	1.00	.50	.30
397	Chuck Cottier	1.00	.50	.30
398	Mets Rookies (Bill Haas, Dick Smith)	1.25	.60	.40
399	Jackie Brandt	1.00	.50	.30
400	Warren Spahn	25.00	12.50	7.50
401	Charlie Maxwell	1.00	.50	.30
402	Tom Sturdivant	1.00	.50	.30
403	Reds Team	3.50	1.75	1.00
404	Tony Martinez	1.00	.50	.30
405	Ken McBride	1.00	.50	.30
406	Al Spangler	1.00	.50	.30
407	Bill Freehan	2.00	1.00	.60
408	Cubs Rookies (Fred Burdette, Jim Stewart)	1.00	.50	.30
409	Bill Fischer	1.00	.50	.30
410	Dick Stuart	1.25	.60	.40
411	Lee Walls	1.00	.50	.30
412	Ray Culp	1.00	.50	.30
413	Johnny Keane	1.00	.50	.30
414	Jack Sanford	1.00	.50	.30
415	Tony Kubek	5.00	2.50	1.50
416	Lee Maye	1.00	.50	.30
417	Don Cardwell	1.00	.50	.30
418	Orioles Rookies (*Darold Knowles*, Les Narum)	1.25	.60	.40
419	*Ken Harrelson*	3.00	1.50	.90
420	Jim Maloney	1.25	.60	.40
421	Camilo Carreon	1.00	.50	.30
422	Jack Fisher	1.25	.60	.40
423	Tops In NL (Hank Aaron, Willie Mays)	50.00	30.00	15.00
424	Dick Bertell	1.00	.50	.30
425	Norm Cash	2.50	1.25	.70
426	Bob Rodgers	1.25	.60	.40

		NR MT	EX	VG
427	Don Rudolph	1.00	.50	.30
428	Red Sox Rookies (Archie Skeen, Pete Smith)	1.00	.50	.30
429	Tim McCarver	3.00	1.50	.90
430	Juan Pizarro	1.00	.50	.30
431	George Alusik	1.00	.50	.30
432	Ruben Amaro	1.00	.50	.30
433	Yankees Team	8.00	4.00	2.50
434	Don Nottebart	1.00	.50	.30
435	Vic Davalillo	1.00	.50	.30
436	Charlie Neal	1.00	.50	.30
437	Ed Bailey	1.00	.50	.30
438	Checklist 430-506	4.00	2.00	1.25
439	Harvey Haddix	1.50	.70	.45
440	Bob Clemente	80.00	40.00	24.00
441	Bob Duliba	1.00	.50	.30
442	Pumpsie Green	1.25	.60	.40
443	Chuck Dressen	1.25	.60	.40
444	Larry Jackson	1.00	.50	.30
445	Bill Skowron	2.50	1.25	.70
446	Julian Javier	1.25	.60	.40
447	Ted Bowsfield	1.00	.50	.30
448	Cookie Rojas	1.25	.60	.40
449	Deron Johnson	1.00	.50	.30
450	Steve Barber	1.00	.50	.30
451	Joe Amalfitano	1.00	.50	.30
452	Giants Rookies (Gil Garrido, *Jim Hart)*	1.25	.60	.40
453	Frank Baumann	1.00	.50	.30
454	Tommie Aaron	1.25	.60	.40
455	Bernie Allen	1.00	.50	.30
456	Dodgers Rookies *(Wes Parker*, John Werhas)	2.00	1.00	.60
457	Jesse Gonder	1.25	.60	.40
458	Ralph Terry	2.00	1.00	.60
459	Red Sox Rookies (Pete Charton, Dalton Jones)	1.00	.50	.30
460	Bob Gibson	20.00	10.00	6.00
461	George Thomas	1.00	.50	.30
462	Birdie Tebbetts	1.00	.50	.30
463	Don Leppert	1.00	.50	.30
464	Dallas Green	1.25	.60	.40
465	Mike Hershberger	1.00	.50	.30
466	Athletics Rookies *(Dick Green*, Aurelio Monteagudo)	1.25	.60	.40
467	Bob Aspromonte	1.00	.50	.30
468	Gaylord Perry	25.00	12.50	7.50
469	Cubs Rookies (Fred Norman, Sterling Slaughter)	1.00	.50	.30
470	Jim Bouton	3.00	1.50	.90
471	*Gates Brown*	1.25	.60	.40
472	Vern Law	1.50	.70	.45
473	Orioles Team	3.00	1.50	.90
474	Larry Sherry	1.00	.50	.30
475	Ed Charles	1.00	.50	.30
476	Braves Rookies *(Rico Carty*, Dick Kelley)	1.25	.60	.40
477	Mike Joyce	.90	.45	.25
478	Dick Howser	2.00	1.00	.60
479	Cardinals Rookies (Dave Bakenhaster, Johnny Lewis)	1.00	.50	.30
480	Bob Purkey	1.00	.50	.30
481	Chuck Schilling	1.00	.50	.30
482	Phillies Rookies *(John Briggs, Danny Cater)*	1.25	.60	.40
483	Fred Valentine	1.00	.50	.30
484	Bill Pleis	1.00	.50	.30
485	Tom Haller	1.25	.60	.40
486	Bob Kennedy	1.00	.50	.30
487	Mike McCormick	1.25	.60	.40
488	Yankees Rookies (Bob Meyer, Pete Mikkelsen)	1.50	.70	.45
489	Julio Navarro	1.00	.50	.30
490	Ron Fairly	1.50	.70	.45
491	Ed Rakow	1.00	.50	.30
492	Colts Rookies (Jim Beauchamp, Mike White)	1.00	.50	.30
493	Don Lee	1.00	.50	.30
494	Al Jackson	1.25	.60	.40
495	Bill Virdon	2.00	1.00	.60
496	White Sox Team	3.00	1.50	.90
497	Jeoff Long	1.00	.50	.30
498	Dave Stenhouse	1.00	.50	.30
499	Indians Rookies (Chico Salmon, Gordon Seyfried)	1.00	.50	.30
500	Camilo Pascual	1.25	.60	.40
501	Bob Veale	1.25	.60	.40
502	Angels Rookies *(Bobby Knoop*, Bob Lee)	1.25	.60	.40
503	Earl Wilson	1.00	.50	.30
504	Claude Raymond	1.00	.50	.30
505	Stan Williams	1.50	.70	.45
506	Bobby Bragan	1.25	.60	.40
507	John Edwards	1.00	.50	.30
508	Diego Segui	1.00	.50	.30
509	Pirates Rookies *(Gene Alley*, Orlando McFarlane)	1.25	.60	.40
510	Lindy McDaniel	1.00	.50	.30
511	Lou Jackson	1.00	.50	.30
512	Tigers Rookies *(Willie Horton, Joe Sparma)*	3.00	1.50	.90
513	Don Larsen	1.50	.70	.45
514	Jim Hickman	1.25	.60	.40
515	Johnny Romano	1.00	.50	.30
516	Twins Rookies (Jerry Arrigo, Dwight Siebler)	1.00	.50	.30
517a	Checklist 507-587 (wrong numbering on back)	7.00	3.50	2.00
517b	Checklist 507-587 (correct numbering on back)	4.50	2.25	1.25
518	Carl Bouldin	1.00	.50	.30
519	Charlie Smith	1.25	.60	.40
520	Jack Baldschun	1.00	.50	.30
521	Tom Satriano	1.00	.50	.30
522	Bobby Tiefenauer	1.00	.50	.30
523	Lou Burdette	6.00	3.00	1.75
524	Reds Rookies (Jim Dickson, Bobby Klaus)	4.00	2.00	1.25
525	Al McBean	4.00	2.00	1.25
526	Lou Clinton	4.00	2.00	1.25
527	Larry Bearnarth	4.50	2.25	1.25
528	Athletics Rookies *(Dave Duncan*, Tom Reynolds)	4.50	2.25	1.25
529	Al Dark	4.50	2.25	1.25
530	Leon Wagner	4.50	2.25	1.25
531	Dodgers Team	8.00	4.00	2.50
532	Twins Rookies (Bud Bloomfield, Joe Nossek)	4.00	2.00	1.25
533	Johnny Klippstein	4.00	2.00	1.25
534	Gus Bell	4.50	2.25	1.25
535	Phil Regan	4.00	2.00	1.25
536	Mets Rookies (Larry Elliot, John Stephenson)	4.50	2.25	1.25
537	Dan Osinski	4.00	2.00	1.25
538	Minnie Minoso	8.00	4.00	2.50
539	Roy Face	5.00	2.50	1.50
540	Luis Aparicio	15.00	7.50	4.50
541	Braves Rookies *(Phil Niekro*, Phil Roof)	150.00	60.00	38.00
542	Don Mincher	4.50	2.25	1.25
543	Bob Uecker	60.00	30.00	17.50
544	Colts Rookies (Steve Hertz, Joe Hoerner)	4.00	2.00	1.25
545	Max Alvis	4.50	2.25	1.25
546	Joe Christopher	4.50	2.25	1.25
547	Gil Hodges	12.00	6.00	3.50
548	N.L. Rookies (Wayne Schurr, Paul Speckenbach)	4.00	2.00	1.25
549	Joe Moeller	4.00	2.00	1.25
550	Ken Hubbs	10.00	5.00	3.00
551	Billy Hoeft	4.00	2.00	1.25
552	Indians Rookies (Tom Kelley, *Sonny Siebert)*	4.50	2.25	1.25
553	Jim Brewer	4.00	2.00	1.25
554	Hank Foiles	4.00	2.00	1.25
555	Lee Stange	4.00	2.00	1.25
556	Mets Rookies (Steve Dillon, Ron Locke)	4.50	2.25	1.25
557	Leo Burke	4.00	2.00	1.25
558	Don Schwall	4.00	2.00	1.25
559	Dick Phillips	4.00	2.00	1.25
560	Dick Farrell	4.00	2.00	1.25
561	Phillies Rookies (Dave Bennett, *Rick Wise)*	4.50	2.25	1.25
562	Pedro Ramos	4.00	2.00	1.25
563	Dal Maxvill	4.50	2.25	1.25
564	A.L. Rookies (Joe McCabe, Jerry McNertney)	4.00	2.00	1.25
565	Stu Miller	4.00	2.00	1.25
566	Ed Kranepool	5.00	2.50	1.50
567	Jim Kaat	8.00	4.00	2.50
568	N.L. Rookies (Phil Gagliano, Cap Peterson)	4.00	2.00	1.25
569	Fred Newman	4.00	2.00	1.25
570	Bill Mazeroski	8.00	4.00	2.50
571	Gene Conley	3.50	1.75	1.00
572	A.L. Rookies (Dick Egan, Dave Gray)	4.00	2.00	1.25
573	Jim Duffalo	4.00	2.00	1.25
574	Manny Jimenez	4.00	2.00	1.25
575	Tony Cloninger	4.50	2.25	1.25
576	Mets Rookies (Jerry Hinsley, Bill Wakefield)	4.50	2.25	1.25
577	Gordy Coleman	4.00	2.00	1.25
578	Glen Hobbie	4.00	2.00	1.25
579	Red Sox Team	6.00	3.00	1.75
580	Johnny Podres	6.00	3.00	1.75
581	Yankees Rookies (Pedro Gonzalez, Archie Moore)	5.00	2.50	1.50
582	Rod Kanehl	4.50	2.25	1.25
583	Tito Francona	4.50	2.25	1.25
584	Joel Horlen	4.00	2.00	1.25
585	Tony Taylor	4.00	2.00	1.25
586	Jim Piersall	6.00	3.00	1.75
587	Bennie Daniels	8.00	2.50	1.25

1964 Topps Coins

The 164 metal coins in this set were issued by Topps as inserts in the company's baseball card wax packs. The series is divided into two principal types, 120 "regular" coins and 44 All-Star coins. The 1-1/2" diameter coins feature a full-color background for the player photos in the "regular" series, while the players in the All-Star series are featured against plain red or blue backgrounds. There are two variations each of the Mantle, Causey and Hinton coins among the All-Star subset.

		NR MT	EX	VG
	Complete Set:	650.00	325.00	200.00
	Common Player:	1.00	.50	.30
1	Don Zimmer	1.00	.50	.30
2	Jim Wynn	1.00	.50	.30
3	Johnny Orsino	1.00	.50	.30
4	Jim Bouton	1.25	.60	.40
5	Dick Groat	1.25	.60	.40
6	Leon Wagner	1.00	.50	.30
7	Frank Malzone	1.00	.50	.30
8	Steve Barber	1.00	.50	.30
9	Johnny Romano	1.00	.50	.30
10	Tom Tresh	1.25	.60	.40
11	Felipe Alou	1.00	.50	.30
12	Dick Stuart	1.00	.50	.30
13	Claude Osteen	1.00	.50	.30
14	Juan Pizarro	1.00	.50	.30
15	Donn Clendenon	1.00	.50	.30
16	Jimmie Hall	1.00	.50	.30
17	Larry Jackson	1.00	.50	.30
18	Brooks Robinson	12.00	6.00	3.50
19	Bob Allison	1.00	.50	.30
20	Ed Roebuck	1.00	.50	.30
21	Pete Ward	1.00	.50	.30
22	Willie McCovey	8.00	4.00	2.50
23	Elston Howard	1.50	.70	.45
24	Diego Segui	1.00	.50	.30
25	Ken Boyer	1.50	.70	.45
26	Carl Yastrzemski	20.00	10.00	6.00
27	Bill Mazeroski	1.50	.70	.45
28	Jerry Lumpe	1.00	.50	.30
29	Woody Held	1.00	.50	.30
30	Dick Radatz	1.00	.50	.30
31	Luis Aparicio	5.00	2.50	1.50
32	Dave Nicholson	1.00	.50	.30
33	Ed Mathews	8.00	4.00	2.50
34	Don Drysdale	10.00	5.00	3.00
35	Ray Culp	1.00	.50	.30
36	Juan Marichal	8.00	4.00	2.50
37	Frank Robinson	8.00	4.00	2.50
38	Chuck Hinton	1.00	.50	.30
39	Floyd Robinson	1.00	.50	.30
40	Tommy Harper	1.00	.50	.30
41	Ron Hansen	1.00	.50	.30
42	Ernie Banks	10.00	5.00	3.00
43	Jesse Gonder	1.00	.50	.30
44	Billy Williams	7.00	3.50	2.00
45	Vada Pinson	1.50	.70	.45
46	Rocky Colavito	1.50	.70	.45
47	Bill Monbouquette	1.00	.50	.30
48	Max Alvis	1.00	.50	.30
49	Norm Siebern	1.00	.50	.30
50	John Callison	1.00	.50	.30
51	Rich Rollins	1.00	.50	.30
52	Ken McBride	1.00	.50	.30
53	Don Lock	1.00	.50	.30
54	Ron Fairly	1.00	.50	.30
55	Bob Clemente	20.00	10.00	6.00
56	Dick Ellsworth	1.00	.50	.30
57	Tommy Davis	1.25	.60	.40
58	Tony Gonzalez	1.00	.50	.30
59	Bob Gibson	10.00	5.00	3.00
60	Jim Maloney	1.00	.50	.30
61	Frank Howard	1.50	.70	.45
62	Jim Pagliaroni	1.00	.50	.30
63	Orlando Cepeda	2.00	1.00	.60
64	Ron Perranoski	1.00	.50	.30
65	Curt Flood	1.25	.60	.40
66	Al McBean	1.00	.50	.30
67	Dean Chance	1.00	.50	.30
68	Ron Santo	1.25	.60	.40
69	Jack Baldschun	1.00	.50	.30
70	Milt Pappas	1.00	.50	.30
71	Gary Peters	1.00	.50	.30
72	Bobby Richardson	1.50	.70	.45
73	Lee Thomas	1.00	.50	.30
74	Hank Aguirre	1.00	.50	.30
75	Carl Willey	1.00	.50	.30
76	Camilo Pascual	1.00	.50	.30
77	Bob Friend	1.00	.50	.30
78	Bill White	1.00	.50	.30
79	Norm Cash	1.25	.60	.40
80	Willie Mays	18.00	9.00	5.50
81	Duke Carmel	1.00	.50	.30
82	Pete Rose	25.00	12.50	7.50
83	Hank Aaron	20.00	10.00	6.00
84	Bob Aspromonte	1.00	.50	.30
85	Jim O'Toole	1.00	.50	.30
86	Vic Davalillo	1.00	.50	.30
87	Bill Freehan	1.00	.50	.30
88	Warren Spahn	8.00	4.00	2.50
89	Ron Hunt	1.00	.50	.30
90	Denis Menke	1.00	.50	.30
91	Turk Farrell	1.00	.50	.30
92	Jim Hickman	1.00	.50	.30
93	Jim Bunning	2.00	1.00	.60
94	Bob Hendley	1.00	.50	.30
95	Ernie Broglio	1.00	.50	.30
96	Rusty Staub	1.50	.70	.45
97	Lou Brock	8.00	4.00	2.50
98	Jim Fregosi	1.00	.50	.30
99	Jim Grant	1.00	.50	.30
100	Al Kaline	15.00	7.50	4.50
101	Earl Battey	1.00	.50	.30
102	Wayne Causey	1.00	.50	.30
103	Chuck Schilling	1.00	.50	.30
104	Boog Powell	1.50	.70	.45
105	Dave Wickersham	1.00	.50	.30
106	Sandy Koufax	15.00	7.50	4.50
107	John Bateman	1.00	.50	.30
108	Ed Brinkman	1.00	.50	.30
109	Al Downing	1.00	.50	.30
110	Joe Azcue	1.00	.50	.30
111	Albie Pearson	1.00	.50	.30
112	Harmon Killebrew	10.00	5.00	3.00
113	Tony Taylor	1.00	.50	.30
114	Alvin Jackson	1.00	.50	.30
115	Billy O'Dell	1.00	.50	.30
116	Don Demeter	1.00	.50	.30
117	Ed Charles	1.00	.50	.30
118	Joe Torre	1.50	.70	.45
119	Don Nottebart	1.00	.50	.30
120	Mickey Mantle	40.00	20.00	12.00
121	Joe Pepitone	1.25	.60	.40
122	Dick Stuart	1.00	.50	.30
123	Bobby Richardson	1.50	.70	.45
124	Jerry Lumpe	1.00	.50	.30
125	Brooks Robinson	10.00	5.00	3.00
126	Frank Malzone	1.00	.50	.30
127	Luis Aparicio	5.00	2.50	1.50
128	Jim Fregosi	1.00	.50	.30
129	Al Kaline	15.00	7.50	4.50
130	Leon Wagner	1.00	.50	.30
131a	Mickey Mantle (batting lefthanded)	45.00	23.00	13.50
131b	Mickey Mantle (batting righthanded)	45.00	23.00	13.50

		NR MT	EX	VG
132	Albie Pearson	1.00	.50	.30
133	Harmon Killebrew	10.00	5.00	3.00
134	Carl Yastrzemski	20.00	10.00	6.00
135	Elston Howard	1.50	.70	.45
136	Earl Battey	1.00	.50	.30
137	Camilo Pascual	1.00	.50	.30
138	Jim Bouton	1.25	.60	.40
139	Whitey Ford	8.00	4.00	2.50
140	Gary Peters	1.00	.50	.30
141	Bill White	1.00	.50	.30
142	Orlando Cepeda	2.00	1.00	.60
143	Bill Mazeroski	1.50	.70	.45
144	Tony Taylor	1.00	.50	.30
145	Ken Boyer	1.50	.70	.45
146	Ron Santo	1.25	.60	.40
147	Dick Groat	1.25	.60	.40
148	Roy McMillan	1.00	.50	.30
149	Hank Aaron	18.00	9.00	4.50
150	Bob Clemente	20.00	10.00	6.00
151	Willie Mays	18.00	9.00	5.50
152	Vada Pinson	1.50	.70	.45
153	Tommy Davis	1.25	.60	.40
154	Frank Robinson	8.00	4.00	2.50
155	Joe Torre	1.50	.70	.45
156	Tim McCarver	1.25	.60	.40
157	Juan Marichal	7.00	3.50	2.00
158	Jim Maloney	1.00	.50	.30
159	Sandy Koufax	15.00	7.50	4.50
160	Warren Spahn	8.00	4.00	2.50
161a	Wayne Causey (N.L. on back)	15.00	7.50	4.50
161b	Wayne Causey (A.L. on back)	1.00	.50	.30
162a	Chuck Hinton (N.L. on back)	15.00	7.50	4.50
162b	Chuck Hinton (A.L. on back)	1.00	.50	.30
163	Bob Aspromonte	1.00	.50	.30
164	Ron Hunt	1.00	.50	.30

1964 Topps Giants

Measuring 3-1/8" by 5-1/4" the Topps Giants were the company's first postcard-size issue. The cards feature large color photographs surrounded by white borders with a white baseball containing the player's name, position and team. Card backs carry another photo of the player surrounded by a newspaper-style explanation of the depicted career highlight. The 60- card set contains primarily stars which means it's an excellent place to find inexpensive cards of Hall of Famers. The '64 Giants were not printed in equal quantity and seven of the cards, including Sandy Koufax and Willie Mays, are significantly scarcer than the remainder of the set.

		NR MT	EX	VG
Complete Set:		75.00	38.00	23.00
Common Player:		.12	.06	.04
1	Gary Peters	.12	.06	.04
2	Ken Johnson	.12	.06	.04
3	Sandy Koufax	15.00	7.50	4.50
4	Bob Bailey	.12	.06	.04
5	Milt Pappas	.25	.13	.08
6	Ron Hunt	.12	.06	.04
7	Whitey Ford	1.75	.90	.50
8	Roy McMillan	.12	.06	.04
9	Rocky Colavito	.40	.20	.12
10	Jim Bunning	.50	.25	.15
11	Bob Clemente	5.00	2.50	1.50
12	Al Kaline	3.00	1.50	.90
13	Nellie Fox	.60	.30	.20
14	Tony Gonzalez	.12	.06	.04
15	Jim Gentile	.12	.06	.04
16	Dean Chance	.12	.06	.04
17	Dick Ellsworth	.12	.06	.04
18	Jim Fregosi	.25	.13	.08
19	Dick Groat	.40	.20	.12
20	Chuck Hinton	.12	.06	.04
21	Elston Howard	.50	.25	.15
22	Dick Farrell	.12	.06	.04
23	Albie Pearson	.12	.06	.04
24	Frank Howard	.50	.25	.15
25	Mickey Mantle	15.00	7.50	4.50
26	Joe Torre	.40	.20	.12
27	Ed Brinkman	.12	.06	.04
28	Bob Friend	2.50	1.25	.70
29	Frank Robinson	1.75	.90	.50
30	Bill Freehan	.25	.13	.08
31	Warren Spahn	1.25	.60	.40
32	Camilo Pascual	.12	.06	.04
33	Pete Ward	.12	.06	.04
34	Jim Maloney	.12	.06	.04
35	Dave Wickersham	.12	.06	.04
36	Johnny Callison	.25	.13	.08
37	Juan Marichal	2.00	1.00	.60
38	Harmon Killebrew	2.00	1.00	.60
39	Luis Aparicio	1.25	.60	.40
40	Dick Radatz	.12	.06	.04
41	Bob Gibson	3.00	1.50	.90
42	Dick Stuart	2.50	1.25	.70
43	Tommy Davis	.40	.20	.12
44	Tony Oliva	.50	.25	.15
45	Wayne Causey	2.50	1.25	.70
46	Max Alvis	.12	.06	.04
47	Galen Cisco	2.50	1.25	.70
48	Carl Yastrzemski	3.00	1.50	.90
49	Hank Aaron	5.00	2.50	1.50
50	Brooks Robinson	2.00	1.00	.60
51	Willie Mays	15.00	7.50	4.50
52	Billy Williams	1.25	.60	.40
53	Juan Pizarro	.12	.06	.04
54	Leon Wagner	.12	.06	.04
55	Orlando Cepeda	.70	.35	.20
56	Vada Pinson	.50	.25	.15
57	Ken Boyer	.60	.30	.20
58	Ron Santo	.40	.20	.12
59	John Romano	.12	.06	.04
60	Bill Skowron	.2.50	1.25	.70

1964 Topps Photo Tatoos

Apparently not content to leave the skin of American children without adornment, Topps jumped back into the tattoo field in 1964 with the release of a new series. Measuring 1-9/16" by 3-1/2," there were 75 tattoos in a complete set. The picture side for the 20 team tattoos gives the team logo and name. For the player tattoos, the picture side has the player's face, name and team.

		NR MT	EX	VG
Complete Set:		600.00	300.00	180.00
Common Player:		3.00	1.50	.90
(1)	Hank Aaron	40.00	20.00	12.50
(2)	H. Aguirre	3.00	1.50	.90
(3)	Max Alvis	3.00	1.50	.90
(4)	Ernie Banks	25.00	12.50	7.50
(5)	S. Barber	3.00	1.50	.90
(6)	K. Boyer	5.00	2.50	1.50
(7)	J. Callison	4.00	2.00	1.25
(8)	Norm Cash	5.00	2.50	1.50
(9)	W. Causey	3.00	1.50	.90
(10)	O. Cepeda	7.00	3.50	2.00
(11)	R. Colavito	7.00	3.50	2.00
(12)	Ray Culp	3.00	1.50	.90
(13)	Davalillo	3.00	1.50	.90
(14)	Drabowsky	3.00	1.50	.90
(15)	Ellsworth	3.00	1.50	.90
(16)	Curt Flood	5.00	2.50	1.50
(17)	B. Freehan	4.00	2.00	1.25
(18)	J. Fregosi	4.00	2.00	1.25
(19)	Bob Friend	4.00	2.00	1.25
(20)	D. Groat	4.00	2.00	1.25
(21)	Woody Held	3.00	1.50	.90
(22)	F. Howard	5.00	2.50	1.50
(23)	Al Jackson	3.00	1.50	.90
(24)	L. Jackson	3.00	1.50	.90
(25)	K. Johnson	3.00	1.50	.90
(26)	Al Kaline	25.00	12.50	7.50
(27a)	Killebrew (green background)	25.00	12.50	7.50
(27b)	Killebrew (red background)	25.00	12.50	7.50
(28)	S. Koufax	35.00	17.50	10.50
(29)	Lock	3.00	1.50	.90
(30)	F. Malzone	3.00	1.50	.90
(31)	M. Mantle	100.00	45.00	27.00
(32)	E. Mathews	15.00	7.50	4.50
(33a)	Willie Mays (yellow background encompasses entire head)	40.00	20.00	12.50
(33b)	Willie Mays (yellow background covers one-half of head)	40.00	20.00	12.50
(34)	Mazeroski	5.00	2.50	1.50
(35)	K. McBride	3.00	1.50	.90
(36)	Monbouquette	3.00	1.50	.90
(37)	Nicholson	3.00	1.50	.90
(38)	C. Osteen	4.00	2.00	1.25
(39)	M. Pappas	4.00	2.00	1.25
(40)	C. Pascual	4.00	2.00	1.25
(41)	A. Pearson	3.00	1.50	.90
(42)	Perranoski	3.00	1.50	.90
(43)	G. Peters	3.00	1.50	.90
(44)	B. Powell	5.00	2.50	1.50
(45)	F. Robinson	20.00	10.00	6.00
(46)	J. Romano	3.00	1.50	.90
(47)	N. Siebern	3.00	1.50	.90
(48)	W. Spahn	15.00	7.50	4.50
(49)	D. Stuart	4.00	2.00	1.25
(50)	Lee Thomas	3.00	1.50	.90
(51)	Joe Torre	5.00	2.50	1.50
(52)	Pete Ward	3.00	1.50	.90
(53)	C. Willey	3.00	1.50	.90
(54)	B. Williams	25.00	12.50	7.50
(55)	Yastrzemski	50.00	25.00	15.00
(56)	Baltimore Orioles Logo	3.00	1.50	.90
(57)	Boston Red Sox Logo	3.00	1.50	.90
(58)	Chicago Cubs Logo	3.00	1.50	.90
(59)	Chicago White Sox Logo	3.00	1.50	.90
(60)	Cincinnati Reds Logo	3.00	1.50	.90
(61)	Cleveland Indians Logo	3.00	1.50	.90
(62)	Detroit Tigers Logo	2.50	1.25	.70
(63)	Houston Colts Logo	3.00	1.50	.90
(64)	Kansas City Athletics Logo	3.00	1.50	.90
(65)	Los Angeles Angels Logo	3.00	1.50	.90
(66)	Los Angeles Dodgers Logo	2.50	1.25	.70
(67)	Milwaukee Braves Logo	3.00	1.50	.90
(68)	Minnesota Twins Logo	3.00	1.50	.90
(69)	New York Mets Logo	2.50	1.25	.70
(70)	New York Yankees Logo	4.00	2.00	1.25
(71)	Philadelphia Phillies Logo	3.00	1.50	.90
(72)	Pittsburgh Pirates Logo	3.00	1.50	.90
(73)	St. Louis Cardinals Logo	2.50	1.25	.70
(74)	San Francisco Giants Logo	3.00	1.50	.90
(75)	Washington Senators Logo	3.00	1.50	.90

1964 Topps Stand-Ups

These 2-1/2" by 3-1/2" cards were the first since the All-Star sets of 1951 to be die-cut. This made it possible for a folded card to stand on display. The 77-cards in the set feature color photographs of the player with yellow and green backgrounds. Directions for folding are on the yellow top background, and when folded only the green background remains. Of the 77 cards, 55 were double-printed while 22 were single-printed, making them twice as scarce. Included in the single-printed group are Warren Spahn, Don Drysdale, Juan Marichal, Willie McCovey and Carl Yastrzemski.

		NR MT	EX	VG
Complete Set:		2400.	1200.	720.00
Common Player:		3.50	1.75	1.00
(1)	Hank Aaron	90.00	45.00	27.00
(2)	Hank Aguirre	3.50	1.75	1.00
(3)	George Altman	3.50	1.75	1.00
(4)	Max Alvis	3.50	1.75	1.00
(5)	Bob Aspromonte	3.50	1.75	1.00
(6)	Jack Baldschun	20.00	10.00	6.00
(7)	Ernie Banks	40.00	20.00	12.00
(8)	Steve Barber	3.50	1.75	1.00
(9)	Earl Battey	3.50	1.75	1.00
(10)	Ken Boyer	6.00	3.00	1.75
(11)	Ernie Broglio	3.50	1.75	1.00
(12)	Johnny Callison	4.00	2.00	1.25
(13)	Norm Cash	25.00	12.50	7.50
(14)	Wayne Causey	3.50	1.75	1.00
(15)	Orlando Cepeda	8.00	4.00	2.50
(16)	Ed Charles	3.50	1.75	1.00
(17)	Bob Clemente	55.00	27.00	16.50
(18)	Donn Clendenon	20.00	10.00	6.00

No.	Player	NR MT	EX	VG
(19)	Rocky Colavito	6.00	3.00	1.75
(20)	Ray Culp	20.00	10.00	6.00
(21)	Tommy Davis	6.00	3.00	1.75
(22)	Don Drysdale	100.00	50.00	30.00
(23)	Dick Ellsworth	3.50	1.75	1.00
(24)	Dick Farrell	3.50	1.75	1.00
(25)	Jim Fregosi	4.00	2.00	1.25
(26)	Bob Friend	4.00	2.00	1.25
(27)	Jim Gentile	3.50	1.75	1.00
(28)	Jesse Gonder	20.00	10.00	6.00
(29)	Tony Gonzalez	20.00	10.00	6.00
(30)	Dick Groat	6.00	3.00	1.75
(31)	Woody Held	3.50	1.75	1.00
(32)	Chuck Hinton	3.50	1.75	1.00
(33)	Elston Howard	7.00	3.50	2.00
(34)	Frank Howard	25.00	12.50	7.50
(35)	Ron Hunt	3.50	1.75	1.00
(36)	Al Jackson	3.50	1.75	1.00
(37)	Ken Johnson	3.50	1.75	1.00
(38)	Al Kaline	40.00	20.00	12.00
(39)	Harmon Killebrew	40.00	20.00	12.00
(40)	Sandy Koufax	40.00	20.00	12.00
(41)	Don Lock	20.00	10.00	6.00
(42)	Jerry Lumpe	20.00	10.00	6.00
(43)	Jim Maloney	3.50	1.75	1.00
(44)	Frank Malzone	3.50	1.75	1.00
(45)	Mickey Mantle	350.00	175.00	105.00
(46)	Juan Marichal	100.00	50.00	30.00
(47)	Ed Mathews	100.00	50.00	30.00
(48)	Willie Mays	90.00	45.00	27.00
(49)	Bill Mazeroski	6.00	3.00	1.75
(50)	Ken McBride	3.50	1.75	1.00
(51)	Willie McCovey	100.00	50.00	30.00
(52)	Claude Osteen	3.50	1.75	1.00
(53)	Jim O'Toole	3.50	1.75	1.00
(54)	Camilo Pascual	3.50	1.75	1.00
(55)	Albie Pearson	20.00	10.00	6.00
(56)	Gary Peters	3.50	1.75	1.00
(57)	Vada Pinson	6.00	3.00	1.75
(58)	Juan Pizarro	3.50	1.75	1.00
(59)	Boog Powell	6.00	3.00	1.75
(60)	Bobby Richardson	7.00	3.50	2.00
(61)	Brooks Robinson	50.00	25.00	15.00
(62)	Floyd Robinson	3.50	1.75	1.00
(63)	Frank Robinson	40.00	20.00	12.00
(64)	Ed Roebuck	20.00	10.00	6.00
(65)	Rich Rollins	3.50	1.75	1.00
(66)	Johnny Romano	3.50	1.75	1.00
(67)	Ron Santo	25.00	12.50	7.50
(68)	Norm Siebern	3.50	1.75	1.00
(69)	Warren Spahn	100.00	50.00	30.00
(70)	Dick Stuart	20.00	10.00	6.00
(71)	Lee Thomas	3.50	1.75	1.00
(72)	Joe Torre	7.00	3.50	2.00
(73)	Pete Ward	3.50	1.75	1.00
(74)	Bill White	20.00	10.00	6.00
(75)	Billy Williams	100.00	50.00	30.00
(76)	Hal Woodeshick	20.00	10.00	6.00
(77)	Carl Yastrzemski	350.00	175.00	105.00

1965 Topps

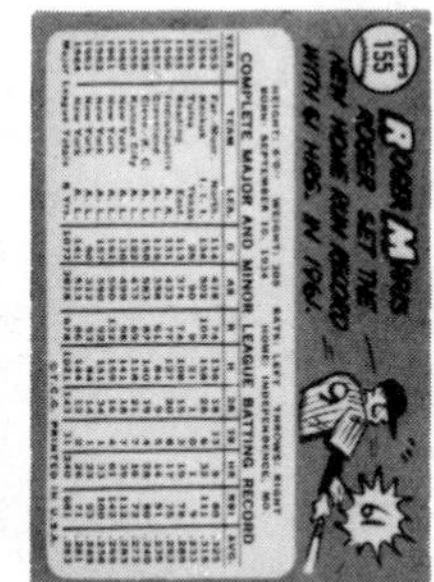

The 1965 Topps set features a large color photograph of the player which was surrounded by a colored, round-cornered frame and a white border. The bottom of the 2-1/2" by 3-1/2" cards include a pennant with a color team logo and name over the left side of a rectangle which features the player's name and position. Backs feature statistics and, if space allowed, a cartoon and headline about the player. There are no multi-player cards in the 1965 set other than the usual team cards and World Series highlights. Rookie cards include team, as well as league groupings from two to four players per card. Also present in the 598-card set are statistical leaders.

	NR MT	EX	VG
Complete Set:	2700.	1350.	775.00
Common Player: 1-198	.70	.35	.20
Common Player: 199-446	.90	.45	.25
Common Player: 447-522	1.25	.60	.40
Common Player: 523-598	4.00	2.00	1.25

No.	Player	NR MT	EX	VG
1	A.L. Batting Leaders (Elston Howard, Tony Oliva, Brooks Robinson)	8.00	3.00	1.25
2	N.L. Batting Leaders (Hank Aaron, Rico Carty, Bob Clemente)	5.00	2.50	1.50
3	A.L. Home Run Leaders (Harmon Killebrew, Mickey Mantle, Boog Powell)	15.00	7.50	4.50
4	N.L. Home Run Leaders (Johnny Callison, Orlando Cepeda, Jim Hart, Willie Mays, Billy Williams)	4.50	2.25	1.25
5	A.L. RBI Leaders (Harmon Killebrew, Mickey Mantle, Brooks Robinson, Dick Stuart)	15.00	7.50	4.50
6	N.L. RBI Leaders (Ken Boyer, Willie Mays, Ron Santo)	4.50	2.25	1.25
7	A.L. ERA Leaders (Dean Chance, Joel Horlen)	2.50	1.25	.70
8	N.L. ERA Leaders (Don Drysdale, Sandy Koufax)	4.50	2.25	1.25
9	A.L. Pitching Leaders (Wally Bunker, Dean Chance, Gary Peters, Juan Pizarro, Dave Wickersham)	4.00	2.00	1.25
10	N.L. Pitching Leaders (Larry Jackson, Juan Marichal, Ray Sadecki)	3.50	1.75	1.00
11	A.L. Strikeout Leaders (Dean Chance, Al Downing, Camilo Pascual)	2.50	1.25	.70
12	N.L. Strikeout Leaders (Don Drysdale, Bob Gibson, Bob Veale)	3.50	1.75	1.00
13	Pedro Ramos	1.00	.50	.30
14	Len Gabrielson	.70	.35	.20
15	Robin Roberts	8.00	4.00	2.50
16	Astros Rookies *(Sonny Jackson, Joe Morgan)*	200.00	100.00	60.00
17	Johnny Romano	.70	.35	.20
18	Bill McCool	.70	.35	.20
19	Gates Brown	.80	.40	.25
20	Jim Bunning	4.00	2.00	1.25
21	Don Blasingame	.70	.35	.20
22	Charlie Smith	.80	.40	.25
23	Bob Tiefenauer	.70	.35	.20
24	Twins Team	4.00	2.00	1.25
25	Al McBean	.70	.35	.20
26	Bobby Knoop	.70	.35	.20
27	Dick Bertell	.70	.35	.20
28	Barney Schultz	.70	.35	.20
29	Felix Mantilla	.70	.35	.20
30	Jim Bouton	2.50	1.25	.70
31	Mike White	.70	.35	.20
32	Herman Franks	.70	.35	.20
33	Jackie Brandt	.70	.35	.20
34	Cal Koonce	.70	.35	.20
35	Ed Charles	.70	.35	.20
36	Bobby Wine	.80	.40	.25
37	Fred Gladding	.70	.35	.20
38	Jim King	.70	.35	.20
39	Gerry Arrigo	.70	.35	.20
40	Frank Howard	2.50	1.25	.70
41	White Sox Rookies (Bruce Howard, Marv Staehle)	.70	.35	.20
42	Earl Wilson	.70	.35	.20
43	Mike Shannon	.80	.40	.25
44	Wade Blasingame	.70	.35	.20
45	Roy McMillan	.80	.40	.25
46	Bob Lee	.70	.35	.20
47	Tommy Harper	.80	.40	.25
48	Claude Raymond	.80	.40	.25
49	Orioles Rookies *(Curt Blefary,* John Miller)	.90	.45	.25
50	Juan Marichal	8.00	4.00	2.50
51	Billy Bryan	.70	.35	.20
52	Ed Roebuck	.70	.35	.20
53	Dick McAuliffe	.80	.40	.25
54	Joe Gibbon	.70	.35	.20
55	Tony Conigliaro	2.50	1.25	.70
56	Ron Kline	.70	.35	.20
57	Cardinals Team	2.25	1.25	.70
58	Fred Talbot	.70	.35	.20
59	Nate Oliver	.70	.35	.20
60	Jim O'Toole	.70	.35	.20
61	Chris Cannizzaro	.80	.40	.25
62	Jim Katt (Kaat)	5.00	2.50	1.50
63	Ty Cline	.70	.35	.20
64	Lou Burdette	2.00	1.00	.60
65	Tony Kubek	4.50	2.25	1.25
66	Bill Rigney	.70	.35	.20
67	Harvey Haddix	.90	.45	.25
68	Del Crandall	.90	.45	.25
69	Bill Virdon	1.25	.60	.40
70	Bill Skowron	1.25	.60	.40
71	John O'Donoghue	.70	.35	.20
72	Tony Gonzalez	.70	.35	.20
73	Dennis Ribant	.80	.40	.25
74	Red Sox Rookies *(Rico Petrocelli,* Jerry Stephenson)	2.50	1.25	.70
75	Deron Johnson	.70	.35	.20
76	Sam McDowell	.90	.45	.25
77	Doug Camilli	.70	.35	.20
78	Dal Maxvill	.80	.40	.25
79a	Checklist 1-88 (61 is C. Cannizzaro)	3.00	1.50	.90
79b	Checklist 1-88 (61 is Cannizzaro)	5.00	2.50	1.50
80	Turk Farrell	.70	.35	.20
81	Don Buford	.80	.40	.25
82	Braves Rookies *(Santos Alomar,* John Braun)	.80	.40	.25
83	George Thomas	.70	.35	.20
84	Ron Herbel	.70	.35	.20
85	Willie Smith	.70	.35	.20
86	Les Narum	.70	.35	.20
87	Nelson Mathews	.70	.35	.20
88	Jack Lamabe	.70	.35	.20
89	Mike Hershberger	.70	.35	.20
90	Rich Rollins	.70	.35	.20
91	Cubs Team	2.25	1.25	.70
92	Dick Howser	1.25	.60	.40
93	Jack Fisher	.80	.40	.25
94	Charlie Lau	.90	.45	.25
95	Bill Mazeroski	2.50	1.25	.70
96	Sonny Siebert	.80	.40	.25
97	Pedro Gonzalez	1.00	.50	.30
98	Bob Miller	.70	.35	.20
99	Gil Hodges	6.00	3.00	1.75
100	Ken Boyer	2.50	1.25	.70
101	Fred Newman	.70	.35	.20
102	Steve Boros	.80	.40	.25
103	Harvey Kuenn	1.25	.60	.40
104	Checklist 89-176	3.00	1.50	.90
105	Chico Salmon	.70	.35	.20
106	Gene Oliver	.70	.35	.20
107	Phillies Rookies *(Pat Corrales,* Costen Shockley)	2.00	1.00	.60
108	Don Mincher	.80	.40	.25
109	Walt Bond	.70	.35	.20
110	Ron Santo	1.50	.70	.45
111	Lee Thomas	.70	.35	.20
112	Derrell Griffith	.70	.35	.20
113	Steve Barber	.70	.35	.20
114	Jim Hickman	.90	.45	.25
115	Bobby Richardson	4.50	2.25	1.25
116	Cardinals Rookies (Dave Dowling, *Bob Tolan)*	1.25	.60	.40
117	Wes Stock	.70	.35	.20
118	*Hal Lanier*	1.50	.70	.45
119	John Kennedy	.70	.35	.20
120	Frank Robinson	20.00	10.00	6.00
121	Gene Alley	.80	.40	.25
122	Bill Pleis	.70	.35	.20
123	Frank Thomas	.70	.35	.20
124	Tom Satriano	.70	.35	.20
125	Juan Pizarro	.70	.35	.20
126	Dodgers Team	4.00	2.00	1.25
127	Frank Lary	.80	.40	.25
128	Vic Davalillo	.80	.40	.25
129	Bennie Daniels	.70	.35	.20
130	Al Kaline	20.00	10.00	6.00
131	Johnny Keane	1.50	.70	.45
132	World Series Game 1 (Cards Take Opener)	2.50	1.25	.70
133	World Series Game 2 (Stottlemyre Wins)	3.00	1.50	.90
134	World Series Game 3 (Mantle's Clutch HR)	18.00	9.00	5.50
135	World Series Game 4 (Boyer's Grand Slam)	2.50	1.25	.70
136	World Series Game 5 (10th Inning Triumph)	2.50	1.25	.70
137	World Series Game 6 (Bouton Wins Again)	3.00	1.50	.90
138	World Series Game 7 (Gibson Wins Finale)	3.50	1.75	1.00
139	World Series Summary (The Cards Celebrate)	2.50	1.25	.70
140	Dean Chance	.80	.40	.25
141	Charlie James	.70	.35	.20
142	Bill Monbouquette	.80	.40	.25
143	Pirates Rookies (John Gelnar, Jerry May)	.70	.35	.20
144	Ed Kranepool	.90	.45	.25
145	*Luis Tiant*	7.00	3.50	2.00
146	Ron Hansen	.70	.35	.20
147	Dennis Bennett	.70	.35	.20
148	Willie Kirkland	.70	.35	.20
149	Wayne Schurr	.70	.35	.20
150	Brooks Robinson	20.00	10.00	6.00
151	Athletics Team	2.25	1.25	.70
152	Phil Ortega	.70	.35	.20
153	Norm Cash	2.00	1.00	.60
154	Bob Humphreys	.70	.35	.20
155	Roger Maris	40.00	20.00	12.00
156	Bob Sadowski	.70	.35	.20
157	Zoilo Versalles	1.50	.70	.45
158	Dick Sisler	.70	.35	.20
159	Jim Duffalo	.70	.35	.20
160	Bob Clemente	75.00	38.00	23.00
161	Frank Baumann	.70	.35	.20
162	Russ Nixon	.70	.35	.20
163	John Briggs	.70	.35	.20
164	Al Spangler	.70	.35	.20
165	Dick Ellsworth	.70	.35	.20
166	Indians Rookies *(Tommie Agee,* George Culver)	1.50	.70	.45
167	Bill Wakefield	.80	.40	.25
168	Dick Green	.80	.40	.25
169	Dave Vineyard	.70	.35	.20
170	Hank Aaron	75.00	38.00	23.00
171	Jim Roland	.70	.35	.20
172	Jim Piersall	1.50	.70	.45
173	Tigers Team	3.25	1.75	1.00
174	Joe Jay	.70	.35	.20
175	Bob Aspromonte	.70	.35	.20
176	Willie McCovey	18.00	9.00	5.50
177	Pete Mikkelsen	1.00	.50	.30
178	Dalton Jones	.70	.35	.20
179	Hal Woodeshick	.70	.35	.20
180	Bob Allison	1.25	.60	.40
181	Senators Rookies (Don Loun, Joe McCabe)	.70	.35	.20
182	Mike de la Hoz	.70	.35	.20
183	Dave Nicholson	.70	.35	.20
184	John Boozer	.70	.35	.20
185	Max Alvis	.70	.35	.20
186	Billy Cowan	.70	.35	.20
187	Casey Stengel	18.00	9.00	5.00
188	Sam Bowens	.70	.35	.20
189	Checklist 177-264	3.00	1.50	.90
190	Bill White	1.25	.60	.40
191	Phil Regan	.70	.35	.20
192	Jim Coker	.70	.35	.20
193	Gaylord Perry	12.00	6.00	3.50
194	Angels Rookies (Bill Kelso, *Rick Reichardt)*	.80	.40	.25
195	Bob Veale	.80	.40	.25
196	Ron Fairly	.80	.40	.25
197	Diego Segui	.70	.35	.20
198	Smoky Burgess	1.25	.60	.40
199	Bob Heffner	.90	.45	.25
200	Joe Torre	2.50	1.25	.70
201	Twins Rookies *(Cesar Tovar,* Sandy Valdespino)	1.00	.50	.30
202	Leo Burke	.90	.45	.25
203	Dallas Green	1.25	.60	.40
204	Russ Snyder	.90	.45	.25
205	Warren Spahn	20.00	10.00	6.00
206	Willie Horton	1.25	.60	.40
207	Pete Rose	150.00	60.00	38.00
208	Tommy John	10.00	5.00	3.00
209	Pirates Team	2.50	1.25	.70
210	Jim Fregosi	1.50	.70	.45
211	Steve Ridzik	.90	.45	.25
212	Ron Brand	.90	.45	.25
213	Jim Davenport	.90	.45	.25
214	Bob Purkey	.90	.45	.25
215	Pete Ward	.90	.45	.25

		NR MT	EX	VG
216	Al Worthington	.90	.45	.25
217	Walt Alston	3.50	1.75	1.00
218	Dick Schofield	.90	.45	.25
219	Bob Meyer	.90	.45	.25
220	Billy Williams	10.00	5.00	3.00
221	John Tsitouris	.90	.45	.25
222	Bob Tillman	.90	.45	.25
223	Dan Osinski	.90	.45	.25
224	Bob Chance	.90	.45	.25
225	Bo Belinsky	1.00	.50	.30
226	Yankees Rookies (Jake Gibbs, Elvio Jimenez)	1.50	.70	.45
227	Bobby Klaus	1.00	.50	.30
228	Jack Sanford	.90	.45	.25
229	Lou Clinton	.90	.45	.25
230	Ray Sadecki	.90	.45	.25
231	Jerry Adair	.90	.45	.25
232	*Steve Blass*	1.00	.50	.30
233	Don Zimmer	1.50	.70	.45
234	White Sox Team	4.00	2.00	1.25
235	Chuck Hinton	.90	.45	.25
236	*Dennis McLain*	12.00	6.00	3.50
237	Bernie Allen	.90	.45	.25
238	Joe Moeller	.90	.45	.25
239	Doc Edwards	1.00	.50	.30
240	Bob Bruce	.90	.45	.25
241	Mack Jones	.90	.45	.25
242	George Brunet	.90	.45	.25
243	Reds Rookies (Ted Davidson, *Tommy Helms)*	1.00	.50	.30
244	Lindy McDaniel	.90	.45	.25
245	Joe Pepitone	3.00	1.50	.90
246	Tom Butters	.90	.45	.25
247	Wally Moon	1.00	.50	.30
248	Gus Triandos	1.00	.50	.30
249	Dave McNally	1.25	.60	.40
250	Willie Mays	90.00	45.00	27.00
251	Billy Herman	2.00	1.00	.60
252	Pete Richert	.90	.45	.25
253	Danny Cater	1.00	.50	.30
254	Roland Sheldon	1.50	.70	.45
255	Camilo Pascual	1.00	.50	.30
256	Tito Francona	1.00	.50	.30
257	Jim Wynn	1.25	.60	.40
258	Larry Bearnarth	1.00	.50	.30
259	Tigers Rookies *(Jim Northrup, Ray Oyler)*	1.25	.60	.40
260	Don Drysdale	15.00	7.50	4.50
261	Duke Carmel	1.50	.70	.45
262	Bud Daley	.90	.45	.25
263	Marty Keough	.90	.45	.25
264	Bob Buhl	1.00	.50	.30
265	Jim Pagliaroni	.90	.45	.25
266	*Bert Campaneris*	4.00	2.00	1.25
267	Senators Team	2.50	1.25	.70
268	Ken McBride	.90	.45	.25
269	Frank Bolling	.90	.45	.25
270	Milt Pappas	1.00	.50	.30
271	Don Wert	.90	.45	.25
272	Chuck Schilling	.90	.45	.25
273	Checklist 265-352	3.25	1.75	1.00
274	Lum Harris	.90	.45	.25
275	Dick Groat	1.75	.90	.50
276	Hoyt Wilhelm	10.00	5.00	3.00
277	Johnny Lewis	1.00	.50	.30
278	Ken Retzer	.90	.45	.25
279	Dick Tracewski	.90	.45	.25
280	Dick Stuart	1.00	.50	.30
281	Bill Stafford	1.50	.70	.45
282	Giants Rookies (Dick Estelle, *Masanori Murakami)*	1.25	.60	.40
283	Fred Whitfield	.90	.45	.25
284	Nick Willhite	.90	.45	.25
285	Ron Hunt	1.00	.50	.30
286	Athletics Rookies (Jim Dickson, Aurelio Monteagudo)	.90	.45	.25
287	Gary Kolb	.90	.45	.25
288	Jack Hamilton	.90	.45	.25
289	Gordy Coleman	.90	.45	.25
290	Wally Bunker	.90	.45	.25
291	Jerry Lynch	.90	.45	.25
292	Larry Yellen	.90	.45	.25
293	Angels Team	2.50	1.25	.70
294	Tim McCarver	2.75	1.50	.80
295	Dick Radatz	1.00	.50	.30
296	Tony Taylor	.90	.45	.25
297	Dave DeBusschere	3.50	1.75	1.00
298	Jim Stewart	.90	.45	.25
299	Jerry Zimmerman	.90	.45	.25
300	Sandy Koufax	90.00	45.00	27.00
301	Birdie Tebbetts	.90	.45	.25
302	Al Stanek	.90	.45	.25
303	Johnny Orsino	.90	.45	.25
304	Dave Stenhouse	.90	.45	.25
305	Rico Carty	1.50	.70	.45
306	Bubba Phillips	.90	.45	.25
307	Barry Latman	.90	.45	.25
308	Mets Rookies *(Cleon Jones*, Tom Parsons)	1.25	.60	.40
309	Steve Hamilton	1.50	.70	.45
310	Johnny Callison	1.25	.60	.40
311	Orlando Pena	.90	.45	.25
312	Joe Nuxhall	1.00	.50	.30
313	Jimmie Schaffer	.90	.45	.25
314	Sterling Slaughter	.90	.45	.25
315	Frank Malzone	1.00	.50	.30
316	Reds Team	2.75	1.50	.80
317	Don McMahon	.90	.45	.25
318	Matty Alou	1.00	.50	.30
319	Ken McMullen	.90	.45	.25
320	Bob Gibson	18.00	9.00	5.50
321	Rusty Staub	3.50	1.75	1.00
322	Rick Wise	1.00	.50	.30
323	Hank Bauer	1.00	.50	.30
324	Bobby Locke	.90	.45	.25
325	Donn Clendenon	1.00	.50	.30
326	Dwight Siebler	.90	.45	.25
327	Denis Menke	.90	.45	.25
328	Eddie Fisher	.90	.45	.25
329	Hawk Taylor	1.00	.50	.30
330	Whitey Ford	18.00	9.00	5.50
331	Dodgers Rookies (Al Ferrara, John Purdin)	1.00	.50	.30
332	Ted Abernathy	.90	.45	.25
333	Tommie Reynolds	.90	.45	.25
334	Vic Roznovsky	.90	.45	.25
335	Mickey Lolich	3.50	1.75	1.00
336	Woody Held	.90	.45	.25
337	Mike Cuellar	1.50	.70	.45
338	Phillies Team	2.50	1.25	.70
339	Ryne Duren	1.00	.50	.30
340	Tony Oliva	3.50	1.75	1.00
341	Bobby Bolin	.90	.45	.25
342	Bob Rodgers	1.00	.50	.30
343	Mike McCormick	1.00	.50	.30
344	Wes Parker	1.00	.50	.30
345	Floyd Robinson	.90	.45	.25
346	Bobby Bragan	1.00	.50	.30
347	Roy Face	1.50	.70	.45
348	George Banks	.90	.45	.25
349	Larry Miller	1.00	.50	.30
350	Mickey Mantle	350.00	140.00	88.00
351	Jim Perry	1.25	.60	.40
352	*Alex Johnson*	1.00	.50	.30
353	Jerry Lumpe	1.00	.50	.30
354	Cubs Rookies (Billy Ott, Jack Warner)	.90	.45	.25
355	Vada Pinson	2.50	1.25	.70
356	Bill Spanswick	.90	.45	.25
357	Carl Warwick	.90	.45	.25
358	Albie Pearson	.90	.45	.25
359	Ken Johnson	.90	.45	.25
360	Orlando Cepeda	5.00	2.50	1.50
361	Checklist 353-429	3.25	1.75	1.00
362	Don Schwall	.90	.45	.25
363	Bob Johnson	.90	.45	.25
364	Galen Cisco	1.00	.50	.30
365	Jim Gentile	1.00	.50	.30
366	Dan Schneider	.90	.45	.25
367	Leon Wagner	1.00	.50	.30
368	White Sox Rookies *(Ken Berry*, Joel Gibson)	1.00	.50	.30
369	Phil Linz	1.50	.70	.45
370	Tommy Davis	1.50	.70	.45
371	Frank Kreutzer	.90	.45	.25
372	Clay Dalrymple	.90	.45	.25
373	Curt Simmons	1.00	.50	.30
374	Angels Rookies *(Jose Cardenal*, Dick Simpson)	1.00	.50	.30
375	Dave Wickersham	.90	.45	.25
376	Jim Landis	.90	.45	.25
377	Willie Stargell	20.00	10.00	6.00
378	Chuck Estrada	.90	.45	.25
379	Giants Team	2.50	1.25	.70
380	Rocky Colavito	3.00	1.50	.90
381	Al Jackson	1.00	.50	.30
382	J.C. Martin	.90	.45	.25
383	Felipe Alou	1.00	.50	.30
384	Johnny Klippstein	.90	.45	.25
385	Carl Yastrzemski	90.00	45.00	27.00
386	Cubs Rookies (Paul Jaeckel, Fred Norman)	.90	.45	.25
387	Johnny Podres	2.00	1.00	.60
388	John Blanchard	1.50	.70	.45
389	Don Larsen	1.25	.60	.40
390	Bill Freehan	1.25	.60	.40
391	Mel McGaha	.90	.45	.25
392	Bob Friend	1.50	.70	.45
393	Ed Kirkpatrick	.90	.45	.25
394	Jim Hannan	.90	.45	.25
395	Jim Hart	1.00	.50	.30
396	Frank Bertaina	.90	.45	.25
397	Jerry Buchek	.90	.45	.25
398	Reds Rookies (Dan Neville, *Art Shamsky)*	1.00	.50	.30
399	Ray Herbert	.90	.45	.25
400	Harmon Killebrew	15.00	7.50	4.50
401	Carl Willey	1.00	.50	.30
402	Joe Amalfitano	.90	.45	.25
403	Red Sox Team	3.00	1.50	.90
404	Stan Williams	.90	.45	.25
405	John Roseboro	1.00	.50	.30
406	Ralph Terry	1.00	.50	.30
407	Lee Maye	.90	.45	.25
408	Larry Sherry	.90	.45	.25
409	Astros Rookies (Jim Beauchamp, *Larry Dierker)*	1.00	.50	.30
410	Luis Aparicio	9.00	4.50	2.75
411	Roger Craig	2.00	1.00	.60
412	Bob Bailey	.90	.45	.25
413	Hal Reniff	1.50	.70	.45
414	Al Lopez	3.00	1.50	.90
415	Curt Flood	1.50	.70	.45
416	Jim Brewer	.90	.45	.25
417	Ed Brinkman	1.00	.50	.30
418	Johnny Edwards	.90	.45	.25
419	Ruben Amaro	.90	.45	.25
420	Larry Jackson	.90	.45	.25
421	Twins Rookies (Gary Dotter, Jay Ward)	.90	.45	.25
422	Aubrey Gatewood	.90	.45	.25
423	Jesse Gonder	1.00	.50	.30
424	Gary Bell	.90	.45	.25
425	Wayne Causey	.90	.45	.25
426	Braves Team	2.50	1.25	.70
427	Bob Saverine	.90	.45	.25
428	Bob Shaw	.90	.45	.25
429	Don Demeter	.90	.45	.25
430	Gary Peters	1.00	.50	.30
431	Cardinals Rookies *(Nelson Briles*, Wayne Spiezio)	1.00	.50	.30
432	Jim Grant	1.00	.50	.30
433	John Bateman	.90	.45	.25
434	Dave Morehead	.90	.45	.25
435	Willie Davis	1.50	.70	.45
436	Don Elston	.90	.45	.25
437	Chico Cardenas	.90	.45	.25
438	Harry Walker	1.00	.50	.30
439	Moe Drabowsky	.90	.45	.25
440	Tom Tresh	2.50	1.25	.70
441	Denver Lemaster	.90	.45	.25
442	Vic Power	.90	.45	.25
443	Checklist 430-506	3.25	1.75	1.00
444	Bob Hendley	.90	.45	.25
445	Don Lock	.90	.45	.25
446	Art Mahaffey	.90	.45	.25
447	Julian Javier	1.25	.60	.40
448	Lee Stange	1.25	.60	.40
449	Mets Rookies (Jerry Hinsley, Gary Kroll)	1.50	.70	.45
450	Elston Howard	5.00	2.50	1.50
451	Jim Owens	1.25	.60	.40
452	Gary Geiger	1.25	.60	.40
453	Dodgers Rookies *(Willie Crawford*, John Werhas)	1.50	.70	.45
454	Ed Rakow	1.25	.60	.40
455	Norm Siebern	1.50	.70	.45
456	Bill Henry	1.25	.60	.40
457	Bob Kennedy	1.25	.60	.40
458	John Buzhardt	1.25	.60	.40
459	Frank Kostro	1.25	.60	.40
460	Richie Allen	6.00	3.00	1.75
461	Braves Rookies *(Clay Carroll*, Phil Niekro)	35.00	17.50	10.50
462	Lew Krausse (photo actually Pete Lovrich)	1.25	.60	.40
463	Manny Mota	1.50	.70	.45
464	Ron Piche	1.25	.60	.40
465	Tom Haller	1.25	.60	.40
466	Senators Rookies (Pete Craig, Dick Nen)	1.25	.60	.40
467	Ray Washburn	1.25	.60	.40
468	Larry Brown	1.25	.60	.40
469	Don Nottebart	1.25	.60	.40
470	Yogi Berra	50.00	30.00	15.00
471	Billy Hoeft	1.25	.60	.40
472	Don Pavletich	1.25	.60	.40
473	Orioles Rookies *(Paul Blair, Dave Johnson)*	10.00	5.00	3.00
474	Cookie Rojas	1.25	.60	.40
475	Clete Boyer	3.00	1.50	.90
476	Billy O'Dell	1.25	.60	.40
477	Cardinals Rookies (Fritz Ackley, *Steve Carlton)*	350.00	175.00	105.00
478	Wilbur Wood	1.00	.50	.30
479	Ken Harrelson	2.50	1.25	.70
480	Joel Horlen	1.25	.60	.40
481	Indians Team	3.00	1.50	.90
482	Bob Priddy	1.25	.60	.40
483	George Smith	1.25	.60	.40
484	Ron Perranoski	1.50	.70	.45
485	Nellie Fox	6.00	3.00	1.75
486	Angels Rookies (Tom Egan, Pat Rogan)	1.25	.60	.40
487	Woody Woodward	1.50	.70	.45
488	Ted Wills	1.25	.60	.40
489	Gene Mauch	1.50	.70	.45
490	Earl Battey	1.50	.70	.45
491	Tracy Stallard	1.25	.60	.40
492	Gene Freese	1.25	.60	.40
493	Tigers Rookies (Bruce Brubaker, Bill Roman)	1.25	.60	.40
494	Jay Ritchie	1.25	.60	.40
495	Joe Christopher	1.50	.70	.45
496	Joe Cunningham	1.25	.60	.40
497	Giants Rookies *(Ken Henderson*, Jack Hiatt)	1.50	.70	.45
498	Gene Stephens	1.25	.60	.40
499	Stu Miller	1.25	.60	.40
500	Ed Mathews	25.00	12.50	7.50
501	Indians Rookies (Ralph Gagliano, Jim Rittwage)	1.25	.60	.40
502	Don Cardwell	1.25	.60	.40
503	Phil Gagliano	1.25	.60	.40
504	Jerry Grote	1.50	.70	.45
505	Ray Culp	1.25	.60	.40
506	Sam Mele	1.25	.60	.40
507	Sammy Ellis	1.25	.60	.40
508a	Checklist 507-598 (large print on front)	6.00	3.00	1.75
508b	Checklist 507-598 (small print on front)	4.00	2.00	1.25
509	Red Sox Rookies (Bob Guindon, Gerry Vezendy)	1.25	.60	.40
510	Ernie Banks	60.00	30.00	18.00
511	Ron Locke	1.50	.70	.45
512	Cap Peterson	1.25	.60	.40
513	Yankees Team	9.00	4.50	2.75
514	Joe Azcue	1.25	.60	.40
515	Vern Law	2.00	1.00	.60
516	Al Weis	1.25	.60	.40
517	Angels Rookies (Paul Schaal, Jack Warner)	1.25	.60	.40
518	Ken Rowe	1.25	.60	.40
519	Bob Uecker	45.00	22.00	13.50
520	Tony Cloninger	1.50	.70	.45
521	Phillies Rookies (Dave Bennett, Morrie Stevens)	1.25	.60	.40
522	Hank Aguirre	1.25	.60	.40
523	Mike Brumley	4.00	2.00	1.25
524	Dave Giusti	4.00	2.00	1.25
525	Eddie Bressoud	4.00	2.00	1.25
526	Athletics Rookies *(Jim Hunter, Rene Lachemann, Skip Lockwood, Johnny Odom)*	125.00	60.00	40.00
527	Jeff Torborg	4.50	2.25	1.25
528	George Altman	4.00	2.00	1.25
529	Jerry Fosnow	4.00	2.00	1.25
530	Jim Maloney	4.50	2.25	1.25
531	Chuck Hiller	4.00	2.00	1.25
532	Hector Lopez	5.00	2.50	1.50
533	Mets Rookies (Jim Bethke, *Tug McGraw*, Dan Napolean, *Ron Swoboda)*	12.00	6.00	3.50
534	John Herrnstein	4.00	2.00	1.25
535	Jack Kralick	4.00	2.00	1.25
536	Andre Rodgers	4.00	2.00	1.25
537	Angels Rookies (Marcelino Lopez, *Rudy May*, Phil Roof)	5.00	2.50	1.50
538	Chuck Dressen	4.50	2.25	1.25
539	Herm Starrette	4.00	2.00	1.25
540	Lou Brock	40.00	20.00	12.00
541	White Sox Rookies (Greg Bollo, Bob Locker)	4.00	2.00	1.25
542	Lou Klimchock	4.00	2.00	1.25
543	Ed Connolly	4.00	2.00	1.25
544	Howie Reed	4.00	2.00	1.25
545	Jesus Alou	4.50	2.25	1.25
546	Indians Rookies (Ray Barker, Bill Davis, Mike Hedlund, Floyd Weaver)	4.00	2.00	1.25
547	Jake Wood	4.00	2.00	1.25

		NR MT	EX	VG
548	Dick Stigman	4.00	2.00	1.25
549	Cubs Rookies (*Glenn Beckert*, Roberto Pena)	5.00	2.50	1.50
550	*Mel Stottlemyre*	15.00	7.50	4.50
551	Mets Team	12.00	6.00	3.50
552	Julio Gotay	4.00	2.00	1.25
553	Astros Rookies (Dan Coombs, Jack McClure, Gene Ratliff)	4.00	2.00	1.25
554	Chico Ruiz	4.00	2.00	1.25
555	Jack Baldschun	4.00	2.00	1.25
556	Red Schoendienst	7.00	3.50	2.00
557	Jose Santiago	4.00	2.00	1.25
558	Tommie Sisk	4.00	2.00	1.25
559	Ed Bailey	4.00	2.00	1.25
560	Boog Powell	6.00	3.00	1.75
561	Dodgers Rookies (Dennis Daboll, *Mike Kekich, Jim Lefebvre*, Hector Valle)	6.00	3.00	1.75
562	Billy Moran	4.00	2.00	1.25
563	Julio Navarro	4.00	2.00	1.25
564	Mel Nelson	4.00	2.00	1.25
565	Ernie Broglio	4.00	2.00	1.25
566	Yankees Rookies (Gil Blanco, Art Lopez, Ross Moschitto)	5.00	2.50	1.50
567	Tommie Aaron	4.50	2.25	1.25
568	Ron Taylor	4.00	2.00	1.25
569	Gino Cimoli	4.00	2.00	1.25
570	Claude Osteen	4.50	2.25	1.25
571	Ossie Virgil	4.00	2.00	1.25
572	Orioles Team	6.00	3.00	1.75
573	Red Sox Rookies (*Jim Lonborg*, Gerry Moses, Mike Ryan, Bill Schlesinger)	8.00	4.00	2.50
574	Roy Sievers	4.50	2.25	1.25
575	Jose Pagan	4.00	2.00	1.25
576	Terry Fox	4.00	2.00	1.25
577	A.L. Rookies (Jim Buschhorn, Darold Knowles, Richie Scheinblum)	4.00	2.00	1.25
578	Camilo Carreon	4.00	2.00	1.25
579	Dick Smith	4.00	2.00	1.25
580	Jimmie Hall	4.00	2.00	1.25
581	N.L. Rookies (Kevin Collins, *Tony Perez*, Dave Ricketts)	80.00	40.00	24.00
582	Bob Schmidt	5.00	2.50	1.50
583	Wes Covington	4.00	2.00	1.25
584	Harry Bright	4.00	2.00	1.25
585	Hank Fischer	4.00	2.00	1.25
586	Tommy McCraw	4.00	2.00	1.25
587	Joe Sparma	4.00	2.00	1.25
588	Lenny Green	4.00	2.00	1.25
589	Giants Rookies (Frank Linzy, Bob Schroder)	4.00	2.00	1.25
590	Johnnie Wyatt	4.00	2.00	1.25
591	Bob Skinner	4.50	2.25	1.25
592	Frank Bork	4.00	2.00	1.25
593	Tigers Rookies (Jackie Moore, John Sullivan)	4.00	2.00	1.25
594	Joe Gaines	4.00	2.00	1.25
595	Don Lee	4.00	2.00	1.25
596	Don Landrum	4.00	2.00	1.25
597	Twins Rookies (Joe Nossek, Dick Reese, John Sevcik)	4.50	2.00	1.25
598	Al Downing	10.00	3.00	1.75

1965 Topps Embossed

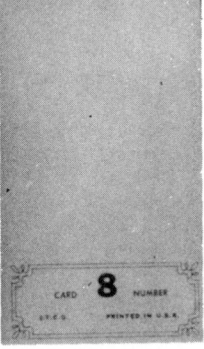

Inserted in regular packs, the 2-1/8" by 3-1/2" Topps Embossed cards are one of the more fascinating issues of the company. The fronts feature an embossed profile portrait on gold foil-like cardboard (some collectors report finding the cards with silver cardboard). The player's name, team and position are below the portrait - which is good, because most of the embossed portraits are otherwise unrecognizeable. There is a gold border with American players framed in blue and National Leaguers in red. The set contains 72 cards divided equally bewteen the leagues. The set provides an inexpensive way to add some interesting cards to a collection. Being special cards, many stars appear in the set.

		NR MT	EX	VG
Complete Set:		70.00	35.00	21.00
Common Player:		.50	.25	.15
1	Carl Yastrzemski	5.00	2.50	1.50
2	Ron Fairly	.50	.25	.15
3	Max Alvis	.50	.25	.15
4	Jim Ray Hart	.50	.25	.15
5	Bill Skowron	.60	.30	.20
6	Ed Kranepool	.50	.25	.15
7	Tim McCarver	.60	.30	.20
8	Sandy Koufax	5.00	2.50	1.50
9	Donn Clendenon	.50	.25	.15
10	John Romano	.50	.25	.15
11	Mickey Mantle	15.00	7.50	4.50
12	Joe Torre	.70	.35	.20
13	Al Kaline	5.00	2.50	1.50
14	Al McBean	.50	.25	.15
15	Don Drysdale	1.50	.70	.45
16	Brooks Robinson	2.00	1.00	.60
17	Jim Bunning	1.00	.50	.30
18	Gary Peters	.50	.25	.15
19	Bob Clemente	5.00	2.50	1.50
20	Milt Pappas	.50	.25	.15
21	Wayne Causey	.50	.25	.15
22	Frank Robinson	2.00	1.00	.60
23	Bill Mazeroski	.60	.30	.20
24	Diego Segui	.50	.25	.15
25	Jim Bouton	.60	.30	.20
26	Ed Mathews	1.50	.70	.45
27	Willie Mays	6.00	3.00	1.75
28	Ron Santo	.60	.30	.20
29	Boog Powell	.60	.30	.20
30	Ken McBride	.50	.25	.15
31	Leon Wagner	.50	.25	.15
32	John Callison	.50	.25	.15
33	Zoilo Versalles	.50	.25	.15
34	Jack Baldschun	.50	.25	.15
35	Ron Hunt	.50	.25	.15
36	Richie Allen	.70	.35	.20
37	Frank Malzone	.50	.25	.15
38	Bob Allison	.50	.25	.15
39	Jim Fregosi	.60	.30	.20
40	Billy Williams	1.50	.70	.45
41	Bill Freehan	.50	.25	.15
42	Vada Pinson	.70	.35	.20
43	Bill White	.50	.25	.15
44	Roy McMillan	.50	.25	.15
45	Orlando Cepeda	1.00	.50	.30
46	Rocky Colavito	.70	.35	.20
47	Ken Boyer	.70	.35	.20
48	Dick Radatz	.50	.25	.15
49	Tommy Davis	.60	.30	.20
50	Walt Bond	.50	.25	.15
51	John Orsino	.50	.25	.15
52	Joe Christopher	.50	.25	.15
53	Al Spangler	.50	.25	.15
54	Jim King	.50	.25	.15
55	Mickey Lolich	.70	.35	.20
56	Harmon Killebrew	2.00	1.00	.60
57	Bob Shaw	.50	.25	.15
58	Ernie Banks	4.00	2.00	1.25
59	Hank Aaron	5.00	2.50	1.50
60	Chuck Hinton	.50	.25	.15
61	Bob Aspromonte	.50	.25	.15
62	Lee Maye	.50	.25	.15
63	Joe Cunningham	.50	.25	.15
64	Pete Ward	.50	.25	.15
65	Bobby Richardson	1.00	.50	.30
66	Dean Chance	.50	.25	.15
67	Dick Ellsworth	.50	.25	.15
68	Jim Maloney	.50	.25	.15
69	Bob Gibson	1.50	.70	.45
70	Earl Battey	.50	.25	.15
71	Tony Kubek	1.00	.50	.30
72	Jack Kralick	.50	.25	.15

1965 Topps Transfers

Issued as strips of three players each as inserts in 1965, the Topps Transfers were 2" by 3" portraits of players. The transfers have blue or red bands at the top and bottom with the team name and position in the top band and the player's name in the bottom. As is so often the case, the superstars in the transfer set can be quite expensive, but like many of Topps non-card products, the transfers are neither terribly expensive or popular today.

		NR MT	EX	VG
Complete Set:		200.00	100.00	60.00
Common Player:		.60	.30	.20
(1)	Hank Aaron	15.00	7.50	4.50
(2)	Richie Allen	.80	.40	.25
(3)	Bob Allison	.70	.35	.20
(4)	Max Alvis	.60	.30	.20
(5)	Luis Aparicio	2.50	1.25	.70
(6)	Bob Aspromonte	.60	.30	.20
(7)	Walt Bond	.60	.30	.20
(8)	Jim Bouton	.80	.40	.25
(9)	Ken Boyer	.80	.40	.25
(10)	Jim Bunning	1.00	.50	.30
(11)	John Callison	.70	.35	.20
(12)	Rico Carty	.70	.35	.20
(13)	Wayne Causey	.60	.30	.20
(14)	Orlando Cepeda	1.00	.50	.30
(15)	Bob Chance	.60	.30	.20
(16)	Dean Chance	.60	.30	.20
(17)	Joe Christopher	.60	.30	.20
(18)	Bob Clemente	15.00	7.50	4.50
(19)	Rocky Colavito	.80	.40	.25
(20)	Tony Conigliaro	.70	.35	.20
(21)	Tommy Davis	.80	.40	.25
(22)	Don Drysdale	4.00	2.00	1.25
(23)	Bill Freehan	.70	.35	.20
(24)	Jim Fregosi	.70	.35	.20
(25)	Bob Gibson	4.00	2.00	1.25
(26)	Dick Groat	.70	.35	.20
(27)	Tom Haller	.60	.30	.20
(28)	Chuck Hinton	.60	.30	.20
(29)	Elston Howard	1.00	.50	.30
(30)	Ron Hunt	.60	.30	.20
(31)	Al Jackson	.60	.30	.20
(32)	Al Kaline	5.00	2.50	1.50
(33)	Harmon Killebrew	5.00	2.50	1.50
(34)	Jim King	.60	.30	.20
(35)	Ron Kline	.60	.30	.20
(36)	Bobby Knoop	.60	.30	.20
(37)	Sandy Koufax	10.00	5.00	3.00
(38)	Ed Kranepool	.60	.30	.20
(39)	Jim Maloney	.60	.30	.20
(40)	Mickey Mantle	60.00	30.00	18.00
(41)	Juan Marichal	4.00	2.00	1.25
(42)	Lee Maye	.60	.30	.20
(43)	Willie Mays	15.00	7.50	4.50
(44)	Bill Mazeroski	.80	.40	.25
(45)	Tony Oliva	.80	.40	.25
(46)	Jim O'Toole	.60	.30	.20
(47)	Milt Pappas	.70	.35	.20
(48)	Camilo Pascual	.70	.35	.20
(49)	Gary Peters	.60	.30	.20
(50)	Vada Pinson	.80	.40	.25
(51)	Juan Pizarro	.60	.30	.20
(52)	Boog Powell	.80	.40	.25
(53)	Dick Radatz	.60	.30	.20
(54)	Bobby Richardson	1.00	.50	.30
(55)	Brooks Robinson	6.00	3.00	1.75
(56)	Frank Robinson	5.00	2.50	1.50
(57)	Bob Rodgers	.70	.35	.20
(58)	John Roseboro	.70	.35	.20
(59)	Ron Santo	.80	.40	.25
(60)	Diego Segui	.60	.30	.20
(61)	Bill Skowron	.70	.35	.20
(62)	Al Spangler	.60	.30	.20
(63)	Dick Stuart	.70	.35	.20
(64)	Luis Tiant	.80	.40	.25
(65)	Joe Torre	.80	.40	.25
(66)	Bob Veale	.60	.30	.20
(67)	Leon Wagner	.60	.30	.20
(68)	Pete Ward	.60	.30	.20
(69)	Bill White	.70	.35	.20
(70)	Dave Wickersham	.60	.30	.20
(71)	Billy Williams	3.00	1.50	.90
(72)	Carl Yastrzemski	25.00	12.50	7.50

1966 Topps

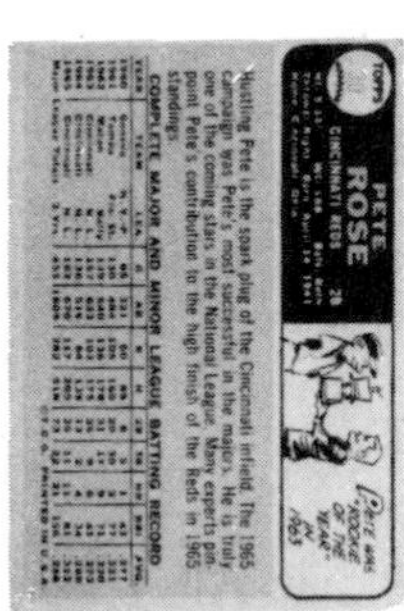

In 1966, Topps produced another 598-card set. The 2-1/2" by 3-1/2" cards feature the almost traditional color photograph with a diagonal strip in the upper left-hand corner carrying the team name. A band at the bottom carries the player's name and position. Multi-player cards returned in 1966 after having had a year's hiatus. The statistical leader cards feature the categorical leader and two runners-up. Most team managers have cards as well. The 1966 set features a handful of cards found with without a notice of the player's sale or trade to another team. Cards without the notice bring higher prices not included in the complete set prices below.

		NR MT	EX	VG
Complete Set:		3800.	1900.	1000.
Common Player: 1-110		.60	.30	.20
Common Player: 111-446		.70	.35	.20
Common Player: 447-522		3.50	1.75	1.00
Common Player Singleprint: 523-598		20.00	10.00	6.00
Common Player: 523-598		15.00	7.50	4.50
1	Willie Mays	200.00	50.00	18.00
2	Ted Abernathy	.80	.30	.20
3	Sam Mele	.60	.30	.20

		NR MT	EX	VG
4	Ray Culp	.60	.30	.20
5	Jim Fregosi	1.00	.50	.30
6	Chuck Schilling	.60	.30	.20
7	Tracy Stallard	.60	.30	.20
8	Floyd Robinson	.60	.30	.20
9	Clete Boyer	1.50	.70	.45
10	Tony Cloninger	.70	.35	.20
11	Senators Rookies (Brant Alyea, Pete Craig)	.60	.30	.20
12	John Tsitouris	.60	.30	.20
13	Lou Johnson	.60	.30	.20
14	Norm Siebern	.70	.35	.20
15	Vern Law	1.00	.50	.30
16	Larry Brown	.70	.35	.20
17	Johnny Stephenson	.70	.35	.20
18	Roland Sheldon	.60	.30	.20
19	Giants Team	2.00	1.00	.60
20	Willie Horton	.80	.40	.25
21	Don Nottebart	.60	.30	.20
22	Joe Nossek	.60	.30	.20
23	Jack Sanford	.60	.30	.20
24	*Don Kessinger*	1.25	.60	.40
25	Pete Ward	.60	.30	.20
26	Ray Sadecki	.60	.30	.20
27	Orioles Rookies (*Andy Etchebarren*, Darold Knowles)	.70	.35	.20
28	Phil Niekro	10.00	5.00	3.00
29	Mike Brumley	.60	.30	.20
30	Pete Rose	60.00	30.00	18.00
31	Jack Cullen	.80	.40	.25
32	Adolfo Phillips	.60	.30	.20
33	Jim Pagliaroni	.60	.30	.20
34	Checklist 1-88	2.00	1.00	.60
35	Ron Swoboda	.80	.40	.25
36	Jim Hunter	25.00	12.50	7.50
37	Billy Herman	1.50	.70	.45
38	Ron Nischwitz	.60	.30	.20
39	Ken Henderson	.60	.30	.20
40	Jim Grant	.60	.30	.20
41	Don LeJohn	.60	.30	.20
42	Aubrey Gatewood	.60	.30	.20
43	Don Landrum	.60	.30	.20
44	Indians Rookies (Bill Davis, Tom Kelley)	.60	.30	.20
45	Jim Gentile	.70	.35	.20
46	Howie Koplitz	.60	.30	.20
47	J.C. Martin	.60	.30	.20
48	Paul Blair	.80	.40	.25
49	Woody Woodward	.70	.35	.20
50	Mickey Mantle	175.00	70.00	44.00
51	Gordon Richardson	.70	.35	.20
52	Power Plus (Johnny Callison, Wes Covington)	1.00	.50	.30
53	Bob Duliba	.60	.30	.20
54	Jose Pagan	.60	.30	.20
55	Ken Harrelson	1.50	.70	.45
56	Sandy Valdespino	.60	.30	.20
57	Jim Lefebvre	.70	.35	.20
58	Dave Wickersham	.60	.30	.20
59	Reds Team	2.25	1.25	.70
60	Curt Flood	1.50	.70	.45
61	Bob Bolin	.60	.30	.20
62a	Merritt Ranew (no sold statement)	15.00	7.50	4.50
62b	Merritt Ranew (with sold statement)	.60	.30	.20
63	Jim Stewart	.60	.30	.20
64	Bob Bruce	.60	.30	.20
65	Leon Wagner	.70	.35	.20
66	Al Weis	.60	.30	.20
67	Mets Rookies (Cleon Jones, Dick Selma)	.80	.40	.25
68	Hal Reniff	.80	.40	.25
69	Ken Hamlin	.60	.30	.20
70	Carl Yastrzemski	60.00	30.00	18.00
71	Frank Carpin	.60	.30	.20
72	Tony Perez	8.00	4.00	2.50
73	Jerry Zimmerman	.60	.30	.20
74	Don Mossi	.70	.35	.20
75	Tommy Davis	1.50	.70	.45
76	Red Schoendienst	1.50	.70	.45
77	Johnny Orsino	.60	.30	.20
78	Frank Linzy	.60	.30	.20
79	Joe Pepitone	2.00	1.00	.60
80	Richie Allen	2.50	1.25	.70
81	Ray Oyler	.60	.30	.20
82	Bob Hendley	.60	.30	.20
83	Albie Pearson	.60	.30	.20
84	Braves Rookies (Jim Beauchamp, Dick Kelley)	.60	.30	.20
85	Eddie Fisher	.60	.30	.20
86	John Bateman	.60	.30	.20
87	Dan Napoleon	.70	.35	.20
88	Fred Whitfield	.60	.30	.20
89	Ted Davidson	.60	.30	.20
90	Luis Aparicio	9.00	4.50	2.75
91a	Bob Uecker (no trade statement)	80.00	40.00	24.00
91b	Bob Uecker (with trade statement)	15.00	7.50	4.50
92	Yankees Team	4.00	2.00	1.25
93	Jim Lonborg	1.00	.50	.30
94	Matty Alou	1.00	.50	.30
95	Pete Richert	.60	.30	.20
96	Felipe Alou	1.00	.50	.30
97	Jim Merritt	.60	.30	.20
98	Don Demeter	.60	.30	.20
99	Buc Belters (Donn Clendenon, Willie Stargell)	3.50	1.75	1.00
100	Sandy Koufax	80.00	40.00	24.00
101a	Checklist 89-176 (115 is Spahn)	7.00	3.50	2.00
101b	Checklist 89-176 (115 is Henry)	3.00	1.50	.90
102	Ed Kirkpatrick	.60	.30	.20
103a	Dick Groat (no trade statement)	20.00	10.00	6.00
103b	Dick Groat (with trade statement)	1.50	.70	.45
104a	Alex Johnson (no trade statement)	15.00	7.50	4.50
104b	Alex Johnson (with trade statement)	.70	.35	.20
105	Milt Pappas	.70	.35	.20
106	Rusty Staub	2.50	1.25	.70
107	Athletics Rookies (Larry Stahl, Ron Tompkins)	.60	.30	.20
108	Bobby Klaus	.70	.35	.20
109	Ralph Terry	.70	.35	.20
110	Ernie Banks	25.00	12.50	7.50
111	Gary Peters	.80	.40	.25
112	Manny Mota	.90	.45	.25
113	Hank Aguirre	.70	.35	.20
114	Jim Gosger	.70	.35	.20
115	Bill Henry	.70	.35	.20
116	Walt Alston	2.50	1.25	.70
117	Jake Gibbs	1.00	.50	.30
118	Mike McCormick	.80	.40	.25
119	Art Shamsky	.70	.35	.20
120	Harmon Killebrew	15.00	7.50	4.50
121	Ray Herbert	.70	.35	.20
122	Joe Gaines	.70	.35	.20
123	Pirates Rookies (Frank Bork, Jerry May)	.70	.35	.20
124	Tug McGraw	3.00	1.50	.90
125	Lou Brock	20.00	10.00	6.00
126	*Jim Palmer*	275.00	137.00	80.00
127	Ken Berry	.70	.35	.20
128	Jim Landis	.70	.35	.20
129	Jack Kralick	.70	.35	.20
130	Joe Torre	2.25	1.25	.70
131	Angels Team	2.25	1.25	.70
132	Orlando Cepeda	3.50	1.75	1.00
133	Don McMahon	.70	.35	.20
134	Wes Parker	.80	.40	.25
135	Dave Morehead	.70	.35	.20
136	Woody Held	.70	.35	.20
137	Pat Corrales	1.00	.50	.30
138	Roger Repoz	1.00	.50	.30
139	Cubs Rookies (Byron Browne, Don Young)	.70	.35	.20
140	Jim Maloney	.80	.40	.25
141	Tom McCraw	.70	.35	.20
142	Don Dennis	.70	.35	.20
143	Jose Tartabull	.70	.35	.20
144	Don Schwall	.70	.35	.20
145	Bill Freehan	.90	.45	.25
146	George Altman	.70	.35	.20
147	Lum Harris	.70	.35	.20
148	Bob Johnson	.70	.35	.20
149	Dick Nen	.70	.35	.20
150	Rocky Colavito	2.50	1.25	.70
151	Gary Wagner	.70	.35	.20
152	Frank Malzone	.80	.40	.25
153	Rico Carty	1.50	.70	.45
154	Chuck Hiller	.80	.40	.25
155	Marcelino Lopez	.70	.35	.20
156	DP Combo (Hal Lanier, Dick Schofield)	1.00	.50	.30
157	Rene Lachemann	.80	.40	.25
158	Jim Brewer	.70	.35	.20
159	Chico Ruiz	.70	.35	.20
160	Whitey Ford	20.00	10.00	6.00
161	Jerry Lumpe	.80	.40	.25
162	Lee Maye	.70	.35	.20
163	Tito Francona	.80	.40	.25
164	White Sox Rookies (Tommie Agee, Marv Staehle)	.90	.45	.25
165	Don Lock	.70	.35	.20
166	Chris Krug	.70	.35	.20
167	Boog Powell	2.50	1.25	.70
168	Dan Osinski	.70	.35	.20
169	Duke Sims	.70	.35	.20
170	Cookie Rojas	.70	.35	.20
171	Nick Willhite	.70	.35	.20
172	Mets Team	3.00	1.50	.90
173	Al Spangler	.70	.35	.20
174	Ron Taylor	.70	.35	.20
175	Bert Campaneris	1.50	.70	.45
176	Jim Davenport	.70	.35	.20
177	Hector Lopez	1.00	.50	.30
178	Bob Tillman	.70	.35	.20
179	Cardinals Rookies (Dennis Aust, Bob Tolan)	.80	.40	.25
180	Vada Pinson	2.50	1.25	.70
181	Al Worthington	.70	.35	.20
182	Jerry Lynch	.70	.35	.20
183a	Checklist 177-264 (large print on front)	2.50	1.25	.70
183b	Checklist 177-264 (small print on front)	4.00	2.00	1.25
184	Denis Menke	.70	.35	.20
185	Bob Buhl	.80	.40	.25
186	Ruben Amaro	1.00	.50	.30
187	Chuck Dressen	.80	.40	.25
188	Al Luplow	.80	.40	.25
189	John Roseboro	.90	.45	.25
190	Jimmie Hall	.70	.35	.20
191	Darrell Sutherland	.80	.40	.25
192	Vic Power	.70	.35	.20
193	Dave McNally	1.00	.50	.30
194	Senators Team	2.25	1.25	.70
195	Joe Morgan	40.00	20.00	12.00
196	Don Pavletich	.70	.35	.20
197	Sonny Siebert	.80	.40	.25
198	*Mickey Stanley*	1.00	.50	.30
199	Chisox Clubbers (Floyd Robinson, Johnny Romano, Bill Skowron)	1.00	.50	.30
200	Ed Mathews	8.00	4.00	2.50
201	Jim Dickson	.70	.35	.20
202	Clay Dalrymple	.70	.35	.20
203	Jose Santiago	.70	.35	.20
204	Cubs Team	2.25	1.25	.70
205	Tom Tresh	2.00	1.00	.60
206	Alvin Jackson	.70	.35	.20
207	Frank Quilici	.70	.35	.20
208	Bob Miller	.70	.35	.20
209	Tigers Rookies (Fritz Fisher, *John Hiller*)	1.25	.60	.40
210	Bill Mazeroski	2.50	1.25	.70
211	Frank Kreutzer	.70	.35	.20
212	Ed Kranepool	1.00	.50	.30
213	Fred Newman	.70	.35	.20
214	Tommy Harper	.80	.40	.25
215	N.L. Batting Leaders (Hank Aaron, Bob Clemente, Willie Mays)	8.00	4.00	2.50
216	A.L. Batting Leaders (Vic Davalillo, Tony Oliva, Carl Yastrzemski)	4.00	2.00	1.25
217	N.L. Home Run Leaders (Willie Mays, Willie McCovey, Billy Williams)	5.00	2.50	1.50
218	A.L. Home Run Leaders (Norm Cash, Tony Conigliaro, Willie Horton)	2.50	1.25	.70
219	N.L. RBI Leaders (Deron Johnson, Willie Mays, Frank Robinson)	4.00	2.00	1.25
220	A.L. RBI Leaders (Rocky Colavito, Willie Horton, Tony Oliva)	2.50	1.25	.70
221	N.L. ERA Leaders (Sandy Koufax, Vern Law, Juan Marichal)	4.00	2.00	1.25
222	A.L. ERA Leaders (Eddie Fisher, Sam McDowell, Sonny Siebert)	2.50	1.25	.70
223	N.L. Pitching Leaders (Tony Cloninger, Don Drysdale, Sandy Koufax)	4.00	2.00	1.25
224	A.L. Pitching Leaders (Jim Grant, Jim Kaat, Mel Stottlemyre)	3.00	1.50	.90
225	N.L. Strikeout Leaders (Bob Gibson, Sandy Koufax, Bob Veale)	4.00	2.00	1.25
226	A.L. Strikeout Leaders (Mickey Lolich, Sam McDowell, Denny McLain, Sonny Siebert)	2.50	1.25	.70
227	Russ Nixon	.70	.35	.20
228	Larry Dierker	.80	.40	.25
229	Hank Bauer	.80	.40	.25
230	Johnny Callison	1.25	.60	.40
231	Floyd Weaver	.70	.35	.20
232	Glenn Beckert	1.00	.50	.30
233	Dom Zanni	.70	.35	.20
234	Yankees Rookies (Rich Beck, *Roy White*)	3.50	1.75	1.00
235	Don Cardwell	.70	.35	.20
236	Mike Hershberger	.70	.35	.20
237	Billy O'Dell	.70	.35	.20
238	Dodgers Team	3.50	1.75	1.00
239	Orlando Pena	.70	.35	.20
240	Earl Battey	.80	.40	.25
241	Dennis Ribant	.80	.40	.25
242	Jesus Alou	.80	.40	.25
243	Nelson Briles	.80	.40	.25
244	Astros Rookies (Chuck Harrison, Sonny Jackson)	.70	.35	.20
245	John Buzhardt	.70	.35	.20
246	Ed Bailey	.70	.35	.20
247	Carl Warwick	.70	.35	.20
248	Pete Mikkelsen	.70	.35	.20
249	Bill Rigney	.70	.35	.20
250	Sam Ellis	.70	.35	.20
251	Ed Brinkman	.80	.40	.25
252	Denver Lemaster	.70	.35	.20
253	Don Wert	.70	.35	.20
254	Phillies Rookies (*Ferguson Jenkins*, Bill Sorrell)	50.00	25.00	15.00
255	Willie Stargell	15.00	7.50	4.50
256	Lew Krausse	.70	.35	.20
257	Jeff Torborg	.80	.40	.25
258	Dave Giusti	.70	.35	.20
259	Red Sox Team	2.50	1.25	.70
260	Bob Shaw	.70	.35	.20
261	Ron Hansen	.70	.35	.20
262	Jack Hamilton	.80	.40	.25
263	Tom Egan	.70	.35	.20
264	Twins Rookies (Andy Kosco, Ted Uhlaender)	.70	.35	.20
265	Stu Miller	.70	.35	.20
266	Pedro Gonzalez	.70	.35	.20
267	Joe Sparma	.70	.35	.20
268	John Blanchard	.70	.35	.20
269	Don Heffner	.70	.35	.20
270	Claude Osteen	.90	.45	.25
271	Hal Lanier	1.00	.50	.30
272	Jack Baldschun	.70	.35	.20
273	Astro Aces (Bob Aspromonte, Rusty Staub)	1.50	.70	.45
274	Buster Narum	.70	.35	.20
275	Tim McCarver	2.50	1.25	.70
276	Jim Bouton	2.50	1.25	.70
277	George Thomas	.70	.35	.20
278	Calvin Koonce	.70	.35	.20
279a	Checklist 265-352 (player's cap black)	4.00	2.00	1.25
279b	Checklist 265-352 (player's cap red)	3.00	1.50	.90
280	Bobby Knoop	.70	.35	.20
281	Bruce Howard	.70	.35	.20
282	Johnny Lewis	.80	.40	.25
283	Jim Perry	1.00	.50	.30
284	Bobby Wine	.80	.40	.25
285	Luis Tiant	2.50	1.25	.70
286	Gary Geiger	.70	.35	.20
287	Jack Aker	.70	.35	.20
288	Dodgers Rookies (*Bill Singer, Don Sutton*)	125.00	56.00	35.00
289	Larry Sherry	.80	.40	.25
290	Ron Santo	2.00	1.00	.60
291	Moe Drabowsky	.70	.35	.20
292	Jim Coker	.70	.35	.20
293	Mike Shannon	.80	.40	.25
294	Steve Ridzik	.70	.35	.20
295	Jim Hart	.80	.40	.25
296	Johnny Keane	1.25	.60	.40
297	Jim Owens	.70	.35	.20
298	Rico Petrocelli	1.25	.60	.40
299	Lou Burdette	2.00	1.00	.60
300	Bob Clemente	70.00	35.00	20.00
301	Greg Bollo	.70	.35	.20
302	Ernie Bowman	.80	.40	.25
303	Indians Team	2.25	1.25	.70
304	John Herrnstein	.70	.35	.20
305	Camilo Pascual	.90	.45	.25
306	Ty Cline	.70	.35	.20
307	Clay Carroll	.80	.40	.25
308	Tom Haller	.80	.40	.25
309	Diego Segui	.70	.35	.20
310	Frank Robinson	30.00	15.00	9.00
311	Reds Rookies (Tommy Helms, Dick Simpson)	.90	.45	.25
312	Bob Saverine	.70	.35	.20

		NR MT	EX	VG
313	Chris Zachary	.70	.35	.20
314	Hector Valle	.70	.35	.20
315	Norm Cash	2.00	1.00	.60
316	Jack Fisher	.80	.40	.25
317	Dalton Jones	.70	.35	.20
318	Harry Walker	.80	.40	.25
319	Gene Freese	.70	.35	.20
320	Bob Gibson	15.00	7.50	4.50
321	Rick Reichardt	.70	.35	.20
322	Bill Faul	.70	.35	.20
323	Ray Barker	1.00	.50	.30
324	John Boozer	.70	.35	.20
325	Vic Davalillo	.80	.40	.25
326	Braves Team	2.25	1.25	.70
327	Bernie Allen	.70	.35	.20
328	Jerry Grote	.90	.45	.25
329	Pete Charton	.70	.35	.20
330	Ron Fairly	.90	.45	.25
331	Ron Herbel	.70	.35	.20
332	Billy Bryan	.70	.35	.20
333	Senators Rookies (*Joe Coleman*, Jim French)	.90	.45	.25
334	Marty Keough	.70	.35	.20
335	Juan Pizarro	.70	.35	.20
336	Gene Alley	.80	.40	.25
337	Fred Gladding	.70	.35	.20
338	Dal Maxvill	.80	.40	.25
339	Del Crandall	1.00	.50	.30
340	Dean Chance	.80	.40	.25
341	Wes Westrum	.90	.45	.25
342	Bob Humphreys	.70	.35	.20
343	Joe Christopher	.70	.35	.20
344	Steve Blass	.80	.40	.25
345	Bob Allison	1.00	.50	.30
346	Mike de la Hoz	.70	.35	.20
347	Phil Regan	.70	.35	.20
348	Orioles Team	3.50	1.75	1.00
349	Cap Peterson	.70	.35	.20
350	Mel Stottlemyre	3.00	1.50	.90
351	Fred Valentine	.70	.35	.20
352	Bob Aspromonte	.70	.35	.20
353	Al McBean	.70	.35	.20
354	Smoky Burgess	1.00	.50	.30
355	Wade Blasingame	.70	.35	.20
356	Red Sox Rookies (Owen Johnson, Ken Sanders)	.70	.35	.20
357	Gerry Arrigo	.70	.35	.20
358	Charlie Smith	.70	.35	.20
359	Johnny Briggs	.70	.35	.20
360	Ron Hunt	.90	.45	.25
361	Tom Satriano	.70	.35	.20
362	Gates Brown	.70	.35	.20
363	Checklist 353-429	3.00	1.50	.90
364	Nate Oliver	.70	.35	.20
365	Roger Maris	75.00	38.00	23.00
366	Wayne Causey	.70	.35	.20
367	Mel Nelson	.70	.35	.20
368	Charlie Lau	.90	.45	.25
369	Jim King	.70	.35	.20
370	Chico Cardenas	.70	.35	.20
371	Lee Stange	.70	.35	.20
372	Harvey Kuenn	1.50	.70	.45
373	Giants Rookies (Dick Estelle, Jack Hiatt)	.70	.35	.20
374	Bob Locker	.70	.35	.20
375	Donn Clendenon	.80	.40	.25
376	Paul Schaal	.70	.35	.20
377	Turk Farrell	.70	.35	.20
378	Dick Tracewski	.70	.35	.20
379	Cardinals Team	2.25	1.25	.70
380	Tony Conigliaro	2.00	1.00	.60
381	Hank Fischer	.70	.35	.20
382	Phil Roof	.70	.35	.20
383	Jackie Brandt	.70	.35	.20
384	Al Downing	1.50	.70	.45
385	Ken Boyer	2.50	1.25	.70
386	Gil Hodges	5.00	2.50	1.50
387	Howie Reed	.70	.35	.20
388	Don Mincher	.80	.40	.25
389	Jim O'Toole	.70	.35	.20
390	Brooks Robinson	15.00	7.50	4.50
391	Chuck Hinton	.70	.35	.20
392	Cubs Rookies (*Bill Hands, Randy Hundley*)	.90	.45	.25
393	George Brunet	.70	.35	.20
394	Ron Brand	.70	.35	.20
395	Len Gabrielson	.70	.35	.20
396	Jerry Stephenson	.70	.35	.20
397	Bill White	1.00	.50	.30
398	Danny Cater	.70	.35	.20
399	Ray Washburn	.70	.35	.20
400	Zoilo Versalles	.80	.40	.25
401	Ken McMullen	.70	.35	.20
402	Jim Hickman	.90	.45	.25
403	Fred Talbot	.70	.35	.20
404	Pirates Team	2.25	1.25	.70
405	Elston Howard	4.00	2.00	1.25
406	Joe Jay	.70	.35	.20
407	John Kennedy	.70	.35	.20
408	Lee Thomas	.70	.35	.20
409	Billy Hoeft	.70	.35	.20
410	Al Kaline	18.00	9.00	5.50
411	Gene Mauch	.90	.45	.25
412	Sam Bowens	.70	.35	.20
413	John Romano	.70	.35	.20
414	Dan Coombs	.70	.35	.20
415	Max Alvis	.70	.35	.20
416	Phil Ortega	.70	.35	.20
417	Angels Rookies (Jim McGlothlin, Ed Sukla)	.70	.35	.20
418	Phil Gagliano	.70	.35	.20
419	Mike Ryan	.70	.35	.20
420	Juan Marichal	8.00	4.00	2.50
421	Roy McMillan	.80	.40	.25
422	Ed Charles	.70	.35	.20
423	Ernie Broglio	.70	.35	.20
424	Reds Rookies (*Lee May*, Darrell Osteen)	2.25	1.25	.70
425	Bob Veale	.80	.40	.25
426	White Sox Team	2.25	1.25	.70
427	John Miller	.70	.35	.20
428	Sandy Alomar	.70	.35	.20
429	Bill Monbouquette	.80	.40	.25
430	Don Drysdale	12.00	6.00	3.50

		NR MT	EX	VG
431	Walt Bond	.70	.35	.20
432	Bob Heffner	.70	.35	.20
433	Alvin Dark	.80	.40	.25
434	Willie Kirkland	.70	.35	.20
435	Jim Bunning	6.00	3.00	1.75
436	Julian Javier	.70	.35	.20
437	Al Stanek	.70	.35	.20
438	Willie Smith	.70	.35	.20
439	Pedro Ramos	1.00	.50	.30
440	Deron Johnson	.70	.35	.20
441	Tommie Sisk	.70	.35	.20
442	Orioles Rookies (Ed Barnowski, Eddie Watt)	.70	.35	.20
443	Bill Wakefield	.80	.40	.25
444a	Checklist 430-506 (456 is R. Sox Rookies)	3.00	1.50	.90
444b	Checklist 430-506 (456 is Red Sox Rookies)	5.00	2.50	1.50
445	Jim Kaat	4.00	2.00	1.25
446	Mack Jones	.70	.35	.20
447	Dick Ellsworth (photo actually Ken Hubbs)	3.50	1.75	1.00
448	Eddie Stanky	3.75	2.00	1.25
449	Joe Moeller	3.50	1.75	1.00
450	Tony Oliva	7.00	3.50	2.00
451	Barry Latman	3.50	1.75	1.00
452	Joe Azcue	3.50	1.75	1.00
453	Ron Kline	3.50	1.75	1.00
454	Jerry Buchek	3.50	1.75	1.00
455	Mickey Lolich	6.00	3.00	1.75
456	Red Sox Rookies (Darrell Brandon, Joe Foy)	3.50	1.75	1.00
457	Joe Gibbon	3.50	1.75	1.00
458	Manny Jiminez (Jimenez)	3.50	1.75	1.00
459	Bill McCool	3.50	1.75	1.00
460	Curt Blefary	3.50	1.75	1.00
461	Roy Face	6.00	3.00	1.75
462	Bob Rodgers	2.50	1.25	.70
463	Phillies Team	6.00	3.00	1.75
464	Larry Bearnarth	3.75	2.00	1.25
465	Don Buford	3.75	2.00	1.25
466	Ken Johnson	3.50	1.75	1.00
467	Vic Roznovsky	3.50	1.75	1.00
468	Johnny Podres	6.00	3.00	1.75
469	Yankees Rookies (*Bobby Murcer*, Dooley Womack)	9.00	4.50	2.75
470	Sam McDowell	4.00	2.00	1.25
471	Bob Skinner	3.50	1.75	1.00
472	Terry Fox	3.50	1.75	1.00
473	Rich Rollins	3.50	1.75	1.00
474	Dick Schofield	3.50	1.75	1.00
475	Dick Radatz	3.75	2.00	1.25
476	Bobby Bragan	3.75	2.00	1.25
477	Steve Barber	3.50	1.75	1.00
478	Tony Gonzalez	3.50	1.75	1.00
479	Jim Hannan	3.50	1.75	1.00
480	Dick Stuart	3.75	2.00	1.25
481	Bob Lee	3.50	1.75	1.00
482	Cubs Rookies (John Boccabella, Dave Dowling)	3.50	1.75	1.00
483	Joe Nuxhall	3.75	2.00	1.25
484	Wes Covington	3.50	1.75	1.00
485	Bob Bailey	3.50	1.75	1.00
486	Tommy John	15.00	7.50	4.50
487	Al Ferrara	3.50	1.75	1.00
488	George Banks	3.50	1.75	1.00
489	Curt Simmons	3.75	2.00	1.25
490	Bobby Richardson	12.00	6.00	3.50
491	Dennis Bennett	3.50	1.75	1.00
492	Athletics Team	5.00	2.50	1.50
493	Johnny Klippstein	3.50	1.75	1.00
494	Gordon Coleman	3.50	1.75	1.00
495	Dick McAuliffe	3.75	2.00	1.25
496	Lindy McDaniel	3.50	1.75	1.00
497	Chris Cannizzaro	3.50	1.75	1.00
498	Pirates Rookies (*Woody Fryman*, Luke Walker)	4.00	2.00	1.25
499	Wally Bunker	3.50	1.75	1.00
500	Hank Aaron	80.00	40.00	24.00
501	John O'Donoghue	3.50	1.75	1.00
502	Lenny Green	3.50	1.75	1.00
503	Steve Hamilton	3.75	2.00	1.25
504	Grady Hatton	3.50	1.75	1.00
505	Jose Cardenal	3.50	1.75	1.00
506	Bo Belinsky	3.75	2.00	1.25
507	John Edwards	3.50	1.75	1.00
508	*Steve Hargan*	3.75	2.00	1.25
509	Jake Wood	3.50	1.75	1.00
510	Hoyt Wilhelm	15.00	7.50	4.50
511	Giants Rookies (Bob Barton, *Tito Fuentes*)	3.75	2.00	1.25
512	Dick Stigman	3.50	1.75	1.00
513	Camilo Carreon	3.50	1.75	1.00
514	Hal Woodeshick	3.50	1.75	1.00
515	Frank Howard	7.00	3.50	2.00
516	Eddie Bressoud	2.00	1.00	.60
517a	Checklist 507-598 (529 is W. Sox Rookies)	9.00	4.50	2.75
517b	Checklist 506-598 (529 is White Sox Rookies)	10.00	5.00	3.00
518	Braves Rookies (Herb Hippauf, Arnie Umbach)	3.50	1.75	1.00
519	Bob Friend	6.00	3.00	1.75
520	Jim Wynn	4.00	2.00	1.25
521	John Wyatt	3.50	1.75	1.00
522	Phil Linz	3.50	1.75	1.00
523	Bob Sadowski	15.00	7.50	4.50
524	Giants Rookies (Ollie Brown, Don Mason)	20.00	10.00	6.00
525	Gary Bell	15.00	7.50	4.50
526	Twins Team	50.00	25.00	15.00
527	Julio Navarro	15.00	7.50	4.50
528	Jesse Gonder	20.00	10.00	6.00
529	White Sox Rookies (*Lee Elia*, Dennis Higgins, Bill Voss)	18.00	9.00	5.50
530	Robin Roberts	35.00	17.50	10.50
531	Joe Cunningham	15.00	7.50	4.50
532	Aurelio Monteagudo	15.00	7.50	4.50
533	Jerry Adair	15.00	7.50	4.50
534	Mets Rookies (Dave Eilers, Rob Gardner)	18.00	9.00	5.50
535	Willie Davis	25.00	12.50	7.50
536	Dick Egan	15.00	7.50	4.50
537	Herman Franks	15.00	7.50	4.50

		NR MT	EX	VG
538	Bob Allen	15.00	7.50	4.50
539	Astros Rookies (Bill Heath, Carroll Sembera)	15.00	7.50	4.50
540	Denny McLain	35.00	17.50	10.50
541	Gene Oliver	15.00	7.50	4.50
542	George Smith	15.00	7.50	4.50
543	Roger Craig	20.00	10.00	6.00
544	Cardinals Rookies (Joe Hoerner, George Kernek, Jimmy Williams)	20.00	10.00	6.00
545	Dick Green	20.00	10.00	6.00
546	Dwight Siebler	15.00	7.50	4.50
547	*Horace Clarke*	20.00	10.00	6.00
548	Gary Kroll	20.00	10.00	6.00
549	Senators Rookies (Al Closter, Casey Cox)	15.00	7.50	4.50
550	Willie McCovey	95.00	45.00	27.00
551	Bob Purkey	20.00	10.00	6.00
552	Birdie Tebbetts	15.00	7.50	4.50
553	Major League Rookies (Pat Garrett, Jackie Warner)	15.00	7.50	4.50
554	Jim Northrup	18.00	9.00	5.50
555	Ron Perranoski	18.00	9.00	5.50
556	Mel Queen	20.00	10.00	6.00
557	Felix Mantilla	15.00	7.50	4.50
558	Red Sox Rookies (Guido Grilli, Pete Magrini, *George Scott*)	18.00	9.00	5.50
559	Roberto Pena	15.00	7.50	4.50
560	Joel Horlen	15.00	7.50	4.50
561	Choo Choo Coleman	20.00	10.00	6.00
562	Russ Snyder	15.00	7.50	4.50
563	Twins Rookies (Pete Cimino, Cesar Tovar)	18.00	9.00	5.50
564	Bob Chance	15.00	7.50	4.50
565	Jimmy Piersall	30.00	15.00	9.00
566	Mike Cuellar	18.00	9.00	5.50
567	Dick Howser	20.00	10.00	6.00
568	Athletics Rookies (Paul Lindblad, Ron Stone)	15.00	7.50	4.50
569	Orlando McFarlane	15.00	7.50	4.50
570	Art Mahaffey	20.00	10.00	6.00
571	Dave Roberts	15.00	7.50	4.50
572	Bob Priddy	15.00	7.50	4.50
573	Derrell Griffith	15.00	7.50	4.50
574	Mets Rookies (Bill Hepler, Bill Murphy)	18.00	9.00	5.50
575	Earl Wilson	15.00	7.50	4.50
576	Dave Nicholson	20.00	10.00	6.00
577	Jack Lamabe	15.00	7.50	4.50
578	Chi Chi Olivo	15.00	7.50	4.50
579	Orioles Rookies (Frank Bertaina, Gene Brabender, Dave Johnson)	20.00	10.00	6.00
580	Billy Williams	70.00	35.00	21.00
581	Tony Martinez	15.00	7.50	4.50
582	Garry Roggenburk	15.00	7.50	4.50
583	Tigers Team	100.00	45.00	27.00
584	Yankees Rookies (Frank Fernandez, *Fritz Peterson*)	18.00	9.00	5.50
585	Tony Taylor	15.00	7.50	4.50
586	Claude Raymond	15.00	7.50	4.50
587	Dick Bertell	15.00	7.50	4.50
588	Athletics Rookies (Chuck Dobson, Ken Suarez)	15.00	7.50	4.50
589	Lou Klimchock	18.00	9.00	5.50
590	Bill Skowron	35.00	17.50	10.50
591	N.L. Rookies (*Grant Jackson*, Bart Shirley)	20.00	10.00	6.00
592	Andre Rodgers	15.00	7.50	4.50
593	Doug Camilli	20.00	10.00	6.00
594	Chico Salmon	15.00	7.50	4.50
595	Larry Jackson	15.00	7.50	4.50
596	Astros Rookies (*Nate Colbert*, Greg Sims)	18.00	9.00	5.50
597	John Sullivan	15.00	7.50	4.50
598	Gaylord Perry	275.00	110.00	69.00

1966 Topps Rub-Offs

Returning to a concept last tried in 1961, Topps tried an expanded version of Rub-Offs in 1966. Measuring 2-1/16" by 3," the Rub-Offs are in vertical format for the 100 players and horizontal for the 20 team pennants. The player Rub-Offs feature a color photo.

	NR MT	EX	VG
Complete Set:	225.00	112.00	67.00
Common Player:	.60	.30	.20

		NR MT	EX	VG
(1)	Hank Aaron	8.00	4.00	2.50
(2)	Jerry Adair	.60	.30	.20
(3)	Richie Allen	1.00	.50	.30
(4)	Jesus Alou	.60	.30	.20
(5)	Max Alvis	.60	.30	.20
(6)	Bob Aspromonte	.60	.30	.20
(7)	Ernie Banks	3.50	1.75	1.00

		NR MT	EX	VG
(8)	Earl Battey	.70	.35	.20
(9)	Curt Blefary	.60	.30	.20
(10)	Ken Boyer	1.00	.50	.30
(11)	Bob Bruce	.60	.30	.20
(12)	Jim Bunning	1.50	.70	.45
(13)	Johnny Callison	.70	.35	.20
(14)	Bert Campaneris	.70	.35	.20
(15)	Jose Cardenal	.60	.30	.20
(16)	Dean Chance	.60	.30	.20
(17)	Ed Charles	.60	.30	.20
(18)	Bob Clemente	7.00	3.50	2.00
(19)	Tony Cloninger	.60	.30	.20
(20)	Rocky Colavito	1.00	.50	.30
(21)	Tony Conigliaro	1.00	.50	.30
(22)	Vic Davalillo	.60	.30	.20
(23)	Willie Davis	.70	.35	.20
(24)	Don Drysdale	3.00	1.50	.90
(25)	Sammy Ellis	.60	.30	.20
(26)	Dick Ellsworth	.60	.30	.20
(27)	Ron Fairly	.70	.35	.20
(28)	Dick Farrell	.60	.30	.20
(29)	Eddie Fisher	.60	.30	.20
(30)	Jack Fisher	.60	.30	.20
(31)	Curt Flood	.70	.35	.20
(32)	Whitey Ford	3.50	1.75	1.00
(33)	Bill Freehan	.70	.35	.20
(34)	Jim Fregosi	.70	.35	.20
(35)	Bob Gibson	3.00	1.50	.90
(36)	Jim Grant	.60	.30	.20
(37)	Jimmie Hall	.60	.30	.20
(38)	Ken Harrelson	.70	.35	.20
(39)	Jim Hart	.60	.30	.20
(40)	Joel Horlen	.60	.30	.20
(41)	Willie Horton	.70	.35	.20
(42)	Frank Howard	1.00	.50	.30
(43)	Deron Johnson	.60	.30	.20
(44)	Al Kaline	4.00	2.00	1.25
(45)	Harmon Killebrew	4.00	2.00	1.25
(46)	Bobby Knoop	.60	.30	.20
(47)	Sandy Koufax	7.00	3.50	2.00
(48)	Ed Kranepool	.60	.30	.20
(49)	Gary Kroll	.60	.30	.20
(50)	Don Landrum	.60	.30	.20
(51)	Vernon Law	.70	.35	.20
(52)	Johnny Lewis	.60	.30	.20
(53)	Don Lock	.60	.30	.20
(54)	Mickey Lolich	1.00	.50	.30
(55)	Jim Maloney	.60	.30	.20
(56)	Felix Mantilla	.60	.30	.20
(57)	Mickey Mantle	40.00	20.00	12.00
(58)	Juan Marichal	3.00	1.50	.90
(59)	Ed Mathews	3.00	1.50	.90
(60)	Willie Mays	8.00	4.00	2.50
(61)	Bill Mazeroski	1.00	.50	.30
(62)	Dick McAuliffe	.60	.30	.20
(63)	Tim McCarver	.70	.35	.20
(64)	Willie McCovey	3.00	1.50	.90
(65)	Sammy McDowell	.70	.35	.20
(66)	Ken McMullen	.60	.30	.20
(67)	Denis Menke	.60	.30	.20
(68)	Bill Monbouquette	.60	.30	.20
(69)	Joe Morgan	2.00	1.00	.60
(70)	Fred Newman	.60	.30	.20
(71)	John O'Donoghue	.60	.30	.20
(72)	Tony Oliva	1.00	.50	.30
(73)	Johnny Orsino	.60	.30	.20
(74)	Phil Ortega	.60	.30	.20
(75)	Milt Pappas	.70	.35	.20
(76)	Dick Radatz	.60	.30	.20
(77)	Bobby Richardson	1.50	.70	.45
(78)	Pete Richert	.60	.30	.20
(79)	Brooks Robinson	4.00	2.00	1.25
(80)	Floyd Robinson	.60	.30	.20
(81)	Frank Robinson	3.50	1.75	1.00
(82)	Cookie Rojas	.60	.30	.20
(83)	Pete Rose	20.00	10.00	6.00
(84)	John Roseboro	.60	.30	.20
(85)	Ron Santo	1.00	.50	.30
(86)	Bill Skowron	.70	.35	.20
(87)	Willie Stargell	3.00	1.50	.90
(88)	Mel Stottlemyre	.70	.35	.20
(89)	Dick Stuart	.60	.30	.20
(90)	Ron Swoboda	.60	.30	.20
(91)	Fred Talbot	.60	.30	.20
(92)	Ralph Terry	.60	.30	.20
(93)	Joe Torre	1.00	.50	.30
(94)	Tom Tresh	.70	.35	.20
(95)	Bob Veale	.60	.30	.20
(96)	Pete Ward	.60	.30	.20
(97)	Bill White	.70	.35	.20
(98)	Billy Williams	2.00	1.00	.60
(99)	Jim Wynn	.70	.35	.20
(100)	Carl Yastrzemski	12.00	6.00	3.50
(101)	Angels Pennant	.60	30	.20
(102)	Astros Pennant	.60	.30	.20
(103)	Athletics Pennant	.60	.30	.20
(104)	Braves Pennant	.60	.30	.20
(105)	Cards Pennant	.60	.30	.20
(106)	Cubs Pennant	.60	.30	.20
(107)	Dodgers Pennant	.60	.30	.20
(108)	Giants Pennant	.60	.30	.20
(109)	Indians Pennant	.60	.30	.20
(110)	Mets Pennant	.60	.30	.20
(111)	Orioles Pennant	.60	.30	.20
(112)	Phillies Pennant	.60	.30	.20
(113)	Pirates Pennant	.60	.30	.20
(114)	Red Sox Pennant	.60	.30	.20
(115)	Reds Pennant	.60	.30	.20
(116)	Senators Pennant	.60	.30	.20
(117)	Tigers Pennant	.60	.30	.20
(118)	Twins Pennant	.60	.30	.20
(119)	White Sox Pennant	.60	.30	.20
(120)	Yankees Pennant	.60	.30	.20

1967 Topps

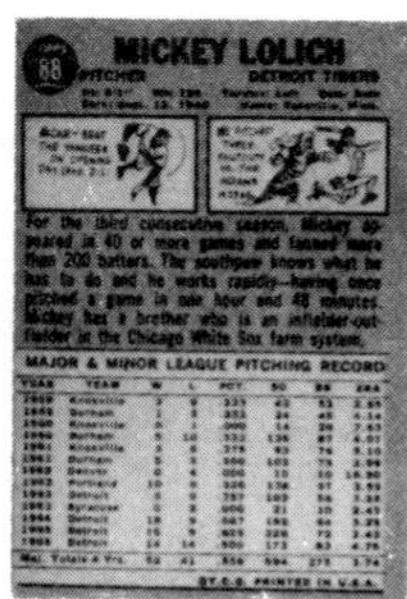

This 609-card set of 2-1/2" by 3-1/2" cards marked the largest set up to that time for Topps. Card fronts feature large color photographs bordered by white. The player's name and position are printed at the top with the team at the bottom. Across the front of the card with the exception of #254 (Milt Pappas) there is a facsimile autograph. The backs were the first to be done vertically, although they continued to carry familiar statistical and biographical information. The only subsets are statistical leaders and World Series highlights. Rookie cards are done by team or league with two players per card. The high numbers (#'s 534-609) in '67 are quite scarce, and while it is known that some are even scarcer, by virtue of having been short-printed in relation to the rest of the series, there is no general agreement on which cards are involved.

		NR MT	EX	VG
	Complete Set:	4000.	2000.	1200.
	Common Player: 1-110	.60	.30	.20
	Common Player: 111-370	.70	.35	.20
	Common Player: 371-457	.80	.40	.25
	Common Player: 458-533	3.00	1.50	.90
	Common Player: 534-609	5.00	2.50	1.50
1	The Champs (Hank Bauer, Brooks Robinson, Frank Robinson)	8.00	4.00	2.50
2	Jack Hamilton	.80	.40	.25
3	Duke Sims	.60	.30	.20
4	Hal Lanier	.80	.40	.25
5	Whitey Ford	12.00	6.00	3.50
6	Dick Simpson	.60	.30	.20
7	Don McMahon	.60	.30	.20
8	Chuck Harrison	.60	.30	.20
9	Ron Hansen	.60	.30	.20
10	Matty Alou	.80	.40	.25
11	Barry Moore	.60	.30	.20
12	Dodgers Rookies (Jimmy Campanis, Bill Singer)	.70	.35	.20
13	Joe Sparma	.60	.30	.20
14	Phil Linz	.60	.30	.20
15	Earl Battey	.70	.35	.20
16	Bill Hands	.60	.30	.20
17	Jim Gosger	.60	.30	.20
18	Gene Oliver	.60	.30	.20
19	Jim McGlothlin	.60	.30	.20
20	Orlando Cepeda	4.00	2.00	1.25
21	Dave Bristol	.60	.30	.20
22	Gene Brabender	.60	.30	.20
23	Larry Elliot	.70	.35	.20
24	Bob Allen	.60	.30	.20
25	Elston Howard	3.00	1.50	.90
26a	Bob Priddy (no trade statement)	8.00	4.00	2.50
26b	Bob Priddy (with trade statement)	.60	.30	.20
27	Bob Saverine	.60	.30	.20
28	Barry Latman	.60	.30	.20
29	Tommy McCraw	.60	.30	.20
30	Al Kaline	20.00	10.00	6.00
31	Jim Brewer	.60	.30	.20
32	Bob Bailey	.60	.30	.20
33	Athletics Rookies (*Sal Bando*, Randy Schwartz)	1.75	.90	.50
34	Pete Cimino	.60	.30	.20
35	Rico Carty	1.00	.50	.30
36	Bob Tillman	.60	.30	.20
37	Rick Wise	.70	.35	.20
38	Bob Johnson	.60	.30	.20
39	Curt Simmons	.80	.40	.25
40	Rick Reichardt	.60	.30	.20
41	Joe Hoerner	.60	.30	.20
42	Mets Team	3.00	1.50	.90
43	Chico Salmon	.60	.30	.20
44	Joe Nuxhall	.80	.40	.25
45	Roger Maris	40.00	20.00	12.00
46	Lindy McDaniel	.60	.30	.20
47	Ken McMullen	.60	.30	.20
48	Bill Freehan	.80	.40	.25
49	Roy Face	1.25	.60	.40
50	Tony Oliva	2.50	1.25	.70
51	Astros Rookies (Dave Adlesh, Wes Bales)	.60	.30	.20
52	Dennis Higgins	.60	.30	.20
53	Clay Dalrymple	.60	.30	.20
54	Dick Green	.60	.30	.20
55	Don Drysdale	12.00	6.00	3.50
56	Jose Tartabull	.60	.30	.20
57	*Pat Jarvis*	.70	.35	.20
58	Paul Schaal	.60	.30	.20
59	Ralph Terry	.80	.40	.25
60	Luis Aparicio	5.00	2.50	1.50
61	Gordy Coleman	.60	.30	.20
62	Checklist 1-109 (Frank Robinson)	3.00	1.50	.90
63	Cards' Clubbers (Lou Brock, Curt Flood)	4.50	2.25	1.25
64	Fred Valentine	.60	.30	.20
65	Tom Haller	.70	.35	.20
66	Manny Mota	.80	.40	.25
67	Ken Berry	.60	.30	.20
68	Bob Buhl	.70	.35	.20
69	Vic Davalillo	.70	.35	.20
70	Ron Santo	1.75	.90	.50
71	Camilo Pascual	.70	.35	.20
72	Tigers Rookies (George Korince, John Matchick)	.60	.30	.20
73	Rusty Staub	2.50	1.25	.70
74	Wes Stock	.60	.30	.20
75	George Scott	1.00	.50	.30
76	Jim Barbieri	.60	.30	.20
77	Dooley Womack	.80	.40	.25
78	Pat Corrales	1.00	.50	.30
79	Bubba Morton	.60	.30	.20
80	Jim Maloney	.70	.35	.20
81	Eddie Stanky	.70	.35	.20
82	Steve Barber	.60	.30	.20
83	Ollie Brown	.60	.30	.20
84	Tommie Sisk	.60	.30	.20
85	Johnny Callison	1.00	.50	.30
86a	Mike McCormick (no trade statement)	9.00	4.50	2.75
86b	Mike McCormick (with trade statement)	.70	.35	.20
87	George Altman	.60	.30	.20
88	Mickey Lolich	2.25	1.25	.70
89	*Felix Millan*	.80	.40	.25
90	Jim Nash	.60	.30	.20
91	Johnny Lewis	.70	.35	.20
92	Ray Washburn	.60	.30	.20
93	Yankees Rookies (*Stan Bahnsen*, Bobby Murcer)	2.50	1.25	.70
94	Ron Fairly	.80	.40	.25
95	Sonny Siebert	.70	.35	.20
96	Art Shamsky	.60	.30	.20
97	Mike Cuellar	.80	.40	.25
98	Rich Rollins	.60	.30	.20
99	Lee Stange	.60	.30	.20
100	Frank Robinson	18.00	9.00	5.50
101	Ken Johnson	.60	.30	.20
102	Phillies Team	2.00	1.00	.60
103a	Checklist 110-196 (Mickey Mantle) (170 is D McAuliffe)	8.00	4.00	2.50
103b	Checklist 110-196 (Mickey Mantle) (170 is D. McAuliffe)	6.00	3.00	1.75
104	Minnie Rojas	.60	.30	.20
105	Ken Boyer	2.00	1.00	.60
106	Randy Hundley	.70	.35	.20
107	Joel Horlen	.60	.30	.20
108	Alex Johnson	.60	.30	.20
109	Tribe Thumpers (Rocky Colavito, Leon Wagner)	1.50	.70	.45
110	Jack Aker	.60	.30	.20
111	John Kennedy	.70	.35	.20
112	Dave Wickersham	.70	.35	.20
113	Dave Nicholson	.70	.35	.20
114	Jack Baldschun	.70	.35	.20
115	Paul Casanova	.70	.35	.20
116	Herman Franks	.70	.35	.20
117	Darrell Brandon	.70	.35	.20
118	Bernie Allen	.70	.35	.20
119	Wade Blasingame	.70	.35	.20
120	Floyd Robinson	.70	.35	.20
121	Ed Bressoud	.80	.40	.25
122	George Brunet	.70	.35	.20
123	Pirates Rookies (Jim Price, Luke Walker)	.70	.35	.20
124	Jim Stewart	.70	.35	.20
125	Moe Drabowsky	.70	.35	.20
126	Tony Taylor	.70	.35	.20
127	John O'Donoghue	.70	.35	.20
128	Ed Spiezio	.70	.35	.20
129	Phil Roof	.70	.35	.20
130	Phil Regan	.70	.35	.20
131	Yankees Team	4.00	2.00	1.25
132	Ozzie Virgil	.70	.35	.20
133	Ron Kline	.70	.35	.20
134	Gates Brown	.70	.35	.20
135	Deron Johnson	.70	.35	.20
136	Carroll Sembera	.70	.35	.20
137	Twins Rookies (Ron Clark, Jim Ollom)	.70	.35	.20
138	Dick Kelley	.70	.35	.20
139	Dalton Jones	.70	.35	.20
140	Willie Stargell	20.00	10.00	6.00
141	John Miller	.70	.35	.20
142	Jackie Brandt	.70	.35	.20
143	Sox Sockers (Don Buford, Pete Ward)	.80	.40	.25
144	Bill Hepler	.80	.40	.25
145	Larry Brown	.70	.35	.20
146	Steve Carlton	75.00	38.00	23.00
147	Tom Egan	.70	.35	.20
148	Adolfo Phillips	.70	.35	.20
149	Joe Moeller	.70	.35	.20
150	Mickey Mantle	200.00	80.00	50.00
151	World Series Game 1 (Moe Mows Down 11)	2.00	1.00	.60
152	World Series Game 2 (Palmer Blanks Dodgers)	3.50	1.75	1.00
153	World Series Game 3 (Blair's Homer Defeats L.A.)	2.00	1.00	.60
154	World Series Game 4 (Orioles Win 4th Straight)	2.00	1.00	.60
155	World Series Summary (The Winners Celebrate)	2.00	1.00	.60
156	Ron Herbel	.70	.35	.20
157	Danny Cater	.70	.35	.20
158	Jimmy Coker	.70	.35	.20
159	Bruce Howard	.70	.35	.20
160	Willie Davis	1.25	.60	.40
161	Dick Williams	1.25	.60	.40
162	Billy O'Dell	.70	.35	.20
163	Vic Roznovsky	.70	.35	.20
164	Dwight Siebler	.70	.35	.20
165	Cleon Jones	.80	.40	.25
166	Ed Mathews	8.00	4.00	2.50
167	Senators Rookies (Joe Coleman, Tim Cullen)	.80	.40	.25
168	Ray Culp	.70	.35	.20
169	Horace Clarke	1.00	.50	.30
170	Dick McAuliffe	.80	.40	.25
171	Calvin Koonce	.70	.35	.20

		NR MT	EX	VG
172	Bill Heath	.70	.35	.20
173	Cardinals Team	2.00	1.00	.60
174	Dick Radatz	.80	.40	.25
175	Bobby Knoop	.70	.35	.20
176	Sammy Ellis	.70	.35	.20
177	Tito Fuentes	.70	.35	.20
178	John Buzhardt	.70	.35	.20
179	Braves Rookies (Cecil Upshaw, Chas. Vaughn)	.70	.35	.20
180	Curt Blefary	.70	.35	.20
181	Terry Fox	.70	.35	.20
182	Ed Charles	.70	.35	.20
183	Jim Pagliaroni	.70	.35	.20
184	George Thomas	.70	.35	.20
185	*Ken Holtzman*	2.75	1.50	.80
186	Mets Maulers (Ed Kranepool, Ron Swoboda)	1.50	.70	.45
187	Pedro Ramos	.70	.35	.20
188	Ken Harrelson	1.50	.70	.45
189	Chuck Hinton	.70	.35	.20
190	Turk Farrell	.70	.35	.20
191a	Checklist 197-283 (Willie Mays) (214 is Dick Kelley)	5.00	2.50	1.50
191b	Checklist 197-283 (Willie Mays) (214 is Tom Kelley)	4.00	2.00	1.25
192	Fred Gladding	.70	.35	.20
193	Jose Cardenal	.80	.40	.25
194	Bob Allison	.90	.45	.25
195	Al Jackson	.70	.35	.20
196	Johnny Romano	.70	.35	.20
197	Ron Perranoski	.80	.40	.25
198	Chuck Hiller	.80	.40	.25
199	Billy Hitchcock	.70	.35	.20
200	Willie Mays	75.00	38.00	23.00
201	Hal Reniff	1.00	.50	.30
202	Johnny Edwards	.70	.35	.20
203	Al McBean	.70	.35	.20
204	Orioles Rookies (*Mike Epstein*, Tom Phoebus)	.90	.45	.25
205	Dick Groat	1.50	.70	.45
206	Dennis Bennett	.70	.35	.20
207	John Orsino	.70	.35	.20
208	Jack Lamabe	.70	.35	.20
209	Joe Nossek	.70	.35	.20
210	Bob Gibson	10.00	5.00	3.00
211	Twins Team	2.00	1.00	.60
212	Chris Zachary	.70	.35	.20
213	*Jay Johnstone*	1.75	.90	.50
214	Tom Kelley	.70	.35	.20
215	Ernie Banks	18.00	9.00	5.50
216	Bengal Belters (Norm Cash, Al Kaline)	3.50	1.75	1.00
217	Rob Gardner	.80	.40	.25
218	Wes Parker	.80	.40	.25
219	Clay Carroll	.80	.40	.25
220	Jim Hart	.80	.40	.25
221	Woody Fryman	.80	.40	.25
222	Reds Rookies (Lee May, Darrell Osteen)	1.00	.50	.30
223	Mike Ryan	.70	.35	.20
224	Walt Bond	.70	.35	.20
225	Mel Stottlemyre	2.25	1.25	.70
226	Julian Javier	.80	.40	.25
227	Paul Lindblad	.70	.35	.20
228	Gil Hodges	5.00	2.50	1.50
229	Larry Jackson	.70	.35	.20
230	Boog Powell	2.50	1.25	.70
231	John Bateman	.70	.35	.20
232	Don Buford	.80	.40	.25
233	A.L. ERA Leaders (Steve Hargan, Joel Horlen, Gary Peters)	2.00	1.00	.60
234	N.L. ERA Leaders (Mike Cuellar, Sandy Koufax, Juan Marichal)	4.00	2.00	1.25
235	A.L. Pitching Leaders (Jim Kaat, Denny McLain, Earl Wilson)	2.50	1.25	.70
236	N.L. Pitching Leaders (Bob Gibson, Sandy Koufax, Juan Marichal, Gaylord Perry)	5.00	2.50	1.50
237	A.L. Strikeout Leaders (Jim Kaat, Sam McDowell, Earl Wilson)	2.50	1.25	.70
238	N.L. Strikeout Leaders (Jim Bunning, Sandy Koufax, Bob Veale)	4.00	2.00	1.25
239	AL 1966 Batting Leaders (Al Kaline, Tony Oliva, Frank Robinson)	4.00	2.00	1.25
240	N.L. Batting Leaders (Felipe Alou, Matty Alou, Rico Carty)	2.00	1.00	.60
241	A.L. RBI Leaders (Harmon Killebrew, Boog Powell, Frank Robinson)	3.50	1.75	1.00
242	N.L. RBI Leaders (Hank Aaron, Richie Allen, Bob Clemente)	5.00	2.50	1.50
243	A.L. Home Run Leaders (Harmon Killebrew, Boog Powell, Frank Robinson)	3.50	1.75	1.00
244	N.L. Home Run Leaders (Hank Aaron, Richie Allen, Willie Mays)	5.00	2.50	1.50
245	Curt Flood	1.50	.70	.45
246	Jim Perry	1.00	.50	.30
247	Jerry Lumpe	.80	.40	.25
248	Gene Mauch	.80	.40	.25
249	Nick Willhite	.70	.35	.20
250	Hank Aaron	75.00	38.00	23.00
251	Woody Held	.70	.35	.20
252	Bob Bolin	.70	.35	.20
253	Indians Rookies (Bill Davis, Gus Gil)	.70	.35	.20
254	Milt Pappas	.80	.40	.25
255	Frank Howard	2.50	1.25	.70
256	Bob Hendley	.70	.35	.20
257	Charley Smith	1.00	.50	.30
258	Lee Maye	.70	.35	.20
259	Don Dennis	.70	.35	.20
260	Jim Lefebvre	.80	.40	.25
261	John Wyatt	.70	.35	.20
262	Athletics Team	2.00	1.00	.60
263	Hank Aguirre	.70	.35	.20
264	Ron Swoboda	.80	.40	.25
265	Lou Burdette	1.50	.70	.45
266	Pitt Power (Donn Clendenon, Willie Stargell)	3.50	1.75	1.00
267	Don Schwall	.70	.35	.20
268	John Briggs	.70	.35	.20
269	Don Nottebart	.70	.35	.20
270	Zoilo Versalles	.80	.40	.25
271	Eddie Watt	.70	.35	.20
272	Cubs Rookies (Bill Connors, Dave Dowling)	.70	.35	.20
273	Dick Lines	.70	.35	.20
274	Bob Aspromonte	.70	.35	.20
275	Fred Whitfield	.70	.35	.20
276	Bruce Brubaker	.70	.35	.20
277	Steve Whitaker	1.00	.50	.30
278	Checklist 284-370 (Jim Kaat)	3.00	1.50	.90
279	Frank Linzy	.70	.35	.20
280	Tony Conigliaro	2.00	1.00	.60
281	Bob Rodgers	.70	.35	.20
282	Johnny Odom	.80	.40	.25
283	Gene Alley	.80	.40	.25
284	Johnny Podres	3.00	1.50	.90
285	Lou Brock	15.00	7.50	4.50
286	Wayne Causey	.70	.35	.20
287	Mets Rookies (Greg Goossen, Bart Shirley)	.80	.40	.25
288	Denver Lemaster	.70	.35	.20
289	Tom Tresh	1.75	.90	.50
290	Bill White	1.00	.50	.30
291	Jim Hannan	.70	.35	.20
292	Don Pavletich	.70	.35	.20
293	Ed Kirkpatrick	.70	.35	.20
294	Walt Alston	3.25	1.75	1.00
295	Sam McDowell	1.00	.50	.30
296	Glenn Beckert	.80	.40	.25
297	Dave Morehead	.70	.35	.20
298	Ron Davis	.70	.35	.20
299	Norm Siebern	.80	.40	.25
300	Jim Kaat	4.50	2.25	1.25
301	Jesse Gonder	.70	.35	.20
302	Orioles Team	2.00	1.00	.60
303	Gil Blanco	.70	.35	.20
304	Phil Gagliano	.70	.35	.20
305	Earl Wilson	.70	.35	.20
306	*Bud Harrelson*	1.75	.90	.50
307	Jim Beauchamp	.70	.35	.20
308	Al Downing	1.25	.60	.40
309	Hurlers Beware (Richie Allen, Johnny Callison)	2.00	1.00	.60
310	Gary Peters	.80	.40	.25
311	Ed Brinkman	.80	.40	.25
312	Don Mincher	.80	.40	.25
313	Bob Lee	.70	.35	.20
314	Red Sox Rookies (*Mike Andrews, Reggie Smith*)	3.00	1.50	.90
315	Billy Williams	8.00	4.00	2.50
316	Jack Kralick	.70	.35	.20
317	Cesar Tovar	.70	.35	.20
318	Dave Giusti	.70	.35	.20
319	Paul Blair	.80	.40	.25
320	Gaylord Perry	8.00	4.00	2.50
321	Mayo Smith	.70	.35	.20
322	Jose Pagan	.70	.35	.20
323	Mike Hershberger	.70	.35	.20
324	Hal Woodeshick	.70	.35	.20
325	Chico Cardenas	.70	.35	.20
326	Bob Uecker	20.00	10.00	6.00
327	Angels Team	2.00	1.00	.60
328	Clete Boyer	.90	.45	.25
329	Charlie Lau	.80	.40	.25
330	Claude Osteen	.80	.40	.25
331	Joe Foy	.70	.35	.20
332	Jesus Alou	.70	.35	.20
333	Ferguson Jenkins	10.00	5.00	3.00
334	Twin Terrors (Bob Allison, Harmon Killebrew)	3.50	1.75	1.00
335	Bob Veale	.80	.40	.25
336	Joe Azcue	.70	.35	.20
337	Joe Morgan	15.00	7.50	4.50
338	Bob Locker	.70	.35	.20
339	Chico Ruiz	.70	.35	.20
340	Joe Pepitone	2.00	1.00	.60
341	Giants Rookies (*Dick Dietz*, Bill Sorrell)	.80	.40	.25
342	Hank Fischer	.70	.35	.20
343	Tom Satriano	.70	.35	.20
344	Ossie Chavarria	.70	.35	.20
345	Stu Miller	.70	.35	.20
346	Jim Hickman	.80	.40	.25
347	Grady Hatton	.70	.35	.20
348	Tug McGraw	2.25	1.25	.70
349	Bob Chance	.70	.35	.20
350	Joe Torre	2.00	1.00	.60
351	Vern Law	1.25	.60	.40
352	Ray Oyler	.70	.35	.20
353	Bill McCool	.70	.35	.20
354	Cubs Team	2.00	1.00	.60
355	Carl Yastrzemski	90.00	45.00	27.00
356	Larry Jaster	.70	.35	.20
357	Bill Skowron	1.50	.70	.45
358	Ruben Amaro	1.00	.50	.30
359	Dick Ellsworth	.70	.35	.20
360	Leon Wagner	.80	.40	.25
361	Checklist 371-457 (Bob Clemente)	4.50	2.25	1.25
362	Darold Knowles	.70	.35	.20
363	Dave Johnson	2.00	1.00	.60
364	Claude Raymond	.70	.35	.20
365	John Roseboro	.80	.40	.25
366	Andy Kosco	.70	.35	.20
367	Angels Rookies (Bill Kelso, Don Wallace)	.70	.35	.20
368	Jack Hiatt	.70	.35	.20
369	Jim Hunter	8.00	4.00	2.50
370	Tommy Davis	1.50	.70	.45
371	Jim Lonborg	1.50	.70	.45
372	Mike de la Hoz	.80	.40	.25
373	White Sox Rookies (Duane Josephson, Fred Klages)	.80	.40	.25
374	Mel Queen	.80	.40	.25
375	Jake Gibbs	1.00	.50	.30
376	Don Lock	.80	.40	.25
377	Luis Tiant	2.25	1.25	.70
378	Tigers Team	3.00	1.50	.90
379	Jerry May	.80	.40	.25
380	Dean Chance	.90	.45	.25
381	Dick Schofield	.80	.40	.25
382	Dave McNally	1.00	.50	.30
383	Ken Henderson	.80	.40	.25
384	Cardinals Rookies (Jim Cosman, Dick Hughes)	.80	.40	.25
385	Jim Fregosi	1.25	.60	.40
386	Dick Selma	.90	.45	.25
387	Cap Peterson	.80	.40	.25
388	Arnold Earley	.80	.40	.25
389	Al Dark	.90	.45	.25
390	Jim Wynn	1.00	.50	.30
391	Wilbur Wood	.90	.45	.25
392	Tommy Harper	.90	.45	.25
393	Jim Bouton	2.25	1.25	.70
394	Jake Wood	.80	.40	.25
395	Chris Short	1.00	.50	.30
396	Atlanta Aces (Tony Cloninger, Denis Menke)	1.00	.50	.30
397	Willie Smith	.80	.40	.25
398	Jeff Torborg	.90	.45	.25
399	Al Worthington	.80	.40	.25
400	Bob Clemente	55.00	28.00	16.50
401	Jim Coates	.80	.40	.25
402	Phillies Rookies (Grant Jackson, Billy Wilson)	.80	.40	.25
403	Dick Nen	.80	.40	.25
404	Nelson Briles	.90	.45	.25
405	Russ Snyder	.80	.40	.25
406	Lee Elia	.90	.45	.25
407	Reds Team	2.50	1.25	.70
408	Jim Northrup	.90	.45	.25
409	Ray Sadecki	.80	.40	.25
410	Lou Johnson	.80	.40	.25
411	Dick Howser	1.50	.70	.45
412	Astros Rookies (Norm Miller, *Doug Rader*)	1.00	.50	.30
413	Jerry Grote	.90	.45	.25
414	Casey Cox	.80	.40	.25
415	Sonny Jackson	.80	.40	.25
416	Roger Repoz	.80	.40	.25
417	Bob Bruce	.80	.40	.25
418	Sam Mele	.80	.40	.25
419	Don Kessinger	.90	.45	.25
420	Denny McLain	3.00	1.50	.90
421	Dal Maxvill	.90	.45	.25
422	Hoyt Wilhelm	8.00	4.00	2.50
423	Fence Busters (Willie Mays, Willie McCovey)	12.00	6.00	3.50
424	Pedro Gonzalez	.80	.40	.25
425	Pete Mikkelsen	.80	.40	.25
426	Lou Clinton	1.00	.50	.30
427	Ruben Gomez	.80	.40	.25
428	Dodgers Rookies (Tom Hutton, *Gene Michael*)	1.00	.50	.30
429	Garry Roggenburk	.80	.40	.25
430	Pete Rose	75.00	37.00	22.00
431	Ted Uhlaender	.80	.40	.25
432	Jimmie Hall	.80	.40	.25
433	Al Luplow	.90	.45	.25
434	Eddie Fisher	.80	.40	.25
435	Mack Jones	.80	.40	.25
436	Pete Ward	.80	.40	.25
437	Senators Team	2.25	1.25	.70
438	Chuck Dobson	.80	.40	.25
439	Byron Browne	.80	.40	.25
440	Steve Hargan	.80	.40	.25
441	Jim Davenport	.80	.40	.25
442	Yankees Rookies (*Bill Robinson*, Joe Verbanic)	1.25	.60	.40
443	Tito Francona	.90	.45	.25
444	George Smith	.80	.40	.25
445	Don Sutton	15.00	7.50	4.50
446	Russ Nixon	.80	.40	.25
447	Bo Belinsky	1.00	.50	.30
448	Harry Walker	.90	.45	.25
449	Orlando Pena	.80	.40	.25
450	Richie Allen	3.00	1.50	.90
451	Fred Newman	.80	.40	.25
452	Ed Kranepool	1.00	.50	.30
453	Aurelio Monteagudo	.80	.40	.25
454a	Checklist 458-533 (Juan Marichal) (left ear shows)	5.00	2.50	1.50
454b	Checklist 458-533 (Juan Marichal) (no left ear)	4.00	2.00	1.25
455	Tommie Agee	.70	.35	.20
456	Phil Niekro	7.00	3.50	2.00
457	Andy Etchebarren	.80	.40	.25
458	Lee Thomas	3.00	1.50	.90
459	Senators Rookies (*Dick Bosman*, Pete Craig)	3.75	2.00	1.25
460	Harmon Killebrew	55.00	28.00	16.50
461	Bob Miller	3.00	1.50	.90
462	Bob Barton	3.00	1.50	.90
463	Tribe Hill Aces (Sam McDowell, Sonny Siebert)	4.00	2.00	1.25
464	Dan Coombs	3.00	1.50	.90
465	Willie Horton	3.75	2.00	1.25
466	Bobby Wine	3.00	1.50	.90
467	Jim O'Toole	3.00	1.50	.90
468	Ralph Houk	4.50	2.25	1.25
469	Len Gabrielson	3.00	1.50	.90
470	Bob Shaw	3.00	1.50	.90
471	Rene Lachemann	3.00	1.50	.90
472	Pirates Rookies (John Gelnar, George Spriggs)	3.00	1.50	.90
473	Jose Santiago	3.00	1.50	.90
474	Bob Tolan	3.75	2.00	1.25
475	Jim Palmer	90.00	45.00	27.00
476	Tony Perez	70.00	35.00	20.00
477	Braves Team	4.75	2.50	1.50
478	Bob Humphreys	3.00	1.50	.90
479	Gary Bell	3.00	1.50	.90
480	Willie McCovey	15.00	7.50	4.50
481	Leo Durocher	4.50	2.25	1.25
482	Bill Monbouquette	3.75	2.00	1.25
483	Jim Landis	3.00	1.50	.90
484	Jerry Adair	3.00	1.50	.90
485	Tim McCarver	4.50	2.25	1.25
486	Twins Rookies (Rich Reese, Bill Whitby)	3.00	1.50	.90
487	Tom Reynolds	3.00	1.50	.90
488	Gerry Arrigo	3.00	1.50	.90
489	Doug Clemens	3.00	1.50	.90
490	Tony Cloninger	3.75	2.00	1.25
491	Sam Bowens	3.00	1.50	.90
492	Pirates Team	4.75	2.50	1.50
493	Phil Ortega	3.00	1.50	.90
494	Bill Rigney	3.00	1.50	.90

		NR MT	EX	VG
495	Fritz Peterson	4.00	2.00	1.25
496	Orlando McFarlane	3.00	1.50	.90
497	Ron Campbell	3.00	1.50	.90
498	Larry Dierker	3.75	2.00	1.25
499	Indians Rookies (George Culver, Jose Vidal)	3.00	1.50	.90
500	Juan Marichal	15.00	7.50	4.50
501	Jerry Zimmerman	3.00	1.50	.90
502	Derrell Griffith	3.00	1.50	.90
503	Dodgers Team	5.00	2.50	1.50
504	Orlando Martinez	3.00	1.50	.90
505	Tommy Helms	3.00	1.50	.90
506	Smoky Burgess	4.00	2.00	1.25
507	Orioles Rookies (Ed Barnowski, Larry Haney)	3.00	1.50	.90
508	Dick Hall	3.00	1.50	.90
509	Jim King	3.00	1.50	.90
510	Bill Mazeroski	4.50	2.25	1.25
511	Don Wert	3.00	1.50	.90
512	Red Schoendienst	6.00	3.00	1.75
513	Marcelino Lopez	3.00	1.50	.90
514	John Werhas	3.00	1.50	.90
515	Bert Campaneris	4.00	2.00	1.25
516	Giants Team	4.75	2.50	1.50
517	Fred Talbot	3.75	2.00	1.25
518	Denis Menke	3.00	1.50	.90
519	Ted Davidson	3.00	1.50	.90
520	Max Alvis	3.00	1.50	.90
521	Bird Bombers (Curt Blefary, Boog Powell)	4.50	2.25	1.25
522	John Stephenson	3.00	1.50	.90
523	Jim Merritt	3.00	1.50	.90
524	Felix Mantilla	3.00	1.50	.90
525	Ron Hunt	3.75	2.00	1.25
526	Tigers Rookies (*Pat Dobson*, George Korince)	3.75	2.00	1.25
527	Dennis Ribant	3.00	1.50	.90
528	Rico Petrocelli	3.75	2.00	1.25
529	Gary Wagner	3.00	1.50	.90
530	Felipe Alou	4.00	2.00	1.25
531	Checklist 534-609 (Brooks Robinson)	5.00	2.50	1.50
532	Jim Hicks	3.00	1.50	.90
533	Jack Fisher	3.00	1.50	.90
534	Hank Bauer	8.00	4.00	2.50
535	Donn Clendenon	6.00	3.00	1.75
536	Cubs Rookies (*Joe Niekro*, Paul Popovich)	30.00	15.00	9.00
537	Chuck Estrada	5.00	2.50	1.50
538	J.C. Martin	8.00	4.00	2.50
539	Dick Egan	5.00	2.50	1.50
540	Norm Cash	25.00	12.50	7.50
541	Joe Gibbon	8.00	4.00	2.50
542	Athletics Rookies (*Rick Monday*, Tony Pierce)	12.00	6.00	3.50
543	Dan Schneider	8.00	4.00	2.50
544	Indians Team	12.00	6.00	3.50
545	Jim Grant	8.00	4.00	2.50
546	Woody Woodward	8.00	4.00	2.50
547	Red Sox Rookies (Russ Gibson, Bill Rohr)	8.00	4.00	2.50
548	Tony Gonzalez	5.00	2.50	1.50
549	Jack Sanford	12.00	6.00	3.50
550	Vada Pinson	6.00	3.00	1.75
551	Doug Camilli	5.00	2.50	1.50
552	Ted Savage	5.00	2.50	1.50
553	Yankees Rookies (Mike Hegan, Thad Tillotson)	15.00	7.50	4.50
554	Andre Rodgers	5.00	2.50	1.50
555	Don Cardwell	8.00	4.00	2.50
556	Al Weis	5.00	2.50	1.50
557	Al Ferrara	12.00	6.00	3.50
558	Orioles Rookies (*Mark Belanger*, Bill Dillman)	25.00	12.50	7.50
559	Dick Tracewski	5.00	2.50	1.50
560	Jim Bunning	40.00	20.00	12.00
561	Sandy Alomar	8.00	4.00	2.50
562	Steve Blass	6.00	3.00	1.75
563	Joe Adcock	18.00	9.00	5.50
564	Astros Rookies (Alonzo Harris, Aaron Pointer)	8.00	4.00	2.50
565	Lew Krausse	8.00	4.00	2.50
566	Gary Geiger	5.00	2.50	1.50
567	Steve Hamilton	8.00	4.00	2.50
568	John Sullivan	8.00	4.00	2.50
569	A.L. Rookies (Hank Allen, *Rod Carew*)	400.00	200.00	125.00
570	Maury Wills	75.00	37.00	22.00
571	Larry Sherry	12.00	6.00	3.50
572	Don Demeter	12.00	6.00	3.50
573	White Sox Team	15.00	7.50	4.50
574	Jerry Buchek	12.00	6.00	3.50
575	*Dave Boswell*	12.00	6.00	3.50
576	N.L. Rookies (Norm Gigon, Ramon Hernandez)	18.00	9.00	5.50
577	Bill Short	8.00	4.00	2.50
578	John Boccabella	8.00	4.00	2.50
579	Bill Henry	8.00	4.00	2.50
580	Rocky Colavito	35.00	17.50	10.50
581	Mets Rookies (Bill Denehy, *Tom Seaver*)	1250.	575.00	350.00
582	Jim Owens	5.00	2.50	1.50
583	Ray Barker	8.00	4.00	2.50
584	Jim Piersall	18.00	9.00	5.50
585	Wally Bunker	8.00	4.00	2.50
586	Manny Jimenez	8.00	4.00	2.50
587	N.L. Rookies (Don Shaw, Gary Sutherland)	15.00	7.50	4.50
588	Johnny Klippstein	5.00	2.50	1.50
589	Dave Ricketts	5.00	2.50	1.50
590	Pete Richert	8.00	4.00	2.50
591	Ty Cline	5.00	2.50	1.50
592	N.L. Rookies (Jim Shellenback, Ron Willis)	7.00	3.50	2.00
593	Wes Westrum	8.00	4.00	2.50
594	Dan Osinski	8.00	4.00	2.50
595	Cookie Rojas	5.00	2.50	1.50
596	Galen Cisco	5.00	2.50	1.50
597	Ted Abernathy	5.00	2.50	1.50
598	White Sox Rookies (Ed Stroud, Walt Williams)	7.00	3.50	2.00
599	Bob Duliba	5.00	2.50	1.50
600	Brooks Robinson	200.00	100.00	60.00
601	Bill Bryan	8.00	4.00	2.50
602	Juan Pizarro	8.00	4.00	2.50
603	Athletics Rookies (Tim Talton, Ramon Webster)	8.00	4.00	2.50
604	Red Sox Team	90.00	45.00	27.00
605	Mike Shannon	6.00	3.00	1.75
606	Ron Taylor	8.00	4.00	2.50
607	Mickey Stanley	6.00	3.00	1.75
608	Cubs Rookies (Rich Nye, John Upham)	6.00	3.00	1.75
609	Tommy John	90.00	30.00	16.50

1967 Topps Pin-Ups

The 5" by 7" "All Star Pin-ups" were inserts to regular 1967 Topps baseball cards. They feature a full color picture with the player's name, position and team in a circle on the lower left side of the front. The numbered set consists of 32 players (generally big names). Even so, they are rather inexpensive. Because the large paper pin-ups had to be folded several times to fit into the wax packs, they are almost never found in true "Mint" condition.

		NR MT	EX	VG
	Complete Set:	40.00	20.00	12.00
	Common Player:	.25	.13	.08
1	Boog Powell	.40	.20	.12
2	Bert Campaneris	.30	.15	.09
3	Brooks Robinson	3.00	1.50	.90
4	Tommie Agee	.25	.13	.08
5	Carl Yastrzemski	3.50	1.75	1.00
6	Mickey Mantle	12.00	6.00	3.50
7	Frank Howard	.50	.25	.15
8	Sam McDowell	.25	.13	.08
9	Orlando Cepeda	.60	.30	.20
10	Chico Cardenas	.25	.13	.08
11	Bob Clemente	5.00	2.50	1.50
12	Willie Mays	5.00	2.50	1.50
13	Cleon Jones	.25	.13	.08
14	John Callison	.25	.13	.08
15	Hank Aaron	5.00	2.50	1.50
16	Don Drysdale	3.00	1.50	.90
17	Bobby Knoop	.25	.13	.08
18	Tony Oliva	.50	.25	.15
19	Frank Robinson	2.00	1.00	.60
20	Denny McLain	.50	.25	.15
21	Al Kaline	5.00	2.50	1.50
22	Joe Pepitone	.40	.20	.12
23	Harmon Killebrew	5.00	2.50	1.50
24	Leon Wagner	.25	.13	.08
25	Joe Morgan	5.00	2.50	1.50
26	Ron Santo	.40	.20	.12
27	Joe Torre	.60	.30	.20
28	Juan Marichal	2.00	1.00	.60
29	Matty Alou	.25	.13	.08
30	Felipe Alou	.25	.13	.08
31	Ron Hunt	.25	.13	.08
32	Willie McCovey	2.00	1.00	.60

1967 Topps Stand-Ups

Never actually issued, no more than a handful of each of these rare test issues has made their way into the hobby market. Designed so that the color photo of the player's head could be popped out of the black background, and the top folded over to create a stand-up display, examples of these 3-1/8" by 5-1/4" cards can be found either die-cut around the portrait or without the cutting. Blank-backed, there are 24 cards in the set, numbered on the front at bottom left. The cards are popular with advanced superstar collectors.

		NR MT	EX	VG
	Complete Set:	6500.	3300.	2000.
	Common Player:	65.00	32.00	19.50
1	Pete Rose	700.00	350.00	210.00
2	Gary Peters	65.00	32.00	19.50
3	Frank Robinson	200.00	100.00	60.00
4	Jim Lonborg	65.00	32.00	19.50
5	Ron Swoboda	65.00	32.00	19.50
6	Harmon Killebrew	200.00	100.00	60.00
7	Bob Clemente	800.00	400.00	240.00
8	Mickey Mantle	1500.	750.00	450.00
9	Jim Fregosi	75.00	37.00	22.00
10	Al Kaline	300.00	150.00	90.00
11	Don Drysdale	250.00	125.00	75.00
12	Dean Chance	65.00	32.00	19.50
13	Orlando Cepeda	75.00	37.00	22.00
14	Tim McCarver	75.00	37.00	22.00
15	Frank Howard	75.00	37.00	22.00
16	Max Alvis	65.00	32.00	19.50
17	Rusty Staub	75.00	37.00	22.00
18	Richie Allen	75.00	37.00	22.00
19	Willie Mays	600.00	300.00	175.00
20	Hank Aaron	600.00	300.00	175.00
21	Carl Yastrzemski	600.00	300.00	180.00
22	Ron Santo	75.00	37.00	22.00
23	Jim Hunter	200.00	100.00	60.00
24	Jim Wynn	65.00	32.00	19.50

1967 Topps Stickers Pirates

Considered a "test" issue, this 33-sticker set of 2-1/2" by 3-1/2" stickers is very similar to the Red Sox stickers which were produced the same year. Player stickers have a color picture (often just the player's head) and the player's name in large "comic book" letters. Besides the players, there are other topics such as "I Love the Pirates," "Bob Clemente for Mayor," and a number of similar sentiments. The stickers have blank backs and are rather scarce.

		NR MT	EX	VG
	Complete Set:	200.00	100.00	60.00
	Common Player:	3.00	1.50	.90
1	Gene Alley	5.00	2.50	1.50
2	Matty Alou	7.00	3.50	2.00
3	Dennis Ribant	3.00	1.50	.90
4	Steve Blass	5.00	2.50	1.50
5	Juan Pizarro	3.00	1.50	.90
6	Bob Clemente	75.00	38.00	23.00
7	Donn Clendenon	5.00	2.50	1.50
8	Roy Face	7.00	3.50	2.00
9	Woody Fryman	3.00	1.50	.90
10	Jesse Gonder	3.00	1.50	.90
11	Vern Law	7.00	3.50	2.00
12	Al McBean	3.00	1.50	.90
13	Jerry May	3.00	1.50	.90
14	Bill Mazeroski	12.00	6.00	3.50
15	Pete Mikkelsen	3.00	1.50	.90
16	Manny Mota	5.00	2.50	1.50
17	Billy O'Dell	3.00	1.50	.90
18	Jose Pagan	3.00	1.50	.90
19	Jim Pagliaroni	3.00	1.50	.90
20	Johnny Pesky	3.00	1.50	.90
21	Tommie Sisk	3.00	1.50	.90
22	Willie Stargell	40.00	20.00	12.50
23	Bob Veale	5.00	2.50	1.50
24	Harry Walker	3.00	1.50	.90
25	I Love The Pirates	3.00	1.50	.90
26	Let's Go Pirates	3.00	1.50	.90
27	Bob Clemente For Mayor	35.00	17.50	10.50
28	National League Batting Champion (Matty Alou)	4.00	2.00	1.25
29	Happiness Is A Pirate Win	3.00	1.50	.90
30	Donn Clendenon Is My Hero	4.00	2.00	1.25
31	Pirates' Home Run Champion (Willie Stargell)	15.00	7.50	4.50

		NR MT	EX	VG
32	Pirates Logo	3.00	1.50	.90
33	Pirates Pennant	3.00	1.50	.90

1967 Topps Stickers Red Sox

Like the 1967 Pirates Stickers, the Red Sox Stickers were part of the same test procedure. The Red Sox Stickers have the same 2-1/2" by 3-1/2" dimensions, color picture and large player's name on the front. A set is complete at 33 stickers. The majority are players, but themes such as "Let's Go Red Sox" are also included.

		NR MT	EX	VG
	Complete Set:	200.00	100.00	60.00
	Common Player:	3.00	1.50	.90
1	Dennis Bennett	3.00	1.50	.90
2	Darrell Brandon	3.00	1.50	.90
3	Tony Conigliaro	10.00	5.00	3.00
4	Don Demeter	3.00	1.50	.90
5	Hank Fischer	3.00	1.50	.90
6	Joe Foy	3.00	1.50	.90
7	Mike Andrews	3.00	1.50	.90
8	Dalton Jones	3.00	1.50	.90
9	Jim Lonborg	9.00	4.50	2.75
10	Don McMahon	3.00	1.50	.90
11	Dave Morehead	3.00	1.50	.90
12	George Smith	3.00	1.50	.90
13	Rico Petrocelli	6.00	3.00	1.75
14	Mike Ryan	3.00	1.50	.90
15	Jose Santiago	3.00	1.50	.90
16	George Scott	6.00	3.00	1.75
17	Sal Maglie	5.00	2.50	1.50
18	Reggie Smith	10.00	5.00	3.00
19	Lee Stange	3.00	1.50	.90
20	Jerry Stephenson	3.00	1.50	.90
21	Jose Tartabull	3.00	1.50	.90
22	George Thomas	3.00	1.50	.90
23	Bob Tillman	3.00	1.50	.90
24	Johnnie Wyatt	3.00	1.50	.90
25	Carl Yastrzemski	75.00	37.00	22.00
26	Dick Williams	6.00	3.00	1.75
27	I Love The Red Sox	3.00	1.50	.90
28	Let's Go Red Sox	3.00	1.50	.90
29	Carl Yastrzemski For Mayor	35.00	17.50	10.50
30	Tony Conigliaro Is My Hero	7.00	3.50	2.00
31	Happiness Is A Boston Win	3.00	1.50	.90
32	Red Sox Logo	3.00	1.50	.90
33	Red Sox Pennant	3.00	1.50	.90

1968 Topps

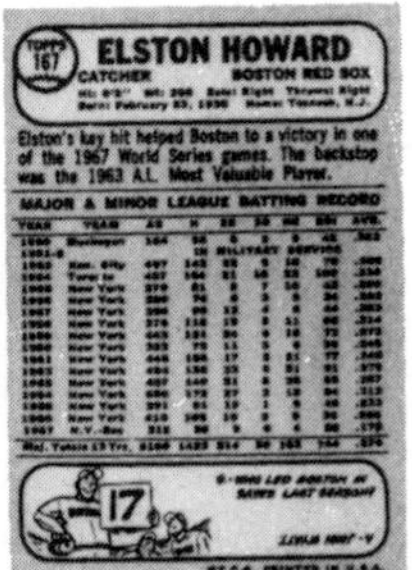

In 1968, Topps returned to a 598-card set of 2-1/2" by 3-1/2" cards. It is not, however, more of the same by way of appearance as the cards feature a color photograph on a background of what appears to be a burlap fabric. The player's name is below the photo but on the unusual background. A colored circle on the lower right carries the team and position. Backs were also changed. While retaining the vertical format introduced the previous year, with stats in the middle and cartoon at the bottom. The set features many of the old favorite subsets, including statistical leaders, World Series highlights, multi-player cards, checklists, rookie cards and the return of All-Star cards.

		NR MT	EX	VG
	Complete Set:	2600.	1300.	750.00
	Common Player: 1-533	.60	.30	.20
	Common Player: 534-598	1.00	.50	.30
1	N.L. Batting Leaders (Matty Alou, Bob Clemente, Tony Gonzalez)	8.00	2.00	1.00
2	A.L. Batting Leaders (Al Kaline, Frank Robinson, Carl Yastrzemski)	4.00	2.00	1.25
3	N.L. RBI Leaders (Hank Aaron, Orlando Cepeda, Bob Clemente)	4.00	2.00	1.25
4	A.L. RBI Leaders (Harmon Killebrew, Frank Robinson, Carl Yastrzemski)	4.00	2.00	1.25
5	N.L. Home Run Leaders (Hank Aaron, Willie McCovey, Ron Santo, Jim Wynn)	4.00	2.00	1.25
6	A.L. Home Run Leaders (Frank Howard, Harmon Killebrew, Carl Yastrzemski)	4.00	2.00	1.25
7	N.L. ERA Leaders (Jim Bunning, Phil Niekro, Chris Short)	2.50	1.25	.70
8	A.L. ERA Leaders (Joe Horlen, Gary Peters, Sonny Siebert)	1.50	.70	.45
9	N.L. Pitching Leaders (Jim Bunning, Ferguson Jenkins, Mike McCormick, Claude Osteen)	2.50	1.25	.70
10a	A.L. Pitching Leaders (Dean Chance, Jim Lonborg, Earl Wilson) ("Lonberg" on back)	3.50	1.75	1.00
10b	A.L. Pitching Leaders (Dean Chance, Jim Lonborg, Earl Wilson) ("Lonborg" on back)	1.50	.70	.45
11	N.L. Strikeout Leaders (Jim Bunning, Ferguson Jenkins, Gaylord Perry)	3.00	1.50	.90
12	A.L. Strikeout Leaders (Dean Chance, Jim Lonborg, Sam McDowell)	1.50	.70	.45
13	Chuck Hartenstein	.60	.30	.20
14	Jerry McNertney	.60	.30	.20
15	Ron Hunt	.70	.35	.20
16	Indians Rookies (Lou Piniella, Richie Scheinblum)	2.50	1.25	.70
17	Dick Hall	.60	.30	.20
18	Mike Hershberger	.60	.30	.20
19	Juan Pizarro	.60	.30	.20
20	Brooks Robinson	12.00	6.00	3.50
21	Ron Davis	.60	.30	.20
22	Pat Dobson	.70	.35	.20
23	Chico Cardenas	.60	.30	.20
24	Bobby Locke	.60	.30	.20
25	Julian Javier	.70	.35	.20
26	Darrell Brandon	.60	.30	.20
27	Gil Hodges	6.00	3.00	1.75
28	Ted Uhlaender	.60	.30	.20
29	Joe Verbanic	.90	.45	.25
30	Joe Torre	2.00	1.00	.60
31	Ed Stroud	.60	.30	.20
32	Joe Gibbon	.60	.30	.20
33	Pete Ward	.60	.30	.20
34	Al Ferrara	.60	.30	.20
35	Steve Hargan	.60	.30	.20
36	Pirates Rookies (Bob Moose, *Bob Robertson)*	.90	.45	.25
37	Billy Williams	7.00	3.50	2.00
38	Tony Pierce	.60	.30	.20
39	Cookie Rojas	.60	.30	.20
40	Denny McLain	3.75	2.00	1.25
41	Julio Gotay	.60	.30	.20
42	Larry Haney	.60	.30	.20
43	Gary Bell	.60	.30	.20
44	Frank Kostro	.60	.30	.20
45	Tom Seaver	150.00	60.00	38.00
46	Dave Ricketts	.60	.30	.20
47	Ralph Houk	1.75	.90	.50
48	Ted Davidson	.60	.30	.20
49a	Ed Brinkman (yellow team letters)	60.00	30.00	18.00
49b	Ed Brinkman (white team letters)	.70	.35	.20
50	Willie Mays	40.00	20.00	12.00
51	Bob Locker	.60	.30	.20
52	Hawk Taylor	.60	.30	.20
53	Gene Alley	.70	.35	.20
54	Stan Williams	.60	.30	.20
55	Felipe Alou	1.00	.50	.30
56	Orioles Rookies (Dave Leonhard, Dave May)	.60	.30	.20
57	Dan Schneider	.60	.30	.20
58	Ed Mathews	9.00	4.50	2.75
59	Don Lock	.60	.30	.20
60	Ken Holtzman	1.00	.50	.30
61	Reggie Smith	1.50	.70	.45
62	Chuck Dobson	.60	.30	.20
63	Dick Kenworthy	.70	.35	.20
64	Jim Merritt	.60	.30	.20
65	John Roseboro	.90	.45	.25
66a	Casey Cox (yellow team letters)	60.00	30.00	18.00
66b	Casey Cox (white team letters)	.60	.30	.20
67	Checklist 1-109 (Jim Kaat)	3.00	1.50	.90
68	Ron Willis	.60	.30	.20
69	Tom Tresh	1.75	.90	.50
70	Bob Veale	.70	.35	.20
71	Vern Fuller	.60	.30	.20
72	Tommy John	5.00	2.50	1.50
73	Jim Hart	.70	.35	.20
74	Milt Pappas	.90	.45	.25
75	Don Mincher	.70	.35	.20
76	Braves Rookies (Jim Britton, *Ron Reed)*	1.00	.50	.30
77	*Don Wilson*	.90	.45	.25
78	Jim Northrup	.70	.35	.20
79	Ted Kubiak	.60	.30	.20
80	Rod Carew	70.00	35.00	21.00
81	Larry Jackson	.60	.30	.20
82	Sam Bowens	.60	.30	.20
83	John Stephenson	.60	.30	.20
84	Bob Tolan	.70	.35	.20
85	Gaylord Perry	8.00	4.00	2.50
86	Willie Stargell	8.00	4.00	2.50
87	Dick Williams	1.00	.50	.30
88	Phil Regan	.60	.30	.20
89	Jake Gibbs	.90	.45	.25
90	Vada Pinson	2.00	1.00	.60
91	Jim Ollom	.60	.30	.20
92	Ed Kranepool	.90	.45	.25
93	Tony Cloninger	.70	.35	.20
94	Lee Maye	.60	.30	.20
95	Bob Aspromonte	.60	.30	.20
96	Senators Rookies (Frank Coggins, Dick Nold)	.60	.30	.20
97	Tom Phoebus	.60	.30	.20
98	Gary Sutherland	.60	.30	.20
99	Rocky Colavito	2.25	1.25	.70
100	Bob Gibson	10.00	5.00	3.00
101	Glenn Beckert	.90	.45	.25
102	Jose Cardenal	.70	.35	.20
103	Don Sutton	6.00	3.00	1.75
104	Dick Dietz	.60	.30	.20
105	Al Downing	1.25	.60	.40
106	Dalton Jones	.60	.30	.20
107	Checklist 110-196 (Juan Marichal)	3.50	1.75	1.00
108	Don Pavletich	.60	.30	.20
109	Bert Campaneris	1.00	.50	.30
110	Hank Aaron	40.00	20.00	12.00
111	Rich Reese	.60	.30	.20
112	Woody Fryman	.70	.35	.20
113	Tigers Rookies (Tom Matchick, Daryl Patterson)	.60	.30	.20
114	Ron Swoboda	.90	.45	.25
115	Sam McDowell	.90	.45	.25
116	Ken McMullen	.60	.30	.20
117	Larry Jaster	.60	.30	.20
118	Mark Belanger	1.00	.50	.30
119	Ted Savage	.60	.30	.20
120	Mel Stottlemyre	2.00	1.00	.60
121	Jimmie Hall	.60	.30	.20
122	Gene Mauch	.90	.45	.25
123	Jose Santiago	.60	.30	.20
124	Nate Oliver	.60	.30	.20
125	Joe Horlen	.60	.30	.20
126	Bobby Etheridge	.60	.30	.20
127	Paul Lindblad	.60	.30	.20
128	Astros Rookies (Tom Dukes, Alonzo Harris)	.60	.30	.20
129	Mickey Stanley	.70	.35	.20
130	Tony Perez	5.00	2.50	1.50
131	Frank Bertaina	.60	.30	.20
132	Bud Harrelson	1.00	.50	.30
133	Fred Whitfield	.60	.30	.20
134	Pat Jarvis	.60	.30	.20
135	Paul Blair	.70	.35	.20
136	Randy Hundley	.60	.30	.20
137	Twins Team	2.00	1.00	.60
138	Ruben Amaro	.90	.45	.25
139	Chris Short	.90	.45	.25
140	Tony Conigliaro	1.50	.70	.45
141	Dal Maxvill	.70	.35	.20
142	White Sox Rookies (Buddy Bradford, Bill Voss)	.60	.30	.20
143	Pete Cimino	.60	.30	.20
144	Joe Morgan	15.00	7.50	4.50
145	Don Drysdale	8.00	4.00	2.50
146	Sal Bando	1.00	.50	.30
147	Frank Linzy	.60	.30	.20
148	Dave Bristol	.60	.30	.20
149	Bob Saverine	.60	.30	.20
150	Bob Clemente	40.00	20.00	12.00
151	World Series Game 1 (Brock Socks 4 Hits In Opener)	3.50	1.75	1.00
152	World Series Game 2 (Yaz Smashes Two Homers)	5.00	2.50	1.50
153	World Series Game 3 (Briles Cools Off Boston)	2.00	1.00	.60
154	World Series Game 4 (Gibson Hurls Shutout!)	3.50	1.75	1.00
155	World Series Game 5 (Lonborg Wins Again!)	2.50	1.25	.70
156	World Series Game 6 (Petrocelli Socks Two Homers)	2.50	1.25	.70
157	World Series Game 7 (St. Louis Wins It!)	2.00	1.00	.60
158	World Series Summary (The Cardinals Celebrate!)	2.00	1.00	.60
159	Don Kessinger	.90	.45	.25
160	Earl Wilson	.70	.35	.20
161	Norm Miller	.60	.30	.20
162	Cardinals Rookies (Hal Gilson, *Mike Torrez)*	1.00	.50	.30
163	Gene Brabender	.60	.30	.20
164	Ramon Webster	.60	.30	.20
165	Tony Oliva	2.50	1.25	.70
166	Claude Raymond	.60	.30	.20
167	Elston Howard	3.00	1.50	.90
168	Dodgers Team	2.50	1.25	.70
169	Bob Bolin	.60	.30	.20
170	Jim Fregosi	1.00	.50	.30
171	Don Nottebart	.60	.30	.20
172	Walt Williams	.60	.30	.20
173	John Boozer	.60	.30	.20
174	Bob Tillman	.60	.30	.20
175	Maury Wills	3.50	1.75	1.00
176	Bob Allen	.60	.30	.20
177	Mets Rookies *(Jerry Koosman, Nolan Ryan)*	1100.	500.00	300.00
178	Don Wert	.70	.35	.20
179	Bill Stoneman	.60	.30	.20
180	Curt Flood	1.50	.70	.45
181	Jerry Zimmerman	.60	.30	.20
182	Dave Giusti	.60	.30	.20
183	Bob Kennedy	.60	.30	.20
184	Lou Johnson	.60	.30	.20
185	Tom Haller	.70	.35	.20
186	Eddie Watt	.60	.30	.20
187	Sonny Jackson	.60	.30	.20
188	Cap Peterson	.60	.30	.20
189	Bill Landis	.60	.30	.20
190	Bill White	1.00	.50	.30
191	Dan Frisella	.70	.35	.20
192a	Checklist 197-283 (Carl Yastrzemski) ("To increase the..." on back)	4.50	2.25	1.25

#	Card	NR MT	EX	VG
192b	Checklist 197-283 (Carl Yastrzemski) ("To increase your..." on back)	6.00	3.00	1.75
193	Jack Hamilton	.60	.30	.20
194	Don Buford	.70	.35	.20
195	Joe Pepitone	2.00	1.00	.60
196	Gary Nolan	.60	.30	.20
197	Larry Brown	.60	.30	.20
198	Roy Face	1.25	.60	.40
199	A's Rookies (Darrell Osteen, Roberto Rodriguez)	.60	.30	.20
200	Orlando Cepeda	4.00	2.00	1.25
201	*Mike Marshall*	1.75	.90	.50
202	Adolfo Phillips	.60	.30	.20
203	Dick Kelley	.60	.30	.20
204	Andy Etchebarren	.60	.30	.20
205	Juan Marichal	8.00	4.00	2.50
206	Cal Ermer	.60	.30	.20
207	Carroll Sembera	.60	.30	.20
208	Willie Davis	1.00	.50	.30
209	Tim Cullen	.60	.30	.20
210	Gary Peters	.70	.35	.20
211	J.C. Martin	.70	.35	.20
212	Dave Morehead	.60	.30	.20
213	Chico Ruiz	.60	.30	.20
214	Yankees Rookies (Stan Bahnsen, Frank Fernandez)	1.00	.50	.30
215	Jim Bunning	4.50	2.25	1.25
216	Bubba Morton	.60	.30	.20
217	Turk Farrell	.60	.30	.20
218	Ken Suarez	.60	.30	.20
219	Rob Gardner	.60	.30	.20
220	Harmon Killebrew	9.00	4.50	2.75
221	Braves Team	2.00	1.00	.60
222	Jim Hardin	.60	.30	.20
223	Ollie Brown	.60	.30	.20
224	Jack Aker	.60	.30	.20
225	Richie Allen	2.25	1.25	.70
226	Jimmie Price	.60	.30	.20
227	Joe Hoerner	.60	.30	.20
228	Dodgers Rookies (*Jack Billingham*, Jim Fairey)	.80	.40	.25
229	Fred Klages	.60	.30	.20
230	Pete Rose	50.00	25.00	15.00
231	Dave Baldwin	.60	.30	.20
232	Denis Menke	.60	.30	.20
233	George Scott	.90	.45	.25
234	Bill Monbouquette	.90	.45	.25
235	Ron Santo	1.50	.70	.45
236	Tug McGraw	1.75	.90	.50
237	Alvin Dark	.90	.45	.25
238	Tom Satriano	.60	.30	.20
239	Bill Henry	.60	.30	.20
240	Al Kaline	10.00	5.00	3.00
241	Felix Millan	.70	.35	.20
242	Moe Drabowsky	.60	.30	.20
243	Rich Rollins	.60	.30	.20
244	John Donaldson	.60	.30	.20
245	Tony Gonzalez	.60	.30	.20
246	Fritz Peterson	1.00	.50	.30
247	Red Rookies (*Johnny Bench*, Ron Tompkins)	300.00	120.00	75.00
248	Fred Valentine	.60	.30	.20
249	Bill Singer	.80	.40	.25
250	Carl Yastrzemski	35.00	17.50	10.50
251	*Manny Sanguillen*	1.25	.60	.40
252	Angels Team	2.00	1.00	.60
253	Dick Hughes	.60	.30	.20
254	Cleon Jones	.90	.45	.25
255	Dean Chance	.70	.35	.20
256	Norm Cash	2.00	1.00	.60
257	Phil Niekro	5.00	2.50	1.50
258	Cubs Rookies (Jose Arcia, Bill Schlesinger)	.60	.30	.20
259	Ken Boyer	1.75	.90	.50
260	Jim Wynn	.90	.45	.25
261	Dave Duncan	.60	.30	.20
262	Rick Wise	.70	.35	.20
263	Horace Clarke	.90	.45	.25
264	Ted Abernathy	.60	.30	.20
265	Tommy Davis	1.50	.70	.45
266	Paul Popovich	.60	.30	.20
267	Herman Franks	.60	.30	.20
268	Bob Humphreys	.60	.30	.20
269	Bob Tiefenauer	.60	.30	.20
270	Matty Alou	1.00	.50	.30
271	Bobby Knoop	.60	.30	.20
272	Ray Culp	.60	.30	.20
273	Dave Johnson	1.75	.90	.50
274	Mike Cuellar	.90	.45	.25
275	Tim McCarver	1.75	.90	.50
276	Jim Roland	.60	.30	.20
277	Jerry Buchek	.70	.35	.20
278a	Checklist 284-370 (Orlando Cepeda) (copyright at right)	3.00	1.50	.90
278b	Checklist 284-370 (Orlando Cepeda) (copyright at left)	5.00	2.50	1.50
279	Bill Hands	.60	.30	.20
280	Mickey Mantle	175.00	87.00	50.00
281	Jim Campanis	.60	.30	.20
282	Rick Monday	1.25	.60	.40
283	Mel Queen	.60	.30	.20
284	John Briggs	.60	.30	.20
285	Dick McAuliffe	.80	.40	.25
286	Cecil Upshaw	.60	.30	.20
287	White Sox Rookies (Mickey Abarbanel, Cisco Carlos)	.60	.30	.20
288	Dave Wickersham	.60	.30	.20
289	Woody Held	.60	.30	.20
290	Willie McCovey	8.00	4.00	2.50
291	Dick Lines	.60	.30	.20
292	Art Shamsky	.80	.40	.25
293	Bruce Howard	.60	.30	.20
294	Red Schoendienst	1.50	.70	.45
295	Sonny Siebert	.60	.30	.20
296	Byron Browne	.60	.30	.20
297	Russ Gibson	.60	.30	.20
298	Jim Brewer	.60	.30	.20
299	Gene Michael	1.00	.50	.30
300	Rusty Staub	2.00	1.00	.60
301	Twins Rookies (George Mitterwald, Rick Renick)	.60	.30	.20
302	Gerry Arrigo	.60	.30	.20
303	Dick Green	.60	.30	.20
304	Sandy Valdespino	.60	.30	.20
305	Minnie Rojas	.60	.30	.20
306	Mike Ryan	.60	.30	.20
307	John Hiller	.90	.45	.25
308	Pirates Team	2.00	1.00	.60
309	Ken Henderson	.60	.30	.20
310	Luis Aparicio	5.00	2.50	1.50
311	Jack Lamabe	.60	.30	.20
312	Curt Blefary	.60	.30	.20
313	Al Weis	.70	.35	.20
314	Red Sox Rookies (Bill Rohr, George Spriggs)	.60	.30	.20
315	Zoilo Versalles	.70	.35	.20
316	Steve Barber	.90	.45	.25
317	Ron Brand	.60	.30	.20
318	Chico Salmon	.60	.30	.20
319	George Culver	.60	.30	.20
320	Frank Howard	2.00	1.00	.60
321	Leo Durocher	2.25	1.25	.70
322	Dave Boswell	.70	.35	.20
323	Deron Johnson	.60	.30	.20
324	Jim Nash	.60	.30	.20
325	Manny Mota	.90	.45	.25
326	Dennis Ribant	.60	.30	.20
327	Tony Taylor	.60	.30	.20
328	Angels Rookies (Chuck Vinson, Jim Weaver)	.60	.30	.20
329	Duane Josephson	.60	.30	.20
330	Roger Maris	25.00	12.50	7.50
331	Dan Osinski	.60	.30	.20
332	Doug Rader	.70	.35	.20
333	Ron Herbel	.60	.30	.20
334	Orioles Team	2.00	1.00	.60
335	Bob Allison	1.00	.50	.30
336	John Purdin	.60	.30	.20
337	Bill Robinson	.90	.45	.25
338	Bob Johnson	.60	.30	.20
339	Rich Nye	.60	.30	.20
340	Max Alvis	.60	.30	.20
341	Jim Lemon	.60	.30	.20
342	Ken Johnson	.60	.30	.20
343	Jim Gosger	.60	.30	.20
344	Donn Clendenon	.70	.35	.20
345	Bob Hendley	.70	.35	.20
346	Jerry Adair	.60	.30	.20
347	George Brunet	.60	.30	.20
348	Phillies Rookies (Larry Colton, Dick Thoenen)	.60	.30	.20
349	Ed Spiezio	.60	.30	.20
350	Hoyt Wilhelm	6.00	3.00	1.75
351	Bob Barton	.60	.30	.20
352	Jackie Hernandez	.60	.30	.20
353	Mack Jones	.60	.30	.20
354	Pete Richert	.60	.30	.20
355	Ernie Banks	15.00	7.50	4.50
356	Checklist 371-457 (Ken Holtzman)	2.50	1.25	.70
357	Len Gabrielson	.60	.30	.20
358	Mike Epstein	.70	.35	.20
359	Joe Moeller	.60	.30	.20
360	Willie Horton	.90	.45	.25
361	Harmon Killebrew AS	5.00	2.50	1.50
362	Orlando Cepeda AS	2.75	1.50	.80
363	Rod Carew AS	8.00	4.00	2.50
364	Joe Morgan AS	3.00	1.50	.90
365	Brooks Robinson AS	6.00	3.00	1.75
366	Ron Santo AS	1.75	.90	.50
367	Jim Fregosi AS	1.00	.50	.30
368	Gene Alley AS	1.00	.50	.30
369	Carl Yastrzemski AS	15.00	7.50	4.50
370	Hank Aaron AS	15.00	7.50	4.50
371	Tony Oliva AS	2.00	1.00	.60
372	Lou Brock AS	5.00	2.50	1.50
373	Frank Robinson AS	5.00	2.50	1.50
374	Bob Clemente AS	15.00	7.50	4.50
375	Bill Freehan AS	1.00	.50	.30
376	Tim McCarver AS	1.50	.70	.45
377	Joe Horlen AS	1.00	.50	.30
378	Bob Gibson AS	5.00	2.50	1.50
379	Gary Peters AS	1.00	.50	.30
380	Ken Holtzman AS	1.00	.50	.30
381	Boog Powell	2.50	1.25	.70
382	Ramon Hernandez	.60	.30	.20
383	Steve Whitaker	.90	.45	.25
384	Reds Rookies (Bill Henry, *Hal McRae*)	6.00	3.00	1.75
385	Jim Hunter	5.00	2.50	1.50
386	Greg Goossen	.70	.35	.20
387	Joe Foy	.60	.30	.20
388	Ray Washburn	.60	.30	.20
389	Jay Johnstone	.90	.45	.25
390	Bill Mazeroski	1.75	.90	.50
391	Bob Priddy	.60	.30	.20
392	Grady Hatton	.60	.30	.20
393	Jim Perry	1.00	.50	.30
394	Tommie Aaron	.90	.45	.25
395	Camilo Pascual	.90	.45	.25
396	Bobby Wine	.60	.30	.20
397	Vic Davalillo	.70	.35	.20
398	Jim Grant	.60	.30	.20
399	Ray Oyler	.70	.35	.20
400a	Mike McCormick (white team letters)	40.00	20.00	12.00
400b	Mike McCormick (yellow team letters)	.70	.35	.20
401	Mets Team	3.25	1.75	1.00
402	Mike Hegan	1.00	.50	.30
403	John Buzhardt	.60	.30	.20
404	Floyd Robinson	.60	.30	.20
405	Tommy Helms	.70	.35	.20
406	Dick Ellsworth	.60	.30	.20
407	Gary Kolb	.60	.30	.20
408	Steve Carlton	40.00	20.00	12.00
409	Orioles Rookies (Frank Peters, Ron Stone)	.60	.30	.20
410	Ferguson Jenkins	3.50	1.75	1.00
411	Ron Hansen	.60	.30	.20
412	Clay Carroll	.70	.35	.20
413	Tommy McCraw	.60	.30	.20
414	Mickey Lolich	2.75	1.50	.80
415	Johnny Callison	1.00	.50	.30
416	Bill Rigney	.60	.30	.20
417	Willie Crawford	.60	.30	.20
418	Eddie Fisher	.60	.30	.20
419	Jack Hiatt	.60	.30	.20
420	Cesar Tovar	.60	.30	.20
421	Ron Taylor	.70	.35	.20
422	Rene Lachemann	.60	.30	.20
423	Fred Gladding	.60	.30	.20
424	White Sox Team	2.00	1.00	.60
425	Jim Maloney	.70	.35	.20
426	Hank Allen	.60	.30	.20
427	Dick Calmus	.60	.30	.20
428	Vic Roznovsky	.60	.30	.20
429	Tommie Sisk	.60	.30	.20
430	Rico Petrocelli	.90	.45	.25
431	Dooley Womack	.90	.45	.25
432	Indians Rookies (Bill Davis, Jose Vidal)	.60	.30	.20
433	Bob Rodgers	.90	.45	.25
434	Ricardo Joseph	.60	.30	.20
435	Ron Perranoski	.70	.35	.20
436	Hal Lanier	.90	.45	.25
437	Don Cardwell	.70	.35	.20
438	Lee Thomas	.60	.30	.20
439	Luman Harris	.60	.30	.20
440	Claude Osteen	.90	.45	.25
441	Alex Johnson	.60	.30	.20
442	Dick Bosman	.60	.30	.20
443	Joe Azcue	.60	.30	.20
444	Jack Fisher	.60	.30	.20
445	Mike Shannon	.70	.35	.20
446	Ron Kline	.60	.30	.20
447	Tigers Rookies (George Korince, Fred Lasher)	.60	.30	.20
448	Gary Wagner	.60	.30	.20
449	Gene Oliver	.60	.30	.20
450	Jim Kaat	4.00	2.00	1.25
451	Al Spangler	.60	.30	.20
452	Jesus Alou	.70	.35	.20
453	Sammy Ellis	.60	.30	.20
454	Checklist 458-533 (Frank Robinson)	4.00	2.00	1.25
455	Rico Carty	1.00	.50	.30
456	John O'Donoghue	.60	.30	.20
457	Jim Lefebvre	.70	.35	.20
458	Lew Krausse	.60	.30	.20
459	Dick Simpson	.60	.30	.20
460	Jim Lonborg	1.00	.50	.30
461	Chuck Hiller	.60	.30	.20
462	Barry Moore	.60	.30	.20
463	Jimmie Schaffer	.60	.30	.20
464	Don McMahon	.60	.30	.20
465	Tommie Agee	.90	.45	.25
466	Bill Dillman	.60	.30	.20
467	Dick Howser	1.50	.70	.45
468	Larry Sherry	.60	.30	.20
469	Ty Cline	.60	.30	.20
470	Bill Freehan	1.00	.50	.30
471	Orlando Pena	.60	.30	.20
472	Walt Alston	2.50	1.25	.70
473	Al Worthington	.60	.30	.20
474	Paul Schaal	.60	.30	.20
475	Joe Niekro	2.25	1.25	.70
476	Woody Woodward	.70	.35	.20
477	Phillies Team	2.00	1.00	.60
478	Dave McNally	1.00	.50	.30
479	Phil Gagliano	.60	.30	.20
480	Manager's Dream (Chico Cardenas, Bob Clemente, Tony Oliva)	15.00	7.50	4.50
481	John Wyatt	.60	.30	.20
482	Jose Pagan	.60	.30	.20
483	Darold Knowles	.60	.30	.20
484	Phil Roof	.60	.30	.20
485	Ken Berry	.60	.30	.20
486	Cal Koonce	.70	.35	.20
487	Lee May	1.25	.60	.40
488	Dick Tracewski	.60	.30	.20
489	Wally Bunker	.60	.30	.20
490	Super Stars (Harmon Killebrew, Mickey Mantle, Willie Mays)	80.00	40.00	24.00
491	Denny Lemaster	.60	.30	.20
492	Jeff Torborg	.70	.35	.20
493	Jim McGlothlin	.60	.30	.20
494	Ray Sadecki	.60	.30	.20
495	Leon Wagner	.70	.35	.20
496	Steve Hamilton	.90	.45	.25
497	Cards Team	3.50	1.75	1.00
498	Bill Bryan	.60	.30	.20
499	Steve Blass	.70	.35	.20
500	Frank Robinson	10.00	5.00	3.00
501	John Odom	.70	.35	.20
502	Mike Andrews	.60	.30	.20
503	Al Jackson	.70	.35	.20
504	Russ Snyder	.60	.30	.20
505	Joe Sparma	.70	.35	.20
506	Clarence Jones	.60	.30	.20
507	Wade Blasingame	.60	.30	.20
508	Duke Sims	.60	.30	.20
509	Dennis Higgins	.60	.30	.20
510	Ron Fairly	.90	.45	.25
511	Bill Kelso	.60	.30	.20
512	Grant Jackson	.60	.30	.20
513	Hank Bauer	.90	.45	.25
514	Al McBean	.60	.30	.20
515	Russ Nixon	.60	.30	.20
516	Pete Mikkelsen	.60	.30	.20
517	Diego Segui	.60	.30	.20
518a	Checklist 534-598 (Clete Boyer) (539 is Maj. L. Rookies)	3.00	1.50	.90
518b	Checklist 534-598 (Clete Boyer) (539 is Amer. L. Rookies)	5.00	2.50	1.50
519	Jerry Stephenson	.60	.30	.20
520	Lou Brock	12.00	6.00	3.50
521	Don Shaw	.70	.35	.20
522	Wayne Causey	.60	.30	.20
523	John Tsitouris	.60	.30	.20
524	Andy Kosco	.90	.45	.25
525	Jim Davenport	.60	.30	.20
526	Bill Denehy	.60	.30	.20
527	Tito Francona	.70	.35	.20
528	Tigers Team	20.00	10.00	6.00
529	Bruce Von Hoff	.60	.30	.20
530	Bird Belters (Brooks Robinson, Frank Robinson)	7.00	3.50	2.00
531	Chuck Hinton	.60	.30	.20
532	Luis Tiant	1.75	.90	.50
533	Wes Parker	.90	.45	.25
534	Bob Miller	1.00	.50	.30

		NR MT	EX	VG
535	Danny Cater	1.00	.50	.30
536	Bill Short	1.25	.60	.40
537	Norm Siebern	1.00	.50	.30
538	Manny Jimenez	1.00	.50	.30
539	Major League Rookies (Mike Ferraro, Jim Ray)	1.25	.60	.40
540	Nelson Briles	1.00	.50	.30
541	Sandy Alomar	1.00	.50	.30
542	John Boccabella	1.00	.50	.30
543	Bob Lee	1.00	.50	.30
544	Mayo Smith	1.25	.60	.40
545	Lindy McDaniel	1.00	.50	.30
546	Roy White	2.50	1.25	.70
547	Dan Coombs	1.00	.50	.30
548	Bernie Allen	1.00	.50	.30
549	Orioles Rookies (Curt Motton, Roger Nelson)	1.00	.50	.30
550	Clete Boyer	1.25	.60	.40
551	Darrell Sutherland	1.00	.50	.30
552	Ed Kirkpatrick	1.00	.50	.30
553	Hank Aguirre	1.00	.50	.30
554	A's Team	3.00	1.50	.90
555	Jose Tartabull	1.00	.50	.30
556	Dick Selma	1.25	.60	.40
557	Frank Quilici	1.00	.50	.30
558	John Edwards	1.00	.50	.30
559	Pirates Rookies (Carl Taylor, Luke Walker)	1.00	.50	.30
560	Paul Casanova	1.00	.50	.30
561	Lee Elia	1.00	.50	.30
562	Jim Bouton	2.50	1.25	.70
563	Ed Charles	1.25	.60	.40
564	Eddie Stanky	1.25	.60	.40
565	Larry Dierker	1.25	.60	.40
566	Ken Harrelson	2.00	1.00	.60
567	Clay Dalrymple	1.00	.50	.30
568	Willie Smith	1.00	.50	.30
569	N.L. Rookies (Ivan Murrell, Les Rohr)	1.25	.60	.40
570	Rick Reichardt	1.00	.50	.30
571	Tony LaRussa	1.75	.90	.50
572	Don Bosch	1.25	.60	.40
573	Joe Coleman	1.25	.60	.40
574	Reds Team	3.00	1.50	.90
575	Jim Palmer	50.00	25.00	15.00
576	Dave Adlesh	1.00	.50	.30
577	Fred Talbot	1.25	.60	.40
578	Orlando Martinez	1.00	.50	.30
579	N.L. Rookies *(Larry Hisle, Mike Lum)*	1.75	.90	.50
580	Bob Bailey	1.00	.50	.30
581	Garry Roggenburk	1.00	.50	.30
582	Jerry Grote	1.25	.60	.40
583	Gates Brown	1.25	.60	.40
584	Larry Shepard	1.00	.50	.30
585	Wilbur Wood	1.25	.60	.40
586	Jim Pagliaroni	1.00	.50	.30
587	Roger Repoz	1.00	.50	.30
588	Dick Schofield	1.00	.50	.30
589	Twins Rookies (Ron Clark, Moe Ogier)	1.00	.50	.30
590	Tommy Harper	1.25	.60	.40
591	Dick Nen	1.00	.50	.30
592	John Bateman	1.00	.50	.30
593	Lee Stange	1.00	.50	.30
594	Phil Linz	1.25	.60	.40
595	Phil Ortega	1.00	.50	.30
596	Charlie Smith	1.25	.60	.40
597	Bill McCool	1.00	.50	.30
598	Jerry May	2.00	.60	.30

1968 Topps Action All-Star Stickers

Still another of the many Topps test issues of the late 1960s, the Action All-Star stickers were sold in a strip of three, with bubblegum, for 10¢. The strip is comprised of three 3-1/4" by 5-1/4" panels, perforated at the joints for separation. The central panel which is numbered, contains a large color picture of a star player. The top and bottom panels contains smaller pictures of three players each. While there are 16 numbered center panels, only 12 of them are different; panels 13-16 show players previously used. Similarly, the triple-player panels at top and bottom of stickers 13-16 repeat panels from #'s 1-4. Prices below are for stickers which have all three panels still joined. Individual panels are priced signicantly lower.

		NR MT	EX	VG
	Complete Set:	1300.	650.00	390.00
	Common Player:	18.00	9.00	5.50
1	Orlando Cepeda, Joe Horlen, Al Kaline, Bill Mazeroski, Claude Osteen, Mel Stottlemyre, Carl Yastrzemski	100.00	50.00	30.00
2	Don Drysdale, Harmon Killebrew, Mike McCormick, Tom Phoebus, George Scott, Ron Swoboda, Pete Ward	30.00	15.00	9.00
3	Hank Aaron, Paul Casanova, Jim Maloney, Joe Pepitone, Rick Reichardt, Frank Robinson, Tom Seaver	35.00	17.50	10.50
4	Bob Aspromonte, Johnny Callison, Dean Chance, Jim Lefebvre, Jim Lonborg, Frank Robinson, Ron Santo	25.00	12.50	7.50
5	Bert Campaneris, Al Downing, Willie Horton, Ed Kranepool, Willie Mays, Pete Rose, Ron Santo	200.00	100.00	60.00
6	Max Alvis, Ernie Banks, Al Kaline, Tim McCarver, Rusty Staub, Walt Williams, Carl Yastrzemski	70.00	35.00	21.00
7	Rod Carew, Tony Gonzalez, Steve Hargan, Mickey Mantle, Willie McCovey, Rick Monday, Billy Williams	300.00	150.00	90.00
8	Clete Boyer, Jim Bunning, Tony Conigliaro, Mike Cuellar, Joe Horlen, Ken McMullen, Don Mincher	18.00	9.00	5.50
9	Orlando Cepeda, Bob Clemente, Jim Fregosi, Harmon Killebrew, Willie Mays, Chris Short, Earl Wilson	40.00	20.00	12.00
10	Hank Aaron, Bob Gibson, Bud Harrelson, Jim Hunter, Mickey Mantle, Gary Peters, Vada Pinson	100.00	50.00	30.00
11	Don Drysdale, Bill Freehan, Frank Howard, Ferguson Jenkins, Tony Oliva, Bob Veale, Jim Wynn	30.00	15.00	9.00
12	Richie Allen, Bob Clemente, Sam McDowell, Jim McGlothlin, Tony Perez, Brooks Robinson, Joe Torre	100.00	50.00	30.00
13	Dean Chance, Don Drysdale, Jim Lefebvre, Tom Phoebus, Frank Robinson, George Scott, Carl Yastrzemski	100.00	50.00	30.00
14	Paul Casanova, Orlando Cepeda, Joe Horlen, Harmon Killebrew, Bill Mazeroski, Rick Reichardt, Tom Seaver	35.00	17.50	10.50
15	Bob Aspromonte, Johnny Callison, Jim Lonborg, Mike McCormick, Frank Robinson, Ron Swoboda, Pete Ward	30.00	15.00	9.00
16	Hank Aaron, Al Kaline, Jim Maloney, Claude Osteen, Joe Pepitone, Ron Santo, Mel Stottlemyre	30.00	15.00	9.00

1968 Topps Discs

One of the scarcest of all Topps collectibles, this 28-player set was apparently a never-completed test issue. These full-color, cardboard discs, which measure approximately 2-1/8" in diameter, were apparently intended to be made into a "pin" set, but for some reason, production was never completed and no actual "pins" are known to exist. Uncut sheets of the player discs have been found, however. The discs include a player portrait photo with the name beneath and

the city and team nickname along the sides. The set includes eight Hall of Famers.

		NR MT	EX	VG
	Complete Set:	3500.	1750.	1050.
	Common Player:	35.00	17.50	10.50
(1)	Hank Aaron	250.00	125.00	75.00
(2)	Richie Allen	60.00	30.00	18.00
(3)	Gene Alley	35.00	17.50	10.50
(4)	Rod Carew	300.00	150.00	90.00
(5)	Orlando Cepeda	60.00	30.00	18.00
(6)	Dean Chance	35.00	17.50	10.50
(7)	Bob Clemente	350.00	175.00	100.00
(8)	Tommy Davis	35.00	17.50	10.50
(9)	Bill Freehan	35.00	17.50	10.50
(10)	Jim Fregosi	35.00	17.50	10.50
(11)	Steve Hargan	35.00	17.50	10.50
(12)	Frank Howard	60.00	30.00	18.00
(13)	Al Kaline	200.00	100.00	60.00
(14)	Harmon Killebrew	150.00	75.00	45.00
(15)	Mickey Mantle	600.00	300.00	175.00
(16)	Willie Mays	300.00	150.00	90.00
(17)	Mike McCormick	35.00	17.50	10.50
(18)	Rick Monday	35.00	17.50	10.50
(19)	Claude Osteen	35.00	17.50	10.50
(20)	Gary Peters	35.00	17.50	10.50
(21)	Brooks Robinson	200.00	100.00	60.00
(22)	Frank Robinson	150.00	75.00	45.00
(23)	Pete Rose	400.00	200.00	125.00
(24)	Ron Santo	60.00	30.00	18.00
(25)	Rusty Staub	60.00	30.00	18.00
(26)	Joe Torre	60.00	30.00	18.00
(27)	Carl Yastrzemski	150.00	75.00	45.00
(28)	Bob Veale	35.00	17.50	10.50

1968 Topps Game

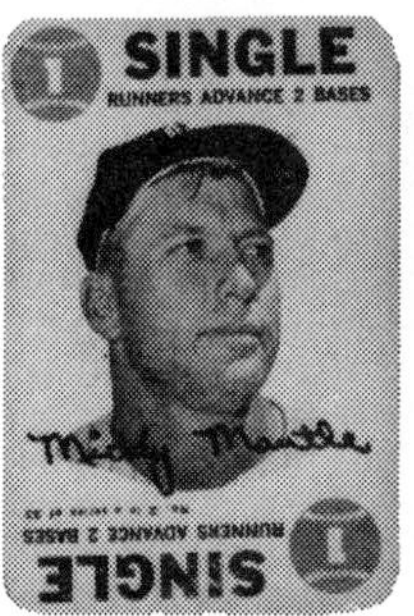

A throwback to the Red and Blue Back sets of 1951, the 33-cards in the 1968 Topps Game set, inserted into packs of regular '68 Topps cards or purchases as a complete boxed set, enable the owner to play a game of baseball based on the game situations on each card. Also on the 2-1/4" by 3-1/4" cards were a color photograph of a player and his facsimile autograph. One redeeming social value of the set (assuming you're not mesmerized by the game) is that it affords an inexpensive way to get big-name cards as the set is loaded with stars, but not at all popular with collectors.

		NR MT	EX	VG
	Complete Set:	50.00	25.00	15.00
	Common Player:	.30	.15	.09
1	Mateo Alou	.50	.25	.15
2	Mickey Mantle	15.00	7.50	4.50
3	Carl Yastrzemski	3.25	1.75	1.00
4	Henry Aaron	3.00	1.50	.90
5	Harmon Killebrew	1.75	.90	.50
6	Roberto Clemente	3.00	1.50	.90
7	Frank Robinson	1.75	.90	.50
8	Willie Mays	3.00	1.50	.90
9	Brooks Robinson	2.00	1.00	.60
10	Tommy Davis	.50	.25	15
11	Bill Freehan	.50	.25	.15
12	Claude Osteen	.40	.20	.12
13	Gary Peters	.30	.15	.09
14	Jim Lonborg	.40	.20	.12
15	Steve Hargan	.30	.15	.09
16	Dean Chance	.40	.20	.12
17	Mike McCormick	.30	.15	.09
18	Tim McCarver	.60	.30	.20
19	Ron Santo	.60	.30	.20
20	Tony Gonzalez	.30	.15	.09
21	Frank Howard	.70	.35	.20

		NR MT	EX	VG
22	George Scott	.40	.20	.12
23	Rich Allen	.70	.35	.20
24	Jim Wynn	.40	.20	.12
25	Gene Alley	.40	.20	.12
26	Rick Monday	.40	.20	.12
27	Al Kaline	2.00	1.00	.60
28	Rusty Staub	.70	.35	.20
29	Rod Carew	2.75	1.50	.80
30	Pete Rose	7.50	3.75	2.25
31	Joe Torre	.70	.35	.20
32	Orlando Cepeda	1.00	.50	.30
33	Jim Fregosi	.50	.25	.15

1968 Topps Plaks

Among the scarcest of the Topps test issues of the late 1960s, the "All Star Baseball Plaks" were plastic busts of two dozen stars of the era which came packaged like model airplane parts. The busts had to be snapped off a sprue and could be inserted into a base which carried the player's name. Packed with the plastic plaks was one of two checklist cards which featured six color photos per side. The 2-1/8" by 4" checklist cards are popular with superstar collectors and are considerably easier to find today than the actual plaks.

		NR MT	EX	VG
Complete Set:		2500.	1250.	750.00
Common Player:		20.00	10.00	6.00
1	Max Alvis	20.00	10.00	6.00
2	Frank Howard	30.00	15.00	9.00
3	Dean Chance	20.00	10.00	6.00
4	Jim Hunter	50.00	25.00	15.00
5	Jim Fregosi	25.00	12.50	7.50
6	Al Kaline	60.00	30.00	18.00
7	Harmon Killebrew	60.00	30.00	18.00
8	Gary Peters	20.00	10.00	6.00
9	Jim Lonborg	20.00	10.00	6.00
10	Frank Robinson	60.00	30.00	18.00
11	Mickey Mantle	800.00	400.00	240.00
12	Carl Yastrzemski	175.00	87.00	52.00
13	Hank Aaron	100.00	50.00	30.00
14	Bob Clemente	100.00	50.00	30.00
15	Richie Allen	30.00	15.00	9.00
16	Tommy Davis	25.00	12.50	7.50
17	Orlando Cepeda	30.00	15.00	9.00
18	Don Drysdale	50.00	25.00	15.00
19	Willie Mays	100.00	50.00	30.00
20	Rusty Staub	30.00	15.00	9.00
21	Tim McCarver	30.00	15.00	9.00
22	Pete Rose	250.00	125.00	75.00
23	Ron Santo	30.00	15.00	9.00
24	Jim Wynn	20.00	10.00	6.00
---	Checklist Card 1-12	250.00	125.00	75.00
---	Checklist Card 13-24	250.00	125.00	75.00

NOTE: A card number in parentheses ( ) indicates the card set is unnumbered.

1968 Topps Posters

Yet another innovation from the creative minds at Topps appeared in 1968; a set of color player posters. Measuring 9-3/4" by 18-1/8," each poster was sold separately with its own piece of gum, rather than as an insert. The posters feature a large color photograph with a star at the bottom containing the player's name, position and team. There are 24 different posters which were folded numerous times to fit into the package they were sold in.

		NR MT	EX	VG
Complete Set:		300.00	150.00	90.00
Common Player:		3.00	1.50	.90
1	Dean Chance	3.00	1.50	.90
2	Max Alvis	3.00	1.50	.90
3	Frank Howard	8.00	4.00	2.50
4	Jim Fregosi	7.00	3.50	2.00
5	Jim Hunter	12.00	6.00	3.50
6	Bob Clemente	25.00	12.50	7.50
7	Don Drysdale	12.00	6.00	3.50
8	Jim Wynn	3.00	1.50	.90
9	Al Kaline	25.00	12.50	7.50
10	Harmon Killebrew	20.00	10.00	6.00
11	Jim Lonborg	3.00	1.50	.90
12	Orlando Cepeda	8.00	4.00	2.50
13	Gary Peters	3.00	1.50	.90
14	Hank Aaron	25.00	12.50	7.50
15	Richie Allen	8.00	4.00	2.50
16	Carl Yastrzemski	20.00	10.00	6.00
17	Ron Swoboda	3.00	1.50	.90
18	Mickey Mantle	50.00	25.00	15.00
19	Tim McCarver	7.00	3.50	2.00
20	Willie Mays	25.00	12.50	7.50
21	Ron Santo	7.00	3.50	2.00
22	Rusty Staub	7.00	3.50	2.00
23	Pete Rose	40.00	20.00	12.00
24	Frank Robinson	15.00	7.50	4.50

1968 Topps 3-D

These are very rare pioneer issues on the part of Topps. The cards measure 2-1/4" by 3-1/2" and were specially printed to simulate a three-dimensional effect. Backgrounds are a purposely blurred stadium scene, in front of which was a normally sharp color player photograph. The outer layer is a thin coating of ribbed plastic. The special process gives the picture the illusion of depth when the card is moved or tilted. As this was done two years before Kellogg's began its 3-D cards, this 12-card test issue really was breaking new ground. Unfortunately, production and distribution were limited making the cards very tough to find.

		NR MT	EX	VG
Complete Set:		9000.	4500.	2500.
Common Player:		350.00	175.00	105.00
(1)	Bob Clemente	2500.	1250.	750.00
(2)	Willie Davis	400.00	200.00	125.00
(3)	Ron Fairly	400.00	200.00	125.00
(4)	Curt Flood	400.00	200.00	125.00
(5)	Jim Lonborg	400.00	200.00	125.00
(6)	Jim Maloney	350.00	175.00	105.00
(7)	Tony Perez	600.00	300.00	175.00
(8)	Boog Powell	500.00	250.00	150.00
(9)	Bill Robinson	350.00	175.00	105.00
(10)	Rusty Staub	450.00	230.00	135.00
(11)	Mel Stottlemyre	400.00	200.00	120.00
(12)	Ron Swoboda	350.00	175.00	105.00

1969 Topps

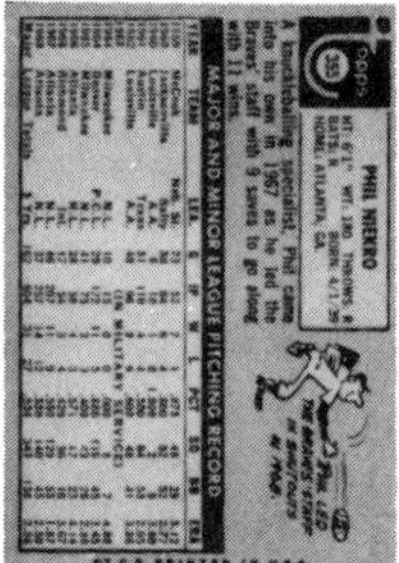

The 1969 Topps set broke yet another record for quantity as the issue is officially a whopping 664 cards. With substantial numbers of variations, the number of possible cards runs closer to 700. The design of the 2-1/2" by 3-1/2" cards in the set feature a color photo with the team name printed in block letters underneath. A circle contains the player's name and position. Card backs returned to a horizontal format. Despite the size of the set, it contains no teamcards. It does, however, have multi-player cards, All-Stars, statistical leaders, and World Series highlights. Most significant among the varieties are white and yellow letter cards from the run of #'s 440-511. The complete set prices below do not include the scarcer and more expensive "white letter" variations.

		NR MT	EX	VG
Complete Set:		1800.	900.00	550.00
Common Player: 1-218		.40	.20	.12
Common Player: 219-327		.90	.45	.25
Common Player: 328-512		.40	.20	.12
Common Player: 513-664		.70	.35	.20
1	A.L. Batting Leaders (Danny Cater, Tony Oliva, Carl Yastrzemski)	7.00	2.00	1.00
2	N.L. Batting Leaders (Felipe Alou, Matty Alou, Pete Rose)	4.00	2.00	1.25
3	A.L. RBI Leaders (Ken Harrelson, Frank Howard, Jim Northrup)	2.00	1.00	.60
4	N.L. RBI Leaders (Willie McCovey, Ron Santo, Billy Williams)	3.50	1.75	1.00
5	A.L. Home Run Leaders (Ken Harrelson, Willie Horton, Frank Howard)	2.00	1.00	.60
6	N.L. Home Run Leaders (Richie Allen, Ernie Banks, Willie McCovey)	3.50	1.75	1.00
7	A.L. ERA Leaders (Sam McDowell, Dave McNally, Luis Tiant)	2.00	1.00	.60
8	N.L. ERA Leaders (Bobby Bolin, Bob Gibson, Bob Veale)	3.00	1.50	.90
9	A.L. Pitching Leaders (Denny McLain, Dave McNally, Mel Stottlemyre, Luis Tiant)	2.00	1.00	.60
10	N.L. Pitching Leaders (Bob Gibson, Fergie Jenkins, Juan Marichal)	3.50	1.75	1.00
11	A.L. Strikeout Leaders (Sam McDowell, Denny McLain, Luis Tiant)	2.00	1.00	.60
12	N.L. Strikeout Leaders (Bob Gibson, Fergie Jenkins, Bill Singer)	3.00	1.50	.90
13	Mickey Stanley	.50	.25	.15
14	Al McBean	.40	.20	.12
15	Boog Powell	2.50	1.25	.70
16	Giants Rookies (Cesar Gutierrez, Rich Robertson)	.40	.20	.12
17	Mike Marshall	1.25	.60	.40
18	Dick Schofield	.40	.20	.12
19	Ken Suarez	.40	.20	.12
20	Ernie Banks	10.00	5.00	3.00
21	Jose Santiago	.40	.20	.12
22	Jesus Alou	.50	.25	.15
23	Lew Krausse	.40	.20	.12
24	Walt Alston	3.00	1.50	.90
25	Roy White	1.25	.60	.40
26	Clay Carroll	.50	.25	.15
27	Bernie Allen	.40	.20	.12

		NR MT	EX	VG
28	Mike Ryan	.40	.20	.12
29	Dave Morehead	.40	.20	.12
30	Bob Allison	1.00	.50	.30
31	Mets Rookies (*Gary Gentry, Amos Otis*)	1.25	.60	.40
32	Sammy Ellis	.40	.20	.12
33	Wayne Causey	.40	.20	.12
34	Gary Peters	.50	.25	.15
35	Joe Morgan	10.00	5.00	3.00
36	Luke Walker	.40	.20	.12
37	Curt Motton	.40	.20	.12
38	Zoilo Versalles	.50	.25	.15
39	Dick Hughes	.40	.20	.12
40	Mayo Smith	.40	.20	.12
41	Bob Barton	.40	.20	.12
42	Tommy Harper	1.00	.50	.30
43	Joe Niekro	1.25	.60	.40
44	Danny Cater	.40	.20	.12
45	Maury Wills	2.50	1.25	.70
46	Fritz Peterson	1.00	.50	.30
47a	Paul Popovich (emblem visible thru airbrush)	4.00	2.00	1.25
47b	Paul Popovich (helmet emblem completely airbrushed)	.40	.20	.12
48	Brant Alyea	.40	.20	.12
49a	Royals Rookies (Steve Jones, Eliseo Rodriquez) (Rodriquez on front)	6.00	3.00	1.75
49b	Royals Rookies (Steve Jones, Eliseo Rodriguez) (Rodriguez on front)	.40	.20	.12
50	Bob Clemente	35.00	17.50	10.50
51	Woody Fryman	.50	.25	.15
52	Mike Andrews	.40	.20	.12
53	Sonny Jackson	.40	.20	.12
54	Cisco Carlos	.40	.20	.12
55	Jerry Grote	1.00	.50	.30
56	Rich Reese	.40	.20	.12
57	Checklist 1-109 (Denny McLain)	3.00	1.50	.90
58	Fred Gladding	.40	.20	.12
59	Jay Johnstone	.70	.35	.20
60	Nelson Briles	.40	.20	.12
61	Jimmie Hall	.40	.20	.12
62	Chico Salmon	.80	.40	.25
63	Jim Hickman	.50	.25	.15
64	Bill Monbouquette	.50	.25	.15
65	Willie Davis	1.00	.50	.30
66	Orioles Rookies (Mike Adamson, *Merv Rettenmund*)	.70	.35	.20
67	Bill Stoneman	.40	.20	.12
68	Dave Duncan	.40	.20	.12
69	Steve Hamilton	.70	.35	.20
70	Tommy Helms	.50	.25	.15
71	Steve Whitaker	.40	.20	.12
72	Ron Taylor	.60	.30	.20
73	Johnny Briggs	.40	.20	.12
74	Preston Gomez	.40	.20	.12
75	Luis Aparicio	5.00	2.50	1.50
76	Norm Miller	.40	.20	.12
77a	Ron Perranoski (LA visible thru airbrush)	4.50	2.25	1.25
77b	Ron Perranoski (cap emblem completely airbrushed)	.50	.25	.15
78	Tom Satriano	.40	.20	.12
79	Milt Pappas	.70	.35	.20
80	Norm Cash	1.75	.90	.50
81	Mel Queen	.40	.20	.12
82	Pirates Rookies (*Rich Hebner, Al Oliver*)	9.00	4.50	2.75
83	Mike Ferraro	.80	.40	.25
84	Bob Humphreys	.40	.20	.12
85	Lou Brock	8.00	4.00	2.50
86	Pete Richert	.40	.20	.12
87	Horace Clarke	.70	.35	.20
88	Rich Nye	.40	.20	.12
89	Russ Gibson	.40	.20	.12
90	Jerry Koosman	2.50	1.25	.70
91	Al Dark	.70	.35	.20
92	Jack Billingham	.50	.25	.15
93	Joe Foy	.40	.20	.12
94	Hank Aguirre	.40	.20	.12
95	Johnny Bench	150.00	60.00	38.00
96	Denver Lemaster	.40	.20	.12
97	Buddy Bradford	.40	.20	.12
98	Dave Giusti	.40	.20	.12
99a	Twins Rookies (Danny Morris, *Graig Nettles*) (black loop above "Twins")	20.00	10.00	6.00
99b	Twins Rookies (Danny Morris, *Graig Nettles*) (no black loop)	12.00	6.00	3.50
100	Hank Aaron	50.00	25.00	15.00
101	Daryl Patterson	.40	.20	.12
102	Jim Davenport	.40	.20	.12
103	Roger Repoz	.40	.20	.12
104	Steve Blass	.50	.25	.15
105	Rick Monday	.80	.40	.25
106	Jim Hannan	.40	.20	.12
107a	Checklist 110-218 (Bob Gibson) (161 is Jim Purdin)	3.00	1.50	.90
107b	Checklist 110-218 (Bob Gibson) (161 is John Purdin)	6.00	3.00	1.75
108	Tony Taylor	.40	.20	.12
109	Jim Lonborg	.80	.40	.25
110	Mike Shannon	.50	.25	.15
111	Johnny Morris	.80	.40	.25
112	J.C. Martin	.70	.35	.20
113	Dave May	.40	.20	.12
114	Yankees Rookies (Alan Closter, John Cumberland)	.70	.35	.20
115	Bill Hands	.40	.20	.12
116	Chuck Harrison	.40	.20	.12
117	Jim Fairey	.40	.20	.12
118	Stan Williams	.40	.20	.12
119	Doug Rader	.50	.25	.15
120	Pete Rose	35.00	17.50	10.50
121	Joe Grzenda	.40	.20	.12
122	Ron Fairly	.80	.40	.25
123	Wilbur Wood	.80	.40	.25
124	Hank Bauer	.80	.40	.25
125	Ray Sadecki	.40	.20	.12
126	Dick Tracewski	.40	.20	.12
127	Kevin Collins	.60	.30	.20
128	Tommie Aaron	.70	.35	.20
129	Bill McCool	.40	.20	.12
130	Carl Yastrzemski	25.00	12.50	7.50
131	Chris Cannizzaro	.40	.20	.12
132	Dave Baldwin	.40	.20	.12
133	Johnny Callison	1.00	.50	.30
134	Jim Weaver	.40	.20	.12
135	Tommy Davis	1.50	.70	.45
136	Cards Rookies (Steve Huntz, Mike Torrez)	.50	.25	.15
137	Wally Bunker	.40	.20	.12
138	John Bateman	.40	.20	.12
139	Andy Kosco	.40	.20	.12
140	Jim Lefebvre	.50	.25	.15
141	Bill Dillman	.40	.20	.12
142	Woody Woodward	.50	.25	.15
143	Joe Nossek	.40	.20	.12
144	Bob Hendley	.60	.30	.20
145	Max Alvis	.50	.25	.15
146	Jim Perry	1.00	.50	.30
147	Leo Durocher	2.25	1.25	.70
148	Lee Stange	.40	.20	.12
149	Ollie Brown	.40	.20	.12
150	Denny McLain	3.00	1.50	.90
151a	Clay Dalrymple (Phillies)	7.00	3.50	2.00
151b	Clay Dalrymple (Orioles)	.40	.20	.12
152	Tommie Sisk	.40	.20	.12
153	Ed Brinkman	.50	.25	.15
154	Jim Britton	.40	.20	.12
155	Pete Ward	.40	.20	.12
156	Astros Rookies (Hal Gilson, Leon McFadden)	.40	.20	.12
157	Bob Rodgers	.70	.35	.20
158	Joe Gibbon	.40	.20	.12
159	Jerry Adair	.40	.20	.12
160	Vada Pinson	2.00	1.00	.60
161	John Purdin	.40	.20	.12
162	World Series Game 1 (Gibson Fans 17; Sets New Record)	3.50	1.75	1.00
163	World Series Game 2 (Tiger Homers Deck The Cards)	2.50	1.25	.70
164	World Series Game 3 (McCarver's Homer Puts St. Louis Ahead)	2.50	1.25	.70
165	World Series Game 4 (Brock's Lead Off Homer Starts Cards' Romp)	3.50	1.75	1.00
166	World Series Game 5 (Kaline's Key Hit Sparks Tiger Rally)	3.50	1.75	1.00
167	World Series Game 6 (Tiger 10-Run Inning Ties Mark)	2.50	1.25	.70
168	World Series Game 7 (Lolich Series Hero, Outduels Gibson)	2.75	1.50	.80
169	World Series Summary (Tigers Celebrate Their Victory)	2.50	1.25	.70
170	Frank Howard	2.00	1.00	.60
171	Glenn Beckert	.80	.40	.25
172	Jerry Stephenson	.40	.20	.12
173	White Sox Rookies (Bob Christian, Gerry Nyman)	.40	.20	.12
174	Grant Jackson	.40	.20	.12
175	Jim Bunning	4.00	2.00	1.25
176	Joe Azcue	.40	.20	.12
177	Ron Reed	.50	.25	.15
178	Ray Oyler	.80	.40	.25
179	Don Pavletich	.40	.20	.12
180	Willie Horton	.80	.40	.25
181	Mel Nelson	.40	.20	.12
182	Bill Rigney	.40	.20	.12
183	Don Shaw	.40	.20	.12
184	Roberto Pena	.40	.20	.12
185	Tom Phoebus	.40	.20	.12
186	John Edwards	.40	.20	.12
187	Leon Wagner	.50	.25	.15
188	Rick Wise	.50	.25	.15
189	Red Sox Rookies (Joe Lahoud, John Thibdeau)	.40	.20	.12
190	Willie Mays	50.00	25.00	15.00
191	Lindy McDaniel	.70	.35	.20
192	Jose Pagan	.40	.20	.12
193	Don Cardwell	.70	.35	.20
194	Ted Uhlaender	.40	.20	.12
195	John Odom	.50	.25	.15
196	Lum Harris	.40	.20	.12
197	Dick Selma	.40	.20	.12
198	Willie Smith	.40	.20	.12
199	Jim French	.40	.20	.12
200	Bob Gibson	12.00	6.00	3.50
201	Russ Snyder	.40	.20	.12
202	Don Wilson	.40	.20	.12
203	Dave Johnson	1.50	.70	.45
204	Jack Hiatt	.40	.20	.12
205	Rick Reichardt	.40	.20	.12
206	Phillies Rookies (Larry Hisle, Barry Lersch)	.80	.40	.25
207	Roy Face	1.25	.60	.40
208a	Donn Clendenon (Expos)	7.00	3.50	2.00
208b	Donn Clendenon (Houston)	.50	.25	.15
209	Larry Haney (photo reversed)	.80	.40	.25
210	Felix Millan	.40	.20	.12
211	Galen Cisco	.40	.20	.12
212	Tom Tresh	1.25	.60	.40
213	Gerry Arrigo	.40	.20	.12
214	Checklist 219-327	2.50	1.25	.70
215	Rico Petrocelli	.80	.40	.25
216	Don Sutton	4.00	2.00	1.25
217	John Donaldson	.40	.20	.12
218	John Roseboro	.60	.30	.20
219	*Freddie Patek*	1.25	.60	.40
220	Sam McDowell	1.25	.60	.40
221	Art Shamsky	1.00	.50	.30
222	Duane Josephson	.90	.45	.25
223	Tom Dukes	.90	.45	.25
224	Angels Rookies (Bill Harrelson, Steve Kealey)	.90	.45	.25
225	Don Kessinger	1.00	.50	.30
226	Bruce Howard	.90	.45	.25
227	Frank Johnson	.90	.45	.25
228	Dave Leonhard	.90	.45	.25
229	Don Lock	.90	.45	.25
230	Rusty Staub	2.50	1.25	.70
231	Pat Dobson	1.00	.50	.30
232	Dave Ricketts	.90	.45	.25
233	Steve Barber	1.00	.50	.30
234	Dave Bristol	.90	.45	.25
235	Jim Hunter	7.00	3.50	2.00
236	Manny Mota	1.00	.50	.30
237	*Bobby Cox*	1.50	.70	.45
238	Ken Johnson	.90	.45	.25
239	Bob Taylor	.90	.45	.25
240	Ken Harrelson	2.00	1.00	.60
241	Jim Brewer	.90	.45	.25
242	Frank Kostro	.90	.45	.25
243	Ron Kline	.90	.45	.25
244	Indians Rookies (*Ray Fosse*, George Woodson)	1.25	.60	.40
245	Ed Charles	1.00	.50	.30
246	Joe Coleman	1.00	.50	.30
247	Gene Oliver	.90	.45	.25
248	Bob Priddy	.90	.45	.25
249	Ed Spiezio	.90	.45	.25
250	Frank Robinson	12.00	6.00	3.50
251	Ron Herbel	.90	.45	.25
252	Chuck Cottier	.90	.45	.25
253	Jerry Johnson	.90	.45	.25
254	Joe Schultz	1.00	.50	.30
255	Steve Carlton	30.00	15.00	9.00
256	Gates Brown	.90	.45	.25
257	Jim Ray	.90	.45	.25
258	Jackie Hernandez	.90	.45	.25
259	Bill Short	.90	.45	.25
260	*Reggie Jackson*	450.00	180.00	113.00
261	Bob Johnson	.90	.45	.25
262	Mike Kekich	1.00	.50	.30
263	Jerry May	.90	.45	.25
264	Bill Landis	.90	.45	.25
265	Chico Cardenas	.90	.45	.25
266	Dodgers Rookies (Alan Foster, Tom Hutton)	.90	.45	.25
267	Vicente Romo	.90	.45	.25
268	Al Spangler	.90	.45	.25
269	Al Weis	1.00	.50	.30
270	Mickey Lolich	3.50	1.75	1.00
271	Larry Stahl	.90	.45	.25
272	Ed Stroud	.90	.45	.25
273	Ron Willis	.90	.45	.25
274	Clyde King	.90	.45	.25
275	Vic Davalillo	.90	.45	.25
276	Gary Wagner	.90	.45	.25
277	*Rod Hendricks*	.90	.45	.25
278	Gary Geiger	.90	.45	.25
279	Roger Nelson	.90	.45	.25
280	Alex Johnson	.90	.45	.25
281	Ted Kubiak	.90	.45	.25
282	Pat Jarvis	.90	.45	.25
283	Sandy Alomar	.90	.45	.25
284	Expos Rookies (Jerry Robertson, Mike Wegener)	.90	.45	.25
285	Don Mincher	1.00	.50	.30
286	*Dock Ellis*	1.25	.60	.40
287	Jose Tartabull	.90	.45	.25
288	Ken Holtzman	1.00	.50	.30
289	Bart Shirley	.90	.45	.25
290	Jim Kaat	4.50	2.25	1.25
291	Vern Fuller	.90	.45	.25
292	Al Downing	1.25	.60	.40
293	Dick Dietz	.90	.45	.25
294	Jim Lemon	.90	.45	.25
295	Tony Perez	4.50	2.25	1.25
296	*Andy Messersmith*	1.25	.60	.40
297	Deron Johnson	.90	.45	.25
298	Dave Nicholson	.90	.45	.25
299	Mark Belanger	1.00	.50	.30
300	Felipe Alou	1.25	.60	.40
301	Darrell Brandon	.90	.45	.25
302	Jim Pagliaroni	.90	.45	.25
303	Cal Koonce	1.00	.50	.30
304	Padres Rookies (Bill Davis, *Clarence Gaston*)	1.00	.50	.30
305	Dick McAuliffe	1.00	.50	.30
306	Jim Grant	.90	.45	.25
307	Gary Kolb	.90	.45	.25
308	Wade Blasingame	.90	.45	.25
309	Walt Williams	.90	.45	.25
310	Tom Haller	1.00	.50	.30
311	*Sparky Lyle*	4.00	2.00	1.25
312	Lee Elia	.90	.45	.25
313	Bill Robinson	1.00	.50	.30
314	Checklist 328-425 (Don Drysdale)	3.50	1.75	1.00
315	Eddie Fisher	.90	.45	.25
316	Hal Lanier	1.00	.50	.30
317	Bruce Look	.90	.45	.25
318	Jack Fisher	.90	.45	.25
319	Ken McMullen	.90	.45	.25
320	Dal Maxvill	1.00	.50	.30
321	Jim McAndrew	1.00	.50	.30
322	Jose Vidal	1.00	.50	.30
323	Larry Miller	.90	.45	.25
324	Tigers Rookies (Les Cain, Dave Campbell)	.90	.45	.25
325	Jose Cardenal	1.00	.50	.30
326	Gary Sutherland	.90	.45	.25
327	Willie Crawford	.90	.45	.25
328	Joe Horlen	.40	.20	.12
329	Rick Joseph	.40	.20	.12
330	Tony Conigliaro	1.50	.70	.45
331	Braves Rookies (Gil Garrido, *Tom House*)	.50	.25	.15
332	Fred Talbot	.80	.40	.25
333	Ivan Murrell	.40	.20	.12
334	Phil Roof	.40	.20	.12
335	Bill Mazeroski	1.75	.90	.50
336	Jim Roland	.40	.20	.12
337	Marty Martinez	.40	.20	.12
338	*Del Unser*	.50	.25	.15
339	Reds Rookies (Steve Mingori, Jose Pena)	.40	.20	.12
340	Dave McNally	.80	.40	.25
341	Dave Adlesh	.40	.20	.12
342	Bubba Morton	.40	.20	.12
343	Dan Frisella	.70	.35	.20
344	Tom Matchick	.40	.20	.12
345	Frank Linzy	.40	.20	.12
346	Wayne Comer	.80	.40	.25
347	Randy Hundley	.40	.20	.12
348	Steve Hargan	.40	.20	.12
349	Dick Williams	.80	.40	.25
350	Richie Allen	2.00	1.00	.60

		NR MT	EX	VG
351	Carroll Sembera	.40	.20	.12
352	Paul Schaal	.40	.20	.12
353	Jeff Torborg	.50	.25	.15
354	Nate Oliver	.80	.40	.25
355	Phil Niekro	5.00	2.50	1.50
356	Frank Quilici	.40	.20	.12
357	Carl Taylor	.40	.20	.12
358	Athletics Rookies (George Lauzerique, Roberto Rodriguez)	.40	.20	.12
359	Dick Kelley	.40	.20	.12
360	Jim Wynn	.80	.40	.25
361	Gary Holman	.40	.20	.12
362	Jim Maloney	.50	.25	.15
363	Russ Nixon	.40	.20	.12
364	Tommie Agee	.80	.40	.25
365	Jim Fregosi	1.00	.50	.30
366	Bo Belinsky	1.00	.50	.30
367	Lou Johnson	.40	.20	.12
368	Vic Roznovsky	.40	.20	.12
369	Bob Skinner	.40	.20	.12
370	Juan Marichal	7.00	3.50	2.00
371	Sal Bando	.80	.40	.25
372	Adolfo Phillips	.40	.20	.12
373	Fred Lasher	.40	.20	.12
374	Bob Tillman	.40	.20	.12
375	Harmon Killebrew	12.00	6.00	3.50
376	Royals Rookies (Mike Fiore, *Jim Rooker*)	.50	.25	.15
377	Gary Bell	.80	.40	.25
378	Jose Herrera	.40	.20	.12
379	Ken Boyer	1.75	.90	.50
380	Stan Bahnsen	.80	.40	.25
381	Ed Kranepool	.80	.40	.25
382	Pat Corrales	.80	.40	.25
383	Casey Cox	.40	.20	.12
384	Larry Shepard	.40	.20	.12
385	Orlando Cepeda	3.50	1.75	1.00
386	Jim McGlothlin	.40	.20	.12
387	Bobby Klaus	.40	.20	.12
388	Tom McCraw	.40	.20	.12
389	Dan Coombs	.40	.20	.12
390	Bill Freehan	.70	.35	.20
391	Ray Culp	.40	.20	.12
392	Bob Burda	.40	.20	.12
393	Gene Brabender	.40	.20	.12
394	Pilots Rookies (Lou Piniella, Marv Staehle)	3.00	1.50	.90
395	Chris Short	.60	.30	.20
396	Jim Campanis	.40	.20	.12
397	Chuck Dobson	.40	.20	.12
398	Tito Francona	.50	.25	.15
399	Bob Bailey	.40	.20	.12
400	Don Drysdale	8.00	4.00	2.50
401	Jake Gibbs	.80	.40	.25
402	Ken Boswell	.70	.35	.20
403	Bob Miller	.40	.20	.12
404	Cubs Rookies (Vic LaRose, Gary Ross)	.40	.20	.12
405	Lee May	1.00	.50	.30
406	Phil Ortega	.40	.20	.12
407	Tom Egan	.40	.20	.12
408	Nate Colbert	.40	.20	.12
409	Bob Moose	.40	.20	.12
410	Al Kaline	12.00	6.00	3.50
411	Larry Dierker	.50	.25	.15
412	Checklist 426-512 (Mickey Mantle)	7.00	3.50	2.00
413	Roland Sheldon	.80	.40	.25
414	Duke Sims	.40	.20	.12
415	Ray Washburn	.40	.20	.12
416	Willie McCovey AS	3.50	1.75	1.00
417	Ken Harrelson AS	1.00	.50	.30
418	Tommy Helms AS	.70	.35	.20
419	Rod Carew AS	4.50	2.25	1.25
420	Ron Santo AS	1.00	.50	.30
421	Brooks Robinson AS	4.00	2.00	1.25
422	Don Kessinger AS	.70	.35	.20
423	Bert Campaneris AS	.80	.40	.25
424	Pete Rose AS	12.00	6.00	3.50
425	Carl Yastrzemski AS	6.00	3.00	1.75
426	Curt Flood AS	1.00	.50	.30
427	Tony Oliva AS	1.50	.70	.45
428	Lou Brock AS	3.50	1.75	1.00
429	Willie Horton AS	.80	.40	.25
430	Johnny Bench AS	10.00	5.00	3.00
431	Bill Freehan AS	.70	.35	.20
432	Bob Gibson AS	3.50	1.75	1.00
433	Denny McLain AS	1.50	.70	.45
434	Jerry Koosman AS	1.00	.50	.30
435	Sam McDowell AS	.80	.40	.25
436	Gene Alley	.70	.35	.20
437	Luis Alcaraz	.40	.20	.12
438	Gary Waslewski	.40	.20	.12
439	White Sox Rookies (Ed Herrmann, Dan Lazar)	.40	.20	.12
440a	Willie McCovey (last name in white)	90.00	45.00	27.00
440b	Willie McCovey (last name in yellow)	20.00	10.00	6.00
441a	Dennis Higgins (last name in white)	10.00	5.00	3.00
441b	Dennis Higgins (last name in yellow)	.40	.20	.12
442	Ty Cline	.40	.20	.12
443	Don Wert	.40	.20	.12
444a	Joe Moeller (last name in white)	10.00	5.00	3.00
444b	Joe Moeller (last name in yellow)	.40	.20	.12
445	Bobby Knoop	.40	.20	.12
446	Claude Raymond	.40	.20	.12
447a	Ralph Houk (last name in white)	15.00	7.50	4.50
447b	Ralph Houk (last name in yellow)	1.50	.70	.45
448	Bob Tolan	.50	.25	.15
449	Paul Lindblad	.40	.20	.12
450	Billy Williams	6.00	3.00	1.75
451a	Rich Rollins (first name in white)	10.00	5.00	3.00
451b	Rich Rollins (first name in yellow)	.80	.40	.25
452a	Al Ferrara (first name in white)	10.00	5.00	3.00
452b	Al Ferrara (first name in yellow)	.40	.20	.12
453	Mike Cuellar	.80	.40	.25
454a	Phillies Rookies (Larry Colton, *Don Money*) (names in white)	10.00	5.00	3.00
454b	Phillies Rookies (Larry Colton, *Don Money*) (names in yellow)	.80	.40	.25
455	Sonny Siebert	.40	.20	.12
456	Bud Harrelson	1.00	.50	.30
457	Dalton Jones	.40	.20	.12
458	Curt Blefary	.40	.20	.12
459	Dave Boswell	.40	.20	.12
460	Joe Torre	1.75	.90	.50
461a	Mike Epstein (last name in white)	10.00	5.00	3.00
461b	Mike Epstein (last name in yellow)	.50	.25	.15
462	Red Schoendienst	1.50	.70	.45
463	Dennis Ribant	.40	.20	.12
464a	Dave Marshall (last name in white)	10.00	5.00	3.00
464b	Dave Marshall (last name in yellow)	.40	.20	.12
465	Tommy John	4.50	2.25	1.25
466	John Boccabella	.40	.20	.12
467	Tom Reynolds	.40	.20	.12
468a	Pirates Rookies (Bruce Dal Canton, Bob Robertson) (names in white)	10.00	5.00	3.00
468b	Pirates Rookies (Bruce Dal Canton, Bob Robertson) (names in yellow)	.50	.25	.15
469	Chico Ruiz	.40	.20	.12
470a	Mel Stottlemyre (last name in white)	15.00	7.50	4.50
470b	Mel Stottlemyre (last name in yellow)	1.50	.70	.45
471a	Ted Savage (last name in white)	10.00	5.00	3.00
471b	Ted Savage (last name in yellow)	.40	.20	.12
472	Jim Price	.40	.20	.12
473a	Jose Arcia (first name in white)	10.00	5.00	3.00
473b	Jose Arcia (first name in yellow)	.40	.20	.12
474	Tom Murphy	.40	.20	.12
475	Tim McCarver	1.50	.70	.45
476a	Red Sox Rookies (*Ken Brett*, Gerry Moses) (names in white)	10.00	5.00	3.00
476b	Red Sox Rookies (*Ken Brett*, Gerry Moses) (names in yellow)	.50	.25	.15
477	Jeff James	.40	.20	.12
478	Don Buford	.60	.30	.20
479	Richie Scheinblum	.40	.20	.12
480	Tom Seaver	90.00	45.00	27.00
481	*Bill Melton*	.80	.40	.25
482a	Jim Gosger (first name in white)	10.00	5.00	3.00
482b	Jim Gosger (first name in yellow)	.80	.40	.25
483	Ted Abernathy	.40	.20	.12
484	Joe Gordon	.50	.25	.15
485a	Gaylord Perry (last name in white)	75.00	38.00	23.00
485b	Gaylord Perry (last name in yellow)	10.00	5.00	3.00
486a	Paul Casanova (last name in white)	10.00	5.00	3.00
486b	Paul Casanova (last name in yellow)	.40	.20	.12
487	Denis Menke	.40	.20	.12
488	Joe Sparma	.40	.20	.12
489	Clete Boyer	.80	.40	.25
490	Matty Alou	1.00	.50	.30
491a	Twins Rookies (Jerry Crider, George Mitterwald) (names in white)	10.00	5.00	3.00
491b	Twins Rookies (Jerry Crider, George Mitterwald) (names in yellow)	.40	.20	.12
492	Tony Cloninger	.50	.25	.15
493a	Wes Parker (last name in white)	10.00	5.00	3.00
493b	Wes Parker (last name in yellow)	.70	.35	.20
494	Ken Berry	.40	.20	.12
495	Bert Campaneris	1.25	.60	.40
496	Larry Jaster	.40	.20	.12
497	Julian Javier	.40	.20	.12
498	Juan Pizarro	.40	.20	.12
499	Astros Rookies (Don Bryant, Steve Shea)	.40	.20	.12
500a	Mickey Mantle (last name in white)	475.00	190.00	119.00
500b	Mickey Mantle (last name in yellow)	175.00	70.00	44.00
501a	Tony Gonzalez (first name in white)	10.00	5.00	3.00
501b	Tony Gonzalez (first name in yellow)	.40	.20	.12
502	Minnie Rojas	.40	.20	.12
503	Larry Brown	.40	.20	.12
504	Checklist 513-588 (Brooks Robinson)	4.00	2.00	1.25
505a	Bobby Bolin (last name in white)	10.00	5.00	3.00
505b	Bobby Bolin (last name in yellow)	.40	.20	.12
506	Paul Blair	.50	.25	.15
507	Cookie Rojas	.40	.20	.12
508	Moe Drabowsky	.40	.20	.12
509	Manny Sanguillen	.50	.25	.15
510	Rod Carew	50.00	25.00	15.00
511a	Diego Segui (first name in white)	10.00	5.00	3.00
511b	Diego Segui (first name in yellow)	.80	.40	.25
512	Cleon Jones	.80	.40	.25
513	Camilo Pascual	.90	.45	.25
514	Mike Lum	.70	.35	.20
515	Dick Green	.70	.35	.20
516	Earl Weaver	3.50	1.75	1.00
517	Mike McCormick	.80	.40	.25
518	Fred Whitfield	.70	.35	.20
519	Yankees Rookies (Len Boehmer, Gerry Kenney)	1.00	.50	.30
520	Bob Veale	.80	.40	.25
521	George Thomas	.70	.35	.20
522	Joe Hoerner	.70	.35	.20
523	Bob Chance	.70	.35	.20
524	Expos Rookies (Jose Laboy, Floyd Wicker)	.70	.35	.20
525	Earl Wilson	.70	.35	.20
526	Hector Torres	.70	.35	.20
527	Al Lopez	3.00	1.50	.90
528	Claude Osteen	.90	.45	.25
529	Ed Kirkpatrick	.70	.35	.20
530	Cesar Tovar	.70	.35	.20
531	Dick Farrell	.70	.35	.20
532	Bird Hill Aces (Mike Cuellar, Jim Hardin, Dave McNally, Tom Phoebus)	1.50	.70	.45
533	Nolan Ryan	300.00	120.00	75.00
534	Jerry McNertney	.90	.45	.25
535	Phil Regan	.70	.35	.20
536	Padres Rookies (Danny Breeden, *Dave Roberts*)	.80	.40	.25
537	Mike Paul	.70	.35	.20
538	Charlie Smith	.70	.35	.20
539	Ted Shows How (Mike Epstein, Ted Williams)	3.25	1.75	1.00
540	Curt Flood	1.50	.70	.45
541	Joe Verbanic	1.00	.50	.30
542	Bob Aspromonte	.70	.35	.20
543	Fred Newman	.70	.35	.20
544	Tigers Rookies (Mike Kilkenny, Ron Woods)	.70	.35	.20
545	Willie Stargell	10.00	5.00	3.00
546	Jim Nash	.70	.35	.20
547	Billy Martin	3.25	1.75	1.00
548	Bob Locker	.70	.35	.20
549	Ron Brand	.70	.35	.20
550	Brooks Robinson	12.00	6.00	3.50
551	Wayne Granger	.70	.35	.20
552	Dodgers Rookies (*Ted Sizemore, Bill Sudakis*)	.80	.40	.25
553	Ron Davis	.70	.35	.20
554	Frank Bertaina	.70	.35	.20
555	Jim Hart	.80	.40	.25
556	A's Stars (Sal Bando, Bert Campaneris, Danny Cater)	1.50	.70	.45
557	Frank Fernandez	1.00	.50	.30
558	*Tom Burgmeier*	.80	.40	.25
559	Cards Rookies (Joe Hague, Jim Hicks)	.70	.35	.20
560	Luis Tiant	1.50	.70	.45
561	Ron Clark	.70	.35	.20
562	*Bob Watson*	1.00	.50	.30
563	Marty Pattin	.90	.45	.25
564	Gil Hodges	6.00	3.00	1.75
565	Hoyt Wilhelm	6.00	3.00	1.75
566	Ron Hansen	.70	.35	.20
567	Pirates Rookies (Elvio Jimenez, Jim Shellenback)	.70	.35	.20
568	Cecil Upshaw	.70	.35	.20
569	Billy Harris	.70	.35	.20
570	Ron Santo	1.75	.90	.50
571	Cap Peterson	.70	.35	.20
572	Giants Heroes (Juan Marichal, Willie McCovey)	7.00	3.50	2.00
573	Jim Palmer	25.00	12.50	7.50
574	George Scott	.90	.45	.25
575	Bill Singer	.80	.40	.25
576	Phillies Rookies (Ron Stone, Bill Wilson)	.70	.35	.20
577	Mike Hegan	1.00	.50	.30
578	Don Bosch	.70	.35	.20
579	*Dave Nelson*	.80	.40	.25
580	Jim Northrup	.80	.40	.25
581	Gary Nolan	.70	.35	.20
582a	Checklist 589-664 (Tony Oliva) (red circle on back)	3.50	1.75	1.00
582b	Checklist 589-664 (Tony Oliva) (white circle on back)	2.50	1.25	.70
583	*Clyde Wright*	.80	.40	.25
584	Don Mason	.70	.35	.20
585	Ron Swoboda	.90	.45	.25
586	Tim Cullen	.70	.35	.20
587	*Joe Rudi*	1.75	.90	.50
588	Bill White	1.00	.50	.30
589	Joe Pepitone	2.00	1.00	.60
590	Rico Carty	1.00	.50	.30
591	Mike Hedlund	.70	.35	.20
592	Padres Rookies (Rafael Robles, Al Santorini)	.70	.35	.20
593	Don Nottebart	.70	.35	.20
594	Dooley Womack	.70	.35	.20
595	Lee Maye	.70	.35	.20
596	Chuck Hartenstein	.70	.35	.20
597	A.L. Rookies (Larry Burchart, *Rollie Fingers*, Bob Floyd)	50.00	25.00	15.00
598	Ruben Amaro	.70	.35	.20
599	John Boozer	.70	.35	.20
600	Tony Oliva	2.25	1.25	.70
601	Tug McGraw	2.00	1.00	.60
602	Cubs Rookies (Alec Distaso, Jim Qualls, Don Young)	.70	.35	.20
603	Joe Keough	.70	.35	.20
604	Bobby Etheridge	.70	.35	.20
605	Dick Ellsworth	.70	.35	.20
606	Gene Mauch	.90	.45	.25
607	Dick Bosman	.70	.35	.20
608	Dick Simpson	1.00	.50	.30
609	Phil Gagliano	.70	.35	.20
610	Jim Hardin	.70	.35	.20
611	Braves Rookies (Bob Didier, Walt Hriniak, Gary Neibauer)	.70	.35	.20
612	Jack Aker	1.00	.50	.30
613	Jim Beauchamp	.70	.35	.20
614	Astros Rookies (Tom Griffin, Skip Guinn)	.70	.35	.20
615	Len Gabrielson	.70	.35	.20
616	Don McMahon	.70	.35	.20
617	Jesse Gonder	.70	.35	.20
618	Ramon Webster	.70	.35	.20
619	Royals Rookies (Bill Butler, *Pat Kelly*, Juan Rios)	.80	.40	.25
620	Dean Chance	.80	.40	.25
621	Bill Voss	.70	.35	.20
622	Dan Osinski	.70	.35	.20

		NR MT	EX	VG
623	Hank Allen	.70	.35	.20
624	N.L. Rookies (Darrel Chaney, Duffy Dyer, Terry Harmon)	.80	.40	.25
625	Mack Jones	.70	.35	.20
626	Gene Michael	1.00	.50	.30
627	George Stone	.70	.35	.20
628	Red Sox Rookies (*Bill Conigliaro*, Syd O'Brien, Fred Wenz)	.90	.45	.25
629	Jack Hamilton	.70	.35	.20
630	*Bobby Bonds*	10.00	5.00	3.00
631	John Kennedy	.90	.45	.25
632	Jon Warden	.70	.35	.20
633	Harry Walker	.80	.40	.25
634	Andy Etchebarren	.70	.35	.20
635	George Culver	.70	.35	.20
636	Woodie Held	.70	.35	.20
637	Padres Rookies (Jerry DaVanon, *Clay Kirby*, Frank Reberger)	.80	.40	.25
638	Ed Sprague	.70	.35	.20
639	Barry Moore	.70	.35	.20
640	Fergie Jenkins	5.00	2.50	1.50
641	N.L. Rookies (Bobby Darwin, Tommy Dean, John Miller)	.70	.35	.20
642	John Hiller	.80	.40	.25
643	Billy Cowan	1.00	.50	.30
644	Chuck Hinton	.70	.35	.20
645	George Brunet	.70	.35	.20
646	Expos Rookies (Dan McGinn, *Carl Morton*)	.90	.45	.25
647	Dave Wickersham	.70	.35	.20
648	Bobby Wine	.70	.35	.20
649	Al Jackson	.90	.45	.25
650	Ted Williams	7.00	3.50	2.00
651	Gus Gil	.90	.45	.25
652	Eddie Watt	.70	.35	.20
653	*Aurelio Rodriguez* (photo actually batboy Leonard Garcia)	1.50	.70	.45
654	White Sox Rookies (*Carlos May*, Rich Morales, Don Secrist)	.90	.45	.25
655	Mike Hershberger	.70	.35	.20
656	Dan Schneider	.70	.35	.20
657	Bobby Murcer	2.25	1.25	.70
658	A.L. Rookies (Bill Burbach, Tom Hall, Jim Miles)	1.00	.50	.30
659	Johnny Podres	1.75	.90	.50
660	Reggie Smith	1.75	.90	.50
661	Jim Merritt	.70	.35	.20
662	Royals Rookies (Dick Drago, Bob Oliver, George Spriggs)	.80	.40	.25
663	Dick Radatz	.90	.45	.25
664	Ron Hunt	2.00	.50	.25

1969 Topps Decals

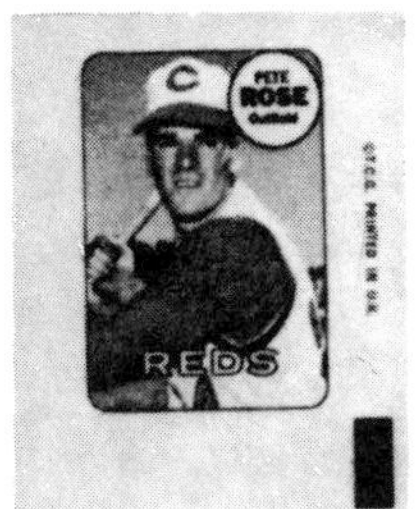

Designed as an insert for 1969 regular issue card packs, these decals are virtually identical in format to the '69 cards. The 48 decals in the set measure 1" by 2-1/2," although they are mounted on white paper backing which measures 1-3/4" by 2-1/8."

		NR MT	EX	VG
	Complete Set:	350.00	175.00	105.00
	Common Player:	4.00	2.00	1.25
(1)	Hank Aaron	40.00	20.00	12.00
(2)	Richie Allen	4.00	2.00	1.25
(3)	Felipe Alou	4.00	2.00	1.25
(4)	Matty Alou	4.00	2.00	1.25
(5)	Luis Aparicio	4.50	2.25	1.25
(6)	Bob Clemente	50.00	25.00	15.00
(7)	Donn Clendenon	4.00	2.00	1.25
(8)	Tommy Davis	4.00	2.00	1.25
(9)	Don Drysdale	7.00	3.50	2.00
(10)	Joe Foy	4.00	2.00	1.25
(11)	Jim Fregosi	4.00	2.00	1.25
(12)	Bob Gibson	7.00	3.50	2.00
(13)	Tony Gonzalez	4.00	2.00	1.25
(14)	Tom Haller	4.00	2.00	1.25
(15)	Ken Harrelson	4.00	2.00	1.25
(16)	Tommy Helms	4.00	2.00	1.25
(17)	Willie Horton	4.00	2.00	1.25
(18)	Frank Howard	4.00	2.00	1.25
(19)	Reggie Jackson	100.00	50.00	30.00
(20)	Fergie Jenkins	6.00	3.00	1.75
(21)	Harmon Killebrew	6.00	3.00	1.75
(22)	Jerry Koosman	4.00	2.00	1.25
(23)	Mickey Mantle	75.00	38.00	23.00
(24)	Willie Mays	35.00	17.50	10.50
(25)	Tim McCarver	4.00	2.00	1.25
(26)	Willie McCovey	7.00	3.50	2.00
(27)	Sam McDowell	4.00	2.00	1.25
(28)	Denny McLain	4.00	2.00	1.25
(29)	Dave McNally	4.00	2.00	1.25
(30)	Don Mincher	4.00	2.00	1.25
(31)	Rick Monday	4.00	2.00	1.25
(32)	Tony Oliva	4.00	2.00	1.25
(33)	Camilo Pascual	4.00	2.00	1.25
(34)	Rick Reichardt	4.00	2.00	1.25
(35)	Pete Rose	25.00	12.50	7.50
(36)	Frank Robinson	7.00	3.50	2.00
(37)	Ron Santo	4.00	2.00	1.25
(38)	Dick Selma	4.00	2.00	1.25
(39)	Tom Seaver	50.00	25.00	15.00
(40)	Chris Short	4.00	2.00	1.25
(41)	Rusty Staub	4.00	2.00	1.25
(42)	Mel Stottlemyre	4.00	2.00	1.25
(43)	Luis Tiant	4.00	2.00	1.25
(44)	Pete Ward	4.00	2.00	1.25
(45)	Hoyt Wilhelm	6.00	3.00	1.75
(46)	Maury Wills	4.00	2.00	1.25
(47)	Jim Wynn	4.00	2.00	1.25
(48)	Carl Yastrzemski	30.00	15.00	9.00

1969 Topps Deckle Edge

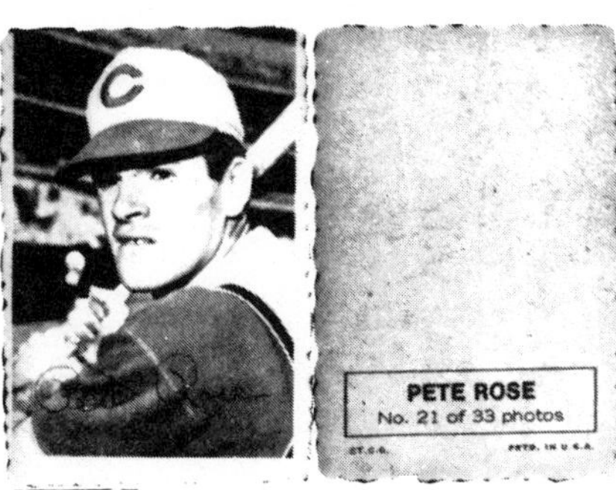

These 2-1/4" by 3-1/4" inch cards take their name from their interesting borders which have a scalloped effect. The fronts have a black and white picture of the player along with a blue facsimile autograph. Backs have the player's name and the card number in light blue ink in a small box at the bottom of the card. Technically, there are only 33 numbered cards, but there are actually 35 possible players; both Jim Wynn and Hoyt Wilhelm cards are found as #11 while cards of Joe Foy and Rusty Staub can be found as #22. Many of the players in the set are stars.

		NR MT	EX	VG
	Complete Set:	100.00	50.00	30.00
	Common Player:	1.00	.50	.30
1	Brooks Robinson	15.00	7.50	4.50
2	Boog Powell	1.00	.50	.30
3	Ken Harrelson	1.00	.50	.30
4	Carl Yastrzemski	15.00	7.50	4.50
5	Jim Fregosi	1.00	.50	.30
6	Luis Aparicio	1.25	.60	.40
7	Luis Tiant	1.00	.50	.30
8	Denny McLain	1.00	.50	.30
9	Willie Horton	1.00	.50	.30
10	Bill Freehan	1.00	.50	.30
11a	Hoyt Wilhelm	10.00	5.00	3.00
11b	Jim Wynn	10.00	5.00	3.00
12	Rod Carew	15.00	7.50	4.50
13	Mel Stottlemyre	1.00	.50	.30
14	Rick Monday	1.00	.50	.30
15	Tommy Davis	1.00	.50	.30
16	Frank Howard	1.00	.50	.30
17	Felipe Alou	1.00	.50	.30
18	Don Kessinger	1.00	.50	.30
19	Ron Santo	1.00	.50	.30
20	Tommy Helms	1.00	.50	.30
21	Pete Rose	10.00	5.00	3.00
22a	Rusty Staub	2.25	1.25	.70
22b	Joe Foy	7.00	3.50	2.00
23	Tom Haller	1.00	.50	.30
24	Maury Wills	1.00	.50	.30
25	Jerry Koosman	1.00	.50	.30
26	Richie Allen	1.00	.50	.30
27	Bob Clemente	15.00	7.50	4.50
28	Curt Flood	1.00	.50	.30
29	Bob Gibson	10.00	5.00	3.00
30	Al Ferrara	1.00	.50	.30
31	Willie McCovey	10.00	5.00	3.00
32	Juan Marichal	7.00	3.50	2.00
33	Willie Mays, Willie Mays	15.00	7.50	4.50

1969 Topps 4-on-1 Mini Stickers

Another in the long line of Topps test issues, the 4-on-1s are 2-1/2" by 3-1/2" cards with blank backs featuring a quartet of miniature stickers in the design of the same cards from the 1969 Topps regular set. There are 25 different cards, for a total of 100 different stickers. As they are not common, Mint cards bring fairly strong prices on today's market. As the set was drawn from the 3rd Series of the regular cards, it includes some rookie stickers and World Series highlight stickers.

		NR MT	EX	VG
	Complete Set:	950.00	475.00	285.00
	Common Player:	15.00	7.50	4.50
(1)	Jerry Adair, Willie Mays, Johnny Morris, Don Wilson	100.00	50.00	30.00
(2)	Tommie Aaron, Jim Britton, Donn Clendenon, Woody Woodward	15.00	7.50	4.50
(3)	World Series Game 4, Tommy Davis, Don Pavletich, Vada Pinson	20.00	10.00	6.00
(4)	Max Alvis, Glenn Beckert, Ron Fairly, Rick Wise	15.00	7.50	4.50
(5)	Johnny Callison, Jim French, Lum Harris, Dick Selma	15.00	7.50	4.50
(6)	World Series Game 3, Bob Gibson, Larry Haney, Rick Reichardt	40.00	20.00	12.00
(7)	Houston Rookie Stars, Wally Bunker, Don Cardwell, Joe Gibbon	15.00	7.50	4.50
(8)	Ollie Brown, Jim Bunning, Andy Kosco, Ron Reed	20.00	10.00	6.00
(9)	Bill Dillman, Jim Lefebvre, John Purdin, John Roseboro	15.00	7.50	4.50
(10)	Bill Hands, Chuck Harrison, Lindy McDaniel, Felix Millan	15.00	7.50	4.50
(11)	Jack Hiatt, Dave Johnson, Mel Nelson, Tommie Sisk	18.00	9.00	5.50
(12)	Clay Dalrymple, Leo Durocher, John Odom, Wilbur Wood	18.00	9.00	5.50
(13)	Hank Bauer, Kevin Collins, Ray Oyler, Russ Snyder	15.00	7.50	4.50
(14)	Red Sox Rookie Stars, World Series Game 7, Gerry Arrigo, Jim Perry	18.00	9.00	5.50
(15)	World Series Game 2, Bill McCool, Roberto Pena, Doug Rader	15.00	7.50	4.50
(16)	Ed Brinkman, Roy Face, Willie Horton, Bob Rodgers	18.00	9.00	5.50
(17)	Dave Baldwin, J.C. Martin, Dave May, Ray Sadecki	15.00	7.50	4.50
(18)	World Series Game 1, Jose Pagan, Tom Phoebus, Mike Shannon	15.00	7.50	4.50
(19)	Pete Rose, Lee Stange, Don Sutton, Ted Uhlaender	275.00	137.00	82.00
(20)	Joe Grzenda, Frank Howard, Dick Tracewski, Jim Weaver	20.00	10.00	6.00
(21)	White Sox Rookie Stars, Joe Azcue, Grant Jackson, Denny McLain	20.00	10.00	6.00
(22)	John Edwards, Jim Fairey, Phillies Rookies, Stan Williams	15.00	7.50	4.50
(23)	World Series Summary, John Bateman, Willie Smith, Leon Wagner	15.00	7.50	4.50
(24)	World Series Game 5, Yankees Rookies, Chris Cannizzaro, Bob Hendley	15.00	7.50	4.50
(25)	Cardinals Rookie Stars, Joe Nossek, Rico Petrocelli, Carl Yastrzemski	175.00	87.00	52.00

1969 Topps Stamps

Topps continued to refine its efforts at baseball stamps in 1969 with the release of 240 player stamps, each measuring 1" by 1-7/16." Each stamp jsd s color photo along with the player's name, position and team. Unlike prior stamp issues, the 1969 stamps have 24 separate albums (one per team). The stamps were issued in strips of 12.

	NR MT	EX	VG
Complete Sheet Set:	250.00	125.00	75.00
Common Sheet:	1.25	.60	.40
Complete Stamp Album Set:	14.00	7.00	4.25

	NR MT	EX	VG
Single Stamp Album:	.50	.25	.15
(1) Tommie Agee, Sandy Alomar, Jose Cardenal, Dean Chance, Joe Foy, Jim Grant, Don Kessinger, Mickey Mantle, Jerry May, Bob Rodgers, Cookie Rojas, Gary Sutherland	18.00	9.00	5.50
(2) Jesus Alou, Mike Andrews, Larry Brown, Moe Drabowsky, Alex Johnson, Lew Krausse, Jim Lefebvre, Dal Maxvill, John Odom, Claude Osteen, Rick Reichardt, Luis Tiant	1.50	.70	.45
(3) Hank Aaron, Matty Alou, Max Alvis, Nelson Briles, Eddie Fisher, Bud Harrelson, Willie Horton, Randy Hundley, Larry Jaster, Jim Kaat, Gary Peters, Pete Ward	7.00	3.50	2.00
(4) Don Buford, John Callison, Tommy Davis, Jackie Hernandez, Fergie Jenkins, Lee May, Denny McLain, Bob Oliver, Roberto Pena, Tony Perez, Joe Torre, Tom Tresh	3.00	1.50	.90
(5) Jim Bunning, Dean Chance, Joe Foy, Sonny Jackson, Don Kessinger, Rick Monday, Gaylord Perry, Roger Repoz, Cookie Rojas, Mel Stottlemyre, Leon Wagner, Jim Wynn	3.00	1.50	.90
(6) Felipe Alou, Gerry Arrigo, Bob Aspromonte, Gary Bell, Clay Dalrymple, Jim Fregosi, Tony Gonzalez, Duane Josephson, Dick McAuliffe, Tony Oliva, Brooks Robinson, Willie Stargell	6.00	3.00	1.75
(7) Steve Barber, Donn Clendenon, Joe Coleman, Vic Davalillo, Russ Gibson, Jerry Grote, Tom Haller, Andy Kosco, Willie McCovey, Don Mincher, Joe Morgan, Don Wilson	4.00	2.00	1.25
(8) George Brunet, Don Buford, John Callison, Danny Cater, Tommy Davis, Willie Davis, John Edwards, Jim Hart, Mickey Lolich, Willie Mays, Roberto Pena, Mickey Stanley	7.00	3.50	2.00
(9) Ernie Banks, Glenn Beckert, Ken Berry, Horace Clarke, Bob Clemente, Larry Dierker, Len Gabrielson, Jake Gibbs, Jerry Koosman, Sam McDowell, Tom Satriano, Bill Singer	3.50	1.75	1.00
(10) Gene Alley, Lou Brock, Larry Brown, Moe Drabowsky, Frank Howard, Tommie John, Roger Nelson, Claude Osteen, Phil Regan, Rick Reichardt, Tony Taylor, Roy White	4.00	2.00	1.25
(11) Bob Allison, John Bateman, Don Drysdale, Dave Johnson, Harmon Killebrew, Jim Maloney, Bill Mazeroski, Gerry McNertney, Ron Perranoski, Rico Petrocelli, Pete Rose, Billy Williams	18.00	9.00	5.50
(12) Bernie Allen, Jose Arcia, Stan Bahnsen, Sal Bando, Jim Davenport, Tito Francona, Dick Green, Ron Hunt, Mack Jones, Vada Pinson, George Scott, Don Wert	1.50	.70	.45
(13) Gerry Arrigo, Bob Aspromonte, Joe Azcue, Curt Blefary, Orlando Cepeda, Bill Freehan, Jim Fregosi, Dave Giusti, Duane Josephson, Tim McCarver, Jose Santiago, Bob Tolan	2.00	1.00	.60
(14) Jerry Adair, Johnny Bench, Clete Boyer, John Briggs, Bert Campaneris, Woody Fryman, Ron Kline, Bobby Knoop, Ken McMullen, Adolfo Phillips, John Roseboro, Tom Seaver	7.00	3.50	2.00
(15) Norm Cash, Ron Fairly, Bob Gibson, Bill Hands, Cleon Jones, Al Kaline, Paul Schaal, Mike Shannon, Duke Sims, Reggie Smith, Steve Whitaker, Carl Yastrzemski	12.00	6.00	3.50
(16) Steve Barber, Paul Casanova, Dick Dietz, Russ Gibson, Jerry Grote, Tom Haller, Ed Kranepool, Juan Marichal, Denis Menke, Jim Nash, Bill Robinson, Frank Robinson	4.00	2.00	1.25
(17) Bobby Bolin, Ollie Brown, Rod Carew, Mike Epstein, Bud Harrelson, Larry Jaster, Dave McNally, Willie Norton, Milt Pappas, Gary Peters, Paul Popovich, Stan Williams	6.00	3.00	1.75
(18) Ted Abernathy, Bob Allison, Ed Brinkman, Don Drysdale, Jim Hardin, Julian Javier, Hal Lanier, Jim McGlothlin, Ron Perranoski, Rich Rollins, Ron Santo, Billy Williams	3.00	1.50	.90
(19) Richie Allen, Luis Aparicio, Wally Bunker, Curt Flood, Ken Harrelson, Jim Hunter, Denver Lemaster, Felix Millan, Jim Northrop (Northrup), Art Shamsky, Larry Stahl, Ted Uhlaender	3.00	1.50	.90
(20) Bob Bailey, Johnny Bench, Woody Fryman, Jim Hannan, Ron Kline, Al McBean, Camilo Pascual, Joe Pepitone, Doug Rader, Ron Reed, John Roseboro, Sonny Siebert	3.00	1.50	.90
(21) Jack Aker, Tommy Harper, Tommy Helms, Dennis Higgins, Jim Hunter, Don Lock, Lee Maye, Felix Millan, Jim Northrop (Northrup), Larry Stahl, Don Sutton, Zoilo Versalles	3.00	1.50	.90
(22) Norm Cash, Ed Charles, Joe Horlen, Pat Jarvis, Jim Lonborg, Manny Mota, Boog Powell, Dick Selma, Mike Shannon, Duke Sims, Steve Whitaker, Hoyt Wilhelm	3.00	1.50	.90
(23) Bernie Allen, Ray Culp, Al Ferrara, Tito Francona, Dick Green, Ron Hunt, Ray Oyler, Tom Phoebus, Rusty Staub, Bob Veale, Maury Wills, Wilbur Wood	2.00	1.00	.60
(24) Ernie Banks, Mark Belanger, Steve Blass, Horace Clarke, Bob Clemente, Larry Dierker, Dave Duncan, Chico Salmon, Chris Short, Ron Swoboda, Cesar Tovar, Rick Wise	3.50	1.75	1.00

NOTE: A card number in parentheses ( ) indicates the set is unnumbered.

1969 Topps Super

These 2-1/4" by 3-1/4" cards are not the bigger "Super" cards which would be seen in following years. Rather, what enabled Topps to dub them "Super Baseball Cards" is their high-gloss finish which enhances the bright color photograph used on their fronts. The only other design element on the front is a facsimile autograph. The backs contain a box at the the bottom which carries the player's name, team, position, a copyright line and the card number. Another unusual feature is that the cards have rounded corners. The 66-card set saw limited production, meaning supplies are tight today. Considering the quality of the cards and the fact that many big names are represented, it's easy to understand why the set is quite expensive and desirable.

		NR MT	EX	VG
Complete Set:		6000.	3000.	1800.
Common Player:		25.00	12.50	7.50
1	Dave McNally	25.00	12.50	7.50
2	Frank Robinson	350.00	175.00	105.00
3	Brooks Robinson	350.00	175.00	105.00
4	Ken Harrelson	25.00	12.50	7.50
5	Carl Yastrzemski	600.00	300.00	180.00
6	Ray Culp	25.00	12.50	7.50
7	James Fregosi	25.00	12.50	7.50
8	Rick Reichardt	25.00	12.50	7.50
9	V. Davalillo	25.00	12.50	7.50
10	Luis Aparicio	35.00	17.50	10.50
11	Pete Ward	25.00	12.50	7.50
12	Joe Horlen	25.00	12.50	7.50
13	Luis Tiant	25.00	12.50	7.50
14	Sam McDowell	25.00	12.50	7.50
15	Jose Cardenal	25.00	12.50	7.50
16	Willie Horton	25.00	12.50	7.50
17	Denny McLain	25.00	12.50	7.50
18	Bill Freehan	25.00	12.50	7.50
19	Harmon Killebrew	200.00	100.00	60.00
20	Tony Oliva	25.00	12.50	7.50
21	Dean Chance	25.00	12.50	7.50
22	Joe Foy	25.00	12.50	7.50
23	Roger Nelson	25.00	12.50	7.50
24	Mickey Mantle	1500.	750.00	450.00
25	Mel Stottlemyre	25.00	12.50	7.50
26	Roy White	25.00	12.50	7.50
27	Rick Monday	25.00	12.50	7.50
28	Reginald Jackson	750.00	375.00	225.00
29	Dagoberto Campaneris	25.00	12.50	7.50
30	Frank Howard	25.00	12.50	7.50
31	Camilo Pascual	25.00	12.50	7.50
32	Tommy Davis	25.00	12.50	7.50
33	Don Mincher	25.00	12.50	7.50
34	Henry Aaron	500.00	250.00	150.00
35	Felipe Rojas Alou	25.00	12.50	7.50
36	Joseph Torre	25.00	12.50	7.50
37	Fergie Jenkins	25.00	12.50	7.50
38	Ronald Santo	25.00	12.50	7.50
39	Billy Williams	40.00	20.00	12.00
40	Tommy Helms	25.00	12.50	7.50
41	Pete Rose	400.00	200.00	120.00
42	Joe Morgan	250.00	125.00	75.00
43	Jim Wynn	25.00	12.50	7.50
44	Curt Blefary	25.00	12.50	7.50
45	Willie Davis	25.00	12.50	7.50
46	Donald Drysdale	250.00	125.00	75.00
47	Tom Haller	25.00	12.50	7.50
48	Rusty Staub	25.00	12.50	7.50
49	Maurice Wills	25.00	12.50	7.50
50	Cleon Jones	25.00	12.50	7.50
51	Jerry Koosman	25.00	12.50	7.50
52	Tom Seaver	600.00	300.00	180.00
53	Rich Allen	25.00	12.50	7.50
54	Chris Short	25.00	12.50	7.50
55	Cookie Rojas	25.00	12.50	7.50
56	Mateo Alou	25.00	12.50	7.50
57	Steve Blass	25.00	12.50	7.50
58	Roberto Clemente	600.00	300.00	180.00
59	Curt Flood	25.00	12.50	7.50
60	Robert Gibson	75.00	38.00	23.00
61	Tim McCarver	25.00	12.50	7.50
62	Dick Selma	25.00	12.50	7.50
63	Ollie Brown	25.00	12.50	7.50
64	Juan Marichal	60.00	30.00	18.00
65	Willie Mays	500.00	250.00	150.00
66	Willie McCovey	60.00	30.00	18.00

1969 Topps Team Posters

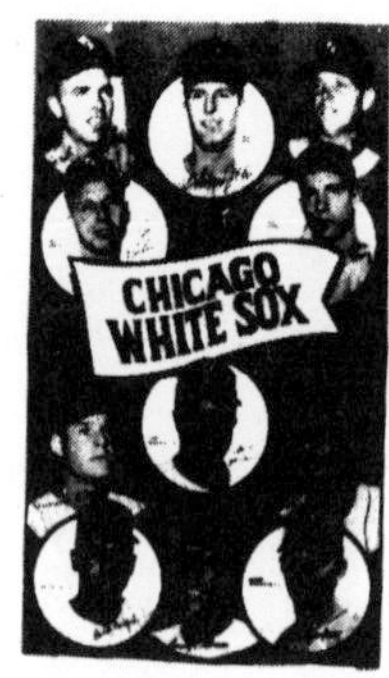

Picking up where the 1968 posters left off, the 1969 poster is larger at about 12" by 20." The posters, 24 in number like the previous year, are very different in style. Each has a team focus with a large pennant carrying the team name, along with nine or ten photos of players. Each of the photos carries a name and a facsimile autograph. Unfortunately, the bigger size of 1969 posters meant they had to be folded to fit in their packages as was the case in 1968. That means that collectors today will have a tough job finding them without fairly heavy creases from the folding.

	NR MT	EX	VG
Complete Set:	800.00	400.00	240.00
Common Poster:	17.00	8.50	5.00
1 Detroit Tigers (Norm Cash, Bill Freehan, Willie Horton, Al Kaline, Mickey Lolich, Dick McAuliffe, Denny McLain, Jim Northrup, Mickey Stanley, Don Wert, Earl Wilson)	40.00	20.00	12.00
2 Atlanta Braves (Hank Aaron, Felipe Alou, Clete Boyer, Rico Carty, Tito Francona, Sonny Jackson, Pat Jarvis, Felix Millan, Phil Niekro, Milt Pappas, Joe Torre)	40.00	20.00	12.00
3 Boston Red Sox (Mike Andrews, Tony Conigliaro, Ray Culp, Russ Gibson, Ken Harrelson, Jim Lonborg, Rico Petrocelli, Jose Santiago, George Scott, Reggie Smith, Carl Yastrzemski)	60.00	30.00	18.00
4 Chicago Cubs (Ernie Banks, Glenn Beckert, Bill Hands, Jim Hickman, Ken Holtzman, Randy Hundley, Fergie Jenkins, Don Kessinger, Adolfo Phillips, Ron Santo, Billy Williams)	35.00	17.50	10.50
5 Baltimore Orioles (Mark Belanger, Paul Blair, Don Buford, Andy Etchebarren, Jim Hardin, Dave Johnson, Dave McNally, Tom Phoebus, Boog Powell, Brooks Robinson, Frank Robinson)	50.00	25.00	15.00
6 Houston Astros (Curt Blefary, Donn Clendenon, Larry Dierker, John Edwards, Denny Lemaster, Denis Menke, Norm Miller, Joe Morgan, Doug Rader, Don Wilson, Jim Wynn)	17.00	8.50	5.00
7 Kansas City Royals (Jerry Adair, Wally Bunker, Mike Fiore, Joe Foy, Jackie Hernandez, Pat Kelly, Dave Morehead, Roger Nelson, Dave Nicholson, Eliseo Rodriguez, Steve Whitaker)	17.00	8.50	5.00
8 Philadelphia Phillies (Richie Allen, Johnny Callison, Woody Fryman, Larry Hisle, Don Money, Cookie Rojas, Mike Ryan, Chris Short, Tony Taylor, Bill White, Rick Wise)	17.00	8.50	5.00
9 Seattle Pilots (Jack Aker, Steve Barber, Gary Bell, Tommy Davis, Jim Gosger, Tommy Harper, Gerry McNertney, Don Mincher, Ray Oyler, Rich Rollins, Chico Salmon)	35.00	17.50	10.50
10 Montreal Expos (Bob Bailey, John Bateman, Jack Billingham, Jim Grant, Larry Jaster, Mack Jones, Manny Mota, Rusty Staub, Gary Sutherland, Jim Williams, Maury Wills)	17.00	8.50	5.00
11 Chicago White Sox (Sandy Alomar, Luis Aparicio, Ken Berry, Buddy Bradford, Joe Horlen, Tommy John, Duane Josephson, Tom McCraw, Bill Melton, Pete Ward, Wilbur Wood)	17.00	8.50	5.00
12 San Diego Padres (Jose Arcia, Danny Breeden, Ollie Brown, Bill Davis, Ron Davis, Tony Gonzalez, Dick Kelley, Al McBean, Roberto Pena, Dick Selma, Ed Spiezio)	17.00	8.50	5.00
13 Cleveland Indians (Max Alvis, Joe Azcue, Jose Cardenal, Vern Fuller, Lou Johnson, Sam McDowell, Sonny Siebert, Duke Sims, Russ Snyder, Luis Tiant, Zoilo Versalles)	17.00	8.50	5.00
14 San Francisco Giants (Bobby Bolin, Jim Davenport, Dick Dietz, Jim Hart, Ron Hunt, Hal Lanier, Juan Marichal, Willie Mays,			

		NR MT	EX	VG
	Willie McCovey, Gaylord Perry, Charlie Smith)	40.00	20.00	12.00
15	Minnesota Twins (Bob Allison, Chico Cardenas, Rod Carew, Dean Chance, Jim Kaat, Harmon Killebrew, Tony Oliva, Jim Perry, John Roseboro, Cesar Tovar, Ted Uhlaender)	40.00	20.00	12.00
16	Pittsburgh Pirates (Gene Alley, Matty Alou, Steve Blass, Jim Bunning, Bob Clemente, Rich Hebner, Jerry May, Bill Mazeroski, Bob Robertson, Willie Stargell, Bob Veale)	40.00	20.00	12.00
17	California Angels (Ruben Amaro, George Brunet, Bob Chance, Vic Davalillo, Jim Fregosi, Bobby Knoop, Jim McGlothlin, Rick Reichardt, Roger Repoz, Bob Rodgers, Hoyt Wilhelm)	20.00	10.00	6.00
18	St. Louis Cardinals (Nelson Briles, Lou Brock, Orlando Cepeda, Curt Flood, Bob Gibson, Julian Javier, Dal Maxvill, Tim McCarver, Vada Pinson, Mike Shannon, Ray Washburn)	35.00	17.50	10.50
19	New York Yankees (Stan Bahnsen, Horace Clarke, Bobby Cox, Jake Gibbs, Mickey Mantle, Joe Pepitone, Fritz Peterson, Bill Robinson, Mel Stottlemyre, Tom Tresh, Roy White)	90.00	45.00	27.00
20	Cincinnati Reds (Gerry Arrigo, Johnny Bench, Tommy Helms, Alex Johnson, Jim Maloney, Lee May, Gary Nolan, Tony Perez, Pete Rose, Bob Tolan, Woody Woodward)	90.00	45.00	27.00
21	Oakland Athletics (Sal Bando, Bert Campaneris, Danny Cater, Dick Green, Mike Hershberger, Jim Hunter, Reggie Jackson, Rick Monday, Jim Nash, John Odom, Jim Pagliaroni)	60.00	30.00	18.00
22	Los Angeles Dodgers (Willie Crawford, Willie Davis, Don Drysdale, Ron Fairly, Tom Haller, Andy Kosco, Jim Lefebvre, Claude Osteen, Paul Popovich, Bill Singer, Bill Sudakis)	35.00	17.50	10.50
23	Washington Senators (Bernie Allen, Brant Alyea, Ed Brinkman, Paul Casanova, Joe Coleman, Mike Epstein, Jim Hannan, Frank Howard, Ken McMullen, Camilo Pascual, Del Unser)	17.00	8.50	5.00
24	New York Mets (Tommie Agee, Ken Boswell, Ed Charles, Jerry Grote, Bud Harrelson, Cleon Jones, Jerry Koosman, Ed Kranepool, Jim McAndrew, Tom Seaver, Ron Swoboda)	100.00	50.00	30.00

1970 Topps

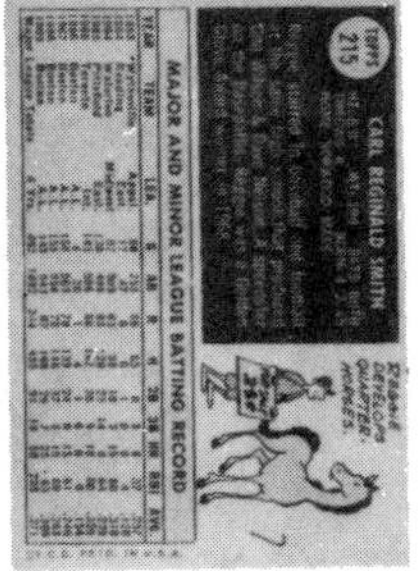

Topps established another set size record by coming out with 720 cards in 1970. The 2-1/2" by 3-1/2" cards have a color photo with a thin white frame. The photo have the player's team overprinted at the top, while the player's name in script and his position are at the bottom. A gray border surrounds the front. Card backs follows the normal design pattern, although they are more readable than some issues of the past. Team cards returned and were joined with many of the usual specialty cards. The World Series highlights were joined by cards with playoff highlights. Statistical leaders and All-Stars are also included in the set. High-numbered cards provide the most expensive cards in the set.

	NR MT	EX	VG
Complete Set:	1500.	750.00	450.00
Common Player: 1-546	.30	.15	.09
Common Player: 547-633	.80	.40	.25
Common Player: 634-720	2.00	1.00	.60

		NR MT	EX	VG
1	World Champions (Mets Team)	10.00	3.00	1.00
2	Diego Segui	.60	.30	.20
3	Darrel Chaney	.30	.15	.09
4	Tom Egan	.30	.15	.09
5	Wes Parker	.40	.20	.12
6	Grant Jackson	.30	.15	.09
7	Indians Rookies (Gary Boyd, Russ Nagelson)	.30	.15	.09
8	Jose Martinez	.30	.15	.09
9	Checklist 1-132	2.50	1.25	.70
10	Carl Yastrzemski	25.00	12.50	7.50
11	Nate Colbert	.30	.15	.09
12	John Hiller	.40	.20	.12
13	Jack Hiatt	.30	.15	.09
14	Hank Allen	.30	.15	.09
15	Larry Dierker	.40	.20	.12
16	Charlie Metro	.30	.15	.09
17	Hoyt Wilhelm	4.00	2.00	1.25
18	Carlos May	.50	.25	.15
19	John Boccabella	.30	.15	.09
20	Dave McNally	.60	.30	.20
21	Athletics Rookies *(Vida Blue, Gene Tenace)*	3.00	1.50	.90
22	Ray Washburn	.30	.15	.09
23	Bill Robinson	.50	.25	.15
24	Dick Selma	.30	.15	.09
25	Cesar Tovar	.30	.15	.09
26	Tug McGraw	1.25	.60	.40
27	Chuck Hinton	.30	.15	.09
28	Billy Wilson	.30	.15	.09
29	Sandy Alomar	.30	.15	.09
30	Matty Alou	.80	.40	.25
31	Marty Pattin	.50	.25	.15
32	Harry Walker	.40	.20	.12
33	Don Wert	.30	.15	.09
34	Willie Crawford	.30	.15	.09
35	Joe Horlen	.30	.15	.09
36	Reds Rookies (Danny Breeden, *Bernie Carbo)*	.50	.25	.15
37	Dick Drago	.30	.15	.09
38	Mack Jones	.30	.15	.09
39	Mike Nagy	.30	.15	.09
40	Rich Allen	1.50	.70	.45
41	George Lauzerique	.30	.15	.09
42	Tito Fuentes	.30	.15	.09
43	Jack Aker	.50	.25	.15
44	Roberto Pena	.30	.15	.09
45	Dave Johnson	1.00	.50	.30
46	Ken Rudolph	.30	.15	.09
47	Bob Miller	.30	.15	.09
48	Gill Garrido (Gil)	.30	.15	.09
49	Tim Cullen	.30	.15	.09
50	Tommie Agee	.40	.20	.12
51	Bob Christian	.30	.15	.09
52	Bruce Dal Canton	.30	.15	.09
53	John Kennedy	.50	.25	.15
54	Jeff Torborg	.40	.20	.12
55	John Odom	.40	.20	.12
56	Phillies Rookies (Joe Lis, Scott Reid)	.30	.15	.09
57	Pat Kelly	.30	.15	.09
58	Dave Marshall	.30	.15	.09
59	Dick Ellsworth	.30	.15	.09
60	Jim Wynn	.60	.30	.20
61	N.L. Batting Leaders (Bob Clemente, Cleon Jones, Pete Rose)	5.00	2.50	1.50
62	A.L. Batting Leaders (Rod Carew, Tony Oliva, Reggie Smith)	2.50	1.25	.70
63	N.L. RBI Leaders (Willie McCovey, Tony Perez, Ron Santo)	2.50	1.25	.70
64	A.L. RBI Leaders (Reggie Jackson, Harmon Killebrew, Boog Powell)	2.50	1.25	.70
65	N.L. Home Run Leaders (Hank Aaron, Lee May, Willie McCovey)	3.00	1.50	.90
66	A.L. Home Run Leaders (Frank Howard, Reggie Jackson, Harmon Killebrew)	2.50	1.25	.70
67	N.L. ERA Leaders (Steve Carlton, Bob Gibson, Juan Marichal)	3.00	1.50	.90
68	A.L. ERA Leaders (Dick Bosman, Mike Cuellar, Jim Palmer)	2.00	1.00	.60
69	N.L. Pitching Leaders (Fergie Jenkins, Juan Marichal, Phil Niekro, Tom Seaver)	2.50	1.25	.70
70	A.L. Pitching Leaders (Dave Boswell, Mike Cuellar, Dennis McLain, Dave McNally, Jim Perry, Mel Stottlemyre)	2.00	1.00	.60
71	N.L. Strikeout Leaders (Bob Gibson, Fergie Jenkins, Bill Singer)	2.50	1.25	.70
72	A.L. Strikeout Leaders (Mickey Lolich, Sam McDowell, Andy Messersmith)	2.00	1.00	.60
73	Wayne Granger	.30	.15	.09
74	Angels Rookies (Greg Washburn, Wally Wolf)	.30	.15	.09
75	Jim Kaat	2.50	1.25	.70
76	Carl Taylor	.30	.15	.09
77	Frank Linzy	.30	.15	.09
78	Joe Lahoud	.30	.15	.09
79	Clay Kirby	.30	.15	.09
80	Don Kessinger	.40	.20	.12
81	Dave May	.30	.15	.09
82	Frank Fernandez	.50	.25	.15
83	Don Cardwell	.30	.15	.09
84	Paul Casanova	.30	.15	.09
85	Max Alvis	.30	.15	.09
86	Lum Harris	.30	.15	.09
87	Steve Renko	.30	.15	.09
88	Pilots Rookies (Dick Baney, Miguel Fuentes)	.50	.25	.15
89	Juan Rios	.30	.15	.09
90	Tim McCarver	1.00	.50	.30
91	Rich Morales	.30	.15	.09
92	George Culver	.30	.15	.09
93	Rick Renick	.30	.15	.09
94	Fred Patek	.40	.20	.12
95	Earl Wilson	.30	.15	.09
96	Cards Rookies (Leron Lee, *Jerry Reuss)*	1.75	.90	.50
97	Joe Moeller	.30	.15	.09
98	Gates Brown	.30	.15	.09
99	Bobby Pfeil	.30	.15	.09
100	Mel Stottlemyre	1.00	.50	.30
101	Bobby Floyd	.30	.15	.09
102	Joe Rudi	.80	.40	.25
103	Frank Reberger	.30	.15	.09
104	Gerry Moses	.30	.15	.09
105	Tony Gonzalez	.30	.15	.09
106	Darold Knowles	.30	.15	.09
107	Bobby Etheridge	.30	.15	.09
108	Tom Burgmeier	.40	.20	.12
109	Expos Rookies (Garry Jestadt, Carl Morton)	.40	.20	.12
110	Bob Moose	.30	.15	.09
111	Mike Hegan	.50	.25	.15
112	Dave Nelson	.30	.15	.09
113	Jim Ray	.30	.15	.09
114	Gene Michael	.60	.30	.20
115	Alex Johnson	.40	.20	.12
116	Sparky Lyle	1.00	.50	.30
117	Don Young	.30	.15	.09
118	George Mitterwald	.30	.15	.09
119	Chuck Taylor	.30	.15	.09
120	Sal Bando	.80	.40	.25
121	Orioles Rookies (Fred Beene, *Terry Crowley)*	.40	.20	.12
122	George Stone	.30	.15	.09
123	Don Gutteridge	.30	.15	.09
124	Larry Jaster	.30	.15	.09
125	Deron Johnson	.30	.15	.09
126	Marty Martinez	.30	.15	.09
127	Joe Coleman	.40	.20	.12
128a	Checklist 133-263 (226 is R Perranoski)	3.00	1.50	.90
128b	Checklist 133-263 (226 is R. Perranoski)	2.50	1.25	.70
129	Jimmie Price	.30	.15	.09
130	Ollie Brown	.30	.15	.09
131	Dodgers Rookies (Ray Lamb, Bob Stinson)	.30	.15	.09
132	Jim McGlothlin	.30	.15	.09
133	Clay Carroll	.40	.20	.12
134	Danny Walton	.50	.25	.15
135	Dick Dietz	.30	.15	.09
136	Steve Hargan	.30	.15	.09
137	Art Shamsky	.30	.15	.09
138	Joe Foy	.30	.15	.09
139	Rich Nye	.30	.15	.09
140	Reggie Jackson	125.00	62.00	37.00
141	Pirates Rookies *(Dave Cash,* Johnny Jeter)	.50	.25	.15
142	Fritz Peterson	.50	.25	.15
143	Phil Gagliano	.30	.15	.09
144	Ray Culp	.30	.15	.09
145	Rico Carty	.80	.40	.25
146	Danny Murphy	.30	.15	.09
147	Angel Hermoso	.30	.15	.09
148	Earl Weaver	1.25	.60	.40
149	Billy Champion	.30	.15	.09
150	Harmon Killebrew	6.00	3.00	1.75
151	Dave Roberts	.30	.15	.09
152	Ike Brown	.30	.15	.09
153	Gary Gentry	.30	.15	.09
154	Senators Rookies (Jan Dukes, Jim Miles)	.30	.15	.09
155	Denis Menke	.30	.15	.09
156	Eddie Fisher	.30	.15	.09
157	Manny Mota	.50	.25	.15
158	Jerry McNertney	.50	.25	.15
159	Tommy Helms	.40	.20	.12
160	Phil Niekro	3.50	1.75	1.00
161	Richie Scheinblum	.30	.15	.09
162	Jerry Johnson	.30	.15	.09
163	Syd O'Brien	.30	.15	.09
164	Ty Cline	.30	.15	.09
165	Ed Kirkpatrick	.30	.15	.09
166	Al Oliver	2.00	1.00	.60
167	Bill Burbach	.50	.25	.15
168	Dave Watkins	.30	.15	.09
169	Tom Hall	.30	.15	.09
170	Billy Williams	4.50	2.25	1.25
171	Jim Nash	.30	.15	.09
172	Braves Rookies *(Ralph Garr,* Garry Hill)	1.00	.50	.30
173	Jim Hicks	.30	.15	.09
174	Ted Sizemore	.30	.15	.09
175	Dick Bosman	.30	.15	.09
176	Jim Hart	.40	.20	.12
177	Jim Northrup	.40	.20	.12
178	Denny Lemaster	.30	.15	.09
179	Ivan Murrell	.30	.15	.09
180	Tommy John	2.75	1.50	.80
181	Sparky Anderson	1.25	.60	.40
182	Dick Hall	.30	.15	.09
183	Jerry Grote	.40	.20	.12
184	Ray Fosse	.40	.20	.12
185	Don Mincher	.50	.25	.15
186	Rick Joseph	.30	.15	.09
187	Mike Hedlund	.30	.15	.09
188	Manny Sanguillen	.40	.20	.12
189	Yankees Rookies (Dave McDonald, *Thurman Munson)*	80.00	40.00	25.00
190	Joe Torre	1.25	.60	.40
191	Vicente Romo	.30	.15	.09
192	Jim Qualls	.30	.15	.09
193	Mike Wegener	.30	.15	.09
194	Chuck Manuel	.30	.15	.09
195	N.L. Playoff Game 1 (Seaver Wins Opener!)	3.00	1.50	.90
196	N.L. Playoff Game 2 (Mets Show Muscle!)	1.75	.90	.50
197	N.L. Playoff Game 3 (Ryan Saves The Day!)	6.00	3.00	1.75
198	N.L. Playoffs Summary (We're Number One!)	1.75	.90	.50
199	A.L. Playoff Game 1 (Orioles Win A Squeaker!)	1.50	.70	.45
200	A.L. Playoff Game 2 (Powell Scores Winning Run!)	1.75	.90	.50
201	A.L. Playoff Game 3 (Birds Wrap It Up!)	1.50	.70	.45
202	A.L. Playoffs Summary (Sweep Twins In Three!)	1.50	.70	.45
203	Rudy May	.40	.20	.12
204	Len Gabrielson	.30	.15	.09
205	Bert Campaneris	.80	.40	.25
206	Clete Boyer	.40	.20	.12
207	Tigers Rookies (Norman McRae, Bob Reed)	.30	.15	.09
208	Fred Gladding	.30	.15	.09
209	Ken Suarez	.30	.15	.09
210	Juan Marichal	8.00	4.00	2.50
211	Ted Williams	7.00	3.50	2.00
212	Al Santorini	.30	.15	.09
213	Andy Etchebarren	.30	.15	.09
214	Ken Boswell	.30	.15	.09
215	Reggie Smith	.60	.30	.20
216	Chuck Hartenstein	.30	.15	.09
217	Ron Hansen	.30	.15	.09
218	Ron Stone	.30	.15	.09
219	Jerry Kenney	.50	.25	.15
220	Steve Carlton	20.00	10.00	6.00

No.	Card	NR MT	EX	VG
221	Ron Brand	.30	.15	.09
222	Jim Rooker	.30	.15	.09
223	Nate Oliver	.30	.15	.09
224	Steve Barber	.50	.25	.15
225	Lee May	.60	.30	.20
226	Ron Perranoski	.40	.20	.12
227	Astros Rookies (*John Mayberry*, Bob Watkins)	1.00	.50	.30
228	Aurelio Rodriguez	.40	.20	.12
229	Rich Robertson	.30	.15	.09
230	Brooks Robinson	10.00	5.00	3.00
231	Luis Tiant	1.25	.60	.40
232	Bob Didier	.30	.15	.09
233	Lew Krausse	.30	.15	.09
234	Tommy Dean	.30	.15	.09
235	Mike Epstein	.40	.20	.12
236	Bob Veale	.40	.20	.12
237	Russ Gibson	.30	.15	.09
238	Jose Laboy	.30	.15	.09
239	Ken Berry	.30	.15	.09
240	Fergie Jenkins	2.50	1.25	.70
241	Royals Rookies (Al Fitzmorris, Scott Northey)	.30	.15	.09
242	Walter Alston	1.75	.90	.50
243	Joe Sparma	.30	.15	.09
244a	Checklist 264-372 (red bat on front)	3.00	1.50	.90
244b	Checklist 264-372 (brown bat on front)	2.50	1.25	.70
245	Leo Cardenas	.30	.15	.09
246	Jim McAndrew	.30	.15	.09
247	Lou Klimchock	.30	.15	.09
248	Jesus Alou	.40	.20	.12
249	Bob Locker	.50	.25	.15
250	Willie McCovey	6.00	3.00	1.75
251	Dick Schofield	.30	.15	.09
252	Lowell Palmer	.30	.15	.09
253	Ron Woods	.50	.25	.15
254	Camilo Pascual	.50	.25	.15
255	*Jim Spencer*	.50	.25	.15
256	Vic Davalillo	.40	.20	.12
257	Dennis Higgins	.30	.15	.09
258	Paul Popovich	.30	.15	.09
259	Tommie Reynolds	.30	.15	.09
260	Claude Osteen	.50	.25	.15
261	Curt Motton	.30	.15	.09
262	Padres Rookies (Jerry Morales, Jim Williams)	.30	.15	.09
263	Duane Josephson	.30	.15	.09
264	Rich Hebner	.40	.20	.12
265	Randy Hundley	.30	.15	.09
266	Wally Bunker	.30	.15	.09
267	Twins Rookies (Herman Hill, Paul Ratliff)	.30	.15	.09
268	Claude Raymond	.30	.15	.09
269	Cesar Gutierrez	.30	.15	.09
270	Chris Short	.40	.20	.12
271	Greg Goossen	.50	.25	.15
272	Hector Torres	.30	.15	.09
273	Ralph Houk	1.00	.50	.30
274	Gerry Arrigo	.30	.15	.09
275	Duke Sims	.30	.15	.09
276	Ron Hunt	.40	.20	.12
277	Paul Doyle	.30	.15	.09
278	Tommie Aaron	.50	.25	.15
279	*Bill Lee*	.50	.25	.15
280	Donn Clendenon	.40	.20	.12
281	Casey Cox	.30	.15	.09
282	Steve Huntz	.30	.15	.09
283	Angel Bravo	.30	.15	.09
284	Jack Baldschun	.30	.15	.09
285	Paul Blair	.40	.20	.12
286	Dodgers Rookies (*Bill Buckner*, Jack Jenkins)	5.00	2.50	1.50
287	Fred Talbot	.30	.15	.09
288	Larry Hisle	.40	.20	.12
289	Gene Brabender	.50	.25	.15
290	Rod Carew	25.00	12.50	7.50
291	Leo Durocher	1.25	.60	.40
292	Eddie Leon	.30	.15	.09
293	Bob Bailey	.30	.15	.09
294	Jose Azcue	.30	.15	.09
295	Cecil Upshaw	.30	.15	.09
296	Woody Woodward	.40	.20	.12
297	Curt Blefary	.50	.25	.15
298	Ken Henderson	.30	.15	.09
299	Buddy Bradford	.30	.15	.09
300	Tom Seaver	55.00	28.00	16.50
301	Chico Salmon	.30	.15	.09
302	Jeff James	.30	.15	.09
303	Brant Alyea	.30	.15	.09
304	*Bill Russell*	1.50	.70	.45
305	World Series Game 1 (Buford Belts Leadoff Homer!)	1.75	.90	.50
306	World Series Game 2 (Clendenon's Homer Breaks Ice!)	1.75	.90	.50
307	World Series Game 3 (Agee's Catch Saves The Day!)	1.75	.90	.50
308	World Series Game 4 (Martin's Bunt Ends Deadlock!)	1.75	.90	.50
309	World Series Game 5 (Koosman Shuts The Door!)	1.75	.90	.50
310	World Series Summary (Mets Whoop It Up!)	1.75	.90	.50
311	Dick Green	.30	.15	.09
312	Mike Torrez	.40	.20	.12
313	Mayo Smith	.30	.15	.09
314	Bill McCool	.30	.15	.09
315	Luis Aparicio	4.50	2.25	1.25
316	Skip Guinn	.30	.15	.09
317	Red Sox Rookies (Luis Alvarado, Billy Conigliaro)	.40	.20	.12
318	Willie Smith	.30	.15	.09
319	Clayton Dalrymple	.30	.15	.09
320	Jim Maloney	.40	.20	.12
321	Lou Piniella	1.50	.70	.45
322	Luke Walker	.30	.15	.09
323	Wayne Comer	.50	.25	.15
324	Tony Taylor	.30	.15	.09
325	Dave Boswell	.30	.15	.09
326	Bill Voss	.30	.15	.09
327	Hal King	.30	.15	.09
328	George Brunet	.30	.15	.09
329	Chris Cannizzaro	.30	.15	.09
330	Lou Brock	6.00	3.00	1.75
331	Chuck Dobson	.30	.15	.09
332	Bobby Wine	.30	.15	.09
333	Bobby Murcer	1.25	.60	.40
334	Phil Regan	.30	.15	.09
335	Bill Freehan	.40	.20	.12
336	Del Unser	.30	.15	.09
337	Mike McCormick	.40	.20	.12
338	Paul Schaal	.30	.15	.09
339	Johnny Edwards	.30	.15	.09
340	Tony Conigliaro	1.25	.60	.40
341	Bill Sudakis	.30	.15	.09
342	Wilbur Wood	.40	.20	.12
343a	Checklist 373-459 (red bat on front)	3.50	1.75	1.00
343b	Checklist 373-459 (brown bat on front)	3.00	1.50	.90
344	Marcelino Lopez	.30	.15	.09
345	Al Ferrara	.30	.15	.09
346	Red Schoendienst	1.25	.60	.40
347	Russ Snyder	.30	.15	.09
348	Mets Rookies (Jesse Hudson, Mike Jorgensen)	.40	.20	.12
349	Steve Hamilton	.50	.25	.15
350	Roberto Clemente	40.00	20.00	12.00
351	Tom Murphy	.30	.15	.09
352	Bob Barton	.30	.15	.09
353	Stan Williams	.30	.15	.09
354	Amos Otis	.50	.25	.15
355	Doug Rader	.30	.15	.09
356	Fred Lasher	.30	.15	.09
357	*Bob Burda*	.30	.15	.09
358	*Pedro Borbon*	.40	.20	.12
359	Phil Roof	.50	.25	.15
360	Curt Flood	1.00	.50	.30
361	Ray Jarvis	.30	.15	.09
362	Joe Hague	.30	.15	.09
363	Tom Shopay	.30	.15	.09
364	Dan McGinn	.30	.15	.09
365	Zoilo Versalles	.40	.20	.12
366	Barry Moore	.30	.15	.09
367	Mike Lum	.30	.15	.09
368	Ed Herrmann	.30	.15	.09
369	Alan Foster	.30	.15	.09
370	Tommy Harper	.70	.35	.20
371	Rod Gaspar	.30	.15	.09
372	Dave Giusti	.30	.15	.09
373	Roy White	1.00	.50	.30
374	Tommie Sisk	.30	.15	.09
375	Johnny Callison	.80	.40	.25
376	Lefty Phillips	.30	.15	.09
377	Bill Butler	.30	.15	.09
378	Jim Davenport	.30	.15	.09
379	Tom Tischinski	.30	.15	.09
380	Tony Perez	3.00	1.50	.90
381	Athletics Rookies (Bobby Brooks, Mike Olivo)	.30	.15	.09
382	Jack DiLauro	.30	.15	.09
383	Mickey Stanley	.40	.20	.12
384	Gary Neibauer	.30	.15	.09
385	George Scott	.40	.20	.12
386	Bill Dillman	.30	.15	.09
387	Orioles Team	1.50	.70	.45
388	Byron Browne	.30	.15	.09
389	Jim Shellenback	.30	.15	.09
390	Willie Davis	.80	.40	.25
391	Larry Brown	.30	.15	.09
392	Walt Hriniak	.30	.15	.09
393	John Gelnar	.50	.25	.15
394	Gil Hodges	4.00	2.00	1.25
395	Walt Williams	.30	.15	.09
396	Steve Blass	.40	.20	.12
397	Roger Repoz	.30	.15	.09
398	Bill Stoneman	.30	.15	.09
399	Yankees Team	2.00	1.00	.60
400	Denny McLain	1.50	.70	.45
401	Giants Rookies (John Harrell, Bernie Williams)	.30	.15	.09
402	Ellie Rodriguez	.30	.15	.09
403	Jim Bunning	3.25	1.75	1.00
404	Rich Reese	.30	.15	.09
405	Bill Hands	.30	.15	.09
406	Mike Andrews	.30	.15	.09
407	Bob Watson	.40	.20	.12
408	Paul Lindblad	.30	.15	.09
409	Bob Tolan	.40	.20	.12
410	Boog Powell	2.00	1.00	.60
411	Dodgers Team	1.50	.70	.45
412	Larry Burchart	.30	.15	.09
413	Sonny Jackson	.30	.15	.09
414	Paul Edmondson	.30	.15	.09
415	Julian Javier	.30	.15	.09
416	Joe Verbanic	.50	.25	.15
417	John Bateman	.30	.15	.09
418	John Donaldson	.50	.25	.15
419	Ron Taylor	.30	.15	.09
420	Ken McMullen	.30	.15	.09
421	Pat Dobson	.40	.20	.12
422	Royals Team	1.25	.60	.40
423	Jerry May	.30	.15	.09
424	Mike Kilkenny	.30	.15	.09
425	Bobby Bonds	1.25	.60	.40
426	Bill Rigney	.30	.15	.09
427	Fred Norman	.30	.15	.09
428	Don Buford	.40	.20	.12
429	Cubs Rookies (Randy Bobb, Jim Cosman)	.30	.15	.09
430	Andy Messersmith	.50	.25	.15
431	Ron Swoboda	.40	.20	.12
432a	Checklist 460-546 ("Baseball" on front in yellow)	4.00	2.00	1.25
432b	Checklist 460-546 ("Baseball" on front in white)	2.50	1.25	.70
433	Ron Bryant	.30	.15	.09
434	Felipe Alou	.70	.35	.20
435	Nelson Briles	.30	.15	.09
436	Phillies Team	1.25	.60	.40
437	Danny Cater	.50	.25	.15
438	Pat Jarvis	.30	.15	.09
439	Lee Maye	.30	.15	.09
440	Bill Mazeroski	1.00	.50	.30
441	John O'Donoghue	.50	.25	.15
442	Gene Mauch	.70	.35	.20
443	Al Jackson	.30	.15	.09
444	White Sox Rookies (Bill Farmer, John Matias)	.30	.15	.09
445	Vada Pinson	1.25	.60	.40
446	*Billy Grabarkewitz*	.40	.20	.12
447	Lee Stange	.30	.15	.09
448	Astros Team	1.25	.60	.40
449	Jim Palmer	15.00	7.50	4.50
450	Willie McCovey AS	3.50	1.75	1.00
451	Boog Powell AS	1.00	.50	.30
452	Felix Millan AS	.50	.25	.15
453	Rod Carew AS	4.00	2.00	1.25
454	Ron Santo AS	.80	.40	.25
455	Brooks Robinson AS	3.50	1.75	1.00
456	Don Kessinger AS	.50	.25	.15
457	Rico Petrocelli AS	.50	.25	.15
458	Pete Rose AS	8.00	4.00	2.50
459	Reggie Jackson AS	8.00	4.00	2.50
460	Matty Alou AS	.70	.35	.20
461	Carl Yastrzemski AS	5.00	2.50	1.50
462	Hank Aaron AS	5.50	2.75	1.75
463	Frank Robinson AS	3.50	1.75	1.00
464	Johnny Bench AS	5.00	2.50	1.50
465	Bill Freehan AS	.50	.25	.15
466	Juan Marichal AS	2.75	1.50	.80
467	Denny McLain AS	.80	.40	.25
468	Jerry Koosman AS	.60	.30	.20
469	Sam McDowell AS	.60	.30	.20
470	Willie Stargell	7.00	3.50	2.00
471	Chris Zachary	.30	.15	.09
472	Braves Team	1.25	.60	.40
473	Don Bryant	.50	.25	.15
474	Dick Kelley	.30	.15	.09
475	Dick McAuliffe	.40	.20	.12
476	Don Shaw	.30	.15	.09
477	Orioles Rookies (Roger Freed, Al Severinsen)	.30	.15	.09
478	Bob Heise	.30	.15	.09
479	Dick Woodson	.30	.15	.09
480	Glenn Beckert	.40	.20	.12
481	Jose Tartabull	.30	.15	.09
482	Tom Hilgendorf	.30	.15	.09
483	Gail Hopkins	.30	.15	.09
484	Gary Nolan	.30	.15	.09
485	Jay Johnstone	.50	.25	.15
486	Terry Harmon	.30	.15	.09
487	Cisco Carlos	.30	.15	.09
488	J.C. Martin	.30	.15	.09
489	Eddie Kasko	.30	.15	.09
490	Bill Singer	.40	.20	.12
491	Graig Nettles	4.00	2.00	1.25
492	Astros Rookies (Keith Lampard, Scipio Spinks)	.30	.15	.09
493	Lindy McDaniel	.50	.25	.15
494	Larry Stahl	.30	.15	.09
495	Dave Morehead	.30	.15	.09
496	Steve Whitaker	.30	.15	.09
497	Eddie Watt	.30	.15	.09
498	Al Weis	.30	.15	.09
499	Skip Lockwood	.50	.25	.15
500	Hank Aaron	25.00	12.50	7.50
501	White Sox Team	1.25	.60	.40
502	Rollie Fingers	4.00	2.00	1.25
503	Dal Maxvill	.40	.20	.12
504	Don Pavletich	.30	.15	.09
505	Ken Holtzman	.40	.20	.12
506	Ed Stroud	.30	.15	.09
507	Pat Corrales	.50	.25	.15
508	Joe Niekro	.70	.35	.20
509	Expos Team	1.25	.60	.40
510	Tony Oliva	1.75	.90	.50
511	Joe Hoerner	.30	.15	.09
512	Billy Harris	.30	.15	.09
513	Preston Gomez	.30	.15	.09
514	Steve Hovley	.50	.25	.15
515	Don Wilson	.30	.15	.09
516	Yankees Rookies (John Ellis, Jim Lyttle)	.50	.25	.15
517	Joe Gibbon	.30	.15	.09
518	Bill Melton	.40	.20	.12
519	Don McMahon	.30	.15	.09
520	Willie Horton	.70	.35	.20
521	Cal Koonce	.30	.15	.09
522	Angels Team	1.25	.60	.40
523	Jose Pena	.30	.15	.09
524	Alvin Dark	.60	.30	.20
525	Jerry Adair	.30	.15	.09
526	Ron Herbel	.30	.15	.09
527	Don Bosch	.30	.15	.09
528	Elrod Hendricks	.30	.15	.09
529	Bob Aspromonte	.30	.15	.09
530	Bob Gibson	8.00	4.00	2.50
531	Ron Clark	.30	.15	.09
532	Danny Murtaugh	.50	.25	.15
533	Buzz Stephen	.50	.25	.15
534	Twins Team	1.50	.70	.45
535	Andy Kosco	.30	.15	.09
536	Mike Kekich	.50	.25	.15
537	Joe Morgan	8.00	4.00	2.50
538	Bob Humphreys	.30	.15	.09
539	Phillies Rookies (*Larry Bowa*, Dennis Doyle)	3.00	1.50	.90
540	Gary Peters	.40	.20	.12
541	Bill Heath	.30	.15	.09
542a	Checklist 547-633 (grey bat on front)	3.50	1.75	1.00
542b	Checklist 547-633 (brown bat on front)	2.50	1.25	.70
543	Clyde Wright	.30	.15	.09
544	Reds Team	1.25	.60	.40
545	Ken Harrelson	1.25	.60	.40
546	Ron Reed	.40	.20	.12
547	Rick Monday	1.00	.50	.30
548	Howie Reed	.80	.40	.25
549	Cardinals Team	1.75	.90	.50
550	Frank Howard	2.25	1.25	.70
551	Dock Ellis	.90	.45	.25
552	Royals Rookies (Don O'Riley, Dennis Paepke, Fred Rico)	.80	.40	.25
553	Jim Lefebvre	.90	.45	.25
554	Tom Timmermann	.80	.40	.25
555	Orlando Cepeda	3.25	1.75	1.00
556	Dave Bristol	.90	.45	.25
557	Ed Kranepool	1.00	.50	.30
558	Vern Fuller	.80	.40	.25

		NR MT	EX	VG
559	Tommy Davis	1.25	.60	.40
560	Gaylord Perry	7.00	3.50	2.00
561	Tom McCraw	.80	.40	.25
562	Ted Abernathy	.80	.40	.25
563	Red Sox Team	2.00	1.00	.60
564	Johnny Briggs	.80	.40	.25
565	Jim Hunter	7.00	3.50	2.00
566	Gene Alley	.90	.45	.25
567	Bob Oliver	.80	.40	.25
568	Stan Bahnsen	.90	.45	.25
569	Cookie Rojas	.80	.40	.25
570	Jim Fregosi	1.00	.50	.30
571	Jim Brewer	.80	.40	.25
572	Frank Quilici	.80	.40	.25
573	Padres Rookies (Mike Corkins, Rafael Robles, Ron Slocum)	.80	.40	.25
574	Bobby Bolin	.90	.45	.25
575	Cleon Jones	.90	.45	.25
576	Milt Pappas	.90	.45	.25
577	Bernie Allen	.80	.40	.25
578	Tom Griffin	.80	.40	.25
579	Tigers Team	2.25	1.25	.70
580	Pete Rose	75.00	37.00	22.00
581	Tom Satriano	.80	.40	.25
582	Mike Paul	.80	.40	.25
583	Hal Lanier	.90	.45	.25
584	Al Downing	.90	.45	.25
585	Rusty Staub	2.00	1.00	.60
586	Rickey Clark	.80	.40	.25
587	Jose Arcia	.80	.40	.25
588a	Checklist 634-720 (666 is Adolpho Phillips)	4.50	2.25	1.25
588b	Checklist 634-720 (666 is Adolfo Phillips)	3.00	1.50	.90
589	Joe Keough	.80	.40	.25
590	Mike Cuellar	.90	.45	.25
591	Mike Ryan	.80	.40	.25
592	Daryl Patterson	.80	.40	.25
593	Cubs Team	1.75	.90	.50
594	Jake Gibbs	.90	.45	.25
595	Maury Wills	2.50	1.25	.70
596	Mike Hershberger	.90	.45	.25
597	Sonny Siebert	.80	.40	.25
598	Joe Pepitone	1.25	.60	.40
599	Senators Rookies (Gene Martin, Dick Stelmaszek, Dick Such)	.80	.40	.25
600	Willie Mays	45.00	23.00	13.50
601	Pete Richert	.80	.40	.25
602	Ted Savage	.80	.40	.25
603	Ray Oyler	.80	.40	.25
604	Clarence Gaston	.80	.40	.25
605	Rick Wise	.90	.45	.25
606	Chico Ruiz	.80	.40	.25
607	Gary Waslewski	.80	.40	.25
608	Pirates Team	1.75	.90	.50
609	*Buck Martinez*	.90	.45	.25
610	Jerry Koosman	1.25	.60	.40
611	Norm Cash	1.50	.70	.45
612	Jim Hickman	.90	.45	.25
613	Dave Baldwin	.90	.45	.25
614	Mike Shannon	.90	.45	.25
615	Mark Belanger	.90	.45	.25
616	Jim Merritt	.80	.40	.25
617	Jim French	.80	.40	.25
618	Billy Wynne	.80	.40	.25
619	Norm Miller	.80	.40	.25
620	Jim Perry	1.00	.50	.30
621	Braves Rookies (*Darrell Evans*, Rick Kester, Mike McQueen)	7.00	3.50	2.00
622	Don Sutton	4.50	2.25	1.25
623	Horace Clarke	.90	.45	.25
624	Clyde King	.80	.40	.25
625	Dean Chance	.90	.45	.25
626	Dave Ricketts	.80	.40	.25
627	Gary Wagner	.80	.40	.25
628	Wayne Garrett	.80	.40	.25
629	Merv Rettenmund	.90	.45	.25
630	Ernie Banks	15.00	7.50	4.50
631	Athletics Team	1.75	.90	.50
632	Gary Sutherland	.80	.40	.25
633	Roger Nelson	.80	.40	.25
634	Bud Harrelson	2.25	1.25	.70
635	Bob Allison	2.25	1.25	.70
636	Jim Stewart	2.00	1.00	.60
637	Indians Team	3.00	1.50	.90
638	Frank Bertaina	2.00	1.00	.60
639	Dave Campbell	2.00	1.00	.60
640	Al Kaline	25.00	12.50	7.50
641	Al McBean	2.00	1.00	.60
642	Angels Rookies (Greg Garrett, Gordon Lund, Jarvis Tatum)	2.00	1.00	.60
643	Jose Pagan	2.00	1.00	.60
644	Gerry Nyman	2.00	1.00	.60
645	Don Money	2.00	1.00	.60
646	Jim Britton	2.00	1.00	.60
647	Tom Matchick	2.00	1.00	.60
648	Larry Haney	2.00	1.00	.60
649	Jimmie Hall	2.00	1.00	.60
650	Sam McDowell	2.50	1.25	.70
651	Jim Gosger	2.00	1.00	.60
652	Rich Rollins	2.25	1.25	.70
653	Moe Drabowsky	2.00	1.00	.60
654	N.L. Rookies (Boots Day, *Oscar Gamble*, Angel Mangual)	2.50	1.25	.70
655	John Roseboro	2.25	1.25	.70
656	Jim Hardin	2.00	1.00	.60
657	Padres Team	4.00	2.00	1.25
658	Ken Tatum	2.00	1.00	.60
659	Pete Ward	2.25	1.25	.70
660	Johnny Bench	150.00	60.00	38.00
661	Jerry Robertson	2.00	1.00	.60
662	Frank Lucchesi	2.00	1.00	.60
663	Tito Francona	2.25	1.25	.70
664	Bob Robertson	2.00	1.00	.60
665	Jim Lonborg	2.25	1.25	.70
666	Adolfo Phillips	2.00	1.00	.60
667	Bob Meyer	2.25	1.25	.70
668	Bob Tillman	2.00	1.00	.60
669	White Sox Rookies (Bart Johnson, Dan Lazar, Mickey Scott)	2.00	1.00	.60
670	Ron Santo	3.25	1.75	1.00
671	Jim Campanis	2.00	1.00	.60
672	Leon McFadden	2.00	1.00	.60
673	Ted Uhlaender	2.00	1.00	.60
674	Dave Leonhard	2.00	1.00	.60
675	Jose Cardenal	2.25	1.25	.70
676	Senators Team	3.25	1.75	1.00
677	Woodie Fryman	2.25	1.25	.70
678	Dave Duncan	2.00	1.00	.60
679	Ray Sadecki	2.00	1.00	.60
680	Rico Petrocelli	2.25	1.25	.70
681	Bob Garibaldi	2.00	1.00	.60
682	Dalton Jones	2.00	1.00	.60
683	Reds Rookies (Vern Geishert, Hal McRae, Wayne Simpson)	2.75	1.50	.80
684	Jack Fisher	2.00	1.00	.60
685	Tom Haller	2.25	1.25	.70
686	Jackie Hernandez	2.00	1.00	.60
687	Bob Priddy	2.00	1.00	.60
688	Ted Kubiak	2.25	1.25	.70
689	Frank Tepedino	2.25	1.25	.70
690	Ron Fairly	2.25	1.25	.70
691	Joe Grzenda	2.00	1.00	.60
692	Duffy Dyer	2.00	1.00	.60
693	Bob Johnson	2.00	1.00	.60
694	Gary Ross	2.00	1.00	.60
695	Bobby Knoop	2.00	1.00	.60
696	Giants Team	3.25	1.75	1.00
697	Jim Hannan	2.00	1.00	.60
698	Tom Tresh	2.75	1.50	.80
699	Hank Aguirre	2.00	1.00	.60
700	Frank Robinson	40.00	20.00	12.00
701	Jack Billingham	2.00	1.00	.60
702	A.L. Rookies (Bob Johnson, Ron Klimkowski, Bill Zepp)	2.25	1.25	.70
703	Lou Marone	2.00	1.00	.60
704	Frank Baker	2.00	1.00	.60
705	Tony Cloninger	2.25	1.25	.70
706	John McNamara	2.50	1.25	.70
707	Kevin Collins	2.00	1.00	.60
708	Jose Santiago	2.00	1.00	.60
709	Mike Fiore	2.00	1.00	.60
710	Felix Millan	2.00	1.00	.60
711	Ed Brinkman	2.25	1.25	.70
712	Nolan Ryan	300.00	120.00	75.00
713	Pilots Team	12.00	6.00	3.50
714	Al Spangler	2.00	1.00	.60
715	Mickey Lolich	5.00	2.50	1.50
716	Cards Rookies (Sal Campisi, *Reggie Cleveland*, Santiago Guzman)	2.25	1.25	.70
717	Tom Phoebus	2.00	1.00	.60
718	Ed Spiezio	2.00	1.00	.60
719	Jim Roland	2.25	.90	.50
720	Rick Reichardt	4.00	1.00	.50

1970 Topps Candy Lids

The 1970 Topps Candy Lids are a test issue that was utilized again in 1973. The set is made up of 24 lids that measure 1-7/8" in diameter and were the tops of small 1.1 oz. tubs of "Baseball Stars Candy." Unlike the 1973 versions, the 1970 lids have no border surrounding the full-color photos. Frank Howard, Tom Seaver and Carl Yastrzemski photos are found on the bottom (inside) of the candy lid.

		NR MT	EX	VG
Complete Set:		2000.	1000.	600.00
Common Player:		30.00	15.00	9.00
(1)	Hank Aaron	200.00	100.00	60.00
(2)	Rich Allen	50.00	25.00	15.00
(3)	Luis Aparicio	80.00	40.00	24.00
(4)	Johnny Bench	200.00	100.00.	60.00
(5)	Ollie Brown	30.00	15.00	9.00
(6)	Willie Davis	30.00	15.00	9.00
(7)	Jim Fregosi	30.00	15.00	9.00
(8)	Mike Hegan	30.00	15.00	9.00
(9)	Frank Howard	50.00	25.00	15.00
(10)	Reggie Jackson	200.00	100.00	60.00
(11)	Fergie Jenkins	60.00	30.00	18.00
(12)	Harmon Killebrew	100.00	50.00	30.00
(13)	Juan Marichal	100.00	50.00	30.00
(14)	Bill Mazeroski	50.00	25.00	15.00
(15)	Tim McCarver	50.00	25.00	15.00
(16)	Sam McDowell	30.00	15.00	9.00
(17)	Denny McLain	50.00	25.00	15.00
(18)	Lou Piniella	50.00	25.00	15.00
(19)	Frank Robinson	100.00	50.00	30.00
(20)	Tom Seaver	175.00	87.00	52.00
(21)	Rusty Staub	50.00	25.00	15.00
(22)	Mel Stottlemyre	50.00	25.00	15.00
(23)	Jim Wynn	30.00	15.00	9.00
(24)	Carl Yastrzemski	150.00	75.00	45.00

1970 Topps Posters

Helping to ease a price increase, Topps included extremely fragile 8-11/16" by 9-5/8" posters in packs of regular cards. The posters feature color portraits and a smaller black and white "action" pose as well as the player's name, team and position at the top. Although there are Hall of Famers in the 24-poster set, all the top names are not represented. Once again, due to folding, heavy creases are a fact of life for today's collector.

		NR MT	EX	VG
Complete Set:		25.00	12.50	7.50
Common Player:		.40	.20	.12
1	Joe Horlen	.40	.20	.12
2	Phil Niekro	1.50	.70	.45
3	Willie Davis	.50	.25	.15
4	Lou Brock	2.00	1.00	.60
5	Ron Santo	.60	.30	.20
6	Ken Harrelson	.50	.25	.15
7	Willie McCovey	2.00	1.00	.60
8	Rick Wise	.40	.20	.12
9	Andy Messersmith	.40	.20	.12
10	Ron Fairly	.50	.25	.15
11	Johnny Bench	3.25	1.75	1.00
12	Frank Robinson	2.50	1.25	.70
13	Tommie Agee	.40	.20	.12
14	Roy White	.50	.25	.15
15	Larry Dierker	.40	.20	.12
16	Rod Carew	3.00	1.50	.90
17	Don Mincher	.40	.20	.12
18	Ollie Brown	.40	.20	.12
19	Ed Kirkpatrick	.40	.20	.12
20	Reggie Smith	.50	.25	.15
21	Bob Clemente	5.00	2.50	1.50
22	Frank Howard	.60	.30	.20
23	Bert Campaneris	.50	.25	.15
24	Denny McLain	.60	.30	.20

1970 Topps Scratch-Offs

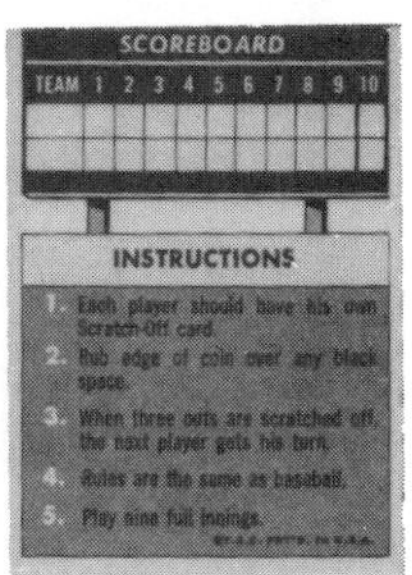

Needing inserts, and having not given up on the idea of a game which could be played with baseball cards, Topps provided a new game - the baseball scratch-off. The set consists of 24 cards. Unfolded, they measure 3-3/8" by 5," and reveal a baseball game of sorts which was played by rubbing the black ink off playing squares which then determined the "action." Fronts of the cards have a player picture as "captain," while backs have instructions and a scoreboard. Inserts with white centers are from 1970 while those with red centers are from 1971.

		NR MT	EX	VG
Complete Set:		20.00	10.00	6.00
Common Player:		.30	.15	.09
(1)	Hank Aaron	2.00	1.00	.60
(2)	Rich Allen	.50	.25	.15
(3)	Luis Aparicio	1.00	.50	.30
(4)	Sal Bando	.30	.15	.09
(5)	Glenn Beckert	.30	.15	.09

		NR MT	EX	VG
(6)	Dick Bosman	.30	.15	.09
(7)	Nate Colbert	.30	.15	.09
(8)	Mike Hegan	.30	.15	.09
(9)	Mack Jones	.30	.15	.09
(10)	Al Kaline	1.50	.70	.45
(11)	Harmon Killebrew	1.50	.70	.45
(12)	Juan Marichal	1.25	.60	.40
(13)	Tim McCarver	.40	.20	.12
(14)	Sam McDowell	.30	.15	.09
(15)	Claude Osteen	.30	.15	.09
(16)	Tony Perez	.60	.30	.20
(17)	Lou Piniella	.40	.20	.12
(18)	Boog Powell	.50	.25	.15
(19)	Tom Seaver	2.00	1.00	.60
(20)	Jim Spencer	.30	.15	.09
(21)	Willie Stargell	1.25	.60	.40
(22)	Mel Stottlemyre	.30	.15	.09
(23)	Jim Wynn	.30	.15	.09
(24)	Carl Yastrzemski	2.25	1.25	.70

1970 Topps Story Booklets

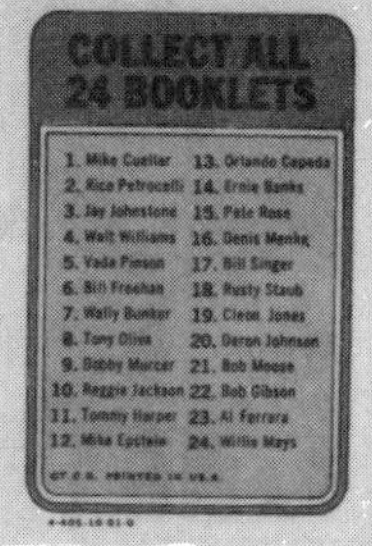

Measuring 2-1/2" by 3-7/16," the Topps Story Booklet was a 1970 regular pack insert. The booklet feature a photo, title and booklet number on the "cover." Inside are six pages of comic book story. The backs give a checklist of other available booklets. Not every star had a booklet as the set is only 24 in number.

		NR MT	EX	VG
Complete Set:		25.00	12.50	7.50
Common Player:		.30	.15	.09
1	Mike Cuellar	.40	.20	.12
2	Rico Petrocelli	.40	.20	.12
3	Jay Johnstone	.40	.20	.12
4	Walt Williams	.30	.15	.09
5	Vada Pinson	.50	.25	.15
6	Bill Freehan	.40	.20	.12
7	Wally Bunker	.30	.15	.09
8	Tony Oliva	.50	.25	.15
9	Bobby Murcer	.40	.20	.12
10	Reggie Jackson	5.00	2.50	1.50
11	Tommy Harper	.30	.15	.09
12	Mike Epstein	.30	.15	.09
13	Orlando Cepeda	.80	.40	.25
14	Ernie Banks	3.00	1.50	.90
15	Pete Rose	8.00	4.00	2.50
16	Denis Menke	.30	.15	.09
17	Bill Singer	.30	.15	.09
18	Rusty Staub	.50	.25	.15
19	Cleon Jones	.30	.15	.09
20	Deron Johnson	.30	.15	.09
21	Bob Moose	.30	.15	.09
22	Bob Gibson	4.00	2.00	1.25
23	Al Ferrara	.30	.15	.09
24	Willie Mays	7.00	3.50	2.00

1970 Topps Super

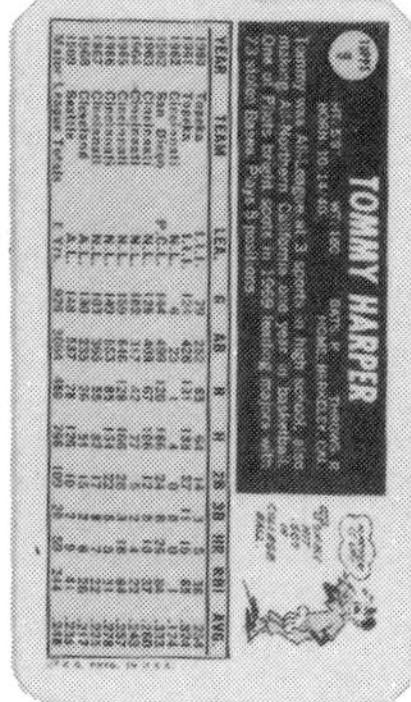

Representing a refinement of the concept begun in 1969, the 1970 Topps Supers had a new 3-1/8" by 5-1/4" postcard size. Printed on heavy stock with rounded corners, card fronts feature a borderless color photograph and facsimile autograph. Card backs are simply an enlarged back from the player's regular 1970 Topps card. The Topps Supers set numbers 42 cards. Probably due to the press sheet configuration eight of the 42 had smaller printings. The most elusive is card #38 (Boog Powell). The set was more widely produced than was the case in 1969, meaning collectors stand a much better chance of affording it.

		NR MT	EX	VG
Complete Set:		200.00	100.00	60.00
Common Player:		.75	.40	.25
1	Claude Osteen	3.00	1.50	.90
2	Sal Bando	3.50	1.75	1.00
3	Luis Aparicio	2.50	1.25	.70
4	Harmon Killebrew	4.00	2.00	1.25
5	Tom Seaver	25.00	12.50	7.50
6	Larry Dierker	.80	.40	.25
7	Bill Freehan	1.00	.50	.30
8	Johnny Bench	15.00	7.50	4.50
9	Tommy Harper	.80	.40	.25
10	Sam McDowell	1.00	.50	.30
11	Louis Brock	4.00	2.00	1.25
12	Roberto Clemente	15.00	7.50	4.50
13	Willie McCovey	4.00	2.00	1.25
14	Rico Petrocelli	.80	.40	.25
15	Philip Niekro	2.25	1.25	.70
16	Frank Howard	1.50	.70	.45
17	Denny McLain	1.25	.60	.40
18	Willie Mays	15.00	7.50	4.50
19	Wilver Stargell	3.50	1.75	1.00
20	Joe Horlen	.80	.40	.25
21	Ronald Santo	1.00	.50	.30
22	Dick Bosman	.80	.40	.25
23	Tim McCarver	1.00	.50	.30
24	Henry Aaron	15.00	7.50	4.50
25	Andy Messersmith	.80	.40	.25
26	Tony Oliva	1.25	.60	.40
27	Mel Stottlemyre	1.00	.50	.30
28	Reginald M. Jackson	18.00	9.00	5.50
29	Carl Yastrzemski	12.00	6.00	3.50
30	James Fregosi	1.00	.50	.30
31	Vada Pinson	1.25	.60	.40
32	Lou Piniella	1.25	.60	.40
33	Robert Gibson	4.00	2.00	1.25
34	Pete Rose	25.00	12.50	7.50
35	Jim Wynn	1.00	.50	.30
36	Ollie Brown	3.00	1.50	.90
37	Frank Robinson	18.00	9.00	5.50
38	John "Boog" Powell	60.00	30.00	18.00
39	Willie Davis	3.50	1.75	1.00
40	Billy Williams	12.00	6.00	3.50
41	Rusty Staub	1.25	.60	.40
42	Tommie Agee	.80	.40	.25

1971 Topps Baseball Tattoos

Topps once again produced baseball tattoos in 1971. This time, the tattoos came in a variety of sizes, shapes and themes. The sheets of tattoos measure 3-1/2" by 14-1/4." Each sheet contains an assortment of tattoos in two sizes, 1-3/4" by 2-3/8," or 1-3/16" by 1-3/4." There are players, facsimile autographed baseballs, team pennants and assorted baseball cartoon figures carried on the 16 different sheets. Listings below are for complete sheets; with the exception of the biggest-name stars, individual tattoos have little or no collector value.

		NR MT	EX	VG
Complete Sheet Set:		175.00	87.00	52.00
Common Sheet:		4.00	2.00	1.25
1	Brooks Robinson Autograph, Montreal Expos Pennant, San Francisco Giants Pennant, Sal Bando, Dick Bosman, Nate Colbert, Cleon Jones, Juan Marichal, B. Robinson	10.00	5.00	3.00
2	Boston Red Sox Pennant, Carl Yastrzemski Autograph, New York Mets Pennant, Glenn Beckert, Tommy Harper, Ken Henderson, Fritz Peterson, Bob Robertson, C. Yastrzemski	18.00	9.00	5.50
3	Jim Fregosi Autograph, New York Yankees Pennant, Philadelphia Phillies Pennant, Orlando Cepeda, Jim Fregosi, Randy Hundley, Reggie Jackson, Jerry Koosman, Jim Palmer	15.00	7.50	4.50
4	Kansas City Royals Pennant, Oakland Athletics Pennant, Sam McDowell Autograph, Dick Dietz, C. Gaston, Dave Johnson, Sam McDowell, Gary Nolan, Amos Otis	3.50	1.75	1.00
5	Al Kaline Autograph, Atlanta Braves Pennant, L.A. Dodgers Pennant, B. Grabarkewitz, Al Kaline, Lee May, Tom Murphy, Vada Pinson, M. Sanguillen	10.00	5.00	3.00
6	Chicago Cubs Pennant, Cincinnati Reds Pennant, Harmon Killebrew Autograph, Luis Aparicio, Paul Blair, C. Cannizzaro, D. Clendenon, Larry Dieker, H. Killebrew	10.00	5.00	3.00
7	Boog Powell Autograph, Cleveland Indians Pennant, Milwaukee Brewers Pennant, Rich Allen, B. Campaneris, Don Money, Boog Powell, Ted Savage, Rusty Staub	5.00	2.50	1.50
8	Chicago White Sox Pennant, Frank Howard Autograph, San Diego Padres Pennant, Leo Cardenas, Bill Hands, Frank Howard, Wes Parker, Reggie Smith, W. Stargell	5.00	2.50	1.50
9	Detroit Tigers Pennant, Henry Aaron Autograph, Hank Aaron, Tommy Agee, Jim Hunter, Dick McAuliffe, Tony Perez, Lou Piniella	15.00	7.50	4.50
10	Baltimore Orioles Pennant, Fergie Jenkins Autograph, R. Clemente, T. Conigliaro, Fergie Jenkins, T. Munson, Gary Peters, Joe Torre	12.00	6.00	3.50
11	Johnny Bench Autograph, Washington Senators Pennant, Johnny Bench, Rico Carty, B. Mazeroski, Bob Oliver, R. Petrocelli, F. Robinson	10.00	5.00	3.00
12	Billy Williams Autograph, Houston Astros Pennant, Bill Freehan, Dave McNally, Felix Millan, M. Stottlemyre, Bob Tolan, Billy Williams	6.00	3.00	1.75
13	Pittsburgh Pirates Pennant, Willie McCovey Autograph, Ray Culp, Bud Harrelson, Mickey Lolich, W. McCovey, Ron Santo, Roy White	9.00	4.50	2.75
14	Minnesota Twins Pennant, Tom Seaver Autograph, Bill Melton, Jim Perry, Pete Rose, Tom Seaver, Maury Wills, Clyde Wright	25.00	12.50	7.50
15	Robert Gibson Autograph, St. Louis Cardinals Pennant, Rod Carew, Bob Gibson, Alex Johnson, Don Kessinger, Jim Merritt, Rick Monday	9.00	4.50	2.75
16	California Angels Pennant, Willie Mays Autograph, Larry Bowa, Mike Cuellar, Ray Fosse, Willie Mays, Carl Morton, Tony Oliva	15.00	7.50	4.50

1971 Topps

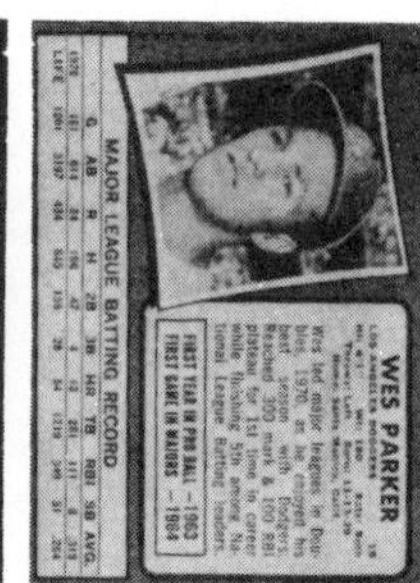

In 1971, Topps again increased the size of its set to 752 cards. These well-liked cards, measuring 2-1/2" by 3-1/2," feature a large color photo which has a thin white frame. Above the picture, in the card's overall black border, is the player's name, team and position. A facsimile autograph completes the front. Backs feature a major change as a black and white "snapshot" of the player appears. Abbreviated statistics, a line giving the player's first pro and major league games and a short biography complete the back of these innovative cards. Specialty cards in this issue are limited. There are statistical leaders as well as World Series and playoff highlights. High numbered cards #644-752 are scarce.

		NR MT	EX	VG
Complete Set:		1500.	750.00	425.00
Common Player: 1-523		.35	.20	.11
Common Player: 524-643		.80	.40	.25
Common Player: 644-752		2.25	1.25	.70
1	World Champions (Orioles Team)	5.00	1.25	.60
2	Dock Ellis	.50	.20	.12
3	Dick McAuliffe	.40	.20	.12
4	Vic Davalillo	.40	.20	.12
5	Thurman Munson	25.00	12.50	7.50
6	Ed Spiezio	.35	.20	.11
7	Jim Holt	.35	.20	.11
8	Mike McQueen	.35	.20	.11
9	George Scott	.50	.25	.15
10	Claude Osteen	.50	.25	.15
11	*Elliott Maddox*	.50	.25	.15
12	Johnny Callison	.60	.30	.20
13	White Sox Rookies (Charlie Brinkman,			

#	Card	NR MT	EX	VG
	Dick Moloney)	.35	.20	.11
14	*Dave Concepcion*	5.00	2.50	1.50
15	Andy Messersmith	.40	.20	.12
16	*Ken Singleton*	1.75	.90	.50
17	Billy Sorrell	.35	.20	.11
18	Norm Miller	.35	.20	.11
19	Skip Pitlock	.35	.20	.11
20	Reggie Jackson	50.00	25.00	15.00
21	Dan McGinn	.35	.20	.11
22	Phil Roof	.35	.20	.11
23	Oscar Gamble	.40	.20	.12
24	Rich Hand	.35	.20	.11
25	Clarence Gaston	.35	.20	.11
26	*Bert Blyleven*	50.00	30.00	15.00
27	Pirates Rookies (Fred Cambria, Gene Clines)	.35	.20	.11
28	Ron Klimkowski	.40	.20	.12
29	Don Buford	.40	.20	.12
30	Phil Niekro	3.25	1.75	1.00
31	Eddie Kasko	.35	.20	.11
32	Jerry DaVanon	.35	.20	.11
33	Del Unser	.35	.20	.11
34	Sandy Vance	.35	.20	.11
35	Lou Piniella	1.25	.60	.40
36	Dean Chance	.40	.20	.12
37	Rich McKinney	.35	.20	.11
38	*Jim Colborn*	.40	.20	.12
39	Tigers Rookies (Gene Lamont, *Lerrin LaGrow)*	.40	.20	.12
40	Lee May	.60	.30	.20
41	Rick Austin	.35	.20	.11
42	Boots Day	.35	.20	.11
43	Steve Kealey	.35	.20	.11
44	Johnny Edwards	.35	.20	.11
45	Jim Hunter	3.75	2.00	1.25
46	Dave Campbell	.35	.20	.11
47	Johnny Jeter	.35	.20	.11
48	Dave Baldwin	.35	.20	.11
49	Don Money	.40	.20	.12
50	Willie McCovey	6.00	3.00	1.75
51	Steve Kline	.40	.20	.12
52	Braves Rookies (Oscar Brown, *Earl Williams)*	.40	.20	.12
53	Paul Blair	.40	.20	.12
54	Checklist 1-132	2.50	1.25	.70
55	Steve Carlton	20.00	10.00	6.00
56	Duane Josephson	.35	.20	.11
57	Von Joshua	.35	.20	.11
58	Bill Lee	.40	.20	.12
59	Gene Mauch	.60	.30	.20
60	Dick Bosman	.35	.20	.11
61	A.L. Batting Leaders (Alex Johnson, Tony Oliva, Carl Yastrzemski)	2.25	1.25	.70
62	N.L. Batting Leaders (Rico Carty, Manny Sanguillen, Joe Torre)	1.25	.60	.40
63	A.L. RBI Leaders (Tony Conigliaro, Frank Howard, Boog Powell)	1.25	.60	.40
64	N.L. RBI Leaders (Johnny Bench, Tony Perez, Billy Williams)	2.25	1.25	.70
65	A.L. Home Run Leaders (Frank Howard, Harmon Killebrew, Carl Yastrzemski)	2.25	1.25	.70
66	N.L. Home Run Leaders (Johnny Bench, Tony Perez, Billy Williams)	2.25	1.25	.70
67	A.L. ERA Leaders (Jim Palmer, Diego Segui, Clyde Wright)	1.25	.60	.40
68	N.L. ERA Leaders (Tom Seaver, Wayne Simpson, Luke Walker)	1.50	.70	.45
69	A.L. Pitching Leaders (Mike Cuellar, Dave McNally, Jim Perry)	1.25	.60	.40
70	N.L. Pitching Leaders (Bob Gibson, Fergie Jenkins, Gaylord Perry)	2.00	1.00	.60
71	A.L. Strikeout Leaders (Bob Johnson, Mickey Lolich, Sam McDowell)	1.25	.60	.40
72	N.L. Strikeout Leaders (Bob Gibson, Fergie Jenkins, Tom Seaver)	2.25	1.25	.70
73	George Brunet	.35	.20	.11
74	Twins Rookies (Pete Hamm, Jim Nettles)	.35	.20	.11
75	Gary Nolan	.35	.20	.11
76	Ted Savage	.35	.20	.11
77	Mike Compton	.35	.20	.11
78	Jim Spencer	.40	.20	.12
79	Wade Blasingame	.35	.20	.11
80	Bill Melton	.40	.20	.12
81	Felix Millan	.35	.20	.11
82	Casey Cox	.35	.20	.11
83	Mets Rookies (Randy Bobb, *Tim Foli)*	.50	.25	.15
84	Marcel Lachemann	.35	.20	.11
85	Billy Grabarkewitz	.35	.20	.11
86	Mike Kilkenny	.35	.20	.11
87	Jack Heidemann	.35	.20	.11
88	Hal King	.35	.20	.11
89	Ken Brett	.35	.20	.11
90	Joe Pepitone	.70	.35	.20
91	Bob Lemon	1.25	.60	.40
92	Fred Wenz	.35	.20	.11
93	Senators Rookies (Norm McRae, Denny Riddleberger)	.35	.20	.11
94	Don Hahn	.35	.20	.11
95	Luis Tiant	1.50	.70	.45
96	Joe Hague	.35	.20	.11
97	Floyd Wicker	.35	.20	.11
98	Joe Decker	.35	.20	.11
99	Mark Belanger	.40	.20	.12
100	Pete Rose	45.00	23.00	13.50
101	Les Cain	.35	.20	.11
102	Astros Rookies *(Ken Forsch*, Larry Howard)	.50	.25	.15
103	Rich Severson	.35	.20	.11
104	Dan Frisella	.35	.20	.11
105	Tony Conigliaro	1.25	.60	.40
106	Tom Dukes	.35	.20	.11
107	Roy Foster	.35	.20	.11
108	John Cumberland	.35	.20	.11
109	Steve Hovley	.35	.20	.11
110	Bill Mazeroski	1.25	.60	.40
111	Yankees Rookies (Loyd Colson, Bobby Mitchell)	.40	.20	.12
112	Manny Mota	.60	.30	.20
113	Jerry Crider	.35	.20	.11
114	Billy Conigliaro	.40	.20	.12
115	Donn Clendenon	.40	.20	.12
116	Ken Sanders	.35	.20	.11
117	*Ted Simmons*	8.00	4.00	2.50
118	Cookie Rojas	.35	.20	.11
119	Frank Lucchesi	.35	.20	.11
120	Willie Horton	.60	.30	.20
121	1971 Rookie Stars (Jim Dunegan, Roe Skidmore)	.35	.20	.11
122	Eddie Watt	.35	.20	.11
123a	Checklist 133-263 (card # on right, orange helmet)	2.50	1.25	.70
123b	Checklist 133-263 (card # on right, red helmet)	2.50	1.25	.70
123c	Checklist 133-263 (card # centered)	3.50	1.75	1.00
124	*Don Gullett*	.70	.35	.20
125	Ray Fosse	.35	.20	.11
126	Danny Coombs	.35	.20	.11
127	*Danny Thompson*	.40	.20	.12
128	Frank Johnson	.35	.20	.11
129	Aurelio Monteagudo	.35	.20	.11
130	Denis Menke	.35	.20	.11
131	Curt Blefary	.40	.20	.12
132	Jose Laboy	.35	.20	.11
133	Mickey Lolich	1.25	.60	.40
134	Jose Arcia	.35	.20	.11
135	Rick Monday	.50	.25	.15
136	Duffy Dyer	.35	.20	.11
137	Marcelino Lopez	.35	.20	.11
138	Phillies Rookies (Joe Lis, *Willie Montanez)*	.50	.25	.15
139	Paul Casanova	.35	.20	.11
140	Gaylord Perry	4.00	2.00	1.25
141	Frank Quilici	.35	.20	.11
142	Mack Jones	.35	.20	.11
143	Steve Blass	.40	.20	.12
144	Jackie Hernandez	.35	.20	.11
145	Bill Singer	.40	.20	.12
146	Ralph Houk	.80	.40	.25
147	Bob Priddy	.35	.20	.11
148	John Mayberry	.50	.25	.15
149	Mike Hershberger	.35	.20	.11
150	Sam McDowell	.70	.35	.20
151	Tommy Davis	.70	.35	.20
152	Angels Rookies (Lloyd Allen, Winston Llenas)	.35	.20	.11
153	Gary Ross	.35	.20	.11
154	Cesar Gutierrez	.35	.20	.11
155	Ken Henderson	.35	.20	.11
156	Bart Johnson	.35	.20	.11
157	Bob Bailey	.35	.20	.11
158	Jerry Reuss	1.00	.50	.30
159	Jarvis Tatum	.35	.20	.11
160	Tom Seaver	30.00	15.00	9.00
161	Coins Checklist	2.50	1.25	.70
162	Jack Billingham	.35	.20	.11
163	Buck Martinez	.35	.20	.11
164	Reds Rookies (Frank Duffy, *Milt Wilcox)*	.60	.30	.20
165	Cesar Tovar	.35	.20	.11
166	Joe Hoerner	.35	.20	.11
167	Tom Grieve	.35	.20	.11
168	Bruce Dal Canton	.35	.20	.11
169	Ed Herrmann	.35	.20	.11
170	Mike Cuellar	.60	.30	.20
171	Bobby Wine	.35	.20	.11
172	Duke Sims	.35	.20	.11
173	Gil Garrido	.35	.20	.11
174	*Dave LaRoche*	.50	.25	.15
175	Jim Hickman	.40	.20	.12
176	Red Sox Rookies (Doug Griffin, Bob Montgomery)	.35	.20	.11
177	Hal McRae	.70	.35	.20
178	Dave Duncan	.35	.20	.11
179	Mike Corkins	.35	.20	.11
180	Al Kaline	12.00	6.00	3.50
181	Hal Lanier	.60	.30	.20
182	Al Downing	.40	.20	.12
183	Gil Hodges	4.00	2.00	1.25
184	Stan Bahnsen	.50	.25	.15
185	Julian Javier	.40	.20	.12
186	Bob Spence	.35	.20	.11
187	Ted Abernathy	.35	.20	.11
188	Dodgers Rookies (Mike Strahler, *Bob Valentine)*	1.75	.90	.50
189	George Mitterwald	.35	.20	.11
190	Bob Tolan	.40	.20	.12
191	Mike Andrews	.35	.20	.11
192	Billy Wilson	.35	.20	.11
193	*Bob Grich*	1.75	.90	.50
194	Mike Lum	.35	.20	.11
195	A.L. Playoff Game 1 (Powell Muscles Twins!)	1.25	.60	.40
196	A.L. Playoff Game 2 (McNally Makes It Two Straight!)	1.25	.60	.40
197	A.L. Playoff Game 3 (Palmer Mows 'Em Down!)	1.75	.90	.50
198	A.L. Playoffs Summary (A Team Effort!)	1.25	.60	.40
199	N.L. Playoff Game 1 (Cline Pinch Triple Decides It!)	1.25	.60	.40
200	N.L. Playoff Game 2 (Tolan Scores For Third Time!)	1.25	.60	.40
201	N.L. Playoff Game 3 (Cline Scores Winning Run!)	1.25	.60	.40
202	N.L. Playoffs Summary (World Series Bound!)	1.25	.60	.40
203	*Larry Gura*	.70	.35	.20
204	Brewers Rookies (George Kopacz, Bernie Smith)	.35	.20	.11
205	Gerry Moses	.35	.20	.11
206a	Checklist 264-393 (orange helmet)	2.50	1.25	.70
206b	Checklist 264-393 (red helmet)	2.50	1.25	.70
207	Alan Foster	.35	.20	.11
208	Billy Martin	1.75	.90	.50
209	Steve Renko	.35	.20	.11
210	Rod Carew	20.00	10.00	6.00
211	Phil Hennigan	.35	.20	.11
212	Rich Hebner	.40	.20	.12
213	Frank Baker	.40	.20	.12
214	Al Ferrara	.35	.20	.11
215	Diego Segui	.35	.20	.11
216	Cards Rookies (Reggie Cleveland, Luis Melendez)	.35	.20	.11
217	Ed Stroud	.35	.20	.11
218	Tony Cloninger	.40	.20	.12
219	Elrod Hendricks	.35	.20	.11
220	Ron Santo	.80	.40	.25
221	Dave Morehead	.35	.20	.11
222	Bob Watson	.40	.20	.12
223	Cecil Upshaw	.35	.20	.11
224	Alan Gallagher	.35	.20	.11
225	Gary Peters	.40	.20	.12
226	Bill Russell	.60	.30	.20
227	Floyd Weaver	.35	.20	.11
228	Wayne Garrett	.35	.20	.11
229	Jim Hannan	.35	.20	.11
230	Willie Stargell	6.00	3.00	1.75
231	Indians Rookies (Vince Colbert, *John Lowenstein)*	.50	.25	.15
232	John Strohmayer	.35	.20	.11
233	Larry Bowa	1.75	.90	.50
234	Jim Lyttle	.40	.20	.12
235	Nate Colbert	.35	.20	.11
236	Bob Humphreys	.35	.20	.11
237	*Cesar Cedeno*	1.50	.70	.45
238	Chuck Dobson	.35	.20	.11
239	Red Schoendienst	1.00	.50	.30
240	Clyde Wright	.35	.20	.11
241	Dave Nelson	.35	.20	.11
242	Jim Ray	.35	.20	.11
243	Carlos May	.40	.20	.12
244	Bob Tillman	.35	.20	.11
245	Jim Kaat	2.50	1.25	.70
246	Tony Taylor	.35	.20	.11
247	Royals Rookies (Jerry Cram, *Paul Splittorff)*	.70	.35	.20
248	Hoyt Wilhelm	3.75	2.00	1.25
249	Chico Salmon	.35	.20	.11
250	Johnny Bench	40.00	20.00	12.00
251	Frank Reberger	.35	.20	.11
252	Eddie Leon	.35	.20	.11
253	Bill Sudakis	.35	.20	.11
254	Cal Koonce	.35	.20	.11
255	Bob Robertson	.35	.20	.11
256	Tony Gonzalez	.35	.20	.11
257	Nelson Briles	.35	.20	.11
258	Dick Green	.35	.20	.11
259	Dave Marshall	.35	.20	.11
260	Tommy Harper	.40	.20	.12
261	Darold Knowles	.35	.20	.11
262	Padres Rookies (Dave Robinson, Jim Williams)	.35	.20	.11
263	John Ellis	.40	.20	.12
264	Joe Morgan	8.00	4.00	2.50
265	Jim Northrup	.40	.20	.12
266	Bill Stoneman	.35	.20	.11
267	Rich Morales	.35	.20	.11
268	Phillies Team	1.25	.60	.40
269	Gail Hopkins	.35	.20	.11
270	Rico Carty	.70	.35	.20
271	Bill Zepp	.35	.20	.11
272	Tommy Helms	.40	.20	.12
273	Pete Richert	.35	.20	.11
274	Ron Slocum	.35	.20	.11
275	Vada Pinson	1.25	.60	.40
276	Giants Rookies (Mike Davison, *George Foster)*	4.00	2.00	1.25
277	Gary Waslewski	.40	.20	.12
278	Jerry Grote	.50	.25	.15
279	Lefty Phillips	.35	.20	.11
280	Fergie Jenkins	3.00	1.50	.90
281	Danny Walton	.35	.20	.11
282	Jose Pagan	.35	.20	.11
283	Dick Such	.35	.20	.11
284	Jim Gosger	.35	.20	.11
285	Sal Bando	.60	.30	.20
286	Jerry McNertney	.35	.20	.11
287	Mike Fiore	.35	.20	.11
288	Joe Moeller	.35	.20	.11
289	White Sox Team	1.25	.60	.40
290	Tony Oliva	1.50	.70	.45
291	George Culver	.35	.20	.11
292	Jay Johnstone	.60	.30	.20
293	Pat Corrales	.50	.25	.15
294	Steve Dunning	.35	.20	.11
295	Bobby Bonds	1.25	.60	.40
296	Tom Timmermann	.35	.20	.11
297	Johnny Briggs	.35	.20	.11
298	Jim Nelson	.35	.20	.11
299	Ed Kirkpatrick	.35	.20	.11
300	Brooks Robinson	9.00	4.50	2.75
301	Earl Wilson	.35	.20	.11
302	Phil Gagliano	.35	.20	.11
303	Lindy McDaniel	.40	.20	.12
304	Ron Brand	.35	.20	.11
305	Reggie Smith	.60	.30	.20
306	Jim Nash	.35	.20	.11
307	Don Wert	.35	.20	.11
308	Cards Team	1.25	.60	.40
309	Dick Ellsworth	.35	.20	.11
310	Tommie Agee	.40	.20	.12
311	Lee Stange	.35	.20	.11
312	Harry Walker	.40	.20	.12
313	Tom Hall	.35	.20	.11
314	Jeff Torborg	.40	.20	.12
315	Ron Fairly	.50	.25	.15
316	Fred Scherman	.35	.20	.11
317	Athletics Rookies (Jim Driscoll, Angel Mangual)	.35	.20	.11
318	Rudy May	.40	.20	.12
319	Ty Cline	.35	.20	.11
320	Dave McNally	.50	.25	.15
321	Tom Matchick	.35	.20	.11
322	Jim Beauchamp	.35	.20	.11
323	Billy Champion	.35	.20	.11
324	Graig Nettles	2.50	1.25	.70
325	Juan Marichal	5.00	2.50	1.50
326	Richie Scheinblum	.35	.20	.11
327	World Series Game 1 (Powell Homers To Opposite Field!)	1.25	.60	.40
328	World Series Game 2 (Buford Goes 2 For-4!)	1.25	.60	.40
329	World Series Game 3 (F. Robinson			

	NR MT	EX	VG
Shows Muscle!)	2.00	1.00	.60
330 World Series Game 4 (Reds Stay Alive!)	1.25	.60	.40
331 World Series Game 5 (B. Robinson Commits Robbery!)	2.00	1.00	.60
332 World Series Summary (Clinching Performance!)	1.25	.60	.40
333 Clay Kirby	.35	.20	.11
334 Roberto Pena	.35	.20	.11
335 Jerry Koosman	1.00	.50	.30
336 Tigers Team	1.75	.90	.50
337 Jesus Alou	.40	.20	.12
338 Gene Tenace	.50	.25	.15
339 Wayne Simpson	.35	.20	.11
340 Rico Petrocelli	.50	.25	.15
341 *Steve Garvey*	80.00	40.00	25.00
342 Frank Tepedino	.40	.20	.12
343 Pirates Rookies (Ed Acosta, *Milt May*)	.40	.20	.12
344 Ellie Rodriguez	.35	.20	.11
345 Joe Horlen	.35	.20	.11
346 Lum Harris	.35	.20	.11
347 Ted Uhlaender	.35	.20	.11
348 Fred Norman	.35	.20	.11
349 Rich Reese	.35	.20	.11
350 Billy Williams	4.50	2.25	1.25
351 Jim Shellenback	.35	.20	.11
352 Denny Doyle	.35	.20	.11
353 Carl Taylor	.35	.20	.11
354 Don McMahon	.35	.20	.11
355 Bud Harrelson	.40	.20	.12
356 Bob Locker	.35	.20	.11
357 Reds Team	1.25	.60	.40
358 Danny Cater	.40	.20	.12
359 Ron Reed	.40	.20	.12
360 Jim Fregosi	.80	.40	.25
361 Don Sutton	3.50	1.75	1.00
362 Orioles Rookies (Mike Adamson, Roger Freed)	.35	.20	.11
363 Mike Nagy	.35	.20	.11
364 Tommy Dean	.35	.20	.11
365 Bob Johnson	.35	.20	.11
366 Ron Stone	.35	.20	.11
367 Dalton Jones	.35	.20	.11
368 Bob Veale	.40	.20	.12
369a Checklist 394-523 (orange helmet)	2.50	1.25	.70
369b Checklist 394-523 (red helmet, black line above ear)	2.50	1.25	.70
369c Checklist 394-523 (red helmet, no line)	2.50	1.25	.70
370 Joe Torre	2.25	1.25	.70
371 Jack Hiatt	.35	.20	.11
372 Lew Krausse	.35	.20	.11
373 Tom McCraw	.35	.20	.11
374 Clete Boyer	.50	.25	.15
375 Steve Hargan	.35	.20	.11
376 Expos Rookies (Clyde Mashore, Ernie McAnally)	.35	.20	.11
377 Greg Garrett	.35	.20	.11
378 Tito Fuentes	.35	.20	.11
379 Wayne Granger	.35	.20	.11
380 Ted Williams	5.00	2.50	1.50
381 Fred Gladding	.35	.20	.11
382 Jake Gibbs	.40	.20	.12
383 Rod Gaspar	.35	.20	.11
384 Rollie Fingers	2.50	1.25	.70
385 Maury Wills	1.25	.60	.40
386 Red Sox Team	1.50	.70	.45
387 Ron Herbel	.35	.20	.11
388 Al Oliver	1.75	.90	.50
389 Ed Brinkman	.40	.20	.12
390 Glenn Beckert	.50	.25	.15
391 Twins Rookies (Steve Brye, Cotton Nash)	.35	.20	.11
392 Grant Jackson	.35	.20	.11
393 Merv Rettenmund	.40	.20	.12
394 Clay Carroll	.40	.20	.12
395 Roy White	.70	.35	.20
396 Dick Schofield	.35	.20	.11
397 Alvin Dark	.50	.25	.15
398 Howie Reed	.35	.20	.11
399 Jim French	.35	.20	.11
400 Hank Aaron	25.00	12.50	7.50
401 Tom Murphy	.35	.20	.11
402 Dodgers Team	1.50	.70	.45
403 Joe Coleman	.40	.20	.12
404 Astros Rookies (Buddy Harris, Roger Metzger)	.35	.20	.11
405 Leo Cardenas	.35	.20	.11
406 Ray Sadecki	.35	.20	.11
407 Joe Rudi	.60	.30	.20
408 Rafael Robles	.35	.20	.11
409 Don Pavletich	.35	.20	.11
410 Ken Holtzman	.40	.20	.12
411 George Spriggs	.35	.20	.11
412 Jerry Johnson	.35	.20	.11
413 Pat Kelly	.35	.20	.11
414 Woodie Fryman	.40	.20	.12
415 Mike Hegan	.35	.20	.11
416 Gene Alley	.40	.20	.12
417 Dick Hall	.35	.20	.11
418 Adolfo Phillips	.35	.20	.11
419 Ron Hansen	.40	.20	.12
420 Jim Merritt	.35	.20	.11
421 John Stephenson	.35	.20	.11
422 Frank Bertaina	.35	.20	.11
423 Tigers Rookies (Tim Marting, Dennis Saunders)	.35	.20	.11
424 Roberto Rodriquez (Rodriguez)	.35	.20	.11
425 Doug Rader	.35	.20	.11
426 Chris Cannizzaro	.35	.20	.11
427 Bernie Allen	.35	.20	.11
428 Jim McAndrew	.35	.20	.11
429 Chuck Hinton	.35	.20	.11
430 Wes Parker	.40	.20	.12
431 Tom Burgmeier	.35	.20	.11
432 Bob Didier	.35	.20	.11
433 Skip Lockwood	.35	.20	.11
434 Gary Sutherland	.35	.20	.11
435 Jose Cardenal	.40	.20	.12
436 Wilbur Wood	.50	.25	.15
437 Danny Murtaugh	.40	.20	.12

	NR MT	EX	VG
438 Mike McCormick	.50	.25	.15
439 Phillies Rookies (*Greg Luzinski*, Scott Reid)	2.00	1.00	.60
440 Bert Campaneris	.70	.35	.20
441 Milt Pappas	.40	.20	.12
442 Angels Team	1.25	.60	.40
443 Rich Robertson	.35	.20	.11
444 Jimmie Price	.35	.20	.11
445 Art Shamsky	.35	.20	.11
446 Bobby Bolin	.35	.20	.11
447 *Cesar Geronimo*	.60	.30	.20
448 Dave Roberts	.35	.20	.11
449 Brant Alyea	.35	.20	.11
450 Bob Gibson	8.00	4.00	2.50
451 Joe Keough	.35	.20	.11
452 John Boccabella	.35	.20	.11
453 Terry Crowley	.35	.20	.11
454 Mike Paul	.35	.20	.11
455 Don Kessinger	.40	.20	.12
456 Bob Meyer	.35	.20	.11
457 Willie Smith	.35	.20	.11
458 White Sox Rookies (Dave Lemonds, Ron Lolich)	.35	.20	.11
459 Jim Lefebvre	.40	.20	.12
460 Fritz Peterson	.50	.25	.15
461 Jim Hart	.40	.20	.12
462 Senators Team	1.50	.70	.45
463 Tom Kelley	.35	.20	.11
464 Aurelio Rodriguez	.40	.20	.12
465 Tim McCarver	.80	.40	.25
466 Ken Berry	.35	.20	.11
467 Al Santorini	.35	.20	.11
468 Frank Fernandez	.35	.20	.11
469 Bob Aspromonte	.35	.20	.11
470 Bob Oliver	.35	.20	.11
471 Tom Griffin	.35	.20	.11
472 Ken Rudolph	.35	.20	.11
473 Gary Wagner	.35	.20	.11
474 Jim Fairey	.35	.20	.11
475 Ron Perranoski	.40	.20	.12
476 Dal Maxvill	.40	.20	.12
477 Earl Weaver	1.00	.50	.30
478 Bernie Carbo	.40	.20	.12
479 Dennis Higgins	.35	.20	.11
480 Manny Sanguillen	.40	.20	.12
481 Daryl Patterson	.35	.20	.11
482 Padres Team	1.25	.60	.40
483 Gene Michael	.50	.25	.15
484 Don Wilson	.35	.20	.11
485 Ken McMullen	.35	.20	.11
486 Steve Huntz	.35	.20	.11
487 Paul Schaal	.35	.20	.11
488 Jerry Stephenson	.35	.20	.11
489 Luis Alvarado	.35	.20	.11
490 Deron Johnson	.35	.20	.11
491 Jim Hardin	.35	.20	.11
492 Ken Boswell	.35	.20	.11
493 Dave May	.35	.20	.11
494 Braves Rookies (Ralph Garr, Rick Kester)	.50	.25	.15
495 Felipe Alou	.60	.30	.20
496 Woody Woodward	.40	.20	.12
497 Horacio Pina	.35	.20	.11
498 John Kennedy	.35	.20	.11
499 Checklist 524-643	2.50	1.25	.70
500 Jim Perry	.60	.30	.20
501 Andy Etchebarren	.35	.20	.11
502 Cubs Team	1.25	.60	.40
503 Gates Brown	.35	.20	.11
504 Ken Wright	.35	.20	.11
505 Ollie Brown	.35	.20	.11
506 Bobby Knoop	.35	.20	.11
507 George Stone	.35	.20	.11
508 Roger Repoz	.35	.20	.11
509 Jim Grant	.35	.20	.11
510 Ken Harrelson	1.25	.60	.40
511 Chris Short	.40	.20	.12
512 Red Sox Rookies (Mike Garman, Dick Mills)	.35	.20	.11
513 Nolan Ryan	90.00	45.00	27.00
514 Ron Woods	.40	.20	.12
515 Carl Morton	.35	.20	.11
516 Ted Kubiak	.35	.20	.11
517 Charlie Fox	.35	.20	.11
518 Joe Grzenda	.35	.20	.11
519 Willie Crawford	.35	.20	.11
520 Tommy John	3.00	1.50	.90
521 Leron Lee	.35	.20	.11
522 Twins Team	1.25	.60	.40
523 John Odom	.40	.20	.12
524 Mickey Stanley	.90	.45	.25
525 Ernie Banks	25.00	12.50	7.50
526 Ray Jarvis	.80	.40	.25
527 Cleon Jones	.90	.45	.25
528 Wally Bunker	.80	.40	.25
529 N.L. Rookies (Bill Buckner, Enzo Hernandez, Marty Perez)	2.50	1.25	.70
530 Carl Yastrzemski	50.00	25.00	15.00
531 Mike Torrez	.90	.45	.25
532 Bill Rigney	.80	.40	.25
533 Mike Ryan	.80	.40	.25
534 Luke Walker	.80	.40	.25
535 Curt Flood	1.75	.90	.50
536 Claude Raymond	.80	.40	.25
537 Tom Egan	.80	.40	.25
538 Angel Bravo	.80	.40	.25
539 Larry Brown	.80	.40	.25
540 Larry Dierker	.90	.45	.25
541 Bob Burda	.80	.40	.25
542 Bob Miller	.80	.40	.25
543 Yankees Team	2.75	1.50	.80
544 Vida Blue	2.50	1.25	.70
545 Dick Dietz	.80	.40	.25
546 John Matias	.80	.40	.25
547 Pat Dobson	.90	.45	.25
548 Don Mason	.80	.40	.25
549 Jim Brewer	.80	.40	.25
550 Harmon Killebrew	12.00	6.00	3.50
551 Frank Linzy	.80	.40	.25
552 Buddy Bradford	.80	.40	.25
553 Kevin Collins	.80	.40	.25
554 Lowell Palmer	.80	.40	.25
555 Walt Williams	.80	.40	.25
556 Jim McGlothlin	.80	.40	.25

	NR MT	EX	VG
557 Tom Satriano	.80	.40	.25
558 Hector Torres	.80	.40	.25
559 A.L. Rookies (Terry Cox, Bill Gogolewski, Gary Jones)	.90	.45	.25
560 Rusty Staub	2.25	1.25	.70
561 Syd O'Brien	.80	.40	.25
562 Dave Giusti	.80	.40	.25
563 Giants Team	2.00	1.00	.60
564 Al Fitzmorris	.80	.40	.25
565 Jim Wynn	1.00	.50	.30
566 Tim Cullen	.80	.40	.25
567 Walt Alston	2.50	1.25	.70
568 Sal Campisi	.80	.40	.25
569 Ivan Murrell	.80	.40	.25
570 Jim Palmer	10.00	5.00	3.00
571 Ted Sizemore	.80	.40	.25
572 Jerry Kenney	.90	.45	.25
573 Ed Kranepool	1.00	.50	.30
574 Jim Bunning	4.00	2.00	1.25
575 Bill Freehan	1.00	.50	.30
576 Cubs Rookies (Brock Davis, Adrian Garrett, Garry Jestadt)	.80	.40	.25
577 Jim Lonborg	1.00	.50	.30
578 Ron Hunt	.90	.45	.25
579 Marty Pattin	.80	.40	.25
580 Tony Perez	4.00	2.00	1.25
581 Roger Nelson	.80	.40	.25
582 Dave Cash	.80	.40	.25
583 Ron Cook	.80	.40	.25
584 Indians Team	2.00	1.00	.60
585 Willie Davis	2.25	1.25	.70
586 Dick Woodson	.80	.40	.25
587 Sonny Jackson	.80	.40	.25
588 Tom Bradley	.80	.40	.25
589 Bob Barton	.80	.40	.25
590 Alex Johnson	.80	.40	.25
591 Jackie Brown	.80	.40	.25
592 Randy Hundley	.80	.40	.25
593 Jack Aker	.90	.45	.25
594 Cards Rookies (Bob Chlupsa, *Al Hrabosky*, Bob Stinson)	2.25	1.25	.70
595 Dave Johnson	1.75	.90	.50
596 Mike Jorgensen	.80	.40	.25
597 Ken Suarez	.80	.40	.25
598 Rick Wise	.90	.45	.25
599 Norm Cash	2.00	1.00	.60
600 Willie Mays	60.00	30.00	18.00
601 Ken Tatum	.80	.40	.25
602 Marty Martinez	.80	.40	.25
603 Pirates Team	3.00	1.50	.90
604 John Gelnar	.80	.40	.25
605 Orlando Cepeda	3.25	1.75	1.00
606 Chuck Taylor	.80	.40	.25
607 Paul Ratliff	.80	.40	.25
608 Mike Wegener	.80	.40	.25
609 Leo Durocher	2.25	1.25	.70
610 Amos Otis	1.00	.50	.30
611 Tom Phoebus	.80	.40	.25
612 Indians Rookies (Lou Camilli, Ted Ford, Steve Mingori)	.80	.40	.25
613 Pedro Borbon	.90	.45	.25
614 Billy Cowan	.80	.40	.25
615 Mel Stottlemyre	1.75	.90	.50
616 Larry Hisle	.90	.45	.25
617 Clay Dalrymple	.80	.40	.25
618 Tug McGraw	2.25	1.25	.70
619a Checklist 644-752 (no copyright on back)	4.50	2.25	1.25
619b Checklist 644-752 (with copyright, no wavy line on helmet brim)	3.00	1.50	.90
619c Checklist 644-752 (with copyright, wavy line on helmet brim)	3.00	1.50	.90
620 Frank Howard	2.25	1.25	.70
621 Ron Bryant	.80	.40	.25
622 Joe Lahoud	.80	.40	.25
623 Pat Jarvis	.80	.40	.25
624 Athletics Team	2.00	1.00	.60
625 Lou Brock	10.00	5.00	3.00
626 Freddie Patek	.90	.45	.25
627 Steve Hamilton	.80	.40	.25
628 John Bateman	.80	.40	.25
629 John Hiller	.90	.45	.25
630 Roberto Clemente	25.00	12.50	7.50
631 Eddie Fisher	.80	.40	.25
632 Darrel Chaney	.80	.40	.25
633 A.L. Rookies (Bobby Brooks, Pete Koegel, Scott Northey)	.80	.40	.25
634 Phil Regan	.80	.40	.25
635 Bobby Murcer	2.00	1.00	.60
636 Denny Lemaster	.80	.40	.25
637 Dave Bristol	.80	.40	.25
638 Stan Williams	.80	.40	.25
639 Tom Haller	.90	.45	.25
640 Frank Robinson	20.00	10.00	6.00
641 Mets Team	3.50	1.75	1.00
642 Jim Roland	.80	.40	.25
643 Rick Reichardt	.80	.40	.25
644 Jim Stewart	2.25	1.25	.70
645 Jim Maloney	2.50	1.25	.70
646 Bobby Floyd	2.25	1.25	.70
647 Juan Pizarro	2.25	1.25	.70
648 Mets Rookies (Rich Folkers, Ted Martinez, *Jon Matlack*)	3.50	1.75	1.00
649 Sparky Lyle	3.00	1.50	.90
650 Rich Allen	9.00	4.50	2.75
651 Jerry Robertson	2.25	1.25	.70
652 Braves Team	3.25	1.75	1.00
653 Russ Snyder	2.25	1.25	.70
654 Don Shaw	2.25	1.25	.70
655 Mike Epstein	2.50	1.25	.70
656 Gerry Nyman	2.25	1.25	.70
657 Jose Azcue	2.25	1.25	.70
658 Paul Lindblad	2.25	1.25	.70
659 Byron Browne	2.25	1.25	.70
660 Ray Culp	2.25	1.25	.70
661 Chuck Tanner	3.00	1.50	.90
662 Mike Hedlund	2.25	1.25	.70
663 Marv Staehle	2.25	1.25	.70
664 Major League Rookies (Archie Reynolds, Bob Reynolds, Ken Reynolds)	2.25	1.25	.70
665 Ron Swoboda	2.25	1.25	.70
666 Gene Brabender	2.25	1.25	.70
667 Pete Ward	2.50	1.25	.70

		NR MT	EX	VG
668	Gary Neibauer	2.25	1.25	.70
669	Ike Brown	2.25	1.25	.70
670	Bill Hands	2.25	1.25	.70
671	Bill Voss	2.25	1.25	.70
672	Ed Crosby	2.25	1.25	.70
673	Gerry Janeski	2.25	1.25	.70
674	Expos Team	3.25	1.75	1.00
675	Dave Boswell	2.25	1.25	.70
676	Tommie Reynolds	2.25	1.25	.70
677	Jack DiLauro	2.25	1.25	.70
678	George Thomas	2.25	1.25	.70
679	Don O'Riley	2.25	1.25	.70
680	Don Mincher	2.50	1.25	.70
681	Bill Butler	2.25	1.25	.70
682	Terry Harmon	2.25	1.25	.70
683	Bill Burbach	2.50	1.25	.70
684	Curt Motton	2.25	1.25	.70
685	Moe Drabowsky	2.25	1.25	.70
686	Chico Ruiz	2.25	1.25	.70
687	Ron Taylor	2.25	1.25	.70
688	Sparky Anderson	3.50	1.75	1.00
689	Frank Baker	2.25	1.25	.70
690	Bob Moose	2.25	1.25	.70
691	Bob Heise	2.25	1.25	.70
692	A.L. Rookies (Hal Haydel, Rogelio Moret, Wayne Twitchell)	2.25	1.25	.70
693	Jose Pena	2.25	1.25	.70
694	Rick Renick	2.25	1.25	.70
695	Joe Niekro	3.25	1.75	1.00
696	Jerry Morales	2.25	1.25	.70
697	Rickey Clark	2.25	1.25	.70
698	Brewers Team	3.50	1.75	1.00
699	Jim Britton	2.25	1.25	.70
700	Boog Powell	4.00	2.00	1.25
701	Bob Garibaldi	2.25	1.25	.70
702	Milt Ramirez	2.25	1.25	.70
703	Mike Kekich	2.50	1.25	.70
704	J.C. Martin	2.25	1.25	.70
705	Dick Selma	2.25	1.25	.70
706	Joe Foy	2.25	1.25	.70
707	Fred Lasher	2.25	1.25	.70
708	Russ Nagelson	2.25	1.25	.70
709	Major League Rookies *(Dusty Baker, Don Baylor, Tom Paciorek)*	30.00	15.00	9.00
710	Sonny Siebert	2.25	1.25	.70
711	Larry Stahl	2.25	1.25	.70
712	Jose Martinez	2.25	1.25	.70
713	Mike Marshall	2.75	1.50	.80
714	Dick Williams	2.75	1.50	.80
715	Horace Clarke	2.50	1.25	.70
716	Dave Leonhard	2.25	1.25	.70
717	Tommie Aaron	2.50	1.25	.70
718	Billy Wynne	2.25	1.25	.70
719	Jerry May	2.25	1.25	.70
720	Matty Alou	2.75	1.50	.80
721	John Morris	2.25	1.25	.70
722	Astros Team	3.25	1.75	1.00
723	Vicente Romo	2.25	1.25	.70
724	Tom Tischinski	2.25	1.25	.70
725	Gary Gentry	2.25	1.25	.70
726	Paul Popovich	2.25	1.25	.70
727	Ray Lamb	2.25	1.25	.70
728	N.L. Rookies (Keith Lampard, Wayne Redmond, Bernie Williams)	2.25	1.25	.70
729	Dick Billings	2.25	1.25	.70
730	Jim Rooker	2.25	1.25	.70
731	Jim Qualls	2.25	1.25	.70
732	Bob Reed	2.25	1.25	.70
733	Lee Maye	2.25	1.25	.70
734	Rob Gardner	2.50	1.25	.70
735	Mike Shannon	2.50	1.25	.70
736	Mel Queen	2.25	1.25	.70
737	Preston Gomez	2.25	1.25	.70
738	Russ Gibson	2.25	1.25	.70
739	Barry Lersch	2.25	1.25	.70
740	Luis Aparicio	15.00	7.50	4.50
741	Skip Guinn	2.25	1.25	.70
742	Royals Team	3.25	1.75	1.00
743	John O'Donoghue	2.25	1.25	.70
744	Chuck Manuel	2.25	1.25	.70
745	Sandy Alomar	2.25	1.25	.70
746	Andy Kosco	2.25	1.25	.70
747	N.L. Rookies (Balor Moore, Al Severinsen, Scipio Spinks)	2.25	1.25	.70
748	John Purdin	2.25	1.25	.70
749	Ken Szotkiewicz	2.25	1.25	.70
750	Denny McLain	6.00	3.00	1.75
751	Al Weis	2.50	1.25	.70
752	Dick Drago	3.75	1.25	.70

1971 Topps Coins

Measuring 1-1/2" in diameter, the latest edition of the Topps coins was a 153-piece set. The coins feature a color photograph surrounded by a colored band on the front. The band carries the player's name, team, position and several stars. Backs have a short biography, the coin number and encour- agement to collect the entire set. Back colors differ, with #'s 1-51 having a brass back, #'s 52-102 chrome backs, and the rest have blue backs. Most of the stars of the period are included in the set.

		NR MT	EX	VG
Complete Set:		400.00	200.00	120.00
Common Player:		.90	.45	.25
1	Clarence Gaston	.90	.45	.25
2	Dave Johnson	1.25	.60	.40
3	Jim Bunning	2.00	1.00	.60
4	Jim Spencer	.90	.45	.25
5	Felix Millan	.90	.45	.25
6	Gerry Moses	.90	.45	.25
7	Fergie Jenkins	2.00	1.00	.60
8	Felipe Alou	1.00	.50	.30
9	Jim McGlothlin	.90	.45	.25
10	Dick McAuliffe	.90	.45	.25
11	Joe Torre	1.50	.70	.45
12	Jim Perry	1.25	.60	.40
13	Bobby Bonds	1.25	.60	.40
14	Danny Cater	.90	.45	.25
15	Bill Mazeroski	1.50	.70	.45
16	Luis Aparicio	5.00	2.50	1.50
17	Doug Rader	.90	.45	.25
18	Vada Pinson	1.50	.70	.45
19	John Bateman	.90	.45	.25
20	Lew Krausse	.90	.45	.25
21	Billy Grabarkewitz	.90	.45	.25
22	Frank Howard	1.50	.70	.45
23	Jerry Koosman	1.25	.60	.40
24	Rod Carew	8.00	4.00	2.50
25	Al Ferrara	.90	.45	.25
26	Dave McNally	1.00	.50	.30
27	Jim Hickman	.90	.45	.25
28	Sandy Alomar	.90	.45	.25
29	Lee May	1.00	.50	.30
30	Rico Petrocelli	1.00	.50	.30
31	Don Money	.90	.45	.25
32	Jim Rooker	.90	.45	.25
33	Dick Dietz	.90	.45	.25
34	Roy White	1.00	.50	.30
35	Carl Morton	.90	.45	.25
36	Walt Williams	.90	.45	.25
37	Phil Niekro	3.25	1.75	1.00
38	Bill Freehan	1.00	.50	.30
39	Julian Javier	.90	.45	.25
40	Rick Monday	1.00	.50	.30
41	Don Wilson	.90	.45	.25
42	Ray Fosse	.90	.45	.25
43	Art Shamsky	.90	.45	.25
44	Ted Savage	.90	.45	.25
45	Claude Osteen	1.00	.50	.30
46	Ed Brinkman	.90	.45	.25
47	Matty Alou	1.00	.50	.30
48	Bob Oliver	.90	.45	.25
49	Danny Coombs	.90	.45	.25
50	Frank Robinson	7.00	3.50	2.00
51	Randy Hundley	.90	.45	.25
52	Cesar Tovar	.90	.45	.25
53	Wayne Simpson	.90	.45	.25
54	Bobby Murcer	1.25	.60	.40
55	Tony Taylor	.90	.45	.25
56	Tommy John	2.50	1.25	.70
57	Willie McCovey	7.00	3.50	2.00
58	Carl Yastrzemski	15.00	7.50	4.50
59	Bob Bailey	.90	.45	.25
60	Clyde Wright	.90	.45	.25
61	Orlando Cepeda	2.00	1.00	.60
62	Al Kaline	7.00	3.50	2.00
63	Bob Gibson	7.00	3.50	2.00
64	Bert Campaneris	1.25	.60	.40
65	Ted Sizemore	.90	.45	.25
66	Duke Sims	.90	.45	.25
67	Bud Harrelson	.90	.45	.25
68	Jerry McNertney	.90	.45	.25
69	Jim Wynn	1.00	.50	.30
70	Dick Bosman	.90	.45	.25
71	Roberto Clemente	15.00	7.50	4.50
72	Rich Reese	.90	.45	.25
73	Gaylord Perry	4.00	2.00	1.25
74	Boog Powell	1.50	.70	.45
75	Billy Williams	5.00	2.50	1.50
76	Bill Melton	.90	.45	.25
77	Nate Colbert	.90	.45	.25
78	Reggie Smith	1.25	.60	.40
79	Deron Johnson	.90	.45	.25
80	Jim Hunter	5.00	2.50	1.50
81	Bob Tolan	.90	.45	.25
82	Jim Northrup	.90	.45	.25
83	Ron Fairly	1.00	.50	.30
84	Alex Johnson	.90	.45	.25
85	Pat Jarvis	.90	.45	.25
86	Sam McDowell	1.00	.50	.30
87	Lou Brock	7.00	3.50	2.00
88	Danny Walton	.90	.45	.25
89	Denis Menke	.90	.45	.25
90	Jim Palmer	7.00	3.50	2.00
91	Tommie Agee	.90	.45	.25
92	Duane Josephson	.90	.45	.25
93	Willie Davis	1.00	.50	.30
94	Mel Stottlemyre	1.00	.50	.30
95	Ron Santo	1.25	.60	.40
96	Amos Otis	1.00	.50	.30
97	Ken Henderson	.90	.45	.25
98	George Scott	1.00	.50	.30
99	Dock Ellis	.90	.45	.25
100	Harmon Killebrew	7.00	3.50	2.00
101	Pete Rose	30.00	15.00	9.00
102	Rick Reichardt	.90	.45	.25
103	Cleon Jones	.90	.45	.25
104	Ron Perranoski	.90	.45	.25
105	Tony Perez	2.50	1.25	.70
106	Mickey Lolich	1.25	.60	.40
107	Tim McCarver	1.25	.60	.40
108	Reggie Jackson	12.00	6.00	3.50
109	Chris Cannizzaro	.90	.45	.25
110	Steve Hargan	.90	.45	.25
111	Rusty Staub	2.50	1.25	.70
112	Andy Messersmith	1.00	.50	.30
113	Rico Carty	1.25	.60	.40
114	Brooks Robinson	7.00	3.50	2.00
115	Steve Carlton	7.00	3.50	2.00
116	Mike Hegan	.90	.45	.25
117	Joe Morgan	4.50	2.25	1.25
118	Thurman Munson	5.00	2.50	1.50
119	Don Kessinger	1.00	.50	.30
120	Joe Horlen	.90	.45	.25
121	Wes Parker	1.00	.50	.30
122	Sonny Siebert	.90	.45	.25
123	Willie Stargell	5.00	2.50	1.50
124	Ellie Rodriguez	.90	.45	.25
125	Juan Marichal	5.00	2.50	1.50
126	Mike Epstein	.90	.45	.25
127	Tom Seaver	8.00	4.00	2.50
128	Tony Oliva	2.50	1.25	.70
129	Jim Merritt	.90	.45	.25
130	Willie Horton	1.00	.50	.30
131	Rick Wise	.90	.45	.25
132	Sal Bando	1.00	.50	.30
133	Ollie Brown	.90	.45	.25
134	Ken Harrelson	1.00	.50	.30
135	Mack Jones	.90	.45	.25
136	Jim Fregosi	1.00	.50	.30
137	Hank Aaron	15.00	7.50	4.50
138	Fritz Peterson	.90	.45	.25
139	Joe Hague	.90	.45	.25
140	Tommy Harper	.90	.45	.25
141	Larry Dierker	.90	.45	.25
142	Tony Conigliaro	1.50	.70	.45
143	Glenn Beckert	1.00	.50	.30
144	Carlos May	.90	.45	.25
145	Don Sutton	3.25	1.75	1.00
146	Paul Casanova	.90	.45	.25
147	Bob Moose	.90	.45	.25
148	Leo Cardenas	.90	.45	.25
149	Johnny Bench	8.00	4.00	2.50
150	Mike Cuellar	1.00	.50	.30
151	Donn Clendenon	.90	.45	.25
152	Lou Piniella	1.25	.60	.40
153	Willie Mays	15.00	7.50	4.50

1971 Topps Greatest Moments

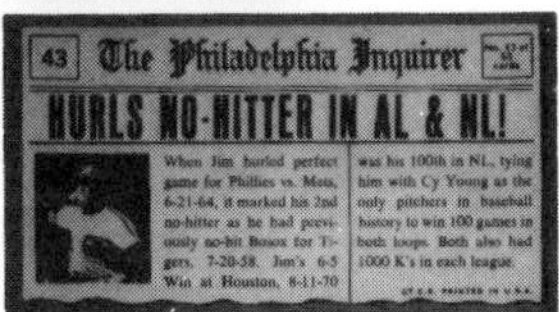
43 The Philadelphia Inquirer

HURLS NO-HITTER IN AL & NL!

When Jim hurled perfect game for Phillies vs. Mets, 6-21-64, it marked his 2nd no-hitter as he had previously no-hit Bosox for Tigers, 7-20-58. Jim's 6-5 Win at Houston, 8-11-70 was his 100th in NL, tying him with Cy Young as the only pitchers in baseball history to win 100 games in both loops. Both also had 1000 K's in each league.

This 55-card set features a great moment from the careers of top players at the time. The front of the 2-1/2" by 4-3/4" cards features a portrait photo of the player at the left and deckle-edge action photo at the right. There is a small headline on the white border of the action photo. The player's name and "One of Baseball's Greatest Moments" along with a black border complete the front. The back features a detail from the front photo and the story of the event. The newspaper style presentation includes the name of real newspapers. Relatively scarce, virtually every card in this set is a star or at least an above-average player.

		NR MT	EX	VG
Complete Set:		1600.	800.00	480.00
Common Player:		4.00	2.00	1.25
1	Thurman Munson	60.00	30.00	18.00
2	Hoyt Wilhelm	30.00	15.00	9.00
3	Rico Carty	15.00	7.50	4.50
4	Carl Morton	4.00	2.00	1.25
5	Sal Bando	5.00	2.50	1.50
6	Bert Campaneris	5.00	2.50	1.50
7	Jim Kaat	20.00	10.00	6.00
8	Harmon Killebrew	60.00	30.00	18.00
9	Brooks Robinson	75.00	37.00	22.00
10	Jim Perry	15.00	7.50	4.50
11	Tony Oliva	20.00	10.00	6.00
12	Vada Pinson	20.00	10.00	6.00
13	Johnny Bench	175.00	87.00	52.00
14	Tony Perez	25.00	12.50	7.50
15	Pete Rose	90.00	45.00	27.00
16	Jim Fregosi	4.00	2.00	1.25
17	Alex Johnson	4.00	2.00	1.25
18	Clyde Wright	4.00	2.00	1.25
19	Al Kaline	25.00	12.50	7.50
20	Denny McLain	20.00	10.00	6.00
21	Jim Northrup	15.00	7.50	4.50
22	Bill Freehan	15.00	7.50	4.50
23	Mickey Lolich	20.00	10.00	6.00
24	Bob Gibson	18.00	9.00	5.50
25	Tim McCarver	5.00	2.50	1.50
26	Orlando Cepeda	7.00	3.50	2.00
27	Lou Brock	18.00	9.00	5.50

		NR MT	EX	VG
28	Nate Colbert	4.00	2.00	1.25
29	Maury Wills	20.00	10.00	6.00
30	Wes Parker	15.00	7.50	4.50
31	Jim Wynn	15.00	7.50	4.50
32	Larry Dierker	15.00	7.50	4.50
33	Bill Melton	15.00	7.50	4.50
34	Joe Morgan	40.00	20.00	12.00
35	Rusty Staub	20.00	10.00	6.00
36	Ernie Banks	25.00	12.50	7.50
37	Billy Williams	50.00	25.00	15.00
38	Lou Piniella	20.00	10.00	6.00
39	Rico Petrocelli	4.00	2.00	1.25
40	Carl Yastrzemski	60.00	30.00	18.00
41	Willie Mays	45.00	22.00	13.50
42	Tommy Harper	15.00	7.50	4.50
43	Jim Bunning	7.00	3.50	2.00
44	Fritz Peterson	15.00	7.50	4.50
45	Roy White	15.00	7.50	4.50
46	Bobby Murcer	15.00	7.50	4.50
47	Reggie Jackson	250.00	125.00	75.00
48	Frank Howard	20.00	10.00	6.00
49	Dick Bosman	15.00	7.50	4.50
50	Sam McDowell	4.00	2.00	1.25
51	Luis Aparicio	12.00	6.00	3.50
52	Willie McCovey	15.00	7.50	4.50
53	Joe Pepitone	15.00	7.50	4.50
54	Jerry Grote	15.00	7.50	4.50
55	Bud Harrelson	15.00	7.50	4.50

1971 Topps Super

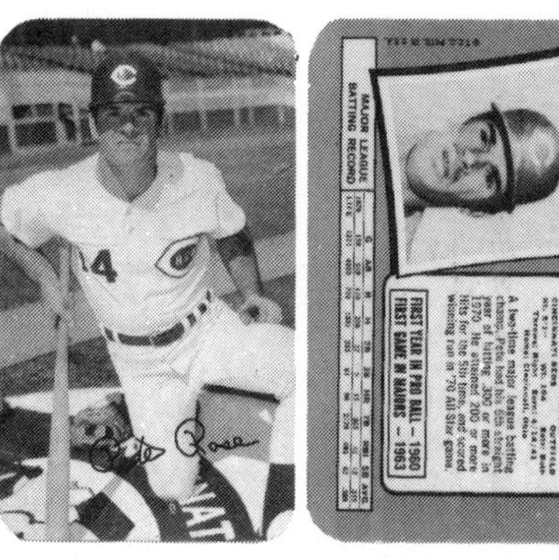

Topps continued to produce its special oversized cards in 1971. The cards, measuring 3-1/8" by 5-1/4," carry a large color photograph with a facsimile autograph on the front. Backs are basically enlargements of the player's regular Topps card. The set size was enlarged to 63 cards in 1971, so there are no short-printed cards as in 1970. Again, Topps included almost every major star who was active at the time, so the set of oversized cards with rounded corners remains an interesting source for those seeking the big names of the era.

		NR MT	EX	VG
Complete Set:		175.00	87.00	52.00
Common Player:		.70	.35	.20
1	Reggie Smith	1.00	.50	.30
2	Gaylord Perry	3.00	1.50	.90
3	Ted Savage	.70	.35	.20
4	Donn Clendenon	.70	.35	.20
5	John "Boog" Powell	1.25	.60	.40
6	Tony Perez	1.75	.90	.50
7	Dick Bosman	.70	.35	.20
8	Alex Johnson	.70	.35	.20
9	Rusty Staub	1.25	.60	.40
10	Mel Stottlemyre	1.00	.50	.30
11	Tony Oliva	1.50	.70	.45
12	Bill Freehan	1.00	.50	.30
13	Fritz Peterson	.70	.35	.20
14	Wes Parker	.70	.35	.20
15	Cesar Cedeno	1.25	.60	.40
16	Sam McDowell	1.00	.50	.30
17	Frank Howard	1.50	.70	.45
18	Dave McNally	1.00	.50	.30
19	Rico Petrocelli	.70	.35	.20
20	Pete Rose	25.00	12.50	7.50
21	Luke Walker	.70	.35	.20
22	Nate Colbert	.70	.35	.20
23	Luis Aparicio	2.50	1.25	.70
24	Jim Perry	1.00	.50	.30
25	Louis Brock	4.50	2.25	1.25
26	Roy White	1.00	.50	.30
27	Claude Osteen	.70	.35	.20
28	Carl W. Morton	.70	.35	.20
29	Ricardo A. Jacabo Carty	1.00	.50	.30
30	Larry Dierker	.70	.35	.20
31	Dagoberto Campaneris	1.00	.50	.30
32	Johnny Bench	8.00	4.00	2.50
33	Felix Millan	.70	.35	.20
34	Tim McCarver	1.25	.60	.40
35	Ronald Santo	1.25	.60	.40
36	Tommie Agee	.70	.35	.20
37	Roberto Clemente	10.00	5.00	3.00
38	Reggie Jackson	15.00	7.50	4.50
39	Clyde Wright	.70	.35	.20
40	Rich Allen	1.50	.70	.45
41	Curt Flood	1.25	.60	.40
42	Fergie Jenkins	1.75	.90	.50
43	Willie Stargell	3.00	1.50	.90
44	Henry Aaron	10.00	5.00	3.00
45	Amos Otis	1.00	.50	.30
46	Willie McCovey	4.50	2.25	1.25
47	William Melton	.70	.35	.20
48	Robert Gibson	3.50	1.75	1.00
49	Carl Yastrzemski	15.00	7.50	4.50
50	Glenn Beckert	1.00	.50	.30
51	Ray Fosse	.70	.35	.20
52	Clarence Gaston	.70	.35	.20
53	Tom Seaver	8.00	4.00	2.50
54	Al Kaline	6.00	3.00	1.75
55	Jim Northrup	.70	.35	.20
56	Willie Mays	10.00	5.00	3.00
57	Sal Bando	1.00	.50	.30
58	Deron Johnson	.70	.35	.20
59	Brooks Robinson	7.00	3.50	2.00
60	Harmon Killebrew	6.00	3.00	1.75
61	Joseph Torre	1.75	.90	.50
62	Lou Piniella	1.25	.60	.40
63	Tommy Harper	.70	.35	.20

1972 Topps

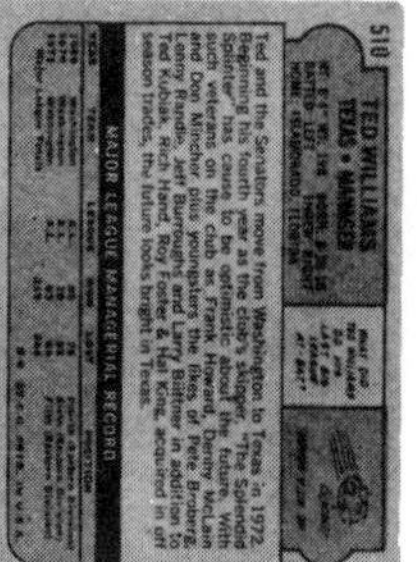

The largest Topps issue of its time appeared in 1972, with the set size reaching the 787 mark. The 2-1/2" by 3-1/2" cards are something special as well. Their fronts have a color photo which is shaped into an arch and surrounded by two different color borders, all of which is inside the overall white border. The player's name is in a white panel below the picture while the team name is above the picture in what might best be described as "superhero" type in a variety of colors. No mention of the player's position appears on the front. Cards backs are tame by comparison, featuring statistics and a trivia question. The set features a record number of specialty card including more than six dozen "In Action" (shown as "IA" in checklists below) cards featuring action shots of popular players. There are the usual statistical leaders, playoff and World Series highlights. Other innovations are 16 "Boyhood Photo" cards which depict scrapbook black and white photos of 1972's top players, and a group of cards depicting the trophies which comprise baseball's major awards. Finally, a group of seven "Traded" cards was included which feature a large "Traded" across the front of the card.

		NR MT	EX	VG
Complete Set:		1300.	650.00	390.00
Common Player: 1-394		.25	.13	.08
Common Player: 395-525		.30	.15	.09
Common Player: 526-656		.70	.35	.20
Common Player: 657-787		2.25	1.25	.70
1	World Champions (Pirates Team)	4.00	.75	.45
2	Ray Culp	.25	.13	.08
3	Bob Tolan	.30	.15	.09
4	Checklist 1-132	2.25	1.25	.70
5	John Bateman	.25	.13	.08
6	Fred Scherman	.25	.13	.08
7	Enzo Hernandez	.25	.13	.08
8	Ron Swoboda	.30	.15	.09
9	Stan Williams	.25	.13	.08
10	Amos Otis	.40	.20	.12
11	Bobby Valentine	.60	.30	.20
12	Jose Cardenal	.30	.15	.09
13	Joe Grzenda	.25	.13	.08
14	Phillies Rookiess (Mike Anderson, Pete Koegel, Wayne Twitchell)	.25	.13	.08
15	Walt Williams	.25	.13	.08
16	Mike Jorgensen	.25	.13	.08
17	Dave Duncan	.25	.13	.08
18a	Juan Pizarro (green under "C" and "S")	3.50	1.75	1.00
18b	Juan Pizarro (yellow under "C" and "S")	.25	.13	.08
19	Billy Cowan	.25	.13	.08
20	Don Wilson	.25	.13	.08
21	Braves Team	.90	.45	.25
22	Rob Gardner	.30	.15	.09
23	Ted Kubiak	.25	.13	.08
24	Ted Ford	.25	.13	.08
25	Bill Singer	.30	.15	.09
26	Andy Etchebarren	.25	.13	.08
27	Bob Johnson	.25	.13	.08
28	Twins Rookies (Steve Brye, Bob Gebhard, Hal Haydel)	.25	.13	.08
29a	Bill Bonham (green under "C" and "S")	3.50	1.75	1.00
29b	Bill Bonham (yellow under "C" and "S")	.30	.15	.09
30	Rico Petrocelli	.50	.25	.15
31	Cleon Jones	.30	.15	.09
32	Cleon Jones IA	.30	.15	.09
33	Billy Martin	1.50	.70	.45
34	Billy Martin IA	.80	.40	.25
35	Jerry Johnson	.25	.13	.08
36	Jerry Johnson IA	.25	.13	.08
37	Carl Yastrzemski	12.00	6.00	3.50
38	Carl Yastrzemski IA	8.00	4.00	2.50
39	Bob Barton	.25	.13	.08
40	Bob Barton IA	.25	.13	.08
41	Tommy Davis	.60	.30	.20
42	Tommy Davis IA	.30	.15	.09
43	Rick Wise	.30	.15	.09
44	Rick Wise IA	.25	.13	.08
45a	Glenn Beckert (green under "C" and "S")	3.50	1.75	1.00
45b	Glenn Beckert (yellow under "C" and "S")	.40	.20	.12
46	Glenn Beckert IA	.30	.15	.09
47	John Ellis	.30	.15	.09
48	John Ellis IA	.30	.15	.09
49	Willie Mays	20.00	10.00	6.00
50	Willie Mays IA	10.00	5.00	3.00
51	Harmon Killebrew	4.00	2.00	1.25
52	Harmon Killebrew IA	2.00	1.00	.60
53	Bud Harrelson	.40	.20	.12
54	Bud Harrelson IA	.30	.15	.09
55	Clyde Wright	.25	.13	.08
56	Rich Chiles	.25	.13	.08
57	Bob Oliver	.25	.13	.08
58	Ernie McAnally	.25	.13	.08
59	*Fred Stanley*	.40	.20	.12
60	Manny Sanguillen	.30	.15	.09
61	Cubs Rookies (Gene Hiser, *Burt Hooton*, Earl Stephenson)	1.00	.50	.30
62	Angel Mangual	.25	.13	.08
63	Duke Sims	.25	.13	.08
64	Pete Broberg	.25	.13	.08
65	Cesar Cedeno	.80	.40	.25
66	Ray Corbin	.25	.13	.08
67	Red Schoendienst	.80	.40	.25
68	Jim York	.25	.13	.08
69	Roger Freed	.25	.13	.08
70	Mike Cuellar	.50	.25	.15
71	Angels Team	.90	.45	.25
72	*Bruce Kison*	.80	.40	.25
73	Steve Huntz	.25	.13	.08
74	Cecil Upshaw	.25	.13	.08
75	Bert Campaneris	.60	.30	.20
76	Don Carrithers	.25	.13	.08
77	Ron Theobald	.25	.13	.08
78	Steve Arlin	.25	.13	.08
79	Red Sox Rookies (*Cecil Cooper, Carlton Fisk*, Mike Garman)	110.00	55.00	33.00
80	Tony Perez	2.00	1.00	.60
81	Mike Hedlund	.25	.13	.08
82	Ron Woods	.25	.13	.08
83	Dalton Jones	.25	.13	.08
84	Vince Colbert	.25	.13	.08
85	N.L. Batting Leaders (Glenn Beckert, Ralph Garr, Joe Torre)	1.25	.60	.40
86	A.L. Batting Leaders (Bobby Murcer, Tony Oliva, Merv Rettenmund)	1.25	.60	.40
87	N.L. RBI Leaders (Hank Aaron, Willie Stargell, Joe Torre)	2.25	1.25	.70
88	A.L. RBI Leaders (Harmon Killebrew, Frank Robinson, Reggie Smith)	2.25	1.25	.70
89	N.L. Home Run Leaders (Hank Aaron, Lee May, Willie Stargell)	2.25	1.25	.70
90	A.L. Home Run Leaders (Norm Cash, Reggie Jackson, Bill Melton)	1.75	.90	.50
91	N.L. ERA Leaders (Dave Roberts, Tom Seaver, Don Wilson)	1.75	.90	.50
92	A.L. ERA Leaders (Vida Blue, Jim Palmer, Wilbur Wood)	1.50	.70	.45
93	N.L. Pitching Leaders (Steve Carlton, Al Downing, Fergie Jenkins, Tom Seaver)	2.00	1.00	.60
94	A.L. Pitching Leaders (Vida Blue, Mickey Lolich, Wilbur Wood)	1.25	.60	.40
95	N.L. Strikeout Leaders (Fergie Jenkins, Tom Seaver, Bill Stoneman)	1.75	.90	.50
96	A.L. Strikeout Leaders (Vida Blue, Joe Coleman, Mickey Lolich)	1.25	.60	.40
97	Tom Kelley	.25	.13	.08
98	Chuck Tanner	.50	.25	.15
99	*Ross Grimsley*	.60	.30	.20
100	Frank Robinson	4.00	2.00	1.25
101	Astros Rookies (Ray Busse, Bill Grief, *J.R. Richard*)	1.00	.50	.30
102	Lloyd Allen	.25	.13	.08
103	Checklist 133-263	2.25	1.25	.70
104	*Toby Harrah*	1.00	.50	.30
105	Gary Gentry	.25	.13	.08
106	Brewers Team	.90	.45	.25
107	*Jose Cruz*	1.75	.90	.50
108	Gary Waslewski	.30	.15	.09
109	Jerry May	.25	.13	.08
110	Ron Hunt	.30	.15	.09
111	Jim Grant	.25	.13	.08
112	Greg Luzinski	.80	.40	.25
113	Rogelio Moret	.25	.13	.08
114	Bill Buckner	1.25	.60	.40
115	Jim Fregosi	.70	.35	.20
116	*Ed Farmer*	.30	.15	.09
117a	Cleo James (green under "C" and "S")	3.50	1.75	1.00
117b	Cleo James (yellow under "C" and "S")	.25	.13	.08
118	Skip Lockwood	.25	.13	.08
119	Marty Perez	.25	.13	.08
120	Bill Freehan	.60	.30	.20
121	Ed Sprague	.25	.13	.08
122	Larry Biittner	.25	.13	.08
123	Ed Acosta	.25	.13	.08
124	Yankees (Alan Closter, Roger Hambright, Rusty Torres)	.30	.15	.09
125	Dave Cash	.25	.13	.08

#	Card	NR MT	EX	VG
126	Bart Johnson	.25	.13	.08
127	Duffy Dyer	.25	.13	.08
128	Eddie Watt	.25	.13	.08
129	Charlie Fox	.25	.13	.08
130	Bob Gibson	5.00	2.50	1.50
131	Jim Nettles	.25	.13	.08
132	Joe Morgan	5.00	2.50	1.50
133	Joe Keough	.25	.13	.08
134	Carl Morton	.25	.13	.08
135	Vada Pinson	.80	.40	.25
136	Darrel Chaney	.25	.13	.08
137	Dick Williams	.50	.25	.15
138	Mike Kekich	.30	.15	.09
139	Tim McCarver	.80	.40	.25
140	Pat Dobson	.30	.15	.09
141	Mets Rookies (Buzz Capra, Jon Matlack, Leroy Stanton)	.40	.20	.12
142	*Chris Chambliss*	1.25	.60	.40
143	Garry Jestadt	.25	.13	.08
144	Marty Pattin	.25	.13	.08
145	Don Kessinger	.40	.20	.12
146	Steve Kealey	.25	.13	.08
147	*Dave Kingman*	3.50	1.75	1.00
148	Dick Billings	.25	.13	.08
149	Gary Neibauer	.25	.13	.08
150	Norm Cash	.70	.35	.20
151	Jim Brewer	.25	.13	.08
152	Gene Clines	.25	.13	.08
153	Rick Auerbach	.25	.13	.08
154	Ted Simmons	1.50	.70	.45
155	Larry Dierker	.30	.15	.09
156	Twins Team	.90	.45	.25
157	Don Gullett	.40	.20	.12
158	Jerry Kenney	.30	.15	.09
159	John Boccabella	.25	.13	.08
160	Andy Messersmith	.40	.20	.12
161	Brock Davis	.25	.13	.08
162	Brewers Rookies (Jerry Bell, *Darrell Porter*, Bob Reynolds) (Bell & Porter photos transposed)	1.00	.50	.30
163	Tug McGraw	.80	.40	.25
164	Tug McGraw IA	.40	.20	.12
165	*Chris Speier*	.80	.40	.25
166	Chris Speier IA	.40	.20	.12
167	Deron Johnson	.25	.13	.08
168	Deron Johnson IA	.25	.13	.08
169	Vida Blue	.80	.40	.25
170	Vida Blue IA	.40	.20	.12
171	Darrell Evans	1.50	.70	.45
172	Darrell Evans IA	.80	.40	.25
173	Clay Kirby	.25	.13	.08
174	Clay Kirby IA	.25	.13	.08
175	Tom Haller	.30	.15	.09
176	Tom Haller IA	.25	.13	.08
177	Paul Schaal	.25	.13	.08
178	Paul Schaal IA	.25	.13	.08
179	Dock Ellis	.30	.15	.09
180	Dock Ellis IA	.25	.13	.08
181	Ed Kranepool	.40	.20	.12
182	Ed Kranepool IA	.30	.15	.09
183	Bill Melton	.30	.15	.09
184	Bill Melton IA	.25	.13	.08
185	Ron Bryant	.25	.13	.08
186	Ron Bryant IA	.25	.13	.08
187	Gates Brown	.25	.13	.08
188	Frank Lucchesi	.25	.13	.08
189	Gene Tenace	.40	.20	.12
190	Dave Giusti	.25	.13	.08
191	*Jeff Burroughs*	.80	.40	.25
192	Cubs Team	.90	.45	.25
193	*Kurt Bevacqua*	.40	.20	.12
194	Fred Norman	.25	.13	.08
195	Orlando Cepeda	2.00	1.00	.60
196	Mel Queen	.25	.13	.08
197	Johnny Briggs	.25	.13	.08
198	Dodgers Rookies (*Charlie Hough*, Bob O'Brien, Mike Strahler)	2.25	1.25	.70
199	Mike Fiore	.25	.13	.08
200	Lou Brock	4.00	2.00	1.25
201	Phil Roof	.25	.13	.08
202	Scipio Spinks	.25	.13	.08
203	*Ron Blomberg*	.50	.25	.15
204	Tommy Helms	.25	.13	.08
205	Dick Drago	.25	.13	.08
206	Dal Maxvill	.30	.15	.09
207	Tom Egan	.25	.13	.08
208	Milt Pappas	.40	.20	.12
209	Joe Rudi	.60	.30	.20
210	Denny McLain	1.25	.60	.40
211	Gary Sutherland	.25	.13	.08
212	Grant Jackson	.25	.13	.08
213	Angels Rookies (Art Kusnyer, Billy Parker, Tom Silverio)	.25	.13	.08
214	Mike McQueen	.25	.13	.08
215	Alex Johnson	.25	.13	.08
216	Joe Niekro	.50	.25	.15
217	Roger Metzger	.25	.13	.08
218	Eddie Kasko	.25	.13	.08
219	*Rennie Stennett*	.40	.20	.12
220	Jim Perry	.60	.30	.20
221	N.L. Playoffs (Bucs Champs!)	1.25	.60	.40
222	A.L. Playoffs (Orioles Champs!)	1.25	.60	.40
223	World Series Game 1	1.25	.60	.40
224	World Series Game 2	1.25	.60	.40
225	World Series Game 3	1.25	.60	.40
226	World Series Game 4	1.50	.70	.45
227	World Series Game 5	1.25	.60	.40
228	World Series Game 6	1.25	.60	.40
229	World Series Game 7	1.25	.60	.40
230	World Series Summary (Series Celebration)	1.25	.60	.40
231	Casey Cox	.25	.13	.08
232	Giants Rookies (Chris Arnold, Jim Barr, Dave Rader)	.30	.15	.09
233	Jay Johnstone	.40	.20	.12
234	Ron Taylor	.25	.13	.08
235	Merv Rettenmund	.30	.15	.09
236	Jim McGlothlin	.25	.13	.08
237	Yankees Team	1.25	.60	.40
238	Leron Lee	.25	.13	.08
239	Tom Timmermann	.25	.13	.08
240	Rich Allen	1.75	.90	.50
241	Rollie Fingers	2.50	1.25	.70
242	Don Mincher	.30	.15	.09
243	Frank Linzy	.25	.13	.08
244	Steve Braun	.25	.13	.08
245	Tommie Agee	.30	.15	.09
246	Tom Burgmeier	.25	.13	.08
247	Milt May	.25	.13	.08
248	Tom Bradley	.25	.13	.08
249	Harry Walker	.30	.15	.09
250	Boog Powell	1.25	.60	.40
251a	Checklist 264-394 (small print on front)	2.25	1.25	.70
251b	Checklist 264-394 (large print on front)	2.25	1.25	.70
252	Ken Reynolds	.25	.13	.08
253	Sandy Alomar	.25	.13	.08
254	Boots Day	.25	.13	.08
255	Jim Lonborg	.40	.20	.12
256	George Foster	1.50	.70	.45
257	Tigers Rookies (Jim Foor, Tim Hosley, Paul Jata)	.25	.13	.08
258	Randy Hundley	.25	.13	.08
259	Sparky Lyle	.70	.35	.20
260	Ralph Garr	.40	.20	.12
261	Steve Mingori	.25	.13	.08
262	Padres Team	.90	.45	.25
263	Felipe Alou	.50	.25	.15
264	Tommy John	2.00	1.00	.60
265	Wes Parker	.30	.15	.09
266	Bobby Bolin	.25	.13	.08
267	Dave Concepcion	1.75	.90	.50
268	A's Rookies (Dwain Anderson, Chris Floethe)	.25	.13	.08
269	Don Hahn	.25	.13	.08
270	Jim Palmer	5.00	2.50	1.50
271	Ken Rudolph	.25	.13	.08
272	*Mickey Rivers*	1.00	.50	.30
273	Bobby Floyd	.25	.13	.08
274	Al Severinsen	.25	.13	.08
275	Cesar Tovar	.25	.13	.08
276	Gene Mauch	.50	.25	.15
277	Elliott Maddox	.30	.15	.09
278	Dennis Higgins	.25	.13	.08
279	Larry Brown	.25	.13	.08
280	Willie McCovey	4.00	2.00	1.25
281	Bill Parsons	.25	.13	.08
282	Astros Team	.90	.45	.25
283	Darrell Brandon	.25	.13	.08
284	Ike Brown	.25	.13	.08
285	Gaylord Perry	4.00	2.00	1.25
286	Gene Alley	.30	.15	.09
287	Jim Hardin	.30	.15	.09
288	Johnny Jeter	.25	.13	.08
289	Syd O'Brien	.25	.13	.08
290	Sonny Siebert	.25	.13	.08
291	Hal McRae	.60	.30	.20
292	Hal McRae IA	.30	.15	.09
293	Danny Frisella	.25	.13	.08
294	Danny Frisella IA	.25	.13	.08
295	Dick Dietz	.25	.13	.08
296	Dick Dietz IA	.25	.13	.08
297	Claude Osteen	.40	.20	.12
298	Claude Osteen IA	.30	.15	.09
299	Hank Aaron	20.00	10.00	6.00
300	Hank Aaron IA	8.00	4.00	2.50
301	George Mitterwald	.25	.13	.08
302	George Mitterwald IA	.25	.13	.08
303	Joe Pepitone	.50	.25	.15
304	Joe Pepitone IA	.30	.15	.09
305	Ken Boswell	.25	.13	.08
306	Ken Boswell IA	.25	.13	.08
307	Steve Renko	.25	.13	.08
308	Steve Renko IA	.25	.13	.08
309	Roberto Clemente	20.00	10.00	6.00
310	Roberto Clemente IA	6.00	3.00	1.75
311	Clay Carroll	.30	.15	.09
312	Clay Carroll IA	.25	.13	.08
313	Luis Aparicio	3.00	1.50	.90
314	Luis Aparicio IA	1.50	.70	.45
315	Paul Splittorff	.30	.15	.09
316	Cardinals Rookies (*Jim Bibby*, Santiago Guzman, Jorge Roque)	.50	.25	.15
317	Rich Hand	.25	.13	.08
318	Sonny Jackson	.25	.13	.08
319	Aurelio Rodriguez	.30	.15	.09
320	Steve Blass	.30	.15	.09
321	Joe Lahoud	.25	.13	.08
322	Jose Pena	.25	.13	.08
323	Earl Weaver	.80	.40	.25
324	Mike Ryan	.25	.13	.08
325	Mel Stottlemyre	.80	.40	.25
326	Pat Kelly	.25	.13	.08
327	*Steve Stone*	1.00	.50	.30
328	Red Sox Team	1.00	.50	.30
329	Roy Foster	.25	.13	.08
330	Jim Hunter	3.50	1.75	1.00
331	Stan Swanson	.25	.13	.08
332	Buck Martinez	.25	.13	.08
333	Steve Barber	.25	.13	.08
334	Rangers Rookies (Bill Fahey, Jim Mason, Tom Ragland)	.25	.13	.08
335	Bill Hands	.25	.13	.08
336	Marty Martinez	.25	.13	.08
337	Mike Kilkenny	.25	.13	.08
338	Bob Grich	.70	.35	.20
339	Ron Cook	.25	.13	.08
340	Roy White	.70	.35	.20
341	Boyhood Photo (Joe Torre)	.50	.25	.15
342	Boyhood Photo (Wilbur Wood)	.40	.20	.12
343	Boyhood Photo (Willie Stargell)	1.50	.70	.45
344	Boyhood Photo (Dave McNally)	.40	.20	.12
345	Boyhood Photo (Rick Wise)	.30	.15	.09
346	Boyhood Photo (Jim Fregosi)	.40	.20	.12
347	Boyhood Photo (Tom Seaver)	2.00	1.00	.60
348	Boyhood Photo (Sal Bando)	.40	.20	.12
349	Al Fitzmorris	.25	.13	.08
350	Frank Howard	1.25	.60	.40
351	Braves Rookies (Jimmy Britton, Tom House, Rick Kester)	.25	.13	.08
352	Dave LaRoche	.30	.15	.09
353	Art Shamsky	.25	.13	.08
354	Tom Murphy	.25	.13	.08
355	Bob Watson	.30	.15	.09
356	Gerry Moses	.25	.13	.08
357	Woodie Fryman	.30	.15	.09
358	Sparky Anderson	.70	.35	.20
359	Don Pavletich	.25	.13	.08
360	Dave Roberts	.25	.13	.08
361	Mike Andrews	.25	.13	.08
362	Mets Team	1.25	.60	.40
363	Ron Klimkowski	.25	.13	.08
364	Johnny Callison	.50	.25	.15
365	Dick Bosman	.25	.13	.08
366	Jimmy Rosario	.25	.13	.08
367	Ron Perranoski	.30	.15	.09
368	Danny Thompson	.30	.15	.09
369	Jim Lefebvre	.30	.15	.09
370	Don Buford	.30	.15	.09
371	Denny Lemaster	.25	.13	.08
372	Royals Rookies (Lance Clemons, Monty Montgomery)	.25	.13	.08
373	John Mayberry	.40	.20	.12
374	Jack Heidemann	.25	.13	.08
375	Reggie Cleveland	.25	.13	.08
376	Andy Kosco	.25	.13	.08
377	Terry Harmon	.25	.13	.08
378	Checklist 395-525	2.25	1.25	.70
379	Ken Berry	.25	.13	.08
380	Earl Williams	.30	.15	.09
381	White Sox Team	.90	.45	.25
382	Joe Gibbon	.25	.13	.08
383	Brant Alyea	.25	.13	.08
384	Dave Campbell	.25	.13	.08
385	Mickey Stanley	.30	.15	.09
386	Jim Colborn	.25	.13	.08
387	Horace Clarke	.30	.15	.09
388	Charlie Williams	.25	.13	.08
389	Bill Rigney	.25	.13	.08
390	Willie Davis	.50	.25	.15
391	Ken Sanders	.25	.13	.08
392	Pirates Rookies (Fred Cambria, *Richie Zisk*)	.70	.35	.20
393	Curt Motton	.25	.13	.08
394	Ken Forsch	.30	.15	.09
395	Matty Alou	.60	.30	.20
396	Paul Lindblad	.30	.15	.09
397	Phillies Team	.90	.45	.25
398	Larry Hisle	.40	.20	.12
399	Milt Wilcox	.40	.20	.12
400	Tony Oliva	1.50	.70	.45
401	Jim Nash	.30	.15	.09
402	Bobby Heise	.30	.15	.09
403	John Cumberland	.30	.15	.09
404	Jeff Torborg	.40	.20	.12
405	Ron Fairly	.50	.25	.15
406	*George Hendrick*	1.00	.50	.30
407	Chuck Taylor	.30	.15	.09
408	Jim Northrup	.40	.20	.12
409	Frank Baker	.40	.20	.12
410	Fergie Jenkins	2.00	1.00	.60
411	Bob Montgomery	.30	.15	.09
412	Dick Kelley	.30	.15	.09
413	White Sox Rookies (Don Eddy, Dave Lemonds)	.30	.15	.09
414	Bob Miller	.30	.15	.09
415	Cookie Rojas	.30	.15	.09
416	Johnny Edwards	.30	.15	.09
417	Tom Hall	.30	.15	.09
418	Tom Shopay	.30	.15	.09
419	Jim Spencer	.30	.15	.09
420	Steve Carlton	15.00	7.50	4.50
421	Ellie Rodriguez	.30	.15	.09
422	Ray Lamb	.30	.15	.09
423	Oscar Gamble	.40	.20	.12
424	Bill Gogolewski	.30	.15	.09
425	Ken Singleton	.70	.35	.20
426	Ken Singleton IA	.40	.20	.12
427	Tito Fuentes	.30	.15	.09
428	Tito Fuentes IA	.30	.15	.09
429	Bob Robertson	.30	.15	.09
430	Bob Robertson IA	.30	.15	.09
431	Clarence Gaston	.30	.15	.09
432	Clarence Gaston IA	.30	.15	.09
433	Johnny Bench	25.00	12.50	7.50
434	Johnny Bench IA	10.00	5.00	3.00
435	Reggie Jackson	25.00	12.50	7.50
436	Reggie Jackson IA	10.00	5.00	3.00
437	Maury Wills	1.50	.70	.45
438	Maury Wills IA	.70	.35	.20
439	Billy Williams	3.50	1.75	1.00
440	Billy Williams IA	1.75	.90	.50
441	Thurman Munson	15.00	7.50	4.50
442	Thurman Munson IA	8.00	4.00	2.50
443	Ken Henderson	.30	.15	.09
444	Ken Henderson IA	.30	.15	.09
445	Tom Seaver	25.00	12.50	7.50
446	Tom Seaver IA	9.00	4.50	2.75
447	Willie Stargell	4.00	2.00	1.25
448	Willie Stargell IA	2.00	1.00	.60
449	Bob Lemon	.90	.45	.25
450	Mickey Lolich	1.25	.60	.40
451	Tony LaRussa	.60	.30	.20
452	Ed Herrmann	.30	.15	.09
453	Barry Lersch	.30	.15	.09
454	A's Team	2.00	1.00	.60
455	Tommy Harper	.40	.20	.12
456	Mark Belanger	.40	.20	.12
457	Padres Rookies (Darcy Fast, Mike Ivie, *Derrel Thomas*)	.40	.20	.12
458	Aurelio Monteagudo	.30	.15	.09
459	Rick Renick	.30	.15	.09
460	Al Downing	.40	.20	.12
461	Tim Cullen	.30	.15	.09
462	Rickey Clark	.30	.15	.09
463	Bernie Carbo	.30	.15	.09
464	Jim Roland	.30	.15	.09
465	Gil Hodges	3.00	1.50	.90
466	Norm Miller	.30	.15	.09
467	Steve Kline	.40	.20	.12
468	Richie Scheinblum	.30	.15	.09
469	Ron Herbel	.30	.15	.09
470	Ray Fosse	.30	.15	.09
471	Luke Walker	.30	.15	.09

		NR MT	EX	VG
472	Phil Gagliano	.30	.15	.09
473	Dan McGinn	.30	.15	.09
474	Orioles Rookies (Don Baylor, Roric Harrison, Johnny Oates)	2.50	1.25	.70
475	Gary Nolan	.30	.15	.09
476	Lee Richard	.30	.15	.09
477	Tom Phoebus	.30	.15	.09
478a	Checklist 526-656 (small print on front)	2.25	1.25	.70
478b	Checklist 526-656 (large printing on front)	2.25	1.25	.70
479	Don Shaw	.30	.15	.09
480	Lee May	.60	.30	.20
481	Billy Conigliaro	.30	.15	.09
482	Joe Hoerner	.30	.15	.09
483	Ken Suarez	.30	.15	.09
484	Lum Harris	.30	.15	.09
485	Phil Regan	.30	.15	.09
486	John Lowenstein	.30	.15	.09
487	Tigers Team	1.50	.70	.45
488	Mike Nagy	.30	.15	.09
489	Expos Rookies (Terry Humphrey, Keith Lampard)	.30	.15	.09
490	Dave McNally	.50	.25	.15
491	Boyhood Photo (Lou Piniella)	.60	.30	.20
492	Boyhood Photo (Mel Stottlemyre)	.40	.20	.12
493	Boyhood Photo (Bob Bailey)	.30	.15	.09
494	Boyhood Photo (Willie Horton)	.40	.20	.12
495	Boyhood Photo (Bill Melton)	.30	.15	.09
496	Boyhood Photo (Bud Harrelson)	.40	.20	.12
497	Boyhood Photo (Jim Perry)	.40	.20	.12
498	Boyhood Photo (Brooks Robinson)	2.00	1.00	.60
499	Vicente Romo	.30	.15	.09
500	Joe Torre	1.25	.60	.40
501	Pete Hamm	.30	.15	.09
502	Jackie Hernandez	.30	.15	.09
503	Gary Peters	.30	.15	.09
504	Ed Spiezio	.30	.15	.09
505	Mike Marshall	.50	.25	.15
506	Indians Rookies (Terry Ley, Jim Moyer, *Dick Tidrow)*	.60	.30	.20
507	Fred Gladding	.30	.15	.09
508	Ellie Hendricks	.30	.15	.09
509	Don McMahon	.30	.15	.09
510	Ted Williams	5.00	2.50	1.50
511	Tony Taylor	.30	.15	.09
512	Paul Popovich	.30	.15	.09
513	Lindy McDaniel	.40	.20	.12
514	Ted Sizemore	.30	.15	.09
515	Bert Blyleven	3.25	1.75	1.00
516	Oscar Brown	.30	.15	.09
517	Ken Brett	.40	.20	.12
518	Wayne Garrett	.30	.15	.09
519	Ted Abernathy	.30	.15	.09
520	Larry Bowa	1.25	.60	.40
521	Alan Foster	.30	.15	.09
522	Dodgers Team	1.25	.60	.40
523	Chuck Dobson	.30	.15	.09
524	Reds Rookies (Ed Armbrister, Mel Behney)	.30	.15	.09
525	Carlos May	.40	.20	.12
526	Bob Bailey	.70	.35	.20
527	Dave Leonhard	.70	.35	.20
528	Ron Stone	.70	.35	.20
529	Dave Nelson	.70	.35	.20
530	Don Sutton	3.50	1.75	1.00
531	Freddie Patek	.70	.35	.20
532	Fred Kendall	.70	.35	.20
533	Ralph Houk	1.25	.60	.40
534	Jim Hickman	.80	.40	.25
535	Ed Brinkman	.80	.40	.25
536	Doug Rader	.70	.35	.20
537	Bob Locker	.70	.35	.20
538	Charlie Sands	.70	.35	.20
539	*Terry Forster*	1.25	.60	.40
540	Felix Millan	.70	.35	.20
541	Roger Repoz	.70	.35	.20
542	Jack Billingham	.70	.35	.20
543	Duane Josephson	.70	.35	.20
544	Ted Martinez	.70	.35	.20
545	Wayne Granger	.70	.35	.20
546	Joe Hague	.70	.35	.20
547	Indians Team	1.50	.70	.45
548	Frank Reberger	.70	.35	.20
549	Dave May	.70	.35	.20
550	Brooks Robinson	15.00	7.50	4.50
551	Ollie Brown	.70	.35	.20
552	Ollie Brown IA	.70	.35	.20
553	Wilbur Wood	.90	.45	.25
554	Wilbur Wood IA	.80	.40	.25
555	Ron Santo	1.50	.70	.45
556	Ron Santo IA	.80	.40	.25
557	John Odom	.70	.35	.20
558	John Odom IA	.70	.35	.20
559	Pete Rose	60.00	30.00	18.00
560	Pete Rose IA	30.00	15.00	9.00
561	Leo Cardenas	.70	.35	.20
562	Leo Cardenas IA	.70	.35	.20
563	Ray Sadecki	.70	.35	.20
564	Ray Sadecki IA	.70	.35	.20
565	Reggie Smith	.90	.45	.25
566	Reggie Smith IA	.80	.40	.25
567	Juan Marichal	6.00	3.00	1.75
568	Juan Marichal IA	3.00	1.50	.90
569	Ed Kirkpatrick	.70	.35	.20
570	Ed Kirkpatrick IA	.70	.35	.20
571	Nate Colbert	.70	.35	.20
572	Nate Colbert IA	.70	.35	.20
573	Fritz Peterson	.80	.40	.25
574	Fritz Peterson IA	.80	.40	.25
575	Al Oliver	2.00	1.00	.60
576	Leo Durocher	1.25	.60	.40
577	Mike Paul	.70	.35	.20
578	Billy Grabarkewitz	.70	.35	.20
579	*Doyle Alexander*	2.75	1.50	.80
580	Lou Piniella	1.75	.90	.50
581	Wade Blasingame	.70	.35	.20
582	Expos Team	2.25	1.25	.70
583	Darold Knowles	.70	.35	.20
584	Jerry McNertney	.70	.35	.20
585	George Scott	.80	.40	.25
586	Denis Menke	.70	.35	.20
587	Billy Wilson	.70	.35	.20
588	Jim Holt	.70	.35	.20
589	Hal Lanier	1.00	.50	.30
590	Graig Nettles	2.50	1.25	.70
591	Paul Casanova	.70	.35	.20
592	Lew Krausse	.70	.35	.20
593	Rich Morales	.70	.35	.20
594	Jim Beauchamp	.70	.35	.20
595	Nolan Ryan	100.00	50.00	30.00
596	Manny Mota	.90	.45	.25
597	Jim Magnuson	.80	.40	.25
598	Hal King	.70	.35	.20
599	Billy Champion	.70	.35	.20
600	Al Kaline	12.00	6.00	3.50
601	George Stone	.70	.35	.20
602	Dave Bristol	.70	.35	.20
603	Jim Ray	.70	.35	.20
604a	Checklist 657-787 (copyright on right)	3.50	1.75	1.00
604b	Checklist 657-787 (copyright on left)	5.00	2.50	1.50
605	Nelson Briles	.70	.35	.20
606	Luis Melendez	.70	.35	.20
607	Frank Duffy	.70	.35	.20
608	Mike Corkins	.70	.35	.20
609	Tom Grieve	.70	.35	.20
610	Bill Stoneman	.70	.35	.20
611	Rich Reese	.70	.35	.20
612	Joe Decker	.70	.35	.20
613	Mike Ferraro	.70	.35	.20
614	Ted Uhlaender	.70	.35	.20
615	Steve Hargan	.70	.35	.20
616	*Joe Ferguson*	.80	.40	.25
617	Royals Team	2.25	1.25	.70
618	Rich Robertson	.70	.35	.20
619	Rich McKinney	.80	.40	.25
620	Phil Niekro	4.50	2.25	1.25
621	Commissioners Award	.90	.45	.25
622	MVP Award	.90	.45	.25
623	Cy Young Award	.90	.45	.25
624	Minor League Player Of The Year Award	.90	.45	.25
625	Rookie Of The Year Award	.90	.45	.25
626	Babe Ruth Award	1.00	.50	.30
627	Moe Drabowsky	.70	.35	.20
628	Terry Crowley	.70	.35	.20
629	Paul Doyle	.70	.35	.20
630	Rich Hebner	.80	.40	.25
631	John Strohmayer	.70	.35	.20
632	Mike Hegan	.70	.35	.20
633	Jack Hiatt	.70	.35	.20
634	Dick Woodson	.70	.35	.20
635	Don Money	.80	.40	.25
636	Bill Lee	.90	.45	.25
637	Preston Gomez	.70	.35	.20
638	Ken Wright	.70	.35	.20
639	J.C. Martin	.70	.35	.20
640	Joe Coleman	.80	.40	.25
641	Mike Lum	.70	.35	.20
642	Denny Riddleberger	.70	.35	.20
643	Russ Gibson	.70	.35	.20
644	Bernie Allen	.80	.40	.25
645	Jim Maloney	.80	.40	.25
646	Chico Salmon	.70	.35	.20
647	Bob Moose	.70	.35	.20
648	Jim Lyttle	.70	.35	.20
649	Pete Richert	.70	.35	.20
650	Sal Bando	1.00	.50	.30
651	Reds Team	2.00	1.00	.60
652	Marcelino Lopez	.70	.35	.20
653	Jim Fairey	.70	.35	.20
654	Horacio Pina	.70	.35	.20
655	Jerry Grote	.80	.40	.25
656	Rudy May	.80	.40	.25
657	Bobby Wine	2.25	1.25	.70
658	Steve Dunning	2.25	1.25	.70
659	Bob Aspromonte	2.25	1.25	.70
660	Paul Blair	2.50	1.25	.70
661	Bill Virdon	2.50	1.25	.70
662	Stan Bahnsen	2.50	1.25	.70
663	Fran Healy	2.25	1.25	.70
664	Bobby Knoop	2.25	1.25	.70
665	Chris Short	2.50	1.25	.70
666	Hector Torres	2.25	1.25	.70
667	Ray Newman	2.25	1.25	.70
668	Rangers Team	3.25	1.75	1.00
669	Willie Crawford	2.25	1.25	.70
670	Ken Holtzman	2.75	1.50	.80
671	Donn Clendenon	2.50	1.25	.70
672	Archie Reynolds	2.25	1.25	.70
673	Dave Marshall	2.25	1.25	.70
674	John Kennedy	2.25	1.25	.70
675	Pat Jarvis	2.25	1.25	.70
676	Danny Cater	2.25	1.25	.70
677	Ivan Murrell	2.25	1.25	.70
678	Steve Luebber	2.25	1.25	.70
679	Astros Rookies (Bob Fenwick, Bob Stinson)	2.25	1.25	.70
680	Dave Johnson	3.50	1.75	1.00
681	Bobby Pfeil	2.25	1.25	.70
682	Mike McCormick	2.50	1.25	.70
683	Steve Hovley	2.25	1.25	.70
684	Hal Breeden	2.25	1.25	.70
685	Joe Horlen	2.25	1.25	.70
686	Steve Garvey	55.00	28.00	16.50
687	Del Unser	2.25	1.25	.70
688	Cardinals Team	3.25	1.75	1.00
689	Eddie Fisher	2.25	1.25	.70
690	Willie Montanez	2.50	1.25	.70
691	Curt Blefary	2.25	1.25	.70
692	Curt Blefary IA	2.25	1.25	.70
693	Alan Gallagher	2.25	1.25	.70
694	Alan Gallagher IA	2.25	1.25	.70
695	Rod Carew	70.00	35.00	21.00
696	Rod Carew IA	25.00	12.50	7.50
697	Jerry Koosman	4.50	2.25	1.25
698	Jerry Koosman IA	2.50	1.25	.70
699	Bobby Murcer	4.00	2.00	1.25
700	Bobby Murcer IA	2.50	1.25	.70
701	Jose Pagan	2.25	1.25	.70
702	Jose Pagan IA	2.25	1.25	.70
703	Doug Griffin	2.25	1.25	.70
704	Doug Griffin IA	2.25	1.25	.70
705	Pat Corrales	2.50	1.25	.70
706	Pat Corrales IA	2.25	1.25	.70
707	Tim Foli	2.25	1.25	.70
708	Tim Foli IA	2.25	1.25	.70
709	Jim Kaat	6.50	3.25	2.00
710	Jim Kaat IA	3.25	1.75	1.00
711	Bobby Bonds	3.75	2.00	1.25
712	Bobby Bonds IA	2.50	1.25	.70
713	Gene Michael	2.50	1.25	.70
714	Gene Michael IA	2.50	1.25	.70
715	Mike Epstein	2.50	1.25	.70
716	Jesus Alou	2.50	1.25	.70
717	Bruce Dal Canton	2.25	1.25	.70
718	Del Rice	2.25	1.25	.70
719	Cesar Geronimo	2.50	1.25	.70
720	Sam McDowell	3.00	1.50	.90
721	Eddie Leon	2.25	1.25	.70
722	Bill Sudakis	2.25	1.25	.70
723	Al Santorini	2.25	1.25	.70
724	A.L. Rookies (John Curtis, Rich Hinton, Mickey Scott)	2.50	1.25	.70
725	Dick McAuliffe	2.50	1.25	.70
726	Dick Selma	2.25	1.25	.70
727	Jose Laboy	2.25	1.25	.70
728	Gail Hopkins	2.25	1.25	.70
729	Bob Veale	2.50	1.25	.70
730	Rick Monday	2.75	1.50	.80
731	Orioles Team	3.25	1.75	1.00
732	George Culver	2.25	1.25	.70
733	Jim Hart	2.50	1.25	.70
734	Bob Burda	2.25	1.25	.70
735	Diego Segui	2.25	1.25	.70
736	Bill Russell	3.00	1.50	.90
737	*Lenny Randle*	2.50	1.25	.70
738	Jim Merritt	2.25	1.25	.70
739	Don Mason	2.25	1.25	.70
740	Rico Carty	3.25	1.75	1.00
741	Major League Rookies (Tom Hutton, *Rick Miller, John Milner)*	2.50	1.25	.70
742	Jim Rooker	2.25	1.25	.70
743	Cesar Gutierrez	2.25	1.25	.70
744	*Jim Slaton*	2.50	1.25	.70
745	Julian Javier	2.25	1.25	.70
746	Lowell Palmer	2.25	1.25	.70
747	Jim Stewart	2.25	1.25	.70
748	Phil Hennigan	2.25	1.25	.70
749	Walter Alston	5.00	2.50	1.50
750	Willie Horton	2.75	1.50	.80
751	Steve Carlton Traded	30.00	15.00	9.00
752	Joe Morgan Traded	25.00	12.50	7.50
753	Denny McLain Traded	6.00	3.00	1.75
754	Frank Robinson Traded	18.00	9.00	5.50
755	Jim Fregosi Traded	2.75	1.50	.80
756	Rick Wise Traded	2.50	1.25	.70
757	Jose Cardenal Traded	2.50	1.25	.70
758	Gil Garrido	2.25	1.25	.70
759	Chris Cannizzaro	2.25	1.25	.70
760	Bill Mazeroski	3.75	2.00	1.25
761	Major League Rookies *(Ron Cey, Ben Oglivie,* Bernie Williams)	12.00	6.00	3.50
762	Wayne Simpson	2.25	1.25	.70
763	Ron Hansen	2.25	1.25	.70
764	Dusty Baker	3.00	1.50	.90
765	Ken McMullen	2.25	1.25	.70
766	Steve Hamilton	2.25	1.25	.70
767	Tom McCraw	2.25	1.25	.70
768	Denny Doyle	2.25	1.25	.70
769	Jack Aker	2.50	1.25	.70
770	Jim Wynn	2.75	1.50	.80
771	Giants Team	3.25	1.75	1.00
772	Ken Tatum	2.25	1.25	.70
773	Ron Brand	2.25	1.25	.70
774	Luis Alvarado	2.25	1.25	.70
775	Jerry Reuss	3.50	1.75	1.00
776	Bill Voss	2.25	1.25	.70
777	Hoyt Wilhelm	15.00	7.50	4.50
778	Twins Rookies (Vic Albury, *Rick Dempsey,* Jim Strickland)	3.25	1.75	1.00
779	Tony Cloninger	2.50	1.25	.70
780	Dick Green	2.25	1.25	.70
781	Jim McAndrew	2.25	1.25	.70
782	Larry Stahl	2.25	1.25	.70
783	Les Cain	2.25	1.25	.70
784	Ken Aspromonte	2.25	1.25	.70
785	Vic Davalillo	2.25	1.25	.70
786	Chuck Brinkman	2.50	1.25	.70
787	Ron Reed	4.50	1.25	.70

1972 Topps Cloth Stickers

Despite the fact they were never actually issued, examples of this test issue can readily be found within the hobby. The set of 33 contains stickers with designs identical to cards found in three contiguous rows of a regular Topps card sheet that year; thus the inclusion of a meaningless checklist card. Sometimes found in complete 33-sticker strips, individual stickers nominally measure 2-1/2" by 3-1/2," though dimensions vary according to the care with which they were cut. Stickers are unnumbered and blank-backed, and do not contain glue.

		NR MT	EX	VG
Complete Set:		175.00	87.00	52.00
Common Player:		3.00	1.50	.90
(1)	Hank Aaron	50.00	25.00	15.00
(2)	Luis Aparicio IA	10.00	5.00	3.00
(3)	Ike Brown	3.00	1.50	.90
(4)	Johnny Callison	5.00	2.50	1.50
(5)	Checklist 264-319	3.00	1.50	.90
(6)	Roberto Clemente IA	25.00	12.50	7.50
(7)	Dave Concepcion	8.00	4.00	2.50
(8)	Ron Cook	3.00	1.50	.90
(9)	Willie Davis	5.00	2.50	1.50
(10)	Al Fitzmorris	3.00	1.50	.90
(11)	Bobby Floyd	3.00	1.50	.90
(12)	Roy Foster	3.00	1.50	.90
(13)	Jim Fregosi Boyhood Photo	4.00	2.00	1.25
(14)	Danny Frisella IA	3.00	1.50	.90
(15)	Woody Fryman	3.50	1.75	1.00
(16)	Terry Harmon	3.00	1.50	.90
(17)	Frank Howard	7.00	3.50	2.00
(18)	Ron Klimkowski	3.00	1.50	.90
(19)	Joe Lahoud	3.00	1.50	.90
(20)	Jim Lefebvre	3.50	1.75	1.00
(21)	Elliott Maddox	3.00	1.50	.90
(22)	Marty Martinez	3.00	1.50	.90
(23)	Willie McCovey	25.00	12.50	7.50
(24)	Hal McRae	6.00	3.00	1.75
(25)	Syd O'Brien	3.00	1.50	.90
(26)	Red Sox Team	4.00	2.00	1.25
(27)	Aurelio Rodriguez	3.50	1.75	1.00
(28)	Al Severinsen	3.00	1.50	.90
(29)	Art Shamsky	3.00	1.50	.90
(30)	Steve Stone	4.00	2.00	1.25
(31)	Stan Swanson	3.00	1.50	.90
(32)	Bob Watson	3.50	1.75	1.00
(33)	Roy White	6.00	3.00	1.75

1972 Topps Posters

Issued as a separate set, rather than as a wax pack insert, the twenty-four 9-7/16" by 18" posters of 1972 feature a borderless full-color picture on the front with the player's name, team and position. Printed on very thin paper, the posters, as happened with earlier issues, were folded for packaging, causing large creases which cannot be removed. Even so, they are good display items for they feature many of stars of the period.

		NR MT	EX	VG
Complete Set:		300.00	150.00	90.00
Common Player:		5.00	2.50	1.50
1	Dave McNally	5.00	2.50	1.50
2	Carl Yastrzemski	30.00	15.00	9.00
3	Bill Melton	5.00	2.50	1.50
4	Ray Fosse	5.00	2.50	1.50
5	Mickey Lolich	6.00	3.00	1.75
6	Amos Otis	5.00	2.50	1.50
7	Tony Oliva	6.00	3.00	1.75
8	Vida Blue	6.00	3.00	1.75
9	Hank Aaron	20.00	10.00	6.00
10	Fergie Jenkins	8.00	4.00	2.50
11	Pete Rose	50.00	25.00	15.00
12	Willie Davis	6.00	3.00	1.75
13	Tom Seaver	20.00	10.00	6.00
14	Rick Wise	5.00	2.50	1.50
15	Willie Stargell	12.00	6.00	3.50
16	Joe Torre	7.00	3.50	2.00
17	Willie Mays	20.00	10.00	6.00
18	Andy Messersmith	5.00	2.50	1.50
19	Wilbur Wood	5.00	2.50	1.50
20	Harmon Killebrew	15.00	7.50	4.50
21	Billy Williams	12.00	6.00	3.50
22	Bud Harrelson	5.00	2.50	1.50
23	Roberto Clemente	20.00	10.00	6.00
24	Willie McCovey	15.00	7.50	4.50

1973 Topps

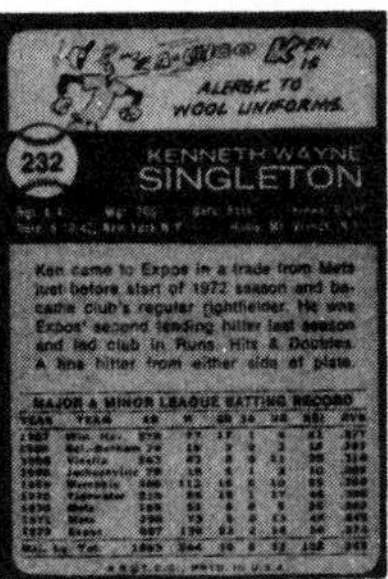

Topps cut back to 660 cards in 1973. The set is interesting for it marks the last time cards were issued by series, a procedure which had produced many a scarce high number card over the years. These 2-1/2" by 3-1/2" cards have a color photo, accented by a silhouette of a player on the front, indicative of his position. Card backs are vertical for the first time since 1968, with the usual statistical and biographical information. Specialty cards begin with card number 1, which depicted Ruth, Mays and Aaron as the all-time home run leaders. It was followed by statistical leaders, although there also were additional all-time leader cards. Also present are playoff and World Series highlights. From the age-and-youth department, the 1973 Topps set has coaches and managers as well as more "Boyhood Photos."

		NR MT	EX	VG
Complete Set:		1000.	450.00	275.00
Common Player: 1-396		.25	.13	.08
Common Player: 397-528		.40	.20	.12
Common Player: 529-660		1.25	.60	.40
1	All Time Home Run Leaders (Hank Aaron, Willie Mays, Babe Ruth)	15.00	7.50	4.50
2	Rich Hebner	.30	.15	.09
3	Jim Lonborg	.40	.20	.12
4	John Milner	.25	.13	.08
5	Ed Brinkman	.30	.15	.09
6	Mac Scarce	.25	.13	.08
7	Rangers Team	.90	.45	.25
8	Tom Hall	.25	.13	.08
9	Johnny Oates	.25	.13	.08
10	Don Sutton	2.00	1.00	.60
11	Chris Chambliss	.70	.35	.20
12a	Padres Mgr./Coaches (Dave Garcia, Johnny Podres, Bob Skinner, Whitey Wietelmann, Don Zimmer) (Coaches background brown)	.50	.25	.15
12b	Padres Mgr./Coaches (Dave Garcia, Johnny Podres, Bob Skinner, Whitey Wietelmann, Don Zimmer) (Coaches background orange)	.40	.20	.12
13	George Hendrick	.70	.35	.20
14	Sonny Siebert	.25	.13	.08
15	Ralph Garr	.30	.15	.09
16	Steve Braun	.25	.13	.08
17	Fred Gladding	.25	.13	.08
18	Leroy Stanton	.25	.13	.08
19	Tim Foli	.25	.13	.08
20a	Stan Bahnsen (small gap in left border)	.50	.25	.15
20b	Stan Bahnsen (no gap)	.25	.13	.08
21	Randy Hundley	.25	.13	.08
22	Ted Abernathy	.25	.13	.08
23	Dave Kingman	1.25	.60	.40
24	Al Santorini	.25	.13	.08
25	Roy White	.40	.20	.12
26	Pirates Team	.90	.45	.25
27	Bill Gogolewski	.25	.13	.08
28	Hal McRae	.50	.25	.15
29	Tony Taylor	.25	.13	.08
30	Tug McGraw	.60	.30	.20
31	*Buddy Bell*	4.00	2.00	1.25
32	Fred Norman	.25	.13	.08
33	Jim Breazeale	.25	.13	.08
34	Pat Dobson	.30	.15	.09
35	Willie Davis	.50	.25	.15
36	Steve Barber	.25	.13	.08
37	Bill Robinson	.25	.13	.08
38	Mike Epstein	.30	.15	.09
39	Dave Roberts	.25	.13	.08
40	Reggie Smith	.50	.25	.15
41	Tom Walker	.25	.13	.08
42	Mike Andrews	.25	.13	.08
43	*Randy Moffitt*	.30	.15	.09
44	Rick Monday	.40	.20	.12
45	Ellie Rodriguez (photo actually Paul Ratliff)	.25	.13	.08
46	Lindy McDaniel	.30	.15	.09
47	Luis Melendez	.25	.13	.08
48	Paul Splittorff	.30	.15	.09
49a	Twins Mgr./Coaches (Vern Morgan, Frank Quilici, Bob Rodgers, Ralph Rowe, Al Worthington) (Coaches background brown)	.50	.25	.15
49b	Twins Mgr./Coaches (Vern Morgan, Frank Quilici, Bob Rodgers, Ralph Rowe, Al Worthington) (Coaches background orange)	.30	.15	.09
50	Roberto Clemente	25.00	12.50	7.50
51	Chuck Seelbach	.25	.13	.08
52	Denis Menke	.25	.13	.08
53	Steve Dunning	.25	.13	.08
54	Checklist 1-132	2.00	1.00	.60
55	Jon Matlack	.40	.20	.12
56	Merv Rettenmund	.30	.15	.09
57	Derrel Thomas	.25	.13	.08
58	Mike Paul	.25	.13	.08
59	*Steve Yeager*	.60	.30	.20
60	Ken Holtzman	.40	.20	.12
61	Batting Leaders (Rod Carew, Billy Williams)	1.75	.90	.50
62	Home Run Leaders (Dick Allen, Johnny Bench)	1.50	.70	.45
63	Runs Batted In Leaders (Dick Allen, Johnny Bench)	1.50	.70	.45
64	Stolen Base Leaders (Lou Brock, Bert Campaneris)	1.25	.60	.40
65	Earned Run Average Leaders (Steve Carlton, Luis Tiant)	1.25	.60	.40
66	Victory Leaders (Steve Carlton, Gaylord Perry, Wilbur Wood)	1.25	.60	.40
67	Strikeout Leaders (Steve Carlton, Nolan Ryan)	2.50	1.25	.70
68	Leading Firemen (Clay Carroll, Sparky Lyle)	.80	.40	.25
69	Phil Gagliano	.25	.13	.08
70	Milt Pappas	.40	.20	.12
71	Johnny Briggs	.25	.13	.08
72	Ron Reed	.30	.15	.09
73	Ed Herrmann	.25	.13	.08
74	Billy Champion	.25	.13	.08
75	Vada Pinson	.80	.40	.25
76	Doug Rader	.25	.13	.08
77	Mike Torrez	.30	.15	.09
78	Richie Scheinblum	.25	.13	.08
79	Jim Willoughby	.25	.13	.08
80	Tony Oliva	1.25	.60	.40
81a	Cubs Mgr./Coaches (Hank Aguirre, Ernie Banks, Larry Jansen, Whitey Lockman, Pete Reiser) (trees in Coaches background)	.70	.35	.20
81b	Cubs Mgr./Coaches (Hank Aguirre, Ernie Banks, Larry Jansen, Whitey Lockman, Pete Reiser) (orange, solid background)	.50	.25	.15
82	Fritz Peterson	.30	.15	.09
83	Leron Lee	.25	.13	.08
84	Rollie Fingers	1.50	.70	.45
85	Ted Simmons	1.25	.60	.40
86	Tom McCraw	.25	.13	.08
87	Ken Boswell	.25	.13	.08
88	Mickey Stanley	.30	.15	.09
89	Jack Billingham	.25	.13	.08
90	Brooks Robinson	5.00	2.50	1.50
91	Dodgers Team	1.00	.50	.30
92	Jerry Bell	.25	.13	.08
93	Jesus Alou	.30	.15	.09
94	Dick Billings	.25	.13	.08
95	Steve Blass	.30	.15	.09
96	Doug Griffin	.25	.13	.08
97	Willie Montanez	.30	.15	.09
98	Dick Woodson	.25	.13	.08
99	Carl Taylor	.25	.13	.08
100	Hank Aaron	20.00	10.00	6.00
101	Ken Henderson	.25	.13	.08
102	Rudy May	.30	.15	.09
103	Celerino Sanchez	.30	.15	.09
104	Reggie Cleveland	.25	.13	.08
105	Carlos May	.30	.15	.09
106	Terry Humphrey	.25	.13	.08
107	Phil Hennigan	.25	.13	.08
108	Bill Russell	.40	.20	.12
109	Doyle Alexander	1.00	.50	.30
110	Bob Watson	.30	.15	.09
111	Dave Nelson	.25	.13	.08
112	Gary Ross	.25	.13	.08
113	Jerry Grote	.30	.15	.09
114	Lynn McGlothen	.25	.13	.08
115	Ron Santo	.80	.40	.25
116a	Yankees Mgr./Coaches (Jim Hegan, Ralph Houk, Elston Howard, Dick Howser, Jim Turner) (Coaches background brown)	1.00	.50	.30
116b	Yankees Mgr./Coaches (Jim Hegan, Ralph Houk, Elston Howard, Dick Howser, Jim Turner) (Coaches background orange)	.70	.35	.20
117	Ramon Hernandez	.25	.13	.08
118	John Mayberry	.40	.20	.12
119	Larry Bowa	.80	.40	.25
120	Joe Coleman	.30	.15	.09
121	Dave Rader	.25	.13	.08
122	Jim Strickland	.25	.13	.08
123	Sandy Alomar	.25	.13	.08
124	Jim Hardin	.25	.13	.08
125	Ron Fairly	.40	.20	.12
126	Jim Brewer	.25	.13	.08
127	Brewers Team	.90	.45	.25
128	Ted Sizemore	.25	.13	.08
129	Terry Forster	.40	.20	.12
130	Pete Rose	20.00	10.00	6.00
131a	Red Sox Mgr./Coaches (Doug Camilli, Eddie Kasko, Don Lenhardt, Eddie Popowski, Lee Stange) (Coaches background brown)	.50	.25	.15
131b	Red Sox Mgr./Coaches (Doug Camilli, Eddie Kasko, Don Lenhardt, Eddie Popowski, Lee Stange) (Coaches background			

No.	Card	NR MT	EX	VG
	orange)	.30	.15	.09
132	Matty Alou	.60	.30	.20
133	Dave Roberts	.25	.13	.08
134	Milt Wilcox	.30	.15	.09
135	Lee May	.50	.25	.15
136a	Orioles Mgr./Coaches (George Bamberger, Jim Frey, Billy Hunter, George Staller, Earl Weaver) (Coaches background brown)	1.00	.50	.30
136b	Orioles Mgr./Coaches (George Bamberger, Jim Frey, Billy Hunter, George Staller, Earl Weaver) (Coaches background orange)	.70	.35	.20
137	Jim Beauchamp	.25	.13	.08
138	Horacio Pina	.25	.13	.08
139	Carmen Fanzone	.25	.13	.08
140	Lou Piniella	.80	.40	.25
141	Bruce Kison	.30	.15	.09
142	Thurman Munson	6.00	3.00	1.75
143	John Curtis	.25	.13	.08
144	Marty Perez	.25	.13	.08
145	Bobby Bonds	.70	.35	.20
146	Woodie Fryman	.30	.15	.09
147	Mike Anderson	.25	.13	.08
148	*Dave Goltz*	.60	.30	.20
149	Ron Hunt	.30	.15	.09
150	Wilbur Wood	.40	.20	.12
151	Wes Parker	.30	.15	.09
152	Dave May	.25	.13	.08
153	Al Hrabosky	.40	.20	.12
154	Jeff Torborg	.30	.15	.09
155	Sal Bando	.70	.35	.20
156	Cesar Geronimo	.30	.15	.09
157	Denny Riddleberger	.25	.13	.08
158	Astros Team	.90	.45	.25
159	Clarence Gaston	.25	.13	.08
160	Jim Palmer	8.00	4.00	2.50
161	Ted Martinez	.25	.13	.08
162	Pete Broberg	.25	.13	.08
163	Vic Davalillo	.30	.15	.09
164	Monty Montgomery	.25	.13	.08
165	Luis Aparicio	2.75	1.50	.80
166	Terry Harmon	.25	.13	.08
167	Steve Stone	.50	.25	.15
168	Jim Northrup	.30	.15	.09
169	Ron Schueler	.25	.13	.08
170	Harmon Killebrew	3.50	1.75	1.00
171	Bernie Carbo	.25	.13	.08
172	Steve Kline	.30	.15	.09
173	Hal Breeden	.25	.13	.08
174	*Rich Gossage*	7.00	3.50	2.00
175	Frank Robinson	5.00	2.50	1.50
176	Chuck Taylor	.25	.13	.08
177	Bill Plummer	.25	.13	.08
178	Don Rose	.25	.13	.08
179a	A's Mgr./Coaches (Jerry Adair, Vern Hoscheit, Irv Noren, Wes Stock, Dick Williams) (Coaches background brown)	.80	.40	.25
179b	A's Mgr./Coaches (Jerry Adair, Vern Hoscheit, Irv Noren, Wes Stock, Dick Williams) (Coaches background orange)	.50	.25	.15
180	Fergie Jenkins	1.50	.70	.45
181	Jack Brohamer	.25	.13	.08
182	*Mike Caldwell*	.50	.25	.15
183	Don Buford	.30	.15	.09
184	Jerry Koosman	.50	.25	.15
185	Jim Wynn	.40	.20	.12
186	Bill Fahey	.25	.13	.08
187	Luke Walker	.25	.13	.08
188	Cookie Rojas	.25	.13	.08
189	Greg Luzinski	.70	.35	.20
190	Bob Gibson	3.50	1.75	1.00
191	Tigers Team	1.25	.60	.40
192	Pat Jarvis	.25	.13	.08
193	Carlton Fisk	10.00	5.00	3.00
194	*Jorge Orta*	.50	.25	.15
195	Clay Carroll	.30	.15	.09
196	Ken McMullen	.25	.13	.08
197	Ed Goodson	.25	.13	.08
198	Horace Clarke	.30	.15	.09
199	Bert Blyleven	1.50	.70	.45
200	Billy Williams	2.75	1.50	.80
201	A.L. Playoffs (Hendrick Scores Winning Run.)	1.00	.50	.30
202	N.L. Playoffs (Foster's Run Decides It.)	1.00	.50	.30
203	World Series Game 1 (Tenace The Menace.)	1.00	.50	.30
204	World Series Game 2 (A's Make It Two Straight.)	1.00	.50	.30
205	World Series Game 3 (Reds Win Squeeker.)	1.00	.50	.30
206	World Series Game 4 (Tenace Singles In Ninth.)	1.00	.50	.30
207	World Series Game 5 (Odom Out At Plate.)	1.00	.50	.30
208	World Series Game 6 (Reds' Slugging Ties Series.)	1.00	.50	.30
209	World Series Game 7 (Campy Starts Winning Rally.)	1.00	.50	.30
210	World Series Summary (World Champions.)	1.00	.50	.30
211	Balor Moore	.25	.13	.08
212	Joe Lahoud	.25	.13	.08
213	Steve Garvey	10.00	5.00	3.00
214	Dave Hamilton	.25	.13	.08
215	Dusty Baker	.50	.25	.15
216	Toby Harrah	.40	.20	.12
217	Don Wilson	.25	.13	.08
218	Aurelio Rodriguez	.30	.15	.09
219	Cardinals Team	.90	.45	.25
220	Nolan Ryan	35.00	17.50	10.50
221	Fred Kendall	.25	.13	.08
222	Rob Gardner	.25	.13	.08
223	Bud Harrelson	.30	.15	.09
224	Bill Lee	.30	.15	.09
225	Al Oliver	1.25	.60	.40
226	Ray Fosse	.25	.13	.08
227	Wayne Twitchell	.25	.13	.08
228	Bobby Darwin	.25	.13	.08
229	Roric Harrison	.25	.13	.08
230	Joe Morgan	5.00	2.50	1.50
231	Bill Parsons	.25	.13	.08
232	Ken Singleton	.40	.20	.12
233	Ed Kirkpatrick	.25	.13	.08
234	*Bill North*	.50	.25	.15
235	Jim Hunter	3.00	1.50	.90
236	Tito Fuentes	.25	.13	.08
237a	Braves Mgr./Coaches (Lew Burdette, Jim Busby, Roy Hartsfield, Eddie Mathews, Ken Silvestri) (Coaches background brown)	1.25	.60	.40
237b	Braves Mgr./Coaches (Lew Burdette, Jim Busby, Roy Hartsfield, Eddie Mathews, Ken Silvestri) (Coaches background orange)	1.00	.50	.30
238	Tony Muser	.25	.13	.08
239	Pete Richert	.25	.13	.08
240	Bobby Murcer	.60	.30	.20
241	Dwain Anderson	.25	.13	.08
242	George Culver	.25	.13	.08
243	Angels Team	.90	.45	.25
244	Ed Acosta	.25	.13	.08
245	Carl Yastrzemski	15.00	7.50	4.50
246	Ken Sanders	.25	.13	.08
247	Del Unser	.25	.13	.08
248	Jerry Johnson	.25	.13	.08
249	Larry Biittner	.25	.13	.08
250	Manny Sanguillen	.30	.15	.09
251	Roger Nelson	.25	.13	.08
252a	Giants Mgr./Coaches (Joe Amalfitano, Charlie Fox, Andy Gilbert, Don McMahon, John McNamara) (Coaches background brown)	.50	.25	.15
252b	Giants Mgr./Coaches (Joe Amalfitano, Charlie Fox, Andy Gilbert, Don McMahon, John McNamara) (Coaches background orange)	.30	.15	.09
253	Mark Belanger	.30	.15	.09
254	Bill Stoneman	.25	.13	.08
255	Reggie Jackson	25.00	12.50	7.50
256	Chris Zachary	.25	.13	.08
257a	Mets Mgr./Coaches (Yogi Berra, Roy McMillan, Joe Pignatano, Rube Walker, Eddie Yost) (Coaches background brown)	1.50	.70	.45
257b	Mets Mgr./Coaches (Yogi Berra, Roy McMillan, Joe Pignatano, Rube Walker, Eddie Yost) (Coaches background orange)	1.25	.60	.40
258	Tommy John	1.75	.90	.50
259	Jim Holt	.25	.13	.08
260	Gary Nolan	.25	.13	.08
261	Pat Kelly	.25	.13	.08
262	Jack Aker	.25	.13	.08
263	George Scott	.30	.15	.09
264	Checklist 133-264	2.00	1.00	.60
265	Gene Michael	.40	.20	.12
266	Mike Lum	.25	.13	.08
267	Lloyd Allen	.25	.13	.08
268	Jerry Morales	.25	.13	.08
269	Tim McCarver	.70	.35	.20
270	Luis Tiant	.80	.40	.25
271	Tom Hutton	.25	.13	.08
272	Ed Farmer	.25	.13	.08
273	Chris Speier	.30	.15	.09
274	Darold Knowles	.25	.13	.08
275	Tony Perez	1.25	.60	.40
276	Joe Lovitto	.25	.13	.08
277	Bob Miller	.25	.13	.08
278	Orioles Team	.90	.45	.25
279	Mike Strahler	.25	.13	.08
280	Al Kaline	4.50	2.25	1.25
281	Mike Jorgensen	.25	.13	.08
282	Steve Hovley	.25	.13	.08
283	Ray Sadecki	.25	.13	.08
284	Glenn Borgmann	.25	.13	.08
285	Don Kessinger	.30	.15	.09
286	Frank Linzy	.25	.13	.08
287	Eddie Leon	.25	.13	.08
288	Gary Gentry	.25	.13	.08
289	Bob Oliver	.25	.13	.08
290	Cesar Cedeno	.40	.20	.12
291	Rogelio Moret	.25	.13	.08
292	Jose Cruz	.80	.40	.25
293	Bernie Allen	.30	.15	.09
294	Steve Arlin	.25	.13	.08
295	Bert Campaneris	.60	.30	.20
296	Reds Mgr./Coaches (Sparky Anderson, Alex Grammas, Ted Kluszewski, George Scherger, Larry Shepard)	.70	.35	.20
297	Walt Williams	.25	.13	.08
298	Ron Bryant	.25	.13	.08
299	Ted Ford	.25	.13	.08
300	Steve Carlton	10.00	5.00	3.00
301	Billy Grabarkewitz	.25	.13	.08
302	Terry Crowley	.25	.13	.08
303	Nelson Briles	.25	.13	.08
304	Duke Sims	.25	.13	.08
305	Willie Mays	20.00	10.00	6.00
306	Tom Burgmeier	.25	.13	.08
307	Boots Day	.25	.13	.08
308	Skip Lockwood	.25	.13	.08
309	Paul Popovich	.25	.13	.08
310	Dick Allen	.80	.40	.25
311	Joe Decker	.25	.13	.08
312	Oscar Brown	.25	.13	.08
313	Jim Ray	.25	.13	.08
314	Ron Swoboda	.30	.15	.09
315	John Odom	.30	.15	.09
316	Padres Team	.90	.45	.25
317	Danny Cater	.25	.13	.08
318	Jim McGlothlin	.25	.13	.08
319	Jim Spencer	.25	.13	.08
320	Lou Brock	3.50	1.75	1.00
321	Rich Hinton	.25	.13	.08
322	*Garry Maddox*	.80	.40	.25
323	Tigers Mgr./Coaches (Art Fowler, Billy Martin, Joe Schultz, Charlie Silvera, Dick Tracewski)	1.00	.50	.30
324	Al Downing	.30	.15	.09
325	Boog Powell	1.00	.50	.30
326	Darrell Brandon	.25	.13	.08
327	John Lowenstein	.25	.13	.08
328	Bill Bonham	.25	.13	.08
329	Ed Kranepool	.30	.15	.09
330	Rod Carew	10.00	5.00	3.00
331	Carl Morton	.25	.13	.08
332	*John Felske*	.30	.15	.09
333	Gene Clines	.25	.13	.08
334	Freddie Patek	.25	.13	.08
335	Bob Tolan	.30	.15	.09
336	Tom Bradley	.25	.13	.08
337	Dave Duncan	.25	.13	.08
338	Checklist 265-396	2.00	1.00	.60
339	Dick Tidrow	.30	.15	.09
340	Nate Colbert	.30	.15	.09
341	Boyhood Photo (Jim Palmer)	1.25	.60	.40
342	Boyhood Photo (Sam McDowell)	.40	.20	.12
343	Boyhood Photo (Bobby Murcer)	.40	.20	.12
344	Boyhood Photo (Jim Hunter)	1.25	.60	.40
345	Boyhood Photo (Chris Speier)	.30	.15	.09
346	Boyhood Photo (Gaylord Perry)	1.25	.60	.40
347	Royals Team	.90	.45	.25
348	Rennie Stennett	.30	.15	.09
349	Dick McAuliffe	.30	.15	.09
350	Tom Seaver	20.00	10.00	6.00
351	Jimmy Stewart	.25	.13	.08
352	*Don Stanhouse*	.40	.20	.12
353	Steve Brye	.25	.13	.08
354	Billy Parker	.25	.13	.08
355	Mike Marshall	.40	.20	.12
356	White Sox Mgr./Coaches (Joe Lonnett, Jim Mahoney, Al Monchak, Johnny Sain, Chuck Tanner)	.50	.25	.15
357	Ross Grimsley	.30	.15	.09
358	Jim Nettles	.25	.13	.08
359	Cecil Upshaw	.25	.13	.08
360	Joe Rudi (photo actually Gene Tenace)	.40	.20	.12
361	Fran Healy	.25	.13	.08
362	Eddie Watt	.25	.13	.08
363	Jackie Hernandez	.25	.13	.08
364	Rick Wise	.30	.15	.09
365	Rico Petrocelli	.40	.20	.12
366	Brock Davis	.25	.13	.08
367	Burt Hooton	.40	.20	.12
368	Bill Buckner	.70	.35	.20
369	Lerrin LaGrow	.25	.13	.08
370	Willie Stargell	3.50	1.75	1.00
371	Mike Kekich	.30	.15	.09
372	Oscar Gamble	.30	.15	.09
373	Clyde Wright	.25	.13	.08
374	Darrell Evans	.70	.35	.20
375	Larry Dierker	.30	.15	.09
376	Frank Duffy	.25	.13	.08
377	Expos Mgr./Coaches (Dave Bristol, Larry Doby, Gene Mauch, Cal McLish, Jerry Zimmerman)	.50	.25	.15
378	Lenny Randle	.25	.13	.08
379	Cy Acosta	.25	.13	.08
380	Johnny Bench	20.00	10.00	6.00
381	Vicente Romo	.25	.13	.08
382	Mike Hegan	.25	.13	.08
383	Diego Segui	.25	.13	.08
384	Don Baylor	1.00	.50	.30
385	Jim Perry	.50	.25	.15
386	Don Money	.30	.15	.09
387	Jim Barr	.25	.13	.08
388	Ben Oglivie	.50	.25	.15
389	Mets Team	1.75	.90	.50
390	Mickey Lolich	.70	.35	.20
391	*Lee Lacy*	.80	.40	.25
392	Dick Drago	.25	.13	.08
393	Jose Cardenal	.30	.15	.09
394	Sparky Lyle	.70	.35	.20
395	Roger Metzger	.25	.13	.08
396	Grant Jackson	.25	.13	.08
397	Dave Cash	.40	.20	.12
398	Rich Hand	.40	.20	.12
399	George Foster	1.50	.70	.45
400	Gaylord Perry	3.00	1.50	.90
401	Clyde Mashore	.40	.20	.12
402	Jack Hiatt	.40	.20	.12
403	Sonny Jackson	.40	.20	.12
404	Chuck Brinkman	.40	.20	.12
405	Cesar Tovar	.40	.20	.12
406	Paul Lindblad	.40	.20	.12
407	Felix Millan	.40	.20	.12
408	Jim Colborn	.40	.20	.12
409	Ivan Murrell	.40	.20	.12
410	Willie McCovey	5.00	2.50	1.50
411	Ray Corbin	.40	.20	.12
412	Manny Mota	.60	.30	.20
413	Tom Timmermann	.40	.20	.12
414	Ken Rudolph	.40	.20	.12
415	Marty Pattin	.40	.20	.12
416	Paul Schaal	.40	.20	.12
417	Scipio Spinks	.40	.20	.12
418	Bobby Grich	.60	.30	.20
419	Casey Cox	.50	.25	.15
420	Tommie Agee	.50	.25	.15
421	Angels Mgr./Coaches (Tom Morgan, Salty Parker, Jimmie Reese, John Roseboro, Bobby Winkles)	.40	.20	.12
422	Bob Robertson	.40	.20	.12
423	Johnny Jeter	.40	.20	.12
424	Denny Doyle	.40	.20	.12
425	Alex Johnson	.40	.20	.12
426	Dave LaRoche	.40	.20	.12
427	Rick Auerbach	.40	.20	.12
428	Wayne Simpson	.40	.20	.12
429	Jim Fairey	.40	.20	.12
430	Vida Blue	.80	.40	.25
431	Gerry Moses	.50	.25	.15
432	Dan Frisella	.40	.20	.12
433	Willie Horton	.60	.30	.20
434	Giants Team	1.00	.50	.30
435	Rico Carty	.60	.30	.20
436	Jim McAndrew	.40	.20	.12
437	John Kennedy	.40	.20	.12

		NR MT	EX	VG
438	Enzo Hernandez	.40	.20	.12
439	Eddie Fisher	.40	.20	.12
440	Glenn Beckert	.50	.25	.15
441	Gail Hopkins	.40	.20	.12
442	Dick Dietz	.40	.20	.12
443	Danny Thompson	.50	.25	.15
444	Ken Brett	.50	.25	.15
445	Ken Berry	.40	.20	.12
446	Jerry Reuss	.60	.30	.20
447	Joe Hague	.40	.20	.12
448	John Hiller	.50	.25	.15
449a	Indians Mgr./Coaches (Ken Aspromonte, Rocky Colavito, Joe Lutz, Warren Spahn) (Spahn's ear pointed)	.50	.25	.15
449b	Indians Mgr./Coaches (Ken Aspromonte, Rocky Colavito, Joe Lutz, Warren Spahn) (Spahn's ear round)	.80	.40	.25
450	Joe Torre	1.00	.50	.30
451	John Vukovich	.40	.20	.12
452	Paul Casanova	.40	.20	.12
453	Checklist 397-528	2.25	1.25	.70
454	Tom Haller	.50	.25	.15
455	Bill Melton	.50	.25	.15
456	Dick Green	.40	.20	.12
457	John Strohmayer	.40	.20	.12
458	Jim Mason	.40	.20	.12
459	Jimmy Howarth	.40	.20	.12
460	Bill Freehan	.60	.30	.20
461	Mike Corkins	.40	.20	.12
462	Ron Blomberg	.50	.25	.15
463	Ken Tatum	.40	.20	.12
464	Cubs Team	1.00	.50	.30
465	Dave Giusti	.40	.20	.12
466	Jose Arcia	.40	.20	.12
467	Mike Ryan	.40	.20	.12
468	Tom Griffin	.40	.20	.12
469	Dan Monzon	.40	.20	.12
470	Mike Cuellar	.60	.30	.20
471	Hit Leader (Ty Cobb)	3.00	1.50	.90
472	Grand Slam Leader (Lou Gehrig)	3.00	1.50	.90
473	Total Base Leader (Hank Aaron)	3.00	1.50	.90
474	R.B.I. Leader (Babe Ruth)	5.00	2.50	1.50
475	Batting Leader (Ty Cobb)	3.00	1.50	.90
476	Shutout Leader (Walter Johnson)	1.25	.60	.40
477	Victory Leader (Cy Young)	1.25	.60	.40
478	Strikeout Leader (Walter Johnson)	1.25	.60	.40
479	Hal Lanier	.60	.30	.20
480	Juan Marichal	3.50	1.75	1.00
481	White Sox Team	1.25	.60	.40
482	*Rick Reuschel*	6.00	3.00	1.75
483	Dal Maxvill	.50	.25	.15
484	Ernie McAnally	.40	.20	.12
485	Norm Cash	.80	.40	.25
486a	Phillies Mgr./Coaches (Carroll Berringer, Billy DeMars, Danny Ozark, Ray Rippelmeyer, Bobby Wine) (Coaches background brown-red)	.70	.35	.20
486b	Phillies Mgr./Coaches (Carroll Beringer, Billy DeMars, Danny Ozark, Ray Rippelmeyer, Bobby Wine) (Coaches background orange)	.50	.25	.15
487	Bruce Dal Canton	.40	.20	.12
488	Dave Campbell	.40	.20	.12
489	Jeff Burroughs	.60	.30	.20
490	Claude Osteen	.60	.30	.20
491	Bob Montgomery	.40	.20	.12
492	Pedro Borbon	.40	.20	.12
493	Duffy Dyer	.40	.20	.12
494	Rich Morales	.40	.20	.12
495	Tommy Helms	.40	.20	.12
496	Ray Lamb	.40	.20	.12
497	Cardinals Mgr./Coaches (Vern Benson, George Kissell, Red Schoendienst, Barney Schultz)	.90	.45	.25
498	Graig Nettles	2.50	1.25	.70
499	Bob Moose	.40	.20	.12
500	A's Team	1.75	.90	.50
501	Larry Gura	.50	.25	.15
502	Bobby Valentine	.60	.30	.20
503	Phil Niekro	3.00	1.50	.90
504	Earl Williams	.40	.20	.12
505	Bob Bailey	.40	.20	.12
506	Bart Johnson	.40	.20	.12
507	Darrel Chaney	.40	.20	.12
508	Gates Brown	.40	.20	.12
509	Jim Nash	.40	.20	.12
510	Amos Otis	.60	.30	.20
511	Sam McDowell	.60	.30	.20
512	Dalton Jones	.40	.20	.12
513	Dave Marshall	.40	.20	.12
514	Jerry Kenney	.40	.20	.12
515	Andy Messersmith	.50	.25	.15
516	Danny Walton	.40	.20	.12
517a	Pirates Mgr./Coaches (Don Leppert, Bill Mazeroski, Dave Ricketts, Bill Virdon, Mel Wright) (Coaches background brown)	1.00	.50	.30
517b	Pirates Mgr./Coaches (Don Leppert, Bill Mazeroski, Dave Ricketts, Bill Virdon, Mel Wright) (Coaches background orange)	.50	.25	.15
518	Bob Veale	.50	.25	.15
519	John Edwards	.40	.20	.12
520	Mel Stottlemyre	.60	.30	.20
521	Braves Team	1.00	.50	.30
522	Leo Cardenas	.40	.20	.12
523	Wayne Granger	.40	.20	.12
524	Gene Tenace	.40	.20	.12
525	Jim Fregosi	.70	.35	.20
526	Ollie Brown	.40	.20	.12
527	Dan McGinn	.40	.20	.12
528	Paul Blair	.50	.25	.15
529	Milt May	1.25	.60	.40
530	Jim Kaat	3.25	1.75	1.00
531	Ron Woods	1.25	.60	.40
532	Steve Mingori	1.25	.60	.40
533	Larry Stahl	1.25	.60	.40
534	Dave Lemonds	1.25	.60	.40
535	John Callison	1.50	.70	.45
536	Phillies Team	2.50	1.25	.70

		NR MT	EX	VG
537	Bill Slayback	1.25	.60	.40
538	Jim Hart	1.50	.70	.45
539	Tom Murphy	1.25	.60	.40
540	Cleon Jones	1.50	.70	.45
541	Bob Bolin	1.25	.60	.40
542	Pat Corrales	1.50	.70	.45
543	Alan Foster	1.25	.60	.40
544	Von Joshua	1.25	.60	.40
545	Orlando Cepeda	3.25	1.75	1.00
546	Jim York	1.25	.60	.40
547	Bobby Heise	1.25	.60	.40
548	Don Durham	1.25	.60	.40
549	Rangers Mgr./Coaches (Chuck Estrada, Whitey Herzog, Chuck Hiller, Jackie Moore)	2.00	1.00	.60
550	Dave Johnson	2.75	1.50	.80
551	Mike Kilkenny	1.25	.60	.40
552	J.C. Martin	1.25	.60	.40
553	Mickey Scott	1.25	.60	.40
554	Dave Concepcion	2.50	1.25	.70
555	Bill Hands	1.25	.60	.40
556	Yankees Team	4.00	2.00	1.25
557	Bernie Williams	1.25	.60	.40
558	Jerry May	1.25	.60	.40
559	Barry Lersch	1.25	.60	.40
560	Frank Howard	2.25	1.25	.70
561	Jim Geddes	1.25	.60	.40
562	Wayne Garrett	1.25	.60	.40
563	Larry Haney	1.25	.60	.40
564	Mike Thompson	1.25	.60	.40
565	Jim Hickman	1.50	.70	.45
566	Lew Krausse	1.25	.60	.40
567	Bob Fenwick	1.25	.60	.40
568	Ray Newman	1.25	.60	.40
569	Dodgers Mgr./Coaches (Red Adams, Walt Alston, Monty Basgall, Jim Gillam, Tom Lasorda)	3.00	1.50	.90
570	Bill Singer	1.50	.70	.45
571	Rusty Torres	1.25	.60	.40
572	Gary Sutherland	1.25	.60	.40
573	Fred Beene	1.50	.70	.45
574	Bob Didier	1.25	.60	.40
575	Dock Ellis	1.50	.70	.45
576	Expos Team	2.50	1.25	.70
577	*Eric Soderholm*	1.50	.70	.45
578	Ken Wright	1.25	.60	.40
579	Tom Grieve	1.25	.60	.40
580	Joe Pepitone	2.00	1.00	.60
581	Steve Kealey	1.25	.60	.40
582	Darrell Porter	1.75	.90	.50
583	Bill Greif	1.25	.60	.40
584	Chris Arnold	1.25	.60	.40
585	Joe Niekro	2.00	1.00	.60
586	Bill Sudakis	1.50	.70	.45
587	Rich McKinney	1.25	.60	.40
588	Checklist 529-660	10.00	5.00	3.00
589	Ken Forsch	1.50	.70	.45
590	Deron Johnson	1.25	.60	.40
591	Mike Hedlund	1.25	.60	.40
592	John Boccabella	1.25	.60	.40
593	Royals Mgr./Coaches (Galen Cisco, Harry Dunlop, Charlie Lau, Jack McKeon)	1.50	.70	.45
594	Vic Harris	1.25	.60	.40
595	Don Gullett	1.50	.70	.45
596	Red Sox Team	2.75	1.50	.80
597	Mickey Rivers	1.75	.90	.50
598	Phil Roof	1.25	.60	.40
599	Ed Crosby	1.25	.60	.40
600	Dave McNally	1.75	.90	.50
601	Rookie Catchers (George Pena, Sergio Robles, Rick Stelmaszek)	1.25	.60	.40
602	Rookie Pitchers (Mel Behney, Ralph Garcia, *Doug Rau*)	1.50	.70	.45
603	Rookie Third Basemen (Terry Hughes, Bill McNulty, *Ken Reitz*)	1.50	.70	.45
604	Rookie Pitchers (Jesse Jefferson, Dennis O'Toole, Bob Strampe)	1.25	.60	.40
605	Rookie First Basemen (Pat Bourque, *Enos Cabell*, Gonzalo Marquez)	1.75	.90	.50
606	Rookie Outfielders (*Gary Matthews*, Tom Paciorek, Jorge Roque)	2.25	1.25	.70
607	Rookie Shortstops (Ray Busse, Pepe Frias, Mario Guerrero)	1.25	.60	.40
608	Rookie Pitchers (*Steve Busby*, Dick Colpaert, *George Medich*)	1.50	.70	.45
609	Rookie Second Basemen (Larvell Blanks, Pedro Garcia, *Dave Lopes*)	3.00	1.50	.90
610	Rookie Pitchers (Jimmy Freeman, Charlie Hough, Hank Webb)	1.75	.90	.50
611	Rookie Outfielders (Rich Coggins, Jim Wohlford, Richie Zisk)	1.50	.70	.45
612	Rookie Pitchers (Steve Lawson, Bob Reynolds, Brent Strom)	1.25	.60	.40
613	Rookie Catchers (*Bob Boone*, Mike Ivie, Skip Jutze)	30.00	15.00	9.00
614	Rookie Outfielders (*Alonza Bumbry, Dwight Evans*, Charlie Spikes)	60.00	30.00	18.00
615	Rookie Third Basemen (Ron Cey, John Hilton, *Mike Schmidt*)	400.00	200.00	125.00
616	Rookie Pitchers (Norm Angelini, Steve Blateric, Mike Garman)	1.50	.70	.45
617	Rich Chiles	1.25	.60	.40
618	Andy Etchebarren	1.25	.60	.40
619	Billy Wilson	1.25	.60	.40
620	Tommy Harper	1.50	.70	.45
621	Joe Ferguson	1.25	.60	.40
622	Larry Hisle	1.50	.70	.45
623	Steve Renko	1.25	.60	.40
624	Astros Mgr./Coaches (Leo Durocher, Preston Gomez, Grady Hatton, Hub Kittle, Jim Owens)	2.25	1.25	.70
625	Angel Mangual	1.25	.60	.40
626	Bob Barton	1.25	.60	.40
627	Luis Alvarado	1.25	.60	.40
628	Jim Slaton	1.50	.70	.45
629	Indians Team	2.50	1.25	.70
630	Denny McLain	3.00	1.50	.90
631	Tom Matchick	1.25	.60	.40
632	Dick Selma	1.25	.60	.40
633	Ike Brown	1.25	.60	.40
634	Alan Closter	1.50	.70	.45

		NR MT	EX	VG
635	Gene Alley	1.50	.70	.45
636	Rick Clark	1.25	.60	.40
637	Norm Niller	1.25	.60	.40
638	Ken Reynolds	1.25	.60	.40
639	Willie Crawford	1.25	.60	.40
640	Dick Bosman	1.25	.60	.40
641	Reds Team	2.75	1.50	.80
642	Jose Laboy	1.25	.60	.40
643	Al Fitzmorris	1.25	.60	.40
644	Jack Heidemann	1.25	.60	.40
645	Bob Locker	1.25	.60	.40
646	Brewers Mgr./Coaches (Del Crandall, Harvey Kuenn, Joe Nossek, Bob Shaw, Jim Walton)	1.75	.90	.50
647	George Stone	1.25	.60	.40
648	Tom Egan	1.25	.60	.40
649	Rich Folkers	1.25	.60	.40
650	Felipe Alou	1.75	.90	.50
651	Don Carrithers	1.25	.60	.40
652	Ted Kubiak	1.25	.60	.40
653	Joe Hoerner	1.25	.60	.40
654	Twins Team	2.50	1.25	.70
655	Clay Kirby	1.25	.60	.40
656	John Ellis	1.25	.60	.40
657	Bob Johnson	1.25	.60	.40
658	Elliott Maddox	1.50	.70	.45
659	Jose Pagan	1.50	.70	.45
660	Fred Scherman	2.25	.70	.45

1973 Topps Candy Lids

A bit out of the ordinary, the Topps Candy Lids were the top of a product called "Baseball Stars Bubble Gum." The bottom (inside) of the lids carry a color photo of a player with a ribbon which contains the name, position and team. The lids are 1-7/8" in diameter. A total of 55 different lids were made, featuring most of the stars of the day.

		NR MT	EX	VG
	Complete Set:	400.00	200.00	120.00
	Common Player:	2.00	1.00	.60
(1)	Hank Aaron	30.00	15.00	9.00
(2)	Dick Allen	4.00	2.00	1.25
(3)	Dusty Baker	2.00	1.00	.60
(4)	Sal Bando	3.00	1.50	.90
(5)	Johnny Bench	20.00	10.00	6.00
(6)	Bobby Bonds	3.00	1.50	.90
(7)	Dick Bosman	2.00	1.00	.60
(8)	Lou Brock	15.00	7.50	4.50
(9)	Rod Carew	20.00	10.00	6.00
(10)	Steve Carlton	20.00	10.00	6.00
(11)	Nate Colbert	2.00	1.00	.60
(12)	Willie Davis	3.00	1.50	.90
(13)	Larry Dierker	2.00	1.00	.60
(14)	Mike Epstein	2.00	1.00	.60
(15)	Carlton Fisk	7.00	3.50	2.00
(16)	Tim Foli	2.00	1.00	.60
(17)	Ray Fosse	2.00	1.00	.60
(18)	Bill Freehan	3.00	1.50	.90
(19)	Bob Gibson	15.00	7.50	4.50
(20)	Bud Harrelson	2.00	1.00	.60
(21)	Jim Hunter	12.00	6.00	3.50
(22)	Reggie Jackson	25.00	12.50	7.50
(23)	Fergie Jenkins	7.00	3.50	2.00
(24)	Al Kaline	15.00	7.50	4.50
(25)	Harmon Killebrew	15.00	7.50	4.50
(26)	Clay Kirby	2.00	1.00	.60
(27)	Mickey Lolich	4.00	2.00	1.25
(28)	Greg Luzinski	3.00	1.50	.90
(29)	Mike Marshall	2.00	1.00	.60
(30)	Lee May	2.00	1.00	.60
(31)	John Mayberry	2.00	1.00	.60
(32)	Willie Mays	30.00	15.00	9.00
(33)	Willie McCovey	15.00	7.50	4.50
(34)	Thurman Munson	15.00	7.50	4.50
(35)	Bobby Murcer	3.00	1.50	.90
(36)	Gary Nolan	2.00	1.00	.60
(37)	Amos Otis	2.00	1.00	.60
(38)	Jim Palmer	12.00	6.00	3.50
(39)	Gaylord Perry	12.00	6.00	3.50
(40)	Lou Piniella	3.00	1.50	.90
(41)	Brooks Robinson	18.00	9.00	5.50
(42)	Frank Robinson	15.00	7.50	4.50
(43)	Ellie Rodriguez	2.00	1.00	.60
(44)	Pete Rose	65.00	32.00	19.50
(45)	Nolan Ryan	18.00	9.00	5.50
(46)	Manny Sanguillen	2.00	1.00	.60
(47)	George Scott	2.00	1.00	.60
(48)	Tom Seaver	20.00	10.00	6.00
(49)	Chris Speier	2.00	1.00	.60
(50)	Willie Stargell	15.00	7.50	4.50
(51)	Don Sutton	12.00	6.00	3.50
(52)	Joe Torre	4.00	2.00	1.25
(53)	Billy Williams	12.00	6.00	3.50
(54)	Wilbur Wood	2.00	1.00	.60
(55)	Carl Yastrzemski	25.00	12.50	7.50

1973 Topps Comics

Strictly a test issue, if ever publicly distributed at all (most are found without any folding which would have occurred had they actually been used to wrap a piece of bubblegum), the 24 players in the 1973 Topps Comics issue appear on 4-5/8" by 3-7/16" waxed paper wrappers. The inside of the wrapper combines a color photo and facsimile autograph with a comic-style presentation of the player's career highlights. The Comics share a checklist with the 1973 Topps Pin-Ups, virtually all star players.

		NR MT	EX	VG
Complete Set:		3000.	1500.	900.00
Common Player:		70.00	35.00	21.00
(1)	Hank Aaron	200.00	100.00	60.00
(2)	Dick Allen	80.00	40.00	24.00
(3)	Johnny Bench	150.00	75.00	45.00
(4)	Steve Carlton	125.00	62.00	37.00
(5)	Nate Colbert	70.00	35.00	21.00
(6)	Willie Davis	80.00	40.00	24.00
(7)	Mike Epstein	70.00	35.00	21.00
(8)	Reggie Jackson	200.00	100.00	60.00
(9)	Harmon Killebrew	125.00	62.00	37.00
(10)	Mickey Lolich	80.00	40.00	24.00
(11)	Mike Marshall	70.00	35.00	21.00
(12)	Lee May	70.00	35.00	21.00
(13)	Willie McCovey	125.00	62.00	37.00
(14)	Bobby Murcer	80.00	40.00	24.00
(15)	Gaylord Perry	100.00	50.00	30.00
(16)	Lou Piniella	80.00	40.00	24.00
(17)	Brooks Robinson	125.00	62.00	37.00
(18)	Nolan Ryan	125.00	62.00	37.00
(19)	George Scott	70.00	35.00	21.00
(20)	Tom Seaver	150.00	75.00	45.00
(21)	Willie Stargell	100.00	50.00	30.00
(22)	Joe Torre	80.00	40.00	24.00
(23)	Billy Williams	100.00	50.00	30.00
(24)	Carl Yastrzemski	250.00	125.00	75.00

1973 Topps Pin-Ups

Another test issue of 1973, the 24 Topps Pin-Ups include the same basic format and the same checklist of star-caliber players as the Comics test issue of the same year. The 3-7/16" by 4-5/8" Pin-Ups are actually the inside of a wrapper for a piece of bubblegum. The color player photo features a decorative lozenge inserted at bottom with the player's name, team and position. There is also a facsimile autograph. Curiously, neither the Pin-Ups nor the Comics of 1973 bear team logos on the players' caps.

		NR MT	EX	VG
Complete Set:		1250.	625.00	375.00
Common Player:		30.00	15.00	9.00
(1)	Hank Aaron	90.00	45.00	27.00
(2)	Dick Allen	35.00	17.50	10.50
(3)	Johnny Bench	70.00	35.00	21.00
(4)	Steve Carlton	60.00	30.00	18.00
(5)	Nate Colbert	30.00	15.00	9.00
(6)	Willie Davis	35.00	17.50	10.50
(7)	Mike Epstein	30.00	15.00	9.00
(8)	Reggie Jackson	90.00	45.00	27.00
(9)	Harmon Killebrew	50.00	25.00	15.00
(10)	Mickey Lolich	35.00	17.50	10.50
(11)	Mike Marshall	30.00	15.00	9.00
(12)	Lee May	30.00	15.00	9.00
(13)	Willie McCovey	50.00	25.00	15.00
(14)	Bobby Murcer	35.00	17.50	10.50
(15)	Gaylord Perry	45.00	22.00	13.50
(16)	Lou Piniella	35.00	17.50	10.50
(17)	Brooks Robinson	55.00	27.00	16.50
(18)	Nolan Ryan	55.00	27.00	16.50
(19)	George Scott	30.00	15.00	9.00
(20)	Tom Seaver	75.00	37.00	22.00
(21)	Willie Stargell	45.00	22.00	13.50
(22)	Joe Torre	35.00	17.50	10.50
(23)	Billy Williams	45.00	22.00	13.50
(24)	Carl Yastrzemski	110.00	55.00	33.00

1973 Topps Team Checklists

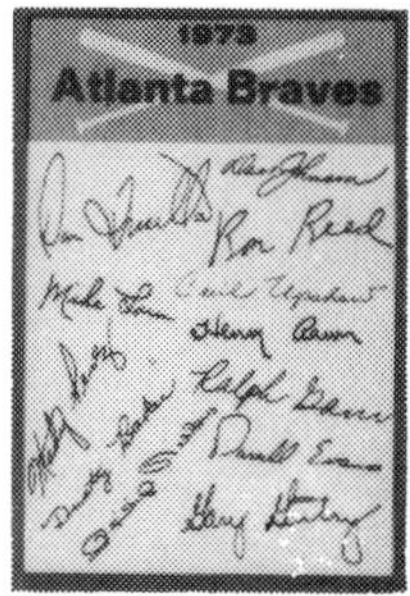

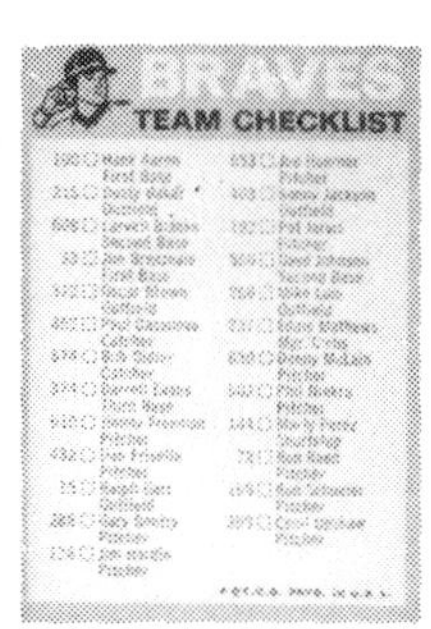

This is a 24-card unnumbered set of 2-1/2" by 3-1/2" cards that is generally believed to have been included with the high-numbered series in 1973, while also being made available in a mail-in offer. The front of the cards have the team name at the top and a white panel with various facsimile autographs takes up the rest of the space except for a blue border. Backs feature the team name and checklist. Relatively scarce, these somewhat mysterious cards are not included by many in their collections despite their obvious relationship to the regular set.

		NR MT	EX	VG
Complete Set:		70.00	35.00	21.00
Common Checklist:		2.50	1.25	.70
(1)	Atlanta Braves	3.00	1.50	.90
(2)	Baltimore Orioles	3.00	1.50	.90
(3)	Boston Red Sox	3.00	1.50	.90
(4)	California Angels	3.00	1.50	.90
(5)	Chicago Cubs	3.00	1.50	.90
(6)	Chicago White Sox	3.00	1.50	.90
(7)	Cincinnati Reds	3.00	1.50	.90
(8)	Cleveland Indians	3.00	1.50	.90
(9)	Detroit Tigers	3.50	1.75	1.00
(10)	Houston Astros	3.00	1.50	.90
(11)	Kansas City Royals	3.00	1.50	.90
(12)	Los Angeles Dodgers	3.00	1.50	.90
(13)	Milwaukee Brewers	3.00	1.50	.90
(14)	Minnesota Twins	3.00	1.50	.90
(15)	Montreal Expos	3.00	1.50	.90
(16)	New York Mets	3.50	1.75	1.00
(17)	New York Yankees	3.50	1.75	1.00
(18)	Oakland A's	3.50	1.75	1.00
(19)	Philadelphia Phillies	3.00	1.50	.90
(20)	Pittsburgh Pirates	3.00	1.50	.90
(21)	St. Louis Cardinals	3.00	1.50	.90
(22)	San Diego Padres	3.00	1.50	.90
(23)	San Francisco Giants	3.00	1.50	.90
(24)	Texas Rangers	3.00	1.50	.90

1974 Topps

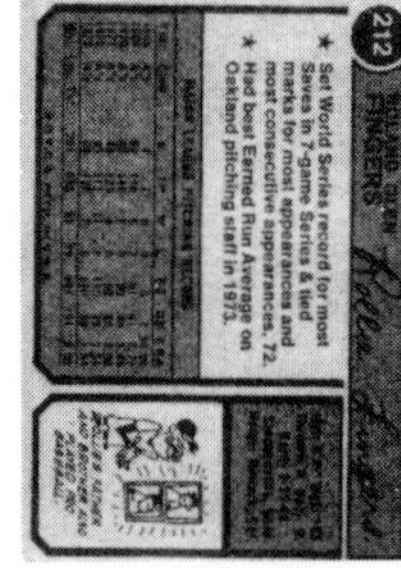

Issued all at once at the beginning of the year, rather than by series throughout the baseball season as had been done since 1952, this 660-card '74 Topps set features a famous group of error cards. At the time the cards were printed, it was uncertain whether the San Diego Padres would move to Washington, D.C., and by the time a decision was made some Padres cards had appeared with a "Washington, Nat'l League" designation on the front. A total of 15 cards were affected, and those with the Washington designation bring prices well in excess of regular cards of the same players (the Washington variations are not included in the complete set prices quoted below). The 2-1/2" by 3-1/2" cards feature color photos (frequently game-action shots) along with the player's name, team and position. Specialty cards abound, starting with a Hank Aaron tribute and running through the usual managers, statistical leaders, playoff and World Series highlights, multi-player rookie cards and All-Stars.

		NR MT	EX	VG
Complete Set:		450.00	230.00	135.00
Common Player:		.20	.10	.06
1	Hank Aaron	30.00	15.00	9.00
2	Aaron Special 1954-57	3.00	1.50	.90
3	Aaron Special 1958-61	3.00	1.50	.90
4	Aaron Special 1962-65	3.00	1.50	.90
5	Aaron Special 1966-69	3.00	1.50	.90
6	Aaron Special 1970-73	3.00	1.50	.90
7	Jim Hunter	3.00	1.50	.90
8	George Theodore	.20	.10	.06
9	Mickey Lolich	.60	.30	.20
10	Johnny Bench	15.00	7.50	4.50
11	Jim Bibby	.25	.13	.08
12	Dave May	.20	.10	.06
13	Tom Hilgendorf	.20	.10	.06
14	Paul Popovich	.20	.10	.06
15	Joe Torre	.80	.40	.25
16	Orioles Team	.80	.40	.25
17	Doug Bird	.20	.10	.06
18	Gary Thomasson	.20	.10	.06
19	Gerry Moses	.25	.13	.08
20	Nolan Ryan	30.00	15.00	8.00
21	Bob Gallagher	.20	.10	.06
22	Cy Acosta	.20	.10	.06
23	Craig Robinson	.20	.10	.06
24	John Hiller	.25	.13	.08
25	Ken Singleton	.30	.15	.09
26	*Bill Campbell*	.40	.20	.12
27	George Scott	.30	.15	.09
28	Manny Sanguillen	.25	.13	.08
29	Phil Niekro	2.00	1.00	.60
30	Bobby Bonds	.50	.25	.15
31	Astros Mgr./Coaches (Roger Craig, Preston Gomez, Grady Hatton, Hub Kittle, Bob Lillis)	.20	.10	.06
32a	John Grubb (Washington)	3.50	1.75	1.00
32b	John Grubb (San Diego)	.25	.13	.08
33	Don Newhauser	.20	.10	.06
34	Andy Kosco	.20	.10	.06
35	Gaylord Perry	2.25	1.25	.70
36	Cardinals Team	.80	.40	.25
37	Dave Sells	.20	.10	.06
38	Don Kessinger	.25	.13	.08
39	Ken Suarez	.20	.10	.06
40	Jim Palmer	5.00	2.50	1.50
41	Bobby Floyd	.20	.10	.06
42	Claude Osteen	.30	.15	.09
43	Jim Wynn	.30	.15	.09
44	Mel Stottlemyre	.40	.20	.12
45	Dave Johnson	.70	.35	.20
46	Pat Kelly	.20	.10	.06
47	*Dick Ruthven*	.25	.13	.08
48	Dick Sharon	.20	.10	.06
49	Steve Renko	.20	.10	.06
50	Rod Carew	5.50	2.75	1.75
51	Bobby Heise	.20	.10	.06
52	Al Oliver	1.00	.50	.30
53a	Fred Kendall (Washington)	3.50	1.75	1.00
53b	Fred Kendall (San Diego)	.25	.13	.08
54	*Elias Sosa*	.25	.13	.08
55	Frank Robinson	3.50	1.75	1.00
56	Mets Team	1.00	.50	.30
57	Darold Knowles	.20	.10	.06
58	Charlie Spikes	.20	.10	.06
59	Ross Grimsley	.25	.13	.08
60	Lou Brock	3.50	1.75	1.00
61	Luis Aparicio	2.50	1.25	.70
62	Bob Locker	.20	.10	.06
63	Bill Sudakis	.20	.10	.06
64	Doug Rau	.20	.10	.06
65	Amos Otis	.30	.15	.09
66	Sparky Lyle	.50	.25	.15
67	Tommy Helms	.20	.10	.06
68	Grant Jackson	.20	.10	.06
69	Del Unser	.20	.10	.06
70	Dick Allen	.80	.40	.25
71	Danny Frisella	.20	.10	.06
72	Aurleio Rodriguez	.25	.13	.08
73	Mike Marshall	.70	.35	.20
74	Twins Team	.80	.40	.25
75	Jim Colborn	.20	.10	.06
76	Mickey Rivers	.30	.15	.09
77a	Rich Troedson (Washington)	3.50	1.75	1.00
77b	Rich Troedson (San Diego)	.25	.13	.08
78	Giants Mgr./Coaches (Joe Amalfitano, Charlie Fox, Andy Gilbert, Don McMahon, John McNamara)	.20	.10	.06
79	Gene Tenace	.30	.15	.09
80	Tom Seaver	7.00	3.50	2.00

		NR MT	EX	VG
81	Frank Duffy	.20	.10	.06
82	Dave Giusti	.20	.10	.06
83	Orlando Cepeda	1.00	.50	.30
84	Rick Wise	.25	.13	.08
85	Joe Morgan	5.00	2.50	1.50
86	Joe Ferguson	.20	.10	.06
87	Fergie Jenkins	1.25	.60	.40
88	Freddie Patek	.20	.10	.06
89	Jackie Brown	.20	.10	.06
90	Bobby Murcer	.40	.20	.12
91	Ken Forsch	.25	.13	.08
92	Paul Blair	.25	.13	.08
93	Rod Gilbreath	.20	.10	.06
94	Tigers Team	.90	.45	.25
95	Steve Carlton	7.00	3.50	2.00
96	*Jerry Hairston*	.40	.20	.12
97	Bob Bailey	.20	.10	.06
98	Bert Blyleven	1.00	.50	.30
99	Brewers Mgr./Coaches (Del Crandall, Harvey Kuenn, Joe Nossek, Jim Walton, Al Widmar)	.25	.13	.08
100	Willie Stargell	3.00	1.50	.90
101	Bobby Valentine	.30	.15	.09
102a	Bill Greif (Washington)	3.50	1.75	1.00
102b	Bill Greif (San Diego)	.25	.13	.08
103	Sal Bando	.40	.20	.12
104	Ron Bryant	.20	.10	.06
105	Carlton Fisk	2.00	1.00	.60
106	Harry Parker	.20	.10	.06
107	Alex Johnson	.20	.10	.06
108	Al Hrabosky	.25	.13	.08
109	Bob Grich	.40	.20	.12
110	Billy Williams	2.75	1.50	.80
111	Clay Carroll	.25	.13	.08
112	Dave Lopes	.40	.20	.12
113	Dick Drago	.20	.10	.06
114	Angels Team	.80	.40	.25
115	Willie Horton	.30	.15	.09
116	Jerry Reuss	.30	.15	.09
117	Ron Blomberg	.25	.13	.08
118	Bill Lee	.25	.13	.08
119	Phillies Mgr./Coaches (Carroll Beringer, Bill DeMars, Danny Ozark, Ray Ripplemeyer, Bobby Wine)	.25	.13	.08
120	Wilbur Wood	.30	.15	.09
121	Larry Lintz	.20	.10	.06
122	Jim Holt	.20	.10	.06
123	Nelson Briles	.20	.10	.06
124	Bob Coluccio	.20	.10	.06
125a	Nate Colbert (Washington)	3.50	1.75	1.00
125b	Nate Colbert (San Diego)	.30	.15	.09
126	Checklist 1-132	1.50	.70	.45
127	Tom Paciorek	.25	.13	.08
128	John Ellis	.20	.10	.06
129	Chris Speier	.25	.13	.08
130	Reggie Jackson	15.00	7.50	4.50
131	Bob Boone	.50	.25	.15
132	Felix Millan	.20	.10	.06
133	*David Clyde*	.30	.15	.09
134	Denis Menke	.20	.10	.06
135	Roy White	.40	.20	.12
136	Rick Reuschel	.80	.40	.25
137	Al Bumbry	.25	.13	.08
138	Ed Brinkman	.25	.13	.08
139	Aurelio Monteagudo	.20	.10	.06
140	Darrell Evans	.60	.30	.20
141	Pat Bourque	.20	.10	.06
142	Pedro Garcia	.20	.10	.06
143	Dick Woodson	.20	.10	.06
144	Dodgers Mgr./Coaches (Red Adams, Walter Alston, Monty Basgall, Jim Gilliam, Tom Lasorda)	1.25	.60	.40
145	Dock Ellis	.25	.13	.08
146	Ron Fairly	.30	.15	.09
147	Bart Johnson	.20	.10	.06
148a	Dave Hilton (Washington)	3.50	1.75	1.00
148b	Dave Hilton (San Diego)	.25	.13	.08
149	Mac Scarce	.20	.10	.06
150	John Mayberry	.30	.15	.09
151	Diego Segui	.20	.10	.06
152	Oscar Gamble	.30	.15	.09
153	Jon Matlack	.30	.15	.09
154	Astros Team	.80	.40	.25
155	Bert Campaneris	.40	.20	.12
156	Randy Moffitt	.20	.10	.06
157	Vic Harris	.20	.10	.06
158	Jack Billingham	.20	.10	.06
159	Jim Ray Hart	.25	.13	.08
160	Brooks Robinson	3.50	1.75	1.00
161	*Ray Burris*	.40	.20	.12
162	Bill Freehan	.40	.20	.12
163	Ken Berry	.20	.10	.06
164	Tom House	.20	.10	.06
165	Willie Davis	.40	.20	.12
166	Royals Mgr./Coaches (Galen Cisco, Harry Dunlop, Charlie Lau, Jack McKeon)	.25	.13	.08
167	Luis Tiant	.50	.25	.15
168	Danny Thompson	.25	.13	.08
169	*Steve Rogers*	.70	.35	.20
170	Bill Melton	.25	.13	.08
171	Eduardo Rodriguez	.20	.10	.06
172	Gene Clines	.20	.10	.06
173a	*Randy Jones* (Washington)	4.00	2.00	1.25
173b	*Randy Jones* (San Diego)	.40	.20	.12
174	Bill Robinson	.20	.10	.06
175	Reggie Cleveland	.20	.10	.06
176	John Lowenstein	.20	.10	.06
177	Dave Roberts	.20	.10	.06
178	Garry Maddox	.40	.20	.12
179	Mets Mgr./Coaches (Yogi Berra, Roy McMillan, Joe Pignatano, Rube Walker, Eddie Yost)	1.25	.60	.40
180	Ken Holtzman	.30	.15	.09
181	Cesar Geronimo	.25	.13	.08
182	Lindy McDaniel	.25	.13	.08
183	Johnny Oates	.20	.10	.06
184	Rangers Team	.80	.40	.25
185	Jose Cardenal	.25	.13	.08
186	Fred Scherman	.20	.10	.06
187	Don Baylor	.70	.35	.20
188	Rudy Meoli	.20	.10	.06

		NR MT	EX	VG
189	Jim Brewer	.20	.10	.06
190	Tony Oliva	.80	.40	.25
191	Al Fitzmorris	.20	.10	.06
192	Mario Guerrero	.20	.10	.06
193	Tom Walker	.20	.10	.06
194	Darrell Porter	.30	.15	.09
195	Carlos May	.25	.13	.08
196	Jim Fregosi	.40	.20	.12
197a	Vicente Romo (Washington)	3.50	1.75	1.00
197b	Vicente Romo (San Diego)	.25	.13	.08
198	Dave Cash	.20	.10	.06
199	Mike Kekich	.20	.10	.06
200	Cesar Cedeno	.40	.20	.12
201	Batting Leaders (Rod Carew, Pete Rose)	3.00	1.50	.90
202	Home Run Leaders (Reggie Jackson, Willie Stargell)	2.00	1.00	.60
203	Runs Batted In Leaders (Reggie Jackson, Willie Stargell)	2.00	1.00	.60
204	Stolen Base Leaders (Lou Brock, Tommy Harper)	1.25	.60	.40
205	Victory Leaders (Ron Bryant, Wilbur Wood)	.50	.25	.15
206	Earned Run Average Leaders (Jim Palmer, Tom Seaver)	2.00	1.00	.60
207	Strikeout Leaders (Nolan Ryan, Tom Seaver)	2.00	1.00	.60
208	Leading Firemen (John Hiller, Mike Marshall)	.50	.25	.15
209	Ted Sizemore	.20	.10	.06
210	Bill Singer	.25	.13	.08
211	Cubs Team	.80	.40	.25
212	Rollie Fingers	1.50	.70	.45
213	Dave Rader	.20	.10	.06
214	Billy Grabarkewitz	.20	.10	.06
215	Al Kaline	3.50	1.75	1.00
216	Ray Sadecki	.20	.10	.06
217	Tim Foli	.20	.10	.06
218	Johnny Briggs	.20	.10	.06
219	Doug Griffin	.20	.10	.06
220	Don Sutton	2.00	1.00	.60
221	White Sox Mgr./Coaches (Joe Lonnett, Jim Mahoney, Alex Monchak, Johnny Sain, Chuck Tanner)	.30	.15	.09
222	Ramon Hernandez	.20	.10	.06
223	Jeff Burroughs	.50	.25	.15
224	Roger Metzger	.20	.10	.06
225	Paul Splittorff	.25	.13	.08
226a	Washington Nat'l. Team	6.00	3.00	1.75
226b	Padres Team	1.00	.50	.30
227	Mike Lum	.20	.10	.06
228	Ted Kubiak	.20	.10	.06
229	Fritz Peterson	.30	.15	.09
230	Tony Perez	1.25	.60	.40
231	Dick Tidrow	.20	.10	.06
232	Steve Brye	.20	.10	.06
233	Jim Barr	.20	.10	.06
234	John Milner	.20	.10	.06
235	Dave McNally	.30	.15	.09
236	Cardinals Mgr./Coaches (Vern Benson, George Kissell, Johnny Lewis, Red Schoendienst, Barney Schultz)	.40	.20	.12
237	Ken Brett	.25	.13	.08
238	Fran Healy	.20	.10	.06
239	Bill Russell	.30	.15	.09
240	Joe Coleman	.25	.13	.08
241a	Glenn Beckert (Washington)	4.00	2.00	1.25
241b	Glenn Beckert (San Diego)	.30	.15	.09
242	Bill Gogolewski	.20	.10	.06
243	Bob Oliver	.20	.10	.06
244	Carl Morton	.20	.10	.06
245	Cleon Jones	.25	.13	.08
246	A's Team	1.25	.60	.40
247	Rick Miller	.20	.10	.06
248	Tom Hall	.20	.10	.06
249	George Mitterwald	.20	.10	.06
250a	Willie McCovey (Washington)	25.00	12.50	7.50
250b	Willie McCovey (San Diego)	4.00	2.00	1.25
251	Graig Nettles	1.50	.70	.45
252	*Dave Parker*	30.00	15.00	9.00
253	John Boccabella	.20	.10	.06
254	Stan Bahnsen	.20	.10	.06
255	Larry Bowa	.40	.20	.12
256	Tom Griffin	.20	.10	.06
257	Buddy Bell	1.25	.60	.40
258	Jerry Morales	.20	.10	.06
259	Bob Reynolds	.20	.10	.06
260	Ted Simmons	.80	.40	.25
261	Jerry Bell	.20	.10	.06
262	Ed Kirkpatrick	.20	.10	.06
263	Checklist 133-264	1.50	.70	.45
264	Joe Rudi	.40	.20	.12
265	Tug McGraw	.60	.30	.20
266	Jim Northrup	.25	.13	.08
267	Andy Messersmith	.30	.15	.09
268	Tom Grieve	.20	.10	.06
269	Bob Johnson	.20	.10	.06
270	Ron Santo	.50	.25	.15
271	Bill Hands	.20	.10	.06
272	Paul Casanova	.20	.10	.06
273	Checklist 265-396	1.50	.70	.45
274	Fred Beene	.25	.13	.08
275	Ron Hunt	.25	.13	.08
276	Angels Mgr./Coaches (Tom Morgan, Salty Parker, Jimmie Reese, John Roseboro, Bobby Winkles)	.20	.10	.06
277	Gary Nolan	.20	.10	.06
278	Cookie Rojas	.20	.10	.06
279	Jim Crawford	.20	.10	.06
280	Carl Yastrzemski	12.00	6.00	3.50
281	Giants Team	.80	.40	.25
282	Doyle Alexander	.40	.20	.12
283	Mike Schmidt	90.00	45.00	30.00
284	Dave Duncan	.20	.10	.06
285	Reggie Smith	.40	.20	.12
286	Tony Muser	.20	.10	.06
287	Clay Kirby	.20	.10	.06
288	*Gorman Thomas*	2.00	1.00	.60
289	Rick Auerbach	.20	.10	.06

		NR MT	EX	VG
290	Vida Blue	.60	.30	.20
291	Don Hahn	.20	.10	.06
292	Chuck Seelbach	.20	.10	.06
293	Milt May	.20	.10	.06
294	Steve Foucault	.20	.10	.06
295	Rick Monday	.30	.15	.09
296	Ray Corbin	.20	.10	.06
297	Hal Breeden	.20	.10	.06
298	Roric Harrison	.20	.10	.06
299	Gene Michael	.30	.15	.09
300	Pete Rose	15.00	7.50	4.50
301	Bob Montgomery	.20	.10	.06
302	Rudy May	.25	.13	.08
303	George Hendrick	.30	.15	.09
304	Don Wilson	.20	.10	.06
305	Tito Fuentes	.20	.10	.06
306	Orioles Mgr./Coaches (George Bamberger, Jim Frey, Billy Hunter, George Staller, Earl Weaver)	.70	.35	.20
307	Luis Melendez	.20	.10	.06
308	Bruce Dal Canton	.20	.10	.06
309a	Dave Roberts (Washington)	3.50	1.75	1.00
309b	Dave Roberts (San Diego)	.25	.13	.08
310	Terry Forster	.30	.15	.09
311	Jerry Grote	.25	.13	.08
312	Deron Johnson	.20	.10	.06
313	Berry Lersch	.20	.10	.06
314	Brewers Team	.80	.40	.25
315	Ron Cey	.60	.30	.20
316	Jim Perry	.40	.20	.12
317	Richie Zisk	.30	.15	.09
318	Jim Merritt	.20	.10	.06
319	Randy Hundley	.20	.10	.06
320	Dusty Baker	.40	.20	.12
321	Steve Braun	.20	.10	.06
322	Ernie McAnally	.20	.10	.06
323	Richie Scheinblum	.20	.10	.06
324	Steve Kline	.25	.13	.08
325	Tommy Harper	.25	.13	.08
326	Reds Mgr./Coaches (Sparky Anderson, Alex Grammas, Ted Kluszewski, George Scherger, Larry Shepard)	.50	.25	.15
327	Tom Timmermann	.20	.10	.06
328	Skip Jutze	.20	.10	.06
329	Mark Belanger	.30	.15	.09
330	Juan Marichal	2.75	1.50	.80
331	All Star Catchers (Johnny Bench, Carlton Fisk)	2.00	1.00	.60
332	All Star First Basemen (Hank Aaron, Dick Allen)	2.00	1.00	.60
333	All Star Second Basemen (Rod Carew, Joe Morgan)	2.00	1.00	.60
334	All Star Third Basemen (Brooks Robinson, Ron Santo)	1.25	.60	.40
335	All Star Shortstops (Bert Campaneris, Chris Speier)	.40	.20	.12
336	All Star Left Fielders (Bobby Murcer, Pete Rose)	2.50	1.25	.70
337	All Star Center Fielders (Cesar Cedeno, Amos Otis)	.40	.20	.12
338	All Star Right Fielders (Reggie Jackson, Billy Williams)	2.00	1.00	.60
339	All Star Pitchers (Jim Hunter, Rick Wise)	.80	.40	.25
340	Thurman Munson	6.00	3.00	1.75
341	*Dan Driessen*	.80	.40	.25
342	Jim Lonborg	.30	.15	.09
343	Royals Team	.80	.40	.25
344	Mike Caldwell	.25	.13	.08
345	Bill North	.25	.13	.08
346	Ron Reed	.25	.13	.08
347	Sandy Alomar	.20	.10	.06
348	Pete Richert	.20	.10	.06
349	John Vukovich	.20	.10	.06
350	Bob Gibson	2.75	1.50	.80
351	Dwight Evans	3.50	1.75	1.00
352	Bill Stoneman	.20	.10	.06
353	Rich Coggins	.20	.10	.06
354	Cubs Mgr./Coaches (Hank Aguirre, Whitey Lockman, Jim Marshall, J.C. Martin, Al Spangler)	.20	.10	.06
355	Dave Nelson	.20	.10	.06
356	Jerry Koosman	.40	.20	.12
357	Buddy Bradford	.20	.10	.06
358	Dal Maxvill	.25	.13	.08
359	Brent Strom	.20	.10	.06
360	Greg Luzinski	.70	.35	.20
361	Don Carrithers	.20	.10	.06
362	Hal King	.20	.10	.06
363	Yankees Team	1.25	.60	.40
364a	Clarence Gaston (Washington)	3.50	1.75	1.00
364b	Clarence Gaston (San Diego)	.25	.13	.08
365	Steve Busby	.25	.13	.08
366	Larry Hisle	.25	.13	.08
367	Norm Cash	.50	.25	.15
368	Manny Mota	.40	.20	.12
369	Paul Lindblad	.20	.10	.06
370	Bob Watson	.25	.13	.08
371	Jim Slaton	.20	.10	.06
372	Ken Reitz	.20	.10	.06
373	John Curtis	.20	.10	.06
374	Marty Perez	.20	.10	.06
375	Earl Williams	.20	.10	.06
376	Jorge Orta	.25	.13	.08
377	Ron Woods	.20	.10	.06
378	Burt Hooton	.30	.15	.09
379	Rangers Mgr./Coaches (Art Fowler, Frank Lucchesi, Billy Martin, Jackie Moore, Charlie Silvera)	.80	.40	.25
380	Bud Harrelson	.25	.13	.08
381	Charlie Sands	.20	.10	.06
382	Bob Moose	.20	.10	.06
383	Phillies Team	.80	.40	.25
384	Chris Chambliss	.40	.20	.12
385	Don Gullett	.25	.13	.08
386	Gary Matthews	.60	.30	.20
387a	Rich Morales (Washington)	3.50	1.75	1.00
387b	Rich Morales (San Diego)	.25	.13	.08
388	Phil Roof	.20	.10	.06
389	Gates Brown	.20	.10	.06

		NR MT	EX	VG
390	Lou Piniella	.70	.35	.20
391	Billy Champion	.20	.10	.06
392	Dick Green	.20	.10	.06
393	Orlando Pena	.20	.10	.06
394	Ken Henderson	.20	.10	.06
395	Doug Rader	.20	.10	.06
396	Tommy Davis	.40	.20	.12
397	George Stone	.20	.10	.06
398	Duke Sims	.25	.13	.08
399	Mike Paul	.20	.10	.06
400	Harmon Killebrew	3.00	1.50	.90
401	Elliott Maddox	.20	.10	.06
402	Jim Rooker	.20	.10	.06
403	Red Sox Mgr./Coaches (Don Bryant, Darrell Johnson, Eddie Popowski, Lee Stange, Don Zimmer)	.25	.13	.08
404	Jim Howarth	.20	.10	.06
405	Ellie Rodriguez	.20	.10	.06
406	Steve Arlin	.20	.10	.06
407	Jim Wohlford	.20	.10	.06
408	Charlie Hough	.40	.20	.12
409	Ike Brown	.20	.10	.06
410	Pedro Borbon	.20	.10	.06
411	Frank Baker	.20	.10	.06
412	Chuck Taylor	.20	.10	.06
413	Don Money	.25	.13	.08
414	Checklist 397-528	1.50	.70	.45
415	Gary Gentry	.20	.10	.06
416	White Sox Team	.80	.40	.25
417	Rich Folkers	.20	.10	.06
418	Walt Williams	.20	.10	.06
419	Wayne Twitchell	.20	.10	.06
420	Ray Fosse	.20	.10	.06
421	Dan Fife	.20	.10	.06
422	Gonzalo Marquez	.20	.10	.06
423	Fred Stanley	.25	.13	.08
424	Jim Beauchamp	.20	.10	.06
425	Pete Broberg	.20	.10	.06
426	Rennie Stennett	.20	.10	.06
427	Bobby Bolin	.20	.10	.06
428	Gary Sutherland	.20	.10	.06
429	Dick Lange	.20	.10	.06
430	Matty Alou	.40	.20	.12
431	*Gene Garber*	.50	.25	.15
432	Chris Arnold	.20	.10	.06
433	Lerrin LaGrow	.20	.10	.06
434	Ken McMullen	.20	.10	.06
435	Dave Concepcion	.70	.35	.20
436	Don Hood	.20	.10	.06
437	Jim Lyttle	.20	.10	.06
438	Ed Herrmann	.20	.10	.06
439	Norm Miller	.20	.10	.06
440	Jim Kaat	1.25	.60	.40
441	Tom Ragland	.20	.10	.06
442	Alan Foster	.20	.10	.06
443	Tom Hutton	.20	.10	.06
444	Vic Davalillo	.25	.13	.08
445	George Medich	.30	.15	.09
446	Len Randle	.20	.10	.06
447	Twins Mgr./Coaches (Vern Morgan, Frank Quilici, Bob Rodgers, Ralph Rowe)	.20	.10	.06
448	Ron Hodges	.20	.10	.06
449	Tom McCraw	.20	.10	.06
450	Rich Hebner	.25	.13	.08
451	Tommy John	1.50	.70	.45
452	Gene Hiser	.20	.10	.06
453	Balor Moore	.20	.10	.06
454	Kurt Bevacqua	.20	.10	.06
455	Tom Bradley	.20	.10	.06
456	*Dave Winfield*	50.00	30.00	15.00
457	Chuck Goggin	.20	.10	.06
458	Jim Ray	.20	.10	.06
459	Reds Team	.90	.45	.25
460	Boog Powell	.90	.45	.25
461	John Odom	.25	.13	.08
462	Luis Alvarado	.20	.10	.06
463	Pat Dobson	.30	.15	.09
464	Jose Cruz	.80	.40	.25
465	Dick Bosman	.20	.10	.06
466	Dick Billings	.20	.10	.06
467	Winston Llenas	.20	.10	.06
468	Pepe Frias	.20	.10	.06
469	Joe Decker	.20	.10	.06
470	A.L. Playoffs	2.00	1.00	.60
471	N.L. Playoffs	.80	.40	.25
472	World Series Game 1	.80	.40	.25
473	World Series Game 2	2.00	1.00	.60
474	World Series Game 3	.80	.40	.25
475	World Series Game 4	.80	.40	.25
476	World Series Game 5	.80	.40	.25
477	World Series Game 6	2.00	1.00	.60
478	World Series Game 7	.80	.40	.25
479	World Series Summary	.80	.40	.25
480	Willie Crawford	.20	.10	.06
481	Jerry Terrell	.20	.10	.06
482	Bob Didier	.20	.10	.06
483	Braves Team	.80	.40	.25
484	Carmen Fanzone	.20	.10	.06
485	Felipe Alou	.40	.20	.12
486	Steve Stone	.40	.20	.12
487	Ted Martinez	.20	.10	.06
488	Andy Etchebarren	.20	.10	.06
489	Pirates Mgr./Coaches (Don Leppert, Bill Mazeroski, Danny Murtaugh, Don Osborn, Bob Skinner)	.30	.15	.09
490	Vada Pinson	.70	.35	.20
491	Roger Nelson	.20	.10	.06
492	Mike Rogodzinski	.20	.10	.06
493	Joe Hoerner	.20	.10	.06
494	Ed Goodson	.20	.10	.06
495	Dick McAuliffe	.25	.13	.08
496	Tom Murphy	.20	.10	.06
497	Bobby Mitchell	.20	.10	.06
498	Pat Corrales	.40	.20	.12
499	Rusty Torres	.20	.10	.06
500	Lee May	.40	.20	.12
501	Eddie Leon	.20	.10	.06
502	Dave LaRoche	.20	.10	.06
503	Eric Soderholm	.20	.10	.06
504	Joe Niekro	.40	.20	.12
505	Bill Buckner	.50	.25	.15
506	Ed Farmer	.20	.10	.06

		NR MT	EX	VG
507	Larry Stahl	.20	.10	.06
508	Expos Team	.80	.40	.25
509	Jesse Jefferson	.20	.10	.06
510	Wayne Garrett	.20	.10	.06
511	Toby Harrah	.30	.15	.09
512	Joe Lahoud	.20	.10	.06
513	Jim Campanis	.20	.10	.06
514	Paul Schaal	.20	.10	.06
515	Willie Montanez	.25	.13	.08
516	Horacio Pina	.20	.10	.06
517	Mike Hegan	.25	.13	.08
518	Derrel Thomas	.20	.10	.06
519	Bill Sharp	.20	.10	.06
520	Tim McCarver	.60	.30	.20
521	Indians Mgr./Coaches (Ken Aspromonte, Clay Bryant, Tony Pacheco)	.20	.10	.06
522	J.R. Richard	.30	.15	.09
523	Cecil Cooper	1.50	.70	.45
524	Bill Plummer	.20	.10	.06
525	Clyde Wright	.20	.10	.06
526	Frank Tepedino	.20	.10	.06
527	Bobby Darwin	.20	.10	.06
528	Bill Bonham	.20	.10	.06
529	Horace Clarke	.25	.13	.08
530	Mickey Stanley	.25	.13	.08
531	Expos Mgr./Coaches (Dave Bristol, Larry Doby, Gene Mauch, Cal McLish, Jerry Zimmerman)	.40	.20	.12
532	Skip Lockwood	.20	.10	.06
533	Mike Phillips	.20	.10	.06
534	Eddie Watt	.20	.10	.06
535	Bob Tolan	.25	.13	.08
536	Duffy Dyer	.20	.10	.06
537	Steve Mingori	.20	.10	.06
538	Cesar Tovar	.20	.10	.06
539	Lloyd Allen	.20	.10	.06
540	Bob Robertson	.20	.10	.06
541	Indians Team	.80	.40	.25
542	Rich Gossage	2.00	1.00	.60
543	Danny Cater	.20	.10	.06
544	Ron Schueler	.20	.10	.06
545	Billy Conigliaro	.20	.10	.06
546	Mike Corkins	.20	.10	.06
547	Glenn Borgmann	.20	.10	.06
548	Sonny Siebert	.20	.10	.06
549	Mike Jorgensen	.20	.10	.06
550	Sam McDowell	.40	.20	.12
551	Von Joshua	.20	.10	.06
552	Denny Doyle	.20	.10	.06
553	Jim Willoughby	.20	.10	.06
554	Tim Johnson	.20	.10	.06
555	Woodie Fryman	.25	.13	.08
556	Dave Campbell	.20	.10	.06
557	Jim McGlothlin	.20	.10	.06
558	Bill Fahey	.20	.10	.06
559	Darrel Chaney	.20	.10	.06
560	Mike Cuellar	.40	.20	.12
561	Ed Kranepool	.30	.15	.09
562	Jack Aker	.20	.10	.06
563	Hal McRae	.40	.20	.12
564	Mike Ryan	.20	.10	.06
565	Milt Wilcox	.25	.13	.08
566	Jackie Hernandez	.20	.10	.06
567	Red Sox Team	.90	.45	.25
568	Mike Torrez	.25	.13	.08
569	Rick Dempsey	.40	.20	.12
570	Ralph Garr	.30	.15	.09
571	Rich Hand	.20	.10	.06
572	Enzo Hernandez	.20	.10	.06
573	Mike Adams	.20	.10	.06
574	Bill Parsons	.20	.10	.06
575	Steve Garvey	12.00	6.00	3.50
576	Scipio Spinks	.20	.10	.06
577	Mike Sadek	.20	.10	.06
578	Ralph Houk	.40	.20	.12
579	Cecil Upshaw	.20	.10	.06
580	Jim Spencer	.20	.10	.06
581	Fred Norman	.20	.10	.06
582	*Bucky Dent*	.90	.45	.25
583	Marty Pattin	.20	.10	.06
584	Ken Rudolph	.20	.10	.06
585	Merv Rettenmund	.25	.13	.08
586	Jack Brohamer	.20	.10	.06
587	*Larry Christenson*	.25	.13	.08
588	Hal Lanier	.40	.20	.12
589	Boots Day	.20	.10	.06
590	Rogelio Moret	.20	.10	.06
591	Sonny Jackson	.20	.10	.06
592	Ed Bane	.20	.10	.06
593	Steve Yeager	.25	.13	.08
594	Leroy Stanton	.20	.10	.06
595	Steve Blass	.25	.13	.08
596	Rookie Pitchers (*Wayne Garland*, Fred Holdsworth, *Mark Littell*, Dick Pole)	.30	.15	.09
597	Rookie Shortstops (Dave Chalk, John Gamble, Pete Mackanin, *Manny Trillo*)	.80	.40	.25
598	Rookie Outfielders (Dave Augustine, *Ken Griffey*, Steve Ontiveros, Jim Tyrone)	5.00	2.50	1.50
599a	Rookie Pitchers (Ron Diorio, Dave Freisleben, Frank Riccelli, Greg Shanahan) (Freisleben- Washington)	.80	.40	.25
599b	Rookie Pitchers (Ron Diorio, Dave Freisleben, Frank Riccelli, Greg Shanahan) (Freisleben- San Diego large print)	3.50	1.75	1.00
599c	Rookie Pitchers (Ron Diorio, Dave Freisleben, Frank Riccelli, Greg Shanahan) (Freisleben- San Diego small print)	6.00	3.00	1.75
600	Rookie Infielders (Ron Cash, Jim Cox, *Bill Madlock*, Reggie Sanders)	2.25	1.25	.70
601	Rookie Outfielders (Ed Armbrister, Rich Bladt, *Brian Downing*, *Bake McBride*)	2.00	1.00	.60
602	Rookie Pitchers (Glenn Abbott, Rick Henninger, Craig Swan, Dan Vossler)	.20	.10	.06
603	Rookie Catchers (Barry Foote, Tom Lundstedt, *Charlie Moore*, Sergio Robles)	.30	.15	.09

		NR MT	EX	VG
604	Rookie Infielders (Terry Hughes, John Knox, *Andy Thornton*, *Frank White*)	4.00	2.00	1.25
605	Rookie Pitchers (Vic Albury, Ken Frailing, Kevin Kobel, *Frank Tanana*)	2.00	1.00	.60
606	Rookie Outfielders (Jim Fuller, Wilbur Howard, Tommy Smith, Otto Velez)	.25	.13	.08
607	Rookie Shortstops (Leo Foster, Tom Heintzelman, Dave Rosello, *Frank Taveras*)	.25	.13	.08
608a	Rookie Pitchers (Bob Apodaco, Dick Baney, John D'Acquisto, Mike Wallace)	2.50	1.25	.70
608b	Rookie Pitchers (Bob Apodaca, Dick Baney, John D'Acquisto, Mike Wallace)	.25	.13	.08
609	Rico Petrocelli	.30	.15	.09
610	Dave Kingman	.90	.45	.25
611	Rick Stelmaszek	.20	.10	.06
612	Luke Walker	.20	.10	.06
613	Dan Monzon	.20	.10	.06
614	Adrian Devine	.20	.10	.06
615	Johnny Jeter	.20	.10	.06
616	Larry Gura	.25	.13	.08
617	Ted Ford	.20	.10	.06
618	Jim Mason	.20	.10	.06
619	Mike Anderson	.20	.10	.06
620	Al Downing	.25	.13	.08
621	Bernie Carbo	.20	.10	.06
622	Phil Gagliano	.20	.10	.06
623	Celerino Sanchez	.25	.13	.08
624	Bob Miller	.20	.10	.06
625	Ollie Brown	.20	.10	.06
626	Pirates Team	.80	.40	.25
627	Carl Taylor	.20	.10	.06
628	Ivan Murrell	.20	.10	.06
629	Rusty Staub	.70	.35	.20
630	Tommie Agee	.25	.13	.08
631	Steve Barber	.20	.10	.06
632	George Culver	.20	.10	.06
633	Dave Hamilton	.20	.10	.06
634	Braves Mgr./Coaches (Jim Busby, Eddie Mathews, Connie Ryan, Ken Silvestri, Herm Starrette)	.90	.45	.25
635	John Edwards	.20	.10	.06
636	Dave Goltz	.25	.13	.08
637	Checklist 529-660	1.50	.70	.45
638	Ken Sanders	.20	.10	.06
639	Joe Lovitto	.20	.10	.06
640	Milt Pappas	.40	.20	.12
641	Chuck Brinkman	.20	.10	.06
642	Terry Harmon	.20	.10	.06
643	Dodgers Team	.90	.45	.25
644	Wayne Granger	.25	.13	.08
645	Ken Boswell	.20	.10	.06
646	George Foster	1.25	.60	.40
647	*Juan Beniquez*	.70	.35	.20
648	Terry Crowley	.20	.10	.06
649	Fernando Gonzalez	.20	.10	.06
650	Mike Epstein	.20	.10	.06
651	Leron Lee	.20	.10	.06
652	Gail Hopkins	.20	.10	.06
653	Bob Stinson	.20	.10	.06
654a	Jesus Alou (no position listed)	5.00	2.50	1.50
654b	Jesus Alou (Outfield)	.40	.20	.12
655	Mike Tyson	.20	.10	.06
656	Adrian Garrett	.20	.10	.06
657	Jim Shellenback	.20	.10	.06
658	Lee Lacy	.30	.15	.09
659	Joe Lis	.20	.10	.06
660	Larry Dierker	.50	.15	.09

1974 Topps Deckle Edge

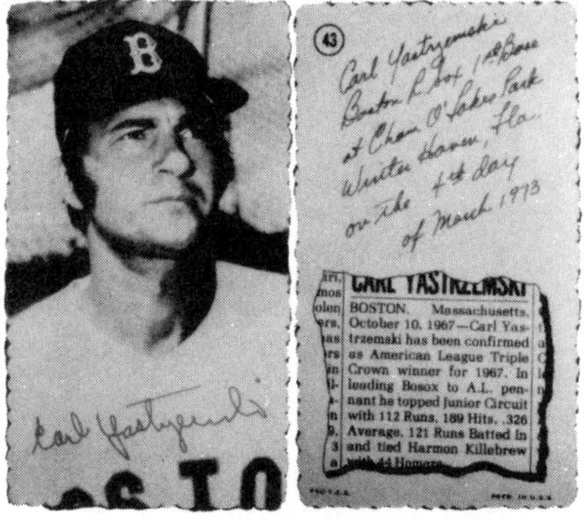

These borderless 2-7/8" by 5" cards feature a black and white photograph with a facsimile autograph on the front. The backs have in handwritten script the player's name, team, position and the date and location of the picture. Below is a mock newspaper clipping providing a detail from the player's career. The cards take their names from their specially cut edges which give them a scalloped appearance. The 72-card set was a test issue and received rather limited distribution.

	NR MT	EX	VG
Complete Set:	2000.	1000.	600.00
Common Player:	10.00	5.00	3.00

		NR MT	EX	VG
1	Amos Otis	10.00	5.00	3.00
2	Darrell Evans	15.00	7.50	4.50
3	Robert Gibson	50.00	25.00	15.00
4	David Nelson	10.00	5.00	3.00
5	Steven N. Carlton	80.00	40.00	25.00
6	Jim "Catfish" Hunter	40.00	20.00	12.00
7	Thurman Munson	50.00	25.00	15.00
8	Bob Grich	15.00	7.50	4.50
9	Tom Seaver	100.00	50.00	30.00
10	Ted L. Simmons	20.00	10.00	6.00
11	Robert J. Valentine	10.00	5.00	3.00
12	Don Sutton	25.00	12.50	7.50
13	Wilbur Wood	10.00	5.00	3.00
14	Douglas Lee Rader	10.00	5.00	3.00
15	Chris Chambliss	10.00	5.00	3.00
16	Pete Rose	200.00	100.00	60.00
17	John F. Hiller	10.00	5.00	3.00
18	Burt Hooton	10.00	5.00	3.00
19	Tim Foli	10.00	5.00	3.00
20	Louis Brock	60.00	30.00	20.00
21	Ron Bryant	10.00	5.00	3.00
22	Manuel Sanguillen	10.00	5.00	3.00
23	Bobby Tolan	10.00	5.00	3.00
24	Greg Luzinski	15.00	7.50	4.50
25	Brooks Robinson	60.00	30.00	18.00
26	Felix Millan	10.00	5.00	3.00
27	Luis Tiant	15.00	7.50	4.50
28	Willie McCovey	60.00	30.00	20.00
29	Chris Speier	10.00	5.00	3.00
30	George Scott	10.00	5.00	3.00
31	Willie Stargell	50.00	25.00	15.00
32	Rod Carew	100.00	50.00	30.00
33	Leslie Charles Spikes	10.00	5.00	3.00
34	Nate Colbert	10.00	5.00	3.00
35	Richie Hebner	10.00	5.00	3.00
36	Bobby Lee Bonds	15.00	7.50	4.50
37	Buddy Bell	15.00	7.50	4.50
38	Claude Osteen	10.00	5.00	3.00
39	Richard A. Allen	15.00	7.50	4.50
40	Bill Russell	10.00	5.00	3.00
41	Nolan Ryan	175.00	87.00	52.00
42	Willie Davis	15.00	7.50	4.50
43	Carl Yastrzemski	125.00	62.00	37.00
44	Jonathon T. Matlack	10.00	5.00	3.00
45	Jim Palmer	30.00	15.00	9.00
46	Dagoberto Campaneris	15.00	7.50	4.50
47	Bert Blyleven	20.00	10.00	6.00
48	Jeff Burroughs	10.00	5.00	3.00
49	James W. Colborn	10.00	5.00	3.00
50	Dave Johnson	15.00	7.50	4.50
51	John Mayberry	10.00	5.00	3.00
52	Don Kessinger	10.00	5.00	3.00
53	Joseph H. Coleman	10.00	5.00	3.00
54	Tony Perez	20.00	10.00	6.00
55	Jose Cardenal	10.00	5.00	3.00
56	Paul Splittorff	10.00	5.00	3.00
57	Henry Aaron	150.00	75.00	45.00
58	David May	10.00	5.00	3.00
59	Fergie Jenkins	30.00	15.00	9.00
60	Ron Blomberg	10.00	5.00	3.00
61	Reggie Jackson	150.00	75.00	45.00
62	Tony Oliva	15.00	7.50	4.50
63	Bobby Ray Murcer	15.00	7.50	4.50
64	Carlton Fisk	20.00	10.00	6.00
65	Stephen Rogers	10.00	5.00	3.00
66	Frank Robinson	40.00	20.00	12.00
67	Joe Ferguson	10.00	5.00	3.00
68	Bill Melton	10.00	5.00	3.00
69	Robert Watson	10.00	5.00	3.00
70	Larry Bowa	15.00	7.50	4.50
71	Johnny Bench	90.00	45.00	27.00
72	Willie Horton	10.00	5.00	3.00

1974 Topps Puzzles

One of many test issues by Topps in the mid-1970s, the 12-player jigsaw puzzle set was an innovation which never caught on with collectors. The 40-piece puzzles (4-3/4" by 7-1/2") feature color photos with a decorative lozenge at bottom naming the player, team and position. The puzzles came in individual wrappers.

	NR MT	EX	VG
Complete Set:	600.00	300.00	200.00
Common Player:	12.00	6.00	3.50

		NR MT	EX	VG
(1)	Hank Aaron	80.00	40.00	25.00
(2)	Dick Allen	12.00	6.00	3.50
(3)	Johnny Bench	75.00	38.00	23.00
(4)	Bobby Bonds	12.00	6.00	3.50
(5)	Bob Gibson	35.00	17.50	10.50
(6)	Reggie Jackson	60.00	30.00	18.00
(7)	Bobby Murcer	12.00	6.00	3.50
(8)	Jim Palmer	50.00	25.00	15.00
(9)	Nolan Ryan	80.00	40.00	24.00
(10)	Tom Seaver	80.00	40.00	24.00
(11)	Willie Stargell	30.00	15.00	9.00
(12)	Carl Yastrzemski	70.00	35.00	21.00

1974 Topps Stamps

Topps continued to market baseball stamps in 1974 through the release of 240 unnumbered stamps featuring color player portraits. The player's name, team and position are found in an oval at the bottom of the 1" by 1-1/2" stamps. The stamps, sold separately rather than issued as an insert, came in strips of six which were then pasted in an appropriate team album designed to hold 10 stamps.

	NR MT	EX	VG
Complete Sheet Set:	100.00	50.00	30.00
Common Sheet:	1.00	.50	.30
Complete Stamp Album Set:	75.00	37.00	22.00
Single Stamp Album:	2.50	1.25	.70

(1) Hank Aaron, Luis Aparicio, Bob Bailey, Johnny Bench, Ron Blomberg, Bob Boone, Lou Brock, Bud Harrelson, Randy Jones, Dave Rader, Nolan Ryan, Joe Torre 6.00 3.00 1.75

(2) Buddy Bell, Steve Braun, Jerry Grote, Tommy Helms, Bill Lee, Mike Lum, Dave May, Brooks Robinson, Bill Russell, Del Unser, Wilbur Wood, Carl Yastrzemski 10.00 5.00 3.00

(3) Jerry Bell, Jerry Bell, Jim Colborn, Toby Harrah, Ken Henderson, John Hiller, Randy Hundley, Don Kessinger, Jerry Koosman, Dave Lopes, Felix Millan, Thurman Munson, Ted Simmons 3.50 1.75 1.00

(4) Jerry Bell, Bill Buckner, Jim Colborn, Ken Henderson, Don Kessinger, Felix Millan, George Mitterwald, Dave Roberts, Ted Simmons, Jim Slaton, Charlie Spikes, Paul Splittorff 1.00 .50 .30

(5) Glenn Beckert, Jim Bibby, Bill Buckner, Jim Lonborg, George Mitterwald, Dave Parker, Dave Roberts, Jim Slaton, Reggie Smith, Charlie Spikes, Paul Splittorff, Bob Watson 3.50 1.75 1.00

(6) Paul Blair, Bobby Bonds, Ed Brinkman, Norm Cash, Mike Epstein, Tommy Harper, Mike Marshall, Phil Niekro, Cookie Rojas, George Scott, Mel Stottlemyre, Jim Wynn 3.50 1.75 1.00

(7) Jack Billingham, Reggie Cleveland, Bobby Darwin, Dave Duncan, Tim Foli, Ed Goodson, Cleon Jones, Mickey Lolich, George Medich, John Milner, Rick Monday, Bobby Murcer 1.00 .50 .30

(8) Steve Carlton, Orlando Cepeda, Joe Decker, Reggie Jackson, Dave Johnson, John Mayberry, Bill Melton, Roger Metzger, Dave Nelson, Jerry Reuss, Jim Spencer, Bobby Valentine 6.00 3.00 1.75

(9) Dan Driessen, Pedro Garcia, Grant Jackson, Al Kaline, Clay Kirby, Carlos May, Willie Montanez, Rogelio Moret, Jim Palmer, Doug Rader, J. R. Richard, Frank Robinson 3.50 1.75 1.00

(10) Pedro Garcia, Ralph Garr, Wayne Garrett, Ron Hunt, Al Kaline, Fred Kendall, Carlos May, Jim Palmer, Doug Rader, Frank Robinson, Rick Wise, Richie Zisk 3.50 1.75 1.00

(11) Dusty Baker, Larry Bowa, Steve Busby, Chris Chambliss, Dock Ellis, Cesar Geronimo, Fran Healy, Deron Johnson, Jorge Orta, Joe Rudi, Mickey Stanley, Rennie Stennett 3.50 1.75 1.00

(12) Bob Coluccio, Ray Corbin, John Ellis, Oscar Gamble, Dave Giusti, Bill Greif, Alex Johnson, Mike Jorgensen, Andy Messersmith, Elias Sosa, Willie Stargell 3.50 1.75 1.00

(13) Ron Bryant, Nate Colbert, Jose Cruz, Dan Driessen, Billy Grabarkewitz, Don Gullett, Willie Horton, Grant Jackson, Clay Kirby, Willie Montanez, Rogelio Moret, J. R. Richard 1.00 .50 .30

(14) Carlton Fisk, Bill Freehan, Bobby Grich, Vic Harris, George Hendrick, Ed Herrmann, Jim Holt, Ken Holtzman, Fergie Jenkins, Lou Piniella, Steve Rogers, Ken Singleton 3.50 1.75 1.00

(15) Stan Bahnsen, Sal Bando, Mark Belanger, David Clyde, Willie Crawford, Burt Hooton, Jon Matlack, Tim McCarver, Joe Morgan, Gene Tenace, Dick Tidrow, Dave Winfield 5.00 2.50 1.50

(16) Hank Aaron, Stan Bahnsen, Bob Bailey, Johnny Bench, Bob Boone, Joe Matlack, Tim McCarver, Joe Morgan, Dave Rader, Gene Tenace, Dick Tidrow, Joe Torre 5.00 2.50 1.50

(17) John Boccabella, Frank Duffy, Darrell Evans, Sparky Lyle, Lee May, Don Money, Bill North, Ted Sizemore, Chris Speier, Wayne Twitchell, Billy Williams, Earl Williams 1.00 .50 .30

(18) John Boccabella, Bobby Darwin, Frank Duffy, Dave Duncan, Tim Foli, Cleon Jones, Mickey Lolich, Sparky Lyle, Lee May, Rick Monday, Bill North, Billy Williams 1.00 .50 .30

(19) Don Baylor, Vida Blue, Tom Bradley, Jose Cardenal, Ron Cey, Greg Luzinski, Johnny Oates, Tony Oliva, Al Oliver, Tony Perez, Darrell Porter, Roy White 3.50 1.75 1.00

(20) Pedro Borbon, Rod Carew, Roric Harrison, Jim Hunter, Ed Kirkpatrick, Garry Maddox, Gene Michael, Rick Miller, Claude Osteen, Amos Otis, Rich Reuschel, Mike Tyson 5.00 2.50 1.50

(21) Sandy Alomar, Bert Campaneris, Tommy Davis, Joe Ferguson, Tito Fuentes, Jerry Morales, Carl Morton, Gaylord Perry, Vada Pinson, Dave Roberts, Ellie Rodriguez 3.50 1.75 1.00

(22) Dick Allen, Jeff Burroughs, Joe Coleman, Terry Forster, Bob Gibson, Harmon Killebrew, Tug McGraw, Bob Oliver, Steve Renko, Pete Rose, Luis Tiant, Otto Velez 13.00 6.50 4.00

(23) Johnny Briggs, Willie Davis, Jim Fregosi, Rich Hebner, Pat Kelly, Dave Kingman, Willie McCovey, Graig Nettles, Freddie Patek, Marty Pattin, Manny Sanguillen, Richie Scheinblum 5.00 2.50 1.50

(24) Bert Blyleven, Nelson Briles, Cesar Cedeno, Ron Fairly, Johnny Grubb, Dave McNally, Aurelio Rodriguez, Ron Santo, Tom Seaver, Bill Singer, Bill Sudakis, Don Sutton 6.00 3.00 1.75

1974 Topps Team Checklists

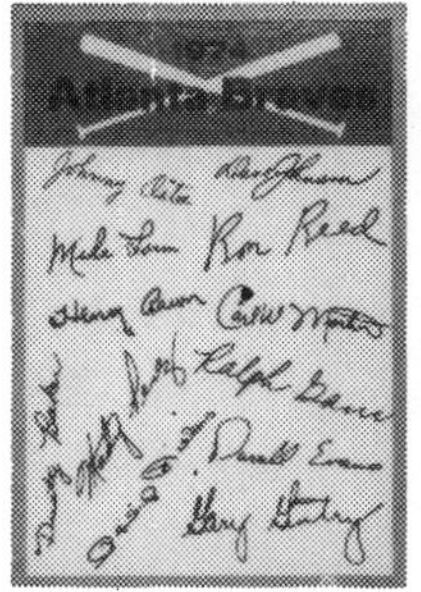

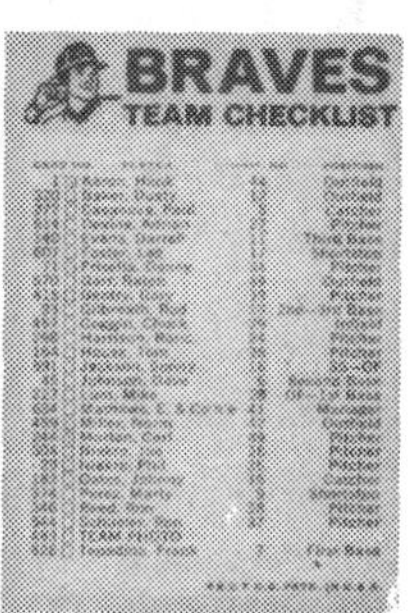

This set is a repeat of the 1973 mystery set in the form of 24 unnumbered 2-1/2" by 3-1/2" checklist cards. As with the 1973 set, the 1974s feature a team name on the front at the top with a white panel and a number of facsimile autographs below. Backs feature the team name and a checklist. The big difference between the 1973 and 1974 checklists is that the 1973s have blue borders while the 1974s have a red border. The 1974s were inserted into packages of the regular issue Topps cards.

	NR MT	EX	VG
Complete Set:	10.00	5.00	3.00
Common Checklist:	.50	.25	.15

		NR MT	EX	VG
(1)	Atlanta Braves	.50	.25	.15
(2)	Baltimore Orioles	.50	.25	.15
(3)	Boston Red Sox	.50	.25	.15
(4)	California Angels	.50	.25	.15
(5)	Chicago Cubs	.50	.25	.15
(6)	Chicago White Sox	.50	.25	.15
(7)	Cincinnati Reds	.50	.25	.15
(8)	Cleveland Indians	.50	.25	.15
(9)	Detroit Tigers	.50	.25	.15
(10)	Houston Astros	.50	.25	.15
(11)	Kansas City Royals	.50	.25	.15
(12)	Los Angeles Dodgers	.50	.25	.15
(13)	Milwaukee Brewers	.50	.25	.15
(14)	Minnesota Twins	.50	.25	.15
(15)	Montreal Expos	.50	.25	.15
(16)	New York Mets	.50	.25	.15
(17)	New York Yankees	.50	.25	.15
(18)	Oakland A's	.50	.25	.15
(19)	Philadelphia Phillies	.50	.25	.15
(20)	Pittsburgh Pirates	.50	.25	.15
(21)	St. Louis Cardinals	.50	.25	.15
(22)	San Diego Padres	.50	.25	.15
(23)	San Francisco Giants	.50	.25	.15
(24)	Texas Rangers	.50	.25	.15

1974 Topps Traded

Appearing late in the season, these 2-1/2" by 3-1/2" cards are basically the same as the regular issue Topps cards. The major change was that a big red panel with the word "Traded" was added below the player photo. Backs feature a "Baseball News" newspaper which contains the details of the trade. Card numbers correspond to the player's regular card number in 1974 except that the suffix "T" is added after the number. The set consists of 43 player cards and a checklist. In most cases, Topps did not obtain pictures of the players in their new uniforms. Instead the Topps artists simply provided the needed changes to existing photos.

		NR MT	EX	VG
Complete Set:		7.00	3.50	2.00
Common Player:		.12	.06	.04
23T	Craig Robinson	.12	.06	.04
42T	Claude Osteen	.15	.08	.05
43T	Jim Wynn	.20	.10	.06
51T	Bobby Heise	.12	.06	.04
59T	Ross Grimsley	.15	.08	.05
62T	Bob Locker	.12	.06	.04
63T	Bill Sudakis	.12	.06	.04
73T	Mike Marshall	.20	.10	.06
123T	Nelson Briles	.12	.06	.04
139T	Aurelio Monteagudo	.12	.06	.04
151T	Diego Segui	.12	.06	.04
165T	Willie Davis	.20	.10	.06
175T	Reggie Cleveland	.12	.06	.04
182T	Lindy McDaniel	.12	.06	.04
186T	Fred Scherman	.12	.06	.04
249T	George Mitterwald	.12	.06	.04
262T	Ed Kirkpatrick	.12	.06	.04
269T	Bob Johnson	.12	.06	.04
270T	Ron Santo	.30	.15	.09
313T	Barry Lersch	.12	.06	.04
319T	Randy Hundley	.12	.06	.04
330T	Juan Marichal	1.25	.60	.40
348T	Pete Richert	.12	.06	.04
373T	John Curtis	.12	.06	.04
390T	Lou Piniella	.50	.25	.15
428T	Gary Sutherland	.12	.06	.04
454T	Kurt Bevacqua	.12	.06	.04
458T	Jim Ray	.12	.06	.04
485T	Felipe Alou	.20	.10	.06
486T	Steve Stone	.20	.10	.06
496T	Tom Murphy	.12	.06	.04
516T	Horacio Pina	.12	.06	.04
534T	Eddie Watt	.12	.06	.04
538T	Cesar Tovar	.12	.06	.04
544T	Ron Schueler	.12	.06	.04
579T	Cecil Upshaw	.12	.06	.04
585T	Merv Rettenmund	.15	.08	.05
612T	Luke Walker	.12	.06	.04
616T	Larry Gura	.15	.08	.05
618T	Jim Mason	.12	.06	.04
630T	Tommie Agee	.15	.08	.05
648T	Terry Crowley	.12	.06	.04
649T	Fernando Gonzalez	.12	.06	.04
---	Traded Checklist	.70	.35	.20

1975 Topps

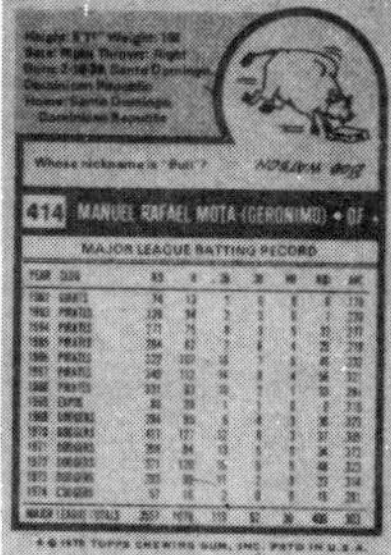

This year Topps produced another 660-card set, one which collectors either seem to like or despise. The 2-1/2" by 3-1/2" cards have a color photo which is framed by a round-cornered white frame. Around that is an eye-catching two-color border in bright colors. The team name appears at the top in bright letters while the player name is at the bottom and his position a baseball at the lower right. A facsimile autograph runs across the picture. The card backs are vertical feature normal statistical and biographical information along with a trivia quiz. Specialty cards include a new 24-card series on MVP winners going back to 1951. Other specialty cards include statistical leaders and post-season highlights. The real highlight of the set, however, are the rookie cards which include their numbers such names as George Brett, Gary Carter, Robin Yount, Jim Rice, Keith Hernandez and Fred Lynn. While the set was released at one time, card numbers 1-132 were printed in somewhat shorter supply than the remainder of the issue.

		NR MT	EX	VG
Complete Set:		650.00	325.00	200.00
Common Player: 1-132		.30	.15	.09
Common Player: 133-660		.20	.10	.06
Complete Mini Set:		1200.	600.00	350.00
Common Mini Player:		.40	.20	.12
1	'74 Highlights (Hank Aaron)	20.00	10.00	6.00
2	'74 Highlights (Lou Brock)	2.00	1.00	.60
3	'74 Highlights (Bob Gibson)	1.75	.90	.50
4	'74 Highlights (Al Kaline)	1.75	.90	.50
5	'74 Highlights (Nolan Ryan)	6.00	3.00	1.75
6	'74 Highlights (Mike Marshall)	.40	.20	.12
7	'74 Highlights (Dick Bosman, Steve Busby, Nolan Ryan)	1.00	.50	.30
8	Rogelio Moret	.30	.15	.09
9	Frank Tepedino	.30	.15	.09
10	Willie Davis	.35	.20	.11
11	Bill Melton	.35	.20	.11
12	David Clyde	.35	.20	.11
13	Gene Locklear	.30	.15	.09
14	Milt Wilcox	.35	.20	.11
15	Jose Cardenal	.35	.20	.11
16	Frank Tanana	.40	.20	.12
17	Dave Concepcion	.60	.30	.20
18	Tigers Team (Ralph Houk)	.90	.45	.25
19	Jerry Koosman	.40	.20	.12
20	Thurman Munson	6.00	3.00	1.75
21	Rollie Fingers	1.50	.70	.45
22	Dave Cash	.30	.15	.09
23	Bill Russell	.35	.20	.11
24	Al Fitzmorris	.30	.15	.09
25	Lee May	.40	.20	.12
26	Dave McNally	.35	.20	.11
27	Ken Reitz	.30	.15	.09
28	Tom Murphy	.30	.15	.09
29	Dave Parker	8.00	4.00	2.50
30	Bert Blyleven	1.00	.50	.30
31	Dave Rader	.30	.15	.09
32	Reggie Cleveland	.30	.15	.09
33	Dusty Baker	.40	.20	.12
34	Steve Renko	.30	.15	.09
35	Ron Santo	.50	.25	.15
36	Joe Lovitto	.30	.15	.09
37	Dave Freisleben	.30	.15	.09
38	Buddy Bell	.80	.40	.25
39	Andy Thornton	.70	.35	.20
40	Bill Singer	.35	.20	.11
41	Cesar Geronimo	.35	.20	.11
42	Joe Coleman	.35	.20	.11
43	Cleon Jones	.35	.20	.11
44	Pat Dobson	.35	.20	.11
45	Joe Rudi	.40	.20	.12
46	Phillies Team (Danny Ozark)	.80	.40	.25
47	Tommy John	1.25	.60	.40
48	Freddie Patek	.30	.15	.09
49	Larry Dierker	.30	.15	.09
50	Brooks Robinson	3.50	1.75	1.00
51	*Bob Forsch*	.80	.40	.25
52	Darrell Porter	.35	.20	.11
53	Dave Giusti	.30	.15	.09
54	Eric Soderholm	.30	.15	.09
55	Bobby Bonds	.50	.25	.15
56	Rick Wise	.35	.20	.11
57	Dave Johnson	.80	.40	.25
58	Chuck Taylor	.30	.15	.09
59	Ken Henderson	.30	.15	.09
60	Fergie Jenkins	1.25	.60	.40
61	Dave Winfield	12.00	6.00	3.50
62	Fritz Peterson	.30	.15	.09
63	Steve Swisher	.30	.15	.09
64	Dave Chalk	.30	.15	.09
65	Don Gullett	.35	.20	.11
66	Willie Horton	.35	.20	.11
67	Tug McGraw	.50	.25	.15
68	Ron Blomberg	.35	.20	.11
69	John Odom	.35	.20	.11
70	Mike Schmidt	50.00	25.00	15.00
71	Charlie Hough	.35	.20	.11
72	Royals Team (Jack McKeon)	.80	.40	.25
73	J.R. Richard	.35	.20	.11
74	Mark Belanger	.35	.20	.11
75	Ted Simmons	.70	.35	.20
76	Ed Sprague	.30	.15	.09
77	Richie Zisk	.35	.20	.11
78	Ray Corbin	.30	.15	.09
79	Gary Matthews	.40	.20	.12
80	Carlton Fisk	2.00	1.00	.60
81	Ron Reed	.35	.20	.11
82	Pat Kelly	.30	.15	.09
83	Jim Merritt	.30	.15	.09
84	Enzo Hernandez	.30	.15	.09
85	Bill Bonham	.30	.15	.09
86	Joe Lis	.30	.15	.09
87	George Foster	1.25	.60	.40
88	Tom Egan	.30	.15	.09

		NR MT	EX	VG
89	Jim Ray	.30	.15	.09
90	Rusty Staub	.60	.30	.20
91	Dick Green	.30	.15	.09
92	Cecil Upshaw	.35	.20	.11
93	Dave Lopes	.40	.20	.12
94	Jim Lonborg	.35	.20	.11
95	John Mayberry	.35	.20	.11
96	Mike Cosgrove	.30	.15	.09
97	Earl Williams	.30	.15	.09
98	Rich Folkers	.30	.15	.09
99	Mike Hegan	.30	.15	.09
100	Willie Stargell	2.50	1.25	.70
101	Expos Team (Gene Mauch)	.80	.40	.25
102	Joe Decker	.30	.15	.09
103	Rick Miller	.30	.15	.09
104	Bill Madlock	1.25	.60	.40
105	Buzz Capra	.30	.15	.09
106	*Mike Hargrove*	.40	.20	.12
107	Jim Barr	.30	.15	.09
108	Tom Hall	.30	.15	.09
109	George Hendrick	.35	.20	.11
110	Wilbur Wood	.35	.20	.11
111	Wayne Garrett	.30	.15	.09
112	Larry Hardy	.30	.15	.09
113	Elliott Maddox	.35	.20	.11
114	Dick Lange	.30	.15	.09
115	Joe Ferguson	.30	.15	.09
116	Lerrin LaGrow	.30	.15	.09
117	Orioles Team (Earl Weaver)	.90	.45	.25
118	Mike Anderson	.30	.15	.09
119	Tommy Helms	.30	.15	.09
120	Steve Busby (photo actually Fran Healy)	.35	.20	.11
121	Bill North	.30	.15	.09
122	Al Hrabosky	.35	.20	.11
123	Johnny Briggs	.30	.15	.09
124	Jerry Reuss	.40	.20	.12
125	Ken Singleton	.40	.20	.12
126	Checklist 1-132	1.50	.70	.45
127	Glen Borgmann	.30	.15	.09
128	Bill Lee	.35	.20	.11
129	Rick Monday	.35	.20	.11
130	Phil Niekro	2.00	1.00	.60
131	Toby Harrah	.35	.20	.11
132	Randy Moffitt	.30	.15	.09
133	Dan Driessen	.30	.15	.09
134	Ron Hodges	.20	.10	.06
135	Charlie Spikes	.20	.10	.06
136	Jim Mason	.25	.13	.08
137	Terry Forster	.30	.15	.09
138	Del Unser	.20	.10	.06
139	Horacio Pina	.20	.10	.06
140	Steve Garvey	6.00	3.00	1.75
141	Mickey Stanley	.25	.13	.08
142	Bob Reynolds	.20	.10	.06
143	*Cliff Johnson*	.40	.20	.12
144	Jim Wohlford	.20	.10	.06
145	Ken Holtzman	.30	.15	.09
146	Padres Team (John McNamara)	.80	.40	.25
147	Pedro Garcia	.20	.10	.06
148	Jim Rooker	.20	.10	.06
149	Tim Foli	.20	.10	.06
150	Bob Gibson	2.50	1.25	.70
151	Steve Brye	.20	.10	.06
152	Mario Guerrero	.20	.10	.06
153	Rick Reuschel	.40	.20	.12
154	Mike Lum	.20	.10	.06
155	Jim Bibby	.20	.10	.06
156	Dave Kingman	.90	.45	.25
157	Pedro Borbon	.20	.10	.06
158	Jerry Grote	.25	.13	.08
159	Steve Arlin	.20	.10	.06
160	Graig Nettles	1.50	.70	.45
161	Stan Bahnsen	.20	.10	.06
162	Willie Montanez	.20	.10	.06
163	Jim Brewer	.20	.10	.06
164	Mickey Rivers	.25	.13	.08
165	Doug Rader	.20	.10	.06
166	Woodie Fryman	.25	.13	.08
167	Rich Coggins	.20	.10	.06
168	Bill Greif	.20	.10	.06
169	Cookie Rojas	.20	.10	.06
170	Bert Campaneris	.40	.20	.12
171	Ed Kirkpatrick	.20	.10	.06
172	Red Sox Team (Darrell Johnson)	1.25	.60	.40
173	Steve Rogers	.30	.15	.09
174	Bake McBride	.25	.13	.08
175	Don Money	.25	.13	.08
176	Burt Hooton	.30	.15	.09
177	Vic Correll	.20	.10	.06
178	Cesar Tovar	.20	.10	.06
179	Tom Bradley	.20	.10	.06
180	Joe Morgan	3.00	1.50	.90
181	Fred Beene	.20	.10	.06
182	Don Hahn	.20	.10	.06
183	Mel Stottlemyre	.40	.20	.12
184	Jorge Orta	.20	.10	.06
185	Steve Carlton	6.00	3.00	1.75
186	Willie Crawford	.20	.10	.06
187	Denny Doyle	.20	.10	.06
188	Tom Griffin	.20	.10	.06
189	1951 - MVPs (Larry (Yogi) Berra, Roy Campanella)	1.50	.70	.45
190	1952 - MVPs (Hank Sauer, Bobby Shantz)	.40	.20	.12
191	1953 - MVPs (Roy Campanella, Al Rosen)	.90	.45	.25
192	1954 - MVPs (Yogi Berra, Willie Mays)	1.50	.70	.45
193	1955 - MVPs (Yogi Berra, Roy Campanella)	1.50	.70	.45
194	1956 - MVPs (Mickey Mantle, Don Newcombe)	6.00	3.00	1.75
195	1957 - MVPs (Hank Aaron, Mickey Mantle)	7.00	3.50	2.00
196	1958 - MVPs (Ernie Banks, Jackie Jensen)	.90	.45	.25
197	1959 - MVPs (Ernie Banks, Nellie Fox)	.90	.45	.25
198	1960 - MVPs (Dick Groat, Roger Maris)	1.25	.60	.40
199	1961 - MVPs (Roger Maris, Frank			

#	Card	NR MT	EX	VG
	Robinson)	1.50	.70	.45
200	1962 - MVPs (Mickey Mantle, Maury Wills)	5.00	2.50	1.50
201	1963 - MVPs (Elston Howard, Sandy Koufax)	1.50	.70	.45
202	1964 - MVPs (Ken Boyer, Brooks Robinson)	1.25	.60	.40
203	1965 - MVPs (Willie Mays, Zoilo Versalles)	1.25	.60	.40
204	1966 - MVPs (Bob Clemente, Frank Robinson)	1.50	.70	.45
205	1967 - MVPs (Orlando Cepeda, Carl Yastrzemski)	1.25	.60	.40
206	1968 - MVPs (Bob Gibson, Denny McLain)	1.25	.60	.40
207	1969 - MVPs (Harmon Killebrew, Willie McCovey)	1.50	.70	.45
208	1970 - MVPs (Johnny Bench, Boog Powell)	1.25	.60	.40
209	1971 - MVPs (Vida Blue, Joe Torre)	.50	.25	.15
210	1972 - MVPs (Rich Allen, Johnny Bench)	1.25	.60	.40
211	1973 - MVPs (Reggie Jackson, Pete Rose)	4.00	2.00	1.25
212	1974 - MVPs (Jeff Burroughs, Steve Garvey)	.90	.45	.25
213	Oscar Gamble	.25	.13	.08
214	Harry Parker	.20	.10	.06
215	Bobby Valentine	.30	.15	.09
216	Giants Team (Wes Westrum)	.80	.40	.25
217	Lou Piniella	.70	.35	.20
218	Jerry Johnson	.20	.10	.06
219	Ed Herrmann	.20	.10	.06
220	Don Sutton	1.50	.70	.45
221	Aurelio Rodriquez (Rodriguez)	.25	.13	.08
222	Dan Spillner	.20	.10	.06
223	*Robin Yount*	150.00	75.00	45.00
224	Ramon Hernandez	.20	.10	.06
225	Bob Grich	.40	.20	.12
226	Bill Campbell	.25	.13	.08
227	Bob Watson	.25	.13	.08
228	*George Brett*	100.00	50.00	27.00
229	Barry Foote	.20	.10	.06
230	Jim Hunter	2.00	1.00	.60
231	Mike Tyson	.20	.10	.06
232	Diego Segui	.20	.10	.06
233	Billy Grabarkewitz	.20	.10	.06
234	Tom Grieve	.20	.10	.06
235	Jack Billingham	.20	.10	.06
236	Angels Team (Dick Williams)	.80	.40	.25
237	Carl Morton	.20	.10	.06
238	Dave Duncan	.20	.10	.06
239	George Stone	.20	.10	.06
240	Garry Maddox	.25	.13	.08
241	Dick Tidrow	.25	.13	.08
242	Jay Johnstone	.25	.13	.08
243	Jim Kaat	1.25	.60	.40
244	Bill Buckner	.50	.25	.15
245	Mickey Lolich	.50	.25	.15
246	Cardinals Team (Red Schoendienst)	.80	.40	.25
247	Enos Cabell	.25	.13	.08
248	Randy Jones	.25	.13	.08
249	Danny Thompson	.25	.13	.08
250	Ken Brett	.25	.13	.08
251	Fran Healy	.20	.10	.06
252	Fred Scherman	.20	.10	.06
253	Jesus Alou	.25	.13	.08
254	Mike Torrez	.25	.13	.08
255	Dwight Evans	4.00	2.00	1.25
256	Billy Champion	.20	.10	.06
257	Checklist 133-264	1.50	.70	.45
258	Dave LaRoche	.20	.10	.06
259	Len Randle	.20	.10	.06
260	Johnny Bench	10.00	5.00	3.00
261	Andy Hassler	.20	.10	.06
262	Rowland Office	.20	.10	.06
263	Jim Perry	.40	.20	.12
264	John Milner	.20	.10	.06
265	Ron Bryant	.20	.10	.06
266	Sandy Alomar	.25	.13	.08
267	Dick Ruthven	.20	.10	.06
268	Hal McRae	.40	.20	.12
269	Doug Rau	.20	.10	.06
270	Ron Fairly	.30	.15	.09
271	Jerry Moses	.20	.10	.06
272	Lynn McGlothen	.20	.10	.06
273	Steve Braun	.20	.10	.06
274	Vicente Romo	.20	.10	.06
275	Paul Blair	.25	.13	.08
276	White Sox Team (Chuck Tanner)	.80	.40	.25
277	Frank Taveras	.20	.10	.06
278	Paul Lindblad	.20	.10	.06
279	Milt May	.20	.10	.06
280	Carl Yastrzemski	10.00	5.00	3.00
281	Jim Slaton	.20	.10	.06
282	Jerry Morales	.20	.10	.06
283	Steve Foucault	.20	.10	.06
284	Ken Griffey	.70	.35	.20
285	Ellie Rodriguez	.20	.10	.06
286	Mike Jorgensen	.20	.10	.06
287	Roric Harrison	.20	.10	.06
288	Bruce Ellingsen	.20	.10	.06
289	Ken Rudolph	.20	.10	.06
290	Jon Matlack	.25	.13	.08
291	Bill Sudakis	.25	.13	.08
292	Ron Schueler	.20	.10	.06
293	Dick Sharon	.20	.10	.06
294	*Geoff Zahn*	.40	.20	.12
295	Vada Pinson	.60	.30	.20
296	Alan Foster	.20	.10	.06
297	Craig Kusick	.20	.10	.06
298	Johnny Grubb	.20	.10	.06
299	Bucky Dent	.40	.20	.12
300	Reggie Jackson	10.00	5.00	3.00
301	Dave Roberts	.20	.10	.06
302	*Rick Burleson*	.50	.25	.15
303	Grant Jackson	.20	.10	.06
304	Pirates Team (Danny Murtaugh)	.80	.40	.25

#	Card	NR MT	EX	VG
305	Jim Colborn	.20	.10	.06
306	Batting Leaders (Rod Carew, Ralph Garr)	.80	.40	.25
307	Home Run Leaders (Dick Allen, Mike Schmidt)	.90	.45	.25
308	Runs Batted In Leaders (Johnny Bench, Jeff Burroughs)	.90	.45	.25
309	Stolen Base Leaders (Lou Brock, Bill North)	.80	.40	.25
310	Victory Leaders (Jim Hunter, Fergie Jenkins, Andy Messersmith, Phil Niekro)	.80	.40	.25
311	Earned Run Average Leaders (Buzz Capra, Jim Hunter)	.50	.25	.15
312	Strikeout Leaders (Steve Carlton, Nolan Ryan)	2.50	1.25	.70
313	Leading Firemen (Terry Forster, Mike Marshall)	.50	.25	.15
314	Buck Martinez	.20	.10	.06
315	Don Kessinger	.25	.13	.08
316	Jackie Brown	.20	.10	.06
317	Joe Lahoud	.20	.10	.06
318	Ernie McAnally	.20	.10	.06
319	Johnny Oates	.20	.10	.06
320	Pete Rose	18.00	9.00	5.50
321	Rudy May	.25	.13	.08
322	Ed Goodson	.20	.10	.06
323	Fred Holdsworth	.20	.10	.06
324	Ed Kranepool	.30	.15	.09
325	Tony Oliva	.80	.40	.25
326	Wayne Twitchell	.20	.10	.06
327	Jerry Hairston	.20	.10	.06
328	Sonny Siebert	.20	.10	.06
329	Ted Kubiak	.20	.10	.06
330	Mike Marshall	.30	.15	.09
331	Indians Team (Frank Robinson)	.90	.45	.25
332	Fred Kendall	.20	.10	.06
333	Dick Drago	.20	.10	.06
334	*Greg Gross*	.30	.15	.09
335	Jim Palmer	5.00	2.50	1.50
336	Rennie Stennett	.20	.10	.06
337	Kevin Kobel	.20	.10	.06
338	Rick Stelmaszek	.20	.10	.06
339	Jim Fregosi	.40	.20	.12
340	Paul Splittorff	.25	.13	.08
341	Hal Breeden	.20	.10	.06
342	Leroy Stanton	.20	.10	.06
343	Danny Frisella	.20	.10	.06
344	Ben Oglivie	.30	.15	.09
345	Clay Carroll	.25	.13	.08
346	Bobby Darwin	.20	.10	.06
347	Mike Caldwell	.20	.10	.06
348	Tony Muser	.20	.10	.06
349	Ray Sadecki	.20	.10	.06
350	Bobby Murcer	.40	.20	.12
351	Bob Boone	.40	.20	.12
352	Darold Knowles	.20	.10	.06
353	Luis Melendez	.20	.10	.06
354	Dick Bosman	.20	.10	.06
355	Chris Cannizzaro	.20	.10	.06
356	Rico Petrocelli	.30	.15	.09
357	Ken Forsch	.25	.13	.08
358	Al Bumbry	.25	.13	.08
359	Paul Popovich	.20	.10	.06
360	George Scott	.30	.15	.09
361	Dodgers Team (Walter Alston)	1.00	.50	.30
362	Steve Hargan	.20	.10	.06
363	Carmen Fanzone	.20	.10	.06
364	Doug Bird	.20	.10	.06
365	Bob Bailey	.20	.10	.06
366	Ken Sanders	.20	.10	.06
367	Craig Robinson	.20	.10	.06
368	Vic Albury	.20	.10	.06
369	Merv Rettenmund	.20	.10	.06
370	Tom Seaver	8.00	4.00	2.50
371	Gates Brown	.20	.10	.06
372	John D'Acquisto	.20	.10	.06
373	Bill Sharp	.20	.10	.06
374	Eddie Watt	.20	.10	.06
375	Roy White	.40	.20	.12
376	Steve Yeager	.20	.10	.06
377	Tom Hilgendorf	.20	.10	.06
378	Derrel Thomas	.20	.10	.06
379	Bernie Carbo	.20	.10	.06
380	Sal Bando	.40	.20	.12
381	John Curtis	.20	.10	.06
382	Don Baylor	.60	.30	.20
383	Jim York	.20	.10	.06
384	Brewers Team (Del Crandall)	.80	.40	.25
385	Dock Ellis	.25	.13	.08
386	Checklist 265-396	1.50	.70	.45
387	Jim Spencer	.20	.10	.06
388	Steve Stone	.30	.15	.09
389	Tony Solaita	.20	.10	.06
390	Ron Cey	.40	.20	.12
391	Don DeMola	.20	.10	.06
392	Bruce Bochte	.40	.20	.12
393	Gary Gentry	.20	.10	.06
394	Larvell Blanks	.20	.10	.06
395	Bud Harrelson	.25	.13	.08
396	Fred Norman	.20	.10	.06
397	Bill Freehan	.40	.20	.12
398	Elias Sosa	.20	.10	.06
399	Terry Harmon	.20	.10	.06
400	Dick Allen	.80	.40	.25
401	Mike Wallace	.25	.13	.08
402	Bob Tolan	.25	.13	.08
403	Tom Buskey	.20	.10	.06
404	Ted Sizemore	.20	.10	.06
405	John Montague	.20	.10	.06
406	Bob Gallagher	.20	.10	.06
407	*Herb Washington*	.30	.15	.09
408	Clyde Wright	.20	.10	.06
409	Bob Robertson	.20	.10	.06
410	Mike Cueller (Cuellar)	.40	.20	.12
411	George Mitterwald	.20	.10	.06
412	Bill Hands	.20	.10	.06
413	Marty Pattin	.20	.10	.06
414	Manny Mota	.30	.15	.09
415	John Hiller	.25	.13	.08
416	Larry Lintz	.20	.10	.06

#	Card	NR MT	EX	VG
417	Skip Lockwood	.20	.10	.06
418	Leo Foster	.20	.10	.06
419	Dave Goltz	.25	.13	.08
420	Larry Bowa	.40	.20	.12
421	Mets Team (Yogi Berra)	1.00	.50	.30
422	Brian Downing	.30	.15	.09
423	Clay Kirby	.20	.10	.06
424	John Lowenstein	.20	.10	.06
425	Tito Fuentes	.20	.10	.06
426	George Medich	.25	.13	.08
427	Clarence Gaston	.20	.10	.06
428	Dave Hamilton	.20	.10	.06
429	*Jim Dwyer*	.30	.15	.09
430	Luis Tiant	.50	.25	.15
431	Rod Gilbreath	.20	.10	.06
432	Ken Berry	.20	.10	.06
433	Larry Demery	.20	.10	.06
434	Bob Locker	.20	.10	.06
435	Dave Nelson	.20	.10	.06
436	Ken Frailing	.20	.10	.06
437	*Al Cowens*	.40	.20	.12
438	Don Carrithers	.20	.10	.06
439	Ed Brinkman	.25	.13	.08
440	Andy Messersmith	.30	.15	.09
441	Bobby Heise	.20	.10	.06
442	Maximino Leon	.20	.10	.06
443	Twins Team (Frank Quilici)	.80	.40	.25
444	Gene Garber	.25	.13	.08
445	Felix Millan	.20	.10	.06
446	Bart Johnson	.20	.10	.06
447	Terry Crowley	.20	.10	.06
448	Frank Duffy	.20	.10	.06
449	Charlie Williams	.20	.10	.06
450	Willie McCovey	3.00	1.50	.90
451	Rick Dempsey	.40	.20	.12
452	Angel Mangual	.20	.10	.06
453	Claude Osteen	.30	.15	.09
454	Doug Griffin	.20	.10	.06
455	Don Wilson	.20	.10	.06
456	Bob Coluccio	.20	.10	.06
457	Mario Mendoza	.20	.10	.06
458	Ross Grimsley	.25	.13	.08
459	A.L. Championships	.80	.40	.25
460	N.L. Championships	.80	.40	.25
461	World Series Game 1	1.50	.70	.45
462	World Series Game 2	.80	.40	.25
463	World Series Game 3	1.00	.50	.30
464	World Series Game 4	.80	.40	.25
465	World Series Game 5	.80	.40	.25
466	World Series Summary	.80	.40	.25
467	Ed Halicki	.20	.10	.06
468	Bobby Mitchell	.20	.10	.06
469	Tom Dettore	.20	.10	.06
470	Jeff Burroughs	.30	.15	.09
471	Bob Stinson	.20	.10	.06
472	Bruce Dal Canton	.20	.10	.06
473	Ken McMullen	.20	.10	.06
474	Luke Walker	.20	.10	.06
475	Darrell Evans	.60	.30	.20
476	*Ed Figueroa*	.30	.15	.09
477	Tom Hutton	.20	.10	.06
478	Tom Burgmeier	.20	.10	.06
479	Ken Boswell	.20	.10	.06
480	Carlos May	.25	.13	.08
481	*Will McEnaney*	.30	.15	.09
482	Tom McCraw	.20	.10	.06
483	Steve Ontiveros	.20	.10	.06
484	Glenn Beckert	.30	.15	.09
485	Sparky Lyle	.40	.20	.12
486	Ray Fosse	.20	.10	.06
487	Astros Team (Preston Gomez)	.80	.40	.25
488	Bill Travers	.20	.10	.06
489	Cecil Cooper	1.00	.50	.30
490	Reggie Smith	.30	.15	.09
491	Doyle Alexander	.40	.20	.12
492	Rich Hebner	.25	.13	.08
493	Don Stanhouse	.20	.10	.06
494	*Pete LaCock*	.25	.13	.08
495	Nelson Briles	.20	.10	.06
496	Pepe Frias	.20	.10	.06
497	Jim Nettles	.20	.10	.06
498	Al Downing	.25	.13	.08
499	Marty Perez	.20	.10	.06
500	Nolan Ryan	30.00	15.00	9.00
501	Bill Robinson	.20	.10	.06
502	Pat Bourque	.20	.10	.06
503	Fred Stanley	.25	.13	.08
504	Buddy Bradford	.20	.10	.06
505	Chris Speier	.25	.13	.08
506	Leron Lee	.20	.10	.06
507	Tom Carroll	.20	.10	.06
508	Bob Hansen	.20	.10	.06
509	Dave Hilton	.20	.10	.06
510	Vida Blue	.50	.25	.15
511	Rangers Team (Billy Martin)	.90	.45	.25
512	Larry Milbourne	.20	.10	.06
513	Dick Pole	.20	.10	.06
514	Jose Cruz	.50	.25	.15
515	Manny Sanguillen	.25	.13	.08
516	Don Hood	.20	.10	.06
517	Checklist 397-528	1.25	.60	.40
518	Leo Cardenas	.20	.10	.06
519	Jim Todd	.20	.10	.06
520	Amos Otis	.30	.15	.09
521	Dennis Blair	.20	.10	.06
522	Gary Sutherland	.20	.10	.06
523	Tom Paciorek	.25	.13	.08
524	John Doherty	.20	.10	.06
525	Tom House	.20	.10	.06
526	Larry Hisle	.25	.13	.08
527	Mac Scarce	.20	.10	.06
528	Eddie Leon	.20	.10	.06
529	Gary Thomasson	.20	.10	.06
530	Gaylord Perry	2.25	1.25	.70
531	Reds Team (Sparky Anderson)	.90	.45	.25
532	Gorman Thomas	.60	.30	.20
533	Rudy Meoli	.20	.10	.06
534	Alex Johnson	.25	.13	.08
535	Gene Tenace	.25	.13	.08
536	Bob Moose	.20	.10	.06
537	Tommy Harper	.25	.13	.08
538	Duffy Dyer	.20	.10	.06

		NR MT	EX	VG
539	Jesse Jefferson	.20	.10	.06
540	Lou Brock	3.00	1.50	.90
541	Roger Metzger	.20	.10	.06
542	Pete Broberg	.20	.10	.06
543	Larry Biittner	.20	.10	.06
544	Steve Mingori	.20	.10	.06
545	Billy Williams	2.25	1.25	.70
546	John Knox	.20	.10	.06
547	Von Joshua	.20	.10	.06
548	Charlie Sands	.20	.10	.06
549	Bill Butler	.20	.10	.06
550	Ralph Garr	.25	.13	.08
551	Larry Christenson	.20	.10	.06
552	Jack Brohamer	.20	.10	.06
553	John Boccabella	.20	.10	.06
554	Rich Gossage	1.25	.60	.40
555	Al Oliver	.80	.40	.25
556	Tim Johnson	.20	.10	.06
557	Larry Gura	.25	.13	.08
558	Dave Roberts	.20	.10	.06
559	Bob Montgomery	.20	.10	.06
560	Tony Perez	1.00	.50	.30
561	A's Team (Alvin Dark)	.90	.45	.25
562	Gary Nolan	.20	.10	.06
563	Wilbur Howard	.20	.10	.06
564	Tommy Davis	.40	.20	.12
565	Joe Torre	.70	.35	.20
566	Ray Burris	.20	.10	.06
567	*Jim Sundberg*	.70	.35	.20
568	Dale Murray	.20	.10	.06
569	Frank White	.40	.20	.12
570	Jim Wynn	.30	.15	.09
571	Dave Lemanczyk	.20	.10	.06
572	Roger Nelson	.20	.10	.06
573	Orlando Pena	.20	.10	.06
574	Tony Taylor	.20	.10	.06
575	Gene Clines	.20	.10	.06
576	Phil Roof	.20	.10	.06
577	John Morris	.20	.10	.06
578	Dave Tomlin	.20	.10	.06
579	Skip Pitlock	.20	.10	.06
580	Frank Robinson	3.00	1.50	.90
581	Darrel Chaney	.20	.10	.06
582	Eduardo Rodriguez	.20	.10	.06
583	Andy Etchebarren	.20	.10	.06
584	Mike Garman	.20	.10	.06
585	Chris Chambliss	.40	.20	.12
586	Tim McCarver	.60	.30	.20
587	Chris Ward	.20	.10	.06
588	Rick Auerbach	.20	.10	.06
589	Braves Team (Clyde King)	.80	.40	.25
590	Cesar Cedeno	.40	.20	.12
591	Glenn Abbott	.20	.10	.06
592	Balor Moore	.20	.10	.06
593	Gene Lamont	.20	.10	.06
594	Jim Fuller	.20	.10	.06
595	Joe Niekro	.40	.20	.12
596	Ollie Brown	.20	.10	.06
597	Winston Llenas	.20	.10	.06
598	Bruce Kison	.20	.10	.06
599	Nate Colbert	.20	.10	.06
600	Rod Carew	6.00	3.00	1.75
601	Juan Beniquez	.30	.15	.09
602	John Vukovich	.20	.10	.06
603	Lew Krausse	.20	.10	.06
604	Oscar Zamora	.20	.10	.06
605	John Ellis	.20	.10	.06
606	Bruce Miller	.20	.10	.06
607	Jim Holt	.20	.10	.06
608	Gene Michael	.30	.15	.09
609	Ellie Hendricks	.20	.10	.06
610	Ron Hunt	.25	.13	.08
611	Yankees Team (Bill Virdon)	1.25	.60	.40
612	Terry Hughes	.20	.10	.06
613	Bill Parsons	.20	.10	.06
614	Rookie Pitchers (Jack Kucek, Dyar Miller, Vern Ruhle, Paul Siebert)	.20	.10	.06
615	Rookie Pitchers (Pat Darcy, *Dennis Leonard, Tom Underwood*, Hank Webb)	.60	.30	.20
616	Rookie Outfielders (Dave Augustine, Pepe Mangual, *Jim Rice*, John Scott)	30.00	15.00	9.00
617	Rookie Infielders (Mike Cubbage, *Doug DeCinces*, Reggie Sanders, Manny Trillo)	1.25	.60	.40
618	Rookie Pitchers (*Jamie Easterly*, Tom Johnson, *Scott McGregor, Rick Rhoden*)	2.25	1.25	.70
619	Rookie Outfielders (Benny Ayala, Nyls Nyman, Tommy Smith, Jerry Turner)	.20	.10	.06
620	Rookie Catchers-Outfielders (*Gary Carter*, Marc Hill, Danny Meyer, Leon Roberts)	35.00	17.50	10.50
621	Rookie Pitchers (*John Denny, Rawly Eastwick, Jim Kern*, Juan Veintidos)	.60	.30	.20
622	Rookie Outfielders (Ed Armbrister, *Fred Lynn*, Tom Poquette, Terry Whitfield)	12.00	6.00	3.50
623	Rookie Infielders (*Phil Garner, Keith Hernandez*, Bob Sheldon, Tom Veryzer)	20.00	10.00	6.00
624	Rookie Pitchers (Doug Konieczny, *Gary Lavelle*, Jim Otten, Eddie Solomon)	.30	.15	.09
625	Boog Powell	.70	.35	.20
626	Larry Haney	.20	.10	.06
627	Tom Walker	.20	.10	.06
628	*Ron LeFlore*	.80	.40	.25
629	Joe Hoerner	.20	.10	.06
630	Greg Luzinski	.70	.35	.20
631	Lee Lacy	.25	.13	.08
632	Morris Nettles	.20	.10	.06
633	Paul Casanova	.20	.10	.06
634	Cy Acosta	.20	.10	.06
635	Chuck Dobson	.20	.10	.06
636	Charlie Moore	.25	.13	.08
637	Ted Martinez	.20	.10	.06
638	Cubs Team (Jim Marshall)	.80	.40	.25
639	Steve Kline	.20	.10	.06
640	Harmon Killebrew	2.50	1.25	.70
641	Jim Northrup	.25	.13	.08
642	Mike Phillips	.20	.10	.06
643	Brent Strom	.20	.10	.06
644	Bill Fahey	.20	.10	.06
645	Danny Cater	.20	.10	.06
646	Checklist 529-660	1.50	.70	.45
647	*Claudell Washington*	2.50	1.25	.70
648	Dave Pagan	.25	.13	.08
649	Jack Heidemann	.20	.10	.06
650	Dave May	.20	.10	.06
651	John Morlan	.20	.10	.06
652	Lindy McDaniel	.20	.10	.06
653	Lee Richards	.20	.10	.06
654	Jerry Terrell	.20	.10	.06
655	Rico Carty	.40	.20	.12
656	Bill Plummer	.20	.10	.06
657	Bob Oliver	.20	.10	.06
658	Vic Harris	.20	.10	.06
659	Bob Apodaca	.20	.10	.06
660	Hank Aaron	20.00	10.00	6.00

1975 Topps Mini

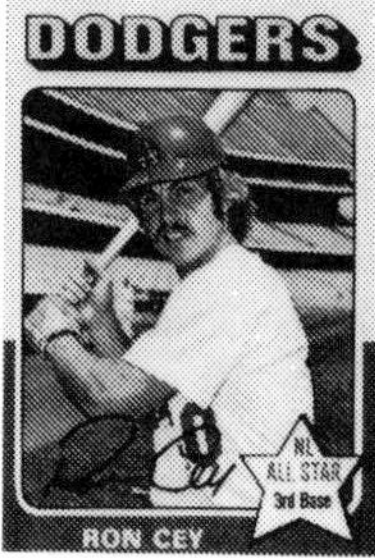

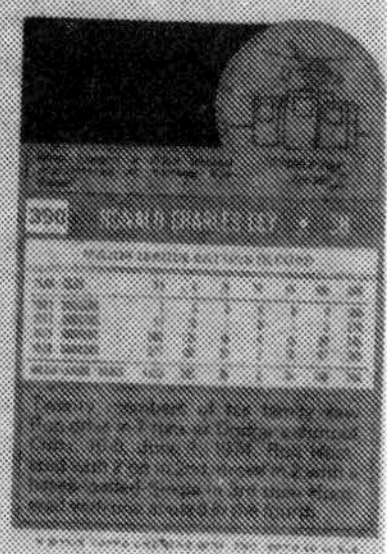

One of the most popular Topps sets of the 1970s is really a test issue. The Topps Minis measure 2-1/4" by 3-1/8," exactly 20 smaller than the regular card size. Other than their size, the Minis are in every way the same as the regular cards. The experiment primarily took place in parts of Michigan and the West Coast, where the Minis were snapped up quickly by collectors.

		NR MT	EX	VG
	Complete Set:	1200.	600.00	350.00
	Common Player:	.40	.20	.12
1	'74 Highlights (Hank Aaron)	25.00	12.50	7.50
2	'74 Highlights (Lou Brock)	3.50	1.75	1.00
3	'74 Highlights (Bob Gibson)	3.25	1.75	1.00
4	'74 Highlights (Al Kaline)	3.25	1.75	1.00
5	'74 Highlights (Nolan Ryan)	3.25	1.75	1.00
6	'74 Highlights (Mike Marshall)	.60	.30	.20
7	'74 Highlights (Dick Bosman, Steve Busby, Nolan Ryan)	1.50	.70	.45
8	Rogelio Moret	.40	.20	.12
9	Frank Tepedino	.40	.20	.12
10	Willie Davis	.60	.30	.20
11	Bill Melton	.40	.20	.12
12	David Clyde	.40	.20	.12
13	Gene Locklear	.40	.20	.12
14	Milt Wilcox	.40	.20	.12
15	Jose Cardenal	.40	.20	.12
16	Frank Tanana	.60	.30	.20
17	Dave Concepcion	.90	.45	.25
18	Tigers Team (Ralph Houk)	1.25	.60	.40
19	Jerry Koosman	.40	.20	.12
20	Thurman Munson	10.00	5.00	3.00
21	Rollie Fingers	3.00	1.50	.90
22	Dave Cash	.40	.20	.12
23	Bill Russell	.60	.30	.20
24	Al Fitzmorris	.40	.20	.12
25	Lee May	.60	.30	.20
26	Dave McNally	.60	.30	.20
27	Ken Reitz	.40	.20	.12
28	Tom Murphy	.40	.20	.12
29	Dave Parker	10.00	5.00	3.00
30	Bert Blyleven	2.00	1.00	.60
31	Dave Rader	.40	.20	.12
32	Reggie Cleveland	.40	.20	.12
33	Dusty Baker	.60	.30	.20
34	Steve Renko	.40	.20	.12
35	Ron Santo	.80	.40	.25
36	Joe Lovitto	.40	.20	.12
37	Dave Freisleben	.40	.20	.12
38	Buddy Bell	1.50	.70	.45
39	Andy Thornton	1.00	.50	.30
40	Bill Singer	.40	.20	.12
41	Cesar Geronimo	.40	.20	.12
42	Joe Coleman	.40	.20	.12
43	Cleon Jones	.40	.20	.12
44	Pat Dobson	.40	.20	.12
45	Joe Rudi	.60	.30	.20
46	Phillies Team (Danny Ozark)	1.25	.60	.40
47	Tommy John	2.50	1.25	.70
48	Freddie Patek	.40	.20	.12
49	Larry Dierker	.40	.20	.12
50	Brooks Robinson	7.00	3.50	2.00
51	Bob Forsch	1.25	.60	.40
52	Darrell Porter	.60	.30	.20
53	Dave Giusti	.40	.20	.12
54	Eric Soderholm	.40	.20	.12
55	Bobby Bonds	.80	.40	.25
56	Rick Wise	.60	.30	.20
57	Dave Johnson	1.25	.60	.40
58	Chuck Taylor	.40	.20	.12
59	Ken Henderson	.40	.20	.12
60	Fergie Jenkins	1.75	.90	.50
61	Dave Winfield	20.00	10.00	6.00
62	Fritz Peterson	.40	.20	.12
63	Steve Swisher	.40	.20	.12
64	Dave Chalk	.40	.20	.12
65	Don Gullett	.40	.20	.12
66	Willie Horton	.60	.30	.20
67	Tug McGraw	.80	.40	.25
68	Ron Blomberg	.40	.20	.12
69	John Odom	.40	.20	.12
70	Mike Schmidt	80.00	40.00	25.00
71	Charlie Hough	.60	.30	.20
72	Royals Team (Jack McKeon)	1.25	.60	.40
73	J.R. Richard	.60	.30	.20
74	Mark Belanger	.60	.30	.20
75	Ted Simmons	1.00	.50	.30
76	Ed Sprague	.40	.20	.12
77	Richie Zisk	.60	.30	.20
78	Ray Corbin	.40	.20	.12
79	Gary Matthews	.60	.30	.20
80	Carlton Fisk	7.00	3.50	2.00
81	Ron Reed	.40	.20	.12
82	Pat Kelly	.40	.20	.12
83	Jim Merritt	.40	.20	.12
84	Enzo Hernandez	.40	.20	.12
85	Bill Bonham	.40	.20	.12
86	Joe Lis	.40	.20	.12
87	George Foster	1.75	.90	.50
88	Tom Egan	.40	.20	.12
89	Jim Ray	.40	.20	.12
90	Rusty Staub	.90	.45	.25
91	Dick Green	.40	.20	.12
92	Cecil Upshaw	.40	.20	.12
93	Dave Lopes	.60	.30	.20
94	Jim Lonborg	.40	.20	.12
95	John Mayberry	.40	.20	.12
96	Mike Cosgrove	.40	.20	.12
97	Earl Williams	.40	.20	.12
98	Rich Folkers	.40	.20	.12
99	Mike Hegan	.40	.20	.12
100	Willie Stargell	7.00	3.50	2.00
101	Expos Team (Gene Mauch)	1.25	.60	.40
102	Joe Decker	.40	.20	.12
103	Rick Miller	.40	.20	.12
104	Bill Madlock	2.00	1.00	.60
105	Buzz Capra	.40	.20	.12
106	Mike Hargrove	.60	.30	.20
107	Jim Barr	.40	.20	.12
108	Tom Hall	.40	.20	.12
109	George Hendrick	.40	.20	.12
110	Wilbur Wood	.40	.20	.12
111	Wayne Garrett	.40	.20	.12
112	Larry Hardy	.40	.20	.12
113	Elliott Maddox	.40	.20	.12
114	Dick Lange	.40	.20	.12
115	Joe Ferguson	.40	.20	.12
116	Lerrin LaGrow	.40	.20	.12
117	Orioles Team (Earl Weaver)	1.25	.60	.40
118	Mike Anderson	.40	.20	.12
119	Tommy Helms	.40	.20	.12
120	Steve Busby (photo actually Fran Healy)	.40	.20	.12
121	Bill North	.40	.20	.12
122	Al Hrabosky	.40	.20	.12
123	Johnny Briggs	.40	.20	.12
124	Jerry Reuss	.60	.30	.20
125	Ken Singleton	.60	.30	.20
126	Checklist 1-132	2.25	1.25	.70
127	Glen Borgmann	.40	.20	.12
128	Bill Lee	.60	.30	.20
129	Rick Monday	.60	.30	.20
130	Phil Niekro	4.00	2.00	1.25
131	Toby Harrah	.40	.20	.12
132	Randy Moffitt	.40	.20	.12
133	Dan Driessen	.60	.30	.20
134	Ron Hodges	.40	.20	.12
135	Charlie Spikes	.40	.20	.12
136	Jim Mason	.40	.20	.12
137	Terry Forster	.40	.20	.12
138	Del Unser	.40	.20	.12
139	Horacio Pina	.40	.20	.12
140	Steve Garvey	12.00	6.00	3.50
141	Mickey Stanley	.40	.20	.12
142	Bob Reynolds	.40	.20	.12
143	Cliff Johnson	.40	.20	.12
144	Jim Wohlford	.40	.20	.12
145	Ken Holtzman	.60	.30	.20
146	Padres Team (John McNamara)	1.25	.60	.40
147	Pedro Garcia	.40	.20	.12
148	Jim Rooker	.40	.20	.12
149	Tim Foli	.40	.20	.12
150	Bob Gibson	7.00	3.50	2.00
151	Steve Brye	.40	.20	.12
152	Mario Guerrero	.40	.20	.12
153	Rick Reuschel	.60	.30	.20
154	Mike Lum	.40	.20	.12
155	Jim Bibby	.40	.20	.12
156	Dave Kingman	1.50	.70	.45
157	Pedro Borbon	.40	.20	.12
158	Jerry Grote	.40	.20	.12
159	Steve Arlin	.40	.20	.12
160	Graig Nettles	2.25	1.25	.70
161	Stan Bahnsen	.40	.20	.12
162	Willie Montanez	.40	.20	.12
163	Jim Brewer	.40	.20	.12
164	Mickey Rivers	.60	.30	.20
165	Doug Rader	.40	.20	.12
166	Woodie Fryman	.40	.20	.12
167	Rich Coggins	.40	.20	.12
168	Bill Greif	.40	.20	.12
169	Cookie Rojas	.40	.20	.12
170	Bert Campaneris	.60	.30	.20
171	Ed Kirkpatrick	.40	.20	.12
172	Red Sox Team (Darrell Johnson)	1.25	.60	.40

No.	Card	NR MT	EX	VG
173	Steve Rogers	.40	.20	.12
174	Bake McBride	.40	.20	.12
175	Don Money	.40	.20	.12
176	Burt Hooton	.40	.20	.12
177	Vic Correll	.40	.20	.12
178	Cesar Tovar	.40	.20	.12
179	Tom Bradley	.40	.20	.12
180	Joe Morgan	10.00	5.00	3.00
181	Fred Beene	.40	.20	.12
182	Don Hahn	.40	.20	.12
183	Mel Stottlemyre	.60	.30	.20
184	Jorge Orta	.40	.20	.12
185	Steve Carlton	20.00	10.00	6.00
186	Willie Crawford	.40	.20	.12
187	Denny Doyle	.40	.20	.12
188	Tom Griffin	.40	.20	.12
189	1951-MVPs (Larry (Yogi) Berra, Roy Campanella)	2.25	1.25	.70
190	1952-MVPs (Hank Sauer, Bobby Shantz)	.60	.30	.20
191	1953-MVPs (Roy Campanella, Al Rosen)	1.25	.60	.40
192	1954-MVPs (Yogi Berra, Willie Mays)	2.25	1.25	.70
193	1955-MVPs (Yogi Berra, Roy Campanella)	2.25	1.25	.70
194	1956-MVPs (Mickey Mantle, Don Newcombe)	9.00	4.50	2.75
195	1957-MVPs (Hank Aaron, Mickey Mantle)	10.00	5.00	3.00
196	1958-MVPs (Ernie Banks, Jackie Jensen)	1.25	.60	.40
197	1959-MVPs (Ernie Banks, Nellie Fox)	1.25	.60	.40
198	1960-MVPs (Dick Groat, Roger Maris)	1.75	.90	.50
199	1961-MVPs (Roger Maris, Frank Robinson)	2.25	1.25	.70
200	1962-MVPs (Mickey Mantle, Maury Wills)	9.00	4.50	2.75
201	1963-MVPs (Elston Howard, Sandy Koufax)	2.25	1.25	.70
202	1964-MVPs (Ken Boyer, Brooks Robinson)	1.75	.90	.50
203	1965-MVPs (Willie Mays, Zoilo Versalles)	1.75	.90	.50
204	1966-MVPs (Bob Clemente, Frank Robinson)	2.25	1.25	.70
205	1967-MVPs (Orlando Cepeda, Carl Yastrzemski)	1.75	.90	.50
206	1968-MVPs (Bob Gibson, Denny McLain)	1.75	.90	.50
207	1969-MVPs (Harmon Killebrew, Willie McCovey)	2.25	1.25	.70
208	1970-MVPs (Johnny Bench, Boog Powell)	1.75	.90	.50
209	1971-MVPs (Vida Blue, Joe Torre)	.80	.40	.25
210	1972-MVPs (Rich Allen, Johnny Bench)	1.75	.90	.50
211	1973-MVPs (Reggie Jackson, Pete Rose)	7.00	3.50	2.00
212	1974-MVPs (Jeff Burroughs, Steve Garvey)	1.25	.60	.40
213	Oscar Gamble	.40	.20	.12
214	Harry Parker	.40	.20	.12
215	Bobby Valentine	.40	.20	.12
216	Giants Team (Wes Westrum)	1.25	.60	.40
217	Lou Piniella	.80	.40	.25
218	Jerry Johnson	.40	.20	.12
219	Ed Herrmann	.40	.20	.12
220	Don Sutton	3.00	1.50	.90
221	Aurelio Rodriquez (Rodriguez)	.40	.20	.12
222	Dan Spillner	.40	.20	.12
223	Robin Yount	200.00	100.00	60.00
224	Ramon Hernandez	.40	.20	.12
225	Bob Grich	.60	.30	.20
226	Bill Campbell	.40	.20	.12
227	Bob Watson	.40	.20	.12
228	George Brett	150.00	75.00	45.00
229	Barry Foote	.40	.20	.12
230	Jim Hunter	4.00	2.00	1.25
231	Mike Tyson	.40	.20	.12
232	Diego Segui	.40	.20	.12
233	Billy Grabarkewitz	.40	.20	.12
234	Tom Grieve	.40	.20	.12
235	Jack Billingham	.40	.20	.12
236	Angels Team (Dick Williams)	1.25	.60	.40
237	Carl Morton	.40	.20	.12
238	Dave Duncan	.40	.20	.12
239	George Stone	.40	.20	.12
240	Garry Maddox	.60	.30	.20
241	Dick Tidrow	.40	.20	.12
242	Jay Johnstone	.60	.30	.20
243	Jim Kaat	2.00	1.00	.60
244	Bill Buckner	.80	.40	.25
245	Mickey Lolich	.80	.40	.25
246	Cardinals Team (Red Schoendienst)	1.25	.60	.40
247	Enos Cabell	.40	.20	.12
248	Randy Jones	.40	.20	.12
249	Danny Thompson	.40	.20	.12
250	Ken Brett	.40	.20	.12
251	Fran Healy	.40	.20	.12
252	Fred Scherman	.40	.20	.12
253	Jesus Alou	.40	.20	.12
254	Mike Torrez	.40	.20	.12
255	Dwight Evans	2.25	1.25	.70
256	Billy Champion	.40	.20	.12
257	Checklist 133-264	2.25	1.25	.70
258	Dave LaRoche	.40	.20	.12
259	Len Randle	.40	.20	.12
260	Johnny Bench	15.00	7.50	4.50
261	Andy Hassler	.40	.20	.12
262	Rowland Office	.40	.20	.12
263	Jim Perry	.60	.30	.20
264	John Milner	.40	.20	.12
265	Ron Bryant	.40	.20	.12
266	Sandy Alomar	.40	.20	.12
267	Dick Ruthven	.40	.20	.12
268	Hal McRae	.60	.30	.20
269	Doug Rau	.40	.20	.12
270	Ron Fairly	.60	.30	.20
271	Jerry Moses	.40	.20	.12
272	Lynn McGlothen	.40	.20	.12
273	Steve Braun	.40	.20	.12
274	Vicente Romo	.40	.20	.12
275	Paul Blair	.60	.30	.20
276	White Sox Team (Chuck Tanner)	1.25	.60	.40
277	Frank Taveras	.40	.20	.12
278	Paul Lindblad	.40	.20	.12
279	Milt May	.40	.20	.12
280	Carl Yastrzemski	15.00	7.50	4.50
281	Jim Slaton	.40	.20	.12
282	Jerry Morales	.40	.20	.12
283	Steve Foucault	.40	.20	.12
284	Ken Griffey	1.00	.50	.30
285	Ellie Rodriguez	.40	.20	.12
286	Mike Jorgensen	.40	.20	.12
287	Roric Harrison	.40	.20	.12
288	Bruce Ellingsen	.40	.20	.12
289	Ken Rudolph	.40	.20	.12
290	Jon Matlack	.40	.20	.12
291	Bill Sudakis	.40	.20	.12
292	Ron Schueler	.40	.20	.12
293	Dick Sharon	.40	.20	.12
294	Geoff Zahn	.40	.20	.12
295	Vada Pinson	.90	.45	.25
296	Alan Foster	.40	.20	.12
297	Craig Kusick	.40	.20	.12
298	Johnny Grubb	.40	.20	.12
299	Bucky Dent	.60	.30	.20
300	Reggie Jackson	20.00	10.00	6.00
301	Dave Roberts	.40	.20	.12
302	Rick Burleson	.80	.40	.25
303	Grant Jackson	.40	.20	.12
304	Pirates Team (Danny Murtaugh)	1.25	.60	.40
305	Jim Colborn	.40	.20	.12
306	Batting Leaders (Rod Carew, Ralph Garr)	1.25	.60	.40
307	Home Run Leaders (Dick Allen, Mike Schmidt)	1.25	.60	.40
308	Runs Batted In Leaders (Johnny Bench, Jeff Burroughs)	1.25	.60	.40
309	Stole Base Leaders (Lou Brock, Bill North)	1.25	.60	.40
310	Victory Leaders (Jim Hunter, Fergie Jenkins, Andy Messersmith, Phil Niekro)	1.25	.60	.40
311	Earned Run Average Leaders (Buzz Capra, Jim Hunter)	.80	.40	.25
312	Strikeout Leaders (Steve Carlton, Nolan Ryan)	2.50	1.25	.70
313	Leading Firemen (Terry Forster, Mike Marshall)	.80	.40	.25
314	Buck Martinez	.40	.20	.12
315	Don Kessinger	.40	.20	.12
316	Jackie Brown	.40	.20	.12
317	Joe Lahoud	.40	.20	.12
318	Ernie McAnally	.40	.20	.12
319	Johnny Oates	.40	.20	.12
320	Pete Rose	40.00	20.00	12.00
321	Rudy May	.40	.20	.12
322	Ed Goodson	.40	.20	.12
323	Fred Holdsworth	.40	.20	.12
324	Ed Kranepool	.40	.20	.12
325	Tony Oliva	1.25	.60	.40
326	Wayne Twitchell	.40	.20	.12
327	Jerry Hairston	.40	.20	.12
328	Sonny Siebert	.40	.20	.12
329	Ted Kubiak	.40	.20	.12
330	Mike Marshall	.60	.30	.20
331	Indians Team (Frank Robinson)	1.25	.60	.40
332	Fred Kendall	.40	.20	.12
333	Dick Drago	.40	.20	.12
334	Greg Gross	.40	.20	.12
335	Jim Palmer	15.00	7.50	4.50
336	Rennie Stennett	.40	.20	.12
337	Kevin Kobel	.40	.20	.12
338	Rick Stelmaszek	.40	.20	.12
339	Jim Fregosi	.60	.30	.20
340	Paul Splittorff	.40	.20	.12
341	Hal Breeden	.40	.20	.12
342	Leroy Stanton	.40	.20	.12
343	Danny Frisella	.40	.20	.12
344	Ben Oglivie	.60	.30	.20
345	Clay Carroll	.40	.20	.12
346	Bobby Darwin	.40	.20	.12
347	Mike Caldwell	.40	.20	.12
348	Tony Muser	.40	.20	.12
349	Ray Sadecki	.40	.20	.12
350	Bobby Murcer	.60	.30	.20
351	Bob Boone	.60	.30	.20
352	Darold Knowles	.40	.20	.12
353	Luis Melendez	.40	.20	.12
354	Dick Bosman	.40	.20	.12
355	Chris Cannizzaro	.40	.20	.12
356	Rico Petrocelli	.40	.20	.12
357	Ken Forsch	.40	.20	.12
358	Al Bumbry	.40	.20	.12
359	Paul Popovich	.40	.20	.12
360	George Scott	.40	.20	.12
361	Dodgers Team (Walter Alston)	1.50	.70	.45
362	Steve Hargan	.40	.20	.12
363	Carmen Fanzone	.40	.20	.12
364	Doug Bird	.40	.20	.12
365	Bob Bailey	.40	.20	.12
366	Ken Sanders	.40	.20	.12
367	Craig Robinson	.40	.20	.12
368	Vic Albury	.40	.20	.12
369	Merv Rettenmund	.40	.20	.12
370	Tom Seaver	25.00	12.50	7.50
371	Gates Brown	.40	.20	.12
372	John D'Acquisto	.40	.20	.12
373	Bill Sharp	.40	.20	.12
374	Eddie Watt	.40	.20	.12
375	Roy White	.60	.30	.20
376	Steve Yeager	.40	.20	.12
377	Tom Hilgendorf	.40	.20	.12
378	Derrel Thomas	.40	.20	.12
379	Bernie Carbo	.40	.20	.12
380	Sal Bando	.60	.30	.20
381	John Curtis	.40	.20	.12
382	Don Baylor	.90	.45	.25
383	Jim York	.40	.20	.12
384	Brewers Team (Del Crandall)	1.25	.60	.40
385	Dock Ellis	.40	.20	.12
386	Checklist 265-396	2.25	1.25	.70
387	Jim Spencer	.40	.20	.12
388	Steve Stone	.60	.30	.20
389	Tony Solaita	.40	.20	.12
390	Ron Cey	.60	.30	.20
391	Don DeMola	.40	.20	.12
392	Bruce Bochte	.40	.20	.12
393	Gary Gentry	.40	.20	.12
394	Larvell Blanks	.40	.20	.12
395	Bud Harrelson	.40	.20	.12
396	Fred Norman	.40	.20	.12
397	Bill Freehan	.60	.30	.20
398	Elias Sosa	.40	.20	.12
399	Terry Harmon	.40	.20	.12
400	Dick Allen	1.25	.60	.40
401	Mike Wallace	.40	.20	.12
402	Bob Tolan	.40	.20	.12
403	Tom Buskey	.40	.20	.12
404	Ted Sizemore	.40	.20	.12
405	John Montague	.40	.20	.12
406	Bob Gallagher	.40	.20	.12
407	Herb Washington	.40	.20	.12
408	Clyde Wright	.40	.20	.12
409	Bob Robertson	.40	.20	.12
410	Mike Cueller (Cuellar)	.60	.30	.20
411	George Mitterwald	.40	.20	.12
412	Bill Hands	.40	.20	.12
413	Marty Pattin	.40	.20	.12
414	Manny Mota	.60	.30	.20
415	John Hiller	.40	.20	.12
416	Larry Lintz	.40	.20	.12
417	Skip Lockwood	.40	.20	.12
418	Leo Foster	.40	.20	.12
419	Dave Goltz	.40	.20	.12
420	Larry Bowa	.60	.30	.20
421	Mets Team (Yogi Berra)	1.50	.70	.45
422	Brian Downing	.60	.30	.20
423	Clay Kirby	.40	.20	.12
424	John Lowenstein	.40	.20	.12
425	Tito Fuentes	.40	.20	.12
426	George Medich	.40	.20	.12
427	Clarence Gaston	.40	.20	.12
428	Dave Hamilton	.40	.20	.12
429	Jim Dwyer	.40	.20	.12
430	Luis Tiant	.80	.40	.25
431	Rod Gilbreath	.40	.20	.12
432	Ken Berry	.40	.20	.12
433	Larry Demery	.40	.20	.12
434	Bob Locker	.40	.20	.12
435	Dave Nelson	.40	.20	.12
436	Ken Frailing	.40	.20	.12
437	Al Cowens	.40	.20	.12
438	Don Carrithers	.40	.20	.12
439	Ed Brinkman	.40	.20	.12
440	Andy Messersmith	.60	.30	.20
441	Bobby Heise	.40	.20	.12
442	Maximino Leon	.40	.20	.12
443	Twins Team (Frank Quilici)	1.25	.60	.40
444	Gene Garber	.40	.20	.12
445	Felix Millan	.40	.20	.12
446	Bart Johnson	.40	.20	.12
447	Terry Crowley	.40	.20	.12
448	Frank Duffy	.40	.20	.12
449	Charlie Williams	.40	.20	.12
450	Willie McCovey	7.00	3.50	2.00
451	Rick Dempsey	.60	.30	.20
452	Angel Mangual	.40	.20	.12
453	Claude Osteen	.40	.20	.12
454	Doug Griffin	.40	.20	.12
455	Don Wilson	.40	.20	.12
456	Bob Coluccio	.40	.20	.12
457	Mario Mendoza	.40	.20	.12
458	Ross Grimsley	.40	.20	.12
459	A.L. Championships	1.25	.60	.40
460	N.L. Championships	1.25	.60	.40
461	World Series Game 1	2.25	1.25	.70
462	World Series Game 2	1.50	.70	.45
463	World Series Game 3	1.50	.70	.45
464	World Series Game 4	1.25	.60	.40
465	World Series Game 5	1.25	.60	.40
466	World Series Summary	1.25	.60	.40
467	Ed Halicki	.40	.20	.12
468	Bobby Mitchell	.40	.20	.12
469	Tom Dettore	.40	.20	.12
470	Jeff Burroughs	.40	.20	.12
471	Bob Stinson	.40	.20	.12
472	Bruce Dal Canton	.40	.20	.12
473	Ken McMullen	.40	.20	.12
474	Luke Walker	.40	.20	.12
475	Darrell Evans	.90	.45	.25
476	Ed Figueroa	.40	.20	.12
477	Tom Hutton	.40	.20	.12
478	Tom Burgmeier	.40	.20	.12
479	Ken Boswell	.40	.20	.12
480	Carlos May	.40	.20	.12
481	Will McEnaney	.40	.20	.12
482	Tom McCraw	.40	.20	.12
483	Steve Ontiveros	.40	.20	.12
484	Glenn Beckert	.40	.20	.12
485	Sparky Lyle	.60	.30	.20
486	Ray Fosse	.40	.20	.12
487	Astros Team (Preston Gomez)	1.25	.60	.40
488	Bill Travers	.40	.20	.12
489	Cecil Cooper	1.50	.70	.45
490	Reggie Smith	.60	.30	.20
491	Doyle Alexander	.60	.30	.20
492	Rich Hebner	.40	.20	.12
493	Doug Stanhouse	.40	.20	.12
494	Pete LaCock	.40	.20	.12
495	Nelson Briles	.40	.20	.12
496	Pepe Frias	.40	.20	.12
497	Jim Nettles	.40	.20	.12
498	Al Downing	.40	.20	.12
499	Marty Perez	.40	.20	.12
500	Nolan Ryan	40.00	20.00	12.00

		NR MT	EX	VG
501	Bill Robinson	.40	.20	.12
502	Pat Bourque	.40	.20	.12
503	Fred Stanley	.40	.20	.12
504	Buddy Bradford	.40	.20	.12
505	Chris Speier	.40	.20	.12
506	Leron Lee	.40	.20	.12
507	Tom Carroll	.40	.20	.12
508	Bob Hansen	.40	.20	.12
509	Dave Hilton	.40	.20	.12
510	Vida Blue	.80	.40	.25
511	Rangers Team (Billy Martin)	1.25	.60	.40
512	Larry Milbourne	.40	.20	.12
513	Dick Pole	.40	.20	.12
514	Jose Cruz	.80	.40	.25
515	Manny Sanguillen	.40	.20	.12
516	Don Hood	.40	.20	.12
517	Checklist 397-528	2.25	1.25	.70
518	Leo Cardenas	.40	.20	.12
519	Jim Todd	.40	.20	.12
520	Amos Otis	.40	.20	.12
521	Dennis Blair	.40	.20	.12
522	Gary Sutherland	.40	.20	.12
523	Tom Paciorek	.40	.20	.12
524	John Doherty	.40	.20	.12
525	Tom House	.40	.20	.12
526	Larry Hisle	.40	.20	.12
527	Mac Scarce	.40	.20	.12
528	Eddie Leon	.40	.20	.12
529	Gary Thomasson	.40	.20	.12
530	Gaylord Perry	6.00	3.00	1.75
531	Reds Team (Sparky Anderson)	1.25	.60	.40
532	Gorman Thomas	.80	.40	.25
533	Rudy Meoli	.40	.20	.12
534	Alex Johnson	.40	.20	.12
535	Gene Tenace	.40	.20	.12
536	Bob Moose	.40	.20	.12
537	Tommy Harper	.40	.20	.12
538	Duffy Dyer	.40	.20	.12
539	Jesse Jefferson	.40	.20	.12
540	Lou Brock	7.00	3.50	2.00
541	Roger Metzger	.40	.20	.12
542	Pete Broberg	.40	.20	.12
543	Larry Biittner	.40	.20	.12
544	Steve Mingori	.40	.20	.12
545	Billy Williams	6.00	3.00	1.75
546	John Knox	.40	.20	.12
547	Von Joshua	.40	.20	.12
548	Charlie Sands	.40	.20	.12
549	Bill Butler	.40	.20	.12
550	Ralph Garr	.40	.20	.12
551	Larry Christenson	.40	.20	.12
552	Jack Brohamer	.40	.20	.12
553	John Boccabella	.40	.20	.12
554	Rich Gossage	1.75	.90	.50
555	Al Oliver	1.25	.60	.40
556	Tim Johnson	.40	.20	.12
557	Larry Gura	.40	.20	.12
558	Dave Roberts	.40	.20	.12
559	Bob Montgomery	.40	.20	.12
560	Tony Perez	1.25	.60	.40
561	A's Team (Alvin Dark)	1.25	.60	.40
562	Gary Nolan	.40	.20	.12
563	Wilbur Howard	.40	.20	.12
564	Tommy Davis	.60	.30	.20
565	Joe Torre	1.00	.50	.30
566	Ray Burris	.40	.20	.12
567	Jim Sundberg	1.00	.50	.30
568	Dale Murray	.40	.20	.12
569	Frank White	.60	.30	.20
570	Jim Wynn	.60	.30	.20
571	Dave Lemanczyk	.40	.20	.12
572	Roger Nelson	.40	.20	.12
573	Orlando Pena	.40	.20	.12
574	Tony Taylor	.40	.20	.12
575	Gene Clines	.40	.20	.12
576	Phil Roof	.40	.20	.12
577	John Morris	.40	.20	.12
578	Dave Tomlin	.40	.20	.12
579	Skip Pitlock	.40	.20	.12
580	Frank Robinson	7.00	3.50	2.00
581	Darrel Chaney	.40	.20	.12
582	Eduardo Rodriguez	.40	.20	.12
583	Andy Etchebarren	.40	.20	.12
584	Mike Garman	.40	.20	.12
585	Chris Chambliss	.60	.30	.20
586	Tim McCarver	.90	.45	.25
587	Chris Ward	.40	.20	.12
588	Rick Auerbach	.40	.20	.12
589	Braves Team (Clyde King)	1.25	.60	.40
590	Cesar Cedeno	.60	.30	.20
591	Glenn Abbott	.40	.20	.12
592	Balor Moore	.40	.20	.12
593	Gene Lamont	.40	.20	.12
594	Jim Fuller	.40	.20	.12
595	Joe Niekro	.60	.30	.20
596	Ollie Brown	.40	.20	.12
597	Winston Llenas	.40	.20	.12
598	Bruce Kison	.40	.20	.12
599	Nate Colbert	.40	.20	.12
600	Rod Carew	18.00	9.00	5.50
601	Juan Beniquez	.40	.20	.12
602	John Vukovich	.40	.20	.12
603	Lew Krausse	.40	.20	.12
604	Oscar Zamora	.40	.20	.12
605	John Ellis	.40	.20	.12
606	Bruce Miller	.40	.20	.12
607	Jim Holt	.40	.20	.12
608	Gene Michael	.40	.20	.12
609	Ellie Hendricks	.40	.20	.12
610	Ron Hunt	.40	.20	.12
611	Yankees Team (Bill Virdon)	1.75	.90	.50
612	Terry Hughes	.40	.20	.12
613	Bill Parsons	.40	.20	.12
614	Rookie Pitchers (Jack Kucek, Dyar Miller, Vern Ruhle, Paul Siebert)	.40	.20	.12
615	Rookie Pitchers (Pat Darcy, Dennis Leonard, Tom Underwood, Hank Webb)	.90	.45	.25
616	Rookie Outfielders (Dave Augustine, Pepe Mangual, Jim Rice, John Scott)	50.00	25.00	15.00

		NR MT	EX	VG
617	Rookie Infielders (Mike Cubbage, Doug DeCinces, Reggie Sanders, Manny Trillo)	2.50	1.25	.70
618	Rookie Pitchers (Jamie Easterly, Tom Johnson, Scott McGregor, Rick Rhoden)	5.00	2.50	1.50
619	Rookie Outfielders (Benny Ayala, Nyls Nyman, Tommy Smith, Jerry Turner)	.40	.20	.12
620	Rookie Catchers-Outfielders (Gary Carter, Marc Hill, Danny Meyer, Leon Roberts)	50.00	25.00	15.00
621	Rookie Pitchers (John Denny, Rawly Eastwick, Jim Kern, Juan Veintidos)	.90	.45	.25
622	Rookie Outfielders (Ed Armbrister, Fred Lynn, Tom Poquette, Terry Whitfield)	15.00	7.50	4.50
623	Rookie Infielders (Phil Garner, Keith Hernandez, Bob Sheldon, Tom Veryzer)	40.00	20.00	12.00
624	Rookie Pitchers (Doug Konieczny, Gary Lavelle, Jim Otten, Eddie Solomon)	.40	.20	.12
625	Boog Powell	1.00	.50	.30
626	Larry Haney	.40	.20	.12
627	Tom Walker	.40	.20	.12
628	Ron LeFlore	1.25	.60	.40
629	Joe Hoerner	.40	.20	.12
630	Greg Luzinski	1.00	.50	.30
631	Lee Lacy	.40	.20	.12
632	Morris Nettles	.40	.20	.12
633	Paul Casanova	.40	.20	.12
634	Cy Acosta	.40	.20	.12
635	Chuck Dobson	.40	.20	.12
636	Charlie Moore	.40	.20	.12
637	Ted Martinez	.40	.20	.12
638	Cubs Team (Jim Marshall)	1.25	.60	.40
639	Steve Kline	.40	.20	.12
640	Harmon Killebrew	6.00	3.00	1.75
641	Jim Northrup	.40	.20	.12
642	Mike Phillips	.40	.20	.12
643	Brent Strom	.40	.20	.12
644	Bill Fahey	.40	.20	.12
645	Danny Cater	.40	.20	.12
646	Checklist 529-660	2.25	1.25	.70
647	Claudell Washington	2.50	1.25	.70
648	Dave Pagan	.40	.20	.12
649	Jack Heidemann	.40	.20	.12
650	Dave May	.40	.20	.12
651	John Morlan	.40	.20	.12
652	Lindy McDaniel	.40	.20	.12
653	Lee Richards	.40	.20	.12
654	Jerry Terrell	.40	.20	.12
655	Rico Carty	.60	.30	.20
656	Bill Plummer	.40	.20	.12
657	Bob Oliver	.40	.20	.12
658	Vic Harris	.40	.20	.12
659	Bob Apodaca	.40	.20	.12
660	Hank Aaron	35.00	17.50	10.50

1976 Topps

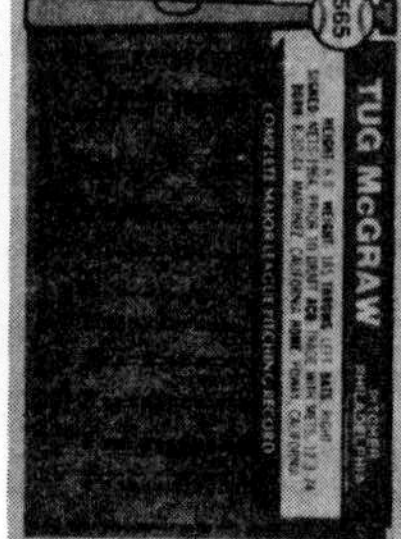

These 2-1/2" by 3-1/2" cards begin a design trend for Topps. The focus was more on the photo quality than in past years with a corresponding trend toward simplicity in the borders. The front of the cards has the player's name and team in two strips while his position is in the lower left corner under a drawing of a player representing that position. The backs have a bat and ball with the card number on the left; statistics and personal information and career highlights on the right. The 660-card set features a number of specialty sets including record-setting performances, statistical leaders, playoff and World Series highlights, the Sporting News All-Time All-Stars and father and son combinations.

	NR MT	EX	VG
Complete Set:	350.00	175.00	100.00
Commmon Player:	.15	.08	.05

		NR MT	EX	VG
1	'75 Record Breaker (Hank Aaron)	12.00	6.00	3.50
2	'75 Record Breaker (Bobby Bonds)	.40	.20	.12
3	'75 Record Breaker (Mickey Lolich)	.35	.20	.11
4	'75 Record Breaker (Dave Lopes)	.35	.20	.11
5	'75 Record Breaker (Tom Seaver)	1.50	.70	.45
6	'75 Record Breaker (Rennie Stennett)	.30	.15	.09
7	Jim Umbarger	.15	.08	.05
8	Tito Fuentes	.15	.08	.05
9	Paul Lindblad	.15	.08	.05
10	Lou Brock	2.50	1.25	.70
11	Jim Hughes	.15	.08	.05
12	Richie Zisk	.20	.10	.06
13	Johnny Wockenfuss	.15	.08	.05
14	Gene Garber	.20	.10	.06
15	George Scott	.25	.13	.08
16	Bob Apodaca	.15	.08	.05
17	Yankees Team (Billy Martin)	1.25	.60	.40
18	Dale Murray	.15	.08	.05
19	George Brett	30.00	15.00	9.00
20	Bob Watson	.20	.10	.06
21	Dave LaRoche	.15	.08	.05
22	Bill Russell	.20	.10	.06
23	Brian Downing	.25	.13	.08
24	Cesar Geronimo	.20	.10	.06
25	Mike Torrez	.20	.10	.06
26	Andy Thornton	.25	.13	.08
27	Ed Figueroa	.15	.08	.05
28	Dusty Baker	.25	.13	.08
29	Rick Burleson	.30	.15	.09
30	*John Montefusco*	.35	.20	.11
31	Len Randle	.15	.08	.05
32	Danny Frisella	.15	.08	.05
33	Bill North	.15	.08	.05
34	Mike Garman	.15	.08	.05
35	Tony Oliva	.60	.30	.20
36	Frank Taveras	.15	.08	.05
37	John Hiller	.20	.10	.06
38	Garry Maddox	.20	.10	.06
39	Pete Broberg	.15	.08	.05
40	Dave Kingman	.80	.40	.25
41	*Tippy Martinez*	.40	.20	.12
42	Barry Foote	.15	.08	.05
43	Paul Splittorff	.20	.10	.06
44	Doug Rader	.15	.08	.05
45	Boog Powell	.60	.30	.20
46	Dodgers Team (Walter Alston)	1.00	.50	.30
47	Jesse Jefferson	.15	.08	.05
48	Dave Concepcion	.40	.20	.12
49	Dave Duncan	.15	.08	.05
50	Fred Lynn	2.00	1.00	.60
51	Ray Burris	.15	.08	.05
52	Dave Chalk	.15	.08	.05
53	Mike Beard	.15	.08	.05
54	Dave Rader	.15	.08	.05
55	Gaylord Perry	2.00	1.00	.60
56	Bob Tolan	.20	.10	.06
57	Phil Garner	.30	.15	.09
58	Ron Reed	.20	.10	.06
59	Larry Hisle	.20	.10	.06
60	Jerry Reuss	.30	.15	.09
61	Ron LeFlore	.30	.15	.09
62	Johnny Oates	.15	.08	.05
63	Bobby Darwin	.15	.08	.05
64	Jerry Koosman	.30	.15	.09
65	Chris Chambliss	.30	.15	.09
66	Father & Son (Buddy Bell, Gus Bell)	.50	.25	.15
67	Father & Son (Bob Boone, Ray Boone)	.40	.20	.12
68	Father & Son (Joe Coleman, Joe Coleman, Jr.)	.20	.10	.06
69	Father & Son (Jim Hegan, Mike Hegan)	.20	.10	.06
70	Father & Son (Roy Smalley, Roy Smalley, Jr.)	.25	.13	.08
71	Steve Rogers	.20	.10	.06
72	Hal McRae	.25	.13	.08
73	Orioles Team (Earl Weaver)	.80	.40	.25
74	Oscar Gamble	.20	.10	.06
75	Larry Dierker	.20	.10	.06
76	Willie Crawford	.15	.08	.05
77	Pedro Borbon	.15	.08	.05
78	Cecil Cooper	1.00	.50	.30
79	Jerry Morales	.15	.08	.05
80	Jim Kaat	.90	.45	.25
81	Darrell Evans	.50	.25	.15
82	Von Joshua	.15	.08	.05
83	Jim Spencer	.15	.08	.05
84	Brent Strom	.15	.08	.05
85	Mickey Rivers	.25	.13	.08
86	Mike Tyson	.15	.08	.05
87	Tom Burgmeier	.15	.08	.05
88	Duffy Dyer	.15	.08	.05
89	Vern Ruhle	.15	.08	.05
90	Sal Bando	.30	.15	.09
91	Tom Hutton	.15	.08	.05
92	Eduardo Rodriguez	.15	.08	.05
93	Mike Phillips	.15	.08	.05
94	Jim Dwyer	.30	.15	.09
95	Brooks Robinson	2.75	1.50	.80
96	Doug Bird	.15	.08	.05
97	Wilbur Howard	.15	.08	.05
98	*Dennis Eckersley*	10.00	5.00	3.00
99	Lee Lacy	.20	.10	.06
100	Jim Hunter	2.00	1.00	.60
101	Pete LaCock	.15	.08	.05
102	Jim Willoughby	.15	.08	.05
103	Biff Pocoroba	.15	.08	.05
104	Reds Team (Sparky Anderson)	.90	.45	.25
105	Gary Lavelle	.15	.08	.05
106	Tom Grieve	.15	.08	.05
107	Dave Roberts	.15	.08	.05
108	Don Kirkwood	.15	.08	.05
109	Larry Lintz	.15	.08	.05
110	Carlos May	.20	.10	.06
111	Danny Thompson	.20	.10	.06
112	*Kent Tekulve*	.80	.40	.25
113	Gary Sutherland	.15	.08	.05
114	Jay Johnstone	.25	.13	.08
115	Ken Holtzman	.25	.13	.08
116	Charlie Moore	.15	.08	.05
117	Mike Jorgensen	.15	.08	.05
118	Red Sox Team (Darrell Johnson)	.90	.45	.25
119	Checklist 1-132	1.25	.60	.40

#	Player	NR MT	EX	VG
120	Rusty Staub	.35	.20	.11
121	Tony Solaita	.15	.08	.05
122	Mike Cosgrove	.15	.08	.05
123	Walt Williams	.20	.10	.06
124	Doug Rau	.15	.08	.05
125	Don Baylor	.50	.25	.15
126	Tom Dettore	.15	.08	.05
127	Larvell Blanks	.15	.08	.05
128	Ken Griffey	.35	.20	.11
129	Andy Etchebarren	.15	.08	.05
130	Luis Tiant	.40	.20	.12
131	Bill Stein	.25	.13	.08
132	Don Hood	.15	.08	.05
133	Gary Matthews	.25	.13	.08
134	Mike Ivie	.15	.08	.05
135	Bake McBride	.20	.10	.06
136	Dave Goltz	.20	.10	.06
137	Bill Robinson	.15	.08	.05
138	Lerrin LaGrow	.15	.08	.05
139	Gorman Thomas	.35	.20	.11
140	Vida Blue	.40	.20	.12
141	*Larry Parrish*	.80	.40	.25
142	Dick Drago	.15	.08	.05
143	Jerry Grote	.20	.10	.06
144	Al Fitzmorris	.15	.08	.05
145	Larry Bowa	.35	.20	.11
146	George Medich	.20	.10	.06
147	Astros Team (Bill Virdon)	.80	.40	.25
148	Stan Thomas	.15	.08	.05
149	Tommy Davis	.30	.15	.09
150	Steve Garvey	4.50	2.25	1.25
151	Bill Bonham	.15	.08	.05
152	Leroy Stanton	.15	.08	.05
153	Buzz Capra	.15	.08	.05
154	Bucky Dent	.30	.15	.09
155	Jack Billingham	.15	.08	.05
156	Rico Carty	.25	.13	.08
157	Mike Caldwell	.15	.08	.05
158	Ken Reitz	.15	.08	.05
159	Jerry Terrell	.15	.08	.05
160	Dave Winfield	6.00	3.00	1.75
161	Bruce Kison	.15	.08	.05
162	Jack Pierce	.15	.08	.05
163	Jim Slaton	.15	.08	.05
164	Pepe Mangual	.15	.08	.05
165	Gene Tenace	.20	.10	.06
166	Skip Lockwood	.15	.08	.05
167	Freddie Patek	.15	.08	.05
168	Tom Hilgendorf	.15	.08	.05
169	Graig Nettles	1.00	.50	.30
170	Rick Wise	.20	.10	.06
171	Greg Gross	.15	.08	.05
172	Rangers Team (Frank Lucchesi)	.80	.40	.25
173	Steve Swisher	.15	.08	.05
174	Charlie Hough	.25	.13	.08
175	Ken Singleton	.30	.15	.09
176	Dick Lange	.15	.08	.05
177	Marty Perez	.15	.08	.05
178	Tom Buskey	.15	.08	.05
179	George Foster	1.00	.50	.30
180	Rich Gossage	1.25	.60	.40
181	Willie Montanez	.20	.10	.06
182	Harry Rasmussen	.15	.08	.05
183	Steve Braun	.15	.08	.05
184	Bill Greif	.15	.08	.05
185	Dave Parker	3.75	1.75	1.00
186	Tom Walker	.15	.08	.05
187	Pedro Garcia	.15	.08	.05
188	Fred Scherman	.15	.08	.05
189	Claudell Washington	.40	.20	.12
190	Jon Matlack	.25	.13	.08
191	N.L. Batting Leaders (Bill Madlock, Manny Sanguillen, Ted Simmons)	.60	.30	.20
192	A.L. Batting Leaders (Rod Carew, Fred Lynn, Thurman Munson)	1.50	.70	.45
193	N.L. Home Run Leaders (Dave Kingman, Greg Luzinski, Mike Schmidt)	1.25	.60	.40
194	A.L. Home Run Leaders (Reggie Jackson, John Mayberry, George Scott)	1.25	.60	.40
195	N.L. Runs Batted In Ldrs. (Johnny Bench, Greg Luzinski, Tony Perez)	1.25	.60	.40
196	A.L. Runs Batted In Ldrs. (Fred Lynn, John Mayberry, George Scott)	.60	.30	.20
197	N.L. Stolen Base Leaders (Lou Brock, Dave Lopes, Joe Morgan)	.90	.45	.25
198	A.L. Stolen Base Leaders (Amos Otis, Mickey Rivers, Claudell Washington)	.50	.25	.15
199	N.L. Victory Leaders (Randy Jones, Andy Messersmith, Tom Seaver)	.80	.40	.25
200	A.L. Victory Leaders (Vida Blue, Jim Hunter, Jim Palmer)	.90	.45	.25
201	N.L. Earned Run Avg. Ldrs. (Randy Jones, Andy Messersmith, Tom Seaver)	.80	.40	.25
202	A.L. Earned Run Avg. Ldrs. (Dennis Eckersley, Jim Hunter, Jim Palmer)	.90	.45	.25
203	N.L. Strikeout Leaders (Andy Messersmith, John Montefusco, Tom Seaver)	.80	.40	.25
204	A.L. Strikeout Leaders (Bert Blyleven, Gaylord Perry, Frank Tanana)	.70	.35	.20
205	Major League Leading Firemen (Rich Gossage, Al Hrabosky)	.50	.25	.15
206	Manny Trillo	.20	.10	.06
207	Andy Hassler	.15	.08	.05
208	Mike Lum	.15	.08	.05
209	Alan Ashby	.35	.20	.11
210	Lee May	.25	.13	.08
211	Clay Carroll	.20	.10	.06
212	Pat Kelly	.15	.08	.05
213	Dave Heaverlo	.15	.08	.05
214	Eric Soderholm	.15	.08	.05
215	Reggie Smith	.25	.13	.08
216	Expos Team (Karl Kuehl)	.80	.40	.25
217	Dave Freisleben	.15	.08	.05
218	John Knox	.15	.08	.05

#	Player	NR MT	EX	VG
219	Tom Murphy	.15	.08	.05
220	Manny Sanguillen	.20	.10	.06
221	Jim Todd	.15	.08	.05
222	Wayne Garrett	.15	.08	.05
223	Ollie Brown	.15	.08	.05
224	Jim York	.15	.08	.05
225	Roy White	.25	.13	.08
226	Jim Sundberg	.25	.13	.08
227	Oscar Zamora	.15	.08	.05
228	John Hale	.15	.08	.05
229	*Jerry Remy*	.30	.15	.09
230	Carl Yastrzemski	7.00	3.50	2.00
231	Tom House	.15	.08	.05
232	Frank Duffy	.15	.08	.05
233	Grant Jackson	.15	.08	.05
234	Mike Sadek	.15	.08	.05
235	Bert Blyleven	1.00	.50	.30
236	Royals Team (Whitey Herzog)	.80	.40	.25
237	Dave Hamilton	.15	.08	.05
238	Larry Biittner	.15	.08	.05
239	John Curtis	.15	.08	.05
240	Pete Rose	15.00	7.50	4.50
241	Hector Torres	.15	.08	.05
242	Dan Meyer	.15	.08	.05
243	Jim Rooker	.15	.08	.05
244	Bill Sharp	.15	.08	.05
245	Felix Millan	.15	.08	.05
246	Cesar Tovar	.15	.08	.05
247	Terry Harmon	.15	.08	.05
248	Dick Tidrow	.20	.10	.06
249	Cliff Johnson	.20	.10	.06
250	Fergie Jenkins	1.00	.50	.30
251	Rick Monday	.30	.15	.09
252	Tim Nordbrook	.15	.08	.05
253	Bill Buckner	.50	.25	.15
254	Rudy Meoli	.15	.08	.05
255	Fritz Peterson	.15	.08	.05
256	Rowland Office	.15	.08	.05
257	Ross Grimsley	.20	.10	.06
258	Nyls Nyman	.15	.08	.05
259	Darrel Chaney	.15	.08	.05
260	Steve Busby	.20	.10	.06
261	Gary Thomasson	.15	.08	.05
262	Checklist 133-264	1.50	.70	.45
263	*Lyman Bostock*	.80	.40	.25
264	Steve Renko	.15	.08	.05
265	Willie Davis	.30	.15	.09
266	Alan Foster	.15	.08	.05
267	Aurelio Rodriguez	.20	.10	.06
268	Del Unser	.15	.08	.05
269	Rick Austin	.15	.08	.05
270	Willie Stargell	3.00	1.50	.90
271	Jim Lonborg	.20	.10	.06
272	Rick Dempsey	.25	.13	.08
273	Joe Niekro	.30	.15	.09
274	Tommy Harper	.20	.10	.06
275	*Rick Manning*	.40	.20	.12
276	Mickey Scott	.15	.08	.05
277	Cubs Team (Jim Marshall)	.80	.40	.25
278	Bernie Carbo	.15	.08	.05
279	Roy Howell	.15	.08	.05
280	Burt Hooton	.20	.10	.06
281	Dave May	.15	.08	.05
282	Dan Osborn	.15	.08	.05
283	Merv Rettenmund	.15	.08	.05
284	Steve Ontiveros	.15	.08	.05
285	Mike Cuellar	.25	.13	.08
286	Jim Wohlford	.15	.08	.05
287	Pete Mackanin	.15	.08	.05
288	Bill Campbell	.15	.08	.05
289	Enzo Hernandez	.15	.08	.05
290	Ted Simmons	.60	.30	.20
291	Ken Sanders	.15	.08	.05
292	Leon Roberts	.15	.08	.05
293	Bill Castro	.15	.08	.05
294	Ed Kirkpatrick	.15	.08	.05
295	Dave Cash	.15	.08	.05
296	Pat Dobson	.20	.10	.06
297	Roger Metzger	.15	.08	.05
298	Dick Bosman	.15	.08	.05
299	Champ Summers	.15	.08	.05
300	Johnny Bench	6.00	3.00	1.75
301	Jackie Brown	.15	.08	.05
302	Rick Miller	.15	.08	.05
303	Steve Foucault	.15	.08	.05
304	Angels Team (Dick Williams)	.80	.40	.25
305	Andy Messersmith	.25	.13	.08
306	Rod Gilbreath	.15	.08	.05
307	Al Bumbry	.20	.10	.06
308	Jim Barr	.15	.08	.05
309	Bill Melton	.20	.10	.06
310	Randy Jones	.30	.15	.09
311	Cookie Rojas	.15	.08	.05
312	Don Carrithers	.15	.08	.05
313	*Dan Ford*	.25	.13	.08
314	Ed Kranepool	.25	.13	.08
315	Al Hrabosky	.20	.10	.06
316	Robin Yount	35.00	17.50	10.50
317	*John Candelaria*	1.75	.90	.50
318	Bob Boone	.30	.15	.09
319	Larry Gura	.20	.10	.06
320	Willie Horton	.25	.13	.08
321	Jose Cruz	.35	.20	.11
322	Glenn Abbott	.15	.08	.05
323	Rob Sperring	.15	.08	.05
324	Jim Bibby	.15	.08	.05
325	Tony Perez	.80	.40	.25
326	Dick Pole	.15	.08	.05
327	Dave Moates	.15	.08	.05
328	Carl Morton	.15	.08	.05
329	Joe Ferguson	.15	.08	.05
330	Nolan Ryan	25.00	12.50	7.50
331	Padres Team (John McNamara)	.80	.40	.25
332	Charlie Williams	.15	.08	.05
333	Bob Coluccio	.15	.08	.05
334	Dennis Leonard	.25	.13	.08
335	Bob Grich	.25	.13	.08
336	Vic Albury	.15	.08	.05
337	Bud Harrelson	.20	.10	.06
338	Bob Bailey	.15	.08	.05
339	John Denny	.25	.13	.08
340	Jim Rice	8.00	4.00	2.50

#	Player	NR MT	EX	VG
341	All Time All-Stars (Lou Gehrig)	3.00	1.50	.90
342	All Time All-Stars (Rogers Hornsby)	1.25	.60	.40
343	All Time All-Stars (Pie Traynor)	.80	.40	.25
344	All Time All-Stars (Honus Wagner)	1.25	.60	.40
345	All Time All-Stars (Babe Ruth)	5.00	2.50	1.50
346	All Time All-Stars (Ty Cobb)	3.00	1.50	.90
347	All Time All-Stars (Ted Williams)	3.00	1.50	.90
348	All Time All-Stars (Mickey Cochrane)	.80	.40	.25
349	All Time All-Stars (Walter Johnson)	1.25	.60	.40
350	All Time All-Stars (Lefty Grove)	1.00	.50	.30
351	Randy Hundley	.15	.08	.05
352	Dave Giusti	.15	.08	.05
353	*Sixto Lezcano*	.30	.15	.09
354	Ron Blomberg	.20	.10	.06
355	Steve Carlton	5.00	2.50	1.50
356	Ted Martinez	.15	.08	.05
357	Ken Forsch	.20	.10	.06
358	Buddy Bell	.50	.25	.15
359	Rick Reuschel	.30	.15	.09
360	Jeff Burroughs	.20	.10	.06
361	Tigers Team (Ralph Houk)	1.00	.50	.30
362	Will McEnaney	.15	.08	.05
363	*Dave Collins*	.40	.20	.12
364	Elias Sosa	.15	.08	.05
365	Carlton Fisk	3.00	1.50	.90
366	Bobby Valentine	.30	.15	.09
367	Bruce Miller	.15	.08	.05
368	Wilbur Wood	.25	.13	.08
369	Frank White	.30	.15	.09
370	Ron Cey	.40	.20	.12
371	Ellie Hendricks	.15	.08	.05
372	Rick Baldwin	.15	.08	.05
373	Johnny Briggs	.15	.08	.05
374	Dan Warthen	.15	.08	.05
375	Ron Fairly	.25	.13	.08
376	Rich Hebner	.20	.10	.06
377	Mike Hegan	.15	.08	.05
378	Steve Stone	.25	.13	.08
379	Ken Boswell	.15	.08	.05
380	Bobby Bonds	.35	.20	.11
381	Denny Doyle	.15	.08	.05
382	Matt Alexander	.15	.08	.05
383	John Ellis	.15	.08	.05
384	Phillies Team (Danny Ozark)	.80	.40	.25
385	Mickey Lolich	.40	.20	.12
386	Ed Goodson	.15	.08	.05
387	Mike Miley	.15	.08	.05
388	Stan Perzanowski	.15	.08	.05
389	Glenn Adams	.15	.08	.05
390	Don Gullett	.20	.10	.06
391	Jerry Hairston	.15	.08	.05
392	Checklist 265-396	1.50	.70	.45
393	Paul Mitchell	.15	.08	.05
394	Fran Healy	.15	.08	.05
395	Jim Wynn	.30	.15	.09
396	Bill Lee	.20	.10	.06
397	Tim Foli	.15	.08	.05
398	Dave Tomlin	.15	.08	.05
399	Luis Melendez	.15	.08	.05
400	Rod Carew	5.00	2.50	1.50
401	Ken Brett	.20	.10	.06
402	Don Money	.20	.10	.06
403	Geoff Zahn	.20	.10	.06
404	Enos Cabell	.20	.10	.06
405	Rollie Fingers	1.25	.60	.40
406	Ed Herrmann	.20	.10	.06
407	Tom Underwood	.15	.08	.05
408	Charlie Spikes	.15	.08	.05
409	Dave Lemanczyk	.15	.08	.05
410	Ralph Garr	.20	.10	.06
411	Bill Singer	.20	.10	.06
412	Toby Harrah	.25	.13	.08
413	Pete Varney	.15	.08	.05
414	Wayne Garland	.15	.08	.05
415	Vada Pinson	.50	.25	.15
416	Tommy John	1.25	.60	.40
417	Gene Clines	.15	.08	.05
418	Jose Morales	.15	.08	.05
419	Reggie Cleveland	.15	.08	.05
420	Joe Morgan	4.00	2.00	1.25
421	A's Team	.80	.40	.25
422	Johnny Grubb	.15	.08	.05
423	Ed Halicki	.15	.08	.05
424	Phil Roof	.15	.08	.05
425	Rennie Stennett	.15	.08	.05
426	Bob Forsch	.25	.13	.08
427	Kurt Bevacqua	.15	.08	.05
428	Jim Crawford	.15	.08	.05
429	Fred Stanley	.20	.10	.06
430	Jose Cardenal	.20	.10	.06
431	Dick Ruthven	.15	.08	.05
432	Tom Veryzer	.15	.08	.05
433	Rick Waits	.15	.08	.05
434	Morris Nettles	.15	.08	.05
435	Phil Niekro	2.00	1.00	.60
436	Bill Fahey	.15	.08	.05
437	Terry Forster	.25	.13	.08
438	Doug DeCinces	.50	.25	.15
439	Rick Rhoden	.60	.30	.20
440	John Mayberry	.25	.13	.08
441	Gary Carter	10.00	5.00	3.00
442	Hank Webb	.15	.08	.05
443	Giants Team	.80	.40	.25
444	Gary Nolan	.15	.08	.05
445	Rico Petrocelli	.25	.13	.08
446	Larry Haney	.15	.08	.05
447	Gene Locklear	.15	.08	.05
448	Tom Johnson	.15	.08	.05
449	Bob Robertson	.15	.08	.05
450	Jim Palmer	4.00	2.00	1.25
451	Buddy Bradford	.15	.08	.05
452	Tom Hausman	.15	.08	.05
453	Lou Piniella	.60	.30	.20

		NR MT	EX	VG
454	Tom Griffin	.15	.08	.05
455	Dick Allen	.50	.25	.15
456	Joe Coleman	.20	.10	.06
457	Ed Crosby	.15	.08	.05
458	Earl Williams	.15	.08	.05
459	Jim Brewer	.15	.08	.05
460	Cesar Cedeno	.30	.15	.09
461	NL & AL Championships	.80	.40	.25
462	1975 World Series	.80	.40	.25
463	Steve Hargan	.15	.08	.05
464	Ken Henderson	.15	.08	.05
465	Mike Marshall	.30	.15	.09
466	Bob Stinson	.15	.08	.05
467	Woodie Fryman	.20	.10	.06
468	Jesus Alou	.20	.10	.06
469	Rawly Eastwick	.15	.08	.05
470	Bobby Murcer	.35	.20	.11
471	Jim Burton	.15	.08	.05
472	Bob Davis	.15	.08	.05
473	Paul Blair	.20	.10	.06
474	Ray Corbin	.15	.08	.05
475	Joe Rudi	.30	.15	.09
476	Bob Moose	.15	.08	.05
477	Indians Team (Frank Robinson)	.80	.40	.25
478	Lynn McGlothen	.15	.08	.05
479	Bobby Mitchell	.15	.08	.05
480	Mike Schmidt	25.00	12.50	7.50
481	Rudy May	.20	.10	.06
482	Tim Hosley	.15	.08	.05
483	Mickey Stanley	.20	.10	.06
484	Eric Raich	.15	.08	.05
485	Mike Hargrove	.20	.10	.06
486	Bruce Dal Canton	.15	.08	.05
487	Leron Lee	.15	.08	.05
488	Claude Osteen	.20	.10	.06
489	Skip Jutze	.15	.08	.05
490	Frank Tanana	.30	.15	.09
491	Terry Crowley	.15	.08	.05
492	Marty Pattin	.15	.08	.05
493	Derrel Thomas	.15	.08	.05
494	Craig Swan	.15	.08	.05
495	Nate Colbert	.15	.08	.05
496	Juan Beniquez	.20	.10	.06
497	Joe McIntosh	.15	.08	.05
498	Glenn Borgmann	.15	.08	.05
499	Mario Guerrero	.15	.08	.05
500	Reggie Jackson	10.00	5.00	3.00
501	Billy Champion	.15	.08	.05
502	Tim McCarver	.50	.25	.15
503	Elliott Maddox	.20	.10	.06
504	Pirates Team (Danny Murtaugh)	.80	.40	.25
505	Mark Belanger	.20	.10	.06
506	George Mitterwald	.15	.08	.05
507	Ray Bare	.15	.08	.05
508	*Duane Kuiper*	.20	.10	.06
509	Bill Hands	.15	.08	.05
510	Amos Otis	.25	.13	.08
511	Jamie Easterly	.15	.08	.05
512	Ellie Rodriguez	.15	.08	.05
513	Bart Johnson	.15	.08	.05
514	Dan Driessen	.30	.15	.09
515	Steve Yeager	.15	.08	.05
516	Wayne Granger	.15	.08	.05
517	John Milner	.15	.08	.05
518	*Doug Flynn*	.20	.10	.06
519	Steve Brye	.15	.08	.05
520	Willie McCovey	2.50	1.25	.70
521	Jim Colborn	.15	.08	.05
522	Ted Sizemore	.15	.08	.05
523	Bob Montgomery	.15	.08	.05
524	Pete Falcone	.15	.08	.05
525	Billy Williams	2.25	1.25	.70
526	Checklist 397-528	1.50	.70	.45
527	Mike Anderson	.15	.08	.05
528	Dock Ellis	.20	.10	.06
529	Deron Johnson	.15	.08	.05
530	Don Sutton	1.50	.70	.45
531	Mets Team (Joe Frazier)	.90	.45	.25
532	Milt May	.15	.08	.05
533	Lee Richard	.15	.08	.05
534	Stan Bahnsen	.15	.08	.05
535	Dave Nelson	.15	.08	.05
536	Mike Thompson	.15	.08	.05
537	Tony Muser	.15	.08	.05
538	Pat Darcy	.15	.08	.05
539	John Balaz	.15	.08	.05
540	Bill Freehan	.25	.13	.08
541	Steve Mingori	.15	.08	.05
542	Keith Hernandez	6.00	3.00	1.75
543	Wayne Twitchell	.15	.08	.05
544	Pepe Frias	.15	.08	.05
545	Sparky Lyle	.35	.20	.11
546	Dave Rosello	.15	.08	.05
547	Roric Harrison	.15	.08	.05
548	Manny Mota	.25	.13	.08
549	Randy Tate	.15	.08	.05
550	Hank Aaron	15.00	7.50	4.50
551	Jerry DaVanon	.15	.08	.05
552	Terry Humphrey	.15	.08	.05
553	Randy Moffitt	.15	.08	.05
554	Ray Fosse	.15	.08	.05
555	Dyar Miller	.15	.08	.05
556	Twins Team (Gene Mauch)	.80	.40	.25
557	Dan Spillner	.15	.08	.05
558	Clarence Gaston	.15	.08	.05
559	Clyde Wright	.15	.08	.05
560	Jorge Orta	.15	.08	.05
561	Tom Carroll	.15	.08	.05
562	Adrian Garrett	.15	.08	.05
563	Larry Demery	.15	.08	.05
564	Bubble Gum Blowing Champ (Kurt Bevacqua)	.30	.15	.09
565	Tug McGraw	.35	.20	.11
566	Ken McMullen	.15	.08	.05
567	George Stone	.15	.08	.05
568	Rob Andrews	.15	.08	.05
569	Nelson Briles	.15	.08	.05
570	George Hendrick	.20	.10	.06
571	Don DeMola	.15	.08	.05
572	Rich Coggins	.20	.10	.06
573	Bill Travers	.15	.08	.05
574	Don Kessinger	.20	.10	.06

		NR MT	EX	VG
575	Dwight Evans	1.00	.50	.30
576	Maximino Leon	.15	.08	.05
577	Marc Hill	.15	.08	.05
578	Ted Kubiak	.15	.08	.05
579	Clay Kirby	.15	.08	.05
580	Bert Campaneris	.30	.15	.09
581	Cardinals Team (Red Schoendienst)	.80	.40	.25
582	Mike Kekich	.15	.08	.05
583	Tommy Helms	.15	.08	.05
584	Stan Wall	.15	.08	.05
585	Joe Torre	.50	.25	.15
586	Ron Schueler	.15	.08	.05
587	Leo Cardenas	.15	.08	.05
588	Kevin Kobel	.15	.08	.05
589	Rookie Pitchers (Santo Alcala, *Mike Flanagan*, Joe Pactwa, Pablo Torrealba)	1.00	.50	.30
590	Rookie Outfielders (Henry Cruz, *Chet Lemon, Ellis Valentine*, Terry Whitfield)	1.00	.50	.30
591	Rookie Pitchers (Steve Grilli, Craig Mitchell, Jose Sosa, George Throop)	.15	.08	.05
592	Rookie Infielders (Dave McKay, *Willie Randolph, Jerry Royster*, Roy Staiger)	5.00	2.50	1.50
593	Rookie Pitchers (Larry Anderson, Ken Crosby, Mark Littell, *Butch Metzger)*	.25	.13	.08
594	Rookie Catchers & Outfielders (Andy Merchant, Ed Ott, Royle Stillman, Jerry White)	.15	.08	.05
595	Rookie Pitchers (Steve Barr, Art DeFilippis, Randy Lerch, Sid Monge)	.15	.08	.05
596	Rookie Infielders (Lamar Johnson, *Johnny LeMaster*, Jerry Manuel, *Craig Reynolds)*	.35	.20	.11
597	Rookie Pitchers *(Don Aase*, Jack Kucek, Frank LaCorte, Mike Pazik)	.50	.25	.15
598	Rookie Outfielders (Hector Cruz, *Jamie Quirk*, Jerry Turner, Joe Wallis)	.20	.10	.06
599	Rookie Pitchers (Rob Dressler, *Ron Guidry, Bob McClure*, Pat Zachry)	10.00	5.00	3.00
600	Tom Seaver	7.00	3.50	2.00
601	Ken Rudolph	.15	.08	.05
602	Doug Konieczny	.15	.08	.05
603	Jim Holt	.15	.08	.05
604	Joe Lovitto	.15	.08	.05
605	Al Downing	.20	.10	.06
606	Brewers Team (Alex Grammas)	.80	.40	.25
607	Rich Hinton	.15	.08	.05
608	Vic Correll	.15	.08	.05
609	Fred Norman	.15	.08	.05
610	Greg Luzinski	.40	.20	.12
611	Rich Folkers	.15	.08	.05
612	Joe Lahoud	.15	.08	.05
613	Tim Johnson	.15	.08	.05
614	Fernando Arroyo	.15	.08	.05
615	Mike Cubbage	.15	.08	.05
616	Buck Martinez	.15	.08	.05
617	Darold Knowles	.15	.08	.05
618	Jack Brohamer	.15	.08	.05
619	Bill Butler	.15	.08	.05
620	Al Oliver	.70	.35	.20
621	Tom Hall	.15	.08	.05
622	Rick Auerbach	.15	.08	.05
623	Bob Allietta	.15	.08	.05
624	Tony Taylor	.15	.08	.05
625	J.R. Richard	.25	.13	.08
626	Bob Sheldon	.15	.08	.05
627	Bill Plummer	.15	.08	.05
628	John D'Acquisto	.15	.08	.05
629	Sandy Alomar	.20	.10	.06
630	Chris Speier	.20	.10	.06
631	Braves Team (Dave Bristol)	.80	.40	.25
632	Rogelio Moret	.15	.08	.05
633	*John Stearns*	.30	.15	.09
634	Larry Christenson	.15	.08	.05
635	Jim Fregosi	.25	.13	.08
636	Joe Decker	.15	.08	.05
637	Bruce Bochte	.20	.10	.06
638	Doyle Alexander	.30	.15	.09
639	Fred Kendall	.15	.08	.05
640	Bill Madlock	1.00	.50	.30
641	Tom Paciorek	.20	.10	.06
642	Dennis Blair	.15	.08	.05
643	Checklist 529-660	1.50	.70	.45
644	Tom Bradley	.15	.08	.05
645	Darrell Porter	.20	.10	.06
646	John Lowenstein	.15	.08	.05
648	Al Cowens	.20	.10	.06
649	Dave Roberts	.15	.08	.05
650	Thurman Munson	6.00	3.00	1.75
651	John Odom	.20	.10	.06
652	Ed Armbrister	.15	.08	.05
653	*Mike Norris*	.30	.15	.09
654	Doug Griffin	.15	.08	.05
655	Mike Vail	.15	.08	.05
656	White Sox Team (Chuck Tanner)	.80	.40	.25
657	*Roy Smalley*	.40	.20	.12
658	Jerry Johnson	.15	.08	.05
659	Ben Oglivie	.25	.13	.08
660	Dave Lopes	.60	.13	.08

1976 Topps Traded

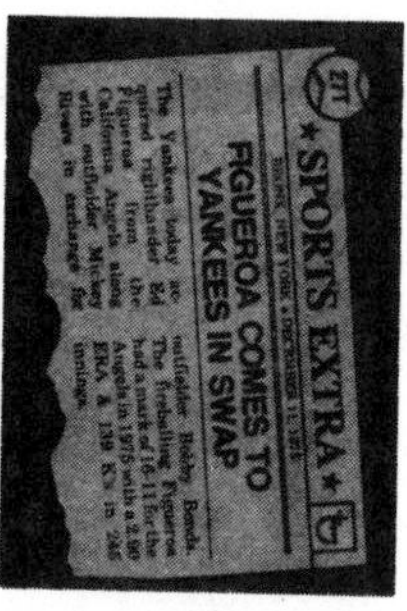

Similar to the Topps Traded set of 1974, the 2-1/2" by 3-1/2" cards feature photos of players traded after the printing deadline. The style of the cards is essentially the same as the regular issue but with a large "Sports Extra" headline announcing the trade and its date. The backs continue in newspaper style to detail the specifics of the trade. There are 43 player cards and one checklist in the set. Numbers remain the same as the player's regular card, with the addition of a "T" suffix.

	NR MT	EX	VG
Complete Set:	8.00	4.00	2.50
Common Player:	.15	.08	.05

		NR MT	EX	VG
27T	Ed Figueroa	.20	.10	.06
28T	Dusty Baker	.35	.20	.11
44T	Doug Rader	.15	.08	.05
58T	Ron Reed	.20	.10	.06
74T	Oscar Gamble	.25	.13	.08
80T	Jim Kaat	.60	.30	.20
83T	Jim Spencer	.15	.08	.05
85T	Mickey Rivers	.30	.15	.09
99T	Lee Lacy	.20	.10	.06
120T	Rusty Staub	.50	.25	.15
127T	Larvell Blanks	.15	.08	.05
146T	George Medich	.15	.08	.05
158T	Ken Reitz	.15	.08	.05
208T	Mike Lum	.15	.08	.05
211T	Clay Carroll	.20	.10	.06
231T	Tom House	.15	.08	.05
250T	Fergie Jenkins	.70	.35	.20
259T	Darrel Chaney	.15	.08	.05
292T	Leon Roberts	.15	.08	.05
296T	Pat Dobson	.20	.10	.06
309T	Bill Melton	.20	.10	.06
338T	Bob Bailey	.15	.08	.05
380T	Bobby Bonds	.35	.20	.11
383T	John Ellis	.15	.08	.05
385T	Mickey Lolich	.50	.25	.15
401T	Ken Brett	.20	.10	.06
410T	Ralph Garr	.20	.10	.06
411T	Bill Singer	.20	.10	.06
428T	Jim Crawford	.15	.08	.05
434T	Morris Nettles	.15	.08	.05
464T	Ken Henderson	.15	.08	.05
497T	Joe McIntosh	.15	.08	.05
524T	Pete Falcone	.15	.08	.05
527T	Mike Anderson	.15	.08	.05
528T	Dock Ellis	.20	.10	.06
532T	Milt May	.15	.08	.05
554T	Ray Fosse	.15	.08	.05
579T	Clay Kirby	.15	.08	.05
583T	Tommy Helms	.15	.08	.05
592T	Willie Randolph	1.00	.50	.30
618T	Jack Brohamer	.15	.08	.05
632T	Rogelio Moret	.15	.08	.05
649T	Dave Roberts	.15	.08	.05
---	Traded Checklist	.80	.40	.25

1977 Topps

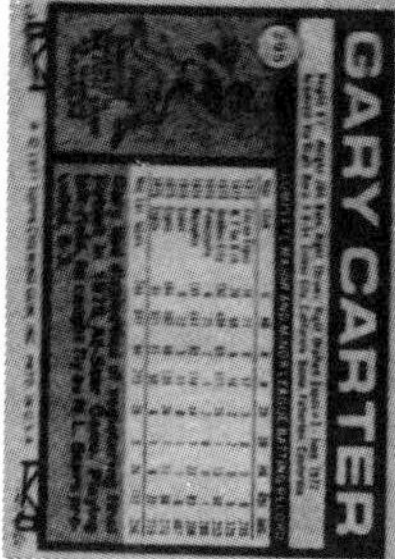

The 1977 Topps Set is a 660-card effort featuring front designs dominated by a color photograph on which there is a facsimile autograph. Above the picture are the player's name, team and position. The backs of the 2-1/2" by 3-1/2" cards include personal and career statistics along with newspaper-style highlights and a cartoon. Specialty cards include statistical leaders, record performances, a new "Turn Back The Clock" feature which highlighted great past moments and a "Big League Brothers" feature.

	NR MT	EX	VG
Complete Set:	350.00	175.00	105.00
Common Player:	.15	.08	.05

No.	Card	NR MT	EX	VG
1	Batting Leaders (George Brett, Bill Madlock)	2.50	.70	.45
2	Home Run Leaders (Graig Nettles, Mike Schmidt)	1.25	.60	.40
3	Runs Batted In Leaders (George Foster, Lee May)	.50	.25	.15
4	Stolen Base Leaders (Dave Lopes, Bill North)	.30	.15	.09
5	Victory Leaders (Randy Jones, Jim Palmer)	.80	.40	.25
6	Strikeout Leaders (Nolan Ryan, Tom Seaver)	3.00	1.50	.90
7	Earned Run Avg. Ldrs. (John Denny, Mark Fidrych)	.30	.15	.09
8	Leading Firemen (Bill Campbell, Rawly Eastwick)	.30	.15	.09
9	Doug Rader	.15	.08	.05
10	Reggie Jackson	8.00	4.00	2.50
11	Rob Dressler	.15	.08	.05
12	Larry Haney	.15	.08	.05
13	Luis Gomez	.15	.08	.05
14	Tommy Smith	.15	.08	.05
15	Don Gullett	.20	.10	.06
16	Bob Jones	.15	.08	.05
17	Steve Stone	.25	.13	.08
18	Indians Team (Frank Robinson)	.80	.40	.25
19	John D'Acquisto	.15	.08	.05
20	Graig Nettles	.90	.45	.25
21	Ken Forsch	.20	.10	.06
22	Bill Freehan	.25	.13	.08
23	Dan Driessen	.25	.13	.08
24	Carl Morton	.15	.08	.05
25	Dwight Evans	2.50	1.25	.70
26	Ray Sadecki	.15	.08	.05
27	Bill Buckner	.35	.20	.11
28	Woodie Fryman	.20	.10	.06
29	Bucky Dent	.25	.13	.08
30	Greg Luzinski	.40	.20	.12
31	Jim Todd	.15	.08	.05
32	Checklist 1-132	1.25	.60	.40
33	Wayne Garland	.15	.08	.05
34	Angels Team (Norm Sherry)	.70	.35	.20
35	Rennie Stennett	.15	.08	.05
36	John Ellis	.15	.08	.05
37	Steve Hargan	.15	.08	.05
38	Craig Kusick	.15	.08	.05
39	Tom Griffin	.15	.08	.05
40	Bobby Murcer	.30	.15	.09
41	Jim Kern	.15	.08	.05
42	Jose Cruz	.30	.15	.09
43	Ray Bare	.15	.08	.05
44	Bud Harrelson	.20	.10	.06
45	Rawly Eastwick	.15	.08	.05
46	Buck Martinez	.15	.08	.05
47	Lynn McGlothen	.15	.08	.05
48	Tom Paciorek	.15	.08	.05
49	Grant Jackson	.15	.08	.05
50	Ron Cey	.35	.20	.11
51	Brewers Team (Alex Grammas)	.70	.35	.20
52	Ellis Valentine	.20	.10	.06
53	Paul Mitchell	.15	.08	.05
54	Sandy Alomar	.20	.10	.06
55	Jeff Burroughs	.25	.13	.08
56	Rudy May	.20	.10	.06
57	Marc Hill	.15	.08	.05
58	Chet Lemon	.30	.15	.09
59	Larry Christenson	.15	.08	.05
60	Jim Rice	4.50	2.25	1.25
61	Manny Sanguillen	.15	.08	.05
62	Eric Raich	.15	.08	.05
63	Tito Fuentes	.15	.08	.05
64	Larry Biittner	.15	.08	.05
65	Skip Lockwood	.15	.08	.05
66	Roy Smalley	.20	.10	.06
67	*Joaquin Andujar*	.60	.30	.20
68	Bruce Bochte	.20	.10	.06
69	Jim Crawford	.15	.08	.05
70	Johnny Bench	6.00	3.00	1.75
71	Dock Ellis	.20	.10	.06
72	Mike Anderson	.15	.08	.05
73	Charlie Williams	.15	.08	.05
74	A's Team (Jack McKeon)	.70	.35	.20
75	Dennis Leonard	.20	.10	.06
76	Tim Foli	.15	.08	.05
77	Dyar Miller	.15	.08	.05
78	Bob Davis	.15	.08	.05
79	Don Money	.15	.08	.05
80	Andy Messersmith	.25	.13	.08
81	Juan Beniquez	.20	.10	.06
82	Jim Rooker	.15	.08	.05
83	Kevin Bell	.15	.08	.05
84	Ollie Brown	.15	.08	.05
85	Duane Kuiper	.15	.08	.05
86	Pat Zachry	.15	.08	.05
87	Glenn Borgmann	.15	.08	.05
88	Stan Wall	.15	.08	.05
89	*Butch Hobson*	.20	.10	.06
90	Cesar Cedeno	.30	.15	.09
91	John Verhoeven	.15	.08	.05
92	Dave Rosello	.15	.08	.05
93	Tom Poquette	.15	.08	.05
94	Craig Swan	.15	.08	.05
95	Keith Hernandez	3.00	1.50	.90
96	Lou Piniella	.40	.20	.12
97	Dave Heaverlo	.15	.08	.05
98	Milt May	.15	.08	.05
99	Tom Hausman	.15	.08	.05
100	Joe Morgan	2.25	1.25	.70
101	Dick Bosman	.15	.08	.05
102	Jose Morales	.15	.08	.05
103	Mike Bacsik	.15	.08	.05
104	*Omar Moreno*	.25	.13	.08
105	Steve Yeager	.15	.08	.05
106	Mike Flanagan	.35	.20	.11
107	Bill Melton	.20	.10	.06
108	Alan Foster	.15	.08	.05
109	Jorge Orta	.15	.08	.05
110	Steve Carlton	4.50	2.25	1.25
111	Rico Petrocelli	.25	.13	.08
112	Bill Greif	.15	.08	.05
113	Blue Jays Mgr./Coaches (Roy Hartsfield, Don Leppert, Bob Miller, Jackie Moore, Harry Warner)	.25	.13	.08
114	Bruce Dal Canton	.15	.08	.05
115	Rick Manning	.20	.10	.06
116	Joe Niekro	.30	.15	.09
117	Frank White	.25	.13	.08
118	Rick Jones	.15	.08	.05
119	John Stearns	.20	.10	.06
120	Rod Carew	5.00	2.50	1.50
121	Gary Nolan	.15	.08	.05
122	Ben Oglivie	.20	.10	.06
123	Fred Stanley	.20	.10	.06
124	George Mitterwald	.15	.08	.05
125	Bill Travers	.15	.08	.05
126	Rod Gilbreath	.15	.08	.05
127	Ron Fairly	.25	.13	.08
128	Tommy John	1.25	.60	.40
129	Mike Sadek	.15	.08	.05
130	Al Oliver	.60	.30	.20
131	Orlando Ramirez	.15	.08	.05
132	Chip Lang	.15	.08	.05
133	Ralph Garr	.20	.10	.06
134	Padres Team (John McNamara)	.70	.35	.20
135	Mark Belanger	.20	.10	.06
136	*Jerry Mumphrey*	.40	.20	.12
137	Jeff Terpko	.15	.08	.05
138	Bob Stinson	.15	.08	.05
139	Fred Norman	.15	.08	.05
140	Mike Schmidt	20.00	10.00	6.00
141	Mark Littell	.15	.08	.05
142	Steve Dillard	.15	.08	.05
143	Ed Herrmann	.15	.08	.05
144	*Bruce Sutter*	2.00	1.00	.70
145	Tom Veryzer	.15	.08	.05
146	Dusty Baker	.25	.13	.08
147	Jackie Brown	.15	.08	.05
148	Fran Healy	.20	.10	.06
149	Mike Cubbage	.15	.08	.05
150	Tom Seaver	6.00	3.00	1.75
151	Johnnie LeMaster	.15	.08	.05
152	Gaylord Perry	2.00	1.00	.60
153	Ron Jackson	.15	.08	.05
154	Dave Giusti	.15	.08	.05
155	Joe Rudi	.25	.13	.08
156	Pete Mackanin	.15	.08	.05
157	Ken Brett	.20	.10	.06
158	Ted Kubiak	.15	.08	.05
159	Bernie Carbo	.15	.08	.05
160	Will McEnaney	.15	.08	.05
161	*Garry Templeton*	.80	.40	.25
162	Mike Cuellar	.25	.13	.08
163	Dave Hilton	.15	.08	.05
164	Tug McGraw	.35	.20	.11
165	Jim Wynn	.25	.13	.08
166	Bill Campbell	.15	.08	.05
167	Rich Hebner	.15	.08	.05
168	Charlie Spikes	.15	.08	.05
169	Darold Knowles	.15	.08	.05
170	Thurman Munson	5.00	2.50	1.50
171	Ken Sanders	.15	.08	.05
172	John Milner	.15	.08	.05
173	Chuck Scrivener	.15	.08	.05
174	Nelson Briles	.15	.08	.05
175	*Butch Wynegar*	.40	.20	.12
176	Bob Robertson	.15	.08	.05
177	Bart Johnson	.15	.08	.05
178	Bombo Rivera	.15	.08	.05
179	Paul Hartzell	.15	.08	.05
180	Dave Lopes	.25	.13	.08
181	Ken McMullen	.15	.08	.05
182	Dan Spillner	.15	.08	.05
183	Cardinals Team (Vern Rapp)	.70	.35	.20
184	Bo McLaughlin	.15	.08	.05
185	Sixto Lezcano	.20	.10	.06
186	Doug Flynn	.15	.08	.05
187	Dick Pole	.15	.08	.05
188	Bob Tolan	.20	.10	.06
189	Rick Dempsey	.20	.10	.06
190	Ray Burris	.15	.08	.05
191	Doug Griffin	.15	.08	.05
192	Clarence Gaston	.15	.08	.05
193	Larry Gura	.15	.08	.05
194	Gary Matthews	.25	.13	.08
195	Ed Figueroa	.20	.10	.06
196	Len Randle	.15	.08	.05
197	Ed Ott	.15	.08	.05
198	Wilbur Wood	.20	.10	.06
199	Pepe Frias	.15	.08	.05
200	Frank Tanana	.30	.15	.09
201	Ed Kranepool	.25	.13	.08
202	Tom Johnson	.15	.08	.05
203	Ed Armbrister	.15	.08	.05
204	Jeff Newman	.15	.08	.05
205	Pete Falcone	.15	.08	.05
206	Boog Powell	.50	.25	.15
207	Glenn Abbott	.15	.08	.05
208	Checklist 133-264	1.25	.60	.40
209	Rob Andrews	.15	.08	.05
210	Fred Lynn	1.50	.70	.45
211	Giants Team (Joe Altobelli)	.70	.35	.20
212	Jim Mason	.15	.08	.05
213	Maximino Leon	.15	.08	.05
214	Darrell Porter	.20	.10	.06
215	Butch Metzger	.15	.08	.05
216	Doug DeCinces	.25	.13	.08
217	Tom Underwood	.15	.08	.05
218	*John Wathan*	.60	.30	.20
219	Joe Coleman	.20	.10	.06
220	Chris Chambliss	.30	.15	.09
221	Bob Bailey	.15	.08	.05
222	Francisco Barrios	.15	.08	.05
223	Earl Williams	.15	.08	.05
224	Rusty Torres	.15	.08	.05
225	Bob Apodaca	.15	.08	.05
226	Leroy Stanton	.15	.08	.05
227	*Joe Sambito*	.25	.13	.08
228	Twins Team (Gene Mauch)	.80	.40	.25
229	Don Kessinger	.20	.10	.06
230	Vida Blue	.40	.20	.12
231	Record Breaker (George Brett)	2.00	1.00	.60
232	Record Breaker (Minnie Minoso)	.35	.20	.11
233	Record Breaker (Jose Morales)	.20	.10	.06
234	Record Breaker (Nolan Ryan)	3.75	1.75	1.10
235	Cecil Cooper	.60	.30	.20
236	Tom Buskey	.15	.08	.05
237	Gene Clines	.15	.08	.05
238	Tippy Martinez	.15	.08	.05
239	Bill Plummer	.15	.08	.05
240	Ron LeFlore	.25	.13	.08
241	Dave Tomlin	.15	.08	.05
242	Ken Henderson	.15	.08	.05
243	Ron Reed	.20	.10	.06
244	John Mayberry	.20	.10	.06
245	Rick Rhoden	.30	.15	.09
246	Mike Vail	.15	.08	.05
247	Chris Knapp	.15	.08	.05
248	Wilbur Howard	.15	.08	.05
249	Pete Redfern	.15	.08	.05
250	Bill Madlock	.40	.20	.12
251	Tony Muser	.15	.08	.05
252	Dale Murray	.15	.08	.05
253	John Hale	.15	.08	.05
254	Doyle Alexander	.30	.15	.09
255	George Scott	.20	.10	.06
256	Joe Hoerner	.15	.08	.05
257	Mike Miley	.15	.08	.05
258	Luis Tiant	.35	.20	.11
259	Mets Team (Joe Frazier)	.80	.40	.25
260	J.R. Richard	.25	.13	.08
261	Phil Garner	.20	.10	.06
262	Al Cowens	.15	.08	.05
263	Mike Marshall	.25	.13	.08
264	Tom Hutton	.15	.08	.05
265	*Mark Fidrych*	.70	.35	.20
266	Derrel Thomas	.15	.08	.05
267	Ray Fosse	.15	.08	.05
268	Rick Sawyer	.15	.08	.05
269	Joe Lis	.15	.08	.05
270	Dave Parker	3.00	1.50	.90
271	Terry Forster	.20	.10	.06
272	Lee Lacy	.15	.08	.05
273	Eric Soderholm	.15	.08	.05
274	Don Stanhouse	.15	.08	.05
275	Mike Hargrove	.20	.10	.06
276	A.L. Championship (Chambliss' Dramatic Homer Decides It)	.70	.35	.20
277	N.L. Championship (Reds Sweep Phillies 3 In Row)	.70	.35	.20
278	Danny Frisella	.15	.08	.05
279	Joe Wallis	.15	.08	.05
280	Jim Hunter	2.00	1.00	.60
281	Roy Staiger	.15	.08	.05
282	Sid Monge	.15	.08	.05
283	Jerry DaVanon	.15	.08	.05
284	Mike Norris	.20	.10	.06
285	Brooks Robinson	2.50	1.25	.70
286	Johnny Grubb	.15	.08	.05
287	Reds Team (Sparky Anderson)	.80	.40	.25
288	Bob Montgomery	.15	.08	.05
289	Gene Garber	.20	.10	.06
290	Amos Otis	.20	.10	.06
291	*Jason Thompson*	.35	.20	.11
292	Rogelio Moret	.15	.08	.05
293	Jack Brohamer	.15	.08	.05
294	George Medich	.15	.08	.05
295	Gary Carter	6.00	3.00	1.75
296	Don Hood	.15	.08	.05
297	Ken Reitz	.15	.08	.05
298	Charlie Hough	.25	.13	.08
299	Otto Velez	.15	.08	.05
300	Jerry Koosman	.30	.15	.09
301	Toby Harrah	.20	.10	.06
302	Mike Garman	.15	.08	.05
303	Gene Tenace	.20	.10	.06
304	Jim Hughes	.15	.08	.05
305	Mickey Rivers	.25	.13	.08
306	Rick Waits	.15	.08	.05
307	Gary Sutherland	.15	.08	.05
308	Gene Pentz	.15	.08	.05
309	Red Sox Team (Don Zimmer)	.80	.40	.25
310	Larry Bowa	.30	.15	.09
311	Vern Ruhle	.15	.08	.05
312	Rob Belloir	.15	.08	.05
313	Paul Blair	.20	.10	.06
314	Steve Mingori	.15	.08	.05
315	Dave Chalk	.15	.08	.05
316	Steve Rogers	.20	.10	.06
317	Kurt Bevacqua	.15	.08	.05
318	Duffy Dyer	.15	.08	.05
319	Rich Gossage	.90	.45	.25
320	Ken Griffey	.30	.15	.09
321	Dave Goltz	.20	.10	.06
322	Bill Russell	.20	.10	.06
323	Larry Lintz	.15	.08	.05
324	John Curtis	.15	.08	.05
325	Mike Ivie	.15	.08	.05
326	Jesse Jefferson	.15	.08	.05
327	Astros Team (Bill Virdon)	.70	.35	.20
328	Tommy Boggs	.15	.08	.05
329	Ron Hodges	.15	.08	.05
330	George Hendrick	.20	.10	.06
331	Jim Colborn	.15	.08	.05
332	Elliott Maddox	.20	.10	.06
333	Paul Reuschel	.15	.08	.05
334	Bill Stein	.15	.08	.05
335	Bill Robinson	.15	.08	.05
336	Denny Doyle	.15	.08	.05
337	Ron Schueler	.15	.08	.05
338	Dave Duncan	.15	.08	.05
339	Adrian Devine	.15	.08	.05
340	Hal McRae	.30	.15	.09
341	Joe Kerrigan	.15	.08	.05
342	Jerry Remy	.15	.08	.05
343	Ed Halicki	.15	.08	.05
344	Brian Downing	.25	.13	.08
345	Reggie Smith	.25	.13	.08
346	Bill Singer	.20	.10	.06
347	George Foster	1.25	.60	.40
348	Brent Strom	.15	.08	.05
349	Jim Holt	.15	.08	.05

		NR MT	EX	VG
350	Larry Dierker	.20	.10	.06
351	Jim Sundberg	.20	.10	.06
352	Mike Phillips	.15	.08	.05
353	Stan Thomas	.15	.08	.05
354	Pirates Team (Chuck Tanner)	.80	.40	.25
355	Lou Brock	2.25	1.25	.70
356	Checklist 265-396	1.25	.60	.40
357	Tim McCarver	.40	.20	.12
358	Tom House	.15	.08	.05
359	Willie Randolph	.80	.40	.25
360	Rick Monday	.25	.13	.08
361	Eduardo Rodriguez	.15	.08	.05
362	Tommy Davis	.30	.15	.09
363	Dave Roberts	.15	.08	.05
364	Vic Correll	.15	.08	.05
365	Mike Torrez	.20	.10	.06
366	Ted Sizemore	.15	.08	.05
367	Dave Hamilton	.15	.08	.05
368	Mike Jorgensen	.15	.08	.05
369	Terry Humphrey	.15	.08	.05
370	John Montefusco	.20	.10	.06
371	Royals Team (Whitey Herzog)	.80	.40	.25
372	Rich Folkers	.15	.08	.05
373	Bert Campaneris	.30	.15	.09
374	Kent Tekulve	.30	.15	.09
375	Larry Hisle	.20	.10	.06
376	Nino Espinosa	.15	.08	.05
377	Dave McKay	.15	.08	.05
378	Jim Umbarger	.15	.08	.05
379	Larry Cox	.15	.08	.05
380	Lee May	.25	.13	.08
381	Bob Forsch	.20	.10	.06
382	Charlie Moore	.15	.08	.05
383	Stan Bahnsen	.15	.08	.05
384	Darrel Chaney	.15	.08	.05
385	Dave LaRoche	.15	.08	.05
386	Manny Mota	.25	.13	.08
387	Yankees Team (Billy Martin)	1.25	.60	.40
388	Terry Harmon	.15	.08	.05
389	Ken Kravec	.15	.08	.05
390	Dave Winfield	4.00	2.00	1.25
391	Dan Warthen	.15	.08	.05
392	Phil Roof	.15	.08	.05
393	John Lowenstein	.15	.08	.05
394	Bill Laxton	.15	.08	.05
395	Manny Trillo	.20	.10	.06
396	Tom Murphy	.15	.08	.05
397	*Larry Herndon*	.40	.20	.12
398	Tom Burgmeier	.15	.08	.05
399	Bruce Boisclair	.15	.08	.05
400	Steve Garvey	5.00	2.50	1.50
401	Mickey Scott	.15	.08	.05
402	Tommy Helms	.15	.08	.05
403	Tom Grieve	.15	.08	.05
404	Eric Rasmussen	.15	.08	.05
405	Claudell Washington	.25	.13	.08
406	Tim Johnson	.15	.08	.05
407	Dave Freisleben	.15	.08	.05
408	Cesar Tovar	.15	.08	.05
409	Pete Broberg	.15	.08	.05
410	Willie Montanez	.15	.08	.05
411	World Series Games 1 & 2	.70	.35	.20
412	World Series Games 3 & 4	.70	.35	.20
413	World Series Summary	.70	.35	.20
414	Tommy Harper	.20	.10	.06
415	Jay Johnstone	.20	.10	.06
416	Chuck Hartenstein	.15	.08	.05
417	Wayne Garrett	.15	.08	.05
418	White Sox Team (Bob Lemon)	.80	.40	.25
419	Steve Swisher	.15	.08	.05
420	Rusty Staub	.35	.20	.11
421	Doug Rau	.15	.08	.05
422	Freddie Patek	.15	.08	.05
423	Gary Lavelle	.15	.08	.05
424	Steve Brye	.15	.08	.05
425	Joe Torre	.40	.20	.12
426	Dick Drago	.15	.08	.05
427	Dave Rader	.15	.08	.05
428	Rangers Team (Frank Lucchesi)	.70	.35	.20
429	Ken Boswell	.15	.08	.05
430	Fergie Jenkins	.80	.40	.25
431	Dave Collins	.25	.13	.08
432	Buzz Capra	.15	.08	.05
433	Turn Back The Clock (Nate Colbert)	.20	.10	.06
434	Turn Back The Clock (Carl Yastrzemski)	2.00	1.00	.60
435	Turn Back The Clock (Maury Wills)	.35	.20	.11
436	Turn Back The Clock (Bob Keegan)	.20	.10	.06
437	Turn Back The Clock (Ralph Kiner)	.50	.25	.15
438	Marty Perez	.15	.08	.05
439	Gorman Thomas	.30	.15	.09
440	Jon Matlack	.20	.10	.06
441	Larvell Blanks	.15	.08	.05
442	Braves Team (Dave Bristol)	.70	.35	.20
443	Lamar Johnson	.15	.08	.05
444	Wayne Twitchell	.15	.08	.05
445	Ken Singleton	.25	.13	.08
446	Bill Bonham	.15	.08	.05
447	Jerry Turner	.15	.08	.05
448	Ellie Rodriguez	.15	.08	.05
449	Al Fitzmorris	.15	.08	.05
450	Pete Rose	9.00	4.50	2.75
451	Checklist 397-528	1.25	.60	.40
452	Mike Caldwell	.15	.08	.05
453	Pedro Garcia	.15	.08	.05
454	Andy Etchebarren	.15	.08	.05
455	Rick Wise	.20	.10	.06
456	Leon Roberts	.15	.08	.05
457	Steve Luebber	.15	.08	.05
458	Leo Foster	.15	.08	.05
459	Steve Foucault	.15	.08	.05
460	Willie Stargell	2.50	1.25	.70
461	Dick Tidrow	.20	.10	.06
462	Don Baylor	.35	.20	.11
463	Jamie Quirk	.15	.08	.05
464	Randy Moffitt	.15	.08	.05
465	Rico Carty	.25	.13	.08
466	Fred Holdsworth	.15	.08	.05
467	Phillies Team (Danny Ozark)	.70	.35	.20
468	Ramon Hernandez	.15	.08	.05
469	Pat Kelly	.15	.08	.05
470	Ted Simmons	.60	.30	.20
471	Del Unser	.15	.08	.05
472	Rookie Pitchers (Don Aase, Bob McClure, Gil Patterson, Dave Wehrmeister)	.25	.13	.08
473	Rookie Outfielders (*Andre Dawson*, Gene Richards, John Scott, *Denny Walling*)	45.00	23.00	13.50
474	Rookie Shortstops (Bob Bailor, Kiko Garcia, Craig Reynolds, Alex Taveras)	.15	.08	.05
475	Rookie Pitchers (Chris Batton, Rick Camp, Scott McGregor, Manny Sarmiento)	.30	.15	.09
476	Rookie Catchers (Gary Alexander, *Rick Cerone, Dale Murphy*, Kevin Pasley)	60.00	30.00	18.00
477	Rookie Infielders (Doug Ault, *Rich Dauer*, Orlando Gonzalez, Phil Mankowski)	.25	.13	.08
478	Rookie Pitchers (Jim Gideon, Leon Hooten, Dave Johnson, Mark Lemongello)	.15	.08	.05
479	Rookie Outfielders (Brian Asselstine, *Wayne Gross*, Sam Mejias, Alvis Woods)	.25	.13	.08
480	Carl Yastrzemski	5.00	2.50	1.50
481	Roger Metzger	.15	.08	.05
482	Tony Solaita	.15	.08	.05
483	Richie Zisk	.20	.10	.06
484	Burt Hooton	.20	.10	.06
485	Roy White	.30	.15	.09
486	Ed Bane	.15	.08	.05
487	Rookie Pitchers (Larry Anderson, Ed Glynn, Joe Henderson, Greg Terlecky)	.15	.08	.05
488	Rookie Outfielders (*Jack Clark, Ruppert Jones, Lee Mazzilli*, Dan Thomas)	20.00	10.00	6.00
489	Rookie Pitchers (*Len Barker*, Randy Lerch, *Greg Minton*, Mike Overy)	.40	.20	.12
490	Rookie Shortstops (*Billy Almon*, Mickey Klutts, Tommy McMillan, Mark Wagner)	.25	.13	.08
491	Rookie Pitchers (Mike Dupree, *Denny Martinez*, Craig Mitchell, Bob Sykes)	1.50	.70	.45
492	Rookie Outfielders (*Tony Armas, Steve Kemp*, Carlos Lopez, Gary Woods)	1.00	.50	.30
493	Rookie Pitchers (*Mike Krukow*, Jim Otten, Gary Wheelock, Mike Willis)	.70	.35	.20
494	Rookie Infielders (Juan Bernhardt, Mike Champion, *Jim Gantner, Bump Wills*)	.50	.25	.15
495	Al Hrabosky	.20	.10	.06
496	Gary Thomasson	.15	.08	.05
497	Clay Carroll	.20	.10	.06
498	Sal Bando	.25	.13	.08
499	Pablo Torrealba	.15	.08	.05
500	Dave Kingman	.60	.30	.20
501	Jim Bibby	.15	.08	.05
502	Randy Hundley	.15	.08	.05
503	Bill Lee	.20	.10	.06
504	Dodgers Team (Tom Lasorda)	1.00	.50	.30
505	Oscar Gamble	.20	.10	.06
506	Steve Grilli	.15	.08	.05
507	Mike Hegan	.15	.08	.05
508	Dave Pagan	.15	.08	.05
509	Cookie Rojas	.15	.08	.05
510	John Candelaria	.80	.40	.25
511	Bill Fahey	.15	.08	.05
512	Jack Billingham	.15	.08	.05
513	Jerry Terrell	.15	.08	.05
514	Cliff Johnson	.15	.08	.05
515	Chris Speier	.15	.08	.05
516	Bake McBride	.15	.08	.05
517	*Pete Vuckovich*	.50	.25	.15
518	Cubs Team (Herman Franks)	.70	.35	.20
519	Don Kirkwood	.15	.08	.05
520	Garry Maddox	.20	.10	.06
521	Bob Grich	.25	.13	.08
522	Enzo Hernandez	.15	.08	.05
523	Rollie Fingers	1.25	.60	.40
524	Rowland Office	.15	.08	.05
525	Dennis Eckersley	2.50	1.25	.70
526	Larry Parrish	.35	.20	.11
527	Dan Meyer	.15	.08	.05
528	Bill Castro	.15	.08	.05
529	Jim Essian	.15	.08	.05
530	Rick Reuschel	.30	.15	.09
531	Lyman Bostock	.25	.13	.08
532	Jim Willoughby	.15	.08	.05
533	Mickey Stanley	.20	.10	.06
534	Paul Splittorff	.20	.10	.06
535	Cesar Geronimo	.20	.10	.06
536	Vic Albury	.15	.08	.05
537	Dave Roberts	.15	.08	.05
538	Frank Taveras	.15	.08	.05
539	Mike Wallace	.15	.08	.05
540	Bob Watson	.20	.10	.06
541	John Denny	.15	.08	.05
542	Frank Duffy	.15	.08	.05
543	Ron Blomberg	.20	.10	.06
544	Gary Ross	.15	.08	.05
545	Bob Boone	.25	.13	.08
546	Orioles Team (Earl Weaver)	.80	.40	.25
547	Willie McCovey	2.00	1.00	.60
548	*Joel Youngblood*	.30	.15	.09
549	Jerry Royster	.15	.08	.05
550	Randy Jones	.20	.10	.06
551	Bill North	.15	.08	.05
552	Pepe Mangual	.15	.08	.05
553	Jack Heidemann	.15	.08	.05
554	Bruce Kimm	.15	.08	.05
555	Dan Ford	.20	.10	.06
556	Doug Bird	.15	.08	.05
557	Jerry White	.15	.08	.05
558	Elias Sosa	.15	.08	.05
559	Alan Bannister	.15	.08	.05
560	Dave Concepcion	.35	.20	.11
561	Pete LaCock	.15	.08	.05
562	Checklist 529-660	1.25	.60	.40
563	Bruce Kison	.15	.08	.05
564	Alan Ashby	.20	.10	.06
565	Mickey Lolich	.50	.25	.15
566	Rick Miller	.15	.08	.05
567	Enos Cabell	.20	.10	.06
568	Carlos May	.20	.10	.06
569	Jim Lonborg	.20	.10	.06
570	Bobby Bonds	.35	.20	.11
571	Darrell Evans	.40	.20	.12
572	Ross Grimsley	.20	.10	.06
573	Joe Ferguson	.15	.08	.05
574	Aurelio Rodriguez	.20	.10	.06
575	Dick Ruthven	.15	.08	.05
576	Fred Kendall	.15	.08	.05
577	Jerry Augustine	.15	.08	.05
578	Bob Randall	.15	.08	.05
579	Don Carrithers	.15	.08	.05
580	George Brett	12.00	6.00	3.50
581	Pedro Borbon	.15	.08	.05
582	Ed Kirkpatrick	.15	.08	.05
583	Paul Lindblad	.15	.08	.05
584	Ed Goodson	.15	.08	.05
585	Rick Burleson	.20	.10	.06
586	Steve Renko	.15	.08	.05
587	Rick Baldwin	.15	.08	.05
588	Dave Moates	.15	.08	.05
589	Mike Cosgrove	.15	.08	.05
590	Buddy Bell	.30	.15	.09
591	Chris Arnold	.15	.08	.05
592	Dan Briggs	.15	.08	.05
593	Dennis Blair	.15	.08	.05
594	Biff Pocoroba	.15	.08	.05
595	John Hiller	.20	.10	.06
596	*Jerry Martin*	.25	.13	.08
597	Mariners Mgr./Coaches (Don Bryant, Jim Busby, Darrell Johnson, Vada Pinson, Wes Stock)	.25	.13	.08
598	Sparky Lyle	.35	.20	.11
599	Mike Tyson	.15	.08	.05
600	Jim Palmer	3.00	1.50	.90
601	Mike Lum	.15	.08	.05
602	Andy Hassler	.15	.08	.05
603	Willie Davis	.25	.13	.08
604	Jim Slaton	.15	.08	.05
605	Felix Millan	.15	.08	.05
606	Steve Braun	.15	.08	.05
607	Larry Demery	.15	.08	.05
608	Roy Howell	.15	.08	.05
609	Jim Barr	.15	.08	.05
610	Jose Cardenal	.20	.10	.06
611	Dave Lemanczyk	.15	.08	.05
612	Barry Foote	.15	.08	.05
613	Reggie Cleveland	.15	.08	.05
614	Greg Gross	.15	.08	.05
615	Phil Niekro	1.50	.70	.45
616	Tommy Sandt	.15	.08	.05
617	Bobby Darwin	.15	.08	.05
618	Pat Dobson	.20	.10	.06
619	Johnny Oates	.15	.08	.05
620	Don Sutton	1.50	.70	.45
621	Tigers Team (Ralph Houk)	.80	.40	.25
622	Jim Wohlford	.15	.08	.05
623	Jack Kucek	.15	.08	.05
624	Hector Cruz	.15	.08	.05
625	Ken Holtzman	.25	.13	.08
626	Al Bumbry	.20	.10	.06
627	Bob Myrick	.15	.08	.05
628	Mario Guerrero	.15	.08	.05
629	Bobby Valentine	.25	.13	.08
630	Bert Blyleven	1.25	.60	.40
631	Big League Brothers (George Brett, Ken Brett)	1.75	.90	.50
632	Big League Brothers (Bob Forsch, Ken Forsch)	.30	.15	.09
633	Big League Brothers (Carlos May, Lee May)	.30	.15	.09
634	Big League Brothers (Paul Reuschel, Rick Reuschel) (names switched)	.30	.15	.09
635	Robin Yount	20.00	10.00	6.00
636	Santo Alcala	.15	.08	.05
637	Alex Johnson	.15	.08	.05
638	Jim Kaat	.80	.40	.25
639	Jerry Morales	.15	.08	.05
640	Carlton Fisk	1.75	.90	.50
641	Dan Larson	.15	.08	.05
642	Willie Crawford	.15	.08	.05
643	Mike Pazik	.15	.08	.05
644	Matt Alexander	.15	.08	.05
645	Jerry Reuss	.25	.13	.08
646	Andres Mora	.15	.08	.05
647	Expos Team (Dick Williams)	.80	.40	.25
648	Jim Spencer	.15	.08	.05
649	Dave Cash	.15	.08	.05
650	Nolan Ryan	25.00	12.50	7.50
651	Von Joshua	.15	.08	.05
652	Tom Walker	.15	.08	.05
653	Diego Segui	.15	.08	.05
654	Ron Pruitt	.15	.08	.05
655	Tony Perez	.80	.40	.25
656	Ron Guidry	2.75	1.50	.80
657	Mick Kelleher	.15	.08	.05
658	Marty Pattin	.15	.08	.05
659	Merv Rettenmund	.15	.08	.05
660	Willie Horton	.40	.13	.08

NOTE: A card number in parentheses ( ) indicates the card set is unnumbered.

1977 Topps Cloth Stickers

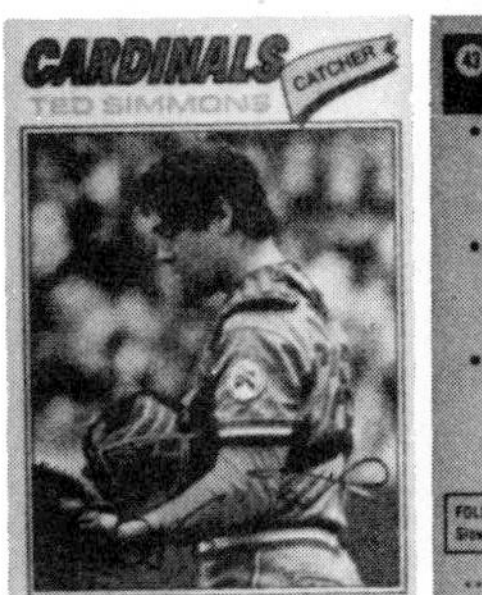

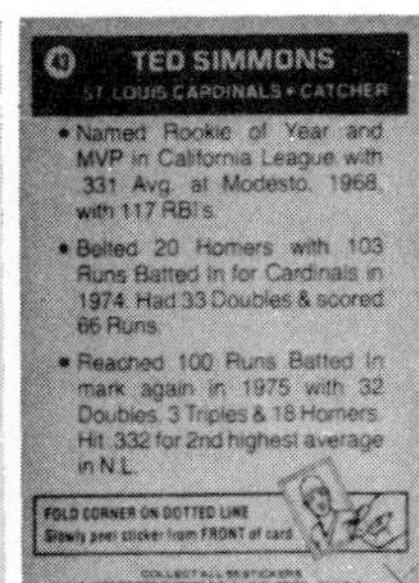

One of the few Topps specialty issues of the late 1970s, the 73-piece set of cloth stickers issued in 1977 includes 55 player stickers and 18 puzzle cards which could be joined to form a photo of the American League or National League All-Star teams. Issued as a separate issue, the 2-1/2" by 3-1/2" stickers have a paper backing which could be removed to allow the cloth to be adhered to a jacket, notebook, etc.

		NR MT	EX	VG
Complete Set:		100.00	50.00	30.00
Common Player:		.20	.10	.06
1	Alan Ashby	.20	.10	.06
2	Buddy Bell	1.00	.50	.30
3	Johnny Bench	5.00	2.50	1.50
4	Vida Blue	.50	.25	.15
5	Bert Blyleven	1.00	.50	.30
6	Steve Braun	.50	.25	.15
7	George Brett	7.00	3.50	2.00
8	Lou Brock	3.00	1.50	.90
9	Jose Cardenal	.20	.10	.06
10	Rod Carew	8.00	4.00	2.50
11	Steve Carlton	6.00	3.00	1.75
12	Dave Cash	.20	.10	.06
13	Cesar Cedeno	1.00	.50	.30
14	Ron Cey	.50	.25	.15
15	Mark Fidrych	.50	.25	.15
16	Dan Ford	.20	.10	.06
17	Wayne Garland	.20	.10	.06
18	Ralph Garr	.20	.10	.06
19	Steve Garvey	4.00	2.00	1.25
20	Mike Hargrove	.20	.10	.06
21	Jim Hunter	3.00	1.50	.90
22	Reggie Jackson	6.00	3.00	1.75
23	Randy Jones	.20	.10	.06
24	Dave Kingman	1.00	.50	.30
25	Bill Madlock	.70	.35	.20
26	Lee May	.50	.25	.15
27	John Mayberry	.20	.10	.06
28	Andy Messersmith	.20	.10	.06
29	Willie Montanez	.20	.10	.06
30	John Montefusco	.50	.25	.15
31	Joe Morgan	3.00	1.50	.90
32	Thurman Munson	3.00	1.50	.90
33	Bobby Murcer	.50	.25	.15
34	Al Oliver	1.25	.60	.40
35	Dave Pagan	.20	.10	.06
36	Jim Palmer	8.00	4.00	2.50
37	Tony Perez	.70	.35	.20
38	Pete Rose	12.00	6.00	3.50
39	Joe Rudi	.50	.25	.15
40	Nolan Ryan	15.00	7.50	4.50
41	Mike Schmidt	12.00	6.00	3.50
42	Tom Seaver	10.00	5.00	3.00
43	Ted Simmons	.70	.35	.20
44	Bill Singer	.20	.10	.06
45	Willie Stargell	1.50	.70	.45
46	Rusty Staub	.50	.25	.15
47	Don Sutton	1.25	.60	.40
48	Luis Tiant	.70	.35	.20
49	Bill Travers	.20	.10	.06
50	Claudell Washington	.50	.25	.15
51	Bob Watson	.20	.10	.06
52	Dave Winfield	3.00	1.50	.90
53	Carl Yastrzemski	4.50	2.25	1.25
54	Robin Yount	10.00	5.00	3.00
55	Richie Zisk	.20	.10	.06

1978 Topps

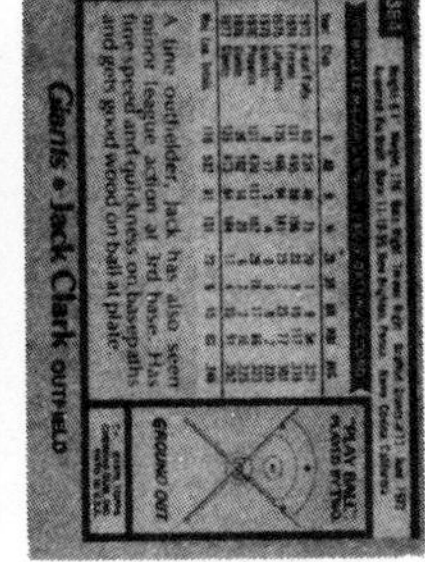

At 726 cards, this was the largest issue from Topps since 1972. In design, the color player photo is slightly larger than usual, with the player's name and team at the bottom. In the upper right-hand corner of the 2-1/2" by 3-1/2" cards there is a small white baseball with the player's position. Most of the starting All-Stars from the previous year had a red, white and blue shield instead of the baseball. Backs feature statistics and a baseball situation which made a card game of baseball possible. Specialty cards include baseball records, statistical leaders and the World Series and playoffs. As one row of cards per sheet had to be double-printed to accommodate the 726-card set size, some cards are more common, yet that seems to have no serious impact on their prices.

		NR MT	EX	VG
Complete Set:		250.00	125.00	75.00
Common Player:		.12	.06	.04
1	Record Breaker (Lou Brock)	2.00	.45	.25
2	Record Breaker (Sparky Lyle)	.25	.13	.08
3	Record Breaker (Willie McCovey)	.70	.35	.20
4	Record Breaker (Brooks Robinson)	.90	.45	.25
5	Record Breaker (Pete Rose)	2.00	1.00	.60
6	Record Breaker (Nolan Ryan)	3.25	1.75	1.00
7	Record Breaker (Reggie Jackson)	1.50	.70	.45
8	Mike Sadek	.12	.06	.04
9	Doug DeCinces	.25	.13	.08
10	Phil Niekro	1.25	.60	.40
11	Rick Manning	.12	.06	.04
12	Don Aase	.20	.10	.06
13	Art Howe	.12	.06	.04
14	Lerrin LaGrow	.12	.06	.04
15	Tony Perez	.25	.13	.08
16	Roy White	.25	.13	.08
17	Mike Krukow	.25	.13	.08
18	Bob Grich	.25	.13	.08
19	Darrell Porter	.20	.10	.06
20	Pete Rose	3.50	1.75	1.00
21	Steve Kemp	.25	.13	.08
22	Charlie Hough	.20	.10	.06
23	Bump Wills	.12	.06	.04
24	Don Money	.12	.06	.04
25	Jon Matlack	.20	.10	.06
26	Rich Hebner	.12	.06	.04
27	Geoff Zahn	.12	.06	.04
28	Ed Ott	.12	.06	.04
29	Bob Lacey	.12	.06	.04
30	George Hendrick	.20	.10	.06
31	Glenn Abbott	.12	.06	.04
32	Garry Templeton	.30	.15	.09
33	Dave Lemanczyk	.12	.06	.04
34	Willie McCovey	2.00	1.00	.60
35	Sparky Lyle	.30	.15	.09
36	*Eddie Murray*	35.00	17.50	10.00
37	Rick Waits	.12	.06	.04
38	Willie Montanez	.12	.06	.04
39	*Floyd Bannister*	1.00	.50	.30
40	Carl Yastrzemski	3.50	1.75	1.00
41	Burt Hooton	.20	.10	.06
42	Jorge Orta	.12	.06	.04
43	Bill Atkinson	.12	.06	.04
44	Toby Harrah	.20	.10	.06
45	Mark Fidrych	.25	.13	.08
46	Al Cowens	.12	.06	.04
47	Jack Billingham	.12	.06	.04
48	Don Baylor	.35	.20	.11
49	Ed Kranepool	.20	.10	.06
50	Rick Reuschel	.40	.20	.12
51	Charlie Moore	.12	.06	.04
52	Jim Lonborg	.20	.10	.06
53	Phil Garner	.12	.06	.04
54	Tom Johnson	.12	.06	.04
55	Mitchell Page	.12	.06	.04
56	Randy Jones	.20	.10	.06
57	Dan Meyer	.12	.06	.04
58	Bob Forsch	.20	.10	.06
59	Otto Velez	.12	.06	.04
60	Thurman Munson	3.00	1.50	.90
61	Larvell Blanks	.12	.06	.04
62	Jim Barr	.12	.06	.04
63	Don Zimmer	.20	.10	.06
64	Gene Pentz	.12	.06	.04
65	Ken Singleton	.25	.13	.08
66	White Sox Team	.50	.25	.15
67	Claudell Washington	.25	.13	.08
68	Steve Foucault	.12	.06	.04
69	Mike Vail	.12	.06	.04
70	Rich Gossage	.70	.35	.20
71	Terry Humphrey	.12	.06	.04
72	Andre Dawson	10.00	5.00	3.00
73	Andy Hassler	.12	.06	.04
74	Checklist 1-121	.90	.45	.25
75	Dick Ruthven	.12	.06	.04
76	Steve Ontiveros	.12	.06	.04
77	Ed Kirkpatrick	.12	.06	.04
78	Pablo Torrealba	.12	.06	.04
79	Darrell Johnson	.12	.06	.04
80	Ken Griffey	.25	.13	.08
81	Pete Redfern	.12	.06	.04
82	Giants Team	.50	.25	.15
83	Bob Montgomery	.12	.06	.04
84	Kent Tekulve	.25	.13	.08
85	Ron Fairly	.20	.10	.06
86	Dave Tomlin	.12	.06	.04
87	John Lowenstein	.12	.06	.04
88	Mike Phillips	.12	.06	.04
89	Ken Clay	.20	.10	.06
90	Larry Bowa	.30	.15	.09
91	Oscar Zamora	.12	.06	.04
92	Adrian Devine	.12	.06	.04
93	Bobby Cox	.12	.06	.04
94	Chuck Scrivener	.12	.06	.04
95	Jamie Quirk	.12	.06	.04
96	Orioles Team	.50	.25	.15
97	Stan Bahnsen	.12	.06	.04
98	Jim Essian	.12	.06	.04
99	*Willie Hernandez*	.70	.35	.20
100	George Brett	5.00	2.50	1.50
101	Sid Monge	.12	.06	.04
102	Matt Alexander	.12	.06	.04
103	Tom Murphy	.12	.06	.04
104	Lee Lacy	.12	.06	.04
105	Reggie Cleveland	.12	.06	.04
106	Bill Plummer	.12	.06	.04
107	Ed Halicki	.12	.06	.04
108	Von Joshua	.12	.06	.04
109	Joe Torre	.30	.15	.09
110	Richie Zisk	.20	.10	.06
111	Mike Tyson	.12	.06	.04
112	Astros Team	.50	.25	.15
113	Don Carrithers	.12	.06	.04
114	Paul Blair	.20	.10	.06
115	Gary Nolan	.12	.06	.04
116	Tucker Ashford	.12	.06	.04
117	John Montague	.12	.06	.04
118	Terry Harmon	.12	.06	.04
119	Denny Martinez	.25	.13	.08
120	Gary Carter	3.00	1.50	.90
121	Alvis Woods	.12	.06	.04
122	Dennis Eckersley	1.50	.70	.45
123	Manny Trillo	.20	.10	.06
124	*Dave Rozema*	.25	.13	.08
125	George Scott	.20	.10	.06
126	Paul Moskau	.12	.06	.04
127	Chet Lemon	.20	.10	.06
128	Bill Russell	.20	.10	.06
129	Jim Colborn	.12	.06	.04
130	Jeff Burroughs	.20	.10	.06
131	Bert Blyleven	.60	.30	.20
132	Enos Cabell	.20	.10	.06
133	Jerry Augustine	.12	.06	.04
134	*Steve Henderson*	.25	.13	.08
135	Ron Guidry	.70	.35	.20
136	Ted Sizemore	.12	.06	.04
137	Craig Kusick	.12	.06	.04
138	Larry Demery	.12	.06	.04
139	Wayne Gross	.12	.06	.04
140	Rollie Fingers	.70	.35	.20
141	Ruppert Jones	.20	.10	.06
142	John Montefusco	.20	.10	.06
143	Keith Hernandez	2.50	1.25	.70
144	Jesse Jefferson	.12	.06	.04
145	Rick Monday	.20	.10	.06
146	Doyle Alexander	.30	.15	.09
147	Lee Mazzilli	.25	.13	.08
148	Andre Thornton	.25	.13	.08
149	Dale Murray	.12	.06	.04
150	Bobby Bonds	.35	.20	.11
151	Milt Wilcox	.12	.06	.04
152	*Ivan DeJesus*	.20	.10	.06
153	Steve Stone	.25	.13	.08
154	Cecil Cooper	.20	.10	.06
155	Butch Hobson	.12	.06	.04
156	Andy Messersmith	.20	.10	.06
157	Pete LaCock	.12	.06	.04
158	Joaquin Andujar	.25	.13	.08
159	Lou Piniella	.35	.20	.11
160	Jim Palmer	3.00	1.50	.90
161	Bob Boone	.25	.13	.08
162	Paul Thormodsgard	.12	.06	.04
163	Bill North	.12	.06	.04
164	Bob Owchinko	.12	.06	.04
165	Rennie Stennett	.12	.06	.04
166	Carlos Lopez	.12	.06	.04
167	Tim Foli	.12	.06	.04
168	Reggie Smith	.25	.13	.08
169	Jerry Johnson	.12	.06	.04
170	Lou Brock	2.00	1.00	.60
171	Pat Zachry	.12	.06	.04
172	Mike Hargrove	.20	.10	.06
173	Robin Yount	10.00	5.00	3.00
174	Wayne Garland	.12	.06	.04
175	Jerry Morales	.12	.06	.04
176	Milt May	.12	.06	.04
177	Gene Garber	.12	.06	.04
178	Dave Chalk	.12	.06	.04
179	Dick Tidrow	.20	.10	.06
180	Dave Concepcion	.35	.20	.11
181	Ken Forsch	.20	.10	.06
182	Jim Spencer	.12	.06	.04
183	Doug Bird	.12	.06	.04
184	Checklist 122-242	.90	.45	.25
185	Ellis Valentine	.20	.10	.06
186	*Bob Stanley*	.25	.13	.08
187	Jerry Royster	.12	.06	.04
188	Al Bumbry	.20	.10	.06
189	Tom Lasorda	.30	.15	.09
190	John Candelaria	.25	.13	.08
191	Rodney Scott	.12	.06	.04
192	Padres Team	.50	.25	.15
193	Rich Chiles	.12	.06	.04
194	Derrel Thomas	.12	.06	.04
195	Larry Dierker	.20	.10	.06
196	Bob Bailor	.12	.06	.04
197	Nino Espinosa	.12	.06	.04
198	Ron Pruitt	.12	.06	.04
199	Craig Reynolds	.12	.06	.04
200	Reggie Jackson	4.50	2.25	1.50
201	Batting Leaders (Rod Carew, Dave Parker)	.80	.40	.25
202	Home Run Leaders (George Foster, Jim Rice)	.25	.13	.08
203	Runs Batted In Ldrs. (George Foster, Larry Hisle)	.25	.13	.08
204	Stolen Base Leaders (Freddie Patek, Frank Taveras)	.12	.06	.04
205	Victory Leaders (Steve Carlton, Dave Goltz, Dennis Leonard, Jim Palmer)	.60	.30	.20
206	Strikeout Leaders (Phil Niekro, Nolan Ryan)	.35	.20	.11
207	Earned Run Avg. Ldrs. (John Candelaria, Frank Tanana)	.12	.06	.04
208	Leading Firemen (Bill Campbell, Rollie			

		NR MT	EX	VG
	Fingers)	.35	.20	.11
209	Dock Ellis	.12	.06	.04
210	Jose Cardenal	.12	.06	.04
211	Earl Weaver	.20	.10	.06
212	Mike Caldwell	.12	.06	.04
213	Alan Bannister	.12	.06	.04
214	Angels Team	.50	.25	.15
215	Darrell Evans	.35	.20	.11
216	Mike Paxton	.12	.06	.04
217	Rod Gilbreath	.12	.06	.04
218	Marty Pattin	.12	.06	.04
219	Mike Cubbage	.12	.06	.04
220	Pedro Borbon	.12	.06	.04
221	Chris Speier	.20	.10	.06
222	Jerry Martin	.12	.06	.04
223	Bruce Kison	.12	.06	.04
224	Jerry Tabb	.12	.06	.04
225	Don Gullett	.12	.06	.04
226	Joe Ferguson	.12	.06	.04
227	Al Fitzmorris	.12	.06	.04
228	Manny Mota	.12	.06	.04
229	Leo Foster	.12	.06	.04
230	Al Hrabosky	.20	.10	.06
231	Wayne Nordhagen	.12	.06	.04
232	Mickey Stanley	.20	.10	.06
233	Dick Pole	.12	.06	.04
234	Herman Franks	.12	.06	.04
235	Tim McCarver	.35	.20	.11
236	Terry Whitfield	.12	.06	.04
237	Rich Dauer	.12	.06	.04
238	Juan Beniquez	.20	.10	.06
239	Dyar Miller	.12	.06	.04
240	Gene Tenace	.20	.10	.06
241	Pete Vuckovich	.20	.10	.06
242	Barry Bonnell	.12	.06	.04
243	Bob McClure	.12	.06	.04
244	Expos Team	.20	.10	.06
245	Rick Burleson	.20	.10	.06
246	Dan Driessen	.20	.10	.06
247	Larry Christenson	.12	.06	.04
248	Frank White	.12	.06	.04
249	Dave Goltz	.12	.06	.04
250	Graig Nettles	.30	.15	.09
251	Don Kirkwood	.12	.06	.04
252	Steve Swisher	.12	.06	.04
253	Jim Kern	.12	.06	.04
254	Dave Collins	.20	.10	.06
255	Jerry Reuss	.20	.10	.06
256	Joe Altobelli	.12	.06	.04
257	Hector Cruz	.12	.06	.04
258	John Hiller	.20	.10	.06
259	Dodgers Team	.80	.40	.25
260	Bert Campaneris	.25	.13	.08
261	Tim Hosley	.12	.06	.04
262	Rudy May	.12	.06	.04
263	Danny Walton	.12	.06	.04
264	Jamie Easterly	.12	.06	.04
265	Sal Bando	.12	.06	.04
266	*Bob Shirley*	.20	.10	.06
267	Doug Ault	.12	.06	.04
268	Gil Flores	.12	.06	.04
269	Wayne Twitchell	.12	.06	.04
270	Carlton Fisk	1.75	.90	.50
271	Randy Lerch	.12	.06	.04
272	Royle Stillman	.12	.06	.04
273	Fred Norman	.12	.06	.04
274	Freddie Patek	.12	.06	.04
275	Dan Ford	.12	.06	.04
276	Bill Bonham	.12	.06	.04
277	Bruce Boisclair	.12	.06	.04
278	Enrique Romo	.12	.06	.04
279	Bill Virdon	.20	.10	.06
280	Buddy Bell	.30	.15	.09
281	Eric Rasmussen	.12	.06	.04
282	Yankees Team	1.00	.50	.30
283	Omar Moreno	.12	.06	.04
284	Randy Moffitt	.12	.06	.04
285	Steve Yeager	.12	.06	.04
286	Ben Oglivie	.20	.10	.06
287	Kiko Garcia	.12	.06	.04
288	Dave Hamilton	.12	.06	.04
289	Checklist 243-363	.90	.45	.25
290	Willie Horton	.20	.10	.06
291	Gary Ross	.12	.06	.04
292	Gene Richard	.12	.06	.04
293	Mike Willis	.12	.06	.04
294	Larry Parrish	.25	.13	.08
295	Bill Lee	.20	.10	.06
296	Biff Pocoroba	.12	.06	.04
297	Warren Brusstar	.12	.06	.04
298	Tony Armas	.25	.13	.08
299	Whitey Herzog	.30	.15	.09
300	Joe Morgan	3.00	1.50	.90
301	Buddy Schultz	.12	.06	.04
302	Cubs Team	.50	.25	.15
303	Sam Hinds	.12	.06	.04
304	John Milner	.12	.06	.04
305	Rico Carty	.20	.10	.06
306	Joe Niekro	.25	.13	.08
307	Glenn Borgmann	.12	.06	.04
308	Jim Rooker	.12	.06	.04
309	Cliff Johnson	.20	.10	.06
310	Don Sutton	1.25	.60	.40
311	Jose Baez	.12	.06	.04
312	Greg Minton	.12	.06	.04
313	Andy Etchebarren	.12	.06	.04
314	Paul Lindblad	.12	.06	.04
315	Mark Belanger	.20	.10	.06
316	Henry Cruz	.12	.06	.04
317	Dave Johnson	.30	.15	.09
318	Tom Griffin	.12	.06	.04
319	Alan Ashby	.12	.06	.04
320	Fred Lynn	.90	.45	.25
321	Santo Alcala	.12	.06	.04
322	Tom Paciorek	.12	.06	.04
323	Jim Fregosi	.12	.06	.04
324	Vern Rapp	.12	.06	.04
325	Bruce Sutter	.50	.25	.15
326	Mike Lum	.12	.06	.04
327	Rick Langford	.12	.06	.04
328	Brewers Team	.50	.25	.15
329	John Verhoeven	.12	.06	.04
330	Bob Watson	.20	.10	.06
331	Mark Littell	.12	.06	.04
332	Duane Kuiper	.12	.06	.04
333	Jim Todd	.12	.06	.04
334	John Stearns	.12	.06	.04
335	Bucky Dent	.30	.15	.09
336	Steve Busby	.20	.10	.06
337	Tom Grieve	.12	.06	.04
338	Dave Heaverlo	.12	.06	.04
339	Mario Guerrero	.12	.06	.04
340	Bake McBride	.12	.06	.04
341	Mike Flanagan	.25	.13	.08
342	Aurelio Rodriguez	.20	.10	.06
343	John Wathan	.12	.06	.04
344	Sam Ewing	.12	.06	.04
345	Luis Tiant	.35	.20	.11
346	Larry Biittner	.12	.06	.04
347	Terry Forster	.20	.10	.06
348	Del Unser	.12	.06	.04
349	Rick Camp	.12	.06	.04
350	Steve Garvey	2.75	1.50	.80
351	Jeff Torborg	.20	.10	.06
352	Tony Scott	.12	.06	.04
353	Doug Bair	.12	.06	.04
354	Cesar Geronimo	.20	.10	.06
355	Bill Travers	.12	.06	.04
356	Mets Team	.70	.35	.20
357	Tom Poquette	.12	.06	.04
358	Mark Lemongello	.12	.06	.04
359	Marc Hill	.12	.06	.04
360	Mike Schmidt	7.00	3.50	2.00
361	Chris Knapp	.12	.06	.04
362	Dave May	.12	.06	.04
363	Bob Randall	.12	.06	.04
364	Jerry Turner	.12	.06	.04
365	Ed Figueroa	.20	.10	.06
366	Larry Milbourne	.12	.06	.04
367	Rick Dempsey	.20	.10	.06
368	Balor Moore	.12	.06	.04
369	Tim Nordbrook	.12	.06	.04
370	Rusty Staub	.30	.15	.09
371	Ray Burris	.12	.06	.04
372	Brian Asselstine	.12	.06	.04
373	Jim Willoughby	.12	.06	.04
374	Jose Morales	.12	.06	.04
375	Tommy John	.90	.45	.25
376	Jim Wohlford	.12	.06	.04
377	Manny Sarmiento	.12	.06	.04
378	Bobby Winkles	.12	.06	.04
379	Skip Lockwood	.12	.06	.04
380	Ted Simmons	.40	.20	.12
381	Phillies Team	.70	.35	.20
382	Joe Lahoud	.12	.06	.04
383	Mario Mendoza	.12	.06	.04
384	Jack Clark	3.25	1.75	1.00
385	Tito Fuentes	.12	.06	.04
386	Bob Gorinski	.12	.06	.04
387	Ken Holtzman	.25	.13	.08
388	Bill Fahey	.12	.06	.04
389	Julio Gonzalez	.12	.06	.04
390	Oscar Gamble	.20	.10	.06
391	Larry Haney	.12	.06	.04
392	Billy Almon	.12	.06	.04
393	Tippy Martinez	.12	.06	.04
394	Roy Howell	.12	.06	.04
395	Jim Hughes	.12	.06	.04
396	Bob Stinson	.12	.06	.04
397	Greg Gross	.12	.06	.04
398	Don Hood	.12	.06	.04
399	Pete Mackanin	.12	.06	.04
400	Nolan Ryan	18.00	9.00	5.50
401	Sparky Anderson	.30	.15	.09
402	Dave Campbell	.12	.06	.04
403	Bud Harrelson	.20	.10	.06
404	Tigers Team	.60	.30	.20
405	Rawly Eastwick	.12	.06	.04
406	Mike Jorgensen	.12	.06	.04
407	Odell Jones	.12	.06	.04
408	Joe Zdeb	.12	.06	.04
409	Ron Schueler	.12	.06	.04
410	Bill Madlock	.50	.25	.15
411	A.L. Championships (Yankees Rally To Defeat Royals)	.70	.35	.20
412	N.L. Championships (Dodgers Overpower Phillies In Four)	.50	.25	.15
413	World Series (Reggie & Yankees Reign Supreme)	1.25	.60	.40
414	Darold Knowles	.12	.06	.04
415	Ray Fosse	.12	.06	.04
416	Jack Brohamer	.12	.06	.04
417	Mike Garman	.12	.06	.04
418	Tony Muser	.12	.06	.04
419	Jerry Garvin	.12	.06	.04
420	Greg Luzinski	.35	.20	.11
421	Junior Moore	.12	.06	.04
422	Steve Braun	.12	.06	.04
423	Dave Rosello	.12	.06	.04
424	Red Sox Team	.70	.35	.20
425	Steve Rogers	.12	.06	.04
426	Fred Kendall	.12	.06	.04
427	*Mario Soto*	.40	.20	.12
428	Joel Youngblood	.20	.10	.06
429	Mike Barlow	.12	.06	.04
430	Al Oliver	.40	.20	.12
431	Butch Metzger	.12	.06	.04
432	Terry Bulling	.12	.06	.04
433	Fernando Gonzalez	.12	.06	.04
434	Mike Norris	.12	.06	.04
435	Checklist 364-484	.90	.45	.25
436	Vic Harris	.12	.06	.04
437	Bo McLaughlin	.12	.06	.04
438	John Ellis	.12	.06	.04
439	Ken Kravec	.12	.06	.04
440	Dave Lopes	.25	.13	.08
441	Larry Gura	.12	.06	.04
442	Elliott Maddox	.12	.06	.04
443	Darrel Chaney	.12	.06	.04
444	Roy Hartsfield	.12	.06	.04
445	Mike Ivie	.12	.06	.04
446	Tug McGraw	.35	.20	.11
447	Leroy Stanton	.12	.06	.04
448	Bill Castro	.12	.06	.04
449	Tim Blackwell	.12	.06	.04
450	Tom Seaver	4.00	2.00	1.25
451	Twins Team	.50	.25	.15
452	Jerry Mumphrey	.20	.10	.06
453	Doug Flynn	.12	.06	.04
454	Dave LaRoche	.12	.06	.04
455	Bill Robinson	.12	.06	.04
456	Vern Ruhle	.12	.06	.04
457	Bob Bailey	.12	.06	.04
458	Jeff Newman	.12	.06	.04
459	Charlie Spikes	.12	.06	.04
460	Jim Hunter	1.75	.90	.50
461	Rob Andrews	.12	.06	.04
462	Rogelio Moret	.12	.06	.04
463	Kevin Bell	.12	.06	.04
464	Jerry Grote	.20	.10	.06
465	Hal McRae	.30	.15	.09
466	Dennis Blair	.12	.06	.04
467	Alvin Dark	.20	.10	.06
468	*Warren Cromartie*	.20	.10	.06
469	Rick Cerone	.20	.10	.06
470	J.R. Richard	.25	.13	.08
471	Roy Smalley	.20	.10	.06
472	Ron Reed	.20	.10	.06
473	Bill Buckner	.30	.15	.09
474	Jim Slaton	.12	.06	.04
475	Gary Matthews	.20	.10	.06
476	Bill Stein	.12	.06	.04
477	Doug Capilla	.12	.06	.04
478	Jerry Remy	.12	.06	.04
479	Cardinals Team	.50	.25	.15
480	Ron LeFlore	.25	.13	.08
481	Jackson Todd	.12	.06	.04
482	Rick Miller	.12	.06	.04
483	Ken Macha	.12	.06	.04
484	Jim Norris	.12	.06	.04
485	Chris Chambliss	.30	.15	.09
486	John Curtis	.12	.06	.04
487	Jim Tyrone	.12	.06	.04
488	Dan Spillner	.12	.06	.04
489	Rudy Meoli	.12	.06	.04
490	Amos Otis	.20	.10	.06
491	Scott McGregor	.20	.10	.06
492	Jim Sundberg	.20	.10	.06
493	Steve Renko	.12	.06	.04
494	Chuck Tanner	.20	.10	.06
495	Dave Cash	.12	.06	.04
496	*Jim Clancy*	.30	.15	.09
497	Glenn Adams	.12	.06	.04
498	Joe Sambito	.12	.06	.04
499	Mariners Team	.50	.25	.15
500	George Foster	.70	.35	.20
501	Dave Roberts	.12	.06	.04
502	Pat Rockett	.12	.06	.04
503	Ike Hampton	.12	.06	.04
504	Roger Freed	.12	.06	.04
505	Felix Millan	.12	.06	.04
506	Ron Blomberg	.12	.06	.04
507	Willie Crawford	.12	.06	.04
508	Johnny Oates	.12	.06	.04
509	Brent Strom	.12	.06	.04
510	Willie Stargell	2.00	1.00	.60
511	Frank Duffy	.12	.06	.04
512	Larry Herndon	.20	.10	.06
513	Barry Foote	.12	.06	.04
514	Rob Sperring	.12	.06	.04
515	Tim Corcoran	.12	.06	.04
516	Gary Beare	.12	.06	.04
517	Andres Mora	.12	.06	.04
518	Tommy Boggs	.12	.06	.04
519	Brian Downing	.25	.13	.08
520	Larry Hisle	.20	.10	.06
521	Steve Staggs	.12	.06	.04
522	Dick Williams	.20	.10	.06
523	*Donnie Moore*	.25	.13	.08
524	Bernie Carbo	.12	.06	.04
525	Jerry Terrell	.12	.06	.04
526	Reds Team	.60	.30	.20
527	Vic Correll	.12	.06	.04
528	Rob Picciolo	.12	.06	.04
529	Paul Hartzell	.12	.06	.04
530	Dave Winfield	2.50	1.25	.70
531	Tom Underwood	.12	.06	.04
532	Skip Jutze	.12	.06	.04
533	Sandy Alomar	.12	.06	.04
534	Wilbur Howard	.12	.06	.04
535	Checklist 485-605	.90	.45	.25
536	Roric Harrison	.12	.06	.04
537	Bruce Bochte	.20	.10	.06
538	Johnnie LeMaster	.12	.06	.04
539	Vic Davalillo	.12	.06	.04
540	Steve Carlton	3.00	1.50	.90
541	Larry Cox	.12	.06	.04
542	Tim Johnson	.12	.06	.04
543	Larry Harlow	.12	.06	.04
544	Len Randle	.12	.06	.04
545	Bill Campbell	.12	.06	.04
546	Ted Martinez	.12	.06	.04
547	John Scott	.12	.06	.04
548	Billy Hunter	.12	.06	.04
549	Joe Kerrigan	.12	.06	.04
550	John Mayberry	.20	.10	.06
551	Braves Team	.50	.25	.15
552	Francisco Barrios	.12	.06	.04
553	*Terry Puhl*	.35	.20	.11
554	Joe Coleman	.20	.10	.06
555	Butch Wynegar	.20	.10	.06
556	Ed Armbrister	.12	.06	.04
557	Tony Solaita	.12	.06	.04
558	Paul Mitchell	.12	.06	.04
559	Phil Mankowski	.12	.06	.04
560	Dave Parker	2.25	1.25	.70
561	Charlie Williams	.12	.06	.04
562	Glenn Burke	.12	.06	.04
563	Dave Rader	.12	.06	.04
564	Mick Kelleher	.12	.06	.04
565	Jerry Koosman	.25	.13	.08
566	Merv Rettenmund	.12	.06	.04
567	Dick Drago	.12	.06	.04
568	Tom Hutton	.12	.06	.04
569	*Lary Sorensen*	.20	.10	.06
570	Dave Kingman	.60	.30	.20
571	Buck Martinez	.12	.06	.04
572	Rick Wise	.20	.10	.06
573	Luis Gomez	.12	.06	.04
574	Bob Lemon	.30	.15	.09
575	Pat Dobson	.20	.10	.06
576	Sam Mejias	.12	.06	.04

		NR MT	EX	VG
577	A's Team	.50	.25	.15
578	Buzz Capra	.12	.06	.04
579	*Rance Mulliniks*	.35	.20	.11
580	Rod Carew	3.00	1.50	.90
581	Lynn McGlothen	.12	.06	.04
582	Fran Healy	.20	.10	.06
583	George Medich	.12	.06	.04
584	John Hale	.12	.06	.04
585	Woodie Fryman	.12	.06	.04
586	Ed Goodson	.12	.06	.04
587	John Urrea	.12	.06	.04
588	Jim Mason	.12	.06	.04
589	*Bob Knepper*	1.00	.50	.30
590	Bobby Murcer	.30	.15	.09
591	George Zeber	.20	.10	.06
592	Bob Apodaca	.12	.06	.04
593	Dave Skaggs	.12	.06	.04
594	Dave Freisleben	.12	.06	.04
595	Sixto Lezcano	.12	.06	.04
596	Gary Wheelock	.12	.06	.04
597	Steve Dillard	.12	.06	.04
598	Eddie Solomon	.12	.06	.04
599	Gary Woods	.12	.06	.04
600	Frank Tanana	.25	.13	.08
601	Gene Mauch	.25	.13	.08
602	Eric Soderholm	.12	.06	.04
603	Will McEnaney	.12	.06	.04
604	Earl Williams	.12	.06	.04
605	Rick Rhoden	.25	.13	.08
606	Pirates Team	.50	.25	.15
607	Fernando Arroyo	.12	.06	.04
608	Johnny Grubb	.12	.06	.04
609	John Denny	.12	.06	.04
610	Garry Maddox	.20	.10	.06
611	Pat Scanlon	.12	.06	.04
612	Ken Henderson	.12	.06	.04
613	Marty Perez	.12	.06	.04
614	Joe Wallis	.12	.06	.04
615	Clay Carroll	.20	.10	.06
616	Pat Kelly	.12	.06	.04
617	Joe Nolan	.12	.06	.04
618	Tommy Helms	.12	.06	.04
619	*Thad Bosley*	.20	.10	.06
620	Willie Randolph	.30	.15	.09
621	Craig Swan	.12	.06	.04
622	Champ Summers	.12	.06	.04
623	Eduardo Rodriguez	.12	.06	.04
624	Gary Alexander	.12	.06	.04
625	Jose Cruz	.25	.13	.08
626	Blue Jays Team	.25	.13	.08
627	Dave Johnson	.12	.06	.04
628	Ralph Garr	.20	.10	.06
629	Don Stanhouse	.12	.06	.04
630	Ron Cey	.25	.13	.08
631	Danny Ozark	.20	.10	.06
632	Rowland Office	.12	.06	.04
633	Tom Veryzer	.12	.06	.04
634	Len Barker	.20	.10	.06
635	Joe Rudi	.25	.13	.08
636	Jim Bibby	.12	.06	.04
637	Duffy Dyer	.12	.06	.04
638	Paul Splittorff	.20	.10	.06
639	Gene Clines	.12	.06	.04
640	Lee May	.12	.06	.04
641	Doug Rau	.12	.06	.04
642	Denny Doyle	.12	.06	.04
643	Tom House	.12	.06	.04
644	Jim Dwyer	.12	.06	.04
645	Mike Torrez	.20	.10	.06
646	Rick Auerbach	.12	.06	.04
647	Steve Dunning	.12	.06	.04
648	Gary Thomasson	.12	.06	.04
649	*Moose Haas*	.25	.13	.08
650	Cesar Cedeno	.25	.13	.08
651	Doug Rader	.12	.06	.04
652	Checklist 606-726	.90	.45	.25
653	Ron Hodges	.12	.06	.04
654	Pepe Frias	.12	.06	.04
655	Lyman Bostock	.20	.10	.06
656	Dave Garcia	.12	.06	.04
657	Bombo Rivera	.12	.06	.04
658	Manny Sanguillen	.12	.06	.04
659	Rangers Team	.50	.25	.15
660	Jason Thompson	.20	.10	.06
661	Grant Jackson	.12	.06	.04
662	Paul Dade	.12	.06	.04
663	Paul Reuschel	.12	.06	.04
664	Fred Stanley	.20	.10	.06
665	Dennis Leonard	.20	.10	.06
666	Billy Smith	.12	.06	.04
667	Jeff Byrd	.12	.06	.04
668	Dusty Baker	.25	.13	.08
669	Pete Falcone	.12	.06	.04
670	Jim Rice	3.50	1.75	1.00
671	Gary Lavelle	.12	.06	.04
672	Don Kessinger	.20	.10	.06
673	Steve Brye	.12	.06	.04
674	*Ray Knight*	.60	.30	.20
675	Jay Johnstone	.20	.10	.06
676	Bob Myrick	.12	.06	.04
677	Ed Herrmann	.12	.06	.04
678	Tom Burgmeier	.12	.06	.04
679	Wayne Garrett	.12	.06	.04
680	Vida Blue	.30	.15	.09
681	Rob Belloir	.12	.06	.04
682	Ken Brett	.20	.10	.06
683	Mike Champion	.12	.06	.04
684	Ralph Houk	.20	.10	.06
685	Frank Taveras	.12	.06	.04
686	Gaylord Perry	1.75	.90	.50
687	*Julio Cruz*	.25	.13	.08
688	George Mitterwald	.12	.06	.04
689	Indians Team	.50	.25	.15
690	Mickey Rivers	.25	.13	.08
691	Ross Grimsley	.20	.10	.06
692	Ken Reitz	.12	.06	.04
693	Lamar Johnson	.12	.06	.04
694	Elias Sosa	.12	.06	.04
695	Dwight Evans	1.50	.70	.45
696	Steve Mingori	.12	.06	.04
697	Roger Metzger	.12	.06	.04
698	Juan Bernhardt	.12	.06	.04
699	Jackie Brown	.12	.06	.04
700	Johnny Bench	5.00	2.50	1.50

		NR MT	EX	VG
701	Rookie Pitchers (*Tom Hume*, Larry Landreth, *Steve McCatty*, Bruce Taylor)	.25	.13	.08
702	Rookie Catchers (Bill Nahorodny, Kevin Pasley, Rick Sweet, Don Werner)	.12	.06	.04
703	Rookie Pitchers (*Larry Andersen*, Tim Jones, Mickey Mahler, *Jack Morris*)	5.00	2.50	1.50
704	Rookie 2nd Basemen (*Garth Iorg*, Dave Oliver, Sam Perlozzo, *Lou Whitaker*)	12.00	6.00	3.50
705	Rookie Outfielders (*Dave Bergman*, Miguel Dilone, *Clint Hurdle*, Willie Norwood)	.25	.13	.08
706	Rookie 1st Basemen (Wayne Cage, Ted Cox, *Pat Putnam*, *Dave Revering*)	.20	.10	.06
707	Rookie Shortstops (Mickey Klutts, *Paul Molitor*, *Alan Trammell*, *U.L. Washington*)	45.00	23.00	13.50
708	Rookie Catchers (*Bo Diaz*, Dale Murphy, *Lance Parrish*, *Ernie Whitt*)	25.00	12.50	7.50
709	Rookie Pitchers (Steve Burke, *Matt Keough*, Lance Rautzhan, *Dan Schatzeder*)	.20	.10	.06
710	Rookie Outfielders (Dell Alston, Rick Bosetti, *Mike Easler*, Keith Smith)	.50	.25	.15
711	Rookie Pitchers (Cardell Camper, Dennis Lamp, Craig Mitchell, Roy Thomas)	.12	.06	.04
712	Bobby Valentine	.25	.13	.08
713	Bob Davis	.12	.06	.04
714	Mike Anderson	.12	.06	.04
715	Jim Kaat	.60	.30	.20
716	Clarence Gaston	.12	.06	.04
717	Nelson Briles	.12	.06	.04
718	Ron Jackson	.12	.06	.04
719	Randy Elliott	.12	.06	.04
720	Fergie Jenkins	.60	.30	.20
721	Billy Martin	.70	.35	.20
722	Pete Broberg	.12	.06	.04
723	Johnny Wockenfuss	.12	.06	.04
724	Royals Team	.70	.35	.20
725	Kurt Bevacqua	.12	.06	.04
726	Wilbur Wood	.40	.10	.06

1979 Topps

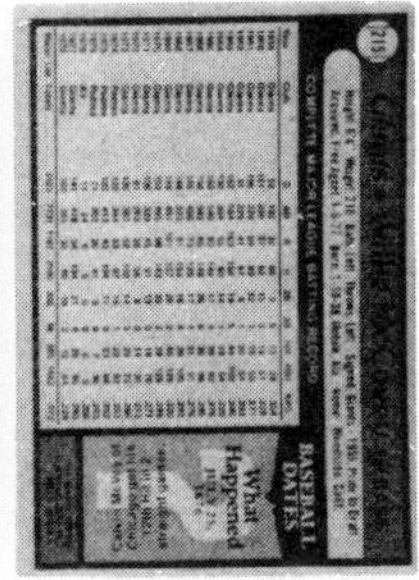

The size of this issue remained the same as in 1978 with 726 cards making their appearance. Actually, the 2-1/2" by 3-1/2" cards have a relatively minor design change from the previous year. The large color photo still dominates the front, with the player's name, team and position below it. The baseball with the player's position was moved to the lower left and the position replaced by a Topps logo. On the back, the printing color was changed and the game situation was replaced by a quiz called "Baseball Dates". Specialty cards include statistical leaders, major league records set during the season and eight cards devoted to career records. For the first time, rookies were arranged by teams under the heading of "Prospects."

		NR MT	EX	VG
	Complete Set:	200.00	100.00	60.00
	Common Player:	.12	.06	.04
1	Batting Leaders (Rod Carew, Dave Parker)	1.50	.40	.25
2	Home Run Leaders (George Foster, Jim Rice)	.50	.25	.15
3	Runs Batted In Leaders (George Foster, Jim Rice)	.50	.25	.15
4	Stolen Base Leaders (Ron LeFlore, Omar Moreno)	.25	.13	.08
5	Victory Leaders (Ron Guidry, Gaylord Perry)	.50	.25	.15
6	Strikeout Leaders (J.R. Richard, Nolan Ryan)	.50	.25	.15
7	Earned Run Avg. Leaders (Ron Guidry, Craig Swan)	.25	.13	.08
8	Leading Firemen (Rollie Fingers, Rich Gossage)	.40	.20	.12
9	Dave Campbell	.12	.06	.04
10	Lee May	.20	.10	.06
11	Marc Hill	.12	.06	.04
12	Dick Drago	.12	.06	.04
13	Paul Dade	.12	.06	.04
14	Rafael Landestoy	.12	.06	.04
15	Ross Grimsley	.20	.10	.06

		NR MT	EX	VG
16	Fred Stanley	.20	.10	.06
17	Donnie Moore	.20	.10	.06
18	Tony Solaita	.12	.06	.04
19	Larry Gura	.12	.06	.04
20	Joe Morgan	.40	.20	.12
21	Kevin Kobel	.12	.06	.04
22	Mike Jorgensen	.12	.06	.04
23	Terry Forster	.20	.10	.06
24	Paul Molitor	4.00	2.00	1.25
25	Steve Carlton	3.00	1.50	.90
26	Jamie Quirk	.12	.06	.04
27	Dave Goltz	.20	.10	.06
28	Steve Brye	.12	.06	.04
29	Rick Langford	.12	.06	.04
30	Dave Winfield	2.50	1.25	.70
31	Tom House	.12	.06	.04
32	Jerry Mumphrey	.12	.06	.04
33	Dave Rozema	.12	.06	.04
34	Rob Andrews	.12	.06	.04
35	Ed Figueroa	.20	.10	.06
36	Alan Ashby	.12	.06	.04
37	Joe Kerrigan	.12	.06	.04
38	Bernie Carbo	.12	.06	.04
39	Dale Murphy	8.00	4.00	2.50
40	Dennis Eckersley	.35	.20	.11
41	Twins Team (Gene Mauch)	.50	.25	.15
42	Ron Blomberg	.12	.06	.04
43	Wayne Twitchell	.12	.06	.04
44	Kurt Bevacqua	.12	.06	.04
45	Al Hrabosky	.20	.10	.06
46	Ron Hodges	.12	.06	.04
47	Fred Norman	.12	.06	.04
48	Merv Rettenmund	.12	.06	.04
49	Vern Ruhle	.12	.06	.04
50	Steve Garvey	1.25	.60	.40
51	Ray Fosse	.12	.06	.04
52	Randy Lerch	.12	.06	.04
53	Mick Kelleher	.12	.06	.04
54	Dell Alston	.12	.06	.04
55	Willie Stargell	2.00	1.00	.60
56	John Hale	.12	.06	.04
57	Eric Rasmussen	.12	.06	.04
58	Bob Randall	.12	.06	.04
59	John Denny	.12	.06	.04
60	Mickey Rivers	.20	.10	.06
61	Bo Diaz	.20	.10	.06
62	Randy Moffitt	.12	.06	.04
63	Jack Brohamer	.12	.06	.04
64	Tom Underwood	.12	.06	.04
65	Mark Belanger	.20	.10	.06
66	Tigers Team (Les Moss)	.60	.30	.20
67	Jim Mason	.12	.06	.04
68	Joe Niekro	.12	.06	.04
69	Elliott Maddox	.12	.06	.04
70	John Candelaria	.25	.13	.08
71	Brian Downing	.20	.10	.06
72	Steve Mingori	.12	.06	.04
73	Ken Henderson	.12	.06	.04
74	*Shane Rawley*	.70	.35	.20
75	Steve Yeager	.12	.06	.04
76	Warren Cromartie	.12	.06	.04
77	Dan Briggs	.12	.06	.04
78	Elias Sosa	.12	.06	.04
79	Ted Cox	.12	.06	.04
80	Jason Thompson	.20	.10	.06
81	Roger Erickson	.12	.06	.04
82	Mets Team (Joe Torre)	.60	.30	.20
83	Fred Kendall	.12	.06	.04
84	Greg Minton	.12	.06	.04
85	Gary Matthews	.20	.10	.06
86	Rodney Scott	.12	.06	.04
87	Pete Falcone	.12	.06	.04
88	Bob Molinaro	.12	.06	.04
89	Dick Tidrow	.20	.10	.06
90	Bob Boone	.25	.13	.08
91	Terry Crowley	.12	.06	.04
92	Jim Bibby	.12	.06	.04
93	Phil Mankowski	.12	.06	.04
94	Len Barker	.12	.06	.04
95	Robin Yount	9.00	4.50	2.75
96	Indians Team (Jeff Torborg)	.50	.25	.15
97	Sam Mejias	.12	.06	.04
98	Ray Burris	.12	.06	.04
99	John Wathan	.20	.10	.06
100	Tom Seaver	2.00	1.00	.60
101	Roy Howell	.12	.06	.04
102	Mike Anderson	.12	.06	.04
103	Jim Todd	.12	.06	.04
104	Johnny Oates	.12	.06	.04
105	Rick Camp	.12	.06	.04
106	Frank Duffy	.12	.06	.04
107	Jesus Alou	.20	.10	.06
108	Eduardo Rodriguez	.12	.06	.04
109	Joel Youngblood	.12	.06	.04
110	Vida Blue	.30	.15	.09
111	Roger Freed	.12	.06	.04
112	Phillies Team (Danny Ozark)	.50	.25	.15
113	Pete Redfern	.12	.06	.04
114	Cliff Johnson	.20	.10	.06
115	Nolan Ryan	10.00	5.00	3.00
116	*Ozzie Smith*	40.00	20.00	12.00
117	Grant Jackson	.12	.06	.04
118	Bud Harrelson	.20	.10	.06
119	Don Stanhouse	.12	.06	.04
120	Jim Sundberg	.20	.10	.06
121	Checklist 1-121	.25	.13	.08
122	Mike Paxton	.12	.06	.04
123	Lou Whitaker	3.00	1.50	.90
124	Dan Schatzeder	.12	.06	.04
125	Rick Burleson	.20	.10	.06
126	Doug Bair	.12	.06	.04
127	Thad Bosley	.12	.06	.04
128	Ted Martinez	.12	.06	.04
129	Marty Pattin	.12	.06	.04
130	Bob Watson	.12	.06	.04
131	Jim Clancy	.25	.13	.08
132	Rowland Office	.12	.06	.04
133	Bill Castro	.12	.06	.04
134	Alan Bannister	.12	.06	.04
135	Bobby Murcer	.25	.13	.08
136	Jim Kaat	.60	.30	.20
137	Larry Wolfe	.12	.06	.04
138	Mark Lee	.12	.06	.04

		NR MT	EX	VG
139	Luis Pujols	.12	.06	.04
140	Don Gullett	.20	.10	.06
141	Tom Paciorek	.12	.06	.04
142	Charlie Williams	.12	.06	.04
143	Tony Scott	.12	.06	.04
144	Sandy Alomar	.12	.06	.04
145	Rick Rhoden	.25	.13	.08
146	Duane Kuiper	.12	.06	.04
147	Dave Hamilton	.12	.06	.04
148	Bruce Boisclair	.12	.06	.04
149	Manny Sarmiento	.12	.06	.04
150	Wayne Cage	.12	.06	.04
151	John Hiller	.20	.10	.06
152	Rick Cerone	.20	.10	.06
153	Dennis Lamp	.12	.06	.04
154	Jim Gantner	.12	.06	.04
155	Dwight Evans	1.00	.50	.30
156	Buddy Solomon	.12	.06	.04
157	U.L. Washington	.12	.06	.04
158	Joe Sambito	.12	.06	.04
159	Roy White	.25	.13	.08
160	Mike Flanagan	.30	.15	.09
161	Barry Foote	.12	.06	.04
162	Tom Johnson	.12	.06	.04
163	Glenn Burke	.12	.06	.04
164	Mickey Lolich	.40	.20	.12
165	Frank Taveras	.12	.06	.04
166	Leon Roberts	.12	.06	.04
167	Roger Metzger	.12	.06	.04
168	Dave Freisleben	.12	.06	.04
169	Bill Nahorodny	.12	.06	.04
170	Don Sutton	1.25	.60	.40
171	Gene Clines	.12	.06	.04
172	Mike Bruhert	.12	.06	.04
173	John Lowenstein	.12	.06	.04
174	Rick Auerbach	.12	.06	.04
175	George Hendrick	.20	.10	.06
176	Aurelio Rodriguez	.20	.10	.06
177	Ron Reed	.20	.10	.06
178	Alvis Woods	.12	.06	.04
179	Jim Beattie	.12	.06	.04
180	Larry Hisle	.20	.10	.06
181	Mike Garman	.12	.06	.04
182	Tim Johnson	.12	.06	.04
183	Paul Splittorff	.20	.10	.06
184	Darrel Chaney	.12	.06	.04
185	Mike Torrez	.20	.10	.06
186	Eric Soderholm	.12	.06	.04
187	Mark Lemongello	.12	.06	.04
188	Pat Kelly	.12	.06	.04
189	*Eddie Whitson*	.50	.25	.15
190	Ron Cey	.25	.13	.08
191	Mike Norris	.12	.06	.04
192	Cardinals Team (Ken Boyer)	.50	.25	.15
193	Glenn Adams	.12	.06	.04
194	Randy Jones	.20	.10	.06
195	Bill Madlock	.40	.20	.12
196	Steve Kemp	.12	.06	.04
197	Bob Apodaca	.12	.06	.04
198	Johnny Grubb	.12	.06	.04
199	Larry Milbourne	.12	.06	.04
200	Johnny Bench	2.00	1.00	.60
201	Record Breaker (Mike Edwards)	.12	.06	.04
202	Record Breaker (Ron Guidry)	.35	.20	.11
203	Record Breaker (J.R. Richard)	.20	.10	.06
204	Record Breaker (Pete Rose)	1.50	.70	.45
205	Record Breaker (John Stearns)	.12	.06	.04
206	Record Breaker (Sammy Stewart)	.12	.06	.04
207	Dave Lemanczyk	.12	.06	.04
208	Clarence Gaston	.12	.06	.04
209	Reggie Cleveland	.12	.06	.04
210	Larry Bowa	.30	.15	.09
211	Denny Martinez	.20	.10	.06
212	*Carney Lansford*	7.00	3.50	2.00
213	Bill Travers	.12	.06	.04
214	Red Sox Team (Don Zimmer)	.60	.30	.20
215	Willie McCovey	1.50	.70	.45
216	Wilbur Wood	.20	.10	.06
217	Steve Dillard	.12	.06	.04
218	Dennis Leonard	.20	.10	.06
219	Roy Smalley	.20	.10	.06
220	Cesar Geronimo	.20	.10	.06
221	Jesse Jefferson	.12	.06	.04
222	Bob Beall	.12	.06	.04
223	Kent Tekulve	.25	.13	.08
224	Dave Revering	.12	.06	.04
225	Rich Gossage	.70	.35	.20
226	Ron Pruitt	.12	.06	.04
227	Steve Stone	.20	.10	.06
228	Vic Davalillo	.12	.06	.04
229	Doug Flynn	.12	.06	.04
230	Bob Forsch	.20	.10	.06
231	Johnny Wockenfuss	.12	.06	.04
232	Jimmy Sexton	.12	.06	.04
233	Paul Mitchell	.12	.06	.04
234	Toby Harrah	.20	.10	.06
235	Steve Rogers	.20	.10	.06
236	Jim Dwyer	.12	.06	.04
237	Billy Smith	.12	.06	.04
238	Balor Moore	.12	.06	.04
239	Willie Horton	.20	.10	.06
240	Rick Reuschel	.25	.13	.08
241	Checklist 122-242	.25	.13	.08
242	Pablo Torrealba	.12	.06	.04
243	Buck Martinez	.12	.06	.04
244	Pirates Team (Chuck Tanner)	.80	.40	.25
245	Jeff Burroughs	.20	.10	.06
246	Darrell Jackson	.12	.06	.04
247	Tucker Ashford	.12	.06	.04
248	Pete LaCock	.12	.06	.04
249	Paul Thormodsgard	.12	.06	.04
250	Willie Randolph	.30	.15	.09
251	Jack Morris	2.00	1.00	.60
252	Bob Stinson	.12	.06	.04
253	Rick Wise	.20	.10	.06

		NR MT	EX	VG
254	Luis Gomez	.12	.06	.04
255	Tommy John	.80	.40	.25
256	Mike Sadek	.12	.06	.04
257	Adrian Devine	.12	.06	.04
258	Mike Phillips	.12	.06	.04
259	Reds Team (Sparky Anderson)	.60	.30	.20
260	Richie Zisk	.20	.10	.06
261	Mario Guerrero	.12	.06	.04
262	Nelson Briles	.12	.06	.04
263	Oscar Gamble	.20	.10	.06
264	*Don Robinson*	.50	.25	.15
265	Don Money	.12	.06	.04
266	Jim Willoughby	.12	.06	.04
267	Joe Rudi	.20	.10	.06
268	Julio Gonzalez	.12	.06	.04
269	Woodie Fryman	.20	.10	.06
270	Butch Hobson	.12	.06	.04
271	Rawly Eastwick	.12	.06	.04
272	Tim Corcoran	.12	.06	.04
273	Jerry Terrell	.12	.06	.04
274	Willie Norwood	.12	.06	.04
275	Junior Moore	.12	.06	.04
276	Jim Colborn	.12	.06	.04
277	Tom Grieve	.12	.06	.04
278	Andy Messersmith	.25	.13	.08
279	Jerry Grote	.12	.06	.04
280	Andre Thornton	.25	.13	.08
281	Vic Correll	.12	.06	.04
282	Blue Jays Team (Roy Hartsfield)	.50	.25	.15
283	Ken Kravec	.12	.06	.04
284	Johnnie LeMaster	.12	.06	.04
285	Bobby Bonds	.30	.15	.09
286	Duffy Dyer	.12	.06	.04
287	Andres Mora	.12	.06	.04
288	Milt Wilcox	.20	.10	.06
289	Jose Cruz	.25	.13	.08
290	Dave Lopes	.25	.13	.08
291	Tom Griffin	.12	.06	.04
292	Don Reynolds	.12	.06	.04
293	Jerry Garvin	.12	.06	.04
294	Pepe Frias	.12	.06	.04
295	Mitchell Page	.12	.06	.04
296	Preston Hanna	.12	.06	.04
297	Ted Sizemore	.12	.06	.04
298	Rich Gale	.12	.06	.04
299	Steve Ontiveros	.12	.06	.04
300	Rod Carew	2.75	1.50	.80
301	Tom Hume	.12	.06	.04
302	Braves Team (Bobby Cox)	.50	.25	.15
303	Lary Sorensen	.12	.06	.04
304	Steve Swisher	.12	.06	.04
305	Willie Montanez	.12	.06	.04
306	Floyd Bannister	.30	.15	.09
307	Larvell Blanks	.12	.06	.04
308	Bert Blyleven	.60	.30	.20
309	Ralph Garr	.20	.10	.06
310	Thurman Munson	2.25	1.25	.70
311	Gary Lavelle	.12	.06	.04
312	Bob Robertson	.12	.06	.04
313	Dyar Miller	.12	.06	.04
314	Larry Harlow	.12	.06	.04
315	Jon Matlack	.20	.10	.06
316	Milt May	.12	.06	.04
317	Jose Cardenal	.12	.06	.04
318	*Bob Welch*	2.50	1.25	.70
319	Wayne Garrett	.12	.06	.04
320	Carl Yastrzemski	2.50	1.25	.70
321	Gaylord Perry	1.50	.70	.45
322	Danny Goodwin	.12	.06	.04
323	Lynn McGlothen	.12	.06	.04
324	Mike Tyson	.12	.06	.04
325	Cecil Cooper	.40	.20	.12
326	Pedro Borbon	.12	.06	.04
327	Art Howe	.12	.06	.04
328	A's Team (Jack McKeon)	.50	.25	.15
329	Joe Coleman	.20	.10	.06
330	George Brett	5.00	2.50	1.50
331	Mickey Mahler	.12	.06	.04
332	Gary Alexander	.12	.06	.04
333	Chet Lemon	.20	.10	.06
334	Craig Swan	.12	.06	.04
335	Chris Chambliss	.25	.13	.08
336	Bobby Thompson	.12	.06	.04
337	John Montague	.12	.06	.04
338	Vic Harris	.12	.06	.04
339	Ron Jackson	.12	.06	.04
340	Jim Palmer	3.00	1.50	.90
341	*Willie Upshaw*	.40	.20	.12
342	Dave Roberts	.12	.06	.04
343	Ed Glynn	.12	.06	.04
344	Jerry Royster	.12	.06	.04
345	Tug McGraw	.30	.15	.09
346	Bill Buckner	.30	.15	.09
347	Doug Rau	.12	.06	.04
348	Andre Dawson	4.00	2.00	1.25
349	Jim Wright	.12	.06	.04
350	Garry Templeton	.20	.10	.06
351	Wayne Nordhagen	.12	.06	.04
352	Steve Renko	.12	.06	.04
353	Checklist 243-363	.60	.30	.20
354	Bill Bonham	.12	.06	.04
355	Lee Mazzilli	.20	.10	.06
356	Giants Team (Joe Altobelli)	.50	.25	.15
357	Jerry Augustine	.12	.06	.04
358	Alan Trammell	4.00	2.00	1.25
359	Dan Spillner	.12	.06	.04
360	Amos Otis	.20	.10	.06
361	Tom Dixon	.12	.06	.04
362	Mike Cubbage	.12	.06	.04
363	Craig Skok	.12	.06	.04
364	Gene Richards	.12	.06	.04
365	Sparky Lyle	.30	.15	.09
366	Juan Bernhardt	.12	.06	.04
367	Dave Skaggs	.12	.06	.04
368	Don Aase	.20	.10	.06
369a	Bump Wills (Blue Jays)	3.00	1.50	.90
369b	Bump Wills (Rangers)	3.50	1.75	1.00
370	Dave Kingman	.35	.20	.11
371	Jeff Holly	.12	.06	.04
372	Lamar Johnson	.12	.06	.04
373	Lance Rautzhan	.12	.06	.04
374	Ed Herrmann	.12	.06	.04

		NR MT	EX	VG
375	Bill Campbell	.12	.06	.04
376	Gorman Thomas	.25	.13	.08
377	Paul Moskau	.12	.06	.04
378	Rob Picciolo	.12	.06	.04
379	Dale Murray	.12	.06	.04
380	John Mayberry	.20	.10	.06
381	Astros Team (Bill Virdon)	.50	.25	.15
382	Jerry Martin	.12	.06	.04
383	Phil Garner	.20	.10	.06
384	Tommy Boggs	.12	.06	.04
385	Dan Ford	.12	.06	.04
386	Francisco Barrios	.12	.06	.04
387	Gary Thomasson	.12	.06	.04
388	Jack Billingham	.12	.06	.04
389	Joe Zdeb	.12	.06	.04
390	Rollie Fingers	.70	.35	.20
391	Al Oliver	.40	.20	.12
392	Doug Ault	.12	.06	.04
393	Scott McGregor	.20	.10	.06
394	Randy Stein	.12	.06	.04
395	Dave Cash	.12	.06	.04
396	Bill Plummer	.12	.06	.04
397	Sergio Ferrer	.12	.06	.04
398	Ivan DeJesus	.12	.06	.04
399	David Clyde	.12	.06	.04
400	Jim Rice	2.50	1.25	.70
401	Ray Knight	.25	.13	.08
402	Paul Hartzell	.12	.06	.04
403	Tim Foli	.12	.06	.04
404	White Sox Team (Don Kessinger)	.50	.25	.15
405	Butch Wynegar	.20	.10	.06
406	Joe Wallis	.12	.06	.04
407	Pete Vuckovich	.20	.10	.06
408	Charlie Moore	.12	.06	.04
409	*Willie Wilson*	1.50	.70	.45
410	Darrell Evans	.30	.15	.09
411	Hits Record Holders (Ty Cobb, George Sisler)	.70	.35	.20
412	Runs Batted In Record Holders (Hank Aaron, Hack Wilson)	.70	.35	.20
413	Home Run Record Holders (Hank Aaron, Roger Maris)	1.00	.50	.30
414	Batting Avg. Record Holders (Ty Cobb, Roger Hornsby)	.70	.35	.20
415	Stolen Bases Record Holders (Lou Brock)	.70	.35	.20
416	Wins Record Holders (Jack Chesbro, Cy Young)	.40	.20	.12
417	Strikeouts Record Holders (Walter Johnson, Nolan Ryan)	.40	.20	.12
418	Earned Run Avg. Record Holders (Walter Johnson, Dutch Leonard)	.20	.10	.06
419	Dick Ruthven	.12	.06	.04
420	Ken Griffey	.25	.13	.08
421	Doug DeCinces	.25	.13	.08
422	Ruppert Jones	.12	.06	.04
423	Bob Montgomery	.12	.06	.04
424	Angels Team (Jim Fregosi)	.60	.30	.20
425	Rick Manning	.12	.06	.04
426	Chris Speier	.20	.10	.06
427	Andy Replogle	.12	.06	.04
428	Bobby Valentine	.25	.13	.08
429	John Urrea	.12	.06	.04
430	Dave Parker	1.50	.70	.45
431	Glenn Borgmann	.12	.06	.04
432	Dave Heaverlo	.12	.06	.04
433	Larry Biittner	.12	.06	.04
434	Ken Clay	.20	.10	.06
435	Gene Tenace	.20	.10	.06
436	Hector Cruz	.12	.06	.04
437	Rick Williams	.12	.06	.04
438	Horace Speed	.12	.06	.04
439	Frank White	.25	.13	.08
440	Rusty Staub	.30	.15	.09
441	Lee Lacy	.12	.06	.04
442	Doyle Alexander	.25	.13	.08
443	Bruce Bochte	.12	.06	.04
444	*Aurelio Lopez*	.20	.10	.06
445	Steve Henderson	.12	.06	.04
446	Jim Lonborg	.20	.10	.06
447	Manny Sanguillen	.12	.06	.04
448	Moose Haas	.12	.06	.04
449	Bombo Rivera	.12	.06	.04
450	Dave Concepcion	.30	.15	.09
451	Royals Team (Whitey Herzog)	.50	.25	.15
452	Jerry Morales	.12	.06	.04
453	Chris Knapp	.12	.06	.04
454	Len Randle	.12	.06	.04
455	Bill Lee	.12	.06	.04
456	Chuck Baker	.12	.06	.04
457	Bruce Sutter	.50	.25	.15
458	Jim Essian	.12	.06	.04
459	Sid Monge	.12	.06	.04
460	Graig Nettles	.50	.25	.15
461	Jim Barr	.12	.06	.04
462	Otto Velez	.12	.06	.04
463	Steve Comer	.12	.06	.04
464	Joe Nolan	.12	.06	.04
465	Reggie Smith	.25	.13	.08
466	Mark Littell	.12	.06	.04
467	Don Kessinger	.12	.06	.04
468	Stan Bahnsen	.12	.06	.04
469	Lance Parrish	3.00	1.50	.90
470	Garry Maddox	.12	.06	.04
471	Joaquin Andujar	.20	.10	.06
472	Craig Kusick	.12	.06	.04
473	Dave Roberts	.12	.06	.04
474	Dick Davis	.12	.06	.04
475	Dan Driessen	.20	.10	.06
476	Tom Poquette	.12	.06	.04
477	Bob Grich	.25	.13	.08
478	Juan Beniquez	.12	.06	.04
479	Padres Team (Roger Craig)	.50	.25	.15
480	Fred Lynn	.70	.35	.20
481	Skip Lockwood	.12	.06	.04
482	Craig Reynolds	.12	.06	.04
483	Checklist 364-484	.25	.13	.08
484	Rick Waits	.12	.06	.04
485	Bucky Dent	.25	.13	.08
486	Bob Knepper	.25	.13	.08
487	Miguel Dilone	.12	.06	.04
488	Bob Owchinko	.12	.06	.04

		NR MT	EX	VG
489	Larry Cox (photo actually Dave Rader)	.12	.06	.04
490	Al Cowens	.12	.06	.04
491	Tippy Martinez	.12	.06	.04
492	Bob Bailor	.12	.06	.04
493	Larry Christenson	.12	.06	.04
494	Jerry White	.12	.06	.04
495	Tony Perez	.60	.30	.20
496	Barry Bonnell	.12	.06	.04
497	Glenn Abbott	.12	.06	.04
498	Rich Chiles	.12	.06	.04
499	Rangers Team (Pat Corrales)	.50	.25	.15
500	Ron Guidry	.90	.45	.25
501	Junior Kennedy	.12	.06	.04
502	Steve Braun	.12	.06	.04
503	Terry Humphrey	.12	.06	.04
504	*Larry McWilliams*	.20	.10	.06
505	Ed Kranepool	.20	.10	.06
506	John D'Acquisto	.12	.06	.04
507	Tony Armas	.20	.10	.06
508	Charlie Hough	.20	.10	.06
509	Mario Mendoza	.12	.06	.04
510	Ted Simmons	.40	.20	.12
511	Paul Reuschel	.12	.06	.04
512	Jack Clark	1.50	.70	.45
513	Dave Johnson	.30	.15	.09
514	Mike Proly	.12	.06	.04
515	Enos Cabell	.12	.06	.04
516	Champ Summers	.12	.06	.04
517	Al Bumbry	.20	.10	.06
518	Jim Umbarger	.12	.06	.04
519	Ben Oglivie	.20	.10	.06
520	Gary Carter	2.50	1.25	.70
521	Sam Ewing	.12	.06	.04
522	Ken Holtzman	.20	.10	.06
523	John Milner	.12	.06	.04
524	Tom Burgmeier	.12	.06	.04
525	Freddie Patek	.12	.06	.04
526	Dodgers Team (Tom Lasorda)	.60	.30	.20
527	Lerrin LaGrow	.12	.06	.04
528	Wayne Gross	.12	.06	.04
529	Brian Asselstine	.12	.06	.04
530	Frank Tanana	.25	.13	.08
531	Fernando Gonzalez	.12	.06	.04
532	Buddy Schultz	.12	.06	.04
533	Leroy Stanton	.12	.06	.04
534	Ken Forsch	.12	.06	.04
535	Ellis Valentine	.12	.06	.04
536	Jerry Reuss	.20	.10	.06
537	Tom Veryzer	.12	.06	.04
538	Mike Ivie	.12	.06	.04
539	John Ellis	.12	.06	.04
540	Greg Luzinski	.30	.15	.09
541	Jim Slaton	.12	.06	.04
542	Rick Bosetti	.12	.06	.04
543	Kiko Garcia	.12	.06	.04
544	Fergie Jenkins	.40	.20	.12
545	John Stearns	.12	.06	.04
546	Bill Russell	.20	.10	.06
547	Clint Hurdle	.12	.06	.04
548	Enrique Romo	.12	.06	.04
549	Bob Bailey	.12	.06	.04
550	Sal Bando	.20	.10	.06
551	Cubs Team (Herman Franks)	.50	.25	.15
552	Jose Morales	.12	.06	.04
553	Denny Walling	.12	.06	.04
554	Matt Keough	.12	.06	.04
555	Biff Pocoroba	.12	.06	.04
556	Mike Lum	.12	.06	.04
557	Ken Brett	.20	.10	.06
558	Jay Johnstone	.20	.10	.06
559	Greg Pryor	.12	.06	.04
560	John Montefusco	.12	.06	.04
561	Ed Ott	.12	.06	.04
562	Dusty Baker	.25	.13	.08
563	Roy Thomas	.12	.06	.04
564	Jerry Turner	.12	.06	.04
565	Rico Carty	.25	.13	.08
566	Nino Espinosa	.12	.06	.04
567	Rich Hebner	.12	.06	.04
568	Carlos Lopez	.12	.06	.04
569	Bob Sykes	.12	.06	.04
570	Cesar Cedeno	.25	.13	.08
571	Darrell Porter	.20	.10	.06
572	Rod Gilbreath	.12	.06	.04
573	Jim Kern	.12	.06	.04
574	Claudell Washington	.20	.10	.06
575	Luis Tiant	.30	.15	.09
576	Mike Parrott	.12	.06	.04
577	Brewers Team (George Bamberger)	.50	.25	.15
578	Pete Broberg	.12	.06	.04
579	Greg Gross	.12	.06	.04
580	Ron Fairly	.20	.10	.06
581	Darold Knowles	.12	.06	.04
582	Paul Blair	.20	.10	.06
583	Julio Cruz	.12	.06	.04
584	Jim Rooker	.12	.06	.04
585	Hal McRae	.25	.13	.08
586	*Bob Horner*	.90	.45	.25
587	Ken Reitz	.12	.06	.04
588	Tom Murphy	.12	.06	.04
589	Terry Whitfield	.12	.06	.04
590	J.R. Richard	.20	.10	.06
591	Mike Hargrove	.20	.10	.06
592	Mike Krukow	.20	.10	.06
593	Rick Dempsey	.20	.10	.06
594	Bob Shirley	.12	.06	.04
595	Phil Niekro	1.25	.60	.40
596	Jim Wohlford	.12	.06	.04
597	Bob Stanley	.20	.10	.06
598	Mark Wagner	.12	.06	.04
599	Jim Spencer	.20	.10	.06
600	George Foster	.60	.30	.20
601	Dave LaRoche	.12	.06	.04
602	Checklist 485-605	.60	.30	.20
603	Rudy May	.12	.06	.04
604	Jeff Newman	.12	.06	.04
605	Rick Monday	.12	.06	.04
606	Expos Team (Dick Williams)	.50	.25	.15
607	Omar Moreno	.12	.06	.04
608	Dave McKay	.12	.06	.04
609	Silvio Martinez	.12	.06	.04
610	Mike Schmidt	8.00	4.00	2.50
611	Jim Norris	.12	.06	.04
612	*Rick Honeycutt*	.30	.15	.09
613	Mike Edwards	.12	.06	.04
614	Willie Hernandez	.20	.10	.06
615	Ken Singleton	.20	.10	.06
616	Billy Almon	.12	.06	.04
617	Terry Puhl	.12	.06	.04
618	Jerry Remy	.12	.06	.04
619	*Ken Landreaux*	.25	.13	.08
620	Bert Campaneris	.25	.13	.08
621	Pat Zachry	.12	.06	.04
622	Dave Collins	.20	.10	.06
623	Bob McClure	.12	.06	.04
624	Larry Herndon	.20	.10	.06
625	Mark Fidrych	.25	.13	.08
626	Yankees Team (Bob Lemon)	.80	.40	.25
627	Gary Serum	.12	.06	.04
628	Del Unser	.12	.06	.04
629	Gene Garber	.12	.06	.04
630	Bake McBride	.12	.06	.04
631	Jorge Orta	.12	.06	.04
632	Don Kirkwood	.12	.06	.04
633	Rob Wilfong	.12	.06	.04
634	Paul Lindblad	.20	.10	.06
635	Don Baylor	.50	.25	.15
636	Wayne Garland	.12	.06	.04
637	Bill Robinson	.12	.06	.04
638	Al Fitzmorris	.12	.06	.04
639	Manny Trillo	.20	.10	.06
640	Eddie Murray	5.00	2.50	1.50
641	*Bobby Castillo*	.12	.06	.04
642	Wilbur Howard	.12	.06	.04
643	Tom Hausman	.12	.06	.04
644	Manny Mota	.20	.10	.06
645	George Scott	.12	.06	.04
646	Rick Sweet	.12	.06	.04
647	Bob Lacey	.12	.06	.04
648	Lou Piniella	.35	.20	.11
649	John Curtis	.12	.06	.04
650	Pete Rose	4.50	2.25	1.25
651	Mike Caldwell	.12	.06	.04
652	Stan Papi	.12	.06	.04
653	Warren Brusstar	.12	.06	.04
654	Rick Miller	.12	.06	.04
655	Jerry Koosman	.30	.15	.09
656	Hosken Powell	.12	.06	.04
657	George Medich	.12	.06	.04
658	Taylor Duncan	.12	.06	.04
659	Mariners Team (Darrell Johnson)	.50	.25	.15
660	Ron LeFlore	.12	.06	.04
661	Bruce Kison	.12	.06	.04
662	Kevin Bell	.12	.06	.04
663	Mike Vail	.12	.06	.04
664	Doug Bird	.12	.06	.04
665	Lou Brock	1.50	.70	.45
666	Rich Dauer	.12	.06	.04
667	Don Hood	.12	.06	.04
668	Bill North	.12	.06	.04
669	Checklist 606-726	.60	.30	.20
670	Jim Hunter	.70	.35	.20
671	Joe Ferguson	.12	.06	.04
672	Ed Halicki	.12	.06	.04
673	Tom Hutton	.12	.06	.04
674	Dave Tomlin	.12	.06	.04
675	Tim McCarver	.30	.15	.09
676	Johnny Sutton	.12	.06	.04
677	Larry Parrish	.25	.13	.08
678	Geoff Zahn	.12	.06	.04
679	Derrel Thomas	.12	.06	.04
680	Carlton Fisk	1.25	.60	.40
681	*John Henry Johnson*	.12	.06	.04
682	Dave Chalk	.12	.06	.04
683	Dan Meyer	.12	.06	.04
684	Jamie Easterly	.12	.06	.04
685	Sixto Lezcano	.12	.06	.04
686	Ron Schueler	.12	.06	.04
687	Rennie Stennett	.12	.06	.04
688	Mike Willis	.12	.06	.04
689	Orioles Team (Earl Weaver)	.70	.35	.20
690	Buddy Bell	.12	.06	.04
691	Dock Ellis	.12	.06	.04
692	Mickey Stanley	.20	.10	.06
693	Dave Rader	.12	.06	.04
694	Burt Hooton	.20	.10	.06
695	Keith Hernandez	2.00	1.00	.60
696	Andy Hassler	.12	.06	.04
697	Dave Bergman	.12	.06	.04
698	Bill Stein	.12	.06	.04
699	Hal Dues	.12	.06	.04
700	Reggie Jackson	2.00	1.00	.60
701	Orioles Prospects (Mark Corey, John Flinn, *Sammy Stewart*)	.20	.10	.06
702	Red Sox Prospects (Joel Finch, Garry Hancock, Allen Ripley)	.12	.06	.04
703	Angels Prospects (Jim Anderson, Dave Frost, Bob Slater)	.12	.06	.04
704	White Sox Prospects (Ross Baumgarten, Mike Colbern, *Mike Squires*)	.20	.10	.06
705	Indians Prospects (*Alfredo Griffin*, Tim Norrid, Dave Oliver)	.70	.35	.20
706	Tigers Prospects (Dave Stegman, Dave Tobik, Kip Young)	.12	.06	.04
707	Royals Prospects (Randy Bass, Jim Gaudet, Randy McGilberry)	.12	.06	.04
708	Brewers Prospects (*Kevin Bass, Eddie Romero*, Ned Yost)	1.25	.60	.40
709	Twins Prospects (Sam Perlozzo, Rick Sofield, Kevin Stanfield)	.12	.06	.04
710	Yankees Prospects (Brian Doyle, *Mike Heath*, Dave Rajsich)	.30	.15	.09
711	A's Prospects (*Dwayne Murphy*, Bruce Robinson, Alan Wirth)	.50	.25	.15
712	Mariners Prospects (Bud Anderson, Greg Biercevicz, Byron McLaughlin)	.12	.06	.04
713	Rangers Prospects (*Danny Darwin*, Pat Putnam, *Billy Sample*)	.40	.20	.12
714	Blue Jays Prospects (Victor Cruz, Pat Kelly, Ernie Whitt)	.20	.10	.06
715	Braves Prospects (*Bruce Benedict, Glenn Hubbard*, Larry Whisenton)	.40	.20	.12
716	Cubs Prospects (Dave Geisel, Karl Pagel, *Scot Thompson*)	.12	.06	.04
717	Reds Prospects (*Mike LaCoss, Ron Oester, Harry Spilman*)	.40	.20	.12
718	Astros Prospects (Bruce Bochy, Mike Fischlin, Don Pisker)	.12	.06	.04
719	Dodgers Prospects (*Pedro Guerrero, Rudy Law*, Joe Simpson)	10.00	5.00	3.00
720	Expos Prospects (Jerry Fry, Jerry Pirtle, *Scott Sanderson*)	.30	.15	.09
721	Mets Prospects (*Juan Berenguer*, Dwight Bernard, Dan Norman)	.30	.15	.09
722	Phillies Prospects (*Jim Morrison, Lonnie Smith*, Jim Wright)	3.00	1.50	.90
723	Pirates Prospects (*Dale Berra*, Eugenio Cotes, Ben Wiltbank)	.20	.10	.06
724	Cardinals Prospects (Tom Bruno, *George Frazier, Terry Kennedy*)	.50	.25	.15
725	Padres Prospects (Jim Beswick, Steve Mura, Broderick Perkins)	.12	.06	.04
726	Giants Prospects (Greg Johnston, Joe Strain, John Tamargo)	.25	.06	.04

1979 Topps Comics

Issued as the 3" by 3-3/4" wax wrapper for a piece of bubblegum, this "test" issue was bought up in great quantities by speculators and remains rather common. It is also inexpensive, because the comic-style player representations were not popular with collectors. The set is complete at 33 pieces.

		NR MT	EX	VG
Complete Set:		6.50	3.25	2.00
Common Player:		.10	.05	.03
1	Eddie Murray	.40	.20	.12
2	Jim Rice	.30	.15	.09
3	Carl Yastrzemski	.60	.30	.20
4	Nolan Ryan	.30	.15	.09
5	Chet Lemon	.10	.05	.03
6	Andre Thornton	.10	.05	.03
7	Rusty Staub	.15	.08	.05
8	Ron LeFlore	.10	.05	.03
9	George Brett	.50	.25	.15
10	Larry Hisle	.10	.05	.03
11	Rod Carew	.35	.20	.11
12	Reggie Jackson	.40	.20	.12
13	Ron Guidry	.20	.10	.06
14	Mitchell Page	.10	.05	.03
15	Leon Roberts	.10	.05	.03
16	Al Oliver	.15	.08	.05
17	John Mayberry	.10	.05	.03
18	Bob Horner	.20	.10	.06
19	Phil Niekro	.25	.13	.08
20	Dave Kingman	.15	.08	.05
21	John Bench	.40	.20	.12
22	Tom Seaver	.40	.20	.12
23	J.R. Richard	.10	.05	.03
24	Steve Garvey	.35	.20	.11
25	Reggie Smith	.15	.08	.05
26	Ross Grimsley	.10	.05	.03
27	Craig Swan	.10	.05	.03
28	Pete Rose	.90	.45	.25
29	Dave Parker	.20	.10	.06
30	Ted Simmons	.15	.08	.05
31	Dave Winfield	.30	.15	.09
32	Jack Clark	.20	.10	.06
33	Vida Blue	.15	.08	.05

1980 Topps

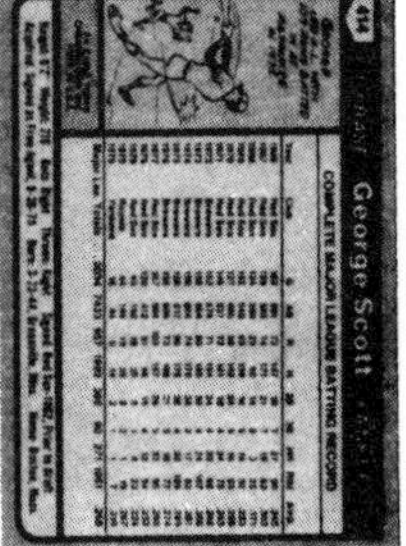

Again numbering 726 cards measuring 2-1/2" by 3-1/2", Topps did make some design changes in 1980. Fronts have the usual color picture with a facsimile autograph. The player's name appears above the picture, while his position is on a pennant at the upper left and his team on another pennant in the lower right. Backs no longer feature games, returning instead to statistics, personal information, a few headlines and a cartoon about the player. Specialty cards include statistical leaders, and previous season highlights. Many rookies again appear in team threesomes.

	NR MT	EX	VG
Complete Set:	190.00	95.00	58.00
Common Player:	.12	.06	.04

No.	Card	NR MT	EX	VG
1	1979 Highlights (Lou Brock, Carl Yastrzemski)	1.50	.70	.45
2	1979 Highlights (Willie McCovey)	.80	.40	.25
3	1979 Highlights (Manny Mota)	.20	.10	.06
4	1979 Highlights (Pete Rose)	2.00	1.00	.60
5	1979 Highlights (Garry Templeton)	.20	.10	.06
6	1979 Highlights (Del Unser)	.12	.06	.04
7	Mike Lum	.12	.06	.04
8	Craig Swan	.12	.06	.04
9	Steve Braun	.12	.06	.04
10	Denny Martinez	.20	.10	.06
11	Jimmy Sexton	.12	.06	.04
12	John Curtis	.12	.06	.04
13	Ron Pruitt	.12	.06	.04
14	Dave Cash	.12	.06	.04
15	Bill Campbell	.12	.06	.04
16	Jerry Narron	.20	.10	.06
17	Bruce Sutter	.35	.25	.14
18	Ron Jackson	.12	.06	.04
19	Balor Moore	.12	.06	.04
20	Dan Ford	.12	.06	.04
21	Manny Sarmiento	.12	.06	.04
22	Pat Putnam	.12	.06	.04
23	Derrel Thomas	.12	.06	.04
24	Jim Slaton	.12	.06	.04
25	Lee Mazzilli	.20	.10	.06
26	Marty Pattin	.12	.06	.04
27	Del Unser	.12	.06	.04
28	Bruce Kison	.12	.06	.04
29	Mark Wagner	.12	.06	.04
30	Vida Blue	.30	.15	.09
31	Jay Johnstone	.20	.10	.06
32	Julio Cruz	.12	.06	.04
33	Tony Scott	.12	.06	.04
34	Jeff Newman	.12	.06	.04
35	Luis Tiant	.30	.15	.09
36	Rusty Torres	.12	.06	.04
37	Kiko Garcia	.12	.06	.04
38	Dan Spillner	.12	.06	.04
39	Rowland Office	.12	.06	.04
40	Carlton Fisk	1.25	.60	.40
41	Rangers Team (Pat Corrales)	.50	.25	.15
42	*Dave Palmer*	.40	.20	.12
43	Bombo Rivera	.12	.06	.04
44	Bill Fahey	.12	.06	.04
45	Frank White	.25	.13	.08
46	Rico Carty	.20	.10	.06
47	Bill Bonham	.12	.06	.04
48	Rick Miller	.12	.06	.04
49	Mario Guerrero	.12	.06	.04
50	J.R. Richard	.20	.10	.06
51	Joe Ferguson	.12	.06	.04
52	Warren Brusstar	.12	.06	.04
53	Ben Oglivie	.20	.10	.06
54	Dennis Lamp	.12	.06	.04
55	Bill Madlock	.40	.20	.12
56	Bobby Valentine	.20	.10	.06
57	Pete Vuckovich	.20	.10	.06
58	Doug Flynn	.12	.06	.04
59	Eddy Putman	.12	.06	.04
60	Bucky Dent	.25	.13	.08
61	Gary Serum	.12	.06	.04
62	Mike Ivie	.12	.06	.04
63	Bob Stanley	.20	.10	.06
64	Joe Nolan	.12	.06	.04
65	Al Bumbry	.20	.10	.06
66	Royals Team (Jim Frey)	.60	.30	.20
67	Doyle Alexander	.25	.13	.08
68	Larry Harlow	.12	.06	.04
69	Rick Williams	.12	.06	.04
70	Gary Carter	2.00	1.00	.60
71	John Milner	.12	.06	.04
72	Fred Howard	.12	.06	.04
73	Dave Collins	.20	.10	.06
74	Sid Monge	.12	.06	.04
75	Bill Russell	.20	.10	.06
76	John Stearns	.12	.06	.04
77	*Dave Stieb*	6.00	3.00	1.75
78	Ruppert Jones	.12	.06	.04
79	Bob Owchinko	.12	.06	.04
80	Ron LeFlore	.20	.10	.06
81	Ted Sizemore	.12	.06	.04
82	Astros Team (Bill Virdon)	.50	.25	.15
83	*Steve Trout*	.30	.15	.09
84	Gary Lavelle	.12	.06	.04
85	Ted Simmons	.40	.20	.12
86	Dave Hamilton	.12	.06	.04
87	Pepe Frias	.12	.06	.04
88	Ken Landreaux	.20	.10	.06
89	Don Hood	.20	.10	.06
90	Manny Trillo	.20	.10	.06
91	Rick Dempsey	.20	.10	.06
92	Rick Rhoden	.25	.13	.08
93	Dave Roberts	.12	.06	.04
94	*Neil Allen*	.30	.15	.09
95	Cecil Cooper	.35	.20	.11
96	A's Team (Jim Marshall)	.50	.25	.15
97	Bill Lee	.20	.10	.06
98	Jerry Terrell	.12	.06	.04
99	Victor Cruz	.12	.06	.04
100	Johnny Bench	3.00	1.50	.90
101	Aurelio Lopez	.12	.06	.04
102	Rich Dauer	.12	.06	.04
103	*Bill Caudill*	.20	.10	.06
104	Manny Mota	.20	.10	.06
105	Frank Tanana	.20	.10	.06
106	*Jeff Leonard*	2.00	1.00	.60
107	Francisco Barrios	.12	.06	.04
108	Bob Horner	.40	.30	.15
109	Bill Travers	.12	.06	.04
110	Fred Lynn	.35	.20	.11
111	Bob Knepper	.20	.10	.06
112	White Sox Team (Tony LaRussa)	.50	.25	.15
113	Geoff Zahn	.12	.06	.04
114	Juan Beniquez	.12	.06	.04
115	Sparky Lyle	.25	.13	.08
116	Larry Cox	.12	.06	.04
117	Dock Ellis	.12	.06	.04
118	Phil Garner	.20	.10	.06
119	Sammy Stewart	.12	.06	.04
120	Greg Luzinski	.30	.15	.09
121	Checklist 1-121	.50	.25	.15
122	Dave Rosello	.12	.06	.04
123	Lynn Jones	.12	.06	.04
124	Dave Lemanczyk	.12	.06	.04
125	Tony Perez	.50	.25	.15
126	Dave Tomlin	.12	.06	.04
127	Gary Thomasson	.12	.06	.04
128	Tom Burgmeier	.12	.06	.04
129	Craig Reynolds	.12	.06	.04
130	Amos Otis	.20	.10	.06
131	Paul Mitchell	.12	.06	.04
132	Biff Pocoroba	.12	.06	.04
133	Jerry Turner	.12	.06	.04
134	Matt Keough	.12	.06	.04
135	Bill Buckner	.30	.15	.09
136	Dick Ruthven	.12	.06	.04
137	*John Castino*	.20	.10	.06
138	Ross Baumgarten	.12	.06	.04
139	*Dane Iorg*	.20	.10	.06
140	Rich Gossage	.60	.30	.20
141	Gary Alexander	.12	.06	.04
142	Phil Huffman	.12	.06	.04
143	Bruce Bochte	.12	.06	.04
144	Steve Comer	.12	.06	.04
145	Darrell Evans	.30	.15	.09
146	Bob Welch	.90	.45	.25
147	Terry Puhl	.12	.06	.04
148	Manny Sanguillen	.12	.06	.04
149	Tom Hume	.12	.06	.04
150	Jason Thompson	.20	.10	.06
151	Tom Hausman	.12	.06	.04
152	John Fulgham	.12	.06	.04
153	Tim Blackwell	.12	.06	.04
154	Lary Sorensen	.12	.06	.04
155	Jerry Remy	.12	.06	.04
156	Tony Brizzolara	.12	.06	.04
157	Willie Wilson	.20	.10	.06
158	Rob Picciolo	.12	.06	.04
159	Ken Clay	.20	.10	.06
160	Eddie Murray	3.00	1.50	.90
161	Larry Christenson	.12	.06	.04
162	Bob Randall	.12	.06	.04
163	Steve Swisher	.12	.06	.04
164	Greg Pryor	.12	.06	.04
165	Omar Moreno	.12	.06	.04
166	Glenn Abbott	.12	.06	.04
167	Jack Clark	1.00	.50	.30
168	Rick Waits	.12	.06	.04
169	Luis Gomez	.12	.06	.04
170	Burt Hooton	.20	.10	.06
171	Fernando Gonzalez	.12	.06	.04
172	Ron Hodges	.12	.06	.04
173	John Henry Johnson	.12	.06	.04
174	Ray Knight	.20	.10	.06
175	Rick Reuschel	.25	.13	.08
176	Champ Summers	.12	.06	.04
177	Dave Heaverlo	.12	.06	.04
178	Tim McCarver	.30	.15	.09
179	*Ron Davis*	.20	.10	.06
180	Warren Cromartie	.12	.06	.04
181	Moose Haas	.12	.06	.04
182	Ken Reitz	.12	.06	.04
183	Jim Anderson	.12	.06	.04
184	Steve Renko	.12	.06	.04
185	Hal McRae	.25	.13	.08
186	Junior Moore	.12	.06	.04
187	Alan Ashby	.12	.06	.04
188	Terry Crowley	.12	.06	.04
189	Kevin Kobel	.12	.06	.04
190	Buddy Bell	.25	.13	.08
191	Ted Martinez	.12	.06	.04
192	Braves Team (Bobby Cox)	.50	.25	.15
193	Dave Goltz	.20	.10	.06
194	Mike Easler	.20	.10	.06
195	John Montefusco	.20	.10	.06
196	Lance Parrish	1.50	.70	.45
197	Byron McLaughlin	.12	.06	.04
198	Dell Alston	.12	.06	.04
199	Mike LaCoss	.20	.10	.06
200	Jim Rice	2.00	1.00	.60
201	Batting Leaders (Keith Hernandez, Fred Lynn)	.50	.25	.15
202	Home Run Leaders (Dave Kingman, Gorman Thomas)	.25	.13	.08
203	Runs Batted In Leaders (Don Baylor, Dave Winfield)	.50	.25	.15
204	Stolen Base Leaders (Omar Moreno, Willie Wilson)	.20	.10	.06
205	Victory Leaders (Mike Flanagan, Joe Niekro, Phil Niekro)	.40	.20	.12
206	Strikeout Leaders (J.R. Richard, Nolan Ryan)	.50	.25	.15
207	Earned Run Avg. Leaders (Ron Guidry, J.R. Richard)	.25	.13	.08
208	Wayne Cage	.12	.06	.04
209	Von Joshua	.12	.06	.04
210	Steve Carlton	3.00	1.50	.90
211	Dave Skaggs	.12	.06	.04
212	Dave Roberts	.12	.06	.04
213	Mike Jorgensen	.12	.06	.04
214	Angels Team (Jim Fregosi)	.50	.25	.15
215	Sixto Lezcano	.12	.06	.04
216	Phil Mankowski	.12	.06	.04
217	Ed Halicki	.12	.06	.04
218	Jose Morales	.12	.06	.04
219	Steve Mingori	.12	.06	.04
220	Dave Concepcion	.30	.15	.09
221	Joe Cannon	.12	.06	.04
222	*Ron Hassey*	.35	.20	.11
223	Bob Sykes	.12	.06	.04
224	Willie Montanez	.12	.06	.04
225	Lou Piniella	.30	.15	.09
226	Bill Stein	.12	.06	.04
227	Len Barker	.12	.06	.04
228	Johnny Oates	.12	.06	.04
229	Jim Bibby	.12	.06	.04
230	Dave Winfield	2.00	1.00	.60
231	Steve McCatty	.12	.06	.04
232	Alan Trammell	3.00	1.50	.90
233	LaRue Washington	.12	.06	.04
234	Vern Ruhle	.12	.06	.04
235	Andre Dawson	3.00	1.50	.90
236	Marc Hill	.12	.06	.04
237	Scott McGregor	.20	.10	.06
238	Rob Wilfong	.12	.06	.04
239	Don Aase	.12	.06	.04
240	Dave Kingman	.40	.20	.12
241	Checklist 122-242	.50	.25	.15
242	Lamar Johnson	.12	.06	.04
243	Jerry Augustine	.12	.06	.04
244	Cardinals Team (Ken Boyer)	.50	.25	.15
245	Phil Niekro	.90	.45	.25
246	Tim Foli	.12	.06	.04
247	Frank Riccelli	.12	.06	.04
248	Jamie Quirk	.12	.06	.04
249	Jim Clancy	.20	.10	.06
250	Jim Kaat	.50	.25	.15
251	Kip Young	.12	.06	.04
252	Ted Cox	.12	.06	.04
253	John Montague	.12	.06	.04
254	Paul Dade	.12	.06	.04
255	Dusty Baker	.12	.06	.04
256	Roger Erickson	.12	.06	.04
257	Larry Herndon	.20	.10	.06
258	Paul Moskau	.12	.06	.04
259	Mets Team (Joe Torre)	.60	.30	.20
260	Al Oliver	.35	.20	.11
261	Dave Chalk	.12	.06	.04
262	Benny Ayala	.12	.06	.04
263	Dave LaRoche	.12	.06	.04
264	Bill Robinson	.12	.06	.04
265	Robin Yount	5.00	2.50	1.50
266	Bernie Carbo	.12	.06	.04
267	Dan Schatzeder	.12	.06	.04
268	Rafael Landestoy	.12	.06	.04
269	Dave Tobik	.12	.06	.04
270	Mike Schmidt	3.00	1.50	.90
271	Dick Drago	.12	.06	.04
272	Ralph Garr	.20	.10	.06
273	Eduardo Rodriguez	.12	.06	.04
274	Dale Murphy	5.50	2.75	1.75
275	Jerry Koosman	.25	.13	.08
276	Tom Veryzer	.12	.06	.04
277	Rick Bosetti	.12	.06	.04
278	Jim Spencer	.20	.10	.06
279	Rob Andrews	.12	.06	.04
280	Gaylord Perry	.90	.45	.25
281	Paul Blair	.20	.10	.06
282	Mariners Team (Darrell Johnson)	.50	.25	.15
283	John Ellis	.12	.06	.04
284	Larry Murray	.12	.06	.04
285	Don Baylor	.35	.20	.11
286	Darold Knowles	.12	.06	.04
287	John Lowenstein	.12	.06	.04
288	Dave Rozema	.12	.06	.04
289	Bruce Bochy	.12	.06	.04
290	Steve Garvey	2.00	1.00	.60
291	Randy Scarbery	.12	.06	.04
292	Dale Berra	.12	.06	.04
293	Elias Sosa	.12	.06	.04
294	Charlie Spikes	.12	.06	.04
295	Larry Gura	.12	.06	.04
296	Dave Rader	.12	.06	.04
297	Tim Johnson	.12	.06	.04
298	Ken Holtzman	.20	.10	.06
299	Steve Henderson	.12	.06	.04
300	Ron Guidry	.70	.35	.20
301	Mike Edwards	.12	.06	.04
302	Dodgers Team (Tom Lasorda)	.60	.30	.20
303	Bill Castro	.12	.06	.04
304	Butch Wynegar	.20	.10	.06
305	Randy Jones	.20	.10	.06
306	Denny Walling	.12	.06	.04
307	Rick Honeycutt	.20	.10	.06
308	Mike Hargrove	.20	.10	.06
309	Larry McWilliams	.12	.06	.04
310	Dave Parker	1.00	.50	.30
311	Roger Metzger	.12	.06	.04
312	Mike Barlow	.12	.06	.04
313	Johnny Grubb	.12	.06	.04
314	*Tim Stoddard*	.20	.10	.06
315	Steve Kemp	.25	.13	.08
316	Bob Lacey	.12	.06	.04
317	Mike Anderson	.12	.06	.04
318	Jerry Reuss	.20	.10	.06
319	Chris Speier	.12	.06	.04
320	Dennis Eckersley	.40	.20	.12
321	Keith Hernandez	1.50	.70	.45
322	Claudell Washington	.20	.10	.06
323	Mick Kelleher	.12	.06	.04
324	Tom Underwood	.12	.06	.04
325	Dan Driessen	.20	.10	.06
326	Bo McLaughlin	.12	.06	.04
327	Ray Fosse	.12	.06	.04
328	Twins Team (Gene Mauch)	.50	.25	.15
329	Bert Roberge	.12	.06	.04
330	Al Cowens	.12	.06	.04
331	Rich Hebner	.12	.06	.04
332	Enrique Romo	.12	.06	.04
333	Jim Norris	.12	.06	.04
334	Jim Beattie	.20	.10	.06
335	Willie McCovey	1.50	.70	.45
336	George Medich	.12	.06	.04

		NR MT	EX	VG
337	Carney Lansford	.30	.15	.09
338	Johnny Wockenfuss	.12	.06	.04
339	John D'Acquisto	.12	.06	.04
340	Ken Singleton	.20	.10	.06
341	Jim Essian	.12	.06	.04
342	Odell Jones	.12	.06	.04
343	Mike Vail	.12	.06	.04
344	Randy Lerch	.12	.06	.04
345	Larry Parrish	.20	.10	.06
346	Buddy Solomon	.12	.06	.04
347	*Harry Chappas*	.20	.10	.06
348	Checklist 243-363	.50	.25	.15
349	Jack Brohamer	.12	.06	.04
350	George Hendrick	.20	.10	.06
351	Bob Davis	.12	.06	.04
352	Dan Briggs	.12	.06	.04
353	Andy Hassler	.12	.06	.04
354	Rick Auerbach	.12	.06	.04
355	Gary Matthews	.20	.10	.06
356	Padres Team (Jerry Coleman)	.50	.25	.15
357	Bob McClure	.12	.06	.04
358	Lou Whitaker	1.25	.60	.40
359	Randy Moffitt	.12	.06	.04
360	Darrell Porter	.12	.06	.04
361	Wayne Garland	.12	.06	.04
362	Danny Goodwin	.12	.06	.04
363	Wayne Gross	.12	.06	.04
364	Ray Burris	.12	.06	.04
365	Bobby Murcer	.25	.13	.08
366	Rob Dressler	.12	.06	.04
367	Billy Smith	.12	.06	.04
368	*Willie Aikens*	.20	.10	.06
369	Jim Kern	.12	.06	.04
370	Cesar Cedeno	.25	.13	.08
371	Jack Morris	1.00	.50	.30
372	Joel Youngblood	.12	.06	.04
373	*Dan Petry*	.30	.15	.09
374	Jim Gantner	.20	.10	.06
375	Ross Grimsley	.12	.06	.04
376	Gary Allenson	.12	.06	.04
377	Junior Kennedy	.12	.06	.04
378	Jerry Mumphrey	.12	.06	.04
379	Kevin Bell	.12	.06	.04
380	Garry Maddox	.20	.10	.06
381	Cubs Team (Preston Gomez)	.50	.25	.15
382	Dave Freisleben	.12	.06	.04
383	Ed Ott	.12	.06	.04
384	Joey McLaughlin	.12	.06	.04
385	Enos Cabell	.12	.06	.04
386	Darrell Jackson	.12	.06	.04
387a	Fred Stanley (name in red)	.20	.10	.06
387b	Fred Stanley (name in yellow)	3.00	1.50	.90
388	Mike Paxton	.12	.06	.04
389	Pete LaCock	.12	.06	.04
390	Fergie Jenkins	.40	.20	.12
391	Tony Armas	.12	.06	.04
392	Milt Wilcox	.12	.06	.04
393	Ozzie Smith	5.00	2.50	1.50
394	Reggie Cleveland	.12	.06	.04
395	Ellis Valentine	.12	.06	.04
396	Dan Meyer	.12	.06	.04
397	Roy Thomas	.12	.06	.04
398	Barry Foote	.12	.06	.04
399	Mike Proly	.12	.06	.04
400	George Foster	.50	.25	.15
401	Pete Falcone	.12	.06	.04
402	Merv Rettenmund	.12	.06	.04
403	Pete Redfern	.12	.06	.04
404	Orioles Team (Earl Weaver)	.60	.30	.20
405	Dwight Evans	.60	.30	.20
406	Paul Molitor	1.50	.70	.45
407	Tony Solaita	.12	.06	.04
408	Bill North	.12	.06	.04
409	Paul Splittorff	.20	.10	.06
410	Bobby Bonds	.25	.13	.08
411	Frank LaCorte	.12	.06	.04
412	Thad Bosley	.12	.06	.04
413	Allen Ripley	.12	.06	.04
414	George Scott	.20	.10	.06
415	Bill Atkinson	.12	.06	.04
416	*Tom Brookens*	.35	.20	.11
417	Craig Chamberlain	.12	.06	.04
418	Roger Freed	.12	.06	.04
419	Vic Correll	.12	.06	.04
420	Butch Hobson	.12	.06	.04
421	Doug Bird	.12	.06	.04
422	Larry Milbourne	.12	.06	.04
423	Dave Frost	.12	.06	.04
424	Yankees Team (Dick Howser)	.70	.35	.20
425	Mark Belanger	.20	.10	.06
426	Grant Jackson	.12	.06	.04
427	Tom Hutton	.12	.06	.04
428	Pat Zachry	.12	.06	.04
429	Duane Kuiper	.12	.06	.04
430	Larry Hisle	.12	.06	.04
431	Mike Krukow	.20	.10	.06
432	Willie Norwood	.12	.06	.04
433	Rich Gale	.12	.06	.04
434	Johnnie LeMaster	.12	.06	.04
435	Don Gullett	.20	.10	.06
436	Billy Almon	.12	.06	.04
437	Joe Niekro	.20	.10	.06
438	Dave Revering	.12	.06	.04
439	Mike Phillips	.12	.06	.04
440	Don Sutton	.90	.45	.25
441	Eric Soderholm	.12	.06	.04
442	Jorge Orta	.12	.06	.04
443	Mike Parrott	.12	.06	.04
444	Alvis Woods	.12	.06	.04
445	Mark Fidrych	.20	.10	.06
446	Duffy Dyer	.12	.06	.04
447	Nino Espinosa	.12	.06	.04
448	Jim Wohlford	.12	.06	.04
449	Doug Bair	.12	.06	.04
450	George Brett	3.50	1.75	1.00
451	Indians Team (Dave Garcia)	.50	.25	.15
452	Steve Dillard	.12	.06	.04
453	Mike Bacsik	.12	.06	.04
454	Tom Donohue	.12	.06	.04
455	Mike Torrez	.20	.10	.06
456	Frank Taveras	.12	.06	.04
457	Bert Blyleven	.50	.25	.15
458	Billy Sample	.12	.06	.04
459	Mickey Lolich	.12	.06	.04
460	Willie Randolph	.25	.13	.08
461	Dwayne Murphy	.20	.10	.06
462	Mike Sadek	.12	.06	.04
463	Jerry Royster	.12	.06	.04
464	John Denny	.12	.06	.04
465	Rick Monday	.20	.10	.06
466	Mike Squires	.12	.06	.04
467	Jesse Jefferson	.12	.06	.04
468	Aurelio Rodriguez	.20	.10	.06
469	Randy Niemann	.12	.06	.04
470	Bob Boone	.20	.10	.06
471	Hosken Powell	.12	.06	.04
472	Willie Hernandez	.20	.10	.06
473	Bump Wills	.12	.06	.04
474	Steve Busby	.12	.06	.04
475	Cesar Geronimo	.12	.06	.04
476	Bob Shirley	.12	.06	.04
477	Buck Martinez	.12	.06	.04
478	Gil Flores	.12	.06	.04
479	Expos Team (Dick Williams)	.50	.25	.15
480	Bob Watson	.20	.10	.06
481	Tom Paciorek	.12	.06	.04
482	*Rickey Henderson*	125.00	62.00	37.00
483	Bo Diaz	.20	.10	.06
484	Checklist 364-484	.50	.25	.15
485	Mickey Rivers	.20	.10	.06
486	Mike Tyson	.12	.06	.04
487	Wayne Nordhagen	.12	.06	.04
488	Roy Howell	.12	.06	.04
489	Preston Hanna	.12	.06	.04
490	Lee May	.20	.10	.06
491	Steve Mura	.12	.06	.04
492	Todd Cruz	.12	.06	.04
493	Jerry Martin	.12	.06	.04
494	Craig Minetto	.12	.06	.04
495	Bake McBride	.12	.06	.04
496	Silvio Martinez	.12	.06	.04
497	Jim Mason	.12	.06	.04
498	Danny Darwin	.20	.10	.06
499	Giants Team (Dave Bristol)	.50	.25	.15
500	Tom Seaver	2.00	1.00	.60
501	Rennie Stennett	.12	.06	.04
502	Rich Wortham	.12	.06	.04
503	Mike Cubbage	.12	.06	.04
504	Gene Garber	.12	.06	.04
505	Bert Campaneris	.20	.10	.06
506	Tom Buskey	.12	.06	.04
507	Leon Roberts	.12	.06	.04
508	U.L. Washington	.12	.06	.04
509	Ed Glynn	.12	.06	.04
510	Ron Cey	.25	.13	.08
511	Eric Wilkins	.12	.06	.04
512	Jose Cardenal	.12	.06	.04
513	Tom Dixon	.12	.06	.04
514	Steve Ontiveros	.12	.06	.04
515	Mike Caldwell	.12	.06	.04
516	Hector Cruz	.12	.06	.04
517	Don Stanhouse	.12	.06	.04
518	Nelson Norman	.12	.06	.04
519	Steve Nicosia	.12	.06	.04
520	Steve Rogers	.20	.10	.06
521	Ken Brett	.12	.06	.04
522	Jim Morrison	.12	.06	.04
523	Ken Henderson	.12	.06	.04
524	Jim Wright	.12	.06	.04
525	Clint Hurdle	.12	.06	.04
526	Phillies Team (Dallas Green)	.70	.35	.20
527	Doug Rau	.12	.06	.04
528	Adrian Devine	.12	.06	.04
529	Jim Barr	.12	.06	.04
530	Jim Sundberg	.12	.06	.04
531	Eric Rasmussen	.12	.06	.04
532	Willie Horton	.20	.10	.06
533	Checklist 485-605	.50	.25	.15
534	Andre Thornton	.25	.13	.08
535	Bob Forsch	.20	.10	.06
536	Lee Lacy	.12	.06	.04
537	*Alex Trevino*	.20	.10	.06
538	Joe Strain	.12	.06	.04
539	Rudy May	.12	.06	.04
540	Pete Rose	4.00	2.00	1.25
541	Miguel Dilone	.12	.06	.04
542	Joe Coleman	.12	.06	.04
543	Pat Kelly	.12	.06	.04
544	*Rick Sutcliffe*	3.25	1.75	1.00
545	Jeff Burroughs	.20	.10	.06
546	Rick Langford	.12	.06	.04
547	John Wathan	.20	.10	.06
548	Dave Rajsich	.12	.06	.04
549	Larry Wolfe	.12	.06	.04
550	Ken Griffey	.25	.13	.08
551	Pirates Team (Chuck Tanner)	.50	.25	.15
552	Bill Nahorodny	.12	.06	.04
553	Dick Davis	.12	.06	.04
554	Art Howe	.12	.06	.04
555	Ed Figueroa	.20	.10	.06
556	Joe Rudi	.20	.10	.06
557	Mark Lee	.12	.06	.04
558	Alfredo Griffin	.25	.13	.08
559	Dale Murray	.12	.06	.04
560	Dave Lopes	.25	.13	.08
561	Eddie Whitson	.20	.10	.06
562	Joe Wallis	.12	.06	.04
563	Will McEnaney	.12	.06	.04
564	Rick Manning	.12	.06	.04
565	Dennis Leonard	.20	.10	.06
566	Bud Harrelson	.20	.10	.06
567	Skip Lockwood	.12	.06	.04
568	*Gary Roenicke*	.25	.13	.08
569	Terry Kennedy	.25	.13	.08
570	Roy Smalley	.20	.10	.06
571	Joe Sambito	.12	.06	.04
572	Jerry Morales	.12	.06	.04
573	Kent Tekulve	.20	.10	.06
574	Scot Thompson	.12	.06	.04
575	Ken Kravec	.12	.06	.04
576	Jim Dwyer	.12	.06	.04
577	Blue Jays Team (Bobby Mattick)	.50	.25	.15
578	Scott Sanderson	.20	.10	.06
579	Charlie Moore	.12	.06	.04
580	Nolan Ryan	10.00	5.00	3.00
581	Bob Bailor	.12	.06	.04
582	Brian Doyle	.20	.10	.06
583	Bob Stinson	.12	.06	.04
584	Kurt Bevacqua	.12	.06	.04
585	Al Hrabosky	.20	.10	.06
586	Mitchell Page	.12	.06	.04
587	Garry Templeton	.20	.10	.06
588	Greg Minton	.12	.06	.04
589	Chet Lemon	.20	.10	.06
590	Jim Palmer	2.00	1.00	.60
591	Rick Cerone	.12	.06	.04
592	Jon Matlack	.20	.10	.06
593	Jesus Alou	.12	.06	.04
594	Dick Tidrow	.12	.06	.04
595	Don Money	.12	.06	.04
596	Rick Matula	.12	.06	.04
597	Tom Poquette	.12	.06	.04
598	Fred Kendall	.12	.06	.04
599	Mike Norris	.12	.06	.04
600	Reggie Jackson	2.50	1.25	.70
601	Buddy Schultz	.12	.06	.04
602	Brian Downing	.20	.10	.06
603	Jack Billingham	.12	.06	.04
604	Glenn Adams	.12	.06	.04
605	Terry Forster	.20	.10	.06
606	Reds Team (John McNamara)	.50	.25	.15
607	Woodie Fryman	.20	.10	.06
608	Alan Bannister	.12	.06	.04
609	Ron Reed	.20	.10	.06
610	Willie Stargell	1.50	.70	.45
611	Jerry Garvin	.12	.06	.04
612	Cliff Johnson	.12	.06	.04
613	Randy Stein	.12	.06	.04
614	John Hiller	.20	.10	.06
615	Doug DeCinces	.20	.10	.06
616	Gene Richards	.12	.06	.04
617	Joaquin Andujar	.20	.10	.06
618	Bob Montgomery	.12	.06	.04
619	Sergio Ferrer	.12	.06	.04
620	Richie Zisk	.20	.10	.06
621	Bob Grich	.20	.10	.06
622	Mario Soto	.20	.10	.06
623	Gorman Thomas	.20	.10	.06
624	Lerrin LaGrow	.12	.06	.04
625	Chris Chambliss	.25	.13	.08
626	Tigers Team (Sparky Anderson)	.60	.30	.20
627	Pedro Borbon	.12	.06	.04
628	Doug Capilla	.12	.06	.04
629	Jim Todd	.12	.06	.04
630	Larry Bowa	.25	.13	.08
631	Mark Littell	.12	.06	.04
632	Barry Bonnell	.12	.06	.04
633	Bob Apodaca	.12	.06	.04
634	Glenn Borgmann	.12	.06	.04
635	John Candelaria	.20	.10	.06
636	Toby Harrah	.20	.10	.06
637	Joe Simpson	.12	.06	.04
638	*Mark Clear*	.20	.10	.06
639	Larry Biittner	.12	.06	.04
640	Mike Flanagan	.25	.13	.08
641	Ed Kranepool	.20	.10	.06
642	Ken Forsch	.12	.06	.04
643	John Mayberry	.20	.10	.06
644	Charlie Hough	.20	.10	.06
645	Rick Burleson	.20	.10	.06
646	Checklist 606-726	.50	.25	.15
647	Milt May	.12	.06	.04
648	Roy White	.20	.10	.06
649	Tom Griffin	.12	.06	.04
650	Joe Morgan	1.50	.70	.45
651	Rollie Fingers	.50	.25	.15
652	Mario Mendoza	.12	.06	.04
653	Stan Bahnsen	.12	.06	.04
654	Bruce Boisclair	.12	.06	.04
655	Tug McGraw	.25	.13	.08
656	Larvell Blanks	.12	.06	.04
657	Dave Edwards	.12	.06	.04
658	Chris Knapp	.12	.06	.04
659	Brewers Team (George Bamberger)	.50	.25	.15
660	Rusty Staub	.30	.15	.09
661	Orioles Future Stars (Mark Corey, Dave Ford, Wayne Krenchicki)	.12	.06	.04
662	Red Sox Future Stars (Joel Finch, Mike O'Berry, Chuck Rainey)	.12	.06	.04
663	Angels Future Stars (Ralph Botting, Bob Clark, *Dickie Thon)*	.30	.15	.09
664	White Sox Future Stars (Mike Colbern, *Guy Hoffman*, Dewey Robinson)	.20	.10	.06
665	Indians Future Stars (Larry Andersen, Bobby Cuellar, Sandy Wihtol)	.12	.06	.04
666	Tigers Future Stars (Mike Chris, Al Greene, Bruce Robbins)	.12	.06	.04
667	Royals Future Stars (Renie Martin, Bill Paschall, *Dan Quisenberry)*	1.00	.50	.30
668	Brewers Future Stars (Danny Boitano, Willie Mueller, Lenn Sakata)	.12	.06	.04
669	Twins Future Stars (Dan Graham, Rick Sofield, *Gary Ward)*	.35	.20	.11
670	Yankees Future Stars (Bobby Brown, Brad Gulden, Darryl Jones)	.20	.10	.06
671	A's Future Stars (Derek Bryant, Brian Kingman, *Mike Morgan)*	.20	.10	.06
672	Mariners Future Stars (Charlie Beamon, Rodney Craig, Rafael Vasquez)	.12	.06	.04
673	Rangers Future Stars (Brian Allard, Jerry Don Gleaton, Greg Mahlberg)	.12	.06	.04
674	Blue Jays Future Stars (Butch Edge, Pat Kelly, Ted Wilborn)	.12	.06	.04
675	Braves Future Stars (Bruce Benedict, Larry Bradford, Eddie Miller)	.12	.06	.04
676	Cubs Future Stars (Dave Geisel, Steve Macko, Karl Pagel)	.12	.06	.04

		NR MT	EX	VG
677	Reds Future Stars (Art DeFreites, *Frank Pastore*, Harry Spilman)	.12	.06	.04
678	Astros Future Stars (Reggie Baldwin, Alan Knicely, *Pete Ladd*)	.12	.06	.04
679	Dodgers Future Stars (Joe Beckwith, *Mickey Hatcher*, Dave Patterson)	.50	.25	.15
680	Expos Future Stars *(Tony Bernazard*, Randy Miller, John Tamargo)	.20	.10	.06
681	Mets Future Stars (Dan Norman, *Jesse Orosco, Mike Scott*)	10.00	5.00	3.00
682	Phillies Future Stars (Ramon Aviles, *Dickie Noles*, Kevin Saucier)	.20	.10	.06
683	Pirates Future Stars (Dorian Boyland, Alberto Lois, Harry Saferight)	.12	.06	.04
684	Cardinals Future Stars (George Frazier, *Tom Herr*, Dan O'Brien)	.50	.40	.20
685	Padres Future Stars (Tim Flannery, Brian Greer, Jim Wilhelm)	.12	.06	.04
686	Giants Future Stars (Greg Johnston, Dennis Littlejohn, Phil Nastu)	.12	.06	.04
687	Mike Heath	.12	.06	.04
688	Steve Stone	.20	.10	.06
689	Red Sox Team (Don Zimmer)	.60	.30	.20
690	Tommy John	.60	.30	.20
691	Ivan DeJesus	.12	.06	.04
692	Rawly Eastwick	.12	.06	.04
693	Craig Kusick	.12	.06	.04
694	Jim Rooker	.12	.06	.04
695	Reggie Smith	.20	.10	.06
696	Julio Gonzalez	.12	.06	.04
697	David Clyde	.12	.06	.04
698	Oscar Gamble	.20	.10	.06
699	Floyd Bannister	.20	.10	.06
700	Rod Carew	1.50	.70	.45
701	*Ken Oberkfell*	.30	.15	.09
702	Ed Farmer	.12	.06	.04
703	Otto Velez	.12	.06	.04
704	Gene Tenace	.20	.10	.06
705	Freddie Patek	.12	.06	.04
706	Tippy Martinez	.12	.06	.04
707	Elliott Maddox	.12	.06	.04
708	Bob Tolan	.12	.06	.04
709	Pat Underwood	.12	.06	.04
710	Graig Nettles	.35	.20	.11
711	Bob Galasso	.12	.06	.04
712	Rodney Scott	.12	.06	.04
713	Terry Whitfield	.12	.06	.04
714	Fred Norman	.12	.06	.04
715	Sal Bando	.20	.10	.06
716	Lynn McGlothen	.12	.06	.04
717	Mickey Klutts	.12	.06	.04
718	Greg Gross	.12	.06	.04
719	Don Robinson	.20	.10	.06
720	Carl Yastrzemski	1.25	.60	.40
721	Paul Hartzell	.12	.06	.04
722	Jose Cruz	.20	.10	.06
723	Shane Rawley	.20	.10	.06
724	Jerry White	.12	.06	.04
725	Rick Wise	.20	.10	.06
726	Steve Yeager	.20	.06	.04

1980 Topps 5x7 Superstar Photos

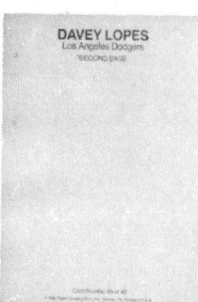

In actuality, these cards measure 4-7/8" by 6-7/8". These were another Topps "test" issue that was bought out almost entirely by investors. The 60 cards have a color photo on the front and a blue ink facsimile autograph. Backs have the player's name, team position and card number. The issue was printed on different cardboard stocks, with the first on thick cardboard with a white back and the second on thinner cardboard with a gray back. Prices below are for the more common gray backs; white backs are valued about three times the figures shown. The issue was distributed in selected geographical areas, but they were hoarded quickly. Those who hoarded them still probably have much of their supply as the set has never taken off, despite the presence of many big-name stars.

		NR MT	EX	VG
	Complete Set:	7.00	3.50	2.00
	Common Player:	.10	.05	.03
1	Willie Stargell	.30	.15	.09
2	Mike Schmidt	.30	.15	.09
3	Johnny Bench	.50	.25	.15
4	Jim Palmer	.35	.20	.11
5	Jim Rice	.40	.20	.12
6	Reggie Jackson	.25	.13	.08
7	Ron Guidry	.20	.10	.06
8	Lee Mazzilli	.10	.05	.03
9	Don Baylor	.15	.08	.05
10	Fred Lynn	.20	.10	.06
11	Ken Singleton	.10	.05	.03
12	Rod Carew	.25	.13	.08
13	Steve Garvey	.25	.13	.08
14	George Brett	.30	.15	.09
15	Tom Seaver	.40	.20	.12
16	Dave Kingman	.15	.08	.05
17	Dave Parker	.10	.05	.03
18	Dave Winfield	.40	.20	.12
19	Pete Rose	1.00	.50	.30
20	Nolan Ryan	.40	.20	.12
21	Graig Nettles	.15	.08	.05
22	Carl Yastrzemski	.60	.30	.20
23	Tommy John	.25	.13	.08
24	George Foster	.15	.08	.05
25	James Rodney Richard	.10	.05	.03
26	Keith Hernandez	.30	.15	.09
27	Bob Horner	.15	.08	.05
28	Eddie Murray	.40	.20	.12
29	Steve Kemp	.10	.05	.03
30	Gorman Thomas	.10	.05	.03
31	Sixto Lezcano	.10	.05	.03
32	Bruce Sutter	.15	.08	.05
33	Cecil Cooper	.15	.08	.05
34	Larry Bowa	.10	.05	.03
35	Al Oliver	.15	.08	.05
36	Ted Simmons	.15	.08	.05
37	Garry Templeton	.10	.05	.03
38	Jerry Koosman	.10	.05	.03
39	Darrell Porter	.10	.05	.03
40	Roy Smalley	.10	.05	.03
41	Craig Swan	.10	.05	.03
42	Jason Thompson	.10	.05	.03
43	Andre Thornton	.10	.05	.03
44	Rick Manning	.10	.05	.03
45	Kent Tekulve	.10	.05	.03
46	Phil Niekro	.30	.15	.09
47	Buddy Bell	.15	.08	.05
48	Randy Jones	.10	.05	.03
49	Brian Downing	.10	.05	.03
50	Amos Otis	.10	.05	.03
51	Rick Bosetti	.10	.05	.03
52	Gary Carter	.40	.20	.12
53	Larry Parrish	.15	.08	.05
54	Jack Clark	.20	.10	.06
55	Bruce Bochte	.10	.05	.03
56	Cesar Cedeno	.15	.08	.05
57	Chet Lemon	.10	.05	.03
58	Dave Revering	.10	.05	.03
59	Vida Blue	.15	.08	.05
60	Davey Lopes	.15	.08	.05

1981 Topps
5x7 Home Team Photos

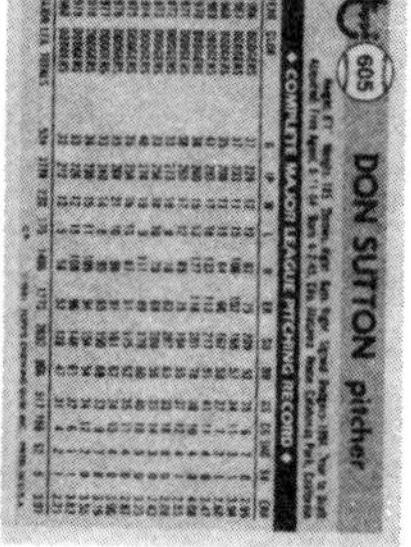

This is another 726-card set of 2-1/2" by 3-1/2" cards from Topps. The cards have the usual color photo with all cards from the same team sharing the same color borders. The player's name appears under the photo with his team and position appearing on a baseball cap at the lower left. The Topps logo returned in a small baseball in the lower right corner. Card backs include the usual stats along with a headline and a cartoon if there was room. Specialty cards include previous season record-breakers, highlights of the playoffs and World Series, along with the final appearance of team cards.

		MT	NR MT	EX
	Complete Set:	100.00	75.00	40.00
	Common Player:	.08	.06	.03
1	Batting Leaders (George Brett, Bill Buckner)	.70	.50	.30
2	Home Run Leaders (Reggie Jackson, Ben Oglivie, Mike Schmidt)	.40	.30	.15
3	Runs Batted In Leaders (Cecil Cooper, Mike Schmidt)	.30	.25	.12
4	Stolen Base Leaders (Rickey Henderson, Ron LeFlore)	.25	.20	.10
5	Victory Leaders (Steve Carlton, Steve Stone)	.20	.15	.08
6	Strikeout Leaders (Len Barker, Steve Carlton)	.20	.15	.08
7	Earned Run Avg. Leaders (Rudy May, Don Sutton)	.15	.11	.06
8	Leading Firemen (Rollie Fingers, Tom Hume, Dan Quisenberry)	.10	.08	.04
9	Pete LaCock	.08	.06	.03
10	Mike Flanagan	.12	.09	.05
11	Jim Wohlford	.08	.06	.03
12	Mark Clear	.08	.06	.03
13	*Joe Charboneau*	.15	.11	.06
14	*John Tudor*	1.25	.90	.50
15	Larry Parrish	.15	.11	.06
16	Ron Davis	.10	.08	.04
17	Cliff Johnson	.08	.06	.03
18	Glenn Adams	.08	.06	.03
19	Jim Clancy	.12	.09	.05
20	Jeff Burroughs	.10	.08	.04
21	Ron Oester	.08	.06	.03
22	Danny Darwin	.08	.06	.03
23	Alex Trevino	.08	.06	.03
24	Don Stanhouse	.08	.06	.03
25	Sixto Lezcano	.08	.06	.03
26	U.L. Washington	.08	.06	.03
27	Champ Summers	.08	.06	.03
28	Enrique Romo	.08	.06	.03
29	Gene Tenace	.10	.08	.04
30	Jack Clark	.50	.40	.20
31	Checklist 1-121	.08	.06	.03
32	Ken Oberkfell	.08	.06	.03
33	Rick Honeycutt	.08	.06	.03
34	Aurelio Rodriguez	.10	.08	.04
35	Mitchell Page	.08	.06	.03
36	Ed Farmer	.08	.06	.03
37	Gary Roenicke	.08	.06	.03
38	Win Remmerswaal	.08	.06	.03
39	Tom Veryzer	.08	.06	.03
40	Tug McGraw	.20	.15	.08
41	Rangers Future Stars (Bob Babcock, John Butcher, Jerry Don Gleaton)	.10	.08	.04
42	Jerry White	.08	.06	.03
43	Jose Morales	.08	.06	.03
44	Larry McWilliams	.08	.06	.03
45	Enos Cabell	.08	.06	.03
46	Rick Bosetti	.08	.06	.03
47	Ken Brett	.10	.08	.04
48	Dave Skaggs	.08	.06	.03
49	Bob Shirley	.08	.06	.03
50	Dave Lopes	.12	.09	.05
51	Bill Robinson	.08	.06	.03
52	Hector Cruz	.08	.06	.03
53	Kevin Saucier	.08	.06	.03
54	Ivan DeJesus	.08	.06	.03
55	Mike Norris	.08	.06	.03
56	Buck Martinez	.08	.06	.03
57	Dave Roberts	.08	.06	.03
58	Joel Youngblood	.08	.06	.03
59	Dan Petry	.12	.09	.05
60	Willie Randolph	.15	.11	.06
61	Butch Wynegar	.08	.06	.03
62	Joe Pettini	.08	.06	.03
63	Steve Renko	.08	.06	.03
64	Brian Asselstine	.08	.06	.03
65	Scott McGregor	.10	.08	.04
66	Royals Future Stars (Manny Castillo, Tim Ireland, Mike Jones)	.08	.06	.03
67	Ken Kravec	.08	.06	.03
68	Matt Alexander	.08	.06	.03
69	Ed Halicki	.08	.06	.03
70	Al Oliver	.15	.11	.06
71	Hal Dues	.08	.06	.03
72	Barry Evans	.08	.06	.03
73	Doug Bair	.08	.06	.03
74	Mike Hargrove	.08	.06	.03
75	Reggie Smith	.15	.11	.06
76	Mario Mendoza	.08	.06	.03
77	Mike Barlow	.08	.06	.03
78	Steve Dillard •	.08	.06	.03
79	Bruce Robbins	.08	.06	.03
80	Rusty Staub	.15	.11	.06
81	Dave Stapleton	.08	.06	.03
82	Astros Future Stars (Danny Heep, Alan Knicely, Bobby Sprowl)	.08	.06	.03
83	Mike Proly	.08	.06	.03
84	Johnnie LeMaster	.08	.06	.03
85	Mike Caldwell	.08	.06	.03
86	Wayne Gross	.08	.06	.03
87	Rick Camp	.08	.06	.03
88	Joe Lefebvre	.08	.06	.03
89	Darrell Jackson	.08	.06	.03
90	Bake McBride	.08	.06	.03
91	Tim Stoddard	.08	.06	.03
92	Mike Easler	.10	.08	.04
93	Ed Glynn	.08	.06	.03
94	Harry Spilman	.08	.06	.03
95	Jim Sundberg	.10	.08	.04
96	A's Future Stars (Dave Beard, *Ernie Camacho*, Pat Dempsey)	.12	.09	.05
97	Chris Speier	.08	.06	.03
98	Clint Hurdle	.08	.06	.03
99	Eric Wilkins	.08	.06	.03
100	Rod Carew	2.00	1.50	.80
101	Benny Ayala	.08	.06	.03
102	Dave Tobik	.08	.06	.03
103	Jerry Martin	.08	.06	.03
104	Terry Forster	.10	.08	.04
105	Jose Cruz	.15	.11	.06
106	Don Money	.08	.06	.03
107	Rich Wortham	.08	.06	.03
108	Bruce Benedict	.08	.06	.03
109	Mike Scott	1.00	.70	.40
110	Carl Yastrzemski	2.00	1.50	.80
111	Greg Minton	.08	.06	.03
112	White Sox Future Stars (Rusty Kuntz, Fran Mullins, Leo Sutherland)	.08	.06	.03
113	Mike Phillips	.08	.06	.03
114	Tom Underwood	.08	.06	.03
115	Roy Smalley	.08	.06	.03
116	Joe Simpson	.08	.06	.03
117	Pete Falcone	.08	.06	.03
118	Kurt Bevacqua	.08	.06	.03
119	Tippy Martinez	.08	.06	.03
120	Larry Bowa	.20	.15	.08
121	Larry Harlow	.08	.06	.03
122	John Denny	.08	.06	.03
123	Al Cowens	.08	.06	.03
124	Jerry Garvin	.08	.06	.03
125	Andre Dawson	.90	.70	.35
126	*Charlie Leibrandt*	.50	.40	.20
127	Rudy Law	.08	.06	.03
128	Gary Allenson	.08	.06	.03
129	Art Howe	.08	.06	.03

#	Card	MT	NR MT	EX
130	Larry Gura	.08	.06	.03
131	*Keith Moreland*	.45	.35	.20
132	Tommy Boggs	.08	.06	.03
133	Jeff Cox	.08	.06	.03
134	Steve Mura	.08	.06	.03
135	Gorman Thomas	.12	.09	.05
136	Doug Capilla	.08	.06	.03
137	Hosken Powell	.08	.06	.03
138	*Rich Dotson*	.30	.25	.12
139	Oscar Gamble	.10	.08	.04
140	Bob Forsch	.10	.08	.04
141	Miguel Dilone	.08	.06	.03
142	Jackson Todd	.08	.06	.03
143	Dan Meyer	.08	.06	.03
144	Allen Ripley	.08	.06	.03
145	Mickey Rivers	.10	.08	.04
146	Bobby Castillo	.08	.06	.03
147	Dale Berra	.08	.06	.03
148	Randy Niemann	.08	.06	.03
149	Joe Nolan	.08	.06	.03
150	Mark Fidrych	.12	.09	.05
151	Claudell Washington	.12	.09	.05
152	John Urrea	.08	.06	.03
153	Tom Poquette	.08	.06	.03
154	Rick Langford	.08	.06	.03
155	Chris Chambliss	.12	.09	.05
156	Bob McClure	.08	.06	.03
157	John Wathan	.12	.09	.05
158	Fergie Jenkins	.30	.25	.12
159	Brian Doyle	.08	.06	.03
160	Garry Maddox	.12	.09	.05
161	Dan Graham	.08	.06	.03
162	Doug Corbett	.08	.06	.03
163	Billy Almon	.08	.06	.03
164	*Lamarr Hoyt (LaMarr)*	.20	.15	.08
165	Tony Scott	.08	.06	.03
166	Floyd Bannister	.12	.09	.05
167	Terry Whitfield	.08	.06	.03
168	Don Robinson	.08	.06	.03
169	John Mayberry	.10	.08	.04
170	Ross Grimsley	.08	.06	.03
171	Gene Richards	.08	.06	.03
172	Gary Woods	.08	.06	.03
173	Bump Wills	.08	.06	.03
174	Doug Rau	.08	.06	.03
175	Dave Collins	.10	.08	.04
176	Mike Krukow	.10	.08	.04
177	Rick Peters	.08	.06	.03
178	Jim Essian	.08	.06	.03
179	Rudy May	.08	.06	.03
180	Pete Rose	3.25	2.50	1.25
181	Elias Sosa	.08	.06	.03
182	Bob Grich	.15	.11	.06
183	Dick Davis	.08	.06	.03
184	Jim Dwyer	.08	.06	.03
185	Dennis Leonard	.10	.08	.04
186	Wayne Nordhagen	.08	.06	.03
187	Mike Parrott	.08	.06	.03
188	Doug DeCinces	.15	.11	.06
189	Craig Swan	.08	.06	.03
190	Cesar Cedeno	.15	.11	.06
191	Rick Sutcliffe	.40	.30	.15
192	Braves Future Stars (*Terry Harper*, Ed Miller, *Rafael Ramirez)*	.25	.20	.10
193	Pete Vuckovich	.10	.08	.04
194	*Rod Scurry*	.10	.08	.04
195	Rich Murray	.08	.06	.03
196	Duffy Dyer	.08	.06	.03
197	Jim Kern	.08	.06	.03
198	Jerry Dybzinski	.08	.06	.03
199	Chuck Rainey	.08	.06	.03
200	George Foster	.25	.20	.10
201	Record Breaker (Johnny Bench)	.40	.30	.15
202	Record Breaker (Steve Carlton)	.40	.30	.15
203	Record Breaker (Bill Gullickson)	.08	.06	.03
204	Record Breaker (Ron LeFlore, Rodney Scott)	.10	.08	.04
205	Record Breaker (Pete Rose)	.80	.60	.30
206	Record Breaker (Mike Schmidt)	.50	.40	.20
207	Record Breaker (Ozzie Smith)	.20	.15	.08
208	Record Breaker (Willie Wilson)	.20	.15	.08
209	Dickie Thon	.10	.08	.04
210	Jim Palmer	2.00	1.50	.80
211	Derrel Thomas	.08	.06	.03
212	Steve Nicosia	.08	.06	.03
213	*Al Holland*	.10	.08	.04
214	Angels Future Stars (Ralph Botting, Jim Dorsey, John Harris)	.08	.06	.03
215	Larry Hisle	.10	.08	.04
216	John Henry Johnson	.08	.06	.03
217	Rich Hebner	.08	.06	.03
218	Paul Splittorff	.08	.06	.03
219	Ken Landreaux	.08	.06	.03
220	Tom Seaver	2.00	1.50	.80
221	Bob Davis	.08	.06	.03
222	Jorge Orta	.08	.06	.03
223	Roy Lee Jackson	.08	.06	.03
224	Pat Zachry	.08	.06	.03
225	Ruppert Jones	.08	.06	.03
226	Manny Sanguillen	.08	.06	.03
227	Fred Martinez	.08	.06	.03
228	Tom Paciorek	.08	.06	.03
229	Rollie Fingers	.60	.45	.25
230	George Hendrick	.10	.08	.04
231	Joe Beckwith	.08	.06	.03
232	Mickey Klutts	.08	.06	.03
233	Skip Lockwood	.08	.06	.03
234	Lou Whitaker	.60	.45	.25
235	Scott Sanderson	.08	.06	.03
236	Mike Ivie	.08	.06	.03
237	Charlie Moore	.08	.06	.03
238	Willie Hernandez	.12	.09	.05
239	Rick Miller	.08	.06	.03
240	Nolan Ryan	3.00	2.25	1.25
241	Checklist 122-242	.08	.06	.03
242	Chet Lemon	.10	.08	.04
243	Sal Butera	.08	.06	.03

#	Card	MT	NR MT	EX
244	Cardinals Future Stars (*Tito Landrum*, Al Olmsted, Andy Rincon)	.15	.11	.06
245	Ed Figueroa	.08	.06	.03
246	Ed Ott	.08	.06	.03
247	Glenn Hubbard	.10	.08	.04
248	Joey McLaughlin	.08	.06	.03
249	Larry Cox	.08	.06	.03
250	Ron Guidry	.50	.40	.20
251	Tom Brookens	.10	.08	.04
252	Victor Cruz	.08	.06	.03
253	Dave Bergman	.08	.06	.03
254	Ozzie Smith	2.00	1.50	.80
255	Mark Littell	.08	.06	.03
256	Bombo Rivera	.08	.06	.03
257	Rennie Stennett	.08	.06	.03
258	*Joe Price*	.12	.09	.05
259	Mets Future Stars (Juan Berenguer, *Hubie Brooks, Mookie Wilson)*	2.50	2.00	1.00
260	Ron Cey	.15	.11	.06
261	Rickey Henderson	20.00	15.00	8.00
262	Sammy Stewart	.08	.06	.03
263	Brian Downing	.12	.09	.05
264	Jim Norris	.08	.06	.03
265	John Candelaria	.12	.09	.05
266	Tom Herr	.15	.11	.06
267	Stan Bahnsen	.08	.06	.03
268	Jerry Royster	.08	.06	.03
269	Ken Forsch	.08	.06	.03
270	Greg Luzinski	.20	.15	.08
271	Bill Castro	.08	.06	.03
272	Bruce Kimm	.08	.06	.03
273	Stan Papi	.08	.06	.03
274	Craig Chamberlain	.08	.06	.03
275	Dwight Evans	.25	.20	.10
276	Dan Spillner	.08	.06	.03
277	Alfredo Griffin	.12	.09	.05
278	Rick Sofield	.08	.06	.03
279	Bob Knepper	.12	.09	.05
280	Ken Griffey	.15	.11	.06
281	Fred Stanley	.08	.06	.03
282	Mariners Future Stars (Rick Anderson, Greg Biercevicz, Rodney Craig)	.08	.06	.03
283	Billy Sample	.08	.06	.03
284	Brian Kingman	.08	.06	.03
285	Jerry Turner	.08	.06	.03
286	Dave Frost	.08	.06	.03
287	Lenn Sakata	.08	.06	.03
288	Bob Clark	.08	.06	.03
289	Mickey Hatcher	.10	.08	.04
290	Bob Boone	.08	.06	.03
291	Aurelio Lopez	.08	.06	.03
292	Mike Squires	.08	.06	.03
293	*Charlie Lea*	.15	.11	.06
294	Mike Tyson	.08	.06	.03
295	Hal McRae	.15	.11	.06
296	Bill Nahorodny	.08	.06	.03
297	Bob Bailor	.08	.06	.03
298	Buddy Solomon	.08	.06	.03
299	Elliott Maddox	.08	.06	.03
300	Paul Molitor	.40	.30	.15
301	Matt Keough	.08	.06	.03
302	Dodgers Future Stars (Jack Perconte, *Mike Scioscia, Fernando Valenzuela)*	5.50	4.25	2.25
303	Johnny Oates	.08	.06	.03
304	John Castino	.08	.06	.03
305	Ken Clay	.08	.06	.03
306	Juan Beniquez	.08	.06	.03
307	Gene Garber	.08	.06	.03
308	Rick Manning	.08	.06	.03
309	*Luis Salazar*	.20	.15	.08
310	Vida Blue	.08	.06	.03
311	Freddie Patek	.08	.06	.03
312	Rick Rhoden	.12	.09	.05
313	Luis Pujols	.08	.06	.03
314	Rich Dauer	.08	.06	.03
315	*Kirk Gibson*	6.00	4.50	2.50
316	Craig Minetto	.08	.06	.03
317	Lonnie Smith	.10	.08	.04
318	Steve Yeager	.08	.06	.03
319	Rowland Office	.08	.06	.03
320	Tom Burgmeier	.08	.06	.03
321	*Leon Durham*	.25	.20	.10
322	Neil Allen	.10	.08	.04
323	Jim Morrison	.08	.06	.03
324	Mike Willis	.08	.06	.03
325	Ray Knight	.12	.09	.05
326	Biff Pocoroba	.08	.06	.03
327	Moose Haas	.08	.06	.03
328	Twins Future Stars (*Dave Engle*, Greg Johnston, Gary Ward)	.12	.09	.05
329	Joaquin Andujar	.12	.09	.05
330	Frank White	.12	.09	.05
331	Dennis Lamp	.08	.06	.03
332	Lee Lacy	.08	.06	.03
333	Sid Monge	.08	.06	.03
334	Dane Iorg	.08	.06	.03
335	Rick Cerone	.08	.06	.03
336	Eddie Whitson	.08	.06	.03
337	Lynn Jones	.08	.06	.03
338	Checklist 243-363	.25	.20	.10
339	John Ellis	.08	.06	.03
340	Bruce Kison	.08	.06	.03
341	Dwayne Murphy	.10	.08	.04
342	Eric Rasmussen	.08	.06	.03
343	Frank Taveras	.08	.06	.03
344	Byron McLaughlin	.08	.06	.03
345	Warren Cromartie	.08	.06	.03
346	Larry Christenson	.08	.06	.03
347	*Harold Baines*	4.00	3.00	1.50
348	Bob Sykes	.08	.06	.03
349	Glenn Hoffman	.08	.06	.03
350	J.R. Richard	.12	.09	.05
351	Otto Velez	.08	.06	.03
352	Dick Tidrow	.08	.06	.03
353	Terry Kennedy	.12	.09	.05
354	Mario Soto	.10	.08	.04
355	Bob Horner	.25	.20	.10
356	Padres Future Stars (George Stablein, Craig Stimac, Tom Tellmann)	.08	.06	.03
357	Jim Slaton	.08	.06	.03
358	Mark Wagner	.08	.06	.03

#	Card	MT	NR MT	EX
359	Tom Hausman	.08	.06	.03
360	Willie Wilson	.30	.25	.12
361	Joe Strain	.08	.06	.03
362	Bo Diaz	.10	.08	.04
363	Geoff Zahn	.08	.06	.03
364	*Mike Davis*	.35	.25	.14
365	Graig Nettles	.12	.09	.05
366	Mike Ramsey	.08	.06	.03
367	Denny Martinez	.10	.08	.04
368	Leon Roberts	.08	.06	.03
369	Frank Tanana	.12	.09	.05
370	Dave Winfield	1.00	.70	.40
371	Charlie Hough	.15	.11	.06
372	Jay Johnstone	.10	.08	.04
373	Pat Underwood	.08	.06	.03
374	Tom Hutton	.08	.06	.03
375	Dave Concepcion	.20	.15	.08
376	Ron Reed	.08	.06	.03
377	Jerry Morales	.08	.06	.03
378	Dave Rader	.08	.06	.03
379	Lary Sorensen	.08	.06	.03
380	Willie Stargell	1.00	.70	.40
381	Cubs Future Stars (Carlos Lezcano, Steve Macko, Randy Martz)	.08	.06	.03
382	*Paul Mirabella*(FC)	.12	.09	.05
383	Eric Soderholm	.08	.06	.03
384	Mike Sadek	.08	.06	.03
385	Joe Sambito	.08	.06	.03
386	Dave Edwards	.08	.06	.03
387	Phil Niekro	.70	.50	.30
388	Andre Thornton	.12	.09	.05
389	Marty Pattin	.08	.06	.03
390	Cesar Geronimo	.08	.06	.03
391	Dave Lemanczyk	.08	.06	.03
392	Lance Parrish	.70	.50	.30
393	Broderick Perkins	.08	.06	.03
394	Woodie Fryman	.10	.08	.04
395	Scot Thompson	.08	.06	.03
396	Bill Campbell	.08	.06	.03
397	Julio Cruz	.08	.06	.03
398	Ross Baumgarten	.08	.06	.03
399	Orioles Future Stars (*Mike Boddicker*, Mark Corey, *Floyd Rayford)*	1.50	1.25	.60
400	Reggie Jackson	2.00	1.50	.80
401	A.L. Championships (Royals Sweep Yankees)	.50	.40	.20
402	N.L. Championships (Phillies Squeak Past Astros)	.40	.30	.15
403	World Series (Phillies Beat Royals In 6)	.25	.20	.10
404	World Series Summary (Phillies Win First World Series)	.25	.20	.10
405	Nino Espinosa	.08	.06	.03
406	Dickie Noles	.08	.06	.03
407	Ernie Whitt	.10	.08	.04
408	Fernando Arroyo	.08	.06	.03
409	Larry Herndon	.10	.08	.04
410	Bert Campaneris	.12	.09	.05
411	Terry Puhl	.08	.06	.03
412	*Britt Burns*	.12	.09	.05
413	Tony Bernazard	.08	.06	.03
414	John Pacella	.08	.06	.03
415	Ben Oglivie	.10	.08	.04
416	Gary Alexander	.08	.06	.03
417	Dan Schatzeder	.08	.06	.03
418	Bobby Brown	.08	.06	.03
419	Tom Hume	.08	.06	.03
420	Keith Hernandez	.80	.60	.30
421	Bob Stanley	.08	.06	.03
422	Dan Ford	.08	.06	.03
423	Shane Rawley	.15	.11	.06
424	Yankees Future Stars (Tim Lollar, Bruce Robinson, Dennis Werth)	.08	.06	.03
425	Al Bumbry	.10	.08	.04
426	Warren Brusstar	.08	.06	.03
427	John D'Acquisto	.08	.06	.03
428	John Stearns	.08	.06	.03
429	Mick Kelleher	.08	.06	.03
430	Jim Bibby	.08	.06	.03
431	Dave Roberts	.08	.06	.03
432	Len Barker	.10	.08	.04
433	Rance Mulliniks	.08	.06	.03
434	Roger Erickson	.08	.06	.03
435	Jim Spencer	.08	.06	.03
436	Gary Lucas	.08	.06	.03
437	Mike Heath	.08	.06	.03
438	John Montefusco	.10	.08	.04
439	Denny Walling	.08	.06	.03
440	Jerry Reuss	.12	.09	.05
441	Ken Reitz	.08	.06	.03
442	Ron Pruitt	.08	.06	.03
443	Jim Beattie	.08	.06	.03
444	Garth Iorg	.08	.06	.03
445	Ellis Valentine	.08	.06	.03
446	Checklist 364-484	.25	.20	.10
447	Junior Kennedy	.08	.06	.03
448	Tim Corcoran	.08	.06	.03
449	Paul Mitchell	.08	.06	.03
450	Dave Kingman	.10	.08	.04
451	Indians Future Stars (Chris Bando, Tom Brennan, Sandy Wihtol)	.12	.09	.05
452	Renie Martin	.08	.06	.03
453	Rob Wilfong	.08	.06	.03
454	Andy Hassler	.08	.06	.03
455	Rick Burleson	.10	.08	.04
456	*Jeff Reardon*	1.25	.90	.50
457	Mike Lum	.08	.06	.03
458	Randy Jones	.10	.08	.04
459	Greg Gross	.08	.06	.03
460	Rich Gossage	.40	.30	.15
461	Dave McKay	.08	.06	.03
462	Jack Brohamer	.08	.06	.03
463	Milt May	.08	.06	.03
464	Adrian Devine	.08	.06	.03
465	Bill Russell	.12	.09	.05
466	Bob Molinaro	.08	.06	.03
467	Dave Stieb	.40	.30	.15
468	Johnny Wockenfuss	.08	.06	.03
469	Jeff Leonard	.20	.15	.08
470	Manny Trillo	.10	.08	.04
471	Mike Vail	.08	.06	.03
472	Dyar Miller	.08	.06	.03
473	Jose Cardenal	.08	.06	.03

		MT	NR MT	EX
474	Mike LaCoss	.08	.06	.03
475	Buddy Bell	.15	.11	.06
476	Jerry Koosman	.15	.11	.06
477	Luis Gomez	.08	.06	.03
478	Juan Eichelberger	.08	.06	.03
479	Expos Future Stars (Bobby Pate, *Tim Raines*, Roberto Ramos)	9.00	6.75	3.50
480	Carlton Fisk	.80	.60	.30
481	Bob Lacey	.08	.06	.03
482	Jim Gantner	.10	.08	.04
483	Mike Griffin	.08	.06	.03
484	Max Venable	.08	.06	.03
485	Garry Templeton	.12	.09	.05
486	Marc Hill	.08	.06	.03
487	Dewey Robinson	.08	.06	.03
488	*Damaso Garcia*	.12	.09	.05
489	John Littlefield (photo actually Mark Riggins)	.08	.06	.03
490	Eddie Murray	1.50	1.25	.60
491	Gordy Pladson	.08	.06	.03
492	Barry Foote	.08	.06	.03
493	Dan Quisenberry	.20	.15	.08
494	*Bob Walk*	.50	.40	.20
495	Dusty Baker	.12	.09	.05
496	Paul Dade	.08	.06	.03
497	Fred Norman	.08	.06	.03
498	Pat Putnam	.08	.06	.03
499	Frank Pastore	.08	.06	.03
500	Jim Rice	1.00	.70	.40
501	Tim Foli	.08	.06	.03
502	Giants Future Stars (Chris Bourjos, Al Hargesheimer, Mike Rowland)	.08	.06	.03
503	Steve McCatty	.08	.06	.03
504	Dale Murphy	2.50	2.00	1.00
505	Jason Thompson	.08	.06	.03
506	Phil Huffman	.08	.06	.03
507	Jamie Quirk	.08	.06	.03
508	Rob Dressler	.08	.06	.03
509	Pete Mackanin	.08	.06	.03
510	Lee Mazzilli	.10	.08	.04
511	Wayne Garland	.08	.06	.03
512	Gary Thomasson	.08	.06	.03
513	Frank LaCorte	.08	.06	.03
514	George Riley	.08	.06	.03
515	Robin Yount	2.75	2.00	1.00
516	Doug Bird	.08	.06	.03
517	Richie Zisk	.10	.08	.04
518	Grant Jackson	.08	.06	.03
519	John Tamargo	.08	.06	.03
520	Steve Stone	.12	.09	.05
521	Sam Mejias	.08	.06	.03
522	Mike Colbern	.08	.06	.03
523	John Fulgham	.08	.06	.03
524	Willie Aikens	.08	.06	.03
525	Mike Torrez	.10	.08	.04
526	Phillies Future Stars (Marty Bystrom, Jay Loviglio, Jim Wright)	.08	.06	.03
527	Danny Goodwin	.08	.06	.03
528	Gary Matthews	.12	.09	.05
529	Dave LaRoche	.08	.06	.03
530	Steve Garvey	1.25	.90	.50
531	John Curtis	.08	.06	.03
532	Bill Stein	.08	.06	.03
533	Jesus Figueroa	.08	.06	.03
534	*Dave Smith*	.40	.30	.15
535	Omar Moreno	.08	.06	.03
536	Bob Owchinko	.08	.06	.03
537	Ron Hodges	.08	.06	.03
538	Tom Griffin	.08	.06	.03
539	Rodney Scott	.08	.06	.03
540	Mike Schmidt	1.50	1.25	.60
541	Steve Swisher	.08	.06	.03
542	Larry Bradford	.08	.06	.03
543	Terry Crowley	.08	.06	.03
544	Rich Gale	.08	.06	.03
545	Johnny Grubb	.08	.06	.03
546	Paul Moskau	.08	.06	.03
547	Mario Guerrero	.08	.06	.03
548	Dave Goltz	.10	.08	.04
549	Jerry Remy	.08	.06	.03
550	Tommy John	.50	.40	.20
551	Pirates Future Stars (*Vance Law, Tony Pena, Pascual Perez*)	2.50	2.00	1.00
552	Steve Trout	.08	.06	.03
553	Tim Blackwell	.08	.06	.03
554	Bert Blyleven	.25	.20	.10
555	Cecil Cooper	.20	.15	.08
556	Jerry Mumphrey	.08	.06	.03
557	Chris Knapp	.08	.06	.03
558	Barry Bonnell	.08	.06	.03
559	Willie Montanez	.08	.06	.03
560	Joe Morgan	.70	.50	.30
561	Dennis Littlejohn	.08	.06	.03
562	Checklist 485-605	.25	.20	.10
563	Jim Kaat	.30	.25	.12
564	Ron Hassey	.08	.06	.03
565	Burt Hooton	.10	.08	.04
566	Del Unser	.08	.06	.03
567	Mark Bomback	.08	.06	.03
568	Dave Revering	.08	.06	.03
569	Al Williams	.08	.06	.03
570	Ken Singleton	.12	.09	.05
571	Todd Cruz	.08	.06	.03
572	Jack Morris	.60	.45	.25
573	Phil Garner	.10	.08	.04
574	Bill Caudill	.08	.06	.03
575	Tony Perez	.35	.25	.14
576	Reggie Cleveland	.08	.06	.03
577	Blue Jays Future Stars (Luis Leal, Brian Milner, *Ken Schrom*)	.20	.15	.08
578	*Bill Gullickson*	.20	.15	.08
579	Tim Flannery	.08	.06	.03
580	Don Baylor	.15	.11	.06
581	Roy Howell	.08	.06	.03
582	Gaylord Perry	.70	.50	.30
583	Larry Milbourne	.08	.06	.03
584	Randy Lerch	.08	.06	.03
585	Amos Otis	.10	.08	.04
586	Silvio Martinez	.08	.06	.03
587	Jeff Newman	.08	.06	.03
588	Gary Lavelle	.08	.06	.03
589	Lamar Johnson	.08	.06	.03
590	Bruce Sutter	.25	.20	.10
591	John Lowenstein	.08	.06	.03

		MT	NR MT	EX
592	Steve Comer	.08	.06	.03
593	Steve Kemp	.12	.09	.05
594	Preston Hanna	.08	.06	.03
595	Butch Hobson	.08	.06	.03
596	Jerry Augustine	.08	.06	.03
597	Rafael Landestoy	.08	.06	.03
598	George Vukovich	.08	.06	.03
599	Dennis Kinney	.08	.06	.03
600	Johnny Bench	1.50	1.25	.60
601	Don Aase	.08	.06	.03
602	Bobby Murcer	.15	.11	.06
603	John Verhoeven	.08	.06	.03
604	Rob Picciolo	.08	.06	.03
605	Don Sutton	.70	.50	.30
606	Reds Future Stars (Bruce Berenyi, Geoff Combe, Paul Householder)	.08	.06	.03
607	Dave Palmer	.08	.06	.03
608	Greg Pryor	.08	.06	.03
609	Lynn McGlothen	.08	.06	.03
610	Darrell Porter	.10	.08	.04
611	Rick Matula	.08	.06	.03
612	Duane Kuiper	.08	.06	.03
613	Jim Anderson	.08	.06	.03
614	Dave Rozema	.08	.06	.03
615	Rick Dempsey	.12	.09	.05
616	Rick Wise	.10	.08	.04
617	Craig Reynolds	.08	.06	.03
618	John Milner	.08	.06	.03
619	Steve Henderson	.08	.06	.03
620	Dennis Eckersley	.20	.15	.08
621	Tom Donohue	.08	.06	.03
622	Randy Moffitt	.08	.06	.03
623	Sal Bando	.12	.09	.05
624	Bob Welch	.20	.15	.08
625	Bill Buckner	.15	.11	.06
626	Tigers Future Stars (Dave Steffen, Jerry Ujdur, Roger Weaver)	.08	.06	.03
627	Luis Tiant	.20	.15	.08
628	Vic Correll	.08	.06	.03
629	Tony Armas	.12	.09	.05
630	Steve Carlton	1.25	.90	.50
631	Ron Jackson	.08	.06	.03
632	Alan Bannister	.08	.06	.03
633	Bill Lee	.10	.08	.04
634	Doug Flynn	.08	.06	.03
635	Bobby Bonds	.15	.11	.06
636	Al Hrabosky	.10	.08	.04
637	Jerry Narron	.08	.06	.03
638	Checklist 606	.25	.20	.10
639	Carney Lansford	.15	.11	.06
640	Dave Parker	.60	.45	.25
641	Mark Belanger	.10	.08	.04
642	Vern Ruhle	.08	.06	.03
643	*Lloyd Moseby*	.90	.70	.35
644	Ramon Aviles	.08	.06	.03
645	Rick Reuschel	.15	.11	.06
646	Marvis Foley	.08	.06	.03
647	Dick Drago	.08	.06	.03
648	Darrell Evans	.25	.20	.10
649	Manny Sarmiento	.08	.06	.03
650	Bucky Dent	.12	.09	.05
651	Pedro Guerrero	1.25	.90	.50
652	John Montague	.08	.06	.03
653	Bill Fahey	.08	.06	.03
654	Ray Burris	.08	.06	.03
655	Dan Driessen	.12	.09	.05
656	Jon Matlack	.10	.08	.04
657	Mike Cubbage	.08	.06	.03
658	Milt Wilcox	.08	.06	.03
659	Brewers Future Stars (John Flinn, Ed Romero, Ned Yost)	.08	.06	.03
660	Gary Carter	1.00	.70	.40
661	Orioles Team (Earl Weaver)	.30	.25	.12
662	Red Sox Team (Ralph Houk)	.30	.25	.12
663	Angels Team (Jim Fregosi)	.25	.20	.10
664	White Sox Team (Tony LaRussa)	.25	.20	.10
665	Indians Team (Dave Garcia)	.25	.20	.10
666	Tigers Team (Sparky Anderson)	.30	.25	.12
667	Royals Team (Jim Frey)	.25	.20	.10
668	Brewers Team (Bob Rodgers)	.25	.20	.10
669	Twins Team (John Goryl)	.25	.20	.10
670	Yankees Team (Gene Michael)	.35	.25	.14
671	A's Team (Billy Martin)	.30	.25	.12
672	Mariners Team (Maury Wills)	.25	.20	.10
673	Rangers Team (Don Zimmer)	.25	.20	.10
674	Blue Jays Team (Bobby Mattick)	.25	.20	.10
675	Braves Team (Bobby Cox)	.25	.20	.10
676	Cubs Team (Joe Amalfitano)	.25	.20	.10
677	Reds Team (John McNamara)	.25	.20	.10
678	Astros Team (Bill Virdon)	.25	.20	.10
679	Dodgers Team (Tom Lasorda)	.35	.25	.14
680	Expos Team (Dick Williams)	.25	.20	.10
681	Mets Team (Joe Torre)	.30	.25	.12
682	Phillies Team (Dallas Green)	.25	.20	.10
683	Pirates Team (Chuck Tanner)	.25	.20	.10
684	Cardinals Team (Whitey Herzog)	.30	.25	.12
685	Padres Team (Frank Howard)	.25	.20	.10
686	Giants Team (Dave Bristol)	.25	.20	.10
687	Jeff Jones	.08	.06	.03
688	Kiko Garcia	.08	.06	.03
689	Red Sox Future Stars (*Bruce Hurst*, Keith MacWhorter, *Reid Nichols*)	2.50	2.00	1.00
690	Bob Watson	.10	.08	.04
691	Dick Ruthven	.08	.06	.03
692	Lenny Randle	.08	.06	.03
693	*Steve Howe*	.20	.15	.08
694	Bud Harrelson	.08	.06	.03
695	Kent Tekulve	.10	.08	.04
696	Alan Ashby	.08	.06	.03

		MT	NR MT	EX
697	Rick Waits	.08	.06	.03
698	Mike Jorgensen	.08	.06	.03
699	Glenn Abbott	.08	.06	.03
700	George Brett	2.25	1.75	.90
701	Joe Rudi	.12	.09	.05
702	George Medich	.08	.06	.03
703	Alvis Woods	.08	.06	.03
704	Bill Travers	.08	.06	.03
705	Ted Simmons	.25	.20	.10
706	Dave Ford	.08	.06	.03
707	Dave Cash	.08	.06	.03
708	Doyle Alexander	.12	.09	.05
709	Alan Trammell	.30	.25	.12
710	Ron LeFlore	.08	.06	.03
711	Joe Ferguson	.08	.06	.03
712	Bill Bonham	.08	.06	.03
713	Bill North	.08	.06	.03
714	Pete Redfern	.08	.06	.03
715	Bill Madlock	.25	.20	.10
716	Glenn Borgmann	.08	.06	.03
717	Jim Barr	.08	.06	.03
718	Larry Biittner	.08	.06	.03
719	Sparky Lyle	.12	.09	.05
720	Fred Lynn	.35	.25	.14
721	Toby Harrah	.10	.08	.04
722	Joe Niekro	.20	.15	.08
723	Bruce Bochte	.08	.06	.03
724	Lou Piniella	.20	.15	.08
725	Steve Rogers	.10	.08	.04
726	Rick Monday	.15	.11	.06

1981 Topps 5x7 National Photos

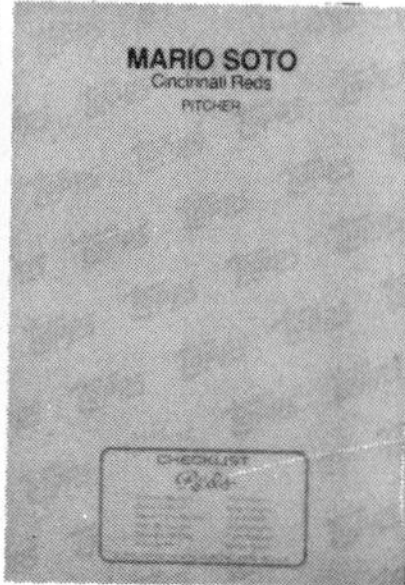

Once again testing the popularity of large cards, Topps issued 4-7/8" by 6-7/8" cards in two different sets. The Home Team cards feature a large color photo, facsimile autograph and white border on the front. Backs have the player's name, team, position and a checklist at the bottom. The 102 cards were sold in limited areas corresponding to the teams' geographic home. It was also possible to order the whole set by mail. Eleven teams are involved in the issue, with the number of players from each team ranging from 6 to 12. Although it is an attractive set featuring many stars, ready availability and many collectors' aversion to large cards keep prices relatively low today.

		MT	NR MT	EX
Complete Set:		40.00	30.00	16.00
Common Player:		.20	.15	.08
(1)	Dusty Baker	.25	.20	.10
(2)	Don Baylor	.40	.30	.15
(3)	Rick Burleson	.20	.15	.08
(4)	Rod Carew	.90	.70	.35
(5)	Ron Cey	.30	.25	.12
(6)	Steve Garvey	.90	.70	.35
(7)	Bobby Grich	.30	.25	.12
(8)	Butch Hobson	.20	.15	.08
(9)	Burt Hooton	.20	.15	.08
(10)	Steve Howe	.20	.15	.08
(11)	Dave Lopes	.25	.20	.10
(12)	Fred Lynn	.50	.40	.20
(13)	Rick Monday	.25	.20	.10
(14)	Jerry Reuss	.25	.20	.10
(15)	Bill Russell	.25	.20	.10
(16)	Reggie Smith	.30	.25	.12
(17)	Bob Welch	.40	.30	.15
(18)	Steve Yeager	.20	.15	.08
(19)	Buddy Bell	.30	.25	.12
(20)	Cesar Cedeno	.30	.25	.12
(21)	Jose Cruz	.30	.25	.12
(22)	Art Howe	.20	.15	.08
(23)	Jon Matlack	.20	.15	.08
(24)	Al Oliver	.40	.30	.15
(25)	Terry Puhl	.20	.15	.08
(26)	Mickey Rivers	.25	.20	.10
(27)	Nolan Ryan	.70	.50	.30
(28)	Jim Sundberg	.25	.20	.10
(29)	Don Sutton	.60	.45	.25
(30)	Bump Wills	.20	.15	.08
(31)	Tim Blackwell	.20	.15	.08
(32)	Bill Buckner	.40	.30	.15
(33)	Britt Burns	.20	.15	.08
(34)	Ivan DeJesus	.20	.15	.08
(35)	Rich Dotson	.25	.20	.10
(36)	Leon Durham	.25	.20	.10
(37)	Ed Farmer	.20	.15	.08
(38)	Lamar Johnson	.20	.15	.08
(39)	Dave Kingman	.40	.30	.15
(40)	Mike Krukow	.25	.20	.10
(41)	Ron LeFlore	.25	.20	.10
(42)	Chet Lemon	.25	.20	.10

		MT	NR MT	EX
(43)	Bob Molinaro	.20	.15	.08
(44)	Jim Morrison	.20	.15	.08
(45)	Wayne Nordhagen	.20	.15	.08
(46)	Ken Reitz	.20	.15	.08
(47)	Rick Reuschel	.30	.25	.12
(48)	Mike Tyson	.20	.15	.08
(49)	Neil Allen	.20	.15	.08
(50)	Rick Cerone	.20	.15	.08
(51)	Bucky Dent	.25	.20	.10
(52)	Doug Flynn	.20	.15	.08
(53)	Rich Gossage	.60	.45	.25
(54)	Ron Guidry	.60	.45	.25
(55)	Reggie Jackson	.90	.70	.35
(56)	Tommy John	.50	.40	.20
(57)	Ruppert Jones	.20	.15	.08
(58)	Rudy May	.20	.15	.08
(59)	Lee Mazzilli	.25	.20	.10
(60)	Graig Nettles	.40	.30	.15
(61)	Willie Randolph	.30	.25	.12
(62)	Rusty Staub	.40	.30	.15
(63)	Frank Taveras	.20	.15	.08
(64)	Alex Trevino	.20	.15	.08
(65)	Bob Watson	.25	.20	.10
(66)	Dave Winfield	.90	.70	.35
(67)	Bob Boone	.25	.20	.10
(68)	Larry Bowa	.40	.30	.15
(69)	Steve Carlton	.70	.50	.30
(70)	Greg Luzinski	.40	.30	.15
(71)	Garry Maddox	.25	.20	.10
(72)	Bake McBride	.20	.15	.08
(73)	Tug McGraw	.40	.30	.15
(74)	Pete Rose	1.75	1.25	.70
(75)	Dick Ruthven	.20	.15	.08
(76)	Mike Schmidt	.90	.70	.35
(77)	Manny Trillo	.25	.20	.10
(78)	Del Unser	.20	.15	.08
(79)	Tom Burgmeier	.20	.15	.08
(80)	Dennis Eckersley	.40	.30	.15
(81)	Dwight Evans	.50	.40	.20
(82)	Carlton Fisk	.60	.45	.25
(83)	Glenn Hoffman	.20	.15	.08
(84)	Carney Lansford	.30	.25	.12
(85)	Tony Perez	.50	.40	.20
(86)	Jim Rice	.70	.50	.30
(87)	Bob Stanley	.20	.15	.08
(88)	Dave Stapleton	.20	.15	.08
(89)	Frank Tanana	.25	.20	.10
(90)	Carl Yastrzemski	1.25	.90	.50
(91)	Johnny Bench	.90	.70	.35
(92)	Dave Collins	.25	.20	.10
(93)	Dave Concepcion	.40	.30	.15
(94)	Dan Driessen	.25	.20	.10
(95)	George Foster	.50	.40	.20
(96)	Ken Griffey	.30	.25	.12
(97)	Tom Hume	.20	.15	.08
(98)	Ray Knight	.25	.20	.10
(99)	Joe Nolan	.20	.15	.08
(100)	Ron Oester	.20	.15	.08
(101)	Tom Seaver	.70	.50	.30
(102)	Mario Soto	.25	.20	.10

1981 Topps

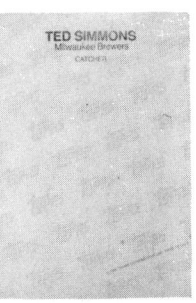

This set is the other half of Topps' efforts with large cards in 1981. Measuring 4-7/8" by 6-7/8", the National photo issue was limited to 15 cards. They were sold in areas not covered by the Home Team sets and feature ten cards which carry the same photos as found in the Home Team set, but with no checklist on the backs. Five cards are unique to the National set: George Brett, Cecil Cooper, Jim Palmer, Dave Parker and Ted Simmons. With their wide distribution and a limited demand, there are currently plenty of these cards to meet the demand, thus keeping prices fairly low.

		MT	NR MT	EX
Complete Set:		5.00	3.75	2.00
Common Player:		.30	.25	.12
(1)	Buddy Bell	.30	.25	.12
(2)	Johnny Bench	.60	.45	.25
(3)	George Brett	.90	.70	.35
(4)	Rod Carew	.60	.45	.25
(5)	Cecil Cooper	.40	.30	.15
(6)	Steve Garvey	.70	.50	.30
(7)	Rich Gossage	.40	.30	.15
(8)	Reggie Jackson	.70	.50	.30
(9)	Jim Palmer	.70	.50	.30
(10)	Dave Parker	.60	.45	.25
(11)	Jim Rice	.50	.40	.20
(12)	Pete Rose	1.25	.90	.50
(13)	Mike Schmidt	.70	.50	.30
(14)	Tom Seaver	.60	.45	.25
(15)	Ted Simmons	.50	.40	.20

1981 Topps Scratchoffs

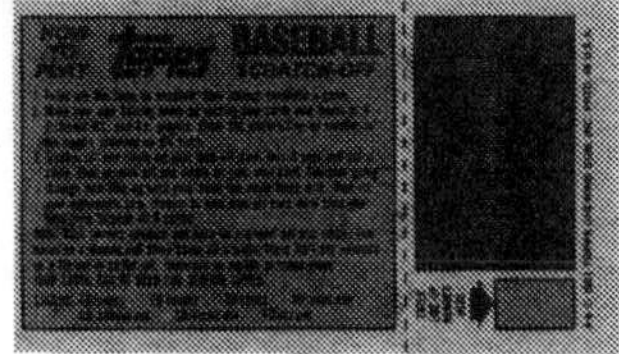

Sold as a separate issue with bubble gum, this 108-card set was issued in three-card panels that measure 3-1/4" by 5-1/4". Each individual card measures 1-13/16" by 3-1/4" and contains a small player photo alongside a series of black dots designed to be scratched off as part of a baseball game. Cards of National League players have a green backgrounds, while American League players have a red background. While there are 108 different players in the set, there are 144 possible panel combinations. An intact panel of three cards is valued approximately 20-25 percent more the sum of the individual cards.

		MT	NR MT	EX
Complete Set:		3.50	2.75	1.50
Common Player:		.02	.02	.01
1	George Brett	.12	.09	.05
2	Cecil Cooper	.04	.03	.02
3	Reggie Jackson	.12	.09	.05
4	Al Oliver	.04	.03	.02
5	Fred Lynn	.06	.05	.02
6	Tony Armas	.02	.02	.01
7	Ben Oglivie	.02	.02	.01
8	Tony Perez	.06	.05	.02
9	Eddie Murray	.10	.08	.04
10	Robin Yount	.08	.06	.03
11	Steve Kemp	.04	.03	.02
12	Joe Charboneau	.04	.03	.02
13	Jim Rice	.10	.08	.04
14	Lance Parrish	.08	.06	.03
15	John Mayberry	.02	.02	.01
16	Richie Zisk	.02	.02	.01
17	Ken Singleton	.04	.03	.02
18	Rod Carew	.10	.08	.04
19	Rick Manning	.02	.02	.01
20	Willie Wilson	.04	.03	.02
21	Buddy Bell	.04	.03	.02
22	Dave Revering	.02	.02	.01
23	Tom Paciorek	.02	.02	.01
24	Champ Summers	.02	.02	.01
25	Carney Lansford	.04	.03	.02
26	Lamar Johnson	.02	.02	.01
27	Willie Aikens	.02	.02	.01
28	Rick Cerone	.02	.02	.01
29	Al Bumbry	.02	.02	.01
30	Bruce Bochte	.02	.02	.01
31	Mickey Rivers	.02	.02	.01
32	Mike Hargrove	.02	.02	.01
33	John Castino	.02	.02	.01
34	Chet Lemon	.04	.03	.02
35	Paul Molitor	.06	.05	.02
36	Willie Randolph	.04	.03	.02
37	Rick Burleson	.02	.02	.01
38	Alan Trammell	.08	.06	.03
39	Rickey Henderson	.10	.08	.04
40	Dan Meyer	.02	.02	.01
41	Ken Landreaux	.02	.02	.01
42	Damaso Garcia	.02	.02	.01
43	Roy Smalley	.02	.02	.01
44	Otto Velez	.02	.02	.01
45	Sixto Lezcano	.02	.02	.01
46	Toby Harrah	.02	.02	.01
47	Frank White	.04	.03	.02
48	Dave Stapleton	.02	.02	.01
49	Steve Stone	.04	.03	.02
50	Jim Palmer	.08	.06	.03
51	Larry Gura	.02	.02	.01
52	Tommy John	.06	.05	.02
53	Mike Norris	.02	.02	.01
54	Ed Farmer	.02	.02	.01
55	Bill Buckner	.04	.03	.02
56	Steve Garvey	.10	.08	.04
57	Reggie Smith	.04	.03	.02
58	Bake McBride	.02	.02	.01
59	Dave Parker	.06	.05	.02
60	Mike Schmidt	.12	.09	.05
61	Bob Horner	.04	.03	.02
62	Pete Rose	.20	.15	.08
63	Ted Simmons	.06	.05	.02
64	Johnny Bench	.12	.09	.05
65	George Foster	.06	.05	.02
66	Gary Carter	.10	.08	.04
67	Keith Hernandez	.08	.06	.03
68	Ozzie Smith	.06	.05	.02
69	Dave Kingman	.06	.05	.02
70	Jack Clark	.06	.05	.02
71	Dusty Baker	.04	.03	.02
72	Dale Murphy	.12	.09	.05
73	Ron Cey	.04	.03	.02
74	Greg Luzinski	.04	.03	.02
75	Lee Mazzilli	.02	.02	.01
76	Gary Matthews	.04	.03	.02
77	Cesar Cedeno	.04	.03	.02
78	Warren Cromartie	.02	.02	.01
79	Steve Henderson	.02	.02	.01
80	Ellis Valentine	.02	.02	.01
81	Mike Easler	.02	.02	.01
82	Garry Templeton	.04	.03	.02
83	Jose Cruz	.04	.03	.02
84	Dave Collins	.02	.02	.01
85	George Hendrick	.02	.02	.01
86	Gene Richards	.02	.02	.01
87	Terry Whitfield	.02	.02	.01
88	Terry Puhl	.02	.02	.01
89	Larry Parrish	.04	.03	.02
90	Andre Dawson	.08	.06	.03
91	Ken Griffey	.04	.03	.02
92	Dave Lopes	.02	.02	.01
93	Doug Flynn	.02	.02	.01
94	Ivan DeJesus	.02	.02	.01
95	Dave Concepcion	.04	.03	.02
96	John Stearns	.02	.02	.01
97	Jerry Mumphrey	.02	.02	.01
98	Jerry Martin	.02	.02	.01
99	Art Howe	.02	.02	.01
100	Omar Moreno	.02	.02	.01
101	Ken Reitz	.02	.02	.01
102	Phil Garner	.02	.02	.01
103	Jerry Reuss	.04	.03	.02
104	Steve Carlton	.10	.08	.04
105	Jim Bibby	.02	.02	.01
106	Steve Rogers	.02	.02	.01
107	Tom Seaver	.10	.08	.04
108	Vida Blue	.04	.03	.02

1981 Topps Stickers

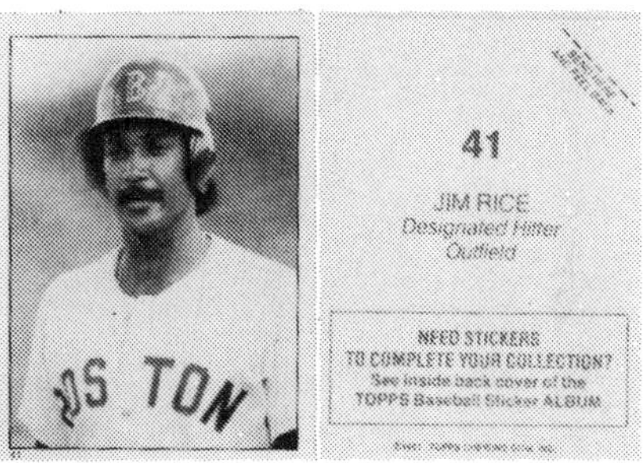

41
JIM RICE
Designated Hitter
Outfield
NEED STICKERS
TO COMPLETE YOUR COLLECTION?
See inside back cover of the
TOPPS Baseball Sticker ALBUM

The 262 stickers in this full-color set measure 1-15/16" by 2-9/16" and are numbered on both the front and back. They were produced for Topps by the Panini Company of Italy. The set includes a series of "All-Star" stickers printed on silver or gold "foil". An album to house the stickers was also available.

		MT	NR MT	EX
Complete Set:		17.00	12.50	6.75
Common Player:		.03	.02	.01
Sticker Album:		.80	.60	.30
1	Steve Stone	.06	.05	.02
2	Tommy John, Mike Norris	.06	.05	.02
3	Rudy May	.03	.02	.01
4	Mike Norris	.03	.02	.01
5	Len Barker	.03	.02	.01
6	Mike Norris	.03	.02	.01
7	Dan Quisenberry	.06	.05	.02
8	Rich Gossage	.10	.08	.04
9	George Brett	.25	.20	.10
10	Cecil Cooper	.08	.06	.03
11	Reggie Jackson, Ben Oglivie	.06	.05	.02
12	Gorman Thomas	.06	.05	.02
13	Cecil Cooper	.08	.06	.03
14	George Brett, Ben Oglivie	.20	.15	.08
15	Rickey Henderson	.25	.20	.10
16	Willie Wilson	.08	.06	.03
17	Bill Buckner	.06	.05	.02
18	Keith Hernandez	.12	.09	.05
19	Mike Schmidt	.25	.20	.10
20	Bob Horner	.10	.08	.04
21	Mike Schmidt	.25	.20	.10
22	George Hendrick	.06	.05	.02
23	Ron LeFlore	.04	.03	.02
24	Omar Moreno	.03	.02	.01
25	Steve Carlton	.20	.15	.08
26	Joe Niekro	.06	.05	.02
27	Don Sutton	.10	.08	.04
28	Steve Carlton	.20	.15	.08
29	Steve Carlton	.20	.15	.08
30	Nolan Ryan	.20	.15	.08
31	Rollie Fingers, Tom Hume	.08	.06	.03
32	Bruce Sutter	.08	.06	.03
33	Ken Singleton	.06	.05	.02
34	Eddie Murray	.20	.15	.08
35	Al Bumbry	.03	.02	.01
36	Rich Dauer	.03	.02	.01
37	Scott McGregor	.04	.03	.02
38	Rick Dempsey	.04	.03	.02
39	Jim Palmer	.15	.11	.06
40	Steve Stone	.06	.05	.02
41	Jim Rice	.20	.15	.08
42	Fred Lynn	.10	.08	.04
43	Carney Lansford	.06	.05	.02
44	Tony Perez	.10	.08	.04
45	Carl Yastrzemski	.30	.25	.12

		MT	NR MT	EX
46	Carlton Fisk	.12	.09	.05
47	Dave Stapleton	.03	.02	.01
48	Dennis Eckersley	.06	.05	.02
49	Rod Carew	.20	.15	.08
50	Brian Downing	.04	.03	.02
51	Don Baylor	.08	.06	.03
52	Rick Burleson	.04	.03	.02
53	Bobby Grich	.06	.05	.02
54	Butch Hobson	.03	.02	.01
55	Andy Hassler	.03	.02	.01
56	Frank Tanana	.04	.03	.02
57	Chet Lemon	.04	.03	.02
58	Lamar Johnson	.03	.02	.01
59	Wayne Nordhagen	.03	.02	.01
60	Jim Morrison	.03	.02	.01
61	Bob Molinaro	.03	.02	.01
62	Rich Dotson	.04	.03	.02
63	Britt Burns	.03	.02	.01
64	Ed Farmer	.03	.02	.01
65	Toby Harrah	.04	.03	.02
66	Joe Charboneau	.04	.03	.02
67	Miguel Dilone	.03	.02	.01
68	Mike Hargrove	.04	.03	.02
69	Rick Manning	.03	.02	.01
70	Andre Thornton	.06	.05	.02
71	Ron Hassey	.03	.02	.01
72	Len Barker	.03	.02	.01
73	Lance Parrish	.12	.09	.05
74	Steve Kemp	.04	.03	.02
75	Alan Trammell	.15	.11	.06
76	Champ Summers	.03	.02	.01
77	Rick Peters	.03	.02	.01
78	Kirk Gibson	.15	.11	.06
79	Johnny Wockenfuss	.03	.02	.01
80	Jack Morris	.12	.09	.05
81	Willie Wilson	.08	.06	.03
82	George Brett	.25	.20	.10
83	Frank White	.06	.05	.02
84	Willie Aikens	.03	.02	.01
85	Clint Hurdle	.03	.02	.01
86	Hal McRae	.06	.05	.02
87	Dennis Leonard	.04	.03	.02
88	Larry Gura	.03	.02	.01
89	American League Pennant Winner (Kansas City Royals Team)	.04	.03	.02
90	American League Pennant Winner (Kansas City Royals Team)	.04	.03	.02
91	Paul Molitor	.10	.08	.04
92	Ben Oglivie	.04	.03	.02
93	Cecil Cooper	.08	.06	.03
94	Ted Simmons	.08	.06	.03
95	Robin Yount	.15	.11	.06
96	Gorman Thomas	.06	.05	.02
97	Mike Caldwell	.03	.02	.01
98	Moose Haas	.03	.02	.01
99	John Castino	.03	.02	.01
100	Roy Smalley	.03	.02	.01
101	Ken Landreaux	.03	.02	.01
102	Butch Wynegar	.04	.03	.02
103	Ron Jackson	.03	.02	.01
104	Jerry Koosman	.04	.03	.02
105	Roger Erickson	.03	.02	.01
106	Doug Corbett	.03	.02	.01
107	Reggie Jackson	.25	.20	.10
108	Willie Randolph	.04	.03	.02
109	Rick Cerone	.03	.02	.01
110	Bucky Dent	.04	.03	.02
111	Dave Winfield	.20	.15	.08
112	Ron Guidry	.12	.09	.05
113	Rich Gossage	.10	.08	.04
114	Tommy John	.10	.08	.04
115	Rickey Henderson	.25	.20	.10
116	Tony Armas	.04	.03	.02
117	Dave Revering	.03	.02	.01
118	Wayne Gross	.03	.02	.01
119	Dwayne Murphy	.04	.03	.02
120	Jeff Newman	.03	.02	.01
121	Rick Langford	.03	.02	.01
122	Mike Norris	.03	.02	.01
123	Bruce Bochte	.03	.02	.01
124	Tom Paciorek	.03	.02	.01
125	Dan Meyer	.03	.02	.01
126	Julio Cruz	.03	.02	.01
127	Richie Zisk	.04	.03	.02
128	Floyd Bannister	.04	.03	.02
129	Shane Rawley	.04	.03	.02
130	Buddy Bell	.06	.05	.02
131	Al Oliver	.06	.05	.02
132	Mickey Rivers	.04	.03	.02
133	Jim Sundberg	.03	.02	.01
134	Bump Wills	.03	.02	.01
135	Jon Matlack	.04	.03	.02
136	Danny Darwin	.03	.02	.01
137	Damaso Garcia	.04	.03	.02
138	Otto Velez	.03	.02	.01
139	John Mayberry	.04	.03	.02
140	Alfredo Griffin	.04	.03	.02
141	Alvis Woods	.03	.02	.01
142	Dave Stieb	.06	.05	.02
143	Jim Clancy	.04	.03	.02
144	Gary Matthews	.06	.05	.02
145	Bob Horner	.08	.06	.03
146	Dale Murphy	.25	.20	.10
147	Chris Chambliss	.04	.03	.02
148	Phil Niekro	.12	.09	.05
149	Glenn Hubbard	.03	.02	.01
150	Rick Camp	.03	.02	.01
151	Dave Kingman	.08	.06	.03
152	Bill Caudill	.03	.02	.01
153	Bill Buckner	.06	.05	.02
154	Barry Foote	.03	.02	.01
155	Mike Tyson	.03	.02	.01
156	Ivan DeJesus	.03	.02	.01
157	Rick Reuschel	.06	.05	.02
158	Ken Reitz	.03	.02	.01
159	George Foster	.08	.06	.03
160	Johnny Bench	.25	.20	.10
161	Dave Concepcion	.06	.05	.02
162	Dave Collins	.04	.03	.02
163	Ken Griffey	.06	.05	.02
164	Dan Driessen	.04	.03	.02
165	Tom Seaver	.20	.15	.08
166	Tom Hume	.03	.02	.01
167	Cesar Cedeno	.06	.05	.02
168	Rafael Landestoy	.03	.02	.01
169	Jose Cruz	.06	.05	.02
170	Art Howe	.03	.02	.01
171	Terry Puhl	.03	.02	.01
172	Joe Sambito	.03	.02	.01
173	Nolan Ryan	.20	.15	.08
174	Joe Niekro	.06	.05	.02
175	Dave Lopes	.04	.03	.02
176	Steve Garvey	.20	.15	.08
177	Ron Cey	.06	.05	.02
178	Reggie Smith	.06	.05	.02
179	Bill Russell	.04	.03	.02
180	Burt Hooton	.03	.02	.01
181	Jerry Reuss	.06	.05	.02
182	Dusty Baker	.04	.03	.02
183	Larry Parrish	.04	.03	.02
184	Gary Carter	.20	.15	.08
185	Rodney Scott	.03	.02	.01
186	Ellis Valentine	.03	.02	.01
187	Andre Dawson	.12	.09	.05
188	Warren Cromartie	.03	.02	.01
189	Chris Speier	.03	.02	.01
190	Steve Rogers	.03	.02	.01
191	Lee Mazzilli	.04	.03	.02
192	Doug Flynn	.03	.02	.01
193	Steve Henderson	.03	.02	.01
194	John Stearns	.03	.02	.01
195	Joel Youngblood	.03	.02	.01
196	Frank Taveras	.03	.02	.01
197	Pat Zachry	.03	.02	.01
198	Neil Allen	.03	.02	.01
199	Mike Schmidt	.25	.20	.10
200	Pete Rose	.40	.30	.15
201	Larry Bowa	.06	.05	.02
202	Bake McBride	.03	.02	.01
203	Bob Boone	.04	.03	.02
204	Garry Maddox	.04	.03	.02
205	Tug McGraw	.06	.05	.02
206	Steve Carlton	.20	.15	.08
207	National League Pennant Winner (Philadelphia Phillies Team)	.04	.03	.02
208	National League Pennant Winner (Philadelphia Phillies Team)	.04	.03	.02
209	Phil Garner	.04	.03	.02
210	Dave Parker	.12	.09	.05
211	Omar Moreno	.03	.02	.01
212	Mike Easler	.04	.03	.02
213	Bill Madlock	.06	.05	.02
214	Ed Ott	.03	.02	.01
215	Willie Stargell	.20	.15	.08
216	Jim Bibby	.03	.02	.01
217	Garry Templeton	.06	.05	.02
218	Sixto Lezcano	.03	.02	.01
219	Keith Hernandez	.12	.09	.05
220	George Hendrick	.04	.03	.02
221	Bruce Sutter	.08	.06	.03
222	Ken Oberkfell	.03	.02	.01
223	Tony Scott	.03	.02	.01
224	Darrell Porter	.04	.03	.02
225	Gene Richards	.03	.02	.01
226	Broderick Perkins	.03	.02	.01
227	Jerry Mumphrey	.03	.02	.01
228	Luis Salazar	.03	.02	.01
229	Jerry Turner	.03	.02	.01
230	Ozzie Smith	.10	.08	.04
231	John Curtis	.03	.02	.01
232	Rick Wise	.03	.02	.01
233	Terry Whitfield	.03	.02	.01
234	Jack Clark	.10	.08	.04
235	Darrell Evans	.08	.06	.03
236	Larry Herndon	.03	.02	.01
237	Milt May	.03	.02	.01
238	Greg Minton	.03	.02	.01
239	Vida Blue	.06	.05	.02
240	Eddie Whitson	.03	.02	.01
241	Cecil Cooper	.20	.15	.08
242	Willie Randolph	.20	.15	.08
243	George Brett	.40	.30	.15
244	Robin Yount	.30	.25	.12
245	Reggie Jackson	.40	.30	.15
246	Al Oliver	.20	.15	.08
247	Willie Wilson	.20	.15	.08
248	Rick Cerone	.15	.11	.06
249	Steve Stone	.15	.11	.06
250	Tommy John	.25	.20	.10
251	Rich Gossage	.25	.20	.10
252	Steve Garvey	.30	.25	.12
253	Phil Garner	.15	.11	.06
254	Mike Schmidt	.40	.30	.15
255	Garry Templeton	.20	.15	.08
256	George Hendrick	.15	.11	.06
257	Dave Parker	.25	.20	.10
258	Cesar Cedeno	.20	.15	.08
259	Gary Carter	.30	.25	.12
260	Jim Bibby	.15	.11	.06
261	Steve Carlton	.30	.25	.12
262	Tug McGraw	.20	.15	.08

1981 Topps Traded

The 132 cards in this extension set are numbered from 727 to 858, technically making them a high-numbered series of the regular Topps set. The set was not packaged in gum packs, but rather placed in a specially designed red box and sold through baseball card dealers only. While many complained about the method, the fact remains, even at higher prices, the set has done well for its owners as it features not only mid-season trades, but also single-player rookie cards of some of the hottest prospects. The cards measure 2-1/2" by 3-1/2".

		MT	NR MT	EX
Complete Set:		30.00	22.00	12.00
Common Player:		.10	.08	.04
727	Danny Ainge(FC)	.50	.40	.20
728	Doyle Alexander	.20	.15	.08
729	Gary Alexander	.10	.08	.04
730	Billy Almon	.10	.08	.04
731	Joaquin Andujar	.15	.11	.06
732	Bob Bailor	.10	.08	.04
733	Juan Beniquez	.10	.08	.04
734	Dave Bergman	.10	.08	.04
735	Tony Bernazard	.10	.08	.04
736	Larry Biittner	.10	.08	.04
737	Doug Bird	.10	.08	.04
738	Bert Blyleven	1.00	.70	.40
739	Mark Bomback	.10	.08	.04
740	Bobby Bonds	.20	.15	.08
741	Rick Bosetti	.10	.08	.04
742	Hubie Brooks	1.25	.90	.50
743	Rick Burleson	.15	.11	.06
744	Ray Burris	.10	.08	.04
745	Jeff Burroughs	.15	.11	.06
746	Enos Cabell	.10	.08	.04
747	Ken Clay	.10	.08	.04
748	Mark Clear	.10	.08	.04
749	Larry Cox	.10	.08	.04
750	Hector Cruz	.10	.08	.04
751	Victor Cruz	.10	.08	.04
752	Mike Cubbage	.10	.08	.04
753	Dick Davis	.10	.08	.04
754	Brian Doyle	.10	.08	.04
755	Dick Drago	.10	.08	.04
756	Leon Durham	.25	.20	.10
757	Jim Dwyer	.10	.08	.04
758	Dave Edwards	.10	.08	.04
759	Jim Essian	.10	.08	.04
760	Bill Fahey	.10	.08	.04
761	Rollie Fingers	.90	.70	.35
762	Carlton Fisk	1.75	1.25	.70
763	Barry Foote	.10	.08	.04
764	Ken Forsch	.10	.08	.04
765	Kiko Garcia	.10	.08	.04
766	Cesar Geronimo	.10	.08	.04
767	Gary Gray	.10	.08	.04
768	Mickey Hatcher	.15	.11	.06
769	Steve Henderson	.10	.08	.04
770	Marc Hill	.10	.08	.04
771	Butch Hobson	.10	.08	.04
772	Rick Honeycutt	.10	.08	.04
773	Roy Howell	.10	.08	.04
774	Mike Ivie	.10	.08	.04
775	Roy Lee Jackson	.10	.08	.04
776	Cliff Johnson	.10	.08	.04
777	Randy Jones	.15	.11	.06
778	Ruppert Jones	.10	.08	.04
779	Mick Kelleher	.10	.08	.04
780	Terry Kennedy	.20	.15	.08
781	Dave Kingman	.40	.30	.15
782	Bob Knepper	.15	.11	.06
783	Ken Kravec	.10	.08	.04
784	Bob Lacey	.10	.08	.04
785	Dennis Lamp	.10	.08	.04
786	Rafael Landestoy	.10	.08	.04
787	Ken Landreaux	.10	.08	.04
788	Carney Lansford	.20	.15	.08
789	Dave LaRoche	.10	.08	.04
790	Joe Lefebvre	.10	.08	.04
791	Ron LeFlore	.15	.11	.06
792	Randy Lerch	.10	.08	.04
793	Sixto Lezcano	.10	.08	.04
794	John Littlefield	.10	.08	.04
795	Mike Lum	.10	.08	.04
796	Greg Luzinski	.25	.20	.10
797	Fred Lynn	.50	.40	.20
798	Jerry Martin	.10	.08	.04
799	Buck Martinez	.10	.08	.04
800	Gary Matthews	.20	.15	.08
801	Mario Mendoza	.10	.08	.04
802	Larry Milbourne	.10	.08	.04
803	Rick Miller	.10	.08	.04
804	John Montefusco	.10	.08	.04
805	Jerry Morales	.10	.08	.04
806	Jose Morales	.10	.08	.04
807	Joe Morgan	2.00	1.50	.80
808	Jerry Mumphrey	.10	.08	.04
809	Gene Nelson(FC)	.30	.25	.12
810	Ed Ott	.10	.08	.04
811	Bob Owchinko	.10	.08	.04
812	Gaylord Perry	1.25	.90	.50
813	Mike Phillips	.10	.08	.04
814	Darrell Porter	.15	.11	.06
815	Mike Proly	.10	.08	.04
816	Tim Raines	8.00	6.00	3.25
817	Lenny Randle	.10	.08	.04
818	Doug Rau	.10	.08	.04
819	Jeff Reardon	.80	.60	.30
820	Ken Reitz	.10	.08	.04
821	Steve Renko	.10	.08	.04
822	Rick Reuschel	.25	.20	.10
823	Dave Revering	.10	.08	.04
824	Dave Roberts	.10	.08	.04
825	Leon Roberts	.10	.08	.04
826	Joe Rudi	.20	.15	.08
827	Kevin Saucier	.10	.08	.04
828	Tony Scott	.10	.08	.04
829	Bob Shirley	.10	.08	.04
830	Ted Simmons	.40	.30	.15
831	Lary Sorensen	.10	.08	.04

		MT	NR MT	EX
832	Jim Spencer	.10	.08	.04
833	Harry Spilman	.10	.08	.04
834	Fred Stanley	.10	.08	.04
835	Rusty Staub	.30	.25	.12
836	Bill Stein	.10	.08	.04
837	Joe Strain	.10	.08	.04
838	Bruce Sutter	.50	.40	.20
839	Don Sutton	1.25	.90	.50
840	Steve Swisher	.10	.08	.04
841	Frank Tanana	.20	.15	.08
842	Gene Tenace	.15	.11	.06
843	Jason Thompson	.10	.08	.04
844	Dickie Thon	.15	.11	.06
845	Bill Travers	.10	.08	.04
846	Tom Underwood	.10	.08	.04
847	John Urrea	.10	.08	.04
848	Mike Vail	.10	.08	.04
849	Ellis Valentine	.10	.08	.04
850	Fernando Valenzuela	4.50	3.50	1.75
851	Pete Vuckovich	.15	.11	.06
852	Mark Wagner	.10	.08	.04
853	Bob Walk	.50	.40	.20
854	Claudell Washington	.15	.11	.06
855	Dave Winfield	2.25	1.75	.90
856	Geoff Zahn	.10	.08	.04
857	Richie Zisk	.15	.11	.06
858	Checklist 727-858	.10	.08	.04

1982 Topps

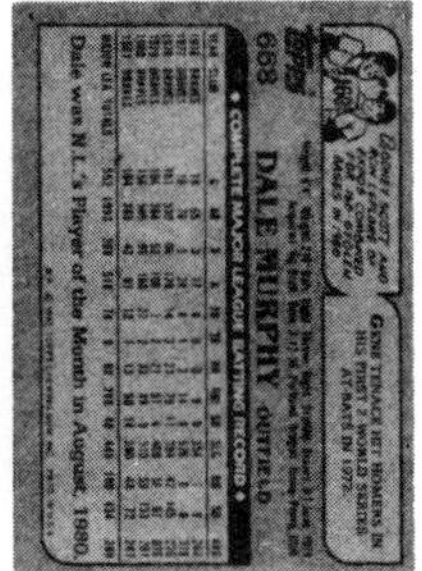

At 792 cards, this was the largest issue produced up to that time, eliminating the need for double- printed cards. The 2-1/2" by 3-1/2" cards feature a front color photo with a pair of stripes down the left side. Under the player's photo are found his name, team and position. A facsimile autograph runs across the front of the picture. Specialty cards include great performances of the previous season, All-Stars, statistical leaders and "In Action" cards (indicated by "IA" in listings below). Managers and hitting/pitching leaders have cards, while rookies are shown as "Future Stars" on group cards.

		MT	NR MT	EX
	Complete Set:	90.00	65.00	35.00
	Common Player:	.08	.06	.03
1	1981 Highlight (Steve Carlton)	.50	.40	.20
2	1981 Highlight (Ron Davis)	.08	.06	.03
3	1981 Highlight (Tim Raines)	.30	.25	.12
4	1981 Highlight (Pete Rose)	.70	.50	.30
5	1981 Highlight (Nolan Ryan)	.30	.25	.12
6	1981 Highlight (Fernando Valenzuela)	.30	.25	.12
7	Scott Sanderson	.08	.06	.03
8	Rich Dauer	.08	.06	.03
9	Ron Guidry	.35	.25	.14
10	Ron Guidry IA	.15	.11	.06
11	Gary Alexander	.08	.06	.03
12	Moose Haas	.08	.06	.03
13	Lamar Johnson	.08	.06	.03
14	Steve Howe	.10	.08	.04
15	Ellis Valentine	.08	.06	.03
16	Steve Comer	.08	.06	.03
17	Darrell Evans	.25	.20	.10
18	Fernando Arroyo	.08	.06	.03
19	Ernie Whitt	.10	.08	.04
20	Garry Maddox	.12	.09	.05
21	Orioles Future Stars (Bob Bonner, *Cal Ripken*, Jeff Schneider)	18.00	13.50	7.25
22	Jim Beattie	.08	.06	.03
23	Willie Hernandez	.10	.08	.04
24	Dave Frost	.08	.06	.03
25	Jerry Remy	.08	.06	.03
26	Jorge Orta	.08	.06	.03
27	Tom Herr	.12	.09	.05
28	John Urrea	.08	.06	.03
29	Dwayne Murphy	.10	.08	.04
30	Tom Seaver	1.00	.70	.40
31	Tom Seaver IA	.30	.25	.12
32	Gene Garber	.08	.06	.03
33	Jerry Morales	.08	.06	.03
34	Joe Sambito	.08	.06	.03
35	Willie Aikens	.08	.06	.03
36	Rangers Batting & Pitching Ldrs. (George Medich, Al Oliver)	.12	.09	.05
37	Dan Graham	.08	.06	.03
38	Charlie Lea	.08	.06	.03
39	Lou Whitaker	.40	.30	.15
40	Dave Parker	.35	.25	.14
41	Dave Parker IA	.15	.11	.06
42	Rick Sofield	.08	.06	.03

		MT	NR MT	EX
43	Mike Cubbage	.08	.06	.03
44	Britt Burns	.08	.06	.03
45	Rick Cerone	.08	.06	.03
46	Jerry Augustine	.08	.06	.03
47	Jeff Leonard	.15	.11	.06
48	Bobby Castillo	.08	.06	.03
49	Alvis Woods	.08	.06	.03
50	Buddy Bell	.15	.11	.06
51	Cubs Future Stars (*Jay Howell*, Carlos Lezcano, Ty Waller)	.40	.30	.15
52	Larry Andersen	.08	.06	.03
53	Greg Gross	.08	.06	.03
54	Ron Hassey	.08	.06	.03
55	Rick Burleson	.10	.08	.04
56	Mark Littell	.08	.06	.03
57	Craig Reynolds	.08	.06	.03
58	John D'Acquisto	.08	.06	.03
59	*Rich Gedman*(FC)	.50	.40	.20
60	Tony Armas	.12	.09	.05
61	Tommy Boggs	.08	.06	.03
62	Mike Tyson	.08	.06	.03
63	Mario Soto	.10	.08	.04
64	Lynn Jones	.08	.06	.03
65	Terry Kennedy	.12	.09	.05
66	Astros Batting & Pitching Ldrs. (Art Howe, Nolan Ryan)	.25	.20	.10
67	Rich Gale	.08	.06	.03
68	Roy Howell	.08	.06	.03
69	Al Williams	.08	.06	.03
70	Tim Raines	1.75	1.25	.70
71	Roy Lee Jackson	.08	.06	.03
72	Rick Auerbach	.08	.06	.03
73	Buddy Solomon	.08	.06	.03
74	Bob Clark	.08	.06	.03
75	Tommy John	.30	.25	.12
76	Greg Pryor	.08	.06	.03
77	Miguel Dilone	.08	.06	.03
78	George Medich	.08	.06	.03
79	Bob Bailor	.08	.06	.03
80	Jim Palmer	.60	.45	.25
81	Jim Palmer IA	.30	.25	.12
82	Bob Welch	.20	.15	.08
83	Yankees Future Stars (*Steve Balboni, Andy McGaffigan, Andre Robertson*)(FC)	.50	.40	.20
84	Rennie Stennett	.08	.06	.03
85	Lynn McGlothen	.08	.06	.03
86	Dane Iorg	.08	.06	.03
87	Matt Keough	.08	.06	.03
88	Biff Pocoroba	.08	.06	.03
89	Steve Henderson	.08	.06	.03
90	Nolan Ryan	4.00	3.00	1.50
91	Carney Lansford	.12	.09	.05
92	Brad Havens	.08	.06	.03
93	Larry Hisle	.10	.08	.04
94	Andy Hassler	.08	.06	.03
95	Ozzie Smith	.40	.30	.15
96	Royals Batting & Pitching Ldrs. (George Brett, Larry Gura)	.35	.25	.14
97	Paul Moskau	.08	.06	.03
98	Terry Bulling	.08	.06	.03
99	Barry Bonnell	.08	.06	.03
100	Mike Schmidt	1.50	1.25	.60
101	Mike Schmidt IA	.70	.50	.30
102	Dan Briggs	.08	.06	.03
103	Bob Lacey	.08	.06	.03
104	Rance Mulliniks	.08	.06	.03
105	Kirk Gibson	1.25	.90	.50
106	Enrique Romo	.08	.06	.03
107	Wayne Krenchicki	.08	.06	.03
108	Bob Sykes	.08	.06	.03
109	Dave Revering	.08	.06	.03
110	Carlton Fisk	.50	.40	.20
111	Carlton Fisk IA	.15	.11	.06
112	Billy Sample	.08	.06	.03
113	Steve McCatty	.08	.06	.03
114	Ken Landreaux	.08	.06	.03
115	Gaylord Perry	.40	.30	.15
116	Jim Wohlford	.08	.06	.03
117	Rawly Eastwick	.08	.06	.03
118	Expos Future Stars (*Terry Francona*, Brad Mills, *Bryn Smith*)(FC)	.25	.20	.10
119	Joe Pittman	.08	.06	.03
120	Gary Lucas	.08	.06	.03
121	Ed Lynch	.08	.06	.03
122	Jamie Easterly	.08	.06	.03
123	Danny Goodwin	.08	.06	.03
124	Reid Nichols	.08	.06	.03
125	Danny Ainge	.20	.15	.08
126	Braves Batting & Pitching Ldrs. (Rick Mahler, Claudell Washington)	.10	.08	.04
127	Lonnie Smith	.10	.08	.04
128	Frank Pastore	.08	.06	.03
129	Checklist 1-132	.12	.09	.05
130	Julio Cruz	.08	.06	.03
131	Stan Bahnsen	.08	.06	.03
132	Lee May	.10	.08	.04
133	Pat Underwood	.08	.06	.03
134	Dan Ford	.08	.06	.03
135	Andy Rincon	.08	.06	.03
136	Lenn Sakata	.08	.06	.03
137	George Cappuzzello	.08	.06	.03
138	Tony Pena	.20	.15	.08
139	Jeff Jones	.08	.06	.03
140	Ron LeFlore	.10	.08	.04
141	Indians Future Stars (Chris Bando, Tom Brennan, *Von Hayes*)(FC)	2.00	1.50	.80
142	Dave LaRoche	.08	.06	.03
143	Mookie Wilson	.12	.09	.05
144	Fred Breining	.08	.06	.03
145	Bob Horner	.20	.15	.08
146	Mike Griffin	.08	.06	.03
147	Denny Walling	.08	.06	.03
148	Mickey Klutts	.08	.06	.03
149	Pat Putnam	.08	.06	.03
150	Ted Simmons	.20	.15	.08
151	Dave Edwards	.08	.06	.03
152	Ramon Aviles	.08	.06	.03
153	Roger Erickson	.08	.06	.03
154	Dennis Werth	.08	.06	.03
155	Otto Velez	.08	.06	.03
156	A's Batting & Pitching Ldrs. (Rickey Henderson, Steve McCatty)	.25	.20	.10

		MT	NR MT	EX
157	Steve Crawford	.08	.06	.03
158	Brian Downing	.12	.09	.05
159	Larry Biittner	.08	.06	.03
160	Luis Tiant	.15	.11	.06
161	Batting Leaders (Carney Lansford, Bill Madlock)	.20	.15	.08
162	Home Run Leaders (Tony Armas, Dwight Evans, Bobby Grich, Eddie Murray, Mike Schmidt)	.35	.25	.14
163	Runs Batted In Leaders (Eddie Murray, Mike Schmidt)	.40	.30	.15
164	Stolen Base Leaders (Rickey Henderson, Tim Raines)	.35	.25	.14
165	Victory Leaders (Denny Martinez, Steve McCatty, Jack Morris, Tom Seaver, Pete Vuckovich)	.20	.15	.08
166	Strikeout Leaders (Len Barker, Fernando Valenzuela)	.20	.15	.08
167	Earned Run Avg. Leaders (Steve McCatty, Nolan Ryan)	.20	.15	.08
168	Leading Relievers (Rollie Fingers, Bruce Sutter)	.20	.15	.08
169	Charlie Leibrandt	.12	.09	.05
170	Jim Bibby	.08	.06	.03
171	Giants Future Stars (*Bob Brenly, Chili Davis*, Bob Tufts)	1.25	.90	.50
172	Bill Gullickson	.10	.08	.04
173	Jamie Quirk	.08	.06	.03
174	Dave Ford	.08	.06	.03
175	Jerry Mumphrey	.08	.06	.03
176	Dewey Robinson	.08	.06	.03
177	John Ellis	.08	.06	.03
178	Dyar Miller	.08	.06	.03
179	Steve Garvey	.80	.60	.30
180	Steve Garvey IA	.40	.30	.15
181	Silvio Martinez	.08	.06	.03
182	Larry Herndon	.10	.08	.04
183	Mike Proly	.08	.06	.03
184	Mick Kelleher	.08	.06	.03
185	Phil Niekro	.50	.40	.20
186	Cardinals Batting & Pitching Ldrs. (Bob Forsch, Keith Hernandez)	.25	.20	.10
187	Jeff Newman	.08	.06	.03
188	Randy Martz	.08	.06	.03
189	Glenn Hoffman	.08	.06	.03
190	J.R. Richard	.12	.09	.05
191	*Tim Wallach*(FC)	3.00	2.25	1.25
192	Broderick Perkins	.08	.06	.03
193	Darrell Jackson	.08	.06	.03
194	Mike Vail	.08	.06	.03
195	Paul Molitor	.35	.25	.14
196	Willie Upshaw	.12	.09	.05
197	Shane Rawley	.15	.11	.06
198	Chris Speier	.08	.06	.03
199	Don Aase	.08	.06	.03
200	George Brett	1.50	1.25	.60
201	George Brett IA	.70	.50	.30
202	Rick Manning	.08	.06	.03
203	Blue Jays Future Stars (*Jesse Barfield*, Brian Milner, Boomer Wells)	4.00	3.00	1.50
204	Gary Roenicke	.08	.06	.03
205	Neil Allen	.08	.06	.03
206	Tony Bernazard	.08	.06	.03
207	Rod Scurry	.08	.06	.03
208	Bobby Murcer	.15	.11	.06
209	Gary Lavelle	.08	.06	.03
210	Keith Hernandez	.60	.45	.25
211	Dan Petry	.10	.08	.04
212	Mario Mendoza	.08	.06	.03
213	*Dave Stewart*(FC)	8.00	6.00	3.25
214	Brian Asselstine	.08	.06	.03
215	Mike Krukow	.10	.08	.04
216	White Sox Batting & Pitching Ldrs. (Dennis Lamp, Chet Lemon)	.10	.08	.04
217	Bo McLaughlin	.08	.06	.03
218	Dave Roberts	.08	.06	.03
219	John Curtis	.08	.06	.03
220	Manny Trillo	.10	.08	.04
221	Jim Slaton	.08	.06	.03
222	Butch Wynegar	.08	.06	.03
223	Lloyd Moseby	.20	.15	.08
224	Bruce Bochte	.08	.06	.03
225	Mike Torrez	.10	.08	.04
226	Checklist 133-264	.12	.09	.05
227	Ray Burris	.08	.06	.03
228	Sam Mejias	.08	.06	.03
229	Geoff Zahn	.08	.06	.03
230	Willie Wilson	.20	.15	.08
231	Phillies Future Stars (*Mark Davis*, Bob Dernier, *Ozzie Virgil*)(FC)	2.00	1.50	.80
232	Terry Crowley	.08	.06	.03
233	Duane Kuiper	.08	.06	.03
234	Ron Hodges	.08	.06	.03
235	Mike Easler	.10	.08	.04
236	John Martin	.08	.06	.03
237	Rusty Kuntz	.08	.06	.03
238	Kevin Saucier	.08	.06	.03
239	Jon Matlack	.10	.08	.04
240	Bucky Dent	.12	.09	.05
241	Bucky Dent IA	.10	.08	.04
242	Milt May	.08	.06	.03
243	Bob Owchinko	.08	.06	.03
244	Rufino Linares	.08	.06	.03
245	Ken Reitz	.08	.06	.03
246	Mets Batting & Pitching Ldrs. (Hubie Brooks, Mike Scott)	.20	.15	.08
247	Pedro Guerrero	.90	.70	.35
248	Frank LaCorte	.08	.06	.03
249	Tim Flannery	.08	.06	.03
250	Tug McGraw	.15	.11	.06
251	Fred Lynn	.30	.25	.12
252	Fred Lynn IA	.15	.11	.06
253	Chuck Baker	.08	.06	.03
254	*Jorge Bell*(FC)	9.00	6.75	3.50
255	Tony Perez	.30	.25	.12
256	Tony Perez IA	.15	.11	.06
257	Larry Harlow	.08	.06	.03
258	Bo Diaz	.10	.08	.04
259	Rodney Scott	.08	.06	.03
260	Bruce Sutter	.20	.15	.08
261	Tigers Future Stars (Howard Bailey, Marty Castillo, Dave Rucker)	.08	.06	.03
262	Doug Bair	.08	.06	.03

		MT	NR MT	EX
263	Victor Cruz	.08	.06	.03
264	Dan Quisenberry	.20	.15	.08
265	Al Bumbry	.10	.08	.04
266	Rick Leach	.15	.11	.06
267	Kurt Bevacqua	.08	.06	.03
268	Rickey Keeton	.08	.06	.03
269	Jim Essian	.08	.06	.03
270	Rusty Staub	.15	.11	.06
271	Larry Bradford	.08	.06	.03
272	Bump Wills	.08	.06	.03
273	Doug Bird	.08	.06	.03
274	*Bob Ojeda*(FC)	.70	.50	.30
275	Bob Watson	.10	.08	.04
276	Angels Batting & Pitching Ldrs. (Rod Carew, Ken Forsch)	.25	.20	.10
277	Terry Puhl	.08	.06	.03
278	John Littlefield	.08	.06	.03
279	Bill Russell	.10	.08	.04
280	Ben Oglivie	.10	.08	.04
281	John Verhoeven	.08	.06	.03
282	Ken Macha	.08	.06	.03
283	Brian Allard	.08	.06	.03
284	Bob Grich	.15	.11	.06
285	Sparky Lyle	.12	.09	.05
286	Bill Fahey	.08	.06	.03
287	Alan Bannister	.08	.06	.03
288	Garry Templeton	.12	.09	.05
289	Bob Stanley	.08	.06	.03
290	Ken Singleton	.12	.09	.05
291	Pirates Future Stars (Vance Law, Bob Long, *Johnny Ray*)(FC)	1.00	.70	.40
292	Dave Palmer	.08	.06	.03
293	Rob Picciolo	.08	.06	.03
294	Mike LaCoss	.08	.06	.03
295	Jason Thompson	.08	.06	.03
296	Bob Walk	.12	.09	.05
297	Clint Hurdle	.08	.06	.03
298	Danny Darwin	.08	.06	.03
299	Steve Trout	.08	.06	.03
300	Reggie Jackson	1.00	.70	.40
301	Reggie Jackson IA	.50	.40	.20
302	Doug Flynn	.08	.06	.03
303	Bill Caudill	.08	.06	.03
304	Johnnie LeMaster	.08	.06	.03
305	Don Sutton	.50	.40	.20
306	Don Sutton IA	.25	.20	.10
307	Randy Bass	.08	.06	.03
308	Charlie Moore	.08	.06	.03
309	Pete Redfern	.08	.06	.03
310	Mike Hargrove	.08	.06	.03
311	Dodgers Batting & Pitching Leaders (Dusty Baker, Burt Hooton)	.12	.09	.05
312	Lenny Randle	.08	.06	.03
313	John Harris	.08	.06	.03
314	Buck Martinez	.08	.06	.03
315	Burt Hooton	.10	.08	.04
316	Steve Braun	.08	.06	.03
317	Dick Ruthven	.08	.06	.03
318	Mike Heath	.08	.06	.03
319	Dave Rozema	.08	.06	.03
320	Chris Chambliss	.10	.08	.04
321	Chris Chambliss IA	.10	.08	.04
322	Garry Hancock	.08	.06	.03
323	Bill Lee	.10	.08	.04
324	Steve Dillard	.08	.06	.03
325	Jose Cruz	.15	.11	.06
326	Pete Falcone	.08	.06	.03
327	Joe Nolan	.08	.06	.03
328	Ed Farmer	.08	.06	.03
329	U.L. Washington	.08	.06	.03
330	Rick Wise	.10	.08	.04
331	Benny Ayala	.08	.06	.03
332	Don Robinson	.10	.08	.04
333	Brewers Future Stars (*Frank DiPino*, Marshall Edwards, Chuck Porter)	.12	.09	.05
334	Aurelio Rodriguez	.10	.08	.04
335	Jim Sundberg	.10	.08	.04
336	Mariners Batting & Pitching Ldrs. (Glenn Abbott, Tom Paciorek)	.10	.08	.04
337	Pete Rose AS	.80	.60	.30
338	Dave Lopes AS	.12	.09	.05
339	Mike Schmidt AS	.60	.45	.25
340	Dave Concepcion AS	.12	.09	.05
341	Andre Dawson AS	.25	.20	.10
342a	George Foster AS (no autograph)	2.25	1.75	.90
342b	George Foster AS (autograph on front)	.40	.30	.15
343	Dave Parker AS	.20	.15	.08
344	Gary Carter AS	.35	.25	.14
345	Fernando Valenzuela AS	.35	.25	.14
346	Tom Seaver AS	.35	.25	.14
347	Bruce Sutter AS	.12	.09	.05
348	Derrel Thomas	.08	.06	.03
349	George Frazier	.08	.06	.03
350	Thad Bosley	.08	.06	.03
351	Reds Future Stars (Scott Brown, Geoff Combe, Paul Householder)	.08	.06	.03
352	Dick Davis	.08	.06	.03
353	Jack O'Connor	.08	.06	.03
354	Roberto Ramos	.08	.06	.03
355	Dwight Evans	.25	.20	.10
356	Denny Lewallyn	.08	.06	.03
357	Butch Hobson	.08	.06	.03
358	Mike Parrott	.08	.06	.03
359	Jim Dwyer	.08	.06	.03
360	Len Barker	.10	.08	.04
361	Rafael Landestoy	.08	.06	.03
362	Jim Wright	.08	.06	.03
363	Bob Molinaro	.08	.06	.03
364	Doyle Alexander	.12	.09	.05
365	Bill Madlock	.20	.15	.08
366	Padres Batting & Pitching Ldrs. (Juan Eichelberger, Luis Salazar)	.10	.08	.04
367	Jim Kaat	.25	.20	.10
368	Alex Trevino	.08	.06	.03
369	Champ Summers	.08	.06	.03
370	Mike Norris	.08	.06	.03
371	Jerry Don Gleaton	.08	.06	.03
372	Luis Gomez	.08	.06	.03
373	*Gene Nelson*	.15	.11	.06
374	Tim Blackwell	.08	.06	.03
375	Dusty Baker	.12	.09	.05
376	Chris Welsh	.08	.06	.03
377	Kiko Garcia	.08	.06	.03
378	Mike Caldwell	.08	.06	.03
379	Rob Wilfong	.08	.06	.03
380	Dave Stieb	.25	.20	.10
381	Red Sox Future Stars (Bruce Hurst, Dave Schmidt, Julio Valdez)	.25	.20	.10
382	Joe Simpson	.08	.06	.03
383a	Pascual Perez (no position on front)	35.00	26.00	14.00
383b	Pascual Perez (position on front)	.12	.09	.05
384	Keith Moreland	.12	.09	.05
385	Ken Forsch	.08	.06	.03
386	Jerry White	.08	.06	.03
387	Tom Veryzer	.08	.06	.03
388	Joe Rudi	.12	.09	.05
389	George Vukovich	.08	.06	.03
390	Eddie Murray	1.25	.90	.50
391	Dave Tobik	.08	.06	.03
392	Rick Bosetti	.08	.06	.03
393	Al Hrabosky	.10	.08	.04
394	Checklist 265-396	.12	.09	.05
395	Omar Moreno	.08	.06	.03
396	Twins Batting & Pitching Ldrs. (Fernando Arroyo, John Castino)	.10	.08	.04
397	Ken Brett	.10	.08	.04
398	Mike Squires	.08	.06	.03
399	Pat Zachry	.08	.06	.03
400	Johnny Bench	.90	.70	.35
401	Johnny Bench IA	.40	.30	.15
402	Bill Stein	.08	.06	.03
403	Jim Tracy	.08	.06	.03
404	Dickie Thon	.10	.08	.04
405	Rick Reuschel	.15	.11	.06
406	Al Holland	.08	.06	.03
407	Danny Boone	.08	.06	.03
408	Ed Romero	.08	.06	.03
409	Don Cooper	.08	.06	.03
410	Ron Cey	.15	.11	.06
411	Ron Cey IA	.10	.08	.04
412	Luis Leal	.08	.06	.03
413	Dan Meyer	.08	.06	.03
414	Elias Sosa	.08	.06	.03
415	Don Baylor	.15	.11	.06
416	Marty Bystrom	.08	.06	.03
417	Pat Kelly	.08	.06	.03
418	Rangers Future Stars (John Butcher, Bobby Johnson, *Dave Schmidt*)(FC)	.20	.15	.08
419	Steve Stone	.12	.09	.05
420	George Hendrick	.10	.08	.04
421	Mark Clear	.08	.06	.03
422	Cliff Johnson	.08	.06	.03
423	Stan Papi	.08	.06	.03
424	Bruce Benedict	.08	.06	.03
425	John Candelaria	.12	.09	.05
426	Orioles Batting & Pitching Ldrs. (Eddie Murray, Sammy Stewart)	.35	.25	.14
427	Ron Oester	.08	.06	.03
428	Lamarr Hoyt (LaMarr)	.08	.06	.03
429	John Wathan	.10	.08	.04
430	Vida Blue	.15	.11	.06
431	Vida Blue IA	.10	.08	.04
432	Mike Scott	.25	.20	.10
433	Alan Ashby	.08	.06	.03
434	Joe Lefebvre	.08	.06	.03
435	Robin Yount	2.00	1.50	.80
436	Joe Strain	.08	.06	.03
437	Juan Berenguer	.08	.06	.03
438	Pete Mackanin	.08	.06	.03
439	*Dave Righetti*(FC)	2.50	2.00	1.00
440	Jeff Burroughs	.10	.08	.04
441	Astros Future Stars (Danny Heep, Billy Smith, Bobby Sprowl)	.08	.06	.03
442	Bruce Kison	.08	.06	.03
443	Mark Wagner	.08	.06	.03
444	Terry Forster	.10	.08	.04
445	Larry Parrish	.12	.09	.05
446	Wayne Garland	.08	.06	.03
447	Darrell Porter	.10	.08	.04
448	Darrell Porter IA	.10	.08	.04
449	*Luis Aguayo*(FC)	.12	.09	.05
450	Jack Morris	.50	.40	.20
451	Ed Miller	.08	.06	.03
452	*Lee Smith*(FC)	.90	.70	.35
453	Art Howe	.08	.06	.03
454	Rick Langford	.08	.06	.03
455	Tom Burgmeier	.08	.06	.03
456	Cubs Batting & Pitching Ldrs. (Bill Buckner, Randy Martz)	.15	.11	.06
457	Tim Stoddard	.08	.06	.03
458	Willie Montanez	.08	.06	.03
459	Bruce Berenyi	.08	.06	.03
460	Jack Clark	.30	.25	.12
461	Rich Dotson	.12	.09	.05
462	Dave Chalk	.08	.06	.03
463	Jim Kern	.08	.06	.03
464	Juan Bonilla	.08	.06	.03
465	Lee Mazzilli	.10	.08	.04
466	Randy Lerch	.08	.06	.03
467	Mickey Hatcher	.10	.08	.04
468	Floyd Bannister	.12	.09	.05
469	Ed Ott	.08	.06	.03
470	John Mayberry	.10	.08	.04
471	Royals Future Stars (*Atlee Hammaker*, Mike Jones, Darryl Motley)	.25	.20	.10
472	Oscar Gamble	.10	.08	.04
473	Mike Stanton	.08	.06	.03
474	Ken Oberkfell	.08	.06	.03
475	Alan Trammell	.50	.40	.20
476	Brian Kingman	.08	.06	.03
477	Steve Yeager	.08	.06	.03
478	Ray Searage	.08	.06	.03
479	Rowland Office	.08	.06	.03
480	Steve Carlton	.80	.60	.30
481	Steve Carlton IA	.40	.30	.15
482	Glenn Hubbard	.10	.08	.04
483	Gary Woods	.08	.06	.03
484	Ivan DeJesus	.08	.06	.03
485	Kent Tekulve	.10	.08	.04
486	Yankees Batting & Pitching Ldrs. (Tommy John, Jerry Mumphrey)	.20	.15	.08
487	Bob McClure	.08	.06	.03
488	Ron Jackson	.08	.06	.03
489	Rick Dempsey	.10	.08	.04
490	Dennis Eckersley	.20	.15	.08
491	Checklist 397-528	.12	.09	.05
492	Joe Price	.08	.06	.03
493	Chet Lemon	.10	.08	.04
494	Hubie Brooks	.20	.15	.08
495	Dennis Leonard	.10	.08	.04
496	Johnny Grubb	.08	.06	.03
497	Jim Anderson	.08	.06	.03
498	Dave Bergman	.08	.06	.03
499	Paul Mirabella	.08	.06	.03
500	Rod Carew	.80	.60	.30
501	Rod Carew IA	.40	.30	.15
502	Braves Future Stars (*Steve Bedrosian, Brett Butler*, Larry Owen)	2.50	2.00	1.00
503	Julio Gonzalez	.08	.06	.03
504	Rick Peters	.08	.06	.03
505	Graig Nettles	.25	.20	.10
506	Graig Nettles IA	.12	.09	.05
507	Terry Harper	.08	.06	.03
508	*Jody Davis*(FC)	.40	.30	.15
509	Harry Spilman	.08	.06	.03
510	Fernando Valenzuela	1.50	1.25	.60
511	Ruppert Jones	.08	.06	.03
512	Jerry Dybzinski	.08	.06	.03
513	Rick Rhoden	.12	.09	.05
514	Joe Ferguson	.08	.06	.03
515	Larry Bowa	.20	.15	.08
516	Larry Bowa IA	.12	.09	.05
517	Mark Brouhard	.08	.06	.03
518	Garth Iorg	.08	.06	.03
519	Glenn Adams	.08	.06	.03
520	Mike Flanagan	.12	.09	.05
521	Billy Almon	.08	.06	.03
522	Chuck Rainey	.08	.06	.03
523	Gary Gray	.08	.06	.03
524	Tom Hausman	.08	.06	.03
525	Ray Knight	.12	.09	.05
526	Expos Batting & Pitching Ldrs. (Warren Cromartie, Bill Gullickson)	.10	.08	.04
527	John Henry Johnson	.08	.06	.03
528	Matt Alexander	.08	.06	.03
529	Allen Ripley	.08	.06	.03
530	Dickie Noles	.08	.06	.03
531	A's Future Stars (Rich Bordi, Mark Budaska, Kelvin Moore)	.08	.06	.03
532	Toby Harrah	.10	.08	.04
533	Joaquin Andujar	.10	.08	.04
534	Dave McKay	.08	.06	.03
535	Lance Parrish	.50	.40	.20
536	Rafael Ramirez	.10	.08	.04
537	Doug Capilla	.08	.06	.03
538	Lou Piniella	.15	.11	.06
539	Vern Ruhle	.08	.06	.03
540	Andre Dawson	.50	.40	.20
541	Barry Evans	.08	.06	.03
542	Ned Yost	.08	.06	.03
543	Bill Robinson	.08	.06	.03
544	Larry Christenson	.08	.06	.03
545	Reggie Smith	.15	.11	.06
546	Reggie Smith IA	.10	.08	.04
547	Rod Carew AS	.35	.25	.14
548	Willie Randolph AS	.12	.09	.05
549	George Brett AS	.60	.45	.25
550	Bucky Dent AS	.12	.09	.05
551	Reggie Jackson AS	.50	.40	.20
552	Ken Singleton AS	.12	.09	.05
553	Dave Winfield AS	.40	.30	.15
554	Carlton Fisk AS	.20	.15	.08
555	Scott McGregor AS	.12	.09	.05
556	Jack Morris AS	.20	.15	.08
557	Rich Gossage AS	.20	.15	.08
558	John Tudor	.30	.25	.12
559	Indians Batting & Pitching Ldrs. (Bert Blyleven, Mike Hargrove)	.15	.11	.06
560	Doug Corbett	.08	.06	.03
561	Cardinals Future Stars (Glenn Brummer, Luis DeLeon, Gene Roof)	.08	.06	.03
562	Mike O'Berry	.08	.06	.03
563	Ross Baumgarten	.08	.06	.03
564	Doug DeCinces	.15	.11	.06
565	Jackson Todd	.08	.06	.03
566	Mike Jorgensen	.08	.06	.03
567	Bob Babcock	.08	.06	.03
568	Joe Pettini	.08	.06	.03
569	Willie Randolph	.15	.11	.06
570	Willie Randolph IA	.10	.08	.04
571	Glenn Abbott	.08	.06	.03
572	Juan Beniquez	.08	.06	.03
573	Rick Waits	.08	.06	.03
574	Mike Ramsey	.08	.06	.03
575	Al Cowens	.08	.06	.03
576	Giants Batting & Pitching Ldrs. (Vida Blue, Milt May)	.15	.11	.06
577	Rick Monday	.12	.09	.05
578	Shooty Babitt	.08	.06	.03
579	*Rick Mahler*(FC)	.30	.25	.12
580	Bobby Bonds	.15	.11	.06
581	Ron Reed	.08	.06	.03
582	Luis Pujols	.08	.06	.03
583	Tippy Martinez	.08	.06	.03
584	Hosken Powell	.08	.06	.03
585	Rollie Fingers	.30	.25	.12
586	Rollie Fingers IA	.15	.11	.06
587	Tim Lollar	.08	.06	.03
588	Dale Berra	.08	.06	.03
589	Dave Stapleton	.08	.06	.03
590	Al Oliver	.20	.15	.08
591	Al Oliver IA	.10	.08	.04
592	Craig Swan	.08	.06	.03
593	Billy Smith	.08	.06	.03
594	Renie Martin	.08	.06	.03
595	Dave Collins	.10	.08	.04
596	Damaso Garcia	.08	.06	.03
597	Wayne Nordhagen	.08	.06	.03
598	Bob Galasso	.08	.06	.03
599	White Sox Future Stars (Jay Loviglio, Reggie Patterson, Leo Sutherland)	.08	.06	.03
600	Dave Winfield	.60	.45	.25
601	Sid Monge	.08	.06	.03

		MT	NR MT	EX
602	Freddie Patek	.08	.06	.03
603	Rich Hebner	.08	.06	.03
604	Orlando Sanchez	.08	.06	.03
605	Steve Rogers	.10	.08	.04
606	Blue Jays Batting & Pitching Ldrs. (John Mayberry, Dave Stieb)	.15	.11	.06
607	Leon Durham	.10	.08	.04
608	Jerry Royster	.08	.06	.03
609	Rick Sutcliffe	.25	.20	.10
610	Rickey Henderson	3.50	2.75	1.50
611	Joe Niekro	.20	.15	.08
612	Gary Ward	.10	.08	.04
613	Jim Gantner	.10	.08	.04
614	Juan Eichelberger	.08	.06	.03
615	Bob Boone	.12	.09	.05
616	Bob Boone IA	.10	.08	.04
617	Scott McGregor	.10	.08	.04
618	Tim Foli	.08	.06	.03
619	Bill Campbell	.08	.06	.03
620	Ken Griffey	.15	.11	.06
621	Ken Griffey IA	.10	.08	.04
622	Dennis Lamp	.08	.06	.03
623	Mets Future Stars (Ron Gardenhire, *Terry Leach, Tim Leary*)(FC)	.90	.70	.35
624	Fergie Jenkins	.25	.20	.10
625	Hal McRae	.15	.11	.06
626	Randy Jones	.10	.08	.04
627	Enos Cabell	.08	.06	.03
628	Bill Travers	.08	.06	.03
629	Johnny Wockenfuss	.08	.06	.03
630	Joe Charboneau	.10	.08	.04
631	Gene Tenace	.10	.08	.04
632	Bryan Clark	.08	.06	.03
633	Mitchell Page	.08	.06	.03
634	Checklist 529-660	.12	.09	.05
635	Ron Davis	.10	.08	.04
636	Phillies Batting & Pitching Ldrs. (Steve Carlton, Pete Rose)	.50	.40	.20
637	Rick Camp	.08	.06	.03
638	John Milner	.08	.06	.03
639	Ken Kravec	.08	.06	.03
640	Cesar Cedeno	.15	.11	.06
641	Steve Mura	.08	.06	.03
642	Mike Scioscia	.10	.08	.04
643	Pete Vuckovich	.10	.08	.04
644	John Castino	.08	.06	.03
645	Frank White	.12	.09	.05
646	Frank White IA	.10	.08	.04
647	Warren Brusstar	.08	.06	.03
648	Jose Morales	.08	.06	.03
649	Ken Clay	.08	.06	.03
650	Carl Yastrzemski	1.25	.90	.50
651	Carl Yastrzemski IA	.60	.45	.25
652	Steve Nicosia	.08	.06	.03
653	Angels Future Stars (*Tom Brunansky*, Luis Sanchez, Daryl Sconiers)	2.50	2.00	1.00
654	Jim Morrison	.08	.06	.03
655	Joel Youngblood	.08	.06	.03
656	Eddie Whitson	.08	.06	.03
657	Tom Poquette	.08	.06	.03
658	Tito Landrum	.08	.06	.03
659	Fred Martinez	.08	.06	.03
660	Dave Concepcion	.15	.11	.06
661	Dave Concepcion IA	.10	.08	.04
662	Luis Salazar	.08	.06	.03
663	Hector Cruz	.08	.06	.03
664	Dan Spillner	.08	.06	.03
665	Jim Clancy	.12	.09	.05
666	Tigers Batting & Pitching Ldrs. (Steve Kemp, Dan Petry)	.15	.11	.06
667	Jeff Reardon	.25	.20	.10
668	Dale Murphy	2.00	1.50	.80
669	Larry Milbourne	.08	.06	.03
670	Steve Kemp	.12	.09	.05
671	Mike Davis	.10	.08	.04
672	Bob Knepper	.12	.09	.05
673	Keith Drumright	.08	.06	.03
674	Dave Goltz	.10	.08	.04
675	Cecil Cooper	.20	.15	.08
676	Sal Butera	.08	.06	.03
677	Alfredo Griffin	.12	.09	.05
678	Tom Paciorek	.08	.06	.03
679	Sammy Stewart	.08	.06	.03
680	Gary Matthews	.12	.09	.05
681	Dodgers Future Stars (*Mike Marshall*, Ron Roenicke, *Steve Sax*)(FC)	4.00	3.00	1.50
682	Jesse Jefferson	.08	.06	.03
683	Phil Garner	.10	.08	.04
684	Harold Baines	.70	.50	.30
685	Bert Blyleven	.20	.15	.08
686	Gary Allenson	.08	.06	.03
687	Greg Minton	.08	.06	.03
688	Leon Roberts	.08	.06	.03
689	Lary Sorensen	.08	.06	.03
690	Dave Kingman	.20	.15	.08
691	Dan Schatzeder	.08	.06	.03
692	Wayne Gross	.08	.06	.03
693	Cesar Geronimo	.08	.06	.03
694	Dave Wehrmeister	.08	.06	.03
695	Warren Cromartie	.08	.06	.03
696	Pirates Batting & Pitching Ldrs. (Bill Madlock, Buddy Solomon)	.15	.11	.06
697	John Montefusco	.08	.06	.03
698	Tony Scott	.08	.06	.03
699	Dick Tidrow	.08	.06	.03
700	George Foster	.25	.20	.10
701	George Foster IA	.12	.09	.05
702	Steve Renko	.08	.06	.03
703	Brewers Batting & Pitching Ldrs. (Cecil Cooper, Pete Vuckovich)	.15	.11	.06
704	Mickey Rivers	.10	.08	.04
705	Mickey Rivers IA	.10	.08	.04
706	Barry Foote	.08	.06	.03
707	Mark Bomback	.08	.06	.03
708	Gene Richards	.08	.06	.03
709	Don Money	.08	.06	.03
710	Jerry Reuss	.12	.09	.05
711	Mariners Future Stars (Dave Edler, *Dave Henderson*, Reggie Walton)	1.25	.90	.50
712	Denny Martinez	.10	.08	.04
713	Del Unser	.08	.06	.03
714	Jerry Koosman	.12	.09	.05
715	Willie Stargell	.70	.50	.30

		MT	NR MT	EX
716	Willie Stargell IA	.30	.25	.12
717	Rick Miller	.08	.06	.03
718	Charlie Hough	.12	.09	.05
719	Jerry Narron	.08	.06	.03
720	Greg Luzinski	.20	.15	.08
721	Greg Luzinski IA	.12	.09	.05
722	Jerry Martin	.08	.06	.03
723	Junior Kennedy	.08	.06	.03
724	Dave Rosello	.08	.06	.03
725	Amos Otis	.10	.08	.04
726	Amos Otis IA	.10	.08	.04
727	Sixto Lezcano	.08	.06	.03
728	Aurelio Lopez	.08	.06	.03
729	Jim Spencer	.08	.06	.03
730	Gary Carter	.70	.50	.30
731	Padres Future Stars (Mike Armstrong, Doug Gwosdz, Fred Kuhaulua)	.08	.06	.03
732	Mike Lum	.08	.06	.03
733	Larry McWilliams	.08	.06	.03
734	Mike Ivie	.08	.06	.03
735	Rudy May	.08	.06	.03
736	Jerry Turner	.08	.06	.03
737	Reggie Cleveland	.08	.06	.03
738	Dave Engle	.08	.06	.03
739	Joey McLaughlin	.08	.06	.03
740	Dave Lopes	.12	.09	.05
741	Dave Lopes IA	.10	.08	.04
742	Dick Drago	.08	.06	.03
743	John Stearns	.08	.06	.03
744	*Mike Witt*(FC)	.80	.60	.30
745	Bake McBride	.08	.06	.03
746	Andre Thornton	.12	.09	.05
747	John Lowenstein	.08	.06	.03
748	Marc Hill	.08	.06	.03
749	Bob Shirley	.08	.06	.03
750	Jim Rice	.90	.70	.35
751	Rick Honeycutt	.08	.06	.03
752	Lee Lacy	.08	.06	.03
753	Tom Brookens	.08	.06	.03
754	Joe Morgan	.50	.40	.20
755	Joe Morgan IA	.20	.15	.08
756	Reds Batting & Pitching Ldrs. (Ken Griffey, Tom Seaver)	.30	.25	.12
757	Tom Underwood	.08	.06	.03
758	Claudell Washington	.12	.09	.05
759	Paul Splittorff	.08	.06	.03
760	Bill Buckner	.15	.11	.06
761	Dave Smith	.12	.09	.05
762	Mike Phillips	.08	.06	.03
763	Tom Hume	.08	.06	.03
764	Steve Swisher	.08	.06	.03
765	Gorman Thomas	.12	.09	.05
766	Twins Future Stars (Lenny Faedo, *Kent Hrbek, Tim Laudner*)(FC)	5.00	3.75	2.00
767	Roy Smalley	.08	.06	.03
768	Jerry Garvin	.08	.06	.03
769	Richie Zisk	.10	.08	.04
770	Rich Gossage	.35	.25	.14
771	Rich Gossage IA	.15	.11	.06
772	Bert Campaneris	.12	.09	.05
773	John Denny	.08	.06	.03
774	Jay Johnstone	.10	.08	.04
775	Bob Forsch	.10	.08	.04
776	Mark Belanger	.10	.08	.04
777	Tom Griffin	.08	.06	.03
778	Kevin Hickey	.08	.06	.03
779	Grant Jackson	.08	.06	.03
780	Pete Rose	2.25	1.75	.90
781	Pete Rose IA	1.00	.70	.40
782	Frank Taveras	.08	.06	.03
783	*Greg Harris*(FC)	.15	.11	.06
784	Milt Wilcox	.08	.06	.03
785	Dan Driessen	.10	.08	.04
786	Red Sox Batting & Pitching Ldrs. (Carney Lansford, Mike Torrez)	.12	.09	.05
787	Fred Stanley	.08	.06	.03
788	Woodie Fryman	.10	.08	.04
789	Checklist 661-792	.12	.09	.05
790	Larry Gura	.08	.06	.03
791	Bobby Brown	.08	.06	.03
792	Frank Tanana	.12	.09	.05

1982 Topps Insert Stickers

5
MIKE SCHMIDT
3rd Base
NEED STICKERS
TO COMPLETE YOUR COLLECTION?
See inside back cover of the
TOPPS Baseball Sticker ALBUM
IT'S
Topps
FOR SPORTS

This 48-player set is actually an abbreviated version of the regular 1982 Topps sticker set with different backs. Used to promote the 1982 sticker set, Topps inserted these stickers in its baseball card wax packs. They are identical to the regular 1982 stickers, except for the backs, which advertise that the Topps sticker album will be "Coming Soon." The 48 stickers retain the same numbers used in the regular sticker set, resulting in the smaller set being skip-numbered.

		MT	NR MT	EX
Complete Set:		2.00	1.50	.80
Common Player:		.03	.02	.01
17	Chris Chambliss	.04	.03	.02
21	Bruce Benedict	.03	.02	.01
25	Leon Durham	.06	.05	.02
29	Bill Buckner	.06	.05	.02
33	Dave Collins	.04	.03	.02
37	Dave Concepcion	.06	.05	.02
41	Nolan Ryan	.15	.11	.06
45	Bob Knepper	.04	.03	.02
49	Ken Landreaux	.03	.02	.01
53	Burt Hooton	.03	.02	.01
57	Andre Dawson	.12	.09	.05
61	Gary Carter	.20	.15	.08
65	Joel Youngblood	.03	.02	.01
69	Ellis Valentine	.03	.02	.01
73	Garry Maddox	.04	.03	.02
77	Bob Boone	.04	.03	.02
81	Omar Moreno	.03	.02	.01
85	Willie Stargell	.20	.15	.08
89	Ken Oberkfell	.03	.02	.01
93	Darrell Porter	.04	.03	.02
97	Juan Eichelberger	.03	.02	.01
101	Luis Salazar	.03	.02	.01
105	Enos Cabell	.03	.02	.01
109	Larry Herndon	.03	.02	.01
143	Scott McGregor	.04	.03	.02
148	Mike Flanagan	.06	.05	.02
151	Mike Torrez	.04	.03	.02
156	Carney Lansford	.06	.05	.02
161	Fred Lynn	.10	.08	.04
166	Rich Dotson	.04	.03	.02
171	Tony Bernazard	.03	.02	.01
176	Bo Diaz	.04	.03	.02
181	Alan Trammell	.15	.11	.06
186	Milt Wilcox	.03	.02	.01
191	Dennis Leonard	.04	.03	.02
196	Willie Aikens	.03	.02	.01
201	Ted Simmons	.08	.06	.03
206	Hosken Powell	.03	.02	.01
211	Roger Erickson	.03	.02	.01
215	Graig Nettles	.06	.05	.02
216	Reggie Jackson	.25	.20	.10
221	Rickey Henderson	.25	.20	.10
226	Cliff Johnson	.03	.02	.01
231	Jeff Burroughs	.04	.03	.02
236	Tom Paciorek	.03	.02	.01
241	Pat Putnam	.03	.02	.01
246	Lloyd Moseby	.06	.05	.02
251	Barry Bonnell	.03	.02	.01

1982 Topps Stickers

The 1982 Topps sticker set is complete at 260 stickers and includes another series of "foil" All-Stars. The stickers measure 1-15/16" by 2-9/16" and feature full-color photos surrounded by a red border for American League players or a blue border for National League players. They are numbered on both the front and back and were designed to be mounted in a special album.

		MT	NR MT	EX
Complete Set:		15.00	11.00	6.00
Common Player:		.03	.02	.01
Sticker Album:		.80	.60	.30
1	Bill Madlock	.06	.05	.02
2	Carney Lansford	.06	.05	.02
3	Mike Schmidt	.25	.20	.10
4	Tony Armas, Dwight Evans, Bobby Grich, Eddie Murray	.12	.09	.05
5	Mike Schmidt	.25	.20	.10
6	Eddie Murray	.20	.15	.08
7	Tim Raines	.03	.02	.01
8	Rickey Henderson	.25	.20	.10
9	Tom Seaver	.20	.15	.08
10	Denny Martinez, Steve McCatty, Jack Morris, Pete Vuckovich	.06	.05	.02
11	Fernando Valenzuela	.15	.11	.06
12	Len Barker	.03	.02	.01
13	Nolan Ryan	.20	.15	.08
14	Steve McCatty	.03	.02	.01
15	Bruce Sutter	.08	.06	.03
16	Rollie Fingers	.10	.08	.04
17	Chris Chambliss	.04	.03	.02
18	Bob Horner	.08	.06	.03
19	Dale Murphy	.25	.20	.10
20	Phil Niekro	.12	.09	.05
21	Bruce Benedict	.03	.02	.01
22	Claudell Washington	.04	.03	.02
23	Glenn Hubbard	.03	.02	.01
24	Rick Camp	.03	.02	.01
25	Leon Durham	.06	.05	.02
26	Ken Reitz	.03	.02	.01
27	Dick Tidrow	.03	.02	.01
28	Tim Blackwell	.03	.02	.01
29	Bill Buckner	.06	.05	.02
30	Steve Henderson	.03	.02	.01
31	Mike Krukow	.04	.03	.02
32	Ivan DeJesus	.03	.02	.01
33	Dave Collins	.04	.03	.02
34	Ron Oester	.03	.02	.01
35	Johnny Bench	.25	.20	.10
36	Tom Seaver	.20	.15	.08
37	Dave Concepcion	.06	.05	.02
38	Ken Griffey	.06	.05	.02
39	Ray Knight	.06	.05	.02
40	George Foster	.08	.06	.03
41	Nolan Ryan	.20	.15	.08
42	Terry Puhl	.03	.02	.01
43	Art Howe	.03	.02	.01
44	Jose Cruz	.06	.05	.02
45	Bob Knepper	.06	.05	.02
46	Craig Reynolds	.03	.02	.01
47	Cesar Cedeno	.06	.05	.02
48	Alan Ashby	.03	.02	.01

		MT	NR MT	EX
49	Ken Landreaux	.03	.02	.01
50	Fernando Valenzuela	.15	.11	.06
51	Ron Cey	.06	.05	.02
52	Dusty Baker	.04	.03	.02
53	Burt Hooton	.04	.03	.02
54	Steve Garvey	.20	.15	.08
55	Pedro Guerrero	.12	.09	.05
56	Jerry Reuss	.06	.05	.02
57	Andre Dawson	.12	.09	.05
58	Chris Speier	.03	.02	.01
59	Steve Rogers	.03	.02	.01
60	Warren Cromartie	.03	.02	.01
61	Gary Carter	.20	.15	.08
62	Tim Raines	.20	.15	.08
63	Scott Sanderson	.03	.02	.01
64	Larry Parrish	.06	.05	.02
65	Joel Youngblood	.03	.02	.01
66	Neil Allen	.03	.02	.01
67	Lee Mazzilli	.04	.03	.02
68	Hubie Brooks	.06	.05	.02
69	Ellis Valentine	.03	.02	.01
70	Doug Flynn	.03	.02	.01
71	Pat Zachry	.03	.02	.01
72	Dave Kingman	.08	.06	.03
73	Garry Maddox	.04	.03	.02
74	Mike Schmidt	.25	.20	.10
75	Steve Carlton	.20	.15	.08
76	Manny Trillo	.04	.03	.02
77	Bob Boone	.04	.03	.02
78	Pete Rose	.40	.30	.15
79	Gary Matthews	.04	.03	.02
80	Larry Bowa	.06	.05	.02
81	Omar Moreno	.03	.02	.01
82	Rick Rhoden	.04	.03	.02
83	Bill Madlock	.06	.05	.02
84	Mike Easler	.04	.03	.02
85	Willie Stargell	.20	.15	.08
86	Jim Bibby	.03	.02	.01
87	Dave Parker	.12	.09	.05
88	Tim Foli	.03	.02	.01
89	Ken Oberkfell	.03	.02	.01
90	Bob Forsch	.04	.03	.02
91	George Hendrick	.04	.03	.02
92	Keith Hernandez	.12	.09	.05
93	Darrell Porter	.04	.03	.02
94	Bruce Sutter	.08	.06	.03
95	Sixto Lezcano	.03	.02	.01
96	Garry Templeton	.04	.03	.02
97	Juan Eichelberger	.03	.02	.01
98	Broderick Perkins	.03	.02	.01
99	Ruppert Jones	.03	.02	.01
100	Terry Kennedy	.04	.03	.02
101	Luis Salazar	.03	.02	.01
102	Gary Lucas	.03	.02	.01
103	Gene Richards	.03	.02	.01
104	Ozzie Smith	.10	.08	.04
105	Enos Cabell	.03	.02	.01
106	Jack Clark	.10	.08	.04
107	Greg Minton	.03	.02	.01
108	Johnnie LeMaster	.03	.02	.01
109	Larry Herndon	.03	.02	.01
110	Milt May	.03	.02	.01
111	Vida Blue	.06	.05	.02
112	Darrell Evans	.08	.06	.03
113	Len Barker	.03	.02	.01
114	Julio Cruz	.03	.02	.01
115	Billy Martin	.08	.06	.03
116	Tim Raines	.20	.15	.08
117	Pete Rose	.40	.30	.15
118	Bill Stein	.03	.02	.01
119	Fernando Valenzuela	.15	.11	.06
120	Carl Yastrzemski	.25	.20	.10
121	Pete Rose	.50	.40	.20
122	Manny Trillo	.15	.11	.06
123	Mike Schmidt	.40	.30	.15
124	Dave Concepcion	.20	.15	.08
125	Andre Dawson	.25	.20	.10
126	George Foster	.20	.15	.08
127	Dave Parker	.25	.20	.10
128	Gary Carter	.30	.25	.12
129	Steve Carlton	.30	.25	.12
130	Bruce Sutter	.25	.20	.10
131	Rod Carew	.40	.30	.15
132	Jerry Remy	.15	.11	.06
133	George Brett	.40	.30	.15
134	Rick Burleson	.15	.11	.06
135	Dwight Evans	.25	.20	.10
136	Ken Singleton	.20	.15	.08
137	Dave Winfield	.30	.25	.12
138	Carlton Fisk	.25	.20	.10
139	Jack Morris	.25	.20	.10
140	Rich Gossage	.25	.20	.10
141	Al Bumbry	.04	.03	.02
142	Doug DeCinces	.06	.05	.02
143	Scott McGregor	.04	.03	.02
144	Ken Singleton	.06	.05	.02
145	Eddie Murray	.20	.15	.08
146	Jim Palmer	.15	.11	.06
147	Rich Dauer	.03	.02	.01
148	Mike Flanagan	.04	.03	.02
149	Jerry Remy	.03	.02	.01
150	Jim Rice	.20	.15	.08
151	Mike Torrez	.04	.03	.02
152	Tony Perez	.10	.08	.04
153	Dwight Evans	.10	.08	.04
154	Mark Clear	.03	.02	.01
155	Carl Yastrzemski	.25	.20	.10
156	Carney Lansford	.06	.05	.02
157	Rick Burleson	.04	.03	.02
158	Don Baylor	.08	.06	.03
159	Ken Forsch	.03	.02	.01
160	Rod Carew	.20	.15	.08
161	Fred Lynn	.10	.08	.04
162	Bob Grich	.06	.05	.02
163	Dan Ford	.03	.02	.01
164	Butch Hobson	.03	.02	.01
165	Greg Luzinski	.08	.06	.03
166	Rich Dotson	.04	.03	.02
167	Billy Almon	.03	.02	.01
168	Chet Lemon	.04	.03	.02
169	Steve Trout	.03	.02	.01
170	Carlton Fisk	.12	.09	.05
171	Tony Bernazard	.03	.02	.01
172	Ron LeFlore	.04	.03	.02

		MT	NR MT	EX
173	Bert Blyleven	.08	.06	.03
174	Andre Thornton	.06	.05	.02
175	Jorge Orta	.03	.02	.01
176	Bo Diaz	.04	.03	.02
177	Toby Harrah	.04	.03	.02
178	Len Barker	.03	.02	.01
179	Rick Manning	.03	.02	.01
180	Mike Hargrove	.04	.03	.02
181	Alan Trammell	.15	.11	.06
182	Al Cowens	.03	.02	.01
183	Jack Morris	.12	.09	.05
184	Kirk Gibson	.15	.11	.06
185	Steve Kemp	.04	.03	.02
186	Milt Wilcox	.03	.02	.01
187	Lou Whitaker	.12	.09	.05
188	Lance Parrish	.12	.09	.05
189	Willie Wilson	.08	.06	.03
190	George Brett	.25	.20	.10
191	Dennis Leonard	.04	.03	.02
192	John Wathan	.04	.03	.02
193	Frank White	.06	.05	.02
194	Amos Otis	.04	.03	.02
195	Larry Gura	.03	.02	.01
196	Willie Aikens	.03	.02	.01
197	Ben Oglivie	.06	.05	.02
198	Rollie Fingers	.10	.08	.04
199	Cecil Cooper	.08	.06	.03
200	Paul Molitor	.10	.08	.04
201	Ted Simmons	.08	.06	.03
202	Pete Vuckovich	.04	.03	.02
203	Robin Yount	.15	.11	.06
204	Gorman Thomas	.04	.03	.02
205	Rob Wilfong	.03	.02	.01
206	Hosken Powell	.03	.02	.01
207	Roy Smalley	.03	.02	.01
208	Butch Wynegar	.04	.03	.02
209	John Castino	.03	.02	.01
210	Doug Corbett	.03	.02	.01
211	Roger Erickson	.03	.02	.01
212	Mickey Hatcher	.03	.02	.01
213	Dave Winfield	.20	.15	.08
214	Tommy John	.10	.08	.04
215	Graig Nettles	.06	.05	.02
216	Reggie Jackson	.25	.20	.10
217	Rich Gossage	.10	.08	.04
218	Rick Cerone	.03	.02	.01
219	Willie Randolph	.06	.05	.02
220	Jerry Mumphrey	.03	.02	.01
221	Rickey Henderson	.20	.15	.08
222	Mike Norris	.03	.02	.01
223	Jim Spencer	.03	.02	.01
224	Tony Armas	.04	.03	.02
225	Matt Keough	.03	.02	.01
226	Cliff Johnson	.03	.02	.01
227	Dwayne Murphy	.04	.03	.02
228	Steve McCatty	.03	.02	.01
229	Richie Zisk	.04	.03	.02
230	Lenny Randle	.03	.02	.01
231	Jeff Burroughs	.04	.03	.02
232	Bruce Bochte	.03	.02	.01
233	Gary Gray	.03	.02	.01
234	Floyd Bannister	.04	.03	.02
235	Julio Cruz	.03	.02	.01
236	Tom Paciorek	.03	.02	.01
237	Danny Darwin	.03	.02	.01
238	Buddy Bell	.06	.05	.02
239	Al Oliver	.06	.05	.02
240	Jim Sundberg	.04	.03	.02
241	Pat Putnam	.03	.02	.01
242	Steve Comer	.03	.02	.01
243	Mickey Rivers	.04	.03	.02
244	Bump Wills	.03	.02	.01
245	Damaso Garcia	.04	.03	.02
246	Lloyd Moseby	.06	.05	.02
247	Ernie Whitt	.03	.02	.01
248	John Mayberry	.03	.02	.01
249	Otto Velez	.03	.02	.01
250	Dave Stieb	.06	.05	.02
251	Barry Bonnell	.03	.02	.01
252	Alfredo Griffin	.04	.03	.02
253	1981 N.L. Championship (Gary Carter)	.10	.08	.04
254	1981 A.L. Championship (Mike Heath, Larry Milbourne)	.03	.02	.01
255	1981 World Champions (Los Angeles Dodgers Team)	.04	.03	.02
256	1981 World Champions (Los Angeles Dodgers Team)	.04	.03	.02
257	1981 World Series - Game 3 (Fernando Valenzuela)	.10	.08	.04
258	1981 World Series - Game 4 (Steve Garvey)	.10	.08	.04
259	1981 World Series - Game 5 (Jerry Reuss, Steve Yeager)	.03	.02	.01
260	1981 World Series - Game 6 (Pedro Guerrero)	.08	.06	.03

1982 Topps Traded

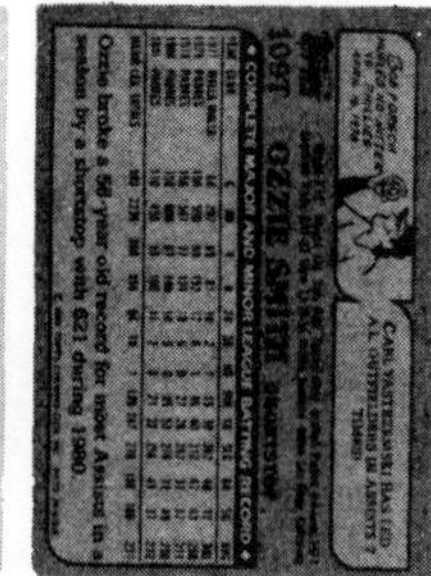

Topps released its second straight 132-card Traded set in September of 1982. Again, the 2-1/2" by 3-1/2" cards feature not only players who had been traded during the season, but also promising rookies who were given their first individual cards. The cards follow the basic design of the regular issues, but have their backs printed in red rather than the regular-issue green. As in 1981, the cards were not available in normal retail outlets and could only be purchased through regular baseball card dealers. Unlike the previous year, the cards are numbered 1-132 with the letter "T" following the number.

		MT	NR MT	EX
Complete Set:		40.00	30.00	15.00
Common Player:		.10	.08	.04
1T	Doyle Alexander	.20	.15	.08
2T	Jesse Barfield	2.25	1.75	.90
3T	Ross Baumgarten	.10	.08	.04
4T	Steve Bedrosian	.80	.60	.30
5T	Mark Belanger	.15	.11	.06
6T	Kurt Bevacqua	.10	.08	.04
7T	Tim Blackwell	.10	.08	.04
8T	Vida Blue	.25	.20	.10
9T	Bob Boone	.20	.15	.08
10T	Larry Bowa	.25	.20	.10
11T	Dan Briggs	.10	.08	.04
12T	Bobby Brown	.10	.08	.04
13T	Tom Brunansky	1.75	1.25	.70
14T	Jeff Burroughs	.15	.11	.06
15T	Enos Cabell	.10	.08	.04
16T	Bill Campbell	.10	.08	.04
17T	Bobby Castillo	.10	.08	.04
18T	Bill Caudill	.10	.08	.04
19T	Cesar Cedeno	.20	.15	.08
20T	Dave Collins	.15	.11	.06
21T	Doug Corbett	.10	.08	.04
22T	Al Cowens	.10	.08	.04
23T	Chili Davis	1.50	1.25	.60
24T	Dick Davis	.10	.08	.04
25T	Ron Davis	.10	.08	.04
26T	Doug DeCinces	.20	.15	.08
27T	Ivan DeJesus	.10	.08	.04
28T	Bob Dernier	.20	.15	.08
29T	Bo Diaz	.15	.11	.06
30T	Roger Erickson	.10	.08	.04
31T	Jim Essian	.10	.08	.04
32T	Ed Farmer	.10	.08	.04
33T	Doug Flynn	.10	.08	.04
34T	Tim Foli	.10	.08	.04
35T	Dan Ford	.10	.08	.04
36T	George Foster	.40	.30	.15
37T	Dave Frost	.10	.08	.04
38T	Rich Gale	.10	.08	.04
39T	Ron Gardenhire	.10	.08	.04
40T	Ken Griffey	.25	.20	.10
41T	Greg Harris	.15	.11	.06
42T	Von Hayes	1.50	1.25	.60
43T	Larry Herndon	.15	.11	.06
44T	Kent Hrbek	5.00	3.75	2.00
45T	Mike Ivie	.10	.08	.04
46T	Grant Jackson	.10	.08	.04
47T	Reggie Jackson	3.00	2.25	1.25
48T	Ron Jackson	.10	.08	.04
49T	Fergie Jenkins	.40	.30	.15
50T	Lamar Johnson	.10	.08	.04
51T	Randy Johnson	.10	.08	.04
52T	Jay Johnstone	.15	.11	.06
53T	Mick Kelleher	.10	.08	.04
54T	Steve Kemp	.15	.11	.06
55T	Junior Kennedy	.10	.08	.04
56T	Jim Kern	.10	.08	.04
57T	Ray Knight	.20	.15	.08
58T	Wayne Krenchicki	.10	.08	.04
59T	Mike Krukow	.15	.11	.06
60T	Duane Kuiper	.10	.08	.04
61T	Mike LaCoss	.10	.08	.04
62T	Chet Lemon	.15	.11	.06
63T	Sixto Lezcano	.10	.08	.04
64T	Dave Lopes	.15	.11	.06
65T	Jerry Martin	.10	.08	.04
66T	Renie Martin	.10	.08	.04
67T	John Mayberry	.15	.11	.06
68T	Lee Mazzilli	.15	.11	.06
69T	Bake McBride	.10	.08	.04
70T	Dan Meyer	.10	.08	.04
71T	Larry Milbourne	.10	.08	.04
72T	Eddie Milner(FC)	.20	.15	.08
73T	Sid Monge	.10	.08	.04
74T	Jose Morales	.10	.08	.04
75T	Keith Moreland	.20	.15	.08
76T	John Montefusco	.10	.08	.04
77T	Jim Morrison	.10	.08	.04
78T	Rance Mulliniks	.10	.08	.04
79T	Steve Mura	.10	.08	.04
80T	Gene Nelson	.10	.08	.04
81T	Joe Nolan	.10	.08	.04
82T	Dickie Noles	.10	.08	.04
83T	Al Oliver	.30	.25	.12
84T	Jorge Orta	.10	.08	.04
85T	Tom Paciorek	.10	.08	.04
86T	Larry Parrish	.20	.15	.08
87T	Jack Perconte	.10	.08	.04
88T	Gaylord Perry	1.50	1.25	.60
89T	Rob Picciolo	.10	.08	.04
90T	Joe Pittman	.10	.08	.04
91T	Hosken Powell	.10	.08	.04
92T	Mike Proly	.10	.08	.04
93T	Greg Pryor	.10	.08	.04
94T	Charlie Puleo(FC)	.15	.11	.06
95T	Shane Rawley	.20	.15	.08
96T	Johnny Ray	.80	.60	.30
97T	Dave Revering	.10	.08	.04
98T	Cal Ripken	16.00	12.00	6.50
99T	Allen Ripley	.10	.08	.04
100T	Bill Robinson	.10	.08	.04
101T	Aurelio Rodriguez	.15	.11	.06
102T	Joe Rudi	.20	.15	.08
103T	Steve Sax	5.00	3.75	2.00
104T	Dan Schatzeder	.10	.08	.04

		MT	NR MT	EX
105T	Bob Shirley	.10	.08	.04
106T	Eric Show(FC)	.70	.50	.30
107T	Roy Smalley	.15	.11	.06
108T	Lonnie Smith	.15	.11	.06
109T	Ozzie Smith	6.00	4.50	2.50
110T	Reggie Smith	.20	.15	.08
111T	Lary Sorensen	.10	.08	.04
112T	Elias Sosa	.10	.08	.04
113T	Mike Stanton	.10	.08	.04
114T	Steve Stroughter	.10	.08	.04
115T	Champ Summers	.10	.08	.04
116T	Rick Sutcliffe	.50	.40	.20
117T	Frank Tanana	.20	.15	.08
118T	Frank Taveras	.10	.08	.04
119T	Garry Templeton	.20	.15	.08
120T	Alex Trevino	.10	.08	.04
121T	Jerry Turner	.10	.08	.04
122T	Ed Vande Berg(FC)	.15	.11	.06
123T	Tom Veryzer	.10	.08	.04
124T	Ron Washington	.10	.08	.04
125T	Bob Watson	.15	.11	.06
126T	Dennis Werth	.10	.08	.04
127T	Eddie Whitson	.15	.11	.06
128T	Rob Wilfong	.10	.08	.04
129T	Bump Wills	.10	.08	.04
130T	Gary Woods	.10	.08	.04
131T	Butch Wynegar	.15	.11	.06
132T	Checklist 1-132	.10	.08	.04

1983 Topps

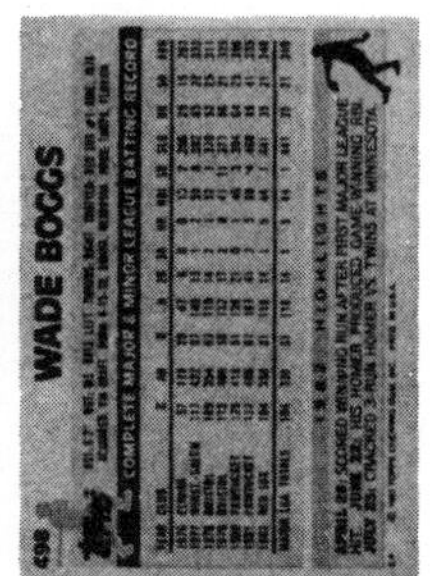

The 1983 Topps set totals 792 cards. Missing among the regular 2-1/2" by 3-1/2" cards are some form of future stars cards, as Topps was saving them for the now-established late season "Traded" set. The 1983 cards carry a large color photo as well as a smaller color photo on the front, quite similar in design to the 1963 set. Team colors frame the card, which, at the bottom, have the player's name, position and team. At the upper right-hand corner is a Topps Logo. The backs are horizontal and include statistics, personal information and 1982 highlights. Specialty cards include record-breaking perfor- mances, league leaders, All-Stars, numbered check- lists "Team Leaders" and "Super Veteran" cards which are horizontal with a current and first-season picture of the honored player.

	MT	NR MT	EX
Complete Set:	110.00	82.00	45.00
Common Player:	.08	.06	.03

		MT	NR MT	EX
1	Record Breaker (Tony Armas)	.12	.09	.05
2	Record Breaker (Rickey Henderson)	.35	.25	.14
3	Record Breaker (Greg Minton)	.08	.06	.03
4	Record Breaker (Lance Parrish)	.20	.15	.08
5	Record Breaker (Manny Trillo)	.08	.06	.03
6	Record Breaker (John Wathan)	.08	.06	.03
7	Gene Richards	.08	.06	.03
8	Steve Balboni	.10	.08	.04
9	Joey McLaughlin	.08	.06	.03
10	Gorman Thomas	.12	.09	.05
11	Billy Gardner	.08	.06	.03
12	Paul Mirabella	.08	.06	.03
13	Larry Herndon	.10	.08	.04
14	Frank LaCorte	.08	.06	.03
15	Ron Cey	.15	.11	.06
16	George Vukovich	.08	.06	.03
17	Kent Tekulve	.10	.08	.04
18	Super Veteran (Kent Tekulve)	.10	.08	.04
19	Oscar Gamble	.10	.08	.04
20	Carlton Fisk	.40	.30	.15
21	Orioles Batting & Pitching Ldrs. (Eddie Murray, Jim Palmer)	.35	.25	.14
22	Randy Martz	.08	.06	.03
23	Mike Heath	.08	.06	.03
24	Steve Mura	.08	.06	.03
25	Hal McRae	.15	.11	.06
26	Jerry Royster	.08	.06	.03
27	Doug Corbett	.08	.06	.03
28	Bruce Bochte	.08	.06	.03
29	Randy Jones	.10	.08	.04
30	Jim Rice	.70	.50	.30
31	Bill Gullickson	.08	.06	.03
32	Dave Bergman	.08	.06	.03
33	Jack O'Connor	.08	.06	.03
34	Paul Householder	.08	.06	.03
35	Rollie Fingers	.30	.25	.12
36	Super Veteran (Rollie Fingers)	.15	.11	.06
37	Darrell Johnson	.08	.06	.03
38	Tim Flannery	.08	.06	.03
39	Terry Puhl	.08	.06	.03
40	Fernando Valenzuela	.50	.40	.20
41	Jerry Turner	.08	.06	.03
42	Dale Murray	.08	.06	.03
43	Bob Dernier	.08	.06	.03
44	Don Robinson	.10	.08	.04
45	John Mayberry	.10	.08	.04
46	Richard Dotson	.12	.09	.05
47	Dave McKay	.08	.06	.03
48	Lary Sorensen	.08	.06	.03
49	*Willie McGee*(FC)	1.25	.90	.50
50	Bob Horner	.20	.15	.08
51	Cubs Batting & Pitching Ldrs. (Leon Durham, Fergie Jenkins)	.15	.11	.06
52	*Onix Concepcion*(FC)	.08	.06	.03
53	Mike Witt	.30	.25	.12
54	Jim Maler	.08	.06	.03
55	Mookie Wilson	.12	.09	.05
56	Chuck Rainey	.08	.06	.03
57	Tim Blackwell	.08	.06	.03
58	Al Holland	.08	.06	.03
59	Benny Ayala	.08	.06	.03
60	Johnny Bench	.60	.45	.25
61	Super Veteran (Johnny Bench)	.30	.25	.12
62	Bob McClure	.08	.06	.03
63	Rick Monday	.12	.09	.05
64	Bill Stein	.08	.06	.03
65	Jack Morris	.35	.25	.14
66	Bob Lillis	.08	.06	.03
67	Sal Butera	.08	.06	.03
68	*Eric Show*	.30	.25	.12
69	Lee Lacy	.08	.06	.03
70	Steve Carlton	.60	.45	.25
71	Super Veteran (Steve Carlton)	.30	.25	.12
72	Tom Paciorek	.08	.06	.03
73	Allen Ripley	.08	.06	.03
74	Julio Gonzalez	.08	.06	.03
75	Amos Otis	.10	.08	.04
76	Rick Mahler	.12	.09	.05
77	Hosken Powell	.08	.06	.03
78	Bill Caudill	.08	.06	.03
79	Mick Kelleher	.08	.06	.03
80	George Foster	.20	.15	.08
81	Yankees Batting & Pitching Ldrs. (Jerry Mumphrey, Dave Righetti)	.15	.11	.06
82	Bruce Hurst	.15	.11	.06
83	*Ryne Sandberg*(FC)	35.00	27.00	15.00
84	Milt May	.08	.06	.03
85	Ken Singleton	.12	.09	.05
86	Tom Hume	.08	.06	.03
87	Joe Rudi	.12	.09	.05
88	Jim Gantner	.10	.08	.04
89	Leon Roberts	.08	.06	.03
90	Jerry Reuss	.12	.09	.05
91	Larry Milbourne	.08	.06	.03
92	Mike LaCoss	.08	.06	.03
93	John Castino	.08	.06	.03
94	Dave Edwards	.08	.06	.03
95	Alan Trammell	.50	.40	.20
96	Dick Howser	.08	.06	.03
97	Ross Baumgarten	.08	.06	.03
98	Vance Law	.10	.08	.04
99	Dickie Noles	.08	.06	.03
100	Pete Rose	1.75	1.25	.70
101	Super Veteran (Pete Rose)	.80	.60	.30
102	Dave Beard	.08	.06	.03
103	Darrell Porter	.10	.08	.04
104	Bob Walk	.08	.06	.03
105	Don Baylor	.15	.11	.06
106	Gene Nelson	.08	.06	.03
107	Mike Jorgensen	.08	.06	.03
108	Glenn Hoffman	.08	.06	.03
109	Luis Leal	.08	.06	.03
110	Ken Griffey	.15	.11	.06
111	Expos Batting & Pitching Ldrs. (Al Oliver, Steve Rogers)	.15	.11	.06
112	Bob Shirley	.08	.06	.03
113	Ron Roenicke	.08	.06	.03
114	Jim Slaton	.08	.06	.03
115	Chili Davis	.20	.15	.08
116	Dave Schmidt	.10	.08	.04
117	Alan Knicely	.08	.06	.03
118	Chris Welsh	.08	.06	.03
119	Tom Brookens	.08	.06	.03
120	Len Barker	.10	.08	.04
121	Mickey Hatcher	.10	.08	.04
122	Jimmy Smith	.08	.06	.03
123	George Frazier	.08	.06	.03
124	Marc Hill	.08	.06	.03
125	Leon Durham	.10	.08	.04
126	Joe Torre	.10	.08	.04
127	Preston Hanna	.08	.06	.03
128	Mike Ramsey	.08	.06	.03
129	Checklist 1-132	.12	.09	.05
130	Dave Stieb	.20	.15	.08
131	Ed Ott	.08	.06	.03
132	Todd Cruz	.08	.06	.03
133	Jim Barr	.08	.06	.03
134	Hubie Brooks	.15	.11	.06
135	Dwight Evans	.25	.20	.10
136	Willie Aikens	.08	.06	.03
137	Woodie Fryman	.10	.08	.04
138	Rick Dempsey	.10	.08	.04
139	Bruce Berenyi	.08	.06	.03
140	Willie Randolph	.12	.09	.05
141	Indians Batting & Pitching Ldrs. (Toby Harrah, Rick Sutcliffe)	.12	.09	.05
142	Mike Caldwell	.08	.06	.03
143	Joe Pettini	.08	.06	.03
144	Mark Wagner	.08	.06	.03
145	Don Sutton	.40	.30	.15
146	Super Veteran (Don Sutton)	.20	.15	.08
147	Rick Leach	.08	.06	.03
148	Dave Roberts	.08	.06	.03
149	Johnny Ray	.15	.11	.06
150	Bruce Sutter	.20	.15	.08
151	Super Veteran (Bruce Sutter)	.12	.09	.05
152	Jay Johnstone	.10	.08	.04
153	Jerry Koosman	.12	.09	.05
154	Johnnie LeMaster	.08	.06	.03
155	Dan Quisenberry	.20	.15	.08
156	Billy Martin	.12	.09	.05
157	Steve Bedrosian	.25	.20	.10
158	Rob Wilfong	.08	.06	.03
159	Mike Stanton	.08	.06	.03
160	Dave Kingman	.20	.15	.08
161	Super Veteran (Dave Kingman)	.10	.08	.04
162	Mark Clear	.08	.06	.03
163	Cal Ripken	4.00	3.00	1.50
164	Dave Palmer	.08	.06	.03
165	Dan Driessen	.10	.08	.04
166	John Pacella	.08	.06	.03
167	Mark Brouhard	.08	.06	.03
168	Juan Eichelberger	.08	.06	.03
169	Doug Flynn	.08	.06	.03
170	Steve Howe	.10	.08	.04
171	Giants Batting & Pitching Ldrs. (Bill Laskey, Joe Morgan)	.15	.11	.06
172	Vern Ruhle	.08	.06	.03
173	Jim Morrison	.08	.06	.03
174	Jerry Ujdur	.08	.06	.03
175	Bo Diaz	.10	.08	.04
176	Dave Righetti	.35	.25	.14
177	Harold Baines	.25	.20	.10
178	Luis Tiant	.15	.11	.06
179	Super Veteran (Luis Tiant)	.10	.08	.04
180	Rickey Henderson	5.00	3.75	2.00
181	Terry Felton	.08	.06	.03
182	Mike Fischlin	.08	.06	.03
183	*Ed Vande Berg*	.12	.09	.05
184	Bob Clark	.08	.06	.03
185	Tim Lollar	.08	.06	.03
186	Whitey Herzog	.10	.08	.04
187	Terry Leach	.12	.09	.05
188	Rick Miller	.08	.06	.03
189	Dan Schatzeder	.08	.06	.03
190	Cecil Cooper	.20	.15	.08
191	Joe Price	.08	.06	.03
192	Floyd Rayford	.08	.06	.03
193	Harry Spilman	.08	.06	.03
194	Cesar Geronimo	.08	.06	.03
195	Bob Stoddard	.08	.06	.03
196	Bill Fahey	.08	.06	.03
197	*Jim Eisenreich*(FC)	.15	.11	.06
198	Kiko Garcia	.08	.06	.03
199	Marty Bystrom	.08	.06	.03
200	Rod Carew	.70	.50	.30
201	Super Veteran (Rod Carew)	.35	.25	.14
202	Blue Jays Batting & Pitching Ldrs. (Damaso Garcia, Dave Stieb)	.12	.09	.05
203	Mike Morgan	.15	.11	.06
204	Junior Kennedy	.08	.06	.03
205	Dave Parker	.40	.30	.15
206	Ken Oberkfell	.08	.06	.03
207	Rick Camp	.08	.06	.03
208	Dan Meyer	.08	.06	.03
209	*Mike Moore*(FC)	2.00	1.50	.70
210	Jack Clark	.30	.25	.12
211	John Denny	.08	.06	.03
212	John Stearns	.08	.06	.03
213	Tom Burgmeier	.08	.06	.03
214	Jerry White	.08	.06	.03
215	Mario Soto	.10	.08	.04
216	Tony LaRussa	.10	.08	.04
217	Tim Stoddard	.08	.06	.03
218	Roy Howell	.08	.06	.03
219	Mike Armstrong	.08	.06	.03
220	Dusty Baker	.12	.09	.05
221	Joe Niekro	.15	.11	.06
222	Damaso Garcia	.08	.06	.03
223	John Montefusco	.08	.06	.03
224	Mickey Rivers	.10	.08	.04
225	Enos Cabell	.08	.06	.03
226	Enrique Romo	.08	.06	.03
227	Chris Bando	.08	.06	.03
228	Joaquin Andujar	.10	.08	.04
229	Phillies Batting & Pitching Ldrs. (Steve Carlton, Bo Diaz)	.20	.15	.08
230	Fergie Jenkins	.25	.20	.10
231	Super Veteran (Fergie Jenkins)	.12	.09	.05
232	Tom Brunansky	.30	.25	.12
233	Wayne Gross	.08	.06	.03
234	Larry Andersen	.08	.06	.03
235	Claudell Washington	.10	.08	.04
236	Steve Renko	.08	.06	.03
237	Dan Norman	.08	.06	.03
238	*Bud Black*(FC)	.25	.20	.10
239	Dave Stapleton	.08	.06	.03
240	Rich Gossage	.30	.25	.12
241	Super Veteran (Rich Gossage)	.15	.11	.06
242	Joe Nolan	.08	.06	.03
243	Duane Walker	.08	.06	.03
244	Dwight Bernard	.08	.06	.03
245	Steve Sax	.35	.25	.14
246	George Bamberger	.08	.06	.03
247	Dave Smith	.12	.09	.05
248	Bake McBride	.08	.06	.03
249	Checklist 133-264	.12	.09	.05
250	Bill Buckner	.15	.11	.06
251	*Alan Wiggins*(FC)	.08	.06	.03
252	Luis Aguayo	.08	.06	.03
253	Larry McWilliams	.08	.06	.03
254	Rick Cerone	.08	.06	.03
255	Gene Garber	.08	.06	.03
256	Super Veteran (Gene Garber)	.08	.06	.03
257	Jesse Barfield	.50	.40	.20
258	Manny Castillo	.08	.06	.03
259	Jeff Jones	.08	.06	.03
260	Steve Kemp	.12	.09	.05
261	Tigers Batting & Pitching Ldrs. (Larry Herndon, Dan Petry)	.10	.08	.04
262	Ron Jackson	.08	.06	.03
263	Renie Martin	.08	.06	.03
264	Jamie Quirk	.08	.06	.03

		MT	NR MT	EX
265	Joel Youngblood	.08	.06	.03
266	Paul Boris	.08	.06	.03
267	Terry Francona	.08	.06	.03
268	*Storm Davis*(FC)	.70	.50	.30
269	Ron Oester	.08	.06	.03
270	Dennis Eckersley	.20	.15	.08
271	Ed Romero	.08	.06	.03
272	Frank Tanana	.12	.09	.05
273	Mark Belanger	.10	.08	.04
274	Terry Kennedy	.12	.09	.05
275	Ray Knight	.12	.09	.05
276	Gene Mauch	.10	.08	.04
277	Rance Mulliniks	.08	.06	.03
278	Kevin Hickey	.08	.06	.03
279	Greg Gross	.08	.06	.03
280	Bert Blyleven	.20	.15	.08
281	Andre Robertson	.08	.06	.03
282	Reggie Smith	.12	.09	.05
283	Super Veteran (Reggie Smith)	.10	.08	.04
284	Jeff Lahti	.08	.06	.03
285	Lance Parrish	.40	.30	.15
286	Rick Langford	.08	.06	.03
287	Bobby Brown	.08	.06	.03
288	*Joe Cowley*(FC)	.12	.09	.05
289	Jerry Dybzinski	.08	.06	.03
290	Jeff Reardon	.15	.11	.06
291	Pirates Batting & Pitching Ldrs. (John Candelaria, Bill Madlock)	.15	.11	.06
292	Craig Swan	.08	.06	.03
293	Glenn Gulliver	.08	.06	.03
294	Dave Engle	.08	.06	.03
295	Jerry Remy	.08	.06	.03
296	Greg Harris	.08	.06	.03
297	Ned Yost	.08	.06	.03
298	Floyd Chiffer	.08	.06	.03
299	George Wright	.08	.06	.03
300	Mike Schmidt	2.25	1.75	.90
301	Super Veteran (Mike Schmidt)	.60	.45	.25
302	Ernie Whitt	.10	.08	.04
303	Miguel Dilone	.08	.06	.03
304	Dave Rucker	.08	.06	.03
305	Larry Bowa	.15	.11	.06
306	Tom Lasorda	.12	.09	.05
307	Lou Piniella	.15	.11	.06
308	Jesus Vega	.08	.06	.03
309	Jeff Leonard	.12	.09	.05
310	Greg Luzinski	.15	.11	.06
311	Glenn Brummer	.08	.06	.03
312	Brian Kingman	.08	.06	.03
313	Gary Gray	.08	.06	.03
314	Ken Dayley(FC)	.15	.11	.06
315	Rick Burleson	.10	.08	.04
316	Paul Splittorff	.08	.06	.03
317	Gary Rajsich	.08	.06	.03
318	John Tudor	.15	.11	.06
319	Lenn Sakata	.08	.06	.03
320	Steve Rogers	.10	.08	.04
321	Brewers Batting & Pitching Ldrs. (Pete Vuckovich, Robin Yount)	.20	.15	.08
322	Dave Van Gorder	.08	.06	.03
323	Luis DeLeon	.08	.06	.03
324	Mike Marshall	.30	.25	.12
325	Von Hayes	.20	.15	.08
326	Garth Iorg	.08	.06	.03
327	Bobby Castillo	.08	.06	.03
328	Craig Reynolds	.08	.06	.03
329	Randy Niemann	.08	.06	.03
330	Buddy Bell	.15	.11	.06
331	Mike Krukow	.10	.08	.04
332	*Glenn Wilson*(FC)	.30	.25	.12
333	Dave LaRoche	.08	.06	.03
334	Super Veteran (Dave LaRoche)	.08	.06	.03
335	Steve Henderson	.08	.06	.03
336	Rene Lachemann	.08	.06	.03
337	Tito Landrum	.08	.06	.03
338	Bob Owchinko	.08	.06	.03
339	Terry Harper	.08	.06	.03
340	Larry Gura	.08	.06	.03
341	Doug DeCinces	.15	.11	.06
342	Atlee Hammaker	.10	.08	.04
343	Bob Bailor	.08	.06	.03
344	Roger LaFrancois	.08	.06	.03
345	Jim Clancy	.10	.08	.04
346	Joe Pittman	.08	.06	.03
347	Sammy Stewart	.08	.06	.03
348	Alan Bannister	.08	.06	.03
349	Checklist 265-396	.12	.09	.05
350	Robin Yount	1.50	1.25	.60
351	Reds Batting & Pitching Ldrs. (Cesar Cedeno, Mario Soto)	.12	.09	.05
352	Mike Scioscia	.10	.08	.04
353	Steve Comer	.08	.06	.03
354	Randy Johnson	.08	.06	.03
355	Jim Bibby	.08	.06	.03
356	Gary Woods	.08	.06	.03
357	*Len Matuszek*(FC)	.08	.06	.03
358	Jerry Garvin	.08	.06	.03
359	Dave Collins	.10	.08	.04
360	Nolan Ryan	3.00	2.25	1.25
361	Super Veteran (Nolan Ryan)	.30	.25	.12
362	Bill Almon	.08	.06	.03
363	*John Stuper*(FC)	.08	.06	.03
364	Brett Butler	.20	.15	.08
365	Dave Lopes	.12	.09	.05
366	Dick Williams	.08	.06	.03
367	Bud Anderson	.08	.06	.03
368	Richie Zisk	.10	.08	.04
369	Jesse Orosco	.15	.11	.06
370	Gary Carter	.50	.40	.20
371	Mike Richardt	.08	.06	.03
372	Terry Crowley	.08	.06	.03
373	Kevin Saucier	.08	.06	.03
374	Wayne Krenchicki	.08	.06	.03
375	Pete Vuckovich	.10	.08	.04
376	Ken Landreaux	.08	.06	.03
377	Lee May	.10	.08	.04
378	Super Veteran (Lee May)	.10	.08	.04
379	Guy Sularz	.08	.06	.03
380	Ron Davis	.08	.06	.03
381	Red Sox Batting & Pitching Ldrs. (Jim Rice, Bob Stanley)	.25	.20	.10

		MT	NR MT	EX
382	Bob Knepper	.12	.09	.05
383	Ozzie Virgil	.10	.08	.04
384	*Dave Dravecky*(FC)	1.25	.90	.50
385	Mike Easler	.10	.08	.04
386	Rod Carew AS	.35	.25	.14
387	Bob Grich AS	.10	.08	.04
388	George Brett AS	.50	.40	.20
389	Robin Yount AS	.25	.20	.10
390	Reggie Jackson AS	.50	.40	.20
391	Rickey Henderson AS	.40	.30	.15
392	Fred Lynn AS	.15	.11	.06
393	Carlton Fisk AS	.15	.11	.06
394	Pete Vuckovich AS	.10	.08	.04
395	Larry Gura AS	.08	.06	.03
396	Dan Quisenberry AS	.12	.09	.05
397	Pete Rose AS	.70	.50	.30
398	Manny Trillo AS	.10	.08	.04
399	Mike Schmidt AS	.60	.45	.25
400	Dave Concepcion AS	.12	.09	.05
401	Dale Murphy AS	.70	.50	.30
402	Andre Dawson AS	.20	.15	.08
403	Tim Raines AS	.35	.25	.14
404	Gary Carter AS	.35	.25	.14
405	Steve Rogers AS	.10	.08	.04
406	Steve Carlton AS	.35	.25	.14
407	Bruce Sutter AS	.12	.09	.05
408	Rudy May	.08	.06	.03
409	Marvis Foley	.08	.06	.03
410	Phil Niekro	.40	.30	.15
411	Super Veteran (Phil Niekro)	.20	.15	.08
412	Rangers Batting & Pitching Ldrs. (Buddy Bell, Charlie Hough)	.15	.11	.06
413	Matt Keough	.08	.06	.03
414	Julio Cruz	.08	.06	.03
415	Bob Forsch	.10	.08	.04
416	Joe Ferguson	.08	.06	.03
417	Tom Hausman	.08	.06	.03
418	Greg Pryor	.08	.06	.03
419	Steve Crawford	.08	.06	.03
420	Al Oliver	.20	.15	.08
421	Super Veteran (Al Oliver)	.12	.09	.05
422	George Cappuzzello	.08	.06	.03
423	*Tom Lawless*(FC)	.10	.08	.04
424	Jerry Augustine	.08	.06	.03
425	Pedro Guerrero	.35	.25	.14
426	Earl Weaver	.10	.08	.04
427	Roy Lee Jackson	.08	.06	.03
428	Champ Summers	.08	.06	.03
429	Eddie Whitson	.08	.06	.03
430	Kirk Gibson	.50	.40	.20
431	*Gary Gaetti*(FC)	5.00	3.75	2.00
432	Porfirio Altamirano	.08	.06	.03
433	Dale Berra	.08	.06	.03
434	Dennis Lamp	.08	.06	.03
435	Tony Armas	.12	.09	.05
436	Bill Campbell	.08	.06	.03
437	Rick Sweet	.08	.06	.03
438	*Dave LaPoint*(FC)	.40	.30	.15
439	Rafael Ramirez	.08	.06	.03
440	Ron Guidry	.30	.25	.12
441	Astros Batting & Pitching Ldrs. (Ray Knight, Joe Niekro)	.12	.09	.05
442	Brian Downing	.12	.09	.05
443	Don Hood	.08	.06	.03
444	Wally Backman(FC)	.25	.20	.10
445	Mike Flanagan	.12	.09	.05
446	Reid Nichols	.08	.06	.03
447	Bryn Smith	.10	.08	.04
448	Darrell Evans	.20	.15	.08
449	*Eddie Milner*	.12	.09	.05
450	Ted Simmons	.20	.15	.08
451	Super Veteran (Ted Simmons)	.12	.09	.05
452	Lloyd Moseby	.15	.11	.06
453	Lamar Johnson	.08	.06	.03
454	Bob Welch	.15	.11	.06
455	Sixto Lezcano	.08	.06	.03
456	Lee Elia	.08	.06	.03
457	Milt Wilcox	.08	.06	.03
458	Ron Washington	.08	.06	.03
459	Ed Farmer	.08	.06	.03
460	Roy Smalley	.08	.06	.03
461	Steve Trout	.08	.06	.03
462	Steve Nicosia	.08	.06	.03
463	Gaylord Perry	.40	.30	.15
464	Super Veteran (Gaylord Perry)	.20	.15	.08
465	Lonnie Smith	.10	.08	.04
466	Tom Underwood	.08	.06	.03
467	Rufino Linares	.08	.06	.03
468	Dave Goltz	.10	.08	.04
469	Ron Gardenhire	.08	.06	.03
470	Greg Minton	.08	.06	.03
471	Royals Batting & Pitching Ldrs. (Vida Blue, Willie Wilson)	.15	.11	.06
472	Gary Allenson	.08	.06	.03
473	John Lowenstein	.08	.06	.03
474	Ray Burris	.08	.06	.03
475	Cesar Cedeno	.12	.09	.05
476	Rob Picciolo	.08	.06	.03
477	Tom Niedenfuer(FC)	.15	.11	.06
478	Phil Garner	.10	.08	.04
479	Charlie Hough	.12	.09	.05
480	Toby Harrah	.10	.08	.04
481	Scot Thompson	.08	.06	.03
482	*Tony Gwynn*(FC)	25.00	20.00	10.00
483	Lynn Jones	.08	.06	.03
484	Dick Ruthven	.08	.06	.03
485	Omar Moreno	.08	.06	.03
486	Clyde King	.08	.06	.03
487	Jerry Hairston	.08	.06	.03
488	Alfredo Griffin	.10	.08	.04
489	Tom Herr	.12	.09	.05
490	Jim Palmer	.50	.40	.20
491	Super Veteran (Jim Palmer)	.20	.15	.08
492	Paul Serna	.08	.06	.03
493	Steve McCatty	.08	.06	.03
494	Bob Brenly	.10	.08	.04
495	Warren Cromartie	.08	.06	.03
496	Tom Veryzer	.08	.06	.03
497	Rick Sutcliffe	.20	.15	.08
498	*Wade Boggs*(FC)	35.00	27.50	15.00
499	Jeff Little	.10	.08	.04

		MT	NR MT	EX
500	Reggie Jackson	.70	.50	.30
501	Super Veteran (Reggie Jackson)	.35	.25	.14
502	Braves Batting & Pitching Ldrs. (Dale Murphy, Phil Niekro)	.50	.40	.20
503	Moose Haas	.08	.06	.03
504	Don Werner	.08	.06	.03
505	Garry Templeton	.12	.09	.05
506	*Jim Gott*(FC)	.25	.20	.10
507	Tony Scott	.08	.06	.03
508	Tom Filer	.15	.11	.06
509	Lou Whitaker	.40	.30	.20
510	Tug McGraw	.15	.11	.06
511	Super Veteran (Tug McGraw)	.10	.08	.04
512	Doyle Alexander	.12	.09	.05
513	Fred Stanley	.08	.06	.03
514	Rudy Law	.08	.06	.03
515	Gene Tenace	.10	.08	.04
516	Bill Virdon	.08	.06	.03
517	Gary Ward	.10	.08	.04
518	Bill Laskey	.08	.06	.03
519	Terry Bulling	.08	.06	.03
520	Fred Lynn	.25	.20	.10
521	Bruce Benedict	.08	.06	.03
522	Pat Zachry	.08	.06	.03
523	Carney Lansford	.12	.09	.05
524	Tom Brennan	.08	.06	.03
525	Frank White	.12	.09	.05
526	Checklist 397-528	.12	.09	.05
527	Larry Biittner	.08	.06	.03
528	Jamie Easterly	.08	.06	.03
529	Tim Laudner	.10	.08	.04
530	Eddie Murray	.80	.60	.30
531	Athletics Batting & Pitching Ldrs. (Rickey Henderson, Rick Langford)	.30	.25	.12
532	Dave Stewart	.80	.60	.30
533	Luis Salazar	.08	.06	.03
534	John Butcher	.08	.06	.03
535	Manny Trillo	.10	.08	.04
536	Johnny Wockenfuss	.08	.06	.03
537	Rod Scurry	.08	.06	.03
538	Danny Heep	.08	.06	.03
539	Roger Erickson	.08	.06	.03
540	Ozzie Smith	.30	.25	.12
541	Britt Burns	.08	.06	.03
542	Jody Davis	.12	.09	.05
543	Alan Fowlkes	.08	.06	.03
544	Larry Whisenton	.08	.06	.03
545	Floyd Bannister	.12	.09	.05
546	Dave Garcia	.08	.06	.03
547	Geoff Zahn	.08	.06	.03
548	Brian Giles	.08	.06	.03
549	*Charlie Puleo*	.15	.11	.06
550	Carl Yastrzemski	.80	.60	.30
551	Super Veteran (Carl Yastrzemski)	.40	.30	.15
552	Tim Wallach	.30	.25	.12
553	Denny Martinez	.10	.08	.04
554	Mike Vail	.08	.06	.03
555	Steve Yeager	.08	.06	.03
556	Willie Upshaw	.10	.08	.04
557	Rick Honeycutt	.08	.06	.03
558	Dickie Thon	.10	.08	.04
559	Pete Redfern	.08	.06	.03
560	Ron LeFlore	.10	.08	.04
561	Cardinals Batting & Pitching Ldrs. (Joaquin Andujar, Lonnie Smith)	.12	.09	.05
562	Dave Rozema	.08	.06	.03
563	Juan Bonilla	.08	.06	.03
564	Sid Monge	.08	.06	.03
565	Bucky Dent	.12	.09	.05
566	Manny Sarmiento	.08	.06	.03
567	Joe Simpson	.08	.06	.03
568	Willie Hernandez	.12	.09	.05
569	Jack Perconte	.08	.06	.03
570	Vida Blue	.15	.11	.06
571	Mickey Klutts	.08	.06	.03
572	Bob Watson	.10	.08	.04
573	Andy Hassler	.08	.06	.03
574	Glenn Adams	.08	.06	.03
575	Neil Allen	.08	.06	.03
576	Frank Robinson	.12	.09	.05
577	Luis Aponte	.08	.06	.03
578	David Green	.08	.06	.03
579	Rich Dauer	.08	.06	.03
580	Tom Seaver	.70	.50	.30
581	Super Veteran (Tom Seaver)	.30	.25	.12
582	Marshall Edwards	.08	.06	.03
583	Terry Forster	.10	.08	.04
584	Dave Hostetler	.08	.06	.03
585	Jose Cruz	.15	.11	.06
586	*Frank Viola*(FC)	8.00	6.00	3.25
587	Ivan DeJesus	.08	.06	.03
588	Pat Underwood	.08	.06	.03
589	Alvis Woods	.08	.06	.03
590	Tony Pena	.12	.09	.05
591	White Sox Batting & Pitching Ldrs. (LaMarr Hoyt, Greg Luzinski)	.15	.11	.06
592	Shane Rawley	.12	.09	.05
593	Broderick Perkins	.08	.06	.03
594	Eric Rasmussen	.08	.06	.03
595	Tim Raines	.50	.40	.20
596	Randy Johnson	.08	.06	.03
597	Mike Proly	.08	.06	.03
598	Dwayne Murphy	.10	.08	.04
599	Don Aase	.08	.06	.03
600	George Brett	1.00	.70	.40
601	Ed Lynch	.08	.06	.03
602	Rich Gedman	.12	.09	.05
603	Joe Morgan	.40	.30	.15
604	Super Veteran (Joe Morgan)	.15	.11	.06
605	Gary Roenicke	.08	.06	.03
606	Bobby Cox	.08	.06	.03
607	Charlie Leibrandt	.10	.08	.04
608	Don Money	.08	.06	.03
609	Danny Darwin	.08	.06	.03
610	Steve Garvey	.70	.50	.30
611	Bert Roberge	.08	.06	.03
612	Steve Swisher	.08	.06	.03
613	Mike Ivie	.08	.06	.03

		MT	NR MT	EX
614	Ed Glynn	.08	.06	.03
615	Garry Maddox	.12	.09	.05
616	Bill Nahorodny	.08	.06	.03
617	Butch Wynegar	.08	.06	.03
618	LaMarr Hoyt	.08	.06	.03
619	Keith Moreland	.10	.08	.04
620	Mike Norris	.08	.06	.03
621	Mets Batting & Pitching Ldrs. (Craig Swan, Mookie Wilson)	.12	.09	.05
622	Dave Edler	.08	.06	.03
623	Luis Sanchez	.08	.06	.03
624	Glenn Hubbard	.10	.08	.04
625	Ken Forsch	.08	.06	.03
626	Jerry Martin	.08	.06	.03
627	Doug Bair	.08	.06	.03
628	Julio Valdez	.08	.06	.03
629	Charlie Lea	.08	.06	.03
630	Paul Molitor	.30	.25	.12
631	Tippy Martinez	.08	.06	.03
632	Alex Trevino	.08	.06	.03
633	Vicente Romo	.08	.06	.03
634	Max Venable	.08	.06	.03
635	Graig Nettles	.20	.15	.08
636	Super Veteran (Graig Nettles)	.12	.09	.05
637	Pat Corrales	.08	.06	.03
638	Dan Petry	.10	.08	.04
639	Art Howe	.08	.06	.03
640	Andre Thornton	.12	.09	.05
641	Billy Sample	.08	.06	.03
642	Checklist 529-660	.12	.09	.05
643	Bump Wills	.08	.06	.03
644	Joe Lefebvre	.08	.06	.03
645	Bill Madlock	.15	.11	.06
646	Jim Essian	.08	.06	.03
647	Bobby Mitchell	.08	.06	.03
648	Jeff Burroughs	.10	.08	.04
649	Tommy Boggs	.08	.06	.03
650	George Hendrick	.10	.08	.04
651	Angels Batting & Pitching Ldrs. (Rod Carew, Mike Witt)	.30	.25	.12
652	Butch Hobson	.08	.06	.03
653	Ellis Valentine	.08	.06	.03
654	Bob Ojeda	.15	.11	.06
655	Al Bumbry	.10	.08	.04
656	Dave Frost	.08	.06	.03
657	Mike Gates	.08	.06	.03
658	Frank Pastore	.08	.06	.03
659	Charlie Moore	.08	.06	.03
660	Mike Hargrove	.08	.06	.03
661	Bill Russell	.10	.08	.04
662	Joe Sambito	.08	.06	.03
663	Tom O'Malley	.08	.06	.03
664	Bob Molinaro	.08	.06	.03
665	Jim Sundberg	.10	.08	.04
666	Sparky Anderson	.12	.09	.05
667	Dick Davis	.08	.06	.03
668	Larry Christenson	.08	.06	.03
669	Mike Squires	.08	.06	.03
670	Jerry Mumphrey	.08	.06	.03
671	Lenny Faedo	.08	.06	.03
672	Jim Kaat	.20	.15	.08
673	Super Veteran (Jim Kaat)	.12	.09	.05
674	Kurt Bevacqua	.08	.06	.03
675	Jim Beattie	.08	.06	.03
676	Biff Pocoroba	.08	.06	.03
677	Dave Revering	.08	.06	.03
678	Juan Beniquez	.08	.06	.03
679	Mike Scott	.20	.15	.08
680	Andre Dawson	.40	.30	.15
681	Dodgers Batting & Pitching Ldrs. (Pedro Guerrero, Fernando Valenzuela)	.25	.20	.10
682	Bob Stanley	.08	.06	.03
683	Dan Ford	.08	.06	.03
684	Rafael Landestoy	.08	.06	.03
685	Lee Mazzilli	.10	.08	.04
686	Randy Lerch	.08	.06	.03
687	U.L. Washington	.08	.06	.03
688	Jim Wohlford	.08	.06	.03
689	Ron Hassey	.08	.06	.03
690	Kent Hrbek	.70	.50	.30
691	Dave Tobik	.08	.06	.03
692	Denny Walling	.08	.06	.03
693	Sparky Lyle	.12	.09	.05
694	Super Veteran (Sparky Lyle)	.10	.08	.04
695	Ruppert Jones	.08	.06	.03
696	Chuck Tanner	.08	.06	.03
697	Barry Foote	.08	.06	.03
698	Tony Bernazard	.08	.06	.03
699	Lee Smith	.20	.15	.08
700	Keith Hernandez	.50	.40	.20
701	Batting Leaders (Al Oliver, Willie Wilson)	.15	.11	.06
702	Home Run Leaders (Reggie Jackson, Dave Kingman, Gorman Thomas)	.25	.20	.10
703	Runs Batted In Leaders (Hal McRae, Dale Murphy, Al Oliver)	.35	.25	.14
704	Stolen Base Leaders (Rickey Henderson, Tim Raines)	.35	.25	.14
705	Victory Leaders (Steve Carlton, LaMarr Hoyt)	.20	.15	.08
706	Strikeout Leaders (Floyd Bannister, Steve Carlton)	.20	.15	.08
707	Earned Run Average Leaders (Steve Rogers, Rick Sutcliffe)	.12	.09	.05
708	Leading Firemen (Dan Quisenberry, Bruce Sutter)	.15	.11	.06
709	Jimmy Sexton	.08	.06	.03
710	Willie Wilson	.20	.15	.08
711	Mariners Batting & Pitching Ldrs. (Jim Beattie, Bruce Bochte)	.12	.09	.05
712	Bruce Kison	.08	.06	.03
713	Ron Hodges	.08	.06	.03
714	Wayne Nordhagen	.08	.06	.03
715	Tony Perez	.25	.20	.10
716	Super Veteran (Tony Perez)	.12	.09	.05
717	Scott Sanderson	.08	.06	.03
718	Jim Dwyer	.08	.06	.03
719	Rich Gale	.08	.06	.03
720	Dave Concepcion	.15	.11	.06
721	John Martin	.08	.06	.03
722	Jorge Orta	.08	.06	.03
723	Randy Moffitt	.08	.06	.03
724	Johnny Grubb	.08	.06	.03
725	Dan Spillner	.08	.06	.03
726	Harvey Kuenn	.10	.08	.04
727	Chet Lemon	.10	.08	.04
728	Ron Reed	.08	.06	.03
729	Jerry Morales	.08	.06	.03
730	Jason Thompson	.08	.06	.03
731	Al Williams	.08	.06	.03
732	Dave Henderson	.15	.11	.06
733	Buck Martinez	.08	.06	.03
734	Steve Braun	.08	.06	.03
735	Tommy John	.25	.20	.10
736	Super Veteran (Tommy John)	.12	.09	.05
737	Mitchell Page	.08	.06	.03
738	Tim Foli	.08	.06	.03
739	Rick Ownbey	.08	.06	.03
740	Rusty Staub	.15	.11	.06
741	Super Veteran (Rusty Staub)	.10	.08	.04
742	Padres Batting & Pitching Ldrs. (Terry Kennedy, Tim Lollar)	.12	.09	.05
743	Mike Torrez	.10	.08	.04
744	Brad Mills	.08	.06	.03
745	Scott McGregor	.10	.08	.04
746	John Wathan	.10	.08	.04
747	Fred Breining	.08	.06	.03
748	Derrel Thomas	.08	.06	.03
749	Jon Matlack	.10	.08	.04
750	Ben Oglivie	.10	.08	.04
751	Brad Havens	.08	.06	.03
752	Luis Pujols	.08	.06	.03
753	Elias Sosa	.08	.06	.03
754	Bill Robinson	.08	.06	.03
755	John Candelaria	.12	.09	.05
756	Russ Nixon	.08	.06	.03
757	Rick Manning	.08	.06	.03
758	Aurelio Rodriguez	.10	.08	.04
759	Doug Bird	.08	.06	.03
760	Dale Murphy	1.50	1.25	.60
761	Gary Lucas	.08	.06	.03
762	Cliff Johnson	.08	.06	.03
763	Al Cowens	.08	.06	.03
764	Pete Falcone	.08	.06	.03
765	Bob Boone	.12	.09	.05
766	Barry Bonnell	.08	.06	.03
767	Duane Kuiper	.08	.06	.03
768	Chris Speier	.08	.06	.03
769	Checklist 661-792	.12	.09	.05
770	Dave Winfield	.50	.40	.20
771	Twins Batting & Pitching Ldrs. (Bobby Castillo, Kent Hrbek)	.20	.15	.08
772	Jim Kern	.08	.06	.03
773	Larry Hisle	.10	.08	.04
774	Alan Ashby	.08	.06	.03
775	Burt Hooton	.10	.08	.04
776	Larry Parrish	.12	.09	.05
777	John Curtis	.08	.06	.03
778	Rich Hebner	.08	.06	.03
779	Rick Waits	.08	.06	.03
780	Gary Matthews	.12	.09	.05
781	Rick Rhoden	.12	.09	.05
782	Bobby Murcer	.12	.09	.05
783	Super Veteran (Bobby Murcer)	.10	.08	.04
784	Jeff Newman	.08	.06	.03
785	Dennis Leonard	.10	.08	.04
786	Ralph Houk	.10	.08	.04
787	Dick Tidrow	.08	.06	.03
788	Dane Iorg	.08	.06	.03
789	Bryan Clark	.08	.06	.03
790	Bob Grich	.12	.09	.05
791	Gary Lavelle	.08	.06	.03
792	Chris Chambliss	.10	.08	.04

1983 Topps All-Star Glossy Set of 40

This set was a "consolation prize" in a scratch-off contest in regular packs of 1983 cards. The 2-1/2" by 3-1/2" cards have a large color photo surrounded by a yellow frame on the front. In very small type on a white border is printed the player's name. Backs carry the player's name, team, position and the card number along with a Topps identification. A major feature is that the surface of the front is glossy, which most collectors find very attractive. With many top stars, the set is a popular one, but the price has not moved too far above the issue price.

		MT	NR MT	EX
	Complete Set:	12.00	9.00	4.75
	Common Player:	.15	.11	.06
1	Carl Yastrzemski	1.00	.70	.40
2	Mookie Wilson	.15	.11	.06
3	Andre Thornton	.15	.11	.06
4	Keith Hernandez	.40	.30	.15
5	Robin Yount	.40	.30	.15
6	Terry Kennedy	.15	.11	.06
7	Dave Winfield	.60	.45	.25
8	Mike Schmidt	1.00	.70	.40
9	Buddy Bell	.20	.15	.08
10	Fernando Valenzuela	.50	.40	.20
11	Rich Gossage	.25	.20	.10
12	Bob Horner	.20	.15	.08
13	Toby Harrah	.15	.11	.06
14	Pete Rose	1.25	.90	.50
15	Cecil Cooper	.20	.15	.08
16	Dale Murphy	1.00	.70	.40
17	Carlton Fisk	.30	.25	.12
18	Ray Knight	.15	.11	.06
19	Jim Palmer	.40	.30	.15
20	Gary Carter	.50	.40	.20
21	Richard Zisk	.15	.11	.06
22	Dusty Baker	.15	.11	.06
23	Willie Wilson	.20	.15	.08
24	Bill Buckner	.15	.11	.06
25	Dave Stieb	.20	.15	.08
26	Bill Madlock	.20	.15	.08
27	Lance Parrish	.30	.25	.12
28	Nolan Ryan	.50	.40	.20
29	Rod Carew	.60	.45	.25
30	Al Oliver	.20	.15	.08
31	George Brett	1.00	.70	.40
32	Jack Clark	.25	.20	.10
33	Rickey Henderson	.70	.50	.30
34	Dave Concepcion	.20	.15	.08
35	Kent Hrbek	.30	.25	.12
36	Steve Carlton	.50	.40	.20
37	Eddie Murray	.60	.45	.25
38	Ruppert Jones	.15	.11	.06
39	Reggie Jackson	.70	.50	.30
40	Bruce Sutter	.20	.15	.08

1983 Topps Foldouts

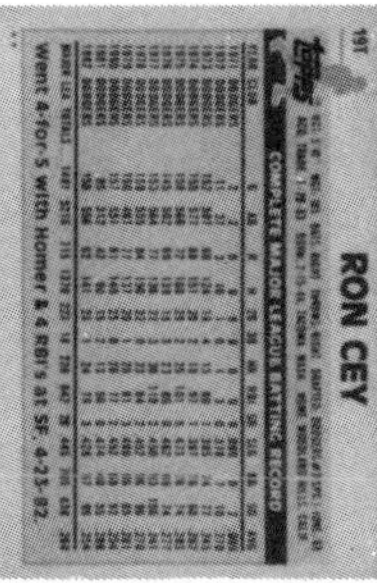

Another Topps test issue, these 3-1/2" by 5-5/16" cards were printed in booklets like souvenier postcards. Each of the booklets have a theme of currently playing statistical leaders in a specific category such as home runs. The cards feature a color player photo on each side. A black strip at the bottom gives the player's name, position and team along with statistics in the particular category. A facsimile autograph crosses the photograph. Booklets carry nine cards, with eight having players on both sides and one doubling as the back cover, for a total of 17 cards per booklet. There are 85 cards in the set, although some players appear in more than one category. Naturally, most of the players pictured are stars. Even so, the set is a problem as it seems to be most valuable when complete and unseparated, so the cards are difficult to display.

		MT	NR MT	EX
	Complete Set:	6.00	4.50	2.50
	Common Folder:	1.00	.70	.40
1	Pitching Leaders (Vida Blue, Bert Blyleven, Steve Carlton, Fergie Jenkins, Tommy John, Jim Kaat, Jerry Koosman, Joe Niekro, Phil Niekro, Jim Palmer, Gaylord Perry, Jerry Reuss, Nolan Ryan, Tom Seaver, Paul Splittorff, Don Sutton, Mike Torrez)	1.75	1.25	.70
2	Home Run Leaders (Johnny Bench, Ron Cey, Darrell Evans, George Foster, Reggie Jackson, Dave Kingman, Greg Luzinski, John Mayberry, Rick Monday, Joe Morgan, Bobby Murcer, Graig Nettles, Tony Perez, Jim Rice, Mike Schmidt, Rusty Staub, Carl Yastrzemski)	2.50	2.00	1.00
3	Batting Leaders (George Brett, Rod Carew, Cecil Cooper, Steve Garvey, Ken Griffey, Pedro Guerrero, Keith Hernandez, Dane Iorg, Fred Lynn, Bill Madlock, Bake McBride, Al Oliver, Dave Parker, Jim Rice, Pete Rose, Lonnie Smith, Willie Wilson)	2.50	2.00	1.00
4	Relief Aces (Tom Burgmeier, Bill Campbell, Ed Farmer, Rollie Fingers, Terry Forster, Gene Garber, Rich Gossage, Jim Kern, Gary Lavelle, Tug McGraw, Greg Minton, Randy Moffitt, Dan Quisenberry, Ron			

		MT	NR MT	EX
	Reed, Elias Sosa, Bruce Sutter, Kent Tekulve)	1.00	.70	.40
5	Stolen Base Leaders (Don Baylor, Larry Bowa, Al Bumbry, Rod Carew, Cesar Cedeno, Dave Concepcion, Jose Cruz, Julio Cruz, Rickey Henderson, Ron LeFlore, Davey Lopes, Garry Maddox, Omar Moreno, Joe Morgan, Amos Otis, Mickey Rivers, Willie Wilson)	1.00	.70	.40

1983 Topps Stickers

Topps increased the number of stickers in its set to 220 in 1983, but retained the same 1-15/16" by 2-9/16" size. The stickers are again numbered on both the front and back. Similar in style to previous sticker issues, the set includes 28 "foil" stickers, and various special stickers highlighting the 1982 season, playoffs and World Series. An album was also available.

	MT	NR MT	EX
Complete Set:	15.00	11.00	6.00
Common Player:	.03	.02	.01
Sticker Album:	.80	.60	.30

No.	Player	MT	NR MT	EX
1	Hank Aaron	.40	.30	.15
2	Babe Ruth	.60	.45	.25
3	Willie Mays	.40	.30	.15
4	Frank Robinson	.30	.25	.12
5	Reggie Jackson	.20	.15	.08
6	Carl Yastrzemski	.25	.20	.10
7	Johnny Bench	.20	.15	.08
8	Tony Perez	.10	.08	.04
9	Lee May	.06	.05	.02
10	Mike Schmidt	.25	.20	.10
11	Dave Kingman	.08	.06	.03
12	Reggie Smith	.06	.05	.02
13	Graig Nettles	.06	.05	.02
14	Rusty Staub	.06	.05	.02
15	Willie Wilson	.06	.05	.02
16	LaMarr Hoyt	.03	.02	.01
17	Reggie Jackson, Gorman Thomas	.15	.11	.06
18	Floyd Bannister	.04	.03	.02
19	Hal McRae	.06	.05	.02
20	Rick Sutcliffe	.08	.06	.03
21	Rickey Henderson	.25	.20	.10
22	Dan Quisenberry	.06	.05	.02
23	Jim Palmer	.30	.25	.12
24	John Lowenstein	.03	.02	.01
25	Mike Flanagan	.04	.03	.02
26	Cal Ripken	.20	.15	.08
27	Rich Dauer	.03	.02	.01
28	Ken Singleton	.06	.05	.02
29	Eddie Murray	.20	.15	.08
30	Rick Dempsey	.04	.03	.02
31	Carl Yastrzemski	.40	.30	.15
32	Carney Lansford	.06	.05	.02
33	Jerry Remy	.03	.02	.01
34	Dennis Eckersley	.06	.05	.02
35	Dave Stapleton	.03	.02	.01
36	Mark Clear	.03	.02	.01
37	Jim Rice	.20	.15	.08
38	Dwight Evans	.08	.06	.03
39	Rod Carew	.20	.15	.08
40	Don Baylor	.08	.06	.03
41	Reggie Jackson	.40	.30	.15
42	Geoff Zahn	.03	.02	.01
43	Bobby Grich	.06	.05	.02
44	Fred Lynn	.10	.08	.04
45	Bob Boone	.04	.03	.02
46	Doug DeCinces	.06	.05	.02
47	Tom Paciorek	.03	.02	.01
48	Britt Burns	.03	.02	.01
49	Tony Bernazard	.03	.02	.01
50	Steve Kemp	.04	.03	.02
51	Greg Luzinski	.20	.15	.08
52	Harold Baines	.10	.08	.04
53	LaMarr Hoyt	.03	.02	.01
54	Carlton Fisk	.12	.09	.05
55	Andre Thornton	.15	.11	.06
56	Mike Hargrove	.04	.03	.02
57	Len Barker	.03	.02	.01
58	Toby Harrah	.04	.03	.02
59	Dan Spillner	.03	.02	.01
60	Rick Manning	.03	.02	.01
61	Rick Sutcliffe	.08	.06	.03
62	Ron Hassey	.03	.02	.01
63	Lance Parrish	.30	.25	.12
64	John Wockenfuss	.03	.02	.01
65	Lou Whitaker	.12	.09	.05
66	Alan Trammell	.15	.11	.06
67	Kirk Gibson	.15	.11	.06
68	Larry Herndon	.03	.02	.01
69	Jack Morris	.12	.09	.05
70	Dan Petry	.04	.03	.02
71	Frank White	.06	.05	.02
72	Amos Otis	.04	.03	.02
73	Willie Wilson	.25	.20	.10
74	Dan Quisenberry	.06	.05	.02
75	Hal McRae	.06	.05	.02
76	George Brett	.25	.20	.10
77	Larry Gura	.03	.02	.01
78	John Wathan	.04	.03	.02
79	Rollie Fingers	.10	.08	.04
80	Cecil Cooper	.08	.06	.03
81	Robin Yount	.30	.25	.12
82	Ben Oglivie	.06	.05	.02
83	Paul Molitor	.10	.08	.04
84	Gorman Thomas	.06	.05	.02
85	Ted Simmons	.06	.05	.02
86	Pete Vuckovich	.04	.03	.02
87	Gary Gaetti	.08	.06	.03
88	Kent Hrbek	.30	.25	.12
89	John Castino	.03	.02	.01
90	Tom Brunansky	.06	.05	.02
91	Bobby Mitchell	.03	.02	.01
92	Gary Ward	.04	.03	.02
93	Tim Laudner	.03	.02	.01
94	Ron Davis	.03	.02	.01
95	Willie Randolph	.06	.05	.02
96	Roy Smalley	.03	.02	.01
97	Jerry Mumphrey	.03	.02	.01
98	Ken Griffey	.06	.05	.02
99	Dave Winfield	.30	.25	.12
100	Rich Gossage	.10	.08	.04
101	Butch Wynegar	.04	.03	.02
102	Ron Guidry	.12	.09	.05
103	Rickey Henderson	.40	.30	.15
104	Mike Heath	.03	.02	.01
105	Dave Lopes	.06	.05	.02
106	Rick Langford	.03	.02	.01
107	Dwayne Murphy	.04	.03	.02
108	Tony Armas	.06	.05	.02
109	Matt Keough	.03	.02	.01
110	Dan Meyer	.03	.02	.01
111	Bruce Bochte	.03	.02	.01
112	Julio Cruz	.03	.02	.01
113	Floyd Bannister	.04	.03	.02
114	Gaylord Perry	.30	.25	.12
115	Al Cowens	.03	.02	.01
116	Richie Zisk	.04	.03	.02
117	Jim Essian	.03	.02	.01
118	Bill Caudill	.03	.02	.01
119	Buddy Bell	.20	.15	.08
120	Larry Parrish	.06	.05	.02
121	Danny Darwin	.03	.02	.01
122	Bucky Dent	.04	.03	.02
123	Johnny Grubb	.03	.02	.01
124	George Wright	.03	.02	.01
125	Charlie Hough	.06	.05	.02
126	Jim Sundberg	.04	.03	.02
127	Dave Stieb	.20	.15	.08
128	Willie Upshaw	.06	.05	.02
129	Alfredo Griffin	.04	.03	.02
130	Lloyd Moseby	.06	.05	.02
131	Ernie Whitt	.03	.02	.01
132	Jim Clancy	.04	.03	.02
133	Barry Bonnell	.03	.02	.01
134	Damaso Garcia	.04	.03	.02
135	Jim Kaat	.08	.06	.03
136	Jim Kaat	.06	.05	.02
137	Greg Minton	.03	.02	.01
138	Greg Minton	.03	.02	.01
139	Paul Molitor	.10	.08	.04
140	Paul Molitor	.08	.06	.03
141	Manny Trillo	.04	.03	.02
142	Manny Trillo	.04	.03	.02
143	Joel Youngblood	.03	.02	.01
144	Joel Youngblood	.03	.02	.01
145	Robin Yount	.15	.11	.06
146	Robin Yount	.12	.09	.05
147	Willie McGee	.08	.06	.03
148	Darrell Porter	.04	.03	.02
149	Darrell Porter	.04	.03	.02
150	Robin Yount	.15	.11	.06
151	Bruce Benedict	.03	.02	.01
152	Bruce Benedict	.03	.02	.01
153	George Hendrick	.04	.03	.02
154	Bruce Benedict	.03	.02	.01
155	Doug DeCinces	.06	.05	.02
156	Paul Molitor	.10	.08	.04
157	Charlie Moore	.03	.02	.01
158	Fred Lynn	.10	.08	.04
159	Rickey Henderson	.20	.15	.08
160	Dale Murphy	.25	.20	.10
161	Willie Wilson	.08	.06	.03
162	Jack Clark	.10	.08	.04
163	Reggie Jackson	.20	.15	.08
164	Andre Dawson	.15	.11	.06
165	Dan Quisenberry	.06	.05	.02
166	Bruce Sutter	.08	.06	.03
167	Robin Yount	.15	.11	.06
168	Ozzie Smith	.10	.08	.04
169	Frank White	.06	.05	.02
170	Phil Garner	.04	.03	.02
171	Doug DeCinces	.06	.05	.02
172	Mike Schmidt	.25	.20	.10
173	Cecil Cooper	.06	.05	.02
174	Al Oliver	.06	.05	.02
175	Jim Palmer	.15	.11	.06
176	Steve Carlton	.15	.11	.06
177	Carlton Fisk	.12	.09	.05
178	Gary Carter	.20	.15	.08
179	Joaquin Andujar	.04	.03	.02
180	Ozzie Smith	.10	.08	.04
181	Cecil Cooper	.06	.05	.02
182	Darrell Porter	.04	.03	.02
183	Darrell Porter	.04	.03	.02
184	Mike Caldwell	.03	.02	.01
185	Mike Caldwell	.03	.02	.01
186	Ozzie Smith	.10	.08	.04
187	Bruce Sutter	.08	.06	.03
188	Keith Hernandez	.12	.09	.05
189	Dane Iorg	.03	.02	.01
190	Dane Iorg	.03	.02	.01
191	Tony Armas	.04	.03	.02
192	Tony Armas	.04	.03	.02
193	Lance Parrish	.12	.09	.05
194	Lance Parrish	.12	.09	.05
195	John Wathan	.04	.03	.02
196	John Wathan	.04	.03	.02
197	Rickey Henderson	.12	.09	.05
198	Rickey Henderson	.12	.09	.05
199	Rickey Henderson	.12	.09	.05
200	Rickey Henderson	.12	.09	.05
201	Rickey Henderson	.12	.09	.05
202	Rickey Henderson	.12	.09	.05
203	Steve Carlton	.15	.11	.06
204	Steve Carlton	.12	.09	.05
205	Al Oliver	.06	.05	.02
206	Dale Murphy, Al Oliver	.20	.15	.08
207	Dave Kingman	.08	.06	.03
208	Steve Rogers			
209	Bruce Sutter	.08	.06	.03
210	Tim Raines	.20	.15	.08
211	Dale Murphy	.40	.30	.15
212	Chris Chambliss	.04	.03	.02
213	Gene Garber	.03	.02	.01
214	Bob Horner	.08	.06	.03
215	Glenn Hubbard	.03	.02	.01
216	Claudell Washington	.04	.03	.02
217	Bruce Benedict	.03	.02	.01
218	Phil Niekro	.12	.09	.05
219	Leon Durham	.20	.15	.08
220	Jay Johnstone	.04	.03	.02
221	Larry Bowa	.06	.05	.02
222	Keith Moreland	.06	.05	.02
223	Bill Buckner	.06	.05	.02
224	Fergie Jenkins	.08	.06	.03
225	Dick Tidrow	.03	.02	.01
226	Jody Davis	.06	.05	.02
227	Dave Concepcion	.06	.05	.02
228	Dan Driessen	.04	.03	.02
229	Johnny Bench	.20	.15	.08
230	Ron Oester	.03	.02	.01
231	Cesar Cedeno	.06	.05	.02
232	Alex Trevino	.03	.02	.01
233	Tom Seaver	.20	.15	.08
234	Mario Soto	.20	.15	.08
235	Nolan Ryan	.30	.25	.12
236	Art Howe	.03	.02	.01
237	Phil Garner	.04	.03	.02
238	Ray Knight	.06	.05	.02
239	Terry Puhl	.03	.02	.01
240	Joe Niekro	.06	.05	.02
241	Alan Ashby	.03	.02	.01
242	Jose Cruz	.06	.05	.02
243	Steve Garvey	.20	.15	.08
244	Ron Cey	.06	.05	.02
245	Dusty Baker	.04	.03	.02
246	Ken Landreaux	.03	.02	.01
247	Jerry Reuss	.06	.05	.02
248	Pedro Guerrero	.12	.09	.05
249	Bill Russell	.04	.03	.02
250	Fernando Valenzuela	.30	.25	.12
251	Al Oliver	.25	.20	.10
252	Andre Dawson	.15	.11	.06
253	Tim Raines	.20	.15	.08
254	Jeff Reardon	.08	.06	.03
255	Gary Carter	.20	.15	.08
256	Steve Rogers	.03	.02	.01
257	Tim Wallach	.08	.06	.03
258	Chris Speier	.03	.02	.01
259	Dave Kingman	.08	.06	.03
260	Bob Bailor	.03	.02	.01
261	Hubie Brooks	.06	.05	.02
262	Craig Swan	.03	.02	.01
263	George Foster	.08	.06	.03
264	John Stearns	.03	.02	.01
265	Neil Allen	.03	.02	.01
266	Mookie Wilson	.20	.15	.08
267	Steve Carlton	.30	.25	.12
268	Manny Trillo	.04	.03	.02
269	Gary Matthews	.06	.05	.02
270	Mike Schmidt	.25	.20	.10
271	Ivan DeJesus	.03	.02	.01
272	Pete Rose	.40	.30	.15
273	Bo Diaz	.04	.03	.02
274	Sid Monge	.03	.02	.01
275	Bill Madlock	.25	.20	.10
276	Jason Thompson	.03	.02	.01
277	Don Robinson	.03	.02	.01
278	Omar Moreno	.03	.02	.01
279	Dale Berra	.03	.02	.01
280	Dave Parker	.10	.08	.04
281	Tony Pena	.06	.05	.02
282	John Candelaria	.06	.05	.02
283	Lonnie Smith	.04	.03	.02
284	Bruce Sutter	.25	.20	.10
285	George Hendrick	.04	.03	.02
286	Tom Herr	.06	.05	.02
287	Ken Oberkfell	.03	.02	.01
288	Ozzie Smith	.10	.08	.04
289	Bob Forsch	.04	.03	.02
290	Keith Hernandez	.15	.11	.06
291	Garry Templeton	.06	.05	.02
292	Broderick Perkins	.03	.02	.01
293	Terry Kennedy	.20	.15	.08
294	Gene Richards	.03	.02	.01
295	Ruppert Jones	.03	.02	.01
296	Tim Lollar	.03	.02	.01
297	John Montefusco	.03	.02	.01
298	Sixto Lezcano	.03	.02	.01
299	Greg Minton	.03	.02	.01
300	Jack Clark	.25	.20	.10
301	Milt May	.03	.02	.01
302	Reggie Smith	.06	.05	.02
303	Joe Morgan	.10	.08	.04
304	John LeMaster	.03	.02	.01
305	Darrell Evans	.08	.06	.03
306	Al Holland	.03	.02	.01
307	Jesse Barfield	.08	.06	.03
308	Wade Boggs	.60	.45	.25
309	Tom Brunansky	.06	.05	.02
310	Storm Davis	.04	.03	.02
311	Von Hayes	.06	.05	.02
312	Dave Hostetler	.03	.02	.01
313	Kent Hrbek	.12	.09	.05
314	Tim Laudner	.03	.02	.01
315	Cal Ripken	.20	.15	.08
316	Andre Robertson	.03	.02	.01
317	Ed Vande Berg	.03	.02	.01
318	Glenn Wilson	.04	.03	.02

		MT	NR MT	EX
319	Chili Davis	.06	.05	.02
320	Bob Dernier	.03	.02	.01
321	Terry Francona	.03	.02	.01
322	Brian Giles	.03	.02	.01
323	David Green	.03	.02	.01
324	Atlee Hammaker	.03	.02	.01
325	Bill Laskey	.03	.02	.01
326	Willie McGee	.12	.09	.05
327	Johnny Ray	.06	.05	.02
328	Ryne Sandberg	.25	.20	.10
329	Steve Sax	.10	.08	.04
330	Eric Show	.04	.03	.02

1983 Topps Stickers Boxes

These eight cards were printed on the back panels of 1983 Topps sticker boxes, on card per box. The blank- backed cards measure the standard 2-1/2" by 3-1/2" and feature a full-color photo with the player's name at the top. The rest of the back panel advertises the sticker album, while the front of the box has an action photo of Reggie Jackson. The boxes are numbered on the front. Prices in the checklist that follows are for complete boxes.

		MT	NR MT	EX
Complete Set:		6.50	5.00	2.50
Common Player:		.75	.60	.30
1	Fernando Valenzuela	1.00	.70	.40
2	Gary Carter	1.25	.90	.50
3	Mike Schmidt	1.25	.90	.50
4	Reggie Jackson	1.25	.90	.50
5	Jim Palmer	1.00	.70	.40
6	Rollie Fingers	.75	.60	.30
7	Pete Rose	1.50	1.25	.60
8	Rickey Henderson	1.25	.90	.50

1983 Topps Traded

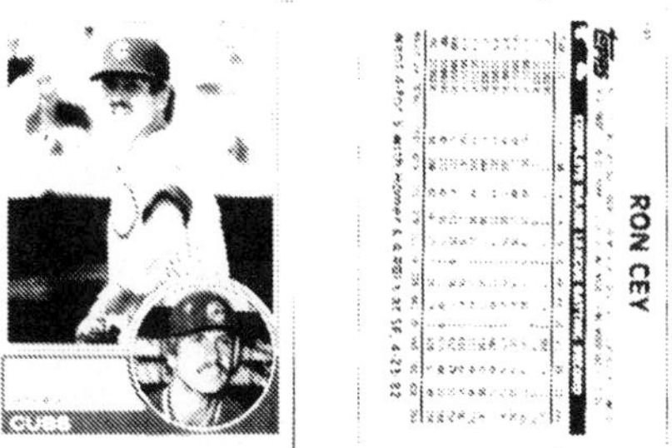

These 2-1/2" by 3-1/2" cards mark a continuation of the traded set introduced in 1981. The 132 cards retain the basic design of the year's regular issue, with their numbering being 1-132 with the "T" suffix. Cards in the set include traded players, new managers and promising rookies. Sold only through dealers, the set was in heavy demand as it contained the first cards of Darryl Strawberry, Ron Kittle, Julio Franco and Mel Hall. While some of those cards were very hot in 1983, it seems likely that some of the rookies may not live up to their initial promise.

		MT	NR MT	EX
Complete Set:		100.00	75.00	40.00
Common Player:		.10	.08	.04
1T	Neil Allen	.10	.08	.04
2T	Bill Almon	.10	.08	.04
3T	Joe Altobelli	.10	.08	.04
4T	Tony Armas	.20	.15	.08
5T	Doug Bair	.10	.08	.04
6T	Steve Baker	.10	.08	.04
7T	Floyd Bannister	.20	.15	.08
8T	Don Baylor	.30	.25	.12
9T	Tony Bernazard	.10	.08	.04
10T	Larry Biittner	.10	.08	.04
11T	Dann Bilardello	.10	.08	.04
12T	Doug Bird	.10	.08	.04
13T	Steve Boros	.10	.08	.04
14T	Greg Brock(FC)	.30	.25	.12
15T	Mike Brown	.10	.08	.04
16T	Tom Burgmeier	.10	.08	.04
17T	Randy Bush(FC)	.20	.15	.08
18T	Bert Campaneris	.20	.15	.08
19T	Ron Cey	.25	.20	.10
20T	Chris Codiroli(FC)	.15	.11	.06
21T	Dave Collins	.15	.11	.06
22T	Terry Crowley	.10	.08	.04
23T	Julio Cruz	.10	.08	.04
24T	Mike Davis	.15	.11	.06
25T	Frank DiPino	.10	.08	.04
26T	Bill Doran(FC)	1.25	.90	.50
27T	Jerry Dybzinski	.10	.08	.04
28T	Jamie Easterly	.10	.08	.04
29T	Juan Eichelberger	.10	.08	.04
30T	Jim Essian	.10	.08	.04
31T	Pete Falcone	.10	.08	.04
32T	Mike Ferraro	.10	.08	.04
33T	Terry Forster	.15	.11	.06
34T	Julio Franco(FC)	4.00	3.00	1.50
35T	Rich Gale	.10	.08	.04
36T	Kiko Garcia	.10	.08	.04
37T	Steve Garvey	1.50	1.25	.60
38T	Johnny Grubb	.10	.08	.04
39T	Mel Hall(FC)	.90	.70	.35
40T	Von Hayes	.50	.40	.20
41T	Danny Heep	.10	.08	.04
42T	Steve Henderson	.10	.08	.04
43T	Keith Hernandez	1.00	.70	.40
44T	Leo Hernandez	.10	.08	.04
45T	Willie Hernandez	.25	.20	.10
46T	Al Holland	.10	.08	.04
47T	Frank Howard	.15	.11	.06
48T	Bobby Johnson	.10	.08	.04
49T	Cliff Johnson	.10	.08	.04
50T	Odell Jones	.10	.08	.04
51T	Mike Jorgensen	.10	.08	.04
52T	Bob Kearney	.10	.08	.04
53T	Steve Kemp	.15	.11	.06
54T	Matt Keough	.10	.08	.04
55T	Ron Kittle(FC)	1.00	.70	.40
56T	Mickey Klutts	.10	.08	.04
57T	Alan Knicely	.10	.08	.04
58T	Mike Krukow	.15	.11	.06
59T	Rafael Landestoy	.10	.08	.04
60T	Carney Lansford	.25	.20	.10
61T	Joe Lefebvre	.10	.08	.04
62T	Bryan Little	.10	.08	.04
63T	Aurelio Lopez	.10	.08	.04
64T	Mike Madden	.10	.08	.04
65T	Rick Manning	.10	.08	.04
66T	Billy Martin	.20	.15	.08
67T	Lee Mazzilli	.15	.11	.06
68T	Andy McGaffigan	.10	.08	.04
69T	Craig McMurtry(FC)	.20	.15	.08
70T	John McNamara	.10	.08	.04
71T	Orlando Mercado	.10	.08	.04
72T	Larry Milbourne	.10	.08	.04
73T	Randy Moffitt	.10	.08	.04
74T	Sid Monge	.10	.08	.04
75T	Jose Morales	.10	.08	.04
76T	Omar Moreno	.10	.08	.04
77T	Joe Morgan	1.75	1.25	.70
78T	Mike Morgan	.10	.08	.04
79T	Dale Murray	.10	.08	.04
80T	Jeff Newman	.10	.08	.04
81T	Pete O'Brien(FC)	1.75	1.25	.70
82T	Jorge Orta	.10	.08	.04
83T	Alejandro Pena(FC)	.60	.45	.25
84T	Pascual Perez	.20	.15	.08
85T	Tony Perez	.60	.45	.25
86T	Broderick Perkins	.10	.08	.04
87T	Tony Phillips(FC)	.20	.15	.08
88T	Charlie Puleo	.10	.08	.04
89T	Pat Putnam	.10	.08	.04
90T	Jamie Quirk	.10	.08	.04
91T	Doug Rader	.10	.08	.04
92T	Chuck Rainey	.10	.08	.04
93T	Bobby Ramos	.10	.08	.04
94T	Gary Redus(FC)	.40	.30	.15
95T	Steve Renko	.10	.08	.04
96T	Leon Roberts	.10	.08	.04
97T	Aurelio Rodriguez	.15	.11	.06
98T	Dick Ruthven	.10	.08	.04
99T	Daryl Sconiers	.10	.08	.04
100T	Mike Scott	.50	.40	.20
101T	Tom Seaver	2.25	1.75	.90
102T	John Shelby(FC)	.40	.30	.15
103T	Bob Shirley	.10	.08	.04
104T	Joe Simpson	.10	.08	.04
105T	Doug Sisk(FC)	.15	.11	.06
106T	Mike Smithson(FC)	.20	.15	.08
107T	Elias Sosa	.10	.08	.04
108T	Darryl Strawberry(FC)	80.00	60.00	33.00
109T	Tom Tellmann	.10	.08	.04
110T	Gene Tenace	.15	.11	.06
111T	Gorman Thomas	.25	.20	.10
112T	Dick Tidrow	.10	.08	.04
113T	Dave Tobik	.10	.08	.04
114T	Wayne Tolleson(FC)	.20	.15	.08
115T	Mike Torrez	.15	.11	.06
116T	Manny Trillo	.15	.11	.06
117T	Steve Trout	.10	.08	.04
118T	Lee Tunnell(FC)	.15	.11	.06
119T	Mike Vail	.10	.08	.04
120T	Ellis Valentine	.10	.08	.04
121T	Tom Veryzer	.10	.08	.04
122T	George Vukovich	.10	.08	.04
123T	Rick Waits	.10	.08	.04
124T	Greg Walker(FC)	.80	.60	.30
125T	Chris Welsh	.10	.08	.04
126T	Len Whitehouse	.10	.08	.04
127T	Eddie Whitson	.15	.11	.06
128T	Jim Wohlford	.10	.08	.04
129T	Matt Young(FC)	.20	.15	.08
130T	Joel Youngblood	.10	.08	.04
131T	Pat Zachry	.10	.08	.04
132T	Checklist 1-132	.10	.08	.04

1984 Topps

Another 792-card regular set from Topps. For the second straight year, the 2-1/2" by 3-1/2" cards featured a color action photo on the front along with a small portrait photo in the lower left. The team name runs in big letters down the left side, while the player's name and position runs under the large action photo. In the upper right-hand corner is the Topps logo. Backs have a team logo in the upper right corner, along with statistics, personal information and a few highlights. The backs have an unusual and hard-to-read red and purple coloring. Specialty cards include past season highlights, team leaders, major league statistical leaders, All-Stars, active career leaders and numbered checklists. Again, promising rookies were saved for the traded set. Late in 1984, Topps introduced a specially boxed "Tiffany" edition of the 1984 set, with the cards printed on white cardboard with a glossy finish. A total of 10,000 sets were produced. Prices for Tiffany edition superstars can run from six to eight times the value of the "regular" edition, while common cards sell in the 40¢ range.

		MT	NR MT	EX
Complete Set:		110.00	83.00	45.00
Common Player:		.08	.06	.03
1	1983 Highlight (Steve Carlton)	.30	.25	.12
2	1983 Highlight (Rickey Henderson)	.30	.25	.12
3	1983 Highlight (Dan Quisenberry)	.10	.08	.04
4	1983 Highlight (Steve Carlton, Gaylord Perry, Nolan Ryan)	.30	.25	.12
5	1983 Highlight (Bob Forsch, Dave Righetti, Mike Warren)	.15	.11	.06
6	1983 Highlight (Johnny Bench, Gaylord Perry, Carl Yastrzemski)	.40	.30	.15
7	Gary Lucas	.08	.06	.03
8	*Don Mattingly*(FC)	30.00	23.00	12.00
9	Jim Gott	.10	.08	.04
10	Robin Yount	1.00	.70	.40
11	Twins Batting & Pitching Leaders (Kent Hrbek, Ken Schrom)	.20	.15	.08
12	Billy Sample	.08	.06	.03
13	Scott Holman	.08	.06	.03
14	Tom Brookens	.08	.06	.03
15	Burt Hooton	.10	.08	.04
16	Omar Moreno	.08	.06	.03
17	John Denny	.08	.06	.03
18	Dale Berra	.08	.06	.03
19	*Ray Fontenot*(FC)	.10	.08	.04
20	Greg Luzinski	.12	.09	.05
21	Joe Altobelli	.08	.06	.03
22	Bryan Clark	.08	.06	.03
23	Keith Moreland	.10	.08	.04
24	John Martin	.08	.06	.03
25	Glenn Hubbard	.10	.08	.04
26	Bud Black	.10	.08	.04
27	Daryl Sconiers	.08	.06	.03
28	Frank Viola	.80	.60	.30
29	Danny Heep	.08	.06	.03
30	Wade Boggs	7.00	5.25	2.75
31	Andy McGaffigan	.08	.06	.03
32	Bobby Ramos	.08	.06	.03
33	Tom Burgmeier	.08	.06	.03
34	Eddie Milner	.08	.06	.03
35	Don Sutton	.30	.25	.12
36	Denny Walling	.08	.06	.03
37	Rangers Batting & Pitching Leaders (Buddy Bell, Rick Honeycutt)	.12	.09	.05
38	Luis DeLeon	.08	.06	.03
39	Garth Iorg	.08	.06	.03
40	Dusty Baker	.12	.09	.05
41	Tony Bernazard	.08	.06	.03
42	Johnny Grubb	.08	.06	.03
43	Ron Reed	.10	.08	.04
44	Jim Morrison	.08	.06	.03
45	Jerry Mumphrey	.08	.06	.03
46	Ray Smith	.08	.06	.03
47	Rudy Law	.08	.06	.03
48	Julio Franco(FC)	1.75	1.25	.70
49	John Stuper	.08	.06	.03
50	Chris Chambliss	.10	.08	.04
51	Jim Frey	.08	.06	.03
52	Paul Splittorff	.08	.06	.03
53	Juan Beniquez	.08	.06	.03
54	Jesse Orosco	.10	.08	.04
55	Dave Concepcion	.15	.11	.06
56	Gary Allenson	.08	.06	.03
57	Dan Schatzeder	.08	.06	.03

		MT	NR MT	EX
58	Max Venable	.08	.06	.03
59	Sammy Stewart	.08	.06	.03
60	Paul Molitor	.20	.15	.08
61	*Chris Codiroli*	.10	.08	.04
62	Dave Hostetler	.08	.06	.03
63	Ed Vande Berg	.08	.06	.03
64	Mike Scioscia	.08	.06	.03
65	Kirk Gibson	.40	.30	.15
66	Astros Batting & Pitching Leaders (Jose Cruz, Nolan Ryan)	.25	.20	.10
67	Gary Ward	.10	.08	.04
68	Luis Salazar	.08	.06	.03
69	Rod Scurry	.08	.06	.03
70	Gary Matthews	.12	.09	.05
71	Leo Hernandez	.08	.06	.03
72	Mike Squires	.08	.06	.03
73	Jody Davis	.10	.08	.04
74	Jerry Martin	.08	.06	.03
75	Bob Forsch	.10	.08	.04
76	Alfredo Griffin	.10	.08	.04
77	Brett Butler	.10	.08	.04
78	Mike Torrez	.10	.08	.04
79	Rob Wilfong	.08	.06	.03
80	Steve Rogers	.10	.08	.04
81	Billy Martin	.12	.09	.05
82	Doug Bird	.08	.06	.03
83	Richie Zisk	.10	.08	.04
84	Lenny Faedo	.08	.06	.03
85	Atlee Hammaker	.08	.06	.03
86	*John Shelby*(FC)	.25	.20	.10
87	Frank Pastore	.08	.06	.03
88	Rob Picciolo	.08	.06	.03
89	*Mike Smithson*(FC)	.15	.11	.06
90	Pedro Guerrero	.35	.25	.14
91	Dan Spillner	.08	.06	.03
92	Lloyd Moseby	.12	.09	.05
93	Bob Knepper	.10	.08	.04
94	Mario Ramirez	.08	.06	.03
95	Aurelio Lopez	.08	.06	.03
96	Royals Batting & Pitching Leaders (Larry Gura, Hal McRae)	.10	.08	.04
97	LaMarr Hoyt	.08	.06	.03
98	Steve Nicosia	.08	.06	.03
99	*Craig Lefferts*(FC)	.20	.15	.08
100	Reggie Jackson	.60	.45	.25
101	Porfirio Altamirano	.08	.06	.03
102	Ken Oberkfell	.08	.06	.03
103	Dwayne Murphy	.10	.08	.04
104	Ken Dayley	.08	.06	.03
105	Tony Armas	.12	.09	.05
106	Tim Stoddard	.08	.06	.03
107	Ned Yost	.08	.06	.03
108	Randy Moffitt	.08	.06	.03
109	Brad Wellman	.08	.06	.03
110	Ron Guidry	.30	.25	.12
111	Bill Virdon	.08	.06	.03
112	Tom Niedenfuer	.10	.08	.04
113	Kelly Paris	.08	.06	.03
114	Checklist 1-132	.08	.06	.03
115	Andre Thornton	.12	.09	.05
116	George Bjorkman	.08	.06	.03
117	Tom Veryzer	.08	.06	.03
118	Charlie Hough	.12	.09	.05
119	Johnny Wockenfuss	.08	.06	.03
120	Keith Hernandez	.40	.30	.15
121	*Pat Sheridan*(FC)	.15	.11	.06
122	Cecilio Guante(FC)	.10	.08	.04
123	Butch Wynegar	.08	.06	.03
124	Damaso Garcia	.08	.06	.03
125	Britt Burns	.08	.06	.03
126	Braves Batting & Pitching Leaders (Craig McMurtry, Dale Murphy)	.25	.20	.10
127	Mike Madden	.08	.06	.03
128	Rick Manning	.08	.06	.03
129	Bill Laskey	.08	.06	.03
130	Ozzie Smith	.20	.15	.08
131	Batting Leaders (Wade Boggs, Bill Madlock)	.50	.40	.20
132	Home Run Leaders (Jim Rice, Mike Schmidt)	.50	.40	.20
133	Runs Batted In Leaders (Cecil Cooper, Dale Murphy, Jim Rice)	.40	.30	.15
134	Stolen Base Leaders (Rickey Henderson, Tim Raines)	.30	.25	.12
135	Victory Leaders (John Denny, LaMarr Hoyt)	.10	.08	.04
136	Strikeout Leaders (Steve Carlton, Jack Morris)	.25	.20	.10
137	Earned Run Average Leaders (Atlee Hammaker, Rick Honeycutt)	.10	.08	.04
138	Leading Firemen (Al Holland, Dan Quisenberry)	.12	.09	.05
139	Bert Campaneris	.12	.09	.05
140	Storm Davis	.12	.09	.05
141	Pat Corrales	.08	.06	.03
142	Rich Gale	.08	.06	.03
143	Jose Morales	.08	.06	.03
144	Brian Harper	.08	.06	.03
145	Gary Lavelle	.08	.06	.03
146	Ed Romero	.08	.06	.03
147	Dan Petry	.10	.08	.04
148	Joe Lefebvre	.08	.06	.03
149	Jon Matlack	.10	.08	.04
150	Dale Murphy	1.00	.70	.40
151	Steve Trout	.08	.06	.03
152	Glenn Brummer	.08	.06	.03
153	Dick Tidrow	.08	.06	.03
154	Dave Henderson	.12	.09	.05
155	Frank White	.12	.09	.05
156	Athletics Batting & Pitching Leaders (Tim Conroy, Rickey Henderson)	.25	.20	.10
157	Gary Gaetti	.70	.50	.30
158	John Curtis	.08	.06	.03
159	Darryl Cias	.08	.06	.03
160	Mario Soto	.10	.08	.04
161	*Junior Ortiz*(FC)	.10	.08	.04
162	Bob Ojeda	.12	.09	.05
163	Lorenzo Gray	.08	.06	.03
164	Scott Sanderson	.08	.06	.03
165	Ken Singleton	.12	.09	.05
166	Jamie Nelson	.08	.06	.03
167	Marshall Edwards	.08	.06	.03
168	Juan Bonilla	.08	.06	.03
169	Larry Parrish	.12	.09	.05

		MT	NR MT	EX
170	Jerry Reuss	.12	.09	.05
171	Frank Robinson	.12	.09	.05
172	Frank DiPino	.08	.06	.03
173	*Marvell Wynne*(FC)	.20	.15	.08
174	Juan Berenguer	.08	.06	.03
175	Graig Nettles	.20	.15	.08
176	Lee Smith	.15	.11	.06
177	Jerry Hairston	.08	.06	.03
178	Bill Krueger	.08	.06	.03
179	Buck Martinez	.08	.06	.03
180	Manny Trillo	.10	.08	.04
181	Roy Thomas	.08	.06	.03
182	*Darryl Strawberry*	18.00	13.50	7.25
183	Al Williams	.08	.06	.03
184	Mike O'Berry	.08	.06	.03
185	Sixto Lezcano	.08	.06	.03
186	Cardinals Batting & Pitching Leaders (Lonnie Smith, John Stuper)	.10	.08	.04
187	Luis Aponte	.08	.06	.03
188	Bryan Little	.08	.06	.03
189	*Tim Conroy*(FC)	.12	.09	.05
190	Ben Oglivie	.10	.08	.04
191	Mike Boddicker	.12	.09	.05
192	*Nick Esasky*(FC)	2.00	1.50	.80
193	Darrell Brown	.08	.06	.03
194	Domingo Ramos	.08	.06	.03
195	Jack Morris	.30	.25	.12
196	Don Slaught(FC)	.12	.09	.05
197	Garry Hancock	.08	.06	.03
198	*Bill Doran*	.60	.45	.25
199	Willie Hernandez	.12	.09	.05
200	Andre Dawson	.35	.25	.14
201	Bruce Kison	.08	.06	.03
202	Bobby Cox	.08	.06	.03
203	Matt Keough	.08	.06	.03
204	*Bobby Meacham*(FC)	.15	.11	.06
205	Greg Minton	.08	.06	.03
206	*Andy Van Slyke*(FC)	3.00	2.25	1.25
207	Donnie Moore	.08	.06	.03
208	*Jose Oquendo*(FC)	.15	.11	.06
209	Manny Sarmiento	.08	.06	.03
210	Joe Morgan	.30	.25	.12
211	Rick Sweet	.08	.06	.03
212	Broderick Perkins	.08	.06	.03
213	Bruce Hurst	.15	.11	.06
214	Paul Householder	.08	.06	.03
215	Tippy Martinez	.08	.06	.03
216	White Sox Batting & Pitching Leaders (Richard Dotson, Carlton Fisk)	.15	.11	.06
217	Alan Ashby	.08	.06	.03
218	Rick Waits	.08	.06	.03
219	Joe Simpson	.08	.06	.03
220	Fernando Valenzuela	.40	.30	.15
221	Cliff Johnson	.08	.06	.03
222	Rick Honeycutt	.08	.06	.03
223	Wayne Krenchicki	.08	.06	.03
224	Sid Monge	.08	.06	.03
225	Lee Mazzilli	.10	.08	.04
226	Juan Eichelberger	.08	.06	.03
227	Steve Braun	.08	.06	.03
228	John Rabb	.08	.06	.03
229	Paul Owens	.08	.06	.03
230	Rickey Henderson	1.50	1.25	.60
231	Gary Woods	.08	.06	.03
232	Tim Wallach	.15	.11	.06
233	Checklist 133-264	.08	.06	.03
234	Rafael Ramirez	.08	.06	.03
235	*Matt Young*	.15	.11	.06
236	Ellis Valentine	.08	.06	.03
237	John Castino	.08	.06	.03
238	Reid Nichols	.08	.06	.03
239	Jay Howell	.10	.08	.04
240	Eddie Murray	.60	.45	.25
241	Billy Almon	.08	.06	.03
242	Alex Trevino	.08	.06	.03
243	Pete Ladd	.08	.06	.03
244	Candy Maldonado(FC)	.25	.20	.10
245	Rick Sutcliffe	.15	.11	.06
246	Mets Batting & Pitching Leaders (Tom Seaver, Mookie Wilson)	.25	.20	.10
247	Onix Concepcion	.08	.06	.03
248	*Bill Dawley*(FC)	.10	.08	.04
249	Jay Johnstone	.10	.08	.04
250	Bill Madlock	.12	.09	.05
251	Tony Gwynn	3.00	2.25	1.25
252	Larry Christenson	.08	.06	.03
253	Jim Wohlford	.08	.06	.03
254	Shane Rawley	.12	.09	.05
255	Bruce Benedict	.08	.06	.03
256	Dave Geisel	.08	.06	.03
257	Julio Cruz	.08	.06	.03
258	Luis Sanchez	.08	.06	.03
259	Sparky Anderson	.12	.09	.05
260	Scott McGregor	.10	.08	.04
261	Bobby Brown	.08	.06	.03
262	*Tom Candiotti*(FC)	.25	.20	.10
263	Jack Fimple	.08	.06	.03
264	Doug Frobel	.08	.06	.03
265	*Donnie Hill*(FC)	.15	.11	.06
266	Steve Lubratich	.08	.06	.03
267	*Carmelo Martinez*(FC)	.25	.20	.10
268	Jack O'Connor	.08	.06	.03
269	Aurelio Rodriguez	.10	.08	.04
270	*Jeff Russell*(FC)	.20	.15	.08
271	Moose Haas	.08	.06	.03
272	Rick Dempsey	.10	.08	.04
273	Charlie Puleo	.08	.06	.03
274	Rick Monday	.10	.08	.04
275	Len Matuszek	.08	.06	.03
276	Angels Batting & Pitching Leaders (Rod Carew, Geoff Zahn)	.20	.15	.08
277	Eddie Whitson	.08	.06	.03
278	Jorge Bell	1.00	.70	.40
279	Ivan DeJesus	.08	.06	.03
280	Floyd Bannister	.12	.09	.05
281	Larry Milbourne	.08	.06	.03
282	Jim Barr	.08	.06	.03
283	Larry Biittner	.08	.06	.03
284	Howard Bailey	.08	.06	.03
285	Darrell Porter	.10	.08	.04
286	Lary Sorensen	.08	.06	.03
287	Warren Cromartie	.08	.06	.03
288	Jim Beattie	.08	.06	.03
289	Randy Johnson	.08	.06	.03

		MT	NR MT	EX
290	Dave Dravecky	.10	.08	.04
291	Chuck Tanner	.08	.06	.03
292	Tony Scott	.08	.06	.03
293	Ed Lynch	.08	.06	.03
294	U.L. Washington	.08	.06	.03
295	Mike Flanagan	.12	.09	.05
296	Jeff Newman	.08	.06	.03
297	Bruce Berenyi	.08	.06	.03
298	Jim Gantner	.10	.08	.04
299	John Butcher	.08	.06	.03
300	Pete Rose	1.50	1.25	.60
301	Frank LaCorte	.08	.06	.03
302	Barry Bonnell	.08	.06	.03
303	Marty Castillo	.08	.06	.03
304	Warren Brusstar	.08	.06	.03
305	Roy Smalley	.08	.06	.03
306	Dodgers Batting & Pitching Leaders (Pedro Guerrero, Bob Welch)	.15	.11	.06
307	Bobby Mitchell	.08	.06	.03
308	Ron Hassey	.08	.06	.03
309	*Tony Phillips*	.15	.11	.06
310	Willie McGee	.35	.25	.14
311	Jerry Koosman	.12	.09	.05
312	Jorge Orta	.08	.06	.03
313	Mike Jorgensen	.08	.06	.03
314	Orlando Mercado	.08	.06	.03
315	Bob Grich	.12	.09	.05
316	Mark Bradley	.08	.06	.03
317	Greg Pryor	.08	.06	.03
318	Bill Gullickson	.08	.06	.03
319	Al Bumbry	.10	.08	.04
320	Bob Stanley	.08	.06	.03
321	Harvey Kuenn	.10	.08	.04
322	Ken Schrom	.08	.06	.03
323	Alan Knicely	.08	.06	.03
324	*Alejandro Pena*	.30	.25	.12
325	Darrell Evans	.15	.11	.06
326	Bob Kearney	.08	.06	.03
327	Ruppert Jones	.08	.06	.03
328	Vern Ruhle	.08	.06	.03
329	Pat Tabler(FC)	.20	.15	.08
330	John Candelaria	.12	.09	.05
331	Bucky Dent	.12	.09	.05
332	*Kevin Gross*(FC)	.35	.25	.14
333	Larry Herndon	.10	.08	.04
334	Chuck Rainey	.08	.06	.03
335	Don Baylor	.15	.11	.06
336	Mariners Batting & Pitching Leaders (Pat Putnam, Matt Young)	.10	.08	.04
337	Kevin Hagen	.08	.06	.03
338	Mike Warren	.08	.06	.03
339	Roy Lee Jackson	.08	.06	.03
340	Hal McRae	.12	.09	.05
341	Dave Tobik	.08	.06	.03
342	Tim Foli	.08	.06	.03
343	Mark Davis	.08	.06	.03
344	Rick Miller	.08	.06	.03
345	Kent Hrbek	.40	.30	.15
346	Kurt Bevacqua	.08	.06	.03
347	Allan Ramirez	.08	.06	.03
348	Toby Harrah	.10	.08	.04
349	Bob Gibson	.08	.06	.03
350	George Foster	.20	.15	.08
351	Russ Nixon	.08	.06	.03
352	Dave Stewart	.90	.70	.50
353	Jim Anderson	.08	.06	.03
354	Jeff Burroughs	.10	.08	.04
355	Jason Thompson	.08	.06	.03
356	Glenn Abbott	.08	.06	.03
357	Ron Cey	.12	.09	.05
358	Bob Dernier	.08	.06	.03
359	*Jim Acker*(FC)	.12	.09	.05
360	Willie Randolph	.12	.09	.05
361	Dave Smith	.10	.08	.04
362	David Green	.08	.06	.03
363	Tim Laudner	.08	.06	.03
364	Scott Fletcher(FC)	.15	.11	.06
365	Steve Bedrosian	.12	.09	.05
366	Padres Batting & Pitching Leaders (Dave Dravecky, Terry Kennedy)	.12	.09	.05
367	Jamie Easterly	.08	.06	.03
368	Hubie Brooks	.15	.11	.06
369	Steve McCatty	.08	.06	.03
370	Tim Raines	.40	.30	.15
371	Dave Gumpert	.08	.06	.03
372	Gary Roenicke	.08	.06	.03
373	Bill Scherrer	.08	.06	.03
374	Don Money	.08	.06	.03
375	Dennis Leonard	.10	.08	.04
376	*Dave Anderson*(FC)	.15	.11	.06
377	Danny Darwin	.08	.06	.03
378	Bob Brenly	.08	.06	.03
379	Checklist 265-396	.08	.06	.03
380	Steve Garvey	.50	.40	.20
381	Ralph Houk	.10	.08	.04
382	Chris Nyman	.08	.06	.03
383	Terry Puhl	.08	.06	.03
384	*Lee Tunnell*	.10	.08	.04
385	Tony Perez	.20	.15	.08
386	George Hendrick AS	.10	.08	.04
387	Johnny Ray AS	.12	.09	.05
388	Mike Schmidt AS	.35	.25	.14
389	Ozzie Smith AS	.15	.11	.06
390	Tim Raines AS	.25	.20	.10
391	Dale Murphy AS	.40	.30	.15
392	Andre Dawson AS	.20	.15	.08
393	Gary Carter AS	.30	.25	.12
394	Steve Rogers AS	.10	.08	.04
395	Steve Carlton AS	.25	.20	.10
396	Jesse Orosco AS	.10	.08	.04
397	Eddie Murray AS	.35	.25	.14
398	Lou Whitaker AS	.20	.15	.08
399	George Brett AS	.35	.25	.14
400	Cal Ripken AS	.35	.25	.14
401	Jim Rice AS	.30	.25	.12
402	Dave Winfield AS	.30	.25	.12
403	Lloyd Moseby AS	.12	.09	.05
404	Ted Simmons AS	.15	.11	.06
405	LaMarr Hoyt AS	.10	.08	.04
406	Ron Guidry AS	.20	.15	.08
407	Dan Quisenberry AS	.12	.09	.05
408	Lou Piniella	.15	.11	.06
409	*Juan Agosto*(FC)	.15	.11	.06
410	Claudell Washington	.10	.08	.04

		MT	NR MT	EX
411	Houston Jimenez	.08	.06	.03
412	Doug Rader	.08	.06	.03
413	*Spike Owen*(FC)	.20	.15	.08
414	Mitchell Page	.08	.06	.03
415	Tommy John	.25	.20	.10
416	Dane Iorg	.08	.06	.03
417	Mike Armstrong	.08	.06	.03
418	Ron Hodges	.08	.06	.03
419	John Henry Johnson	.08	.06	.03
420	Cecil Cooper	.15	.11	.06
421	Charlie Lea	.08	.06	.03
422	Jose Cruz	.12	.09	.05
423	Mike Morgan	.08	.06	.03
424	Dann Bilardello	.08	.06	.03
425	Steve Howe	.10	.08	.04
426	Orioles Batting & Pitching Leaders (Mike Boddicker, Cal Ripken)	.25	.20	.10
427	Rick Leach	.08	.06	.03
428	Fred Breining	.08	.06	.03
429	*Randy Bush*	.15	.11	.06
430	Rusty Staub	.12	.09	.05
431	Chris Bando	.08	.06	.03
432	*Charlie Hudson*(FC)	.20	.15	.08
433	Rich Hebner	.08	.06	.03
434	Harold Baines	.25	.20	.10
435	Neil Allen	.08	.06	.03
436	Rick Peters	.08	.06	.03
437	Mike Proly	.08	.06	.03
438	Biff Pocoroba	.08	.06	.03
439	Bob Stoddard	.08	.06	.03
440	Steve Kemp	.10	.08	.04
441	Bob Lillis	.08	.06	.03
442	Byron McLaughlin	.08	.06	.03
443	Benny Ayala	.08	.06	.03
444	Steve Renko	.08	.06	.03
445	Jerry Remy	.08	.06	.03
446	Luis Pujols	.08	.06	.03
447	Tom Brunansky	.20	.15	.08
448	Ben Hayes	.08	.06	.03
449	Joe Pettini	.08	.06	.03
450	Gary Carter	.40	.30	.15
451	Bob Jones	.08	.06	.03
452	Chuck Porter	.08	.06	.03
453	Willie Upshaw	.10	.08	.04
454	Joe Beckwith	.08	.06	.03
455	Terry Kennedy	.10	.08	.04
456	Cubs Batting & Pitching Leaders (Fergie Jenkins, Keith Moreland)	.15	.11	.06
457	Dave Rozema	.08	.06	.03
458	Kiko Garcia	.08	.06	.03
459	Kevin Hickey	.08	.06	.03
460	Dave Winfield	.40	.30	.15
461	Jim Maler	.08	.06	.03
462	Lee Lacy	.08	.06	.03
463	Dave Engle	.08	.06	.03
464	Jeff Jones	.08	.06	.03
465	Mookie Wilson	.12	.09	.05
466	Gene Garber	.08	.06	.03
467	Mike Ramsey	.08	.06	.03
468	Geoff Zahn	.08	.06	.03
469	Tom O'Malley	.08	.06	.03
470	Nolan Ryan	3.00	2.25	1.25
471	Dick Howser	.08	.06	.03
472	Mike Brown	.08	.06	.03
473	Jim Dwyer	.08	.06	.03
474	Greg Bargar	.08	.06	.03
475	*Gary Redus*	.25	.20	.10
476	Tom Tellmann	.08	.06	.03
477	Rafael Landestoy	.08	.06	.03
478	Alan Bannister	.08	.06	.03
479	Frank Tanana	.12	.09	.05
480	Ron Kittle(FC)	.40	.30	.15
481	*Mark Thurmond*(FC)	.10	.08	.04
482	Enos Cabell	.08	.06	.03
483	Fergie Jenkins	.20	.15	.08
484	Ozzie Virgil	.08	.06	.03
485	Rick Rhoden	.12	.09	.05
486	Yankees Batting & Pitching Leaders (Don Baylor, Ron Guidry)	.15	.11	.06
487	Ricky Adams	.08	.06	.03
488	Jesse Barfield	.25	.20	.10
489	Dave Von Ohlen	.08	.06	.03
490	Cal Ripken	.60	.45	.25
491	Bobby Castillo	.08	.06	.03
492	Tucker Ashford	.08	.06	.03
493	Mike Norris	.08	.06	.03
494	Chili Davis	.12	.09	.05
495	Rollie Fingers	.25	.20	.10
496	Terry Francona	.08	.06	.03
497	Bud Anderson	.08	.06	.03
498	Rich Gedman	.10	.08	.04
499	Mike Witt	.15	.11	.06
500	George Brett	.70	.50	.30
501	Steve Henderson	.08	.06	.03
502	Joe Torre	.08	.06	.03
503	Elias Sosa	.08	.06	.03
504	Mickey Rivers	.10	.08	.04
505	Pete Vuckovich	.10	.08	.04
506	Ernie Whitt	.10	.08	.04
507	Mike LaCoss	.08	.06	.03
508	Mel Hall	.20	.15	.08
509	Brad Havens	.08	.06	.03
510	Alan Trammell	.40	.30	.15
511	Marty Bystrom	.08	.06	.03
512	Oscar Gamble	.10	.08	.04
513	Dave Beard	.08	.06	.03
514	Floyd Rayford	.08	.06	.03
515	Gorman Thomas	.10	.08	.04
516	Expos Batting & Pitching Leaders (Charlie Lea, Al Oliver)	.12	.09	.05
517	John Moses	.12	.09	.05
518	*Greg Walker*	.45	.35	.20
519	Ron Davis	.08	.06	.03
520	Bob Boone	.10	.08	.04
521	Pete Falcone	.08	.06	.03
522	Dave Bergman	.08	.06	.03
523	Glenn Hoffman	.08	.06	.03
524	Carlos Diaz	.08	.06	.03
525	Willie Wilson	.15	.11	.06
526	Ron Oester	.08	.06	.03
527	Checklist 397-528	.08	.06	.03
528	Mark Brouhard	.08	.06	.03
529	*Keith Atherton*(FC)	.20	.15	.08
530	Dan Ford	.08	.06	.03

		MT	NR MT	EX
531	Steve Boros	.08	.06	.03
532	Eric Show	.12	.09	.05
533	Ken Landreaux	.08	.06	.03
534	*Pete O'Brien*	1.00	.70	.40
535	Bo Diaz	.10	.08	.04
536	Doug Bair	.08	.06	.03
537	Johnny Ray	.12	.09	.05
538	Kevin Bass	.15	.11	.06
539	George Frazier	.08	.06	.03
540	George Hendrick	.10	.08	.04
541	Dennis Lamp	.08	.06	.03
542	Duane Kuiper	.08	.06	.03
543	*Craig McMurtry*	.12	.09	.05
544	Cesar Geronimo	.08	.06	.03
545	Bill Buckner	.15	.11	.06
546	Indians Batting & Pitching Leaders (Mike Hargrove, Lary Sorensen)	.10	.08	.04
547	Mike Moore	.10	.08	.04
548	Ron Jackson	.08	.06	.03
549	*Walt Terrell*	.50	.40	.20
550	Jim Rice	.40	.30	.15
551	Scott Ullger	.08	.06	.03
552	Ray Burris	.08	.06	.03
553	Joe Nolan	.08	.06	.03
554	Ted Power(FC)	.12	.09	.05
555	Greg Brock	.15	.11	.06
556	Joey McLaughlin	.08	.06	.03
557	Wayne Tolleson	.10	.08	.04
558	Mike Davis	.10	.08	.04
559	Mike Scott	.20	.15	.08
560	Carlton Fisk	.30	.25	.12
561	Whitey Herzog	.10	.08	.04
562	Manny Castillo	.08	.06	.03
563	Glenn Wilson	.10	.08	.04
564	Al Holland	.08	.06	.03
565	Leon Durham	.10	.08	.04
566	Jim Bibby	.08	.06	.03
567	Mike Heath	.08	.06	.03
568	Pete Filson	.08	.06	.03
569	Bake McBride	.08	.06	.03
570	Dan Quisenberry	.12	.09	.05
571	Bruce Bochy	.08	.06	.03
572	Jerry Royster	.08	.06	.03
573	Dave Kingman	.15	.11	.06
574	Brian Downing	.12	.09	.05
575	Jim Clancy	.10	.08	.04
576	Giants Batting & Pitching Leaders (Atlee Hammaker, Jeff Leonard)	.10	.08	.04
577	Mark Clear	.08	.06	.03
578	Lenn Sakata	.08	.06	.03
579	Bob James	.08	.06	.03
580	Lonnie Smith	.10	.08	.04
581	*Jose DeLeon*(FC)	.60	.45	.25
582	Bob McClure	.08	.06	.03
583	Derrel Thomas	.08	.06	.03
584	Dave Schmidt	.08	.06	.03
585	Dan Driessen	.10	.08	.04
586	Joe Niekro	.15	.11	.06
587	Von Hayes	.15	.11	.06
588	Milt Wilcox	.08	.06	.03
589	Mike Easler	.10	.08	.04
590	Dave Stieb	.15	.11	.06
591	Tony LaRussa	.10	.08	.04
592	Andre Robertson	.08	.06	.03
593	Jeff Lahti	.08	.06	.03
594	Gene Richards	.08	.06	.03
595	Jeff Reardon	.15	.11	.06
596	Ryne Sandberg	4.00	3.00	1.50
597	Rick Camp	.08	.06	.03
598	Rusty Kuntz	.08	.06	.03
599	*Doug Sisk*	.10	.08	.04
600	Rod Carew	.50	.40	.20
601	John Tudor	.12	.09	.05
602	John Wathan	.10	.08	.04
603	Renie Martin	.08	.06	.03
604	John Lowenstein	.08	.06	.03
605	Mike Caldwell	.08	.06	.03
606	Blue Jays Batting & Pitching Leaders (Lloyd Moseby, Dave Stieb)	.15	.11	.06
607	Tom Hume	.08	.06	.03
608	Bobby Johnson	.08	.06	.03
609	Dan Meyer	.08	.06	.03
610	Steve Sax	.20	.15	.08
611	Chet Lemon	.10	.08	.04
612	Harry Spilman	.08	.06	.03
613	Greg Gross	.08	.06	.03
614	Len Barker	.10	.08	.04
615	Garry Templeton	.12	.09	.05
616	Don Robinson	.10	.08	.04
617	Rick Cerone	.08	.06	.03
618	Dickie Noles	.08	.06	.03
619	Jerry Dybzinski	.08	.06	.03
620	Al Oliver	.20	.15	.08
621	Frank Howard	.10	.08	.04
622	Al Cowens	.08	.06	.03
623	Ron Washington	.08	.06	.03
624	Terry Harper	.08	.06	.03
625	Larry Gura	.10	.08	.04
626	Bob Clark	.08	.06	.03
627	Dave LaPoint	.10	.08	.04
628	Ed Jurak	.08	.06	.03
629	Rick Langford	.08	.06	.03
630	Ted Simmons	.15	.11	.06
631	Denny Martinez	.10	.08	.04
632	Tom Foley	.08	.06	.03
633	Mike Krukow	.10	.08	.04
634	Mike Marshall	.15	.11	.06
635	Dave Righetti	.25	.20	.10
636	Pat Putnam	.08	.06	.03
637	Phillies Batting & Pitching Leaders (John Denny, Gary Matthews)	.10	.08	.04
638	George Vukovich	.08	.06	.03
639	Rick Lysander	.08	.06	.03
640	Lance Parrish	.35	.25	.14
641	Mike Richardt	.08	.06	.03
642	Tom Underwood	.08	.06	.03
643	Mike Brown	.08	.06	.03
644	Tim Lollar	.08	.06	.03
645	Tony Pena	.12	.09	.05
646	Checklist 529-660	.08	.06	.03
647	Ron Roenicke	.08	.06	.03
648	Len Whitehouse	.08	.06	.03
649	Tom Herr	.12	.09	.05
650	Phil Niekro	.30	.25	.12

		MT	NR MT	EX
651	John McNamara	.08	.06	.03
652	Rudy May	.08	.06	.03
653	Dave Stapleton	.08	.06	.03
654	Bob Bailor	.08	.06	.03
655	Amos Otis	.10	.08	.04
656	Bryn Smith	.08	.06	.03
657	Thad Bosley	.08	.06	.03
658	Jerry Augustine	.08	.06	.03
659	Duane Walker	.08	.06	.03
660	Ray Knight	.12	.09	.05
661	Steve Yeager	.08	.06	.03
662	Tom Brennan	.08	.06	.03
663	Johnnie LeMaster	.08	.06	.03
664	Dave Stegman	.08	.06	.03
665	Buddy Bell	.15	.11	.06
666	Tigers Batting & Pitching Leaders (Jack Morris, Lou Whitaker)	.15	.11	.06
667	Vance Law	.10	.08	.04
668	Larry McWilliams	.08	.06	.03
669	Dave Lopes	.10	.08	.04
670	Rich Gossage	.25	.20	.10
671	Jamie Quirk	.08	.06	.03
672	Ricky Nelson	.08	.06	.03
673	Mike Walters	.08	.06	.03
674	Tim Flannery	.08	.06	.03
675	Pascual Perez	.10	.08	.04
676	Brian Giles	.08	.06	.03
677	Doyle Alexander	.12	.09	.05
678	Chris Speier	.08	.06	.03
679	Art Howe	.08	.06	.03
680	Fred Lynn	.25	.20	.10
681	Tom Lasorda	.12	.09	.05
682	Dan Morogiello	.08	.06	.03
683	*Marty Barrett*(FC)	1.00	.70	.40
684	Bob Shirley	.08	.06	.03
685	Willie Aikens	.08	.06	.03
686	Joe Price	.08	.06	.03
687	Roy Howell	.08	.06	.03
688	George Wright	.08	.06	.03
689	Mike Fischlin	.08	.06	.03
690	Jack Clark	.25	.20	.10
691	*Steve Lake*(FC)	.10	.08	.04
692	Dickie Thon	.10	.08	.04
693	Alan Wiggins	.08	.06	.03
694	Mike Stanton	.08	.06	.03
695	Lou Whitaker	.40	.30	.15
696	Pirates Batting & Pitching Leaders (Bill Madlock, Rick Rhoden)	.15	.11	.06
697	Dale Murray	.08	.06	.03
698	Marc Hill	.08	.06	.03
699	Dave Rucker	.08	.06	.03
700	Mike Schmidt	.80	.60	.30
701	NL Active Career Batting Leaders (Bill Madlock, Dave Parker, Pete Rose)	.35	.25	.14
702	NL Active Career Hit Leaders (Tony Perez, Pete Rose, Rusty Staub)	.35	.25	.14
703	NL Active Career Home Run Leaders (Dave Kingman, Tony Perez, Mike Schmidt)	.30	.25	.12
704	NL Active Career RBI Leaders (Al Oliver, Tony Perez, Rusty Staub)	.15	.11	.06
705	NL Active Career Stolen Bases Leaders (Larry Bowa, Cesar Cedeno, Joe Morgan)	.12	.09	.05
706	NL Active Career Victory Leaders (Steve Carlton, Fergie Jenkins, Tom Seaver)	.30	.25	.12
707	NL Active Career Strikeout Leaders (Steve Carlton, Nolan Ryan, Tom Seaver)	.35	.25	.14
708	NL Active Career ERA Leaders (Steve Carlton, Steve Rogers, Tom Seaver)	.25	.20	.10
709	NL Active Career Save Leaders (Gene Garber, Tug McGraw, Bruce Sutter)	.12	.09	.05
710	AL Active Career Batting Leaders (George Brett, Rod Carew, Cecil Cooper)	.30	.25	.12
711	AL Active Career Hit Leaders (Bert Campaneris, Rod Carew, Reggie Jackson)	.30	.25	.12
712	AL Active Career Home Run Leaders (Reggie Jackson, Greg Luzinski, Graig Nettles)	.20	.15	.08
713	AL Active Career RBI Leaders (Reggie Jackson, Graig Nettles, Ted Simmons)	.20	.15	.08
714	AL Active Career Stolen Bases Leaders (Bert Campaneris, Dave Lopes, Omar Moreno)	.10	.08	.04
715	AL Active Career Victory Leaders (Tommy John, Jim Palmer, Don Sutton)	.25	.20	.10
716	AL Active Strikeout Leaders (Bert Blyleven, Jerry Koosman, Don Sutton)	.15	.11	.06
717	AL Active Career ERA Leaders (Rollie Fingers, Ron Guidry, Jim Palmer)	.15	.11	.06
718	AL Active Career Save Leaders (Rollie Fingers, Rich Gossage, Dan Quisenberry)	.15	.11	.06
719	Andy Hassler	.08	.06	.03
720	Dwight Evans	.20	.15	.08
721	Del Crandall	.08	.06	.03
722	Bob Welch	.15	.11	.06
723	Rich Dauer	.08	.06	.03
724	Eric Rasmussen	.08	.06	.03
725	Cesar Cedeno	.12	.09	.05
726	Brewers Batting & Pitching Leaders (Moose Haas, Ted Simmons)	.12	.09	.05
727	Joel Youngblood	.08	.06	.03
728	Tug McGraw	.12	.09	.05
729	Gene Tenace	.10	.08	.04
730	Bruce Sutter	.20	.15	.08
731	Lynn Jones	.08	.06	.03
732	Terry Crowley	.08	.06	.03
733	Dave Collins	.10	.08	.04
734	Odell Jones	.08	.06	.03
735	Rick Burleson	.10	.08	.04
736	Dick Ruthven	.08	.06	.03
737	Jim Essian	.08	.06	.03
738	*Bill Schroeder*(FC)	.20	.15	.08

		MT	NR MT	EX
739	Bob Watson	.10	.08	.04
740	Tom Seaver	.50	.40	.20
741	Wayne Gross	.08	.06	.03
742	Dick Williams	.08	.06	.03
743	Don Hood	.08	.06	.03
744	Jamie Allen	.08	.06	.03
745	Dennis Eckersley	.15	.11	.06
746	Mickey Hatcher	.10	.08	.04
747	Pat Zachry	.08	.06	.03
748	Jeff Leonard	.12	.09	.05
749	Doug Flynn	.08	.06	.03
750	Jim Palmer	.50	.40	.20
751	Charlie Moore	.08	.06	.03
752	Phil Garner	.10	.08	.04
753	Doug Gwosdz	.08	.06	.03
754	Kent Tekulve	.10	.08	.04
755	Garry Maddox	.10	.08	.04
756	Reds Batting & Pitching Leaders (Ron Oester, Mario Soto)	.10	.08	.04
757	Larry Bowa	.15	.11	.06
758	Bill Stein	.08	.06	.03
759	Richard Dotson	.12	.09	.05
760	Bob Horner	.15	.11	.06
761	John Montefusco	.08	.06	.03
762	Rance Mulliniks	.08	.06	.03
763	Craig Swan	.08	.06	.03
764	Mike Hargrove	.08	.06	.03
765	Ken Forsch	.08	.06	.03
766	Mike Vail	.08	.06	.03
767	Carney Lansford	.12	.09	.05
768	Champ Summers	.08	.06	.03
769	Bill Caudill	.08	.06	.03
770	Ken Griffey	.12	.09	.05
771	Billy Gardner	.08	.06	.03
772	Jim Slaton	.08	.06	.03
773	Todd Cruz	.08	.06	.03
774	Tom Gorman	.08	.06	.03
775	Dave Parker	.30	.25	.12
776	Craig Reynolds	.08	.06	.03
777	Tom Paciorek	.08	.06	.03
778	*Andy Hawkins*(FC)	.40	.30	.15
779	Jim Sundberg	.10	.08	.04
780	Steve Carlton	.50	.40	.20
781	Checklist 661-792	.08	.06	.03
782	Steve Balboni	.10	.08	.04
783	Luis Leal	.08	.06	.03
784	Leon Roberts	.08	.06	.03
785	Joaquin Andujar	.10	.08	.04
786	Red Sox Batting & Pitching Leaders (Wade Boggs, Bob Ojeda)	.40	.30	.15
787	Bill Campbell	.08	.06	.03
788	Milt May	.08	.06	.03
789	Bert Blyleven	.20	.15	.08
790	Doug DeCinces	.12	.09	.05
791	Terry Forster	.10	.08	.04
792	Bill Russell	.10	.08	.04

1984 Topps All-Star Glossy Set of 22

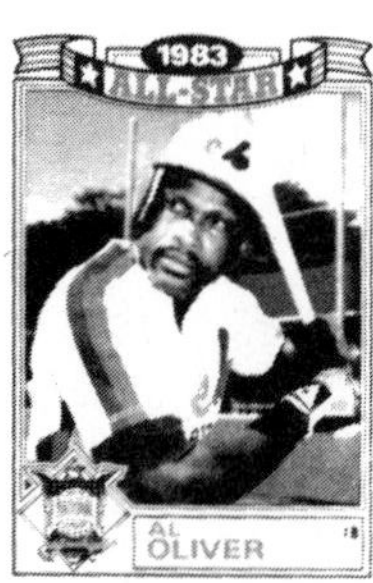

These 2-1/2" by 3-1/2" cards were a result of the success of Topps' efforts the previous year with glossy cards on a mail-in basis. A 22-card set, the cards are divided evenly between the two leagues. Each All-Star Game starter for both leagues, the managers and the honorary team captains have an All-Star Glossy card. The cards feature a large color photo on the front with an All-Star banner across the top and the league emblem in the lower left. The player's name and position appear below the photo. Backs have a name, team, position and card number along with the phrase "1983 All-Star Game Commemorative Set". The '84 Glossy All-Stars were distributed one card per pack in Topps rack packs that year.

		MT	NR MT	EX
Complete Set:		6.00	4.50	2.50
Common Player:		.20	.15	.08
1	Harvey Kuenn	.20	.15	.08
2	Rod Carew	.50	.40	.20
3	Manny Trillo	.20	.15	.08
4	George Brett	.80	.60	.30
5	Robin Yount	.40	.30	.15
6	Jim Rice	.50	.40	.20
7	Fred Lynn	.25	.20	.10
8	Dave Winfield	.50	.40	.20
9	Ted Simmons	.25	.20	.10
10	Dave Stieb	.25	.20	.10
11	Carl Yastrzemski	.80	.60	.30
12	Whitey Herzog	.20	.15	.08
13	Al Oliver	.25	.20	.10
14	Steve Sax	.30	.25	.12
15	Mike Schmidt	.80	.60	.30
16	Ozzie Smith	.30	.25	.12
17	Tim Raines	.50	.40	.20
18	Andre Dawson	.35	.25	.14
19	Dale Murphy	.80	.60	.30
20	Gary Carter	.50	.40	.20
21	Mario Soto	.20	.15	.08
22	Johnny Bench	.60	.45	.25

1984 Topps All-Star Glossy Set of 40

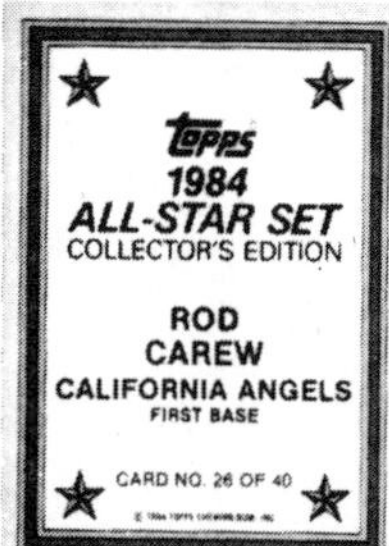

For the second straight year in 1984, Topps produced a 40-card All-Star "Collector's Edition" set as a "consolation prize" for its sweepstakes game. By collecting game cards and sending them in with a bit of cash, the collector could receive one of eight different five-card series. As the previous year, the 2-1/2" by 3-1/2" cards feature a nearly full-frame color photo on its glossy finish front. Backs are printed in red and blue.

		MT	NR MT	EX
Complete Set:		16.00	12.00	6.50
Common Player:		.15	.11	.06
1	Pete Rose	1.25	.90	.50
2	Lance Parrish	.30	.25	.12
3	Steve Rogers	.15	.11	.06
4	Eddie Murray	.60	.45	.25
5	Johnny Ray	.20	.15	.08
6	Rickey Henderson	.70	.50	.30
7	Atlee Hammaker	.15	.11	.06
8	Wade Boggs	3.00	2.25	1.25
9	Gary Carter	.50	.40	.20
10	Jack Morris	.30	.25	.12
11	Darrell Evans	.20	.15	.08
12	George Brett	1.00	.70	.40
13	Bob Horner	.20	.15	.08
14	Ron Guidry	.30	.25	.12
15	Nolan Ryan	.50	.40	.20
16	Dave Winfield	.60	.45	.25
17	Ozzie Smith	.25	.20	.10
18	Ted Simmons	.20	.15	.08
19	Bill Madlock	.20	.15	.08
20	Tony Armas	.15	.11	.06
21	Al Oliver	.20	.15	.08
22	Jim Rice	.50	.40	.20
23	George Hendrick	.15	.11	.06
24	Dave Stieb	.20	.15	.08
25	Pedro Guerrero	.25	.20	.10
26	Rod Carew	.60	.45	.25
27	Steve Carlton	.50	.40	.20
28	Dave Righetti	.30	.25	.12
29	Darryl Strawberry	3.00	2.25	1.25
30	Lou Whitaker	.30	.25	.12
31	Dale Murphy	1.00	.70	.40
32	LaMarr Hoyt	.15	.11	.06
33	Jesse Orosco	.15	.11	.06
34	Cecil Cooper	.20	.15	.08
35	Andre Dawson	.35	.25	.14
36	Robin Yount	.40	.30	.15
37	Tim Raines	.50	.40	.20
38	Dan Quisenberry	.15	.11	.06
39	Mike Schmidt	1.00	.70	.40
40	Carlton Fisk	.30	.25	.12

1984 Topps Gallery of Immortals

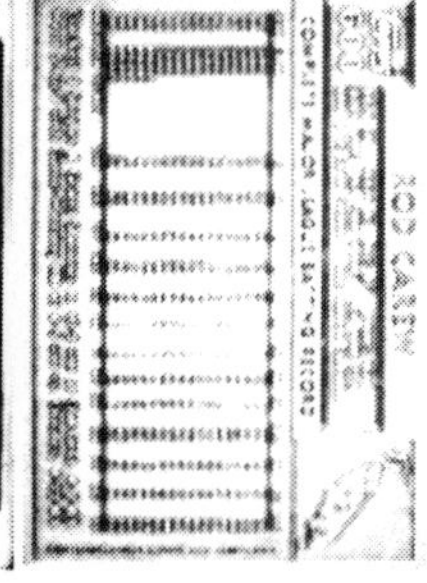

The Gallery of Immortals set of aluminum, bronze and silver replicas was the first miniature set of 12 from Topps and the start of an annual tradition (in 1985, the name was changed to Gallery of Champions) .Each mini is an exact replica (one- quarter scale) of the featured player's official Topps baseball card card, both front and back, in minute detail. The bronze and silver sets include a dozen three-dimensional raised metal cards packaged in a velvet-lined case that bears the title of the set in gold-embossed letters. A certificate of authenticity is included with each set. A Tom Seaver pewter metal mini-card was given as a premium to dealers who purchsed bronze and silver sets (value $75). A Darryl Strawberry bronze was given as a premium to dealers who purchased cases of the 1984 Topps Traded sets (value $12). Additionally, a Steve Carlton bronze was issued as a premium in 1983 to dealers who purchased 1983 Topps Traded sets (value $50).

		MT	NR MT	EX
Complete Aluminum Set:		30.00	22.00	12.00
Complete Bronze Set:		175.00	131.00	70.00
Complete Silver Set:		600.00	450.00	240.00
(1a)	George Brett (aluminum)	1.50	1.25	.60
(1b)	George Brett (bronze)	15.00	11.00	6.00
(1c)	George Brett (silver)	80.00	60.00	32.00
(2a)	Rod Carew (aluminum)	1.25	.90	.50
(2b)	Rod Carew (bronze)	12.50	9.50	5.00
(2c)	Rod Carew (silver)	50.00	37.00	20.00
(3a)	Steve Carlton (aluminum)	1.25	.90	.50
(3b)	Steve Carlton (bronze)	12.50	9.50	5.00
(3c)	Steve Carlton (silver)	50.00	37.00	20.00
(4a)	Rollie Fingers (aluminum)	1.00	.70	.40
(4b)	Rollie Fingers (bronze)	10.00	7.50	4.00
(4c)	Rollie Fingers (silver)	20.00	15.00	8.00
(5a)	Steve Garvey (aluminum)	1.25	.90	.50
(5b)	Steve Garvey (bronze)	12.50	9.50	5.00
(5c)	Steve Garvey (silver)	50.00	37.00	20.00
(6a)	Reggie Jackson (aluminum)	1.50	1.25	.60
(6b)	Reggie Jackson (bronze)	15.00	11.00	6.00
(6c)	Reggie Jackson (silver)	80.00	60.00	32.00
(7a)	Joe Morgan (aluminum)	1.00	.70	.40
(7b)	Joe Morgan (bronze)	10.00	7.50	4.00
(7c)	Joe Morgan (silver)	20.00	15.00	8.00
(8a)	Jim Palmer (aluminum)	1.00	.70	.40
(8b)	Jim Palmer (bronze)	10.00	7.50	4.00
(8c)	Jim Palmer (silver)	20.00	15.00	8.00
(9a)	Pete Rose (aluminum)	2.50	2.00	1.00
(9b)	Pete Rose (bronze)	25.00	18.50	10.00
(9c)	Pete Rose (silver)	110.00	82.00	44.00
(10a)	Nolan Ryan (aluminum)	1.25	.90	.50
(10b)	Nolan Ryan (bronze)	12.50	9.50	5.00
(10c)	Nolan Ryan (silver)	50.00	37.00	20.00
(11a)	Mike Schmidt (aluminum)	1.50	1.25	.60
(11b)	Mike Schmidt (bronze)	15.00	11.00	6.00
(11c)	Mike Schmidt (silver)	80.00	60.00	32.00
(12a)	Tom Seaver (aluminum)	1.25	.90	.50
(12b)	Tom Seaver (bronze)	12.50	9.50	5.00
(12c)	Tom Seaver (silver)	50.00	37.00	20.00

1984 Topps Rub Downs

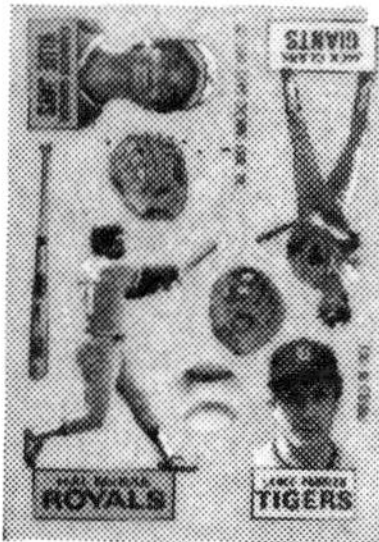

This set, produced by Topps in 1984, consists of 32 "Rub Down" sheets featuring 112 different players. Each sheet measures 2-3/8" by 3-15/16" and includes small, color baseball player figures along with bats, balls and gloves. The pictures can be transferred to another surface by rubbing the paper backing. The sheets, which were sold as a separate issue, are somewhat reminiscent of earlier tattoo sets issued by Topps. The sheets are not numbered.

		MT	NR MT	EX
Complete Set:		9.00	6.75	3.50
Common Player:		.10	.08	.04
(1)	Tony Armas, Harold Baines, Lonnie Smith	.10	.08	.04
(2)	Don Baylor, George Hendrick, Ron Kittle, Johnnie LeMaster	.10	.08	.04
(3)	Buddy Bell, Ray Knight, Lloyd Moseby	.10	.08	.04
(4)	Bruce Benedict, Atlee Hammaker, Frank White	.10	.08	.04
(5)	Wade Boggs, Rick Dempsey, Keith Hernandez	.60	.45	.25
(6)	George Brett, Andre Dawson, Paul Molitor, Alan Wiggins	.30	.25	.12
(7)	Tom Brunansky, Pedro Guerrero, Darryl Strawberry	.40	.30	.15
(8)	Bill Buckner, Rich Gossage, Dave Stieb,			

	MT	NR MT	EX
Rick Sutcliffe	.15	.11	.06
(9) Rod Carew, Carlton Fisk, Johnny Ray, Matt Young	.25	.20	.10
(10) Steve Carlton, Bob Horner, Dan Quisenberry	.25	.20	.10
(11) Gary Carter, Phil Garner, Ron Guidry	.25	.20	.10
(12) Ron Cey, Steve Kemp, Greg Luzinski, Kent Tekulve	.10	.08	.04
(13) Chris Chambliss, Dwight Evans, Julio Franco	.15	.11	.06
(14) Jack Clark, Damaso Garcia, Hal McRae, Lance Parrish	.20	.15	.08
(15) Dave Concepcion, Cecil Cooper, Fred Lynn, Jesse Orosco	.15	.11	.06
(16) Jose Cruz, Gary Matthews, Jack Morris, Jim Rice	.20	.15	.08
(17) Ron Davis, Kent Hrbek, Tom Seaver	.25	.20	.10
(18) John Denny, Carney Lansford, Mario Soto, Lou Whitaker	.10	.08	.04
(19) Leon Durham, Dave Lopes, Steve Sax	.15	.11	.06
(20) George Foster, Gary Gaetti, Bobby Grich, Gary Redus	.15	.11	.06
(21) Steve Garvey, Bill Russell, Jerry REmy, George Wright	.20	.15	.08
(22) Moose Haas, Bruce Sutter, Dickie Thon, Andre Thornton	.10	.08	.04
(23) Toby Harrah, Pat Putnam, Tim Raines, Mike Schmidt	.30	.25	.12
(24) Rickey Henderson, Dave Righetti, Pete Rose	.70	.50	.30
(25) Steve Henderson, Bill Madlock, Alan Trammell	.20	.15	.08
(26) LaMarr Hoyt, Larry Parrish, Nolan Ryan	.25	.20	.10
(27) Reggie Jackson, Eric Show, Jason Thompson	.30	.25	.12
(28) Tommy John, Terry Kennedy, Eddie Murray, Ozzie Smith	.25	.20	.10
(29) Jeff Leonard, Dale Murphy, Ken Singleton, Dave Winfield	.30	.25	.12
(30) Craig McMurtry, Cal Ripken, Steve Rogers, Willie Upshaw	.25	.20	.10
(31) Ben Oglivie, Jim Palmer, Darrell Porter	.20	.15	.08
(32) Tony Pena, Fernando Valenzuela, Robin Yount	.20	.15	.08

1984 Topps Stickers

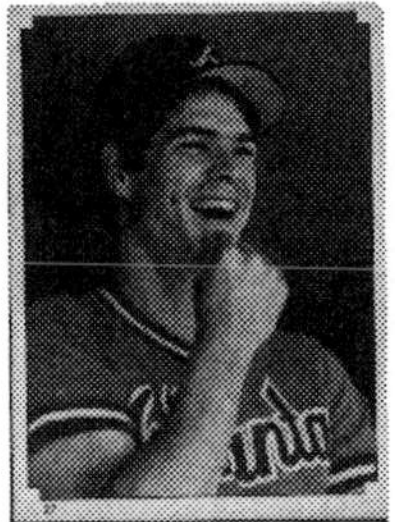

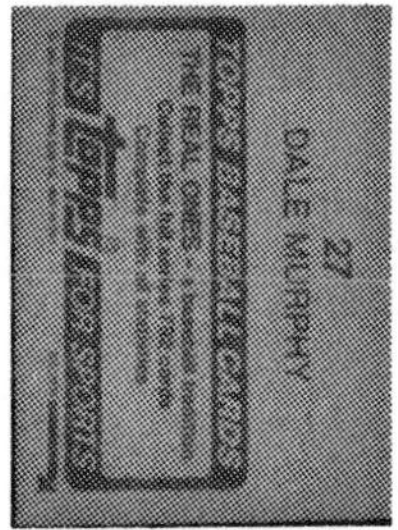

The largest sticker set issued by Topps, the 1984 set consists of 386 stickers, each measuring 1-15/16" by 2-9/16". The full color photos have stars in each of the corners and are numbered on both the front and the back. The back includes information about the sticker album and a promotion to order stickers through the mail.

	MT	NR MT	EX
Complete Set:	15.00	11.00	6.00
Common Player:	.03	.02	.01
Sticker Album:	.80	.60	.30

No.	Player	MT	NR MT	EX
1	Steve Carlton	.15	.11	.06
2	Steve Carlton	.12	.09	.05
3	Rickey Henderson	.20	.15	.08
4	Rickey Henderson	.15	.11	.06
5	Fred Lynn	.12	.09	.05
6	Fred Lynn	.10	.08	.04
7	Greg Luzinski	.08	.06	.03
8	Greg Luzinski	.06	.05	.02
9	Dan Quisenberry	.08	.06	.03
10	Dan Quisenberry	.06	.05	.02
11	1983 Championship (LaMarr Hoyt)	.03	.02	.01
12	1983 Championship (Mike Flanagan)	.04	.03	.02
13	1983 Championship (Mike Boddicker)	.04	.03	.02
14	1983 Championship (Tito Landrum)	.03	.02	.01
15	1983 Championship (Steve Carlton)	.12	.09	.05
16	1983 Championship (Fernando Valenzuela)	.12	.09	.05
17	1983 Championship (Charlie Hudson)	.03	.02	.01
18	1983 Championship (Gary Matthews)	.04	.03	.02
19	1983 World Series (John Denny)	.03	.02	.01
20	1983 World Series (John Lowenstein)	.03	.02	.01
21	1983 World Series (Jim Palmer)	.10	.08	.04
22	1983 World Series (Benny Ayala)	.03	.02	.01
23	1983 World Series (Rick Dempsey)	.03	.02	.01
24	1983 World Series (Cal Ripken)	.15	.11	.06
25	1983 World Series (Sammy Stewart)	.03	.02	.01
26	1983 World Series (Eddie Murray)	.15	.11	.06
27	Dale Murphy	.25	.20	.10
28	Chris Chambliss	.04	.03	.02
29	Glenn Hubbard	.04	.03	.02
30	Bob Horner	.08	.06	.03
31	Phil Niekro	.12	.09	.05
32	Claudell Washington	.04	.03	.02
33	Rafael Ramirez	.03	.02	.01
34	Bruce Benedict	.04	.03	.02
35	Gene Garber	.03	.02	.01
36	Pascual Perez	.04	.03	.02
37	Jerry Royster	.03	.02	.01
38	Steve Bedrosian	.06	.05	.02
39	Keith Moreland	.06	.05	.02
40	Leon Durham	.06	.05	.02
41	Ron Cey	.06	.05	.02
42	Bill Buckner	.06	.05	.02
43	Jody Davis	.06	.05	.02
44	Lee Smith	.06	.05	.02
45	Ryne Sandberg	.10	.08	.04
46	Larry Bowa	.04	.03	.02
47	Chuck Rainey	.04	.03	.02
48	Fergie Jenkins	.06	.05	.02
49	Dick Ruthven	.03	.02	.01
50	Jay Johnstone	.04	.03	.02
51	Mario Soto	.06	.05	.02
52	Gary Redus	.04	.03	.02
53	Ron Oester	.04	.03	.02
54	Cesar Cedeno	.06	.05	.02
55	Dan Driessen	.04	.03	.02
56	Dave Concepcion	.06	.05	.02
57	Dann Bilardello	.03	.02	.01
58	Joe Price	.03	.02	.01
59	Tom Hume	.03	.02	.01
60	Eddie Milner	.03	.02	.01
61	Paul Householder	.04	.03	.02
62	Bill Scherrer	.04	.03	.02
63	Phil Garner	.04	.03	.02
64	Dickie Thon	.04	.03	.02
65	Jose Cruz	.06	.05	.02
66	Nolan Ryan	.15	.11	.06
67	Terry Puhl	.03	.02	.01
68	Ray Knight	.06	.05	.02
69	Joe Niekro	.06	.05	.02
70	Jerry Mumphrey	.10	.08	.04
71	Bill Dawley	.03	.02	.01
72	Alan Ashby	.04	.03	.02
73	Denny Walling	.04	.03	.02
74	Frank DiPino	.04	.03	.02
75	Pedro Guerrero	.12	.09	.05
76	Ken Landreaux	.03	.02	.01
77	Bill Russell	.04	.03	.02
78	Steve Sax	.10	.08	.04
79	Fernando Valenzuela	.15	.11	.06
80	Dusty Baker	.04	.03	.02
81	Jerry Reuss	.04	.03	.02
82	Alejandro Pena	.04	.03	.02
83	Rick Monday	.06	.05	.02
84	Rick Honeycutt	.03	.02	.01
85	Mike Marshall	.06	.05	.02
86	Steve Yeager	.04	.03	.02
87	Al Oliver	.06	.05	.02
88	Steve Rogers	.03	.02	.01
89	Jeff Reardon	.08	.06	.03
90	Gary Carter	.20	.15	.08
91	Tim Raines	.15	.11	.06
92	Andre Dawson	.12	.09	.05
93	Manny Trillo	.04	.03	.02
94	Tim Wallach	.06	.05	.02
95	Chris Speier	.03	.02	.01
96	Bill Gullickson	.04	.03	.02
97	Doug Flynn	.04	.03	.02
98	Charlie Lea	.03	.02	.01
99	Bill Madlock	.06	.05	.02
100	Wade Boggs	.25	.20	.10
101	Mike Schmidt	.15	.11	.06
102a	Jim Rice	.06	.05	.02
102b	Reggie Jackson	.06	.05	.02
103	Hubie Brooks	.06	.05	.02
104	Jesse Orosco	.04	.03	.02
105	George Foster	.08	.06	.03
106	Tom Seaver	.20	.15	.08
107	Keith Hernandez	.15	.11	.06
108	Mookie Wilson	.06	.05	.02
109	Bob Bailor	.03	.02	.01
110	Walt Terrell	.04	.03	.02
111	Brian Giles	.06	.05	.02
112	Jose Oquendo	.06	.05	.02
113	Mike Torrez	.03	.02	.01
114	Junior Ortiz	.03	.02	.01
115	Pete Rose	.40	.30	.15
116	Joe Morgan	.12	.09	.05
117	Mike Schmidt	.25	.20	.10
118	Gary Matthews	.06	.05	.02
119	Steve Carlton	.15	.11	.06
120	Bo Diaz	.04	.03	.02
121	Ivan DeJesus	.04	.03	.02
122	John Denny	.03	.02	.01
123	Garry Maddox	.03	.02	.01
124	Von Hayes	.08	.06	.03
125	Al Holland	.03	.02	.01
126	Tony Perez	.06	.05	.02
127	John Candelaria	.06	.05	.02
128	Jason Thompson	.03	.02	.01
129	Tony Pena	.06	.05	.02
130	Dave Parker	.12	.09	.05
131	Bill Madlock	.08	.06	.03
132	Kent Tekulve	.04	.03	.02
133	larry McWilliams	.03	.02	.01
134	Johnny Ray	.04	.03	.02
135	Marvell Wynne	.03	.02	.01
136	Dale Berra	.03	.02	.01
137	Mike Easler	.03	.02	.01
138	Lee Lacy	.03	.02	.01
139	George Hendrick	.04	.03	.02
140	Lonnie Smith	.04	.03	.02
141	Willie McGee	.08	.06	.03
142	Tom Herr	.06	.05	.02
143	Darrell Porter	.04	.03	.02
144	Ozzie Smith	.10	.08	.04
145	Bruce Sutter	.06	.05	.02
146	Dave LaPoint	.03	.02	.01
147	Neil Allen	.03	.02	.01
148	Ken Oberkfell	.04	.03	.02
149	David Green	.03	.02	.01
150	Andy Van Slyke	.04	.03	.02
151	Garry Templeton	.06	.05	.02
152	Juan Bonilla	.03	.02	.01
153	Alan Wiggins	.03	.02	.01
154	Terry Kennedy	.04	.03	.02
155	Dave Dravecky	.04	.03	.02
156	Steve Garvey	.15	.11	.06
157	Bobby Brown	.04	.03	.02
158	Ruppert Jones	.03	.02	.01
159	Luis Salazar	.03	.02	.01
160	Tony Gwynn	.12	.09	.05
161	Gary Lucas	.10	.08	.04
162	Eric Show	.04	.03	.02
163	Darrell Evans	.08	.06	.03
164	Gary Lavelle	.03	.02	.01
165	Atlee Hammaker	.03	.02	.01
166	Jeff Leonard	.06	.05	.02
167	Jack Clark	.10	.08	.04
168	Johnny LeMaster	.03	.02	.01
169	Duane Kuiper	.03	.02	.01
170	Tom O'Malley	.06	.05	.02
171	Chili Davis	.06	.05	.02
172	Bill Laskey	.03	.02	.01
173	Joel Youngblood	.06	.05	.02
174	Bob Brenly	.06	.05	.02
175	Atlee Hammaker	.15	.11	.06
176	Rick Honeycutt	.15	.11	.06
177	John Denny	.06	.05	.02
178	LaMarr Hoyt	.03	.02	.01
179	Tim Raines	.30	.25	.12
180	Dale Murphy	.40	.30	.15
181	Andre Dawson	.25	.20	.10
182	Steve Rogers	.15	.11	.06
183	Gary Carter	.30	.25	.12
184	Steve Carlton	.25	.20	.10
185	George Hendrick	.15	.11	.06
186	Johnny Ray	.15	.11	.06
187	Ozzie Smith	.20	.15	.08
188	Mike Schmidt	.40	.30	.15
189	Jim Rice	.30	.25	.12
190	Dave Winfield	.30	.25	.12
191	Lloyd Moseby	.15	.11	.06
192	LaMarr Hoyt	.15	.11	.06
193	Ted Simmons	.15	.11	.06
194	Ron Guidry	.20	.15	.08
195	Eddie Murray	.40	.30	.15
196	Lou Whitaker	.25	.20	.10
197	Cal Ripken	.40	.30	.15
198	George Brett	.40	.30	.15
199	Dale Murphy	.15	.11	.06
200a	Cecil Cooper	.03	.02	.01
200b	Jim Rice	.25	.20	.10
201	Tim Raines	.10	.08	.04
202	Rickey Henderson	.15	.11	.06
203	Eddie Murray	.20	.15	.08
204	Cal Ripken	.20	.15	.08
205	Gary Roenicke	.03	.02	.01
206	Ken Singleton	.06	.05	.02
207	Scott McGregor	.04	.03	.02
208	Tippy Martinez	.03	.02	.01
209	John Lowenstein	.04	.03	.02
210	Mike Flanagan	.04	.03	.02
211	Jim Palmer	.10	.08	.04
212	Dan Ford	.12	.09	.05
213	Rick Dempsey	.04	.03	.02
214	Rich Dauer	.03	.02	.01
215	Jerry Remy	.03	.02	.01
216	Wade Boggs	.50	.40	.20
217	Jim Rice	.20	.15	.08
218	Tony Armas	.06	.05	.02
219	Dwight Evans	.08	.06	.03
220	Bob Stanley	.04	.03	.02
221	Dave Stapleton	.06	.05	.02
222	Rich Gedman	.04	.03	.02
223	Glenn Hoffman	.06	.05	.02
224	Dennis Eckersley	.08	.06	.03
225	John Tudor	.06	.05	.02
226	Bruce Hurst	.04	.03	.02
227	Rod Carew	.20	.15	.08
228	Bobby Grich	.06	.05	.02
229	Doug DeCinces	.06	.05	.02
230	Fred Lynn	.10	.08	.04
231	Reggie Jackson	.20	.15	.08
232	Tommy John	.10	.08	.04
233	Luis Sanchez	.03	.02	.01
234	Bob Boone	.04	.03	.02
235	Bruce Kison	.04	.03	.02
236	Brian Downing	.04	.03	.02
237	Ken Forsch	.03	.02	.01
238	Rick Burleson	.04	.03	.02
239	Dennis Lamp	.03	.02	.01
240	LaMarr Hoyt	.03	.02	.01
241	Richard Dotson	.04	.03	.02
242	Harold Baines	.10	.08	.04
243	Carlton Fisk	.12	.09	.05
244	Greg Luzinski	.08	.06	.03
245	Rudy Law	.06	.05	.02
246	Tom Paciorek	.03	.02	.01
247	Floyd Bannister	.04	.03	.02
248	Julio Cruz	.04	.03	.02
249	Vance Law	.03	.02	.01
250	Scott Fletcher	.04	.03	.02
251	Toby Harrah	.04	.03	.02
252	Pat Tabler	.04	.03	.02
253	Gorman Thomas	.06	.05	.02
254	Rick Sutcliffe	.08	.06	.03
255	Andre Thornton	.06	.05	.02
256	Bake McBride	.03	.02	.01
257	Alan Bannister	.03	.02	.01
258	Jamie Easterly	.03	.02	.01
259	Lary Sorenson	.03	.02	.01
260	Mike Hargrove	.03	.02	.01
261	Bert Blyleven	.06	.05	.02
262	Ron Hassey	.04	.03	.02
263	Jack Morris	.12	.09	.05

		MT	NR MT	EX
264	Larry Herndon	.03	.02	.01
265	Lance Parrish	.12	.09	.05
266	Alan Trammell	.15	.11	.06
267	Lou Whitaker	.12	.09	.05
268	Aurelio Lopez	.03	.02	.01
269	Dan Petry	.04	.03	.02
270	Glenn Wilson	.04	.03	.02
271	Chet Lemon	.04	.03	.02
272	Kirk Gibson	.06	.05	.02
273	Enos Cabell	.04	.03	.02
274	Johnny Wockenfuss	.03	.02	.01
275	George Brett	.25	.20	.10
276	Willie Aikens	.03	.02	.01
277	Frank White	.04	.03	.02
278	Hal McRae	.06	.05	.02
279	Dan Quisenberry	.06	.05	.02
280	Willie Wilson	.08	.06	.03
281	Paul Splitorff	.03	.02	.01
282	U.L. Washington	.03	.02	.01
283	Bud Black	.06	.05	.02
284	John Wathan	.04	.03	.02
285	Larry Gura	.03	.02	.01
286	Pat Sheridan	.03	.02	.01
287a	Rusty Staub	.06	.05	.02
287b	Dave Righetti	.25	.20	.10
288a	Bob Forsch	.03	.02	.01
288b	Mike Warren	.06	.05	.02
289	Al Holland	.10	.08	.04
290	Dan Quisenberry	.15	.11	.06
291	Cecil Cooper	.06	.05	.02
292	Moose Haas	.03	.02	.01
293	Ted Simmons	.08	.06	.03
294	Paul Molitor	.10	.08	.04
295	Robin Yount	.15	.11	.06
296	Ben Oglivie	.04	.03	.02
297	Tom Tellmann	.50	.40	.20
298	Jim Gantner	.04	.03	.02
299	Rick Manning	.03	.02	.01
300	Don Sutton	.06	.05	.02
301	Charlie Moore	.04	.03	.02
302	Jim Slaton	.03	.02	.01
303	Gary Ward	.04	.03	.02
304	Tom Brunansky	.08	.06	.03
305	Kent Hrbek	.12	.09	.05
306	Gary Gaetti	.10	.08	.04
307	John Castino	.03	.02	.01
308	Ken Schrom	.03	.02	.01
309	Ron Davis	.03	.02	.01
310	Lenny Faedo	.03	.02	.01
311	Darrell Brown	.06	.05	.02
312	Frank Viola	.06	.05	.02
313	Dave Engle	.03	.02	.01
314	Randy Bush	.03	.02	.01
315	Dave Righetti	.12	.09	.05
316	Rich Gossage	.12	.09	.05
317	Ken Griffey	.06	.05	.02
318	Ron Guidry	.12	.09	.05
319	Dave Winfield	.15	.11	.06
320	Don Baylor	.08	.06	.03
321	Butch Wynegar	.03	.02	.01
322	Omar Moreno	.03	.02	.01
323	Andre Robertson	.03	.02	.01
324	Willie Randolph	.04	.03	.02
325	Don Mattingly	.50	.40	.20
326	Graig Nettles	.06	.05	.02
327	Rickey Henderson	.25	.20	.10
328	Carney Lansford	.08	.06	.03
329	Jeff Burroughs	.04	.03	.02
330	Chris Codiroli	.03	.02	.01
331	Dave Lopes	.06	.05	.02
332	Dwayne Murphy	.04	.03	.02
333	Wayne Gross	.03	.02	.01
334	Bill Almon	.03	.02	.01
335	Tom Underwood	.04	.03	.02
336	Dave Beard	.03	.02	.01
337	Mike Heath	.03	.02	.01
338	Mike Davis	.04	.03	.02
339	Pat Putnam	.03	.02	.01
340	Tony Bernazard	.03	.02	.01
341	Steve Henderson	.03	.02	.01
342	Richie Zisk	.04	.03	.02
343	Dave Henderson	.06	.05	.02
344	Al Cowens	.03	.02	.01
345	Bill Caudill	.03	.02	.01
346	Jim Beattie	.06	.05	.02
347	Ricky Nelson	.04	.03	.02
348	Roy Thomas	.06	.05	.02
349	Spike Owen	.04	.03	.02
350	Jamie Allen	.03	.02	.01
351	Buddy Bell	.06	.05	.02
352	Billy Sample	.03	.02	.01
353	George Wright	.03	.02	.01
354	Larry Parrish	.06	.05	.02
355	Jim Sundberg	.04	.03	.02
356	Charlie Hough	.06	.05	.02
357	Pete O'Brien	.06	.05	.02
358	Wayne Tolleson	.03	.02	.01
359	Danny Darwin	.03	.02	.01
360	Dave Stewart	.04	.03	.02
361	Mickey Rivers	.04	.03	.02
362	Bucky Dent	.04	.03	.02
363	Willie Upshaw	.06	.05	.02
364	Damaso Garcia	.04	.03	.02
365	Lloyd Moseby	.06	.05	.02
366	Cliff Johnson	.03	.02	.01
367	Jim Clancy	.04	.03	.02
368	Dave Stieb	.06	.05	.02
369	Alfredo Griffin	.04	.03	.02
370	Barry Bonnell	.04	.03	.02
371	Luis Leal	.03	.02	.01
372	Jesse Barfield	.06	.05	.02
373	Ernie Whitt	.03	.02	.01
374	Rance Mulliniks	.06	.05	.02
375	Mike Boddicker	.06	.05	.02
376	Greg Brock	.06	.05	.02
377	Bill Doran	.06	.05	.02
378	Nick Esasky	.06	.05	.02
379	Julio Franco	.08	.06	.03
380	Mel Hall	.06	.05	.02
381	Bob Kearney	.03	.02	.01
382	Ron Kittle	.06	.05	.02
383	Carmelo Martinez	.06	.05	.02
384	Craig McMurtry	.03	.02	.01
385	Darryl Strawberry	.30	.25	.12
386	Matt Young	.04	.03	.02

1984 Topps Stickers Boxes

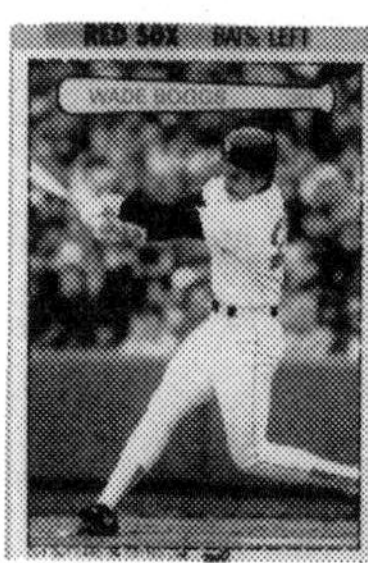

For the second straight year, Topps printed baseball cards on the back of its sticker boxes. The 1984 set, titled "The Super Bats" features 24 hitting leaders. The cards are blank-backed and measure 2-1/2" by 3-1/2". Two cards were printed on each of 12 different boxes. The player's name appears inside a bat above his photo. Prices listed are for complete boxes.

		MT	NR MT	EX
Complete Set:		8.50	6.50	3.50
Common Player:		.75	.60	.30
1	Al Oliver, Lou Whitaker	1.00	.70	.40
2	Ken Oberkfell, Ted Simmons	.75	.60	.30
3	Hal McRae, Alan Wiggins	.75	.60	.30
4	Lloyd Moseby, Tim Raines	1.00	.70	.40
5	Lonnie Smith, Willie Wilson	.75	.60	.30
6	Keith Hernandez, Robin Yount	.75	.60	.30
7	Wade Boggs, Johnny Ray	1.50	1.25	.60
8	Willie McGee, Ken Singleton	.75	.60	.30
9	Ray Knight, Alan Trammell	1.00	.70	.40
11	Rod Carew, George Hendrick	1.25	.90	.50
12	Bill Madlock, Eddie Murray	1.25	.90	.50
13	Jose Cruz, Cal Ripken, Jr.	1.25	.90	.50

1984 Topps Super

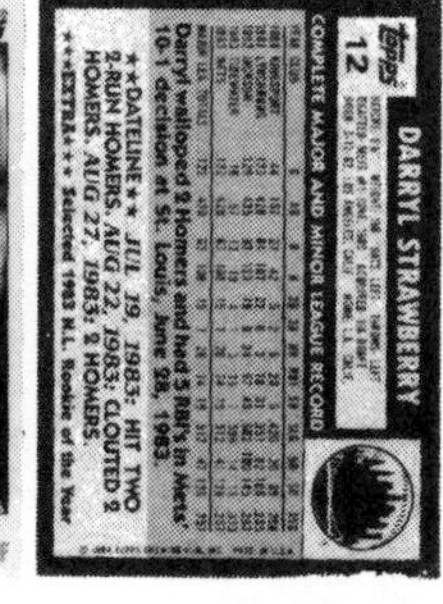

The next installment in Topps' continuing produc- tion of large-format cards, these 4-7/8" by 6-7/8" cards were sold in cellophane packs with a complete set being 30 cards. Other than their size and the change in card number on the back, there is nothing to distinguish the Supers from the regular 1984 Topps cards of the same players. One plus is that the players are all big name stars, and are likely to remain in demand.

		MT	NR MT	EX
Complete Set:		10.00	7.50	4.00
Common Player:		.20	.15	.08
1	Cal Ripken	.70	.50	.30
2	Dale Murphy	.90	.70	.35
3	LaMarr Hoyt	.20	.15	.08
4	John Denny	.20	.15	.08
5	Jim Rice	.50	.40	.20
6	Mike Schmidt	.90	.70	.35
7	Wade Boggs	1.25	.90	.50
8	Bill Madlock	.20	.15	.08
9	Dan Quisenberry	.20	.15	.08
10	Al Holland	.20	.15	.08
11	Ron Kittle	.20	.15	.08
12	Darryl Strawberry	1.25	.90	.50
13	George Brett	.90	.70	.35
14	Bill Buckner	.25	.20	.10
15	Carlton Fisk	.30	.25	.12
16	Steve Carlton	.50	.40	.20
17	Ron Guidry	.35	.25	.14
18	Gary Carter	.50	.40	.20
19	Rickey Henderson	.70	.50	.30
20	Andre Dawson	.35	.25	.14
21	Reggie Jackson	.60	.45	.25
22	Steve Garvey	.50	.40	.20
23	Fred Lynn	.30	.25	.12
24	Pedro Guerrero	.25	.20	.10
25	Eddie Murray	.60	.45	.25
26	Keith Hernandez	.50	.40	.20
27	Dave Winfield	.50	.40	.20
28	Nolan Ryan	.50	.40	.20
29	Robin Yount	.40	.30	.15
30	Fernando Valenzuela	.40	.30	.15

1984 Topps Traded

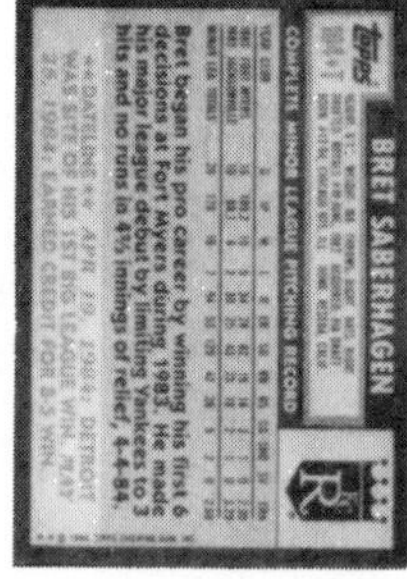

The popular Topps Traded set returned for its fourth year in 1984 with another 132-card set. The 2-1/2" by 3-1/2" cards have an identical design to the regular Topps cards except that the back cardboard is white and the card numbers carry a "T" suffix. As before, the set was sold only through hobby dealers. Also as before, players who changed teams, new managers and promis- ing rookies are included in the set. The presence of several promising young rookies in especially high demand from investors and speculators had made this one of the most expensive Topps issues of recent years. A glossy-finish "Tiffany" version of the set was also issued, valued at four to five times the price of the normal Traded cards.

		MT	NR MT	EX
Complete Set:		110.00	82.00	45.00
Common Player:		.10	.08	.04
1T	Willie Aikens	.10	.08	.04
2T	Luis Aponte	.10	.08	.04
3T	Mike Armstrong	.10	.08	.04
4T	Bob Bailor	.10	.08	.04
5T	Dusty Baker	.20	.15	.08
6T	Steve Balboni	.20	.15	.08
7T	Alan Bannister	.10	.08	.04
8T	Dave Beard	.10	.08	.04
9T	Joe Beckwith	.10	.08	.04
10T	Bruce Berenyi	.10	.08	.04
11T	Dave Bergman	.10	.08	.04
12T	Tony Bernazard	.10	.08	.04
13T	Yogi Berra	.20	.15	.08
14T	Barry Bonnell	.10	.08	.04
15T	Phil Bradley(FC)	1.75	1.25	.70
16T	Fred Breining	.10	.08	.04
17T	Bill Buckner	.25	.20	.10
18T	Ray Burris	.10	.08	.04
19T	John Butcher	.10	.08	.04
20T	Brett Butler	.20	.15	.08
21T	Enos Cabell	.10	.08	.04
22T	Bill Campbell	.10	.08	.04
23T	Bill Caudill	.10	.08	.04
24T	Bob Clark	.10	.08	.04
25T	Bryan Clark	.10	.08	.04
26T	Jaime Cocanower	.10	.08	.04
27T	Ron Darling(FC)	6.00	4.50	2.50
28T	Alvin Davis(FC)	7.00	5.25	2.75
29T	Ken Dayley	.10	.08	.04
30T	Jeff Dedmon(FC)	.15	.11	.06
31T	Bob Dernier	.10	.08	.04
32T	Carlos Diaz	.10	.08	.04
33T	Mike Easler	.15	.11	.06
34T	Dennis Eckersley	.30	.25	.12
35T	Jim Essian	.10	.08	.04
36T	Darrell Evans	.25	.20	.10
37T	Mike Fitzgerald(FC)	.15	.11	.06
38T	Tim Foli	.10	.08	.04
39T	George Frazier	.10	.08	.04
40T	Rich Gale	.10	.08	.04
41T	Barbaro Garbey	.15	.11	.06
42T	Dwight Gooden(FC)	45.00	34.00	18.00
43T	Rich Gossage	.40	.30	.15
44T	Wayne Gross	.10	.08	.04
45T	Mark Gubicza(FC)	6.00	4.50	2.50
46T	Jackie Gutierrez	.10	.08	.04
47T	Mel Hall	.20	.15	.08
48T	Toby Harrah	.15	.11	.06
49T	Ron Hassey	.10	.08	.04
50T	Rich Hebner	.10	.08	.04
51T	Willie Hernandez	.30	.25	.12
52T	Ricky Horton(FC)	.40	.30	.15
53T	Art Howe	.10	.08	.04
54T	Dane Iorg	.10	.08	.04
55T	Brook Jacoby(FC)	2.50	2.00	1.00
56T	Mike Jeffcoat(FC)	.15	.11	.06
57T	Dave Johnson	.15	.11	.06
58T	Lynn Jones	.10	.08	.04
59T	Ruppert Jones	.10	.08	.04
60T	Mike Jorgensen	.10	.08	.04

		MT	NR MT	EX
61T	Bob Kearney	.10	.08	.04
62T	Jimmy Key(FC)	3.00	2.25	1.25
63T	Dave Kingman	.40	.30	.15
64T	Jerry Koosman	.25	.20	.10
65T	Wayne Krenchicki	.10	.08	.04
66T	Rusty Kuntz	.10	.08	.04
67T	Rene Lachemann	.10	.08	.04
68T	Frank LaCorte	.10	.08	.04
69T	Dennis Lamp	.10	.08	.04
70T	Mark Langston(FC)	18.00	13.50	7.25
71T	Rick Leach	.10	.08	.04
72T	Craig Lefferts	.15	.11	.06
73T	Gary Lucas	.10	.08	.04
74T	Jerry Martin	.10	.08	.04
75T	Carmelo Martinez	.25	.20	.10
76T	Mike Mason(FC)	.15	.11	.06
77T	Gary Matthews	.25	.20	.10
78T	Andy McGaffigan	.10	.08	.04
79T	Larry Milbourne	.10	.08	.04
80T	Sid Monge	.10	.08	.04
81T	Jackie Moore	.10	.08	.04
82T	Joe Morgan	1.50	1.25	.60
83T	Graig Nettles	.50	.40	.20
84T	Phil Niekro	1.00	.70	.40
85T	Ken Oberkfell	.10	.08	.04
86T	Mike O'Berry	.10	.08	.04
87T	Al Oliver	.30	.25	.12
88T	Jorge Orta	.10	.08	.04
89T	Amos Otis	.15	.11	.06
90T	Dave Parker	.80	.60	.30
91T	Tony Perez	.60	.45	.25
92T	Gerald Perry(FC)	1.25	.90	.50
93T	Gary Pettis(FC)	.25	.20	.10
94T	Rob Picciolo	.10	.08	.04
95T	Vern Rapp	.10	.08	.04
96T	Floyd Rayford	.10	.08	.04
97T	Randy Ready(FC)	.25	.20	.10
98T	Ron Reed	.15	.11	.06
99T	Gene Richards	.10	.08	.04
100T	Jose Rijo(FC)	1.50	1.25	.60
101T	Jeff Robinson(FC)	.50	.40	.20
102T	Ron Romanick(FC)	.20	.15	.08
103T	Pete Rose	7.00	5.25	2.75
104T	Bret Saberhagen(FC)	25.00	20.00	10.00
105T	Juan Samuel(FC)	2.50	2.00	1.00
106T	Scott Sanderson	.10	.08	.04
107T	Dick Schofield(FC)	.35	.25	.14
108T	Tom Seaver	3.25	2.50	1.25
109T	Jim Slaton	.10	.08	.04
110T	Mike Smithson	.10	.08	.04
111T	Lary Sorensen	.10	.08	.04
112T	Tim Stoddard	.10	.08	.04
113T	Champ Summers	.10	.08	.04
114T	Jim Sundberg	.15	.11	.06
115T	Rick Sutcliffe	.50	.40	.20
116T	Craig Swan	.10	.08	.04
117T	Tim Teufel(FC)	.30	.25	.12
118T	Derrel Thomas	.10	.08	.04
119T	Gorman Thomas	.25	.20	.10
120T	Alex Trevino	.10	.08	.04
121T	Manny Trillo	.15	.11	.06
122T	John Tudor	.25	.20	.10
123T	Tom Underwood	.10	.08	.04
124T	Mike Vail	.10	.08	.04
125T	Tom Waddell	.10	.08	.04
126T	Gary Ward	.10	.08	.04
127T	Curt Wilkerson	.10	.08	.04
128T	Frank Williams(FC)	.25	.20	.10
129T	Glenn Wilson	.20	.15	.08
130T	Johnny Wockenfuss	.10	.08	.04
131T	Ned Yost	.10	.08	.04
132T	Checklist 1-132	.10	.08	.04

1985 Topps

Holding the line at 792 cards, Topps did initiate some major design changes in its 2-1/2" by 3-1/2" cards in 1985. The use of two photos on the front was discontinued in favor of one large color photo. The Topps logo appears in the upper left-hand corner. At the bottom runs a diagonal rectangular box with the team name. It joins a team logo, and below that point runs the player's position and name. The backs feature statistics, biographical information and a trivia question. Some interesting specialty sets were introduced in 1985, including the revival of the father/son theme from 1976, a subset of the 1984 U.S. Olympic Baseball Team members and a set featuring #1 draft choices since the inception of the baseball draft in 1965. Again in 1985, a glossy-finish "Tiffany" edition of the regular set was produced, though the number was cut back to 5,000 sets. Values range from four times regular value for common cards to five-six times for high-demand stars and rookie cards.

		MT	NR MT	EX
	Complete Set:	100.00	75.00	40.00
	Common Player:	.06	.05	.02
1	Record Breaker (Carlton Fisk)	.15	.11	.06
2	Record Breaker (Steve Garvey)	.20	.15	.08
3	Record Breaker (Dwight Gooden)	1.00	.70	.40
4	Record Breaker (Cliff Johnson)	.08	.06	.03
5	Record Breaker (Joe Morgan)	.15	.11	.06
6	Record Breaker (Pete Rose)	.60	.45	.25
7	Record Breaker (Nolan Ryan)	.30	.25	.12
8	Record Breaker (Juan Samuel)(FC)	.20	.15	.08
9	Record Breaker (Bruce Sutter)	.12	.09	.05
10	Record Breaker (Don Sutton)	.20	.15	.08
11	Ralph Houk	.08	.06	.03
12	Dave Lopes	.08	.06	.03
13	Tim Lollar	.06	.05	.02
14	Chris Bando	.06	.05	.02
15	Jerry Koosman	.10	.08	.04
16	Bobby Meacham	.06	.05	.02
17	Mike Scott	.15	.11	.06
18	Mickey Hatcher	.06	.05	.02
19	George Frazier	.06	.05	.02
20	Chet Lemon	.08	.06	.03
21	Lee Tunnell	.06	.05	.02
22	Duane Kuiper	.06	.05	.02
23	*Bret Saberhagen*	6.00	4.50	2.50
24	Jesse Barfield	.25	.20	.10
25	Steve Bedrosian	.12	.09	.05
26	Roy Smalley	.06	.05	.02
27	Bruce Berenyi	.06	.05	.02
28	Dann Bilardello	.06	.05	.02
29	Odell Jones	.06	.05	.02
30	Cal Ripken	.50	.40	.20
31	Terry Whitfield	.06	.05	.02
32	Chuck Porter	.06	.05	.02
33	Tito Landrum	.06	.05	.02
34	Ed Nunez(FC)	.08	.06	.03
35	Graig Nettles	.15	.11	.06
36	Fred Breining	.06	.05	.02
37	Reid Nichols	.06	.05	.02
38	Jackie Moore	.06	.05	.02
39	Johnny Wockenfuss	.06	.05	.02
40	Phil Niekro	.25	.20	.10
41	Mike Fischlin	.06	.05	.02
42	Luis Sanchez	.06	.05	.02
43	Andre David	.06	.05	.02
44	Dickie Thon	.08	.06	.03
45	Greg Minton	.06	.05	.02
46	Gary Woods	.06	.05	.02
47	Dave Rozema	.06	.05	.02
48	Tony Fernandez(FC)	1.25	.90	.50
49	Butch Davis	.06	.05	.02
50	John Candelaria	.10	.08	.04
51	Bob Watson	.08	.06	.03
52	Jerry Dybzinski	.06	.05	.02
53	Tom Gorman	.06	.05	.02
54	Cesar Cedeno	.10	.08	.04
55	Frank Tanana	.10	.08	.04
56	Jim Dwyer	.06	.05	.02
57	Pat Zachry	.06	.05	.02
58	Orlando Mercado	.06	.05	.02
59	Rick Waits	.06	.05	.02
60	George Hendrick	.08	.06	.03
61	Curt Kaufman	.06	.05	.02
62	Mike Ramsey	.06	.05	.02
63	Steve McCatty	.06	.05	.02
64	*Mark Bailey*(FC)	.10	.08	.04
65	Bill Buckner	.12	.09	.05
66	Dick Williams	.06	.05	.02
67	*Rafael Santana*(FC)	.20	.15	.08
68	Von Hayes	.10	.08	.04
69	*Jim Winn*(FC)	.10	.08	.04
70	Don Baylor	.12	.09	.05
71	Tim Laudner	.06	.05	.02
72	Rick Sutcliffe	.12	.09	.05
73	Rusty Kuntz	.06	.05	.02
74	Mike Krukow	.08	.06	.03
75	Willie Upshaw	.08	.06	.03
76	Alan Bannister	.06	.05	.02
77	Joe Beckwith	.06	.05	.02
78	Scott Fletcher	.08	.06	.03
79	Rick Mahler	.06	.05	.02
80	Keith Hernandez	.30	.25	.12
81	Lenn Sakata	.06	.05	.02
82	Joe Price	.06	.05	.02
83	Charlie Moore	.06	.05	.02
84	Spike Owen	.08	.06	.03
85	Mike Marshall	.15	.11	.06
86	Don Aase	.06	.05	.02
87	David Green	.06	.05	.02
88	Bryn Smith	.06	.05	.02
89	Jackie Gutierrez	.06	.05	.02
90	Rich Gossage	.20	.15	.08
91	Jeff Burroughs	.08	.06	.03
92	Paul Owens	.06	.05	.02
93	*Don Schulze*(FC)	.10	.08	.04
94	Toby Harrah	.08	.06	.03
95	Jose Cruz	.10	.08	.04
96	Johnny Ray	.12	.09	.05
97	Pete Filson	.06	.05	.02
98	Steve Lake	.06	.05	.02
99	Milt Wilcox	.06	.05	.02
100	George Brett	.50	.40	.20
101	Jim Acker	.06	.05	.02
102	Tommy Dunbar	.06	.05	.02
103	Randy Lerch	.06	.05	.02
104	Mike Fitzgerald	.08	.06	.03
105	Ron Kittle	.10	.08	.04
106	Pascual Perez	.08	.06	.03
107	Tom Foley	.06	.05	.02
108	Darnell Coles(FC)	.15	.11	.06
109	Gary Roenicke	.06	.05	.02
110	Alejandro Pena	.08	.06	.03
111	Doug DeCinces	.10	.08	.04
112	Tom Tellmann	.06	.05	.02
113	Tom Herr	.10	.08	.04
114	Bob James	.06	.05	.02
115	Rickey Henderson	1.00	.70	.40
116	Dennis Boyd(FC)	.15	.11	.06
117	Greg Gross	.06	.05	.02
118	Eric Show	.08	.06	.03
119	Pat Corrales	.06	.05	.02
120	Steve Kemp	.08	.06	.03
121	Checklist 1-132	.06	.05	.02
122	Tom Brunansky	.12	.09	.05
123	Dave Smith	.08	.06	.03
124	Rich Hebner	.06	.05	.02
125	Kent Tekulve	.08	.06	.03
126	Ruppert Jones	.06	.05	.02
127	*Mark Gubicza*	1.25	.90	.50
128	Ernie Whitt	.08	.06	.03
129	Gene Garber	.06	.05	.02
130	Al Oliver	.12	.09	.05
131	Father - Son (Buddy Bell, Gus Bell)	.12	.09	.05
132	Father - Son (Dale Berra, Yogi Berra)	.20	.15	.08
133	Father - Son (Bob Boone, Ray Boone)	.12	.09	.05
134	Father - Son (Terry Francona, Tito Francona)	.08	.06	.03
135	Father - Son (Bob Kennedy, Terry Kennedy)	.08	.06	.03
136	Father - Son (Bill Kunkel, Jeff Kunkel)(FC)	.08	.06	.03
137	Father - Son (Vance Law, Vern Law)	.10	.08	.04
138	Father - Son (Dick Schofield, Dick Schofield)	.08	.06	.03
139	Father - Son (Bob Skinner, Joel Skinner)	.08	.06	.03
140	Father - Son (Roy Smalley, Roy Smalley)	.08	.06	.03
141	Father - Son (Dave Stenhouse, Mike Stenhouse)	.08	.06	.03
142	Father - Son (Dizzy Trout, Steve Trout)	.08	.06	.03
143	Father - Son (Ossie Virgil, Ozzie Virgil)	.08	.06	.03
144	Ron Gardenhire	.06	.05	.02
145	*Alvin Davis*	2.00	1.50	.80
146	Gary Redus	.08	.06	.03
147	Bill Swaggerty	.06	.05	.02
148	Steve Yeager	.06	.05	.02
149	Dickie Noles	.06	.05	.02
150	Jim Rice	.35	.25	.14
151	Moose Haas	.06	.05	.02
152	Steve Braun	.06	.05	.02
153	Frank LaCorte	.06	.05	.02
154	Argenis Salazar(FC)	.06	.05	.02
155	Yogi Berra	.12	.09	.05
156	Craig Reynolds	.06	.05	.02
157	Tug McGraw	.10	.08	.04
158	Pat Tabler	.08	.06	.03
159	Carlos Diaz	.06	.05	.02
160	Lance Parrish	.25	.20	.10
161	Ken Schrom	.06	.05	.02
162	*Benny Distefano*(FC)	.10	.08	.04
163	Dennis Eckersley	.12	.09	.05
164	Jorge Orta	.06	.05	.02
165	Dusty Baker	.08	.06	.03
166	Keith Atherton	.06	.05	.02
167	Rufino Linares	.06	.05	.02
168	Garth Iorg	.06	.05	.02
169	Dan Spillner	.06	.05	.02
170	George Foster	.15	.11	.06
171	Bill Stein	.06	.05	.02
172	Jack Perconte	.06	.05	.02
173	Mike Young(FC)	.12	.09	.05
174	Rick Honeycutt	.06	.05	.02
175	Dave Parker	.25	.20	.10
176	Bill Schroeder	.06	.05	.02
177	Dave Von Ohlen	.06	.05	.02
178	Miguel Dilone	.06	.05	.02
179	Tommy John	.20	.15	.08
180	Dave Winfield	.35	.25	.14
181	*Roger Clemens*(FC)	10.00	7.50	4.00
182	Tim Flannery	.06	.05	.02
183	Larry McWilliams	.06	.05	.02
184	Carmen Castillo(FC)	.10	.08	.04
185	Al Holland	.06	.05	.02
186	Bob Lillis	.06	.05	.02
187	Mike Walters	.06	.05	.02
188	Greg Pryor	.06	.05	.02
189	Warren Brusstar	.06	.05	.02
190	Rusty Staub	.12	.09	.05
191	Steve Nicosia	.08	.06	.03
192	Howard Johnson(FC)	4.00	3.00	1.50
193	*Jimmy Key*	1.00	.70	.40
194	Dave Stegman	.06	.05	.02
195	Glenn Hubbard	.06	.05	.02
196	Pete O'Brien	.12	.09	.05
197	Mike Warren	.06	.05	.02
198	Eddie Milner	.06	.05	.02
199	Denny Martinez	.08	.06	.03
200	Reggie Jackson	.40	.30	.15
201	Burt Hooton	.08	.06	.03
202	Gorman Thomas	.10	.08	.04
203	Bob McClure	.06	.05	.02
204	Art Howe	.06	.05	.02
205	Steve Rogers	.08	.06	.03
206	Phil Garner	.08	.06	.03
207	Mark Clear	.06	.05	.02
208	Champ Summers	.06	.05	.02
209	Bill Campbell	.06	.05	.02
210	Gary Matthews	.10	.08	.04
211	Clay Christiansen	.06	.05	.02
212	George Vukovich	.06	.05	.02
213	Billy Gardner	.06	.05	.02
214	John Tudor	.10	.08	.04
215	Bob Brenly	.06	.05	.02
216	Jerry Don Gleaton	.06	.05	.02
217	Leon Roberts	.06	.05	.02
218	Doyle Alexander	.10	.08	.04

		MT	NR MT	EX
219	Gerald Perry	.35	.25	.14
220	Fred Lynn	.20	.15	.08
221	Ron Reed	.06	.05	.02
222	Hubie Brooks	.10	.08	.04
223	Tom Hume	.06	.05	.02
224	Al Cowens	.06	.05	.02
225	Mike Boddicker	.10	.08	.04
226	Juan Beniquez	.06	.05	.02
227	Danny Darwin	.06	.05	.02
228	Dion James(FC)	.20	.15	.08
229	Dave LaPoint	.08	.06	.03
230	Gary Carter	.35	.25	.14
231	Dwayne Murphy	.08	.06	.03
232	Dave Beard	.06	.05	.02
233	Ed Jurak	.06	.05	.02
234	Jerry Narron	.06	.05	.02
235	Garry Maddox	.10	.08	.04
236	Mark Thurmond	.06	.05	.02
237	Julio Franco	.50	.40	.20
238	*Jose Rijo*	.40	.30	.15
239	Tim Teufel	.12	.09	.05
240	Dave Stieb	.12	.09	.05
241	Jim Frey	.06	.05	.02
242	Greg Harris	.06	.05	.02
243	Barbaro Garbey	.10	.08	.04
244	Mike Jones	.06	.05	.02
245	Chili Davis	.10	.08	.04
246	Mike Norris	.06	.05	.02
247	Wayne Tolleson	.06	.05	.02
248	Terry Forster	.08	.06	.03
249	Harold Baines	.15	.11	.06
250	Jesse Orosco	.08	.06	.03
251	Brad Gulden	.06	.05	.02
252	Dan Ford	.06	.05	.02
253	*Sid Bream*(FC)	.40	.30	.15
254	Pete Vuckovich	.08	.06	.03
255	Lonnie Smith	.08	.06	.03
256	Mike Stanton	.06	.05	.02
257	Brian Little (Bryan)	.06	.05	.02
258	Mike Brown	.06	.05	.02
259	Gary Allenson	.06	.05	.02
260	Dave Righetti	.20	.15	.08
261	Checklist 133-264	.06	.05	.02
262	*Greg Booker*(FC)	.12	.09	.05
263	Mel Hall	.08	.06	.03
264	Joe Sambito	.06	.05	.02
265	Juan Samuel(FC)	.50	.40	.20
266	Frank Viola	.20	.15	.08
267	*Henry Cotto*(FC)	.15	.11	.06
268	Chuck Tanner	.06	.05	.02
269	*Doug Baker*(FC)	.10	.08	.04
270	Dan Quisenberry	.10	.08	.04
271	1968 #1 Draft Pick (Tim Foli)	.08	.06	.03
272	1969 #1 Draft Pick (Jeff Burroughs)	.08	.06	.03
273	1974 #1 Draft Pick (Bill Almon)	.08	.06	.03
274	1976 #1 Draft Pick (Floyd Bannister)	.10	.08	.04
275	1977 #1 Draft Pick (Harold Baines)	.15	.11	.06
276	1978 #1 Draft Pick (Bob Horner)	.15	.11	.06
277	1979 #1 Draft Pick (Al Chambers)	.08	.06	.03
278	1980 #1 Draft Pick (Darryl Strawberry)	1.25	.90	.50
279	1981 #1 Draft Pick (Mike Moore)(FC)	.20	.15	.08
280	1982 #1 Draft Pick (*Shawon Dunston*)(FC)	3.00	2.25	1.25
281	1983 #1 Draft Pick (Tim Belcher)(FC)	2.00	1.50	.80
282	1984 #1 Draft Pick (*Shawn Abner*)(FC)	.60	.45	.25
283	Fran Mullins	.06	.05	.02
284	Marty Bystrom	.06	.05	.02
285	Dan Driessen	.08	.06	.03
286	Rudy Law	.06	.05	.02
287	Walt Terrell	.08	.06	.03
288	*Jeff Kunkel*(FC)	.10	.08	.04
289	Tom Underwood	.06	.05	.02
290	Cecil Cooper	.12	.09	.05
291	Bob Welch	.12	.09	.05
292	Brad Komminsk(FC)	.08	.06	.03
293	*Curt Young*(FC)	.35	.25	.14
294	*Tom Nieto*(FC)	.10	.08	.04
295	Joe Niekro	.10	.08	.04
296	Ricky Nelson	.06	.05	.02
297	Gary Lucas	.06	.05	.02
298	Marty Barrett	.15	.11	.06
299	Andy Hawkins	.08	.06	.03
300	Rod Carew	.40	.30	.15
301	John Montefusco	.06	.05	.02
302	Tim Corcoran	.06	.05	.02
303	*Mike Jeffcoat*	.08	.06	.03
304	Gary Gaetti	.25	.20	.10
305	Dale Berra	.06	.05	.02
306	Rick Reuschel	.10	.08	.04
307	Sparky Anderson	.08	.06	.03
308	John Wathan	.08	.06	.03
309	Mike Witt	.12	.09	.05
310	Manny Trillo	.08	.06	.03
311	Jim Gott	.06	.05	.02
312	Marc Hill	.06	.05	.02
313	Dave Schmidt	.06	.05	.02
314	Ron Oester	.06	.05	.02
315	Doug Sisk	.06	.05	.02
316	John Lowenstein	.06	.05	.02
317	*Jack Lazorko*(FC)	.10	.08	.04
318	Ted Simmons	.12	.09	.05
319	Jeff Jones	.06	.05	.02
320	Dale Murphy	.60	.45	.25
321	*Ricky Horton*	.30	.25	.12
322	Dave Stapleton	.06	.05	.02
323	Andy McGaffigan	.06	.05	.02
324	Bruce Bochy	.06	.05	.02
325	John Denny	.06	.05	.02
326	Kevin Bass	.10	.08	.04
327	Brook Jacoby	.30	.25	.12
328	Bob Shirley	.06	.05	.02
329	Ron Washington	.06	.05	.02
330	Leon Durham	.08	.06	.03

		MT	NR MT	EX
331	Bill Laskey	.06	.05	.02
332	Brian Harper	.06	.05	.02
333	Willie Hernandez	.08	.06	.03
334	Dick Howser	.06	.05	.02
335	Bruce Benedict	.06	.05	.02
336	Rance Mulliniks	.06	.05	.02
337	Billy Sample	.06	.05	.02
338	Britt Burns	.06	.05	.02
339	Danny Heep	.06	.05	.02
340	Robin Yount	.60	.45	.25
341	Floyd Rayford	.06	.05	.02
342	Ted Power	.06	.05	.02
343	Bill Russell	.08	.06	.03
344	Dave Henderson	.10	.08	.04
345	Charlie Lea	.06	.05	.02
346	*Terry Pendleton*(FC)	.70	.50	.30
347	Rick Langford	.06	.05	.02
348	Bob Boone	.08	.06	.03
349	Domingo Ramos	.06	.05	.02
350	Wade Boggs	3.50	2.75	1.50
351	Juan Agosto	.06	.05	.02
352	Joe Morgan	.30	.25	.12
353	Julio Solano	.06	.05	.02
354	Andre Robertson	.06	.05	.02
355	Bert Blyleven	.12	.09	.05
356	Dave Meier	.06	.05	.02
357	Rich Bordi	.06	.05	.02
358	Tony Pena	.10	.08	.04
359	Pat Sheridan	.06	.05	.02
360	Steve Carlton	.40	.30	.15
361	Alfredo Griffin	.08	.06	.03
362	Craig McMurtry	.06	.05	.02
363	Ron Hodges	.06	.05	.02
364	Richard Dotson	.10	.08	.04
365	Danny Ozark	.06	.05	.02
366	Todd Cruz	.06	.05	.02
367	Keefe Cato	.06	.05	.02
368	Dave Bergman	.06	.05	.02
369	*R.J. Reynolds*(FC)	.25	.20	.10
370	Bruce Sutter	.12	.09	.05
371	Mickey Rivers	.08	.06	.03
372	Roy Howell	.06	.05	.02
373	Mike Moore	.06	.05	.02
374	Brian Downing	.10	.08	.04
375	Jeff Reardon	.12	.09	.05
376	Jeff Newman	.06	.05	.02
377	Checklist 265-396	.06	.05	.02
378	Alan Wiggins	.06	.05	.02
379	Charles Hudson	.08	.06	.03
380	Ken Griffey	.10	.08	.04
381	Roy Smith	.06	.05	.02
382	Denny Walling	.06	.05	.02
383	Rick Lysander	.06	.05	.02
384	Jody Davis	.10	.08	.04
385	Jose DeLeon	.08	.06	.03
386	*Dan Gladden*(FC)	.30	.25	.12
387	*Buddy Biancalana*(FC)	.12	.09	.05
388	Bert Roberge	.06	.05	.02
389	1984 United States Baseball Team (Rod Dedeaux)	.06	.05	.02
390	1984 United States Baseball Team (Sid Akins)(FC)	.10	.08	.04
391	1984 United States Baseball Team (Flavio Alfaro)	.06	.05	.02
392	1984 United States Baseball Team (Don August)(FC)	.40	.30	.15
393	1984 United States Baseball Team (Scott Bankhead)(FC)	.90	.70	.35
394	1984 United States Baseball Team (Bob Caffrey)(FC)	.08	.06	.03
395	1984 United States Baseball Team (Mike Dunne)(FC)	.40	.30	.15
396	1984 United States Baseball Team (Gary Green)(FC)	.08	.06	.03
397	1984 United States Baseball Team (John Hoover)	.06	.05	.02
398	1984 United States Baseball Team (Shane Mack)(FC)	.40	.30	.15
399	1984 United States Baseball Team (John Marzano)(FC)	.20	.15	.08
400	1984 United States Baseball Team (Oddibe McDowell)(FC)	.80	.60	.30
401	1984 United States Baseball Team (Mark McGwire)(FC)	18.00	13.50	7.25
402	1984 United States Baseball Team (Pat Pacillo)(FC)	.20	.15	.08
403	1984 United States Baseball Team (Cory Snyder)(FC)	4.00	3.00	1.50
404	1984 United States Baseball Team (Billy Swift)(FC)	.30	.25	.12
405	Tom Veryzer	.06	.05	.02
406	Len Whitehouse	.06	.05	.02
407	Bobby Ramos	.06	.05	.02
408	Sid Monge	.06	.05	.02
409	Brad Wellman	.06	.05	.02
410	Bob Horner	.15	.11	.06
411	Bobby Cox	.06	.05	.02
412	Bud Black	.06	.05	.02
413	Vance Law	.08	.06	.03
414	Gary Ward	.08	.06	.03
415	Ron Darling	1.25	.90	.50
416	Wayne Gross	.06	.05	.02
417	*John Franco*(FC)	1.00	.70	.40
418	Ken Landreaux	.06	.05	.02
419	Mike Caldwell	.06	.05	.02
420	Andre Dawson	.30	.25	.12
421	Dave Rucker	.06	.05	.02
422	Carney Lansford	.10	.08	.04
423	Barry Bonnell	.06	.05	.02
424	*Al Nipper*(FC)	.15	.11	.06
425	Mike Hargrove	.06	.05	.02
426	Verne Ruhle	.06	.05	.02
427	Mario Ramirez	.06	.05	.02
428	Larry Andersen	.06	.05	.02
429	Rick Cerone	.06	.05	.02
430	Ron Davis	.06	.05	.02
431	U.L. Washington	.06	.05	.02
432	Thad Bosley	.06	.05	.02
433	Jim Morrison	.06	.05	.02
434	Gene Richards	.06	.05	.02
435	Dan Petry	.08	.06	.03
436	Willie Aikens	.06	.05	.02
437	Al Jones	.06	.05	.02
438	Joe Torre	.08	.06	.03

		MT	NR MT	EX
439	Junior Ortiz	.06	.05	.02
440	Fernando Valenzuela	.30	.25	.12
441	Duane Walker	.06	.05	.02
442	Ken Forsch	.06	.05	.02
443	George Wright	.06	.05	.02
444	Tony Phillips	.06	.05	.02
445	Tippy Martinez	.06	.05	.02
446	Jim Sundberg	.08	.06	.03
447	Jeff Lahti	.06	.05	.02
448	Derrel Thomas	.06	.05	.02
449	*Phil Bradley*	.80	.60	.30
450	Steve Garvey	.40	.30	.15
451	Bruce Hurst	.12	.09	.05
452	John Castino	.06	.05	.02
453	Tom Waddell	.06	.05	.02
454	Glenn Wilson	.08	.06	.03
455	Bob Knepper	.08	.06	.03
456	Tim Foli	.06	.05	.02
457	Cecilio Guante	.06	.05	.02
458	Randy Johnson	.06	.05	.02
459	Charlie Leibrandt	.08	.06	.03
460	Ryne Sandberg	1.00	.70	.40
461	Marty Castillo	.06	.05	.02
462	Gary Lavelle	.06	.05	.02
463	Dave Collins	.08	.06	.03
464	*Mike Mason*(FC)	.10	.08	.04
465	Bob Grich	.10	.08	.04
466	Tony LaRussa	.08	.06	.03
467	Ed Lynch	.06	.05	.02
468	Wayne Krenchicki	.06	.05	.02
469	Sammy Stewart	.06	.05	.02
470	Steve Sax	.20	.15	.08
471	Pete Ladd	.06	.05	.02
472	Jim Essian	.06	.05	.02
473	Tim Wallach	.12	.09	.05
474	Kurt Kepshire	.06	.05	.02
475	Andre Thornton	.10	.08	.04
476	*Jeff Stone*(FC)	.12	.09	.05
477	Bob Ojeda	.10	.08	.04
478	Kurt Bevacqua	.06	.05	.02
479	Mike Madden	.06	.05	.02
480	Lou Whitaker	.30	.25	.12
481	Dale Murray	.06	.05	.02
482	Harry Spilman	.06	.05	.02
483	Mike Smithson	.06	.05	.02
484	Larry Bowa	.10	.08	.04
485	Matt Young	.06	.05	.02
486	Steve Balboni	.08	.06	.03
487	*Frank Williams*	.15	.11	.06
488	Joel Skinner(FC)	.08	.06	.03
489	Bryan Clark	.06	.05	.02
490	Jason Thompson	.06	.05	.02
491	Rick Camp	.06	.05	.02
492	Dave Johnson	.08	.06	.03
493	*Orel Hershiser*(FC)	7.00	5.25	2.75
494	Rich Dauer	.06	.05	.02
495	Mario Soto	.08	.06	.03
496	Donnie Scott	.06	.05	.02
497	Gary Pettis	.15	.11	.06
498	Ed Romero	.06	.05	.02
499	Danny Cox(FC)	.20	.20	.10
500	Mike Schmidt	.60	.45	.25
501	Dan Schatzeder	.06	.05	.02
502	Rick Miller	.06	.05	.02
503	Tim Conroy	.06	.05	.02
504	Jerry Willard	.06	.05	.02
505	Jim Beattie	.06	.05	.02
506	*Franklin Stubbs*(FC)	.25	.20	.10
507	Ray Fontenot	.06	.05	.02
508	John Shelby	.08	.06	.03
509	Milt May	.06	.05	.02
510	Kent Hrbek	.25	.20	.10
511	Lee Smith	.10	.08	.04
512	Tom Brookens	.06	.05	.02
513	Lynn Jones	.06	.05	.02
514	Jeff Cornell	.06	.05	.02
515	Dave Concepcion	.12	.09	.05
516	Roy Lee Jackson	.06	.05	.02
517	Jerry Martin	.06	.05	.02
518	Chris Chambliss	.08	.06	.03
519	Doug Rader	.06	.05	.02
520	LaMarr Hoyt	.06	.05	.02
521	Rick Dempsey	.08	.06	.03
522	Paul Molitor	.15	.11	.06
523	Candy Maldonado	.10	.08	.04
524	Rob Wilfong	.06	.05	.02
525	Darrell Porter	.08	.06	.03
526	Dave Palmer	.06	.05	.02
527	Checklist 397-528	.06	.05	.02
528	Bill Krueger	.06	.05	.02
529	Rich Gedman	.10	.08	.04
530	Dave Dravecky	.08	.06	.03
531	Joe Lefebvre	.06	.05	.02
532	Frank DiPino	.06	.05	.02
533	Tony Bernazard	.06	.05	.02
534	Brian Dayett(FC)	.06	.05	.02
535	Pat Putnam	.06	.05	.02
536	*Kirby Puckett*(FC)	15.00	11.00	6.00
537	Don Robinson	.08	.06	.03
538	Keith Moreland	.08	.06	.03
539	Aurelio Lopez	.06	.05	.02
540	Claudell Washington	.08	.06	.03
541	Mark Davis	.06	.05	.02
542	Don Slaught	.06	.05	.02
543	Mike Squires	.06	.05	.02
544	Bruce Kison	.06	.05	.02
545	Lloyd Moseby	.10	.08	.04
546	Brent Gaff	.06	.05	.02
547	Pete Rose	.60	.45	.25
548	Larry Parrish	.10	.08	.04
549	Mike Scioscia	.08	.06	.03
550	Scott McGregor	.08	.06	.03
551	Andy Van Slyke	.35	.25	.14
552	Chris Codiroli	.06	.05	.02
553	Bob Clark	.06	.05	.02
554	Doug Flynn	.06	.05	.02
555	Bob Stanley	.06	.05	.02
556	Sixto Lezcano	.06	.05	.02
557	Len Barker	.08	.06	.03
558	Carmelo Martinez	.08	.06	.03
559	Jay Howell	.08	.06	.03
560	Bill Madlock	.12	.09	.05
561	Darryl Motley	.06	.05	.02
562	Houston Jimenez	.06	.05	.02

		MT	NR MT	EX
563	Dick Ruthven	.06	.05	.02
564	Alan Ashby	.06	.05	.02
565	Kirk Gibson	.35	.25	.14
566	Ed Vande Berg	.06	.05	.02
567	Joel Youngblood	.06	.05	.02
568	Cliff Johnson	.06	.05	.02
569	Ken Oberkfell	.06	.05	.02
570	Darryl Strawberry	3.00	2.25	1.25
571	Charlie Hough	.08	.06	.03
572	Tom Paciorek	.06	.05	.02
573	*Jay Tibbs*(FC)	.15	.11	.06
574	Joe Altobelli	.06	.05	.02
575	Pedro Guerrero	.25	.20	.10
576	Jaime Cocanower	.06	.05	.02
577	Chris Speier	.06	.05	.02
578	Terry Francona	.06	.05	.02
579	*Ron Romanick*	.10	.08	.04
580	Dwight Evans	.12	.09	.05
581	Mark Wagner	.06	.05	.02
582	Ken Phelps(FC)	.20	.15	.08
583	Bobby Brown	.06	.05	.02
584	Kevin Gross	.10	.08	.04
585	Butch Wynegar	.06	.05	.02
586	Bill Scherrer	.06	.05	.02
587	Doug Frobel	.06	.05	.02
588	Bobby Castillo	.06	.05	.02
589	Bob Dernier	.06	.05	.02
590	Ray Knight	.10	.08	.04
591	Larry Herndon	.08	.06	.03
592	*Jeff Robinson*	.30	.25	.12
593	Rick Leach	.06	.05	.02
594	Curt Wilkerson(FC)	.08	.06	.03
595	Larry Gura	.06	.05	.02
596	Jerry Hairston	.06	.05	.02
597	Brad Lesley	.06	.05	.02
598	Jose Oquendo	.06	.05	.02
599	Storm Davis	.10	.08	.04
600	Pete Rose	1.00	.70	.40
601	Tom Lasorda	.10	.08	.04
602	*Jeff Dedmon*	.12	.09	.05
603	Rick Manning	.06	.05	.02
604	Daryl Sconiers	.06	.05	.02
605	Ozzie Smith	.15	.11	.06
606	Rich Gale	.06	.05	.02
607	Bill Almon	.06	.05	.02
608	Craig Lefferts	.08	.06	.03
609	Broderick Perkins	.06	.05	.02
610	Jack Morris	.25	.20	.10
611	Ozzie Virgil	.06	.05	.02
612	Mike Armstrong	.06	.05	.02
613	Terry Puhl	.06	.05	.02
614	Al Williams	.06	.05	.02
615	Marvell Wynne	.06	.05	.02
616	Scott Sanderson	.06	.05	.02
617	Willie Wilson	.12	.09	.05
618	Pete Falcone	.06	.05	.02
619	Jeff Leonard	.10	.08	.04
620	*Dwight Gooden*	9.00	6.75	3.50
621	Marvis Foley	.06	.05	.02
622	Luis Leal	.06	.05	.02
623	Greg Walker	.12	.09	.05
624	Benny Ayala	.06	.05	.02
625	*Mark Langston*	3.50	2.75	1.50
626	German Rivera	.06	.05	.02
627	*Eric Davis*(FC)	15.00	11.00	6.00
628	Rene Lachemann	.06	.05	.02
629	Dick Schofield	.12	.09	.05
630	Tim Raines	.35	.25	.14
631	Bob Forsch	.08	.06	.03
632	Bruce Bochte	.06	.05	.02
633	Glenn Hoffman	.06	.05	.02
634	Bill Dawley	.06	.05	.02
635	Terry Kennedy	.08	.06	.03
636	Shane Rawley	.10	.08	.04
637	Brett Butler	.08	.06	.03
638	*Mike Pagliarulo*(FC)	.80	.60	.30
639	Ed Hodge	.06	.05	.02
640	Steve Henderson	.06	.05	.02
641	Rod Scurry	.06	.05	.02
642	Dave Owen	.06	.05	.02
643	Johnny Grubb	.06	.05	.02
644	Mark Huismann(FC)	.06	.05	.02
645	Damaso Garcia	.06	.05	.02
646	Scot Thompson	.06	.05	.02
647	Rafael Ramirez	.06	.05	.02
648	Bob Jones	.06	.05	.02
649	Sid Fernandez(FC)	.90	.70	.35
650	Greg Luzinski	.10	.08	.04
651	Jeff Russell	.08	.06	.03
652	Joe Nolan	.06	.05	.02
653	Mark Brouhard	.06	.05	.02
654	Dave Anderson	.06	.05	.02
655	Joaquin Andujar	.08	.06	.03
656	Chuck Cottier	.06	.05	.02
657	Jim Slaton	.06	.05	.02
658	Mike Stenhouse	.06	.05	.02
659	Checklist 529-660	.06	.05	.02
660	Tony Gwynn	.80	.60	.30
661	Steve Crawford	.06	.05	.02
662	Mike Heath	.06	.05	.02
663	Luis Aguayo	.06	.05	.02
664	*Steve Farr*(FC)	.30	.25	.12
665	Don Mattingly	10.00	7.50	4.00
666	Mike LaCoss	.06	.05	.02
667	Dave Engle	.06	.05	.02
668	Steve Trout	.06	.05	.02
669	Lee Lacy	.06	.05	.02
670	Tom Seaver	.30	.25	.12
671	Dane Iorg	.06	.05	.02
672	Juan Berenguer	.06	.05	.02
673	Buck Martinez	.06	.05	.02
674	Atlee Hammaker	.06	.05	.02
675	Tony Perez	.15	.11	.06
676	*Albert Hall*(FC)	.15	.11	.06
677	Wally Backman	.08	.06	.03
678	Joey McLaughlin	.06	.05	.02
679	Bob Kearney	.06	.05	.02
680	Jerry Reuss	.08	.06	.03
681	Ben Oglivie	.08	.06	.03
682	Doug Corbett	.06	.05	.02
683	Whitey Herzog	.08	.06	.03
684	Bill Doran	.12	.09	.05
685	Bill Caudill	.06	.05	.02
686	Mike Easler	.08	.06	.03

		MT	NR MT	EX
687	Bill Gullickson	.06	.05	.02
688	Len Matuszek	.06	.05	.02
689	Luis DeLeon	.06	.05	.02
690	Alan Trammell	.35	.25	.14
691	Dennis Rasmussen(FC)	.30	.25	.12
692	Randy Bush	.06	.05	.02
693	Tim Stoddard	.06	.05	.02
694	Joe Carter(FC)	2.75	2.00	1.00
695	Rick Rhoden	.10	.08	.04
696	John Rabb	.06	.05	.02
697	Onix Concepcion	.06	.05	.02
698	Jorge Bell	.40	.30	.15
699	Donnie Moore	.06	.05	.02
700	Eddie Murray	.50	.40	.20
701	Eddie Murray AS	.30	.25	.12
702	Damaso Garcia AS	.08	.06	.03
703	George Brett AS	.35	.25	.14
704	Cal Ripken AS	.30	.25	.12
705	Dave Winfield AS	.20	.15	.08
706	Rickey Henderson AS	.30	.25	.12
707	Tony Armas AS	.08	.06	.03
708	Lance Parrish AS	.15	.11	.06
709	Mike Boddicker AS	.08	.06	.03
710	Frank Viola AS	.12	.09	.05
711	Dan Quisenberry AS	.10	.08	.04
712	Keith Hernandez AS	.20	.15	.08
713	Ryne Sandberg AS	.20	.15	.08
714	Mike Schmidt AS	.30	.25	.12
715	Ozzie Smith AS	.12	.09	.05
716	Dale Murphy AS	.35	.25	.14
717	Tony Gwynn AS	.35	.25	.14
718	Jeff Leonard AS	.10	.08	.04
719	Gary Carter AS	.20	.15	.08
720	Rick Sutcliffe AS	.12	.09	.05
721	Bob Knepper AS	.08	.06	.03
722	Bruce Sutter AS	.10	.08	.04
723	Dave Stewart	.12	.09	.05
724	Oscar Gamble	.08	.06	.03
725	Floyd Bannister	.10	.08	.04
726	Al Bumbry	.08	.06	.03
727	Frank Pastore	.06	.05	.02
728	Bob Bailor	.06	.05	.02
729	Don Sutton	.30	.25	.12
730	Dave Kingman	.15	.11	.06
731	Neil Allen	.06	.05	.02
732	John McNamara	.06	.05	.02
733	Tony Scott	.06	.05	.02
734	John Henry Johnson	.06	.05	.02
735	Garry Templeton	.08	.06	.03
736	Jerry Mumphrey	.06	.05	.02
737	Bo Diaz	.08	.06	.03
738	Omar Moreno	.06	.05	.02
739	Ernie Camacho	.06	.05	.02
740	Jack Clark	.20	.15	.08
741	John Butcher	.06	.05	.02
742	Ron Hassey	.06	.05	.02
743	Frank White	.10	.08	.04
744	Doug Bair	.06	.05	.02
745	Buddy Bell	.12	.09	.05
746	Jim Clancy	.08	.06	.03
747	Alex Trevino	.06	.05	.02
748	Lee Mazzilli	.08	.06	.03
749	Julio Cruz	.06	.05	.02
750	Rollie Fingers	.20	.15	.08
751	Kelvin Chapman	.06	.05	.02
752	Bob Owchinko	.06	.05	.02
753	Greg Brock	.08	.06	.03
754	Larry Milbourne	.06	.05	.02
755	Ken Singleton	.08	.06	.03
756	Rob Picciolo	.06	.05	.02
757	Willie McGee	.30	.25	.12
758	Ray Burris	.06	.05	.02
759	Jim Fanning	.06	.05	.02
760	Nolan Ryan	1.00	.70	.40
761	Jerry Remy	.06	.05	.02
762	Eddie Whitson	.06	.05	.02
763	Kiko Garcia	.06	.05	.02
764	Jamie Easterly	.06	.05	.02
765	Willie Randolph	.10	.08	.04
766	Paul Mirabella	.06	.05	.02
767	Darrell Brown	.06	.05	.02
768	Ron Cey	.10	.08	.04
769	Joe Cowley	.06	.05	.02
770	Carlton Fisk	.40	.30	.15
771	Geoff Zahn	.06	.05	.02
772	Johnnie LeMaster	.06	.05	.02
773	Hal McRae	.10	.08	.04
774	Dennis Lamp	.06	.05	.02
775	Mookie Wilson	.10	.08	.04
776	Jerry Royster	.06	.05	.02
777	Ned Yost	.06	.05	.02
778	Mike Davis	.08	.06	.03
779	Nick Esasky	.08	.06	.03
780	Mike Flanagan	.10	.08	.04
781	Jim Gantner	.08	.06	.03
782	Tom Niedenfuer	.08	.06	.03
783	Mike Jorgensen	.06	.05	.02
784	Checklist 661-792	.06	.05	.02
785	Tony Armas	.10	.08	.04
786	Enos Cabell	.06	.05	.02
787	Jim Wohlford	.06	.05	.02
788	Steve Comer	.06	.05	.02
789	Luis Salazar	.06	.05	.02
790	Ron Guidry	.25	.20	.10
791	Ivan DeJesus	.06	.05	.02
792	Darrell Evans	.12	.09	.05

1985 Topps All-Star Glossy Set of 22

This was the second straight year for this set of 22 cards featuring the starting players, the honorary captains and the managers in the All-Star Game. The set is virtually identical to that of the previous year in design with a color photo, All-Star banner, league emblem, and player's name and position on the front. What makes the cards special is their high gloss finish. The cards

were available as inserts in Topps rack packs. With their combination of attractive appearance and big-name stars, these 2-1/2" by 3-1/2" cards will probably continue to enjoy a great deal of popularity.

		MT	NR MT	EX
	Complete Set:	6.00	4.50	2.50
	Common Player:	.20	.15	.08
1	Paul Owens	.20	.15	.08
2	Steve Garvey	.50	.40	.20
3	Ryne Sandberg	.40	.30	.15
4	Mike Schmidt	.60	.45	.25
5	Ozzie Smith	.30	.25	.12
6	Tony Gwynn	.60	.45	.25
7	Dale Murphy	.80	.60	.30
8	Darryl Strawberry	1.00	.70	.40
9	Gary Carter	.50	.40	.20
10	Charlie Lea	.20	.15	.08
11	Willie McCovey	.40	.30	.15
12	Joe Altobelli	.20	.15	.08
13	Rod Carew	.50	.40	.20
14	Lou Whitaker	.30	.25	.12
15	George Brett	.80	.60	.30
16	Cal Ripken	.60	.45	.25
17	Dave Winfield	.50	.40	.20
18	Chet Lemon	.20	.15	.08
19	Reggie Jackson	.60	.45	.25
20	Lance Parrish	.30	.25	.12
21	Dave Stieb	.25	.20	.10
22	Hank Greenberg	.20	.15	.08

1985 Topps All-Star Glossy Set of 40

Similar to previous years' glossy sets, the 1985 All-Star "Collector's Edition" glossy set of 40 could be obtained through the mail in eight five-card subsets. To obtain the 2-1/2" by 3-1/2" cards, collectors had to accumulate sweepstakes insert cards from Topps packs, and pay 75¢ postage and handling. Under the circumstances, the complete set of 40 cards was not inexpensive. They are however, rather attractive and popular cards, and the set size enabled Topps to include some players who didn't make their 22-card set.

		MT	NR MT	EX
	Complete Set:	15.00	11.00	6.00
	Common Player:	.15	.11	.06
1	Dale Murphy	1.00	.70	.40
2	Jesse Orosco	.15	.11	.06
3	Bob Brenly	.15	.11	.06
4	Mike Boddicker	.15	.11	.06
5	Dave Kingman	.25	.20	.10
6	Jim Rice	.50	.40	.20
7	Frank Viola	.30	.25	.12
8	Alvin Davis	.35	.25	.14
9	Rick Sutcliffe	.20	.15	.08
10	Pete Rose	1.25	.90	.50
11	Leon Durham	.15	.11	.06
12	Joaquin Andujar	.15	.11	.06
13	Keith Hernandez	.40	.30	.15
14	Dave Winfield	.60	.45	.25
15	Reggie Jackson	.70	.50	.30
16	Alan Trammell	.35	.25	.14
17	Bert Blyleven	.20	.15	.08
18	Tony Armas	.15	.11	.06
19	Rich Gossage	.25	.20	.10
20	Jose Cruz	.15	.11	.06
21	Ryne Sandberg	.40	.30	.15
22	Bruce Sutter	.20	.15	.08

		MT	NR MT	EX
23	Mike Schmidt	1.00	.70	.40
24	Cal Ripken	.70	.50	.30
25	Dan Petry	.15	.11	.06
26	Jack Morris	.30	.25	.12
27	Don Mattingly	3.50	2.75	1.50
28	Eddie Murray	.60	.45	.25
29	Tony Gwynn	.60	.45	.25
30	Charlie Lea	.15	.11	.06
31	Juan Samuel	.30	.25	.12
32	Phil Niekro	.35	.25	.14
33	Alejandro Pena	.15	.11	.06
34	Harold Baines	.25	.20	.10
35	Dan Quisenberry	.15	.11	.06
36	Gary Carter	.50	.40	.20
37	Mario Soto	.15	.11	.06
38	Dwight Gooden	2.50	2.00	1.00
39	Tom Brunansky	.20	.15	.08
40	Dave Stieb	.20	.15	.08

1985 Topps All-Time Record Holders

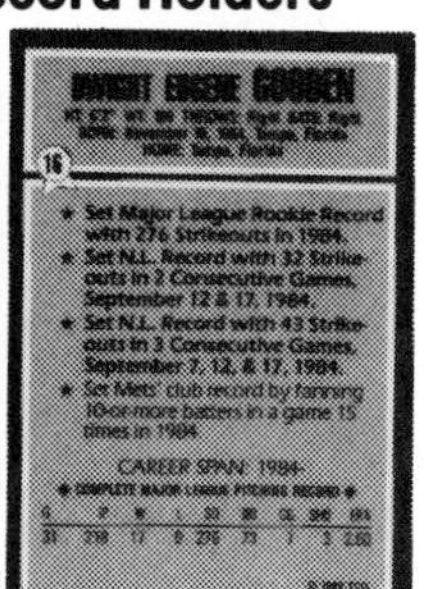

This 44-card boxed set was produced by Topps for the Woolworth's chain stores. Many hobbyists refer to this as the "Woolworth's" set, but that name does not appear anywhere on the cards. Featuring a combination of black and white and color photos of baseball record holders from all eras, the set is in the standard 2-1/2" by 3-1/2" format. Backs, printed in blue and orange, give career details and personal data. Because it combined old-timers with current players, the set did not achieve a great deal of collector popularity.

		MT	NR MT	EX
	Complete Set:	5.00	3.75	2.00
	Common Player:	.05	.04	.02
1	Hank Aaron	.25	.20	.10
2	Grover Alexander	.10	.08	.04
3	Ernie Banks	.12	.09	.05
4	Yogi Berra	.15	.11	.06
5	Lou Brock	.12	.09	.05
6	Steve Carlton	.12	.09	.05
7	Jack Chesbro	.07	.05	.03
8	Ty Cobb	.30	.25	.12
9	Sam Crawford	.07	.05	.03
10	Rollie Fingers	.07	.05	.03
11	Whitey Ford	.12	.09	.05
12	Johnny Frederick	.05	.04	.02
13	Frankie Frisch	.07	.05	.03
14	Lou Gehrig	.30	.25	.12
15	Jim Gentile	.05	.04	.02
16	Dwight Gooden	.60	.45	.25
17	Rickey Henderson	.15	.11	.06
18	Rogers Hornsby	.12	.09	.05
19	Frank Howard	.07	.05	.03
20	Cliff Johnson	.05	.04	.02
21	Walter Johnson	.15	.11	.06
22	Hub Leonard	.05	.04	.02
23	Mickey Mantle	1.00	.70	.40
24	Roger Maris	.12	.09	.05
25	Christy Mathewson	.12	.09	.05
26	Willie Mays	.20	.15	.08
27	Stan Musial	.20	.15	.08
28	Dan Quisenberry	.05	.04	.02
29	Frank Robinson	.12	.09	.05
30	Pete Rose	.40	.30	.15
31	Babe Ruth	.60	.45	.25
32	Nolan Ryan	.12	.09	.05
33	George Sisler	.10	.08	.04
34	Tris Speaker	.10	.08	.04
35	Ed Walsh	.07	.05	.03
36	Lloyd Waner	.07	.05	.03
37	Earl Webb	.05	.04	.02
38	Ted Williams	.30	.25	.12
39	Maury Wills	.07	.05	.03
40	Hack Wilson	.07	.05	.03
41	Owen Wilson	.05	.04	.02
42	Willie Wilson	.07	.05	.03
43	Rudy York	.05	.04	.02
44	Cy Young	.12	.09	.05

1985 Topps Gallery of Champions

This second annual aluminum, bronze, and silver miniature issues honors 12 award winners from the previous season (MVP, Cy Young, Rookie of Year, Fireman, etc.). Each mini is an exact reproduction, at one-quarter scale of the player's

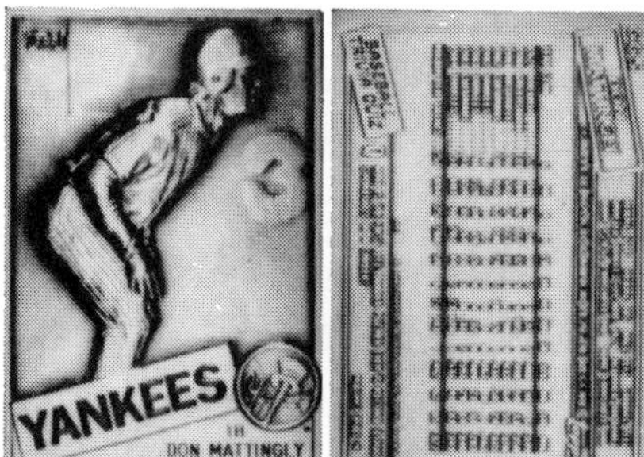

official Topps baseball card, both front and back. The bronze and silver sets were issued in a specially-designed velvet-like case. Aluminum sets came cello-wrapped. A Dwight Gooden pewter replica was given as a premium to dealers who bought bronze and silver sets (value $75). A Pete Rose bronze was issued as a premium to dealers purchasing cases of 1985 Topps Traded sets (value $12).

	MT	NR MT	EX
Complete Aluminum Set:	30.00	22.00	12.00
Complete Bronze Set:	175.00	131.00	70.00
Complete Silver Set:	600.00	450.00	240.00
(1a) Tony Armas (aluminum)	.70	.50	.30
(1b) Tony Armas (bronze)	7.50	5.75	3.00
(1c) Tony Armas (silver)	20.00	15.00	8.00
(2a) Alvin Davis (aluminum)	1.00	.70	.40
(2b) Alvin Davis (bronze)	10.00	7.50	4.00
(2c) Alvin Davis (silver)	30.00	22.00	12.00
(3a) Dwight Gooden (aluminum)	3.00	2.25	1.25
(3b) Dwight Gooden (bronze)	25.00	18.50	10.00
(3c) Dwight Gooden (silver)	125.00	94.00	50.00
(4a) Tony Gwynn (aluminum)	1.25	.90	.50
(4b) Tony Gwynn (bronze)	12.00	9.00	4.75
(4c) Tony Gwynn (silver)	50.00	37.00	20.00
(5a) Willie Hernandez (aluminum)	.70	.50	.30
(5b) Willie Hernandez (bronze)	7.50	5.75	3.00
(5c) Willie Hernandez (silver)	20.00	15.00	8.00
(6a) Don Mattingly (aluminum)	8.00	6.00	3.25
(6b) Don Mattingly (bronze)	50.00	37.00	20.00
(6c) Don Mattingly (silver)	200.00	150.00	80.00
(7a) Dale Murphy (aluminum)	1.50	1.25	.60
(7b) Dale Murphy (bronze)	15.00	11.00	6.00
(7c) Dale Murphy (silver)	80.00	60.00	32.00
(8a) Dan Quisenberry (aluminum)	.70	.50	.30
(8b) Dan Quisenberry (bronze)	7.50	5.75	3.00
(8c) Dan Quisenberry (silver)	20.00	15.00	8.00
(9a) Ryne Sandberg (aluminum)	1.25	.90	.50
(9b) Ryne Sandberg (bronze)	12.50	9.50	5.00
(9c) Ryne Sandberg (silver)	50.00	37.00	20.00
(10a) Mike Schmidt (aluminum)	1.50	1.25	.60
(10b) Mike Schmidt (bronze)	15.00	11.00	6.00
(10c) Mike Schmidt (silver)	80.00	60.00	32.00
(11a) Rick Sutcliffe (aluminum)	.70	.50	.30
(11b) Rick Sutcliffe (bronze)	7.50	5.75	3.00
(11c) Rick Sutcliffe (silver)	20.00	15.00	8.00
(12a) Bruce Sutter (aluminum)	.70	.50	.30
(12b) Bruce Sutter (bronze)	7.50	5.75	3.00
(12c) Bruce Sutter (silver)	20.00	15.00	8.00

1985 Topps Rub Downs

Similar in size and design to the Rub Downs of the previous year, the 1985 set again consisted of 32 unnumbered sheets featuring 112 different players. The set was sold by Topps as a separate issue.

	MT	NR MT	EX
Complete Set:	8.00	6.00	3.25
Common Player:	.10	.08	.04
(1) Tony Armas, Harold Baines, Lonnie Smith	.10	.08	.04
(2) Don Baylor, George Hendrick, Ron Kittle, Johnnie LeMaster	.10	.08	.04
(3) Buddy Bell, Tony Gwynn, Lloyd Moseby	.25	.20	.10
(4) Bruce Benedict, Atlee Hammaker, Frank White	.10	.08	.04
(5) Mike Boddicker, Rod Carew, Carlton Fisk, Johnny Ray	.25	.20	.10
(6) Wade Boggs, Rick Dempsey, Keith Hernandez	.60	.45	.25
(7) George Brett, Andre Dawson, Paul Molitor, Alan Wiggins	.30	.25	.12
(8) Tom Brunansky, Pedro Guerrero, Darryl Strawberry	.40	.30	.15
(9) Bill Buckner, Tim Raines, Ryne Sandberg, Mike Schmidt	.30	.25	.12
(10) Steve Carlton, Bob Horner, Dan Quisenberry	.25	.20	.10
(11) Gary Carter, Phil Garner, Ron Guidry	.25	.20	.10
(12) Jack Clark, Damaso Garcia, Hal McRae, Lance Parrish	.20	.15	.08
(13) Dave Concepcion, Cecil Cooper, Fred Lynn, Jesse Orosco	.15	.11	.06
(14) Jose Cruz, Jack Morris, Jim Rice, Rick Sutcliffe	.20	.15	.08
(15) Alvin Davis, Steve Kemp, Greg Luzinski, Kent Tekulve	.20	.15	.08
(16) Ron Davis, Kent Hrbek, Juan Samuel	.20	.15	.08
(17) John Denny, Carney Lansford, Mario Soto, Lou Whitaker	.15	.11	.06
(18) Leon Durham, Willie Hernandez, Steve Sax	.15	.11	.06
(19) Dwight Evans, Julio Franco, Dwight Gooden	.40	.30	.15
(20) George Foster, Gary Gaetti, Bobby Grich, Gary Redus	.15	.11	.06
(21) Steve Garvey, Jerry Remy, Bill Russell, George Wright	.20	.15	.08
(22) Kirk Gibson, Rich Gossage, Don Mattingly, Dave Stieb	.90	.70	.35
(23) Moose Haas, Bruce Sutter, Dickie Thon, Andre Thornton	.10	.08	.04
(24) Rickey Henderson, Dave Righetti, Pete Rose	.70	.50	.30
(25) Steve Henderson, Bill Madlock, Alan Trammell	.15	.11	.06
(26) LaMarr Hoyt, Larry Parrish, Nolan Ryan	.25	.20	.10
(27) Reggie Jackson, Eric Show, Jason Thompson	.30	.25	.12
(28) Terry Kennedy, Eddie Murray, Tom Seaver, Ozzie Smith	.25	.20	.10
(29) Mark Langston, Ben Oglivie, Darrell Porter	.15	.11	.06
(30) Jeff Leonard, Gary Matthews, Dale Murphy, Dave Winfield	.30	.25	.12
(31) Craig McMurtry, Cal Ripken, Steve Rogers, Willie Upshaw	.25	.20	.10
(32) Tony Pena, Fernando Valenzuela, Robin Yount	.20	.15	.08

1985 Topps Stickers

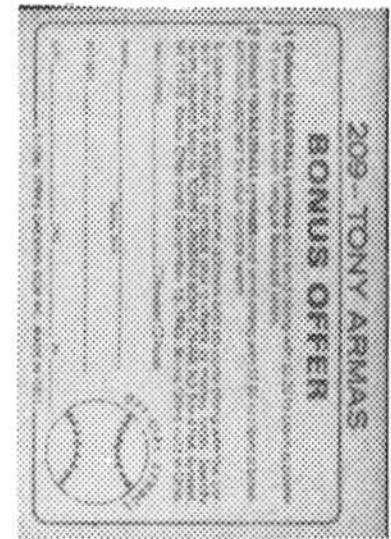

Topps went to a larger size for its stickers in 1985. Each of the 376 stickers measures 2-1/8" by 3" and is numbered on both the front and the back. The backs contain either an offer to obtain an autographed team ball or a poster. An album was also available.

		MT	NR MT	EX
	Complete Set:	16.00	12.00	6.50
	Common Player:	.03	.02	.01
	Sticker Album:	.80	.60	.30
1	Steve Garvey	.25	.20	.10
2	Steve Garvey	.25	.20	.10
3	Dwight Gooden	.25	.20	.10
4	Dwight Gooden	.25	.20	.10
5	Joe Morgan	.10	.08	.04
6	Joe Morgan	.10	.08	.04
7	Don Sutton	.10	.08	.04
8	Don Sutton	.10	.08	.04
9	1984 A.L. Championships (Jack Morris)	.06	.05	.02
10	1984 A.L. Championships (Milt Wilcox)	.03	.02	.01
11	1984 A.L. Championships (Kirk Gibson)	.08	.06	.03
12	1984 N.L. Championships (Gary Matthews)	.04	.03	.02
13	1984 N.L. Championships (Steve Garvey)	.10	.08	.04
14	1984 N.L. Championships (Steve Garvey)	.15	.11	.06
15	1984 World Series (Jack Morris)	.06	.05	.02
16	1984 World Series (Kurt Bevacqua)	.03	.02	.01

		MT	NR MT	EX
17	1984 World Series (Milt Wilcox)	.03	.02	.01
18	1984 World Series (Alan Trammell)	.08	.06	.03
19	1984 World Series (Kirk Gibson)	.08	.06	.03
20	1984 World Series (Alan Trammell)	.12	.09	.05
21	1984 World Series (Chet Lemon)	.03	.02	.01
22	Dale Murphy	.25	.20	.10
23	Steve Bedrosian	.10	.08	.04
24	Bob Horner	.10	.08	.04
25	Claudell Washington	.06	.05	.02
26	Rick Mahler	.06	.05	.02
27	Rafael Ramirez	.04	.03	.02
28	Craig McMurtry	.04	.03	.02
29	Chris Chambliss	.04	.03	.02
30	Alex Trevino	.03	.02	.01
31	Bruce Benedict	.04	.03	.02
32	Ken Oberkfell	.03	.02	.01
33	Glenn Hubbard	.04	.03	.02
34	Ryne Sandberg	.15	.11	.06
35	Rick Sutcliffe	.08	.06	.03
36	Leon Durham	.06	.05	.02
37	Jody Davis	.06	.05	.02
38	Bob Dernier	.04	.03	.02
39	Keith Moreland	.06	.05	.02
40	Scott Sanderson	.04	.03	.02
41	Lee Smith	.06	.05	.02
42	Ron Cey	.06	.05	.02
43	Steve Trout	.06	.05	.02
44	Gary Matthews	.06	.05	.02
45	Larry Bowa	.04	.03	.02
46	Mario Soto	.06	.05	.02
47	Dave Parker	.12	.09	.05
48	Dave Concepcion	.06	.05	.02
49	Gary Redus	.06	.05	.02
50	Ted Power	.06	.05	.02
51	Nick Esasky	.04	.03	.02
52	Duane Walker	.06	.05	.02
53	Eddie Milner	.03	.02	.01
54	Ron Oester	.03	.02	.01
55	Cesar Cedeno	.04	.03	.02
56	Joe Price	.03	.02	.01
57	Pete Rose	.20	.15	.08
58	Nolan Ryan	.15	.11	.06
59	Jose Cruz	.06	.05	.02
60	Jerry Mumphrey	.04	.03	.02
61	Enos Cabell	.03	.02	.01
62	Bob Knepper	.04	.03	.02
63	Dickie Thon	.04	.03	.02
64	Phil Garner	.04	.03	.02
65	Craig Reynolds	.06	.05	.02
66	Frank DiPino	.03	.02	.01
67	Terry Puhl	.03	.02	.01
68	Bill Doran	.06	.05	.02
69	Joe Niekro	.04	.03	.02
70	Pedro Guerrero	.12	.09	.05
71	Fernando Valenzuela	.15	.11	.06
72	Mike Marshall	.08	.06	.03
73	Alejandro Pena	.04	.03	.02
74	Orel Hershiser	.10	.08	.04
75	Ken Landreaux	.06	.05	.02
76	Bill Russell	.06	.05	.02
77	Steve Sax	.06	.05	.02
78	Rick Honeycutt	.03	.02	.01
79	Mike Scioscia	.03	.02	.01
80	Tom Niedenfuer	.06	.05	.02
81	Candy Maldonado	.03	.02	.01
82	Tim Raines	.15	.11	.06
83	Gary Carter	.20	.15	.08
84	Charlie Lea	.03	.02	.01
85	Jeff Reardon	.08	.06	.03
86	Andre Dawson	.06	.05	.02
87	Tim Wallach	.04	.03	.02
88	Terry Francona	.04	.03	.02
89	Steve Rogers	.03	.02	.01
90	Bryn Smith	.03	.02	.01
91	Bill Gullickson	.04	.03	.02
92	Dan Driessen	.03	.02	.01
93	Doug Flynn	.03	.02	.01
94	Mike Schmidt	.20	.15	.08
95	Tony Armas	.30	.25	.12
96	Dale Murphy	.15	.11	.06
97	Rick Sutcliffe	.10	.08	.04
98	Keith Hernandez	.12	.09	.05
99	George Foster	.08	.06	.03
100	Darryl Strawberry	.30	.25	.12
101	Jesse Orosco	.04	.03	.02
102	Mookie Wilson	.04	.03	.02
103	Doug Sisk	.03	.02	.01
104	Hubie Brooks	.06	.05	.02
105	Ron Darling	.04	.03	.02
106	Wally Backman	.04	.03	.02
107	Dwight Gooden	.15	.11	.06
108	Mike Fitzgerald	.04	.03	.02
109	Walt Terrell	.03	.02	.01
110	Ozzie Virgil	.04	.03	.02
111	Mike Schmidt	.25	.20	.10
112	Steve Carlton	.15	.11	.06
113	Al Holland	.03	.02	.01
114	Juan Samuel	.06	.05	.02
115	Von Hayes	.04	.03	.02
116	Jeff Stone	.06	.05	.02
117	Jerry Koosman	.04	.03	.02
118	Al Oliver	.04	.03	.02
119	John Denny	.03	.02	.01
120	Charles Hudson	.03	.02	.01
121	Garry Maddox	.06	.05	.02
122	Bill Madlock	.06	.05	.02
123	John Candelaria	.06	.05	.02
124	Tony Pena	.06	.05	.02
125	Jason Thompson	.03	.02	.01
126	Lee Lacy	.04	.03	.02
127	Rick Rhoden	.06	.05	.02
128	Doug Frobel	.06	.05	.02
129	Kent Tekulve	.04	.03	.02
130	Johnny Ray	.04	.03	.02
131	Marvell Wynne	.08	.06	.03
132	Larry McWilliams	.03	.02	.01
133	Dale Berra	.03	.02	.01
134	George Hendrick	.06	.05	.02
135	Bruce Sutter	.08	.06	.03

		MT	NR MT	EX
136	Joaquin Andujar	.04	.03	.02
137	Ozzie Smith	.10	.08	.04
138	Andy Van Slyke	.04	.03	.02
139	Lonnie Smith	.06	.05	.02
140	Darrell Porter	.03	.02	.01
141	Willie McGee	.06	.05	.02
142	Tom Herr	.04	.03	.02
143	Dave LaPoint	.03	.02	.01
144	Neil Allen	.04	.03	.02
145	David Green	.03	.02	.01
146	Tony Gwynn	.20	.15	.08
147	Rich Gossage	.12	.09	.05
148	Terry Kennedy	.04	.03	.02
149	Steve Garvey	.15	.11	.06
150	Alan Wiggins	.03	.02	.01
151	Garry Templeton	.08	.06	.03
152	Ed Whitson	.04	.03	.02
153	Tim Lollar	.03	.02	.01
154	Dave Dravecky	.04	.03	.02
155	Graig Nettles	.04	.03	.02
156	Eric Show	.03	.02	.01
157	Carmelo Martinez	.03	.02	.01
158	Bob Brenly	.03	.02	.01
159	Gary Lavelle	.03	.02	.01
160	Jack Clark	.10	.08	.04
161	Jeff Leonard	.04	.03	.02
162	Chili Davis	.06	.05	.02
163	Mike Krukow	.03	.02	.01
164	Johnnie LeMaster	.03	.02	.01
165	Atlee Hammaker	.03	.02	.01
166	Dan Gladden	.06	.05	.02
167	Greg Minton	.03	.02	.01
168	Joel Youngblood	.03	.02	.01
169	Frank Williams	.04	.03	.02
170	Tony Gwynn	.20	.15	.08
171	Don Mattingly	.30	.25	.12
172	Bruce Sutter	.15	.11	.06
173	Dan Quisenberry	.10	.08	.04
174	Tony Gwynn	.40	.30	.15
175	Ryne Sandberg	.35	.25	.14
176	Steve Garvey	.30	.25	.12
177	Dale Murphy	.40	.30	.15
178	Mike Schmidt	.40	.30	.15
179	Darryl Strawberry	.50	.40	.20
180	Gary Carter	.30	.25	.12
181	Ozzie Smith	.20	.15	.08
182	Charlie Lea	.15	.11	.06
183	Lou Whitaker	.25	.20	.10
184	Rod Carew	.30	.25	.12
185	Cal Ripken	.40	.30	.15
186	Dave Winfield	.30	.25	.12
187	Reggie Jackson	.40	.30	.15
188	George Brett	.40	.30	.15
189	Lance Parrish	.25	.20	.10
190	Chet Lemon	.15	.11	.06
191	Dave Stieb	.15	.11	.06
192	Gary Carter	.20	.15	.08
193	Mike Schmidt	.30	.25	.12
194	Tony Armas	.15	.11	.06
195	Mike Witt	.10	.08	.04
196	Eddie Murray	.20	.15	.08
197	Cal Ripken	.20	.15	.08
198	Scott McGregor	.04	.03	.02
199	Rick Dempsey	.04	.03	.02
200	Tippy Martinez	.08	.06	.03
201	Ken Singleton	.04	.03	.02
202	Mike Boddicker	.06	.05	.02
203	Rich Dauer	.03	.02	.01
204	John Shelby	.04	.03	.02
205	Al Bumbry	.04	.03	.02
206	John Lowenstein	.04	.03	.02
207	Mike Flanagan	.04	.03	.02
209	Tony Armas	.04	.03	.02
210	Wade Boggs	.60	.45	.25
211	Bruce Hurst	.06	.05	.02
212	Dwight Evans	.06	.05	.02
213	Mike Easler	.04	.03	.02
214	Bill Buckner	.04	.03	.02
215	Bob Stanley	.04	.03	.02
216	Jackie Gutierrez	.03	.02	.01
217	Rich Gedman	.04	.03	.02
218	Jerry Remy	.03	.02	.01
219	Marty Barrett	.04	.03	.02
220	Reggie Jackson	.20	.15	.08
221	Geoff Zahn	.03	.02	.01
222	Doug DeCinces	.06	.05	.02
223	Rod Carew	.20	.15	.08
224	Brian Downing	.04	.03	.02
225	Fred Lynn	.06	.05	.02
226	Gary Pettis	.04	.03	.02
227	Mike Witt	.06	.05	.02
228	Bob Boone	.06	.05	.02
229	Tommy John	.06	.05	.02
230	Bobby Grich	.06	.05	.02
231	Ron Romanick	.04	.03	.02
232	Ron Kittle	.06	.05	.02
233	Richard Dotson	.06	.05	.02
234	Harold Baines	.08	.06	.03
235	Tom Seaver	.15	.11	.06
236	Greg Walker	.06	.05	.02
237	Roy Smalley	.04	.03	.02
238	Greg Luzinski	.06	.05	.02
239	Julio Cruz	.03	.02	.01
240	Scott Fletcher	.03	.02	.01
241	Rudy Law	.04	.03	.02
242	Vance Law	.03	.02	.01
243	Carlton Fisk	.20	.15	.08
244	Andre Thornton	.06	.05	.02
245	Julio Franco	.08	.06	.03
246	Brett Butler	.06	.05	.02
247	Bert Blyleven	.08	.06	.03
248	Mike Hargrove	.04	.03	.02
249	George Vukovich	.04	.03	.02
250	Pat Tabler	.04	.03	.02
251	Brook Jacoby	.06	.05	.02
252	Tony Bernazard	.03	.02	.01
253	Ernie Camacho	.03	.02	.01
254	Mel Hall	.06	.05	.02
255	Carmen Castillo	.04	.03	.02
256	Jack Morris	.12	.09	.05
257	Willie Hernandez	.06	.05	.02
258	Alan Trammell	.15	.11	.06
259	Lance Parrish	.12	.09	.05
260	Chet Lemon	.10	.08	.04

		MT	NR MT	EX
261	Lou Whitaker	.06	.05	.02
262	Howard Johnson	.06	.05	.02
263	Barbaro Garbey	.06	.05	.02
264	Dan Petry	.03	.02	.01
265	Aurelio Lopez	.03	.02	.01
266	Larry Herndon	.03	.02	.01
267	Kirk Gibson	.06	.05	.02
268	George Brett	.25	.20	.10
269	Dan Quisenberry	.06	.05	.02
270	Hal McRae	.06	.05	.02
271	Steve Balboni	.06	.05	.02
272	Pat Sheridan	.06	.05	.02
273	Jorge Orta	.04	.03	.02
274	Frank White	.04	.03	.02
275	Bud Black	.03	.02	.01
276	Darryl Motley	.03	.02	.01
277	Willie Wilson	.04	.03	.02
278	Larry Gura	.03	.02	.01
279	Don Slaught	.03	.02	.01
280	Dwight Gooden	.20	.15	.08
281	Mark Langston	.30	.25	.12
282	Tim Raines	.15	.11	.06
283	Rickey Henderson	.10	.08	.04
284	Robin Yount	.15	.11	.06
285	Rollie Fingers	.10	.08	.04
286	Jim Sundberg	.03	.02	.01
287	Cecil Cooper	.06	.05	.02
288	Jaime Cocanower	.04	.03	.02
289	Mike Caldwell	.03	.02	.01
290	Don Sutton	.06	.05	.02
291	Rick Manning	.04	.03	.02
292	Ben Oglivie	.04	.03	.02
293	Moose Haas	.15	.11	.06
294	Ted Simmons	.04	.03	.02
295	Jim Gantner	.03	.02	.01
296	Kent Hrbek	.12	.09	.05
297	Ron Davis	.03	.02	.01
298	Dave Engle	.03	.02	.01
299	Tom Brunansky	.06	.05	.02
300	Frank Viola	.06	.05	.02
301	Mike Smithson	.04	.03	.02
302	Gary Gaetti	.06	.05	.02
303	Tim Teufel	.04	.03	.02
304	Mickey Hatcher	.04	.03	.02
305	John Butcher	.03	.02	.01
306	Darrell Brown	.03	.02	.01
307	Kirby Puckett	.06	.05	.02
308	Dave Winfield	.15	.11	.06
309	Phil Niekro	.12	.09	.05
310	Don Mattingly	.70	.50	.30
311	Don Baylor	.08	.06	.03
312	Willie Randolph	.04	.03	.02
313	Ron Guidry	.06	.05	.02
314	Dave Righetti	.06	.05	.02
315	Bobby Meacham	.04	.03	.02
316	Butch Wynegar	.04	.03	.02
317	Mike Pagliarulo	.08	.06	.03
318	Joe Cowley	.03	.02	.01
319	John Montefusco	.03	.02	.01
320	Dave Kingman	.08	.06	.03
321	Rickey Henderson	.20	.15	.08
322	Bill Caudill	.03	.02	.01
323	Dwayne Murphy	.04	.03	.02
324	Steve McCatty	.04	.03	.02
325	Joe Morgan	.06	.05	.02
326	Mike Heath	.03	.02	.01
327	Chris Codiroli	.06	.05	.02
328	Ray Burris	.04	.03	.02
329	Tony Phillips	.03	.02	.01
330	Carney Lansford	.04	.03	.02
331	Bruce Bochte	.03	.02	.01
332	Alvin Davis	.15	.11	.06
333	Al Cowens	.03	.02	.01
334	Jim Beattie	.03	.02	.01
335	Bob Kearney	.03	.02	.01
336	Ed Vande Berg	.03	.02	.01
337	Mark Langston	.08	.06	.03
338	Dave Henderson	.04	.03	.02
339	Spike Owen	.03	.02	.01
340	Matt Young	.04	.03	.02
341	Jack Perconte	.04	.03	.02
342	Barry Bonnell	.03	.02	.01
343	Mike Stanton	.03	.02	.01
344	Pete O'Brien	.08	.06	.03
345	Charlie Hough	.06	.05	.02
346	Larry Parrish	.06	.05	.02
347	Buddy Bell	.08	.06	.03
348	Frank Tanana	.06	.05	.02
349	Curt Wilkerson	.03	.02	.01
350	Jeff Kunkel	.03	.02	.01
351	Billy Sample	.03	.02	.01
352	Danny Darwin	.03	.02	.01
353	Gary Ward	.03	.02	.01
354	Mike Mason	.03	.02	.01
355	Mickey Rivers	.04	.03	.02
356	Dave Stieb	.08	.06	.03
357	Damaso Garcia	.04	.03	.02
358	Willie Upshaw	.06	.05	.02
359	Lloyd Moseby	.08	.06	.03
360	George Bell	.08	.06	.03
361	Luis Leal	.04	.03	.02
362	Jesse Barfield	.06	.05	.02
363	Dave Collins	.03	.02	.01
364	Roy Lee Jackson	.04	.03	.02
365	Doyle Alexander	.04	.03	.02
366	Alfredo Griffin	.04	.03	.02
367	Cliff Johnson	.04	.03	.02
368	Alvin Davis	.15	.11	.06
369	Juan Samuel	.10	.08	.04
370	Brook Jacoby	.08	.06	.03
371	Dwight Gooden, Mark Langston	.30	.25	.12
372	Mike Fitzgerald	.04	.03	.02
373	Jackie Gutierrez	.03	.02	.01
374	Dan Gladden	.08	.06	.03
375	Carmelo Martinez	.06	.05	.02
376	Kirby Puckett	.20	.15	.08

NOTE: A card number in parentheses ( ) indicates the set is unnumbered.

1985 Topps Super

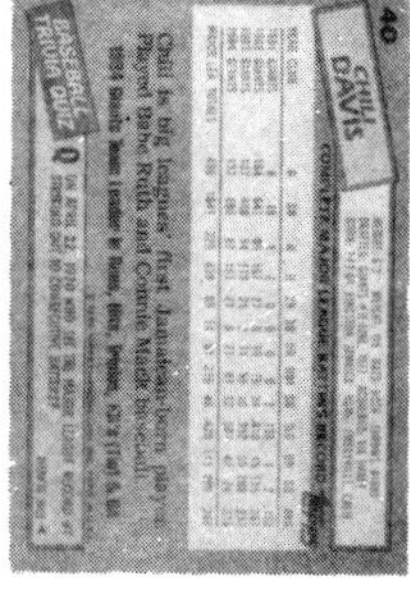

Still trying to sell collectors on the idea of jumbo-sized cards, Topps returned for a second year with its 4-7/8" by 6-7/8" "Super" set. In fact, the set size was doubled from the previous year, to 60 cards. The Supers are identical to the regular-issue 1985 cards of the same players, only the card numbers on back were changed. The cards were again sold three per pack for 50¢.

		MT	NR MT	EX
Complete Set:		14.00	10.50	5.50
Common Player:		.20	.15	.08
1	Ryne Sandberg	.50	.40	.20
2	Willie Hernandez	.20	.15	.08
3	Rick Sutcliffe	.25	.20	.10
4	Don Mattingly	2.25	1.75	.90
5	Tony Gwynn	.70	.50	.30
6	Alvin Davis	.35	.25	.14
7	Dwight Gooden	2.00	1.50	.80
8	Dan Quisenberry	.20	.15	.08
9	Bruce Sutter	.25	.20	.10
10	Tony Armas	.20	.15	.08
11	Dale Murphy	.90	.70	.35
12	Mike Schmidt	.90	.70	.35
13	Gary Carter	.50	.40	.20
14	Rickey Henderson	.70	.50	.30
15	Tim Raines	.50	.40	.20
16	Mike Boddicker	.20	.15	.08
17	Alejandro Pena	.20	.15	.08
18	Eddie Murray	.60	.45	.25
19	Gary Matthews	.20	.15	.08
20	Mark Langston	.30	.25	.12
21	Mario Soto	.20	.15	.08
22	Dave Stieb	.20	.15	.08
23	Nolan Ryan	.50	.40	.20
24	Steve Carlton	.50	.40	.20
25	Alan Trammell	.40	.30	.15
26	Steve Garvey	.50	.40	.20
27	Kirk Gibson	.35	.25	.14
28	Juan Samuel	.35	.25	.14
29	Reggie Jackson	.60	.45	.25
30	Darryl Strawberry	.90	.70	.35
31	Tom Seaver	.50	.40	.20
32	Pete Rose	1.25	.90	.50
33	Dwight Evans	.30	.25	.12
34	Jose Cruz	.20	.15	.08
35	Bert Blyleven	.25	.20	.10
36	Keith Hernandez	.50	.40	.20
37	Robin Yount	.40	.30	.15
38	Joaquin Andujar	.20	.15	.08
39	Lloyd Moseby	.20	.15	.08
40	Chili Davis	.20	.15	.08
41	Kent Hrbek	.35	.25	.14
42	Dave Parker	.30	.25	.12
43	Jack Morris	.35	.25	.14
44	Pedro Guerrero	.30	.25	.12
45	Mike Witt	.20	.15	.08
46	George Brett	.90	.70	.35
47	Ozzie Smith	.30	.25	.12
48	Cal Ripken	.70	.50	.30
49	Rich Gossage	.25	.20	.10
50	Jim Rice	.50	.40	.20
51	Harold Baines	.25	.20	.10
52	Fernando Valenzuela	.40	.30	.15
53	Buddy Bell	.25	.20	.10
54	Jesse Orosco	.20	.15	.08
55	Lance Parrish	.35	.25	.14
56	Jason Thompson	.20	.15	.08
57	Tom Brunansky	.25	.20	.10
58	Dave Righetti	.30	.25	.12
59	Dave Kingman	.25	.20	.10
60	Dave Winfield	.50	.40	.20

1985 Topps 3-D

These 4-1/4" by 6" cards were something new. Printed on plastic, rather than paper, the player picture on the card is actually raised above the surface much like might be found on a relief map; a true 3-D baseball card. The plastic cards include the player's name, a Topps logo and card number across the top, and a team logo on the side. The backs are blank but have two peel-off adhesive strips so that the card may be attached to a flat surface. There are 30 cards in the set, the bulk of whom are stars.

		MT	NR MT	EX
Complete Set:		14.00	10.50	5.50
Common Player:		.20	.15	.08
1	Mike Schmidt	.90	.70	.35
2	Eddie Murray	.70	.50	.30
3	Dale Murphy	.90	.70	.35
4	George Brett	.90	.70	.35
5	Pete Rose	1.25	.90	.50
6	Jim Rice	.60	.45	.25
7	Ryne Sandberg	.50	.40	.20
8	Don Mattingly	2.50	2.00	1.00
9	Darryl Strawberry	.90	.70	.35
10	Rickey Henderson	.80	.60	.30
11	Keith Hernandez	.50	.40	.20
12	Dave Kingman	.20	.15	.08
13	Tony Gwynn	.80	.60	.30
14	Reggie Jackson	.70	.50	.30
15	Gary Carter	.60	.45	.25
16	Cal Ripken	.80	.60	.30
17	Tim Raines	.50	.40	.20
18	Dave Winfield	.60	.45	.25
19	Dwight Gooden	2.00	1.50	.80
20	Dave Stieb	.20	.15	.08
21	Fernando Valenzuela	.50	.40	.20
22	Mark Langston	.30	.25	.12
23	Bruce Sutter	.25	.20	.10
24	Dan Quisenberry	.20	.15	.08
25	Steve Carlton	.60	.45	.25
26	Mike Boddicker	.20	.15	.08
27	Goose Gossage	.30	.25	.12
28	Jack Morris	.40	.30	.15
29	Rick Sutcliffe	.25	.20	.10
30	Tom Seaver	.60	.45	.25

1985 Topps Traded

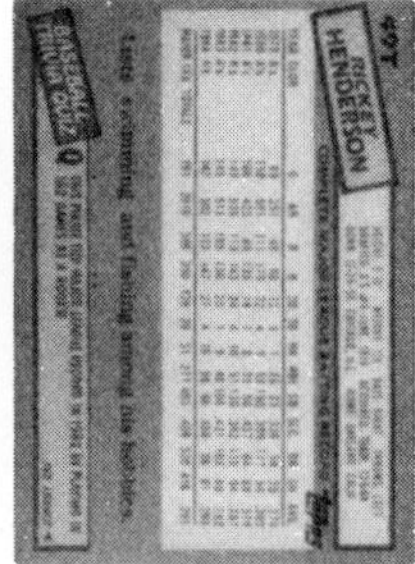

By 1985, the Topps Traded set had become a yearly feature, and Topps continued the tradition with another 132-card set. The 2-1/2" by 3-1/2" cards followed the pattern of being virtually identical in design to the regular cards issued by Topps. Sold only through established hobby dealers, the set features traded veterans and promising rookies. A glossy-finish "Tiffany" edition of the set is valued at four times normal Traded card value for commons, up to five or six times normal value for superstars and hot rookies.

		MT	NR MT	EX
Complete Set:		18.00	13.50	7.25
Common Player:		.10	.08	.04
1T	Don Aase	.10	.08	.04
2T	Bill Almon	.10	.08	.04
3T	Benny Ayala	.10	.08	.04
4T	Dusty Baker	.15	.11	.06
5T	George Bamberger	.10	.08	.04
6T	Dale Berra	.10	.08	.04
7T	Rich Bordi	.10	.08	.04
8T	Daryl Boston(FC)	.20	.15	.08
9T	Hubie Brooks	.25	.20	.10
10T	Chris Brown(FC)	.25	.20	.10
11T	Tom Browning(FC)	1.25	.90	.50
12T	Al Bumbry	.10	.08	.04
13T	Ray Burris	.10	.08	.04
14T	Jeff Burroughs	.15	.11	.06
15T	Bill Campbell	.10	.08	.04
16T	Don Carman(FC)	.40	.30	.15
17T	Gary Carter	.70	.50	.30
18T	Bobby Castillo	.10	.08	.04
19T	Bill Caudill	.10	.08	.04
20T	Rick Cerone	.10	.08	.04
21T	Bryan Clark	.10	.08	.04
22T	Jack Clark	.35	.25	.14
23T	Pat Clements(FC)	.20	.15	.08
24T	Vince Coleman(FC)	4.00	3.00	1.50
25T	Dave Collins	.15	.11	.06
26T	Danny Darwin	.15	.11	.06
27T	Jim Davenport	.10	.08	.04
28T	Jerry Davis	.10	.08	.04
29T	Brian Dayett	.10	.08	.04
30T	Ivan DeJesus	.10	.08	.04
31T	Ken Dixon	.10	.08	.04
32T	Mariano Duncan(FC)	.20	.15	.08
33T	John Felske	.10	.08	.04
34T	Mike Fitzgerald	.10	.08	.04
35T	Ray Fontenot	.10	.08	.04
36T	Greg Gagne(FC)	.35	.25	.14
37T	Oscar Gamble	.15	.11	.06
38T	Scott Garrelts(FC)	.50	.40	.20
39T	Bob Gibson	.10	.08	.04
40T	Jim Gott	.10	.08	.04
41T	David Green	.10	.08	.04
42T	Alfredo Griffin	.15	.11	.06
43T	Ozzie Guillen(FC)	2.00	1.50	.80
44T	Eddie Haas	.10	.08	.04
45T	Terry Harper	.10	.08	.04
46T	Toby Harrah	.15	.11	.06
47T	Greg Harris	.10	.08	.04
48T	Ron Hassey	.10	.08	.04
49T	Rickey Henderson	2.00	1.50	.80
50T	Steve Henderson	.10	.08	.04
51T	George Hendrick	.15	.11	.06
52T	Joe Hesketh(FC)	.20	.15	.08
53T	Teddy Higuera(FC)	2.25	1.75	.90
54T	Donnie Hill	.10	.08	.04
55T	Al Holland	.10	.08	.04
56T	Burt Hooton	.15	.11	.06
57T	Jay Howell	.15	.11	.06
58T	Ken Howell(FC)	.15	.11	.06
59T	LaMarr Hoyt	.10	.08	.04
60T	Tim Hulett(FC)	.15	.11	.06
61T	Bob James	.10	.08	.04
62T	Steve Jeltz(FC)	.15	.11	.06
63T	Cliff Johnson	.10	.08	.04
64T	Howard Johnson	2.00	1.50	.80
65T	Ruppert Jones	.10	.08	.04
66T	Steve Kemp	.15	.11	.06
67T	Bruce Kison	.10	.08	.04
68T	Alan Knicely	.10	.08	.04
69T	Mike LaCoss	.10	.08	.04
70T	Lee Lacy	.10	.08	.04
71T	Dave LaPoint	.20	.15	.08
72T	Gary Lavelle	.10	.08	.04
73T	Vance Law	.15	.11	.06
74T	Johnnie LeMaster	.10	.08	.04
75T	Sixto Lezcano	.10	.08	.04
76T	Tim Lollar	.10	.08	.04
77T	Fred Lynn	.30	.25	.12
78T	Billy Martin	.20	.15	.08
79T	Ron Mathis	.10	.08	.04
80T	Len Matuszek	.10	.08	.04
81T	Gene Mauch	.15	.11	.06
82T	Oddibe McDowell	.60	.45	.25
83T	Roger McDowell(FC)	.90	.70	.35
84T	John McNamara	.10	.08	.04
85T	Donnie Moore	.10	.08	.04
86T	Gene Nelson	.10	.08	.04
87T	Steve Nicosia	.10	.08	.04
88T	Al Oliver	.30	.25	.12
89T	Joe Orsulak(FC)	.20	.15	.08
90T	Rob Picciolo	.10	.08	.04
91T	Chris Pittaro	.10	.08	.04
92T	Jim Presley(FC)	1.00	.70	.40
93T	Rick Reuschel	.25	.20	.10
94T	Bert Roberge	.10	.08	.04
95T	Bob Rodgers	.10	.08	.04
96T	Jerry Royster	.10	.08	.04
97T	Dave Rozema	.10	.08	.04
98T	Dave Rucker	.10	.08	.04
99T	Vern Ruhle	.10	.08	.04
100T	Paul Runge(FC)	.15	.11	.06
101T	Mark Salas(FC)	.15	.11	.06
102T	Luis Salazar	.10	.08	.04
103T	Joe Sambito	.10	.08	.04
104T	Rick Schu(FC)	.20	.15	.08
105T	Donnie Scott	.10	.08	.04
106T	Larry Sheets(FC)	.50	.40	.20
107T	Don Slaught	.10	.08	.04
108T	Roy Smalley	.15	.11	.06
109T	Lonnie Smith	.15	.11	.06
110T	Nate Snell	.10	.08	.04
111T	Chris Speier	.10	.08	.04
112T	Mike Stenhouse	.10	.08	.04
113T	Tim Stoddard	.10	.08	.04
114T	Jim Sundberg	.15	.11	.06
115T	Bruce Sutter	.25	.20	.10
116T	Don Sutton	.60	.45	.25
117T	Kent Tekulve	.15	.11	.06
118T	Tom Tellmann	.10	.08	.04
119T	Walt Terrell	.15	.11	.06
120T	Mickey Tettleton(FC)	1.25	.90	.50
121T	Derrel Thomas	.10	.08	.04
122T	Rich Thompson	.10	.08	.04
123T	Alex Trevino	.10	.08	.04
124T	John Tudor	.25	.20	.10
125T	Jose Uribe(FC)	.25	.20	.10
126T	Bobby Valentine	.10	.08	.04
127T	Dave Von Ohlen	.10	.08	.04
128T	U.L. Washington	.10	.08	.04
129T	Earl Weaver	.15	.11	.06
130T	Eddie Whitson	.10	.08	.04
131T	Herm Winningham(FC)	.20	.15	.08
132T	Checklist 1-132	.10	.08	.04

1986 Topps

The 1986 Topps set consists of 792 cards. Fronts of the 2-1/2" by 3-1/2" cards feature color photos with the Topps logo in the upper right-hand corner while the player's position is in the lower left-hand corner. Above the picture is the team name, while below it is the player's

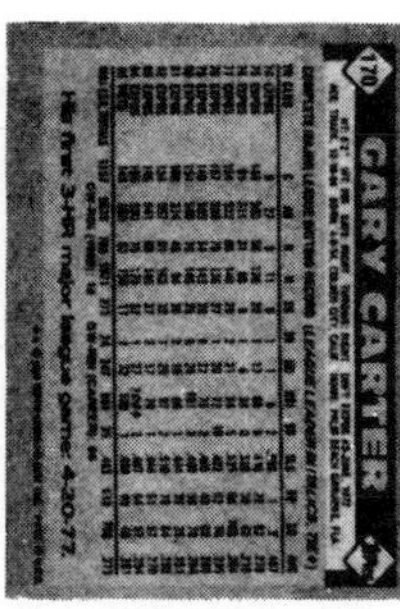

name. The borders are a departure from previous practice, as the top 7/8" is black, while the remainder was white. There are no card numbers 51 and 171 in the set; the card that should have been #51, Bobby Wine, shares #57 with Bill Doran, while #171, Bob Rodgers, shares #141 with Chuck Cottier. Once again, a 5,000-set glossy-finish "Tiffany" edition was produced. Values are four to six times higher than the same card in the regular issue.

		MT	NR MT	EX
	Complete Set:	40.00	30.00	15.00
	Common Player:	.05	.04	.02
1	Pete Rose	.90	.70	.35
2	Rose Special 1963-66	.30	.25	.12
3	Rose Special 1967-70	.30	.25	.12
4	Rose Special 1971-74	.30	.25	.12
5	Rose Special 1975-78	.30	.25	.12
6	Rose Special 1979-82	.30	.25	.12
7	Rose Special 1983-85	.30	.25	.12
8	Dwayne Murphy	.07	.05	.03
9	Roy Smith	.05	.04	.02
10	Tony Gwynn	.40	.30	.15
11	Bob Ojeda	.07	.05	.03
12	*Jose Uribe*(FC)	.20	.15	.08
13	Bob Kearney	.05	.04	.02
14	Julio Cruz	.05	.04	.02
15	Eddie Whitson	.05	.04	.02
16	Rick Schu(FC)	.07	.05	.03
17	Mike Stenhouse	.05	.04	.02
18	Brent Gaff	.05	.04	.02
19	Rich Hebner	.05	.04	.02
20	Lou Whitaker	.25	.20	.10
21	George Bamberger	.05	.04	.02
22	Duane Walker	.05	.04	.02
23	*Manny Lee*(FC)	.15	.11	.06
24	Len Barker	.07	.05	.03
25	Willie Wilson	.12	.09	.05
26	Frank DiPino	.05	.04	.02
27	Ray Knight	.07	.05	.03
28	Eric Davis	2.50	2.00	1.00
29	Tony Phillips	.05	.04	.02
30	Eddie Murray	.40	.30	.15
31	Jamie Easterly	.05	.04	.02
32	Steve Yeager	.05	.04	.02
33	Jeff Lahti	.05	.04	.02
34	Ken Phelps(FC)	.07	.05	.03
35	Jeff Reardon	.12	.09	.05
36	Tigers Leaders (Lance Parrish)	.12	.09	.05
37	Mark Thurmond	.05	.04	.02
38	Glenn Hoffman	.05	.04	.02
39	Dave Rucker	.05	.04	.02
40	Ken Griffey	.10	.08	.04
41	Brad Wellman	.05	.04	.02
42	Geoff Zahn	.05	.04	.02
43	Dave Engle	.05	.04	.02
44	*Lance McCullers*(FC)	.25	.20	.10
45	Damaso Garcia	.05	.04	.02
46	Billy Hatcher(FC)	.20	.15	.08
47	Juan Berenguer	.05	.04	.02
48	Bill Almon	.05	.04	.02
49	Rick Manning	.05	.04	.02
50	Dan Quisenberry	.07	.05	.03
51	Not Issued			
52	Chris Welsh	.05	.04	.02
53	*Len Dykstra*(FC)	1.25	.90	.50
54	John Franco	.12	.09	.05
55	Fred Lynn	.15	.11	.06
56	Tom Niedenfuer	.07	.05	.03
57a	Bobby Wine	.05	.04	.02
57b	Bill Doran	.10	.08	.04
58	Bill Krueger	.05	.04	.02
59	Andre Thornton	.07	.05	.03
60	Dwight Evans	.12	.09	.05
61	Karl Best	.05	.04	.02
62	Bob Boone	.07	.05	.03
63	Ron Roenicke	.05	.04	.02
64	Floyd Bannister	.10	.08	.04
65	Dan Driessen	.07	.05	.03
66	Cardinals Leaders (Bob Forsch)	.07	.05	.03
67	Carmelo Martinez	.07	.05	.03
68	Ed Lynch	.05	.04	.02
69	Luis Aguayo	.05	.04	.02
70	Dave Winfield	.30	.25	.12
71	Ken Schrom	.05	.04	.02
72	Shawon Dunston	.20	.15	.08
73	Randy O'Neal(FC)	.07	.05	.03
74	Rance Mulliniks	.05	.04	.02
75	Jose DeLeon	.07	.05	.03
76	Dion James	.07	.05	.03
77	Charlie Leibrandt	.07	.05	.03
78	Bruce Benedict	.05	.04	.02
79	Dave Schmidt	.07	.05	.03
80	Darryl Strawberry	.70	.50	.30
81	Gene Mauch	.07	.05	.03
82	Tippy Martinez	.05	.04	.02
83	Phil Garner	.07	.05	.03
84	Curt Young	.07	.05	.03
85	Tony Perez	.15	.11	.06
86	Tom Waddell	.05	.04	.02
87	Candy Maldonado	.10	.08	.04
88	Tom Nieto	.05	.04	.02
89	Randy St. Claire(FC)	.07	.05	.03
90	Garry Templeton	.07	.05	.03
91	Steve Crawford	.05	.04	.02
92	Al Cowens	.05	.04	.02
93	Scot Thompson	.05	.04	.02
94	Rick Bordi	.05	.04	.02
95	Ozzie Virgil	.05	.04	.02
96	Blue Jay Leaders (Jim Clancy)	.07	.05	.03
97	Gary Gaetti	.20	.15	.08
98	Dick Ruthven	.05	.04	.02
99	Buddy Biancalana	.05	.04	.02
100	Nolan Ryan	.70	.50	.30
101	Dave Bergman	.05	.04	.02
102	*Joe Orsulak*	.15	.11	.06
103	Luis Salazar	.05	.04	.02
104	Sid Fernandez	.12	.09	.05
105	Gary Ward	.07	.05	.03
106	Ray Burris	.05	.04	.02
107	Rafael Ramirez	.05	.04	.02
108	Ted Power	.05	.04	.02
109	Len Matuszek	.05	.04	.02
110	Scott McGregor	.07	.05	.03
111	Roger Craig	.07	.05	.03
112	Bill Campbell	.05	.04	.02
113	U.L. Washington	.05	.04	.02
114	Mike Brown	.05	.04	.02
115	Jay Howell	.07	.05	.03
116	Brook Jacoby	.10	.08	.04
117	Bruce Kison	.05	.04	.02
118	Jerry Royster	.05	.04	.02
119	Barry Bonnell	.05	.04	.02
120	Steve Carlton	.30	.25	.12
121	Nelson Simmons	.05	.04	.02
122	Pete Filson	.05	.04	.02
123	Greg Walker	.10	.08	.04
124	Luis Sanchez	.05	.04	.02
125	Dave Lopes	.07	.05	.03
126	Mets Leaders (Mookie Wilson)	.07	.05	.03
127	*Jack Howell*(FC)	.30	.25	.12
128	John Wathan	.07	.05	.03
129	Jeff Dedmon(FC)	.05	.04	.02
130	Alan Trammell	.30	.25	.12
131	Checklist 1-132	.05	.04	.02
132	Razor Shines	.05	.04	.02
133	Andy McGaffigan	.05	.04	.02
134	Carney Lansford	.10	.08	.04
135	Joe Niekro	.10	.08	.04
136	Mike Hargrove	.05	.04	.02
137	Charlie Moore	.05	.04	.02
138	Mark Davis	.05	.04	.02
139	Daryl Boston	.10	.08	.04
140	John Candelaria	.10	.08	.04
141a	Bob Rodgers	.05	.04	.02
141b	Chuck Cottier	.05	.04	.02
142	Bob Jones	.05	.04	.02
143	Dave Van Gorder	.05	.04	.02
144	Doug Sisk	.05	.04	.02
145	Pedro Guerrero	.20	.15	.08
146	Jack Perconte	.05	.04	.02
147	Larry Sheets	.20	.15	.08
148	Mike Heath	.05	.04	.02
149	Brett Butler	.07	.05	.03
150	Joaquin Andujar	.07	.05	.03
151	Dave Stapleton	.05	.04	.02
152	Mike Morgan	.05	.04	.02
153	Ricky Adams	.05	.04	.02
154	Bert Roberge	.05	.04	.02
155	Bob Grich	.10	.08	.04
156	White Sox Leaders (Richard Dotson)	.07	.05	.03
157	Ron Hassey	.05	.04	.02
158	Derrel Thomas	.05	.04	.02
159	Orel Hershiser	1.00	.70	.40
160	Chet Lemon	.07	.05	.03
161	Lee Tunnell	.05	.04	.02
162	Greg Gagne	.10	.08	.04
163	Pete Ladd	.05	.04	.02
164	Steve Balboni	.07	.05	.03
165	Mike Davis	.07	.05	.03
166	Dickie Thon	.07	.05	.03
167	Zane Smith(FC)	.15	.11	.06
168	Jeff Burroughs	.07	.05	.03
169	George Wright	.05	.04	.02
170	Gary Carter	.25	.20	.10
171	Not Issued			
172	Jerry Reed	.05	.04	.02
173	Wayne Gross	.05	.04	.02
174	Brian Snyder	.05	.04	.02
175	Steve Sax	.15	.11	.06
176	Jay Tibbs	.05	.04	.02
177	Joel Youngblood	.05	.04	.02
178	Ivan DeJesus	.05	.04	.02
179	*Stu Cliburn*(FC)	.10	.08	.04
180	Don Mattingly	3.50	2.75	1.50
181	Al Nipper	.05	.04	.02
182	Bobby Brown	.05	.04	.02
183	Larry Andersen	.05	.04	.02
184	Tim Laudner	.05	.04	.02
185	Rollie Fingers	.20	.15	.08
186	Astros Leaders (Jose Cruz)	.07	.05	.03
187	Scott Fletcher	.07	.05	.03
188	Bob Dernier	.05	.04	.02
189	Mike Mason	.05	.04	.02
190	George Hendrick	.07	.05	.03
191	Wally Backman	.07	.05	.03
192	Milt Wilcox	.05	.04	.02
193	Daryl Sconiers	.05	.04	.02
194	Craig McMurtry	.05	.04	.02
195	Dave Concepcion	.12	.09	.05
196	Doyle Alexander	.10	.08	.04
197	Enos Cabell	.05	.04	.02
198	Ken Dixon	.05	.04	.02
199	Dick Howser	.05	.04	.02
200	Mike Schmidt	.50	.40	.20
201	Record Breaker (Vince Coleman)(FC)	.30	.25	.12
202	Record Breaker (Dwight Gooden)	.40	.30	.15
203	Record Breaker (Keith Hernandez)	.20	.15	.08
204	Record Breaker (Phil Niekro)	.15	.11	.06
205	Record Breaker (Tony Perez)	.10	.08	.04
206	Record Breaker (Pete Rose)	.50	.40	.20
207	Record Breaker (Fernando Valenzuela)	.20	.15	.08
208	Ramon Romero	.05	.04	.02
209	Randy Ready	.10	.08	.04
210	Calvin Schiraldi(FC)	.10	.08	.04
211	Ed Wojna	.05	.04	.02
212	Chris Speier	.05	.04	.02
213	Bob Shirley	.05	.04	.02
214	Randy Bush	.05	.04	.02
215	Frank White	.10	.08	.04
216	A's Leaders (Dwayne Murphy)	.07	.05	.03
217	Bill Scherrer	.05	.04	.02
218	Randy Hunt	.05	.04	.02
219	Dennis Lamp	.05	.04	.02
220	Bob Horner	.10	.08	.04
221	Dave Henderson	.10	.08	.04
222	Craig Gerber	.05	.04	.02
223	Atlee Hammaker	.05	.04	.02
224	Cesar Cedeno	.10	.08	.04
225	Ron Darling	.15	.11	.06
226	Lee Lacy	.05	.04	.02
227	Al Jones	.05	.04	.02
228	Tom Lawless	.05	.04	.02
229	Bill Gullickson	.05	.04	.02
230	Terry Kennedy	.07	.05	.03
231	Jim Frey	.05	.04	.02
232	Rick Rhoden	.10	.08	.04
233	Steve Lyons(FC)	.07	.05	.03
234	Doug Corbett	.05	.04	.02
235	Butch Wynegar	.05	.04	.02
236	Frank Eufemia	.05	.04	.02
237	Ted Simmons	.12	.09	.05
238	Larry Parrish	.10	.08	.04
239	Joel Skinner	.05	.04	.02
240	Tommy John	.20	.15	.08
241	Tony Fernandez	.20	.15	.08
242	Rich Thompson	.05	.04	.02
243	Johnny Grubb	.05	.04	.02
244	Craig Lefferts	.05	.04	.02
245	Jim Sundberg	.07	.05	.03
246	Phillies Leaders (Steve Carlton)	.15	.11	.06
247	Terry Harper	.05	.04	.02
248	Spike Owen	.05	.04	.02
249	Rob Deer(FC)	.40	.30	.15
250	Dwight Gooden	2.00	1.50	.80
251	Rich Dauer	.05	.04	.02
252	Bobby Castillo	.05	.04	.02
253	Dann Bilardello	.05	.04	.02
254	*Ozzie Guillen*	.70	.50	.30
255	Tony Armas	.07	.05	.03
256	Kurt Kepshire	.05	.04	.02
257	Doug DeCinces	.10	.08	.04
258	*Tim Burke*(FC)	.25	.20	.10
259	Dan Pasqua(FC)	.20	.15	.08
260	Tony Pena	.10	.08	.04
261	Bobby Valentine	.05	.04	.02
262	Mario Ramirez	.05	.04	.02
263	Checklist 133-264	.05	.04	.02
264	*Darren Daulton*(FC)	.12	.09	.05
265	Ron Davis	.05	.04	.02
266	Keith Moreland	.07	.05	.03
267	Paul Molitor	.15	.11	.06
268	Mike Scott	.15	.11	.06
269	Dane Iorg	.05	.04	.02
270	Jack Morris	.20	.15	.08
271	Dave Collins	.07	.05	.03
272	Tim Tolman	.05	.04	.02
273	Jerry Willard	.05	.04	.02
274	Ron Gardenhire	.05	.04	.02
275	Charlie Hough	.08	.06	.03
276	Yankees Leaders (Willie Randolph)	.07	.05	.03
277	Jaime Cocanower	.05	.04	.02
278	Sixto Lezcano	.05	.04	.02
279	Al Pardo	.05	.04	.02
280	Tim Raines	.30	.25	.12
281	Steve Mura	.05	.04	.02
282	Jerry Mumphrey	.05	.04	.02
283	Mike Fischlin	.05	.04	.02
284	Brian Dayett	.05	.04	.02
285	Buddy Bell	.10	.08	.04
286	Luis DeLeon	.05	.04	.02
287	*John Christensen*(FC)	.10	.08	.04
288	Don Aase	.05	.04	.02
289	Johnnie LeMaster	.05	.04	.02
290	Carlton Fisk	.30	.25	.12
291	Tom Lasorda	.07	.05	.03
292	Chuck Porter	.05	.04	.02
293	Chris Chambliss	.07	.05	.03
294	Danny Cox	.10	.08	.04
295	Kirk Gibson	.30	.25	.12
296	Geno Petralli(FC)	.07	.05	.03
297	Tim Lollar	.05	.04	.02
298	Craig Reynolds	.05	.04	.02
299	Bryn Smith	.05	.04	.02
300	George Brett	.50	.40	.20
301	Dennis Rasmussen	.12	.09	.05
302	Greg Gross	.05	.04	.02
303	Curt Wardle	.05	.04	.02
304	*Mike Gallego*(FC)	.12	.09	.05
305	Phil Bradley	.15	.11	.06
306	Padres Leaders (Terry Kennedy)	.07	.05	.03
307	Dave Sax	.05	.04	.02
308	Ray Fontenot	.05	.04	.02
309	John Shelby	.05	.04	.02
310	Greg Minton	.05	.04	.02
311	Dick Schofield	.05	.04	.02
312	Tom Filer	.05	.04	.02
313	Joe DeSa	.05	.04	.02
314	Frank Pastore	.05	.04	.02
315	Mookie Wilson	.10	.08	.04
316	Sammy Khalifa	.05	.04	.02

		MT	NR MT	EX
317	Ed Romero	.05	.04	.02
318	Terry Whitfield	.05	.04	.02
319	Rick Camp	.05	.04	.02
320	Jim Rice	.30	.25	.12
321	Earl Weaver	.07	.05	.03
322	Bob Forsch	.07	.05	.03
323	Jerry Davis	.05	.04	.02
324	Dan Schatzeder	.05	.04	.02
325	Juan Beniquez	.05	.04	.02
326	Kent Tekulve	.07	.05	.03
327	Mike Pagliarulo	.20	.15	.08
328	Pete O'Brien	.10	.08	.04
329	Kirby Puckett	3.00	2.25	1.25
330	Rick Sutcliffe	.12	.09	.05
331	Alan Ashby	.05	.04	.02
332	Darryl Motley	.05	.04	.02
333	Tom Henke(FC)	.15	.11	.06
334	Ken Oberkfell	.05	.04	.02
335	Don Sutton	.25	.20	.10
336	Indians Leaders (Andre Thornton)	.07	.05	.03
337	Darnell Coles	.07	.05	.03
338	Jorge Bell	.25	.20	.10
339	Bruce Berenyi	.05	.04	.02
340	Cal Ripken	.40	.30	.15
341	Frank Williams	.05	.04	.02
342	Gary Redus	.05	.04	.02
343	Carlos Diaz	.05	.04	.02
344	Jim Wohlford	.05	.04	.02
345	Donnie Moore	.05	.04	.02
346	Bryan Little	.05	.04	.02
347	*Teddy Higuera*	1.00	.70	.40
348	Cliff Johnson	.05	.04	.02
349	Mark Clear	.05	.04	.02
350	Jack Clark	.20	.15	.08
351	Chuck Tanner	.05	.04	.02
352	Harry Spilman	.05	.04	.02
353	Keith Atherton	.05	.04	.02
354	Tony Bernazard	.05	.04	.02
355	Lee Smith	.10	.08	.04
356	Mickey Hatcher	.05	.04	.02
357	Ed Vande Berg	.05	.04	.02
358	Rick Dempsey	.07	.05	.03
359	Mike LaCoss	.05	.04	.02
360	Lloyd Moseby	.10	.08	.04
361	Shane Rawley	.10	.08	.04
362	Tom Paciorek	.05	.04	.02
363	Terry Forster	.07	.05	.03
364	Reid Nichols	.05	.04	.02
365	Mike Flanagan	.10	.08	.04
366	Reds Leaders (Dave Concepcion)	.07	.05	.03
367	Aurelio Lopez	.05	.04	.02
368	Greg Brock	.07	.05	.03
369	Al Holland	.05	.04	.02
370	*Vince Coleman*	1.50	1.25	.60
371	Bill Stein	.05	.04	.02
372	Ben Oglivie	.07	.05	.03
373	*Urbano Lugo*(FC)	.07	.05	.03
374	Terry Francona	.05	.04	.02
375	Rich Gedman	.10	.08	.04
376	Bill Dawley	.05	.04	.02
377	Joe Carter	.30	.25	.12
378	Bruce Bochte	.05	.04	.02
379	Bobby Meacham	.05	.04	.02
380	LaMarr Hoyt	.05	.04	.02
381	Ray Miller	.05	.04	.02
382	*Ivan Calderon*(FC)	.40	.30	.15
383	*Chris Brown*	.30	.25	.12
384	Steve Trout	.05	.04	.02
385	Cecil Cooper	.10	.08	.04
386	*Cecil Fielder*(FC)	5.00	2.50	1.50
387	Steve Kemp	.07	.05	.03
388	Dickie Noles	.05	.04	.02
389	Glenn Davis(FC)	3.50	2.75	1.50
390	Tom Seaver	.40	.30	.15
391	Julio Franco	.10	.08	.04
392	John Russell(FC)	.10	.08	.04
393	Chris Pittaro	.05	.04	.02
394	Checklist 265-396	.05	.04	.02
395	Scott Garrelts	.07	.05	.03
396	Red Sox Leaders (Dwight Evans)	.07	.05	.03
397	*Steve Buechele*(FC)	.20	.15	.08
398	*Earnie Riles*(FC)	.15	.11	.06
399	Bill Swift	.12	.09	.05
400	Rod Carew	.30	.25	.12
401	Turn Back The Clock (Fernando Valenzuela)	.15	.11	.06
402	Turn Back The Clock (Tom Seaver)	.15	.11	.06
403	Turn Back The Clock (Willie Mays)	.20	.15	.08
404	Turn Back The Clock (Frank Robinson)	.15	.11	.06
405	Turn Back The Clock (Roger Maris)	.20	.15	.08
406	Scott Sanderson	.05	.04	.02
407	Sal Butera	.05	.04	.02
408	Dave Smith	.07	.05	.03
409	*Paul Runge*	.07	.05	.03
410	Dave Kingman	.15	.11	.06
411	Sparky Anderson	.07	.05	.03
412	Jim Clancy	.07	.05	.03
413	Tim Flannery	.05	.04	.02
414	Tom Gorman	.05	.04	.02
415	Hal McRae	.10	.08	.04
416	Denny Martinez	.07	.05	.03
417	R.J. Reynolds	.07	.05	.03
418	Alan Knicely	.05	.04	.02
419	Frank Wills	.05	.04	.02
420	Von Hayes	.10	.08	.04
421	Dave Palmer	.05	.04	.02
422	Mike Jorgensen	.05	.04	.02
423	Dan Spillner	.05	.04	.02
424	Rick Miller	.05	.04	.02
425	Larry McWilliams	.05	.04	.02
426	Brewers Leaders (Charlie Moore)	.07	.05	.03
427	Joe Cowley	.05	.04	.02
428	Max Venable	.05	.04	.02
429	Greg Booker	.05	.04	.02
430	Kent Hrbek	.20	.15	.08
431	George Frazier	.05	.04	.02
432	Mark Bailey	.05	.04	.02
433	Chris Codiroli	.05	.04	.02
434	Curt Wilkerson	.05	.04	.02
435	Bill Caudill	.05	.04	.02
436	Doug Flynn	.05	.04	.02
437	Rick Mahler	.05	.04	.02
438	Clint Hurdle	.05	.04	.02
439	Rick Honeycutt	.05	.04	.02
440	Alvin Davis	.30	.25	.12
441	Whitey Herzog	.07	.05	.03
442	Ron Robinson(FC)	.12	.09	.05
443	Bill Buckner	.10	.08	.04
444	Alex Trevino	.05	.04	.02
445	Bert Blyleven	.12	.09	.05
446	Lenn Sakata	.05	.04	.02
447	Jerry Don Gleaton	.05	.04	.02
448	*Herm Winningham*	.15	.11	.06
449	Rod Scurry	.05	.04	.02
450	Graig Nettles	.15	.11	.06
451	Mark Brown	.05	.04	.02
452	Bob Clark	.05	.04	.02
453	Steve Jeltz	.07	.05	.03
454	Burt Hooton	.07	.05	.03
455	Willie Randolph	.10	.08	.04
456	Braves Leaders (Dale Murphy)	.25	.20	.10
457	*Mickey Tettleton*	.60	.45	.25
458	Kevin Bass	.10	.08	.04
459	Luis Leal	.05	.04	.02
460	Leon Durham	.07	.05	.03
461	Walt Terrell	.07	.05	.03
462	Domingo Ramos	.05	.04	.02
463	Jim Gott	.05	.04	.02
464	Ruppert Jones	.05	.04	.02
465	Jesse Orosco	.07	.05	.03
466	Tom Foley	.05	.04	.02
467	Bob James	.05	.04	.02
468	Mike Scioscia	.07	.05	.03
469	Storm Davis	.10	.08	.04
470	Bill Madlock	.12	.09	.05
471	Bobby Cox	.05	.04	.02
472	Joe Hesketh	.07	.05	.03
473	Mark Brouhard	.05	.04	.02
474	John Tudor	.10	.08	.04
475	Juan Samuel	.12	.09	.05
476	Ron Mathis	.05	.04	.02
477	Mike Easler	.07	.05	.03
478	Andy Hawkins	.05	.04	.02
479	*Bob Melvin*(FC)	.12	.09	.05
480	*Oddibe McDowell*	.30	.25	.12
481	Scott Bradley(FC)	.10	.08	.04
482	Rick Lysander	.05	.04	.02
483	George Vukovich	.05	.04	.02
484	Donnie Hill	.05	.04	.02
485	Gary Matthews	.10	.08	.04
486	Angels Leaders (Bob Grich)	.07	.05	.03
487	Bret Saberhagen	.70	.50	.30
488	Lou Thornton	.05	.04	.02
489	Jim Winn	.05	.04	.02
490	Jeff Leonard	.07	.05	.03
491	Pascual Perez	.07	.05	.03
492	Kelvin Chapman	.05	.04	.02
493	Gene Nelson	.05	.04	.02
494	Gary Roenicke	.05	.04	.02
495	Mark Langston	.20	.15	.08
496	Jay Johnstone	.07	.05	.03
497	John Stuper	.05	.04	.02
498	Tito Landrum	.05	.04	.02
499	Bob Gibson	.05	.04	.02
500	Rickey Henderson	.40	.30	.15
501	Dave Johnson	.07	.05	.03
502	Glen Cook	.05	.04	.02
503	Mike Fitzgerald	.05	.04	.02
504	Denny Walling	.05	.04	.02
505	Jerry Koosman	.10	.08	.04
506	Bill Russell	.07	.05	.03
507	*Steve Ontiveros*(FC)	.12	.09	.05
508	Alan Wiggins	.05	.04	.02
509	Ernie Camacho	.05	.04	.02
510	Wade Boggs	2.25	1.75	.90
511	Ed Nunez	.05	.04	.02
512	Thad Bosley	.05	.04	.02
513	Ron Washington	.05	.04	.02
514	Mike Jones	.05	.04	.02
515	Darrell Evans	.12	.09	.05
516	Giants Leaders (Greg Minton)	.07	.05	.03
517	*Milt Thompson*(FC)	.25	.20	.10
518	Buck Martinez	.05	.04	.02
519	Danny Darwin	.05	.04	.02
520	Keith Hernandez	.30	.25	.12
521	Nate Snell	.05	.04	.02
522	Bob Bailor	.05	.04	.02
523	Joe Price	.05	.04	.02
524	Darrell Miller(FC)	.07	.05	.03
525	Marvell Wynne	.05	.04	.02
526	Charlie Lea	.05	.04	.02
527	Checklist 397-528	.05	.04	.02
528	Terry Pendleton	.15	.11	.06
529	Marc Sullivan	.05	.04	.02
530	Rich Gossage	.20	.15	.08
531	Tony LaRussa	.07	.05	.03
532	*Don Carman*	.25	.20	.10
533	Billy Sample	.05	.04	.02
534	Jeff Calhoun	.05	.04	.02
535	Toby Harrah	.07	.05	.03
536	Jose Rijo	.10	.08	.04
537	Mark Salas	.07	.05	.03
538	Dennis Eckersley	.12	.09	.05
539	Glenn Hubbard	.05	.04	.02
540	Dan Petry	.07	.05	.03
541	Jorge Orta	.05	.04	.02
542	Don Schulze	.05	.04	.02
543	Jerry Narron	.05	.04	.02
544	Eddie Milner	.05	.04	.02
545	Jimmy Key	.15	.11	.06
546	Mariners Leaders (Dave Henderson)	.07	.05	.03
547	*Roger McDowell*	.40	.30	.15
548	Mike Young	.05	.04	.02
549	Bob Welch	.12	.09	.05
550	Tom Herr	.10	.08	.04
551	Dave LaPoint	.07	.05	.03
552	Marc Hill	.05	.04	.02
553	Jim Morrison	.05	.04	.02
554	Paul Householder	.05	.04	.02
555	Hubie Brooks	.10	.08	.04
556	John Denny	.05	.04	.02
557	Gerald Perry	.12	.09	.05
558	Tim Stoddard	.05	.04	.02
559	Tommy Dunbar	.05	.04	.02
560	Dave Righetti	.20	.15	.08
561	Bob Lillis	.05	.04	.02
562	Joe Beckwith	.05	.04	.02
563	Alejandro Sanchez	.05	.04	.02
564	Warren Brusstar	.05	.04	.02
565	Tom Brunansky	.12	.09	.05
566	Alfredo Griffin	.07	.05	.03
567	Jeff Barkley	.05	.04	.02
568	Donnie Scott	.05	.04	.02
569	Jim Acker	.05	.04	.02
570	Rusty Staub	.10	.08	.04
571	Mike Jeffcoat	.05	.04	.02
572	Paul Zuvella	.05	.04	.02
573	Tom Hume	.05	.04	.02
574	Ron Kittle	.10	.08	.04
575	Mike Boddicker	.07	.05	.03
576	Expos Leaders (Andre Dawson)	.12	.09	.05
577	Jerry Reuss	.07	.05	.03
578	Lee Mazzilli	.07	.05	.03
579	Jim Slaton	.05	.04	.02
580	Willie McGee	.15	.11	.06
581	Bruce Hurst	.12	.09	.05
582	Jim Gantner	.07	.05	.03
583	Al Bumbry	.05	.04	.02
584	*Brian Fisher*(FC)	.30	.25	.12
585	Garry Maddox	.07	.05	.03
586	Greg Harris	.05	.04	.02
587	Rafael Santana	.05	.04	.02
588	Steve Lake	.05	.04	.02
589	Sid Bream	.10	.08	.04
590	Bob Knepper	.07	.05	.03
591	Jackie Moore	.05	.04	.02
592	Frank Tanana	.10	.08	.04
593	Jesse Barfield	.20	.15	.08
594	Chris Bando	.05	.04	.02
595	Dave Parker	.20	.15	.08
596	Onix Concepcion	.05	.04	.02
597	Sammy Stewart	.05	.04	.02
598	Jim Presley	.25	.20	.10
599	*Rick Aguilera*(FC)	.20	.15	.08
600	Dale Murphy	.50	.40	.20
601	Gary Lucas	.05	.04	.02
602	*Mariano Duncan*	.15	.11	.06
603	Bill Laskey	.05	.04	.02
604	Gary Pettis	.05	.04	.02
605	Dennis Boyd	.07	.05	.03
606	Royals Leaders (Hal McRae)	.07	.05	.03
607	Ken Dayley	.05	.04	.02
608	Bruce Bochy	.05	.04	.02
609	Barbaro Garbey	.05	.04	.02
610	Ron Guidry	.15	.11	.06
611	Gary Woods	.05	.04	.02
612	Richard Dotson	.10	.08	.04
613	Roy Smalley	.05	.04	.02
614	Rick Waits	.05	.04	.02
615	Johnny Ray	.10	.08	.04
616	Glenn Brummer	.05	.04	.02
617	Lonnie Smith	.07	.05	.03
618	Jim Pankovits	.05	.04	.02
619	Danny Heep	.05	.04	.02
620	Bruce Sutter	.12	.09	.05
621	John Felske	.05	.04	.02
622	Gary Lavelle	.05	.04	.02
623	Floyd Rayford	.05	.04	.02
624	Steve McCatty	.05	.04	.02
625	Bob Brenly	.05	.04	.02
626	Roy Thomas	.05	.04	.02
627	Ron Oester	.05	.04	.02
628	*Kirk McCaskill*(FC)	.35	.25	.14
629	*Mitch Webster*(FC)	.25	.20	.10
630	Fernando Valenzuela	.30	.25	.12
631	Steve Braun	.05	.04	.02
632	Dave Von Ohlen	.05	.04	.02
633	Jackie Gutierrez	.05	.04	.02
634	Roy Lee Jackson	.05	.04	.02
635	Jason Thompson	.05	.04	.02
636	Cubs Leaders (Lee Smith)	.07	.05	.03
637	Rudy Law	.05	.04	.02
638	John Butcher	.05	.04	.02
639	Bo Diaz	.07	.05	.03
640	Jose Cruz	.10	.08	.04
641	Wayne Tolleson	.05	.04	.02
642	Ray Searage	.05	.04	.02
643	Tom Brookens	.05	.04	.02
644	Mark Gubicza	.12	.09	.05
645	Dusty Baker	.07	.05	.03
646	Mike Moore	.05	.04	.02
647	Mel Hall	.07	.05	.03
648	Steve Bedrosian	.10	.08	.04
649	Ronn Reynolds	.05	.04	.02
650	Dave Stieb	.12	.09	.05
651	Billy Martin	.12	.09	.05
652	Tom Browning	.25	.20	.10
653	Jim Dwyer	.05	.04	.02
654	Ken Howell	.07	.05	.03
655	Manny Trillo	.07	.05	.03
656	Brian Harper	.05	.04	.02
657	Juan Agosto	.05	.04	.02
658	Rob Wilfong	.05	.04	.02
659	Checklist 529-660	.05	.04	.02
660	Steve Garvey	.30	.25	.12
661	Roger Clemens	3.00	2.25	1.25
662	Bill Schroeder	.05	.04	.02
663	Neil Allen	.05	.04	.02
664	Tim Corcoran	.05	.04	.02
665	Alejandro Pena	.07	.05	.03
666	Rangers Leaders (Charlie Hough)	.07	.05	.03
667	Tim Teufel	.05	.04	.02
668	Cecilio Guante	.05	.04	.02
669	Ron Cey	.10	.08	.04
670	Willie Hernandez	.07	.05	.03
671	Lynn Jones	.05	.04	.02
672	Rob Picciolo	.05	.04	.02
673	Ernie Whitt	.07	.05	.03

		MT	NR MT	EX
674	Pat Tabler	.07	.05	.03
675	Claudell Washington	.07	.05	.03
676	Matt Young	.05	.04	.02
677	Nick Esasky	.07	.05	.03
678	Dan Gladden	.07	.05	.03
679	Britt Burns	.05	.04	.02
680	George Foster	.15	.11	.06
681	Dick Williams	.05	.04	.02
682	Junior Ortiz	.05	.04	.02
683	Andy Van Slyke	.15	.11	.06
684	Bob McClure	.05	.04	.02
685	Tim Wallach	.12	.09	.05
686	Jeff Stone	.05	.04	.02
687	Mike Trujillo	.05	.04	.02
688	Larry Herndon	.07	.05	.03
689	Dave Stewart	.12	.09	.05
690	Ryne Sandberg	.35	.25	.14
691	Mike Madden	.05	.04	.02
692	Dale Berra	.05	.04	.02
693	Tom Tellmann	.05	.04	.02
694	Garth Iorg	.05	.04	.02
695	Mike Smithson	.05	.04	.02
696	Dodgers Leaders (Bill Russell)	.07	.05	.03
697	Bud Black	.05	.04	.02
698	Brad Komminsk	.05	.04	.02
699	Pat Corrales	.05	.04	.02
700	Reggie Jackson	.35	.25	.14
701	Keith Hernandez AS	.15	.11	.06
702	Tom Herr AS	.07	.05	.03
703	Tim Wallach AS	.07	.05	.03
704	Ozzie Smith AS	.10	.08	.04
705	Dale Murphy AS	.30	.25	.12
706	Pedro Guerrero AS	.12	.09	.05
707	Willie McGee AS	.12	.09	.05
708	Gary Carter AS	.20	.15	.08
709	Dwight Gooden AS	.40	.30	.15
710	John Tudor AS	.07	.05	.03
711	Jeff Reardon AS	.07	.05	.03
712	Don Mattingly AS	.90	.70	.35
713	Damaso Garcia AS	.05	.04	.02
714	George Brett AS	.30	.25	.12
715	Cal Ripken AS	.25	.20	.10
716	Rickey Henderson AS	.25	.20	.10
717	Dave Winfield AS	.20	.15	.08
718	Jorge Bell AS	.20	.15	.08
719	Carlton Fisk AS	.12	.09	.05
720	Bret Saberhagen AS	.15	.11	.06
721	Ron Guidry AS	.10	.08	.04
722	Dan Quisenberry AS	.07	.05	.03
723	Marty Bystrom	.05	.04	.02
724	Tim Hulett	.07	.05	.03
725	Mario Soto	.07	.05	.03
726	Orioles Leaders (Rick Dempsey)	.07	.05	.03
727	David Green	.05	.04	.02
728	Mike Marshall	.12	.09	.05
729	Jim Beattie	.05	.04	.02
730	Ozzie Smith	.15	.11	.06
731	Don Robinson	.07	.05	.03
732	*Floyd Youmans*(FC)	.20	.15	.08
733	Ron Romanick	.05	.04	.02
734	Marty Barrett	.10	.08	.04
735	Dave Dravecky	.07	.05	.03
736	Glenn Wilson	.07	.05	.03
737	Pete Vuckovich	.07	.05	.03
738	Andre Robertson	.05	.04	.02
739	Dave Rozema	.05	.04	.02
740	Lance Parrish	.20	.15	.08
741	Pete Rose	.40	.30	.15
742	Frank Viola	.15	.11	.06
743	Pat Sheridan	.05	.04	.02
744	Lary Sorensen	.05	.04	.02
745	Willie Upshaw	.07	.05	.03
746	Denny Gonzalez	.05	.04	.02
747	Rick Cerone	.05	.04	.02
748	Steve Henderson	.05	.04	.02
749	Ed Jurak	.05	.04	.02
750	Gorman Thomas	.10	.08	.04
751	Howard Johnson	.12	.09	.05
752	Mike Krukow	.07	.05	.03
753	Dan Ford	.05	.04	.02
754	*Pat Clements*	.12	.09	.05
755	Harold Baines	.15	.11	.06
756	Pirates Leaders (Rick Rhoden)	.07	.05	.03
757	Darrell Porter	.07	.05	.03
758	Dave Anderson	.05	.04	.02
759	Moose Haas	.05	.04	.02
760	Andre Dawson	.20	.15	.08
761	Don Slaught	.05	.04	.02
762	Eric Show	.07	.05	.03
763	Terry Puhl	.05	.04	.02
764	Kevin Gross	.07	.05	.03
765	Don Baylor	.12	.09	.05
766	Rick Langford	.05	.04	.02
767	Jody Davis	.10	.08	.04
768	Vern Ruhle	.05	.04	.02
769	*Harold Reynolds*(FC)	.60	.45	.25
770	Vida Blue	.10	.08	.04
771	John McNamara	.05	.04	.02
772	Brian Downing	.07	.05	.03
773	Greg Pryor	.05	.04	.02
774	Terry Leach	.05	.04	.02
775	Al Oliver	.10	.08	.04
776	Gene Garber	.05	.04	.02
777	Wayne Krenchicki	.05	.04	.02
778	Jerry Hairston	.05	.04	.02
779	Rick Reuschel	.10	.08	.04
780	Robin Yount	.50	.40	.20
781	Joe Nolan	.05	.04	.02
782	Ken Landreaux	.05	.04	.02
783	Ricky Horton	.07	.05	.03
784	Alan Bannister	.05	.04	.02
785	Bob Stanley	.05	.04	.02
786	Twins Leaders (Mickey Hatcher)	.07	.05	.03
787	Vance Law	.07	.05	.03
788	Marty Castillo	.05	.04	.02
789	Kurt Bevacqua	.05	.04	.02
790	Phil Niekro	.25	.20	.10
791	Checklist 661-792	.05	.04	.02
792	Charles Hudson	.06	.05	.02

1986 Topps All-Star Glossy Set of 22

As in previous years, Topps continued to make the popular glossy-surfaced cards as an insert in rack packs. The All-Star Glossy set of 22 2-1/2" by 3-1/2" cards shows little design change from previous years. Cards feature a front color photo and All-Star banner at the top. The bottom has the player's name and position. The set includes the All-Star starting teams as well as the managers and honorary captains.

		MT	NR MT	EX
Complete Set:		6.00	4.50	2.50
Common Player:		.20	.15	.08
1	Sparky Anderson	.20	.15	.08
2	Eddie Murray	.50	.40	.20
3	Lou Whitaker	.30	.25	.12
4	George Brett	.80	.60	.30
5	Cal Ripken	.60	.45	.25
6	Jim Rice	.50	.40	.20
7	Rickey Henderson	.60	.45	.25
8	Dave Winfield	.50	.40	.20
9	Carlton Fisk	.30	.25	.12
10	Jack Morris	.30	.25	.12
11	A.L. All-Star Team	.20	.15	.08
12	Dick Williams	.20	.15	.08
13	Steve Garvey	.50	.40	.20
14	Tom Herr	.20	.15	.08
15	Graig Nettles	.20	.15	.08
16	Ozzie Smith	.30	.25	.12
17	Tony Gwynn	.60	.45	.25
18	Dale Murphy	.80	.60	.30
19	Darryl Strawberry	.80	.60	.30
20	Terry Kennedy	.20	.15	.08
21	LaMarr Hoyt	.20	.15	.08
22	N.L. All-Star Team	.20	.15	.08

1986 Topps All-Star Glossy Set of 40

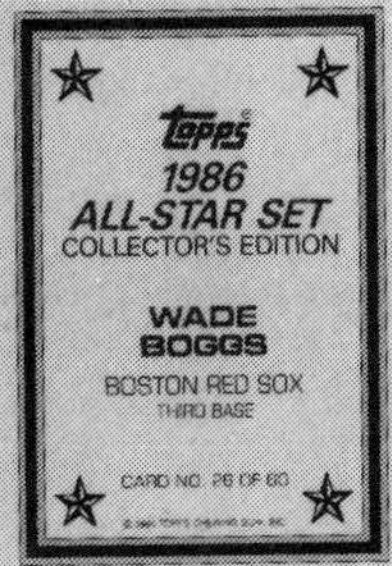

The Topps All-Star & Hot Prospects Glossy Set of 60 cards represents an expansion of a good idea. The 2-1/2" by 3-1/2" cards had a good following when they were limited to stars, but Topps realized that the addition of top young players would spice up the set even further, so in 1986 it was expanded from 40 to 60 cards. The cards themselves are basically all color glossy pictures with the player's name in very small print in the lower left-hand corner. To obtain the set, it was necessary to send $1 plus six special offer cards from wax packs to Topps for each series. At 60 cards, that meant the process had to be repeated six times as there were 10 cards in each series, making the set quite expensive from the outset.

		MT	NR MT	EX
Complete Set:		15.00	11.00	6.00
Common Player:		.15	.11	.06
1	Oddibe McDowell	.25	.20	.10
2	Reggie Jackson	.70	.50	.30
3	Fernando Valenzuela	.35	.25	.14
4	Jack Clark	.25	.20	.10
5	Rickey Henderson	.70	.50	.30
6	Steve Balboni	.15	.11	.06
7	Keith Hernandez	.40	.30	.15
8	Lance Parrish	.30	.25	.12
9	Willie McGee	.25	.20	.10
10	Chris Brown	.40	.30	.15
11	Darryl Strawberry	.90	.70	.35
12	Ron Guidry	.30	.25	.12
13	Dave Parker	.25	.20	.10
14	Cal Ripken	.70	.50	.30
15	Tim Raines	.50	.40	.20
16	Rod Carew	.60	.45	.25
17	Mike Schmidt	.90	.70	.35
18	George Brett	.90	.70	.35
19	Joe Hesketh	.15	.11	.06
20	Dan Pasqua	.20	.15	.08
21	Vince Coleman	1.00	.70	.40
22	Tom Seaver	.50	.40	.20
23	Gary Carter	.50	.40	.20
24	Orel Hershiser	.40	.30	.15
25	Pedro Guerrero	.30	.25	.12
26	Wade Boggs	1.25	.90	.50
27	Bret Saberhagen	.30	.25	.12
28	Carlton Fisk	.25	.20	.10
29	Kirk Gibson	.35	.25	.14
30	Brian Fisher	.20	.15	.08
31	Don Mattingly	3.00	2.25	1.25
32	Tom Herr	.15	.11	.06
33	Eddie Murray	.60	.45	.25
34	Ryne Sandberg	.40	.30	.15
35	Dan Quisenberry	.15	.11	.06
36	Jim Rice	.50	.40	.20
37	Dale Murphy	.90	.70	.35
38	Steve Garvey	.50	.40	.20
39	Roger McDowell	.25	.20	.10
40	Earnie Riles	.15	.11	.06
41	Dwight Gooden	1.25	.90	.50
42	Dave Winfield	.50	.40	.20
43	Dave Stieb	.20	.15	.08
44	Bob Horner	.20	.15	.08
45	Nolan Ryan	.50	.40	.20
46	Ozzie Smith	.25	.20	.10
47	Jorge Bell	.50	.40	.20
48	Gorman Thomas	.15	.11	.06
49	Tom Browning	.25	.20	.10
50	Larry Sheets	.20	.15	.08
51	Pete Rose	1.25	.90	.50
52	Brett Butler	.15	.11	.06
53	John Tudor	.20	.15	.08
54	Phil Bradley	.20	.15	.08
55	Jeff Reardon	.20	.15	.08
56	Rich Gossage	.25	.20	.10
57	Tony Gwynn	.60	.45	.25
58	Ozzie Guillen	.25	.20	.10
59	Glenn Davis	.35	.25	.14
60	Darrell Evans	.15	.11	.06

1986 Topps Box Panels

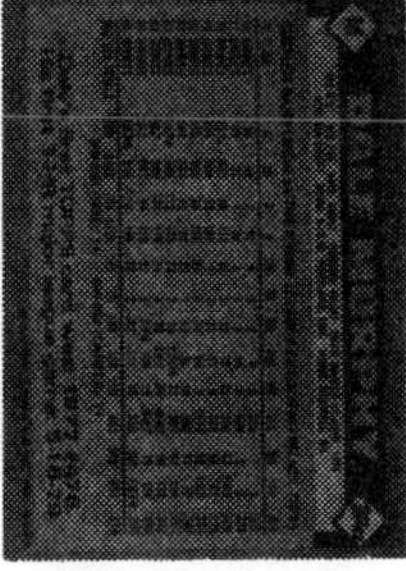

Following the lead of Donruss, which introduced the concept in 1985, Topps produced special cards on the bottom panels of wax boxes. Individual cards measure 2-1/2" by 3-1/2", the same as regular cards. Design of the cards is virtually identical with regular '86 Topps, though the top border is in red, rather than black. The cards are lettered "A" through "P", rather than numbered on the back.

		MT	NR MT	EX
Complete Panel Set:		12.00	9.00	4.75
Complete Singles Set:		4.75	3.50	2.00
Common Panel:		2.00	1.50	.80
Common Single Player:		.15	.11	.06
Panel		3.50	2.75	1.50
A	Jorge Bell	.20	.15	.08
B	Wade Boggs	.60	.45	.25
C	George Brett	.35	.25	.14
D	Vince Coleman	.35	.25	.14
Panel		2.00	1.50	.80
E	Carlton Fisk	.15	.11	.06
F	Dwight Gooden	.40	.30	.15
G	Pedro Guerrero	.15	.11	.06
H	Ron Guidry	.15	.11	.06
Panel		3.50	2.75	1.50
I	Reggie Jackson	.30	.25	.12
J	Don Mattingly	.90	.70	.35
K	Oddibe McDowell	.15	.11	.06
L	Willie McGee	.15	.11	.06
Panel		3.00	2.25	1.25
M	Dale Murphy	.35	.25	.14
N	Pete Rose	.50	.40	.20
O	Bret Saberhagen	.15	.11	.06
P	Fernando Valenzuela	.20	.15	.08

1986 Topps Gallery of Champions

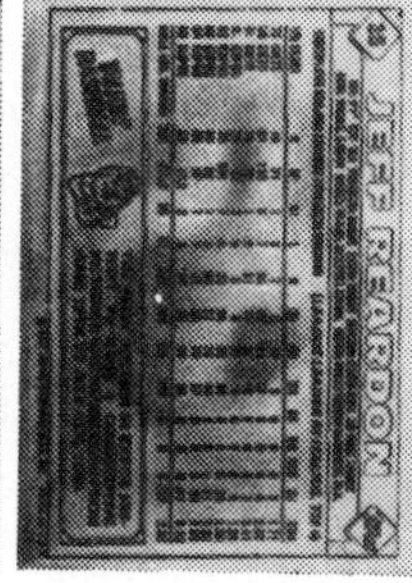

For the third consecutive year Topps issued 12 "metal mini-cards" as a dealer-ordering incentive. The metal replicas were minted 1/4-size (approxima- tely 1-1/4" by 1-3/4") of the regular cards and come in silver, aluminum and bronze. The bronze and silver sets were issued in leather-like velvet-lined display cases. A bronze 1952 Topps Mickey Mantle was given as a premium for dealers purchasing 1986 Traded sets, while a pewter Don Mattingly was issued as a premium to those ordering the aluminum, bronze and silver sets. The Mantle bronze is valued at $12 and the Mattingly pewter at $100.

		MT	NR MT	EX
Complete Aluminum Set:		30.00	22.00	12.00
Complete Bronze Set:		175.00	131.00	70.00
Complete Silver Set:		650.00	487.00	260.00
(1a)	Wade Boggs (aluminum)	3.00	2.25	1.25
(1b)	Wade Boggs (bronze)	25.00	18.50	10.00
(1c)	Wade Boggs (silver)	125.00	94.00	50.00
(2a)	Vince Coleman (aluminum)	1.25	.90	.50
(2b)	Vince Coleman (bronze)	12.00	9.00	4.75
(2c)	Vince Coleman (silver)	50.00	37.00	20.00
(3a)	Darrell Evans (aluminum)	.70	.50	.30
(3b)	Darrell Evans (bronze)	7.50	5.75	3.00
(3c)	Darrell Evans (silver)	20.00	15.00	8.00
(4a)	Dwight Gooden (aluminum)	2.00	1.50	.80
(4b)	Dwight Gooden (bronze)	20.00	15.00	8.00
(4c)	Dwight Gooden (silver)	100.00	75.00	40.00
(5a)	Ozzie Guillen (aluminum)	.70	.50	.30
(5b)	Ozzie Guillen (bronze)	7.50	5.75	3.00
(5c)	Ozzie Guillen (silver)	20.00	15.00	8.00
(6a)	Don Mattingly (aluminum)	8.00	6.00	3.25
(6b)	Don Mattingly (bronze)	50.00	37.00	20.00
(6c)	Don Mattingly (silver)	200.00	150.00	80.00
(7a)	Willie McGee (aluminum)	1.00	.70	.40
(7b)	Willie McGee (bronze)	10.00	7.50	4.00
(7c)	Willie McGee (silver)	30.00	22.00	12.00
(8a)	Dale Murphy (aluminum)	1.50	1.25	.60
(8b)	Dale Murphy (bronze)	15.00	11.00	6.00
(8c)	Dale Murphy (silver)	80.00	60.00	32.00
(9a)	Dan Quisenberry (aluminum)	.70	.50	.30
(9b)	Dan Quisenberry (bronze)	7.50	5.75	3.00
(9c)	Dan Quisenberry (silver)	20.00	15.00	8.00
(10a)	Jeff Reardon (aluminum)	.70	.50	.30
(10b)	Jeff Reardon (bronze)	7.50	5.75	3.00
(10c)	Jeff Reardon (silver)	20.00	15.00	8.00
(11a)	Pete Rose (aluminum)	2.50	2.00	1.00
(11b)	Pete Rose (bronze)	25.00	18.50	10.00
(11c)	Pete Rose (silver)	110.00	82.00	44.00
(12a)	Bret Saberhagen (aluminum)	1.00	.70	.40
(12b)	Bret Saberhagen (bronze)	10.00	7.50	4.00
(12c)	Bret Saberhagen (silver)	30.00	22.00	12.00

1986 Topps Mini League Leaders

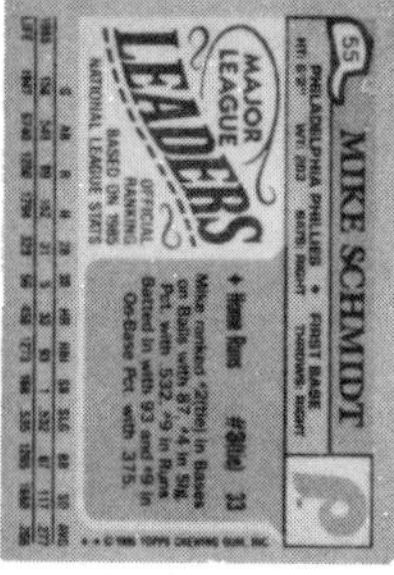

Topps had long experimented with bigger cards, but in 1986, they also decided to try smaller ones. These 2-1/8" by 2-15/16" cards feature top players in a number of categories. Sold in plastic packs as a regular Topps issue, the 66-card set is attractive as well as innovative. The cards feature color photos and a minimum of added information on the fronts where only the player's name and Topps logo appear. Backs limited information as well, but do feature whatever information was required to justify the player's inclusion in a set of league leaders.

		MT	NR MT	EX
Complete Set:		6.50	5.00	2.50
Common Player:		.09	.07	.04
1	Eddie Murray	.40	.30	.15
2	Cal Ripken	.40	.30	.15
3	Wade Boggs	.80	.60	.30
4	Dennis Boyd	.09	.07	.04
5	Dwight Evans	.15	.11	.06
6	Bruce Hurst	.15	.11	.06
7	Gary Pettis	.09	.07	.04
8	Harold Baines	.15	.11	.06
9	Floyd Bannister	.09	.07	.04
10	Britt Burns	.09	.07	.04
11	Carlton Fisk	.20	.15	.08
12	Brett Butler	.15	.11	.06
13	Darrell Evans	.15	.11	.06
14	Jack Morris	.25	.20	.10
15	Lance Parrish	.25	.20	.10
16	Walt Terrell	.09	.07	.04
17	Steve Balboni	.09	.07	.04
18	George Brett	.50	.40	.20
19	Charlie Leibrandt	.09	.07	.04
20	Bret Saberhagen	.20	.15	.08
21	Lonnie Smith	.09	.07	.04
22	Willie Wilson	.15	.11	.06
23	Bert Blyleven	.15	.11	.06
24	Mike Smithson	.09	.07	.04
25	Frank Viola	.20	.15	.08
26	Ron Guidry	.20	.15	.08
27	Rickey Henderson	.40	.30	.15
28	Don Mattingly	1.25	.90	.50
29	Dave Winfield	.30	.25	.12
30	Mike Moore	.09	.07	.04
31	Gorman Thomas	.09	.07	.04
32	Toby Harrah	.09	.07	.04
33	Charlie Hough	.09	.07	.04
34	Doyle Alexander	.09	.07	.04
35	Jimmy Key	.15	.11	.06
36	Dave Stieb	.15	.11	.06
37	Dale Murphy	.50	.40	.20
38	Keith Moreland	.09	.07	.04
39	Ryne Sandberg	.30	.25	.12
40	Tom Browning	.15	.11	.06
41	Dave Parker	.20	.15	.08
42	Mario Soto	.09	.07	.04
43	Nolan Ryan	.30	.25	.12
44	Pedro Guerrero	.20	.15	.08
45	Orel Hershiser	.30	.25	.12
46	Mike Scioscia	.09	.07	.04
47	Fernando Valenzuela	.25	.20	.10
48	Bob Welch	.15	.11	.06
49	Tim Raines	.30	.25	.12
50	Gary Carter	.30	.25	.12
51	Sid Fernandez	.15	.11	.06
52	Dwight Gooden	.70	.50	.30
53	Keith Hernandez	.25	.20	.10
54	Juan Samuel	.20	.15	.08
55	Mike Schmidt	.50	.40	.20
56	Glenn Wilson	.09	.07	.04
57	Rick Reuschel	.15	.11	.06
58	Joaquin Andujar	.09	.07	.04
59	Jack Clark	.20	.15	.08
60	Vince Coleman	.60	.45	.25
61	Danny Cox	.09	.07	.04
62	Tom Herr	.09	.07	.04
63	Willie McGee	.15	.11	.06
64	John Tudor	.15	.11	.06
65	Tony Gwynn	.40	.30	.15
66	Checklist	.09	.07	.04

1986 Topps Stickers

The 1986 Topps stickers are 2-1/8" by 3". The 200- piece set features 316 different subjects, with some stickers including two or three players. Numbers run only to 315, however. The set includes some specialty stickers such as League Championships and World Series themes. Stickers are numbered both front and back and included a chance to win a trip to spring training as well as an offer to buy a complete 1986 Topps regular set. An album for the stickers was available in stores.

		MT	NR MT	EX
Complete Set:		15.00	11.00	6.00
Common Player:		.03	.02	.01
Sticker Album:		.70	.50	.30
1	Pete Rose	.25	.20	.10
2	Pete Rose	.25	.20	.10
3	George Brett	.12	.09	.05
4	Rod Carew	.10	.08	.04
5	Vince Coleman	.12	.09	.05
6	Dwight Gooden	.15	.11	.06
7	Phil Niekro	.08	.06	.03
8	Tony Perez	.06	.05	.02
9	Nolan Ryan	.10	.08	.04
10	Tom Seaver	.10	.08	.04
11	N.L. Championship Series (Ozzie Smith)	.06	.05	.02
12	N.L. Championship Series (Bill Madlock)	.04	.03	.02
13	N.L. Championship Series (Cardinals Celebrate)	.03	.02	.01
14	A.L. Championship Series (Al Oliver)	.04	.03	.02
15	A.L. Championship Series (Jim Sundberg)	.03	.02	.01
16	A.L. Championship Series (George Brett)	.10	.08	.04
17	World Series (Bret Saberhagen)	.06	.05	.02
18	World Series (Dane Iorg)	.03	.02	.01
19	World Series (Tito Landrum)	.03	.02	.01
20	World Series (John Tudor)	.04	.03	.02
21	World Series (Buddy Biancalana)	.03	.02	.01
22	World Series (Darryl Motley, Darrell Porter)	.03	.02	.01
23	World Series (George Brett, Frank White)	.10	.08	.04
24	Nolan Ryan	.15	.11	.06
25	Bill Doran	.08	.06	.03
26	Jose Cruz	.04	.03	.02
27	Mike Scott	.08	.06	.03
28	Kevin Bass	.04	.03	.02
29	Glenn Davis	.10	.08	.04
30	Mark Bailey	.06	.05	.02
31	Dave Smith	.10	.08	.04
32	Phil Garner	.03	.02	.01
33	Dickie Thon	.06	.05	.02
34	Bob Horner	.12	.09	.05
35	Dale Murphy	.25	.20	.10
36	Glenn Hubbard	.04	.03	.02
37	Bruce Sutter	.08	.06	.03
38	Ken Oberkfell	.04	.03	.02
39	Claudell Washington	.04	.03	.02
40	Steve Bedrosian	.04	.03	.02
41	Terry Harper	.03	.02	.01
42	Rafael Ramirez	.06	.05	.02
43	Rick Mahler	.03	.02	.01
44	Joaquin Andujar	.06	.05	.02
45	Willie McGee	.10	.08	.04
46	Ozzie Smith	.06	.05	.02
47	Vince Coleman	.12	.09	.05
48	Danny Cox	.04	.03	.02
49	Tom Herr	.04	.03	.02
50	Jack Clark	.08	.06	.03
51	Andy Van Slyke	.04	.03	.02
52	John Tudor	.08	.06	.03
53	Terry Pendleton	.03	.02	.01
54	Keith Moreland	.06	.05	.02
55	Ryne Sandberg	.15	.11	.06
56	Lee Smith	.04	.03	.02
57	Steve Trout	.06	.05	.02
58	Jody Davis	.08	.06	.03
59	Gary Matthews	.04	.03	.02
60	Leon Durham	.04	.03	.02
61	Rick Sutcliffe	.06	.05	.02
62	Dennis Eckersley	.04	.03	.02
63	Bob Dernier	.03	.02	.01
64	Fernando Valenzuela	.15	.11	.06
65	Pedro Guerrero	.12	.09	.05
66	Jerry Reuss	.06	.05	.02
67	Greg Brock	.06	.05	.02
68	Mike Scioscia	.03	.02	.01
69	Ken Howell	.04	.03	.02
70	Bill Madlock	.04	.03	.02
71	Mike Marshall	.06	.05	.02
72	Steve Sax	.06	.05	.02
73	Orel Hershiser	.06	.05	.02
74	Andre Dawson	.12	.09	.05
75	Tim Raines	.12	.09	.05
76	Jeff Reardon	.06	.05	.02
77	Hubie Brooks	.04	.03	.02
78	Bill Gullickson	.04	.03	.02
79	Bryn Smith	.04	.03	.02
80	Terry Francona	.04	.03	.02
81	Vance Law	.03	.02	.01
82	Tim Wallach	.04	.03	.02
83	Herm Winningham	.04	.03	.02
84	Jeff Leonard	.06	.05	.02
85	Chris Brown	.20	.15	.08
86	Scott Garrelts	.03	.02	.01
87	Jose Uribe	.04	.03	.02
88	Manny Trillo	.04	.03	.02
89	Dan Driessen	.04	.03	.02
90	Dan Gladden	.06	.05	.02
91	Mark Davis	.04	.03	.02
92	Bob Brenly	.03	.02	.01
93	Mike Krukow	.04	.03	.02
94	Dwight Gooden	.35	.25	.14
95	Darryl Strawberry	.25	.20	.10
96	Gary Carter	.10	.08	.04
97	Wally Backman	.06	.05	.02
98	Ron Darling	.06	.05	.02
99	Keith Hernandez	.12	.09	.05
100	George Foster	.06	.05	.02
101	Howard Johnson	.06	.05	.02
102	Rafael Santana	.04	.03	.02
103	Roger McDowell	.06	.05	.02
104	Steve Garvey	.15	.11	.06
105	Tony Gwynn	.20	.15	.08
106	Graig Nettles	.06	.05	.02
107	Rich Gossage	.10	.08	.04
108	Andy Hawkins	.04	.03	.02
109	Carmelo Martinez	.04	.03	.02
110	Garry Templeton	.04	.03	.02
111	Terry Kennedy	.06	.05	.02
112	Tim Flannery	.08	.06	.03
113	LaMarr Hoyt	.03	.02	.01

		MT	NR MT	EX
114	Mike Schmidt	.25	.20	.10
115	Ozzie Virgil	.06	.05	.02
116	Steve Carlton	.10	.08	.04
117	Garry Maddox	.03	.02	.01
118	Glenn Wilson	.06	.05	.02
119	Kevin Gross	.03	.02	.01
120	Von Hayes	.04	.03	.02
121	Juan Samuel	.06	.05	.02
122	Rick Schu	.08	.06	.03
123	Shane Rawley	.06	.05	.02
124	Johnny Ray	.06	.05	.02
125	Tony Pena	.06	.05	.02
126	Rick Reuschel	.12	.09	.05
127	Sammy Khalifa	.06	.05	.02
128	Marvell Wynne	.04	.03	.02
129	Jason Thompson	.03	.02	.01
130	Rick Rhoden	.04	.03	.02
131	Bill Almon	.03	.02	.01
132	Joe Orsulak	.06	.05	.02
133	Jim Morrison	.06	.05	.02
134	Pete Rose	.40	.30	.15
135	Dave Parker	.12	.09	.05
136	Mario Soto	.03	.02	.01
137	Dave Concepcion	.10	.08	.04
138	Ron Oester	.03	.02	.01
139	Buddy Bell	.06	.05	.02
140	Ted Power	.03	.02	.01
141	Tom Browning	.06	.05	.02
142	John Franco	.08	.06	.03
143	Tony Perez	.06	.05	.02
144	Willie McGee	.08	.06	.03
145	Dale Murphy	.15	.11	.06
146	Tony Gwynn	.40	.30	.15
147	Tom Herr	.15	.11	.06
148	Steve Garvey	.30	.25	.12
149	Dale Murphy	.40	.30	.15
150	Darryl Strawberry	.40	.30	.15
151	Graig Nettles	.15	.11	.06
152	Terry Kennedy	.15	.11	.06
153	Ozzie Smith	.20	.15	.08
154	LaMarr Hoyt	.15	.11	.06
155	Rickey Henderson	.40	.30	.15
156	Lou Whitaker	.25	.20	.10
157	George Brett	.40	.30	.15
158	Eddie Murray	.40	.30	.15
159	Cal Ripken	.40	.30	.15
160	Dave Winfield	.30	.25	.12
161	Jim Rice	.30	.25	.12
162	Carlton Fisk	.25	.20	.10
163	Jack Morris	.25	.20	.10
164	Wade Boggs	.15	.11	.06
165	Darrell Evans	.06	.05	.02
166	Mike Davis	.06	.05	.02
167	Dave Kingman	.08	.06	.03
168	Alfredo Griffin	.04	.03	.02
169	Carney Lansford	.04	.03	.02
170	Bruce Bochte	.10	.08	.04
171	Dwayne Murphy	.08	.06	.03
172	Dave Collins	.04	.03	.02
173	Chris Codiroli	.10	.08	.04
174	Mike Heath	.03	.02	.01
175	Jay Howell	.12	.09	.05
176	Rod Carew	.20	.15	.08
177	Reggie Jackson	.20	.15	.08
178	Doug DeCinces	.10	.08	.04
179	Bob Boone	.12	.09	.05
180	Ron Romanick	.15	.11	.06
181	Bob Grich	.08	.06	.03
182	Donnie Moore	.06	.05	.02
183	Brian Downing	.10	.08	.04
184	Ruppert Jones	.10	.08	.04
185	Juan Beniquez	.04	.03	.02
186	Dave Stieb	.06	.05	.02
187	Jorge Bell	.20	.15	.08
188	Willie Upshaw	.08	.06	.03
189	Tom Henke	.04	.03	.02
190	Damaso Garcia	.10	.08	.04
191	Jimmy Key	.06	.05	.02
192	Jesse Barfield	.10	.08	.04
193	Dennis Lamp	.03	.02	.01
194	Tony Fernandez	.06	.05	.02
195	Lloyd Moseby	.04	.03	.02
196	Cecil Cooper	.08	.06	.03
197	Robin Yount	.15	.11	.06
198	Rollie Fingers	.08	.06	.03
199	Ted Simmons	.04	.03	.02
200	Ben Oglivie	.04	.03	.02
201	Moose Haas	.04	.03	.02
202	Jim Gantner	.03	.02	.01
203	Paul Molitor	.06	.05	.02
204	Charlie Moore	.03	.02	.01
205	Danny Darwin	.06	.05	.02
206	Brett Butler	.06	.05	.02
207	Brook Jacoby	.08	.06	.03
208	Andre Thornton	.12	.09	.05
209	Tom Waddell	.04	.03	.02
210	Tony Bernazard	.04	.03	.02
211	Julio Franco	.08	.06	.03
212	Pat Tabler	.04	.03	.02
213	Joe Carter	.08	.06	.03
214	George Vukovich	.03	.02	.01
215	Rich Thompson	.04	.03	.02
216	Gorman Thomas	.06	.05	.02
217	Phil Bradley	.10	.08	.04
218	Alvin Davis	.06	.05	.02
219	Jim Presley	.08	.06	.03
220	Matt Young	.04	.03	.02
221	Mike Moore	.04	.03	.02
222	Dave Henderson	.06	.05	.02
223	Ed Nunez	.04	.03	.02
224	Spike Owen	.03	.02	.01
225	Mark Langston	.06	.05	.02
226	Cal Ripken	.20	.15	.08
227	Eddie Murray	.20	.15	.08
228	Fred Lynn	.06	.05	.02
229	Lee Lacy	.03	.02	.01
230	Scott McGregor	.04	.03	.02
231	Storm Davis	.04	.03	.02
232	Rick Dempsey	.06	.05	.02
233	Mike Boddicker	.06	.05	.02
234	Mike Young	.06	.05	.02
235	Sammy Stewart	.06	.05	.02
236	Pete O'Brien	.08	.06	.03
237	Oddibe McDowell	.15	.11	.06
238	Toby Harrah	.04	.03	.02
239	Gary Ward	.04	.03	.02
240	Larry Parrish	.04	.03	.02
241	Charlie Hough	.04	.03	.02
242	Burt Hooton	.03	.02	.01
243	Don Slaught	.04	.03	.02
244	Curt Wilkerson	.04	.03	.02
245	Greg Harris	.03	.02	.01
246	Jim Rice	.15	.11	.06
247	Wade Boggs	.60	.45	.25
248	Rich Gedman	.04	.03	.02
249	Dennis Boyd	.04	.03	.02
250	Marty Barrett	.04	.03	.02
251	Dwight Evans	.06	.05	.02
252	Bill Buckner	.04	.03	.02
253	Bob Stanley	.03	.02	.01
254	Tony Armas	.04	.03	.02
255	Mike Easler	.10	.08	.04
256	George Brett	.25	.20	.10
257	Dan Quisenberry	.06	.05	.02
258	Willie Wilson	.06	.05	.02
259	Jim Sundberg	.06	.05	.02
260	Bret Saberhagen	.12	.09	.05
261	Bud Black	.06	.05	.02
262	Charlie Leibrandt	.06	.05	.02
263	Frank White	.04	.03	.02
264	Lonnie Smith	.06	.05	.02
265	Steve Balboni	.06	.05	.02
266	Kirk Gibson	.15	.11	.06
267	Alan Trammell	.15	.11	.06
268	Jack Morris	.10	.08	.04
269	Darrell Evans	.04	.03	.02
270	Dan Petry	.04	.03	.02
271	Larry Herndon	.04	.03	.02
272	Lou Whitaker	.06	.05	.02
273	Lance Parrish	.08	.06	.03
274	Chet Lemon	.03	.02	.01
275	Willie Hernandez	.10	.08	.04
276	Tom Brunansky	.08	.06	.03
277	Kent Hrbek	.12	.09	.05
278	Mark Salas	.03	.02	.01
279	Bert Blyleven	.06	.05	.02
280	Tim Teufel	.03	.02	.01
281	Ron Davis	.04	.03	.02
282	Mike Smithson	.06	.05	.02
283	Gary Gaetti	.08	.06	.03
284	Frank Viola	.06	.05	.02
285	Kirby Puckett	.12	.09	.05
286	Carlton Fisk	.12	.09	.05
287	Tom Seaver	.15	.11	.06
288	Harold Baines	.06	.05	.02
289	Ron Kittle	.04	.03	.02
290	Bob James	.03	.02	.01
291	Rudy Law	.04	.03	.02
292	Britt Burns	.03	.02	.01
293	Greg Walker	.06	.05	.02
294	Ozzie Guillen	.06	.05	.02
295	Tim Hulett	.03	.02	.01
296	Don Mattingly	.70	.50	.30
297	Rickey Henderson	.20	.15	.08
298	Dave Winfield	.10	.08	.04
299	Butch Wynegar	.03	.02	.01
300	Don Baylor	.06	.05	.02
301	Eddie Whitson	.03	.02	.01
302	Ron Guidry	.06	.05	.02
303	Dave Righetti	.08	.06	.03
304	Bobby Meacham	.06	.05	.02
305	Willie Randolph	.08	.06	.03
306	Vince Coleman	.15	.11	.06
307	Oddibe McDowell	.15	.11	.06
308	Larry Sheets	.06	.05	.02
309	Ozzie Guillen	.06	.05	.02
310	Earnie Riles	.04	.03	.02
311	Chris Brown	.10	.08	.04
312	Brian Fisher, Roger McDowell	.08	.06	.03
313	Tom Browning	.04	.03	.02
314	Glenn Davis	.10	.08	.04
315	Mark Salas	.03	.02	.01

1986 Topps Super

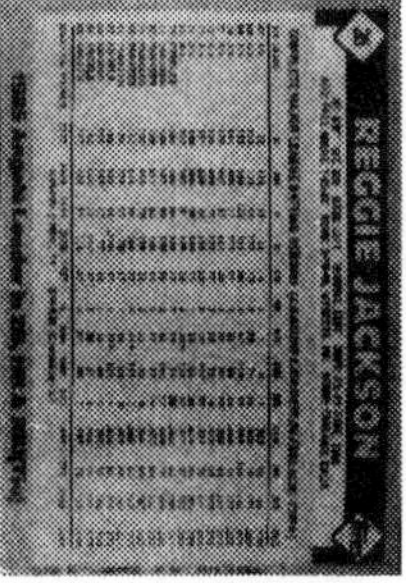

A third year of oversize, 4-7/8" by 6-7/8", versions of Topps' regular issue cards saw the set once again hit the 60-card mark. Besides being four times the size of a normal card, the Supers differ only in the number on the back of the card.

		MT	NR MT	EX
	Complete Set:	9.00	6.75	3.50
	Common Player:	.20	.15	.08
1	Don Mattingly	2.25	1.75	.90
2	Willie McGee	.35	.25	.14
3	Bret Saberhagen	.35	.25	.14
4	Dwight Gooden	1.50	1.25	.60
5	Dan Quisenberry	.20	.15	.08
6	Jeff Reardon	.25	.20	.10
7	Ozzie Guillen	.25	.20	.10
8	Vince Coleman	.70	.50	.30
9	Harold Baines	.25	.20	.10
10	Jorge Bell	.50	.40	.20
11	Bert Blyleven	.25	.20	.10
12	Wade Boggs	1.25	.90	.50
13	Phil Bradley	.25	.20	.10
14	George Brett	.80	.60	.30
15	Hubie Brooks	.20	.15	.08
16	Tom Browning	.25	.20	.10
17	Bill Buckner	.20	.15	.08
18	Brett Butler	.20	.15	.08
19	Gary Carter	.50	.40	.20
20	Cecil Cooper	.25	.20	.10
21	Darrell Evans	.25	.20	.10
22	Dwight Evans	.20	.15	.08
23	Carlton Fisk	.30	.25	.12
24	Steve Garvey	.50	.40	.20
25	Kirk Gibson	.35	.25	.14
26	Rich Gossage	.25	.20	.10
27	Pedro Guerrero	.30	.25	.12
28	Ron Guidry	.30	.25	.12
29	Tony Gwynn	.70	.50	.30
30	Rickey Henderson	.70	.50	.30
31	Keith Hernandez	.50	.40	.20
32	Tom Herr	.20	.15	.08
33	Orel Hershiser	.50	.40	.20
34	Jay Howell	.20	.15	.08
35	Reggie Jackson	.60	.45	.25
36	Bob James	.20	.15	.08
37	Charlie Leibrandt	.20	.15	.08
38	Jack Morris	.35	.25	.14
39	Dale Murphy	.80	.60	.30
40	Eddie Murray	.60	.45	.25
41	Dave Parker	.35	.25	.14
42	Tim Raines	.50	.40	.20
43	Jim Rice	.50	.40	.20
44	Dave Righetti	.30	.25	.12
45	Cal Ripken	.70	.50	.30
46	Pete Rose	1.00	.70	.40
47	Nolan Ryan	.50	.40	.20
48	Ryne Sandberg	.50	.40	.20
49	Mike Schmidt	.80	.60	.30
50	Tom Seaver	.50	.40	.20
51	Bryn Smith	.20	.15	.08
52	Lee Smith	.20	.15	.08
53	Ozzie Smith	.30	.25	.12
54	Dave Stieb	.20	.15	.08
55	Darryl Strawberry	.80	.60	.30
56	Gorman Thomas	.20	.15	.08
57	John Tudor	.20	.15	.08
58	Fernando Valenzuela	.40	.30	.15
59	Willie Wilson	.25	.20	.10
60	Dave Winfield	.50	.40	.20

1986 Topps Super Star

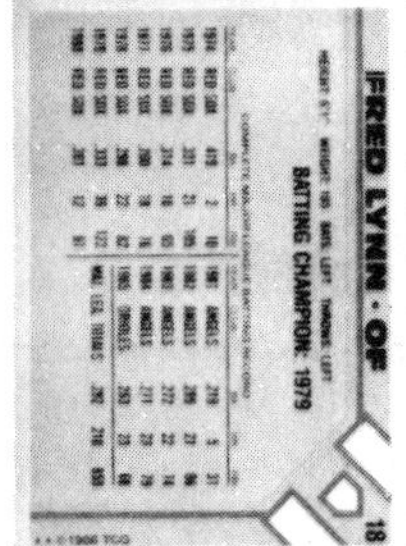

Labeled "Topps' Collector Series" in a red band at the top of the front, this set marked the second year of Topps' production of a special boxed set for the Woolworth chain of stores, though Woolworth's name does not appear anywhere on the card. The cards, which measure 2-1/2" by 3-1/2", feature a color photo with its lower right corner rolled up to reveal the words "Super Star" on a bright yellow border. The player's name appears in the lower left corner. The 66-card set features stars and retains a certain measure of popularity on that basis.

		MT	NR MT	EX
	Complete Set:	5.00	3.75	2.00
	Common Player:	.09	.07	.04
1	Tony Armas	.09	.07	.04
2	Don Baylor	.12	.09	.05
3	Wade Boggs	1.00	.70	.40
4	George Brett	.40	.30	.15
5	Bill Buckner	.09	.07	.04
6	Rod Carew	.30	.25	.12
7	Gary Carter	.30	.25	.12
8	Cecil Cooper	.12	.09	.05
9	Darrell Evans	.12	.09	.05
10	Dwight Evans	.15	.11	.06
11	George Foster	.12	.09	.05
12	Bobby Grich	.09	.07	.04
13	Tony Gwynn	.35	.25	.14
14	Keith Hernandez	.25	.20	.10
15	Reggie Jackson	.30	.25	.12
16	Dave Kingman	.12	.09	.05
17	Carney Lansford	.09	.07	.04
18	Fred Lynn	.12	.09	.05
19	Bill Madlock	.12	.09	.05

		MT	NR MT	EX
20	Don Mattingly	2.00	1.50	.80
21	Willie McGee	.20	.15	.08
22	Hal McRae	.09	.07	.04
23	Dale Murphy	.40	.30	.15
24	Eddie Murray	.35	.25	.14
25	Ben Oglivie	.09	.07	.04
26	Al Oliver	.12	.09	.05
27	Dave Parker	.20	.15	.08
28	Jim Rice	.30	.25	.12
29	Pete Rose	.90	.70	.35
30	Mike Schmidt	.40	.30	.15
31	Gorman Thomas	.09	.07	.04
32	Willie Wilson	.12	.09	.05
33	Dave Winfield	.30	.25	.12

1986 Topps Tattoos

Topps returned to tattoos in 1986, marketing a set of 24 different tattoo sheets. Each sheet of tattoos measures 3-7/16" by 14" and includes both player and smaller action tattoos. As the action tattoos were uniform and not of any particular player, they add little value to the sheet. The player tattoos measure 1-3/16" by 2-3/8". With 24 sheets, eight players per sheet, there are 192 players represented in the set. The sheets are numbered.

	MT	NR MT	EX
Complete Set:	5.00	3.75	2.00
Common Player:	.20	.15	.08

		MT	NR MT	EX
1	Julio Franco, Rich Gossage, Keith Hernandez, Charlie Leibrandt, Jack Perconte, Lee Smith, Dickie Thon, Dave Winfield	.25	.20	.10
2	Jesse Barfield, Shawon Dunston, Dennis Eckersley, Brian Fisher, Moose Haas, Mike Moore, Dale Murphy, Bret Saberhagen	.30	.25	.12
3	George Bell, Bob Brenly, Steve Carlton, Jose DeLeon, Bob Horner, Bob James, Dan Quisenberry, Andre Thornton	.25	.20	.10
4	Mike Davis, Leon Durham, Darrell Evans, Glenn Hubbard, Johnny Ray, Cal Ripken, Ted Simmons	.25	.20	.10
5	John Candelaria, Rick Dempsey, Steve Garvey, Ozzie Guillen, Gary Matthews, Jesse Orosco, Tony Pena	.25	.20	.10
6	Bruce Bochte, George Brett, Cecil Cooper, Sammy Khalifa, Ron Kittle, Scott McGregor, Pete Rose, Mookie Wilson	.45	.35	.20
7	John Franco, Carney Lansford, Don Mattingly, Graig Nettles, Rick Reuschel, Mike Schmidt, Larry Sheets, Don Sutton	.45	.35	.20
8	Cecilio Guante, Willie Hernandez, Mike Krukow, Fred Lynn, Phil Niekro, Ed Nunez, Ryne Sandberg, Pat Tabler	.25	.20	.10
9	Brett Butler, Chris Codiroli, Jim Gantner, Charlie Hough, Dave Parker, Rick Rhoden, Glenn Wilson, Robin Yount	.20	.15	.08
10	Tom Browning, Ron Darling, Von Hayes, Chet Lemon, Tom Seaver, Mike Smithson, Bruce Sutter, Alan Trammell	.25	.20	.10
11	Tony Armas, Jose Cruz, Jay Howell, Rick Mahler, Jack Morris, Rafael Ramirez, Dave Righetti, Mike Young	.20	.15	.08
12	Alvin Davis, Doug DeCinces, Andy Hawkins, Dennis Lamp, Keith Moreland, Jim Presley, Mario Soto, John Tudor	.20	.15	.08
13	Hubie Brooks, Jody Davis, Dwight Evans, Ron Hassey, Charles Hudson, Kirby Puckett, Jose Uribe	.20	.15	.08
14	Tony Bernazard, Phil Bradley, Bill Buckner, Brian Downing, Dan Driessen, Ron Guidry, LaMarr Hoyt, Garry Maddox	.20	.15	.08
15	Buddy Bell, Joe Carter, Tony Fernandez, Tito Landrum, Jeff Leonard, Hal McRae, Willie Randolph, Juan Samuel	.20	.15	.08
16	Dennis Boyd, Vince Coleman, Scott Garrelts, Alfredo Griffin, Donnie Moore, Tony Perez, Ozzie Smith, Frank White	.25	.20	.10
17	Rich Gedman, Kent Hrbek, Reggie Jackson, Mike Marshall, Terry Pendleton, Tim Raines, Mark Salas, Claudell Washington	.25	.20	.10
18	Chris Brown, Tom Brunansky, Glenn Davis, Ron Davis, Burt Hooton, Darryl Strawberry, Frank Viola, Tim Wallach	.30	.25	.12
19	Jack Clark, Bill Doran, Toby Harrah, Bill Madlock, Pete O'Brien, Larry Parrish, Mike Scioscia, Garry Templeton	.20	.15	.08
20	Gary Carter, Andre Dawson, Dwight Gooden, Orel Hershiser, Oddibe McDowell, Roger McDowell, Dwayne Murphy, Jim Rice	.40	.30	.15
21	Steve Balboni, Mike Easler, Charlie Lea, Lloyd Moseby, Steve Sax, Rick Sutcliffe, Gary Ward, Willie Wilson	.20	.15	.08
22	Wade Boggs, Dave Concepcion, Kirk Gibson, Tom Herr, Lance Parrish, Jeff Reardon, Bryn Smith, Gorman Thomas	.30	.25	.12
23	Carlton Fisk, Bob Grich, Pedro Guerrero, Willie McGee, Paul Molitor, Mike Scott, Dave Stieb, Lou Whitaker	.20	.15	.08
24	Bert Blyleven, Damaso Garcia, Phil Garner, Tony Gwynn, Rickey Henderson, Ben Oglivie, Nolan Ryan, Fernando Valenzuela	.30	.25	.12

1986 Topps Traded

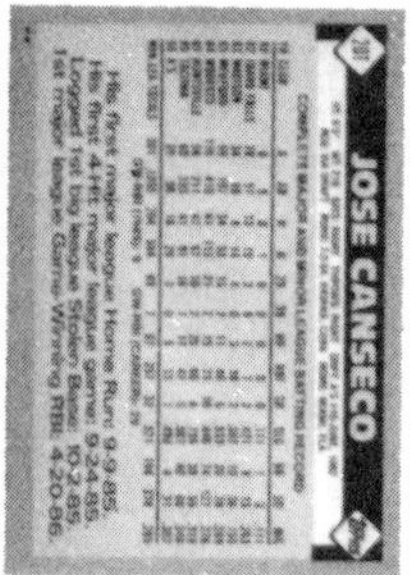

This 132-card set of 2-1/2" by 3-1/2" cards is one of the most popular sets of recent times. As always, the set features traded veterans, including such players as Phil Niekro and Tom Seaver. They are not, however, the reason for the excitement. The demand is there because of a better than usual crop of rookies who also appear in the sets. Among those are Jose Canseco, Wally Joyner, Pete Incaviglia, Todd Worrell and the first card of Bo Jackson. As in the previous two years, a glossy-finish "Tiffany" edition of 5,000 Traded sets was produced. The "Tiffany" cards are worth four to six times the value of the regular Traded cards.

	MT	NR MT	EX
Complete Set:	30.00	22.50	12.50
Common Player:	.08	.06	.03

		MT	NR MT	EX
1T	Andy Allanson(FC)	.20	.15	.08
2T	Neil Allen	.08	.06	.03
3T	Joaquin Andujar	.10	.08	.04
4T	Paul Assenmacher(FC)	.20	.15	.08
5T	Scott Bailes(FC)	.20	.15	.08
6T	Don Baylor	.15	.11	.06
7T	Steve Bedrosian	.15	.11	.06
8T	Juan Beniquez	.08	.06	.03
9T	Juan Berenguer	.08	.06	.03
10T	Mike Bielecki(FC)	.50	.40	.20
11T	Barry Bonds(FC)	1.75	1.25	.70
12T	Bobby Bonilla(FC)	1.75	1.25	.70
13T	Juan Bonilla	.08	.06	.03
14T	Rich Bordi	.08	.06	.03
15T	Steve Boros	.08	.06	.03
16T	Rick Burleson	.10	.08	.04
17T	Bill Campbell	.08	.06	.03
18T	Tom Candiotti	.08	.06	.03
19T	John Cangelosi(FC)	.20	.15	.08
20T	Jose Canseco(FC)	15.00	11.00	6.00
21T	Carmen Castillo	.08	.06	.03
22T	Rick Cerone	.08	.06	.03
23T	John Cerutti(FC)	.20	.15	.08
24T	Will Clark(FC)	12.00	9.00	4.75
25T	Mark Clear	.08	.06	.03
26T	Darnell Coles	.12	.09	.05
27T	Dave Collins	.10	.08	.04
28T	Tim Conroy	.08	.06	.03
29T	Joe Cowley	.08	.06	.03
30T	Joel Davis(FC)	.12	.09	.05
31T	Rob Deer	.15	.11	.06
32T	John Denny	.08	.06	.03
33T	Mike Easler	.10	.08	.04
34T	Mark Eichhorn(FC)	.20	.15	.08
35T	Steve Farr	.08	.06	.03
36T	Scott Fletcher	.15	.11	.06
37T	Terry Forster	.10	.08	.04
38T	Terry Francona	.08	.06	.03
39T	Jim Fregosi	.08	.06	.03
40T	Andres Galarraga(FC)	1.75	1.25	.70
41T	Ken Griffey	.12	.09	.05
42T	Bill Gullickson	.08	.06	.03
43T	Jose Guzman(FC)	.35	.25	.14
44T	Moose Haas	.08	.06	.03
45T	Billy Hatcher	.20	.15	.08
46T	Mike Heath	.08	.06	.03
47T	Tom Hume	.08	.06	.03
48T	Pete Incaviglia(FC)	.50	.40	.20
49T	Dane Iorg	.08	.06	.03
50T	Bo Jackson(FC)	10.00	7.50	4.00
51T	Wally Joyner(FC)	2.50	2.00	1.00
52T	Charlie Kerfeld(FC)	.15	.11	.06
53T	Eric King(FC)	.20	.15	.08
54T	Bob Kipper(FC)	.12	.09	.05
55T	Wayne Krenchicki	.08	.06	.03
56T	John Kruk(FC)	.40	.30	.15
57T	Mike LaCoss	.08	.06	.03
58T	Pete Ladd	.08	.06	.03
59T	Mike Laga	.08	.06	.03
60T	Hal Lanier	.08	.06	.03
61T	Dave LaPoint	.12	.09	.05
62T	Rudy Law	.08	.06	.03
63T	Rick Leach	.08	.06	.03
64T	Tim Leary	.08	.06	.03
65T	Dennis Leonard	.10	.08	.04
66T	Jim Leyland	.08	.06	.03
67T	Steve Lyons	.12	.09	.05
68T	Mickey Mahler	.08	.06	.03
69T	Candy Maldonado	.15	.11	.06
70T	Roger Mason(FC)	.10	.08	.04
71T	Bob McClure	.08	.06	.03
72T	Andy McGaffigan	.08	.06	.03
73T	Gene Michael	.08	.06	.03
74T	Kevin Mitchell(FC)	7.00	5.25	2.75
75T	Omar Moreno	.08	.06	.03
76T	Jerry Mumphrey	.08	.06	.03
77T	Phil Niekro	.40	.30	.15
78T	Randy Niemann	.08	.06	.03
79T	Juan Nieves(FC)	.25	.20	.10
80T	Otis Nixon(FC)	.12	.09	.05
81T	Bob Ojeda	.12	.09	.05
82T	Jose Oquendo	.08	.06	.03
83T	Tom Paciorek	.08	.06	.03
84T	Dave Palmer	.08	.06	.03
85T	Frank Pastore	.08	.06	.03
86T	Lou Piniella	.12	.09	.05
87T	Dan Plesac(FC)	.40	.30	.15
88T	Darrell Porter	.10	.08	.04
89T	Rey Quinones(FC)	.20	.15	.08
90T	Gary Redus	.10	.08	.04
91T	Bip Roberts	.08	.06	.03
92T	Billy Jo Robidoux(FC)	.15	.11	.06
93T	Jeff Robinson	.12	.09	.05
94T	Gary Roenicke	.08	.06	.03
95T	Ed Romero	.08	.06	.03
96T	Argenis Salazar	.08	.06	.03
97T	Joe Sambito	.08	.06	.03
98T	Billy Sample	.08	.06	.03
99T	Dave Schmidt	.08	.06	.03
100T	Ken Schrom	.08	.06	.03
101T	Tom Seaver	.60	.45	.25
102T	Ted Simmons	.20	.15	.08
103T	Sammy Stewart	.08	.06	.03
104T	Kurt Stillwell(FC)	.30	.25	.12
105T	Franklin Stubbs	.12	.09	.05
106T	Dale Sveum(FC)	.25	.20	.10
107T	Chuck Tanner	.08	.06	.03
108T	Danny Tartabull(FC)	1.00	.70	.40
109T	Tim Teufel	.08	.06	.03
110T	Bob Tewksbury(FC)	.15	.11	.06
111T	Andres Thomas(FC)	.30	.25	.12
112T	Milt Thompson	.12	.09	.05
113T	Robby Thompson(FC)	.50	.40	.20
114T	Jay Tibbs	.08	.06	.03
115T	Wayne Tolleson	.08	.06	.03
116T	Alex Trevino	.08	.06	.03
117T	Manny Trillo	.10	.08	.04
118T	Ed Vande Berg	.08	.06	.03
119T	Ozzie Virgil	.08	.06	.03
120T	Bob Walk	.08	.06	.03
121T	Gene Walter(FC)	.12	.09	.05
122T	Claudell Washington	.12	.09	.05
123T	Bill Wegman(FC)	.20	.15	.08
124T	Dick Williams	.08	.06	.03
125T	Mitch Williams(FC)	.70	.50	.30
126T	Bobby Witt(FC)	.40	.30	.15
127T	Todd Worrell(FC)	.60	.45	.25
128T	George Wright	.08	.06	.03
129T	Ricky Wright	.08	.06	.03
130T	Steve Yeager	.08	.06	.03
131T	Paul Zuvella	.08	.06	.03
132T	Checklist	.08	.06	.03

1986 Topps 3-D

This set is a second effort in the production of over-size (4-1/2" by 6") plastic cards on which the player figure is embossed. Cards were sold one per pack for approximately 50¢. The 30 players in the set are among the game's top stars. The embossed color photo is bordered at bottom by a strip of contrasting color on which the player name appears. At the top, a row of white baseballs each contain a letter of the team nickname. Backs have no printing, and contain two self-adhesive strips with which the cards can be attached to a hard surface.

		MT	NR MT	EX
	Complete Set:	11.00	8.25	4.50
	Common Player:	.20	.15	.08
1	Bert Blyleven	.30	.25	.12
2	Gary Carter	.60	.45	.25
3	Wade Boggs	1.25	.90	.50
4	Dwight Gooden	1.00	.70	.40
5	George Brett	.80	.60	.30
6	Rich Gossage	.30	.25	.12
7	Darrell Evans	.20	.15	.08
8	Pedro Guerrero	.30	.25	.12
9	Ron Guidry	.30	.25	.12
10	Keith Hernandez	.50	.40	.20
11	Rickey Henderson	.70	.50	.30
12	Orel Hershiser	.50	.40	.20
13	Reggie Jackson	.60	.45	.25
14	Willie McGee	.30	.25	.12
15	Don Mattingly	2.25	1.75	.90
16	Dale Murphy	.80	.60	.30
17	Jack Morris	.30	.25	.12
18	Dave Parker	.30	.25	.12
19	Eddie Murray	.60	.45	.25
20	Jeff Reardon	.30	.25	.12
21	Dan Quisenberry	.20	.15	.08
22	Pete Rose	1.00	.70	.40
23	Jim Rice	.50	.40	.20
24	Mike Schmidt	.80	.60	.30
25	Bret Saberhagen	.30	.25	.12
26	Darryl Strawberry	.80	.60	.30
27	Dave Stieb	.20	.15	.08
28	John Tudor	.20	.15	.08
29	Dave Winfield	.50	.40	.20
30	Fernando Valenzuela	.40	.30	.15

1987 Topps

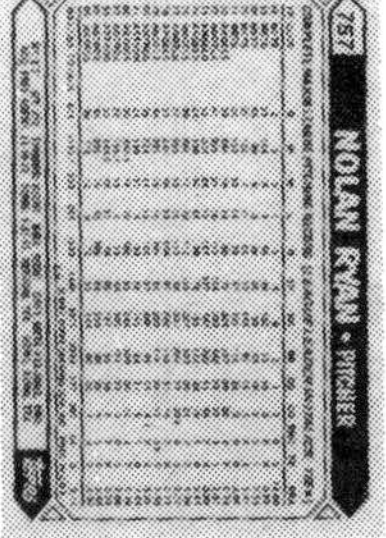

Many collectors feel that Topps' 1987 set of 792 card is a future classic. The 2-1/2" by 3-1/2" design is closely akin to the 1962 set in that the player photo is set against a woodgrain border. Instead of a rolling corner, as in 1962, the player photos in '87 feature a couple of clipped corners at top left and bottom right, where the team logo and player name appear. The player's position is not given on the front of the card. For the first time in several years, the trophy which designates members of Topps All-Star Rookie Team returned to the card design. As in the previous three years, Topps issued a glossy-finish "Tiffany" edition of their 792-card set. However, it was speculated that as many as 50,000 sets were produced as opposed to the 5,000 sets printed in 1985 and 1986. Because of the large print run, the values for the Tiffany cards are only 3-4 times higher than the same card in the regular issue.

		MT	NR MT	EX
	Complete Set:	40.00	30.00	15.00
	Common Player:	.05	.04	.02
1	Record Breaker (Roger Clemens)	.35	.25	.14
2	Record Breaker (Jim Deshaies)	.07	.05	.03
3	Record Breaker (Dwight Evans)	.07	.05	.03
4	Record Breaker (Dave Lopes)	.07	.05	.03
5	Record Breaker (Dave Righetti)	.07	.05	.03
6	Record Breaker (Ruben Sierra)	.25	.20	.10
7	Record Breaker (Todd Worrell)	.07	.05	.03
8	Terry Pendleton	.07	.05	.03
9	Jay Tibbs	.05	.04	.02
10	Cecil Cooper	.10	.08	.04
11	Indians Leaders (Jack Aker, Chris Bando, Phil Niekro)	.07	.05	.03
12	*Jeff Sellers*(FC)	.15	.11	.06
13	Nick Esasky	.07	.05	.03
14	Dave Stewart	.12	.09	.05
15	Claudell Washington	.07	.05	.03
16	Pat Clements	.05	.04	.02
17	Pete O'Brien	.10	.08	.04
18	Dick Howser	.05	.04	.02
19	Matt Young	.05	.04	.02
20	Gary Carter	.20	.15	.08
21	Mark Davis	.05	.04	.02
22	Doug DeCinces	.07	.05	.03
23	Lee Smith	.10	.08	.04
24	Tony Walker	.05	.04	.02
25	Bert Blyleven	.12	.09	.05
26	Greg Brock	.07	.05	.03
27	Joe Cowley	.05	.04	.02
28	Rick Dempsey	.07	.05	.03
29	Jimmy Key	.10	.08	.04
30	Tim Raines	.25	.20	.10
31	Braves Leaders (Glenn Hubbard, Rafael Ramirez)	.07	.05	.03
32	Tim Leary	.07	.05	.03
33	Andy Van Slyke	.12	.09	.05
34	Jose Rijo	.07	.05	.03
35	Sid Bream	.07	.05	.03
36	*Eric King*	.25	.20	.10
37	Marvell Wynne	.05	.04	.02
38	Dennis Leonard	.07	.05	.03
39	Marty Barrett	.07	.05	.03
40	Dave Righetti	.12	.09	.05
41	Bo Diaz	.07	.05	.03
42	Gary Redus	.05	.04	.02
43	Gene Michael	.05	.04	.02
44	Greg Harris	.05	.04	.02
45	Jim Presley	.10	.08	.04
46	Danny Gladden	.05	.04	.02
47	Dennis Powell	.07	.05	.03
48	Wally Backman	.07	.05	.03
49	Terry Harper	.05	.04	.02
50	Dave Smith	.07	.05	.03
51	Mel Hall	.07	.05	.03
52	Keith Atherton	.05	.04	.02
53	Ruppert Jones	.05	.04	.02
54	Bill Dawley	.05	.04	.02
55	Tim Wallach	.10	.08	.04
56	Brewers Leaders (Jamie Cocanower, Paul Molitor, Charlie Moore, Herm Starrette)	.07	.05	.03
57	*Scott Nielsen*(FC)	.10	.08	.04
58	Thad Bosley	.05	.04	.02
59	Ken Dayley	.05	.04	.02
60	Tony Pena	.07	.05	.03
61	*Bobby Thigpen*(FC)	.35	.25	.14
62	Bobby Meacham	.05	.04	.02
63	Fred Toliver(FC)	.07	.05	.03
64	Harry Spilman	.05	.04	.02
65	Tom Browning	.10	.08	.04
66	Marc Sullivan	.05	.04	.02
67	Bill Swift	.05	.04	.02
68	Tony LaRussa	.07	.05	.03
69	Lonnie Smith	.07	.05	.03
70	Charlie Hough	.07	.05	.03
71	*Mike Aldrete*(FC)	.20	.15	.08
72	Walt Terrell	.07	.05	.03
73	Dave Anderson	.05	.04	.02
74	Dan Pasqua	.10	.08	.04
75	Ron Darling	.12	.09	.05
76	Rafael Ramirez	.05	.04	.02
77	Bryan Oelkers	.05	.04	.02
78	Tom Foley	.05	.04	.02
79	Juan Nieves	.10	.08	.04
80	*Wally Joyner*	1.50	1.25	.70
81	Padres Leaders (Andy Hawkins, Terry Kennedy)	.07	.05	.03
82	*Rob Murphy*(FC)	.15	.11	.06
83	Mike Davis	.07	.05	.03
84	Steve Lake	.05	.04	.02
85	Kevin Bass	.07	.05	.03
86	Nate Snell	.05	.04	.02
87	Mark Salas	.05	.04	.02
88	Ed Wojna	.05	.04	.02
89	Ozzie Guillen	.25	.20	.10
90	Dave Stieb	.10	.08	.04
91	Harold Reynolds	.10	.08	.04
92a	Urbano Lugo (no trademark on front)	.30	.25	.12
92b	Urbano Lugo (trademark on front)	.07	.05	.03
93	Jim Leyland	.05	.04	.02
94	Calvin Schiraldi	.05	.04	.02
95	Oddibe McDowell	.07	.05	.03
96	Frank Williams	.05	.04	.02
97	Glenn Wilson	.07	.05	.03
98	Bill Scherrer	.05	.04	.02
99	Darryl Motley	.05	.04	.02
100	Steve Garvey	.20	.15	.08
101	*Carl Willis*(FC)	.10	.08	.04
102	Paul Zuvella	.05	.04	.02
103	Rick Aguilera	.06	.05	.02
104	Billy Sample	.05	.04	.02
105	Floyd Youmans	.07	.05	.03
106	Blue Jays Leaders (George Bell, Willie Upshaw)	.07	.05	.03
107	John Butcher	.05	.04	.02
108	Jim Gantner (photo reversed)	.07	.05	.03
109	R.J. Reynolds	.05	.04	.02
110	John Tudor	.10	.08	.04
111	Alfredo Griffin	.07	.05	.03
112	Alan Ashby	.05	.04	.02
113	Neil Allen	.05	.04	.02
114	Billy Beane	.05	.04	.02
115	Donnie Moore	.05	.04	.02
116	Bill Russell	.07	.05	.03
117	Jim Beattie	.05	.04	.02
118	Bobby Valentine	.05	.04	.02
119	Ron Robinson	.05	.04	.02
120	Eddie Murray	.30	.25	.12
121	*Kevin Romine*(FC)	.12	.09	.05
122	Jim Clancy	.07	.05	.03
123	*John Kruk*	.35	.25	.14
124	Ray Fontenot	.05	.04	.02
125	Bob Brenly	.05	.04	.02
126	*Mike Loynd*(FC)	.15	.11	.06
127	Vance Law	.07	.05	.03
128	Checklist 1-132	.05	.04	.02
129	Rick Cerone	.05	.04	.02
130	Dwight Gooden	.80	.60	.30
131	Pirates Leaders (Sid Bream, Tony Pena)	.07	.05	.03
132	*Paul Assenmacher*	.15	.11	.06
133	Jose Oquendo	.05	.04	.02
134	*Rich Yett*(FC)	.12	.09	.05
135	Mike Easler	.07	.05	.03
136	Ron Romanick	.05	.04	.02
137	Jerry Willard	.05	.04	.02
138	Roy Lee Jackson	.05	.04	.02
139	*Devon White*(FC)	1.25	.90	.50
140	Bret Saberhagen	.15	.11	.06
141	Herm Winningham	.05	.04	.02
142	Rick Sutcliffe	.10	.08	.04
143	Steve Boros	.05	.04	.02
144	Mike Scioscia	.07	.05	.03
145	Charlie Kerfeld	.07	.05	.03
146	*Tracy Jones*(FC)	.25	.20	.10
147	Randy Niemann	.05	.04	.02
148	Dave Collins	.07	.05	.03
149	Ray Searage	.05	.04	.02
150	Wade Boggs	1.25	.90	.50
151	Mike LaCoss	.05	.04	.02
152	Toby Harrah	.07	.05	.03
153	*Duane Ward*(FC)	.12	.09	.05
154	Tom O'Malley	.05	.04	.02
155	Eddie Whitson	.05	.04	.02
156	Mariners Leaders (Bob Kearney, Phil Regan, Matt Young)	.07	.05	.03
157	Danny Darwin	.05	.04	.02
158	Tim Teufel	.05	.04	.02
159	Ed Olwine	.05	.04	.02
160	Julio Franco	.10	.08	.04
161	Steve Ontiveros	.05	.04	.02
162	*Mike LaValliere*	.25	.20	.10
163	Kevin Gross	.07	.05	.03
164	Sammy Khalifa	.05	.04	.02
165	Jeff Reardon	.10	.08	.04
166	Bob Boone	.07	.05	.03
167	*Jim Deshaies*	.25	.20	.10
168	Lou Piniella	.07	.05	.03
169	Ron Washington	.05	.04	.02
170	Future Stars *(Bo Jackson)*	4.00	3.00	1.50
171	*Chuck Cary*(FC)	.10	.08	.04
172	Ron Oester	.05	.04	.02
173	Alex Trevino	.05	.04	.02
174	Henry Cotto	.05	.04	.02
175	Bob Stanley	.05	.04	.02
176	Steve Buechele	.07	.05	.03
177	Keith Moreland	.07	.05	.03
178	Cecil Fielder	1.00	.70	.40
179	Bill Wegman	.10	.08	.04
180	Chris Brown	.07	.05	.03
181	Cardinals Leaders (Mike LaValliere, Ozzie Smith, Ray Soff)	.07	.05	.03
182	Lee Lacy	.05	.04	.02
183	Andy Hawkins	.05	.04	.02
184	*Bobby Bonilla*	2.00	1.50	.80
185	Roger McDowell	.10	.08	.04
186	Bruce Benedict	.05	.04	.02
187	Mark Huismann	.05	.04	.02
188	Tony Phillips	.05	.04	.02
189	Joe Hesketh	.05	.04	.02
190	Jim Sundberg	.07	.05	.03
191	Charles Hudson	.05	.04	.02
192	Cory Snyder(FC)	.70	.50	.30
193	Roger Craig	.07	.05	.03
194	Kirk McCaskill	.07	.05	.03
195	Mike Pagliarulo	.10	.08	.04
196	Randy O'Neal	.05	.04	.02
197	Mark Bailey	.05	.04	.02
198	Lee Mazzilli	.07	.05	.03
199	Mariano Duncan	.05	.04	.02
200	Pete Rose	.60	.45	.25
201	*John Cangelosi*	.12	.09	.05
202	Ricky Wright	.05	.04	.02
203	*Mike Kingery*(FC)	.15	.11	.06
204	Sammy Stewart	.05	.04	.02
205	Graig Nettles	.10	.08	.04
206	Twins Leaders (Tim Laudner, Frank Viola)	.07	.05	.03
207	George Frazier	.05	.04	.02
208	John Shelby	.05	.04	.02
209	Rick Schu	.05	.04	.02
210	Lloyd Moseby	.07	.05	.03
211	John Morris(FC)	.07	.05	.03
212	Mike Fitzgerald	.05	.04	.02
213	*Randy Myers*(FC)	.50	.40	.20
214	Omar Moreno	.05	.04	.02
215	Mark Langston	.12	.09	.05
216	Future Stars *(B.J. Surhoff)*(FC)	.50	.40	.20
217	Chris Codiroli	.05	.04	.02
218	Sparky Anderson	.07	.05	.03
219	Cecilio Guante	.05	.04	.02
220	Joe Carter	.12	.09	.05
221	Vern Ruhle	.05	.04	.02
222	Denny Walling	.05	.04	.02
223	Charlie Leibrandt	.07	.05	.03
224	Wayne Tolleson	.05	.04	.02
225	Mike Smithson	.05	.04	.02
226	Max Venable	.05	.04	.02
227	*Jamie Moyer*(FC)	.20	.15	.08
228	Curt Wilkerson	.05	.04	.02
229	*Mike Birkbeck*(FC)	.15	.11	.06
230	Don Baylor	.10	.08	.04
231	Giants Leaders (Bob Brenly, Mike Krukow)	.07	.05	.03
232	*Reggie Williams*	.10	.08	.04
233	*Russ Morman*(FC)	.10	.08	.04
234	Pat Sheridan	.05	.04	.02
235	Alvin Davis	.10	.08	.04
236	Tommy John	.15	.11	.06
237	Jim Morrison	.05	.04	.02
238	Bill Krueger	.05	.04	.02
239	Juan Espino	.05	.04	.02
240	Steve Balboni	.07	.05	.03
241	Danny Heep	.05	.04	.02
242	Rick Mahler	.05	.04	.02
243	Whitey Herzog	.07	.05	.03
244	Dickie Noles	.05	.04	.02
245	Willie Upshaw	.07	.05	.03
246	Jim Dwyer	.05	.04	.02
247	Jeff Reed(FC)	.07	.05	.03
248	Gene Walter	.07	.05	.03
249	Jim Pankovits	.05	.04	.02
250	Teddy Higuera	.15	.11	.06
251	Rob Wilfong	.05	.04	.02
252	Denny Martinez	.05	.04	.02
253	Eddie Milner	.05	.04	.02
254	*Bob Tewksbury*	.12	.09	.05
255	Juan Samuel	.10	.08	.04
256	Royals Leaders (George Brett, Frank White)	.10	.08	.04
257	Bob Forsch	.07	.05	.03
258	Steve Yeager	.05	.04	.02

		MT	NR MT	EX
259	*Mike Greenwell*(FC)	3.00	2.25	1.25
260	Vida Blue	.07	.05	.03
261	*Ruben Sierra*(FC)	3.50	2.75	1.50
262	Jim Winn	.05	.04	.02
263	Stan Javier(FC)	.07	.05	.03
264	Checklist 133-264	.05	.04	.02
265	Darrell Evans	.10	.08	.04
266	*Jeff Hamilton*(FC)	.25	.20	.10
267	Howard Johnson	.10	.08	.04
268	Pat Corrales	.05	.04	.02
269	Cliff Speck	.05	.04	.02
270	Jody Davis	.07	.05	.03
271	Mike Brown	.05	.04	.02
272	Andres Galarraga	1.00	.70	.40
273	Gene Nelson	.05	.04	.02
274	*Jeff Hearron*(FC)	.05	.04	.02
275	LaMarr Hoyt	.05	.04	.02
276	Jackie Gutierrez	.05	.04	.02
277	Juan Agosto	.05	.04	.02
278	Gary Pettis	.05	.04	.02
279	*Dan Plesac*	.30	.25	.12
280	Jeffrey Leonard	.07	.05	.03
281	Reds Leaders (Bo Diaz, Bill Gullickson, Pete Rose)	.10	.08	.04
282	Jeff Calhoun	.05	.04	.02
283	*Doug Drabek*(FC)	.35	.25	.14
284	John Moses	.05	.04	.02
285	Dennis Boyd	.07	.05	.03
286	Mike Woodard(FC)	.07	.05	.03
287	Dave Von Ohlen	.05	.04	.02
288	Tito Landrum	.05	.04	.02
289	Bob Kipper	.07	.05	.03
290	Leon Durham	.07	.05	.03
291	*Mitch Williams*(FC)	.60	.45	.25
292	Franklin Stubbs	.07	.05	.03
293	Bob Rodgers	.05	.04	.02
294	Steve Jeltz	.05	.04	.02
295	Len Dykstra	.12	.09	.05
296	*Andres Thomas*	.25	.20	.10
297	Don Schulze	.05	.04	.02
298	Larry Herndon	.05	.04	.02
299	Joel Davis	.07	.05	.03
300	Reggie Jackson	.30	.25	.12
301	*Luis Aquino*(FC)	.10	.08	.04
302	Bill Schroeder	.05	.04	.02
303	Juan Berenguer	.05	.04	.02
304	Phil Garner	.05	.04	.02
305	John Franco	.10	.08	.04
306	Red Sox Leaders (Rich Gedman, John McNamara, Tom Seaver)	.07	.05	.03
307	*Lee Guetterman*(FC)	.15	.11	.06
308	Don Slaught	.05	.04	.02
309	Mike Young	.05	.04	.02
310	Frank Viola	.15	.11	.06
311	Turn Back The Clock (Rickey Henderson)	.10	.08	.04
312	Turn Back The Clock (Reggie Jackson)	.10	.08	.04
313	Turn Back The Clock (Roberto Clemente)	.15	.11	.06
314	Turn Back The Clock (Carl Yastrzemski)	.10	.08	.04
315	Turn Back The Clock (Maury Wills)	.07	.05	.03
316	Brian Fisher	.07	.05	.03
317	Clint Hurdle	.05	.04	.02
318	Jim Fregosi	.05	.04	.02
319	*Greg Swindell*(FC)	1.00	.70	.40
320	*Barry Bonds*	2.00	1.50	.80
321	Mike Laga	.05	.04	.02
322	Chris Bando	.05	.04	.02
323	*Al Newman*	.07	.05	.03
324	Dave Palmer	.05	.04	.02
325	Garry Templeton	.07	.05	.03
326	Mark Gubicza	.10	.08	.04
327	*Dale Sveum*	.20	.15	.08
328	Bob Welch	.10	.08	.04
329	Ron Roenicke	.05	.04	.02
330	Mike Scott	.12	.09	.05
331	Mets Leaders (Gary Carter, Keith Hernandez, Dave Johnson, Darryl Strawberry)	.10	.08	.04
332	Joe Price	.05	.04	.02
333	Ken Phelps	.07	.05	.03
334	*Ed Correa*	.15	.11	.06
335	Candy Maldonado	.07	.05	.03
336	*Allan Anderson*(FC)	.25	.20	.10
337	Darrell Miller	.05	.04	.02
338	Tim Conroy	.05	.04	.02
339	Donnie Hill	.05	.04	.02
340	Roger Clemens	1.00	.70	.40
341	Mike Brown	.05	.04	.02
342	Bob James	.05	.04	.02
343	Hal Lanier	.05	.04	.02
344a	Joe Niekro (copyright outside yellow on back)	.30	.25	.12
344b	Joe Niekro (copyright inside yellow on back)	.07	.05	.03
345	Andre Dawson	.20	.15	.08
346	Shawon Dunston	.07	.05	.03
347	Mickey Brantley(FC)	.07	.05	.03
348	Carmelo Martinez	.07	.05	.03
349	Storm Davis	.10	.08	.04
350	Keith Hernandez	.20	.15	.08
351	Gene Garber	.05	.04	.02
352	Mike Felder(FC)	.07	.05	.03
353	Ernie Camacho	.05	.04	.02
354	Jamie Quirk	.05	.04	.02
355	Don Carman	.07	.05	.03
356	White Sox Leaders (Ed Brinkman, Julio Cruz)	.07	.05	.03
357	*Steve Fireovid*(FC)	.07	.05	.03
358	Sal Butera	.05	.04	.02
359	Doug Corbett	.05	.04	.02
360	Pedro Guerrero	.15	.11	.06
361	Mark Thurmond	.05	.04	.02
362	*Luis Quinones*(FC)	.12	.09	.05
363	Jose Guzman	.12	.09	.05
364	Randy Bush	.05	.04	.02
365	Rick Rhoden	.07	.05	.03
366	*Mark McGwire*	3.00	2.25	1.25
367	Jeff Lahti	.05	.04	.02
368	John McNamara	.05	.04	.02
369	Brian Dayett	.05	.04	.02
370	Fred Lynn	.15	.11	.06
371	*Mark Eichhorn*	.15	.11	.06
372	Jerry Mumphrey	.05	.04	.02
373	Jeff Dedmon	.05	.04	.02
374	Glenn Hoffman	.05	.04	.02
375	Ron Guidry	.12	.09	.05
376	Scott Bradley	.05	.04	.02
377	John Henry Johnson	.05	.04	.02
378	Rafael Santana	.05	.04	.02
379	John Russell	.05	.04	.02
380	Rich Gossage	.15	.11	.06
381	Expos Leaders (Mike Fitzgerald, Bob Rodgers)	.07	.05	.03
382	Rudy Law	.05	.04	.02
383	Ron Davis	.05	.04	.02
384	Johnny Grubb	.05	.04	.02
385	Orel Hershiser	.30	.25	.12
386	Dickie Thon	.07	.05	.03
387	*T.R. Bryden*(FC)	.10	.08	.04
388	Geno Petralli	.05	.04	.02
389	Jeff Robinson	.07	.05	.03
390	Gary Matthews	.07	.05	.03
391	Jay Howell	.07	.05	.03
392	Checklist 265-396	.05	.04	.02
393	Pete Rose	.40	.30	.15
394	Mike Bielecki	.07	.05	.03
395	Damaso Garcia	.05	.04	.02
396	Tim Lollar	.05	.04	.02
397	Greg Walker	.07	.05	.03
398	Brad Havens	.05	.04	.02
399	Curt Ford(FC)	.07	.05	.03
400	George Brett	.35	.25	.14
401	Billy Jo Robidoux	.07	.05	.03
402	Mike Trujillo	.05	.04	.02
403	Jerry Royster	.05	.04	.02
404	Doug Sisk	.05	.04	.02
405	Brook Jacoby	.10	.08	.04
406	Yankees Leaders (Rickey Henderson, Don Mattingly)	.15	.11	.06
407	Jim Acker	.05	.04	.02
408	John Mizerock	.05	.04	.02
409	Milt Thompson	.07	.05	.03
410	Fernando Valenzuela	.25	.20	.10
411	Darnell Coles	.07	.05	.03
412	Eric Davis	.90	.70	.35
413	Moose Haas	.05	.04	.02
414	Joe Orsulak	.05	.04	.02
415	*Bobby Witt*	.30	.25	.12
416	Tom Nieto	.05	.04	.02
417	Pat Perry(FC)	.07	.05	.03
418	Dick Williams	.05	.04	.02
419	*Mark Portugal*(FC)	.10	.08	.04
420	*Will Clark*	5.00	3.75	2.00
421	Jose DeLeon	.07	.05	.03
422	Jack Howell	.07	.05	.03
423	Jaime Cocanower	.05	.04	.02
424	Chris Speier	.05	.04	.02
425	Tom Seaver	.30	.25	.12
426	Floyd Rayford	.05	.04	.02
427	Ed Nunez	.05	.04	.02
428	Bruce Bochy	.05	.04	.02
429	Future Stars (*Tim Pyznarski*)(FC)	.10	.08	.04
430	Mike Schmidt	.40	.30	.15
431	Dodgers Leaders (Tom Niedenfuer, Ron Perranoski, Alex Trevino)	.07	.05	.03
432	Jim Slaton	.05	.04	.02
433	*Ed Hearn*(FC)	.10	.08	.04
434	Mike Fischlin	.05	.04	.02
435	Bruce Sutter	.12	.09	.05
436	*Andy Allanson*	.15	.11	.06
437	Ted Power	.05	.04	.02
438	*Kelly Downs*(FC)	.30	.25	.12
439	Karl Best	.05	.04	.02
440	Willie McGee	.10	.08	.04
441	*Dave Leiper*(FC)	.10	.08	.04
442	Mitch Webster	.07	.05	.03
443	John Felske	.05	.04	.02
444	Jeff Russell	.05	.04	.02
445	Dave Lopes	.07	.05	.03
446	*Chuck Finley*(FC)	.12	.09	.05
447	Bill Almon	.05	.04	.02
448	*Chris Bosio*(FC)	.25	.20	.10
449	Future Stars (*Pat Dodson*)(FC)	.10	.08	.04
450	Kirby Puckett	.30	.25	.12
451	Joe Sambito	.05	.04	.02
452	Dave Henderson	.10	.08	.04
453	*Scott Terry*(FC)	.12	.09	.05
454	Luis Salazar	.05	.04	.02
455	Mike Boddicker	.07	.05	.03
456	A's Leaders (Carney Lansford, Tony LaRussa, Mickey Tettleton, Dave Von Ohlen)	.07	.05	.03
457	Len Matuszek	.05	.04	.02
458	Kelly Gruber(FC)	.90	.70	.35
459	Dennis Eckersley	.10	.08	.04
460	Darryl Strawberry	.35	.25	.14
461	Craig McMurtry	.05	.04	.02
462	Scott Fletcher	.07	.05	.03
463	Tom Candiotti	.05	.04	.02
464	Butch Wynegar	.05	.04	.02
465	Todd Worrell	.30	.25	.12
466	Kal Daniels(FC)	1.25	.90	.50
467	Randy St. Claire	.05	.04	.02
468	George Bamberger	.05	.04	.02
469	*Mike Diaz*(FC)	.15	.11	.06
470	Dave Dravecky	.07	.05	.03
471	Ronn Reynolds	.05	.04	.02
472	Bill Doran	.07	.05	.03
473	Steve Farr	.05	.04	.02
474	Jerry Narron	.05	.04	.02
475	Scott Garrelts	.05	.04	.02
476	Danny Tartabull	.90	.70	.35
477	Ken Howell	.05	.04	.02
478	Tim Laudner	.05	.04	.02
479	*Bob Sebra*(FC)	.10	.08	.04
480	Jim Rice	.25	.20	.10
481	Phillies Leaders (Von Hayes, Juan Samuel, Glenn Wilson)	.07	.05	.03
482	Daryl Boston	.05	.04	.02
483	Dwight Lowry	.05	.04	.02
484	Jim Traber(FC)	.15	.11	.06
485	Tony Fernandez	.10	.08	.04
486	Otis Nixon	.05	.04	.02
487	Dave Gumpert	.05	.04	.02
488	Ray Knight	.07	.05	.03
489	Bill Gullickson	.05	.04	.02
490	Dale Murphy	.40	.30	.15
491	*Ron Karkovice*(FC)	.10	.08	.04
492	Mike Heath	.05	.04	.02
493	Tom Lasorda	.07	.05	.03
494	*Barry Jones*(FC)	.12	.09	.05
495	Gorman Thomas	.10	.08	.04
496	Bruce Bochte	.05	.04	.02
497	*Dale Mohorcic*(FC)	.15	.11	.06
498	Bob Kearney	.05	.04	.02
499	*Bruce Ruffin*(FC)	.20	.15	.08
500	Don Mattingly	2.25	1.75	.90
501	Craig Lefferts	.05	.04	.02
502	Dick Schofield	.05	.04	.02
503	Larry Andersen	.05	.04	.02
504	Mickey Hatcher	.05	.04	.02
505	Bryn Smith	.05	.04	.02
506	Orioles Leaders (Rich Bordi, Rick Dempsey, Earl Weaver)	.07	.05	.03
507	Dave Stapleton	.05	.04	.02
508	*Scott Bankhead*	.25	.20	.10
509	Enos Cabell	.05	.04	.02
510	Tom Henke	.07	.05	.03
511	Steve Lyons	.05	.04	.02
512	*Dave Magadan*(FC)	.70	.50	.30
513	Carmen Castillo	.05	.04	.02
514	Orlando Mercado	.05	.04	.02
515	Willie Hernandez	.07	.05	.03
516	Ted Simmons	.10	.08	.04
517	Mario Soto	.07	.05	.03
518	Gene Mauch	.07	.05	.03
519	Curt Young	.07	.05	.03
520	Jack Clark	.15	.11	.06
521	Rick Reuschel	.10	.08	.04
522	Checklist 397-528	.05	.04	.02
523	Earnie Riles	.05	.04	.02
524	Bob Shirley	.05	.04	.02
525	Phil Bradley	.10	.08	.04
526	Roger Mason	.05	.04	.02
527	Jim Wohlford	.05	.04	.02
528	Ken Dixon	.05	.04	.02
529	*Alvaro Espinoza*(FC)	.07	.05	.03
530	Tony Gwynn	.35	.25	.14
531	Astros Leaders (Yogi Berra, Hal Lanier, Denis Menke, Gene Tenace)	.07	.05	.03
532	Jeff Stone	.05	.04	.02
533	Argenis Salazar	.05	.04	.02
534	Scott Sanderson	.05	.04	.02
535	Tony Armas	.07	.05	.03
536	*Terry Mulholland*(FC)	.10	.08	.04
537	Rance Mulliniks	.05	.04	.02
538	Tom Niedenfuer	.07	.05	.03
539	Reid Nichols	.05	.04	.02
540	Terry Kennedy	.07	.05	.03
541	*Rafael Belliard*(FC)	.10	.08	.04
542	Ricky Horton	.07	.05	.03
543	Dave Johnson	.07	.05	.03
544	Zane Smith	.07	.05	.03
545	Buddy Bell	.07	.05	.03
546	Mike Morgan	.05	.04	.02
547	Rob Deer	.10	.08	.04
548	*Bill Mooneyham*(FC)	.10	.08	.04
549	Bob Melvin	.05	.04	.02
550	*Pete Incaviglia*	.40	.30	.15
551	Frank Wills	.05	.04	.02
552	Larry Sheets	.07	.05	.03
553	*Mike Maddux*(FC)	.15	.11	.06
554	Buddy Biancalana	.05	.04	.02
555	Dennis Rasmussen	.10	.08	.04
556	Angels Leaders (Bob Boone, Marcel Lachemann, Mike Witt)	.07	.05	.03
557	*John Cerutti*	.15	.11	.06
558	Greg Gagne	.05	.04	.02
559	Lance McCullers	.07	.05	.03
560	Glenn Davis	.25	.20	.10
561	*Rey Quinones*	.15	.11	.06
562	*Bryan Clutterbuck*(FC)	.10	.08	.04
563	John Stefero	.05	.04	.02
564	Larry McWilliams	.05	.04	.02
565	Dusty Baker	.07	.05	.03
566	Tim Hulett	.05	.04	.02
567	*Greg Mathews*(FC)	.20	.15	.08
568	Earl Weaver	.07	.05	.03
569	Wade Rowdon(FC)	.07	.05	.03
570	Sid Fernandez	.10	.08	.04
571	Ozzie Virgil	.05	.04	.02
572	Pete Ladd	.05	.04	.02
573	Hal McRae	.07	.05	.03
574	Manny Lee	.05	.04	.02
575	Pat Tabler	.07	.05	.03
576	Frank Pastore	.05	.04	.02
577	Dann Bilardello	.05	.04	.02
578	Billy Hatcher	.07	.05	.03
579	Rick Burleson	.07	.05	.03
580	Mike Krukow	.07	.05	.03
581	Cubs Leaders (Ron Cey, Steve Trout)	.07	.05	.03
582	Bruce Berenyi	.05	.04	.02
583	Junior Ortiz	.05	.04	.02
584	Ron Kittle	.07	.05	.03
585	*Scott Bailes*	.15	.11	.06
586	Ben Oglivie	.07	.05	.03
587	Eric Plunk(FC)	.10	.08	.04
588	Wallace Johnson	.05	.04	.02
589	Steve Crawford	.05	.04	.02
590	Vince Coleman	.25	.20	.10
591	Spike Owen	.05	.04	.02
592	Chris Welsh	.05	.04	.02
593	Chuck Tanner	.05	.04	.02
594	Rick Anderson	.05	.04	.02
595	Keith Hernandez AS	.12	.09	.05
596	Steve Sax AS	.07	.05	.03
597	Mike Schmidt AS	.20	.15	.08
598	Ozzie Smith AS	.07	.05	.03
599	Tony Gwynn AS	.20	.15	.08
600	Dave Parker AS	.10	.08	.04
601	Darryl Strawberry AS	.20	.15	.08
602	Gary Carter AS	.15	.11	.06
603a	Dwight Gooden AS (no trademark on front)	.80	.60	.30

		MT	NR MT	EX
603b	Dwight Gooden AS (trademark on front)	.30	.25	.12
604	Fernando Valenzuela AS	.12	.09	.05
605	Todd Worrell AS	.10	.08	.04
606a	Don Mattingly AS (no trademark on front)	1.75	1.25	.70
606b	Don Mattingly AS (trademark on front)	.70	.50	.30
607	Tony Bernazard AS	.05	.04	.02
608	Wade Boggs AS	.40	.30	.15
609	Cal Ripken AS	.15	.11	.06
610	Jim Rice AS	.15	.11	.06
611	Kirby Puckett AS	.15	.11	.06
612	George Bell AS	.12	.09	.05
613	Lance Parrish AS	.10	.08	.04
614	Roger Clemens AS	.30	.25	.12
615	Teddy Higuera AS	.10	.08	.04
616	Dave Righetti AS	.10	.08	.04
617	Al Nipper	.05	.04	.02
618	Tom Kelly	.05	.04	.02
619	Jerry Reed	.05	.04	.02
620	Jose Canseco	6.00	4.50	2.50
621	Danny Cox	.07	.05	.03
622	*Glenn Braggs*(FC)	.40	.30	.15
623	*Kurt Stillwell*(FC)	.35	.25	.14
624	Tim Burke	.05	.04	.02
625	Mookie Wilson	.07	.05	.03
626	Joel Skinner	.05	.04	.02
627	Ken Oberkfell	.05	.04	.02
628	Bob Walk	.05	.04	.02
629	Larry Parrish	.07	.05	.03
630	John Candelaria	.07	.05	.03
631	Tigers Leaders (Sparky Anderson, Mike Heath, Willie Hernandez)	.07	.05	.03
632	Rob Woodward(FC)	.07	.05	.03
633	Jose Uribe	.07	.05	.03
634	Future Stars *(Rafael Palmeiro)*(FC)	1.25	.90	.50
635	Ken Schrom	.05	.04	.02
636	Darren Daulton	.05	.04	.02
637	Bip Roberts	.05	.04	.02
638	Rich Bordi	.05	.04	.02
639	Gerald Perry	.10	.08	.04
640	Mark Clear	.05	.04	.02
641	Domingo Ramos	.05	.04	.02
642	Al Pulido	.05	.04	.02
643	Ron Shepherd	.05	.04	.02
644	John Denny	.05	.04	.02
645	Dwight Evans	.12	.09	.05
646	Mike Mason	.05	.04	.02
647	Tom Lawless	.05	.04	.02
648	*Barry Larkin*	2.75	2.00	1.00
649	Mickey Tettleton	.05	.04	.02
650	Hubie Brooks	.07	.05	.03
651	Benny Distefano	.05	.04	.02
652	Terry Forster	.07	.05	.03
653	*Kevin Mitchell*	4.00	3.00	1.50
654	Checklist 529-660	.05	.04	.02
655	Jesse Barfield	.15	.11	.06
656	Rangers Leaders (Bobby Valentine, Rickey Wright)	.07	.05	.03
657	Tom Waddell	.05	.04	.02
658	*Robby Thompson*	.30	.25	.12
659	Aurelio Lopez	.05	.04	.02
660	Bob Horner	.10	.08	.04
661	Lou Whitaker	.15	.11	.06
662	Frank DiPino	.05	.04	.02
663	Cliff Johnson	.05	.04	.02
664	Mike Marshall	.10	.08	.04
665	Rod Scurry	.05	.04	.02
666	Von Hayes	.07	.05	.03
667	Ron Hassey	.05	.04	.02
668	Juan Bonilla	.05	.04	.02
669	Bud Black	.05	.04	.02
670	Jose Cruz	.07	.05	.03
671a	Ray Soff (no "D" before copyright line)	.20	.15	.08
671b	Ray Soff ("D" before copyright line)	.05	.04	.02
672	Chili Davis	.07	.05	.03
673	Don Sutton	.15	.11	.06
674	Bill Campbell	.05	.04	.02
675	Ed Romero	.05	.04	.02
676	Charlie Moore	.05	.04	.02
677	Bob Grich	.07	.05	.03
678	Carney Lansford	.07	.05	.03
679	Kent Hrbek	.15	.11	.06
680	Ryne Sandberg	.25	.20	.10
681	George Bell	.25	.20	.10
682	Jerry Reuss	.07	.05	.03
683	Gary Roenicke	.05	.04	.02
684	Kent Tekulve	.07	.05	.03
685	Jerry Hairston	.05	.04	.02
686	Doyle Alexander	.07	.05	.03
687	Alan Trammell	.25	.20	.10
688	Juan Beniquez	.05	.04	.02
689	Darrell Porter	.07	.05	.03
690	Dane Iorg	.05	.04	.02
691	Dave Parker	.15	.11	.06
692	Frank White	.07	.05	.03
693	Terry Puhl	.05	.04	.02
694	Phil Niekro	.20	.15	.08
695	Chico Walker	.05	.04	.02
696	Gary Lucas	.05	.04	.02
697	Ed Lynch	.05	.04	.02
698	Ernie Whitt	.07	.05	.03
699	Ken Landreaux	.05	.04	.02
700	Dave Bergman	.05	.04	.02
701	Willie Randolph	.07	.05	.03
702	Greg Gross	.05	.04	.02
703	Dave Schmidt	.05	.04	.02
704	Jesse Orosco	.07	.05	.03
705	Bruce Hurst	.10	.08	.04
706	Rick Manning	.05	.04	.02
707	Bob McClure	.05	.04	.02
708	Scott McGregor	.07	.05	.03
709	Dave Kingman	.10	.08	.04
710	Gary Gaetti	.15	.11	.06
711	Ken Griffey	.07	.05	.03
712	Don Robinson	.07	.05	.03
713	Tom Brookens	.05	.04	.02
714	Dan Quisenberry	.07	.05	.03
715	Bob Dernier	.05	.04	.02
716	Rick Leach	.05	.04	.02
717	Ed Vande Berg	.05	.04	.02
718	Steve Carlton	.25	.20	.10
719	Tom Hume	.05	.04	.02
720	Richard Dotson	.07	.05	.03
721	Tom Herr	.07	.05	.03
722	Bob Knepper	.07	.05	.03
723	Brett Butler	.07	.05	.03
724	Greg Minton	.05	.04	.02
725	George Hendrick	.07	.05	.03
726	Frank Tanana	.07	.05	.03
727	Mike Moore	.05	.04	.02
728	Tippy Martinez	.05	.04	.02
729	Tom Paciorek	.05	.04	.02
730	Eric Show	.07	.05	.03
731	Dave Concepcion	.10	.08	.04
732	Manny Trillo	.07	.05	.03
733	Bill Caudill	.05	.04	.02
734	Bill Madlock	.10	.08	.04
735	Rickey Henderson	.30	.25	.12
736	Steve Bedrosian	.10	.08	.04
737	Floyd Bannister	.07	.05	.03
738	Jorge Orta	.05	.04	.02
739	Chet Lemon	.07	.05	.03
740	Rich Gedman	.07	.05	.03
741	Paul Molitor	.12	.09	.05
742	Andy McGaffigan	.05	.04	.02
743	Dwayne Murphy	.07	.05	.03
744	Roy Smalley	.05	.04	.02
745	Glenn Hubbard	.05	.04	.02
746	Bob Ojeda	.07	.05	.03
747	Johnny Ray	.07	.05	.03
748	Mike Flanagan	.07	.05	.03
749	Ozzie Smith	.15	.11	.06
750	Steve Trout	.07	.05	.03
751	Garth Iorg	.05	.04	.02
752	Dan Petry	.07	.05	.03
753	Rick Honeycutt	.05	.04	.02
754	Dave LaPoint	.07	.05	.03
755	Luis Aguayo	.05	.04	.02
756	Carlton Fisk	.20	.15	.08
757	Nolan Ryan	.40	.30	.15
758	Tony Bernazard	.05	.04	.02
759	Joel Youngblood	.05	.04	.02
760	Mike Witt	.07	.05	.03
761	Greg Pryor	.05	.04	.02
762	Gary Ward	.07	.05	.03
763	Tim Flannery	.05	.04	.02
764	Bill Buckner	.07	.05	.03
765	Kirk Gibson	.20	.15	.08
766	Don Aase	.05	.04	.02
767	Ron Cey	.07	.05	.03
768	Dennis Lamp	.05	.04	.02
769	Steve Sax	.15	.11	.06
770	Dave Winfield	.25	.20	.10
771	Shane Rawley	.07	.05	.03
772	Harold Baines	.12	.09	.05
773	Robin Yount	.35	.25	.14
774	Wayne Krenchicki	.05	.04	.02
775	Joaquin Andujar	.07	.05	.03
776	Tom Brunansky	.10	.08	.04
777	Chris Chambliss	.07	.05	.03
778	Jack Morris	.20	.15	.08
779	Craig Reynolds	.05	.04	.02
780	Andre Thornton	.07	.05	.03
781	Atlee Hammaker	.05	.04	.02
782	Brian Downing	.07	.05	.03
783	Willie Wilson	.10	.08	.04
784	Cal Ripken	.30	.25	.12
785	Terry Francona	.05	.04	.02
786	Jimy Williams	.05	.04	.02
787	Alejandro Pena	.07	.05	.03
788	Tim Stoddard	.05	.04	.02
789	Dan Schatzeder	.05	.04	.02
790	Julio Cruz	.05	.04	.02
791	Lance Parrish	.15	.11	.06
792	Checklist 661-792	.05	.04	.02

1987 Topps All-Star Glossy Set of 22

For the fourth consecutive year, Topps produced an All-Star Game commemorative set of 22 cards. The glossy cards, which measure 2-1/2" by 3-1/2", were included in rack packs. Using the same basic card design as in previous efforts with a few minor changes, the 1987 edition features American and National League logos on the card fronts. Card #'s 1- 12 feature representatives from the American League, while #'s 13-22 are National Leaguers.

		MT	NR MT	EX
	Complete Set:	5.00	3.75	2.00
	Common Player:	.15	.11	.06
1	Whitey Herzog	.15	.11	.06
2	Keith Hernandez	.40	.30	.15
3	Ryne Sandberg	.40	.30	.15
4	Mike Schmidt	.70	.50	.30
5	Ozzie Smith	.30	.25	.12
6	Tony Gwynn	.50	.40	.20
7	Dale Murphy	.80	.60	.30
8	Darryl Strawberry	.80	.60	.30
9	Gary Carter	.40	.30	.15
10	Dwight Gooden	.60	.45	.25
11	Fernando Valenzuela	.30	.25	.12
12	Dick Howser	.15	.11	.06
13	Wally Joyner	1.25	.90	.50
14	Lou Whitaker	.30	.25	.12
15	Wade Boggs	1.00	.70	.40
16	Cal Ripken	.50	.40	.20
17	Dave Winfield	.40	.30	.15
18	Rickey Henderson	.50	.40	.20
19	Kirby Puckett	.40	.30	.15
20	Lance Parrish	.30	.25	.12
21	Roger Clemens	.60	.45	.25
22	Teddy Higuera	.30	.25	.12

1987 Topps All-Star Glossy Set of 60

Using the same design as the previous year, the 1987 Topps All-Star Glossy set includes 48 All-Star performers plus 12 potential superstars branded as "Hot Prospects". The card fronts are uncluttered, save the player's name found in very small print at the bottom. The set was available via a mail-in offer. Six subsets make up the 60-card set, with each subset being available for $1.00 plus six special offer cards that were found in wax packs.

		MT	NR MT	EX
	Complete Set:	14.00	10.50	5.50
	Common Player:	.15	.11	.06
1	Don Mattingly	3.50	2.75	1.50
2	Tony Gwynn	.60	.45	.25
3	Gary Gaetti	.25	.20	.10
4	Glenn Davis	.30	.25	.12
5	Roger Clemens	.70	.50	.30
6	Dale Murphy	.90	.70	.35
7	Lou Whitaker	.30	.25	.12
8	Roger McDowell	.15	.11	.06
9	Cory Snyder	.50	.40	.20
10	Todd Worrell	.20	.15	.08
11	Gary Carter	.50	.40	.20
12	Eddie Murray	.60	.45	.25
13	Bob Knepper	.15	.11	.06
14	Harold Baines	.20	.15	.08
15	Jeff Reardon	.20	.15	.08
16	Joe Carter	.25	.20	.10
17	Dave Parker	.25	.20	.10
18	Wade Boggs	1.25	.90	.50
19	Danny Tartabull	.35	.25	.14
20	Jim Deshaies	.20	.15	.08
21	Rickey Henderson	.70	.50	.30
22	Rob Deer	.15	.11	.06
23	Ozzie Smith	.25	.20	.10
24	Dave Righetti	.25	.20	.10
25	Kent Hrbek	.30	.25	.12
26	Keith Hernandez	.40	.30	.15
27	Don Baylor	.15	.11	.06
28	Mike Schmidt	.90	.70	.35
29	Pete Incaviglia	.50	.40	.20
30	Barry Bonds	.50	.40	.20
31	George Brett	.90	.70	.35
32	Darryl Strawberry	.90	.70	.35
33	Mike Witt	.15	.11	.06
34	Kevin Bass	.15	.11	.06
35	Jesse Barfield	.20	.15	.08
36	Bob Ojeda	.15	.11	.06
37	Cal Ripken	.70	.50	.30
38	Vince Coleman	.25	.20	.10
39	Wally Joyner	1.75	1.25	.70
40	Robby Thompson	.20	.15	.08
41	Pete Rose	1.25	.90	.50
42	Jim Rice	.50	.40	.20
43	Tony Bernazard	.15	.11	.06
44	Eric Davis	1.00	.70	.40
45	George Bell	.50	.40	.20
46	Hubie Brooks	.15	.11	.06
47	Jack Morris	.30	.25	.12
48	Tim Raines	.50	.40	.20
49	Mark Eichhorn	.20	.15	.08
50	Kevin Mitchell	.25	.20	.10
51	Dwight Gooden	.80	.60	.30
52	Doug DeCinces	.15	.11	.06
53	Fernando Valenzuela	.35	.25	.14
54	Reggie Jackson	.70	.50	.30
55	Johnny Ray	.15	.11	.06
56	Mike Pagliarulo	.20	.15	.08
57	Kirby Puckett	.50	.40	.20

		MT	NR MT	EX
58	Lance Parrish	.30	.25	.12
59	Jose Canseco	3.00	2.25	1.25
60	Greg Mathews	.25	.20	.10

1987 Topps Baseball Highlights

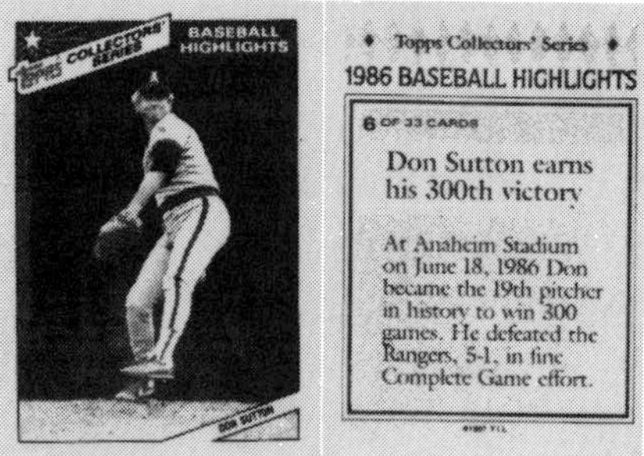

The "Baseball Highlights" boxed set of 33 cards was prepared by Topps for distribution at stores in the Woolworth's chain. Each card measures 2-1/2" by 3-1/2" in size and features a memorable baseball event that occurred during the 1986 season. The glossy set sold for $1.99 in Woolworth's stores.

		MT	NR MT	EX
	Complete Set:	5.00	3.75	2.00
	Common Player:	.09	.07	.04
1	Steve Carlton	.30	.25	.12
2	Cecil Cooper	.12	.09	.05
3	Rickey Henderson	.35	.25	.14
4	Reggie Jackson	.30	.25	.12
5	Jim Rice	.25	.20	.10
6	Don Sutton	.20	.15	.08
7	Roger Clemens	.50	.40	.20
8	Mike Schmidt	.35	.25	.14
9	Jesse Barfield	.15	.11	.06
10	Wade Boggs	.70	.50	.30
11	Tim Raines	.30	.25	.12
12	Jose Canseco	1.00	.70	.40
13	Todd Worrell	.15	.11	.06
14	Dave Righetti	.15	.11	.06
15	Don Mattingly	1.25	.90	.50
16	Tony Gwynn	.35	.25	.14
17	Marty Barrett	.09	.07	.04
18	Mike Scott	.12	.09	.05
19	World Series Game #1 (Bruce Hurst)	.12	.09	.05
20	World Series Game #1 (Calvin Schiraldi)	.09	.07	.04
21	World Series Game #2 (Dwight Evans)	.12	.09	.05
22	World Series Game #2 (Dave Henderson)	.09	.07	.04
23	World Series Game #3 (Len Dykstra)	.12	.09	.05
24	World Series Game #3 (Bob Ojeda)	.09	.07	.04
25	World Series Game #4 (Gary Carter)	.30	.25	.12
26	World Series Game #4 (Ron Darling)	.15	.11	.06
27	Jim Rice	.30	.25	.12
28	Bruce Hurst	.09	.07	.04
29	World Series Game #6 (Darryl Strawberry)	.35	.25	.14
30	World Series Game #6 (Ray Knight)	.09	.07	.04
31	World Series Game #6 (Keith Hernandez)	.25	.20	.10
32	World Series Games #7 (Mets Celebrate)	.12	.09	.05
33	Ray Knight	.09	.07	.04

1987 Topps Box Panels

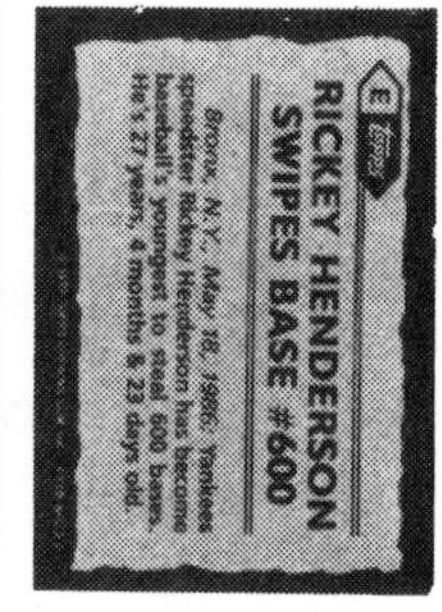

Offering baseball cards on retail boxes for a second straight year, Topps reduced the size of the cards to 2-1/8" by 3". Four different wax pack boxes were available, each featuring two cards that were placed on the sides of the boxes. The card fronts are identical in design to the regular issue cards. The backs are printed in blue and yellow and carry a commentary imitating a newspaper format. The cards are numbered A through H.

		MT	NR MT	EX
	Complete Panel Set:	5.00	3.75	2.00
	Complete Singles Set:	2.00	1.50	.80
	Common Panel:	.75	.60	.30
	Common Single Player:	.15	.11	.06
Panel		1.25	.90	.50
A	Don Baylor	.15	.11	.06
B	Steve Carlton	.30	.25	.12
Panel		.75	.60	.30
C	Ron Cey	.15	.11	.06
D	Cecil Cooper	.15	.11	.06
Panel		1.75	1.25	.70
E	Rickey Henderson	.40	.30	.15
F	Jim Rice	.25	.20	.10
Panel		1.25	.90	.50
G	Don Sutton	.20	.15	.08
H	Dave Winfield	.30	.25	.12

1987 Topps Coins

For the first time since 1971, Topps issued a set of baseball "coins". Similar in design to the 1964 edition of Topps coins, the metal discs measure 1-1/2" in diameter. The aluminum coins were sold on a limited basis in retail outlets. Three coins and three sticks of gum were found in a pack. The coin fronts feature a full-color photo along with the player's name, team ans position in a white band at the bottom of the coin. Gold-colored rims are found for American League players; National League players have silver-colored rims. Backs are silver in color and carry the coin number, player's name and personal and statistical information.

		MT	NR MT	EX
	Complete Set:	10.00	7.50	4.00
	Common Player:	.15	.11	.06
1	Harold Baines	.15	.11	.06
2	Jesse Barfield	.15	.11	.06
3	George Bell	.20	.15	.08
4	Wade Boggs	.70	.50	.30
5	George Brett	.30	.25	.12
6	Jose Canseco	1.00	.70	.40
7	Joe Carter	.15	.11	.06
8	Roger Clemens	.40	.30	.15
9	Alvin Davis	.15	.11	.06
10	Rob Deer	.15	.11	.06
11	Kirk Gibson	.20	.15	.08
12	Rickey Henderson	.25	.20	.10
13	Kent Hrbek	.20	.15	.08
14	Pete Incaviglia	.20	.15	.08
15	Reggie Jackson	.25	.20	.10
16	Wally Joyner	.60	.45	.25
17	Don Mattingly	1.25	.90	.50
18	Jack Morris	.20	.15	.08
19	Eddie Murray	.25	.20	.10
20	Kirby Puckett	.30	.25	.12
21	Jim Rice	.25	.20	.10
22	Dave Righetti	.20	.15	.08
23	Cal Ripken	.25	.20	.10
24	Cory Snyder	.25	.20	.10
25	Danny Tartabull	.20	.15	.08
26	Dave Winfield	.25	.20	.10
27	Hubie Brooks	.15	.11	.06
28	Gary Carter	.25	.20	.10
29	Vince Coleman	.20	.15	.08
30	Eric Davis	.70	.50	.30
31	Glenn Davis	.15	.11	.06
32	Steve Garvey	.25	.20	.10
33	Dwight Gooden	.40	.30	.15
34	Tony Gwynn	.30	.25	.12
35	Von Hayes	.15	.11	.06
36	Keith Hernandez	.20	.15	.08
37	Dale Murphy	.30	.25	.12
38	Dave Parker	.20	.15	.08
39	Tony Pena	.15	.11	.06
40	Nolan Ryan	.25	.20	.10
41	Ryne Sandberg	.20	.15	.08
42	Steve Sax	.15	.11	.06
43	Mike Schmidt	.30	.25	.12
44	Mike Scott	.15	.11	.06
45	Ozzie Smith	.15	.11	.06
46	Darryl Strawberry	.40	.30	.15
47	Fernando Valenzuela	.20	.15	.08
48	Todd Worrell	.15	.11	.06

1987 Topps Gallery of Champions

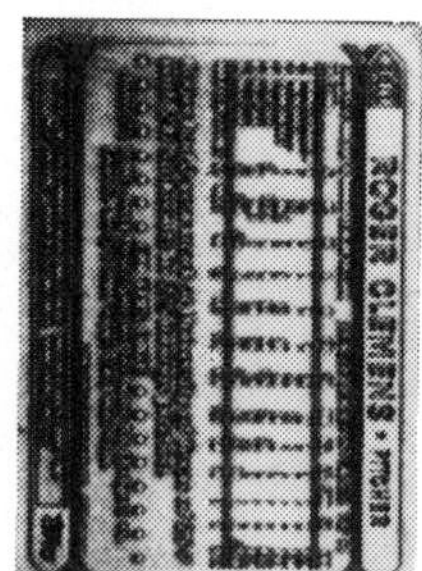

Designed as a tribute to the 1986 season's winners of baseball's most prestigious awards, the Gallery of Champions are metal "cards" that are one-quarter size replicas of the regular issue Topps cards. The bronze and silver sets were issued in leather-like velvet-lined display cases; the aluminum sets came cello-wrapped. Hobby dealers who purchased one bronze set or a 16-set case of aluminum "cards" received one free Jose Canseco pewter metal mini-card (value $60). The purchase of a silver set included five Canseco pewters. A 1953 Willie Mays bronze was given to dealers who brought cases of 1987 Topps Traded sets (value $10).

		MT	NR MT	EX
	Complete Aluminum Set:	30.00	22.00	12.00
	Complete Bronze Set:	175.00	131.00	70.00
	Complete Silver Set:	700.00	525.00	280.00
(1a)	Jesse Barfield (aluminum)	.70	.50	.30
(1b)	Jesse Barfield (bronze)	7.50	5.75	3.00
(1c)	Jesse Barfield (silver)	20.00	15.00	8.00
(2a)	Wade Boggs (aluminum)	3.00	2.25	1.25
(2b)	Wade Boggs (bronze)	25.00	18.50	10.00
(2c)	Wade Boggs (silver)	125.00	94.00	50.00
(3a)	Jose Canseco (aluminum)	3.00	2.25	1.25
(3b)	Jose Canseco (bronze)	25.00	18.50	10.00
(3c)	Jose Canseco (silver)	125.00	94.00	50.00
(4a)	Joe Carter (aluminum)	.70	.50	.30
(4b)	Joe Carter (bronze)	7.50	5.75	3.00
(4c)	Joe Carter (silver)	20.00	15.00	8.00
(5a)	Roger Clemens (aluminum)	2.00	1.50	.80
(5b)	Roger Clemens (bronze)	20.00	15.00	8.00
(5c)	Roger Clemens (silver)	90.00	67.00	36.00
(6a)	Tony Gwynn (aluminum)	1.25	.90	.50
(6b)	Tony Gwynn (bronze)	12.00	9.00	4.75
(6c)	Tony Gwynn (silver)	50.00	37.00	20.00
(7a)	Don Mattingly (aluminum)	8.00	6.00	3.25
(7b)	Don Mattingly (bronze)	50.00	37.00	20.00
(7c)	Don Mattingly (silver)	200.00	150.00	80.00
(8a)	Tim Raines (aluminum)	1.00	.70	.40
(8b)	Tim Raines (bronze)	10.00	7.50	4.00
(8c)	Tim Raines (silver)	30.00	22.00	12.00
(9a)	Dave Righetti (aluminum)	1.00	.70	.40
(9b)	Dave Righetti (bronze)	10.00	7.50	4.00
(9c)	Dave Righetti (silver)	30.00	22.00	12.00
(10a)	Mike Schmidt (aluminum)	1.50	1.25	.60
(10b)	Mike Schmidt (bronze)	15.00	11.00	6.00
(10c)	Mike Schmidt (silver)	80.00	60.00	32.00
(11a)	Mike Scott (aluminum)	.70	.50	.30
(11b)	Mike Scott (bronze)	7.50	5.75	3.00
(11c)	Mike Scott (silver)	20.00	15.00	8.00
(12a)	Todd Worrell (aluminum)	.70	.50	.30
(12b)	Todd Worrell (bronze)	10.00	7.50	4.00
(12c)	Todd Worrell (silver)	20.00	15.00	8.00

1987 Topps Glossy Rookies

The 1987 Topps Glossy Rookies set of 22 cards was introduced with Topps' new 100-card "Jumbo Packs". Intended for sale in supermarkets, the jumbo packs contained one glossy card. Measuring the standard 2-1/2" by 3-1/2" size, the special insert cards feature the top rookies from the previous season.

		MT	NR MT	EX
Complete Set:		10.00	7.50	4.00
Common Player:		.20	.15	.08
1	Andy Allanson	.20	.15	.08
2	John Cangelosi	.20	.15	.08
3	Jose Canseco	3.00	2.25	1.25
4	Will Clark	1.50	1.25	.60
5	Mark Eichhorn	.40	.30	.15
6	Pete Incaviglia	.70	.50	.30
7	Wally Joyner	2.00	1.50	.80
8	Eric King	.30	.25	.12
9	Dave Magadan	.60	.45	.25
10	John Morris	.20	.15	.08
11	Juan Nieves	.40	.30	.15
12	Rafael Palmeiro	1.00	.70	.40
13	Billy Jo Robidoux	.20	.15	.08
14	Bruce Ruffin	.40	.30	.15
15	Ruben Sierra	1.25	.90	.50
16	Cory Snyder	.80	.60	.30
17	Kurt Stillwell	.60	.45	.25
18	Dale Sveum	.40	.30	.15
19	Danny Tartabull	.80	.60	.30
20	Andres Thomas	.40	.30	.15
21	Robby Thompson	.40	.30	.15
22	Todd Worrell	.40	.30	.15

1987 Topps Mini League Leaders

Returning for 1987, the Topps "Major League Leaders" set was increased in size from 66 to 76 cards. The 2-1/8" by 3" cards feature wood grain borders that encompass a white-bordered full-color photo. The card backs are printed in yellow, orange and brown and list the player's official ranking based on his 1986 American or National League statistics. The players featured are those who finished the top five in their leagues' various batting and pitching statistics. The cards were sold in plastic-wrapped packs, seven cards plus a game card per pack.

		MT	NR MT	EX
Complete Set:		6.00	4.50	2.50
Common Player:		.09	.07	.04
1	Bob Horner	.20	.15	.08
2	Dale Murphy	.50	.40	.20
3	Lee Smith	.09	.07	.04
4	Eric Davis	.60	.45	.25
5	John Franco	.15	.11	.06
6	Dave Parker	.20	.15	.08
7	Kevin Bass	.09	.07	.04
8	Glenn Davis	.20	.15	.08
9	Bill Doran	.15	.11	.06
10	Bob Knepper	.09	.07	.04
11	Mike Scott	.20	.15	.08
12	Dave Smith	.09	.07	.04
13	Mariano Duncan	.09	.07	.04
14	Orel Hershiser	.30	.25	.12
15	Steve Sax	.20	.15	.08
16	Fernando Valenzuela	.25	.20	.10
17	Tim Raines	.30	.25	.12
18	Jeff Reardon	.15	.11	.06
19	Floyd Youmans	.09	.07	.04
20	Gary Carter	.30	.25	.12
21	Ron Darling	.20	.15	.08
22	Sid Fernandez	.15	.11	.06
23	Dwight Gooden	.60	.45	.25
24	Keith Hernandez	.25	.20	.10
25	Bob Ojeda	.09	.07	.04
26	Darryl Strawberry	.50	.40	.20
27	Steve Bedrosian	.15	.11	.06
28	Von Hayes	.15	.11	.06
29	Juan Samuel	.20	.15	.08
30	Mike Schmidt	.50	.40	.20
31	Rick Rhoden	.09	.07	.04
32	Vince Coleman	.20	.15	.08
33	Danny Cox	.09	.07	.04
34	Todd Worrell	.15	.11	.06
35	Tony Gwynn	.40	.30	.15
36	Mike Krukow	.09	.07	.04
37	Candy Maldonado	.09	.07	.04
38	Don Aase	.09	.07	.04
39	Eddie Murray	.40	.30	.15
40	Cal Ripken	.40	.30	.15
41	Wade Boggs	.80	.60	.30
42	Roger Clemens	.60	.45	.25
43	Bruce Hurst	.15	.11	.06
44	Jim Rice	.30	.25	.12
45	Wally Joyner	.80	.60	.30
46	Donnie Moore	.09	.07	.04
47	Gary Pettis	.09	.07	.04
48	Mike Witt	.09	.07	.04
49	John Cangelosi	.09	.07	.04
50	Tom Candiotti	.09	.07	.04
51	Joe Carter	.20	.15	.08
52	Pat Tabler	.09	.07	.04
53	Kirk Gibson	.25	.20	.10
54	Willie Hernandez	.09	.07	.04
55	Jack Morris	.25	.20	.10
56	Alan Trammell	.30	.25	.12
57	George Brett	.50	.40	.20
58	Willie Wilson	.15	.11	.06
59	Rob Deer	.09	.07	.04
60	Teddy Higuera	.15	.11	.06
61	Bert Blyleven	.15	.11	.06
62	Gary Gaetti	.20	.15	.08
63	Kirby Puckett	.35	.25	.14
64	Rickey Henderson	.40	.30	.15
65	Don Mattingly	1.25	.90	.50
66	Dennis Rasmussen	.15	.11	.06
67	Dave Righetti	.20	.15	.08
68	Jose Canseco	1.00	.70	.40
69	Dave Kingman	.15	.11	.06
70	Phil Bradley	.15	.11	.06
71	Mark Langston	.15	.11	.06
72	Pete O'Brien	.09	.07	.04
73	Jesse Barfield	.15	.11	.06
74	George Bell	.25	.20	.10
75	Tony Fernandez	.15	.11	.06
76	Tom Henke	.09	.07	.04
77	Checklist	.09	.07	.04

1987 Topps Stickers

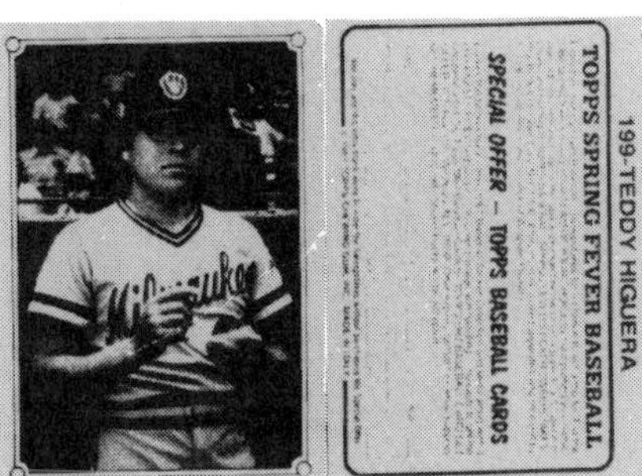

For the seventh consecutive year, Topps issued stickers to be housed in a specially designed yearbook. The stickers, which measure 2-1/8" by 3", offer a full-color front with a peel-off back printed in blue ink on white stock. The sticker fronts feature either one full-size player picture or two half-size individual stickers. The sticker yearbook measures 9" by 10-3/4" and contains 36 glossy, magazine-style pages, all printed in full color. Mike Schmidt, 1986 National League MVP, is featured on the cover. The yearbook sold in retail outlets for 35¢, while stickers were sold five in a pack for 25¢. The number in parentheses in the following checklist is the sticker number the player shares the sticker with.

		MT	NR MT	EX
Complete Set:		18.00	13.50	7.25
Common Player:		.03	.02	.01
Sticker Album:		.70	.50	.30
1	1986 Highlights (Jim Deshaies) (172)	.04	.03	.02
2	1986 Highlights (Roger Clemens) (175)	.15	.11	.06
3	1986 Highlights (Roger Clemens) (176)	.15	.11	.06
4	1986 Highlights (Dwight Evans) (177)	.06	.05	.02
5	1986 Highlights (Dwight Gooden) (178)	.15	.11	.06
6	1986 Highlights (Dwight Gooden) (180)	.15	.11	.06
7	1986 Highlights (Dave Lopes) (181)	.03	.02	.01
8	1986 Highlights (Dave Righetti) (182)	.06	.05	.02
9	1986 Highlights (Dave Righetti) (183)	.10	.08	.04
10	1986 Highlights (Ruben Sierra) (185)	.15	.11	.06
11	1986 Highlights (Todd Worrell) (186)	.06	.05	.02
12	1986 Highlights (Todd Worrell) (187)	.06	.05	.02
13	N.L. Championship Series (Lenny Dykstra)	.06	.05	.02
14	N.L. Championship Series (Gary Carter)	.08	.06	.03
15	N.L. Championship Series (Mike Scott)	.06	.05	.02
16	A.L. Championship Series (Gary Pettis)	.03	.02	.01
17	A.L. Championship Series (Jim Rice)	.08	.06	.03
18	A.L. Championship Series (Bruce Hurst)	.04	.03	.02
19	1986 World Series (Bruce Hurst)	.04	.03	.02
20	1986 World Series (Wade Boggs)	.15	.11	.06
21	1986 World Series (Lenny Dykstra)	.06	.05	.02
22	1986 World Series (Gary Carter)	.08	.06	.03
23	1986 World Series (Dave Henderson)	.04	.03	.02
24	1986 World Series (Howard Johnson)	.04	.03	.02
25	1986 World Series (Mets Celebrate)	.08	.06	.03
26	Glenn Davis	.15	.11	.06
27	Nolan Ryan (188)	.10	.08	.04
28	Charlie Kerfeld (189)	.03	.02	.01
29	Jose Cruz (190)	.04	.03	.02
30	Phil Garner (191)	.06	.05	.02
31	Bill Doran (192)	.06	.05	.02
32	Bob Knepper (195)	.03	.02	.01
33	Denny Walling (196)	.10	.08	.04
34	Kevin Bass (197)	.04	.03	.02
35	Mike Scott	.10	.08	.04
36	Dale Murphy	.25	.20	.10
37	Paul Assenmacher (198)	.06	.05	.02
38	Ken Oberkfell (200)	.06	.05	.02
39	Andres Thomas (201)	.08	.06	.03
40	Gene Garber (202)	.03	.02	.01
41	Bob Horner	.08	.06	.03
42	Rafael Ramirez (203)	.03	.02	.01
43	Rick Mahler (204)	.03	.02	.01
44	Omar Moreno (205)	.03	.02	.01
45	Dave Palmer (206)	.03	.02	.01
46	Ozzie Smith	.12	.09	.05
47	Bob Forsch (207)	.03	.02	.01
48	Willie McGee (209)	.06	.05	.02
49	Tom Herr (210)	.06	.05	.02
50	Vince Coleman (211)	.08	.06	.03
51	Andy Van Slyke (212)	.06	.05	.02
52	Jack Clark (215)	.08	.06	.03
53	John Tudor (216)	.04	.03	.02
54	Terry Pendleton (217)	.03	.02	.01
55	Todd Worrell	.10	.08	.04
56	Lee Smith	.06	.05	.02
57	Leon Durham (218)	.03	.02	.01
58	Jerry Mumphrey (219)	.06	.05	.02
59	Shawon Dunston (220)	.06	.05	.02
60	Scott Sanderson (221)	.06	.05	.02
61	Ryne Sandberg	.15	.11	.06
62	Gary Matthews (222)	.04	.03	.02
63	Dennis Eckersley (225)	.06	.05	.02
64	Jody Davis (226)	.06	.05	.02
65	Keith Moreland (227)	.04	.03	.02
66	Mike Marshall (228)	.06	.05	.02
67	Bill Madlock (229)	.06	.05	.02
68	Greg Brock (230)	.04	.03	.02
69	Pedro Guerrero (231)	.08	.06	.03
70	Steve Sax	.12	.09	.05
71	Rick Honeycutt (232)	.03	.02	.01
72	Franklin Stubbs (235)	.03	.02	.01
73	Mike Scioscia (236)	.10	.08	.04
74	Mariano Duncan (237)	.03	.02	.01
75	Fernando Valenzuela	.15	.11	.06
76	Hubie Brooks	.06	.05	.02
77	Andre Dawson (238)	.08	.06	.03
78	Tim Burke (240)	.04	.03	.02
79	Floyd Youmans (241)	.03	.02	.01
80	Tim Wallach (242)	.04	.03	.02
81	Jeff Reardon (243)	.06	.05	.02
82	Mitch Webster (244)	.15	.11	.06
83	Bryn Smith (245)	.03	.02	.01
84	Andres Galarraga (246)	.12	.09	.05
85	Tim Raines	.15	.11	.06
86	Chris Brown	.08	.06	.03
87	Bob Brenly (247)	.03	.02	.01
88	Will Clark (249)	.25	.20	.10
89	Scott Garrelts (250)	.04	.03	.02
90	Jeffrey Leonard (251)	.06	.05	.02
91	Robby Thompson (252)	.06	.05	.02
92	Mike Krukow (255)	.03	.02	.01
93	Danny Gladden (256)	.03	.02	.01
94	Candy Maldonado (257)	.04	.03	.02
95	Chili Davis	.04	.03	.02
96	Dwight Gooden	.30	.25	.12
97	Sid Fernandez (258)	.04	.03	.02
98	Len Dykstra (259)	.06	.05	.02
99	Bob Ojeda (260)	.04	.03	.02
100	Wally Backman (261)	.04	.03	.02
101	Gary Carter	.15	.11	.06
102	Keith Hernandez (262)	.10	.08	.04
103	Darryl Strawberry (265)	.15	.11	.06
104	Roger McDowell (266)	.08	.06	.03
105	Ron Darling (267)	.08	.06	.03
106	Tony Gwynn	.20	.15	.08
107	Dave Dravecky (268)	.04	.03	.02
108	Terry Kennedy (269)	.08	.06	.03
109	Rich Gossage (270)	.10	.08	.04
110	Garry Templeton (271)	.04	.03	.02
111	Lance McCullers (272)	.04	.03	.02
112	Eric Show (275)	.04	.03	.02
113	John Kruk (276)	.12	.09	.05
114	Tim Flannery (277)	.06	.05	.02
115	Steve Garvey	.15	.11	.06
116	Mike Schmidt	.25	.20	.10
117	Glenn Wilson (278)	.06	.05	.02
118	Kent Tekulve (280)	.06	.05	.02
119	Gary Redus (281)	.08	.06	.03
120	Shane Rawley (282)	.03	.02	.01
121	Von Hayes	.06	.05	.02
122	Don Carman (283)	.04	.03	.02
123	Bruce Ruffin (285)	.04	.03	.02
124	Steve Bedrosian (286)	.06	.05	.02
125	Juan Samuel (287)	.06	.05	.02
126	Sid Bream (288)	.06	.05	.02
127	Cecilio Guante (289)	.03	.02	.01
128	Rick Reuschel (290)	.04	.03	.02
129	Tony Pena (291)	.04	.03	.02
130	Rick Rhoden	.06	.05	.02
131	Barry Bonds (292)	.10	.08	.04

		MT	NR MT	EX
132	Joe Orsulak (295)	.03	.02	.01
133	Jim Morrison (296)	.12	.09	.05
134	R.J. Reynolds (297)	.04	.03	.02
135	Johnny Ray	.06	.05	.02
136	Eric Davis	.30	.25	.12
137	Tom Browning (298)	.10	.08	.04
138	John Franco (300)	.06	.05	.02
139	Pete Rose (301)	.20	.15	.08
140	Bill Gullickson (302)	.04	.03	.02
141	Ron Oester (303)	.04	.03	.02
142	Bo Diaz (304)	.40	.30	.15
143	Buddy Bell (305)	.04	.03	.02
144	Eddie Milner (306)	.08	.06	.03
145	Dave Parker	.10	.08	.04
146	Kirby Puckett	.35	.25	.14
147	Rickey Henderson	.40	.30	.15
148	Wade Boggs	.60	.45	.25
149	Lance Parrish	.25	.20	.10
150	Wally Joyner	.70	.50	.30
151	Cal Ripken	.40	.30	.15
152	Dave Winfield	.30	.25	.12
153	Lou Whitaker	.25	.20	.10
154	Roger Clemens	.50	.40	.20
155	Tony Gwynn	.40	.30	.15
156	Ryne Sandberg	.25	.20	.10
157	Keith Hernandez	.25	.20	.10
158	Gary Carter	.30	.25	.12
159	Darryl Strawberry	.50	.40	.20
160	Mike Schmidt	.40	.30	.15
161	Dale Murphy	.40	.30	.15
162	Ozzie Smith	.20	.15	.08
163	Dwight Gooden	.50	.40	.20
164	Jose Canseco	.80	.60	.30
165	Curt Young (307)	.04	.03	.02
166	Alfredo Griffin (308)	.12	.09	.05
167	Dave Stewart (309)	.06	.05	.02
168	Mike Davis (310)	.06	.05	.02
169	Bruce Bochte (311)	.03	.02	.01
170	Dwayne Murphy (312)	.04	.03	.02
171	Carney Lansford (313)	.20	.15	.08
172	Joaquin Andujar (1)	.04	.03	.02
173	Dave Kingman	.08	.06	.03
174	Wally Joyner	.40	.30	.15
175	Gary Pettis (2)	.15	.11	.06
176	Dick Schofield (3)	.15	.11	.06
177	Donnie Moore (4)	.06	.05	.02
178	Brian Downing (5)	.15	.11	.06
179	Mike Witt	.06	.05	.02
180	Bob Boone (6)	.15	.11	.06
181	Kirk McCaskill (7)	.03	.02	.01
182	Doug DeCinces (8)	.06	.05	.02
183	Don Sutton (9)	.10	.08	.04
184	Jessie Barfield	.10	.08	.04
185	Tom Henke (10)	.15	.11	.06
186	Willie Upshaw (11)	.06	.05	.02
187	Mark Eichhorn (12)	.06	.05	.02
188	Damaso Garcia (27)	.10	.08	.04
189	Jim Clancy (28)	.03	.02	.01
190	Lloyd Moseby (29)	.04	.03	.02
191	Tony Fernandez (30)	.06	.05	.02
192	Jimmy Key (31)	.06	.05	.02
193	George Bell	.20	.15	.08
194	Rob Deer	.06	.05	.02
195	Mark Clear (32)	.03	.02	.01
196	Robin Yount (33)	.10	.08	.04
197	Jim Gantner (34)	.04	.03	.02
198	Cecil Cooper (37)	.06	.05	.02
199	Teddy Higuera	.08	.06	.03
200	Paul Molitor (38)	.08	.06	.03
201	Dan Plesac (39)	.08	.06	.03
202	Billy Jo Robidoux (40)	.03	.02	.01
203	Earnie Riles (42)	.03	.02	.01
204	Ken Schrom (43)	.03	.02	.01
205	Pat Tabler (44)	.03	.02	.01
206	Mel Hall (45)	.03	.02	.01
207	Tony Bernazard (47)	.03	.02	.01
208	Joe Carter	.10	.08	.04
209	Ernie Camacho (48)	.06	.05	.02
210	Julio Franco (49)	.06	.05	.02
211	Tom Candiotti (50)	.08	.06	.03
212	Brook Jacoby (51)	.06	.05	.02
213	Cory Snyder	.30	.25	.12
214	Jim Presley	.08	.06	.03
215	Mike Moore (52)	.08	.06	.03
216	Harold Reynolds (53)	.04	.03	.02
217	Scott Bradley (54)	.03	.02	.01
218	Matt Young (57)	.03	.02	.01
219	Mark Langston (58)	.06	.05	.02
220	Alvin Davis (59)	.06	.05	.02
221	Phil Bradley (60)	.06	.05	.02
222	Ken Phelps (62)	.04	.03	.02
223	Danny Tartabull	.20	.15	.08
224	Eddie Murray	.20	.15	.08
225	Rick Dempsey (63)	.06	.05	.02
226	Fred Lynn (64)	.06	.05	.02
227	Mike Boddicker (65)	.04	.03	.02
228	Don Aase (66)	.06	.05	.02
229	Larry Sheets (67)	.06	.05	.02
230	Storm Davis (68)	.04	.03	.02
231	Lee Lacy (69)	.08	.06	.03
232	Jim Traber (71)	.03	.02	.01
233	Cal Ripken	.20	.15	.08
234	Larry Parrish	.06	.05	.02
235	Gary Ward (72)	.03	.02	.01
236	Pete Incaviglia (73)	.10	.08	.04
237	Scott Fletcher (74)	.03	.02	.01
238	Greg Harris (77)	.08	.06	.03
239	Pete O'Brien	.06	.05	.02
240	Charlie Hough (78)	.04	.03	.02
241	Don Slaught (79)	.03	.02	.01
242	Steve Buechele (80)	.04	.03	.02
243	Oddibe McDowell (81)	.06	.05	.02
244	Roger Clemens (82)	.15	.11	.06
245	Bob Stanley (83)	.03	.02	.01
246	Tom Seaver (84)	.12	.09	.05
247	Rich Gedman (87)	.03	.02	.01
248	Jim Rice	.15	.11	.06
249	Dennis Boyd (88)	.25	.20	.10
250	Bill Buckner (89)	.04	.03	.02
251	Dwight Evans (90)	.06	.05	.02
252	Don Baylor (91)	.06	.05	.02
253	Wade Boggs	.40	.30	.15
254	George Brett	.25	.20	.10
255	Steve Farr (92)	.03	.02	.01
256	Jim Sundberg (93)	.03	.02	.01
257	Dan Quisenberry (94)	.04	.03	.02
258	Charlie Leibrandt (97)	.04	.03	.02
259	Argenis Salazar (98)	.06	.05	.02
260	Frank White (99)	.04	.03	.02
261	Willie Wilson (100)	.04	.03	.02
262	Lonnie Smith (102)	.10	.08	.04
263	Steve Balboni	.04	.03	.02
264	Darrell Evans	.06	.05	.02
265	Johnny Grubb (103)	.15	.11	.06
266	Jack Morris (104)	.08	.06	.03
267	Lou Whitaker (105)	.08	.06	.03
268	Chet Lemon (107)	.04	.03	.02
269	Lance Parrish (108)	.08	.06	.03
270	Alan Trammell (109)	.10	.08	.04
271	Darnell Coles (110)	.04	.03	.02
272	Willie Hernandez (111)	.04	.03	.02
273	Kirk Gibson	.15	.11	.06
274	Kirby Puckett	.20	.15	.08
275	Mike Smithson (112)	.04	.03	.02
276	Mickey Hatcher (113)	.12	.09	.05
277	Frank Viola (114)	.06	.05	.02
278	Bert Blyleven (117)	.06	.05	.02
279	Gary Gaetti	.10	.08	.04
280	Tom Brunansky (118)	.06	.05	.02
281	Kent Hrbek (119)	.08	.06	.03
282	Roy Smalley (120)	.03	.02	.01
283	Greg Gagne (122)	.04	.03	.02
284	Harold Baines	.10	.08	.04
285	Ron Hassey (123)	.04	.03	.02
286	Floyd Bannister (124)	.06	.05	.02
287	Ozzie Guillen (125)	.06	.05	.02
288	Carlton Fisk (126)	.06	.05	.02
289	Tim Hulett (127)	.03	.02	.01
290	Joe Cowley (128)	.04	.03	.02
291	Greg Walker (129)	.04	.03	.02
292	Neil Allen (131)	.10	.08	.04
293	John Cangelosi	.04	.03	.02
294	Don Mattingly	.90	.70	.35
295	Mike Easler (132)	.03	.02	.01
296	Rickey Henderson (133)	.12	.09	.05
297	Dan Pasqua (134)	.04	.03	.02
298	Dave Winfield (137)	.10	.08	.04
299	Dave Righetti	.12	.09	.05
300	Mike Pagliarulo (138)	.06	.05	.02
301	Ron Guidry (139)	.20	.15	.08
302	Willie Randolph (140)	.04	.03	.02
303	Dennis Rasmussen (141)	.04	.03	.02
304	Jose Canseco (142)	.40	.30	.15
305	Andres Thomas (143)	.04	.03	.02
306	Danny Tartabull (144)	.08	.06	.03
307	Robby Thompson (165)	.04	.03	.02
308	Pete Incaviglia, Cory Snyder (166)	.12	.09	.05
309	Dale Sveum (167)	.06	.05	.02
310	Todd Worrell (168)	.06	.05	.02
311	Andy Allanson (169)	.03	.02	.01
312	Bruce Ruffin (170)	.04	.03	.02
313	Wally Joyner (171)	.20	.15	.08

1987 Topps Traded

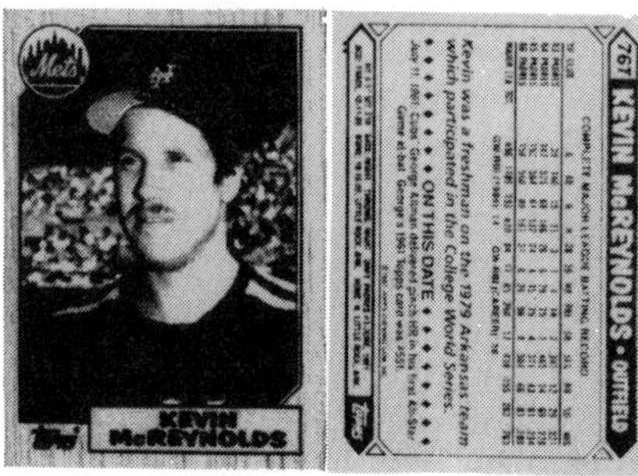

The Topps Traded set consists of 132 cards as have all Traded sets issued by Topps since 1981. The cards measure the standard 2 1/2" by 3 1/2" and are identical in design to the regular edition set. The purpose of the set is to update player trades and feature rookies not included in the regular issue. As they had done the previous three years, Topps produced a glossy-coated "Tiffany" edition of the Traded set. The Tiffany edition cards are valued at two to three times greater than the regular Traded cards.

		MT	NR MT	EX
	Complete Set:	15.00	11.00	6.00
	Common Player:	.06	.05	.02
1T	Bill Almon	.06	.05	.02
2T	Scott Bankhead	.08	.06	.03
3T	Eric Bell(FC)	.15	.11	.06
4T	Juan Beniquez	.06	.05	.02
5T	Juan Berenguer	.06	.05	.02
6T	Greg Booker	.06	.05	.02
7T	Thad Bosley	.06	.05	.02
8T	Larry Bowa	.10	.08	.04
9T	Greg Brock	.10	.08	.04
10T	Bob Brower(FC)	.15	.11	.06
11T	Jerry Browne(FC)	.30	.25	.12
12T	Ralph Bryant(FC)	.12	.09	.05
13T	DeWayne Buice(FC)	.15	.11	.06
14T	Ellis Burks(FC)	2.00	1.50	.80
15T	Ivan Calderon	.12	.09	.05
16T	Jeff Calhoun	.06	.05	.02
17T	Casey Candaele(FC)	.10	.08	.04
18T	John Cangelosi	.06	.05	.02
19T	Steve Carlton	.30	.25	.12
20T	Juan Castillo(FC)	.06	.05	.02
21T	Rick Cerone	.06	.05	.02
22T	Ron Cey	.10	.08	.04
23T	John Christensen	.06	.05	.02
24T	Dave Cone(FC)	1.25	.90	.50
25T	Chuck Crim(FC)	.15	.11	.06
26T	Storm Davis	.06	.05	.02
27T	Andre Dawson	.40	.30	.15
28T	Rick Dempsey	.08	.06	.03
29T	Doug Drabek	.10	.08	.04
30T	Mike Dunne	.40	.30	.15
31T	Dennis Eckersley	.20	.15	.08
32T	Lee Elia	.06	.05	.02
33T	Brian Fisher	.10	.08	.04
34T	Terry Francona	.06	.05	.02
35T	Willie Fraser(FC)	.15	.11	.06
36T	Billy Gardner	.06	.05	.02
37T	Ken Gerhart(FC)	.15	.11	.06
38T	Danny Gladden	.06	.05	.02
39T	Jim Gott	.06	.05	.02
40T	Cecilio Guante	.06	.05	.02
41T	Albert Hall	.06	.05	.02
42T	Terry Harper	.06	.05	.02
43T	Mickey Hatcher	.06	.05	.02
44T	Brad Havens	.06	.05	.02
45T	Neal Heaton	.06	.05	.02
46T	Mike Henneman(FC)	.30	.25	.12
47T	Donnie Hill	.06	.05	.02
48T	Guy Hoffman	.06	.05	.02
49T	Brian Holton(FC)	.15	.11	.06
50T	Charles Hudson	.06	.05	.02
51T	Danny Jackson(FC)	.30	.25	.12
52T	Reggie Jackson	.50	.40	.20
53T	Chris James(FC)	.40	.30	.15
54T	Dion James	.10	.08	.04
55T	Stan Jefferson(FC)	.20	.15	.08
56T	Joe Johnson(FC)	.08	.06	.03
57T	Terry Kennedy	.08	.06	.03
58T	Mike Kingery	.08	.06	.03
59T	Ray Knight	.10	.08	.04
60T	Gene Larkin(FC)	.30	.25	.12
61T	Mike LaValliere	.10	.08	.04
62T	Jack Lazorko	.06	.05	.02
63T	Terry Leach	.06	.05	.02
64T	Tim Leary	.06	.05	.02
65T	Jim Lindeman(FC)	.15	.11	.06
66T	Steve Lombardozzi(FC)	.06	.05	.02
67T	Bill Long(FC)	.20	.15	.08
68T	Barry Lyons(FC)	.15	.11	.06
69T	Shane Mack	.20	.15	.08
70T	Greg Maddux(FC)	.60	.45	.25
71T	Bill Madlock	.15	.11	.06
72T	Joe Magrane(FC)	1.25	.90	.50
73T	Dave Martinez(FC)	.25	.20	.10
74T	Fred McGriff(FC)	2.00	1.50	.80
75T	Mark McLemore(FC)	.10	.08	.04
76T	Kevin McReynolds(FC)	.60	.45	.25
77T	Dave Meads(FC)	.15	.11	.06
78T	Eddie Milner	.06	.05	.02
79T	Greg Minton	.06	.05	.02
80T	John Mitchell(FC)	.15	.11	.06
81T	Kevin Mitchell	1.75	1.25	.70
82T	Charlie Moore	.06	.05	.02
83T	Jeff Musselman(FC)	.25	.20	.10
84T	Gene Nelson	.06	.05	.02
85T	Graig Nettles	.12	.09	.05
86T	Al Newman	.06	.05	.02
87T	Reid Nichols	.06	.05	.02
88T	Tom Niedenfuer	.08	.06	.03
89T	Joe Niekro	.10	.08	.04
90T	Tom Nieto	.06	.05	.02
91T	Matt Nokes(FC)	.70	.50	.30
92T	Dickie Noles	.06	.05	.02
93T	Pat Pacillo	.15	.11	.06
94T	Lance Parrish	.20	.15	.08
95T	Tony Pena	.10	.08	.04
96T	Luis Polonia(FC)	.30	.25	.12
97T	Randy Ready	.06	.05	.02
98T	Jeff Reardon	.12	.09	.05
99T	Gary Redus	.08	.06	.03
100T	Jeff Reed	.06	.05	.02
101T	Rick Rhoden	.10	.08	.04
102T	Cal Ripken, Sr.	.06	.05	.02
103T	Wally Ritchie(FC)	.15	.11	.06
104T	Jeff Robinson(FC)	.40	.30	.15
105T	Gary Roenicke	.06	.05	.02
106T	Jerry Royster	.06	.05	.02
107T	Mark Salas	.06	.05	.02
108T	Luis Salazar	.06	.05	.02
109T	Benny Santiago(FC)	1.25	.90	.50
110T	Dave Schmidt	.08	.06	.03
111T	Kevin Seitzer(FC)	.70	.50	.30
112T	John Shelby	.06	.05	.02
113T	Steve Shields(FC)	.08	.06	.03
114T	John Smiley(FC)	.40	.30	.15
115T	Chris Speier	.06	.05	.02
116T	Mike Stanley(FC)	.20	.15	.08
117T	Terry Steinbach(FC)	.70	.50	.30
118T	Les Straker(FC)	.20	.15	.08
119T	Jim Sundberg	.08	.06	.03
120T	Danny Tartabull	.35	.25	.14
121T	Tom Trebelhorn	.08	.06	.03
122T	Dave Valle(FC)	.12	.09	.05
123T	Ed Vande Berg	.06	.05	.02
124T	Andy Van Slyke	.20	.15	.08
125T	Gary Ward	.06	.05	.02
126T	Alan Wiggins	.06	.05	.02
127T	Bill Wilkinson(FC)	.15	.11	.06
128T	Frank Williams	.08	.06	.03
129T	Matt Williams(FC)	3.25	2.50	1.25
130T	Jim Winn	.06	.05	.02
131T	Matt Young	.06	.05	.02
132T	Checklist 1T-132T	.06	.05	.02

NOTE: A card number in parentheses ( ) indicates the set is unnumbered.

1988 Topps

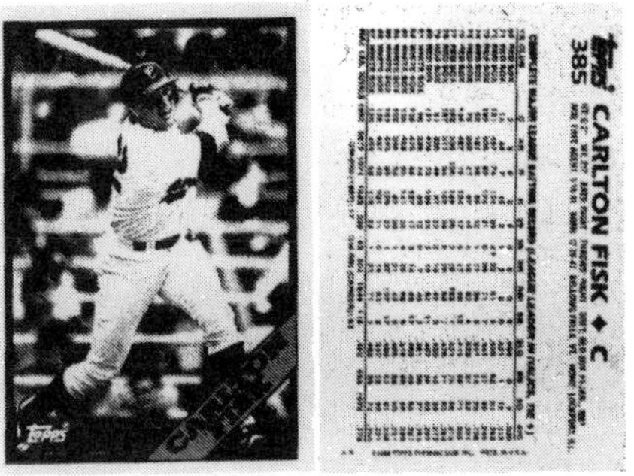

The 1988 Topps set features a clean, attractive design that should prove to be very popular with collectors for many years to come. The full-color player photo is surrounded by a thin yellow frame which is encompassed by a white border. The player's name appears in the lower right corner in a colored band which appears to wrap around the player photo. The player's team nickname is located in large letters at the top of the card. The Topps logo is placed in the lower left corner of the card. The card backs feature black print on orange and gray stock and includes the usual player personal and career statistics. Many of the cards contain a new feature entitled "This Way To The Clubhouse", which explains how the player joined his current team, be it by trade, free agency, etc. The 792-card set includes a number of special subsets including "Future Stars", "Turn Back The Clock", All-Star teams, All-Star rookie selections, and Record Breakers. All cards measure 2-1/2" by 3-1/2". For the fifth consecutive year, Topps issued a glossy "Tiffany" edition of its 792-card regular-issue set. The Tiffany cards have a value of 3-4 times greater than the same card in the regular issue. The Tiffany edition could be purchased by collectors directly from Topps for $99. The company placed ads for the Tiffany set in publications such as USA Today and The Sporting News.

		MT	NR MT	EX
Complete Set:		25.00	20.00	10.00
Common Player:		.04	.03	.02
1	'87 Record Breakers (Vince Coleman)	.08	.06	.03
2	'87 Record Breakers (Don Mattingly)	.60	.45	.25
3a	'87 Record Breakers (Mark McGwire) (white triangle by left foot)	.70	.50	.30
3b	'87 Record Breakers (Mark McGwire) (no triangle by left foot)	.50	.40	.20
4a	'87 Record Breakers (Eddie Murray) (no mention of record on front)	.10	.08	.04
4b	'87 Record Breakers (Eddie Murray) (record stated on card front)	2.00	1.50	.80
5	'87 Record Breakers (Joe Niekro, Phil Niekro)	.10	.08	.04
6	'87 Record Breakers (Nolan Ryan)	.10	.08	.04
7	'87 Record Breakers (Benito Santiago)	.15	.11	.06
8	Kevin Elster(FC)	.25	.20	.10
9	Andy Hawkins	.04	.03	.02
10	Ryne Sandberg	.15	.11	.06
11	Mike Young	.04	.03	.02
12	Bill Schroeder	.04	.03	.02
13	Andres Thomas	.06	.05	.02
14	Sparky Anderson	.06	.05	.02
15	Chili Davis	.06	.05	.02
16	Kirk McCaskill	.06	.05	.02
17	Ron Oester	.04	.03	.02
18a	*Al Leiter* (no "NY" on shirt, photo actually Steve George)(FC)	.80	.60	.30
18b	*Al Leiter* ("NY" on shirt, correct photo)(FC)	.60	.45	.25
19	*Mark Davidson*(FC)	.12	.09	.05
20	Kevin Gross	.06	.05	.02
21	Red Sox Leaders (Wade Boggs, Spike Owen)	.15	.11	.06
22	Greg Swindell	.15	.11	.06
23	Ken Landreaux	.04	.03	.02
24	Jim Deshaies	.06	.05	.02
25	Andres Galarraga	.12	.09	.05
26	Mitch Williams	.06	.05	.02
27	R.J. Reynolds	.04	.03	.02
28	*Jose Nunez*(FC)	.20	.15	.08
29	Argenis Salazar	.04	.03	.02
30	Sid Fernandez	.08	.06	.03
31	Bruce Bochy	.04	.03	.02
32	Mike Morgan	.04	.03	.02
33	Rob Deer	.06	.05	.02
34	Ricky Horton	.06	.05	.02
35	Harold Baines	.10	.08	.04
36	Jamie Moyer	.06	.05	.02
37	Ed Romero	.04	.03	.02
38	Jeff Calhoun	.04	.03	.02
39	Gerald Perry	.08	.06	.03
40	Orel Hershiser	.20	.15	.08
41	Bob Melvin	.04	.03	.02
42	*Bill Landrum*(FC)	.10	.08	.04

		MT	NR MT	EX
43	Dick Schofield	.04	.03	.02
44	Lou Piniella	.06	.05	.02
45	Kent Hrbek	.12	.09	.05
46	Darnell Coles	.06	.05	.02
47	Joaquin Andujar	.06	.05	.02
48	Alan Ashby	.04	.03	.02
49	Dave Clark(FC)	.10	.08	.04
50	Hubie Brooks	.08	.06	.03
51	Orioles Leaders (Eddie Murray, Cal Ripken)	.12	.09	.05
52	Don Robinson	.06	.05	.02
53	Curt Wilkerson	.04	.03	.02
54	Jim Clancy	.06	.05	.02
55	Phil Bradley	.08	.06	.03
56	Ed Hearn	.04	.03	.02
57	*Tim Crews*(FC)	.15	.11	.06
58	Dave Magadan	.10	.08	.04
59	Danny Cox	.06	.05	.02
60	Rickey Henderson	.25	.20	.10
61	*Mark Knudson*(FC)	.10	.08	.04
62	Jeff Hamilton	.08	.06	.03
63	Jimmy Jones(FC)	.10	.08	.04
64	*Ken Caminiti*(FC)	.30	.25	.12
65	Leon Durham	.06	.05	.02
66	Shane Rawley	.06	.05	.02
67	Ken Oberkfell	.04	.03	.02
68	Dave Dravecky	.06	.05	.02
69	*Mike Hart*(FC)	.10	.08	.04
70	Roger Clemens	.50	.40	.20
71	Gary Pettis	.04	.03	.02
72	Dennis Eckersley	.10	.08	.04
73	Randy Bush	.04	.03	.02
74	Tom Lasorda	.06	.05	.02
75	Joe Carter	.10	.08	.04
76	Denny Martinez	.04	.03	.02
77	Tom O'Malley	.04	.03	.02
78	Dan Petry	.06	.05	.02
79	Ernie Whitt	.06	.05	.02
80	Mark Langston	.10	.08	.04
81	Reds Leaders (John Franco, Ron Robinson)	.06	.05	.02
82	*Darrel Akerfelds*(FC)	.12	.09	.05
83	Jose Oquendo	.04	.03	.02
84	Cecilio Guante	.04	.03	.02
85	Howard Johnson	.08	.06	.03
86	Ron Karkovice	.04	.03	.02
87	Mike Mason	.04	.03	.02
88	Earnie Riles	.04	.03	.02
89	*Gary Thurman*(FC)	.20	.15	.08
90	Dale Murphy	.30	.25	.12
91	*Joey Cora*(FC)	.12	.09	.05
92	Len Matuszek	.04	.03	.02
93	Bob Sebra	.04	.03	.02
94	*Chuck Jackson*(FC)	.15	.11	.06
95	Lance Parrish	.12	.09	.05
96	*Todd Benzinger*(FC)	.35	.25	.14
97	Scott Garrelts	.04	.03	.02
98	*Rene Gonzales*(FC)	.15	.11	.06
99	Chuck Finley	.06	.05	.02
100	Jack Clark	.12	.09	.05
101	Allan Anderson	.06	.05	.02
102	Barry Larkin	.35	.25	.14
103	Curt Young	.06	.05	.02
104	Dick Williams	.04	.03	.02
105	Jesse Orosco	.06	.05	.02
106	*Jim Walewander*(FC)	.12	.09	.05
107	Scott Bailes	.06	.05	.02
108	Steve Lyons	.04	.03	.02
109	Joel Skinner	.04	.03	.02
110	Teddy Higuera	.08	.06	.03
111	Expos Leaders (Hubie Brooks, Vance Law)	.06	.05	.02
112	*Les Lancaster*(FC)	.15	.11	.06
113	Kelly Gruber	.04	.03	.02
114	Jeff Russell	.04	.03	.02
115	Johnny Ray	.06	.05	.02
116	Jerry Don Gleaton	.04	.03	.02
117	*James Steels*(FC)	.10	.08	.04
118	Bob Welch	.08	.06	.03
119	*Robbie Wine*(FC)	.12	.09	.05
120	Kirby Puckett	.40	.30	.15
121	Checklist 1-132	.04	.03	.02
122	Tony Bernazard	.04	.03	.02
123	Tom Candiotti	.04	.03	.02
124	Ray Knight	.06	.05	.02
125	Bruce Hurst	.08	.06	.03
126	Steve Jeltz	.04	.03	.02
127	Jim Gott	.04	.03	.02
128	Johnny Grubb	.04	.03	.02
129	Greg Minton	.04	.03	.02
130	Buddy Bell	.08	.06	.03
131	Don Schulze	.04	.03	.02
132	Donnie Hill	.04	.03	.02
133	Greg Mathews	.06	.05	.02
134	Chuck Tanner	.04	.03	.02
135	Dennis Rasmussen	.08	.06	.03
136	Brian Dayett	.04	.03	.02
137	Chris Bosio	.06	.05	.02
138	Mitch Webster	.06	.05	.02
139	Jerry Browne	.06	.05	.02
140	Jesse Barfield	.10	.08	.04
141	Royals Leaders (George Brett, Bret Saberhagen)	.12	.09	.05
142	Andy Van Slyke	.10	.08	.04
143	Mickey Tettleton	.04	.03	.02
144	*Don Gordon*(FC)	.08	.06	.03
145	Bill Madlock	.08	.06	.03
146	*Donell Nixon*(FC)	.15	.11	.06
147	Bill Buckner	.08	.06	.03
148	Carmelo Martinez	.06	.05	.02
149	Ken Howell	.04	.03	.02
150	Eric Davis	.60	.45	.25
151	Bob Knepper	.06	.05	.02
152	*Jody Reed*(FC)	.40	.30	.15
153	John Habyan	.04	.03	.02
154	Jeff Stone	.04	.03	.02
155	Bruce Sutter	.10	.08	.04
156	Gary Matthews	.06	.05	.02
157	Atlee Hammaker	.04	.03	.02
158	Tim Hulett	.04	.03	.02
159	*Brad Arnsberg*(FC)	.12	.09	.05
160	Willie McGee	.10	.08	.04
161	Bryn Smith	.06	.05	.02
162	Mark McLemore	.06	.05	.02

		MT	NR MT	EX
163	Dale Mohorcic	.04	.03	.02
164	Dave Johnson	.06	.05	.02
165	Robin Yount	.20	.15	.08
166	*Rick Rodriguez*(FC)	.10	.08	.04
167	Rance Mulliniks	.04	.03	.02
168	Barry Jones	.04	.03	.02
169	*Ross Jones*(FC)	.12	.09	.05
170	Rich Gossage	.12	.09	.05
171	Cubs Leaders (Shawon Dunston, Manny Trillo)	.06	.05	.02
172	*Lloyd McClendon*(FC)	.10	.08	.04
173	Eric Plunk	.04	.03	.02
174	Phil Garner	.04	.03	.02
175	Kevin Bass	.06	.05	.02
176	Jeff Reed	.04	.03	.02
177	Frank Tanana	.06	.05	.02
178	Dwayne Henry(FC)	.06	.05	.02
179	Charlie Puleo	.04	.03	.02
180	Terry Kennedy	.06	.05	.02
181	Dave Cone	.80	.60	.30
182	Ken Phelps	.06	.05	.02
183	Tom Lawless	.04	.03	.02
184	Ivan Calderon	.08	.06	.03
185	Rick Rhoden	.06	.05	.02
186	Rafael Palmeiro	.35	.25	.14
187	Steve Kiefer(FC)	.06	.05	.02
188	John Russell	.04	.03	.02
189	*Wes Gardner*(FC)	.20	.15	.08
190	Candy Maldonado	.06	.05	.02
191	John Cerutti	.06	.05	.02
192	Devon White	.20	.15	.08
193	Brian Fisher	.06	.05	.02
194	Tom Kelly	.04	.03	.02
195	Dan Quisenberry	.06	.05	.02
196	Dave Engle	.04	.03	.02
197	Lance McCullers	.06	.05	.02
198	Franklin Stubbs	.06	.05	.02
199	*Dave Meads*	.12	.09	.05
200	Wade Boggs	.80	.60	.30
201	Rangers Leaders (Steve Buechele, Pete Incaviglia, Pete O'Brien, Bobby Valentine)	.06	.05	.02
202	Glenn Hoffman	.04	.03	.02
203	Fred Toliver	.04	.03	.02
204	Paul O'Neill(FC)	.12	.09	.05
205	*Nelson Liriano*(FC)	.20	.15	.08
206	Domingo Ramos	.04	.03	.02
207	*John Mitchell, John Mitchell*(FC)	.20	.15	.08
208	Steve Lake	.04	.03	.02
209	Richard Dotson	.06	.05	.02
210	Willie Randolph	.06	.05	.02
211	Frank DiPino	.04	.03	.02
212	Greg Brock	.06	.05	.02
213	Albert Hall	.04	.03	.02
214	Dave Schmidt	.04	.03	.02
215	Von Hayes	.06	.05	.02
216	Jerry Reuss	.06	.05	.02
217	Harry Spilman	.04	.03	.02
218	Dan Schatzeder	.04	.03	.02
219	Mike Stanley	.08	.06	.03
220	Tom Henke	.06	.05	.02
221	Rafael Belliard	.04	.03	.02
222	Steve Farr	.04	.03	.02
223	Stan Jefferson	.08	.06	.03
224	Tom Trebelhorn	.04	.03	.02
225	Mike Scioscia	.06	.05	.02
226	Dave Lopes	.06	.05	.02
227	Ed Correa	.04	.03	.02
228	Wallace Johnson	.04	.03	.02
229	Jeff Musselman	.08	.06	.03
230	Pat Tabler	.06	.05	.02
231	Pirates Leaders (Barry Bonds, Bobby Bonilla)	.10	.08	.04
232	Bob James	.04	.03	.02
233	Rafael Santana	.04	.03	.02
234	Ken Dayley	.04	.03	.02
235	Gary Ward	.06	.05	.02
236	Ted Power	.04	.03	.02
237	Mike Heath	.04	.03	.02
238	*Luis Polonia*	.20	.15	.08
239	Roy Smalley	.04	.03	.02
240	Lee Smith	.08	.06	.03
241	Damaso Garcia	.04	.03	.02
242	Tom Niedenfuer	.06	.05	.02
243	Mark Ryal(FC)	.04	.03	.02
244	Jeff Robinson	.04	.03	.02
245	Rich Gedman	.06	.05	.02
246	*Mike Campbell*(FC)	.20	.15	.08
247	Thad Bosley	.04	.03	.02
248	Storm Davis	.08	.06	.03
249	Mike Marshall	.10	.08	.04
250	Nolan Ryan	.40	.30	.15
251	Tom Foley	.04	.03	.02
252	Bob Brower	.06	.05	.02
253	Checklist 133-264	.04	.03	.02
254	Lee Elia	.04	.03	.02
255	Mookie Wilson	.06	.05	.02
256	Ken Schrom	.04	.03	.02
257	Jerry Royster	.04	.03	.02
258	Ed Nunez	.04	.03	.02
259	Ron Kittle	.06	.05	.02
260	Vince Coleman	.15	.11	.06
261	Giants Leaders (Will Clark, Candy Maldonado, Kevin Mitchell, Robby Thompson, Jose Uribe)	.10	.08	.04
262	Drew Hall(FC)	.12	.09	.05
263	Glenn Braggs	.08	.06	.03
264	*Les Straker*	.15	.11	.06
265	Bo Diaz	.06	.05	.02
266	Paul Assenmacher	.04	.03	.02
267	*Billy Bean*(FC)	.10	.08	.04
268	Bruce Ruffin	.06	.05	.02
269	*Ellis Burks*	1.25	.90	.50
270	Mike Witt	.06	.05	.02
271	Ken Gerhart	.06	.05	.02
272	Steve Ontiveros	.04	.03	.02
273	Garth Iorg	.04	.03	.02
274	Junior Ortiz	.04	.03	.02
275	Kevin Seitzer	.60	.45	.25
276	Luis Salazar	.04	.03	.02
277	Alejandro Pena	.06	.05	.02
278	Jose Cruz	.06	.05	.02
279	Randy St. Claire	.04	.03	.02

No.	Player	MT	NR MT	EX
280	Pete Incaviglia	.12	.09	.05
281	Jerry Hairston	.04	.03	.02
282	Pat Perry	.04	.03	.02
283	Phil Lombardi(FC)	.06	.05	.02
284	Larry Bowa	.06	.05	.02
285	Jim Presley	.08	.06	.03
286	*Chuck Crim*	.12	.09	.05
287	Manny Trillo	.06	.05	.02
288	*Pat Pacillo*	.15	.11	.06
289	Dave Bergman	.04	.03	.02
290	Tony Fernandez	.10	.08	.04
291	Astros Leaders (Kevin Bass, Billy Hatcher)	.06	.05	.02
292	Carney Lansford	.08	.06	.03
293	*Doug Jones*(FC)	.35	.25	.14
294	*Al Pedrique*(FC)	.12	.09	.05
295	Bert Blyleven	.10	.08	.04
296	Floyd Rayford	.04	.03	.02
297	Zane Smith	.06	.05	.02
298	Milt Thompson	.04	.03	.02
299	Steve Crawford	.04	.03	.02
300	Don Mattingly	1.50	1.25	.60
301	Bud Black	.04	.03	.02
302	Jose Uribe	.04	.03	.02
303	Eric Show	.06	.05	.02
304	George Hendrick	.06	.05	.02
305	Steve Sax	.12	.09	.05
306	Billy Hatcher	.06	.05	.02
307	Mike Trujillo	.04	.03	.02
308	Lee Mazzilli	.06	.05	.02
309	*Bill Long*	.15	.11	.06
310	Tom Herr	.06	.05	.02
311	Scott Sanderson	.04	.03	.02
312	Joey Meyer(FC)	.30	.25	.12
313	Bob McClure	.04	.03	.02
314	Jimy Williams	.04	.03	.02
315	Dave Parker	.12	.09	.05
316	Jose Rijo	.06	.05	.02
317	Tom Nieto	.04	.03	.02
318	Mel Hall	.06	.05	.02
319	Mike Loynd	.04	.03	.02
320	Alan Trammell	.15	.11	.06
321	White Sox Leaders (Harold Baines, Carlton Fisk)	.08	.06	.03
322	*Vicente Palacios*(FC)	.15	.11	.06
323	Rick Leach	.04	.03	.02
324	Danny Jackson	.20	.15	.08
325	Glenn Hubbard	.04	.03	.02
326	Al Nipper	.04	.03	.02
327	Larry Sheets	.06	.05	.02
328	*Greg Cadaret*(FC)	.15	.11	.06
329	Chris Speier	.04	.03	.02
330	Eddie Whitson	.04	.03	.02
331	Brian Downing	.06	.05	.02
332	Jerry Reed	.04	.03	.02
333	Wally Backman	.06	.05	.02
334	Dave LaPoint	.06	.05	.02
335	Claudell Washington	.06	.05	.02
336	Ed Lynch	.04	.03	.02
337	Jim Gantner	.04	.03	.02
338	Brian Holton	.08	.06	.03
339	Kurt Stillwell	.08	.06	.03
340	Jack Morris	.15	.11	.06
341	Carmen Castillo	.04	.03	.02
342	Larry Andersen	.04	.03	.02
343	Greg Gagne	.04	.03	.02
344	Tony LaRussa	.04	.03	.02
345	Scott Fletcher	.06	.05	.02
346	Vance Law	.06	.05	.02
347	Joe Johnson	.04	.03	.02
348	Jim Eisenreich	.04	.03	.02
349	Bob Walk	.04	.03	.02
350	Will Clark	1.00	.70	.40
351	Cardinals Leaders (Tony Pena, Red Schoendienst)	.06	.05	.02
352	*Billy Ripken*(FC)	.20	.15	.08
353	Ed Olwine	.04	.03	.02
354	Marc Sullivan	.04	.03	.02
355	Roger McDowell	.08	.06	.03
356	Luis Aguayo	.04	.03	.02
357	Floyd Bannister	.06	.05	.02
358	Rey Quinones	.04	.03	.02
359	Tim Stoddard	.04	.03	.02
360	Tony Gwynn	.25	.20	.10
361	Greg Maddux	.35	.25	.14
362	Juan Castillo	.04	.03	.02
363	Willie Fraser	.06	.05	.02
364	Nick Esasky	.06	.05	.02
365	Floyd Youmans	.04	.03	.02
366	Chet Lemon	.06	.05	.02
367	Tim Leary	.06	.05	.02
368	*Gerald Young*(FC)	.30	.25	.12
369	Greg Harris	.04	.03	.02
370	Jose Canseco	1.75	1.25	.70
371	Joe Hesketh	.04	.03	.02
372	*Matt Williams*	1.75	1.25	.70
373	Checklist 265-396	.04	.03	.02
374	Doc Edwards	.04	.03	.02
375	Tom Brunansky	.08	.06	.03
376	*Bill Wilkinson*	.12	.09	.05
377	*Sam Horn*(FC)	.20	.15	.08
378	*Todd Frohwirth*(FC)	.15	.11	.06
379	Rafael Ramirez	.04	.03	.02
380	*Joe Magrane*	.40	.30	.15
381	Angels Leaders (Jack Howell, Wally Joyner)	.12	.09	.05
382	*Keith Miller*(FC)	.20	.15	.08
383	Eric Bell	.06	.05	.02
384	Neil Allen	.04	.03	.02
385	Carlton Fisk	.20	.15	.08
386	Don Mattingly AS	.60	.45	.25
387	Willie Randolph AS	.06	.05	.02
388	Wade Boggs AS	.35	.25	.14
389	Alan Trammell AS	.08	.06	.03
390	George Bell AS	.10	.08	.04
391	Kirby Puckett AS	.12	.09	.05
392	Dave Winfield AS	.12	.09	.05
393	Matt Nokes AS	.15	.11	.06
394	Roger Clemens AS	.15	.11	.06
395	Jimmy Key AS	.06	.05	.02
396	Tom Henke AS	.06	.05	.02
397	Jack Clark AS	.06	.05	.02
398	Juan Samuel AS	.06	.05	.02
399	Tim Wallach AS	.06	.05	.02

No.	Player	MT	NR MT	EX
400	Ozzie Smith AS	.08	.06	.03
401	Andre Dawson AS	.10	.08	.04
402	Tony Gwynn AS	.15	.11	.06
403	Tim Raines AS	.12	.09	.05
404	Benny Santiago AS	.10	.08	.04
405	Dwight Gooden AS	.15	.11	.06
406	Shane Rawley AS	.06	.05	.02
407	Steve Bedrosian AS	.08	.06	.03
408	Dion James	.06	.05	.02
409	Joel McKeon(FC)	.04	.03	.02
410	Tony Pena	.06	.05	.02
411	Wayne Tolleson	.04	.03	.02
412	Randy Myers	.10	.08	.04
413	John Christensen	.04	.03	.02
414	John McNamara	.04	.03	.02
415	Don Carman	.06	.05	.02
416	Keith Moreland	.06	.05	.02
417	*Mark Ciardi*(FC)	.10	.08	.04
418	Joel Youngblood	.04	.03	.02
419	Scott McGregor	.06	.05	.02
420	Wally Joyner	.35	.25	.14
421	Ed Vande Berg	.04	.03	.02
422	Dave Concepcion	.06	.05	.02
423	*John Smiley*	.30	.25	.12
424	Dwayne Murphy	.06	.05	.02
425	Jeff Reardon	.08	.06	.03
426	Randy Ready	.04	.03	.02
427	*Paul Kilgus*(FC)	.20	.15	.08
428	John Shelby	.04	.03	.02
429	Tigers Leaders (Kirk Gibson, Alan Trammell)	.08	.06	.03
430	Glenn Davis	.12	.09	.05
431	Casey Candaele	.04	.03	.02
432	Mike Moore	.04	.03	.02
433	*Bill Pecota*(FC)	.15	.11	.06
434	Rick Aguilera	.04	.03	.02
435	Mike Pagliarulo	.08	.06	.03
436	Mike Bielecki	.04	.03	.02
437	*Fred Manrique*(FC)	.12	.09	.05
438	*Rob Ducey*(FC)	.12	.09	.05
439	Dave Martinez	.08	.06	.03
440	Steve Bedrosian	.10	.08	.04
441	Rick Manning	.04	.03	.02
442	*Tom Bolton*(FC)	.15	.11	.06
443	Ken Griffey	.06	.05	.02
444	Cal Ripken, Sr.	.04	.03	.02
445	Mike Krukow	.06	.05	.02
446	Doug DeCinces	.06	.05	.02
447	*Jeff Montgomery*(FC)	.30	.25	.12
448	Mike Davis	.06	.05	.02
449	*Jeff Robinson*	.35	.25	.14
450	Barry Bonds	.10	.08	.04
451	Keith Atherton	.04	.03	.02
452	Willie Wilson	.08	.06	.03
453	Dennis Powell	.04	.03	.02
454	Marvell Wynne	.04	.03	.02
455	*Shawn Hillegas*(FC)	.15	.11	.06
456	Dave Anderson	.04	.03	.02
457	Terry Leach	.04	.03	.02
458	Ron Hassey	.04	.03	.02
459	Yankees Leaders (Willie Randolph, Dave Winfield)	.08	.06	.03
460	Ozzie Smith	.12	.09	.05
461	Danny Darwin	.04	.03	.02
462	Don Slaught	.04	.03	.02
463	*Fred McGriff*	1.00	.70	.40
464	Jay Tibbs	.04	.03	.02
465	Paul Molitor	.10	.08	.04
466	Jerry Mumphrey	.04	.03	.02
467	Don Aase	.04	.03	.02
468	Darren Daulton	.04	.03	.02
469	Jeff Dedmon	.04	.03	.02
470	Dwight Evans	.10	.08	.04
471	Donnie Moore	.04	.03	.02
472	Robby Thompson	.06	.05	.02
473	Joe Niekro	.06	.05	.02
474	Tom Brookens	.04	.03	.02
475	Pete Rose	.20	.15	.08
476	Dave Stewart	.08	.06	.03
477	Jamie Quirk	.04	.03	.02
478	Sid Bream	.06	.05	.02
479	Brett Butler	.06	.05	.02
480	Dwight Gooden	.40	.30	.15
481	Mariano Duncan	.04	.03	.02
482	Mark Davis	.04	.03	.02
483	*Rod Booker*(FC)	.12	.09	.05
484	Pat Clements	.04	.03	.02
485	Harold Reynolds	.06	.05	.02
486	*Pat Keedy*(FC)	.10	.08	.04
487	Jim Pankovits	.04	.03	.02
488	Andy McGaffigan	.04	.03	.02
489	Dodgers Leaders (Pedro Guerrero, Fernando Valenzuela)	.08	.06	.03
490	Larry Parrish	.06	.05	.02
491	B.J. Surhoff	.10	.08	.04
492	Doyle Alexander	.06	.05	.02
493	Mike Greenwell	1.00	.70	.40
494	*Wally Ritchie*	.12	.09	.05
495	Eddie Murray	.25	.20	.10
496	Guy Hoffman	.04	.03	.02
497	Kevin Mitchell	.30	.25	.12
498	Bob Boone	.06	.05	.02
499	Eric King	.06	.05	.02
500	Andre Dawson	.15	.11	.06
501	Tim Birtsas(FC)	.06	.05	.02
502	Danny Gladden	.04	.03	.02
503	*Junior Noboa*(FC)	.10	.08	.04
504	Bob Rodgers	.04	.03	.02
505	Willie Upshaw	.06	.05	.02
506	John Cangelosi	.04	.03	.02
507	Mark Gubicza	.10	.08	.04
508	Tim Teufel	.04	.03	.02
509	Bill Dawley	.04	.03	.02
510	Dave Winfield	.20	.15	.08
511	Joel Davis	.04	.03	.02
512	Alex Trevino	.04	.03	.02
513	Tim Flannery	.04	.03	.02
514	Pat Sheridan	.04	.03	.02
515	Juan Nieves	.06	.05	.02
516	Jim Sundberg	.06	.05	.02
517	Ron Robinson	.04	.03	.02
518	Greg Gross	.04	.03	.02
519	Mariners Leaders (Phil Bradley, Harold Reynolds)	.06	.05	.02

No.	Player	MT	NR MT	EX
520	Dave Smith	.06	.05	.02
521	Jim Dwyer	.04	.03	.02
522	*Bob Patterson*(FC)	.12	.09	.05
523	Gary Roenicke	.04	.03	.02
524	Gary Lucas	.04	.03	.02
525	Marty Barrett	.06	.05	.02
526	Juan Berenguer	.04	.03	.02
527	Steve Henderson	.04	.03	.02
528a	Checklist 397-528 (#455 is Steve Carlton)	.40	.30	.15
528b	Checklist 397-528 (#455 is Shawn Hillegas)	.06	.05	.02
529	Tim Burke	.04	.03	.02
530	Gary Carter	.15	.11	.06
531	Rich Yett	.04	.03	.02
532	Mike Kingery	.04	.03	.02
533	*John Farrell*(FC)	.30	.25	.12
534	John Wathan	.06	.05	.02
535	Ron Guidry	.12	.09	.05
536	John Morris	.04	.03	.02
537	Steve Buechele	.04	.03	.02
538	Bill Wegman	.04	.03	.02
539	Mike LaValliere	.06	.05	.02
540	Bret Saberhagen	.25	.20	.10
541	Juan Beniquez	.04	.03	.02
542	*Paul Noce*(FC)	.10	.08	.04
543	Kent Tekulve	.06	.05	.02
544	Jim Traber	.06	.05	.02
545	Don Baylor	.08	.06	.03
546	John Candelaria	.06	.05	.02
547	*Felix Fermin*(FC)	.12	.09	.05
548	*Shane Mack*	.15	.11	.06
549	Braves Leaders (Ken Griffey, Dion James, Dale Murphy, Gerald Perry)	.08	.06	.03
550	Pedro Guerrero	.15	.11	.06
551	Terry Steinbach	.15	.11	.06
552	Mark Thurmond	.04	.03	.02
553	Tracy Jones	.10	.08	.04
554	Mike Smithson	.04	.03	.02
555	Brook Jacoby	.08	.06	.03
556	*Stan Clarke*(FC)	.12	.09	.05
557	Craig Reynolds	.04	.03	.02
558	Bob Ojeda	.06	.05	.02
559	*Ken Williams*(FC)	.20	.15	.08
560	Tim Wallach	.08	.06	.03
561	Rick Cerone	.04	.03	.02
562	Jim Lindeman	.10	.08	.04
563	Jose Guzman	.06	.05	.02
564	Frank Lucchesi	.04	.03	.02
565	Lloyd Moseby	.06	.05	.02
566	*Charlie O'Brien*(FC)	.12	.09	.05
567	Mike Diaz	.06	.05	.02
568	Chris Brown	.06	.05	.02
569	Charlie Leibrandt	.06	.05	.02
570	Jeffrey Leonard	.06	.05	.02
571	*Mark Williamson*(FC)	.12	.09	.05
572	Chris James	.15	.11	.06
573	Bob Stanley	.04	.03	.02
574	Graig Nettles	.08	.06	.03
575	Don Sutton	.12	.09	.05
576	*Tommy Hinzo*(FC)	.12	.09	.05
577	Tom Browning	.08	.06	.03
578	Gary Gaetti	.10	.08	.04
579	Mets Leaders (Gary Carter, Kevin McReynolds)	.08	.06	.03
580	Mark McGwire	1.00	.70	.40
581	Tito Landrum	.04	.03	.02
582	*Mike Henneman*	.20	.15	.08
583	Dave Valle(FC)	.06	.05	.02
584	Steve Trout	.04	.03	.02
585	Ozzie Guillen	.06	.05	.02
586	Bob Forsch	.06	.05	.02
587	Terry Puhl	.04	.03	.02
588	*Jeff Parrett*(FC)	.20	.15	.08
589	Geno Petralli	.04	.03	.02
590	George Bell	.20	.15	.08
591	Doug Drabek	.06	.05	.02
592	Dale Sveum	.06	.05	.02
593	Bob Tewksbury	.04	.03	.02
594	Bobby Valentine	.04	.03	.02
595	Frank White	.06	.05	.02
596	John Kruk	.08	.06	.03
597	Gene Garber	.04	.03	.02
598	Lee Lacy	.04	.03	.02
599	Calvin Schiraldi	.04	.03	.02
600	Mike Schmidt	.40	.30	.15
601	Jack Lazorko	.04	.03	.02
602	Mike Aldrete	.06	.05	.02
603	Rob Murphy	.06	.05	.02
604	Chris Bando	.04	.03	.02
605	Kirk Gibson	.15	.11	.06
606	Moose Haas	.04	.03	.02
607	Mickey Hatcher	.04	.03	.02
608	Charlie Kerfeld	.04	.03	.02
609	Twins Leaders (Gary Gaetti, Kent Hrbek)	.08	.06	.03
610	Keith Hernandez	.15	.11	.06
611	Tommy John	.12	.09	.05
612	Curt Ford	.04	.03	.02
613	Bobby Thigpen	.08	.06	.03
614	Herm Winningham	.04	.03	.02
615	Jody Davis	.06	.05	.02
616	*Jay Aldrich*(FC)	.10	.08	.04
617	Oddibe McDowell	.06	.05	.02
618	Cecil Fielder	.60	.45	.25
619	*Mike Dunne*	.20	.15	.08
620	Cory Snyder	.15	.11	.06
621	Gene Nelson	.04	.03	.02
622	Kal Daniels	.15	.11	.06
623	Mike Flanagan	.06	.05	.02
624	Jim Leyland	.04	.03	.02
625	Frank Viola	.12	.09	.05
626	Glenn Wilson	.06	.05	.02
627	*Joe Boever*(FC)	.12	.09	.05
628	Dave Henderson	.08	.06	.03
629	Kelly Downs	.08	.06	.03
630	Darrell Evans	.08	.06	.03
631	Jack Howell	.06	.05	.02
632	*Steve Shields*	.12	.09	.05
633	*Barry Lyons*	.12	.09	.05
634	Jose DeLeon	.06	.05	.02
635	Terry Pendleton	.06	.05	.02
636	Charles Hudson	.04	.03	.02

		MT	NR MT	EX
637	*Jay Bell*(FC)	.25	.20	.10
638	Steve Balboni	.06	.05	.02
639	Brewers Leaders (Glenn Braggs, Tony Muser)	.06	.05	.02
640	Garry Templeton	.06	.05	.02
641	Rick Honeycutt	.04	.03	.02
642	Bob Dernier	.04	.03	.02
643	*Rocky Childress*(FC)	.12	.09	.05
644	Terry McGriff(FC)	.06	.05	.02
645	*Matt Nokes*	.50	.40	.20
646	Checklist 529-660	.04	.03	.02
647	Pascual Perez	.06	.05	.02
648	Al Newman	.04	.03	.02
649	*DeWayne Buice*	.15	.11	.06
650	Cal Ripken	.25	.20	.10
651	*Mike Jackson*(FC)	.15	.11	.06
652	Bruce Benedict	.04	.03	.02
653	Jeff Sellers	.06	.05	.02
654	Roger Craig	.06	.05	.02
655	Len Dykstra	.08	.06	.03
656	Lee Guetterman	.04	.03	.02
657	Gary Redus	.04	.03	.02
658	Tim Conroy	.04	.03	.02
659	Bobby Meacham	.04	.03	.02
660	Rick Reuschel	.08	.06	.03
661	Turn Back The Clock (Nolan Ryan)	.08	.06	.03
662	Turn Back The Clock (Jim Rice)	.08	.06	.03
663	Turn Back The Clock (Ron Blomberg)	.04	.03	.02
664	Turn Back The Clock (Bob Gibson)	.08	.06	.03
665	Turn Back The Clock (Stan Musial)	.12	.09	.05
666	Mario Soto	.06	.05	.02
667	Luis Quinones	.04	.03	.02
668	Walt Terrell	.06	.05	.02
669	Phillies Leaders (Lance Parrish, Mike Ryan)	.06	.05	.02
670	Dan Plesac	.08	.06	.03
671	Tim Laudner	.04	.03	.02
672	*John Davis*(FC)	.15	.11	.06
673	Tony Phillips	.04	.03	.02
674	Mike Fitzgerald	.04	.03	.02
675	Jim Rice	.20	.15	.08
676	Ken Dixon	.04	.03	.02
677	Eddie Milner	.04	.03	.02
678	Jim Acker	.04	.03	.02
679	Darrell Miller	.04	.03	.02
680	Charlie Hough	.06	.05	.02
681	Bobby Bonilla	.12	.09	.05
682	Jimmy Key	.08	.06	.03
683	Julio Franco	.08	.06	.03
684	Hal Lanier	.04	.03	.02
685	Ron Darling	.10	.08	.04
686	Terry Francona	.04	.03	.02
687	Mickey Brantley	.04	.03	.02
688	Jim Winn	.04	.03	.02
689	*Tom Pagnozzi*(FC)	.12	.09	.05
690	Jay Howell	.06	.05	.02
691	Dan Pasqua	.08	.06	.03
692	Mike Birkbeck	.06	.05	.02
693	Benny Santiago	.60	.45	.25
694	*Eric Nolte*(FC)	.12	.09	.05
695	Shawon Dunston	.08	.06	.03
696	Duane Ward	.04	.03	.02
697	Steve Lombardozzi	.08	.06	.03
698	Brad Havens	.04	.03	.02
699	Padres Leaders (Tony Gwynn, Benny Santiago)	.12	.09	.05
700	George Brett	.30	.25	.12
701	Sammy Stewart	.04	.03	.02
702	Mike Gallego	.04	.03	.02
703	Bob Brenly	.04	.03	.02
704	Dennis Boyd	.06	.05	.02
705	Juan Samuel	.10	.08	.04
706	Rick Mahler	.04	.03	.02
707	Fred Lynn	.10	.08	.04
708	Gus Polidor(FC)	.06	.05	.02
709	George Frazier	.04	.03	.02
710	Darryl Strawberry	.30	.25	.12
711	Bill Gullickson	.04	.03	.02
712	John Moses	.04	.03	.02
713	Willie Hernandez	.06	.05	.02
714	Jim Fregosi	.04	.03	.02
715	Todd Worrell	.08	.06	.03
716	Lenn Sakata	.04	.03	.02
717	Jay Baller(FC)	.06	.05	.02
718	Mike Felder	.04	.03	.02
719	Denny Walling	.04	.03	.02
720	Tim Raines	.20	.15	.08
721	Pete O'Brien	.06	.05	.02
722	Manny Lee	.04	.03	.02
723	Bob Kipper	.04	.03	.02
724	Danny Tartabull	.15	.11	.06
725	Mike Boddicker	.06	.05	.02
726	Alfredo Griffin	.06	.05	.02
727	Greg Booker	.04	.03	.02
728	Andy Allanson	.06	.05	.02
729	Blue Jays Leaders (George Bell, Fred McGriff)	.10	.08	.04
730	John Franco	.08	.06	.03
731	Rick Schu	.04	.03	.02
732	Dave Palmer	.04	.03	.02
733	Spike Owen	.04	.03	.02
734	Craig Lefferts	.04	.03	.02
735	Kevin McReynolds	.20	.15	.08
736	Matt Young	.04	.03	.02
737	Butch Wynegar	.04	.03	.02
738	Scott Bankhead	.04	.03	.02
739	Daryl Boston	.04	.03	.02
740	Rick Sutcliffe	.08	.06	.03
741	Mike Easler	.06	.05	.02
742	Mark Clear	.04	.03	.02
743	Larry Herndon	.04	.03	.02
744	Whitey Herzog	.06	.05	.02
745	Bill Doran	.06	.05	.02
746	*Gene Larkin*	.25	.20	.10
747	Bobby Witt	.08	.06	.03
748	Reid Nichols	.04	.03	.02
749	Mark Eichhorn	.06	.05	.02
750	Bo Jackson	1.25	.90	.50
751	Jim Morrison	.04	.03	.02
752	Mark Grant	.04	.03	.02
753	Danny Heep	.04	.03	.02
754	Mike LaCoss	.04	.03	.02
755	Ozzie Virgil	.04	.03	.02
756	Mike Maddux	.06	.05	.02
757	*John Marzano*	.15	.11	.06
758	*Eddie Williams*(FC)	.20	.15	.08
759	A's Leaders (Jose Canseco, Mark McGwire)	.40	.30	.15
760	Mike Scott	.10	.08	.04
761	Tony Armas	.06	.05	.02
762	Scott Bradley	.04	.03	.02
763	Doug Sisk	.04	.03	.02
764	Greg Walker	.06	.05	.02
765	Neal Heaton	.06	.05	.02
766	Henry Cotto	.04	.03	.02
767	*Jose Lind*(FC)	.25	.20	.10
768	Dickie Noles	.04	.03	.02
769	Cecil Cooper	.08	.06	.03
770	Lou Whitaker	.20	.15	.08
771	Ruben Sierra	.50	.40	.20
772	Sal Butera	.04	.03	.02
773	Frank Williams	.04	.03	.02
774	Gene Mauch	.06	.05	.02
775	Dave Stieb	.08	.06	.03
776	Checklist 661-792	.04	.03	.02
777	Lonnie Smith	.06	.05	.02
778a	*Keith Comstock* (white team letters)(FC)	7.00	5.25	2.75
778b	*Keith Comstock* (blue team letters)(FC)	.25	.20	.10
779	*Tom Glavine*(FC)	.35	.25	.14
780	Fernando Valenzuela	.15	.11	.06
781	*Keith Hughes*(FC)	.15	.11	.06
782	*Jeff Ballard*(FC)	.30	.25	.12
783	Ron Roenicke	.04	.03	.02
784	Joe Sambito	.04	.03	.02
785	Alvin Davis	.10	.08	.04
786	Joe Price	.04	.03	.02
787	Bill Almon	.04	.03	.02
788	Ray Searage	.04	.03	.02
789	Indians Leaders (Joe Carter, Cory Snyder)	.08	.06	.03
790	Dave Righetti	.12	.09	.05
791	Ted Simmons	.08	.06	.03
792	John Tudor	.08	.06	.03

1988 Topps All-Star Glossy Set of 22

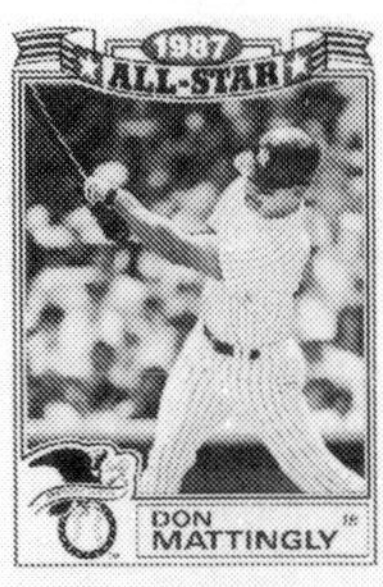

The fifth edition of Topps' special All-Star inserts (22 cards) was included in the company's 1988 rack packs. The 1987 American and National League All-Star lineup, plus honorary captains Jim Hunter and Billy Williams, are featured on the standard-size All-Star inserts. The glossy full-color card fronts contain player photos centered between a red and yellow "1987 All-Star" logo printed across the card top and the player name (also red and yellow) which is printed across the bottom margin. A National or American League logo appears in the lower left corner. Card backs are printed in red and blue on a white background, with the title and All-Star logo emblem printed above the player name and card number.

		MT	NR MT	EX
Complete Set:		4.00	3.00	1.50
Common Player:		.15	.11	.06
1	John McNamara	.15	.11	.06
2	Don Mattingly	1.50	1.25	.60
3	Willie Randolph	.15	.11	.06
4	Wade Boggs	.80	.60	.30
5	Cal Ripken	.50	.40	.20
6	George Bell	.30	.25	.12
7	Rickey Henderson	.50	.40	.20
8	Dave Winfield	.40	.30	.15
9	Terry Kennedy	.15	.11	.06
10	Bret Saberhagen	.25	.20	.10
11	Jim Hunter	.25	.20	.10
12	Davey Johnson	.15	.11	.06
13	Jack Clark	.25	.20	.10
14	Ryne Sandberg	.40	.30	.15
15	Mike Schmidt	.60	.45	.25
16	Ozzie Smith	.25	.20	.10
17	Eric Davis	.60	.45	.25
18	Andre Dawson	.25	.20	.10
19	Darryl Strawberry	.60	.45	.25
20	Gary Carter	.40	.30	.15
21	Mike Scott	.15	.11	.06
22	Billy Williams	.25	.20	.10

1988 Topps All-Star Glossy Set of 60

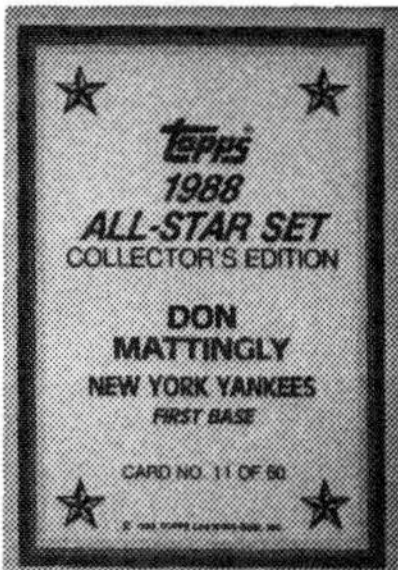

This standard-size collectors set includes 60 full-color glossy cards featuring All-Stars and Prospects in six separate 10-card sets. In 1986, Topps issued a similar set that included only All-Stars. Card fronts have a white border and a thin red line framing the player photo, with the player's name in the lower left corner. Card backs, in red and blue, include very basic player information (name, team and position), along with the card set logo and card number. Topps glossy collector sets were marketed via a special offer printed on a card packaged in all Topps wax packs. For six special offer cards and $1.25, collectors received one of the six 10-card sets; 18 special offer cards and $7.50 earned the entire 60-card collection.

		MT	NR MT	EX
Complete Set:		14.00	10.50	5.50
Common Player:		.15	.11	.06
1	Andre Dawson	.30	.25	.12
2	Jesse Barfield	.20	.15	.08
3	Mike Schmidt	.70	.50	.30
4	Ruben Sierra	.40	.30	.15
5	Mike Scott	.20	.15	.08
6	Cal Ripken	.70	.50	.30
7	Gary Carter	.50	.40	.20
8	Kent Hrbek	.30	.25	.12
9	Kevin Seitzer	.70	.50	.30
10	Mike Henneman	.25	.20	.10
11	Don Mattingly	3.50	2.75	1.50
12	Tim Raines	.40	.30	.15
13	Roger Clemens	.80	.60	.30
14	Ryne Sandberg	.40	.30	.15
15	Tony Fernandez	.20	.15	.08
16	Eric Davis	.80	.60	.30
17	Jack Morris	.30	.25	.12
18	Tim Wallach	.20	.15	.08
19	Mike Dunne	.25	.20	.10
20	Mike Greenwell	1.00	.70	.40
21	Dwight Evans	.20	.15	.08
22	Darryl Strawberry	.80	.60	.30
23	Cory Snyder	.30	.25	.12
24	Pedro Guerrero	.25	.20	.10
25	Rickey Henderson	.60	.45	.25
26	Dale Murphy	.70	.50	.30
27	Kirby Puckett	.50	.40	.20
28	Steve Bedrosian	.20	.15	.08
29	Devon White	.25	.20	.10
30	Benny Santiago	.25	.20	.10
31	George Bell	.40	.30	.15
32	Keith Hernandez	.40	.30	.15
33	Dave Stewart	.15	.11	.06
34	Dave Parker	.25	.20	.10
35	Tom Henke	.15	.11	.06
36	Willie McGee	.20	.15	.08
37	Alan Trammell	.30	.25	.12
38	Tony Gwynn	.60	.45	.25
39	Mark McGwire	1.25	.90	.50
40	Joe Magrane	.25	.20	.10
41	Jack Clark	.25	.20	.10
42	Willie Randolph	.15	.11	.06
43	Juan Samuel	.25	.20	.10
44	Joe Carter	.25	.20	.10
45	Shane Rawley	.15	.11	.06
46	Dave Winfield	.50	.40	.20
47	Ozzie Smith	.25	.20	.10
48	Wally Joyner	.70	.50	.30
49	B.J. Surhoff	.20	.15	.08
50	Ellis Burks	.80	.60	.30
51	Wade Boggs	1.25	.90	.50
52	Howard Johnson	.20	.15	.08
53	George Brett	.70	.50	.30
54	Dwight Gooden	.80	.60	.30
55	Jose Canseco	2.50	2.00	1.00
56	Lee Smith	.15	.11	.06
57	Paul Molitor	.20	.15	.08
58	Andres Galarraga	.30	.25	.12
59	Matt Nokes	.40	.30	.15
60	Casey Candaele	.15	.11	.06

1988 Topps American Baseball

This 88-card set, unlike Topps' United Kingdom football cards, was made available for distribution by U.S. hobby dealers. The cards were packaged in checklist-backed boxes with an American flag on the top flap. The 2-1/4" by 3" cards feature full-color player photos printed on white stock

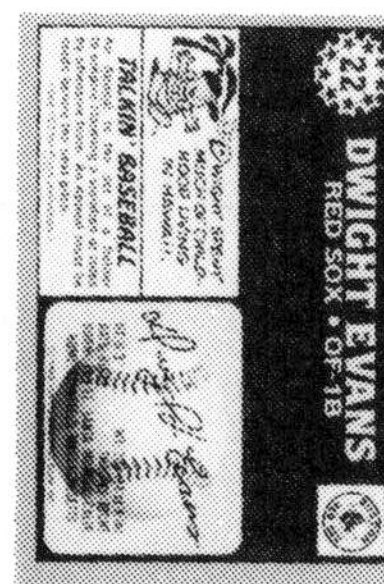

with a red line framing the photo. The team name, printed in individual team colors, intersects the red frame at the top of the card. A bright yellow name banner appears below the photo. Card backs have bright blue borders and cartoon-style horizontal layouts. The card number appears within a circle of red stars upper left, beside the player's name and team logo. A red banner containing the player career stats runs the length of the card back. The lower half of the flip side features a caricature of the player and a one-line caption. Below the cartoon, a short "Talkin' Baseball" paragraph provides elementary baseball information, obviously designed to acquaint soccer-playing European collectors with American baseball rules and terminology. A glossy edition of the set was issued and is valued at 2-3 times greater than the regular issue.

		MT	NR MT	EX
Complete Set:		7.00	5.25	2.75
Common Player:		.08	.06	.03
1	Harold Baines	.15	.11	.06
2	Steve Bedrosian	.10	.08	.04
3	George Bell	.25	.20	.10
4	Wade Boggs	1.00	.70	.40
5	Barry Bonds	.20	.15	.08
6	Bob Boone	.08	.06	.03
7	George Brett	.40	.30	.15
8	Hubie Brooks	.08	.06	.03
9	Ivan Calderon	.10	.08	.04
10	Jose Canseco	1.25	.90	.50
11	Gary Carter	.30	.25	.12
12	Joe Carter	.15	.11	.06
13	Jack Clark	.20	.15	.08
14	Will Clark	.50	.40	.20
15	Roger Clemens	.60	.45	.25
16	Vince Coleman	.20	.15	.08
17	Alvin Davis	.15	.11	.06
18	Eric Davis	.70	.50	.30
19	Glenn Davis	.20	.15	.08
20	Andre Dawson	.25	.20	.10
21	Mike Dunne	.15	.11	.06
22	Dwight Evans	.10	.08	.04
23	Tony Fernandez	.15	.11	.06
24	John Franco	.10	.08	.04
25	Gary Gaetti	.20	.15	.08
26	Kirk Gibson	.25	.20	.10
27	Dwight Gooden	.60	.45	.25
28	Pedro Guerrero	.20	.15	.08
29	Tony Gwynn	.35	.25	.14
30	Billy Hatcher	.08	.06	.03
31	Rickey Henderson	.35	.25	.14
32	Tom Henke	.08	.06	.03
33	Keith Hernandez	.25	.20	.10
34	Orel Hershiser	.30	.25	.12
35	Teddy Higuera	.10	.08	.04
36	Charlie Hough	.08	.06	.03
37	Kent Hrbek	.25	.20	.10
38	Brook Jacoby	.10	.08	.04
39	Dion James	.08	.06	.03
40	Wally Joyner	.50	.40	.20
41	John Kruk	.15	.11	.06
42	Mark Langston	.15	.11	.06
43	Jeffrey Leonard	.08	.06	.03
44	Candy Maldonaldo	.08	.06	.03
45	Don Mattingly	2.00	1.50	.80
46	Willie McGee	.15	.11	.06
47	Mark McGwire	1.00	.70	.40
48	Kevin Mitchell	.08	.06	.03
49	Paul Molitor	.15	.11	.06
50	Jack Morris	.15	.11	.06
51	Lloyd Moseby	.10	.08	.04
52	Dale Murphy	.40	.30	.15
53	Eddie Murray	.30	.25	.12
54	Matt Nokes	.40	.30	.15
55	Dave Parker	.20	.15	.08
56	Larry Parrish	.08	.06	.03
57	Kirby Puckett	.35	.25	.14
58	Tim Raines	.30	.25	.12
59	Willie Randolph	.08	.06	.03
60	Harold Reynolds	.08	.06	.03
61	Cal Ripken	.35	.25	.14
62	Nolan Ryan	.25	.20	.10
63	Bret Saberhagen	.20	.15	.08
64	Juan Samuel	.15	.11	.06
65	Ryne Sandberg	.25	.20	.10
66	Benny Santiago	.15	.11	.06
67	Mike Schmidt	.40	.30	.15
68	Mike Scott	.10	.08	.04
69	Kevin Seitzer	.40	.30	.15
70	Larry Sheets	.08	.06	.03
71	Ruben Sierra	.15	.11	.06
72	Ozzie Smith	.15	.11	.06
73	Zane Smith	.08	.06	.03
74	Cory Snyder	.15	.11	.06
75	Dave Stewart	.10	.08	.04
76	Darryl Strawberry	.50	.40	.20
77	Rick Sutcliffe	.15	.11	.06
78	Danny Tartabull	.20	.15	.08
79	Alan Trammell	.25	.20	.10
80	Fernando Valenzuela	.20	.15	.08
81	Andy Van Slyke	.15	.11	.06
82	Frank Viola	.15	.11	.06
83	Greg Walker	.10	.08	.04
84	Tim Wallach	.10	.08	.04
85	Dave Winfield	.30	.25	.12
86	Mike Witt	.08	.06	.03
87	Robin Yount	.25	.20	.10
88	Checklist	.08	.06	.03

1988 Topps Big Baseball

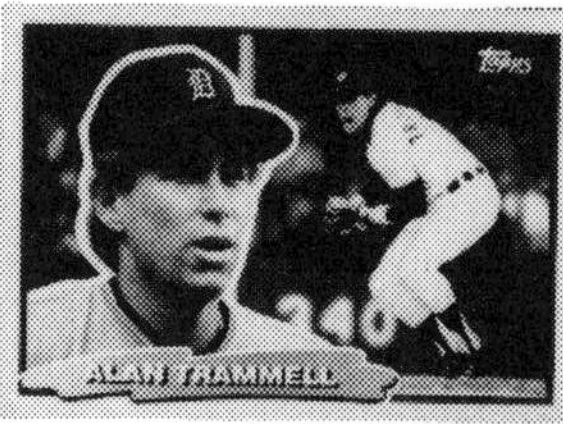

1988 Topps Big Baseball cards (2-5/8" by 3-3/4") were issued in three series, 88 cards per series (a total set of 264 cards). Each series features current star players, sold in 7-card packages. The glossy cards are similar in format, both front and back, to the 1956 Topps 340-card set. Each card features a posed head shot and a close-up action photo on the front, framed by a wide white border and a dark blue inner border. A white outlines highlights the player closeup. The player's name appears below his head shot, in reversed type on a splash of color that fades from yellow to orange to red to pink. On the card back, the player's name is printed in large red letters across the top, followed by his team name and position in black. Personal info is printed in a red rectangle beside a Topps baseball logo bearing the card number. A triple cartoon strip, in full-color, illustrates career highlights, performance, personal background, etc. A red, white and blue statistics box (pitching, batting, fielding) is printed across the bottom.

		MT	NR MT	EX
Complete Set:		22.00	16.50	8.75
Common Player:		.05	.04	.02
1	Paul Molitor	.12	.09	.05
2	Milt Thompson	.05	.04	.02
3	Billy Hatcher	.05	.04	.02
4	Mike Witt	.05	.04	.02
5	Vince Coleman	.12	.09	.05
6	Dwight Evans	.10	.08	.04
7	Tim Wallach	.10	.08	.04
8	Alan Trammell	.15	.11	.06
9	Will Clark	.25	.20	.10
10	Jeff Reardon	.08	.06	.03
11	Dwight Gooden	.50	.40	.20
12	Benny Santiago	.12	.09	.05
13	Jose Canseco	1.25	.90	.50
14	Dale Murphy	.30	.25	.12
15	George Bell	.20	.15	.08
16	Ryne Sandberg	.20	.15	.08
17	Brook Jacoby	.08	.06	.03
18	Fernando Valenzuela	.15	.11	.06
19	Scott Fletcher	.05	.04	.02
20	Eric Davis	.60	.45	.25
21	Willie Wilson	.10	.08	.04
22	B.J. Surhoff	.10	.08	.04
23	Steve Bedrosian	.08	.06	.03
24	Dave Winfield	.25	.20	.10
25	Bobby Bonilla	.15	.11	.06
26	Larry Sheets	.08	.06	.03
27	Ozzie Guillen	.08	.06	.03
28	Checklist 1-88	.05	.04	.02
29	Nolan Ryan	.20	.15	.08
30	Bob Boone	.05	.04	.02
31	Tom Herr	.08	.06	.03
32	Wade Boggs	.90	.70	.35
33	Neal Heaton	.05	.04	.02
34	Doyle Alexander	.05	.04	.02
35	Candy Maldonado	.08	.06	.03
36	Kirby Puckett	.25	.20	.10
37	Gary Carter	.20	.15	.08
38	Lance McCullers	.08	.06	.03
39a	Terry Steinbach (black Topps logo on front)	.12	.09	.05
39b	Terry Steinbach (white Topps logo on front)	.12	.09	.05
40	Gerald Perry	.10	.08	.04
41	Tom Henke	.05	.04	.02
42	Leon Durham	.05	.04	.02
43	Cory Snyder	.12	.09	.05
44	Dale Sveum	.05	.04	.02
45	Lance Parrish	.12	.09	.05
46	Steve Sax	.12	.09	.05
47	Charlie Hough	.05	.04	.02
48	Kal Daniels	.15	.11	.06
49	Bo Jackson	.25	.20	.10
50	Ron Guidry	.10	.08	.04
51	Bill Doran	.08	.06	.03
52	Wally Joyner	.40	.30	.15
53	Terry Pendleton	.08	.06	.03
54	Marty Barrett	.08	.06	.03
55	Andres Galarraga	.15	.11	.06
56	Larry Herndon	.05	.04	.02
57	Kevin Mitchell	.08	.06	.03
58	Greg Gagne	.05	.04	.02
59	Keith Hernandez	.15	.11	.06
60	John Kruk	.10	.08	.04
61	Mike LaValliere	.08	.06	.03
62	Cal Ripken	.30	.25	.12
63	Ivan Calderon	.08	.06	.03
64	Alvin Davis	.10	.08	.04
65	Luis Polonia	.08	.06	.03
66	Robin Yount	.20	.15	.08
67	Juan Samuel	.12	.09	.05
68	Andres Thomas	.05	.04	.02
69	Jeff Musselman	.05	.04	.02
70	Jerry Mumphrey	.05	.04	.02
71	Joe Carter	.12	.09	.05
72	Mike Scioscia	.05	.04	.02
73	Pete Incaviglia	.10	.08	.04
74	Barry Larkin	.15	.11	.06
75	Frank White	.08	.06	.03
76	Willie Randolph	.08	.06	.03
77	Kevin Bass	.05	.04	.02
78	Brian Downing	.08	.06	.03
79	Willie McGee	.10	.08	.04
80	Ellis Burks	.40	.30	.15
81	Hubie Brooks	.08	.06	.03
82	Darrell Evans	.08	.06	.03
83	Robby Thompson	.05	.04	.02
84	Kent Hrbek	.15	.11	.06
85	Ron Darling	.12	.09	.05
86	Stan Jefferson	.05	.04	.02
87	Teddy Higuera	.10	.08	.04
88	Mike Schmidt	.30	.25	.12
89	Barry Bonds	.15	.11	.06
90	Jim Presley	.08	.06	.03
91	Orel Hershiser	.25	.20	.10
92	Jesse Barfield	.10	.08	.04
93	Tom Candiotti	.05	.04	.02
94	Bret Saberhagen	.12	.09	.05
95	Jose Uribe	.05	.04	.02
96	Tom Browning	.10	.08	.04
97	Johnny Ray	.08	.06	.03
98	Mike Morgan	.05	.04	.02
100	Jim Sundberg	.05	.04	.02
101	Roger McDowell	.08	.06	.03
102	Randy Ready	.05	.04	.02
103	Mike Gallego	.05	.04	.02
104	Steve Buechele	.05	.04	.02
105	Greg Walker	.08	.06	.03
106	Jose Lind	.12	.09	.05
107	Steve Trout	.05	.04	.02
108	Rick Rhoden	.08	.06	.03
109	Jim Pankovits	.05	.04	.02
110	Ken Griffey	.08	.06	.03
111	Danny Cox	.08	.06	.03
112	Franklin Stubbs	.05	.04	.02
113	Lloyd Moseby	.08	.06	.03
114	Mel Hall	.08	.06	.03
115	Kevin Seitzer	.25	.20	.10
116	Tim Raines	.25	.20	.10
117	Juan Castillo	.05	.04	.02
118	Roger Clemens	.50	.40	.20
119	Mike Aldrete	.08	.06	.03
120	Mario Soto	.05	.04	.02
121	Jack Howell	.05	.04	.02
122	Rick Schu	.05	.04	.02
123	Jeff Robinson	.10	.08	.04
124	Doug Drabek	.08	.06	.03
125	Henry Cotto	.05	.04	.02
126	Checklist 89-176	.05	.04	.02
127	Gary Gaetti	.12	.09	.05
128	Rick Sutcliffe	.10	.08	.04
129	Howard Johnson	.08	.06	.03
130	Chris Brown	.08	.06	.03
131	Dave Henderson	.08	.06	.03
132	Curt Wilkerson	.05	.04	.02
133	Mike Marshall	.10	.08	.04
134	Kelly Gruber	.05	.04	.02
135	Julio Franco	.10	.08	.04
136	Kurt Stillwell	.12	.09	.05
137	Donnie Hill	.05	.04	.02
138	Mike Pagliarulo	.10	.08	.04
139	Von Hayes	.08	.06	.03
140	Mike Scott	.10	.08	.04
141	Bob Kipper	.05	.04	.02
142	Harold Reynolds	.08	.06	.03
143	Bob Brenly	.05	.04	.02
144	Dave Concepcion	.08	.06	.03
145	Devon White	.12	.09	.05
146	Jeff Stone	.05	.04	.02
147	Chet Lemon	.05	.04	.02
148	Ozzie Virgil	.05	.04	.02
149	Todd Worrell	.10	.08	.04
150	Mitch Webster	.05	.04	.02
151	Rob Deer	.08	.06	.03
152	Rich Gedman	.08	.06	.03
153	Andre Dawson	.15	.11	.06
154	Mike Davis	.05	.04	.02
155	Nelson Liriano	.08	.06	.03
156	Greg Swindell	.10	.08	.04
157	George Brett	.30	.25	.12
158	Kevin McReynolds	.15	.11	.06
159	Brian Fisher	.08	.06	.03
160	Mike Kingery	.05	.04	.02
161	Tony Gwynn	.25	.20	.10
162	Don Baylor	.10	.08	.04
163	Jerry Browne	.05	.04	.02

		MT	NR MT	EX
164	Dan Pasqua	.08	.06	.03
165	Rickey Henderson	.25	.20	.10
166	Brett Butler	.08	.06	.03
167	Nick Esasky	.05	.04	.02
168	Kirk McCaskill	.05	.04	.02
169	Fred Lynn	.10	.08	.04
170	Jack Morris	.12	.09	.05
171	Pedro Guerrero	.12	.09	.05
172	Dave Stieb	.10	.08	.04
173	Pat Tabler	.08	.06	.03
174	Floyd Bannister	.05	.04	.02
175	Rafael Belliard	.05	.04	.02
176	Mark Langston	.10	.08	.04
177	Greg Mathews	.08	.06	.03
178	Claudell Washington	.05	.04	.02
179	Mark McGwire	1.00	.70	.40
180	Bert Blyleven	.10	.08	.04
181	Jim Rice	.20	.15	.08
182	Mookie Wilson	.08	.06	.03
183	Willie Fraser	.05	.04	.02
184	Andy Van Slyke	.10	.08	.04
185	Matt Nokes	.10	.08	.04
186	Eddie Whitson	.05	.04	.02
187	Tony Fernandez	.10	.08	.04
188	Rick Reuschel	.08	.06	.03
189	Ken Phelps	.05	.04	.02
190	Juan Nieves	.08	.06	.03
191	Kirk Gibson	.20	.15	.08
192	Glenn Davis	.15	.11	.06
193	Zane Smith	.05	.04	.02
194	Jose DeLeon	.08	.06	.03
195	Gary Ward	.05	.04	.02
196	Pascual Perez	.05	.04	.02
197	Carlton Fisk	.12	.09	.05
198	Oddibe McDowell	.08	.06	.03
199	Mark Gubicza	.10	.08	.04
200	Glenn Hubbard	.05	.04	.02
201	Frank Viola	.15	.11	.06
202	Jody Reed	.12	.09	.05
203	Len Dykstra	.08	.06	.03
204	Dick Schofield	.05	.04	.02
205	Sid Bream	.05	.04	.02
206	Guillermo Hernandez	.05	.04	.02
207	Keith Moreland	.05	.04	.02
208	Mark Eichhorn	.05	.04	.02
209	Rene Gonzales	.08	.06	.03
210	Dave Valle	.05	.04	.02
211	Tom Brunansky	.10	.08	.04
212	Charles Hudson	.05	.04	.02
213	John Farrell	.10	.08	.04
214	Jeff Treadway	.12	.09	.05
215	Eddie Murray	.25	.20	.10
216	Checklist 177-264	.05	.04	.02
217	Greg Brock	.08	.06	.03
218	John Shelby	.05	.04	.02
219	Craig Reynolds	.05	.04	.02
220	Dion James	.05	.04	.02
221	Carney Lansford	.08	.06	.03
222	Juan Berenguer	.05	.04	.02
223	Luis Rivera	.08	.06	.03
224	Harold Baines	.12	.09	.05
225	Shawon Dunston	.08	.06	.03
226	Luis Aguayo	.05	.04	.02
227	Pete O'Brien	.08	.06	.03
228	Ozzie Smith	.12	.09	.05
229	Don Mattingly	1.50	1.25	.60
230	Danny Tartabull	.15	.11	.06
231	Andy Allanson	.05	.04	.02
232	John Franco	.08	.06	.03
233	Mike Greenwell	.80	.60	.30
234	Bob Ojeda	.08	.06	.03
235	Chili Davis	.08	.06	.03
236	Mike Dunne	.12	.09	.05
237	Jim Morrison	.05	.04	.02
238	Carmelo Martinez	.05	.04	.02
239	Ernie Whitt	.05	.04	.02
240	Scott Garrelts	.05	.04	.02
241	Mike Moore	.05	.04	.02
242	Dave Parker	.10	.08	.04
243	Tim Laudner	.05	.04	.02
244	Bill Wegman	.05	.04	.02
245	Bob Horner	.08	.06	.03
246	Rafael Santana	.05	.04	.02
247	Alfredo Griffin	.05	.04	.02
248	Mark Bailey	.05	.04	.02
249	Ron Gant	.12	.09	.05
250	Bryn Smith	.05	.04	.02
251	Lance Johnson	.10	.08	.04
252	Sam Horn	.10	.08	.04
253	Darryl Strawberry	.40	.30	.15
254	Chuck Finley	.05	.04	.02
255	Darnell Coles	.08	.06	.03
256	Mike Henneman	.10	.08	.04
257	Andy Hawkins	.08	.06	.03
258	Jim Clancy	.08	.06	.03
259	Atlee Hammaker	.05	.04	.02
260	Glenn Wilson	.05	.04	.02
261	Larry McWilliams	.05	.04	.02
262	Jack Clark	.12	.09	.05
263	Walt Weiss	.80	.60	.30
264	Gene Larkin	.08	.06	.03

1988 Topps Box Panels

After a one-year hiatus during which they appeared on the sides of Topps wax pack display boxes, Topps retail box cards returned to box bottoms in 1988. Topps first issued box-bottom cards in 1986, following the introduction of the concept by Donruss in 1985. Topps 1988 box-bottom series includes 16 standard-size baseball cards, four cards per each of four different display boxes. Card fronts follow the same design as the 1988 Topps basic issue; full-color player photos, framed in yellow, surrounded by a white border; diagonal player name lower right; team name in large letters at the top of the card front. Card backs are

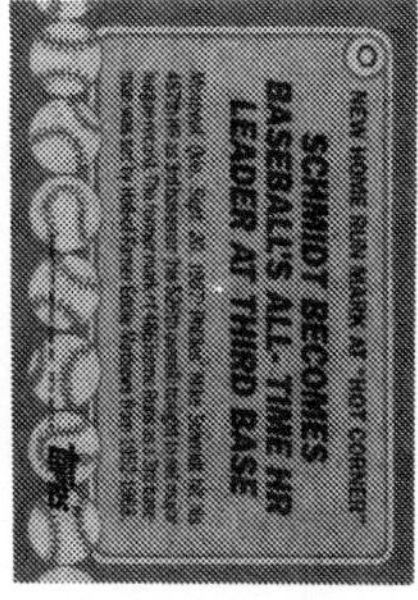

"numbered" A through P and are printed in black and orange.

		MT	NR MT	EX
Complete Panel Set:		7.00	5.25	2.75
Complete Singles Set:		2.50	2.00	1.00
Common Panel:		1.00	.70	.40
Common Single Player:		.08	.06	.03
Panel		1.00	.70	.40
A	Don Baylor	.12	.09	.05
B	Steve Bedrosian	.12	.09	.05
C	Juan Beniquez	.08	.06	.03
D	Bob Boone	.08	.06	.03
Panel		1.75	1.25	.70
E	Darrell Evans	.12	.09	.05
F	Tony Gwynn	.30	.25	.12
G	John Kruk	.15	.11	.06
H	Marvell Wynne	.08	.06	.03
Panel		2.75	2.00	1.00
I	Joe Carter	.15	.11	.06
J	Eric Davis	.50	.40	.20
K	Howard Johnson	.12	.09	.05
L	Darryl Strawberry	.35	.25	.14
Panel		2.50	2.00	1.00
M	Rickey Henderson	.20	.15	.08
N	Nolan Ryan	.35	.25	.14
O	Mike Schmidt	.08	.06	.03
P	Kent Tekulve	.08	.06	.03

1988 Topps Coins

This edition of 60 lightweight metal coins is similar in design to Topps' 1964 set. The 1988 coins are 1-1/2" in diameter and feature full-color player closeups under crimped edges in silver, gold and pink. Curved under the photo is a red and white player name banner pinned by two gold stars. Coin backs list the coin number, player name, personal information and career summary in black letters on a silver background.

		MT	NR MT	EX
Complete Set:		8.00	6.00	3.25
Common Player:		.10	.08	.04
1	George Bell	.25	.20	.10
2	Roger Clemens	.40	.30	.15
3	Mark McGwire	.60	.45	.25
4	Wade Boggs	.70	.50	.30
5	Harold Baines	.15	.11	.06
6	Ivan Calderon	.10	.08	.04
7	Jose Canseco	.80	.60	.30
8	Joe Carter	.15	.11	.06
9	Jack Clark	.15	.11	.06
10	Alvin Davis	.15	.11	.06
11	Dwight Evans	.15	.11	.06
12	Tony Fernandez	.15	.11	.06
13	Gary Gaetti	.15	.11	.06
14	Mike Greenwell	.40	.30	.15
15	Charlie Hough	.10	.08	.04
16	Wally Joyner	.30	.25	.12
17	Jimmy Key	.10	.08	.04
18	Mark Langston	.15	.11	.06
19	Don Mattingly	1.00	.70	.40
20	Paul Molitor	.15	.11	.06
21	Jack Morris	.15	.11	.06
22	Eddie Murray	.20	.15	.08
23	Kirby Puckett	.25	.20	.10
24	Cal Ripken	.25	.20	.10
25	Bret Saberhagen	.15	.11	.06
26	Ruben Sierra	.15	.11	.06
27	Cory Snyder	.15	.11	.06
28	Terry Steinbach	.15	.11	.06
29	Danny Tartabull	.15	.11	.06
30	Alan Trammell	.15	.11	.06
31	Devon White	.15	.11	.06
32	Robin Yount	.15	.11	.06
33	Andre Dawson	.15	.11	.06
34	Steve Bedrosian	.15	.11	.06
35	Benny Santiago	.15	.11	.06
36	Tony Gwynn	.25	.20	.10
37	Bobby Bonilla	.15	.11	.06
38	Will Clark	.30	.25	.12
39	Eric Davis	.40	.30	.15
40	Mike Dunne	.15	.11	.06
41	John Franco	.10	.08	.04
42	Dwight Gooden	.40	.30	.15
43	Pedro Guerrero	.15	.11	.06
44	Dion James	.10	.08	.04
45	John Kruk	.15	.11	.06
46	Jeffrey Leonard	.10	.08	.04
47	Carmelo Martinez	.10	.08	.04
48	Dale Murphy	.30	.25	.12
49	Tim Raines	.20	.15	.08
50	Nolan Ryan	.20	.15	.08
51	Juan Samuel	.15	.11	.06
52	Ryne Sandberg	.20	.15	.08
53	Mike Schmidt	.30	.25	.12
54	Mike Scott	.15	.11	.06
55	Ozzie Smith	.15	.11	.06
56	Darryl Strawberry	.40	.30	.15
57	Rick Sutcliffe	.15	.11	.06
58	Fernando Valenzuela	.15	.11	.06
59	Tim Wallach	.15	.11	.06
60	Todd Worrell	.15	.11	.06

1988 Topps Gallery of Champions

These bronze replicas are exact reproductions at one-quarter scale of Topps official 1988 cards, both front and back. The set includes 12 three-dimensional raised metal cards packaged in a velvet-lined case that bears the title of the set in gold embossed letters. A deluxe limited edition of the set (1,000) was produced in sterling silver and an economy version in aluminum. Topps first issued the metal mini-cards in 1984 (the initial set was called Gallery of Immortals). Since 1985, the metal cards have honored award-winning players from the previous season. A Mark McGwire pewter replica was given as a premium to dealers ordering the aluminum, bronze and silver sets ($50 value). The special pewter card is distinguished from the regular issue by a diagonal name banner in the lower right corner (regular) replicas have a rectangular name banner printer parallel to the lower edge of the card). A 1955 Topps Duke Snider bronze (value $10) was available to dealers purchasing cases of the 1988 Topps Traded sets.

		MT	NR MT	EX
Complete Aluminum Set:		20.00	15.00	8.00
Complete Bronze Set:		125.00	94.00	50.00
Complete Silver Set:		500.00	375.00	200.00
(1a)	Steve Bedrosian (aluminum)	.70	.50	.30
(1b)	Steve Bedrosian (bronze)	7.50	5.75	3.00
(1c)	Steve Bedrosian (silver)	20.00	15.00	8.00
(2a)	George Bell (aluminum)	1.00	.70	.40
(2b)	George Bell (bronze)	10.00	7.50	4.00
(2c)	George Bell (silver)	20.00	15.00	8.00
(3a)	Wade Boggs (aluminum)	3.00	2.25	1.25
(3b)	Wade Boggs (bronze)	25.00	18.50	10.00
(3c)	Wade Boggs (silver)	125.00	94.00	50.00
(4a)	Jack Clark (aluminum)	1.00	.70	.40
(4b)	Jack Clark (bronze)	10.00	7.50	4.00
(4c)	Jack Clark (silver)	20.00	15.00	8.00
(5a)	Roger Clemens (aluminum)	2.00	1.50	.80
(5b)	Roger Clemens (bronze)	20.00	15.00	8.00
(5c)	Roger Clemens (silver)	90.00	67.00	36.00
(6a)	Andre Dawson (aluminum)	1.00	.70	.40
(6b)	Andre Dawson (bronze)	10.00	7.50	4.00
(6c)	Andre Dawson (silver)	20.00	15.00	8.00
(7a)	Tony Gwynn (aluminum)	1.25	.90	.50
(7b)	Tony Gwynn (bronze)	12.00	9.00	4.75
(7c)	Tony Gwynn (silver)	50.00	37.00	20.00
(8a)	Mark Langston (aluminum)	.70	.50	.30
(8b)	Mark Langston (bronze)	7.50	5.75	3.00
(8c)	Mark Langston (silver)	20.00	15.00	8.00
(9a)	Mark McGwire (aluminum)	3.00	2.25	1.25
(9b)	Mark McGwire (bronze)	25.00	18.50	10.00
(9c)	Mark McGwire (silver)	125.00	94.00	50.00
(10a)	Dave Righetti (aluminum)	1.00	.70	.40
(10b)	Dave Righetti (bronze)	10.00	7.50	4.00
(10c)	Dave Righetti (silver)	20.00	15.00	8.00
(11a)	Nolan Ryan (aluminum)	1.00	.70	.40
(11b)	Nolan Ryan (bronze)	10.00	7.50	4.00
(11c)	Nolan Ryan (silver)	20.00	15.00	8.00

	MT	NR MT	EX
(12a) Benny Santiago (aluminum)	1.00	.70	.40
(12b) Benny Santiago (bronze)	10.00	7.50	4.00
(12c) Benny Santiago (silver)	20.00	15.00	8.00

1988 Topps Glossy Rookies

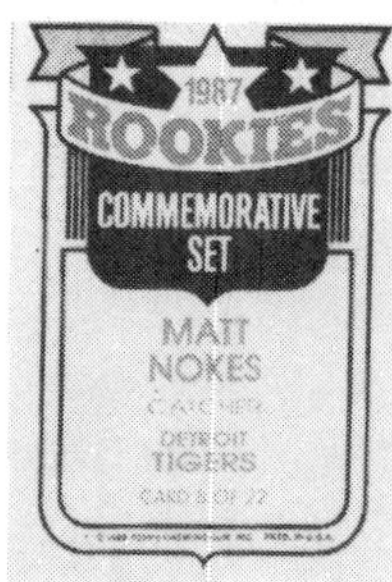

The Topps 1988 Rookies special insert cards follow the same basic design as the All-Star inserts. The set consists of 22 standard-size cards. Large, glossy color player photos are printed on a white background below a red, yellow and blue "1987 Rookies" banner. A red and yellow player name appears beneath the photo. Red, white and blue card backs bear the title of the special insert set, the Rookies logo emblem, player name and card number.

		MT	NR MT	EX
Complete Set:		10.00	7.50	4.00
Common Player:		.20	.15	.08
1	Billy Ripken	.30	.25	.12
2	Ellis Burks	1.50	1.25	.60
3	Mike Greenwell	2.00	1.50	.80
4	DeWayne Buice	.20	.15	.08
5	Devon White	.40	.30	.15
6	Fred Manrique	.20	.15	.08
7	Mike Henneman	.40	.30	.15
8	Matt Nokes	.60	.45	.25
9	Kevin Seitzer	1.25	.90	.50
10	B.J. Surhoff	.40	.30	.15
11	Casey Candaele	.20	.15	.08
12	Randy Myers	.60	.45	.25
13	Mark McGwire	2.00	1.50	.80
14	Luis Polonia	.25	.20	.10
15	Terry Steinbach	.40	.30	.15
16	Mike Dunne	.40	.30	.15
17	Al Pedrique	.20	.15	.08
18	Benny Santiago	.70	.50	.30
19	Kelly Downs	.40	.30	.15
20	Joe Magrane	.40	.30	.15
21	Jerry Browne	.20	.15	.08
22	Jeff Musselman	.25	.20	.10

1988 Topps Mini League Leaders

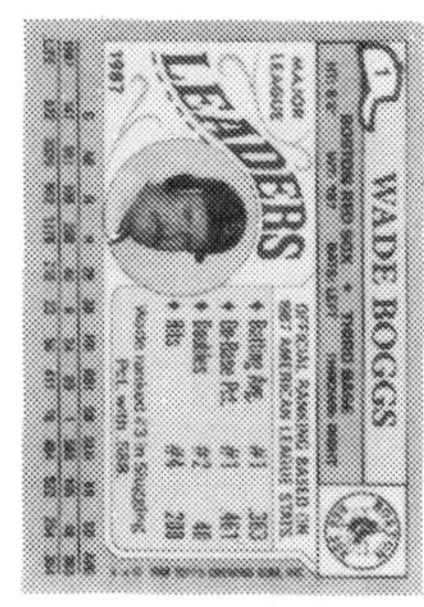

The third consecutive issue of Topps mini-cards (2-1/8" by 3") includes 77 cards spotlighting the top five ranked pitchers and batters. This set is unique in that it was the first time Topps included full-color player photos on both the front and back. Glossy action shots on the card fronts fade into a white border with a Topps logo in an upper corner. The player's name is printed in bold black letters beneath the photo. Horizontal reverses feature circular player photos on a blue and white background with the card number, player name, personal information, 1987 ranking and lifetime/1987 stats printed in red, black and yellow lettering.

		MT	NR MT	EX
Complete Set:		6.00	4.50	2.50
Common Player:		.09	.07	.04
1	Wade Boggs	.80	.60	.30
2	Roger Clemens	.60	.45	.25
3	Dwight Evans	.15	.11	.06
4	DeWayne Buice	.09	.07	.04
5	Brian Downing	.09	.07	.04
6	Wally Joyner	.60	.45	.25
7	Ivan Calderon	.15	.11	.06
8	Carlton Fisk	.20	.15	.08
9	Gary Redus	.09	.07	.04
10	Darrell Evans	.15	.11	.06
11	Jack Morris	.25	.20	.10
12	Alan Trammell	.30	.25	.12
13	Lou Whitaker	.20	.15	.08
14	Bret Saberhagen	.20	.15	.08
15	Kevin Seitzer	.50	.40	.20
16	Danny Tartabull	.25	.20	.10
17	Willie Wilson	.15	.11	.06
18	Teddy Higuera	.15	.11	.06
19	Paul Molitor	.20	.15	.08
20	Dan Plesac	.15	.11	.06
21	Robin Yount	.25	.20	.10
22	Kent Hrbek	.25	.20	.10
23	Kirby Puckett	.35	.25	.14
24	Jeff Reardon	.15	.11	.06
25	Frank Viola	.20	.15	.08
26	Rickey Henderson	.40	.30	.15
27	Don Mattingly	1.25	.90	.50
28	Willie Randolph	.15	.11	.06
29	Dave Righetti	.20	.15	.08
30	Jose Canseco	1.00	.70	.40
31	Mark McGwire	.90	.70	.35
32	Dave Stewart	.09	.07	.04
33	Phil Bradley	.15	.11	.06
34	Mark Langston	.15	.11	.06
35	Harold Reynolds	.09	.07	.04
36	Charlie Hough	.09	.07	.04
37	George Bell	.25	.20	.10
38	Tom Henke	.09	.07	.04
39	Jimmy Key	.15	.11	.06
40	Dion James	.09	.07	.04
41	Dale Murphy	.50	.40	.20
42	Zane Smith	.09	.07	.04
43	Andre Dawson	.25	.20	.10
44	Lee Smith	.09	.07	.04
45	Rick Sutcliffe	.15	.11	.06
46	Eric Davis	.60	.45	.25
47	John Franco	.15	.11	.06
48	Dave Parker	.20	.15	.08
49	Billy Hatcher	.09	.07	.04
50	Nolan Ryan	.25	.20	.10
51	Mike Scott	.20	.15	.08
52	Pedro Guerrero	.20	.15	.08
53	Orel Hershiser	.30	.25	.12
54	Fernando Valenzuela	.25	.20	.10
55	Bob Welch	.15	.11	.06
56	Andres Galarraga	.25	.20	.10
57	Tim Raines	.30	.25	.12
58	Tim Wallach	.15	.11	.06
59	Len Dykstra	.15	.11	.06
60	Dwight Gooden	.60	.45	.25
61	Howard Johnson	.15	.11	.06
62	Roger McDowell	.15	.11	.06
63	Darryl Strawberry	.50	.40	.20
64	Steve Bedrosian	.15	.11	.06
65	Shane Rawley	.09	.07	.04
66	Juan Samuel	.20	.15	.08
67	Mike Schmidt	.50	.40	.20
68	Mike Dunne	.15	.11	.06
69	Jack Clark	.25	.20	.10
70	Vince Coleman	.20	.15	.08
71	Willie McGee	.15	.11	.06
72	Ozzie Smith	.20	.15	.08
73	Todd Worrell	.15	.11	.06
74	Tony Gwynn	.40	.30	.15
75	John Kruk	.20	.15	.08
76	Rick Rueschel	.15	.11	.06
77	Checklist	.09	.07	.04

1988 Topps Stickercards

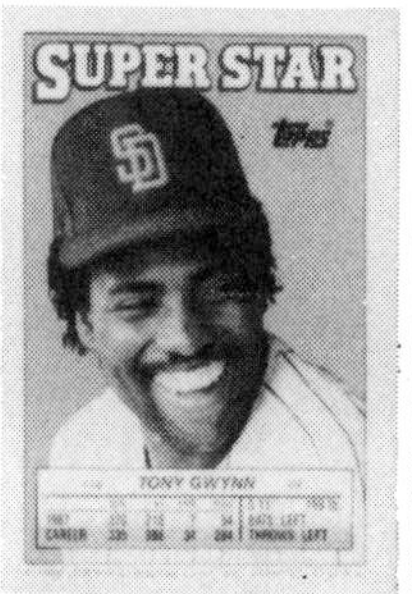

Actually a part of the 1988 Topps Stickers issue, this set consists of 67 cards. The cards are the backs of the peel-off stickers and measure 2-1/8" by 3". To determine total value, combine the prices of the stickers (found in the 1988 Topps Stickers checklist) on the stickercard front with the value assigned to the stickercard in the following checklist.

		MT	NR MT	EX
Complete Set:		2.00	1.50	.80
Common Player:		.02	.02	.01
1	Jack Clark	.03	.02	.01
2	Andres Galarraga	.03	.02	.01
3	Keith Hernandez	.04	.03	.02
4	Tom Herr	.02	.02	.01
5	Juan Samuel	.03	.02	.01
6	Ryne Sandberg	.04	.03	.02
7	Terry Pendleton	.02	.02	.01
8	Mike Schmidt	.06	.05	.02
9	Tim Wallach	.02	.02	.01
10	Hubie Brooks	.02	.02	.01
11	Shawon Dunston	.02	.02	.01
12	Ozzie Smith	.03	.02	.01
13	Andre Dawson	.04	.03	.02
14	Eric Davis	.06	.05	.02
15	Pedro Guerrero	.03	.02	.01
16	Tony Gwynn	.05	.04	.02
17	Jeffrey Leonard	.02	.02	.01
18	Dale Murphy	.06	.05	.02
19	Dave Parker	.03	.02	.01
20	Tim Raines	.04	.03	.02
21	Darryl Strawberry	.06	.05	.02
22	Gary Carter	.04	.03	.02
23	Jody Davis	.02	.02	.01
24	Ozzie Virgil	.02	.02	.01
25	Dwight Gooden	.08	.06	.03
26	Mike Scott	.02	.02	.01
27	Rick Sutcliffe	.02	.02	.01
28	Sid Fernandez	.02	.02	.01
29	Neal Heaton	.02	.02	.01
30	Fernando Valenzuela	.03	.02	.01
31	Steve Bedrosian	.02	.02	.01
32	John Franco	.02	.02	.01
33	Lee Smith	.02	.02	.01
34	Wally Joyner	.06	.05	.02
35	Don Mattingly	.12	.09	.05
36	Mark McGwire	.08	.06	.03
37	Willie Randolph	.02	.02	.01
38	Lou Whitaker	.03	.02	.01
39	Frank White	.02	.02	.01
40	Wade Boggs	.10	.08	.04
41	George Brett	.06	.05	.02
42	Paul Molitor	.02	.02	.01
43	Tony Fernandez	.02	.02	.01
44	Cal Ripken	.06	.05	.02
45	Alan Trammell	.04	.03	.02
46	Jesse Barfield	.03	.02	.01
47	George Bell	.04	.03	.02
48	Jose Canseco	.10	.08	.04
49	Joe Carter	.03	.02	.01
50	Dwight Evans	.02	.02	.01
51	Rickey Henderson	.05	.04	.02
52	Kirby Puckett	.05	.04	.02
53	Cory Snyder	.03	.02	.01
54	Dave Winfield	.04	.03	.02
55	Terry Kennedy	.02	.02	.01
56	Matt Nokes	.03	.02	.01
57	B.J. Surhoff	.02	.02	.01
58	Roger Clemens	.08	.06	.03
59	Jack Morris	.03	.02	.01
60	Bret Saberhagen	.03	.02	.01
61	Ron Guidry	.03	.02	.01
62	Bruce Hurst	.02	.02	.01
63	Mark Langston	.02	.02	.01
64	Tom Henke	.02	.02	.01
65	Dan Plesac	.02	.02	.01
66	Dave Righetti	.03	.02	.01
67	Checklist	.02	.02	.01

1988 Topps Stickers

This set of 313 stickers (on 198 cards) offers a new addition for 1988 - 66 different players are pictured on the reverse of the sticker cards. The stickers come in two sizes (2-1/8" by 3" or 1-1/2" by 2-1/8"). Larger stickers fill an entire card, smaller ones are attached in pairs. A 36-page sticker yearbook produced by Topps has a designated space inside for each sticker,with one page per team and special pages of 1987 Highlights, World Series, All-Stars and Future Stars. No printing appears on the full-color action shot stickers except for a small black number in the lower left corner. Sticker card backs carry a Super Star header, player close-up and stats. Stickers were sold in packages of five (with gum) for 25 cents per pack. Unlike the 1987 Topps Stickers set, different pairings can be found, rather than the same two players/numbers always sharing the same sticker. To determine total value, combine the value of the stickercard (found in the 1988 Topps Stickercard checklist) with the values assigned the stickers in the following checklist.

	MT	NR MT	EX
Complete Set:	15.00	11.00	6.00
Common Player:	.02	.02	.01
Sticker Album:	.60	.45	.25

		MT	NR MT	EX
1	1987 Highlights (Mark McGwire)	.20	.15	.08
2	1987 Highlights (Benny Santiago)	.04	.03	.02
3	1987 Highlights (Don Mattingly)	.25	.20	.10
4	1987 Highlights (Vince Coleman)	.04	.03	.02
5	1987 Highlights (Bob Boone)	.02	.02	.01
6	1987 Highlights (Steve Bedrosian)	.02	.02	.01
7	1987 Highlights (Nolan Ryan)	.08	.06	.03
8	1987 Highlights (Darrell Evans)	.02	.02	.01
9	1987 Highlights (Mike Schmidt)	.10	.08	.04
10	1987 Highlights (Don Baylor)	.04	.03	.02
11	1987 Highlights (Eddie Murray)	.08	.06	.03
12	1987 Highlights (Juan Beniquez)	.02	.02	.01
13	1987 Championship Series (John Tudor)	.04	.03	.02
14	1987 Championship Series (Jeff Reardon)	.04	.03	.02
15	1987 Championship Series (Tom Brunansky)	.06	.05	.02
16	1987 Championship Series (Jeffrey Leonard)	.04	.03	.02
17	1987 Championship Series (Gary Gaetti)	.10	.08	.04
18	1987 Championship Series (Cardinals Celebrate)	.04	.03	.02
19	1987 World Series (Danny Gladden)	.04	.03	.02
20	1987 World Series (Bert Blyleven)	.08	.06	.03
21	1987 World Series (John Tudor)	.06	.05	.02
22	1987 World Series (Tom Lawless)	.04	.03	.02
23	1987 World Series (Curt Ford)	.04	.03	.02
24	1987 World Series (Kent Hrbek)	.12	.09	.05
25	1987 World Series (Frank Viola)	.10	.08	.04
26	Dave Smith	.02	.02	.01
27	Jim Deshaies	.02	.02	.01
28	Billy Hatcher	.02	.02	.01
29	Kevin Bass	.02	.02	.01
30	Mike Scott	.04	.03	.02
31	Danny Walling	.02	.02	.01
32	Alan Ashby	.02	.02	.01
33	Ken Caminiti	.02	.02	.01
34	Bill Doran	.02	.02	.01
35	Glenn Davis	.12	.09	.05
36	Ozzie Virgil	.02	.02	.01
37	Ken Oberkfell	.02	.02	.01
38	Ken Griffey	.02	.02	.01
39	Albert Hall	.02	.02	.01
40	Zane Smith	.02	.02	.01
41	Andres Thomas	.02	.02	.01
42	Dion James	.02	.02	.01
43	Jim Acker	.02	.02	.01
44	Tom Glavine	.04	.03	.02
45	Dale Murphy	.25	.20	.10
46	Jack Clark	.10	.08	.04
47	Vince Coleman	.04	.03	.02
48	Ricky Horton	.02	.02	.01
49	Terry Pendleton	.02	.02	.01
50	Tom Herr	.02	.02	.01
51	Joe Magrane	.04	.03	.02
52	Tony Pena	.02	.02	.01
53	Ozzie Smith	.04	.03	.02
54	Todd Worrell	.04	.03	.02
55	Willie McGee	.10	.08	.04
56	Andre Dawson	.15	.11	.06
57	Ryne Sandberg	.06	.05	.02
58	Keith Moreland	.02	.02	.01
59	Greg Maddux	.04	.03	.02
60	Jody Davis	.02	.02	.01
61	Rick Sutcliffe	.08	.06	.03
62	Jamie Moyer	.02	.02	.01
63	Leon Durham	.02	.02	.01
64	Lee Smith	.02	.02	.01
65	Shawon Dunston	.02	.02	.01
66	Franklin Stubbs	.02	.02	.01
67	Mike Scioscia	.02	.02	.01
68	Orel Hershiser	.06	.05	.02
69	Mike Marshall	.04	.03	.02
70	Fernando Valenzuela	.15	.11	.06
71	Mickey Hatcher	.02	.02	.01
72	Matt Young	.02	.02	.01
73	Bob Welch	.04	.03	.02
74	Steve Sax	.04	.03	.02
75	Pedro Guerrero	.12	.09	.05
76	Tim Raines	.15	.11	.06
77	Casey Candaele	.02	.02	.01
78	Mike Fitzgerald	.02	.02	.01
79	Andres Galarraga	.04	.03	.02
80	Neal Heaton	.02	.02	.01
81	Hubie Brooks	.02	.02	.01
82	Floyd Youmans	.02	.02	.01
83	Herm Winningham	.02	.02	.01
84	Denny Martinez	.02	.02	.01
85	Tim Wallach	.08	.06	.03
86	Jeffrey Leonard	.04	.03	.02
87	Will Clark	.10	.08	.04
88	Kevin Mitchell	.04	.03	.02
89	Mike Aldrete	.02	.02	.01
90	Scott Garrelts	.02	.02	.01
91	Jose Uribe	.02	.02	.01
92	Bob Brenly	.02	.02	.01
93	Robby Thompson	.02	.02	.01
94	Don Robinson	.02	.02	.01
95	Candy Maldonado	.04	.03	.02
96	Darryl Strawberry	.25	.20	.10
97	Keith Hernandez	.06	.05	.02
98	Ron Darling	.04	.03	.02
99	Howard Johnson	.04	.03	.02

		MT	NR MT	EX
100	Roger McDowell	.02	.02	.01
101	Dwight Gooden	.30	.25	.12
102	Kevin McReynolds	.04	.03	.02
103	Sid Fernandez	.02	.02	.01
104	Dave Magadan	.04	.03	.02
105	Gary Carter	.08	.06	.03
106	Carmelo Martinez	.02	.02	.01
107	Eddie Whitson	.02	.02	.01
108	Tim Flannery	.02	.02	.01
109	Stan Jefferson	.02	.02	.01
110	John Kruk	.10	.08	.04
111	Chris Brown	.04	.03	.02
112	Benny Santiago	.04	.03	.02
113	Garry Templeton	.02	.02	.01
114	Lance McCullers	.02	.02	.01
115	Tony Gwynn	.20	.15	.08
116	Steve Bedrosian	.06	.05	.02
117	Von Hayes	.02	.02	.01
118	Kevin Gross	.02	.02	.01
119	Bruce Ruffin	.02	.02	.01
120	Juan Samuel	.04	.03	.02
121	Shane Rawley	.02	.02	.01
122	Chris James	.04	.03	.02
123	Lance Parrish	.04	.03	.02
124	Glenn Wilson	.02	.02	.01
125	Mike Schmidt	.25	.20	.10
126	Andy Van Slyke	.08	.06	.03
127	Jose Lind	.04	.03	.02
128	Al Pedrique	.02	.02	.01
129	Bobby Bonilla	.04	.03	.02
130	Sed Bream	.02	.02	.01
131	Mike LaValliere	.02	.02	.01
132	Mike Dunne	.04	.03	.02
133	Jeff Robinson	.02	.02	.01
134	Doug Drabek	.02	.02	.01
135	Barry Bonds	.10	.08	.04
136	Dave Parker	.08	.06	.03
137	Nick Esasky	.02	.02	.01
138	Buddy Bell	.02	.02	.01
139	Kal Daniels	.04	.03	.02
140	Barry Larkin	.04	.03	.02
141	Eric Davis	.25	.20	.10
142	John Franco	.02	.02	.01
143	Bo Diaz	.02	.02	.01
144	Ron Oester	.02	.02	.01
145	Dennis Rasmussen	.02	.02	.01
146	Eric Davis	.40	.30	.15
147	Ryne Sandberg	.30	.25	.12
148	Andre Dawson	.20	.15	.08
149	Mike Schmidt	.40	.30	.15
150	Jack Clark	.20	.15	.08
151	Darryl Strawberry	.40	.30	.15
152	Gary Carter	.30	.25	.12
153	Ozzie Smith	.20	.15	.08
154	Mike Scott	.20	.15	.08
155	Rickey Henderson	.40	.30	.15
156	Don Mattingly	.90	.70	.35
157	Wade Boggs	.60	.45	.25
158	George Bell	.30	.25	.12
159	Dave Winfield	.30	.25	.12
160	Cal Ripken	.40	.30	.15
161	Terry Kennedy	.15	.11	.06
162	Willie Randolph	.15	.11	.06
163	Bret Saberhagen	.25	.20	.10
164	Mark McGwire	.35	.25	.14
165	Tony Phillips	.02	.02	.01
166	Jay Howell	.02	.02	.01
167	Carney Lansford	.02	.02	.01
168	Dave Stewart	.02	.02	.01
169	Alfredo Griffin	.02	.02	.01
170	Dennis Eckersley	.04	.03	.02
171	Mike Davis	.02	.02	.01
172	Luis Polonia	.02	.02	.01
173	Jose Canseco	.60	.45	.25
174	Mike Witt	.06	.05	.02
175	Jack Howell	.02	.02	.01
176	Greg Minton	.02	.02	.01
177	Dick Schofield	.02	.02	.01
178	Gary Pettis	.02	.02	.01
179	Wally Joyner	.25	.20	.10
180	DeWayne Buice	.02	.02	.01
181	Brian Downing	.02	.02	.01
182	Bob Boone	.02	.02	.01
183	Devon White	.04	.03	.02
184	Jim Clancy	.02	.02	.01
185	Willie Upshaw	.02	.02	.01
186	Tom Henke	.02	.02	.01
187	Ernie Whitt	.02	.02	.01
188	George Bell	.20	.15	.08
189	Lloyd Moseby	.02	.02	.01
190	Jimmy Key	.02	.02	.01
191	Dave Stieb	.02	.02	.01
192	Jesse Barfield	.04	.03	.02
193	Tony Fernandez	.10	.08	.04
194	Paul Molitor	.06	.05	.02
195	Jim Gantner	.02	.02	.01
196	Teddy Higuera	.04	.03	.02
197	Glenn Braggs	.02	.02	.01
198	Rob Deer	.02	.02	.01
199	Dale Sveum	.02	.02	.01
200	Bill Wegman	.02	.02	.01
201	Robin Yount	.06	.05	.02
202	B.J. Surhoff	.04	.03	.02
203	Dan Plesac	.06	.05	.02
204	Pat Tabler	.04	.03	.02
205	Mel Hall	.02	.02	.01
206	Scott Bailes	.02	.02	.01
207	Julio Franco	.04	.03	.02
208	Cory Snyder	.06	.05	.02
209	Chris Bando	.02	.02	.01
210	Greg Swindell	.04	.03	.02
211	Brook Jacoby	.02	.02	.01
212	Brett Butler	.02	.02	.01
213	Joe Carter	.10	.08	.04
214	Mark Langston	.08	.06	.03
215	Rey Quinones	.02	.02	.01
216	Ed Nunez	.02	.02	.01
217	Jim Presley	.02	.02	.01
218	Phil Bradley	.04	.03	.02
219	Alvin Davis	.10	.08	.04
220	Dave Valle	.02	.02	.01
221	Harold Reynolds	.02	.02	.01
222	Scott Bradley	.02	.02	.01
223	Gary Matthews	.02	.02	.01

		MT	NR MT	EX
224	Eric Bell	.02	.02	.01
225	Terry Kennedy	.02	.02	.01
226	Dave Schmidt	.02	.02	.01
227	Billy Ripken	.04	.03	.02
228	Cal Ripken	.20	.15	.08
229	Ray Knight	.02	.02	.01
230	Larry Sheets	.02	.02	.01
231	Mike Boddicker	.02	.02	.01
232	Tom Niedenfuer	.02	.02	.01
233	Eddie Murray	.20	.15	.08
234	Ruben Sierra	.12	.09	.05
235	Steve Buechele	.02	.02	.01
236	Charlie Hough	.02	.02	.01
237	Oddibe McDowell	.02	.02	.01
238	Mike Stanley	.02	.02	.01
239	Pete Incaviglia	.04	.03	.02
240	Pete O'Brien	.02	.02	.01
241	Scott Fletcher	.02	.02	.01
242	Dale Mohorcic	.02	.02	.01
243	Larry Parrish	.04	.03	.02
244	Wade Boggs	.35	.25	.14
245	Dwight Evans	.04	.03	.02
246	Sam Horn	.04	.03	.02
247	Jim Rice	.06	.05	.02
248	Marty Barrett	.02	.02	.01
249	Mike Greenwell	.15	.11	.06
250	Ellis Burks	.10	.08	.04
251	Roger Clemens	.12	.09	.05
252	Rich Gedman	.02	.02	.01
253	Bruce Hurst	.06	.05	.02
254	Bret Saberhagen	.15	.11	.06
255	Frank White	.02	.02	.01
256	Dan Quisenberry	.02	.02	.01
257	Danny Tartabull	.06	.05	.02
258	Bo Jackson	.08	.06	.03
259	George Brett	.25	.20	.10
260	Charlie Leibrandt	.02	.02	.01
261	Kevin Seitzer	.10	.08	.04
262	Mark Gubicza	.04	.03	.02
263	Willie Wilson	.04	.03	.02
264	Frank Tanana	.02	.02	.01
265	Darrell Evans	.02	.02	.01
266	Bill Madlock	.04	.03	.02
267	Kirk Gibson	.06	.05	.02
268	Jack Morris	.12	.09	.05
269	Matt Nokes	.06	.05	.02
270	Lou Whitaker	.04	.03	.02
271	Eric King	.02	.02	.01
272	Jim Morrison	.02	.02	.01
273	Alan Trammell	.20	.15	.08
274	Kent Hrbek	.12	.09	.05
275	Tom Brunansky	.04	.03	.02
276	Bert Blyleven	.04	.03	.02
277	Gary Gaetti	.04	.03	.02
278	Tim Laudner	.04	.03	.02
279	Gene Larkin	.02	.02	.01
280	Jeff Reardon	.02	.02	.01
281	Danny Gladden	.02	.02	.01
282	Frank Viola	.04	.03	.02
283	Kirby Puckett	.20	.15	.08
284	Ozzie Guillen	.06	.05	.02
285	Ivan Calderon	.02	.02	.01
286	Donnie Hill	.02	.02	.01
287	Ken Williams	.04	.03	.02
288	Jim Winn	.02	.02	.01
289	Bob James	.02	.02	.01
290	Carlton Fisk	.04	.03	.02
291	Richard Dotson	.02	.02	.01
292	Greg Walker	.02	.02	.01
293	Harold Baines	.10	.08	.04
294	Willie Randolph	.06	.05	.02
295	Mike Pagliarulo	.04	.03	.02
296	Ron Guidry	.04	.03	.02
297	Rickey Henderson	.10	.08	.04
298	Rick Rhoden	.02	.02	.01
299	Don Mattingly	.70	.50	.30
300	Dave Righetti	.04	.03	.02
301	Claudell Washington	.02	.02	.01
302	Dave Winfield	.08	.06	.03
303	Gary Ward	.02	.02	.01
304	Al Pedrique	.02	.02	.01
305	Casey Candaele	.02	.02	.01
306	Kevin Seitzer	.10	.08	.04
307	Mike Dunne	.04	.03	.02
308	Jeff Musselman	.02	.02	.01
309	Mark McGwire	.20	.15	.08
310	Ellis Burks	.10	.08	.04
311	Matt Nokes	.06	.05	.02
312	Mike Greenwell	.15	.11	.06
313	Devon White	.04	.03	.02

1988 Topps Traded

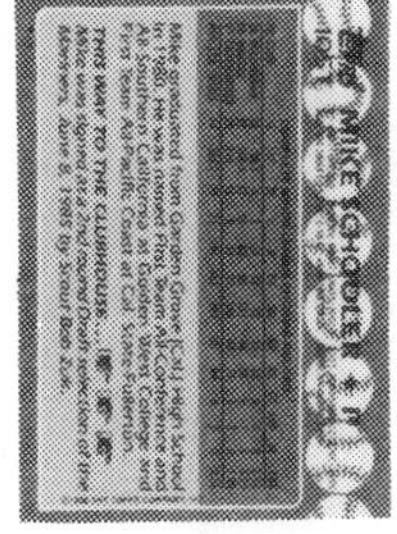

In addition to new players and traded veterans, 21 members of the U.S.A. Olympic Baseball team are showcased in this 132-card set, numbered 1T-132T. The standard-size (2-1/2" by 3-1/2")

set follows the same design as the basic Topps issue - white borders, large full-color photos, team name (or U.S.A.) in large bold letters at the top of the card face, player name on a diagonal stripe across the lower right corner. Topps has issued its traded series each year since 1981 in boxed complete sets available through hobby dealers.

		MT	NR MT	EX
Complete Set:		35.00	27.00	15.00
Common Player:		.06	.05	.02
1T	Jim Abbott (U.S.A.)(FC)	10.00	7.50	4.00
2T	Juan Agosto	.06	.05	.02
3T	Luis Alicea(FC)	.15	.11	.06
4T	Roberto Alomar(FC)	2.25	1.75	.90
5T	Brady Anderson(FC)	.40	.30	.15
6T	Jack Armstrong(FC)	1.50	1.25	.60
7T	Don August	.15	.11	.06
8T	Floyd Bannister	.08	.06	.03
9T	Bret Barberie (U.S.A.)(FC)	.40	.30	.15
10T	Jose Bautista(FC)	.15	.11	.06
11T	Don Baylor	.10	.08	.04
12T	Tim Belcher	.20	.15	.08
13T	Buddy Bell	.10	.08	.04
14T	Andy Benes (U.S.A.)(FC)	3.50	2.75	1.50
15T	Damon Berryhill(FC)	.25	.20	.10
16T	Bud Black	.06	.05	.02
17T	Pat Borders(FC)	.20	.15	.08
18T	Phil Bradley	.10	.08	.04
19T	Jeff Branson (U.S.A.)(FC)	.40	.30	.15
20T	Tom Brunansky	.12	.09	.05
21T	Jay Buhner(FC)	.25	.20	.10
22T	Brett Butler	.08	.06	.03
23T	Jim Campanis (U.S.A.)(FC)	.40	.30	.15
24T	Sil Campusano(FC)	.25	.20	.10
25T	John Candelaria	.08	.06	.03
26T	Jose Cecena(FC)	.15	.11	.06
27T	Rick Cerone	.06	.05	.02
28T	Jack Clark	.15	.11	.06
29T	Kevin Coffman(FC)	.10	.08	.04
30T	Pat Combs (U.S.A.)(FC)	2.00	1.50	.80
31T	Henry Cotto	.06	.05	.02
32T	Chili Davis	.08	.06	.03
33T	Mike Davis	.08	.06	.03
34T	Jose DeLeon	.08	.06	.03
35T	Richard Dotson	.10	.08	.04
36T	Cecil Espy(FC)	.08	.06	.03
37T	Tom Filer	.06	.05	.02
38T	Mike Fiore (U.S.A.)(FC)	.60	.45	.25
39T	Ron Gant(FC)	.80	.60	.30
40T	Kirk Gibson	.15	.11	.06
41T	Rich Gossage	.15	.11	.06
42T	Mark Grace(FC)	6.00	4.50	2.50
43T	Alfredo Griffin	.08	.06	.03
44T	Ty Griffin (U.S.A.)(FC)	1.25	.90	.50
45T	Bryan Harvey(FC)	.30	.25	.12
46T	Ron Hassey	.06	.05	.02
47T	Ray Hayward(FC)	.08	.06	.03
48T	Dave Henderson	.10	.08	.04
49T	Tom Herr	.10	.08	.04
50T	Bob Horner	.10	.08	.04
51T	Ricky Horton	.08	.06	.03
52T	Jay Howell	.08	.06	.03
53T	Glenn Hubbard	.06	.05	.02
54T	Jeff Innis(FC)	.15	.11	.06
55T	Danny Jackson	.15	.11	.06
56T	Darrin Jackson(FC)	.10	.08	.04
57T	Roberto Kelly(FC)	.50	.40	.20
58T	Ron Kittle	.10	.08	.04
59T	Ray Knight	.08	.06	.03
60T	Vance Law	.08	.06	.03
61T	Jeffrey Leonard	.08	.06	.03
62T	Mike Macfarlane(FC)	.20	.15	.08
63T	Scotti Madison(FC)	.15	.11	.06
64T	Kirt Manwaring(FC)	.20	.15	.08
65T	Mark Marquess (U.S.A.)	.06	.05	.02
66T	Tino Martinez (U.S.A.)(FC)	1.50	1.25	.60
67T	Billy Masse (U.S.A.)(FC)	.40	.30	.15
68T	Jack McDowell(FC)	.20	.15	.08
69T	Jack McKeon	.06	.05	.02
70T	Larry McWilliams	.06	.05	.02
71T	Mickey Morandini (U.S.A.)(FC)	.60	.45	.25
72T	Keith Moreland	.08	.06	.03
73T	Mike Morgan	.06	.05	.02
74T	Charles Nagy (U.S.A.)(FC)	.40	.30	.15
75T	Al Nipper	.06	.05	.02
76T	Russ Nixon	.06	.05	.02
77T	Jesse Orosco	.08	.06	.03
78T	Joe Orsulak	.06	.05	.02
79T	Dave Palmer	.06	.05	.02
80T	Mark Parent(FC)	.20	.15	.08
81T	Dave Parker	.12	.09	.05
82T	Dan Pasqua	.10	.08	.04
83T	Melido Perez(FC)	.40	.30	.15
84T	Steve Peters(FC)	.15	.11	.06
85T	Dan Petry	.08	.06	.03
86T	Gary Pettis	.08	.06	.03
87T	Jeff Pico(FC)	.20	.15	.08
88T	Jim Poole (U.S.A.)(FC)	.40	.30	.15
89T	Ted Power	.06	.05	.02
90T	Rafael Ramirez	.06	.05	.02
91T	Dennis Rasmussen	.10	.08	.04
92T	Jose Rijo	.08	.06	.03
93T	Earnie Riles	.06	.05	.02
94T	Luis Rivera(FC)	.08	.06	.03
95T	Doug Robbins (U.S.A.)(FC)	.40	.30	.15
96T	Frank Robinson	.10	.08	.04
97T	Cookie Rojas	.06	.05	.02
98T	Chris Sabo(FC)	2.25	1.75	.90
99T	Mark Salas	.06	.05	.02
100T	Luis Salazar	.06	.05	.02
101T	Rafael Santana	.06	.05	.02
102T	Nelson Santovenia(FC)	.20	.15	.08
103T	Mackey Sasser(FC)	.10	.08	.04
104T	Calvin Schiraldi	.06	.05	.02
105T	Mike Schooler(FC)	.30	.25	.12
106T	Scott Servais (U.S.A.)(FC)	.40	.30	.15
107T	Dave Silvestri (U.S.A.)(FC)	.40	.30	.15
108T	Don Slaught	.06	.05	.02
109T	Joe Slusarski (U.S.A.)(FC)	.40	.30	.15
110T	Lee Smith	.10	.08	.04
111T	Pete Smith(FC)	.10	.08	.04
112T	Jim Snyder	.06	.05	.02
113T	Ed Sprague (U.S.A.)(FC)	.60	.45	.25
114T	Pete Stanicek(FC)	.15	.11	.06
115T	Kurt Stillwell	.10	.08	.04
116T	Todd Stottlemyre(FC)	.30	.25	.12
117T	Bill Swift	.06	.05	.02
118T	Pat Tabler	.08	.06	.03
119T	Scott Terry(FC)	.10	.08	.04
120T	Mickey Tettleton	.06	.05	.02
121T	Dickie Thon	.08	.06	.03
122T	Jeff Treadway(FC)	.20	.15	.08
123T	Willie Upshaw	.08	.06	.03
124T	Robin Ventura(FC)	2.50	2.00	1.00
125T	Ron Washington	.06	.05	.02
126T	Walt Weiss(FC)	.70	.50	.30
127T	Bob Welch	.10	.08	.04
128T	David Wells(FC)	.08	.06	.03
129T	Glenn Wilson	.08	.06	.03
130T	Ted Wood (U.S.A.)(FC)	.60	.45	.25
131T	Don Zimmer	.06	.05	.02
132T	Checklist 1T-132T	.06	.05	.02

1989 Topps

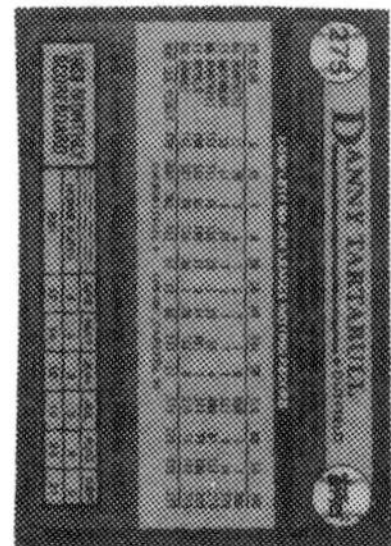

Ten top young players who led the June 1988 draft picks are featured on "#1 Draft Pick" cards in this full-color basic set of 792 standard-size baseball cards. An additional five cards salute 1989 Future Stars, 22 cards highlight All-Stars, seven contain Record Breakers, five are designated Turn Back The Clock, and six contain checklists. This set features the familiar white borders, but two inner photo corners (upper left and lower right) have been rounded off and the rectangular player name was replaced by a curved name banner in bright red or blue that leads to the team name in large script in the lower right corner. The card backs are printed in black on a red background and include personal information and complete minor and major league stats. Another new addition in this set is the special Monthly Scoreboard chart that lists monthly stats (April through September) in two of several categories (hits, run, home runs, stolen bases, RBIs, wins, strikeouts, games or saves).

		MT	NR MT	EX
Complete Set:		22.00	16.50	8.75
Common Player:		.03	.02	.01
1	Record Breaker (George Bell)	.08	.06	.03
2	Record Breaker (Wade Boggs)	.35	.25	.14
3	Record Breaker (Gary Carter)	.10	.08	.04
4	Record Breaker (Andre Dawson)	.08	.06	.03
5	Record Breaker (Orel Hershiser)	.10	.08	.04
6	Record Breaker (Doug Jones)	.06	.05	.02
7	Record Breaker (Kevin McReynolds)	.08	.06	.03
8	*Dave Eiland*(FC)	.20	.15	.08
9	Tim Teufel	.03	.02	.01
10	Andre Dawson	.15	.11	.06
11	Bruce Sutter	.08	.06	.03
12	Dale Sveum	.06	.05	.02
13	Doug Sisk	.03	.02	.01
14	Tom Kelly	.03	.02	.01
15	Robby Thompson	.06	.05	.02
16	Ron Robinson	.03	.02	.01
17	Brian Downing	.06	.05	.02
18	Rick Rhoden	.06	.05	.02
19	Greg Gagne	.03	.02	.01
20	Steve Bedrosian	.08	.06	.03
21	White Sox Leaders (Greg Walker)	.06	.05	.02
22	Tim Crews	.06	.05	.02
23	Mike Fitzgerald	.03	.02	.01
24	Larry Andersen	.03	.02	.01
25	Frank White	.06	.05	.02
26	Dale Mohorcic	.03	.02	.01
27	*Orestes Destrade*(FC)	.12	.09	.05
28	Mike Moore	.03	.02	.01
29	Kelly Gruber	.03	.02	.01
30	Doc Gooden	.40	.30	.15
31	Terry Francona	.03	.02	.01
32	Dennis Rasmussen	.08	.06	.03
33	B.J. Surhoff	.08	.06	.03
34	Ken Williams	.06	.05	.02
35	John Tudor	.08	.06	.03
36	Mitch Webster	.06	.05	.02
37	Bob Stanley	.03	.02	.01
38	Paul Runge	.03	.02	.01
39	Mike Maddux	.03	.02	.01
40	Steve Sax	.12	.09	.05
41	Terry Mulholland	.03	.02	.01
42	Jim Eppard(FC)	.08	.06	.03
43	Guillermo Hernandez	.06	.05	.02
44	Jim Snyder	.03	.02	.01
45	Kal Daniels	.12	.09	.05
46	Mark Portugal	.03	.02	.01
47	Carney Lansford	.06	.05	.02
48	Tim Burke	.03	.02	.01
49	*Craig Biggio*(FC)	.70	.50	.30
50	George Bell	.20	.15	.08
51	Angels Leaders (Mark McLemore)	.06	.05	.02
52	Bob Brenly	.03	.02	.01
53	Ruben Sierra	.30	.25	.12
54	Steve Trout	.03	.02	.01
55	Julio Franco	.08	.06	.03
56	Pat Tabler	.06	.05	.02
57	Alejandro Pena	.06	.05	.02
58	Lee Mazzilli	.06	.05	.02
59	Mark Davis	.03	.02	.01
60	Tom Brunansky	.10	.08	.04
61	Neil Allen	.03	.02	.01
62	Alfredo Griffin	.06	.05	.02
63	Mark Clear	.03	.02	.01
64	Alex Trevino	.03	.02	.01
65	Rick Reuschel	.08	.06	.03
66	Manny Trillo	.03	.02	.01
67	Dave Palmer	.03	.02	.01
68	Darrell Miller	.03	.02	.01
69	Jeff Ballard	.06	.05	.02
70	Mark McGwire	.60	.45	.25
71	Mike Boddicker	.06	.05	.02
72	John Moses	.03	.02	.01
73	Pascual Perez	.06	.05	.02
74	Nick Leyva	.03	.02	.01
75	Tom Henke	.06	.05	.02
76	*Terry Blocker*(FC)	.12	.09	.05
77	Doyle Alexander	.06	.05	.02
78	Jim Sundberg	.06	.05	.02
79	Scott Bankhead	.03	.02	.01
80	Cory Snyder	.15	.11	.06
81	Expos Leaders (Tim Raines)	.08	.06	.03
82	Dave Leiper	.03	.02	.01
83	Jeff Blauser(FC)	.15	.11	.06
84	#1 Draft Pick *(Bill Bene)*(FC)	.25	.20	.10
85	Kevin McReynolds	.12	.09	.05
86	Al Nipper	.03	.02	.01
87	Larry Owen	.03	.02	.01
88	*Darryl Hamilton*(FC)	.12	.09	.05
89	Dave LaPoint	.06	.05	.02
90	Vince Coleman	.12	.09	.05
91	Floyd Youmans	.03	.02	.01
92	Jeff Kunkel	.03	.02	.01
93	Ken Howell	.03	.02	.01
94	Chris Speier	.03	.02	.01
95	Gerald Young	.10	.08	.04
96	Rick Cerone	.03	.02	.01
97	Greg Mathews	.06	.05	.02
98	Larry Sheets	.06	.05	.02
99	*Sherman Corbett*(FC)	.12	.09	.05
100	Mike Schmidt	.35	.25	.14
101	Les Straker	.06	.05	.02
102	Mike Gallego	.03	.02	.01
103	Tim Birtsas	.03	.02	.01
104	Dallas Green	.03	.02	.01
105	Ron Darling	.10	.08	.04
106	Willie Upshaw	.06	.05	.02
107	Jose DeLeon	.06	.05	.02
108	Fred Manrique	.06	.05	.02
109	*Hipolito Pena*(FC)	.12	.09	.05
110	Paul Molitor	.12	.09	.05
111	Reds Leaders (Eric Davis)	.10	.08	.04
112	Jim Presley	.06	.05	.02
113	Lloyd Moseby	.06	.05	.02
114	Bob Kipper	.03	.02	.01
115	Jody Davis	.06	.05	.02
116	Jeff Montgomery	.06	.05	.02
117	Dave Anderson	.03	.02	.01
118	Checklist 1-132	.03	.02	.01
119	Terry Puhl	.03	.02	.01
120	Frank Viola	.12	.09	.05
121	Garry Templeton	.06	.05	.02
122	Lance Johnson(FC)	.10	.08	.04
123	Spike Owen	.03	.02	.01
124	Jim Traber	.06	.05	.02
125	Mike Krukow	.06	.05	.02
126	Sid Bream	.06	.05	.02
127	Walt Terrell	.06	.05	.02
128	Milt Thompson	.03	.02	.01
129	*Terry Clark*(FC)	.20	.15	.08
130	Gerald Perry	.08	.06	.03
131	Dave Otto(FC)	.08	.06	.03
132	Curt Ford	.03	.02	.01
133	Bill Long	.06	.05	.02
134	Don Zimmer	.03	.02	.01
135	Jose Rijo	.06	.05	.02
136	Joey Meyer	.08	.06	.03
137	Geno Petralli	.03	.02	.01
138	Wallace Johnson	.03	.02	.01
139	Mike Flanagan	.06	.05	.02
140	Shawon Dunston	.08	.06	.03
141	Indians Leaders (Brook Jacoby)	.06	.05	.02
142	Mike Diaz	.06	.05	.02
143	Mike Campbell	.08	.06	.03
144	Jay Bell	.06	.05	.02
145	Dave Stewart	.08	.06	.03
146	Gary Pettis	.03	.02	.01
147	DeWayne Buice	.03	.02	.01
148	Bill Pecota	.06	.05	.02
149	*Doug Dascenzo*(FC)	.25	.20	.10
150	Fernando Valenzuela	.15	.11	.06
151	Terry McGriff	.03	.02	.01
152	Mark Thurmond	.03	.02	.01
153	Jim Pankovits	.03	.02	.01
154	Don Carman	.06	.05	.02

No.	Player	MT	NR MT	EX
155	Marty Barrett	.06	.05	.02
156	*Dave Gallagher*(FC)	.20	.15	.08
157	Tom Glavine	.08	.06	.03
158	Mike Aldrete	.06	.05	.02
159	Pat Clements	.03	.02	.01
160	Jeffrey Leonard	.06	.05	.02
161	#1 Draft Pick *(Gregg Olson)*(FC)	1.00	.70	.40
162	John Davis	.03	.02	.01
163	Bob Forsch	.06	.05	.02
164	Hal Lanier	.03	.02	.01
165	Mike Dunne	.08	.06	.03
166	*Doug Jennings*(FC)	.20	.15	.08
167	Future Star *(Steve Searcy)*(FC)	.25	.20	.10
168	Willie Wilson	.08	.06	.03
169	Mike Jackson	.06	.05	.02
170	Tony Fernandez	.10	.08	.04
171	Braves Leaders (Andres Thomas)	.06	.05	.02
172	Frank Williams	.03	.02	.01
173	Mel Hall	.06	.05	.02
174	*Todd Burns*(FC)	.25	.20	.10
175	John Shelby	.03	.02	.01
176	Jeff Parrett	.08	.06	.03
177	#1 Draft Pick *(Monty Fariss)*(FC)	.50	.40	.20
178	Mark Grant	.03	.02	.01
179	Ozzie Virgil	.03	.02	.01
180	Mike Scott	.10	.08	.04
181	*Craig Worthington*(FC)	.40	.30	.15
182	Bob McClure	.03	.02	.01
183	Oddibe McDowell	.06	.05	.02
184	*John Costello*	.20	.15	.08
185	Claudell Washington	.06	.05	.02
186	Pat Perry	.03	.02	.01
187	Darren Daulton	.03	.02	.01
188	Dennis Lamp	.03	.02	.01
189	Kevin Mitchell	.50	.40	.20
190	Mike Witt	.06	.05	.02
191	*Sil Campusano*	.20	.15	.08
192	Paul Mirabella	.03	.02	.01
193	Sparky Anderson	.06	.05	.02
194	*Greg Harris*(FC)	.25	.20	.10
195	Ozzie Guillen	.06	.05	.02
196	Denny Walling	.03	.02	.01
197	Neal Heaton	.03	.02	.01
198	Danny Heep	.03	.02	.01
199	*Mike Schooler*	.30	.25	.12
200	George Brett	.30	.25	.12
201	Blue Jays Leaders (Kelly Gruber)	.06	.05	.02
202	*Brad Moore*(FC)	.12	.09	.05
203	Rob Ducey	.03	.02	.01
204	Brad Havens	.03	.02	.01
205	Dwight Evans	.10	.08	.04
206	Roberto Alomar	.50	.40	.20
207	Terry Leach	.03	.02	.01
208	Tom Pagnozzi	.06	.05	.02
209	*Jeff Bittiger*(FC)	.12	.09	.05
210	Dale Murphy	.30	.25	.12
211	Mike Pagliarulo	.08	.06	.03
212	Scott Sanderson	.03	.02	.01
213	Rene Gonzales	.06	.05	.02
214	Charlie O'Brien	.03	.02	.01
215	Kevin Gross	.06	.05	.02
216	Jack Howell	.06	.05	.02
217	Joe Price	.03	.02	.01
218	Mike LaValliere	.06	.05	.02
219	Jim Clancy	.06	.05	.02
220	Gary Gaetti	.12	.09	.05
221	Cecil Espy	.08	.06	.03
222	#1 Draft Pick *(Mark Lewis)*(FC)	.50	.40	.20
223	Jay Buhner	.10	.08	.04
224	Tony LaRussa	.06	.05	.02
225	*Ramon Martinez*(FC)	1.00	.70	.40
226	Bill Doran	.06	.05	.02
227	John Farrell	.08	.06	.03
228	*Nelson Santovenia*	.25	.20	.10
229	Jimmy Key	.08	.06	.03
230	Ozzie Smith	.12	.09	.05
231	Padres Leaders (Roberto Alomar)	.10	.08	.04
232	Ricky Horton	.06	.05	.02
233	Future Star (Gregg Jefferies)(FC)	2.25	1.75	.90
234	Tom Browning	.08	.06	.03
235	John Kruk	.06	.05	.02
236	Charles Hudson	.03	.02	.01
237	Glenn Hubbard	.03	.02	.01
238	Eric King	.03	.02	.01
239	Tim Laudner	.03	.02	.01
240	Greg Maddux	.10	.08	.04
241	Brett Butler	.06	.05	.02
242	Ed Vande Berg	.03	.02	.01
243	Bob Boone	.06	.05	.02
244	Jim Acker	.03	.02	.01
245	Jim Rice	.20	.15	.08
246	Rey Quinones	.03	.02	.01
247	Shawn Hillegas	.06	.05	.02
248	Tony Phillips	.03	.02	.01
249	Tim Leary	.06	.05	.02
250	Cal Ripken	.30	.25	.12
251	*John Dopson*(FC)	.25	.20	.10
252	Billy Hatcher	.06	.05	.02
253	*Jose Alvarez*(FC)	.12	.09	.05
254	Tom LaSorda	.06	.05	.02
255	Ron Guidry	.12	.09	.05
256	Benny Santiago	.12	.09	.05
257	Rick Aguilera	.03	.02	.01
258	Checklist 133-264	.03	.02	.01
259	Larry McWilliams	.03	.02	.01
260	Dave Winfield	.25	.20	.10
261	Cardinals Leaders (Tom Brunansky)	.06	.05	.02
262	*Jeff Pico*	.20	.15	.08
263	Mike Felder	.03	.02	.01
264	*Rob Dibble*(FC)	.30	.25	.12
265	Kent Hrbek	.15	.11	.06
266	Luis Aquino	.03	.02	.01
267	Jeff Robinson	.06	.05	.02
268	Keith Miller	.06	.05	.02
269	Tom Bolton	.06	.05	.02
270	Wally Joyner	.20	.15	.08
271	Jay Tibbs	.03	.02	.01
272	Ron Hassey	.03	.02	.01
273	Jose Lind	.08	.06	.03
274	Mark Eichhorn	.06	.05	.02
275	Danny Tartabull	.15	.11	.06
276	Paul Kilgus	.08	.06	.03
277	Mike Davis	.06	.05	.02
278	Andy McGaffigan	.03	.02	.01
279	Scott Bradley	.03	.02	.01
280	Bob Knepper	.06	.05	.02
281	Gary Redus	.03	.02	.01
282	*Cris Carpenter*(FC)	.25	.20	.10
283	Andy Allanson	.03	.02	.01
284	Jim Leyland	.03	.02	.01
285	John Candelaria	.06	.05	.02
286	Darrin Jackson	.08	.06	.03
287	Juan Nieves	.06	.05	.02
288	Pat Sheridan	.03	.02	.01
289	Ernie Whitt	.06	.05	.02
290	John Franco	.08	.06	.03
291	Mets Leaders (Darryl Strawberry)	.12	.09	.05
292	*Jim Corsi*(FC)	.15	.11	.06
293	Glenn Wilson	.06	.05	.02
294	Juan Berenguer	.03	.02	.01
295	Scott Fletcher	.06	.05	.02
296	Ron Gant	.10	.08	.04
297	*Oswald Peraza*(FC)	.15	.11	.06
298	Chris James	.08	.06	.03
299	*Steve Ellsworth*(FC)	.12	.09	.05
300	Darryl Strawberry	.35	.25	.14
301	Charlie Leibrandt	.06	.05	.02
302	Gary Ward	.06	.05	.02
303	Felix Fermin	.06	.05	.02
304	Joel Youngblood	.03	.02	.01
305	Dave Smith	.06	.05	.02
306	Tracy Woodson(FC)	.10	.08	.04
307	Lance McCullers	.06	.05	.02
308	Ron Karkovice	.03	.02	.01
309	Mario Diaz(FC)	.10	.08	.04
310	Rafael Palmeiro	.20	.15	.08
311	Chris Bosio	.03	.02	.01
312	Tom Lawless	.03	.02	.01
313	Denny Martinez	.06	.05	.02
314	Bobby Valentine	.03	.02	.01
315	Greg Swindell	.10	.08	.04
316	Walt Weiss	.50	.40	.20
317	*Jack Armstrong*	.50	.40	.20
318	Gene Larkin	.08	.06	.03
319	Greg Booker	.03	.02	.01
320	Lou Whitaker	.15	.11	.06
321	Red Sox Leaders (Jody Reed)	.06	.05	.02
322	John Smiley	.10	.08	.04
323	Gary Thurman	.10	.08	.04
324	*Bob Milacki*(FC)	.25	.20	.10
325	Jesse Barfield	.08	.06	.03
326	Dennis Boyd	.06	.05	.02
327	*Mark Lemke*(FC)	.20	.15	.08
328	Rick Honeycutt	.03	.02	.01
329	Bob Melvin	.03	.02	.01
330	Eric Davis	.35	.25	.14
331	Curt Wilkerson	.03	.02	.01
332	Tony Armas	.06	.05	.02
333	Bob Ojeda	.06	.05	.02
334	Steve Lyons	.03	.02	.01
335	Dave Righetti	.10	.08	.04
336	Steve Balboni	.06	.05	.02
337	Calvin Schiraldi	.03	.02	.01
338	Jim Adduci(FC)	.06	.05	.02
339	Scott Bailes	.03	.02	.01
340	Kirk Gibson	.15	.11	.06
341	Jim Deshaies	.03	.02	.01
342	Tom Brookens	.03	.02	.01
343	Future Star *(Gary Sheffield)*(FC)	1.50	1.25	.60
344	Tom Trebelhorn	.03	.02	.01
345	Charlie Hough	.06	.05	.02
346	Rex Hudler(FC)	.06	.05	.02
347	John Cerutti	.06	.05	.02
348	Ed Hearn	.03	.02	.01
349	*Ron Jones*(FC)	.30	.25	.12
350	Andy Van Slyke	.12	.09	.05
351	Giants Leaders (Bob Melvin)	.06	.05	.02
352	Rick Schu	.03	.02	.01
353	Marvell Wynne	.03	.02	.01
354	Larry Parrish	.06	.05	.02
355	Mark Langston	.08	.06	.03
356	Kevin Elster	.08	.06	.03
357	Jerry Reuss	.06	.05	.02
358	*Ricky Jordan*(FC)	1.25	.90	.50
359	Tommy John	.10	.08	.04
360	Ryne Sandberg	.20	.15	.08
361	Kelly Downs	.08	.06	.03
362	Jack Lazorko	.03	.02	.01
363	Rich Yett	.03	.02	.01
364	Rob Deer	.06	.05	.02
365	Mike Henneman	.08	.06	.03
366	Herm Winningham	.03	.02	.01
367	*Johnny Paredes*(FC)	.20	.15	.08
368	Brian Holton	.06	.05	.02
369	Ken Caminiti	.06	.05	.02
370	Dennis Eckersley	.10	.08	.04
371	Manny Lee	.03	.02	.01
372	Craig Lefferts	.03	.02	.01
373	Tracy Jones	.08	.06	.03
374	John Wathan	.06	.05	.02
375	Terry Pendleton	.08	.06	.03
376	Steve Lombardozzi	.03	.02	.01
377	Mike Smithson	.03	.02	.01
378	Checklist 265-396	.03	.02	.01
379	Tim Flannery	.03	.02	.01
380	Rickey Henderson	.30	.25	.12
381	Orioles Leaders (Larry Sheets)	.06	.05	.02
382	*John Smoltz*(FC)	.40	.30	.15
383	Howard Johnson	.08	.06	.03
384	Mark Salas	.03	.02	.01
385	Von Hayes	.08	.06	.03
386	Andres Galarraga AS	.08	.06	.03
387	Ryne Sandberg AS	.10	.08	.04
388	Bobby Bonilla AS	.08	.06	.03
389	Ozzie Smith AS	.08	.06	.03
390	Darryl Strawberry AS	.15	.11	.06
391	Andre Dawson AS	.10	.08	.04
392	Andy Van Slyke AS	.08	.06	.03
393	Gary Carter AS	.10	.08	.04
394	Orel Hershiser AS	.12	.09	.05
395	Danny Jackson AS	.08	.06	.03
396	Kirk Gibson AS	.08	.06	.03
397	Don Mattingly AS	.60	.45	.25
398	Julio Franco AS	.06	.05	.02
399	Wade Boggs AS	.35	.25	.14
400	Alan Trammell AS	.08	.06	.03
401	Jose Canseco AS	.50	.40	.20
402	Mike Greenwell AS	.20	.15	.08
403	Kirby Puckett AS	.12	.09	.05
404	Bob Boone AS	.06	.05	.02
405	Roger Clemens AS	.15	.11	.06
406	Frank Viola AS	.08	.06	.03
407	Dave Winfield AS	.12	.09	.05
408	Greg Walker	.06	.05	.02
409	Ken Dayley	.03	.02	.01
410	Jack Clark	.12	.09	.05
411	Mitch Williams	.06	.05	.02
412	Barry Lyons	.03	.02	.01
413	Mike Kingery	.03	.02	.01
414	Jim Fregosi	.03	.02	.01
415	Rich Gossage	.10	.08	.04
416	Fred Lynn	.10	.08	.04
417	Mike LaCoss	.03	.02	.01
418	Bob Dernier	.03	.02	.01
419	Tom Filer	.03	.02	.01
420	Joe Carter	.10	.08	.04
421	Kirk McCaskill	.06	.05	.02
422	Bo Diaz	.06	.05	.02
423	Brian Fisher	.06	.05	.02
424	Luis Polonia	.06	.05	.02
425	Jay Howell	.06	.05	.02
426	Danny Gladden	.03	.02	.01
427	Eric Show	.06	.05	.02
428	Craig Reynolds	.03	.02	.01
429	Twins Leaders (Greg Gagne)	.06	.05	.02
430	Mark Gubicza	.08	.06	.03
431	Luis Rivera	.06	.05	.02
432	*Chad Kreuter*(FC)	.20	.15	.08
433	Albert Hall	.03	.02	.01
434	*Ken Patterson*(FC)	.15	.11	.06
435	Len Dykstra	.08	.06	.03
436	Bobby Meacham	.03	.02	.01
437	#1 Draft Pick *(Andy Benes)*	1.25	.90	.50
438	Greg Gross	.03	.02	.01
439	Frank DiPino	.03	.02	.01
440	Bobby Bonilla	.10	.08	.04
441	Jerry Reed	.03	.02	.01
442	Jose Oquendo	.03	.02	.01
443	*Rod Nichols*(FC)	.15	.11	.06
444	Moose Stubing	.03	.02	.01
445	Matt Nokes	.15	.11	.06
446	Rob Murphy	.03	.02	.01
447	Donell Nixon	.03	.02	.01
448	Eric Plunk	.03	.02	.01
449	Carmelo Martinez	.03	.02	.01
450	Roger Clemens	.40	.30	.15
451	Mark Davidson	.06	.05	.02
452	*Israel Sanchez*	.12	.09	.05
453	Tom Prince(FC)	.08	.06	.03
454	Paul Assenmacher	.03	.02	.01
455	Johnny Ray	.06	.05	.02
456	Tim Belcher	.08	.06	.03
457	Mackey Sasser	.06	.05	.02
458	*Donn Pall*(FC)	.20	.15	.08
459	Mariners Leaders (Dave Valle)	.06	.05	.02
460	Dave Stieb	.08	.06	.03
461	Buddy Bell	.06	.05	.02
462	Jose Guzman	.08	.06	.03
463	Steve Lake	.03	.02	.01
464	Bryn Smith	.03	.02	.01
465	Mark Grace	2.00	1.50	.80
466	Chuck Crim	.03	.02	.01
467	Jim Walewander	.03	.02	.01
468	Henry Cotto	.03	.02	.01
469	*Jose Bautista*	.20	.15	.08
470	Lance Parrish	.12	.09	.05
471	*Steve Curry*(FC)	.20	.15	.08
472	Brian Harper	.03	.02	.01
473	Don Robinson	.03	.02	.01
474	Bob Rodgers	.03	.02	.01
475	Dave Parker	.10	.08	.04
476	Jon Perlman(FC)	.06	.05	.02
477	Dick Schofield	.03	.02	.01
478	Doug Drabek	.06	.05	.02
479	*Mike Macfarlane*	.20	.15	.08
480	Keith Hernandez	.20	.15	.08
481	Chris Brown	.06	.05	.02
482	*Steve Peters*	.12	.09	.05
483	Mickey Hatcher	.03	.02	.01
484	Steve Shields	.03	.02	.01
485	Hubie Brooks	.08	.06	.03
486	Jack McDowell	.08	.06	.03
487	Scott Lusader(FC)	.08	.06	.03
488	Kevin Coffman	.06	.05	.02
489	Phillies Leaders (Mike Schmidt)	.12	.09	.05
490	*Chris Sabo*	1.00	.70	.40
491	Mike Birkbeck	.03	.02	.01
492	Alan Ashby	.03	.02	.01
493	Todd Benzinger	.10	.08	.04
494	Shane Rawley	.06	.05	.02
495	Candy Maldonado	.06	.05	.02
496	Dwayne Henry	.03	.02	.01
497	Pete Stanicek	.12	.09	.05
498	Dave Valle	.03	.02	.01
499	*Don Heinkel*(FC)	.15	.11	.06
500	Jose Canseco	1.25	.90	.50
501	Vance Law	.06	.05	.02
502	Duane Ward	.03	.02	.01
503	Al Newman	.03	.02	.01
504	Bob Walk	.03	.02	.01
505	Pete Rose	.20	.15	.08
506	Kirt Manwaring	.10	.08	.04
507	Steve Farr	.03	.02	.01
508	Wally Backman	.06	.05	.02

		MT	NR MT	EX
509	Bud Black	.03	.02	.01
510	Bob Horner	.08	.06	.03
511	Richard Dotson	.06	.05	.02
512	Donnie Hill	.03	.02	.01
513	Jesse Orosco	.06	.05	.02
514	Chet Lemon	.06	.05	.02
515	Barry Larkin	.20	.15	.08
516	Eddie Whitson	.03	.02	.01
517	Greg Brock	.06	.05	.02
518	Bruce Ruffin	.03	.02	.01
519	Yankees Leaders (Willie Randolph)	.03	.02	.01
520	Rick Sutcliffe	.08	.06	.03
521	Mickey Tettleton	.03	.02	.01
522	*Randy Kramer*(FC)	.12	.09	.05
523	Andres Thomas	.06	.05	.02
524	Checklist 397-528	.03	.02	.01
525	Chili Davis	.06	.05	.02
526	Wes Gardner	.06	.05	.02
527	Dave Henderson	.08	.06	.03
528	*Luis Medina*(FC)	.25	.20	.10
529	Tom Foley	.03	.02	.01
530	Nolan Ryan	.35	.25	.14
531	Dave Hengel(FC)	.08	.06	.03
532	Jerry Browne	.03	.02	.01
533	Andy Hawkins	.03	.02	.01
534	Doc Edwards	.03	.02	.01
535	Todd Worrell	.08	.06	.03
536	Joel Skinner	.03	.02	.01
537	Pete Smith	.08	.06	.03
538	Juan Castillo	.03	.02	.01
539	Barry Jones	.03	.02	.01
540	Bo Jackson	.50	.40	.20
541	Cecil Fielder	.25	.20	.10
542	Todd Frohwirth	.06	.05	.02
543	Damon Berryhill	.15	.11	.06
544	Jeff Sellers	.03	.02	.01
545	Mookie Wilson	.06	.05	.02
546	Mark Williamson	.06	.05	.02
547	Mark McLemore	.03	.02	.01
548	Bobby Witt	.08	.06	.03
549	Cubs Leaders (Jamie Moyer)	.03	.02	.01
550	Orel Hershiser	.20	.15	.08
551	Randy Ready	.03	.02	.01
552	Greg Cadaret	.06	.05	.02
553	Luis Salazar	.03	.02	.01
554	Nick Esasky	.06	.05	.02
555	Bert Blyleven	.10	.08	.04
556	Bruce Fields(FC)	.06	.05	.02
557	*Keith Miller*(FC)	.15	.11	.06
558	Dan Pasqua	.08	.06	.03
559	Juan Agosto	.03	.02	.01
560	Rock Raines	.25	.20	.10
561	Luis Aguayo	.03	.02	.01
562	Danny Cox	.06	.05	.02
563	Bill Schroeder	.03	.02	.01
564	Russ Nixon	.03	.02	.01
565	Jeff Russell	.03	.02	.01
566	Al Pedrique	.03	.02	.01
567	David Wells	.08	.06	.03
568	Mickey Brantley	.03	.02	.01
569	*German Jimenez*(FC)	.08	.06	.03
570	Tony Gwynn	.30	.25	.12
571	Billy Ripken	.06	.05	.02
572	Atlee Hammaker	.03	.02	.01
573	#1 Draft Pick *(Jim Abbott)*	1.50	1.25	.60
574	Dave Clark	.06	.05	.02
575	Juan Samuel	.10	.08	.04
576	Greg Minton	.03	.02	.01
577	Randy Bush	.03	.02	.01
578	John Morris	.03	.02	.01
579	Astros Leaders (Glenn Davis)	.08	.06	.03
580	Harold Reynolds	.06	.05	.02
581	Gene Nelson	.03	.02	.01
582	Mike Marshall	.10	.08	.04
583	*Paul Gibson*(FC)	.15	.11	.06
584	Randy Velarde(FC)	.10	.08	.04
585	Harold Baines	.10	.08	.04
586	Joe Boever	.03	.02	.01
587	Mike Stanley	.03	.02	.01
588	*Luis Alicea*	.15	.11	.06
589	Dave Meads	.03	.02	.01
590	Andres Galarraga	.12	.09	.05
591	Jeff Musselman	.06	.05	.02
592	John Cangelosi	.03	.02	.01
593	Drew Hall	.10	.08	.04
594	Jimy Williams	.03	.02	.01
595	Teddy Higuera	.08	.06	.03
596	Kurt Stillwell	.06	.05	.02
597	*Terry Taylor*(FC)	.12	.09	.05
598	Ken Gerhart	.06	.05	.02
599	Tom Candiotti	.03	.02	.01
600	Wade Boggs	.90	.70	.35
601	Dave Dravecky	.06	.05	.02
602	Devon White	.10	.08	.04
603	Frank Tanana	.06	.05	.02
604	Paul O'Neill	.03	.02	.01
605a	Bob Welch (missing Complete Major League Pitching Record line)	2.50	2.00	1.00
605b	Bob Welch (contains Complete Major League Pitching Record line)	.08	.06	.03
606	Rick Dempsey	.06	.05	.02
607	#1 Draft Pick *(Willie Ansley)*(FC)	.50	.40	.20
608	Phil Bradley	.08	.06	.03
609	Tigers Leaders (Frank Tanana)	.06	.05	.02
610	Randy Myers	.08	.06	.03
611	Don Slaught	.03	.02	.01
612	Dan Quisenberry	.06	.05	.02
613	*Gary Varsho*(FC)	.20	.15	.08
614	Joe Hesketh	.03	.02	.01
615	Robin Yount	.25	.20	.10
616	*Steve Rosenberg*(FC)	.15	.11	.06
617	*Mark Parent*	.15	.11	.06
618	Rance Mulliniks	.03	.02	.01
619	Checklist 529-660	.03	.02	.01
620	Barry Bonds	.10	.08	.04
621	Rick Mahler	.03	.02	.01
622	Stan Javier	.03	.02	.01
623	Fred Toliver	.03	.02	.01
624	Jack McKeon	.03	.02	.01

		MT	NR MT	EX
625	Eddie Murray	.25	.20	.10
626	Jeff Reed	.03	.02	.01
627	Greg Harris	.03	.02	.01
628	Matt Williams	.10	.08	.04
629	Pete O'Brien	.06	.05	.02
630	Mike Greenwell	.50	.40	.20
631	Dave Bergman	.03	.02	.01
632	*Bryan Harvey*	.20	.15	.08
633	Daryl Boston	.03	.02	.01
634	Marvin Freeman(FC)	.08	.06	.03
635	Willie Randolph	.06	.05	.02
636	Bill Wilkinson	.06	.05	.02
637	Carmen Castillo	.03	.02	.01
638	Floyd Bannister	.06	.05	.02
639	Athletics Leaders (Walt Weiss)	.15	.11	.06
640	Willie McGee	.10	.08	.04
641	Curt Young	.06	.05	.02
642	Argenis Salazar	.03	.02	.01
643	*Louie Meadows*(FC)	.12	.09	.05
644	Lloyd McClendon	.03	.02	.01
645	Jack Morris	.12	.09	.05
646	Kevin Bass	.06	.05	.02
647	*Randy Johnson*(FC)	.50	.40	.20
648	Future Star *(Sandy Alomar)*(FC)	1.25	.90	.50
649	Stewart Cliburn	.03	.02	.01
650	Kirby Puckett	.25	.20	.10
651	Tom Niedenfuer	.06	.05	.02
652	Rich Gedman	.06	.05	.02
653	*Tommy Barrett*(FC)	.12	.09	.05
654	Whitey Herzog	.06	.05	.02
655	Dave Magadan	.08	.06	.03
656	Ivan Calderon	.06	.05	.02
657	Joe Magrane	.08	.06	.03
658	R.J. Reynolds	.03	.02	.01
659	Al Leiter	.15	.11	.06
660	Will Clark	.50	.40	.20
661	Turn Back The Clock (Dwight Gooden)	.20	.15	.08
662	Turn Back The Clock (Lou Brock)	.08	.06	.03
663	Turn Back The Clock (Hank Aaron)	.15	.11	.06
664	Turn Back The Clock (Gil Hodges)	.06	.05	.02
665	Turn Back The Clock (Tony Oliva)	.06	.05	.02
666	Randy St. Claire	.03	.02	.01
667	Dwayne Murphy	.06	.05	.02
668	Mike Bielecki	.03	.02	.01
669	Dodgers Leaders (Orel Hershiser)	.12	.09	.05
670	Kevin Seitzer	.25	.20	.10
671	Jim Gantner	.03	.02	.01
672	Allan Anderson	.06	.05	.02
673	Don Baylor	.08	.06	.03
674	Otis Nixon	.03	.02	.01
675	Bruce Hurst	.08	.06	.03
676	Ernie Riles	.03	.02	.01
677	Dave Schmidt	.03	.02	.01
678	Dion James	.03	.02	.01
679	Willie Fraser	.03	.02	.01
680	Gary Carter	.15	.11	.06
681	Jeff Robinson	.10	.08	.04
682	Rick Leach	.03	.02	.01
683	*Jose Cecena*	.15	.11	.06
684	Dave Johnson	.06	.05	.02
685	Jeff Treadway	.10	.08	.04
686	Scott Terry	.08	.06	.03
687	Alvin Davis	.10	.08	.04
688	Zane Smith	.06	.05	.02
689	Stan Jefferson	.03	.02	.01
690	Doug Jones	.10	.08	.04
691	Roberto Kelly	.25	.20	.10
692	Steve Ontiveros	.03	.02	.01
693	*Pat Borders*	.20	.15	.08
694	Les Lancaster	.06	.05	.02
695	Carlton Fisk	.20	.15	.08
696	Don August	.08	.06	.03
697	Franklin Stubbs	.03	.02	.01
698	Keith Atherton	.03	.02	.01
699	Pirates Leaders (Al Pedrique)	.06	.05	.02
700	Don Mattingly	1.25	.90	.50
701	Storm Davis	.08	.06	.03
702	Jamie Quirk	.03	.02	.01
703	Scott Garrelts	.03	.02	.01
704	*Carlos Quintana*(FC)	.40	.30	.15
705	Terry Kennedy	.06	.05	.02
706	Pete Incaviglia	.08	.06	.03
707	Steve Jeltz	.03	.02	.01
708	Chuck Finley	.03	.02	.01
709	Tom Herr	.06	.05	.02
710	Dave Cone	.30	.25	.12
711	*Candy Sierra*(FC)	.12	.09	.05
712	Bill Swift	.03	.02	.01
713	#1 Draft Pick *(Ty Griffin)*	.70	.50	.25
714	Joe Morgan	.03	.02	.01
715	Tony Pena	.06	.05	.02
716	Wayne Tolleson	.03	.02	.01
717	Jamie Moyer	.03	.02	.01
718	Glenn Braggs	.06	.05	.02
719	Danny Darwin	.03	.02	.01
720	Tim Wallach	.08	.06	.03
721	*Ron Tingley*(FC)	.12	.09	.05
722	Todd Stottlemyre	.15	.11	.06
723	Rafael Belliard	.03	.02	.01
724	Jerry Don Gleaton	.03	.02	.01
725	Terry Steinbach	.08	.06	.03
726	Dickie Thon	.03	.02	.01
727	Joe Orsulak	.03	.02	.01
728	Charlie Puleo	.03	.02	.01
729	Rangers Leaders (Steve Buechele)	.06	.05	.02
730	Danny Jackson	.12	.09	.05
731	Mike Young	.03	.02	.01
732	Steve Buechele	.03	.02	.01
733	*Randy Bockus*(FC)	.06	.05	.02
734	Jody Reed	.10	.08	.04
735	Roger McDowell	.08	.06	.03
736	Jeff Hamilton	.06	.05	.02
737	*Norm Charlton*(FC)	.35	.25	.14
738	Darnell Coles	.06	.05	.02

		MT	NR MT	EX
739	Brook Jacoby	.08	.06	.03
740	Dan Plesac	.08	.06	.03
741	Ken Phelps	.06	.05	.02
742	Future Star *(Mike Harkey)*(FC)	.40	.30	.15
743	Mike Heath	.03	.02	.01
744	Roger Craig	.06	.05	.02
745	Fred McGriff	.40	.30	.15
746	*German Gonzalez*(FC)	.20	.15	.08
747	Wil Tejada(FC)	.06	.05	.02
748	Jimmy Jones	.03	.02	.01
749	Rafael Ramirez	.03	.02	.01
750	Bret Saberhagen	.12	.09	.05
751	Ken Oberkfell	.03	.02	.01
752	Jim Gott	.03	.02	.01
753	Jose Uribe	.03	.02	.01
754	Bob Brower	.03	.02	.01
755	Mike Scioscia	.06	.05	.02
756	*Scott Medvin*(FC)	.20	.15	.08
757	*Brady Anderson*	.30	.25	.12
758	Gene Walter	.03	.02	.01
759	Brewers Leaders (Rob Deer)	.06	.05	.02
760	Lee Smith	.08	.06	.03
761	*Dante Bichette*(FC)	.25	.20	.10
762	Bobby Thigpen	.08	.06	.03
763	Dave Martinez	.06	.05	.02
764	#1 Draft Pick *(Robin Ventura)*	1.00	.70	.40
765	Glenn Davis	.20	.15	.08
766	Cecilio Guante	.03	.02	.01
767	*Mike Capel*(FC)	.15	.11	.06
768	Bill Wegman	.03	.02	.01
769	Junior Ortiz	.03	.02	.01
770	Alan Trammell	.15	.11	.06
771	Ron Kittle	.06	.05	.02
772	Ron Oester	.03	.02	.01
773	Keith Moreland	.06	.05	.02
774	Frank Robinson	.08	.06	.03
775	Jeff Reardon	.08	.06	.03
776	Nelson Liriano	.06	.05	.02
777	Ted Power	.03	.02	.01
778	Bruce Benedict	.03	.02	.01
779	Craig McMurtry	.03	.02	.01
780	Pedro Guerrero	.12	.09	.05
781	*Greg Briley*(FC)	.70	.50	.30
782	Checklist 661-792	.03	.02	.01
783	*Trevor Wilson*(FC)	.15	.11	.06
784	#1 Draft Pick *(Steve Avery)*(FC)	1.25	.90	.50
785	Ellis Burks	.50	.40	.20
786	Melido Perez	.08	.06	.03
787	*Dave West*(FC)	.50	.40	.20
788	Mike Morgan	.03	.02	.01
789	Royals Leaders (Bo Jackson)	.15	.11	.06
790	Sid Fernandez	.08	.06	.03
791	Jim Lindeman	.03	.02	.01
792	Rafael Santana	.03	.02	.01

A player's name in italic type indicates a rookie card.

1989 Topps All-Star Glossy Set of 22

Bearing the same design and style of the past two years, Topps featured the top first-year players from the 1988 season in this glossy set. The full-color player photos appears beneath the "1988 Rookies" banner. The player's name is displayed beneath the photo. The flip side features the "1988 Rookies Commemorative Set" logo followed by the player's name, position, team, and card number. The glossy All-Stars are included in the Topps 1989 Jumbo Paks.

		MT	NR MT	EX
Complete Set:		3.50	2.75	1.50
Common Player:		.15	.11	.06
1	Roberto Alomar	.25	.20	.10
2	Brady Anderson	.20	.15	.08
3	Tim Belcher	.20	.15	.08
4	Damon Berryhill	.15	.11	.06
5	Jay Buhner	.20	.15	.11
6	Kevin Elster	.15	.11	.06
7	Cecil Espy	.15	.11	.06
8	Dave Gallagher	.15	.11	.06
9	Ron Gant	.15	.11	.06
10	Paul Gibson	.15	.11	.06
11	Mark Grace	.90	.70	.35
12	Darrin Jackson	.15	.11	.06
13	Gregg Jefferies	1.00	.70	.40
14	Ricky Jordan	.50	.40	.20
15	Al Leiter	.15	.11	.06
16	Melido Perez	.15	.11	.06
17	Chris Sabo	.35	.25	.14
18	Nelson Santovenia	.20	.15	.08
19	Mackey Sasser			

1989 Topps All-Star Glossy Set of 60

For the seventh straight year Topps issued this "send-away" glossy set. Divided into six 10-card sets, it was available only by sending in special offer cards from the 1989 Topps wax packs. The 2-1/2" by 3-1/2" cards feature full-color photos bordered in white with a thin yellow frame. The player's name appears in small print in the lower right corner. Red-and-blue-printed flip sides provide basic information including player's name, team, and position. Any of the six 10-card sets were available for $1.25 and six special offer cards. The set was also made available in its complete 60-card set form for $7.50 and 18 special offer cards.

		MT	NR MT	EX
Complete Set:		12.00	9.00	4.75
Common Player:		.15	.11	.06
1	Kirby Puckett	.50	.40	.20
2	Eric Davis	.70	.50	.30
3	Joe Carter	.20	.15	.08
4	Andy Van Slyke	.20	.15	.08
5	Wade Boggs	1.00	.70	.40
6	Dave Cone	.25	.20	.10
7	Kent Hrbek	.15	.11	.06
8	Darryl Strawberry	.70	.50	.30
9	Jay Buhner	.15	.11	.06
10	Ron Gant	.15	.11	.06
11	Will Clark	1.00	.70	.40
12	Jose Canseco	1.50	1.25	.60
13	Juan Samuel	.15	.11	.06
14	George Brett	.25	.20	.10
15	Benny Santiago	.20	.15	.08
16	Dennis Eckersley	.15	.11	.06
17	Gary Carter	.15	.11	.06
18	Frank Viola	.20	.15	.08
19	Roberto Alomar	.30	.25	.12
20	Paul Gibson	.15	.11	.06
21	Dave Winfield	.20	.15	.08
22	Howard Johnson	.35	.25	.14
23	Roger Clemens	.40	.30	.15
24	Bobby Bonilla	.25	.20	.10
25	Alan Trammell	.20	.15	.08
26	Kevin McReynolds	.20	.15	.08
27	George Bell	.20	.15	.08
28	Bruce Hurst	.15	.11	.06
29	Mark Grace	1.00	.70	.40
30	Tim Belcher	.20	.15	.08
31	Mike Greenwell	.80	.60	.30
32	Glenn Davis	.15	.11	.06
33	Gary Gaetti	.15	.11	.06
34	Ryne Sandberg	.30	.25	.12
35	Rickey Henderson	.35	.25	.14
36	Dwight Evans	.15	.11	.06
37	Doc Gooden	.50	.40	.20
38	Robin Yount	.25	.20	.10
39	Damon Berryhill	.15	.11	.06
40	Chris Sabo	.20	.15	.11
41	Mark McGwire	1.00	.70	.40
42	Ozzie Smith	.25	.20	.10
43	Paul Molitor	.20	.15	.08
44	Andres Galarraga	.30	.25	.12
45	Dave Stewart	.15	.11	.06
46	Tom Browning	.15	.11	.06
47	Cal Ripken	.50	.40	.20
48	Orel Hershiser	.40	.30	.15
49	Dave Gallagher	.20	.15	.08
50	Walt Weiss	.20	.15	.08
51	Don Mattingly	2.50	2.00	1.00
52	Tony Fernandez	.20	.15	.08
53	Rock Raines	.20	.15	.08
54	Jeff Reardon	.15	.11	.06
55	Kirk Gibson	.20	.15	.08
56	Jack Clark	.20	.15	.08
57	Danny Jackson	.15	.11	.06
58	Tony Gwynn	.60	.45	.25
59	Cecil Espy	.15	.11	.06
60	Jody Reed	.15	.11	.06

1989 Topps American Baseball

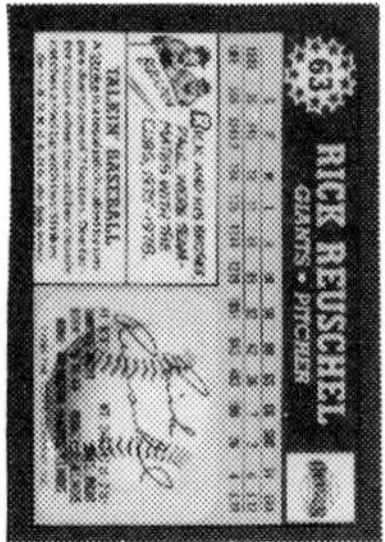

For the second consecutive year Topps released an 88-card set of baseball cards available in both the United States and the United Kingdom. The mini-sized cards (2-1/4" by 3") feature full-color photos on the card fronts. The cards are printed on white stock with a low gloss finish. The player action photo is outlined in red, white, and blue and framed in white. The card backs are printed horizontally and include a characterization cartoon along with biographical information and statistics. The cards are sold in packs of five cards with a stick of bubble gum.

		MT	NR MT	EX
Complete Set:		7.00	5.25	2.75
Common Player:		.08	.06	.03
1	Brady Anderson	.08	.06	.03
2	Harold Baines	.15	.11	.06
3	George Bell	.15	.11	.06
4	Wade Boggs	1.00	.70	.40
5	Barry Bonds	.20	.15	.08
6	Bobby Bonilla	.20	.15	.08
7	George Brett	.15	.11	.06
8	Hubie Brooks	.08	.06	.03
9	Tom Brunansky	.08	.06	.03
10	Jay Buhner	.08	.06	.03
11	Brett Butler	.08	.06	.03
12	Jose Canseco	1.25	.90	.50
13	Joe Carter	.15	.11	.06
14	Jack Clark	.08	.06	.03
15	Will Clark	.80	.60	.30
16	Roger Clemens	.30	.25	.12
17	Dave Cone	.08	.06	.03
18	Alvin Davis	.08	.06	.03
19	Eric Davis	.30	.25	.12
20	Glenn Davis	.08	.06	.03
21	Andre Dawson	.12	.09	.05
22	Bill Doran	.08	.06	.03
23	Dennis Eckersley	.08	.06	.03
24	Dwight Evans	.08	.06	.03
25	Tony Fernandez	.08	.06	.03
26	Carlton Fisk	.08	.06	.03
27	John Franco	.08	.06	.03
28	Andres Galarraga	.15	.11	.06
29	Ron Gant	.08	.06	.03
30	Kirk Gibson	.08	.06	.03
31	Doc Gooden	.25	.20	.10
32	Mike Greenwell	.50	.40	.20
33	Mark Gubicza	.08	.06	.03
34	Pedro Gurrero	.12	.09	.05
35	Ozzie Guillen	.08	.06	.03
36	Tony Gwynn	.15	.11	.06
37	Rickey Henderson	.15	.11	.06
38	Orel Hershiser	.15	.11	.06
39	Teddy Higuera	.08	.06	.03
40	Charlie Hough	.08	.06	.03
41	Kent Hrbek	.12	.09	.05
42	Bruce Hurst	.08	.06	.03
43	Bo Jackson	.50	.40	.20
44	Gregg Jefferies	.60	.45	.25
45	Ricky Jordan	.25	.20	.10
46	Wally Joyner	.15	.11	.06
47	Mark Langston	.12	.09	.05
48	Mike Marshall	.08	.06	.03
49	Don Mattingly	2.00	1.50	.80
50	Fred McGriff	.35	.25	.14
51	Mark McGwire	1.00	.70	.40
52	Kevin McReynolds	.15	.11	.06
53	Paul Molitor	.08	.06	.03
54	Jack Morris	.08	.06	.03
55	Dale Murphy	.15	.11	.06
56	Eddie Murray	.10	.08	.04
57	Pete O'Brien	.08	.06	.03
58	Rafael Palmeiro	.08	.06	.03
59	Gerald Perry	.08	.06	.03
60	Kirby Puckett	.30	.25	.12
61	Rock Raines	.15	.11	.06
62	Johnny Ray	.08	.06	.03
63	Rick Reuschel	.08	.06	.03
64	Cal Ripken	.15	.11	.06
65	Chris Sabo	.15	.11	.06
66	Juan Samuel	.08	.06	.03
67	Ryane Sandberg	.15	.11	.06
68	Benny Santiago	.15	.11	.06
69	Steve Sax	.08	.06	.03
70	Mike Schmidt	.20	.15	.11
71	Ruben Sierra	.20	.15	.11
72	Ozzie Smith	.15	.11	.06
73	Cory Snyder	.08	.06	.03
74	Dave Stewart	.08	.06	.03
75	Darryl Strawberry	.25	.20	.10
76	Greg Swindell	.15	.11	.06
77	Alan Trammell	.15	.11	.06
78	Fernando Valenzuela	.08	.06	.03
79	Andy Van Slyke	.20	.15	.08
80	Frank Viola	.20	.15	.08
81	Claudell Washington	.08	.06	.03
82	Walt Weiss	.08	.06	.03
83	Lou Whitaker	.08	.06	.03
84	Dave Winfield	.20	.15	.08
85	Mike Witt	.08	.06	.03
86	Gerald Young	.08	.06	.03
87	Robin Yount	.20	.15	.08
88	Checklist	.08	.06	.03

NOTE: A card number in parentheses ( ) indicates the set is unnumbered.

The values quoted are intended to reflect the market price.

1989 Topps Batting Leaders

For the second straight year, Topps issued an 88-card set of mini (2-1/4" by 3") cards aimed at the Great Britain hobby market. The fronts of the cards display a red, white and blue color scheme, with the player's name below the photo and his team and position above. The colorful backs of the cards include 1988 and lifetime stats, brief biographical data and a cartoon panel illustrating some fact about the player. Beneath the cartoon, a baseball term is explained under a "Talkin' Baseball" heading. The set, which features the game's top stars, was intended to introduce fans in Great Britain to America's Pastime, but the sets were also available from hobby dealers in the U.S. The active career batting leaders are showcased in this 22-card set. The standard-size cards are printed on super glossy stock with full-color photos. A unique left-handed or right-handed batter creates one of the vertical borders. The Topps logo appears in the upper left portion of the photo, while a "Top Active Career Batting Leaders" cup is displayed in the lower left. The player's name appears above the photo. This set is specially numbered in accordance to career batting average. Wade Boggs is featured on card number one as the top active career batting leader. The flip sides present batting statistics. One batting leader card was included in each K-mart blister pack, which also includes 100 cards from the 1989 regular Topps set.

Complete Set:
Common Player:

1 Wade Boggs

1989 Topps Big Baseball

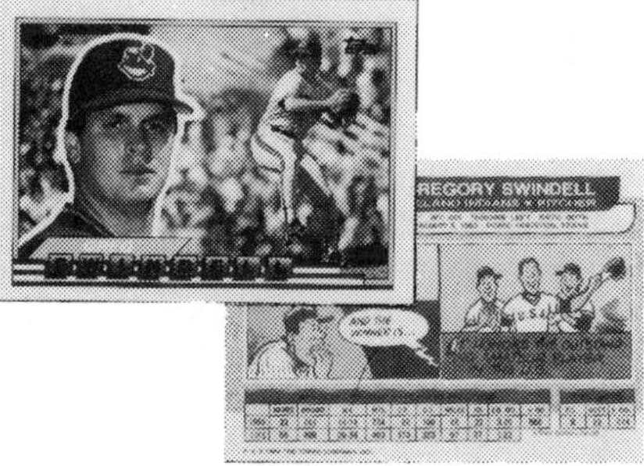

Known by collectors as Topps "Big Baseball," the cards in this 330-card set measure 2-5/8" by 3-3/4" and are patterned after the 1956 Topps cards. The glossy card fronts are horizontally-designed and include two photos of each player, a posed head shot alongside an action photo. The backs include 1988 and career stats, but are dominated by a color cartoon featuring the player. The set was issued in three series of 110 cards each.

		MT	NR MT	EX
Complete Set:		25.00	20.00	10.00
1	Common Player:, Orel Hershiser	.15	.11	.06
2	Harold Reynolds	.08	.06	.03
3	Jody Davis	.05	.04	.02
4	Greg Walker	.05	.04	.02
5	Barry Bonds	.08	.06	.03
6	Bret Saberhagen	.12	.09	.05
7	Johnny Ray	.05	.04	.02
8	Mike Fiore	.20	.15	.08
9	Juan Castillo	.05	.04	.02
10	Todd Burns	.05	.04	.02
11	Carmelo Martinez	.05	.04	.02
12	Geno Petralli	.05	.04	.02

		MT	NR MT	EX
13	Mel Hall	.05	.04	.02
14	Tom Browning	.08	.06	.03
15	Fred McGriff	.15	.11	.06
16	Kevin Elster	.05	.04	.02
17	Tim Leary	.05	.04	.02
18	Jim Rice	.05	.04	.02
19	Bret Barberie	.15	.11	.06
20	Jay Buhner	.05	.04	.02
21	Atlee Hammaker	.05	.04	.02
22	Lou Whitaker	.05	.04	.02
23	Paul Runge	.05	.04	.02
24	Carlton Fisk	.08	.06	.03
25	Jose Lind	.05	.04	.02
26	Mark Gubicza	.08	.06	.03
27	Billy Ripken	.05	.04	.02
28	Mike Pagliarulo	.05	.04	.02
29	Jim Deshaies	.05	.04	.02
30	Mark McLemore	.05	.04	.02
31	Scott Terry	.05	.04	.02
32	Franklin Stubbs	.05	.04	.02
33	Don August	.05	.04	.02
34	Mark McGwire	1.00	.70	.40
35	Eric Show	.05	.04	.02
36	Cecil Espy	.05	.04	.02
37	Ron Tingley	.05	.04	.02
38	Mickey Brantley	.05	.04	.02
39	Paul O'Neill	.05	.04	.02
40	Ed Sprague	.35	.25	.14
41	Len Dykstra	.05	.04	.02
42	Roger Clemens	.25	.20	.10
43	Ron Gant	.05	.04	.02
44	Dan Pasqua	.05	.04	.02
45	Jeff Robinson	.05	.04	.02
46	George Brett	.15	.11	.06
47	Bryn Smith	.05	.04	.02
48	Mike Marshall	.05	.04	.02
49	Doug Robbins	.15	.11	.06
50	Don Mattingly	1.50	1.25	.60
51	Mike Scott	.08	.06	.03
52	Steve Jeltz	.05	.04	.02
53	Dick Schofield	.05	.04	.02
54	Tom Brunansky	.08	.06	.03
55	Gary Sheffield	1.00	.70	.40
56	Dave Valle	.05	.04	.02
57	Carney Lansford	.08	.06	.03
58	Tony Gwynn	.15	.11	.06
59	Checklist	.05	.04	.02
60	Damon Berryhill	.05	.04	.02
61	Jack Morris	.05	.04	.02
62	Brett Butler	.05	.04	.02
63	Mickey Hatcher	.05	.04	.02
64	Bruce Sutter	.05	.04	.02
65	Robin Ventura	.80	.60	.30
66	Junior Oritiz	.05	.04	.02
67	Pat Tabler	.05	.04	.02
68	Greg Swindell	.08	.06	.03
69	Jeff Branson	.20	.15	.08
70	Manny Lee	.05	.04	.02
71	Dave Magadan	.05	.04	.02
72	Rich Gedman	.05	.04	.02
73	Rock Raines	.08	.06	.03
74	Mike Maddux	.05	.04	.02
75	Jim Presley	.05	.04	.02
76	Chuck Finley	.05	.04	.02
77	Jose Oquendo	.05	.04	.02
78	Rob Deer	.05	.04	.02
79	Jay Howell	.05	.04	.02
80	Terry Steinbach	.08	.06	.03
81	Eddie Whitson	.05	.04	.02
82	Ruben Sierra	.20	.15	.08
83	Bruce Benedict	.05	.04	.02
84	Fred Manrique	.05	.04	.02
85	John Smiley	.05	.04	.02
86	Mike Macfarlane	.05	.04	.02
87	Rene Gonzales	.05	.04	.02
88	Charles Hudson	.05	.04	.02
90	Les Straker	.05	.04	.02
91	Carmen Castillo	.05	.04	.02
92	Tracy Woodson	.05	.04	.02
93	Tino Martinez	.70	.50	.30
94	Herm Winningham	.05	.04	.02
95	Kelly Gruber	.05	.04	.02
96	Terry Leach	.05	.04	.02
97	Jody Reed	.05	.04	.02
98	Nelson Santovenia	.05	.04	.02
99	Tony Armas	.05	.04	.02
100	Greg Brock	.05	.04	.02
101	Dave Stewart	.05	.04	.02
102	Roberto Alomar	.08	.06	.03
103	Jim Sundberg	.05	.04	.02
104	Albert Hall	.05	.04	.02
105	Steve Lyons	.05	.04	.02
106	Sid Bream	.05	.04	.02
107	Danny Tartabull	.08	.06	.03
108	Rick Dempsey	.05	.04	.02
109	Rich Renteria	.05	.04	.02
110	Ozzie Smith	.08	.06	.03
111	Steve Sax	.08	.06	.03
112	Kelly Downs	.05	.04	.02
113	Larry Sheets	.05	.04	.02
114	Andy Benes	1.00	.70	.40
115	Pete O'Brien	.05	.04	.02
116	Kevin McReynolds	.08	.06	.03
117	Juan Berenguer	.05	.04	.02
118	Billy Hatcher	.05	.04	.02
119	Rick Cerone	.05	.04	.02
120	Andre Dawson	.08	.06	.03
121	Storm Davis	.05	.04	.02
122	Devon White	.05	.04	.02
123	Alan Trammell	.08	.06	.03
124	Vince Coleman	.08	.06	.03
125	Al Leiter	.05	.04	.02
126	Dale Sveum	.05	.04	.02
127	Pete Incaviglia	.05	.04	.02
128	Dave Stieb	.08	.06	.03
129	Kevin Mitchell	.30	.25	.12
130	Dave Schmidt	.05	.04	.02
131	Gary Redus	.05	.04	.02
132	Ron Robinson	.05	.04	.02
133	Darnell Coles	.05	.04	.02
134	Benny Santiago	.08	.06	.03
135	John Farrell	.05	.04	.02
136	Willie Wilson	.05	.04	.02
137	Steve Bedrosian	.05	.04	.02
138	Don Slaught	.05	.04	.02
139	Darryl Strawberry	.25	.20	.10
140	Frank Viola	.10	.08	.04
141	Dave Silvestri	.20	.15	.08
142	Carlos Quintana	.05	.04	.02
143	Vance Law	.05	.04	.02
144	Dave Parker	.05	.04	.02
145	Tim Belcher	.05	.04	.02
146	Will Clark	.90	.70	.35
147	Mark Williamson	.05	.04	.02
148	Ozzie Guillen	.05	.04	.02
149	Kirk McCaskill	.05	.04	.02
150	Pat Sheridan	.05	.04	.02
151	Terry Pendleton	.05	.04	.02
152	Roberto Kelly	.05	.04	.02
153	Joey Meyer	.05	.04	.02
154	Mark Grant	.05	.04	.02
155	Joe Carter	.08	.06	.03
156	Steve Buechele	.05	.04	.02
157	Tony Fernandez	.08	.06	.03
158	Jeff Reed	.05	.04	.02
159	Bobby Bonilla	.08	.06	.03
160	Henry Cotto	.05	.04	.02
161	Kurt Stillwell	.05	.04	.02
162	Mickey Morandini	.25	.20	.10
163	Robby Thompson	.05	.04	.02
164	Rick Schu	.05	.04	.02
165	Stan Jefferson	.05	.04	.02
166	Ron Darling	.05	.04	.02
167	Kirby Puckett	.25	.20	.10
168	Bill Doran	.05	.04	.02
169	Dennis Lamp	.05	.04	.02
170	Ty Griffin	.60	.45	.25
171	Ron Hassey	.05	.04	.02
172	Dale Murphy	.08	.06	.03
173	Andres Galarraga	.08	.06	.03
174	Tim Flannery	.05	.04	.02
175	Cory Snyder	.05	.04	.02
176	Checklist	.05	.04	.02
177	Tommy Barrett	.05	.04	.02
178	Dan Petry	.05	.04	.02
179	Billy Masse	.20	.15	.08
180	Terry Kennedy	.05	.04	.02
181	Joe Orsulak	.05	.04	.02
182	Doyle Alexander	.05	.04	.02
183	Willie McGee	.05	.04	.02
184	Jim Gantner	.05	.04	.02
185	Keith Hernandez	.05	.04	.02
186	Greg Gagne	.05	.04	.02
187	Kevin Bass	.05	.04	.02
188	Mark Eichhorn	.05	.04	.02
189	Mark Grace	.25	.20	.10
190	Jose Canseco	1.00	.70	.40
191	Bobby Witt	.05	.04	.02
192	Rafael Santana	.05	.04	.02
193	Dwight Evans	.05	.04	.02
194	Greg Booker	.05	.04	.02
195	Brook Jacoby	.05	.04	.02
196	Rafael Belliard	.05	.04	.02
197	Candy Maldonado	.05	.04	.02
198	Mickey Tettleton	.08	.06	.03
199	Barry Larkin	.08	.06	.03
200	Frank White	.05	.04	.02
201	Wally Joyner	.15	.11	.06
202	Chet Lemon	.05	.04	.02
203	Joe Magrane	.05	.04	.02
204	Glenn Braggs	.05	.04	.02
205	Scott Fletcher	.05	.04	.02
206	Gary Ward	.05	.04	.02
207	Nelson Liriano	.05	.04	.02
208	Howard Johnson	.15	.11	.06
209	Kent Hrbek	.08	.06	.03
210	Ken Caminiti	.05	.04	.02
211	Mike Greenwell	.50	.40	.20
212	Ryne Sandberg	.25	.20	.10
213	Joe Slusarski	.25	.20	.10
214	Donnell Nixon	.05	.04	.02
215	Tim Wallach	.05	.04	.02
216	John Kruk	.05	.04	.02
217	Charles Nagy	.25	.20	.10
218	Alvin Davis	.08	.06	.03
219	Oswald Peraza	.05	.04	.02
220	Mike Schmidt	.30	.25	.12
221	Spike Owen	.05	.04	.02
222	Mike Smithson	.05	.04	.02
223	Dion James	.05	.04	.02
224	Ernie Whitt	.05	.04	.02
225	Mike Davis	.05	.04	.02
226	Gene Larkin	.05	.04	.02
227	Pat Combs	.50	.40	.20
228	Jack Howell	.05	.04	.02
229	Ron Oester	.05	.04	.02
230	Paul Gibson	.05	.04	.02
231	Mookie Wilson	.05	.04	.02
232	Glenn Hubbard	.05	.04	.02
233	Shawon Dunston	.05	.04	.02
234	Otis Nixon	.05	.04	.02
235	Melido Perez	.05	.04	.02
236	Jerry Browne	.05	.04	.02
237	Rick Rhoden	.05	.04	.02
238	Bo Jackson	.50	.40	.20
239	Randy Velarde	.05	.04	.02
240	Jack Clark	.05	.04	.02
241	Wade Boggs	.80	.60	.30
242	Lonnie Smith	.05	.04	.02
243	Mike Flanagan	.05	.04	.02
244	Willie Randolph	.05	.04	.02
245	Oddibe McDowell	.05	.04	.02
246	Ricky Jordan	.35	.25	.14
247	Greg Briley	.20	.15	.08
248	Rex Hudler	.05	.04	.02
249	Robin Yount	.20	.15	.08
250	Lance Parrish	.05	.04	.02
251	Chris Sabo	.20	.15	.08
252	Mike Henneman	.05	.04	.02
253	Gregg Jefferies	1.00	.70	.40
254	Curt Young	.05	.04	.02
255	Andy Van Slyke	.08	.06	.03
256	Rod Booker	.05	.04	.02
257	Rafael Palmeiro	.05	.04	.02
258	Jose Uribe	.05	.04	.02
259	Ellis Burks	.20	.15	.08
260	John Smoltz	.10	.08	.04
261	Tom Foley	.05	.04	.02
262	Lloyd Moseby	.05	.04	.02
263	Jim Poole	.15	.11	.06
264	Gary Gaetti	.08	.06	.03
265	Bob Dernier	.05	.04	.02
266	Harold Baines	.08	.06	.03
267	Tom Candiotti	.05	.04	.02
268	Rafael Ramirez	.05	.04	.02
269	Bob Boone	.05	.04	.02
270	Buddy Bell	.05	.04	.02
271	Rickey Henderson	.15	.11	.06
272	Willie Fraser	.05	.04	.02
273	Eric Davis	.25	.20	.10
274	Jeff Robinson	.05	.04	.02
275	Damaso Garcia	.05	.04	.02
276	Sid Fernandez	.05	.04	.02
277	Stan Javier	.05	.04	.02
278	Marty Barrett	.05	.04	.02
279	Gerald Perry	.05	.04	.02
280	Rob Ducey	.05	.04	.02
281	Mike Scioscia	.05	.04	.02
282	Randy Bush	.05	.04	.02
283	Tom Herr	.05	.04	.02
284	Glenn Wilson	.05	.04	.02
285	Pedro Guerrero	.10	.08	.04
286	Cal Ripken	.10	.08	.04
287	Randy Johnson	.15	.11	.06
288	Julio Franco	.08	.06	.03
289	Ivan Calderon	.05	.04	.02
290	Rich Yett	.05	.04	.02
291	Scott Servais	.20	.15	.08
292	Bill Pecota	.05	.04	.02
293	Ken Phelps	.05	.04	.02
294	Chili Davis	.05	.04	.02
295	Manny Trillo	.05	.04	.02
296	Mike Boddicker	.05	.04	.02
297	Geronimo Berroa	.05	.04	.02
298	Todd Stottlemyre	.05	.04	.02
299	Kirk Gibson	.05	.04	.02
300	Wally Backman	.05	.04	.02
301	Hubie Brooks	.05	.04	.02
302	Von Hayes	.05	.04	.02
303	Matt Nokes	.05	.04	.02
304	Doc Gooden	.20	.15	.08
305	Walt Weiss	.10	.08	.04
306	Mike LaValliere	.05	.04	.02
307	Cris Carpenter	.10	.08	.04
308	Ted Wood	.20	.15	.08
309	Jeff Russell	.05	.04	.02
310	Dave Gallagher	.05	.04	.02
311	Andy Allanson	.05	.04	.02
312	Craig Reynolds	.05	.04	.02
313	Kevin Seitzer	.08	.06	.03
314	Dave Winfield	.10	.08	.04
315	Andy McGaffigan	.05	.04	.02
316	Nick Esasky	.05	.04	.02
317	Jeff Blauser	.05	.04	.02
318	George Bell	.10	.08	.04
319	Eddie Murray	.10	.08	.04
320	Mark Davidson	.05	.04	.02
321	Juan Samuel	.05	.04	.02
322	Jim Abbott	1.00	.70	.40
323	Kal Daniels	.05	.04	.02
324	Mike Brumley	.05	.04	.02
325	Gary Carter	.05	.04	.02
326	Dave Henderson	.05	.04	.02
327	Checklist •	.05	.04	.02
328	Garry Templeton	.05	.04	.02
329	Pat Perry	.05	.04	.02
330	Paul Molitor	.08	.06	.03

1989 Topps Box Panels

Continuing its practice of printing baseball cards on the bottom panels of its wax pack boxes, Topps in 1989 issued a special 16-card set, printing four cards on each of four different box-bottom panels. The cards are identical in design to the regular 1989 Topps cards. They are designated by letter (from A through P) rather than by number.

		MT	NR MT	EX
Complete Panel Set:		5.00	3.75	2.00
Complete Singles Set:		2.00	1.50	.80
Common Panel:		.50	.40	.20
Common Single Player:		.08	.06	.03
Panel		.50	.40	.20
A	George Brett	.25	.20	.10
B	Bill Buckner	.08	.06	.03
C	Darrell Evans	.08	.06	.03
D	Rich Gossage	.08	.06	.03
Panel		1.00	.70	.40
E	Greg Gross	.08	.06	.03
F	Rickey Henderson	.30	.25	.12
G	Keith Hernandez	.15	.11	.06

		MT	NR MT	EX
H	Tom Lasorda	.08	.06	.03
Panel		2.50	2.00	1.00
I	Jim Rice	.15	.11	.06
J	Cal Ripken	.35	.25	.14
K	Nolan Ryan	.50	.40	.20
L	Mike Schmidt	.25	.20	.10
Panel		1.00	.70	.40
M	Bruce Sutter	.15	.11	.06
N	Don Sutton	.10	.08	.04
O	Kent Tekulve	.08	.06	.03
P	Dave Winfield	.25	.20	.10

1989 Topps Dream Team

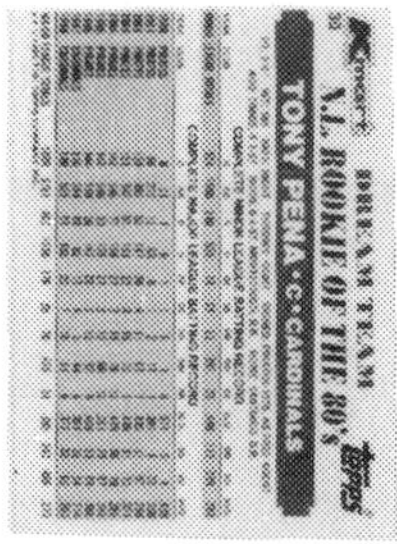

This 33-card, glossy set was produced by Topps for K-Mart, where it was sold in stores nationwide. The standard-size cards feature mostly action shots on the front, and include the Topps "Dream Team" logo at the top, with the K-Mart logo in the lower right corner. The first 11 cards in the set picture the top rookies of 1988, while next 11 picture the top A.L. rookies of the '80s, and the final 11 cards highlight the top N.L. rookies of the decade.

		MT	NR MT	EX
Complete Set:		5.00	3.75	2.00
Common Player:		.10	.08	.04
1	Mark Grace	.70	.50	.30
2	Ron Gant	.15	.11	.06
3	Chris Sabo	.15	.11	.06
4	Walt Weiss	.15	.11	.06
5	Jay Buhner	.15	.11	.06
6	Cecil Espy	.10	.08	.04
7	Dave Gallagher	.15	.11	.06
8	Damon Berryhill	.10	.08	.04
9	Tim Belcher	.20	.15	.08
10	Paul Gibson	.10	.08	.04
11	Gregg Jefferies	.90	.70	.40
12	Don Mattingly	1.50	1.25	.60
13	Harold Reynolds	.15	.11	.06
14	Wade Boggs	.80	.60	.30
15	Cal Ripken	.25	.20	.10
16	Kirby Puckett	.40	.30	.15
17	George Bell	.15	.11	.06
18	Jose Canseco	.50	.40	.20
19	Terry Steinbach	.20	.15	.08
20	Roger Clemens	.40	.30	.15
21	Mark Langston	.20	.15	.08
22	Harold Baines	.15	.11	.06
23	Will Clark	.50	.40	.20
24	Ryne Sanberg	.25	.20	.10
25	Tim Wallach	.10	.08	.04
26	Shawon Dunston	.10	.08	.04
27	Rock Raines	.15	.11	.06
28	Darryl Strawberry	.35	.25	.14
29	Tony Gwynn	.35	.25	.14
30	Tony Pena	.10	.08	.04
31	Doc Gooden	.35	.25	.12
32	Fernando Valenzuela	.15	.11	.06
33	Pedro Guerrero	.15	.11	.06

1989 Topps Highlights

This 33-card set was produced by Topps for the Woolworth store chain and was sold in a special box with a checklist on the back. The glossy-coated cards commemorate the most memorable moments in baseball from the the 1988 season, and include the logo "Woolworth's Baseball Highlights" along the top. The player photos are framed in red, yellow and white and feature the player's name beneath the photo. The backs include a description of the various highlights. Orel Hershiser is pictured on four of the cards, and Jose Canseco appears on two.

		MT	NR MT	EX
Complete Set:		6.00	4.50	2.50
Common Player:		.09	.07	.04
1	Jose Canseco	1.25	.90	.50
2	Kirk Gibson	.15	.11	.06
3	Frank Viola	.15	.11	.06
4	Orel Hershiser	.15	.11	.06
5	Walt Weiss	.20	.15	.11
6	Chris Sabo	.20	.15	.11
7	George Bell	.15	.11	.06
8	Wade Boggs	1.00	.70	.40
9	Tom Browning	.12	.09	.05
10	Gary Carter	.12	.09	.05
11	Andre Dawson	.15	.11	.06
12	John Franco	.09	.07	.04
13	Randy Johnson	.15	.11	.06
14	Doug Jones	.09	.07	.04
15	Kevin McReynolds	.20	.15	.11
16	Gene Nelson	.09	.07	.04
17	Jeff Reardon	.09	.07	.04
18	Pat Tabler	.09	.07	.04
19	Tim Belcher	.25	.20	.10
20	Dennis Eckersley	.15	.11	.06
21	Orel Hershiser	.20	.15	.08
22	Gregg Jefferies	1.00	.70	.40
23	Jose Canseco	1.25	.90	.50
24	Kirk Gibson	.20	.15	.08
25	Orel Hershiser	.20	.15	.08
26	Mike Marshall	.09	.07	.04
27	Mark McGwire	1.00	.70	.40
28	Rick Honeycutt	.09	.07	.04
29	Tim Belcher	.20	.15	.08
30	Jay Howell	.12	.09	.05
31	Mickey Hatcher	.09	.07	.04
32	Mike Davis	.09	.07	.04
33	Orel Hershiser	.15	.11	.06

1989 Topps Mini League Leaders

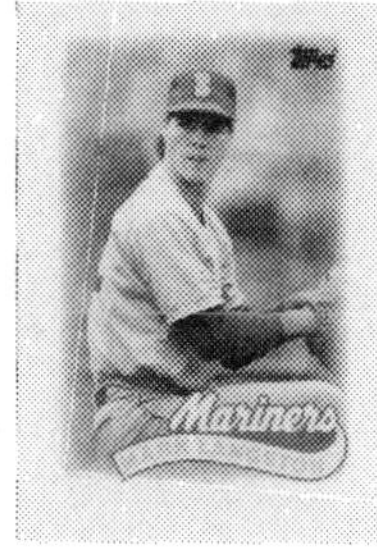

This 77-card set from Topps features baseball's statistical leaders from the 1988 season, and is referred to as a "mini" set because of the cards' small (2-1/8" by 3") size. The glossy cards feature action photos that have a soft focus on all edges. The player's team and name appear along the bottom of the card. The back features a head-shot of the player along with his 1988 season ranking and stats.

		MT	NR MT	EX
Complete Set:		5.00	3.75	2.00
Common Player:		.09	.07	.04
1	Dale Murphy	.35	.25	.14
2	Gerald Perry	.09	.07	.04
3	Andre Dawson	.20	.15	.08
4	Greg Maddux	.20	.15	.08
5	Rafael Palmeiro	.15	.11	.06
6	Tom Browning	.12	.09	.05
7	Kal Daniels	.15	.11	.06
8	Eric Davis	.60	.45	.25
9	John Franco	.09	.07	.04
10	Danny Jackson	.09	.07	.04
11	Barry Larkin	.15	.11	.06
12	Jose Rijo	.12	.09	.05
13	Chris Sabo	.20	.15	.08
14	Mike Scott	.09	.07	.04
15	Nolan Ryan	.50	.40	.20
16	Gerald Young	.09	.07	.04
17	Kirk Gibson	.12	.09	.05
18	Orel Hershiser	.25	.20	.10
19	Steve Sax	.12	.09	.05
20	John Tudor	.09	.07	.04
21	Hubie Brooks	.09	.07	.04
22	Andres Galarraga	.15	.11	.06
23	Otis Nixon	.09	.07	.04
24	Dave Cone	.15	.11	.06
25	Sid Fernandez	.12	.09	.05
26	Doc Gooden	.30	.25	.12
27	Kevin McReynolds	.20	.15	.08
28	Darryl Strawberry	.35	.25	.14
29	Juan Samuel	.09	.07	.04
30	Bobby Bonilla	.12	.09	.05
31	Sid Bream	.09	.07	.04
32	Andy Van Slyke	.12	.09	.05
33	Vince Coleman	.12	.09	.05
34	Jose DeLeon	.09	.07	.04
35	Joe Magrane	.12	.09	.05
36	Ozzie Smith	.12	.09	.05
37	Todd Worrell	.09	.07	.04
38	Tony Gwynn	.30	.25	.12
39	Brett Butler	.12	.09	.05
40	Will Clark	1.00	.70	.40
41	Jim Gott	.09	.07	.04
42	Rick Reuschel	.12	.09	.05
43	Checklist	.09	.07	.04
44	Eddie Murray	.20	.15	.08
45	Wade Boggs	.80	.60	.30
46	Roger Clemens	.30	.25	.12
47	Dwight Evans	.12	.09	.05
48	Mike Greenwell	.70	.50	.30
49	Bruce Hurst	.12	.09	.05
50	Johnny Ray	.09	.07	.04
51	Doug Jones	.09	.07	.04
52	Greg Swindell	.15	.11	.06
53	Gary Pettis	.09	.07	.04
54	George Brett	.15	.11	.06
55	Mark Gubicza	.15	.11	.06
56	Willie Wilson	.09	.07	.04
57	Teddy Higuera	.12	.09	.05
58	Paul Molitor	.15	.11	.06
59	Robin Yount	.25	.20	.10
60	Allan Anderson	.09	.07	.04
61	Gary Gaetti	.12	.09	.04
62	Kirby Puckett	.40	.30	.15
63	Jeff Reardon	.09	.07	.04
64	Frank Viola	.12	.09	.05
65	Jack Clark	.12	.09	.05
66	Rickey Henderson	.25	.20	.10
67	Dave Winfield	.15	.11	.06
68	Jose Canseco	1.00	.70	.40
69	Dennis Eckersley	.12	.09	.05
70	Mark McGwire	.80	.60	.30
71	Dave Stewart	.12	.09	.05
72	Alvin Davis	.12	.09	.05
73	Mark Langston	.12	.09	.05
74	Harold Reynolds	.12	.09	.05
75	George Bell	.15	.11	.06
76	Tony Fernandez	.15	.11	.06
77	Fred McGriff	.25	.20	.10

1989 Topps Traded

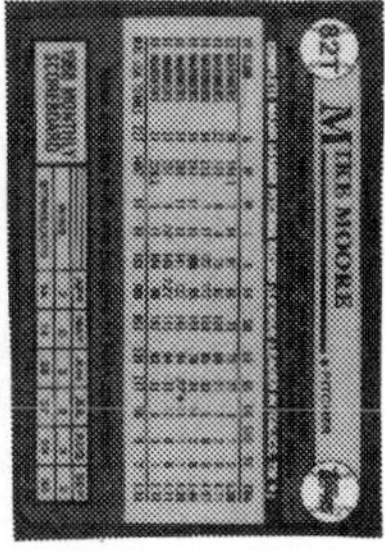

For the ninth straight year, Topps issued its annual 132-card "Traded" set at the end of the 1989 baseball season. The set, which was packaged in a special box and sold by hobby dealers, includes traded players and rookies who were not in the regular 1989 Topps set.

		MT	NR MT	EX
Complete Set:		13.00	9.75	5.25
Common Player:		.05	.04	.02
1T	Don Aase	.05	.04	.02
2T	Jim Abbott	1.00	.70	.40
3T	Kent Anderson(FC)	.25	.20	.10
4T	Keith Atherton	.05	.04	.02
5T	Wally Backman	.05	.04	.02
6T	Steve Balboni	.05	.04	.02
7T	Jesse Barfield	.05	.04	.02
8T	Steve Bedrosian	.05	.04	.02
9T	Todd Benzinger	.05	.04	.02
10T	Geronimo Berroa(FC)	.10	.08	.04
11T	Bert Blyleven	.05	.04	.02
12T	Bob Boone	.05	.04	.02
13T	Phil Bradley	.08	.06	.03
14T	Jeff Brantley(FC)	.25	.20	.10
15T	Kevin Brown(FC)	.20	.15	.08
16T	Jerry Browne	.05	.04	.02
17T	Chuck Cary	.20	.15	.08
18T	Carmen Castillo	.05	.04	.02
19T	Jim Clancy	.05	.04	.02
20T	Jack Clark	.10	.08	.04
21T	Bryan Clutterbuck	.05	.04	.02
22T	Jody Davis	.05	.04	.02
23T	Mike Devereaux(FC)	.10	.08	.04
24T	Frank DiPino	.05	.04	.02
25T	Benny Distefano	.05	.04	.02
26T	John Dopson	.20	.15	.08
27T	Len Dykstra	.10	.08	.04
28T	Jim Eisenreich	.05	.04	.02
29T	Nick Esasky	.08	.06	.03
30T	Alvaro Espinoza	.25	.20	.10
31T	Darrell Evans	.08	.06	.03
32T	Junior Felix(FC)	.80	.60	.30
33T	Felix Fermin	.05	.04	.02
34T	Julio Franco	.15	.11	.06
35T	Terry Francona	.05	.04	.02
36T	Cito Gaston	.05	.04	.02
37T	Bob Geren (incorrect photo)(FC)	.50	.40	.20
38T	Tom Gordon(FC)	1.00	.70	.40

		MT	NR MT	EX
39T	Tommy Gregg(FC)	.25	.20	.10
40T	Ken Griffey	.15	.11	.06
41T	Ken Griffey, Jr.(FC)	6.00	4.50	2.50
42T	Kevin Gross	.05	.04	.02
43T	Lee Guetterman	.05	.04	.02
44T	Mel Hall	.05	.04	.02
45T	Erik Hanson(FC)	.30	.25	.12
46T	Gene Harris(FC)	.25	.20	.10
47T	Andy Hawkins	.05	.04	.02
48T	Rickey Henderson	.35	.25	.14
49T	Tom Herr	.05	.04	.02
50T	Ken Hill(FC)	.20	.15	.08
51T	Brian Holman(FC)	.30	.25	.12
52T	Brian Holton	.10	.08	.04
53T	Art Howe	.05	.04	.03
54T	Ken Howell	.05	.04	.02
55T	Bruce Hurst	.05	.04	.02
56T	Chris James	.05	.04	.02
57T	Randy Johnson(FC)	1.25	.90	.50
58T	Jimmy Jones	.05	.04	.02
59T	Terry Kennedy	.05	.04	.02
60T	Paul Kilgus	.05	.04	.02
61T	Eric King	.08	.06	.03
62T	Ron Kittle	.08	.06	.03
63T	John Kruk	.08	.06	.03
64T	Randy Kutcher(FC)	.08	.06	.03
65T	Steve Lake	.05	.04	.02
66T	Mark Langston	.25	.20	.10
67T	Dave LaPoint	.05	.04	.02
68T	Rick Leach	.05	.04	.02
69T	Terry Leach	.05	.04	.02
70T	Jim Levebvre	.05	.04	.02
71T	Al Leiter	.05	.04	.02
72T	Jeffrey Leonard	.05	.04	.02
73T	Derek Lilliquist(FC)	.25	.20	.10
74T	Rick Mahler	.05	.04	.02
75T	Tom McCarthy(FC)	.25	.20	.10
76T	Lloyd McClendon	.20	.15	.08
77T	Lance McCullers	.05	.04	.02
78T	Oddibe McDowell	.05	.04	.02
79T	Roger McDowell	.05	.04	.02
80T	Larry McWilliams	.05	.04	.02
81T	Randy Milligan(FC)	1.25	.90	.50
82T	Mike Moore	.15	.11	.06
83T	Keith Moreland	.05	.04	.02
84T	Mike Morgan	.05	.04	.02
85T	Jamie Moyer	.05	.04	.02
86T	Rob Murphy	.05	.04	.02
87T	Eddie Murray	.30	.25	.12
88T	Pete O'Brien	.05	.04	.02
89T	Gregg Olson	.80	.60	.30
90T	Steve Ontiveros	.05	.04	.02
91T	Jesse Orosco	.05	.04	.02
92T	Spike Owen	.05	.04	.02
93T	Rafael Palmeiro	.08	.06	.03
94T	Clay Parker(FC)	.20	.15	.08
95T	Jeff Parrett	.05	.04	.02
96T	Lance Parrish	.05	.04	.02
97T	Dennis Powell	.05	.04	.02
98T	Rey Quinones	.05	.04	.02
99T	Doug Rader	.05	.04	.02
100T	Willie Randolph	.08	.06	.03
101T	Shane Rawley	.05	.04	.02
102T	Randy Ready	.05	.04	.02
103T	Bip Roberts	.05	.04	.02
104T	Kenny Rogers(FC)	.25	.20	.10
105T	Ed Romero	.05	.04	.02
106T	Nolan Ryan	1.25	.90	.50
107T	Luis Salazar	.05	.04	.02
108T	Juan Samuel	.08	.06	.03
109T	Alex Sanchez(FC)	.20	.15	.08
110T	Deion Sanders(FC)	.90	.70	.35
111T	Steve Sax	.15	.11	.06
112T	Rick Schu	.05	.04	.02
113T	Dwight Smith(FC)	1.50	1.25	.60
114T	Lonnie Smith	.05	.04	.02
115T	Billy Spiers(FC)	.40	.30	.15
116T	Kent Tekulve	.05	.04	.02
117T	Walt Terrell	.05	.04	.02
118T	Milt Thompson	.05	.04	.02
119T	Dickie Thon	.05	.04	.02
120T	Jeff Torborg	.05	.04	.02
121T	Jeff Treadway	.05	.04	.02
122T	Omar Vizquel(FC)	.30	.25	.12
123T	Jerome Walton(FC)	2.50	2.00	1.00
124T	Gary Ward	.05	.04	.02
125T	Claudell Washington	.05	.04	.02
126T	Curt Wilkerson	.05	.04	.02
127T	Eddie Williams	.05	.04	.02
128T	Frank Williams	.05	.04	.02
129T	Ken Williams	.05	.04	.02
130T	Mitch Williams	.15	.11	.06
131T	Steve Wilson(FC)	.20	.15	.08
132T	Checklist	.05	.04	.02

1990 Topps

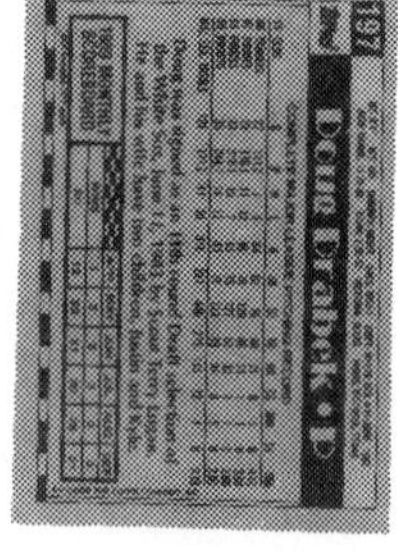

The 1990 Topps set again included 792 cards, and sported a newly-designed front that featured six different color schemes. The set led off with a special four-card salute to Nolan Ryan, and featured various other specials, including All-Stars, Number 1 Draft Picks, Record Breakers, manager cards, rookies, and "Turn Back the Clock" cards. The set also includes a special card commemorating A. Bartlett Giamatti, the late Baseball Commissioner. The backs are printed in black on a chartreuse background with the card number in the upper left corner. The set features 725 different individual player cards, the most ever, including 138 players making their first appearance in a regular Topps set.

		MT	NR MT	EX
Complete Set:		25.00	20.00	10.00
Common Player:		.03	.02	.01
1	Nolan Ryan	.35	.25	.14
2	Nolan Ryan (The Mets Years)	.20	.15	.08
3	Nolan Ryan (The Angels Years)	.20	.15	.08
4	Nolan Ryan (The Astros Years)	.20	.15	.08
5	Nolan Ryan (The Rangers)	.20	.15	.08
6	1989 Record Breaker (Vince Coleman)	.10	.08	.04
7	1989 Record Breaker (Rickey Henderson)	.20	.15	.08
8	1989 Record Breaker (Cal Ripken)	.15	.11	.06
9	Eric Plunk	.03	.02	.01
10	Barry Larkin	.15	.11	.06
11	Paul Gibson	.04	.03	.02
12	Joe Girardi(FC)	.15	.11	.06
13	Mark Williamson	.03	.02	.01
14	*Mike Fetters*(FC)	.20	.15	.08
15	Teddy Higuera	.06	.05	.02
16	*Kent Anderson*	.10	.08	.04
17	Kelly Downs	.05	.04	.02
18	Carlos Quintana	.09	.07	.04
19	Al Newman	.03	.02	.01
20	Mark Gubicza	.12	.09	.05
21	Jeff Torborg	.03	.02	.01
22	Bruce Ruffin	.03	.02	.01
23	Randy Velarde	.07	.05	.03
24	Joe Hesketh	.03	.02	.01
25	Willie Randolph	.08	.06	.03
26	Don Slaught	.03	.02	.01
27	Rick Leach	.03	.02	.01
28	Duane Ward	.04	.03	.02
29	John Cangelosi	.03	.02	.01
30	David Cone	.10	.08	.04
31	Henry Cotto	.03	.02	.01
32	John Farrell	.05	.04	.02
33	Greg Walker	.05	.04	.02
34	*Tony Fossas*(FC)	.07	.05	.03
35	Benito Santiago	.12	.09	.05
36	John Costello	.04	.03	.02
37	Domingo Ramos	.03	.02	.01
38	Wes Gardner	.04	.03	.02
39	Curt Ford	.04	.03	.02
40	Jay Howell	.06	.05	.02
41	Matt Williams	.15	.11	.06
42	Jeff Robinson	.05	.04	.02
43	Dante Bichette	.07	.05	.03
44	#1 Draft Pick *(Roger Salkeld)*(FC)	.30	.25	.12
45	Dave Parker	.09	.07	.04
46	Rob Dibble	.07	.05	.03
47	Brian Harper	.04	.03	.02
48	Zane Smith	.03	.02	.01
49	Tom Lawless	.03	.02	.01
50	Glenn Davis	.08	.06	.03
51	Doug Rader	.03	.02	.01
52	*Jack Daugherty*(FC)	.20	.15	.08
53	Mike LaCoss	.04	.03	.02
54	Joel Skinner	.04	.03	.02
55	Darrell Evans	.05	.04	.02
56	Franklin Stubbs	.04	.03	.02
57	*Greg Vaughn*(FC)	1.25	.90	.50
58	Keith Miller	.10	.08	.04
59	Ted Power	.03	.02	.01
60	George Brett	.15	.11	.06
61	*Deion Sanders*	.40	.30	.15
62	Ramon Martinez	.10	.08	.04
63	Mike Pagliarulo	.04	.03	.02
64	Danny Darwin	.03	.02	.01
65	Devon White	.07	.05	.03
66	*Greg Litton*(FC)	.25	.20	.10
67	Scott Sanderson	.04	.03	.02
68	Dave Henderson	.06	.05	.02
69	Todd Frohwirth	.03	.02	.01
70	Mike Greenwell	.30	.25	.12
71	Allan Anderson	.05	.04	.02
72	*Jeff Huson*(FC)	.25	.20	.10
73	Bob Milacki	.05	.04	.02
74	#1 Draft Pick *(Jeff Jackson)*(FC)	.30	.25	.12
75	Doug Jones	.05	.04	.02
76	Dave Valle	.03	.02	.01
77	Dave Bergman	.03	.02	.01
78	Mike Flanagan	.04	.03	.02
79	Ron Kittle	.05	.04	.02
80	Jeff Russell	.05	.04	.02
81	Bob Rodgers	.03	.02	.01
82	Scott Terry	.04	.03	.02
83	Hensley Meulens	.30	.25	.12
84	Ray Searage	.03	.02	.01
85	Juan Samuel	.05	.04	.02
86	Paul Kilgus	.03	.02	.01
87	*Rick Luecken*(FC)	.15	.11	.06
88	Glenn Braggs	.05	.04	.02
89	*Clint Zavaras*(FC)	.15	.11	.06
90	Jack Clark	.06	.05	.02
91	*Steve Frey*(FC)	.20	.15	.08
92	Mike Stanley	.03	.02	.01
93	Shawn Hillegas	.03	.02	.01
94	Herm Winningham	.03	.02	.01
95	Todd Worrell	.05	.04	.02
96	Jody Reed	.04	.03	.02

		MT	NR MT	EX
97	Curt Schilling(FC)	.10	.08	.04
98	Jose Gonzalez(FC)	.10	.08	.04
99	*Rich Monteleone*(FC)	.15	.11	.06
100	Will Clark	.70	.50	.30
101	Shane Rawley	.04	.03	.02
102	Stan Javier	.04	.03	.02
103	Marvin Freeman	.09	.07	.04
104	Bob Knepper	.03	.02	.01
105	Randy Myers	.05	.04	.02
106	Charlie O'Brien	.03	.02	.01
107	Fred Lynn	.05	.04	.02
108	Rod Nichols	.04	.03	.02
109	Roberto Kelly	.08	.06	.03
110	Tommy Helms	.03	.02	.01
111	Ed Whited	.20	.15	.08
112	Glenn Wilson	.03	.02	.01
113	Manny Lee	.03	.02	.01
114	Mike Bielecki	.05	.04	.02
115	Tony Pena	.06	.05	.02
116	Floyd Bannister	.04	.03	.02
117	Mike Sharperson(FC)	.09	.07	.04
118	Erik Hanson	.10	.08	.04
119	Billy Hatcher	.04	.03	.02
120	John Franco	.05	.04	.02
121	Robin Ventura	.35	.25	.14
122	Shawn Abner	.03	.02	.01
123	Rich Gedman	.04	.03	.02
124	Dave Dravecky	.04	.03	.02
125	Kent Hrbek	.07	.05	.03
126	Randy Kramer	.03	.02	.01
127	Mike Devereaux	.06	.05	.02
128	Checklist 1-132	.03	.02	.01
129	Ron Jones	.10	.08	.04
130	Bert Blyleven	.05	.04	.02
131	Matt Nokes	.06	.05	.02
132	Lance Blankenship(FC)	.10	.08	.04
133	Ricky Horton	.03	.02	.01
134	#1 Draft Pick *(Earl Cunningham)*(FC)	.50	.40	.20
135	Dave Magadan	.05	.04	.02
136	Kevin Brown	.06	.05	.02
137	*Marty Pevey*(FC)	.15	.11	.06
138	Al Leiter	.04	.03	.02
139	Greg Brock	.04	.03	.02
140	Andre Dawson	.12	.09	.05
141	John Hart	.05	.04	.02
142	*Jeff Wetherby*(FC)	.20	.15	.08
143	Rafael Belliard	.03	.02	.01
144	Bud Black	.03	.02	.01
145	Terry Steinbach	.07	.05	.03
146	*Rob Richie*(FC)	.20	.15	.08
147	Chuck Finley	.04	.03	.02
148	Edgar Martinez(FC)	.09	.07	.04
149	Steve Farr	.04	.03	.02
150	Kirk Gibson	.09	.07	.04
151	Rick Mahler	.03	.02	.01
152	Lonnie Smith	.05	.04	.02
153	Randy Milligan	.05	.04	.02
154	Mike Maddux	.05	.04	.02
155	Ellis Burks	.25	.20	.10
156	Ken Patterson	.04	.03	.02
157	Craig Biggio	.15	.11	.06
158	Craig Lefferts	.04	.03	.02
159	Mike Felder	.03	.02	.01
160	Dave Righetti	.06	.05	.02
161	Harold Reynolds	.06	.05	.02
162	*Todd Zeile*(FC)	1.25	.90	.50
163	Phil Bradley	.05	.04	.02
164	#1 Draft Pick *(Jeff Juden)*(FC)	.35	.25	.14
165	Walt Weiss	.08	.06	.03
166	Bobby Witt	.04	.03	.02
167	*Kevin Appier*(FC)	.35	.25	.14
168	Jose Lind	.04	.03	.02
169	Richard Dotson	.03	.02	.01
170	George Bell	.12	.09	.05
171	Russ Nixon	.03	.02	.01
172	Tom Lampkin(FC)	.10	.08	.04
173	Tim Belcher	.12	.09	.05
174	Jeff Kunkel	.03	.02	.01
175	Mike Moore	.07	.05	.02
176	Luis Quinones	.03	.02	.01
177	Mike Henneman	.05	.04	.02
178	Chris James	.06	.05	.02
179	Brian Holton	.04	.03	.02
180	Rock Raines	.10	.08	.04
181	Juan Agosto	.03	.02	.01
182	Mookie Wilson	.05	.04	.02
183	Steve Lake	.03	.02	.01
184	Danny Cox	.04	.03	.02
185	Ruben Sierra	.20	.15	.08
186	Dave LaPoint	.03	.02	.01
187	*Rick Wrona*(FC)	.12	.09	.05
188	Mike Smithson	.03	.02	.01
189	Dick Schofield	.04	.03	.02
190	Rick Reuschel	.06	.05	.02
191	Pat Borders	.08	.06	.03
192	Don August	.04	.03	.02
193	Andy Benes	.35	.25	.14
194	Glenallen Hill(FC)	.25	.20	.10
195	Tim Burke	.05	.04	.02
196	Gerald Young	.04	.03	.02
197	Doug Drabek	.07	.05	.03
198	Mike Marshall	.06	.05	.02
199	*Sergio Valdez*(FC)	.20	.15	.08
200	Don Mattingly	.90	.70	.35
201	Cito Gaston	.03	.02	.01
202	Mike Macfarlane	.03	.02	.01
203	*Mike Roesler*(FC)	.15	.11	.06
204	Bob Dernier	.03	.02	.01
205	Mark Davis	.09	.07	.04
206	Nick Esasky	.07	.05	.02
207	Bob Ojeda	.04	.03	.02
208	Brook Jacoby	.04	.03	.02
209	Greg Mathews	.04	.03	.02
210	Ryne Sandberg	.15	.11	.06
211	John Cerutti	.04	.03	.02
212	Joe Orsulak	.03	.02	.01
213	Scott Bankhead	.05	.04	.02
214	Terry Francona	.03	.02	.01
215	Kirk McCaskill	.04	.03	.02
216	Ricky Jordan	.30	.25	.12
217	Don Robinson	.04	.03	.02

		MT	NR MT	EX
218	Wally Backman	.04	.03	.02
219	Donn Pall	.03	.02	.01
220	Barry Bonds	.10	.08	.04
221	*Gary Mielke*(FC)	.20	.15	.08
222	Kurt Stillwell	.05	.04	.02
223	Tommy Gregg	.06	.05	.02
224	*Delino DeShields*(FC)	.70	.50	.30
225	Jim Deshaies	.05	.04	.02
226	Mickey Hatcher	.03	.02	.01
227	*Kevin Tapani*(FC)	.30	.25	.12
228	Dave Martinez	.03	.02	.01
229	David Wells	.03	.02	.01
230	Keith Hernandez	.07	.05	.03
231	Jack McKeon	.03	.02	.01
232	Darnell Coles	.04	.03	.02
233	Ken Hill	.10	.08	.06
234	Mariano Duncan	.05	.04	.02
235	Jeff Reardon	.04	.03	.02
236	Hal Morris(FC)	.10	.08	.06
237	*Kevin Ritz*(FC)	.20	.15	.08
238	Felix Jose(FC)	.10	.08	.04
239	Eric Show	.04	.03	.02
240	Mark Grace	.40	.30	.15
241	Mike Krukow	.04	.03	.02
242	Fred Manrique	.03	.02	.01
243	Barry Jones	.03	.02	.01
244	Bill Schroeder	.03	.02	.01
245	Roger Clemens	.25	.20	.10
246	Jim Eisenreich	.03	.02	.01
247	Jerry Reed	.03	.02	.01
248	Dave Anderson	.03	.02	.01
249	*Mike Smith*(FC)	.20	.15	.08
250	Jose Canseco	.70	.50	.30
251	Jeff Blauser	.05	.04	.02
252	Otis Nixon	.03	.02	.01
253	Mark Portugal	.03	.02	.01
254	Francisco Cabrera	.25	.20	.10
255	Bobby Thigpen	.07	.05	.03
256	Marvell Wynne	.03	.02	.01
257	Jose DeLeon	.07	.05	.03
258	Barry Lyons	.03	.02	.01
259	Lance McCullers	.05	.04	.02
260	Eric Davis	.30	.25	.12
261	Whitey Herzog	.03	.02	.01
262	Checklist 133-264	.03	.02	.01
263	*Mel Stottlemyre, Jr.*(FC)	.15	.11	.06
264	Bryan Clutterbuck	.03	.02	.01
265	Pete O'Brien	.06	.05	.02
266	German Gonzalez	.04	.03	.02
267	Mark Davidson	.03	.02	.01
268	Rob Murphy	.03	.02	.01
269	Dickie Thon	.03	.02	.01
270	Dave Stewart	.08	.06	.03
271	Chet Lemon	.05	.04	.02
272	Bryan Harvey	.04	.03	.02
273	Bobby Bonilla	.15	.11	.06
274	*Goose Gozzo*(FC)	.20	.15	.08
275	Mickey Tettleton	.07	.05	.03
276	Gary Thurman	.03	.02	.01
277	Lenny Harris(FC)	.12	.09	.05
278	Pascual Perez	.04	.03	.02
279	Steve Buechele	.04	.03	.02
280	Lou Whitaker	.07	.05	.03
281	Kevin Bass	.05	.04	.02
282	Derek Lilliquist	.10	.08	.04
283	*Joey Belle*(FC)	.80	.60	.30
284	*Mark Gardner*(FC)	.30	.25	.12
285	Willie McGee	.06	.05	.02
286	Lee Guetterman	.03	.02	.01
287	Vance Law	.03	.02	.01
288	Greg Briley	.15	.11	.06
289	Norm Charlton	.10	.08	.04
290	Robin Yount	.20	.15	.08
291	Dave Johnson	.03	.02	.01
292	Jim Gott	.04	.03	.02
293	Mike Gallego	.04	.03	.02
294	Craig McMurtry	.03	.02	.01
295	Fred McGriff	.25	.20	.10
296	Jeff Ballard	.07	.05	.03
297	Tom Herr	.06	.05	.02
298	Danny Gladden	.05	.04	.02
299	Adam Peterson(FC)	.09	.07	.04
300	Bo Jackson	.50	.40	.20
301	Don Aase	.03	.02	.01
302	*Marcus Lawton*(FC)	.08	.06	.03
303	Rick Cerone	.03	.02	.01
304	Marty Clary(FC)	.08	.06	.03
305	Eddie Murray	.15	.11	.06
306	Tom Niedenfuer	.03	.02	.01
307	Bip Roberts	.08	.06	.03
308	Jose Guzman	.05	.04	.02
309	*Eric Yelding*(FC)	.20	.15	.08
310	Steve Bedrosian	.05	.04	.02
311	Dwight Smith	.90	.70	.35
312	Dan Quisenberry	.05	.04	.02
313	Gus Polidor	.03	.02	.01
314	#1 Draft Pick *(Donald Harris)*(FC)	.30	.25	.12
315	Bruce Hurst	.06	.05	.02
316	Carney Lansford	.06	.05	.02
317	*Mark Guthrie*(FC)	.20	.15	.08
318	Wallace Johnson	.03	.02	.01
319	Dion James	.04	.03	.02
320	Dave Steib	.07	.05	.03
321	Joe Morgan	.03	.02	.01
322	Junior Ortiz	.03	.02	.01
323	Willie Wilson	.04	.03	.02
324	Pete Harnisch(FC)	.10	.08	.04
325	Robby Thompson	.06	.05	.02
326	*Tom McCarthy*	.10	.08	.04
327	Ken Williams	.03	.02	.01
328	Curt Young	.03	.02	.01
329	Oddibe McDowell	.06	.05	.02
330	Ron Darling	.09	.07	.04
331	*Juan Gonzalez*(FC)	.40	.30	.15
332	Paul O'Neill	.07	.05	.03
333	Bill Wegman	.03	.02	.01
334	Johnny Ray	.05	.04	.02
335	Andy Hawkins	.05	.04	.02
336	Ken Griffey, Jr.	2.50	2.00	1.00
337	Lloyd McClendon	.06	.05	.02
338	Dennis Lamp	.03	.02	.01
339	Dave Clark	.04	.03	.02
340	Fernando Valenzuela	.06	.05	.02
341	Tom Foley	.03	.02	.01
342	Alex Trevino	.03	.02	.01
343	Frank Tanana	.04	.03	.02
344	*George Canale*(FC)	.25	.20	.10
345	Harold Baines	.09	.07	.04
346	Jim Presley	.04	.03	.02
347	*Junior Felix*	.40	.30	.15
348	*Gary Wayne*(FC)	.12	.09	.05
349	*Steve Finley*(FC)	.30	.25	.12
350	Bret Saberhagen	.10	.08	.04
351	Roger Craig	.03	.02	.01
352	Bryn Smith	.05	.04	.02
353	Sandy Alomar	.25	.20	.10
354	*Stan Belinda*(FC)	.20	.15	.08
355	Marty Barrett	.05	.04	.02
356	Randy Ready	.03	.02	.01
357	Dave West	.20	.15	.08
358	Andres Thomas	.04	.03	.02
359	Jimmy Jones	.03	.02	.01
360	Paul Molitor	.09	.07	.04
361	*Randy McCament*(FC)	.25	.20	.10
362	Damon Berryhill	.06	.05	.02
363	Dan Petry	.03	.02	.01
364	Rolando Roomes(FC)	.15	.11	.06
365	Ozzie Guillen	.05	.04	.02
366	Mike Heath	.03	.02	.01
367	Mike Morgan	.03	.02	.01
368	Bill Doran	.06	.05	.02
369	Todd Burns	.04	.03	.02
370	Tim Wallach	.07	.05	.03
371	Jimmy Key	.08	.06	.03
372	Terry Kennedy	.03	.02	.01
373	Alvin Davis	.08	.06	.03
374	*Steve Cummings*(FC)	.20	.15	.08
375	Dwight Evans	.08	.06	.03
376	Checklist 265-396	.03	.02	.01
377	*Mickey Weston*(FC)	.20	.15	.08
378	Luis Salazar	.03	.02	.01
379	Steve Rosenberg	.03	.02	.01
380	Dave Winfield	.15	.11	.06
381	Frank Robinson	.03	.02	.01
382	Jeff Musselman	.03	.02	.01
383	John Morris	.04	.03	.02
384	*Pat Combs*	.50	.40	.20
385	Fred McGriff AS	.20	.15	.08
386	Julio Franco AS	.10	.08	.04
387	Wade Boggs AS	.20	.15	.08
388	Cal Ripken AS	.15	.11	.06
389	Robin Yount AS	.20	.15	.08
390	Ruben Sierra AS	.20	.15	.08
391	Kirby Puckett AS	.20	.15	.08
392	Carlton Fisk AS	.08	.06	.03
393	Bret Saberhagen AS	.10	.08	.04
394	Jeff Ballard AS	.08	.06	.03
395	Jeff Russell AS	.08	.06	.03
396	A. Bartlett Giamatti	.30	.25	.12
397	Will Clark AS	.25	.20	.10
398	Ryne Sandberg AS	.15	.11	.06
399	Howard Johnson AS	.15	.11	.06
400	Ozzie Smith AS	.10	.08	.04
401	Kevin Mitchell AS	.20	.15	.08
402	Eric Davis AS	.20	.15	.08
403	Tony Gwynn AS	.15	.11	.06
404	Craig Biggio AS	.15	.11	.06
405	Mike Scott AS	.08	.06	.03
406	Joe Magrane AS	.08	.06	.03
407	Mark Davis AS	.08	.06	.03
408	Trevor Wilson	.06	.05	.02
409	Tom Brunansky	.09	.07	.04
410	Joe Boever	.06	.05	.02
411	Ken Phelps	.03	.02	.01
412	Jamie Moyer	.04	.03	.02
413	*Brian DuBois*(FC)	.20	.15	.08
414	#1 Draft Pick *(Frank Thomas)*(FC)	.60	.45	.25
415	Shawon Dunston	.06	.05	.02
416	*Dave Johnson*(FC)	.12	.09	.05
417	Jim Gantner	.06	.05	.02
418	Tom Browning	.08	.06	.03
419	*Beau Allred*(FC)	.30	.25	.12
420	Carlton Fisk	.08	.06	.03
421	Greg Minton	.03	.02	.01
422	Pat Sheridan	.03	.02	.01
423	Fred Toliver	.03	.02	.01
424	Jerry Reuss	.05	.04	.02
425	Bill Landrum	.05	.04	.02
426	Jeff Hamilton	.05	.04	.02
427	Carmem Castillo	.03	.02	.01
428	*Steve Davis*(FC)	.12	.09	.05
429	Tom Kelly	.03	.02	.01
430	Pete Incaviglia	.06	.05	.02
431	Randy Johnson	.10	.08	.04
432	Damaso Garcia	.03	.02	.01
433	*Steve Olin*(FC)	.12	.08	.04
434	Mark Carreon(FC)	.09	.07	.04
435	Kevin Seitzer	.09	.07	.04
436	Mel Hall	.05	.04	.02
437	Les Lancaster	.05	.04	.02
438	Greg Myers(FC)	.10	.08	.04
439	Jeff Parrett	.06	.05	.02
440	Alan Trammell	.09	.07	.04
441	Bob Kipper	.03	.02	.01
442	Jerry Browne	.07	.05	.02
443	Cris Carpenter	.09	.07	.04
444	*Kyle Abbott* (Number 1 Daft Pick)(FC)	.30	.25	.12
445	Danny Jackson	.05	.04	.02
446	Dan Pasqua	.05	.04	.02
447	Atlee Hammaker	.03	.02	.01
448	Greg Gagne	.04	.03	.02
449	Dennis Rasmussen	.04	.03	.02
450	Rickey Henderson	.20	.15	.08
451	Mark Lemke(FC)	.10	.08	.04
452	Luis de los Santos(FC)	.10	.08	.04
453	Jody Davis	.03	.02	.01
454	Jeff King(FC)	.15	.11	.06
455	Jeffrey Leonard	.06	.05	.02
456	Chris Gwynn(FC)	.09	.07	.03
457	Gregg Jefferies	.50	.40	.20
458	Bob McClure	.03	.02	.01
459	Jim Lefebvre	.03	.02	.01
460	Mike Scott	.09	.07	.03
461	*Carlos Martinez*(FC)	.25	.20	.10
462	Denny Walling	.03	.02	.01
463	Drew Hall	.03	.02	.01
464	*Jerome Walton*	1.00	.70	.40
465	Kevin Gross	.06	.05	.02
466	Rance Mulliniks	.03	.02	.01
467	Juan Nieves	.04	.03	.02
468	Billy Ripken	.04	.03	.02
469	John Kruk	.07	.05	.02
470	Frank Viola	.09	.07	.04
471	Mike Brumley	.03	.02	.01
472	Jose Uribe	.04	.03	.02
473	Joe Price	.03	.02	.01
474	Rich Thompson	.04	.03	.02
475	Bob Welch	.06	.05	.02
476	Brad Komminsk	.03	.02	.02
477	Willie Fraser	.03	.02	.02
478	Mike LaValliere	.04	.03	.02
479	Frank White	.06	.05	.02
480	Sid Fernandez	.09	.07	.04
481	Garry Templeton	.05	.04	.02
482	*Steve Carter*(FC)	.20	.15	.08
483	Alejandro Pena	.04	.03	.02
484	Mike Fitzgerald	.03	.02	.01
485	John Candelaria	.05	.04	.02
486	Jeff Treadway	.05	.04	.02
487	Steve Searcy	.05	.04	.02
488	Ken Oberkfell	.03	.02	.01
489	Nick Leyva	.03	.02	.01
490	Dan Plesac	.07	.05	.03
491	*Dave Cochrane*(FC)	.20	.15	.08
492	Ron Oester	.04	.03	.02
493	*Jason Grimsley*(FC)	.25	.20	.10
494	Terry Puhl	.03	.02	.01
495	Lee Smith	.06	.05	.02
496	Cecil Espy	.06	.05	.02
497	Dave Schmidt	.03	.02	.01
498	Rick Schu	.03	.02	.01
499	Bill Long	.04	.03	.02
500	Kevin Mitchell	.35	.25	.14
501	Matt Young	.03	.02	.01
502	Mitch Webster	.04	.03	.02
503	Randy St. Claire	.03	.02	.01
504	Tom O'Malley	.03	.02	.01
505	Kelly Gruber	.08	.06	.03
506	Tom Glavine	.10	.08	.04
507	Gary Redus	.04	.03	.02
508	Terry Leach	.03	.02	.01
509	Tom Pagnozzi	.03	.02	.01
510	Doc Gooden	.25	.20	.10
511	Clay Parker	.07	.05	.03
512	Gary Pettis	.03	.02	.01
513	Mark Eichhorn	.03	.02	.01
514	Andy Allanson	.03	.02	.01
515	Len Dykstra	.06	.05	.02
516	Tim Leary	.05	.04	.02
517	Roberto Alomar	.15	.11	.06
518	Bill Krueger	.03	.02	.01
519	Bucky Dent	.03	.02	.01
520	Mitch Williams	.09	.07	.03
521	Craig Worthington	.15	.11	.06
522	Mike Dunne	.04	.03	.02
523	Jay Bell	.03	.02	.01
524	Daryl Boston	.03	.02	.01
525	Wally Joyner	.20	.15	.08
526	Checklist 397-528	.03	.02	.01
527	Ron Hassey	.03	.02	.01
528	*Kevin Wickander*(FC)	.20	.15	.08
529	Greg Harris	.03	.02	.01
530	Mark Langston	.10	.08	.04
531	Ken Caminiti	.06	.05	.02
532	Cecilio Guante	.03	.02	.01
533	Tim Jones(FC)	.07	.05	.03
534	Louie Meadows	.07	.05	.03
535	John Smoltz	.15	.11	.06
536	*Bob Geren*	.15	.11	.06
537	Mark Grant	.03	.02	.01
538	*Billy Spiers*	.20	.15	.08
539	Neal Heaton	.03	.02	.01
540	Danny Tartabull	.09	.07	.03
541	Pat Perry	.03	.02	.01
542	Darren Daulton	.03	.02	.01
543	Nelson Liriano	.03	.02	.01
544	Dennis Boyd	.05	.04	.02
545	Kevin McReynolds	.09	.07	.04
546	Kevin Hickey	.05	.04	.02
547	Jack Howell	.05	.04	.02
548	Pat Clements	.03	.02	.01
549	Don Zimmer	.03	.02	.01
550	Julio Franco	.09	.07	.04
551	Tim Crews	.03	.02	.01
552	*Mike Smith*(FC)	.15	.11	.06
553	*Scott Scudder*(FC)	.20	.15	.11
554	Jay Buhner	.08	.06	.03
555	Jack Morris	.07	.05	.03
556	Gene Larkin	.03	.02	.01
557	*Jeff Innis*	.15	.11	.08
558	Rafael Ramirez	.04	.03	.02
559	Andy McGaffigan	.04	.03	.02
560	Steve Sax	.08	.06	.03
561	Ken Dayley	.03	.02	.01
562	Chad Kreuter	.10	.08	.04
563	Alex Sanchez	.10	.08	.04
564	#1 Draft Pick *(Tyler Houston)*(FC)	.50	.40	.20
565	Scott Fletcher	.05	.04	.02
566	Mark Knudson	.06	.05	.02
567	Ron Gant	.08	.06	.03
568	John Smiley	.07	.05	.03
569	Ivan Calderon	.05	.04	.02
570	Cal Ripken	.15	.11	.06
571	Brett Butler	.06	.05	.02
572	Greg Harris	.09	.07	.04
573	Danny Heep	.03	.02	.01
574	Bill Swift	.04	.03	.02
575	Lance Parrish	.07	.05	.03
576	*Mike Dyer*(FC)	.20	.15	.08
577	Charlie Hayes(FC)	.10	.08	.04
578	Joe Magrane	.09	.07	.04
579	Art Howe	.03	.02	.01
580	Joe Carter	.15	.11	.06
581	Ken Griffey	.05	.04	.02
582	Rick Honeycutt	.03	.02	.01
583	Bruce Benedict	.03	.02	.01
584	*Phil Stephenson*(FC)	.09	.07	.04

		MT	NR MT	EX
585	Kal Daniels	.10	.08	.04
586	Ed Nunez	.03	.02	.01
587	Lance Johnson	.08	.06	.03
588	Rick Rhoden	.03	.02	.01
589	Mike Aldrete	.03	.02	.01
590	Ozzie Smith	.10	.08	.04
591	Todd Stottlemyre	.08	.06	.03
592	R.J. Reynolds	.03	.02	.01
593	Scott Bradley	.03	.02	.01
594	*Luis Sojo*(FC)	.20	.15	.08
595	Greg Swindell	.10	.08	.04
596	Jose DeJesus(FC)	.10	.08	.04
597	Chris Bosio	.07	.05	.03
598	Brady Anderson	.05	.04	.02
599	Frank Williams	.03	.02	.01
600	Darryl Strawberry	.30	.15	.08
601	Luis Rivera	.04	.03	.02
602	Scott Garrelts	.07	.05	.03
603	Tony Armas	.03	.02	.01
604	Ron Robinson	.03	.02	.01
605	Mike Scioscia	.07	.05	.03
606	Storm Davis	.07	.05	.03
607	Steve Jeltz	.03	.02	.01
608	*Eric Anthony*(FC)	1.75	1.25	.70
609	Sparky Anderson	.03	.02	.01
610	Pedro Guerrero	.12	.09	.05
611	Walt Terrell	.05	.04	.02
612	Dave Gallagher	.07	.05	.02
613	Jeff Pico	.04	.03	.02
614	Nelson Santovenia	.09	.07	.04
615	Rob Deer	.07	.05	.03
616	Brian Holman	.10	.08	.04
617	Geronimo Berroa	.08	.06	.03
618	Eddie Whitson	.05	.04	.02
619	Rob Ducey	.08	.06	.03
620	*Tony Castillo*(FC)	.20	.15	.08
621	Melido Perez	.07	.05	.03
622	Sid Bream	.05	.04	.02
623	Jim Corsi	.05	.04	.02
624	Darrin Jackson	.04	.03	.02
625	Roger McDowell	.07	.05	.03
626	Bob Melvin	.03	.02	.01
627	Jose Rijo	.07	.05	.03
628	Candy Maldonado	.04	.03	.02
629	Eric Hetzel(FC)	.10	.08	.04
630	Gary Gaetti	.10	.08	.04
631	*John Wetteland*(FC)	.20	.15	.08
632	Scott Lusader	.06	.05	.02
633	Dennis Cook(FC)	.25	.20	.10
634	Luis Polonia	.06	.05	.02
635	Brian Downing	.06	.05	.02
636	Jesse Orosco	.03	.02	.01
637	Craig Reynolds	.03	.02	.01
638	Jeff Montgomery	.07	.05	.03
639	Tony LaRussa	.03	.02	.01
640	Rick Sutcliffe	.06	.05	.02
641	*Doug Strange*(FC)	.15	.11	.06
642	Jack Armstrong	.04	.03	.02
643	Alfredo Griffin	.04	.03	.02
644	Paul Assenmacher	.04	.03	.02
645	Jose Oquendo	.06	.05	.02
646	Checklist 529-660	.03	.02	.01
647	Rex Hudler	.03	.02	.01
648	Jim Clancy	.03	.02	.01
649	*Dan Murphy*(FC)	.15	.11	.06
650	Mike Witt	.06	.05	.02
651	Rafael Santana	.06	.05	.02
652	Mike Boddicker	.06	.05	.02
653	John Moses	.03	.02	.01
654	#1 Draft Pick *(Paul Coleman)*(FC)	.30	.25	.12
655	Gregg Olson	.30	.25	.12
656	Mackey Sasser	.05	.04	.02
657	Terry Mulholland	.06	.05	.02
658	Donell Nixon	.03	.02	.01
659	Greg Cadaret	.03	.02	.01
660	Vince Coleman	.10	.08	.04
661	Turn Back The Clock - 1985 (Dick Howser)	.07	.05	.03
662	Turn Back The Clock - 1980 (Mike Schmidt)	.07	.05	.03
663	Turn Back The Clock - 1975 (Fred Lynn)	.07	.05	.03
664	Turn Back The Clock - 1970 (Johnny Bench)	.07	.05	.03
665	Turn Back The Clock - 1965 (Sandy Koufax)	.07	.05	.03
666	Brian Fisher	.05	.04	.02
667	Curt Wilkerson	.03	.02	.01
668	*Joe Oliver*(FC)	.30	.25	.12
669	Tom Lasorda	.03	.02	.01
670	Dennis Eckersley	.09	.07	.04
671	Bob Boone	.09	.07	.04
672	Roy Smith	.03	.02	.01
673	Joey Meyer	.03	.02	.01
674	Spike Owen	.05	.04	.02
675	Jim Abbott	.80	.60	.30
676	Randy Kutcher(FC)	.07	.05	.03
677	Jay Tibbs	.03	.02	.01
678	Kirt Manwaring	.10	.08	.04
679	Gary Ward	.04	.03	.02
680	Howard Johnson	.15	.11	.06
681	Mike Schooler	.07	.05	.03
682	Dann Bilardello	.03	.02	.01
683	*Kenny Rogers*	.10	.08	.04
684	*Julio Machado*(FC)	.20	.15	.08
685	Tony Fernandez	.09	.07	.04
686	Carmelo Martinez	.06	.05	.02
687	Tim Birtsas	.03	.02	.01
688	Milt Thompson	.06	.05	.02
689	Rich Yett	.03	.02	.01
690	Mark McGwire	.50	.40	.20
691	Chuck Cary	.03	.02	.01
692	Sammy Sosa	.50	.40	.20
693	Calvin Schiraldi	.03	.02	.01
694	*Mike Stanton*(FC)	.15	.11	.06
695	Tom Henke	.06	.05	.02
696	B.J. Surhoff	.07	.05	.03
697	Mike Davis	.03	.02	.01
698	*Omar Vizquel*	.10	.08	.04
699	Jim Leyland	.03	.02	.01
700	Kirby Puckett	.25	.20	.10
701	*Bernie Williams*(FC)	.25	.20	.10
702	Tony Phillips	.04	.03	.02

		MT	NR MT	EX
703	*Jeff Brantley*	.12	.09	.05
704	*Chip Hale*(FC)	.20	.15	.08
705	Claudell Washington	.07	.05	.03
706	Geno Petralli	.03	.02	.01
707	Luis Aquino	.03	.02	.01
708	Larry Sheets	.03	.02	.01
709	Juan Berenguer	.03	.02	.01
710	Von Hayes	.09	.07	.04
711	Rick Aguilera	.05	.04	.02
712	Todd Benzinger	.09	.07	.04
713	*Tim Drummond*(FC)	.15	.11	.06
714	*Marquis Grissom*(FC)	.80	.60	.30
715	Greg Maddux	.15	.11	.06
716	Steve Balboni	.03	.02	.01
717	Ron Kakovice	.03	.02	.01
718	Gary Sheffield	.50	.40	.20
719	*Wally Whitehurst*(FC)	.15	.11	.06
720	Andres Galarraga	.15	.11	.06
721	Lee Mazzilli	.03	.02	.01
722	Felix Fermin	.03	.02	.01
723	Jeff Robinson	.05	.04	.02
724	Juan Bell(FC)	.10	.08	.04
725	Terry Pendleton	.07	.05	.03
726	Gene Nelson	.03	.02	.01
727	Pat Tabler	.05	.04	.02
728	Jim Acker	.03	.02	.01
729	Bobby Valentine	.03	.02	.01
730	Tony Gwynn	.20	.15	.08
731	Don Carman	.05	.04	.02
732	Ernie Riles	.03	.02	.01
733	John Dopson	.09	.07	.04
734	Kevin Elster	.06	.05	.02
735	Charlie Hough	.06	.05	.02
736	Rick Dempsey	.03	.02	.01
737	Chris Sabo	.15	.11	.06
738	*Gene Harris*	.10	.08	.04
739	Dale Sveum	.04	.03	.02
740	Jesse Barfield	.08	.06	.03
741	Steve Wilson	.10	.08	.04
742	Ernie Whitt	.05	.04	.02
743	Tom Candiotti	.05	.04	.02
744	*Kelly Mann*(FC)	.20	.15	.08
745	Hubie Brooks	.06	.05	.02
746	Dave Smith	.06	.05	.02
747	Randy Bush	.03	.02	.01
748	Doyle Alexander	.06	.05	.02
749	Mark Parent	.04	.03	.02
750	Dale Murphy	.10	.08	.04
751	Steve Lyons	.04	.03	.02
752	Tom Gordon	.50	.40	.20
753	Chris Speier	.03	.02	.01
754	Bob Walk	.05	.04	.02
755	Rafael Palmeiro	.08	.06	.03
756	Ken Howell	.03	.02	.01
757	*Larry Walker*(FC)	.30	.25	.12
758	Mark Thurmond	.03	.02	.01
759	Tom Trebelhorn	.03	.02	.01
760	Wade Boggs	.40	.30	.15
761	Mike Jackson	.05	.04	.02
762	Doug Dascenzo	.07	.05	.03
763	Denny Martinez	.07	.05	.03
764	Tim Teufel	.05	.04	.02
765	Chili Davis	.07	.05	.03
766	Brian Meyer(FC)	.10	.08	.04
767	Tracy Jones	.06	.05	.02
768	Chuck Crim	.04	.03	.02
769	*Greg Hibbard*(FC)	.30	.25	.12
770	Cory Snyder	.09	.07	.04
771	Pete Smith	.06	.05	.02
772	Jeff Reed	.03	.02	.01
773	Dave Leiper	.03	.02	.01
774	*Ben McDonald*(FC)	2.00	1.50	.80
775	Andy Van Slyke	.09	.07	.04
776	Charlie Leibrandt	.04	.03	.02
777	Tim Laudner	.03	.02	.01
778	Mike Jeffcoat	.03	.02	.01
779	Lloyd Moseby	.06	.05	.02
780	Orel Hershiser	.15	.11	.06
781	Mario Diaz	.03	.02	.01
782	Jose Alvarez	.03	.02	.01
783	Checklist 661-792	.03	.02	.01
784	Scott Bailes	.03	.02	.01
785	Jim Rice	.07	.05	.03
786	Eric King	.04	.03	.02
787	Rene Gonzales	.03	.02	.01
788	Frank DiPino	.03	.02	.01
789	John Wathan	.03	.02	.01
790	Gary Carter	.07	.05	.03
791	Alvaro Espinoza	.15	.11	.06
792	Gerald Perry	.06	.05	.02

1987 Toys "R" Us

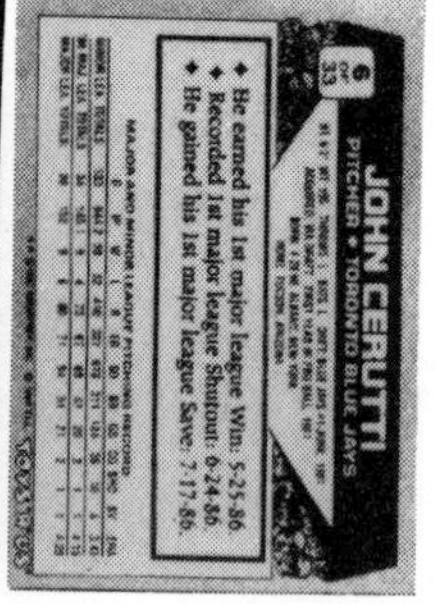

Marked as a collectors' edition set and titled "Baseball Rookies," the 1987 Toys "R" Us issue was produced by Topps for the toy store chain. The set is comprised of 33 glossy-coated cards, each measur ing 2-1/2" by 3-1/2". The card fronts are very colorful, employing nine different colors including deep black borders. The backs, printed in blue and orange, contain career highlights and composite minor and major league statistics. The set was distributed in a specially designed box and sold for **$1.99** in retail outlets.

		MT	NR MT	EX
	Complete Set:	5.00	3.75	2.00
	Common Player:	.09	.07	.04
1	Andy Allanson	.12	.09	.05
2	Paul Assenmacher	.12	.09	.05
3	Scott Bailes	.12	.09	.05
4	Barry Bonds	.30	.25	.12
5	Jose Canseco	1.50	1.25	.60
6	John Cerutti	.15	.11	.06
7	Will Clark	.90	.70	.35
8	Kal Daniels	.25	.20	.10
9	Jim Deshaies	.15	.11	.06
10	Mark Eichhorn	.12	.09	.05
11	Ed Hearn	.09	.07	.04
12	Pete Incaviglia	.40	.30	.15
13	Bo Jackson	.60	.45	.25
14	Wally Joyner	1.00	.70	.40
15	Charlie Kerfeld	.09	.07	.04
16	Eric King	.12	.09	.05
17	John Kruk	.40	.30	.15
18	Barry Larkin	.30	.25	.12
19	Mike LaValliere	.15	.11	.06
20	Greg Mathews	.15	.11	.06
21	Kevin Mitchell	.20	.15	.08
22	Dan Plesac	.20	.15	.08
23	Bruce Ruffin	.15	.11	.06
24	Ruben Sierra	.50	.40	.20
25	Cory Snyder	.40	.30	.15
26	Kurt Stillwell	.20	.15	.08
27	Dale Sveum	.12	.09	.05
28	Danny Tartabull	.30	.25	.12
29	Andres Thomas	.15	.11	.06
30	Robby Thompson	.15	.11	.06
31	Jim Traber	.09	.07	.04
32	Mitch Williams	.15	.11	.06
33	Todd Worrell	.30	.25	.12

1988 Toys "R" Us

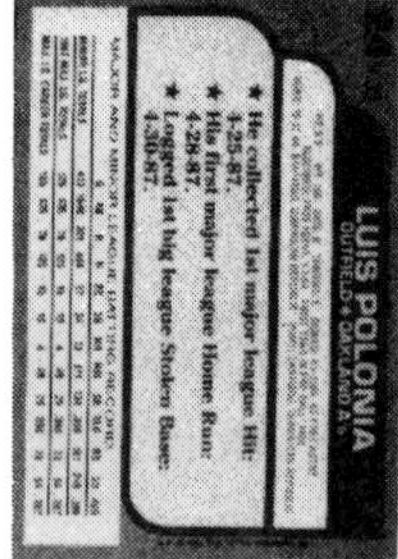

This 33-card boxed edition was produced by Topps for exclusive distribution at Toys "R" Us stores. The glossy standard-size cards spotlight rookies in both closeups and action photos on a bright blue background inlaid with yellow. The Toys "R" Us logo frames the top left corner, above a curving white banner that reads "Topps 1988 Collectors' Edition Rookies". A black Topps logo hugs the upper right-hand edge of the photo. The player name, red-lettered on a tube of yellow, frames the bottom. Card backs are horizontal, blue and pink on a bright pink background and include the player name, personal information and career highlights and stats.

		MT	NR MT	EX
	Complete Set:	5.00	3.75	2.00
	Common Player:	.09	.07	.04
1	Todd Benzinger	.20	.15	.08
2	Bob Brower	.09	.07	.04
3	Jerry Browne	.09	.07	.04
4	DeWayne Buice	.09	.07	.04
5	Ellis Burks	.70	.50	.30
6	Ken Caminiti	.12	.09	.05
7	Casey Candaele	.09	.07	.04
8	Dave Cone	.50	.40	.20
9	Kelly Downs	.20	.15	.08
10	Mike Dunne	.15	.11	.06
11	Ken Gerhart	.12	.09	.05
12	Mike Greenwell	.70	.50	.30
13	Mike Henneman	.12	.09	.05
14	Sam Horn	.20	.15	.08
15	Joe Magrane	.20	.15	.08
16	Fred Manrique	.12	.09	.05
17	John Marzano	.12	.09	.05
18	Fred McGriff	.15	.11	.06
19	Mark McGwire	1.00	.70	.40
20	Jeff Musselman	.12	.09	.05
21	Randy Myers	.20	.15	.08
22	Matt Nokes	.40	.30	.15
23	Al Pedrique	.12	.09	.05
24	Luis Polonia	.15	.11	.06
25	Billy Ripken	.25	.20	.10
26	Benny Santiago	.25	.20	.10
27	Kevin Seitzer	.70	.50	.30

		MT	NR MT	EX
28	John Smiley	.20	.15	.08
29	Mike Stanley	.09	.07	.04
30	Terry Steinbach	.20	.15	.08
31	B.J. Surhoff	.25	.20	.10
32	Bobby Thigpen	.12	.09	.05
33	Devon White	.25	.20	.10

1989 Toys "R" Us

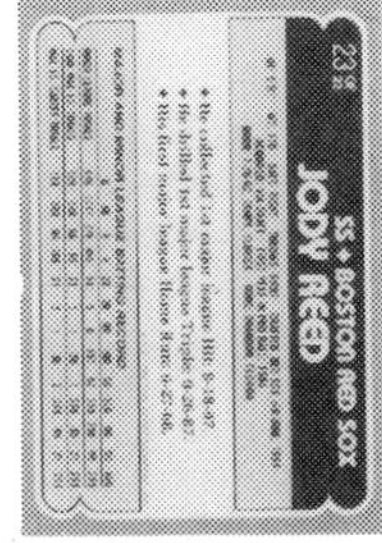

This glossy set of 33 top rookies was produced by Topps for the Toys 'R' Us chain and was sold in a special box. Each player's name and position appear below the full-color photo, while the Toys 'R' Us logo and "Topps 1989 Collector's Edition" appear along the top. Major and minor league stats are on the back. The set is numbered alphabetically.

		MT	NR MT	EX
	Complete Set:	5.00	3.75	2.00
	Common Player:	.09	.07	.04
1	Roberto Alomar	.20	.15	.08
2	Brady Anderson	.09	.07	.04
3	Tim Belcher	.20	.15	.08
4	Damon Berryhill	.12	.09	.05
5	Jay Buhner	.12	.09	.05
6	Sherman Corbett	.09	.07	.04
7	Kevin Elster	.12	.09	.05
8	Cecil Espy	.12	.09	.05
9	Dave Gallagher	.12	.09	.05
10	Ron Gant	.12	.09	.05
11	Paul Gibson	.09	.07	.04
12	Mark Grace	.90	.70	.35
13	Bryan Harvey	.12	.09	.05
14	Darrin Jackson	.09	.07	.04
15	Gregg Jefferies	1.00	.70	.40
16	Ron Jones	.15	.11	.06
17	Ricky Jordan	.70	.50	.30
18	Roberto Kelly	.25	.20	.10
19	Al Leiter	.09	.07	.04
20	Jack McDowell	.09	.07	.04
21	Melido Perez	.12	.09	.05
22	Jeff Pico	.09	.07	.04
23	Jody Reed	.12	.09	.05
24	Chris Sabo	.25	.20	.10
25	Nelson Santovenia	.15	.11	.06
26	Mackey Sasser	.09	.07	.04
27	Mike Schooler	.12	.09	.05
28	Gary Sheffield	.90	.70	.35
29	Pete Smith	.12	.09	.05
30	Pete Stanicek	.09	.07	.04
31	Jeff Treadway	.09	.07	.04
32	Walt Weiss	.25	.20	.10
33	Dave West	.35	.25	.14

1969 Transogram

Produced by the Transogram toy company, the 2-1/2" by 3-1/2" cards were printed on the bottom of toy baseball player statue boxes. The cards feature a color photo of the player surrounded by a rounded white border. Below the photo is the player's name in red and his team and other personal details all printed in black. The overall background is yellow. The cards were designed to be cut off the box, but collectors prefer to find the box intact and better still, with the statue inside. Although the 60-card set features a lot of stars, and is fairly scarce, it does not not have a lot of popularity today.

		NR MT	EX	VG
	Complete Set:	550.00	275.00	160.00
	Common Player:	.80	.40	.25
(1)	Hank Aaron	30.00	15.00	9.00
(2)	Richie Allen	4.00	2.00	1.25
(3)	Felipe Alou	3.00	1.50	.90
(4)	Matty Alou	3.00	1.50	.90
(5)	Luis Aparicio	15.00	7.50	4.50
(6)	Joe Azcue	2.00	1.00	.60
(7)	Ernie Banks	10.00	5.00	3.00
(8)	Lou Brock	20.00	10.00	6.00
(9)	John Callison	3.00	1.50	.90
(10)	Jose Cardenal	2.00	1.00	.60
(11)	Danny Cater	2.00	1.00	.60
(12)	Roberto Clemente	25.00	12.50	7.50
(13)	Willie Davis	1.00	.50	.30
(14)	Mike Epstein	2.00	1.00	.60
(15)	Jim Fregosi	1.00	.50	.30
(16)	Bob Gibson	8.00	4.00	2.50
(17)	Tom Haller	2.00	1.00	.60
(18)	Ken Harrelson	3.00	1.50	.90
(19)	Willie Horton	3.00	1.50	.90
(20)	Frank Howard	1.50	.70	.45
(21)	Tommy John	8.00	4.00	2.50
(22)	Al Kaline	10.00	5.00	3.00
(23)	Harmon Killebrew	10.00	5.00	3.00
(24)	Bobby Knoop	2.00	1.00	.60
(25)	Jerry Koosman	.80	.40	.25
(26)	Jim Lefebvre	2.00	1.00	.60
(27)	Mickey Mantle	125.00	62.00	37.00
(28)	Juan Marichal	8.00	4.00	2.50
(29)	Lee May	3.00	1.50	.90
(30)	Willie Mays	30.00	15.00	9.00
(31)	Bill Mazeroski	4.00	2.00	1.25
(32)	Tim McCarver	4.00	2.00	1.25
(33)	Willie McCovey	10.00	5.00	3.00
(34)	Denny McLain	1.50	.70	.45
(35)	Dave McNally	3.00	1.50	.90
(36)	Rick Monday	3.00	1.50	.90
(37)	Blue Moon Odom	.80	.40	.25
(38)	Tony Oliva	1.50	.70	.45
(39)	Camilo Pascual	3.00	1.50	.90
(40)	Tony Perez	7.00	3.50	2.00
(41)	Rico Petrocelli	1.00	.50	.30
(42)	Rick Reichardt	.80	.40	.25
(43)	Brooks Robinson	25.00	12.50	7.50
(44)	Frank Robinson	8.00	4.00	2.50
(45)	Cookie Rojas	2.00	1.00	.60
(46)	Pete Rose	30.00	15.00	9.00
(47)	Ron Santo	1.50	.70	.45
(48)	Tom Seaver	10.00	5.00	3.00
(49)	Rusty Staub	4.00	2.00	1.25
(50)	Mel Stottlemyre	1.00	.50	.30
(51)	Ron Swoboda	.80	.40	.25
(52)	Luis Tiant	3.00	1.50	.90
(53)	Joe Torre	4.00	2.00	1.25
(54)	Cesar Tovar	2.00	1.00	.60
(55)	Pete Ward	2.00	1.00	.60
(56)	Roy White	3.00	1.50	.90
(57)	Billy Williams	15.00	7.50	4.50
(58)	Don Wilson	2.00	1.00	.60
(59)	Jim Wynn	.80	.40	.25
(60)	Carl Yastrzemski	25.00	12.50	7.50

1970 Transogram

Like the 1969 cards, the 1970 Transogram cards were available on boxes of Transogram baseball statues. The cards are slightly larger at 2-9/16" by 3- 1/2". The 30-card set has the same pictures as the 1969 set except for Joe Torre. All players in the '70 set were included in the '69 Transogram issue except for Reggie Jackson, Sam McDowell and Boog Powell. Three cards and three statues were part of each Transogram box in 1970. When available, most collectors prefer to find the cards as uncut panels of three, better yet, as complete boxes.

		NR MT	EX	VG
	Complete Set:	275.00	150.00	80.00
	Common Player:	.80	.40	.25
(1)	Hank Aaron	30.00	15.00	9.00
(2)	Ernie Banks	8.00	4.00	2.50
(3)	Roberto Clemente	25.00	12.50	6.00
(4)	Willie Davis	1.00	.50	.30
(5)	Jim Fregosi	1.00	.50	.30
(6)	Bob Gibson	8.00	4.00	2.50
(7)	Frank Howard	1.50	.70	.45
(8)	Reggie Jackson	40.00	20.00	12.00
(9)	Cleon Jones	.80	.40	.25
(10)	Al Kaline	10.00	5.00	3.00
(11)	Harmon Killebrew	10.00	5.00	3.00
(12)	Jerry Koosman	.80	.40	.25
(13)	Willie McCovey	10.00	5.00	3.00
(14)	Sam McDowell	3.00	1.50	.90
(15)	Denny McLain	1.50	.70	.45
(16)	Juan Marichal	8.00	4.00	2.50
(17)	Willie Mays	30.00	15.00	9.00
(18)	Blue Moon Odom	.80	.40	.25
(19)	Tony Oliva	1.50	.70	.45
(20)	Rico Petrocelli	1.00	.50	.30
(21)	Boog Powell	4.00	2.00	1.25
(22)	Rick Reichardt	.80	.40	.25
(23)	Frank Robinson	10.00	5.00	3.00
(24)	Pete Rose	30.00	15.00	9.00
(25)	Ron Santo	1.50	.70	.45
(26)	Tom Seaver	10.00	5.00	3.00
(27)	Mel Stottlemyre	1.00	.50	.30
(28)	Joe Torre	4.00	2.00	1.25
(29)	Jim Wynn	.80	.40	.25
(30)	Carl Yastrzemski	25.00	12.50	7.50

1970 Transogram Mets

The Transogram Mets set is a second set that the company produced in 1970. The cards are 2-9/16" by 3-1/2" and feature members of the World Champions Mets team. There are 15 cards in the set which retains the basic color picture with player's names in red and team, position and biographical details in ablack format. As with the other Transogram sets, the cards are most valuable when they are still part of their original box with the statues. Values decrease for them if the cards are removed from the box. While the Mets set does not have the attraction of many Hall of Famers as was the case with the regular set, it does make a very nice item for the Mets team collector.

		NR MT	EX	VG
	Complete Set:	110.00	55.00	35.00
	Common Player:	.80	.40	.25
(1)	Tommie Agee	3.00	1.50	.90
(2)	Ken Boswell	2.00	1.00	.60
(3)	Donn Clendenon	3.00	1.50	.90
(4)	Gary Gentry	2.00	1.00	.60
(5)	Jerry Grote	3.00	1.50	.90
(6)	Bud Harrelson	3.00	1.50	.90
(7)	Cleon Jones	.80	.40	.25
(8)	Jerry Koosman	.80	.40	.25
(9)	Ed Kranepool	3.00	1.50	.90
(10)	Tug McGraw	7.00	3.50	2.00
(11)	Nolan Ryan	75.00	38.00	23.00
(12)	Art Shamsky	2.00	1.00	.60
(13)	Tom Seaver	15.00	7.50	4.50
(14)	Ron Swoboda	.80	.40	.25
(15)	Al Weis	2.00	1.00	.60

1983 True Value White Sox

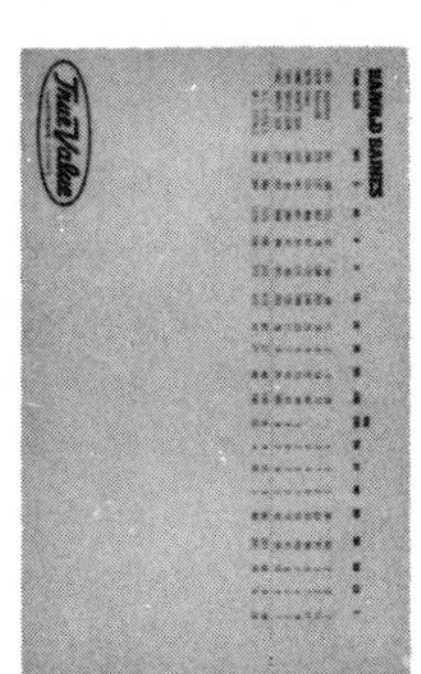

Issued by the Chicago White Sox and True Value hardware stores, these 2-5/8" by 4-1/8" cards are a rather expensive and scarce regional set. The 23-card set was originally scheduled as part of a promotion in which cards were given out at special Tuesday night games. The idea was sound, but rainouts forced the cancellation of some games so those scheduled cards were never given out. They were, however, smuggled out to hobby channels making it possible, although not easy, to assemble complete sets. The cards feature a large color photo with a wide white border. A red and blue White Sox logo is in the lower left corner, while the player's name, position and team number are in the lower right. Backs feature a True Value ad along with statistics. The three cards which were never given out through the normal channels are considered more scarce than the others. They are Marc Hill, Harold Baines and Salome Barojas.

		MT	NR MT	EX
Complete Set:		30.00	22.00	12.00
Common Player:		.40	.30	.15
1	Scott Fletcher	.60	.45	.25
2	Harold Baines	5.00	3.75	2.00
5	Vance Law	.50	.40	.20
7	Marc Hill	3.25	2.50	1.25
10	Tony LaRussa	.50	.40	.20
11	Rudy Law	.40	.30	.15
14	Tony Bernazard	.40	.30	.15
17	Jerry Hairston	.40	.30	.15
19	Greg Luzinski	1.00	.70	.40
24	Floyd Bannister	.60	.45	.25
25	Mike Squires	.40	.30	.15
30	Salome Barojas	3.25	2.50	1.25
31	LaMarr Hoyt	.50	.40	.20
34	Richard Dotson	.70	.50	.30
36	Jerry Koosman	.70	.50	.30
40	Britt Burns	.50	.40	.20
41	Dick Tidrow	.40	.30	.15
42	Ron Kittle	1.75	1.25	.70
44	Tom Paciorek	.40	.30	.15
45	Kevin Hickey	.40	.30	.15
53	Dennis Lamp	.40	.30	.15
67	Jim Kern	.40	.30	.15
72	Carlton Fisk	2.25	1.75	.90

1984 True Value White Sox

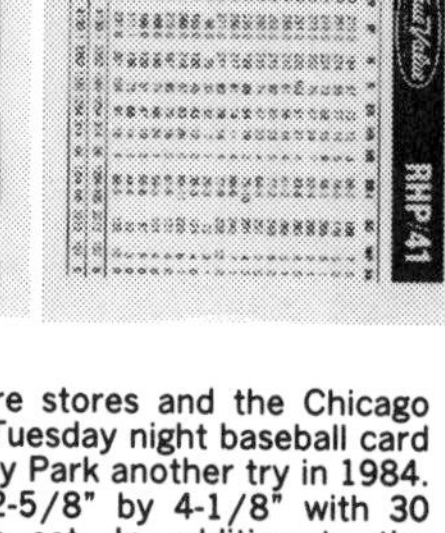

True Value hardware stores and the Chicago White Sox gave their Tuesday night baseball card promotion at Comiskey Park another try in 1984. The cards measure 2-5/8" by 4-1/8" with 30 cards comprising the set. In addition to the players, there are cards for manager Tony LaRussa, the coaching staff, and former Sox greats Luis Aparicio and Minnie Minoso. Cards designs are very similar to the 1983 cards. As the cards were given out two at a time, it was very difficult to acquire a complete set. Additionally, as numbers available vary because of attendance, some cards are scarcer than others.

		MT	NR MT	EX
Complete Set:		25.00	18.50	10.00
Common Player:		.40	.30	.15
1	Scott Fletcher	.60	.45	.25
3	Harold Baines	2.25	1.75	.90
5	Vance Law	.50	.40	.20
7	Marc Hill	.40	.30	.15
8	Dave Stegman	.40	.30	.15
10	Tony LaRussa	.50	.40	.20
11	Rudy Law	.40	.30	.15
16	Julio Cruz	.40	.30	.15
17	Jerry Hairston	.40	.30	.15
19	Greg Luzinski	.90	.70	.35
20	Jerry Dybzinski	.40	.30	.15
24	Floyd Bannister	.60	.45	.25
25	Mike Squires	.40	.30	.15
27	Ron Reed	.40	.30	.15
29	Greg Walker	1.50	1.25	.60
30	Salome Barojas	.40	.30	.15
31	LaMarr Hoyt	.50	.40	.20
32	Tim Hulett	1.00	.70	.40
34	Richard Dotson	.70	.50	.30
40	Britt Burns	.40	.30	.15
41	Tom Seaver	3.00	2.25	1.25
42	Ron Kittle	1.00	.70	.40
44	Tom Paciorek	.40	.30	.15
50	Juan Agosto	.40	.30	.15
59	Tom Brennan	1.00	.70	.40
72	Carlton Fisk	2.00	1.50	.80
---	Minnie Minoso	2.00	1.50	.80
---	Luis Aparicio	2.00	1.50	.80
---	Nancy Faust (organist)	1.00	.70	.40
---	The Coaching Staff (Ed Brinkman, Dave Duncan, Art Kusnyer, Tony LaRussa, Jim Leyland, Dave Nelson, Joe Nossek)	.40	.30	.15

1986 True Value

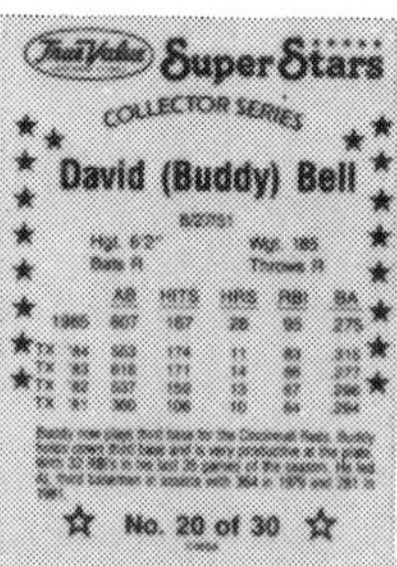

A 30-card set of 2-1/2" by 3-1/2" cards was available in three-card packets at True Value hardware stores with a purchase of $5 or more. Cards feature a photo enclosed by stars and a ball and bat at the bottom. The player's name and team are in the lower left while his position and a Major League Baseball logo are in the lower right. The True Value logo is in the upper left. Above the picture runs the phrase "Collector Series." Backs feature some personal information and brief 1985 statistics. Along with the player cards, the folders contained a sweepstakes card offering trips to post-season games and other prizes.

		MT	NR MT	EX
Complete Panel Set:		9.00	6.75	3.50
Complete Singles Set:		3.00	2.25	1.25
Common Panel:		.40	.30	.15
Common Single Player:		.05	.04	.02
Panel		1.00	.70	.40
1	Pedro Guerrero	.08	.06	.03
2	Steve Garvey	.15	.11	.06
3	Eddie Murray	.20	.15	.08
Panel		2.75	2.00	1.00
4	Pete Rose	.30	.25	.12
5	Don Mattingly	.80	.60	.30
6	Fernando Valenzuela	.10	.08	.04
Panel		.60	.45	.25
7	Jim Rice	.15	.11	.06
8	Kirk Gibson	.10	.08	.04
9	Ozzie Smith	.08	.06	.03
Panel		1.00	.70	.40
10	Dale Murphy	.20	.15	.08
11	Robin Yount	.10	.08	.04
12	Tom Seaver	.15	.11	.06
Panel		.80	.60	.30
13	Reggie Jackson	.15	.11	.06
14	Ryne Sandberg	.10	.08	.04
15	Bruce Sutter	.05	.04	.02
Panel		1.00	.70	.40
16	Gary Carter	.15	.11	.06
17	George Brett	.20	.15	.08
18	Rick Sutcliffe	.05	.04	.02
Panel		.40	.30	.15
19	Dave Stieb	.05	.04	.02
20	Buddy Bell	.05	.04	.02
21	Alvin Davis	.08	.06	.03
Panel		.60	.45	.25
22	Cal Ripken, Jr.	.20	.15	.08
23	Bill Madlock	.05	.04	.02
24	Kent Hrbek	.10	.08	.04
Panel		.50	.40	.20
25	Lou Whitaker	.08	.06	.03
26	Nolan Ryan	.15	.11	.06
27	Dwayne Murphy	.05	.04	.02
Panel		1.75	1.25	.70
28	Mike Schmidt	.20	.15	.08
29	Andre Dawson	.10	.08	.04
30	Wade Boggs	.50	.40	.20

1932 U.S. Caramel

Produced by the U.S. Caramel Company, Boston, this set is not limited to baseball. Rather, it is a set of 31 "Famous Athletes" of which some 27 are baseball players. The 2-1/2" by 3" cards have a black and white picture on the front with a red background and white border. The player's name appears in white above the picture. The backs feature the player's name, position, team and league as well as a redemption ad and card number. The cards were among the last of the caramel card sets and are very scarce today. The cards could be redeemed for a baseball and

baseball glove. Card #16 was recently discovered and is not included in the complete set price.

		NR MT	EX	VG
Complete Set:		20000.	10000.	6000.
Common Player:		450.00	225.00	135.00
1	Edward T. (Eddie) Collins	650.00	325.00	200.00
2	Paul (Big Poison) Waner	500.00	250.00	150.00
4	William (Bill) Terry	500.00	250.00	150.00
5	Earl B. Combs (Earle)	500.00	250.00	150.00
6	William (Bill) Dickey	650.00	325.00	200.00
7	Joseph (Joe) Cronin	675.00	337.00	202.00
8	Charles (Chick) Hafey	500.00	250.00	150.00
10	Walter (Rabbit) Maranville	500.00	250.00	150.00
11	Rogers (Rajah) Hornsby	900.00	450.00	275.00
12	Gordon (Mickey) Cochrane	500.00	250.00	150.00
13	Lloyd (Little Poison) Waner	500.00	250.00	150.00
14	Tyrus (Ty) Cobb	2000.	1000.	600.00
16	Charles (Lindy) Lindstrom	25000.	12500.	7500.
17	Al. Simmons	500.00	250.00	150.00
18	Anthony (Tony) Lazzeri	500.00	250.00	150.00
19	Walter (Wally) Berger	450.00	225.00	135.00
20	Charles (Large Charlie) Ruffing	500.00	250.00	150.00
21	Charles (Chuck) Klein	500.00	250.00	150.00
23	James (Jimmy) Foxx	650.00	325.00	195.00
24	Frank J. (Lefty) O'Doul	450.00	225.00	135.00
26	Henry (Lou) Gehrig	2000.	1000.	600.00
27	Robert (Lefty) Grove	750.00	375.00	225.00
28	Edward Brant (Brandt)	450.00	225.00	135.00
29	George Earnshaw	450.00	225.00	135.00
30	Frank (Frankie) Frisch	675.00	337.00	202.00
31	Vernon (Lefty) Gomez	675.00	337.00	202.00
32	George (Babe) Ruth	3000.	1500.	900.00

1989 Upper Deck

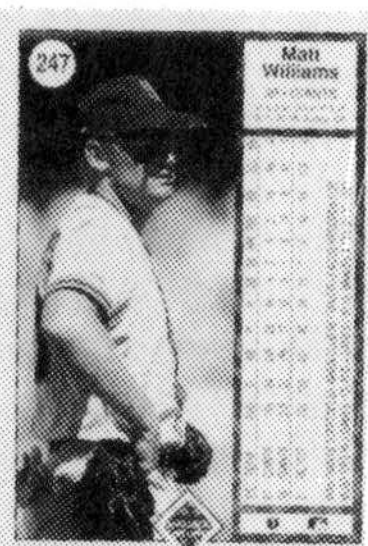

This premiere "Collector's Choice' issue from Upper Deck contains 700 cards (2-1/2" by 3-1/2") with full-color photos on both sides. The first 26 cards feature Star Rookies. The set also includes 26 special portrait cards with team checklist backs and seven numberical checklist cards (one for each 100 numbers). Team Checklist cards feature individual player portraits by artist Vernon Wells. Major 1988 award winners (Cy Young, Rookie of Year, MVP) are honored on 10 cards in the set, in addition to their individual player cards. There are also special cards for the Most Valuable Players in both League Championship series and the World Series. The card fronts feature head-and-shoulder poses framed by a white border. A vertical brown and green artist's rendition of the runner's lane that leads from home plate to first base is found along the right margin. The backs carry full-color action poses that fill the card back, except for a compact (yet complete) stats chart. A high-number series, cards 701-800, featuring rookies and traded players, was released in mid- season in foil packs mixed within the complete set, in boxed complete sets and in high number set boxes.

	MT	NR MT	EX
Complete Set: 1-700	50.00	37.00	20.00
Common Player: 1-700	.08	.06	.03
Complete Set: 1-800	70.00	50.00	30.00
Common Player: 701-800	.10	.08	.04

		MT	NR MT	EX
1	Star Rookie *(Ken Griffey, Jr.)*	25.00	18.50	10.00
2	Star Rookie *(Luis Medina)*	.30	.25	.12
3	Star Rookie *(Tony Chance)*	.20	.15	.08
4	Star Rookie (Dave Otto)	.08	.06	.03
5	Star Rookie *(Sandy Alomar, Jr.)*	3.00	2.25	1.25
6	Star Rookie *(Rolando Roomes)*	.40	.30	.15
7	Star Rookie *(David West)*	.40	.30	.15
8	Star Rookie *(Cris Carpenter)*	.30	.25	.12
9	Star Rookie (Gregg Jefferies)	3.00	2.25	1.25
10	Star Rookie *(Doug Dascenzo)*	.25	.20	.10
11	Star Rookie *(Ron Jones)*	.35	.25	.14
12	Star Rookie *(Luis de los Santos)*	.25	.20	.10
13a	Star Rookie *(Gary Sheffield)* (SS position on front is upside down)	4.00	3.00	1.50
13b	Star Rookie *(Gary Sheffield)* (SS position on front is correct)	2.25	1.75	.90
14	Star Rookie *(Mike Harkey)*	.50	.40	.20
15	Star Rookie *(Lance Blankenship)*	.25	.20	.10
16	Star Rookie *(William Brennan)*	.20	.15	.08
17	Star Rookie *(John Smoltz)*	1.00	.70	.40
18	Star Rookie *(Ramon Martinez)*	3.00	2.25	1.25
19	Star Rookie *(Mark Lemke)*	.20	.15	.08
20	Star Rookie *(Juan Bell)*	.50	.40	.20
21	Star Rookie *(Rey Palacios)*	.20	.15	.08
22	Star Rookie *(Felix Jose)*	.60	.45	.25
23	Star Rookie *(Van Snider)*	.25	.20	.10
24	Star Rookie *(Dante Bichette)*	.40	.30	.15
25	Star Rookie *(Randy Johnson)*	.60	.45	.25
26	Star Rookie *(Carlos Quintana)*	.50	.40	.20
27	Star Rookie Checklist 1-26	.08	.06	.03
28	*Mike Schooler*	.40	.30	.15
29	Randy St. Claire	.08	.06	.03
30	*Jerald Clark*	.25	.20	.10
31	Kevin Gross	.08	.06	.03
32	*Dan Firova*	.20	.15	.08
33	Jeff Calhoun	.08	.06	.03
34	Tommy Hinzo	.08	.06	.03
35	*Ricky Jordan*	1.75	1.25	.70
36	Larry Parrish	.08	.06	.03
37	Bret Saberhagen	.15	.11	.06
38	Mike Smithson	.08	.06	.03
39	Dave Dravecky	.08	.06	.03
40	Ed Romero	.08	.06	.03
41	Jeff Musselman	.08	.06	.03
42	Ed Hearn	.08	.06	.03
43	Rance Mulliniks	.08	.06	.03
44	Jim Eisenreich	.08	.06	.03
45	*Sil Campusano*	.20	.15	.08
46	Mike Krukow	.08	.06	.03
47	*Paul Gibson*	.20	.15	.08
48	Mike LaCoss	.08	.06	.03
49	Larry Herndon	.08	.06	.03
50	Scott Garrelts	.08	.06	.03
51	Dwayne Henry	.08	.06	.03
52	Jim Acker	.08	.06	.03
53	Steve Sax	.15	.11	.06
54	Pete O'Brien	.08	.06	.03
55	Paul Runge	.08	.06	.03
56	Rick Rhoden	.08	.06	.03
57	*John Dopson*	.25	.20	.10
58	Casey Candaele	.08	.06	.03
59	Dave Righetti	.12	.09	.05
60	Joe Hesketh	.08	.06	.03
61	Frank DiPino	.08	.06	.03
62	Tim Laudner	.08	.06	.03
63	Jamie Moyer	.08	.06	.03
64	Fred Toliver	.08	.06	.03
65	Mitch Webster	.08	.06	.03
66	John Tudor	.10	.08	.04
67	John Cangelosi	.08	.06	.03
68	Mike Devereaux	.15	.11	.06
69	Brian Fisher	.08	.06	.03
70	Mike Marshall	.12	.09	.05
71	Zane Smith	.08	.06	.03
72a	Brian Holton (ball not visible on card front, photo actually Shawn Hillegas)	2.00	1.50	.80
72b	Brian Holton (ball visible, correct photo)	.15	.11	.06
73	Jose Guzman	.10	.08	.04
74	Rick Mahler	.08	.06	.03
75	John Shelby	.08	.06	.03
76	Jim Deshaies	.08	.06	.03
77	Bobby Meacham	.08	.06	.03
78	Bryn Smith	.08	.06	.03
79	Joaquin Andujar	.08	.06	.03
80	Richard Dotson	.08	.06	.03
81	Charlie Lea	.08	.06	.03
82	Calvin Schiraldi	.08	.06	.03
83	Les Straker	.08	.06	.03
84	Les Lancaster	.08	.06	.03
85	Allan Anderson	.08	.06	.03
86	Junior Ortiz	.08	.06	.03
87	Jesse Orosco	.08	.06	.03
88	Felix Fermin	.08	.06	.03
89	Dave Anderson	.08	.06	.03
90	Rafael Belliard	.08	.06	.03
91	Franklin Stubbs	.08	.06	.03
92	Cecil Espy	.08	.06	.03
93	Albert Hall	.08	.06	.03
94	Tim Leary	.08	.06	.03
95	Mitch Williams	.08	.06	.03
96	Tracy Jones	.10	.08	.04
97	Danny Darwin	.08	.06	.03
98	Gary Ward	.08	.06	.03
99	Neal Heaton	.08	.06	.03
100	Jim Pankovits	.08	.06	.03
101	Bill Doran	.08	.06	.03
102	Tim Wallach	.10	.08	.04
103	Joe Magrane	.10	.08	.04
104	Ozzie Virgil	.08	.06	.03
105	Alvin Davis	.12	.09	.05
106	Tom Brookens	.08	.06	.03
107	Shawon Dunston	.10	.08	.04
108	Tracy Woodson	.10	.08	.04
109	Nelson Liriano	.08	.06	.03
110	Devon White	.12	.09	.05
111	Steve Balboni	.08	.06	.03
112	Buddy Bell	.08	.06	.03
113	*German Jimenez*	.08	.06	.03
114	Ken Dayley	.08	.06	.03
115	Andres Galarraga	.15	.11	.06
116	Mike Scioscia	.08	.06	.03
117	Gary Pettis	.08	.06	.03
118	Ernie Whitt	.08	.06	.03
119	Bob Boone	.08	.06	.03
120	Ryne Sandberg	.25	.20	.10
121	Bruce Benedict	.08	.06	.03
122	Hubie Brooks	.10	.08	.04
123	Mike Moore	.08	.06	.03
124	Wallace Johnson	.08	.06	.03
125	Bob Horner	.10	.08	.04
126	Chili Davis	.08	.06	.03
127	Manny Trillo	.08	.06	.03
128	Chet Lemon	.08	.06	.03
129	John Cerutti	.08	.06	.03
130	Orel Hershiser	.25	.20	.10
131	Terry Pendleton	.10	.08	.04
132	Jeff Blauser	.10	.08	.04
133	Mike Fitzgerald	.08	.06	.03
134	Henry Cotto	.08	.06	.03
135	Gerald Young	.12	.09	.05
136	Luis Salazar	.08	.06	.03
137	Alejandro Pena	.08	.06	.03
138	Jack Howell	.08	.06	.03
139	Tony Fernandez	.12	.09	.05
140	Mark Grace	1.75	1.25	.70
141	Ken Caminiti	.08	.06	.03
142	Mike Jackson	.08	.06	.03
143	Larry McWilliams	.08	.06	.03
144	Andres Thomas	.08	.06	.03
145	Nolan Ryan	1.25	.90	.50
146	Mike Davis	.08	.06	.03
147	DeWayne Buice	.08	.06	.03
148	Jody Davis	.08	.06	.03
149	Jesse Barfield	.10	.08	.04
150	Matt Nokes	.20	.15	.08
151	Jerry Reuss	.08	.06	.03
152	Rick Cerone	.08	.06	.03
153	Storm Davis	.10	.08	.04
154	Marvell Wynne	.08	.06	.03
155	Will Clark	.80	.60	.30
156	Luis Aguayo	.08	.06	.03
157	Willie Upshaw	.08	.06	.03
158	Randy Bush	.08	.06	.03
159	Ron Darling	.12	.09	.05
160	Kal Daniels	.15	.11	.06
161	Spike Owen	.08	.06	.03
162	Luis Polonia	.08	.06	.03
163	Kevin Mitchell	.50	.40	.20
164	*Dave Gallagher*	.25	.20	.10
165	Benito Santiago	.15	.11	.06
166	Greg Gagne	.08	.06	.03
167	Ken Phelps	.08	.06	.03
168	Sid Fernandez	.10	.08	.04
169	Bo Diaz	.08	.06	.03
170	Cory Snyder	.15	.11	.06
171	Eric Show	.08	.06	.03
172	Rob Thompson	.08	.06	.03
173	Marty Barrett	.08	.06	.03
174	Dave Henderson	.10	.08	.04
175	Ozzie Guillen	.08	.06	.03
176	Barry Lyons	.08	.06	.03
177	*Kelvin Torve*(FC)	.20	.15	.08
178	Don Slaught	.08	.06	.03
179	Steve Lombardozzi	.08	.06	.03
180	*Chris Sabo*	.80	.60	.30
181	Jose Uribe	.08	.06	.03
182	Shane Mack	.08	.06	.03
183	Ron Karkovice	.08	.06	.03
184	Todd Benzinger	.12	.09	.05
185	Dave Stewart	.10	.08	.04
186	Julio Franco	.10	.08	.04
187	Ron Robinson	.08	.06	.03
188	Wally Backman	.08	.06	.03
189	Randy Velarde	.08	.06	.03
190	Joe Carter	.12	.09	.05
191	Bob Welch	.10	.08	.04
192	Kelly Paris	.08	.06	.03
193	Chris Brown	.08	.06	.03
194	Rick Reuschel	.10	.08	.04
195	Roger Clemens	.50	.40	.20
196	Dave Concepcion	.10	.08	.04
197	Al Newman	.08	.06	.03
198	Brook Jacoby	.10	.08	.04
199	Mookie Wilson	.08	.06	.03
200	Don Mattingly	1.50	1.25	.60
201	Dick Schofield	.08	.06	.03
202	Mark Gubicza	.10	.08	.04
203	Gary Gaetti	.15	.11	.06
204	Dan Pasqua	.10	.08	.04
205	Andre Dawson	.20	.15	.08
206	Chris Speier	.08	.06	.03
207	Kent Tekulve	.08	.06	.03
208	Rod Scurry	.08	.06	.03
209	Scott Bailes	.08	.06	.03
210	Rickey Henderson	.35	.25	.14
211	Harold Baines	.12	.09	.05
212	Tony Armas	.08	.06	.03
213	Kent Hrbek	.20	.15	.08
214	Darrin Jackson	.08	.06	.03
215	George Brett	.35	.25	.14
216	Rafael Santana	.08	.06	.03
217	Andy Allanson	.08	.06	.03
218	Brett Butler	.08	.06	.03
219	Steve Jeltz	.08	.06	.03
220	Jay Buhner	.10	.08	.04
221	Bo Jackson	.60	.45	.25
222	Angel Salazar	.08	.06	.03
223	Kirk McCaskill	.08	.06	.03
224	Steve Lyons	.08	.06	.03
225	Bert Blyleven	.10	.08	.04
226	Scott Bradley	.08	.06	.03
227	Bob Melvin	.08	.06	.03
228	Ron Kittle	.08	.06	.03
229	Phil Bradley	.10	.08	.04
230	Tommy John	.12	.09	.05
231	Greg Walker	.08	.06	.03
232	Juan Berenguer	.08	.06	.03
233	Pat Tabler	.08	.06	.03
234	*Terry Clark*	.20	.15	.08
235	Rafael Palmeiro	.25	.20	.10
236	Paul Zuvella	.08	.06	.03
237	Willie Randolph	.08	.06	.03
238	Bruce Fields	.08	.06	.03
239	Mike Aldrete	.08	.06	.03
240	Lance Parrish	.15	.11	.06
241	Greg Maddux	.12	.09	.05
242	John Moses	.08	.06	.03
243	Melido Perez	.10	.08	.04
244	Willie Wilson	.10	.08	.04
245	Mark McLemore	.08	.06	.03
246	Von Hayes	.10	.08	.04
247	Matt Williams	.12	.09	.05
248	John Candelaria	.08	.06	.03
249	Harold Reynolds	.08	.06	.03
250	Greg Swindell	.12	.09	.05
251	Juan Agosto	.08	.06	.03
252	Mike Felder	.08	.06	.03
253	Vince Coleman	.15	.11	.06
254	Larry Sheets	.08	.06	.03
255	George Bell	.25	.20	.10
256	Terry Steinbach	.10	.08	.04
257	*Jack Armstrong*	1.00	.70	.40
258	Dickie Thon	.08	.06	.03
259	Ray Knight	.08	.06	.03
260	Darryl Strawberry	.40	.30	.15
261	Doug Sisk	.08	.06	.03
262	Alex Trevino	.08	.06	.03
263	Jeff Leonard	.08	.06	.03
264	Tom Henke	.08	.06	.03
265	Ozzie Smith	.15	.11	.06
266	Dave Bergman	.08	.06	.03
267	Tony Phillips	.08	.06	.03
268	Mark Davis	.08	.06	.03
269	Kevin Elster	.10	.08	.04
270	Barry Larkin	.20	.15	.08
271	Manny Lee	.08	.06	.03
272	Tom Brunansky	.12	.09	.05
273	*Craig Biggio*	.80	.60	.30
274	Jim Gantner	.08	.06	.03
275	Eddie Murray	.25	.20	.10
276	Jeff Reed	.08	.06	.03
277	Tim Teufel	.08	.06	.03
278	Rick Honeycutt	.08	.06	.03
279	Guillermo Hernandez	.08	.06	.03
280	John Kruk	.10	.08	.04
281	*Luis Alicea*	.20	.15	.08
282	Jim Clancy	.08	.06	.03
283	Billy Ripken	.08	.06	.03
284	Craig Reynolds	.08	.06	.03
285	Robin Yount	.35	.25	.14
286	Jimmy Jones	.08	.06	.03
287	Ron Oester	.08	.06	.03
288	Terry Leach	.08	.06	.03
289	Dennis Eckersley	.12	.09	.05
290	Alan Trammell	.20	.15	.08
291	Jimmy Key	.10	.08	.04
292	Chris Bosio	.08	.06	.03
293	Jose DeLeon	.08	.06	.03
294	Jim Traber	.08	.06	.03
295	Mike Scott	.12	.09	.05
296	Roger McDowell	.10	.08	.04
297	Garry Templeton	.08	.06	.03
298	Doyle Alexander	.08	.06	.03
299	Nick Esasky	.08	.06	.03
300	Mark McGwire	.70	.50	.30
301	*Darryl Hamilton*	.20	.15	.08
302	Dave Smith	.08	.06	.03
303	Rick Sutcliffe	.10	.08	.04
304	Dave Stapleton	.08	.06	.03
305	Alan Ashby	.08	.06	.03
306	Pedro Guerrero	.15	.11	.06
307	Ron Guidry	.12	.09	.05
308	Steve Farr	.08	.06	.03
309	Curt Ford	.08	.06	.03
310	Claudell Washington	.08	.06	.03
311	Tom Prince	.08	.06	.03
312	*Chad Kreuter*	.20	.15	.08
313	Ken Oberkfell	.08	.06	.03
314	Jerry Browne	.08	.06	.03
315	R.J. Reynolds	.08	.06	.03
316	Scott Bankhead	.08	.06	.03
317	Milt Thompson	.08	.06	.03
318	Mario Diaz	.10	.08	.04
319	Bruce Ruffin	.08	.06	.03
320	Dave Valle	.08	.06	.03
321a	*Gary Varsho* (batting righty on card back, photo actually Mike Bielecki)	2.00	1.50	.80
321b	*Gary Varsho* (batting lefty on card back, correct photo)	.30	.25	.12
322	Paul Mirabella	.08	.06	.03
323	Chuck Jackson	.08	.06	.03
324	Drew Hall	.10	.08	.04
325	Don August	.10	.08	.04
326	*Israel Sanchez*	.20	.15	.08
327	Denny Walling	.08	.06	.03
328	Joel Skinner	.08	.06	.03
329	Danny Tartabull	.20	.15	.08
330	Tony Pena	.08	.06	.03
331	Jim Sundberg	.08	.06	.03
332	Jeff Robinson	.12	.09	.05
333	Odibbe McDowell	.08	.06	.03
334	Jose Lind	.10	.08	.04
335	Paul Kilgus	.10	.08	.04
336	Juan Samuel	.12	.09	.05
337	Mike Campbell	.10	.08	.04
338	Mike Maddux	.08	.06	.03
339	Darnell Coles	.08	.06	.03

No.	Player	MT	NR MT	EX
340	Bob Dernier	.08	.06	.03
341	Rafael Ramirez	.08	.06	.03
342	Scott Sanderson	.08	.06	.03
343	B.J. Surhoff	.10	.08	.04
344	Billy Hatcher	.08	.06	.03
345	Pat Perry	.08	.06	.03
346	Jack Clark	.15	.11	.06
347	Gary Thurman	.12	.09	.05
348	*Timmy Jones*	.20	.15	.08
349	Dave Winfield	.30	.25	.12
350	Frank White	.08	.06	.03
351	Dave Collins	.08	.06	.03
352	Jack Morris	.15	.11	.06
353	Eric Plunk	.08	.06	.03
354	Leon Durham	.08	.06	.03
355	Ivan DeJesus	.08	.06	.03
356	*Brian Holman*	.30	.25	.12
357a	Dale Murphy (photo on card front reversed)	130.00	98.00	52.00
357b	Dale Murphy (correct photo)	.35	.25	.14
358	Mark Portugal	.08	.06	.03
359	Andy McGaffigan	.08	.06	.03
360	Tom Glavine	.10	.08	.04
361	Keith Moreland	.08	.06	.03
362	Todd Stottlemyre	.15	.11	.06
363	Dave Leiper	.08	.06	.03
364	Cecil Fielder	.80	.60	.30
365	Carmelo Martinez	.08	.06	.03
366	Dwight Evans	.10	.08	.04
367	Kevin McReynolds	.15	.11	.06
368	Rich Gedman	.08	.06	.03
369	Len Dykstra	.10	.08	.04
370	Jody Reed	.12	.09	.05
371	Jose Canseco	1.25	.90	.50
372	Rob Murphy	.08	.06	.03
373	Mike Henneman	.10	.08	.04
374	Walt Weiss	.40	.30	.15
375	*Rob Dibble*	.25	.20	.10
376	Kirby Puckett	.30	.25	.12
377	Denny Martinez	.08	.06	.03
378	Ron Gant	.12	.09	.05
379	Brian Harper	.08	.06	.03
380	*Nelson Santovenia*	.20	.15	.08
381	Lloyd Moseby	.08	.06	.03
382	Lance McCullers	.08	.06	.03
383	Dave Stieb	.10	.08	.04
384	Tony Gwynn	.30	.25	.12
385	Mike Flanagan	.08	.06	.03
386	Bob Ojeda	.08	.06	.03
387	Bruce Hurst	.10	.08	.04
388	Dave Magadan	.10	.08	.04
389	Wade Boggs	1.00	.70	.40
390	Gary Carter	.25	.20	.10
391	Frank Tanana	.08	.06	.03
392	Curt Young	.08	.06	.03
393	Jeff Treadway	.10	.08	.04
394	Darrell Evans	.10	.08	.04
395	Glenn Hubbard	.08	.06	.03
396	Chuck Cary	.08	.06	.03
397	Frank Viola	.15	.11	.06
398	Jeff Parrett	.10	.08	.04
399	*Terry Blocker*	.15	.11	.06
400	Dan Gladden	.08	.06	.03
401	*Louie Meadows*	.20	.15	.08
402	Tim Raines	.25	.20	.10
403	Joey Meyer	.10	.08	.04
404	Larry Andersen	.08	.06	.03
405	Rex Hudler	.08	.06	.03
406	Mike Schmidt	.70	.50	.30
407	John Franco	.10	.08	.04
408	*Brady Anderson*	.30	.25	.12
409	Don Carman	.08	.06	.03
410	Eric Davis	.40	.30	.15
411	Bob Stanley	.08	.06	.03
412	Pete Smith	.10	.08	.04
413	Jim Rice	.25	.20	.10
414	Bruce Sutter	.10	.08	.04
415	Oil Can Boyd	.08	.06	.03
416	Ruben Sierra	.40	.30	.15
417	Mike LaValliere	.08	.06	.03
418	Steve Buechele	.08	.06	.03
419	Gary Redus	.08	.06	.03
420	Scott Fletcher	.08	.06	.03
421	Dale Sveum	.08	.06	.03
422	Bob Knepper	.08	.06	.03
423	Luis Rivera	.08	.06	.03
424	Ted Higuera	.10	.08	.04
425	Kevin Bass	.08	.06	.03
426	Ken Gerhart	.08	.06	.03
427	Shane Rawley	.08	.06	.03
428	Paul O'Neill	.08	.06	.03
429	Joe Orsulak	.08	.06	.03
430	Jackie Gutierrez	.08	.06	.03
431	Gerald Perry	.10	.08	.04
432	Mike Greenwell	.60	.45	.25
433	Jerry Royster	.08	.06	.03
434	Ellis Burks	.60	.45	.25
435	Ed Olwine	.08	.06	.03
436	Dave Rucker	.08	.06	.03
437	Charlie Hough	.08	.06	.03
438	Bob Walk	.08	.06	.03
439	Bob Brower	.08	.06	.03
440	Barry Bonds	.12	.09	.05
441	Tom Foley	.08	.06	.03
442	Rob Deer	.08	.06	.03
443	Glenn Davis	.15	.11	.06
444	Dave Martinez	.08	.06	.03
445	Bill Wegman	.08	.06	.03
446	Lloyd McClendon	.08	.06	.03
447	Dave Schmidt	.08	.06	.03
448	Darren Daulton	.08	.06	.03
449	Frank Williams	.08	.06	.03
450	Don Aase	.08	.06	.03
451	Lou Whitaker	.15	.11	.06
452	Goose Gossage	.12	.09	.05
453	Ed Whitson	.08	.06	.03
454	Jim Walewander	.08	.06	.03
455	Damon Berryhill	.12	.09	.05
456	Tim Burke	.08	.06	.03
457	Barry Jones	.08	.06	.03
458	Joel Youngblood	.08	.06	.03
459	Floyd Youmans	.08	.06	.03
460	Mark Salas	.08	.06	.03
461	Jeff Russell	.08	.06	.03
462	Darrell Miller	.08	.06	.03
463	Jeff Kunkel	.08	.06	.03
464	*Sherman Corbett*	.20	.15	.08
465	Curtis Wilkerson	.08	.06	.03
466	Bud Black	.08	.06	.03
467	Cal Ripken, Jr.	.35	.25	.14
468	John Farrell	.10	.08	.04
469	Terry Kennedy	.08	.06	.03
470	Tom Candiotti	.08	.06	.03
471	Roberto Alomar	.40	.30	.15
472	Jeff Robinson	.12	.09	.05
473	Vance Law	.08	.06	.03
474	Randy Ready	.08	.06	.03
475	Walt Terrell	.08	.06	.03
476	Kelly Downs	.10	.08	.04
477	*Johnny Paredes*	.20	.15	.08
478	Shawn Hillegas	.08	.06	.03
479	Bob Brenly	.08	.06	.03
480	Otis Nixon	.08	.06	.03
481	Johnny Ray	.08	.06	.03
482	Geno Petralli	.08	.06	.03
483	Stu Cliburn	.08	.06	.03
484	Pete Incaviglia	.10	.08	.04
485	Brian Downing	.08	.06	.03
486	Jeff Stone	.08	.06	.03
487	Carmen Castillo	.08	.06	.03
488	Tom Niedenfuer	.08	.06	.03
489	Jay Bell	.08	.06	.03
490	Rick Schu	.08	.06	.03
491	*Jeff Pico*	.25	.20	.10
492	*Mark Parent*	.20	.15	.08
493	Eric King	.08	.06	.03
494	Al Nipper	.08	.06	.03
495	Andy Hawkins	.08	.06	.03
496	Daryl Boston	.08	.06	.03
497	Ernie Riles	.08	.06	.03
498	Pascual Perez	.08	.06	.03
499	Bill Long	.08	.06	.03
500	Kirt Manwaring	.10	.08	.04
501	Chuck Crim	.08	.06	.03
502	Candy Maldonado	.08	.06	.03
503	Dennis Lamp	.08	.06	.03
504	Glenn Braggs	.08	.06	.03
505	Joe Price	.08	.06	.03
506	Ken Williams	.08	.06	.03
507	Bill Pecota	.08	.06	.03
508	Rey Quinones	.08	.06	.03
509	*Jeff Bittiger*	.15	.11	.06
510	Kevin Seitzer	.30	.25	.12
511	Steve Bedrosian	.10	.08	.04
512	Todd Worrell	.10	.08	.04
513	Chris James	.10	.08	.04
514	Jose Oquendo	.08	.06	.03
515	David Palmer	.08	.06	.03
516	John Smiley	.12	.09	.05
517	Dave Clark	.08	.06	.03
518	Mike Dunne	.10	.08	.04
519	Ron Washington	.08	.06	.03
520	Bob Kipper	.08	.06	.03
521	Lee Smith	.10	.08	.04
522	Juan Castillo	.08	.06	.03
523	Don Robinson	.08	.06	.03
524	Kevin Romine	.08	.06	.03
525	Paul Molitor	.15	.11	.06
526	Mark Langston	.10	.08	.04
527	Donnie Hill	.08	.06	.03
528	Larry Owen	.08	.06	.03
529	Jerry Reed	.08	.06	.03
530	Jack McDowell	.10	.08	.04
531	Greg Mathews	.08	.06	.03
532	John Russell	.08	.06	.03
533	Don Quisenberry	.08	.06	.03
534	Greg Gross	.08	.06	.03
535	Danny Cox	.08	.06	.03
536	Terry Francona	.08	.06	.03
537	Andy Van Slyke	.15	.11	.06
538	Mel Hall	.08	.06	.03
539	Jim Gott	.08	.06	.03
540	Doug Jones	.10	.08	.04
541	Criag Lefferts	.08	.06	.03
542	Mike Boddicker	.08	.06	.03
543	Greg Brock	.08	.06	.03
544	Atlee Hammaker	.08	.06	.03
545	Tom Bolton	.08	.06	.03
546	*Mike Macfarlane*	.20	.15	.08
547	*Rich Renteria*	.15	.11	.06
548	John Davis	.08	.06	.03
549	Floyd Bannister	.08	.06	.03
550	Mickey Brantley	.08	.06	.03
551	Duane Ward	.08	.06	.03
552	Dan Petry	.08	.06	.03
553	Mickey Tettleton	.08	.06	.03
554	Rick Leach	.08	.06	.03
555	Mike Witt	.08	.06	.03
556	Sid Bream	.08	.06	.03
557	Bobby Witt	.10	.08	.04
558	Tommy Herr	.08	.06	.03
559	Randy Milligan	.08	.06	.03
560	*Jose Cecena*	.20	.15	.08
561	Mackey Sasser	.08	.06	.03
562	Carney Lansford	.08	.06	.03
563	Rick Aguilera	.08	.06	.03
564	Ron Hassey	.08	.06	.03
565	Dwight Gooden	.50	.40	.20
566	Paul Assenmacher	.08	.06	.03
567	Neil Allen	.08	.06	.03
568	Jim Morrison	.08	.06	.03
569	Mike Pagliarulo	.10	.08	.04
570	Ted Simmons	.10	.08	.04
571	Mark Thurmond	.08	.06	.03
572	Fred McGriff	.40	.30	.15
573	Wally Joyner	.25	.20	.10
574	*Jose Bautista*	.20	.15	.08
575	Kelly Gruber	.08	.06	.03
576	Cecilio Guante	.08	.06	.03
577	Mark Davidson	.08	.06	.03
578	Bobby Bonilla	.12	.09	.05
579	Mike Stanley	.08	.06	.03
580	Gene Larkin	.10	.08	.04
581	Stan Javier	.08	.06	.03
582	Howard Johnson	.10	.08	.04
583a	Mike Gallego (photo on card back reversed)	2.00	1.50	.80
583b	Mike Gallego (correct photo)	.15	.11	.06
584	David Cone	.35	.25	.14
585	*Doug Jennings*	.20	.15	.08
586	Charlie Hudson	.08	.06	.03
587	Dion James	.08	.06	.03
588	Al Leiter	.15	.11	.06
589	Charlie Puleo	.08	.06	.03
590	Roberto Kelly	.25	.20	.10
591	Thad Bosley	.08	.06	.03
592	Pete Stanicek	.10	.08	.04
593	*Pat Borders*	.25	.20	.10
594	*Bryan Harvey*	.25	.20	.10
595	Jeff Ballard	.10	.08	.04
596	Jeff Reardon	.10	.08	.04
597	Doug Drabek	.08	.06	.03
598	Edwin Correa	.08	.06	.03
599	Keith Atherton	.08	.06	.03
600	Dave LaPoint	.08	.06	.03
601	Don Baylor	.10	.08	.04
602	Tom Pagnozzi	.08	.06	.03
603	Tim Flannery	.08	.06	.03
604	Gene Walter	.08	.06	.03
605	Dave Parker	.12	.09	.05
606	Mike Diaz	.08	.06	.03
607	Chris Gwynn	.10	.08	.04
608	Odell Jones	.08	.06	.03
609	Carlton Fisk	.15	.11	.06
610	Jay Howell	.08	.06	.03
611	Tim Crews	.08	.06	.03
612	Keith Hernandez	.20	.15	.08
613	Willie Fraser	.08	.06	.03
614	Jim Eppard	.08	.06	.03
615	Jeff Hamilton	.08	.06	.03
616	Kurt Stillwell	.08	.06	.03
617	Tom Browning	.10	.08	.04
618	Jeff Montgomery	.08	.06	.03
619	Jose Rijo	.08	.06	.03
620	Jamie Quirk	.08	.06	.03
621	Willie McGee	.12	.09	.05
622	Mark Grant	.08	.06	.03
623	Bill Swift	.08	.06	.03
624	Orlando Mercado	.08	.06	.03
625	*John Costello*	.20	.15	.08
626	Jose Gonzalez	.08	.06	.03
627a	Bill Schroeder (putting on shin guards on card back, photo actually Ronn Reynolds)	2.00	1.50	.80
627b	Bill Schroeder (arms crossed on card back, correct photo)	.15	.11	.06
628a	Fred Manrique (throwing on card back, photo actually Ozzie Guillen)	2.00	1.50	.80
628b	Fred Manrique (batting on card back, correct photo)	.15	.11	.06
629	Ricky Horton	.08	.06	.03
630	Dan Plesac	.10	.08	.04
631	Alfredo Griffin	.08	.06	.03
632	Chuck Finley	.08	.06	.03
633	Kirk Gibson	.20	.15	.08
634	Randy Myers	.10	.08	.04
635	Greg Minton	.08	.06	.03
636	Herm Winningham	.08	.06	.03
637	Charlie Leibrandt	.08	.06	.03
638	Tim Birtsas	.08	.06	.03
639	Bill Buckner	.10	.08	.04
640	Danny Jackson	.15	.11	.06
641	Greg Booker	.08	.06	.03
642	Jim Presley	.08	.06	.03
643	Gene Nelson	.08	.06	.03
644	Rod Booker	.08	.06	.03
645	Dennis Rasmussen	.10	.08	.04
646	Juan Nieves	.08	.06	.03
647	Bobby Thigpen	.10	.08	.04
648	Tim Belcher	.10	.08	.04
649	Mike Young	.08	.06	.03
650	Ivan Calderon	.08	.06	.03
651	*Oswaldo Peraza*	.20	.15	.08
652a	Pat Sheridan (no position on front)	40.00	30.00	15.00
652b	Pat Sheridan (position on front)	.08	.06	.03
653	Mike Morgan	.08	.06	.03
654	Mike Heath	.08	.06	.03
655	Jay Tibbs	.08	.06	.03
656	Fernando Valenzuela	.20	.15	.08
657	Lee Mazzilli	.08	.06	.03
658	Frank Viola	.08	.06	.03
659	Jose Canseco	.08	.06	.03
660	Walt Weiss	.08	.06	.03
661	Orel Hershiser	.08	.06	.03
662	Kirk Gibson	.08	.06	.03
663	Chris Sabo	.08	.06	.03
664	Dennis Eckersley	.08	.06	.03
665	Orel Hershiser	.08	.06	.03
666	Kirk Gibson	.08	.06	.03
667	Orel Hershiser	.08	.06	.03
668	Angels Checklist (Wally Joyner)	.08	.06	.03
669	Astros Checklist (Nolan Ryan)	.08	.06	.03
670	Athletics Checklist (Jose Canseco)	.08	.06	.03
671	Blue Jays Checklist (Fred McGriff)	.08	.06	.03
672	Braves Checklist (Dale Murphy)	.08	.06	.03
673	Brewers Checklist (Paul Molitor)	.08	.06	.03
674	Cardinals Checklist (Ozzie Smith)	.08	.06	.03
675	Cubs Checklist (Ryne Sandberg)	.08	.06	.03
676	Dodgers Checklist (Kirk Gibson)	.08	.06	.03
677	Expos Checklist (Andres Galarraga)	.08	.06	.03
678	Giants Checklist (Will Clark)	.08	.06	.03
679	Indians Checklist (Cory Snyder)	.08	.06	.03
680	Mariners Checklist (Alvin Davis)	.08	.06	.03
681	Mets Checklist (Darryl Strawberry)	.08	.06	.03
682	Orioles Checklist (Cal Ripken, Jr.)			

		MT	NR MT	EX
		.08	.06	.03
683	Padres Checklist (Tony Gwynn)			
		.08	.06	.03
684	Phillies Checklist (Mike Schmidt)			
		.08	.06	.03
685	Pirates Checklist (Andy Van Slyke)			
		.08	.06	.03
686	Rangers Checklist (Ruben Sierra)			
		.08	.06	.03
687	Red Sox Checklist (Wade Boggs)			
		.08	.06	.03
688	Reds Checklist (Eric Davis)	.08	.06	.03
689	Royals Checklist (George Brett)			
		.08	.06	.03
690	Tigers Checklist (Alan Trammell)			
		.08	.06	.03
691	Twins Checklist (Frank Viola)			
		.08	.06	.03
692	White Sox Checklist (Harold Baines)			
		.08	.06	.03
693	Yankees Checklist (Don Mattingly)			
		.08	.06	.03
694	Checklist 1-100	.08	.06	.03
695	Checklist 101-200	.08	.06	.03
696	Checklist 201-300	.08	.06	.03
697	Checklist 301-400	.08	.06	.03
698	Checklist 401-500	.08	.06	.03
699	Checklist 501-600	.08	.06	.03
700	Checklist 601-700	.08	.06	.03
701	Checklist 701-800	.20	.15	.08
702	Jessie Barfield	.10	.08	.04
703	Walt Terrell	.10	.08	.04
704	Dickie Thon	.10	.08	.04
705	Al Leiter	.10	.08	.04
706	Dave LaPoint	.10	.08	.04
707	Charlie Hayes(FC)	.15	.11	.06
708	Andy Hawkins	.10	.08	.04
709	Mickey Hatcher	.10	.08	.04
710	Lance McCullers	.10	.08	.04
711	Ron Kittle	.10	.08	.04
712	Bert Blyleven	.10	.08	.04
713	Rick Dempsey	.10	.08	.04
714	Ken Williams	.10	.08	.04
715	Steve Rosenberg(FC)	.15	.11	.06
716	Joe Skalski(FC)	.20	.15	.08
717	Spike Owen	.10	.08	.04
718	Todd Burns	.10	.08	.04
719	Kevin Gross	.10	.08	.04
720	Tommy Herr	.10	.08	.04
721	Rob Ducey	.10	.08	.04
722	Gary Green(FC)	.15	.11	.06
723	Gregg Olson(FC)	3.25	2.50	1.25
724	Greg Harris(FC)	.15	.11	.06
725	Craig Worthington(FC)	.50	.40	.20
726	Tom Howard(FC)	.35	.25	.14
727	Dale Mohorcic	.10	.08	.04
728	Rich Yett	.10	.08	.04
729	Mel Hall	.10	.08	.04
730	Floyd Youmans	.10	.08	.04
731	Lonnie Smith	.15	.11	.06
732	Wally Backman	.10	.08	.04
733	Trevor Wilson	.10	.08	.04
734	Jose Alvarez	.10	.08	.04
735	Bob Milacki(FC)	.15	.11	.06
736	Tom Gordon(FC)	2.50	2.00	1.00
737	Wally Whitehurst(FC)	.25	.20	.10
738	Mike Aldrete	.10	.08	.04
739	Keith Miller	.10	.08	.04
740	Randy Milligan	.10	.08	.04
741	Jeff Parrett	.10	.08	.04
742	Steve Finley(FC)	.35	.25	.14
743	Junior Felix(FC)	2.00	1.50	.80
744	Pete Harnisch(FC)	.25	.20	.10
745	Bill Spiers(FC)	.50	.40	.20
746	Hensley Meulens(FC)	.70	.50	.30
747	Juan Bell	.20	.15	.08
748	Steve Sax	.15	.11	.06
749	Phil Bradley	.10	.08	.04
750	Rey Quinones	.10	.08	.04
751	Tommy Gregg(FC)	.15	.11	.06
752	Kevin Brown(FC)	.10	.08	.04
753	Derek Lilliquist(FC)	.15	.11	.06
754	Todd Zeile(FC)	7.00	5.25	2.75
755	Jim Abbott(FC)	6.00	4.50	2.50
756	Ozzie Canseco(FC)	.70	.50	.30
757	Nick Esasky	.10	.08	.04
758	Mike Moore	.15	.11	.06
759	Rob Murphy	.10	.08	.04
760	Rick Mahler	.10	.08	.04
761	Fred Lynn	.10	.08	.04
762	Kevin Blankenship(FC)	.10	.08	.04
763	Eddie Murray	.15	.11	.06
764	Steve Searcy(FC)	.10	.08	.04
765	Jerome Walton(FC)	7.00	5.25	2.75
766	Erik Hanson(FC)	.25	.20	.10
767	Bob Boone	.15	.11	.06
768	Edgar Martinez(FC)	.60	.45	.25
769	Jose DeJesus(FC)	.10	.08	.04
770	Greg Briley(FC)	1.25	.90	.50
771	Steve Peters(FC)	.10	.08	.04
772	Rafael Palmeiro	.15	.11	.06
773	Jack Clark	.15	.11	.06
774	Nolan Ryan	4.00	3.00	1.50
775	Lance Parrish	.10	.08	.04
776	Joe Girardi(FC)	.35	.25	.14
777	Willie Randolph	.10	.08	.04
778	Mitch Williams	.30	.25	.12
779	Dennis Cook(FC)	.40	.30	.15
780	Dwight Smith(FC)	3.00	2.25	1.25
781	Lenny Harris(FC)	.20	.15	.08
782	Torey Lovullo(FC)	.15	.11	.06
783	Norm Charlton(FC)	.10	.08	.04
784	Chris Brown	.10	.08	.04
785	Todd Benzinger	.10	.08	.04
786	Shane Rawley	.10	.08	.04
787	Omar Vizquel(FC)	.25	.20	.10
788	LaVel Freeman(FC)	.25	.20	.10
789	Jeffrey Leonard	.10	.08	.04
790	Eddie Williams(FC)	.10	.08	.04
791	Jamie Moyer	.10	.08	.04
792	Bruce Hurst	.10	.08	.04
793	Julio Franco	.15	.11	.06
794	Claudell Washington	.10	.08	.04
795	Jody Davis	.10	.08	.04
796	Odibbe McDowell	.10	.08	.04
797	Paul Kilgus	.10	.08	.04
798	Tracy Jones	.10	.08	.04
799	Steve Wilson(FC)	.25	.20	.10
800	Pete O'Brien,			

1990 Upper Deck

Following the success of its first issue, Upper Deck released the first 700 cards of the 1990 set. The cards contain full-color photos on both sides and are 2-1/2" by 3-1/2" in size. The artwork of Vernon Wells is featured on the front of all team checklist cards. The 1990 set also introduces two new Wells illustrations - a tribute to Mike Schmidt upon his retirement and one commemorating Nolan Ryan's 5,000 career strikeouts. The cards are similar in design to the 1989 issue. The Wade Boggs card depicts the Red Sox star in four stages of his batting swing via a quad-action photograph, much like the Jim Abbott card of 1989. A high- number series (701-800) is expected to become available mid-season.

		MT	NR MT	EX
Complete Set:		45.00	35.00	18.00
Common Player:		.06	.05	.02
1	Star Rookie Checklist	.06	.05	.02
2	*Randy Nosek*(FC)	.15	.11	.06
3	*Tom Dress*(FC)	.15	.11	.06
4	Curt Young	.06	.05	.02
5	Angels Checklist	.06	.05	.02
6	Luis Salazar	.06	.05	.02
7	Phillies Checklist	.06	.05	.02
8	Jose Bautista	.08	.06	.03
9	*Marquis Grissom*(FC)	1.25	.90	.50
10	Dodgers Checklist	.06	.05	.02
11	Rick Aguilera	.08	.06	.03
12	Padres Checklist	.06	.05	.02
13	*Deion Sanders*(FC)	.50	.40	.20
14	Marvell Wynne	.06	.05	.02
15	David West	.15	.11	.06
16	Pirates Checklist	.06	.05	.02
17	*Sammy Sosa*(FC)	.80	.60	.30
18	Yankees Checklist	.06	.05	.02
19	Jack Howell	.06	.05	.02
20	Mike Schmidt (Special Card)			
		1.50	1.25	.60
21	Robin Ventura(FC)	.70	.50	.30
22	Brian Meyer(FC)	.20	.15	.08
23	*Blaine Beatty*(FC)	.20	.15	.08
24	Mariners Checklist	.06	.05	.02
25	*Greg Vaughn*(FC)	2.00	1.50	.80
26	*Xavier Hernandez*(FC)	.15	.11	.06
27	*Jason Grimsley*(FC)	.25	.20	.10
28	*Eric Anthony*(FC)	2.50	2.00	1.00
29	Expos Checklist	.06	.05	.02
30	David Wells	.06	.05	.02
31	Hal Morris(FC)	.15	.11	.06
32	Royals Checklist	.25	.20	.10
33	*Kelly Mann*(FC)	.15	.11	.06
34	Nolan Ryan (Special Card)	1.75	1.25	.70
35	*Scott Service*(FC)	.20	.15	.08
36	Athletics Checklist	.06	.05	.02
37	*Tino Martinez*(FC)	.60	.45	.25
38	Chili Davis	.09	.07	.04
39	Scott Sanderson	.06	.05	.02
40	Giants Checklist	.06	.05	.02
41	Tigers Checklist	.06	.05	.02
42	*Scott Coolbaugh*(FC)	.40	.30	.15
43	*Jose Cano*(FC)	.15	.11	.06
44	*Jose Vizcaino*(FC)	.40	.30	.15
45	*Bob Hamelin*(FC)	1.25	.90	.50
46	*Jose Offerman*(FC)	1.50	1.25	.60
47	Kevin Blankenship	.10	.08	.04
48	Twins Checklist	.06	.05	.02
49	*Tommy Greene*(FC)	.90	.70	.35
50	Will Clark (Special Card)	.40	.30	.15
51	Rob Nelson(FC)	.09	.07	.04
52	*Chris Hammond*(FC)	.15	.11	.06
53	Indians Checklist	.06	.05	.02
54a	*Ben McDonald* (Orioles Logo)(FC)			
		50.00	37.00	20.00
54b	*Ben McDonald* (Rookies Logo)(FC)			
		3.50	2.75	1.50
55	Andy Benes(FC)	1.00	.70	.40
56	*John Olerud*(FC)	4.00	3.00	1.50
57	Red Sox Checklist	.06	.05	.02
58	Tony Armas	.06	.05	.02
59	*George Canale*(FC)	.50	.40	.20
60a	Orioles Checklist (Jamie Weston)			
		10.00	7.50	4.00
60b	Orioles Checklist (Mickey Weston)			
		.08	.06	.03
61	*Mike Stanton*(FC)	.15	.11	.06
62	Mets Checklist	.06	.05	.02
63	*Kent Mercker*(FC)	.90	.70	.35
64	*Francisco Cabrera*(FC)	.30	.25	.20
65	Steve Avery(FC)	1.00	.70	.40
66	Jose Canseco	.90	.70	.50
67	*Matt Merullo*(FC)	.15	.11	.06
68	Cardinals Checklist	.06	.05	.02
69	Ron Karkovice	.06	.05	.02
70	*Kevin Maas*(FC)	.50	.40	.20
71	Dennis Cook	.10	.08	.04
72	*Juan Gonzalez*(FC)	1.00	.70	.40
73	Cubs Checklist	.06	.05	.02
74	*Dean Palmer*(FC)	.40	.30	.15
75	Bo Jackson (Special Card)	.80	.60	.30
76	*Rob Richie*(FC)	.20	.15	.08
77	*Bobby Rose*(FC)	.40	.30	.15
78	*Brian DuBois*(FC)	.15	.11	.06
79	White Sox Checklist	.06	.05	.02
80	Gene Nelson	.06	.05	.02
81	Bob McClure	.06	.05	.02
82	Rangers Checklist	.06	.05	.02
83	Greg Minton	.06	.05	.02
84	Braves Checklist	.06	.05	.02
85	Willie Fraser	.06	.05	.02
86	Neal Heaton	.06	.05	.02
87	*Kevin Tapani*(FC)	.30	.25	.12
88	Astros Checklist	.06	.05	.02
89a	Jim Gott (Incorrect Photo)			
		11.00	8.25	4.50
89b	Jim Gott (Photo of Gott)	.10	.08	.04
90	Lance Johnson(FC)	.09	.07	.04
91	Brewers Checklist	.06	.05	.02
92	Jeff Parrett	.08	.06	.03
93	*Julio Machado*(FC)	.25	.20	.10
94	Ron Jones	.10	.08	.04
95	Blue Jays Checklist	.06	.05	.02
96	Jerry Reuss	.06	.05	.02
97	Brian Fisher	.06	.05	.02
98	*Kevin Ritz*(FC)	.25	.20	.10
99	Reds Checklist	.06	.05	.02
100	Checklist 1-100	.06	.05	.02
101	Gerald Perry	.06	.05	.02
102	*Kevin Appier*(FC)	.30	.15	.08
103	Julio Franco	.10	.08	.04
104	Craig Biggio	.30	.25	.12
105	Bo Jackson	.90	.70	.35
106	*Junior Felix*	.70	.50	.30
107	Mike Harkey(FC)	.30	.25	.12
108	Fred McGriff	.25	.20	.10
109	Rick Sutcliffe	.08	.06	.03
110	Pete O'Brien	.08	.06	.03
111	Kelly Gruber	.10	.08	.04
112	Pat Borders	.10	.08	.04
113	Dwight Evans	.10	.08	.04
114	Dwight Gooden	.20	.15	.08
115	*Kevin Batiste*(FC)	.15	.11	.06
116	Eric Davis	.25	.20	.10
117	Kevin Mitchell	.40	.30	.15
118	Ron Oester	.06	.05	.02
119	Brett Butler	.09	.07	.04
120	Danny Jackson	.06	.05	.02
121	Tommy Gregg	.06	.05	.02
122	Ken Caminiti	.08	.06	.03
123	Kevin Brown	.10	.08	.04
124	George Brett	.15	.11	.06
125	Mike Scott	.10	.08	.04
126	Cory Snyder	.10	.08	.04
127	George Bell	.15	.11	.06
128	Mark Grace	.50	.40	.20
129	Devon White	.10	.08	.04
130	Tony Fernandez	.15	.11	.06
131	Dan Aase	.06	.05	.02
132	Rance Mulliniks	.06	.05	.02
133	Marty Barrett	.08	.06	.03
134	Nelson Liriano	.07	.05	.03
135	Mark Carreon(FC)	.15	.11	.06
136	Candy Maldonado	.06	.05	.02
137	Tim Birtsas	.06	.05	.02
138	Tom Brookens	.06	.05	.02
139	John Franco	.08	.06	.03
140	Mike LaCoss	.06	.05	.02
141	Jeff Treadway	.07	.05	.03
142	Pat Tabler	.07	.05	.03
143	Darrell Evans	.06	.05	.02
144	Rafael Ramirez	.06	.05	.02
145	Oddibe McDowell	.09	.07	.04
146	Brian Downing	.09	.07	.04
147	Curtis Wilkerson	.06	.05	.02
148	Ernie Whitt	.07	.05	.02
149	Bill Schroeder	.06	.05	.02
150	Domingo Ramos	.06	.05	.02
151	Rick Honeycutt	.06	.05	.02
152	Don Slaught	.06	.05	.02
153	Mitch Webster	.06	.05	.02
154	Tony Phillips	.07	.05	.02
155	Paul Kilgus	.06	.05	.02
156	Ken Griffey, Jr.	3.50	2.75	1.50
157	Gary Sheffield	.50	.40	.20
158	Wally Backman	.06	.05	.02
159	B.J. Surhoff	.08	.06	.03
160	Louie Meadows	.08	.06	.03
161	Paul O'Neill	.09	.07	.04
162	*Jeff McKnight*(FC)	.20	.15	.08
163	Alvaro Espinoza(FC)	.15	.11	.06
164	*Scott Scudder*(FC)	.20	.15	.08
165	Jeff Reed	.06	.05	.02
166	Gregg Jefferies	.60	.45	.25
167	Barry Larkin	.15	.11	.06
168	Gary Carter	.10	.08	.04
169	Robby Thompson	.09	.07	.04
170	Rolando Roomes	.15	.11	.06
171	Mark McGwire	.50	.40	.20
172	Steve Sax	.10	.08	.04
173	Mark Williamson	.06	.05	.02
174	Mitch Williams	.15	.11	.06
175	Brian Holton	.06	.05	.02
176	Rob Deer	.08	.06	.03
177	Tim Raines	.12	.09	.05
178	Mike Felder	.06	.05	.02
179	Harold Reynolds	.10	.08	.04
180	Terry Francona	.06	.05	.02
181	Chris Sabo	.15	.11	.06

		MT	NR MT	EX
182	Darryl Strawberry	.20	.15	.08
183	Willie Randolph	.10	.08	.04
184	Billy Ripken	.06	.05	.02
185	Mackey Sasser	.08	.06	.03
186	Todd Benzinger	.08	.06	.03
187	Kevin Elster	.07	.05	.03
188	Jose Uribe	.06	.05	.02
189	Tom Browning	.10	.08	.04
190	Keith Miller	.09	.07	.04
191	Don Mattingly	.80	.60	.30
192	Dave Parker	.12	.09	.05
193	Roberto Kelly	.12	.09	.05
194	Phil Bradley	.09	.07	.04
195	Ron Hassey	.07	.05	.03
196	Gerald Young	.06	.05	.02
197	Hubie Brooks	.08	.06	.03
198	Bill Doran	.09	.07	.04
199	Al Newman	.06	.05	.02
200	Checklist 101-200	.06	.05	.02
201	Terry Puhl	.06	.05	.02
202	Frank DiPino	.06	.05	.02
203	Jim Clancy	.06	.05	.02
204	Bob Ojeda	.07	.05	.03
205	Alex Trevino	.06	.05	.02
206	Dave Henderson	.10	.08	.04
207	Henry Cotto	.06	.05	.02
208	Rafael Belliard	.06	.05	.02
209	Stan Javier	.07	.05	.03
210	Jerry Reed	.06	.05	.02
211	Doug Dascenzo	.08	.06	.03
212	Andres Thomas	.07	.05	.03
213	Greg Maddux	.20	.15	.08
214	Mike Schooler	.09	.07	.04
215	Lonnie Smith	.09	.07	.04
216	Jose Rijo	.10	.08	.04
217	Greg Gagne	.08	.06	.03
218	Jim Gantner	.08	.06	.03
219	Allan Anderson	.09	.07	.04
220	Rick Mahler	.06	.05	.02
221	Jim Deshaies	.09	.07	.04
222	Keith Hernandez	.10	.08	.04
223	Vince Coleman	.12	.09	.05
224	David Cone	.20	.15	.08
225	Ozzie Smith	.20	.15	.08
226	Matt Nokes	.10	.08	.04
227	Barry Bonds	.10	.08	.04
228	Felix Jose	.10	.08	.04
229	Dennis Powell	.06	.05	.02
230	Mike Gallego	.06	.05	.02
231	Shawon Dunston	.09	.07	.04
232	Ron Gant	.10	.08	.04
233	*Omar Vizquel*	.10	.08	.04
234	Derek Lilliquist	.10	.08	.04
235	Erik Hanson	.10	.08	.04
236	Kirby Puckett	.50	.40	.20
237	*Bill Spiers*	.25	.20	.10
238	Dan Gladden	.07	.05	.03
239	Bryan Clutterbuck(FC)	.07	.05	.03
240	John Moses	.06	.05	.02
241	Ron Darling	.12	.09	.05
242	Joe Magrane	.12	.09	.05
243	Dave Magadan	.09	.07	.03
244	Pedro Guerrero	.15	.11	.06
245	Glenn Davis	.10	.08	.04
246	Terry Steinbach	.12	.09	.05
247	Fred Lynn	.09	.07	.04
248	Gary Redus	.06	.05	.02
249	Kenny Williams	.06	.05	.02
250	Sid Bream	.06	.05	.02
251	Bob Welch	.08	.06	.03
252	Bill Buckner	.07	.05	.03
253	Carney Lansford	.09	.07	.04
254	Paul Molitor	.12	.09	.05
255	Jose DeJesus	.15	.11	.06
256	Orel Hershiser	.25	.20	.10
257	Tom Brunansky	.10	.08	.04
258	Mike Davis	.06	.05	.02
259	Jeff Ballard	.12	.09	.05
260	Scott Terry	.09	.07	.04
261	Sid Fernandez	.10	.08	.04
262	Mike Marshall	.08	.06	.03
263	Howard Johnson	.20	.15	.08
264	Kirk Gibson	.09	.07	.04
265	Kevin McReynolds	.15	.11	.06
266	Cal Ripken, Jr.	.15	.11	.06
267	Ozzie Guillen	.07	.05	.03
268	Jim Traber	.06	.05	.02
269	Bobby Thigpen	.09	.07	.04
270	Joe Orsulak	.06	.05	.02
271	Bob Boone	.09	.07	.04
272	Dave Stewart	.09	.07	.04
273	Tim Wallach	.09	.07	.04
274	Luis Aquino	.06	.05	.02
275	Mike Moore	.10	.08	.04
276	Tony Pena	.08	.06	.03
277	Eddie Murray	.15	.11	.06
278	Milt Thompson	.07	.05	.03
279	Alejandro Pena	.06	.05	.02
280	Ken Dayley	.06	.05	.02
281	Carmen Castillo	.06	.05	.02
282	Tom Henke	.08	.06	.03
283	Mickey Hatcher	.06	.05	.02
284	Roy Smith(FC)	.06	.05	.02
285	Manny Lee	.06	.05	.02
286	Dan Pasqua	.07	.05	.02
287	Larry Sheets	.06	.05	.02
288	Garry Templeton	.07	.05	.03
289	Eddie Williams	.07	.05	.03
290	Brady Anderson	.07	.05	.03
291	Spike Owen	.07	.05	.03
292	Storm Davis	.09	.07	.04
293	Chris Bosio	.09	.07	.04
294	Jim Eisenreich	.07	.05	.03
295	Don August	.07	.05	.03
296	Jeff Hamilton	.07	.05	.03
297	Mickey Tettleton	.10	.08	.04
298	Mike Scioscia	.09	.07	.04
299	Kevin Hickey(FC)	.06	.05	.02
300	Checklist 201-300	.06	.05	.02
301	Shawn Abner	.06	.05	.02
302	Kevin Bass	.08	.06	.03
303	Bip Roberts(FC)	.08	.06	.03
304	Joe Girardi	.10	.08	.04
305	Danny Darwin	.06	.05	.02

		MT	NR MT	EX
306	Mike Heath	.06	.05	.02
307	Mike Macfarlane	.06	.05	.02
308	Ed Whitson	.08	.06	.03
309	Tracy Jones	.07	.05	.02
310	Scott Fletcher	.07	.05	.02
311	Darnell Coles	.07	.05	.02
312	Mike Brumley	.06	.05	.02
313	Bill Swift	.06	.05	.02
314	Charlie Hough	.07	.05	.03
315	Jim Presley	.08	.06	.03
316	Luis Polonia	.07	.05	.03
317	Mike Morgan	.06	.05	.02
318	Lee Guetterman	.06	.05	.02
319	Jose Oquendo	.08	.06	.03
320	Wayne Tollenson	.06	.05	.02
321	Jody Reed	.07	.05	.03
322	Damon Berryhill	.09	.07	.04
323	Roger Clemens	.40	.30	.15
324	Ryne Sandberg	.15	.11	.06
325	Benito Santiago	.10	.08	.04
326	Bret Saberhagen	.15	.11	.06
327	Lou Whitaker	.10	.08	.04
328	Dave Gallagher	.10	.08	.04
329	Mike Pagliarulo	.07	.05	.03
330	Doyle Alexander	.07	.05	.03
331	Jeffrey Leonard	.09	.07	.04
332	Torey Lovullo	.20	.15	.08
333	Pete Incaviglia	.09	.07	.04
334	Rickey Henderson	.15	.11	.06
335	Rafael Palmeiro	.10	.08	.04
336	Ken Hill	.10	.08	.04
337	Dave Winfield	.12	.09	.05
338	Alfredo Griffin	.07	.05	.03
339	Andy Hawkins	.07	.05	.03
340	Ted Power	.06	.05	.02
341	Steve Wilson	.10	.08	.04
342	Jack Clark	.10	.08	.04
343	Ellis Burks	.25	.20	.10
344	Tony Gwynn	.20	.15	.08
345	*Jerome Walton*	1.25	.90	.50
346	Roberto Alomar	.10	.08	.04
347	*Carlos Martinez*(FC)	.15	.11	.06
348	Chet Lemon	.07	.05	.03
349	Willie Wilson	.07	.05	.03
350	Greg Walker	.07	.05	.03
351	Tom Bolton	.06	.05	.02
352	German Gonzalez(FC)	.08	.06	.03
353	Harold Baines	.10	.08	.04
354	Mike Greenwell	.50	.40	.20
355	Ruben Sierra	.20	.15	.08
356	Anres Galarraga	.12	.09	.05
357	Andre Dawson	.15	.11	.06
358	*Jeff Brantley*(FC)	.10	.08	.04
359	Mike Bielecki	.08	.06	.03
360	Ken Oberkfell	.06	.05	.02
361	Kurt Stillwell	.07	.05	.03
362	Brian Holman	.09	.07	.04
363	Kevin Seitzer	.12	.09	.05
364	Alvin Davis	.15	.11	.06
365	Tom Gordon	.70	.50	.30
366	Bobby Bonilla	.10	.08	.04
367	Carlton Fisk	.10	.08	.04
368	*Steve Carter*(FC)	.15	.11	.06
369	Joel Skinner	.06	.05	.02
370	John Cangelosi	.06	.05	.02
371	Cecil Espy	.08	.06	.03
372	*Gary Wayne*(FC)	.25	.20	.10
373	Jim Rice	.08	.06	.03
374	*Mike Dyer*(FC)	.15	.11	.06
375	Joe Carter	.12	.09	.05
376	Dwight Smith	.60	.45	.25
377	*John Wetteland*(FC)	.25	.20	.10
378	Ernie Riles	.06	.05	.02
379	Otis Nixon	.06	.05	.02
380	Vance Law	.06	.05	.02
381	Dave Bergman	.06	.05	.02
382	Frank White	.07	.05	.03
383	Scott Bradley	.06	.05	.02
384	Israel Sanchez	.06	.05	.02
385	Gary Pettis	.06	.05	.02
386	Donn Pall(FC)	.06	.05	.02
387	John Smiley	.10	.08	.04
388	Tom Candiotti	.07	.05	.03
389	Junior Ortiz	.06	.05	.02
390	Steve Lyons	.06	.05	.02
391	Brian Harper	.06	.05	.02
392	Fred Manrique	.06	.05	.02
393	Lee Smith	.08	.06	.03
394	Jeff Kunkel	.06	.05	.02
395	Claudell Washington	.08	.06	.03
396	John Tudor	.07	.05	.03
397	Terry Kennedy	.07	.05	.03
398	Lloyd McClendon	.09	.07	.04
399	Craig Lefferts	.06	.05	.02
400	Checklist 301-400	.06	.05	.02
401	Keith Moreland	.06	.05	.02
402	Rich Gedman	.07	.05	.03
403	Jeff Robinson	.07	.05	.03
404	Randy Ready	.06	.05	.02
405	Rick Cerone	.06	.05	.02
406	Jeff Blauser	.07	.05	.03
407	Larry Andersen	.06	.05	.02
408	Joe Boever	.08	.06	.03
409	Felix Fermin	.06	.05	.02
410	Glenn Wilson	.06	.05	.02
411	Rex Hudler	.06	.05	.02
412	Mark Grant	.06	.05	.02
413	Dennis Martinez	.08	.06	.03
414	Darrin Jackson	.06	.05	.02
415	Mike Aldrete	.06	.05	.02
416	Roger McDowell	.09	.07	.04
417	Jeff Reardon	.10	.08	.04
418	Darren Daulton	.06	.05	.02
419	Tim Laudner	.08	.06	.03
420	Don Carman	.07	.05	.03
421	Lloyd Moseby	.09	.07	.04
422	Doug Drabek	.09	.07	.04
423	Lenny Harris	.09	.07	.04
424	Jose Lind	.07	.05	.03
425	*Dave Johnson*(FC)	.30	.25	.12
426	Jerry Browne	.09	.07	.04
427	*Eric Yelding*(FC)	.12	.09	.05
428	Brad Komminsk(FC)	.06	.05	.02
429	Jody Davis	.06	.05	.02

		MT	NR MT	EX
430	Mariano Duncan(FC)	.09	.07	.04
431	Mark Davis	.12	.09	.05
432	Nelson Santovenia	.10	.08	.04
433	Bruce Hurst	.10	.08	.04
434	*Jeff Huson*(FC)	.25	.20	.10
435	Chris James	.09	.07	.04
436	*Mark Guthrie*(FC)	.15	.11	.06
437	Charlie Hayes(FC)	.10	.08	.04
438	Shane Rawley	.08	.06	.03
439	Dickie Thon	.06	.05	.02
440	Juan Berenguer	.06	.05	.02
441	Kevin Romine	.06	.05	.02
442	Bill Landrum	.09	.07	.04
443	Todd Frohwirth	.07	.05	.03
444	Craig Worthington	.10	.08	.04
445	Fernando Valenzuela	.09	.07	.04
446	*Joey Belle*(FC)	1.00	.70	.40
447	*Ed Whited*(FC)	.15	.11	.06
448	Dave Smith	.09	.07	.04
449	Dave Clark	.07	.05	.03
450	Juan Agosto	.06	.05	.02
451	Dave Valle	.06	.05	.02
452	Kent Hrbek	.15	.11	.06
453	Von Hayes	.10	.08	.04
454	Gary Gaetti	.15	.11	.06
455	Greg Briley	.40	.30	.15
456	Glenn Braggs	.08	.06	.03
457	Kirt Manwaring	.10	.08	.04
458	Mel Hall	.07	.05	.03
459	Brook Jacoby	.08	.06	.03
460	Pat Sheridan	.06	.05	.02
461	Rob Murphy	.06	.05	.02
462	Jimmy Key	.10	.08	.04
463	Nick Esasky	.10	.08	.04
464	Rob Ducey	.09	.07	.04
465	Carlos Quintana	.09	.07	.04
466	*Larry Walker*(FC)	.50	.40	.20
467	Todd Worrell	.10	.08	.04
468	Kevin Gross	.09	.07	.04
469	Terry Pendleton	.09	.07	.04
470	Dave Martinez	.07	.05	.02
471	Gene Larkin	.06	.05	.02
472	Len Dykstra	.09	.07	.04
473	Barry Lyons	.06	.05	.02
474	Terry Mulholland(FC)	.10	.08	.04
475	*Chip Hale*(FC)	.15	.11	.06
476	Jesse Barfield	.08	.06	.03
477	Dan Plesac	.09	.07	.04
478a	Scott Garrelts (Photo actually Bill Bathe)	5.00	3.75	2.00
478b	Scott Garrelts (Correct photo)	.10	.08	.04
479	Dave Righetti	.10	.08	.04
480	Gus Polidor(FC)	.06	.05	.02
481	Mookie Wilson	.09	.07	.04
482	Luis Rivera	.06	.05	.02
483	Mike Flanagan	.07	.05	.03
484	Dennis "Oil Can" Boyd	.07	.05	.03
485	John Cerutti	.07	.05	.03
486	John Costello	.07	.05	.03
487	Pascual Perez	.07	.05	.03
488	Tommy Herr	.09	.07	.04
489	Tom Foley	.06	.05	.02
490	Curt Ford	.06	.05	.02
491	Steve Lake	.06	.05	.02
492	Tim Teufel	.06	.05	.02
493	Randy Bush	.06	.05	.02
494	Mike Jackson	.06	.05	.02
495	Steve Jeltz	.06	.05	.02
496	Paul Gibson	.08	.06	.03
497	Steve Balboni	.06	.05	.02
498	Bud Black	.06	.05	.02
499	Dale Sveum	.06	.05	.02
500	Checklist 401-500	.06	.05	.02
501	Timmy Jones	.06	.05	.02
502	Mark Portugal	.06	.05	.02
503	Ivan Calderon	.07	.05	.03
504	Rick Rhoden	.06	.05	.02
505	Willie McGee	.09	.07	.04
506	Kirk McCaskill	.08	.06	.03
507	Dave LaPoint	.07	.05	.03
508	Jay Howell	.10	.08	.04
509	Johnny Ray	.08	.06	.03
510	Dave Anderson	.06	.05	.02
511	Chuck Crim	.06	.05	.02
512	Joe Hesketh	.06	.05	.02
513	Dennis Eckersley	.10	.08	.04
514	Greg Brock	.08	.06	.03
515	Tim Burke	.08	.06	.03
516	Frank Tanana	.07	.05	.03
517	Jay Bell	.07	.05	.03
518	Guillermo Hernandez	.07	.05	.03
519	Randy Kramer(FC)	.08	.06	.03
520	Charles Hudson	.06	.05	.02
521	Jim Corsi(FC)	.08	.06	.03
522	Steve Rosenberg	.08	.06	.03
523	Cris Carpenter	.10	.08	.04
524	*Matt Winters*(FC)	.12	.09	.05
525	Melido Perez	.08	.06	.03
526	Chris Gwynn	.08	.06	.03
527	Bert Blyleven	.09	.07	.04
528	Chuck Cary	.07	.05	.03
529	Daryl Boston	.06	.05	.02
530	Dale Mohorcic	.06	.05	.02
531	Geronimo Berroa(FC)	.09	.07	.04
532	Edgar Martinez	.09	.07	.04
533	Dale Murphy	.15	.11	.06
534	Jay Buhner	.09	.07	.04
535	John Smoltz	.15	.11	.06
536	Andy Van Slyke	.15	.11	.06
537	Mike Henneman	.09	.07	.04
538	Miguel Garcia(FC)	.07	.05	.03
539	Frank Williams	.06	.05	.02
540	R.J. Reynolds	.06	.05	.02
541	Shawn Hillegas	.06	.05	.02
542	Walt Weiss	.10	.08	.04
543	*Greg Hibbard*(FC)	.15	.11	.06
544	Nolan Ryan	1.00	.70	.40
545	*Todd Zeile*	2.25	1.75	.90
546	Hensley Meulens	.20	.15	.08
547	Tim Belcher	.10	.08	.04
548	Mike Witt	.08	.06	.03
549	Greg Cadaret	.06	.05	.02
550	Franklin Stubbs	.06	.05	.02

		MT	NR MT	EX
551	*Tony Castillo*(FC)	.12	.09	.05
552	Jeff Robinson	.08	.06	.03
553	*Steve Olin*(FC)	.12	.09	.05
554	Alan Trammell	.10	.08	.04
555	Wade Boggs	.70	.50	.30
556	Will Clark	1.00	.70	.40
557	Jeff King(FC)	.10	.08	.04
558	Mike Fitzgerald	.06	.05	.02
559	Ken Howell	.06	.05	.02
560	Bob Kipper	.06	.05	.02
561	Scott Bankhead	.09	.07	.04
562a	*Jeff Innis* (Photo actually David West)(FC)	5.00	3.75	2.00
562b	*Jeff Innis* (Corrected)(FC)	.20	.15	.08
563	Randy Johnson	.10	.08	.04
564	*Wally Whitehurst*	.10	.08	.04
565	*Gene Harris*(FC)	.10	.08	.04
566	Norm Charlton	.09	.07	.04
567	Robin Yount	.40	.30	.15
568	*Joe Oliver*(FC)	.35	.25	.14
569	Mark Parent	.07	.05	.03
570	John Farrell	.07	.05	.03
571	Tom Glavine	.10	.08	.04
572	Rod Nichols(FC)	.06	.05	.02
573	Jack Morris	.09	.07	.04
574	Greg Swindell	.12	.09	.05
575	Steve Searcy(FC)	.09	.07	.04
576	Ricky Jordan	.50	.40	.20
577	Matt Williams	.35	.25	.14
578	Mike LaValliere	.07	.05	.03
579	Bryn Smith	.08	.06	.03
580	Bruce Ruffin	.06	.05	.02
581	Randy Myers	.08	.06	.03
582	*Rick Wrona*(FC)	.15	.11	.06
583	Juan Samuel	.09	.07	.04
584	Les Lancaster	.07	.05	.03
585	Jeff Musselman	.07	.05	.03
586	Rob Dibble	.09	.07	.04
587	Eric Show	.07	.05	.03
588	Jesse Orosco	.06	.05	.02
589	Herm Winningham	.06	.05	.02
590	Andy Allanson	.06	.05	.02
591	Dion James	.06	.05	.02
592	Carmelo Martinez	.08	.06	.03
593	Luis Quinones(FC)	.08	.06	.03
594	Dennis Rasmussen	.08	.06	.03
595	Rich Yett	.06	.05	.02
596	Bob Walk	.08	.06	.03
597	Andy McGaffigan	.07	.05	.03
598	Billy Hatcher	.07	.05	.03
599	Bob Knepper	.06	.05	.02
600	Checklist 501-600	.06	.05	.02
601	Joey Cora(FC)	.10	.08	.04
602	*Steve Finley*	.15	.11	.06
603	Kal Daniels	.10	.08	.04
604	Gregg Olson	.50	.40	.20
605	Dave Steib	.09	.07	.04
606	*Kenny Rogers*(FC)	.15	.11	.06
607	Zane Smith	.06	.05	.02
608	*Bob Geren*(FC)	.25	.20	.10
609	Chad Kreuter	.10	.08	.04
610	Mike Smithson	.06	.05	.02
611	*Jeff Wetherby*(FC)	.15	.11	.06
612	*Gary Mielke*(FC)	.15	.11	.06
613	Pete Smith	.08	.06	.03
614	*Jack Daugherty*(FC)	.15	.11	.06
615	Lance McCullers	.08	.06	.03
616	Don Robinson	.06	.05	.02
617	Jose Guzman	.06	.05	.02
618	Steve Bedrosian	.08	.06	.03
619	Jamie Moyer	.06	.05	.02
620	Atlee Hammaker	.06	.05	.02
621	*Rick Luecken*(FC)	.15	.11	.06
622	Greg W. Harris	.09	.07	.04
623	Pete Harnisch	.10	.08	.04
624	Jerald Clark	.10	.08	.04
625	Jack McDowell	.07	.05	.03
626	Frank Viola	.12	.09	.05
627	Ted Higuera	.09	.07	.04
628	*Marty Pevey*(FC)	.15	.11	.06
629	Bill Wegman	.06	.05	.02
630	Eric Plunk	.06	.05	.02
631	Drew Hall	.06	.05	.02
632	Doug Jones	.08	.06	.03
633	Geno Petralli	.06	.05	.02
634	Jose Alvarez	.06	.05	.02
635	Bob Milacki(FC)	.10	.08	.04
636	Bobby Witt	.07	.05	.03
637	Trevor Wilson	.08	.06	.03
638	Jeff Russell	.08	.06	.03
639	Mike Krukow	.07	.05	.03
640	Rick Leach	.06	.05	.02
641	Dave Schmidt	.06	.05	.02
642	Terry Leach	.06	.05	.02
643	Calvin Schiraldi	.06	.05	.02
644	Bob Melvin	.06	.05	.02
645	Jim Abbott	1.00	.70	.40
646	*Jaime Navarro*(FC)	.20	.15	.08
647	Mark Langston	.10	.08	.04
648	Juan Nieves	.08	.06	.03
649	Damaso Garcia	.06	.05	.02
650	Charlie O'Brien	.06	.05	.02
651	Eric King	.06	.05	.02
652	Mike Boddicker	.08	.06	.03
653	Duan Ward	.07	.05	.03
654	Bob Stanley	.06	.05	.02
655	Sandy Alomar, Jr.	.50	.40	.20
656	Danny Tartabull	.10	.08	.04
657	Randy McCament	.15	.11	.06
658	Charlie Leibrandt	.07	.05	.03
659	Dan Quisenberry	.07	.05	.03
660	Paul Assenmacher	.06	.05	.02
661	Walt Terrell	.07	.05	.03
662	Tim Leary	.07	.05	.03
663	Randy Milligan	.08	.06	.03
664	Bo Diaz	.06	.05	.02
665	Mark Lemke	.07	.05	.03
666	Jose Gonzalez	.08	.06	.03
667	Chuck Finley	.07	.05	.03
668	John Kruk	.08	.06	.03
669	Dick Schofield	.07	.05	.03
670	Tim Crews	.06	.05	.02
671	John Dopson	.09	.07	.04
672	*John Orton*(FC)	.15	.11	.06
673	Eric Hetzel(FC)	.10	.08	.04
674	Lance Parrish	.08	.06	.03
675	Ramon Martinez	.10	.08	.04
676	Mark Gubicza	.10	.08	.04
677	Greg Litton	.20	.15	.08
678	Greg Mathews	.07	.05	.03
679	Dave Dravecky	.07	.05	.03
680	Steve Farr	.07	.05	.03
681	Mike Devereaux	.09	.07	.04
682	Ken Griffey, Sr.	.08	.06	.03
683a	*Mickey Weston* (Jamie)(FC)	10.00	7.50	4.00
683b	*Mickey Weston* (corrected)(FC)	.30	.25	.12
684	Jack Armstrong	.07	.05	.03
685	Steve Buechele	.07	.05	.03
686	Bryan Harvey	.07	.05	.03
687	Lance Blankenship	.09	.07	.04
688	Dante Bichette	.09	.07	.04
689	Todd Burns	.09	.07	.04
690	Dan Petry	.06	.05	.02
691	*Kent Anderson*(FC)	.15	.11	.06
692	Todd Stottlemyre	.08	.06	.03
693	Wally Joyner	.15	.11	.06
694	Mike Rochford(FC)	.10	.08	.04
695	Floyd Bannister	.07	.05	.03
696	Rick Reuschel	.09	.07	.04
697	Jose DeLeon	.09	.07	.04
698	Jeff Montgomery	.08	.06	.03
699	Jeff Montgomery	.08	.06	.03
700a	Checklist 601-700 (Jamie Weston)	10.00	7.50	4.00
700b	Checklist 601-700 (Mickey Weston)	.10	.08	.04

1921 V61
Neilson's Chocolate

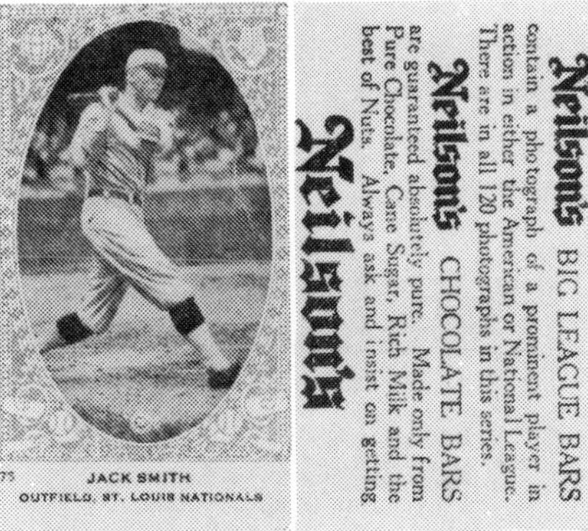

Another set closely related to the popular 1922 American Caramel set (E120), this 120-card set was issued by Neilson's Chocolate Bars and carries the American Card Catalog designation V61. The front of the black and white cards are very similar to the E120 set, while the backs contain an ad for Neilson's Chocolates. Backs exist with the Nielson's name printed in Old English type or in regular printing.

		NR MT	EX	VG
	Complete Set:	9500.	4750.	2850.
	Common Player:	55.00	27.00	16.50
1	George Burns	55.00	27.00	16.50
2	John Tobin	55.00	27.00	16.50
3	J.T. Zachary	55.00	27.00	16.50
4	"Bullet" Joe Bush	75.00	37.00	22.00
5	Lu Blue	55.00	27.00	16.50
6	Clarence (Tillie) Walker	55.00	27.00	16.50
7	Carl Mays	75.00	37.00	22.00
8	Leon Goslin	125.00	62.00	37.00
9	Ed Rommel	55.00	27.00	16.50
10	Charles Robertson	55.00	27.00	16.50
11	Ralph (Cy) Perkins	55.00	27.00	16.50
12	Joe Sewell	125.00	62.00	37.00
13	Harry Hooper	125.00	62.00	37.00
14	Urban (Red) Faber	125.00	62.00	37.00
15	Bib Falk ((Bibb))	55.00	27.00	16.50
16	George Uhle	55.00	27.00	16.50
17	Emory Rigney	55.00	27.00	16.50
18	George Dauss	55.00	27.00	16.50
19	Herman Pillette	55.00	27.00	16.50
20	Wallie Schang	55.00	27.00	16.50
21	Lawrence Woodall	55.00	27.00	16.50
22	Steve O'Neill	55.00	27.00	16.50
23	Edmund (Bing) Miller	55.00	27.00	16.50
24	Sylvester Johnson	55.00	27.00	16.50
25	Henry Severeid	55.00	27.00	16.50
26	Dave Danforth	55.00	27.00	16.50
27	Harry Heilmann	125.00	62.00	37.00
28	Bert Cole	55.00	27.00	16.50
29	Eddie Collins	125.00	62.00	37.00
30	Ty Cob (Cobb)	1000.	500.00	300.00
31	Bill Wambsganss	75.00	37.00	22.00
32	George Sisler	125.00	62.00	37.00
33	Bob Veach	55.00	27.00	16.50
34	Earl Sheely	55.00	27.00	16.50
35	T.P. (Pat) Collins	55.00	27.00	16.50
36	Frank (Dixie) Davis	55.00	27.00	16.50
37	Babe Ruth	1200.	600.00	360.00
38	Bryan Harris	55.00	27.00	16.50
39	Bob Shawkey	75.00	37.00	22.00
40	Urban Shocker	55.00	27.00	16.50
41	Martin McManus	55.00	27.00	16.50
42	Clark Pittenger	55.00	27.00	16.50
43	"Deacon" Sam Jones	55.00	27.00	16.50
44	Waite Hoyt	125.00	62.00	37.00
45	Johnny Mostil	55.00	27.00	16.50
46	Mike Menosky	55.00	27.00	16.50
47	Walter Johnson	600.00	300.00	180.00
48	Wallie Pipp	80.00	40.00	24.00
49	Walter Gerber	55.00	27.00	16.50
50	Ed Gharrity	55.00	27.00	16.50
51	Frank Ellerbe	55.00	27.00	16.50
52	Kenneth Williams	75.00	37.00	22.00
53	Joe Hauser	55.00	27.00	16.50
54	Carson Bigbee	55.00	27.00	16.50
55	Emil (Irish) Meusel	55.00	27.00	16.50
56	Milton Stock	55.00	27.00	16.50
57	Wilbur Cooper	55.00	27.00	16.50
58	Tom Griffith	55.00	27.00	16.50
59	Clarence (Shovel) Hodge	55.00	27.00	16.50
60	Gene (Bubbles) Hargrave	55.00	27.00	16.50
61	Russell Wrightstone	55.00	27.00	16.50
62	Frank Frisch	125.00	62.00	37.00
63	Jack Peters	55.00	27.00	16.50
64	Walter (Dutch) Reuther	55.00	27.00	16.50
65	Bill Doak	55.00	27.00	16.50
66	Marty Callaghan	55.00	27.00	16.50
67	Sammy Bohne	55.00	27.00	16.50
68	Earl Hamilton	55.00	27.00	16.50
69	Grover C. Alexander	250.00	125.00	75.00
70	George Burns	55.00	27.00	16.50
71	Max Carey	125.00	62.00	37.00
72	Adolfo Luque	55.00	27.00	16.50
73	Walt Barbare	55.00	27.00	16.50
74	Vic Aldridge	55.00	27.00	16.50
75	Jack Smith	55.00	27.00	16.50
76	Bob O'Farrell	55.00	27.00	16.50
77	Pete Donohue	55.00	27.00	16.50
78	Ralph Pinelli	75.00	37.00	22.00
79	Eddie Roush	125.00	62.00	37.00
80	Norman Boeckel	55.00	27.00	16.50
81	Rogers Hornsby	500.00	250.00	150.00
82	George Toporcer	55.00	27.00	16.50
83	Ivy Wingo	55.00	27.00	16.50
84	Virgil Cheeves	55.00	27.00	16.50
85	Vern Clemons	55.00	27.00	16.50
86	Lawrence (Hack) Miller	55.00	27.00	16.50
87	Johnny Kelleher	55.00	27.00	16.50
88	Heinie Groh	55.00	27.00	16.50
89	Burleigh Grimes	125.00	62.00	37.00
90	"Rabbit" Maranville	125.00	62.00	37.00
91	Charles (Babe) Adams	55.00	27.00	16.50
92	Lee King	55.00	27.00	16.50
93	Art Nehf	55.00	27.00	16.50
94	Frank Snyder	55.00	27.00	16.50
95	Raymond Powell	55.00	27.00	16.50
96	Wilbur Hubbell	55.00	27.00	16.50
97	Leon Cadore	55.00	27.00	16.50
98	Joe Oeschger	55.00	27.00	16.50
99	Jake Daubert	75.00	37.00	22.00
100	Will Sherdel	55.00	27.00	16.50
101	Hank DeBerry	55.00	27.00	16.50
102	Johnny Lavan	55.00	27.00	16.50
103	Jesse Haines	125.00	62.00	37.00
104	Joe (Goldie) Rapp	55.00	27.00	16.50
105	Oscar Ray Grimes	55.00	27.00	16.50
106	Ross Young (Youngs)	125.00	62.00	37.00
107	Art Fletcher	55.00	27.00	16.50
108	Clyde Barnhart	55.00	27.00	16.50
109	Louis (Pat) Duncan	55.00	27.00	16.50
110	Charlie Hollocher	55.00	27.00	16.50
111	Horace Ford	55.00	27.00	16.50
112	Bill Cunningham	55.00	27.00	16.50
113	Walter Schmidt	55.00	27.00	16.50
114	Joe Schultz	55.00	27.00	16.50
115	John Morrison	55.00	27.00	16.50
116	Jimmy Caveney	55.00	27.00	16.50
117	Zach Wheat	125.00	62.00	37.00
118	Fred (Cy) Williams	75.00	37.00	22.00
119	George Kelly	125.00	62.00	37.00
120	Jimmy Ring	55.00	27.00	16.50

1923 V100
Willard Chocolate

Issued circa 1923, this set was produced by the Willard Chocolate Company of Canada and features sepia-toned photographs on cards measuring 3-1/4" by 2-1/16". The cards are blank-backed and feature the player's name in script on the front. The set is complete at 180 cards and nearly one-fourth of the photos used in the set are identical to the better known E120 American Caramel set. The Willard set is identified as V100 in the American Card Catalog.

		NR MT	EX	VG
Complete Set:		11000.	5500.	3300.
Common Player:		50.00	25.00	15.00
(1)	Chas. B. Adams	50.00	25.00	15.00
(2)	Grover C. Alexander	65.00	32.00	19.50
(3)	J.P. Austin	50.00	25.00	15.00
(4)	J.C. Bagby	50.00	25.00	15.00
(5)	J. Franklin Baker	225.00	112.00	67.00
(6)	David J. Bancroft	225.00	112.00	67.00
(7)	Turner Barber	50.00	25.00	15.00
(8)	Jesse L. Barnes	50.00	25.00	15.00
(9)	J.C. Bassler	50.00	25.00	15.00
(10)	L.A. Blue	50.00	25.00	15.00
(11)	Norman D. Boeckel	50.00	25.00	15.00
(12)	F.L. Brazil (Brazill)	50.00	25.00	15.00
(13)	G.H. Burns	50.00	25.00	15.00
(14)	Geo. J. Burns	50.00	25.00	15.00
(15)	Leon Cadore	50.00	25.00	15.00
(16)	Max G. Carey	225.00	112.00	67.00
(17)	Harold G. Carlson	50.00	25.00	15.00
(18)	Lloyd R Christenberry (Christenbury)	50.00	25.00	15.00
(19)	Vernon J. Clemons	50.00	25.00	15.00
(20)	T.R. Cobb	1000.	500.00	300.00
(21)	Bert Cole	50.00	25.00	15.00
(22)	John F. Collins	50.00	25.00	15.00
(23)	S. Coveleskie (Coveleski)	225.00	112.00	67.00
(24)	Walton E. Cruise	50.00	25.00	15.00
(25)	G.W. Cutshaw	50.00	25.00	15.00
(26)	Jacob E. Daubert	75.00	37.00	22.00
(27)	Geo. Dauss	50.00	25.00	15.00
(28)	F.T. Davis	50.00	25.00	15.00
(29)	Chas. A. Deal	50.00	25.00	15.00
(30)	William L. Doak	50.00	25.00	15.00
(31)	William E. Donovan	50.00	25.00	15.00
(32)	Hugh Duffy	225.00	112.00	67.00
(33)	J.A. Dugan	75.00	37.00	22.00
(34)	Louis B. Duncan	50.00	25.00	15.00
(35)	James Dykes	75.00	37.00	22.00
(36)	H.J. Ehmke	50.00	25.00	15.00
(37)	F.R. Ellerbe	50.00	25.00	15.00
(38)	E.G. Erickson	50.00	25.00	15.00
(39)	John J. Evers	225.00	112.00	67.00
(40)	U.C. Faber	225.00	112.00	67.00
(41)	B.A. Falk	50.00	25.00	15.00
(42)	Max Flack	50.00	25.00	15.00
(43)	Lee Fohl	50.00	25.00	15.00
(44)	Jacques F. Fournier	50.00	25.00	15.00
(45)	Frank F. Frisch	225.00	112.00	67.00
(46)	C.E. Galloway	50.00	25.00	15.00
(47)	W.C. Gardner	50.00	25.00	15.00
(48)	E.P. Gharrity	50.00	25.00	15.00
(49)	Geo. Gibson	50.00	25.00	15.00
(50)	Wm. Gleason	50.00	25.00	15.00
(51)	William Gleason	50.00	25.00	15.00
(52)	Henry M. Gowdy	50.00	25.00	15.00
(53)	I.M. Griffin	50.00	25.00	15.00
(54)	Griffith	225.00	112.00	67.00
(55)	Burleigh A. Grimes	225.00	112.00	67.00
(56)	Charles J. Grimm	75.00	37.00	22.00
(57)	Jesse J. Haines	75.00	37.00	22.00
(58)	S.R. Harris	225.00	112.00	67.00
(59)	W.B. Harris	50.00	25.00	15.00
(60)	R.K. Hasty	50.00	25.00	15.00
(61)	H.E. Heilman (Heilmann)	225.00	112.00	67.00
(62)	Walter J. Henline	50.00	25.00	15.00
(63)	Walter L. Holke	50.00	25.00	15.00
(64)	Charles J. Hollocher	50.00	25.00	15.00
(65)	H.B. Hooper	225.00	112.00	67.00
(66)	Rogers Hornsby	400.00	200.00	120.00
(67)	W.C. Hoyt	225.00	112.00	67.00
(68)	Miller Huggins	225.00	112.00	67.00
(69)	W.C. Jacobsen (Jacobson)	50.00	25.00	15.00
(70)	C.D. Jamieson	50.00	25.00	15.00
(71)	Ernest Johnson	50.00	25.00	15.00
(72)	W.P. Johnson	600.00	300.00	180.00
(73)	James H. Johnston	50.00	25.00	15.00
(74)	R.W. Jones	50.00	25.00	15.00
(75)	Samuel Pond Jones	50.00	25.00	15.00
(76)	J.I. Judge	50.00	25.00	15.00
(77)	James W. Keenan	50.00	25.00	15.00
(78)	Geo. L. Kelly	225.00	112.00	67.00
(79)	Peter J. Kilduff	50.00	25.00	15.00
(80)	William Killefer	50.00	25.00	15.00
(81)	Lee King	50.00	25.00	15.00
(82)	Ray Kolp	50.00	25.00	15.00
(83)	John Lavan	50.00	25.00	15.00
(84)	H.L. Leibold	50.00	25.00	15.00
(85)	Connie Mack	300.00	150.00	90.00
(86)	J.W. Mails	50.00	25.00	15.00
(87)	Walter J. Maranville	225.00	112.00	67.00
(88)	Richard W. Marquard	225.00	112.00	67.00
(89)	C.W. Mays	75.00	37.00	22.00
(90)	Geo. F. McBride	50.00	25.00	15.00
(91)	H.M. McClellan	50.00	25.00	15.00
(92)	John J. McGraw	250.00	125.00	75.00
(93)	Austin B. McHenry	50.00	25.00	15.00
(94)	J. McInnis	50.00	25.00	15.00
(95)	Douglas McWeeney (McWeeny)	50.00	25.00	15.00
(96)	M. Menosky	50.00	25.00	15.00
(97)	Emil F. Meusel	50.00	25.00	15.00
(98)	R. Meusel	75.00	37.00	22.00
(99)	Henry W. Meyers	50.00	25.00	15.00
(100)	J.C. Milan	50.00	25.00	15.00
(101)	John K. Miljus	50.00	25.00	15.00
(102)	Edmund J. Miller	50.00	25.00	15.00
(103)	Elmer Miller	50.00	25.00	15.00
(104)	Otto L. Miller	50.00	25.00	15.00
(105)	Fred Mitchell	50.00	25.00	15.00
(106)	Geo. Mogridge	50.00	25.00	15.00
(107)	Patrick J. Moran	50.00	25.00	15.00
(108)	John D. Morrison	50.00	25.00	15.00
(109)	J.A. Mostil	50.00	25.00	15.00
(110)	Clarence F. Mueller	50.00	25.00	15.00
(111)	A. Earle Neale	175.00	87.00	52.00
(112)	Joseph Oeschger	50.00	25.00	15.00
(113)	Robert J. O'Farrell	50.00	25.00	15.00
(114)	J.C. Oldham	50.00	25.00	15.00
(115)	I.M. Olson	50.00	25.00	15.00
(116)	Geo. M. O'Neil	50.00	25.00	15.00
(117)	S.F. O'Neill	50.00	25.00	15.00
(118)	Frank J. Parkinson	50.00	25.00	15.00
(119)	Geo. H. Paskert	50.00	25.00	15.00
(120)	R.T. Peckinpaugh	50.00	25.00	15.00
(121)	H.J. Pennock	225.00	112.00	67.00
(122)	Ralph Perkins	50.00	25.00	15.00
(123)	Edw. J. Pfeffer	50.00	25.00	15.00
(124)	W.C. Pipp	175.00	87.00	52.00
(125)	Charles Elmer Ponder	50.00	25.00	15.00
(126)	Raymond R. Powell	50.00	25.00	15.00
(127)	D.B. Pratt	50.00	25.00	15.00
(128)	Joseph Rapp	50.00	25.00	15.00
(129)	John H. Rawlings	50.00	25.00	15.00
(130)	E.S. Rice (should be E.C.)	225.00	112.00	67.00
(131)	Rickey	300.00	150.00	90.00
(132)	James J. Ring	50.00	25.00	15.00
(133)	Eppa J. Rixey	225.00	112.00	67.00
(134)	Davis A. Robertson	50.00	25.00	15.00
(135)	Edwin Rommel	50.00	25.00	15.00
(136)	Edd J. Roush	225.00	112.00	67.00
(137)	Harold Ruel (Herold)	50.00	25.00	15.00
(138)	Allen Russell	50.00	25.00	15.00
(139)	G.H. Ruth	1100.	550.00	330.00
(140)	Wilfred D. Ryan	50.00	25.00	15.00
(141)	Henry F. Sallee	50.00	25.00	15.00
(142)	W.H. Schang	50.00	25.00	15.00
(143)	Raymond H. Schmandt	50.00	25.00	15.00
(144)	Everett Scott	50.00	25.00	15.00
(145)	Henry Severeid	50.00	25.00	15.00
(146)	Jos. W. Sewell	225.00	112.00	67.00
(147)	Howard S. Shanks	50.00	25.00	15.00
(148)	E.H. Sheely	50.00	25.00	15.00
(149)	Ralph Shinners	50.00	25.00	15.00
(150)	U.J. Shocker	50.00	25.00	15.00
(151)	G.H. Sisler	225.00	112.00	67.00
(152)	Earl L. Smith	50.00	25.00	15.00
(153)	Earl S. Smith	50.00	25.00	15.00
(154)	Geo. A. Smith	50.00	25.00	15.00
(155)	J.W. Smith	50.00	25.00	15.00
(156)	Tris E. Speaker	250.00	125.00	75.00
(157)	Arnold Staatz	50.00	25.00	15.00
(158)	J.R. Stephenson	75.00	37.00	22.00
(159)	Milton J. Stock	50.00	25.00	15.00
(160)	John L. Sullivan	50.00	25.00	15.00
(161)	H.F. Tormahlen	50.00	25.00	15.00
(162)	Jas. A. Tierney	50.00	25.00	15.00
(163)	J.T. Tobin	50.00	25.00	15.00
(164)	Jas. L. Vaughn	50.00	25.00	15.00
(165)	R.H. Veach	50.00	25.00	15.00
(166)	C.W. Walker	50.00	25.00	15.00
(167)	A.L. Ward	50.00	25.00	15.00
(168)	Zack D. Wheat	225.00	112.00	67.00
(169)	George B. Whitted	50.00	25.00	15.00
(170)	Irvin K. Wilhelm	50.00	25.00	15.00
(171)	Roy H. Wilkinson	50.00	25.00	15.00
(172)	Fred C. Williams	75.00	37.00	22.00
(173)	K.R. Williams	75.00	37.00	22.00
(174)	Sam'l W. Wilson	50.00	25.00	15.00
(175)	Ivy B. Wingo	50.00	25.00	15.00
(176)	L.W. Witt	50.00	25.00	15.00
(177)	Joseph Wood	75.00	37.00	22.00
(178)	E. Yaryan	50.00	25.00	15.00
(179)	R.S. Young	50.00	25.00	15.00
(180)	Ross Young (Youngs)	225.00	112.00	67.00

1936 V355 World Wide Gum

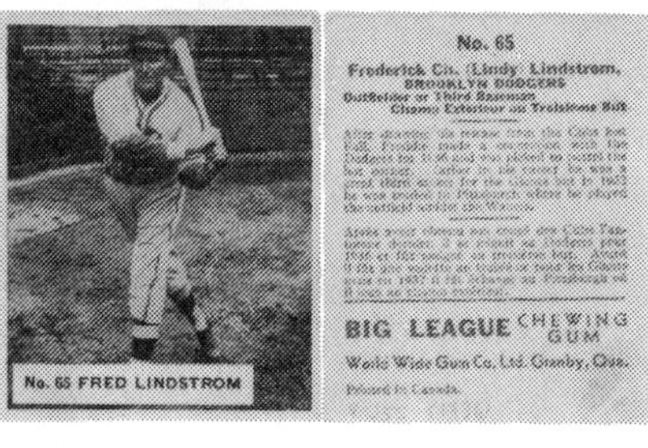

This black and white Canadian set was issued by World Wide Gum in 1936. The cards measure approximately 2-1/2" by 2-7/8", and the set includes both portrait and action photos. The card number and player's name (appearing in all capital letters) are printed inside a white box below the photo.

		NR MT	EX	VG
Complete Set:		20000.	10000.	6000.
Common Player:		110.00	55.00	33.00
1	Jimmy Dykes	125.00	62.00	37.00
2	Paul Waner	250.00	125.00	75.00
3	Cy Blanton	110.00	55.00	33.00
4	Sam Leslie	110.00	55.00	33.00
5	Johnny Louis Vergez	110.00	55.00	33.00
6	Arky Vaughan	250.00	125.00	75.00
7	Bill Terry	300.00	150.00	90.00
8	Joe Moore	110.00	55.00	33.00
9	Gus Mancuso	110.00	55.00	33.00
10	Fred Marberry	110.00	55.00	33.00
11	George Selkirk	110.00	55.00	33.00
12	Spud Davis	110.00	55.00	33.00
13	Chuck Klein	250.00	125.00	75.00
14	Fred Fitzsimmons	110.00	55.00	33.00
15	Bill Delancey	110.00	55.00	33.00
17	George Davis	110.00	55.00	33.00
20	Roy Parmelee	110.00	55.00	33.00
21	Vic Sorrell	110.00	55.00	33.00
22	Harry Danning	110.00	55.00	33.00
23	Hal Schumacher	110.00	55.00	33.00
24	Cy Perkins	110.00	55.00	33.00
25	Speedy Durocher	300.00	150.00	90.00
26	Glenn Myatt	110.00	55.00	33.00
27	Bob Seeds	110.00	55.00	33.00
28	Jimmy Ripple	110.00	55.00	33.00
29	Al Schacht	90.00	45.00	27.00
31	Del Baker	110.00	55.00	33.00
32	Flea Clifton	110.00	55.00	33.00
33	Tommy Bridges	110.00	55.00	33.00
34	Bill Dickey	400.00	200.00	120.00
35	Wally Berger	110.00	55.00	33.00
36	Slick Castleman	110.00	55.00	33.00
37	Dick Bartell	110.00	55.00	33.00
38	Red Rolfe	110.00	55.00	33.00
39	Waite Hoyt	250.00	125.00	75.00
40	Wes Ferrell	110.00	55.00	33.00
41	Hank Greenberg	400.00	200.00	120.00
42	Charlie Gehringer	250.00	125.00	75.00
43	Goose Goslin	250.00	125.00	75.00
44	Schoolboy Rowe	90.00	45.00	27.00
45	Mickey Cochrane	300.00	150.00	90.00
46	Joe Cronin	300.00	150.00	90.00
48	Jerry Walker	110.00	55.00	33.00
49	Charlie Gelbert	110.00	55.00	33.00
50	Roy Hayworth (Ray)	110.00	55.00	33.00
51	Joe DiMaggio	1500.	750.00	450.00
52	Billy Rogell	110.00	55.00	33.00
53	Joe McCarthy	300.00	150.00	90.00
54	Phil Cavaretta (Cavarretta)	90.00	45.00	27.00
55	Kiki Cuyler	250.00	125.00	75.00
56	Lefty Gomez	300.00	150.00	90.00
57	Gabby Hartnett	250.00	125.00	75.00
59	Burgess Whitehead	110.00	55.00	33.00
60	Whitey Whitehill	110.00	55.00	33.00
61	Buckey Walters	110.00	55.00	33.00
62	Luke Sewell	110.00	55.00	33.00
63	Joey Kuhel	110.00	55.00	33.00
64	Lou Finney	110.00	55.00	33.00
65	Fred Lindstrom	250.00	125.00	75.00
66	Paul Derringer	110.00	55.00	33.00
67	Steve O'Neil (O'Neill)	110.00	55.00	33.00
68	Mule Haas	110.00	55.00	33.00
69	Freck Owen	110.00	55.00	33.00
70	Wild Bill Hallahan	110.00	55.00	33.00
72	Dan Taylor	110.00	55.00	33.00
74	Jo-Jo White	110.00	55.00	33.00
75	Mickey Medwick (Ducky)	250.00	125.00	75.00
76	Joe Vosmik	110.00	55.00	33.00
77	Al Simmons	250.00	125.00	75.00
78	Shag Shaughnessy	110.00	55.00	33.00
79	Harry Smythe	110.00	55.00	33.00
80	Benny Tate	110.00	55.00	33.00
81	Billy Rhiel	110.00	55.00	33.00
82	Lauri Myllykangas	110.00	55.00	33.00
83	Ben Sankey	110.00	55.00	33.00
85	Jim Bottomley	250.00	125.00	75.00
87	Ossie Bluege	110.00	55.00	33.00
88	Lefty Grove	300.00	150.00	90.00
89	Charlie Grimm	90.00	45.00	27.00
90	Ben Chapman	110.00	55.00	33.00
91	Frank Crosetti	200.00	100.00	60.00
92	John Pomorski	110.00	55.00	33.00
93	Jesse Haines	250.00	125.00	75.00
94	Chick Hafey	250.00	125.00	75.00
95	Tony Piet	110.00	55.00	33.00
96	Lou Gehrig	1800.	900.00	550.00
97	Bill Jurges	110.00	55.00	33.00
98	Smead Jolley	110.00	55.00	33.00
99	Jimmy Wilson	110.00	55.00	33.00
100	Lonnie Warneke	110.00	55.00	33.00
101	Lefty Tamulis	110.00	55.00	33.00
103	Earl Grace	110.00	55.00	33.00
104	Rox Lawson	110.00	55.00	33.00
105	Stan Hack	110.00	55.00	33.00
106	August Galan	110.00	55.00	33.00
107	Frank Frisch	250.00	125.00	75.00
108	Bill McKechnie	250.00	125.00	75.00
109	Bill Lee	110.00	55.00	33.00
110	Connie Mack	300.00	150.00	90.00
111	Frank Reiber	110.00	55.00	33.00
112	Zeke Bonura	110.00	55.00	33.00
113	Luke Appling	250.00	125.00	75.00
114	Monte Pearson	110.00	55.00	33.00
115	Bob O'Farrell	110.00	55.00	33.00
116	Marvin Duke	110.00	55.00	33.00
117	Paul Florence	110.00	55.00	33.00
118	John Berley	110.00	55.00	33.00
119	Tom Oliver	110.00	55.00	33.00
120	Norman Kies	110.00	55.00	33.00
121	Hal King	110.00	55.00	33.00
122	Tom Abernathy	110.00	55.00	33.00
123	Phil Hensick	110.00	55.00	33.00
124	Roy Schalk (Ray)	250.00	125.00	75.00
125	Paul Dunlap	110.00	55.00	33.00
126	Benny Bates	110.00	55.00	33.00
127	George Puccinelli	110.00	55.00	33.00
128	Stevie Stevenson	110.00	55.00	33.00
129	Rabbit Maranville	250.00	125.00	75.00
130	Bucky Harris	250.00	125.00	75.00
132	Buddy Myer	110.00	55.00	33.00

NOTE: A card number in parentheses ( ) indicates the card set is unnumbered.

		NR MT	EX	VG
133	Cliff Bolton	110.00	55.00	33.00
134	Estel Crabtree	110.00	55.00	33.00

1989 Very Fine Pirates

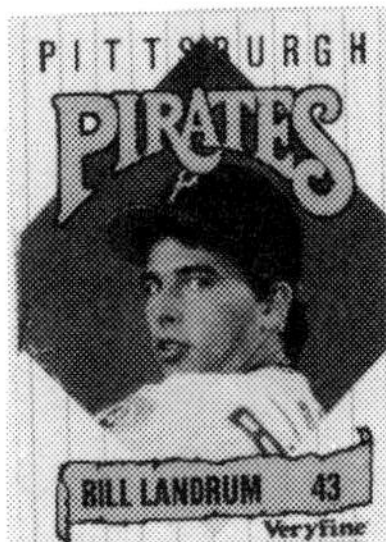

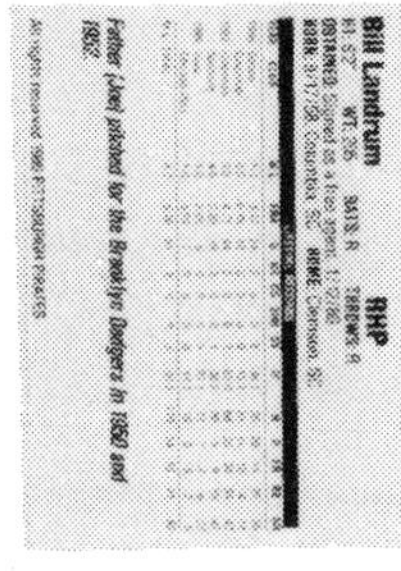

This 30-card set Pittsburgh Pirates team set was sponsored by Veryfine fruit juices, and was issued in the form of two uncut, perforated panels, each containing 15 standard-size cards. A third panel featured color action photographs. The panels were distributed in a stadium promotion to fans attending the April 23 Pirates game at Three Rivers Stadium. The cards display the Pirates traditional black and gold color scheme, and include the player's names and uniform number along the bottom. The "Veryfine" logo appears in the lower right corner. The backs include player data and complete stats.

		MT	NR MT	EX
Complete 3-Panel Set:		20.00	15.00	8.00
Complete Singles Card Set:		12.00	9.00	4.75
Common Player:		.20	.15	.08
0	Junior Ortiz	.20	.15	.08
2	Gary Redus	.30	.25	.12
3	Jay Bell	.30	.25	.12
5	Sid Bream	.30	.25	.12
6	Rafael Belliard	.25	.20	.10
10	Jim Leyland	.30	.25	.12
11	Glenn Wilson	.30	.25	.12
12	Mike La Valliere	.30	.25	.12
13	Jose Lind	.40	.30	.15
14	Ken Oberkfell	.25	.20	.10
15	Doug Drabek	.50	.40	.20
16	Bob Kipper	.20	.15	.08
17	Bob Walk	.25	.20	.10
18	Andy Van Slyke	1.00	.70	.40
23	R.J. Reynolds	.30	.25	.12
24	Barry Bonds	1.25	.90	.50
25	Bobby Bonilla	1.25	.90	.50
26	Neal Heaton	.30	.25	.12
30	Benny Distefano	.30	.25	.12
35	Jim Gott	.35	.25	.14
41	Mike Dunne	.30	.25	.12
43	Bill Landrum	.40	.30	.15
44	John Cangelosi	.25	.20	.10
49	Jeff Robinson	.35	.25	.12
52	Dorn Taylor	.60	.45	.25
54	Brian Fisher	.25	.20	.10
57	John Smiley	.50	.40	.20
---	Ray Miller, Tommy Sandt (31-37)	.20	.15	.08
---	Bruce Kimm (32-36)	.20	.15	.08
---	Gene Lamont (32-36)	.20	.15	.08
---	Milt May (39-45)	.20	.15	.08
---	Rich Donnelly (39-45)	.20	.15	.08

1922 W501

This "strip card" set, known as W501 in the American Card Catalog, is closely connected to the more popular E121 American Caramel set of 1921 and 1922. Measuring the same 2" by 3-1/2", the cards are actually reproductions of the E121 120-card series distributed as strip cards. The W501 cards are numbered in the upper left corner and have the notation "G-4-22" in the upper right corner, apparently indicating the cards were issued in April of 1922.

		NR MT	EX	VG
Complete Set:		5200.	2600.	1560.
Common Player:		20.00	10.00	6.00
1	Ed Rounnel (Rommel)	20.00	10.00	6.00
2	Urban Shocker	20.00	10.00	6.00
3	Dixie Davis	20.00	10.00	6.00
4	George Sisler	40.00	20.00	12.00
5	Bob Veach	20.00	10.00	6.00
6	Harry Heilman (Heilmann)	40.00	20.00	12.00
7a	Ira Falgstead (name incorrect)	20.00	10.00	6.00
7b	Ira Flagstead (name correct)	20.00	10.00	6.00
8	Ty Cobb	600.00	300.00	180.00
9	Oscar Vitt	20.00	10.00	6.00
10	Muddy Ruel	20.00	10.00	6.00
11	Derrill Pratt	20.00	10.00	6.00
12	Ed Gharrity	20.00	10.00	6.00
13	Joe Judge	20.00	10.00	6.00
14	Sam Rice	40.00	20.00	12.00
15	Clyde Milan	20.00	10.00	6.00
16	Joe Sewell	40.00	20.00	12.00
17	Walter Johnson	200.00	100.00	60.00
18	Jack McInnis	20.00	10.00	6.00
19	Tris Speaker	60.00	30.00	18.00
20	Jim Bagby	20.00	10.00	6.00
21	Stanley Coveleskie (Coveleski)	40.00	20.00	12.00
22	Bill Wambsganss	25.00	12.50	7.50
23	Walter Mails	20.00	10.00	6.00
24	Larry Gardner	20.00	10.00	6.00
25	Aaron Ward	20.00	10.00	6.00
26	Miller Huggins	40.00	20.00	12.00
27	Wally Schang	20.00	10.00	6.00
28	Tom Rogers	20.00	10.00	6.00
29	Carl Mays	25.00	12.50	7.50
30	Everett Scott	20.00	10.00	6.00
31	Robert Shawkey	25.00	12.50	7.50
32	Waite Hoyt	40.00	20.00	12.00
33	Mike McNally	20.00	10.00	6.00
34	Joe Bush	25.00	12.50	7.50
35	Bob Meusel	25.00	12.50	7.50
36	Elmer Miller	20.00	10.00	6.00
37	Dick Kerr	20.00	10.00	6.00
38	Eddie Collins	40.00	20.00	12.00
39	Kid Gleason	20.00	10.00	6.00
40	Johnny Mostil	20.00	10.00	6.00
41	Bib Falk (Bibb)	20.00	10.00	6.00
42	Clarence Hodge	20.00	10.00	6.00
43	Ray Schalk	40.00	20.00	12.00
44	Amos Strunk	20.00	10.00	6.00
45	Eddie Mulligan	20.00	10.00	6.00
46	Earl Sheely	20.00	10.00	6.00
47	Harry Hooper	40.00	20.00	12.00
48	Urban Faber	40.00	20.00	12.00
49	Babe Ruth	700.00	350.00	210.00
50	Ivy B. Wingo	20.00	10.00	6.00
51	Earle Neale	25.00	12.50	7.50
52	Jake Daubert	25.00	12.50	7.50
53	Ed Roush	40.00	20.00	12.00
54	Eppa J. Rixey	40.00	20.00	12.00
55	Elwood Martin	20.00	10.00	6.00
56	Bill Killifer (Killefer)	20.00	10.00	6.00
57	Charles Hollocher	20.00	10.00	6.00
58	Zeb Terry	20.00	10.00	6.00
59	Grover Alexander	60.00	30.00	18.00
60	Turner Barber	20.00	10.00	6.00
61	John Rawlings	20.00	10.00	6.00
62	Frank Frisch	40.00	20.00	12.00
63	Pat Shea	20.00	10.00	6.00
64	Dave Bancroft	40.00	20.00	12.00
65	Cecil Causey	20.00	10.00	6.00
66	Frank Snyder	20.00	10.00	6.00
67	Heinie Groh	20.00	10.00	6.00
68	Ross Young (Youngs)	40.00	20.00	12.00
69	Fred Toney	20.00	10.00	6.00
70	Arthur Nehf	20.00	10.00	6.00
71	Earl Smith	20.00	10.00	6.00
72	George Kelly	40.00	20.00	12.00
73	John J. McGraw	50.00	25.00	15.00
74	Phil Douglas	20.00	10.00	6.00
75	Bill Ryan	20.00	10.00	6.00
76	Jess Haines	40.00	20.00	12.00
77	Milt Stock	20.00	10.00	6.00
78	William Doak	20.00	10.00	6.00
79	George Toporcer	20.00	10.00	6.00
80	Wilbur Cooper	20.00	10.00	6.00
81	George Whitted	20.00	10.00	6.00
82	Chas. Grimm	25.00	12.50	7.50
83	Rabbit Maranville	40.00	20.00	12.00
84	Babe Adams	20.00	10.00	6.00
85	Carson Bigbee	20.00	10.00	6.00
86	Max Carey	40.00	20.00	12.00
87	Whitey Glazner	20.00	10.00	6.00
88	George Gibson	20.00	10.00	6.00
89	Bill Southworth	20.00	10.00	6.00
90	Hank Gowdy	20.00	10.00	6.00
91	Walter Holke	20.00	10.00	6.00
92	Joe Oeschger	20.00	10.00	6.00
93	Pete Kilduff	20.00	10.00	6.00
94	Hy Myers	20.00	10.00	6.00
95	Otto Miller	20.00	10.00	6.00
96	Wilbert Robinson	40.00	20.00	12.00
97	Zach Wheat	40.00	20.00	12.00
98	Walter Ruether	20.00	10.00	6.00
99	Curtis Walker	20.00	10.00	6.00
100	Fred Williams	25.00	12.50	7.50
101	Dave Danforth	20.00	10.00	6.00
102	Ed Rounnel (Rommel)	20.00	10.00	6.00
103	Carl Mays	25.00	12.50	7.50
104	Frank Frisch	40.00	20.00	12.00
105	Lou DeVormer	20.00	10.00	6.00
106	Tom Griffith	20.00	10.00	6.00
107	Harry Harper	20.00	10.00	6.00
108a	John Lavan	20.00	10.00	6.00
108b	John J. McGraw	60.00	30.00	18.00
109	Elmer Smith	20.00	10.00	6.00
110	George Dauss	20.00	10.00	6.00
111	Alexander Gaston	20.00	10.00	6.00
112	John Graney	20.00	10.00	6.00
113	Emil Muesel	20.00	10.00	6.00
114	Rogers Hornsby	100.00	50.00	30.00
115	Leslie Nunamaker	20.00	10.00	6.00
116	Steve O'Neill	20.00	10.00	6.00
117	Max Flack	20.00	10.00	6.00
118	Bill Southworth	20.00	10.00	6.00
119	Arthur Nehf	20.00	10.00	6.00
120	Chick Fewster	20.00	10.00	6.00

1928 W502

Issued in 1927, this 63-card set is closely related to the York Caramel set (E210) of the same year. The black and white cards measure 1-3/8" by 2-1/2" and display the player's name at the bottom in capital letters preceded by a number in parenthesis. The backs of the cards read either "One Bagger," "Three Bagger" or "Home Run", and were apparently designed to be used as part of a baseball game. There are two cards known to exist for card numbers 26, 38, 40, 55 and 59. The set carries the American Card Catalog designation W502.

		NR MT	EX	VG
Complete Set:		3100.	1550.	930.00
Common Player:		20.00	10.00	6.00
1	Burleigh Grimes	45.00	22.00	13.50
2	Walter Reuther	20.00	10.00	6.00
3	Joe Dugan	25.00	12.50	7.50
4	Red Faber	45.00	22.00	13.50
5	Gabby Hartnett	45.00	22.00	13.50
6	Babe Ruth	600.00	300.00	180.00
7	Bob Meusel	25.00	12.50	7.50
8	Herb Pennock	45.00	22.00	13.50
9	George Burns (photo is George J., not George H. Burns)	20.00	10.00	6.00
10	Joe Sewell	45.00	22.00	13.50
11	George Uhle	20.00	10.00	6.00
12	Bob O'Farrell	20.00	10.00	6.00
13	Rogers Hornsby	125.00	62.00	37.00
14	Pie Traynor	45.00	22.00	13.50
15	Clarence Mitchell	20.00	10.00	6.00
16	Eppa Rixey	45.00	22.00	13.50
17	Carl Mays	25.00	12.50	7.50
18	Adolfo Luque	20.00	10.00	6.00
19	Dave Bancroft	45.00	22.00	13.50
20	George Kelly	45.00	22.00	13.50
21	Earl Combs (Earle)	45.00	22.00	13.50
22	Harry Heilmann	45.00	22.00	13.50
23	Ray W. Schalk	45.00	22.00	13.50
24	Johnny Mostil	20.00	10.00	6.00
25	Hack Wilson (photo actually Art Wilson)	45.00	22.00	13.50
26a	Lou Gehrig	500.00	250.00	150.00
26b	Stanley Harris	20.00	10.00	6.00
27	Ty Cobb	500.00	250.00	150.00
28	Tris Speaker	90.00	45.00	27.00
29	Tony Lazzeri	35.00	17.50	10.50
30	Waite Hoyt	45.00	22.00	13.50
31	Sherwood Smith	20.00	10.00	6.00
32	Max Carey	45.00	22.00	13.50
33	Eugene Hargrave	20.00	10.00	6.00
34	Miguel L. Gonzales	20.00	10.00	6.00
35	Joe Judge	20.00	10.00	6.00
36	E.C. (Sam) Rice	45.00	22.00	13.50
37	Earl Sheely	20.00	10.00	6.00
38a	Sam Jones	20.00	10.00	6.00
38b	Emory E. Rigney	20.00	10.00	6.00
39	Bib A. Falk (Bibb)	20.00	10.00	6.00
40a	Nick Altrock	20.00	10.00	6.00
40b	Willie Kamm	20.00	10.00	6.00
42	John J. McGraw	90.00	45.00	27.00

		NR MT	EX	VG
43	Artie Nehf	20.00	10.00	6.00
44	Grover Alexander	90.00	45.00	27.00
45	Paul Waner	45.00	22.00	13.50
46	William H. Terry	70.00	35.00	21.00
47	Glenn Wright	20.00	10.00	6.00
48	Earl Smith	20.00	10.00	6.00
49	Leon (Goose) Goslin	45.00	22.00	13.50
50	Frank Frisch	45.00	22.00	13.50
51	Joe Harris	20.00	10.00	6.00
52	Fred (Cy) Williams	25.00	12.50	7.50
53	Eddie Roush	45.00	22.00	13.50
54	George Sisler	45.00	22.00	13.50
55a	Ed Rommel	20.00	10.00	6.00
55b	L. Waner (photo actually Paul Waner)	45.00	22.00	13.50
56	Roger Peckinpaugh	20.00	10.00	6.00
57	Stanley Coveleskie (Coveleski)	45.00	22.00	13.50
58	Lester Bell	20.00	10.00	6.00
59a	Dave Bancroft	45.00	22.00	13.50
59b	L. Waner	45.00	22.00	13.50
60	John P. McInnis	20.00	10.00	6.00

1922 W503

Issued circa 1923, this 64-card set of blank-backed cards, measuring 1-3/4" by 2-3/4", feature black and white player photos surrounded by a white border. The player's name and team appear on the card, along with a card number in either the left or right bottom corner. There is no indication of the set's producer, although it is believed the cards were issued with candy or gum. The set carries a W503 American Card Catalog designation.

		NR MT	EX	VG
	Complete Set:	3700.	1850.	1110.
	Common Player:	35.00	17.50	10.50
1	Joe Bush	25.00	12.50	7.50
2	Wally Schang	35.00	17.50	10.50
3	Dave Robertson	35.00	17.50	10.50
4	Wally Pipp	80.00	40.00	24.00
5	Bill Ryan	35.00	17.50	10.50
6	George Kelly	90.00	45.00	27.00
7	Frank Snyder	35.00	17.50	10.50
8	Jimmy O'Connell	35.00	17.50	10.50
9	Bill Cunningham	35.00	17.50	10.50
10	Norman McMillan	35.00	17.50	10.50
11	Waite Hoyt	90.00	45.00	27.00
12	Art Nehf	35.00	17.50	10.50
13	George Sisler	90.00	45.00	27.00
14	Al DeVormer	35.00	17.50	10.50
15	Casey Stengel	200.00	100.00	60.00
16	Ken Williams	35.00	17.50	10.50
17	Joe Dugan	35.00	17.50	10.50
18	"Irish" Meusel	35.00	17.50	10.50
19	Bob Meusel	35.00	17.50	10.50
20	Carl Mays	35.00	17.50	10.50
22	Jess Barnes	35.00	17.50	10.50
23	Walter Johnson	90.00	45.00	27.00
24	Claude Jonnard	35.00	17.50	10.50
25	Dave Bancroft	90.00	45.00	27.00
26	Johnny Rawlings	35.00	17.50	10.50
27	"Pep" Young	35.00	17.50	10.50
28	Earl Smith	35.00	17.50	10.50
29	Willie Kamm	35.00	17.50	10.50
30	Art Fletcher	35.00	17.50	10.50
31	"Kid" Gleason	35.00	17.50	10.50
32	"Babe" Ruth	900.00	450.00	270.00
33	Guy Morton	35.00	17.50	10.50
34	Heinie Groh	35.00	17.50	10.50
35	Leon Cadore	35.00	17.50	10.50
36	Joe Tobin	35.00	17.50	10.50
37	"Rube" Marquard	90.00	45.00	27.00
38	Grover Alexander	125.00	62.00	37.00
39	George Burns	35.00	17.50	10.50
40	Joe Oeschger	35.00	17.50	10.50
41	"Chick" Shorten	35.00	17.50	10.50
42	Roger Hornsby (Rogers)	200.00	100.00	60.00
43	Adolfo Luque	35.00	17.50	10.50
44	Zack Wheat	125.00	62.00	37.00
45	Herb Pruett (Hub)	35.00	17.50	10.50
46	Rabbit Maranville	125.00	62.00	37.00
47	Jimmy Ring	35.00	17.50	10.50
48	Sherrod Smith	35.00	17.50	10.50
49	Lea Meadows (Lee)	35.00	17.50	10.50
50	Aaron Ward	35.00	17.50	10.50
51	Herb Pennock	125.00	62.00	37.00
52	Carlson Bigbee (Carson)	35.00	17.50	10.50
53	Max Carey	125.00	62.00	37.00
54	Charles Robertson	35.00	17.50	10.50
55	Urban Shocker	35.00	17.50	10.50
56	Dutch Ruether	35.00	17.50	10.50
57	Jake Daubert	35.00	17.50	10.50
58	Louis Guisto	35.00	17.50	10.50
59	Ivy Wingo	35.00	17.50	10.50
60	Bill Pertica	35.00	17.50	10.50
61	Luke Sewell	35.00	17.50	10.50
62	Hank Gowdy	35.00	17.50	10.50
63	Jack Scott	35.00	17.50	10.50
64	Stan Coveleskie (Coveleski)	125.00	62.00	37.00

1926 W512

One of the many "strip card" sets of the period (so-called because the cards were sold in strips), the W512 set was issued in 1926 and includes 20 baseball players among its 60 cards. Also featured are boxers, golfers, tennis players, aviators, movie stars and other celebrities. The tiny (1-3/8" by 2-1/4") cards feature rather crude color drawings of the subjects with their names below. The card number appears in the lower left corner. Baseball players lead off the set and are numbered from 1 to 20. Eight of the players are Hall of Famers. Like most strip cards, they have blank backs.

		NR MT	EX	VG
	Complete Set:	500.00	250.00	150.00
	Common Player:	15.00	7.50	4.50
1	Dave Bancroft	40.00	20.00	12.00
2	Grover Alexander	65.00	32.00	19.50
3	"Ty" Cobb	175.00	87.00	52.00
4	Tris Speaker	65.00	32.00	19.50
5	Glen Wright (Glenn)	15.00	7.50	4.50
6	"Babe" Ruth	200.00	100.00	60.00
7	Everett Scott	15.00	7.50	4.50
8	Frank Frisch	40.00	20.00	12.00
9	Rogers Hornsby	80.00	40.00	24.00
10	Dazzy Vance	40.00	20.00	12.00

1926 W513

This "strip card" set, issued in 1928 was actually a continuation of the W512 set issued two years earlier and is numbered starting with number 61 where the W512 set ended. The blank-backed cards measure 1-3/8" by 2-1/4" and display color drawings of the various celebrities featured in the set, which includes the 26 baseball players listed here. (Ten are Hall of Famers.) The cards are numbered in the lower left corner.

		NR MT	EX	VG
	Complete Set:	550.00	275.00	165.00
	Common Player:	15.00	7.50	4.50
61	Eddie Roush	30.00	15.00	9.00
62	Waite Hoyt	30.00	15.00	9.00
63	"Gink" Hendrick	15.00	7.50	4.50
64	"Jumbo" Elliott	15.00	7.50	4.50
65	John Miljus	15.00	7.50	4.50
66	Jumping Joe Dugan	18.00	9.00	5.50
67	Smiling Bill Terry	40.00	20.00	12.00
68	Herb Pennock	30.00	15.00	9.00
69	Rube Benton	15.00	7.50	4.50
70	Paul Waner	30.00	15.00	9.00
71	Adolfo Luque	15.00	7.50	4.50
72	Burleigh Grimes	30.00	15.00	9.00
73	Lloyd Waner	30.00	15.00	9.00
74	Hack Wilson	30.00	15.00	9.00
75	Hal Carlson	15.00	7.50	4.50
76	L. Grantham	15.00	7.50	4.50
77	Wilcey Moore (Wilcy)	15.00	7.50	4.50
78	Jess Haines	30.00	15.00	9.00
79	Tony Lazzeri	18.00	9.00	5.50
80	Al DeVormer	15.00	7.50	4.50
81	Joe Harris	15.00	7.50	4.50
82	Pie Traynor	30.00	15.00	9.00
83	Mark Koenig	15.00	7.50	4.50
84	Babe Herman	18.00	9.00	5.50
85	George Harper	15.00	7.50	4.50
86	Earl Coombs (Earle Combs)	30.00	15.00	9.00

1919 W514

Consisting of 120 cards, the W514 set is the largest of the various "strip card" issues, so called because the cards were sold in strips. Dating to 1919, it is also one of the earliest and most widely-collected. The color drawings measure 1-3/8" by 2-1/2" and display the card number in the lower corner inside the frame that surrounds the picture. The player's name, position and team appear in the bottom border of the blank-backed cards. The set contains two dozen Hall of Famers and holds an additional interest for baseball historians because it includes seven of the eight Chicago "Black Sox" who were banned from baseball for their alleged role in throwing the 1919 World Series. The most famous of them, "Shoeless" Joe Jackson, makes his only strip card appearance in this set.

		NR MT	EX	VG
	Complete Set:	2900.	1450.	870.00
	Common Player:	15.00	7.50	4.50
1	Ira Flagstead	15.00	7.50	4.50
2	Babe Ruth	350.00	175.00	105.00
3	Happy Felsch	18.00	9.00	5.50
4	Doc Lavan	15.00	7.50	4.50
5	Phil Douglas	15.00	7.50	4.50
6	Earle Neale	18.00	9.00	5.50
7	Leslie Nunamaker	15.00	7.50	4.50
8	Sam Jones	15.00	7.50	4.50
9	Claude Hendrix	15.00	7.50	4.50
10	Frank Schulte	15.00	7.50	4.50
11	Cactus Cravath	18.00	9.00	5.50
12	Pat Moran	15.00	7.50	4.50
13	Dick Rudolph	15.00	7.50	4.50
14	Arthur Fletcher	15.00	7.50	4.50
15	Joe Jackson	325.00	162.00	97.00
16	Bill Southworth	15.00	7.50	4.50
17	Ad Luque	15.00	7.50	4.50
18	Charlie Deal	15.00	7.50	4.50
19	Al Mamaux	15.00	7.50	4.50
20	Stuffy McInness (McInnis)	15.00	7.50	4.50
21	Rabbit Maranville	30.00	15.00	9.00
22	Max Carey	30.00	15.00	9.00
23	Dick Kerr	15.00	7.50	4.50
24	George Burns	15.00	7.50	4.50
25	Eddie Collins	30.00	15.00	9.00
26	Steve O'Neil (O'Neill)	15.00	7.50	4.50
27	Bill Fisher	15.00	7.50	4.50
28	Rube Bressler	15.00	7.50	4.50
29	Bob Shawkey	18.00	9.00	5.50
30	Donie Bush	15.00	7.50	4.50
31	Chick Gandil	18.00	9.00	5.50
32	Ollie Zeider	15.00	7.50	4.50
33	Vean Gregg	15.00	7.50	4.50
34	Miller Huggins	30.00	15.00	9.00
35	Lefty Williams	18.00	9.00	5.50

		NR MT	EX	VG
36	Tub Spencer	15.00	7.50	4.50
37	Lew McCarty	15.00	7.50	4.50
38	Hod Eller	15.00	7.50	4.50
39	Joe Gedeon	15.00	7.50	4.50
40	Dave Bancroft	30.00	15.00	9.00
41	Clark Griffith	30.00	15.00	9.00
42	Wilbur Cooper	15.00	7.50	4.50
43	Ty Cobb	300.00	150.00	90.00
44	Roger Peckinpaugh	15.00	7.50	4.50
45	Nic Carter (Nick)	15.00	7.50	4.50
46	Bob Roth	15.00	7.50	4.50
47	Heinie Groh	15.00	7.50	4.50
48	Frank Davis	15.00	7.50	4.50
49	Leslie Mann	15.00	7.50	4.50
50	Fielder Jones	15.00	7.50	4.50
51	Bill Doak	15.00	7.50	4.50
52	John J. McGraw	20.00	10.00	6.00
53	Charles Hollocher	15.00	7.50	4.50
54	Babe Adams	15.00	7.50	4.50
55	Dode Paskert	15.00	7.50	4.50
56	Roger Hornsby (Rogers)	15.00	7.50	4.50
57	Max Rath	60.00	30.00	18.00
58	Jeff Pfeffer	15.00	7.50	4.50
59	Nick Cullop	15.00	7.50	4.50
60	Ray Schalk	30.00	15.00	9.00
61	Bill Jacobson	15.00	7.50	4.50
62	Nap Lajoie	25.00	12.50	7.50
63	George Gibson	15.00	7.50	4.50
64	Harry Hooper	30.00	15.00	9.00
65	Grover Alexander	20.00	10.00	6.00
66	Ping Bodie	15.00	7.50	4.50
67	Hank Gowdy	15.00	7.50	4.50
68	Jake Daubert	18.00	9.00	5.50
69	Red Faber	30.00	15.00	9.00
70	Ivan Olson	15.00	7.50	4.50
71	Pickles Dilhoefer	15.00	7.50	4.50
72	Christy Mathewson	60.00	30.00	18.00
73	Ira Wingo (Ivy)	15.00	7.50	4.50
74	Fred Merkle	18.00	9.00	5.50
75	Frank Baker	30.00	15.00	9.00
76	Bert Gallia	15.00	7.50	4.50
77	Milton Watson	15.00	7.50	4.50
78	Bert Shotten (Shotton)	15.00	7.50	4.50
79	Sam Rice	30.00	15.00	9.00
80	Dan Greiner	15.00	7.50	4.50
81	Larry Doyle	15.00	7.50	4.50
82	Eddie Cicotte	18.00	9.00	5.50
83	Hugo Bezdek	15.00	7.50	4.50
84	Wally Pipp	12.00	6.00	3.50
85	Eddie Rousch (Roush)	30.00	15.00	9.00
86	Slim Sallee	15.00	7.50	4.50
87	Bill Killifer (Killefer)	15.00	7.50	4.50
88	Bob Veach	15.00	7.50	4.50
89	Jim Burke	15.00	7.50	4.50
90	Everett Scott	15.00	7.50	4.50
91	Buck Weaver	18.00	9.00	5.50
92	George Whitted	15.00	7.50	4.50
93	Ed Konetchy	15.00	7.50	4.50
94	Walter Johnson	60.00	30.00	18.00
95	Sam Crawford	30.00	15.00	9.00
96	Fred Mitchell	15.00	7.50	4.50
97	Ira Thomas	15.00	7.50	4.50
98	Jimmy Ring	15.00	7.50	4.50
99	Wally Shange (Schang)	15.00	7.50	4.50
100	Benny Kauff	15.00	7.50	4.50
101	George Sisler	30.00	15.00	9.00
102	Tris Speaker	20.00	10.00	6.00
103	Carl Mays	18.00	9.00	5.50
104	Buck Herzog	15.00	7.50	4.50
105	Swede Risberg	18.00	9.00	5.50
106	Hugh Jennings	30.00	15.00	9.00
107	Pep Young	15.00	7.50	4.50
108	Walter Reuther	15.00	7.50	4.50
109	Joe Gharrity	15.00	7.50	4.50
110	Zach Wheat	30.00	15.00	9.00
111	Jim Vaughn	15.00	7.50	4.50
112	Kid Gleason	15.00	7.50	4.50
113	Casey Stengel	60.00	30.00	18.00
114	Hal Chase	18.00	9.00	5.50
115	Oscar Stange (Stanage)	15.00	7.50	4.50
116	Larry Shean	15.00	7.50	4.50
117	Steve Pendergast	15.00	7.50	4.50
118	Larry Kopf	15.00	7.50	4.50
119	Charles Whiteman	15.00	7.50	4.50
120	Jess Barnes	15.00	7.50	4.50

1923 W515

Cards in the 60-card "strip set" measure 1-5/8" by 2-3/8" and feature color drawings. The card number along with the player's name, position and team appear in the bottom border. Most cards also display a "U&U" copyright line, indicating that the drawings for the blank-backed set were provided by Underwood & Underwood, a major news photo service of the day. The set has a heavy emphasis on New York players with 39 of the 60 cards depicting members of the Yankees, Dodgers or Giants. Babe Ruth appears on two cards and two other cards picture two players each. The set includes 23 Hall of Famers.

		NR MT	EX	VG
Complete Set:		1750.	875.00	525.00
Common Player:		15.00	7.50	4.50
1	Bill Cunningham	15.00	7.50	4.50
2	Al Mamaux	15.00	7.50	4.50
3	"Babe" Ruth	350.00	175.00	105.00
4	Dave Bancroft	25.00	12.50	7.50
5	Ed Rommel	15.00	7.50	4.50
6	"Babe" Adams	15.00	7.50	4.50
7	Clarence Walker	15.00	7.50	4.50
8	Waite Hoyt	25.00	12.50	7.50
9	Bob Shawkey	18.00	9.00	5.50
10	"Ty" Cobb	300.00	150.00	90.00
11	George Sisler	25.00	12.50	7.50
12	Jack Bentley	15.00	7.50	4.50
13	Jim O'Connell	15.00	7.50	4.50
14	Frank Frisch	25.00	12.50	7.50
15	Frank Baker	25.00	12.50	7.50
16	Burleigh Grimes	25.00	12.50	7.50
17	Wally Schang	15.00	7.50	4.50
18	Harry Heilman (Heilmann)	25.00	12.50	7.50
19	Aaron Ward	15.00	7.50	4.50
20	Carl Mays	18.00	9.00	5.50
21	The Meusel Bros (Bob Meusel, Irish Meusel)	20.00	10.00	6.00
22	Arthur Nehf	15.00	7.50	4.50
23	Lee Meadows	15.00	7.50	4.50
24	"Casey" Stengel	55.00	27.00	16.50
25	Jack Scott	15.00	7.50	4.50
26	Kenneth Williams	18.00	9.00	5.50
27	Joe Bush	18.00	9.00	5.50
28	Tris Speaker	45.00	22.00	13.50
29	Ross Young (Youngs)	15.00	7.50	4.50
30	Joe Dugan	18.00	9.00	5.50
31	The Barnes Bros. (Jesse Barnes, Virgil Barnes)	18.00	9.00	5.50
32	George Kelly	25.00	12.50	7.50
33	Hugh McQuillen (McQuillan)	15.00	7.50	4.50
34	Hugh Jennings	25.00	12.50	7.50
35	Tom Griffith	15.00	7.50	4.50
36	Miller Huggins	25.00	12.50	7.50
37	"Whitey" Witt	15.00	7.50	4.50
38	Walter Johnson	55.00	27.00	16.50
39	"Wally" Pipp	20.00	10.00	6.00
40	"Dutch" Reuther	15.00	7.50	4.50
41	Jim Johnston	15.00	7.50	4.50
42	Willie Kamm	15.00	7.50	4.50
43	Sam Jones	15.00	7.50	4.50
44	Frank Snyder	15.00	7.50	4.50
45	John McGraw	45.00	22.00	13.50
46	Everett Scott	15.00	7.50	4.50
47	"Babe" Ruth	350.00	175.00	105.00
48	Urban Shocker	15.00	7.50	4.50
49	Grover Alexander	45.00	22.00	13.50
50	"Rabbit" Maranville	25.00	12.50	7.50
51	Ray Schalk	25.00	12.50	7.50
52	"Heinie" Groh	15.00	7.50	4.50
53	Wilbert Robinson	25.00	12.50	7.50
54	George Burns	15.00	7.50	4.50
55	Rogers Hornsby	50.00	25.00	15.00
56	Zack Wheat	25.00	12.50	7.50
57	Eddie Roush	25.00	12.50	7.50
58	Eddie Collins	25.00	12.50	7.50
59	Charlie Hollocher	15.00	7.50	4.50
60	Red Faber	25.00	12.50	7.50

1920 W516-1

This "strip card" set consists of 30 cards featuring color drawings - either portraits or full-length action poses. The blank-backed cards measure 1-1/2" by 2-1/2". The player's name, position and team appear beneath the photo, along with the card number. The set can be identified by an "IFS" copyright symbol, representing International Feature Service. The set includes a dozen Hall of Famers.

		NR MT	EX	VG
Complete Set:		1050.	525.00	315.00
Common Player:		18.00	9.00	5.50
1	Babe Ruth	350.00	175.00	105.00
2	Heinie Groh	18.00	9.00	5.50
3	Ping Bodie	18.00	9.00	5.50
4	Ray Shalk (Schalk)	30.00	15.00	9.00
5	Tris Speaker	45.00	22.00	13.50
6	Ty Cobb	300.00	150.00	90.00
7	Roger Hornsby (Rogers)	55.00	27.00	16.50
8	Walter Johnson	55.00	27.00	16.50
9	Grover Alexander	45.00	22.00	13.50
10	George Burns	18.00	9.00	5.50
11	Jimmy Ring	18.00	9.00	5.50
12	Jess Barnes	18.00	9.00	5.50
13	Larry Doyle	18.00	9.00	5.50
14	Arty Fletcher	18.00	9.00	5.50
15	Dick Rudolph	18.00	9.00	5.50
16	Benny Kauf (Kauff)	18.00	9.00	5.50
17	Art Nehf	18.00	9.00	5.50
18	Babe Adams	18.00	9.00	5.50
19	Will Cooper	18.00	9.00	5.50
20	R. Peckinpaugh	18.00	9.00	5.50
21	Eddie Cicotte	20.00	10.00	6.00
22	Hank Gowdy	18.00	9.00	5.50
23	Eddie Collins	30.00	15.00	9.00
24	Christy Mathewson	55.00	27.00	16.50
25	Clyde Milan	18.00	9.00	5.50
26	M. Kelley (should be G. Kelly)	15.00	7.50	4.50
27	Ed Hooper (Harry)	15.00	7.50	4.50
28	Pep. Young	18.00	9.00	5.50
29	Eddie Rousch (Roush)	30.00	15.00	9.00
30	Geo. Bancroft (Dave)	55.00	27.00	16.50

1921 W516-2

This set is essentially a re-issue of the W516-1 set of the previous year with one major change. The cards are identical to the W516-1 set, except the numbers have been changed and the pictures have all been reversed. The blank-backed cards measure 1-1/2" by 2-1/2" and feature color drawings with the player's name, position and team beneath the picture, along with the card number. The cards display an "IFS" copyright symbol.

		NR MT	EX	VG
Complete Set:		1200.	600.00	360.00
Common Player:		18.00	9.00	5.50
1	George Burns	18.00	9.00	5.50
2	Grover Alexander	90.00	45.00	27.00
3	Walter Johnson	150.00	75.00	45.00
4	Roger Hornsby (Rogers)	100.00	50.00	30.00
5	Ty Cobb	325.00	162.00	97.00
6	Tris Speaker	90.00	45.00	27.00
7	Ray Shalk (Schalk)	40.00	20.00	12.00
8	Ping Bodie	18.00	9.00	5.50
9	Heinie Groh	18.00	9.00	5.50
10	Babe Ruth	400.00	200.00	120.00
11	R. Peckinpaugh	18.00	9.00	5.50
12	Will. Cooper	18.00	9.00	5.50
13	Babe Adams	18.00	9.00	5.50
14	Art Nehf	18.00	9.00	5.50
15	Benny Kauf (Kauff)	18.00	9.00	5.50
16	Dick Rudolph	18.00	9.00	5.50
17	Arty. Fletcher	18.00	9.00	5.50
18	Larry Doyle	18.00	9.00	5.50
19	Jess Barnes	18.00	9.00	5.50
20	Jimmy Ring	18.00	9.00	5.50
21	George Bancroft (Dave)	30.00	15.00	9.00
22	Eddie Rousch (Roush)	40.00	20.00	12.00
23	Pep Young	18.00	9.00	5.50
24	Ed Hooper (Harry)	30.00	15.00	9.00
25	M. Kelley (should be G. Kelly)	30.00	15.00	9.00
26	Clyde Milan	18.00	9.00	5.50
27	Christy Mathewson	150.00	75.00	45.00
28	Eddie Collins	40.00	20.00	12.00
29	Hank Gowdy	18.00	9.00	5.50
30	Eddie Cicotte	15.00	7.50	4.50

Definitions for grading conditions are located in the Introduction section at the front of this book.

1931 W517

The 54-card W517 set is a scarce issue of 3" by 4" cards which are generally found in a sepia color. There are, however, other known colors of W517s, and they tend to bring higher prices from specialists. The cards feature a player picture as well as his name and team. The card number appears in a small circle on the front, while the backs are blank. The set is heavy in stars of the period including two Babe Ruths (#'s 4 and 20). Not actively collected by many, the set is a relatively inexpensive way to obtain cards of many contemporary Hall of Famers.

		NR MT	EX	VG
Complete Set:		3400.	1700.	1020.
Common Player:		55.00	27.00	16.50
1	Earl Combs (Earle)	65.00	32.00	19.50
2	Pie Traynor	55.00	27.00	16.50
3	Eddie Rausch (Roush)	55.00	27.00	16.50
4	Babe Ruth	450.00	225.00	135.00
5a	Chalmer Cissell (Chicago)	55.00	27.00	16.50
5b	Chalmer Cissell (Cleveland)	55.00	27.00	16.50
6	Bill Sherdel	55.00	27.00	16.50
7	Bill Shore	55.00	27.00	16.50
8	Geo. Earnshaw	55.00	27.00	16.50
9	Bucky Harris	45.00	22.00	13.50
10	Charlie Klein	55.00	27.00	16.50
11a	Geo. Kelly (Reds)	55.00	27.00	16.50
11b	Geo. Kelly (Brooklyn)	55.00	27.00	16.50
12	Travis Jackson	55.00	27.00	16.50
13	Willie Kamm	55.00	27.00	16.50
14	Harry Heilman (Heilmann)	55.00	27.00	16.50
15	Grover Alexander	65.00	32.00	19.50
16	Frank Frisch	55.00	27.00	16.50
17	Jack Quinn	55.00	27.00	16.50
18	Cy Williams	35.00	17.50	10.50
19	Kiki Cuyler	55.00	27.00	16.50
20	Babe Ruth	450.00	225.00	135.00
21	Jimmie Foxx	85.00	42.00	25.00
22	Jimmy Dykes	55.00	27.00	16.50
23	Bill Terry	65.00	32.00	19.50
24	Freddy Lindstrom	55.00	27.00	16.50
25	Hughey Critz	55.00	27.00	16.50
26	Pete Donahue	55.00	27.00	16.50
27	Tony Lazzeri	45.00	22.00	13.50
28	Heine Manush (Heinie)	55.00	27.00	16.50
29a	Chick Hafey (Cardinals)	55.00	27.00	16.50
29b	Chick Hafey (Cincinnati)	55.00	27.00	16.50
30	Melvin Ott	75.00	37.00	22.00
31	Bing Miller	55.00	27.00	16.50
32	Geo. Haas	55.00	27.00	16.50
33a	Lefty O'Doul (Phillies)	35.00	17.50	10.50
33b	Lefty O'Doul (Brooklyn)	35.00	17.50	10.50
34	Paul Waner	55.00	27.00	16.50
35	Lou Gehrig	325.00	162.00	97.00
36	Dazzy Vance	55.00	27.00	16.50
37	Mickey Cochrane	55.00	27.00	16.50
38	Rogers Hornsby	90.00	45.00	27.00
39	Lefty Grove	65.00	32.00	19.50
40	Al Simmons	55.00	27.00	16.50
41	Rube Walberg	55.00	27.00	16.50
42	Hack Wilson	55.00	27.00	16.50
43	Art Shires	55.00	27.00	16.50
44	Sammy Hale	55.00	27.00	16.50
45	Ted Lyons	55.00	27.00	16.50
46	Joe Sewell	55.00	27.00	16.50
47	Goose Goslin	55.00	27.00	16.50
48	Lou Fonseca (Lew)	35.00	17.50	10.50
49	Bob Muesel (Meusel)	35.00	17.50	10.50
50	Lu Blue	55.00	27.00	16.50
52	Eddy Collins (Eddie)	65.00	32.00	19.50
53	Joe Judge	55.00	27.00	16.50
54	Mickey Cochrane	225.00	112.00	67.00

1920 W519 - Numbered

Cards in this 20-card "strip set" measure 1-1/2" by 2-1/2" and feature player drawings set against a background of either red, blue, orange, yellow, violet or green. The card number appears in the lower left corner followed by the player's name, which is printed in all capital letters. The player drawings are all posed portraits, except for Joe Murphy and Ernie Kreuger, who are shown catching. Like all strip cards, the cards were sold in strips and have blank backs. The W519 set was issued circa 1920.

		NR MT	EX	VG
Complete Set:		575.00	287.00	172.00
Common Player:		15.00	7.50	4.50
1	Guy Morton	15.00	7.50	4.50
2	Rube Marquard	50.00	25.00	15.00
3	Gabby Cravath (Gavvy)	18.00	9.00	5.50
4	Ernie Krueger	15.00	7.50	4.50
5	Babe Ruth	300.00	150.00	90.00
6	George Sisler	50.00	25.00	15.00
7	Rube Benton	15.00	7.50	4.50
8	Jimmie Johnston	15.00	7.50	4.50
9	Wilbur Robinson (Wilbert)	50.00	25.00	15.00
10	Johnny Griffith	15.00	7.50	4.50
11	Frank Baker	50.00	25.00	15.00
12	Bob Veach	15.00	7.50	4.50
13	Jesse Barnes	15.00	7.50	4.50
14	Leon Cadore	15.00	7.50	4.50
15	Ray Schalk	50.00	25.00	15.00
16	Kid Gleasen (Gleason)	15.00	7.50	4.50
17	Joe Murphy	15.00	7.50	4.50
18	Frank Frisch	50.00	25.00	15.00
19	Eddie Collins	50.00	25.00	15.00
20	Wallie Schang	15.00	7.50	4.50

1920 W519 - Unnumbered

Cards in this 10-card set are identical in design and size (1-1/2" by 2-1/2") to the W519 Numbered set, except the player drawings are all set against a blue background and the cards are not numbered. With the lone exception of Eddie Cicotte, all of the subjects in the unnumbered set also appear in the numbered set.

		NR MT	EX	VG
Complete Set:		175.00	87.00	52.00
Common Player:		15.00	7.50	4.50
(1)	Eddie Cicotte	18.00	9.00	5.50
(2)	Eddie Collins	50.00	25.00	15.00
(3)	Gabby Cravath (Gavvy)	18.00	9.00	5.50
(4)	Frank Frisch	50.00	25.00	15.00
(5)	Kid Gleasen (Gleason)	15.00	7.50	4.50
(6)	Ernie Kreuger	15.00	7.50	4.50
(7)	Rube Marquard	50.00	25.00	15.00
(8)	Guy Morton	15.00	7.50	4.50
(9)	Joe Murphy	15.00	7.50	4.50
(10)	Babe Ruth	300.00	150.00	90.00

1920 W520

Another "strip card" set issued circa 1920, cards in this set measure 1-3/8" by 2-1/4" and are numbered in the lower right corner from 1 to 20. The first nine cards in the set display portrait poses, while the rest are full-length action poses. Some of the poses in this set are the same as those in the W516 issue with the pictures reversed. The player's last name appears in the border beneath the picture. The cards are blank-backed.

		NR MT	EX	VG
Complete Set:		1400.	700.00	420.00
Common Player:		30.00	15.00	9.00
1	Dave Bancroft	90.00	45.00	27.00
2	Christy Mathewson	225.00	112.00	67.00
3	Larry Doyle	30.00	15.00	9.00
4	Jess Barnes	30.00	15.00	9.00
5	Art Fletcher	30.00	15.00	9.00
6	Wilbur Cooper	30.00	15.00	9.00
7	Mike Gonzales	30.00	15.00	9.00
8	Zach Wheat	90.00	45.00	27.00
9	Tris Speaker	150.00	75.00	45.00
10	Benny Kauff	30.00	15.00	9.00
11	Zach Wheat	90.00	45.00	27.00
12	Phil Douglas	30.00	15.00	9.00
13	Babe Ruth	500.00	250.00	150.00
14	Stan Koveleski (Coveleski)	90.00	45.00	27.00
15	Goldie Rapp	30.00	15.00	9.00
16	Pol Perritt	30.00	15.00	9.00
17	Otto Miller	30.00	15.00	9.00
18	George Kelly	90.00	45.00	27.00
19	Mike Gonzales	30.00	15.00	9.00
20	Les Nunamaker	30.00	15.00	9.00

1921 W521

This issue is closely related to the W519 Numbered set. In fact, it uses the same color drawings as that set with the pictures reversed, resulting in a mirror-image of the W519 cards. The player poses and the numbering system are identical, as are the various background colors. The W521 cards are blank-backed and were sold in strips.

		NR MT	EX	VG
Complete Set:		500.00	250.00	150.00
Common Player:		15.00	7.50	4.50
1	Guy Morton	15.00	7.50	4.50
2	Rube Marquard	40.00	20.00	12.00
3	Gabby Cravath (Gavvy)	10.00	5.00	3.00
4	Ernie Krueger	15.00	7.50	4.50
5	Babe Ruth	300.00	150.00	90.00
6	George Sisler	40.00	20.00	12.00
7	Rube Benton	15.00	7.50	4.50
8	Jimmie Johnston	15.00	7.50	4.50
9	Wilbur Robinson (Wilbert)	40.00	20.00	12.00
10	Johnny Griffith	15.00	7.50	4.50
11	Frank Baker	40.00	20.00	12.00
12	Bob Veach	15.00	7.50	4.50
13	Jesse Barnes	15.00	7.50	4.50
14	Leon Cadore	15.00	7.50	4.50
15	Ray Schalk	40.00	20.00	12.00
16	Kid Gleasen (Gleason)	15.00	7.50	4.50
17	Joe Murphy	15.00	7.50	4.50
18	Frank Frisch	40.00	20.00	12.00
19	Eddie Collins	40.00	20.00	12.00
20	Wallie Schang	15.00	7.50	4.50

1918 W522

The 20 cards in this "strip card" set, issued circa 1920, are numbered from 31-50 and use the same players and drawings as the W520 set, issued about the same time. The cards measure 1-3/8" by 2-1/4" and are numbered in the lower left corner followed by the player's name. The cards have blank backs.

		NR MT	EX	VG
Complete Set:		1200.	600.00	360.00
Common Player:		30.00	15.00	9.00
31	Benny Kauf (Kauff)	30.00	15.00	9.00
32	Tris Speaker	100.00	50.00	30.00
33	Zach Wheat	30.00	15.00	9.00
34	Mike Gonzales	30.00	15.00	9.00
35	Wilbur Cooper	30.00	15.00	9.00
36	Art Fletcher	30.00	15.00	9.00
37	Jess Barnes	30.00	15.00	9.00
38	Larry Doyle	30.00	15.00	9.00
39	Christy Mathewson	225.00	112.00	67.00
40	Dave Bancroft	75.00	37.00	22.00
41	Les Nunamaker	30.00	15.00	9.00
42	Mike Gonzales	30.00	15.00	9.00
43	George Kelly	75.00	37.00	22.00
44	Otto Miller	30.00	15.00	9.00
45	Pol Perritt	30.00	15.00	9.00
46	Goldie Rapp	30.00	15.00	9.00
47	Stan Koveleski (Coveleski)	75.00	37.00	22.00
48	Babe Ruth	500.00	250.00	150.00
49	Phil Douglas	30.00	15.00	9.00
50	Zach Wheat	75.00	37.00	22.00

1922 W551

Antoher "strip set" issued circa 1920, these ten cards measure 1-3/8" by 2-1/4" and feature color drawings. The cards are unnumbered and blank-backed.

		NR MT	EX	VG
Complete Set:		1250.	625.00	375.00
Common Player:		45.00	22.00	13.50
(1)	Frank Baker	100.00	50.00	30.00
(2)	Dave Bancroft	100.00	50.00	30.00
(3)	Jess Barnes	45.00	22.00	13.50
(4)	Ty Cobb	400.00	200.00	120.00
(5)	Walter Johnson	200.00	100.00	60.00
(6)	Wally Pipp	65.00	32.00	19.50
(7)	Babe Ruth	425.00	212.00	127.00
(8)	George Sisler	100.00	50.00	30.00
(9)	Tris Speaker	150.00	75.00	45.00
(10)	Casey Stengel	200.00	100.00	60.00

1907 W555

Designated as W555 in the American Card Catalog, very little is known about this obscure set. The nearly square cards measure a tiny 1-1/8" by 1-3/16" and feature a sepia-colored player photo. Sixty-six different cards have been discovered to date, but more are very likely to exist. The manufacturer of the set is unknown, but the sets appear to be related to a series of four early candy cards that carry the ACC designations of E93, E94, E97 and E98, because, with only two exceptions, the players and poses are the same. It is not known how the cards were issued. There is speculation that they may have been issued as "strip" cards or as part of a candy box.

		NR MT	EX	VG
Complete Set:		4300.	2150.	1290.
Common Player:		45.00	22.00	13.50
(1)	Red Ames	45.00	22.00	13.50
(2)	Jimmy Austin	45.00	22.00	13.50
(3)	Johnny Bates	45.00	22.00	13.50
(4)	Chief Bender	125.00	62.00	37.00
(5)	Bob Bescher	45.00	22.00	13.50
(6)	Joe Birmingham	45.00	22.00	13.50
(7)	Bill Bradley	45.00	22.00	13.50
(8)	Kitty Bransfield	45.00	22.00	13.50
(9)	Mordecai Brown	125.00	62.00	37.00
(10)	Bobby Byrne	45.00	22.00	13.50
(11)	Frank Chance	60.00	30.00	18.00
(12)	Hal Chase	70.00	35.00	21.00
(13)	Ed Cicotte	55.00	27.00	16.50
(14)	Fred Clarke	125.00	62.00	37.00
(15)	Ty Cobb	800.00	400.00	240.00
(16)	Eddie Collins (dark uniform)	125.00	62.00	37.00
(17)	Eddie Collins (light uniform)	125.00	62.00	37.00
(18)	Harry Coveleskie (Coveleski)	45.00	22.00	13.50
(19)	Sam Crawford	125.00	62.00	37.00
(20)	Harry Davis	45.00	22.00	13.50
(21)	Jim Delehanty	45.00	22.00	13.50
(22)	Art Devlin	45.00	22.00	13.50
(23)	Josh Devore	45.00	22.00	13.50
(24)	Wild Bill Donovan	45.00	22.00	13.50
(25)	Red Dooin	45.00	22.00	13.50
(26)	Mickey Doolan	45.00	22.00	13.50
(27)	Bull Durham	45.00	22.00	13.50
(28)	Jimmy Dygert	45.00	22.00	13.50
(29)	Johnny Evers	125.00	62.00	37.00
(30)	Russ Ford	45.00	22.00	13.50
(31)	George Gibson	45.00	22.00	13.50
(32)	Clark Griffith	125.00	62.00	37.00
(33)	Topsy Hartsell (Hartsel)	45.00	22.00	13.50
(34)	Bill Heinchman (Hinchman)	45.00	22.00	13.50
(35)	Ira Hemphill	45.00	22.00	13.50
(36)	Hughie Jennings	125.00	62.00	37.00
(37)	Davy Jones	45.00	22.00	13.50
(38)	Addie Joss	125.00	62.00	37.00
(39)	Wee Willie Keeler	45.00	22.00	13.50
(40)	Red Kleinow	45.00	22.00	13.50
(41)	Nap Lajoie	200.00	100.00	60.00
(42)	Joe Lake	45.00	22.00	13.50
(43)	Tommy Leach	45.00	22.00	13.50
(44)	Sherry Magee	55.00	27.00	16.50
(45)	Christy Mathewson	225.00	112.00	67.00
(46)	Amby McConnell	45.00	22.00	13.50
(47)	John McGraw	175.00	87.00	52.00
(48)	Chief Meyers	45.00	22.00	13.50
(49)	Earl Moore	45.00	22.00	13.50
(50)	Mike Mowery	45.00	22.00	13.50
(51)	George Mullin	45.00	22.00	13.50
(52)	Red Murray	45.00	22.00	13.50
(53)	Nichols	45.00	22.00	13.50
(54)	Jim Pastorious (Pastorius)	45.00	22.00	13.50
(55)	Deacon Phillippi (Phillippe)	45.00	22.00	13.50
(56)	Eddie Plank	55.00	27.00	16.50
(57)	Fred Snodgrass	45.00	22.00	13.50
(58)	Harry Steinfeldt	55.00	27.00	16.50
(59)	Joe Tinker	125.00	62.00	37.00
(60)	Hippo Vaughn	45.00	22.00	13.50
(61)	Honus Wagner	600.00	300.00	180.00
(62)	Rube Waddell	125.00	62.00	37.00
(63)	Hooks Wiltse	45.00	22.00	13.50
(64a)	Cy Young (standing, full name on front)	175.00	87.00	52.00
(64b)	Cy Young (standing, last name on front)	175.00	87.00	52.00
(65)	Cy Young (portrait)	175.00	87.00	52.00

1927 W560

Although assigned a "W" number, this set is not a "strip card" issue in the same sense as the rest of the "W" sets, although W560 cards are frequently found in uncut sheets of three or four across or down. Uncut sheets of 16 cards, in four rows of four cards each, are also known to exist. Cards in the W560 set measure 1-3/4" by 2-3/4" and are designed like a deck of playing cards, with the pictures on the various suits - either hearts, clubs, spades, diamonds or jokers. The set includes movie stars, aviators and other athletes, in addition to baseball players. Because they are designed as a deck of playing cards, the cards are printed in either red or black.

		NR MT	EX	VG
Complete Set:		2800.	1400.	840.00
Common Player:		25.00	12.50	7.50
(1)	Vic Aldridge	25.00	12.50	7.50
(2)	Lester Bell	25.00	12.50	7.50
(3)	Larry Benton	25.00	12.50	7.50
(4)	Max Bishop	25.00	12.50	7.50
(5)	Del Bissonette	25.00	12.50	7.50
(6)	Jim Bottomley	55.00	27.00	16.50
(7)	Guy Bush	25.00	12.50	7.50
(8)	W. Clark	25.00	12.50	7.50
(9)	Andy Cohen	25.00	12.50	7.50
(10)	Mickey Cochrane	55.00	27.00	16.50
(11)	Hugh Critz	25.00	12.50	7.50
(12)	Kiki Cuyler	55.00	27.00	16.50
(13)	Taylor Douthit	25.00	12.50	7.50
(14)	Fred Fitzsimmons	25.00	12.50	7.50
(15)	Jim Foxx	225.00	112.00	67.00
(16)	Lou Gehrig	500.00	250.00	150.00
(17)	Goose Goslin	55.00	27.00	16.50
(18)	Sam Gray	25.00	12.50	7.50
(19)	Lefty Grove	150.00	75.00	45.00
(20)	Jesse Haines	55.00	27.00	16.50
(21)	Babe Herman	18.00	9.00	5.50
(22)	Roger Hornsby (Rogers)	200.00	100.00	60.00
(23)	Waite Hoyt	55.00	27.00	16.50
(24)	Henry Johnson	25.00	12.50	7.50
(25)	Walter Johnson	200.00	100.00	60.00
(26)	Willie Kamm	25.00	12.50	7.50
(27)	Fred Lindstrom	55.00	27.00	16.50
(28)	Fred Maguire	25.00	12.50	7.50
(29)	Fred Marberry	25.00	12.50	7.50
(30)	Johnny Mostil	25.00	12.50	7.50
(31)	Buddy Myer	25.00	12.50	7.50
(32)	Herb Pennock	55.00	27.00	16.50
(33)	George Pipgras	25.00	12.50	7.50
(34)	Flint Rhem	25.00	12.50	7.50
(35)	Babe Ruth	650.00	325.00	195.00
(36)	Luke Sewell	25.00	12.50	7.50
(37)	Willie Sherdel	25.00	12.50	7.50
(38)	Al Simmons	55.00	27.00	16.50
(39)	Thomas Thevenow	25.00	12.50	7.50
(40)	Fresco Thompson	25.00	12.50	7.50
(41)	George Uhle	25.00	12.50	7.50
(42)	Dazzy Vance	55.00	27.00	16.50
(43)	Rube Walberg	25.00	12.50	7.50
(44)	Lloyd Waner	55.00	27.00	16.50
(45)	Paul Waner	55.00	27.00	16.50
(46)	Fred "Cy" Williams	18.00	9.00	5.50
(47)	Jim Wilson	25.00	12.50	7.50
(48)	Glen Wright (Glenn)	25.00	12.50	7.50

1923 W572

This set, designated as W572 by the American Card Catalog, measures 1-3/8" by 2-1/2" and are blank-backed. These "strip cards" feature black and white player photos, although some sepia-toned cards have also been found. The set is closely related to the popular E120 American Caramel set issued in 1922 and, with the exception of Ty Cobb, it uses the same photos. The cards were originally issued as strips of ten, with five baseball players and five boxers. They are found on either a white, slick stock or a dark, coarser one. The player's name on the front of the card appears in script. To date 119 different subjects have been found, although it is likely one more exists.

		NR MT	EX	VG
Complete Set:		4000.	2000.	1200.
Common Player:		18.00	9.00	5.50
(1)	Eddie Ainsmith	18.00	9.00	5.50
(2)	Vic Aldridge	18.00	9.00	5.50
(3)	Grover Alexander	65.00	32.00	19.50
(4)	Walt Barbare	18.00	9.00	5.50

		NR MT	EX	VG
(5)	Jess Barnes	18.00	9.00	5.50
(6)	John Bassler	18.00	9.00	5.50
(7)	Lu Blue	18.00	9.00	5.50
(8)	Norman Boeckel	18.00	9.00	5.50
(9)	George Burns	18.00	9.00	5.50
(10)	Joe Bush	20.00	10.00	6.00
(11)	Leon Cadore	18.00	9.00	5.50
(12)	Virgil Cheevers (Cheeves)	18.00	9.00	5.50
(13)	Ty Cobb	700.00	350.00	210.00
(14)	Eddie Collins	50.00	25.00	15.00
(15)	John Collins	18.00	9.00	5.50
(16)	Wilbur Cooper	18.00	9.00	5.50
(17)	Stanley Coveleski	50.00	25.00	15.00
(18)	Walton Cruise	18.00	9.00	5.50
(19)	Dave Danforth	18.00	9.00	5.50
(20)	Jake Daubert	20.00	10.00	6.00
(21)	Hank DeBerry	18.00	9.00	5.50
(22)	Lou DeVormer	18.00	9.00	5.50
(23)	Bill Doak	18.00	9.00	5.50
(24)	Pete Donohue	18.00	9.00	5.50
(25)	Pat Duncan	18.00	9.00	5.50
(26)	Jimmy Dykes	20.00	10.00	6.00
(27)	Urban Faber	50.00	25.00	15.00
(28)	Bib Falk (Bibb)	18.00	9.00	5.50
(29)	Frank Frisch	50.00	25.00	15.00
(30)	C. Galloway	18.00	9.00	5.50
(31)	Ed Gharrity	18.00	9.00	5.50
(32)	Chas. Glazner	18.00	9.00	5.50
(33)	Hank Gowdy	18.00	9.00	5.50
(34)	Tom Griffith	18.00	9.00	5.50
(35)	Burleigh Grimes	50.00	25.00	15.00
(36)	Ray Grimes	18.00	9.00	5.50
(37)	Heinie Groh	18.00	9.00	5.50
(38)	Joe Harris	18.00	9.00	5.50
(39)	Stanley Harris	50.00	25.00	15.00
(40)	Joe Hauser	18.00	9.00	5.50
(41)	Harry Heilmann	50.00	25.00	15.00
(42)	Walter Henline	18.00	9.00	5.50
(43)	Chas. Hollocher	18.00	9.00	5.50
(44)	Harry Hooper	50.00	25.00	15.00
(45)	Rogers Hornsby	150.00	75.00	45.00
(46)	Waite Hoyt	50.00	25.00	15.00
(47)	Wilbur Hubbell	18.00	9.00	5.50
(48)	Wm. Jacobson	18.00	9.00	5.50
(49)	Chas. Jamieson	18.00	9.00	5.50
(50)	S. Johnson	18.00	9.00	5.50
(51)	Walter Johnson	150.00	75.00	45.00
(52)	Jimmy Johnston	18.00	9.00	5.50
(53)	Joe Judge	18.00	9.00	5.50
(54)	Geo. Kelly	50.00	25.00	15.00
(55)	Lee King	18.00	9.00	5.50
(56)	Larry Kopff (Kopf)	18.00	9.00	5.50
(57)	Geo. Leverette	18.00	9.00	5.50
(58)	Al Mamaux	18.00	9.00	5.50
(59)	"Rabbit" Maranville	50.00	25.00	15.00
(60)	"Rube" Marquard	50.00	25.00	15.00
(61)	Martin McManus	18.00	9.00	5.50
(62)	Lee Meadows	18.00	9.00	5.50
(63)	Mike Menosky	18.00	9.00	5.50
(64)	Bob Meusel	30.00	15.00	9.00
(65)	Emil Meusel	18.00	9.00	5.50
(66)	Geo. Mogridge	18.00	9.00	5.50
(67)	John Morrison	18.00	9.00	5.50
(68)	Johnny Mostil	18.00	9.00	5.50
(69)	Roliene Naylor	18.00	9.00	5.50
(70)	Art Nehf	18.00	9.00	5.50
(71)	Joe Oeschger	18.00	9.00	5.50
(72)	Bob O'Farrell	18.00	9.00	5.50
(73)	Steve O'Neill	18.00	9.00	5.50
(74)	Frank Parkinson	18.00	9.00	5.50
(75)	Ralph Perkins	18.00	9.00	5.50
(76)	H. Pillette	18.00	9.00	5.50
(77)	Ralph Pinelli	20.00	10.00	6.00
(78)	Wallie Pipp	35.00	17.50	10.50
(79)	Ray Powell	18.00	9.00	5.50
(80)	Jack Quinn	18.00	9.00	5.50
(81)	Goldie Rapp	18.00	9.00	5.50
(82)	Walter Reuther	18.00	9.00	5.50
(83)	Sam Rice	50.00	25.00	15.00
(84)	Emory Rigney	18.00	9.00	5.50
(85)	Eppa Rixey	50.00	25.00	15.00
(86)	Ed Rommel	18.00	9.00	5.50
(87)	Eddie Roush	50.00	25.00	15.00
(88)	Babe Ruth	900.00	450.00	270.00
(89)	Ray Schalk	18.00	9.00	5.50
(90)	Wallie Schang	18.00	9.00	5.50
(91)	Walter Schmidt	18.00	9.00	5.50
(92)	Joe Schultz	18.00	9.00	5.50
(93)	Hank Severeid	18.00	9.00	5.50
(94)	Joe Sewell	50.00	25.00	15.00
(95)	Bob Shawkey	20.00	10.00	6.00
(96)	Earl Sheely	18.00	9.00	5.50
(97)	Will Sherdel	18.00	9.00	5.50
(98)	Urban Shocker	18.00	9.00	5.50
(99)	George Sisler	50.00	25.00	15.00
(100)	Earl Smith	18.00	9.00	5.50
(101)	Elmer Smith	18.00	9.00	5.50
(102)	Jack Smith	18.00	9.00	5.50
(103)	Bill Southworth	18.00	9.00	5.50
(104)	Tris Speaker	65.00	32.00	19.50
(105)	Milton Stock	18.00	9.00	5.50
(106)	Jim Tierney	18.00	9.00	5.50
(107)	Harold Traynor	18.00	9.00	5.50
(108)	Geo. Uhle	50.00	25.00	15.00
(109)	Bob Veach	18.00	9.00	5.50
(110)	Clarence Walker	18.00	9.00	5.50
(111)	Curtis Walker	18.00	9.00	5.50
(112)	Bill Wambsganss	20.00	10.00	6.00
(113)	Aaron Ward	18.00	9.00	5.50
(114)	Zach Wheat	50.00	25.00	15.00
(115)	Fred Williams	30.00	15.00	9.00
(116)	Ken Williams	30.00	15.00	9.00
(117)	Ivy Wingo	18.00	9.00	5.50
(118)	Joe Wood	30.00	15.00	9.00
(119)	J.T. Zachary	18.00	9.00	5.50

A player's name in *italic* type indicates a rookie card. An (FC) indicates a player's first card for that particular card company.

1922 W573

CLARENCE MITCHELL
PITCHER, BROOKLYN NATIONALS

These cards, identified as W573 in the American Card Catalog, appear to be blank-backed versions of the popular E120 American Caramel set. In reality they were "strip cards," produced in 1923 and sold in strips of ten for a penny. The cards feature black and white photos. To date 144 different subjects have been found, but it is likely that all 240 poses from the E120 set actually exist.

		NR MT	EX	VG
Complete Set:		4500.	2250.	1350.
Common Player:		25.00	12.50	7.50
(1)	Babe Adams	25.00	12.50	7.50
(2)	Eddie Ainsmith	25.00	12.50	7.50
(3)	Vic Aldridge	25.00	12.50	7.50
(4)	Grover Alexander	80.00	40.00	24.00
(5)	Home Run Baker	60.00	30.00	18.00
(6)	Dave Bancroft	60.00	30.00	18.00
(7)	Walt Barbare	25.00	12.50	7.50
(8)	Turner Barber	25.00	12.50	7.50
(9)	Jess Barnes	25.00	12.50	7.50
(10)	John Bassler	25.00	12.50	7.50
(11)	Carson Bigbee	25.00	12.50	7.50
(12)	Lu Blue	25.00	12.50	7.50
(13)	Norman Boeckel	25.00	12.50	7.50
(14)	Geo. Burns (Boston)	25.00	12.50	7.50
(15)	Geo. Burns (Cincinnati)	25.00	12.50	7.50
(16)	Marty Callaghan	25.00	12.50	7.50
(17)	Max Carey	60.00	30.00	18.00
(18)	Jimmy Caveney	25.00	12.50	7.50
(19)	Virgil Cheeves	25.00	12.50	7.50
(20)	Vern Clemons	25.00	12.50	7.50
(21)	Ty Cobb	750.00	375.00	225.00
(22)	Bert Cole	25.00	12.50	7.50
(23)	Eddie Collins	60.00	30.00	18.00
(24)	Pat Collins	25.00	12.50	7.50
(25)	Wilbur Cooper	25.00	12.50	7.50
(26)	Elmer Cox	25.00	12.50	7.50
(27)	Bill Cunningham	25.00	12.50	7.50
(28)	George Cutshaw	25.00	12.50	7.50
(29)	Dave Danforth	25.00	12.50	7.50
(30)	George Dauss	25.00	12.50	7.50
(31)	Dixie Davis	25.00	12.50	7.50
(32)	Hank DeBerry	25.00	12.50	7.50
(33)	Lou DeVormer	25.00	12.50	7.50
(34)	Bill Doak	25.00	12.50	7.50
(35)	Joe Dugan	40.00	20.00	12.00
(36)	Howard Ehmke	25.00	12.50	7.50
(37)	Frank Ellerbe	25.00	12.50	7.50
(38)	Urban Faber	60.00	30.00	18.00
(39)	Bib Falk (Bibb)	25.00	12.50	7.50
(40)	Max Flack	25.00	12.50	7.50
(41)	Ira Flagstead	25.00	12.50	7.50
(42)	Art Fletcher	25.00	12.50	7.50
(43)	Horace Ford	25.00	12.50	7.50
(44)	Jack Fournier	25.00	12.50	7.50
(45)	Frank Frisch	60.00	30.00	18.00
(46)	Ollie Fuhrman	25.00	12.50	7.50
(47)	C. Galloway	25.00	12.50	7.50
(48)	Walter Gerber	25.00	12.50	7.50
(49)	Ed Gharrity	25.00	12.50	7.50
(50)	Chas. Glazner	25.00	12.50	7.50
(51)	Leon Goslin	60.00	30.00	18.00
(52)	Hank Gowdy	25.00	12.50	7.50
(53)	John Graney	25.00	12.50	7.50
(54)	Ray Grimes	25.00	12.50	7.50
(55)	Heinie Groh	25.00	12.50	7.50
(56)	Jesse Haines	60.00	30.00	18.00
(57)	Earl Hamilton	25.00	12.50	7.50
(58)	Bubbles Hargrave	25.00	12.50	7.50
(59)	Bryan Harris	25.00	12.50	7.50
(60)	Cliff Heathcote	25.00	12.50	7.50
(61)	Harry Heilmann	60.00	30.00	18.00
(62)	Clarence Hodge	25.00	12.50	7.50
(63)	Chas. Hollocher	25.00	12.50	7.50
(64)	Harry Hooper	60.00	30.00	18.00
(65)	Rogers Hornsby	125.00	62.00	37.00
(66)	Waite Hoyt	60.00	30.00	18.00
(67)	Ernie Johnson	25.00	12.50	7.50
(68)	S. Johnson	25.00	12.50	7.50
(69)	Walter Johnson	25.00	12.50	7.50
(70)	Doc Johnston	135.00	67.00	40.00
(71)	Sam Jones	25.00	12.50	7.50
(72)	Ben Karr	25.00	12.50	7.50
(73)	Johnny Lavan	25.00	12.50	7.50
(74)	Geo. Leverette	25.00	12.50	7.50
(75)	"Rabbit" Maranville	60.00	30.00	18.00
(76)	Cliff Markle	25.00	12.50	7.50
(77)	Carl Mays	40.00	20.00	12.00
(78)	Hervey McClellan	25.00	12.50	7.50
(79)	Martin McManus	25.00	12.50	7.50
(80)	Lee Meadows	25.00	12.50	7.50
(81)	Mike Menosky	25.00	12.50	7.50
(82)	Emil Meusel	25.00	12.50	7.50
(83)	Clyde Milan	25.00	12.50	7.50
(84)	Bing Miller	25.00	12.50	7.50
(85)	Elmer Miller	25.00	12.50	7.50
(86)	Lawrence Miller	25.00	12.50	7.50
(87)	Clarence Mitchell	25.00	12.50	7.50
(88)	Geo. Mogridge	25.00	12.50	7.50
(89)	John Morrison	25.00	12.50	7.50
(90)	Johnny Mostil	25.00	12.50	7.50
(91)	Elmer Meyers	25.00	12.50	7.50
(92)	Roliene Naylor	25.00	12.50	7.50
(93)	Les Nunamaker	25.00	12.50	7.50
(94)	Bob O'Farrell	25.00	12.50	7.50
(95)	George O'Neil	25.00	12.50	7.50
(96)	Steve O'Neill	25.00	12.50	7.50
(97)	Herb Pennock	60.00	30.00	18.00
(98)	Ralph Perkins	25.00	12.50	7.50
(99)	Tom Phillips	25.00	12.50	7.50
(100)	Val Picinich	25.00	12.50	7.50
(101)	H. Pillette	25.00	12.50	7.50
(102)	Ralph Pinelli	25.00	12.50	7.50
(103)	Wallie Pipp	40.00	20.00	12.00
(104)	Clark Pittenger	25.00	12.50	7.50
(105)	Derrill Pratt	25.00	12.50	7.50
(106)	Goldie Rapp	25.00	12.50	7.50
(107)	John Rawlings	25.00	12.50	7.50
(108)	Walter Reuther	25.00	12.50	7.50
(109)	Emory Rigney	25.00	12.50	7.50
(110)	Charles Robertson	25.00	12.50	7.50
(111)	Ed Rommel	25.00	12.50	7.50
(112)	Muddy Ruel	25.00	12.50	7.50
(113)	Babe Ruth	1000.	500.00	300.00
(114)	Ray Schalk	60.00	30.00	18.00
(115)	Wallie Schang	25.00	12.50	7.50
(116)	Ray Schmidt	25.00	12.50	7.50
(117)	Walter Schmidt	25.00	12.50	7.50
(118)	Joe Schultz	25.00	12.50	7.50
(119)	Hank Severeid	25.00	12.50	7.50
(120)	Joe Sewell	60.00	30.00	18.00
(121)	Bob Shawkey	40.00	20.00	12.00
(122)	Earl Sheely	25.00	12.50	7.50
(123)	Ralph Shinner	25.00	12.50	7.50
(124)	Urban Shocker	25.00	12.50	7.50
(125)	George Sisler	60.00	30.00	18.00
(126)	Earl Smith (Washington)	25.00	12.50	7.50
(127)	Earl Smith (New York)	25.00	12.50	7.50
(128)	Jack Smith	25.00	12.50	7.50
(129)	Al Sothoron	25.00	12.50	7.50
(130)	Tris Speaker	80.00	40.00	24.00
(131)	Amos Strunk	25.00	12.50	7.50
(132)	Jim Tierney	25.00	12.50	7.50
(133)	John Tobin	25.00	12.50	7.50
(134)	George Toporcer	25.00	12.50	7.50
(135)	Geo. Uhle	25.00	12.50	7.50
(136)	Bob Veach	25.00	12.50	7.50
(137)	John Watson	25.00	12.50	7.50
(138)	Zach Wheat	60.00	30.00	18.00
(139)	Fred Williams	40.00	20.00	12.00
(140)	Ken Williams	25.00	12.50	7.50
(141)	Lawrence Woodall	25.00	12.50	7.50
(142)	Russell Wrightstone	25.00	12.50	7.50
(143)	Ross Young (Youngs)	60.00	30.00	18.00
(144)	J.T. Zachary	25.00	12.50	7.50

1932 W574

Issued circa 1932, cards in the W574 set measure 2-1/4" by 2-7/8". They are unnumbered and are listed here in alphabetical order.

		NR MT	EX	VG
Complete Set:		1600.	800.00	480.00
Common Player:		45.00	22.00	13.50
(1)	Dale Alexander	45.00	22.00	13.50
(2)	Luke Appling	125.00	62.00	37.00
(3)	Earl Averill	125.00	62.00	37.00
(4)	Ivy Paul Andrews	45.00	22.00	13.50
(5)	Geore Blaeholder	45.00	22.00	13.50
(6)	Irving Burns	45.00	22.00	13.50
(7)	Pat Caraway	45.00	22.00	13.50
(8)	Chalmer Cissell	45.00	22.00	13.50
(9)	Harry Davis	45.00	22.00	13.50
(10)	Jimmy Dykes	70.00	35.00	21.00
(11)	George Earnshaw	45.00	22.00	13.50
(12)	Urban Faber	125.00	62.00	37.00
(13)	Lewis Fonseca	45.00	22.00	13.50
(14)	Jimmy Foxx	225.00	112.00	67.00
(15)	Victor Frasier	45.00	22.00	13.50
(16)	Robert Grove	200.00	100.00	60.00
(17)	Frank Grube	45.00	22.00	13.50
(18)	Irving Hadley	45.00	22.00	13.50
(19)	Willie Kamm	45.00	22.00	13.50
(20)	Bill Killefer	45.00	22.00	13.50
(21)	Ralph Kress	45.00	22.00	13.50
(22)	Fred Marberry	45.00	22.00	13.50
(23)	Roger Peckinpaugh	45.00	22.00	13.50
(24)	Frank Reiber	45.00	22.00	13.50

		NR MT	EX	VG
(25)	Carl Reynolds	45.00	22.00	13.50
(26)	Al Simmons	125.00	62.00	37.00
(27)	Joe Vosmik	45.00	22.00	13.50
(28)	Gerald Walker	45.00	22.00	13.50
(29)	Whitlow Wyatt	45.00	22.00	13.50

1922 W575-1

Designated as W575 in the American Card Catalog, these "strip cards" are blank-backed. Issued circa 1922, cards in this set measure 2" by 3-1/4". The subjects for the set were taken from the E121 set and include representatives of all 16 major league teams, with heavier emphasis on the New York teams.

		NR MT	EX	VG
	Complete Set:	8500.	4250.	2550.
	Common Player:	30.00	15.00	9.00
(1)	Chas. "Babe" Adams	30.00	15.00	9.00
(2)	G.C. Alexander	100.00	50.00	30.00
(3)	Grover Alexander	100.00	50.00	30.00
(4)	Jim Bagby	30.00	15.00	9.00
(5a)	J. Franklin Baker	85.00	42.00	25.00
(5b)	Frank Baker	85.00	42.00	25.00
(6)	Dave Bancroft (batting)	85.00	42.00	25.00
(7)	Dave Bancroft (fielding)	85.00	42.00	25.00
(8)	Jesse Barnes	30.00	15.00	9.00
(9)	Howard Berry	30.00	15.00	9.00
(10)	L. Bigbee (should be C.)	30.00	15.00	9.00
(11)	Ping Bodie	30.00	15.00	9.00
(13)	"Ed" Brown	30.00	15.00	9.00
(14)	George Burns	30.00	15.00	9.00
(15)	Geo. J. Burns	30.00	15.00	9.00
(16)	"Bullet Joe" Bush	30.00	15.00	9.00
(17)	Owen Bush	30.00	15.00	9.00
(18)	Max Carey (batting)	85.00	42.00	25.00
(19)	Max Carey (hands on hips)	85.00	42.00	25.00
(20)	Ty Cobb	750.00	375.00	225.00
(21)	Eddie Collins	100.00	50.00	30.00
(22)	"Rip" Collins	30.00	15.00	9.00
(23)	Stanley Coveleskie (Coveleski)	85.00	42.00	25.00
(24)	Bill Cunningham	30.00	15.00	9.00
(25)	Jake Daubert	40.00	20.00	12.00
(26)	George Dauss	30.00	15.00	9.00
(27)	"Dixie" Davis	30.00	15.00	9.00
(28)	Charles Deal (dark uniform)	30.00	15.00	9.00
(29)	Charles Deal (light uniform)	30.00	15.00	9.00
(30)	Lou DeVormer	30.00	15.00	9.00
(31)	William Doak	30.00	15.00	9.00
(32)	Bill Donovan	30.00	15.00	9.00
(33)	"Phil" Douglas	30.00	15.00	9.00
(34a)	Johnny Evers (Mgr.)	85.00	42.00	25.00
(34b)	Johnny Evers (Manager)	85.00	42.00	25.00
(35a)	Urban Faber (dark uniform)	85.00	42.00	25.00
(35b)	Urban Faber (white uniform)	85.00	42.00	25.00
(36)	Bib Falk (Bibb)	30.00	15.00	9.00
(37)	Alex Ferguson	30.00	15.00	9.00
(38)	Wm. Fewster	30.00	15.00	9.00
(39)	Eddie Foster	30.00	15.00	9.00
(40)	Frank Frisch	85.00	42.00	25.00
(41)	W.L. Gardner	30.00	15.00	9.00
(42)	Alexander Gaston	30.00	15.00	9.00
(43)	E.P. Gharrity	30.00	15.00	9.00
(44)	Chas. "Whitey" Glazner	30.00	15.00	9.00
(45)	"Kid" Gleason	30.00	15.00	9.00
(46)	"Mike" Gonzalez	30.00	15.00	9.00
(47)	Hank Gowdy	30.00	15.00	9.00
(48a)	John Graney (Util. o.f.)	30.00	15.00	9.00
(49b)	John Graney (O.F.)	30.00	15.00	9.00
(50)	Tom Griffith	30.00	15.00	9.00
(51)	Chas. Grimm	40.00	20.00	12.00
(52a)	Heinie Groh (Cincinnati)	30.00	15.00	9.00
(52b)	Heinie Groh (New York)	30.00	15.00	9.00
(53)	Jess Haines	85.00	42.00	25.00
(54)	Harry Harper	30.00	15.00	9.00
(55)	"Chicken" Hawks	30.00	15.00	9.00
(56)	Harry Heilman (Heilmann) (holding bat)	85.00	42.00	25.00
(57)	Harry Heilman (Heilmann) (running)	85.00	42.00	25.00
(58)	Fred Hoffman	30.00	15.00	9.00
(59a)	Walter Holke (1st B., portrait)	30.00	15.00	9.00
(59b)	Walter Holke (1B, portrait)	30.00	15.00	9.00
(60)	Walter Holke (throwing)	30.00	15.00	9.00
(61a)	Charles Hollacher (name incorrect)	30.00	15.00	9.00
(61b)	Charles Hollocher (name correct)	30.00	15.00	9.00
(62)	Harry Hooper	30.00	15.00	9.00
(63a)	Rogers Hornsby (2nd B.)	150.00	75.00	45.00
(63b)	Rogers Hornsby (O.F.)	150.00	75.00	45.00
(64)	Waite Hoyt	85.00	42.00	25.00
(65)	Miller Huggins	85.00	42.00	25.00
(66)	Wm. C. Jacobson	30.00	15.00	9.00
(67)	Hugh Jennings	30.00	15.00	9.00
(68)	Walter Johnson (arms at chest)	200.00	100.00	60.00
(69)	Walter Johnson (throwing)	200.00	100.00	60.00
(70)	James Johnston	30.00	15.00	9.00
(71)	Joe Judge (batting)	30.00	15.00	9.00
(73a)	George Kelly (1st B.)	85.00	42.00	25.00
(73b)	George Kelly (1B.)	85.00	42.00	25.00
(74)	Dick Kerr	30.00	15.00	9.00
(75)	P.J. Kilduff	30.00	15.00	9.00
(76)	Bill Killefer	30.00	15.00	9.00
(77)	John Lavan	30.00	15.00	9.00
(78)	"Nemo" Leibold	30.00	15.00	9.00
(79)	Duffy Lewis	30.00	15.00	9.00
(80)	Al. Mamaux	30.00	15.00	9.00
(81)	"Rabbit" Maranville	85.00	42.00	25.00
(81b)	Carl Mays (name correct)	40.00	20.00	12.00
(82a)	Carl May (name incorrect)	40.00	20.00	12.00
(83)	John McGraw	110.00	55.00	33.00
(84)	Jack McInnis	30.00	15.00	9.00
(85)	M.J. McNally	30.00	15.00	9.00
(86)	Emil Muesel	30.00	15.00	9.00
(87)	R. Meusel	50.00	25.00	15.00
(88)	Clyde Milan	30.00	15.00	9.00
(89)	Elmer Miller	30.00	15.00	9.00
(90)	Otto Miller	30.00	15.00	9.00
(91a)	John Mitchell (S.S.)	30.00	15.00	9.00
(91b)	John Mitchell (3rd B.)	30.00	15.00	9.00
(92)	Guy Morton	30.00	15.00	9.00
(94)	Eddie Mulligan	30.00	15.00	9.00
(95)	Eddie Murphy	30.00	15.00	9.00
(96a)	"Hy" Myers (C.F./O.F.)	30.00	15.00	9.00
(96b)	Hy Myers (O.F.)	30.00	15.00	9.00
(97)	A.E. Neale	60.00	30.00	18.00
(98)	Arthur Nehf	30.00	15.00	9.00
(99)	Joe Oeschger	30.00	15.00	9.00
(100)	Chas. O'Leary	30.00	15.00	9.00
(101)	Steve O'Neill	30.00	15.00	9.00
(101a)	Jeff Pfeffer (Brooklyn)	30.00	15.00	9.00
(101b)	Jeff Pfeffer (St. Louis)	30.00	15.00	9.00
(102a)	Roger Peckinbaugh (name incorrect)	30.00	15.00	9.00
(102b)	Roger Peckinpaugh (name correct)	30.00	15.00	9.00
(104)	Walter Pipp	60.00	30.00	18.00
(105)	Jack Quinn	30.00	15.00	9.00
(106a)	John Rawlings (2nd B.)	30.00	15.00	9.00
(106b)	John Rawlings (2B.)	30.00	15.00	9.00
(107a)	E.S. Rice (name incorrect)	85.00	42.00	25.00
(107b)	E.C. Rice (name correct)	85.00	42.00	25.00
(108)	Eppa Rixey, Jr.	85.00	42.00	25.00
(109)	Wilbert Robinson	85.00	42.00	25.00
(110)	Tom Rogers	30.00	15.00	9.00
(111)	Ed Rounnel (Rommel)	30.00	15.00	9.00
112	Robert Roth (Rommel)	30.00	15.00	9.00
(113a)	Ed Roush (O.F.)	85.00	42.00	25.00
(113b)	Ed Roush (C.F.)	85.00	42.00	25.00
(114)	"Muddy" Ruel	30.00	15.00	9.00
(115a)	"Babe" Ruth (R.F.)	900.00	450.00	270.00
(115b)	Babe Ruth (L.F.)	900.00	450.00	270.00
(116)	Bill Ryan	30.00	15.00	9.00
(117)	"Slim" Sallee (ball in hand)	30.00	15.00	9.00
(118)	"Slim" Sallee (no ball in hand)	30.00	15.00	9.00
(119)	Ray Schalk (bunting)	85.00	42.00	25.00
(120)	Ray Schalk (catching)	85.00	42.00	25.00
(121a)	Walter Schang	30.00	15.00	9.00
(121b)	Wally Schang	30.00	15.00	9.00
(122a)	Fred Schupp (name incorrect)	30.00	15.00	9.00
(122b)	Ferd Schupp (name correct)	30.00	15.00	9.00
(123a)	Everett Scott (Boston)	30.00	15.00	9.00
(123b)	Everett Scott (New York)	30.00	15.00	9.00
(124)	Hank Severeid	30.00	15.00	9.00
(125)	Robert Shawkey	40.00	20.00	12.00
(126a)	"Pat" Shea	30.00	15.00	9.00
(126b)	Pat Shea	30.00	15.00	9.00
(127)	Earl Sheely	30.00	15.00	9.00
(128)	Urban Shocker	30.00	15.00	9.00
(129)	George Sisler (batting)	100.00	50.00	30.00
(130)	George Sisler (throwing)	100.00	50.00	30.00
(131)	Earl Smith	30.00	15.00	9.00
(132)	Elmer Smith	30.00	15.00	9.00
(133)	Frank Snyder	30.00	15.00	9.00
(134a)	Tris Speaker (large projection)	110.00	55.00	33.00
(134b)	Tris Speaker (small projection)	110.00	55.00	33.00
(135)	Charles Stengel (batting)	225.00	112.00	67.00
(136)	Charles Stengel (portrait)	225.00	112.00	67.00
(137)	Milton Stock	30.00	15.00	9.00
(138a)	Amos Strunk (C.F.)	30.00	15.00	9.00
(138b)	Amos Strunk (O.F.)	30.00	15.00	9.00
(139)	Zeb Terry	30.00	15.00	9.00
(140)	Chester Thomas	30.00	15.00	9.00
(141)	Fred Toney (both feet on ground)	30.00	15.00	9.00
(142)	Fred Toney (one foot in air)	30.00	15.00	9.00
(143)	George Toporcer	30.00	15.00	9.00
(144)	George Tyler	30.00	15.00	9.00
(145)	Jim Vaughn (plain uniform)	30.00	15.00	9.00
(146)	Jim Vaughn (striped uniform)	30.00	15.00	9.00
(147)	Bob Veach (arm raised)	30.00	15.00	9.00
(148)	Bob Veach (arms folded)	30.00	15.00	9.00
(149)	Oscar Vitt	30.00	15.00	9.00
(150)	Curtis Walker	30.00	15.00	9.00
(151)	W. Wambsganss	40.00	20.00	12.00
(152)	Zach Wheat	85.00	42.00	25.00
(153)	George Whitted	30.00	15.00	9.00
(154)	Fred Williams	40.00	20.00	12.00
(155)	Ivy B. Wingo	30.00	15.00	9.00
(156)	Lawton Witt	30.00	15.00	9.00
(157)	Joe Wood	40.00	20.00	12.00
(158)	Pep Young	30.00	15.00	9.00
(159)	Ross Young (Youngs)	85.00	42.00	25.00

1922 W575-2

The black and white cards in this set measure 2-1/8" by 3-3/8". Because of the design of the cards the set is sometimes called the "autograph on shoulder" series.

		NR MT	EX	VG
	Complete Set:	2900.	1450.	870.00
	Common Player:	35.00	17.50	10.50
(1)	Dave Bancroft	75.00	37.00	22.00
(2)	Johnnie Bassler	35.00	17.50	10.50
(3)	Joe Bush	40.00	20.00	12.00
(4)	Ty Cobb	750.00	375.00	225.00
(5)	Eddie Collins	75.00	37.00	22.00
(6)	Stan Coveleskie (Coveleski)	75.00	37.00	22.00
(7)	Jake Daubert	40.00	20.00	12.00
(8)	Joe Dugan	40.00	20.00	12.00
(9)	Red Faber	75.00	37.00	22.00
(10)	Frank Frisch	75.00	37.00	22.00
(11)	Walter H. Gerber	35.00	17.50	10.50
(12)	Harry Heilmann	75.00	37.00	22.00
(13)	Harry Hooper	75.00	37.00	22.00
(14)	Rogers Hornsby	250.00	125.00	75.00
(15)	Waite Hoyt	75.00	37.00	22.00
(16)	Joe Judge	35.00	17.50	10.50
(17)	Geo. Kelly	75.00	37.00	22.00
(18)	Rabbit Maranville	75.00	37.00	22.00
(19)	Rube Marquard	75.00	37.00	22.00
(20)	Guy Morton	35.00	17.50	10.50
(21)	Art Nehf	35.00	17.50	10.50
(22)	Derrill B. Pratt	35.00	17.50	10.50
(23)	Jimmy Ring	35.00	17.50	10.50
(24)	Eppa Rixey	75.00	37.00	22.00
(25)	Gene Robertson	35.00	17.50	10.50
(26)	Ed Rommell (Rommel)	35.00	17.50	10.50
(27)	Babe Ruth	1000.	500.00	300.00
(28)	Wally Schang	35.00	17.50	10.50
(29)	Everett Scott	35.00	17.50	10.50
(30)	Henry Severeid	35.00	17.50	10.50
(31)	Joe Sewell	75.00	37.00	22.00
(32)	Geo. Sisler	75.00	37.00	22.00
(33)	Tris Speaker	100.00	50.00	30.00
(34)	Riggs Stephenson	40.00	20.00	12.00
(35)	Zeb Terry	35.00	17.50	10.50
(36)	Bobbie Veach	35.00	17.50	10.50
(37)	Clarence Walker	35.00	17.50	10.50
(38)	Johnnie Walker	35.00	17.50	10.50
(39)	Zach Wheat	75.00	37.00	22.00
(40)	Kenneth Williams	40.00	20.00	12.00

1950-56 W576
Callahan Hall of Fame

These cards, which feature drawings of Hall of Famers, were produced from 1950 through 1956 and sold by the Baseball Hall of Fame in Cooperstown. The cards measure 1-3/4" by 2-1/2" and include a detailed player biography on the back. When introduced in 1950 the set included all members of the Hall of Fame up to that time, and then new cards were added each year as more players were elected. Therefore, cards of players appearing in all previous editions are lesser in value than those players who appeared in just one or two years. When the set was discontinued in 1956 it consisted of 82 cards, which is now considered a complete set. The cards are not numbered and are listed here

KENESAW MOUNTAIN LANDIS
Elected to the Hall of Fame, 1944. First High Commissioner of Baseball; born at Millville, Ohio, November 20, 1866; died November 25, 1944, age 78.

Lean, dynamic, white-haired Judge Landis brought to baseball one of the greatest and fairest legal minds in America, plus a fanatical love for the game and uncompromising insistence on all-inclusive cleanness and honesty. The Judge knew baseball and knew human nature just as thoroughly. For many years, prior to his appointment as Commissioner he served distinctively and fearlessly on the Federal Bench.

As baseball's High Commissioner, Landis ruled the game impartially and understandingly—but with an iron hand—from 1920 until his death. To him must go the credit for rebuilding a strong and enduring foundation for baseball and restoring public confidence in its integrity after the disrupting "Black Sox" scandal following the 1919 Chicago-Cincinnati World Series. His verdict in that case barred 8 White Sox players—including several of the game's brightest stars—from organized ball for life.

Scores of his decisions were tough to take, but all were made for the everlasting good of the game. The Judge's constructive work raised high the standard of baseball, set basic ideals which will endure as long as the game endures.

alphabetically.

		NR MT	EX	VG
Complete Set:		450.00	230.00	135.00
Common Player:		3.00	1.50	.90
(1)	Grover Alexander	5.00	2.50	1.50
(2)	"Cap" Anson	5.00	2.50	1.50
(3)	J. Franklin "Home Run" Baker	6.00	3.00	1.75
(4)	Edward G. Barrow	6.00	3.00	1.75
(5a)	Charles "Chief" Bender (different biography)	6.00	3.00	1.75
(5b)	Charles "Chief" Bender (different biography)	6.00	3.00	1.75
(6)	Roger Bresnahan	3.00	1.50	.90
(7)	Dan Brouthers	3.00	1.50	.90
(8)	Mordecai Brown	3.00	1.50	.90
(9)	Morgan G. Bulkeley	3.00	1.50	.90
(10)	Jesse Burkett	3.00	1.50	.90
(11)	Alexander Cartwright	3.00	1.50	.90
(12)	Henry Chadwick	3.00	1.50	.90
(13)	Frank Chance	3.00	1.50	.90
(14)	Albert B. Chandler	20.00	10.00	6.00
(15)	Jack Chesbro	3.00	1.50	.90
(16)	Fred Clarke	3.00	1.50	.90
(17)	Ty Cobb	30.00	15.00	9.00
(18a)	Mickey Cochran (name incorrect)	30.00	15.00	9.00
(18b)	Mickey Cochrane (name correct)	5.00	2.50	1.50
(19a)	Eddie Collins (different biography)	5.00	2.50	1.50
(19b)	Eddie Collins (different biography)	5.00	2.50	1.50
(20)	Jimmie Collins	3.00	1.50	.90
(21)	Charles A. Comiskey	3.00	1.50	.90
(22)	Tom Connolly	6.00	3.00	1.75
(23)	"Candy" Cummings	3.00	1.50	.90
(24)	Dizzy Dean	20.00	10.00	6.00
(25)	Ed Delahanty	3.00	1.50	.90
(26a)	Bill Dickey (different biography)	20.00	10.00	6.00
(26b)	Bill Dickey (different biography)	20.00	10.00	6.00
(27)	Joe DiMaggio	70.00	35.00	21.00
(28)	Hugh Duffy	3.00	1.50	.90
(29)	Johnny Evers	3.00	1.50	.90
(30)	Buck Ewing	3.00	1.50	.90
(31)	Jimmie Foxx	6.00	3.00	1.75
(32)	Frank Frisch	3.00	1.50	.90
(33)	Lou Gehrig	30.00	15.00	9.00
(34)	Charles Gehringer	3.00	1.50	.90
(35)	Clark Griffith	3.00	1.50	.90
(36)	Lefty Grove	5.00	2.50	1.50
(37)	Leo "Gabby" Hartnett	6.00	3.00	1.75
(38)	Harry Heilmann	3.00	1.50	.90
(39)	Rogers Hornsby	6.00	3.00	1.75
(40)	Carl Hubbell	5.00	2.50	1.50
(41)	Hughey Jennings	3.00	1.50	.90
(42)	Ban Johnson	3.00	1.50	.90
(43)	Walter Johnson	6.00	3.00	1.75
(44)	Willie Keeler	3.00	1.50	.90
(45)	Mike Kelly	3.00	1.50	.90
(46)	Bill Klem	6.00	3.00	1.75
(47)	Napoleon Lajoie	3.00	1.50	.90
(48)	Kenesaw M. Landis	3.00	1.50	.90
(49)	Ted Lyons	6.00	3.00	1.75
(50)	Connie Mack	6.00	3.00	1.75
(51)	Walter Maranville	6.00	3.00	1.75
(52)	Christy Mathewson	6.00	3.00	1.75
(53)	Tommy McCarthy	3.00	1.50	.90
(54)	Joe McGinnity	3.00	1.50	.90
(55)	John McGraw	5.00	2.50	1.50
(56)	Charles Nichols	3.00	1.50	.90
(57)	Jim O'Rourke	3.00	1.50	.90
(58)	Mel Ott	5.00	2.50	1.50
(59)	Herb Pennock	3.00	1.50	.90
(60)	Eddie Plank	3.00	1.50	.90
(61)	Charles Radbourne	3.00	1.50	.90
(62)	Wilbert Robinson	3.00	1.50	.90
(63)	Babe Ruth	70.00	35.00	21.00
(64)	Ray "Cracker" Schalk	6.00	3.00	1.75
(65)	Al Simmons	6.00	3.00	1.75
(66a)	George Sisler (different biography)	3.00	1.50	.90
(66b)	George Sisler (different biography)	3.00	1.50	.90
(67)	A. G. Spalding	3.00	1.50	.90
(68)	Tris Speaker	3.00	1.50	.90
(69)	Bill Terry	6.00	3.00	1.75
(70)	Joe Tinker	3.00	1.50	.90
(71)	"Pie" Traynor	3.00	1.50	.90
(72)	Clarence A. "Dizzy" Vance	6.00	3.00	1.75
(73)	Rube Waddell	3.00	1.50	.90
(74)	Hans Wagner	20.00	10.00	6.00
(75)	Bobby Wallace	6.00	3.00	1.75
(76)	Ed Walsh	3.00	1.50	.90
(77)	Paul Waner	5.00	2.50	1.50
(78)	George Wright	3.00	1.50	.90
(79)	Harry Wright	6.00	3.00	1.75
(80)	Cy Young	6.00	3.00	1.75

	NR MT	EX	VG
---a) Museum Exterior View (different biography)	6.00	3.00	1.75
---b) Museum Exterior View (different biography)	6.00	3.00	1.75
---a) Museum Interior View (different biography)	6.00	3.00	1.75
---b) Museum Interior View (different biography)	6.00	3.00	1.75

1938 W711-1 Reds

WALLY BERGER
Outfielder
Ever since he came into the league in 1930 Berger has been one of the circuit's most dangerous hitters. Led the league in home runs in 1935 and has hit more homers than any player in the league except Mel Ott and Chuck Klein. Was acquired by the Reds in a trade with the Giants in June.

This 32-card set is a challenging one of particular interest to Cincinnati team collectors. The 2" by 3" cards were sold at the ballpark. Fronts feature a picture of the player while backs have the player's name, position and a generally flattering description of the player's talents. The cards are not numbered.

		NR MT	EX	VG
Complete Set:		300.00	150.00	90.00
Common Player:		10.00	5.00	3.00
(1)	Wally Berger ("... in a trade with the Giants in June.")	15.00	7.50	4.50
(2)	Joe Cascarella	25.00	12.50	7.50
(3)	Allen "Dusty" Cooke	25.00	12.50	7.50
(4)	Harry Craft	10.00	5.00	3.00
(5)	Ray "Peaches" Davis	10.00	5.00	3.00
(6)	Paul Derringer ("Won 22 games ... this season.")	15.00	7.50	4.50
(7)	Linus Frey ("... only 25 now.")	25.00	12.50	7.50
(8)	Lee Gamble ("... Syracuse last year.")	25.00	12.50	7.50
(9)	Ival Goodman (no mention of 30 homers)	25.00	12.50	7.50
(10)	Harry "Hank" Gowdy	10.00	5.00	3.00
(11)	Lee Grissom (no mention of 1938)	25.00	12.50	7.50
(12)	Willard Hershberger	15.00	7.50	4.50
(13)	Ernie Lombardi (no mention of 1938 MVP)	30.00	15.00	9.00
(14)	Frank McCormick	15.00	7.50	4.50
(15)	Bill McKechnie ("Last year he led ...")	25.00	12.50	7.50
(16)	Lloyd "Whitey" Moore ("... last year with Syracuse.")	25.00	12.50	7.50
(17)	Billy Myers ("... in his fourth year.")	25.00	12.50	7.50
(18)	Lee Riggs ("... in his fourth season ...")	25.00	12.50	7.50
(19)	Eddie Roush	25.00	12.50	7.50
(20)	Gene Schott	25.00	12.50	7.50
(21)	Johnny Vander Meer (pitching pose)	20.00	10.00	6.00
(22)	Wm. "Bucky" Walter ("... won 14 games ...")	15.00	7.50	4.50
(23)	Jim Weaver	10.00	5.00	3.00

1939 W711-1 Reds

WALLY BERGER
Outfielder
Ever since he came into the league in 1930, Berger has been one of the circuit's most dangerous hitters. Led the league in home runs in 1935 and has hit more homers than any player in the league except Mel Ott and Chuck Klein. Was acquired by the Reds in a trade with the Giants in June, 1938.

An updating by one season of the team-issued 1938 W711-1 issue, most of the players and poses on the 2" by 3" cards remained the same. A close study of the career summary on the card's back is necessary to determine which year of issue is at hand.

		NR MT	EX	VG
Complete Set:		400.00	200.00	120.00
Common Player:		20.00	10.00	6.00
(1)	Wally Berger ("... in a trade with the Giants in June, 1938.")	30.00	15.00	9.00
(2)	Nino Bongiovanni	30.00	15.00	9.00
(3)	Stanley 'Frenchy' Bordagaray	30.00	15.00	9.00
(4)	Harry Craft	20.00	10.00	6.00
(5)	Ray "Peaches" Davis	20.00	10.00	6.00
(6)	Paul Derringer ("Won 22 games ... last year.")	30.00	15.00	9.00
(7)	Linus Frey ("... only 26 now.")	12.00	6.00	3.50
(8)	Lee Gamble ("... Syracuse in 1937.")	12.00	6.00	3.50
(9)	Ival Goodman (mentions hitting 30 homers)	12.00	6.00	3.50
(10)	Harry "Hank" Gowdy	20.00	10.00	6.00
(11)	Lee Grissom (mentions 1938)	12.00	6.00	3.50
(12)	Willard Hershberger	30.00	15.00	9.00
(13)	Eddie Joost	12.00	6.00	3.50
(14)	Wes Livengood	80.00	40.00	24.00
(15)	Ernie Lombardi (mentions MVP of 1938)	30.00	15.00	9.00
(16)	Frank McCormick	30.00	15.00	9.00
(17)	Bill McKechnie ("In 1937 he led ...")	50.00	25.00	15.00
(18)	Lloyd "Whitey" Moore ("... in 1937 with Syracuse.")	12.00	6.00	3.50
(19)	Billy Myers ("... in his fifth year ...")	12.00	6.00	3.50
(20)	Lee Riggs ("... in his fifth season...")	12.00	6.00	3.50
(21)	Les Scarsella	30.00	15.00	9.00
(22)	Eugene "Junior" Thompson	12.00	6.00	3.50
(23)	Johnny Vander Meer (portrait)	20.00	10.00	6.00
(24)	Wm. "Bucky" Walters ("Won 15 games ...")	30.00	15.00	9.00
(25)	Jim Weaver	20.00	10.00	6.00
(26)	Bill Werber	12.00	6.00	3.50
(27)	Jimmy Wilson	12.00	6.00	3.50

1940 W711-2 Harry Hartman Reds

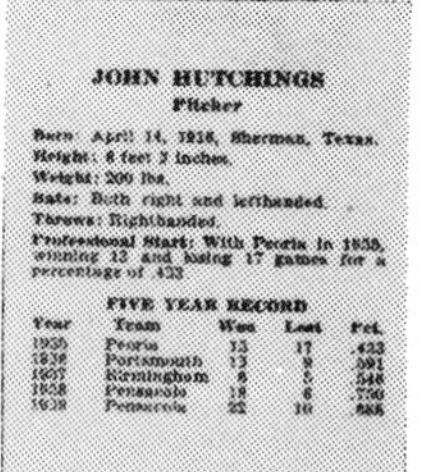

JOHN HUTCHINGS
Pitcher
FIVE YEAR RECORD
Year Team Won Lost Pct.

Another early set of the Cincinnati Reds, this 32- card set of 2-1/8" by 2-5/8" cards contains a number of interesting items. The black and white cards carry no numbers and feature a picture of the player on the front and name, position and biographical information on the back. As the Reds were World Champions in 1940 after defeating Detroit in four games to three, the set features special cards for the World Series title, making it one of the first to feature events as well as individuals. The set takes it name from Reds' announcer Harry Hartman, who has a card in the issue and supposedly was instrumental in its issue.

		NR MT	EX	VG
Complete Set:		450.00	225.00	135.00
Common Player:		12.00	6.00	3.50
(1)	Morris Arnovich	12.00	6.00	3.50
(2)	William (Bill) Baker	12.00	6.00	3.50
(3)	Joseph Beggs	12.00	6.00	3.50
(4)	Harry Craft	12.00	6.00	3.50
(5)	Paul Derringer	20.00	10.00	6.00
(6)	Linus Frey	12.00	6.00	3.50
(7)	Ival Goodman	12.00	6.00	3.50
(8)	Harry (Hank) Gowdy	12.00	6.00	3.50
(9)	Witt Guise	12.00	6.00	3.50
(10)	Harry (Socko) Hartman	12.00	6.00	3.50
(11)	Willard Hershberger	15.00	7.50	4.50
(12)	John Hutchings	12.00	6.00	3.50
(13)	Edwin Joost	12.00	6.00	3.50
(14)	Ernie Lombardi	45.00	22.00	13.50
(15)	Frank McCormick	20.00	10.00	6.00
(16)	Myron McCormick	12.00	6.00	3.50
(17)	William Boyd McKechnie	30.00	15.00	9.00
(18)	Lloyd (Whitey) Moore	12.00	6.00	3.50
(19)	William (Bill) Myers	12.00	6.00	3.50
(20)	Lewis Riggs	12.00	6.00	3.50
(21)	Elmer Riddle	12.00	6.00	3.50
(22)	James A. Ripple	12.00	6.00	3.50
(23)	Milburn Shoffner	12.00	6.00	3.50
(24)	Eugene Thompson	12.00	6.00	3.50
(25)	James Turner	12.00	6.00	3.50
(26)	John Vander Meer	30.00	15.00	9.00
(27)	Wm. (Bucky) Walters	20.00	10.00	6.00
(28)	William (Bill) Werber	12.00	6.00	3.50

		NR MT	EX	VG
(29)	James Wilson	15.00	7.50	4.50
(30)	The Cincinnati Reds	12.00	6.00	3.50
(31)	The Cincinnati Reds World Champions	12.00	6.00	3.50
(32)	Tell The World About The Cincinnati Reds	12.00	6.00	3.50
(33)	Tell The World About The Cincinnati Reds World (Champions)	12.00	6.00	3.50
(34)	Results 1940 World's Series	15.00	7.50	4.50
(35)	Debt of Gratitude to Wm. Koehl Co.	12.00	6.00	3.50

1941 W753 St. Louis Browns

Measuring 2-1/8" by 2-5/8", this unnumbered set of cards features the St. Louis Browns in black and white portrait photos. There are 29 cards in the set which featured a photo on the front and the player's name, position and personal and statistical informa- tion. There are also cards for coaches and one of the the club's two managers that season (Luke Sewell). As the Browns weren't much of a team in 1941 (or in most seasons for that matter) there are no major stars in the set.

		NR MT	EX	VG
	Complete Set:	400.00	200.00	120.00
	Common Player:	12.00	6.00	3.50
(1)	Johnny Allen	12.00	6.00	3.50
(2)	Elden Auker (Eldon)	12.00	6.00	3.50
(3)	Donald L Barnes	12.00	6.00	3.50
(4)	Johnny Berardino	20.00	10.00	6.00
(5)	George Caster	12.00	6.00	3.50
(6)	Harlond Benton (Darky) Clift	12.00	6.00	3.50
(7)	Roy J. Cullenbine	12.00	6.00	3.50
(8)	William O. DeWitt	12.00	6.00	3.50
(9)	Roberto Estalella	12.00	6.00	3.50
(10)	Richard Benjamin (Rick) Ferrell	50.00	25.00	15.00
(11)	Dennis W. Galehouse	12.00	6.00	3.50
(12)	Joseph L. Grace	12.00	6.00	3.50
(13)	Frank Grube	12.00	6.00	3.50
(14)	Robert A. Harris	12.00	6.00	3.50
(15)	Donald Henry Heffner	12.00	6.00	3.50
(16)	Fred Hofmann	12.00	6.00	3.50
(17)	Walter Franklin Judnich	12.00	6.00	3.50
(18)	John Henry (Jack) Kramer	12.00	6.00	3.50
(19)	Chester (Chet) Laabs	12.00	6.00	3.50
(20)	John Lucadello	12.00	6.00	3.50
(21)	George Hartley McQuinn	12.00	6.00	3.50
(22)	Robert Cleveland Muncrief, Jr.	12.00	6.00	3.50
(23)	John Niggeling	12.00	6.00	3.50
(24)	Fred Raymond (Fritz) Ostermueller	20.00	10.00	6.00
(25)	James Luther (Luke) Sewell	12.00	6.00	3.50
(26)	Alan Cochran Strange (Cochrane)	12.00	6.00	3.50
(27)	Robert Virgil (Bob) Swift	12.00	6.00	3.50
(28)	James W. (Zack) Taylor	12.00	6.00	3.50
(29)	William Felix (Bill) Trotter	12.00	6.00	3.50
(30)	Presentation Card/Order Form	25.00	12.50	7.50

1941 W754 St. Louis Cardinals

A companion set to W753, this time featuring the other team in St. Louis. Cards measure 2-1/8" by 2-5/8" and are unnumbered. Like the Browns set, there are 29 cards featuring black and white photos on the front and the individual's name, position and personal and statistical information on the back. One interesting addition to the set is a card of Branch Rickey which, coupled with cards of Enos Slaughter and Johnny Mize, gives the set a bit more appeal than the Browns set.

		NR MT	EX	VG
	Complete Set:	450.00	225.00	135.00
	Common Player:	12.00	6.00	3.50
(1)	Sam Breadon	12.00	6.00	3.50
(2)	James Brown	12.00	6.00	3.50
(3)	Morton Cooper	12.00	6.00	3.50
(4)	William Walker Cooper	12.00	6.00	3.50
(5)	Estel Crabtree	12.00	6.00	3.50
(6)	Frank Crespi	12.00	6.00	3.50
(7)	William Crouch	12.00	6.00	3.50
(8)	Miguel Mike Gonzalez	12.00	6.00	3.50
(9)	Harry Gumbert	12.00	6.00	3.50
(10)	John Hopp	12.00	6.00	3.50
(11)	Ira Hutchinson	12.00	6.00	3.50
(12)	Howard Krist	12.00	6.00	3.50
(13)	Edward E. Lake	12.00	6.00	3.50
(14)	Hubert Max Lanier	20.00	10.00	6.00
(15)	Gus Mancuso	12.00	6.00	3.50
(16)	Martin Marion	25.00	12.50	7.50
(17)	Steve Mesner	12.00	6.00	3.50
(18)	John Mize	50.00	25.00	15.00
(19)	Capt. Terry Moore	20.00	10.00	6.00
(20)	Sam Nahem	12.00	6.00	3.50
(21)	Don Padgett	12.00	6.00	3.50
(22)	Branch Rickey	50.00	25.00	15.00
(23)	Clyde Shoun	12.00	6.00	3.50
(24)	Enos Slaughter	50.00	25.00	15.00
(25)	William H. (Billy) Southworth	12.00	6.00	3.50
(26)	Herman Coaker Triplett	12.00	6.00	3.50
(27)	Clyde Buzzy Wares	12.00	6.00	3.50
(28)	Lou Warneke	12.00	6.00	3.50
(29)	Ernest White	12.00	6.00	3.50
(30)	Presentation Card/Order Form	25.00	12.50	7.50

1888 WG1
Base Ball Playing Cards

This little-known set of playing cards featuring drawings of real baseball players in action poses was issued in 1888 and includes members of the eight National League teams in existence at the time. Each club is represented by nine players - one at each position - making the set complete at 72 cards. The cards measure 2-1/2" by 3-1/2" and have a blue-patterned design on the back. The cards were sold as a complete set packed in their own separate box. They were designed to resemble a deck of regular playing cards, and the various positions were all assigned the same denomination (for example, all of the pitchers were kings, catchers were aces, etc.). There are no cards numbered either two, three, four or five; and rather than the typical hearts, clubs, diamonds and spades, each team represents a different "suit." The actual rules of the game remain open to speculation because no instructions have ever been found. The set has an American Card Catalog designation of WG1.

		NR MT	EX	VG
	Complete Set:	16000.	8000.	4800.
	Common Player:	150.00	75.00	45.00
(1)	Ed Andrews	150.00	75.00	45.00
(2)	Cap Anson	1100.	550.00	325.00
(3)	Charles Bassett	150.00	75.00	45.00
(4)	Charles Bastian	150.00	75.00	45.00
(5)	Charles Bennett	150.00	75.00	45.00
(6)	Handsome Boyle	150.00	75.00	45.00
(7)	Dan Brouthers	500.00	250.00	150.00
(8)	Thomas Brown	150.00	75.00	45.00
(9)	Thomas Burns	150.00	75.00	45.00
(10)	Frederick Carroll	150.00	75.00	45.00
(11)	Daniel Casey	250.00	125.00	75.00
(12)	John Clarkson	500.00	250.00	150.00
(13)	Jack Clements	150.00	75.00	45.00
(14)	John Coleman	150.00	75.00	45.00
(15)	Roger Connor	500.00	250.00	150.00
(16)	Abner Dalrymple	150.00	75.00	45.00
(17)	Jerry Denny	150.00	75.00	45.00
(18)	Jim Donelly	150.00	75.00	45.00
(19)	Sure Shot Dunlap	150.00	75.00	45.00
(20)	Dude Esterbrook	150.00	75.00	45.00
(21)	Buck Ewing	500.00	250.00	150.00
(22)	Sid Farrar	150.00	75.00	45.00
(23)	Silver Flint	150.00	75.00	45.00
(24)	Jim Fogarty	150.00	75.00	45.00
(25)	Elmer Foster	150.00	75.00	45.00
(26)	Pud Galvin	500.00	250.00	150.00
(27)	Charlie Getzein	150.00	75.00	45.00
(28)	Pebbly Jack Glasscock	250.00	125.00	75.00
(29)	Piano Legs Gore	150.00	75.00	45.00
(30)	Ned Hanlon	150.00	75.00	45.00
(31)	Paul Hines	150.00	75.00	45.00
(32)	Joe Hornung	150.00	75.00	45.00
(33)	Dummy Hoy	250.00	125.00	75.00
(34)	Cutrate Irwin (Philadelphia)	150.00	75.00	45.00
(35)	John Irwin (Washington)	150.00	75.00	45.00
(36)	Dick Johnston	150.00	75.00	45.00
(37)	Tim Keefe	500.00	250.00	150.00
(38)	King Kelly	500.00	250.00	150.00
(39)	Willie Kuehne	150.00	75.00	45.00
(40)	Connie Mack	750.00	375.00	225.00
(41)	Smiling Al Maul	150.00	75.00	45.00
(42)	Al Meyers (Myers) (Washington)	150.00	75.00	45.00
(43)	George Meyers (Myers) (Indianapolis)	150.00	75.00	45.00
(44)	Honest John Morrill	150.00	75.00	45.00
(45)	Joseph Mulvey	150.00	75.00	45.00
(46)	Billy Nash	150.00	75.00	45.00
(47)	Billy O'Brien	150.00	75.00	45.00
(48)	Orator Jim O'Rourke	500.00	250.00	150.00
(49)	Bob Pettit	150.00	75.00	45.00
(50)	Fred Pfeffer	150.00	75.00	45.00
(51)	Danny Richardson (New York)	150.00	75.00	45.00
(52)	Hardy Richardson (Detroit)	150.00	75.00	45.00
(53)	Jack Rowe	150.00	75.00	45.00
(54)	Jimmy Ryan	150.00	75.00	45.00
(55)	Emmett Seery	150.00	75.00	45.00
(56)	George Shoch	150.00	75.00	45.00
(57)	Otto Shomberg (Schomberg)	150.00	75.00	45.00
(58)	Pap Smith	150.00	75.00	45.00
(59)	Marty Sullivan	150.00	75.00	45.00
(60)	Billy Sunday	500.00	250.00	150.00
(61)	Ezra Sutton	150.00	75.00	45.00
(62)	Big Sam Thompson	500.00	250.00	150.00
(63)	Silent Mike Tiernan	150.00	75.00	45.00
(64)	Larry Twitchell	150.00	75.00	45.00
(65)	Rip Van Haltren	150.00	75.00	45.00
(66)	Monte Ward	500.00	250.00	150.00
(67)	Deacon White	150.00	75.00	45.00
(68)	Grasshopper Whitney	150.00	75.00	45.00
(69)	Ned Williamson	150.00	75.00	45.00
(70)	Watt Wilmot	150.00	75.00	45.00
(71)	Medoc Wise	150.00	75.00	45.00
(72)	George "Dandy" Wood	150.00	75.00	45.00

1904 WG2 Fan Craze
American League

One of the earliest 20th Century baseball card sets, this 1904 issue from the Fan Craze Company of Cincinnati was designed like a deck of playing cards and was intended to be used as a baseball table game. Separate sets were issued for the National League, which are printed in red, and the American League, which are blue. Both sets feature sepia-toned, black and white player portraits inside an oval with the player's name and team below. The top of the card indicates one of many various baseball plays, such as "Single," "Out at First," "Strike," "Stolen Base," etc. The unnumbered cards measure 2-1/2" by 3-1/2" and are identified as "An Artistic Constellation of Great Stars."

		NR MT	EX	VG
	Complete Set:	5000.	2500.	1500.
	Common Player:	50.00	25.00	15.00
(1)	Nick Altrock	50.00	25.00	15.00
(2)	Jim Barrett	50.00	25.00	15.00
(3)	Harry Bay	50.00	25.00	15.00
(4)	Albert Bender	100.00	50.00	30.00

		NR MT	EX	VG
(5)	Bill Bernhardt	50.00	25.00	15.00
(6)	W. Bradley	50.00	25.00	15.00
(7)	Jack Chesbro	250.00	125.00	75.00
(8)	Jimmy Collins	100.00	50.00	30.00
(9)	Sam Crawford	100.00	50.00	30.00
(10)	Lou Criger	50.00	25.00	15.00
(11)	Lave Cross	50.00	25.00	15.00
(12)	Monte Cross	50.00	25.00	15.00
(13)	Harry Davis	50.00	25.00	15.00
(14)	Bill Dinneen	50.00	25.00	15.00
(15)	Pat Donovan	50.00	25.00	15.00
(16)	Pat Dougherty	50.00	25.00	15.00
(17)	Norman Elberfield (Elberfeld)	50.00	25.00	15.00
(18)	Hoke Ferris (Hobe)	50.00	25.00	15.00
(19)	Elmer Flick	100.00	50.00	30.00
(20)	Buck Freeman	50.00	25.00	15.00
(21)	Fred Glade	50.00	25.00	15.00
(22)	Clark Griffith	100.00	50.00	30.00
(23)	Charley Hickman	50.00	25.00	15.00
(24)	Wm. Holmes	50.00	25.00	15.00
(25)	Harry Howell	50.00	25.00	15.00
(26)	Frank Isbel (Isbell)	50.00	25.00	15.00
(27)	Albert Jacobson	50.00	25.00	15.00
(28)	Ban Johnson	125.00	62.00	37.00
(29)	Fielder Jones	50.00	25.00	15.00
(30)	Adrian Joss	100.00	50.00	30.00
(31)	Billy Keeler	150.00	75.00	45.00
(32)	Napolean Lajoie	350.00	175.00	105.00
(33)	Connie Mack	325.00	162.00	100.00
(34)	Jimmy McAleer	50.00	25.00	15.00
(35)	Jim McGuire	50.00	25.00	15.00
(36)	Earl Moore	50.00	25.00	15.00
(37)	George Mullen (Mullin)	50.00	25.00	15.00
(38)	Billy Owen	50.00	25.00	15.00
(39)	Fred Parent	50.00	25.00	15.00
(40)	Case Patten	50.00	25.00	15.00
(41)	Ed Plank	50.00	25.00	15.00
(42)	Ossie Schreckengost	50.00	25.00	15.00
(43)	Jake Stahl	50.00	25.00	15.00
(44)	Fred Stone	50.00	25.00	15.00
(45)	Wm. Sudhoff	50.00	25.00	15.00
(46)	Roy Turner	50.00	25.00	15.00
(47)	G.E. Waddell	100.00	50.00	30.00
(48)	Bob Wallace	100.00	50.00	30.00
(49)	G. Harris White	50.00	25.00	15.00
(50)	Geo. Winters	50.00	25.00	15.00
(51)	Cy Young	450.00	225.00	135.00

1904 WG2 Fan Craze National League

Identical in size and format to the American League set, this series of unnumbered cards was issued by the Fan Craze Company of Cincinnati in 1904 and was designed like a deck of playing cards. The cards were intended to be used in playing a baseball table game. The National League cards are printed in red.

		NR MT	EX	VG
Complete Set:		5000.	2500.	1500.
Common Player:		50.00	25.00	15.00
(1)	Leon Ames	50.00	25.00	15.00
(2)	Clarence Beaumont	50.00	25.00	15.00
(3)	Jake Beckley	100.00	50.00	30.00
(4)	Billy Bergen	50.00	25.00	15.00
(5)	Roger Bresnahan	150.00	75.00	45.00
(6)	George Brown (Browne)	50.00	25.00	15.00
(7)	Mordacai Brown	200.00	100.00	60.00
(8)	Jas. Casey	50.00	25.00	15.00
(9)	Frank Chance	200.00	100.00	60.00
(10)	Fred Clarke	100.00	50.00	30.00
(11)	Thos. Corcoran	50.00	25.00	15.00
(12)	Bill Dahlen	50.00	25.00	15.00
(13)	Mike Donlin	50.00	25.00	15.00
(14)	Charley Dooin	50.00	25.00	15.00
(15)	Mickey Doolin (Doolan)	50.00	25.00	15.00
(16)	Hugh Duffy	100.00	50.00	30.00
(17)	John E. Dunleavy	50.00	25.00	15.00
(18)	Bob Ewing	50.00	25.00	15.00
(19)	"Chick" Fraser	50.00	25.00	15.00
(20)	J. Edward Hanlon	50.00	25.00	15.00
(21)	G.E. Howard	50.00	25.00	15.00
(22)	Miller Huggins	100.00	50.00	30.00
(23)	Joseph Kelley	100.00	50.00	30.00
(24)	John Kling	50.00	25.00	15.00
(25)	Tommy Leach	50.00	25.00	15.00
(26)	Harry Lumley	50.00	25.00	15.00
(27)	Carl Lundgren	50.00	25.00	15.00
(28)	Bill Maloney	50.00	25.00	15.00
(29)	Dan McGann	50.00	25.00	15.00
(30)	Joe McGinnity	125.00	62.00	37.00
(31)	John J. McGraw	325.00	167.00	100.00
(32)	Harry McIntire (McIntyre)	50.00	25.00	15.00
(33)	Charley Nichols	50.00	25.00	15.00
(34)	Mike O'Neil (O'Neill)	50.00	25.00	15.00
(35)	Orville Overall (Orval)	50.00	25.00	15.00
(36)	Frank Pfeffer	50.00	25.00	15.00
(37)	Deacon Phillippe	50.00	25.00	15.00
(38)	Charley Pittinger	50.00	25.00	15.00
(39)	Harry C. Pulliam	50.00	25.00	15.00
(40)	Claude Ritchey	50.00	25.00	15.00
(41)	Ed Ruelbach (Reulbach)	50.00	25.00	15.00
(42)	J. Bentley Seymour	50.00	25.00	15.00
(43)	Jim Sheckard	50.00	25.00	15.00
(44)	Jack Taylor	50.00	25.00	15.00
(45)	Luther H. Taylor	50.00	25.00	15.00
(46)	Fred Tenny (Tenney)	50.00	25.00	15.00
(47)	Harry Theilman	50.00	25.00	15.00
(48)	Roy Thomas	50.00	25.00	15.00
(49)	Hans Wagner	500.00	250.00	150.00
(50)	Jake Weimer	50.00	25.00	15.00
(51)	Bob Wicker	50.00	25.00	15.00
(52)	Victor Willis	50.00	25.00	15.00
(53)	Lew Wiltsie	50.00	25.00	15.00
(54)	Irving Young	50.00	25.00	15.00

1985 Wendy's Tigers

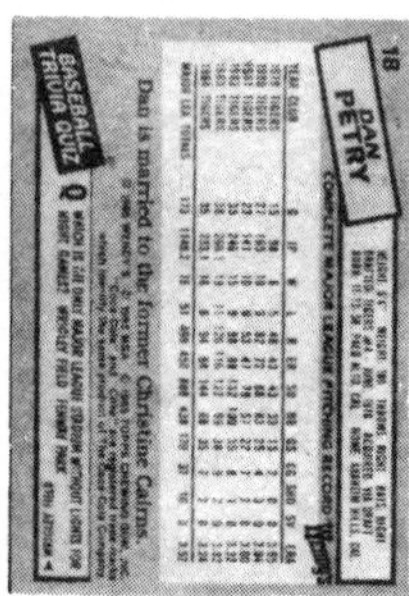

This 22-card set of cards measuring 2-1/2" by 3-1/2", which carry both Wendy's Hamburgers and Coca-Cola logos was produced by Topps. The cards feature a color photo with the player's team, name and position underneath the picture and the Wendy's logo in the lower left and Coke logo in the upper right. Backs are identical to 1985 Topps cards except they have different card numbers and are done in a red and black color scheme. Cards were distributed three to a pack along with a "Header" checklist in a cellophane package at selected Wendy's outlets in Michigan only.

		MT	NR MT	EX
Complete Set:		8.00	6.00	3.25
Common Player:		.15	.11	.06
1	Sparky Anderson	.30	.25	.12
2	Doug Bair	.15	.11	.06
3	Juan Berenguer	.15	.11	.06
4	Dave Bergman	.15	.11	.06
5	Tom Brookens	.15	.11	.06
6	Marty Castillo	.15	.11	.06
7	Darrell Evans	.40	.30	.15
8	Barbaro Garbey	.15	.11	.06
9	Kirk Gibson	1.00	.70	.40
10	Johnny Grubb	.15	.11	.06
11	Willie Hernandez	.25	.20	.10
12	Larry Herndon	.15	.11	.06
13	Rusty Kuntz	.15	.11	.06
14	Chet Lemon	.25	.20	.10
15	Aurelio Lopez	.15	.11	.06
16	Jack Morris	.80	.60	.30
17	Lance Parrish	.80	.60	.30
18	Dan Petry	.25	.20	.10
19	Bill Scherrer	.15	.11	.06
20	Alan Trammell	1.00	.70	.40
21	Lou Whitaker	.80	.60	.30
22	Milt Wilcox	.15	.11	.06

1974 Weston Expos

This 10-card set features members of the Montreal Expos. Each full-color card measures 3-1/2" by 5-1/2" and includes a facsimile autograph in black ink with the player's name printed along the bottom. The backs are distinct because they are divided in half. The top of the card lists player data and 1973 statistics in English, while the bottom carries the same information in French. The cards are numbered according to the player's uniform number.

		NR MT	EX	VG
Complete Set:		4.00	2.00	1.25
Common Player:		.40	.20	.12
3	Bob Bailey	.40	.20	.12
8	Boots Day	.40	.20	.12

		NR MT	EX	VG
12	John Boccabella	.40	.20	.12
16	Mike Jorgensen	.40	.20	.12
18	Steve Renko	.40	.20	.12
19	Tim Foli	.40	.20	.12
21	Ernie McAnally	.40	.20	.12
26	Bill Stoneman	.40	.20	.12
29	Ken Singleton	.60	.30	.20
33	Ron Hunt	.40	.20	.12

1935 Wheaties - Series 1

This set of 25 major leaguers was issued on the back of Wheaties cereal boxes in 1935 and, because of its design, is known as "Fancy Frame with Script Signature." The unnumbered cards measure 6" by 6-1/4" with frame, and 5" by 5-1/2" without the frame. The player photo is tinted blue, while the background is blue and orange. A facsimile autograph appears at the bottom of the photo.

		NR MT	EX	VG
Complete Set:		1500.	750.00	450.00
Common Player:		25.00	12.50	7.50
(1)	Jack Armstrong (batting)	25.00	12.50	7.50
(2)	Jack Armstrong (throwing)	25.00	12.50	7.50
(3)	Wally Berger	25.00	12.50	7.50
(4)	Tommy Bridges	25.00	12.50	7.50
(5a)	Mickey Cochrane (black hat)	50.00	25.00	15.00
(5b)	Michey Cochrane (white hat)	250.00	125.00	75.00
(6)	James "Rip" Collins	25.00	12.50	7.50
(7)	Dizzy Dean	100.00	50.00	30.00
(8)	Dizzy Dean, Paul Dean	70.00	35.00	21.00
(9)	Paul Dean	30.00	15.00	9.00
(10)	William Delancey	25.00	12.50	7.50
(11)	"Jimmie" Foxx	70.00	35.00	21.00
(12)	Frank Frisch	40.00	20.00	12.00
(13)	Lou Gehrig	300.00	150.00	90.00
(14)	Goose Goslin	40.00	20.00	12.00
(15)	Lefty Grove	60.00	30.00	18.00
(16)	Carl Hubbell	50.00	25.00	15.00
(17)	Travis C. Jackson	40.00	20.00	12.00
(18)	"Chuck" Klein	40.00	20.00	12.00
(19)	Gus Mancuso	25.00	12.50	7.50
(20)	Johnny "Pepper" Martin	30.00	15.00	9.00
(21)	Pepper Martin	30.00	15.00	9.00
(22)	Joe Medwick	40.00	20.00	12.00
(23)	Melvin Ott	60.00	30.00	18.00
(24)	Harold Schumacher	25.00	12.50	7.50
(25)	Al Simmons	40.00	20.00	12.00
(26)	"Jo Jo" White	25.00	12.50	7.50

1936 Wheaties - Series 3

Consisting of 12 unnumbered cards, this set is similar in size (6" by 6-1/4" with frame) and design to the Wheaties set of the previous year, but is known as "Fancy Frame with Printed Name and Data" because the cards also include a few printed words describing the player.

	NR MT	EX	VG
Complete Set:	700.00	350.00	210.00
Common Player:	25.00	12.50	7.50
(1) Earl Averill	40.00	20.00	12.00
(2) Mickey Cochrane	50.00	25.00	15.00
(3) Jimmy Foxx	60.00	30.00	18.00
(4) Lou Gehrig	300.00	150.00	90.00
(5) Hank Greenberg	50.00	25.00	15.00
(6) "Gabby" Hartnett	40.00	20.00	12.00
(7) Carl Hubbell	50.00	25.00	15.00
(8) "Pepper" Martin	20.00	10.00	6.00
(9) Van L. Mungo	25.00	12.50	7.50
(10) "Buck" Newsom	25.00	12.50	7.50
(11) "Arky" Vaughan	40.00	20.00	12.00
(12) Jimmy Wilson	25.00	12.50	7.50

1936 Wheaties - Series 4

This larger size (8-1/2" by 6") card also made up the back of a Wheaties box, and because of its distinctive border which featured drawings of small athletic figures, it is referred to as "Thin Orange Border/Figures in Border." Twelve major leaguers are pictured in the unnumbered set. The photos are enclosed in a 4" by 6-1/2" box. Below the photo is an endorsement for Wheaties, the "Breakfast of Champions," and a facsimile autograph.

	NR MT	EX	VG
Complete Set:	700.00	350.00	210.00
Common Player:	25.00	12.50	7.50
(1) Curt Davis	25.00	12.50	7.50
(2) Lou Gehrig	300.00	150.00	90.00
(3) Charley Gehringer	50.00	25.00	15.00
(4) Lefty Grove	60.00	30.00	18.00
(5) Rollie Hemsley	25.00	12.50	7.50
(6) Billy Herman	40.00	20.00	12.00
(7) Joe Medwick	40.00	20.00	12.00
(8) Mel Ott	60.00	30.00	18.00
(9) Schoolboy Rowe	25.00	12.50	7.50
(10) Arky Vaughan	40.00	20.00	12.00
(11) Joe Vosmik	25.00	12.50	7.50
(12) Lon Warneke	25.00	12.50	7.50

1936 Wheaties - Series 5

Often referred to as "How to Play Winning Baseball", this 12-card set features a large player photo surrounded by blue and white drawings that illustrate various playing tips. Different major leaguers offer advice on different aspects of the game. The cards again made up the back panel of a Wheaties box and measure 8-1/2" by 6-1/2". The cards are numbered from 1 through 12, and some of the panels are also found with a small number "28" followed by a letter from "A" through "L."

	NR MT	EX	VG
Complete Set:	600.00	300.00	180.00
Common Player:	25.00	12.50	7.50
1 Lefty Gomez	50.00	25.00	15.00
2 Billy Herman	40.00	20.00	12.00
3 Luke Appling	40.00	20.00	12.00
4 Jimmie Foxx	60.00	30.00	18.00
5 Joe Medwick	40.00	20.00	12.00
6 Charles Gehringer	40.00	20.00	12.00
7a Mel Ott (tips in vertical sequence)	60.00	30.00	18.00
7b Mel Ott (tips in two horizontal rows)	60.00	30.00	18.00
8 Odell Hale	25.00	12.50	7.50
9 Bill Dickey	60.00	30.00	18.00
10 "Lefty" Grove	60.00	30.00	18.00
11 Carl Hubbell	50.00	25.00	15.00
12 Earl Averill	40.00	20.00	12.00

1937 Wheaties - Series 6

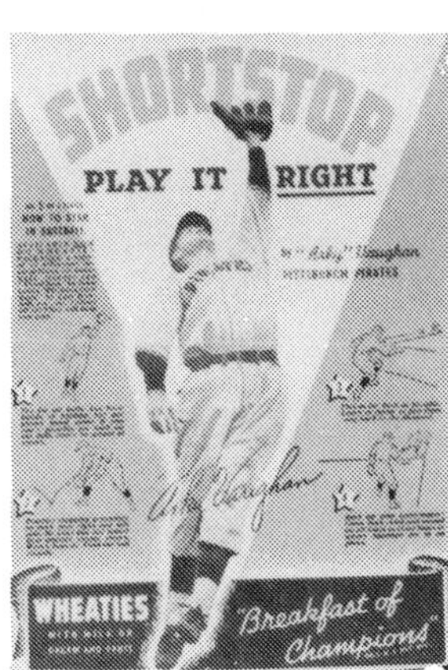

Similar to the Series 5 set, this numbered, 12-card series is known as "How to Star in Baseball" and again includes a large player photo with small instructional drawings to illustrate playing tips. The cards measure 8-1/4" by 6" and include a facsimile autograph.

	NR MT	EX	VG
Complete Set:	750.00	375.00	225.00
Common Player:	25.00	12.50	7.50
1 Bill Dickey	60.00	30.00	18.00
2 Red Ruffing	40.00	20.00	12.00
3 Zeke Bonura	25.00	12.50	7.50
4 Charlie Gehringer	50.00	25.00	15.00
5 "Arky" Vaughn (Vaughan)	25.00	12.50	7.50
6 Carl Hubbell	50.00	25.00	15.00
7 John Lewis	25.00	12.50	7.50
8 Heinie Manush	40.00	20.00	12.00
9 "Lefty" Grove	60.00	30.00	18.00
10 Billy Herman	40.00	20.00	12.00
11 Joe DiMaggio	300.00	150.00	90.00
12 Joe Medwick	40.00	20.00	12.00

1937 Wheaties - Series 7

This 15-card set of 6" by 8-1/4" panels contains several different card designs. One style (picturing Lombardi, Travis and Mungo) has a white background with an orange border and a large orange circle behind the player. Another design (showing Bonura, DiMaggio and Bridges) has the player outlined against a bright orange background with a Wheaties endorsement along

the bottom. A third format (picturing Moore, Radcliff and Martin) has a distinctive red, white and blue border. And a fourth design (featuring Trosky, Demaree and Vaughan) has a tilted picture against an orange background framed in blue and white. The set also includes three Pacific Coast League Players. The cards are numbered with a small "29" followed by a letter from "A" through "P." Card number "29N," which may be another PCL player, is unknown.

	NR MT	EX	VG
Complete Set:	650.00	325.00	195.00
Common Player:	25.00	12.50	7.50
29A "Zeke" Bonura	25.00	12.50	7.50
29B Cecil Travis	25.00	12.50	7.50
29C Frank Demaree	25.00	12.50	7.50
29D Joe Moore	25.00	12.50	7.50
29E Ernie Lombardi	40.00	20.00	12.00
29F John L. "Pepper" Martin	30.00	15.00	9.00
29G Harold Trosky	25.00	12.50	7.50
29H Raymond Radcliff	25.00	12.50	7.50
29I Joe DiMaggio	300.00	150.00	90.00
29J Tom Bridges	25.00	12.50	7.50
29K Van L. Mungo	25.00	12.50	7.50
29L "Arky" Vaughn (Vaughan)	40.00	20.00	12.00
29M Arnold Statz	200.00	100.00	60.00
29N Unknown	25.00	12.50	7.50
29O Fred Muller (Mueller)	200.00	100.00	60.00
29P Gene Lillard	200.00	100.00	60.00

1937 Wheaties - Series 8

Another series printed on the back of Wheaties boxes in 1937, the eight cards in this set are unnumbered and measure 8-1/2" by 6". There are several different designs, but in all of them the player photo is surrounded by speckles of color, causing this series to be known as the "Speckled Orange, White and Blue" series. A facsimile autograph is included, along with brief printed 1936 season statistics.

	NR MT	EX	VG
Complete Set:	675.00	337.00	202.00
Common Player:	40.00	20.00	12.00
(1) Luke Appling	40.00	20.00	12.00
(2) Earl Averill	40.00	20.00	12.00
(3) Joe DiMaggio	300.00	150.00	90.00
(4) Robert Feller	110.00	55.00	33.00
(5) Chas. Gehringer	50.00	25.00	15.00
(6) Lefty Grove	60.00	30.00	18.00
(7) Carl Hubbell	50.00	25.00	15.00
(8) Joe Medwick	40.00	20.00	12.00

1937 Wheaties - Series 9

This unnumbered set includes one player from each of the 16 major league teams and is generally referred to as the "Color Series." The cards measure 8-1/2" by 6" and were the back panels of Wheaties boxes. The player photos are shown inside or against large stars, circles, "V" shapes, rectangles and other geometrical designs. A facsimile autograph and team designation are printed near the photo, while a Wheaties endorsement and a line of player stats appear along the bottom.

		NR MT	EX	VG
Complete Set:		900.00	450.00	270.00
Common Player:		25.00	12.50	7.50
(1)	Zeke Bonura	25.00	12.50	7.50
(2)	Tom Bridges	25.00	12.50	7.50
(3)	Harland Clift (Harlond)	25.00	12.50	7.50
(4)	Kiki Cuyler	40.00	20.00	12.00
(5)	Joe DiMaggio	300.00	150.00	90.00
(6)	Robert Feller	110.00	55.00	33.00
(7)	Lefty Grove	60.00	30.00	18.00
(8)	Billy Herman	40.00	20.00	12.00
(9)	Carl Hubbell	50.00	25.00	15.00
(10)	Buck Jordan	25.00	12.50	7.50
(11)	"Pepper" Martin	20.00	10.00	6.00
(12)	John Moore	25.00	12.50	7.50
(13)	Wally Moses	25.00	12.50	7.50
(14)	Van L. Mungo	25.00	12.50	7.50
(15)	Cecil Travis	25.00	12.50	7.50
(16)	Arky Vaughan	40.00	20.00	12.00

1937 Wheaties - Series 14

Much reduced in size (2-5/8" by 3-7/8"), these unnumbered cards made up the back panels of single-serving size Wheaties boxes. The player photo (which is sometimes identical to the photos used in the larger series) is set against an orange or white background. The player's name appears in large capital letters with his position and team in smaller capitals. A facsimile autograph and Wheaties endorsement is also included. Some cards are also found with the number "29" followed by a letter.

		NR MT	EX	VG
Complete Set:		1350.	675.00	405.00
Common Player:		50.00	25.00	15.00
(1)	"Zeke" Bonura	50.00	25.00	15.00
(2)	Tom Bridges	50.00	25.00	15.00
(3)	Dolph Camilli	50.00	25.00	15.00
(4)	Frank Demaree	50.00	25.00	15.00
(5)	Joe DiMaggio	400.00	200.00	120.00
(6)	Billy Herman	90.00	45.00	27.00
(7)	Carl Hubbell	100.00	50.00	30.00
(8)	Ernie Lombardi	90.00	45.00	27.00
(9)	"Pepper" Martin	60.00	30.00	18.00
(10)	Joe Moore	50.00	25.00	15.00
(11)	Van Mungo	50.00	25.00	15.00
(12)	Mel Ott	125.00	62.00	37.00
(13)	Raymond Radcliff	50.00	25.00	15.00
(14)	Cecil Travis	50.00	25.00	15.00
(15)	Harold Trosky	50.00	25.00	15.00
(16a)	"Arky" Vaughan (29L on card)	90.00	45.00	27.00
(16b)	"Arky" Vaughan (no 29L on card)	90.00	45.00	27.00

1938 Wheaties - Series 10

One player from each major league team is included in this 16-card set, referred to as the "Biggest Thrills in Baseball" series. Measuring 8-1/2" by 6", each numbered card was the back panel of a Wheaties box and pictures a player along with a printed description of his biggest thrill in baseball and facsimile autograph. All 16 cards in this series have also been found on paper stock.

		NR MT	EX	VG
Complete Set:		550.00	275.00	165.00
Common Player:		25.00	12.50	7.50
1	Bob Feller	110.00	55.00	33.00
2	Cecil Travis	25.00	12.50	7.50
3	Joe Medwick	40.00	20.00	12.00
4	Gerald Walker	25.00	12.50	7.50
5	Carl Hubbell	50.00	25.00	15.00
6	Bob Johnson	25.00	12.50	7.50
7	Beau Bell	25.00	12.50	7.50
8	Ernie Lombardi	40.00	20.00	12.00
9	Lefty Grove	60.00	30.00	18.00
10	Lou Fette	25.00	12.50	7.50
11	Joe DiMaggio	300.00	150.00	90.00
12	Art Whitney	25.00	12.50	7.50
13	Dizzy Dean	110.00	55.00	33.00
14	Charley Gehringer	50.00	25.00	15.00
15	Paul Waner	40.00	20.00	12.00
16	Dolf Camilli	25.00	12.50	7.50

1938 Wheaties - Series 11

Cards in this unnumbered, eight-card series measure 8-1/4" by 6" and show the players in street clothes either eating or getting ready to enjoy a bowl of Wheaties. Sometimes a waitress or other person also appears in the photo. The set is sometimes called the "Dress Clothes" or" Civies" series.

		NR MT	EX	VG
Complete Set:		225.00	112.00	67.00
Common Player:		25.00	12.50	7.50
(1)	Lou Fette	25.00	12.50	7.50
(2)	Jimmie Foxx	75.00	37.00	22.00
(3)	Charlie Gehringer	50.00	25.00	15.00
(4)	Lefty Grove	60.00	30.00	18.00
(5)	Hank Greenberg, Roxie Lawson	50.00	25.00	15.00
(6)	Lee Grissom, Ernie Lombardi	40.00	20.00	12.00
(7)	Joe Medwick	40.00	20.00	12.00
(8)	Lon Warneke	25.00	12.50	7.50

1938 Wheaties - Series 15

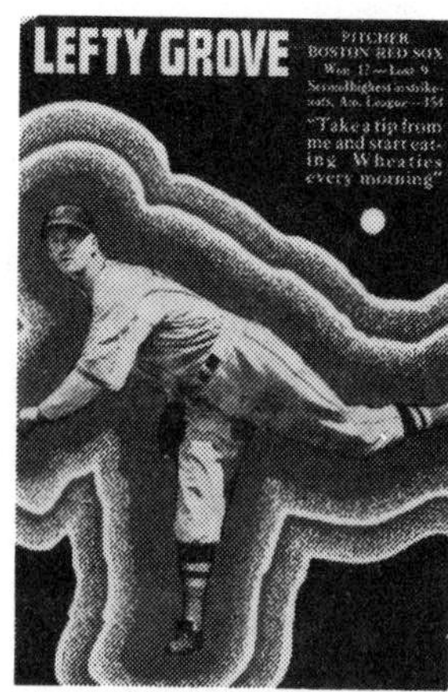

Another set of small (2-5/8" by 3-7/8") cards, the photos in this unnumbered series made up the back panels of single-serving size Wheaties boxes. The panels have orange, blue and white backgrounds, and some of the photos are the same as those used in the larger Wheaties panels.

		NR MT	EX	VG
Complete Set:		1400.	700.00	420.00
Common Player:		50.00	25.00	15.00
(1)	"Zeke" Bonura	50.00	25.00	15.00
(2)	Joe DiMaggio	400.00	200.00	120.00
(3)	Charles Gehringer (batting)	125.00	62.00	37.00
(4)	Chas. Gehringer (leaping)	125.00	62.00	37.00
(5)	Hank Greenberg	125.00	62.00	37.00
(6)	Lefty Grove	150.00	75.00	45.00
(7)	Carl Hubbell	110.00	55.00	33.00
(8)	John (Buddy) Lewis	50.00	25.00	15.00
(9)	Heinie Manush	90.00	45.00	27.00
(10)	Joe Medwick	90.00	45.00	27.00
(11)	Arky Vaughan	90.00	45.00	27.00

1939 Wheaties - Series 12

The nine cards in this numbered series, known as the "Personal Pointers" series, measure 8-1/4" by 6" and feature an instructional format similar to earlier Wheaties issues. The cards feature a player photo along with printed tips on various aspects of hitting and pitching.

	NR MT	EX	VG
Complete Set:	450.00	225.00	135.00

		NR MT	EX	VG
Common Player:		25.00	12.50	7.50
1	Ernie Lombardi	40.00	20.00	12.00
2	Johnny Allen	25.00	12.50	7.50
3	Lefty Gomez	45.00	22.00	13.50
4	Bill Lee	25.00	12.50	7.50
5	Jimmie Foxx	90.00	45.00	27.00
6	Joe Medwick	40.00	20.00	12.00
7	Hank Greenberg	60.00	30.00	18.00
8	Mel Ott	60.00	30.00	18.00
9	Arky Vaughn (Vaughan)	40.00	20.00	12.00

1939 Wheaties - Series 13

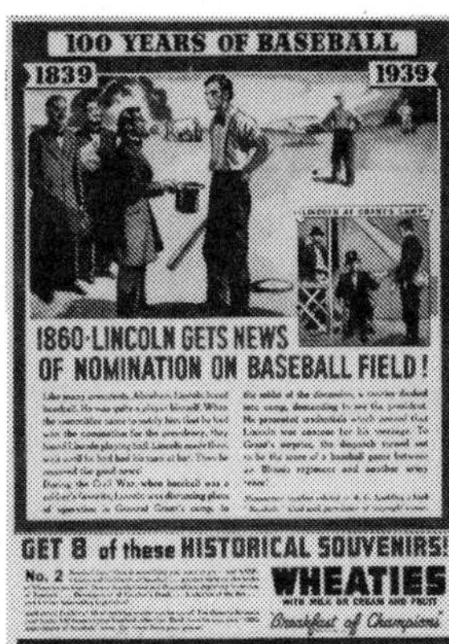

Issued in baseball's centennial year of 1939, this set of eight 6" by 6-3/4" cards commemorates "100 Years of Baseball," and each of the numbered panels illustrates a significant event in baseball history.

		NR MT	EX	VG
Complete Set:		200.00	100.00	60.00
Common Panel:		25.00	12.50	7.50
1	Design of First Diamond - 1838 (Abner Doubleday)	25.00	12.50	7.50
2	Gets News of Nomination on Field - 1860 (Abraham Lincoln)	25.00	12.50	7.50
3	Crowd Boos First Baseball Glove - 1869	25.00	12.50	7.50
4	Curve Ball Just an Illusion - 1877	25.00	12.50	7.50
5	Fencer's Mask is Pattern - 1877	25.00	12.50	7.50
6	Baseball Gets "All Dressed Up" - 1895	25.00	12.50	7.50
7	Modern Bludgeon Enters Game - 1895	25.00	12.50	7.50
8	"Casey at the Bat"	25.00	12.50	7.50

1940 Wheaties Champs of the USA

This numbered set consists of 13 panels, each picturing one baseball player and two other athletes (football stars, golfers, skaters, racers, etc.). The entire panel measures approximately 8-1/4" by 6", while the actual card measures approximately 6" square. Each athlete is pictured in what looks like a postage stamp with a serrated edge. A brief biography appears alongside the "stamp." Some variations are known to exist among the first nine panels. The cards are numbered in the upper right corner.

		NR MT	EX	VG
Complete Set:		850.00	425.00	255.00
Common Panel:		25.00	12.50	7.50
1A	Bob Feller, Lynn Patrick, Charles "Red" Ruffling	75.00	37.00	22.00
1B	Leo Durocher, Lynn Patrick, Charles "Red" Ruffing	50.00	25.00	15.00
2A	Joe DiMaggio, Don Duge, Hank Greenberg	200.00	100.00	60.00
2B	Joe DiMaggio, Mel Ott, Ellsworth Vines	200.00	100.00	60.00
3	Bernie Bierman, Bill Dickey, Jimmie Foxx	75.00	37.00	22.00
4	Morris Arnovich, Capt R.K. Baker, Earl "Dutch" Clark	25.00	12.50	7.50
5	Madison (Matty) Bell, Ab Jenkins, Joe Medwick	25.00	12.50	7.50
6A	Ralph Guldahl, John Mize, Davey O'Brien	25.00	12.50	7.50
6B	Bob Feller, John Mize, Rudy York	50.00	25.00	15.00
6C	Ralph Guldahl, Gabby Hartnett, Davey O'Brien	25.00	12.50	7.50
7A	Joe Cronin, Cecil Isbell, Byron Nelson	25.00	12.50	7.50
7B	Joe Cronin, Hank Greenberg, Byron Nelson	40.00	20.00	12.00
7C	Paul Derringer, Cecil Isbell, Byron Nelson	25.00	12.50	7.50
8A	Ernie Lombardi, Jack Manders, George I. Myers	25.00	12.50	7.50
8B	Paul Derringer, Ernie Lombardi, George I. Myers	25.00	12.50	7.50
9	Bob Bartlett, Captain R.C. Hanson, Terrell Jacobs	25.00	12.50	7.50
10	Lowell "Red" Dawson, Billy Herman, Adele Inge	25.00	12.50	7.50
11	Dolph Camilli, Antoinette Concello, Wallace Wade	25.00	12.50	7.50
12	Luke Appling, Stanley Hack, Hugh McManus	25.00	12.50	7.50
13	Felix Adler, Hal Trosky, Mabel Vinson	25.00	12.50	7.50

1941 Wheaties Champs of the USA

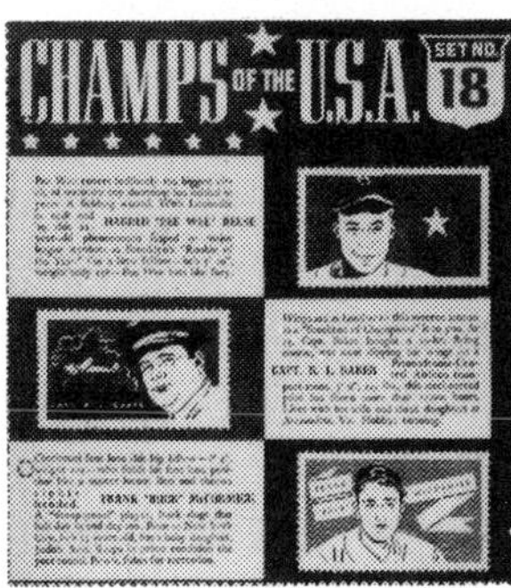

This eight-card series is actually a continuation of the previous year's Wheaties set, and the format is identical. The set begins with number 14, starting where the 1940 set ended.

		NR MT	EX	VG
Complete Set:		375.00	187.00	112.00
Common Panel:		25.00	12.50	7.50
14	Felix Adler, Jimmie Foxx, Capt. R.G. Hanson	50.00	25.00	15.00
15	Bernie Bierman, Bob Feller, Jessie McLeod	50.00	25.00	15.00
16	Lowell "Red" Dawson, Hank Greenberg, J.W. Stoker	30.00	15.00	9.00
17	Antoinette Concello, Joe DiMaggio, Byron Nelson	200.00	100.00	60.00
18	Capt. R.L. Baker, Frank "Buck" McCormick, Harold "Pee Wee" Reese	50.00	25.00	15.00
19	William W. Robbins, Gene Sarazen, Gerald "Gee" Walker	25.00	12.50	7.50
20	Harry Danning, Barney McCosky, Bucky Walters	25.00	12.50	7.50
21	Joe "Flash" Gordon, Stan Hack, George I. Myers	25.00	12.50	7.50

1951 Wheaties

Printed as the backs of single-serving size boxes of Wheaties, the six-card 1951 set includes three baseball players and one football player, basketball player and golfer. Well-trimmed cards measure 2-1/2" by 3-1/4". The cards feature blue line drawings of the athletes with a facsimile autograph and descriptive title below. There is a wide white border.

		NR MT	EX	VG
Complete Set:		600.00	300.00	180.00
Common Player:		50.00	25.00	15.00
(1)	Bob Feller (baseball)	125.00	62.00	37.00
(2)	John Lujack (football)	75.00	38.00	23.00
(3)	George K. Mikan (basketball)	125.00	62.00	37.00
(4)	Stan Musial (baseball)	150.00	75.00	45.00
(5)	Sam Snead (golfer)	50.00	25.00	15.00
(6)	Ted Williams (baseball)	200.00	100.00	60.00

1952 Wheaties

These 2" by 2-3/4" cards appeared on the back of the popular cereal boxes. Actually, sports figures had been appearing on the backs of the boxes for many years, but in 1952, of the 30 athletes depicted, 10 were baseball players. That means there are 20 baseball cards, as each player appears in both a portrait and an action drawing. The cards have a blue line drawing on an orange background with a white border. The player's name, team, and position appear at the bottom. The cards have rounded corners and are not widely collected because they have an outdated look, are mixed with other athletes and are often poorly cut from the boxes.

		NR MT	EX	VG
Complete Set:		800.00	400.00	240.00
Common Player:		15.00	7.50	4.50
(1)	Larry "Yogi" Berra (portrait)	50.00	25.00	15.00
(2)	Larry "Yogi" Berra (action pose)	50.00	25.00	15.00
(3)	Roy Campanella (portrait)	50.00	25.00	15.00
(4)	Roy Campanella (action pose)	50.00	25.00	15.00
(5)	Bob Feller (portrait)	40.00	20.00	12.00
(6)	Bob Feller (action pose)	40.00	20.00	12.00
(7)	George Kell (portrait)	18.00	9.00	5.50
(8)	George Kell (action pose)	18.00	9.00	5.50
(9)	Ralph Kiner (portrait)	25.00	12.50	7.50
(10)	Ralph Kiner (action pose)	25.00	12.50	7.50
(11)	Bob Lemon (portrait)	25.00	12.50	7.50
(12)	Bob Lemon (action pose)	25.00	12.50	7.50
(13)	Stan Musial (portrait)	75.00	37.00	22.00
(14)	Stan Musial (action pose)	75.00	37.00	22.00
(15)	Phil Rizzuto (portrait)	30.00	15.00	9.00
(16)	Phil Rizzuto (action pose)	30.00	15.00	9.00
(17)	Elwin "Preacher" Roe (portrait)	15.00	7.50	4.50
(18)	Elwin "Preacher" Roe (action pose)	15.00	7.50	4.50
(19)	Ted Williams (portrait)	80.00	40.00	24.00
(20)	Ted Williams (action pose)	80.00	40.00	24.00

1982 Wheaties Indians

These 2-13/16" by 4-1/8" cards were given out ten at a time during three special promotional games; later the complete set was placed on sale at the Indians' gift shop. The 30-card set represented the first time in 30 years that Wheaties had been associated with a baseball card set. The cards feature color photos surrounded by a wide white border with the player's name and position below the picture. The Indians logo is in the lower left corner while the Wheaties logo is in the lower right. Card backs have a Wheaties ad.

	MT	NR MT	EX
Complete Set:	10.00	7.50	4.00
Common Player:	.25	.20	.10

EATIES FOR WHEATIES
—that undeniable, irresistible urge for the crispy, crunchy whole wheat taste of

		NR MT	EX	VG
(1)	Chris Bando	.25	.20	.10
(2)	Alan Bannister	.25	.20	.10
(3)	Len Barker	.40	.30	.15
(4)	Bert Blyleven	.90	.70	.35
(5)	Tom Brennan	.25	.20	.10
(6)	Joe Charboneau	.40	.30	.15
(7)	Rodney Craig	.25	.20	.10
(8)	John Denny	.40	.30	.15
(9)	Miguel Dilone	.25	.20	.10
(10)	Jerry Dybzinski	.25	.20	.10
(11)	Mike Fischlin	.25	.20	.10
(12)	Dave Garcia	.25	.20	.10
(13)	Johnny Goryl	.25	.20	.10
(14)	Mike Hargrove	.40	.30	.15
(15)	Toby Harrah	.40	.30	.15
(16)	Ron Hassey	.25	.20	.10
(17)	Von Hayes	1.25	.90	.50
(18)	Dennis Lewallyn	.25	.20	.10
(19)	Rick Manning	.25	.20	.10
(20)	Bake McBride	.25	.20	.10
(21)	Tommy McCraw	.25	.20	.10
(22)	Jack Perconte	.25	.20	.10
(23)	Mel Queen	.25	.20	.10
(24)	Dennis Sommers	.25	.20	.10
(25)	Lary Sorensen	.25	.20	.10
(26)	Dan Spillner	.25	.20	.10
(27)	Rick Sutcliffe	.90	.70	.35
(28)	Andre Thornton	.50	.40	.20
(29)	Rick Waits	.25	.20	.10
(30)	Eddie Whitson	.50	.40	.20

1983 Wheaties Indians

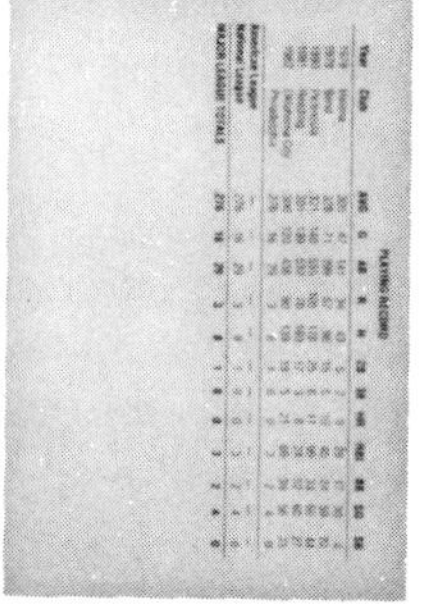

A 32-card set marked the second year of Wheaties involvement with the Indians. Distribution of the 2- 13/16" by 4-1/8" cards changed slightly in that the entire set was given away on the day of the special promotional game. As happened in 1982, the set was then placed on sale at the team's gift shop. The set includes 27 players, four coaches and the manager. The format of the cards remained basically the same on the front although the backs of player cards were changed to include complete major and minor league statistics.

		MT	NR MT	EX
Complete Set:		8.00	6.00	3.25
Common Player:		.15	.11	.06
(1)	Bud Anderson	.15	.11	.06
(2)	Jay Baller	.20	.15	.08
(3)	Chris Bando	.15	.11	.06
(4)	Alan Bannister	.15	.11	.06
(5)	Len Barker	.25	.20	.10
(6)	Bert Blyleven	.60	.45	.25
(7)	Wil Culmer	.15	.11	.06
(8)	Miguel Dilone	.15	.11	.06
(9)	Juan Eichelberger	.15	.11	.06
(10)	Jim Essian	.15	.11	.06
(11)	Mike Ferraro	.15	.11	.06
(12)	Mike Fischlin	.15	.11	.06
(13)	Julio Franco	1.25	.90	.50
(14)	Ed Glynn	.15	.11	.06
(15)	Johnny Goryl	.15	.11	.06
(16)	Mike Hargrove	.25	.20	.10
(17)	Toby Harrah	.25	.20	.10
(18)	Ron Hassey	.15	.11	.06
(19)	Neal Heaton	.35	.25	.14
(20)	Rick Manning	.15	.11	.06
(21)	Bake McBride	.15	.11	.06

		NR MT	EX	VG
(22)	Don McMahon	.15	.11	.06
(23)	Ed Napoleon	.15	.11	.06
(24)	Broderick Perkins	.15	.11	.06
(25)	Dennis Sommers	.15	.11	.06
(26)	Lary Sorensen	.15	.11	.06
(27)	Dan Spillner	.15	.11	.06
(28)	Rick Sutcliffe	.60	.45	.25
(29)	Andre Thornton	.50	.40	.20
(30)	Manny Trillo	.25	.20	.10
(31)	George Vukovich	.15	.11	.06
(32)	Rick Waits	.15	.11	.06

1984 Wheaties Indians

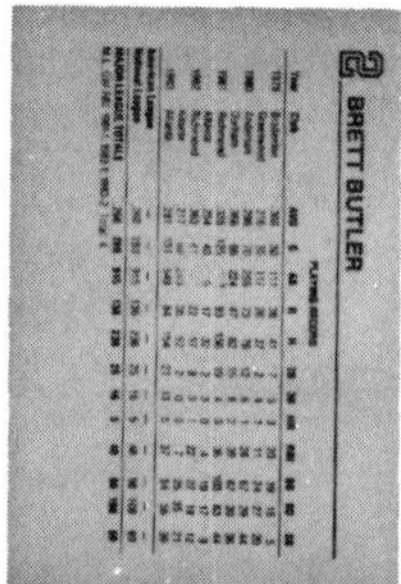

The 2-13/16" by 4-1/8" cards again were given out at Municipal Stadium as part of a promotion involving Wheaties and the Indians on July 22. The set was down from 32 cards in 1983 to 29. There are 26 players as well as cards for the manager, coaches and team mascot, Tom-E-Hawk. Designs of the cards are identical to prior years. The 1984 set is numbered by uniform number. A total of 15,000 sets were printed and any left over from the promotion were placed on sale in the team's gift shop.

		MT	NR MT	EX
Complete Set		9.00	6.75	3.50
Common Player		.15	.11	.06
2	Brett Butler	.40	.30	.15
4	Tony Bernazard	.20	.15	.08
8	Carmelo Castillo	.15	.11	.06
10	Pat Tabler	.50	.40	.20
13	Ernie Camacho	.15	.11	.06
14	Julio Franco	1.00	.70	.40
15	Broderick Perkins	.15	.11	.06
16	Jerry Willard	.15	.11	.06
18	Pat Corrales	.15	.11	.06
21	Mike Hargrove	.25	.20	.10
22	Mike Fischlin	.15	.11	.06
23	Chris Bando	.15	.11	.06
24	George Vukovich	.15	.11	.06
26	Brook Jacoby	.80	.60	.30
27	Steve Farr	.25	.20	.10
28	Bert Blyleven	.60	.45	.25
29	Andre Thornton	.50	.40	.20
30	Joe Carter	1.50	1.25	.60
31	Steve Comer	.15	.11	.06
33	Roy Smith	.15	.11	.06
34	Mel Hall	.40	.30	.15
36	Jamie Easterly	.15	.11	.06
37	Don Schulze	.20	.15	.08
38	Luis Aponte	.15	.11	.06
44	Neal Heaton	.25	.20	.10
46	Mike Jeffcoat	.15	.11	.06
54	Tom Waddell	.20	.15	.08
---	Coaching Staff (Bobby Bonds, John Goryl, Don McMahon, Ed Napoleon, Dennis Sommers)	.15	.11	.06
---	Tom-E-Hawk (mascot)	.15	.11	.06

1954 Wilson Franks

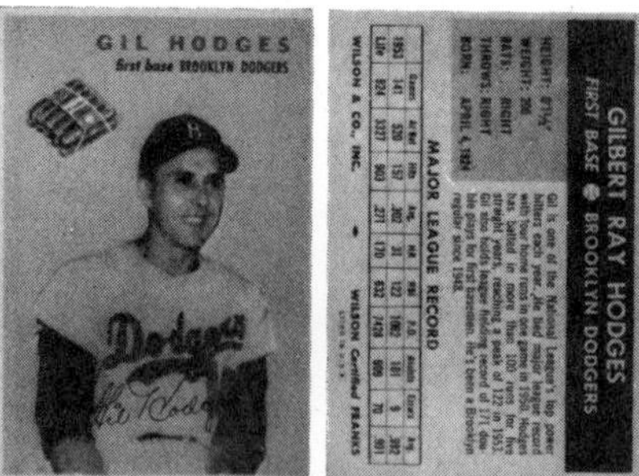

first base BROOKLYN DODGERS

FIRST BASE ◆ BROOKLYN DODGERS

The 2-5/8" by 3-3/4" cards are among the most popular and difficult to find baseball card sets issued with hot dogs during the 1950s. The cards feature color-added photos on the front where the player's name, team and position appear at the top. The front also has a facsimile autograph and a color picture of a package of Wilson's frankfurters. The card backs feature personal information, a short career summary and 1953 and career statistics. The 20-card set includes players from a number of teams and was distributed nationally in the frankfurter packages. The problem with such distribution is that the cards are very tough to find without grease stains from the hot dogs.

		NR MT	EX	VG
Complete Set:		6500.	3250.	1950.
Common Player:		175.00	87.00	52.00
(1)	Roy Campanella	750.00	375.00	225.00
(2)	Del Ennis	175.00	87.00	52.00
(3)	Carl Erskine	200.00	100.00	60.00
(4)	Ferris Fain	175.00	87.00	52.00
(5)	Bob Feller	600.00	300.00	180.00
(6)	Nelson Fox	300.00	150.00	90.00
(7)	Johnny Groth	175.00	87.00	52.00
(8)	Stan Hack	175.00	87.00	52.00
(9)	Gil Hodges	500.00	250.00	150.00
(10)	Ray Jablonski	175.00	87.00	52.00
(11)	Harvey Kuenn	200.00	100.00	60.00
(12)	Roy McMillan	175.00	87.00	52.00
(13)	Andy Pafko	175.00	87.00	52.00
(14)	Paul Richards	175.00	87.00	52.00
(15)	Hank Sauer	175.00	87.00	52.00
(16)	Red Schoendienst	200.00	100.00	60.00
(17)	Enos Slaughter	400.00	200.00	120.00
(18)	Vern Stephens	175.00	87.00	52.00
(19)	Sammy White	175.00	87.00	52.00
(20)	Ted Williams	3000.	1500.	900.00

1988 Woolworth

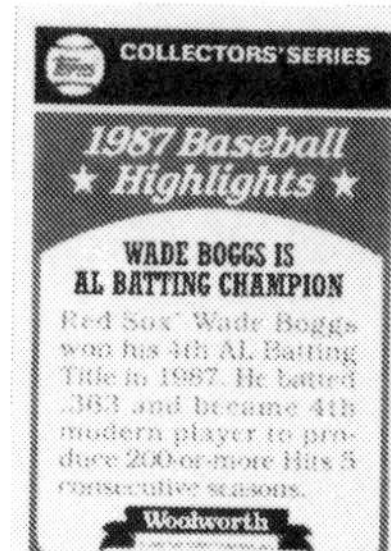

COLLECTORS' SERIES
1987 Baseball
★ Highlights ★
WADE BOGGS IS
AL BATTING CHAMPION
Red Sox' Wade Boggs won his 4th AL Batting Title in 1987. He batted .363 and became 4th modern player to produce 200-or-more Hits 5 consecutive seasons.
Woolworth

This 33-card boxed set was produced by Topps for exclusive distribution at Woolworth stores. The set includes 18 individual player cards and 15 World Series game action photo cards. World Series cards include two for each game of the Series, plus a card of 1987 Series MVP Frank Viola. Card front carry a Woolworth's Baseball Highlights heading on a red and yellow banner above the blue-bordered super glossy player photo. A white-lettered caption beneath the photo consists of either the player's name or a World Series game notation. Card backs are red, white and blue and contain the Topps logo, card number and "Collector's Series" label above a "1987 Baseball Highlights" logo and a brief description of the photo on the front.

		MT	NR MT	EX
Complete Set:		5.00	3.75	2.00
Common Player:		.09	.07	.04
1	Don Baylor	.12	.09	.05
2	Vince Coleman	.15	.11	.06
3	Darrell Evans	.12	.09	.05
4	Don Mattingly	1.50	1.25	.60
5	Eddie Murray	.30	.25	.12
6	Nolan Ryan	.30	.25	.12
7	Mike Schmidt	.35	.25	.14
8	Andre Dawson	.20	.15	.08
9	George Bell	.25	.20	.10
10	Steve Bedrosian	.12	.09	.05
11	Roger Clemens	.50	.40	.20
12	Tony Gwynn	.35	.25	.14
13	Wade Boggs	1.00	.70	.40
14	Benny Santiago	.35	.25	.14
15	Mark McGwire	.80	.60	.30
16	Dave Righetti	.15	.11	.06
17	Jeffrey Leonard	.09	.07	.04
18	Gary Gaetti	.12	.09	.05
19	World Series Game #1 (Frank Viola)	.12	.09	.05
20	World Series Game #1 (Dan Gladden)	.09	.07	.04
21	World Series Game #2 (Bert Blyleven)	.12	.09	.05
22	World Series Game #2 (Gary Gaetti)	.12	.09	.05
23	World Series Game #3 (John Tudor)	.12	.09	.05
24	World Series Game #3 (Todd Worrell)	.12	.09	.05
25	World Series Game #4 (Tom Lawless)	.09	.07	.04
26	World Series Game #4 (Willie McGee)			

		NR MT	EX	VG
		.12	.09	.05
27	World Series Game #5 (Danny Cox)	.09	.07	.04
28	World Series Game #5 (Curt Ford)	.09	.07	.04
29	World Series Game #6 (Don Baylor)	.12	.09	.05
30	World Series Game #6 (Kent Hrbek)	.15	.11	.06
31	World Series Game #7 (Kirby Puckett)	.25	.20	.10
32	World Series Game #7 (Greg Gagne)	.09	.07	.04
33	World Series MVP (Frank Viola)	.12	.09	.05

1928 Yeungling's Ice Cream

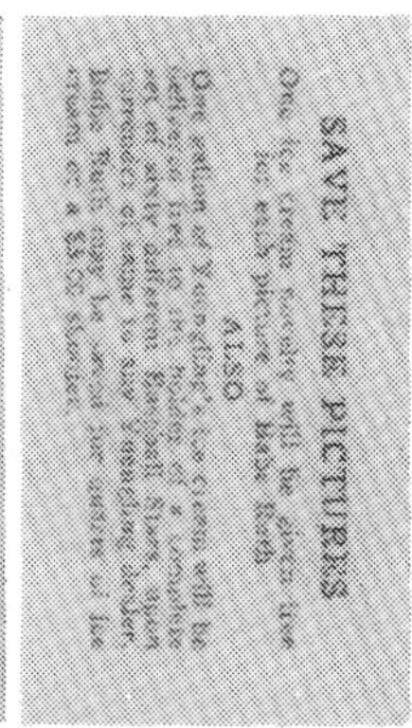

Issued in 1928, the Yeungling's Ice Cream issue consists of 60 black and white cards that measure 1-3/8" by 2-1/2". The photos are similar to those used in the E210 and W502 sets. Other ice cream companies such as Harrington's and Tharp's produced sets closely related to the Yeungling's issue. Collectors could redeem an entire set of Yeungling's cards for a gallon of ice cream or turn in a Babe Ruth card from the set for quarts of ice cream or a scooter valued at $5.

		NR MT	EX	VG
Complete Set:		2000.	1000.	600.00
Common Player:		12.00	6.00	3.50
1	Burleigh Grimes	25.00	12.50	7.50
2	Walter Reuther	12.00	6.00	3.50
3	Joe Dugan	15.00	7.50	4.50
4	Red Faber	25.00	12.50	7.50
5	Gabby Hartnett	25.00	12.50	7.50
6	Babe Ruth	350.00	175.00	105.00
7	Bob Meusel	15.00	7.50	4.50
8	Herb Pennock	25.00	12.50	7.50
9	George Burns	12.00	6.00	3.50
10	Joe Sewell	25.00	12.50	7.50
11	George Uhle	12.00	6.00	3.50
12	Bob O'Farrell	12.00	6.00	3.50
13	Rogers Hornsby	75.00	37.00	22.00
14	"Pie" Traynor	25.00	12.50	7.50
15	Clarence Mitchell	12.00	6.00	3.50
16	Eppa Rixey	25.00	12.50	7.50
17	Carl Mays	15.00	7.50	4.50
18	Adolfo Luque	12.00	6.00	3.50
19	Dave Bancroft	25.00	12.50	7.50
20	George Kelly	25.00	12.50	7.50
21	Earl Combs (Earle)	25.00	12.50	7.50
22	Harry Heilmann	25.00	12.50	7.50
23	Ray W. Schalk	25.00	12.50	7.50
24	Johnny Mostil	12.00	6.00	3.50
25	Hack Wilson	25.00	12.50	7.50
26	Lou Gehrig	200.00	100.00	60.00
27	Ty Cobb	200.00	100.00	60.00
28	Tris Speaker	35.00	17.50	10.50
29	Tony Lazzeri	20.00	10.00	6.00
30	Waite Hoyt	25.00	12.50	7.50
31	Sherwood Smith	12.00	6.00	3.50
32	Max Carey	25.00	12.50	7.50
33	Eugene Hargrave	12.00	6.00	3.50
34	Miguel L. Gonzales	12.00	6.00	3.50
35	Joe Judge	12.00	6.00	3.50
36	E.C. (Sam) Rice	25.00	12.50	7.50
37	Earl Sheely	12.00	6.00	3.50
38	Sam Jones	12.00	6.00	3.50
39	Bib A. Falk (Bibb)	12.00	6.00	3.50
40	Willie Kamm	12.00	6.00	3.50
41	Stanley Harris	25.00	12.50	7.50
42	John J. McGraw	30.00	15.00	9.00
43	Artie Nehf	12.00	6.00	3.50
44	Grover Alexander	35.00	17.50	10.50
45	Paul Waner	25.00	12.50	7.50
46	William H. Terry	30.00	15.00	9.00
47	Glenn Wright	12.00	6.00	3.50
48	Earl Smith	12.00	6.00	3.50
49	Leon (Goose) Goslin	25.00	12.50	7.50
50	Frank Frisch	25.00	12.50	7.50
51	Joe Harris	12.00	6.00	3.50
52	Fred (Cy) Williams	15.00	7.50	4.50
53	Eddie Roush	25.00	12.50	7.50
54	George Sisler	25.00	12.50	7.50
55	Ed. Rommel	12.00	6.00	3.50
56	Roger Peckinpaugh	12.00	6.00	3.50
57	Stanley Coveleskie (Coveleski)	25.00	12.50	7.50
58	Lester Bell	12.00	6.00	3.50
59	L. Waner	25.00	12.50	7.50
60	John P. McInnis	12.00	6.00	3.50

Z

1982 Zellers Expos

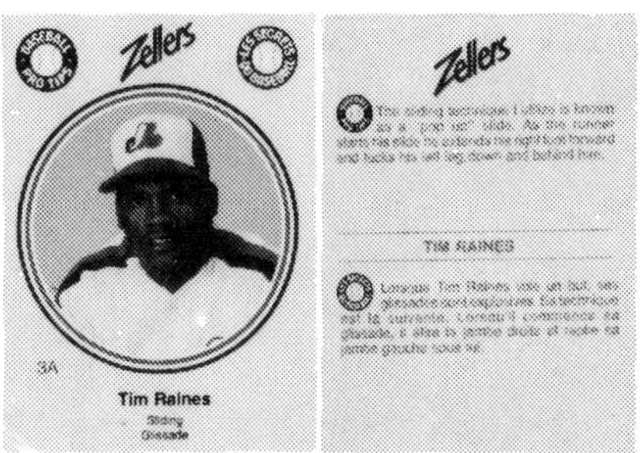

Produced and distributed by the Zellers department stores in Canada, this 60-card set was produced in the form of 20 three-card panels. The cards feature a photo of the player surrounded by rings and a yellow background. A red "Zellers" is above the photo and on either side of it are the words "Baseball Pro Tips" in English on the left and in French on the right. The player's name and the title of the playing tip are under the photo. Backs have the playing tip in both languages. Single cards measure 2-1/2" by 3-1/2" while the whole panel is 7-1/2" by 3-1/2". Although a number of stars are depicted, this set is not terribly popular as collectors do not generally like the playing tips idea. Total panels are worth more than separated cards.

		MT	NR MT	EX
Complete Set:		12.00	9.00	4.75
Common Player:		.40	.30	.15
1	Gary Carter (Catching Position)	1.00	.70	.40
2	Steve Rogers (Pitching Stance)	.50	.40	.20
3	Tim Raines (Sliding)	1.00	.70	.40
4	Andre Dawson (Batting Stance)	.80	.60	.30
5	Terry Francona (Contact Hitting)	.40	.30	.15
6	Gary Carter (Fielding Pop Fouls)	1.00	.70	.40
7	Warren Cromartie (Fielding at First Base)	.40	.30	.15
8	Chris Speier (Fielding at Shortstop)	.40	.30	.15
9	Billy DeMars (Signals)	.40	.30	.15
10	Andre Dawson (Batting Stroke)	.80	.60	.30
11	Terry Francona (Outfield Throws)	.40	.30	.15
12	Woodie Fryman (Holding the Runner-Left Handed)	.40	.30	.15
13	Gary Carter (Fielding Low Balls)	1.00	.70	.40
14	Andre Dawson (Playing Centerfield)	.80	.60	.30
15	Bill Gullickson (The Slurve)	.50	.40	.20
16	Gary Carter (Catching Stance)	1.00	.70	.40
17	Scott Sanderson (Fielding as a Pitcher)	.40	.30	.15
18	Warren Cromartie (Handling Bad Throws)	.40	.30	.15
19	Gary Carter (Hitting Stride)	1.00	.70	.40
20	Ray Burris (Holding the Runner-Right Handed)	.40	.30	.15

A player's name in *italic* type indicates a rookie card. An (FC) indicates a player's first card for that particular card company.

M.L. TEAM ADDRESSES

Collectors often request the addresses of M.L. teams so they may direct autograph requests to players. Here they are:

American League

Baltimore Orioles: Memorial Stadium, Baltimore, MD 21218.

Boston Red Sox: Fenway Park, 24 Yawkey Way, Boston, MA 02215.

California Angels: Anaheim Stadium, 2000 State College Blvd., Anaheim, CA 92806.

Chicago White Sox: Comiskey Park, 324 W. 35th St., Chicago, IL 60616.

Cleveland Indians: Boudreau Blvd., Cleveland, OH 44114.

Detroit Tigers: Tiger Stadium, Detroit, MI 48216.

Kansas City Royals: P.O. Box 419969, Kansas City, MO 64141.

Milwaukee Brewers: Milw. County Stadium, Milwaukee, WI 53214.

Minnesota Twins: 501 Chicago Ave. S., Minneapolis, MN 55415.

New York Yankees: Yankee Stadium, Bronx, NY 10451.

Oakland A's: Oakland Alameda Co. Coliseum, P.O. Box 2220, Oakland, CA 94621.

Seattle Mariners: P.O. Box 4100, Seattle, WA 98104.

Texas Rangers: P.O. Box 1111, Arlington, TX 76010.

Toronto Blue Jays: Skydome, 300 The Esplanade West, Suite #3200, Toronto, Ont., Canada M5V 3B3.

National League

Atlanta Braves: P.O. Box 4064, Atlanta, GA 30302.

Chicago Cubs: Wrigley Field, 1060 W. Addison St., Chicago, IL 60613.

Cincinnati Reds: Riverfront Stadium, Cincinnati, OH 45202.

Houston Astros: P.O. Box 288, Houston, TX 77001.

Los Angeles Dodgers: Dodger Stadium, 1000 Elysian Park Ave., L.A., CA 90012.

Montreal Expos: P.O. Box 500, Station M, Montreal, Quebec, Canada H1V 3P2.

New York Mets: Shea Stadium, Flushing, NY 11368.

Philadelphia Phillies: P.O. Box 7575, Philadelphia, PA 19101

Pittsburgh Pirates: Three Rivers Stadium, 600 Stadium Circle, Pittsburgh, PA 15212

St. Louis Cardinals: 250 Stadium Plaza, St. Louis, MO 63102.

San Diego Padres: P.O. Box 2000, San Diego, CA 92120.

San Francisco Giants: Candlestick Park, San Francisco, CA 94124.

MINOR LEAGUES ISSUES

This section of the *Standard Catalog of Baseball Cards* contains most minor league sets issued from 1970 through 1989. Minor league sets issued prior to 1970 (such as the T210, Zeenuts, etc.) can be found in the regular alphabetical listings.

Note that only complete set prices are given for minor league sets. Individual cards are not priced, because it is uncommon for dealers to buy or sell minor league cards as singles. Plus, due to the possible counterfeiting of key minor league cards, it is recommended that minor league cards be bought, sold or traded only as complete sets. It is less likely that entire sets of minor league cards would be counterfeited.

The listings in this section were provided by Don Harrison of the 10th Inning of Hampton, Va., one of the hobby's leading authorities on minor league cards. The set values were determined through various sources.

Preceding each listing will be special notes about the set, plus the team's Major League affiliation and classification (AAA, AA, A or Rookie League).

1974 Caruso Hawaii Islanders

	NR MT	EX	VG
Complete Set:	10.00	5.00	3.00

101 Gene Locklear
102 Gary Jestadt
103 Hector Torres
104 Ed Acosta
105 Pat Corrales
106 Bill Almon
107 Rich Chiles
108 Roy Hartsfield

1974 Caruso Phoenix Giants

	NR MT	EX	VG
Complete Set:	17.50	8.75	5.25

80 Skip James
81 Mike Sadek
82 Leon Brown
83 Glenn Redmon
84 Ed Sukla
85 Glenn Adams
86 Bruce Christiansen
87 Jimmy Rosario
88 Frank Johnson
89 Glenn Ezell
90 Rocky Bridges

1974 Caruso Sacramento Solons

	NR MT	EX	VG
Complete Set:	17.50	8.75	5.25

46 Tom Reynolds
47 Art Kusnyer
48 Gorman Thomas
49 Bill Mc Nulty
50 Tom Bianco
51 Gary Cavallo
52 Tom Hausman
53 Roger Miller
54 Tom King
55 Craig Glassco
56 Jose Salado
57 Sixto Lezcano
58 Steve Mc Cartney
59 Juan Lopez
60 Jack Lind
61 Rob Ellis
62 Bob Lemon
63 Bob Sheldon

1974 Caruso Salt Lake City Angels

91 Rudy Meoli
92 Bob Marcano
93 Frankie George
94 Dave Chorley
95 Morrie Nettles
96 Bruce Bochte
97 Norm Sherry
98 Jerry Bell
99 Paul Dade
100 Danny Briggs

1974 Caruso Spokane Indians

	NR MT	EX	VG
Complete Set:	17.50	8.75	5.25

28 Steve Dunning
29 Bob Johnson
30 Rick Henninger
31 Jim Schellenback
32 Rick Waits
33 Dave Driscione
34 Bill Fahey
35 Don Castle
36 Bob Jones
37 Dave Moates
38 Tom Robson
39 Mike Cubbage
40 Steve Greenberg
41 Roy Howell
42 Pete Mackanin
43 Vern Wilkens
44 Marty Martinez
45 Del Wilber

1974 Caruso Tacoma Twins

	NR MT	EX	VG
Complete Set:	17.50	8.75	5.25

1 Jim Obradovich
2 Dale Soderholm
3 Craig Kusick
4 Cal Ermer
5 Eddie Bane
6 Dan Fife
7 Jim Hughes
8 Mike Pazik
9 Frank Schuster
10 Coley Smith
11 Earl Stephenson
12 Juan Vientidos
13 Dan Vossler
14 Mark Wiley
15 Sam Ceci
16 George Pena
17 Sergio Ferrer
18 Doug Howard
19 Bill Ralston
20 Rick Renick
21 Jim Van Wyck
22 Mike Adams
23 Lyman Bostock
24 Jim Fairey
25 Tom Kelly
26 Ed Palat
27 Danny Walton

1974 TCMA Cedar Rapids Astros

6
1974
CEDAR
RAPIDS
ASTROS
T.C.M.A. LTD. Box 2 AMAWALK N.Y.

(Houston Astros, A)

	NR MT	EX	VG
Complete Set:	95.00	47.50	29.00

1 Bob Renninger
2 Bob Youse
3 Jesus Reyes
4 Arturo Gonzalez
5 Tom Rima
6 Joe Sambito
7 Dave Aloi
8 Mike Jones
9 Calvin Partley
10 Alejandro Taveras
11 Luis Pujols
12 Eric Brown
13 Luis Sanchez
14 Jose Alfaro
15 Jorge Moreno
16 Fred Mims
17 Fernando Tatis
18 Tom Twellman
19 Kevin Drake
20 Guillermo Foster
21 Pastor Perez
22 Bob Cluck
23 Larry Elenes
24 Jose Sosa
25 Leo Posada
26 Mike Holland
27 Paulo DeLeon
28 Don Buchheister

1974 TCMA Cedar Rapids Astros

(Houston Astros, A) (cards are slightly smaller than the standard 2-1/2" by 3-1/2" size)

	NR MT	EX	VG
Complete Set:	90.00	45.00	25.00

1 Arturo Gonzales
2 Ramon Perez
3 Al Williams
4 Guillermo Forster
5 Bob Dean
6 Fred Mims
7 Art Gardner
8 Jesus Reyes
9 Don Buchheister
10 Neil Rasmussen
11 Luis Pujols
12 George Vasquez
13 Paulo DeLeon
14 Mike Stanton
15 Luis Sanchez
16 Jose Sosa
17 Luis Melendez
18 Steve Englishby
19 Rafael Tatis
20 Richard Williams
21 Alfredo Javier
22 Romalde Blanco
23 Bob Youse
24 Heleno Cuen
25 Leo Posada
26 Team Photo
27 Pancho Lopez
28 Jorge Moreno

1974 TCMA Cedar Rapids Cardinals

(St. Louis Cardinals, A) (complete set price includes the scarce team photo card which measures 3-1/4" by 5")

	NR MT	EX	VG
Complete Set:	180.00	90.00	54.00

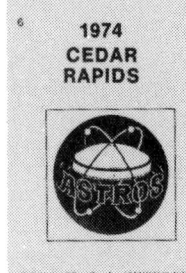

1 Bill Pinkham
2 Mark Hale
3 Tom Zimmer
4 Don Buchheister
5 Jethro Mills
6 John Sawatski
7 Jim Gregory
8 Duke Wheeler
9 Victor Diaz
10 Jim Dunham
11 Mike Carmuso
12 Bruce Henderson
13 Manny Abreu
14 Luis Gonzales
15 Gary Trumbauer
16 Randy Rencor
17 Gary Geiger
18 Burt Nordstrom
19 Mike Proffitt

20 Milo Voskovitch
21 Jim Silvey
22 Joe Mazzella
23 Craig Burns
24 Leon Lee
25 Larry Aubel
26 Mark Mueller
27 Tony Velasquez
28 Bill Poe
29 Monte Bolinger
30 Team Photo

1974 TCMA Gastonia Rangers

(Texas Rangers, A)

	NR MT	EX	VG
Complete Set:	120.00	60.00	35.00

(1) Curt Arnett
(2) Jon Astroth
(3) Mike Bacsik
(4) Len Barker
(5) Don Bodenhamer
(6) Don Bright
(7) Gary Cooper
(8) Rich Donnelly
(9) Dan Duran
(10) Dave Fendrick
(11) Lindsey Graham
(12) Tim Murphy
(13) Fred Nichols
(14) Drew Nickerson
(15) Ed Nottle
(16) Wally Pontiff
(17) Ray Rainbolt
(18) Rich Shubert
(19) Rick Simon
(20) Keith Smith
(21) John Sutton
(22) Mark Tanner
(23) Don Thomas
(24) Bobby Thompson

1975

1975 Chong Albuquerque Dukes

	NR MT	EX	VG
Complete Set:	12.00	6.00	3.50

1 Orlando Alvarez
2 Joe Simpson
3 Jerry Royster
4 Lee Robinson
5 John Hale
6 Bobby Randall
7 Terry McDermott
8 Terry Collins
9 Cleo Smith
10 Wayne Burney
11 Dick Selma
12 Greg Shanahan
13 Rex Hudson
14 Stan Wasiak
15 Pablo Peguero
16 Rick Nitz
17 Stan Wall
18 Jim Allen
19 Jim Haller
20 Dennis Lewallyn
21 Wayne Miller

1975 Chong Hawaii Islanders

	NR MT	EX	VG
Complete Set:	20.00	10.00	6.00

1 Gus Gil
2 Steve Huntz
3 Bob Davis
4 Randy Elliott
5 Dave Roberts
6 Rod Gaspar
7 Jim Fairey
8 Jerry Turner
9 Marv Galliher
10 Sonny Jackson
11 Bill Almon
12 Brent Strom
13 Frank Linzy
14 Jim Shellenback
15 Larry Hardy
16 Gary Ross
17 Bob Strampe
18 Jerry Johnson
19 Butch Metzer
20 Dave Wehrmeister
21 Bob Miller

1975 Circle K Foods Phoenix Giants

	NR MT	EX	VG
Complete Set:	7.00	3.50	2.10

1 Rocky Bridges
2 Jack Mull
3 Mike Sadek
4 Bob Nolan
5 Tony Gonzalez
6 Ed Sukla
7 Don Rose
8 Greg Minton
9 Tom Bradley
10 Bob Knepper
11 Rob Dressler
12 John Le Master
13 Glen Redmon
14 Skip James
15 Bruce Christiansen
16 Mike Eden
17 Tom Heintzelman
18 Tony Pepper
19 Jim Williams
20 Larry Herndon
21 Leon Brown
22 Horace Speed
23 Frank Johnson
24 Henry K Jordan
25 Ethan Blackaby
26 Michael J Cramer

1975 Sussman Ft. Lauderdale Yankees

	NR MT	EX	VG
Complete Set:	90.00	45.00	25.00

1 Scott Norris
2 Mike Ferraro
3 Benny Perez
4 Neil Liebovitz
5 Dave Wright
6 Rich Meltz
7 Dave Rajsick
8 Greg Diehl
9 Tony Derosa
10 Rick Fleshman
11 Pat Peterson
12 Jim Sullivan
13 Marv Thompson
14 Joe Alvarez
15 Ken Kruppa
16 Jim Bierman
17 Doug Melvin
18 Joe Kwasny
19 Mike Heath
20 Sheldon Gill
21 Dennis Werth
22 Jesus Figueroa
23 Wilson Plunkett
24 Jose Alcantara
25 Leo Pasada
26 Garth Iorg
27 Scott Delgatti
28 Mike Rusk
29 Team Photo
30 Jerry Narron

1975 Sussman West Palm Beach Expos

	NR MT	EX	VG
Complete Set:	25.00	12.00	7.00

1 Julio Perez
2 Gary Gingrich
3 Jim Baby
4 1975 Expos
5 Mark Ewell
6 Jose Bastian
7 Roberto Ramos
8 Carlos Ledezma
9 Joe Kerrigan
10 Hal Dues
11 Marcel Lacheman
12 Godfrey Evans
13 Jerry Fry
14 Ron Staggs
15 Mike Curran
16 William Welsh
17 Gordon Mac Kenzie
18 Chris Wood
19 Mike Grabowski
20 Bob Woodland
21 Shane Rawley
22 Gary Horstmann
23 Mike Finlayson
24 Dave Mac Quarrie
25 Larry Horn
26 Mark Knose
27 Ron Sorey
28 Guy Krause
29 Antonio Bernazand

1975 TCMA Anderson Rangers

(Texas Rangers, A)

		NR MT	EX	VG
Complete Set:		70.00	35.00	27.00
1	Tommy Smith			
2	Rick Lisi			
3	Mark Miller			
8	Tim Brookens			
9	Keath Chauncey			
10	Glenn Purvis			
15	Gary Grey			
16	Curt Runyon			
17	Terry Olson			
18	Jim Crall			
20	Dave McCarthy			
23	Kerry Getter			
25	Danny Tidwell			
28	Wes Goodale			
29	Jeff Byrd			
32	Jim Clancy			
37	Bob Carroll			
39	Bill Patten			
42	Freeman Evans			
43	Don Bright			
46	Joe Russell			
47	Ward Smith			
57	Drew Nickerson			
67	Darrel Frolin			
---	Ed Nottle	60.00	30.00	18.00

1975 TCMA Appleton Foxes

(Chicago White Sox, A)

	NR MT	EX	VG
Complete Set:	65.00	33.00	19.00

(1) Fred Anyzeski
(2) Kevin Bell
(3) Robert Bianco
(4) Paul Bock
(5) Bobby Combs
(6) Roy Coulter
(7) Bob Flynn
(8) Bill Kautzer
(9) Tom King
(10) Bob Klein
(11) Odie Koehnke
(12) Tony Komadina
(13) Juan Leonardo
(14) Ted Loehr
(15) Gordon Lund
(16) Bobby McClellan
(17) Candy Mercado
(18) Larry Monroe
(19) Johnny Narron
(20) Phil Nerone
(21) Ed Olszta
(22) Bob Palmer
(23) Harris Price
(24) Scott Richartz
(25) Silvano Robles
(26) Eric Thomas
(27) Tom Toman
(28) Ed Wheeler
(29) Batboys

1975 TCMA Burlington Bees

(Milwaukee Brewers, A)

	NR MT	EX	VG
Complete Set:	70.00	35.00	21.00

(1) John Buffamoyer
(2) Gary Conn

(3) Barry Cort
(4) Marty DeMerritt
(5) "Butch" Edge
(6) Terry Erwin
(7) Matt Galante
(8) Miguel Garcia
(9) Frank Gaton
(10) "Moose" Hass (Haas)
(11) Dennis Holmberg
(12) Sam Jones
(13) Sam Killingsworth
(14) Esteban Maria
(15) Victor Marichal
(16) Marcos Majias
(17) Sam Monteau
(18) Willie Mueller
(19) Abelino Pena
(20) Neil Rasmussen
(21) Alex Rodriquez
(22) Sal Rosario
(23) Pedro Sanchez
(24) Carey Scarborough
(25) Joe Slaymaker
(26) Ron Smith
(27) Gil Stafford
(28) Dave Sylvia
(29) John Whiting

1975 TCMA Cedar Rapids Giants

(San Francisco Giants, A)

	NR MT	EX	VG
Complete Set:	75.00	37.00	22.00

1 Tom Hughes
2 Mike Wilbins
3 Steve Cline
4 Joe Heinen
5 German de los Santos
6 John Riddle
7 Bob Thompson
8 Jeff Yurak
9 Terry Lee
10 Dan Beitey
11 John Nix
12 Don Sasser
13 Brian Felda
14 John Johnson
15 Mike Cash
16 Jim Ray
17 Dan Smith
18 Don Buchheister, Bob Hartsfield
19 Bob Hartsfield
20 Barney Wilson
21 Frank Ferrell
22 Mike Dodd
23 Jim Ayers
24 Jerry Stamps
25 Mark Woodbrey
26 Don Benedetti
27 Ron Hodges
28 Wayne Bradley
29 Calvin Moore
30 Garet Strong
31 Terry Kenny
32 Ernie Young

1975 TCMA Clinton Pilots

(Detroit Tigers, A)

	NR MT	EX	VG
Complete Set:	75.00	37.00	22.00

1 Jim Leyland
2 Dave Rozema
3 Dwight Carter
4 Brian Kelly
5 Greg Kline
6 Steve Gamby
7 Bill Michael
8 Randy Haas
9 Issac Gimenez
10 Ray Gimenez
11 Jim Murray
12 John Dinkelmeyer
13 Larry Feola
14 Tom Lantz
16 Mike Uremovich
17 Kevin Slattery
18 Mark Wagner
19 Ben Hunt
20 Greg Shippy
21 Luis Atilano
22 Tom Perkins
23 Al Baker
24 Steve Trella
24a Jose Centeno
24b Steve Trella
25 Harry Schulz
26 Not Issued
27 Mike Bartell
28 Al Callis
29 Venoy Garrison
30 Jeff Reinke
--- Dave Holm

1975 TCMA Dubuque Packers

(Houston Astros, A)

	NR MT	EX	VG
Complete Set:	75.00	37.00	22.00

1 Clancy (Mascot)
2 Terry Puhl
3 Jeff Smith
4 Tom Rima
5 Arnaldo Alvarado
6 Fay Thompson
7 Bob Dean
8 Mike Mendoza
9 John McLaren
10 Bob Cluck
11 Romo Blanco
12 Roger Polanco
13 Eleno Cuen
14 Rick Haynes
15 J.J. Cannon
16 Fernando Tatis
17 Mike Weeber
18 Alan Knicely
19 Tom Dixon
20 Paulo DeLeon
21 Luis Pujols
22 Jose Alfaro
23 Gordon Pladson
24 Dave Aloi
25 Jorge Moreno
26 Tom Twellman
27 George Lazarique (Lauzerique)
28 Arnie Costell
29 Kevin Drake
30 Mike Hasley
31 Jack Goetz
32 Alvin Osofsky

1975 TCMA International League

(AAA) (this set has been counterfeited and care should be taken when making a purchase)

	NR MT	EX	VG
Complete Set:	195.00	97.00	58.00

1 Jerry White
2 Dyar Miller
3 Mike Krizmanich
4 Earl Stephenson
5 Mike Reinbach
6 Jerry White
7 John Stearns
8 Lee Elia
9 Dave Pagan
10 Rob Andrews
11 Jim Hutto
12 Chris Coletta
13 Ron Clark
14 Bill Kirkpatrick
15 Fred Frazier
16 Joe Altobelli
17 Jim Hutto
18 Mike Willis
19 Glenn Stitzel
20 Fred Frazier
21 Gary Carter
22 Steve Dillard
23 Mike Krizmanich
24 Hank Webb
25 Karl Kuehl
26 Lee Elia
27 Chris Coletta
28 Mike Willis
29 Bob Gebhard
30 Dick Wissel
31 Dick Wissel

1975 TCMA Iowa Oaks

(Houston Astros, AAA)

	NR MT	EX	VG
Complete Set:	145.00	72.00	43.00

(1) Carlos Alfonso
(2) Ron Boone
(3) Ray Busse
(4) Mike Cosgrove
(5) Jerry Davannon (DaVanon)
(6) Bob Didier
(7) Mike Easler
(8) Art Gardner
(9) Alfredo Javier
(10) Jesus de la Rosa
(11) Ramon de los Santos
(12) Joe Niekro
(13) George Pena
(14) Ramon Perez
(15) Russ Rothermal
(16) Ron Roznovsky
(17) Pual Siebert
(18) Joe Sparks
(19) Scipio Spinks
(20) Mike Stanton
(21) Alejandro Taveras

1975 TCMA Lafayette Drillers

(San Francisco, AA)

	NR MT	EX	VG
Complete Set:	185.00	92.00	55.00

1 Chico Del Orbe
2 Wendell Kim
3 Joey Martin
4 Scott Wolfe
5 Tommy Smith
6 Jake Brown
7 Gary Atwell
8 Ernie Young
9 Craig Barnes
10 John Yeglinski
11 Tom Stedman
12 Gary Alexander
13 Jack Clark
14 Reggie Walton
15 Frank Riccelli
16 Rob Dressler
17 Kyle Hypes
18 Jay Dillard
19 Jeff Little
20 Julio Divison
21 Silvano Quezada
22 David Fuqua
23 Terry Cornutt
24 John Steigerwald
25 Bob Drew
26 Don Steele
27 Al Stuckeman
28 Dan Adams
29 Ducky Crandall
30 Denny Sommers
31 Clark Field
32 Batboys

1975 TCMA Lynchburg Rangers

(Texas Rangers, A)

	NR MT	EX	VG
Complete Set:	75.00	37.00	22.00

(1) Rich Albert
(2) Curt Arnett
(3) George Ban
(4) Mel Barrow
(5) Larry Bradford
(6) Bobby Buford
(7) Bobby Cuellar
(8) Amado Dinzey
(9) Brian Doyle
(10) Dan Duran
(11) Chuck Hammond
(12) Eddie Holman
(13) William Johnson
(14) Jerome Johnson
(15) Robert Long
(16) Ken Miller
(17) Brian Nakamoto
(18) Pat Putnam
(19) Ray Rainbolt
(20) Ron Rockhill
(21) Jeff Scott
(22) Glenn Smith
(23) Mark Tanner
(24) Wayne Terwilliger
(25) Don Thomas

(26) Bobby Thompson

1975 TCMA Quad City Angels

(California Angels, A)

	NR MT	EX	VG
Complete Set:	70.00	35.00	21.00

1 Rick Young
2 Ralph Botting
3 Willie Aikens
4 Bryant Fahrow
5 Stan Cliburn
6 Bobby Knoop
7 Jim Dorsey
8 Julio Cruz
9 Carl Person
10 Steve Mulliniks
11 Alex Guerrero
12 Manuel Jiminez
13 Rafael Kelly
14 Mike Howard
15 Carl Meche
16 Carlos Perez
17 Pat Kelly
18 John Hund
19 Mark Wulfemeyer
20 Steve Powers
21 John Roslund
22 Doug Slettvet
23 Billy Taylor
24 Mal Washington
25 Paul Hartzell
26 Steve Kelley
27 Andy Castillo
28 Danny Miller
29 Thad Bosley
30 Steve Brisbin
31 Kim Allen
32 Mark Stipetich
33 Mike Martinson
34 John Caneira

1975 TCMA San Antonio Brewers

WIL AARON INF/OF

(Cleveland Indians, AA)

	NR MT	EX	VG
Complete Set:	65.00	32.00	19.50

(1) Wil Aaron
(2) Ed Arsenault
(3) Jerry Bell
(4) Mike Brooks
(5) Gary Cleverly
(6) Joe Garcia
(7) Bob Grossman
(8) Rich Guerra
(9) Mike Hannah
(10) Bob Hickey
(11) Bill Hiss
(12) Dennis Kinney
(13) Manny Lantigua
(14) Tom Linnert
(15) Tony Manning
(16) Steve Rametta
(17) Andy Rodriguez
(18) Ron Salyer
(19) Woody Smith
(20) Paul Starkovich
(21) Gary Weese
(22) Norm Werd

1975 TCMA Shreveport Captains

(Pittsburgh Pirates, AA)

	NR MT	EX	VG
Complete Set:	75.00	37.00	22.00

(1) Paul Djakonow
(2) Mike Edwards
(3) Mike Gonzalez
(4) Frank Grundler
(5) Randy Hopkins
(6) Tim Jones
(7) Mike Kavanagh
(8) Rick Langford
(9) Don Leshnock
(10) Ken Melvin
(11) Ron Mitchell
(12) Tim Murtaugh
(13) Dave Nelson
(14) Doug Nelson
(15) Steve Nicosa (Nicosia)
(16) Max Oliveras
(17) Mitchell Page
(18) Harry Saferight
(19) Randy Sealy
(20) Jim Sexton
(21) Rich Standart
(22) Tom Thomas
(23) Steve Williams

1975 TCMA Waterbury Dodgers

WATERBURY
Dodgers
LANDESTOY, RAFAEL INF
Age-21 Ht-5'10" Wt-165 B&T-R
Home -Bani, Dominican Rep.
1974 G HR RBI BA
Orngbg 134 2 49 .274

Rafael Landestoy INF

(Los Angeles Dodgers, AA) (black and white)

	NR MT	EX	VG
Complete Set:	70.00	35.00	21.00

(1) Tom Badcock
(2) Jose Baez
(3) Glenn Burke
(4) Larry Corrigan
(5) bob Detherage
(6) Mike Dimmel
(7) Art Fischetti
(8) Dewey Forry
(9) Rafael Landestoy
(10) Dave Lanfair
(11) Don LeJohn
(12) Bob Lesslie
(13) Rich Magner
(14) Barney Mestek
(15) Steve Patchin
(16) Thad Philyaw
(17) Lance Rautzham
(18) Jim Riggleman
(19) Don Standley
(20) Tim Steele
(21) Jim Van Der Beck
(22) Marvin Webb

1975 TCMA Waterloo Royals

(Kansas City Royals, A) (complete set price includes both Barranca variations)

	NR MT	EX	VG
Complete Set:	85.00	42.00	25.00

(1a) German Barranca (Waterloo Royals logo on back)
(1b) German Barranca (Dubuque Packers logo and #17 on back)
(2) Al Bartlinski
(3) John Bass
(4) Charlie Beamon
(5) Roy Branch
6 Brenda Brunk
(6) Dave Brunk
(7) Willie Clark
(8) Pat Curran
(9) Karel Deleeuw
(10) Bobby Edmonson
(11) Bobby Falcon
(12) Craig Flanders
(13) Joe Gates
(14) Luis Gonzalez
(15) John Hart
(16) Dave Hrovat
(17) Steve Lacy
(18) Kevin Lahey
(19) Tom Laseter
(20) Manuel Moreta
(21) Lou Olsen
(22) Darrell Parker
(23) Jerry Peterson
(24) Dan Quisenberry
(25) Ed Sempsprott
(26) Luis Silverio
(27) Dick Smotherman
(28) Mark Souza
(29) John Sullivan
(30) Roy Tanner
(31) Hal Thomasson
(32) Gary Williams
(33) Mike Williams
(34) Willie Wilson

1975 Team Oklahoma City 89'ers

	NR MT	EX	VG
Complete Set:	12.00	6.00	3.50

1 Robert Grossman
2 Barry Lersch
3 Thomas Mc Gough
4 Richard Henninger
5 Thomas Brennan
6 Bruce Ellingsen
7 Larry Andersen
8 James Kern
9 James Strickland
10 Rick Waits
11 John Siracusa
12 Benjamin Heise
13 Orlando Gonzalez
14 Brian Ostrosser
15 Tommy Smith
16 Thomas Mc Millan
17 James Norris
18 Mike Hannah
19 Nelson Garcia
20 Joseph Lis
21 Gene Dusan
22 Michael Brooks
23 John Davis
24 Rex Rosser

1975 Team Tucson Toros

	NR MT	EX	VG
Complete Set:	12.00	6.00	3.50

Autograph Card
1 Hank Aguirre
2 Charlie Chant
3 Juan Gomez
4 Bill Grabarkewitz
5 Alan Griffin
6 Leon Hooten
7 Lew Krausse
8 Chester Lemon
9 Skip Lockwood
10 Leo Mazzone
11 Rich Mc Kinney
12 Craig Mitchell
13 Roger Nelson
14 Buzz Nitschke
15 Orlando Pena
16 Galyen Pitts
17 Charlie Sands
18 Tom Sandt
19 Dale Sanner
20 Mike Weathers
21 Ramon Webster
22 Larry Davis
23 Freddie The Toro

1976

1976 Caruso Hawaii Islanders

(San Diego Padres, AAA) (black & white) (cards are appromimately 3-5/8" x 2-3/4" in size.

	NR MT	EX	VG
Complete Set:	25.00	12.50	7.50

1 Chuck Hartenstein
2 Jim Shellenback
3 Eddie Watt
4 Roy Hartsfield
5 Dave Roberts
6 Bobby Valentine
7 John Scott
8 Jerry Stone
9 Dave Hilton
10 Bill Almon
11 Joe Pepitone
12 Gaylen Mc Spadden
13 Gene Richards
14 Ken Reynolds
15 Jim Fairey
16 Dave Freisleben

17 Kala Kaaihue
18 Rod Gaspar
19 Jerry Johnson
20 Steve Huntz
21 Mike Champion

1976 Caruso Phoenix Giants

(San Francisco Giants, AAA) (black & white) (yellow card stock) This set is approximately 10/16" x 2-3/4" in size.

	NR MT	EX	VG
Complete Set:	22.50	11.25	6.75

1 John Le Master
2 Bruce Christensen
3 Kyle Hypes
4 Silvano Quezada
5 Skip James
6 Rocky Bridges
7 Frank Riccelli
8 Horace Speed
9 Terry Cornutt
10 Mike Wegener
11 Gary Alexander
12 Tommy Toms
13 Bob Gallagher
14 Mike Eden
15 Bob Knepper
16 Tom Heintzelman
17 Joey Martin
18 Ed Plank
19 Jack Clark
20 Bruce Miller

1976 Caruso Sacramento Solons

(Texas Rangers, AAA) (black & white)

	NR MT	EX	VG
Complete Set:	25.00	12.50	7.50

1 Dave Criscione
2 Keith Smith
3 Dave Moharter
4 Craig Skok
5 Bob Jones
6 Mike Bacsik
7 Tommy Cruz
8 Tommy Boggs
9 Doug Ault
10 Greg Pryor
11 Charlie Bordes
12 Art De Filippis
13 John Sutton
14 Ed Nottle
15 Jim Gideon
16 Don Thomas
17 Bump Wills
18 Lew Beasley
19 Jerry Bostic
20 Len Barker
21 David Clyde
22 Rick Donnelly
23 Greg Mohlberg

1976 Caruso Salt Lake City Gulls

(California Angels, AAA) (black & white) This set is identifiable by its green border.

	NR MT	EX	VG
Complete Set:	12.50	6.25	3.75

1 Darrell Darrow
2 Gary Wheelock
3 Mike Overy
4 Frankie George
5 Carlos Lopez
6 Mike Miley
7 Mike Martinson
8 Ed Kurpici
9 Billy Smith
10 Pat Cristelli
11 Orlando Alvarez
12 Ike Hampton
13 Chuck Hockenbery
14 Wayne Simpson
15 Dick Lange
16 Skip Pitlock
17 Luis Quintana
18 Paul Dade
19 Dave Collins
20 Dan Briggs
21 Charlie Hudson
22 Gil Flores

Definitions for grading conditions are located in the Introduction section at the front of this book.

1976 Caruso Spokane Indians

(Milwaukee Brewers, AAA) (black & white)

	NR MT	EX	VG
Complete Set:	25.00	12.50	7.50

1 Bobby Sheldon
2 Jimy Rosario
3 Sam Ceci
4 Tom Widmar
5 Ron Jacobs
6 Bob Ellis
7 Juan Lopez
8 Kevin Kobel
9 Bob Stampe
10 Moose Haas
11 Perry Danforth
12 Art Kuysner
13 Frank Howard
14 Gary Beare
15 Kurt Bevacqua
16 Tommie Reynolds
17 Bob Hansen
18 Steve Bowling
19 Lenn Sakata
20 Toby Bianco
21 Rick Austin

1976 Caruso Tucson Toros

(Texas Rangers, AAA) (black & white)

	NR MT	EX	VG
Complete Set:	12.00	6.00	3.50

1 Bob Picciolo
2 Don Hopkins
3 Keith Lieppman
4 Gary Woods
5 Mike Weathers
6 Angel Manguel
7 Bob Lacey
8 Rich McKinney
9 Harry Bright
10 Wayne Gross
11 Jim Holt
12 Leon Hooten
13 Alan Griffin
14 Gaylen Pitts
15 Craig Mitchell
16 Tom Bradley
17 Rick Lysander
18 Charlie Hudson
19 Jeff Newman
20 Charlie Sands

1976 Coke Phoenix Giants

(San Francisco Giants, AAA) This black and white set lists no positions, is approximately 4-3/8 x 3-3/8 inches in size, and has a Coca-Cola emblem on each card. Stamped autographs appear on the card fronts, backs are blank.

	NR MT	EX	VG
Complete Set:	12.00	6.00	3.50

(1) Alexander Gary
(2) Bruce Christensen
(3) Jack Clark
(4) Terry Cornutt
(5) Rob Dressler
(6) Mike Eden
(7) Bob Gallagher
(8) Tom Heintzelman
(9) Larry Herndon
(10) Kyle Hypes
(11) Bob Knepper
(12) Johnnie Lemaster
(13) Bruce Miller
(14) Jack Mull
(15) Ed Plank
(16) Silvano Quezada
(17) Frank Riccelli
(18) Horace Speed
(19) Tommy Toms
(20) Mike Wegener
(21a) Rocky Bridges
(21b) Rocky Bridges
(22a) Skip James
(22b) Skip James

1976 Cramer Phoenix Giants

(San Fransico Giants, AAA) This set is numbered as it appears on the backs on the cards.

	NR MT	EX	VG
Complete Set:	35.00	17.50	10.50

2 Johnnie LeMaster
10 Jack Mull
11 Larry Herndon
14 Bruce Miller
15 Skip James
17 Bruce Christensen
18 Bob Gallagher
19 Mike Eden
20 Horace Speed

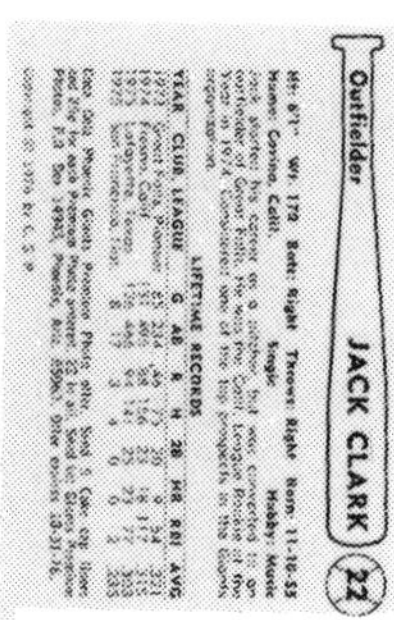

22 Jack Clark
23 Tom Heintzelman
25 Gary Alexander
26 Rocky Bridges
28 Ed Plank
30 Frank Ricelli
32 Silvano Quezoda
33 Tommy Toms
34 Bob Knepper
35 WMike Wegener
36 Kyle Hypes
37 Rob Dressler
38 Terry Cornutt
--- Ethan Blackaby, Trainer/Stad. Super. Card, Checklist

1976 Cramer Seattle Rainiers

(No Affiliations, A) (black & white, 2"x3")

	NR MT	EX	VG
Complete Set:	12.00	6.00	3.50

2 Steve Stillwell
5 Doug Peterson
6 Steve Watson
7 Bob Kraft
8 Russ Attebery
9 Terry Sheehan
11 George Benson
12 Dave Stewart
14 Paul Gilmartin
17 Ken May
18 Kevin Gilmartin
19 Ken Kanikeberg
20 Xavier Dixon
21 Vince Barbisan
23 Ken Peters
26 Dave Sloan
27 Jimmy Williams
30 Danny Miller
35 Art Peterson
37 Dennis Peterson

1976 Dairy Queen Tacoma Twins

(Minnesota Twins, AAA) (black & white)

	NR MT	EX	VG
Complete Set:	32.50	16.25	9.75

Paul Ausman, Randy Bass, Bill Butler

Larry Cox
Tom Epperly
Cal Ermer
Jim Gideon
Bob Gorinski
Tom Johnson
Jack Maloof
Bob Maneely
Davis May
Dave Mc Kay
Willie Norwood

Mike Pazik
Rick Rennick
Tommy Sain
Dale Solderholm
Jim Van Wyck
Juan Vientidos
Mark Wiley
Rob Wilfong
Al Woods

1976 Goof's Pants Tulsa Oilers

(St. Louis Cardinals, AAA) (black & white)

	NR MT	EX	VG
Complete Set:	100.00	50.00	30.00

1 Ken Boyer
2 Lloyd Allen
3 Tom Harmon
4 Stan Butkus
5 Doug Clary
6 Mike Easler
7 Doug Capilla
8 Stan Mejias
9 Ed Crosby
10 Jimmy Freeman
11 JOhn Tamargo
12 Leon Lee
13 Leron Lagrow
14 Luis Alvarado
15 Mike Potter
16 Mike Proly
17 Bill Rothan
18 Garry Templeton
19 Tom Walker
20 Charlie Chant
21 Steve Waterbury
22 Randy Wiles
23 Satchel Paige (autographed)
24 Paul Dean (autogrpahed)
25 Earl Bass
26 Lee Landers

1976 Knowlton's San Antonio Brewers

(Texas Rangers, AA) (black & white)

	NR MT	EX	VG
Complete Set:	75.00	37.00	22.00

Mel Barrow
Frank Bolick
Don Bright
Mike Bucci
Jeffrey Byrd
Keith Chauncey
Jim Clancy
Bobby Cuellar
Doug Duncan
Dan Duran
Gary Gray
Ed Holman
Rudy Jaramillo
Marty Martinez
Brian Nakamoto
Ron Norman
Wayne Pinkerton
John Poloni
Ray Rainbolt
Rich Shubert
Mike Steen
Blair Stouffer
Don G. Thomas
Jim Thomas
Bobby Thompson
Dan Wheat

1976 Sussman Ft. Lauderdale Yankees

(New York Yankees, A) (black & white) All cards in this set have blank backs.

	NR MT	EX	VG
Complete Set:	75.00	37.00	22.00

1 Jesus Figueroa
2 Duke Drawdy
3 Jerry Narron
4 Joe Alcantara
5 Jim Mc Donald
6 Tom Davis
7 Bernardo Estevez
8 Jim Lysgaard
9 Domingo Ramos
10 Ken Kruppa
11 Nate Chapman
12 Antonio Bautista
13 Darnell Waters
14 Mike Heath
15 Damaso Garcia
16 Marty Caffrey
17 Mike Ferraro
18 Orlando Pena
19 Dave Wright
20 Greg Diehl
21 Willie Upshaw
22 Roger Slagle
23 Rick Stenholm
24 Benny Perez
25 Tim Lewis
26 Bevan Luis
27 Doug Melvin
28 Randy Niemann
29 Juan Espino
30 Sandy Valdespino

1976 TCMA Appleton Foxes

(Chicago White Sox, A) (black and white)

	NR MT	EX	VG
Complete Set:	50.00	25.00	15.00

(1) Jay Attardi
(2) Roy Coulter
(3) Curt Etchandy
(4) Rick Evans
(5) Mike Farrell
(6) Bob Flynn
(7) Jim Handley
(8) Marshal Harper
(9) Tom Jyce
(10) Bill Kautzer
(11) Bill Lehman
(12) Mitch Lukevics
(13) Bob Madden
(14) Pete Maropis
(15) Candy Mercado
(16) Phil Nerone
(17) Mike Nored
(18) Ed Olszta
(19) Harris Price
(20) Curt Ramstack
(21) Scott Richartz
(22) Silvano Robles
(23) Ted Schultz
(24) Randy Seltzer
(25) Mike Smith
(26) Tommy Toman
(27) Ed Yesenchak
(28) Ed Holtz, Jim Napier
(29) Batboys

1976 TCMA Arkansas Travelers

(St. Louis Cardinals, AA) (cards are slightly larger than the standard 2-1/2" by 3-1/2" size)

	NR MT	EX	VG
Complete Set:	150.00	75.00	45.00

(1) Cardell Camper
(2) Manny Castillo
(3) Bill Caudill
(4) Jack Krol
(5) Ryan Kurosaki
(6) Terry Landrum
(7) Ken Oberkfell
(8) Mike Ramsey
(9) John Urrea
(10) Bill Valentine
(11) Randy Wiles
(12) John Young

1976 TCMA Asheville Tourists

(Texas Rangers, A) (black & white)

	NR MT	EX	VG
Complete Set:	135.00	67.00	40.00

1 Joe Russell
2 Randy Reynolds
3 Paul Mirabella
4 David Rivera
5 Bob Carroll
6 Bill Stone
7 Riccardo Lisi
8 Ward Smith
9 Harold Kelly
10 David McCarthy
11 Wayne Pinkerton
12 Richard Couch
13 Mike Arrington
14 Jerry Gaines
15 Patrick Putnam
16 Patrick Moock
17 Mark Miller
18 Larue Washington
19 Danny Tidwell
20 Wayne Terwilliger
21 Glenn Furvis
22 Len Glowzenski
23 Mark Soroko
24 Edward Miller
25 Joseph Stewart

1976 TCMA Baton Rouge Cougars

(No affiliation ,A) (black & white)

	NR MT	EX	VG
Complete Set:	60.00	30.00	18.00

(1) Sterling Allen
(2) Nick Baltz
(3) Matt Batts
(4) Randy Benson
(5) Mike Brooks
(6) Tom Brown
(7) Jim Carruth
(8) Winston Cole
(9) Robbie Cox
(10) Kevin Fogg
(11) Gary Grunsky
(12) Larry Keenum
(13) Paul Kennemur
(14) Terry Leach
(15) Mickey Miller
(16) Dave Obal
(17) Ken Palmer
(18) Gerry Poche
(19) Ed Stephenson
(20) Bob Taylor
(21) Curtis Wallace

1976 TCMA Burlington Bees

(Milwaukee Brewers, A) (black & white)

	NR MT	EX	VG
Complete Set:	65.00	32.50	19.50

(1) Greg Anderson
(2) Gary Conn
(3) Roger Danson
(4) John Dempsey
(5) Bill Dick
(6) Alvin Edge
(7) Butch Edge
(8) Miguel Encarcion
(9) Adalberto Flores
(10) Rich Ford
(11) Elliott Franklin
(12) Geroge Frazier
(13) Matt Galante
(14) Frank Gaton
(15) Gary Gingrich
(16) Dave Globig
(17) John Hannon
(18) Dennis Holmberg
(19) Sam Jones
(20) Gary Larocque
(21) Shawn McCarthy
(22) Sam Monteau
(23) Willie Mueller
(24) Rick O'Keeffe
(25) Jay Passmore
(26) Abelino Pena
(27) Eric Restin
(28) Edgardo Romero
(29) Chuck Ross
(30) Dave Smith
(31) Ron Smith
(32) Talmage Tanks
(33) Ron Wrona

1976 TCMA Cedar Rapids Giants

(San Francisco Giants, A) (complete set price includes all variations)

	NR MT	EX	VG
Complete Set:	50.00	25.00	15.00

(1) Terry Adams
(2) Dave Anderson
(3) Ted Barnicle
(4) Jose Barrios
(5) Ken Barton
(6) Bryan Boyne
(7) Don Buchheister
(8) Ken Burton
(9) Wayne Cato
(10) Mike Glinatsis
(11a) Steve Grimes (incorrect name on back)

(11b) Steve Grimes (correct name on back)

(12) Ron Hodges
(13) John Johnson
(14) Steven McKown
(15) Dave Mendoza
(16) Stan Moline
(17) Dick Murray
(18) Billy Ray Parker
(19) Francis Parker
(20) Wayne Pechek
(21) Tim Peterson
(22) Jim Pryor
(23) Mike Rex
(24) Pat Roy
(25) German de los Santos
(26) Don Sasser
(27) Ted Schoenhaus
(28) Steve Sherman
(29) Bill Tullish
(30) Lozando Washington
(31) STeve Watson
(32) Steve Wilkins
(33) Barney Wilson
(34a) Mark Woodbrey (incorrect name on back)

(34b) Mark Woodbrey (correct name on back)

(35) Ernie Young
(36) Jeff Yurak
(37) Team Photo

1976 TCMA Clinton Pilots

Silvano Robles OF

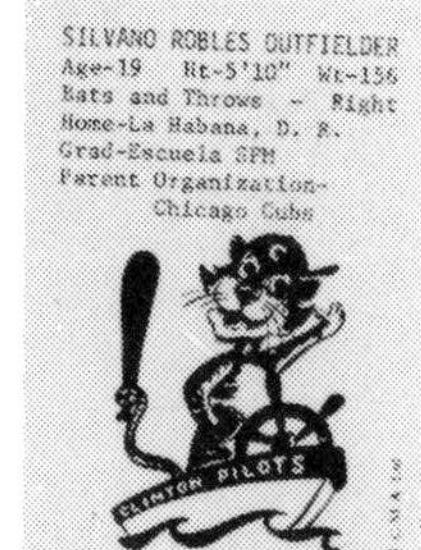

(Detroit Tigers, A) (complete set price includes scarce Kline and Robles cards)

	NR MT	EX	VG
Complete Set:	150.00	75.00	45.00

(1) Phil Bauer
(2) Mike Bigusiak
(3) Ken Bokek
(4) Bobby Buford
(5) Davy Burress
(6) Felan Byrd
(7) Tom Carlson
(8) George Davis
(9) Fred DePietro
(10) Julian Ditto
(11) Tim Doerr
(12) Mike Elders
(13) Freeman Evans
(14) Popilio Fermin
(15) Don Fletcher
(16) Miguel Garcia
(17) Kerry Getter
(18) Juan Gonzalez
(19) Bob Hartsfield
(20) Kent Hunziker
(21) Joe Jackson
(22) Tom King
(23) Greg Kline
(24) Willie Mueller
(25) Denzil Palmer
(26) Jack Parish
(27) Gene Quick
(28) Silvano Robles
(29) Phil Trucks
(30) Jackie Uhey
(31) Mike Vaughn
(32) Paul Vavruska
(33) Larry Walbring
(34) Mal Washington
(35) Ward Wilson
(36) Dave Wood
(37) Donna Colschen, Fritz Colschen

1976 TCMA Dubuque Packers

(Houston Astros, A) (black & white)

	NR MT	EX	VG
Complete Set:	50.00	25.00	15.00

(1) Jose Alvarez
(2) Edward Anderson
(3) Reno Aragon
(4) Bruce Boehy
(5) Leroy Clark
(6) John Clothery
(7) Robert Cluck
(8) Neal Cooper
(9) Martin DeMerritt
(10) Jeff Ellison
(11) Larry Eubanks
(12) Barry Glabman
(13) Larry Green
(14) Robert Hallgren
(15) Michael Hasley
(16) Ray Hutchinson
(17) Alan Knicely
(18) Kenneth Lahonta
(19) George Lauzerique
(20) John Lee
(21) William Melendez
(22) Michael Mendoza
(23) Richard Miller
(24) Raul Nieves
(25) Martin Perez
(26) Donald Pisker
(27) Joseph Pittman
(28) Gordon Pladson
(29) Pedro Prieto
(30) Bill Roberts
(31) Alberto Rondon
(32) Simon Rosario
(33) Randy Rouse
(34) Jeffrey Smith
(35) Fay Thompson
(36) Tom Twellman
(37) Michael Tyler
(38) Jerry Willeford
(39) Gary Wilson
(40) Robert Cluck, Steve Greenberg, George Lauzerique

1976 TCMA Quad City Angels

(California Angels, A) (black & white)

	NR MT	EX	VG
Complete Set:	135.00	67.50	40.50

(1) Dan Beerbrower
(2) Ned Bergert
(3) Ralph Botting
(4) Bob Boyd
(5) Gary Boyle
(6) Rich Brewster
(7) Jim Brown
(8) Jerry Brust
(9) Bob Clark
(10) Mark Clear
(11) Stan Cliburn
(12) Steve Eddy
(13) Bill Ewing
(14) Bob Ferris
(15) John Flannery
(16) David Hollifield
(17) Rafael Kelly
(18) Carney Lansford
(19) Joe Maddon
(20) Mike Martinson
(21) Manuel Mercedes
(22) Scott Moffit
(23) Don Mraz
(24) Mystery Infielder
(25) Jim Officer
(26) Harry Pells
(27) Charles Porter
(28) Jerry Quigley
(29) John Ricanelli
(30) Bob Slater
(31) Doug Slettvet
(32) Randy Smith
(33) Bob Starks
(34) Dave Steck
(35) Larry Stubing
(36) Billy Taylor
(37) Steve Tebbetts
(38) Richard Thon
(39) Steve Whitehead
(40) Ken Wright

1976 TCMA Shreveport Captains

(Pittsburgh Pirates, AA) (complete set price includes scarce Weinberg card) (Pittsburgh Pirates) (black & white)

	NR MT	EX	VG
Complete Set:	125.00	62.00	37.00

1 Gary Hargis
2 Rich Standart
3 Rich Anderson
4 Doug Nelson
5 Luke Wrenn
6 Mike Gonzalez
7 Rod Scurry
8 Jim Sexton
9 Paul Djakonow
10 Dave Nelson
11 Mike Edwards
12 Randy Sealy
13 John Lipon
14 Albert Louis
15 Silvio Martinez
16 Steve Blomberg
17 Frank Grundler
18 Harry Saferight
19 Chet Gunter
20 Rafael Cariel
21 Ron Mitchell
22 Randy Hopkins
23 Barry Weinberg
--- Tim Murtaugh

1976 TCMA Waterloo Royals

(Kansas City Royals, A) (black & white)

	NR MT	EX	VG
Complete Set:	85.00	42.00	25.00

(1) Bob Barr
(2) German Barranca
(3) Steve Beene
(4) Kent Cvejdlik
(5) Karel De Leeuw
(6) Rich Dubee
(7) Craig Eaton
(8) Richard Gale
(9) Danny Garcia
(10) Kevin Gillen
(11) Dale Hrovat
(12) Jack Hudson
(13) Clint Hurdle
(14) Bryan Jones
(15) Ron Kainer
(16) Steve Lacy
(17) Tom Laseter
(18) Fernando Llodrat
(19) Manuel Moreta
(20) Darrell Parker
(21) Ricky Passalacqua
(22) Jerry Peterson
(23) Ken Phelps
(24) Dan Quisenberry
(25) Ed Sempsrott
(26) Luis Silverio
(27) Ron Smith
(28) Mark Souza
(29) John Sullivan
(30) Roy Tanner
(31) Hal Thomasson
(32) Alan Viebrock
(33) Mike Williams

1976 TCMA Wausau Mets

Mario Ramirez Inf

(New York Mets, A) (black & white)

	NR MT	EX	VG
Complete Set:	80.00	40.00	24.00

(1) Gene Bardot
(2) Bob Barger
(3) Dave Bedrosian
(4) Butch Benton
(5) Keith Bodie
(6) Randy Brown
(7) Paul Cacciatore
(8) Larry Calufetti
(9) Ed Cipot
(10) Russell Clark
(11) Steve Darnell
(12) Tony Echols
(13) Ed Hicks
(14) Steve Kessels
(15) Steve Love
(16) Luis Lunar
(17) Jeryl McIves
(18) Jim Mills
(19) Juan Monasterio
(20) Bill Monbouquette
(21) Ted O'Neill
(22) Mario Ramirez
(23) Willie Simon
(24) Fred Westfall
(25) Jim Brown, Mike Feder

1976 TCMA Williamsport Tomahawks

(Cleveland Indians, AA) (black & white)

	NR MT	EX	VG
Complete Set:	70.00	35.00	21.00

(1) Wil Aaron
(2) Ed Arsenault
(3) Stan Bockewitz
(4) Wayne Cage
(5) Red Davis
(6) Bob Grossman
(7) Rich Guerra
(8) Mike Hannah
(9) Tom Linnert
(10) Tom McGough
(11) Mike Dolf
(12) Lou Isaac
(13) Pete Ithier
(14) Dennis Kinney
(15) George Mahan
(16) Tim Norrid
(17) Rick Oliver
(18) Bob Servoss
(19) Glenn Redmon
(20) Pat Wasko
(21) Gary Weese
(22) Kris Yoder
(23) Checklist

1976 Team Batavia Trojans

(Cleveland Indians, A) (black & white) (back of cards are blank)

	NR MT	EX	VG
Complete Set:	150.00	75.00	45.00

(1) Ron Arp
(2) John Brown
(3) Rocky Bullard
(4) John Buszka
(5) Al Cajide
(6) Jack Cassini
(7) Denny Doss
(8) Dave Fowlkes
(9) Ray Gault
(10) Tim Glass
(11) Larry Harmon
(12) Craig Harvey
(13) Kevin Jeansonne
(14) Bill Mitchell
(15) Steve Narleski
(16) Ken Preseren
(17) Nate Puryear
(18) Julian Rodriguez
(19) Mike Rowe
(20) Reggie Smith
(21) John Spence
(22) Sam Spence
(23) Paul Tasker
(24) John Teising
(25) Jeff Tomski
(26) Tony Toups
(27) Terry Tyson
(28) Troy Wilder
(29) Bubba Wilson

1976 Team Indianapolis Indians

(Cincinnati Reds, AAA) (color) (co-sponsored by Tom Aikens)

	NR MT	EX	VG
Complete Set:	40.00	20.00	12.00

Checklist
1 Jim Snyder
2 Larry Payne
3 Ray Knight
4 Arturo De Freites
5 Joe Henderson
6 Tom Spencer
7 Dave Revering
8 Jeff Sovern
9 Tom Hume
10 Rudy Meoli
11 Sonny Ruberto
12 Tom Carroll
13 Junior Kennedy
14 Lorin Grow
15 Dave Schneck
16 Manny Sarmiento
17 Don Werner
18 Mike Thompson
19 Keith Marshall
20 Rich Hinton
21 John Knox
22 Carlos Alfonso

Definitions for grading conditions are located in the Introduction section at the front of this book.

23 Tony Franklin
24 Mac Scarce
25 Ron Mc Clain

1976 Team Oklahoma City 89'ers

(Philadelphia Phillies, AAA) (black & white) This set is numbered as it appears on the cards.

	NR MT	EX	VG
Complete Set:	70.00	35.00	21.00

1 Terry R Jones
2 Sergio Ferrer
3 Ronald B Clark
4 Lonnie Smith
6 James F Morrison
7 Mickael T Buskey
8 Dane C Iorg
10 Richard A Bosetti
12 Fred Jr Andrews
14 James P D Bunning
15 Randy L Lerch
16 Danny J Boitano
18 Willie Hernandez
19 William G Nahorodny
20 Ruben Amaro
21 David Wallace
22 Wayne O Nordhagen
23 Quency Hill
24 John M Bastable
25 John E Montague
26 Manuel M Seoane
28 Larry G Kiser
30 Robert L Oliver

1976 Team Tucson Toros

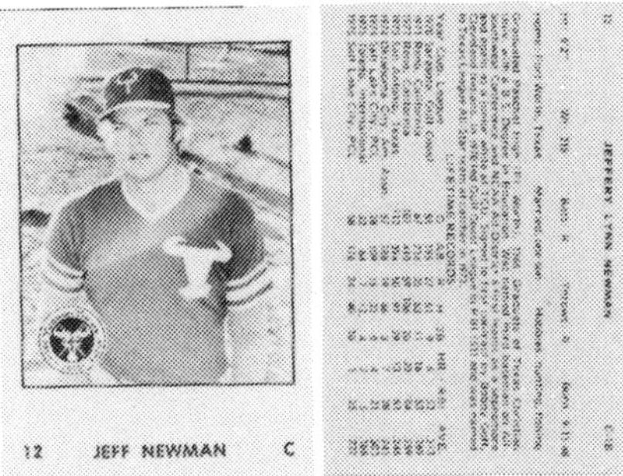

(Texas Rangers, AAA) (black and white, 2-3/8" x 3-1/2") This set is numbered as it appears on the cards.

	NR MT	EX	VG
Complete Set:	12.00	6.00	3.50

2 Mike Weathers
3 Gary Woods
6 Keith Lieppman
8 Angel Manguel
9 Rob Picciolo
10 Chris Batton
11 Don Hopkins
12 Jeff Newman
14 Dale Sanner
15 Wayne Kirby
16 Leon Hooten
19 Bob Lacey
22 Rich McKinney
23 Harry Bright
25 Wayne Gross
28 Rick Lysander
32 Craig Mitchell
33 Juan Gomez
34 Alan Griffin
35 Tom Bradley
37 Jim Holt
39 Charlie Sands
42 Gaylen Pitts
44 Skip Pitlock

1976 Top Trophies Omaha Royals

(Kansas City Royals, AAA) (black & white) (cards are 8"x10" in size and have blank backs)

	NR MT	EX	VG
Complete Set:	100.00	50.00	30.00

Hall Of Fame Members
Hal Baird
Cowboy (Mark Ballinger)
Tom Bruno
Jerry Cram
Dave Cripe
Dave Hasbach
Bob Johnson
Ruppert Jones
Gary Lance
Sheldon Mallory
Gary Martz
Bob Mc Clure
Lynn Mc Kinney
Brian Murphy
Roger Nelson
Lew Olsen
Moose (Frank Ortenzio)
Steve Patchin
Max Patkin
Craig Perkins
Steve Staggs
Bill Sudakis
George Throop
U. L. Washington
Duke (John Wathan)
Joe Zdeb

1976 Valley Nat'l Bank Phoenix Giants

(San Francisco Giants, AAA) (black & white) This set lists no positions. Cards are approximately 4-3/8"x3-3/8" in size. All cards in this set have blank backs and stamped autographs on their fronts.

	NR MT	EX	VG
Complete Set:	17.50	8.75	5.25

(1) Gary Alexander
(2) Rocky Bridges (Sitting in dugout)
(3) Rocky Bridges (Standing in field)
(4) Bruce Christiansen (Standing in field)
(5) Jack Clark (Standing in field)
(6) Terry Cornutt (Standing in field)
(7) Jay Dillard (Standing in field)
(8) Bob Gallagher (Standing in field)
(9) Don Hahn (Standing in field)
(10) Tom Heintzelman (Standing in field)
(11) Kyle Hypes (Standing in field)
(12) Skip James (fielding)
(13) Skip James (Throwing)
(14) Harry Jordan (Throwing)
(15) Bob Knepper (Throwing)
(16) Johnny Le Master (Throwing)
(17) Joey Martin (Throwing)
(18) Bruce Miller (Throwing)
(19) Greg Minton (Throwing)
(20) Jack Mull (Throwing)
(21) Ed Plank (Throwing)
(22) Silvano Quezoda (Throwing)
(23) Frank Ricelli (Throwing)
(24) Horace Speed (Throwing)
(25) Tommy Toms (Throwing)
(26) Mike Wegener (Throwing)

1977

1977 Caruso Hawaii Islanders

(San Diego Padres, AAA) (black & white) This set is numbered as they appear on the cards.

	NR MT	EX	VG
Complete Set:	20.00	10.00	6.00

1 Manny Estrada
3 Jim Wilhelm
4 Lin Hamilton
5 Luis Melendez
7 Pedro Garcia
8 Warren Hacker
9 Kala Kaaihu
10 Chuck Baker
11 Jerry Stone
12 Jim Fairey
14 John D'Acquisto
15 Jay Franklin
16 Dick Phillips
17 Bob Kammeyer
18 Rick Sweet
20 John Mc Allen
21 Mike Du Pree
22 Steve Mura
23 Vic Bernal
24 Clay Kirby
25 Mark Wiley
28 Steve Huntz
29 Eddie Watt
30 Chris Ward

1977 Chong Hawaii Islanders

	NR MT	EX	VG
Complete Set:	17.50	8.75	5.25

1 Manny Estrada
3 Jim Wilhelm
4 Lin Hamilton
5 Luis Melendez
7 Pedro Garcia
8 Warren Hacker
9 Kala Kaaihu
10 Chuck Baker
11 Jerry Stone
12 Jim Fairey
14 John D'Acquisto
15 Jay Franklin

16 Dick Phillips
17 Bob Kammeyer
18 Rick Sweet
20 John McAllen
21 Mike DuPree
22 Steve Mura
23 Vic Bernal
24 Clay Kirby
25 Mark Wiley
28 Steve Huntz
29 Eddie Watt
30 Chris Ward

1977 Chong Modesto A's

(Oakland A's, A) (black & white)

	NR MT	EX	VG
Complete Set:	600.00	300.00	180.00

1 Ted Smith
2 Barry Wright
3 Craig Minetto
4 Dominic Scala
5 Rickey Henderson
6 Jesse Wright
7 Mike Rodriguez
8 Ernie Camacho
9 Pat Dempsey
10 Randy Green
11 Mike Patterson
12 Mace Harrison
13 Rod Patterson
14 Monte Bothwell
15 Bart Braun
16 Rich Oziemiela
17 Tom Trebelhorn
18 Rod Mc Neely
19 Ron Beaurivage
20 Brian Meyl
21 John Eisinger
22 Juan Gomez, Tom Trebelhorn

1977 Cramer Phoenix Giants

(San Francisco Giants, AAA) (color, 2-3/8" by 3-1/2") (co-sponsored by Coca-Cola) (set is numbered as it appears on backs of cards)

	NR MT	EX	VG
Complete Set:	6.00	3.00	1.80

2 Wendell Kim
4 Vic Harris
6 Junior Kennedy
7 Greg Minton
9 Garry Jestadt
10 Rick Sanderlin
11 Don Hahn
12 Frank Riccelli
15 Skip James
16 Rob Dressler
17 Chris Arnold
18 Rick Bradley
20 Horace Speed
21 Bob Knepper
22 Michael Wegener
23 Tommy Toms
24 Dave Heaverlo
25 Gary Alexander
26 Rocky Bridges
27 Joey Martin
28 Ed Plank
29 Kyle Hypes
--- Ethan Blackaby
--- Harry Jordan

1977 Cramer Phoenix Giants

(San Francisco Giants, AAA) (color, 2-3/8" by 3-1/2") (co-sponsored by Coca-Cola) (set is numbered as it appears on backs of cards)

	NR MT	EX	VG
Complete Set:	6.00	3.00	1.80

2 Wendell Kim
4 Vic Harris
6 Junior Kennedy
7 Greg Minton
9 Garry Jestadt
10 Rick Sanderlin
11 Don Hahn
12 Frank Riccelli
15 Skip James
16 Rob Dressler
17 Chris Arnold
18 Rick Bradley
20 Horace Speed
21 Bob Knepper
22 Michael Wegener
23 Tommy Toms
24 Dave Heaverlo
25 Gary Alexander
26 Rocky Bridges
27 Joey Martin
28 Ed Plank
29 Kyle Hypes
--- Ethan Blackaby
--- Harry Jordan

1977 Cramer Salt Lake City Gulls

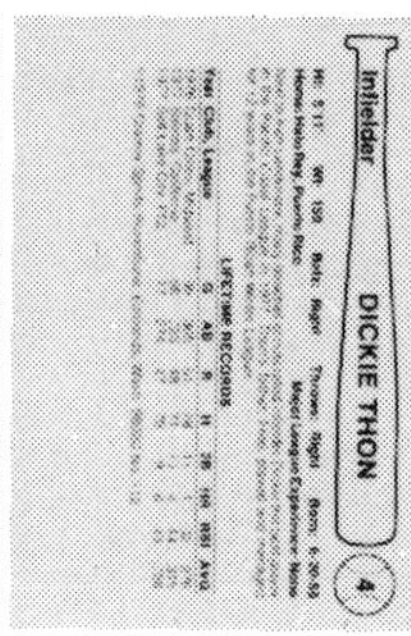

(California Angels, AAA) (color, 2-3/8" by 3-1/2") (co-sponsored by Coca-Cola)

	NR MT	EX	VG
Complete Set:	7.50	3.75	2.25

1 Jimy Williams
2 Fred Frazier
4 Rance Mulliniks
5 Gilberto Flores
6 Chuck Dobson
7 Danny Goodwin
8 Tom Donohue
9 Thad Bosley
10 Pat Cristelli
11 Dave Machemer
12 Fred Kuhaulua
13 Orlando Alvarez
14 Frankie George
15 Bob Nolan
16 Luis Quintana
17 Stan Perzanowski
18 John Caneira
19 Frank Panick
20 Dick Lange
21 Mike Barlow
22 Willie Aikens
24 Mike Overy
25 Butch Alberts
--- Leonard Garcia

1977 Cramer Spokane Indians

(Milwaukee Brewers, AAA) (color, 2-3/8" by 3-1/2") (co-sponsored by Cola-Cola)

	NR MT	EX	VG
Complete Set:	9.50	4.75	2.85

1 Duane Espy
2 Bill McLaurine
4 Jim Gantner
6 Bill Sharp
7 Perry Danforth
8 Steve Ruling
10 Art Kusnyer
11 Lenn Sakata
12 Bob Sheldon
13 Gorman Thomas
14 Juan Lopez
15 Tommie Reynolds
16 Ron Diggle
17 Sam Hinds
18 Tom Hausman
19 Lary Sorensen
20 Ken Sanders
21 Dick Davis
22 Kevin Kobel
24 Bob Ellis
25 Roger Miller
26 John Felske
28 Rich Folkers
--- Mark Voorhees

1977 Cramer Tucson Toros

(Texas Rangers, AAA) (color, 2-3/8" by 3-1/2") (co-sponsored by Orange Crush)

	NR MT	EX	VG
Complete Set:	7.00	3.50	2.10

2 Dave Moates
4 Lew Beasley
5 Ken Pape
6 Wayne Pinkerton
7 Larue Washington
8 Greg Mahlberg
11 Keith Smith
12 Keathel Chauncey
13 David Moharter
14 Rich Donnelly
17 Rick Stelmaszek
19 Gary Gray
20 Bob Babcock
27 Ed Nottle
32 David Clyde
33 Kurt Bevacqua
35 John Poloni
40 Len Barker
45 Mark Soroko
51 Pat Putnam
52 Mike Bacsik
53 Bobby Cuellar
59 David Harper
--- Chip Steger

1977 Dairy Queen Tacoma Twins

(Minnesota Twins, AAA) (black & white)

	NR MT	EX	VG
Complete Set:	27.50	13.75	8.25

1 Jim Van Wyck
2a Luis Gomez
2b Wayne Caughey
3 Dave Edwards
4 Sam Perlozzo
5 Sam Perlozzo
6 Hosken Powell
7 Tommy Sain
8 Willie Norwood
9 John Lonchar
10 Tom Kelly
11 Eddie Bane
12 Davis May
13 Tom Hall
14 Gregg Bemis
15 Gary Ward
16 Gary Serum
17 Mike Proly
18 Steve Luebber
19 Art DeFillippis
20 Jim Gideon
21 Jim Hughes
22 Juan Veintidos
23 Randy Bass
24 Bill Butler
25 Dan Graham
26 Del Wilber

1977 McCurdy's Rochester Red Wings

(Baltimore Orioles, AAA) This black and white set was also produced in the form of 4 uncut sheets measuring 7-1/2 x 11 inches in size. The listing is typed as the players appear on the uncut sheets (six players per sheet).

	NR MT	EX	VG
Complete Set:	125.00	62.50	37.50

(1) David Criscione
(3) Pedro Liranzo
(4) Michael Parrott
(5) Taylor Duncan
(6) David Ford
(7) Earl Stephenson
(8) Blake Doyle
(9) Richard Bladt
(10) Terry Crowley
(11) Tony Chavez
(12) John Flinn
(13) Larry Harlow
(14) John O'Rear
(15) Randy Miller
(16) Mike Fiore
(17) Creighton Tevlin
(18) Ed Farmer
(19) John McCall
(20) Myrl Smith
(21) Gersan Jarquin
(22) Dave Harper
(23) Dennis Blair
(24) Kevin Kennedy
(25) Ken Boyer

1977 Mr. Chef's San Jose Missions

(Oakland A's, AAA) (color)

	NR MT	EX	VG
Complete Set:	12.00	6.00	3.50

1 Team Card/Checklist
2 Rene Lachemann
3 Blue Moon Odom
4 Derek Bryant
5 Milt Ramirez
6 Mark Williams
7 Jim Tyrone
8 Greg Sinatro
9 Charlie Beamon
10 Tim Hosley
11 Denny Haines
12 Mike Weathers
13 Don Hopkins
14 Bob Lacey
15 Craig Mitchell
16 Randy Boyd
17 Denny Walling
18 Randy Scarbery
19 Brian Kingman

20 Ron Bell
21 Randy Taylor
22 Jimmy Sexton
23 Brian Abraham
24 Dave Johnson
25 Paul Mitchell

1977 Sussman Ft. Lauderdale Yankees

(New York Yankees, A) (black & white) (all cards have blank backs)

	NR MT	EX	VG
Complete Set:	100.00	50.00	30.00

1 Pat Callahan
2 Woody Keys
3 Johnny Crawford
4 Jose Alcantara
5 Mark Theil
6 Joe Le Febvre
7 Beban Luis
8 Ted Wilborn
9 Gerry Gaube
10 Nat Showalter
11 Mark Softy
12 Jose Paulino
13 Roger Holt
14 Jim Mc Donald
15 Tim Kibbee
16 Tim Guess
17 Sam Ellis
18 Pat Tabler
19 Dave Wright
20 Steve Peters
21 Don Hogestyn
22 Scott Delgatti
23 Don Fisk
24 Stan Saleski
25 Jimmy De Paola
26 Mark Burlingame
27 Gus Gil
28 Butch Riggar
29 Juan Espino
30 Tony Cameron
31 Eddie Napoleon

1977 TCMA Appleton Foxes

(Chicago White Sox, A) (complete set price includes scarce Minoso variation)

	NR MT	EX	VG
Complete Set:	195.00	97.00	58.00

(1) Tim Bright
(2) Brad Calhoun
(3) Bobby Combs
(4) Marvis Foley
(5) Lorenzo Gray
(6) Marshal Harper
(7) Greg Herman
(8) Clay Hicks
(9) A.J. Hill
(10) Fred Howard
(11) Kent Hunziker
(12) Bob Madden
(13) John Martin
(14) Candy Mercado
(15a) Orestes Minosi, Jr. (name incorrect)
(15b) Orestes Minoso, Jr. (name correct)
(16) Ed Olszta
(17) Andy Pasillas
(18) Joel Perez
(19) Carlos Rios
(20) Keith Rokosz
(21) Randy Seltzer
(22) Michael Sivik
(23) Paul Soth
(24) Leo Sutherland
(25) Rick Thoren
(26) Steve Trout
(27) Mike Tulacz
(28) Ed Yesenchak
(29) Appleton Foxes Staff

NOTE: A card number in parentheses ( ) indicates the set is unnumbered.

1977 TCMA Arkansas Travelers

(St. Louis Cardinals, AA) (complete set includes all variations) (black & white)

	NR MT	EX	VG
Complete Set:	225.00	112.50	67.50

(1) Carlton Roy Keller
(2) Carlton Roy Keller
(3) Ryan Kurosaki
(4) Ryan Kurosaki
(5) Terry Landrum
(6) Teto Landrum
(7) Nick Leyva
(8) Nick Leyva
(9) Mike Murphy
(10) Mike Ramsey
(11) Mike Ramsey
(12) Andy Replogle
(13) Andy Replogle
(14) Jim Riggleman
(15) Jim Riggleman
(16) Steve Staniland
(17) John Yeglinski
(18) John Yeglinski
(19) John Young
(20) John Young
(21) Ray Winder Field

1977 TCMA Asheville Tourists

(Texas Rangers, A) (black & white)

	NR MT	EX	VG
Complete Set:	40.00	20.00	12.00

(1) Bryan Allard
(2) Steve Bianchi
(3) Richard Couch
(4) Dennis Doyle
(5) Steve Finch
(6) Jerry Gaines
(7) Mike Griffin
(8) Mike Hicks
(9) Mike Jaccar
(10) Stan Jakubowski
(11) Greg Jemison
(12) Kerry Keenan
(13) Vic Mabee
(14) Dave McCarthy
(15) Arnold McCrary
(16) Ron Patrick
(17) Scott Peterson
(18) Dave Rivera
(19) Phil Roddy
(20) Jeff Scott
(21) Bill Simpson
(22) John Takas
(23) Wayne Terwilliger
(24) Al Thomson
(25) Phil Watson
(26) Len Whitehouse
(27) Wayne Wilkerson
(28) Glenn Williams
(29) Mike Williamson

1977 TCMA Bristol Red Sox

(Boston Red Sox, A) (black & white)

	NR MT	EX	VG
Complete Set:	250.00	125.00	75.00

(1) Erwin Bryant
(2) Mark Buba
(3) Jose Caldera
(4) Tom Farias
(5) Joel Finch
(6) Glenn Fisher
(7) Otis Foster
(8) Ken Huizenga
(9) Ed Jurak
(10) Dave Koza
(11) Joe Kranich
(12) Dave Labossiere
(13) Breen Newcomer
(14) Mike O'Berry
(15) Gary Purcell
(16) Win Remmerswael (Remmerswaal)
(17) Burke Suter
(18) Steve Tarbell
(19) John Tudor
(20) Rich Waller

1977 TCMA Burlington Bees

(Milwaukee Brewers, A) (complete set price includes scarce Halls and Mercado cards) (black & white)

	NR MT	EX	VG
Complete Set:	150.00	75.00	45.00

(1) Daryl Bailey
(2) Tim Bannister
(3) Mike Dempsey
(4) Bill Dick
(5) Gary Donovan
(6) Larry Edwards
(7) Bert Flores
(8) Richard Ford
(9) Gary Gingerich
(10) Steve Greene
(11) Gary Halls
(12) Dave Hersh
(13) Al Manning
(14) Brad Meagher
(15) Candy Mercado
(16) Dennis Menke
(17) Larry Montgomery
(18) Willie Mueller
(19) Jose Oppenheimer
(20) Glenn Partridge
(21) Jay Passmore
(22) Rene Quinones
(23) Eric Restin
(24) Chuck Ross
(25) Terry Shoebridge
(26) Steve Splitt
(27) Jesus Vega

1977 TCMA Cedar Rapids Giants

(San Francisco Giants, A) (complete set price includes scarce Laubhan card)

	NR MT	EX	VG
Complete Set:	150.00	75.00	45.00

1 Rich Murray
2 Bob Brenly
3 Dave Anderson
4 John Sylvester
5 Ken Feinburg
6 Brian Moulton
7 Phil Nastu
8 Henry Marcias
9 Gary Ledbetter
10 Ken Barton
11 Jack Mull
12 Drew Nickerson
13 Jim Pryor
14 Mike Wardlow
15 Dave Myers
16 Bart Bass
17 Steve Sherman
18 Jon Harper
19 Don Buchheister
20 Mark Kuecker
21 Dan Hartwig
22 Chris Bourjos
23 Jeff Shourds
24 Steve Pearce
--- John Laubhan

1977 TCMA Charleston Patriots

(Pittsburgh Pirates, A) (black & white)

	NR MT	EX	VG
Complete Set:	45.00	22.50	13.50

(1) Tom Burke III
(2) Jorge Carty
(3) Arcadio Cruz
(4) Bienvenido de la Rosa
(5) Rick Evans
(6) Stan Floyd
(7) Skip Leech
(8) Jim Mahoney
(9) Jim Miller
(10) Adalberto Ortiz
(11) Jim Parke
(12) Pascual Perez
(13) Eric Peterson
(14) Fred Rein
(15) Martin Rivas
(16) Bob Rock
(17) Richard Rodriquez
(18) Chuck Rouse
(19) Simon Santana
(20) Brian Schwerman
(21) Bob Semerano
(22) Jim Smith
(23) Alfredo Torres
(24) Candido Ventura
(25) Jerry Yandrick

1977 TCMA Clinton Dodgers

(Los Angeles Dodgers, A) (black & white)

	NR MT	EX	VG
Complete Set:	175.00	87.50	52.50

(1) Paul Bain
(2) Paul Bock
(3) Dave Cohea
(4) Gerry de la Cruz
(5) Jim Del Vecchio
(6) Charles Dorgan
(7) Jim Evans
(8) Chuck Gardner
(9) Rich Goulding
(10) Dan Henry
(11) Tim Jones
(12) George Kaage

(13) Ron Kittle
(14) Mark Kryka
(15) Mickey Lashley
(16) Don LeJohn, Jr.
(17) Dick McLaughlin
(18) Damon Middleton
(19) Jim Peterson
(20) Jose Reyes
(21) Tim Roche
(22) Eric Schmidt
(23) Mike Scioscia
(24) Hilario Soriano
(25) Dave Stewart
(26) Bill Swoope
(27) Ken Townsend
(28) Max Venable
(29) Mike Wilson

1977 TCMA Cocoa Astros

(Houston Astros, A) (black & white)

	NR MT	EX	VG
Complete Set:	40.00	20.00	12.00

(1) Ed Anderson
(2) Reno Aragon
(3) Bruce Bochy
(4) Jeff Ellison
(5) Larry Eubanks
(6) Bob Hallgren
(7) Don Harkness
(8) Phil Klimas
(9) Randy Lamb
(10) Ramon Leader
(11) Diago Melendez
(12) Mark Miggins
(13) Dennis Miscik
(14) Jose Mota
(15) Jim Pankovits
(16) Gordy Pladson
(17) George Ploucher
(18) Pete Prieto
(19) Gary Rajsich
(20) Bert Roberge
(21) Simon Rosario
(22) Randy Rouse
(23) Dave Smith
(24) Tom Wiedenbauer
(25) Cocoa Astros Staff

1977 TCMA Columbus Clippers

(Pittsburgh Pirates, AAA) (complete set price includes variations) (black & white)

	NR MT	EX	VG
Complete Set:	350.00	175.00	105.00

(1) Dave Augustine
(2) Chris Batton
(3) Dale Berra
(4) Mike Easler
(5) Mike Edwards
(6) Gary Hargis
(7) Red Hartman
(8) Randy Hopkins
(9) Tim Jones
(10a) Alberto Lois (photo actually Lowell Palmer)
(10b) Alberto Lois (correct photo)

(11) Ken Macha
(12) Ron Mitchell
(13) Tim Murtaugh
(14) Doug Nelson
(15) Jim Nettles
(16) Steve Nicosa (Nicosia)
(17) Bob Oliver
(18a) Lowell Palmer (photo actually Alberto Lois)
(18b) Lowell Palmer (correct photo)

(19) Ray Price
(20) Fred Scherman
(21) Rich Standart
(22) Ed Whitson

NOTE: A card number in parentheses ( ) indicates the set is unnumbered.

1977 TCMA Daytona Beach Islanders

(Kansas City Royals, A) (black & white)

	NR MT	EX	VG
Complete Set:	37.50	18.75	11.25

(1) Steve Beene
(2) Ed Cowan
(3) Rich Dubee
(4) Craig Eaton
(5) Bob Engelmeyer
(6) Jack Fleming
(7) Henry Greene
(8) Ben Grzybeck
(9) John Hoscheidt
(10) Sam Jones
(11) Tom Krattli
(12) Steve Lacey
(13) Mel Lowman
(14) Jose Martinez
(15) Ken Phelps
(16) Ray Prince
(17) Phil Pulido
(18) Tim Riley
(19) Cliff Roberts
(20) Juan Rodriquez
(21) Ed Sempsrott
(22) Marty Serrano
(23) Brad Simmons
(24) Paul Stevens
(25) Roy Tanner
(26) Hal Thomasson
(27) Buddy Yarbrough

1977 TCMA Evansville Triplets

(Detroit Tigers, AAA) (black & white)

	NR MT	EX	VG
Complete Set:	400.00	200.00	120.00

(1) Bob Adams
(2) Julio Alonso
(3) Tom Bianco
(4) Tom Brookens
(5) George Cappuzzello
(6) Tim Corcoran
(7) Charles Day
(8) Pio DiSalva
(9) Jim Eschen
(10) Gary Geiger
(11) Eddie Glynn
(12) Dan Gonzales
(13) Glenn Gulliver
(14) Frank Harris
(15) Roric Harrison
(16) Artie James
(17) Marvin Lane
(18) Jerry Manuel
(19) Bob Molinaro
(20) Jack Morris
(21) Les Moss
(22) Lance Parrish
(23) Bruce Taylor
(24) John Valle
(25) Milt Wilcox

1977 TCMA Holyoke Millers

(Milwaukee Brewers, AA) (black & white)

	NR MT	EX	VG
Complete Set:	30.00	15.00	9.00

(1) Ike Blessitt
(2) Mark Bomback
(3) John Buffamoyer
(4) Doug Clarey
(5) Garry Conn
(6) Gene Delyon
(7) Bill Dick
(8) Greg Erardi
(9) Rick Ford
(10) George Frazier
(11) Matt Galante
(12) John Hannon
(13) Lynn B. Herzig
(14) Gary Holle
(15) Dale Hrovat
(16) Ron Jacobs
(17) Tom Kayser
(18) Gary LaRocque
(19) Lanny Phillips
(20) Neil Rasmussen
(21) Ed Rasmussen
(22) Ed Romero
(23) Bill Severns
(24) Rich Shubert
(25) Dave Smith
(26) Ron Wrona
(27) Jeff Yurak

1977 TCMA Jacksonville Suns

(Kansas City Royals, AA) (black & white)

	NR MT	EX	VG
Complete Set:	90.00	45.00	27.00

(1) Mark Ballanger
(2) German Barranca
(3) Steve Burke
(4) Mike Denevi
(5) Rich Gale
(6) Joe Gates
(7) Jim Gaudet
(8) Kevin Gillen
(9) Bobby Glass
(10) Tim Ireland
(11) Dennis Kaspryzak
(12) Pete Koegel
(13) Gordon MacKenzie
(14) Frank McCann
(15) Randy McGilberry
(16) Lew Olsen
(17) Darrell Parker
(18) Bill Paschall
(19) Ken Phelps
(20) Dan Quisenberry
(21) Luis Silverio
(22) Gary Williams

1977 TCMA Lodi Dodgers

(Los Angeles Dodgers, A) (black & white)

	NR MT	EX	VG
Complete Set:	95.00	47.00	28.00

(1) Charles Barrett
(2) Mark Bradley
(3) Merv Garrison
(4) Brad Gulden
(5) Dan Henry
(6) Ubaldo Heredia
(7) Hank Jones
(8) Mike Lake
(9) Rudy Law
(10) Tony Martin
(11) Dave Patterson
(12) Pable Peguero
(13) Jack Perconte
(14) Charlie Phillips
(15) Don Ruzek
(16) Rick Sander
(17) Ed Santos
(18) Rod Scheller
(19) Steve Shirley
(20) Kelly Snider
(21) Mike Tennant
(22) Miguel Vallaran
(23) Stan Wasiak
(24) Myron White
(25) Mike Williams

1977 TCMA Lynchburg Mets

(New York Mets, A) (complete set price includes scarce Reardon card plus Greenstein variations) (black & white)

	NR MT	EX	VG
Complete Set:	400.00	200.00	120.00

(1) Jack Aker
(2a) Neil Allen (Pirates logo)
(2b) Neil Allen (Mets Logo)
(3) Gene Bardot
(4a) Butch Benton (knee showing)

(4b) Butch Benton (ankle showing)

(5) George Bradbury
(6) Mike Brown
(7) Randy Brown
(8) Robert Bryant
(9) Russell Clark
(10) Carmen Coppol
(11) Dave Covert
(12) Curt Fisher
(13) Ron Gill
(14) Scott Goodfarb
(15) Bob Grant
(16) Stu Greenstein (knee to head photo)

(17) Stu Greenstein (waist to head photo)

(18) Bob Healy
(19) Steve Keesses
(20) Jerry McIver
(21) Juan Monasterio
(22) Ted O'Neill
(23) Pacho Perez
(24) Mario Ramirez
(25) Jeff Reardon

(26) Bob Rossen
(27) Cliff Speck
(28) Randy Tate
(29) David Von Ohlen
(30) Fred Westfall
(31) Ward Wilson
(32) Steve Yost

1977 TCMA Newark Co-Pilots

(Milwaukee Brewers, A) (black & white)

	NR MT	EX	VG
Complete Set:	40.00	20.00	12.00

(1) Kevin Bass
(2) Manuel Betemit
(3) Rick Broas
(4) Ronald Buggs
(5) Chris Carstensen
(6) Pablo Caudillo
(7) Stan Davis
(8) Steve Day
(9) Tom DeRosa
(10) Ron Driver
(11) Gerry Erb
(12) Brian Fisher
(13) Adalberto Flores
(14) Bill Foley
(15) Eric Frey
(16) Jeff Harryman
(17) Dennis Holmberg
(18) Gary House
(19) Jerry Jenkins
(20) Tim Jordan
(21) David LaPoint
(22) Joe Mitchell
(23) Steve Manderfield
(24) Chester Nelson
(25) Rick Nicholson
(26) Joe Polese
(27) James Quinn
(28) John Roesch
(29) John Skorockocki

1977 TCMA Orlando Twins

(Minnesota Twins, AA) (black & white)

	NR MT	EX	VG
Complete Set:	175.00	87.00	52.00

(1) Archie Amerson
(2) Paul Ausman
(3) Terry Bulling
(4) John Castino
(5) Wayne Caughey
(6) Julian Ditto
(7) Tom Epperly
(8) Frank Estes
(9) John Felton
(10) Greg Field
(11) Mike Gatlin
(12) John Goryl
(13) Bill Harris
(14) Bruce MacPherson
(15) Dennis Mantick
(16) Johnny Pittman
(17) Brian Rothrock
(18) Gary Serum
(19) Dale Soderholm
(20) Mark Souza
(21) Greg Thayer
(22) Steve Wagner
(23) Jeff Youngbauer

1977 TCMA Quad City Angels

(California Angels, A) (black & white)

	NR MT	EX	VG
Complete Set:	55.00	27.50	16.50

(1) Jim Ball
(2) Gary Balla
(3) Ned Bergert
(4) Mike Bishop
(5) Arturo Bonitto
(6) Bob Boyd
(7) Rich Brewster
(8) Scott Carnes
(9) Mark Clear
(10) Keith Comstock
(11) Frank Coppenbarger
(12) Chuck Cottier
(13) Joel Crisler
(14) John Harris
(15) Bob Healy
(16) John Henderson
(17) Craig Hendrickson
(18) Dave Hollifield
(19) Greg Johnson
(20) Donny Jones
(21) Scott Moffitt
(22) Steve Oliva
(23) Harry Pells
(24) Ken Schrom
(25) Rick Sentlinger
(26) Doug Slettvet
(27) Fernando Tarin
(28) Steve Tebbetts
(29) Ken Wright

1977 TCMA Reading Phillies

(Philadelphia Phillies, AA) (black & white)

	NR MT	EX	VG
Complete Set:	375.00	187.50	112.50

(1) Gary Begnaud
(2) George Benson
(3) Todd Brenizer
(4) Franco Ciammachilli
(5) Narda Contreras
(6) Rafael Contreras
(7) Phil Convertino
(8) Todd Cruz
(9) Bobby Demeo
(10) Lee Elia
(11) Dan Greenhalgh
(12) Glenn Gregson
(13) John Guarnaccia
(14) Jesus Hernaiz
(15) Mark Klein
(16) Pete Manos
(17) Jose Moreno
(18) Ed Olivaros
(19) Mel Roberts
(20) Kevin Saucier
(21) Tom Siliacato
(22) Rocky Skalisky
(23) Tom White

1977 TCMA St. Petersburg Cardinals

(St. Louis Cardinals, A) (black & white)

	NR MT	EX	VG
Complete Set:	95.00	47.00	28.00

1 Kelly Parris (Paris)
2 William Bowman
3 Felipe Zayas
4 John Littlefield
5 Denzel Martindale
6 John Fulgham
7 Raymond Searage
8 Frank Hundsacker
9 Michael Stone
10 Terry Gray
11 Daniel O'Brien
12 Jorge Arazamendi
13 Hub Kittle
14 Thomas Herr
15 Raymond Donaghue
16 Henry Mays
17 Scott Boras
18 Claude Crockett
19 Michael Pisarkiewicz
20 Robert Harrison
21 Hector Eduardo
22 Alfred Meyer
23 David Pennial
24 Benny Joe Edelen
25 Ralph Miller, Jr.

1977 TCMA Salem Pirates

(Pittsburgh Pirates, A) (complete set price includes variations) (black & white)

	NR MT	EX	VG
Complete Set:	250.00	125.00	75.00

(1) Paul Anthony
(2) Jim Brady
(3) Randy Bryandt
(4) Bryan Clark
(5) Casey Clatk
(6) Stewart Cliburn
(7) Wink Cole
(8) Eugenio Cotes
(9) Pablo Cruz (no shadow on face)
(10) Pablo Cruz (shadow on face)
(11) Dennis Davis
(12) John Dean (waist to cap photo)
(13) John Dean (chest to cap photo)
(14) Dan DeBattista
(15) Steve Demeter
(16) Bob Mazur
(17) Jerry McDonald (waist to cap photo)
(18) Jerry McDonald (chest to cap photo)
(19) Ossie Oliveras (chest to cap photo)
(20) Ossie Oliveras (batting)
(21) Tony Pena
(22) Alphie Perdue
(23) Jeff Pinkus
(24) Steve Powers (logo on left)
(25) Steve Powers (logo on right)
(26) Fred Rein
(27) Dave Rodgers
(28) Luis Salazar
(29) Chuck Valley
(30) Rafael Vasquez
(31) Dick Walterhouse (logo on right)
(32) Dick Walterhouse (logo on left)
(33) Bob Weismiller (logo on left)
(34) Bob Weismiller (logo on right)
(35) Ernie Young

1977 TCMA Shreveport Captains

(Pittsburgh Pirates, AA) (black & white)

	NR MT	EX	VG
Complete Set:	95.00	47.00	28.00

(1) Doe Boyland
(2) Fred Breining
(3) Jim Busby
(4) Juan Deliza
(5) Paul Djakonow
(6) Chet Gunter
(7) Al Holland
(8) Rick Honeycutt
(9) Rusty Johnston
(10) Mike Kavanagh
(11) Jim Kidder
(12) John Lipon
(13) Larry Littleton
(14) Tim Murtaugh
(15) Doug Nelson
(16) Nelson Norman
(17) Leo Ortiz
(18) Don Robinson
(19) Felix Rodriquez
(20) Harry Saferight
(21) Rod Scurry
(22) Tommy Thomas
(23) Luke Wrenn

1977 TCMA Spartanburg Phillies

(Philadelphia Phillies, A) (black & white)

	NR MT	EX	VG
Complete Set:	125.00	62.50	37.50

1 Pablo Minier
2 Tom Brunswick
3 Marty Bystrom
4 Jim Nickerson
5 Jarrell Whaley
6 Wally Nunn
7 Henry Mack
8 Jim Lasek
9 Joe Jones
10 Nick Popovich
11 Ricky Burdette
12 Armand Abreu
13 Ronnie Mattson
14 Glenn Ballard
15 Tony Gonzalez
16 Brian Watts
17 Elijah Bonaparte
18 Jeff Kraus
19 Mike Comptom
20 Bob Roman
21 Ozzie Virgil
22 Barry Janney
23 Sam Welborn
24 Ken Berger

1977 TCMA Visalia Oaks

(Minnesota Twins, A) (black & white)

	NR MT	EX	VG
Complete Set:	37.50	18.75	11.25

(1) John Altman
(2) Leland Byrd
(3) Bob Carroll
(4) Tim Costello
(5) Doug Duncan
(6) Rick Green
(7) James LaFountain
(8) Roy McMillan
(9) Dean Olson
(10) Glenn Purvis
(11) Frank Quintero
(12) Charlie Renneau
(13) Ray Smith
(14) Rick Sofield
(15) Kevin Stanfield
(16) Joe Stewart
(17) Bill Stone

1977 TCMA Waterloo Indians

(Cleveland Indians, A) (complete set price includes scarce Arnold and Strickfaden cards plus Brennan variations)

	NR MT	EX	VG
Complete Set:	250.00	125.00	75.00

(1) Craig Adams
(2) John Arnold
(3a) Thomas Brennan (Texas League logo on front)
(3b) Thomas Brennan (Midwest League logo on front)
(4) John Buszka
(5) Norman Churchhill
(6) Dennis Doss
(7) Gene Dusan
(8) David Fowlkes
(9) Pedro Garcia
(10) Raymond Gault
(11) Craig Harvey
(12) William Hiss
(13) Rick Howerton
(14) Kevin Jeansonne
(15) Steven Narleski
(16) Thomas Pulchinski
(17) Nathaniel Puryear
(18) Junior Roman
(19) David Schuler
(20) Daniel Skiba
(21) Forest Smith
(22) Samuel Spence
(23) Dave Strickfaden
(24) Jeffery Tomski
(25) Tony Toups
(26) Terry Tyson
(27) Michael Vaughn
(28) Patrick Washko
(29) Steven Widner
(30) Al Wihtal (Whitol)
(31) Dwain Wilson

1977 TCMA Wausau Mets

(New York Mets, A) (black & white)

	NR MT	EX	VG
Complete Set:	70.00	35.00	21.00

(1) Kevan Aman
(2) Rick Armer
(3) Paul Cacciatore
(4) Buddy Cardwell
(5) Kelvin Chapman
(6) Alexander Coghan
(7) Gary Corrado
(8) Tom Egan
(9) Bob Grant
(10) James Hammer
(11) Randy Holman
(12) Luis Lunar
(13) Bill Muth
(14) Bob Pappageorgas
(15) Rick Patterson
(16) Don Pearson
(17) Dennis Sandoval
(18) Kim Seaman
(19) Keith Shermeyer
(20) Tony Thomas
(21) Tom Thurberg
(22) Alex Trevino
(23) Charlie Warren
(24) Rick Wolf

1977 TCMA West Haven Yankees

(New York Yankees, AA) (black & white)

	NR MT	EX	VG
Complete Set:	275.00	137.00	82.00

(1) Richard Anderson
(2) Antonie Bautista
(3) Jim Beattie
(4) Donald Castle
(5) Steven Coulson
(6) Duke Drawdy
(7) Michael Ferraro
(8) Jesus Figueroa
(9) Richard Fleshman
(10) Damaso Garcia
(11) Michael Heath
(12) Lloyd Kern
(13) Timothy Lewis
(14) Jim Lysgaard
(15) Douglas Melvin
(16) Carl Merrill
(17) Jerry Narron
(18) Nelson Pichardo
(19) Domingo Ramos
(20) Roger Slagle
(21) Garry Smith
(22) Richard Stenholm
(23) Sandy Valdespino
(24) Will Verhoeff
(25) Bob Zeig

1977 Team Indianapolis Indians

(Cincinnati Reds, AAA) (color)

	NR MT	EX	VG
Complete Set:	15.00	7.50	4.50

2 Roy Majtyka
3 Joe Henderson
4 Dave Revering
5 Tom Hume
6 Ron Oester
7 Larry Payne
8 Don Werner
9 Paul Moskau
10 Dan Norman
11 Mike LaCoss
12 Mike Grace
13 Dan Dumoulin
14 Steve Henderson
15 Mac Scarce
16 Tommy Mutz
17 Larry Rothschild
18 Rudy Meoli
19 Raul Ferreyra
20 Arturo DeFreites
21 Mario Soto
22 Hugh Yancy
23 Barry Moss
24 Jack Maloof
25 Manny Sarmiento
26 Ron McClain
--- Checklist,

1977 Top Trophies Omaha Royals

(Kansas City Royals, AAA) (black & white) (cards are approximately 6-1/2" x 8-1/4" in size)

	NR MT	EX	VG
Complete Set:	75.00	37.50	22.50

Mark Ballinger
Steve Barr
Charlie Beamon
Jerry Cram
Dave Cripe
Rich Gale
Dave Hasbach
Clint Hurdle
Rudy Kinard
Pete Koegel
Joe Lahoud
Gary Lance
Lynn Mc Kinney
Ken Melvin
Brian Murphy
Greg Shanahan
John Sullivan
U. L. Washington
Gary Wright

NOTE: A card number in parentheses ( ) indicates the set is unnumbered.

1977 Valley Nat'l Bank Phoenix Giants

(San Francisco Giants, AAA) (black & white) This lists no positions and is approximately 4-3/8" x 3-3/8" in size. It can further be identified by its blue bottom border. Also all cards are stamped with autographs except the Rick Bradley card.

	NR MT	EX	VG
Complete Set:	27.50	13.75	8.25

Chris Arnold
Rick Bradley
Rocky Bridges
Terry Cornutt
Rob Dressler
Monroe Greenfield
Don Hahn
Randy Hammon
Tom Heintzelman
Kyle Hypes
Skip James
Garry Jestadt
Harry Jordan
Junior Kennedy
Wendell Kim
Bob Knepper
Joey Martin
Greg Minton
Ed Plank
Frank Riccelli
Rick Sanderlin
Horace Speed
Tommy Toms
Mike Wegener

1978

1978 Brittling's Memphis Chicks

(Montreal Expos, AA) (black & white, 3-7/8" x 2-13/16")

	NR MT	EX	VG
Complete Set:	20.00	10.00	6.00

(1) Felipe Alou
(2) Ray Crowley
(3) Godfrey Evans
(4) Larry Goldetsky
(5) Warren Hemm
(6) Dale McMullen
(7) Julio Perez
(8) Joe Pettini
(9) John Scoras
(10) Rick Williams

1978 Chong Modesto A's

(Oakland A's, A) (black & white)

	NR MT	EX	VG
Complete Set:	75.00	37.50	22.50

1 Pat Dempsey
2 Ed Nottle
3 Mike Davis
4 Bruce Fournier
5 Dana Berry
6 Dave Mc Carthy
7 Doug Hunt
8 Dave Beard
9 Shooty Babbit
10 Dennis Wysznski
11 Mike Mc Lellan
12 Don Van Marter
13 Don Schubert
14 Craig Harris
15 Paul Mize
16 Chip Kniss
17 Tom Eagan
18 Jim Bennett
19 Robert Moore
20 John Lavery
21 Ken Palmer
22 Eric Attaway
23 Bob Markham
24 Dan Darichuk
25 Ted Nowakowski
26 Gaylen Pitts

1978 Cramer Albuquerque Dukes

(Los Angeles Dodgers, AAA) (color, 2-3/8" by 3-1/2") This set is numbered as they appear on the backs of the cards.

	NR MT	EX	VG
Complete Set:	32.50	16.25	9.75

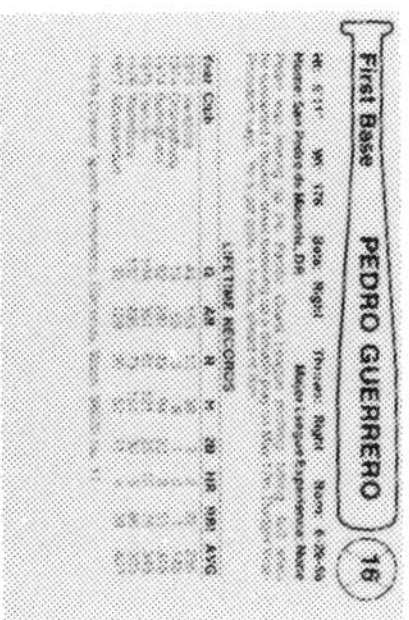

1 Dell Crandall (Del)
2 Terry Collins
3 Rudy Law
4 Enzo Hernandez
5 Ron Washington
6 Joe Simpson
7 Rafael Landestoy
9 Pablo Peguero
11 Bob Welch
12 John O'Rear
13 Hank Webb
14 Dennis Lewallyn
16 Pedro Guerrero
17 Joe Beckwith
19 Claude Westmoreland
20 Brad Gulden
21 Rick Sutcliffe
24 Kevin Keefe
29 Bill Butler
--- Team Logo & Schedule

1978 Cramer Phoenix Giants

(San Francisco Giants, AAA) (color, 2-3/8" by 3-1/2") (co-sponsored by Pepsi-Cola)

	NR MT	EX	VG
Complete Set:	8.00	4.00	2.50

2 Wendell Kim
3 Greg Johnston
5 Howie Mitchell
6 Joe Strain
7 Greg Minton
10 Rick Sanderlin
11 Guy Sularz
12 Phil Nastu
13 Rocky Bridges
14 Mike Rowland
15 Mike Cash
16 Rob Dressler
17 Casey Parsons
18 Randy Hammon
19 Terry Cornutt
21 Jeff Little
22 Rich Murray
23 Don Carrithers
24 Art Gardner
25 Rick Bradley
27 Dennis Littlejohn
28 Ed Plank
29 Kyle Hypes
--- Ethan Blackaby
--- Harry Jordan

1978 Cramer Salt Lake City Gulls

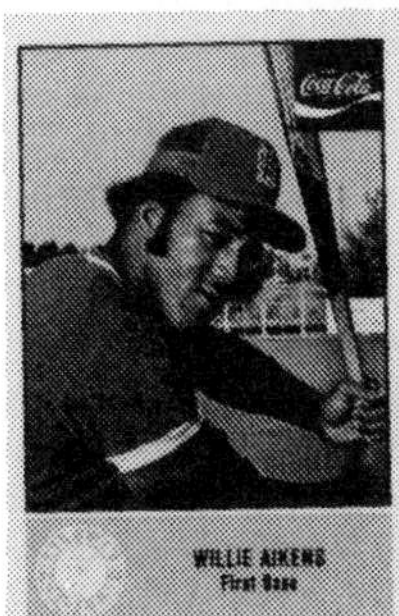

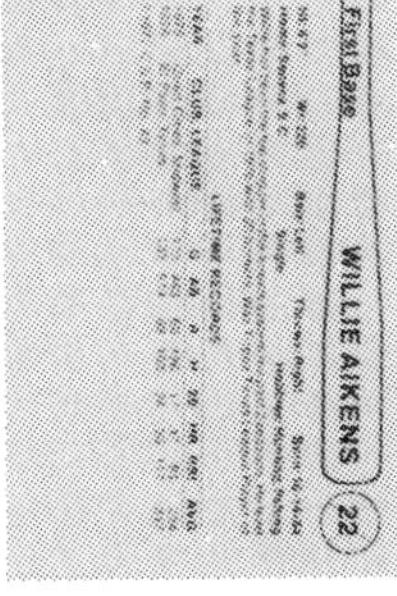

(California Angels, AAA) (color, 2-3/8" by 3-1/2") (co-sponsored by Coca-Cola) (California Angels, AAA) (color) This set is numbered as it appears on the cards. It is also identified by the Meadow Gold emblem in the upper right corner.

	NR MT	EX	VG
Complete Set:	9.00	4.50	2.70

1 Tommy Smith
2 Jim Anderson
3 Dave Machemer
4 Dickie Thon
5 Kim Allen
6 Gil Flores
7 Deron Johnson
8 Tom Donohue
9 Steve Stroughter
10 Pat Cristelli
11 John Racanelli
14 Stan Cliburn
15 Bobby Jones
16 Gil Kubski
17 Chuck Porter
18 John Caneira
19 Bob Ferris
20 Dave Schuler
21 Mike Barlow
22 Willie Aikens
24 Mike Overy
25 Dave Frost
26 Carlos Perez
--- Leonard Garcia

1978 Cramer Spokane Indians

(Milwaukee Brewers, AAA) (black and white, 2-3/8" by 3-1/2")

	NR MT	EX	VG
Complete Set:	7.00	3.50	2.00

1 Duane Espy
2 William L. McLaurine
3 Ronnie Jay "Ron" Diggle
4 Dale M. Hrovat
5 James P. Quirk
6 Lanny A. Phillips
7 Billy E. Severns
8 Tony Muser
9 Jack S. Heidemann
10 Edgardo Romero
11 Stephen M. Ruling
12 Creighton J. Tevlin
13 (I.) Juan Lopez
14 Not Issued
15 Tommie D. Reynolds
16 Not Issued
17 Ron R. Wrona
18 Barry L. Cort
19 Samuel H. Hinds
20 John A. Buffamoyer
21 Robert J. Galasso, Jr.
22 Edward J. Farmer
23 Not Issued
24 Lynn E. McKinney
25 Not Issued
26 John F. Felske
27 Gary R. Beare
28 Edgar F. "Ned" Yost

1978 Cramer Tacoma Yankees

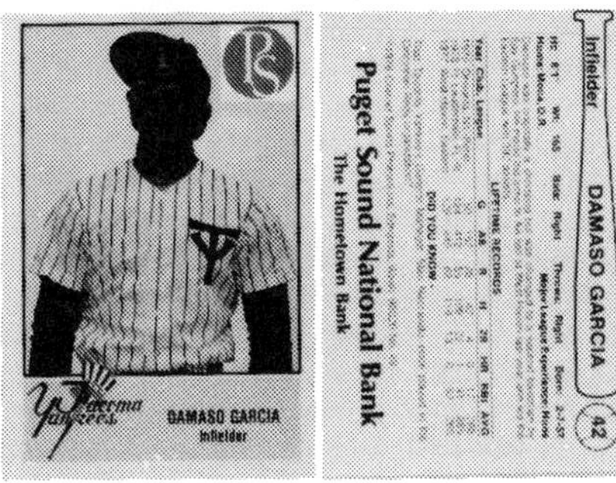

(New York Yankees, AAA) (color, 2-3/8" by 3-1/2") (co-sponsored by Puget Sound National Bank)

	NR MT	EX	VG
Complete Set:	9.00	4.50	2.75

1 Mike Ferraro
8 Ed Napoleon
9 Dennis Werth
10 Roger Slagle
14 Dennis Irwin
15 Darryl Jones
17 Domingo Ramos
18 Jim Lysgaard
19 Jim Curnal
20 George Zeber
21 Bob Kammeyer
22 Marv Thompson
23 Roy Staiger
25 Steve Taylor
27 Dell Alston (Del)
28 Dave Rajsich
29 Larry McCall
38 Jerry Narron
39a Brian Doyle
39b Garry Smith
42 Damaso Garcia
43 Bob Polinsky
44 Tommy Cruz
47 Hoyt Wilhelm
54 Neal Mersch

1978 Cramer Tucson Toros

(Texas Rangers, AAA) (color, 2-3/8" by 3-1/2") (co-sponsored by Orange Crush)

	NR MT	EX	VG
Complete Set:	7.50	3.75	2.25

2 Larue Washington
4 Nelson Norman
9 Wayne Pinkerton
10 Paul Mirabella
12 Keathel Chauncey
13 David Moharter
14 Bill Fahey
15a Mike Bucci
15b Keith Smith
19 Bill Sample
20 Bob Babcock
21 Don Bright
22 Stan Thomas
24 Greg Mahlberg
27 Gary Gray
28 Danny Darwin
32 Pat Putnam
35 Rusty Torres
39 Jackie Brown
42 Rich Donnelly
45 Mike Bacsik
46 Bobby Cuellar
48 Jerry Reedy
59a David Harper
59b Jim Hughes

1978 Mr. Chef's San Jose Missions

(Seattle Mariners, AAA) (color)

	NR MT	EX	VG
Complete Set:	35.00	17.50	10.50

1 Team logo & checklist
2 Rene Lachemann
3 Greg Biercevicz
4 Frank Mac Cormack
5 Ed Crosby
6 Joe Decker
7 Jose Elguezabal
8 Gary Wheelock
9 Alan Griffin
10 Pete Ithier
11 Rick Baldwin
12 Charlie Beamon
13 Juan Berhnardt
14 Luis Delgado
15 Steve Hamrick
16 Tom Brown
17 Byron Mc Laughlin
18 Tommy Mc Millan
19 Bill Plummer
20 George Mitterwald
21 Archie Amerson
22 Manny Estrada
23 Jack Pierce
24 Mike Kekich

1978 Richard West Springfield Redbirds

(St. Louis Cardinals, AAA) This set is numbered as it appears on the cards.

	NR MT	EX	VG
Complete Set:	75.00	37.50	22.50

2 Ron Farkas
3 Mike Potter
4 John Scott
5 Mike Ramsey
6 Nyls Nyman
7 David Bialas
8 Benny Ayala
9 Manny Castillo
10 John Tamargo
11 Eddie Daves
12 Lee Landers
13 Jimy Williams
14 Tommy Toms
15 Al Autry
16 Tom Bruno
17 Frank Riccelli
18 Silvio Martinez
19 Bill Rothan
20 Gregory Terlecky
21 Ron Selak
22 Aurelio Lopez
24 Ken Rudolph

1978 TCMA Appleton Foxes

(Chicago White Sox, A) (black and white)

	NR MT	EX	VG
Complete Set:	75.00	37.00	22.00

(1) Rod Allen
(2) Edward Bahns
(3) Phil Bauer

(4) Ross Baumgarten
(5) Harry Chappas
(6) Roy Coulter
(7) David Daniels
(8) Mark Esser
(9) Curt Etchandy
(10) Lorenzo Gray
(11) John Hanely
(12) Dave Hersh
(13) Clay Hicks
(14) Lamar Hoyt (LaMarr)
(15) Dewey Robinson
(16) Mike Sivik
(17) Jackie Smith
(18) Paul Soth
(19) Leo Sutherland
(20) Richard Thoren
(21) Tom Toman
(22) Phil Trucks
(23) Michael Tulacz
(24) Jeffery Vuksan
(25) Victor Walters

1978 TCMA Arkansas Travelers

(St. Louis Cardinals, AA) (black and white)

	NR MT	EX	VG
Complete Set:	250.00	125.00	75.00

(1) Jose Aranzamendi
(2) Earl Bass
(3) Dave Boyer
(4) Glenn Brummer
(5) Mike Calise
(6) Roy Donaghue
(7) Gene Dotson
(8) Leon Durham
(9) Joe Edelen
(10) John Fulgham
(11) Nelson Garcia
(12) R.J. Harrison
(13) Terry Herr (Tommy)
(14) Terry Kennedy
(15) Ryan Kurosaki
(16) Jim Lentine
(17) John Littlefield
(18) Dan O'Brien
(19) Dave Penniall
(20) Len Strelitz
(21) Randy Thomas
(22) Tommy Thompson
(23) Fred Tisdale

1978 TCMA Asheville Tourists

(Texas Rangers, A) (black and white)

	NR MT	EX	VG
Complete Set:	45.00	22.50	13.50

(1) Jim Barbe
(2) John Butch
(3) Jim Capowski
(4) Ron Carney
(5) Joe Carrol
(6) Ted Davis
(7) Luis Gonzalez
(8) Issie Gutierrez
(9) Bob Hallgren
(10) Dave Hibner
(11) Mike Jirschele
(12) Bobby Johnson
(13) Chuck Lamson
(14) Bill LaRosa
(15) Ed Lynch
(16) Jim Mathews
(17) Arnold McCrary
(18) Mark Mercer
(19) Linvel Mosby
(20) Pat Nelson
(21) Steve Nielsen
(22) Scott Peterson
(23) Miguel Pizarro
(24) Steve Righetti
(25) Bill Simpson
(26) Mike Vickers
(27) Len Whitehouse
(28) Arnold Wilhoite
(29) George Wright

1978 TCMA Burlington Bees

(Milwaukee Brewers, A) (black and white)

	NR MT	EX	VG
Complete Set:	50.00	25.00	15.00

(1) John Adam
(2) Daryl Bailey
(3) Tim Bannister
(4) Kevin Bass
(5) Manuel Betemit
(6) Terry Bevington
(7) Chris Cartensen
(8) Tom DeRosa
(9) Bill Dick
(10) Frank DiPino
(11) Alvin Edge
(12) Larry Edwards
(13) Bill Foley
(14) Ed Gilliam
(15) Jeff Harryman
(16) Jerry Jenkins
(17) Jim Jordan
(18) David LaPoint
(19) Doug Loman
(20) Melvin Manning
(21) Larry Montgomery
(22) Steve Reed
(23) Ivan Rodriquez
(24) Terry Shoebridge
(25) Lee Sigman
(26) John Skorochocki
(27) Bob Smith
(28) Weldon Swift

1978 TCMA Cedar Rapids Giants

(San Francisco Giants, A) (black and white)

	NR MT	EX	VG
Complete Set:	100.00	50.00	30.00

(1) Pat Alexander
(2) Darnell Baker
(3) Jeff Borruel
(4) De Wayne Buice
(5) Don Buchheister
(6) Raymondo Cosio
(7) Charles (Chili) Davis
(8) Ken Feinberg
(9) Rob Henderson
(10) Craig Hedrick
(11) Steve Holman
(12) Bob Kearney
(13) Craig Landis
(14) Doug Landuyt
(15) Javier Lopez
(16) Henry Macias
(17) Louis Marietta
(18) Jack Mull
(19) Venice Murray
(20) Bob Omo
(21) Juan Oppenheimer
(22) Ron Pisel
(23) Francisco Rojas
(24) Alfonso Rosario
(25) John Smith
(26) Jeff Stadler
(27) Jeff Stember
(28) Frankie Thon
(29) Veterans Memorial Stadium

1978 TCMA Clinton Dodgers

(Los Angeles Dodgers, A) (black and white)

	NR MT	EX	VG
Complete Set:	65.00	32.50	19.50

(1) Jan Bach, Rich Bach
(2) Jerry Bass
(3) Rocky Cordova
(4) Dean Craig
(5) Mark Elliott
(6) Larry Ferst
(7) Rick Ford
(8) Doug Foster
(9) Miguel Franjul
(10) Doug Harrison
(11) Leonardo Hernandez
(12) Mike Holt
(13) Mike Howard
(14) Tim Jones
(15) Kevin Joyce
(16) Mark Kryka
(17) Don LeJohn
(18) Jack Littrell
(19) Evon Martinson
(20) Rusty McDonald
(21) Dick McLaughlin
(22) Chris Mulden
(23) Rick Ollar
(24) Joe Purpura
(25) German Rivera
(26) Mike Stone
(27) Steve Sunker
(28) Bill Swoope
(29) Mark Van Bever
(30) Mitch Webster
(31) Larry Wright
(32) Clinton Batboys
(33) Clinton's Riverview Stadium

1978 TCMA Columbus Clippers

(Pittsburgh Pirates, AAA) (color)

	NR MT	EX	VG
Complete Set:	20.00	10.00	6.00

(1) Dale Berra
(2) Dorian Boyland
(3) Fred Breining
(4) Cot Deal
(5) Mike Easler
(6) Mike Fiore

(7) Jim Fuller
(8) Fernando Gonzales (Gonzalez)
(9) Gary Hargis
(10) Al Holland
(11) Randy Hopkins
(12) Odell Jones
(13) John Lipon
(14) Alberto Lois
(15) Ken Macha
(16) Ron Mitchell
(17) Roger Nelson
(18) Steve Nicosia
(19) Ossie Olivares
(20) Dave Pagan
(21) Harry Saferight
(22) Mickey Scott
(23) Rod Scurry
(24) Tom Shopay
(25) Randy Tate
(26) Tom Walker
(27) Ed Whitson

1978 TCMA Daytona Beach Astros

(Houston Astros, A) (black and white)

	NR MT	EX	VG
Complete Set:	40.00	20.00	12.00

(1) Ricky Adams
(2) Rick Aponte
(3) Julio Beltran
(4) Al Cajide
(5) John Cloherty
(6) Paul Cooper
(7) Steve Englishby
(8) George Gross
(9) Don Harkness
(10) Pete Hernandez
(11) Kevin Houston
(12) Doug Jackson
(13) Ramon Leader
(14) Del Leatherwood
(15) Stan Leland
(16) Scott Loucks
(17) Jim MacDonald
(18) Diego Melendez
(19) Fred Morris
(20) Jose Mota
(21) Leo Posado
(22) Simon Rosario
(23) Randy Rouse
(24) Billy Smith
(25) Jose Turnes
(26) Randy Walraven

1978 TCMA Dunedin Blue Jays

(Toronto Blue Jays, A) (black and white)

	NR MT	EX	VG
Complete Set:	135.00	67.50	40.50

(1) Jesse Barfield
(2) Larry Bullard
(3) Jeff Carsley
(4) Rick Counts
(5) Tom Dejak
(6) Eduardo Dennis
(7) Wayne DeWright
(8) Roberto Galvez
(9) Miguel Gomez
(10) Scott Gregory
(11) Rick Hertel
(12) Darryl Hill
(13) Jack Hollis
(14) Dennis Homberg
(15) Mike Lebo
(16) Denis Menke
(17) Benny Perez
(18) Jay Robertson
(19) Dave Rohm
(20) Jose Rosario
(21) Pete Rowe
(22) Ron Sorey
(23) Fay Thompson
(24) Greg Wells
(25) Ralph Wheeler
(26) Randy Wiens
(27) Andre Wood

1978 TCMA Greenwood Braves

(Atlanta Braves, A) (black and white)

	NR MT	EX	VG
Complete Set:	25.00	12.50	7.50

(1) Terry Abbot
(2) Tom Ballard
(3) Tim Barr
(4) Clete Boyer
(5) Smokey Burgess
(6) Tim Cole
(7) Joe Cowley
(8) John Dyer
(9) Andre Forbes
(10) Alan Gallagher
(11) Bill Haley
(12) Steve Hammond
(13) Bill Haslerig
(14) Danny Lucia
(15) Jeff Matthews
(16) Tommy Mee
(17) Alvin Moore
(18) Felix Pettaway
(19) Bob Porter
(20) Rafael Ramirez
(21) George Ramos
(22) Andre Sams
(23) Brian Snitker
(24) Scott Thayer
(25) Bruce Tonascia
(26) Wyatt Tonkin
(27) William Tucker
(28) Bob Veale
(29) Richard Wieters

1978 TCMA Holyoke Millers

(Milwaukee Brewers, AA) (color)

	NR MT	EX	VG
Complete Set:	20.00	10.00	6.00

(1) Jeff Barker
(2) Ken Biggerstaff
(3) Ed Carroll
(4) Mike Dempsey
(5) Bill Dick
(6) Ronnie Driver
(7) Marshall Edwards
(8) George Farson
(9) Steve Green
(10) Steve Grimes
(11) Mike Henderson
(12) Lynn B. Herzig
(13) Gary Holle
(14) Ron Jacobs
(15) Bernado Leonard
(16) Willie Mueller
(17) Rick Nicholson
(18) Neil Rasmussen
(19) Chuck Ross
(20) Dave Smith
(21) Steve Splitt
(22) Esteban Texidor
(23) Don Whiting
(24) Jeff Yurak

1978 TCMA Knoxville Knox Sox

(Chicago White Sox, AA) (black and white)

	NR MT	EX	VG
Complete Set:	300.00	150.00	90.00

(1) Harold Baines
(2) Richard Barnes
(3) Richard Dotson
(4) Marvis Foley
(5) Ken Frailing
(6) Fred Frazier
(7) Joe Gates
(8) Quency Hill
(9) Fred Howard
(10) Rusty Kuntz
(11) Tony LaRussa
(12) Mitch Lukevics
(13) Larry Monroe
(14) Bill Moran
(15) Mark Naehring
(16) Chris Nyman
(17) Andy Pasillas
(18) Donn Seidholz
(19) Duane Shaffer
(20) Ken Silvestri
(21) Tom Spencer
(22) Willie Thompson
(23) Tommy Toman
(24) Steve Trout
(25) Mike Wolf

1978 TCMA Lodi Dodgers

(Los Angeles Dodgers, A) (black and white)

	NR MT	EX	VG
Complete Set:	45.00	22.00	13.50

(1) Paul Bain
(2) Bobby Brown
(3) H.P. Drake
(4) Larry Fobbs
(5) Marv Garrison
(6) Rick Goulding
(7) Brian Hayes
(8) Ubalso Heredia
(9) Hank Jones
(10) George Kaage
(11) Mike Lake
(12) Mickey Lashley
(13) Dave Richards
(14) Tim Roche
(15) Ron Roenicke
(16) Don Ruzek
(17a) Rod Scheller (incorrect name on back)

(17b) Rod Scheller (correct name on back)

(18) Eric Schmidt
(19) Steve Shirley
(20) John Shoemaker
(21) Mike Stone
(22) Ken Townsend
(23) Max Venable
(24) John Walker
(25) Stan Wasiak

1978 TCMA Newark Wayne Co-Pilots

(Milwaukee Brewers, A) (black and white)

	NR MT	EX	VG
Complete Set:	50.00	25.00	15.00

(1) Bert Acosta
(2) Sally Beal
(3) Randy Boyce
(4) Eddie Brunson
(5) Ron Bugga
(6) Pablo Cavallo
(7) Rafael Cuevas
(8) Stan Davis
(9) Greg Dellart
(10) Jorge DeJesus
(11) Roberto Diaz
(12) Duke Duncan
(13) Lance Ediger
(14) Willie Flowers
(15) Steve Gibson
(16) Sam Gierhan
(17) Dan Gilmartin
(18) Dean Hall
(19) Rocky Hall
(20) Nick Hernandez
(21) Doug Jones
(22) Tim Jordan
(23) Eliqio Kelly
(24) Harvey Kuenn
(25) David Lebron
(26) Jerry Lewis
(27) Steve Manderfield
(28) Ray Manship
(29) Dan Maxson
(30) Tom McLish
(31) Steve Norwood
(32) Rick Olsen
(33) Jim Padula
(34) Vince Pone
(35) Luis Ramirez
(36) Russell Ramirez
(37) Kenny Richardson
(38) Jim Robinson
(39) John Roesch
(40) Pat Seegers
(41) Tom Soto
(42) John Stevenson
(43) Al Wesolowski
(44) Nick Wilhite
(45) Porter Wyatt

1978 TCMA Orlando Twins

(Minnesota Twins, AA) (black and white)
(Minnesota Twins, AA) (black & white)

	NR MT	EX	VG
Complete Set:	30.00	15.00	9.00

(1) Terry Bulling
(2) John Castino
(3) Mark Clapham
(4) Rich Dalton
(5) Rick Duncan
(6) Frank Estes
(7) John Goryl
(8) Jeff Holly
(9) Darrell Jackson
(10) Curt Lewis
(11) Bruce MacPherson
(12) Dennis Mantick
(13) Marty Maxwell
(14) Kevin McWhinter
(15) Warren Mertens
(16) Frank Quintero
(17) Tom Sain
(18) Terry Sheehan
(19) Ray Smith
(20) Dan Spain
(21) Jesus Vega
(22) Steve Wagner
(23) Kurt Whittmayer

NOTE: A card number in parentheses ( ) indicates the set is unnumbered.

1978 TCMA Quad City Angels

(California Angels, A) (black and white)

	NR MT	EX	VG
Complete Set:	100.00	50.00	30.00

(1) Gary Balla
(2) Ned Bergert
(3) Jeff Bertoni
(4) Joe Blyleven
(5) Arturo Bonnitto
(6) Bob Border
(7) Jeff Connor
(8) Brian Harper
(9) Brad Havens
(10) Mike Heaton
(11) Don Jones
(12) Guy Jones
(13) Monte Mendenhall
(14) Mark Miller
(15) Charles Nash
(16) Steve Oliva
(17) Harry Pells
(18) John Pound
(19) Melvin Quarles
(20) Bran Riffle (Riffel)
(21) Greg Ris
(22) Andy Rodriguez
(23) Wade Schexnayder
(24) Darryl Sconiers
(25) Mike Stover
(26) Doug Thompson
(27) Jim Vallone
(28) Steve Van Deren
(29) Alan Wiggins
(30) Waterloo Municipal Stadium

1978 TCMA Richmond Braves

(Atlanta Braves, AAA) (color)

	NR MT	EX	VG
Complete Set:	25.00	12.50	7.50

(1) Tommie Aaron
(2) James Arline
(3) Bruce Benedict
(4) Larry Bradford
(5) Glenn Hubbard
(6) Frank LaCorte
(7) Michael Macha
(8) Jerry Maddox
(9) Richard Mahler
(10) Joey McLaughlin
(11) Edward Miller
(12) Jon Richardson
(13) Chico Ruiz
(14) John Sain
(15) Hank Small
(16) Duane Theiss
(17) Larry Whisenton
(18) Kris Yoder
(19) Front Office
(20) Chief Powa Hitta, Seymore Baseball (Team mascots)

1978 TCMA Rochester Red Wings

(Baltimore Orioles, AAA) (color)

	NR MT	EX	VG
Complete Set:	25.00	12.50	7.50

(1) Ray Bare
(2) Tom Bianco
(3) Don Cardoza
(4) Tony Chevez
(5) Tom Chism
(6) Dave Criscione
(7) Mike Dimmel
(8) Blake Doyle
(9) Skeeter Jarquin
(10) Kevin Kennedy
(11) Wayne Krenchicki
(12) Rafael Liranzo
(13) Marty Parrill
(14) Jeff Rineer
(15) Frank Robinson
(16) Earl Stephenson
(17) Tim Stoddard

1978 TCMA St. Petersburg Cardinals

(St. Louis Cardinals, A) (black and white)

	NR MT	EX	VG
Complete Set:	50.00	25.00	15.00

(1) Fulvio Bertolotti
(2) Jack Boag
(3) Mark Bumstead
(4) Tom Chamberlain
(5) Donnie Chesire
(6) Dennis Cirbo
(7) Glenn Comoletti
(8) Chris Davis
(9) Hector Eduardo
(10) Neil Fiala
(11) Julian Gutierrez
(12) Brett Houser
(13) Dave Johnson
(14) Dave Jorn
(15) Arno Kirchenwitz
(16) Terry Landrum
(17) Hal Lanier
(18) Chris Lombardo
(19) Ralph Miller, Jr.
(20) Kelly Paris
(21) Mike Pisarkiewicz
(22) Mike Pope
(23) Jim Reeves
(24) Gene Roof
(25) Larry Silver
(26) Elliot Waller
(27) Ray Williams
(28) Hal Witt
(29) Felipe Zayas

1978 TCMA Salem Pirates

(Pittsburgh Pirates, A) (black and white)

	NR MT	EX	VG
Complete Set:	32.00	16.00	9.50

(1) Juan Arias
(2) Pablo Cruz
(3) Phil Cyburt
(4) Rickey Evans
(5) Marc Gelinas
(6) Sandy Hill
(7) Rick Lancelotti
(8) Robert Long
(9) Jim Mahoney
(10) Frank Miloszewski
(11) Bob Parsons
(12) Rick Peterson
(13) Luis Salazar
(14) Dean Rick
(15) Bob Rock
(16) Luis Salazar
(17) Rick Peterson
(18) Alfredo Torres
(19) Chich Valley
(20) Ben Wiltbank

1978 TCMA Syracuse Chiefs

(Toronto Blue Jays, AAA) (color)

	NR MT	EX	VG
Complete Set:	27.50	13.75	8.25

(1) Danny Ainge
(2) Butch Alberts
(3) Vern Benson
(4) Jeff Byrd
(5) Victor Cruz
(6) Mike Darr
(7) Andy Dyes
(8) Butch Edge
(9) Sam Ewing
(10) Chuck Fore
(11) Steve Grilli
(12) pat Kelly
(13) Sheldon Mallory
(14) Luis Melendez
(15) Ken Pape
(16) Ken Reynolds
(17) Tom Sandt
(18) Mike Stanton
(19) Hector Torres
(20) Ernie Whitt
(21) Alvis Woods
(22) Gary Woods

1978 TCMA Tidewater Tides

(New York Mets, AAA) (color) (complete set price includes scarce Verdi card)

	NR MT	EX	VG
Complete Set:	27.50	13.75	8.25

(1) Neil Allen
(2) Fred Andrews
(3) Juan Berenguer
(4) Dwight Bernard
(5) Marshall Brant
(6) Mike Bruhart
(7) Ed Cipot
(8) Mardie Cornejo
(9) Sergio Ferrer
(10) Tom Hausman
(11) Roy Lee Jackson
(12) Ed Kurpiel
(13) Pepe Mangual
(14) Rich Miller
(15) Bob Myrick
(16) Dan Norman
(17) John Pacella
(18) Greg Pavlick
(19) Marty Perez
(20) Mario Ramirez
(21) Randy Rogers
(22) Luis Rosado
(23) Mike Scott
(24) Dan Smith
(25) Alex Trevino
(26) Mike Van De Casteele
(27) Frank Verdi

1978 TCMA Waterloo Indians

(Cleveland Indians, A) (black and white)

	NR MT	EX	VG
Complete Set:	30.00	15.00	9.00

(1) Tom Anderson
(2) Ken Bolek
(3) Juan Bonilla
(4) Tim Brill
(5) John Buszka
(6) Bob Conley
(7) Sammy Davis
(8) Jack DuBeau
(9) Jerry Dybzinski
(10) Robin Fuson
(11) Tim Glass
(12) Vic Homstedt
(13) Don Hubbard
(14) Angelo Lo Grande
(15) Carl Nicholson
(16) Thomas Pulchinski
(17) Al Rauch
(18) Kevin Rhomberg
(19) Ramon Romero
(20) Ed Saavedra
(21) Forest Smith
(22) Sam Spence
(23) John Teising
(24) Lloyd Turner
(25) Glenn Wendt
(26) Troy Wilder

1978 TCMA Wausau Mets

(New York Mets, A) (black and white)

	NR MT	EX	VG
Complete Set:	70.00	35.00	21.00

(1) Curt Baker
(2) Don Brazell
(3) Stewart Bringhurst
(4) Greg Brown
(5) Bill Chamberlain
(6) Al Coghen
(7) Ed Cuervo
(8) Bruce Ferguson
(9) Jeff Franklin
(10) Brent Gaff
(11) John Hinkel
(12) Chris Jones
(13) Ken Jones
(14) Chris Kirby
(15) Randy Lamb
(16) Steve Lowe
(17) Mike Lowry
(18) Dan Monzon
(19) Jim Noonan
(20) Darryl Paquette
(21) Don Pearson
(22) Junior Roman
(23) Frank Sanchez
(24) Keith Shermeyer
(25) John McDonald Stadium

1978 TCMA Wisconsin Rapids Twins

(Minnesota Twins, A) (black and white)

	NR MT	EX	VG
Complete Set:	30.00	15.00	9.00

(1) Greg Allen
(2) Paul Croft
(3) George Dierburger
(4) Gary Dobbs
(5) Mark Funderburk
(6) Michael Gustave
(7) Lance Hallberg
(8) Elmore Hill
(9) Joe Keith Isaac
(10) Abner Johnson
(11) Elmer Lingerman
(12) Ronnie Mears
(13) John Minarcin
(14) Dean Moranda
(15) Eric Prevost
(16) Clyde Reichard
(17) Harold Rowe
(18) Richard Stelmaszek

1978 Team Geneva Cubs

(Chicago Cubs, A) This set is numbered as it appears on the cards. It was also produced in a set of 4 uncut sheets.

	NR MT	EX	VG
Complete Set:	215.00	107.50	64.50

4 Jeff Doyle
7 Bob Hartsfield
8 Mike Turgeon
10 Bill Morgan
11 Jerry Ahlert
14 Bubba Kizer
18 J.W. Mitchell
21 Joe Cole
22 Bill Ross
25 Joe Hicks
26 Mike Godley
27 Mark Parker
28 Ted Trevino
29 Mark Gilbert
30 Lou Whetstone
31 Ted May
37 Joe McClain
39a Ennis Lamont
39b Doug McCracken
41 Tom Spino
44 Bill Earley
45 Randy Clark
49 Joe Stethers

1978 Team Indianapolis Indians

(Cincinnati Reds, AAA) (color) This set was co-sponsored by Tom Aikens.

	NR MT	EX	VG
Complete Set:	25.00	12.50	7.50

1 Team Photo
2 Roy Majtyka
3 Paul Moskau
4 Harry Spilman
5 Mike LaCoss
6 Ron Oester
7 Dan Dumoulin
8 Ed ARmbrister
9 Mario Soto
10 Tommy Mutz
11 Dave Moore
12 John Summers
13 Larry Payne
14 John Valle
15 George Cappuzzello
16 Mike Grace
17 Rafael Santo Domingo
18 Angel Torres
19 Vic Correll
20 Lynn Jones
21 Raul Ferreyra
22 Arturo Defreites
23 Frank Pastore
24 Randy Davidson
25 Jeff Sovern
26 Ron McClain
27 Checklist

1978 Team Oklahoma City 89'ers

(Philadelphia Phillies, AAA)

	NR MT	EX	VG
Complete Set:	75.00	37.50	22.50

1 Fred Ray Beene
3 Ramon Aviles
4 Lonnie Smith
5 Robert Michael DeMeo
6 James Forrest Morrison
7 Michael T. Buskey
8 Kerry Michael Dineen
9 Rogers Lee Brown
10 Steven Craig Waterbury
11 Orlando Alvarez
12 Todd Ruben Cruz
14 Saucier Kevin Andrew
15 Mike Anderson
16 Danny Jon Boitano
17 Charles Edward Kniffin
18 Daniel Dean Warthen
19 Bobby Keith Moreland
20 Orlando Gonzalez
21 Michael Sherman Wallace
22 John C. Vukovich
23 John William Poff
25 Jackson A. Todd
26 Arnaldo Contreras, Jr.
27 Michael James Ryan
28 Tom Harmon
29 William Connors

1978 Tiefel & Associates Denver Bears

(Montreal Expos, AAA) (color)

	NR MT	EX	VG
Complete Set:	10.00	5.00	3.00

1 Tony Bernazard
2 Tony Bernazard ("6 for 6")
3 Ossie Blanco
4 Leonel Carrion
5 Joe Carroll
6 Ed Creech
7 Don Demola
8 Doc Edwards
9 Jerry Fry
10 Dave Gronlund
11 Mike Hart
12 Tim Jones
13 Joe Keener
14 Larry Landreth
15 Pete Mackanin
16 Randy Miller
17 Frank Ortenzio
18 Bob Pate
19 Roberto Ramos
20 Steve Ratzer
21 Rick REnick
22 Ken Rushing
23 Dan Schatzeder
24 Bryn Smith
25 Frank Orenzio, Bobby Pate, Rick Resnick

1979

1979 Chong Modesto A's

(Oakland A's, A) (black and white) (cards are gold on front, and have blank backs)

	NR MT	EX	VG
Complete Set:	50.00	25.00	15.00

Logo Card
1 Gaylen Pitts
2 Rich Morales
3 Frank Kneuer
4 Pat Dempsey
5 Fred Devito
6 Dana Berry
7 Paul Stevens
8 Mike Woodard
9 Jay Greb
10 Kelvin Moore
11 Mike Davis
12 Bob Markham
13 Don Morris
14 Don Schubert
15 Craig Harris
16 Mike Yesenchak
17 Chuck Dougherty
18 Don Van Marter
19 Walt Bigos
20 John Gosse
21 Fritz Lund
22 Dave Mc Carthy
23 Ron Jensen

1979 Chong Hawaii Islanders

	NR MT	EX	VG
Complete Set:	7.50	3.75	2.25

3 Al Zarilla
5 Sam Perlozzo
8 Tucker Ashford
9 Steve Brye
10 Vic Bernal
11 Chuck Baker
12 Bob Mitcherll
13 Juan Eichelberger
14 Craig Stimac
16 Tom Tellman
17 Dennis Kinney
18 Rick Sweet
19 Al Fitzmorris
20 Lynn McKinney
21 Jim Beswick
22 Randy Fierbaugh
23 Fred Kuhaulua
24 Dick Phillips
25 Jim Wilhelm
26 Gary Lucas
27 Tony Castillo
28 Andy Dyes
29 Dave Wehrmeister
--- Team Logo/Schedule

1979 Cramer Hawaii Islanders

(San Diego Padres, AAA) (color, 2-3/8" by 3-1/2") (co-sponsored by 7-Up)

	NR MT	EX	VG
Complete Set:	7.50	3.75	2.25

3 Al Zarilla
5 Sam Perlozzo
8 Tucker Ashford
9 Steve Brye
10 Vic Bernal
11 Chuck Baker
12 Bob Mitchell
13 Juan Eichelberger

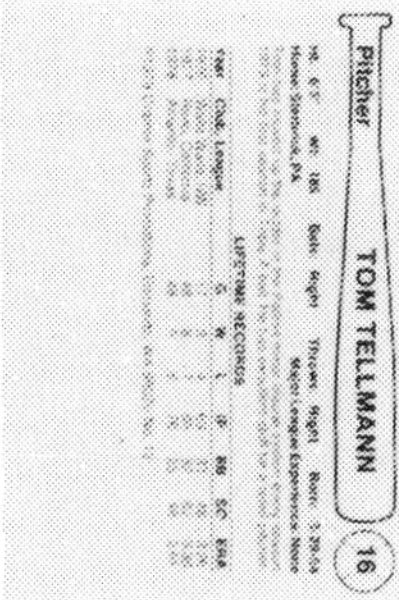

14 Craig Stimac
16 Tom Tellmann
17 Dennis Kinney
18 Rick Sweet
19 Al Fitzmorris
20 Lynn McKinney
21 Jim Beswick
22 Randy Fierbaugh
23 Fred Kuhaulua
24 Dick Phillips
25 Jim Wilhelm
26 Gary Lucas
27 Tony Castillo
28 Andy Dyes
29 Dave Wehrmeister
--- Team Logo & Schedule

1979 Cramer Phoenix Giants

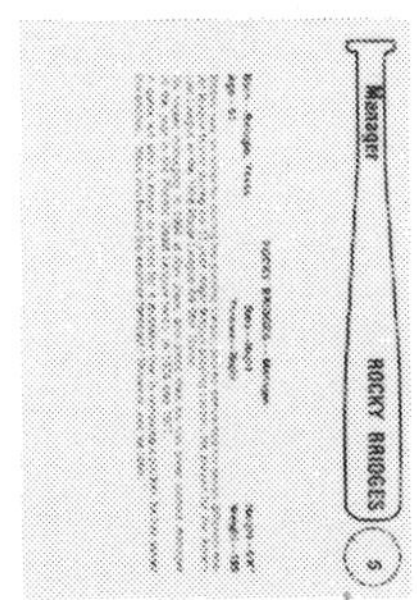

San Francisco Giants, AAA) (color, 2-7/16" by 3-1/2") (co-sponsored by Valley National Bank)

	NR MT	EX	VG
Complete Set:	7.50	3.75	2.25

1 Doug Schafer
2 Kyle Hypes
3 Mike Rowland
4 Jeff Little
5 Rocky Bridges
6 Phil Nastu
7 Bill Bordley
8 Ed Plank
9 Joe Strain
10 Greg Johnston
11 Don Carrithers
12 Tom Heintzelman
13 Randy Harmon
14 Rick Bradley
15 Terry Cornutt
16 Chris Bourjos
17 Casey Parsons
18 Rich Murray
19 Dennis Littlejohn
20 Mark Kuecker
21 Rick Sanderlin
22 Guy Sularz
23 Mike Rex
24 Ethan Blackaby
--- Tommy Gonzales
--- Harry Jordan

1979 Police Iowa Oaks

(Chicago White Sox, AAA) (black and white)

	NR MT	EX	VG
Complete Set:	185.00	92.50	55.50

(1) Lloyd Allen
(2) Harold Baines
(3) Kevin Bell
(4) Harry Chappas
(5) Mike Colbern
(6) Fred Frazier
(7) Guy Hoffman
(8) Dewey Hoyt
(9) Art Kusnyer
(10) Tony LaRussa
(11) Bob Molinaro
(12) Chris Nyman
(13) Dewey Robinson
(14) John Sutton

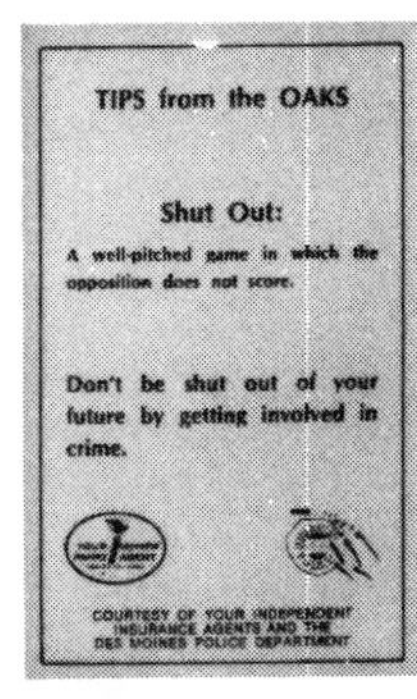
TIPS from the OAKS

Shut Out:

A well-pitched game in which the opposition does not score.

Don't be shut out of your future by getting involved in crime.

COURTESY OF YOUR INDEPENDENT INSURANCE AGENTS AND THE DES MOINES POLICE DEPARTMENT

1979 TCMA Albuquerque Dukes

(Los Angeles Dodgers, AAA) (color)

	NR MT	EX	VG
Complete Set:	50.00	25.00	15.00

1 Pablo Peguero
2 Mike Tennent
3 Mike Williams
4 Bill Swiacki
5 Dave Stewart
6 Dave Patterson
7 Dennis Lewallyn
8 Kevin Keefe
9 Gerry Hannahs
10 Mike Scioscia
11 Mickey Hatcher
12 John O'Rear
13 Jack Perconte
14 Kelly Snider
15 Alex Taveras
16 Pedro Guerrero
17 Rich Magner
18 Bobby Mitchell
19 Rudy Law
20 Joe Beckwith
21 Claude Westmoreland
22 Bobby Castillo
23 Bobby Padilla

1979 TCMA Appleton Foxes

(Chicago White Sox, A) (black and white)

	NR MT	EX	VG
Complete Set:	95.00	47.00	28.00

1 Paul Soth
2 Dennis Keating
3 Vito Lucarelli
4 Ed Bahns
5 Dave White
6 Kevin Hickey
7 Clancy Woods
8 Jeff Vuksan
9 Lorenzo Gray
10 Mike Johnson
11 Dave Daniels
12 Ivan Mesa
13 Mike Sivik
14 Phil Bauer
15 Mart Teutsch
16 Luis Estrada
17 Jim Breazeale
18 Vince Bienek
19 Bob Umdenstock
20 Mike Maitland
21 Duane Shaffer
22 Mark Platel
23 Don Kraeger
24 Vic Walters
25 Paul Gbur

1979 TCMA Arkansas Travelers

(St. Louis Cardinals, AA) (color)

	NR MT	EX	VG
Complete Set:	20.00	10.00	6.00

1 Arno Kirchenwitz
2 Len Strelitz
3 Raymond Williams
4 Terry Landrum
5 Jim Riggleman
6 John Littlefield
7 Thomas N. Thompson
8 Joseph Dotson
9 Elliott Waller
10 Joseph DeSa
11 Fred Tisdale
12 Jorge Aranzamendi
13 Neil Fiala
14 Mike McCormick
15 Fulvio Bertolotti
16 Dennis Delany
17 Chris Davis
18 Randy Thomas
19a Tom Chamberlain

19b Hector Eduardo
20 Ray Searage
21 David Johnson
22 Gene Roof

1979 TCMA Asheville Tourists

(Texas Rangers, A) (black and white)

	NR MT	EX	VG
Complete Set:	185.00	92.00	55.00

1 Luis Gonzalez
2 Tracy Cowger
3 Tom McGivney
4 Lynvel Mosby
5 Wayne Terwilliger
6 Jim Farr
7 Dave Chapman
8 Andy Tam
9 Jeff Zitek
10 George Wright
11 Dave Miller
12 Wes Williams
13 Jim McWilliams
14 Al Ortiz
15 Steve Righetti
16 Bobby Tanzi
17 Amos Lewis
18 Arnold Wilhoite
19 Pat Nelson
20 Mike Childs
21 Mike Vickers
22 Jeff Scott
23 Dan Dixon
24 Chuck Kwolek
25 Dave Hibner
26 Mike Richardt
27 Stan Reese
28 Gene Nelson

1979 TCMA Buffalo Bisons

(Pittsburgh Pirates, AA) (black and white)

	NR MT	EX	VG
Complete Set:	125.00	62.00	37.00

1 Dave Dravecky
2 Stu Cliburn
3 Rick Lancellotti
4 Joe Galante
5 Tony Pena
6 Jerry McDonald
7 Steve Demeter
8 Ernie Young
9 Bubba Evans
10 Marc Galinas
11 Juan Arias
12 Harry Dorish, Bob Weismiller
13 Fred Breining
14 Chick Valley
15 Tom McMillan
16 Luis Salazar
17 Jim Smith
18 Al Torres
19 Dick Walterhouse
20 Robert Long
21 Paul Djakonow

1979 TCMA Burlington Bees

(Milwaukee Brewers, A) (black and white)

	NR MT	EX	VG
Complete Set:	30.00	15.00	9.00

1 Larry Edwards
2 Russell Ramirez
3 Pat Seegers
4 Jim Robinson
5 Sam Gierham
6 Rocky Hall
7 Willie Lozado
8 Nick Hernandez
9 Ron Buggs
10 Dan Gilmartin
11 Mark Lepson
12 Doug Jones
13 Steve Gibson
14 Bob Gibson
15 Johnny Evans
16 Roberto Diaz
17 Duane Espy
18 Vince Bailey
19 Randy Boyce
20 Greg DeHart
21 Stan Davis
22 Vince Pone
23 Jim Padula
24 Steve Norwood
25 Steve Manderfield

Definitions for grading conditions are located in the Introduction section at the front of this book.

1979 TCMA Cedar Rapids Giants

(San Francisco Giants, A) (black and white)

	NR MT	EX	VG
Complete Set:	115.00	57.50	34.50

1 Steve Duckhorn
2 Jesus Cruz
3 Mark Benson
4 Jorge Mundroig
5 John Rabb
6 Robbie Henderson
7 Jeff Stadler
8 Matt Sutherland
9 Francisco Fojas
10 Rick Doss
11 Bruce Oliver
12 Bill Bellomo
13 Glenn Fisher
14 Bud Curran
15 Wayne Cato
16 Jeff Stember
17 Paul Plinski
18 Jose Chue
19 Rick Kean
20 George Torassa
21 Ned Raines
22 Lou Merietta
23 Craig Hedrick
24 Kelly Anderson
25 Harry Wing
26 Juan Oppenhiemer
27 Ray Cosio
28 Bob Deer (Rob)
29 Don Buchheister
30 Phil Sutton
31 Doug Linduyt
32 Bob Cummins

1979 TCMA Charleston Charlies

(Houston Astros, AAA) (color) (complete set price includes variations)

	NR MT	EX	VG
Complete Set:	40.00	20.00	12.00

1 Keith Drumright
2 Jim Beauchamp
3 Russ Rothermel
4 Reggie Baldwin
5 Gary Woods
6 Mike Fischlin
7 Mike Tyler
8 Dave Bergman
9 Ramon Perez
10a Mark Miggins (Dave Smith photo, no mustache)
10b Mark Miggins (correct photo, with mustache)
11a David Smith (Mark Miggins photo, with mustache)
11b David Smith (correct photo, no mustache)
12 Dave Augustine
13 Gordy Pladson
14 Luis Pujols
15 Larry Hardy
16 Rob Sperring
17 Wilbur Howard
18 Gary Wilson
19 Mike Mendoza

1979 TCMA Clinton Dodgers

(Los Angeles Dodgers, A) (black and white)

	NR MT	EX	VG
Complete Set:	165.00	82.50	49.50

1 Mark Eliott
2 Clay Smith
3 Johnny Lee Robbins
4 Roberto Alexander
5 Matt Reeves
6 Alan Wiggins
7 Otis Bradley
8 Paul Popovich
9 Alejandro Pena
10 Steve Sax
11 Mitch Webster
12 Eric Schmidt
13 Chris Gancy
14 Kent Johnson
15 Marcos Rodriguez
16 Leonardo Hernandez
17 Dick McLaughlin
18 Dave Sax
19 Dave LaPointe
20 Rod Nelson
21 Bob Giesecke
22 Larry Wright
23 Steve Maples
24 Kevin Joyce
25 Bob White
26 Candido Maldonado
27 Frank Wilczewski
28 Larry Ferst

NOTE: A card number in parentheses ( ) indicates the set is unnumbered.

1979 TCMA Columbus Clippers

(New York Yankees, AAA) (color)

	NR MT	EX	VG
Complete Set:	20.00	10.00	6.00

1 Brad Gulden
2 Roy Staiger
3 Paul Semall
4 Damaso Garcia
5 Garry Smith
6 Stan Williams
7 Gene Michael
8 Jim Beattie
9 Gerry McNertney
10 Dennis Werth
11 Mark Letendre
12 Marvin Thompson
13 Tommy Cruz
14 Ron Davis
15 Bob Polinsky
16 Bruce Robinson
17 Gerg Cochran
18 Rodger Holt
19 Dennis Sherrill
20 Steve Taylor
21 Rich Anderson
22 Nathan Chapman
23 Bob Kammeyer
24 Chris Welsh
25 Howard Cassidy
26 Paul Mirabella
27 Bobby Brown
28 Daryl Jones
29 Mickey Vernon

1979 TCMA Elmira Pioneers

(Boston Red Sox, A) (black and white)

	NR MT	EX	VG
Complete Set:	110.00	55.00	33.00

1 Lloyd Bessard
2 Jay Fredlund
3 ken Hagemann
4 Danny Huffstickler
5 Arturo Samaniego
6 Glenn Eddins, Jr.
7 Joaquin Gutierrez
8 Tom McCarthy
9 Steve Fortune
10 Don Hayford
11 Eddie Lee
12 Russell Lee Pruitt
13 Scott Gering
14 Dave Holt
15 Steve Schaefer
16 Tony Cleary
17 Andy Serrano
18 Francisco Vasquez
19 Gus Malespin
20 Hal Natupsky
21 Dick Berardino
22 Ed Berroa
23 Bill Limoncelli
24 Bob Birrell
25 Wayne Tremblay
26 Tom Brunner
27 Tom DeSanto
28 Mark Saunders

1979 TCMA Hawaii Islanders

(San Diego Padres, AAA) (color)

	NR MT	EX	VG
Complete Set:	13.00	6.50	4.00

1 Bob Mitchell
2 Lynn McKinney
3 Rick Sweet
4 Craig Stimac
5 Andy Dyes
6 Dick Phillips
7 Jim Wilhelm
8 Vic Bernal
9 Gary Lucas
10 Jim Beswick
11 Sam Perlozzo
12 Steve Brye
13 Don Reynolds
14 Steve Smith
15 Al Zarilla
16 Chuck Baker
17 Alan Fitzmorris
18 Dennis Kinney
19 Mike Dupree
20 Fred Kuhaulua
21 Juan Eichelberger
22 Dennis Blair
23 Tom Tellmann
24 Tony Castillo

1979 TCMA Holyoke Millers

(Milwaukee Brewers, AA) (color)

	NR MT	EX	VG
Complete Set:	13.00	6.50	4.00

1 Rene Quinones
2 Terry Bevington
3 Bill Foley
4 Ed Carroll
5 Kevin Bass
6 Bobby Smith
7 Mark Schuster
8 George Farson
9 Rick Olsen
10 Tom Soto
11 Ron Driver
12 Tom Cook
13 Gersan Jarquin
14 Rick Duran
15 Don Whiting
16 Brian Thorson
17 Mike Henderson
18 Butch Riggar
19 Steve Splitt
20 Larry Rush
21 Steve Reed
22 Darryl Bailey
23 Weldon Swift
24 Rocky Hall
25 Lance Rautzhan
26 Barry Cort
27 "Duke" Duncan
28 Jeff Yurak
29 Sam Hinds
30 Tom Kayser

1979 TCMA Jackson Mets

(New York Mets, AA) (color)

	NR MT	EX	VG
Complete Set:	20.00	10.00	6.00

1 "Paco" Perez
2 Wally Backman
3 Hubie Brooks
4 Wayne Sexton
5 Paul Wiener
6 Bob Wellman
7 Jodie Davis
8 Bob Grote
9 Sergio Beltre
10 Paul Cacciatore
11 Keith Bodie
12 Pete Hamner
13 Luis Lunar
14 Mike Howard
15 Dave Von Ohlen
16 Rick Anderson
17 Dan Smith
18 Rich Miller, Jr.
19 Bobby Bryant
20 Russell Clark
21 Greg Harris
22a Front Office Staff
22b Stan Hough
23 Ronald MacDonald
24 Fred Martinez

1979 TCMA Knoxville White Sox

(Chicago White Sox, AA) (black and white)

	NR MT	EX	VG
Complete Set:	165.00	82.00	49.00

1 Mark Naehring
2 Phil Trucks
3 Luis Guzman
4 Gordy Lund
5 Richard Barnes
6 Britt Burns
7 Leo Sutherland
8 Richard Dotson
9 Don Seidholz
10 John Flannery
11 Mitch Lukevics
12 Ron Kittle
13 Willie Gutierrez
14 Larry Monroe
15 John Hanley
16 Joel Perez
17 Jackie Smith
18 Bruce Dal Canton
19 Ray Murillo
20 Andy Pasillas
21 Ted Barnicle
22 A.J. Hill
23 Ray Torres
24 Rod Allen
25 Tom Spencer
26 Willie Thompson

1979 TCMA Lodi Dodgers

(Los Angeles Dodgers, A) (black and white)

	NR MT	EX	VG
Complete Set:	110.00	55.00	33.00

1 Rod Kemp
2 Augie Ruiz
3 Paul Bain
4 Alfredo Mejia
5 Skip Mann
6 Mike Marshall
7 Rocky Cordova
8 Steve Perry
9 Jesse Baez
10 Jim Nobles
11 Larry Powers
12 Johnny Walker
13 Bill Swoope
14 Stan Wasiak
15 Miguel Franjul
16 Jerry Bass
17 Bob Foster
18 Chris Malden
19 Brian Hayes
20 Hank Jones
21 Evon Martinson

1979 TCMA Memphis Chicks

(Montreal Expos, AA) (black and white)

	NR MT	EX	VG
Complete Set:	275.00	137.50	82.50

1 Steve Lovins
2 Steve Michael
3 Bill Armstrong
4 Julio Perez
5 Bryn Smith
6 Larry Goldetsky
7 Doug Simunic
8 Charlie Lea
9 Dave Hostetler
10 Anthony Johnson
11 Randy Schafer
12 Mike Finlayson
13 Rick Williams
14 Rick Engle
15 Bob Teneini
16 Ray Crowley
17 John Scoras
18 Jeff Gingrich
19 Dennis Sherow
20 Tim Raines
21 Billy Gardner
22 Pat Rooney
23 Warren Hemm
24 Godfrey Evans

1979 TCMA Newark Co-Pilots

(No affiliation, A) (black and white)

	NR MT	EX	VG
Complete Set:	40.00	20.00	12.00

1 Tom Dann
2 Steve Nicastro
3 Joe Rigoli
4 Bob Bill
5 Mike Overton
6 Mike Fichman
7 Steve Dembowski
8 Mal Oleksak
9 Don Clatterbuck
10 Michael LaCasse
11 Kevin MacDonald
12 Joe McCann
13 Harry White
14 Mark Grier
15 Carl Adams
16 Bob Cross
17 Billy Clay
18 Keith Gainer
19 Richard Block
20 Kevin Rose
21 Mitch Wright
22 Len Spicer
23 Lance Viola
24 Andy Pascarella

1979 TCMA Ogden A's

(Oakland A's, AAA) (color)

	NR MT	EX	VG
Complete Set:	175.00	87.50	52.50

1 Terry Enyart
2 Tim Hosley
3 Mike Morgan
4 Mike Rodriguez
5 Craig Mitchell
6 Jose Pagan
7 Mack Harrison
8 Dennis Haines
9 Rickey Henderson
10 Brian Abraham
11 Richard Lysander
12 Jeff Cox
13 Brian Kingman
14 Royle Stillman
15 Danny Goodwin
16 Rya Cosey
17 Mark Souza
18 Mark Budaska
19 Frank Kolarek
20 Pat Dempsey
21 Craig Mitchell
22 Allen Wirth
23 Jeff Jones
24 Mike Patterson
25 Bob Grandas
26 Keith Liepman

1979 TCMA Portland Beavers

(Pittsburgh Pirates, AAA) (color)

	NR MT	EX	VG
Complete Set:	15.00	7.50	4.50

1 Al Holland
2 Ossie Oliveras
3 Greg Field
4 Ben Wiltbank
5 Vance Law
6 Tom Sandt
7 Dorian Boyland
8 Ron Mitchell
9 John Lipon
10 Gene Cotes
11 Joe Coleman
12 Gene Pentz
13 Gary Hargis
14 Alberto Lois
15 Mike Garman
16 Manny Lantigua
17 Dan Warthen
18 Craig Cacek
19 Larry Littleton
20 Pascual Perez
21 Harry Saferight
22 Rod Scurry
23 Rick Jones
24 Rod Gilbreath

1979 TCMA Quad City Cubs

(Chicago Cubs, A) (black and white)

	NR MT	EX	VG
Complete Set:	85.00	42.00	25.00

1 Mike Wright
2 Ed Mohr
3 Ed Moore
4 Roger Crow
5 Bill Morgan
6 Wayne Rohlfing
7 Ted May
8 Joe McClain
9 Rich McClure
10 J.W. Mitchell
11 Joe Hicks
12 Mark Gilbert
13 Joey Cole
14 Randy Clark
15 Hal Kizer
16 Craig Kornfeld
17 Bob Maddon
18 Gordon Hodgson
19 John Bargfeldt
20 Andy Walker
21 Freddy Forgeur
22 Jim Napier
23 Tom Spino
24 Mike Shepston
25 Steve Viskas
26 Bob Oliver
27 Norm Churchill

1979 TCMA Richmond Braves

(Atlanta Braves, AAA) (color)

	NR MT	EX	VG
Complete Set:	13.00	6.50	4.00

1 Joey McLaughlin
2 Mike Reynolds
3 John Sain
4 Larry Whisenton
5 Larry Owen
6 Jerry Maddox
7 Jon Richardson
8 Seymour Baseball, Chief Powa-Hitta (Team Mascots)
9 Radio Voices
10 Front Office
11 Jamie Easterly
12 Roger Alexander
13 Chico Ruiz
14 Terry Harper
15 Tom Burgess
16 Duane Thesis
17 Larry Bradford
18 Dan Morogiello
19 Jerry Keller

20 Pat Rockett
21 Rick Camp
22 Tommy Boggs
23 Jim Arline
24 Ed Miller
25 Tony Brizzolara

1979 TCMA Rochester Red Wings

(Baltimore Orioles, AAA) (color)

	NR MT	EX	VG
Complete Set:	13.00	6.50	4.00

1 Jeff Youngbauer
2 Joe Kerrigan
3 Kevin Kennedy
4 Blake Doyle
5 Willie Royster
6 Art James
7 Tony Franklin
8 Carlos Lopez
9 Mike Eden
10 Howard Edwards
11 Tom Bianco
12 Gerry Pirtle
13 Jim Smith
14 Ken Diggle
15 Mark Corey
16 Jeff Rineer
17 Jose Bastian
18 Tom Chism
19 Tony Chevez
20 Dave Ford

1979 TCMA Salt Lake City Gulls

(California Angels, AAA) (color)

	NR MT	EX	VG
Complete Set:	15.00	7.50	4.50

9 Mike Overy
10 Bob Ferris
11 Rance mulliniks
12 Bob Clark
13 Bill Ewing
14 Jim Dorsey
15 Joel Crisler
16a John Harris
16b Gil Kubski
17a Darrell Darrow
17b Dave Schuler
18a Rick Foley
18b Carlos Perez
19a Chuck Porter
19b Dan Whitmer
20a Jay Peters
20b Floyd Rayford
21a Bobby Ramos
21b Bob Slater
22a Pepe Manguel
22b Jim Williams
23a Daniel Boone
23b Leonard Garcia

1979 TCMA Savannah Braves

(Atlanta Braves, AA) (color)

	NR MT	EX	VG
Complete Set:	25.00	12.50	7.50

1 Dom Chiti
2 Gary Cooper
4 Bill Haslerig
5 Brian Snitker
6 Tim Brill
7 Tim Graven
8 Sonny Jackson
9 Mike Shields
10 Greg Johnson
11 Clay Elliott
12 Jose Alvarez
13 Kris Yoder
14 Steve Bedrosian
15 Joe Cowley
16 Richard Witers (correct picture, wrong name & stats)
17 Leo Mazzone
18 Eddie Hass (correct picture, wrong name & stats)
19 Terry Leach
20 Tim Cole
21 Louis Pratt
22 Bob Porter
23 Rafael Ramirez
24 Kenny Smith
25 Mike Miller
26 Jim Wessinger
--- Rufino Linares

1979 TCMA Spokane Indians

(Seattle Mariners, AAA) (color)

	NR MT	EX	VG
Complete Set:	13.00	6.50	4.00

1 Ed Crosby
2 Royle Stillman
3 Mike Potter
4 Danny Walton
5 Rod Craig
6 Charlie Beamon
7 Jack L. Pierce
8 Ken Pape
9 Reggie Walton
10 Bill Plummer
11 Gary Lance
12 George Decker
13 Jim Lewis
14 Mike Davey
15 Jack Heidemann
16 Rene Lachemann
17 Gary Wheelock
18 Rob Pietroburgo
19 Rob Dressler
20 Karl Anderson
21 Greg Biercevicz
22 Steve Burke
23 Terry Bulling
24 Moncho Berhardt
25 Manny Estrada

1979 TCMA Syracuse Chiefs

(Toronto Blue Jays, AAA) (color)

	NR MT	EX	VG
Complete Set:	20.00	10.00	6.00

1 Greg Wells
2 Vern Benson
3 Ernie Whitt
4 Willie Upshaw
5 Mark Wiley
6 Domingo Ramos
7 Joe Cannon
8 Don Pisker
9 Butch Edge
10 Mike Sember
11 Dave Baker
12 Garth Iorg
13 Jackson Todd
14 Chuck Fore
15 Doug Ault
16 Davis May
17 Steve Grilli
18 Luis Rosado
19 Ken Raynolds
20 Steve Luebber

1979 TCMA Tacoma Tugs

(Cleveland Indians, AAA) (color)

	NR MT	EX	VG
Complete Set:	20.00	10.00	6.00

1 Ron Hassey
2 Tom Brown
3 Rick Borchers
4 larry Andersen
5 Tom Brennan
6 Juan Berenguer
7 Bobby Cuellar
8 Todd Heimer
9 Gary Melson
10 Hugh Yancy
11 Sal Rende
12 Dave Oliver
13 Jerry Dybzinski
14 Mike Champion
15 Bob Allietta
16 Sandy Whitol
17 Nate Puryear
18 Carl Nicholson
19 Del Alston
20 Rich Chiles
21 Sheldon Mallory
22 Tim Norrid
23 Rob Ellis
24 Gene Dusan
25 Fred Gladding
26 Wayne Cage

1979 TCMA Tidewater Tides

(New York Mets, AAA) (color)

	NR MT	EX	VG
Complete Set:	30.00	15.00	9.00

1 Roy Lee Jackson
2 John Pacella
3 Jose Moreno
4 Frank Verdi
5 Jeff Reardon
6 Dwight Bernard
7 Mookie Wilson
8 Butch Benton
9 Ron Washington
10 Jim Buckner
11 Dan Norman
12 Mario Ramirez
13 Marshall Brant
14 Ed Cipot
15 Mike Scott
16 Stan Hough
17 Scott Holman
18 Kelvin Chapman
19 Mike Van De Casteele
20 Greg Pavlick
21 Bobby Bryant
22 Russell Clark
23 Jesse Orosco
24 Bob Gorinski
25 Earl Stephenson

1979 TCMA Toledo Mud Hens

(Minnesota Twins, AAA) (color)

	NR MT	EX	VG
Complete Set:	13.00	6.50	4.00

1 Gary Ward
2 Paul Thormodsgard
3 Cal Ermer
4 Archie Amerson
5 Kevin Stanfield
6 Dan Graham
7 Dave Engle
8 Sal Butera
9 Terry Felton
10 Terry Sheehan
11 Wayne Caughey
12 John Verhoeven
13 Buck Chamberlin
14 Jim Buckner
15 Tom Sain
16 Greg Thayer
17 Dave Coleman
18 Darrell Jackson
19 Frank Vilorio
20 Jesus Vega
21 Dennis Mantick
22 Ray Smith

1979 TCMA Tucson Toros

(Texas Rangers, AAA) (color)

	NR MT	EX	VG
Complete Set:	13.50	6.75	4.00

1 Gary Gray
2 Myrl Smith
3 Mike Bruhardt
4 Brian Allard
5 Mike Bucci
6 Stan Jakubowski
7 Ron Gooch
8 Rich Donnelly
9 Steve Bianchi
10 Marty Scott
11 Don Kainer
12 Wayne Pinkerton
13 Fla Strawn
14 Tom Grieve
15 Greg Mahlberg
16 Dave Moharter
17 Mike Hart
18 Odie Davis
19 Keathel Chauncey
20 Ed Lynch
21 Bob Myrick
22 Mel Barrow
23 Larry McCall
24 Jim Umbarger

1979 TCMA Tulsa Drillers

(Texas Rangers, AA) (color)

	NR MT	EX	VG
Complete Set:	15.00	7.50	4.50

1 Wayne Tolleson
2 Joe Russell
3 Len Whitehouse
4 Jim Capowski
5 Fla Strawn
6 Steve Finch
7 Dan Dixon
8 Ray Rainbolt
9 Steve Nielsen
10 Mark Mercer
11 Ron Gooch
12 Jack Ramirez
13 Jim Schaffer
14 Rick Lisi
15 Terry Bogener
16 John Butcher
17 Jim Barbe
18 Ron Carney
19 Dave Crutcher
20 Nick Capra
21 Mel Barrow
22 Hal Kelly
23 Bill Rollings
24 Roy Clark

1979 TCMA Vancouver Canadians

(Milwaukee Brewers, AAA) (color)

	NR MT	EX	VG
Complete Set:	13.00	6.50	4.00

1 Skip James

2 Vic Harris
3 Ron Jacobs
4 Marshall Edwards
5 Craig Ryan
6 Tim Nordbrook
7 Mark Bomback
8 Andy Replogle
9 Danny Boitano
10 Rickey Keeton
11 Gus Quiros
12 Juan Lopez
13 Ned Yost
14 Clay Carroll
15 Kuni Ogawa
16 Randy Stein
17 Ed Romero
18 Jeff Yurak
19 Sam Hinds
20 John Felske
21 Billy Severns
22a Kent Biggerstaff
22b Lenn Sakata
23a Willie Mueller
23b Creighton Tevlin

1979 TCMA Waterbury A's

(Oakland A's, AA) (black and white)

	NR MT	EX	VG
Complete Set:	95.00	47.00	28.00

1 Dennis De Barr
2 Rick Tronerud
3 Walt Horn
4 Bart Braun
5 Dennis Wysznaski
6 Keith Atherton
7 Leroy Robbins
8 Frank Kolarek
9 Ed Nottle
10 Al Armstead
11 Shooty Babitt
12 Randy Green
13 Bob Klebba
14 Mike Patterson
15 Mike Davis
16 Al Minker
17 Larry Groover
18 Paul Mize
19 Bruce Fournier
20 Bob Grandas
21 Ron McNeely
22 Tim Conroy
23 Scott Meyer
24 Dave Beard
25 Robert Moore

1979 TCMA Waterloo Indians

(Cleveland Indians, A) (black and white)

	NR MT	EX	VG
Complete Set:	150.00	75.00	45.00

1a Matt Bullinger
1b Lynn Garrett
2a Lou Ganci
2b Tim Glass
3a Bill Hallstrom
3b Ron Linfonte
4a Keith Hendry
4b Jeff Klein
5 Troy Wilder
6 Jerry Stuzrien
7 Frank Regan
8 Gary Hinson
9 Steve McMurray
10 Sammy Davis
11 Rick Barnhart
12 John Asbell
13 Tom Anderson
14 Dane Anthony
15 Reid Cassidy
16 Scott Dwyer
17 Randy Rambis
18 Marcus Clark
19 Carmelo Castello (Castillo)
20 Rick Colzie
21 Ed Saavedra
22 Bob Diering
23 Mel Queen
24 Cal Emory
25 Peter Peltz
26 Tommy Martinez
27 Robbie Alvarez
28 John Walters
29 Dave Hudgins
30 Greg Johnson
31 Rod Hudson
32 Ray Richard

1979 TCMA Wausau Timbers

(No affiliation, A) (black and white)

	NR MT	EX	VG
Complete Set:	40.00	20.00	12.00

1 Brent Gaff
2 Jerry Stutzriem
3 Todd Winterfeldt
4 Kerry keenan
5 Dave Stockstill
6 Vic Mabee
7 Israel Gutierrez
8 Wally Goff
9 Joe Nemeth
10 Lloyd Turner
11 John Zisk
12 Bob Johnson
13 Rick Barnhart
14 Ramon Romero
15 Jack Littrell
16 Tom Robson
17 Donald Lowe
18 Dean Craig
19 Alex Christianson
20 Ted Davis
21 Mike Jirschele
22 Cameron Killebrew
23 Arnold McCrary
24 Jim Payne
25 Tom Owens

1979 TCMA West Haven Yankees

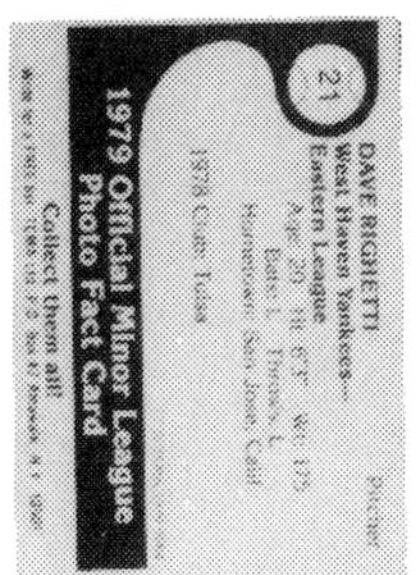

(New York Yankees, AA) (color)

	NR MT	EX	VG
Complete Set:	70.00	35.00	21.00

1 Mark Johnston
2 Ed Napoleon
3 Don Cooper
4 Brian Dayett
5 Dan Schmitz
6 Pat Callahan
7 Nat Showalter
8 Carl Merrill
9 Dan Ledduke
10 Jim McDonald
11 Tom Filer
12 Kenny Baker
13 Willie McGee
14 Andy McGaffigan
15 Greg Jemison
16 Mark Softy
17 Mike Griffin
18 Tim Lewis
19 Steve Donohue
20 Tim Lollar
21 Dave Righetti
22 Batboys
23 Robert Zeig
24 Juan Espino
25 Joe Lefebvre
26 Mark Harris
27 Hoyt Wilhelm
28 Lloyd Kern
29 Front Office Staff
30 Neal Mersch

1979 TCMA Wisconsin Rapids Twins

(Minnesota Twins, A) (black and white)

	NR MT	EX	VG
Complete Set:	85.00	42.00	25.00

1 Antonio Lopez
2 Mike Ungs
3 Mike Riley
4 George Dierberger
5 Bob Blake
6 Alex Dovalis
7 Ron Grout
8 Matt Henderson
9 Steve Mapel
10 John Minarcin
11 Kim Nelson
12 Scott Stoltenberg
13 Bob Bohnet
14 Tarry Boelter
15 Gary Dobbs
16 Stan Cannon
17 Luis Bravo
18 Rubio Malone
19 Ted Kromy
20 Chuck Belk
21 Jose Rodriques
22 Jack Schumate
23 Rich Stelmaszek

1979 Team Indianapolis Indians

(Cincinnati Reds, AAA) (color)

	NR MT	EX	VG
Complete Set:	30.00	15.00	9.00

1 Team Photo
2 Roy Majtyka
3 Ron Oester
4 Dave Moore
5 Harry Spilman
6 The Outfielders
7 Charlie Leibrandt
8 Tommy Mutz
9 Larry Rothschild
10 Eddie Milner
11 The Infielders
12 Doug Corbett
13 Randy Davidson
14 Bruce Berenyl
15 Don Lyle
16 George Cappuzzello
17 The Catchers
18 Mike Grace
19 Geoff Combe
20 Steve Bowling
21 Manny Sarmiento
22 Don Werner
23 The Relievers
24 Jay Howell
25 John Valle
26 Dan Dumoulin
27 Mickey Duval
28 Mario Soto
29 The Starters
30 Ron McClain
31 Bush Stadium
32 Checklist

1979 Team Nashville Sounds

(Cincinnati Reds, AA) (color) (co-sponsored by Sundrop)

	NR MT	EX	VG
Complete Set:	30.00	15.00	9.00

1979 Soundettes
Team Photo
Mike Armstrong
Skeeter Barnes
Scott Brown
Geoff W. Combe
Bill Dawley
Rick Duncan
Rayl Ferreyra
Bob Hamilton
Paul Householder
Greg Hughes
Bill Kelly
Bob Mayer
Gene Menees
Mark Miller
Eddie Milner
Farrell Owens
Joe Price
R. Santo Domingo
George R. Scherger
Larry Schmittoy
Tom Sohns
Dave Van Gorder
Duane Walker

1979 Team Oklahoma City 89'ers

(Philadelphia Phillies, AAA) This set is numbered as it appears on the cards.

	NR MT	EX	VG
Complete Set:	60.00	30.00	18.00

1 Fred Ray Beene
3 Ramon Aviles
4 Lee Constantine Elia
5 Robert Michael DeMeo
6 James Forrest Morrison
7 Orlando Isales
8 Kerry Michael Dineen
9 Bobby Keith Moreland
10 Luis Aguayo
11 Jose Luis Martinez
14 Kevin Andrew Saucier
16 Carlos Ruben Arroyo
17 Dickie Ray Noles
18 Daniel James Larson
20 Orlando Gonzalez
21 Donald Ross McCormack
22 John C. Vukovich
23 John William Poff
24 John Andrew Kucek
25 Pete Charles Manos
26 Martin Eugene Bystrom
28 Ellis Fergason Deal
29 Gary Ray Beare

1979 Team Syracuse Chiefs

(Toronto Blue Jays, AAA) This set is numbered

as it appears on the cards. Cards are approximately 4x6 inches in size with blank backs. No positions are listed.

	NR MT	EX	VG
Complete Set:	20.00	10.00	6.00

1 Domingo Ramos
2 Papo Rosado
3 Chuck Scrivener
4 Danny Ainge
5 Dave Baker
6 Pat Kelly
7 Don Pisker
8 Vern Benson
9 Garth Iorg
10 Mike Sember
12 Ernie Whitt
14 Butch Alberts
15 Ken Reynolds
16 Jackson Todd
17 Doug Ault
19 Butch Edge
21 Steve Grilli
22 Davis May
23 Joe Cannon
25 Jerry Garvin
26 Willie Upshaw
27 Mark Wiley
29 Tom Buskey
31 Steve Luebber

1979 University Volkswagen Albuquerque Dukes

(Los Angeles Dodgers, AAA)

	NR MT	EX	VG
Complete Set:	215.00	107.50	64.50

(1) Joe Beckwith
(2) Robert Castillo
(3) Del Crandall
(4) Pedro Guerrero
(5) Gerald Hannahs
(6) Mickey Hatcher
(7) Kevin Keefe
(8) Rudy Law
(9) Dennis Lewallyn
(10) Rich Magner
(11) Bobby Mitchell
(12) John O'Rear
(13) Dave Patterson
(14) Pablo Peguero
(15) Jack Perconte
(16) Mike Scioscia
(17) Kelly Snider
(18) Dave Stewart
(19) Bill Swiacki
(20) Alex Taveras
(21) Mike Tennant
(22) Claude Westmoreland
(23) Mike Williams

1979 Valley Nat'l Bank Phoenix Giants

	NR MT	EX	VG
Complete Set:	7.50	3.75	2.25

1 Doug Schaefer
2 Kyle Hypes
3 Mike Rowland
4 Jeff Little
5 Rocky Bridges
6 Phil Nastu
7 Bill Bordley
8 Ed Plank
9 Joe Strain
10 Greg Johnston
11 Don Carrithers
12 Tom Heintzelman
13 Randy Hammon
14 Rick Bradley
15 Terry Cornutt
16 Chris Bourjos
17 Casey Parsons
18 Rich Murray
19 Dennis Littlejohn
20 Mark Kuecker
21 Rick Sanderlin
22 Gut Sularz
23 Mike Rex
24 Ethan Blackaby, Tommy Gonzales, Harry Jordan

1980

1980 Chong Modesto A's

(Oakland A's, A)

	NR MT	EX	VG
Complete Set:	40.00	20.00	12.00

1 Don Schubert
2 Steve Gelfarb
3 Mike Woodard
4 Paul Stockley
5 Gordon Eakin
6 Kevin Jacobson
7 Al Armstead
8 Jim Bennett
9 Lynn Garrett
10 Bob Garrett
11 Rich Hatcher
12 Jim Durrman
13 Frank Kneuer
14 Frank Kolarek
15 John Gosse
16 Ron Mantsch
17 Rick Holloway
18 Ken Corzel
19 Don Van Marter
20 Chuck Dougherty
21 Tom Brunswick
22 Ed Retzer
23 Mark Ferguson
24 Roy Moretti
25 Keith Call
26 Bob Wood
27 Keith Lieppman
28 Brad Fischer
29 Dan Kiser

1980 Jack In The Box San Jose Missions

(No affiliation, AAA) (2" x 3")

	NR MT	EX	VG
Complete Set:	37.50	18.75	11.25

1 Bill Plummer
2 Ed Aponte
3 Mark Batten
4 Bud Black
5 Mark Chellette
6 Ramon Estepa
7 Chris Flammang
8 Bill Gaffney
9 Rick Graser
10 Tim Hallgren
11 Tracy Harris
12 Steve Knight
13 Chris Krajewski
14 Jed Murray
15 Tito Nanni
16 Brian Snyder
18 Jeff Stottlemyre
19 Scott Stranski
20 Dave Valle
21 Checklist

1980 Police Charlotte O's

(Baltimore Orioles, AA) (set is bordered in orange)

	NR MT	EX	VG
Complete Set:	1250.	625.00	375.00

(1) Larry Anderson
(2) John Buffamoyer
(3) Brooks Carey
(4) Doc Cole
(5) John Denman
(6) Tommy Eaton
(7) Kurt Fabrizio
(8) Will George
(9) Jose Gonzales
(10) Drungo Hazewood
(11) Marshall Hester
(12) Dave Huppert
(13) Minnie Mendoza
(14) Edwin Neal
(15) Russ Pensiero
(16) Billy Presley
(17) Luis Quintana
(18) Dan Ramirez
(19) Cal Ripken, Jr.
(20) Willie Royster
(21) John Shelby
(22) Tommy Smith
(23) Don Welchel
(24) Cat Whitfield
(25) Jimmy Williams
(26) "The Pepper Girls"
(27) Team Logo
(28) Team Photo

1980 Police Iowa Oaks

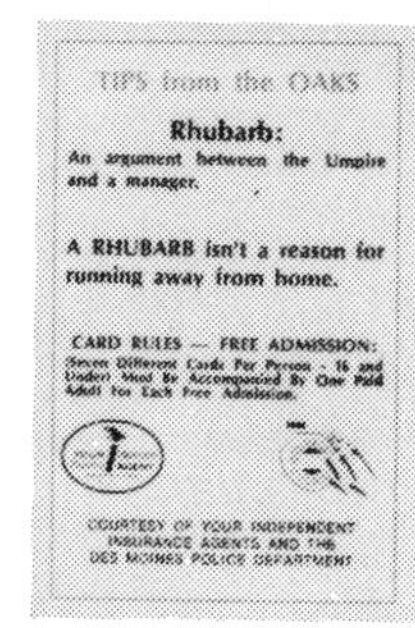

(Chicago White Sox, AAA)

	NR MT	EX	VG

Complete Set:, Richard Barnes, Nardi Contreras, Henry Cruz, Fred Frazier, Joe Gates, Guy Hoffman, Lamar Hoyt, Chris Nyman, Dewey Robinson, Leo Sutherland, Pete Ward, Mike Wolf.
a) Mike Colbern, Raymundo Torres (RHUBARB)
b) Mike Colbern, Raymundo Torres (A WALK)

1980 TCMA Albuquerque Dukes

(Los Angeles Dodgers, AAA) (color)

	NR MT	EX	VG
Complete Set:	50.00	25.00	15.00

1 Dave Stewart
2 Joe Beckwith
3 Pablo Peguero
4 Kelly Snider
5 Bill Swiacki
6 Ron Roenicke
7 John O'Rear
8 Dennis Lewallyn
9 Doug Harrison
10 Dave Patterson
11 Claude Westmoreland
12 Myron White
13 Gary Weiss
14 Teddy Martinez
15 Mike Wilson
16 Jack Perconte
17 Kevin Keefe
18 Wayne Caughey
19 Terry Collins
20 Bobby Mitchell
21 Mark Nipp
22 Ted Power
23 Del Crandall
24 Paul Padilla
25 Gerald Hannahs
26 Mike Scioscia
27 Don Crow

1980 TCMA Anderson Braves

(Atlanta Braves, A) (color)

	NR MT	EX	VG
Complete Set:	32.50	16.25	9.75

1 Dan Church
2 Arcilio Castaigne
3 Duane Theiss
4 Tim Fuller
5 Larry Edwards
6 Tim Alexander
7 Dave Coghill
8 Sonny Jackson
9 Scott Patterson
10 Ken Ames
11 Felipe Arroyo
12 Dave Chase
13 Mark Moses

14 Bill Nice
15 Mike Payne
16 Carlos Rymer
17 Buddy Bailey
18 Roy North
19 Randy Whistler
20 Eric Ayala
21 Mike Koperda
22 Mike Garcia
23 Ken Scanlon
24 Miguel Sosa
25 Harold Williams
26 Brett Butler
27 Brook Jacoby
28 Brad Komminsk
29 Rafael Quezada

1980 TCMA Appleton Foxes

(Chicago White Sox, A) (black and white)

	NR MT	EX	VG
Complete Set:	185.00	92.00	55.00

1 Luis Estrada
2 Bob Fallon
3 Diego Melendez
4 William Mills
5 Rick Naumann
6 J.B. Brown
7 Jeff Vuksan
8 Vito Lucarelli
9 Ron Kittle
10 Larry Wright
11 Dennis Vasquez
12 Nelson Rodreguez
13 Steve Pastrovich
14 Daniel Ortega
15 Keith Brown
16 Jim English
17 A.J. Hill
18 Mitch Olson
19 Greg Stewart
20 Greg Walker
21 David White
22 Tim Carroll
23 Dave Daniels
24 Dennis Keatting
25 Bill Luzinski
26 Lary Doby
27 Larry Hall
28 Mike Maitland
29 Gordy Lund
30 Ron Wollenhaupt

1980 TCMA Arkansas Travelers

(St. Louis Cardinals, AA) (color)

	NR MT	EX	VG
Complete Set:	17.00	8.50	5.10

1 Benny (Joe) Edelen
2 George Bjorkman
3 Jorge Aranzamendi
4 Jame Riggleman
5 John Ruberto
6 Mike Calise
7 Luis DeLeon
8 Mike Dimmel
9 Andrew Rincon
10 Dave Penniall
11 Alan Olmsted
12 James McIntyre
13 Ryan Kurosaki
14 David Johnson
15 Frank Hunsaker
16 Julian Gutierrez
17 Nelson Garcia
18 Freddie Tisdale
19 Felipe Zayas
20 Ray Williams
21 John Murphy
22 Kelly Paris
23 Bill Valentine
24 Mike McCormick
25 David Jorn

1980 TCMA Asheville Tourists

(Texas Rangers, A) (color)

	NR MT	EX	VG
Complete Set:	27.50	13.75	8.25

1 Billy Goodman
2 Tom Robson
3 George Gomez
4 Melvin Gilliam
5 Andy Hancock
6 Jim Schaefer
7 Toni Fossas
8 Dave Hibner
9 Ron McKee
10 Bobby Ball
11 Jimmy Tjader
12 Joe Nemeth
13 Pete O'Brien
14 Ron Carney
15 Kerry Kenan
16 Jim Maxwell
17 Jay Pettibone
18 Bill Taylor
19 Daryl Smith

20 Linvel Mosby
21 Donnie Scott
22 Larry Donofrio
23 Frank Garcia
24 Rick Burdette
25 Dave Schmidt
26 Greg Eason
27 Shelton McMath
28 Mike Jirschele

1980 TCMA Batavia Trojans

(Cleveland Indians, A) (black and white)

	NR MT	EX	VG
Complete Set:	100.00	50.00	30.00

1 Angelo Gilbert
2 Terry Norman
3 Mark Bajus
4 Todd Richards
5 Mike Kolodny
6 Kirk Jones
7 Tom Blackmon
8 Tom Burns
9 Monty Holland
10 Mike Schwarber
11 Orestes Moldes
12 Chuck Hollowell
13 Tom Stiboro
14 Brian Meier
15 Rick Elkin
16 Luis Duarte
17 Chuck Melito
18 Darold Ellison
19 Kevin Malone
20 Andy Alvis
21 Kelly Gruber
22 Rick Colzie
23 Justo Saavedra
24 Matt Minium
25 Dave Gallagher
26 Pat Grady
27 Chris Rehbaum
28 Jeff Moronko
29 Nelson Ruiz
30 Mark Wright

1980 TCMA Buffalo Bisons

(Pittsburgh Pirates, AA) (color)

	NR MT	EX	VG
Complete Set:	17.50	8.75	5.25

Al Ortiz, Jr.
1 Mike Barnes
2 Ron Mitchell
3 Rick Federici
4 Dave Dravecky
5 Jim Buckner
6 Drew Macauley
7 Steve Farr
8 Rick Evans
10 Paul Djakonow
11 Mike Allen
12 Bob Rock
13 Al Torres
14 Larry Nicholson
15 Ed Vargas
16 Steve Demeter

1980 TCMA Burlington Bees

(Milwaukee Brewers, A) (black and white)

	NR MT	EX	VG
Complete Set:	47.50	23.75	14.25

1 Steve Gibson
2 Kevin McCoy
3 Mike Donovan
4 Mark Lepson
5 Dave Grier
6 Greg Dehart
7 Orlando Gonzalez
8 Steve Manderfield
9 Brian Thorson
10 Duane Espy
11 Vince Pone
12 Jesse Vasquez

13 Al Walker
14 Ty Coleman
15 Steve Norwood
16 Rich Bach
17 Greg Cicotte
18 Mike Anderson
19 Kurt Kingsolver
20 Walt Steele
21 Jorge DeJesus
22 Juan Castillo
23 Mark Higgins
24 Kirk Downs
25 John Evans
26 Curt Watanabe
27 Stan Levi
28 Karl McKay
29 Bengie Biggus

1980 TCMA Cedar Rapids Reds

(Chicago White Sox, A) (color)

	NR MT	EX	VG
Complete Set:	10.00	5.00	3.00

1 Mark Moore
2 Newt Box
3 Dave Hoenstine
4 Emil Drzayich
5 Larry Buckle
6 Carlos Porte
7 Eski Viltz
8 Steve Hughes
9 Tony Masone
10 Bob Lapple
11 Rick Jendra
12 Charlie McKinney
13 Jose Mota
14 Steve Skaggs
15 Frank DeJulio
16 Mark Miller
17 Les Straker
18 Paul Gibson
19 Jeff Jones
20 Mike Messaros
21 Don "Bucky" Buchheister
22 Jim Lett
23 Mike Kripner
24 Steve Daniels
25 Kevin Waller
26 Wayne Guinn

1980 TCMA Charleston Charlies

(Texas Rangers, AAA) (color)

	NR MT	EX	VG
Complete Set:	15.00	7.50	4.50

1 Tom Burgess
2 Mark Scott
3 Wayne Pinkerton
4 Nelson Norman
5 Brian Allard
6 Greg Mahlberg
7 Dave Moharter
8 Mike Richardt
9 Richard Lisi
10 Mike Hart
11 Mark Mercer
12 Dan Duran
13 John Butcher
14 Fla Strawn
15 Odie Davis
16 Tucker Ashford
17 Bob Babcock

1980 TCMA Clinton Giants

(San Francisco Giants, A) (black and white)

	NR MT	EX	VG
Complete Set:	125.00	62.00	37.00

1 Dave Wilhelmi
2 Dennis Rathjen
3 Jose Chue
4 Ramon Bautista
5 Jerry Stoval
6 Chris Goodchild
7 Ron Matrisciano
8 Ken Schwab
9 Tim Hagemann
10 Scott Garrelts
11 Art Maebe
12 Kevin Johnson
13 David Fonseca
14 Randy Kutcher
15 Tim Painton
16 Chris Brown
17 Frank Thon
18 Rafael Estepan
19 Glen Moon
20 Rob Deer
21 Ron Perodin
22 Stan Morton
23 Richard Figueroa
24 Bob Cummings
25 Gilbert Albright
26 Wayne Cato
27 Tommy Jones

1980 TCMA Columbus Astros

(Houston Astros, AA) (black and white)

	NR MT	EX	VG
Complete Set:	75.00	37.00	22.00

1 Greg Cypret
2 Val Primmante
3 Tim Tolman
4 Stan Leland
5 Del Letherwood
6 Chick Valley
7 Johnny Ray
8 Bert Pena
9 Doug Stokke
10 Matt Galante
11 Greg Dahl
12 Rod Boxberger
13 John Hessler
14 Simone Rosario
15 Reggie Waller
16 Riccardo Aponte
17 Scott Loucks
18 Keith Bodie
19 Ron Meredith
20 Jim MacDonald
21 Mark Miggins
22 Rex Jones

1980 TCMA Columbus Clippers

(New York Yankees, AAA) (color)

	NR MT	EX	VG
Complete Set:	65.00	32.00	19.50

1 Tim Lollar
2 Roger Slagle
3 Chris Welsh
4 Wayne Harer
5 Garry Smith
6 Brad Gulden
7 Roger Holt
8 Joe Altobelli
9 Roy Staiger
10 Bob Kammeyer
11 Jim McDonald
12 Jim Nettles
13 Brian Doyle
14 Sammy Ellis
15 Bruce Robinson
16 Jim Lewis
17 Dave Righetti
19 Dave Coleman
20 Marshall Brant
21 Greg Cochran
22 Jerry McNertney
23 Dennis Sherrill
24 Marv Thompson
25 Dave Wehrmeister
26 Joe Lefebvre
27 George Sisler, Jr.
28 Juan Espino

1980 TCMA Elmira Pioneers

(Boston Red Sox, A) (black and white)

	NR MT	EX	VG
Complete Set:	125.00	62.00	37.00

1 Alan Banes
2 Tom Bolton
3 Allan Bowlin
4 Dennis Boyd
5 Brice Cote
6 Steve Garrett
7 George Greco
8 Ty Herman
9 Ron Hill
10 Kevin Keenan
11 Jeff Hall
12 John Ackley
13 Mark Weinbrecht
14 Bob Sandling
15 Brandon Plainte
16 George Mecerod
17 Tom McCarthy
18 Mitch Johnson
19 Don Leach
20 Tim Duncan
21 Jeff Hunter
22 Tony Stevens
23 Ron Oddo
24 Wolf Ramos
25 Mike Bryant
26 Gus Burgess
27 Mike Ciampa
28 Simon Glenn
29 Dick Berardino
30 Parker Wilson
31 Brian Zell
32 Gilberto Gonzalez
33 Bob Crandall
34 Marve Handler
34a Marve Handler
34b Bill Limoncelli
35 Brian Butera
36 Sam Mele
37 Frank Malzone
38 Charlie Wagner
39 Jay La Bare
40 Charlie Lynch
41 Alan Mintz
42 Rodolfo Santana
43 Miguel Valdez

1980 TCMA El Paso Diablos

(California Angels, AA) (color)

	NR MT	EX	VG
Complete Set:	20.00	10.00	6.00

1 Brandt Humphrey
2 Dennis Gilbert
3 Scott Garnes
4 Rick Steirer
5 Tom Chevolek
6 Rich Rommel
7 Jim Saul
8 Mark Miller
9 Brian Harper
10 Bob Border
11 Joel Crisler
12 Mike Bishop
13 Tom Bhagwat
14 Daryl Sconiers
15 Don Smelser
16 Steve Brown
17 Tom Brunansky
18 Donny Jones
19 Perry Morrison
20 Rich Brewster
21 Rick Adams
22 Mike Walters
23 Jamie Hamilton
24 Charlie Phillips

1980 TCMA Evansville Triplets

(Detroit Tigers, AAA) (color)

	NR MT	EX	VG
Complete Set:	12.00	6.00	3.50

1 Roger Weaver
2 Mark DeJohn
3 James Gaudet
4 David Steffen
5 Michael Chris
6 Mark Fidrych
7 Ed Putnam
8 Altar Greene
9 David Rucker
10 Gerald Ujdur
11 Darrell Brown
12 Steve Baker
13 Go Giannotta
14 John Martin
15 Ralph Treuel
16 David Machemer
17 Jim Leyland
18 Bruce Robbins
19 Martin Castillo
20 Dan Gonzales
21 Glenn Gulliver
22 Steve Patchin
23 Juan Lopez
24 Richard Leach

Definitions for grading conditions are located in the Introduction of this price guide.

1980 TCMA Glens Falls White Sox

(Chicago White Sox, AA) (black and white)

	NR MT	EX	VG
Complete Set:	250.00	125.00	75.00

1 Steve Pastrovich
2 Len Bradley
3 Tom Johnson
4 Randy Evans
5 Mark Platel
6 Luis Rois
7 Rick Seilheimer
8 Ray Torres
9 Reggie Patterson
10 Kevin Hickey
11 Ted Barnicle
12 Rick Wieters
13 Mark Teutsch
14 Mark Esser
15 Andy Pasillas
16 Julio Perez
17 Ron Perry
18 Randy Johnson
19 Dom Fucci
20 Vince Bienek
21 A.J. Hill
22 Lorenzo Gray
23 Fran Mullins
24 Mike Pazik
25 Duane Shaffer
26 Orlando Cepeda
27 Allan Haines
28 Batboys
29 Bob Bolster

1980 TCMA Glens Falls White Sox

(Chicago White Sox, AA) (color)

	NR MT	EX	VG
Complete Set:	30.00	15.00	9.00

1 Ron Perry
2 Len Bradley
3 Mark Teutsch
4 Randy Johnson
5 Mark Esser
6 Andy Pasillas
7 Kevin Hickey
8 Rick Seilheimer
9 Mark Platel
10 Julio Perez
11 Vince Bienek
12 Fran Mullins
13 Rick Wieters
14 Dom Fucci
15 Randy Evans
16 Steve Pastrovich
17 Luis Rois
18 Reggie Patterson
19 Ted Barnicle
20 Sox Infield (Don Fucci, Lorenzo Gray, A.J. Hill)
21 Mike Pazik
22 Allan Haines
23 Bob Bolster
24 Duane Shaffer
25 Orlando Cepeda
26 Lorenzo Gray
27 Ray Torres
28 Tom Johnson
29 Batboys
30 A.J. Hill

1980 TCMA Hawaii Islanders

(San Diego Padres, AAA) (color)

	NR MT	EX	VG
Complete Set:	12.00	6.00	3.50

1 Chuck Baker
2 Doug Rader
3 Bob Duensing
4 Juan Eichelberger
5 Eric Mustad
6 Craig Stimac
7 Graig Kusick
8 Jim Beswick
9 Dennis Blair
10 Bobby Mitchell
11 Chuck Hartenstein
12 John Yandle
13 Greg Wilkes
14 Tom Tellmann
15 George Stablein
16 Mike Armstrong
17 Mark Lee
18 Steve Smith
19 Tim Flannery
20 Rick Sweet
21 Tony Castillo
22 Broderick Perkins
23 Don Reynolds
24 Andy Dyes
25 Fred Kuhaulua

1980 TCMA Holyoke Millers

(Milwaukee Brewers, AA) (color)

	NR MT	EX	VG
Complete Set:	13.00	6.50	4.00

1 Rick Kranitz
2 John Skorochocki
3 Mark Schuster
4 Barry Cort
5 Frank Thomas
6 Ivan Rodriguez
7 Eddie Brunson
8 Kuni Ogawa
9 Terry Shoebridge
10 Tom Kayser
11 Weldon Swift
12 Frank DiPino
13 Kevin Bass
14 David Green
15 Doug Loman
16 John Adams
17 Steve Lake
18 Steve Reed
19 Ed Carroll
20 Larry Montgomery
21 Terry Lee
22 Dave Curran
23 Gerald Ako
24 Tony Torres
25 Lee Stigman

1980 TCMA Knoxville Blue Jays

(Toronto Blue Jays, AA) (black and white)

	NR MT	EX	VG
Complete Set:	275.00	137.00	82.00

1 Chuck Fore
2 Gene Petralli
3 John Poloni
4 Pete Rowe
5 Paul Hodgson
6 Mark Stober
7 Davis May
8 Jesse Flores
9 Bob Silverman
10 Shaun McCarthy
11 Ralph Santana
12 Mike Cuellar, Jr.
13 Jesse Barfield
14 Ed Dennis
15 Tim Thompson
16 Tom Dejak
17 Pedro Hernandez
18 Larry Hardy
19 Dave Gibson
20 Jesus de la Rosa
21 Charlie Puelo
22 Andre Wood
23 Keith Walker
24 "Rocket" Wheeler
25 Bob Humphreys
26 Rick Morgan
27 Duane Larson
28 Ed Holtz

1980 TCMA Lynn Sailors

(Seattle Mariners, AA) (color)

	NR MT	EX	VG
Complete Set:	20.00	10.00	6.00

1 Mike Moore
2 Larry Patterson
3 Rodney Hobbs
4 Bobby Floyd
5 Chuck Lindsay
6 Rob Simond
7 Mike Hart
8 Don Minnick
9 Orlando Mercado
10 Miguel Negron
11 Karl Best
12 Jeff Cary
13 Manny Estrada
14 Gary Pellant
15 Mickey Bowers
16 Tom Hunt
17 Joe Georger
18 Jammie Allen
19 R.J. Harrison
20 Roy Clark
21 Sam Welborn
22 Lloyd Kern
23 Ron Musselman

1980 TCMA Memphis Chicks

(Montreal Expos, AA) (black and white)

	NR MT	EX	VG
Complete Set:	50.00	25.00	15.00

1 Steve Lovins
2 Charlie Lea
3 Anthony Johnson
4 Tom Gorman
5 Greg Bargar
6 Joe Abone
7 Larry Goldetsky
8 Larry Bearnarth
9 Mike Gates
10 Glen Franklin
11 Ray Crowley
12 Leonel Carrion
13 Terry Francona
14 Kevin Mendon
15 Brad Mills
16 Tony Phillips
17 Pat Rooney
18 Dennis Sherow
19 Tommy Joe Shimp
20 Bryn Smith
21 Chris Smith
22 Doug Simunic
23 Bob Tenenini
24 Grayling Tobias
25 Tom Wieghaus
26 Rick Williams
27 Steve Winfield
28 Frank Wren
29 Bud Yanus
30 Audie Thor

1980 TCMA Ogden A's

(Oakland A's, AAA) (color)

	NR MT	EX	VG
Complete Set:	12.00	6.00	3.50

1 Tim Hosley
2 Ray Cosey
3 Craig Minetto
4 Derek Bryant
5 Randy Green
6 Rich Lysander
7 Mark Busaska
8 Terry Enyart
9 Brian Abraham
10 Mark Souza
11 Bob Grandas
12 Frank Harris
13 John Sutton
14 Milt Ramirez
15 David Beard
16 Bruce Fournier
17 Allen Wirth
18 Royle Stillman
19 Jeff Cox
20 Kelvin Moore
21 "Shooty" Babbitt (Babitt)
22 Pat Dempsey
23 Jose Pagan

1980 TCMA Orlando Twins

(Minnesota Twins, AA) (black and white)

	NR MT	EX	VG
Complete Set:	195.00	97.00	58.00

1 Wade Adamson
2 Tim Barr
3 Tom Biko
4 Steve Green
5 Eddie Hodge
6 Steve Mapel
7 Jose Reyes
8 Lance Hallberg
9 F. Estes
10 Lenny Faedo
11 Steve Benson
12 Tim Laudner
13 A. Cadahia
14 G. Ballard
15 Mike Ungs
16 Terry Sheehan
17 Steve McManaman
18 Alex Ramirez
19 Mark Funderburk
20 Kevin McWhirter
21 Scott Ullger
22 Roy McMillan

1980 TCMA Peninsula Pilots

(Philadelphia Phillies, A) (black and white) (complete set price includes scarce Bill Dancy card)

	NR MT	EX	VG
Complete Set:	75.00	37.50	22.50

1 Phil Teston
2 Daryl Adams
3 Carlos Cabassa
4 Miguel Alicea
5 Fred Warner
6 Kelly Faulk
7 Wally Goff
8 Wil Culmer
9 Keith Washington
10 Bob Tiefenauer
11 Don Carman
12 Roy Smith
13 Jim Wright
14 Randy Greer
15 Joe Bruno
16 Al White
17 Paul Kiess
18 Russ Hamric
19 Ray Borucki
20 Ron Smith
21 Julio Franco
22 Jeff Ulrich
23 Herb Orensky
24 John Fierro
25 Bob Neal
26 Frank Funk
27 Bill Dancy

1980 TCMA Peninsula Pilots

(Philadelphia Phillies, A) (color)

	NR MT	EX	VG
Complete Set:	40.00	20.00	12.00

1 Phil Teston
2 Daryl Adams
3 Carlos Cabassa
4 Roy Smith
5 Don Carman
6 Miguel Alicea
7 Jim Wright
8 Fred Warner
9 Bob Neal
10 John Fierro
11 George Farson
12 Bill Dancy
13 Kelly Faulk
14 Wally Goff
15 Herb Orensky
16 Jeff Ulrich
17 Julio Franco
18 Keith Washington
19 Wil Culmer
20 Randy Greer
21 Joe Bruno
22 Al White
23 Paul Kiess
24 Russ Hamric
25 Ray Borucki
26 Ron Smith
27 Bob Tiefenauer

1980 TCMA Portland Beavers

(Pittsburgh Pirates, AAA) (color)

	NR MT	EX	VG
Complete Set:	20.00	10.00	6.00

1 Mike Tyler
2 Dorian Boyland
3 Craig Cacek
4 Jerry McDonald
5 Rob Ellis
6 Jim Mahoney
7 Pascual Perez
8 Tommy Sandt
9 Vance Law
10 Mickey Mahler
11 Dick Pole
12 Bill Fortinberry
13 Stewart Cliburn
14 Harry Dorish
15 Gary Hargis
17 Odell Jones
18 Tom Trebelhorn
19 Mike Davey
20 Rick Lancellotti
21 Robert Long
22 Rod Gilbreath
23 Larry Anderson (Andersen)
24 Tony Pena
25 Gene Pentz
26 Dan Warthen
27 Rick Rhoden

1980 TCMA Quad City Cubs

(Chicago Cubs, A) (black and white)

	NR MT	EX	VG
Complete Set:	125.00	62.00	37.00

1 Mike Thompson
2 Gerry Mims
3 Tim Millner
4 Ed Moore
5 Tom Morris
6 Glenn Swaggerty

7 Ray Soff
8 Carlos Gil
9 Richard Renwick
10 Mark Wilkins
11 Bob Maddon
12 Norm Churchill
13 Mike Diaz
14 Pete Bazan
15 Ted Trevino
16 Jack Upton
17 Craig Kornfeld
18 Jim Payne
19 Glenn Millhauser
20 Bruce Compton
21 Mike Kelley
22 Dennis Mork
23 Gordy Hodgson
24 Wayne Rohlfing
25 Phil Belmonte
26 Mike Wilson
27 Rich DeLoach
28 John Stockstill
29 Carmelo Martinez
30 Jim Napier
31 Davey Nesmoe
32 Roger Crow

1980 TCMA Reading Phillies

(Philadelphia Phillies, AA) (black and white)

	NR MT	EX	VG
Complete Set:	500.00	250.00	150.00

1 Wayne Williams
2 Jose Castro
3 Ozzie Virgil
4 Mark Davis
5 Don Fowler
6 Miguel Ibarra
7 Joe Jones
8 Jeff Kraus
9 Tommy Hart
10 Ernie Gause
11 Darren Burroughs
12 Tom Lombarski
13 Jorge Bell
14 John Devincenzo
15 Bob Dernier
16 Manny Abreu
17 Ron Clark
18 Rollie Dearmas
19 Cliff Speck
20 Dan Prior
21 Tony McDonald
22 Ryne Sandberg
23 Steve Curry

1980 TCMA Richmond Braves

(Atlanta Braves, AAA) (color)

	NR MT	EX	VG
Complete Set:	13.00	6.50	4.00

1 Danny Morogiello
2 Rafael Ramirez
3 Butch Edge
4 Larry Whisenton
5 Fred Hatfield
6 Steve Hammond
7 Tony Brizzolara
8 Gary Melson
9 John Sain
10 Danny O'Brien
11 Rick Mahler
12 Charlie Keller
13 Butch Metzger
14 Horace Speed
15 Glenn Hubbard
16 Harry Saferight
17 Terry Harper
18 Ken Smith
19 Bob Beall
20 Craig Skok
21 Jim Wessinger
22 Eddie Miller
23 Bo McLaughlin

Definitions for grading conditions are located in the Introduction of this price guide.

1980 TCMA Rochester Red Wings

(Baltimore Orioles, AAA) (color)

	NR MT	EX	VG
Complete Set:	12.00	6.00	3.50

1 Bob Bonner
2 Dallas Williams
3 Vern Thomas
4 Dan Logan
5 Mark Corey
6 Mike Boddicker
7 Larry Jones
8 Jeff Rineer
9 Tom Rowe
10 Jeff Schneider
11 Kevin Kennedy
12 Mike Eden
13 Doc Edwards
14 John Valle
15 Steve Luebber
16 Wayne Krenchicki
17 Jim Smith
18 Floyd Rayford
19 Tom Smith
20 Larry Johnson
21 Pete Torrez

1980 TCMA Salt Lake City Gulls

(California Angels, AAA) (color) (complete set price includes scarce card #'s 18-21)

	NR MT	EX	VG
Complete Set:	15.00	7.50	4.50

1 Ralph Botting
2 Dan Whitmer
3 Craig Eaton
4 Scott Moffitt
5 Mark Nocciolo
6 Dave Schuler
7 Ken Schrom
8 Charlie Phillips
9 Jeff Bertoni
10 Rick Oliver
11 Jay Peters
12 John Harris
13 Carlos Perez
14 Steve Lubratich
15 Rick Foley
16 Jim Dorsey
17 Steve Eddy
18 Moose Stubing
19 Leonard Garcia
20 Sterling Gull
21 Gil Kubski
22 Pete Mangual
23 Bob Clark
24 Bob Ferris
25 Fernando Gonzalez
26 Mike Overy

1980 TCMA Spokane Indians

(Seattle Mariners, AAA) (color)

	NR MT	EX	VG
Complete Set:	20.00	10.00	6.00

1 Bob Stoddard
2 Dave Smith
3 Greg Biercevicz
4 Carlos Diaz
5 Joe Coleman
6 Ron McGee
7 Roy Branch
8 Bryan Clark
9 Vance McHenry
10 Terry Bulling
11 Kip young
12 Manny Sarmiento
13 Randy Stein
14 Jim Maler
15 Dave Elder
16 Dave Henderson
17 Gary Wheelock
18 Rene Lachemann
19 Kim Allen
20 Rich Anderson
21 Reggie Walton
22 Dan Firova
23 Steve Stroughter
24 Charlie Beamon

1980 TCMA Syracuse Chiefs

(Toronto Blue Jays, AAA) (color)

	NR MT	EX	VG
Complete Set:	27.50	13.75	8.25

1 Garth Iorg
2 Doug Ault
3 Kevin Pasley
4 Jackson Todd
5 Pat Rockett
6 Jay Robertson
7 Mike Willis
8 Tom Brown
9 Phil Huffman
10 Butch Alberts
11 Jack Kucek
12 Mitchell Webster
13 Mike Barlow
14 Greg Wells
15 Pat Kelly
16 Lloyd Moseby
17 Dave Baker
18 Randy Benson
19 Harry Warner
20 Danny Ainge
21 Willie Upshaw
22 Domingo Ramos
23 Don Pisker

1980 TCMA Tacoma Tigers

(Cleveland Indians, AAA) (color)

	NR MT	EX	VG
Complete Set:	12.00	6.00	3.50

1 Not Issued
2 Tim Norrid
3 Larry Littleton
4 Wayne Cage
5 Don Collins
6 Bobby Cuellar
7 Mel Queen
8 Larry McCall
9 Raphael Vasquez
10 Sandy Whitol
11 Bob Allietta
12 Tom Brennan
13 Mike Bucci
14 Sal Rende
15 Dave Oliver
16 Mike Champion
17 Gary Gray
18 Todd Heimer
19 John Bonilla
20 Kevin Rhomberg
21 Rick Borchers
22 Art Popham
23 Gene Dusan
24 Del Alston
25 Eric Wilkins
26 Steve Ciszczon
27 Miek Paxton
27a Louis DeLeon
27b Mike Paxton
--- Rob Pietroburgo

1980 TCMA Tidewater Tides

(New York Mets, AAA) (color)

	NR MT	EX	VG
Complete Set:	35.00	17.50	10.50

1 Dave Von Ohlen
2 Jose Moreno
3 Juan Berenguer
4 Wally Backman
5 Sergio Ferrer
6 Gil Flores
7 Ed Cipot

8 Butch Benton
9 Ron MacDonald
10 Dyar Miller
11 Greg Harris
12 Tom Dixon
13 Reggie Baldwin
14 Fred Beene
15 Hubie Brooks
17 Mookie Wilson
18 Kelvin Chapman
19 Roy Lee Jackson
20 Jimmy Smith
21 Ed Lynch
22 Papo Rosado
23 Mike Scott
24 Frank Verdi
25 Randy McGilberry

1980 TCMA Toledo Mud Hens

(Minnesota Twins, AAA) (color)

	NR MT	EX	VG
Complete Set:	12.50	6.25	3.75

1 Steve Mapel
2 Bob Randall
3 Cal Ermer
4 Bruce MacPherson
5 Gary Serum
6 Ron Washington
7 Terry Felton
8 Randy Bush
9 John Walker
10 Willie Norwood
11 Jesus Vega
12 Wilfredo Sarmiento
13 Steve Herz
14 Buck Chamberlin
15 Dave Engle
16 Ray Smith
17 Al williams
18 Jeff Brueggemann
19 Bob Veselic
20 Kurt Seibert

1980 TCMA Tucson Toros

(Houston Astros, AAA) (color)

	NR MT	EX	VG
Complete Set:	12.00	6.00	3.50

1 Danny Heep
2 Jimmy Sexton
3 Joe Pittman
4 Rick Williams
5 Gary Wilson
6 Bob Sprowl
7 Jack Fleming
8 Tom Wiedenbauer
9 Jimmy Johnson
10 George Gross
11 Billy Smith
12 Dave LaBossiere
13 Dennis Miscik
14 Alan Knicely
15 Tom Spencer
16 Gary Rajsich
17 Mike Fischlin
18 Gordy Pladson
19 Jim Pankovits
20 Brent Strom
21 Mike Mendoza
22 Gary Woods
23 Bert Roberge
24 Doug Stokke

1980 TCMA Tulsa Drillers

(Texas Rangers, AA) (color)

	NR MT	EX	VG
Complete Set:	12.00	6.00	3.50

1 Jerry Gleaton
2 Dave Crutcher
3 Tony Hudson
4 Ted Davis
5 Mike Roberts
6 Jack Lozorko
7 Jim Farr
8 Nick Capra
9 Larry Reynolds
10 George Wright
11 Mel Barrow
12 Frank Garcia
13 Phil Klimas
14 Luis Gonzalez
15 Mike Jirschele
16 Wayne Tolleson
17 Ronnie Gooch
18 Tracy Cowger
19 Steve Nielsen
20 Chuck Lamson
21 Bobby Johnson
22 Dave Schmidt
23 Darrell Ortiz
24 Wayne Terwilliger
25 Mike Vickers
26 Mitch Fletcher

1980 TCMA Utica Blue Jays

(Toronto Blue Jays, A) (black and white)

	NR MT	EX	VG
Complete Set:	60.00	30.00	18.00

1 Larry Hardy
2 Rich White
3 Carlos Cabrera
4 Jim Baker
5 Felix Feliciano
6 Rafael Harris
7 Tom Norko
8 Silverio Valdez
9 Jon Woodworth
10 Bob Wilbur
11 Hector Torres
12 Tomas Castillo
13 Juan Castillo
14 Roberto Cerrud
15 Jose Escobar
16 Tony Gilmore
17 Luis Guzman
18 Toby Hernandez
19 Mark Holton
20 Dennis Howard
21 Miguel Ortiz
22 Tom O'Dowd
23 Al Montgomery
24 Bob McNair
25 Tom Lukish
26 Herman Lewis
27 Carlos Leal
28 Paul Langfield
29 Mike Hurdle
30 Bill Reade
31 Rafael Rivas
32 Miguel Rodriguez
33 Rico Sutton

1980 TCMA Vancouver Canadians

(Milwaukee Brewers, AAA) (color)

	NR MT	EX	VG
Complete Set:	15.00	7.50	4.50

1 Lawrence Rush
2 Willie Mueller
3 Ned Yost
4 Gus Quiros
5 Bobby Glen Smith
6 Terry Bevington
7 Dave LaPoint
8 Billy Severns
9 Lance Rautzhan
10 Tim Nordbrook
11 Bob Didier
12 Kent Biggerstaff
13 Ed Romero
14 Dan Boitano
15 Craig Ryan
16 Rene Quinones
17 Mike Henderson
18 Fred Holdsworth
19 Marshall Edwards
20 Bob Galasso
21 Vic Harris
22 Rick Olsen

1980 TCMA Waterbury Reds

(Cincinnati Reds, AA) (black and white)

	NR MT	EX	VG
Complete Set:	135.00	67.50	40.50

1 Nick Fiorillo
2 Jeff Lahti
3 Steve Christmas
4 Doug Neuenschwander
5 Paul Herring
6 Randy Town
7 Bill Scherer (Scherrer)
8 Scott Dye
9 Lee Garrett
10 Mike Compton
11 Rick O'Keefe
12 Jose Brito
13 Bob Hamilton
14 Mark Gilbert
15 Skeeter Barnes
16 Tom Sohns
17 Dan Sarrett
18 Tom Lawless
19 Tom Foley
20 Russ Aldrich
21 Nick Esasky
22 Greg Hughes

1980 TCMA Waterloo Indians

(Cleveland Indians, A) (black and white)

	NR MT	EX	VG
Complete Set:	140.00	70.00	42.00

1 John Hoban
2 Dane Anthony
3 Ron Leach
4 Larry White
5 Tim Glass
6 Ramon Romero
7 Alan Willis
8 Jack Nuismer
9 John Bohnet
10 John Asbell
11 Larry Hrynko
12 Kirk Jones
13 Rick Barnhart
14 Daryl Fazzio
15 Bryan Meier
16 Chris Rehbaum
17 Sammy Torres
18 Bruce Chaney
19 Erik Peterson
20 George Cechetti
21 Robert Bohnet
22 Don Nicolet
23 Gary Hinson
24 Frank Regan
25 Everett Rey
26 Rick Baker
27 Carmelo Castillo
28 Tommy Martinez
29 Mike Taylor
30 Cal Emery
31 Chuck Stobbs
32 Bob Gariglio
33 Rich Blumeyer
34 Wes Mitchell
35 Von Hayes

1980 TCMA Wausau Timbers

(Seattle Mariners, A) (black and white)

	NR MT	EX	VG
Complete Set:	110.00	55.00	33.00

1 Tom Brennan
2 John Burden
3 Mark Cahill
4 Tony Jordan
5 Martin Little
6 Edwin Nunez
7 Steve Roche
8 Elias Salva
9 Mark Softy
10 John Zisk
11 Takashi Upshur
12 Bobby Tanzi
13 Jimmy Presley
14 Mario Diaz
15 Enrique Diaz
16 Mike Hood
17 Chris Henry
18 Rick Graser
19 Mike Frierson
20 Kevin King
21 Werner Lajszky
22 Arnie McCrary
23 Orlando Martinez

1980 TCMA West Haven White Caps

(Oakland A's, AA) (color)

	NR MT	EX	VG
Complete Set:	13.00	6.50	4.00

1 Al Minker
2 Dennis Wyszynski
3 Leroy Robbins
4 Don Morris
5 Bruce Fournier
6 Rob Klebba
7 Paul Stevens
8 Paul Mize
9 Scott Meyer
10 Bert Bradley
11 Craig Harris
12 Bobby Markham
13 Fred Devito
14 Darryl Ciaz
15 Mike Patterson
16 Keith Atherton
17 Shooty Babbitt (Babitt)
18a Nick Beamon
18b Staff
19a Keith Comstock
19b John Gosse
20a David Goldstein
20b Ed Nottle
21a Keathel Chauncey
21b Rich Lynch
21c Bob Moore
22a Tim Conroy
22b Aggie Maggio
23a Coach Benson
23b Randy Sealy
24 Rick Tronerud

1980 TCMA Wichita Aeros

(Chicago Cubs, AAA) (color)

	NR MT	EX	VG
Complete Set:	17.50	8.75	5.25

1 Karl Pagel
2 Jim Tracy
3 Kim Buettemeyer
4 Mark Parker
5 Bill Hayes
6 Danny Rohn
7 Randy martz
8 Jack Hiatt
9 Jesus Figeroa
10 Ignacio Javier
11 Mike Turgeon
12 Lee Smith
13 Mike Allen
14 Jesus Alfaro
15 Paul Semall
16 Jared Martin
17 Brian Rosinski
18 Steve Macko
19 Vince Valentini
20 George Riley
21 Manny Seoane
22 Mark Lemongello

1980 TCMA Wisconsin Rapids Twins

(Minnesota Twins, A) (black and white)

	NR MT	EX	VG
Complete Set:	295.00	147.00	88.00

1 Sam Arrington
2 Luis Santos
3 Robert Mulilgan
4 Larry May
5 Manuel Lunar
6 William Lamkey
7 Bob Konepa
8 Hal Jackson
9 Ken Francingues
10 Conrad Everett
11 Chris Thomas
12 Paul Voight
13 Richard Ray Austin
14 Glenn Ballard
15 James Christensen
16 Manuel Colletti
17 Gary Gaetti
18 Kent Hrbek
19 Kevin Miller
20 Norberto Molina
21 Brad Carlson
22 Matt Henderson
23 Joe Kubit
24 Bruce Stocker
25 Ray Stein
26 Rich Stelmaszek
27 Tony Oliva

1980 Team Columbus Clippers

(New York Yankees, AAA)

	NR MT	EX	VG
Complete Set:	20.00	10.00	6.00

(1) Joe Altibelli
(2) Marshall Brandt
(3) Ken Clay
(4) Greg Cochan
(5) Dave Coleman
(6) Brian Doyle
(7) Brad Gulden
(8) Roger Holt
(9) Bob Kammeyer
(10) Joe Lefebvre
(11) Jim Lewis
(12) Tim Lollar
(13) Jim McDonald
(14) Jim Nettles
(15) Dave Righetti
(16) Bruce Robinson
(17) Dennis Sherrill
(18) George H. Sisler Jr.
(19) Roger Slagle
(20) Roy Staiger
(21) Marv Thompson
(22) Dave Wehrmeister
(23) Chris Welsh
(24) Coaches/Trainer Card (Jerry McNertney, Sammy Ellis, Mark Letendre)
(25) Garry Smith

Definitions for grading conditions are located in the introduction of this price guide.

1980 Team Indianapolis Indians

(Cincinnati Reds, AAA)

	NR MT	EX	VG
Complete Set:	32.50	16.25	9.75

1 Team Photo
2 Jim Beauchamp
3 Sheldon Burnside
4 Mike Grace
5 Joe Price
6 John Hale
7 Geoff Combe
8 Dave Van Gorder
9 Bruce Berenyi
10 Eddie Milner
11 Jay Howell
12 Paul O'Neill
13 The Braintrust
14 Larry Rothschild
15 Paul Householder
16 The Relievers
17 Scott Brown
18 Mark Milner
19 The Starters
20 Blake Doyle
21 Gene Menees
22 Rafael Santo Domingo
23 Bill Kelly
24 Don Lyle
25 Bill Dawley
26 Duane Walker
27 Angel Torres
28 The Catchers
29 The Infielders
30 The Outfielders
31 John Young
32 Checklist

1980 Team Nashville Sounds

(New York Yankees, AA)

	NR MT	EX	VG
Complete Set:	30.00	15.00	9.00

(1) Ken Baker
(2) Steve Balboni
(3) Paul Boris
(4) Pat Callahan
(5) Nate Chapman
(6) Don Cooper
(7) Brian Dayett
(8) Pat Dobson
(9) Brad Gulden
(10) Greg Jemison
(11) Dan Ledduke
(12) Andy Mc Gaffigan
(13) Willie Mc Gee
(14) Stump (Carl Merrill)
(15) Eddie Napoleon
(16) Brian Ryder
(17) Brian Ryder
(18) Rafel Santana (S/B RAFAEL)
(19) Danny Schmitz
(20) Buck Showalter
(21) Roger Slagle
(22) Pat Tabler
(23) Steve Taylor
(24) James Werly
(25) Ted Wilborn

1980 Team Oklahoma City 89'ers

(Philadelphia Phillies, AAA) This set is numbered as it appears on the cards.

	NR MT	EX	VG
Complete Set:	60.00	30.00	18.00

1 John Paul Loviglio
3 Luis Aguayo
4 Mike Anderson
6 Jim Snyder
7 Orlando Isales
8 Billy Edward Smith
9 Luis Ernesto Rodriguez
10 Ramon Antonio Lora
11 Jose Luis Martinez
12 Leonard James Matuszek
14 Orlando Sanchez
15 Elijah B. Bonaparte
16 Ruben Carlos Arroyo
17 Paul G. Thormodsgard
18 Scott A. Munninghoff
19 Porfirio Altamirano
20 Orlando E. Gonzalez
21 Donald Ross McCormack
22 Robert Clifford Speck
23 John William Poff
24 James L. Wright Jr.
25 William Burke Suter Jr.
26 Martin Eugene Bystrom
28 Jerry Maxwell Reed

1980 Team Omaha Royals

(Kansas City Royals, AAA) Cards have police tips on their backs.

	NR MT	EX	VG
Complete Set:	60.00	30.00	18.00

(1) Dave Augustine
(2) German Barranca
(3) Leon Brown
(4) Steve Busby
(5) Manny Castillo
(6) Craig Chamberlain
(7) Jerry Cram
(8) Ken Cvejdlik
(9) Bob Detherage
(10) Keith Drumright
(11) Dan Fischer
(12) Danny Garcia
(13) Jim Gaudet
(14) Kelly Heath
(15) Tim Ireland
(16) Bill Laskey
(17) Randy McGilberry
(18) Mike Morley
(19) Tom Mutz
(20) Bill Paschall
(21) Ken Phelps
(22) Jeff Schattinger
(23) Joe Sparks
(24) Jeff Twitty

1980 Team Syracuse Chiefs

(Toronto Blue Jays, AAA) This set is numbered as it appears on the cards, is 3-1/4 x 5 inches in size, with blank backs.

	NR MT	EX	VG
Complete Set:	50.00	25.00	15.00

Tony DeRosa ((Trainer))
4 Don Pisker
5 Dave Baker
9 Garth lorg
11 Kevin Pasley
12 Steve Davis
14 Butch Alberts
15 Lloyd Moseby
16 Jackson Todd
17 Mitchell Webster
18 Pat Rockett
19 Tom Brown
20 Jack Kucek
21 Steve Grilli
22 Phil Huffman
23 Mike Willis
24 Harry Warner
25 Doug Ault
26 Pat Kelly
27 Randy Benson
28 Luis Leal
29 Mike Barlow
30 Jay Robertson
32 Greg Wells

1980 Syracuse Chiefs

	NR MT	EX	VG
Complete Set:	50.00	25.00	15.00

(1) Butch Alberts
(2) Doug Ault
(3) Dave Baker
(4) Mike Barlow
(5) Randy Benson
(6) Tom Brown, Steve Davis
(7) Tony De Rosa
(8) Steve Grilli
(9) Phil Huffman
(10) Garth lorg
(11) Pat Kelly
(12) Jack Kucek
(13) Luis Leal
(14) Lloyd Moseby
(15) Kevin Pasley
(16) Don Pisker
(17) Jay Robertson
(18) Pat Rockett
(19) Jackson Todd
(20) Harry Warner
(21) Mitchell Webster
(22) Greg (Boomer) Well
(23) Mike Willis

1980 Valley Nat'l Bank Phoenix Giants

(San Francisco Giants, AAA) (2" x 5")

	NR MT	EX	VG
Complete Set:	6.00	3.00	1.80

1 Mike Williams
2 Bob Tufts
3 Doug Schaefer
4 Mike Rowland
5 Larry Prewitt
6 Ed Plank
7 Phil Nastu
8 Terry Cornutt
9 Fred Breining
10 Bill Bordley
11 Chris Bourjos
12 Max Venable
13 Casey Parsons
14 Craig Landis
15 Bob Kearney
16 Dennis Littlejohn
17 Jose Barrios
18 Mike Rex
19 Rich Murray
20 Joe Pettini
21 Guy Sularz
22 Rocky Bridges
23 Jim Duffalo
24 Ethan Blackaby
25 Tommy Gonzales
26 Harry Jordan

1980 WBTV Charlotte O's

(Baltimore Orioles, AA)

	NR MT	EX	VG
Complete Set:	300.00	150.00	90.00

1 John Shelby
3 John Buffamoyer
4 Tommy Eaton
6 Cat Whitfield
9 Tommy Smith
11 Curt Fabrizio
13 Willie Royster
14 Drungo Hazewood
16 Cal Ripken Jr.
17 John Denman
18 Larry Anderson
19 David Huppert
20 Billy Presley
21 Brooks Carey
22 Russ Pensiero
24 Dan Ramierz
25 Jose Gonzales
27 Luis Quintans
30 Don Welchel
31 George Will
32 Edwin Neal
---) . . . Minnie Mendoza, Doc Cole, Marshall Hester

1981

1981 Arby's Nashville Sounds

(New York Yankees, AA)

	MT	NR MT	EX
Complete Set:	40.00	30.00	16.50

(1) Manager, Trainer & Coaches
(2) Team Photo
(3) Rod Boxberger
(4) Pat Callahan
(5) Nate Chapman
(6) Brian Dayett
(7) Dan Hanggie
(8) Bob Jamison
(9) Curt Kaufman
(10) Dan Led Duke
(11) Don Mattingly
(12) Willie Mc Gee
(13) Mike Morgan
(14) Otis Nixon
(15) Erik Peterson
(16) Brian Poldberg
(17) Frank Ricci
(18) Wes Robbins
(19) Buck Showalter
(20) Roger Slagle
(21) Jeff Taylor
(22) Steve Taylor
(23) Rafael Villaman
(24) Jamie Werly
(25) Ted Wilborn

1981 Chong Modesto A's

(Oakland A's, A)

	MT	NR MT	EX
Complete Set:	30.00	22.50	12.25

1 Rick Arnold
2 Ron Mantsch
3 Robert Moore
4 Ed Retzer
5 Don Van Marter
6 Robert Wood
7 Mark Ferguson
8 Ron Jensen
9 Bill Kreuger
10 Greg Mine
11 Mike Altobelli
12 Gordon Eakin
13 Terry Byrum
14 Paul Stockley
15 Monte Mc Abee
16 Selwyn Young
17 Kevin Jacobson
18 Joe Williams
19 Tom Colburn
20 Terry Harper
21 Jay Schellin
22 Dennis Stowe
23 Joe Soprano
24 Wayne Rudolph
25 Frank Harris
26 Keith Lieppman
27 Brad Fischer
28 Dwight Adams
29 Phil Danielson
30 Rod Murphy

1981 Police Columbus Clippers

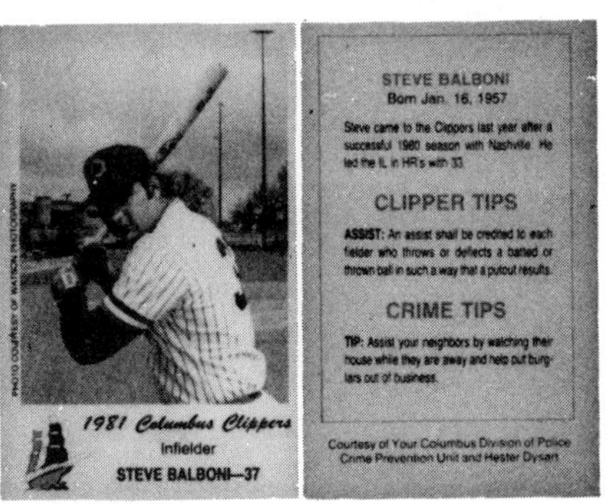

(New York Yankees, AAA)

	MT	NR MT	EX
Complete Set:	15.00	11.25	6.00

(1) Tucker Ashford
(2) Steve Balboni
(3) Paul Boris
(4) Marshall Brant
(5) Pat Callahan
(6) Greg Cochran
(7) Dave Coleman
(8) Juan Espino
(9) Mike Griffin
(10) Wayne Harer
(11) Jim Lewis
(12) John Pacella
(13) Dave Righetti
(14) Andre Robertson
(15) Brian Ryder
(16) Dan Schmitz
(17) Buck Showalter
(18) George H. Sisler Jr.
(19) Garry Smith
(20) Rick Stenholm
(21) Pat Tabler
(22) Frank Verdi
(23) Dave Wehrmeister
(24) Coaches/Trainer Card (Jerry McNertney, Sammy Ellis, Mark Letendre)
(25) Sgt. Dick Hoover (Columbus Police Dept.)

1981 Red Rooster Edmonton Trappers

(Chicago White Sox, AAA)

	MT	NR MT	EX
Complete Set:	6.00	4.50	2.50

1 Gary Holle
2 John Poff
3 Dan Williams
4 Nardi Contreras
5 Juan Agosto
6 Guy Hoffman
7 Chris Nyman
8 Gord Lund
9 Vern Thomas
10 Rich Barnes
11 John Flannery
12 Bill Atkinson
13 Hector Eduardo
14 Leo Sutherland
15 Ray Murillo
16 Joe Gates
17 Julio Perez
18 Marv Foley
19 Mike Colbern
20 Fran Mullins
21 Rod Allen
22 Reggie Patterson
23 Jay Loviglio
24 Mark Teutsch

1981 TCMA Albuquerque Dukes

(Los Angeles Dodgers, AAA) (color)

	MT	NR MT	EX
Complete Set:	175.00	131.00	72.00

1 Dave Moore
2 Dave Patterson
3 Steve Shirley
4 Alejandro Pena
5 Ted Power
6 Bill Swiacki
7 Ricky Wright
8 Dave Richards
9 Ron Roenicke
10 Brian Holton
11 Kevin Keefe
12 Brent Strom
13 Don Crow
14 Wayne Caughey
15 Larry Fobbs
16 Mike Marshall
17 Jack Perconte
18 Alex Taveras
19 Gary Weiss
20 Rudy Law
21 Candy Maldonado
22 Bobby Mitchell
23a Sandy Koufax
23b Tack Wilson
24 Del Crandall
25 Dick McLaughlin

1981 TCMA Appleton Foxes

(Chicago White Sox, A) (color)

	MT	NR MT	EX
Complete Set:	15.00	11.25	6.00

1 Jesse Anderson
2 Jeff Barnard
3 keith Desjarlais
4 Kevin Flannery
5 Tom Mullen
6 Rick Naumann
7 Dan Ortega
8 Steve Pastrovich
9 Mark Platel
10 Jim Siwy
11 Roy Schumacher
12 Wayne Schukert
13 Larry Donofrio
14 Cecil Espy
15 Leo Garcia
16 Ike Golden
17 John Hanley
18 A.J. Hill
19 Scott Meier
20 Mike Morse
21 Dave Nix
22 Gary Robinette
23 Ramon Romero
24 Mark Seeger
25 Ray Torres
26 Wes Kent
27 Dave Wall
28 Sam Ewing
29 Doug Wiesner

1981 TCMA Arkansas Travelers

(St. Louis Cardinals, AA) (black and white)

	MT	NR MT	EX
Complete Set:	27.50	20.50	11.25

1 Felipe Zayas
2 Steve Turco
3 Donald Moore
4 Dennis Delany
5 Fred Tisdale
6 Rhadames Mills
7 Jeffrey Doyle
8 Jorge Aranzamendi
9 David Kable
10 Kerry Burchett
11 Jerry Johnson
12 David Jorn
13 Rafael Pimentel
14 Mark Riggins
15 Daniel Winslow
16 Kevin Hagen
17 James Cott
18 Ralph Citarella
19 James Riggleman
20 Louis Pratt
21 Gaylen Pitts
22 Jerry McKune
23 Arkansas Travelerettes

1981 TCMA Batavia Trojans

(Cleveland Indians, A) (black and white)

	MT	NR MT	EX
Complete Set:	30.00	22.00	12.00

1 Mark Bajus
2 Tom Burns
3 Jose Roman
4 Steve Cushing
5 Mike Poindexter
6 Todd Richard
7 Brian Silvas
8 Phil Deriso
9 Bart Mackie
10 Adalberto Nieves
11 Rick Elkin
12 Arnold Cochran
13 Ray Martinez
14 Jerry Nalley
15 Junior Noboa
16 Ed Tanner
17 Sam Martin
18 John Merchant
19 Scott Collins
20 Bernardo Brito
21 Gary Holden
22 Eric Jones
23 Chris Rehbaum
24 Randy Washington
25 George Alpert
26 Miguel Roman
27 Dave Oliver
28 Luis Isaac
29 Paul Seymour
30 John Jakubowski

1981 TCMA Birmingham Barons

(Detroit Tigers, AA) (black and white)

	MT	NR MT	EX
Complete Set:	175.00	131.00	72.00

1 John Lackey
2 Roy Majtyka
3 Dwight Lowry
4 Manny Seoane
5 Ron Mathis
6 Bruce Robbins
7 Mark Dacko
8 Mike Laga
9 Frank Hunsaker
10 Glenn Wilson
11 Gary Bozich
12 Howard Johnson
13 Jeff Kenaga
14 Bob Nandin
15 Jack Smith
16 Bruce Chaney
17 Stan Younger
18 Nick O'Connor
19 Dick Pole
20 Stine Poole
21 Darrell Woodard
22 Barbaro Garbey
23 Augie Ruiz
24 Paul Josephson
25 Mike Beecroft

1981 TCMA Bristol Red Sox

(Boston Red Sox, AA) (color)

	MT	NR MT	EX
Complete Set:	16.00	12.00	6.50

1 Craig Brooks
2 Bill Moloney
3 Kevin Kane
4 Gene Gentile
5 Reggie Whittemore
6 Jim Wilson
7 Brian Denman
8 Tony Torchia
9 Dave Schoppee
10 Rick Colbert
11 Chuck Sandberg
12 Ed Jurak
13 Jerry King
14 Kenny Young
15 Jay Fredlund
16 Erwin Bryant
17 Steve Shields
18 Glenn Eddins
19 Dave Tyler
20 Clint Johnson
21 Dennis Burtt
22 Jim Watkins

1981 TCMA Buffalo Bisons

(Pittsburgh Pirates, AA) (color)

	MT	NR MT	EX
Complete Set:	10.00	7.50	4.00

1 John Lipon
2 John Holland
3 Doug Britt
4 Jose DeLeon
5 Ben Wiltbank
6 Benny de la Rosa
7 Drew Macauley
8 Carlos Ledezema
9 Stew Cliburn
10 Bob Rock
11 Rafael Vasquez
12 Dan Wortham
13 Jose Rodriguez
14 Billy Waag
15 Gary Hargis
16 Jose Calderon
17 Angel Barez
18 Steve Farr
19 Carlos Rios
20 Tony Incavigua
21 Terry Salazar
22 Doug Frobel
23 Eddie Vargas
24 Frank Riccelli
25 Reggie Buchanan

1981 TCMA Burlington Bees

(Milwaukee Brewers, A) (black and white)

	MT	NR MT	EX
Complete Set:	40.00	30.00	16.50

1 Dave Morris
2 Vince Pone
3 Kevin McCoy
4 Steve Noewood
5 Gene Smith
6 Raymond Gallo
7 Craig Herberholz
9 Mark Lepson
10 Tim Crews
11 Steve Gibson
12 Johnson Wood
13 Murphy Susa
14 Angel Morris
15 Henry Contreras
16 Steve Jordan
17 Randy Ready
18 Butch Kirby
19 Mike Samuel
20 Juan Castillo
21 Brad DeKraai
22 Carlos Ponce
23 Mark Higgins
24 Gerry Miller
25 Ronnie Jones
26 Karl McKay
27 Joel Parker
28 Bill Nowlan
29 Lawrence Avery
30 Terry Bevington

1981 TCMA Cedar Rapids Reds

(Cincinnati Reds, A) (color)

	MT	NR MT	EX
Complete Set:	32.50	24.25	13.25

1 Larry Jackson
2 Kurt Kepshire
3 Brad Lesley
4 Rick Myles
5 Mike Raines
6 Don Robinson
7 Mark Rothey
8 Ray Corbett
9 Dave Miley
10 Emil Drzavich
11 Kevin Hinds
12 Dave Hoenstine
13 Dean Seats
14 Mike Sorel
15 Tom Wesley
16 Jeff Jones
17 Ken Scarpace
18 Scott Terry
19 Randy Davidson
20 Don Buchheister
21 Jeff Clay
22 Mark Bowden
23 Bob Buchanan
24 Scott Ender
25 Greg McKinney
26 Dave Hall

1981 TCMA Charleston Charlies

(Cleveland Indians, AAA) (color)

	MT	NR MT	EX
Complete Set:	27.50	20.50	11.25

1 Tom Brennan
2 Bobby Cuellar
3 Gordy Glaser
4 Ed Glynn
5 Mike Paxton
6 Eric Wilkins
7 Sandy Whitol
8 Chris Bando
9 Tim Norrid
10 Kenny Barton
11 Mike Bucci
12 Len Faedo
13 Mike Fischlin
14 Angelo Logrande
15 Von Hayes
16 Odie Davis
17 Jim Lentine
18 Karl Pagel
19 Rodney Craig
20 Vassie Gardner
21 Mel Queen
22 Nate Puryear
23 Rob Petroburgo
24 Cal Emery

1981 TCMA Charleston Royals

(Kansas City Royals, A) (black and white)

	MT	NR MT	EX
Complete Set:	20.00	15.00	8.25

1 Greg Jonson
2 Hector Arroyo
3 David Wong
4 Mike Olson
5 Hal Hatcher
6 Roger Hansen
7 Glenn Ray
8 Theo Shaw
9 Dave Albright
10 Bob Hegman
11 Fran Cutty
12 Doug Cook
13 Russell Stephans
14 Chuck McMichael
15 Ben Cadahia
16 Cliff Pastornicky
17 Jeff Gladden
18 Mark Huismann
19 Abner Johnson
20 Randy Meyer
21 Bill Best
22 Larry Grahek
23 Rick Risso
24 Tad Venger
25 Willie Neal
26 Rick Mathews

1981 TCMA Chattanooga Lookouts

(Cleveland Indians, AA) (black and white)

	MT	NR MT	EX
Complete Set:	25.00	18.75	10.25

1 Robert Gariglio
2 John Burden
3 Robbie Alvarez
4 Luis DeLeon
5 Steve Narleski
6 Matt Bullinger
7 Jack Nuismer
8 Steve Roche
9 Everett Rey
10 Todd Heimer
11 Tim Glass
12 Jeff Moronko
13 John Bohnet
14 George Cecchetti
15 Ricky Baker
16 Carmelo Castillo
17 Sal Rende
18 Rick Burchers
19 Chuck Stobbs
20 Craig Adams
21 Larry White
22 Jeff Tomski
23 Kevin Rhomberg
24 Woody Smith
25 Bud Anderson

1981 TCMA Clinton Giants

(San Francisco Giants, A) (black and white)

	MT	NR MT	EX
Complete Set:	30.00	22.00	12.00

1 Joe Banach
2 Wendell Kim
3 Steve Cline
4 Dave Wilhelmi
5 Bruce Oliver
6 Ben Callo
7 Jose Chue
8 Art Gomez
9 Kevin Smay
10 Greg Bangert
11 Mark O'Connell
12 Matt Young
13 Dennis Schafer
14 Louis D'Amore
15 Gus Stokes
16 Kirk Ortega
17 John Taylor
18 Ken Frazier
19 James Johnson
20 Sean Toerner
21 Dave Wilson
22 Joe Henderson
23 Mike Lenti
24 Tom McLaughlin

25 Greg McSparron
26 Rolloa Adams
27 Lance Junker
28 Rich Figueroa
29 Mark Tudor

1981 TCMA Columbus Clippers

(New York Yankees, AAA) (color)

	MT	NR MT	EX
Complete Set:	45.00	34.00	18.00

1 Dick Stenholm
2 Tucker Ashford
3 Andre Robertson
4 Pat Callahan
5 Danny Schmitz
6 Jim Lewis
7 Paul Boris
8 Andy McGaffigan
9 Dave Righetti
10 Mike Griffin
11 Steve Balboni
12 Greg Cochran
13 Marshall Bryant
14 Brian Ryder
15 Juan Espino
16 Pat Tabler
17 Frank Verdi
18 Dave Coleman
19 Wayne Harer
20 Bill Showalter
21 Gary Smith
22 John Pacella
23 Dave Wehrmister (Wehrmeister)
24 Tom Filer
25 Mark Letenore
26 Sam Ellis
27 George H. Sisler
28 Jerry McNertney

1981 TCMA Durham Bulls

(Atlanta Braves, A) (black and white)

	MT	NR MT	EX
Complete Set:	27.50	20.50	11.25

1 Miguel Sosa
2 Mike Garcia
3 Kevin Rigby
4 Ken Scanlon
5 Tommy Thompson
6 Gary Cooper
7 Tom Hayes
8 Harold Williams
9 Keith Hagman
10 Brad Komminsk
11 Glen Bockhorn
12 Jeff Vuksan
13 Alvin Moore
14 Alan Gallagher
15 Rick Behenna
16 Rick Coatney
17 Jeff Dedmon
18 Glen Germer
19 Hoot Gibson
20 Danny Lucia
21 Roy North
22 Scott Patterson
23 Mike Payne
24 Gary Reiter

1981 TCMA El Paso Diablos

(Milwaukee Brewers, AA) (color)

	MT	NR MT	EX
Complete Set:	12.50	9.25	5.00

1 Ed Irvine
2 Willie Lozado
3 Al Manning
4 John Skorochocki
5 Terry Showbridge
6 Stan Davis
7 Jerry Lane
8 Doug Loman
9 Gerry Ako
10 Jim Koontz
11 Doug Jones
12 Larry Motgomery
13 Bill Schroeder
14 Mike Madden
15 Bob Skubbe (Skube)
16 Chick Valley
17 Rick Krantiz
18 Tony Torres
19 Weldon Swift
20 Tim Cook
21 Johnny Evans
22 Tom Candiotti
23 Tony Muser
24 Al Price

1981 TCMA Evansville Triplets

(Detroit Tigers, AAA) (color)

	MT	NR MT	EX
Complete Set:	12.00	9.00	4.75

1 Jim Leyland
2 George Cappuzzello
3 Mike Chris
4 Mark Fidrych
5 Larry Pashnick
6 Larry Rothschild
7 Manny Seoane
8 Jerry Ujdur
9 Pat Underwood
10 Roger Weaver
11 Marty Castillo
12 Larry Johnson
13 Mark DeJohn
14 Vern Followell
15 Glenn Gulliver
16 Craig Kusick
17 Juan Lopez
18 Tim Corcoran
19 Les Filkins
20 Eddie Gates
21 Ken Houston
22 Dennis Kinney

1981 TCMA Glens Falls White Sox

(Chicago White Sox, AA) (color)

	MT	NR MT	EX
Complete Set:	40.00	30.00	16.00

1 Luis Estrada
2 Randy Evans
3 Robert Fallon
4 Chuck Johnson
5 Mickey Maitland
6 Tom Mullen
7 Dennis Vasquez
8 Richard Wieters
9 Ricky Seilheimer
10 Andy Pasillas
11 Dom Fucci
12 Tim Hulett
13 Ivan Mesa
14 Peter Peltz
15 Ron Perry
16 Greg Walker
17 Vince Bienek
18 Randy Johnson
19 Ron Kittle
20 Luis Rois
21 Raymundo Torres
22 Jim Mahoney
23 Len Bradley
24 Larry Edwards

1981 TCMA Hawaii Islanders

(San Diego Padres, AAA) (color)

	MT	NR MT	EX
Complete Set:	11.00	8.25	4.50

1 Tim Flannery
2 Jose Moreno
3 Gary Ashby
4 Steve Smith
5 Doug Gwosdz
6 Tony Castillo
7 Jim Beswick
8 Alan Wiggins
9 Rick Lancellotti
10 Curtis Reed
11 Mike Armstrong
12 Steve Fireovid
13 Alan Olmsted
14 George Stablein
15 Tom Tellmann
16 Kim Seaman
17 Fred Kuhualua
18 Floyd Chiffer
19 Eric Show
20 Larry Duensing
21 Doug Rader
22 Chuck Hartenstein
23 Mario Ramirez

1981 TCMA Holyoke Millers

(California Angels, AA) (color) (California Angels, AA) (color)

	MT	NR MT	EX
Complete Set:	15.00	11.00	6.00

1 Ed Rodriguez
2 Jim Saul
3 Tom Kayser
4 T.J. Byrne
5 D. Comforti, D. Thomas
6 John Yandle
7 Ricky Adams
8 Mike Brown
9 Chris Clark
10 Dennis Gilbert
11 Curt Brown
12 Jeff Connor
13 Lonnie Dugger
14 Dave Duran
15 Rick Foley
16 Pat Keedy
17 Darrell Miller
18 Mark Nocciolo
19 Les Pearsey
20 Gary Pettis
21 Gustavo Polidor
22 Brandt Humphry
23 Bill Mooneyham
24 Perry Morrison
25 Dennis Rasmussen
26 Rick Rommell

1981 TCMA Lynn Sailors

(Seattle Mariners, AA) (color)

	MT	NR MT	EX
Complete Set:	22.50	17.00	9.25

1 Karl Best
2 Bud Black
3 Mark Cahill
4 Joe Georger
5 Tracy Harris
6 R.J. Harrison
7 Steve Krueger
8 Jed Murray
9 Dave Sheriff
10 Rob simond
11 Dave Smith
12 Matt Young
13 Jim Nelson
14 Dave Valle
15 Edwin Aponte
16 Billy Crone
17 Mario Diaz
18 Paul Serna
19 Mike White
20 Al Chambers
21 Ramon Estepa
22 Rodney Hobbs
23 Tito Nanni
24 Bobby Floyd
25 Mickey Bowers
26 Bob Randolph
27 Jeff Stottlemyre
28 Clark Crist

1981 TCMA Miami Orioles

(Baltimore Orioles, A) (black and white) (complete set price includes scarce Willsher and Young cards)

	MT	NR MT	EX
Complete Set:	125.00	94.00	50.00

1 Ron Dillard
2 Al Pardo
3 Freddie Smith
4 Mark Brown
5 Don Murelli
6 Minnie Mendoza
7 John DeLeon
8 Pat Dumouchelle
9 Satch Sanders
10 Francisco Oliveras
11 Mike Alvarez
12 Skip Clark
13 Andy Timko
14 Frank Ferroni
15 Lonnie Ivie
16 Neal Herrick
17 Leon Hoke
18 Tim Maples
19 Jeff Williams
20 Bret Gold
21 Scott Johnson
22 Chris Willsher
23 Mike Young

1981 TCMA Oklahoma City 89'ers

(Philadelphia Phillies, AAA) (color)

	MT	NR MT	EX
Complete Set:	65.00	48.75	26.50

1 Porfirio Altamirano

2 Carlos Arroyo
3 Eli Bonaparte
4 Warren Brusstar
5 Bob Dernier
6 Mark Davis
7 Dan Larsen
8 Orlando Isales
9 Don McCormack
10 Lenny Matuszek
11 Dennis Miscik
12 Manny McDonald
13 Scott Munninghoff
14 Dickie Noles
15 Jon Reelhorn
16 Luis Rodriguez
17 Ryne Sandberg
18 Bill Suter
19 Osvaldo (Ozzie) Virgil
20 George Vukovich
21 Bob Demeo
22 Ellis Deal
23 Jim Snyder
24 Jose Castro
25 Jim Rasmussen
26 Jeff Ulrich

1981 TCMA Omaha Royals

(Kansas City Royals, AAA) (color)

	MT	NR MT	EX
Complete Set:	15.00	11.25	6.00

1 Joe Sparks
2 Jerry Cram
3 Paul McGannon
4 Craig Chamberlain
5 Gary Christenson
6 Altee Hammaker
7 Dan Fischer
8 Don Hood
9 Mike Jones
10 Bill Laskey
11 Bill Paschall
12 Jeff Schattinger
13 Jim Gaudet
14 Greg Keatley
15 Manny Castillo
16 Onix Concepcion
17 Kelly Heath
18 Tim Ireland
19 Ron Johnson
20 Jim Buckner
21 Bob Detherage
22 Darryl Motley
23 Bombo Rivera
24 Pat Sheridan

1981 TCMA Pawtucket Red Sox

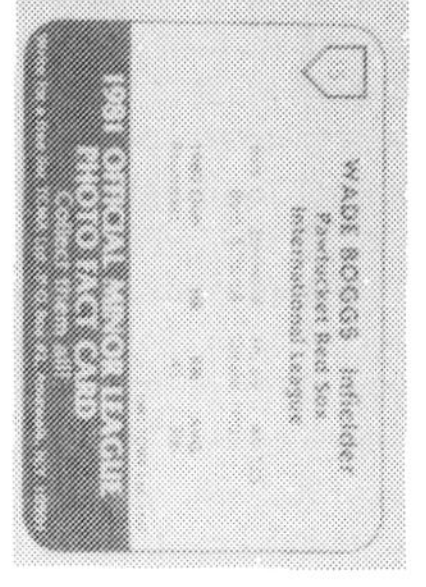

(Boston Red Sox, AAA) (color)

	MT	NR MT	EX
Complete Set:	100.00	75.00	41.00

1 Joel Finch
2 Mike Howard
3 Bruce Hurst
4 Keith MacWhorther
5 Bob Ojeda
6 Danny Parks
7 Win Remmerswaal
8 Luis Aponte
9 Jim Dorsey
10 Manny Sarmiento
11 Mike Smithson
12 Joe Morgan
13 Dale Robertson
14 Marty Barrett
15 Wade Boggs
16 Dave Koza
17 Julio Valdez
18 Sam Bowen
19 Lee Graham
20 Russ Laribee
21 Mike Ongarato
22 Chico Walker
23 Roger LaFrancois
24 Rich Gedman

1981 TCMA Portland Beavers

(Pittsburgh Pirates, AAA) (color)

	MT	NR MT	EX
Complete Set:	50.00	37.00	20.00

1 Pete Ward
2 Tom Trebelhorn
3 Santo Alcala
4 Matt Alexander
5 Mike Anderson
6 Dave Augustine
7 Bob Beall
8 Doe Boyland
9 Craig Cacek
10 Cecilio Guante
11 Dave Hilton
12 Willie Horton
13 Odell Jones
14 Vance Law
15 Mark Lee
16 Robert Long
17 Dale Mohorgic
18 Bobby Mitchell
19 Junior Ortiz
20 Pascual Perez
21 Tommy Sandt
22 Jimmy Smith
23 Luis Tiant
24 Alfredo Torres
25 Rusty Torres
26 Eleno Cuen
27 Kent Biggerstaff

1981 TCMA Quad City Cubs

(Chicago Cubs, A) (black and white)

	MT	NR MT	EX
Complete Set:	12.50	9.25	5.00

1 Dave Pagel
2 Don Hyman
3 Greg Tarnow
4 Rusty Piggot
5 Fritz Connally
6 Mike Buckley
7 Shane Allen
8 Mickey Tenney
9 Dennis Webb
10 Kevin Schoendienst
11 Jim Walsh
12 Terry Austin
13 Tom Johnson
14 Gary Monroe
15 Henry Cotto
16 Dan Cataline
17 Mike King
18 Tom Smith
19 Stan Kyles
20 Joe Housey
21 John Miglio
22 Ken Pryce
23 Ray Soff
24 Mark Vaji
25 Glenn Swaggerty
26 Craig Weissman
27 Jim Gerlach
28 Mark Wilkins
29 Don Schultze
30 Rich Morales
31 Gene Oliver
32 Roger Crow
33 Mike Palmer

1981 TCMA Reading Phillies

(Philadelphia Phillies, AA) (black and white)

	MT	NR MT	EX
Complete Set:	195.00	146.00	78.00

1 Jerry Reed
2 Kelly Faulk
3 Tom Hart
4 Darren Burroughs
5 Dan Prior
6 Miguel Alicea
7 Leroy Smith
8 Don Carman
9 Carlos Cabassa
10 Wally Goff
11 Herb Orensky
12 Miguel Ibarra
13 Jim Wright
14 Russ Hamric
15 Ron Smith
16 Tom Lombarski
17 Julio Franco
18 Ray Borucki
19 Keith Washington
20 Joe Bruno
21 Wil Culmer
22 Al Sanchez
23 Ron Clark
24 George Culver

1981 TCMA Redwood Pioneers

(California Angels, A) (black and white)

	MT	NR MT	EX
Complete Set:	15.00	11.00	6.00

1 Robert Bastian
2 Brian Buckley
3 Tom Crisler
4 Jay Kibbe
5 Ron Romanick
6 Jeff Smith
7 Ron Sylvia
8 Mike Venezia
9 Doug Rau
10 Aldo Bagiotti
11 Duffy Ryan
12 Wade Schexnayder
13 Harry Francis
14 Matt Gundelfinger
15 Ron Hunt
16 Marion Hunter
17 Tim Krauss
18 Mark Sproesser
19 Leo Lemon
20 Ken Tillman
21 Luis Zambrana
22 Warren Spahn
23 Tom Leonard
24 Kathy Leonard
25 David Levinson
26 Ralph Hartman
27 Chris Bankowski
28 Chris Cannizzaro
29 Barton Braun
30 Steve Levinson

1981 TCMA Richmond Braves

(Atlanta Braves, AAA) (color)

	MT	NR MT	EX
Complete Set:	30.00	22.50	12.25

1 John Sain
2 Tony Brizzolara
3 Jerry Keller
4 Ken Smith
5 Cragi Landis
6 Larry Whisenton
7 Bob Porter
8 Brett Butler
9 Chico Ruiz
10 Paul Runge
11 Butch Edge
12 Steve Bedrosian
13 Carlos Diaz
14 Larry McWilliams
15 Jose Alvarez
16 Steve Hammond
17 Steve Curry
18 Dan O'Brien
19 Ken Dayley
20 Matt Sinatro
21 Eddie Haas
22 Randy Johnson
23 Craig Robinson
24 Harry Saferight
25 Sam Ayoub

1981 TCMA Rochester Red Wings

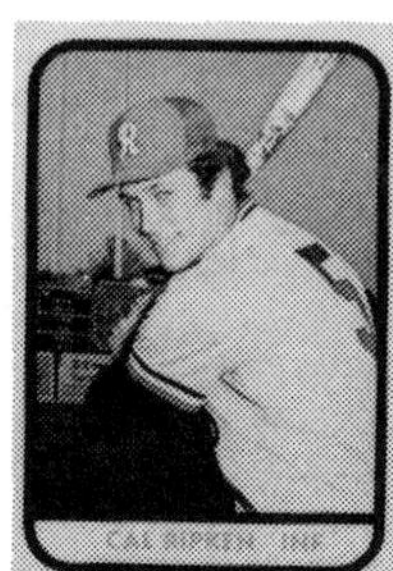

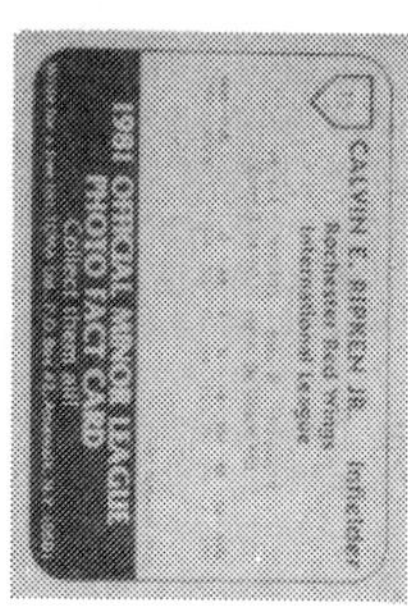

(Baltimore Orioles, AAA) (color)

	MT	NR MT	EX
Complete Set:	60.00	45.00	24.75

1 Mike Boddicker
2 Bill Bonner
3 Brooks Carey
4 Tom Chism
5 Tom Eaton
6 Johnny Hale
7 Mike Hart
8 Drungo Hazewood
9 Dave Huppert
10 Kevin Kennedy
11 Dan Logan
12 Steve Luebber
13 Ed Putnam
14 Floyd Rayford
15 Cal Ripken, Jr.
16 Tom Rowe
17 John Valle
18 Don Welchel
19 Larry Jones
20 Richie Bancells
21 Chris Bourjos
22 Doc Edwards
23 Dallas Williams

1981 TCMA Salt Lake City Gulls

(California Angels, AAA) (color)

	MT	NR MT	EX
Complete Set:	20.00	15.00	8.25

1 Leonard Garcia
2 Ralph Botting
3 Steve Brown
4 Craig Eaton
5 Bob Ferris
6 Dave Frost
7 Christian Knapp
8 Mike Mahler
9 Alfredo Martinez
10 Carlos Perez
11 Dave Schuler
12 Ricky Steirer
13 Mike Walters
14 Mike Bishop
15 Brian Harper
16 Jeff Bertoni
17 Scott Carnes
18 Fernando Gonzalez
19 Steve Lubratich
20 Daryl Sconier
21 Tom Brunansky
22 Pepe Mangual
23 Scott Moffitt
24 Don Pisker
25 Moose Stubing
26 Bob Davis

1981 TCMA Shreveport Captains

(Pittsburgh Pirates, AA) (black and white)

	MT	NR MT	EX
Complete Set:	20.00	15.00	8.00

1 Jack Mull
2 John Rabb
3 Jim Dunn
4 Tom O'Malley
5 Jim Wojcik
6 Glenn Fisher
7 Alan Fowlkes
8 Mike Tucker
9 Dan Gladden
10 Brad Bauman
11 Mark Dempsey
12 Paul Szymarek
13 Jim Duffalo
14 Doug Landuyt
15 Doran Perdue
16 Greg Baker
17 Ron Quick
18 Doug Wabeke
19 Jim Rothford
20 Scott Garrelts
21 Mark Lohuis
22 Greg Moyer
23 Pat Alexander

1981 TCMA Spokane Indians

(Seattle Mariners, AAA) (color)

	MT	NR MT	EX
Complete Set:	10.00	7.50	4.00

1 Chris Flammang
2 Manny Estrada
3 Scott Stranski
4 Sam Welborn
5 Orlando Mercado
6 Roy Clark
7 Mike Hart
8 Greg Biercevicz
9 Bob Galasso
10 Brian Allard
11 Steve Finch
12 Doug Merrifield
13 Rene Lachemann
14 Reggie Walton
15 Ed Vande Berg
16 Ted Cox
17 Ron Musselman
18 Bob Stoddard
19 Joe Coleman
20 Vance McHenry
21 Ken Pape
22 Jim Mahler
23 Larry Patterson
24 Randy Stein
25 Allen Wirth
26 Casey Parsons
27 Kim Allen
28 Rich Anderson
29 Jim Beattie
30 Brad Gulden
31 Jamie Allen
32 Marty Martinez

1981 TCMA Syracuse Chiefs

(Toronto Blue Jays, AAA) (color)

	MT	NR MT	EX
Complete Set:	10.00	7.50	4.00

1 Steve Baker
2 Tom Brown
3 Chuck Fore
4 Steve Grilli
5 Phil Huffman
6 Jack Kucek
7 Dale Murray
8 Kevin Pasley
9 Gene Petralli
10 Ramon Lora
11 Dave Baker
12 Charlie Beamon
13 Keith Chapman
14 Mike Davis
15 Pedro Hernandez
16 Greg Wells
17 Joe Cannon
18 Gil Kubski
19 Creighton Tevlin
20 Marv Thomson
21 Ken Schrom
22 Dave Tomlin
23 Bob Humphreys
24 Tony DeRosa

1981 TCMA Tacoma Tigers

(Oakland A's, AAA) (color)

	MT	NR MT	EX
Complete Set:	12.00	9.00	5.00

1 Larry Davis
2 Rick Randahl
3 Art Popham
4 Eric Mustad
5 Bob Kearney
6 Ed Nottle
7 Pat Dempsey
8 Dave Hamilton
9 Derek Bryant
10 Rich Bordi
11 Mike Davis
12 Jim Nettles
13 Mark Budaska
14 Don Fowler
15 Jim Sexton
16 Paul Mize
17 Keith Drumright
18 Kelvin Moore
19 Jeff Cox
20 Roy Thomas
21 Fred Holdsworth
22 Mark Souza
23 Rick Lysander
24 Dave Beard
25 Kevin Bell
26 Dave Heaverlo
27 Bob Grandas
28 Tigers Mascot
29 Batboys
30 Stan Naccarato
31 Jim Perry
32 Ed Figueroa

1981 TCMA Tidewater Tides

(New York Mets, AAA) (color)

	MT	NR MT	EX
Complete Set:	20.00	15.00	8.00

1 Ricky Sweet
2 Bruce Bochy
3 Ronald McDonald
4 Brian Giles
5 Ron Gardenhire
6 Phil Mankowski
7 Todd Winterfeldt
8 Wally Backman
9 Gary Rajsich
10 Sergio Beltre
11 Gil Flores
12 Mike Howard
13 Charlie Puleo
14 Tom Dixon
15 Scott Dye
16 Ed Lynch
17 Brent Gaff
18 Dave Von Ohlen
19 Mike Mendoza
20 Jesse Orosco
21 Jack Aker
22 Sam Perlozzo
23 Greg Harris
24 Ray Searage
25 Mark Daly
26 Rick Anderson
27 Danny Boitano
28 Dan Norman
29 Terry Leach

1981 TCMA Toledo Mud Hens

(Minnesota Twins, AAA) (color)

	MT	NR MT	EX
Complete Set:	10.00	7.50	4.00

1 Cal Ermer
2 Buck Chamberlin
3 Jose Bastian
4 Terry Felton
5 Gerry Hannahs
6 Mike Kinnunen
7 Buce MacPherson
8 Wally Sarmiento
9 Bob Veselic
10 Ric Williams
11 Aurelio Cadahia
12 Steve Herz
13 Dave Machemer
14 Kurt Seibert
15 Kelly Snider
16 Jesus Vega
17 John Walker
18 Ron Washington
19 Keathel Chauncey
20 Ed Cipot
21 Frank Estes
22 Steve Stroughter

1981 TCMA Tucson Toros

(Houston Astros, AAA) (color)

	MT	NR MT	EX
Complete Set:	40.00	30.00	16.00

1 Greg Cyprt
2 Dell Leayherwood
3 Joe Pittman
4 Alan Knicely
5 Bob Cluck
6 Tom Vessey
7 Bert Pena
8 Simon Rosario
9 Mark Miggins
10 Johnny Ray
11 Scott Loucks
12 Jimmy Johnson
13 Tom Spencer
14 Dave Labossiere
15 Stan Leland
16 Ron Meredith
17 Jim Pankovits
18 Gordon Pladson
19 Pete Ladd
20 Tim Tolman
21 Bert Roberge
22 George Gross
23 Jim MacDonald
24 Billy Smith
25 Jack Donovan
26 Tom Wiedenbauer

1981 TCMA Tulsa Drillers

(Texas Rangers, AA) (color)

	MT	NR MT	EX
Complete Set:	27.50	20.50	11.25

1 George Wright
2 Tracy Cowger
3 Phil Klimas
4 Marty Scott
5 Dave Stockstill
6 Mel Barrow
7 Larry Reynolds
8 Ted Davis
9 Steve Nielsen
10 Ron Carney
11 Joe Nemeth
12 Walt Terrell
13 Don Scott
14 Dennis Long
15 Dave Crutcher
16a Tony Fossas
16b Pete O'Brien
17 Mike Roberts
18 Ron Darling
19 Jack Lazorko
20 Tom Burgess
21 Tony Hudson
22 Kevin Richards
23 Greg Hughes
24 Brooks Wallace
25 Lindy Duncan
26 Bobby Ball
27 Joe Russell
28 Ron Gooch
29 Mike Jirschele

1981 TCMA Vancouver Canadians

(Milwaukee Brewers, AAA) (color)

	MT	NR MT	EX
Complete Set:	13.00	9.75	5.25

1 Jamie Cocanower
2 Chuck Porter
3 Doug Wanz
4 Dwight Bernard
5 Mark Schuster
6 Frank Thomas
7 Brian Thorson
8 Ivan Rodriguez
9 Gil Kubski
10 Baylor Moore
11 Gus Quiros
12 Larry Rush

13 Rich Olsen
14 Terry Lee
15 Willie Mueller
16 Andy Replogle
17 Frank DiPino
18 Rene Quinones
19 Bobby Smith
20 Lee Stigman
21 John Flinn
22 Gerry Ako
23 Tom Soto
24 Kevin Bass
25 Steve Lake

1981 TCMA Vero Beach Dodgers

(Los Angeles Dodgers, A) (black and white)

	MT	NR MT	EX
Complete Set:	30.00	22.50	12.25

1 Ed Amelung
2 Paul Bard
3 Frank Bryant
4 John Debus
5 Dan Forer
6 Art Hammond
7 Bobby Kenyon
8 Tony Lachowetz
9 Dave Lanning
10 Skip Mann
11 Holly Martin
12 Mike O'Malley
13 Felix Oroz
14 Steve Perry
15 Pat Raimondo
16 Curtis Reade
17 R.J. Reynolds
18 Greg Smith
19 Bill Sobbe
20 Terry Sutcliffe
21 Ricky Thomas
22 Brad Thorp
23 Juan Villaescusa
24 Brett Wise
25 David Wallace
26 John Shoemaker
27 Stan Wasiak

1981 TCMA Waterbury Reds

(Cincinnati Reds, AA) (black and white)

	MT	NR MT	EX
Complete Set:	32.50	24.25	13.50

1 Rich Carlucci
2 Keefe Cato
3 Mike Dowless
4 Ken Jones
5 Doug Neuenschwander
6 Rick O'Keefe
7 Bill Scherrer
8 Lester Straker
9 Mike Sullivan
10 Randy Town
11 Anthony Walker
12 Steve Christmas
13 Adolfo Feliz
14 Tom Lawless
15 Gary Redus
16 Hector Rincones
17 Eski Viltz
18 Russ Aldrich
19 Mark Gilbert
20 Dave Bisceglia
21 Tony Walker
22 George Scherger
23 Lee Garrett

1981 TCMA Waterloo Indians

(Cleveland Indians, A) (black and white)

	MT	NR MT	EX
Complete Set:	32.50	24.25	13.50

1 Gomer Hodge
2 Rick Colzie
3 Dennis Brogna
4 Larry Hrynko
5 John Asbell
6 Mark Bajus
7 Tom Burns
8 Mike Dixon
9 John Hoban
10 Mike Jeffcoat
11 Ricky Lintz
12 Tom Owens
13 Greg Pope
14 Ramon Romero
15 Mike Schwarber
16 Rich Thompson
18 Jack Fimple
19 John Malkin
20 Arnold Cochran
21 Shanie Dugas
22 Kelly Gruber
23 Marlin Methven
24 Juan Pacho
25 Larry Dotson
26 Dave Gallagher

27 Ed Saavedra
28 Mike Taylor
29 Winston Ficklin
30 Adalberto Nieves
31 Bernardo Brito
32 Steve Cushing
33 Ralph Elpin
34 Bob Feller
--- Louis Duarte

1981 TCMA Wausau Timbers

(Seattle Mariners, A) (black and white)

	MT	NR MT	EX
Complete Set:	85.00	64.00	34.00

1 Kevin Steger
2 Jeff Stottlemyre
3 Bob Hudson
4 Edwin Nunez
5 Tom Brennan
6 Mark Pedersen
7 Brian Snyder
8 Mark Batten
9 CHris Hunger
10 Don McKenzie
11 David Blume
12 Eddie Yampierre
13 Jesse Baez
14 Rick Adair
15 Jeff Cary
16 Enrique Diaz
17 Donnell Nixon
18 Harold Reynolds
19 Darnell Coles
20 Jimmy Presley
21 Clark Crist
22 Omar Minaya
23 Mark Chelette
24 Glenn Walker
25 John Moses
26 Ivan Calderon
27 Kevin King
28 Tom Hunt
29 Bill Plummer

1981 TCMA West Haven A's

(Oakland A's, AA) (color)

	MT	NR MT	EX
Complete Set:	13.00	9.75	5.25

1 Robert Didier
2 Keith Atherton
3 Bert Bradley
4 DeWayne Buice
5 Darryl Cias
6 Keith Comstock
7 Tim Conroy
8 Jim Durrman
9 Bobby Garrett
10 Bruce Fournier
11 Lynn Garrett
12 Steve Gelfarb
13 Rick Holloway
14 Tony Phillips
15 Ricky Troneru d
16 Don Morris
17 Mike Woodard
18 Alan Abraham
19 Dennis Sherow
20 Gorman Heimueller
21 Scott Meyer
22 Dick Lynch
23 Scott Pyle

1981 TCMA Wisconsin Rapids Twins

(Minnesota Twins, A) (black and white)

	MT	NR MT	EX
Complete Set:	45.00	33.50	18.00

1 Ken Staples
2 Tom Leix
3 Smokey Everett
4 Tony Guerrero
5 Larry Harris
6 Kirby Krueger
7 Jeorge Ortiz
8 Adriano Pena
9 Luis Suarez
10 Mike Ungs
11 Mark Wright
12 Richard Yett
13 Ken Chandler
14 Jeff Reed
15 Michael Cole
16 Ken Foster
17 Jim Payne
18 Bill Price
19 Mandy Smith
20 Talbot Aiello
21 Jim Eisenreich
22 John Palica
23 Nelson Suarez

1981 Team Charlotte O's

(Baltimore Orioles, AA)

	MT	NR MT	EX
Complete Set:	75.00	56.25	31.00

(1) Juan Arias
(2) Don Bowman
(3) Scott Budner
(4) Storm Davis
(5) John Denman
(6) Tim Derryberry
(7) Allen Edwards
(8) Will George
(9) Tim Graven
(10) Drungo Hazewood
(11) Ricky Jones
(12) Mark Naehring
(13) Earl Neal
(14) Paul O'Neill
(15) Victor Rodriguez
(16) Willie Royster
(17) John Shelby
(18) Mark Smith
(19) Cliff Speck
(20) Bill Swaggerty
(21) Don Welchel
(22) Cat Whitfield
(23) Mark Wiley
(24) "The Pepper Girls"
(25) Team Logo

1981 Team Holyoke Millers

(California Angels, AA) This set features blank back cards, and was also produced in the form of an uncut poster.

	MT	NR MT	EX
Complete Set:	70.00	52.50	28.75

(1) Rick Adams
(2) Mike Brown
(3) T.J. Byrne
(4) Chris Clark
(5) Jeff Connor
(6) Lonnie Dugger
(7) Dave Duran
(8) Rick Foley
(9) Dennis Gilbert
(10) Brandt Humphry
(11) Tom Kayser
(12) Pat Keedy
(13) Darrell Miller
(14) Bill Mooneyham
(15) Jerry Morrison
(16) Mark Nocciolo
(17) Les Pearsey
(18) Gary Pettis
(19) Gustavo Polidor
(20) Dennis Rasmussen
(21) Ed Rodriguez
(22) Rich Rommel
(23) Jim Saul
(24) Dave Thomas
(25) John Yandle

1981 Team Indianapolis Indians

(Cincinnati Reds, AAA) (co-sponsored by Tom Aikens)

	MT	NR MT	EX
Complete Set:	25.00	18.50	10.00

1 Team Photo
2 Jim Beauchamp
3 Geoff Combe
4 Paul Householder
5 Charlie Leibrandt
6 Dave Van Gorder
7 Tom Foley
8 Kip Young
9 Eddie Milner
10 The Relievers
11 Jose Brito
12 Greg Mahlberg
13 Bill Bohnam
14 The Teachers
15 Nick Esasky
16 Jeff Lahti
17 The Lightening Squad
18 Gene Menees
19 Scott Brown
20 The Outfielders

21 Duane Walker
22 Bill Kelly
23 The Infielders
24 Joe Kerrigan
25 German Barranca
26 The Starters
27 Paul Herring
28 Bill Dawley
29 Skeeter Barnes
30 The Catchers
31 Sergio Ferrer
32 John Young

1981 Team Syracuse Chiefs

(Toronto Blue Jays, AAA) All cards are postcard size with blank backs.

	MT	NR MT	EX
Complete Set:	42.50	31.75	17.50

2 Pedro Hernandez
3 Kelvin Chapman
5 Steve Baker
6 Domingo Ramos
8 Dan Whitmer
9 Gere Petralli
10 Charlie Beamon
12 Steve Davis
14 Paul Mirabella
15 Ramon Lora
16 Dave Tomlin
17 Creighton Tevlin
19 Tom Brown
20 Jack Kucek
22 Marv Thompson
23 J.J. Cannon
24 Phil Huffman
25 Bob Humphreys
26 Jim Wright
27 Dale Murray
28 Steve Baker
29 Ken Schrom
31 Chuck Fore
32 "Boomer" Wells

1981 Valley Nat'l Bank Phoenix Giants

(San Francisco Giants, AAA) (3-3/8" x 2-1/4")

	MT	NR MT	EX
Complete Set:	12.50	9.50	5.25

1 Phoenix Booster Rooster/Checklist

2 Harry Jordan
3 Bob Tufts
4 Bob Brenly
5 Jeff Stember
6 Max Venable
7 Doug Shaefer
8 Mike Williams
9 Mark Clavert
10 Mike Rowland
11 Mike Rex
12 Jose Barrios
13 Al Hargesheimer
14 Dave Wiggins
15 Guy Sularz
16 Tommy Jones
17 Phil Hinrichs
18 Dennis Littlejohn
19 Wayne Pechek
20 Gene Pentz
21 Joe Pettini
22 Jeff Ransom
23 Tom Runnells
24 Rich Murray
25 Rocky Bridges
26 Tommy Gonzales
27 Ethan Blackaby

1981 WTF Co. Rochester Red Wings

(Baltimore Orioles, AAA)

	MT	NR MT	EX
Complete Set:	85.00	64.00	34.00

1 Calvin Ripken Jr.
2 Dallas Williams
3 Chris Bourjos
4 Mark Corey
5 Doc Edwards
6 Thomas Rowe
7 Jeffrey Schneider
8 James Umbarger
9 Don Welchel
10 Larry Jones
11 Dan Logan
12 Steve Luebber
13 Eddy Putman
14 Floyd Rayford
15 David Huppert
16 Drungo Hazewood
17 James Hart
18 John Hale
19 Tom Eaton
20 Checklist
21 Bob Bonner
22 Brooks Carey
23 Mike Boddicker
24 Thomas Chism
25 Silver Stadium

1982

1982 Arby's Nashville Sounds

(New York Yankees, AA)

	MT	NR MT	EX
Complete Set:	10.00	7.50	4.00

1 Dave Banes
2 Mike Browning
3 Brian Butterfield
4 Ben Callahan
5 Pat Callahan
6 Nate Chapman
7 Clay Christiansen
8 Dean Craig
9 Brian Dayett
10 Tommie Dodd
11 Guy Elston
12 Ray Fontenot
13 Paul Grayner
14 Rex Hudler
15 Tim Knight
16 Chris Lein
17 Erik Peterson
18 Brian Poldberg
19 Frank Ricci
20 Mark Salas
21 Dan Schmitz
22 Buck Showalter
23 Roger Slagle
24 Garry Smith
25 Bob Sykes
26 Rafael Villaman
27 Stefan Wever
--- Manager & Coaches (Hoyt Wilhelm, John Oates, Eddie Napoleon)

1982 Chong Modesto A's

(Oakland A's, A)

	MT	NR MT	EX
Complete Set:	32.50	24.25	13.50

1 Dave Hudgens
2 Rod Murphy
3 Selwyn Young
4 Tom Copeland
5 Thad Reece
6 Rick Tronerud
7 Terry Harper
8 John Hotchkiss
9 Jimmy Camacho
10 Aurdie Colbert
11 Mickey Tettleton
12 Curt Young
13 Wayne Palicia
14 Ed Retzer
15 Paul Josephson
16 Mike Lynes
17 Mark Ferguson
18 Tony Herron
19 Gary Dawson
20 Tim Conroy
21 Rick Rodriguez
22 Don Van Marter
23 Wayne Rudolph
24 Pete Whisenant
25 Jim Durrman
26 Phil Danielson
27 Dan Kiser

1982 Ehrler's Dairy Louisville Redbirds

(St. Louis Cardinals, AAA)

	MT	NR MT	EX
Complete Set:	22.50	16.50	9.00

(1) George A. Bjorkman
(2) Jose Oscar Brito
(3) Glen E. Brummer
(4) Michael S. Calise
(5) Ralph A. Citarella
(6) Joseph De Sa
(7) Jeffrey D. Doyle
(8) Joseph F. Frazier
(9) John T. Fulgham
(10) David A. Green
(11) Ricky N. Horton
(12) David B. Kable
(13) Jeffrey Allen Lahti
(14) William Allen Lyons
(15) John R. Martin
(16) Willie D. Mc Gee
(17) Jerry Mc Kune
(18) Dyar K. Miller
(19) Gotay Mills
(20) Daniel J. Morogiello
(21) Alan R. Olmsted
(22) Kelly J. Paris
(23) Gaylen R. Pitts
(24) Andrew J. Rinson
(25) Gene (Eugene L. Roof)
(26) Orlando Sanchez
(27) Rafael Santana
(28) Jed Smith
(29) John A. Stuper
(30) Steven W. Winfield

1982 Fritsch Appleton Foxes

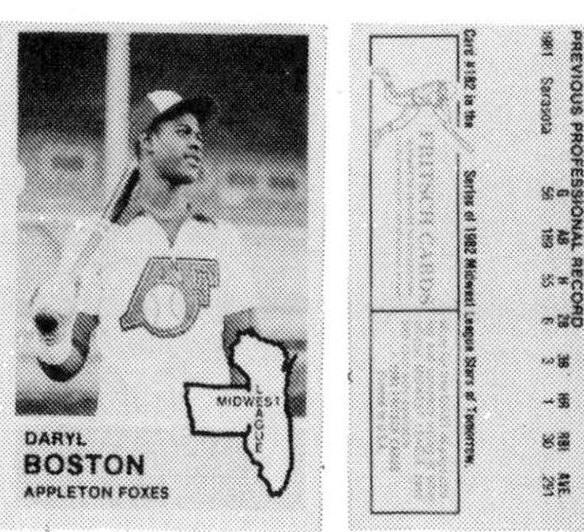

(Chicago White Sox, A)

	MT	NR MT	EX
Complete Set:	15.00	11.25	6.00

1 Team Logo/Checklist
2 Jeff Overton
3 Leo Garcia
4 Jim Sutton
5 Wade L. Rowdon
6 Ramon Romero
7a Al Jones (leg showing) (sample card)
7b Al Jones (no leg showing) (regular issue)
8 John Taylor
9 Scott Meier
10 Jess Anderson
11 Steve Pastrovich
12 Curt Reed
13 Wes Kent
14 John Skinner
15 Dave Nix
16 Joseph J. Paglino
17 Don Koch
18 Wayne Schuckert
19 Bill Babcock
20 Eddie Miles
21a Kevin Flannery (elbow showing) (sample card)
21b Kevin Flannery (elbow not showing) (regular issue)
22 Scott Gibson
23 Art Niemann
24 Daryl Boston
25 Michael J. Tanzi
26 Michael J. Buggs
27 Pat Adams
28 Al Heath
29 Doug Wiesner
30 Mike Pazik
31 Adrian Garrett

1982 Fritsch Beloit Brewers

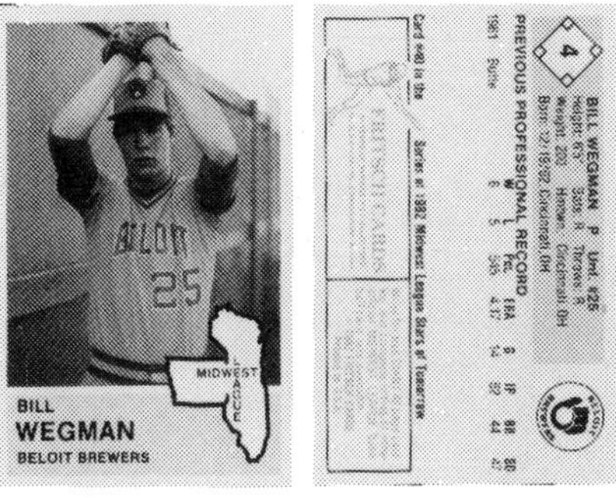

(Milwaukee Brewers, A)

	MT	NR MT	EX
Complete Set:	17.50	13.00	7.00

1 Team Logo/Checklist
2a Joe Henderson (catching) (sample card)
2b Joe Henderson (batting) (regular issue)
3 Gerry Miller
4 Bill Wegman
5 Johnson C. Wood

6 Ty Van Burkleo
7 John Hoban
8 John Gibbons
9 Fritz Fedor
10 Marcos Gomez
11 Dewey James
12 Mike Myerchin
13 Collin Tanabe
14 Kenny Clayton
15 Butch Kirby
16 Joe Edwin Morales
17 Gary Evans
18 Danny Gilmartin
19 Mike Samuel
20 Bryan Clutterbuck
21 Bill Max
22 Brad DeKraai
23 Martin Antunez
24 Terry Bevington
25 Bill Nowlan
26 Angel Morris Jr.
27a Ted Pallas (glove above head) (sample card)
27b Ted Pallas (glove at waist) (regular issue)

1982 Fritsch Burlington Rangers

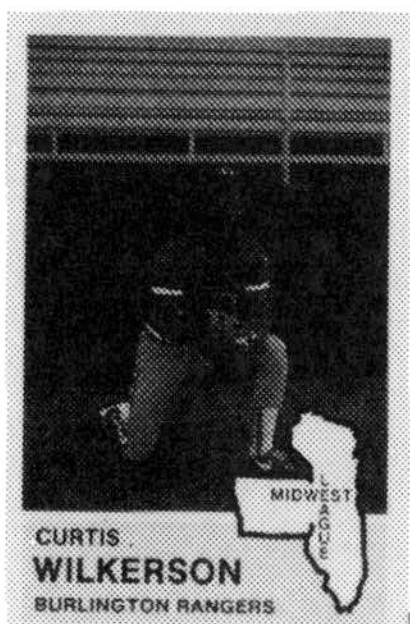

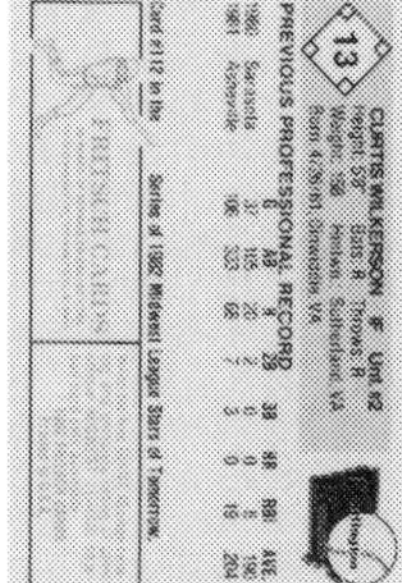

(Texas Rangers, A)

	MT	NR MT	EX
Complete Set:	8.00	6.00	3.25

1 Team Logo/Checklist
2 Lawrence Avery
3 Kevin Buckley
4 Dwayne Henry
5 Al Hartman
6 Tony Triplett
7 Ray Warren
8 Frank Brosious
9 Garry Venner
10 Keith Jones
11 Rod Hodde
12 Jorge Gomez
13 Curtis Wilkerson
14 Tim Henry
15 Greg Tabor
16 Chuckie Canady
17 Mark Gammage
18 Mike Schmid
19 Gary Sharp
20 Larry McLane
21 Tony Hudson
22 Doug Davis
23 Glen Cook
24 Whitney Harry
25 Jim Jeffries
26 Greg Campbell
27 Otto Gonzalez
28 Marty Scott
29 Tim Maki
30 Steve Nielsen

1982 Fritsch Clinton Giants

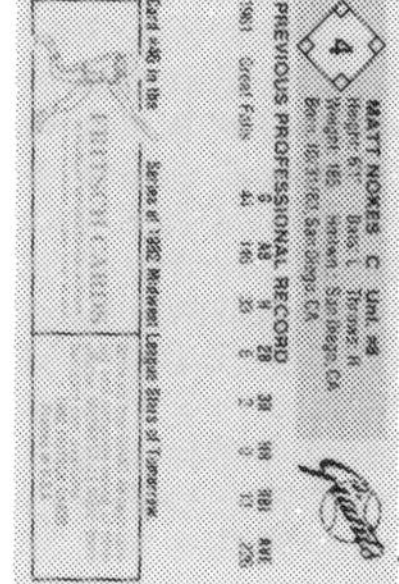

(San Francisco Giants, A)

	MT	NR MT	EX
Complete Set:	20.00	15.00	8.00

1 Team Logo/Checklist
2 Wendell Kim
3 Steve Cline
4 Matt Nokes
5 Phil Ouellette
6 Glenn Barling
7 Michael Jones
8 Todd Zacher
9 David Nenad
10 Everett Graham
11 Steve Wilcox
12 Randy Saunier
13 Ramon Bautista
14 Mike Dunn
15 Marty Baier
16 Kernan Ronan
17 Gene Lambert
18 Allen Smoot
19 Larry Crews
20 Brian Murtha
21 Glenn Jones
22 Eric Erickson
23 Mark Grant
24 Randy Ebersberger
25 Bob O'Connor
26 Mark Tudor
27 Gus Stokes
28 John Marks
29 Jim Weir
30 Mickey Swenson
31 Mark Swenson
32 Mark Swenson, Mickey Swenson

1982 Fritsch Danville Suns

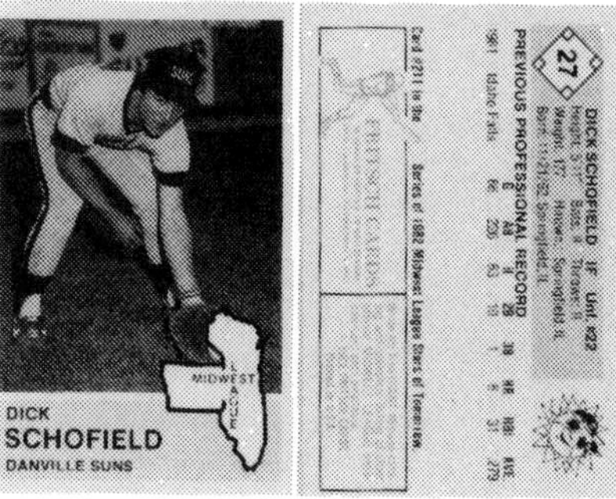

(California Angels, A)

	MT	NR MT	EX
Complete Set:	22.50	16.50	9.00

1 Team Logo/Checklist
2 Gus Gil
3 Jeff Ahern
4 T.R. Bryden
5 Mark Bingham
6 Bill White
7a Rick Turner (no glove) (sample card)
7b Rick Turner (with glove) (regular issue)
8 Jack Crawford
9 Kevin Price
10 Butch Dowies
11 Carlos Matos
12 Doug Lindsey
13 Tony Gonzalez
14 Marcel Lachemann
15 Richard Zaleski
16 Scott Oliver
17 Ellie Barros
18 Willie D. Williams
19 Freddy Machuca
20 Bill Worden
21 Devon White
22 Joe King
23 Mike Saverino
24 Brian Hartsock
25 Mark Bonner
26 Rafel Lugo
27 Dick Schofield
28 Norman Carrasco

1982 Fritsch Madison Muskies

(Oakland A's, A)

	MT	NR MT	EX
Complete Set:	8.00	6.00	3.25

1 Team Logo/Checklist
2 Joel Boni
3 Steve Kiefer
4 Mike Flinn
5 John "Duke" Smith
6 Chuck Kolotka
7 Kevin Coughlon
8 Tom Heckman
9 Gene Ransom
10 Scott Anderson
11 Scot Mitchell

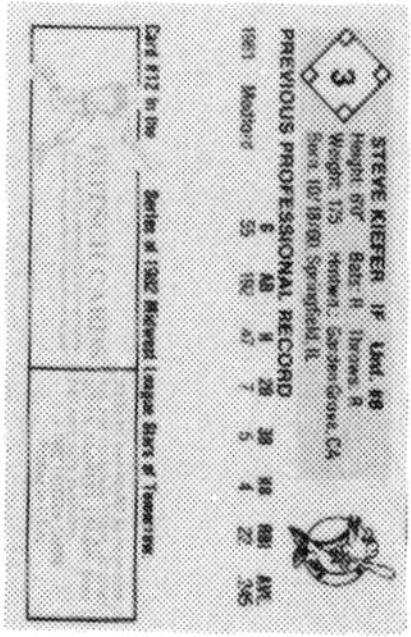

12 Mark Jarrett
13 Jeff Tipton
14 Mark Fellows
15 Monte R. McAbee
16 Ron Wilkinson
17 Allen Edwards
18 Frank Harris
19 Brad Fischer
20 James Feeley
21 Ron Harrison
22 Kevin D. Waller
23 Mike Ashman
24 Rob Vavrock
25 Jeff Kobernus
26 Keith Call
27a Pat O'Hara (batting) (sample card)
27b Pat O'Hara (catching) (regular issue)
28 Thomas Romano
29 Mark "Mac" McDonald
30 Bruce Amador
31 Jeff Cary
32 Hector Perez
33 Ed Janus
34 Bob Drew, Michael Duval

1982 Fritsch Springfield Cardinals

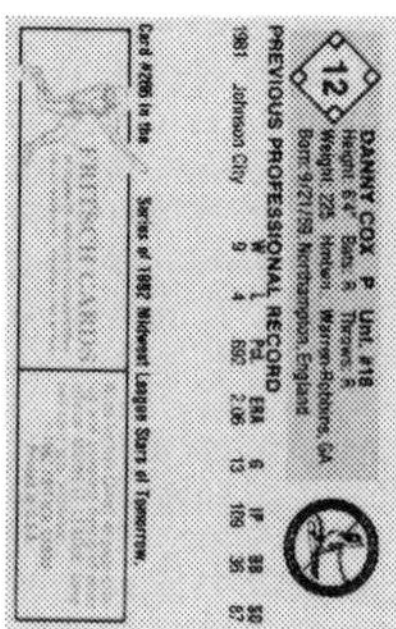

(St. Louis Cardinals, AAA)

	MT	NR MT	EX
Complete Set:	12.50	9.50	5.25

1 Team Logo/Checklist
2 Dave Bialas
3 Bruce "Pic" Miller
4 Bill Lyons
5 Mike Pittman
6 Freddie Silva
7 Robert Hicks
8 Tom Epple
9a Dan Stryffeler (bat on shoulder) (sample card))
9b Dan Stryffeler (bat off shoulder) (regular issue)
10 Gus Malespin
11 Steve Winfield
12 Danny Cox
13 Greg Dunn
14 Bobby Kish
15 Tom Dozier
16 Marty Mason
17 Alan Hunsinger
18 Don Collins
19 Mike Harris
20 Randy Hunt
21 Deron Thomas
22 Harry McCulla
23 Brad Bennett
24 Francisco Batista

1982 Fritsch Waterloo Indians

(Cleveland Indians, A)

	MT	NR MT	EX
Complete Set:	8.00	6.00	3.25

1 Team Logo/Checklist
2 Gomer Hodge
3 Vic Albury
4 Ron Wollenhaupt
5a Rickey Lintz (left wrist not showing) (sample card))
5b Rickey Lintz (left wrist showing) (regular issue)
6 Jerry Nalley
7 Phil Wilson
8 Rod McDonald
9 Rod Carraway
10 Steve Roche
11 Dave Gallagher
12 Ralph Elpin
13 Dave Wick
14 Mike Gertz
15 Steve Cushing
16 John Miglio
17 Chris Rehbaum
18 Marlin Methven
19 Winston Ficklin
20 John Malkin
21 Sammy Martin
22 Ed Tanner
23 Rich Doyle
24 Jose Roman
25 Wayne Johnson
26 Randy Washington
27 George Alpert
28 Junior Noboa

1982 Fritsch Wausau Timbers

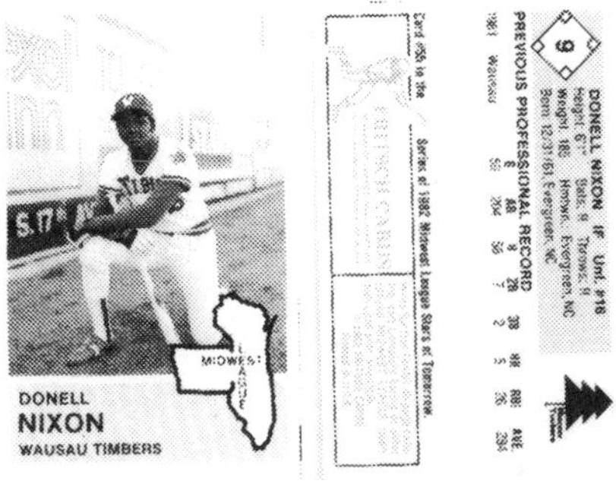

(Seattle Mariners, A)

	MT	NR MT	EX
Complete Set:	12.50	9.50	5.25

1 Team Logo/Checklist
2 Team Photo
3 Jack Roeder
4 Stan Edmonds
5 Curtis Kouba
6 Bart Mackie
7 Joe Benes
8 Randy Meier
9 Donell Nixon
10 Ivan Calderon
11 Eric Parent
12 Mike Bucci
13 Bret McAfee
14 Ronn Dixon
15 Martin O. Enriquez
16 Luis Trinidad H. Castillo
17 R.J. Harrison
18 Mike Johnson
19 Mitch Zwolensky
20 Donny Holland
21 Jay Michael Erdahl
22 Mike Evans
23 Gary Pellant
24 Don Diego Pierce
25 Angel Vicente Fonseca
26 Bill Taylor
27 Ric Wilson
28 Chip Conklin
29 Terry Hayes
30 Tom Hunt
31 Bob Gisselman

NOTE: A card number in parentheses ( ) indicates the set is unnumbered.

1982 Fritsch Wisconsin Rapids Twins

(Minnesota Twins, A)

	MT	NR MT	EX
Complete Set:	12.50	9.50	5.25

1 Team Logo/Checklist
2 Greg Kipfer
3 Ken Staples
4 Mike Weiermiller
5 Dave Hoyt
6 Mark Wright
7 Alvaro "Espi" Espinoza
8 Paul Fleming
9 Johnny Salery
10 Herbert Carter
11 Rick Scheetz
12 Larry James Mikesell
13 Sebby Borriello
14 Mark Portugal
15 Jose Gil
16 Barry "B.C." Houston
17 Dick Henkemeyer
18 Phil Franko
19 John Foster
20 Eric Porter
21 Willi Flores
22 Mark Larcom
23 Steve Aragon
24 Marc J. Page
25 Jeff Arney
26 Craig Henderson
27 Rhett Whisman

1982 Police Columbus Clippers

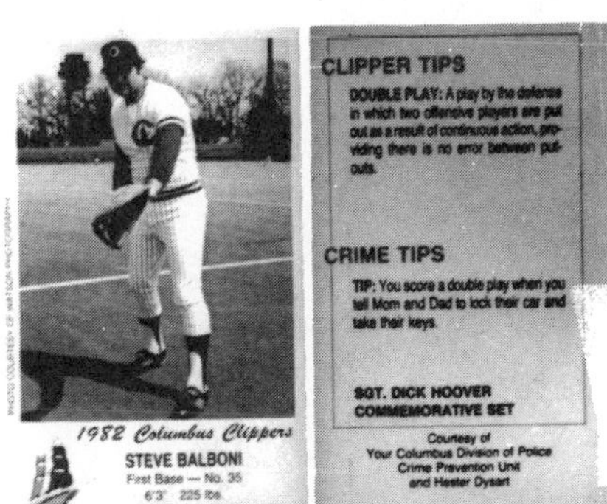

(New York Yankees, AAA)

	MT	NR MT	EX
Complete Set:	50.00	37.50	20.50

(1) Tucker Ashford
(2) Steve Balboni
(3) Marshall Brant
(4) Mike Bruhert
(5) Greg Cochran
(6) Juan Espino
(7) Pete Filson
(8) Wayne Harper
(9) Curt Kaufman
(10) Jim Lewis
(11) Don Mattingly
(12) John Pacella
(13) Mike Patterson
(14) Scott Patterson
(15) Bobby Ramos
(16) Andre Robertson
(17) Dan Schmitz
(18) George H. Sisler Jr.
(19) Garry Smith
(20) Dave Stegman
(21) Bob Sykes
(22) Frank Verdi
(23) Dave Wehrmeister
(24) Jamie Werly
(25) Coaches/Trainer Card (Sammy Ellis, Jerry McNertney, Steve Donohue)

1982 TCMA Albuquerque Dukes

(Los Angeles Dodgers, AAA) (color) (complete set price includes scarce Koufax card)

	MT	NR MT	EX
Complete Set:	75.00	56.00	30.00

1 Joe Beckwith
2 John Franco
3 Burt Geiger
4 Orel Hershiser
5 Brian Holton
6 Dave Moore
7 Tom Niedenfuer
8 Steve Shirley
9 Rick Rodas
10 Larry White
11 Rick Wright
12 Don Crow
13 Dave Sax
14 Dave Anderson
15 Greg Brock
16 Larry Fobbs
17 Ross Jones
18 Alex Taveras
19 Mark Bradley
20 Dave Holman
21 Candy Maldonado
22 Mike Marshall
23 Tack Wilson
24 Del Crandall
25 Dave Cohea
26 Dick McLaughlin
27 Brent Strom

1982 TCMA Alexandria Dukes

(Pittsburgh Pirates, A) (black and white)

	MT	NR MT	EX
Complete Set:	32.00	24.00	13.00

1 Johnny Taylor
2 Lee Marcheskie
3 Larry Lamonde
4 Ray Krawczyk
5 Jeffrey Horne
6 Christopher Green
7 Fernando Gonzales
8 Lance Dodd
9 Wilfrido Cordoba
10 Mike Quade
11 Brad Garnett
12 Marvin Clack
13 Nick Castaneda
14 Pete Rowe
15 Burk Goldthorn
16 James Churchill
17 Jeffrey Zaske
18 Timothy Wheeler
19 Brian McCann
20 Dan Warthen
21 John Lipon
22 Joe Orsulak
23 Ken Ford
24 Jim Felt
25 Nelson de la Rosa
26 Andy Smith
27 Rick Renteria

1982 TCMA Amarillo Gold Sox

(San Diego Padres, AA) (black and white)

	MT	NR MT	EX
Complete Set:	32.00	24.00	13.00

1 George Hinshaw
2 Brian Greer
3 John Stevenson
4 Joe Scherger
5 Gerry Davis
6 Bob Macias
7 Jeff Ronk
8 Don Purpura
9 Mike Martin
10 Mark Parent
11 James Steels
12 Jim Coffman
13 John White
14 Tom Biko
15 Neil Bryant
16 Mike Couchee
17 Steve Stone
18 Bill Long
19 Willie Hardwick
20 Marty Kain
21 Randy Kaczmarski
22 Rick Shaw
23 Glen Ezell
24 Mike Hebrard
25 Tom House

NOTE: A card number in parentheses ( ) indicates the card set is unnumbered.

1982 TCMA Arkansas Travelers

(St. Louis Cardinals, AA) (black and white)

	MT	NR MT	EX
Complete Set:	105.00	79.00	42.00

1 Scott Arigoni
2 Kevin Hagen
3 Rickey Horton
4 Jeff Keener
5 Rafael Pimentel
6 Gerry Perry
7 Mark Riggins
8 Ed Sanford
9 Buddy Schultz
10 Tom Thurberg
11 Mark Salas
12 Tom Nieto
13 Jose Gonzales
14 Greg Guin
15 Peachy Guiterrez
16 Luis Ojeda
17 Don Moore
18 Jim Adduci
19 Andy Van Slyke
20 Jack Ayer
21 Larry Reynolds
22 Gaylen Pitts
23 Dave England
24 Jorge Aranzamendi

1982 TCMA Auburn Astros

(Houston Astros, A) (black and white)

	MT	NR MT	EX
	20.00	15.00	8.00

1 Tom Roarke
2 Bob hartsfield
3 Jeff Jacobson
4 Mike Stellern
5 Ray Perkins
6 Eric Anderson
7 Jeff Meadows
8 Mike Hogan
9 Larry McIver
10 Bob Hinson
11 Jeff Datz
12 Tracy Dophied
13 Rich Bombard
14 Craig Kizer
15 Tom Riewerts
16 Steve Swain
17 Ricardo Rivera
18 Carlos Alfonso
19 Rick Thompson

1982 TCMA Birmingham Barons

(Detroit Tigers, AA) (color)

	MT	NR MT	EX
Complete Set:	14.00	10.50	5.50

1 Stan Younger
2 Barbaro Garbey
3 Darrell Woodard
4 Homer Moncrief
5 Dave Gumpert
6 Mike Beecroft
7 Bob Melvin
8 Randy O'Neal
9 Chuck Cary
10 Kenny Baker
11 Bruce Fields
12 Randy Harvey
13 Rondal Rollins
14 Gary Hinson
15 John Flannery
16 Dave Hawarney
17 Kevin Pasley
18 Jerry Bass
19 Frank McCann
20 Steve Quealey
21 Charlie Nail
22 Emilio Carrasquel
23 Paul Gibson
24 Ed Brinkman

1982 TCMA Buffalo Bisons

(Pittsburgh Pirates, AA) (color)

	MT	NR MT	EX
Complete Set:	17.00	12.75	7.00

1 Rich Leggat
2 Bob Misak
3 Connor McGeehee
4 Drew McCauley
5 Greg Pastors
6 John Schaive
7 Al Torres
8 Keith Thibodeaux
9 Tim Wheeler
10 Kevin Houston
11 Ron Wotus
12 John Holland
13 Steve Farr

14 Eleno Cuen
15 Tim Burke
16 Mike Bielecki
17 Rick Peterson
18 Tom Sandt

1982 TCMA Burlington Rangers

(Texas Rangers, A) (black and white) (complete set price includes scarce Avery card)

	MT	NR MT	EX
Complete Set:	100.00	75.00	40.00

1 Timothy Henry
2 Rodney Hodde
3 Anthony Hudson
4 James Jeffries
5 Keith Jones
6 Timothy Maki
7 Larry McLane
8 Michael Schmid
9 Gary Sharp
10 Gregory Tabor
11 Antonio Triplett
12 Raymond Warren
13 Curtis Wilkerson
14 Frank Brosiuos
15 Kevin Buckley
16 Chuckie Canady
17 Glen Cook
18 Douglas Davis
19 Mark Gammage
20 Jorge Gomez
21 Otto Gonzalez
22 Whitney Harry
23 Albert Hartman
24 Dwayne Henry
25 Martin Scott
26 Steven Nielsen
27 Larry Avery

1982 TCMA Cedar Rapids Reds

(Cincinnati Reds, A) (color)

	MT	NR MT	EX
Complete Set:	75.00	56.00	30.00

1 Mark Rothey
2 Rob Murphy
3 Curt Heidenreich
4 Steve Lowrey
5 Kurt Kepshire
6 Mike Riley
7 Freddie Toliver
8 Mike Ferguson
9 Mike Hennessy
10 Jim Pettibone
11 Larry Freeburg
12 Danny Lamar
13 Mark Matzen
14 Paul Kirsch
15 Adolfo Feliz
16 Tony Burley
17 Byron Peyton
18 Bill Metil
19 Dave Hall
20 Eric Davis
21 Paul O'Neill
22 Tim Stout
23 Scott Terry
24 Jeff Jones
25 Randy Davidson
26 David Clay
27 Don Buchheister

1982 TCMA Charleston Charlies

(Cleveland Indians, AAA) (color)

	MT	NR MT	EX
Complete Set:	17.50	13.00	7.00

1 Bud Anderson
2 John Bohnet
3 Gordy Glaser
4 Ed Glynn
5 Neal Heaton
6 Larry Hrynko
7 Silvio Martinez
8 Jack Nuismer
9 Rob Pietroburgo
10 Ray Searage
11 Bill Nahorodny
12 Tim Norrid
13 Craig Stimac
14 Luis DeLeon
15 Angelo LoGrande
16 Rich Murray
17 Kevin Rhomberg
18 Dave Rosello
19 Carmelo Castillo
20 Larry Littleton
21 Karl Pagel
22 Dave Riviera
23 Doc Edwards
24 Chuck Estrada

1982 TCMA Charleston Royals

(Kansas City Royals, A) (black and white) (Cone and Psaltis cards have transposed backs)

	MT	NR MT	EX
Complete Set:	55.00	41.25	22.50

1 Jim Miner
2 Roger Hausen
3 Mike Sorrel
4 Tom McHugh
5 John Bryant
6 Danny Jackson
7 Mitch Ashmore
8 Perry Swanson
9 Bert Johnson
10 Chris Bryeans
11 Bob Umdenstock
12 Mike Kingery
13 Tim Ballard
14 Dick Vitato
15 Ron Krauss
16 Ken Patterson
17 Roland Oruna
18 Den Swank
19 Spiro Psaltis (Dave Cone name & bio on card)
20 Dave Cone (Spiro Psaltis name & bio on card)
21 Cliff Pastornicky
22 Willie Neal
23 Mark Farnsworth
24 Roy Tanner

1982 TCMA Chattanooga Lookouts

(Cleveland Indians, AA) (black and white)

	MT	NR MT	EX
Complete Set:	37.50	28.00	15.50

1 Nate Puryear
2 Scott Munninghoff
3 Everett Rey
4 Ed Saavedra
5 Richard Thompson
6 Tim Glass

7 Ricky Baker
8 Dane Anthony
9 Tom Owens
10 Mike Schwarber
11 Sal Rende
12 Marlin Methvin
13 Shanie Dugas
14 George Cecchetti
15 Steve Roche
16 Kelly Gruber
17 Dave Gallagher
18 Robin Fuson
19 Steve Narleski
20 Rick Borchers
21 Jeff Moronko
22 Craig Adams
23 Al Gallagher
24 Chuck Stobbs
25 Hank Gaughan

1982 TCMA Columbus Clippers

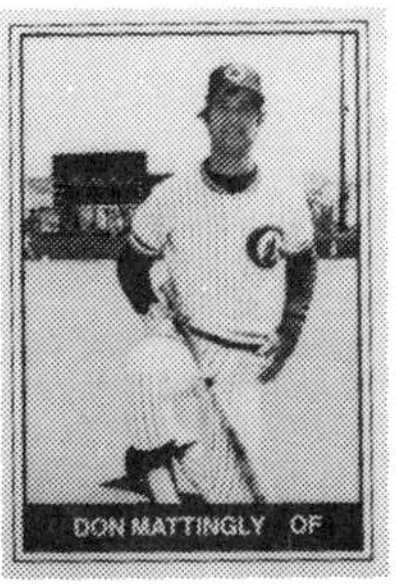

(New York Yankees, AAA) (color)

	MT	NR MT	EX
Complete Set:	350.00	262.00	140.00

1 John Pacella
2 Tucker Ashford
3 Wayne Harer
4 Steve Balboni
5 Curt Kaufman
6 Marshall Brant
7 Mike Bruhert
8 Greg Cochran
9 Pete Filson
10 Jamie Werley
11 Dave Wehrmeister
12 Bob Sykes
13 David Stegman
14 Garry Smith
15 Dick Scott
16 Dan Schmitz
17 Andre Robertson
18 Bobby Ramos
19 Scott Patterson
20 Mike Patterson
21 Don Mattingly
22 Jim Lewis
23 Juan Espino
24 Steve Donohue, Sammy Ellis, Jerry McNertney
25 Frank Verdi
26 George H. Sisler, Jr.

1982 TCMA Daytona Beach Astros

(Houston Astros, A) (black and white)

	MT	NR MT	EX
Complete Set:	65.00	48.75	26.50

1 Guillermo Castro
2 Mitch Coplon
3 Joe Ferrante
4 Scott Gardner
5 Manny Hernandez
6 Uvaldo Regalado
7 Rex Schimpf
8 Ben Snyder
9 Roberto Yan
10 Doug Britt
11 Steve Dunnegan
12 Eric Bullock
13 Ty Gainey
14 Ira Lane
15 Neil Simons
16 Eric Swanson
17 Mark Campbell
18 Robbie McGorkle
19 Jamie Williams
20 Glenn Davis
21 Jim McKnight
22 Val Medina
23 Larry Simcox
24 Phil Smith
25 Mark Strucher

1982 TCMA Durham Bulls

(Atlanta Braves, A) (black and white)

	MT	NR MT	EX
Complete Set:	100.00	75.00	41.00

1 Mike Garcia
2 Keith Hagman
3 Scott Hood
4 Joe Lorenz
5 Bob Luzon
6 Bryan Neal
7 Ken Scanlon
8 Rick Siriano
9 Miguel Sosa
10 Jim Stefanski
11 Tommy Thompson
12 Freddy Tiburcio
13 Bob Tumpane
14 Dave Clay
15 Rick Coatney
16 Jeff Dedmon
17 Brian Fisher
18 Rick Hatcher
19 Mike Payne
20 Gary Reiter
21 Andre Treadway
22 Bruce Dal Canton
23 Buddy Bailey
24 Gene Lane
25 Bob Dews

1982 TCMA Edmonton Trappers

(Chicago White Sox, AAA) (color)

	MT	NR MT	EX
Complete Set:	25.00	18.50	10.00

1 Carlos Ibarra
2 Jose Castro
3 Jim Siwy
4 Steve Dillard
5 Chris Nyman
6 Guy Hoffman
7 Keith Desjarlais
8 Jay Loviglio
9 Fran Mullins
10 Lorenzo Gray
11 Leo Sutherland
12 Woody Agosto
13 Ron Kittle
14 Nardi Contreras
15 Reggie Patterson
16 David Hogg
17 Len Bradley
18 Dom Fucci
19 Rich Barnes
20 Rusty Kuntz
21 Rick Seilheimer
22 Gordy Lund
23 Geoff Combe
24 Dave Grossman
25 Jeff Schattinger

1982 TCMA El Paso Diablos

(Milwaukee Brewers, AA) (color)

	MT	NR MT	EX
Complete Set:	20.00	15.00	8.00

1 Eric Peyton
2 Dion James
3 Ron Koenigsfeld
4 Kurt Kingsolver
5 Dan Davidsmeier
6 Bill Foley
7 Randy Ready
8 Mark Schuster
9 Don Whiting
10 Mark Johnston
11 Joe Hansen
12 Steve Michael
13 Jerry Jenkins
14 Andy Beene
15 Steve Manderfield
16 Bob Schroeck
17 Dave Grier
18 Jack Uhey
19 Steve Parrott
20 Jim Koontz
21 Bob Gibson
22 Derek Tatsuno
23 Tony Muser
24 Al Price

1982 TCMA Evansville Triplets

(Detroit Tigers, AAA) (color)

	MT	NR MT	EX
Complete Set:	14.00	10.50	5.50

1 Howard Bailey
2 Juan Berenguer
3 Mark Dacko
4 Mark Lee
5 Rick Matula
6 Bruce Robbins
7 Larry Rothschild
8 Dave Rucker
9 Augie Ruez
10 Gerald Ujdur
11 Marty Castillo
12 Don McCormack
13 Stine Poole
14 Jeff Cox
15 Paul Djakonow
16 Mike Laga
17 Juan Lopez
18 Vern Followell
19 Les Filkins
20 Eddie Gates
21 Ray Hampton
22 Jeff Kenaga
23 Mark Corey
24 Ken Houston
25 Roy Majtyka

1982 TCMA Fort Myers Royals

(Kansas City Royals, A) (black and white)

	MT	NR MT	EX
Complete Set:	17.50	13.00	7.00

1 Rick Rizzo
2 Hal Hatcher
3 Tommy Thompson
4 Benny Gadahia
5 Warren Oliver
6 Greg Jonson
7 Nick Harsh
8 Mickey Palmer
9 Rick Plautz
10 Duane Gustavson
11 Tony Ferreira
12 Mike Alvarez
13 Jeff Gladden
14 Dave Wong
15 Fran Cutty
16 Mark Huismann
17 James Gleissner
18 Bill Best
19 Lester Strode
20 Mark Newman
21 Bill Pecota
22 Rick Mathews
23 Steve Morrow

1982 TCMA Glens Falls White Sox

(Chicago White Sox, AA) (black and white)

	MT	NR MT	EX
Complete Set:	195.00	146.00	78.00

1 Vince Bienek
2 J.B. Brown
3 Ed Cipot
4 Larry Donofrid
5 Dom Fucci
6 Tim Hulett
7 Phil Klimas
8 Mike Morse
9 Pete Peltz
10 Joel Skinner
11 Vern Thomas
12 Dan Williams
13 Dave Yobs
14 Not Issued
15 Not Issued
16 Larry Edwards
17 Bob Fallopn

18 Jack Hardy
19 Chuck Johnson
20 John Lackey
21 Mike Maitland
22 Tom Mullen
23 Mark Teutsch
24 Mike Withrow
25 Jim Mahoney

1982 TCMA Hawaii Islanders

(San Diego Padres, AAA) (color)

	MT	NR MT	EX
Complete Set:	75.00	56.00	30.00

1 Ron Tingley
2 Dave Richards
3 Steve Smith
4 Jim Pankovits
5 Jerry Johnson
6 Joe Lansford
7 Jerry De Simone
8 Dan Gausepohl
9 Aaron Cain
10 Tony Gwynn
11 Rick Lancellotti
12 Jeff Pyburn
13 Steve Fireovid
14 Andy Hawkins
15 George Stablein
16 Ron Meredith
17 Fred Kuhaulua
18 Tim Hamm
19 Tom Tellmann
20 Dave Dravecky
21 Mark Thurmond
22 Kim Seaman
23 Doug Rader
24 Chuck Hartenstein
25 Larry Duensing

1982 TCMA Holyoke Millers

(California Angels, AA) (color)

	MT	NR MT	EX
Complete Set:	14.00	10.50	5.50

1 Michael Barba
2 Brian Buckely
3 Jeff Conner
4 Lonnie Dugger
5 Dave Duran
6 Bill Mooneyham
7 Perry Morrison
8 Ron Romanick
9 David A. Smith
10 David W. Smith
11 Bob Palmer
12 Larry Patterson
13 Rick Adams
14 Bob Bohnet
15 Ron Hunt
16 Pat Keedy
17 Tim Krauss
18 Gus Polidor
19 Chris Clark
20 Harry Francis
21 Dennis Gilbert
22 Darrell Miller
23 Jack Hiatt
24 Marc Terrazas
25 George Como
26 Ben Surner

1982 TCMA Idaho Falls Athletics

(Oakland A's, A) (black and white)

	MT	NR MT	EX
Complete Set:	20.00	15.00	8.00

1 Dave Baehr
2 Jim Bailey
3 Mark Border
4 Eric Brown
5 Tom Conquest
6 Doug Farrow
7 Todd Fischer
8 Angelo Gilbert
9 Mark Kochanski
10 Tim Lambert
11 Dave Leiper
12 Tenoa Stevenson
13 Steve Travers
14 Shawn Gill
15 Russ Wortmann
16 Leon Baham
17 Bill Davis
18 Mark Dye
19 John Michel
20 Clemente Oropeza
21 Greg Robles
22 Kenny Clayton
23 Steve Campbell
24 Rob Loscalzo
25 Eddie Malone
26 Gary McGraw
27 Jorge Oquendo
28 Ricky Thomas
29 Dave Wilder

30 Keith Lieppman
31 Grady Fuson
32 Mark Doberenz
33 Dave Sheriff

1982 TCMA Iowa Cubs

(Chicago Cubs, AAA) (color)

	MT	NR MT	EX
Complete Set:	27.50	20.50	11.25

1 Alfred Benton
2 Scott Fletcher
3 Tom Grant
4 Mel Hall
5 Bill Hayes
6 Randy LaVigne
7 Jared Martin
8 Danny Rohn
9 Joe Strain
10 Pat Tabler
11 Scot Thompson
12 Jack Upton
13 Elliott Waller
14 Robert Blyth
15 Tom Filer
16 Jay Howell
17 Larry Jones
18 Chris Knapp
19 Ken Kravec
20 Craig Lefferts
21 Mark Parker
22 Mike Proly
23 Herman Segelke
24 Randy Stein
25 Jim Napier
26 Scott Breeden
27 Ken Grandquist
28 Bob Reynolds
29 Tom Butts
30 Frank Macy
31 Kim Hart
32 Dr. Richard Evans

1982 TCMA Jackson Mets

(New York Mets, AA) (color)

	MT	NR MT	EX
Complete Set:	200.00	150.00	80.00

1 Jeff Bittiger
2 Matt Bullinger
3 Ted Davis
4 Scott Dye
5 Steve Ibarguen
6 Jody Johnston
7 Brain Kolbe
8 Jose Rodriguez
9 John Semprini
10 Doug Sisk
11 Ronn Reynolds
12 Dave Duff
13 Rick Poe
14 Mike Anicich
15 Rick McMullen
16 Al Pedrique
17 Jim Woodward
18 Bill Rittweger
19 Billy Beane
20 Terry Blocker
21 Darryl Strawberry
22 Gene Dusan
23 Bob Apodaca
24 Bob Sikes
25 Bill Walberg

1982 TCMA Knoxville Blue Jays

(Toronto Blue Jays, AA) (black and white)

	MT	NR MT	EX
Complete Set:	20.00	15.00	8.00

1 Team Photo
2 Scott Elam
3 Randy Ford
4 Dennis Howard
5 Tom Lukish
6 Colin McLaughlin
7 Keith Walker
8 Matt Williams
9 Brian Stemberger
10 Brian Milner
11 Dan Whitmer
12 Tim Thompson
13 Paul Hodgson
14 Andre Wood
15 Carlos Rios
16 Ed Dennis
17 Vern Ramie
18 J.J. Cannon
19 Vassie Gardner
20 Ron Shepherd
21 Larry Hardy
22 Hector Torres
23 John Woodworth

Definitions for grading conditions are located in the introduction of this price guide.

1982 TCMA Lynchburg Mets

(New York Mets, A) (black and white)

	MT	NR MT	EX
Complete Set:	125.00	94.00	52.00

1 Danny Monzon
2 Laschelle Tarver
3 Herman Winningham
4 John De Imonte
5 Bruce Kastelic
6 Kevin Mitchell
7 DeWayne Vaughn
8 Ed Rech
9 Jeff Sunderlage
10 Paul Wilmet
11 Tom Miller
12 Roger Frash
13 Duane Evans
14 Chuck Schonoor
15 Randy Milligan
16 Lloyd McClendon
17 Rick Myles
18 Roger Begue
19 Jay Tibbs
20 Bill Fultz
21 Rich Webster
22 Jody Johnston
23 John Raeside

1982 TCMA Lynn Sailors

(Seattle Mariners, AA) (black and white)

	MT	NR MT	EX
Complete Set:	37.50	28.00	15.25

1 Rick Adair
2 Carl Best (Karl)
3 Kevin Dukes
4 Joe Georger
5 Steve Krueger
6 Jed Murray
7 Jeff Stottlemyre
8 Scott Stranski (photo actually Jeff Stottlemyre)
9 Jim Nelson
10 Clark Crist
11 Bill Crone (photo actually John Moses)
12 Mario Diaz
13 Jim Presley
14 Ramon Estepa (photo acutally Tito Nanni)
15 Tito Nanni
16 Glenn Walker
17 Harold Reynolds
18 Mickey Bowers

1982 TCMA Miami Marlins

(Baltimore Orioles, A) (black and white)

	MT	NR MT	EX
Complete Set:	20.00	15.00	8.00

1 Will George
2 Mike Glinatsis
3 Marcos Gonzalez
4 Brian McDonough
5 Carlos Moreno
6 Joel Pyfrom
7 Tony Wadley
8 Jose Caballero
9 Ron Cardieri
10 Jorge Curbelo
11 Jorge Llano
12 Robbie Alvarez
13 Julio Beltran
14 Bob Boyce
15 Edgar Castro
16 Rick Rembielak
17 Angel Valdez
18 Raul Tovar
19 Lee Granger
20 Mike Kutner
21 Frank Contreras
22 John Tamargo

1982 TCMA Oklahoma City 89'ers

(Philadelphia Phillies, AAA) (color)

	MT	NR MT	EX
Complete Set:	35.00	26.25	14.50

1 Mike Willis
2 Rowland Office
3 Tim Corcoran
4 Ramon Aviles
5 Ellis Deal
6 Ron Clark
7 Al Sanchez
8 Len Matuszek
9 Jerry Reed
10 Rusty Hamric
11 Julio Franco
12 Mark Davis

13 Joe Kerrigan
14 Tom Lombarski
15 Tony McDonald
16 Luis Rodriguez
17 Jeff Ulrich
18 Jim Rasmussen
19 Jon Reelhorn
20 Herb Orensky
21 Kelly Downs
22 Marty Decker
23 Darren Burroughs
24 Don Carman
25 Wil Culmer

1982 TCMA Omaha Royals

(Kansas City Royals, AAA) (color) (complete set price includes variations)

	MT	NR MT	EX
Complete Set:	60.00	45.00	24.00

1 Mike Armstrong
2 Ralph Botting
3 Keith Creel
4 Dan Fischer
5 Don Hood
6 Phil Huffman
7 Bill Kelly
8 Dave Schuler
9 Bob Tufts
10 Frank Wills
11 Greg Keatley
12 Don Slaught
13 Mitch Ashmore
14 Buddy Biancalana
15 Manuel Colletti
16 Dave Edler
17a Ron Johnson (blue uinform, photo actually Dan Weiser)
17b Ron Johnson (white uniform, correct photo)
18a Dan Weiser (white uniform, photo actually Ron Johnson)
18b Dan Weiser (blue uniform, correct photo)
19 Darryl Motley
20 Bombo Rivera
21 Mark Ryal
22 Pat Sheridan
23 Luis Silverio
24 Bill Gorman
25 Joe Sparks
26 Jerry Cram
27 Paul McGannon

1982 Tcma Oneonta Yankees

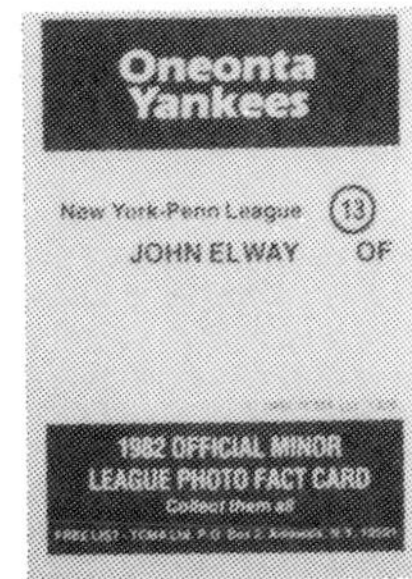

(New York Yankees, A) (black and white)

	MT	NR MT	EX
Complete Set:	175.00	131.00	72.00

1 Orestes Destrade
2 Jim Riggs
3 Brent Giesdal
4 Ken Berry
5 Dan O'Regan
6 Q.V. Lowe
7 Stan Sanders
8 Tim Birtsas
9 Steve Campagno
10 Pat Bone
11 Tim Byron
12 Jesus Alcala
13 John Elway
14 Mike Fennell
15 Jim Ferguson
16 Mike Gatlin
17 Pedro Medina

1982 TCMA Orlando Twins

(Minnesota Twins, AA) (black and white)

	MT	NR MT	EX
Complete Set:	32.50	24.25	13.50

1 Kevin Williams
2 Lee Belanger
3 Eric Broersma

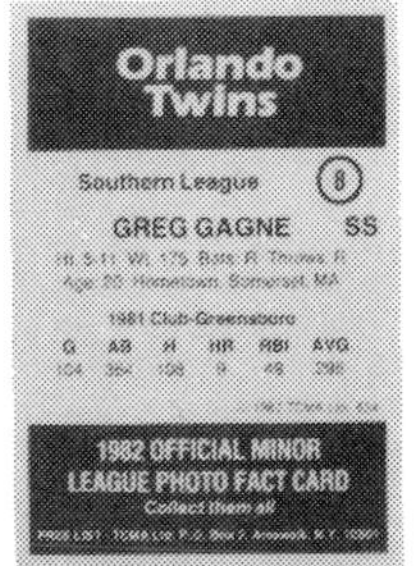

4 Smokey Everett
5 Jack Hobbs
6 Bob Konopa
7 Mark Funderburk
8 Greg Gagne
9 Dave Meier
10 Mike McCain
11 Tony Pilla
12 Tim Teufel
13 Tom Kelly
14 Rick Austin
15 Chino Cadahia
16 Andre David
17 Steve Douglas
18 Ken Foster
19 Ted Kromy
20 Larry May
21 Bob Mulligan
22 Jay Pettibone
23 Sam Arrington
24 Eddie Hodge

1982 TCMA Orland Twins Southern League Champs

(Minnesota Twins, AA) (black and white) (set features players from 1981 championship season)

	MT	NR MT	EX
Complete Set:	70.00	52.50	29.00

1 Rod Booker
2 Randy Bush
3 Chino Cadahia
4 Manny Colletti
5 Andre David
6 Steve Douglas
7 Gary Gaetti
8 Tim Laudner
9 Tim Teufel
10 Scott Ulger
11 Lance Hallberg
12 Tom Kelly
13 Eric Broersma
14 Scott Gleckel
15 Steve Green
16 Brad Havens
17 Jack Hobbs
18 Bob Konopa
19 Ted Kromy
20 STeve Mapel
21 Bob Mulligan
22 Jose Reyes
23 Gary Serum
24 Frank Viola

1982 TCMA Portland Beavers

(Pittsburgh Pirates, AAA) (color)

	MT	NR MT	EX
Complete Set:	18.00	13.50	7.50

1 Jose DeLeon
2 Butch Edge
3 Cecilio Guante
4 Odell Jones
5 Robert Long
6 Randy Nieman
7 Pasqual Perez (Pascual)
8 Manny Sarmiento
9 Lee Tunnell
10 Stan Cliburn
11 Junior Ortiz
12 Wayne Caughey
13 Denny Gonzalez
14 Willie Horton
15 Bobby Mitchell
16 Nelson Norman
17 Eddie Vargas
18 Dave Augustine
19 Trench Davis
20 Doug Frobel
21 Jose Rodriguez
22 Reggie Walton
23 Jim Saul
24 Vern Law, Jim Saul
25 Not Issued
26 Carlos Lezedma

1982 TCMA Quad City Cubs

(Chicago Cubs, A) (black and white)

	MT	NR MT	EX
Complete Set:	20.00	15.00	8.00

1 Darryl Banks
2 Allen Black
3 Russ Brahms
4 Rich Buonantony
5 Jorge Carpio
6 Tim Clarke
7 Mitch Cooke
8 Jeff Fruge
9 Ron Kaufman
10 Vance Lovelace
11 Mike Shulleetta
12 Roger Crow
13 Criag Weissman
14 Lee George
15 Wendell Henderson
16 Jeff Remo
17 James Allen
18 Ken Arnerich
19 Jeff Rutledge
20 Otis Tramble
21 Antonio Cordova
22 Darrin Jackson
23 Scott Miller
24 Rolando Roomes
25 Jim Walsh
26 George Enright
27 Quency Hill
28 Randy Roetter

1982 TCMA Reading Phillies

(Philadelphia Phillies, AA) (black and white)

	MT	NR MT	EX
Complete Set:	45.00	34.00	18.00

1 Jay Baller
2 Kelly Faulk
3 Butch Hughes
4 Kyle Money
5 John Palmieri
6 Dan Prior
7 Jim Rasmussen
8 Leroy Smith
9 Dennis Thomas
10 Richard Wortham
11 Gerry Willard
12 Al Velasquez
13 Dave Enos
14 Paul Fryer
15 Steve Jeltz
16 Jon Lindsey
17 Joe Nemeth
18 Randy Salava
19 Keith Washington
20 Steve Harvey
21 Tony McDonald
22 John Felske

1982 TCMA Redwood Pioneers

(California Angels, A) (black and white)

	MT	NR MT	EX
Complete Set:	20.00	15.00	8.00

1 Michael Brooks
2 Steven Eakes
3 Craig Gerber
4 Kevin Halicki
5 Gordon Jones
6 Tim Kammeyer
7 Steve Liddle
8 James Randall
9 Esmyel Romero
10 Michael Saatzer
11 Mark Smelko
12 Jeff Smith
13 Mark Sproesser
14 Darryl Stephens
15 Richard Sundberg
16 Ronald Sylvia
17 Paul Wright
18 Luis Zambrana
19 Harry Oliver
20 Glen Fisher
21 Ronald Hunt
22 Terry Harper
23 Kevin Jacobson
24 Barton Barun
25 Chris Cannizzaro
26 Brian Parfrey
27 Ralph Hartman

1982 TCMA Richmond Braves

(Atlanta Braves, AAA) (color) (complete set price includes both Brizzolara cards)

	MT	NR MT	EX
Complete Set:	75.00	56.00	30.00

1 Jose Alvarez
2a Tony Brizzolara (catching)
2b Tony Brizzolara (portrait)
3 Tim Cole
4 John D'Acquisto
5 Carlos Diaz
6 Craig McMurtry
7 Donnie Moore
8 Jeff Twitty

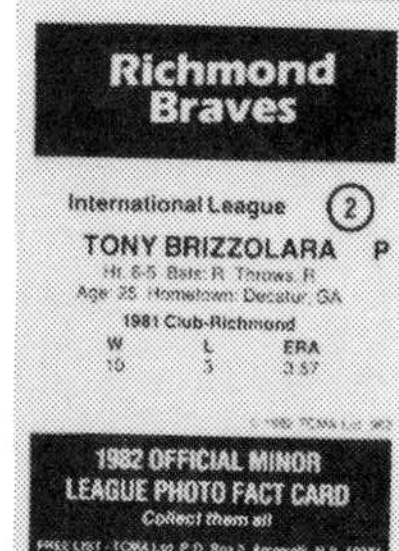

9 Roger Weaver
10 Jerry Keller
11 Larry Owen
12 Matt Sinatro
13 Brook Jacoby
14 Gerald Perry
15 Chico Ruiz
16 Paul Runge
17 Paul Zuvella
18 Mike Reynolds
19 Albert Hall
20 Leonel Vargas
21 Bob Porter
22 Mike Colbern
23 Ken Smith
24 Terry Harper
25 Ken Dayley
26 Mike Smith
27 Eddie Haas
28 Johnny Sain
29 Craig Robinson
30 Sam Ayoub
31 Albert Hall, Terry Harper, Brook Jacoby, Gerald Perry, Roger Weaver

1982 TCMA Rochester Red Wings

(Baltimore Orioles, AAA) (color)

	MT	NR MT	EX
Complete Set:	17.50	13.00	7.00

1 Mike Boddicker
2 John Flinn
3 Bruce MacPherson
4 Craig Minetto
5 Allan Ramirez
6 Cliff Speck
7 Bill Swaggerty
8 Don Welchel
9 Tim Derryberry
10 Dan Graham
11 Willie Royster
12 Glenn Gulliver
13 Rick Jones
14 Rick Lisi
15 Dan Logan
16 Vic Rodriguez
17 John Shelby
18 John Valle
19 Mike Young
20 Lance Nichols
21 Tom Chism
22 Ken Rowe

1982 TCMA Salt Lake City Gulls

(Seattle Mariners, AAA) (color)

	MT	NR MT	EX
Complete Set:	14.00	10.50	5.50

1 Doug Merrifield
2 Jamie Allen
3 Rod Allen
4 Rich Bordi
5 Al Chambers
6 Bryan Clark
7 Roy Clark
8 Steve Finch
9 Gary Gray
10 Tracy Harris
11 Mike Hart
12 Vance McHenry
13 Orlando Mercado
14 Ron Musselman
15 Casey Parsons
16 Domingo Ramos
17 Brian Snyder
18 Bob Stoddard
19 Roy Thomas
20 Dave Valle
21 Sammye Welborn
22 Matt Young
23 Manny Estrada
24 Bobby Floyd
25 Joe Decker

Definitions for grading conditions are located in the Introduction of this price guide.

1982 TCMA Spokane Indians

(California Angels, AAA) (color)

	MT	NR MT	EX
Complete Set:	15.00	11.25	6.00

1 Steve Brown
2 Craig Eaton
3 Rick Foley
4 Mickey Mahler
5 Fred Martinez
6 Paul Olden
7 Jeff Schneider
8 Rick Steirer
9 Mike Walters
10 Mike Bishop
11 Steve Herz
12 Jerry Narron
13 Jeff Bertoni
14 Craig Cacer
15 Scott Carnes
16 John Harris
17 Steve Lubratich
18 Les Pearsey
19 Mike Brown
20 Tom Brunansky
21 Ron Jackson
22 Pepe Mangual
23 Gary Pettis
24 Moose Stubing
25 Joe Coleman
26 Leonard Garcia

1982 TCMA Syracuse Chiefs

(Toronto Blue Jays, AAA) (color) (complete set price includes scarce Larson, O'Keefe and Whitmer cards)

	MT	NR MT	EX
Complete Set:	100.00	75.00	40.00

1 Mike Barlow
2 Tom Dixon
3 Mark Eichhorn
4 Mark Geisel
5 John Littlefield
6 Frank Ricelli
7 Ken Schrom
8 Steve Senteney
9 Jackson Todd
10 Jim Wright
11 Jim Gaudet
12 Ramon Lora
13 Gene Petralli
14 Dave Baker
15 Charlie Beamon
16 Brian Doyle
17 Tony Fernandez
18 Fred Manrique
19 Glenn Adams
20 George Bell
21 Pedro Hernandez
22 Creighton Tevlin
23 Mitch Webster
24 Doug Ault
25 Tom Craig
26 Jim Beauchamp
27a Duane Larson
27b Rick O'Keefe
28 Dan Whitmer

1982 TCMA Tacoma Tigers

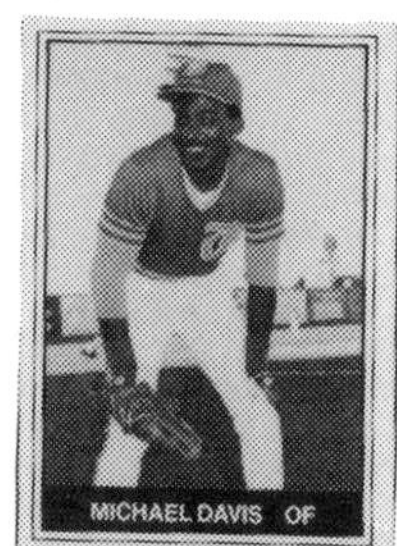

(Oakland A's, AAA) (color) (complete set price includes scarce Comstock and Sexton cards)

	MT	NR MT	EX
Complete Set:	60.00	45.00	24.00

1 DeWayne Bruce
2 Don Fowler
3 Dave Heaverlo
4 Bill Castro
5 Gorman Heimueller
6 Dennis Kinney
7 Eric Mustad
8 Dave Patterson
9 Bill Swiacki
10 Ed Figueroa
11 Darryl Cias
12 Tim Hosley
13 Kevin Bell
14 Danny Goodwin
15 Paul Mize
16 Johnny Evans
17 Jim Nettles
18 Dennis Sherow
19 Ed Nottle
20 Larry Davis
21 Art Popham
22 Stan Naccarato
23 Keith Atherton
24 Jeff Jones
25 Brian Kingman
26 Pat Dempsey
27 Robert Kearney
28 Mack Babitt
29 Keith Drumright
30 Mike Gallego
31 Kelvin Moore
32 Tony Phillips
33 Rick Bosetti
34 Michael Davis
35 Bob Grandas
36 Mitchell Page
37 Tigers Mascot
38 Johnny Sexton
39 Keith Comstock

1982 TCMA Tidewater Tides

(New York Mets, AAA) (color) (complete set price includes scarce Cubbage cards)

	MT	NR MT	EX
Complete Set:	40.00	30.00	16.00

1 Rick Ownbey
2 Kelvin Chapman
3 Mike Davis
4 Mike Fitzgerald
5 Mike Howard
6 Bruce Bochy
7 Gil Flores
8 Brian Giles
9 Phil Mankowski
10 Ronald MacDonald
11 Rusty Tillman
12 Rick Anderson
13 Ron Darling
14 Terry Leach
15 Jose Oquendo
16 Marvell Wynne
17 Greg Biercevicz
18 Scott Holman
19 Jack Aker
20 Brent Gaff
21 Steve Ratzer
22 Bob Schaefer
23 Dave Von Ohlen
24 Walt Terrell
25 Mike Anicich
26 Mike Cubbage

1982 TCMA Toledo Mud Hens

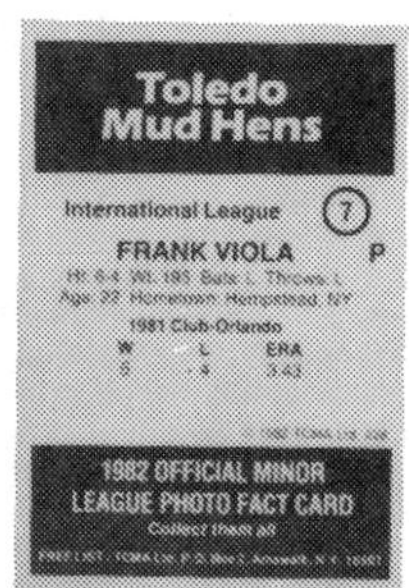

(Minnesota Twins, AAA) (color) (complete set price includes scarce #'s 26-28)

	MT	NR MT	EX
Complete Set:	110.00	82.50	45.25

1 Don Cooper
2 Glenn Dooner
3 Steve Korczyk
4 Jeff Little
5 Jack O'Connor
6 Bob Veselic
7 Frank Viola
8 Mike Walters
9 Rick Williams
10 Harry Saferight
11 Ray Smith
12 Rod Booker
13 Jim Christensen
14 Dave Machemer
15 Ivan Mesa
16 Kelly Snider
17 Greg Wells
18 Mike Sodders
19 Elijah Bonaparte
20 Randy Bush
21 Rick Sofield
22 Scott Ulger
23 Cal Ermer
24 Buck Chamberlin
26 Pete Filson
27 Doug Fregin
28 Bob Mitchell

1982 TCMA Tucson Toros

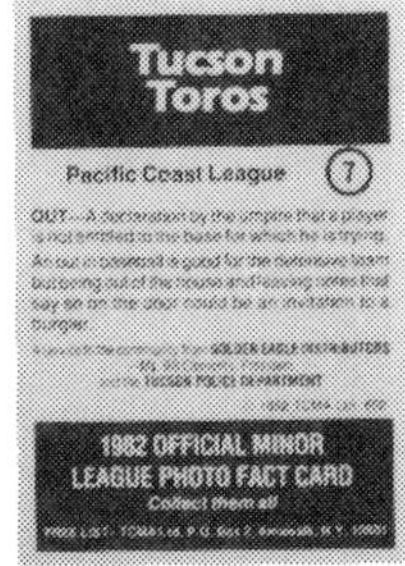

(Houston Astros, AAA) (color)

	MT	NR MT	EX
Complete Set:	22.50	16.50	9.00

1 Bert Pena
2 Chris Jones
3 Mark Ross
4 Tom Vessey
5 Steve Lake
6 Greg Cypret
7 Billy Doran
8 Tim Tolman
9 Jim Tracy
10 Larry Ray
11 Harry Spillman (Spilman)
12 Jim McDonald
13 Rickey Keeton
14 Zacarias Paris
15 Bert Roberge
16 Rick Lysander
17 Mark Miggins
18 Billy Smith
19 Bobby Sprowl
20 George Cappuzzello
21 Gordy Pladson
22 Bill Wood
23 James Hand
24 Jim Johnson
25 Gary Tuck
26 Dennis Menke (Denis)
27 Dave Labossiere
28 Batboys

1982 TCMA Tulsa Drillers

(Texas Rangers, AA) (color) (complete set price includes scarce #'s 25-28)

	MT	NR MT	EX
Complete Set:	90.00	67.00	36.00

1 Tom Henke
2 Brad Mengwasser
3 Martin Leach
4 Dennis Long
5 Mike Mason
6 Tim Henry
7 Al Lachowicz
8 Kevin Richards
9 Jim Gideon
10 Tom Dunbar
11 Don Scott
12 Tracy Cowger
13 Steve Moore
14 Carmelo Aguayo
15 Dave STockstill
16 Oscar Majia
17 Dan Murphy
18 Ron Dillard
19 Mike Jirschele
20 Gerry Neufang
21 Robert Ball
22 Tom Burgess
23 Orlando Gomez
24 Joe Nemeth
25 Curtis Wilkerson
26 Brett Benza
27 Steve Buechele
28 Mike Rubel

1982 TCMA Vancouver Canadians

(Milwaukee Brewers, AAA) (color)

	MT	NR MT	EX
Complete Set:	14.00	10.50	5.50

1 Bob Skube
2 Frank Thomas
3 Bill Schroder (Schroeder)
4 Kevin Bass
5 Willie Lozada (Lozado)
6 John Skorochocki
7 Lawrence Rush
8 Ed Irvine
9 Stan Davis
10 Doug Loman
11 Steve Herz
12 Tim Cook
13 Doug Jones
14 Mike Madden
15 Rich Olsen
16 Frank DiPino
17 Pete Ladd
18 Chuck Valley
19 Rick Kranitz
20 Jaimie Cocanower (Jamie)
21 Chuck Porter
22 Mike Anderson
23 Eli Grba
24 Brian Thorson

1982 TCMA Vero Beach Dodgers

(Los Angeles Dodgers, A) (black and white)

	MT	NR MT	EX
Complete Set:	165.00	124.00	68.00

1 Roberto Alexandro
2 Ernie Borbon
3 Paul Cozzolino
4 Dave Daniel
5 Rich Felt
6 Sid Fernandez
7 Robert Kenyon
8 Steve Martin
9 Peyton Mosher
10 Matt Reeves
11 Robert Slezak
12 Paul Bard
13 Steve Boncore
14 Jack Fimple
15 Robert Allen
16 Carmelo Alvarez
17 Jerry Bendorf
18 Sid Bream
19 Harold Perkins
20 Larry See
21 Ralph Bryant
22 Cecil Espy
23 Tony Lachowetz
24 Stu Pederson
25 Bob Seymour
26 Terry Collins
27 Rob Giesecke
28 Dave Wallace
29 John Shoemaker

1982 TCMA Waterbury Reds

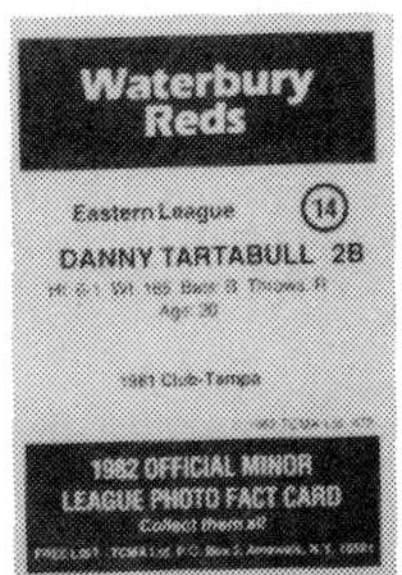

(Cincinnati Reds, AA) (color)

	MT	NR MT	EX
Complete Set:	40.00	30.00	16.00

1 Bill Landrum
2 Larry Buckle
3 Keefe Cato
4 Kenneth Jones
5 Gene Menees
6 Clem Freeman
7 Bob Buchanan
8 Jeff Russell
9 Ronald Robinson
10 Nicholas Fiorillo
11 Raymond Corbett
12 Michael Kripner
13 Skeeter Barnes
14 Danny Tartabull
15 Eski Viltz
16 Paul Herring
17 Glen Franklin
18 Mark Gilbert
19 Kenneth Scarpace
20 Tony Walker
21 Ronald Little
22 Crestwell Pratt
23 Jim Lett

1982 TCMA Waterloo Indians

(Cleveland Indians, A) (black and white) (set includes scarce #'s 26-28)

	MT	NR MT	EX
Complete Set:	95.00	71.00	38.00

1 Steve Cushing
2 Rich Doyle
3 Ralph Elpin
4 Mike Jeffcoat
5 Wayne Johnson
6 Ricky Lintz
7 Rodney McDonald
8 John Miglio
9 Ramon Romero
10 David Wick
11 Alan Willis
12 John Malkin
13 Phillip Wilson
14 Rod Carraway
15 Winston Ficklin
16 Mike Gertz
17 Sam Martin
18 Junior Noboa
19 Ed Tanner
20 George Albert
21 Jerry Nalley
22 Chris Rehbaum
23 Dwight Taylor
24 Mike Taylor
25 Randy Washington
26 Gomer Hodge
27 Vic Albury
28 Ron Wollenhaupt

1982 TCMA West Haven A's

(Oakland A's, AA) (black and white)

	MT	NR MT	EX
Complete Set:	20.00	15.00	8.00

1 Brian Abraham
2 Bert Bradley
3 Jeff Carey
4 Chris Codiroli
5 Keith Comstock
6 Chuck Hensley
7 Bill Krueger
8 Lou Marietta
9 Jack Smith
10 Bill Bathe
11 Chuck Fick
12 Mike Gallego
13 Steve Gelfarb
14 Donnie Hill
15 Monte McAbee
16 Paul Mize
17 Tim Pyznarski
18 Ron Wilkerson
19 Mike Woodard
20 Jim Bennett
21 Lynn Garrett
22 Rodney Hobbs
23 Rusty McNealy
24 Luis Rojas
25 Dennis Sherow
26 Bob Didier
27 Keith Lieppman
28 Scot Pyle
29 Walt Horn

1982 Team Charlotte O's "Heroes Aren't Hard"

(Baltimore Orioles, AA) (orange and blue border)

	MT	NR MT	EX
Complete Set:	65.00	48.75	26.50

The Heroes
Jesus Alfaro
Juan Arias
Tony Arnold
Chris Bourjos
Don Bowman
Randy Boyd
Mark Brown
Carlos Cabassa
Mark Corey
Dan Craven
John Denman
H. Shelton Drum

Drungo Hazewood
Leo Hernandez
Eddie Hook
Dave Huppert
Bruce Mac Pherson
Minnie Mendoza
Mark Naehring
Phil Nastu
Paul O'Neill
Francisco Oliveras
Russ Pensiero
Julio Perez
Tom Rowe
Jeff Schaeffer
Mark Smith
John Stefero
Matt Tyner
Mark Wiley

1982 Team Holyoke Millers

(California Angels, AA) This set was also produced in the form of a poster. The cards were bordered by stars and measured approximately 1-7/8 x 2-7/8 inches in size.

	MT	NR MT	EX
Complete Set:	50.00	37.00	20.00

(1) Mike Barba
(2) Jim Beswick
(3) Bob Bohnet
(4) Rod Boxberger
(5) Brian Buckley
(6) Chris Clark
(7) Jeff Conner
(8) Harry Francis
(9) Dennis Gilbert
(10) Mike Gordon
(11) Jack Hiatt
(12) Pat Keedy
(13) Jay Kibbe
(14) Tim Krauss
(15) Steve Liddle
(16) Mark McCormack
(17) Darrell Miller
(18) Bill Mooneyham
(19) Bob Palmer
(20) Larry Patterson
(21) Gustavo Polidor
(22) Ron Romanick
(23) David A. Smith
(24) D.W. Smith
(25) Mark Sproesser
(26) Marc Terrasaz
(27) Craig Thomas
(28) Mike Venezia
(29) Matt Wroth

1982 Team Indianapolis Indians

(Cincinnati Reds, AAA) (co-sponsored by Tom Aikens)

	MT	NR MT	EX
Complete Set:	20.00	15.00	8.00

1 Team Photo
2 George Scherger
3 Kip Young
4 Nick Esasky
5 Brad Lesley
6 Duane Walker
7 Bill Dawley
8 The Instructors
9 Brooks Carey
10 Orlando Isales
11 Brian Ryder
12 Dave Van Gorder
13 Greg Harris
14 The Bullpen
15 Tom Lawless
16 Mike Dowless
17 Gary Redus
18 The Catchers
19 Rich Carlucci
20 Tom Foley
21 Ben Hayes
22 Steve Christmas
23 The Outfielders
24 Ron Farkas
25 Dave Tomlin
26 Dallas Williams
27 The Infielders
28 Gil Kubski
29 Neil Fiala
30 The Starting Pitchers
31 Lee Garrett
32 Behind The Scenes

1982 Team Wichita Aeros

(Montreal Expos, AAA)

	MT	NR MT	EX
Complete Set:	17.50	13.00	7.00

(1) Joseph Abone
(2) Felipe Alou
(3) Douglas Capilla
(4) Michael Gates
(5) Thomas Gorman
(6) Batting Leaders (Roy Johnson)
(7) Roy Johnson
(8) Wally Johnson
(9) Richard Little
(10) Willard Mueller
(11) Richard Murray
(12) Batting Leaders (Ken Phelps)
(13) Kenneth Phelps
(14) Luis Quintana
(15) Richard Ramos
(16) Pat Rooney
(17) William Sattler
(18) Kim Seaman
(19) Christopher Smith
(20) Michael Stenhouse
(21) Thomas Weighaus

1982 Valley Nat'l Bank Phoenix Giants

(San Francisco Giants, AAA)

	MT	NR MT	EX
Complete Set:	7.50	5.50	3.00

1 Team Photo
2 Mike Chris
3 Ted Wilborn
4 Mike Rowland
5 John Rabb
6 Paul Szymarek
7 Rocky Bridges
8 Dave Roberts
9 Tommy Gonzales, Harry Jordan
10 Mike Tucker
11 Ethan Blackaby
12 Craig Chamberlain
13 Ron Pruitt
14 Mark Dempsey
15 Dorian Boyland
16 Jeff Stember
17 Mike Turgeon
18 Giantettes
19 Andy Mc Gaffigan
20 Kelly Smith
21 Tom Runnells
22 Dan Gladden
23 Tom O'Malley
24 Jose Barrios
25 Bill Martin
26 Mike Rex
27 Al Hergesheimer

1983

1983 BHN Las Vegas Stars

(San Diego Padres, AAA)

	MT	NR MT	EX
Complete Set:	25.00	18.50	10.00

Greg Booker
Bobby Brown
Larry Brown
Tim Cook
Gerry Davis
Gerry De Simone
Harry Dunlop
Steve Fireovid
Larry Harlow
Geroge Hinshaw
Tom House
Jerry Johnson
Joe Lansford
Bill Long
Kevin Mc Reynolds
Felix Oroz
Joe Pittman
Larry Rothschild
Cecilio Ruiz
James Steels
Mark Thurmond
Ron Tingley

1983 BHN Phoenix Giants

(San Francisco Giants, AAA)

	MT	NR MT	EX
Complete Set:	20.00	15.00	8.00

1 John Rabb
2 Mark Calvert
3 Scott Garrelts
4 Brian Asselstine
5 Jeff Ransom
6 Rich Murray
7 Jeff Cornell
8 Dan Gladden
9 Tom Runnells
10 Kernan Ronan
11 Phil Hinrichs
12 Kelvin Torve
13 Herman Segelke
14 Guy Sularz
15 Randy Kutcher
16 Ted Wilborn
17 Mike Brecht
18 Butch Hughes
19 Ron Pisel
20 Mark Davis
21 Mark Dempsey
22 Chris Smith
23 Craig Chamberlain
24 Jack Mull
25 Doug Landuyt
26 Ethan Blackaby
27 Phoenix Giants Rooster
28 Tommy Gonzalez

1983 Chong Modesto A's

(Oakland A's, A)

	MT	NR MT	EX
Complete Set:	27.50	20.50	11.25

1 Bruce Amador
2 Eric Barry
3 Bob Bathe
4 Tommy Copeland
5 Kevin Coughlon
6 James Eppard
7 Charles Fick
8 Mike Gorman
9 Tony Herron
10 Rodney Hobbs, Mark Jarrett
11 Mark Jarrett
12 Jeff Kaiser
13 Jeff Kobernus
14 Tim Lambert
15 Rod Murphy
16 Ed Myers
17 Davis Peterson
18 Tab Rojas
19 Phil Strom
20 Mickey Tettleton
21 Raymond Thoma
22 Ricky Thomas
23 Robert Vavrock
24 Thomas Zmudosky
25 George Mitterwald
26 Rick Tronerud
27 Keith Lieppman
28 Phil Danielson
29 Dan Kiser
30 Davis Fry

1983 B. Colla San Jose Bees

(No affiliation, AAA)

	MT	NR MT	EX
Complete Set:	10.00	7.50	4.00

1 Frank Verdi
2 Hiromi Wada
3 Charlie Bertucio
4 Lee Granger
5 Brian Mc Donough
6 Gary Springer
7 Dan Mc Inerny
8 Osamu Abe
9 Yukiichi Komazaki
10 Hiro Shirahata
11 Mark Butler
12 Mark Jacob
13 Kerry Cook
14 Bruce Fields
15 Gary Legumina
16 Sadahito Ueda
17 Kraig Priessman
18 Katsuya Soma
19 Mike Daughterty
20 Carl Nichols
21 Jeff Gilbert
22 Jeff Summers
23 Leon Hoke
24 Kurt Leiter
25 Greg Dehart
26 Harry Steve

1983 Dog-N-Shake Wichita Aeros

(Montreal Expos, AAA)

	MT	NR MT	EX
Complete Set:	17.00	12.75	7.00

1 Checklist
2 Felipe Alou
3 Shooty Babitt
4 Greg Bargar
5 Butch Benton
6 Tom Dixon
7 Mike Fuentes
8 Mike Gates
9 Gene Glynn
10 Dick Grapenthin
11 Bob James
12 Roy Johnson
13 Brad Mills
14 Eric Mustad
15 Luis Quintana

16 Rick Ramos
17 Bob Reece
18 Pat Rooney
19 Angel Salazar
20 Bill Sattler
21 Mike Stenhouse
22 Rennie Stennett
23 Tom Wieghaus
24 1982 Batting Title (Roy Johnson)

1983 Fritsch Appleton Foxes

(Chicago White Sox, A) (Chicago White Sox, A)

	MT	NR MT	EX
Complete Set:	14.00	10.50	5.75

1 Bill Smith
2 Mike Trujillo
3 Dave McLaughlin
4 Kim Christensen
5 Joel Mc Keon
6 Jim Best
7 Rich DeVincenzo
8 Pat Adams
9 Steve Noworyta
10 Craig Smajstrla
11 Mike Henley
12 Rolando Pino
13 John Cangelosi
14 Ken Williams
15 Team Photo
16 Team Photo
17 Edwin Correa
18 Ed Sedar
19 Bill Atkinson
20 Al Jones
21 Greg Tarnow
22 Ron Karkovice
23 David Kinsel
24 Johnny Moses
25 John Boles
26 Garry Keeton
27 Don Ruzek
28 Bill Sandry
29 Al Heath
30 Team Logo/Checklist

1983 Fritsch Beloit Brewers

(Milwaukee Brewers, A)

	MT	NR MT	EX
Complete Set:	20.00	15.00	8.00

1 Butch Kirby
2 Woolsey Rice
3 Dewey James
4 Jeff Gyarmati
5 John Mitchell
6 John Antonelli
7 Hank Landers
8 Jay Aldrich
9 Bruce Williams
10 Mark Johnston
11 Doug Norton
12 Steve Anderson
13 Bill Nowlan
14 Don Whiting
15 Team Logo/Checklist
16 Tim Nordbrook
17 Dave Tarrolly
18 Brian Finley
19 Jim Teahan
20 Tim Utecht
21 Billy Joe Robidoux
22 Chuck Crim
23 Edgar Diaz
24 Fritz Fedor
25 Dan Scarpetta
26 Hector Quinones
27 Chris Bosio
28 Stan Boroski
29 Joel Weatherford
--- Team Logo/Checklist

1983 Fritsch Burlington Rangers

(Texas Rangers, A)

	MT	NR MT	EX
Complete Set:	8.00	6.00	3.25

1 Bob Hausladen
2 Todd Schulte
3 Sam Sorce
4 George Crum
5 Randy Kramer
6 Antonio Triplett
7 Jose Guzman
8 Elijah Ben
9 Barry Bass
10 Terry Johnson
11 Bobby Brower
12 Glen Cook
13 Bob Gergen
14 Ron Dillard
15 Whitney J. Harry
16 Chris Joslin
17 Otto Gonzalez
18 Brendan Hennessy
19 Tim Maki
20 John Buckley
21 Mark Sutton
22 Kevin Stock
23 David Hopkins
24 Jeff Mace
25 Greg Campbell
26 Greg Jemison
28 Team Logo/Checklist
29 Team Logo/Fritsch Ad
30 Sponsor Card

1983 Fritsch Cedar Rapids Reds

(Cincinnati Reds, A)

	MT	NR MT	EX
Complete Set:	18.00	13.50	7.50

1 Tim Reynolds
2 Buddy Pryor
3 Tim Scott
4 Joe Stalp
5 Tom Riley
6 Wayne Harmon
7 Jay Munson
8 Dave Lochner
9 Mike Knox
10 Billy Hawley
11 Dave Haberle
12 Louie Trujillo
13 Terry Lee
14 Mike Konderla
15 Jeff Rhodes
16 Glenn Spagnola
17 Kal Daniels
18 Scott Jones
19 Vin Rover
20 Mike Manfre
21 Scott Radloff
22 Bruce Kimm
23 Orsino Hill
24 Rob Murphy
25 Steve Padia
26 Team Logo/Checklist

1983 Fritsch Clinton Giants

(San Francisco Giants, A)

	MT	NR MT	EX
Complete Set:	10.00	7.50	4.00

1 Bill Kuehn, Gus Stokes
2 Eric Halberg
3 Scott Norman
4 Billy Cabell
5 Jim Weir
6 Greg Lynn
7 Marty Baier
8 Ramon Bautista
9 Scott Rainey
10 Gene Lambert
11 Orlando Blackwell
12 Davis Tavarez
13 Bob Naber
14 Alonzo Powell
15 Mike Empting
16 John Hughes
17 Brian Bargerhuff
18 Alan Marr
19 Ken Mills
20 Kelvin Smith
21 Van Sowards
22 Kurt Mattson
23 Ed Stewart
24 Dennie Taft
25 Marty DeMerritt
26 Scott Blanke
27 Randy Weibel
28 Jeff Gladden
29 Bill Lachemann
30 Team Logo/Checklist

1983 Fritsch Madison Muskies

(Oakland A's, A)

	MT	NR MT	EX
Complete Set:	45.00	33.50	18.00

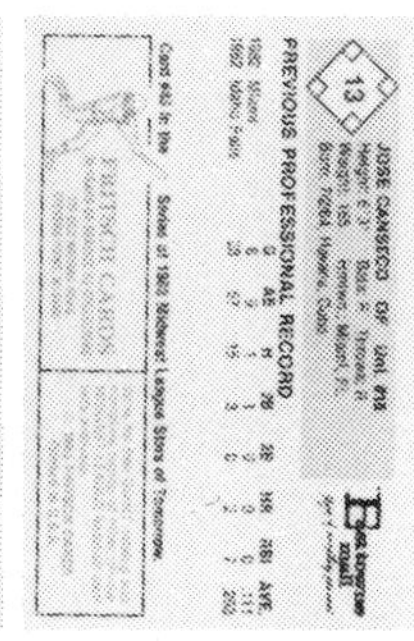

1 B. Drew, E. Janus
2 S. Charry, M. Du Val
3 Dave Collins
4 Todd Fischer
5 Dave Wilder
6 Ray Alonzo
7 Dennis Gonsalves
8 Jorge Diaz
9 Thad Reece
10 Ed Retzer
11 Shawn Gill
12 Tom Conquest
13 Jose Canseco
14 Keith Call
15 Bob Loscalzo
16 Bob Hallas
17 Eddie Escribano
18 Gene Ransom
19 John Michel
20 Mikki Jackson
21 Juan Cruz
22 Greg Robles
23 Pete Kendrick
24 Gary Dawson
25 Glenn Godwin
26 John Huey
27 Dave Leiper
28 Brian Graham
29 Hector Perez
30 Frank Trucchio
31 Brad Fischer
32 Team Logo/Checklist

1983 Fritsch Peoria Suns

(California Angels, A)

	MT	NR MT	EX
Complete Set:	15.00	11.25	6.00

1 Ray Jimenez
2 Joe King
3 Kevin Davis
4 Scott Glanz
5 Donald Groh
6 Dave Heath
7 Kris Kline
8 Doug McKenzie
9 Mark McLemore
10 Tom Smith
11 Rick Stromer
12 Jose Valdez
13 Don Timberlake
14 Mike Rizzo
15 Jack Crawford
16 Tom Rentschler
17 Jeff Salazar
18 Jay Lewis
19 Al Cristy
20 Rafael Lugo
21 Scott Suehr
22 Devon White
23 Julian Gonzalez
24 Brian Hartsock
25 Bob Kipper
26 Ron Phipps
27 Mike Saverino
28 Eddie Rodriguez
29 Joe Coleman
30 Team Logo/Checklist

1983 Fritsch Springfield Cardinals

(St. Louis Cardinals, A)

	MT	NR MT	EX
Complete Set:	17.00	12.75	7.00

1 Pete Stoll
2 David Clements
3 Paul Cherry
4 Sammy Martin
5 Dave Droschak
6 Curtis Ford
7 Marty Mason
8 Ed Tanner
9 Scott Arigoni
10 Brett Benza
11 Mick Shade
12 Joe Silkwood
13 Bob Geren
14 Greg Dunn
15 John Young
16 Dave Hoyt

17 Harry McCulla
18 Matt Gundelfinger
19 Randy Martinez
20 Mike Pittman
21 Dan Stryffeler
22 Dave Bialas
23 Mike Gambeski
24 Allen Morlock
25 Gus Malespin
26 Team Logo/Checklist

1983 Fritsch Visalia Oaks

(Minnesota Twins, A)

	MT	NR MT	EX
Complete Set:	100.00	75.00	41.00

1 Lee Belanger
2 Jeff Arney
3 Steve Aragon
4 Sam Arrington
5 Phil,Franko
6 Kirby Puckett
7 Frank Ramppen
8 Bob DeCosta
9 Jack McMahon
10 Stan Holmes
11 Frank Eufemia
12 Ron McKelvie
13 Harry Warner
14 Jeff Brueggemann
15 Erez Borowsky
16 Mark Cartwright
17 Joe Kubit
18 Curt Wardle
19 Bennie Richie
20 Craig Henderson
21 Greg Howe
22 Curt Kindred
23 Alvaro Espinoza
24 Mark Portugal
25 Brian Rupe

1983 Fritsch Waterloo Indians

(Cleveland Indians, A)

	MT	NR MT	EX
Complete Set:	7.00	5.25	2.75

1 Randy Washington
2 Edwin Aponte
3 Ben Piphus
4 Eddie Diaz
5 Andy Ortiz
6 Juan Lopez
7 Nelson Pedraza
8 Junior Noboa
9 Jay Keeler
10 Wilson Valera
11 John Miglio
12 Jose Roman
13 Miguel Roman
14 Phil Wilson
15 Reggie Ritter
16 Pookie Bernstine
17 Bernardo Brito
18 Winston Ficklin
19 Ray Martinez
20 Jeff Barkley
21 Dane Anthony
22 Mike Gertz
23 Wes Pierorazio
24 Mike Poindexter
25 Rich Diaz
26 Rick Henke
27 Vic Albury
28 Gomer Hodge
29 Team Logo/Checklist Card

1983 Fritsch Wausau Timbers

(Seattle Mariners, A)

	MT	NR MT	EX
Complete Set:	7.00	5.25	2.75

1 K.R. Houston
2 John Poloni
3 Gary Pellant
4 Tom Burns
5 Martin Enriquez
6 Brian David
7 Ronn Dixon
8 Tim Slavin
9 Terry Taylor
10 Eric Parent
11 Chip Conklin
12 David Myers
13 Kevin Roy
14 Todd Francis
15 Randy Meier
16 Robby Vollmer
17 Jesse Baez
18 Scott Barnhouse
19 Paul Schneider
20 Scott Roebuck
21 Tom Duggan
22 Bob Baldrick
23 Sam Haley
24 Ron Sismondo
25 Randy Newman
26 John Duncan
27 Dave Smith
28 Wray Begendahl
29 Kenny Briggs
30 R.J. Harrison
31 Team Logo/Checklist Card

1983 Fritsch Wisconsin Rapids Twins

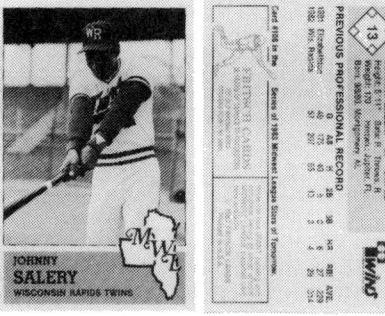

(Minnesota Twins, A)

	MT	NR MT	EX
Complete Set:	14.00	10.50	5.75

1 Coe Brier
2 Ronnie Scheer
3 Allan Anderson
4 Jeff Wilson
5 Joe Sain
6 Paul Felix
7 Carson Carroll
8 David Steinberg
9 Tim Graupmann
10 John Kearns
11 Bob Ferro
12 Mark Larcom
13 Johnny Salery
14 Bob Costello
15 Leo Cardenas, Jr.
16 Danny Clay
17 Brian Hobaugh
18 Mike Maack
19 Luis Cruz
20 Jim Burnos
21 Ken Klump
22 Paul Mancuso
23 Brad Skoglund
24 Michael Moreno
25 David Baehr
26 John Marks
27 Charlie Manuel
28 Team Logo/Checklist

1983 Riley's Louisville Redbirds

(St. Louis Cardinals, AAA)

	MT	NR MT	EX
Complete Set:	17.00	12.75	7.00

1 Jim Fregosi
2 Gaylen Pitts
3 Jerry Mc Kune
4 Dyar Miller
5 Gene Roof
6 Kevin Hagen
7 Joe De Sa
8 David Von Ohlen
9 Tom Nieto
10 Jeff Keener
11 Jeff Doyle
12 Tito Landrum
13 Jose Gonzalez
14 Jose Brito
15 Gene Dotson
16 Ralph Citarella
17 Andy Rincon
18 Andy Van Slyke
19 Jim Adduci
20 John Fulgham
21 Mike Calise
22 Dennis Werth
23 Ricky Horton
24 Orlando Sanchez
25 Tom Thurberg
26 Todd Worrell
27 Bill Lyons
28 Dave Kable
29 Doyle Harris
30 Jed Smith

1983 TCMA Albany-Colonie A's

(Oakland A's, AA) (black and white)

	MT	NR MT	EX
Complete Set:	175.00	131.00	72.00

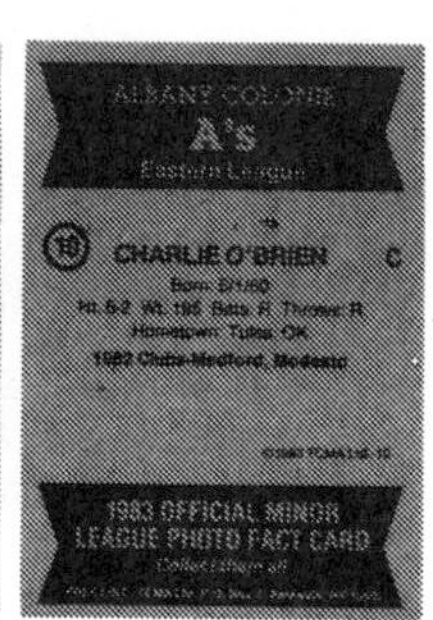

1 Jesse Anderson
2 Allen Edwards
3 Mark Fellows
4 Mark Ferguson
5 Paul Josephson
6 Mike Lynes
7 Steve Ontiveros
8 Gary Wex
9 Jim Durrman
10 Charlie O'Brien
11 Mike Ashman
12 Steve Kiefer
13 Tim Pyznarski
14 Luis Quinones
15 Phil Stephenson
16 Sly Young
17 Luis Bravo
18 Ron Harrison
19 Tom Romano
20 Pete Whisenant

1983 TCMA Albuquerque Dukes

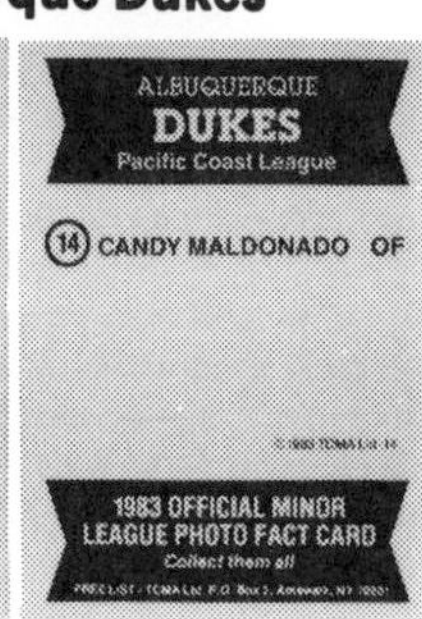

(Los Angeles Dodgers, AAA) (color)

	MT	NR MT	EX
Complete Set:	70.00	52.50	28.75

1 Franklin Stubbs
2 Bert Geiger
3 Orel Hershiser
4 Brian Holton
5 Dean Rennicke
6 Rich Rodas
7 Paul Voigt
8 Larry White
9 Steve Perry
10 Alex Taveras
11 Jack Fimple
12 Scotti Madison
13 Brent Strom
14 Candy Maldonado
15 Sid Bream
16 Ross Jones
17 German Rivera
18 Greg Schultz
19 Ed Amelung
20 Tony Brewer
21 Ernesto Borbon
22 Lemmie Miller
23 Del Crandall
24 Dave Cohea
25 Dick McLaughlin

1983 TCMA Alexandria Dukes

(Pittsburgh Pirates, A) (black and white)

	MT	NR MT	EX
Complete Set:	70.00	52.50	28.75

1 Bobby Lyons
2 Sam Khalifa
3 Chuck Meadows
4 Scott Borland
5 Nick Castaeda
6 Jim Opie
7 Marvin Clack
8 Pete Rice
9 Art Ray
10 Scott Bailes
11 John Lipon
12 Johnny Taylor
13 Jim Aulenback

14 CHris Lein
15 David Tumbas
16 Roberto Bonilla
17 Thomas Martinez
18 Sean Faherty
19 Craig Brown
20 David Johnson
21 Steve Susce
22 Jim Felt
23 Nelson de la Rosa
24 Eric Zimmerman
25 Steve Lewis
26 Rubin Rodriguez
27 Ravelo Manzanillo
28 Mike Quade
29 Jim Buckmier
30 Dorn Taylor
31 Lorenzo Bundy

1983 TCMA Anderson Braves

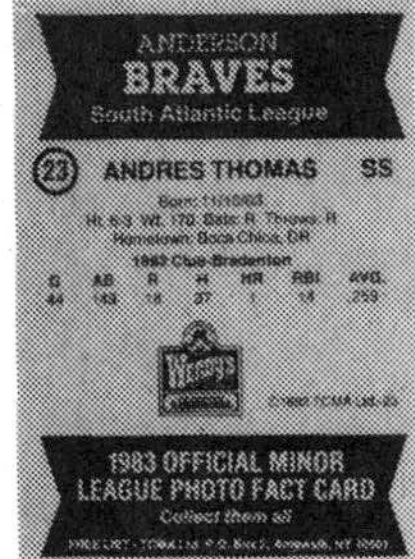

(Atlanta Braves, A) (color)

	MT	NR MT	EX
Complete Set:	20.00	15.00	8.00

1 Bill MacKay
2 Rick Albert
3 Skip Weisman
4 Randy Ingle
5 Dave May
6 Buzz Capra
7 John Baker
8 Jose Cano
9 Al Candelaria
10 Chip Reese
11 Ken Lynn
12 Charlie Morelock
13 John Mortillaro
14 Jim Rivera
15 Randy Rogers
16 Maximo Rosario
17 Rudy Torres
18 Sylverio Valdez
19 Ramon Vargas
20 Dave Griffin
21 Ralph Giansanti
22 Jay Palma
23 Andres Thomas
24 Dave Van Horn
25 Russ Anglin
26 Clint Brill
27 Jerry Ragsdale
28 Paul Llewellyn
29 Dave Morris
30 Larry Moser
31 Jay Roberts
32 Rich Thompson
33 Jeff Wagner

1983 TCMA Arkansas Travelers

(St. Louis Cardinals, AA) (black and white)

	MT	NR MT	EX
Complete Set:	100.00	75.00	41.00

1 Mike Rhodes
2 Ruben Gotay
3 Terry Clark
4 Kurt Kepshire
5 Walter Pierce
6 Mike Barba
7 Bill Thomas
8 Steve Winfield
9 Jerry Johnson
10 John Adams
11 Randy Hunt
12 Mark Salas
13 Mike Harris
14 Mike Wolters
15 Terry Pendelton
16 Luis Ojeda
17 Greg Guin
18 Alan Hunsinger
19 Rod Booker
20 Fran Batista
21 Gotay Mills
22 Larry Reynolds
23 Nick Leyva
24 Jorge Aranzamendi
25 Dave England

1983 TCMA Beaumont Golden Gators

(San Diego Padres, AA) (black and white) (card #3 of Steve Johnson is rarely found in mint condition)

	MT	NR MT	EX
Complete Set:	135.00	101.00	54.00

1 Mike Martin
2 Ozzie Guillen
3 Steve Johnson
4 Randy Kaczmarski
5 Walt Vanderbush
6 Jim Leopold
7 Bob Patterson
8 Mark Williamson
9 Marty Lain
10 Dan Purpura
11 John Kruk
12 Steve Garcia
13 Mark Parent
14 Jeff Ronk
15 Mark Gillaspie
16 Pat Casey
17 Frank Ricci
18 Willie Hardwick
19 Ray Haywood, Jr.
20 James Steels
21 Jack Maloof
22 Allen Gerhardt
23 Gene Confreda

1983 TCMA Birmingham Barons

(Detroit Tigers, AA) (color)

	MT	NR MT	EX
Complete Set:	12.00	9.00	4.75

1 Raul Tovar
2 Don Gordon
3 Dan Williams
4 Dwight Lowry
5 Stan Younger
6 Dave Hawarny
7 Mark Smith
8 Doug Baker
9 Don Heinker
10 Bruce Robbins
11 George Foussianes
12 Bob Melvin
13 Greg Norman
14 Chuck Cary
15 Scott Tabor
16 Nelson Simmons
17 Scottie Earl
18 Ted Davis
19 Colin Ward
20 Jon Furman
21 Pedro Chavez
22 Keith Comstock
23 Troy Dixon
24 Roger Mason
25 Roy Majtyka

1983 TCMA Buffalo Bisons

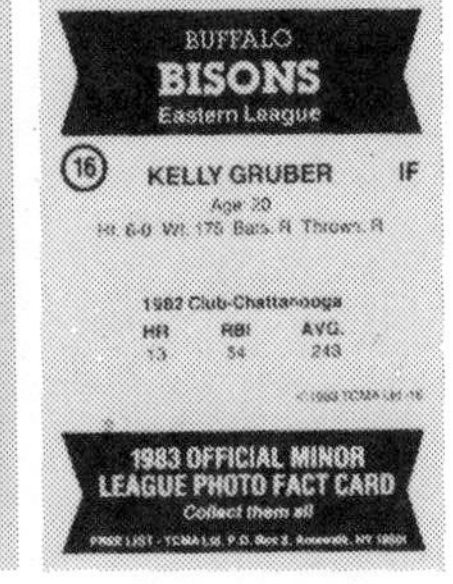

(Cleveland Indians, AA) (color)

	MT	NR MT	EX
Complete Set:	16.00	12.00	6.50

1 Robin Fuson
2 Wayne Johnson
3 Rich Doyle
4 Gordie Glaser
5 Rod McDonald
6 Tom Owens
7 Rich Thompson
8 Jeff Green
9 Ramon Romero
10 John Malkin
11 Tim Glass
12 Everett Rey
13 Sal Rende
14 Jim Wilson
15 Shanie Dugas
16 Kelly Gruber
17 Jeff Moronko
18 Rene Quinones
19 Dave Gallagher
20 Ed Saavedra
21 Dwight Taylor
22 George Cecchetti
23 Joe Charboneau
24 Al Gallagher
25 Jack Aker

1983 TCMA Burlington Rangers

(Texas Rangers, A) (color)

	MT	NR MT	EX
Complete Set:	15.00	11.25	6.00

1 Barry Bass
2 John Buckley
3 Glenn Cook
4 Jose Guzman
5 Dave Hopkins
6 Terry Johnson
7 Chris Joslin
8 Randy Kramer
9 Tim Maki
10 Todd Schulte
11 Mike Soper
12 Elijah Ben
13 Bob Brower
14 George Crum
15 Ron Dillard
16 Bob Gergen
17 Otto Gonzales
18 Whitney Harry
19 Bob Hausladen
20 Brendan Hennessey
21 Jeff Mace
22 Sam Sorce
23 Kevin Stock
24 Mark Sutton
25 Tony Triplett
26 Orlando Gomez
27 Greg Jemison
28 Greg Campbell

1983 TCMA Butte Copper Kings

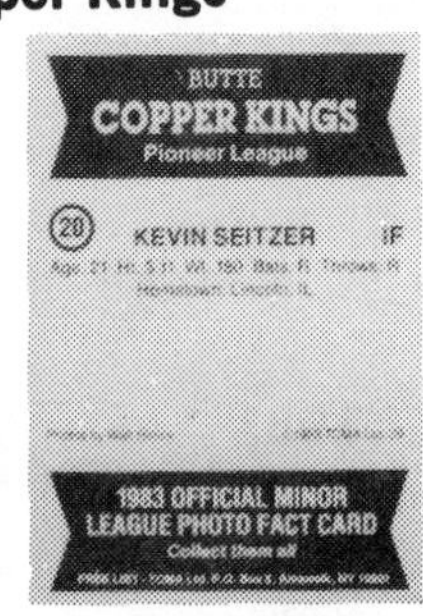

(Kansas City Royals, Rookie) (black and white)

	MT	NR MT	EX
Complete Set:	50.00	37.50	20.50

1 Dennis Boatright
2 Dan Chelini
3 Dave Digirolama
4 Tom Edens
5 Phil George
6 Gary Klein
7 Stefan Lipson
8 Charley Luman
9 Randy Robinson
10 John Serritella
11 Jose Torres
12 Rob Vodvarka
13 Dave Landrith
14 Tom Niemann
15 Stan Oxner
16 Jim Bagnall
17 Vic Davila
18 Jere Longenecker
19 Mike Miller
20 Kevin Seitzer

21 Kevin Stanley
22 Mark Van Blaricom
23 Edward Allen
24 John Devich
25 Tommy Mohr
26 Dave Rooker
27 John Rubel
28 Jeff Schulz
29 Joe Kasunick
30 Tommy Jones
31 Guy Hansen
32 Bruce Piatt
33 Tom Osowski

1983 TCMA Cedar Rapids Reds

(Cincinnati Reds, A) (color)

	MT	NR MT	EX
Complete Set:	40.00	30.00	16.00

1 Bruce Kimm
2 Scott Jones
3 Dave Lochner
4 Mike Knox
5 Glenn Spagnola
6 Billy Hawley
7 Mike Konderla
8 Tim Scott
9 Tim Reynolds
10 Joe Stalp
11 Louie Trujillo
12 Steve Padia
13 Rob Murphy
14 Buddy Pryor
15 Scott Radloff
16 Tom Riley
17 Delwyn Young
18 Dave Haberle
19 Terry Lee
20 Mike Manfre
21 Vince Rover
22 Kal Daniels
23 Orsino Hill
24 Jeff Rhodes
25 Jay Munson
26 Don Buchheister
27 Batboys
28 Wayne Harmon

1983 TCMA Charleston Charlies

(Cleveland Indians, AAA) (color)

	MT	NR MT	EX
Complete Set:	12.00	9.00	4.75

1 Jay Baller
2 Mike Jeffcoat
3 Larry Hrynko
4 Jerry Reed
5 Roy Smith
6 Sandy Whitol
7 Doug Simunic
8 Jerry Willard
9 Luis DeLeon
10 Angelo Logrande
11 Juan Pacho
12 Karl Pagel
13 Jack Perconte
14 Tim Norrid
15 Rodney Craig
16 Wil Culmer
17 Kevin Rhomberg
18 Otto Velez
19 Ed Glynn
20 Vic Albury
21 Steve Cisczon
22 Doc Edwards

1983 TCMA Charleston Royals

(Kansas City Royals, A) (black and white)

	MT	NR MT	EX
Complete Set:	25.00	18.50	10.00

1 Mark Pirruccello
2 Nicky Richards
3 Joe Szekely
4 Jim Bagnall
5 Chris Bryeans
6 Craig Goodin
7 Keith Hempfield
8 Bill Phillips
9 Rich Vitato
10 Edward Allen
11 Roland Oruna
12 Jack Shuffield
13 Van Snider
14 Richard Aube
15 John Bryant
16 Doug Cook
17 John Davis
18 Bob De Bord
19 Tom Drizmala
20 Rich Goodin
21 Ron McCormack
22 Israel Sanchez
23 John Serritella
24 Roy Tanner
25 Duane Gustavson
26 Mark Farnsworth

1983 TCMA Chattanooga Lookouts

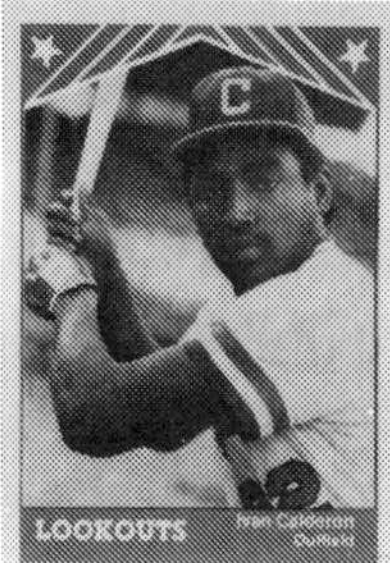

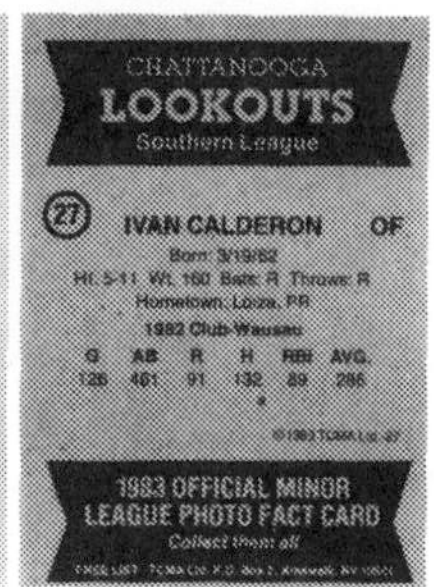

(Seattle Mariners, AA) (black and white)

	MT	NR MT	EX
Complete Set:	225.00	169.00	90.00

1 Darnell Coles
2 Paul Serna
3 Chris Hunger
4 Joe Whitmer
5 Ramon Estepa
6 Danny Tartabull
7 Vic Martin
8 Alvin Davis
9 Mike Bucci
10 Miguel Negron
11 Mark Langston
12 Mickey Bowers
13 Bob Randolph
14 Robert Hudson
15 Don (Clay) Hill
16 Jeff Stottlemyre
17 Tracy Harris
18 Kevin King
19 Kevin Dukes
20 John Burden
21 Mark Cahill
22 Kevin Steger
23 Tom Hunt
24 Chief Lookout
25 Harry Landreth
26 Dave Valle
27 Ivan Calderon
--- Team Photo

1983 TCMA Columbus Astros

(Houston Astros, AA) (black and white)

	MT	NR MT	EX
Complete Set:	85.00	64.00	34.00

1 George Bjorkman
2 Ed Cuervo
3 John Csefalvay
4 Mike Grace
5 Jim Sherman
6 Mark Strucher
7 Larry Simcox
8 Steve Benson
9 Eric Bullock
10 Ty Gainey
11 Glenn Davis
12 Fransisco Jabalera
13 Jeff Calhoun
14 Jeff Heathcock
15 Jim MacDonald
16 Tim Meckes
17 Zac Paris
18 Pat Perry
19 Ben Snyder
20 Jack Smith
21 Bob Sprowl
22 Jack Hiatt
23 Ken Bolek
24 Rex Jones

1983 TCMA Columbus Clippers

(New York Yankees, AAA) (color)

	MT	NR MT	EX
Complete Set:	65.00	49.00	26.00

1 Johnny Oates
2 Coaching Staff
3 Juan Espino
4 Bradley Gulden
5 Silton Fontenot
6 David Wehrmeister
7 Timothy Burke
8 Dennis Rasmussen
9 Clay Christiansen
10 Stefan Wever
11 Curt Kaufman
12 Jesus Hernaiz
13 Guy Elston
14 Benjamin Callahan III
15 Stephen Balboni
16 Marshall Brant
17 Bert Campaneris
18 Edwin Rodriguez
19 Barry Evans
20 Robert Meacham
21 Clell Hobson, Jr.
22 Michael Patterson
23 Matthew Winters
24 James Hart
25 Otis Nixon
26 Brian Dayett
27 Rowland Office

1983 TCMA Daytona Beach Astros

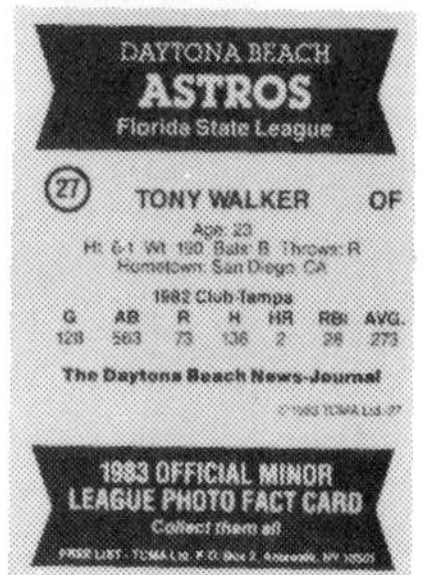

(Houston Astros, A) (black and white)

	MT	NR MT	EX
Complete Set:	30.00	22.00	12.00

1 Dave Cripe
2 Stan Hough
3 Rich Bombard
4 Mike Callahan
5 Guillermo Castro
6 Manny Hernandez
7 Mark Knudson
8 Mike Hogan
9 Uvaldo Regaldo
10 Ed Reilly
11 Rex Schimpf
12 Jamey Shouppe
13 Tom Wiedenbauer
14 Don Berti
15 Jeff Datz
16 Jamie Williams
17 Randy Braun
18 Glenn Carpenter
19 Juan Delgado
20 Gary D'Onofrio
21 Steve McAllister
22 Ricardo Rivera
23 Jim Thomas
24 Mike Botkin
25 Curtis Burke
26 Louie Meadows
27 Tony Walker

1983 TCMA Durham Bulls

(Atlanta Braves, A) (color)

	MT	NR MT	EX
Complete Set:	13.00	9.75	5.25

1 Chip Childress
2 Steve Chmil
3 Terry Cormack
4 Inocencio Guerrero
5 Johnny Hatcher
6 Pat Hodge
7 Scott Hood
8 Mike Knox
9 Bob Luzon
10 Bryan Neal
11 Tony Neuendorff
12 Ken Scanlon
13 Rick Siriano
14 Freddy Tiburcio
15 Bob Tumpane
16 Mike Bormann
17 Dave Clay
18 Tim Cole
19 Mark Lance
20 Rich Leggatt
21 Dennis Lubert
22 Ike Pettaway
23 Allen Sears
24 Zane Smith
25 Duane Ward
26 Matt West
27 Tim Alexander
28 Brian Snitker
29 Leo Mazzone

1983 TCMA El Paso Diablos

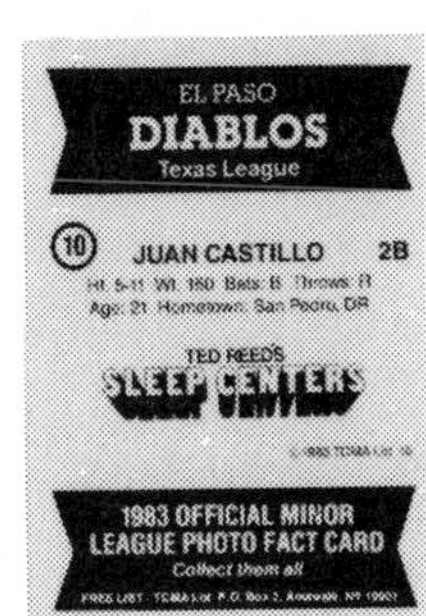

(Milwaukee Brewers, AA) (color)

	MT	NR MT	EX
Complete Set:	20.00	15.00	8.00

1 Dan Burns
2 Eric Peyton
3 Joe Henderson
4 Jim Paciorek
5 Bryan Duquette
6 Stan Davis
7 Mark Effrig
8 Rene Quinones
9 Mike Felder
10 Juan Castillo
11 Stan Levi
12 Garrett Nago
13 Bill Max
14 Ray Gallo
15 Bryan Clutterbuck
16 Steve Parrott
17 Tim Crews
18 Al Price
19 Carlos Ponce
20 Kevin McCoy
21 Earnest Riles
22 Frank Thomas
23 Jack Lazorko
24 Bob Schroeck
25 Lee Sigman

1983 TCMA Erie Cardinals

(St. Louis Cardinals, A) (color)

	MT	NR MT	EX
Complete Set:	30.00	22.00	12.00

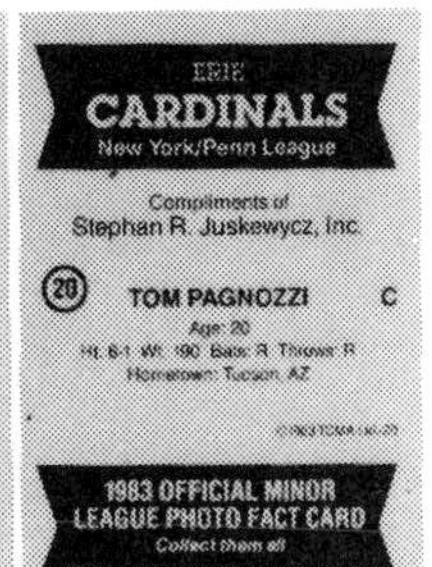

1 Paul Mangiardi
2 Joe Rigoli
3 John Rigos
4 Jim ReBoulet
5 Wilfredo Martinez
6 Bill Packer
7 Mark Dougherty
8 Keith Turnbull
9 Jamie Brisco
10 Brian Farley
11 Mike Behrend
12 Mark Angelo
13 Jeff Pasquali
14 Scott Pleis
15 Chuck McGrath
16 Jeff Gass
17 Phil Burwell
18 John Costello
19 Tim Kavanaugh
20 Tom Pagnozzi
21 Tom Rossi
22 Ernie Carrasco
23 Tom Caulfield
24 Mike Robinson
25 Kurt Kaull

1983 TCMA Evansville Triplets

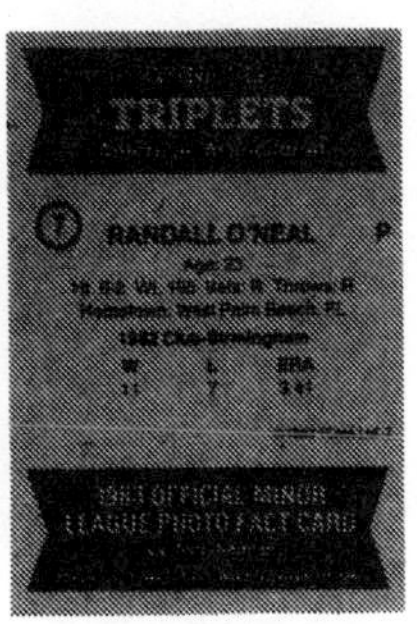

(Detroit Tigers, AAA) (color)

	MT	NR MT	EX
Complete Set:	13.00	9.75	5.25

1 Mark Dacko
2 Craig Eaton
3 David Gumpert
4 Bryan Kelly
5 Steven Luebber
6 Charles Nail
7 Randall O'Neill
8 Larry Pashnick
9 Davis Rucker
10 Patrick Underwood
11 Martin Castillo
12 Willie Royster
13 Jeffery Bertoni
14 Julio Gonzales
15 Mike Laga
16 Juan Lopez
17 Kenneth Baker
18 Barbaro Garbey
19 Bob Grandas
20 Jeffrey Kenaga
21 Darryl Motley
22 Gordon MacKenzie
23 William Armstrong
24 Mark DeJohn
25 German Barranca

1983 TCMA Glens Falls White Sox

(Chicago White Sox, AA) (black and white)

	MT	NR MT	EX
Complete Set:	95.00	71.00	38.00

1 Darryl Boston
2 J.B. Brown
3 Wes Kent
4 Monte McAbee
5 Scott Meier
6 Ed Miles

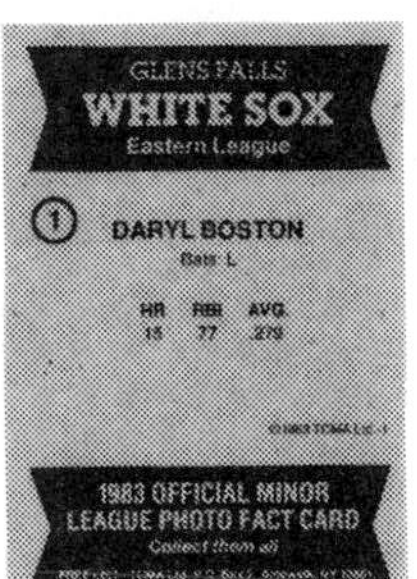

7 Mike Morse
8 Dave Nix
9 Curt Reed
10 Ramon Romero
11 Pat Kelly
12 Tom Brennan
13 Keith Desjarlais
14 Mike Maitland
15 Homer Moncrief
16 Robert Moore
17 Tom Mullen
18 Steve Pastrovich
19 Wayne Schuckert
20 Mike Tanzi
21 Mike Withrow
22 Adrian Garrett
23 Lori Corcoran
24 Dick Manning

1983 TCMA Greensboro Hornets

(New York Yankees, A) (color)

	MT	NR MT	EX
Complete Set:	50.00	37.00	20.00

1 Johnny Baldwin
2 Scott Beahan
3 Ozzie Canseco
4 Jim Corsi
5 Logan Easley
6 John Caston
7 Steve George
8 Randy Graham
9 Rich Gumbert
10 Daryl Humphrey
11 Steve Ray
12 Dick Seidel
13 Randy White
14 Fredi Gonzalez
15 Phil Lombardi
16 Mark Blaser
17 Maurice Ching
18 Mike Fennell
19 Roberto Kelly
20 Pedro Medina
21 Felix Perdomo
22 Jim Riggs
23 Jose Rivera
24 Stan Javier
25 Joe MacKay
26 Tony Russell
27 Carlos Tosca
28 Bill Evers
29 Q.V. Lowe
30 Don McGann

1983 TCMA Idaho Falls Athletics

(Oakland A's, A) (black and white)

	MT	NR MT	EX
Complete Set:	30.00	22.00	12.00

1 Steve Bowens
2 Steve Chasteen
3 Oscar DeChavez
4 Wayne Giddings
5 Dave Hanna
6 Darel Hansen
7 Perry Johnson

8 Mark Leonette
9 Wade Mangum
10 Camilo Pascual
11 Larry Smith
12 Bob Vantrease
13 Tony Wadley
14 Joe Law
15 Eric Garrett
16 Matt Held
17 Mike Rojas
18 Steve Chumas
19 Darrell Dull
20 Rich Borowski
21 Twayne Harris
22 Rob Nelson
23 Felix Pagan
24 Mike Rantz
25 Mike Wilder
26 Maurice Castain
27 Steve Howard
28 Sly Humphrey
29 Tony Moncrief
30 Jim Nettles
31 Grady Fuson
32 Gary Lance
33 Mark Doberenz
34 Dave Sheriff

1983 TCMA Iowa Cubs

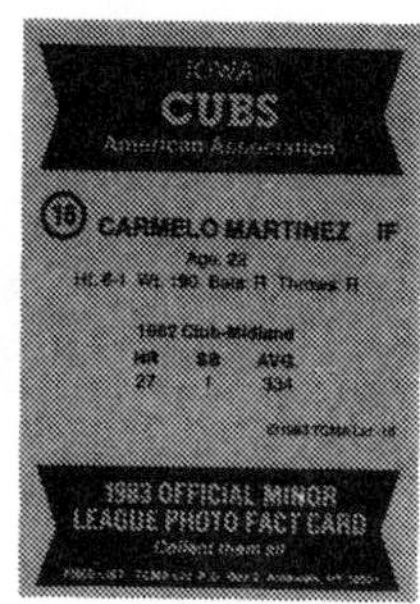

(Chicago Cubs, AAA) (color)

	MT	NR MT	EX
Complete Set:	85.00	64.00	35.00

1 Rich Bordi
2 Bill Earley
3 Tom Filer
4 Alan Hargesheimer
5 Larry Jones
6 Dan Larson
7 Reggie Patterson
8 John Perlman (Jon)
9 Don Schulze
10 Randy Stein
11 Mike Diaz
12 Bill Hayes
13 Fritz Connally
14 Joe Hicks
15 Jay Loviglio
16 Carmelo Martinez
17 Jerry Manuel
18 Dave Owen
19 Dan Rohn
20 Joe Carter
21 Henry Cotto
22 Tom Grant
23 Carlos Lezcano
24 Steve Carroll
25 Front Office Team
26 Jim Narier
27 Scott Breeden
28 Kim Hart
29 Ken Grandquist
--- Cubby (team mascot)

1983 TCMA Knoxville Blue Jays

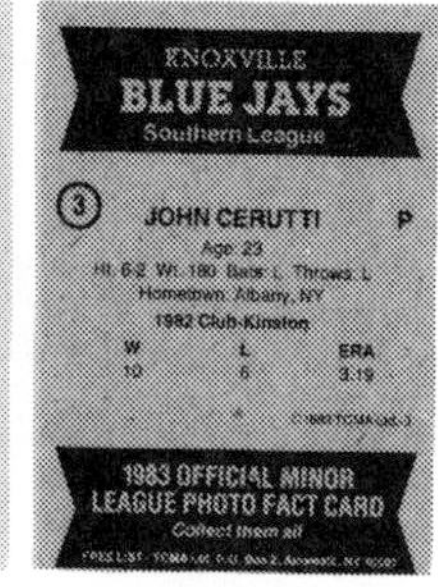

(Toronto Blue Jays, AA) (black and white)

	MT	NR MT	EX
Complete Set:	20.00	15.00	8.00

1 Tom Blackmon
2 Stan Clarke
3 John Cerutti
4 Mercedes Esquer
5 Jack McKnight
6 Chris Phillips
7 Dave Shipanoff
8 Bill Pinkham
9 Dan Whitmer
10 Carry Harris
11 Chris Johnston
12 Augie Schmidt
13 Andre Wood
14 Chris Shaddy
15 Kevin Aitcheson
16 Eddie Dennis
17 Greg Griffin
18 Paul Hodgson
19 John McLaren
20 Doug Ault
21 John Woodworth
22 Gary McCune

1983 TCMA Lynchburg Mets

(New York Mets, A) (black and white)

	MT	NR MT	EX
Complete Set:	95.00	71.00	39.00

1 Reggie Jackson
2 Larry McNutt
3 Bill Latham
4 Jeff Bettendorf
5 Bill Fultz
6 Darryl Denby
7 Randy Milligan
8 Greg Olson
9 Bruce Morrison
10 Dwight Gooden
11 Sam Perlozzo
12 Not Issued
13 John Cumberland
14a Mark Carreon
14b Dave Cochrane
15 Lenny Dykstra
16 Jay Tibbs
17 John Heller
18 Jeff Sunderlage
19 Dave Wyatt
20 Joe Graves
21 Rich Pickett
22 Ed Hearn
23 Wes Gardner

1983 TCMA Lynn Pirates

(Pittsburgh Pirates, AA) (black and white)

	MT	NR MT	EX
Complete Set:	60.00	45.00	24.00

1 Mike Bielecki
2 Wilfredo Cordoba
3 Fernando Gonzalez
4 John Lackey
5 Lee Marcheskie
6 Dale Mahorcic
7 Craig Pippin
8 Keith Thibodeaux
9 Tim Wheeler
11 Stan Cliburn
12 Burke Goldthorn
13 Peter Rowe
14 Rafael Belliard
15 Nelson Norman
16 Greg Pastors
17 Rich Renteria
18 John Schaive
19 Benny Distefano
20 Ken Ford
21 Connor McGeehee
22 Jose Rodriguez
23 Tommy Sandt
24 Frank Leger
25 Brian McCann
26 Thomas Lynn
27 Gary Fitzpatrick
28 Jay Walsh

1983 TCMA Memphis Chicks

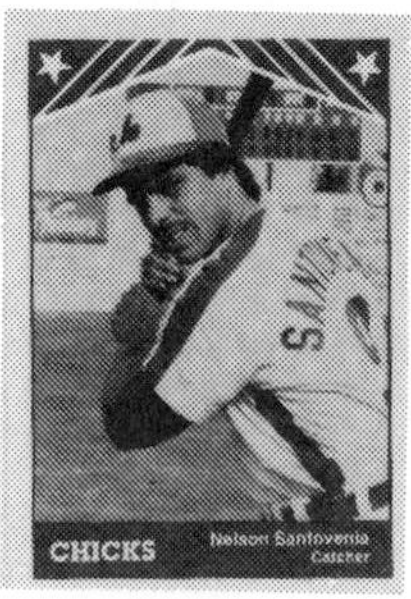

(Montreal Expos, AA) (black and white)

	MT	NR MT	EX
Complete Set:	35.00	26.25	14.50

1 Shooty Babitt
2 Georgie Cruz
3 Rene Gonzales
4 John Damon
5 Jeff Carl
6 Larry Goldetsky
7 Don Carter
8 Nelson Santovenia
9 Dave Hoeksema
10 Tommy Joe Shimp
11 Tim Cates
12 Bud Yanus
13 Rod Nealeigh
14 Jeff Taylor
15 Leonel Carrion
16 Jim Auten
17 Bob Tenenini
18 Larry Glasscock
19 Joe Hesketh
20 Greg Bargar
21 Razor Shines
22 Jeff Porter
23 Rick Renick
24 Mike Kinnvnen

1983 TCMA Miami Marlins

(San Diego Padres, A) (black and white)

	MT	NR MT	EX
Complete Set:	250.00	187.00	100.00

1 Will George
2 Mike McClain
3 Scott Gardner
4 Francisco Cota
5 Gene Walter
6 Sergio Del Rosario
7 Bill Gerhardt
8 Chuck Kolotka
9 Greg Raymer
10 Kevin Rhodas
11 Jeff Dean
12 Ray Nodell
13 Billy Ireland
14 Jose Gomez
15 Dan Jones
16 Al Simmons
17 Paul Noce
18 Manny Del Rosario
19 John Frierson
20 Benito Santiago
21 Bob Allinger
22 Tim Cannon
23 Tommy Francis
24 Steve Sayles
25 Jim Breazeale
26 Mark Miggins
27 Dennis Maley
28 Todd Hutcheson

1983 TCMA Midland Cubs

(Chicago Cubs, AA) (black and white)

	MT	NR MT	EX
Complete Set:	25.00	18.50	10.00

1 Bill Schammel
2 Tommy Harmon

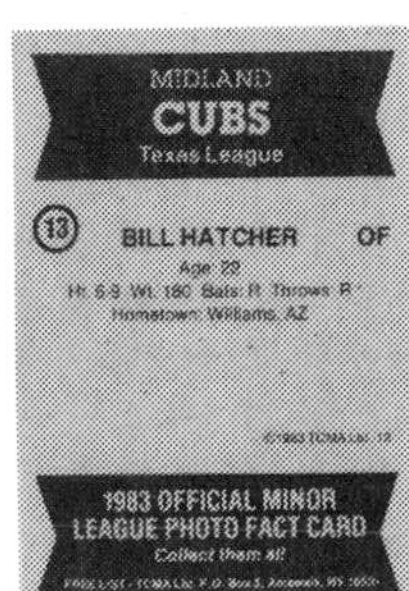

3 Glen Gregson
4 Jim Walsh
5 Neil Bryant
6 Dennis Brogna
7 Carlos Gil
8 Doug Weleno
9 Tim Millner
10 Bruce Chanye
11 Ken Pryce
12 Darrel Banks
13 Bill Hatcher
14 Tom Lombarski
15 George Borges
16 Trey Brooks
17 Don Hyman
18 Ron Richardson
19 Stan Kyles
20 Mike Anicich
21 Jim Gerlach
22 Ray Soff
23 Tom Johnson
24 Randy LaVigne
25 Rick Baker
26 A.J. Hill

1983 TCMA Nashua Angels

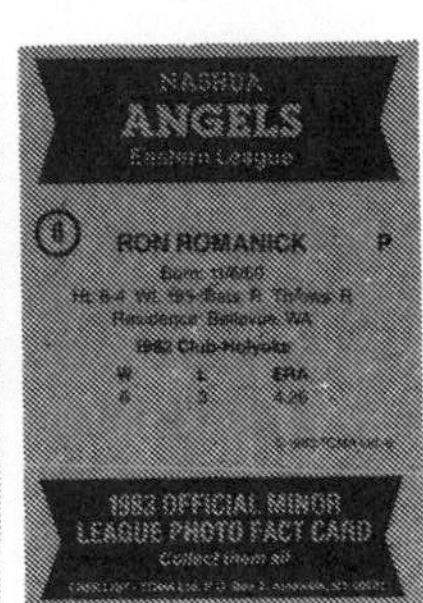

(California Angels, AA) (black and white) (mint cards of Cliburn and Connor are scarce)

	MT	NR MT	EX
Complete Set:	15.00	11.00	6.00

1 Bob Bastian
2 Rod Boxberger
3 Stewart Cliburn
4 Jeff Connor
5 Bill Mooneyham
6 Ron Romanick
7 Mickey Saatzer
8 D.W. Smith
9 Ron Sylvia
10 Steve Liddle
11 Larry Patterson
12 Harry Francis
13 Craig Gerber
14 Gustavo Polidor
15 Darryl Stephens
16 Frank Viloria
17 Jim Beswick
18 Sap Randall
19 Al Romero
20 Winston Llenas
21 Frank Reberger
22 Richard Zaleski
23 Mark McCormack
24 Ben Surner
25 Jerry Mileur
26 George Como
27 Nashua Angels Chicken

1983 TCMA Oklahoma City 89'ers

(Texas Rangers, AAA) (color)

	MT	NR MT	EX
Complete Set:	15.00	11.25	6.00

1 Bill Stearns
2 Tommy Burgess

3 Terry Bogener
4 Nick Capra
5 Tracy Cowger
6 Victor Cruz
7 Tommy Dunbar
8 Mike Griffin
9 Thomas Henke
10 Michael Jirschele
11 Robert Jones
12 Peter MacKanin
13 Mark Mercer
14 Ron Musselman
15 David Rajsich
16 Paul Semall
17 David Stockstill
18 Don Werner
19 Curt Wilkerson
20 Mike Mason
21 Joe Strain
22 Jim Farr
23 Don Scott
24 Danny Wheat

1983 TCMA Omaha Royals

(Kansas City Royals, AAA) (color)

	MT	NR MT	EX
Complete Set:	30.00	22.50	12.25

1 Mike Alvarez
2 Bud Black
3 Derek Botelho
4 Scott Brown
5 Keith Creel
6 Danny Jackson
7 Mike Parrott
8 Dan St. Clair
9 Dave Schuler
10 Vince Yuhas
11 Brian Poldberg
12 Russ Stephans
13 Buddy Biancalana
14 Jeff Cox
15 Mark Funderburk
16 Kelly Heath
17 Cliff Pastornicky
18 Steve Hammond
19 Bombo Rivera
20 Mark Ryal
21 Pat Sheridan
22 Dave Leeper
23 Bill Gorman
24 Joe Sparks
25 Jerry Cram
26 Paul McCannon

1983 TCMA Orlando Twins

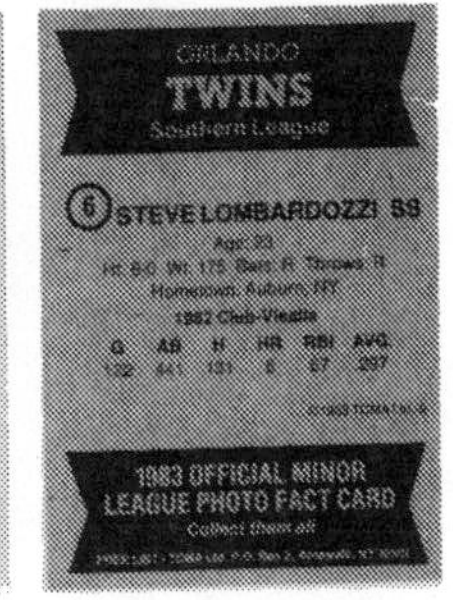

(Minnesota Twins, AA) (color) (complete set price includes scarce Carroll card)

	MT	NR MT	EX
Complete Set:	195.00	146.00	78.00

1 Phil Roof
2 Tony Pilla
3 Jim Weaver
4 Kevin Williams
5 Jeff Reed
6 Steve Lombardozzi
7 Mike McCain
8 John Palica
9 Mike Sodders
10 Chino Cadahia
11 Ken Foster
12 Jerry Lomastro
13 Manny Pena
14 Jay Pettibone
15 Rich Yett
16 Jack Hobbs
17 Ted Kromy
18 Kirby Krueger
19 Eric Broersma
20 Paul Gibson
21 Mike Giordano
22 Tony Guerrero
25 Carson Carroll

1983 TCMA Pawtucket Red Sox

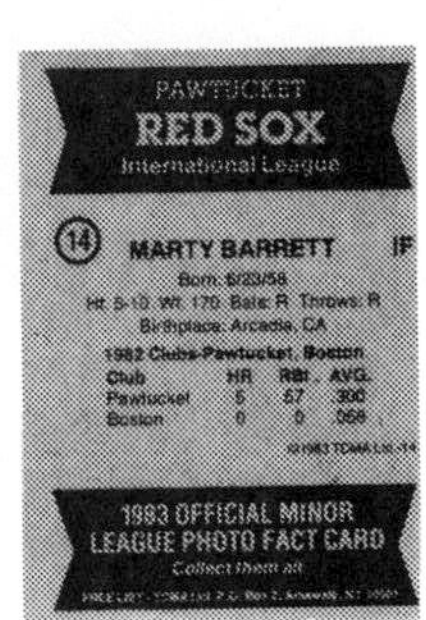

(Boston Red Sox, AAA) (color)

	MT	NR MT	EX
Complete Set:	85.00	64.00	34.00

1 Bob Birrell
2 Dennis Boyd
3 Dennis Burtt
4 Steve Crawford
5 Brian Denman
6 Jim Dorsey
7 Mark Fidrych
8 Keith MacWhorter
9 Bill Moloney
10 Dave Schoppee
11 Steve Shields
12 Roger LaFrancois
13 John Lickert
14 Marty Barrett
15 Juan Bustabad
16 Mike Davis
17 Dave Koza
18 Jim Wilson
19 Reggie Whittemore
20 Gus Burgess
21 Geno Gentile
22 Lee Graham
23 Juan Pautt
24 Chico Walker
25 Tony Torchia
26 Mike Roarke

1983 TCMA Portland Beavers

(Philadelphia Phillies, AAA) (black and white) (complete set price includes scarce #'s 23-25)

	MT	NR MT	EX
Complete Set:	195.00	146.00	78.00

1 Luis Aguayo
2 Juan Samuel
3 Larry Andersen
4 Kyle Money
5 Kevin Gross
6 Steve Jeltz
7 Jerry Keller
8 Len Matuszek
9 Kelly Downs
10 Ramon Aviles
11 Tim Corcoran
12 George Culver
13 John Felske
14 Chris Bourjos
15 Porfi Altamirano
16 Dick Davis
17 John Russell

18 Marty Decker
19 Charlie Hudson
20 Ed Miller
21 Ron Pruitt
22 Alejandro Sanchez
23 Stan Bahnsen
24 Larry Bradford
25 Kiko Garcia

1983 TCMA Quad City Cubs

(Chicago Cubs, A) (black and white)

	MT	NR MT	EX
Complete Set:	85.00	64.00	34.00

1 Roger Crow
2 Larry Cox
3 Dick Pole
4 Mario Panetta
5 David Barber, Kyle Benjamin

6 Mark Baker
7 Steve Balmer
8 Brad Blevins
9 Mitch Cook
10 Jeff Fruge
11 Rene German
12 Tim Grachen
13 Randy Lockie
14 Rudy Serafini
15 Brian Tuller
16 Steven Roadcap
17 Juan Velazquez
18 Jim Allen
19 Steve Cordner
20 Shawon Dunston
21 Gary Jones
22 Tony Woods
23 Jose Rivera
24 Stan Boderick
25 Damon Farmar
26 Dave Martinez
27 Rolando Roomes

1983 TCMA Reading Phillies

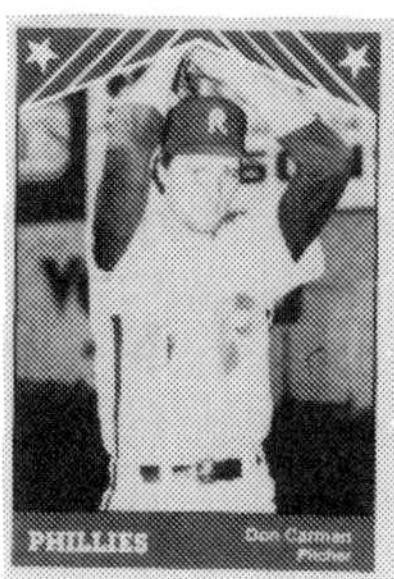

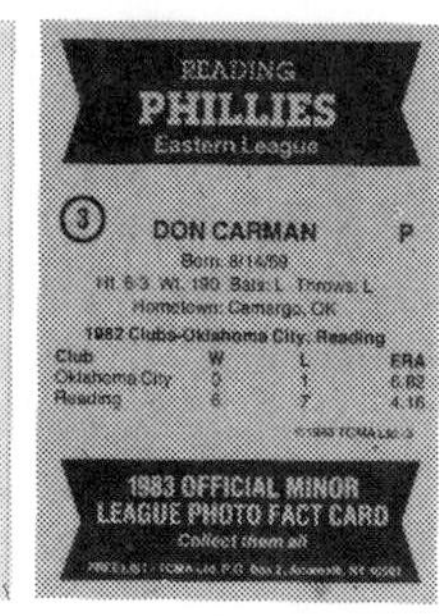

(Philadelphia Phillies, AA) (black and white)

	MT	NR MT	EX
Complete Set:	195.00	146.00	78.00

1 Bud Bartholow
2 Darren Burroughs
3 Don Carman
4 Jay Davisson
5 Rich Gaynor
6 Frankie Griffin
7 Bill Johnson
8 George Riley
9 Denny Thomas
10 Ed Wojna
11 Darren Daulton
12 Mike LaValliere
13 Den Dowell
14 Greg Legg
15 Francisco Melendez
16 Julio Perez
17 Juan Samuel
18 Willie Darkis
19 Randy Salava
20 Jeff Stone
21 Keith Washington
22 Mel Williams
23 Bill Dancy
24 Bob Tiefenauer

1983 TCMA Redwood Pioneers

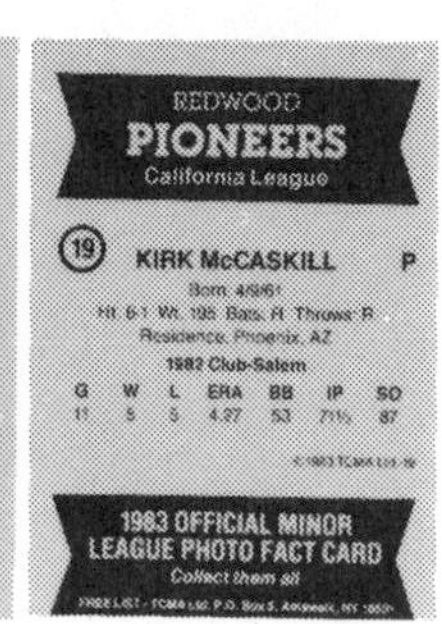

(California Angels, A) (color)

	MT	NR MT	EX
Complete Set:	17.00	12.75	7.00

1 Jeff Ahern
2 Ken Angulo
3 Kris Bankowski
4 Mark Bonner
5 Norman Carrasco
6 Dave Brady
7 T.R. Bryden
8 Kevin Davis
9 Steve Enkes
10 Lonnie Garza
11 Dennis Gilbert
12 Terry Harper
13 Lee Jones
14 Lance Junker
15 Tim Kammeyer
16 Greg Key
17 Tony Mack
18 Mike Madril
19 Kirk McCaskill
20 Scott Oliver
21 Kevin Price
22 Tom Rentschuler
23 Mark Smelko
24 Rick Turner
25 Bill Worden
26 Goldie Wright
27 Luis Zambrana
28 Don Rowe
29 Bernie Smith
30 Jack Lind
31 Mark Terrazas
32 Pioneer Pete (team mascot)

1983 TCMA Richmond Braves

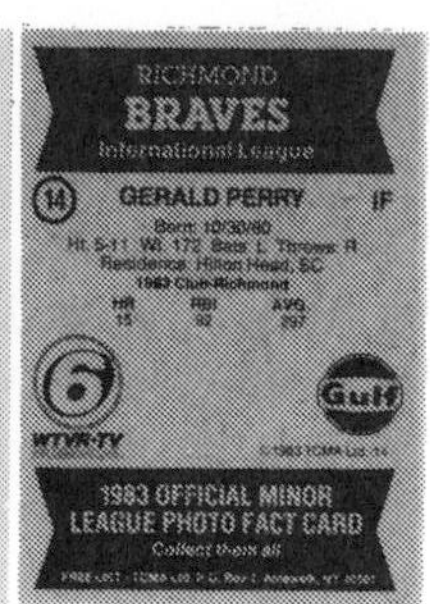

(Atlanta Braves, AAA) (color)

	MT	NR MT	EX
Complete Set:	22.50	16.75	9.25

1 Jose Alvarez
2 Tony Brizzolara
3 Joe Cowley
4 Ken Daley
5 Greg Field
6 Chuck Fore
7 Sam Ayoub
8 Gary Reiter
9 Augie Ruiz
10 Bob Walk
11 Matt Sinatro
12 Steve Swisher
13 Brook Jacoby
14 Gerald Perry
15 Chico Ruiz
16 Paul Runge
17 Paul Zuvella
18 Albert Hall
19 Brad Komminsk
20 Bob Porter
21 Leonel Vargas
22 Larry Whisenton
23 Eddie Haas
24 Craig Robinson
25 Johnny Sain

1983 TCMA Rochester Redwings

(Baltimore Orioles, AAA) (color)

	MT	NR MT	EX
Complete Set:	40.00	30.00	16.00

1 Lance Nichols
2 Mark Brown
3 John Flinn
4 Dave Ford
5 Craig Minetto
6 Dan Morogiello
7 Allan Ramirez
8 Mark Smith
9 Cliff Speck
10 Bill Swaggerty
11 Dave Huppert
12 Al Pardo
13 Floyd Rayford
14 Bob Bonner
15 Glenn Gulliver
16 Rick Jones
17 Dan Logan
18 John Valle
19 Elijah Bonaparte
20 Drungo Hazewood
21 Ric Lisi
22 Mike Young
23 Tom Chism
24 Richie Bancells
25 Mark Wiley

1983 TCMA St. Petersburg Cardinals

(St. Louis Cardinals, A) (black and white)

	MT	NR MT	EX
Complete Set:	30.00	22.00	12.00

1 Joseph Boever
2 Javier Carranza
3 Henry Carson
4 Danny Cox
5 Thomas Dozier
6 Thomas Epple
7 Michael Hartley
8 Robert Kish
9 John Martin
10 Christian Martinez
11 Mark Riggins
12 Freddie Silva
13 Scott Young
14 Randall Champion
15 Timothy Wallace
16 James Burns
17 Frank Garcia
18 Brad Luther
19 Deron Thomas
20 Francisco Batista
21 Robert Helsom
22 Richard James
23 Jose Rodriguez
24 Barry Sayler
25 Steve F. Turco
26 Stephen Turgion
27 Ralph Miller, Jr.
28 Karl Rogozenski
29 James Riggleman
30 Dave Link

1983 TCMA Salt Lake City Gulls

(Seattle Mariners, AAA) (color)

	MT	NR MT	EX
Complete Set:	22.50	16.75	9.25

1 Edwin Nunez
2 Jerry Gleaton
3 Robert Babcock
4 Brian Snyder
5 Karl Best
6 Brian Allard
7 Mike Moore
8 Rick Adair
9 Jed Murray

10 Joe Decker
11 Phil Bradley
12 Mark Woodmansee
13 Tito Nanni
14 Rod Allen
15 Bud Bulling
16 Jamie Nelson
17 Jim Maler
18 Bill Crone
19 John Moses
20 Glen Walker
21 Al Chambers
22 Harold Reynolds
23 Spike Owen
24 Bobby Floyd
25 Doug Merrifield
26a Manny Estrada
26b Manny Estrada

1983 TCMA Syracuse Chiefs

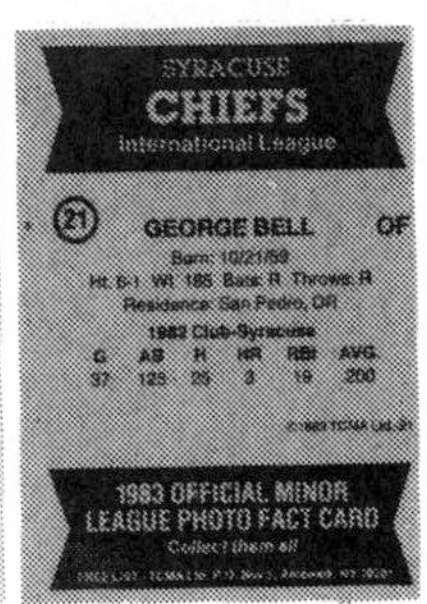

(Toronto Blue Jays, AAA) (color)

	MT	NR MT	EX
Complete Set:	52.50	39.25	21.50

1 Jim Beauchamp
2 Bernie Beckman
3 Tommy Craig
4 Jim Baker
5 Mark Bomback
6 Don Cooper
7 Mark Eichhorn
8 Dennis Howard
9 Tom Lukish
10 Colin McLaughlin
11 Jeff Schneider
12 Keith Walker
13 Matt Williams
14 Toby Hernandez
15 Geno Petralli
16 Tony Fernandez
17 Fred Manrique
18 Bob Nandin
19 Jeff Reynolds
20 Tim Thompson
21 George Bell
22 Anthony Johnson
23 Vern Ramie
24 Ron Shepherd
25 Mitch Webster
26 Bob Humphreys

1983 TCMA Tacoma Tigers

(Oakland A's, AAA) (color) (complete set price includes scarce cards of McKay, Moore, Perry, Retzer and Rodriguez)

	MT	NR MT	EX
Complete Set:	150.00	112.00	60.00

1 Keith Atherton
2 Bert Bradley
3 DeWayne Buice
4 Gorman Heimueller
5 Chuck Hensley
6 Jerome King
7 Russ McDonald
8 Curt Young
9 Daryl Cias
10 Bill Bathe
11 Donnie Hill
12 John Hotchkiss
13 Mike Woodard
14 Jim Bennett
15 Lynn Garrett
16 Dave Hudgens
17 Rusty McNealy
18 Bob Didier
19 Stan Naccarato
20 Jim Nettles
21 Dave Heaverlo
22 Larry Davis
23 Art Popham
24 Tigers Mascot
25a Bob Christofferson
25b Danny Goodwin
26 Scott Pyle
27 Dennis Sherow
28 Jeff Jones
29a Dave McKay
29b Rickey Peters
30a Jim Christiansen
30b Dave Rodriguez
31 Ed Retzer
32 Kelvin Moore
33 Shawn Perry

1983 TCMA Tampa Tarpons

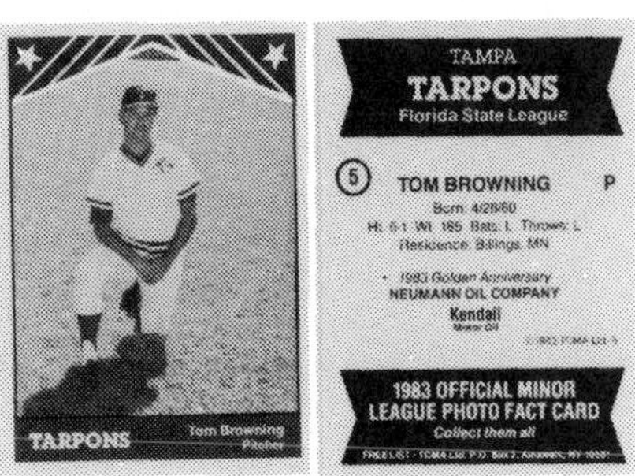

(Cincinnati Reds, A) (black and white) (complete sets usually include many miscut cards)

	MT	NR MT	EX
Complete Set:	45.00	33.50	18.00

1 Tony Burley
2 Virg Conley
3 L.C. Culver
4 Tony Evans
5 Tom Browning
7 Tim Dodd
8 Jason Felice
9 Adolfo Feliz
10 Fergy Ferguson
11 Jack Foley
12 Clem Freeman, Jr.
13 Orlando Gonzalez
14 Dave Hall
15 Ty Hubbard, III
16 Danny LaMar
17 Ted Langdon
18 Terrence McGriff
19 Paul O'Neil
20 Cressy Pratt
21 Kevin Steinmetz
22 Allen Swindle
23 Scott Terry
24 Tony Threatt
25 Steve Watson
26 Tracy Jones
27 Nick Fiorillo
28 Jim Hoff
29 Mike Sims
30 Bull Norman

1983 TCMA Tidewater Tides

(New York Mets, AAA) (color)

	MT	NR MT	EX
Complete Set:	90.00	67.50	37.00

1 Ron Darling
2 Mike Fitzgerald
3 Wally Backman
4 Clint Hurdle
5 Terry Leach
6 Mike Bishop
7 Kelvin Chapman

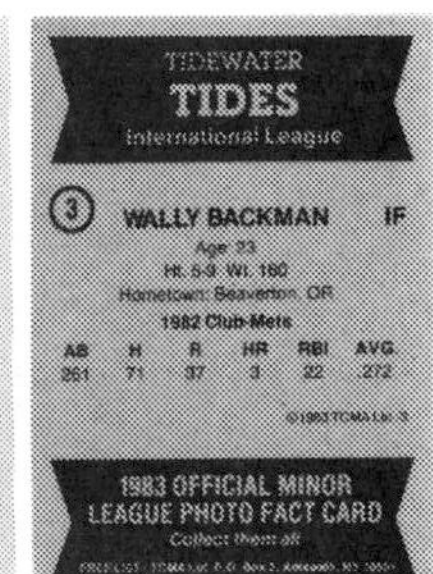

8 Gary Rajsich
9 Tim Leary
10 Steve Senteney
11 Tom Gorman
12 Walt Terrell
13 Jeff Bittiger
14 Scott Dye
15 Greg Biercevicz
16 Brent Gaff
17 Dan Schmitz
18 Mike Howard
19 Rusty Tillman
20 Ron Gardenhire
21 Marvell Wynne
22 Gil Flores
23 Davey Johnson
24 Al Jackson
25 Josh Wakana
26 Tucker Ashford
27 Bob Sikes
28 Darryl Strawberry
29 Jose Oquendo

1983 TCMA Toledo Mud Hens

(Minnesota Twins, AAA) (color) (complete set price includes scarce #'s 26-29)

	MT	NR MT	EX
Complete Set:	150.00	112.00	60.00

1 Paul Boris
2 Terry Felton
3 Kevin Flannery
4 Ed Hodge
5 Steve Korczyk
6 Jim Lewis
7 Jeff Little
8 Bob Mulligan
9 Ken Schrom
10 Mike Walters
11 Rick Austin
12 Stine Poole
13 Dave Baker
14 Greg Gagne
15 Houston Jimenez
16 Tim Teufel
17 Jesus Vega
18 Michael Wilson
19 Andre David
20 Mike Hart
21 Randy Johnson
22 Dave Meier
23 Cal Ermer
24 Tim Agan, Kevin Flannery
25 Scott Tellgren
26 Eric Broersma
27 Mike McCain
28 Bryan Oelkers
29 Jack O'Conner

1983 TCMA Tri-Cities Triplets

(Texas Rangers, A) (black and white)

	MT	NR MT	EX
Complete Set:	22.00	16.50	9.00

1 Bob Sebra
2 Steve Kordish
3 Bruce Kipper
4 Kerry Burns
5 Dennis Knight
6 Mark Cipres
7 John Munley
8 Robin Keathley
9 Nick Esposito

10 John Fryhoff
11 Dan Lindquist
12 Jim Allison
13 Bill Hance
14 Tony Carlucci
15 Reggie Mosley
16 Mark Gile
17 Ron Hansen
18 Mike Keehn
19 Vince Sakowski
20 Bert Martinez
21 Greg Bailey
22 Danny Simpson
23 Jim Cesario
24 Brendan Hennessy
25 Clint Curry
26 Dave Oliver
27 Gary Venner
28 Bob Bill

1983 TCMA Tucson Toros

(Houston Astros, AAA) (color)

	MT	NR MT	EX
Complete Set:	13.00	9.75	5.25

1 Ed Bonine
2 Dan Boone
3 Buster Keeton
4 Ron Mathis
5 Ron Meredith
6 Jeff Morris
7 Gordie Pladson
8 Bert Roberge
9 Bob Veselic
10 Sam Welborn
11 Julio Solano
12 Steve Christmas
13 Luis Pujols
14 Wes Clements
15 Greg Cypret
16 Jim Pankovits
17 Bert Pena
18 Cliff Wherry
19 Chris Jones
20 Larry Ray
21 Bob Pate
22 Scott Loucks
23 Matt Galante
24 Gary Tuck
25 Dave Labossiere
26 Ruben Robles

1983 TCMA Tulsa Drillers

(Texas Rangers, AA) (color)

	MT	NR MT	EX
Complete Set:	15.00	11.00	6.00

1 Jorge Gomez
2 Glen Cook
3 Tony Fossas
4 Rob Clark
5 Billy Taylor
6 Larry McLane
7 Daryl Smith
8 Dennis Long
9 Mitch Zwolensky
10 Tim Henry
11 Dwayne Henry
12 Kirk Killingsworth
13 Bob Brower
14 Chuckie Canady
15 Mike Rubel
16 John Buckley
17 Tracy Cowger
18 Steve Nielsen
19 Joe Nemeth
20 Jim Foit
21 Dan Murphy
22 Steve Buechele
23 Jerry Neufang
24 Terry Johnson
25 Marty Scott

1983 TCMA Vero Beach Dodgers

(Los Angeles Dodgers, A) (black and white)

	MT	NR MT	EX
Complete Set:	27.50	20.50	11.25

1 Mike Beuder
2 Tom Duffy
3 Rick Felt
4 Mike Gentle
5 Brian Innis
6 Charlie Jones
7 Vance Lovelace
8 Morris Madden
9 Rafael Montalvo
10 Bill Scudder
11 Chris Thomas
12 Rob Slezak
13 Luis Rivera
14 Steve Boncore
15 Bob Gilles
16 Mariano Duncan
17 John Gregory
18 Hector Guzman
19 Gary Newsom
20 Harold Perkins
21 Billy White
22 Ralph Bryant
23 Jerald Cain
24 Dan Cataline
25 Reggie Williams
26 John Shoemaker
27 Rob Giesecke
28 Stan Wasiak
29 Dennis Lewallyn

1983 TCMA Waterbury Reds

(Cincinnati Reds, AA) (black and white)

	MT	NR MT	EX
Complete Set:	115.00	86.25	47.50

1 Keefe Cato
2 Bryan Funk
3 Curt Heidenreich
4 Ken Jones
5 Bill Landrum
6 Jim Pettibone
7 Mark Rothey
8 Lester Straker
9 Lloyd McClendon
10 Dave Miley
11 Adolfo Feliz
12 Carlos Porte
13 Hector Rincones
14 Wade Rowdon
15 Eric Davis
16 Dexter Day
17 Leo Garcia
18 Ruben Guzman
19 Jim Lett

1983 Team Indianapolis Indians

(Cincinnati Reds, AAA) (co-sponsored by Tom Aikens)

	MT	NR MT	EX
Complete Set:	12.50	9.50	5.25

1 Indians Team
2 "Last Season We Won It All"
3 Roy Hartsfield
4 Charlie Leibrandt
5 Nick Esasky
6 Greg Harris
7 Dallas Williams
8 Joe Edelen
9 The Starters (Mike Dowless, Greg Harris, Charlie Leibrandt, Jeff Russell, Freddie Toliver)
10 Willie Lozado
11 Brian Ryder
12 Tom Lawless
13 The Bullpen (Bob Buchanan, Rich Carlucci, Joe Edelen, Brad Lesley, Brian Ryder)
14 Jeff Russell
15 Ray Corbett
16 Rich Carlucci
17 The Infielders (Skeeter Barnes, Nick Esasky, Glen Franklin, John Harris, Tom Lawless, Willie Lozado)
18 Orlando Isales
19 Freddie Toliver
20 Ron Little
21 The Catchers (Ray Corabett, Dave Van Gorder)
22 Mark Gilbert
23 Mike Dowless
24 Glen Franklin
25 The Outfielders (Mark Gilbert, Orlando Isales, Ron Little, Dallas Williams)
26 Brad Lesley
27 Dave Van Gorder
28 Bob Buchanan
29 John Harris
30 The Instructors (Ted Kluszewski, Fred Norman)
31 Skeeter Barnes
32 Lee Garrett

1983 Team Nashville Sounds

(New York Yankees, AA)

	MT	NR MT	EX
Complete Set:	14.00	10.50	5.75

(1) Scott Bradley
(2) Mike Browning
(3) Tim Burke
(4) Ben Callahan
(5) Pete Dalena
(6) Matt Gallegos
(7) Paul Grayner
(8) Doug Holmquist
(9) Frank Kneuer
(10) Tim Knight
(11) Vic Mata
(12) Derwin Mc Nealy
(13) Ed Olwine
(14) Mike Pagliarulo
(15) Scott Patterson
(16) Erik Peterson
(17) Mike Reddish
(18) Jim Saul
(19) Kelly Scott
(20) Mark Shifflett
(21) Buck Showalter
(22) Mark Silva
(23) Keith Smith
(24) Dave Szymczak
(25) Hoyt Wilhelm

1983 Tony Kelly Kinston Blue Jays

(Toronto Blue Jays, A)

	MT	NR MT	EX
Complete Set:	125.00	93.75	51.50

(1) Jim Bishop
(2) J.J. Cannon
(3) Ron Clark
(4) Scot Elam
(5) Jose Escobar
(6) Keith Gilliam
(7) Devallon Harper
(8) Moe Hazelette
(9) Ken Kinnard
(10) Chris Knapp
(11) Tom Layton
(12) Tom Layton
(13) Perry Lychak
(14) Peery Mader
(15) Alex Marte
(16) Mark Poole
(17) Joe Pursell
(18) Steve Reish
(19) Derrick Reutter
(20) Ralph Rivas
(21) Tim Rodgers
(22) Randy Romagna
(23) Eddie Santos
(24) Jay Schroeder
(25) Mike Sharperson
(26) Rico Sutton
(27) Bernie Tatis
(28) Guillermo Valenzuela
(29) Dave Wells

1984

1984 Chong Modesto A's

(Oakland A's, A)

	MT	NR MT	EX
Complete Set:	175.00	131.25	72.00

1 Eric Barry
2 Mark Bauer
3 Paul Bradley
4 Greg Cadaret
5 Jose Canseco

6 Chip Conklin
7 Ron Cummings
8 Rocky Coyle
9 Oscar De Chavez
10 Brian Dorsett
11 Mark Ferguson
12 Eric Garret
13 Mike Gorman
14 Juan Cruz
15 Brian Guinn
16 Stan Hilton
17 Joe Law
18 Dave Leiper
19 Tony Moncrief
20 Doug Scherer
21 Keith Thrower
22 Jose Tolentino
23 George Mitterwald
24 Jeff Kobernus
25 Mark Doberenz
26 Dan Kiser
27 Dave Fry
28 Tom Zmudosky

1984 Cramer Albuquerque Dukes

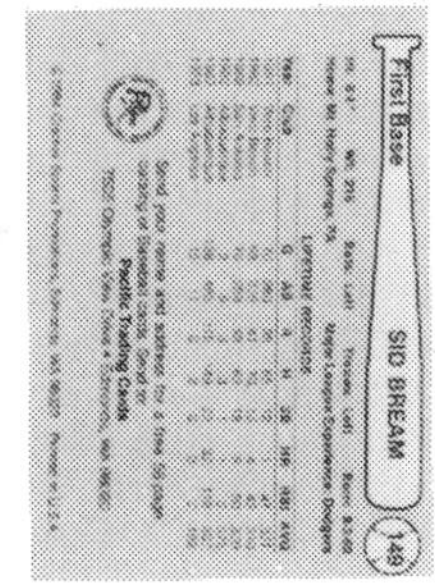

(Los Angeles Dodgers, AAA)

	MT	NR MT	EX
Complete Set:	10.00	7.50	4.00

146 Jack Fimple
147 Rich Rodas
148 R.J. Reynolds
149 Sid Bream
150 Lemmie Miller
151 Franklin Stubbs
152 Dave Sax
153 Alex Taveras
154 Steve Perry
155 Don Smith
156 Robbie Allen
157 Greg Schultz
158 Larry White
159 Ernesto Borbon
160 Dean Rennicke
161 Tony Brewer
162 Larry See
163 Ed Amelung
164 John Debus
165 Ken Howell
166 Roberto Alexander
167 Terry Collins
168 Brian Holton
169 Dick McLaughlin
245 Dave Wallace
246 Mark Sheehy

1984 Cramer Edmonton Trappers

(California Angels, AAA) (color)

	MT	NR MT	EX
Complete Set:	7.00	5.25	2.75

97 Moose Stubing
98 Tim Krauss
99 Angel Moreno
100 Marty Kain
101 Sap Randall
102 Rick Steirer
103 Dave W. Smith
104 Rick Adams
105 Craig Gerber
106 Steve Finch
107 Steve Liddle
108 Chris Clark
109 Darrell Miller
110 Bill Mooneyham
111 Doug Corbett
112 Steve Lubratich
113 Stu Cliburn
114 Mike Browning
115 Joe Simpson
116 Reggie West
117 Mike Brown
118 Pat Keedy
119 Jay Kibbe
120 Ed Ott
242 Frank Reberger
249 Steve Lubratich

1984 Cramer Everett Giants

(San Francisco Giants, Rookie) (black and white)

	MT	NR MT	EX
Complete Set:	7.00	5.25	2.75

1 Greg Litton
2 Lyle Swepson
3a Mike Cicione
3b Darin James
4 Joe Olker
5 Harry Davis
6 Greg Gilbert
7 Kent Cooper
8 Steve Cottrell
9 Kevin Woodhouse
10 Keith Silver
11 Dave Hornsby
12 Stuart Tate
13 Rob Cosby
14 Sixto Martes
15 Rod Rush
16 Dave Hinnrichs
17 Francisco Echevarria
18 Chris Stangel
19 Paul Blair
20 Terry Mulholland
21 T.J. McDonald
22 Brad Porter
23 Francis Calzado
24 Jim Wasem
25 John Grimes
26 Todd Moriaty
27a John Ackerman
27b Tony Perezchica
28 Rocky Bridges
29 Tom Wetzel
30 Tom Messier

1984 Cramer Hawaii Islanders

(Pittsburgh Pirates, AAA) (color)

	MT	NR MT	EX
Complete Set:	7.50	5.50	3.00

121 Al Pulido
122 Jeff Zaske
123 Kelly Paris
124 Larry Lamonde
125 Paul Semall
126 Dave Tomlin
127 Lorenzo Bundy
128 Ron Wotus
129 Ray Krawczyk
130 Denny Gonzales
131 Mike Bielecki
132 Stan Cliburn
133 Nelson Norman
134 Chuck Hartenstein
135 Mike Howard
136 Bob Miscik
137 Tom Sandt
138 Jim Winn
139 Trench Davis
140 Tim Wheeler
141 Bob Walk
142 Steve Herz
143 Carlos Ledezma
144 Benny Distefano
145 John Malkin

1984 Cramer Las Vegas Stars

(San Diego Padres, AAA) (color) This set is numbered as they appear on the backs of the cards.

	MT	NR MT	EX
Complete Set:	17.50	13.00	7.00

218 Greg Booker
219 Ray Hayward
220 Joe Lansford
221 Bob Patterson
222 Jerry Davis
223 Jerry DeSimone
224 Fritz Connally
225 Bruce Bochy
226 Marty Decker
227 Mike Martin
228 John Kruk
229 Walt Vanderbush
230 Rick Lancellotti
231 Ed Wojna
232 Tom House
233 Felix Oroz
234 George Hinshaw
235 Darren Burroughs
236 Ozzie Guillen
237 Ron Roenicke
238 Larry Brown
239 Bob Cluck
240 Ed Rodriguez
244 Larry Duensing
250 John Kruk

Definitions for grading conditions are located in the Introduction of this price guide.

1984 Cramer Phoenix Giants

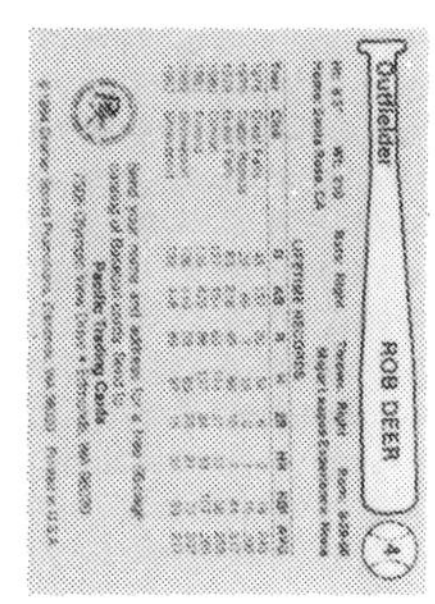

(San Francisco Giants, AAA) (color)

	MT	NR MT	EX
Complete Set:	12.00	9.00	4.75

1 Phil Oullette
2 Mark Calvert
3 Mark Grant
4 Rob Deer
5 Scott Garrelts
6 Rich Murray
7 Mark Schuster
8 Alejandro Sanchez
9 Jim Farr
10 Herman Segelke
11 Tom O'Malley
12 Jeff Cornell
13 Joe Pettini
14 Tip Lefebvre
15 Brian Kingman
16 Alan Fowlkes
17 Dan Gladden
18 Randy Kutcher
19 Jeff Blobaum
20 Randy Gomez
21 Colin Ward
22 Guy Sularz
23 Chris Brown
24 Jack Mull
241 Tim Blackwell

1984 Cramer Portland Beavers

(Philadelphia Phillies, AAA) (color) (co-sponsored by Coca-Cola)

	MT	NR MT	EX
Complete Set:	12.00	9.00	4.75

195 Dave Wehrmeister
196 Stephen Mura
197 Jeff Stone
198 Darren Daulton
199 Francisco Melendez
200 Lee Elia
201 Kelly Downs
202 Bobby Mitchell
203 Randy Salava
204 Don Carman
205 Steve Jeltz
206 George Riley
207 Jose Calderon
208 John Russell
209 Rick Schu
210 Ken Dowell
211 Willie Darkis
212 Richard Gaynor
213 Jay Davisson
214 Steve Fireovid
215 George Culver
216 Russ Hamric

1984 Cramer Salt Lake City Gulls

(Seattle Mariners, AAA) (color) (co-sponsored by Pennzoil)

	MT	NR MT	EX
Complete Set:	22.00	16.50	8.75

170 Danny Tartabull
171 Brian Allard
172 Bill Crone
173 Ivan Calderon
174 Tito Nanni
175 Dave Geisel
176 Dave Valle
177 Jed Murray
178 Brian Snyder
179 Robert Long
180 Jim Lewis
181 Bill Nahorodny
182 Jamie Allen
183 Edwin Nunez
184 Jim Presley
185 Harold Reynolds
186 Jerry Gleaton
187 Glen Walker
188 Al Chambers
189 Karl Best
190 Darnell Coles

191 Bobby Floyd
192 Bobby Cuellar
193 Brad Boylan

1984 Cramer Tacoma Tigers

(Oakland A's, AAA) (color) This set is numbered as it appears on the backs of the cards.

	MT	NR MT	EX
Complete Set:	7.00	5.25	2.75

73 Bruce Robinson
74 Dave Hudgens
75 Ron Arnold
76 Ramon de los Santos
77 Tom Romano
78 Steve Kiefer
79 Carlos Lezcano
80 Bill Bathe
81 Mike Gallego
82 Jeff Jones
83 Steve Ontiveros
84 Bill Krueger
85 Curt Young
86 Chuck Hensley
87 Tim Pyznarski
88 Phil Stephenson
89 Mark Wagner
90 Ed Nottle
91 Danny Goodwin
92 Bert Bradley
93 John Hotchkiss
94 Dave Ford
95 Gorman Heimueller
96 Dan Meyer
247 Ed Farmer

1984 Cramer Tucson Toros

(Houston Astros, AAA) (color) This set is numbered as it appears on the backs of the cards.

	MT	NR MT	EX
Complete Set:	15.00	11.25	6.00

49 Eric Rasmussen
50 Matt Galante
51 Jose Alvarez
52 Chris Jones
53 Wes Clements
54 Greg Cypert
55 Dwight Bernard
56 Rex Jones
57 Tim Tolman
58 Jaime Williams
59 Manny Hernandez
60 Tye Waller
61 Jim Pankovits
62 Glenn Davis
63 Julio Solano
64 Eddie Bonine
65 Jeff Heathcock
66 Ruben Robles
67 Bert Pena
68 Mark Ross
69 Craig Minetto
70 Larry Ray
71 Luis Pujols
72 Ron Mathis
248 Gary Tuck

1984 Cramer Vancouver Canadians

(Milwaukee Brewers, AAA) (color) (co-sponsored by Orange Crush)

	MT	NR MT	EX
Complete Set:	7.00	5.25	2.75

25 Ron Koenigsfeld
26 Andy Beene
27 Tony Muser
28 Doug Loman
29 Dan Davidsmeier
30 Ray Searage
31 Kelvin Moore
32 Tom Candiotti
33 Frankie Thomas
34 Carlos Ponce
35 Earnie Riles
36 Dan Boone
37 Dave Huppert
38 Hoskin Powell
39 Doug Jones
40 Bob Gibson
41 Eric Peyton
42 Scott Roberts
43 Jamie Nelson
44 Ed Irvine
45 Jim Koontz
46 Mike Anderson
47 Marshall Edwards
48 Jack Lazorko
243 Don Rowe

Definitions for grading conditions are located in the Introduction of this price guide.

1984 1st Base Sports Shreveport Captains

(No affiliation, AA)

	MT	NR MT	EX
Complete Set:	15.00	11.25	6.00

(1) Kevin Bates
(2) Orlando Blackwell
(3) Randy Bockus
(4) Steve Cline
(5) Larry Crews
(6) Bob Cumming
(7) Duane Espy
(8) Bob Gendron
(9) Mike Jones
(10) Chuck Lusted
(11) Kurt Mattson
(12) Bobby Moore
(13) Randy Morse
(14) Matt Nokes
(15) Bob O'Connor
(16) Jessie Reid
(17) Kernan Ronan
(18) Steve Smith
(19) Bryan Snyder
(20) Van Sowards
(21) Steve Stanicek
(22) John Stevenson
(23) Kelvin Torve
(24) Dave Wilhelmi

1984 Forestry Jackson Mets

(New York Mets, AA) (3" x 4") This set lists the major league team each player signed with.

	MT	NR MT	EX
Complete Set:	75.00	56.00	30.00

(1) Neil Allen (Cardinals)
(2) Wally Backman (Mets)
(3) Hubie Brooks (Mets)
(4) Jody Davis (Cubs)
(5) Brian Giles (Mets)
(6) Tim Leary (Mets)
(7) Lee Mazzilli (Pirates)
(8) Jesse Orosco (Mets)
(9) Jeff Reardon (Expos)
(10) Doug Sisk (Mets)
(11) Darryl Strawberry (Mets)
(12) Mookie Wilson (Mets)
(13) Marvel Wynne (Pirates)
(14) Ned Yost (Rangers)
(15) Davey Johnson (Mets)

1984 Pizza Hut Greenville Braves

	MT	NR MT	EX
Complete Set:	50.00	37.50	20.50

David Clay
1 Mike Cole
2 Freddie Tiburcio
5 Carlos Rios
6 Joe Johnson
9 Steve Chmil
10 Marty Clary
11 Randy Ingle
12 Glen Bockhorn
14 Augie Ruiz
15 Matt Sinatro
16 Rich Leggett
18 Matt West
19 Doc Estes
20 Bobby Dews
22 Steve Curry
23 Roy North
24 Tommy Thompson
25 Inocencio Guerrero
26 Bob Luzon
27 Leo Mazzone, Duane Ward
28 Tim Cole
29 Mike Bormann
30 Andre Treadway

1984 Riley's Louisville Redbirds

(St. Louis Cardinals, AAA)

	MT	NR MT	EX
Complete Set:	17.00	12.75	7.00

1 Jim Fregosi
2 Gaylen Pitts
3 Jerry Mc Kune
4 Dyar Miller
5 Gene Roof
6 Gary Rajsich
7 Doyle Harris
8 Tom Nieto
9 Dave Von Ohlen
10 Jed Smith
11 Kevin Hagen
12 Rod Booker
13 Jose Gonazlez
14 Bill LyONs
15 Terry Pendleton
16 Ralph Citarella
17 Kurt Kenshire
18 Vic Harris
19 Jim Aducci
20 Vince Coleman
21 Jack Ayer
22 Jeff Keener
23 Rick Ownbey
24 Terry Clark
25 Steve Baker
26 Jerry Johnson
27 Mark Salas
28 Mickey Mahler
29 Dave Kable
30 Dennis Werth

1984 Rock's Dugout Wichita Aeros

(Montreal Expos, AAA)

	MT	NR MT	EX
Complete Set:	75.00	56.00	30.00

Checklist
1 Charlie Puleo
2 Dave Miley
3 Hector Rincones
4 Leo Garcia
5 Tom Browning
6 Charlie Nail
7 Wayne Krenchicki
8 Ron Robinson
9 Curt Heidenrich
10 Dave Van Gorder
11 Tom Runnells
12 Mark Gilbert
13 Terry Bogener
14 Keefe Cato
15 Eric Davis
16 Skeeter Barner
17 Bill Landrum
18 Alan Knicely
19 John Franco
20 Fred Toliver
21 Wade Rowdon
22 Gene Dusan

1984 T&J SC Madison Muskies

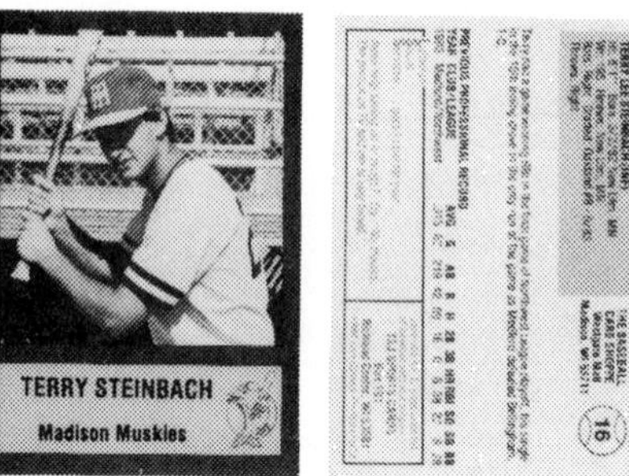

(Oakland A's, A) (black and white)

	MT	NR MT	EX
Complete Set:	20.00	15.00	8.00

1 Darrel Akerfelds
2 Larry Beardman
3 Rich Borowski
4 Maurice Castain
5 Kevin Coughlon
6 Mike Fulmer
7 Eric Garrett
8 Wayne Giddings
9 Shawn Gill
10 Dennis Gonsalves
11 Darel Hansen
12 Jim Jones
13 Bob Loscalzo
14 John Marquardt
15 Rob Nelson
16 Terry Steinbach
17 Tim Belcher
18 Al Heath
19 Luis Polonia
20 Joe Odom
21 Scotty Lee Whaley
22 Mike Wilder
23 Dave Schober
24 Gary Lance
25 Brad Fischer

1984 TCMA Albany-Colonie A'S

(Oakland A's, AA) (color)

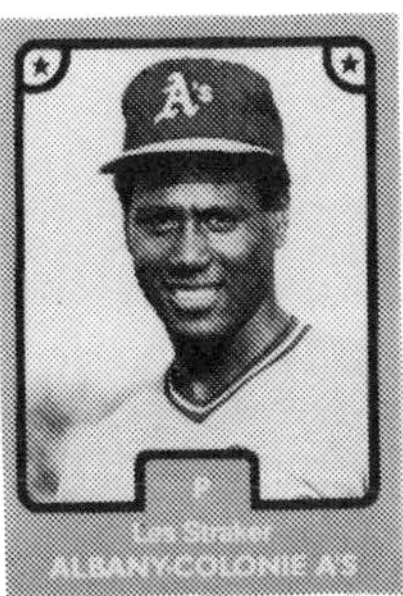

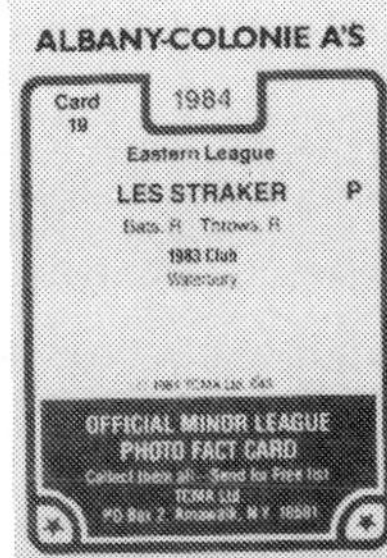

	MT	NR MT	EX
Complete Set:	17.50	13.00	7.00

1 Jim Bennett
2 Ron Arnold
3 Gene Gentile
4 Rodney Hobbs
5 Thad Reece
6 Brian Graham
7 Keith Lieppman
8 Rick Tronerud
9 Brian Thorson
10 John Liburdi
11 Tom Dozier
12 Todd Fischer
13 Bob Hallas
14 Pete Kendrick
15 Stan Kyles
16 Erik Bernard
17 Tim Lambert
18 Ed Myers
19 Les Straker
20 Tom Zmudosky
21 Mike Ashman
22 Mickey Tettleton
23 Bob Bathe
24 Jim Eppard
25 Greg Robles
26 Ray Thoma

1984 TCMA Arkansas Travelers

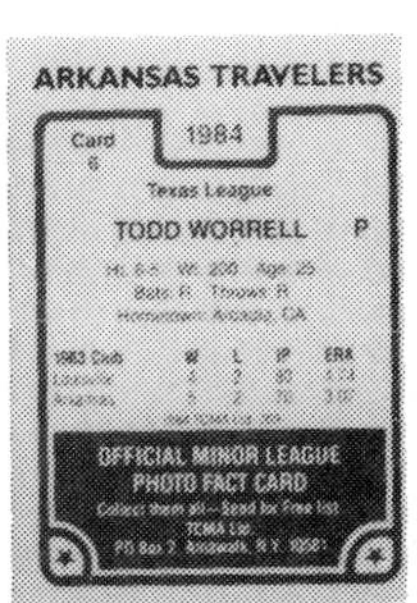

(St. Louis Cardinals, AA) (color)

	MT	NR MT	EX
Complete Set:	20.00	15.00	8.00

1 Eddie Tanner
2 Dave Clements
3 Dan Stryffeler
4 Deron Thomas
5 Tim Wallace
6 Todd Worrell
7 Bob Helson
8 Al Morlock
9 Larry Reynolds
10 Greg Guin
11 Bob Geren
12 John Adams
13 Mark Schulte
14 Dave Bialas
15 Willie Hardwick
16 Curt Ford
17 John Martin
18 Pat Perry
19 Marty Mason
20 Joe Silkwood
21 Gotay Mills
22 John Young
23 Pete Stoll
24 Walt Pierce
25 Andy Hassler
26 Mike Harris

1984 TCMA Beaumont Golden Gators

(San Diego Padres, AA) (color)

	MT	NR MT	EX
Complete Set:	12.00	9.00	5.00

1 Jimmy Jones
2 Pete Kutsukos
3 James Steels
4 Al Newman

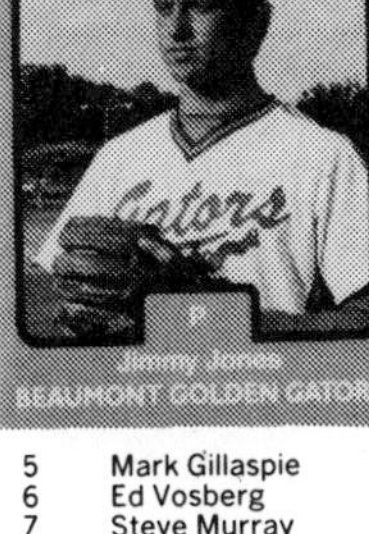

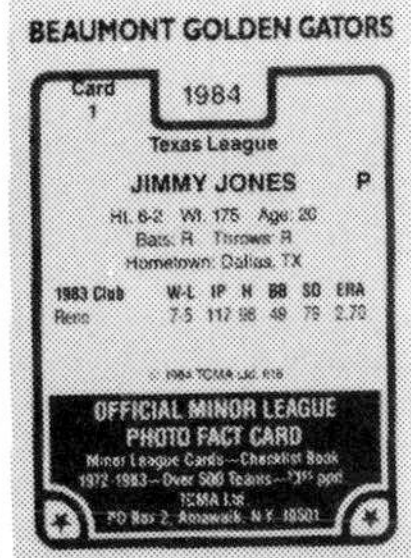

5 Mark Gillaspie
6 Ed Vosberg
7 Steve Murray
8 Mark Parent
9 Gene Walter
10 Kevin Towers
11 Bill Long
12 Tim Cook
13 Steve Schefsky
14 Jim Leopold
15 Jimmy Thomas
16 Pat Casey
17 Mark Wasinger
18 Steve Garcia
19 Jerry Johnson
20 Steve Johnson
21 Bobby Tolan
22 Chuck Kolotka
23 Todd Hutcheson
24 Ray Etchebarren
25 Jeff Ronk

1984 TCMA Buffalo Bisons

(Cleveland Indians, AA) (color)

	MT	NR MT	EX
Complete Set:	12.00	9.00	5.00

1 Jeff Moronko
2 George Cecchetti
3 Tim Glass
4 "Junior" Naboa
5 Rene Quinones
6 Doug Simonic
7 Andy allanson
8 Jose Roman
9 Jay Baller
10 Alec McCullock
11 Rich Doyle
12 Rich Thompson
13 Dave Szymczak
14 John Bohnet
15 Andy Ortiz
16 Ramon Romero
17 Steve Mardsen
18 Jack Aker
19 Ed Aponte
20 Randy Washington
21 Don Carter
22 Ed Saavedra
23 Poolie Bernstine
24 Robin Fuson
25 Doug Helmquist

1984 TCMA Butte Copper Kings

(Seattle Mariners, A) (color)

	MT	NR MT	EX
Complete Set:	17.00	12.50	6.75

1 Manny Estrada
2 John Anderson
3 James Bowden
4 Dan Clark
5 Mike Wood
6 Tom Osowski
7 Carl Moesche
8 Greg Brinkman
9 Tony Diaz
10 Charlie Fonville
11 Steve French
12 Richard Hayden
13 Brad Kinney
14 Dan Larson
15 Mark Machalec
16 Rafael Matos
17 Pablo Monceratt
18 Arvid Morfin
19 Kevin Ochs
20 Bill O'Leary
21 Bregg Ray
22 Paul Steinert
23 Gregg Thienpont
24 George Uribe
25 Nestor Valiente
26 Lazaro Vilella
27 Logan White

Definitions for grading conditions are located in the Introduction of this price guide.

1984 TCMA Cedar Rapids Reds

(Cincinnati Reds, A) (color)

	MT	NR MT	EX
Complete Set:	25.00	18.50	10.00

1 Robbie Phillips
2 Ted Langdon
3 Jim Pettibone
4 Doug Barba
5 Paul Kirsch
6 Brian Funk
7 Hugh Kemp
8 Virgil Conley
9 Mike Konderla
10 Jordan Berge
11 Tim Dodd
12 Jim Lett
13 Dexter Day
14 Joe Oliver
15 Tom Riley
16 Lanell Culver
17 Kurt Stillwell
18 Danny LaMar
19 Don Buchheister
20 ronnie Giddens
21 Mike Manfre
22 Scott Loseke
23 Rod Lich
24 Mike Dowless
25 Lenny Harris
26 Gary Denbo
27 Ron Henika
28 Dave Haberle

1984 TCMA Charlotte O'S

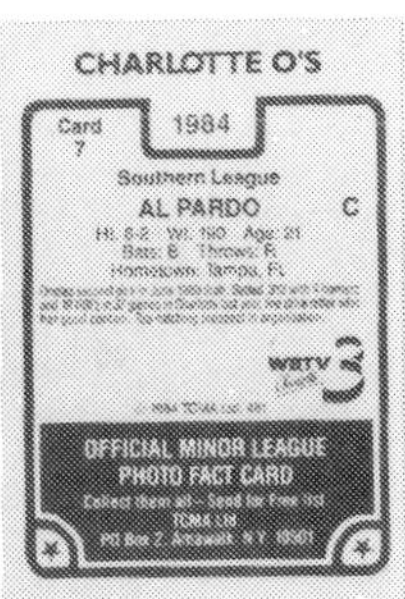

(Baltimore Orioles, AA) (color)

	MT	NR MT	EX
Complete Set:	12.50	9.50	5.25

1 Bob Hice
2 Terry Mauney
3 Charlie Frederick
4 Ronni Salcedo
5 Paul Cameron
6 Carlos Concepcion
7 Al Pardo
8 Jeff Kenaga
9 Peter Torrez
10 Grady Little
11 Chris Willsher
12 Bobby Mariano
13 Pat Dumouchelle
14 Jamie Reed
15 Bob Konopa
16 Dave Falcone
17 Kenny Dixon
18 Jeff Gilbert
19 Jesus Alfaro
20 Jeff Williams
21 Paul Bard
22 Ken Gerhart
23 Kurt Leiter
24 John Tutt
25 Jeff Summers
26 Tony Arnold
27 Herbie Oliveras

NOTE: A card number in parentheses ( ) indicates the set is unnumbered.

1984 TCMA Chattanooga Lookouts

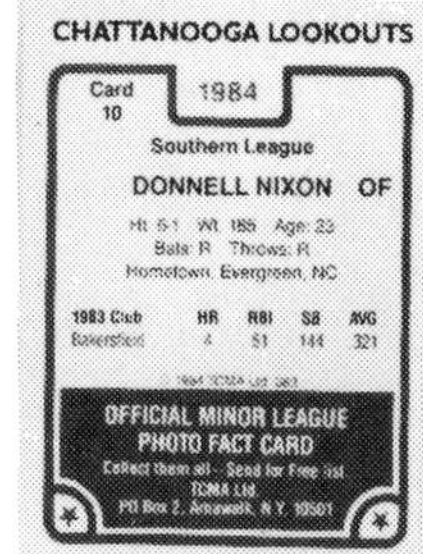

(Seattle Mariners, AA) (color)

	MT	NR MT	EX
Complete Set:	14.00	10.50	5.75

1a Mike Evans
1b Kevin King
2 Ramon Estepa
3 Dan Hanggie
4 Brick Smith
5 Ed Holtz
6 Clark Crist
7 Ross Grimsley
8 Bill Plummer
9 Tom Hunt
10 Donnell Nixon (Donell)
11 John Semprini
12 Paul Serna
13 Mike Johnson
14 Harry Landreth
15 Lee Guetterman
16 Joe Whitmer
18 Rick Luecken
19 Tom Rowe
20 A.J. Hill
21 Randy Ramirez
22 Ric Wilson
23 Rick Adair
24 John Moses
25 Mario Diaz
26 Mickey Brantley
27 Don Clay Hill
28 Jeff McDonald
29 Greg Bartley

1984 TCMA Columbus Clippers

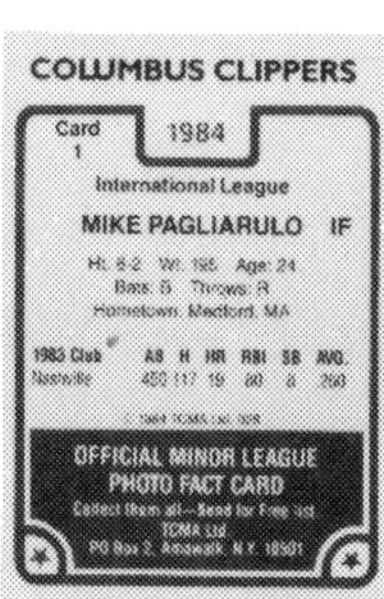

(New York Yankees, AAA) (color)

	MT	NR MT	EX
Complete Set:	25.00	18.50	10.00

1 Mike Pagliarulo
2 Kelly Heath
3 Pat rooney
4 Brian Dayett
5 Dan Briggs
6 Don Fowler
7 George Cappuzzello
8 Rex Hudler
9 Andre Robertson
10 Victor Mata
11 Scott Bradley
12 Clay Christianson
13 Joe Cowley
14 Scott Patterson
15 Curt Brown
16 Butch Hobson
17 Don Cooper
18 Pete Dalena
19 Kelly Scott
20 Mike O'Berry
21 Coach, Trainer, & Manager
22 Matt Winters
23 Stump Merrill
24 George Sisler, Jr.
25 Dennis Rasmussen

1984 TCMA Durham Bulls

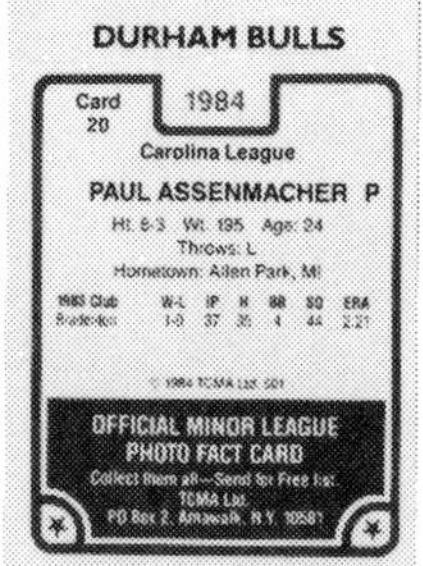

(Atlanta Braves, A) (color)

	MT	NR MT	EX
Complete Set:	16.00	12.00	6.50

1 Simon Rosario
2 Mark Lance
3 Mike Yastrzemski
4 Pat Hodge
5 Johnny Hatcher
6 Terry Cormack
7 Jeff Wagner
8 Dave Griffin
9 Leo Mazzone
10 Tim Alexander
11 Rafael Barbosa
12 Bob Tumpane
13 Chip Childress
14 Andres Thomas
15 Mike Knox
16 Tony Neuendorff
17 Scott Hood
18 Rich Leggatt
19 Todd Lamb
20 Paul Assenmacher
21 Paul Josephson
22 Jose Cano
23 Steve Ziem
24 John Mortillaro
25 Brian Aviles
26 Jim Rivera
27 Marty Schreiber
28 Brian Snitker
29 Randy Ingle
30 Sonny Jackson

1984 TCMA El Paso Diablos

(Milwaukee Brewers, AA) (color)

	MT	NR MT	EX
Complete Set:	25.00	18.50	10.00

1 Mark Effrig
2 Johnson Wood
3 Bob Schroeck
4 Steve Michael
5 Bryan Clutterbuck
6 Chuck Grim
7 Doug Jones
8 Mike Villegas
9 Mike Samuel
10 Tim Crews
11 Bryan Duquette
12 Terry Bevington
13 Kelvin Moore
14 STan Davis
15 Ted Higuera
16 Juan Castillo
17 Dan Plante
18 Dave Klipstein
19 Alan Cartwright
20 Paul Hartzell
21 Joe Morales
22 Cam Walker
23 Mike Felder
24 Dale Sveum
25 Garrett Nago

1984 TCMA Evansville Triplets

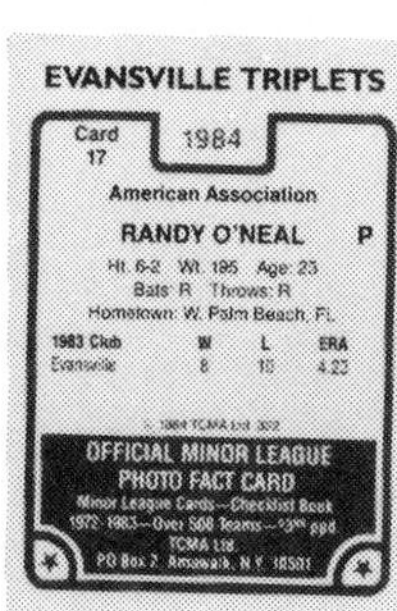

(Detroit Tigers, AAA) (color)

	MT	NR MT	EX
Complete Set:	11.00	8.25	4.50

1 Juan Lopez
2 Howard Bailey
3 Rondal Rollin
4 Gordon McKenzie
5 Pat Larkin
6 Mark Dacko
7 Stan Younger
8 Dave Gumpert
9 Nelson Simmons
10 Len Faedo
11 Bob Melvin
12 Dallas Williams
13 Doug Baker
14 Scotty Earl
15 John Harris
16 Mike Laga
17 Randy O'Neal
18 Jeff Conner
19 Don Heinkel
20 Bill Armstrong
21 Roger Mason
22 Carl Willis

1984 TCMA Greensboro Hornets

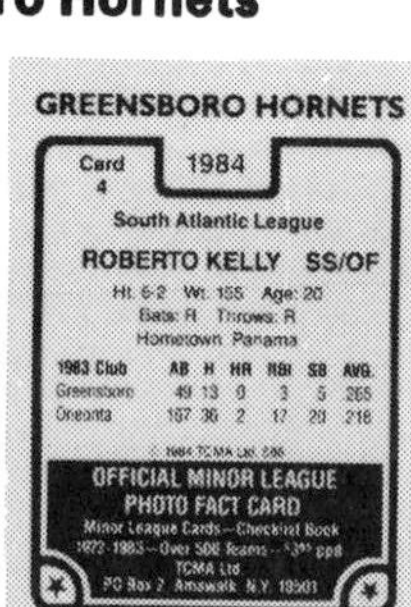

(New York Yankees, A) (color)

	MT	NR MT	EX
Complete Set:	27.50	20.50	11.25

1 Carlos Tosca
2 Ray Fortaleza
3 Brad Winler
4 Roberto Kelly
5 Jeff Horne
6 Fredi Gonzalez
7 Nattie George
8 Joey MacKay
9 Doug Carpenter
10 Brad Arnsberg
11 Chris Fedor
12 Bill Bulton
13 Dave Smalley
14 Tim Williams
15 Chuck Mathison
16 Eric Parent
17 Ricky Torres
18 Steve George
19 Mark Ferguson
20 Jonis Rodriguez
21 Bob Devlin
22 Moe Ching
23 Pedro Medina
24 Rich Mattocks
25 Mitch Seoane
26 Bill Englehart

1984 TCMA Iowa Cubs

(Chicago Cubs, AA) (color)

	MT	NR MT	EX
Complete Set:	42.50	31.75	17.50

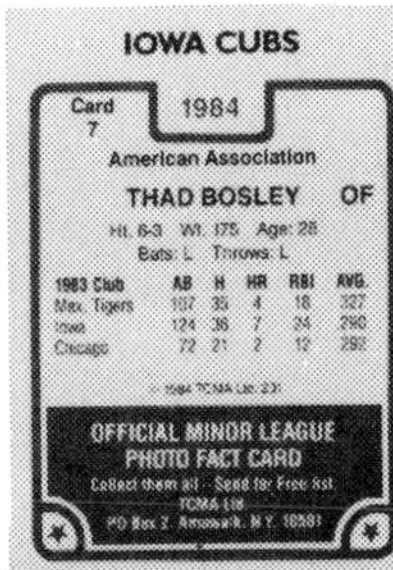

1 Ken Pryce
2 Bill Earley
3 Cubby (team mascot)
4 Dick Easter
5 Ken Grandquist
6 Jon Perlman
7 Thad Bosley
8 Don Rohn
9 Joe Hicks
10 B. Holden, F. Macy
11 Jim Napier
12 Pete Mackanin
13 S. Bernabe, M. Schimming
14 Trey Brooks
15 Bill Hayes
16 Don Werner
17 Tom Lombarski
18 Dave Owen
19 B. Bielenberg, C. McCullough
20 Gil Carlos
21 Dick Cummings
22 Don Schulze
23 Porfirio Altamirano
24 Billy Hatcher
25 Joe Carter
27 Ron Meredith
28 Tom Filer
29 Bill Johnson
30 Tom Grant
31 Reggie Patterson
--- Derek Botelho

1984 TCMA Jackson Mets

(New York Mets, AA) (color)

	MT	NR MT	EX
Complete Set:	42.50	31.75	17.50

1 DeWayne Vaughn
2 Rick Myles
3 Mark Lockenmeyer
4 Calvin Schiraldi
5 Reggie Jackson
6 Jeff Innis
7 Bill Fultz
8 Joe Graves
9 Jeff Bettendorf
10 Greg Pavlick
11 Staff (B. Hetrick, S. Massengale, R. Rainer)
12 Bill Max
15 Floyd Youmans
16 Sam Perlozzo
17 Billy Beane
18 Lenny Dykstra
19 Daryl Denby
20 Mark Carreon
21 Dave Cochran
22 Steve Springer
23 Al Pedrique
24 Fermin Ubri
25 Randy Milligan
--- Ed Hearn
--- Greg Olson

1984 TCMA Little Falls Mets

(New York Mets, A) (color)

	MT	NR MT	EX
Complete Set:	30.00	22.00	12.00

1 Will Stiles
2 Keith Belcik
3 Mike Westbrook
4 Scott Little
5 Chuck Friedel
6 Ralph Adams
7 Jeff Karr
8 Ray Pereira
9 Keith Traylor
10 Shane Young
11 Owen Moreland, III
12 Jeff Howes
13 Bud Harrelson
14 Terence Johnson
15 Craig Kiley
16 Jeff Ciszkowski
17 Hector Perez
18 Bucky Autry
19 Kevin Elster
20 Alan Wilson
21 Mauro Gozzo
22 Mark Davis
23 Lew Graham
24 David West
25 Rich Rodriguez
26 Ron Dominco

1984 TCMA Maine Guides

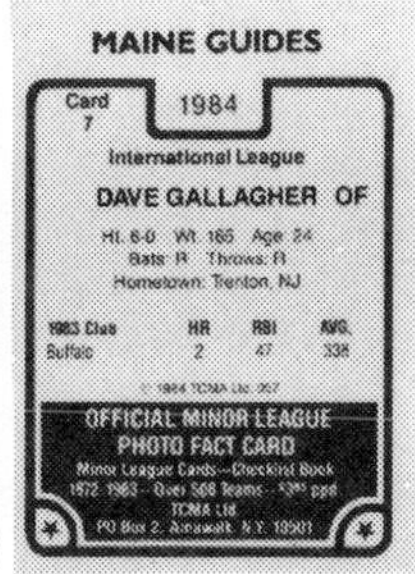

(Cleveland Indians, AAA) (color)

	MT	NR MT	EX
Complete Set:	12.50	9.50	5.25

1 Ramon Romero
2 Jerry Reed
3 Roy Smith
4 Steve Farr
5 Doug Simunic
6 Richard Barnes
7 Dave Gallagher
8 Bud Anderson
9 Vic Albury
10 Doc Edwards
11 Picky DeLeon
12 Lorenzo Gray
13 Guy Elston
14 Wil Culmer
15 Jeff Barkley
16 Karl Pagel
17 Juan Espino
18 Dwight Taylor
19 Rod Craig
20 Luis Quinones
21 Keith MacWhorter
22 Ed Glynn
23 Shanie Dugas

1984 TCMA Memphis Chicks

(Kansas City Royals, AA) (color)

	MT	NR MT	EX
Complete Set:	9.00	6.75	3.50

1 Rick Mathews
2 Rich Dubee
3 Rick Rizzo
4 Art Hartinez
5 Billy Best
6 Reggie Wyatt
7 Mike Kingery
8 Mitch Ashmore
9 Van Snider
10 Jeff Neuzil
11 Bill Wilder
12 Doug Cook
13 Bob Hegman
14 Lester Strode
15 Vinnie Yuhas
16 Jim Miner
17 Steve Reish
18 Roger Hansen
19 Doug Gilcrease
20 Hal Hatcher
21 Jose Reyes
22 Steve Morrow
23 Mark Pirruccello
24 Bill Pecota
25 Dave Cone

1984 TCMA Midland Cubs

(Chicago Cubs, AA) (color)

	MT	NR MT	EX
Complete Set:	42.50	31.75	17.50

1 Joe Henderson
2 Antonio Cordova
3 Don Hyman
4 Jim Boudreau
5 John Huey
6 Jorge Carpio
7 Joe Housey
8 Darryl Banks
9 Ray Soff
10 Mike Capel
11 Jeff Moscaret
12 Doug Potestio
13 Dennis Brogna
14 Glenn Gregson
15 George Enright
16 Darrin Jackson
17 Danny Norman
18 Ricky Baker
19 Jim Auten
20 Jeff Jones
21 Paul Noce
22 Shawon Dunston
23 Gary Varsho
24 Tony Woods

1984 TCMA Newark Orioles

(Baltimore Orioles, A) (color)

	MT	NR MT	EX
Complete Set:	14.00	10.50	5.50

1 Randy Riley
2 Eric Bell
3 Troy Howerton
4 David Dahse
5 Dan Mickan
6 Wayne Wilson
7 Dan Fizpatrick
8 Alan Ennis
9 Rich Bair
10 Greg Wirth
11 David Smith
12 Mike Whalen
13 Dan Hayes
14 Tim Smith
15 Frank Velleggia
16 Jim Rooney
17 Rich Caldwell
18 Henry Gonzales
19 Larry Heise
20 Gerry Adams
21 Bob Gutierrez
22 Randy Wilson
23 Jim Hutto
24 Bob Kline
25 Jeff Arnold

1984 TCMA Oklahoma City 89'ers

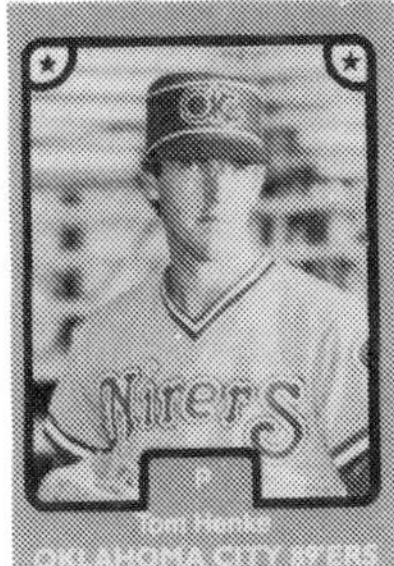

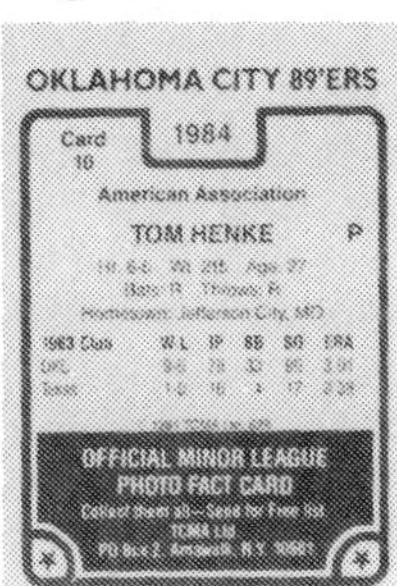

(Texas Rangers, AAA) (color)

	MT	NR MT	EX
Complete Set:	12.00	9.00	5.00

1 Al Lachowicz
2 Rob Clark

3 Tommy Burgess
4 Cliff Wherry
5 Rusty Gerhardt
6 Dan Larson
7 Mike Griffin
8 Dave Stockstill
9 Mike Jirschele
10 Tom Henke
11 Nick Capra
12 Tony Fossas
13 Steve Buechele
14 Mike Rubel
15 Barry Brunkenkant
16 Kevin Buckley
17 Chuckie Canady
18 Tommy Dunbar
19 Don Scott
20 Victor Cruz
21 Mitch Zwolensky
22 Glenn Cook
23 Dan Murphy
24 German Barranca

1984 TCMA Omaha Royals

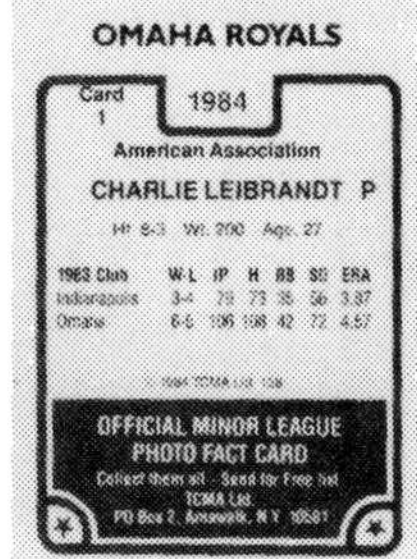

(Kansas City Royals, AAA) (color)

	MT	NR MT	EX
Complete Set:	12.00	9.00	5.00

1 Charlie Leibrandt
2 Gene Lamont
3 Tony Ferreira
4 Al Hargesheimer
5 Frank Wills
6 Rickey Keeton
7 Nick Swartz
8 John Morris
9 Mike Brewer
10 Steve Hammond
11 Mike Parrott
12 Marty Wilkerson
13 Jerry Cram
14 Bill Gorman
15 Keith Creel
16 Vinnie Yuhas
17 Theo Shaw
18 Dan St. Clair
19 Mike Alvarez
20 Mike Jones
21 Cliff Pastornicky
22 Dave Leeper
23 Brian Poldberg
24 Mark Ryal
25 Rondin Johnson
26 Russ Stephens
27 Jim Scranton
28 Frank Mancuso
29 Matt Bassett
30 Terry Wendlandt

1984 TCMA Pawtucket Red Sox

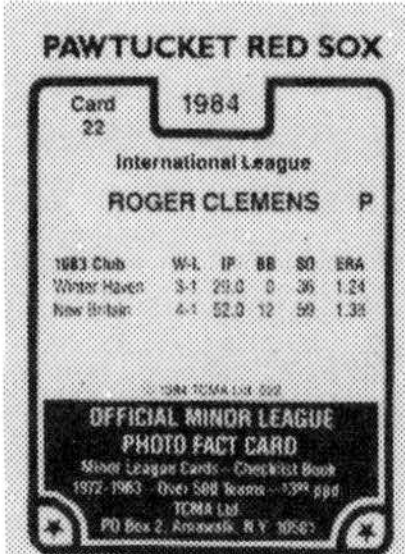

(Boston Red Sox, AAA) (color)

	MT	NR MT	EX
Complete Set:	80.00	60.00	32.00

1 Charlie Mitchell
2 Lee Graham
3a Tony Torcia (name incorrect)
3b Tony Torchia (name correct)
4 Dale Robertson
5 Dennis Burtt
6 Jim Dorsey
7 Chuck Davis (photo actually Mike Davis)
8 Paul Gnacinski
9 Gus Burgess
10a Paul Hundhammer (incorrect name on back)
10b Paul Hundhammer (correct name on back)
11a Tony Herron (incorrect name on back)
11b Tony Herron (correct name on back)
12 Juan Pautt
13 Kevin Romine
14 Steve Crawford
15 Reggie Whittemore
16 Chico Walker
17 Dave Malpeso
18 Steve Lyons
19 Pat Dodson
20 Marc Sullivan
21 Mike Rochford
22 Roger Clemens
23 Rich Gale
24 Brian Denman
25 Juan Bustabad
26 Mike Davis

1984 TCMA Prince William Pirates

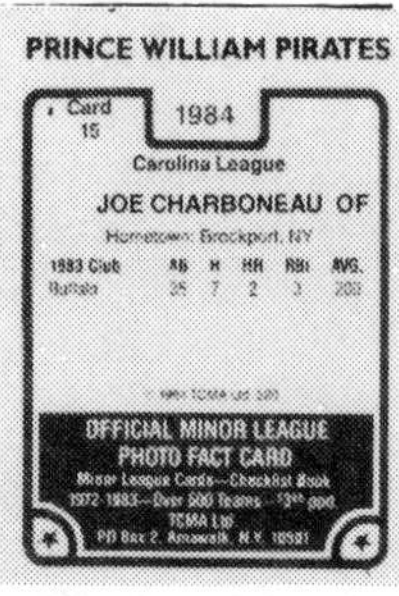

(Pittsburgh Pirates, A) (color)

	MT	NR MT	EX
Complete Set:	13.50	10.00	5.50

1 Leon Roberts
2 Jim Buckmier
3 Sean Faherty
4 Shawn Holman
5 Jim Felt
6 Dorn Taylor
7 Mike Berger
8 Pete Piskol
9 John Pavlik
10 Brian Buckley
11 Eric Fink
12 Dorley Downs
13 Wilfredo Cordoba
14 Jim Aulenback
15 Joe Charboneau
16 Felix Fermin
17 Jeff Patton
18 Scott Borland
19 Steve Lewis
20 Don Williams
21 Shawn Stone
22 Sam Haro
23 Rich Sauveur
24 Mitch McKelvey
25 Kim Christenson
26 Craig Brown
27 David Tumbas
28 Leo Sanchez
29 John Lipon
30 Dave Johnson
31 Nick Castaneda
32 Kerry Baker
33 George Borges
34 Stacy Pettis

1984 TCMA Richmond Braves

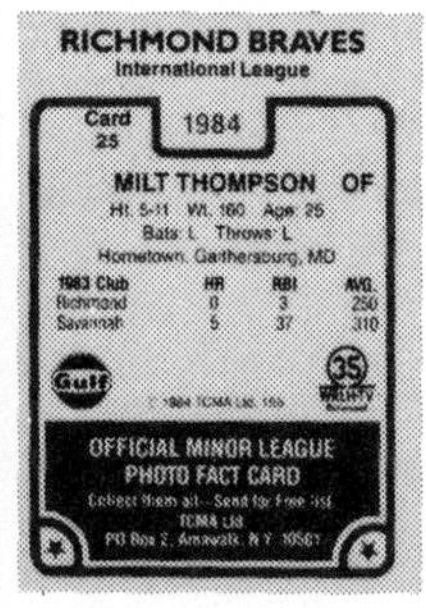

(Atlanta Braves, AAA) (color)

	MT	NR MT	EX
Complete Set:	12.50	9.50	5.25

1 Mike Reynolds
2 Rufino Linares
3 Ken Smith
4 Paul Boris
5 Larry Whisenton
6 Tom Hayes
7 Vic Lisi
8 Larry Owen
9 Tony Brizzolara
10 Brad Komminsk, Leo Vargas
11 Brad Komminsk
12 Leo Vargas
13 Craig Jones
14 Roger LaFrancois
15 Gary Reiter
16 Bob Galasso
17 Steve Shields
18 Randy Martz
19 Terry Leach
20 Brian Fisher
21 Joe Johnson
22 Sam Ayoub
23 Paul Zuvella
24 Paul Runge
25 Milt Thompson
26 Johnny Sain
27 Eddie Haas

1984 TCMA Rochester Red Wings

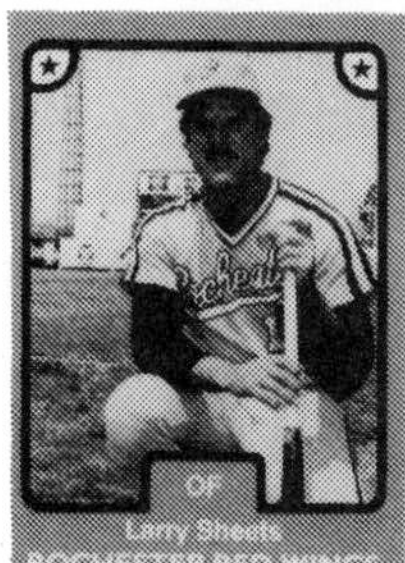

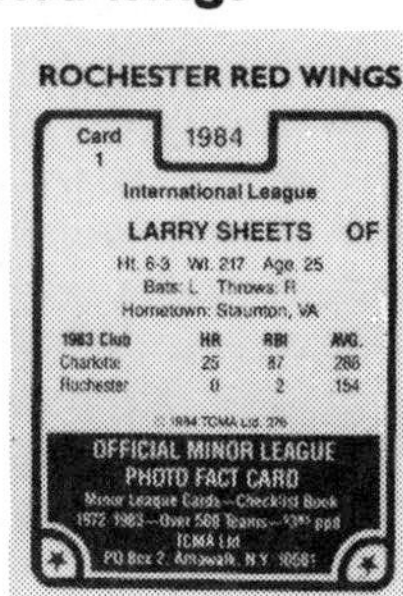

(Baltimore Orioles, AAA) (color)

	MT	NR MT	EX
Complete Set:	15.00	11.00	6.00

1 Larry Sheets
2 Rich Carlucci
3 Mark Wiley
4 Jim Hutto
5 Mike Calise
6 John Valle
7 Lee Granger
8 Ismael Oquendo
9 Frank Verdi
10 Jeff Shaefer
11 Glenn Gulliver
12 Luis Rosado
13 Bob Bonner
14 Don Welchel
15 Leo Hernandez
16 Allan Ramirez
17 Bill Swaggerty
18 Joe Kucharski
19 Mike Young

1984 TCMA Savannah Cardinals

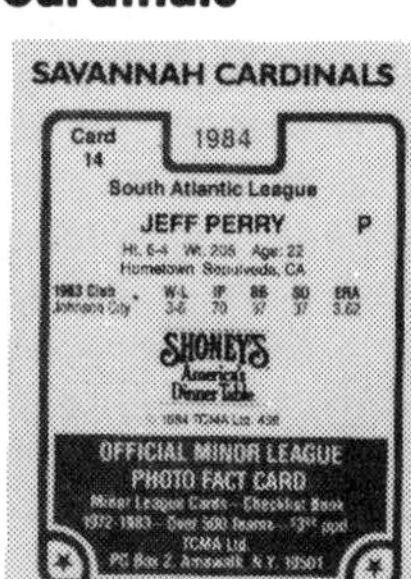

(St. Louis Cardinals, A) (color)

	MT	NR MT	EX
Complete Set:	12.50	9.50	5.25

1 Sonny James

2 Jeff Lauck
3 Barry McPherson
4 John Costello
5 Kurt Kaull
6 Chuck McGrath
7 Ken Huth
8 Hans Herzog
9 Ted Milner
10 Jim Reboulet
11 Mark Angelo
12 Bob Kish
13 Jamie Brisco
14 Jeff Perry
15 Ernie Carrasco
16 Harry McCulla
17 Bill Packer
18 Glenn Harris
19 Victor Paulino
20 George Vogel
21 Lloyd Merritt
22 Sal Agostinelli
23 Ted Carson
24 Miguel Soto
25 Ken Sinclair
26 Mike Behrend

1984 TCMA Syracuse Chiefs

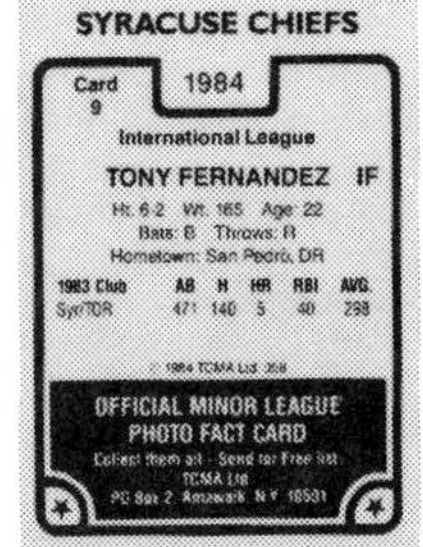

(Toronto Blue Jays, AAA) (color)

	MT	NR MT	EX
Complete Set:	32.50	24.25	13.50

1 Jim Beauchamp
2 Larry Hardy
3 Tommy Craig
4 Dennis Howard
5 Ron Shephard
6 Rick Leach
7 Anthony Johnson
8 Augie Schmidt
9 Tony Fernandez
10 Jerry Keller
11 Matt Williams
12 Fred Manrique
13 Bobby Nandin
14 Al Woods
15 Toby Hernandez
16 Mike Proly
17 Tim Rodgers
18 Mark Eichhorn
19 Stan Clarke
20 Tom Lukish
21 David Walsh
22 Mike Morgan
23 Mark Bomback
24 Manny Castillo
25 Dave Shipanoff
26 Dave Stenhouse
27 Kelly Gruber
28 Dale Holman
29 Jim Baker
30 Tim Thompson
31 John Cerutti
32 Batboys

1984 TCMA Tidewater Tides

(New York Mets, AAA) (color)

	MT	NR MT	EX
Complete Set:	40.00	30.00	16.00

1 Scott Holman
2 Sid Fernandez
3 Wes Gardner
4 John Christensen
5 Herman Winningham
6 Bill Latham
7 Gil Flores
8 Brent Gaff
9 Rusty Tillman
10 Bob Schaefer
11 Ed Olwine
12 Rich Pickett
13 Jeff Bittiger
14 Tom Gorman
15 Jay Tibbs
16 Rafael Santana
17 Bob Sikes
18 Ross Jones
19 Rick Anderson
20 Terry Blocker
21 Laschelle Tarver
22 Al Jackson
23 Kevin Mitchell
24 Brian Giles
25 Ronn Reynolds
26 Terry Leach
27 Kelvin Chapman
28 Clint Hurdle

1984 TCMA Toledo Mud Hens

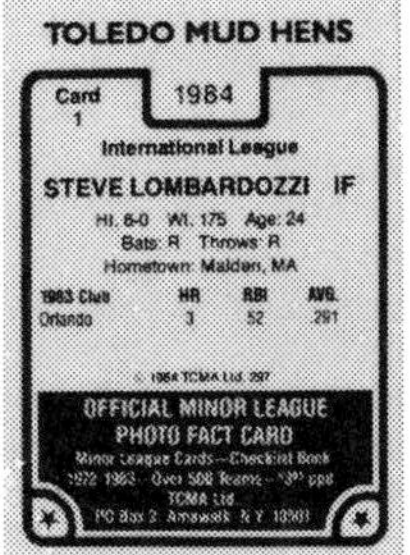

(Minnesota Twins, AAA) (color)

	MT	NR MT	EX
Complete Set:	10.00	7.50	4.00

1 Steve Lombardozzi
2 Jeffrey Reed
3 Alvaro Espinoza
4 Ray Smith
5 Rich Yett
6 Cal Ermer
7 Dan Schmitz
8 Brad Havens
9 Bob Mulligan
10 Bob Mitchell
11 Andre David
12 Scott Ulger
13 James Weaver
14 Tom Klawitter
15 Jack O'Connor
16 Keith Comstock
17 Eric Broersma
18 Greg Field
19 Tim Agan
20 Dave Baker
21 Jim Shellenback
22 Tack Wilson
23 Rick Lysander
24 Jay Pettibone

1984 TCMA Visalia Oaks

(Minnesota Twins, A) (color)

	MT	NR MT	EX
Complete Set:	17.00	12.75	7.00

1 Bennie Richie
2 Curt Kindred
3 Erez Borowsky
4 Alexis Marte
5 Vincent Ferraro
6 Osvaldo Alfonzo
7 Corey Elliot
8 Phillip Sheppard
9 Leonard Braddy
10 John Hilton
11 Timothy Thompson
12 Brian Hobaugh
13 Tom Reed
14 Jeffrey Schugel
15 Carson Carroll
16 Tim Graupmann
17 Matthew Butcher
18 Paul Mancuso
19 Antonio Codinach
20 Allan Anderson
21 Ronald Scheer
22 Scott Gibson
23 Joseph Tarangelo
--- Steven Aragon
--- Dan Lindquist

1984 Team Columbus Clippers

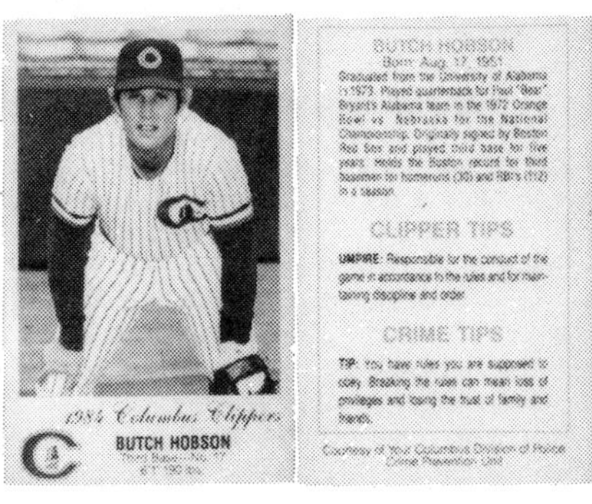

(New York Yankees, AAA)

	MT	NR MT	EX
Complete Set:	7.50	5.50	3.00

(1) Dan Briggs
(2) Curt Brown
(3) George Cappuzzello
(4) Clay Christiansen
(5) Don Cooper
(6) Joe Cowley
(7) Pete Dalena
(8) Brian Dayett
(9) Don Fowler
(10) Kelly Heath
(11) Butch Hobson
(12) Rex Hudler
(13) Victor Mata
(14) "Stump" Merrill
(15) Mike O'Berry
(16) Mike Pagliarulo
(17) Scott Patterson
(18) Dennis Rasmussen
(19) Andre Robertson
(20) Pat Rooney
(21) Kelly Scott
(22) George H. Sisler Jr.
(23) Matt Winters
(24) Coaches/Trainer Card (Mark Connor, Mickey Vernon, Gil Patterson, Steve Donohue)

1984 Team Daytona Beach Astros

(Houston Astros, A)

	MT	NR MT	EX
Complete Set:	70.00	52.50	28.75

1 Dave Cripe
2 Stan Hough
3 Rich Bombard
4 Mik Crefin
5 Mike Friederich
6 Chuck Mathews
7 Greg Mize
8 Raynor Noble
9 Ray Perkins
10 Uvaldo Reglado
11 Doug Shaab
12 Don Berti
13 Jeff Datz
14 Robbie Wine
15 Glenn Carpenter
16 Bobby Falls
17 Ramon Rodriguez
18 Nelson Rood
19 Jim Sherman
20 Mike Botkin
21 Curtis Burke
22 Juan Delgado
23 Louis Meadows
24 Mike Stellern
25 Larry Lasky

1984 Team Idaho Falls A's

(Oakland A's, A)

	MT	NR MT	EX
Complete Set:	85.00	64.00	34.00

(1) Russ Applegate
(2) Eldridge Armstrong
(3) Darren Balsley
(4) Mickey Boyer
(5) Adan Brito
(6) Antonio Cabrera
(7) Mike Cupples
(8) Arturo Ferreira
(9) Mark Gillespie
(10) John Gonzalez
(11) Bob Hassel
(12) Jesus Hernaz
(13) James Jackson
(14) Tony Johnson
(15) Felix Jose
(16) Mark Leonette
(17) Scott LeVander
(18) Jim Nettles
(19) Ramon Nunez
(20) Ken Patterson
(21) Ted Polakowski
(22) Basilio Reyes
(23) Kevin Russ
(24) Scott Sabo
(25) David Sheriff
(26) Bob Vantrease
(27) Camilo Veras
(28) Mike Walker
(29) Mark Warren
(30) James Wilridge

1984 Team Indianapolis Indians

(Montreal Expos, AAA) (co-sponsored by Tom Aikens)

	MT	NR MT	EX
Complete Set:	10.00	7.50	4.00

1 1984 Indianapolis Indians

2 Bob Rodgers
3 Leonel Carrion
4 Chris Welsh
5 Sal Butera
6 Joe Hesketh
7 Roy Johnson
8 Craig Eaton
9 Brad Mills
10 The Catchers (George Bjorkman, Sal Butera)
11 Eric Mustad
12 Mike Fuentes
13 Greg Bargar
14 Shooty Babitt
15 The Outfielders (Shooty Babitt, Mike Fuentes, Roy Johnson, Max Venable)

16 Dick Grapenthin
17 Razor Shines
18 The Starting Pitchers (Greg Bargar, Tim Burke, Joe Hesketh, Eric Mustad, Chris Welsh)
19 Bill Sattler
20 George Bjorkman
21 The Relief Pitchers (Darren Dilks, Craig Eaton, Dick Grapenthin, Bill Sattler)

22 Gene Glynn
23 Tim Burke
24 Ron Johnson
25 Rene Gonzales
26 The Infielders (Mike Gates, Gene Glynn, Rene Gonzales, Ron Johnson, Brad Mills, Razor Shines)
27 Darren Dilks
28 Max Venable
29 Mike Gates
30 Mike Stenhouse
31 Jeff Porter
32 Bush Stadium

1984 Team Tulsa Drillers

(Texas Rangers, AA) This set is numbered as it appears on the cards.

	MT	NR MT	EX
Complete Set:	15.00	11.25	6.00

4 Jorge Gomez
6 Keith Jones
7 Oscar Mejia
14 Greg Jemison
16 Dan Murphy
18 Randy Asadoor
19 Greg Tabor
20 Whitney Harry
22 Barry Bass
23 Orlando Gomez
24 Tim Meckes
26 Bob Gergen
27 John Buckley
28 Bill Hance
29 Jose Guzman
30 Steve Kordish
31 Javier Ortiz
32 Billy Taylor
34 Terry Johnson
36 Dwayne Henry
37 Tommy Joe Shimp
---) Greg Campbell

1985

1985 Chong Modesto A's

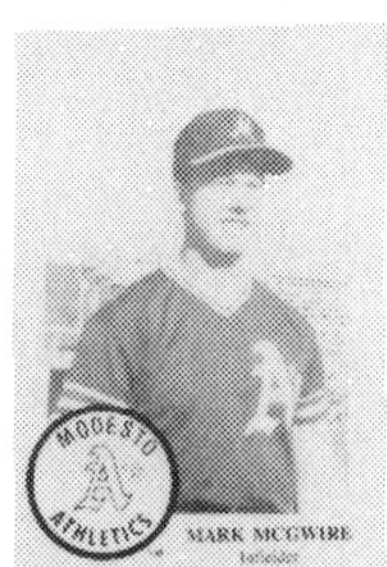

(Oakland A's, A) Only 200 of the error sets were produced. (misspelled McGwire)

	MT	NR MT	EX
Complete Set:	80.00	60.00	33.00

1 Kevin Stock
2 Paul Bradley
3 Antonio Cabrera
4 Twayne Harris
5 Oscar De Chavez
6 Eric Garrett
7 Brian Guinn
8 Allan Heath
9 Joe Strong
10 Mike Fulmer
11 Randy Harvey
12 Kevin Coughlon
13 Jim Eppard
14 Pete Kendrick
15 Jim Jones
16 Steve Howard
17a Mark McGuire (misspelled)
17b Mark McGwire (corrected)
18 Rick Rodriguez
19 Mark Bauer
20 Damon Farmar
21 Dave Wilder
22 Stan Hilton
23 Doug Scherer
24 Bob Loscalzo
25 Joe Odom
26 George Mitterwald
27 Rick Tronerud
28 John Cartelli

1985 Cramer Albuquerque Dukes

(Los Angeles Dodgers, AAA) (color)

	MT	NR MT	EX
Complete Set:	8.00	6.00	3.25

151 Dean Rennicke
152 Tony Brewer
153 Joe Vavra
154 Dennis Powell
155 Craig Shipley
156 Terry Collins
157 Hector Rincones
158 Ed Amelung
159 Erik Sonberg
160 Dick McLaughlin
161 Ralph Bryant
162 German Rivera
163 Jack Fimple
164 Brian Holton
165 Lemmie Miller
166 Bill Scudder
167 Stu Pederson
168 Larry White
169 Tim Meeks
170 Gil Reyes
171 Don Smith
172 Steve Martin
173 Rafael Montalvo
174 Rich Rodas
175 Franklin Stubbs

1985 Cramer Bend Phillies

(Philadelphia Phillies, A) (black and white, 2" x 3")

	MT	NR MT	EX
Complete Set:	11.00	8.25	4.50

(1) Dion Beck
(2) Ben Blackmun
(3) Steve Bowden
(4) Rodney Brunelle
(5) Tim Collins
(6) Luis Faccio
(7) Kenley Graves
(8) Nat Green
(9) Jason Grimsley
(10) Steve Harris
(11) Vince Holyfield
(13) Ron Jones
(14) Bruce Luttrull
(15) Trey McCall
(16) John McKinney
(17) Robert Nazabal
(18) Rick Parker
(19) Mario Perez
(20) Ernie Rodriguez
(21) Floyd Rossum
(22) Steve Sharts
(23) Clifton Walker
(24) Carlos Zayas

1985 Cramer Calgary Cannons

(Seattle Mariners, AAA) (color)

	MT	NR MT	EX
Complete Set:	25.00	18.50	10.00

76 Karl Best
77 Jim Lewis
78 Bobby Floyd
79 Paul Serna
80 Al Chambers
81 Don Scott
82 Roy Thomas
83 John Moses
84 Bobby Cuellar
85 Frank Wills
86 Pat Casey
87 Dave Tobik
88 Mickey Brantley
89 Paul Mirabella
90 Bob Stoddard
91 Ricky Nelson
92 Brian Snyder
93 Bill Crone
94 Danny Tartabull
95 Bob Long
96 Darnell Coles
97 Ron Tingley
98 Rick Luecken
99 Joe Whitmer
100 Clay Hill

1985 Cramer Edmonton Trappers

(California Angels, AAA) (color)

	MT	NR MT	EX
Complete Set:	25.00	18.50	10.00

1 Pat Keedy
2 Wally Joyner
3 Mike Madril
4 Don Groh
5 Scott Oliver
6 Tony Mack
7 Kirk McCaskill
8 Reggie West
9 Rafael Lugo
10 James Randall
11 Marty Kain
12 Gus Polidor
13 Steve Liddle
14 Winston Llenas
15 Bob Ramos
16 Dave Smith
17 Tim Krauss
18 Chris Clark
19 Stewart Cliburn
20 Curt Kaufman
21 Bob Bastian
22 Norman Carrasco
23 Frank Reberger
24 Jack Howell
25 Al Romero

1985 Cramer Everett Giants - Series I

(San Francisco Giants, A) (black and white) (cards measure 2" by3")

	MT	NR MT	EX
Complete Set:	5.00	3.75	2.00

(1) David Blakely
(2) George Bonilla (pitching)
(3) George Bonilla (portrait)

(4) Ty Dabney
(5) Tom Ealy
(6) Kim Flowers (portrait)
(7) Kim Flowers (with glove)
(8) George Jones (portrait)
(9) George Jones (with bat)
(10) Joe Kmak
(11) Alan Marr
(12) Willie Mijares
(13) Todd Miller
(14) Rick Nelson (holding bat)
(15) Rick Nelson (swinging bat)
(16) Tom Osowski
(17) Darren Pearson (standing in shadow)
(18) Darren Pearson (sunlight on right side)
(19) Brian Petty
(20) Steve Santora
(21) Howard Townsend (portrait)
(22) Howard Townsend (with glove)
(23) John Verducci
(24) Mike Whitt

1985 Cramer Everett Giants - Series II

(San Francisco Giants, A) (black and white) (cards measure 2" by3")

	MT	NR MT	EX
Complete Set:	5.00	3.75	2.00

1 Jeff Carter
2 Mike Dandos
3 Bruce Graham
4 Dave Hornsby
5 Lloyd Jackson
6 Robert Jackson
7 Darrin James
8 Joe Jordan
9 Randy McCament
10 Timber Mead
11 Dave Morris
12 Curt Motton
13 Brian Ohnoutka
14 Doug Robertson
15 Darrell Rodgers
16 Steve Santora
17 Billy Smith
18 Joe Strain
19 Jack Uhey
20 John Van Kempen
21 Paul Van Stone
22 Mike Whitt
23 Rick Wilson
24 Trevor Wilson

1985 Cramer Hawaii Islanders

(Pittsburgh Pirates, AAA) (color)

	MT	NR MT	EX
Complete Set:	10.00	7.50	4.00

226 Jim Opie
227 Sam Khalifa
228 Scott Loucks
229 Denio Gonzalez
230 Rick Reuschel
231 Benny Distefano
232 Paul Semall
233 Tommy Sandt
234 Mitchell Page
235 Steve Shirley
236 Hedi Vargas
237 Jim Winn
238 Trench Davis
239 Bobby Miscik
240 Chris Green
241 Dave Tomlin
242 Stan Cliburn
243 Bob Walk
244 Steve Herz
245 Ray Krawczyk
246 John Henry Johnson
247 John Malkin
248 Manny Sarmiento
249 Jeff Zaske
250 Jerry Dybzinski

1985 Cramer Las Vegas Stars

(San Diego Padres, AAA) (color)

	MT	NR MT	EX
Complete Set:	11.50	8.50	4.75

101 Victor Rodriguez
102 Rusty Tillman
103 John Kruk
104 Ray Hayward
105 Mark Parent
106 Steve Lubratich
107 Marty Decker
108 Ed Rodriguez
109 Lance McCullers
110 Bob Cluck
111 Walt Vanderbush
112 Gene Walter
113 George Hinshaw
114 Ray Smith
115 Steve Garcia
116 Randy Asadoor
117 Bob Patterson
118 Keefe Cato
119 Jim Leopold
120 Ed Wojna
121 Sonny Siebert
122 Tim Pyznarski
123 Mike Couchee
125 James Steels

1985 Cramer Phoenix Giants

(San Francisco Giants, AAA) (color)

	MT	NR MT	EX
Complete Set:	8.50	6.25	3.50

176 Jack Lazorko
177 Randy Kutcher
178 Larry Crews
179 Randy Gomez
180 Fran Mullins
181 Mike Woodard
182 Phil Oullette
183 John Rabb
184 Jeff Robinson
185 Mark Schuster
186 Pat Adams
187 Jim Lefebvre
188 Ricky Adams
189 Kelly Downs
190 Roger Mason
191 Bob Lacey
192 Doug Mansalino
193 Kevin Rhomberg
194 Augie Schmidt
195 Tack Wilson
196 Greg Schultz
197 Bobby Cummings
198 Colin Ward
199 Mark Grant
200 Jeff Cornell

1985 Cramer Portland Beavers

(Philadelphia Phillies, AAA) (color)

	MT	NR MT	EX
Complete Set:	22.50	16.50	9.00

26 David Rucker
27 Gib Seibert
28 Dave Shipanoff
29 Chris James
30 Steve Moses
31 Rocky Childress
32 Alan LeBoeuf
33 Arturo Gonzalez
34 Rick Schu
35 Bill Dancy
36 Jim Olander
37 Randy Salava
38 Mike Maddux
39 Bill Nahorodny
40 Tony Ghelfi
41 Jay Davisson
42 Darren Daulton
43 Francisco Melendez
44 Ralph Citarella
45 Rodger Cole
46 Ken Dowell
47 Bob Tiefenauer
48 Greg Legg
49 Rick Surhoff
50 Mike Diaz

1985 Cramer Spokane Indians

(San Diego Padres, A) (black and white) (cards measure 2" by 3")

	MT	NR MT	EX
Complete Set:	8.00	6.00	3.25

(1) Eric Bauer
(2) Bill Blount
(3) Jerald Clark
(4) Joey Cora
(5) Adam Ging
(6) Greg Hall
(7) Greg Harris
(8) Nate Hill
(9) Chris Knabenshue
(10) Glen Kuiper
(11) Joe Lynch
(12) Jack Maloof
(13) Matt Maysey
(14) Tom Meagher
(15) Maurice Morton
(16) Jay Nieporte
(17) Eric Nolte
(18) Juan Paris
(19) Jeff Parks
(20) Ramon Rodriguez
(21) Norm Sherry
(22) Bill Stevenson
(23) Jorge Suris
(24) Jim Tatum

1985 Cramer Spokane Indians All-Time Greats

(black and white) (cards measure 2" by 3")

	MT	NR MT	EX
Complete Set:	8.00	6.00	3.25

(1) Doyle Alexander
(2) John Billingham
(3) Bill Buckner
(4) Willie Crawford
(5) Jim Fairey
(6) Alan Foster
(7) Steve Garvey
(8) Charlie Hough
(9) Tommy Hutton
(10) Von Joshua
(11) Ray Lamb
(12) Tom Lasorda
(13) Dave Lopes
(14) Joe Moeller
(15) Tom Paciorek
(16) John Purdin
(17) Bill Russell
(18) Ted Sizemore
(19) Gus Sposito
(20) Jack Spring
(21) Bob Stinson
(22) Bob Valentine
(23) Sandy Vance
(24) Geoff Zahn

1985 Cramer Tacoma Tigers

(Oakland A's, AAA) (color)

	MT	NR MT	EX
Complete Set:	9.50	7.00	3.75

126 Keith Lieppman
127 Jose Tolentino
128 Keith Thrower
129 Chuck Estrada
130 Ricky Peters
131 Tom Romano
132 Phil Stephenson
133 Jose Rijo
134 Danny Goodwin
135 Thad Reece
136 Mike Ashman
137 Ron Harrison
138 Stan Kyles
139 Steve Kiefer
140 Tim Lambert
141 Doug Scherer
142 Steve Ontiveros
143 Bob Bathe
144 Bob Owchinko
145 Tom Dozier
146 Joe Lansford
147 Steve Mura
148 Bill Bathe
149 Mike Chris
150 Tom Tellman (Tellmann)

1985 Cramer Tucson Toros

(Houston Astros, AAA) (color)

	MT	NR MT	EX
Complete Set:	15.00	11.00	6.00

51 Chris Jones
52 Eric Bullock
53 Jimmy Johnson
54 Mark Ross
55 Larry Acker
56 Manny Hernandez
57 Vern Followell
58 Larry Montgomery
59 Rick Colbert
60 Mark Knudson
61 Rafael Landestoy
62 Stan Hough
63 Mike Calise
64 Tye Waller
65 Glenn Davis
66 Randy Martz
67 Chuck Jackson
68 John Mizerock
69 Ty Gainey
70 Eddie Bonine
71 Pedro Hernandez
72 James Miner
73 Charlie Kerfeld
74 Rex Jones
75 Brad Mills

1985 Cramer Vancouver Canadians

(Milwaukee Brewers, AAA) (color)

	MT	NR MT	EX
Complete Set:	11.50	8.50	4.75

201 Dan Davidsmeier
202 Brad Lesley
203 Tim Leary

204 Bobby Clark
205 Juan Castillo
206 Jim Aducci
207 Earnie Riles
208 Mike Paul
209 Dale Sveum
210 Jaime Cocanower
211 Mike Felder
212 Brian Duquette
213 Jim Paciorek
214 Bob Skube
215 Tom Trebelhorn
216 Bill Wegman
217 Mike Martin
218 Scott Roberts
219 Rick Waits
220 Chuck Crim
221 Jaime Nelson
222 Brian Clutterbuck
223 Garret Nago
224 Carlos Ponce
225 Al Price

1985 Pizza Hut Greenville Braves

(Atlanta Braves, AA) This set is numbered as it appears on the backs of the cards, and is in the form of a poster. The complete poster is approximately 16-1/2 x 21 inches in size.

	MT	NR MT	EX
Complete Set:	30.00	22.50	12.25

Bob Tumpane
Ken Smith
Team logo card (in white)
Team logo card (in navy blue)
4a Bob Luzon
4b Bill Slack
5 Mike Knox
6 Maximo Rosario
7 Tom Hayes
8 Andres Thomas
11 Jeff Ransom
12 Glen Bockhorn
14 Randy Ingle
15 Rich Leggatt
16 Paul Assenmacher
17 Rick Albert
19 Todd Lamb
20 Tommy Thompson
22 Leo Vargas
25 Inocencio Guerrero
27 Steve Ziem
30 Andre Treadway
31 Larry Bradford
32 Jim Beauchamp
40 Ben Callahan
55 Luke Appling

1985 Pro Cards Reading Phillies

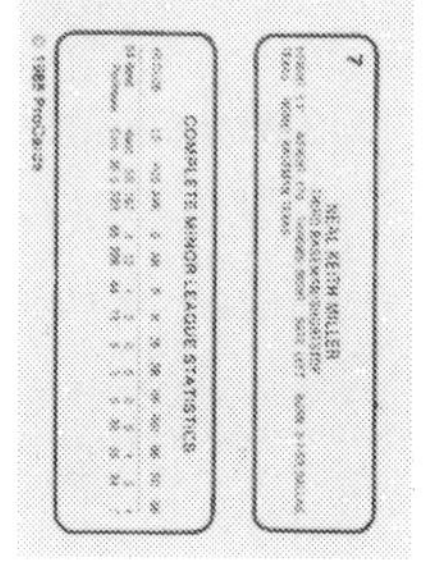

(Philadelphia Phillies, AA) This was the first and only set produced by ProCards in 1985.

	MT	NR MT	EX
Complete Set:	7.50	5.50	3.00

1 George Culver
2 Randy Day
3 Marvin Freeman
4 Bruce Long
5 Ramon Caraballo
6 Kevin Ward
7 Keith Mille,
8 Jose Escobar
9 Ken Kinnard
10 Todd Soares
11 Greg Jelks
12 Ken Jackson
13 Tony Brown
14 Joe Cipolloni
15 Wilfredo Tejada
16 Rob Hicks
17 Scott Wright
18 Bryan Hobbie
19 Mark Bowden
20 Jim Olson
21 Steve Labay
22 Tony Evetts
23 Darryl Menard
24 Rich Gaynor
25 Barney Nugent

1985 Pro Cards Vancouver Canadians

	MT	NR MT	EX
Complete Set:	10.00	7.50	4.00

(2) Terry Bevington
(3) Mike Birkbeck
(4) Chris Bosio
(5) Glen Braggs
(6) Mark Ciardi
(7) Bryan Clutterbuck
(8) Chuck Crim
(9) Dan Davidsmeier
(10) Ed Diaz
(11) Bryan Duquette
(12) Bob Gibson
(13) Dion James
(14) John Johnson
(15) Steve Kiefer
(16) Dave Klipstein
(17) Joe Meyer
(18) Ed Myers
(19) Charlie O'Brien
(20) Jim Paciorek
(21) Mike Paul
(22) Chuck Porter
(23) Ray Searage
(24) B.J. Surhoff
(25) Dale Sveum
(26) Rich Thompson
(27) Rick Waits

1985 Riley's Louisville Redbirds

(St. Louis Cardinals, AAA)

	MT	NR MT	EX
Complete Set:	17.50	13.00	7.00

1 Jim Fregosi
2 Joe Rigoli
3 Frank Evans
4 Jerry Mc Kune
5 Vince Coleman
6 Andy Hassler
7 Kevin Hagen
8 Jeff Keener
9 Dave Kable
10 Jed Smith
11 Randy Hunt
12 Joe Pettini
13 Curt Ford
14 Dave Clements
15 Jose Oquendo
16 Matt Keough
17 Bill Lyons
18 Pat Perry
19 Willie Lozado
20 Fred Martinez
21 Jack Ayer
22 Mike Lavalliere
23 John Morris
24 Mick Shade
25 Ben Hayes
26 Rick Ownby
27 Casey Parsons
28 Todd Worrell
29 Mike Anderson
30 Ron Jackson

1985 Smokey Fresno Giants

	MT	NR MT	EX
Complete Set:	65.00	48.75	26.50

1 Wendell Kim
2 Marty De Merritt
3 Charles Culberson
4 Angel Escobar
5 Dave Allen
6 Mike Jones
7 Jim Wasem
8 Mackey Sasser
9 Deron Mc Cue
10 Greg Gilbert
11 Charlie Hayes
13 Romy Cucjen
14 John Grimes
15 Ed Puikunas
16 Dan Winters
18 Jay Reid
19 Stuart Tate
20 Al Candelaria
21 Todd Kuhn
22 John Burkett
23 Steve Smith
24 Rich Henning
25 Tommy Alexander
26 Todd Oakes
27 Don Wolfe
29 Bill Thompson
30 Curt Goldgrabe

1985 T&J SC Madison Muskies

(Oakland A's, A)

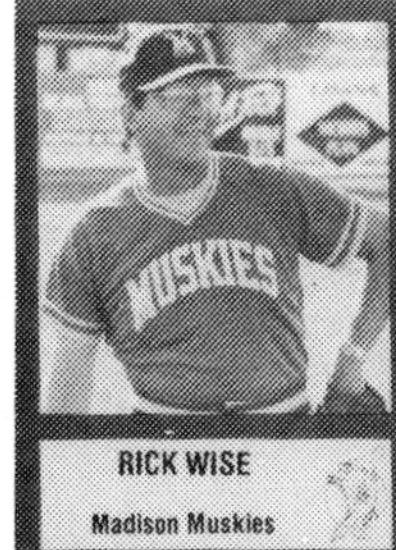

	MT	NR MT	EX
Complete Set:	10.00	7.50	4.00

1 Roy Anderson
2 Russ Applegate
3 Tony Arias
4 Greg Brake
5 Todd Burns
6 Brian Criswell
7 Mike Cupples
8 Brian Dorsett
9 P.J. Dietrick
10 Arturo Ferreira
11 Bob Gould
12 Darel Hansen
13 Mark Howie
14 Felix Jose
15 John Kanter
16 Russ Kibler
17 Joe Kramer
18 Andy Krause
19 Mark Leonette
20 Jim Nettles
21 Scott Sabo
22 Faustoe Santos
23 Dave Schober
24 Scotty Lee Whaley
25 Rick Wise

1985 TCMA Albany-Colonie Yankees

(New York Yankees, AA) (complete set price includes scarce Lindsey and Hughes cards)

	MT	NR MT	EX
Complete Set:	50.00	37.00	20.00

1 Brad Arnsberg
2 Tim Byron
3 Darin Cloninger
4 Doug Drabek
5 Logan Easley
6 Mark Ferguson
7 Steve Frey
8 Randy Graham
9 Scott Nielsen
10 Scott Patterson
11 Bob Tewksbury
12 Bill Lindsey
13 Phil Lombardi
14 Mark Blaser
15 Ron Chapman
16 Orestes Destrade
17 Rafael Landestoy
18 Jim Riggs
19 Dick Scott
20 Doug Carpenter
21 Tony Russell
22 Brad Winkler
23 Barry Foote
24 Dave LaRoche
25 Jim Saul
26 Mike Fennell
27 Kevin Rand
28 Bernard Bremer
29 Erik Bernard
30 S. Hayes, J. Lemperle
31 Phil Pivnick
32 John Hawkins
33 Tim Knight
34 John Liburdi
35 Keith Hughes

1985 TCMA Beaumont Golden Gators

(San Diego Padres, AA) (color)

	MT	NR MT	EX
Complete Set:	32.50	24.25	13.50

1 Jeffrey Childers
2 Rickey Coleman
3 Mark Williamson
4 Shane Mack
5 Edward Vosberg
6 Gregory Smith
7 Peter Kutsukos
8 Jimmy Jones
9 Ulises Sierra
10 Rigo Rodriguez
11 Steven Schefsky

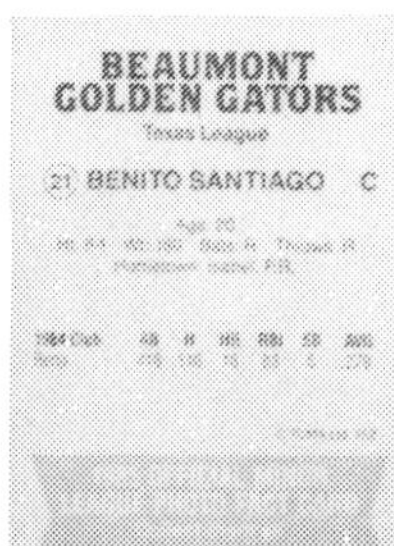

12 Michael McClain
13 Edward Miller
14 Thomas Brassil
15 Frank Castro
16 Mark Poston
17 Michael Mills
18 Gary Green
19 Mark Wasinger
20 David Corman
21 Benito Santiago
22 John Tutt
23 Todd Hutcheson
24 Jack Lamabe
25 Bobby Tolan

1985 TCMA Beloit Brewers

(Milwaukee Brewers, A) (color)

	MT	NR MT	EX
Complete Set:	17.50	13.00	7.00

1 Mike Samuel
2 Walt Pohle
3 Joe Mitchell
4 Jim Rowe
5 Mike Coin
6 Bob Simonson
7 Rob Dewolf
8 Mike Gobbo
9 Tom Steinbach
10 Angel Rodriguez
11 Frank Mattox
12 Bernard Kent
13 Darryel Walters
14 Wes Clements
15 Dean Freeland
16 Mike Frew
17 Greg Simmons
18 Alex Madrid
19 John Ludy
20 Gary Kanwisher
21 Alan Sadler
22 Martin Montano
23 Derek Diaz
24 Miguel Alicea
25 Rob Derksen
26 Dave Machemer

1985 TCMA Buffalo Bisons

(Chicago White Sox, AAA) (color)

	MT	NR MT	EX
Complete Set:	10.00	7.50	4.00

1 John Boles
2 Nardi Contreras
3 Greg Latta
4 Steve Christmas
5 Rick Seltheimer
6 Joel Skinner
7 Nelson Barrera
8 Jose Castro
9 Bryan Little
10 Kelvin Moore
11 Ramon Romero
12 Alex Taveras
13 Mark Gilbert
14 Randy Johnson
15 Mark Ryal
16 Dave Yobs
17 Bob Fallon
18 Steve Fireovid
19 Jerry Gleaton
20 Jim Hickey
21 Bill Long
22 Joel McKeon
23 Tom Mullen
24 Scott Stranski
25 Bruce Tanner
26 Dave Wehrmeister

1985 TCMA Burlington Rangers

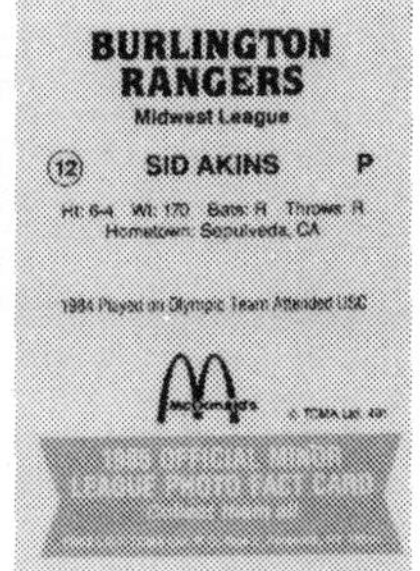

(Texas Rangers, A) (color)

	MT	NR MT	EX
Complete Set:	10.00	7.50	4.00

1 Joe Grayston
2 Mike Page
3 Larry Klein
4 Brad Hill
5 Steve Cullers
6 Neil Reilly
7 Dale Lanok
8 George Threadgill
9 Dave Darretta
10 Mike Bucci
11 Steve Neilsen
12 Sid Akins
13 Angelo Vasquez
14 Tim Owen
15 Jim St. Laurent
16 Bob O'Hearn
17 Jim Jagnow
18 Mark Kramer
19 Carlos Hernandez
20 Bryan Dial
21 Ty Harden
22 Robin Keathley
23 Stu Rogers
24 Darrell Whitaker
25 Steve Daniel
26 Ross Jones
27 Jim Allison
28 Jim Bridges

1985 TCMA Cedar Rapids Reds

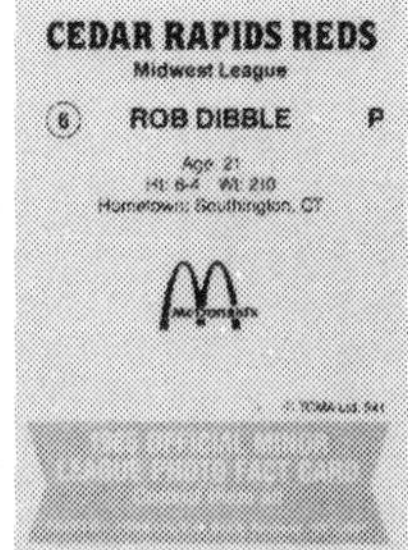

(Cincinnati Reds, A) (color)

	MT	NR MT	EX
Complete Set:	22.50	16.50	9.00

1 John Boyles
2 Mark Cieslak
3 Mike Coffey
4 Virgil Conley
5 Clay Daniel
6 Rob Dibble
7 Barry Fick
8 Mike Goedde
9 Doug Kampsen
10 Steve Oliverio
11 Jim Pettibone
12 Danny Smith
13 Ozzie Soto
14 Mark Berry
15 Greg Toler
16 Gary Denbo
17 Gerg Monda
18 Carlos Porte
19 Brian Robinson
20 Eddie Williams
21 Dan Boever
22 Elvin Fulgencio
23 Tubby Pace
24 Darren Riley
25 Allen Sigler
26 Paul Kirsch
27 Jay Ward
28 Don Buchheister
29 Rod Licht
30 Bud Curren
31 Tom Riley
32 Scott Breeden

1985 TCMA Charlotte O'S

(Baltimore Orioles, A) (complete set price includes scarce Gilbert and Nichols cards)

	MT	NR MT	EX
Complete Set:	16.00	12.00	6.50

1 Kenny Gerhart
2 Lee Granger
3 Jeff Jacobson
4 Rick Lockwood
5 John Stefero
6 Dave Thielker
7 Kelvin Torve
8 Tony Arnold
9 Carl Nichols
10 Mike Reddish
11 Ron Salcedo
12 Jeff Schaefer
13 Dom Chiti
14 John Hart
15 Francisco Oliveras
16 Jeff Summers
17 Jeff Wood
18 Bobby Mariano
19 Rich Caldwell
20 Jeff Gilbert
21 John Babyan
22 John Hoover
23 Ricky Jones
24 John Flinn
25 Alan Ramirez
26 Jose Brito
27 Bob Hice
28 Terry Mauney
29 Charlie Frederick
30 Paul Cameron
31 Mike Couche

1985 TCMA Columbus Clippers

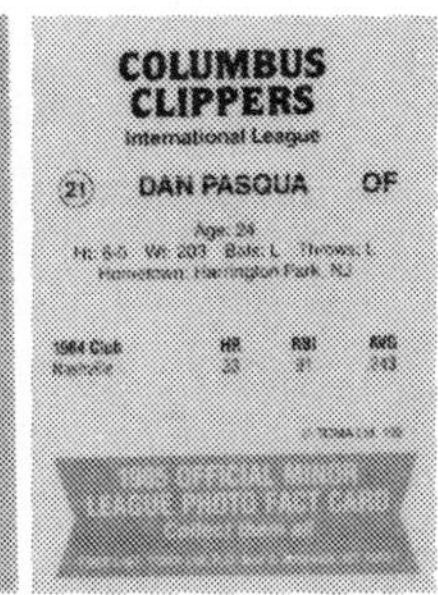

(New York Yankees, AAA) (complete set price includes scarce Bonilla and Mata cards)

	MT	NR MT	EX
Complete Set:	31.00	23.00	12.50

1 Vic Mata
2 Bert Bradley
3 Curt Brown
4 Clay Christiansen
5 Don Cooper
6 Kelly Faulk
7 Brian Fisher
8 Alphonso Pulido
9 Kelly Scott
10 Al Williams
11 Juan Espino
12 Mike O'Berry
13 Tom Barrett
14 Dan Briggs
15 Pete Dalena
16 Kelly Heath
17 Butch Hobson
18 Rex Hudler
19 Keith Smith
20 Tim Knight
21 Dan Pasqua
22 Matt Winters
23 Jim Deshaies
24 Mark Silva
25 Doug Holmquist
26 Juan Bonilla
29 George Sisler
--- Coaches (Steve Donohue, Q.V. Lowe, Jerry McNertney, Mickey Vernon)

Definitions for grading conditions are located in the Introduction of this price guide.

1985 TCMA Durham Bulls

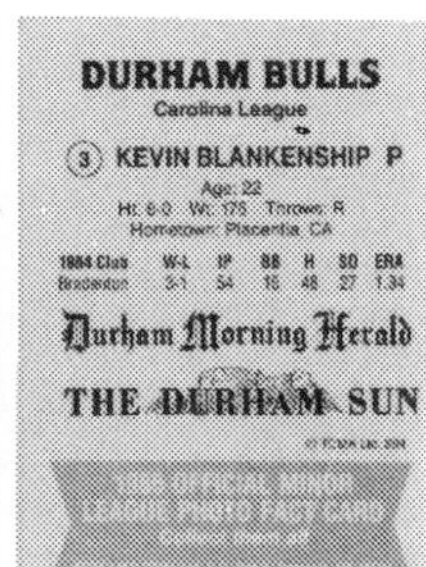

(Atlanta Braves, A) (color)

	MT	NR MT	EX
Complete Set:	15.00	11.25	6.00

1 Paul Assenmacher
2 Vince Barger
3 Kevin Blankenship
4 Mike Bormann
5 Kevin Coffman
6 Maximo Del Rosario
7 David Jones
8 Dave Morris
9 Mac Rogers
10 Not Issued
11 Mike Santiago
12 Marty Schrieber
13 Troy Tomsick
14 Harry Bright
15 Jim Grant
16 Bob Porter
17 Mike Delao
18 Flavio alfaro
19 Chris Baird
20 Chip Childress
21 Terry Cormack
22 Sal D'Alessandro
23 Juan Fredymond
24 Dave Griffin
25 Wayne Harrison
26 Johnny Hatcher
27 Roger LaFrancois
28 Mike Nipper
29 Bob Posey
30 Mike Reynolds
31 Jeff Wagner
32 Mike Yastrzemski

1985 TCMA Elmira Pioneers

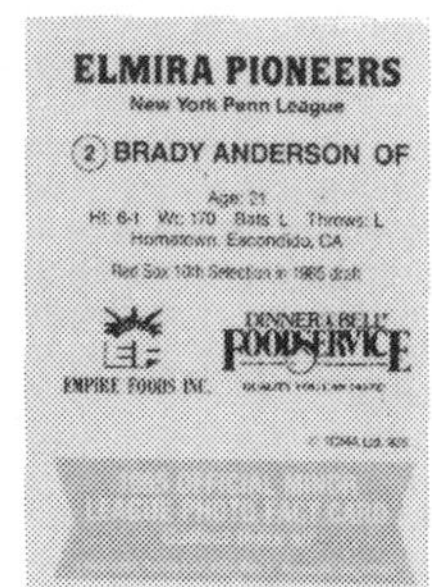

(Boston Red Sox, A) (color)

	MT	NR MT	EX
Complete Set:	30.00	22.00	12.00

1 John Abbot
2 Brady Anderson
3 Mike Carista
4 Dell Carter
5 Jim Cox
6 Roberto Fuentes
7 Dan Gabriele
8 Gary Gouldrup
9 Brock Knight
10 Eric Laseke
11 Derek Livernois
12 Greg Lotzar
13 Greg Magistri
14 Josias Manzanillo
15 Donnie McGowan
16 Bill Plante
17 Todd Pratt
18 Catlos Quintana
19 Marte Rogers
20 Victor Rosario
21 Tim Speakman
22 John Toale
23 Luis Vasquez
24 Kerman Williams
25 Bill Zupka

Definitions for grading conditions are located in the introduction of this price guide.

1985 TCMA Ft. Myers Royals

(Kansas City Royals, A) (color)

	MT	NR MT	EX
Complete Set:	35.00	26.00	14.00

1 Ed Bass
2 Todd Mabe
3 Brad Davis
4 Craig Walter
5 Don Sparling
6 Tom Niemann
7 Angel Morris
8 Jeff Hull
9 Kevin Seitzer
10 Mark Van Blaricom
11 Phil George
12 Jose DeJesus
13 Jose Nunez
14 Jeff Brown
15 Israel Sanchez
16 Chito Martinez
17 Doug Gilcrease
18 Gary Thurman
19 Tommy Mohr
20 Theo Shaw
21 Mark Farnsworth
22 Steve DeSalvo
23 Mike Keckler
24 Jackie Blackburn
25 Jim Moore
26 Duane Gustavson
27 Mike Alvarez
28 Luis Santos
29 Derek Vanacore
30 Jose Rodiles

1985 TCMA Greensboro Hornets

(Boston Red Sox, A) (color)

	MT	NR MT	EX
Complete Set:	10.00	7.50	4.00

1 Doug Camilli
2 Alan Ashikinazy
3 Tary Scott
4 Manuel Jose
5 Thomas Bonk
6 Bruce Lockhart
7 Christopher Moritz
8 Joseph Skripko
9 Zachary Crouch
10 Roberto Zambrano
11 Joseph Stephenson
12 Wayne Tremblay
13 Eduardo Zambrano
14 Pat Dewechter
15 Roy Hall
16 James Corsi
17 Daryl Irvine
18 Eric Hetzel
19 David Peterson
20 Daniel Cakeler
21 Ernest Abril
22 Patrick Jelks
23 Jose Flores
24 Eugene Barrios
25 Anthony DeFrancesco
26 Leverne Jackson
27 Bradley Mettler
28 John DePrimo

1985 TCMA International League All-Stars

(AAA) (complete set price includes includes scarce Greenwell, Mitchell and Slider cards)

	MT	NR MT	EX
Complete Set:	50.00	37.50	20.50

1 Bob Shaffer
2 Bob Tumpane
3 Miguel Sosa
4 Kevin Mitchell
5 Carlos Rios
6 Lasbelle Tarver
7 Billy Beane
8 Doc Estes

9 Larry Owen
10 Ed Hearn
11 Tony Brizzolara
12 John Rabb
13 Billy Springer (Steve Springer)
14 Al Pedrique
15 John Gibbons
16 Terry Blocker
17 Joe Johnson
18 Charlie Mitchell (withdrawn from set - scarce)
19 Rick Anderson
20 Jeff Bittiger
21 Wes Gardner
22 Roy Majtyka
23 Bruce Dal Canton
24 Doc Edwards
25 Jim Wilson
26 Juan Bonilla
27 Scott Ullger
28 Kelly Paris
29 Rick Leach
30 Mike Hart
31 Kelly Heath
32 Juan Espino
33 Dan Briggs
34 Jim Deshaies
35 Dave Gallagher
36 Dan Rohn
37 Kelly Gruber
38 Jeff Reed
39 Dennis Burtt
40 Brad Havens
41 Tom Henke
42 Tom Rowe
43 Brian Allard
44 Mike Greenwell (withdrawn from set scarce)
45 Rac Slider (withdrawn from set - scarce)

1985 TCMA Iowa Cubs

(Chicago Cubs, AAA) (color)

	MT	NR MT	EX
Complete Set:	17.00	12.75	7.00

1 Tony Castillo
2 Bill Hayes
3 Trey Brooks
4 Tom Lombarski
5 Paul Noce
6 Dave Owen
7 Julio Valdez
8 Brian Dayett
9 Tom Grant
10 Billy Hatcher
11 Chico Walker
12 Jay Baller
13 Derek Botelho
14 Dave Gumpert
15 Scott Holman
16 Bill Johnson
17 Ron Meridith
18 Sam Bernabe
19 Jon Perlman
20 Ken Pryce
21 Larry Rothschild
22 Mark Gillaspie
23 Dave Hostetler
24 Greg Hoffmann
25 Dick Cummings
26 Ken Grandquist
27 Don Silverman
28 Larry Cox
29 Jim Colborn
30 Steve Carroll
31 Steve Weck
33 Bruce Bielenberg
34 Not Issued
35 Cubby (mascot), Del Roy Smith (batboy), Danny Woolis (batboy)
36 Steve Rodiles

1985 TCMA Kingston Blue Jays

(Toronto Blue Jays, A) (color)

	MT	NR MT	EX
Complete Set:	25.00	18.50	10.00

1 Mark Clemons
2 Omar Bencomo
3 Tony Castillo
4 Mike Cullen
5 Mark Dickman

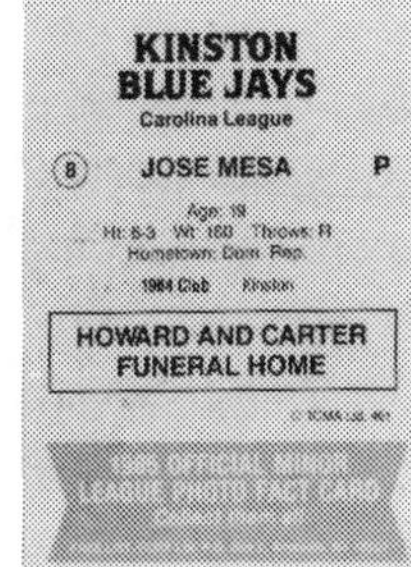

6 Perry Lychak
7 Alan McKay
8 Jose Mesa
9 Pablo Reyes
10 Jose Segura
11 Willie Shanks
12 Mark Cooper
13 Nelson Liriano
14 Randy Romagna
15 Pat Borders
16 Webster Garrison
17 Omar Malave
18 Joselito Reyes
19 Glen-Allen Hill
20 Drex Roberts
21 Geronimo berroa
22 Ken Whitfield
23 Eric Yelding
24 Grady Little
25 Rocket Wheeler
26 Tex Drake

1985 TCMA Little Falls Mets

(New York Mets, A) (color)

	MT	NR MT	EX
Complete Set:	17.50	13.00	7.00

1 Mike Anderson
2 Kevin Armstrong
3 Steve Brueggemann
4 Ron Dominico
5 Brian Givens
6 Lorin Jundy
7 Kelvin Page
8 Chris Rauth
9 Jeff Richardson
10 John Touzzo
11 Tom Wachs
12 Todd Welborn
13 Mark Brunswick
14 Ron Narcisse
15 Rob Colescott
16 Kurt DeLuca
17 Andres Espinoza
18 Dave Gelatt
19 T.J. Johnson
20 Luis Natera
21 Craig Repoz
22 Joaquin Contreras
23 Cliff Gonzalez
24 Maury Gooden
25 Dean Johnson
26 Johnny Monell
27 Bryant Robertson

1985 TCMA Lynchburg Mets

(New York Mets, A) (color)

	MT	NR MT	EX
Complete Set:	40.00	30.00	16.00

1 Mike Cubbage
2 Jim Bibby
3 Dave Tresch
4 Jeff Innis
5 Reggie Dobie
6 Mickey Weston
7 Wray Bergendahl
8 Dave Jensen
9 Jose Bautista
10 David Wyatt
11 Tom Burns
12 Kyle Hartshorn
13 Joe Klink
14 Kevin Burrell
15 Al Carmichael
16 Steve Philips
17 Chris Maloney
18 Keith Miller
19 Kevin Elster
20 Frank Moscat
21 Wilmer Caraballo
22 Andy Lawrence
23 Rey Martinez
24 John Wilson
25 Shawn Abner
26 George Doggett
27 Scott Little

Definitions for grading conditions are located in the Introduction of this price guide.

1985 TCMA Madison Muskies

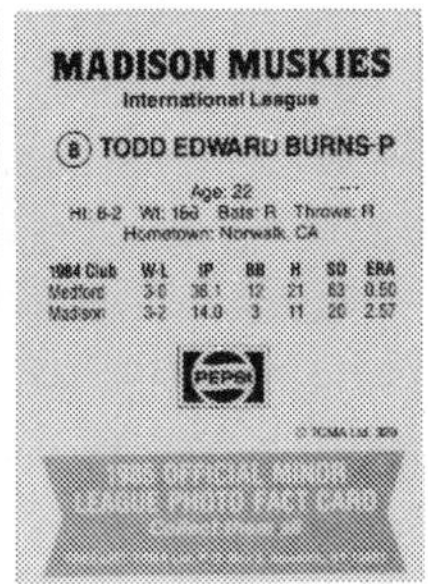

(Oakland A's, A) (color)

	MT	NR MT	EX
Complete Set:	15.00	11.25	6.00

1 Scott Sabo
2 Faustoe Santos
3 Scott Whaley
4 Roy Anderson
5 Russell Appletgate
6 Antionio Arlas
7 Gregory Brake
8 Todd Burns
9 Brian Criswell
10 Michael Cupples
11 Brian Dorsett
12 Patrick Dietrick
13 Jose Ferreira
14 Robert Gould
15 Darel Hansen
16 Mark Howie
17 Domingo Jose
18 John Kanter
19 Russell Kibler
20 Joseph Kramer
21 Andrew Krause
22 Mark Leonette
23 James Nettles
24 Richard Wise
25 David Schober

1985 TCMA Maine Guides

(Cleveland Indians, AAA) (color)

	MT	NR MT	EX
Complete Set:	12.50	9.50	5.25

1 Jeff Barkley
2 Dave Beard
3 Jose Calderon
4 Mark Calvert
5 Bryan Clark
6 Keith Creel
8 Jerry Reed
9 Tommy Rowe
10 Roy Smith
11 Rich Thompson
12 Jim Siwy
13 Jose Roman
14 Pat Dempsey
15 Kevin Buckley
16 Geno Petralli
17 Shanie Dugas
18 Barry Evans
19 Jeff Moronko
20 Junior Noboa
21 Luis Quinones
22 Danny Rohn
23 Orlando Sanchez
24 Jim Wilson
26 Mike Brewer
27 Dave Gallagher
28 Dwight Taylor
29 Doc Edwards
30 Brian Allard
31 Steve Ciszczon
32 Scott Tellgren

1985 TCMA Tigers De Mexico

(Mexican League, AAA) (color)

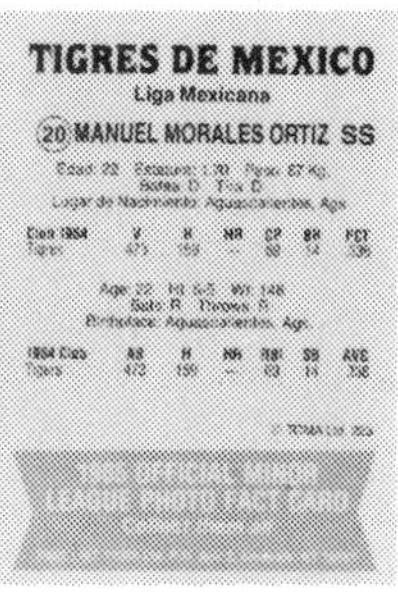

	MT	NR MT	EX
Complete Set:	8.50	6.25	3.50

1 Jesus Rios
2 Roberto Mendez
3 Maurillo Arangure
4 Oswaldo Alvarez
5 Martin Buitimea
6 Ramon Villegas
7 Rodolfo Dimas
8 Francisco Montano
9 Ildefonso Velazquel
10 Lorenzo Retes
11 Francisco Coto
12 Juan Palafox
13 Martin Torres
14 Jose Aguilar
15 Jose Alvarado
16 Ismael Jaime
17 Homar Rojas
18 Adulfo Camacho
19 Jose De Jesus
20 Manuel Morales
21 Amado Peralta
22 Ricardo Renteria
23 Nicolas Castaneda
24 Antionio Castro
25 Matias Caprillo
26 Javier Cruz
27 Juan Bellacetin
28 Luis Ibarra
29 "Chano" & The Chicken

1985 TCMA Midland Angels

(California Angels, AA) (color)

	MT	NR MT	EX
Complete Set:	22.50	16.50	9.00

1 Tito Nanni
2 Bryan Price
3 Greg Key
4 Fred Wilburn
5 Mark Bonner
6 David Heath
7 Doug McKenzie
8 Devon White
9 Dan Murphy
10 Joe Maddon
11 Tom Bryden
12 Don Timberlake
13 Steve Finch
14 Doug Davis
15 Ken Angulo
16 Spiro Psaltis
17 Mark McLemore
18 Kevin Davis
19 Billie Merrifield
20 Aurelio Monteagudo
21 Scott Suehr
22 Ed Delzer
23 Juan Cruz
24 Reggie Montgomery
25 Julian Gonzalez

1985 TCMA Nashua Pirates

(Pittsburgh Pirates, AA) (color)

	MT	NR MT	EX
Complete Set:	15.00	11.25	6.00

1 Scott Bailes
2 Kerry Baker
3 Mike Berger
4 Craig Brown
5 Kim Christenson
6 Nelson de la Rosa
7 Dorley Downs
8 Stan Fansler
9 Felix Fermin
10 Ken Ford
11 Sam Haro
12 Dave Johnson
13 Tony Laird
14 Larry Lamonde
15 Ravelo Manzanillo
16 Lee Marcheskie
17 Steve McAllister
18 Mitch McKelvy
19 Pete Rice
20 Leon Roberts
21 Ruben Rodriguez
22 Leo Sanchez
23 Rich Sauveur
24 Don Taylor
25 Dave Tumbas
26 Donald Williams
27 John Lipon
28 George Como
29 Jerome Mileur

1985 TCMA Newark Orioles

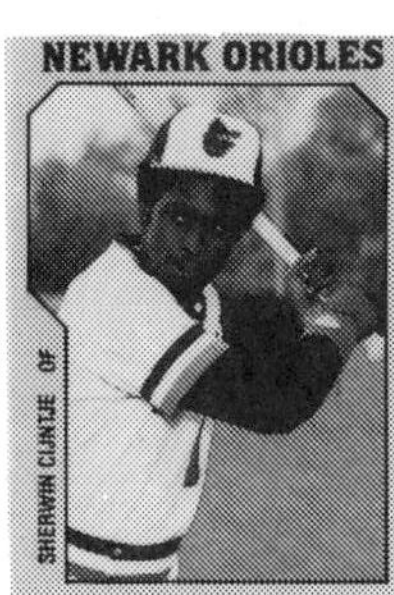

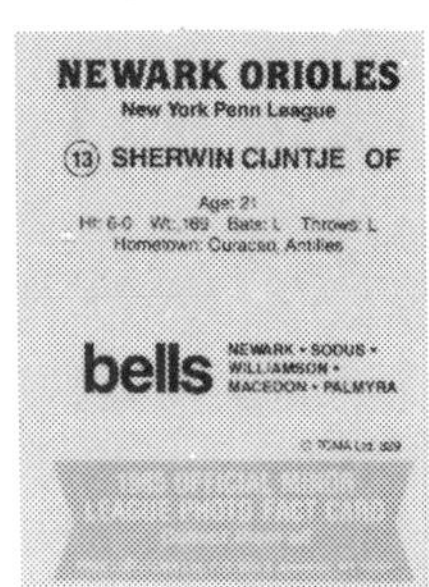

(Baltimore Orioles, A) (color)

	MT	NR MT	EX
Complete Set:	10.00	7.50	4.00

1 Scott Williams
2 Randy King
3 Ty Nichols
4 Greg Talamantez
5 Jeff Tackett
6 Hemmy McFarlane
7 Tony Rohan
8 Mike Holm
9 Gerald Adams
10 Henry Gonzalez
11 Wayne Wilson
12 Benny Bautista
13 Sherwin Cijntje
14 Rico Rossy
15 Robert Gutierrez
16 Mark Schockman
17 Rob Dromerhauser
18 Ray Crone
19 Chris Gaeta
20 Pat Van Heyningen
21 Pete Mancini
22 Jesse Vazquez
23 Matt Skinner
24 Kevin Burke
25 Frank Bellino

1985 TCMA Oklahoma City 89'ers

(Texas Rangers, AAA) (color)

	MT	NR MT	EX
Complete Set:	25.00	18.50	10.00

1 Orlando Mercado
2 Mitch Zwolensky
3 Jeff Kunkel
4 Mike Jirchele

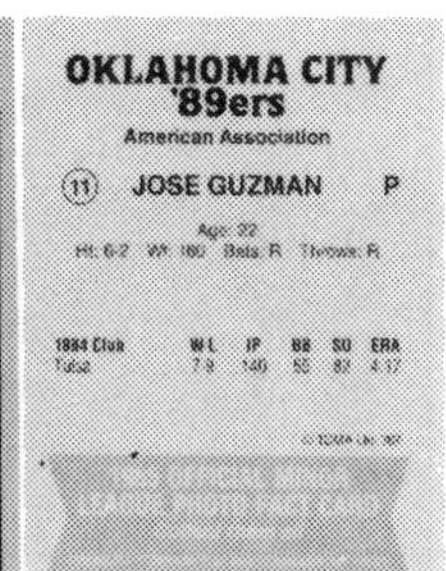

5 Geno Petralli
6 Jim Anderson
7 Tommy Boggs
8 Glen Cook
9 Ricky Wright
10 Tony Fossas
11 jose Guzman
12 Mike Parrott
13 Tommy Shimp
14 Greg Cambell
15 Dave Oliver
16 George Wright
17 Steve Buechele
18 Oddibie McDowell
19 Bob Sebra
20 Jim Maler
21 Bob Brower
22 Mike Rubel
23 Dave Stockstill
24 Rusty Gerhardt
25 Nick Capra
26 Dale Mohorcic
27 Dale Murray
28 Greg Tabor
29 Chuckie Canady
30 Bill Earley

1985 TCMA Omaha Royals

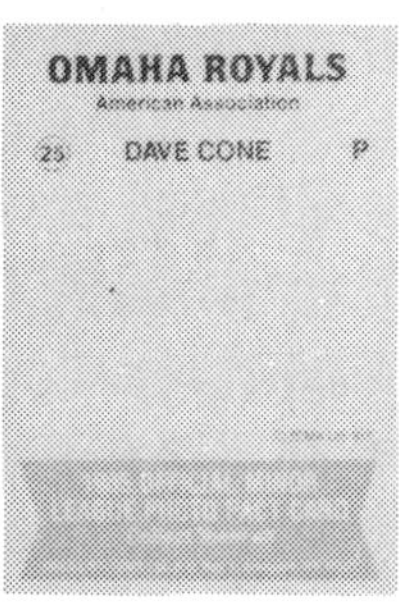

(Kansas City Royals, AAA) (color)

	MT	NR MT	EX
Complete Set:	30.00	22.50	12.25

1 Bil Gorman
2 Matt Bassett
3 Nick Swartz
4 Frank Mancuso
5 Terry Wendlandt
6 Gus Cherry
7 Les Strode
8 Rich Murray
9 Pat Putnam
10 Tony Ferreira
11 Rich Dubee
12 Butch Davis
13 Mike Griffin
14 Renie Martin
15 Mark Huismann
16 Jamie Quirk
17 Jim Scranton
18 Mike Kinnunen
19 John Morris
20 Marty Wilkerson
21 Rondin Johnson
22 Gene Lamont
23 Mike Kingery
24 Dave Leeper
25 Dave Cone
26 Al Hargesheimer
27 Kenny Baker
28 Buster Keeton
29 Bill Pecota
30 Bob Hegman
31 Brian Pohlberg

1985 TCMA Orlando Twins

(Minnesota Twins, AA) (color)

	MT	NR MT	EX
Complete Set:	10.00	7.50	4.00

1 Steve Aragon

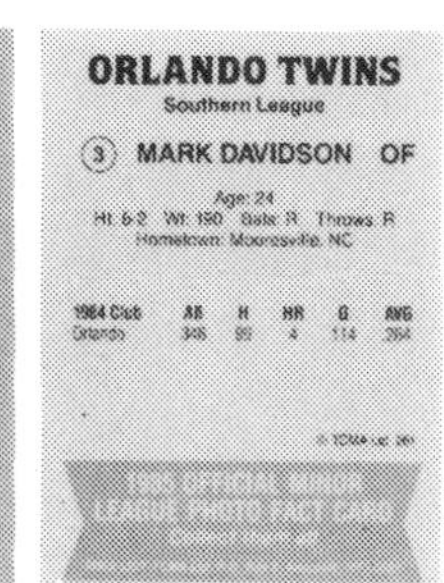

2 Erez Borowsky
3 Mark Davison
4 Paul Felix
5 Mark Funderburk
6 Dan Hanggie
7 Alexis Marte
8 Mike Moreno
9 Greg Morhardt
10 Bobby Ralston
11 Sam Sorce
12 Jeff Trout
13 Mike Verkuilen
14 Ossie Alfonzo
15 Al Cardwood
16 Danny Clay
17 Ken Klump
18 Paul Mancuso
19 Bob Mulligan
20 Les Straker
21 Tim Wiseman
22 Charlie Manuel
23 Wayne Hattaway
24 Dave Williams
25 Gorman Heimueller
26 Craig Henderson

1985 TCMA Pawtucket Red Sox

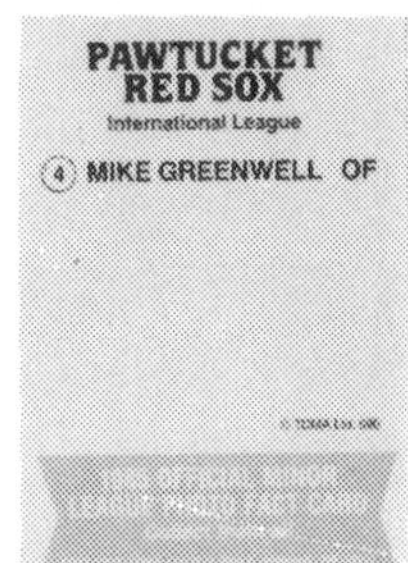

(Boston Red Sox, AAA) (color)

	MT	NR MT	EX
Complete Set:	75.00	56.00	30.00

1 Gus Burgess
2 Juan Bustabad
3 Pat Dodson
4 Mike Greenwell
5 Paul Hundhammer
7 Dave Malpeso
8 Mike Mesh
9 Garry Miller-Jones
10 Sam Nattile
11 Kevin Romine
12 Danny Sheaffer
13 Robin Fuson
14 Rac Slider
15 Dave Sax
16 Tony Herron
17 Tom McCarthy
18 Kevin Kane
19 Mitch Johnson
20 Charlie Mitchell
21 George Mercerod

1985 TCMA Prince William Pirates

(Pittsburgh Pirates, A) (color)

	MT	NR MT	EX
Complete Set:	15.00	11.25	6.00

1 Orlando Lind
2 Scott Neal
3 Barry Jones
4 Jose Melendez
5 Chip Cunningham
6 Terry Adkins
7 Robby Russell
8 Dimas Gutierrez
9 Steve Lewis
10 Jim Neidlinger
11 Steve Barnard

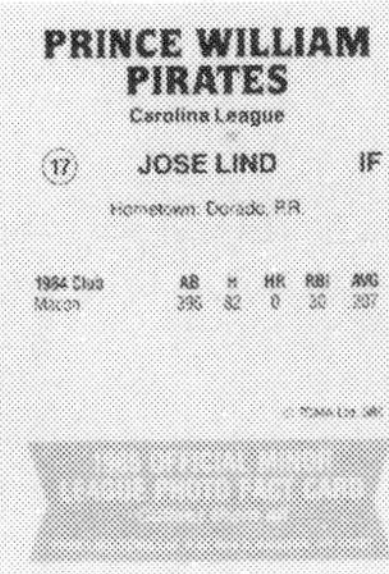

12 Mike Folga
13 Chris Lein
14 Lance Belen
15 Scott Borland
16 Shawn Holman
17 Jose Lind
18 Tony Blasucci
19 Gary Grudzinski
20 Reggie Barringer
21 Kevin Gordon
22 John Smiley
23 Ed Ott
24 Mike Stevens
25 Van Evans
26 Frank Klopp
27 J.B. Moore
28 Dave Butters
29 Scott Knox
30 Burk Goldthorn
31 Brian Jones

1985 TCMA Richmond Braves

(Atlanta Braves, AAA) (color)

	MT	NR MT	EX
Complete Set:	12.00	9.00	5.00

1 Tony Brizzolara
2 Marty Clary
3 David Clay
4 Jeff Dedmon
5 Dan Morogiello
6 Mike Payne
7 Gary Reiter
8 Dave Schuler
9 Steve Shields
10 Matt West
11 John Lickert
12 Larry Owen
13 Glenn Gulliver
14 Randy Johnson
15 Carlos Rios
16 Ken Smith
17 Miguel Sosa
18 Doc Estes
19 Lee Graham
20 Gene Roof
21 Milt Thompson
22 John Rabb
23 Bruce Dal Canton
24 Sam Ayoub
25 Sonny Jackson
26 Roy Majtyka

1985 TCMA Rochester Red Wings

(Baltimore Orioles, AAA) (complete set price includes scarce Biercevicz and Bjorkman cards)

	MT	NR MT	EX
Complete Set:	20.00	15.00	8.00

1 Raymond Corbett
2 Al Pardo
3 Luis Rosado
4 Dave Falcone
5 Leonardo Hernandez
6 Ricky Jones
7 Nelson Norman
8 Kelly Paris
9 James Traber
10 Roderick Allen

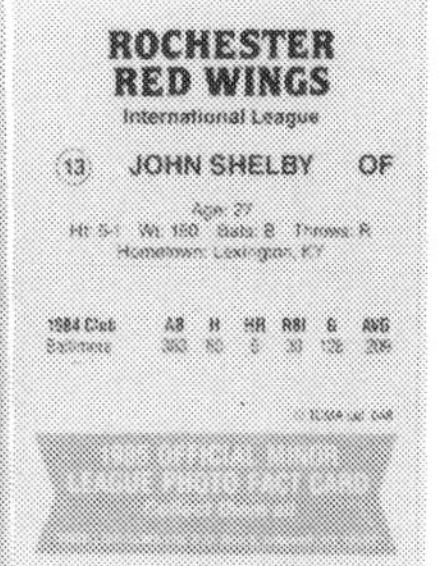

11 Darrel Brown
12 Robert Molinaro
13 John Shelby
14 Gerald Augustine
15 Jose Brito
16 Bradley Havens
17 Phillip Huffman
18 Jerry Johnson
19 Odell Jones
20 Joseph Kucharski
21 David Rajsich
22 William Swaggerty
23 Donald Welchel
24 Frank Verdi
25 Sandy Valdespino
26 "The Braintrust"
27 D. Gordon, J. Kurcharski
28 Jamie Reed
29 Mark Wiley
30 Greg Biercevicz
31 George Bjorkman

1985 TCMA Springfield Cardinals

(St. Louis Cardinals, A) (color)

	MT	NR MT	EX
Complete Set:	11.00	8.25	4.50

1 John Rigos
2 Rich Embser
3 Jim Fregosi
4 Jim Van Houten
5 John Costello
6 Todd Demeter
7 John Digioia
8 Greg Dunn
9 John Fassero
10 Lloyd Merrit
11 Mike Fitzgerald
12 Craig Wilson
13 Mike Hartley
14 Matt Kinzer
15 Ron Leon
16 Brad Luther
17 Harry McCulla
18 Steve Turco
19 Steve Turgeon
20 Charles McGrath
21 Jay North
22 Angleo Nunley
23 Pete Stoll
25 Mike Robinson
30 Paul Wilmet

1985 TCMA Syracuse Chiefs

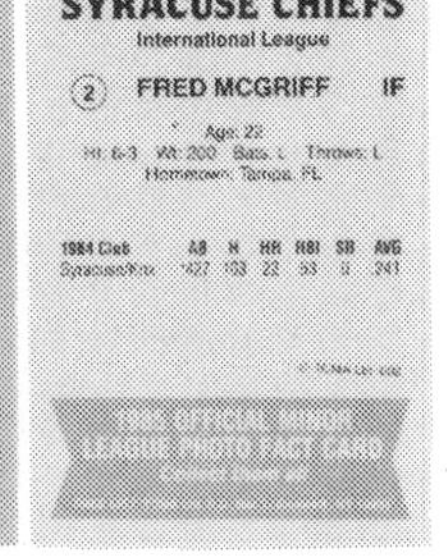

(Toronto Blue Jays, AAA) (color)

	MT	NR MT	EX
Complete Set:	72.50	54.25	30.00

1 Gibson Alba
2 Fred McGriff
3 Gary Allenson
4 Stan Clark (Clarke)
5 Dale Holman
6 Tom Filer
7 Keith Gilliam
8 Tom Henke
9 Dennis Howard
10 John Woodworth
11 Rick Leach
12 Matt Williams
13 Don Gordon
14 Alex Infante
15 Colin McLaughlin
16 Pat Rooney
17 Mark Poole
18 Jerry Keller
19 Mike Sharperson
20 John Mayberry
21 Doug Ault
22 Kelly Gruber
23 Vance McHenry
24 "Red" Coughlin
25 Dale Holman, Fred McGriff
26 Batboys
27 John Cerutti
28 Dennis Homberg
29 Derwin McNealy
30 Cloyd Boyer
31 Dave Stegman

1985 TCMA Tidewater Tides

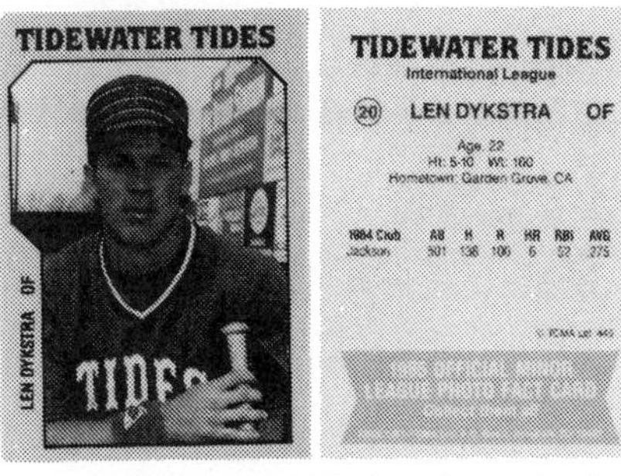

(New York Mets, AAA) (complete set price includes scarce card #16)

	MT	NR MT	EX
Complete Set:	60.00	45.00	24.75

1 Rick Lancellotti
2 Terry Leach
3 Sid Fernandez
4 Jeff Bettendorf
5 Calvin Schiraldi
6 Rick Anderson
7 Randy Niemann
8 Jeff Bittiger
9 Wes Gardner
10 Bill Latham
11 Rick Aguilera
12 Ed Olwine
13 Laschelle Tarver
14 Billy Beane
15 John Gibbons
16 Steve Springer (black bat, photo actually Ed Hearn)
17 Steve Springer (white bat, correct photo)
18 Kevin Mitchell
19 Terry Blocker
20 Len Dykstra
21 Ed Hearn
22 Ross Jones
23 Mike Davis
24 Alfredo Pedrique
25 Mark Carreon
26 John Cumberland
27 Bob Schaefer
28 Rick Rainer

1985 TCMA Toldeo Mud Hens

(Minnesota Twins, AAA) (complete set price includes scarce Chiffer card)

	MT	NR MT	EX
Complete Set:	17.50	13.00	7.00

1 Allan Anderson
2 Eric Broersma
3 Mark Brown
4 Dennis Burtt
5 Not Issued
6 Frank Eufemia
8 Ed Hodge

9 Not Issued
10 Mark Portugal
11 Mike Walters
12 Len Whitehouse
13 Toby Hernandez
14 Jeff Reed
15 Alvaro Espinoza
16 Houston Jiminez
17 Steve Lombardozzi
18 Scott Ullger
19 Reggie Whittemore
20 Andre David
21 Mike Hart
22 Stan Holmes
23 Greg Howe
24 Jerry Lomastro
25 Al Woods
26 Cal Ermer
27 Jim Shellenback
30 Rich Yett
32 Floyd Cliffer

1985 TCMA Utica Blue Sox

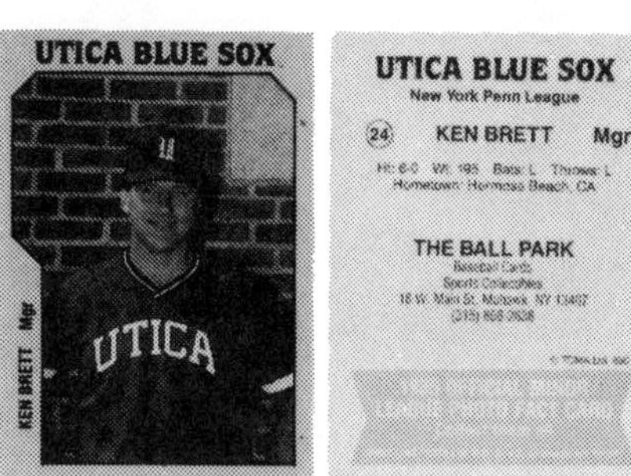

(No Affiliation, A) (color) Although the Utica Blue Jays set is classified as a Co-op team, players were furnished from the Expos, Phillies, Rangers and Tigers.

	MT	NR MT	EX
Complete Set:	25.00	18.50	10.00

1 Jim Allison
2 Ross Jones
3 Dave Linton
4 Paulino Paixao
5 Bob Sudo
6 Darren Travels
7 Sergio Valdez
8 Rob Williams
9 Roger Dean
10 Pancho Hedfelt
11 Al Hibbs
12 Esteben Beltre
13 Rodney Clark
14 Jeff Scheaffer
15 Alfonso Traverez
16 Larry Walker
17 Bob Brown
18 Andy Donatelli
19 Ray Garcia
20 Raymond Noble
21 Fred Perez
22 Troy Ricker
23 Steve St. Claire
24 Ken Brett
25 Gene Glynn
26 Dan Gazzilli

1985 TCMA Vero Beach Dodgers

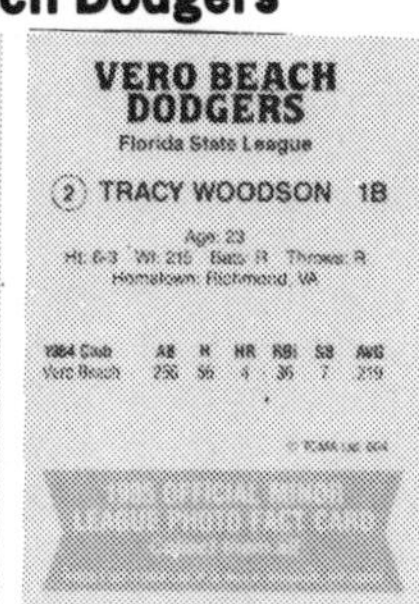

(Los Angeles Dodgers, A) (color)

	MT	NR MT	EX
Complete Set:	12.00	9.00	5.00

1 Bobby Hamilton
2 Tracy Woodson
3 John Schlichting
4 Gary Newsom
5 Manuel Francois
6 Joe Szekley
7 Felipe Gutierrez
8 Wayne Kirby
9 Gary Legumina
10 Ed Jacobo
11 Henry Gatewood
12 Norberto Flores
13 Harry Ritch
14 Joe Karmeris
15 William Brennan
16 Bob Jacobsen
17 Vince Beringhele
18 Mike Schweignoffer
19 Bary Wohler
20 Greg Mayberry
21 Luis Lopez
22 Mike Pesavento
23 Mike Cherry
24 Rob Giesecke
25 Dennis Lewallyn
26 Stan Wasiak
27 John Shoemaker

1985 TCMA Visalia Oaks

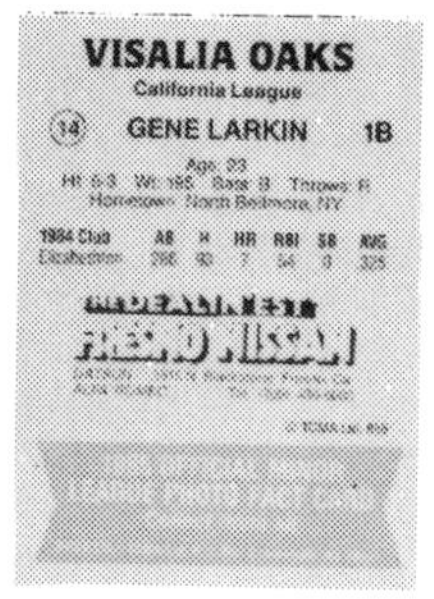

(Minnesota Twins, A) (color)

	MT	NR MT	EX
Complete Set:	10.00	7.50	4.00

1 Phil Wilson
2 Doug Palmer
3 Perry Husband
4 Bill O'Connor
5 Sal Nicolosi
6 Jeff Schugel
7 Brad Bierley
8 Jay Bell
9 Chris Forgione
10 Robert Calley
11 Tom DiCeglio
12 Chris Calvert
13 Dave Vetsch
14 Gene Larkin
15 Bob Lee
16 Ray Velasquez
17 Todd Budke
18 Jeff Rojas
19 Wes Pierorazio
20 Neil Landmark
21 Tony Guerrero
22 Jose Dominguez
23 Scott Klingbell
24 Troy Galloway
25 Danny Schmitz

1985 TCMA Waterbury Indians

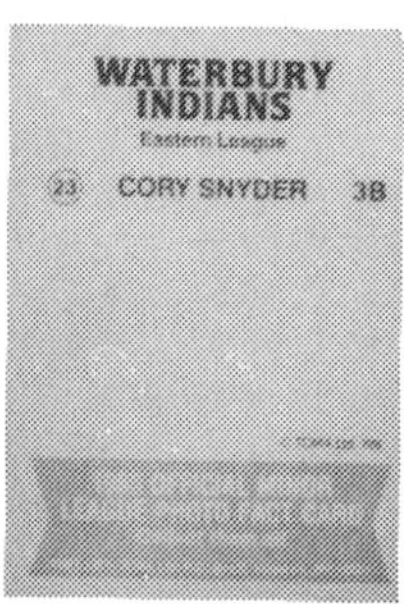

(Cleveland Indians, AA) (color)

	MT	NR MT	EX
Complete Set:	25.00	18.50	10.00

1 Nelson Pedraza
2 Wilson Valera
3 Randy Washington
4 Winston Ficklin
5 Glenn Edwards
6 Richard Doyle
7 Mickey Street
8 John Miglio
9 Cal Santarelli
10 Wayne Johnson
11 Reggie Ritter
12 Doug Jones
13 Marty Leach
14 Jeff Arney
15 Dave Clark
16 Ron Wallenhaupt
17 German Barranca
18 Tim Glass
19 Jim Driscoll
20 George Cecchetti
21 John Farrell
22 Jack Aker
23 Cory Snyder
24 Andy Allanson
25 Dain Syverson

1985 Team Birmingham Barons

(Detroit Tigers, AA)

	MT	NR MT	EX
Complete Set:	45.00	33.50	18.00

(1) Ricky Barlow
(2) Cary Golbert
(3) Curt Cornwell
(4) Mark Dejohn
(5) Steve Eagar
(6) Bruce Fields
(7) Paul Gibson
(8) Mike Henneman
(9) William Hinz
(10) John Hotchkiss
(11) Duane James
(12) Al Labozzetta
(13) Gordon Mackenzie
(14) Scotti Madison
(15) Steve McInnery
(16) Craig Mills
(17) Dan Norman
(18) Ramon Pena
(19) Joe Perrotte
(20) Jeff Robinson
(21) Ronald Rollin
(22) Benny Ruiz
(23) Gary Springer
(24) Dan St. Clair
(25) Reggie Thomas

1985 Team Chattanooga Lookouts

(Seattle Mariners, AAA) All cards have blank backs.

	MT	NR MT	EX
Complete Set:	75.00	56.00	30.00

(1) Rick Adair
(2) Brian Bargerhuff
(3) Greg Bartley
(4) Randy Braun
(5) Renard Brown
(6) Jim Bryant
(7) Clark Crist
(8) Brian David
(9) Mario Diaz
(10) Mike Evans
(11) Dan Firova
(12) Ross Grimsley
(13) Dave Hengel
(14) Paul Hollins
(15) Tom "Radar" Hunt
(16) Ken Jones
(17) Vic Martin
(18) Jeff McDonald
(19) Rusty McNealy
(20) Jed Murray
(21) Dave Myers
(22) Randy Newman
(23) Bill Plummer
(24) Brick Smith
(25) Terry Taylor
(26) Ric Wilson

1985 Team Columbus Clippers

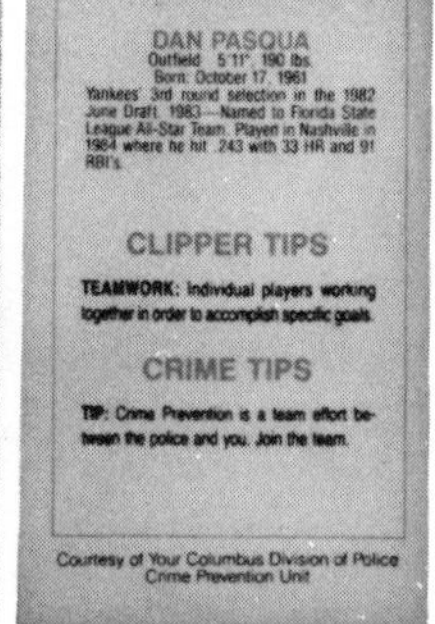

(New York Yankees, AAA)

	MT	NR MT	EX
Complete Set:	6.00	4.50	2.50

(1) Tom Barrett
(2) Bert Bradley
(3) Dan Briggs
(4) Curt Brown
(5) Clay Christiansen
(6) Don Cooper
(7) Pete Dalena
(8) Jim Deshaies
(9) Juan Espino
(10) Kelly Faulk
(11) Brian Fisher
(12) Kelly Heath
(13) Butch Hobson
(14) Rex Hudler
(15) Tim Knight
(16) Carl "Stump" Merrill
(17) Dan Pasqua
(18) Alphonso Pulido
(19) Kelly Scott
(20) Mark Silva
(21) George H. Sisler Jr.
(22) Keith Smith
(23) Al Williams
(24) Matt Winters
(25) Coaches/Trainer Card (Q.V. Lowe, Jerry McNertney, Mickey Vernon, Steve Donohue)

1985 Team Dayton Beach Islanders

(Cleveland Indians, A) This set is numbered as they appear on the cards.

	MT	NR MT	EX
Complete Set:	37.50	28.00	15.25

1 Tim Haller
2 Michael Holm
3 Dave Murray
4 Mike Halasaz
5 Ray Corbett
6 Jeff Hubbard
7 Perry Hill
8 Kurt Beamesderfer
10 Rick Poznanski
11 Tony Triplett
12 Bill Ripken
14 Pat Vanheyningen
15 Dan Van Cleve
16 Larry Heise
17 Jim Hutto
18 Tim Smith
19 Robert Gutierrez
20 Rob Amble
22 Chris Willsher
23 Eric Dersin
24 Rich Rice
25 Jeff Melrose
26 Carm Lo Sauro
27 Edward Rohan
28 Ben Bianchi
29 Justin Gannon
30 Bruce Kipper
31 Ron Johnson
--- Brian Robinson
--- Thomas Petrizzo

1985 Team Greenville Braves

(Atlanta Braves, AA)

	MT	NR MT	EX
Complete Set:	32.50	24.25	13.50

(1) Rick Albert
(2) Brian Aviles
(3) Jim Beauchamp
(4) Glen Bockhorn
(5) Larry Bradford
(6) Inocencio Guerrero
(7) Tom Hayes
(8) Randy Ingle
(9) Joe Johnson
(10) Mike Knox
(11) Todd Lamb
(12) Rich Leggatt
(13) Bob Luzon
(14) Simon Rosario
(15) Matt Sinatro
(16) Bill Slack
(17) Jeff Taylor
(18) Andre Thomas
(19) Tommy Thompson
(20) Freddie Tiburcio
(21) Andre Treadway
(22) Bob Tumpane
(23) Leo Vargas
(24) Duane Ward
(25) Larry Whisenton
(26) Steve Ziem

1985 Team Huntsville Stars

(Oakland A's, AA) (co-sponsored by Burger King)

	MT	NR MT	EX
Complete Set:	10.00	7.50	4.00

Brian Thorson
11 Luis Polonia
14 Brian Graham
15 Tom Dozier
16 Terry Steinbach
17 Chip Conklin
18 John Marquardt
19 Ray Thoma
20 Stan Javier
21 Bill Monneyham
22 Brian Dorsett
23 Scott Whaley
24 Gary lance
25 Brad Fischer
26 Mark Bauer
30 Larry Smith
31 Tim Belcher
32 Darrel Akerfelds
33 Eric Plunk
34 Greg Cadaret
40 Joe Law
41 Rob Nelson
42 Wayne Giddings
43 Rick Stromer
44 Jose Canseco

1985 Team Indianapolis Indians

(Cincinnati Reds, AAA)

	MT	NR MT	EX
Complete Set:	27.50	20.50	11.25

1 Team photo
2 Felipe Alou
3 Andres Galarraga
4 Rich Stoll
5 Roy Johnson
6 Steve Baker
7 Mike Fuentes
8 Tim Cates
9 Max Venable
10 Fred Breining
11 Rene Gonzales
12 Fred Manrique
13 Greg Bargar
14 Al Newman
15 Sal Butera
16 Mickey Mahler
17 Dave Hostetler
18 Paul Hertzler
19 Randy St. Claire
20 George Bjorkman
21 Wally Johnson
22 Jack O'Connor
23 Dave Hocksema
24 Steve Brown
25 Casey Candaele
26 Coaches/Trainer Card
27 The Broadcasters
28 Ray Knight (Indianapolis alumni)
29 Dave Revering (Indianapolis alumni)
30 Ron Oester (Indianapolis alumni)
31 Mario Soto (Indianapolis alumni)
32 Bruce Berenyi (Indianapolis alumni)
33 Charlie Leibrandt (Indianapolis alumni)
34 Gary Redus (Indianapolis alumni)
35 Nick Esasky (Indianapolis alumni)
36 Bob Rodgers (Indianapolis alumni)

1985 Team Nashville Sounds

(Detroit Tigers, AA)

	MT	NR MT	EX
Complete Set:	7.00	5.25	2.75

(1) Doug Baker
(2) Darrell Brown
(3) Chuck Cary
(4) Jeff Conner
(5) Brian Denman
(6) Scott Earl
(7) Bryan Kelly
(8) Rusty Kuntz
(9) Mike Laga
(10) Dwight Lowry
(11) Scotti Madison
(12) Don Mc Gann
(13) Gordy Mc Kenzie
(14) Dan Meyer
(15) Bobby Mitchell
(16) Rich Monteleone
(17) John Pacella
(18) Chris Pittaro
(19) Joe Pittman
(20) Leon Roberts
(21) Steve Shirley
(22) Nelson Simmons
(23) Robert Stoddard
(24) Paul Voight
(25) Don Werner

1985 Team Osceola Astros

(Houston Astros, A)

	MT	NR MT	EX
Complete Set:	80.00	60.00	33.00

(1) Troy Afenir
(2) Karl Allaire
(3) Mark Baker
(4) Curtis Burke
(5) Ken Caminiti
(6) Earl Cash
(7) Mike Cerefin
(8) Dave Cripe
(9) Greg Dube
(10) Mike Friederich
(11) Tony Hampton
(12) Scott Houp
(13) Ryan Job
(14) Kevin Jones
(15) Kirk Jones
(17) Larry Lasky
(18) Arbrey Lucas
(19) Rob Mallicoat
(20) Mark Mangham
(21) Chuck Mathews
(22) Jim O'Dell
(23) Bob Parker
(24) Mark Reynolds
(25) David Rosen
(26) Doug Shaab
(27) Glenn Sherlock
(28) Mike Stellern
(29) Charley Taylor
(30) Gerald Young
(126) Clarke Lange

1985 Team Tulsa Drillers

(Texas Rangers, AA) This set is numbered as it appears on the backs of the cards.

	MT	NR MT	EX
Complete Set:	160.00	120.00	66.00

Ken Reitz
4 George Crum
6 George Foussianes
7 Oscar Mejia
9 Jamie Doughty
10 Mark Gile
12 Ruben Sierra
14 Barry Brunenkant
17 Larry Pott
18 Bobby Witt
19 Duane James
20 Tony Hudson
22 Jeff Moronko
23 Orlando Gomez
24 Jeff Mace
25 Bob Gergen
26 Barry Bass
27 Rob Clark
28 Bill Fahey

29 Dwayne Henry
30 Terry Johnson
31 Javier Ortiz
32 Kirk Killingsworth
33 Scott Anderson
34 Bill Taylor
35 Otto Gonzalez
36 Al Lachowicz
37 Clyde Reichard

1986

1986 Chong Modesto A's

(Oakland A's, A)

	MT	NR MT	EX
Complete Set:	12.50	9.50	5.25

1 Roy Anderson
2 Russ Applegate
3 Darren Baisley
4 Bo Kent
5 Tyler Brilinski
6 Pat Dietrick
7 Mike Duncan
8 Darel Hansen
9 Twayne Harris
10 Steve Howard
11 James Jones
12 Felix Jose
13 Lance Blankenship
14 Richard Martig
15 Shannon Mendenhall
16 Jerome Nelson
17 Jose Peguero
18 Bob Sharpnack
19 Mark Tortorice
20 Bruce Walton
21 Joe Xavier
22 Kevin Tapani
23 Mark Beavers
24 Butch Hughes
25 Tommie Reynolds
26 John Cartelli
27 Jeff Koryta

1986 Cramer Bellingham Mariners

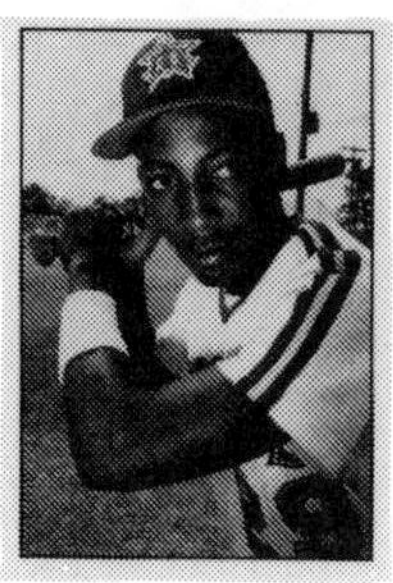

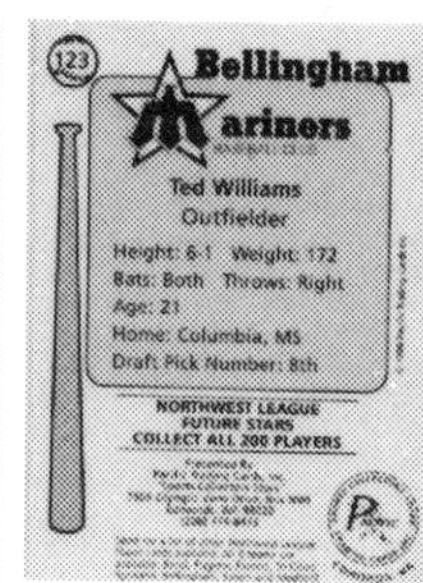

(Seattle Mariners, Rookie)

	MT	NR MT	EX
Complete Set:	8.00	6.00	3.25

101 David Hartnett
102 Jim Bowie, Jr.
103 Michael McDonald
104 Jose Bennet
105 Deron Johnson, Jr.
106 Wendell Bolar
107 Gregory Briley
108 Jose Tartabull, Jr.
109 Thomas Little
110 Jerry Goff
111 Michael Thorpe
112 Brad Rohde
113 James Pritikin
114 Bret Simmermacher
115 Tim Fortugno
116 Arvid Morfin
117 Jody Ryan
118 Troy Williams
119 Randy Little
120 James Blueberg
121 Richard DeLuca
122 Daniel Disher
123 Ted Williams
124 Raul Mendez
125 Fausto Ramirez
126 Clay Gunn
127 Rudy Webster
128 Patrick Lennon
129 Mark Wooden

1986 Cramer Bend Phillies

(Philadelphia Phillies, A)

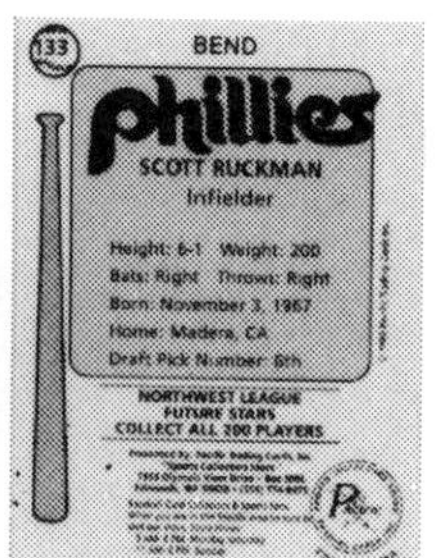

	MT	NR MT	EX
Complete Set:	6.00	4.50	2.50

130 Roderick Robertson
131 Quinn Williams
132 Al Hibbs
133 Scott Ruckman
134 Doug Hodo
135 Stephen Scarsone
136 Charles Malone
137 Keith Greene
138 Donald Church
139 Andrew Ashby
140 Elvis Romero
141 Glen Anderson
142 Kenny Miller
143 Fred Christopher
144 Brad Moore
145 Leroy Ventress
146 John Gianukakis
147 Chris Limbach
148 Tim Sossamon
149 Ryan Silva
150 Gary Berman
151 Bubba Allison
152 Juan Ascencio
153 Jeff Myaer
154 Garland Kiser

1986 Cramer Eugene Emeralds

(Kansas City Royals, A) This set is numbered as they appear on the cards.

	MT	NR MT	EX
Complete Set:	7.00	5.25	2.75

26 Rob Wolkoys
27 David Tinkle
28 Brian McRae
29 Mike Oblesbee
30 Carlos Escalera
31 Pat Bailey
32 Tim Goff
33 Ondra Ford
34 Robert Bell
35 John Larios
36 Jim Larsen
37 Kenny Jackson
38 Sean Berry
39 Randy Goodenenough
40 Mike Butcher
41 Kevin Karcher
42 Chuck Mount
43 Greg Hibbard
44 Boo Champagne
45 Gary Blouin
46 Ken Adams
47 Gus Jones
48 Joe Skodny
49 Mike Tresmer
50 Dennis Moeller

1986 Cramer Everett Giants - Color

(San Francisco Giants, A) (color)

	MT	NR MT	EX
Complete Set:	10.00	7.50	4.00

1 Kevin Fitzgerald
2 Paul McClellan
3 Matt Williams
4 Brad Gambee
5 Gregg Ritchie
6 Kevin Redick
7 John Toal
8 Russ Swan
9 Drew Ricker
10 Jim McNamara
11 Andrew Dixon
12 David Patterson
13 Tim McCoy
14 James Pena
15 Marty Newton
16 Chuck Tate
17 Jim Massey
18 Chris Stubberfield
19 John Rannow
20 Shaun MacKenzie
21 Tod Ronson
22 Chris Shultis
23 Brock Birch
24 Keith Krafve
25 James Jones
180 Joe Strain
181 Todd Wilson
182 Mark Leonard
183 Robin Riemer
184 David Nash
185 Chuck Higso
186 Matt Walker

1986 Cramer Everett Giants - Black/White

(San Francisco Giants, A) (2" x 3")

	MT	NR MT	EX
Complete Set:	10.00	7.50	4.00

(1) James "Earl" Averill
(2) Brock Birch
(3) Andrew Dixon
(4) Kevin Fitzgerald
(5) Ricky Fleming
(6) Brad Gambee
(7) Bruce Graham
(8) Chuck Higson
(9) James Jones
(10) Keith Krafve
(11) Mark Leonard
(12) Shaun MacKenzie
(13) Jim Massey
(14) Paul McClellan
(15) Tim McCoy
(16) Jim McNamara
(17) Willie Mijares
(18) Dave Nash
(19) Marty Newton
(20) Dave Patterson
(21) James Pena
(22) John Rannow
(23) Kevin Redick
(24) Drew Ricker
(25) Robin Reimer
(26) Gregg Ritchie
(27) Tod Ronson
(28) Chris Shultis
(29) Damon Skyta
(30) Joe Strain
(31) Chris Stubberfield
(32) Chuck Tate
(33) John Toal
(34) Jack Uhey
(35) Matt Walker
(36) Todd Wilson

1986 Cramer Medford A's

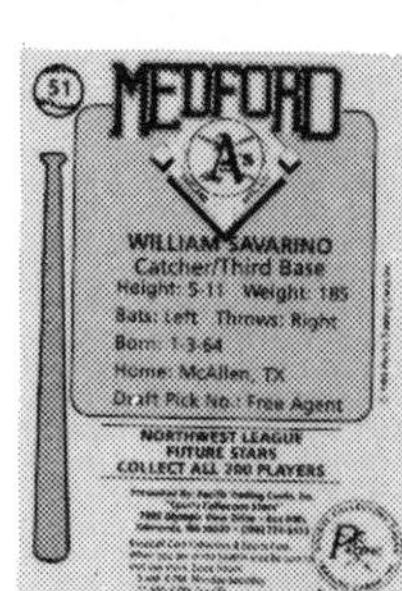

(Oakland A's, A) This set is numbered as it appears on the backs of the cards.

	MT	NR MT	EX
Complete Set:	7.50	5.50	3.00

51 William Savarino
52 James Reiser
53 David Veres
54 Mark Stancel
55 Mark Beavers
56 William Reynolds
57 Luis Martinez
58 Bill Coonan
59 Pat Gilbert
60 Larry Ritchey
61 Glenn Hoffinger
62 Robbie Gilbert
63 Todd Hartley

64 Kevin Tapani
65 Weston Weber
66 Jeff Kopyta
67 Dann Howitt
68 Jeff Glover
69 Lance Blankenship
70 Kevin Kunkel
71 James Carroll
72 Darrin Duffy
73 John Kent
74 Vincent Teixeira
75 Keith Wentz

1986 Cramer Salem Angels

(California Angels, A) This set is numbered as it appears on the backs of the cards.

	MT	NR MT	EX
Complete Set:	7.50	5.50	3.00

76 Colin Charland
77 Giovanny Reyes
78 Jeff Gay
79 Julio Granco
80 Brandy Vann
81 Alan Mills
82 Gary Gorski
83 Bobby Cabello
84 Bill Vanderwel
85 Greg Jackson
86 Scott Cerny
87 Michael Knapp
88 Daryl Green
89 Colby Ward
90 James Bisceglia
91 Greg Fix
92 Luis Merejo
93 Tony Bonura
94 David Grilione
95 Terence Carr
96 Lee Stevens
97 Michael Fetters
98 Santiaga Espinosa
99 Mike Spearnock
100 Roberto Hernandez

1986 Cramer Spokane Indians

(San Diego Padres, A) This set is numbered as it appears on the backs of the cards.

	MT	NR MT	EX
Complete Set:	7.50	5.50	3.00

155 Brian Wood
156 Bob Lutticken
157 Jim Navilliat
158 Carl Holmes
159 Ronald Moore
160 George Brett
161 Greg Harris
162 Dave Brockil
163 Ricky Bones
164 Brian Harrison
165 Paul Quinzer
166 Mark Sampson
167 Mike Basso
168 Craig Cooper
169 Tom Levasseur
170 Terry McDevitt
171 Thomas Howard
172 Tony Pellegrino
173 Keith Harrison
174 Warren Newson
175 Kevin Coentopp
176 Jeff Yurtin
177 Rob Picciolo
178 James Austin
179 William Taylor

1986 Cramer Tri-Cities Triplets

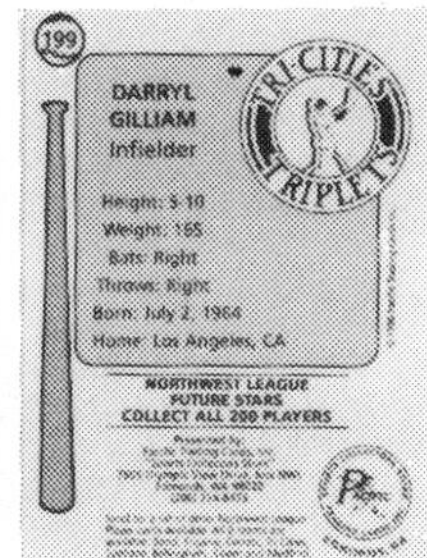

(No Affiliation, A)

	MT	NR MT	EX
Complete Set:	6.00	4.50	2.50

180 Joe Strain
181 Tod Wilson
182 Mark Leonard
183 Robin Riomer
184 David Nash
185 Chuck Higso
186 Matt Walker.
187 Andy Naworski
188 Kevin Brockway
189 Bruce Carter
190 Dan Adriance
191 Tony Rasmus
192 Kendall Walling
193 Eric Pawling
194 Joe Giola
195 John Jaha
196 Daron Connelly
197 David Connelly
198 Andy Hall
199 Darryl Gilliam
200 Thomas Ealy

1986 Donn Jennings Albuquerque Dukes

(AA) All cards in this set are listed as 1986 All Stars with the exception of Jose Canseco, listed as 1985 MVP, and Bo Jackson, listed as 1986 Future Star.

	MT	NR MT	EX
Complete Set:	12.50	9.50	5.25

1 Bill Ripken (Char.)
2 Mike Yastrzemski (Birm.)
3 Mark McGwire (Hunt.)
4 Gary Thurman (Mem.)
5 Karkovice Ron (Birm.)
6 Jose Tolentino (Hunt.)
7 Chris Padget (Char.)
8 Brian Guinn (Hunt.)
9 Luis De Los Santos (Mem.)
10 Terry Steinback (Hunt.)
11 Larry Ray (Colum.)
12 Tom Dodd (Char.)
13 Bo Jackson (Mem.)
14 Jose Canseco (Hunt.)
15 Alonzo Powell (Jack.)
16 Glenallen Hill (Knox.)
17 Brick Smith (Chatta.)
18 Todd Burns (Hunt.)
19 Dave White (Birm.)
20 Paul Schneider (Chatta.)
21 Brian Holman (Jack.)
22 Anthony Kelly (Colum.)
23 Tom Glavine (Green.)
24 Cliff Young (Knox.)
25 Kevin Price (Jack.)

1986 Pro Cards Albuquerque Dukes

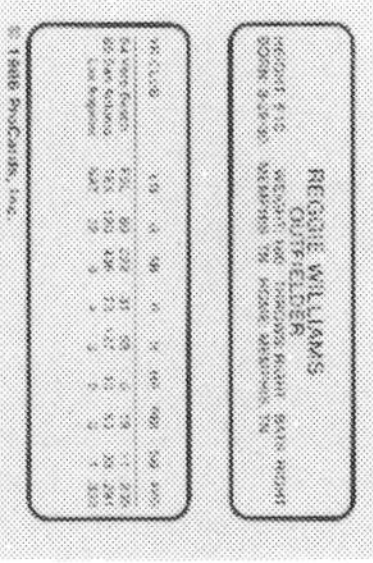

(Los Angeles Dodgers, AAA)

	MT	NR MT	EX
Complete Set:	9.00	6.75	3.50

(1) Ed Amelung
(2) Ralph Bryant
(3) Terry Collins
(4) Lenny Currier
(5) Jon Debus
(6) Dave Eichhorn
(7) Jack Fimple
(8) Balvino Galvez
(9) Jose Gonzalez
(10) Jeff Hamilton
(11) Mark Heuer
(12) Brian Holton
(13) Dennis Livingston
(14) Scott May
(15) Dick McLaughlin
(16) Adrian Meagher
(17) Tim Meeks
(18) Gary Newsom
(19) Stu Pederson
(20) Mike Schweighoffer
(21) Larry See
(22) Craig Shipley
(23) Steve Shirley
(24) Joe Vavra
(25) Dave Wallace
(26) Mike Watters
(27) Reggie Williams

Definitions for grading conditions are located in the introduction of this price guide.

1986 Pro Cards Appleton Foxes

(Chicago White Sox, A)

	MT	NR MT	EX
Complete Set:	7.00	5.25	2.75

(1) Tony Bartolomucci
(2) John Boling
(3) Glen Braxton
(4) Kurt Brown
(5) Buzz Capra
(6) Tony Cento
(7) William Eveline
(8) James Filippi
(9) Cornelio Garcia
(10) Tom Hartley
(11) Richard Issac
(12) Scott Kershaw
(13) William Magallanes
(14) Steve McLaughlin
(15) Eric Milholand
(16) Steve Moran
(17) Donn Pall
(18) Luis Peraza
(19) David Reynolds
(20) Jesus Sandoval
(21) Ron Scruggs
(22) Dave Sheldon
(23) Duke Sims
(24) John Stein
(25) George Stone
(26) Randy Velarde
(27) Aubrey Waggoner
(28) Marty Warren

1986 Pro Cards Arkansas Travelers

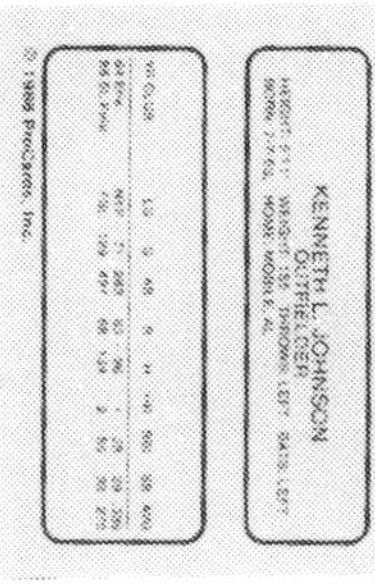

(St. Louis Cardinals, AA)

	MT	NR MT	EX
Complete Set:	17.50	13.00	7.00

(1) Tom Almante
(2) Rod Booker
(3) Ernie Carrasco
(4) Paul Cherry
(5) Dave Clements
(6) Mark Dougherty
(7) Rich Embser
(8) Lance Johnson
(9) Dave Kable
(10) Jeff Kenner
(11) Jeff Ledbetter
(12) Joe Magrane
(13) John Martin
(14) Henry McCulla
(15) Curt Metzger
(16) Allen Morlock
(17) Mike Rhodes
(18) Mark Riggins
(19) James Riggleman
(20) Mike Robinson
(21) Jose Rodriguez
(22) Mark Schulte
(23) Ray Soff
(24) Eddie Tanner
(25) Tim Wallace
(26) Scott Young

1986 Pro Cards Asheville Tourists

(Houston Astros, A)

	MT	NR MT	EX
Complete Set:	12.00	9.00	5.00

(1) Tim Arnsburg
(2) Jeff Baldwin
(3) Ken Bolek
(4) Chris Clawson
(5) Carlo Colombino
(6) Todd Credeur
(7) Pedro DeLeon
(8) Cameron Drew
(9) Jeff Edwards
(10) John Elliot
(11) Stan Fascher
(12) Fred Gladding
(13) Neder Horta

(14) Bert Hunter
(15) Blaise Ilsley
(16) Richard Johnson
(17) Larry Lasky
(18) Scott Markley
(19) David Meads
(20) Tony Metoyer
(21) Gary Murphy
(22) Carlos Reyes
(23) A. Rodriguez
(24) Ron Roebuck
(25) Wayne Rogalski
(26) Joe Schulte
(27) Shawn Talbott
(28) Dan Walters
(29) Terry Wells

1986 Pro Cards Auburn Astros

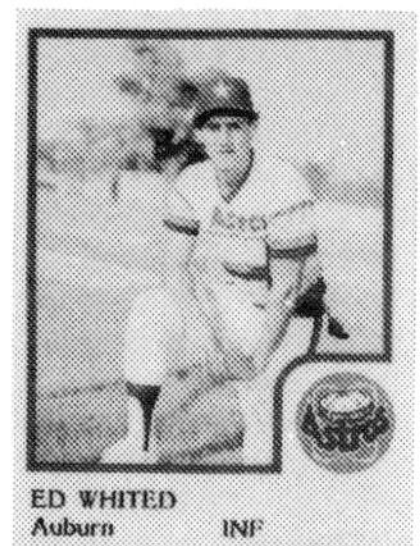

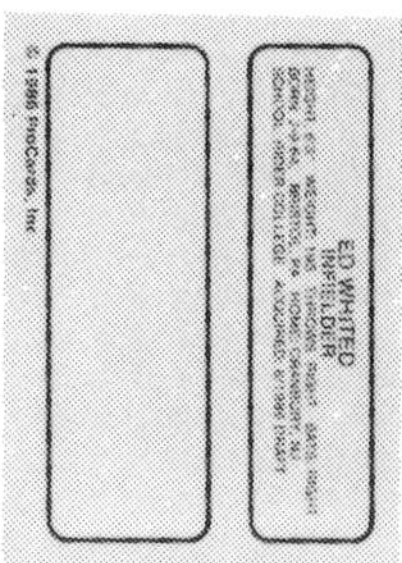

(Houston Astros, A)

	MT	NR MT	EX
Complete Set:	9.00	6.75	3.50

(1) Troy Aleshire
(2) Dave Banks
(3) Keith Bodie
(4) Daven Bond
(5) Bill Bonham
(6) Damon Brooks
(7) Gary Cooper
(8) Jeff Edwards
(9) Joel Estes
(10) Scott Gray
(11) Carl Grovom
(12) Trent Hubbard
(13) Bert Hunter
(14) Gayron Jackson
(15) Rusty Kryzanowski
(16) Brian Meyer
(17) Guy Nomrand
(18) Jimmy Olson
(19) Dave Potts
(20) Ron Roebuck
(21) Dave Rohde
(22) Pedro Sanchez
(23) Richie Simon
(24) Matt Stennett
(25) Jim Vike
(26) Kevin Wasilewski
(27) Ed Whited

1986 Pro Cards Bakersfield Dodgers

(Los Angeles Dodgers, A)

	MT	NR MT	EX
Complete Set:	35.00	26.25	14.50

(1) Dave Alarid
(2) Mike Batesole
(3) Manuel Benitez
(4) Mike Burke
(5) Dave Carlucci
(6) Jovon Edwards
(7) Mike Fiala
(8) Bert Flores
(9) Rick Gahbrielson
(10) Rene Garcia
(11) Darryl Gilliam
(12) Anthony Hardwick
(13) Ted Holcomb
(14) Jay Hornacek
(15) Ron Jackson
(16) Stan Jonston
(17) Tim Kelly
(18) Brian Kopetsky
(19) Don "Ducky" LeJohn
(20) Ramon Martinez
(21) Andy Naworski
(22) Jeff Nelson
(23) Jay Ray
(24) Jack Savage
(25) Bryan Smith
(26) Dan Smith
(27) Walt Stull
(28) John Wetteland

1986 Pro Cards Beaumont Golden Gators

(Houston Astros, AA)

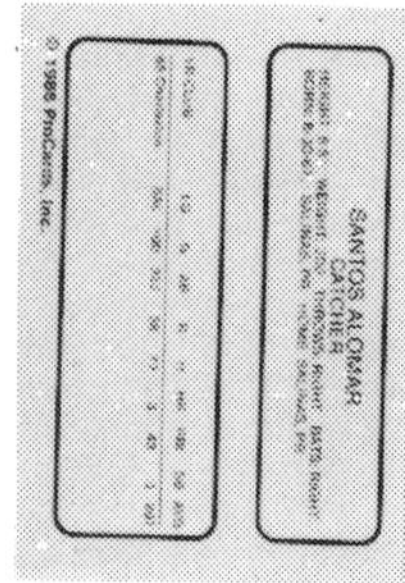

	MT	NR MT	EX
Complete Set:	25.00	18.50	10.00

(1) Santos Alomar
(2) Joe Bitker
(3) Tom Brassil
(4) Randy Byers
(5) Frank Castro
(6) Joe Chavez
(7) Joey Cora
(8) Mike Costello
(9) Mike Debutch
(10) Rich Doyle
(11) Rich Doyle
(12) Rusty Ford
(13) Brent Gjesdal
(14) Eric Hardgrave
(15) Steve Lubratich
(16) Steve Luebber
(17) Shane Mack
(18) Paul Mancuso
(19) Mike McClain
(20) Mike Mills
(21) Mark Poston
(22) Candy Sierra
(23) Todd Simmons
(24) Steve Smith
(25) Eric Varoz
(26) Bill Wrona

1986 Pro Cards Beloit Brewers

(Milwaukee Brewers, A)

	MT	NR MT	EX
Complete Set:	7.00	5.25	2.75

(1) Shon Ashley
(2) Rich Bosley
(3) Bob Caci
(4) Isaiah Clark
(5) Carlos Escalera
(6) Frank Fazzini
(7) Dan Fitzpatrick
(8) Ed Greene
(9) Joe Haney
(10) Doug Henry
(11) Gomer Hodge
(12) Tom Kleean
(13) Lance Lincoln
(14) Rusty McGinnis
(15) Charlie McGrew
(16) Carl Moraw
(17) Ray Ojeda
(18) Warren Olson
(19) Juan Reyes
(20) Jim Rowe
(21) Greg Simmons
(22) Bob Simonson
(23) Jeff Smith
(24) Jose Ventura
(25) Randy Veres
(26) Larry Whitford

1986 Pro Cards Buffalo Bisons

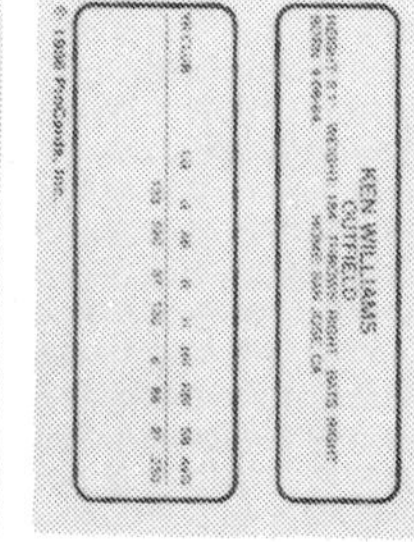

(Chicago White Sox, AAA)

	MT	NR MT	EX
Complete Set:	8.00	6.00	3.25

(1) Glen Bockhorn
(2) Dick Bosman
(3) Daryl Boston
(4) Scott Bradley
(5) Tony Brizzolara
(6) Darren Burroughs
(7) Nick Capra
(8) Bryan Clark
(9) Joe Cowley
(10) Pete Filson
(11) Jerry Don Gleaton
(12) Al Jones
(13) Tim Krauss
(14) Greg Latta
(15) Bill Long
(16) Jim Marshall
(17) Steve McCatty
(18) Russ Morman
(19) Chris Nyman
(20) Bruce Tanner
(21) Tom Thomson
(22) Dave Wehrmeister
(23) Ken Williams
(24) Matt Winters
(25) Dave Yobs

1986 Pro Cards Burlington Expos

(Montreal Expos, Kansas City Royals, A)

	MT	NR MT	EX
Complete Set:	12.50	9.50	5.25

(1) Tom Arrington
(2) Daryl Asbe
(3) Luis Corcino
(4) Matt Crouch
(5) Geff Davis
(6) Pat Dougherty
(7) Fritz Fedor
(8) Cesar Hernandez
(9) Jim Hunter
(10) Jeff Huson
(11) Juan Jimenez
(12) Tom Johnson
(13) Frank Laureano
(14) Tim Lemons
(15) Andy Leonard
(16) J.R. Miner
(17) Melido Perez
(18) Jose Rodriguez
(19) Brad Shores
(20) Joe Slotnick
(21) Stuart Stauffacher
(22) Bob Sudd
(23) Scott Sundgren
(24) Alfonso Tavarez
(25) Larry Walker
(26) Bob Williams
(27) John Williams
(28) Team Photo

1986 Pro Cards Calgary Cannons

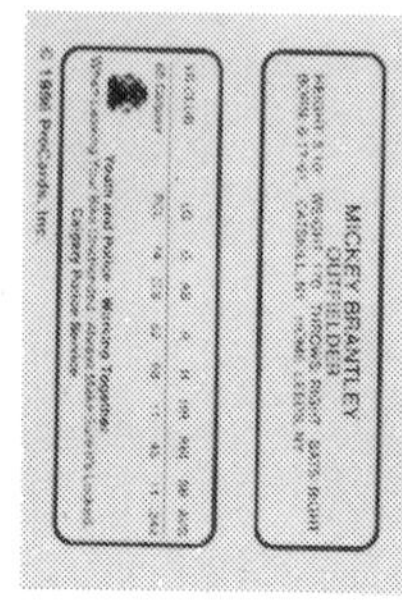

(Seattle Mariners, AAA)

	MT	NR MT	EX
Complete Set:	11.00	8.25	4.50

(1) Greg Bartley
(2) Mickey Brantley
(3) Randy Braun
(4) Pat Casey
(5) Bill Crone
(6) Mario Diaz
(7) Jerry Dybzinski
(8) Steve Fireovid
(9) Dan Firova
(10) Ross Grimsley
(11) Dave Hengel
(12) Clay Hill
(13) Vic Martin
(14) Doug Merrifield
(15) Rich Montelone
(16) John Moses
(17) Jed Murray
(18) Ricky Nelson
(19) Randy Newman
(20) Jack O'conner
(21) Bill Plummer
(22) Jerry Reed
(23) Harold Reynolds
(24) Dave Valle
(25) Bill Wilkinson
(26) Joe Witmer

1986 Pro Cards Charleston Rainbows

(San Diego Padres, A)

	MT	NR MT	EX
Complete Set:	10.00	7.50	4.00

(1) Carlos Baerega
(2) Miguel Batista (with bat)
(3) Miguel Batista (with glove)
(4) Billy Blount
(5) Victor Cabrera
(6) Rafael Chaves
(7) Jeff Cisco
(8) Roberto Clemente, Jr.
(9) Jim Daniel
(10) Carl Ferraro
(11) Greg Harris
(12) Pat Kelly
(13) Chris Knabenshue
(14) Jim Lewis
(15) Bill Marx
(16) Matt Maysey
(17) Rod Mccray
(18) Tom Meagher
(19) Jaime Moreno
(20) Eric Nolte
(21) Juan Paris
(22) Joe Pleasac
(23) Ramon Rodriguez
(24) Greg Sparks
(25) Bill Stevenson
(26) Jim Tatum
(27) Kevin Towers
(28) Rafael Valez
(29) Jim Wasem

1986 Pro Cards Chattanooga Lookouts

(Seattle Mariners, AA)

	MT	NR MT	EX
Complete Set:	10.50	7.75	4.25

(1) Ben Amaya
(2) Bob Baldrick
(3) Brian Bargerhuff
(4) Terry Bell
(5) Jim Bryant
(6) John Burden
(7) Scott Buss
(8) Brian David
(9) John Duncun
(10) Bob Gunnarson
(11) Matt Hall
(12) R.J. Harrison
(13) Paul Hollins
(14) Tom Hunt
(15) Ross Jones
(16) Rick Luecken
(17) Edgar Martinez
(18) Jeff McDonald
(19) Rusty McNealy
(20) Rick Moore
(21) Dave Myers
(22) Paul Schneider
(23) Brick Smith
(24) Terry Taylor
(25) Mike Wishnevski

1986 Pro Cards Clearwater Phillies

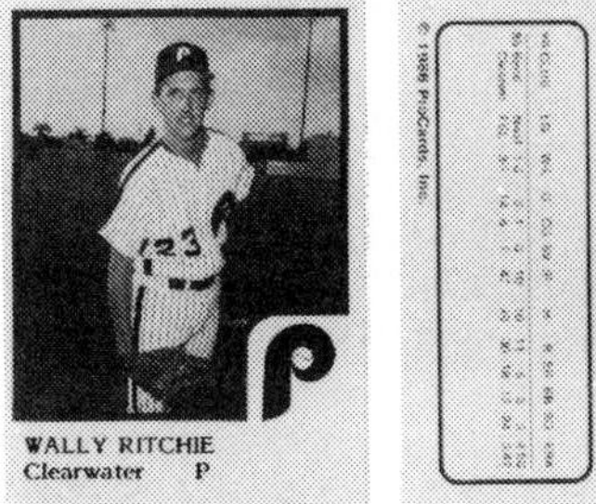

(Philadelphia Phillies, A)

	MT	NR MT	EX
Complete Set:	10.00	7.50	4.00

(1) Carlos Arroyo
(2) Bruce Carter
(3) Travis Chambers
(4) Ron Clark
(5) Pat Coveney
(6) Shawn Dantzler
(7) Greg Edge
(8) Jim Fortenberry
(9) Todd Frohwirth
(10) Billy Jester
(11) Ronald Jones
(12) Bart Kaiser
(13) Jeff Kaye
(14) Jeff Knox
(15) Ken Kraft
(16) Scott Madden
(17) Mike Miller
(18) Tom Newell
(19) Segio Perez
(20) Mark Pottinger
(21) Walley Ritchie
(22) Bob Scanlan
(23) Scott Steen
(24) Rodney Wheeler
(25) Steven Williams
(26) Ted Zipeto

1986 Pro Cards Clinton Giants

(San Francisco Giants, A)

	MT	NR MT	EX
Complete Set:	7.00	5.25	2.75

(1) John Barry
(2) Dave Blakely
(3) George Bonilla
(4) Jeff Carter
(5) Todd Cash
(6) Tom Ealy
(7) Bill Evers
(8) Perry Flowers
(9) Dean Freeland
(10) Dave Hornsby
(11) Lloyd Jackson
(12) Timber Mead
(13) Todd Miller
(14) Dave Morris
(15) Jack Mull
(16) Rick Nelson
(17) Eric Pawling
(18) Darren Pearson
(19) Jose Pena
(20) C.L. Penigar
(21) Eric Pilkington
(22) Doug Robertson
(23) Dobie Swepson
(24) Howard Townsend
(25) Paul Van Stone
(26) Matt Walker
(27) Mike Whitt
(28) Trevor Wilson
(29) Team Photo

1986 Pro Cards Columbia Mets

(New York Mets, AA)

	MT	NR MT	EX
Complete Set:	100.00	75.00	41.00

(1) Bob Apodaca
(2) Jaime Archibald
(3) Kevin Armstrong
(4) Brandon Bailey
(5) Chris Bayer
(6) Mark Brunswick
(7) Joaquin Contreras
(8) Kurt Deluca
(9) Tom Doyle
(10) Dave Gelatt
(11) Brian Givens (blue jersey)
(12) Brian Givens (white jersey)
(13) Alan Hayden
(14) Barry Hightower
(15) Troy James
(16) Scott Jaster
(17) Greg Jeffries (Jefferies)
(18) Geary Jones
(19) Johnny Monell
(20) Felix Perdomo
(21) Chris Rauth
(22) Craig Repoz
(23) Robert Rinehart, Jr.
(24) Daniel Siblerud
(25) William Stiles
(26) john Thozzo
(27) Thomas Wachs
(28) Mark Willoughby

1986 Pro Cards Columbus Astros

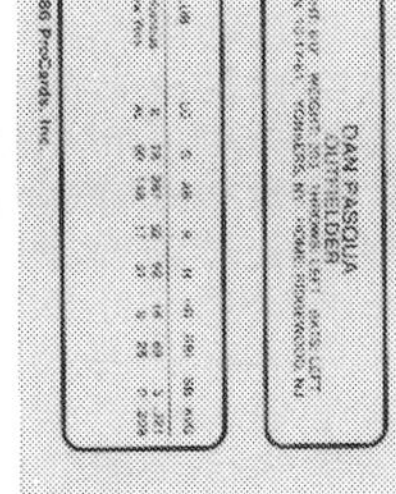

(Houston Astros, AA)

	MT	NR MT	EX
Complete Set:	11.00	8.25	4.50

(1) Troy Afenir
(2) Karl Allaire
(3) Mark Baker
(4) Jeff Bettendorf
(5) Rich Bombard
(6) Pen Caminiti
(7) Mitch Cook
(8) Dave Cripe
(9) Jeff Datz
(10) Juan Delgado
(11) Ed Duke
(12) Bobby Falls
(13) Mike Friederich
(14) Tom Funk
(15) Ryan Job
(16) Tony Kelley
(17) Rob Mallicoat
(18) Chuck Mathews
(19) Joe Mikulik
(20) Jim O'Dell
(21) Bob Parker
(22) Larry Ray
(23) Roger Samuels
(24) Chuck Taylor
(25) Gerald Young

1986 Pro Cards Columbus Clippers

(New York Yankees, AAA)

	MT	NR MT	EX
Complete Set:	12.00	9.00	4.75

(1) Mike Armstrong
(2) Brad Arnsburg
(3) Clay Christiansen
(4) Pete Dalena
(5) Orestes Destrade
(6) Doug Drabek
(7) Juam Espino
(8) Kelly Faulk
(9) Barry Foote
(10) Randy Graham
(11) Leo Hernandez
(12) Al Holland
(13) Brian Butterfield, Dave LaRoche, Kevin Rand
(14) Phil Lombardi
(15) Victor Mata
(16) Derwin McNealy
(17) Dan Pasqua
(18) Scott Patterson
(19) Jeff Pries
(20) Alfonso Pulido
(21) Andre Robertson
(22) Mark Silva
(23) Keith Smith
(24) Mike Soper
(25) Miguel Sosa
(26) Dave Stegman

1986 Pro Cards Daytona Beach Islanders

(No Affiliation, A)

	MT	NR MT	EX
Complete Set:	7.00	5.25	2.75

(1) Jim Allison
(2) Regan Bass
(3) Warren Busick
(4) Chino Cadihia
(5) Tony Clark
(6) Rafael Cruz
(7) Mike Dotzler
(8) Darrin Garner
(9) Otto Gonzalez
(10) Ty Harden
(11) David Hausterman
(12) Perry W. Hill
(13) Paul James
(14) Ross Jones
(15) Mark Kramer
(16) Dave Linton
(17) Carmen Losauro
(18) Jimmy Meadows
(19) Jeff Melrose
(20) Tim Owen
(21) Larry Pardo
(22) Dave Rolland
(23) Ron Russell
(24) Travis Sheffield
(25) Ed Soto
(26) Jim St. Laurent
(27) George Threadgill
(28) Tom West

1986 Pro Cards Durham Bulls

(Atlanta Braves, A)

	MT	NR MT	EX
Complete Set:	12.50	9.50	5.25

(1) Buddy Bailey
(2) Jeff Blauser

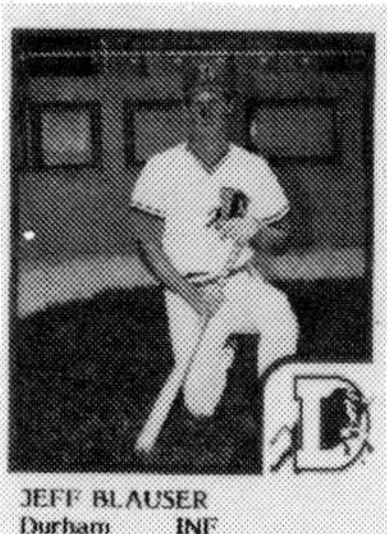

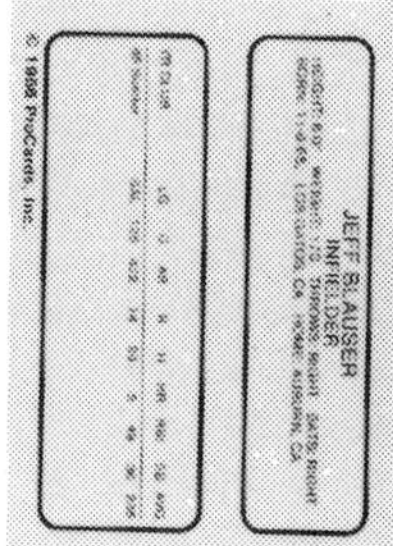

(3) Johnny Cash
(4) Bill Clossen
(5) Kevin Coffman
(6) Tim Criswell
(7) Chris Cron
(8) Maximo Del Rosario
(9) Drew Denson
(10) Todd Dewey
(11) Juan Fredymond
(12) Ronnie Gant
(13) Wayne Harrison
(14) Larry Jaster
(15) Cesar Jiminez
(16) John Kilner
(17) Todd Lamb
(18) Mike Merrill
(19) Charlie Morelock
(20) Mike Nipper
(21) Bob Posey
(22) Mike Reynolds
(23) Jim Rockey
(24) Mac Rogers
(25) Rick Siebert
(26) Gerald Wagner
(27) Phil Wellman

1986 Pro Cards Edmonton Trappers

(California Angels, AAA)

	MT	NR MT	EX
Complete Set:	10.00	7.50	4.00

(1) Robert Bastien
(2) Norman Carrasco
(3) Ray Chadwick
(4) Bobby Clark
(5) The Cliburns (Stan Cliburn, Stewart Cliburn)
(6) Stan Cliburn
(7) Stewart Cliburn
(8) Steven Finch
(9) Todd Fischer
(10) Tony Fossas
(11) Alan Kim Fowlkes
(12) Leonard Garcia
(13) Craig Gerber
(14) Chris Green
(15) Jack Howell
(16) Pat Keedy
(17) Steven Liddle
(18) Rufino Linares
(19) Winston Llenas
(20) Tony Lynn Mack
(21) Reggie Montgomery
(22) Gus Polidor
(23) Frank Reberger
(24) Al Romero
(25) Mark Ryal
(26) David Wayne Smith
(27) Devon White

1986 Pro Cards Elmira Pioneers

(Boston Red Sox, A)

	MT	NR MT	EX
Complete Set:	13.50	10.00	5.50

(1) Mike Baker
(2) Steve Bast
(3) Ken Bourne
(4) Tim Buheller
(5) Mike Coffey
(6) Scott Cooper
(7) Roger Haggerty
(8) Bart Haley
(9) Keith Harrison
(10) Tony Hill
(11) Joe Marchese
(12) Dave Milstien
(13) Jim Morrison
(14) Glen O'Donnell
(15) Lem Pilkinton
(16) Chris Rawdon
(17) Julio Rosario
(18) Ken Ryan
(19) Ed Sardinha
(20) Curt Schilling
(21) Thom Sepela
(22) Scott Sommers
(23) Joaquin Tejada
(24) Al Thorton
(25) David Walters
(26) Ron Warren
(27) Stuart Weidie
(28) Mike Whiting
(29) Kerman Williams
(30) Paul Williams

1986 Pro Cards El Paso Diablos

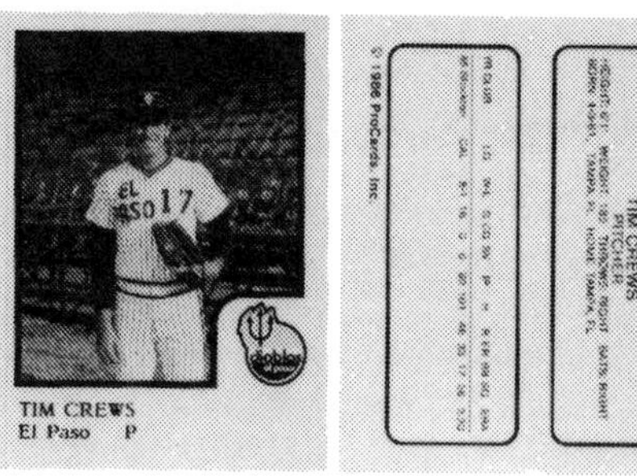

(Milwaukee Brewers, AA)

	MT	NR MT	EX
Complete Set:	15.00	11.00	6.00

(1) Jay Aldrich
(2) Robby Allen
(3) Jesus Alfaro
(4) Bill Bates
(5) Alan Cartwright
(6) Dave Clay
(7) Tim Crews
(8) Derek Diaz
(9) Duffy Dyer
(10) Brian Finley
(11) Lavell Freeman
(12) John Gibbons
(13) Dave Huppert
(14) Pete Hendrick
(15) Pete Kolb
(16) Dan Murphy
(17) Garrett Nago
(18) Bob Nandin
(19) Steve Stanicek
(20) Dave Stapleton
(21) John Thorton
(22) Jackson Todd
(23) Cam Walker

1986 Pro Cards Erie Cardinals

(St. Louis Cardinals, A) (complete set price includes scarce Hershman card)

	MT	NR MT	EX
Complete Set:	45.00	33.50	18.00

(1) Luis Alicea
(2) Tom Baine
(3) Mark Behny
(4) Brad Bluestone
(5) Randy Butts
(6) Rick Christain
(7) Bien Figueroa
(8) Robert Glisson
(9) Stephen Graff
(10) Kerry Griffith
(11) John Hackett
(12) Scott Hamilton
(13) William Hershman
(14) Eric Hohn
(15) Joe Hollinshed
(16) David Horton
(17) Glen Kuiper
(18) Scott Lawrence
(19) Roberto Marte
(20) Steve Meyer
(21) Carey Nemeth
(22) Robert Nettles
(23) Carrol Parker
(24) Francisco Perez
(25) Kyle Reese
(26) Joe Rigoli
(27) Steve Shade
(28) Greg Smith
(29) Steve Turgeon
(30) Stanley Zaltsman
(31) Todd Zeile

1986 Pro Cards Florida State League All-Stars

(Class A) (A)

	MT	NR MT	EX
Complete Set:	45.00	33.50	18.00

(1) Odie Abril
(2) Julio Alcala
(3) Chris Alvarez
(4) Brady Anderson
(5) Scott Arnold
(6) Tim Arnold
(7) Mark Berry
(8) Dave Bialas
(9) Marc Bombard
(10) Norman Brock
(11) Alax Cole
(12) Rufus Ellis
(13) Jeff Fassero
(14) Jeff Fischer
(15) John Fishel
(16) Jim Fortenberry
(17) Pete Geist
(18) Otto Gonzalez
(19) Maurice Guercio
(20) Matt Harrison
(21) John Hawkins
(22) Brad Henderson
(23) Ted Higgins
(24) Dave Holt
(25) Jim Jefferson
(26) Ron Johns
(27) Ron Jones
(28) Dan Juenke
(29) Tim Leiper
(30) Joel Lono
(31) Luis Lopez
(32) Rob Lopez
(33) Greg Lotzar
(34) Walt McConnell
(35) Jim Meadows
(36) Chris Morgan
(37) Max Oliveras
(38) Ray Perkins
(39) Dody Rather
(40) Jim Reboulet
(41) Darren Riley
(42) Don Rowland
(43) Tary Scott
(44) Mike Sears
(45) Doug Strange
(46) George Threadgill
(47) Shane Turner
(48) Luis Vasquez
(49) Tom West
(50) John Wockenfuss

1986 Pro Cards Ft. Lauderdale Yankees

(New York Yankees, A)

	MT	NR MT	EX
Complete Set:	12.00	9.00	4.75

(1) Chris Alverez
(2) Anthony Balabon
(3) Douglas Carpenter
(4) Chris Carroll
(5) Gary Cathcart
(6) Mike Christopher
(7) Ysidro Giron
(8) Fred Gonzalez
(9) Robert Green
(10) Maurice Guerico
(11) Mathew Harrison
(12) Johnny Hawkins
(13) Theodore Higgins
(14) Harvey Lee
(15) Jason Maas
(16) Michael McClear
(17) Kenneth Patterson
(18) Johnnie Pleicones
(19) Norman Santiago
(20) Robert Sepanek
(21) Scott Shaw
(22) Aristarco Tirado
(23) Shane Turner

1986 Pro Cards Ft. Myers Royals

(Kansas City Royals, A)

	MT	NR MT	EX
Complete Set:	8.00	6.00	3.25

(1) Julio Alcala
(2) Mike Alvarez
(3) Jeff Bedell
(4) Stan Boroski
(5) Pete Carey
(6) Bob Davis
(7) Jose DeJesus
(8) Rafael DeLeon
(9) Rufus Ellis
(10) Mark Farnsworth
(11) Phil George
(12) Carlos Gonzalez
(13) Duane Gustavson
(14) Jeff Hull
(15) Chris Jelic
(16) Kevin Koslofski
(17) Deric Ladnier
(18) Mike Loggins
(19) Mitch McKelvey
(20) Bill Mulligan
(21) Geoff Peterson
(22) Henry Robinson
(23) Ricky Rojas
(24) Gregg Schmidt
(25) Mark Van Blaricom
(26) Bob Van Vuren
(27) Troy Watkins
(28) Dejon Watson
(29) Don Woyce

1986 Pro Cards Geneva Cubs

(Chicago Cubs, A)

	MT	NR MT	EX
Complete Set:	8.00	6.00	3.25

(1) Jim Bullinger
(2) Todd Cloninger
(3) Tony Collins
(4) Mike Curtis
(5) Sergio Espinal
(6) Jimmie Gardner
(7) John Green
(8) Tony Hamza
(9) Derrick Hardamon
(10) Phil Harrison
(11) Clint Harwick
(12) Joe Housey
(13) Ced Landrum
(14) Jerry Lapenta
(15) Tony LaPoint
(16) Jay Loviglio
(17) Kelly Mann
(18) Jim Matas
(19) Steve Melendez
(20) Chuck Oertli
(21) Brian Otten
(22) Randy Penvose
(23) Parnell Perry
(24) Harry Shelton
(25) Jose Soto
(26) Bob Strickland
(27) Fernando Zarranz

1986 Pro Cards Glens Falls Tigers

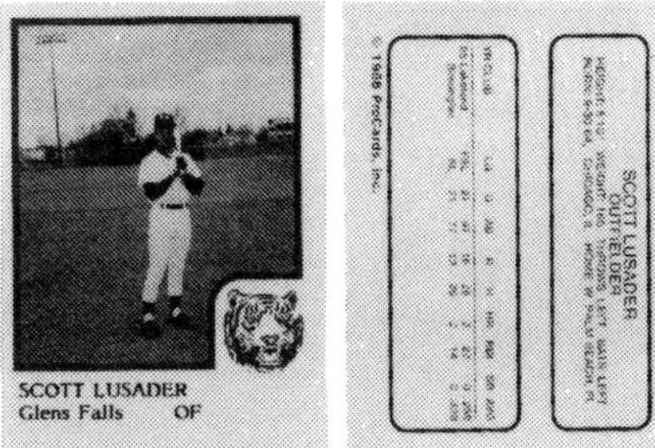

(Detroit Tigers, AAA)

	MT	NR MT	EX
Complete Set:	8.00	6.00	3.25

(1) Ricky Barlow
(2) Willie Darkins
(3) Allen Duffy
(4) Paul Felix
(5) Marty Freeman
(6) Paul Gibson
(7) Mike Gorman
(8) Ruben Guzman
(9) Jeff Herman
(10) John Hiller
(11) Al Labozzetta
(12) Scott Lusader
(13) Morris Madden
(14) Frank Masters
(15) Steve McInerney
(16) Craig Mills
(17) Rey Palacios
(18) Roman Pena
(19) Benny Ruiz
(20) Bob Schaefer
(21) Steve Searcy
(22) Max Soto
(23) James Walewander
(24) Craig Weissmann

1986 Pro Cards Greensboro Hornets

(Boston Red Sox, A)

	MT	NR MT	EX
Complete Set:	12.00	9.00	5.00

(1) John Abbott
(2) Alan Ashkinazy
(3) Doug Camilli
(4) Kevin Camilli
(5) Jose Flores
(6) Dan Gabriele
(7) Chris Gaeckle
(8) Dan Gakeler
(9) Mike Goff
(10) Dan Hale
(11) Ray Hansen
(12) Tom Kane
(13) Derek Livernois
(14) Don McGowan
(15) Jim Orsag
(16) Billy Plante
(17) Todd Pratt
(18) Carlos Quintana
(19) Ray Revak
(20) John Roberts
(21) Victor Rosario
(22) Larry Shikles
(23) John Toale
(24) Paul Toutsis
(25) Pete Youngman
(26) Eddie Zambrano
(27) Bill Zupka

1986 Pro Cards Greenville Braves

(Atlanta Braves, AA) The set was also produced in the form of a 16 x 20 inch poster with a logo card included. The regular set does not contain the logo card.

	MT	NR MT	EX
Complete Set:	10.00	7.50	4.00

(1) Rick Albert
(2) Jose Alvarez
(3) Jim Beauchamp
(4) Kevin Blankenship
(5) Chip Childress
(6) Steve Curry
(7) Sal D'Alessandro
(8) Darryl Denby
(9) Tom Glavine
(10) Paul Gnacinski
(11) Dave Griffin
(12) Jeff Groves
(13) Inocencio Guerrero
(14) Randy Ingle
(15) Carlos Rios
(16) Mike Scott
(17) Bill Slack
(18) Pete Smith
(19) Thornton Stringfellow
(20) Freddy Tiburcio
(21) Greg Tubbs
(22) Bob Tumpane
(23) Steve Ziem
(24) Logo card (featured in poster set only)

1986 Pro Cards Hagerstown Suns

(Baltimore Orioles, A)

	MT	NR MT	EX
Complete Set:	13.00	9.75	5.25

(1) Jeff Ballard
(2) Frank Bellino
(3) Mickey Billmeyer
(4) Sherwin Clintje
(5) Brian Dudois
(6) Chris Eagelston
(7) Glenn Gulliver
(8) Scott Khoury
(9) Tom Magrann
(10) Paul McNeal
(11) Bob Milacki
(12) Bob Molinaro
(13) Ty Nichols
(14) Pete Palermo
(15) Tim Richardson
(16) Norman Roberts
(17) Geraldo Sanchez
(18) Dana Smith
(19) Chuck Stanhope
(20) Pete Stanicek
(21) Earl Stephenson
(22) Scott Stranski
(23) Craig Strobel
(24) Greg Talamantez
(25) Paul Thorpe
(26) Jesse Vasquez
(27) Ted Wilborn
(28) Wayne Wilson
(29) Craig Worthington

1986 Pro Cards Hawaii Islanders

(Pittsburgh Pirates, AAA)

	MT	NR MT	EX
Complete Set:	10.00	7.50	4.00

(1) Jackie Brown
(2) Glenn Brummer
(3) Trench Davis
(4) Benny Distefano
(5) Cecil Espy
(6) Tom Fandt
(7) Stan Fansler
(8) Ed Farmer
(9) Felix Fermin
(10) Burk Goldthorn
(11) Sam Haro
(12) Dave Johnson
(13) Barry Jones
(14) Ray Krawczyk
(15) Carlos Ledezma
(16) Dave Leeper
(17) Bobby Miscik
(18) Scott Neal
(19) Bob Patterson
(20) Rick Renteria
(21) Lee Tunnell
(22) Ron Wotus
(23) Jeff Zaske

1986 Pro Cards Iowa Cubs

(Chicago Cubs, AAA)

	MT	NR MT	EX
Complete Set:	10.00	7.50	4.00

(1) Johnny Abrego
(2) Bob Bathe
(3) Pookie Berustine
(4) Trey Brooks
(5) Mike Brumley
(6) Steve Christmas
(7) Jim Colborn
(8) Jeff Cornell
(9) Larry Cox
(10) Steve Engel
(11) Terry Francona
(12) Dave Grossman
(13) Dave Gumpert
(14) Steve Hammond
(15) Joe Hicks
(16) Guy Hoffman
(17) Dave Martinez
(18) Ron Meridith
(19) Brad Mills
(20) Paul Noce
(21) Gary Parmenter
(22) Doug Potestio
(23) Ken Pryce
(24) Bobby Ramos
(25) Julio Valdez
(26) Chico Walker

1986 Pro Cards Jamestown Expos

(Montreal Expos, A)

	MT	NR MT	EX
Complete Set:	20.00	15.00	8.00

(1) Michael Blowers
(2) Don Burke
(3) C. Scott Clemo
(4) William D'Boever
(5) Kody Duey
(6) Jerome Duke
(7) Kenneth Fox
(8) Paul Frye
(9) Chan Galbato
(10) Robert Gaylor
(11) Michael Haines
(12) Mark Hardy
(13) Gene Harris
(14) Steven King
(15) Paul Peter Martineau
(16) James McDonald
(17) David Morrow
(18) Jeffrey Oller
(19) Troy Ricker
(20) Michael Robertson
(21) Dean Rockweiler
(22) Robert Shannon
(23) Steve St. Claire
(24) Joe Beely Sims
(25) Jeffrey Tabaka
(26) Darren Travels
(27) Sal Vaccaro
(28) Jeffrey Wedvick

(29) Frank Welborn
(30) Yippee (team mascot)

1986 Pro Cards Kenosha Twins

(Minnesota Twins, A)

	MT	NR MT	EX
Complete Set:	10.00	7.50	4.00

(1) Paul Abbott
(2) Larry Blackwell
(3) Jeff Bumgarner
(4) James Cook
(5) Mark Davis
(6) Tom DiCeglio
(7) Julio Delancer
(8) Rafael DeLima
(9) Tom Fiore
(10) Steven Gasser
(11) Marty Lanoux
(12) Bob Lee
(13) Don Leppert
(14) Jerry Mack
(15) Howard Manzon
(16) Ted Miller
(17) Edgar Naveda
(18) Tim O'Conner
(19) Yorkis Perez
(20) Bob Perry
(21) Mike Redding
(22) Bob Strube
(23) Luis Tapais
(24) Gary Thomason
(25) Leonard Webster

1986 Pro Cards Kinston Eagles

(No Affiliation, A)

	MT	NR MT	EX
Complete Set:	7.00	5.25	2.75

(1) Howard Akers
(2) Bubba Brevell
(3) Scott Cannon
(4) Ed Delzer
(5) Van Evans
(6) Bruce Fischback
(7) Gene Gentile
(8) Al Heath
(9) Mike Ingle
(10) Lindsey Johnson
(11) Roger Johnson
(12) Randy Kramer
(13) Dan Larsen
(14) Perry Lychak
(15) Scott Melvin
(16) Paul Moralez
(17) Marty Reed
(18) Emmett Robinson
(19) Gabriel Robles
(20) Randy Romagna
(21) Melvin Rosario
(22) John Schofield
(23) Dave Trembley
(24) Ken Whitfield

1986 Pro Cards Knoxville Blue Jays

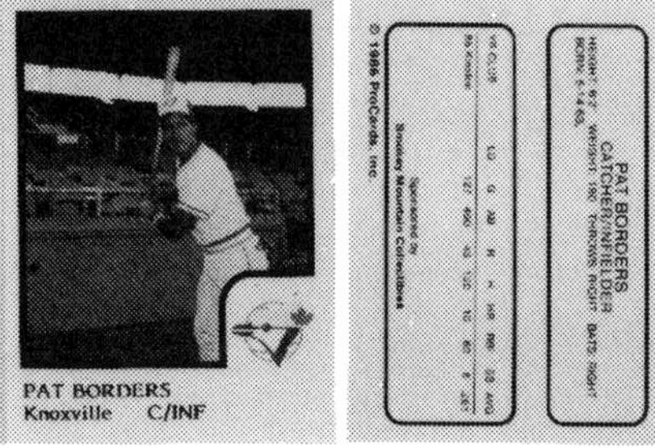

(Toronto Blue Jays, AA)

	MT	NR MT	EX
Complete Set:	10.00	7.50	4.00

(1) Kash Beauchamp
(2) Jim Bishop
(3) Pat Borders
(4) Sal Campusano
(5) J.J. Cannon
(6) Eddie Dennis
(7) Tim Englund
(8) Keith Gilliam
(9) Larry Hardy
(10) Glenallen Hill
(11) Randy Holland
(12) Jim Howard
(13) Tony Hudson
(14) Manny Lee
(15) Nelson Liriano
(16) Colin McLaughlin
(17) Greg Moore
(18) Oswald Peraza
(19) Jose Segura
(20) Chris Shaddy
(21) Kevin Sliwinski
(22) Matt Stark
(23) Bernie Tatis
(24) Norm Tonnucci
(25) Dave Walsh
(26) Mike Yearout
(27) Cliff Young

1986 Pro Cards Lakeland Tigers

(Detroit Tigers, A)

	MT	NR MT	EX
Complete Set:	17.50	13.00	7.00

(1) Jeff Agar
(2) Bernie Anderson
(3) Tommy Burgess
(4) Bill Cooper
(5) Steve Eagar
(6) Ken Gohmann
(7) Keith Hoskinson
(8) Mark Lee
(9) Tim Leiper
(10) Al Liebert
(11) Tony Long
(12) Porfi Martinez
(13) Chip McHugh
(14) Jeff Minick
(15) Dave Minnema
(16) Chris Morgan
(17) Rod Poissant
(18) Laney Prioleau
(19) Art Raubolt
(20) Donnie Rowland
(21) Joseph Slavic
(22) Terry Smith
(23) John Smoltz
(24) Doug Strange
(25) Mike York

1986 Pro Cards Las Vegas Stars

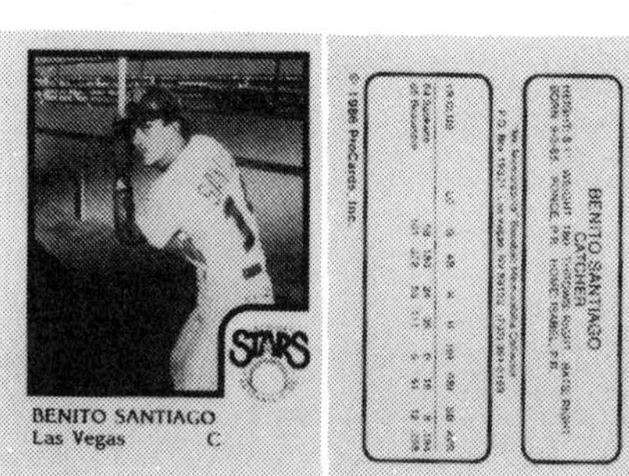

(San Diego Padres, AAA) Las Vegas sets sold through ProCards dealer distributions did not include Larry Bowa Manager card.

	MT	NR MT	EX
Complete Set:	17.00	12.50	6.75

Larry Bowa (included only in ballpark giveaway sets)
(1) Randy Asadoor
(2) Greg Booker
(3) Steve Garcia
(4) Dick Grapenthin
(5) Gary Green
(6) Ray Hayward
(7) Todd Hutcheson
(8) Jimmy Jones
(9) Steve Kemp
(10) Steve Lubratich
(11) Mark Parent
(12) Tim Pyznarski
(13) Edwin Rodriguez
(14) Benito Santiago
(15) James Siwy
(16) Gregory Smith
(17) Brian Snyder
(18) James Steels
(19) Bob Stoddard
(20) John Tutt
(21) Ed Vosberg
(22) Mark Wasinger
(23) Mark Williamson
(24) Ed Wojna
(25) Gary Woods

1986 Pro Cards Little Falls Mets

(New York Mets, A)

	MT	NR MT	EX
Complete Set:	18.00	13.50	7.25

(1) Mike Anderson
(2) Pete Bauer
(3) Lou Berge
(4) Rick Brown
(5) Genaro Castro
(6) Rob Colescott
(7) Pat Crosby
(8) Mark DiVincenzo
(9) Rick Duant
(10) Ken Farmer
(11) Mark Fiedler
(12) Cliff Gonzalez
(13) Ceoric Hawkins
(14) Rob Hernandez
(15) Alex Jiminez
(16) Lorin Jundy
(17) Rich Lundahl
(18) Dan McMurtrie
(19) Rich Miller
(20) Rodney Murrel
(21) Ron Narcisse
(22) Luis Natera
(23) Fritz Polka
(24) Jaime Roseboro
(25) Joel Sklar
(26) Heath Slocumb
(27) Andy Taylor
(28) Tony Thompson
(29) Todd Welborn

1986 Pro Cards Lynchburg Mets

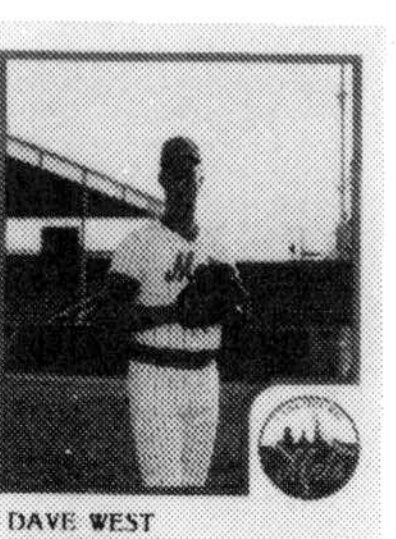

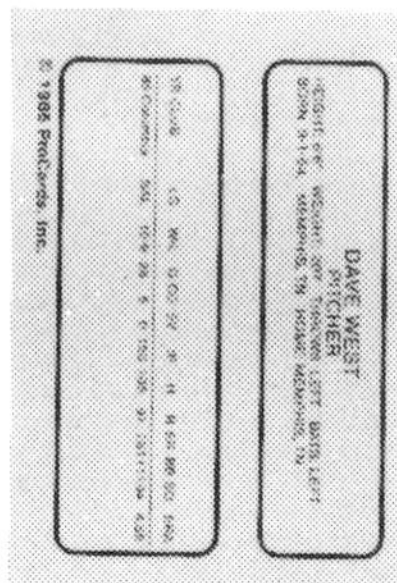

(New York Mets, A)

	MT	NR MT	EX
Complete Set:	17.50	13.00	7.00

(1) Ralph Adams
(2) Jim Bibby
(3) Desi Brooks
(4) Kevin Brown
(5) Wilmer Caraballo
(6) Al Carmichael
(7) Jeff Ciszkowski
(8) Angelo Cuevas
(9) Bobby Floyd
(10) Jeff Gardner
(11) Steve Gay
(12) Ronnie Gideon
(13) Mauro Gozzo
(14) Marcus Lawton
(15) Chuck Lynn
(16) Hector Perez
(17) Steve Phillips
(18) Jeff Richardson
(19) Rich Rodriguez
(20) Zoilo Sanchez
(21) Eric Stampel
(22) Dave Tresch
(23) Wilson Valera
(24) Juan Villanueva
(25) Dave West
(26) Mike Westbrook
(27) Dan Winters
(28) Shane Young

1986 Pro Cards Macon Pirates

(Pittsburgh Pirates, A)

	MT	NR MT	EX
Complete Set:	7.00	5.25	2.75

(1) Ben Abner
(2) Kevin Andersh
(3) Kirk Berry
(4) Dwight Bernard
(5) Octavio Cepeda
(6) Tony Chance
(7) Jim Davins
(8) Dorley Downs
(9) Kevin Franchi
(10) Ron Giddens
(11) Andy Hall
(12) Todd Hansen
(13) Rob Hatfield
(14) Guillermo Mercedes
(15) Orlando Merced
(16) Douglas Moreno
(17) Rafael Muratti
(18) Luis Pena
(19) Julio Perez
(20) Mike Quade
(21) Gilbert Roca

(22) Jeff Satzinger
(23) Brian Stackhouse
(24) Mike Stevanus
(25) Keith Swartzlander
(26) Jay Wollenburg
(27) Joey Zellner

1986 Pro Cards Madison Muskies

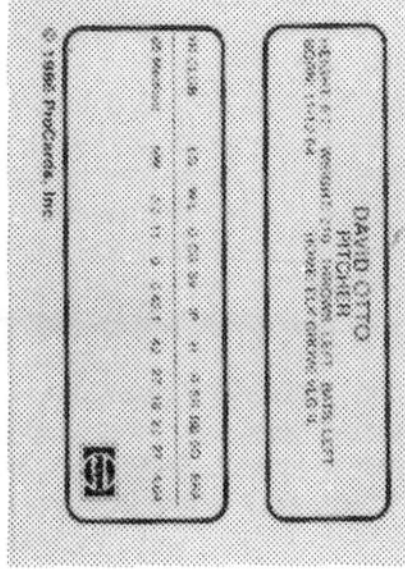

(Oakland A's, A)

	MT	NR MT	EX
Complete Set:	12.50	9.50	5.25

(1) Douglas Ames
(2) Tony Arias
(3) Larry Arnot
(4) Antonio Cabrera
(5) Ron Carter
(6) Brian Criswell
(7) Michael Cupples
(8) Patrick Dietrick
(9) Bobby Gould
(10) Marty Hall
(11) Mark Howie
(12) Andre Jacas
(13) Russell Kibler
(14) Kirk McDonald
(15) James Nettles
(16) Dave Nix
(17) David Otis
(18) Kevin Russ
(19) Scott Sabo
(20) Dave Schober
(21) Jeffrey Shaver
(22) Dave Shillinglaw
(23) Nelson Silverio
(24) Robert Stocker
(25) Camilo Veras
(26) Walter Weiss
(27) Walter Whitehurst
(28) Rick Wise

1986 Pro Cards Maine Guides

(Cleveland Indians, AAA)

	MT	NR MT	EX
Complete Set:	17.50	13.00	7.00

(1) Barry Bruenkant
(2) Kevin Buckley
(3) George Cecchetti
(4) Steve Ciszczon
(5) Dave Clark
(6) Steve Commer
(7) Keith Creel
(8) Barry Evans
(9) Dave Gallagher
(10) Kevin Hagen
(11) Doug Jones
(12) Jim Napier
(13) Junior Noboa
(14) Bryan Oelkers
(15) Craig Pippen
(16) Reggie Ritter
(17) Scott Roberts
(18) Jose Roman
(19) Tommy Rowe
(20) Cory Snyder
(21) Curt Wardle
(22) Randy Washington
(23) Jim Weaver
(24) Frank Wills
(25) Jim Wilson
(26) Rich Yett

1986 Pro Cards Miami Marlins

(Baltimore Orioles, A)

	MT	NR MT	EX
Complete Set:	7.00	5.25	2.75

(1) German Bautista
(2) Juan Bellver
(3) Mike Browning
(4) Rick Carrano
(5) Tim Dulin
(6) Todd Edwards
(7) Marc Estes
(8) John Harrington
(9) Fred Hatfield
(10) Tommy Hearn
(11) Alan Hixon
(12) Lance Hudson
(13) Dan Juenke
(14) Bob Latmore
(15) Kurt Leiter
(16) Pedro Llanes
(17) Jerry Miller
(18) Curt Morgan
(19) Luis Ojeda
(20) Ray Perkins
(21) Eric Rasmussen
(22) Elem Rossy
(23) Todd Smith
(24) Phil Taylor
(25) Dave Van Ohlen
(26) Greg Wallace
(27) Phil Wielegman
(28) Roger Wilson
(29) John Wockenfuss

1986 Pro Cards Midland Angels

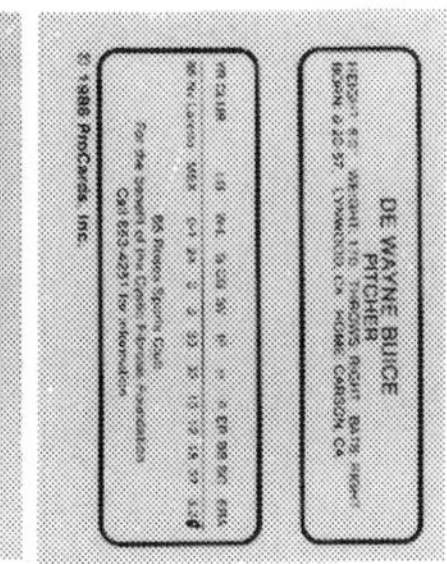

(California Angels, AA)

	MT	NR MT	EX
Complete Set:	38.00	28.00	15.00

(1) Doug Banning
(2) Brian Brady
(3) DeWayne Buice
(4) Vinicio Cedeno
(5) Terry Clark
(6) Mike Cook
(7) Sherman Corbett
(8) Doug Davis
(9) Brian Hartsock
(10) Dave Heath
(11) John Hotchkiss
(12) Kevin King
(13) Vance Lovelace
(14) Joe Maddon
(15) Mike Madril
(16) Mark McLemore
(17) Bill Merriefield
(18) Aurelio Monteagudo
(19) Rafael Pimental
(20) James Randall
(21) Jeff Schaffer
(22) Don Timberlake
(23) Raul Tovar
(24) Phil Venturino
(25) Glen Walker
(26) Richard Zaleski

1986 Pro Cards Modesto A's

(Oakland A's, A)

	MT	NR MT	EX
Complete Set:	25.00	18.50	10.00

(1) Roy Anderson (catching)
(2) Roy Anderson (with bat)
(3) Russell Applegate
(4) Darren Balsley
(5) Tyler Brilinski
(6) John "Doc" Cartelli
(7) Jerry Deguero
(8) Mike Duncan
(9) Vic Figueroa
(10) Darel Hansen
(11) Twayne Harris
(12) Mike Hogan
(13) Steve Howard
(14) Butch Hughes
(15) Jim Jones
(16) Felix Jose
(17) John Kanter
(18) Rich Martig
(19) Jerome Nelson
(20) Tommie Reynolds
(21) Bob Sharpnack
(22) Jim Strichek
(23) Joe Strong
(24) Mark Tortorice
(25) Bruce Walton

1986 Pro Cards Nashua Pirates

(Pittsburgh Pirates, AA)

	MT	NR MT	EX
Complete Set:	10.00	7.50	4.00

(1) Mike Ashman
(2) Kerry Baker
(3) Mike Berger
(4) Craig Brown
(5) Matias Carrillo
(6) Scott Fiepke
(7) Ken Ford
(8) Kevin Gordon
(9) Tommy Gregg
(10) Dimas Gutierrez
(11) Reggie Hammonds
(12) Martin Hernandez
(13) Shawn Holman
(14) Tony Laird
(15) Jim Leopold
(16) Jose Lind
(17) Orlando Lind
(18) Steve McAllister
(19) Jim Neidlinger
(20) Jim Opie
(21) Hipolito Pena
(22) Pete Rice
(23) Ruben Rodriguez
(24) Dennis Rogers
(25) Rich Sauveur
(26) Dorn Taylor
(27) Spin Williams
(28) "H" Williams

1986 Pro Cards New Britain Red Sox

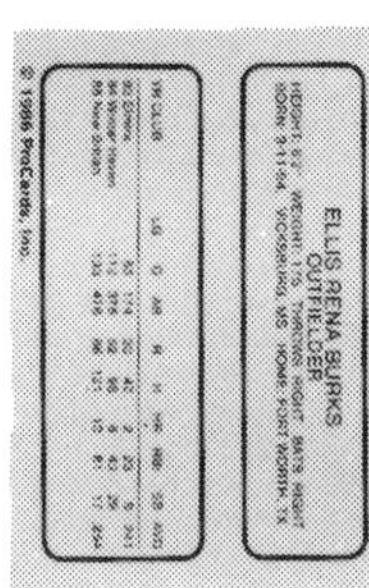

(Boston Red Sox, AA)

	MT	NR MT	EX
Complete Set:	45.00	33.50	18.00

(1) Andy Araujo
(2) Tony Beal
(3) Jose Birriel
(4) Ellis Burks
(5) Pete Cappadona
(6) Robert Chadwick
(7) Jim Corsi
(8) Steve Curry
(9) Chuck Davis
(10) Steve Ellsworth
(11) Eduardo Estrada
(12) Demarlo Hale
(13) Sam Horn
(14) Pat Jelks
(15) Dana Kiecker
(16) John Marzano
(17) Bill McInnis
(18) Mark Meleski
(19) Sam Nattile
(20) Dave Peterson
(21) Jody Reed
(22) Paul Slifko
(23) Hector Steward
(24) Tony Torchia
(25) Scott Wade

1986 Pro Cards Oklahoma City 89'ers

(Texas Rangers, AAA)

	MT	NR MT	EX
Complete Set:	9.00	6.75	3.50

(1) Bob Brower
(2) Greg Campbell
(3) Rob Clark
(4) Glen Cook
(5) Tommy Dunbar
(6) Dave Geisel
(7) Rusty Gerhardt
(8) Bobby Jones
(9) Jeff Kunkel
(10) Willie Lozado
(11) Jim Maler
(12) Orlando Mercado
(13) Dale Mohoric (Mohorcic)
(14) Jeff Moronko
(15) Dave Oliver
(16) Dave Owen
(17) Mike Parrott
(18) Luis Pujols
(19) Jeff Russell
(20) Tommy Joe Shimp

(21) Ruben Sierra
(22) Rick Surhoff
(23) Greg Tabor
(24) Don Welchel
(25) Don Werner
(26) Matt Williams

1986 Pro Cards Omaha Royals

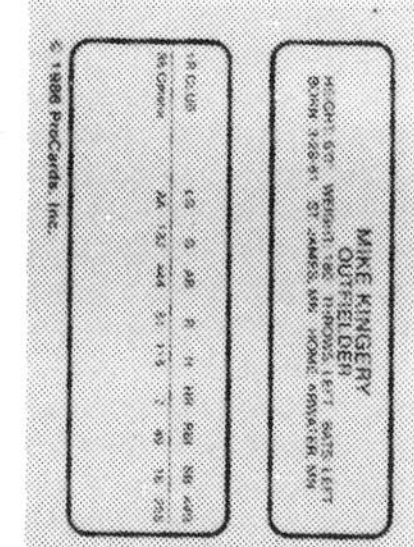

(Kansas City Royals, AAA)

	MT	NR MT	EX
Complete Set:	20.00	15.00	8.00

(1) Scott Bankhead
(2) John Boles
(3) Mike Brewer
(4) Keefe Cato
(5) Joe Citari
(6) David Cone
(7) Frank Funk
(8) Mike Griffin
(9) Roger Hansen
(10) Bill Hayes
(11) Bob Hegman
(12) Rondin Johnson
(13) Mike Kingery
(14) Renie Martin
(15) Mike Miller
(16) Tom Mullen
(17) Bill Pecota
(18) Jose Reyes
(19) Dave Schuler
(20) Jeff Schulz
(21) Jim Scranton
(22) Kevin Seitzer
(23) Theo Shaw
(24) Russ Stephans
(25) Lester Strode
(26) Nick Swartz
(27) Scott Taber
(28) Mike Warren
(29) Marty Wilkerson

1986 Pro Cards Orlando Twins

(Minnesota Twins, AA)

	MT	NR MT	EX
Complete Set:	8.00	6.00	3.25

(1) Steve Aragon
(2) Brad Bierley
(3) Todd Budke
(4) Mark Clemons
(5) Jose Dominguez
(6) Troy Galloway
(7) Steve Gomez
(8) Stan Holmes
(9) Joe Klink
(10) Gene Larkin
(11) John Marquardt
(12) George Mitterwald
(13) Greg Morhardt
(14) Steve Padia
(15) Doug Palmer
(16) Ray Ramirez
(17) Robbie Smith
(18) Alan Sontag
(19) Sam Sorce
(20) Jeff Taylor
(21) Jeff Trout
(22) Dave Vetsch
(23) Kevin Wiggins
(24) Phil Wilson

1986 Pro Cards Osceola Astros

(Houston Astros, A)

	MT	NR MT	EX
Complete Set:	7.00	5.25	2.75

(1) Norman Brock
(2) Mike Brown
(3) Scott Camp
(4) Jesus Carrion
(5) Earl Cash
(6) Don Dunster
(7) Francois Durocher
(8) John Fishel
(9) Terry Green
(10) Anthony Hampton
(11) Geysi Heredia
(12) Stan Hough
(13) Ken Houston
(14) Chris Huchingson
(15) Calvin James
(16) Joe Kwolek
(17) Jeff Livin
(18) Dyrryl Menard
(19) Pete Mueller
(20) Randy Randle
(21) Dody Rather
(22) Marty Schreiber
(23) Glenn Sherlock
(24) Doug Snyder
(25) Mel Stottlemyre
(26) Gary Tuck
(27) Jose Vargas
(28) Tom Wiedenbauer
(29) Jamie Williams

1986 Pro Cards Palm Springs Angels

(California Angels, A)

	MT	NR MT	EX
Complete Set:	8.00	6.00	3.25

(1) Kent Anderson
(2) Bobby Bell
(3) Dante Bichette
(4) Paul Bilak
(5) Mike Butler
(6) Richie Carter
(7) Pete Coachman
(8) Larry Cook
(9) Barry Dacus
(10) John DiGioia
(11) Mark Doran
(12) Todd Eggertsen
(13) William Fraser
(14) Miguel Garcia
(15) Billy Geivett
(16) Bryan Harvey
(17) Chuck Hernandez
(18) Doug Jennings
(19) Tom Kotchman
(20) Reggie Lambert
(21) Scott Marrott
(22) David Martinez
(23) Dave Montanari
(24) Dario Nunez
(25) Erik Pappas
(26) Stacey Pettis
(27) Bryan Price
(28) Mike Romanovsky
(29) Ty Van Burkleo

1986 Pro Cards Pawtucket Red Sox

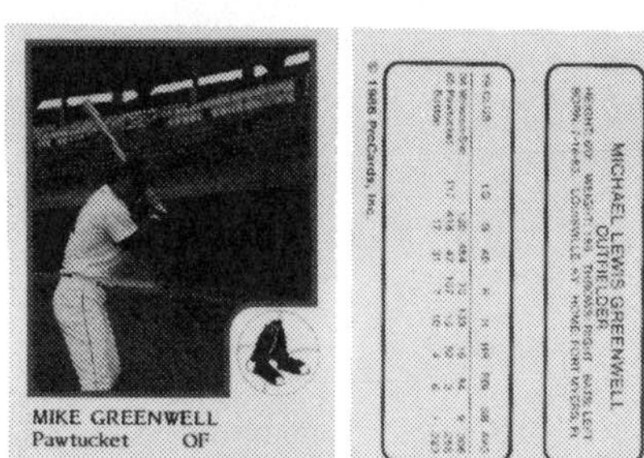

(Boston Red Sox, AAA)

	MT	NR MT	EX
Complete Set:	55.00	41.25	22.50

(1) Dick Berardino
(2) Todd Benzinger
(3) Mike Brown
(4) Chris Cannizzaro
(5) John Christensen (glove on right hand)
(6) John Christensen (glove on left hand)
(7) Tony Cleary
(8) Mike Dalton
(9) Pat Dodson
(10) Mike Greenwell
(11) Mitch Johnson
(12) John Leister
(13) George Mecerod
(14) Mike Mesh
(15) Gary Miller-Jones
(16) Ed Nottle
(17) Rey Quinonez
(18) Mike Rochford
(19) Kevin Romine
(20) Calvin Schiraldi
(21) Jeff Sellers
(22) Danny Sheaffer
(23) Mike Stenhouse
(24) Laschelle Tarver
(25) Gary Tremblay
(26) Mike Trujillo
(27) Dana Williams
(28) Rob Woodard

1986 Pro Cards Peninsula White Sox

(Chicago White Sox, A)

	MT	NR MT	EX
Complete Set:	9.00	6.75	3.50

(1) Jorge Alcazar
(2) Larry Allen
(3) Jeff Anderson
(4) Bob Bailey
(5) Jerry Bertolani
(6) Virgil Conley
(7) Dan Cronkright
(8) Tom Drees
(9) Wayne Edwards
(10) Duane Engram
(11) Chuck Hartenstein
(12) Mark Henry
(13) Tom Hildebrand
(14) Chris Jefts
(15) Tom Lahrman
(16) Jim Markert
(17) Glen McElroy
(18) Mike Moore
(19) John Pawlowski
(20) Adam Peterson
(21) Darrell Pruitt
(22) Kevin Renz
(23) Ron Scheer
(24) Ed Sedar
(25) Pete Venturini
(26) Dave Wallwork
(27) Eric wilson
(28) Jim Winters

1986 Pro Cards Peoria Chiefs

(Chicago Cubs, A)

	MT	NR MT	EX
Complete Set:	75.00	56.00	30.00

(1) Scott Anders
(2) Dick Canan
(3) Tony Collins
(4) Leonard Damian
(5) Bill Danek
(6) John Fierro
(7) Jim Gardner
(8) Mark Grace
(9) John Green
(10) Tony Hamza
(11) Jeff Hirsch
(12) Greg Kallevig
(13) Joe Kraemer
(14) John Lewis
(15) Dave Liddell
(16) Tom Lombarski
(17) Pete Mackanin
(18) Bob Mandeville
(19) Bill Phillips
(20) Kris Roth
(21) Tad Scowik
(22) Jeff Small
(23) Dwight Smith
(24) John Turner
(25) Tim Wallace
(26) Jim Wright
(27) Fernando Zarranz

1986 Pro Cards Phoenix Firebirds

(San Francisco Giants, AAA)

	MT	NR MT	EX
Complete Set:	10.00	7.50	4.00

(1) Rick Adams
(2) Mike Aldrete
(3) Randy Bockus
(4) Kelly Downs
(5) Duane Espy
(6) Randy Gomez

(7) Everett Graham
(8) Mark Grant
(9) Chuck Hensley
(10) Mike Jeffcoat
(11) Randy Johnson
(12) Cris Jones
(13) Randy Kutcher
(14) Rick Lancellotti
(15) Jim Lefebvre
(16) Jack McNight
(17) Bob Moore
(18) Terry Mulholland
(19) Phil Ouellette
(20) Jon Perlman
(21) Luis Quinones
(22) Jesse Reid
(23) Cliff Shidawara
(24) Frank Williams
(25) Jack Wilson
(26) Mike Woodard

1986 Pro Cards Pittsfield Cubs

(Chicago Cubs, AA)

	MT	NR MT	EX
Complete Set:	37.50	28.00	15.25

(1) Rich Amaral
(2) Damon Berryhill
(3) Mike Capel
(4) Bruce Crabbe
(5) Luis Cruz
(6) Jackie Davidson
(7) Jim Dickerson
(8) Drew Hall
(9) Carl Hamilton
(10) Darrin Jackson
(11) Dave Kopf
(12) Mike Lacer
(13) Dave Lenderman
(14) Greg Maddux
(15) Mike Martin
(16) Allen McKay
(17) Jamie Moyer
(18) Rafael Palmeiro
(19) Dick Pole
(20) Steve Roadcap
(21) Jeff Rutledge
(22) Tom Spencer
(23) Phil Stephenson
(24) Gary Varsho
(25) Tony Woods

1986 Pro Cards Portland Beavers

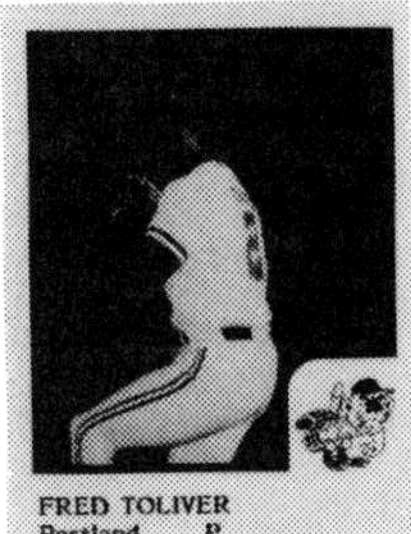

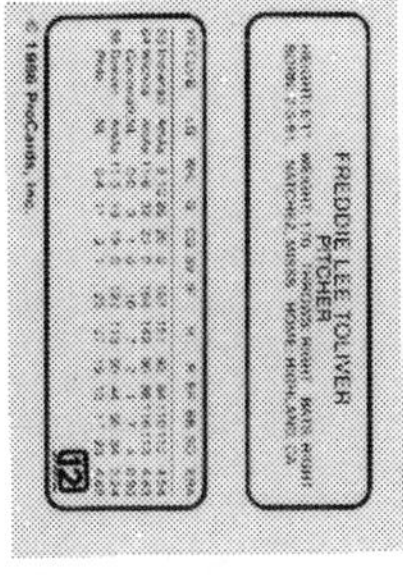

(Philadelphia Phillies, AAA)

	MT	NR MT	EX
Complete Set:	35.00	26.00	14.00

(1) Jeff Bittiger
(2) Dave Bulls
(3) Joe Cipolloni
(4) Randy Day
(5) Ken Dowell
(6) Arturo Gonzalez
(7) Tom Gorman
(8) Kevin Hickey
(9) Rob Hicks
(10) Chris James
(11) Greg Jelks
(12) Tim Knight
(13) Alan LeBoeuf
(14) Randy Lerch
(15) Mike Maddux
(16) Francisco Melendez
(17) Keith Miller
(18) Kyle Money
(19) Ronn Reynolds
(20) Dave Shipanoff
(21) Jeff Stone
(22) Bobby Tiefenauer
(23) Fred Toliver

1986 Pro Cards Prince William Pirates

(Pittsburgh Pirates, A)

	MT	NR MT	EX
Complete Set:	10.00	7.50	4.00

(1) Reggie Barringer
(2) Lance Belen
(3) Tony Blasucci
(4) Rocky Bridges
(5) Tony Chance
(6) Carey Cheek
(7) Jeff Cook
(8) Ron Delucchi
(9) Tim Drummond
(10) Sal Ferreiras
(11) Brett Gideon
(12) Mike Goodwin
(13) Brian Jones
(14) Bob Koopman
(15) Tim McMillan
(16) Jose Melendez
(17) Larry Melton
(18) Page Odle
(19) Chris Pierce
(20) Tom Prince
(21) Chris Ritter
(22) Dave Rooker
(23) Rob Russell
(24) John Smiley
(25) Greg Stading
(26) Mike Stevens
(27) Kyle Todd

1986 Pro Cards Quad City Angels

(California Angels, A)

	MT	NR MT	EX
Complete Set:	10.00	7.50	4.00

(1) Edgar Alfonso
(2) Tom Alfredson
(3) Bob Auth
(4) Gerald Baker
(5) Mark Ban
(6) Tim Burcham
(7) Chris Collins
(8) Frank DiMichele
(9) Santiago Espinosha
(10) Andres Esponisa (Espinoza)
(11) Chuck Finley
(12) Ken Grant
(13) Dan Grunard
(14) Randy Harvey
(15) Dave Johnson
(16) Sam Joseph
(17) Scott Kannenberg
(18) Bill Lachemann
(19) Jeff Manto
(20) Mark Marino
(21) Ed Marquez
(22) Steve McGuire
(23) Glenn Meyers
(24) Richerd Morehouse
(25) Gary Nalls
(26) Giovanny Reyes
(27) Edwin Rivera
(28) Ed Rodriguez
(29) Robert Rose
(30) Mickey Saatzer
(31) Glenn Washington
(32) Roger Zottneck
(33) Team Card

1986 Pro Cards Reading Phillies

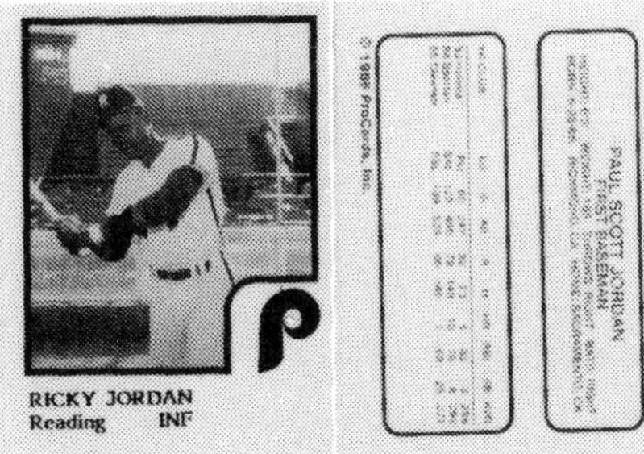

(Philadelphia Phillies, AA)

	MT	NR MT	EX
Complete Set:	30.00	22.50	12.25

(1) Ramon Aviles
(2) Shawn Barton
(3) Mark Bowden
(4) Tony Brown
(5) Jose Cecena
(6) George Culver
(7) Steve DeAngelis
(8) Marvin Freeman
(9) Ramon Henderson
(10) Ken Jackson
(11) Michael Jackson
(12) Rickey Jordan
(13) Steve Labay
(14) Jose Leiva
(15) Bruce Long
(16) Darren Loy
(17) Keith Miller
(18) Steve Moses
(19) Howard Nichols, Jr.
(20) Barney Nugent
(21) Jim Olander
(22) Ray Ramon
(23) Bruce Ruffin
(24) Mike Shelton
(25) Kevin Ward
(26) Lenny Watts

1986 Pro Cards Richmond Braves

(Atlanta Braves, AAA)

	MT	NR MT	EX
Complete Set:	9.00	6.75	3.50

(1) Sam Ayoub
(2) Dave Beard
(3) Steve Curry
(4) Bruce Dal Canton
(5) Juan Eichelberger
(6) Doc Estes
(7) Lee Graham
(8) Al Hall
(9) Kelly Heath
(10) Mike Jones
(11) Brad Komminsk
(12) Robert Long
(13) Roy Majtyka
(14) Ed Olwine
(15) Larry Owen
(16) Gerald Perry
(17) Charlie Puleo
(18) John Rabb
(19) Paul Runge
(20) Steve Shields
(21) Cliff Speck
(22) Mark Strucher
(23) Ron Tingley
(24) Andre Treadway
(25) Matt West
(26) Paul Zuvella

1986 Pro Cards Rochester Red Wings

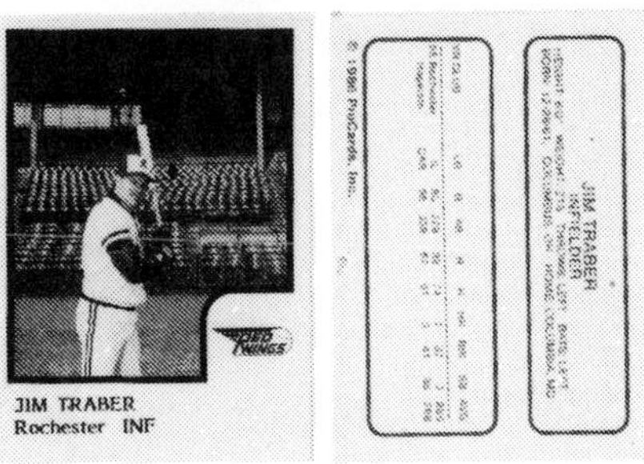

(Baltimore Orioles, AAA)

	MT	NR MT	EX
Complete Set:	8.00	6.00	3.25

(1) Tony Arnold
(2) Dom Chiti
(3) Ken Gerhart
(4) Glenn Gulliver
(5) John Habyan
(6) John Hart
(7) Moke Hart
(8) Rex Hudler
(9) Phil Hoffman
(10) Odell Jones
(11) Rick Jones
(12) Mick Kinnunen
(13) Curt Motton
(14) Tom O'Malley
(15) Al Pardo
(16) Kelly Paris
(17) Eric Rasmussen
(18) Mike Reddish
(19) Don Scott
(20) Nelson Simmons
(21) Mike Skinner
(22) Ken Smith
(23) Kelvin Torve
(24) Jim Traber
(25) Jeff Williams

1986 Pro Cards St. Petersburg Cards

(St. Louis Cardinals, A)

	MT	NR MT	EX
Complete Set:	12.00	9.00	4.75

(1) Sal Agostinelli

(2) Scott Arnold
(3) Richard Arzola
(4) David Bilalis
(5) Henry Carson
(6) Alex Cole
(7) John Costello
(8) Jeff Fassero
(9) Jim Fregosi, Jr.
(10) Brad Henderson
(11) Hans Herzog
(12) Stephen Hill
(13) Howard Hilton
(14) Ken Infante
(15) Ronald Johns
(16) Bill Jones
(17) Matt Kinzer
(18) Martin Mason
(19) Charles McGrath
(20) Jesus Mendez
(21) Scott Murray
(22) Jay North
(23) Mauricio Nunez
(24) Steven Petitt
(25) Jim Puzey
(26) Jim Reboulet
(27) John Rigos
(28) Roy Silver
(29) Mike Theisen

1986 Pro Cards Salem Red Birds

(Texas Rangers, A)

	MT	NR MT	EX
Complete Set:	7.50	5.50	3.00

(1) Kevin Bootay
(2) Mike Bucci
(3) Joel Cartaya
(4) Jeff Clay
(5) Bryan Dial
(6) Tom Duggan
(7) Riley Epps
(8) Al Farmer
(9) Greg Ferlenda
(10) Stephen Glasker
(11) Tim Hallgren
(12) Brad Hill
(13) Duane James
(14) Ron King
(15) Steve Kordish
(16) Chad Kreuter
(17) Steve Lankard
(18) Jeff Mays
(19) Tim McLoughlin
(20) Bob Mortimer
(21) Dave Murray
(22) Bob O'Hearn
(23) Kevin Reimer
(24) Dave Satnat
(25) Mitch Thomas
(26) Jose Vargas
(27) Jim Vlcek
(28) Darrell Whitaker
(29) Mike Winbush

1986 Pro Cards San Jose Bees

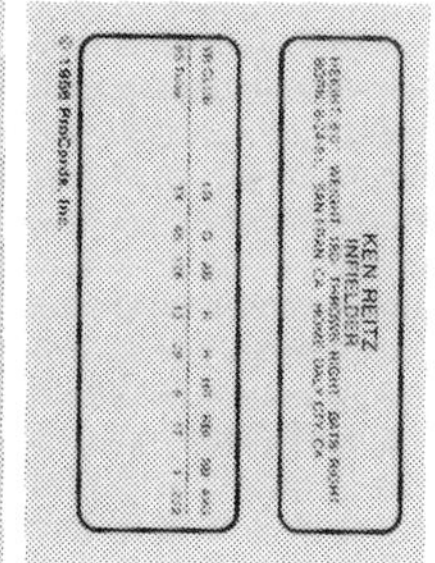

(No Affiliation, A)

	MT	NR MT	EX
Complete Set:	7.00	5.25	2.75

(1) Freddie Arroyo
(2) Shawn Barton
(3) Mike Bigusiak
(4) Randy Bispo
(5) James Bolt
(6) Darryl Cias
(7) Ken Foster
(8) Darren Garrick
(9) Lorenzo Gray
(10) Steven Howe
(11) Brian Kubala
(12) Edward McCarter
(13) Ted Milner
(14) Yoshi Nakashima
(15) Mike Nittoli
(16) Dave Okubo
(17) Ken Reitz
(18) Daryl Sconiers
(19) Harry Steve
(20) Nori Tanabe
(21) Jim Tinkey
(22) Mike Verdi
(23) Hank Wada
(24) Mickey Yamano
(25) George Yokota

1986 Pro Cards Shreveport Captains

(San Francisco Giants, AA)

	MT	NR MT	EX
Complete Set:	8.00	6.00	3.25

(1) Jeff Brantley
(2) John Burkett
(3) Kevin Burrell
(4) Alan Cockrell
(5) Charlie Corbell
(6) Marty Demerritt
(7) Angel Escobar
(8) George Ferran
(9) John Grimes
(10) Dean Hummel
(11) Charlie Hayes
(12) Mike Jones
(13) Wendell Kim
(14) Demerritt Kim
(15) Greg Litton
(16) Daryl Masuyama
(17) Deron McCue
(18) Scott Medvin
(19) Steve Miller
(20) Brian Ohnoutka
(21) Ed Phikunas
(22) Mackey Sasser
(23) Keith Silver
(24) Stu Tate
(25) Todd Thomas
(26) John Verducci
(27) Colin Ward
(28) Team Card

1986 Pro Cards Stockton Ports

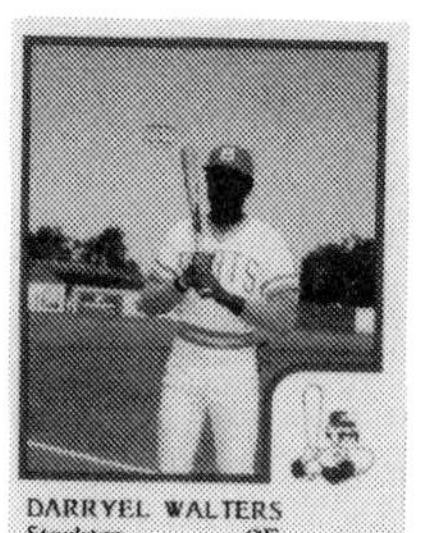

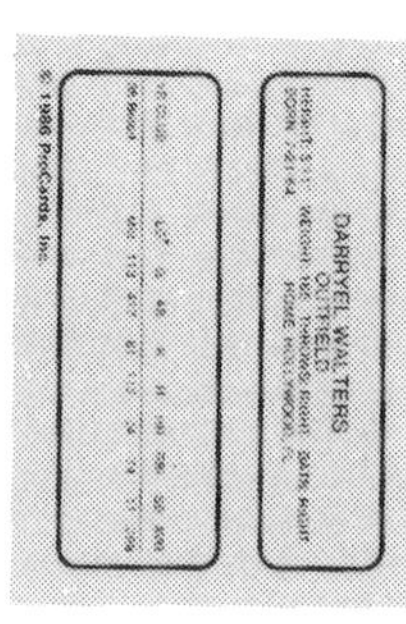

(Milwaukee Brewers, A)

	MT	NR MT	EX
Complete Set:	7.00	5.25	2.75

(1) John Beuerlein
(2) Jamie Brisco
(3) Todd Brown
(4) Tim Casey
(5) Rob Derksen
(6) Rob DeWolf
(7) Todd France
(8) Mike Frew
(9) Mike Fulmer
(10) Mike Gobbo
(11) Gary Kanwisher
(12) Matt Kent
(13) John Ludy
(14) Dave Machaemer
(15) Joe Mitchell
(16) Mario Monico
(17) Martin Montano
(18) Frank Mattox
(19) Doug Norton
(20) Jeff Peterek
(21) Walter Pohle
(22) Danny Ratliff
(23) Jeff Reece
(24) Alan Sadler
(25) Darryel Walters
(26) Fred Williams

1986 Pro Cards Sumter Braves

(Atlanta Braves, A)

	MT	NR MT	EX
Complete Set:	10.00	7.50	4.00

(1) Tom Abrell
(2) John Alva
(3) Ron Bianco
(4) Johnny Cuevas
(5) Shawn Frazier
(6) Jeff Greene
(7) Tom Greene
(8) Kevin Harmon
(9) Mike Hennessy
(10) Dennis Hood
(11) Dodd Johnson
(12) Barry Jones
(13) Clarence Jones
(14) David Jones
(15) Dave Justice
(16) Mark Lemke
(17) Al Martin
(18) Ed Mathews
(19) Leo Mazzone
(20) Bob McNally
(21) Bob Pfaff
(22) Ellis Roby
(23) Matt Rowe
(24) Jim Salisbury
(25) David Seitz
(26) Brian Snitker
(27) Andy Tomberlain
(28) Rob Tomberlain
(29) Danny Weems
(30) Jeff Wetherby

1986 Pro Cards Syracuse Chiefs

(Toronto Blue Jays, AAA)

	MT	NR MT	EX
Complete Set:	18.50	13.75	7.50

(1) Gibson Alba
(2) Luis Aquino
(3) Doug Ault
(4) Joe Beckwith
(5) Stan Clarke
(6) Rich Carlucci
(7) Jose Castro
(8) John Cerutti
(9) Don Cooper
(10) Red Coughlin
(11) Otis Green
(12) Dale Holman
(13) Dennis Howard
(14) Alex Infante
(15) Joe Johnston
(16) Luis Leal
(17) Manny Lee
(18) Fred McGriff
(19) Steve Mingori
(20) Ron Musselman
(21) Mark Poole
(22) Mike Sharperson
(23) Ron Shepherd
(24) Dave Stenhouse
(25) Lou Thornton
(26) Rockett Wheeler
(27) John Woodworth

1986 Pro Cards Tacoma Tigers

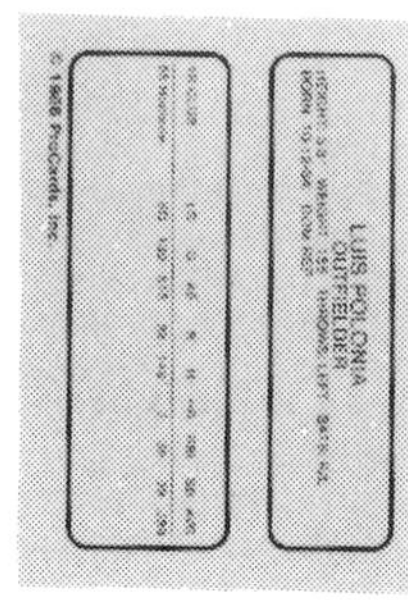

(Oakland A's, AAA)

	MT	NR MT	EX
Complete Set:	8.50	6.25	3.50

(1) Darrel Ackerfelds
(2) Ralph Citarella
(3) Brian Dorsett
(4) Tom Dozier
(5) Jim Eppard
(6) Chuck Estrada
(7) Mike Gallego
(8) Walt Horn
(9) Brian Javier
(10) Jeff Kaiser
(11) Tim Lambert
(12) Dave Leiper
(13) Keith Lieppman
(14) Joey McLaughlin
(15) Rob Nelson
(16) Eric Plunk
(17) Luis Polonia
(18) Thad Reece
(19) Rick Rodriguez
(20) Lenn Sakata
(21) Ray Smith
(22) Keith Thrower
(23) Rusty Tillman
(24) Jerry Willard
(25) Curt Young

1986 Pro Cards Tampa Tarpons

(Cincinnati Reds, A)

	MT	NR MT	EX
Complete Set:	7.00	5.25	2.75

(1) Carlos Acosta
(2) Tim Barker
(3) Mark Berry
(4) Phil Dolf
(5) Chuck Donahue
(6) Jeff Hayward
(7) Jim Jefferson
(8) Dave Keller
(9) Ted Langdon
(10) Rod Lich
(11) Joel Lond
(12) Rob Lopez
(13) Tim Mirabito
(14) Angelo Nunley
(15) Mike Ramsey
(16) Darren Riley
(17) Dusty Rogers
(18) Isidro Rondon
(19) Francisco Riverio
(20) Jack Smith
(21) Ozzie Soto
(22) Tom Summer
(23) Francisco Tenacen
(24) Don Wakamatsu
(25) Brant Weatherford
(26) Jeff Wilson
(27) Tom Wilson

1986 Pro Cards Tidewater Tides/Tides Emblem

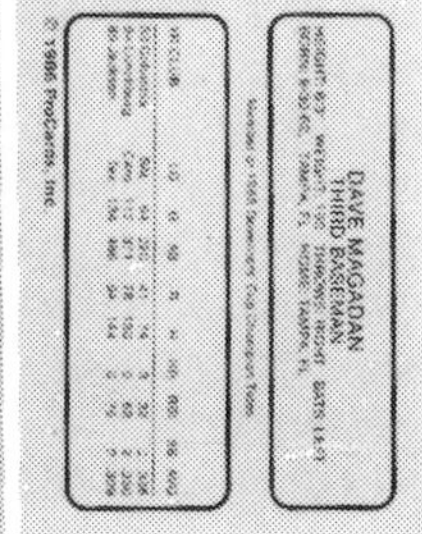

(New York Mets, AAA)

	MT	NR MT	EX
Complete Set:	12.50	9.50	5.25

(1) Rick Anderson
(2) Terry Blocker
(3) Tom Bupus
(4) Mark Carreon
(5) Tim Corcoran
(6) John Cumberland
(7) Mike Davis
(8) Tony Ferreira
(9) Doug Frobel
(10) Ron Gardenhire
(11) John Gibbons
(12) Ed Glynn
(13) Ed Hearn
(14) Stan Jefferson
(15) Terry Leach
(16) Barry Lyons
(17) Dave Magadan
(18) Tom McCarthy
(19) Marlin McPhail
(20) Randy Milligan
(21) John Mitchell
(22) Randy Myers
(23) Alfredo Pedrique
(24) Sam Perlozzo
(25) Rick Rainer
(26) Doug Sisk
(27) Steve Springer
(28) DeWayne Vaughn
(29) Dave Wyatt

1986 Pro Cards Tidewater Tides/Mets Emblem

(New York Mets, AAA)

	MT	NR MT	EX
Complete Set:	12.50	9.50	5.25

(1) Richard Anderson
(2) Terry Blocker
(3) Tom Burns
(4) Mark Carreon
(5) Tim Corcoran
(6) John Cumberland
(7) Michael Davis
(8) Tony Ferreira
(9) Doug Frobel

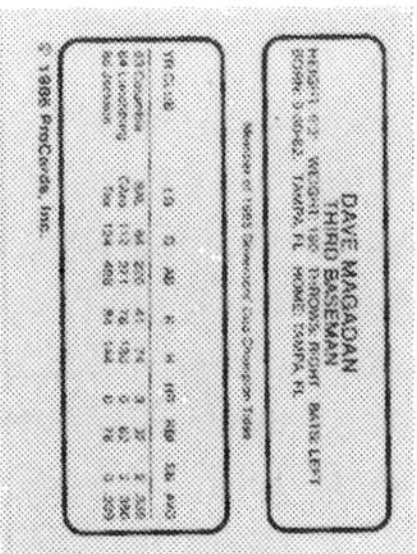

(10) Ronald Gardenhire
(11) John Gibbons
(12) Edward Glynn
(13) Edward Hearn
(14) Stanley Jefferson
(15) Terry Leach
(16) Barry Lyons
(17) David Magadan
(18) Marlin McPhail
(19) Tom McCarthy
(20) Randy Milligan
(21) John Mitchell
(22) Randy Myers
(23) Sam Perlozzo
(24) Alfredo Pedrique
(25) Rick Rainer
(26) Doug Sisk
(27) Steven Springer
(28) DeWayne Vaughn
(29) David Wyatt

1986 Pro Cards Toledo Mud Hens

(Houston Astros, AAA)

	MT	NR MT	EX
Complete Set:	7.50	5.50	3.00

(1) Allen Anderson
(2) Brad Boylan
(3) Eric Broersma
(4) Glen Carpenter
(5) Danny Clay
(6) Mark Davidson
(7) Andre David
(8) Pat Dempsey
(9) Alvaro Espinosa
(10) Frank Eufemia
(11) Mark Funderburk
(12) Gorman Heimueller
(13) Richard Leggatt
(14) Jerry Lomastro
(15) Charlie Manuel
(16) Alax Morte
(17) Charlie Mitchell
(18) Bob Ralston
(19) Mario Ramirez
(20) Ramon Romero
(21) Les Straker
(22) Scott Ullger
(23) Ron Washington
(24) Al Woods

1986 Pro Cards Tucson Toros

(Houston Astros, AAA)

	MT	NR MT	EX
Complete Set:	7.00	5.25	2.75

(1) Larry Acker
(2) Carlos Alfonso
(3) Don August
(4) Mark Brown
(5) Ty Gainey
(6) Jeff Heathcock
(7) Manny Hernandez
(8) Chuck Jackson
(9) Rex Jones
(10) Mark Knudson
(11) Rob Mallicoat
(12) Ron Mathis
(13) Louie Meadows
(14) Jim Miner
(15) John Mizerock
(16) Rafael Montalvo
(17) Ray Noble
(18) Bert Pena
(19) Nelson Rood
(20) Mark Ross
(21) Jim Sherman
(22) Jim Thomas
(23) Duane Walker
(24) Ty Waller
(25) Eddie Watt
(26) Robbie Wine

1986 Pro Cards Vancouver Canadians

(Milwaukee Brewers, AAA)

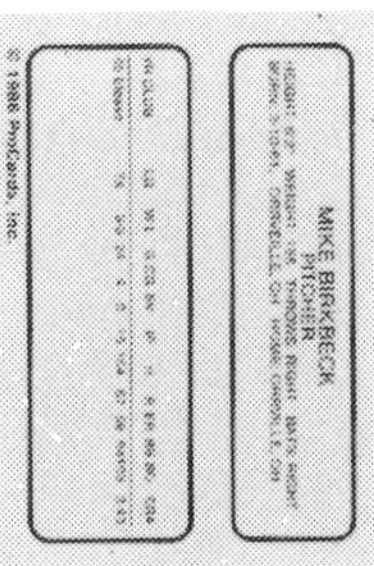

	MT	NR MT	EX
Complete Set:	20.00	15.00	8.00

(1) Jim Adduci
(2) Terry Bevington
(3) Mike Birkbeck
(4) Chris Bosio
(5) Glenn Braggs
(6) Mark Ciardi
(7) Bryan Clutterbuck
(8) Chuck Crim
(9) Dan Davidsmeier
(10) Ed Diaz
(11) Bryan Duquette
(12) Bob Gibson
(13) Dion James
(14) John Johnson
(15) Steve Kiefer
(16) Dave Klipstein
(17) Joe Meyer
(18) Ed Myers
(19) Charlie O'Brien
(20) Jim Paciorek
(21) Mike Paul
(22) Chuck Porter
(23) Ray Searage
(24) B.J. Surhoff
(25) Dale Sveum
(26) Rich Thompson
(27) Rick Waits

1986 Pro Cards Ventura Gulls

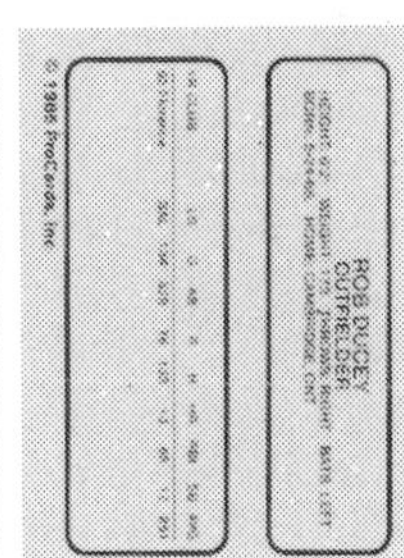

(Toronto Blue Jays, A)

	MT	NR MT	EX
Complete Set:	13.00	9.75	5.25

(1) Geronimo Berroa
(2) Hugh Bringson
(3) Francisco Cabera
(4) Mark Dickmon
(5) Rob Ducey
(6) Oscar Escobar
(7) Glenn Ezell
(8) Sandy Guerrero
(9) Mike Jones
(10) Ken Kinnard
(11) Darryl Landrum
(12) Omar Malave
(13) Domingo Martinez
(14) Jose Mesa
(15) Steve Mumaw
(16) Jeff Musselman
(17) Greg Myers
(18) Al Olsen
(19) Alfredo Ortiz
(20) Zack Paris
(21) Todd Provence
(22) Pablo Reyes
(23) Luis Reyna
(24) Willie Shanks
(25) Todd Stottlemyre
(26) Tom Wasilewski
(27) Dave Wells
(28) Eric Yelding

1986 Pro Cards Vermont Reds

(Cincinnati Reds, AA)

	MT	NR MT	EX
Complete Set:	15.00	11.00	6.00

(1) Jordan Berge
(2) John Boyles

(3) Norm Charlton
(4) Jeff Cox
(5) Clay Daniel
(6) Gary Denbo
(7) Rob Diaale
(8) Jeff Gray
(9) Lenny Harris
(10) Billy Hawley
(11) Ron Henika
(12) Mike Manfre
(13) Greg Monda
(14) Steve Oliverio
(15) Buddy Pryor
(16) Brian Robinson
(17) Jim Scott
(18) Brooks Shumake
(19) Mike Sims
(20) Danny Smith
(21) Glen Spagnola
(22) Jeff Treadway
(23) Jay Ward
(24) Delwyn Young

1986 Pro Cards Vero Beach Dodgers

(Los Angeles Dodgers, A)

	MT	NR MT	EX
Complete Set:	7.00	5.25	2.75

(1) Andy Anthony
(2) Kevin Ayers
(3) Michael Cherry
(4) Carl Cox
(5) Kevin Devine
(6) Peter Geist
(7) Rob Giesecke
(8) Juan Guzman
(9) Jeff Hartman
(10) Darren Holmes
(11) Michael Hoff
(12) Ed Jacobo
(13) Robert Jacobsen
(14) Wayne Kirby
(15) Ken Lampert
(16) Luis Lopez
(17) Walt McConnell
(18) Domingo Michel
(19) Jon Pequignot
(20) Rod Rochie
(21) John Schlichting
(22) Jorge Sepulveda
(23) John Shoemaker
(24) Felix Tejeda
(25) Bob Tucker
(26) Jesus Vila
(27) Stan Wasiak

1986 Pro Cards Visalia Oaks

(Minnesota Twins, A)

	MT	NR MT	EX
Complete Set:	7.00	5.25	2.75

(1) Mike Adams
(2) Joey Aragon
(3) Ben Bianchi
(4) Gary Borg
(5) Bob Callfy
(6) Alfredo Cardwood
(7) DeWayne Coleman
(8) Rob Cramer
(9) Chris Forgione
(10) Henry Gatewood
(11) Donnie Iasparro
(12) Chris Kroener
(13) Sal Nicolosi
(14) Bill O'Conner
(15) Wes Pierorazio
(16) Shannon Raybon
(17) Scott Rohlof
(18) Danny Schmitz
(19) Tom Schwarz
(20) Tim Senne
(21) Bob Tabeling
(22) Tom Thomas
(23) Ray Velasquez
(24) Eddie Yanes

1986 Pro Cards Waterbury Indians

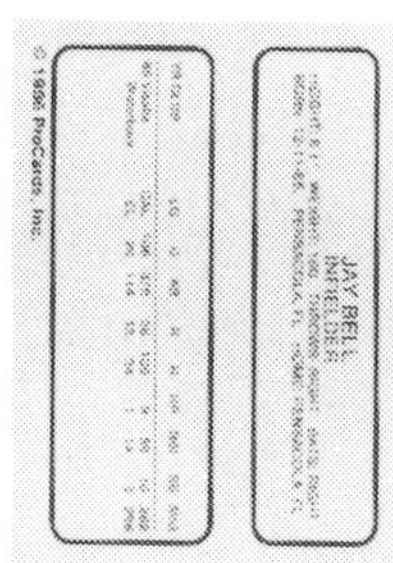

(Cleveland Indians, AA)

	MT	NR MT	EX
Complete Set:	9.00	6.75	3.50

(1) Jeff Arney
(2) Chris Beasley
(3) Mike Bellaman
(4) Jay Bell
(5) Bernardo Brito
(6) George Crum
(7) Jim Driscoll
(8) Luis Encarnacion
(9) John Farrell
(10) Winston Ficklin
(11) Orlando Gomez
(12) Milt Harper
(13) Rick Henke
(14) Bob Link
(15) Don Lovell
(16) Oscar Mejia
(17) Kent Murphy
(18) Michael Murphy
(19) Cliff Pastornicky
(20) Miguel Roman
(21) Cal Santarelli
(22) Craig Smajstra
(23) Daryl Smith
(24) Dain Syverson
(25) Steve Whitmyer
(26) Bill Worden

1986 Pro Cards Waterloo Indians

(Cleveland Indians, A)

	MT	NR MT	EX
Complete Set:	9.00	6.75	3.50

(1) Brian Allard
(2) David Alvis
(3) Keith Bennett
(4) Dave Bresnahan
(5) Claudio Carrasco
(6) Glen Fairchild
(7) Mike Farr
(8) Myron Gardner
(9) Andy Ghelfi
(10) John Githens
(11) Mark Higgins
(12) Trey Hillman
(13) Steve Johnson
(14) Scott Jordan
(15) Greg Karpik
(16) Lee Kuntz
(17) Greg LaFever
(18) Luis Medina
(19) Manny Mercado
(20) Rod Nichols
(21) Mike Poehl
(22) John Power
(23) Mike Rountree
(24) Don Santo
(25) Charles Scott
(26) Rob Swain
(27) Steve Swisher
(28) Chuck Todd
(29) Kevin Trudeau
(30) Casey Webster
(31) Greg Williamson
(32) Mike Workman

1986 Pro Cards Watertown Pirates

(Pittsburgh Pirates, A)

	MT	NR MT	EX
Complete Set:	7.50	5.50	3.00

(1) Steve Adams
(2) Moises Alou
(3) Jeff BAnister
(4) Daryl Boyd
(5) Lawrence Brady
(6) Guy Conti
(7) Bill Copp
(8) Jeff Gurtcheff
(9) Craig Heakins
(10) Mike Khoury
(11) Tim Kirk
(12) Blaine Lockley
(13) Dino Moran
(14) Douglas Moreno
(15) Steve Moser
(16) Ed Ott
(17) Al Quintana
(18) Randy Robicheaux
(19) Carl Rose
(20) Scott Runge
(21) Bill Samen
(22) Butch Schlopy
(23) Tom Shields
(24) Tracy Toy
(25) Glenn Trudd
(26) Miguel Varverde
(27) Mike Walker

Definitions for grading conditions are located in the Introduction of this price guide.

1986 Pro Cards Wausau Timbers

(Seattle Mariners, A)

	MT	NR MT	EX
Complete Set:	7.00	5.25	2.75

(1) Robert Bernardo
(2) Fremio Cabrera
(3) John Clem
(4) Don Cohoon
(5) Bobby Cuellar
(6) Mike Darby
(7) Bret Davis
(8) William Diaz
(9) Tom Eccleston
(10) Joe Georger
(11) Bob Gibree
(12) Dan Larson
(13) Benito Malave
(14) Brian McCann
(15) Dave McCorkle
(16) Tim McLain
(17) Pablo Moncerratt
(18) Clay Parker
(19) Jeff Roberts
(20) Brad Rohde
(21) Mike Schooler
(22) Rich Slominski
(23) Paul Serna
(24) Bob Siegel
(25) Dave Snell
(26) Jorge Uribe
(27) Omar Visquel
(28) Anthony Woods
(29) Clint Zavarras

1986 Pro Cards West Palm Beach Expos

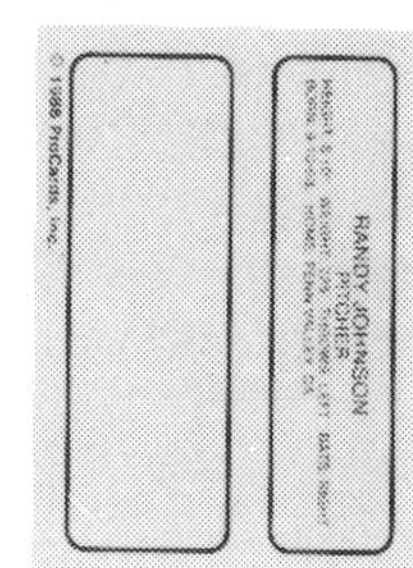

(Montreal Expos, A)

	MT	NR MT	EX
Complete Set:	14.00	10.50	5.75

(1) Felipe Alou
(2) Tim Arnold
(3) Scott Ayers
(4) Kent Bachman
(5) Esteban Beltre
(6) Mark Blaser
(7) Edgar Caceres
(8) Allen Collins
(9) Kerry Cook
(10) Bill Cunningham
(11) Mike Day
(12) Bob Devlin
(13) Eddie Dixon
(14) Kevin Dunton
(15) Jeff Fischer
(16) George Flower
(17) Keith Foley
(18) Gene Glynn
(19) Sam Haley
(20) Melvin Houston
(21) Randy Johnson
(22) Jim Kahmann
(23) Scott Mann
(24) Alonzo Powell
(25) Iggy Rodriguez
(26) Tim Thiessen
(27) Gary Wayne
(28) Bud Yanus

1986 Pro Cards Winston-Salem Spirits

(Chicago Cubs, A)

	MT	NR MT	EX
Complete Set:	10.00	7.50	4.00

(1) Bob Bafia
(2) Greg Bell
(3) Brent Casteel
(4) Doug Dacenzo (Dascenzo)
(5) Jim Essian
(6) Ron Ewart
(7) Rick Hopkins
(8) Brian House
(9) Rick Krantiz

(10) Lester Lancaster
(11) Dave Masters
(12) Steve Maye
(13) Julius McDougal
(14) Mark McMorris
(15) William Menendez
(17) David Pavlas
(18) Jim Phillip
(19) Jeff Pico
(20) Cohen Renfroe
(21) Tim Rice
(22) Don Richardson
(23) Rolando Roomes
(24) Mike Tullier
(25) Hector Villanueva
(26) Darcy Walker
(27) Rick Wrona
(28) Ernie Shore Stadium
(29) Ernie Shore Stadium
(30) Team Photo

1986 Pro Cards Winter Haven Red Sox

(Boston Red Sox, A)

	MT	NR MT	EX
Complete Set:	20.00	15.00	8.00

(1) Odie Abril
(2) Brady Anderson
(3) Gregg Barrios
(4) Greg Bochesa
(5) Mike Carista
(6) Mike Clarkin
(7) Tony DeFrancesco
(8) Robert Fuentes
(9) Angel Gonzalez
(10) Dave Holt
(11) Daryl Irvine
(12) Laverne Jackson
(13) Manny Jose
(14) Eric Laseke
(15) Bruce Lockhart
(16) Greg Lotzar
(17) Tim McGee
(18) Chris Moritz
(19) Rob Parkins
(20) John Sanderski
(21) Tary Scott
(22) Mike Sears
(23) Scott Skripko
(24) Jim Snediker
(25) Dan Sullivan
(26) Luis Vasquez
(27) Robert Zambrano

1986 Smokey Bear Fresno Giants

(San Francisco Giants, A)

	MT	NR MT	EX
Complete Set:	45.00	33.50	18.00

1 Tim Blackwell (manager)
2 Gary Davenport (coach)
3 Vince Sferrazza (trainer)
4 Gary Jones
5 Felipe Gonzalez
6 Joe Kmak
7 Greg Gilbert
8 Sam Moore
9 Mike Villa
10 Tom Messier
11 Randy McCament
12 Joe Olker
13 Dave Hinnrichs
14 Eric Erickson
15 Darrell Rodgers
16 Dennis Cook
17 Steve Smith
18 Hector Quinones
19 Ty Dabney
20 Tony Perezchica
21 Scott Thompson
22 Tom Mathews
23 John Skurla
24 T.J. McDonald
25 Charles Culberson
26 Harry Davis
27 Kenny Compton (batboy)
28 Tony Vitale (groundskeeper)
29 Smokey Bear (batting)
30 Smokey Bear (throwing)
31 Smokey Bear (saluting)
--- Introductory Card

1986 Smokey Bear Palm Springs Angels

(California Angels, A)

	MT	NR MT	EX
Complete Set:	19.00	14.25	7.75

1 Tom Osowski (general manager)
2 Tom Kotchman (manager)
3 Chuck Hernandez (coach)
4 Paul Bilak (trainer)
5 Bobby Bell
6 Eric Pappas
7 John DiGioia
8 Miguel Garcia
9 William Fraser
10 Mike Romanovsky
11 Larry Cook
12 Bryan Harvey
13 Scott Marrett
14 Richie Carter
15 Bryan Price
16 Todd Eggertson
17 Mick Butler
18 Phil Venturino
19 Barry Dacus
20 Ty Van Burkleo
21 David Montanari
22 Pete Coachman
23 Billy Geivett
24 Mitch Seoane
25 Dario Nunez
26 Doug Jennings
27 Reggie Lambert
--- Introductory Card

1986 Daniels Madison Muskies

(Oakland A's, A)

	MT	NR MT	EX
Complete Set:	12.50	9.50	5.25

1 Doug Ames
2 Tony Arias
3 Larry Arndt
4 Tony Cabrera
5 Ron Carter
6 Brian Criswell
7 Mike Cupples
8 Pat Dietrick
9 Bobby Gould
10 Marty Hall
11 Mark Howie
12 Andre Jacas
13 Russ Kibler
14 Kirk McDonald
15 Dave Nix
16 Dave Otto
17 Scott Sabo
18 Jeff Shaver
19 Nelson Silverio
20 Bob Stocker
21 Camilo Veras
22 Walt Weiss
23 Wally Whitehurst
24 Jim Nettles
25 Dave Schober
26 Dave Schillinglaw
27 Rick Wise

1986 TCMA Albany Colonie Yankees

(New York Yankees, AA) (color)

	MT	NR MT	EX
Complete Set:	10.00	7.50	4.00

1 Jim Riggs
2 Roberto Kelly
3 Carson Carroll
4 Miguel Sosa
5 Tom Barrett
6 Ferdi Gonzalez
7 Keith Hughes
8 Bill Monobouquette
9 Carlos Martinez
10 Tony Russell
11 Mike Heifferon
12 Eric Bernard
13 John Liburdi
14 Eric Dersin
15 Jeff Pries
16 Jim Saul
17 Logan Easley
18 Mo Ching
19 John Lemperle
20 Chuck Yaeger
21 Eric Schmidt
22 Bill Lindsey
23 Darren Reed
24 John Kennedy
25 Aris Tirado
26 Bill Fulton
27 Joe Impagliazzo
28 Clay Christensen
29 Steve George
30 Brent Blum
31 Bob Davidson
32 Bullpen Action (Brent Blum, Logan Easley, Bill Monobouquette)

1986 TCMA Cedar Rapids Reds

(Cincinnati Reds, A) (color)

	MT	NR MT	EX
Complete Set:	10.00	7.50	4.00

1 Dan Belinskas
2 Brad Brusky
3 Mike Converse
4 Mike Campbell
5 Tim Deltz
6 Curt Kindred
7 Gino Mintelli
8 Mike Roesler
9 Greg Simpson
10 Mike Smith
11 Greg Toler
12 Mike Vincent
13 Rod Zeratsky
14 Marty Brown
15 Joe Dunlap
16 Mark Germann
17 Scott Hilgenberg
18 Randy Hindman
19 Cal Cain
20 Mark Jackson
21 Chris Jones
22 Allen Sigler
23 John Bryant
24 Paul Kirsch
25 Gene Dusan
26 Neal Davenport
27 "Bucky" Buchheister
28 Lamar the Dog (mascot)

1986 TCMA Jackson Mets

(New York Mets, AA) (color)

	MT	NR MT	EX
Complete Set:	20.00	15.00	8.00

1 Jim Adamczak
2 Reggie Dobie
3 Wray Bergendahl
4 Tom Edens
5 Kyle Hartshorn
6 Jeff Innis
7 Kurt Lundgren
8 Ed Pruitt
9 Mike Santiago
10 Mickey Weston
11 Doug Gwosdz
12 Greg Olson
13 Kevin Elster
14 Dennis Glynn
15 Paul Hertzler
16 Andy Lawrence
17 Jeff McKnight
18 Rick Lockwood
19 Shawn Abner
20 Jason Felice
21 Scott Little
22 Johnny Wilson
23 Sam McCrary
24 Mike Cubbage
25 Glenn Abbott
26 Randy Milligan
27 Keith Miller

1986 TCMA Jacksonville Expos

(Montreal Expos, AA) (color)

	MT	NR MT	EX
Complete Set:	12.00	9.00	5.00

1 Tony Nicometi
2 Johnny Paredes

3 Jim Cecchini
4 Armando Moreno
5 Tom Traen
6 Peter Camelo
7 John Trautwein
8 Nelson Santovenia
9 Leonel Carrion
10 Q.V. Lowe
11 Joe Graves
12 Greg Raymer
13 Matt Sferrazza
14 Kevin Price
15 Mark Gardner
16 Troy McKay
17 Gary Weinberger
18 Wilfredo Tejada
19 Tommy Thompson
20 Mark Corey
21 Jeff Reynolds
22 Norman Nelson
23 Brian Holman
24 Bill Cutshall
25 Jack Daugherty
26 Tim McCormack

1986 Tcma Omaha Royals

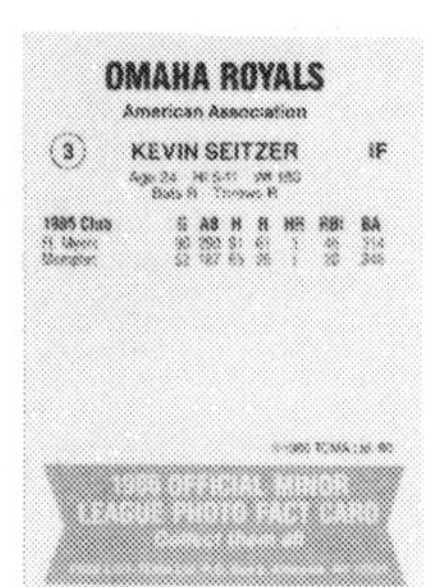

(Kansas City Royals, AA) (color)

	MT	NR MT	EX
Complete Set:	25.00	18.50	10.00

1 Bill Hayes
2 Ron Johnson
3 Kevin Seitzer
4 Mike Kingery
5 Roger Hansen
6 Jeff Schultz
7 Jim Scranton
8 Bob Hegman
9 Marty Wilkerson
10 Russ Stephans
11 Dwight Taylor
12 Bill Pecota
13 Mike Brewer
14 Joe Citari
15 Mike Griffin
16 Dave Cone
17 Scott Tabor
18 Jim Strode
19 Dave Schuler
20 Theo Shaw
21 Alan Hargesheimer
22 Tom Mullen
23 John Boles
24 Frank Funk
25 Scott Bankhead

1986 TCMA Stars Of The Future Post Card Set

	MT	NR MT	EX
Complete Set:	15.00	11.25	6.00

1 Cooper Stadium Home of the Clippers

2 Team & Barry Foote, Mgr.
3 Pitchers (Alfonso Pulido, Doug Drabek, Mike Armstrong, Brad Arnsberg)

4 Catchers (Juan Espino, Phil Lombardi)

5 1st base, 2nd base shortstop (Orestes Destrade, Andre Robertson, Mike Soper)

6 Doug Potestio
7 Julio Valdez
8 Dave Martinez, Steve Hammond, son, Mike Soper Mike Brumley, Bobby Ramosond, son, Mike Soper
9 Dave Gumpert Ken Price
10 Trey Brooks
11 Joe Hicks
12 Pookie Bernstine
13 Johnny Abrego
14 Dennis Livingston
15 Mike Watters (2nd base)
16 Stu Pederson (Outfielder)
17 Ralph Bryant
18 Jeff Hamilton (3rd base)
19 Balvino Galvez (Pitcher)
20 Ed Amelung (Outfielder)
21 Alvis Woods
22 Scott Ullger
23 Andre David
24 Dennis Burtt
25 Geraldo "Jerry" Lomastro
26 Fred McGriff
27 Alex Infante
28 Stan Clarke
29 Chris Johnston
30 Jeff Hearron
31 Stan Jefferson
32 Dave Magadan
33 John Gibbons
34 John Mitchell
35 Tony Ferreira
36 Jesse Reid
37 Jim Lefebvre
38 Mike Aldrete
39 Terry Mulholland
40 Mark Grant

1986 Team Birmingham Barons

(Chicago White Sox, AA)

	MT	NR MT	EX
Complete Set:	30.00	22.50	12.25

1 Steve Oswald
2 Manny Salinas
3 Ken Reed
4 Dave White
5 Troy Thomas
6 Tony Menendez
7 Tom Moritz
8 Ron Karkovice
9 John Johnson
10 Mike Harris
11 Dave Cochrane
12 Rolando Pino
13 Mike Taylor
14 Rick Seilheimer
15 Tom Forrester
16 Jack Hardy
17 Mike Yastrzemski
18 Jim Hickey
19 Bobby Thigpen
20 Bob Bolin (coach)
21 Mark Williams
22 Kurt Walker
23 Marv Foley
24 Ken Koch (trainer)
25 Tom Haller (manager)
26 Sam Hairston (coach)
27 Rich DeVincenzo

1986 Team Columbus Clippers

(New York Yankees, AAA)

	MT	NR MT	EX
Complete Set:	7.00	5.25	2.75

(1) Mike Armstrong
(2) Brad Arnsberg
(3) Clay Christiansen
(4) Pete Dalena
(5) Orastes Destrade
(6) Doug Drabek
(7) Juan Espino
(8) Kelly Faulk
(9) Randy Graham
(10) Leo Hernandez
(11) Al Holland
(12) Phil Lombardi
(13) Victor Mata
(14) Derwin McNealy
(15) Dan Pasqua
(16) Scott Patterson
(17) Jeff Pries
(18) Alfonso Pulido
(19) Andre Robertson
(20) Mark Silva
(21) Keith Smith
(22) Mike Soper
(23) Dave Stegman
(24) Manager Card (George Sisler Jr., Barry Foote)
(25) Coaches/Trainer Card (Dave La Roche, Brian Butterfield, Kevin Rand)

1986 Team Huntsville Stars

(Oakland A's, AA)

	MT	NR MT	EX
Complete Set:	12.50	9.50	5.25

10 Amin David
11 Gary Jones
12 Dave Nix
14 Dave Wilder
15 Rocky Coyle
16 Terry Steinbach
18 Damon Farmar
19 Ray Thoma
20 Brian Guinn
21 Todd Burns
22 Stan Hilton
23 Wally Whitehurst
24 Jose Tolentino
25 Brad Fischer
26 Mark Leonette
30 Stan Kyles
31 Tim Belcher
32 Scott Whaley
33 Mark McGwire
34 Greg Cadaret
40 Doug Scherer
41 John Cox
42 Kirk McDonald
44 Rick Tronerud
45 Roy Johnson

1986 Team Indianapolis Indians

(Montreal Expos, AAA)

	MT	NR MT	EX
Complete Set:	12.50	9.50	5.25

1 Team logo & promo card
2 Owen J. Bush (past player/memorialized)

3 Joe Sparks
4 Rich Stoll
5 Jack Glasscock (past player memorialized)
6 Randy Hunt
7 Tom Romano
8 Amos Rusie (past player/memorialized)

9 Bob Owchinko
10 Rene Gonzales
11 Authentic document
12 John Dopson
13 Derrell Baker
14 1928 Indianapolis team photo

15 Randy St. Claire
16 "Skeeter" Barnes
17 Rodger Cole
18 "Lefty Bob" Logan (past player memorialized)
19 Wally Johnson
20 Len Barker
21 Al Lopez (past player/memorialized)

22 Mike Hocutt
23 Bob Sebra
24 Herb Score (past player/memorialized)

25 Curt Brown
26 Dallas Williams
27 Larry Groves
28 Luis Rivera
29 Don Buford (past player/memorialized)

30 Tom Nieto
31 Dave Tomlin
32 "Champ" Summers
33 Candaele
34 Tim Barrett
35 Billy Moore
36 Coaches/Trainer card (Jerry Manuel, Lee Garrett, Rick Williams)

1986 Team Louisville Redbirds

(St. Louis Cardinals, AAA)

	MT	NR MT	EX
Complete Set:	14.00	10.50	5.75

-1 Jim Fregosi
-2 Dyar Miller
-3 David Hudson
-4 Jack Ayer
-5 Steve Braun
-6 Joe Boever
7 Rod Booker
8 Rich Buonantony
9 Ralph Citarella
10 Greg Dunn
11 Mike Dunne
12 Bill Farley
13 Curt Ford
14 Kurt Kepshire
15 Alan Knicely
16 Jim Linde3man
17 Bill Lyons
18 Fred Manrique
19 Fred Martinez
20 John Morris
21 Tom Pagnozzi
22 Casey Parsons
23 Joe Pettini
24 Marty Pevey
25 Dave Rajsich
26 Ray Soff
27 Dan Stryffeler
28 Tim Wallace
29 Jed Smith
30 Mascots (B. Johnson & D. Harris)

1986 Team Nashville Sounds

(Detroit Tigers, AAA)

	MT	NR MT	EX
Complete Set:	10.00	7.50	4.00

(1) Doug Baker
(2) Fred Breining
(3) Chuck Cary
(4) Pedro Chavez
(5) Jeff Conner
(6) Brian Denman
(7) Scott Earl
(8) Bruce Fields
(9) Paul Gibson
(10) Brian Harper
(11) Don Heinkel
(12) Mike Henneman
(13) Rodney Hobbs
(14) Bryan Kelly
(15) Jack Lazorko
(16) Scotti Madison
(17) Don McGann
(18) Matt Nokes
(19) Chris Nyman
(20) German Rivera
(21) Leon Roberts
(22) Jeff Robinson
(23) Gene Roof
(24) Tim Tolman

1986 Team Pittsfield Cubs

(Chicago Cubs, AA) This set is in the form of a 10-7/8 x 16-3/4 poster.

	MT	NR MT	EX
Complete Set:	40.00	30.00	16.00

(1) Rich (Amarel)
(2) Damon Berryhill
(3) Brad Blevins
(4) Mike Capel
(5) Troy Chestnut
(6) Bruce Crabbe
(7) Luis Cruz
(8) Jackie Davidson
(9) Drew Hall
(10) Carl Hamilton
(11) Darrin Jackson
(12) Dave Kopf
(13) Tom Layton
(14) Dave Lenderman
(15) Mike Martin
(16) Alan McKay
(17) Paul Noce
(18) Rafael Palmeiro
(19) Rolando Roomes
(20) Phil Stephenson
(21) Gary Varsho
(22) Tony Woods

1986 Team Tulsa Drillers

(Texas Rangers, AA)

	MT	NR MT	EX
Complete Set:	13.50	10.00	5.50

1 Mark Poole
2 Tony Triplett
3 Kirk Killingsworth
4 Mike Couchee
5 Art Gardner
6 Bill Stearns
7 Tim Rodgers
8 Mike Loynd
9a Jerry Browne
9b Rick Knapp
10 Steve Wilson
11 Jamie Doughty
12 Benny Cadahia
14 Bob Gergen
15 Greg Ferlenda
16 Kevin Bootay
17 Javier Ortiz
18 Greg Bailey
19 Dan Olsson
20 Paul Kilgus
21 Jeff Melrose
22 Rick Raether
23 Randy Kramer
24 Larry Klein
25 Mike Stanley
26 Bob Bill
27 Jose Mota

1986 Time Out Sports Memphis Chicks

(Kansas City Royals, AA) This set is numbered as it appears on the cards. It was produced as a silver set, and a gold set.

	MT	NR MT	EX
Complete Set:	42.50	31.75	17.50

Steve Morrow
1 Tommy Jones
3 Gary Thurman
5 Gene Morgan
6 Mike Miller
7 Hector Rincones
9 Van Snider
10 Chito Martinez
11 Phil George
12 Art Martinez
14 Israel Sanchez
15 Doug Gilcrease
16 Jere Longenecker
18 Joe Jarrell
20 Angel Morris
21 Mitch McKelvey
23 Rick Goodin
24 Jimmy Daniel
25 Rich Dubee
26 Ken Crew
27 Terry Bell
28 Bo Jackson
29 John Davis
32 Jose Rodiles
33 Luis De Los Santos
35 Mike McFarlane

1986 University of Hawaii Rainbows

1 Guy Ogawa
2 Nelson Inabata
3 Kelsey Isa
4 Paul List
5 Jeff Vierra
6 John Matias
7 Keith Ishibashi
8 Todd Crosby
9 Norman Holt
10 Steve Morris
11 Mark Kawakami
12 Dan Nyssen
13 Mike Ponio
14 Mark Furtak
15 Mike Reitzel
16 Markus Owens
17 Louis Calvert
18 Joey Vierra
19 Greg Burlingame
20 Roberts Muhammad
21 Mark McWherter
22 Monty Vold
23 Colin Franker
24 Randy Oyama
25 Phil Williams
26 Larry Gonzales
27 Les Murakami (head coach)
28 Carl Furutani (assistant coach)
29 Ron Nomura (assistant coach)
30 Howard Dashefsky

1986 WBTV Charlotte O's

(Baltimore Orioles, AA)

	MT	NR MT	EX
Complete Set:	22.00	16.50	9.00

(1) Kurt Beamesderfer
(2) Eric Bell
(3) Greg Biagini
(4) Terry Bogner
(5) Jim Boudreau
(6) Mark Brown
(7) Paul Cameron (sportscaster)
(8) Tom Dodd
(9) Dave Falcone
(10) John Flinn
(11) Charlie Frederick (sportscaster)
(12) Lee Granger
(13) Bob Hice (sportscaster)
(14) Jerry Holtz
(15) John Hoover
(16) Joe Kucharski
(17) Terry Mauney (sportscaster)
(18) Carl Nichols
(19) Francisco Oliveras
(20) Chris Padget
(21) Mike Raczka
(22) Joe Redfield
(23) Rich Rice
(24) Billy Ripken
(25) Rico Rossy
(26) Ron Salcedo
(27) Dave Smith
(28) Scott Stranski
(29) Jeff Wood
(30) O's Fans

1987

1987 Best Birmingham Barons

(Chicago White Sox, AA)

	MT	NR MT	EX
Complete Set:	7.50	5.50	3.00

1 Rico Petrocelli
2 Sam Hairston, Sr.
3 Moe Drabowsky
4 James Wesley (Jim) O'Dell
5 Marlin McPhail
6 Wil Caraballo
7 Rondal Rollin
8 Larry Acker
9 Jeff Bettendorf
10 Antonio G. (Tony) Menendez
11 Richard Kent (Rich) Gaynor
12 John Robert Boling
13 Adam Charles Peterson
14 Gardner C. (Grady) Hall
15 Donn Steven Pall
16 James Joseph (Jim) Hickey
17 John Pawlowski
18 John Graydon (Jack) Hardy
19 Rolando Pino
20 Kenton Craig (Kent) Torve
21 Darrell Ray Pruitt
22 Peter Paul Venturini
23 Manual Victor Salinas
24 James A. (Jim) Winters
25 Troy Gene Thomas
26 William Donald (Bill) Lindsey
27 Jorge Enrique Alcazar
28 Rick DeHart (trainer)

1987 Best Chattanooga Lookouts

(Seattle Mariners, AA) A second identical set was also printed in a limited quantity of 1,000 with the cards featuring Coca-Cola emblems.

	MT	NR MT	EX
Complete Set:	10.00	7.50	4.00

1 Sal Rende
2 Dan Warthen
3 Gregory Bartley
4 James Parker
5 James Walker
6 Calvin Jones
7 James Bryant
8 Michael Schooler
9 Douglas Givler
10 Erik Hanson
11 Michael Christ
12 Kenneth Spratke
13 Robert Gunnarson
14 Roger Hansen
15 Bill McGuire
16 Eric Fox
17 Greg Briley
18 Gregory Fulton
19 Nesi Balelo
20 David Myers
21 Matthew Hall
22 John Gibbons
23 Brian David
24 William Mendek
25 Andre Robertson
26 Tom Hunt (trainer)

1987 Best Greenville Braves

(Atlanta Braves, AA)

	MT	NR MT	EX
Complete Set:	11.50	8.50	4.75

1 James Beauchamp
2 Leo D. Mazzone
3 Roland T. Jackson
4 Randy Ingle
5 Carlos Rafael Rios
6 Ronald Nipper
7 Andrew Denson
8 Adrian Charles Wills
9 David Justice
10 Todd Alan Dewey
11 Willie John Childress
12 Edgar Yost
13 Ronald Edwin Gant
14 John Steven Kilner
15 Brian Keith Aviles
16 Bryan Pierce Farmer
17 Inocencio Guerrero
18 Maximo Del Rosario
19 Kevin Blankenship
20 Kevin Reese Coffman
21 Jeffrey Wetherby
22 Larry Wayne Heise
23 Ira Thomas Greene
24 Peter John Smith
25 Johnny Hatcher
26 Gregory Alan Tubbs
27 Kenneth Joe Kinnard
28 Michael William Scott

1987 Best Memphis Chicks

(Kansas City Royals, AA)

	MT	NR MT	EX
Complete Set:	8.00	6.00	3.25

1 Bob Schaefer

2 Duane Gustavson
3 Rich Dubee
4 Jose Rivera
5 Julio Alcala
6 Mark Van Blaricom
7 Jim Bennett
8 Ken Crew
9 Jose DeJesus
10 Scott Stranski
11 Phil George
12 Theo Shaw
13 Mark Shiflett
14 Don Sparling
15 Mike Miller
16 Tim Lambert
17 Gene Morgan
18 Mike Loggins
19 Jere Longenecker
20 Mauro Gozza
21 Jim Eisenreich
22 Rick Luecken
23 Terry Bell
24 Matt Winters
25 Mike Fuentes
26 Jamie Nelson
27 Steve Morrow (trainer)

1987 Best Springfield Cardinals

(St. Louis Cardinals, A)

	MT	NR MT	EX
Complete Set:	20.00	15.00	8.00

1 Gaylen Pitts
2 Mark A. Riggins
3 Alexander Ojea
4 Stephen W. Meyer
5 James W. Puzey
6 Ronald M. Johns
7 Tim Lemons
8 John T. Baine
9 Jeffrey L. Graham
10 William E. Bivens
11 Robert J. Faron
12 Stephen F. Hill
13 Howard Hilton
14 David Takach
15 Michael I. Perez
16 David J. Sala
17 Scott W. Hamilton
18 Robert A. Glisson
19 Michael S. Raziano
20 Brian Farley
21 Larry R. Breedlove
22 Bienvendo Figueroa
23 Vincent L. Kindred
24 Scott Melvin
25 Otis B. Gilkey
26 Todd E. Zeile
27 Bluestone Brad
28 Scott Norman

1987 Bob's Photo Richmond Braves

(Atlanta Braves, AAA) This team issued set measures 5 x 3-78 inches in size.

	MT	NR MT	EX
Complete Set:	40.00	30.00	16.00

(1) Chuck Cary
(2) Floyd Chiffer
(3) Marty Clary
(4) Sal D'Alessandro
(5) Trench Davis
(6) Juan Eichelberger
(7) Mike Fischlin
(8) Tom Glavine
(9) Dave Griffin
(10) Inocencio Guerrero
(11) Kelly Heath
(12) Chuck Hensley
(13) Dale Holman
(14) John Mizerock
(15) Darryl Motley
(16) Ed Olwine
(17) John Rabb
(18) Paul Runge
(19) Cliff Speck
(20) Matt West
(21) Steve Ziem

1987 Chong Modesto A's

(Oakland A's, A)

	MT	NR MT	EX
Complete Set:	10.00	7.50	4.00

1 Mike Bordick, Mike Bordick, Tony LaRussa (Pro Sportsworld Special Edition card)
2 Pat Britt, Pat Britt, Joe Rudi (Pro Sportsworld Special Edition card)

3 Jim Corsi, Jim Corsi, Dave Duncan (Pro Sportsworld Special Edition card)

4 David Gavin, David Gavin, Dave Leiper (Pro Sportsworld Special Edition card)

5 Robert Gould, Robert Gould
6 Scott Holcomb, Scott Holcomb

7 Dann Howitt, Dann Howitt
8 Steve Iannini, Steve Ianini
9 Bo Kent, Bob Kent
10 Joe Law, Joe Law
11 John Minch, John Minch
12 Jerome Nelson, Jerome Nelson

13 Jose Peguero, Jose Peguero

14 Bill Savarino, Jamie Reiser, Bill Savarino

15 Kevin Tapini
16 David Veres, David Veres
17 Bruce Walton, Bruce Walton

18 Kevin Williamson, Kevin Williamson

19 Chris Hayes, Vinnie Teixeira
20 Frank Masters, Camilo Veras

21 Jeff Whitney, Jeff Whitney
22 Drew Stratton, Drew Stratton

23 Tommie Reynolds, Dave Schober

24 Butch Huges
25 John Cartelli
26 Bob Fingers
27 Gary Gorski
28 The Pro Sportsworld Team

1987 Cramer Everett Giants

(San Francisco Giants, A)

	MT	NR MT	EX
Complete Set:	11.00	8.25	4.50

1 Matt Walker
2 Gilbert Heredia
3 Scott Goins
4 Anthony Piazza
5 Lonnie Phillips
6 Richard Aldrete
7 Andy Rohn
8 Kip Southland
9 Jamie Cooper
10 Glenn Abraham
11 Randy Lind
12 Joe Strain
13 Eric Gunderson
14 Chris Kocman
15 Tony Michalak
16 Tom Hostetler
17 Michael Ham
18 Todd Hawkins
19 Jimmy Terrill
20 Shaun MacKenzie
21 Jim Massey
22 Rob Wilson
23 Donn Perno
24 Gary Geiger
25 Bill Bluhm
26 Jeff Morris
27 Brad Comstock
28 Dickens Benoit
29 Brad Gambee
30 Mark Owens
31 Mike Remlinger
32 Mark Dewey
33 Bruce Graham
34 Checklist

1987 Crown Oil Richmond Braves

(Atlanta Braves, AAA) This set is numbered as it appears on the cards. Also, originally in the form of a perforated 11" by 28-1/2" sheet.

	MT	NR MT	EX
Complete Set:	12.50	9.50	5.25

Sam Ayoub
1 Kelly Heath
2 Jeff Baluser
5 Mark Strueher
6 Roy Majtyka
8 John Mizerock
9 Bob Tumpane
10 Sal D'Alessandro
12 Paul Runge
14 Tom Glavine
15 Juan Elchelberger
18 Miko Feschlin
19 Steve Ziem
20 John Rabb
24 DAvid Griffin
25 Dale Holman
26 Rick Albert
28 Floyd Chiffer
29 STan Cliburn
30 Darryl Motley
31 BEan Stringfellow
32 Treuch Davis
34 Marty Clary
37 Chuck Hensley
39 Cliff speck
42 Mike Brown
43 Nardi Contreras
45 Matt West
47 Chuck Cary

1987 Donn Jennings Southern League All-Stars

(AA)

	MT	NR MT	EX
Complete Set:	7.50	5.50	3.00

1 Dave Falcone
2 Rondal Rollin
3 Geronimo Berroa
4 Bernie Tatis
5 Nelson Santovenia
6 Tom Dodd
7 Cameron Drew
8 Larry Walker
9 Matt Winters
10 Ken Caminiti
11 Dave Myers
12 Jimmy Jones
13 Ronnie Gant
14 John Trautwein
15 Rob Mallicoat
16 Randy Johnson
17 Kevin Price
18 Steve Gasser
19 Kevin Coffman
20 Adam Peterson
21 Jeff Bettendorf
22 Jim Beauchamp (manager)
23 Rico Petrocelli (coach)
24 Greg Biagini (coach)
25 Leo Mazzone (coach)

1987 Jones Photo Tucson Toros

(Houston Astros, AAA) No positions are listed on these cards which measure 3 x 5-1/8 inches in size. Each set comes in a protective miniature binder.

	MT	NR MT	EX
Complete Set:	55.00	41.25	22.50

(1) Dale Berra
(2) Eric Bullock
(3) Glenn Carpenter
(4) Bill Crone
(5) Bob Dider
(6) Jeff Edwards
(7) Tom Funk
(8) TY Gainey
(9) Jeff Heathcock
(10) Manny Hernandez
(11) Paul Householder
(12) Chuck Jackson
(13) Anthony Kelley
(14) Ron Mathis
(15) Louie Meadows
(16) Jim Miner
(17) Rafael Montaivo
(18) Raynor Noble
(19) Ronn Reynolds
(20) Nelson Rood
(21) Tye Waller
(22) Ed Watt
(23) Robbie Wine
(24) Gerald Young

1987 Pizza World Peoria Chiefs

(Chicago Cubs, A) This set is 5-1/2" by 4-1/2" in size and is co-sponsored by station WCT-106.

	MT	NR MT	EX
Complete Set:	75.00	56.00	30.00

(1) Butch Garcia
(2) Pat Gomez
(3) John Green
(4) Steve Hill
(5) Jerome Walton
(6) Chief Rainout

1987 Police Salinas Spurs

(A)

	MT	NR MT	EX
Complete Set:	75.00	56.00	30.00

1 Keith Foley
2 Jorge Uribe
3 Dave Snell
4 Maryann Hudson
5 Mike Brants
6 William Diaz
7 Andrea Fine
8 Dave "Doc" Mosley
9 John Clem
10 Rick Moore
11 Greg Brinkman
12 Dave McCorkle
13 Bob Bernardo
14 Tom Eccelston
15 Danny Larson
16 Jovan Edwads
17 Michael Darby
18 Buddy Meachum
19 Omar Visquel
20 Robert Gibree
21 Tom Krause
22 Steve Murray
23 Pablo Moncerratt
24 Tom Newberg
25 Jeff Hull
26 Tim Fortugno
27 Jeff Nelson
28 Mike Kolovitz
29 John Burden
30 Clint Zavaras
31 Smokey Bear
32 Greg Mahlberg

1987 Pro Cards Albany-Colonie Yankees

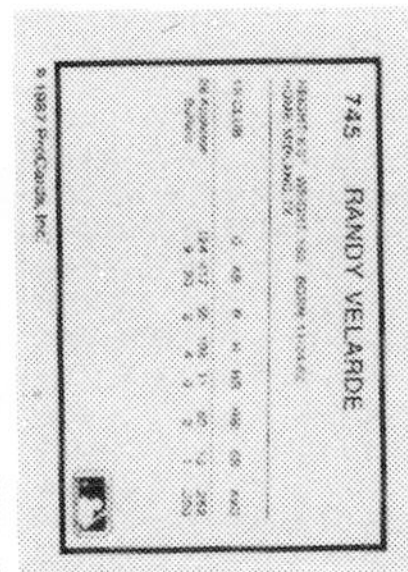

(New York Yankees, AA)

	MT	NR MT	EX
Complete Set:	10.00	7.50	4.00

739 Steve Rosenberg
740 Tony Russell
741 Bob Barker
742 Eric Schmidt
743 Robert Geren
744 Maurice Guercio
745 Randy Velarde
746 Ted Higgins
747 Gary Cathcart
749 Tim Layana
750 Jim Howard
751 Matthew Harrison
752 Carson Carroll
753 Chris Alvarez
754 Darren Reed
755 Jeff Knox
756 Jeffrey Pries
757 Tommy Jones
758 Fredi Gonzalez
759 Hal Morris
760 Brent Blum
761 Steve Frey
762 Jerry McNertney

1987 Pro Cards Appleton Foxes

(Kansas City Royals, A)

	MT	NR MT	EX
Complete Set:	7.00	5.25	2.75

513 Chuck Mount
514 Bill Gilmore
515 John Larios
516 Pete Capello
517 D.J. Watson
518 Carlos Escalera
519 Frank Laureano
520 Deric Ladnier
521 Mike Tresemer
522 Mike Butcher
523 Joe Skodny
524 Darren Watkins
525 Ben Lee
526 Carlos Gonzalez
527 Charlie Eisenreich
528 Tom Gilles
529 Brian Poldberg
530 Mike Alvarez
531 Pat Bailey
532 Jose Rodriquez
533 Rob Wolkovs
534 Mike Leon
535 Tony Pickett
536 Ken Barry
537 Luke Nocas
538 Dennis Moeller
539 Greg Hibbard
540 Kenny Jackson
541 Phil McKinzie
542 Jim Willis

1987 Pro Cards Arkansas Travelers

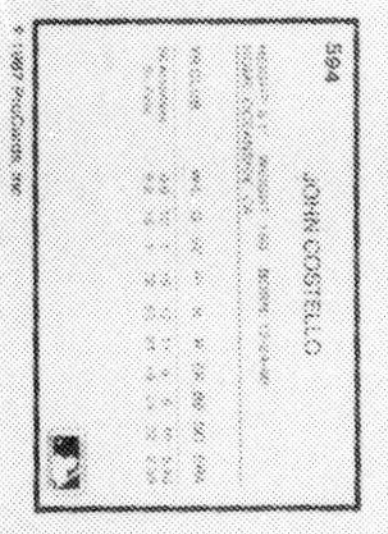

(St. Louis Cardinals, AA)

	MT	NR MT	EX
Complete Set:	9.00	6.75	3.50

570 Dennis Carter
571 Mike Robinson
572 Charles McGrath
573 Jose Calderon
574 Kennedy Infante
575 Jeff Passero
576 James Riggleman
577 Randall Champion
578 Steven Peters
579 Paul Wilmet
580 James Fregosi
581 Roy Silver
582 Scott Arnold
583 Tim Jones
584 Sal Agostinelli
585 Luis Alicea
586 Craig Weissmann
587 Jeff Oyster
588 Kenneth Hill
589 Alex Cole
590 Mike Fitzgerald
591 Ray Stevens
592 James Reboult
593 Brad Henderson
594 John Costello

1987 Pro Cards Asheville Tourists

(Houston Astros, A)

	MT	NR MT	EX
Complete Set:	8.00	6.00	3.25

1818 Karl Rhodes
1819 Trent Hubbard
1820 Gene Confreda
1821 Keith Bodie
1822 Ryan Bowen
1823 Daven Bond
1824 Lou Frazier
1825 Doug Gonring
1826 Jim Olson
1827 Marty Hall
1828 Charlie Taylor
1829 Kevin Wasilewski
1830 Guy Normand
1831 Mike Stoker
1832 Nedar Horta
1833 Bert Hunter
1834 Mike Simms
1835 Shawn Talbott
1836 Victor Hithe
1837 Sam August
1838 Todd McClure
1839 Mike Oglesbee
1840 Lou Deiley
1841 Ed Whited
1842 Jeff Edwards
1843 Gorky Perez
1844 Pedro Sanchez
1845 John Sheehan

1987 Pro Cards Auburn Astros

(Houston Astros, A)

	MT	NR MT	EX
Complete Set:	7.00	5.25	2.75

2446 John Massarelli
2447 Rusty Harris
2448 Todd McClure
2449 Not Issued
2450 Damon Brooks
2451 Billy Paul Carver
2452 Andres Mota
2453 Dan Lewis
2454 Steve Polverini
2455 Randy Hennis
2456 Chris Hawkins
2457 Gary Tuck
2458 Dan Nyssen
2459 Carlos Laboy
2460 Gorky Perez
2461 Robert Romo
2462 Todd Newman
2463 Greg Johnson
2464 Rick Aponte
2465 Hector Herrera
2466 Ken Dickson
2467 Al Osuna
2468 Edison Renteria
2469 Dean Hartgraves
2470 Richie Simon
2471 Douglas Royalty

1987 Pro Cards Bakersfield Dodgers

(Los Angeles Dodgers, A)

	MT	NR MT	EX
Complete Set:	10.50	7.75	4.25

1406 Mike Hartley
1407 Dan Montgomery
1408 Macario Gastelum
1409 Miguel Mota
1410 Juan Guzman
1411 Billy Brooks
1412 Juan Bell
1413 Todd Kroll
1414 John Stein
1415 Luis Lopez
1416 Jim Kating
1417 Mike White
1418 Doug Cox
1419 Stan Johnston
1420 Kevin Kennedy
1421 Mark Sheehy
1422 Rod Roche
1423 Ted Holcomb
1424 Eric Managham
1425 Fred Farwell
1426 Dave Hansen
1427 Tim Anderson
1428 Wayne Kirby
1429 Paul Moralez
1430 Carlos Hernandez
1431 Mike Siler
1432 Mike Munoz
1433 Mike Pitz
1434 Willie Pinelli

1987 Pro Cards Beloit Brewers

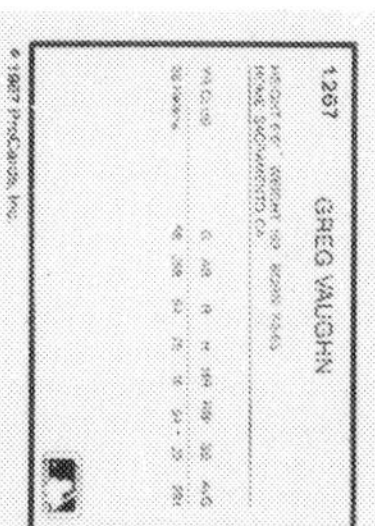

(Milwaukee Brewers, A)

	MT	NR MT	EX
Complete Set:	18.00	13.50	7.25

1266 Randy Veres
1267 Greg Vaughn
1268 John Jaha
1269 Shon Ashley

1270 Steve Monson
1271 Steve Kostichka
1272 Jamie Cangemi
1273 Robert Jones
1274 Brian Stone
1275 Brian Drahman
1276 Jim Rowe
1277 Doug Henry
1278 Rusty McGinnis
1279 Lance Lincoln
1280 Terry Brown
1281 Ron Harrison
1282 Tim Barker
1283 Gomer Hodge
1284 Dave Carley
1285 Hector Alberro
1286 Tim Watkins
1287 Ray Ojeda
1288 Dan Adriance
1289 Manny Chireno
1290 Dave Taylor
1291 Tim McIntosh

1987 Pro Cards Burlington Expos

(Montreal Expos, A)

	MT	NR MT	EX
Complete Set:	7.00	5.25	2.75

1067 Leonard Kelly
1068 James Vincent Olson
1069 Nels Jacobsen
1070 Tony Welborn
1071 Kent Bottenfield
1072 Sal Vaccaro
1073 Doug Duke
1074 Jeff Oller
1075 Mike Dull
1076 Jose Alou
1077 Steven St. Claire
1078 Ben Spitale
1079 Kevin Finigan
1080 Russ Schueler
1081 Delwyn Young
1082 Jeff Wedvick
1083 David Morrow
1084 Bobby Gaylor
1085 Mike Ishmael
1086 Mark Hardy
1087 Buzz Capra
1088 John Howes
1089 Bobby Pate
1090 J.R. Miner
1091 Sean Cunningham
1092 Dan Larson
1093 Mel Rojas
1094 Robin DeYoung
1095 Doug Vontz

1987 Pro Cards Calgary Cannons

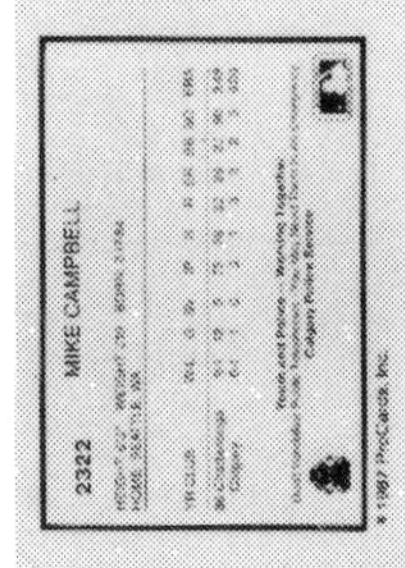

(Seattle Mariners, AAA)

	MT	NR MT	EX
Complete Set:	9.00	6.75	3.50

2309 Edgar Martinez
2310 Mike Watters
2311 Jim Weaver
2312 Bill Plummer
2313 Ross Grimsley
2314 Dennis Powell
2315 Mike Brown
2316 Paul Schneider
2317 Dave Hengel
2318 Karl Best
2319 Mario Diaz
2320 Brick Smith
2321 Roy Thomas
2322 Mike Campbell
2323 Randy Braun
2324 Mike Wishnevski
2325 Terry Taylor
2326 Stan Clarke
2327 Donell Nixon
2328 Tony Ferreira
2329 Jerry Narron
2330 Dave Gallagher
2331 Doug Gwosdz
2332 Rich Monteleone

1987 Pro Cards Cedar Rapids Reds

(Cincinnati Reds, A)

	MT	NR MT	EX
Complete Set:	9.00	6.75	3.50

1010 Al Lobozzetta
1011 Phil Dale
1012 Scott Willis
1013 Curt Kindred
1014 Joe Lazor
1015 Joel Lono
1016 Scott Scudder
1017 Ron Mullins
1018 Mendy Espinal
1019 Keith Brown
1020 Dusty Rogers
1021 Joe Bruno
1022 Keith Lockhart
1023 Reggie Jefferson
1024 Greg Lonigro
1025 Don Wakamatsu
1026 Brian Robinson
1027 Cal Cain
1028 Mike Vincent
1029 Ted Wilborn
1030 John Stewart
1031 Don Brown
1032 Francisco Silverio
1033 Paul Kirsch
1034 Bernie Walker
1035 Rich Bombard
1036 Jim Knudtson
1037 Lamar (mascot)

1987 Pro Cards Charleston Rainbows

(San Diego Padres, A)

	MT	NR MT	EX
Complete Set:	8.00	6.00	3.25

1984 Brian Brooks
1985 Carlos Baerga
1986 Gregg S. Harris
1987 Michael J. King
1988 Gregory Hall
1989 William Taylor
1990 James P. Austin
1991 Brian Lee Harrison
1992 Gary Lance
1993 Mike Young
1994 James Navilliat
1995 Terry McDevitt
1996 Omar Olivares
1997 Matt Maysey
1998 Rafael Valdez
1999 Warren Newson
2000 Tony Torchia
2001 Jamie Norena
2002 Jimmy Tatum, Jr.
2003 Michael A. Basso
2004 Ricardo Bones
2005 Keith Harrison
2006 Doug Brocail

1987 Pro Cards Charleston Wheelers

(No Affiliation, A)

	MT	NR MT	EX
Complete Set:	8.00	6.00	3.25

2135 William Melvin
2136 James Hendrix
2137 Gilbert Villaueva
2138 Alan Wilson
2139 Steven Scarsone
2140 Peter Callas
2141 Rodney Brunelle
2142 Bob Gsellman
2143 Steven Mehl
2144 Gary Pifer
2145 Larry Allen
2146 John Knapp
2147 Danny Weems
2148 Hal Dyer
2149 Carl Grovom
2150 Kevin Main
2151 Timothy McMillian
2152 Robert Strickland
2153 J. Anthony LaPoint
2154 Jimmie Gardiver
2155 Steven O'Quinn
2156 Christopher Keshock
2157 L. Timothy Sossamon
2158 Jack Peel
2159 Norberto Martin
2160 Thomas Abrell
2161 Randall Robinson
2162 Doyle Balthazar

1987 Pro Cards Clearwater Phillies

(Philadelphia Phillies, A)

	MT	NR MT	EX
Complete Set:	7.00	5.25	2.75

1521 Rick Parker
1522 Brad Moore
1523 Curt Befort
1524 Chuck Malone
1525 Olen Parker
1526 Carlos Zayas
1527 Bobby Behnsch
1528 Jeff Kaye
1529 Harvey Brumfield
1530 Shawn Dantzier
1531 Ramon Caraballo
1532 Eric Boudreaux
1533 Garry Clark
1534 Warren Magec
1535 Carlos Arroyo
1536 Steve Sharts
1537 Gary White
1538 Gary Berman
1539 Rollie DeArmas
1540 Dave Brundage
1541 Julio Machado
1542 Juan Sanchez
1543 Brad Brink
1544 Allen Wisdom
1545 Bart Kaiser
1546 Todd Howey
1547 Travis Warren

1987 Pro Cards Clinton Giants

(San Francisco Giants, A)

	MT	NR MT	EX
Complete Set:	7.00	5.25	2.75

981 Doug Robertson
982 John Toal
983 Dave Patterson
984 Gregg Ritchie
985 Jim Anderson
986 Willie Mijares
987 Felipe Gonzales
988 Tod Ronson
989 Jim McNamara
990 John Rannow
991 Bill Carlson
992 Tom Ealy
993 Kevin Redick
994 Mark Leonard
995 Dee Dixon
996 Kim Flowers
997 Bill Evers
998 Todd Oakes
999 Jim Pena
1000 Brock Birch
1001 Paul McClellan
1002 Drew Ricker
1003 Sam Moore
1004 Daron Connelly
1005 Bob Richmond
1006 Ray Velasquaz
1007 Trevor Wilson
1008 Bryan Hickerson
1009 Team Photo

1987 Pro Cards Columbia Mets

(New York Mets, AA)

	MT	NR MT	EX
Complete Set:	9.00	6.75	3.50

1623 Barry Hightower
1624 Bob Apodaca
1625 Brandon Bailey
1626 Cliff Gonzalez
1627 David Lau
1628 Jaime Roseboro
1629 Rich Lundahl
1630 Adam Ging
1631 Johnny Monell
1632 Butch Hobson
1633 Steve Kennelley
1634 Rick Brown
1635 David Liddell
1636 Luis Natera
1637 Bobby Hernandez
1638 Victor Garcia
1639 Scott Henion
1640 Juan Marina
1641 Dan McMurtrie
1642 Mike Anderson
1643 Fritz Polka
1644 Rodney Murrell
1645 Tom Doyle
1646 Danny Naughton
1647 Rick Durant
1648 Julio Valera
1649 Rob Colescott
1650 Alex Jiminez
1651 Todd Welborn

Definitions for grading conditions are located in the introduction of this price guide.

1987 Pro Cards Columbus Astros

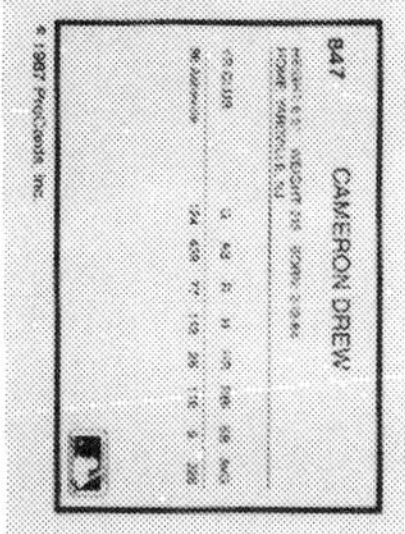

(Houston Astros, AA)

	MT	NR MT	EX
Complete Set:	10.00	7.50	4.00

841 Al Chambers
842 Jeff Datz
843 Fred Gladding
844 Troy Afenir
845 Jim Thomas
846 Mel Stottlemyre
847 Cameron Drew
848 Blaise Isley
849 Mitch Cook
850 Rob Parker
851 Jim Van Houten
852 John Fishel
853 Mark Baker
854 Karl Allaire
855 Joe Mikulik
856 Tom Wiedenbauer
857 Dody Rather
858 Jose Rodiles
859 Earl Cash
860 Jeff Livin
861 Larry Lasky
862 Rob Mallicoat
863 Rich Johnson
864 Norman Brock
865 Ken Caminiti

1987 Pro Cards Columbus Clippers

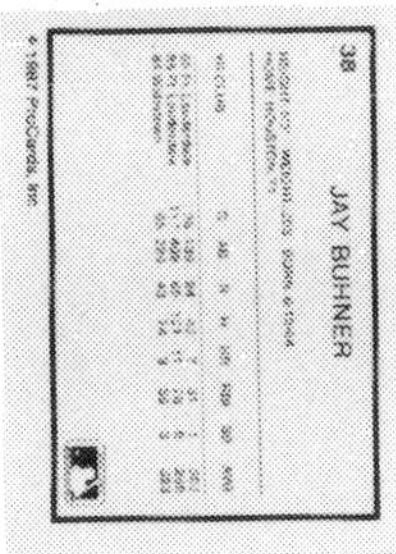

(New York Yankees, AAA)

	MT	NR MT	EX
Complete Set:	12.00	9.00	4.75

24 Bucky Dent
25 Clete Boyer, Jerry McNertney, Kevin Rand, Ken Rowe, Champ Summers

26 Glenn Sherlock
27 Juan Espino
28 Mitch Lyden
29 Bobby Meacham
30 Pete Dalena
31 Orestes Destrade
32 Shane Turner
33 Bryan Little
34 Jeff Moronko
35 Phil Lombardi
36 Dick Scott
37 Roberto Kelly
38 Jay Buhner
39 Henry Cotto
40 Keith Hughes
41 Rich Bordi
42 Randy Graham
43 Alfonso Pulido
44 Mike Armstrong
45 Al Holland
46 Ron Romanick
47 Brad Arnsberg
48 Pete Filson
49 Al Leiter
50 Bill Fulton

1987 Pro Cards Daytona Beach Admirals

(Chicago White Sox, A)

	MT	NR MT	EX
Complete Set:	7.00	5.25	2.75

2283 Todd Trafton
2284 Carl Sullivan
2285 Eric Milholland
2286 Tom Drees
2287 Tony Blasucci
2288 Carlos de la Cruz
2289 Ken Reed
2290 Doug Little
2291 James Brennen
2292 Mark Henry
2293 Francisco Abreu
2294 Conde Cortez
2295 Patrick Coveny
2296 Matt Mercullo
2297 Wayne Edwards
2298 Chris Jefts
2299 Frank Potesto
2300 Billy Eveline
2301 Ed Sedar
2302 Chris Cota
2303 Gralyn Engram
2304 Jerry Bertolani
2305 Andy Nieto
2306 Dan Cronkright
2307 Mike Gellinger
2308 Glen McElroy

1987 Pro Cards Denver Zephyrs

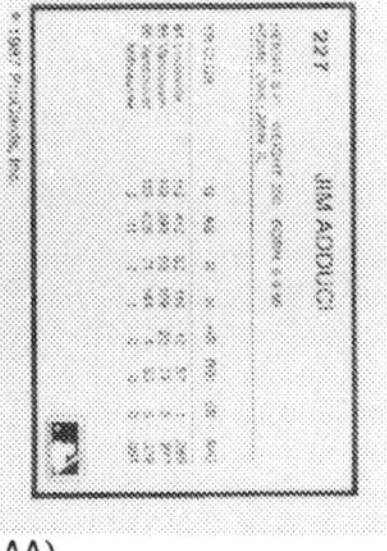

(Milwaukee Brewers, AAA)

	MT	NR MT	EX
Complete Set:	9.00	6.75	3.50

212 David Clay
213 Tim Pyznarski
214 Al Price
215 Jay Aldrich
216 Joey Meyer
217 Brad Komminsk
218 Billy Bates
219 Ron Harrison
220 Paul Mirabella
221 Alex Madrid
222 Dave Schuler
223 Dave Klipstein
224 Terry Bevington
225 John Beuerlein
226 Dan Scarpetta
227 Jim Adduci
228 Don August
229 Steve Kiefer
230 Alan Cartwright
231 Mark Knudson
232 Jackson Todd
233 David Davidsmeier
234 Bryan Clutterbuck
235 Charlie O'Brien
236 Keith Smith
237 Al Jones
238 Steve Stanicek

1987 Pro Cards Dunedin Blue Jays

(Toronto Blue Jays, A)

	MT	NR MT	EX
Complete Set:	7.00	5.25	2.75

923 Carlos Diaz
924 Steve Cummings
925 Bob Watts
926 Mike Jones
927 Hugh Brinson
928 Bob Bailor
929 Dennis Holmberg
930 Dana Johnson
931 Darren Baisley
932 Steve Mumaw
933 Daryl Landrum
934 Tony Castillo
935 Steve Mingori
936 Ric Moreno
937 Webster Garrison
938 Hector de la Cruz
939 Chris Jones
940 Ray Young
941 Kevin Batiste
942 Greg David
943 Shawn Jeter
944 Willie Blair
945 Domingo Martinez
946 Earl Sanders
947 Jerry Schunk
948 Pedro Munoz
949 Ken Rivers
950 Derek Ware
951 Pat Saitta

1987 Pro Cards Durham Bulls

(Atlanta Braves, A)

	MT	NR MT	EX
Complete Set:	8.50	6.25	3.50

1652 Cesar Jimenez
1653 Barry Jones
1654 Jeff Weiss
1655 Bob Pfaff
1656 Sid Akins
1657 Brian G. Smitker
1658 Tim Criswell
1659 Johnny Cuevas
1660 Gary Newsom
1661 Ellis Roby
1662 Dave Miller
1663 Kent Mercker
1664 John Stewart
1665 Alex Smith
1666 Bill Slack
1667 Eddie Matthews (Mathews)
1668 Mike Merrill
1669 Rick Siebert
1670 Gary Eave
1671 Rick Morris
1672 Juan Fredymond
1673 Jeff Greene
1674 D.J. Jones
1675 Jim Salisbury
1676 John Alva
1677 Mark Lemke
1678 Dennis Hood
1679 Dodd Johnson

1987 Pro Cards Edmonton Trappers

(California Angels, AAA)

	MT	NR MT	EX
Complete Set:	7.00	5.25	2.75

2061 Jim Eppard
2062 Jack Lazorko
2063 David Heath
2064 Bobby Misick
2065 Dave Shippanoff (Shipanoff)

2066 Michael Ramsey
2067 Doug Banning
2068 Kevin King
2069 Allen Morelock
2070 Tack Wilson
2071 Ed Amelung
2072 Tom Kotchman
2073 Pete Coachman
2074 Bill Merrifield
2075 Richard Zaleski
2076 James Randall
2077 Frank Reberger
2078 Sherman Corbett
2079 Norm Carrasco
2080 Tony Fossas
2081 T.R. Bryden
2082 Terry Clark
2083 Jack Fimple

1987 Pro Cards El Paso Diablos

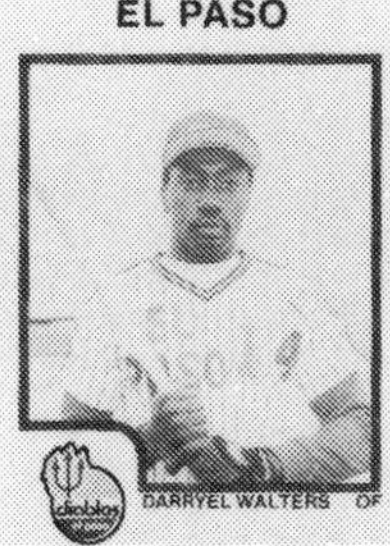

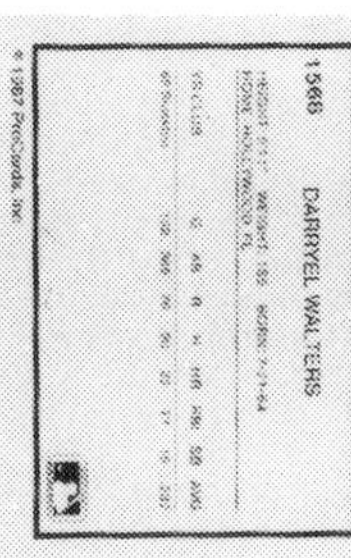

(Milwaukee Brewers, AA)

	MT	NR MT	EX
Complete Set:	14.00	10.50	5.50

1548 Lavell Freeman
1549 Joseph Mitchell
1550 Donald Scott
1551 Peter Kendrick
1552 Garrett Nago
1553 Robert DeWolf
1554 Eric Hardgrave
1555 Frank Mattox
1556 Pete Kolb

1557 Jamie Brisco
1558 Mark Ambrose
1559 John Miglio
1560 Tim Casey
1561 Duffy Dyer
1562 Jesus Alfaro
1563 Derek Diaz
1564 Todd Brown
1565 Cameron Walker
1566 Walter Pohle
1567 Paul Lindblad
1568 Darryel Walters
1569 Daniel Murphy, Jr.
1570 Jeffrey Peterek
1571 Alan Sadler
1572 Ramon Serna
1573 Michael Gobbo
1574 Barry Bass

1987 Pro Cards Erie Cardinals

(St. Louis Cardinals, A)

	MT	NR MT	EX
Complete Set:	10.00	7.50	4.00

2566 Rick Christian
2567 Opie Moran
2568 Joe Rigoli
2569 Reed Olmstead
2570 Ron Leon
2571 Steve Jeffers
2572 Eddie Carter
2573 Steve Jongewaard
2574 Ernie Radcliffe
2575 Roberto Marte
2576 Gregg Smith
2577 Antron Grier
2578 Keith Bennett
2579 Tim Meamber
2580 Scott Broadfoot
2581 Tony Russo
2582 Mike Evans
2583 Orlando Thomas
2584 Brad Harvick
2585 Kevin Robinson
2586 Dave Payton
2587 Scott Halama
2588 Jerry Daniels
2589 Chris Houser
2590 Darren Nelson
2591 Jeremy Hernandez
2592 Pat Moore
2593 Mike Hinkle
2594 Tim Redman

1987 Pro Cards Eugene Emeralds

(Kansas City Royals, A)

	MT	NR MT	EX
Complete Set:	32.50	24.25	13.50

2648 Darryl Robinson
2649 Antoine Pickett
2650 Doug Hupke
2651 Erv Houston
2652 Stu Cole
2653 Bob Moore
2654 James Campbell
2655 Archie Smith
2656 Doug Bock
2657 Doug Nelson
2658 Ben Pierce
2659 Keith Shibata
2660 Pete Alborano
2661 Brian McCormack
2662 Trey Gainous
2663 Derek Sholl
2664 Darren Watkins
2665 Bud Adams
2666 Luis Mallea
2667 Tony Clements
2668 Jorge Pedre
2669 Juan Berrios
2670 Montie Phillips
2671 Jim Hudson
2672 Kevin Appier
2673 Tom Gordon
2674 Terry Shumpert
2675 Don Wright
2676 Kevin Pickens
2677 Dennis Studeman

1987 Pro Cards Fayetteville Generals

(Detroit Tigers, A)

	MT	NR MT	EX
Complete Set:	8.00	6.00	3.25

1292 Hector Berrios
1293 Jose Ramos
1294 Dan O'Neill
1295 Steve Parascand
1296 Basilio Cabrera
1297 Ramon Solano
1298 Zach Doster
1299 Milt Cuyler
1300 Wade Phillips
1301 Darryl Martin
1302 Scott Aldred
1303 Manny Mantrana
1304 Darren Hursey
1305 Carlos Rivera
1306 Allen Liebert
1307 Paul Foster
1308 John Lipon
1309 Juan Lopez
1310 Arnie Beyeler
1311 Marcos Gonzalez
1312 Liliano Castro
1313 Luis Melendez
1314 Phil Clark
1315 Ron Rightnowar
1316 Ken Williams
1317 Rob Friesen
1318 Glenn Belcher

1987 Pro Cards Ft. Lauderdale Yankees

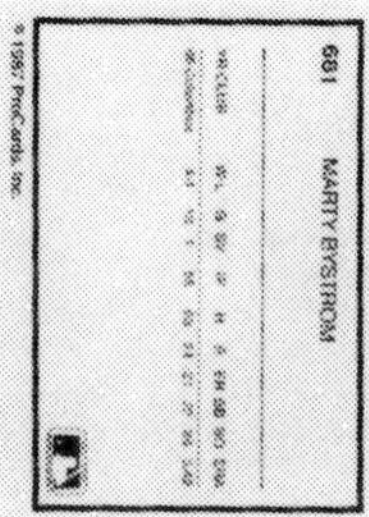

(New York Yankees, A)

	MT	NR MT	EX
Complete Set:	10.00	7.50	4.00

669 Jose Laboy
680 Tim Becker
681 Marty Bystrom
682 Steve Frey
683 Troy Evers
684 Chris Carroll
685 Bob Green
686 Scott Shaw
687 Mike Christopher
688 Dana Ridenour
689 Andy Stankiewicz
690 George Berube
691 Max Ward
692 Dan Arendas
693 Paul Lassard
694 Ron Rub
695 Bill Voeltz
696 Scott Gay
697 Rich Scheid
698 Kevin Mass
700 Bernie Williams
701 Steve Adkins
702 John Johnson
703 Jim Leyritz
704 Jeff Hellman
705 Mel Rosario
706 Mark Manering
707 Steve Brow
708 Fred Carter
709 Ken Patterson

1987 Pro Cards Ft. Myers Royals

(Kansas City Royals, A)

	MT	NR MT	EX
Complete Set:	17.50	13.00	7.00

2220 Bill Mulligan
2221 Stan Boroski
2222 Gary Blouin
2223 Mike Trapp
2224 David Tinkle
2225 Greg Hibbard
2226 Sean Berry
2227 Boo Champagne
2228 Andy Naworski
2229 Tim Odom
2230 Jesus DeLeon
2231 Mark Schulte
2232 Dennis Studeman
2233 Gus Jones
2234 Charles Culberson
2235 Vasquez Aquedo
2236 Tim Goff
2237 Rufus Ellis
2238 Tom Johnson
2239 Ricky Rojas
2240 Terry Jones
2241 Luis Corcino
2242 Randy Goodenough
2243 Kevin Koslofski
2244 Tom Gordon
2245 Brian McRae
2246 Kyle Reese
2247 Ken Kravec
2248 Jerry Terrell
2249 Angel Morris
2250 Mark Farnsworth
2251 David Howard
2252 Jacob Brumfield
2253 Ron Johnson

1987 Pro Cards Gastonia Rangers

(Texas Rangers, A)

	MT	NR MT	EX
Complete Set:	35.00	26.25	14.50

1761 Felipe Castillo
1762 Glenn Patterson
1763 Aurelio Cadania
1764 Juan Gonzalez
1765 Bob Gross
1766 Saul M. Barretto
1767 Phil Bryant
1768 Dean Palmer
1769 Rivert (Ortiz) Lino
1770 Allen Gerhardt
1771 Bob Malloy
1772 Gus Meizosa
1773 Raphael Cruz
1774 Ed Soto
1775 Roger Pavlik
1776 Paul Postier
1777 Ross Jones
1778 Wayne Rosenthal
1779 Michael Scanlin
1780 Ronald Jackson
1781 James McCutcheon
1782 Darrin Garner
1783 Richard Ramirez
1784 Art Gardner
1785 Jose Velez
1786 Darrell Whitaker
1787 John Burgos
1788 Francisco Sanchez
1789 Samuel Sosa

1987 Pro Cards Geneva Cubs

(Chicago Cubs, A)

	MT	NR MT	EX
Complete Set:	7.00	5.25	2.75

2622 Mike Aspray
2623 Brett Robinson
2624 Mark North
2625 Tom Spencer
2626 Steve Melendez
2627 Ken Reynolds
2628 Rick Wilkins
2629 Herberto Andrade
2630 Ray Mullino
2631 Fernando Ramsey
2632 Derrick Moore
2633 Mike Boswell
2634 Marty Rivero
2635 Mike Reeder
2636 Gabby Rodriguez
2637 Bill Melvin
2638 Henry Gomez
2639 Ed Caballero
2640 Kevin Main
2641 Phil Hannon
2642 Eddie Williams
2643 Jeff Massicotte
2644 Simeon Mejias
2645 Vaughn Williams
2646 Glenn Sullivan
2647 Steve Owens

1987 Pro Cards Glens Falls Tigers

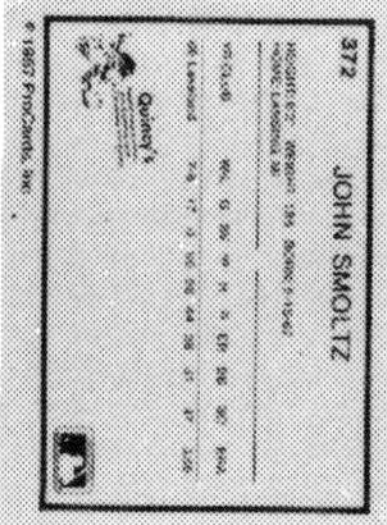

(Detroit Tigers, AA)

	MT	NR MT	EX
Complete Set:	8.50	6.25	3.50

349 Ruben Guzman

350 Chris Hoiles
351 Tom Burgess
352 Jeff Jones
353 Wes Clements
354 Kevin Ritz
355 Steve McInerney
356 Bill Cooper
357 Tim Leiper
358 Doug Strange
359 Ron Marigny
360 Jeff Agar
361 Matt Sferrazza
362 Benny Ruiz
363 Mark Lee
364 Rod Poissant
365 Chris Morgan
366 Jeff Hermann
367 Paul Felix
368 Ramon Pena
369 Pedro Chavez
370 Dan DiMascio
371 John Duffy
372 John Smoltz
373 Chip McHugh

1987 Pro Cards Greensboro Hornets

(Boston Red Sox, A)

	MT	NR MT	EX
Complete Set:	10.00	7.50	4.00

1704 Tom Kane
1705 Curt Schilling
1706 Dick Bererdino
1707 Pete Youngman
1708 Mike Carista
1709 Ken Ryan
1710 Chuck Wacha
1711 John Roberts
1712 Scott Summers
1713 Scott Cooper
1714 Joe Marchese
1715 Juan Paris
1716 Juan Molero
1717 Tony Hill
1718 Gilberto Martinez
1719 Tim McGee
1720 Ray Hansen
1721 Alex Flores
1722 Victor Rosario
1723 Dan Hale
1724 Mike Baker
1725 Jim Morrison
1726 Lern Pilkinton
1727 John Sanderski
1728 Chris Gaeckle
1729 David Walters

1987 Pro Cards Hagerstown Suns

(Baltimore Orioles, A)

	MT	NR MT	EX
Complete Set:	9.00	6.75	3.50

1465 Mike Borgatti
1466 Paul McNeal
1467 Will George
1468 Brian Dubois
1469 Leo Gomez
1470 Benny Bautista
1471 Gerry Lomastro
1472 Craig Strobel
1473 Randy Struek
1474 Tim Dulin
1475 Glenn Gulliver
1476 Blaine Beatty
1477 John Posey
1478 Louie Paulino
1479 Steve Bowden
1480 Wayne Wilson
1481 Pete Palermo
1482 Rick Carriger
1483 Tim Richardson
1484 Kevin Burke
1485 Frank Bellino
1486 Rafael Skeetl
1487 Paul Thorpe
1488 Mel Mallinak
1489 Gordon Dillard
1490 Scott Khoury
1491 Ernie Young
1492 Geraldo Sanchez
1493 Doug Cinnella

1987 Pro Cards Harrisburg Senators

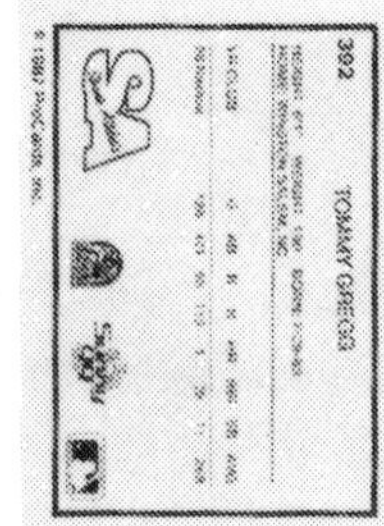

(Pittsburgh Pirates, AA)

	MT	NR MT	EX
Complete Set:	10.00	7.50	4.00

374 Shawn Holman
375 Dave Trembley
376 Tom Prince
377 David Rooker
378 Jose Melendez
379 Felix Fermin
380 Craig Brown
382 Scott Neal
383 Jeff Cook
384 Lance Belen
385 Rob Russell
386 Kyle Todd
387 Orlando Lind
388 Don Williams
389 Dave Douglas
390 Brian Jones
391 Brett Gideon
392 Tommy Gregg
393 Jim Neidlinger
394 Gino Gentile
395 Dimas Gutierrez
396 Mike Walker
397 Rich Sauveur
398 Chris Ritter
399 Ben Abner

1987 Pro Cards Hawaii Islanders

(Chicago White Sox, AAA)

	MT	NR MT	EX
Complete Set:	10.00	7.50	4.00

185 Mike Yastrzemski
186 Ken Williams
187 Jack Hardy
188 David White
189 Derek Tatsuno
190 Ralph Citarella
191 Tom Forrester
192 Brian Giles
193 Tommy Thompson
194 Don Rowe
195 Jim Rasmussen
196 Mike Taylor
197 Dave Cochrane
198 Tim Scott
199 Scott Nielson
200 Bill Long
201 Ray Krawczyk
202 Kevin Hickey
203 Joey McLaughlin
204 Kala Kaaihue
205 Carlos Martinez
206 Russ Norman
207 Tim Krauss
208 Randy Gomez
209 Greg Latta
210 Bob Bailey
211 Pat Keedy

1987 Pro Cards Idaho Falls Braves

(Atlanta Braves, A)

	MT	NR MT	EX
Complete Set:	7.00	5.25	2.75

2595 Mike Wilson
2596 Anthony Ferrebee
2597 Phillip Maldonado
2598 Mark Martin
2599 Jeff Allison
2600 Richard Duke
2601 Chuck Lavrusky
2602 Kevin McNees
2603 Rod Gilbreath
2604 Teddy Williams
2605 Walter Hawkins
2606 Chris Bryant
2607 A.J. Waznik
2608 Mike Lomeli
2609 Gregg Gilbert
2610 Jim Procopio
2611 Bill Wright
2612 Herb Hippauf
2613 Matthew Williams
2614 Joe Koh
2615 Daerren Cox
2616 Steve Glass
2617 Frank Ramirez
2618 John Mitchell
2619 Jeff Dodig
2620 Pat Abbatiello
2621 Greg Ziegler

1987 Pro Cards Jacksonville Expos

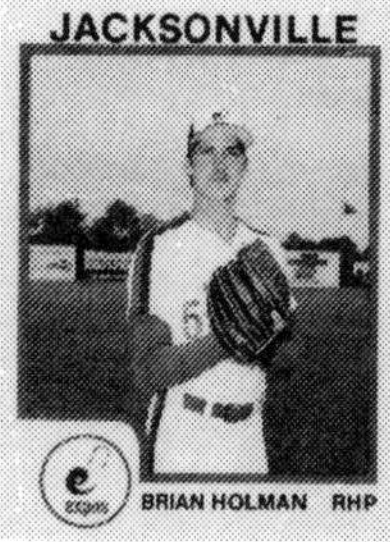

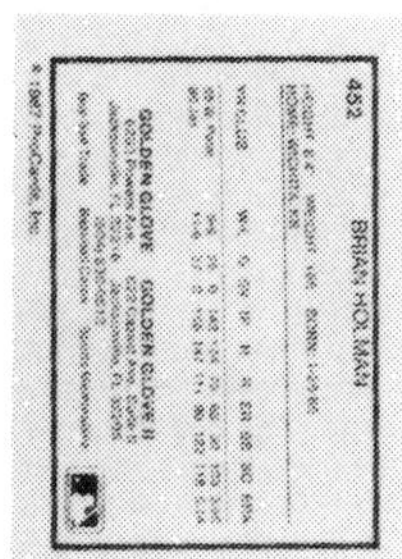

(Montreal Expos, AA)

	MT	NR MT	EX
Complete Set:	11.00	8.25	4.50

429 Larry Walker
430 Tim Arnold
431 Norm Santiago
432 Pete Camelo
433 Nelson Santovenia
434 Mike Berger
435 Andy Lawrence
436 Scott Mann
437 Edgar Caceres
438 Gary Weinberger
439 Esteban Beltre
440 Armando Moreno
441 James Opie
442 Mike Shade
443 Dave Graybill
444 Mike Payne
445 Bill Cunningham
446 Bob Devlin
447 Bob Sudo
448 Kevin Price
449 John Trautwein
450 Gary Wayne
451 Randy Johnson
452 Brian Holman
453 Tommy Thompson
454 Joe Kerrigan
455 Mike Quade
456 Jim Kahmann
457 Team Photo

1987 Pro Cards Jamestown Expos

(Montreal Expos, A)

	MT	NR MT	EX
Complete Set:	7.00	5.25	2.75

2538 Russ Martin
2539 Angelo Cianfrocco
2540 Michael Ishmael
2541 Scott McHugh
2543 Jesus Paredes
2544 F. Boi Rodriguez
2545 Joe B. Sims
2546 Larry Doss
2547 Terrel E. Hansen
2548 Jorge Mitchell
2549 Kelvin Shephard
2550 Troy Landon Ricker
2551 Corey Viltz
2553 Gene Glynn
2554 Brian Braden
2555 Bob Natal
2556 Scott Ayers
2557 Mario Brito
2558 Bob Kerrigan
2559 Gilles Bergeron
2560 Danilo Leon
2561 Howard Earl Farmer
2562 Matt Shiflett

2563 Kevin Cavalier
2564 Jeff Carter
2565 Chris Marchok
2678 Q.V. Lowe
2679 Jeff Wedrick

1987 Pro Cards Kenosha Twins

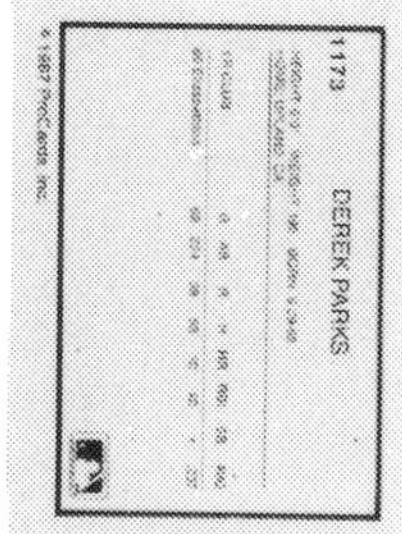

(Minnesota Twins, A)

	MT	NR MT	EX
Complete Set:	7.00	5.25	2.75

1155 Jim Davins
1156 Robert Hernandez
1157 Michael Randle
1158 Kendall Snyder
1159 Edgar Naveda
1160 Rafael DeLima
1161 Buddy Buzzard
1162 Burt Beattie
1163 Rusty Kryzanowski
1164 Michael Lexa
1165 Mike Dyer
1166 David Jacas
1167 Robert Tinkey
1168 Jarvis Brown
1169 Dana Heinle
1170 Dwight Bernard
1171 Jeff Satzinger
1172 Carl Thomas
1173 Derek Parks
1174 Lenny Webster
1175 Scott Leius
1176 Chris Forgione
1177 Elvis Romero
1178 Paul Abbott
1179 Miguel
1180 German Gonzalez
1181 Don Leppert
1182 John Skelton
1183 Enrique Rios

1987 Pro Cards Kinston Indians

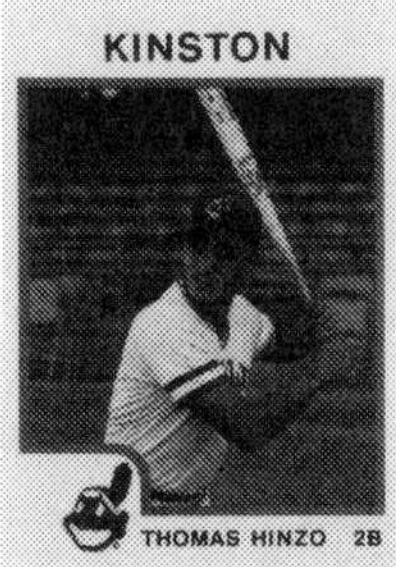

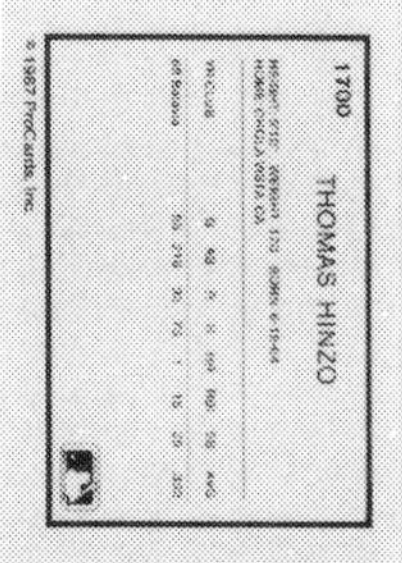

(Cleveland Indians, A)

	MT	NR MT	EX
Complete Set:	10.00	7.50	4.00

1680 Bill Shamblin
1681 Kevin Wickander
1682 Mark Gilles
1683 Charles Soos
1684 Scott Buss
1685 Phillip Dillmore
1686 Lewis Kent
1687 Jim Grossman
1688 Michael Poehl
1689 Fritz Fedor
1690 Brian Graham
1691 Scott Jordan
1692 Casey Webster
1693 Michael Workman
1694 Michael Farr
1695 Andrew Ghelfi
1696 James Bruske
1697 Robert Swain
1698 Trey Hillman
1699 Doyle Wilson
1700 Thomas Hinzo
1701 Milton Harper
1702 Kerry Richardson
1703 Rodney Nichols

1987 Pro Cards Knoxville Blue Jays

(Toronto Blue Jays, AA)

	MT	NR MT	EX
Complete Set:	9.50	7.00	3.75

1494 Jose Mesa
1495 Chris Shaddy
1496 Mike Yearout
1497 Omar Malave
1498 Aurelio Monteagudo
1499 Rocky Coyle
1500 Troy Chestnut
1501 Tim Englund
1502 Luis Reyna
1503 Kevin Silwinski
1504 Todd Provence
1505 Eric Yelding
1506 Keith Gilliam
1507 Omar Bencomo
1508 Geronimo Berroa
1509 Bernie Tatis
1510 Enrique Burgos
1511 Oswald Peraza
1512 Dave Walsh
1513 Pat Borders
1514 Jeff Hearron
1515 Randy Holland
1516 Glenn Ezell
1517 Kevin Kierst
1518 Norm Tomucci
1519 J.J. Cannon
1520 Cliff Young

1987 Pro Cards Lakeland Tigers

(Detroit Tigers, A)

	MT	NR MT	EX
Complete Set:	7.00	5.25	2.75

2333 Wayne Housie
2334 Keith Nicholson
2335 Craig Mills
2336 Rich Wieligman
2337 Scott Schultz
2338 Donnie Rowland
2339 Kevin Bradshaw
2340 Doyle Balthazar
2341 Ron Marigny
2342 Bernie Anderson
2343 Terry Smith
2344 Rocky Cusack
2345 Richard Carter
2346 Rich Lacko
2347 Wade Phillips
2348 Mike Hansen
2349 Mark Lee
2350 Pat Austin
2351 Bob Thomson
2352 Mark Pottinger
2353 Robinson Garces
2354 Blane Fox
2355 Dave Cooper
2356 Adam Dempsay
2357 Paul Wenson
2358 Ken Gohmann

1987 Pro Cards Las Vegas Stars

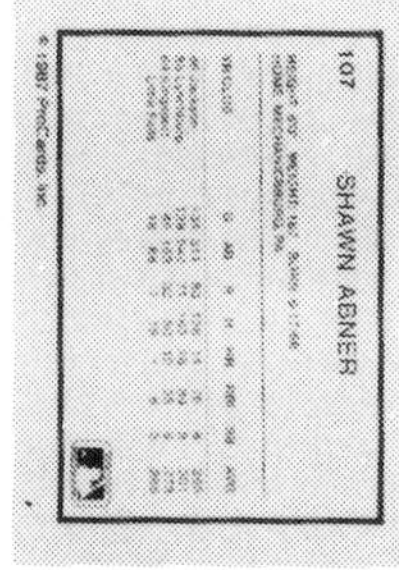

(San Diego Padres, AAA)

	MT	NR MT	EX
Complete Set:	19.00	14.00	7.50

106 Joe Bitker
107 Shawn Abner
108 Jack Kroll
109 Joe Lansford
110 Scott Parsons
111 Sonny Seibert
112 Randy Asadoor
113 Kevin John Buckley
114 Rusty Ford
115 Mark Poston
116 Todd Simmons
117 Ray Hayward
118 Todd Hutcheson
119 Randell Byers
120 Brian Snyder
121 Bill Blount
122 Jimmy Jones
123 Shane Mack
124 Edwin Rodriguez
125 Steve Garcia
126 Craig Wiley
127 Gary Green
128 Roberts Leon
129 Ed Vosberg
130 James Siwy
131 Rob Piccolo
132 Mark Wasinger

1987 Pro Cards Little Falls Mets

(New York Mets, A)

	MT	NR MT	EX
Complete Set:	10.50	7.75	4.25

2382 Terry Bross
2383 Pat Disabato
2384 Terry Griffin
2385 Eric Hillman
2386 Lorin Jundy
2387 Steve LaRose
2388 Jim McAnarney
2389 Mike Miller
2390 Steve Newton
2391 Jeff Smith
2392 Dave Trautwein
2393 Butch Wallen
2394 Anthony Young
2395 Javier Gonzalez
2396 Todd Hundley
2397 Tim Bogar
2398 Ron Height
2399 Alex Jiminez (Jimenez)
2400 Dave Joiner
2401 Bob Olah
2402 Radhames Polanco
2403 Rob Lemle
2404 Terry McDaniel
2405 Danny Naughton
2406 Titi Roche
2407 Jim Tesmer
2409 Rich Miller
2410 Al Jackson
2411 Rick McWane

1987 Pro Cards Lynchburg Mets

(New York Mets, A)

	MT	NR MT	EX
Complete Set:	10.00	7.50	4.00

2163 Craig Repoz
2164 Juan Villanueva
2165 Tom Wachs
2166 Chris Jelic
2167 Kip Gross
2168 Desi Brooks
2169 Eric Erickson
2170 Jamie Archibald
2172 Hector Perez
2173 Alan Hayden
2174 Felix Perdomo
2175 Jeff Ciszkowski
2176 Pete Bauer
2177 Chris Rauth
2178 Bill Stiles
2179 Geary Jones
2180 Dave Gelatt
2181 Rich Rodriguez
2182 Jim Bibby
2183 Scott Jaster
2184 John Tamargo
2185 Troy James
2186 Jeff Richardson
2187 Mark Brunswick
2188 Wilson Valera
2189 Scott Lawrenson
2190 Brian Givens

1987 Pro Cards Macon Pirates

(Pittsburgh Pirates, A)

	MT	NR MT	EX
Complete Set:	9.50	7.00	3.75

1184 Ernesto Santana
1185 Tracy Toy
1186 Joel Forrest
1187 Jeff Banister
1188 Tony Mealy
1189 John Love
1190 Mike York
1191 Tony Longmire
1192 Tim Vaughn
1193 Richard Reed

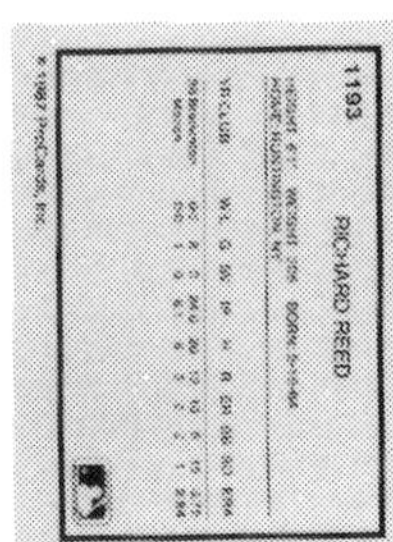

1194 Pete Murphy
1195 Blane Lockley
1196 Steve Adams
1197 Julio Perez
1198 Doug Ellis
1199 Julio Peguero
1200 Stan Belinda
1201 Damon Hansel
1202 Craig Heakins
1203 Ed Yacopino
1204 Glenn Trudo
1205 Scott Ruskin
1206 Tonny Cohen
1207 Dennis Rogers
1208 Dave Moharter

1987 Pro Cards Madison Muskies

(Oakland A's, A)

	MT	NR MT	EX
Complete Set:	12.00	9.00	5.00

488 Bert Bradley
489 David D. Schober
490 Scott Hemond
491 James Nettles
492 Vince Teixeira
493 Ozzie Canseco
494 Pat Gilbert
495 Luis Martinez
496 Doug Ortman
497 Jamie Reiser
498 Weston Weber
499 Gerry Barragan
500 Leland Maddox
501 Ken Jones
502 Camilo Veras
503 Mike Cupples
504 Jeffrey Glover
505 Jeff Kopyta
506 Kevin Kunkel
507 Mark Beavers
508 Jim Carroll
509 Blaine Deabenderfer, Jr.
510 Reese Lambert
511 Luis Salcedo
512 Bob Sharpnack

1987 Pro Cards Maine Guides

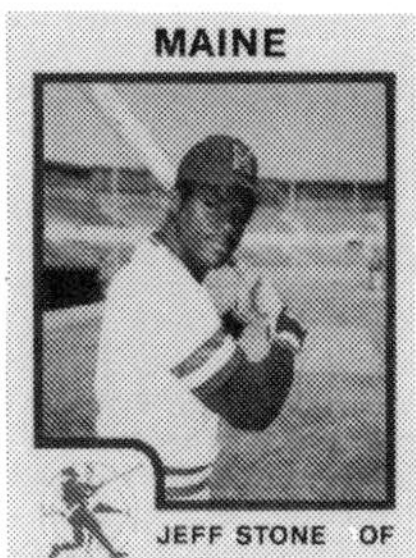

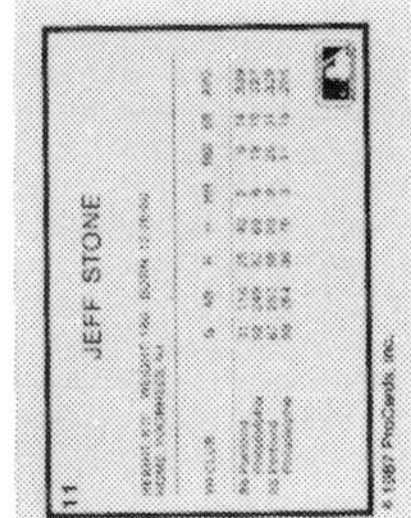

(Philadelphia Phillies, AAA)

	MT	NR MT	EX
Complete Set:	10.50	7.75	4.25

1 Jim Olander
2 Doug Bair
3 Len Watts
4 Greg Legg
5 Fred Tolliver (Toliver)
6 Shawn Barton
7 Ken Jackson
8 Keith Miller
9 Greg Jelks
10 Barney Nugent
11 Jeff Stone
12 Marvin Freeman
13 Steve DeAngelis
14 Jeff Calhoun
15 Gib Seibert
16 Ken Dowell
17 Wally Ritchie
18 Joe Cipolloni
19 Travis Chambers
20 Tom Newell
21 Darren Loy
22 Alan LeBoeuf
23 Ron Jones

1987 Pro Cards Memphis Chicks

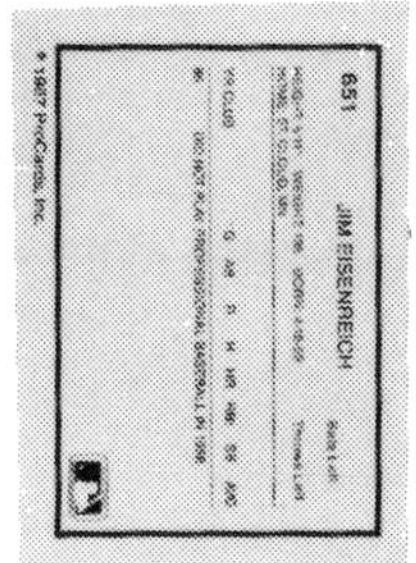

(Kansas City Royals, AA)

	MT	NR MT	EX
Complete Set:	10.00	7.50	4.00

625 Mike Fuentes
626 Phil George
627 Mauro Gozzo
628 Mike Loggins
629 Jose DeJesus
630 Mark Shiflett
631 Matt Winters
632 Jamie Nelson
633 Jere Longenecker
634 Bob Schafer
635 Rich Dubee
636 Mark Van Blaricom
637 Tim Lambert
638 Scott Stranski
639 Theo Shaw
640 Gene Morgan
641 Terry Bell
642 Rick Luecken
643 Don Sparling
644 Ken Crew
645 Duane Gustavson
646 Mike Miller
647 Jose Rivera
648 Julio Alcala
649 Jim Bennett
650 Steve Morrow
651 Jim Eisenreich

1987 Pro Cards Miami Marlins

(Baltimore Orioles, A)

	MT	NR MT	EX
Complete Set:	7.00	5.25	2.75

710 Kenny King
711 Jim Falzone
712 Stacey Burdick
713 Scott Evans
714 Tony Woods
716 Doug Carpenter
717 Rick Richardi
718 Tony Rohan
719 Bobby Latmore
720 Mickey Billmeyer
721 Masahito Watanabe
722 Shuji Inagaki
723 Scott Diez
724 Mike Browning
725 Frank Colston
727 Ken Adderly
728 Greg Daniels
729 John Harrington
730 Fred de la Mata
731 Hideharu Matsuo
732 Larry Mims
733 Tom Magrann
734 Toshimitsu Suetsugu
735 Luis Ojeda

1987 Pro Cards Midland Angels

(California Angels, AA)

	MT	NR MT	EX
Complete Set:	8.50	6.25	3.50

595 Miguel Garcia
596 David Martinez
597 Bill Geivett
598 Chris Collins
599 Brian Brady
600 Doug Banning

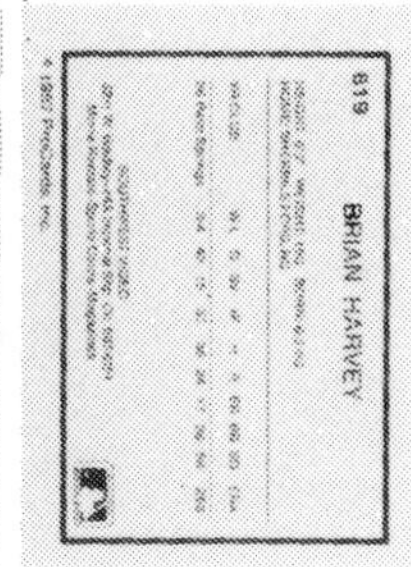

601 Ty Van Burkleo
602 Vinicio Cedeno
603 Al Olson
604 Doug Davis
605 John Hotchkiss
606 Edwin Marquez
607 Joe Redfield
608 Damon Farmar
609 Max Oliveras
610 Doug Jennings
611 Stan Holmes
612 Chuck Hernandez
613 Toby Mack
614 Mitch Seoane
615 Mark Doran
616 Mike Romanovsky
617 Robbie Allen
618 Vance Lovelace
619 Brian Harvey
620 Steve McGuire
621 Marty Reed
622 Barry Dacus
623 Phil Venturino
624 Team Photo

1987 Team Wichita Pilots

(San Diego Padres, AAA)

	MT	NR MT	EX
Complete Set:	20.00	15.00	8.00

10 Mike Debutch
11 Kevin Armstrong
12 Tommy Alexander
14 Roberto Alomar
15 Sandy Alomar, Jr.
17 Nate Colbert
18 Chris Knabenshue
19 Brad Pounders
20 Steve Smith
21 Joe Lynch
22 Greg Harris
23 Eric Nolte
24 Thomas Howard
25 Jeff Reece
26 Mike Costello
27 Scott Rainey
28 Jeff Stewart
29 Dave Cortez
30 Tom Brassil
31 Candy Sierra
32 Kevin Brown
33 Eric Bauer
42 Steve Luebber
43 Jerald Clark
44 Cam Walker

1987 Pro Cards Modesto A's

(Oakland A's, A)

	MT	NR MT	EX
Complete Set:	7.00	5.25	2.75

266 John Kent
267 William Savarino III
268 David Veres
269 Michael Duncan
270 Jerome Nelson
271 Michael Bordick
272 John Minch
273 Steve Gokey
274 Butch Hughes
275 Lance Blankenship
276 Robert Gould
277 Kevin Tapani
278 Chris Hayes
279 Bruce Walton
280 Steve Iannini
281 Kevin Williamson
282 Jerry Peguero
283 Bob Fingers
284 Joseph Law
285 Dann Howitt
286 Patrick Britt
287 John Cartelli
288 Tommie D. Reynolds
289 Scott Holcomb
290 Jim Corsi

1987 Pro Cards Myrtle Beach Blue Jays

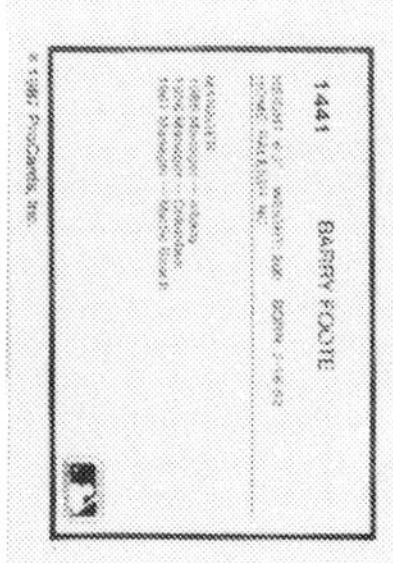

(Toronto Blue Jays, A)

	MT	NR MT	EX
Complete Set:	16.00	12.00	6.50

1435 Julian Yan
1436 Oscar Escobar
1437 Jose Diaz
1438 Darren Hall
1439 Doug Linton
1440 Vince Horsman
1441 Barry Foote
1442 Mike Murray
1443 Leroy Stanton
1444 Patrick Hentgen
1445 Tom Quinlan
1446 Randy Knorr
1447 Dennis Jones
1448 Cesar Mejia
1449 Lindsay Foster
1450 Jim Tracy
1451 John Poloni
1452 John Shea
1453 Rocket Wheeler
1454 Wayne Davis
1455 Junior Felix
1456 Rich Depastino
1457 Victor Diaz
1458 Mark Whiten
1459 Joe Humphries
1460 Bob Guehther
1461 Andy Dziadkowiec
1462 Francisco Cabrera
1463 Luis Sojo
1464 Paul Rodgers

1987 Pro Cards Newark Orioles

(Baltimore Orioles, A)

	MT	NR MT	EX
Complete Set:	10.00	7.50	4.00

2769 David Esquer
2770 Mike Lehman
2771 Mike Hart
2772 Earl Stephenson
2773 John Oliphant
2774 Gary Arnold
2775 Jack Voigt
2776 Tom Michno
2777 Frank Bryan
2778 Craig Lopez
2779 Steve Culkar
2780 Mike Sander
2781 Bob Shoulders
2782 Joe Gast
2783 Bob Williams
2784 Mike Elmore
2785 Chaun Wilson
2786 Danny Hartline
2787 Don Buford, Jr.
2788 Jeff Ahr
2789 Steven Finley
2790 Dickie Winzenread
2791 Scott Evans
2792 Mike Eberle
2793 Ernie Young
2794 Thomas Shannon
2795 Randy Strijek
2796 Tom Harms
2797 Luis Pena

1987 Pro Cards New Britain Red Sox

(Boston Red Sox, AA)

	MT	NR MT	EX
Complete Set:	15.00	11.00	6.00

763 Mike Clarkin
764 Zach Crouch
765 Bill Zupka
766 Angel Gonzalez
767 Luis Vasquez
768 Greg Lotzar
769 Brady Anderson
770 Bill McInnis
771 Bob Chadwick
772 Scott Skripko
773 Steve Bast

774 Carlos Quintana
775 Greg Bochesa
776 Daryl Irvine
777 Tony DeFrancesco
778 Dana Williams
779 Dana Kiecker
780 Dave Holt
781 Dan Gakeler
782 Roberto Zambrano
783 Josias Manzanillo
784 Tary Scott
785 Chris Mortiz
786 Jose Birriel
787 Ed Estrada

1987 Pro Cards Oklahoma City 89'ers

(Texas Rangers, AAA)

	MT	NR MT	EX
Complete Set:	10.00	7.50	4.00

133 Paul Kilgus
134 Gary Wheelock
135 Dave Owen
136 Frank Pastore
137 Don Werner
138 Dave Meier
139 Keith Creel
140 Mike Stanley
141 Kirk Killingsworth
142 Mike Jeffcoat
143 Steve Kemp
144 Toby Harrah
145 Ron Meridith
146 Glen Cook
147 Javier Ortiz
148 Cecil Espy
149 Tim Rodgers
150 Dwayne Henry
151 Greg Smith
152 Tom O'Malley
153 Greg Tabor
154 Alan Knicely
155 Nick Capra
156 Ray Ramirez
157 Bill Taylor
158 Jeff Zaske
159 Dave Rucker

1987 Pro Cards Omaha Royals

(Kansas City Royals, AAA)

	MT	NR MT	EX
Complete Set:	10.00	7.50	4.00

2084 Frank Funk
2085 Jose Angero
2086 John Wathan
2087 VAn Snider
2088 Nick Swartz
2089 Gary Thurman
2090 Chito Martinez
2091 Dwight Taylor
2092 Joe Citari
2093 Derek Botelho
2094 Rondin Johnson
2095 Bob Stoddard
2096 Al Hargesheimer
2097 Steve Shirley
2098 Craig Pippin
2099 Adrian Garrett
2100 Scott Madison
2101 Israel Sanchez
2102 John Davis
2103 Ron Wotus
2104 Bobby Ramos
2105 Rick Anderson
2106 Jeff Schulz
2107 Mike MacFarlane (Macfarlane)

2108 Luis Delos de las Santos
2109 Tom Muller

1987 Pro Cards Oneonta Yankees

	MT	NR MT	EX
Complete Set:	13.00	9.75	5.25

2505 Lew Hill
2506 Anthony Morrison
2507 Darrel Tingle
2508 Bernie Williams
2509 Hector Vargas
2510 Gerald Williams
2511 Dan Roman
2512 Steve Erickson
2513 Tom Popplewell
2514 Doug Gogolewski
2515 Bill DaCoste
2516 David Turgeon
2517 Tom Weeks
2518 Brian Butterfield
2519 Freddie Hailey
2520 Julio Ramon
2521 Dave Eiland
2522 Jay Makemson
2523 Bill Voeltz
2524 Chris Byrnes
2525 Randy Foster
2526 Mark Mitchell
2527 Ron Ehrhard
2528 Gary Allenson
2529 Rod Imes
2530 Mark Marris
2531 Bobby Dickerson
2532 Tim Bishop
2533 Dean Kelley
2534 Ed Martel
2535 Luc Berube
2536 Jack Gills
2537 Tom Cloninger

1987 Pro Cards Orlando Twins

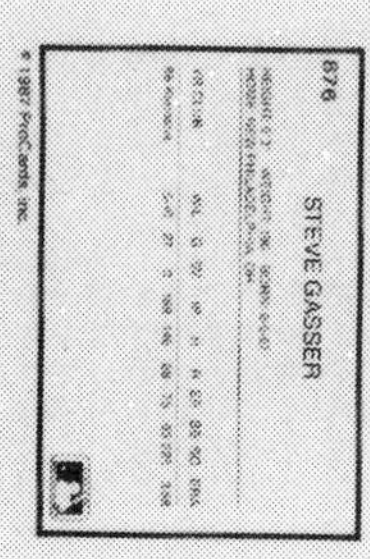

(Minnesota Twins, AA)

	MT	NR MT	EX
Complete Set:	7.00	5.25	2.75

866 Jeff Bumgarner
867 Robbie Smith
868 Dan Smith
869 John Eccles
870 Henry Gatewood
871 Bobby Ralston
872 Jim Shellenback
873 Ken Koch
874 George Mitterwald
875 Mark Clemons
876 Steve Glassor
877 Toby Nivens
878 Steve Gomez
879 Brad Bierley
880 Jeff Reboulet
881 Gary Borg
882 Doug Palmer
883 Tom Schwarz
884 Eddie Yanes
886 Jeff Bronkey
887 Wes Pierorazio
888 Allan Sontag
889 Darrell Higgs
890 Mark Funderburk
891 Larry Blackwell
892 Dave Vetsch

76590

1987 Pro Cards Osceola Astros

(Houston Astros, A)

	MT	NR MT	EX
Complete Set:	7.00	5.25	2.75

952 Terry Wells
953 Juan Lopez
954 Mike Brown
955 Carlo Colobino
956 Randy Randle
957 Ken Bolek
958 Calvin James
959 Dan Walters
960 Doug Snyder
961 Jeff Baldwin
962 Stan Fascher
963 Tony Metoyer
964 Brian Meyer
965 Joe Schulte

966 Jose Vargas
967 David Potts
968 John Elliott
969 Jack Billingham
970 Don Dunster
971 Joel Estes
972 Gary Cooper
973 Juan Delgrado
974 Scott Markley
975 Ken Houston
976 Terry Green
977 Tim Arnsberg
978 Jose Cano
979 Todd Credeur
980 David Rohde

1987 Pro Cards Palm Springs Angels

(California Angels, A)

	MT	NR MT	EX
Complete Set:	20.00	15.00	8.00

291 Mike Spearnock
292 Al Heath
293 David Johnson
294 Jeff Manto
295 Reggie Lambert
296 Paul Bilak
297 Kenny Grant
298 Dan Grunhard
299 Colin Charland
300 Mike Shull
301 Paul Sorrento
302 Lee Stevens
303 Bill Vanderwel
304 Colby Ward
305 Glenn Washington
306 Roger Zottneck
307 Bill Lachemann
308 Tim Kelly
309 Tom Alfredson
310 Edgar Alfonso
311 Tim Burham
312 Dario Nunez
313 Erik Pappas
314 Michael Anderson
315 Bobby Bell
316 Mike Fetters
317 Frank DiMichele
318 Richard Morehouse
319 Todd Eggertsen
320 Mark Marino
321 Andres Espinoza
322 Gary Nalls

1987 Pro Cards Pawtucket Red Sox

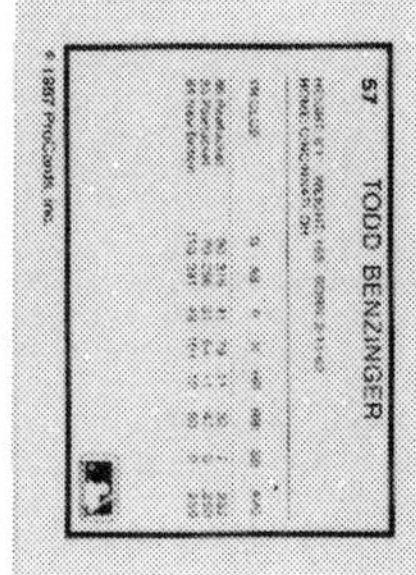

(Boston Red Sox, AAA)

	MT	NR MT	EX
Complete Set:	7.00	5.25	2.75

51 John Marzano
52 Sam Horn
53 Stephen Curry
54 Kevin Romine
55 John Leister
56 Jody Reed
57 Todd Benzinger
58 Mitchell Johnson
59 Mike Rochford
60 LaSchelle Tarver
61 Hector Stewart
62 Tom Bolten
63 Glenn Hoffman
64 Andy Araujo
65 Tony Cleary
66 Mike Dalton
67 Steve Ellsworth
68 Mike Mesh
69 Gary Miller-Jones
70 Gary Tremblay
71 Scott Wade
72 Ed Nottle
73 Ellis Burks
74 Chuck Davis
75 Mark Meleski
76 Dana Williams
77 Chris Cannizzaro

1987 Pro Cards Peninsula White Sox

(Chicago White Sox, A)

	MT	NR MT	EX
Complete Set:	9.00	6.75	3.50

1872 Mark Davis
1873 Kevin Renz
1874 Chet Diemidc
1875 Mark Foley
1876 Daniel Tauken
1877 Joe Singley
1878 Dewey Robinson
1879 Aubrey Waggoner
1880 Mike Ollom
1881 Craig Grebeck
1882 Dave Reynolds
1883 Scott Radinsky
1884 Miguel Audain
1885 Bruce Hulstrom
1886 Tom Sutryk
1887 Glenn Braxton
1888 Ron Scheer
1889 Dave Wallwork
1890 Tom Reichel
1891 Jeff Greene
1892 Kelsey Isa
1893 Tom Lahrman
1894 Bo Kennedy
1895 Todd Hall
1896 Ron Scruggs
1897 Kurt Brown
1898 Virgil Conley
1899 Tony Cento
1900 Dan Wagner

1987 Pro Cards Peoria Chiefs

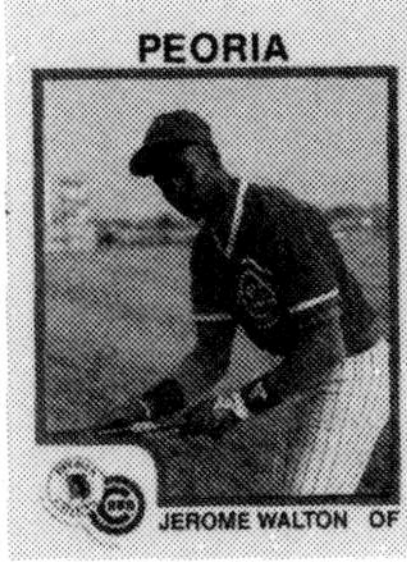

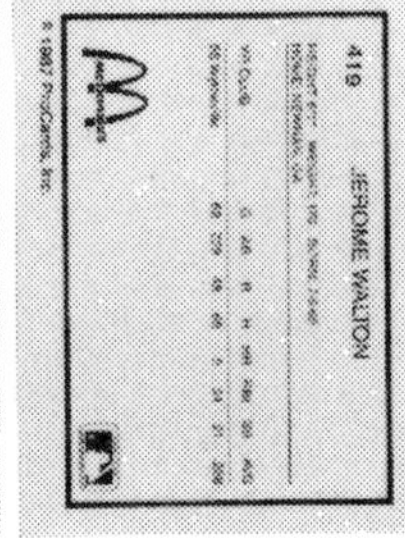

(Chicago Cubs, A)

	MT	NR MT	EX
Complete Set:	60.00	45.00	24.75

400 Ray Mullino
401 Butch Garcia
402 John Green
403 Sergio Espinal
404 Dick Canan
405 Jerry Lapenta
406 Steve Hill
407 Shawn Boskie
408 Greg Iaverone
409 John Berringer
410 Joe Housey
411 Derrick May
412 Pat Gomez
413 Greg Smith
414 Brian Otten
415 David Rosario
416 Elvin Paulino
417 Edwards Williams
418 Harry Shelton
419 Jerome Walton
420 Simeon Mejias
421 Parnell Perry
422 Phil Harrison
423 Steve Parker
424 Kelly Mann
425 Mike Folga
426 Jim Tracy
427 William Kazmierczak
428 Fernando Zarranz

1987 Pro Cards Phoenix Firebirds

(San Francisco Giants, AAA)

	MT	NR MT	EX
Complete Set:	12.00	9.00	5.00

78 Chris Jones
79 Matt Williams
80 Randy Bockus
81 George Ferran
82 Terry Mulholland
83 Charlie Corbell
84 Angel Escobar
85 Kevin Burrell
86 Colin Ward
87 Mike Woodard
88 Larry Hardy
89 Randy Kutcher
90 Jon Perlman
91 Jack McKnight
92 Alan Cockrell
93 Jessie Reid
94 Joe Price
95 John Verducci
96 Cliff Shidawara
97 Mackey Sasser
98 Pat Adams
99 Duane Espy
100 Wendell Kim
101 Atlee Hammaker
102 Francisco Melendez
103 Steve Miller
104 Mike Rubel
105 Jeff Brantly

1987 Pro Cards Pittsfield Cubs

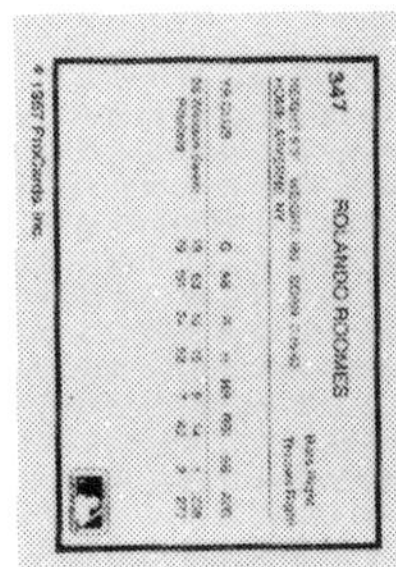

(Chicago Cubs, A)

	MT	NR MT	EX
Complete Set:	60.00	45.00	24.75

323 Ray Thoma
324 Greg Bell
325 Hector Villanueva
326 Jim Essian
327 Jim Wright
328 Brian McCann
329 Brian House
330 Laddy Renfroe
331 Mike Miller
332 Mark Grace
333 Brian Guinn
334 Jim Phillips
335 Leonard Damian
336 Dave Masters
338 Mark Leonette
339 Rick Wrona
340 David Wilder
341 Jeff Pico
342 Rick Hopkins
343 Roger Williams
344 Rich Amaral
345 Doug Dascenzo
346 Tim Rice
347 Rolando Roomes
348 Dwight Smith

1987 Pro Cards Port Charlotte Rangers

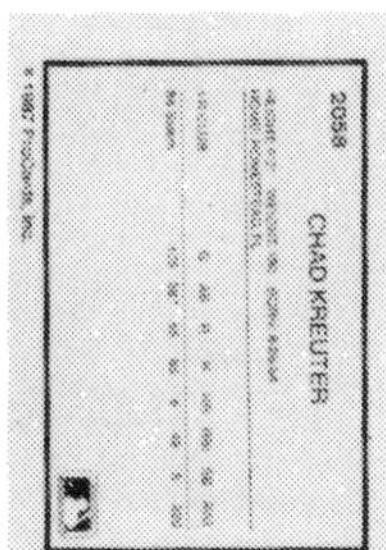

(Texas Rangers, A)

	MT	NR MT	EX
Complete Set:	7.50	5.50	3.00

2034 Ken Clawson
2035 John Schofield
2036 Steve Lankard
2037 Scott Morse
2038 John Barfield
2039 Mitch Thomas
2040 Marty Cerny
2041 Edwin Morales

2042 Rick Raether
2043 Steve Wilson
2044 Jeff Mays
2045 Jeff Andrews
2046 Greg Harrell
2047 Fred Samson
2048 Stephen Glasker
2049 Mick Billmeyer
2050 Jose Vargas
2051 Rick Bernardo
2052 Mark Kramer
2053 Julio DeLeon
2054 Joel Cartaya
2055 Chris Colon
2056 Gar Millay
2057 Jim Skaalen
2058 Chad Kreuter
2059 Kevin Reimer
2060 Joe Pearn

1987 Pro Cards Portland Beavers

(Minnesota Twins, AAA)

	MT	NR MT	EX
Complete Set:	7.50	5.50	3.00

160 Jeff Bittiger
161 Pat Dempsey
162 Randy Niemann
163 Allan Anderson
164 Billy Beane
165 Chris Pittaro
166 Pat Casey
167 Roy Smith
168 Phil Wilson
169 Steve Liddle
170 Danny Clay
171 Julius McDougal
172 Kevin Hagen
173 Alvaro Espinosa
174 Kevin Trudeau
175 Ben Bianchi
176 Alex Marte
177 Bill Latham
178 Gene Larkin
179 Greg Morhardt
180 Ron Musselman
181 Charlie Manuel
182 Ken Silvestri
183 Brad Boylan
184 Ron Gardenhire

1987 Pro Cards Prince William Yankees

(New York Yankees, A)

	MT	NR MT	EX
Complete Set:	16.00	12.00	6.50

2254 Hensley Meulens
2255 Yanko Hauradou
2256 Bob Davidson
2257 Ricky Torres
2258 Ralph Kraus
2259 Scott Kamieniecki
2260 Alan Mills
2261 Art Calvert
2262 Rick Balabon
2263 Rob Sepanek, Jr.
2264 Chris Howard
2265 Mickey Tresh
2266 Chris Lombardozzi
2267 Mike Heifferon
2268 Bill Clossen
2269 Bill Voeltz
2270 Ysidro Giron
2271 Aris Tirado
2272 Amalio Carreno
2273 Steve Adkins
2274 Hector Vargas
2275 Fernando Figuerda (Figueroa)
2276 Ramon Manon
2277 Jason Maas
2278 Rob Lambert
2279 Joe Hicks
2280 Tony Gwinn
2281 John Ramos
2282 William Morales

1987 Pro Cards Quad City Angels

(California Angels, A)

	MT	NR MT	EX
Complete Set:	7.00	5.25	2.75

1096 Terrence Carr
1097 Troy Giles
1098 Edgar Rodriguez
1099 Santiago Espinosa
1100 Giovanny Reyes
1101 Lawrence Pardo
1102 Jose Tapia
1103 Roberto Hernandez
1104 Scott Kannenberg
1105 Daryl Green
1106 Luis Merejo
1107 Brandy Vann
1108 Mike Kelser
1109 Jim Bisceglia
1110 Rafael Pineda
1111 Elvin Rivera
1112 Greg Fix
1113 Eddie Rodriguez
1114 Don Long
1115 Gary Ruby
1116 Jim McCollom
1117 Chris Graves
1118 Chris Cron
1119 Scott Cerney
1120 Kendall Walling
1121 Jeff Gay
1122 Michael Knapp
1123 Ken Bandy
1124 Dave Grilione
1125 Greg Jackson
1126 Luis Gallardo

1987 Pro Cards Reading Phillies

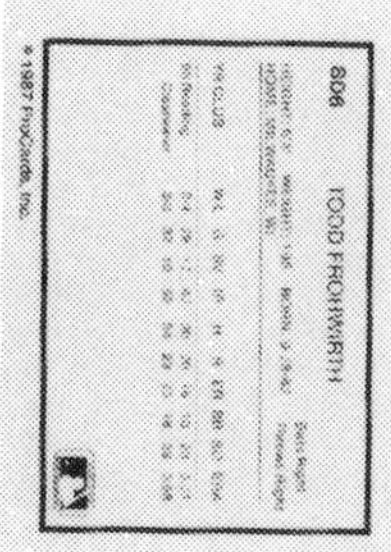

(Philadelphia Phillies, AA)

	MT	NR MT	EX
Complete Set:	17.50	13.00	7.00

788 George Culver
789 Tony Brown
790 Joe Lefebvre
791 Greg Edge
792 Miguel Vargas
793 Dan Giesen
794 Tom Barrett
795 Dion Beck
796 Mike Shelton
797 Bruce Long
798 Ray Roman
799 Kevin Ward
800 Rick Lundblade
801 Howard Nichols
802 Ramon Henderson
803 Ricky Jordan
804 Mark Bowden
805 Steve Blackshear
806 Todd Frohwirth
807 Bob Scanlon
808 Jim Fortenberry
809 Jose Leiva
810 John McLarnan
811 Steve Williams
812 Michael Miller
813 Rob Hicks

1987 Pro Cards Rochester Red Wings

(Baltimore Orioles, AAA)

	MT	NR MT	EX
Complete Set:	9.50	7.00	3.75

1901 Phil Hoffman
1902 Dave Van Gorder
1903 John Hart
1904 Ron Salcedo
1905 Mike Skinner
1906 Chris Padget
1907 Scott Ullger
1908 Eric Rasmussen
1909 Mike Griffin
1910 Mike Hart
1911 Carl Nichols
1912 Bill Ripken
1913 Curt Motton
1914 D.L. Smith
1915 Dom Chiti
1916 Luis DeLeon
1917 Brad Havens
1918 Nelson Simmons
1919 Ron Washington
1920 Jack O'Connor
1921 Kelvin Torve
1922 Jamie Reed
1923 Craig Worthington
1924 John Habyan
1925 Jeff Ballard
1926 Jim Traber
1927 Bob Molinaro

1987 Pro Cards St. Petersburg Cardinals

(St. Louis Cardinals, A)

	MT	NR MT	EX
Complete Set:	10.00	7.50	4.00

2007 Dave Osteen
2008 Craig Wilson
2009 Jesus Mendez
2010 Mike Sassone
2011 Mike Robertson
2012 Mauricio Nunez
2013 Brett Harrison
2014 Joe Cunningham
2015 Michael Senne
2016 Tom Amante
2017 Mike Fox
2018 Dave Horton
2019 John Murphy
2020 David DeCordova
2021 Chris Forrest
2022 Hans Herzog
2023 Tom Mauch
2024 Dave Bialas
2025 Marty Mason
2026 Crucito Lara
2027 William Hershmann
2028 Benito Malave
2029 Gregory Becker
2030 Randy Butts
2031 Jay North
2032 Pete Fagan
2033 Rob Livchak

1987 Pro Cards Salem Angels

(California Angels, A)

	MT	NR MT	EX
Complete Set:	8.00	6.00	3.25

2412 Edgar Rodriguez
2413 Gary Buckels
2414 Jay Bobel, Jr.
2415 Troy Giles
2416 Robert Wassenaar
2417 John Orton
2418 Mario Molina
2419 Bill Robinson
2420 Greg Jackson
2421 Eric Reinholtz
2422 Jorge Montero
2423 Ramon Martinez
2424 Reed Peters
2425 Tony Rasmus
2426 Jim Townsend
2427 Frnak Mutz
2428 Ruben Amaro
2429 Santiago Espinosa
2430 Wiley Lee, Jr.
2431 Paul List
2432 Rafael Pineda
2433 Kevin Flora
2434 Mikael Musolino
2435 Mike Erb
2436 Luis Gallardo
2437 Cary Grubb
2438 Lanny Abshier
2439 Freddie Davis, Jr.
2440 Scott Randolph
2441 Jeff Goettsch
2442 Jesse Flores
2443 Mark Weidemaier
2444 Chris Smith
2445 Derek Winchell

1987 Pro Cards Salem Buccaneers

(Pittsburgh Pirates, A)

	MT	NR MT	EX
Complete Set:	10.00	7.50	4.00

1236 Kevin Franchi
1237 Mike Stevens
1238 Larry Melton
1239 Rob Hatfield
1240 Octavio Cepeda
1241 Greg Stading
1242 Pete Rice
1243 Tim Kirk
1244 Ben Morrow
1245 Matias Carrillo
1246 Martin Hernandez
1247 Mike Dotzher
1248 Steve Moser
1249 John Rigos
1250 Harold Williams
1251 Gilberto Roca
1252 Rafael Muratti
1253 Jim Thrift
1254 Bill Copp
1255 Bob Koopmann
1256 Bill Sampen
1257 Mike Stevanus
1258 Reggie Barringer
1259 Jeff King
1260 Tony Chance
1261 Todd Smith
1262 Doug Pittman
1263 Chris Lein

1987 Pro Cards San Bernadino Spirits

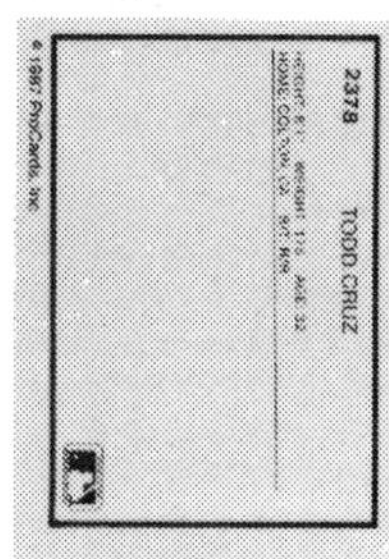

(No Affiliation, A)

	MT	NR MT	EX
Complete Set:	10.00	7.50	4.00

2359 Steve Walker
2360 Larry Smith
2361 Jeff Edwards
2362 Don Stearns
2363 Randy Harvey
2364 Stan Sanchez
2365 Rich Dauer
2366 Ron Carter
2367 Mark Combs
2368 James Filippi
2369 Delwyn Young
2370 Vince Shinholster
2371 Brian Hartsock
2372 Leon Baham
2373 Scott Marrett
2374 Mike Brocki
2375 Brian Morrison
2376 Walt Stull
2377 Robert Greenlee
2378 Todd Cruz
2379 Tony Triplett
2380 Todd Hayes
2381 Tom Thompson

1987 Pro Cards San Jose Bees

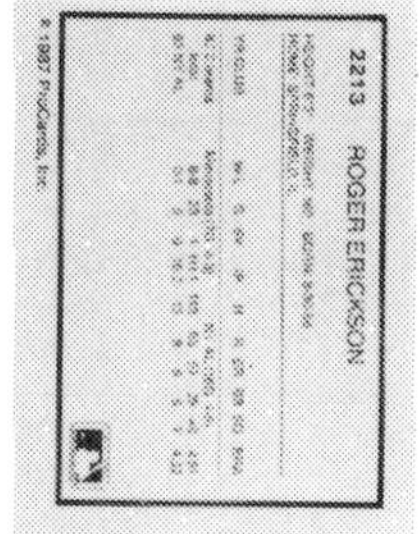

(No Affiliation, A)

	MT	NR MT	EX
Complete Set:	7.00	5.25	2.75

2191 Sam Hirose
2192 Hector Nakamura
2193 Ken Reitz
2194 Sal Vaccaro
2195 Harvey Lee
2196 Charlie Moore
2197 Rocky Osaka
2198 Kat Kamei
2199 Frank Bryan
2200 Ted Haraguchi
2201 Mickey Yamano
2202 Dan Mori
2203 Tom Nabekawa
2204 Rattoo Akimoto
2205 David Rolland
2206 Mark Seay
2207 Paco Burgos
2208 Elias Sosas
2209 Mike Verdi
2210 Rick Tracy
2211 Warren Brusstar
2212 Lawrence Feola
2213 Roger Erickson
2214 Julian Gonzales
2215 Eddie Gonzales
2216 Steve McCatty
2217 Rusty McNealy
2218 Daryl Sconiers
2219 Shawn Barton
--- Brian Kubala

1987 Pro Cards Savannah Cardinals

(St. Louis Cardinals, A)

	MT	NR MT	EX
Complete Set:	7.00	5.25	2.75

1846 Bobby DeLoach
1847 Chuck Johnson
1848 David Krebs
1849 Geronimo Pena
1850 Eric Hahn
1851 Scott Nichols
1852 Jay Martel
1853 Greg Ward
1854 Pat Hewes
1855 Mike Henry
1856 Mark Grater
1857 Mark Davis
1858 Pedro Llanes
1859 Carroll Parker
1860 Chico Singletary
1861 Carey Nemeth
1862 Reed Olmstead
1863 Eddie Looper
1864 Julian Martinez
1865 Franklin Abreu
1866 Don Dumas
1867 Stan Zaltsman
1868 Lenny Picota
1869 Mark Behny
1870 Scott Lawrence
1871 Mark DeJohn

1987 Pro Cards Shreveport Captains

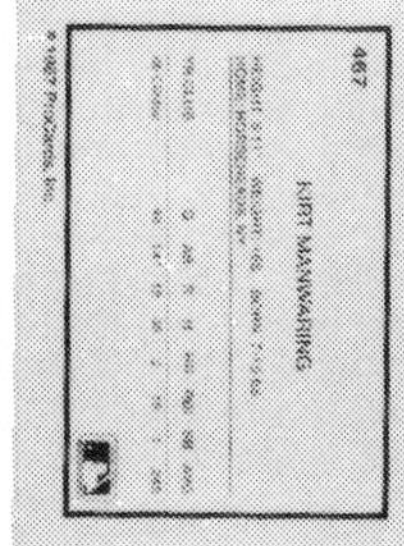

(San Francisco Giants, AA)

	MT	NR MT	EX
Complete Set:	9.00	6.75	3.50

458 Everett Graham
459 Paul Meyers
460 Ty Dabney
461 Dennis Cook
462 Dean Freeland
463 Tony Perezchica
464 Scott Medvin
465 Greg Litton
466 Romy Cucjen
467 Kirt Manwaring
468 Brian Ohnoutka
470 Jeff Brantley
471 John Burkett
472 Ed Puikunas
473 Randy McCament
474 Charlie Hayes
475 T.J. McDonald
476 Deron McCue
477 Stuart Tate
478 Tom Wailewski
479 John Grimes
480 Vince Sferazza
481 Marty DeMerritt
482 Jack Mull

1987 Pro Cards Spartanburg Phillies

(Philadelphia Phillies, A)

	MT	NR MT	EX
Complete Set:	9.00	6.75	3.50

1705 Mark Sims
1790 Jim Platts
1791 Peter Maldonado
1792 Gene Bierscheid
1793 Jeff Stark
1794 Charles McElroy
1796 Garry Clark
1797 Keith Greene
1798 Kenny Miller
1799 Michel Lamarche
1800 Ramon Aviles
1801 Ron Nelson
1802 Andy Ashby
1803 Trey McCall
1804 Todd Crosby
1805 Cliff Walker
1806 Martin Foley
1807 Luis Iglesias
1808 Elbi Romero
1809 Vince Holyfield
1810 Jeff Grotewald
1811 Bob Tiefanauer
1812 Vladimir Perez
1813 Phillip Price
1814 Scott Hufford
1816 Fred Christopher
1817 Mike Colpitt

1987 Pro Cards Spokane Indians

(San Diego Padres, A)

	MT	NR MT	EX
Complete Set:	7.00	5.25	2.75

2680 Osvaldo Sanchez
2681 Darrin Reichle
2682 Tony Lewis
2683 Saul Soltero
2684 Jay Estrada
2685 Rich Holsman
2686 Andy Skeels
2687 David Hollins
2688 Charles Hilleman
2689 Steve Lubratich
2690 Reggie Farmer
2691 Monte Brooks
2692 Bobby Sheridan
2693 Kevin Farmer
2694 Francisco de la Cruz
2695 David Bond
2696 Paul Faries
2697 Bob Lutticken
2698 Terry Gilmore
2699 Pedro Aquino
2700 Todd Torchia
2701 Steve Hendricks
2702 Jose Valentin
2703 Mike Myers
2704 Dustin Picciolo, Rob Picciolo

1987 Pro Cards Stockton Ports

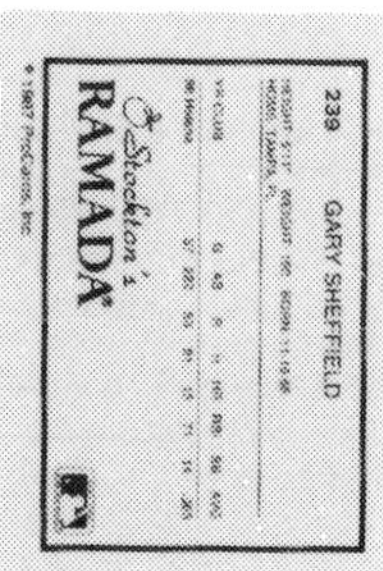

(Milwaukee Brewers, A)

	MT	NR MT	EX
Complete Set:	20.00	15.00	8.00

239 Gary Sheffield
240 Rob Derksen
241 Dave Machemer
242 Sandy Guerrero
243 Todd France
244 Danny Fitzpatrick
245 Mario Monico
246 Daryl Hamilton
247 Renard Brown
248 Angel Rodriguez
249 Isaiah Clark
250 Charley McGrew
251 Martin Montano
252 Ruben Escalera
253 Mike Frew
254 John Ludy
255 Luis Castillo
256 George Canale
257 Jim Hunter
258 Keith Fleming
259 Carl Moraw
260 Tim Torricelli
261 Jim Morris
263 Gary Kanwisher
264 Fred Williams
265 Ed Puig

1987 Pro Cards Sumter Braves

(Atlanta Braves, A)

	MT	NR MT	EX
Complete Set:	7.50	5.50	3.00

1349 Jerald Frost
1350 William Turner
1351 Miguel Sabino
1352 Walt Williams
1353 Bob McNally
1354 Clarence Jones
1355 Kevin Brown
1356 Rusty Richards
1357 Paul Marak
1358 Buddy Bailey
1359 Mark Clark
1360 Kevin Harmon
1361 David Plumb
1362 Carl Jones
1363 Rich Longuil
1364 Mike Bell
1365 Jesse Minton
1366 Rich Maloney
1367 Jim Czajkowski
1368 Jim Lemasters
1369 Larry Jaster
1370 Danny Rogers
1371 Ken Pennington
1372 Al Martin
1373 James Nowlin
1374 Brian Deak
1375 Sean Ross
1376 Gerald Wagner
1377 David Butts
1378 Jay Johnson

1987 Pro Cards Syracuse Chiefs

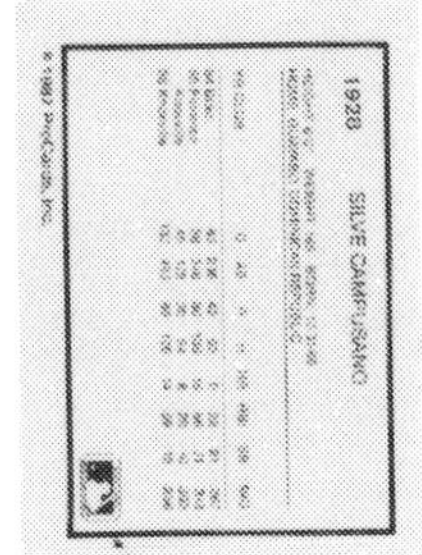

(Toronto Blue Jays, AAA)

	MT	NR MT	EX
Complete Set:	10.00	7.50	4.00

1928 Silve Campusano
1929 Nelson Liriano
1930 Lou Thornton
1931 Greg Myers
1932 Don Gordon
1933 Steve Firevoid
1934 Doug Ault
1935 Alex Infante
1936 Jose Segura
1937 Luis Aquino
1938 Todd Stottlemyre
1939 Tony Hudson
1940 Dave Stenhouse
1941 Manny Lee
1942 Otis Green
1943 Rob Ducey
1944 Jose Escobar
1945 Jose Castro
1946 Dave LaRoche
1947 Hector Torres
1948 Steve Davis
1949 Doc Estes
1950 Glenallen Hill

1987 Pro Cards Tacoma Tigers

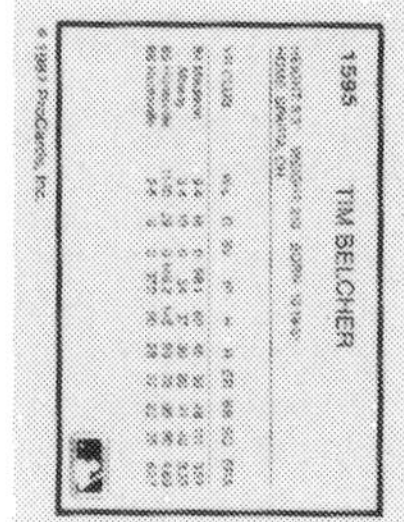

(Oakland A's, AAA)

	MT	NR MT	EX
Complete Set:	7.00	5.25	2.75

1575 Tim Dozier
1576 Darrel Akerfelds
1577 Stan Kyles
1578 Bobby Clark
1579 Gary Jones
1580 Wayne Krenchicki
1581 Dave Van Ohlen
1582 Bruce Tanner
1583 Matt Sinatro
1584 Thad Reece
1585 Eric Broersma
1586 Chuck Estrada
1587 Steve Henderson
1588 Keith Liepman
1589 Roy Johnson
1591 Jose Tolentino
1592 Bill Mooneyham
1593 Jerry Willard
1594 Alejandro Sanchez
1595 Tim Belcher
1596 Brian Dorsett
1597 Tim Birtsas

1987 Pro Cards Tampa Tarpons

(Cincinnati Reds, A)

	MT	NR MT	EX
Complete Set:	7.50	5.50	3.00

1319 Gary Denbo
1320 Pete Carey
1321 Mike Converse
1322 Ken Huseby
1323 Mike Roesler
1324 Kevin Pearson
1325 Juan Pinol
1326 Marc Bombard
1327 Tim Swob
1328 Dwayne Williams
1329 Tom Novak
1330 Jeff Richardson
1331 Bret Williamson
1332 Jack Smith
1333 Chris Hammond
1334 Timber Mead
1335 Kent Willis
1336 Mark Jackson
1337 Steve Davis
1338 Gino Minutelli
1339 Mike Campbell
1340 Chris Fernandez
1341 Neal Davenport
1342 Scott Hilgenberg
1343 Jeff Forney
1344 Billy Hawley
1345 Pete Beeler
1346 Rod Zeratsky
1347 Rich Sapienza
1348 Mike Villa

1987 Pro Cards Tidewater Tides

(New York Mets, AAA)

	MT	NR MT	EX
Complete Set:	10.00	7.50	4.00

2472 Clint Hurdle
2473 DeWayne Vaugh
2474 Reggie Dobie
2475 Jeff McKnight
2476 Terry Blocker
2477 John Gibbons
2478 Jason Felice
2479 Jeff Innis
2480 Tom Edens
2481 Keith Miller
2482 Steve Springer
2483 Mike Cubbage
2484 Tom McCarthy
2485 Dave Wyatt
2486 Ed Glynn
2487 Ricky Nelson
2488 Tom Lombarski
2489 John Cumberland
2490 Greg Olson
2491 John Mitchell
2492 Mark Carreon
2493 Bill Latham
2494 Jose Roman
2495 Andre David
2496 Don Schulze
2497 Bob Buchanan
2498 Gene Walter
2499 Randy Milligan
2500 Rob Evans
2501 Rick Rainer
2502 Dwight Gooden
2503 Kevin Elster
2504 Bob Gibson

1987 Pro Cards Toledo Mud Hens

(Detroit Tigers, AAA)

	MT	NR MT	EX
Complete Set:	9.00	6.75	3.50

1954 Scott Earl
1955 Steve Searcy
1956 Scott Lusader
1957 German Rivera
1958 Jim Walewander

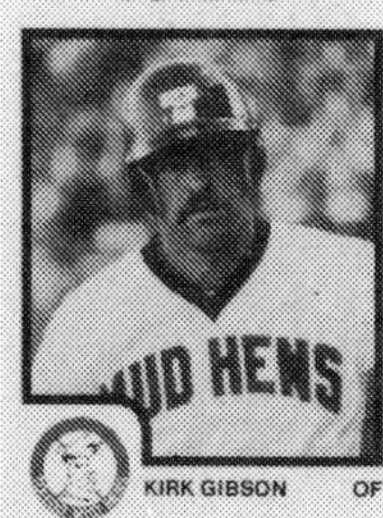

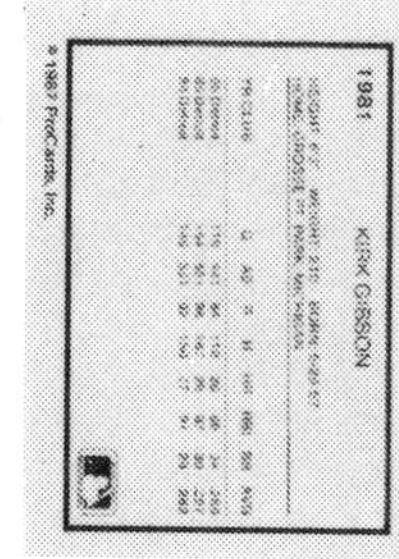

1959 Ricky Wright
1960 Don Heinkel
1961 John Pacella
1962 Ricky Barlow
1963 Paul Gibson
1964 Fred Tiburcio
1965 Tim Tolman
1966 Jed Murray
1967 Bruce Fields
1968 Rey Palacios
1969 Mike Henneman
1970 Doug Baker
1971 Morris Madden
1972 Mike Stenhouse
1973 Leon Roberts
1974 Bill Laskey
1975 Gene Roof
1976 Don McGann
1977 Jeff Ransom
1978 John Hiller
1979 Billy Bean
1980 Willie Hernandez
1981 Kirk Gibson
1982 Bryan Kelly

76880

1987 Pro Cards Tucson Toros

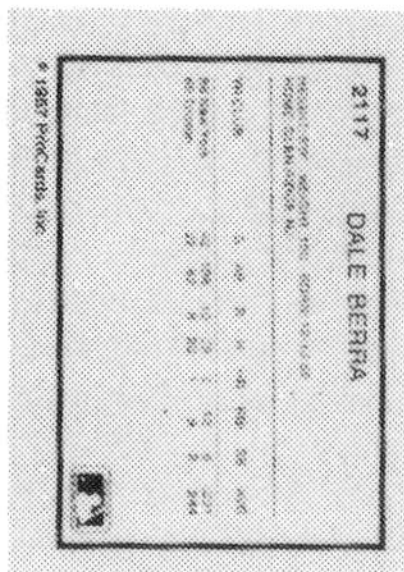

(Houston Astros, AAA)

	MT	NR MT	EX
Complete Set:	8.00	6.00	3.25

2110 Juan Agosto
2111 Glenn Carpenter
2112 Robbie Wine
2113 Bill Crone
2114 Rafael Montalvo
2115 Tye Waller
2116 Manny Hernandez
2117 Dale Berra
2118 Louie Meadows
2119 Rocky Childress
2120 Gerald Young
2121 Ray Fontenot
2122 Jim Miner
2123 Ron Mathis
2124 Nelson Rood
2125 Bert Pena
2126 Kevin Hagen
2127 Jeff Heathcock
2128 Eric Bullock
2129 Ronn Reynolds
2130 Anthony Kelley
2131 Eddie Watt
2132 Ty Gainey
2133 Bob Didier
2134 Tom Funk

1987 Pro Cards Utica Blue Sox

(Philadelphia Phillies, A)

	MT	NR MT	EX
Complete Set:	10.00	7.50	4.00

2705 Manlio Perez
2706 Leroy Ventress
2707 Rafael Bustamante
2708 Kim Batiste
2709 Scott Ruckman

2710 Shelby McDonald
2711 Troy Zerb
2712 Robert Jones
2713 Jim Vatcher
2714 Doug Lindsey
2715 Jeffrey Scott
2716 Gary White
2717 Mark Cobb
2718 Bob Chadwick
2719 David Monterio
2720 Marc Lopez
2721 Rick Trlicek
2722 Steve Kirkpatrick
2723 Darrell Coulter
2724 Scott Reaves
2725 Joe Williams
2726 Royal Thomas
2727 John LaRosa
2728 Timothy Peek
2729 Andy Ashby
2730 Matt Rambo
2731 Jaime Barragan
2732 Robert Hurta
2733 Phil Fagnano
2734 Corey Smith
2735 Ike Galloway
2736 Dave Allen
2737 Greg McCarthy

1987 Pro Cards Vancouver Canadians

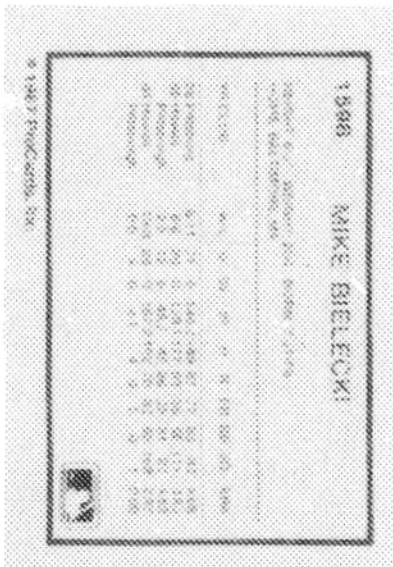

(Pittsburgh Pirates, AAA)

	MT	NR MT	EX
Complete Set:	13.00	9.75	5.25

1598 Mike Bielecki
1599 Jackie Brown
1600 Jeff Cox
1601 Carlos LeDezma
1602 Mark Ross
1603 Tommy Dunbar
1604 Stan Fansler
1605 Rocky Bridges
1606 Dave Johnson
1607 Sammy Haro
1608 Sammy Khalifa
1609 Houston Jimenez
1610 Tim Drummond
1611 Dave Leeper
1612 Mike Dunne
1613 Randy Kramer
1614 Butch Davis
1615 Hipolito Pena
1616 Jose Lind
1617 Larry Ray
1618 Danny Bilardello
1619 Vincente Palacios
1620 Ruben Rodriquez
1621 Dorn Taylor
1622 U.L. Washington

1987 Pro Cards Vermont Reds

(Cincinnati Reds, A)

	MT	NR MT	EX
Complete Set:	7.00	5.25	2.75

814 Brad Brusky
815 Jim Jefferson
816 Ted Langdon
817 Francisco Tenacen
818 Marty Brown
819 Greg Simpson
820 Ramon Sambo
821 Tim Mirabito
822 Rob Lopez
823 Joe Dunlap
824 Tom Dietz
825 Mike Smith
826 Angelo Nunley
827 Steve Oliverio
828 John Bryant
829 Tom Runnells
830 Dave Miley
831 Glenn Spagnolia
832 Joe Oliver
833 Mark Germann
834 Greg Monita
835 Chris Jones
837 Mark Berry
838 Darren Riley
839 Marvin Haynes
840 Rod Lich

1987 Pro Cards Vero Beach Dodgers

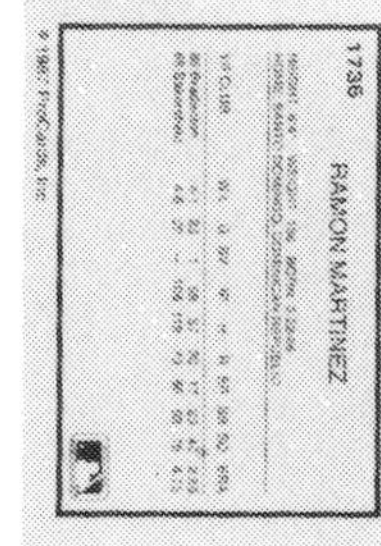

(Los Angeles Dodgers, A)

	MT	NR MT	EX
Complete Set:	20.00	15.00	8.00

1730 John Wetteland
1731 Jose Tapia
1732 Joe Spagnuolo
1733 Dan Pena
1734 Darren Holmes
1735 Pete Feist
1736 Ramon Martinez
1737 Pat Zachry
1738 Fred Gegan
1739 Ken Lambert
1740 Manny Francois
1741 Mancy Benitez
1742 Mike Garner
1743 Tom Thomas
1744 Mike Batesole
1745 Jeff Brown
1746 Kevin Campbell
1747 Rob Giesecke
1748 Joe Kesselmark
1749 Jay Hornacek
1750 Felipe Esteban
1751 Tom Beyers
1752 Kevin Devine
1753 Bryan Smith
1754 Mike Burke
1755 Bill Bartels
1756 Rene Garcia
1757 Lee Langley
1758 Kevin Shea
1759 John Shoemaker
1760 Phil Torres

1987 Pro Cards Visalia Oaks

(Minnesota Twins, A)

	MT	NR MT	EX
Complete Set:	7.00	5.25	2.75

543 Jamie Williams
544 Glen Myers
545 Kenny Morgan
546 Tim Cota
547 Bob Strube
548 Bob Lee
549 Jeff Perry
550 Kurt Walker
551 Troy Galloway
552 Dave Blakely
553 Park Pittman
554 Ike Goldstein
555 Chris Calvert
556 Tim Senne
557 Kenny Davis
558 Mike Redding
559 Tim O'Connor
560 Todd Burke
561 Joey Aragon
562 Joey Zellner
563 John Pust
564 Mike Adams
565 Marty Lanoux
566 Gordon Heimueller
567 Dan Schmitz
568 Clark Lange
569 Shannon Raybon

1987 Pro Cards Waterloo Indians

(Cleveland Indians, A)

	MT	NR MT	EX
Complete Set:	7.00	5.25	2.75

1038 Fidel Compres
1039 Manny Mercado
1040 Jim Richardson
1041 Steve Johnigan
1042 Brad Wolten
1043 Mark Pike
1044 Dave Alvis
1045 Tom Gamba
1046 Scott Johnson

WATERLOO

LENNY RANDLE COACH

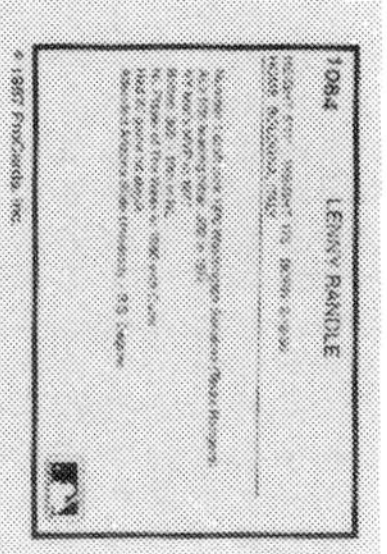

1047 Glenn Adams
1048 Todd Gonzales
1049 Kevin Kuykendall
1050 John Githens
1052 Mike Walker
1053 Jeff Shaw
1054 Carl Chambers
1055 Rudy Seanez
1056 Paul Kuzniar
1057 Don Santos
1058 Keith Seifert
1059 Ray Williamson
1060 Tom Lampkin
1061 Riley Polk
1062 Glenn Fairchild
1063 Claudio Carrasco
1064 Lenny Randle
1065 Dan Redmond
1066 Rick Adair

1987 Pro Cards Watertown Pirates

(Pittsburgh Pirates, A)

	MT	NR MT	EX
Complete Set:	7.00	5.25	2.75

2798 Ben Webb
2799 Rodger Castner
2800 Robert Harris
2801 Ed Shea
2802 Scott Runge
2803 Chip Duncan
2804 Scott Barczi
2805 Keith Raisanen
2806 Pete Freeman
2807 Steve Carter
2808 Kevin Burdick
2809 Wesley Chamberlain
2810 Domingo Merejo
2811 Junior Vizcaino
2812 Keith Shepherd
2813 Ed Hartman
2814 Jose Acosta
2815 Jim Garrison
2816 Jody Williams
2817 Mark Thomas
2818 Rob Barnwell
2819 Jeff Griffith
2820 Joe Pacholec
2821 Pete Murphy
2822 Mark Koller
2823 Joe Macavage
2824 Moises Alou
2825 Doug Torberg
2826 Charlie Green
2827 Jeff Cox
2828 Mike Sandoval

1987 Pro Cards Wausau Timbers

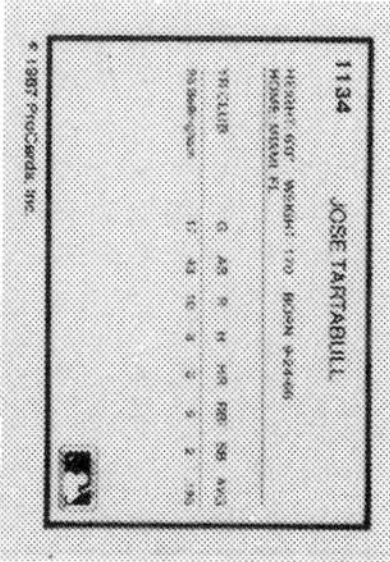

(Seattle Mariners, A)

	MT	NR MT	EX
Complete Set:	7.00	5.25	2.75

1127 Bobby Cuellar
1128 Jim Bluerberg
1129 Jody Ryan
1130 Dan Disher

1131 Howard Townsend
1132 Troy Williams
1133 Patrick Lennon
1134 Jose Tartabull
1135 Wendell Bolar
1136 Clay Gunn
1137 Jose Bennett
1138 Ted Williams
1139 Anthony Woods
1140 Drew Kosco
1141 Jim Bowie
1142 Mark Wooden
1143 Jerry Goff
1144 Deron Johnson
1145 Mike Thorpe
1146 Michael McDonald
1147 Trent Intorcia
1148 Dave Hartnott
1149 Mark Gold
1150 Pat Rice
1151 Rudy Webster
1152 Unidentified Player
1153 Ric Wilson
1154 Tim Erickson

1987 Pro Cards West Palm Beach Expos

(Montreal Expos, A)

	MT	NR MT	EX
Complete Set:	8.00	6.00	3.25

652 Rob Leary
653 Tim Touma
654 Paul Frye
655 Alfredo Cardwood
656 Jeff Tabaka
657 Rob Williams
658 Derrell Baker
659 Pat Sipe
660 Kevin Dean
661 Bob Caffrey
662 Bud Yanus
663 Don Burke
664 Mike Blowers
665 Cesar Hernandez
666 Al Collins
667 Yorkis Perez
668 Charlie Lea
669 Omer Munoz
670 Mel Houston
671 Tommy Traen
672 Eddie Dixon
673 Kevin Kristan
674 Jeff Huson
675 Don Burke
676 Steve Rousey
677 Gene Harris
678 Geff Davis
679 John Spinosa

1987 Pro Cards Williamsport Bills

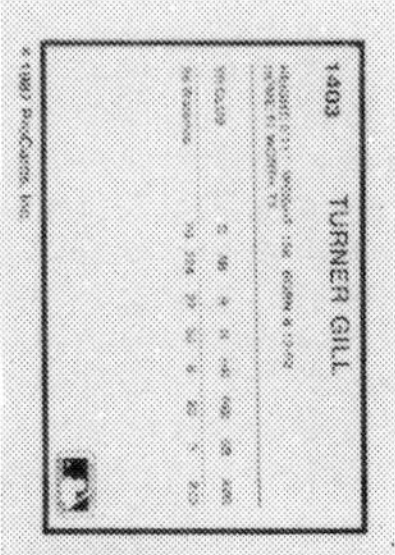

(Cleveland Indians, AA)

	MT	NR MT	EX
Complete Set:	7.00	5.25	2.75

1379 Dain Syverson
1380 Keith Bennett
1381 Winston Ficklin
1382 Oscar Mejia
1383 Luis Encarnacion
1384 Steve Moses
1385 Bobby Link
1386 Jim Bishop
1387 Mark Higgins
1388 Mike Bellaman
1389 Ivan Murrell
1390 Daryl Smith
1391 Miguel Roman
1392 Dave Bresnahan
1393 Rick Henke
1394 Brian Allard
1395 Greg LaFever
1396 Steve Swosher
1397 Greg Dube
1398 Scott Sabo
1399 Roger Wilson
1400 Chris Beasley
1401 Bernardo Brito
1402 Luis Medina
1403 Turner Gill
1404 Greg Karpuк
1405 Joe Skalski

1987 Pro Cards Winston-Salem Spirits

(Chicago Cubs, A)

	MT	NR MT	EX
Complete Set:	7.00	5.25	2.75

1209 Mark McMorris
1210 Greg Kallevig
1211 Todd Cloninger
1212 Cedric Landrum
1213 Bill Danek
1214 Phil Hannon
1215 Heath Slocumb
1216 Bob Bafia
1217 Luis Cruz
1218 Jim Bullinger
1219 Tad Slowik
1220 Glenn Gregson
1221 Jay Loviglio
1222 Lee Grimes
1223 Tim Wallace
1224 John Lewis
1225 Joe Girardi
1226 Gabby Robles
1227 Mike Tullier
1228 Mike Miller
1229 Chuck Oertli
1230 Kris Roth
1231 Jeff Hirsch
1232 Jeff Small
1233 DeWayne Coleman
1234 Jim Matas
1235 Mike Curtis

1987 Pro Cards Winter Haven Red Sox

(Boston Red Sox, A)

	MT	NR MT	EX
Complete Set:	13.00	9.75	5.25

893 Tim Buheller
894 Felix Dedos
895 Livio Padilla
896 Larry Shikles
897 Ronnie McGowan
898 Bart Haley
899 Erik Laseke
900 Leverne Jackson
901 Daniel Sullivan
902 Dan Gabrielle
903 Mike Coffey
904 Stuart Weidie
905 Bruce Lockhart
906 David Milstein
907 Odie Abril
908 John Toale
909 Manny Jose
910 Wayne Murphy
911 Mike Sears
912 Paul Slifko
913 Eduardo Zambrano
914 Eric Hetzel
915 Derek Livernois
916 Doug Camilli
917 Mike Ickes
918 Roger Haggerty
919 Paul Thoutsis
920 Jim Orsag
921 Todd Pratt
922 Dana Gomez

1987 Pro Cards Wytheville Cubs

(Chicago Cubs, A)

	MT	NR MT	EX
Complete Set:	7.00	5.25	2.75

2738 Anthony Whitson
2739 Matt Walbeck
2740 Horace Tucker
2741 Scott Taylor
2742 Derek Stroud
2743 Dave Sommer
2744 Jossy Rosario
2745 Victor Quiles
2746 Eric Perry
2747 Elvin Paulino
2748 Nelson Nunex
2749 Greg Jackson
2750 John Gardner
2751 Edger Galarza
2752 Henry Fleming
2753 Matthew Franco
2754 Francisco Espino
2755 Darren Eggleston
2756 Jay Eddings
2757 Braz Davis
2758 Frank Castillo
2759 Danny Carpenter
2760 Carlos Canino
2761 Frank Campos
2762 Matt Cakora
2763 Warren Arrington
2764 Alex Arias
2765 Tom King
2766 Rick Kranitz
2767 Brad Mills
2768 Team Photo

1987 T&J SC Madison Muskies

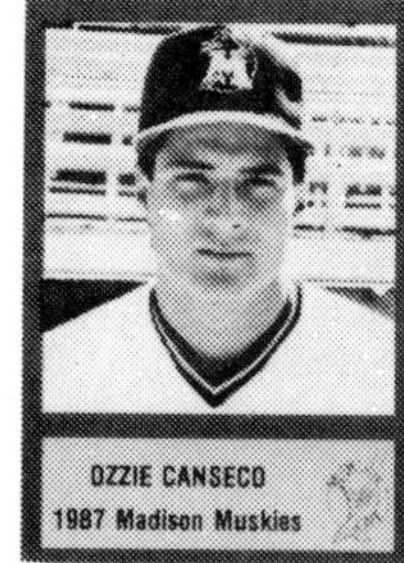

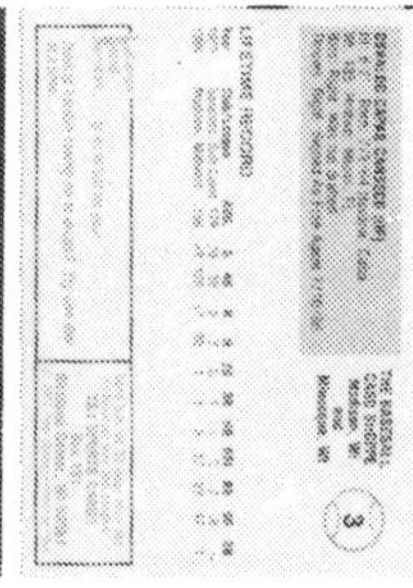

(Madison Muskies, A)

	MT	NR MT	EX
Complete Set:	10.00	7.50	4.00

1 Gerry Barragan
2 Mark Beavers
3 Ozzie Canseco
4 Jim Carroll
5 Mike Cupples
6 Blaine Deabenberfer
7 Pat Gilbert
8 Jeff Glover
9 Scott Hemond
10 Jeff Kopyta
11 Kevin Kunkel
12 Luis Martinez
13 Doug Ortman
14 Dave Otto
15 Jamie Reiser
16 Luis Salcedo
17 Bob Sharpnack
18 Bob Stocker
19 Vinnie Teixeira
20 Camilo Veras
21 Wes Weber
22 Jim Nettles
23 Dave Schober

1987 TCMA Columbus Clippers

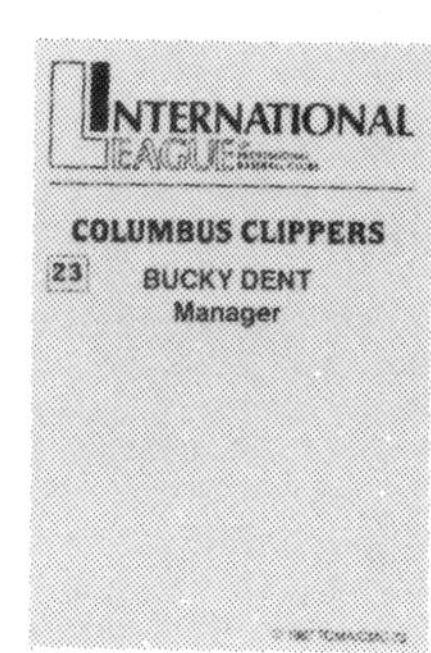

(New York Yankees, AAA)

	MT	NR MT	EX
Complete Set:	9.00	6.75	3.50

1 Brad Arnsberg
2 Rich Bordi
3 Pete Filson
4 Bill Fulton
5 Randy Graham
6 Al Holland
7 Alfonso Pulido
8 Ron Romanick
9 Bob Tewksbury
10 Juan Espino
11 Mitch Lyden
12 Pete Dalena
13 Orestes Destrade
14 Bryan Little
15 Phil Lombardi
16 Bobby Meacham
17 Jeff Moronko
18 Shane Turner
19 Jay Buhner
20 Henry Cotto
21 Keith Hughes
22 Roberto Kelly
23 Bucky Dent
24 Jerry McNertney, Kevin Rand, Ken Rowe, Champ Summers
25 Glenn Sherlock

1987 TCMA International League All-Stars

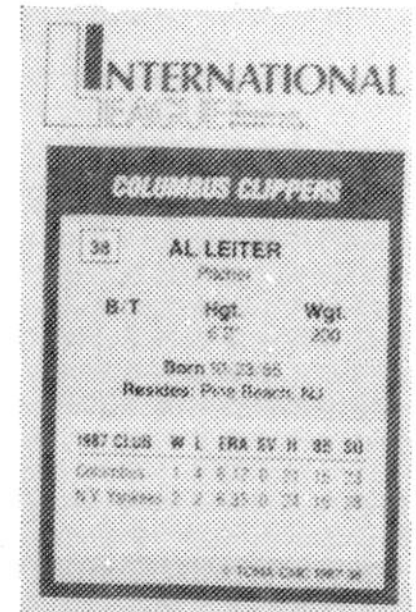

(AAA)

Complete Set:	MT	NR MT	EX
	14.00	10.50	5.50

1 Jeff Moronko
2 Jay Buhner
3 Brad Arnsberg
4 Roberto Kelly
5 Randy Milligan
6 Kevin Elster
7 Sam Horn
8 Nelson Liriano
9 Ed Nottle
10 Don Gordon
11 Rey Palacios
12 Mark Carreon
13 Randy Velarde
14 Bruce Fields
15 Mike Henneman
16 Scott Lusader
17 Jim Walewander
18 Keith Miller
19 John Marzano
20 Todd Benzinger
21 Jody Reed
22 Tom Bolton
23 Orestes Destrade
24 Sylvester Campusano
25 Todd Stottlemyre
26 Rob Ducey
27 Bill Ripken
28 Jeff Ballard
29 Pete Stanicek
30 Craig Worthington
31 Chris Padget
32 Tom Glavine
33 Jeff Blauser
34 Marty Clary
35 David Griffin
36 Keith Miller
37 Travis Chambers
38 Al Leiter
39 Columbus Clippers Team

40 Tidewater Tides Team
41 Pawtucket Red Sox Team

42 Syracuse Chiefs Team
43 Toledo Mud Hens Team

44 Rochester Red Wings Team

45 Maine Guides Team

1987 TCMA Maine Guides

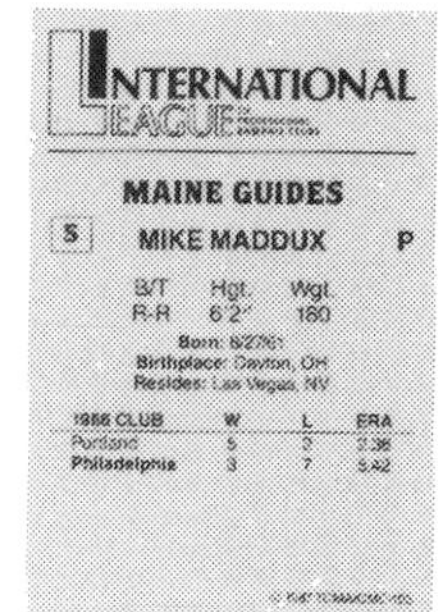

(Philadelphia Phillies, AAA) Withdrawn cards #'s 26 & 27 are quite scarce.

Complete Set:	MT	NR MT	EX
	10.00	7.50	4.00

1 Shawn Barton
2 Jeff Calhoun
3 Travis Chambers
4 Marvin Freeman
5 Mike Maddux
6 Tom Newell
7 Fred Toliver
8 Joe Cipolloni
9 Darren Loy
10 Ken Dowell
11 Ken Jackson
12 Greg Jelks
13 Alan LeBoeuf
14 Greg Legg
15 Keith Miller
16 Gib Seibert
17 Ron Jones
18 Jim Olander
19 Jeff Stone
20 Len Watts
21 Darren Daulton
22 Kevin Ward
23 Bill Dancy
24 Tim Corcoran
25 Mike Willis

1987 TCMA Pawtucket Red Sox

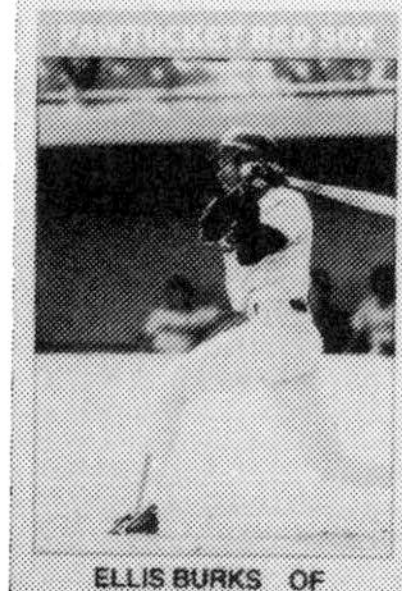

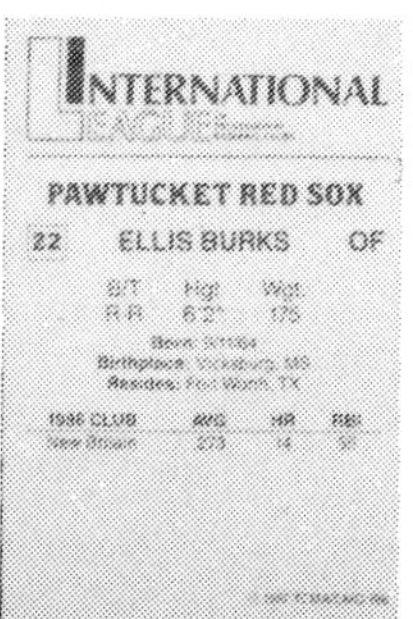

(Boston Red Sox, AAA) (S. Horn, J. Marzano, E. Burks and other young prospects appear in the 1987 Pawtucket Red Sox set.

Complete Set:	MT	NR MT	EX
	20.00	15.00	8.00

1 Andy Araujo
2 Chris Cannizzaro
3 Steve Curry
4 Mike Dalton
5 Chuck Davis
6 Steve Ellsworth
7 Mitch Johnson
8 Danny Sheaffer
9 Mike Rochford
10 Hector Stewart
11 John Marzano
12 Gary Tremblay
13 Todd Benzinger
14 Sam Horn
15 Mike Mesh
16 Gary Miller-Jones
17 Jody Reed
18 Kevin Romine
19 LaSchelle Tarver
20 Scott Wade
21 Ed Nottle
22 Ellis Burks
23 Rob Woodard
24 Pat Dodson
25 Dave Sax
26 John Leister
27 Tom Bolton
28 Mark Meleski

1987 TCMA Richmond Braves

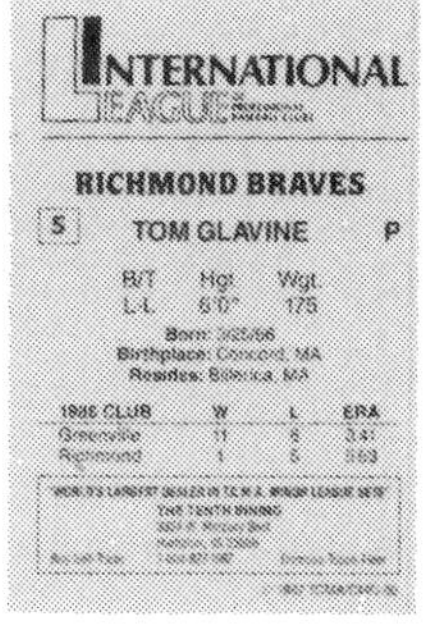

(Atlanta Braves, AAA)

Complete Set:	MT	NR MT	EX
	35.00	26.00	14.00

1 Chuck Cary
2 Floyd Chiffer
3 Marty Clary
4 Juan Eichelberger
5 Tom Glavine
6 Chuck Hensley
7 Bean Stringfellow
8 Matt West
9 Steve Ziem
10 John Mizerock
11 Jeff Blauser
12 Mike Fischlin
13 David Griffin
14 Paul Runge
15 Mark Strucher
16 Bob Tumpane
17 Trench Davis
18 Kelly Heath
19 Darryl Motley
20 John Rabb
21 Roy Majtyka
22 Nardi Contreras
23 Dale Holman
24 Jim McManus
25 Cliff Speck
26 Rich Albert
27 Mike Brown
28 Stan Cliburn
29 Sam Ayoub

1987 TCMA Rochester Red Wings

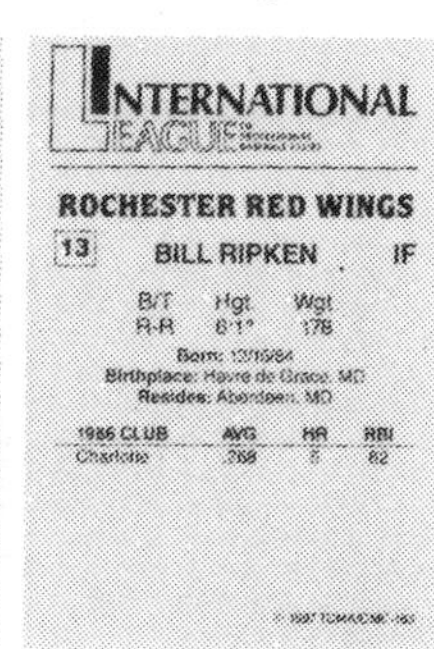

(Baltimore Orioles, AAA)

Complete Set:	MT	NR MT	EX
	13.00	9.75	5.25

1 Jeff Ballard
2 Luis DeLeon
3 Mike Griffin
4 John Habyan
5 Brad Havens
6 Phil Huffman
7 Jack O'Connor
8 Eric Rasmussen
9 Mike Skinner
10 Carl Nichols
11 Dave Van Gorder
12 Chris Padget
13 Bill Ripken
14 David Lee Smith
15 Kelvin Torve
16 Ron Washington
17 Craig Worthington
18 Mike Hart
19 Ron Salcedo
20 Jim Traber
21 Scott Ullger
22 Chris Green
23 Curt Motton
24 John Hart
25 Dom Chiti
26 Jerry Lomastro
27 Joe Kucharski
28 Rex Mudler
29 Don Gordon, Joe Kucharski

1987 TCMA Syracuse Chiefs

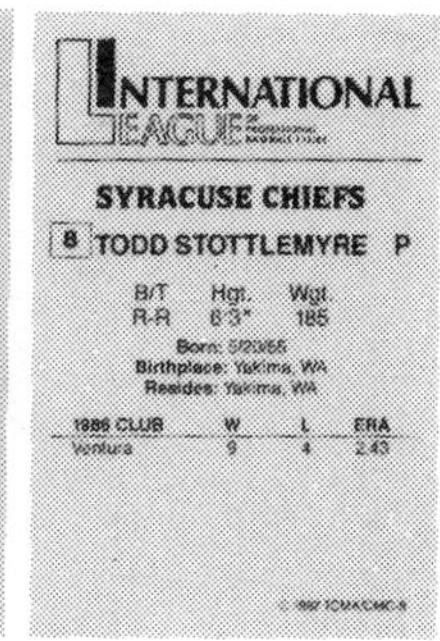

(Toronto Blue Jays, AAA)

Complete Set:	MT	NR MT	EX
	13.00	9.75	5.25

1 Luis Aquino
2 Steve Davis
3 Jeff Hearron
4 Don Gordon
5 Odell Jones

6 Colin McLaughlin
7 Jose Segura
8 Todd Stottlemyre
9 David Wells
10 Greg Myers
11 Dave Stenhouse
12 Jose Castro
13 Jose Escobar
14 Otis Green
15 Alex Infante
16 Manny Lee
17 Nelson Liriano
18 Silvester Campusano
19 Rob Ducey
20 Glenallen Hill
21 Lou Thornton
22 Doc Estes
23 Doug Ault
24 Dave LaRoche
25 Hector Torres
26 Don Gordon, Joe Kucharski
27 Joseph Coyle
28 Mel Queen
29 Kash Beauchamp
30 Steve Fireovid
31 Randy Day
32 Eddie Mahar
33 Red Coughlin

1987 TCMA Tidewater Tides

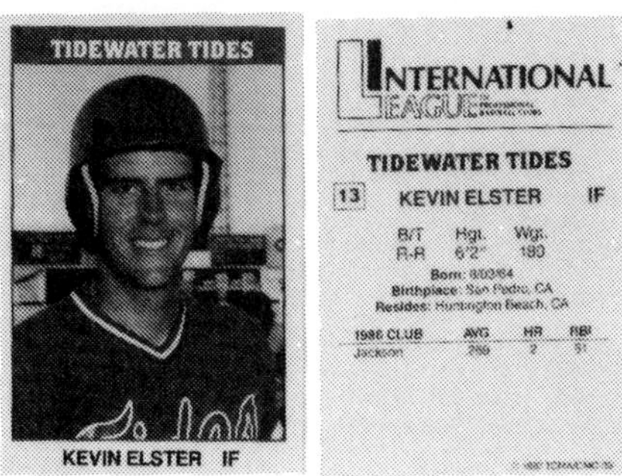

(New York Mets, AAA)

	MT	NR MT	EX
Complete Set:	15.00	11.00	6.00

1 Reggie Dobie
2 Tom Edens
3 Bob Gibson
4 Ed Glynn
5 Jeff Innis
6 Tom McCarthy
7 John Mitchell
8 DeWayne Vaughn
9 Dave Wyatt
10 John Gibbons
11 Greg Olson
12 Andre David
13 Kevin Elster
14 Tom Lombarski
15 Jeff McKnight
16 Keith Miller
17 Randy Milligan
18 Steve Springer
19 Terry Blocker
20 Mark Carreon
21 Gene Walter
22 Clint Hurdle
23 Mike Cubbage
24 John Cumberland
25 Rick Rainer
26 Don Schulze
27 Bob Buchanan
28 Bill Latham
29 Jose Roman
30 Dwight Gooden

1987 TCMA Toledo Mud Hens

(Detroit Tigers, AAA)

	MT	NR MT	EX
Complete Set:	13.00	9.75	5.25

1 Rey Palacios
2 Don Heinkel
3 German Rivera
4 Bill Laskey
5 Mike Stenhouse
6 Fred Tiburcio
7 Jim Walewander
8 Scott Lusader
9 Bruce Fields
10 Scott Earl
11 Jeff Ransom
12 James R. Wright
13 Mike Henneman
14 John Pacella
15 Morris Madden
16 Steve Searcy
17 Paul Gibson
18 Jed Murray
19 Ricky Barlow

20 Doug Baker
21 Leon Roberts
22 Gene Roof
23 Tim Tolman
24 Jerry Davis
25 Dwight Lowry

1987 Team Albuquerque Dukes

(Los Angeles Dodgers, AAA)

	MT	NR MT	EX
Complete Set:	12.50	9.50	5.25

1 Terry Collins (manager)
2 Ben Hines (coach)
3 Brent Strom (coach)
4 Lenny Currier (trainer)
5 William Brennan
6 Dennis Burtt
7 Jaime Cocanower
8 Tim Crews
9 Jeff Edwards
10 Hector Heredia
11 Shawn Hillegas
12 Pete Ladd
13 Dennis Livingston
14 Tim Meeks
15 Jon Debus
16 Orlando Mercado
17 Gilberto Reyes
18 Shanie Dugas
19 Jeff Hamilton
20 Jack Perconte
21 Larry See
22 Craig Shipley
23 Brad Wellman
24 Tracy Woodson
25 Ralph Bryant
26 Jose Gonzalez
27 Chris Gwynn
28 George Hinshaw
29 Stu Pederson
30 Mike Ramsey

1987 Team Bellingham Mariners

(Seattle Mariners, A)

	MT	NR MT	EX
Complete Set:	32.00	24.00	13.00

1 Jeffrey Hooper
2 Erick Bryant
3 Brian Wilkerson
4 Dorian Daughtry
5 Kevin Reichardt
6 Keith Helton
7 John Hoffman
8 Victor Manguel
9 Chuck Carr
10 Tom Peters
11 Todd Haney
12 Joe Georger
13 Jeff Morrison
14 Wade Taylor
15 Ken Griffey, Jr.
16 Spyder Webb
17 Otis Patrick
18 Mike Goff
19 Brian Baldwin
20 Tony Cayson
21 Mike Sisco
22 Mike McGuire
23 Ruben Gonzalez
24 Rick Sweet
25 Daryl Burrus
26 Scott Stoerck
27 Fausto Ramirez
28 Salty Parker
29 Steve Bieksha
30 Paul Togneri
31 Corey Paul
32 Chris VanBuren
33 Team Photo
--- Marty Reese
--- Team Logo Card

1987 Team Buffalo Bisons

(Cleveland Indians, AAA) (co-sponsored by Pucko)

	MT	NR MT	EX
Complete Set:	10.00	7.50	4.00

1 Don Lovell
2 Kent Murphy
3 Andy Allanson
4 Jay Bell
5 Barry Brunkenkant
6 Dave Clark
7 Doug Frobel
8 Junior Noboa
9 Casey Parsons
10 Craig Smajstria
11 Ron Tingley
12 Randy Washington
13 Eddie Williams
14 Gibson Alba
15 John Farrell
16 Jeff Kaiser
17 Mike Murphy
18 Bryan Oelkers
19 Reggie Ritter
20 Scott Roberts
21 Jose Roman
22 Don Shulze
23 Frank Wills
24 Rod Allen
25 Orlando Gomez
26 Mike Bucci, Rick Peterson
27 Mike Billoni
28 Donald "Butcher" Palmer
29 John Murphy, Pete Weber

1987 Team Charlotte O's

(Baltimore Orioles, AA)

	MT	NR MT	EX
Complete Set:	12.00	9.00	5.00

(1) Miguel Alicea
(2) Kurt Beamesderfer
(3) Greg Biagini
(4) Paul Cameron
(5) erwin Cijntle
(6) Matt Cimo
(7) Jim Daniel
(8) Tom Dodd
(9) Dave Falcone
(10) John Flinn
(11) Charlie Frederick
(12) Bob Hice
(13) Jerry Holtz
(14) John Hoover
(15) Paul Householder
(16) Joe Jarrell
(17) Ricky Jones
(18) Joe Kucharski
(19) Robert Long
(20) Terry Mauney
(21) Bob Milacki
(22) Francisco Javier Oliveras
(23) Mike Raczka
(24) Rico Rossy
(25) Chester Durwood Stanhope
(26) Pete STanicek
(27) Jack Tackett
(28) Greg Talamantez
(29) Jeff Wood
(30) Crockett Park

1987 Team Columbus Clippers

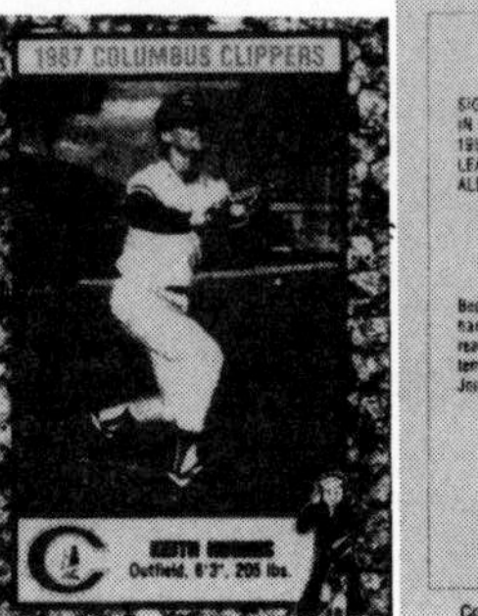

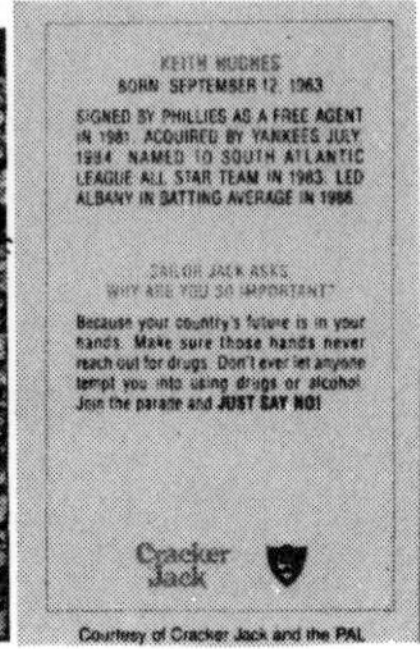

(New York Yankees, AAA) (Withdrawn cards in this set are very scarce - generally not found in many sets.

	MT	NR MT	EX
Complete Set:	7.00	5.25	2.75

(1) Mike Armstrong
(2) Brad Arnsberg
(3) Rich Bordi
(4) Jay Buhner
(5) Pete Dalena
(6) Bucky Dent
(7) Oretes Destrade
(8) Juan Espino
(9) Pete Filson
(10) Bill Fulton
(11) Randy Graham
(12) Al Holland
(13) Keith Hughes
(14) Roberto Kelly
(15) Al Leiter
(16) Bryan Little
(17) Phil Lombardi
(18) Phil Lombardi (variation - withdrawn from set)
(19) Mitch Lyden
(20) Bobby Meacham
(21) Jeff Moronko (withdrawn from set)
(22) Pulido Alfonso

(23) Ron Romanick
(24) Glenn Sherlock
(25) George Sisler
(26) Shane Turner
(27) Coaches card (Clete Boyer, John Summers, Jerry McNertney, Ken Rowe)

1987 Team Elmira Pioneers - Black

(Boston Red Sox, A)

	MT	NR MT	EX
Complete Set:	8.00	6.00	3.25

1 Clyde Smoll (president/general manager)

2 Bill Limoncelli (manager)
3 Dave Sullivan (assistant general manager)

4 Miguel Monegro
5 Larry Scanneli
6 Kendrick Bourne
7 Robert Echevarria
8 Julio Rosario
9 Brian Warfel
10 Terry Marrs
11 Sam Melton
12 Scott Powers
13 Al Thornton
14 Luis Dorante
15 Mike Kelly
16 Vincent Degifico
17 Tony Mosley
18 Craig Wilson
19 Steve Michael
20 Thom Sepela
21 Tony Romero
22 Jhonny Diaz
23 Greg McCollum
24 Edward Banasiak
25 Joaquin Tejeda
26 Jose Pemberton
27 Ronnie Richardson
28 Bernie Stento
29 Al Bumbry (instructor)
30 Felix Maldonado (instructor)

31 Frank Malzone (instructor)
32 Eddie Popowski (instructor)
33 Charlie Wagner (instructor)
34 Paul Brown

1987 Team Elmira Pioneers - Red

(Boston Red Sox, A)

	MT	NR MT	EX
Complete Set:	22.00	16.50	9.00

1 Clyde Smoll
2 Bill Limoncelli
3 Dave Sullivan
4 Miguel Monegro
5 Larry Scanneli
6 Kendrick Bourne
7 Robert Echevarria
8 Julio Rosario
9 Brian Warfel
10 Terry Marrs
11 Sam Melton
12 Scott Powers
13 Al Thornton
14 Luis Dorante
15 Mike Kelly
16 Vincent Degifico
17 Tony Mosley
18 Craig Wilson
19 Steve Michael
20 Thom Sepela
21 Tony Romero
22 Johnny Diaz
23 Greg McCollum
24 Edward Banasiak
25 Joaquin Tejeda
26 Jose Pemberton
27 Ronnie Richardson
28 Bernie Stento
29 Al Bumbry
30 Reggie Harris
31 Bob Zupcic
32 Mike Dillard
33 Mickey Pine
34 Phillip Plantier
35 Checklist
36 Checklist

1987 Team Huntsville Stars

(Oakland A's, AA)

	MT	NR MT	EX
Complete Set:	8.50	6.25	3.50

1 Roy Anderson
2 Larry Arndt
3 Tim Birtsas
4 Lance Blankenship
5 Tyler Brilinski
6 Todd Burns
7 Jim Corsi
8 Brian Criswell
9 Pat Dietrick
10 Darrin Duffy
11 Brad Fischer
12 Scott Hemond
13 Steve Howard
14 Mark Howie
15 Jimmy Jones
16 Felix Jose
17 Russ Kibler
18 Joe Kramer
19 Reese Lambert
20 Doug Scherer
21 Jeff Shaver
22 Jose Tolentino
23 Walt Weiss
24 Wally Whitehurst
25 Joe Xavier

1987 Team Indianapolis Indians

(Montreal Expos, AAA) (co-sponsored by Tom Aikens) All cards in this set have a Pepsi-Cola emblem on the front.

	MT	NR MT	EX
Complete Set:	10.50	7.75	4.25

1 Team Photo
2 It Was Magic
3 The Magic Continues
4 Joe Sparks (manager)
5 Jerry Manuel (coach)
6 Luis Pujols
7 Dave Tomlin
8 Razor Shines
9 Tim Barrett
10 Jack Daugherty
11 Ubaldo Heredia
12 Ron Shepherd
13 Curt Brown
14 Tom Romano
15 Jeff Fischer
16 Jeff Reynolds
17 Jeff Parrett
18 Billy Moore
19 Mark Gardner
20 Johnny Paredes
21 Sergio Valdez
22 Dallas Williams
23 Mike Smith
24 Kelly Faulk
25 Wilfredo Tejada
26 Pascual Perez
27 Luis Rivera
28 Scott Clemo
29 Nelson Norman
30 Mark Corey
31 Dennis Martinez
32 Tim McCormack (trainer)
33 Alonzo Powell
34 The Voices of the Indians (Tom Akins, Howard Kellman)
35 The Bat Boys (Kenny Akins, Sean Schnaiter, Mark Schumacher)
36 Bill Rowley (clubhouse man)

1987 Team Jackson Mets

(New York Mets, AA)

	MT	NR MT	EX
Complete Set:	17.50	13.00	7.00

1 Dan Winters
2 Jeff McKnight
3 Jose Bautista
4 Tucker Ashford
5 Tom McCarthy
6 Zoilo Sanchez
7 Shane Young
8 Kurt Lundgren
9 Jeff Gardner
10 Mike Hocutt
11 MIckey Weston
12 Al CArmichael
13 Sam McCrary
14 Ed Pruitt
15 Joaquin Contreras
16 Marcus Lawton
17 Johnny Wilson
18 Steve Phillips
19 Kyle Hartshorn
20 Glenn Abbott
21 Tom Burns
22 Alan Hayden
23 Dave West
24 Gregg Jefferies
25 Mike Santiago

1987 Team Louisville Redbirds

(St. Louis Cardinals, AAA)

	MT	NR MT	EX
Complete Set:	12.50	9.50	5.25

1 Mike Jorgensen
2 Joe Pettini
3 Jack Ayer
4 Greg Bargar
5 Joe Boever
6 Rod Booker
7 Rich Buontatony
8 Jose Calderon
9 Paul Cherry
10 Rick Colbert
11 Mark Dougherty

12 Dan Driessen
13 Bill Earley
14 Dick CGrapenthin
15 David Green
16 Lance Johnson
17 Tim Jones
18 Mickey Mahler
19 John A. Martin
20 John Morris
21 John Murphy
22 Tom Pagnozzi
23 Mike Laga
24 Bill Lyons
25 Joe Magrane
26 Victor Rodriguez
27 Ray Soff
28 Duane Walker
29 David "Hap" Hudson
30 Billy Johnson

1987 Team Nashville Sounds

(Cincinnati Reds, AA)

	MT	NR MT	EX
Complete Set:	10.00	7.50	4.00

(1) Mark Berry
(2) Norm Charlton
(3) Bill Cutshall
(4) Rob Dibble
(5) Leo Garcia
(6) Wayne Garland
(7) Orlando Gonzalez
(8) Jeff Gray
(9) Lenny Harris
(10) Ron Henika
(11) Bob Jamison
(12) Duncan Stewart
(13) Hugh Kemp
(14) Mike Konderla
(15) Jack Lind
(16) Mike Manfre
(17) Jeff Montgomery
(18) Pat Pacillo
(19) Buddy pryor
(20) Chris Sabo
(21) Eddie Tanner
(22) Scott Terry
(23) Jeff Treadway
(24) Max Venable
(25) Carl Willis
(26) John Young

1987 Team Salt Lake City Trappers

(No affiliation, A)

	MT	NR MT	EX
Complete Set:	10.00	7.50	4.00

1 Kurt Strange
2 Michael Malinak
3 Kent Hetrick
4 Jon Beuder
5 Neil Reynolds
6 James Ferguson
7 Coach/Bat Boys (Lance Bagshaw, Ryan Bagshaw, Andy Iacona, Reuben Rodriguez) (coach)
8 John Groennert
9 Isaac Alleyne
10 Todd Noonan
11 Jim Gilligan (manager)
12 David Ward
13 Ed Citronnelli
14 General Manager/Public Relations (Steve Pearson, Glenn Seninger)
15 Kouichi Ikeue
16 Mike Humphrey
17 Niles Creekmore
18 Frank Colston
19 Adam Casillas
20 Yasuhiro Hiyama
21 Trainer/Announcer (Steve Fong, Randy Kerdoon)
22 Anthony Blackmon
23 Matt Huff
24 Jon Leake
25 Tim Peters
26 Steve Scott
27 David Poss
28 Team Photo/Checklist

--- Baseball Cards, Etc. (Kim & Joie Casey)

1987 Team San Antonio Dodgers

(Los Dodgers, Sets

	MT	NR MT	EX
Complete Set:	8.00	6.00	3.25

1 Jeff Schaefer
2 Andres Mena
3 Manager/Coaches (Gary LaRocque, Dennis Lewallyn, Jim Stoeckel)
4 Tim Scott
5 Alonzo Tellez
6 Rob Rowen
7 Domingo Michel
8 Barry Wohler
9 Juan Bustabad
10 Mike Devereaux
11 Scott May
12 Jeff Brown
13 Mike Schweighoffer
14 Walt McConnell
15 Felix Tejeda
16 Mike Huff
17 Joe Szekely
18 Bob Hamilton
19 Jon Pequignot
20 Dave Eichhorn
21 Homar Rojas
22 Jack Savage
23 Ken Harvey
24 Mark Heuer

1987 Team Tulsa Drillers

(Texas Rangers, AA)

	MT	NR MT	EX
Complete Set:	9.00	6.75	3.50

1 Dave Murray
2 Brad Hill
3 Mike Jirschele
4 Bobby Jones
5 Mike couchee
6 Bill Stearns
7 Dave Harman
8 Greg Ferlenda
9 Jeff Melrose
10 Otto Gonzalez
11 Eddie Jurak
12 Jim ST. Laurent
13 Howard Hilton, Dave Pavlas
14 Ruben Guzman
15 Tom Duggan
16 George Threadgill
17 Ken Rogers
18 Rick Knapp
19 Jose Cecena
20 Bob Malloy
21 Darrell Whitaker
22 Rick Odekirk
23 Larry Klein
24 Tommy West
25 Jose Mota
26 Gary Mielke
27 Rob Bill
28 Rod Lung

1987 Texas League All-Stars

(Detroit Tigers, AAA)

	MT	NR MT	EX
Complete Set:	17.50	13.00	7.00

1 Mike Debutch
2 Roy Silver
3 Joe Lynch
4 Doug Jennings
5 Brad Pounders
6 Jack Mull
7 Jeff Gardner
8 Roberto Alomar
9 Ed Jurak
10 Sandy Alomar, Jr.
11 Gregg Jefferies
12 Joe Redfield
13 Steve Smith
14 Shane Young
15 Marty Reed
16 Joaquin Contreras
17 Jim St. Laurent
18 Thomas Howard
19 Steve Peters
20 John Miglio
21 Scott Arnold
22 Kirt Manwaring
23 Greg Harris
24 Marcus Lawton
25 Lavel Freeman
26 Mike Fitzgerald
27 Charlie Hayes
28 Mike Devereaux
29 David West
30 Jesus Alfaro
31 Ray Stephens
32 Ty Dabney
33 John Burkett
34 Jack Savage
35 Joe Szckely

1988

1988 Best Birmingham Barons

(Chicago White Sox, AA)

	MT	NR MT	EX
Complete Set:	7.00	5.25	2.75

1 Wayne Edwards
2 Tony Biasucci
3 Tom Drees
4 Ray Chadwick
5 Jim Markert
6 Dave Wallwork
7 Moe Drabowsky
8 Rico Petrocelli
9 Todd Trafton
10 Tommy Tompson
11 Pete Venturini
12 Tom Forrester
13 Dan Wagner
14 Mark Davis
15 Rick Pollack
16 Carlos Martinez
17 Rich Gaynor
18 John Boling
19 Daryl Smith
20 Tony Menedez
21 Dan Cronkright
22 Matt Merullo
23 Jerry Bertolani
24 Craig Grebeck
25 Willie Magallanes
26 Doug Little
27 Chuck Mount
28 Kevin Renz
29 Checklist/Hoover Metro Stadium

1988 Best Charleston Wheelers

(Chicago Cubs, A)

	MT	NR MT	EX
Complete Set:	7.00	5.25	2.75

1 Matt Walbeck
2 Brad Mills
3 Greg Mahlberg
4 Scott Taylor
5 Mike Reeder
6 Lee Grimes
7 Eric Perry
8 Steve Owens
9 Alex Arias
10 Darren Eggleston
11 Tony Duenas
12 Jay Eddings
13 Patrick Gomez
14 Henry Gomez
15 John Gardner
16 Marcus Lopez
17 Matt Cakora
18 Don Cohoon
19 DeWayne Coleman
20 Braz Davis
21 Harry Shelton
22 Fernando Ramsey
23 Elio Jose
24 Frank Campos
25 Ray Mullino
26 Nick Rameriez
27 Bob Grimes
28 Checklist/Wheelers Stadium

1988 Best Chattanooga Lookouts

(Cincinnati Reds, AA)

	MT	NR MT	EX
Complete Set:	7.00	5.25	2.75

1 Timber Mead
2 Chris Hammond
3 Keith Brown
4 Joe Lazor
5 Rich Bombard
6 Chris Jones
7 Tony DeFrancasco
8 Hedi Vargas
9 Keith Lockhart
10 Mark Germann
11 Darrell Pruitt
12 Don Wakamatsu
13 Brian Finley
14 Tom Runnells
15 Tim Deitz
16 Gino Minutelli
17 Joe Bruno
18 Phil Dale
19 Jim Jefferson
20 Lary Sorenson
21 Mike Smith
22 Jeff Richardson
23 Bernie Walker
24 Darren Riley
25 Angelo Nunley
26 Logo & checklist card

1988 Best Columbus Astros

(Houston Astros, AA)

	MT	NR MT	EX
Complete Set:	7.00	5.25	2.75

1 Charlie Kerfeld
2 Don Dunster
3 Terry Wells
4 Glenn Spagnola
5 Brian Meyer
6 Ken Crew
7 Doug Givler
8 Jose Vargas
9 Kyle Todd
10 Juan Lopez
11 David Rohde
12 Dan Walters
13 John Elliott
14 Rich Johnson
15 Larry Lasky
16 Jeff Edwards
17 Blaise Ilsley
18 Tom Funk
19 Carlo Colombino
20 Fred Gladding
21 Gary Cooper
22 Terry Green
23 Troy Afenir
24 Dayton Preston
25 Tom Wiedenbauer
26 Clavin James
27 Norman Brock
28 Team photo & checklist card

1988 Best El Paso Diablos

(Milwaukee Brewers, AA)

	MT	NR MT	EX
Complete Set:	20.00	15.00	8.00

1 Gary Sheffield
2 Donald Scott
3 Daniel Scarpetta
4 Jamie Brisco
5 George Canale
6 Dave Machemer
7 Ramon Serna
8 Luis Castillo
9 Bill Mooneyham
10 Paul Lindblad
11 Jim Rowe
12 Matias Carrillo

13 Alan Cartwright
14 Robert DeWolf
15 Mark Ambrose
16 Andy Anderson
17 Barry Bass
18 Bradley Wheeler
19 Fred Williams
20 Gregory Vaughn
21 Jeffrey Peterek
22 Edward Puig
23 Angel Rodriguez
24 Adrian Meagher
25 Joseph Mitchell
26 Mario Monico
27 Rob Hicks
28 James Hunter
29 Frankie Mattox
30 Checklist/Dudley Dome

1988 Best El Paso Diablos Limited Edition

(Milwaukee Brewers, AA) This set includes the same players as listed in the regular set. The fronts of the cards are silver & black and the backs of the cards are royal blue as opposed to the gray backs of the regular set. Only 1,300 of these sets were made.

	MT	NR MT	EX
Complete Set:	25.00	18.50	10.00

1988 Best Eugene Emeralds

(Kansas City Royals, A)

	MT	NR MT	EX
Complete Set:	9.50	7.00	3.75

1 Bob Hamblin
2 Steve Hoeme
3 Greg Harvey
4 Steve Otto
5 Bill Drohan
6 Hector Wagner
7 Kyle Irvin
8 Jim Smith
9 Brad Hopper
10 Randy Vaughn
11 Joel Johnston
12 David Rolls
13 Rob Buchanan
14 Jeff Hulse
15 Fred Russell
16 Jeff Garber
17 Kelvin Davis
18 Ron Collins
19 Bill Gardner
20 Steve Preston
21 Karl Drezek
22 Bobby Holley
23 Frank Henderson
24 John Gilcrist
25 Derek Sholl
26 Gerald Ingram
27 Milt Richardson
28 Frankie Watson
29 Keith Shibata
30 Logo & checklist card

1988 Best Greenville Braves

(Atlanta Braves, AA)

	MT	NR MT	EX
Complete Set:	7.50	5.50	3.00

1 Ed Whited
2 Terry Bell
3 Sal D'Alessandro
4 Inocencio Guerrero
5 Dennis Hood
6 John Alva
7 Miguel Sabino
8 Barry Jones
9 Drew Denson
10 Mark Lemke
11 Jim Lovell
12 Dale Polley
13 Bryan Farmer
14 Dave Miller
15 Steve Ziem
16 Kevin Blankenship
17 Maximo Del Rosario
18 Tom Dozier
19 Andy Nezelek
20 John Kilner
21 Tom Dunbar
22 Eddie Mathews
23 Mike Fischlin
24 Logo & checklist card

1988 Best Jacksonville Expos

(Montreal Expos, AA)

	MT	NR MT	EX
Complete Set:	8.00	6.00	3.25

1 Rick Carriger
2 Mike Shade
3 Rich Sauver
4 John Hoover
5 Gene Harris
6 Eddie Dixon
7 Mark Gardner
8 Mark Clemons
9 Tommy Alexander
10 Richie Lewis
11 Yorkis Perez
12 Orsino Hill
13 Kevin Dean
14 Derrell Baker
15 Bill Mann
16 Mike Blowers
17 Esteban Beltre
18 Jeff Huson
19 Andy Lawrence
20 Pat Sipe
21 Randy Braun
22 Doug Duke
23 Nardi Contreras
24 Tommy Thompson
25 Bob Caffrey
26 Jim Yalmann
27 Armando Moreno
28 Gary Engelkin
29 Checklist/Sam W. Wolfson Stadium

1988 Best Knoxville Blue Jays

(Toronto Blue Jays, AA)

	MT	NR MT	EX
Complete Set:	8.00	6.00	3.25

1 Alex Sanchez
2 Sanchez Felix
3 John Shea
4 Mike Jones
5 Jimy Kelly
6 Domingo Martinez
7 Kevin Batiste
8 Hector Delacruz
9 Kash Beauchamp
10 Darren Balsley
11 Doug Scherer
12 Carlos Diaz
13 Jose Escobar
14 Ken Rivers
15 Doug Linton
16 Chris Jones
17 Omar Bencomo
18 Correa Guzman
19 Dennis Jones
20 Steve Cummings
21 Gary McCune
22 Tim Ringler
23 John Poloni
24 Hugh Brinson
25 Tom Quinlan
26 Logo & checklist card

1988 Best Memphis Chicks

(Kansas City Royals, AA)

	MT	NR MT	EX
Complete Set:	7.00	5.25	2.75

1 Mel Stottlemyre
2 Rich Thompson
3 Mark Van Blaricom
4 Steve Morrow
5 Ken Bowen
6 Jacob Brumfield
7 Larry Acker
8 Matt Crouch
9 Casey Parson
10 Jim Campbell
11 Kevin Burrell
12 Luis Encarnacion
13 Mark Gillaspie
14 Ken Kravec
15 Randy Hunt
16 Mauro Gozzo
17 Charlie Culberson
18 Jose DeJesus
19 Matt Winters
20 Rick Lueken
21 Chito Martinez
22 Mike Miller
23 Ken Spratke
24 Thad Reece
25 Jose Rivera
26 Sal Rende
27 Tim McCarver Stadium
28 che, Checklist card

1988 Best Orlando Twins

(Minnesota Twins, AA)

	MT	NR MT	EX
Complete Set:	7.00	5.25	2.75

1 Derek Parks
2 Tim O'Connor
3 Duane Gustavson
4 Eddie Yanes
5 Mark Funderburk
6 Toby Nivens
7 Steven Comer
8 James Pittman
9 Mike Dyer
10 Jaime Williams
11 Joey Aragon
12 Gary Borg
13 Jeff Satzinger
14 Kevin Trudeau
15 Terry Jorgensen
16 Chris Forgione
17 German Gonzalez
18 Chip Hale
19 Jeff Reboulet
20 Larry Casian
21 Mike Dotzler
22 Rafael DeLima
23 Steve Gasser
24 Francisco Oliveras
25 Shannon Raybon
26 Wayne Hattaway
27 Bill Cutshall
28 Bernardo Brito
29 Checklist/Tinker Field

1988 Best San Antonio Missions

(Los Angeles Dodgers, AA)

	MT	NR MT	EX
Complete Set:	20.00	15.00	8.00

1 Ramon Martinez
2 Barry Wohler
3 Michael Pitz
4 Greg LaFever
5 Tony Mack
6 Domingo Michel
7 Michael Munoz
8 Wayne Kirby
9 Jim Kating
10 Mike Schweighoffer
11 Joe Kesselmark
12 Juan Bustabad
13 David Eichhorn
14 Manuel Francois
15 Darrin Fletcher
16 Walter McConnell
17 Phil Torres
18 Jose Manuel
19 Mike Huff
20 Joe Humphries
21 John Wetteland
22 Javier Ortiz
23 Kevin Kennedy
24 Juan Bell
25 Mark Sheehy
26 Luis Lopez
27 Pat Zachry
28 Logo & checklist card

1988 Best San Antonio Missions Ltd Edition

(Los Angeles Dodgers, AA) The set contains the same players as listed in the regular set. The fronts of the cards are silver & black and the backs of the cards are royal blue as opposed to the gray backs of the regular set. Only 1,300 of these sets were made.

	MT	NR MT	EX
Complete Set:	20.00	15.00	8.00

1988 Best San Bernadino Spirit

(Seattle Mariners, A)

Complete Set:	25.00	18.50	10.00

1 Ken Griffey Jr.
2 Don Reynolds
3 Lee Townsend
4 Ted Williams
5 Anthony Woods
6 Pat Rice
7 Jody Ryan
8 Rich DeLucia
9 William Diaz
10 Dan Disher
11 Ted Eldredge
12 Jerry Goff
13 Jose Tartabull
14 Ralph Dick
15 Jim Blueburg
16 Jim Bowie Jr.
17 Dave Burba
18 Clay Gunn
19 Keith Helton
20 Steve Hisey
21 Joe Kemp
22 Bryan King
23 Jeff Nelson
24 Rich Doyle
25 Todd Hayes
26 Mike Brocki
27 Bobby Cuellar
28 Checklist/Fiscalini Field

1988 Best San Bernadino Spirit Ltd Edition

This set features the same players as listed in the regular set. Fronts of cards are silver & black and the backs are royal blue as opposed to the gray backs of the regular set. Only 1,300 of these sets were made.

	MT	NR MT	EX
Complete Set:	35.00	26.25	14.50

1988 Best Springfield Cardinals

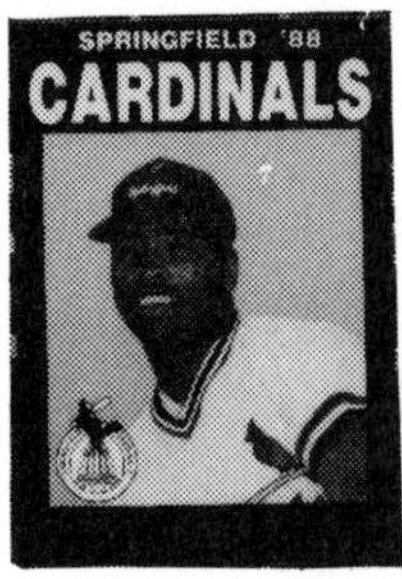

(St. Louis Cardinals, A)

	MT	NR MT	EX
Complete Set:	9.00	6.75	3.50

1 Robert Glisson
2 Mark Grater
3 Jeremy Hernandez
4 Michael Henry
5 Gregory Becker
6 Shawn Hathaway
7 William Bivens
8 Andrew Taylor
9 James Gibbs
10 Frank Postio
11 Bob Sudo
12 Charles Johnson
13 Bernard Gilkey
14 Raymond Lankford
15 David Payton
16 Michael Raziano
17 Alex Ojea
18 Stephen Meyer
19 Rodney Brewer
20 Steven Jeffers
21 Franklin Abreu
22 John Murphy
23 Gary Nichols
24 Ed Fulton
25 Chris Maloney
26 Mark De John
27 Brad Bluestone
28 Logo & checklist card

1988 Best/Pro Cards Baseball Am. AA Prospects

(AA)

	MT	NR MT	EX
Complete Set:	22.00	16.50	9.00

1AA Hensley Meulens (Albany)
2AA Mike Harkey (Pittsfield)
3AA Rob Ritchie (Glens Falls)
4AA Omar Vizquel (Vermont)
5AA Jerome Walton (Pittsfield)
6AA Chuck Malone (Reading)
7AA Tom Lampkin (Williamsport)

8AA Joe Girardi (Pittsfield)
9AA Kevin Wickander (Williamsport)

10AA Bill McGuire (Vermont)
11AA Pete Harnisch (Charlotte)
12AA Derek Park (Orlando)
13AA Alex Sanchez (Knoxville)
14AA Jose DeJesus (Memphis)
15AA Rafael DeLima (Orlando)
16AA Mark Lemke (Greenville)
17AA Chris Hammond (Chattanooga)

18AA German Gonzalez (Orlando)
19AA Dennis Jones (Knoxville)
20AA Francisco Cabrera (Knoxville)

21AA Ramon Martinez (San Antonio)

22AA Gary Sheffield (El Paso)
23AA Juan Bell (San Antonio)
24AA Greg Vaughn (El Paso)
25AA Kevin Brown (Tulsa)
26AA Mike Munoz (San Antonio)
27AA Trevor Wilson (Shreveport)
28AA John Wetteland (San Antonio)

29AA Jeff Manto (Midland)
30AA Buddy Bailey (Greenville)

1988 Bob's Photo Richmond Braves

(Atlanta Braves, AAA) (3-7/8" x 5")

	MT	NR MT	EX
Complete Set:	50.00	37.50	20.50

1 Joe Boever
2 Bean Stringfellow
3 Carlos Rios
4 Sid Akins
5 Lonnie Smith
6 Jeff Blauser
7 Derek Lilliquist
8 John Smoltz
9 Juan Espino
10 John Mizerock
11 Marty Clary
12 Mike Fischlin
13 David Justice
14 Dave Griffin
15 Tommy Greene
16 Alex Smith
17 Jeff Wetherby
18 Gary Eave
19 Greg Tubbs
20 Dave Miller
21 Kevin Coffman
22 Tommy Dunbar
23 John Grubb
24 Barry Jones

1988 Cain Elmira Pioneers

(Boston Red Sox, A)

	MT	NR MT	EX
Complete Set:	8.00	6.00	3.25

1 Logo card
2 Alberto Pratts
3 Steve Michael
4 Scott Taylor
5 Bernie Dzafic
6 Dan Kite
7 John Dolan
8 Peter Estrada
9 Tim Stange
10 Al Sanders
11 Carlos Rivera
12 Luis Dorante
13 John Flaherty
14 Pedro Matilla
15 David Monegro
16 Lou Munoz
17 Tim Naehring
18 Julio Rosario
19 Willie Tatum
20 Al Thornton
21 Chris Whitehead
22 Terry Marrs
23 Mickey Rivers Jr.
24 Larry Scannell
25 John Spencer
26 Brian Warfel
27 Bill Limoncelli
28 John Post
29 Dennis Robarge
30 Clyde Smoll

1988 Cal Cards Bakersfield Dodgers

(Los Angeles Dodgers, A)

	MT	NR MT	EX
Complete Set:	5.00	3.75	2.00

234 Jeff Brown
235 Dan Henley
236 John Knapp
237 Alan Lewis
238 Dan Montgomery
239 Jose Munoz
240 Jose Vizcaino
241 Amilcar Valdez
242 Adam Brown
243 Carlos Hernandez
244 Billy Argo
245 Jay Hornacek
246 John Beuder
247 Bruce Dostal
248 Steve Green
249 Wayne Kirby
250 Billy Brooks
251 Carlos Carrasco
252 Chris Cerny
253 Chris Gettler
254 Ken King
255 Todd Kroll
256 Lee Langley
257 Dan Pena
258 Tim Scott
259 Zak Shinall
260 Dennis Springer
261 John Wanish
262 Gary La Rogue
263 Guy Conti
264 Stan Johnston
265 Tommy Davis
266 Jack Patton
267 Rick Smith

1988 Cal Cards California League All Stars

(A)

	MT	NR MT	EX
Complete Set:	17.50	13.00	7.00

1 Jose Offerman
2 Eric Karros
3 Mark Merchant
4 Willie Banks
5 Lance Rice
6 Carlos Capellan
7 Jose Valentin
8 Dave Jacas
9 Braulio Castillo
10 Mike Humphreys
11 Wiley Lee
12 Ruben Gonzalez
13 Johnny Ard
14 Mike Goff
15 Jeff Hartsock
16 James Wray
17 Doug Simons
18 Jerry Brooks
19 Eddie Pye
20 Andy Skeels
21 Sean Snedeker
22 Steve Finken
23 Tim Johnson
24 Guy Conti
25 Scott Ullger
26 Tim Terrio
27 Bill Weiss
28 Don Drysdale
29 Charlie Montoyo
30 Jim Jones
31 Stan Royer
32 Bobby Jones
33 Darren Lewis
34 Gary Borg
35 Steve Hecht
36 Gary Nalls
37 John Dalfanz
38 Chris George
39 Mike Ignasiak
40 Kevin Meier
41 Joe Strong
42 Shawn Barton
43 Mark Dewey
44 Bill Savarino
45 John Jaha
46 Joe Kmak
47 Steve Lienhard
48 Greg Sparks
49 Duane Espy
50 Todd Oakes
51 Scott Wilson
52 Brent Howard
53 Erik DeSonnaville
54 Bob Brooks
55 George Ulrich
56 Joe Gagliardi

1988 Cal Cards Fresno Suns

(A)

	MT	NR MT	EX
Complete Set:	5.00	3.75	2.00

1 Tony Triplett
2 Marc Combs
3 Joe Mancini
4 Jon Hobbs
5 Ernie Young

6 Dan Simonds
7 Tracy Pancoski
8 Frank Bellino
9 Todd Hawkins
10 John Barry
11 Kim Flowers
12 Jim Malseed
13 Dave Nash
14 Richard Yagi
15 Hector Miyauchi
16 Steve Bowden
17 Frank Bryan
18 John Bilello
19 Rob Rowen
20 Anthony Tagi
21 Bullet Manabe
22 Chuck Higson
23 Gary Geiger
24 Rocco Buffalino
25 Brad Comstock
26 Dean Treanor
27 Tom Bell

1988 Cal Cards Modesto A;s

(Oakland A's, A)

	MT	NR MT	EX
Complete Set:	6.50	4.75	2.50

56 David Veres
57 David Shotkoski
58 Ray Young
59 Kevin Williamson
60 Jeff Glover
61 Mark Beavers
62 Gary Gorski
63 Jeff Kopyta
64 Scott Chiamparino
65 Mark Stancel
66 Steve Maye
67 Dann Howitt
68 Jorge Brito
69 Drew Stratton
70 David Finley
71 Keith Watkins
72 Ron Coomer
73 Gerry Barragan
74 Luis Martinez
75 Bill Savarino
76 Heriberto Done
77 Randy Randle
78 Francis Ciprian
79 Patrick Gilbert
80 Vince Teixeira
81 Jeff Newman
82 Pete Richert
83 Dave Hollenback

1988 Cal Cards Palm Springs Angels

(California Angels, A)

	MT	NR MT	EX
Complete Set:	6.50	4.75	2.50

85 Colin Charland
86 Mike Erb
87 John Fritz
88 Scott Kannenberg
89 Jim Long
90 Luis Merejo
91 Rich Morehouse
92 Jeff Richardson
93 Jose Tapia
94 Bill Vanderwel
95 Dan Ward
96 Edgar Alfonzo
97 Ruben Amaro
98 Mike Anderson
99 Mark Baca
100 Jeff Barns
101 Scott Cerny
102 Cris Cron
103 Ted Dyson
104 Jim McAnany
105 Mike Musolino
106 Gary Nalls
107 John Orton
108 Reed Peters
109 Giovanny Reyes
110 Paul Sorrento
111 Glenn Washington
112 Bill Lachemann

1988 Cal Cards Reno Silver Sox

(No affiliation) (A)

	MT	NR MT	EX
Complete Set:	5.00	3.75	2.00

268 Alan Fowlkes
269 Elvin Rivera
270 Tony LaCerra
271 Reggie Glover
272 Bill Shamblin
273 Scott Madden
274 Joe Strong
275 John Savage
276 Frank Mutz
277 Mike Garner
278 Kinney Sims 279.00
279 Jamie Allison
280 Jim Aylward
281 Cary Grubb
282 Chris Holmes
283 Robbie Rogers
284 Mike Rountree
285 Joe Ortiz
286 Gregg Ward
287 Dave Liddell
288 Jim Pace
289 Pete Houston
290 Fred Carter
291 Nate Oliver

1988 Cal Cards Riverside Red Wave

(A)

	MT	NR MT	EX
Complete Set:	5.00	3.75	2.00

206 Kevin Armstrong
207 James Austin
208 Ricky Bones
209 Rafael Chaves
210 Brian Harrison
211 Richard Holsman
212 James Lewis
213 Steve Loubier
214 Bill Marx
215 Brian Wood
216 Brian Brooks
217 Paul Faries
218 Kevin Farmer
219 Greg Hall
220 Kevin Garner
221 Steve Hendricks
222 Dave Hollins
223 Tom Levasseur
224 Terry McDevitt
225 Warren Newsom
226 Andy Skeels
227 Bill Taylor
228 Pat Jelks
229 Tony Torchia
230 William Blount
231 Jim Danile

1988 Cal Cards San Bernadino Spirit

(Seattle Mariners, A)

	MT	NR MT	EX
Complete Set:	35.00	26.25	14.50

28 Bryan King
29 Steve Murray
30 Jim Bowie Jr.
31 Dan Disher
32 Clay Gunn
33 Jerry Goff
34 Ken Griffey Jr.
35 Joe Kemp
36 Jose Tartabull
37 William Diaz
38 Ted Williams
39 Steve Hisey
40 Mike Brocki
41 Ted Eldredge
42 Jody Ryan
43 Pat Rice
44 Keith Helton
45 Howard Townsend
46 Tim McLain
47 Jim Blueberg
48 Jeff Nelson
49 David Burba
50 Rich DeLucia
51 Todd Hayes
52 Rich Doyle
53 Ralph Dick
54 Bobby Cuellar

1988 Cal Cards San Jose Giants

(San Francisco Giants, A)

	MT	NR MT	EX
Complete Set:	5.00	3.75	2.00

116 Rich Aldrete
117 Paul Blair
118 Greg Conner
119 Tad Hanyuda
120 Joe Jodo
121 Gary Jones
122 Mark Leonard
123 Jim McNamara
124 William Mijares
125 Scott Murray
126 Dave Patterson
127 Gregg Ritchie
128 Tod Ronson
129 Ken Suzuki
130 Daron Connelly
131 Eric Gunderson
132 Gil Heredia
133 Koji Maeda
134 Tom Meagher
135 Kevin Meier
136 Eric Pilkington
137 Doug Robertson
138 Russ Swan
139 Ray Velasquez
140 Masa Yamamoto
141 Duane Espy
142 Sam Hirose
143 Todd Oakes
144 Lance Hutchins

1988 Cal Cards Stockton Ports

(Milwaukee Brewers, A)

	MT	NR MT	EX
Complete Set:	6.50	4.75	2.50

175 Steve Monson
176 Ron Romanick
177 Doug henry
178 Brian Stone
179 Randy Veres
180 Angel Miranda
181 Alan Sadler
182 Jaime Navarro
183 Narcisco Elvira
184 Carl Moraw
185 Keith Fleming
186 Brian Drahman
187 Danny Fitzpatrick
188 Gil Villanueva
189 Tim McIntosh
190 Robert Jones
191 Mark Aguilar
192 Robert Smith
193 John Jaha
194 Shon Ashley
195 Dave Taylor
196 Sandy Guerrero
197 Bill Spiers
198 Angel Rodriguez
199 Charlie Montoyo
200 Ruben Escalera
201 Rob Derksen
202 Dave Huppert
203 Jay Williams
204 Don Miller
205 Dan Chapman

1988 Cal Cards Visalia Oaks

(Minnesota Twins, A)

	MT	NR MT	EX
Complete Set:	5.00	3.75	2.00

145 Kenny Davis
146 Ken Morgan
147 Mike Randle
148 Joey Zellner
149 Tim Arnold
150 John Eccles
151 Shawn Gilbert
152 Kenny Grant
153 Marty Lanoux
154 Scott Leius
155 Jose Marzan
156 Ed Naveda
157 A.J. Richardson
158 Doug Snyder
159 Larry Blackwell
160 Mike Reddings

161 Steve Scanlon
162 Bob Strube
163 Jim Williams
164 Troy James
165 Paul Abbott
166 Jeff Bronkey
167 Mark Guthrie
168 Dana Heinle
169 Doug Kline
170 Scott Ullger
171 Bruce Bucz
172 Andy Seidensticker
173 Mark Jones
174 Gorman Heimueller

1988 CMC Albuquerque Dukes

(Los Angeles Dodgers, AAA)

	MT	NR MT	EX
Complete Set:	6.00	4.50	2.50

1 Shawn Hillegas
2 Stan Kyles
3 Bill Krueger
4 Ray Searage
5 Tony Arnold
6 Bill Brennan
7 Dennis Burtt
8 Tim Crews
9 Mike Hartley
10 Chuck Hensley
11 Hector Heredia
12 Chris Gwynn
13 Hinshaw George
14 Mike Ramsey
15 Jon Debus
16 Mike Sharperson
17 Tracy Woodson
18 Mike Devereaux
19 Jose Gonzalez
20 John Gibbons
21 Gil Reyes
22 Shanie Dugas
23 Mariano Duncan
24 Steve Garcia
25 Terry Collins

1988 CMC Buffalo Bisons

(Pittsburgh Pirates, AAA)

	MT	NR MT	EX
Complete Set:	7.00	5.25	2.75

1 Logan Easley
2 Stan Fansler
3 Brett Gideon
4 Dave Johnson
5 Randy Kramer
6 Morris Madden
7 Bob Patterson
8 Dave Rucker
9 Dorn Taylor
10 Scott Medvin
11 Benny Distefano
12 Tommy Gregg
13 Tom Romano
14 Bernie Tatis
15 Denny Gonzalez
16 Bryan Little
17 Jim Reboulet
18 Rico Rossy
19 Tom Prince
20 Orestes Destrade
21 Felix Fermin
22 Dave Sax
23 Skeeter Barnes
24 Stan Cliburn
25 Rocky Bridges

1988 CMC Calgary Cannons

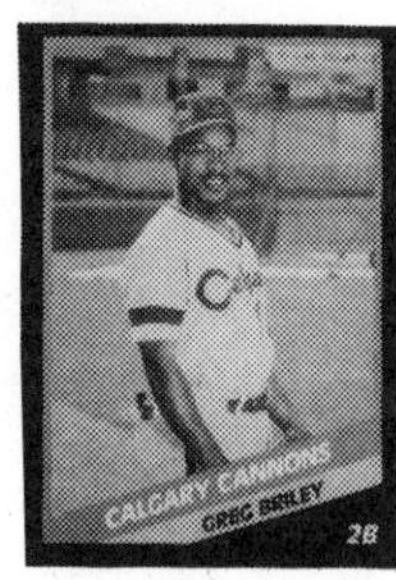

(Seattle Mariners, AAA)

	MT	NR MT	EX
Complete Set:	7.50	5.50	3.00

1 Darren Burroughs
2 Paul Schneider
3 Rich Monteleone
4 Dennis Powell
5 Jay Baller
6 Mike Christ
7 Jim Walker
8 Matt West
9 Mike Schooler
10 Rod Scurry
11 Donell Nixon
12 Phil Ouellette
13 Greg Briley
14 Dave Cochrane
15 Brian Giles
16 Edgar Martinez
17 John Christensen
18 Dave Hengel
19 Nelson Simmons
20 Mike Wishnevski
21 Roger Hansen
22 Doug Merrifield
23 Mike Watters
24 Bill Plummer
25 Dan Warthen

1988 CMC Colorado Springs Sky Sox

(Cleveland Indians, AAA)

	MT	NR MT	EX
Complete Set:	7.00	5.50	3.00

1 Darrel Akerfelds
2 Mike Brown
3 Don Gordon
4 Jeff Kaiser
5 Ron Mathis
6 Jon Perlman
7 Reggie Ritter
8 Rick Rodrigez
9 Charlie Scott
10 Joe Skalski
11 John Stefano
12 Ron Tingley
13 Mark Higgins
14 Tommy Hinzo
15 Don Lovell
16 Domingo Ramos
17 Eddie Williams
18 Paul Zuvella
19 Rod Allen
20 Terry Francona
21 Luis Medina
22 Randy Washington
23 Reggie Williams
24 Steve Swisher
25 Aurelio Rodriguez

1988 CMC Columbus Clippers

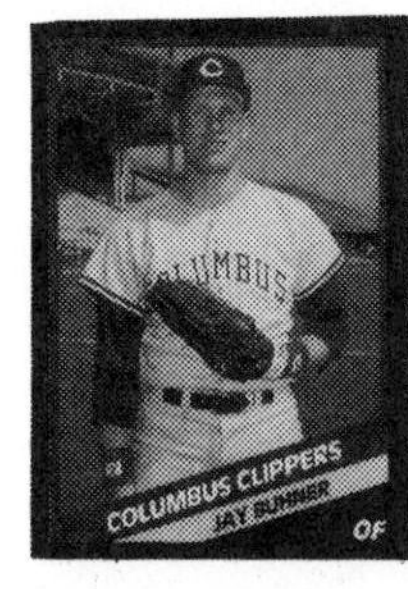

(New York Yankees, AAA)

	MT	NR MT	EX
Complete Set:	8.00	6.00	3.25

1 Pat Clements
2 Clay Parker
3 Scott Nielsen
4 Bill Fulton
5 Matt Harrison
6 Steve Shields
7 Hipolito Pena
8 Eric Schmidt
9 Mike Kinnuenen
10 Rick Langford
11 Bob Geren
12 Jamie Nelson
13 Berton Pena
14 Rob Lambert
15 Alvaro Espinoza
16 Pete Dalena
17 Randy Velarde
18 Jeff Moronko
19 Turner Ward
20 Hal Morris
21 Casey Close
22 Cliff Speck
23 Jay Buhner
24 Chris Alvarez
25 Bucky Dent
26 Governors Cup

1988 CMC Denver Zephyrs

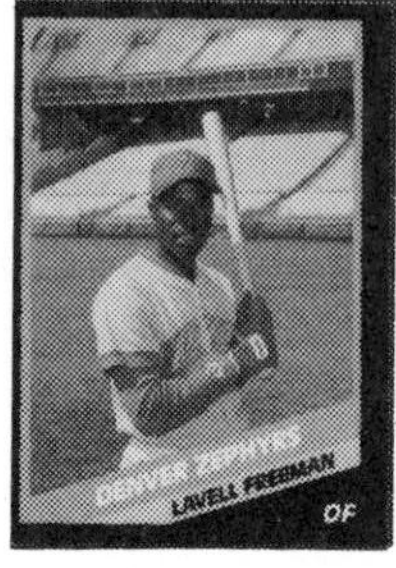

(Milwaukee Brewers, AAA)

	MT	NR MT	EX
Complete Set:	7.50	5.50	3.00

1 Mark Knudson
2 Mike Konderla
3 Alex Madrid
4 John Miglio
5 Paul Mirabella
6 Tim Watkins
7 Jay Aldrich
8 Don August
9 Mark Ciardi
10 Tom Filer
11 Tim Pyznarski
12 German Rivera
13 Billy Jo Robidoux
14 Keith Smith
15 Charlie O'Brian
16 Ronn Reynolds
17 Billy Bates
18 Kiki Diaz
19 Todd Brown
20 Lavell Freeman
21 Brad Komminsk
22 Steve Stanicek
23 Darryel Walters
24 Darryl Hamilton
25 Duffy Dyer

1988 CMC Edmonton Trappers

(California Angels, AAA)

	MT	NR MT	EX
Complete Set:	7.50	5.50	3.00

1 Terry Clark
2 Mike Cook
3 Jack Lazorko
4 Vance Lovelace
5 Bryan Harvey
6 Urbano Lugo
7 Joe Johnson
8 Philip Venturino
9 Marty Reed
10 Barry Dacus
11 Miguel Alicea
12 Darrell Miller
13 Pete Coachman
14 Stan Holmes
15 Bob Miscik
16 Brian Brady
17 Kent Anderson
18 Doug Davis
19 Edwin Marquez
20 Joe Redfield
21 Jim Eppard
22 Tom Kotchman
23 Dante Bichette
24 Mark Doran
25 Kevin King

1988 CMC Indianapolis Indians

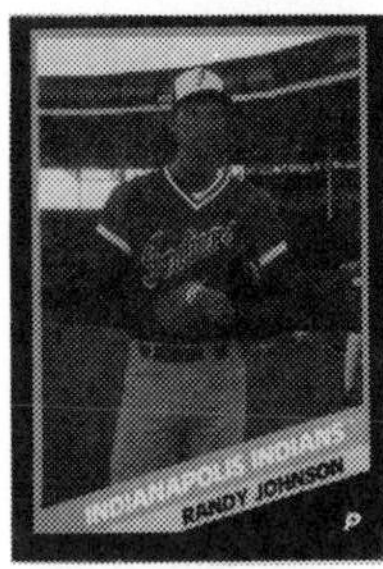

(Montreal Expos, AAA)

	MT	NR MT	EX
Complete Set:	7.50	5.50	3.00

1 Randy Johnson
2 Kurt Kepshire
3 Bob Sebra
4 Steve Shirley
5 Tim Barrett
6 Jeff Fischer
7 Mike Smith
8 Sergio Valdez
9 Brian Holman
10 Rex Hudler
11 Johnny Paredes
12 Razor Shines
13 Billy Moore
14 Otis Nixon
15 Alonzo Powell
16 Ron Shepherd
17 Tim Hulett
18 Nelson Santovenia
19 Wilfredo Tejada
20 Mike Berger
21 Jack Daugherty
22 Garrett Nago
23 Mel Houston
24 Joe Sparks
25 Mike Colbern, Joe Kerrigan, Nelson Norman

1988 CMC Iowa Cubs

(Chicago Cubs, AAA)

	MT	NR MT	EX
Complete Set:	17.50	13.00	7.00

1 Mike Capel
2 Len Damian
3 Jeff Pico
4 Laddie Renfroe
5 Bob Tewksbury
6 Jeff Hirsch
7 Joe Kraemer
8 Bill Landrum
9 Dave Masters
10 Rich Surhoff
11 Roger Williams
12 Damon Berryhill
13 Bruce Crabbe
14 Mark Grace
15 Brian Guinn
16 Paul Noce
17 Phil Stephenson
18 Greg Tabor
19 Doug Dascenzo
20 Dave Meier
21 Dwight Smith
22 Gary Varsho
23 Bill Bathe
24 Pete Mackanin
25 Jim Wright

1988 CMC Las Vegas Stars

(San Diego Padres, AAA)

	MT	NR MT	EX
Complete Set:	10.00	7.50	4.00

1 Joe Bitker
2 Keith Comstock
3 Greg Harris
4 Joel McKeon
5 Pete Roberts
6 Todd Simmons
7 Ed Vosberg
8 Kevin Towers
9 Joe Lynch
10 Shane Mack
11 Thomas Howard
12 Jerald Clark
13 Randy Byers
14 Bip Roberts
15 Brad Pounders
16 Rob Nelson
17 Gary Green
18 Joey Cora
19 Mike Brumley
20 Roberto Alomar
21 Bruce Bochy
22 Sandy Alomar, Jr.
23 Tom Brassil
24 Steve Smith
25 Sonny Siebert

1988 CMC Louisville Redbirds

(St Louis Cardinals, AAA)

	MT	NR MT	EX
Complete Set:	9.00	6.75	3.50

1 John Costello
2 Dick Grapenthin
3 John Martin
4 Randy O'Neal
5 Tim Conroy
6 Gibson Alba
7 Rich Buonantony
8 Chris Carpenter (Cris)
9 Dave Rajsich
10 Jim Leopold
11 Alex Cole
12 Bill Lyons
13 Tim Jones
14 David Green
15 Craig Wilson
16 John Murphy
17 Duane Walker
18 Mike Fitzgerald
19 Carl Ray Stephens
20 Luis Alicea
21 Sal Agostinelli
22 Roy Silver
23 Mark Dougherty
24 Joe Pettini
25 Mike Jorgenson (Jorgensen)

1988 CMC Maine Phillies

(Philedelphia Phillies, AAA)

	MT	NR MT	EX
Complete Set:	9.00	6.75	3.50

1 Marty Bystrom
2 Travis Chambers
3 Barney Nugent
4 Marvin Freeman
5 Brad Brink
6 John McLarnan
7 Mike Shelton
8 Tom Newell
9 Bob Scanlan
10 Todd Frohwirth
11 Ricky Jordon (Jordan)
12 John Russell
13 Shane Turner
14 Ron Jones
15 Rick Lundblade
16 Tommy Barrett
17 Kenny Jackson
18 Greg Jelks
19 Ramon Henderson
20 Keith Miller
21 Jim Olander
22 Kevin Ward
23 George Culver
24 Ramon Aviles
25 Joe Lefebvre

1988 CMC Nashville Sounds

(Cincinnati Reds, AAA)

	MT	NR MT	EX
Complete Set:	7.00	5.25	2.75

1 Jack Armstrong
2 Tim Birtsas
3 Norm Charlton
4 Rob Dibble
5 Jeff Gray
6 Mike Jones
7 Hugh Kemp
8 Rob Lopez
9 Steve Oliverio
10 Pat Pacillo
11 Mike Roesler
12 Lenny Harris
13 Greg Monda
14 Luis Quinones
15 Dan Boever
16 Doug Gwosdz
17 Joe Oliver
18 Marty Brown
19 Scott Earl
20 Dave Klipstein
21 Ron Roenicke
22 Van Snider
23 Jack Lind
24 Wayne Garland
25 John Young

1988 CMC Oklahoma City 89'ers

(Texas Rangers, AAA)

	MT	NR MT	EX
Complete Set:	6.00	4.50	2.50

1 Scott Anderson
2 Dwayne Henry
3 Scott May
4 Craig McMurtry
5 Gary Mielke
6 Ferguson Jenkins
7 Ray Hayward
8 Ed Vande Berg
9 Tony Fossas
10 Rick Odekirk
11 Darrell Whitaker
12 Otto Gonzalez
13 Gar Millay
14 Jose Tolentino
15 Bill Merrifield
16 Barbaro Garbey
17 Larry Klein
18 Jeff Kunkel
19 Tom O'Malley
20 Dan Rohn
21 Don Werner
22 Robby Wine
23 Jim St. Laurent
24 James Steels
25 Toby Harrah

1988 CMC Pawtucket Red Sox

(Boston Red Sox, AAA)

	MT	NR MT	EX
Complete Set:	7.00	5.25	2.75

1 Rob Woodward
2 Mike Rochford
3 Mitch Johnson
4 John Leister
5 Andy Araujo
6 Zack Crouch
7 Steve Curry
8 Eric Hetzel
9 Tom Bolton
10 Dana Kiecker
11 Randy Kutcher
12 Bill McInnis
13 Glenn Hoffman
14 Tony Cleary
15 Chris Cannizzaro
16 Pat Dodson
17 Angel Gonzalez
18 Mike Mesh
19 Gary Miller-Jones
20 Carlos Quintana
21 Dana Williams
22 Gary Tremblay
23 Scott Wade
24 Ed Nottie
25 Mark Meleski

1988 CMC Portland Beavers

(Minnesota Twins, AAA)

	MT	NR MT	EX
Complete Set:	7.00	5.25	2.75

1 Andy Anderson
2 Karl Best
3 T.R. Bryden
4 Jeff Bumgarner
5 Mark Portugal
6 Roy Smith
7 Ray Soff
8 Freddie Toliver
9 Jim Winn
10 Jim Davins
11 Brian Harper
12 Steve Liddle
13 Doug Baker
14 Ricky Jones
15 Kelvin Torve
16 Brad Bierly
17 Eric Bullock
18 Winston Ficklin
19 Chris Pittaro
20 Vic Rodriguez
21 Robby Ralston
22 John Moses
23 Phil Wilson
24 Jim Mahoney
25 Jim Shellenback

1988 CMC Omaha Royals

(Kansas City Royals, AAA)

	MT	NR MT	EX
Complete Set:	6.00	4.50	2.50

1 Rick Anderson
2 Luis Aquino
3 Bob Buchanan
4 Steve Fireovid
5 Jerry Don Gleaton
6 Al Hargesheimer
7 Jeff Montgomery
8 Tom Mullen
9 Bill Swaggerty
10 Rondin Johnson
11 Israel Sanchez
12 Nick Capra
13 Mike Loggins
14 Gary Thurman
15 Jeff Schulz
16 Dave Owen
17 Dann Bilardello
18 Larry Owen
19 Tom Dodd
20 Buddy Biancalana
21 Joe Citari
22 Luis de los Santos
23 Rich Dubee
24 Jose Castro
25 Glenn Ezell

1988 CMC Phoenix Firebirds

(San Francisco Giants, AAA)

	MT	NR MT	EX
Complete Set:	10.00	7.50	4.00

1 Randy Bockus
2 John Burkett
3 Dennis Cook
4 Roger Mason
5 Jeff Brantley
6 Mike Hogan
7 Brian Ohnoutka
8 Roger Samuels
9 Randy McCament
10 Terry Mullholland
11 Ed Puikunas
12 Kirt Manwaring
13 Bobby Ramos
14 Angel Escobar
15 Charlie Hayes
16 Tony Perezchica
17 Mark Wasinger
18 Matt Williams
19 Alan Cockrell
20 Everett Graham
21 Rusty Tillman
22 Ty Dabney
23 Deron McCue
24 Wendell Kim
25 Tim Blackwell, Marty DeMarrite

1988 CMC Richmond Braves

(Atlanta Braves, AAA)

	MT	NR MT	EX
Complete Set:	7.00	5.25	2.75

1 Tommy Green
2 Derek Lilliquist
3 John Smoltz
4 Bean Stringfellow
5 Gary Eave
6 Juan Eichelberger
7 Sid Akins
8 Jose Alvarez
9 Joe Boever
10 Marty Clary
11 Todd Dewey
12 Ron Gant
13 Alex Smith
14 Lonnie Smith
15 Greg Tubbs
16 Jeff Wetherby
17 David Justice
18 Carlos Rios
19 Dave Griffin
20 Juan Espino
21 John Mizerock
22 Jeff Blauser
23 Jim Beauchamp
24 Leo Mazzone
25 Clarence Jones

1988 CMC Rochester Red Wings

(Baltimore Orioles, AAA)

	MT	NR MT	EX
Complete Set:	7.00	5.25	2.75

1 Jeff Ballard
2 Eric Bell
3 Jose Mesa
4 Mark Bowden
5 Bob Gibson
6 John Habyan
7 Mike Griffin
8 Dickie Noles
9 Bill Scherrer
10 Jay Tibbs
11 Matt Cimo
12 Dale Berra
13 Chris Padget
14 Jerry Narron
15 Keith Hughes
16 Ron Salcedo
17 David Lee Smith
18 Pete Stanicek
19 Craig Worthington
20 Sherwin Cinjtje
21 Mickey Tettleton
22 Tito Landrum
23 Vic Mata
24 Johnny Oates
25 Curt Motton

1988 CMC Syracuse Chiefs

(Toronto Blue Jays, AAA)

	MT	NR MT	EX
Complete Set:	7.00	5.25	2.75

1 Steve Davis
2 Randy Holland
3 Colin McLaughlin
4 Jose Nunez
5 Mark Ross
6 Norm Tonucci
7 Bob Shirley
8 Cliff Young
9 Doug Bair
10 Jack O'Connor
11 Frank Wills
12 Luis Reyna
13 Geronimo Berroa
14 Rob Ducey
15 Glenallen Hill
16 Sal Butera
17 Eric Yelding
18 Greg Myers
19 Otis Green
20 Kelly Heath
21 Alexis Infante
22 Chris Shaddy
23 Hector Torres
24 Bob Bailor
25 Galen Cisco

1988 CMC Tacoma Tigers

(Oakland A's, AAA)

	MT	NR MT	EX
Complete Set:	7.50	5.50	3.00

1 Rich Bordi
2 Todd Burns
3 Charlie Corbell
4 Reese Lambert
5 Tim Meeks
6 Jeff Zaske
7 Jim Corsi
8 Jeff Shaver
9 Brian Snyder
10 Bob Stoddard
11 Lance Blakenship
12 Tyler Brilinski
13 Ed Jurak
14 Wayne Krenchicki
15 Roy Johnson
16 Luis Polonia
17 Alex Sanchez
18 Matt Sinatro
19 Andre Robertson
20 Kevin Sliwinski
21 Jimmy Jones
22 Orlando Mercado
23 Gary Jones
24 Felix Jose
25 Joe Xavier

NOTE: A card number in parentheses ( ) indicates the card set is unnumbered.

1988 CMC Tidewater Tides

(New York Mets, AAA)

	MT	NR MT	EX
Complete Set:	25.00	18.50	10.00

1 Jack Savage
2 David West
3 Jeff Innis
4 Tim Drummond
5 Tom Edens
6 Steve Frey
7 Tom McCarthy
8 John Mitchell
9 Jose Roman
10 Randy Niemann
11 Wally Whitehurst
12 Phil Lombardi
13 Greg Olson
14 Ken Dowell
15a Gregg Jeffries (misspelled)
15b Greg Jefferies (corrected)
16 Darren Reed
17 Joaquin Contreras
18 Andre David
19 Jeff McKnight
20 Keith Miller
21 Steve Springer
22 Mark Carreon
23 Tim Tolman
24 Mike Cubbage
25 John Cumberland
26 Rich Miler

1988 CMC Toledo Mud Hens

(Detroit Tigers, AAA)

	MT	NR MT	EX
Complete Set:	6.00	4.50	2.50

1 Dave Beard
2 Stan Clarke
3 Don Schulze
4 Steve Searcy
5 Eric King
6 Roman Pena
7 Mike Trujillo
8 Dave Cooper
9 Paul Cherry
10 John Duffy
11 Mark Huisman
12 Billy Bean
13 Scott Lusader
14 Doug Strange
15 Jeff Reynolds
16 Benny Ruis
17 Pedro Chavez
18 Rey Palacios
19 Chris Hoiles
20 Paul Felix
21 Tim Leiper
22 Donnie Rowland
23 Pete Rice
24 Mike Brown
25 Pat Corrales

1988 CMC Triple A All Stars

(AAA)

	MT	NR MT	EX
Complete Set:	17.50	13.00	7.00

1 Bill Bathe (Iowa)
2 Luis De Los Santos (Omaha)
3 Johnny Paredes (Indianapolis)
4 Tom O'Malley (Oklahoma City)
5 Felix Fermin (Buffalo)
6 Billy Moore (Indianapolis)
7 Ronaldo Roomes (Iowa)
8 Van Snider (Nashville)
9 German Rivera (Denver)
10 Lavell Freeman (Denver)
11 Dorn Taylor (Buffalo)
12 Norm Charlton (Nashville)
13 Randy Johnson (Indianapolis)
14 Gary Sheffield (Denver)
15 Mike Harkey (Iowa)
16 Bob Geren (Columbus)
17 Dave Griffin (Richmond)
18 Tom Barrett (Maine)
19 Craig Worthington (Rochester)
20 Randy Velarde (Columbus)
21 Steve Finley (Rochester)
22 Carlos Quintana (Pawtucket)
23 Mark Carreon (Tidewater)
24 Lonnie Smith (Richmond)
25 Steve Searcy (Toledo)
26 Mark Huismann (Toledo)
27 Gregg Jefferies (Tidewater)
28 Ricky Jordan (Maine)
29 Dave West (Tidewater)
30 John Smoltz (Richmond)
31 Sandy Alomar Jr. (Las Vegas)
32 Francisco Melendez (Phoenix)
33 Mike Woodard (Vancouver)
34 Edgar Martinez (Calgary)
35 Mike Brumley (Las Vegas)
36 Mike Deverax (Albuquerque)
37 Cameron Drew (Tucson)
38 Luis Medina (Colorado Springs)
39 Rod Allen (Colorado Springs)
40 George Henshaw (Albuquerque)
41 Bill Brenna (Albuquerque)
42 Bill Krueger (Albuquerque)
43 Karl Best (Portland)
44 Juan Bell (Albuquerque)
45 Ramon Martinez (Albuquerque)

1988 CMC Tucson Toros

(Houston Astros, AAA)

	MT	NR MT	EX
Complete Set:	7.50	5.50	3.00

1 Manny Hernandez
2 Anthony Kelley
3 Mike Loynd
4 Dave Meads
5 Kevin Hagen
6 Rafael Montalvo
7 Jose Cano
8 Rocky Childress
9 Jeff Datz
10 Luis DeLeon
11 Ken Caminiti
12 Glenn Carpenter
13 Nelson Rood
14 Cameron Drew
15 Craig Biggio
16 Alex Trevino
17 Karl Allaire
18 Joe Mikulik
19 John Fishel
20 Louie Meadows
21 Jim Weaver
22 Pat Keedy
23 Craig Smajstrla
24 Bob Didier
25 Eddie Watt

1988 CMC Vancouver Canadians

(Chicago White Sox, AAA)

	MT	NR MT	EX
Complete Set:	6.00	4.50	2.50

1 Jeff Bittiger
2 Joel Davis
3 Steve Rosenberg
4 Carl Willis
5 Ed Wojna
6 Ken Patterson
7 Adam Peterson
8 Grady Hall
9 Donn Pall
10 Jack Hardy
11 Greg Hibbard
12 Kelly Paris
13 Santiago Garcia
14 Mike Woodwood
15 Ron Karkovice
16 Bill Lindsey
17 Russ Morman
18 Troy Thomas
19 Mike Yastrzemski
20 James Randall
21 Jeff Schafer
22 Daryl Sconiers
23 Jorge Alcazar
24 Dave Gallagher
25 Marlin McPhail

1988 Donn Jennings Southern League All Stars

(AA)

Complete Set:	MT	NR MT	EX
	6.00	4.50	2.50

1 Matt Winters (Memphis)
2 Kevin Burrell (Memphis)
3 Steve Howard (Huntsville)
4 Mike Bordick (Huntsville)
5 Keith Lockhart (Chattanooga)
6 Darrell Pruitt (Chattanooga)
7 Matt Merullo (Birmingham)
8 Jerry Bertolani (Birmingham)
9 Tim Dulin (Charlotte)
10 Carlo Columbino (Columbus)
11 Rafael Delima (Orlando)
12 Derek Parks (Orlando)
13 Bernardo Brito (Orlando)
14 Barry Jones (Greenville)
15 Mark Lemke (Greenville)
16 Ed Whited (Greenville)
17 Drew Denson (Greenville)
18 Jeff Huson (Jacksonville)
19 Bob Caffrey (Jackson)
20 Randy Braun (Jackson)
21 Armando Moreno (Jackson)
22 Frrancisco Cabreba (Knoxville)
23 Webster Garrison (Knoxville)
24 Junior Felix (Knoxville)
25 Domingo Martinez (Knoxville)
26 Alex Sanchez (Knoxville)
27 Steve Cummings (Knoxville)
28 Kevin Blankenship (Greenville)
29 Larry Casian (Orlando)
30 German Gonzales (Orlando)
31 Brian Meyer (Columbus)
32 Pete Harnisch (Charlotte)
33 Brian Householder (Charlotte)
34 Tom Drees (Birmingham)
35 Joe Lazor (Chattanooga)
36 Chris Hammond (Chattanooga)
37 Joe Bruno (Chattanooga)
38 Rico Petrocelli (Birmingham)
39 Tommy Thompson (Jacksonville)
40 Nardi Contreres (Jacksonville)

1988 Grand Slam Arkansas Travelers

(St. Louis Cardinals, AA)

Complete Set:	MT	NR MT	EX
	10.00	7.50	4.00

1 Rick Colbert
2 Brad Henderson
3 Steve Engel
4 Jim Riggleman
5 Jeff Fassero
6 Bien Figueroa
7 Todd Zeile
8 Tom Baine
9 Bob Faron
10 Mauricio Nunez
11 Ken Infante
12 Howard Hilton
13 Brett Harrison
14 Matt Kinzer
15 Jesus Mendez
16 Jim Fregosi
17 Benito Malave
18 Mike Sassone
19 Mike Robinson
20 Mike Robertson
21 Mike Perez
22 Jim Puzey
23 Dave Osteen
24 Jeff Oyster
25 Mike Senne

1988 Grand Slam Beloit Brewers

(Milwaukee Brewers, A)

Complete Set:	MT	NR MT	EX
	5.00	3.75	2.00

1 Gomer Hodge
2 Gary Robson
3 Jim Poulin
4 Frank Bolick
5 Tim Raley
6 Dan Adriance
7 Charlie McGrew
8 Juan Uribe
9 Bob Simonson
10 Mark Chapman
11 Bob Sobczyk
12 Bryan Foster
13 Kent Hetrick
14 Torricelli Tim
15 Mike Guerrero
16 Curt Krippner
17 Tim Wahl
18 Leonardo Perez
19 Dave Nilsson
20 Dan Peters
21 Randy Moore
22 Mike Whitlock
23 Chris Cassels
24 Steve Sparks
25 Chris Johnson

1988 Grand Slam Columbia Mets

(New York Mets, A)

Complete Set:	MT	NR MT	EX
	6.00	4.50	2.50

1 Butch Hobson
2 Pete Bauer
3 Rick Durant
4 Rocky Elli
5 Eric Hillman
6 Steve Larose
7 Juan Marina
8 James McAnarney
9 Mike Miller
10 Kevin Ponder
11 Julio Valera
12 Javier Gonzalez
13 David Lau
14 Alex Diaz
15 Alex Jimenez
16 David Joiner
17 Rodney Murrell
18 Fred Hina
19 Manny Mantrana
20 Scott Spoolstra
21 Rob Lemle
22 Terry McDaniel
23 Danny Naughton
24 Jaime Roseboro
25 Scott Jaster
26 Chris Donnels
28 Joel Horlen

1988 Grand Slam Jackson Mets

(New York Mets, AA)

Complete Set:	MT	NR MT	EX
	6.00	4.50	2.50

1 Ron Gideon
2 Zoilo Sanchez
3 Geary Jones
4 Tucker Ashford
5 Glenn Abbott
6 Kyle Hartshorn
7 Tom Doyle
8 Chris Jelic
9 Mike Santiago
10 Jeff Gardner
11 Virgil Conley
12 Craig Shipley
13 Rich Rodriguez
14 Brian Given
15 Blaine Beatty
16 Todd Welborn
17 Miguel Roman
18 Manny Salinas
19 Shawn Barton
20 Joaquin Contreras
21 Angelo Cuevas
22 Mickey Weston
23 Kevin Tapani
24 Felix Perdomo
25 Alan Hayden

1988 Grand Slam Midland Angels

(California Angels, AA)

Complete Set:	MT	NR MT	EX
	6.00	4.50	2.50

1 Max Oliveras
2 Kurt Walker
3 Tim Kelly
4 Vinicio Cedeno
5 Shane Young
6 Tim Burcham
7 Chris Collins
8 Frank Dimichelle
9 Todd Eggertsen
10 Mike Fetters
11 Colby Ward
12 Steve McGuire
13 Mike Knapp
14 Erik Pappas
15 Tom Alfredson
16 Danny Grunhard
17 C.L. Penigar
18 Lee Stevens
19 Jesus Alfaro
20 David Martinez
21 Jeff Manto
22 Jim McCollom
23 Jim Thomas
24 Craig Gerber
25 Norm Carrasco

1988 Grand Slam Midwest League All Stars

(A)

Complete Set:	MT	NR MT	EX
	12.50	9.50	5.25

1 Mark Owens (Clinton)
2 Andres Santana (Clinton)
3 Erik Johnson (Clinton)
4 Jamie Cooper (Clinton)
5 Rod Beck (Clinton)
6 Stephen Connolly (Clinton)
7 Tom Hostetler (Clinton)
8 Pete Beeler (Cedar Rapids)
9 Greg Lonigro (Cedar Rapids)
10 Jeff Forney (Cedar Rapids)
11 Bill Dodd (Cedar Rapids)
12 Butch Henry (Cedar Rapids)
13 Darrell Rodgers (Cedar Rapids)
14 Scott Scudder (Cedar Rapids)
15 Marc Bombard (Cedar Rapids)
16 Brian Deak (Burlington)
17 Rich Casarotti (Burlington)
18 Brian Hunter (Burlington)
19 Al Martin (Burlington)
20 Jim Lemasters (Burlington)
21 Troy Neel (Waterloo)
22 Tommy Kramer (Waterloo)
23 Bob Rose (Quad City)
24 Wiley Lee (Quad City)
25 Gary Buckels (Quad City)
26 Ray Lankford (Springfield)
27 Greg Becker (Springfield)
28 Greg Kallevig (Peoria)
29 Fernando Zarranz (Peoria)
30 Steve Olin (Waterloo)
31 Lenny Webster (Kenosha)
32 Shawn Gilbert (Kenosha)
33 Jarvis Brown (Kenosha)
34 Pat Bangston (Kenosha)
35 Pete Delkus (Kenosha)
36 Ron Gardenhire (Kenosha)
37 Jorge Pedre (Appleton)
38 Darryl Robinson (Appleton)
39 Jesus Deleon (Appleton)
40 Tom Gordon (Appleton)
41 Bobby Knecht (Appleton)
42 Greg Colbrunn (Rockford)
43 John Mello (Rockford)
44 Delino DeShields (Rockford)
45 Mario Brito (Rockford)
46 Howard Farmer (Rockford)
47 Tim Peters (Rockford)
48 Mike Maksudian (S. Bend)
49 Ray Payton (S. Bend)
50 Scott Brosius (Madison)
51 Ozzie Canseco (Madison)
52 Jim Chenevey (Madison)
53 Pat Wernig (Madison)
54 Will Schock (Madison)
55 Mike McDonald (Wausau)
56 Chuck Carr (Wausau)
57 Mike Goff (Wausau)
58 Kurt Stange (Wausau)
59 Mark Chapman (Beloit)

1988 Grand Slam Quad City Angels

(California Angels, A)

Complete Set:	MT	NR MT	EX
	6.00	4.50	2.50

1 Eddie Rodriguez
2 Mike Couchee
3 Bill Zick
4 Wiley Lee
5 Kevin Flora
6 Larry Pardo
7 Edgal Rodriguez
8 Bill Robinson
9 Terence Carr
10 Steve Dunn
11 David Holdridge
12 Frank Mutz
13 Daryl Green
14 Bob Rose
15 Troy Giles
16 Rod Lung
17 Jim Townsend
18 Mario Molina

19 Edgar Alfonzo
20 Roberto Hernandez
21 Kenny Grant
22 Jim Aylward
23 Cesar DeLaRosa
24 Charlie Romero
25 Rob Wassenaar
26 Tim McKinnis
27 Chris Graves
28 Gary Buckels
29 Brandy Vann
30 Mike Musolino

1988 Grand Slam South Bend White Sox

(A)

	MT	NR MT	EX
Complete Set:	6.00	4.50	2.50

1 Cesar Bernhardt
2 Larry Allen
3 Javier Ocasio
4 Kevin Murdock
5 Ed Smith
6 Ray Payton
7 Dwayne Hosey
8 Rod McCray
9 Kinnis Pledger
10 Mike Maksudian
11 Wilson Valera
12 Bernando Cruz
13 Kurt Brown
14 Don Cooper
15 Steve Dillard
16 Jim Reinebold
17 Ed Sedar
18 Argenis Conde
19 Mike Girouard
20 Julian Gonzalez
21 Curt Hasler
22 John Hudek
23 Bo Kennedy
24 Rob Resnikoff
25 Randy Robinson
26 Steve Schrenik
27 Mark Tortorice
28 Stanley Coveleski

1988 Grand Slam South Atlantic League All Stars

(A)

	MT	NR MT	EX
Complete Set:	8.00	6.00	3.25

1 Richie Hebner (Myrtle Beach)

2 Mel Roberts (Spartanburg)
3 Ned Yost (Sumter)
4 Bill Paul Carver (Asheville)
5 Ron Downs (Augusta)
6 Eddie Taubensee (Greensboro)

7 Brian Lane (Greensboro)
8 Joe Turek (Greensboro)
9 Ron Mullins (Greensboro)
10 Omar Olivares (Charleston)
11 Darrin Reichle (Charleston)
12 Guillermo Velazquez
13 Alex Arias (Charleston)
14 Mike Miller (Columbia)
15 Anthony Toney (Fayetteville)

16 Brant Alyea (Gastonia)
17 Williams Suero (Myrtle Beach)

18 Luis Sojo (Myrtle Beach)
19 Greg Vella (Myrtle Beach)
20 Derek Bell (Myrtle Beach)
21 Xavier Hernandez (Myrtle Beach)

22 Jimmy Rogers (Myrtle Beach)

23 Denis Boucher (Myrtle Beach)

24 Rob Colescott (Savannah)
25 John Sellick (Sumter)
26 James Vatcher (Spartanburg)

27 Andy Carter (Spartanburg)
28 Dennis Burlingame (Sumter)

1988 Grand Slam Texas League All Stars

(AA)

	MT	NR MT	EX
Complete Set:	10.00	7.50	4.00

1 Jack Mull (Shreveport)
2 Todd Zeile (Arkansas)
3 Chad Kreuter (Tulsa)
4 Gary Alexander (Tulsa)
5 Steve Wilson (Tulsa)
6 Dan Scarpetta (El Paso)
7 John Wetteland (San Antonio)
8 Joe Olker (Shreveport)
9 Kevin Bootay (Tulsa)
10 Angelo Cuevas (Jackson)
11 Mike Benjamin (Shreveport)

12 Scott Coolbaugh (Tulsa)
13 Brett Harrison (Arkansas)
14 Manny Salinas (Jackson)
15 John Skurla (Shreveport)
16 Tom Baine (Arkansas)
17 John Barfield (Tulsa)
18 Blaine Beatty (Jackson)
19 Jose Dominguez (Shreveport)

20 Scott Arnold (Arkansas)
21 Dave Pavlas (Tulsa)
22 Kevin Kennedy (San Antonio)

23 Mike Basso (Wichita)
24 Mario Monico (El Paso)
25 Fred Williams (El Paso)
26 Gary Sheffield (El Paso)
27 Jim McCollom (Midland)
28 Ramon Martinez (San Antonio)

29 Terry Gilmore (Wichita)
30 Mike Munoz (San Antonio)
31 Ed Puig (El Paso)
32 Carlos Baerga (Wichita)
33 Mike Huff (San Antonio)
34 Chris Knabenshue (Wichita)
35 Greg Vaughn (El Paso)
36 Mike Knapp (Midland)
37 Luis Lopez (San Antonio)
38 Frank Mattox (El Paso)
39 Jeff Manto (Midland)

1988 Grand Slam Wausau Timbers

(Seattle Mariners, A)

	MT	NR MT	EX
Complete Set:	6.00	4.50	2.50

1 Rick Sweet
2 Chuck Kniffen
3 Fausto Ramirez
4 Chris Doll
5 Lorenzo Sisney
6 Ruben Gonzalez
7 Keith Frink
8 Chuck Carr
9 John Hoffman
10 Kurt Stange
11 Mike McDonald
12 Jim Pritikin
13 Ray Williams
14 Todd Haney
15 Todd Azar
16 Jeff Hooper
17 Rudy Webster
18 Steve Bieksha
19 Chuck Webb
20 Mike McGuire
21 Brian Baldwin
22 Tony Woods
23 Scott Stoerick
24 Frank Colston
25 Mike Gardiner
26 Dru Kosco
27 Mike Goff
28 Randy Roetter

1988 Jones Photo Tucson Toros

(Houston Astros, AAA) No positions are listed on cards which measure 3 x 5-1/8 inches in size. Each set comes in a protective miniature binder.

	MT	NR MT	EX
Complete Set:	45.00	33.50	18.00

(1) Karl Allaire
(2) Craig Biggio
(3) Ken Caminiti
(4) Jose Cano
(5) Glenn Carpenter
(6) Rocky Childress
(7) Jeff Datz
(8) Luis DeLeon
(9) Bob Didier
(10) Drew Cameron
(11) John Fishel
(12) Kevin Hagen
(13) Manny Hernandez
(14) Pat Keedy
(15) Anthony Kelley
(16) Dave Meads
(17) Joe Mikulik
(18) Rafael Montalvo
(19) Nelson Rood
(20) Joe Sambito
(21) Alex Trevino
(22) Eddie Watt
(23) Jim Weaver
(24) Craig Smajstria

1988 Legoe Bellingham Mariners

(Seattle Mariners, A)

	MT	NR MT	EX
Complete Set:	6.00	4.50	2.50

Logo card
1 Ricky Candelari
2 Dorian Daughtry
3 Tony Cayson
4 Ellerton Maynard
5 Mike McLaughlin
6 Tom McNamara
7 Greg Prikl
8 Julio Reyan
9 Jeff Miller
10 Pete Schmidt
11 Tim Stargell
12 Gary Wheelock
13 Brian Wilkinson
14 Lee Hancock
15 John Kohli
16 Jim Kosnik
17 Tom Liss
18 Victor Mangual
19 Scott Pitcher
20 Keith Barrett
21 Scott Stoerck
22 Nick Felix
23 Ted Eldredge
24 Chris Doll
25 Erick Bryant
26 Mike Beiras
27 Otis Patrick
28 P.J. Carey
29 Donnie Reynolds
30 Batboys (Jeff Crnich, Mike Thompson)

31 Spyder Webb

1988 Police Columbus Clippers

(New York Yankees, AAA) This is also a police set.

	MT	NR MT	EX
Complete Set:	7.00	5.25	2.75

(1) Chris Alvarez
(2) Jay Buhner
(3) Pat Clements
(4) Casey Close
(5) Pete Dalena
(6) Alvaro Espinoza
(7) Bill Fulton
(8) Bob Geren
(9) Matt Harrison
(10) Mike Kinnunen
(11) Rick Langford
(12) Jeff Moronko
(13) Hal Morris
(14) Jamie Nelson
(15) Scott Nielson
(16) Clay Parker
(17) Bert Pena
(18) Hipolito Pena
(19) Eric Schmidt
(20) Steve Shields
(21) Cliff Speck
(22) Randy Velarde
(23) Ward Turner
(24) Coaches/Trainer card (Champ Summers, Kevin Rand, Ken Rowe)
(25) Managers card (George Sisler, Bucky Dent)

1988 Pro Cards Albany-Colonie Yankees

(New York Yankees, AA)

	MT	NR MT	EX
Complete Set:	8.00	6.00	3.25

1329 Amalio Carreno
1330 Andy Stankiewicz
1331 Bob Green
1332 Rob Sepanek
1333 Tim Layana
1334 Bobby Davidson
1335 Gary Cathcart
1336 Dave Eiland
1337 Mike Christopher

1338 Rick Torres
1339 Tony Ferreira
1340 Troy Evers
1341 Tim Becker
1342 Dana Ridenour
1343 Melvin Rosario
1344 Jim Leyritz
1345 Scott Shaw
1346 Jason Mass
1347 Oscar Azocar
1348 Aris Tirado
1349 Hensley Meulens
1350 Dickie Scott
1351 Deron Johnson
1352 Tommy Jones
1353 Tony Cloninger
1354 Mike Heifferon
--- Checklist

1988 Pro Cards Albuquerque Dukes

(Los Angeles Dodgers, AAA)

	MT	NR MT	EX
Complete Set:	6.00	4.50	2.50

249 Steve Garcia
250 Bill Brennan
251 Brent Strom
252 Mike Devereaux
253 Mike Sharperson
254 Von Joshua
255 Mariano Duncan
256 Tracy Woodson
257 Gilberto Reyes
258 Jose Gonzalez
259 Chris Gwynn
260 John Gibbons
261 Tony Arnold
262 Ray Searage
263 Mike Hartley
264 Tim Crews
265 Shawn Hillegas
266 Shanie Dugas
267 Mike Ramsey
268 George Hinshaw
269 Jon Debus
270 Terry Collins
271 Bill Krueger
272 Lenny Currier
273 Chuck Hensley
274 Hector Heredia
275 Stan Kyles
276 Dennis Burtt
--- Checklist

1988 Pro Cards Appleton Foxes

(Kansas City Royals, A)

	MT	NR MT	EX
Complete Set:	15.00	11.25	6.00

137 Jorge Pedre
138 Luis Mallea
139 Brian Meyers
140 Kevin Shaw
141 Doug Nelson
142 Terry Shumpert
143 Linton Dyer
144 Darryl Robinson
145 Dave Howard
146 Don Wright
147 Bill Stonikas
148 Karl Drezek
149 Tom Gordon
150 Tim Odom
151 Trey Gainous
152 Brian McCormack
153 Keith Shibata
154 Frank Henderson
155 Jesus DeLeon
156 Chris Gurchiek
157 Doug Bock
158 Jeff Baum
159 Andre Rabouin
160 Dennis Moeller
161 Bobby Knecht
162 Brian Poldberg
163 Mike Leon
164 Larry Dawson
165 Team Photo Card
--- Checklist

1988 Pro Cards Asheville Tourists

(Houston Astros, A)

	MT	NR MT	EX
Complete Set:	6.00	4.50	2.50

1049 Billy Carver
1050 Kenny Dickson
1051 Greg Johnson
1052 Andy Harter
1053 Ramon Cedeno
1054 Mike Beams
1055 Joe Charno
1056 Carlos Laboy
1057 Neder Horta
1058 Ed Renteria
1059 Chris Lee
1060 Harold Allen
1061 Dan Lewis
1062 Gorky Perez
1063 Fred Costello
1064 Joe Locke
1065 Doug Royalty
1066 Joe Ortiz
1067 Charley Taylor
1068 Gary Tuck
1069 Richie Simon
1070 Dennis Tafoya
1071 Danny Newman
1072 Dean Hartgraves
1073 Mike Hook
1074 Carlos Henry
1075 Dave Cunningham
1076 Gene Confreda
1077 Ron McKee
1078 Todd Weber
--- Checklist

1988 Pro Cards Auburn Astros

(Houston Astros, A)

	MT	NR MT	EX
Complete Set:	7.00	5.25	2.75

1947 Larry Lamphere
1948 Scott Spurgeon
1949 Chris Small
1950 Wally Trice
1951 Dennis Tafoya
1952 Pat Penafeather
1953 Kenny Lofton
1954 Ron Porterfield
1955 Rodney Windes
1956 Harry Fuller
1957 Ken Morris
1958 Dave Shermet
1959 Bernie Jenkins
1960 Rod Scheckla
1961 John Massarelli
1962 Mike Beams
1963 Rick Wise
1964 Bob Neal
1965 Neder Horta
1966 Andy Mota
1967 Frank Cacciatore
1968 Jim DeSapio
1969 Rick Dunnum
1970 Gordy Farmer
1971 John Graham
1972 David Klinefelter
1973 Luis Gonzalez
1974 Mica Lewis
--- Checklist

1988 Pro Cards Augusta Pirates

(Pittsburgh Pirates, A)

	MT	NR MT	EX
Complete Set:	6.00	4.50	2.50

359 Wes Chamberlain
360 Moises Alou
361 Miguel Valverde
362 Mickey Peyton
363 Jeff Griffith
364 Orlando Merced
365 Carlos Garcia
366 Eddie Hartman
367 Pete Freeman
368 Scott Barczi
369 Jimmy Garrison
370 Ben Shelton
371 Jose Acosta
372 Joe Macavage
373 Joe Pacholec
374 Butch Schlopy
375 Keith Shepherd
376 Scott Runge
377 Willie Smith
378 Ron Downs
379 Tracy Toy
380 Tonny Cohen
381 Joel Forrest
382 Jeff Cox
383 Dave Moharter
384 Glenn Trudo
385 S. Carter
386 Robert Harris
387 Jmaes Rhoades
388 Paul Day
389 Len Monheimer
1576 Mark Merchant
--- Checklist

1988 Pro Cards Batavia Clippers

(Philadelphia Phillies, A)

	MT	NR MT	EX
Complete Set:	5.00	3.75	2.00

Checklist
1662 Bob Tiefenauer
1663 Dave Cash
1664 Don McCormack
1665 Tony Trevino
1666 Leroy Ventress
1667 Nicio Martinez
1668 Scott Drury
1669 Wayne Fuller
1670 Rick Trlicek
1671 Eric Enos
1672 Mark Bradford
1673 Erik Bratlien
1674 Tim Dell
1675 Mike Owens
1676 Tom Marsh
1677 Chris Walker
1678 Nick Santa Cruz
1679 Joe Tenhunfeld
1680 Ike Galloway
1681 Rich Walker
1682 Todd Elam
1683 Matt Viggiano
1684 Dave Allen
1685 Rich Tracy
1686 Fred Felton III
1687 Andy Barrick
1688 Gary Wilson
1689 Brian Cummings
1690 Troy Zerb
1691 Brad Rogers

1988 Pro Cards Billings Mustangs

(Cincinnati Reds, A)

	MT	NR MT	EX
Complete Set:	5.00	3.75	2.00

Checklist
1802 David Keller
1803 David Keller
1804 Jim Brune
1805 Duane Mulville
1806 Glenn Sutko
1807 Scott Sellner
1808 Michael Mulvaney
1809 Doug Bond
1810 Steve Reyes
1811 Tony Terzarial
1812 Dante Johnson
1813 Danny Perozo
1814 Scott Economy
1815 John Groennert
1816 Tomas Rodriguez
1817 Steve McCarthy
1818 Steve Foster
1819 Brian Nichols
1820 Brian Landy
1821 Jerry Spradlin
1822 Reggie Sanders
1823 C.L. Thomas
1824 Vicente Javier
1825 Johnny Almaraz
1826 Carl Stewart
1827 Jim Hoff
1828 Kurt Dempster
1829 Michael Songini
1830 Benny Colvard
1831 Carl Nordstrom

1988 Pro Cards Boise Hawks

(No affiliation, A)

	MT	NR MT	EX
Complete Set:	5.00	3.75	2.00

Checklist
1605 John Bilello
1606 Michael Tate
1607 Wendell Bolar
1608 Michael Moore
1609 Christopher Gurchiek
1610 James Qualls
1611 Mike Shambaugh
1612 Edward Holub
1613 Christopher Shultis
1614 Barry Griffin
1615 Larry Lundeen

1616 Jeff Mace
1617 Earl Malone
1618 Jerry Backus
1619 Randy Janikowski
1620 Michael Larson
1621 Chuck Lavrusky
1622 Michael Lomeli
1623 Bill Wenrick
1624 Charles Douglas
1625 Mark Krumback
1626 Joseph Mancini
1627 Daren De Pew
1628 Keven Bottenfield
1629 Tim MacKinnon
1630 Frank Jury
1631 Robert Winterburn
1632 Mal Fichman

1988 Pro Cards Bristol Tigers

	MT	NR MT	EX
Complete Set:	6.50	4.75	2.50

1862 Rick Mag
1863 Carlos Maldonado
1864 Doug Biggs
1865 Tim Brader
1866 Juan Estevez
1867 Bob Frassa
1868 Rusty Meacham
1869 Julio Rosa
1870 Ron Howard
1871 Mike Davidson
1872 Rich Rowland
1873 Freddy Padilla
1874 Jimmy Hayes
1875 Chris Gollehon
1876 Eric Shoup
1877 Mike Rendina
1878 Duane Walker
1879 Blaine Rudolph
1880 Mike Koller
1881 Tom Aldrich
1882 Marcos Bentances
1883 Mick Delas
1884 Bret Roach
1885 Rico Brogna
1886 Ed Ferm
1887 Kurt Shea
1888 Rob Thomas
1889 Mike Jones
1890 Paul Nozling
1891 Tookie Spann
1892 Benny Castillo
--- Checklist

1988 Pro Cards Buffalo Bisons

(Pittsburgh Pirates, AAA)

	MT	NR MT	EX
Complete Set:	6.00	4.50	2.50

1464 Randy Kramer
1465 Felix Fermin
1466 Morris Madden
1467 Bob Patterson
1468 Dorn Taylor
1469 Stan Fansler
1470 Jim Reboulet
1471 Rico Rossy
1472 Dave Rucker
1473 Denny Gonzalez
1474 Tommy Gregg
1475 Bernie Tatis
1476 Dave Johnson
1477 Donald Palmer
1478 Rocky Bridges
1479 Jackie Brown
1480 Stan Cliburn
1481 Carlos Ledezma
1482 Kevin Hodge
1483 Dave Sax
1484 Scott Medvin
1485 Tom Romano
1486 Orestes Destrade
1487 Skeeter Barnes
1488 Tom Prince
1489 Benny Distefano
1490 Logan Easley
1491 Bryan Little
1492 Brett Gideon
1493 Pilot Field
--- Checklist

1988 Pro Cards Burlington Braves

(Atlanta Braves, A)

	MT	NR MT	EX
Complete Set:	6.00	4.50	2.50

1106 Lynn Robinson
1107 Carl Pointer-Jones
1108 Mike Stanton
1109 Chad Smith
1110 Matt Turner
1111 Pat Tilman
1112 Brian Murphy
1113 Jerald Frost
1114 Steve Glass
1115 Brian Champion
1116 Grady Little
1117 Brian Cummings
1118 Jim Lemasters
1119 Jeff Greene
1120 Jim Nowlin
1121 Dave Karasinski
1122 Jaime Cuesta
1123 Dave Grilone
1124 Albert Martin
1125 Sean Ross
1126 Rich Casarotti
1127 Rick Berg
1128 Eduardo Perez
1129 Andy Tomberlin
1130 Brian Hunter
1131 Gil Garrido, Jr.
1132 Brian Deak
1133 John Mitchell
1134 Jack Aker
1135 Paul Egins III
--- Checklist

1988 Pro Cards Burlington Indians

(Cleveland Indians, A)

	MT	NR MT	EX
Complete Set:	25.00	18.50	10.00

Checklist
1772 Brent Roberts
1773 Rick Falkner
1774 Lenny Gilmore
1775 Martin Eddy
1776 Randy Mazey
1777 Vince Barranco
1778 Sean Baron
1779 Jeff Bonchek
1780 Rouglas Odor
1781 Axel Castillo
1782 Todd Butler
1783 Carlos Mota
1784 Scott Allen
1785 Charles Alexander
1786 Mike Bucci
1787 Pedro Arias
1788 Pablo Gomez
1789 David Oliveras
1790 Doug Piatt
1791 Barry Blundin
1792 Jeff Mutis
1793 Mike Ashworth
1794 Bob Kairls
1795 Brett Merriman
1796 Greg McMichael
1797 Andre Halle
1798 Brian Johnson
1799 Dan Williams
1800 Mark Lewis
1801 Ray Borowicz

1988 Pro Cards Calgary Cannons

(Seattle Mariners, AAA) This is also a police set.

	MT	NR MT	EX
Complete Set:	7.50	5.50	3.00

779 Rod Scurry
780 Darren Burroughs
781 Terry Taylor
782 Edgar Martinez
783 Mike Wishnevski
784 Brian Giles
785 Dave Cocrane
786 Erik Hanson
787 Doug Merrifield
788 Matt West
789 Dan Warthen
790 Roger Hansen
791 Jim Walker
792 Jay Baller
793 Paul Schneider
794 John Christensen
795 Mike Schooler
796 Dennis Powell
797 Rich Monteleone
798 Mike Watters
799 Greg Briley
800 Bill Plummer
801 Phil Ouellette
802 Nelson Simmons
803 Brick Smith
804 Mario Diaz
1550 Dave Hengel
--- Checklist

1988 Pro Cards Cedar Rapids Reds

(Cincinnati Reds, A)

	MT	NR MT	EX
Complete Set:	7.00	5.25	2.75

1136 Don Buchheister
1137 Greg Simpson
1138 Bill Dodd
1139 Mike Moscrey
1140 Sandy Krume
1141 Chico Fernandez
1142 Freddy Benavides
1143 Gary Denbo
1144 Marc Bombard
1145 Bruce Colson
1146 Reggie Jefferson
1147 Pete Beeler
1148 Rich Sapienza
1149 Ramon Sambo
1150 Steve Davis
1151 Jeff Forney
1152 Greg Lonigro
1153 Doug Eastman
1154 Jim Brune
1155 Eddie Rush
1156 Brad Brusky
1157 Scott Scudder
1158 Carl Nordstrom
1159 Butch Henry
1160 Sam Chavez
1161 Bud Curran
1162 Darrell Rodgers
1163 Milton Hill
1164 Mike Malinak
1165 Jim Bishop
--- Checklist

1988 Pro Cards Charleston Rainbows

(San Diego Padres, A)

	MT	NR MT	EX
Complete Set:	6.00	4.50	2.50

1193 Willie Forbes
1194 Tony Pellegrino
1195 Jim Wasem
1196 David Bond
1197 Charles Hillemann
1198 Jose Valentin
1199 Mike Myers
1200 Osvaldo Sanchez
1201 Rafael Valdez
1202 Mike King
1203 Guillermo Velazquez
1204 Monte Brooks
1205 Mark Kleven
1206 Todd Hansen
1207 Keith Harrison
1208 Darrin Reichle
1209 Todd Torchia
1210 Omar Olivares
1211 Doug Brocail
1212 Gary Lance
1213 Jay Estrada
1214 Tony Lewis
1215 Saul Soltero
1216 Reggie Farmer
1217 Bob Lutticken
1218 Jaime Moreno
1219 Jack Krol
1220 Nelson Silverio
1221 Tim Barker
--- Checklist

1988 Pro Cards Clinton Giants

(San Francisco Giants, A)

	MT	NR MT	EX
Complete Set:	6.00	4.50	2.50

693 John Vuz
694 Steve Lienhard
695 Rod Beck
696 Steve Connelly
697 Tom Hostetler

698 Scott Nelson
699 Mark Poling
700 Bill Carlson
701 Juan Guerrero
702 Jimmy Terrill
703 Jim Anderson
704 Mark Owens
705 Andres Santana
706 Todd Miller
707 Craig Colbert
708 Erik Johnson
709 Mike Ham
710 Tony Michalak
711 Mark Dewey
712 Bill Evers
713 Mike Stanfield
714 Robert Lucero
715 Jamie Cooper
716 Elanis Westbrooks
717 Jeff Morris
718 Tom Ealy
719 Mike Villa
720 Lonnie Phillips
--- Checklist

1988 Pro Cards Colorado Springs Sky Sox

(Cleveland Indians, AAA)

	MT	NR MT	EX
Complete Set:	6.00	4.50	2.50

1522 John Stefero
1523 Don Lovell
1524 Reggie Williams
1525 Randy Washington
1526 Mike Brown
1527 Tommy Hinzo
1528 Paul Zuvella
1529 Charles Scott
1530 Rick Peterson
1531 Jeff Kaiser
1532 Ron Tingley
1533 Joe Skalski
1534 Domingo Ramos
1535 Keith Bennett
1536 Aurelio Rodriguez
1537 Darrel Akerfelds
1538 Don Gordon
1539 Steve Ciszczon
1540 Reggie Ritter
1541 Terry Francona
1542 Jon Perlman
1543 Luis Medina
1544 Mark Higgins
1545 Rod Allen
1546 Steve Swisher
1547 Eddie Williams
1548 Ron Mathis
1549 Rick Rodriguez
--- Checklist

1988 Pro Cards Columbus Clippers

(New York Yankees, AAA)

	MT	NR MT	EX
Complete Set:	7.00	5.25	2.75

303 Bob Geren
304 Glenn Sherlock
305 Jamie Nelson
306 Bucky Dent
307 Field Staff
308 Rick Langford
309 Clay Parker
310 Scott Nielsen
311 Cliff Speck
312 Bill Fulton
313 Eric Schmidt
314 Steve Shields
315 Hipolito Pena
316 Mike Kinnunen
317 Matt Harrison
318 Pat Clements
319 Rob Lambert
320 Alvaro Espinoza
321 Pete Dalena
322 Berto Pena
323 Chris Alvarez
324 Randy Velarde
325 Casey Close
326 Max Ward
327 Hal Morris
328 Jeff Moronko
329 Jay Buhner
330 Team Photo
--- Checklist

1988 Pro Cards Denver Zephyrs

(Milwaukee Brewers, AAA)

	MT	NR MT	EX
Complete Set:	7.00	5.25	2.75

1250 Todd Jackson
1251 Alex Madrid
1252 Peter Kolb
1253 German Rivera
1254 Bill Mooneyham
1255 Darryel Walters
1256 Kiki Diaz
1257 Tom Filer
1258 Paul Mirabella
1259 Don August
1260 John Miglio
1261 Keith Smith
1262 Ronn Reynolds
1263 Brad Komminsk
1264 Duffy Dyer
1265 Tim Watkins
1266 Steve Stanicek
1267 Billy Jo Robidoux
1268 Charlie O'Brien
1269 Pete Kendrick
1270 Jay Aldrich
1271 Billy Bates
1272 Mark Ciardi
1273 Tim Pyznarski
1274 Darryl Hamilton
1275 Mark Knudson
1276 Mike Konderla
1277 Lavell Freeman
1278 Todd Brown
--- Checklist

1988 Pro Cards Eastern League All Stars

(Class AA)

	MT	NR MT	EX
Complete Set:	15.00	11.25	6.00

1 Dave Eiland
2 Kevin Maas
3 Hensley Meulens
4 Dana Ridenour
5 Andy Stankiewicz
6 Dan Dimascio
7 Shawn Holman
8 Tobey Lovullo
9 Julius McDougal
10 Cesar Mejia
11 Rob Richie
12 Delwyn Young
13 Jeff Cook
14 Kevin Davis
15 Dimas Gutierrez
16 Jeff King
17 Larry Melton
18 Paul Wilmet
19 Jose Birriel
20 Mike Carista
21 Ed Estrada
22 Todd Pratt
23 John Roberts
24 Luis Vasquez
25 Joe Girardi
26 Mike Harkey
27 Bryan House
28 Hector Villanueva
29 Jerome Walton
30 Dean Wilkins
31 Tony Brown
32 Greg Edge
33 Warren Magee
34 Chuck Malone
35 Jeff Hull
36 Ricky Rojas
37 Omar Vizquel
38 Jim Wilson
39 Mark Howie
40 Scott Jordan
41 Tom Lampkin
42 Mike Poehl
43 Casey Webster
44 Kevin Wickander
45 Dave Trembley
46 Harold Williams
47 Jim Essian
48 Grant Jackson
49 Brian McCann
50 Brian Allard
51 Brian Graham
52 Mike Hargroce

1988 Pro Cards Edmonton Trappers

(California Angels, AAA)

	MT	NR MT	EX
Complete Set:	7.50	5.50	3.00

555 Joe Redfield
556 Jack Lazorko
557 Vance Lovelace
558 Jim Eppard
559 Doug Davis
560 Joe Johnson
561 Chico Walker
562 Marty Reed
563 Chuck Hernandez
564 Junior Noboa
565 Frank Dimichele
566 Phil Venturino
567 Mike Cook
568 Barry Dacus
569 Terry Clark
570 Mark Doran
571 Stan Holmes
572 Brian Brady
573 Kevin King
574 Kent Anderson
575 Edwin Marquez
576 Dante Bichette
577 Bobby Miscik
578 Pete Coachman
579 Darrell Miller
580 Tom Kotchman
581 Urbano Lugo
582 Miguel Alicea
583 Craig Gerber
584 Al Olson
--- Checklist

1988 Pro Cards Fayetteville Generals

(Detroit Tigers, A)

	MT	NR MT	EX
Complete Set:	6.00	4.50	2.50

1079 Keith Nicholson
1080 Glenn Belcher
1081 Steve Pegues
1082 Andy Toney
1083 Luis Melendez
1084 Larry Coker
1085 Mark Adler
1086 Jose Ramos
1087 Robinson Garces
1088 Steve Parascand
1089 Chuck Duquette
1090 Zack Doster
1091 Duben Bello
1092 Charles Steward
1093 Felix Liriano
1094 Travis Fryman
1095 Dave Richards
1096 Ron Cook
1097 Chris Schnurbursh
1098 Randy Luciani
1099 Kevin Camilli
1100 Miguel Murphy
1101 Liliano Castro
1102 Bill Henderson
1103 Michael Wilkins
1104 Leon Roberts
1105 Mike DeLao
--- Checklist

1988 Pro Cards Fresno Suns

(No Affiliation, A)

	MT	NR MT	EX
Complete Set:	6.00	4.50	2.50

1222 Frank Bryan
1223 Kim Flowers
1224 John Bilello
1225 Chuck Higson
1226 Brad Comstock
1227 John Barry
1228 Dave Nash
1229 Gary Geiger
1230 Dan Simonds
1231 Rocco Buffolino
1232 Jim Malseed
1233 H Miyauchi
1234 Antony Tagi
1235 Bullet Manabe
1236 Dean Treanor
1237 Jon Hobbs
1238 Joe Ueda
1239 Richard Yagi
1240 Tracey Pancoski
1241 Ernie Young
1242 Todd Hawkins
1243 Tony Triplett
1244 Rob Rowen
1245 Marty Montano
1246 George Omachi
1247 Joe Mancini
1248 Tom Bell
1249 Donna Van Duzer
--- Checklist

1988 Pro Cards Gastonia Rangers

(Texas Rangers, A)

	MT	NR MT	EX
Complete Set:	7.50	5.50	3.00

995 Marv Rockman
996 Bob Lavender
997 Bill Findlay
998 Mike Taylor
999 Jay Baker
1000 Rick Knapp
1001 Chris Shiflett
1002 Luke Sable
1003 Robb Nan
1004 Jim McCutcheon
1005 Cris Colon
1006 Joe Pearn
1007 Brant Alyea
1008 Felipe Castillo
1009 Orlando Gomez
1010 Kevin Belcher
1011 Jose Velez
1012 Jeff Melrose
1013 Bill Losa
1014 Pat Garman
1015 Brad Meyer
1016 Marty Cerny
1017 Wilson Alvarez
1018 Brian Steiner
1019 Spencer Wilkinson
1020 Roger Pavlik
1021 Glenn Patterson
1022 Saul Barretto
1023 Chuck Marguardt
--- Checklist

1988 Pro Cards Geneva Cubs

(Chicago Cubs, A)

	MT	NR MT	EX
Complete Set:	6.00	4.50	2.50

1633 Eric Perry
1634 Nick Ramirez
1635 Eric Williams
1636 Gary Arnold
1637 Ray Figueroa
1638 Jim Murphy
1639 Skip Eggleston
1640 Rick Mundy
1641 Dave Goodwin
1642 Mike Sodders
1643 Tim Ellis
1644 Dan Johnston
1645 Matt Leonard
1646 Eligio Rodriguez
1647 Tracy Smith
1648 Francisco Espino
1649 Derrick Stroud
1650 Bill St. Peter
1651 Scott Taylor
1652 Ben Shreve
1653 Chris Lutz
1654 Bill Hayes
1655 Carlos Canino
1656 Ken Shepard
1657 George Brzezinski
1658 Marty Owens
1659 Dave Oster
1660 Sheila Arnold
1661 Quinn's Cards
--- Checklist

1988 Pro Cards Glens Falls Tigers

(Detroit Tigers, AA)

	MT	NR MT	EX
Complete Set:	7.00	5.25	2.75

913 Wayne Housie
914 Pat Austin
915 Eric Hardgrave
916 Delwyn Young
917 John Wockenfuss
918 Ken Williams
919 Julius McDougal
920 Rich Lacko
921 Paul Wenson
922 Rich Wieligman
923 Torey Lovullo
924 Cesar Mejia
925 Rob Richie
926 Kevin Ritz
927 Mike Schwabe
928 Bernie Anderson
929 Shawn Holman
930 Ken Gotmann
931 Dan Dimascio
932 Adam Dempsay
933 Bill Cooper
934 Kevin Bradshaw
935 Hector Berrios
936 Jeff Jones
937 Robert Link
938 Tim Leiper
--- Checklist

1988 Pro Cards Greensboro Hornets

(Cincinnati Reds, A)

	MT	NR MT	EX
Complete Set:	6.00	4.50	2.50

1551 Bill Risley
1552 Quinn Marsh
1553 Scott Jeffery
1554 Keith Thomas
1555 Brian Lane
1556 Shane Letterio
1557 Brad Robinson
1558 Eddie Taubenese
1559 Joe Turek
1560 Kevin Pearson
1561 Ron Mullins
1562 Adam Casillias
1563 Tony Mealy
1564 Ken Huseby
1565 Scott Westermann
1566 Mack Jenkins
1567 Rosario Rodriguez
1568 Andy Rickman
1569 Jack Smith
1570 Steve Hester
1571 Jimmy Mee
1572 Don Brown
1573 Keith Kaiser
1574 Joey Vierra
1575 Mark Berry
--- Checklist

1988 Pro Cards Hamilton Redbirds

(St. Louis Cardinals, A)

	MT	NR MT	EX
Complete Set:	6.00	4.50	2.50

Checklist
1719 Chris Houser
1720 Scott Halama
1721 John Cebuhar
1722 Brad Duvall
1723 Antron Grier
1724 Rick Christian
1725 Mark Battell
1726 Lee Plemel
1727 Mike Ross
1728 Dale Kisten
1729 Tim Redman
1730 Kevin Robinson
1731 Cory Saterfield
1732 Dan Radison
1733 Luis Melendez
1734 Mike Evans
1735 Randy Butts
1736 Mark Clark
1737 John Lepley
1738 Joe Federico
1739 Steve Fanning
1740 Rodney Brooks
1741 Tom Malchesky
1742 Ed Lampe
1743 J.P. Gentleman
1744 Dean Weese
1745 Steve Graham
1746 Frank Moran
1747 Joe Hall

1988 Pro Cards Harrisburg Senators

(Pittsburgh Pirates, AA)

	MT	NR MT	EX
Complete Set:	6.00	4.50	2.50

834 John Rigos
835 Jeff Cook
836 Tommy Shields
837 Kevin Davis
838 Scott Little
839 Spin Williams
840 Rick Reed
841 Dimas Gutierrez
842 Jim Neidlinger
843 Mike Curtis
844 Lance Belen
845 Chris Ritter
846 Dave Trembley
847 Orlando Lind
848 Jose Melendez
849 Ron Johns
850 Mike Walker
851 Gilberto Roca
852 Paul Wilmet
853 Bill Copp
854 Tony Chance
855 Jeff Banister
856 Gino Gentile
857 Larry Melton
858 Robby Russell
859 Jeff King
860 Clay Daniel
861 Harold Williams
862 Scott Kautz
--- Checklist

1988 Pro Cards Idaho Falls Braves

(Atlanta Braves, A)

	MT	NR MT	EX
Complete Set:	6.00	4.50	2.50

Checklist
1832 The Clubhouse
1833 Team photo & checklist
1834 Daryl Blanks
1835 Marco Paddy
1836 Gary Schoonover
1837 Glenn Mitchell
1838 Rodney Richey
1839 John Albertson
1840 Lamar Hall
1841 Dave Monteiro
1842 Matthew Williams
1843 Chris Jones
1844 Ramces Guerrero
1845 Donovan Campbell
1846 Kevin henry
1847 Greg Harper
1848 Al Bacosa
1849 Pat Stivers
1850 Keith LeClair
1851 Eric Kuhlman
1852 Rai Henninger
1853 Jim Procopio
1854 Paul Opdyke
1855 Rudy Gardey
1856 Mark Eskins
1857 Daniel Lehnerz
1858 Jim Kortright
1859 Steve Lopez
1860 Herb Hippauf
1861 Rich Pohle

1988 Pro Cards Indianapolis Indians

(Montreal Expos, AAA)

	MT	NR MT	EX
Complete Set:	8.00	6.00	3.25

496 Joe Sparks
497 Billy Moore
498 Tim McCormack
499 Mike Colbern, Joe Kerrigan
500 Nelson Santovenia
501 Sergio Valdez
502 Tim Barrett
503 Jeff Fischer
504 Brian Holman
505 Steve Shirley
506 Kurt Kepshire
507 Mel Houston
508 Gary Wayne
509 Mike Smith
510 Randy Johnson
511 Bob Sebra
512 Joe Hesketh
513 Rex Hudler
514 Razor Shines
515 Garrett Nago
516 Johnny Paredes
517 Nelson Norman
518 Otis Nixon
519 Mike Berger
520 Alonzo Powell
521 Jack Daugherty
522 Tim Hulett
523 Wil Tejada
524 Ron Shepherd
525 Tom Akins, Howard Kellman
--- Checklist

1988 Pro Cards Iowa Cubs

(Chicago Cubs, AAA)

	MT	NR MT	EX
Complete Set:	15.00	11.25	6.00

526 Brian Guinn
527 Bill Bathe
528 Doug Dascenzo
529 Rick Surhoff
530 Dwight Smith
531 Dave Grossman
532 Jeff Hirsch
533 Dave Masters
534 Bob Tewksbury
535 Gary Varsho
536 Dave Meier
537 Damon Berryhill
538 Paul Noce
539 Mark Grace
540 Phil Stephenson
541 Bill Landrum
542 Jim Wright
543 Pete Mackanin
544 Leonard Damian
545 Roger Williams
546 Jeff Pico
547 Mike Capel
548 Greg Tabor
549 Joe Kraemer
550 Bruce Crabbe
551 Laddie Renfroe
552 Front Office
553 More Front Office
554 Cubbie Bear (mascot)
--- Checklist

1988 Pro Cards Jacksonville Expos

(Montreal Expos, AA)

	MT	NR MT	EX
Complete Set:	7.50	5.50	3.00

964 Scott Mann
965 Orsino Hill
966 Jeffrey Huson
967 Eddie Dixon
968 Derrell Baker
969 Nardi Contreras
970 Doug Duke
971 Tommy Thompson
972 Andy Lawrence
973 Yorkis Perez
974 Jim Kahmann
975 Mike Blowers
976 Randy Braun
977 Mark Clemons
978 Todd Soares
979 Bob Caffrey
980 Gene Harris
981 Pat Sipe
982 Tommy Alexander
983 Armando Moreno
984 Kevin Dean
985 Mike Shade
986 Rich Sauver
987 Mark Gardner
988 Rick Carriger
989 John Hoover
990 Gary Engelkin
991 Esteban Belter
992 Richie Lewis
993 Team Photo
994 Sam Molfson Park
--- Checklist

1988 Pro Cards Jamestown Expos

(Montreal Expos, A)

	MT	NR MT	EX
Complete Set:	22.00	16.50	9.00

Checklist
1893 Kevin P. Malone
1894 Roger LaFrancois
1895 Wilfredo Nieva
1896 Bryn Kosco
1897 Bret Davis
1898 Rob Kerrigan
1899 Daniel Freed
1900 Angel Rivera
1901 Jeff Atha
1902 Tim Piechowski
1903 Isaac Alleyne
1904 Tim Laker
1905 Rodney Boddie
1906 Idaiberto Echemendia
1907 Brian Sajonia
1908 Joe Siddall
1909 Joe Klancnik
1910 Marquis Grissom
1911 Keith Kaub
1912 Jose Solarte
1913 Danilo Leon
1914 Steve Overeem
1915 Kevin Finigan
1916 Jorge Mitchell
1917 Javan Reagans
1918 Darrin Winston
1920 Dan Archibald
1921 Martin Robitaille
2039 Q.V. Lowe

1988 Pro Cards Kenosha Twins

(Minnesota Twins, A)

	MT	NR MT	EX
Complete Set:	7.50	5.50	3.00

1379 Bob Tinkey
1380 Willie Banks
1381 Dwight Bernard
1382 Fred White
1383 Rusty Kryzanowski
1384 Steve Stowell
1385 Alex Perez
1386 Chad Swanson
1387 Tom Gilles
1388 Doug Pittman
1389 Dave Jacas
1390 Jarvis Brown
1391 David Smith
1392 Lenny Webster
1393 Frank Valdez
1394 Mark Ericson
1395 Michael Lexa
1396 Carlos Capellan
1397 Chris Martin
1398 Pete Delkus
1399 Don Leppert
1400 John Skelton
1401 Jenny Shane
1402 Ron Gardenhire
1403 Bob Lee
1404 Basil Meyer
1405 Tom Marten
1406 Pat Bangtson
--- Checklist

1988 Pro Cards Las Vegas Stars

(San Diego Padres, AAA)

	MT	NR MT	EX
Complete Set:	8.50	6.25	3.50

222 Edward Vosberg
223 Joe Lynch
224 Randell Byers
225 Joel McKeon
226 Todd Hutcheson
227 Greg Harris
228 Pete Roberts
229 Jerald Clark
230 Joe Bitker
231 Roberto Alomar
232 Gary Green
233 Shane Mack
234 Joey Cora
235 Mike Brumley
236 Sandy Alomar
237 Rob Nelson
238 Tom Brassil
239 Thomas Howard
240 Todd Simmons
241 Bruce Bochy
242 Kevin Towers
243 Steve Lubratich
244 Steve Smith
245 Bip Roberts
246 Keith Comstock
247 Brad Pounders
248 Sonny Siebert
--- Checklist

1988 Pro Cards Louisville Redbirds

(St. Louis Cardinals, AAA)

	MT	NR MT	EX
Complete Set:	9.00	6.75	3.50

421 David Green
422 Carl Ray Stephens
423 John Martin
424 Sal Agostinelli
425 Duane Walker
426 Dick Grapenthin
427 Mike Fitzgerald
428 Chris Carpenter (Cris)
429 John Murphy
430 Randy O'Neal
431 Roy Silver
432 Bill Lyons
433 Tim Jones
434 David Hudson
435 Joe Pettini
436 Luis Alicea
437 Jim Leopold
438 Alex Cole
439 Craig Wilson
440 John Costello
441 Mike Jorgenson (Jorgensen)

442 Gibson Alba
443 Dave Rajsich
444 Mark Dougherty
445 Rich Bounantony
--- Checklist

1988 Pro Cards Maine Phillies

(Philadelphia Phillies, AAA)

	MT	NR MT	EX
Complete Set:	6.00	4.50	2.50

277 Jim Olander
278 Kevin Ward
279 Marvin Freeman
280 Ron Jones
281 John McLarnan
282 Mike Shelton
283 Travis Chambers
284 Tom Barrett
285 John Russell
286 Ricky Jordan
287 Ken Jackson
288 Shane Turner
289 Brad Brink
290 Keith Miller
291 Rick Lundblade
292 Marty Bystrom
293 Tom Newell
294 Bob Scanlan
295 Ramon Henderson
296 Todd Frohwirth
297 Danny Clay
298 Greg Jelks
299 Barney Nugent
300 George Culver
301 Joe Lefebvre
302 Ramon Aviles
--- Checklist

1988 Pro Cards Myrtle Beach Blue Jays

(Toronto Blue Jays, A)

	MT	NR MT	EX
Complete Set:	10.00	7.50	4.00

1166 Steve Wapnick
1167 Graeme LLoyd
1168 Denis Boucher
1169 Bernardino Nunez
1170 Edgar Marquez
1171 Derek Bell
1172 Steve Woide
1173 Chris Floyd
1174 Nate Cromwell
1175 Juan de la Rosa
1176 Greg David
1177 Dan Etzweiler
1178 Xavier Hernandez
1179 Mike Murray
1180 Leroy Stanton
1181 Omar Malave
1182 Randy Knorr
1183 Greg Vella
1184 Mike Timlin
1185 Steve Towey
1186 Williams Suero
1187 Allan Silverstein
1188 Richard Hebner
1189 Luis Sojo
1190 Jimmy Rogers
1191 Rob MacDonald
1192 Todd Provence
--- Checklist

1988 Pro Cards Nashville Sounds

(Cincinnati Reds, AAA)

	MT	NR MT	EX
Complete Set:	7.50	5.50	3.00

471 Scott Earl
472 Pat Pacillo
473 Van Snider
474 Dave Klipstein
475 Ron Roenicke
476 Dan Boever
477 Tim Birtsas
478 Jeff Gray
479 Hugh Kemp
480 Doug Gwosdz
481 Marty Brown
482 Steve Oliverio
483 Joe Oliver
484 Jack Armstrong
485 Mike Jones
486 Jack Lind
487 Rob Lopez
488 Norm Charlton
489 Lenny Harris
490 Luis Quinones
491 Greg Monda
492 Mike Roesler
493 Robbie Dibble
494 Wayne Garland
495 John R. Young
--- Checklist

1988 Pro Cards New Britain Red Sox

(Boston Red Sox, AA)

	MT	NR MT	EX
Complete Set:	6.00	4.50	2.50

889 Luis Vasquez
890 Daryl Irvine
891 Mike Clarkin
892 Doug Palmer
893 Bob Chadwick
894 John Roberts
895 Eduardo Zambrano
896 Mike Dalton
897 Manny Jose
898 Dan Gabrielle
899 Larry Shikles
900 Greg Bochesa
901 Tim McGee
902 Jose Birriel
903 Ed Estrada
904 Dan Gakeler
905 Tito Stewart
906 Todd Pratt
907 Chris Moritz
908 Curt Schilling
909 Mike Carista
910 Angel Gonzalez
911 Roberto Zambrano
912 Jason Jackson
--- Checklist

1988 Pro Cards Oneonta Yankees

(New York Yankees, A)

	MT	NR MT	EX
Complete Set:	6.00	4.50	2.50

Checklist
2040 Ed Martel
2041 Andy Cook
2042 Todd Brill
2043 Pat Kelly
2044 Bob DeJardin
2045 Jason Bridges
2046 Herb Erhardt
2047 Ken Greer
2048 Skip Nelloms
2049 Hector Vargas
2050 John Seeburger
2051 Craig Brink
2052 Jeff Livesey
2053 Rey Fernandez
2054 Miguel Torres
2055 Jorge Candelaria
2056 Bob Hunter
2057 Jeff Hoffman
2058 Bob Zeihen
2059 Mike Draper
2060 Art Canestro
2061 Bruce Prybylinski
2062 Jerry Nielsen
2063 Jay Makemson
2064 Gary & Kelvin Allenson
2065 Tim Weston
2066 Alan Warren
2067 Jay Knoblauh
2068 Mark Martin
2069 Jeff Johnson
2070 Jeff Taylor
2071 Frank Seminara
2072 Rod Ehrhard

1988 Pro Cards Oklahoma City 89'ers

(Texas Rangers, AAA) Cards in this set have a Pizza Hut emblem on their backs.

	MT	NR MT	EX
Complete Set:	6.00	4.50	2.50

27 Scott May
28 Bill Taylor
29 Rick Odekirk
30 Jeff Kunkel
31 Dan Rohn
32 Larry Klein
33 Dwayne Henry
34 Tony Fossas
35 Gary Mielke
36 Bill Merrifield
37 Don Werner
38 James Steels
39 Jim St Laurent
40 Gar Millay
41 Jose Tolentino
42 Robbie Wine
43 Darrell Whitaker
44 Craig McMurtry
45 Barbaro Garbey
46 Toby Harrah
47 Otto Gonzalez
48 Tom O'Malley
49 Ray Hayward
50 Ferguson Jenkins
51 Ray Ramirez
52 Ed Vande Berg
--- Checklist

1988 Pro Cards Reading Phillies

(Philadelphia Phillies, AA)

	MT	NR MT	EX
Complete Set:	6.00	4.50	2.50

863 Tom Schwarz
864 Alan Leboeuf
865 Steve Sharts
866 Brad Moore
867 Tony Brown
868 Scott Service
869 Chuck Malone
870 Tim Sossamon
871 Warren Magee
872 Jeff Kaye
873 Gary Berman
874 Dan Giesen
875 CHuck McElroy
876 Tim Fortugno
877 Steve Deangelis
878 Rick Parker
879 Howard Nichols
880 Greg Edge
881 Harvey Brumfield
882 Greg Legg
883 Vince Holyfield
884 Jose Leiva
885 Ray Roman
886 Chris Calvert
887 Tim Corcoran
888 Carlos Arroyo
--- Checklist

1988 Pro Cards Omaha Royals

(Kansas City Royals, AAA)

	MT	NR MT	EX
Complete Set:	6.00	4.50	2.50

1494 Rich Dubee
1495 Tom Poquette
1496 Israel Sanchez
1497 Jerry Gleaton
1498 Bill Swaggerty
1499 Nick Capra
1500 Nick Swartz
1501 Jeff Montgomery
1502 Buddy Biancalana
1503 Glenn Ezell
1504 Mike Loggins
1505 Tom Dodd
1506 Luis de los Santos
1507 Tom Mullen
1508 Jeff Schulz
1509 Jose Castro
1510 Dave Owen
1511 Don Welchel
1512 Rick Anderson
1513 Steve Fireovid
1514 Bob Buchanan
1515 Ron Johnson
1516 Larry Owen
1517 Al Hargesheimer
1518 Dann Bilardello
1519 Joe Citari
1520 Luis Aquino
1521 Gary Thurman
--- Checklist

1988 Pro Cards Palm Springs Angels

(California Angels, A)

	MT	NR MT	EX
Complete Set:	6.00	4.50	2.50

1433 John Orton
1434 Ruben Amaro
1435 J. Gary Ruby
1436 Bill Lacheman
1437 Luis Merejo
1438 Mike Anderson
1439 Reed Peters
1440 Scott Cerny
1441 Chris Cron
1442 Dan Ward
1443 Mike Erb
1444 Scott Kannenberg
1445 John Fritz
1446 Jose Tapia
1447 Colin Charland
1448 Dario Nunez
1449 Richard Morehouse
1450 Paul Sorrento
1451 Jeff Barns
1452 Jim McAnany
1453 Tim Dyson
1454 Gary Nalls
1455 Glenn Washington
1456 Mark Baca
1457 Bill Vanderwel
1458 Jim Bisceglia
1459 Bobby Bell
1460 Jimmy Long
1461 Reggie Lambert
1462 Bill Durney
1463 Jeff Richardson
--- Checklist

1988 Pro Cards Pawtucket Red Sox

(Boston Red Sox, AAA)

	MT	NR MT	EX
Complete Set:	6.00	4.50	2.50

446 Andy Araujo
447 Mike Rochford
448 Rob Woodward
449 Eric Hetzel
450 Gary Tremblay
451 Chris Cannizzaro
452 Tom Bolton
453 Carlos Quintana
454 Mark Meleski
455 Mitch Johnson
456 Bill McInnis
457 Zack Crouch
458 Scott Wade
459 Gary Miller-Jones
460 Dana Williams
461 Dana Kiecker
462 Angel Gonzalez
463 Mike Mesh
464 Randy Kutcher
465 Glenn Hoffman
466 Pat Dodson
467 Tony Cleary
468 Steve Curry
469 Ed Nottle
470 John Leister
--- Checklist

1988 Pro Cards Phoenix Firebirds

(San Francisco Giants, AAA)

	MT	NR MT	EX
Complete Set:	6.00	4.50	2.50

53 Tim Blackwell
54 Mark Wasinger
55 Randy Bockus
56 Matt Williams
57 Charlie Hayes
58 Deron McCue
59 Rusty Tillman
60 Everett Graham
61 Kirt Manwaring
62 Roger Mason
63 Angel Escobar
64 Francisco Melendez
65 Wendell Kim
66 CLiff Shidawara
67 Marty DeMerritt
68 Alan Cockrell
69 Bobby Ramos
70 Roger Samuels
71 Randy McCament
72 Ty Dabney
73 Mike Hogan
74 Ed Puikunas
75 Tony Perezchica
76 John Burkett
77 Terry Mulholland
78 Jeff Brantley
79 Brian Ohnoutka
80 Dennis Cook
--- Checklist

1988 Pro Cards Pittsfield Cubs

(Chicago Cubs, AA)

	MT	NR MT	EX
Complete Set:	20.00	15.00	8.00

1355 Hector Villanueva
1356 Mitch Zwolensky
1357 Julio Valdez
1358 Ray Thoma
1359 Joe Girardi
1360 Jim Essian
1361 Bryan House
1362 Rich Amaral
1363 Bob Bafia
1364 Brian McCann
1365 Mike Tullier
1366 Jerry Lapenta
1367 Jim Bullinger
1368 Dean Wilkins
1369 Steve Parker
1370 Ced Landrum
1371 Mark Leonette
1372 Rich Scheid
1373 Dave Kopf
1374 Jerome Walton
1375 Jackie Davidson
1376 Kris Roth
1377 Mike Harkey
1378 Gary Parmenter
--- Checklist

1988 Pro Cards Pocatello Giants

(San Francisco Giants, R)

	MT	NR MT	EX
Complete Set:	6.00	4.50	2.50

Checklist
2073 Don Brock
2074 David Wuthrich
2075 Andre George
2076 Jim Myers
2077 Carlos Sanchez
2078 Francisco (Arias)
2079 Sean Thompson
2080 Scott Ebert
2081 Adam Hilpert
2082 Steve Reed
2083 Lance Burnett
2084 Dave Edwards
2085 Marino Hernandez
2086 Greg Lee
2087 Reuben Smiley
2088 Daris Toussaint
2089 Victor Cruz
2090 Brett Hewatt
2091 Kevin Rodgers
2092 Adam Smith
2093 Kevin Hall
2094 David Slavin
2095 Dobie (Swepson)
2096 Jesus Laya
2097 Joey Speaks
2098 David Booth
2099 Carl Hanselman
2100 Diego Segui
2101 Jack Hiatt
2102 Jack Penrod

1988 Pro Cards Portland Beavers

(Minnesota Twins, AAA)

	MT	NR MT	EX
Complete Set:	6.00	4.50	2.50

639 Brad Bierley
640 Eric Bullock
641 Kelvin Torve
642 Jim Winn
643 John Moses
644 Jim Shellenback
645 Roy Smith
646 Karl Best
647 Doug Baker
648 Brad Boylan
649 Vic Rodrigeuz
650 Jim Mahoney
651 Brian Harper
652 Winston Ficklin
653 Chris Pittaro
654 Allan Anderson
655 Steve Liddle
656 Ricky Jones
657 Bobby Ralston
658 Mark Portugai
659 Jeff Bumgarner
660 Jim Davins
661 Phil Wilson
662 Ray Soff
663 T.R. Bryden
664 Fred Toliver
--- Checklist

1988 Pro Cards Pulaski Braves

(Atlanta Braves, R)

	MT	NR MT	EX
Complete Set:	6.00	4.50	2.50

Checklist
1748 Phillip Wellman
1749 Fred Koenig
1750 Smoky Burgess
1751 Scott Goselin
1752 Scott Grove
1753 John Greenwood
1754 Tom Rizzo
1755 Steve Wendell
1756 Glen Gardner
1757 David Reis
1758 Errol Flynn
1759 Paul Reis
1760 Calvain Culberson
1761 Ricky Rigsby
1762 Brent McCoy
1763 Chris Mitta
1764 Mike Urman
1765 David Piela
1766 Roger Hailey
1767 Robert Minaya
1768 Randy Simmons
1769 Ron Thomas
1770 Cloyd Boyer
1771 Don Bowman

1988 Pro Cards Richmond Braves

(Atlanta Braves, AAA)

	MT	NR MT	EX
Complete Set:	6.00	4.50	2.50

1 Lonnie Smith
2 Tommy Greene
3 Ronnie Gant
4 Todd Dewey
5 Greg Tubbs
6 Sam Ayoub
7 Juan Espino
8 Carlos Rios
9 Jeff Wetherby
10 Juan Eichelberger
11 Marty Clary
12 Jose Alvarez
13 Bean Stringfellow
14 Sid Akins
15 Jim Beauchamp
16 Leo Mazzone
17 Clarence Jones
18 Jeff Blauser
19 John Mizerock
20 Dave Griffin
21 Derek Lilliquist
22 Joe Boever
23 John Smoltz
24 Dave Justice
25 Alex Smith
26 Gary Eave
--- Checklist

1988 Pro Cards Riverside Red Wave

(San Diego Padres, A)

	MT	NR MT	EX
Complete Set:	6.00	4.50	2.50

1407 Ron Oglesby
1408 Kevin Farmer
1409 Steve Hendricks
1410 Brian Brooks
1411 Pat Jelks
1412 Jim Daniel
1413 Tony Torchia
1414 Tye Waller
1415 Greg Hall
1416 Warren Newson
1417 Tom Levasseur
1418 Dave Hollins
1419 Bill Taylor
1420 Brian Wood
1421 Bill Blount
1422 Paul Faries
1423 Jim Lewis
1424 Bill Marx
1425 Andy Skeels
1426 Ricky Bones
1427 Rich Holsman
1428 Brian Harrison
1429 Rafel Chavez
1430 Terry McDevitt
1431 Kevin Garner
1432 Steve Loubier
--- Checklist

1988 Pro Cards Rochester Red Wings

(Baltimore Orioles, AAA)

	MT	NR MT	EX
Complete Set:	6.00	4.50	2.50

193 Dale Berra
194 Eric Bell
195 Dave Smith
196 Bob Gibson
197 Vic Mata
198 Sherwin Cinjntje
199 Jeff Ballard
200 Ron Salcedo
201 Jay Tibbs
202 Mickey Tettleton
203 Matt Cimo
204 Chris Padget
205 Pete Stanicek
206 Jose Mesa
207 Reg Montgomery
208 Mark Bowden
209 Bill Scherrer
210 Mike Griffin
211 Johnny Oates
212 Dom Chiti
213 Keith Hughes
214 Jamie Reed
215 John Habyan
216 Jerry Narron
217 Craig Worthington
218 Curt Motton
219 Dickie Noles
220 Jay Colley
221 Silver Stadium
--- Checklist

1988 Pro Cards St. Catharines Blue Jays

(Toronto Blue Jays, A)

	MT	NR MT	EX
Complete Set:	6.00	4.50	2.50

Checklist
2005 Armando Pagliari
2006 Luis Salazar
2007 Timothy Brown
2008 Jose Villa
2009 Benigno Placeres
2010 Brad Evaschuk
2011 Jose Guarache
2012 Pablo Castro
2013 Donn Wolfe
2014 Eddie Dennis
2015 Mike McAlpin
2016 Timithy Hodge
2017 Nigel Wilson
2018 Daniel Dodd
2019 Greg Williams
2020 Greg McCutcheon
2021 Robert Montalvo
2022 Curtis Johnson
2023 David Weathers
2024 Jose Martinez
2025 Edgar Marquez
2026 Rafael Martinez
2027 Jason Townley
2028 Marcos Tavaras
2029 Greg Harding
2030 Bryan Dixon
2031 Mike Jockish
2032 Mike Taylor
2033 Rick Vaughn
2034 Anthony Ward
2035 Ryan Thompson
2036 Darrin Wade
2037 Armando Serra
2038 Patrick Guerrero

1988 Pro Cards San Jose Giants

(San Francisco Giants, A)

	MT	NR MT	EX
Complete Set:	6.00	4.50	2.50

108 Koli Maeda
109 Paul Blair
110 Willie Mijares
111 Dave Peterson
112 Gary Jones
113 Scott Murray
114 Eric Gunderson
115 Doug Robertson
116 Ray Velasquez
117 Masa Yamamoto
118 Russ Swan
119 Rich Aldrete
120 Tom Meagher
121 Ken Suzuki
122 Todd Oakes
123 Sam Hirose
124 Lance Hutchins
125 Duane Espy
126 Tod Ronson
127 Eric Pilkington
128 Tad Hanyuda
129 Greg Conner
130 Gil Heredia
131 Gregg Ritchie
132 Kevin Meier
133 Jim McNamara
134 Mark Leonard
135 Daron Connelly
136 Joe Johdo
--- Checklist

1988 Pro Cards Savannah Cardinals

(St. Louis Cardinals, A)

	MT	NR MT	EX
Complete Set:	6.00	4.50	2.50

331 Mike Hinkle
332 Ken Smith
333 Tony Russo
334 Tim Sherrill
335 Rob Colescott
336 Martin Mason
337 Keith Champion
338 Dave Krebs
339 Mark Behny
340 Bill Hershman
341 Roberto Marte
342 Hal Hempen
343 Clint Horsley
344 Tim Meamber
345 Brad Harvick
346 Reed Olmstead
347 John Sellick
348 Jim Ferguson
349 Stan Barrs
350 Eddie Looper
351 Kris Huffman
352 Ryan Johnston
353 Mike Alvarez
354 Eddie Carter
355 Antron Grier
356 Jean Gentleman
357 Greg Doss
358 Francisco Rosario
--- Checklist

1988 Pro Cards Shreveport Captains

(San Francisco Giants, AA)

	MT	NR MT	EX
Complete Set:	6.00	4.50	2.50

1279 Jack Mull
1280 Joe Kmak
1281 Jose Dominguez
1282 Joe Olker
1283 Mike Benjamin
1284 Vince Sferrazza
1285 Dean Freeland
1286 Steve Cline
1287 Andy Dixon
1288 Paul Meyers
1289 George Bonilla
1290 Paul McClellan
1291 Jeff Carter
1292 Jose Pena
1293 Romy Cucjen
1294 Rick Nelson
1295 Stuart Tate
1296 Mike Remlinger
1297 John Skurla
1298 Trevor Wilson
1299 Harry Davis
1300 Tim McCoy
1301 Ed Puikunas
1302 T.J. McDonald
--- Checklist

1988 Pro Cards Southern Oregon A's

(Oakland A's, A)

	MT	NR MT	EX
Complete Set:	7.50	5.50	3.00

Checklist
1692 Jim Buccheri
1693 Tim Vannaman
1694 Richard Rozman
1695 Nick Venuto
1696 Tony Ariola
1697 Joel Smith
1698 DeWayne Jones
1699 Tom Carcione
1700 Josue Espinal
1701 Stan Royer
1702 Rod Correia
1703 Joel Chimelis
1704 Mike Messerly
1705 Dean Borelli
1706 Lee Tinsley
1707 Tony Floyd
1708 Greg Ferguson
1709 Kevin MacLeod
1710 Mike Mungin
1711 Dan Eskew
1712 Jim Lawson
1713 Ray Harris
1714 J.P. Ricciardi
1715 Jerry Rizza
1716 Joe Hillman
1717 Lenny Sakata
1718 Jesus Hernaiz

1988 Pro Cards Spartanburg Phillies

(Philadelphia Phillies, A)

	MT	NR MT	EX
Complete Set:	6.00	4.50	2.50

1024 Jeff Stark
1025 Matt Rambo
1026 Bob Hurta
1027 Tim Peek
1028 Greg McCarthy
1029 Darrell Coulter
1030 Shelby McDonald
1031 John Larosa
1032 Phil Fagnano
1033 Mel Roberts
1034 Rod Robertson
1035 Kim Batista
1036 Jaime Barragan
1037 Scott Ruckman
1038 Marty Foley
1039 Carlos Zayas
1040 Tony Trevino
1041 Gary Maasberg
1042 Doug Lindsey
1043 Todd Felton
1044 Gary White
1045 Jim Vatcher
1046 Bob Britt
1047 Buzz Capra
1048 Jim Platts
--- Checklist

1988 Pro Cards Spokane Indians

(San Diego Padres, A)

	MT	NR MT	EX
Complete Set:	6.00	4.50	2.50

Checklist
Checklist
1922 Greg Conley, Greg Conley
1923 Tye Waller, Tye Waller
1924 Rob Cantwell, Rob Cantwell
1925 Kelly Lifgren, Kelly Lifgren
1926 Mike Humphreys, Mike Humphreys
1927 Squeezer Thompson, Squeezer Thompson
1928 Steve Lubratich, Steve Lubratich
1929 Pedro Aquino, Pedro Aquino
1930 Luis Lopez, Luis Lopez
1931 Craig Bigham, Craig Bigham
1932 Greg Smith, Greg Smith
1933 A.J. Sager, A.J. Sager
1934 John Kuehl, John Kuehl
1935 Chad Kuhn, Chad Kuhn
1936 Nicko Riesgo, Nicko Riesgo
1937 Brad Hoyer, Brad Hoyer
1938 David Briggs, David Briggs
1939 Bob Curnow, Bob Curnow
1940 Brian Cisarik, Brian Cisarik
1941 Renay Bryand, Renay Bryand
1942 Barry Hightower, Barry Hightower
1943 Mark Verstandig, Mark Verstandig
1944 Craig Proctor, Craig Proctor
1945 Chris Haslock, Chris Haslock
1946 Ron Morton, Ron Morton

1988 Pro Cards Stockton Ports

(Milwaukee Brewers, A)

	MT	NR MT	EX
Complete Set:	7.50	5.50	3.00

721 Rob Derkson
722 Steve Monson
723 Mark Aguilar
724 Shon Ashley
725 Keith Fleming
726 Alan Sadler
727 Snady Guerrero
728 Gil Villanueva
729 Dave Taylor
730 Randy Veres
731 Ron Romanick
732 Bobby Jones
733 Tim McIntosh
734 Brian Drahman
735 Ruben Escalera
736 Jaime Navarro
737 Charlie Montoyo
738 Bill Spiers
739 Brian Stone
740 Dave Hoppert
741 Rob Smith
742 Angel Rodriguez
743 John Jaha
744 Jay Williams
745 Danny Fitzpatrick
746 Carl Moraw
747 Doug Henry
748 Narcisso Elvira
749 Angel Miranda
750 Don Miller
751 Dan Chapman
752 Mike Conroy, Mark Marine
--- Checklist

1988 Pro Cards Sumter Braves

(Atlanta Braves, A)

	MT	NR MT	EX
Complete Set:	6.00	4.50	2.50

390 Keith Mitchell
391 Tony Baldwin
392 Bob Cole
393 Dennis Burlingame
394 John Reilley
395 Wes Currin
396 Mark Davis
397 Johnny Cuevas
398 Jesus Mendoza
399 Jose Valencia
400 Winnie Relaford
401 Greg Harper
402 Rick Siebert
403 Marcos Vezquez
404 Skipper Wright
405 Gregg Gilbert
406 Greg Cloninger
407 A J Waznik
408 Glenn Mitchell
409 Juan Fredymond
410 Ben Rivera
411 David Colon
412 Tom Redington
413 Dave Nied
414 Ned Yost
415 Larry Jaster
416 Rick Albert
417 Willy Johnson
418 Ralph Meister
419 Teddy Williams
420 Ed Holtz
--- Checklist

1988 Pro Cards Syracuse Chiefs

(Toronto Blue Jays, AAA)

	MT	NR MT	EX
Complete Set:	7.50	5.50	3.00

805 Jack O'Connor
806 Luis Leal
807 Cliff Young
808 Geronimo Berroa
809 Norm Tonucci
810 Luis Reyna
811 Kelly Hetah
812 Glenallen Hill
813 Alexis Infante
814 Steve Davis
815 Enrique Burgos
816 Doug Bair
817 Bob Bailor
818 Galen Cisco
819 Red Coughlin
820 Jose Nunez
821 Greg Myers
822 Hector Torres
823 Colin McLaughlin
824 Mark Ross
825 Rob Ducey
826 Sal Butera
827 Bob Shirley
828 Marc DeBottis
829 Randy Holland
830 Frank Wills
831 Otis Green
832 Eric Yelding
833 Chris Shaddy
--- Checklist

1988 Pro Cards Tacoma Tigers

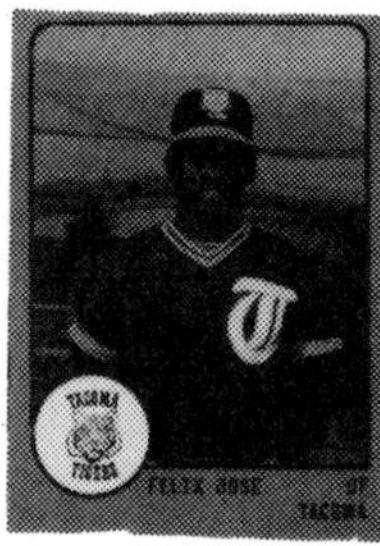

(Oakland A's, AAA)

	MT	NR MT	EX
Complete Set:	7.00	5.25	2.75

612 Gary Jones
613 Joe Xavier
614 Felix Jose
615 Eddie Jurak
616 Matt Sinatro
617 Tyler Brilinski
618 Jim Jones
619 Jeff Shaver
620 Stan Naccarato
621 Roy Johnson
622 Brad Fischer
623 Chuck Estrada
624 Orlando Mercado
625 Jim Corsi
626 Kevin Sliwinski
627 Rich Bordi
628 Bob Stoddard
629 Brian Snyder
630 Lance Blankenship
631 Reese Lambert
632 Todd Burns
633 Tim Meeks
634 Andre Robertson
635 Wayne Krenchicki
636 Charlie Corbell
637 Alex Sanchez
638 Luis Polonia
--- Checklist

1988 Pro Cards Tidewater Tides

(New York Mets, AAA)

	MT	NR MT	EX
Complete Set:	16.00	12.00	6.50

1577 John Mitchell
1578 Phil Lombardi
1579 John Cumberland
1580 Sam McCrary
1581 Tom Edens
1582 Jeff Innis
1583 Jack Savage
1584 Tim Tolman
1585 Rich Miller
1586 Mike Cubbage
1587 Jeff McKnight
1588 Mark Carren
1589 Wally Whitehurst
1590 Reggie Dobie
1591 Marcus Lawton
1592 Dave West
1593 Tim Drummond
1594 Al Pardo
1595 Ken Dowell
1596 Andre David
1597 Greg Olson
1598 Steve Springer
1599 Tom McCarthy
1600 Gregg Jefferies
1601 Jose Roman
1602 Steve Frey
1603 Darren Reed
1604 Keith Miller
--- Checklist

1988 Pro Cards Toledo Mud Hens

(Detroit Tigers, AAA)

	MT	NR MT	EX
Complete Set:	6.00	4.50	2.50

585 Jeff Reynolds
586 Dave Beard
587 Doug Strange
588 Mark Huismann
589 Donnie Rowland
590 Pat Corrales
591 Paul Cherry
592 Eric King
593 Mike Trujillo
594 Scott Lusader
595 Billy Bean
596 John Duffy
597 Chris Hoiles
598 Pete Rice
599 Gene Roof
600 Paul Felix
601 Pedro Chavez
602 Benny Ruiz
603 Tim Leiper
604 Don Schulze
605 Rey Palacios
606 Don McGann
607 Stan Clarke
608 Dave Cooper
609 Steve Searcy
610 Ramon Pena
611 Mike Brown
--- Checklist

1988 Pro Cards Triple-A All-Stars

(AAA) AAA precedes all card numbers on the backs of the cards.

	MT	NR MT	EX
Complete Set:	15.00	11.25	6.00

1 Mike Devereaux
2 Chris Gwynn
3 Tracy Woodson
4 Benny Distefano
5 Tom Prince
6 Eddie Jurak
7 Phil Ouellette
8 Luis Medina
9 Bob Geren
10 Mike Kinnunen
11 Scott Nielsen
12 Lavell Freeman
13 Tim Pyznarski
14 German Rivera
15 Urbano Lugo
16 Bill Bathe
17 Bob Sebra
18 Mike Bielecki
19 Dwight Smith
20 Sandy Alomar
21 Mike Brumley
22 Joey Cora
23 Greg Harris
24 Dick Grapenthin
25 Mike Shelton
26 Marty Brown
27 Hugh Kemp
28 Tom O'Malley
29 Steve Finley
30 Luis de los Santos
31 Steve Curry
32 Tony Perezchica
33 Roy Smith
34 Joe Boever
35 Bob Milacki
36 Geronimo Berroa
37 Eric Yelding
38 Lance Blankenship
39 Mark Carreon
40 Gregg Jefferies
41 David West
42 Mark Huismann
43 Rey Palacios
44 Cameron Drew
45 Donn Pall
46 Sap Randall
47 Terry Collins
48 Carlos Ledezma
49 Bill Plummer
50 Joe Sparks
51 Toby Harrah
52 Ed Nottle
53 Randy Holland
54 Mike Cubbage
--- Checklist

1988 Pro Cards Tucson Toros

(Houston Astros, AAA)

	MT	NR MT	EX
Complete Set:	7.50	5.50	3.00

166 Craig Biggio
167 Karl Allaire
168 Craig Smajstrla
169 Manny Hernandez
170 Rafael Montalvo
171 Jose Cano
172 Jim Weaver
173 Glenn Carpenter
174 Luis DeLeon
175 Pat Keedy
176 Joe Mikulik
177 Louie Meadows
178 John Fishel
179 Clay Christiansen
180 Kevin Hagen
181 Rocky Childress
182 Ken Caminiti
183 Dave Meads
184 Eddie Watt
185 Mike Loynd
186 Anthony Kelley
187 Jeff Datz
188 Cameron Drew
189 Ernie Camacho
190 Bob Didier
191 Nelson Rood
192 Rex Jones
--- Checklist

1988 Pro Cards Vancouver Canadians

(Chicago White Sox, AAA)

	MT	NR MT	EX
Complete Set:	6.00	4.50	2.50

753 Jeff Schaefer
754 Steve Rosenberg
755 Jack Hardy
756 Edward Wojna
757 Ken Patterson
758 Bill Lindsey
759 Donn Pall
760 Russ Morman
761 Grady Hall
762 Carl Willis
763 Joel Davis
764 Santiago Garcia
765 James Randall
766 Daryl Sconiers
767 Mike Woodard
768 Ron Jackson
769 Eli Grba
770 Greg Hibbard
771 Dave Gallagher
772 Jorge Alcazar
773 Ron Karkovice
774 Mike Yastrzemski
775 Troy Thomas
776 Adam Peterson
777 Marlin McPhail
778 Terry Bevington
--- Checklist

1988 Pro Cards Vermont Mariners

(Seattle Mariners, AA)

	MT	NR MT	EX
Complete Set:	6.00	4.50	2.50

939 Mark Wooden
940 Bryan Price
941 Dave Schuler
942 Greg Fulton
943 Bill McGuire
944 Jim Wilson
945 Eric Fox
946 Omar Vizquel
947 Pat Lennon
948 Keith Foley
949 Nezi Balelo
950 John Gibbons
951 Dave Brundage
952 Dave Myers
953 Jorge Uribe
954 Rich Morales
955 Tom Newberg
956 Dave Snell
957 Greg Brinkman
958 Bill Mendek
959 Ricky Rojas
960 Clint Zavaras
961 Jeff Hull
962 Calvin Jones
963 Dave McCorkle
--- Checklist

1988 Pro Cards Visalia Oaks

(Minnesota Twins, A)

	MT	NR MT	EX
Complete Set:	6.00	4.50	2.50

Checklist
81 Kenny Davis
82 Dana Heinle
83 Larry Blackwell
84 John Eccles
85 Mike Randle
86 Kenny Grant
87 A.J. Richardson
88 Troy James
89 Jose Marzan
90 Kenny Morgan
91 Shawn Gilbert
92 Paul Abbott
93 Mike Redding
94 Steve Scanlon
95 Jeff Bronkey
96 Slim Williams
97 Tim Arnold
98 Joey Zellner
99 Scott Ullger
100 Doug Snyder
101 Bob Strube
102 Scott Leius
103 Edgar Naveda
104 Marty Lanoux
105 Gorman Heimueller
106 Andy Seidensticker
107 Doug Kline

1988 Pro Cards Waterloo Indians

(Cleveland Indians, A)

	MT	NR MT	EX
Complete Set:	6.00	4.50	2.50

665 Tommy Kurczewski
666 Andy Casano
667 Angel Ortiz
668 Bill Bluhm
669 John Stutz
670 Willie Garza
671 Jim Baxter
672 Scott Khoury
673 T.J. Gamba
674 Bill Narleski
675 Julio Liriano
676 Ramon Bautista
677 Ivan McBride
678 Keith Seifert
679 Steve Colavito
680 Sam Ferretti
681 Troy Neel
682 Peter Kuld
683 Mark Pike
684 Keith Bennett
685 Roger Hill
686 Eric Rasmussen
687 Ken Bolek
688 Steve Olin
689 Tom Kramer
690 Tony Scaglione
691 Greg Roscoe
692 Rudy Seanez
--- Checklist

1988 Pro Cards Williamsport Bills

(Cleveland Indians, AA)

	MT	NR MT	EX
Complete Set:	6.00	4.50	2.50

1303 Lee Kuntz
1304 Tom Lampkin
1305 Kent Murphy
1306 Mike Hargrove
1307 Mike Farr
1308 Andy Ghelfi
1309 Jeff Shaw
1310 Mike Walker
1311 Brian Allard
1312 Turner Gill
1313 Brian Graham
1314 Tony Ghelfi
1315 Kevin Wickander
1316 Stan Hilton
1317 Casey Webster
1318 Theo Shaw
1319 Darryl Landrum
1320 Claudio Carrasco
1321 Paul Kuzniar
1322 Mark Howie
1323 Jim Bruske
1324 Doyle Wilson
1325 Mike Poehl
1326 Scott Jordan
1327 Milt Harper
1328 Kerry Richardson
--- Checklist

1988 Pro Cards Wytheville Cubs

	MT	NR MT	EX
Complete Set:	6.00	4.50	2.50

1975 Milciades Uribe
1976 Rob Bonneau
1977 Wayne Weinheimer
1978 Kevin Roberson
1979 Brad Huff
1980 Victor Cancel
1981 Sean Reed
1982 Marvin Cole
1983 Bill Paynter
1984 Tony Whitson
1985 Daren Burns
1986 Roberto Smalls
1987 Bubba Browder
1988 Julio Valdez
1989 Bill Earley
1990 Woody Smith
1991 Steve Roadcap
1992 Benny Shreve
1993 Mike Galdu
1994 Kenny Holley
1995 Ivan Marteniz
1996 Matt Leonard
1997 Jason Doss
1999 Marc Caosielli
2000 Billy Gamble
2001 Ronnie Rasp
2002 Jerome Williams
2003 Troy Bailey
2004 Team Photo
--- Checklist

1988 Pucko Little Falls Mets

(New York Mets, A)

	MT	NR MT	EX
Complete Set:	5.00	3.75	2.00

1 Lee May
2 Kevin Baez
3 Tom Bales
4 Tom Becker
5 Ron Height
6 Todd Hundley
7 Michael Noelke
8 Bob Olah
9 Steve Piskor
10 Radhames Polanco
11 Titi Roche
12 Sammye Sanchez
13 Greg Turtletaub
14 Lonnie Walker
15 Terry Bross
16 Terry Griffin
17 Chris Hill
18 Steve Newton
19 Vladimir Perez
20 Dale Plummer
21 Dave Proctor
22 Pete Schourek
23 John Wenrick
24 Anthony Young
25 Brian Zimmerman
26 Bill Stein
27 Al Jackson
28 Rick McWane
29 Frenk Minnissale

1988 Pucko Rochester Red Wings

(Baltimore Orioles, AAA)

	MT	NR MT	EX
Complete Set:	12.50	9.50	5.25

1 Rochester Red Wings
2 Mark Bowden
3 Dale Berra
4 Curt Brown
5 Matt Cimo
6 Gordon Dillard
7 Steve Finley
8 Mike Griffin
9 John Habyan
10 Pete Harnisch
11 Kevin Hickey
12 Gerry Holtz
13 Keith Hughes
14 Ken Landreaux
15 Vic Mata
16 Bob Milacki
17 Jerry Narron
18 Carl Nichols
19 Dickie Noles
20 Chris Padget
21 Tim Pyznarski
22 Mike Raczka
23 Wade Rowdon
24 Ron Salcedo
25 Chuck Stanhope
26 Jeff Stone
27 Craig Worthington
28 Dom Chiti
29 Curt Motton
30 Johnny Oates
31 Jamie Reed
32 Bob Goughan
33 Rochester Red Wings
34 Rochester Red Wings
35 Rochester Red Wings
36 Rochester Red Wings

1988 Pucko Utica Blue Sox

(Chicago White Sox, A)

	MT	NR MT	EX
Complete Set:	5.00	3.75	2.00

1 Rob Lukachyk
2 Clemente Alvarez
3 Brett Berry
4 Mark Chasey
5 Paul Fuller
6 Vince Harris
7 Derek Lee
8 Steve Mehl
9 Jesus Merejo
10 Eugenio Tejada
11 Marcus Trammell
12 Randy Warren
13 John Zaksek
14 John Chafin
15 Virgil Cooper
16 Fred Dabney
17 Carlos De LaCruz
18 Keith Felden
19 Scott Fuller
20 Mike Galvan
21 Pat Mehrtens
22 Frank Merigliano
23 Jose Pena
24 Ron Stephens
25 Ed Walsh
26 Rick Patterson
27 Preston Douglas
28 Steve Jessup
29 Joanne Gerace

1988 Pucko Watertown Pirates

(Pittsburgh Pirates, A)

	MT	NR MT	EX
Complete Set:	6.00	4.50	2.50

1 Keith Richardson, Keith Richardson
2 Joe Ausanio, Joe Ausanio
3 Steve Buckholz, Steve Buckholz
4 Rodger Castner, Rodger Castner
5 Joel Forrest, Joel Forrest
6 Tim Holmes, Tim Holmes
7 Mark Koller, Mark Koller
8 Craig Lewis, Craig Lewis
9 Dan Nielson, Dan Nielson
10 Ernesto Santana, Ernesto Santana
11 Mike Stevanus, Mike Stevanus
12 Randy Tomlin, Randy Tomlin
13 Bobby Underwood, Bobby Underwood
14 Bryan Arnold, Bryan Arnold
15 Jay Bluthardt, Jay Bluthardt
16 Ken Buksa, Ken Buksa
17 Ralph Denkenberger, Ralph Denkenberger
18 Chris Estep, Chris Estep
19 Mike Huyler, Mike Huyler
20 Deron Johnson, Deron Johnson
21 Domingo Merejo, Domingo Merejo
22 Steve Montejo, Steve Montejo
23 Darwin Pennye, Darwin Pennye
24 Paul Spalt, Paul Spalt
25 Dave Stone, Dave Stone
26 Mike Valla, Mike Valla
27 Tim Wakefield, Tim Wakefield
28 John Wehner, John Wehner
29 Flavio Williams, Flavio Williams
30 John Young, John Young
31 Stan Cliburn, Stan Cliburn
32 Tom Barnard, Tom Barnard
33 Robert Bill, Robert Bill
34 Gene Sunnen, Gene Sunnen
35 Bob Burgess & Bob Morgia, Bob Burgess & Bob Morgia

1988 Rock's Dugout Wichita Pilots

(San Diego Padres, AA) This set is numbered by the player's uniforms.

	MT	NR MT	EX
Complete Set:	7.50	5.50	3.00

Matt Maysey
Logo card
10 Mike DeButch
11 Jeff Yurtin
12 Craig Wiley
14 Chris Knabenshue
15 Carlos Baerga
16 Mike Basso
17 Nate Colbert
18 Jim Tatum
19 Gregg Harris
20 Terry Gilmore
21 Bill Wrona
22 Jimmy Lester
23 Paul Quinzer
24 Craig Cooper
25 James Austin
26 Mike Costello
27 Jeff Hermann
28 Pat Jelks
29 Bill Stevenson
30 Jeff Childers
31 Mike Mills
32 Kevin Brown
33 Eric Bauer
40 Pat Kelly
41 Rusty Ford
42 Steve Luebber
43 Matt Maysey

1988 SG & CC Tidewater Tides

(New York Mets, AAA) This set is numbered as it appears on the cards. The set is also in the form of a perforated uncut sheet. The team photo measure approximately 9-1/2 x 11 inches in size.

	MT	NR MT	EX
Complete Set:	25.00	18.50	10.00

Sam McCrary
Dave Rosenfield
R.C. Reuteman
Tony Mercurio
Team photo
4 Steve Frey
5 Ken Dowell
9 Gregg Jeffries
10 Steve Springer
11 Darren Reed
16 Tim Tolman
17 Andre David
18 Jeff McKnight
19 Jose Roman
21 Wally Whitehurst
22 Joaquin Contreras
23 Jack Savage
25 Keith Miller
26 Mike Cubbage
27 John Miller
28 Tom Edens
29 Greg Olson
30 Dave West
31 Mark Carreon
33 Phil Lombardi
34 John Cumberland
35 Tim Drummond
36 Tom McCarthy
37 Rich Miller
39 Randy Niemann
40 Jeff Innis

1988 Sport Pro Butte Copper Kings

(Texas Rangers, R)

	MT	NR MT	EX
Complete Set:	12.00	9.00	5.00

1 Mike Hamilton
2 Jim Hivizda
3 Greg Kuzman
4 Tim MacNeil
5 Robb Nen
6 Ken Penland
7 Carl Randle
8 Bill Schorr
9 Cedrick Shaw
10 Kyle Spencer
11 Kenny Shiozaki
12 Denny Tomori
13 Bill Losa
14 Jeff Frye
15 Rob Maurer
16 Dom Pierce
17 Joe Wardlow
18 Trey McCoy
19 Rod Morris
20 Mike Spear
21 Thayer Swain
22 Monty Farriss
23 Travis Law
24 Brad Fontes
25 Jeff Hainline
26 Steve Allen
27 Ev Cunningham
28 Ernie Rodriquez
29 Bump Wills

1988 Star Co. Baseball City Royals

(Kansas City Royals, A)

	MT	NR MT	EX
Complete Set:	10.00	7.50	4.00

1 Bud Adams
2 Ken Adams
3 Jon Alexander
4 Jose Anglero
5 Kevin Appier
6 Sean Berry
7 Mike Butcher
8 Dera Clark
9 Tony Bridges-Clements
10 Jeff Conine
11 Carlos Escalera
12 Carlos Gonzalez
13 Dan Harlan
14 Kenny Jackson
15 Kevin Koslofski
16 Richie LeBlanc Jr.
17 Brian McRae
18 Bobby Moore
19 Harvey Pulliam Jr.
20a Tom Rice
20b Luis Silverio (late issue, misnumbered, gold rather than blue border)
21 Joe Skodny
22 Mike Tresemer
23a Aguedo Vasquez (correct name & stats, wrong picture)
23b Aguedo Vasquez (corrected)
24a Steve Walker (correct name & stats, wrong picture)
24b Steve Walker (corrected)
25 DeJon Watson

1988 Star Co. Carolina League All-Stars

(A)

	MT	NR MT	EX
Complete Set:	10.50	7.75	4.25

1 Jay Ward
2 Mike Hart
3 Stan Belinda
4 Royal Clayton
5 Scott Cooper
6 Brian DuBois
7 Mike Eberle
8 Andy Hall
9 Chris Howard
10 Dean Kelley
11 Tim Kirk
12 Joe Marchese
13 Jim Orsag
14 Julio Peguero
15 John Ramos
16 Enrique Rios
17 Randy Strijek
18 Junior Vizcaino
19 Bernie Williams
20 Bob Zupcic
21 Glenn Adams
22 Pete Alborano
23 Beau Allred
24 Kevin Bearse
25 Mike Bell
26 Luis Cruz
27 Butch Garcia
28 Phil Harrison
29 Allen Liebert
30 Kelly Mann
31 Kent Mercker
32 Rick Morris
33 Charles Ogden
34 Dave Plumb
35 Greg Smith
36 Rob Swain
37 Theron Todd
38 Mike Twardoski
39 Danny Weems
40 Mike Westbrook

1988 Star Co. Clearwater Phillies

(Philadelphia Phillies, A)

	MT	NR MT	EX
Complete Set:	7.00	5.25	2.75

1 Steve Bates
2 Cliff Brantley
3 Rod Brunelle
4 Pete Callas
5a Chris Calvert
5b Luis Iglesias (misnumbered)
6 Ramon Caraballo
7 Fred Christopher
8 Garry Clark
9 Todd Crosby
10 Shawn Dantzler
11 Kevin Fynan
12a Jason Grimsley
12b Travis Walden (late issue, misnumbered, gold rather than red border)
13 Jeff Grotewold
14 Todd Howey
16 Steve Kirkpatrick
17 Chris Limbach
18 Pete Maldonado
19 Trey McCall
20 Scott Reaves
21 Mark Sims
22 Steve Scarsone
23 Brad Smith
24 Tim Taft
25 Royal Thomas
26 Travis Walden

1988 Star Co. Dunedin Blue Jays

(Toronto Blue Jays, A)

	MT	NR MT	EX
Complete Set:	7.00	5.25	2.75

1 Francisco Cabrera
2 Tony Castillo
3a Wayne Davis
3b Doug Ault (late issue, misnumbered, gold rather than aqua border)
4 Jose Diaz
5 Richard DePastino
6 Lindsay Foster
7 Peter Geist
8 Darren Hall
9 Pat Hentgen
10 Vince Horsman
11 Shawn Jeter
12 Steve Mumaw
13 Pedro Munoz
14 Paul Rodgers
15 Earl Sanders
16 Jerry Schunk
17 Jason Townley
18 Tracy James
19 Darrin Wade
20 Bob Watts
21 Mark Whiten
22 Bob Wishnevski
23 Julian Yan
24 Mark Young

1988 Star Co. Durham Bulls (Orange)

(Atlanta Braves, A)

	MT	NR MT	EX
Complete Set:	8.50	6.25	3.50

1 Michael Bell
2 Scott Bohlke
3 David Butts
4 Jim Czajowski
5 Jeff Dodig
6 Mike Fowler
7 Ted Holcomb
8 Cesar Jimenez
9 Dodd Johnson
10 Rich Longuil
11 Phil Maldonado
12 Rich Maloney
13 Paul Marak
14 Kent Mercker
15 Rick Morris
16 Kenneth Pennington
17 Dave Plumb
18 Ellis Roby
19 Doug Stockam
20 Mike Stoker
21 Theron Todd

22 Lee Upshaw
23 Danny Weems
24 Walt Williams
25 Buddy Bailey
26 Kevin Costner

1988 Star Co. Durham Bulls

(Atlanta Braves, A) The Costner Gold cards in this set were issued late and are misnumbered. Many of them were sold as single cards and not included in sets. The Gold card in sets should be considered quite scare. The Costner no number card was re-issued as a blue card at the request of the ball club and again were sold as singles even though they should be included in the sets.

	MT	NR MT	EX
Complete Set:	12.00	9.00	5.00

Kevin Costner (Blue)
1 Michael Bell
2 Scott Bohlke
3 David Butts
4a Jim Czajowski
4b Buddy Bailey (Gold)
5 Jeff Dodig
6 Mike Fowler
7 Ted Holcomb
8 Cesar Jimenez
9a Dodd Johnson
9b Kevin Costner (Gold)
10 Rich Longuil
11 Phil Maldinado
12 Rich Maloney
13 Paul Marak
14 Kent Mercker
15 Rick Morris
16 Kenneth Pennington
17 Dave Plumb
18 Ellis Roby
19 Doug Stockam
20 Mike Stoker
21 Theron Todd
22 Lee Upshaw
23 Danny Weems
24 Walt Williams

1988 Star Co. Florida State All-Stars

(A)

	MT	NR MT	EX
Complete Set:	7.50	5.50	3.00

1 John Shoemaker
2 Felipe Alou
3 Keith Bodie
4 Doug Cinnella
5 Scott Diez
6 Kip Gross
7 Dave Hansen
8 Randy Hennis
9 Nels Jacobsen
10 Chris Limbach
11 Luis Martinez
12 Todd McClure
13 Brian Morrison
14 Bob Natal
15 Chris Nichting
16 Geronimo Pena
17 Fritz Polka
18 Karl Rhodes
19 Homar Rojas
20 Miguel Santana
21 Mike Simms
22 Greg Talamantez
23 John Vanderwal
24 Juan Villaneuva
25 Mike White
26 Masahiro Yamaoto
27 Buck Showalter
28 John Lipon
29 Russ Meyer
30 Luis Silverio
31 Phil Clark
32 Milt Cuyler
33 Jose Diaz
34 Carlos Escalera
35 Greg Everson
36 Blame Fox
37 Cornelio Garcia
38 Darrin Garner
39 Mike Hansen
40 Brent Knackert
41 Adam Lamle
42 Richie LeBlanc
43 Ravelo Manzanillo
44 Kevin Mmahat
45 Tony Morrison
46 Livio Padilla
47 Dean Palmer
48 Dan Rohrmeier
49 Carl Sullivan
50 Aquedo Vasquez
51 Don Vesling
52 Julian Yan

1988 Star Co. Ft. Lauderdale Yankees

(New York Yankees, A)

	MT	NR MT	EX
Complete Set:	7.00	5.25	2.75

1 Dan Arendas
2 Luc Berube
3 Art Clavert
4 Darrin Chapin
5 Bob Dickerson
6 Jim Ehrhard
7 Steve Erickson
8 Fernando Figueroa
9 Scott Gay
10 Doug Gogolewski
11 Fred Hailey
12 Rodney Imes
13 Scoitt Kamieniecki
14 Ralph Kraus
15 Mark Mitchell
16 Kevin Mmahat
17 Tony Morrison
18 Carlos Rodriguez
19a Gabriel Rodriguez
19b Buck Showalter (late issue, misnumbered, gold rather than purple border)
20 Dan Roman
21 Wade Taylor
22 David Turgeon
23 Bill Voeltz
24 Thomas Weeks

1988 Star Co. Hagerstown Suns

(Baltimore Orioles, AA)

	MT	NR MT	EX
Complete Set:	7.00	5.25	2.75

1 Jeff Ahr
2 Dave Bettendorf
3 Don Buford Jr.
4 Mike Eberle
5 Scott Evans
6 Craig Faulkner
7 Steve Finley
8 Tom Harms
9 Walt Harris
10 Bob Latmore
11a Kevin McNees
11b Mike Hart (late issue, misnumbered, gold rather than orange border)
12 Larry Mims
13 Chris Myers
14 Matt Nowak
15 Louie Paulino
16a Pete Palermo (correct name & stats, wrong picture)
16b Pete Palermo (corrected picture, however listed as Carolina League rather than Hagerstown)
17a Chris Pinder (correct name & stats, wrong picture)
17b Chris Pinder (corrected picture, however listed as Carlina League rather than Hagerstown)
18 Mike Sander
19 David Secui
20 Steve Sonneberger
21 Randy Strijek
22 Anthony Telford
23 Jack Voigt
24 Bob Williams
25 Chaun Wilson

1988 Star Co. Kinston Indians

(Cleveland Indians, A)

	MT	NR MT	EX
Complete Set:	15.00	11.25	6.00

1a Beau Allread
1b Glen Adams (late issue, misnumbered, gold rathern than violet border)

2 Kevin Bearse
3 Joey Belle
4 Steven Bird
5 Glenn Fairchild
6 Greg Ferlinda
7 Mark Gilles
8 John Githens
9 Todd Gonzales
10 David Harwell
11 Christopher Isaacson
12 Scott Johnson
13 Carl Kelipuleole
14 Lewis Kent
15 Allen Liebert
16 Everado Magallanes
17 Mark Maloney
18 Charles Ogden
19 James Richardson
20 Charles Soos
21 Robert Swain
22 Michael Twardoski
23 Michael Westbrook
24 Raymond Williamson

1988 Star Co. Lakeland Tigers

(Detroit Tigers, A)

	MT	NR MT	EX
Complete Set:	7.00	5.25	2.75

1 Scott Aldred
2 Doyle Balthazar
3 Arnie Beyeler
4 Basilio Cabrera
5 Luis Galindo
6 Richard Carter
7 Phil Clark
8 Milt Cuyler
9 Dean Decillis
10 Gregory Everson
11 Paul Foster
12 Blane Fox
13 Mike Hansen
14 Lance Hudson
15a Scott Hufford
15b John Lipon (late issue, misnumbered, gold rather than violet border)
16 Darren Hursey
17 Mark Lee
18 Randy Nosek
19 Dan O'Neill
20 Wade Phillips
21 Gary Pifer
22 Ron Rightnowar
23 Joseph Slavik
24 Bob Thomson
25 Donald Vesling

1988 Star Co. Lynchburg Red Sox

(Boston Red Sox, A)

	MT	NR MT	EX
Complete Set:	12.00	9.00	5.00

Team logo card
1 Billy Bartels
2 Paul Brown
3 Tim Buheller
4 Randy Cina
5a Scott Cooper
5b Dick Berardino (late issue, misnumbered, gold rather than sea-green border)

6 Paul Devlin
7 David Gray
8 Bart Haley
9 Reggie Harris
10 Joseph Marchese
11 Gilberto Martinez
12 Gregory McCollum
13 Timothy McGee
14 Shannon Mendenhall
15 Juan Molero
16 Jim Orsag
17 Mickey Pina
18 Jeffrey Plympton
19 Scott Powers
20 Ronnie Richardson
21 Enrique Rios
22 Kenneth Ryan
23 Scott Sommers
24 David Walters
25 Stuart Weidie
26 Craig Wilson
27 Robert Zupcic

1988 Star Co. Martinsville Phillies

(Philadelphia Phillies, R)

	MT	NR MT	EX
Complete Set:	25.00	18.50	10.00

1 John Anderson
2 Kenneth Bean
3 Al Bennett
4 Toby Borland
5 Greg Breaux
6 Tim Churchill
7 Dan Coccia
8 Matt Current
9 Mike Dafforn
10 Rollie DeArmas
11 Tom Doyle
12 Donnie Elliot

13 John Escobar
14 Paul Fletcher
15 Reggie Garcia
16 Brian Harper
17 Dennis Hoffman
18 Luther Johnson
19 Craig Johnston
20 Troy Kent
21 Darrell Lindsey
22 Antonio Linares
23 Aurelio Llanos
24 Chris Lowe
25 Nick Macaluso
26 John Marshall
27 Eulogio Perez
28 Edwin Rosado
29 Victor Rosario
30 Francisco Tejada
31 Chris Toney
32 Ray Walker

1988 Star Co. Miami Marlins

(A)

	MT	NR MT	EX
Complete Set:	6.00	4.50	2.50

1 Jeff Allison
2 Mick Billmeyer
3 Ron Brevell
4 Mike Browning
5 Hector Cotto
6 Tony Diaz
7 Scott Diez
8 Orlando Gonzalez
9 Clay Hill
10 Matt Huff
11 Kanenori Tarumi
12 Shuji Inagaki
13 Trent Intorcia
14 Masao Kida
15 Brian Morrison
16 Rafael Muratti
17a Mitsuru Ogiwara
17b Jose Santiago (late issue, misnumbered, gold rather than green border)
18 Julio Perez
19 Arnie Prieto
20 Rick Richardi
21 Sal Roldan
22 Tony Rohan
23 Motokuni Sano
24 Dave Von Ohlen

1988 Star Co. Osceola Astros

(Houston Astros, A)

	MT	NR MT	EX
Complete Set:	7.00	5.25	2.75

1 Manuel Acta
2 Samuel August
3 Jeff Baldwin
4 Daven Bond
5 Ryan Bowen
6 Todd Credeur
7a Louis Deiley
7b Keith Bodie (late issue, misnumbered, gold rather than orange border)

8 Pedro DeLeon
9 Tony Eusebio
10 Lou Frazier
11 Carl Grovom
12 Rusty Harris
13 Randall Hennis
14 Victor Hithe
15 Trent Hubbard
16 Bert Hunter
17 Todd McClure
18 Guy Normand
19 Dan Nyssen
20 Alfonso Osuna
21 David Potts
22 Karl Rhodes
23 Pedro Sanchez
24 John Sheenan
25 Mike Simms

1988 Star Co. Port Charlotte Rangers

(Texas Rangers, A) Team is located in Port Charlotte, Florida.

	MT	NR MT	EX
Complete Set:	12.50	9.25	5.00

1 Rick Bernardo
2 Brian Bohanon
3 Omar Brewer
4 Phil Bryant
5 Paco Burgos
6 Rufus Ellis
7 Darrin Garner
8 Juan Gonzalez
9 Bill Haselman
10 Jonathan Hurst
11 Mark Kramer
12 Adam Lamle
13 Darren Loy
14a Barry Manuel
14b Bobby Jones (late issue, misnumbered)

15 Terry Mathews
16 Jeff Mays
17 Darren Niethammer
18 Dean Palmer
19 Mark Petkovsek
20 Lino Rivera
21 Wayne Rosenthal
22 Tony Scruggs
23 Sammy Sosa
--- Rey Sanchez

1988 Star Co. Prince William Yankees

(New York Yankees, A) There was no manager card produced in this set.

	MT	NR MT	EX
Complete Set:	7.50	5.50	3.00

1 Steve Adkins
2 Tim Bishop
3 Brent Blum
4 Dennis Brow
5 Ken Brown
6 Royal Clayton
7 Bill Dacosta
8 Luis Faccio
9 Reynaldo Fernandez
10 Randy Foster
11 Victor Garcia
12 Chris Howard
13 Dean Kelly
14 Jose Laboy
15 Kevin Maas
16 Mark Marris
17 Alan Mills
18 William Morales
19 Tom Popplewell
20 John Ramos
21 Jerry Rub
22 Darrell Tingle
23 Mickey Tresh
24 Bernie Williams
25 Gerald Williams

1988 Star Co. St. Lucie Mets

(New York Mets, A)

	MT	NR MT	EX
Complete Set:	7.00	5.25	2.75

1 Brandon Bailey
2 Chris Bayer
3 Kevin Brown
4 Rick Brown
5 Jeff Ciszkowski
6 Chris Donnels
7 Jovon Edwards
8 Dave Gelatt
9 Adam Ging
10 Kip Gross
11 Rob Hernandez
12 Andre Jacas
13a Scott Jaster
13b Clint Hurdle (late issue, misnumbered, gold rather than violet border)
14 Geary Jones
15 Manny Mantrana
16 Gus Meizoso
17 Doug Myres
18 Hector Perez
19 Fritz Polka
20 Craig Repoz
21 Bill Stiles
22 Greg Talamantez
23 John Toale
24 Dave Trautwein
25 Juan Villanueva

1988 Star Co. St. Petersburg Cardinals

(St. Louis Cardinals, A)

	MT	NR MT	EX
Complete Set:	7.00	5.50	3.00

1 John Balfanz
2 Scott Braodfoot
3 Dennis Carter
4 Jerry Daniels
5 Jerry Daniels
6a Terry Elliot
6b David Bialas (late issue, misnumbered, gold rather than red border)
7 James Fernandez
8 Scott Hamilton
9 Patrick Hews
10 Stephen Hill
11 Crucito Lara
12 Scott Lawrence
13 Robert Livchak
14 Lonnie Maclin
15 Julian Martinez
16 Thomas Mauch
17 Kevin Maxey
18 Scott Melvin
19 Darren Nelson
20 Jay North
21 Geronimo Pena
22 Lenin Picota
23 Larry Pierson
24 Terrence Thomas
25 Stanley Zaltsman
26 Mark Riggins (late issue)
27 Pete Fagan (late issue)

1988 Star Co. Salem Buccaneers

(Pittsburgh Pirates, A)

	MT	NR MT	EX
Complete Set:	7.00	5.25	2.75

1 Steve Adams
2 Stan Belinda
3 Kevin Burdick
4 Terry Crowley
5 Chip Duncan
6 Oscar Escobar
7 Andy Hall
8 Scott Henion
9 Tim Kirk
10 Tony Longmire
11 John Love
12 Tim McKinley
13 Tim McMillan
14 Pete Murphy
15 Julio Peguero
16 Keith Raisanen
17 Richard Reed
18 Scott Ruskin
19 Mike Stevanus
20 Dave Takach
21a Doug Torborg
21b Jay Ward (late issue, misnumbered, gold rather than aqua border)
22 Junior Vizcaino
23 Ben Webb
24 Ed Yacopino
25 Mike York

1988 Star Co. Spartanburg Phillies

(Philadelphia Phillies, A)

	MT	NR MT	EX
Complete Set:	7.00	5.25	2.75

1 Jimmy Barragan
2 Kim Batiste
3 Andy Carter
4 Mark Cobb
5 Darrell Coulter
6 Paul Ellison
7 Martin Foley
8 Bobby Hurta
9 Stephen Kirkpatrick
10 John Larosa
11 Doug Lindsey
12 Tim Mauser
13 Greg McCarthy
14 Sheebie McDonald
15 Timothy Peek
16 Matt Rambo
17 Scott Reaves
18 Rod Robertson
19 Scott Ruckman
20 Royal Thomas Jr.
21 James Vatcher
22 Mel Roberts
23 Buzz Capra
24 Brett Massie

1988 Star Co. Tampa Tarpons

(Chicago White Sox, A)

	MT	NR MT	EX
Complete Set:	6.00	4.50	2.50

Team logo card
1 Hernan Adames
2 Leon Baham
3 Kurt Brown
4 Chris Cauley

5 Brian Davis
6 Bill Eveline
7 Cornelio Garcia
8 Jeff Greene
9 Buddy Groom
10a Todd Hall
10b Marv Foley (late issue, misnumbered, gold rather than navy border)
11 Brent Knackert
12 Jerry Kutzler
13 Tom Lahrman
14 Ravelo Manzanillo
15 Norberto Martin
16 Pat Mehrtens
17 Eric Milholland
18 Kevin Murdock
19 Mike Ollom
20 Jack Peel
21 Dave Reynolds
22 Dan Rohrmeier
23 Carl Sullivan
24 Tony Woods

1988 Star Co. Vero Beach Dodgers

(Los Angeles Dodgers, A)

	MT	NR MT	EX
Complete Set:	10.00	7.50	4.00

1 Michael Batesole
2 Kevin Campbell
3 Timothy Cash
4 Doug Cox
5 Thomas DeMerit
6 Felipe Esteban
7 Howard Freiling
8 Henry Goshay
9 David Hansen
10 Jeffrey Hartman
11 Gordon Hershiser
12 Carl Johnson
13 Eric Mangham
14 Angel Martinez
15 Gregory Mayberry
16 Frank Mustari
17 Jeffrey Mons
18a Christopher Nichting
18b John Shoemaker (late issue, misnumbered, gold rather than red border)
19 Hioetsugu Nishimura
20 Douglas Noch
21 Jay Ray
22 Homar Rojas
23 Miguel Santana
24 Mike White
25 Stephen Wood
26 Masahiro Yamamoto

1988 Star Co. Virginia Generals

(A)

	MT	NR MT	EX
Complete Set:	10.00	7.50	4.00

Team logo card
1 Pete Alborano
2 Mike Borgatti
3 Kevin Brooks
4 Pete Capelio
5 Lee Carballo
6 Luis Corcino
7 Steve Culkaf
8a Brian Dubois
8b Joe Breeden (late issue, misnumbered, gold rather than navy border)
9 Kent Headley
10 Jimi Hendrix
11 Tom Johnson
12a John Joslyn (correct name & stats, wrong picture)
12b John Joslyn (corrected)
13 Frank Laureano
14 Carmelo Losauro
15 Pat McKinley
16 Angel Morris
17 Gregory Papageorge
18 Phil Price
19 Ruben Pujois
20 Ernest Radcliffe Jr.
21 Kyle Reese
22 Kent Willis
23 Ondra Ford
--- Gilinda Phillippe (late issue - very scarce)

1988 Star Co. West Palm Beach Expos

(Montreal Expos, A)

	MT	NR MT	EX
Complete Set:	6.00	4.50	2.50

1 Pat Adams
2a Jose Alou
2b Felipe Alou (late issue, misnumbered, gold rather than sea-green border)
3 Kent Bottenfield
4 Kevin Cavalier
5 Doug Cinnella
6 Scott Clemo
7 Al Collins
8 Rob DeYoung
9 Mike Dull
10 Bobby Gaylor
11 John Howes
12 Nels Jacobsen
13 Ross Jones
14 Tyrone Kingwood
15 Danilo Leon
16 Guinn Mack
17 Rob Mason
18 Omer Munoz
19 Bob Natal
20 Jeff Oller
21 Boi Rodriguez
22 Norm Santiago
23 Jeff Tabaka
24 John Vanderwal
25 Corey Viltz
26 Tony Welborn

1988 Star Co. Winston-Salem Spirits

(Chicago Cubs, A)

	MT	NR MT	EX
Complete Set:	6.00	4.50	2.50

1 John Berringer
2 Luis Cruz
3 Victor Garcia
4 Henry Gatewood
5 Phil Harrison
6 Steve Hill
7 Bill Kazmierczak
8 John Lewis
9 Kelly Mann
10 Jim Matas
11 Derrick May
12 Tom Michno
13 Brian Otten
14 Gregg Patterson
15 David Rosario
16a Heath Slocumb
16b Jay Loviglio (late issue, misnumbered, gold rather than green border)
17 Greg Smith
18 Glen Sullivan
19 Jeff Schwarz
20 Francisco Tenacen
21 Tim Waliace
22 Eric Woods

1988 Star Co. Winter Haven Red Sox

(Boston Red Sox, A)

	MT	NR MT	EX
Complete Set:	7.00	5.25	2.75

1 John Abbott
2 Odie Abril
3 Mike Baker
4 Eddie Banasiak
5 Ken Bourne
6 Dale Burgo
7 Johnny Diaz
8 Donald Florence
9 Roger Haggerty
10 Michael Kelly
11 Jorge Kuilan
12 Donnie McGowan
13 David Milstien
14 Miguel Monegro
15 Tony Mosley
16 Luis Munoz
17 Warren Olson
18 Livio Padilla
19 Juan Paris
20 Phil Plantier
21 Carlos Rivera
22 Julio Rosario
23 Michael Thompson
24 Doug Treadway
25 Leslie Wallin
26 Brian Warfel
27 Paul Williams Jr.

1988 T&J SC Madison Muskies

(Oakland A's, A) (color, 2-3/8" by 3-3/8")

	MT	NR MT	EX
Complete Set:	10.00	7.50	4.00

1 Rob Alexander
2 Bruce Arola
3 Pedro Baez
4 Bert Bradley
5 Scott Brosius
6 Nasusel Cabrera
7 Ozzie Canseco
8 Felix Caraballo
9 Jim Carroll
10 Jim Chenevey
11 Dave Gavin
12 Chris Gust
13 Demarlo Hale
14 Fred Hanker
15 Frank Masters
16 Jim Nettles
17 Bob Parry
18 Jamie Reiser
19 Dion Reyna
20 Marteese Robinson
21 Will Schock
22 Matt Siuda
23 Bob Stocker
24 Brian Thorson
25 Pat Wernig

1988 Team Bellingham Mariners

	MT	NR MT	EX
Complete Set:	6.00	4.50	2.50

1 Jeff Hooper
2 Erick Bryant
3 Brian Wilkinson
4 Dorian Daughty
5 Kevin Reichardt
6 Keith Helton
7 John Hoffman
8 Victor Mangual
9 Chuck Carr
10 Tom Peters
11 Todd Haney
12 Joe Georger
13 Jeff Morrison
14 Wade Taylor
15 Ken Griffey, Jr.
16 Spyder Webb
17 Otis Patrick
18 Mike Goff
19 Brian Baldwin
20 Tony Cayson
21 Mike Sisco
22 Mike McGuire
23 Ruben Gonzalez
24 Rick Sweet
25 Daryl Burrus
26 Scott Stoerck
27 Fausto Ramirez
28 Salty Parker
29 Steve Beiksha
30 Paul Togneri
31 Corey Paul
32 Chris Van Buren
33 Team Photo/Checklist

1988 Team Buffalo Bisons

(Pittsburgh Pirates, AAA) This set is in the form of a 14 x 14 inch poster.

	MT	NR MT	EX
Complete Set:	15.00	11.25	6.00

(1) Rocky Bridges
(2) Benny Distefano
(3) Dave Johnson
(4) Bryan Little
(5) Morris Madden
(6) Jim Reboulet
(7) Tom Romano
(8) Dorn Taylor

1988 Team Charlotte Knights

(Baltimore Orioles, AA)

	MT	NR MT	EX
Complete Set:	10.00	7.50	4.00

1 Brian Householder
2 Bob Williams
3 Butch Davis
4 Kevin Price
5 Tim Dulin
6 Rob Walton
7 Jim O'Dell
8 Jeff Tackett
9 Joe Jarrell
10 Jeff Wood
11 John Posey
12 Craig Chamberlain
13 Rocky Cusak
14 Mike Pazik
15 Rafel Skeete
16 Jim Daniel
17 Paul Thorpe
18 PEte Harnish
19 Jerry Holtz
20 Gordon Dillard
21 Dana Smith
22 Ty Nichols
23 Greg Biagini
24 Curt Brown
25 Sherwin Cijntje

1988 Team Chattanooga Lookout Legends #l

(Cincinnati Reds, AA)

	MT	NR MT	EX
Complete Set:	25.00	18.50	10.00

(1) Chris Bando
(2) Juan Bonilla
(3) Joe Charboneau
(4) Pat Corrales
(5) Ellis Clary
(6) Gil Coan
(7) Jeff Cox
(8) Sonny Dixon
(9) Lee Elia
(10) Joe Engel
(11) Engel Stadium
(12) Cal Ermer
(13) Don Grate
(14) Roy Hawes
(15) "Spook" Jacobs
(16) Jim Kaat
(17) Matt Keough
(18) Harmon Killebrew
(19) Rene Lacheman
(20) Hillis Layne
(21) Jesse Levan
(22) Frank Lucchesi
(23) Jackie Mitchell
(24) Louis "Bobo" Newsom
(25) Sal Rende
(26) Kevin Rhomberg
(27) Costen Shockley
(28) Al Sima
(29) Buck Varner
(30) Gene Verble
(31) Junior Wooten
(32) Checklist

1988 Team Great Falls Dodgers

(Los Angeles Dodgers, R)

	MT	NR MT	EX
Complete Set:	25.00	18.50	10.00

1 Bill Bene
2 Eric Karros
3 Brett Magnusson
4 Ernie Carr
5 Chris Morrow
6 Mike McHugh
7 Lance Rice
8 Jeff Castillo
9 Eddie Pye
10 Dan Opperman
11 Jerry Brooks
12 Don Carroll
13 Jim Wray
14 John Braase
15 Steve Finken
16 Brock McMurray
17 Bill Wengert
18 John Huebner
19 Bryan Beals
20 Sean Snedeker
21 Jeff Hartsock
22 Jose Oferman
23 Mike James
24 Cam Biberdorf
25 Ramon Valdes
26 Tim Johnson
27 Goose Gregson

1988 Team Huntsville Stars

(Oakland A's, A)

	MT	NR MT	EX
Complete Set:	5.00	3.75	2.00

(2) Scott Chiamparino
(3) Brian Criswell
(4) Pat Dietrick
(5) DeMarlo Hale
(6) Scott Hemond
(7) Scott Holcomb
(8) Steve Howard
(9) Jimmy Jones
(10) Bo Kent
(11) Kirk McDonald
(12) John Minch
(13) Jerome Nelson
(14) Jerry Peguero
(15) Tommie Reynolds
(16) Andre Robertson
(17) Will Schock
(18) Bob Sharpnack
(19) Dave Shotkoski
(20) Kevin Sliwinski
(21) Greg Sparks
(22) Bruce Tanner
(23) Camilo Veras
(24) Dave Veres
(25) Bruce Walton
(26) Mike Bordick

1988 Team Louisville Redbirds

(St. Louis Cardinals, AAA)

	MT	NR MT	EX
Complete Set:	12.50	9.50	5.25

Logo card
1 Mike Jorgensen
2 Joe Pettini
3 Darold Knowles
4 Steve Braun
5 Sal Agostinelli
6 Gibson Alba
7 Luis Alicea
8 Scott Arnold
9 Greg Bargar
10 Rod Booker
11 Derek Botelho
12 Rich Buonantony
13 Cris Carpenter
14 Alex Cole
15 Tim Conroy
16 John Costello
17 Danny Cox
18 Mark Dougherty
19 Mike Fitzgerald
20 Dick Grapenthin
21 David Green
22 Mike Hocutt
23 Tim Jones
24 Matt Kinzer
25 Wayne Krenchicki
26 Mike Laga
27 Jim Leopold
28 Jim Lindeman
29 Rick Lockwood
30 Bill Lyons
31 Joe Magrane
32 John A. Martin
33 Greg Mathews
34 Ron Meridith
35 John Morris
36 John V. Murphy
37 Randy O'Neal
38 Jeff Oyster
39 Steve Peters
40 Jim Puzey
41 Dave Rajsich
42 Mike Robinson
43 Mark Ryal
44 Roy Silver
45 Carl Ray Stephens
46 Lester Strode
47 Scott Terry
48 Lee Tunnell
49 Duane Walker
50 Craig Wilson
51 David "Hap" Hudson
52 Billy "Bird" Johnson
53 Billings & Burnett
54 Checklist

1988 Team Modesto A's

(Oakland A's, A)

	MT	NR MT	EX
Complete Set:	6.00	4.50	2.50

1 Jeff Newman
2 Pete Richert
3 Dave Hollenback
4 Rich Berg
5 Felix Caraballo
6 Jim Carroll
7 Jeff Childers
8 Scott Chiamparino
9 Jim Foley
10 Jeff Glover
11 Gary Gorski
12 Jeff Kopta
13 Steve Maye
14 Mark Stancel
15 Weston Weber
16 Ray Young
17 Jorge Brito
18 Francis Ciprian
19 Tony Arias
20 Isaiah Clark
21 Ron Coomer
22 Darrin Duffy
23 Dave Finley
24 Angel Martinez
25 Dan Russell
26 Pat Gilbert
27 Dann Howitt
28 Antoine Pickett
29 Drew Stratton
30 Steve Gokey
31 Dave Shotkoski
32 David Veres
33 Mike Gallego
34 Walt Weiss
35 Greg Cadaret
36 Team Checklist

1988 Team Nashville Sounds

(Cincinnati Reds, AAA)

	MT	NR MT	EX
Complete Set:	7.00	5.25	2.75

(1) Jack Armstrong
(2) Skeeter Barnes
(3) Dan Boever
(4) Marty Brown
(5) Norm Charlton
(6) Tony DeFrancesco
(7) Rob Dibble
(8) Scottie Earl
(9) Jeff Gray
(10) Doug Gwosdz
(11) Lenny Harris
(12) Jim Jefferson
(13) Mike Jones
(14) Hugh Kemp
(15) Terry McGriff
(16) Charlie Mitchell
(17) Steve Oliverio
(18) Luis Quinones
(19) Ron Roenicke
(20) Candy Sierra
(21) Van Snider
(22) Eddie Tanner
(23) Hedi Vargas
(24) Manager/Coach/Trainer card (John Young, Frank Lucchesi, Wayne Garland)

1988 Team Peoria Chiefs

(Chicago Cubs, AA)

	MT	NR MT	EX
Complete Set:	17.50	13.00	7.00

(1) Herbie Andrade
(2) Warren Arrington
(3) Mike Aspray
(4) Lenny Bell
(5) Pookie Bernstine
(6) Mike Boswell
(7) Ed Caballero
(8) Chiefs' Alumni
(9) Rusty Crockett
(10) Sergio Espinal
(11) Mark Grace
(12) Carl Hamilton
(13) Phil Hannon
(14) Hersey Hawkins
(15) Greg Kallevig
(16) Rick Kranitz
(17) Jerry Lapenta
(18) Greg Maddux
(19) Jeff Massicotte
(20) Steve Melendez
(21) Bill Melvin
(22) Mark North
(23) Rafael Palmeiro
(24) Elvin Pulino
(25) Pete & Harry
(26) Jeff Pico
(27) Marty Rivero
(28) Brett Robinson
(29) Gabby Rodriguez
(30) Stars of the Future
(31) Jim Tracy
(32) Rick Wilkins
(33) Eddie Williams
(34) Jerome Walton
(35) Fernando Zarranz

1988 Team Pittsfield Cubs

(Chicago Cubs, AA) This set is in the form of a 10-7/8 x 16-3/4 poster.

Complete Set:

(1) Rich Amaral
(2) Bob Bafia
(3) Jim Bullinger
(4) Jackie Davidson
(5) Jim Essian
(6) Joe Girardi (not pictured)
(7) Mike Harkey
(8) Bryan House
(9) Grant Jackson (not pictured)
(10) Dave Kopf
(11) Cedric Landrum
(12) Jerry LaPenta
(13) Mark Leonette
(14) Brian McCann
(15) Alan McKay
(16) E.J. Narcise (not pictured)

(17) Steve Parker
(18) Gary Parmenter
(19) Kris Roth
(20) Rich Scheid
(21) Jeff Small
(22) Ray Thoma
(23) Mike Tullier (not pictured)
(24) Hector Villanueva
(25) Robin Wadsworth (not pictured)

(26) Jerome Walton (not pictured)

(27) Matt & Ben Webber
(28) Dean Wilkens
(29) Rick Wrona
(30) Mitch Zwolensky

1988 Team Richmond Braves

(Atlanta Braves, AAA) This set is also sponsored by station 35-WRLH.

Complete Set:

Sam Ayoub
Team Photo
2 Jeff Blauser
4 Mike Fischlin
5 Lonnie Smith
6 Carlos Rios
9 Jim Beauchamp
14 Terry Bell
15 Greg Tubbs
16 Sid Akins
18 Dave Justice
19 Bean Strinfellow
20 Dave Miller
22 Jeff Wetherby
24 Derek Lilliquist
25 John Mizerock
26 John Smoltz
27 Johnny Grubb
28 Steve Ziem
29 Juan Espino
30 Alex Smith
31 Gary Eave
32 Marty Clary
33 Tommy Greene
34 Dave Griffin
36 Joe Boever

1988 Team Rochester Red Wings

(Baltimore Orioles, AAA)

	MT	NR MT	EX
Complete Set:	7.00	5.25	2.75

(1) Jeff Ballard
(2) Eric Bell
(3) Dale Berra
(4) Mark Bowden
(5) Dom Chiti
(6) Sherwin Cijntje
(7) Matt Cimo
(8) Bob Gibson
(9) Mike Griffin
(10) John Habyan
(11) Keith Hughes
(12) Vic Mata
(13) Jose Mesa
(14) Curt Motton
(15) Jerry Narron
(16) Dickie Noles
(17) Johnny Oates
(18) Chris Padget
(19) Ron Salcedo
(20) Bill Scherrer
(21) Dave (D.L.) Smith
(22) Pete Stanicek
(23) Mickey Tettleton
(24) Jay Tibbs
(25) Jim Traber
(26) Craig Worthington

1988 Team Rockford Expos

(Montreal Expos, A)

	MT	NR MT	EX
Complete Set:	17.50	13.00	7.00

Nate Minchey
(1) Alan Bannister
(2) Mario Brito
(3) Scott Bromby
(4) John Cain
(5) Jeff Carter
(6) Archi Cianfrocco
(7) Dave Clark
(8) Greg Colbrunn
(9) Sean Cunningham
(10) Delino DeShields
(11) Dan Deweerdt
(12) Howard Farmer
(13) James Faulk
(14) Paul Frye
(15) Gene Glynn
(16) Jeff Hauser
(17) Cesar Hernandez
(18) Rob Kerrigan
(19) Scott Lane
(20) Chris Lariviere
(21) Bill Larsen
(22) Rob Leary
(23) Chris Marchok
(24) John Mello
(25) Jesus Paredes
(26) Mike Parrott
(27) Steve Pearse
(28) Trevor Penn
(29) Chris Pollack
(30) Troy Ricker
(31) Thomas Shannon
(32) Kevin Sheary
(33) Kent Willis

1988 Team Salt Lake City Trappers

(A)

	MT	NR MT	EX
Complete Set:	6.00	4.50	2.50

1 Patrick Waid
2 Murray Brothers
3 Coaches
4 Front office & announcer
5 Chris Sloniger
6 Bullpen Coach & Bat boys
7 Ray Karczewski
8 Kelly Zane
9 Jeff Allison
10 Tommy Boyce
11 Bobby Edwards
12 Rick L. Hurni
13 Will Ambos
14 Greg "Tank" Ehmig
15 Michael Gibbons
16 Promo/Bus mgr & Scout
17 Kerry Shaw
18 Barry Moss
19 Doug Howard
20 Myron "Pops" Gardner
21 Fred Riscen
22 Martin Peralta
23 Terence "T-Can" Glover
24 Tim McKercher
25 Mando Verdugo
26 Bill Wenrick
27 Sal Roldan
28 Lee Carballo
29 Sean Johnson
30 Bill Murray

1988 Team Tulsa Drillers

(Texas Rangers, AA)

	MT	NR MT	EX
Complete Set:	17.00	12.75	7.00

1 Mike Scanlin
2 George Threadgill
3 Monty Fariss
4 Mitch Thomas
5 Efrain Valdez
6 Darrell Whitaker
7 Jose Vargas
8 Steve Wilson
9 Jeff Andrews
10 Jim Skaalen
11 Stan Hough
12 GARY Alexander
13 Kevin Bootay
14 John Barfield
15 Kevin Brown
16 Joel Cartaya
17 Bubba Jackson
18 Scott Coolbaugh
19 Chad Kreuter
20 Steve Lankard
21 Gar Millay
22 Bob Malloy
23 Dave Pavlas
24 Paul Fostier
25 Kevin Reimer
26 Rick Raether
27 Greg Harrel
28 Kenny Rogers

Definitions for grading conditions are located in the Introduction of this price guide.

1989

1989 Best Albany Yankees

(New York Yankees, AA) (color)

	MT	NR MT	EX
Complete Set:	12.00	9.00	5.00

1 Deion Sanders
2 Jim Leyritz
3 Bob Davidson
4 Scott Shaw
5 Tim Layana
6 Royal Clayton
7 Glenn Sherlock
8 Buck Showalter
9 Rob Sepanek
10 Bob Green
11 Ricky Torres
12 Jerry Rub
13 John Ramos
14 Mitch Lyden
15 Andy Stankiewicz
16 Bobby Dickerson
17 Hensley Meulens
18 Aris Tirado
19 Oscar Azocar
20 Tim Becker
21 Rodney Imes
22 Mike Christopher
23 Kevin Mmahat
24 Jason Maas
25 Scott Kamieniecki
26 Dale McConachie
27 Russ Meyer
28 Bob Mariano
29 Tim Weston
30 Checklist

1989 Best (Limited Edition) Albany-Colonie Yankees

(New York Yankees, A) This Limited Edition set has a platinum colored border as opposed to the white border of the regular set. Also the backs of the cards are blue & white as opposed to the yellow backs of the regular set.

	MT	NR MT	EX
Complete Set:	15.00	11.25	6.00

1 Deion Sanders
2 Jim Leyritz
3 Bob Davidson
4 Scott Shaw
5 Tim Layana
6 Royal Clayton
7 Glenn Sherlock
8 Buck Showalter
9 Rob Sepanek
10 Bob Green
11 Ricky Torres
12 Jerry Rub
13 John Ramos
14 Mitch Lyden
15 Andy Stankiewicz
16 Bobby Dickerson
17 Hensley Meulens
18 Aris Tirado
19 Oscar Azocar
20 Tim Becker
21 Rodney Immes
22 Mike Christopher
23 Kevin Mmahat
24 Jason Maas
25 Scott Kamieniecki
26 Dale McConachie
27 Russ Meyer
28 Bob Mariano
29 Tim Weston
30 Checklist

1989 Best(All Decade) Albany Yankees

(New York Yankees, A)

	MT	NR MT	EX
Complete Set:	7.50	5.50	3.00

1 Delon Sanders
2 Mike Ashman
3 Kelly Roberto
4 Bob Geren
5 Logan Easley
6 Jim Leyritz
7 Steve Ontiveros
8 Matt Harrison
9 Scott Nielsen
10 Royal Clayton
11 Tim Layana
12 Kevin Maas
13 Bob Tewksbury
14 Phil Stephenson
15 Tom Barrett
16 Rod Imes
17 Andy Stankiewicz
18 Hal Morris
19 Randy Velarde
20 Darren Reed
21 Orestes Destrade
22 Doug Drabeck
23 Hensley Meulens
24 Tim Lambert
25 Kevin Mmahat
26 Dave Elland
27 Brad Arnsberg
28 Steve Adkins
29 Rob Spanek
30 Steve Rosenberg
31 Mickey Tettleton
32 Keith Hughes
33 Bernie Williams
34 Mitch Lyden
35 Thad Reece
36 Logo & checklist card

1989 Best/Procards Baseball America Prospect

	MT	NR MT	EX
Complete Set:	15.00	11.25	6.00

Checklist card
1 Wes Chamberlain
2 Edwin Valentin
3 Steve Adkins
4 Jason Grimsley
5 Bernie Williams
6 Tino Martinez
7 Beau Allred
8 Rodney Imes
9 Scott Cooper
10 Pat Combs
11 Eric Anthony
12 Darryl Kile
13 Steve Avery
14 Marquis Grissom
15 Delino Deshields
16 Brian Lane
17 Bob Hamelin
18 Scott Leius
19 Paul Sorrento
20 Howard Farmer
21 Robin Ventura
22 Wayne Edwards
23 Ray Lankford
24 Andy Benes
25 Jose Offerman
26 Juan Gonzalez
27 Dean Palmer
28 Julio Valera
29 Sammy Sosa
30 Gary Disarcina

1989 Best Birmingham Barons

(Chicago White Sox, AA) (color)

	MT	NR MT	EX
Complete Set:	10.00	7.50	4.00

1 Robin Ventura
2 Mike Ollom
3 Tony Menendez
4 Victor Diaz
5 Dan Wagner
6 Kevin Davis
7 Doug Frobel
8 Aubrey Waggoner
9 Chidez Garcia
10 Tony Blasucci
11 Grady Hall
12 Jerry Bertolani
13 Ravelo Manzanillo
14 Rich Amaral
15 Jerry Kutzler
16 Don Wakamatsu
17 Craig Grebeck
18 Chuck Mount
19 Todd Trafton
20 Ken Berry
21 Wayne Edwards
22 Doug Little
23 C.L. Penigar
24 Buddy Groom
25 Dave Wallwork
26 Ron Jackson
27 Tommy Thompson
28 Rick Peterson
29 Sam Hairston
30 Checklist

1989 Best (Limited Edition) Birmingham Barons

(Chicago White Sox, AA) This set has a platinum colored border as opposed to the white border of the regular set. Also the backs of the cards are white as opposed to the yellow & white backs of the regular set.

	MT	NR MT	EX
Complete Set:	12.00	9.00	5.00

1 Robin Ventura
2 Mike Ollom
3 Tony Menendez
4 Victor Diaz
5 Dan Wagner
6 Kevin Davis
7 Doug Frobel
8 Aubrey Waggoner
9 Chidez Garcia
10 Tony Blasucci
11 Grady Hall
12 Jerry Bertolani
13 Ravelo Manzanillo
14 Rich Amaral
15 Jerry Kutzler
16 Don Wakamatsu
17 Craig Grebeck
18 Chuck Mount
19 Todd Trafton
20 Ken Berry
21 Wayne Edwards
22 Doug Little
23 C.L. Penigar
24 Buddy Groom
25 Dave Wallwork
26 Ron Jackson
27 Tommy Thompson
28 Rick Peterson
29 Sam Hairston
30 Checklist

1989 (All Decade) Birmingham Barons

(Chicago White Sox, AA)

	MT	NR MT	EX
Complete Set:	7.00	5.25	2.75

1 Robin Ventura
2 Howard Johnson
3 Ken Berry
4 Doug Baker
5 Keith Comstock
6 Ken Baker
7 Tom Drees
8 Scotty Earl
9 Wayne Edwards
10 Bruce Fields
11 Tom Forrester
12 George Foussianes
13 Barbaro Garbey
14 Paul Gibson
15 Craig Grebeck
16 Dave Gumpert
17 Don Heinkel
18 Mike Henneman
19 Ron Karkovice
20 Mike Laga
21 Roy Majtyka
22 Carlos Martinez
23 Bob Melvin
24 Tony Menendez
25 Matt Merullo
26 Donn Pall
27 Adam Peterson
28 Rico Petrocelli
29 Rondall Rollin
30 Bobby Thigpen
31 Glenn Wilson
32 Mike Yastrzemski
33 Stan Younger
34 Logo & checklist card

1989 Best Canton-Akron Indians

(Cleveland Indians, AA) (color)

	MT	NR MT	EX
Complete Set:	6.50	4.75	2.50

1 Kevin Bearse
2 Julius McDougal
3 Jeff Shaw
4 Beau Allred
5 Casey Webster
6 Efrain Valdez
7 Dan Boever
8 William Williams
9 Dan Redmond
10 Tom Magrann
11 Eric Rasmussen
12 Michael Twardoski
13 Mark Gilles
14 Gregory Ferlenda
15 Lindsay Foster
16 Todd Gonzales
17 Bob Molinaro
18 Carl Keliipuleole
19 Scott Khoury
20 Paul Kuzniar
21 Allen Liebert
22 Jose Leiva
23 Everado Magallanes
24 Gregory McMichael
25 Troy Neel
26 Robert Swain
27 Charles Ogden
28 Checklist

1989 Best Cedar Rapids Reds

(Cincinnati Reds, A) (color)

	MT	NR MT	EX
Complete Set:	6.00	4.50	2.50

1 Jeff Branson
2 Stephen Foster
3 Scott Jeffrey
4 Quinn Marsh
5 Michael Myers
6 William Risley
7 Joseph Turek
8 Joseph Vierra
9 Scott Economy
10 Steve McCarthy
11 Duane Mulville
12 Eddie Taubensee
13 Andy Rickman
14 Adam Casillas
15 Kennedy Infante
16 Chris Schnurbusch
17 Scott Sellner
18 Norm Brock
19 Benny Colvard
20 Doug Eastman
21 Tony Mealy
22 Dave Miley
23 Gerry Groninger
24 Don Buchheister
25 Tom Spencer
26 Larry Rothchild
27 Tony Vasquez
28 Chris Lombardozzi
29 Steve Hester
30 Checklist

1989 Best (All Decade) Cedar Rapids Reds

(Cincinnati Reds, A)

	MT	NR MT	EX
Complete Set:	7.50	5.50	3.00

1 Eric Davis
2 Kal Daniels
3 Lenny Harris
4 Chris Sabo
5 Paul O'Neill
6 Kurt Stillwell
7 Scott Terry
8 Joe Oliver
9 Riggie Jefferson
10 Eddie Williams
11 Eddie Taubensee
12 Kieth Lockhart
13 Bob Murphy
14 Ron Robinson
15 Scott Scudder
16 Rob Dibble
17 Ron Henika
18 Adam Casillas
19 Jeff Jones
20 Jeff Branson
21 Brad Lesley
22 Phil Dale
23 Butch Henry
24 Rosario Rodriquez
25 Ray Corbett
26 Eski Viltz
27 Bruce Kimm
28 Marc Bombard
29 Marty Brown
30 Scott Bryant
31 Ross Powell
32 Keith Brown
33 Dan Boever
34 Don Buchheister
35 Lamar
36 Team photo & checklist

1989 Best Charleston Wheelers

(Chicago Cubs, A) (color)

	MT	NR MT	EX
Complete Set:	6.00	4.50	2.50

1 Wayne Weinheimer
2 Eric Williams
3 Miliciades Uribe
4 Kraig Washington
5 Scott Taylor
6 William St. Peter
7 Kevin Roberson
8 Jossy Rosario
9 Mathew Leonard
10 James Murphy
11 Matthew Franco
12 Luis Benitez
13 Herberto Andrade
14 Anthony Whitson
15 Roberto Smalls
16 Sean Reed
17 Ronnie Rasp
18 David Goodwin
19 John Gardner
20 Jason Doss
21 Jay Eddings
22 Matthew Cakora
23 Frank Campos
24 William Earley

25 Greg Mahlberg
26 Jim O'Reilly
27 Watt Powell Park

1989 Best Columbia Mets

(Cincinnati Reds, AA) (color) (New York Mets, A) (color)

	MT	NR MT	EX
Complete Set:	6.50	4.75	2.75

1 Reggie Jefferson, Todd Hundley
2 Keith Kaiser, Vladimir Perez
3 Tony DeFrancesco, Derrick Young
4 Brian Lane, Rob Lemle
5 Joe Lazor, Archie Corbin
6 Milton Hill, Dan Furmanik
7 Jim Tracy, Bob Olah
8 Rich Bombard, Dave Joiner
9 Butch Henry, Michael Noelke
10 Terry Lee, Lee May
11 Pete Beeler, Eric Hillman
12 Alfredo Benavides, Kevin Baez
13 Timber Mead, Chris Hill
14 Bill Dodd, Pete Schourek
15 Darrell Rodgers, Jim Morrisette
16 Greg Lonigro, Anthony Young
17 Chris Lombardozzi, John Wenrick
18 Kevin Pearson, Steve Newton
19 Mike Moscrey, Andy Reich
20 Bernie Walker, Doug Saunders
21 Joe Bruno, Radhames Polanco
22 Don Brown, Bill Stein
23 Jerome Nelson, Jack Fisher
24 Sandy Krum, Pat Hyman
25 Alan Hayden, Rich Bomgardner
26 , Frank Harris
27 Lonnie Walker
28 Kevin Maloney
29 Al Jimenez
30 Checklist

1989 Best Columbus Mudcats

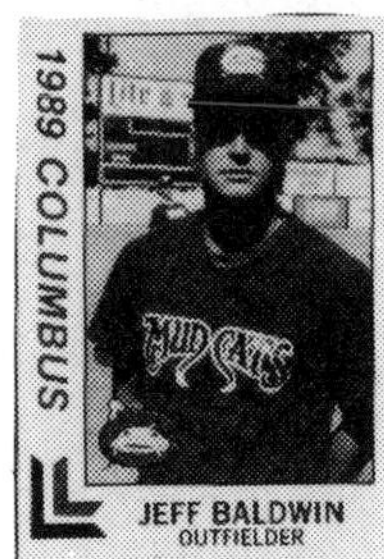

(Houston Astros, AA) (color)

	MT	NR MT	EX
Complete Set:	14.00	10.50	5.75

1 Eric Anthony
2 Manny Acta
3 Garret Nago
4 Darryl Kile
5 David Salaiz
6 Pedro Sanchez
7 Michael Simms
8 Tom Weidenbrauer
9 Randy Hennis
10 Fred Gladding
11 Doug Givler
12 Lou Frazier
13 Jeff Baldwin
14 Blane Fox
15 Tony Eusebio
16 Fred Costello
17 Mike Browning
18 Ryan Bowen
19 Jim Hickey
20 Bobby Ramos
21 David Rohde
22 Karl Rhodes
23 Billy Carter
24 Steve Oliverio
25 Jose Cano
26 Todd Credeur
27 Phil Torres
28 Checklist

Definitions for grading conditions are located in the Introduction of this price guide.

1989 Best (Limited Edition) Columbus Mudcats

(Houston Astros, AA)

	MT	NR MT	EX
Complete Set:	20.00	15.00	8.00

1 Eric Anthony
2 Manny Acta
3 Garret Nago
4 Darryl Kile
5 David Salaiz
6 Pedro Sanchez
7 Michael Simms
8 Tom Weidenbrauer
9 Randy Hennis
10 Fred Gladding
11 Doug Givler
12 Lou Frazier
13 Jeff Baldwin
14 Blane Fox
15 Tony Eusebio
16 Fred Costello
17 Mike Browning
18 Ryan Bowen
19 Jim Hickey
20 Bobby Ramos
21 David Rohde
22 Karl Rhodes
23 Billy Carter
24 Steve Oliverio
25 Jose Cano
26 Todd Credeur
27 Phil Torres
28 Checklist

1989 Best Eugene Emeralds

(Kansas City Royals, A) (color)

	MT	NR MT	EX
Complete Set:	5.00	3.75	2.00

1 Chris Schaeffer
2 Mike Webster
3 Kirk Baldwin
4 Jake Jacobs
5 Don Lindsey
6 Matt Karchner
7 Scott Centala
8 Ben Pardo
9 Ed Pierce
10 Kirk Thompson
11 Dave Ritchie
12 David Solseth
13 Colin Ryan
14 Kevin Long
15 Javier Alvarez
16 Rich Tunison
17 Kerwin Moore
18 Milt Richardson
19 Fred Russell
20 Ron Collins
21 Rob Buchanan
22 John Gilcrist
23 Brian Ahern
24 Sean Collins
25 Checklist

1989 Best Greenville Braves

(Atlanta Braves, AA) (color)

	MT	NR MT	EX
Complete Set:	10.00	7.50	4.00

1 Dennis Hood
2 Brian Hunter
3 Darrell Pruitt
4 Mike Bell
5 Rick Morris
6 Edwin Alicea
7 John Alva
8 Juan Pacho
9 Ellis Roby
10 Jim Lemasters
11 Maximo Del Rosario
12 Tim Deitz
13 Danny Weems
14 Mike Stanton
15 Dale Polley
16 Doug Stockam
17 Paul Marak
18 Bill Slack
19 Terry Bell
20 Buddy Bailey
21 Randy Ingle
22 Jim Lovell
23 German Jimenez
24 Jimmy Kremers
25 Dave Plumb
26 Tommy Dunbar
27 Miguel Sabino
28 Steven Avery
29 Checklist

1989 Best Hagerstown Suns

(Baltimore Orioles, AA) (color)

	MT	NR MT	EX
Complete Set:	6.00	4.50	2.50

1 Leo Gomez
2 John Githens
3 Jose Mesa
4 Robert Latmore
5 Victor Hithe
6 Maduro Garces
7 Sherwin Cijntje
8 Steve Culkar
9 Dave Bettendorf
10 Jimmie Schaffer
11 Tom Brown
12 Mike Eberle
13 Brian Dubois
14 Craig Faulkner
15 Don Buford
16 Brian Ebel
17 Chuck Stanhope
18 Erik Sonberg
19 Paul Thorpe
20 Randy Strijek
21 Dana Smith
22 Rafel Skeete
23 Dan Simonds
24 Jeff Schwarz
25 Mike Sander
26 John Posey
27 Chris Pinder
28 Ty Nichols
29 Checklist

1989 Best Hagerstown Suns

(Baltimore Orioles, AA)

	MT	NR MT	EX
Complete Set:	7.00	5.25	2.75

1 Jeff Ballard
2 Blaine Beatty
3 Eric Bell
4 Dave Bettendorf
5 Dave Corman
6 Paul Croft
7 Brian Dubois
8 Pat Dumouchelle
9 Dave Falcone
10 Steve Finley
11 Ken Gerhart
12 Leo Gomez
13 Ed Hook
14 Bob Konopa
15 Mike Linskey
16 Grady Little
17 Bob Mollinaro
18 Chris Myers
19 Gregg Olson
20 Al Pardo
21 Tim Richardson
22 Bill Ripken
23 Ramon Romero
24 Ron Salcedo
25 Mike Sander
26 Dave Segui
27 Larry Sheets
28 Chuck Stanhope
29 Pete Stanicek
30 John Stefero
31 Scott Stranski
32 Andy Timko
33 Jim Traber
34 Matt Tyner
35 Craig Worthington
36 Logo & checklist card

1989 Best Huntsville Stars

(Oakland A's, AA) (color)

	MT	NR MT	EX
Complete Set:	8.00	6.00	3.25

1 Scott Hemond
2 William Schock
3 Troy Afenir
4 William Savarino
5 David Veres
6 Jim Kating
7 Dann Howitt
8 Robert Strocker
9 Eric Fox
10 Stephen Maye
11 Robert Sharpnack
12 Scott Brosius
13 Weston Weber
14 Tim Casey
15 David Shotkoski
16 Scott Holcomb
17 Gary Jones
18 Rick Tronerud
19 Dave Schober
20 Jeffrey Newman
21 Pat Gilbert
22 Kevin Ward
23 Patrick Wernig
24 Raymond Young
25 Angel Escobar
26 Jose Mota
27 Joe Klink
28 Ozzie Canseco
29 Checklist

1989 Best Jacksonville Expos

(Montreal Expos, AA) (color)

	MT	NR MT	EX
Complete Set:	12.50	9.50	5.25

1 Marquis Grissom
2 Alan Bannister
3 Mel Houston
4 Chris Marchok
5 Eddie Dixon
6 Doug Duke
7 Mike Dull
8 Pat Sipe
9 Kent Bottenfield
10 Travis Chambers
11 Archie Cianfrocco
12 Howard Farmer
13 Tim Peters
14 Quinn Mack
15 Delino Deshields
16 Boi Rodriguez
17 Rob Natal
18 Fred Williams
19 Rick Carriger
20 Gomer Hodge
21 Danilo Leon
22 Sean Cunningham
23 Peter Bragan
24 Dan Gakeler
25 John Vanderwal
26 Nardi Contreas
27 Gene Glynn
28 Melquiades Rojas
29 Checklist (Rojas)

1989 Best Knoxville Blue Jays

(Toronto Blue Jays, AA)

	MT	NR MT	EX
Complete Set:	7.00	5.25	2.75
Complete Set: (corrected)			

1 Derek Bell
2 Kevin Batiste
3 Darren Balsley
4 Carlos Diaz
5 Jose Diaz
6 Webster Garrison
7 Tom Gilles
8 Mauro Gozzo
9 Xavier Hernandez
10 Shawn Jeter
11 Chris Jones
12 Dennis Jones
13 Rob MacDonald
14 Omar Malave
15 Domingo Martinez
16 Mike Mills
17 Brian Morrison
18 Pedro Munoz
19 Joe Newcomb
20 Tom Quinlan
21 Ken Rivers
22 Jimmy Rogers (Schunk pictured on card's back.)
23 Jerry Schunk (Rogers pictured on card's back.)
24 John Shea
25 J.J. Cannon
26 Mark Whiten
27 Bob Wisheuski
28 Barry Foote
29 John Poloni
30 Tim Ringler
31 Logo & checklist card

1989 Best Knoxville Blue Jays

(Toronto Blue Jays, AA) (corrected set)

1 Derek Bell
2 Kevin Batiste
3 Darren Balsley
4 Carlos Diaz
5 Jose Diaz
6 Webster Garrison
7 Tom Gilles
8 Mauro Gozzo
9 Xavier Hernandez
10 Shawn Jeter
11 Chris Jones
12 Dennis Jones
13 Rob MacDonald
14 Omar Malave
15 Domingo Martinez
16 Mike Mills
17 Brian Morrison
18 Pedro Munoz
19 Joe Newcomb
20 Tom Quinlan
21 Ken Rivers
22 Jimmy Rogers
23 Jerry Schunk
24 John Shea
25 J.J. Cannon
26 Mark Whiten
27 Bob Wisheuski
28 Barry Foote
29 John Poloni
30 Tim Ringler
31 Logo & Checklist

1989 Best Medford A's

(Oakland A's, A) (color)

	MT	NR MT	EX
Complete Set:	7.00	5.25	2.75

1 Michael Conte
2 Scott Schockey
3 Frank Harris
4 James Gibbs
5 Scott Erwin
6 Mike Grimes
7 Brad Eagar
8 Scott Lydy
9 Fred Cooley
10 Dionini Guzman
11 Pedro Pena
12 Dave Latter
13 Darin Kracl
14 Nick Venuto
15 Ken Ritter
16 Trent Weaver
17 Lorenzo Furcal
18 Grady Fuson
19 Steve Lemuth
20 Steve Chitren
21 Russ Cormier
22 Craig Paquette
23 Tim Annee
24 Marco Armas
25 Jimmy Waggoner
26 Enoch Simmons
27 Kurt Abbott
28 Dana Allison
29 Galvin Osteen
30 Todd Smith
31 Checklist

1989 Best Memphis Chicks

(Kansas City Royals, AA) (color)

	MT	NR MT	EX
Complete Set:	8.00	6.00	3.25

1 Bob Hamelin
2 John Duffy
3 Jacob Brunfield
4 Mark Lee
5 Aguedo Vasquez
6 Julio Alcala
7 Tony Bridges-Clement
8 Kenny Bowen
9 Stewart Cole
10 Carlos Escalera
11 Deric Ladnier
12 Chito Martinez
13 Brian McRae
14 Angel Morris
15 Harvey Pulliam
16 Kyle Reese
17 Jim Campbell
18 Dora Clark
19 Victor Cole
20 Luis Encarnacion
21 Mike Magnante
22 Mike Tresemer
23 Steve Walker
24 Jeff Cox
25 Joe Breeden
26 Guy Hansen
27 Mike Leon
28 Checklist

1989 Best Orlando Twins

(Minnesota Twins, AA) (color)

	MT	NR MT	EX
Complete Set:	7.00	5.25	2.75

1 Paul Sorrento
2 Jimmy Williams
3 Mark Funderburk
4 Dwight Bernard
5 Ron Garderhire
6 Jim Kahmann
7 Paul Abbott
8 Tim Arnold
9 Pat Bangston
10 Ben Bianchi
11 Larry Blackwell
12 Jeff Bronkey
13 Pete Delkus
14 Mark Guthrie
15 Terry Jorgensen
16 Scott Leius
17 Ken Morgan
18 Edger Naveda
19 Derek Parkes
20 Park Pittman
21 Mike Randle
22 Mike Redding
23 A.J. Richardson
24 Jeff Satzinger
25 Doug Snyder
26 Marty Lanoux
27 Wayne Hattaway
28 Shereen Samonds
29 Jamie Lowe
30 Greg Brinkman
31 Checklist

1989 Best Quad City Angels

(California Angels, A) (color)

	MT	NR MT	EX
Complete Set:	6.00	4.50	2.50

1 Glenn Carter
2 Eddie Rodriquez
3 Joe Georger
4 Bill Zick
5 Jeff Oberdank
6 Kevin Flora
7 David Esquer
8 Jim Aylward
9 Mark Holzemer
10 Mike Erb
11 Justin Martin
12 Larry Pardo
13 Frank Mutz
14 Steve McGuire
15 Bill Vanderwel
16 Gary Murrhy
17 Mark Zappelli
18 John Marchese
19 Bruce Vegely
20 Mike Musolino
21 Larry Gonzales
22 J.R. Phillips
23 Claudio Carrasco
24 Dave Partrick
25 Mitch Seoane
26 Bill Eveline
27 Jim Edmonds
28 Beban Perez
29 Steve De Angelis
30 Ruben Amaro, Jr.
31 Checklist

1989 Best Reading Phillies

(Philadelphia Phillies, AA) (color)

	MT	NR MT	EX
Complete Set:	7.00	5.25	2.75

1 Chuck McElroy
2 Warren Magee
3 Chuch Malone
4 Steve Scarsone
5 Stephen Sharts
6 Scott Service
7 Jeff Tabaka
8 Bob Scanlan
9 Rick Parker
10 Jason Grimsley
11 Cliff Brantley
12 Shane Turner
13 Ramon Henderson
14 Vince Holyfield
15 Martin Foley
16 Gregory Edge
17 Bobby Edmonds
18 Frank Bellinio
19 Eric Boudreaux
20 Harvey Brumfield
21 Chris Calvert
22 Sal Agostinelli
23 Jeffrey Williams
24 Mark Ruffner
25 Ramon Aviles
26 Mike Hart
27 Checklist

1989 Best Riverside Red Wave

(San Diego Padres, A) (color)

	MT	NR MT	EX
Complete Set:	6.00	4.50	2.50

1 Bob Lutticken
2 Mark Beavers
3 Scott Bigham
4 Jay Estrada
5 Kevin Farmer
6 Todd Hansen
7 Brian Harrison
8 Mike Humphreys
9 Tony Lewis
10 Kelly Lifgren
11 Stephen Loubier
12 Bill Marx
13 Tim McWilliam
14 Darrin Reichle

15 Andy Skeels
16 Saul Soltero
17 William Taylor
18 Rafael Valdez
19 Jose Valentin
20 Guillermo Valasquez
21 Mike Young
22 Steve Lubratich
23 Joh Matlack
24 Nate Colbert
25 Bruce Bochy
26 Greg Hall
27 Monte Brooks
28 Jim Daniel
29 Isaiah Clark
30 Checklist

1989 Best San Antonio Missions

(Los Angeles Dodgers, AA) (color)

	MT	NR MT	EX
Complete Set:	7.50	5.50	3.00

1 Mike White
2 Manuel Francois
3 Eric Mangham
4 Darren Holmes
5 Tony Arnold
6 Kevin Armstrong
7 Gordon Hershiser
8 Wayne Kirby
9 Joseph Kesselmark
10 Adam Brown
11 Brian Traxler
12 Dan Henley
13 Carlos Hernandez
14 Louie Martinez
15 Louie Lopez
16 Isidrio Marquez
17 Dave Hansen
18 Dan Scarpetta
19 Greg Mayberry
20 Dennis Springer
21 Homar Rojas
22 Chris Nichting
23 Michael Pitz
24 Tim Scott
25 John Shoemaker
26 Claude Osteen
27 Offerman
28 Checklist

1989 Best San Bernadino Spirit

(Seattle Mariners, A) (color)

	MT	NR MT	EX
Complete Set:	7.00	5.25	2.75

1 Jim Companis
2 Dorian Daughtry
3 Richard Carter
4 Rick Balabon
5 Greg Burlingame
6 Jim Blueburg
7 Daniel Barbara
8 Brian Baldwin
9 Willie Ambos
10 Chuck Kniffin
11 Ralph Dick
12 Jorge Uribe
13 Kurt Stange
14 Jim Pritikin
15 Steve Hill
16 Lee Hancock
17 Anthony Woods
18 Jose Tarabull
19 Scott Runge
20 Bryan King
21 Jody Ryan
22 Mike McDonald
23 Ruben Gonzalez
24 Mike Goff
25 Todd Haney
26 Stan Sanchez
27 Mark Merchant
28 Rich Dauer, Mark Harmon
29 Checklist

1989 Best San Jose Giants

(San Francisco Giants, A) (color)

	MT	NR MT	EX
Complete Set:	6.50	4.75	2.50

1 Andres Santana
2 Rod Beck
3 Jamie Cooper
4 James Terrill
5 Lonnie Phillips
6 Don Brock
7 Mark Dewey
8 Dan Fernandez
9 Bill Carlson
10 David Booth
11 Steve Decker
12 Montie Phillips
13 Elanis Westbrook
14 Tom Ealy
15 Bryan Hickerson
16 James Pena
17 Scott Wilson
18 Kevin Meier
19 Tom Hostetler
20 Steve Lienhard
21 Juan Guerrero
22 James Malseed
23 Jim Jones
24 Steve Hecht
25 T.J. McDonald
26 Mike Ham
27 Scott Goins
28 Duanne Espy
29 Todd oakes
30 Ernie Sierra
31 Checklist

1989 Best Springfield Cardinals

(St. Louis Cardinals, A) (color)

	MT	NR MT	EX
Complete Set:	6.50	4.75	2.50

1 Mike Fiore
2 Dave Grimes
3 Antron Grier
4 Brad DuVall
5 Bob Colescott
6 Scott Broadfoot
7 Luis Faccio
8 Winston Brown
9 Kris Huffman
10 Michael Ross
11 Lee Plemel
12 Jeff Shireman
13 Scott Lawrence
14 John Sellick
15 David Payton
16 David Richardson
17 Charlie White
18 Cory Satterfield
19 Tom Malchesky
20 Dale Kisten
21 Roberto Marte
22 Ti Meamber
23 Edward Looper
24 Fred Langiotti
25 Lonnie Maclin
26 Vince Sferrezza
27 Rick Colbert
28 Dan Moushon
29 Dan Radison
30 Checklist

1989 Best (All Decade) Springfield Cardinals

(St. Louis Cardinals, A) (color)

	MT	NR MT	EX
Complete Set:	7.50	5.50	3.00

1 Todd Zeile
2 Craig Wislon
3 Harry McCulla
4 Tom Amante
5 Frankie Batista
6 Ed Tanner
7 Alan Hunsinger
8 Tom Dozier
9 Danny Cox
10 John Costello
11 Jeff Oyster
12 John Young
13 Matt Kinzer
14 Joe Boever
15 Mike Hartley
16 Paul Wilmet
17 Pat Perry
18 Scott Arnold
19 Dale Kisten
20 Steve Peters
21 Robert Faron
22 Dave Bialas
23 Tom Baine
24 Ray Lankford
25 Mike Perez
26 Mike Milchin
27 Gaylen Pitts
28 Bob Geren
29 Jim Lindeman
30 Curt Ford
31 Vince Coleman
32 Bill Lyons
33 Randy Hunt
34 Mike Fitzgerald
35 Tom Pagnozzi
36 Logo & Checklist card

1989 Best Stockton Ports

(Milwaukee Brewers, A) (color)

	MT	NR MT	EX
Complete Set:	6.00	4.50	2.50

1 Dave Nilsson
2 Chris George
3 Mike Ignasiak
4 Steve Monson
5 Carl Moraw
6 Jamie Cangemi
7 Richard Durant
8 Steve Sparks
9 Kent Hetrick
10 Mark Ambrose
11 Jeff Ciszekowski
12 Danny Fitzpatrick
13 Leo Perez
14 Charlie Montoyo
15 Larry Oedewaldt
16 John Jaha
17 Randy Snyder
18 Gary Borg
19 Chris Cassels
20 Tim Raley
21 Bryan Foster
22 Pat Listach
23 Rob Smith
24 Bobby Jones
25 Jim Poulin
26 Batboys (Chris Moreno, Mike Wickhan)
27 Don Miller
28 Dan Chapman
29 Dave Huppert
30 Rob Derksen
31 (Mark Marino, Mike Conroy)

32 Checklist

1989 Best Tulsa Drillers

(Texas Rangers, AA)

	MT	NR MT	EX
Complete Set:	7.00	5.25	2.75

1 Scott Collbaugh
2 Chuckie Canady
3 Wayne Tolleson
4 Pete O'Brien
5 Dean Palmer
6 Mike Stanley
7 Jim St. Laurent
8 Bob Sebra
9 Steve Wilson
10 Rick Raether
11 Walt Terrell
12 Mike Rubel
13 Jack Lazorko
14 Kevin Buckley
15 Steve Buechele
16 David Lynch
17 Jerry Gleaton
18 Ron Darling
19 Tom Henke
20 Mike Jirschele
21 Eddie Jurak
22 Phil Klimas
23 Chad Kreuter
24 Tommy Dunbar
25 Juan Gonzalez
26 Mel Barrow
27 Jerry Browne
28 Tom Burgess
29 Jim Skaalen
30 Kevin Reimer
31 Sammy Sosa
32 Kevin Brown
33 Rob Clark
34 Marty Scott
35 Ruben Sierra
36 Logo & checklist card

1989 Bob's Photo Richmond Braves

(Atlanta Braves, AAA) (color)

	MT	NR MT	EX
Complete Set:	12.00	9.00	5.00

1 Andy Nezelek
2 Carlos Rios
3 Terry Blocker
4 Kent Mercker
5 Eddie Mathews
6 Kash Beauchamp
7 Bryan Farmer
8 Gary Eave
9 Chris Shaddy
10 Dwayne Henry
11 Tommy Greene
12 Ed Whited
13 Dave Justice
14 Rusty Richards
15 Robbie Wine
16 John Mizerock

17 Mark Lemke
18 Barry Jones
19 Alex Smith
20 Drew Denson
21 Jim Beauchamp
22 Leo Mazzone
23 Sonny Jackson
24 John Grubb
25 Greg Tubbs
26 Joel McKeon
27 Steve Ziem
28 Dave Plumb
29 Charlie Puleo

1989 CMC Albuquerque Dukes

(Los Angeles Dodgers, AAA) (color)

	MT	NR MT	EX
Complete Set:	8.50	6.25	3.50

1 William Brennan
2 Dennis Burtt
3 Jeff Fischer
4 Mike Hartley
5 Hector Heredia
6 Dave Eichhorn
7 Ramon Martinez
8 Mike Munoz
9 Jim Neidlinger
10 Dave Walsh
11 John Wetteland
12 Jon Debus
13 Shanie Dugas
14 Mike Sharperson
15 Chris Gwynn
16 Tracy Woodson
17 Jose Gonzalez
18 Darrin Fletcher
19 Joe Szekely
20 Juan Bustabad
21 Walt McConnell
22 Domingo Michel
23 Jose Vizcaino
24 Mike Huff
25 Javier Ortiz

1989 CMC Buffalo Bisons

(Pittsburgh Pirates, AAA) (color)

	MT	NR MT	EX
Complete Set:	6.00	4.50	2.50

1 Mike Billoni
2 Bill Landrum
3 Carlos Ledezma
4 Jay Bell
5 Dave Rucker
6 Scott Medvin
7 Miguel Garcia
8 Larry Melton
9 Rick Reed
10 Andy Hall
11 Benny Distefano
12 Mascot (Buster T. Bison)
13 Dann Bilardello
14 Steve Henderson
15 Sammy Khalifa
16 Jeff King
17 Bobby Meacham
18 Jim Pankovits
19 Ron Krauza
20 Scott Little
21 Tom Romano
22 Lue Thornton
23 Reggie Williams
24 Terry Collins
25 Jackie Brown

1989 CMC Calgary Cannons

(Seattle Mariners, AAA) (color)

	MT	NR MT	EX
Complete Set:	6.00	4.50	2.50

1 Luis DeLeon
2 Chuck Hensley
3 Colin McLaughlin
4 Steve Oliverio
5 Reggie Dobie
6 Bill Wilkinson
7 Rich Doyle
8 Jeff Hull
9 Bryan Price
10 Glenn Spagnola
11 Clint Zavaras
12 Dan Boever
13 Jay Buhner
14 Dave Cochrane
15 Roger Hansen
16 Paul Noce
17 Jim Bowie
18 Joe Dunlap
19 Bruce Fields
20 Mike Kingery
21 Bill McGuire
22 Jim Wilson
23 Omar Visquel
24 Rich Morales
25 Dan Warthen

1989 CMC Colorado Springs Sky Sox

(Cleveland Indians, AAA) (color)

	MT	NR MT	EX
Complete Set:	6.00	4.50	2.50

1 Steve Davis
2 Don Gordon
3 Jeff Kaiser
4 Ed Wonjna
5 Kevin Wickander
6 Neil Allen
7 Joel Davis
8 Charles Scott
9 Joe Skalski
10 Mike Hargrove
11 Ron Tingley
12 Pete Dalena
13 Brian Giles
14 Denny Gonzales
15 Mark Higgins
16 Tommy Hinzo
17 Paul Zuvella
18 Dave Hengel
19 Dwight Taylor
20 Mark Salas
21 Danny Sheaffer
22 Ty Gainey
23 Rick Adair
24 Rich Dauer
25 Steve Ciczczon

1989 CMC Columbus Clippers

(New York Yankees, AAA) (color)

	MT	NR MT	EX
Complete Set:	6.50	4.75	2.50

1 Bill Fulton
2 Scott Nielsen
3 Dickie Noles
4 Clay Parker
5 Hipolito Pena
6 Don Schultze
7 Chuck Cary
8 Dave Eiland
9 Jimmy Jones
10 Balvino Galvez
11 Bob Geren
12 Mike Woodard
13 Randy Velarde
14 Brian Dorsett
15 Steve Kiefer
16 Hal Morris
17 Kevin Maas
18 John Fishel
19 Darrell Miller
20 Bob Green
21 Bernie Williams
22 Mark Wasinger
23 Dick Grapenthin
24 Coach Staff (Ken Rowe, Champ Summers, Gary Tuck, Mike Heifferon)
25 Bucky Dent
26 Dave Sax
27 Dave Griffin
28 Stanley Jefferson
29 Mark Leiter
30 Darrin Chapin

1989 CMC Denver Zephyrs

(Milwaukee Brewers, AAA) (color)

	MT	NR MT	EX
Complete Set:	7.50	5.50	3.00

1 Jay Aldrich
2 Tim Watkins
3 Tony Fossas
4 Mike Kinnuenen
5 Mike Costello
6 Donnie Scott
7 Ray Krawczyk
8 Jeff Petarek
9 Al Sadler
10 Todd Simmons
11 Bob Stoddard
12 Kiki Diaz
13 Darryl Hamilton
14 Lavell Freeman
15 Billy Bates
16 Darryel Walters
17 Jimmy Jones
18 Ruben Rodriguez
19 George Canale
20 Joe Mitchell
21 Joe Xavier
22 Matias Carrillo
23 Greg Vaughn
24 Jackson Todd
25 Dave Machemer

1989 CMC Edmonton Trappers

(California Angels, AAA) (color)

	MT	NR MT	EX
Complete Set:	6.00	4.50	2.50

1 Jack Lazorko
2 Rich Monteleone
3 Carl Willis
4 Cliff Young
5 Tim Burcham
6 Colin Charland
7 Stu Cliburn (edmonton)
8 Sherman Corbett
9 Mike Fetters
10 Colby Ward
11 Stan Holmes
12 Pete Coachman
13 Edwin Marquez
14 Jim Eppard
15 Doug Davis
16 Mike Ramsey
17 Kent Anderson
18 Mike Brown
19 Jamie Nelson
20 Jeff Manto
21 Lee Stevens
22 Jim Thomas
23 Max Venable
24 Chuck Hernandez
25 Tom Kotchman

1989 CMC Indianapolis Indians

(Montreal Expos, AAA) (color)

	MT	NR MT	EX
Complete Set:	7.00	5.25	2.75

1 Tim Barrett
2 Sergio Valdez
3 Steve Frey
4 Pat Pacillo
5 Brett Gideon
6 Scott Anderson
7 Jay Baller
8 Mark Gardner
9 Tim McCormack
10 Rich Thompson
11 Gil Reyes
12 Razor Shines
13 Billy Moore
14 Mike Blowers
15 Marty Pevey
16 Randy Braun
17 Lorenzo Bundy
18 Jeff Huson
19 Armando Moreno
20 Junio Noboa
21 Kevin Dean
22 Darryl Motley
23 Larry Walker
24 Coaching Staff (Dave Van Gorder, Joe Kerrigan, Nelson Norman)
25 Tom Runnells

1989 CMC Iowa Cubs

(Chicago Cubs, AAA) (color)

	MT	NR MT	EX
Complete Set:	7.50	5.50	3.00

1 Mike Capel
2 Len Damian
3 Joe Kraemer
4 Ed Vande Berg
5 Mike Harkey
6 Dave Masters
7 Kevin Blankenship
8 Lester Lancaster
9 Rich Scheid
10 Dean Wilkins
11 Butch Garcia
12 Lloyd McClendon
13 Hector Villanueva
14 Bruce Crabbe
15 Luis Cruz
16 Brian Guinn
17 Bryan House
18 Howard Nichols
19 Dave Owen
20 Doug Dascenzo
21 Winston Ficklin
22 Dwight Smith
23 Mike Tullier
24 Jim Wright
25 Pete Mackanin

1989 CMC Las Vegas Stars

(San Diego Padres, AAA) (color)

	MT	NR MT	EX
Complete Set:	7.00	5.25	2.75

1 Joe Bitker
2 Keith Comstock
3 Joe Lynch
4 Terry Gilmore
5 Tony Ghelfi
6 Matt Maysey
7 Dan Murphy
8 Eric Nolte
9 Pete Roberts
10 Bill Taylor
11 Sandy Alomar

12 Randy Byers
13 Jerald Clark
14 Joey Cora
15 Thomas Howard
16 Rob Nelson
17 Jeff Hearron
18 Carlos Baerga
19 Bill Wrona
20 Jeff Yurtin
21 Paul Runge
22 Shawn Abner
23 Chris Knabenshue
24 Steve Smith
25 Coaching Staff (Tony Torchia, Steve Luebber)

1989 CMC Nashville Sounds

(Cincinnati Reds, AA) (color)

	MT	NR MT	EX
Complete Set:	7.00	5.25	2.75

1 Charlie Mitchell
2 Keith Brown
3 Jeff Gray
4 Mike Griffin
5 Hugh Kemp
6 Rob Lopez
7 Mike Roesler
8 Scott Scudder
9 John Young
10 Luis Vasquez
11 Doug Gwosdz
12 Joe Oliver
13 Skeeter Barnes
14 Marty Brown
15 Mark Germann
16 Keith Lockhart
17 Luis Quinones
18 Jeff Richardson
19 Eddie Tanner
20 Chris Jones
21 Scotti Madison
22 Rolando Roomes
23 Van Snider
24 Ray Rippelmeyer
25 Frank Lucchesi

1989 CMC Oklahoma City 89'ers

(Texas Rangers, AAA) (color)

	MT	NR MT	EX
Complete Set:	6.00	4.50	2.50

1 Darrel Akerfelds
2 John Barfield
3 Bill Scherrer
4 Mike Jeffcoat
5 Scott May
6 Gary Mielke
7 Dave Miller
8 Dave Pavlas
9 Paul Wilmet
10 Darrell Whitaker
11 Mike Berger
12 John Gibbons
13 Jack Daugherty
14 Andre Robertson
15 Dan Rohn
16 Ron Roenicke
17 Jim St. Laurent
18 Rey Sanchez
19 Kevin Reimer
20 Darren Loy
21 Scott Coolbaugh
22 Tack Wilson
23 Jim Skaalen
24 Stan Hough
25 Ferguson Jenkins

1989 CMC Omaha Royals

(Kansas City Royals, AAA) (color)

	MT	NR MT	EX
Complete Set:	6.00	4.50	2.50

1 Bob Buchanan
2 Stan Clarke
3 Steve Fireovid
4 Kevin Appier
5 Matt Crouch
6 Jose DeJesus
7 Rikc Luecken
8 Ed Olwine
9 Ken Spratke
10 Kevin Burrell
11 Tom Dodd
12 Ed hearn
13 Nick Castaneda
14 Jose Castro
15 Bill Pecota
16 Mike Mesh
17 Mike Jirschele
18 Terry Shumpert
19 Nick Capra
20 Mike Loggins
21 Matt Winters
22 Jeff Schulz
23 Sal Rende
24 Steve Morrow
25 Coaching Staff (Tom Poquette, Rich Dubee)

1989 CMC Pawtucket Red Sox

(Boston Red Sox, AAA) (color)

	MT	NR MT	EX
Complete Set:	6.00	4.50	2.50

1 Tom Bolton
2 Steve Currey
3 Eric Hetzel
4 Dana Kiecker
5 John Leister
6 Mike Rochford
7 Steve Ellsworth
8 Andy Araujjo
9 John Trautwein
10 Rob Woodward
11 Chris Canizzaro
12 Gary Miller-Jones
13 Carlos Quintana
14 Gary Tremblay
15 Scott Wade
16 Dana Williams
17 John Marzano
18 Kevin Romine
19 Jackie Gutierrez
20 Luis Rivera
21 John Roberts
22 Angel Gonzales
23 Eduardo Estrade
24 Mark Meleski
25 Ed Nottle

1989 CMC Phoenix Firebirds

(San Francisco Giants, AAA) (color)

	MT	NR MT	EX
Complete Set:	8.00	6.00	3.25

1 John Burkett
2 Ed Puikunas
3 Dennis Cook
4 Terry Mullholland
5 Mark Leonard
6 Ernie Camacho
7 Marty DeMarrite
8 Joe Olker
9 Stu Tate
10 Trevor Wilson
11 Bill Bathe
12 Wilfredo Tejada
13 Charlie Hayes
14 Tony Perezchica
15 Rusty Tillman
16 Mike Benjamin
17 Mike Laga
18 Matt Williams
19 Ron Wotus
20 Ken Gerhart
21 Jack Mull
22 Paul Meyers
23 John Skurla
24 George Wright
25 Gordie McKenzie

1989 CMC Portland Beavers

(Minnesota Twins, AAA) (color)

	MT	NR MT	EX
Complete Set:	6.00	4.50	2.50

1 Jim Davins
2 Manny Hernandez
3 Kurt Kepshire
4 Steve Shields
5 Ray Soff
6 Lee Tunnell
7 Larry Cadian
8 Mike Dyer
9 Francisco Oliveras
10 Les Straker
11 Randy St. Claire
12 Orlando Mercado
13 Greg Olson
14 Doug Baker
15 Bobby Ralston
16 Kelvin Torve
17 Vic Rodriquez
18 Brad Bierly
19 John Christensen
20 Alan Cockrell
21 Bernardo Brito
22 Mark Davidson
23 Rafael Delima
24 Chip Hale
25 Jim Shellenback

1989 CMC Richmond Braves

(Atlanta Braves, AAA) (color)

	MT	NR MT	EX
Complete Set:	7.00	5.25	2.75

1 Marty Clary
2 Gary Eave
3 Tommy Green
4 Dwayne Henry
5 Kent Mercker
6 Andy Nezelek
7 Rusty Richards
8 Bryan Farmer
9 Bob Black
10 Eddie Mathews
11 Robby Wine
12 John Mizerock
13 Carlos Rios
14 Sam Ayoub
15 David Justice
16 Jeff Wetherby
17 Terry Blocker
18 Drew Denson
19 Mark Lemke
20 Barry Jones
21 Ed Whited
22 Chris Shaddy
23 Kash Beauchamp
24 Coaching Staff (Leo Mazzone, Sonny Jackson, John Grubb)
25 Jim Beauchamp

1989 CMC Rochester Red Wings

(Baltimore Orioles, AAA) (color)

	MT	NR MT	EX
Complete Set:	6.00	4.50	2.50

1 Mike Jones
2 Chuck Stanhope
3 Francisco Melendez
4 Cesar Mejia
5 Mike Raczka
6 Mickey Weston
7 Curt Shilling
8 Mike Smith (Height 6'1")
9 Mike Smith (Height 6'3")
10 Mark Huismann
11 Dave Johnson
12 John Posey
13 Keith Hughes
14 Chris Padget
15 Sherwin Cijntje
16 Tim Hulett
17 Jeff Tackett
18 Harold Perkins
19 Waly Harris
20 Tim Dulin
21 Juan Bell
22 Butch Davis
23 Rick Schu
24 Rick Bosman
25 Greg Biagini

1989 CMC Scranton-Wilkes Red Barons

(Philadelphia Phillies, AAA) (color)

	MT	NR MT	EX
Complete Set:	6.00	4.50	2.50

1 Marvin Freeman
2 Barney Nugent
3 John Martin
4 Bob Sebra
5 Alex Madrid
6 Dave Cash
7 Gordon Dillard
8 Brad Moore
9 Wally Ritchie
10 Randy O'Neal
11 Tommy Barrett
12 Steve Stanicek
13 Keith Miller
14 Matt Cimo
15 Jim Olander
16 Ron Salcedo
17 Ken Jackson
18 Joe LaFebvre
19 Greg Legg
20 Joe Redfield
21 Al Pardo
22 Floyd Rayford
23 Victor Rosario
24 Kevin Bootay
25 Bill Dancy

1989 CMC Syracuse Chiefs

(Toronto Blue Jays, AAA) (color)

	MT	NR MT	EX
Complete Set:	8.00	6.00	3.25

1 Doug Bair
2 Joe Nunez
3 Jack O'Connor
4 Mark Ross
5 Frank Wills
6 Willie Blair
7 Steve Cummings
8 DeWayne Buice
9 Juan Guzman
10 Alex Sanchez
11 Sal Butera
12 Otis Green
13 Randy Holland

14 Tim Tolman
15 Glenallen Hill
16 Stu Pederson
17 Kelly Heath
18 Hector De La Cruz
19 Junio Felix
20 Frank Cabrera
21 Sil Campusano
22 Luis Sojo
23 Chico Walker
24 Coaching Staff (Galen Cisco, Hector Torres)
25 Bob Bailor

1989 CMC Tacoma Tigers

(Oakland A's, AAA) (color)

	MT	NR MT	EX
Complete Set:	6.00	4.50	2.50

1 Rich Bordi
2 Jim Corsi
3 Reese Lambert
4 Brian Snyder
5 Bill Dawley
6 Joe Law
7 Bryan Clark
8 Bruce Walton
9 Chuck Estrada
10 Dave Otto
11 Jeff Shaver
12 Lance Blankenship
13 Tyler Brilinski
14 Felix Jose
15 Buddy Pryor
16 Russ McGinnis
17 Jessie Reid
18 Donnie Hill
19 Doug Jennings
20 Dick Scott
21 Steve Howard
22 Larry Arndt
23 Mike Bordick
24 Pat Dietrick
25 Brad Fischer

1989 CMC Tidewater Tides

(New York Mets, AAA) (color)

	MT	NR MT	EX
Complete Set:	6.00	4.50	2.50

1 Tim Drummond
2 Tom Edens
3 Jeff Innis
4 John Mitchell
5 Jack Savage
6 Wally Whitehurst
7 Dave West
8 Shawn Barton
9 Blaine Beatty
10 Kevin Tapini
11 Ken Dowell
12 Phil Lombardi
13 Jeff McKnight
14 Keith Miller
15 Tom O'Malley
16 Joaquin Contreras
17 Darren Reed
18 Dave Liddell
19 Rick Lundblade
20 Jeff Gardner
21 Mike Cubbage
22 Craig Shipley
23 Marcus Lawton
24 Mark Carreon
25 Rich Miller
26 Glenn Abbott
27 Tony Brown
28 Sam McCrary
29 Mark Bailey

1989 CMC Toledo Mud Hens

(Detroit Tigers, AAA) (color)

	MT	NR MT	EX
Complete Set:	6.00	4.50	2.50

1 Randy Bockus
2 Ramon Pena
3 Mike Trujillo
4 Dave Palmer
5 Shawn Holman
6 Bob Link
7 Kevin Ritz
8 Paul Wenson
9 Kenny Williams
10 Dave Beard
11 Jeff Datz
12 Dave Griffin
13 Doug Strange
14 Larry See
15 Jim Walewander
16 Leo Garcia
17 Dan Dimascio
18 Pat Austin
19 Kevin Bradshaw
20 Norman Carrasco
21 Milt Cuyler
22 Delwyn Young
23 Rich Wieligman
24 Steve McInerney
25 John Wockenfuss

1989 CMC AAA All Stars

(AAA) (color)

	MT	NR MT	EX
Complete Set:	12.50	9.50	5.25

1 Todd Zeile
2 Luis de los Santos
3 Junior Noboa
4 Jeff Huson
5 Scott Coolbaugh
6 Skeeter Barnes
7 Larry Walker
8 Greg Vaughn
9 Steve Henderson
10 Mark Gardner
11 Morris Madden
12 Jack Armstrong
13 Stan Belinda
14 Alex Cole
15 Orlando Merced
16 Frank Cabrera
17 Hal Morris
18 Mark Lemke
19 Randy Velarde
20 Tom O'Malley
21 Butch Davis
22 Glenallen Hill
23 Greg Tubbs
24 Kevin Maas
25 Alex Sanchez
26 Mark Eichhorn
27 Mickey Pina
28 Julio Machado
29 Rob Richie
30 Tim Naehring
31 Sandy Alomar
32 Kelvin Torve
33 Joey Cora
34 Paul Zuvella
35 Matt Williams
36 Bruce Fields
37 Jerald Clark
38 Mike Huff
39 Jim Wilson
40 Ramon Martinez
41 Bryan Clark
42 Steve Olin
43 Andy Benes
44 Lee Stevens
45 Adam Peterson

1989 CMC Tucson Toros

(Houston Astros, AAA) (color)

	MT	NR MT	EX
Complete Set:	6.00	4.50	2.50

1 Rocky Childress
2 Mitch Johnson
3 Anthony Kelley
4 Roger Mason
5 Dave Meads
6 Ed Vosberg
7 Jeff Heathcock
8 Charlie Kerfeld
9 Brian Meyer
10 Dan Schatzeder
11 Matt Sinatro
12 Craig Smajstrla
13 Jose Tolentino
14 Louie Meadows
15 Carl Nichols
16 Casey Candaele
17 Brick Smith
18 Harry Spillman
19 Ron Washington
20 Chuck Jackson
21 Carlo Columbino
22 Gary Cooper
23 Steve Lombardozzi
24 Coaching Staff (Eddie Watt, Frank Cacciatore)
25 Bob Skinner

1989 CMC Vancouver Canadians

(Chicago White Sox, AAA) (color)

	MT	NR MT	EX
Complete Set:	6.00	4.50	2.50

1 Jeff Bittiger
2 Adam Peterson
3 Greg Hibbard
4 Tom McCarthy
5 Jack Hardy
6 Jose Segura
7 John Pawlowski
8 Rick Rodriguez
9 John Davis
10 Tom Drees
11 Kelly Paris
12 Steve Springer
13 Keith Smith
14 Jim Weaver
15 Marlin McPhail
16 Russ Morman
17 Carlos Martinez
18 Lance Johnson
19 Jerry Willard
20 Tom Forrester
21 Cal Emery
22 Mark Davis
23 Marv Foley
24 Jeff Schaefer
25 Moe Drabowsky

1989 Cal League Bakersfield Dodgers

(Los Angeles Dodgers, A) (color)

	MT	NR MT	EX
Complete Set:	8.00	6.00	3.25

180 David Dawson
181 Sean Snedeker
182 Kevin Campbell
183 Jeff Hartsock
184 Bill Bene
185 Macario Gastelum
186 Mike James
187 Rob Piscetta
188 Bill Wengert
189 James Wray
190 Cam Biberdorf
191 Bill Parham
192 Lance Rice
193 Eric Boddie
194 Jose Offerman
195 Scott Marabell
196 John Huebner
197 Bryan Beals
198 Eddie Pye
199 K.G. White
200 Ernie Carr
201 Eric Karros
202 Braulio Castillo
203 Jerry Brooks
204 Chris Morrow
205 Steve Finken
206 Tim Johnson
207 Guy Conti
208 Tim Terrio

1989 California League All Stars

(A) (color)

	MT	NR MT	EX
Complete Set:	9.00	6.75	3.50

1 Jose Offerman
2 Eric Karros
3 Mark Merchant
4 Willie Banks
5 Lance Rice
6 Carlos Capellan
7 Jose Valentin
8 David Jacas
9 Braulio Castillo
10 Mike Humphreys
11 Miley Lee
12 Ruben Gonzelez
13 Johnny Ard
14 Mike Goff
15 Jeff Hartsock
16 James Wray
17 Doug Simons
18 Jerry Brooks
19 Eddie Pye
20 Andy Skeels
21 Sean Snedeker
22 Steve Finken
23 Tim Johnson
24 Guy Conti
25 Scott Ullger
26 Tim Terrio
27 Bill Weiss
28 Don Drysdale
29 Charlie Montoyo
30 Jim Jones
31 Stan Royer
32 Bobby Jones
33 Darren Lewis
34 Gary Borg
35 Steve Hecht
36 Gary Nalls
37 John Balfanz
38 Chris George
39 Mike Ignasiak
40 Kevin Meier
41 Joe Strong
42 Shawn Barton
43 Mark Dewey
44 Bill Savarino
45 John Jaha
46 Joe Kmak
47 Steve Lienhard
48 Greg Sparks
49 Duane Espy
50 Todd Oakes
51 Scott Wilson
52 Brent Howard
53 Erik deSonnaville
54 Bob Brooks
55 George Ulrich
56 Joe Gagliardi

Definitions for grading conditions are located in the Introduction of this price guide.

1989 Cal League Palm Springs Angels

(California Angels, A) (color)

	MT	NR MT	EX
Complete Set:	6.00	4.50	2.50

32 Troy Giles
33 Dave Sturdivant
34 Jeff Gay
35 Ronnie Ortegon
36 Charlie Romero
37 Mario Marlina
38 Ramon Martinez
39 Wiley Lee
40 Christopher Graves
41 Ed Rodriquez
42 Christopher Threadgill
43 Cesar DeLaRosa
44 Edgar Alfonzo
45 Fred Carter
46 Jose Valez
47 Frank Bryan
48 James Townsend
49 David Neal
50 Donald Vidmar
51 Jeffrey Richardson
52 James Bisceglia
53 Brandy Vann
54 Steve McGuire
55 Miguel Alicia
56 Todd James
57 Tim McCoy
58 Chris Beardsley
59 David Graybill
60 Don Long
61 Al Olson
62 Kernan Ronan
63 Bill Lacheman

1989 Cal League Reno Silver Sox

(No affiliation, A) (color)

	MT	NR MT	EX
Complete Set:	6.00	4.50	2.50

239 Mike Anderson
240 Bob Ayrault
241 John Bilelo
242 Jeorge Candelaria
243 Carlos Carrasco
244 Tim Fortugno
245 Joe Strong
246 Brian Sullivan
247 Gil Villanueva
248 Mike Warren
249 Brian Hartsock
250 Gary Nalls
251 Mike Westbrook
252 Joe Kmak
253 Mike Bosco
254 Doug Carpenter
255 Terence Carr
256 Framl Dominguez
257 Kaha Wong
258 Brian Palma
259 Claudio Carrasco
260 Shawn Barton
261 John Balfanz
262 Bill Bluhm
263 Jack Patton
264 Jerry Maldonado
265 Eli Grba

1989 Cal League Riverside Red Wave

(San Diego Padres, A) (color)

	MT	NR MT	EX
Complete Set:	6.00	4.50	2.50

1 Scott Bigham
2 Tim McWilliams
3 Gil Valasquez
4 Rafael Valdez
5 Mike Humphreys
6 Greg Hall
7 Kevin Farmer
8 Jose Varentin
9 Isaiah Clark
10 Montie Brooks
11 Bob Lutticken
12 Andy Skeels
13 Will Taylor
14 Bill Marx
15 Darren Reichle
16 Kelly Lifgren
17 Brian Harrison
18 Mike Young
19 Bobby Sheridan
20 Steve Loubier
21 Jay Estrada
22 Todd Hansen
23 Mark Beavers
24 Tony Lewis
25 Steve Lubratich
26 Jon Matlack
27 Nate Colbert
28 Jim Daniels
29 Bruce Bochy
30 Tye Waller
31 Saul Soltero

1989 Cal League Salinas Spurs

(No affiliation, A) (color)

	MT	NR MT	EX
Complete Set:	6.00	4.50	2.50

123 Ray Velasquez
124 Dan Adriance
125 Doug Messer
126 Larry Carter
127 Scott Nelson
128 Dave Horan
129 Dave Cantrell
130 Yuki Kaseda
131 Chikada Toyotoshi
132 Dragon Taguchi
133 Yuji Yamaguchi
134 Masa Kuoda
135 Yasu Suzuki
136 Toshi Yoshinaga
137 Dickens Benoit
138 Pat Brady
139 Mark Standford
140 Matt Williams
141 Greg Lee
142 Jeff Kaiser
143 Tod Ronson
144 Kerry Shaw
145 Jim McNamara
146 Tim Ireland
147 Jerry Nyman
148 Ken Kajima
149 Brian Castello

1989 Cal League San Bernadino Spirit

(Seattle Mariners, A) (color)

	MT	NR MT	EX
Complete Set:	6.00	4.50	2.50

64 Calvin Jones
65 Troy Evans
66 Will Ambos
67 Jody Ryan
68 Richard Carter
69 Kurt Strange
70 Greg Burlingame
71 Lee Hancock
72 Mike Goff
73 Brian Baldwin
74 Rick Balabon
75 Rodney Poissant
76 Dan Barbara
77 John Hoffman
78 Jorge Uribe
79 Jose Tartebull
80 Bryan King
81 Todd Haney
82 Ruben Gonzalez
83 Anthony Woods
84 Steve Hill
85 Jim Campanis
86 Jim Pritikin
87 Mike McDonald
88 Dorian Daughtry
89 Chuck Kniffen
90 Ralph Dick
91 Stan Sanchez
92 Chris Verna
93 Mark Merchant
--- The Bug (mascot)

1989 Cal League San Jose Giants

(San Francisco Giants, A) (color)

	MT	NR MT	EX
Complete Set:	6.50	4.75	2.50

209 Rod Beck
210 Don Brock
211 Mark Dewey
212 Bryan Hickerson
213 Tom Hostetler
214 Steve Leinhard
215 Kevin Meier
216 Jim Pena
217 Lonnie Phillips
218 Jim Terrill
219 Juan Guerrero
220 Mike Ham
221 Steve Hecht
222 Jim Jones
223 Jim Malseed
224 T.J. McDonald
225 Elanis Westbrooks
226 Andrew Santana
227 Steve Decker
228 David Booth
229 Bill Carlson
230 Jamie Cooper
231 Tom Ealy
232 Dan Fernandez
233 Scoot Goins
234 Scott Wilson
235 Duane Espy
236 Todd Oakes
237 Harry Steve
238 Dave Hilton

1989 Cal League Stockton Ports

(Milwaukee Brewers, A) (color)

	MT	NR MT	EX
Complete Set:	6.00	4.50	2.50

150 Jaime Cangemi
151 Dan Fitzpatrick
152 Steve Sparks
153 Chris George
154 Jeff Ciszkowski
155 Rick Durant
156 Carl Moraw
157 Mike Ignasiak
158 Leo Perez
159 Mark Ambrose
160 Steve Monson
161 Kent Hetrick
162 Dave Nillson
163 Chris Cassels
164 Gary Borg
165 John Jaha
166 Bobby Jones
167 Larry Oedewaldt
168 Rob Smith
169 Tim Raley
170 Randy Snyder
171 Bryan Foster
172 Charlie Montoya
173 Pat Listach
174 Dan Chapman
175 Don "Killer" Miller
176 Dave Huppert
177 Rob Derkson
178 Jim Poulin
179 Julio Cruz

1989 Cal League Visalia Oaks

(Minnesota Twins, A) (color)

	MT	NR MT	EX
Complete Set:	6.00	4.50	2.50

94 Basil Meyer
95 Doug Simons
96 Johnny Ard
97 Steve Stowell
98 Rob Wassenaar
99 Bob Strube
100 Howard Townsend
101 Willie Banks
102 Fred White
103 Kiyoshi Sagawa
104 Shawn Gilbert
105 Mike Dotzler
106 Jarvis Brown
107 Loy McBride
108 Frank Valdez
109 Dave Jacas
110 Lenny Webster
111 Jose Marzan
112 Carlos Capellan
113 Vince Teixeira
114 Kouichi Ozawa
115 Minoru Yojo
116 Ken Fujimoto
117 David Smith
118 Scott Ullger
119 Gorman Heimueller
120 Takashi Yoshida
121 Acey Kohlogi
122 Rick McWane

1989 Candl Coins Fold Out Set Tidewater Tides

(New York Mets, AAA) (color) This set is in calendar form and measures approximately 11" x 28-1/2".

	MT	NR MT	EX
Complete Set:	7.00	5.25	2.75

1987 Tides Team photo,
1 Danny Frisella
2 Roy Foster
3 Jon Matlack
4 Amos Otis
5 Choo Choo Coleman
6 Mike Vail
7 Nino Espinosa
8 George Theodore
9 Craig Swan
10 Roy Staiger
11 Don Schuize
12 Clint Hurdle
13 Randy Milligan
14 Mark Carreon
15 Kevin Elster

1989 Chong Modesto A's

(Oakland A's, A) (black and white)

	MT	NR MT	EX
Complete Set:	10.00	7.50	4.00

1 Ted Kubiak
2 Pete Richert
3 Dave Hollenback
4 Dan Kiser
5 Mike Cobleigh
6 Steve Gokey
7 Rob Alexander
8 Pedro Baez
9 Steve Dye
10 Dan Eskew
11 Daryl Green
12 Gary Gorski
13 Kirk McDonald
14 William Perez
15 Joe Slusarski
16 Steve Towey
17 Brian Veilleux
18 Weston Weber
19 Tom Carcione
20 Henry Mercedes
21 Bill Savarino
22 Joel Chimelis
23 Rod Correia
24 Francisco Matos
25 Stan Royer
26 Daryl Vice
27 Ron Witmeyer
28 David Gavin
29 Joe Hillman
30 Darren Lewis
31 Bob Parry
32 Keith Thomas
33 Ricky Henderson
34 Jose Canseco
35 Mark McGwire
36 Checklist

1989 Donn Jennings Southern League All Stars

(AA) (color)

	MT	NR MT	EX
Complete Set:	6.00	4.50	2.50

1 Harvey Pulliam
2 Robin Ventura
3 Eric Anthony
4 Kelly Mann
5 Delino DeShields
6 Scott Leius
7 Bernie Walker
8 Jimmy Kremers
9 Bob Hamelin
10 Todd Trafton
11 Greg Smith
12 Terry Jorgensen
13 Paul Sorrento
14 Paul Abbott
15 Jerry Kutzler
16 Wayne Edwards
17 Buddy Groom
18 Joe Bruno
19 Mark Guthrie
20 Mel Rojas
21 Rob Wishnevski
22 Luis Encarnacion
23 Buddy Bailey
24 Barry Foote
25 Jeff Newman

1989 Dunkin' Donuts Pawtucket Red Sox

(Boston Red Sox, AAA) This set is in the form of an 11"x19" perforated poster.

	MT	NR MT	EX
Complete Set:	10.00	7.50	4.00

(1) Andy Araujo
(2) Steve Bast
(3) Tom Bolton
(4) Chris Cannizzaro
(5) Tony Cleary
(6) Steve Curry
(7) Mike Dalton
(8) Steve Ellsworth
(9) Angel Gonzalez
(10) Jackie Gutierrez
(11) Eric Hetzel
(12) Dana Kiecker
(13) Rick Lancellotti
(14) John Leister
(15) John Marzano
(16) Mark Meleski
(17) Gary Miller-Jones
(18) Ed Nottle
(19) Carlos Quintana
(20) Luis Rivera
(21) John Roberts
(22) Mike Rochford
(23) Kevin Romine
(24) Lee Stange
(25) Gary Trautwein
(26) Gary Tremblay
(27) Scott Wade
(28) Dana Williams
(29) Rob Woodward
(30) Logo card
(31) Team card

1989 Grand Slam Arkansas Travelers

(St. Louis Cardinals, AA) (color)

	MT	NR MT	EX
Complete Set:	6.00	4.50	2.50

1 Gaylen Pitts
2 Chris Maloney
3 Rod Brewer
4 Dennis Carter
5 Mike Fox
6 Bernard Gilkey
7 Steve Hill
8 Mike Hinkle
9 Ray Lankford
10 John Lepley
11 Julian Martinez
12 Chuck McGarth
13 Opie Moran
14 Steve Mumaw
15 Dave Osteen
16 Jeff Oyster
17 Mike Perez
18 Len Picota
19 Frank Potestio
20 Andy Rincon
21 Mike Robertson
22 Roy Silver
23 Ray Stephens
24 Craig Weissmann
25 Craig Wilson

1989 Grand Slam Chattanooga Lookouts

(Cincinnati Reds, AA) (color)

	MT	NR MT	EX
Complete Set:	6.00	4.50	2.50

1 Jim Tracy
2 Rich Bombard
3 Sandy Krum
4 Pete Beeler
5 Fred Benavides
6 Don Brown
7 Joe Bruno
8 Tony DeFrancesco
9 Bill Dodd
10 Milton Hill
11 Butch Henry
12 Reggie Jefferson
13 Keith kaiser
14 Brian Lane
15 Joe Lazor
16 Terry Lee
17 Greg Lonigro
18 Mike Moscrey
19 Jerome Nelson
20 Kevin Pearson
21 Darrell Rodgers
22 Bernie Walker
23 Alan Hayden
24 Timber Mead
25 Chris Lombardozzi

1989 Grand Slam Columbia Mets

(New York Mets, A) (color)

	MT	NR MT	EX
Complete Set:	6.00	4.50	2.50

Team logo
1 Bill Stein
2 Jack Fisher
3 Rich Bomgardner
4 Skip Weisman
5 Kevin Maloney
6 Kevin Baez
7 Archie Corbin
8 Dan Furmanik
9 Chris Hill
10 Eric Hillman
11 Todd Hundley
12 Alex Jimenez
13 Dave Joiner
14 Rob Lemle
15 Lee May
16 James Morrisette
17 Steve Newton
18 Mike Noelke
19 Bob Olah
20 Vladimir Perez
21 Radhames Polanco
22 Andy Reich
23 Doug Saunders
24 Pete Schourek
25 Julian Vasquez
26 Lonnie Walker
27 John Wenrick
28 Anthony Young
29 Derrick Young

Definitions for grading conditions are located in the introduction of this price guide.

1989 Grand Slam El Paso Diablos

(Milwaukee Brewers, AA) (color)

	MT	NR MT	EX
Complete Set:	6.00	4.50	2.50

1 Marc Bombard
2 Paul Lindblad
3 James Austin
4 Mark Chapman
5 Mike Costello
6 Brian Drahman
7 Keith Fleming
8 Doug Henry
9 Jim Hunter
10 John Miglio
11 Steve Monson
12 Carl Moraw
13 Jaime Navarro
14 Ed Puig
15 Tim Watkins
16 Teddy Higuera
17 Randy Veres
18 Tim McIntosh
19 Tim Torricelli
20 Jesus Alfaro
21 Greg Edge
22 Sandy Guerrero
23 Frank Mattox
24 D.L. Smith
25 Shon Ashley
26 Andre David
27 Ruben Escalera
28 Ramon Sambo
29 Darryel Walters
30 Mario Monico

1989 Grand Slam Jackson Mets

(New York Mets, AA) (color)

	MT	NR MT	EX
Complete Set:	6.00	4.50	2.50

1 Greg Talamantez
2 Chuck Carr
3 Tim Bogar
4 Craig Repoz
5 Chris Jelic
6 Toby Nivens
7 Todd Welborn
8 Dave Trautwein
9 Gus Meizoso
10 Jeff Bumgarner
11 Julio Machado
12 Juan Villanueva
13 Manny Salinas
14 Angelo Cuevas
15 Zoilo Sanchez
16 Johnny Monell
17 Gilberto Roca
18 Howie Freiling
19 Mike DeButch
20 Steve Swisher
21 Bob Apodaca
22 Kip Gross
23 Pete Bauer
24 Chris Rauth
25 Dave Liddell
26 Kevin Brown
27 Brian Givens
28 Dale Plummer
29 Julio Valera
30 Alan Hayden

1989 Grand Slam Midland Angels

(California Angels, A) (color)

	MT	NR MT	EX
Complete Set:	6.00	4.50	2.50

1 Max Oliveras
2 Nate Oliver
3 Gary Ruby
4 Tom Alfredson
5 Jeff Barns
6 Gary Buckels
7 Tim Burcham
8 Mike Butcher
9 Vinicio Cedeno
10 Scott Cerny
11 Chris Cron
12 Frank DiMichele
13 Gary DiSarcina
14 Mark Doran
15 Otto Gonzalez
16 Everett Graham
17 Danny Grunhard
18 Roberto Hernandez
19 Mark Howie
20 Mike Knapp
21 Scott Lewis
22 David Martinez
23 Luis Merejo
24 Rich Morehouse
25 John Orton
26 Reed Peters
27 Bobby Rose
28 Kevin Trudeau

29 Hediberto Vargas
30 Shane Young

1989 Grand Slam Quad City Angels

(California Angels, A) (color)

	MT	NR MT	EX
Complete Set:	7.50	5.50	3.00

1 Eddie Rogriguez
2 Mitch Seoane
3 Joe Georger
4 Bill Zick
5 Mark Zappelli
6 Jim Edmonds
7 J.R. Phillips
8 Glenn Carter
9 Dave Patrick
10 John Marchese
11 Kevin Flora
12 Bruce Vegely
13 Kyle Abbott
14 Mike Erb
15 Mike Musolino
16 Bill Vanderwel
17 Steve McGuire
18 Ruben Amaro, Jr.
19 Gary Murphy
20 Jeff Oberdank
21 Mark Holzemer
22 Frank Mutz
23 Beban Perez
24 Larry Pardo
25 David Esquer
26 Steve Deangelis
27 Jim Aylward
28 Larry Gonzales
29 Claudio Carrasco
30 Bill Eveline

1989 Grand Slam South Atlantic League All Stars

(A) (color)

	MT	NR MT	EX
Complete Set:	7.00	5.25	2.75

1 Stan Cliburn
2 Orlando Gomez
3 Willie Ansley
4 Larry Lamphere
5 Greg Sims
6 Glen McNabb
7 Jeff Neely
8 Brian Wood
9 Keith Raisanen
10 Mandy Romero
11 Pedro Martinez
12 John Kuehl
13 Scott Taylor
14 Matt Franco
15 Chris Hill
16 Andy Reich
17 Todd Hundley
18 Bob Olah
19 Kevin Baez
20 James Morrisette
21 Lino Rivera
22 Anthony Young
23 Reggie Sanders
24 Darren Oliver
25 Jim Hvizda
26 Ivan Rodriguez
27 Jeff Frye
28 Trey McCoy
29 Doug Cronk
30 Kevin Belcher
31 Mo Sanford
32 Dave McAuliffe
33 Mike Mulvaney
34 Lavell Codjo
35 Ray Giannelli
36 John Ericks
37 Gabriel Ozuna
38 Mauricio Nunez
39 Darryl Martin
40 Francisco Valdez
41 Leroy Ventress
42 Glen Gardner
43 Everett Cunningham
44 Randy Simmons
45 Pete Blohm
46 Jeff Osborne

1989 Grand Slam South Bend White Sox

(Chicago White Sox, A) (color)

	MT	NR MT	EX
Complete Set:	7.00	5.25	2.75

1 Craig Wallin
2 Rick Patterson
3 Jim Reinebold
4 Roger LaFrancois
5 Kirk Champion
6 Scott Johnson
7 Scott Radinsky
8 Frank Merigliano
9 Sam Chavez
10 Virgil Cooper
11 Fred Dabney
12 Carlos Delacruz
13 Bret Marshall
14 Mike Mitchner
15 Steve Schrenk
16 Jose Ventura
17 Randy Warren
18 Steve Mehl
19 Kinnis Pledger
20 John Zaksek
21 Mark Chasey
22 Rob Lukachyk
23 Wayne Busby
24 Cesar Bernhardt
25 Eugenio Tejada
26 Greg Roth
27 Derek Lee
28 Ed Smith
29 Jay Hornacek
30 Clemente Alvarez

1989 Grand Slam Texas League All Stars

(AA) (color)

	MT	NR MT	EX
Complete Set:	8.00	6.00	3.25

1 Pat Kelly
2 Chris Cron
3 Bobby Rose
4 Gary Disarcina
5 Scott Lewis
6 Luis Merejo
7 Paul Faries
8 Warren Newson
9 Charlie Hillemann
10 Andy Benes
11 Omar Olivares
12 Rich Holsman
13 Tim McIntosh
14 Shon Ashley
15 Ramon Sambo
16 D.L. Smith
17 Carlos Hernandez
18 Dennis Springer
19 Gaylon Pitts, Chris Mahoney

20 Julian Martinez
21 Ray Stephens
22 Ray Lankford
23 Dave Osteen
24 Mike Perez
25 Bill Bivens
26 Julio Valera
27 Dave Trautwein
28 Chuck Carr
29 Jeff Carter
30 Craig Colbert
31 Gary Alexander
32 Dean Palmer
33 Bill Haselman
34 Juan Gonzalez
35 Steve Lankard
36 Mark Petkovsek
37 Bob Malloy
38 Roy Silver
39 Not used
40 Carl Sawatski
--- League Logo

1989 Grand Slam Tulsa Drillers

(Texas Rangers, AA) (color)

	MT	NR MT	EX
Complete Set:	7.50	5.50	3.00

1 Tommy Thompson
2 Walt Williams
3 Jeff Andrews
4 Greg Harrel
5 Gary Alexander
6 Phil Bryant
7 Felipe Castillo
8 Monty Fariss
9 Darrin Garner
10 Juan Gonzalez
11 Bill Haselman
12 Adam Lamle
13 Steve Lankard
14 David Lynch
15 Bob Malloy
16 Barry Manuel
17 Terry Mathews
18 Gar Millay
19 Dean Palmer
20 Mark Petkovsek
21 Paul Postier
22 Marv Rockman
23 Fred Samson
24 Tony Scruggs
25 Sammy Sosa
26 George Threadgill

1989 Grand Slam Wausau Timbers

(Seattle Mariners, A) (color)

	MT	NR MT	EX
Complete Set:	6.00	4.50	2.50

1 Mike McGuire
2 Tommy Jones
3 Ernest Castro
4 Bob Burton
5 John Reilley
6 John Boyles
7 Ellerton Maynard
8 Scott Pitcher
9 Ted Eldridge
10 Ben Burnau
11 Scott Taylor
12 Mark Razook
13 Brian Wilkinson
14 Scott Stoerck
15 Jeremy Matthews
16 Nick Felix
17 Jim Bennett
18 Hunter Hoffman
19 Jorge Robles
20 Steve Murray
21 Rick Candelari
22 Kevin Kerkes
23 Jeff Miller
24 Jeff Keitges
25 Erick Bryant
26 Tim Stargell
27 Chris Howard
28 Mike Gardner

1989 Jones Photo Tucson Toros

(Houston Astros, AAA) (color)

	MT	NR MT	EX
Complete Set:	45.00	33.50	18.00

(1) Eric Anthony
(2) Frank Cacciatore
(3) Casey Candaele
(4) Rocky Childress
(5) Carlo Colombino
(6) Gary Cooper
(7) Jeff Heathcock
(8) Chuck Jackson
(9) Mitch Johnson
(10) Anthony Kelley
(11) Charley Kerfeld
(12) Darryl Kile
(13) Steve Lombardozzi
(14) Roger Mason
(15) Louie Meadows
(16) Dave Meads
(17) Brian Meyer
(18) Carl Nichols
(19) Dave Rohde
(20) Dan Schatzede
(21) Craig Smajstrla
(22) Brick Smith
(23) Harry Spilman
(24) Jose Tolentino
(25) Ed Vosberg
(26) Ron Washington

1989 Kodak Gold 200 Peoria Chiefs

(Chicago Cubs, A) (color) (corrected set)

	MT	NR MT	EX
Complete Set:	9.50	7.00	3.75

1 Ty Griffin
2 Braz Davis
3 Frankie Espino
4 Marcos Lopez
5 Jeff Massicotte
6 Jay Eddings
7 Brett Robinson
8 John Salles
9 Heathcliff Slocumb
10 Mike Sodders
11 Derek Stroud
12 Rick Mundy
13 Billy Paynter
14 Chicago's Future,
15 Matt Walbeck
16 Juan Adames
17 Alex Arias
18 Eddie Williams
19 Eric Perry
20 Tracy Smith
21 , Fernando Ramsey, Ty Griffin

22 Woddy Smith
23 Warren Arrington
24 Elvin Paulino
25 Fernando Ramsey
26 Harry Shelton
27 Greg Eberle
28 Jeff Pico, Greg Maddux, Paul Kilgus

29 Pookie Bernstine
30 Brad Mills
31 Rick Kranitz
32 Bob Grimes
33 Clar Krusinski
34 Front Office Staff
--- McDonalds Coupon

1989 Legoe Bellingham Mariners

(Seattle Mariners, A)

	MT	NR MT	EX
Complete Set:	6.50	4.75	2.50

1 Greg Pirki
2 Julio Reyan
3 Keith Bryant
4 Jeff Darwin
5 Anthony Gordon
6 Jim Gutierrez
7 Michael LeBlanc
8 Tom Liss
9 Richard Lodding
10 Scott Lodgek
11 Darin Loe
12 Oscar Rivas
13 Roger Salkeld
14 Glenn Twardy
15 Johnny Wiggs
16 Kerry Woodson
17 Lash Bailey
18 Doug Davis
19 Pedro Roa
20 Brian Turang
21 Mark Brakebill
22 Jeremy Mathews
23 Bonel Chevalier
24 Alvin Rittman
25 Tony Cayson
26 Rich Hanlin
27 Corey Paul
28 Willie Romay
29 Dave Smith
30 P.J. Carey
31 Mauro Mazzotti
32 Gary Wheelock
33 Spyder Webb
34 Bill Tucker
35 Jerry Walker
36 Batboys & checklist card-Logo card

1989 Legoe Bend Bucks Independent

	MT	NR MT	EX
Complete Set:	6.50	4.75	2.50

1 Erik Bennett
2 Marvin Cobb
3 Chris Cota
4 Wayne Helm
5 James Jones
6 Jaun Reyes
7 Fili Martinez
8 Marcus Moore
9 David Rice
10 Paul Swingle
11 Willie Warrecker
12 Joe Warren
13 David Neville
14 Richard Parker
15 Tom Rudstrom
16 Damion Easley
17 Corey Kapano
18 Jeff Kipila
19 Brian Specyalski
20 Rick hirtensteiner
21 Bobby Jones
22 Jeff Kelso
23 Tim Salmon
24 Terry Taylor
25 Russell Lundgren
26 Don Long
27 Howie Gershberg
28 Rick Ingalls
29 Bill Durney
30 Bucky (Mascot)

1989 Police Columbus Clippers

(New York Yankees, AAA) (color)

	MT	NR MT	EX
Complete Set:	6.00	4.50	2.50

1 Chuck Cary
2 Dave Eiland
3 Bill Fulton
4 Balvino Galvez
5 Dick Grapethin
6 Jimmy Jones
7 Scott Nielsen
8 Duckie Noles
9 Clay Parker
10 Hipolito Pena
11 Don Schulze
12 Brian Dorsett
13 Bob Geren
14 Darrell Miller
15 Steve Kiefer
16 Hal Morris
17 Randy Velarde
18 Mark Wasinger
19 Mike Woodard
20 John Fishel
21 Bobby Green
22 Kevin Maas
23 Bernie Williams
24 Coaching Staff (Ken Rowe, Champ Summers, Mike Heifferon, Gary Tuck)

25 (George Sisler, Bucky Dent)

1989 Procards Albany Yankees

(New York Yankees, A) (color)

	MT	NR MT	EX
Complete Set:	10.00	7.50	4.00

313 Checklist
314 Rodney Imes
315 Tim Becker
316 Scott Kamieniecki
317 Scott Shaw
318 Royal Clayton
319 Bobby Dickerson
320 Mitch Lyden
321 Mike Christopher
322 Russ Meyer
323 Tim Weston
324 Bob Mariano
325 Jim Leyritz
326 Buck Showalter
327 Bobby Davidson
328 Jerry Rub
329 Tim Layana
330 Rob Sepanek
331 Aris Tirado
332 Oscar Azocar
333 Andy Stankiewicz
334 Jason Maas
335 Ricky Torres
336 John Ramos
337 Hensley Meulens
338 Deion Sanders
339 Glenn Sherlock
340 Darrin Chapin
341 Kevin Mmahat

1989 Procards Albuquerque Dukes

(Los Angeles Dodgers, AAA)

	MT	NR MT	EX
Complete Set:	8.50	6.25	3.50

58 Darrin Fletcher
59 Mike Sharperson
60 Brent Strom
61 Dave Eichhorn
62 Mike Munoz
63 John Wetteland
64 Chris Gwynn
65 William Brennan
66 Hector Heredia
67 Mike Hartley
68 Dennis Burtt
69 Ramon Martinez
70 Dave Walsh
71 Jim Neidlinger
72 Kevin Kennedy
73 Von Joshua
74 Stan Johnston
75 Tracy Woodson
76 Jon Debus
77 Joe Szekely
78 Juan Bustabad
79 Mike Huff
80 Jose Gonzalez
81 Domingo Michel
82 Jose Vizcaino
83 Walt McConnell
84 Javier Ortiz
85 Shanie Dugas
86 Jeff Fischer
87 Checklist

1989 Procards Appleton Foxes

(Kansas City Royals, A) (color)

	MT	NR MT	EX
Complete Set:	6.00	4.50	2.50

848 Checklist
849 Hector Wagner
850 Randy Vaughn
851 Dennis Studeman
852 Steve Hoeme
853 Greg Harvey
854 Bill Drohan
855 Don Wright
856 Hugh Walker
857 Frank Henderson
858 Greg Prusia
859 Ondra Ford
860 Darryl Robinson
861 Steve Preston
862 Chris Garibaldo
863 Jeff Garber
864 Mike Beall
865 Pete Capello
866 Jeff Hulse
867 Linton Dyer
868 Rob Buchanan
869 Brad Shores
870 Allard Baird
871 Andre Rabouin
872 Brian Poldberg
873 John McCormick
874 Ben Pierce
875 Mark Parnell
876 Steve Otto
877 Luke Nocas
878 John Hofer

1989 Procards Asheville Tourists

(Houston Astros, A) (color)

	MT	NR MT	EX
Complete Set:	13.50	10.00	5.50

939 Checklist
940 Matthew McKee
941 Vitas Laniauskas
942 Ron McKee
943 Kevin Day
944 Charley Taylor
945 John Massarelli
946 Roddy Scheckla
947 Rodney Windes
948 Dave Shermet
949 Rafael Campos
950 Willie Ansley
951 Pedro Delossantos
952 Andujar Cedeno
953 Gordon Farmer
954 Brian Bennett
955 Brian Griffiths
956 Troy Dovey
957 Harry Fuller
958 Scott Spurgeon
959 Gregory Johnson
960 Dean Hartgraves
961 Jim Coveney
962 Joe Charno
963 Francisco Perez
964 Rick Dunnum
965 Carlos Henry
966 Mica Lewis
967 Lawrence Lamphere
968 Mike Beams

1989 Procards Auburn Astros

(Houston Astros, A) (color)

	MT	NR MT	EX
Complete Set:	6.50	4.75	2.50

2159 Checklist
2160 Edwin Valentin
2161 Shane Reynolds
2162 Teo Campusano
2163 Scott Makarewicz
2164 Lance Madsen
2165 Jose Santana
2166 Ken Lofton
2167 Toncie Reed
2168 Reggie Waller
2169 Brian Porter
2170 Cole Hyson
2171 Ben Gonzalez
2172 Jim Desapio
2173 Mike McDowell
2174 Francisco Perez
2175 Howard Prager
2176 Luther Johnson
2177 John Graham
2178 Bob Neal
2179 Darin Bruehl
2180 P.J. Riley
2181 Roger Marrero
2182 Donne Wall
2183 Kevin Scott
2184 Doug Simunic
2185 Dave Henderson
2186 Mica Lewis
2187 Rick Wise
2188 Mark Small
2189 Daryl Wooten

1989 Procards (Poster) Auburn Astros

(Houston Astros, A)

Complete Set:

2159 Checklist card
2160 Edwin Valentin
2161 Shane Reynolds
2162 Ted Campusano
2163 Scott Makarewicz
2164 Lance Madsen
2165 Jose Santana
2166 Ken Lofton
2167 Toncie Reed
2168 Reggie Waller
2169 Brian Porter
2170 Cole Hyson
2171 Ben Gonzales
2172 Jim Desapio
2173 Mike McDowell
2174 Francisco Perez
2175 Howard Prager

2176 Luther Johnson
2177 John Graham
2178 Bob Neal
2179 Darin Bruehl
2180 P.J. Riley
2181 Roger Marrero
2182 Donne Wall
2183 Kevin Scott
2184 Doug Simunic
2185 Dave Henderson
2186 Mica Lewis
2187 Rick Wise
2188 Mark Small
2189 Daryl Wooten

1989 Procards Augusta Pirates

(Pittsburgh Pirates, A) (color)

	MT	NR MT	EX
Complete Set:	6.00	4.50	2.50

490 Checklist
491 Jeff Kuder
492 Jose Acosta
493 Tim Odom
494 Jeff Osborne
495 Jeff Neely
496 Mark Merchant
497 Felix Antigua
498 Mandy Romero
499 Chris Estep
500 Bobby Underwood
501 Jeff Stout
502 Mike Stevanus
503 Ken Huseby
504 Darwin Pennye
505 Flavio Williams
506 Keith Raisanen
507 Mark Thomas
508 Glenn McNabb
509 Mike Huyler
510 Antonio Felix
511 Ben Shelton
512 Kevin Andersh
513 Bruce Klein
514 Stan Cliburn
515 Terry Abbott
516 Pete Blohm
517 Greg Sims
518 Rod Byerly
519 Jay Snead
520 Chris Scheuer
521 Kyle Fisher

1989 Procards Batavia Clippers

(Philadelphia Phillies, A) (color)

	MT	NR MT	EX
Complete Set:	6.00	4.50	2.50

1915 Checklist
1916 Tony Lozinski
1917 Jeff Etheredge
1918 Robert Mendonca
1919 Tim Churchill
1920 Albert Bennett
1921 Paul Fletcher
1922 Joe Millette
1923 Steve Parris
1924 Matt Stevens
1925 Donnie Elliott
1926 David Agado
1927 Todd Goergen
1928 Robert Gaddy
1929 Mike Sullivan
1930 Michael Owens
1931 Mickey Hyde
1932 Dana Brown
1933 Joe Urbon
1934 Steve Bieser
1935 Field Staff
1936 Pat Woodruff
1937 Sam Taylor
1938 Greg Gunderson
1939 Eduardo Ortega
1940 John Escobar
1941 Eric Bratlein
1942 Josh Lowery
1943 Brian Cummings
1944 Edwin Rosado
1945 Robby Corsaro

1989 Procards Billings Mustangs

(Cincinnati Reds, A) (color)

	MT	NR MT	EX
Complete Set:	6.50	4.75	2.50

2038 Checklist
2039 Kevin Hudson
2040 Travis Teegarden
2041 Trey Wilburn
2042 K.C. Gillum
2043 Brian Nichols
2044 Tomas Rodriquez
2045 Rick Allen
2046 Chris Gill
2047 Kyle Reagan
2048 David Keller
2049 Mike Goedde
2050 Brian Parrotte
2051 Brian Fry
2052 Sean Doty
2053 Kurt Dempster
2054 Mark Cerny
2055 Rob Dombrowski
2056 Andy Duke
2057 Steve Vondran
2058 Danny Perozo
2059 Harry Henderson IV
2060 Bob Blankenship
2061 Eric Bates
2062 Chris Keim
2063 Scott Pose
2064 Tim Pugh
2065 Gill Galloway
2066 Mark Borcherding
2067 Darron Cox
2068 Trevor Hoffman

1989 Procards Birmingham Barons

(Chicago White Sox, A) (color)

	MT	NR MT	EX
Complete Set:	10.50	7.75	4.25

88 Checklist
89 Ken Berry
90 Dan Wagner
91 Rich Amaral
92 Chuck Mount
93 Doug Little
94 Tony Blasucci
95 Mike Ollom
96 Dave Wallwork
97 Todd Trafton
98 Kevin Davis
99 Rick Peterson
100 Jerry Bertolani
101 Victor Diaz
102 Cornelio Garcia
103 Tony Menendez
104 Tommy Thompson
105 Doug Frobel
106 Robin Ventura
107 Don Wakamatsu
108 Grady Hall
109 Buddy Groom
110 Wayne Edwards
111 Craig Grebeck
112 Sam Airston, Sr.
113 Ron Jackson
114 Aubrey Waggoner
115 C.L. Penigar
116 Glen McElroy
117 Jerry Kutzler
118 Hoover Stadium

1989 Procards Boise Hawks

(No affiliation, A) (color)

	MT	NR MT	EX
Complete Set:	6.00	4.50	2.50

1976 Checklist
1977 Jeff Mace
1978 Boise Batboys (J.D. Schmidt, Nick Baltes, Kevin Kuenzi, Bill Church)
1979 Chip Reese
1980 Scott Jurgens
1981 David Perry
1982 Stan Cook
1983 Eric Doucet
1984 Tommy Griffith
1985 Jeff Byarmati
1986 Darrell MacMillan
1987 Rod Tafoya
1988 Jeff Thrams
1989 Steve Mattingly
1990 Jack Malone
1991 Joe Mancini
1992 Ruben Rodriguez
1993 Bob Sobczyk
1994 Tim Wallace
1995 Dan Olson
1996 Bruce Arola
1997 John Bilello
1998 Jorge Candelaria
1999 Chris Cerny
2000 Brian Currie
2001 Chris Forreset
2002 Steve King
2003 Michael Larson
2004 Mike Lomeli
2005 Garry Wurm
2006 Paul Cluff

1989 Procards Buffalo Bisons

(Pittsburgh Pirates, AAA) (color)

	MT	NR MT	EX
Complete Set:	6.00	4.50	2.50

1661 Checklist
1662 Dave Rucker
1663 Bobby Meacham
1664 Jim Pankovits
1665 Steve Carter
1666 mascot (Buster T. Bison)
1667 Sammy Khalifa
1668 Terry Collins
1669 Lou Thornton
1670 Tom Romano
1671 Jeff King
1672 Andy Hall
1673 Larry Melton
1674 Bill Landrum
1675 Rick Reed
1676 Steve Henderson
1677 Dann Bilardello
1678 Carlos Ledezma
1679 Jay Bell
1680 Scott Medvin
1681 Scott Little
1682 Benny Distefano
1683 Jackie Brown
1684 Bob Patterson
1685 Reggie Williams
1686 Miguel Garcia
1687 Orestes Destrade

1989 Procards Burlington Braves

(Atlanta Braves, A) (color)

	MT	NR MT	EX
Complete Set:	6.00	4.50	2.50

1596 Checklist
1597 Johnny Cuevas
1598 Lee Upshaw
1599 Mark Davis
1600 Joe Saccomanno
1601 Greg Cloninger
1602 Gary Schoonover
1603 Tom Kurczewski
1604 Preston Watson
1605 Jesus Mendoza
1606 Bob Pfaff
1607 Steve Glass
1608 Tony Baldwin
1609 Keith Mitchell
1610 Tom Redington
1611 Dave Karasinski
1612 Allan Waznik
1613 Steve Curry
1614 Ross Grimsley
1615 Jim Saul
1616 Steve Wendell
1617 Chris Czarnik
1618 Brian Cummings
1619 Dave Reis
1620 Don Campbell
1621 Daryl Blanks
1622 Teddy Williams
1623 Kevin Kelly
1624 Rich Longuil
1625 Paul C. Egins, III
1626 Skipper Wright
1627 Robert Cole

1989 Procards Calgary Cannons

(Seattle Mariners, AAA) (color)

	MT	NR MT	EX
Complete Set:	6.00	4.50	2.50

522 Checklist
523 Dan Warthen
524 Greg Fulton
525 Jim Bowie
526 Jeff Hull
527 Glenn Spagnola
528 Reggie Dobie
529 Joe Dunlap
530 Roger Hansen
531 Chuck Hensley
532 Colin McLaughlin
533 Bill McGuire
534 Bruce Fields
535 Dan Boever
536 Jim Wilson
537 Omar Vizquel
538 Rich Morales
539 Paul Noce
540 Bryan Price
541 Rich Doyle
542 Dave Cochrane
543 Steve Oliverio
544 Jay Buhner
545 Mike Kingery

1989 Procards Canton-Akron Indians

(Cleveland Indians, AA) (color)

	MT	NR MT	EX
Complete Set:	6.50	4.75	2.50

1297 Checklist
1298 Jeff Shaw
1299 Mike Twardoski

1300 Carl Keliipueole
1301 Not Used
1302 Beau Allred
1303 Rob Swain
1304 Lindsay Foster
1305 Paul Kuznair
1306 Kevin Bearse
1307 Sam Ferretti
1308 Eric Rasmussen
1309 Everado Magallanes
1310 Scott Khoury
1311 Efrain Valdez
1312 Jose Leiva
1313 Tom Magrann
1314 Allen Liebert
1315 Greg McMichael
1316 Jeff Edwards
1317 Billy Williams
1318 Casey Webster
1319 Bob Molinaro
1320 Todd Gonzales
1321 Julius McDougal
1322 Todd Ogden
1323 Mark Gilles
1324 Troy Neel
1325 Dan Boever

1989 Procards Cedar Rapids Reds

(Cincinnati Reds, A) (color)

6.50 4.75 (2.50)

910 Checklist
911 Mike Malinak
912 Bill Risley
913 Scott Jeffery
914 Steve McCarthy
915 Joey Vierra
916 Benny Colvard
917 Tom Spencer
918 Mike Myers
919 Steve Hester
920 Joe Turek
921 Scott Eonomy
922 Adam Casillas
923 Doug Eastman
924 Duane Mulville
925 Scott Bellner
926 Tony Mealy
927 Dave Miley
928 Jeff Branson
929 Quinn Marsh
930 Gerry Groninger
931 Don Buchheister
932 Andy Rickman
933 Larry Rothschild
934 Chris Schnurbusch
935 Chris Lombardozzi
936 Steve Foster
937 Eddie Taubensee
938 Norm Brock

1989 Procards Charleston Rainbows

(San Diego Padres, A) (color)

	MT	NR MT	EX
Complete Set:	6.00	4.50	2.50

969 Checklist
970 Team picture
971 A.J. Sager
972 Vance Tucker
973 Bob Brucato
974 Greg Conley
975 Brian Span
976 Vince Harris
977 Stan Tukes
978 Ron Oglesby
979 Greg Smith
980 Gerard Cifarelli
981 Chris Haslock
982 Joe Murdock
983 Bryce Florie
984 Luis Lopez
985 Matt Witkowski
986 John Kuehl
987 Jeff hart
988 Scot Welish
989 Jimmy Lester
990 Mark Verstandig
991 Jack Krol
992 Pedro Martinez
993 David Bond
994 Dave Briggs
995 Nicko Riesgo
996 Renay Bryand

1989 Procards Charleston Wheelers

(Chicago Cubs, A) (color)

	MT	NR MT	EX
Complete Set:	6.00	4.50	2.50

1743 Checklist
1744 Miliciades Uribe
1745 James Murphy
1746 Jim O'Reilly
1747 Kevin Roberson
1748 Matt Franco
1749 Luis Benitez
1750 Jossy Rosario
1751 Wayne Weinheimer
1752 Kraig Washington
1753 Bill Saint Peter
1754 Bill Earley
1755 Greg Mahlberg
1756 Eric Williams
1757 Scott Taylor
1758 Mathew Leonard
1759 Herberto Andrade
1760 Christopher Lutz
1761 Roberto Smalls
1762 Sean Reed
1763 Tony Whitson
1764 Ronnie Rasp
1765 Jason Doss
1766 Jay Eddings
1767 Frank Campos
1768 David Goodwin
1769 John Gardner
1770 Matt Cakora

1989 Procards Clinton Giants

(San Francisco Giants, A) (color)

	MT	NR MT	EX
Complete Set:	6.00	4.50	2.50

879 Checklist
880 Dave Bohnenkamp
881 Kevin Temperly
882 Adell Davenport
883 Adam Hilpert
884 Marino Hernandez
885 Chris Fye
886 Jimmy Myers
887 Gary Sharko
888 Karl Breitenbucher
890 Chris Hancock
891 Kevin Rogers
892 Jeffry Bonner
893 Reggie Williams
894 Rueben Smiley
895 Royce Clayton
896 Robbie Kemper
897 Scooter Tucker
898 Keith Bodie
899 Steve Gray
900 Julio Fernandez
901 Jeff Morris
902 Shannon Coppell
903 Carl Hanselman
904 Dominick Johnson
905 Domingo Delarosa
906 Steve Reed
907 Bill Gibbons
908 Steve Pratt
909 Dave Slavin
8889 Shane (Borchert)

1989 Procards Columbus Clippers

(New York Yankees, AAA) (color) (Cleveland Indians, AAA) (color)

	MT	NR MT	EX
Complete Set:	6.50	4.75	2.50

233 Checklist
234 Dwight Taylor
235 Pete Dalena
236 Ed Wojna
237 Joel Davis
238 Kevin Wickander
239 Mike Walker
240 Mark Salas
241 Danny Sheaffer
242 Rich Dauer
243 Dave Hengel
244 Stan Hilton
245 Paul Zuvella
246 Mike Hargrove
247 Rick Adair
248 Denny Gonzalez
249 Steve Davis
250 Steve Ciszczon
251 Mike Young
252 Steve Olin
253 Brian Giles
254 Tom Lampkin
255 Mark Higgins
256 Tommy Hinzo
257 Ron Tingley
258 Ty Gainey
259 Theo Shaw
260 Don Gordon
732 Checklist
733 Darrel Miller
734 Bobby Green
735 John Fishel
736 Bernie Williams
737 Kevin Maas
738 Mark Wasinger
739 Chris Alvarez
740 Steve Kiefer
741 Randy Velarde
742 Mike Woodard
743 Hal Morris
744 Hipolito Pena
745 Chuck Cary
746 Bill Fulton
747 Dick Grapenthin
748 Balvino Galvez
749 Dickie Noles
750 Dave Eiland
751 Clay Parker
752 Jimmy Jones
753 Don Schulze
754 Scott Nielsen
755 Field Staff (Ken Rowe, Bucky Dent, Champ Summers, Mike Heifferon, Gary Tuck)
756 Dave Sax
757 Bucky Dent
758 Bob Geren
759 Brian Dorsett

1989 Procards Columbus Mudcats

(Houston Astros, AA) (color)

	MT	NR MT	EX
Complete Set:	11.50	8.50	4.75

119 Checklist
120 Team Logo
121 Bobby Ramos
122 Mike Browning
123 Dave Rohde
124 Doug Givler
125 Tony Eusebio
126 Ryan Bowen
127 Pedro Sanchez
128 Joel Estes
129 Fred Costello
130 Tom Wiedenbauer
131 Rob Mallicoat
132 Trent Hubbard
133 Darryl Kile
134 Eric Anthony
135 Jeff Baldwin
136 Manny Acta
137 Randy Hennis
138 David Salaiz
139 Fred Gladding
140 Sam August
141 Mike Simms
142 Karl Rhodes
143 Blane Fox
144 Terry Wells
145 Lou Frazier
146 Garrett Nago
147 Mike Loynd
148 Bert Hunter
149 Team Picture

1989 Procards Denver Zephyrs

(Milwaukee Brewers, AAA) (color)

	MT	NR MT	EX
Complete Set:	9.00	6.75	3.50

30 Todd Simmons
31 Bob Stoddard
32 Ray Krawczyk
33 Mike Kinnunen
34 Ruben Rodriguez
35 George Canale
36 Greg Vaughn
37 Dave Machemer
38 Billy Bates
39 Darryl Hamilton
40 Jim Jones
41 Tim Watkins
42 Jay Aldrich
43 Joe Mitchell
44 Alan Sadler
45 Mike Costello
46 Jeff Peterek
47 Kiki Diaz
48 Lavell Freeman
49 Matias Carrillo
50 Peter Kolb
51 Jackson Todd
52 Donnie Scott
53 Joe Xavier
54 Darryel Walters
55 Tony Fossas
56 Norm Jones
57 Checklist

1989 Procards Eastern League All Stars

(AA)

	MT	NR MT	EX
Complete Set:	8.50	6.25	3.50

1 Index
2 Andy Stankiewicz
3 Leo Gomez
4 Travis Fryman
5 Wes Chamberlain

6 Beau Allred
7 Troy Neel
8 Rob Sepanek
9 Jim Leyritz
10 Rodney Imes
11 Steve Adkins
12 Daryl Irvine
13 Dan Gabriele
14 Tim Layana
15 Scott Kamieniecki
16 Jason Grimsley
17 Josias Manzanillo
18 Tino Martinez
19 Casey Webster
20 Jack Smith
21 Victor Hithe
22 John Ramos
23 Jeff Bannister
24 Tim Mauser
25 Rick Parker
26 Buck Showalter

1989 Procards Eastern League Diamond Dipolmacy

(AA)

	MT	NR MT	EX
Complete Set:	8.00	6.00	3.25

1 Index
2 Vitalyi Romanov
3 German Gulbit
4 Sergey Korolev
5 Vadim Kulakov
6 Evgenyi Puchkov
7 Alexei Koshevoy
8 Sergey Zhigalov
9 Edmuntas Matusyavichus
10 Alexander Dundik
11 Sergei Onichuk
12 Boris Rogascozv
13 Andrei Fzelykovskyi
14 Alexander Krupenchenkov
15 Leonid Korneev
16 Roman Stepanov
17 Ilya Bogatyrev
18 Alexander Kozyrez
19 Timur Tritonenkov
20 Audrey Popov
21 Igor Mahambitov
22 Kevin Burdick
23 Dave Milstien
24 Dave Walters
25 Steve Scarsone
26 Tommy Shields
27 Steve Adams
28 Jeff Banister
29 Dan Simonds
30 Joe Dunlap
31 Leverne Jackson
32 Rich Doyle
33 Glenn Spagnola
34 Chris Calvert
35 Mike Twardoski
36 Ted Williams
37 Troy Neel
38 Don Buford
39 Frank Bellino
40 Mike Sander
41 Jeff Edwards
42 Eastern League group photo
43 Rich Gale
44 Stump Merrill
45 Rob Thomson
46 Dave Trembley
47 Dick Groch
48 Potter, Fitzgerald, Kellogg
49 Kevin Rand
50 David Hays

1989 Procards Edmonton Trappers

(California Angels, AAA) (color)

	MT	NR MT	EX
Complete Set:	6.00	4.50	2.50

546 Checklist
547 Sherm Corbett
548 Jim Eppard
549 Tom Kotchman
550 Jim Thomas
551 Doug Davis
552 Edwin Marquez
553 Tim Burcham
554 Lee Stevens
555 Stan Holmes
556 Max Venable
557 Cliff Young
558 Mike Brown
559 Vance Lovelace
560 Don McGann
561 Mike Ramsey
562 Chuck Hernandez
563 Pete Coachman
564 Rich Monteleone
565 Colin Charland
566 Stewart Cliburn
567 Carl Willis
568 Colby Ward
569 Jamie Nelson
570 Jeff Manto

1989 Procards Fayetteville Generals

(Detroit Tigers, A) (color)

	MT	NR MT	EX
Complete Set:	6.00	4.50	2.50

1567 Checklist
1568 Glenn Belcher
1569 Leo Torres
1570 Jeff Jones
1571 Rob Thomas
1572 Linty Ingram
1573 Lino Rivera
1574 Marcos Betances
1575 Rusty Meacham
1576 Mike Koller
1577 Gene Roof
1578 Rich Rowland
1579 Blaine Rudolph
1580 Benny Castillo
1581 Randy Marshall
1582 Kurt Shea
1583 Tim Brader
1584 Mike Rendina
1585 Darryl Martin
1586 Jim Murphy
1587 Julio Rosa
1588 Freddy Torres
1589 Brett Roach
1590 Micky Delas
1591 Paul Nozling
1592 Ron Howard
1593 Mike Davidson
1594 Steve Peques
1595 Freddy Padilla

1989 Procards Gastonia Rangers

(Texas Rangers, A) (color)

	MT	NR MT	EX
Complete Set:	6.50	4.75	2.50

997 Checklist
998 Joe Wardlow
999 Spencer Wilkinson
1000 Everett Cunningham
1001 Dominic Pierce
1002 Kyle Spencer
1003 Robb Nen
1004 Kevin Belcher
1005 Carl Randle
1006 Ivan Rodriguez
1007 Joe Lewis
1008 Eric McCray
1009 Anthony Berry
1010 Chuck Marquardt
1011 Jim McCutcheon
1012 Trey McCoy
1013 Doug Cronk
1014 Cris Colon
1015 Jim Crawford
1016 Ronaldo Romero
1017 Orlando Gomez
1018 Jose Hernandez
1019 Jim Hvizda
1020 Francisco Valdez
1021 Darren Oliver
1022 Steve Allen
1023 Jeff Frye
1024 Tim MacNeil
1025 Oscar Acosta
1026 Mike Mendazona

1989 Procards Geneva Cubs

(Chicago Cubs, A) (color)

	MT	NR MT	EX
Complete Set:	7.00	5.25	2.75

1856 Checklist
1857 Quinn's Cards
1858 Front Office Staff
1859 Grounds Crew (Ed Smaldone, Dave Mungo)
1860 Frankie Espino
1861 Ed Smaldone
1862 Rene Francisco
1863 Darrin Beep
1864 Doug Welch
1865 Kevin Gore
1866 David Swartzbaugh
1867 Travis Willis
1868 Jeff Cesari
1869 Jeff Ludwig
1870 Luis Benitez
1871 Richie Grayum
1872 Kalani Bush
1873 Jim Sweeney
1874 Al Stacey
1875 Tony Colon
1876 Chris Ebright
1877 Gary Scott
1878 Mark Linden
1879 Pablo Delgado
1880 Micah Murphy
1881 Shannon Jones
1882 Gregg Patterson
1883 Rick Mundy
1884 Billy White
1885 Ken Reynolds
1886 Pookie Bernstine

1989 Procards Greensboro Hornets

(Cincinnati Reds, A) (color)

	MT	NR MT	EX
Complete Set:	6.00	4.50	2.50

403 Checklist
404 Gary Denbo
405 Mark Berry
406 Lavell Cudjo
407 Victor Garcia
408 Igor Baez
409 Danny Perozo
410 Mike Mulvaney
411 Dave McAuliffe
412 Brian Landy
413 Jerry Spradlin
414 Jason Satre
415 Reggie Sanders
416 Eugene Jones
417 Dante Johnson
418 Eddie Rush
419 Jim Wolfer
420 Glenn Sutko
421 Mike Songini
422 Vicente Javier
423 Mo Sanford
424 Mike Malley
425 Mark Krumback
426 Kurt Dempster
427 Phil Dale
428 Mike Anderson
429 Carl Nordstrom
430 Tom Iverson
431 Johnny Almaraz

1989 Procards Greenville Braves

(Atlanta Braves, AA) (color)

	MT	NR MT	EX
Complete Set:	6.50	4.75	2.50

1150 Checklist
1151 Sid Adkins
1152 Greg Tubbs
1153 German Jimenez
1154 John Alva
1155 Juan Pacho
1156 Edwin Alicea
1157 Danny Weems
1158 Brian Hunter
1159 Ellis Roby
1160 Dale Polley
1161 Maximo Delrosario
1162 Terry Bell
1163 Jimmy Kremers
1164 Dale Plumb
1165 Doug Stockam
1166 Mike Stanton
1167 Jim Lovell
1168 Bill Slack
1169 Dennis Hood
1170 Miguel Sabino
1171 Darrell Pruitt
1172 Rick Morris
1173 Mike Bell
1174 Paul Marak
1175 Tim Deitz
1176 Jim Lemasters
1177 Randy Ingle
1178 Buddy Bailey
1179 Tommy Dunbar

1989 Procards Hagerstown Suns

(Baltimore Orioles, AA) (color)

	MT	NR MT	EX
Complete Set:	6.00	4.50	2.50

261 Checklist
262 John Githens
263 Jeff Schwarz
264 Larry Mims
265 Randy Strijek
266 Craig Faulkner
267 Erik Sonberg
268 Chris Pinder
269 Chuck Stanhope
270 Mike Eberle
271 Bob Latmore
272 Victor Hithe
273 Dave Bettendorf
274 Brian Dubois
275 Mike Sander
276 Steve Culkar
277 Don Buford
278 Rafel Skeete

279 Ty Nichols
280 Leo Gomez
281 Robinson Garces
282 Jim Schaffer
283 Tom Brown
284 Brian Ebel
285 Paul Thorpe
286 Dana Smith

1989 Procards Harrisburg Senators

(Pittsburgh Pirates, AA) (color)

	MT	NR MT	EX
Complete Set:	6.00	4.50	2.50

287 Checklist
288 TIm Conroy
289 Rico Rossy
290 Bill Sampen
291 Ed Yacopino
292 Dave Trembley
293 Junior Vizcaino
294 Julio Peguero
295 Steve Adams
296 Wes Chamberlain
297 Kevin Burdick
298 Tommy Shields
299 Orlando Merced
300 Orlando Lind
301 Chris Lein
302 Harold Williams
303 Robby Russell
304 Jeff Cook
305 Stan BElinda
306 Jeff Banister
307 Julio Perez
308 Pete Murphy
309 Jim Tracy
310 Mike York
311 Ben Webb
312 Tim McKinley

1989 Procards Idaho Falls Braves

(Atlanta Braves, R) (color)

	MT	NR MT	EX
Complete Set:	7.50	5.50	3.00

2007 Checklist
2008 Field Staff (Mike Boyer, Randy Smith, Cloyd Boyer)
2009 Brian Wright
2010 Ramces Guerrero
2011 Jimmie Pullins
2012 Lionel Adams III
2013 Rickey Rigsby
2014 Ken Harring, Jr.
2015 Jose Olmeda
2016 Fred Lopez
2017 Ricky Gore
2018 Daniel Sims, Jr.
2019 Dave Waldenberger
2020 Billy Miller
2021 Tyler Houston
2022 Chris Burton
2023 Michael Sweeney
2024 Chris Sparrow
2025 Jim Baranoski
2026 Tony Valle
2027 Doug Rogers
2028 Eric Kuhlman
2029 Jeff Zona
2030 Tom Eckhardt
2031 Jim Kortright
2032 Scott Osmon
2033 Don Lemon
2034 Randy White
2035 Mike Parker
2036 Tom Newman
2037 Kevin Haeberle

1989 Procards Indianapolis Indians

(Montreal Expos, AAA) (color)

	MT	NR MT	EX
Complete Set:	6.50	4.75	2.50

1209 Checklist
1210 Alonzo Powell
1211 Billy Moore
1212 Joel McKeon
1213 Randy Braun
1214 Jeff Dedmon
1215 Sergio Valdez
1216 Howard Kellman, Tom Akins

1217 Marty Pevey
1218 Steve Frey
1219 Razor Shines
1220 Tom Runnells
1221 Mike Blowers
1222 Armando Moreno
1223 Lorenzo Bundy
1224 Mark Gardner
1225 Kevin Dean
1226 Tim McCormack
1227 Coaching Staff (Dave Van Gorder, Joe Kerrigan, Nelson Normanan)
1228 Rich Sauveur
1229 Tim Barrett
1230 Brett Gideon
1231 Jay Baller
1232 Urbano Lugo
1233 Jeff Huson
1234 Scott Anderson
1235 Junior Noboa
1236 Pat Picillo
1237 Rich Thompson
1238 Darryl Motley
1239 Larry Walker
1240 Gilberto Reyes

1989 Procards Iowa Cubs

(Chicago Cubs, AAA) (color)

	MT	NR MT	EX
Complete Set:	8.00	6.00	3.25

1688 Checklist
1689 Les Lancaster
1690 Dean Wilkins
1691 Roger Williams
1692 Luis Cruz
1693 Butch Garcia
1694 Dave Owen
1695 Lloyd McClendon
1696 Hector Villanueva
1697 Jim Wright
1698 Dave Masters
1699 Kevin Blankenship
1700 Bryan House
1701 Mike Tullier
1702 Doug Dascenzo
1703 Dave Grossman
1704 Mike Harkey
1705 Len Damian
1706 Mike Capel
1707 Pete Mackanin
1708 Dwight Smith
1709 Brian Guinn
1710 Ed Vandeberg
1711 Winston Ficklin
1712 Howard Nichols
1713 Rich Scheid
1714 Bruce Crabbe
1715 Joe Kraemer

1989 Procards Jacksonville Expos

(Montreal Expos, AA) (color)

	MT	NR MT	EX
Complete Set:	12.50	9.50	5.25

150 Checklist
151 Alan Bannister
152 Delino Deshields
153 Quinn Mack
154 Tim Peters
155 Howard Farmer
156 Mel Rojas
157 Dan Gakeler
158 Sean Cunningham
159 Eddie Dixon
160 Archie Cianfrocco
161 John Vanderwal
162 Travis Chambers
163 Kent Bottenfield
164 Mike Dull
165 Pat Sipe
166 Chris Marchok
167 Doug Duke
168 Rick Carriger
169 Danilo Leon
170 Mel Houston
171 Phil Wilson
172 Fred Williams
173 Nardi Contreras
174 Gene Glynn
175 Marquis Grissom
176 Rob Natal
177 Boi Rodriguez
178 Team Photo

1989 Procards Jamestown Expos

(Montreal Expos, A) (color)

	MT	NR MT	EX
Complete Set:	6.00	4.50	2.50

2129 Checklist
2130 Dale Buzzard
2131 Buena Rodriquez
2132 F.P. Santangelo
2133 Robert Small
2134 Tyrone Woods
2135 Paul Ciaglo
2136 Pete Young
2137 Tim Laker
2138 Gary Pipik
2139 Troy Wessel
2140 Steve Whitehead
2141 Matt Stairs
2142 Dan Archibald
2143 Pat Heiderscheit
2144 David Sommer
2145 Scott Davison
2146 Todd Mayo
2147 Isaac Elder
2148 Ken Lake
2149 Gary Engelken
2150 Don Werner
2151 Steve Mandl
2152 Q.V. Lowe
2153 Alejandro Tejada
2154 Gary Regira
2155 Joe Klancnik
2156 Rusty Kilgo
2157 John Thoden
2158 Joe Logan, Jr.

1989 Procards Kenosha Twins

(Minnesota Twins, A) (color)

	MT	NR MT	EX
Complete Set:	6.50	4.75	2.50

1057 Checklist
1058 Bob Lee
1059 Mike Mathiot
1060 Steve Morris
1061 Mark North
1062 Brad Fontes
1063 Jay Kvasnicka
1064 Deryk Gross
1065 Carl Johnson
1066 Dom Rovasio
1067 Pat Mahomes
1068 Terry Brown
1069 Bryan Roskom
1070 Don Leppert
1071 Mike Misuraca
1072 J.P. Wright
1073 Steve Dunn
1074 J.T. Bruett
1075 Gary Resetar
1076 Rich Garces
1077 Rusty Kryzanowski
1078 Chad Swanson
1079 Steve Muh
1080 Brian Allard
1081 Mike Pomeranz
1082 Rolando Pino
1083 Cheo Garcia
1084 Steve Liddle
1085 Dan Fox

1989 Procards Knoxville Blue Jays

(Toronto Blue Jays, AA) (color)

	MT	NR MT	EX
Complete Set:	6.50	4.75	2.50

1119 Checklist
1120 Bill Dyke
1121 Gary McCune
1122 Tim Ringler
1123 Tom Quinlan
1124 Kevin Batiste
1125 Carlos Diaz
1126 Pedro Munoz
1127 Omar Malave
1128 Barry Foote
1129 J.J. Cannon
1130 Shawn Jeter
1131 Webster Garrison
1132 Ken Rivers
1133 Jimmy Rogers
1134 Chris Jones
1135 Joe Newcomb
1136 Dennis Jones
1137 Darren Balsley
1138 Bob Wishnevski
1139 Rob MacDonald
1140 John Shea
1141 Mike Mills
1142 Jerry Schunk
1143 Tom Gilles
1144 Xavier Hernandez
1145 Goose Gozzo
1146 Brian Morrison
1147 John Paul Poloni
1148 Domingo Martinez
1149 Derek Bell

1989 Procards Las Vegas Stars

(San Diego Padres, AAA) (color)

	MT	NR MT	EX
Complete Set:	6.50	4.75	2.50

1 Tony Ghelfi
2 Dan Murphy
3 Billy Taylor
4 Joe Bitker
5 Matt Maysey
6 Randy Byers

7 Sandy Alomar
8 Thomas Howard
9 Carlos Baerga
10 Jerald Clark
11 Jeff Hearron
12 Eric Nolte
13 Pete Roberts
14 Keith Comstock
15 Pat Clements
16 Terry Gilmore
17 Roger Smithberg
18 Billy Wrona
19 Chris Knabenshue
20 Jeff Yurtin
21 Shawn Abner
22 Joe Lynch
23 Joey Cora
24 Rob Nelson
25 Steve Smith
26 Steve Luebber
27 Tony Torchia
28 Todd Hutcheson
29 Checklist

1989 Procards London Tigers

(Detroit Tigers, AA) (color)

	MT	NR MT	EX
Complete Set:	6.50	4.75	2.50

1356 Checklist
1357 Steve Howe
1358 Bob Gilson
1359 Bob Eaman
1360 Bill Wilkinson
1361 Dan Ross
1362 Dave Cooper
1363 Donnie Rowland
1364 Bernie Anderson
1365 John Toale
1366 Travis Fryman
1367 Mike DeLao
1368 Scott Aldred
1369 Ron Rightnowar
1370 Darren Hursey
1371 Arnie Beyeler
1372 Dean Decillis
1373 Tim Leiper
1374 Don Vesling
1375 Mike Schwabe
1376 Mike Hansen
1377 Randy Nosek
1378 Chris Chambliss
1379 Rob Thomson
1380 Greg Everson
1381 Scott Livingstone
1382 Wayne Housie
1383 Phil Clark
1384 Doyle Balthazar
1385 Manny Jose
1386 Tom Aldrich
1387 Jose Ramos

1989 Procards Louisville Redbirds

(St. Louis Cardinals, AAA) (color)

	MT	NR MT	EX
Complete Set:	8.50	6.25	3.50

1241 Checklist
1242 Roger Erickson
1243 Jim Puzey
1244 Bryan Oelkers
1245 Randy Byers
1246 Jeff Fassero
1247 Steve Peters
1248 Scott Arnold
1249 Ted Power
1250 Bob Tewksbury
1251 Howard Hilton
1252 Gibson Alba
1253 David "Hap" Hudson
1254 Mark Riggins
1255 Matt Kinzer
1256 Mike Jorgensen
1257 Romy Cucjen
1258 Greg Jelks
1259 Mike Fitzgerald
1260 Leon Durham
1261 Ron Shepherd
1262 Bien Figueroa
1263 Luis Alicea
1264 Rod Booker
1265 Tom Baine
1266 Alex Cole
1267 Todd Zeile
1268 Ken Hill

1989 Procards Memphis Chicks

(Kansas City Royals, AA) (color)

	MT	NR MT	EX
Complete Set:	6.50	4.75	2.50

1180 Checklist
1181 John Duffy
1182 Carlos Escalera
1183 Julio Alcala
1184 Stu Cole
1185 Victor Cole
1186 Aguedo Vasquez
1187 Luis Encarnacion
1188 Jacob Brumfield
1189 Deric Ladnier
1190 Mark Lee
1191 Mike Leon
1192 Guy Hansen
1193 Joe Breeden
1194 Jim Campbell
1195 Jeff Cox
1196 Steve Walker
1197 Mike Tresemer
1198 Mike Magnante
1199 Dera Clark
1200 Chito Martinez
1201 Rob Hamelin
1202 Tony Bridges-Clements
1203 Angel Morris
1204 Harvey Pulliam
1205 Brian McRae
1206 Kyle Reese
1207 Ken Bowen

1989 Procards Myrtle Beach Blue Jays

(Toronto Blue Jays, A) (color)

	MT	NR MT	EX
Complete Set:	6.00	4.50	2.50

1450 Checklist
1451 Leroy Stanton
1452 Mark Young
1453 Eddie Mendez
1454 Greg David
1455 Todd Provence
1456 Domingo Cedeno
1457 Tim Hodge
1458 Juan DeLaRosa
1459 Jose Monzon
1460 Eric Brooks
1461 Mike Seal
1462 Mike Taylor
1463 Mike Ogliaruso
1464 Tim Brown
1465 Mike Fischlin
1466 Bill Monbouquette
1467 Rafael Martinez
1468 Greg Harding
1469 Ray Giannelli
1470 Curtis Johson
1471 Dan Dodd
1472 Jose Olivares
1473 Jesse Cross
1474 Terry Wilson
1475 David Weathers
1476 Mike Brady
1628 Rich Depastino
1629 Rick Vaughan
1630 Anthony Ward

1989 Procards Nashville Sounds

(Cincinnati Reds, AA) (color)

	MT	NR MT	EX
Complete Set:	6.50	4.75	2.50

1269 Checklist
1270 Jeff Sellers
1271 Scotti Madison
1272 Luis Quinones
1273 Charlie Mitchell
1274 Mike Griffin
1275 Mark Germann
1276 John Young
1277 Doug Gwosdz
1278 Keith Lockhart
1279 Chris Hammond
1280 Ray Rippelmeyer
1281 Van Snider
1282 Mike Roesler
1283 Joe Oliver
1284 Frank Lucchesi
1285 Luis Vasquez
1286 Rolando Roomes
1287 Eddie Tanner
1288 Jeff Gray
1289 Skeeter Barnes
1290 Chris Jones
1291 Jeff Richardson
1292 Marty Brown
1293 Scott Scudder
1294 Hugh Kemp
1295 Rob Lopez
1296 Keith Brown

1989 Procards New Britain Red Sox

(Boston Red Sox, AA) (color)

	MT	NR MT	EX
Complete Set:	7.50	5.50	3.00

598 Checklist
599 Ed Zambrano
600 Bob Zupcic
601 Pete Youngman
602 Rich Gale
603 Chris Moritz
604 Dan Gabriele
605 Mike Carista
606 Josias Manzanillo
607 Mike Dalton
608 Steve Bast
609 Scott Cooper
610 Jim Orsag
611 Daryl Irvine
612 Zach Crouch
613 Larry Shikles
614 Dave Walters
615 Leverne Jackson
616 Joe Marchese
617 Butch Hobson
618 Randy Randle
619 Mickey Pina
620 Livio Padilla
621 Dave Milstien
622 Jeff Plympton
623 Scott Sommers
624 Todd Pratt

1989 Procards Oklahoma City 89'ers

(Texas Rangers, AAA) (color)

	MT	NR MT	EX
Complete Set:	6.00	4.50	2.50

1506 Checklist
1507 (Abner 89er)
1508 Jim Skaalen
1509 Paul Wilmet
1510 Jeff Stone
1511 Rey Sanchez
1512 Scott Coolbaugh
1513 Ferguson Jenkins
1514 Andre Robertson
1515 Mike Berger
1516 Darrel Whitaker
1517 Drew Hall
1518 John Barfield
1519 Ron Roanicke
1520 Mike Jeffcoat
1521 Stan Hough
1522 Dave Miller
1523 Scott May
1524 Jim St. Laurent
1525 Jack Daugherty
1526 Darren Loy
1527 Kevin Reimer
1528 Gary Mielke
1529 Dave Pavlas
1530 Dan Rohn
1531 John Gibbons
1532 Darrel Akerfelds
1533 Ray Ramirez
1534 Tack Wilson

1989 Procards Omaha Royals

(Kansas City Royals, AAA) (color)

	MT	NR MT	EX
Complete Set:	6.00	4.50	2.50

1716 Checklist
1717 Matt Crouch
1718 Steve Fireovid
1719 Ken Spratke
1720 Kevin Appier
1721 Terry Shumpert
1722 Nick Casteneoa
1723 Steve Morrow
1724 Bob Buchanan
1725 Ed Olwine
1726 Tim Pyznarski
1727 Tom Dodd
1728 Matt Winters
1729 Luis Delossantos
1730 Mike Mesh
1731 Jose Castro
1732 Ed Hearn
1733 Kevin Burrell
1734 Rick Luecken
1735 Jose DeJesus
1736 Jeff Schulz
1737 Stan Clarke
1738 Mike Loggins
1739 Rich Dubee
1740 Sal Rende
1741 Tom Poquette
1742 Nick Capra

1989 Procards Oneonta Yankees

(New York Yankees, A) (color)

	MT	NR MT	EX
Complete Set:	6.50	4.75	2.50

2097 Checklist
2098 Brian Butterfield
2099 John Barrilleaux
2100 Enrique Hernandez
2101 Jeff Taylor

2102 Sherman Obando
2103 Mike Gardella
2104 Art Canestro
2105 James Moody
2106 Larry Stanford
2107 Scott Chase
2108 Kelly Sharitt
2109 Russ Davis
2110 Brad Ausmus
2111 Lew Hill
2112 J.T. Snow
2113 David Howell
2114 Ken Juarbe
2115 Aaron Van Scoyoc
2116 Ricky STrickland
2117 Richard Barnwell
2118 Mark Hutton
2119 Dave Kent
2120 Rich Arena
2121 Frank Seminara
2122 Todd Malone
2123 Ricky Rhodes
2124 Orlando Miller
2125 Joe Ross
2126 Jose Vazquez
2127 Paul Oster
2128 John Brubaker

1989 Procards Orlando Twins

(Minnesota Twins, AA) (color)

	MT	NR MT	EX
Complete Set:	6.50	4.75	2.50

1326 Checklist
1327 Doug Snyder
1328 Marty Lanoux
1329 Ben Bianchi
1330 Jeff Gatzinger
1331 Pete Delkus
1332 Scott Leius
1333 Mike Redding
1334 Park Pittman
1335 Mark Guthrie
1336 Wayne Hattaway
1337 Jeff Bronkey
1338 Pat Bangston
1339 Mike Randle
1340 Larry Blackwell
1341 Ken Morgan
1342 Dwight Bernard
1343 Paul Sorrento
1344 Mike Funderburk
1345 Jeff Reboulet
1346 A.J. Richardson
1347 Edgar Naveda
1348 Paul Abbott
1349 Jim Kahmann
1350 Derek Parks
1351 John Eccles
1352 Terry Jorgensen
1353 Tim Arnold
1354 Jimmy Williams
1355 Ron Gardenhire

1989 Procards Palm Springs Angels

(California Angels, A) (color)

	MT	NR MT	EX
Complete Set.	6.00	4.50	2.50

462 Checklist
463 Jim Townsend
464 Edgar Alfonzo
465 Edgar Rodriguez
466 Jeff Gay
467 Ramon Martinez
468 Tim McCoy
469 Jeff Richardson
470 Charlie Romero
471 Brandy Vann
472 Chris Treadgill
473 Troy Giles
474 Dave Neal
475 Cesar DeLaRosa
476 Don Long
477 Mario Molina
478 Ronnie Ortegon
479 Fred Carter
480 Al Olson
481 Keenan Ronan
482 Don Vidmar
483 Chris Graves
484 Jose Velez
485 Wiley Lee
486 Dave Sturdivant
487 Frank Bryan
488 Chris Beasley
489 Bill Lachemann

1989 Procards Pawtucket Red Sox

(Boston Red Sox, AAA) (color)

	MT	NR MT	EX
Complete Set:	6.00	4.50	2.50

677 Checklist
678 Ed Nottle
679 Andy Araujo
680 Tom Bolton
681 John Leister
682 Kevin Romine
683 Tony Cleary
684 Angel Gonzalez
685 John Troutwein
686 Chris Cannizzaro
687 John Marzano
688 Carlos Quintana
689 Gary Miller-Jones
690 Dana Williams
691 Steve Curry
692 Lee Stange
693 John Roberts
694 Jackie Gutierrez
695 Scott Wade
696 Mark Meleski
697 Luis Rivera
698 Ed Estrada
699 Rob Woodward
700 Mike Rochford
701 Dana Kiecker
702 Gary Tremblay
703 Eric Hetzel
704 Steve Ellsworth

1989 Procards Phoenix Firebirds

(San Francisco Giants, AAA) (color)

	MT	NR MT	EX
Complete Set:	9.00	6.75	3.50

207 Checklist
208 Chip Hale
209 Orlando Mercado
210 Victor Rodriquez
211 Jim Davins
212 Bernardo Brito
213 Randy St. Claire
214 John Christensen
215 Kurt Kepshire
216 Ray Soff
217 Lee Tunnell
218 Steve Shields
219 Lester Straker
220 Kelvin Torve
221 Manny Hernandez
222 Rafael Delima
223 Larry Casian
224 Alan Cockrell
225 Greg Olson
226 Jim Shellenback
227 Mark Davidson
228 Mike Dyer
229 Francisco Oliveras
230 Doug Baker
231 Brad Bierley
232 Bobby Ralston
1477 Checklist
1478 Mike Hamm
1479 Rusty Tillman
1480 Terry Mulholland
1481 Trevor Wilson
1482 Dennis Cook
1483 John Burkett
1484 George Wright
1485 Matt Williams
1486 Marty DeMerritt
1487 Charlie Hayes
1488 Bruce Graham
1489 Wil Tejada
1490 Paul Meyers
1491 Stu Tate
1492 Ed Puikunas
1493 Mike Laga
1494 Ernie Camacho
1495 Bill Bathe
1496 John Skurla
1497 Joe Olker
1498 Mark Leonard
1499 Ken Gerhart
1500 Mike Benjamin
1501 Ron Wotus
1502 Tony Perezchica
1503 Jack Mull
1504 Gordy MacKenzie
1505 Ron Davis

1989 Procards Pulaski Braves

(Atlanta Braves, R) (color)

	MT	NR MT	EX
Complete Set:	6.50	4.75	2.50

1887 Checklist
1888 Dave Dickman
1889 Ron Thomas
1890 Mike Pisacreta
1891 Bat Boys (Council Compton, Chris Dishon)
1892 Javier Lopez
1893 Melvin Nieves
1894 Brent McCoy
1895 Don Strange
1896 Dan Snover
1897 Earl Jewett
1898 Shaun Sottile
1899 Tab Brown
1900 Fred Koenig
1901 Phillip Wellman
1902 Matt West
1903 Mike Cerame
1904 Ton Tarasco
1905 Darren Ritter
1906 Jarrod Parker
1907 Roger Hailey
1908 Mark Wohlers
1909 Sean Hutchinson
1910 Jeff Clark
1911 Lee Heath
1912 Greg Arnold
1913 John Kupsey
1914 Steve Swail

1989 Procards Reading Phillies

(Philadelphia Phillies, AA) (color)

	MT	NR MT	EX
Complete Set:	6.50	4.75	2.50

650 Checklist
651 Steve Sharts
652 Bob Scanlan
653 Ramon Henderson
654 Sal Agostinelli
655 Shane Turner
656 Chuck Malone
657 Scott Service
658 Mike Hart
659 Frank Bellino
660 Rick Parker
661 Vince Holyfield
662 Cliff Brantley
663 Jeff Tabaka
664 Chris Calvert
665 Steve Scarsone
666 Greg Edge
667 Harvey Brumfield
668 Eric Boudreaux
669 Chuck McElroy
670 Jason Grimsley
671 Ramon Aviles
672 Marty Foley
673 Bobby Joe Edmonds
674 Warren Magee
675 Jeff Williams
676 Pat Combs

1989 Procards Richmond Braves

MARK LEMKE
Third Base
Richmond Braves

(Atlanta Braves, AAA) (color)

	MT	NR MT	EX
Complete Set:	6.00	4.50	2.50

817 Checklist
818 Team Photo
819 Clubhouse Managers (Tex Drake, Steve Barden)
820 Sam Ayoub
821 John Grubb
822 Jim Beauchamp
823 Greg Tubbs
824 Chris Shaddy
825 Mark Eichhorn
826 Mark Clary
827 John Mizerock
828 Gary Eave
829 Rusty Richards
830 Mark Lemke
831 Tommy Greene
832 Sonny Jackson
833 Leo D. Mazzone
834 Bryan Farmer
835 Kent Mercker
836 Kash Beauchamp
837 Ed Whited
838 Dave Justice
839 Andy Nezelek
840 Jeff Wetherby
841 Alex Smith
842 Carlos Rios
843 Robbie Wine
844 Dwayne Henry
845 Eddie Mathews
846 Barry Jones
847 Drew Denson

Definitions for grading conditions are located in the introduction of this price guide.

1989 Procards Riverside Red Wave

(San Diego Padres, A) (color)

	MT	NR MT	EX
Complete Set:	6.00	4.50	2.50

1388 Checklist
1389 Steve Loubier
1390 Mark Beavers
1391 Nate Colbert
1392 Kelly Lifgren
1393 Darrin Reichle
1394 Guillermo Valazquez
1395 Tony Lewis
1396 Scott Bigham
1397 Greg Hall
1398 Rafael Valdez
1399 Mike Young
1400 Mike Humphreys
1401 Tim McWilliams
1402 Will Taylor
1403 Bob Lutticken
1404 Isaiah Clark
1405 Bruce Bochy
1406 Saul Soltero
1407 Jim Daniels
1408 Jon Matlack
1409 Jay Estrada
1410 Brian Harrison
1411 Steve Lubratich
1412 Kevin Farmer
1413 Todd Hansen
1414 Andy Skeels
1415 Jose Valentin
1416 Bill Marx
1417 Monte Brooks
1418 Bobby Sheridan

1989 Procards Rochester Red Wings

(Baltimore Orioles, A) (color)

	MT	NR MT	EX
Complete Set:	6.00	4.50	2.50

1631 Checklist
1632 Sherwin Cijntje
1633 Jay Tibbs
1634 Mike Smith (height 6'1")
1635 Cesar Mejia
1636 Jose Mesa
1637 Mike Smith (height 6'3")
1638 Micky Weston
1639 Steve Finley
1640 Chris Hoyles
1641 Dick Bosman
1642 Rick Schu
1643 Harold Perkins
1644 Chris Padget
1645 Jeff Tackett
1646 Tim Dulin
1647 Billy Moore
1648 Mike Raszka
1649 Pete Harnisch
1650 Mark Huismann
1651 Walt Harris
1652 Butch Davis
1653 Tim Hulett
1654 Francisco Melendez
1655 Curt Schilling
1656 Dave Johnson
1657 Mike Jones
1658 Juan Bell
1659 Keith Hughes
1660 Greg Biagini

1989 Procards St. Catharines Blue Jays

(Toronto Blue Jays, A) (color)

	MT	NR MT	EX
Complete Set:	6.00	4.50	2.50

2069 Checklist
2070 Gregg Martin
2071 Bill Abere
2072 Ryan Thompson
2073 Daren Brown
2074 Scott Hutson
2075 Oscar Garcia
2076 Daren Kizziah
2077 Carlos Delgado
2078 Mike Jockish
2079 Greg O'Halloran
2080 Hector Mercedes
2081 Nigel Wilson
2082 Billy Parese
2083 Gonzalo Vargas
2084 Anton Mobley
2085 Chris Beacom
2086 John Wanish
2087 Ernesto Santana
2088 Rob Blumberg
2089 Sterling Stock
2090 Greg Bicknell
2091 Jeff Kent
2092 Armondo Pagliardi
2093 Mike McAlpin
2094 Greg McCutcheon
2095 Bob Shirley
2096 Rick Holifield

1989 Procards Salinas Spurs

(No affiliation, A) (color)

	MT	NR MT	EX
Complete Set:	6.00	4.50	2.50

1799 Checklist
1800 Dave Horan
1801 Mark Standiford
1802 Steve Gray
1803 Kerry Shaw
1804 Masa Kuoda
1805 Jeff Kaiser
1806 Greg Lee
1807 Ray Valasquez
1808 Yuki Kaseda
1809 Dragon Taguchi
1810 Yoshi Yoshinaga
1811 Jim McNamara
1812 Honen Chikida
1813 Yuji Yamaguchi
1814 Yasu Suzuki
1815 Pat Brady
1816 Larry Carter
1817 Doug Messer
1818 Dan Adriance
1819 Greg Sparks
1820 Jerry Nyman
1821 Tod Ronson
1822 Tim Ireland
1823 Scott Gay
1824 Scott Nelson
1825 Matt Williams
1826 Dave Cantrell
1827 Dickens Benoit
1828 Brian John Costello

1989 Procards San Jose Giants

(San Francisco Giants, A) (color)

	MT	NR MT	EX
Complete Set:	6.50	4.75	2.50

432 Checklist
433 Montie Phillips
434 Tom Ealy
435 Elanis Westbrooks
436 T.J. McDonald
437 Jim Malseed
438 Scott Goins
439 Bill Carlson
440 David Booth
441 Dan Fernandez
442 Don Brock
443 Bryan Hickerson
444 Tom Hostetler
445 Jim Pena
446 Steve Decker
447 Kevin Meier
448 Mark Dewey
449 Jim Terrill
450 Andres Santana
451 Juan Guerrero
452 Lonnie Phillips
453 Duane Espy
454 Scott Wilson
455 Todd Oakes
456 Steve Lienhard
457 Steve Hecht
458 Jamie Cooper
459 Rod Beck
460 Jim Jones
461 Mike Ham

1989 Procards Savannah Cardinals

(St. Louis Cardinals, A) (color)

	MT	NR MT	EX
Complete Set:	6.00	4.50	2.50

342 Checklist
343 Jay North
344 Keith Champion
345 Gabriel Ozuna
346 Bobby Deloach
347 Dan Doyel
348 Dean Weese
349 Orlando Thomas
350 Luis Martinez
351 John Burgos
352 Tim Pettengill
353 Ahmed Rodriguez
354 Jim Ferguson
355 Vince Kindred
356 Juan Belbru
357 Mauricio Nunez
358 Eddie Carter
359 Mateo Ozuna
360 Lorenzo Calzado
361 Julio Mendez
362 Al Biggers
363 Steve Fanning
364 Mike Hensley
365 Brad Harvick
366 Bill Hershman
367 David Sala
368 Andy Taylor
369 Dan Hitt
370 Mark Clark
371 John Ericks

1989 Procards Scranton-Wilkes Red Barons

(Philadelphia Phillies, AAA) (color)

	MT	NR MT	EX
Complete Set:	6.00	4.50	2.50

705 Checklist
706 Danny Clay
707 Ron Salcedo
708 Greg Legg
709 Brad Moore
710 Victor Rosario
711 Al Pardo
712 Barney Nugent
713 Kevin Bootay
714 Gordon Dillard
715 Wally Ritchie
716 Keith Miller
717 Steve Stanicek
718 Bob Sebra
719 John Martin
720 Alex Madrid
721 Brad Brink
722 Joe LeFebvre
723 Jim Olander
724 George Culver
725 Tommy Barrett
726 Randy O'Neal
727 Floyd Rayford
728 Bruce Ruffin
729 Ken Johnson
730 Matt Cimo
731 Joe Redfield
1208 Bill Dancy

1989 Procards Shreveport Captains

(San Francisco Giants, AA) (color)

	MT	NR MT	EX
Complete Set:	6.00	4.50	2.50

1829 Checklist
1830 Steve Connolly
1831 Russ Swan
1832 Mike Remlinger
1833 Eric Gunderson
1834 Paul Blair
1835 Jim Anderson
1836 Dee Dixon
1837 Steve Cline
1838 Bill Evers
1839 Greg Connor
1840 Mike Senne
1841 Gregg Ritchie
1842 Ted Wood
1843 David Patterson
1844 Craig Colbert
1845 Erik Johnson
1846 Jeff Carter
1847 Rich Aldrete
1848 Jose Pena
1849 Markus Owens
1850 Paul McClellan
1851 Doug Robertson
1852 Dean Freeland
1853 Randy McCament
1854 Jose Dominquez
1855 George Bonilla

1989 Procards Spartanburg Phillies

(Philadelphia Phillies, A) (color)

	MT	NR MT	EX
Complete Set:	6.50	4.75	2.50

1027 Checklist
1028 Todd Elam
1029 Ed Rosado
1030 Mickey Morandini
1031 Jon Szynal
1032 Rick Jones
1033 Troy Kent
1034 Greg McCarthy
1035 Mike Carlin
1036 Gary Wilson
1037 Toby Borland
1038 Jason Backs
1039 Reggie Garcia
1040 Darrell Lindsey
1041 Paul Ellison
1042 Darrell Coulter
1043 Nick Santacruz
1044 Leroy Ventress
1045 John Marshall
1046 Antonio Linares
1047 Tom Marsh

1048 Reed Olmstead
1049 Chris Sementelli
1050 Mel Roberts
1051 Pedro Zayas
1052 Tim Dell
1053 Tim Churchill
1054 John Larosa
1055 Steve Keller
1056 Don "Moose" DeMuth

1989 Procards Stockton Ports

(Milwaukee Brewers, A) (color)

	MT	NR MT	EX
Complete Set:	6.00	4.50	2.50

372 Checklist
373 Leo Perez
374 Dave Nilsson
375 Larry Oedewaldt
376 Kent Hetrick
377 Mark Ambrose
378 Carl Moraw
379 Pat Listach
380 John Jaha
381 Charlie Montoyo
382 Randy Snyder
383 Bobby Jones
384 Steve Monson
385 Rob Derksen
386 Dave Huppert
387 Jim Poulin
388 Rick Durant
389 Jamie Cangemi
390 Steve Sparks
391 Chris George
392 Chris Cassels
393 Bryan Foster
394 Rob Smith
395 Dan Fitzpatrick
396 Gary Borg
397 Don Miller
398 Dan Chapman
399 Jeff Ciszkowski
400 Mike Ignasiak
401 Tim Raley
402 Compliment Card

1989 Procards Sumter Braves

(Atlanta Braves, R) (color)

	MT	NR MT	EX
Complete Set:	6.00	4.50	2.50

1086 Checklist
1087 Tom Rizzo
1088 Ed Holtz
1089 Billy Partin
1090 Paul Reis
1091 Ralph Rowe
1092 Willy Johnson
1093 Elias Sosa
1094 Gil Garrido
1095 Ned Yost
1096 Steve Lopez
1097 Glen Gardner
1098 Lionel Adams
1099 Mark Wohlers
1100 Dave Dickman
1101 Calvain Culberson
1102 Judd Johnson
1103 Winnie Relaford
1104 Rod Richey
1105 Johnny Maldonado
1106 Lamar Hall
1107 Scott Goselin
1108 Chad Smith
1109 Mike Urman
1110 Randy Simmons
1111 Roberto Minaya
1112 Eduardo Perez
1113 Roberto DeLeon
1114 Scott Grove
1115 Marcos Vazquez
1116 Glenn Mitchell
1117 Greg Harper
1118 Jeff Meier

1989 Procards Syracuse Chiefs

(Toronto Blue Jays, AAA) (color)

	MT	NR MT	EX
Complete Set:	8.50	6.25	3.50

790 Checklist
791 Francisco Cabrera
792 Chico Walker
793 Otis Green
794 Frank Wills
795 Randy Holland
796 Bob Bailor
797 Juan Guzman
798 Stu Pederson
799 Galen Cisco
800 Kelly Heath
801 Hector Torres
802 Sal Butera
803 Steve Cummings
804 Glenallen Hill
805 Willie Blair
806 Jose Nunez
807 Doug Bair
808 Sil Campusano
809 Luis Sojo
810 Junior Felix
811 DeWayne Buice
812 Jack O'Connor
813 Alex Sanchez
814 Mark Ross
815 Tim Tolman
816 Hector Delacruz

1989 Procards Tacoma Tigers

(Oakland A's, AAA) (color)

	MT	NR MT	EX
Complete Set:	6.50	4.75	2.50

1535 Checklist
1536 Jose Canseco
1537 Mark McGwire
1538 Walt Weiss
1539 Lance Blankenship
1540 Bruce Tanner
1541 Doug Jennings
1542 Felix Jose
1543 Walt Horn
1544 Rich Bordi
1545 Brian Snyder
1546 Bruce Walton
1547 Dave Otto
1548 Reese Lambert
1549 Jessie Reid
1550 Joe Law
1551 Brad Fischer
1552 Steve Howard
1553 Pat Dietrick
1554 Dickie Scott
1555 Bill Dawley
1556 Russ McGinnis
1557 Larry Arndt
1558 Buddy Pryor
1559 Jeff Shaver
1560 Jim Corsi
1561 Tyler Brilinski
1562 Donnie Hill
1563 Bryan Clark
1564 Chuck Estrada
1565 Mike Bordick
1566 Stan Naccaratto

1989 Procards Tidewater Tides

(New York Mets, AAA) (color)

	MT	NR MT	EX
Complete Set:	7.00	5.25	2.75

1946 Checklist
1947 Field Staff (Mike Cubbage, Glenn Abbott, Sam McCrary, Rich Miller)
1948 Keith Miller
1949 Mark Bailey
1950 Jeff Innis
1951 Manny Salinas
1952 Tim Drummond
1953 Jeff McKnight
1954 Lou Thornton
1955 Bill Scherrer
1956 Tom Edens
1957 Darren Reed
1958 Wally Whitehurst
1959 Mike DeButch
1960 Joaquin Contreras
1961 Craig Shipley
1962 Kevin Brown
1963 Ken Dowell
1964 Blaine Beatty
1965 Tom O'Malley
1966 Jeff Gardner
1967 Marcus Lawton
1968 Rick Lundblade
1969 Shawn Barton
1970 John Mitchell
1971 Jack Savage
1972 Kevin Tapani
1973 Dave West
1974 Tony Brown
1975 Phil Lombardi

1989 Procards Toledo Mud Hens

(Detroit Tigers, AAA) (color)

	MT	NR MT	EX
Complete Set:	6.00	4.50	2.50

760 Checklist
761 Jeff Datz
762 Steve McInerney
763 Kenny Williams
764 Delwyn Young
765 Rob Richie
766 Pat Austin
767 Leo Garcia
768 Norman Carrasco
769 Randy Bockus
770 Jim Walewander
771 John Wockenfuss
772 Billy Bean
773 Edwin Nunez
774 Ivan DeJesus
775 Rich Wieligman
776 Mike Trujillo
777 Dave Beard
778 Bob Link
779 Ramon Pena
780 Paul Wenson
781 Shawn Holman
782 Doug Strange
783 Kevin Bradshaw (toledo)
784 Larry See
785 Dave Griffin
786 Kevin Ritz
787 Milt Cuyler
788 Dan DeMascio
789 Dave Palmer

1989 Procards Triple A All Star Game

(AAA) (color)

	MT	NR MT	EX
Complete Set:	14.00	10.50	5.75

1 Checklist
2 Scotti Madison
3 Mike Heifferon
4 Ed Hearn
5 Kent Mercker
6 Sandy Alomar
7 Jay Bell
8 Junior Noboa
9 Dorn Taylor
10 Mark Gardner
11 Jeff Huson
12 Hap Hudson
13 Tom O'Malley
14 Todd Zeile
15 Skeeter Barnes
16 Francisco Cabrera
17 Tom Bolton
18 Kevin Maas
19 Randy Velarde
20 Hal Morris
21 Bucky Dent
22 Steve Henderson
23 Keith Hughes
24 Keith Miller
25 Mike Trujillo
26 Scott Coolbaugh
27 Terry Clark
28 Tom Kotchman
29 Tom Drees
30 Lance Johnson
31 Glenallen Hill
32 Jim Wilson
33 Paul Zuvella
34 Steve Olin
35 Tom Lampkin
36 Pete Dalena
37 Sal Rende
38 Rick Luecken
39 Bryan Clark
40 Victor Rodriguez
41 Billy Bates
42 Greg Vaughn
43 Pete Mackanin
44 Kevin Blankenship
45 Carl Nichols
46 Javier Ortiz
47 Ramon Martinez
48 Mike Huff
49 Jerald Clark
50 Steve Smith
51 Matt Williams
52 Stu Tate
53 Jim Beauchamp
54 Tommy Greene
55 Mark Lemke

1989 Procards Tucson Toros

(Houston Astros, AAA) (color)

	MT	NR MT	EX
Complete Set:	6.00	4.50	2.50

179 Checklist
180 Dave Meads
181 Steve Lombardozzi
182 Larry Lasky
183 Jose Tolentino
184 Gary Cooper
185 Carl Nichols
186 Anthony Kelly
187 Mitch Johnson
188 Charley Kerfeld
189 Brian Meyer
190 Ron Washington
191 Louie Meadows
192 Ed Vosberg
193 Brick Smith
194 Rocky Childress
195 Roger Mason
196 Jeff Heathcock
197 Casey Candaele
198 Dan Schatzeder
199 Harry Spilman
200 Craig Smajstrla
201 Matt Sinatro
202 Frank Cacciatore
203 Bob Skinner

204 Eddie Watt
205 Chuck Jackson
206 Carlo Colombino

1989 Procards Vancouver Canadians

(Chicago White Sox, AAA) (color)

	MT	NR MT	EX
Complete Set:	6.00	4.50	2.50

571 Checklist
572 Cal Emery
573 Marv Foley
574 Greg Latta
575 Doug Mansolino
576 Lance Johnson
577 Jack McDowell
578 Keith Smith
579 Carlos Martinez
580 Rick Rodriguez
581 Moe Drabowsky
582 John Davis
583 Jim Weaver
584 Greg Hibbard
585 Mark Davis
586 Jack Hardy
587 Jerry Willard
588 Tom Drees
589 Adam Peterson
590 Russ Morman
591 Jose Segura
592 Steve Springer
593 Tom McCarthy
594 Kelly Paris
595 John Pawlowski
596 Marlin McPhail
597 Tom Forrester

1989 Procards Visalia Oaks

(Minnesota Twins, A) (color)

	MT	NR MT	EX
Complete Set:	6.50	4.75	2.50

1419 Checklist
1420 Gorman Heimueller
1421 Howard Townsend
1422 Kouichi Ozawa
1423 Vince Teixeira
1424 Minoru Yojo
1425 Rob Wassenaar
1426 Willie Banks
1427 Johnny Ard
1428 Greg Brinkman
1429 Bob Strube
1430 Takashi Yoshida
1431 Rick McWane
1432 Kenji Fujimoto
1433 Scott Ullger
1434 Kiyoshi Sagawa
1435 Doug Simons
1436 Todd McClure
1437 Jarvis Brown
1438 Mike Dotzler
1439 Shawn Gilbert
1440 Frank Valdez
1441 Carlos Capellan
1442 Lenny Webster
1443 Jose Marzan
1444 Steve Stowell
1445 Basil Meyer
1446 Fred White
1447 David Jacas
1448 David Smith
1449 Loy McBride

1989 Procards Waterloo Diamonds

(No affiliation, A) (color)

	MT	NR MT	EX
Complete Set:	6.00	4.50	2.50

1771 Checklist
1772 Steve Hendricks
1773 Scott Meadows
1774 Alexis Figueroa
1775 Jose LeBron
1776 Dave Gavin
1777 Bob Curnow
1778 James Nolan
1779 Tim Holland
1780 Rob Cantwell
1781 Jeff Hart
1782 Ron Morton
1783 Chuck Ricci
1784 Mark Littell
1785 Jamie Moreno
1786 Osvaldo Sanchez
1787 Mike King
1788 Billy Reed
1789 Luis Galindez
1790 Pedro Lopez
1791 Ray Holbert
1792 Don Fowler
1793 Mike Borgatti
1794 Brad Hoyer
1795 Dave Cunningham
1796 Reggie Farmer
1797 Chad Kuhn
1798 Rich Slomkowski

1989 Procards Williamsport Bills

(Seattle Mariners, AA) (color)

	MT	NR MT	EX
Complete Set:	8.50	6.25	3.50

625 Checklist
626 Dru Kosco
627 Bobby Cuellar
628 Mark Wooden
629 Mike Brocki
630 David Burba
631 Jerry Goff
632 Pat Lennon
633 Jose Melendez
634 Randy Roetter
635 Tino Martinez
636 Ted Williams
637 Jeff Nelson
638 Scott Runge
639 Jeff Hooper
640 William Diaz
641 Harry Davis
642 Dave Brundage
643 Jack Smith
644 Brad Brusky
645 Keith Helton
646 Pat Rice
647 Dana Ridenour
648 Greg Fulton
649 Rich Delucia

1989 Pucko Elmira Pioneers

(Boston Red Sox) (color)

	MT	NR MT	EX
Complete Set:	10.50	7.75	4.25

1 Dave Alvarez
2 Johnny Diaz
3 Luis Dorante
4 Chris Hanks
5 Pete Hoy
6 Garrett Jenkins
7 Steve Michael
8 Jim Morrison
9 Bart Moore
10 Frank Morelli
11 Tony Mosley
12 Lou Munoz
13 Ender Perozo
14 Ed Riley
15 Carlos Rivera
16 Julio Rosario
17 Chris Rosfelder
18 Andy Rush
19 Al Sanders
20 John Spencer
21 Richard Witherspoon
22 Mike Verdi
23 Dave Kennedy
24 Dunn Field
25 Clyde Smoll
26 Dennis Robarge
27 Kevin Morton
28 Michael Thompson
29 John Locker
30 Jeff McNeely
31 Paul Quantrill
32 Eric Wedge

1989 Pucko Niagara Falls Rapids

(Detroit Tigers, A) (color)

	MT	NR MT	EX
Complete Set:	6.50	4.75	2.50

1 Don Pedersen
2 Eric Albright
3 Marcos Betances
4 Brian Cornelius
5A Luis Ivan Cruz, Dave Keating
6 John DeSilva
7 John Doherty
8 Mark Ettles
9 Jeff Goodale
10 Jim Heins
11 Tim Herrmann
12 Jody Hurst
13 Kieth Kimberlin
14 Keith Langston
15 Matt Logue
16 Doug Marcero
17 Craig Middlekauff
18 Mario Moccia
19 Gustavo Pinto
20 Bob Reimink
21 Rick Sellers
22 Freddy Torres
23 Craig Wiley
24 David Wilson
25 Rick Magnante
26 Juan Lopez
27 Ron Ross
28 Tom Prohaska
29 San Maglie Stadium

1989 Pucko Utica Blue Sox

(Chicago White Sox, A) (color)

	MT	NR MT	EX
Complete Set:	6.50	4.75	2.50

1 Dave Van Winkle
2 Glen Braxton
3 Kenny Burroughs
4 Ken Coleman
5 Mike Davino
6 Brian Davis
7 John Furch
8 Mike Galvan
9 Dave Gorman
10 Keith Harris
11 Jeff Ingram
12 Brian Keyser
13 Greg Kobza
14 Rich Long
15 Pat Mehrtens
16 Jesus Merejo
17 Greg Perschke
18 Ron Plemmons
19 Johnny Ruffin
20 Lance Sanders
21 Joe Singley
22 John Smith
23 Scott Stevens
24 Dean Tatarain
25 Robert Thompson
26 Dennis Walker
27 Jerry Wolak
28 Ron Vaughn
29 Bill Ballou
30 Mike Gelllinger
31 Rick Ray
32 Joanne Gerace
33 Strike-O
34 Murnane Field

1989 Pucko Welland Pirates

(Pittsburgh Pirates, A) (color)

	MT	NR MT	EX
Complete Set:	6.50	4.75	2.50

1 William Pennyfeather
2 Scott Arvesen
3 Robert Bailey, Jr.
4 Angel Beltram
5 David Bird
6 Mike Brewington
7 Kim Broome
8 Rod Byerly
9 Nelson Caraballo
10 Tom Deller
11 Raymond Doss
12 Mike Fortuna
13 Valentine Henderson
14 Deron Johnson
15 Paul Keefer
16 Jeff Kuder
17 John Latham
18 Javier Magria
19 Erik Nelson
20 Rob Peterson
21 Winston Seymour
22 Garland Slaughter
23 Mark Thomas
24 Ken Trusky
25 Tom Tuholski
26 Paul Wagner
27 Tim Wakefield
28 Ron Way
29 Flavio Williams
30 U.L. Washington
31 Larry Smith
32 Paul Allen
33 Bill Kuehn
34 Bob Burgess
35 John Belford, Norma Chaney

1989 Rock's Dugout Wichita Wranglers

(San Diego Padres, AA) (color)

	MT	NR MT	EX
Complete Set:	10.50	7.75	4.25

(1) Mike Basso
(2) Andy Benes
(3) Ricky Bones
(4) Doug Brocail
(5) Brian Brooks
(6) Joe Chavez
(7) Rafael Chavez
(8) Brian Cisarik
(9) Craig Cooper
(10) Robert DeWolf
(11) Paul Faries
(12) Kevin Garner
(13) Greg Harris
(14) Charlie Hillemann
(15) David Hollins
(16) Rich Holsman
(17) Pat Kelly
(18) Gary Lance
(19) Tom LeVasseur
(20) Jim Lewis
(21) Bryan Little
(22) Warren Newson
(23) Omar Olivares
(24) Tony Pellegrino
(25) Paul Quinzer
(26) Rich Rodriguez
(27) Dan Walters
(28) Brian Wood
(29) Team Logo
(30) Rock's Dugout Card

1989 Rock's Dugout Wichita Wranglers

(San Diego Padres, AA) (color) (stadium set)

	MT	NR MT	EX
Complete Set:	10.50	7.75	4.25

1 Compliment Card
2 Warren Nelson
3 Tony Pellegrino
4 Charlie Hillemann
5 Brian Cisarik
6 Larry Mims
7 Steve Hendricks
8 Andy Benes
9 Mike Basso
10 Compliment Card
11 Omar Olivares
12 Dave Hollins
13 Doug Brocail
14 Jim Lewis
15 Pat Kelly
16 Ricky Bones
17 Kevin Garner
18 Paul Faries
19 Rich Rodriguez
20 Rich Holsman
21 Compliment Card
22 Title Card
23 Saul Soltero
24 Steve Loubier
25 Rafael Chavez
26 Tom LeVasseur
27 Bryan Little
28 Gary Lance
29 Cookie (mascot)
30 Compliment

1989 Rock's Dugout Wichita Wranglers

(San Diego Padres, AA) (color) (highlight set)

	MT	NR MT	EX
Complete Set:	10.50	7.75	4.25

1 Title Card
2 Home Run Threats (Warren Newson, Rob DeWolf, Brian Brooks, Kevin Garner)

3 Wranglers Celebrate
4 Pitching Round-Up (Rich Rogriguez, Rich Holsman, Doug Brocial, Brian Wood, Omar Olivares, Rafael Chavez)
5 Paul Faries
6 Tribute to A. Bartlett Giamatti

7 Jose Mota
8 300 Club (Warren Newson, Brian Cisarik, Rob DeWolf, Tom LeVasseur, Paul Faries)
9 Tom LeVasseur
10 Mike Basso
11 Dave Hollins
12 Warren Newson
13 Newson Scoring
14 Holson's Wind Up
15 Kelly's Direction
16 Pitching Sensation (Valdez)

17 DeWolf's Grand Slam
18 Omar Olivares
19 Benes Delivers
20 Ricky Bones

1989 Rock's Dugout Wichita Wranglers Update

(San Diego Padres, AA) (color) (update set)

	MT	NR MT	EX
Complete Set:	10.50	7.75	4.25

1 Title Card
2 Pat Kelly
3 Paul Faries
4 Omar Olivares
5 Andy Benes
6 Charlie Hillemann
7 Warren Newson
8 Craig Cooper
9 Saul Soltero
10 Rafael Valdez
11 Jose Mota
12 Brian Brooks
13 Larry Mims
14 Steve Loubler
15 Rob DeWolf
16 Paul Quinzer
17 Home Run Threats (Warren Newson, Rob DeWolf, Brian Brooks, Kevin Garner)

18 Jose Valentin
19 Andy Benes
20 Rich Holsman

1989 Sport Pro Butte Copper Kings

(Texas Rangers, R) (color)

	MT	NR MT	EX
Complete Set:	10.00	7.50	4.00

1 Stacy Parker
2 David Perez
3 Brian Roper
4 Donald Harris
5 Eric Bickhardt
6 Brian Romero
7 Barry Winford
8 Brian Crowley
9 Jose Borges
10 Steve Rowley
11 Jim Clinton
12 Jose Oliva
13 Joe Eischen
14 Chris Shiflett
15 Geoff Flinn
16 Troy Eklund
17 Jay Franklin
18 Brian Steiner
19 Manny Garcia
20 Randy Marshall
21 John Graves
22 Mark Young
23 Darrin Hays
24 Bump Wills
25 Buddy Micheu
26 Timmie Morrow
27 Dan Peltier
28 Ernie Rodriguez
29 Marvin White
30 Dave Freisleben

1989 Sport Pro Helena Brewers

(Milwaukee Brewers, A) (color)

	MT	NR MT	EX
Complete Set:	9.00	6.75	3.50

1 Joe Andrzejewski
2 Angel Diaz
3 Reggie Brown
4 Pat Rehwinkel
5 Tim Wilson
6 Rusty Rugg
7 Troy Haugen
8 Tony Diggs
9 Bill Brakeley
10 Greg Landry
11 Troy O'Leary
12 David Volt
13 Joe Roebuck
14 Gustavo Federico
15 Ramser Correa
16 Reed Charpia
17 Bo Dodson
18 Bob Vancho
19 Bob Kappesser
20 Eric Patton
21 David Weldin
22 Sam Drake
23 Kevin Tannahill
24 Scott Muscat
25 Darrin White
26 Ray Burris
27 Dusty Rhodes

1989 Sport Pro Great Falls Dodgers

(Los Angeles Dodgers, R) (color)

	MT	NR MT	EX
Complete Set:	20.00	15.00	8.00

1 Tom Goodwin
2 Michael Frame
3 Rich Crane
4 Michael Potthoff
5 Jamie McAndrew
6 Tony Helmick
7 Javier Loera
8 Audelle Cummings
9 Joe Vavra
10 Jason Brosnan
11 Ray Bielanin
12 Michael Wismer
13 Yale Fowler
14 Tim Barker
15 Joey Seals
16 Lee DeLoach
17 John Deutsch
18 Kiki Jones
19 Bryan Baar
20 Barry Parisotto
21 Frank Humber
22 Anthony Collier
23 Mathew Howard
24 Erik Madsen
25 Stephen O'Donnell
26 Rod Harvell
27 Bobby Fletcher
28 Mike Galle
29 Craig White
30 Ray Calhoun
31 Bill Miller
32 Matt Wilson
33 Goose Gregson

1989 Sport Pro Spokane Indians

(San Diego Padres, A) (color)

	MT	NR MT	EX
Complete Set:	10.00	7.50	4.00

1 Dave Staton
2 Eddie Zinter
3 Rod Billingsley
4 Bruce Bochy
5 Tony McGee
6 John Phelan
7 Joe Buckley
8 Greg Hall
9 Terry Rupp
10 Dan Deville
11 Rick Davis
12 Bill Johnson
13 Tom Brassel
14 Kerry Knox
15 Brian Span
16 Scot Welish
17 Troy Cunningham
18 Steve Martin
19 Kevin Higgins
20 Chris Gollehon
21 Jeff Barton
22 Bobby Sheridan
23 Kevin Towers
24 Rico Coleman
25 Steve Bethea
26 Darrell Sherman

1989 Star Co. Albany-Colonie Yankees

(New York Yankees, AA) (color)

	MT	NR MT	EX
Complete Set:	10.50	7.75	4.25

1 Oscar Azocar
2 Tim Becker
3 Darrin Chapin
4 Mike Christopher
5 Royal Clayton
6 Bobby Davidson
7 Bobby Dickerson
8 Rodney Imes
9 Tim Layana
10 Jim Leyritz
11 Mitch Lyden
12 Jason Maas
13 Hensley Meulens
14 Kevin Mmahat
15 John Ramos
16 Jerry Rub
17 Rob Sepanek
18 Scott Shaw
19 Andy Stankiewicz
20 Aris Tirado
21 Ricky Torres
22 Buck Showalter
23 Deion Sanders (Last Issue)

Definitions for grading conditions are located in the Introduction of this price guide.

1989 Star Co. Baseball City Royals

(Kansas City Royals, A) (color)

	MT	NR MT	EX
Complete Set:	7.00	5.25	2.75

1 Ken Adams
2 Pete Alborano
3 Jon Alexander
4 Jose Anglero
5 Sean Berry
6 Jeff Conine
7 Carlos Gonzalez
8 Kevin Shaw
9 Dave Howard
10 Jim Hudson
11 Tom Johnson
12 Joel Johnston
13 Lorin Jundy
14 Kevin Koslofski
15 Francisco Laureano
16 Brian McCormack
17 Dennis Moeller
18 Bobby Moore
19 Doug Nelson
20 Jorge Pedre
21 Kevin Pickens
22 Ruben Pujols
23 Keith Shepherd
24 Bill Stonikas
25 Not Issued
26 DeJon Watson (Late Issue)
27 Coaches card (Luis Silverio, Ron Johnson, Mike Alvarez)

1989 Star Beloit Brewers

(Milwaukee Brewers, A)

	MT	NR MT	EX
Complete Set:	6.00	4.50	2.50

1 Frank Bolick
2 Kevin Carmody
3 Don Erickson
4 John Faccio
5 Dave Fitzgerald
6 Librado Garcia
7 Mike Grayson
8 Mike Guerrero
9 Bert Hefferman
10 Chris Johnson
11 Mark Kiefer
12 Ken Kremer
13 Greg Landry
14 Heath Lane
15 Oreste Marrero
16 Vilato Marrero
17 Don Meyett
18 Bob Muhammad
19 Troy O'Leary
20 Joe Ortiz
21 Jose Peguero
22 Rich Pfaff
23 Dave Voit
24 Tim Wahl
25 Bob Watts
26 (Alex Taveras & Gary Robson)

1989 Star Co. Beloit Brewers

(Milwaukee Brewers, A)

	MT	NR MT	EX
Complete Set:	6.00	4.50	2.50

1 Frank Bolick
2 Arthur Butcher
3 John Byington
4 Jamie Cangemi
5 Kevin Carmody
6 Larry Carter
7 Steve Diaz
8 Calvin Eldred
9 John Finn
10 Dave Fitzgerald
11 Librado Garcia
12 Ron Hanisch
13 Mitch Hannahs
14 Bert Heffernan
15 Kenny Jackson
16 Chris Johnson
17 Mark Kiefer
18 Ken Kremer
19 Curt Krippner
20 Vilato Marrero
21 Don Meyett
22 Angel Miranda
23 Rich Pfaff
24 Guillermo Sandoval

1989 Star Co. Bluefield Orioles

(Baltimore Orioles, R) (color)

	MT	NR MT	EX
Complete Set:	6.50	4.75	2.50

1 Eric Alexander
2 Manny Alexander
3 Chris Batiste
4 Mattie Belen
5 Cristian Benitez
6 Sergio Cairo
7 Bo Davis
8 Cesar Devares
9 John Fowler
10 Israel Frias
11 Shawn Heiden
12 Keith Kessinger
13 T.R. Lewis
14 John Marett
15 Tom Martin
16 Victor Medina
17 Jimmy Roso
18 Brad Pennington
19 Arron Norwood
20 Keith Schmidt
21 Al Sieradzki
22 Rob Stiegele
23 Doug Sutton
24 Tommy Taylor
25 Alex Taveras, Joe Teixeira
26 Mat Anderson (Late Issue)
27 Daryl Noore (Late Issue)
28 Bob Wheatcroft (Late Issue)

29 Coaching Staff (Jose Soto, Mike Young, Chet Nichols)

1989 Star Co. Bristol Tigers

(Detroit Tigers, A) (color)

	MT	NR MT	EX
Complete Set:	6.00	4.50	2.50

1 Michael Bowman
2 Jeff Braley
3 Aurturo Caines
4 Pedro Checo
5 Matthew Coleman
6 Lance Daniels
7 Robert Davis
8 Fredie Gamble
9 Mike Garcia
10 Jose Guzman
11 Chris Hall
12 Ricky Ibarguen
13 Travis Kinyoun
14 Ken Lewis
15 Ron Maietta
16 Steve Matchett
17 Kasy McKeon
18 Joe Neidinger
19 Kelley O'Neal
20 Rudy Pemberton
21 Mike Rendina
22 Juan Reyes
23 Eddie Rodriguez
24 Jose Rodriquez
25 Brian Rountree
26 Mac Siebert
27 Mario Stefani
28 Brad Wilson
29 Ruben Amaro
30 Steve Webber
31 Boyce Cox

1989 Star Co. Burlington Braves

(Atlanta Braves, A) (color)

	MT	NR MT	EX
Complete Set:	6.00	4.50	2.50

1 Tony Baldwin
2 Daryl Blanks
3 Donovan Campbell
4 Greg Cloninger
5 Bob Cole
6 Johnny Cuevas
7 Brian Cummings
8 Chris Czarnik
9 Mark Davis
10 Steve Glass
11 Dave Karasinski
12 Kevin Kelly
13 Jesus Mendoza
14 Rich Longuil
15 Keith Mitchell
16 Bob Pfaff
17 Thomas Redington
18 David Reis
19 Joseph Saccomanno
20 Gary Schoonover
21 Lee Upshaw
22 Preston Watson
23 Allen Waznik
24 Steven Wendell
25 Teddy Williams
26 Skipper Wright
27 Jim Saul
28 Ross Grimsely
29 Steve Curry
30 Not Issued

1989 Star Co. Burlington Indians

(Cleveland Indians, A) (color)

	MT	NR MT	EX
Complete Set:	6.00	4.50	2.50

Robert Persons (Last Issue)
1 Chad Allen
2 Andy Baker
3 Stacy Brown
4 Mark Charbonnet
5 Chris Cole
6 John Cotton
7 Mike Davis
8 Anthony Dela Cruz
9 Mark Delpiano
10 Carey Elston
11 Mike Gonzalez
12 Brian Hart
13 Avery Johnson
14 Tom Lachmann
15 Nolan Lane
16 Jesse Levis
17 Dean Meddaugh
18 David Nebraska
19 Ramon Ortiz
20 Cecil Pettiford
21 Clyde Pough
22 Roberto Rivera
23 Tommy Tillman
24 Ramon Torres
25 Reynaldo Ventura
26 Olonzo Woodfin (Late Issue)
27 Jim Cabella (Last Issue)
28 Coach Staff (Mark Oestreich, Stan Hilton)
29 Teddy Blackwell (Last Issue)

1989 Star Co. Canton-Akron Indians

(Cleveland Indians, AA) (color)

	MT	NR MT	EX
Complete Set:	6.50	4.75	2.50

1 Beau Allred
2 Coaching Staff (Bob Molinaro, Eric Rasmussen, Billy Williams)
3 Dan Boever
4 Jeff Edwards
5 Greg Ferlenda
6 Lindsay Foster
7 Mark Gilles
8 Todd Gonzales
9 Carl Keliipuleole
10 Scott Khoury
11 Paul Kuzniar
12 Allen Liebert
13 Everado Magallanes
14 Tom Magrann
15 Julius McDougal
16 Greg McMichael
17 Troy Neel
18 Todd Ogden
19 Jeff Shaw
20 Rob Swain
21 Mike Twardoski
22 Efrain Valdez
23 Casey Webster
24 Jose Leiva
25 Joey Belle

1989 Star Co. Cedar Rapids Reds

(Cincinnati Reds, A) (color)

	MT	NR MT	EX
Complete Set:	6.00	4.50	2.50

1 Jeff Branson
2 Norm Brock
3 Adam Casillas
4 Benny Colvard
5 Doug Eastman
6 Scott Eonomy
7 Steve Foster
8 Steve Hester
9 Scott Jeffery
10 Quinn Marsh
11 Steve McCarthy
12 Tony Mealy
13 Duane Mulville
14 Mike Myers
15 Andy Rickman
16 Bill Risley
17 Chris Schnurbusch
18 Scott Sellner
19 Eddie Taubensee
20 Joe Turek
21 Joey Vierra
22 Dave Miley
23 Gerry Groninger
24 Tom Spencer
25 Pete Beeler
26 Don Brown
27 Steve Hester
28 Kennedy Infante
29 Mike Malinak
30 Ross Powell

Definitions for grading conditions are located in the introduction of this price guide.

1989 Star Co. Charlotte Rangers

(Texas Rangers, A)

	MT	NR MT	EX
Complete Set:	6.00	4.50	2.50

Jonathon Hurst, Rob Lavender, Rob Maurer (Late issue, corrected cards)

1 Wilson Alvarez
2 Rick Bernardo
3 Mick Billmeyer
4 Paco Burgos
5 Joel Cartaya
6 Felipe Castillo
7 Brian Evans
8 Pat Garman
9 Stephan Glaskar
10 Not Issued
11 Not Issued
12 Travis Law
13 Bruce Lipscomb
14 Bill Losa
15 Not Issued
16 Rod Morris
17 Scott Morse
18 Ed Ohman
19 Roger Pavlik
20 Wayne Rosenthal
21 Luke Sable
22 Cedric Shaw
23 Jeff Shore
24 John Sipple
25 Mike Taylor
26 Bobby Jones
27 Rusty Gerhardt
28 Jeff Hubbard

1989 Star Co. Clearwater Phillies

(Philadelphia Phillies, A) (color)

	MT	NR MT	EX
Complete Set:	6.50	4.75	2.50

Clearwater Phillies 5th Anniversary Card

1 Jaime Barragan
2 Kim Batiste
3 Kendrick Bourne
4 Jim Carroll
5 Andy Carter
6 Fred Christopher
7 Mark Cobb
8 Pat Combs
9 Kevin Fynan
10 Jeff Grotewold
11 Dave Holdridge
12 Steve Kirkpatrick
13 Lee Langley
14 Tim Mauser
15 Trey McCall
16 Shelby McDonald
17 Matt Rambo
18 Scott Reaves
19 Rod Robertson
20 Mark Sims
21 Royal Thomas
22 Tony Trevino
23 Jim Vatcher
24 Chris Walker
25 Carlos Zayas
26 (Glenn Bulliver & Tim Corcoran Last Issue)

1989 Star Co. Columbus Mudcats

(Houston Astros, AA) (color)

	MT	NR MT	EX
Complete Set:	10.50	7.75	4.25

1 Manny Acta
2 Eric Anthony
3 Jeff Baldwin
4 Ryan Bowen
5 Mike Browning
6 Fred Costello
7 Joel Estes
8 Tony Eusebio
9 Blane Fox
10 Lou Frazier
11 Doug Givier
12 Randy Hennis
13 Trent Hubbard
14 Bert Hunter
15 Darryl Kile
16 Mike Loynd
17 Rob Mallicoatt
18 Garret Nago
19 Karl Rhodes
20 David Rohde
21 Pedro Sanchez
22 Mike William
23 Terry Wells
24 Coaching Staff (Tom Wiedenbauer, Bobby Ramos, Fred Gladding)

1989 Star Co. Columbus Mudcats

(Houston Astros, AA) Platinum set.

	MT	NR MT	EX
Complete Set:	12.00	9.00	5.00

1 Manny Acta
2 Eric Anthony
3 Jeff Baldwin
4 Ryan Bowen
5 Mike Browning
6 Fred Costello
7 Joel Estes
8 Tony Eusebio
9 Blane Fox
10 Lou Frazier
11 Doug Givier
12 Randy Hennis
13 Trent Hubbard
14 Bert Hunter
15 Darryl Kile
16 Mike Loynd
17 Rob Mallicoat
18 Garret Nago
19 Karl Rhodes
20 David Rohde
21 Pedro Sanchez
22 Mike William
23 Terry Wells
24 Coaching Staff (Tom Wiedenbauer, Bobby Ramos, Fred Gladding)

1989 Star Co. Dunedin Blue Jays

(Toronto Blue Jays, A) (color)

	MT	NR MT	EX
Complete Set:	6.50	4.75	2.50

1 Denis Boucher
2 Enrique Burgos
3 Nate Cromwell
4 Andy Dziadkowiec
5 Henry Lee Goshay
6 Darren Hall
7 Pat Hentgen
8 Vince Horsman
9 Jimy Kelly
10 Randy Knorr
11 Mike Mills
12 Bernardino Nunez
13 Paul Rodgers
14 Earl Sanders
15 Al Silverstein
16 Ed Sprague
17 Williams Suero
18 Marcos Taveras
19 Mike Tomlin
20 Relito Uribe
21 Greg Vella
22 Steve Wapnick
23 Woody Williams
24 Julian Yan
25 Mark Young
26 Coaching Staff (Doug Ault, Dennis Holmberg, Steve Mingori - Late Issue)

1989 Star Co. Durham Bulls

(Atlanta Braves, A) (color) (Atlanta Braves, A) (color)

	MT	NR MT	EX
Complete Set:	7.50	5.50	3.00

1 Steve Avery, Steve Avery
2 Dennis Burlingame, Dennis Burlingame
3 David Butts, David Butts
4 Rich Casarotti, Rich Casarotti
5 Brian Champion, Brian Champion
6 Jamie Cuesta, Jamie Cuesta
7 Wes Currin, Wes Currin
8 Jim Czajkowski, Jim Czajkowski
9 Brian Deak, Brian Deak
10 Todd Dewey, Todd Dewey
11 Mike Fowler, Mike Fowler
12 Jerald Frost, Jerald Frost
13 Phil McDonald, Phil McDonald
14 Rich Maloney, Rich Maloney
15 Al Martin, Al Martin
16 David Nied, David Nied
17 Ken Pennington, Ken Pennington
18 Ben Rivera, Ben Rivera
19 Sean Ross, Sean Ross
20 Mike Stoker, Mike Stoker
21 Pat Tilmon, Pat Tilmon
22 Theron Todd, Theron Todd
23 Andy Tomberlin, Andy Tomberlin
24 Matt Turner, Matt Turner
25 Steve Ziem, Steve Ziem
26 Grady Little, Grady Little
27 Larry Jaster, Larry Jaster
28 Inocencio Guerrero, Inocencio Guerrero
29 Kevin Costner, Kevin Costner

1989 Star Co. Elizabethton Twins

(Minnesota Twins, A) (color)

	MT	NR MT	EX
Complete Set:	6.00	4.50	2.50

1 Bryan Asp
2 Tom Benson
3 Jayson Best
4 David Bigham
5 Marty Cordoua
6 Sandy Diaz
7 Steve Dunn
8 Rick Freeman
9 Randy Gentile
10 Jody Harrington
11 Mike Hinde
12 Mike House, Karl Johnson
13 Karl Johnson
14 Jose Leon
15 Mike Lloyd
16 Angel Lugo
17 Bob McCreary
18 Jeff Milene
19 Mike Misuraca
20 Steve Morris
21 Willie Mota
22 Dennis Neagle
23 Tim Nedin
24 Rex De La Nuez
25 Kerry Taylor
26 Amadeo Garcia
27 Wade Wacker
28 Phil Wiese
29 Ray Smith
30 Coaching Staff (Rick Tomlin, Jim Lemon,)
31 Jeff Chambers

1989 Star Co. Erie Orioles

(Baltimore Orioles, A) (color)

	MT	NR MT	EX
Complete Set:	9.00	6.75	3.50

1 Tony Beasley
2 Dan Berthel
3 John Bowen
4 Dave Brown
5 Pat Hedge
6 John Hemmerly
7 Aman Hicks
8 Brad Hildreth
9 Ed Horowitz
10 Zack Kerr
11 Pat Leinen
12 Rich Meek
13 Carey Metts
14 Cary Moore
15 Steve Nicosia
16 Mike Oquist
17 Jamie Pena
18 Doug Reynolds
19 Art Rhodes
20 Mike Richardson
21 David Riddle
22 Pete Rose Jr.
23 Mark Rupp
24 Gary Shingledecker
25 Melvin Wearing
26 Steve Williams (Late issue)
27 Bobby Tolan (Late issue)
28 Mark Brown (Late issue)
29 Dave Werner (Late issue)

1989 Star Co. Everett Giants

(San Francisco Giants, A) (color)

	MT	NR MT	EX
Complete Set:	6.00	4.50	2.50

1 Maximo Aleys
2 Clayton Bellinger
3 Steve Callahan
4 Teodoro Cespedes
5 Ron Crowe
6 Brian Dour
7 Scott Ebert
8 Mike Grahovac
9 Edward Gustafson
10 Kevin Hall
11 Chris Hancock
12 Carl Hanselman
13 Dan Hendrickson
14 David Hocking
15 Steve Hosey
16 Randy Johnson
17 Kevin Jones
18 Kevin Kasper
19 Jesus Laya
20 Mike McDonald
21 Troy Mentzer
22 Dan Montes
23 Vince Palyan
24 Ed Quesada
25 Jon Schiller
26 Greg Brummett
27 Greg Lund
28 Jason McFarlin
29 Glen Warren
30 Joe Strain
31 Diego Segui
32 Bryce Welch

1989 Star Co. Fort Lauderdale Yankees

(New York Yankees, A) (color)

	MT	NR MT	EX
Complete Set:	6.00	4.50	2.50

1 Yankees (Steve Adkins)
2 Yankees (Russell Davis)
3 Yankees (Herb Erhardt)
4 Yankees (Steve Erickson)
5 Yankees (Victor Garcia)
6 Yankees (Doug Gogolewski)
7 Yankees (John Green)
8 Yankees (Freddie Hailey)
9 Yankees (Mike Hook)
10 Yankees (Chris Howard)
11 Yankees (Dean Kelly)
12 Yankees (Ralph Kraus)
13 Yankees (Mark Leiter)
14 Yankees (Ramon Manon)
15 Yankees (Ed Martel)
16 Yankees (Alan Mills)
17 Yankees (Red Morrison)
18 Yankees (Skip Nelloms)
19 Yankees (Tom Popplewell)
20 Yankees (Mike Rhodes)
21 Yankees (Carlos Rodriguez)
22 Yankees (Garriel Rodriguez)
23 Yankees (Dan Roman)
24 Yankees (Melvin Rosario)
25 Yankees (John Seeburger)
26 Yankees (Bob Zeihen)
27 Yankees (Clete Boyer)
28 Yankees (Jack Hubbard)
29 Yankees (David Schuler)

1989 Star Co. Frederick Keys

(Baltimore Orioles, A) (color)

	MT	NR MT	EX
Complete Set:	10.00	7.50	4.00

1 Stacey Burdick
2 Mike Cavers
3 Andres Constant
4 Francisco Dela Rosa
5 Mike Deutsch
6 Oneri Fleita
7 Roy Gilbert
8 Ricky Gutierrez
9 Tom Harms
10 Paris Hayden
11 Stacey Jones
12 Mike Lehman
13 Mike Linskey
14 Rodney Lofton
15 Scott Meadows
16 Luis Mercedes
17 Dave Miller
18 Steve Mondile
19 Chris Myers
20 Luis Paulino
21 David Segui
22 Dan Simonds
23 Anthony Telford
24 Jack Voight
25A Jerry Narron ((Error) with glasses, late issue)
25B Jerry Narron (Corrected)
26 Mike Pazik (Late issue)
27 Pete Rose, Jr. (Late issue)

1989 Star Co. Gastonia Rangers

(Texas Rangers, A) (color)

	MT	NR MT	EX
Complete Set:	6.00	4.50	2.50

1 Steve Allen
2 Kevin Belcher
3 Tony Berry
4 Cris Colon
5 Doug Cronk
6 Everett Cunningham
7 Jeff Frye
8 Jose Hernandez
9 Jim Hvizda
10 Joe Lewis
11 Tim MacNeil
12 Trey McCoy
13 Eric McCray
14 Jim McCutchen
15 Mike Mendazona
16 Robb Nen
17 Darren Oliver
18 Dominic Pierce
19 Carl Randle
20 Ivan Rodriguez
21 Rolando Romero
22 Kyle Spencer
23 Frank Valdez
24 Joe Wardlow
25 Spencer Wilkinson
26 Not Known

1989 Star Co. Greenville Braves

(Atlanta Braves, AA) (color)

	MT	NR MT	EX
Complete Set:	7.00	5.25	2.75

1 Edwin Alicea
2 John Alva
3 Mike Bell
4 Terry Bell
5 Tim Dietz
6 Maximo Del Rosario
7 Tommy Dunbar
8 Dennis Hood
9 Brian Hunter
10 German Jimenez
11 John Kilner
12 Jimmy Kremers
13 Jim Lemasters
14 Paul Marak
15 Rick Morris
16 Juan Pacho
17 Dave Plumb
18 Dale Polley
19 Darrell Pruitt
20 Ellis Roby
21 Miguel Sabino
22 Mike Stanton
23 Dopug Stockam
24 Danny Weems
25 Coaching Staff (Buddy Bailey, Bill Slack, Randy Ingle)

1989 Star Co. Hagerstown Suns

(Baltimore Orioles, AA) (color)

	MT	NR MT	EX
Complete Set:	6.00	4.50	2.50

1 Dave Bettendorf
2 Don Buford
3 Sherwin Cijntje
4 Steve Culkar
5 Brian Dubois
6 Mike Eberle
7 Craig Faulkner
8 Robinson Garces
9 John Githens
10 Leo Gomez
11 Victor Hithe
12 Bob Latmore
13 Ty Nichols
14 John Posey
15 Mike Sander
16 Jeff Schwarz
17 Rafel Skeete
18 Dana Smith
19 Randy Strijek
20 Pete Stanicek
21 Paul Thorpe
22 Coaching Staff (Jimmie Schaffer, Tom Brown)

1989 Star Co. Hamilton Redbirds

(St. Louis Cardinals, A) (color)

	MT	NR MT	EX
Complete Set:	6.00	4.50	2.50

1 Scott Banton
2 Mark Battell
3 Allan Biggers
4 Mark Bowlan
5 David Boss
6 Cliff Brannon
7
8 John Cebuhar
9 David Cassidy
10 Tripp Cromer
11 Jose Fernandez
12 Randy Berlin
13 Steve Graham
14 Larry Gryskevich
15 Chris Gorton
16 Brian Golden
17 Sean Grubb
18 Don Green
19 Tom Infante
20 Tim Lata
21 Mike Milchin
22 Tim Redman
23 Dan Shannon
24 Jose Trujillo
25 Stan Tukes
26 Mark Wilson
27 Joseph Pettini
28 Joseph Cunningham
29 Mike Evans

1989 Star Co. Harrisburg Senators

(Pittsburgh Pirates, AA) (color)

	MT	NR MT	EX
Complete Set:	6.00	4.50	2.50

1 Steve Adams
2 Jeff Banister
3 Stan Belinda
4 Kevin Burdick
5 Wes Chamberlain
6 Jeff Cook
7 Orlando Lind
8 Tim McKinley
9 Orlando Merced
10 Pete Murphy
11 Julio Peguero
12 Julio Perez
13 Rico Rossy
14 Rob Russell
15 Bill Sampen
16 Tommy Shields
17 Jim Tracy
18 Junior Vizcaino
19 Ben Webb
20 Ed Yacopino
21 Mike York
22 Dave Trembley
23 Chris Lein

1989 Star Co. Johnson City Cardinals

(St. Louis Cardinals, R) (color)

	MT	NR MT	EX
Complete Set:	7.50	5.50	3.00

1 Jim Allen
2 Juan Andujar
3 Alan Botkin
4 Johnny Calzado
5 Frank Cimorelli
6 Paul Coleman
7 Ernie Baker
8 Steve Dixon
9 Chuck Edwards
10 Bryan Eversgerd
11 Willie Espinal
12 Bill Felitz
13 Jeff Fayne
14 Scott Halama
15 Mike Kraft
16 Tony Ochs
17 Al Pacheco
18 Ahmed Rodriguez

19 Odails Savinon
20 Richard Shackle
21 John Stevens
22 Ron Weber
23 Denny Wiseman
24 Coaching Staff (Mark DeJohn, Dick Sisler)
25 Alfredo Ortiz
26 Robert Harrison

1989 Star Co. Kenosha Twins

(Minnesota Twins, A) (color)

	MT	NR MT	EX
Complete Set:	6.00	4.50	2.50

1 Tom Boyce
2 Terry Brown
3 J.T. Bruett
4 Steve Dunn
5 Brad Fontes
6 Rich Garces
7 Cheo Garcia
8 Deryk Gross
9 Carl Johnson
10 Rusty Kryzanowski
11 Jay Kvasnicka
12 Pat Mahomes
13 Mike Mathiot
14 Todd McClure
15 Mike Misuraca
16 Steve Morris
17 Steve Muh
18 Mark North
19 Rolando Pino
20 Mike Pomeranz
21 Gary Resetar
22 Bryan Roskom
23 Dom Rovasio
24 J.P. Wright
25 Steve Liddle
26 Dan Fox
27 Brian Allard

1989 Star Co. Kingsport Mets

(New York Mets, R) (color)

	MT	NR MT	EX
Complete Set:	6.50	4.75	2.50

1 Dan Auchard
2 Tim Buhe
3 Chris Butle
4 Hector Carrasco
5 Albert Castillo
6 Nick Davis
7 Alberto Diaz
8 Tom Engle
9 Andy Fidler
10 Brook Fordyce
11 Rob Guzik
12 James Harris
13 Reid Hartmann
14 Craig Johnston
15 Mike Lehnerz
16 Tim McClinton
17 Wallace Minnifield
18 Rich Ostopowicz
19 Nicolas Polanco
20 Deron Sample
21 Craig Scott
22 Jim Sheffler
23 Eric Thornton
24 Ed Vazquez
25 Kyle Washington
26 Jim Eschen
27 Dan Norman
28 Mike Murray
29 Bat Boys (Tyler Hobbs, Josh Brickey, Ben Smith, Travis Nelson)
30 Dottie Elsea

1989 Star Co. Kinston Indians

(Cleveland Indians, A) (color)

	MT	NR MT	EX
Complete Set:	6.50	4.75	2.50

1 Jamie Allison
2 Ramon Bautista
3 Barry Blackwell
4 Jim Bruske
5 Andy Casano
6 Daren Epley
7 Richard Falkner
8 Greg Ferlenda
9 Sam Ferretti
10 Brian Johnson
11 Tommy Kramer
12 Mark Lewis
13 Jeff Mutis
14 Charles Nagy
15 Rouglas Odor
16 David Oliveras
17 Angel Ortiz
18 Doug Piatt
19 Mark Pike
20 Jim Richardson
21 Greg Roscoe
22 Tony Scaglione
23 Rudy Seanez
24 Ken Whitfield
25 Ken Bolek
26 Mike Brown
27 Will George

1989 Star Co. Knoxville Blue Jays

(Toronto Blue Jays, AA)

	MT	NR MT	EX
Complete Set:	6.50	4.75	2.50

1 Derek Bell
2 Carlos Diaz
3 Jose Diaz
4 Webster Garrison
5 Darren Balsley
6 Goose Gozzo
7 Kevin Batiste
8 Shawn Jeter
9 Chris Jones
10 Dennis Jones
11 Rob MacDonald
12 Domingo Martinez
13 Omar Malave
14 Pedro Munoz
15 Joe Dean Newcomb
16 Tom Quinlan
17 Ken Rivers
18 Jimmy Rogers
19 Jerry Schunk
20 John Shea
21 Mark Whiten
22 Bob Wishnevski
23 Mike Mills
24 J.J. Cannon
25 John Poloni

1989 Star Co. Lakeland Tigers

(Detroit Tigers, A) (color)

	MT	NR MT	EX
Complete Set:	6.50	4.75	2.50

1 Marcos Adler
2 Jim Baxter
3 Rico Brogna
4 Basilio Cabrera
5 Ron Cook
6 Luis Gilindo
7 Dave Haas
8 Shawn Hare
9 Bill Henderson
10 Riccardo Ingram
11 Mike Jones
12 John Kiely
13 Kurt Knudsen
14 Mike Lumley
15 Ron Marigny
16 Dan O'Neill
17 Dan Raley
18 Dave Richards
19 Tookie Spann
20 Chuck Steward
21 Eric Stone
22 Steve Strong
23 Andy Toney
24 Mike Wilkins
25 Marty Willis
26 John Lipon
27 Kenn Cunningham
28 Ralph Treuel

1989 Star Co. Lynchburg Red Sox

(Boston Red Sox, A) (color)

	MT	NR MT	EX
Complete Set:	6.50	4.75	2.50

1 Mike Baker
2 Jose Birriel
3 Tim Buheller
4 Dale Burgo
5 Fred Davis
6 Paul Devlin
7 John Dolan
8 Tom Fischer
9 Dave Gray
10 Bart Haley
11 Mike Kelly
12 Derek Livernois
13 Gil Martinez
14 Juan Molero
15 Tim Naehring
16 David Owen
17 Juan Paris
18 Phil Plantier
19 Scott Powers
20 Leslie Wallin
21 Stu Weidie
22 Craig Wilson
23 Gary Allenson
24 Jim Bibby
25 Scott Skripko
26 Roger Hagger
27 Zack Dzafic
28 Ronnie Richardson
29 Rodney Taylor

1989 Star Co. Madison Muskies

(Oakland A's, A) (color)

	MT	NR MT	EX
Complete Set:	6.00	4.50	2.50

1 Mark Aguilar
2 Tony Ariola
3 Rich Berg
4 Dean Borelli
5 James Buccheri
6 Tom Carcione
7 Mike Messerly
8 Jim Foley
9 Lorenzo Furcal
10 Apolinar Garcia
11 Dwayne Hosey
12 Jim Lawson
13 Will Love
14 Angel Martinez
15 Frank Masters
16 Luis Mateo
17 Jim Nettles
18 Bronswell Patrick
19 Ed Ricks
20 Billy Taylor
21 Lee Tinsley
22 Tim Vannaman

1989 Star Co. Martinsville Phillies

(Philadelphia Phillies, R) (color)

	MT	NR MT	EX
Complete Set:	6.50	4.75	2.50

1 Al Baur
2 Kenneth Bean
3 Luis Brito
4 Williams Carmona
5 Paul Carson
6 Cancio Casado
7 Jim Cosman
8 Ismael Cruz
9 Matt Current
10 Mike Current
11 Larar Foster
12 Darrell Goedhart
13 Elliot Gray
14 Tom Hardgrove
15 Charles Aurst
16 Jeff Jackson
17 Aurelio Llanos
18 Stewart Lovdal
19 Chris Lowe
20 Facanel Medina
21 Rick Meyer
22 Sixto Montero
23 Jeff Patterson
24 Eulogio Perez
25 Jimmy Phillips
26 Mark Randall
27 David Ross
28 Chuck Shive
29 Calvin Talford
30 Cory Thomas
31 Gil Valencia
32 Julio Vargas
33 Dan Welch
34 Scott Wiegandt
35 Coaching Staff (Roly DeArmas, Al LeBoeuf, John Martin)

1989 Star Co. Memphis Chicks

(Kansas City Royals, AA) (color)

	MT	NR MT	EX
Complete Set:	6.50	4.75	2.50

1 Julio Alcala
2 Kenny Bowen
3 Tony Bridge-Clements
4 Jacob Brumfield
5 Jim Campbell

6 Dera Clark
7 Stu Cole
8 Victor Cole
9 John Duffy
10 Luis Encarnacion
11 Carlos Escalera
12 Bob Hamelin
13 Deric Ladnier
14 Mark Lee
15 Mike Magnante
16 Chito Martinez
17 Brian McRae
18 Angel Morris
19 Harvey Pulliam
20 Kyle Reese
21 Mike Tresemer
22 Aguedo Vasquez
23 Steve Walker
24 Coaching Staff (Jeff Cox, Guy Hansen, Joe Breeden)

1989 Star Co. Miami Miracle

(No affiliation, A)

	MT	NR MT	EX
Complete Set:	6.00	4.50	2.50

1 Rick Bernardo
2 Tommy Boyce
3 Not issued
4 Fernando Figueroa
5 Longo Garcia
6 Jim Gattis
7 Lindsey Johnson
8 Randy Kotchman
9 Mark Kramer
10 Adam Lamle
11 Shane Letterio
12 Tony Mack
13 Tony Metoyer
14 Ronald Mullins
15 Michael Maksudian
16 Kevin Ponder
17 Chris Sloniger
18 Doug Torborg
19 Al Torres
20 Luis Verdugo
21 Front Office
22 Miracle team photo
--- Marty Cerny

1989 Star Co. New Britain Red Sox

(Boston Red Sox, AA) (color)

	MT	NR MT	EX
Complete Set:	9.50	7.00	3.75

1 Ed Estrada
2 Leverne Jackson
3 Scott Cooper
4 Zach Crouch
5 Titi Srewart
6 Don Gabriele
7 Daryl Irvine
8 Josias Manzanillo
9 Joe Marchese
10 David Milstien
11 Chris Moritz
12 Jim Orsag
13 Lavid Padilla
14 Mickey Pina
15 Todd Pratt
16 Jeff Plympton
17 Randy Randle
18 Larry Shikles
19 Scott Sommers
20 David Walters
21 Ed Zambrano
22 Robert Zupcic
23 Butch Hobson
24 Rich Gale
25 Pete Youngman

1989 Star Co. Osceola Astros

(Houston Astros, A) (color)

	MT	NR MT	EX
Complete Set:	6.50	4.75	2.50

1 Harold Allen
2 David Bond
3 Billy Paul Carver
4 Ramon Cedeno
5 Todd Credeur
6 Luis Gonzalez
7 Rusty Harris
8 Blaise Ilsley
9 Bernie Jenkins
10 Carlos Laboy
11 Dan Lewis
12 Andy Mota
13 Guy Normand
14 Dan Nyssen
15 Joe Ortiz
16 Al Osuna
17 Gorky Perez
18 David Potts
19 Ed Renteria
20 Scott Servais
21 John Sheehan
22 Dave Silvestri
23 Richie Simon
24 Dennis Tafoya
25 Willie Trice
26 Jose Vargas (Late Issue)
27 Rick Sweet (Late Issue)

1989 Star Co. Peninsula Pilots

(No affiliation, A) (color)

	MT	NR MT	EX
Complete Set:	6.00	4.50	2.50

1 Dave Bauer
2 Chris Bushing
3 Jeff Champ
4 Hernan Cortes
5 Tom Fine
6 Joe Gast
7 Pat Hewes
8 Dodd Johnson
9 Tim Kirk
10 Jay Knoblaugh
11 Al Lombardi
12 Julian Machado
13 Jay Makemson
14 Sam Manti
15 Matt Michael
16 Rodney Murrell
17 Greg Papageorge
18 Hector Perez
19 Lem Pilkenton
20 Tad Powers
21 Clyde Reichard
22 Rick Seibert
23 Todd Stephan
24 Len Thigpen
25 Micky Tresh
26 Coaching Staff (Jim Thrift, Clyde Reichard - Late Issue)

1989 Star Co. Pittsfield Mets

(New York Mets, A) (color)

	MT	NR MT	EX
Complete Set:	7.00	5.25	2.75

1 Chris Butterfield
2 Stanton Cameron
3 Joe Dellicarri
4 Chris Dorn
5 Steve Gasser
6 Dennis Harriger
7 Mike Hemmerich
8 Derek Henderson
9 Tim Hines
10 Tim Howard
11 Pat Howell
12 Paul Johnson
13 John Johnstone
14 Greg Langbehn
15 Medina Luciano
16 Lee May, Jr.
17 Joe McCann
18 Norberto Navarro
19 Steve Piskor
20 Curtis Pride
21 Ryan Richmond
22 Dave Telgheder
23 Mark Willoughby
24 Tim Blackwell
25 Dan Sequi
26 Steve Jacobucci
27 Jamie Hoffner
28 Jim Tesmer
29 Alan Zinter

1989 Star Co. Princeton Pirates

(Pittsburgh Pirates, R) (color)

	MT	NR MT	EX
Complete Set:	6.00	4.50	2.50

1 Adrian Adkins
2 Felix Antiqua
3 Tim Curley
4 John Curtis
5 Alberto De Los Santos
6 Marvin Dooley
7 Marc Biordano
8 Z.B. Hamilton
9 Bill Holmes
10 David Howard
11 Wade Lytle
12 Ramon Martinez
13 Troy Mooney
14 Eric Parkinson
15 Darryl Ratliff
16 Andre Redmond
17 Jose Rodriquez
18 Roman Rodriquez
19 Delvy Santiago
20 Bruce Schreiber
21 Jesse Torres
22 Ramon Valdez
23 Dave Watson
24 Bobby West
25 Kelly Woods
26 Julio Garcia
27 Tom Dettore
28 Ken Crenshaw

1989 Star Co. Prince William Cannons

(New York Yankees, A) (color)

	MT	NR MT	EX
Complete Set:	6.50	4.75	2.50

1 Jason Bridges
2 Dennis Brow
3 Andy Cook
4 Bob DeJardin
5 Pedro DeLeon
6 Mike Draper
7 Rob Ehrhard
8 Ken Greer
9 Jeff Johnson
10 Pat Kelly
11 Jeff Livesey
12 Mark Marris
13 Bill Masse
14 Gerald Nielsen
15 Mark Ohlms
16 Vince Phillips
17 Bruce Prybylin
18 Frank Seminara
19 Don Sparks
20 Don Stanford
21 Wade Taylor
22 Dave Turgeon
23 Hector Vargas
24 Tom Weeks
25 Gerald William
26 Mauricio Zazue (Late Issue)
27 Mark Weidemaie (Late Issue)

28 Dave Jorn (Late Issue)
29 Trey Hillman (Late Issue)

1989 Star Co. Reading Phillies

(Philadelphia Phillies, AA)

	MT	NR MT	EX
Complete Set:	7.00	5.25	2.75

1 Sal Agostinelli
2 Frank Bellino
3 Erik Bratlien
4 Harvey Brumfield
5 Chris Calvert
6 Amalio Carreno
7 Fred Christopher
8 Joe Citari
9 Pat Combs
10 Bobby Joe Edmonds
11 Marty Foley
12 Jason Grimsley
13 Ramon Henderson
14 Gerald Holtz
15 Vince Holyfield
16 Warren Magee
17 Chuck Malone
18 Chuck McElroy
19 Rick Parker
20 Victor Rosario
21 Bob Scanlan
22 Steve Scarone
23 Scott Service
24 Shane Turner
25 Jeff Williams
26 Coaching Staff (Mike Hart, Ramon Aviles, George Culver)

1989 Star Co. St. Petersburg Cardinals

(St. Louis Cardinals, A) (color)

	MT	NR MT	EX
Complete Set:	6.00	4.50	2.50

1 Franklin Abreu
2 Greg Becker

3 Bill Bivens
4 Art Calvert
5 Greg Carmona
6 Ric Christian
7 Alex Cole
8 Rheal Cormier
9 Todd Crosby
10 Terry Elliot
11 Joe Federico
12 Joey Fernandez
13 Ed Fulton
14 Mark Grater
15 Joe Hall
16 Shawn Hathaway
17 Jeremy Hernandez
18 Rich Hoffman
19 Chuck Johnson
20 Scott Melvin
21 Scott Nichols
22 Larry Pierson
23 Tony Russo
24 Tim Sherrill
25 Ken Smith
26 Paul Thoutsis (Late Issue)
27 Dave Bialas (Late Issue)
28 Marty Mason (Late Issue)
29 Team Photo (Late Issue)

1989 Star Co. Saint Lucie Mets

(New York Mets, A) (color)

	MT	NR MT	EX
Complete Set:	6.50	4.75	2.50

1 Brant Alyea
2 Terry Bross
3 Alex Diaz
4 Tony Diaz
5 Chris Donnels
6 Clint Hurdle
7 Ron Gideon
8 Terry Griffin
9 Rudy Hernandez
10 Tin Hines
11 Scott Jaster
12 Crucito Lara
13 Steve Larose
14 David Lau
15 Juan Marina
16 Terry McDaniel
17 Mike Miller
18 Danny Naughton
19 Dale Plummer
20 Dave Proctor
21 Titi Roche
22 Jamie Roseboro
23 Julio Valera
24 Mike Whitlock
25 Vince Zawaski
26 Joel Horlen
27 Fred Hina

1989 Star Co. Salem Buccaneers

(Pittsburgh Pirates, A) (color)

	MT	NR MT	EX
Complete Set:	6.50	4.75	2.50

Robert Harris (Late Issue)
1 Moises Alou
2 Fernando Arguelles
3 Joe Ausanio
4 Scott Barczi
5 Terry Crowley
6 Ron Downs
7 Chip Duncan
8 Mike Fortuna
9 Carlos Garcia
10 Ed Hartman
11 Trent Jewett
12 Domingo Merejo
13 Paul Miller
14 Blas Minor
15 Albert Molina
16 Joseph Pacholec
17 Keith Richardson
18 Scott Ruskin
19 Butch Schlopy
20 Winston Seymour
21 Willie Smith
22 Randy Tomlin
23 Miguel Valverde
24 John Wehner
25 Rocky Bridges
26 Julio Garcia (Late Issue)
27 Spin Williams (Late Issue)

1989 Star Co. San Jose Giants

(San Francisco Giants, A) (color)

	MT	NR MT	EX
Complete Set:	7.00	5.25	2.75

1 Rod Beck
2 Dave Booth
3 Don Brock
4 Bill Carlson
5 Jamie Cooper
6 Steve Decker
7 Mark Dewey
8 Tom Ealy
9 Dan Fernandez
10 Scott Goins
11 Juan Guerrero
12 Mike Ham
13 Steven Hecht
14 Bryan Hickerson
15 Tom Hostetler
16 Jim Jones
17 Steve Lienhard
18 James Malseed
19 T.J. McDonald
20 Kevin Meier
21 James Pena
22 Montie Phillips
23 Andres Santana
24 James Terrill
25 Elanis Westbrooks
26 Todd Oakes
27 Duane Espy
28 Scott Wilson

1989 Star Co. Sarasota White Sox

(Chicago White Sox, R) (color)

	MT	NR MT	EX
Complete Set:	6.00	4.50	2.50

1 Kurt Brown
2 Eddie Caceres
3 Darrin Campbell
4 Chris Cauley
5 Bob Fletcher
6 Paul Fuller
7 Ken Gohmann
8 Cliff Gonzalez
9 Todd Hall
10 Curt Hasler
11 John Hudek
12 Bo Kennedy
13 Brent Knackert
14 Rodney McCray
15 Jim Morris
16 Javier Ocasio
17 Raymond Payton
18 Jack Peel
19 Bob Resnikoff
20 Dave Reynolds
21 Dan Rohrmeier
22 Ron Stephens
23 Carl Sullivan
24 Scott Tedder
25 Coaching Staff (Tony Franklin, Don Cooper, Pat Roessler)

1989 Star Co. Spartanburg Phillies

(Philadelphia Phillies, A) (color)

	MT	NR MT	EX
Complete Set:	6.50	4.75	2.50

1 Jason Backs
2 Toby Borland
3 Mike Carlin
4 Tim Churchill
5 Darrell Coulter
6 Tim Dell
7 Todd Elam
8 Paul Ellison
9 Reggie Garcia
10 Steve Keller
11 Troy Kent
12 John LaRosa
13 Antonio Linares
14 Darrell Lindsey
15 Tom Marsh
16 John Marshall
17 Greg McCarthy
18 Mike Morandini
19 Reed Olmstead
20 Ed Rosado
21 Nick Santa Cruz
22 Jon Szynal
23 Leory Ventress
24 Gary Wilson
25 Pedro Zayas
26 Coaching Staff (Mel Roberts, Rick Jones, Buzz Capra - Late Issue)

1989 Star Co. Stockton Ports

(Los Angeles Dodgers, A) (color)

	MT	NR MT	EX
Complete Set:	6.00	4.50	2.50

1 Gary Borg
2 Larry Oedewaldt
3 John Jaha
4 Pat Listach
5 Mike Ignasiak
6 Elvira Narciso
7 Tim Fortugno
8 Chris George
9 Tim Raley
10 Kent Hetrick
11 Steve Sparks
12 Charlie Montoyo
13 Jamie Cangemi
14 Chris Cassels
15 Bobby Jones
16 Randy Synder
17 Jeff Ciszkowski
18 Ron Smith
19 Richard Durrant
20 Bryan Foster
21 Dave Nilsson
22 Dave Huppert, James Poole
23 Dan Chapman
24 Don Miller
25 Rob Derksen
26 (Marsh/Wickam)
27 Jim Poulin
28 (Marino/Conroy)

1989 Star Co. Vero Beach Dodgers

(Los Angeles Dodgers, A) (color)

	MT	NR MT	EX
Complete Set:	6.00	4.50	2.50

1 William Argo
2 Anthony Barron
3 Rafael Bournigal
4 Albert Bustillos
5 J. Dale Coleman
6 Sherman Collins
7 Bruce Dostal
8 Dino Ebel
9 Stephen Green
10 Mark Griffin
11 Dana Heinle
12 Masaki Kamanaka
13 Yasuhiro Kawabata
14 John Knapp
15 Alan Lewis
16 Brett Magnusson
17 Danny Montgomery
18a Jose Munoz
18b Jose Monoz (corrected)
19a Douglas Noch
19b Douglas Noch (corrected)
20a Daniel Opperman
20b Daniel Opperman (corrected)
21a Hector Ortiz
21b Hector Ortiz (corrected)
22a James Poole
22b James Poole (corrected)
23a Henry Rodriguez
23b Henry Rodriguez (corrected)
24a Michael Sampson
24b Michael Sampson (corrected)
25a Zakary Shinall
25b Zakary Shinall (corrected)
26 Jeff Van Zytveld
27 Joe Alvarez
28 Dennis Lewallyn
29 Jun Arisawa
--- Compliment card

1989 Star Co. Waterloo Diamonds

(No affiliation, A) (color)

	MT	NR MT	EX
Complete Set:	6.00	4.50	2.50

1 Mike Borgatti
2 Rob Cantwell
3 Dave Cunningham
4 Bob Curnow
5 Reggie Farmer
6 Alex Figueroa
7 Don Fowler
8 Luis Galindez
9 Anthony Witson
10 Darrin Hart
11 Steve Hendricks
12 Ray Holbert
13 Tim Holland
14 Brad Hoyer
15 Mike King
16 Chad Kuhn

17 Jose LeBron
18 Pedro Lopez
19 Rich Slomkowski
20 Scott Meadows
21 Ron Morton
22 James Noland
23 Billy Reed
24 Chuck Ricci
25 Osvaldo Sanchez
26 Jaime Moreno
27 Mark Littell
28 George Paulis
29 Mark Gieseke
30 Darrin Hart
31 Terry McDivitt
32 Scott McNaney

1989 Star Co. Watertown Indians

(Cleveland Indians, A) (color)

	MT	NR MT	EX
Complete Set:	6.00	4.50	2.50

1 Chuck Alexander
2 Keith Bevenour
3 Jerry Dipoto
4 Martin Durkin
5 Bruce Egloff
6 Alex Farran
7 Cornell Foggie
8 Fabio Gomez
9 Jeff Hancock
10 Joey James
11 Brian Graham
12 Garland Kiser
13 Ty Kovach
14 Brett Merriman
15 Carlos Mota
16 Scott Neill
17 Rouglas Odor
18 Doug Piatt
19 Tim Riemer
20 Greg Roscoe
21 Marc Tepper
22 Will Vespe
23 Dan Williams
24 Don Young
25 Erik Young
26 Ken Silvertri
27 Frank Kelbe
28 Rich Saint John
29 Brad DesJardins

1989 Star Co. West Palm Beach Expos

(Montreal Expos, A) (color)

	MT	NR MT	EX
Complete Set:	5.50	4.00	2.25

1 Jose Alou
2 Bret Barberie
3 Chris Bennett
4 Daryl Boyd
5 Jeff Carter
6 Doug Cinnella
7 Greg Colbrunn
8 Will Cordero
9 Rob DeYoung
10 Bert Echemendia
11 Jim Fregosi
12 Scott Henion
13 Ross Jones
14 Doug Kline
15 Rob Leary
16 John Mello
17 Yorkis Perez
18 Alonzo Powell
19 Troy Ricker
20 Hector Rivera
21 Trevor Penn
22 Matt Stairs
23 Corey Viltz
24 David Wainhouse
25 Pat Murphy
26 , Luis Puljols
27 Felipe Alou
28 Dave Tomlin
29 Dave Jauss
--- Team Logo

1989 Star Co. Williamsport Bills

(Seattle Mariners, AA) (color)

	MT	NR MT	EX
Complete Set:	8.50	6.25	3.50

1 Dave Brundage
2 Brad Brusky
3 Bobby Cuellar
4 Harry Davis
5 Rich DeLucia
6 William Diaz
7 Jeff Goff
8 Todd Haney
9 Keith Helton
10 Jeff Hooper
11 Calvin Jones
12 Patrick Lennon
13 Tino Martinez
14 Jose Melendez
15 Jeff Nelson
16 Bryan Price
17 Mark Razook
18 Patrick Rice
19 Richardo Rojas
20 Jack Smith
21 Glen Spagnola
22 Ted Williams
23 Mark Wooden
24 Jay Ward
25 David Burba (Late Issue)

1989 Star Co. Winston-Salem Spirit

(Chicago Cubs, A) (color)

	MT	NR MT	EX
Complete Set:	6.00	4.50	2.50

Team Photo
1 Lenney Bell
2 Ed Caballero
3 Dick Canan
4 Frank Castillo
5 Don Cohoon
6 Rusty Crockett
7 Darren Duffy
8 Pat Gomez
9 Phillip Hannon
10 John Jensen
11 Dan Kennedy
12 Ray Mullino
13 Steve Parker
14 Marty Rivero
15 Bob Strickland
16 Francisco Tenacen
17 Rick Wilkins
18 Eric Woods
19 Jay Loviglio
20 Joe Housey
21 Steve Melendez

1989 Star Co. Winter Haven Red Sox

(Boston Red Sox, A) (color)

	MT	NR MT	EX
Complete Set:	6.00	4.50	2.50

1 Odie Abril
2 Jim Byrd
3 Felix DeDos
4 Vincent Degifico
5 Bernie Dzafic
6 Peter Estrada
7 John Flaherty
8 Donald Florence
9 Chris Hanks
10 Reggie Harris
11 Howard Landry
12 Erik Laseke
13 Chris Leach
14 Terry Marrs
15 Pedro Matilla
16 Meredith Moore
17 Alfredo Pratts
18 Micky Rivers
19 Ken Ryan
20 Al Sanders
21 Larry Scannell
22 Hector Stewart
23 Willie Tatum
24 Mike Thompson
25 John Valentin
26 Charles Wacha
27 James Whitehead
28 Doug Camilli
29 David Holt,

1989 Star Co. Wytheville Cubs

(Chicago Cubs, R) (color)

	MT	NR MT	EX
Complete Set:	9.00	6.75	3.50

1 Newland Aponte
2 Troy Bailey
3 Ronnie Brown
4 Victor Cancel
5 Pedro Castelland
6 Amilcar Correa
7 Dale Craig
8 Earl Cunningham
9 Kevin Dalson
10 Eddie Fowler
11 Jac Gelb
12 Don Gillespie
13 Fred Hill
14 Brad Huff
15 Calvin Ford
16 Jesse Hollins
17 Eric Jaques
18 Dan Kennedy
19 Greg Kessler
20 Mike Little
21 Raymond Mack
22 Recardo Medina
23 Leo Perez
24 Randy Sodders
25 Aaron Taylor
26 Scott Teague (Late Issue)
27 Paul Torres (Late Issue)
28 Clinton Write (Late Issue)
29 Coaching Staff (Late Issue)
30 Greg Keuter (Late Issue)

1989 Team Chattanooga Lookouts

(Cincinnati Reds, AA) (black and white)

	MT	NR MT	EX
Complete Set:	12.50	9.50	5.25

1 Ted Abernathy
2 Bob Allison
4 Jimmy Bragen
5 Mickey Brantley
6 Kieth Brown
7 Bob Costas
8 Alan Davis
9 Kid Elberfeld
10 Dave Gallagher
11 Erik Hanson
12 Dave Hengel
13 Grant Jackson
14 Ferguson Jenkins
15 Bill Lee
16 Charlie Letchas
17 Robert Long
18 Jim Morgan
19 Jeff Moronko
20 Al Neiger
21 Sammy Stang Nicklin
22 Bob Oldis
23 Ernie Oravetz
24 Jim Presley
25 Tom Runnells
26 Frank Sacka
27 Mike Schooler
28 Brick Smith
29 Danny Tartabull
30 Dave Valle
31 Hedi Vargas
32 Denny Walling
--- Chattanooga Regional History Museum

1989 Team Charlotte Knights

(Chicago Cubs, AA) (color)

	MT	NR MT	EX
Complete Set:	12.50	9.50	5.25

1 Laddie Renfroe
2 Jim Essian
3 Grant Jackson
4 Ced Lanorum
5 Derrick May
6 Jim Bullinger
7 Butch Garcia
8 Luis Cruz
9 Kelly Mann
10 Glenn Sullivan
11 Greg Smith
12 Erik Pappas
13 David Rosario
14 Ty Griffin
15 Tom Michno
16 Greg Kallevig
17 Shawn Boskie
18 Jeff Hirsch
19 Jackie Davidson
20 Matt Cakora
21 Phil Harrison
22 Bob Bafia
23 Brian McCann
24 Orsino Hill
25 Pablo Rivera

1989 Team Durham Bulls

(Atlanta Braves, A) (color) (co-sponsored by 28 WPTF-TV & Kodak)

	MT	NR MT	EX
Complete Set:	17.50	13.00	7.00

(1) Team Photo
(2) Steve Avery
(3) Dennis Burlingame
(4) David Butts
(5) Rich Casarotti

(6) Brian Champion
(7) Jamie Cuesta
(8) Wes Currin
(9) Jim Czajkowski
(10) Brian Deak
(11) Todd Dewey
(12) Mike Fowler
(13) Jerald Frost
(14) Phil Maldonado
(15) Rich Maloney
(16) David Nied
(17) Al Martin
(18) Ken Pennington
(19) Ben Rivera
(20) Sean Ross
(21) Mike Stoker
(22) Pat Tilmon
(23) Theron Todd
(24) Andy Tomberlin
(25) Matt Turner
(26) Steve Ziem
(27) Ino Guerrero
(28) Larry Jaster
(29) Grady Little

1989 Team Fayetteville Generals

(Detroit Tigers, A)

	NR MT	EX	VG
Complete Set:	5.00	3.75	2.00

(1) Mark Cole
(2) John DeSilva
(3) Don Erickson
(4) Mark Ettles
(5) Ed Ferm
(6) Greg Gohr
(7) Pat Pesavento
(8) Dan Raley
(9) Andy Toney
(10) Duane Walker

1989 Team Louisville Redbirds

(St. Louis Cardinals, AAA) Only 1,000 sets were produced. All sets have high gloss fronts and stats on back are printed in regular ink.

	MT	NR MT	EX
Complete Set:	15.50	11.50	6.25

1 Billy Bird (mascot)
2 Todd Zeile
3 Todd Zeile
4 Todd Zeile
5 Todd Zeile
6 Mike Jorgensen
7 Gibson Alba
8 Luis Alicea
9 Scott Arnold
10 Tom Baine
11 Rod Booker
12 Randell Byers
13 Cris Carpenter
14 Alex Cole
15 Romy Cucjen
16 Leon Durham
17 Roger Erickson
18 Jeff Fassero
19 Bien Figueroa
20 Mike Fitzgerald
21 Don Heinkel
22 Ken Hill
23 Howard Hilton
24 Greg Jelks
25 Matt Kinzer
26 Jim Lindeman
27 Willie McGee
28 Chuck McGrath
29 Bryan Oelkers
30 Steve Peters
31 Frank Potestio
32 Ted Power
33 Jim Puzey
34 Ron Shepherd
35 Bob Tewksbury
36 Craig Wilson
37 Todd Worrell
38 Hap Hudson

1989 Team Nashville Sounds

(New York Yankees, AA)

	MT	NR MT	EX
Complete Set:	5.00	3.75	2.00

1 Skeeter Barnes
2 Freddie Benavides
3 Keith Brown
4 Marty Brown
5 George Dyce
6 Jeff Gray
7 Mike Griffin
8 Doug Gwosdz
9 Chris Hammond
10 Alan Hayden
11 Hugh Kemp
12 Tito Landrum
13 Keith Lockhart
14 Rob Lopez
15 Frank Lucchesi
16 Scotti Madison
17 Terry McGriff
18 Charlie Mitchell
19 Joe Oliver
20 Kevin Pearson
21 Jeff Reynolds
22 Jeff Richardson
23 (Ray Rippelmeyer & John Young)
24 Mike Roesler
25 Larry Schmittou
26 Scott Scudder
27 Van Snider
28 Eddie Tanner
29 Luis Vasquez
30 (Bob Walters & Bob Jamison)

1989 Team Peoria Chiefs

(Chicago Cubs, A) (color) (error set)

	MT	NR MT	EX
Complete Set:	9.50	7.00	3.75

1 Ty Griffin
2 Braz Davis
3 Frankie Espino
4 Marcos Lopez
5 Jeff Massicotte
6 Jay Eddings
7 Brett Robinson
8 John Salles
9 Heathcliff Slocumb
10 Mike Sodders
11 Derek Stroud
12 Rick Mundy
13 Billy Paynter
14 Peoria's Past Chicago's Future
15 Matt Walbeck
16 Jaun Adames
17 Alex Arias
18 Eddie Williams
19 Eric Perry
20 Tracy Smith
21 Peoria's Olympic Stars (Fernando Ramsey, Ty Griffin)
22 Woody Smith
23 Warren Arrington
24 Elvin Paulino
25 Fernando Ramsey
26 Harry Shelton
27 Greg Eberle
28 (Jeff Pico, Greg Maddux, Paul Kilgus)
29 Pookie Bernstine
30 Brad Mills
31 Rick Kranitz
32 Bob Grimes
33 Clar Krusinski
34 Front Office Staff
--- McDonalds Coupon

1989 Team Richmond Braves

(Atlanta Braves, AAA) (color)

	MT	NR MT	EX
Complete Set:	6.00	4.50	2.50

(1) Team Photo
(2) Jim Beauchamp
(3) Coaching Staff (John Grubb)
(4) Coaching Staff (Leo Mazzone)
(5) Coaching Staff (Sonny Jackson)
(6) Coaching Staff (Sam Ayoub)
(7) Carlos Rios
(8) Kash Beauchamp
(9) Chris Shaddy
(10) Bryan Farmer
(11) Alex Smith
(12) Mark Lemke
(13) Barry Jones
(14) Terry Blocker
(15) Dave Justice
(16) Jeff Weatherby
(17) Kent Mercker
(18) John Mizerock
(19) Eddie Mathews
(20) Robbie Wine
(21) John Kilner
(22) Gary Eave
(23) Marty Clary
(24) Tommy Greene
(25) Andy Nezelek
(26) Ed Whited
(27) Dwayne Henry
(28) Drew Denson
(29) Rusty Richards

1989 Team Rockford Expos

(Montreal Expos, A)

	MT	NR MT	EX
Complete Set:	6.00	4.50	2.50

(1) Isaac Alleyne
(2) Derrell Baker
(3) Esteban Beltre
(4) Rod Boddie
(5) Scott Bromby
(6) Reid Cornelius
(7) Bret Davis
(8) Kevin Foster
(9) Dan Freed
(10) Michael Gibbons
(11) Terrel Hansen
(12) Dan Hargis
(13) Ben Howze
(14) Keith Kaub
(15) Rob Kerrigan
(16) Bryn Kosco
(17) Rob Mason
(18) Nate Minchey
(19) Chris Nabholz
(20) Dave Oropeza
(21) Jesus Paredes
(22) Mike Parrott
(23) Mike Quade
(24) Kelvin Shephard
(25) Matt Shiflett
(26) Joe Siddall
(27) Joel Smith
(28) Adam Terris
(29) Jay Williams
(30) Darrin Williams
(31) Kelly Zane

1989 Team Salem Dodgers

(Los Angeles Dodgers, A)

	MT	NR MT	EX
Complete Set:	6.00	4.50	2.50

1 Tom Beyers
2 Burt Hooton
3 Anthony Garcia
4 Geoff Clark
5 Jorge Alvarez
6 Garrett Beard
7 Bill Bene
8 Paul Branconier
9 Don Carroll
10 Clayton Enno
11 Gary Forrester
12 Larry Gonzalez
13 Sebastian Goodlow
14 John Kries
15 Ken Luckham
16 Brock McMurray
17 Bill Miller
18 Chris Morrow
19 Robin Nina
20 Hector Ortiz
21 Jorge Pascual
22 Jose Perez
23 Pedro Perez
24 Rex Peters
25 Mike Piazza
26 Rafael Rijo
27 Napoleon Robinson
28 Chris Sperry
29 Dan Stupur
30 Ramon Taveras

1989 Tribune Albuquerque Dukes

(Los Angeles Dodgers, AAA) (co-sponsored by the Albuquerque Tribune)

	MT	NR MT	EX
Complete Set:	40.00	30.00	16.00

(1) Bill Brennan
(2) Dennis Burtt
(3) Juan Bustabad
(4) Jon Debus
(5) Shanie Dugas
(6) Dave Eichhorn
(7) Jeff Fischer
(8) Darrin Fletcher
(9) Jose Gonzalez
(10) Chris Gwynn
(11) Mike Hartley
(12) Stan Johnson
(13) Von Joshua
(14) Kevin Kennedy
(15) Ramon Martinez
(16) Walt McConnell
(17) Domingo Michel
(18) Mike Munoz
(19) Jim Neidlinger
(20) Javier Ortiz
(21) Mike Sharperson
(22) Brent Strom
(23) Joe Szekely
(24) Jose Vizcaino
(25) Dave Walsh
(26) John Wetteland
(27) Tracy Woodson

NOTE: A card number in parentheses ( ) indicates the set is unnumbered.

BASEBALL HALL OF FAME ROSTER

Hank Aaron, 1982
Grover Alexander, 1938
Walter Alston, 1983 (manager)
Cap Anson, 1939
Luis Aparicio, 1984
Luke Appling, 1964
Earl Averill, 1975
Home Run Baker, 1955
Dave Bancroft, 1971
Ernie Banks, 1977
Al Barlick, 1989 (umpire)
Ed Barrow, 1953 (executive)
Jake Beckley, 1971
Cool Papa Bell, 1974 (Negro Leagues)
Johnny Bench, 1989
Chief Bender, 1953
Yogi Berra, 1972
Jim Bottomley, 1974
Lou Boudreau, 1970
Roger Bresnahan, 1945
Lou Brock, 1985
Dan Brouthers, 1945
Three Finger Brown, 1949
Morgan Bulkeley, 1973 (executive)
Jesse Burkett, 1946
Roy Campanella, 1969
Max Carey, 1961
Alexander Cartwright, 1938 (organizer)
Henry Chadwick, 1938 (organizer)
Frank Chance, 1946
Happy Chandler, 1982 (executive)
Oscar Charleston, 1976 (Negro Leagues)
Jack Chesbro, 1946
Fred Clarke, 1945
John Clarkson, 1963
Roberto Clemente, 1973
Ty Cobb, 1936
Mickey Cochrane, 1947
Eddie Collins, 1939
Jimmy Collins, 1945
Earle Combs, 1970
Charley Comiskey, 1939 (manager)
Jocko Conlan, 1974 (umpire)
Tommy Connolly, 1953 (umpire)
Roger Connor, 1976
Stan Coveleski, 1969
Sam Crawford, 1957
Joe Cronin, 1956
Candy Cummings, 1968
Ray Dandridge, 1987 (Negro Leagues)
Dizzy Dean, 1953
Ed Delahanty, 1945
Bill Dickey, 1954
Martin Dihigo, 1977 (Negro Leagues)
Joe DiMaggio, 1955
Bobby Doerr, 1986
Don Drysdale, 1984
Hugh Duffy, 1945
Billy Evans, 1973 (umpire)
Johnny Evers, 1946
Buck Ewing, 1939
Red Faber, 1964
Bob Feller, 1962
Rick Ferrell, 1984
Elmer Flick, 1963
Whitey Ford, 1974
Rube Foster, 1981 (Negro Leagues)
Jimmie Foxx, 1951
Ford Frick, 1970 (executive)
Frank Frisch, 1947
Pud Galvin, 1965
Lou Gehrig, 1939
Charley Gehringer, 1949
Bob Gibson, 1981
Josh Gibson, 1972 (Negro Leagues)
Warren Giles, 1979 (executive)
Lefty Gomez, 1972
Goose Goslin, 1968
Hank Greenberg, 1956
Clark Griffith, 1946 (manager)
Burleigh Grimes, 1964
Lefty Grove, 1947
Chick Hafey, 1971
Jesse Haines, 1970
Billy Hamilton, 1961
Will Harridge, 1972 (executive)
Bucky Harris, 1975
Gabby Hartnett, 1955
Harry Heilmann, 1952
Billy Herman, 1975
Harry Hooper, 1971
Rogers Hornsby, 1942
Waite Hoyt, 1969
Cal Hubbard, 1976 (umpire)
Carl Hubbell, 1947
Miller Huggins, 1964 (manager)
Catfish Hunter, 1987
Monte Irvin, 1973 (Negro Leagues)
Travis Jackson, 1982
Hugh Jennings, 1945
Ban Johnson, 1937 (executive)
Judy Johnson, 1975 (Negro Leagues)
Walter Johnson, 1936
Addie Joss, 1978
Al Kaline, 1980
Tim Keefe, 1964
Willie Keeler, 1939
George Kell, 1983
Joe Kelley, 1971
George Kelly, 1973
Mike Kelly, 1945
Harmon Killebrew, 1984
Ralph Kiner, 1975
Chuck Klein, 1980
Bill Klem, 1953 (umpire)
Sandy Koufax, 1972
Nap Lajoie, 1937
Kenesaw Mountain Landis, 1944 (exec.)
Bob Lemon, 1976
Buck Leonard, 1972 (Negro Leagues)
Fred Lindstrom, 1976
John Henry Lloyd, 1977 (Negro Leagues)
Ernie Lombardi, 1986
Al Lopez, 1977 (manager)
Ted Lyons, 1955
Connie Mack, 1937 (manager)
Larry MacPhail, 1978 (executive)
Mickey Mantle, 1974
Heinie Manush, 1964
Rabbit Maranville, 1954
Juan Marichal, 1983
Rube Marquard, 1971
Eddie Mathews, 1978
Christy Mathewson, 1936
Willie Mays, 1979
Joe McCarthy, 1957 (manager)
Tommy McCarthy, 1946
Willie McCovey, 1986
Joe McGinnity, 1946
John McGraw, 1937 (manager)
Bill McKechnie, 1962 (manager)
Joe Medwick, 1968
Johnny Mize, 1981
Joe Morgan, 1990
Stan Musial, 1969
Kid Nichols, 1949
Jim O'Rourke, 1945
Mel Ott, 1951
Satchel Paige, 1971 (Negro Leagues)
Jim Palmer, 1990
Herb Pennock, 1948
Eddie Plank, 1946
Hoss Radbourn, 1939
Pee Wee Reese, 1984
Sam Rice, 1963
Branch Rickey, 1967 (executive)
Eppa Rixey, 1963
Robin Roberts, 1976
Brooks Robinson, 1983
Frank Robinson, 1982
Jackie Robinson, 1962
Wilbert Robinson, 1945 (manager)
Edd Roush, 1962
Red Ruffing, 1967
Amos Rusie, 1977
Babe Ruth, 1936
Ray Schalk, 1955
Red Schoendienst, 1989
Joe Sewell, 1977
Al Simmons, 1953
George Sisler, 1939
Enos Slaughter, 1985
Duke Snider, 1980
Warren Spahn, 1973
Al Spalding, 1939
Tris Speaker, 1937
Willie Stargell, 1988
Casey Stengel, 1966 (manager)
Bill Terry, 1954
Sam Thompson, 1974
Joe Tinker, 1946
Pie Traynor, 1948
Dazzy Vance, 1955
Arky Vaughan, 1985
Rube Waddell, 1946
Honus Wagner, 1936
Bobby Wallace, 1953
Ed Walsh, 1946
Lloyd Waner, 1967
Paul Waner, 1952
John Montgomery Ward, 1964
George Weiss, 1971 (executive)
Mickey Welch, 1973
Zack Wheat, 1959
Hoyt Wilhelm, 1985
Billy Williams, 1987
Ted Williams, 1966
Hack Wilson, 1979
George Wright, 1937 (manager)
Harry Wright, 1953 (manager)
Early Wynn, 1972
Carl Yastrzemski, 1989
Tom Yawkey, 1980 (executive)
Cy Young, 1937
Ross Youngs, 1972

1887-1890 N172 Old Judge

Complete checklist with all known variations

One of the most fascinating of all card sets, these cards were issued by the Goodwin & Co. tobacco firm in their Old Judge and, to a lesser extent, Gypsy Queen cigarettes. Players from more than 40 major and minor league teams are pictured on the 1-1/2" by 2-1/2" cards, with some 518 different players known to exist. Up to 17 different pose and team variations exist for some players, and the cards were issued both with and without dates on the card fronts, numbered and unnumbered, and with both handwritten and machine-printed names. Known variations number in the thousands. The cards themselves are blank-backed, sepia-toned photographs pasted onto thick cardboard. The listings are based on the recordings in the The Cartophilic Society's World Index, Part IV, compiled by E.C. Wharton-Tigar with the help of many collectors, especially Donald J. McPherson and Lew Lipset. The list below includes all known variations for each player in the set. Current values for the N172 Old Judge set are found under the regular listings beginning on page 244.

1-1a Gus Albert (bat at 45 degrees, Clevelands)
1-1b Gus Albert (bat at 45 degrees, Milwaukees)
1-2a Gus Albert (bat over shoulder, Clevelands)
1-2b Gus Albert (bat over shoulder, Milwaukees)
1-3 Gus Albert (fielding grounder)
1-4a Gus Albert (throwing, Cleveland's)
1-4b Gus Albert (throwing, Milwaukees)
2-1a Alcott (hands on hips, St. Louis Whites)
2-1b Alcott (hands on hips, Mansfields)
2-2 Alcott (ball in hand above head)
2-3a Alcott (bat at ready position, left arm across belt, 3d B., St. Louis Whites)
2-3b Alcott (bat at ready position, left arm across belt, 3rd B., St. Louis Whites)
2-3c Alcott (bat at ready position, left arm across belt, Mansfields)
2-4 Alcott (bat at ready position, left arm clear of belt)
2-5 Alcott (fielding grounder)
3-1 Alexander (ball in hands at chest)
3-2a Alexander (ball in hand above head, Des Moines)
3-2b Alexander (ball in hand above head, Des Moine)
3-3 Alexander (ball in hand head-high)
3-4 Alexander (batting)
4-1 Myron Allen (fielding high ball, well clear of glove, Kansas City)
4-2 Myron Allen (fielding high ball, touching glove, Kansas City)
4-3 Myron Allen (stooping, feet apart, looking at ball, Kansas City)
4-4 Myron Allen (stooping, right foot behind left leg, Kansas City)
4-5 Myron Allen (ball in hand head-high, Kansas City)
4-6 Myron Allen (batting, Kansas City)
5-1 Bob Allen (batting, Pittsburghs)
5-2 Bob Allen (hands on thighs, Philadelphia N.L.)
5-3 Bob Allen (hands clasped at waist, Pittsburghs)
5-4a Bob Allen (fielding, hands at waist, Pittsburghs)

Note: Values for the N172 Old Judge set appear on page 244 of the regular listings.

5-4b Bob Allen (fielding, hands at waist, Philadelphia N.L.)
5-5 Bob Allen (fielding grounder, Pittsburghs)
6-1 Uncle Bill Alvord (fielding grounder)
6-2 Uncle Bill Alvord (batting)
6-3 Uncle Bill Alvord (sliding)
7-1 Varney Anderson (pitching, right hand head-high)
7-2 Varney Anderson (batting)
7-3 Varney Anderson (pitching, hands chest high)
8-1 Wally Andrews (fielding, stretching to right, Omaha)
8-2 Wally Andrews (fielding, hands by right shoulder, Omaha)
8-3 Wally Andrews (batting, Omaha)
9-1a Ed Andrews (bat in hand at side, Phila)
9-1b Ed Andrews (bat in hand at side, Phila's)
9-2a Ed Andrews (striking ball, bat nearly horizontal, Phila)
9-2b Ed Andrews (striking ball, bat nearly horizontal, Philadelphias)
9-3 Ed Andrews (bat at ready position, no bal visible, Phila's)
9-4 Ed Andrews (right hand above head, left hand behind at side, Phila)
9-5a Ed Andrews (fielding, hands shoulder high, Phila's)
9-5b Ed Andrews (fielding, hands shoulder high, Philadelphias)
9-6a Ed Andrews, Buster Hoover (Andrews being tagged by Hoover, Phila)
9-6b Ed Andrews, Buster Hoover (Andrews being tagged by Hoover, Phila's)
10-1a Bill Annis (bat in hand at side, Worcesters)
10-1b Bill Annis (bat in hand at side, Omaha)
10-2 Bill Annis (striking ball, bat nearly horizontal)
10-3 Bill Annis (lying on ground by base)
11-1a Cap Anson (portrait, no arms visible, Chicagoes)
11-1b Cap Anson (portrait, no arms visible, Chicagos)
11-1c Cap Anson (portrait, no arms visible, Chicagos N.L.)
11-2 Cap Anson (portrait, arms folded)
12-1 Old Hoss Ardner (throwing)
12-2 Old Hoss Ardner (hands on hips)
12-3 Old Hoss Ardner (batting)
13-1 Tug Arundel (fielding, hands head-high)
13-2 Tug Arundel (ball in hands thigh-high)
13-3 Tug Arundel (bat in hand at side)
13-4 Tug Arundel (bat at ready position)
13-5 Tug Arundel (throwing)
14-1a Jersey Bakley (Bakely) (pitching, hands at chest, Clevelands)
14-1b Jersey Bakley (Bakely) (pitching, hands at chest, Cleveland's)
14-2a Jersey Bakley (Bakely) (pitching, left arm half concealing face, Cleveland's)
14-2b Jersey Bakley (Bakely) (pitching, left arm half concealing face, Clevelands)
14-3a Jersey Bakley (Bakely) (pitching, right hand head-high, Cleveland's)
14-3b Jersey Bakley (Bakely) (pitching, right hand head-high, Clevelands)
14-4 Jersey Bakley (Bakely) (batting, feet together)
14-5 Jersey Bakley (Bakely) (batting, feet apart)
15-1a Fido Baldwin (portrait, P. Chicago)
15-1b Fido Baldwin (portrait, P., Chicago)
15-1c Fido Baldwin (portrait, P. (PL))
15-2a Fido Baldwin (pitching, right hand in back waist-high, Chicago)
15-2b Fido Baldwin (pitching, right hand in back waist-high, Columbus)
15-3a Fido Baldwin (pitching, hands neck-high, Chicago)
15-3b Fido Baldwin (pitching, hands neck-high, Columbus)
15-4 Fido Baldwin (pitching, right hand above head, Chicago)
15-5 Fido Baldwin (batting, heels together, Chicago)
15-6 Fido Baldwin (batting, right foot behind left foot)
15-7a Fido Baldwin (bat in hand at side, Chicago)
15-7b Fido Baldwin (bat in hand at side, Chicagos)
16-1a Kid Baldwin (ball in hands head-high, Cincinnati)
16-1b Kid Baldwin (ball in hands head-high, Cincinnatti)
16-2a Kid Baldwin (ball in right hand head-high, Cincinnati)
16-2b Kid Baldwin (ball in right hand head-high, Cincinnatis)
16-2c Kid Baldwin (ball in right hand head-high, Cincinnatti)
16-3a Kid Baldwin (batting, Cincinnati)
16-3b Kid Baldwin (batting, Cincinnatis)
16-4 Kid Baldwin (fielding ball by right foot, Cincinnati)
16-5a Kid Baldwin (ball falling in hands above head, Cincinnati)
16-5b Kid Baldwin (ball falling in hands above head, Cincinnatti)
17-1 Lady Baldwin (batting, Detroits)
17-2 Lady Baldwin (pitching, hands neck-high Detroits)
17-3a Lady Baldwin (pitching, left hand thigh high, Detroits)
17-3b Lady Baldwin (pitching, left hand thigh high, Cincinnati)
17-4 Lady Baldwin (pitching, left hand head high, Detroits)
18-1 James Banning (hands on knees)
18-2 James Banning (fielding, hands above head)
18-3 James Banning (throwing)
18-4 James Banning (batting)
18-5 James Banning (stooping, hands by left foot)
19-1a Sam Barkley (portrait, 2d B.)
19-1b Sam Barkley (portrait, 2d Base)
19-2a Sam Barkley (fielding, right hand above head, 2d B., Pittsburg)
19-2b Sam Barkley (fielding, right hand above head, 2d Base, Pittsburg)
19-2c Sam Barkley (fielding, right hand above head, Kansas City)
19-2d Sam Barkley (fielding, right hand above head, 2nd B., Pittsburgh)
19-3a Sam Barkley (throwing, 2d B.)
19-3b Sam Barkley (throwing, 2d Base)
19-3c Sam Barkley (throwing, 2nd B.)
19-4a Sam Barkley (tagging player on ground, 2d B. Pittsburg)
19-4b Sam Barkley (tagging player on ground, 2d Base, Pittsburg)
19-4c Sam Barkley (tagging player on ground, 2d B., Kansas City)
19-4d Sam Barkley (tagging player on ground, 2nd B.. Pittsburg)
19-5a Sam Barkley (fielding grounder, 2d B.)
19-5b Sam Barkley (fielding grounder, 2d Base)
19-5c Sam Barkley (fielding grounder, 2nd B.)
19-6a Sam Barkley (batting, 2d B.)
19-6b Sam Barkley (batting, 2d Base)
20-1a John Barnes (portrait, bare head, St. Pauls)
20-1b John Barnes (portrait, bare head, St. Paul)
20-2a John Barnes (portrait, top hat, St. Pauls)
20-2b John Barns (Barnes) (portrait, top hat, St Paul)
21-1 Bald Billy Barnie (portrait)
22-1a Charles Bassett (bat at ready position, Indianapolis)
22-1b Charles Bassett (bat at ready position, New Yorks (N.L.))
22-2a Charles Bassett (bat in hand at side, 2d B.)
22-2b Charles Bassett (bat in hand at side, 2nd B.)
23-1 Charles Bastian (batting, looking at camera)
23-2 Charles Bastian (batting, looking at ball)
23-3a Charles Bastian (bat over shoulder, Phila)
23-3b Charles Bastian (bat over shoulder, Chicagos)
23-3c Charles Bastian (bat over shoulder, Chicagos (PL))
23-4 Charles Bastian (fielding, hands chest high)
23-5 Charles Bastian (stooping for low ball)
23-6 Charles Bastian, Pop Schriver (Schriver tagging Bastian)
24-1a Ed Beatin (pitching, hands at chest, name correct)
24-1b Ed Beattin (Beatin) (pitching, hands at chest, name incorrect)
24-2 Ed Beatin (pitching, chin concealed behind left arm)
24-4 Ed Beatin (batting)
25-1a Jake Beckley (batting, "O" just visible on shirt, St. Louis Whites)
25-1b Jake Beckley (batting, "O" just visible on shirt, Pittsburghs)
25-1c Jake Beckley (batting, "O" just visible on shirt, Pittsburgs)
25-2 Jake Beckley (batting, "TLO" visible on shirt)
25-3a Jake Beckley (fielding, hands neck-high, St. Louis Whites)
25-3b Jake Beckley (fielding, hands neck-high, Pittsburghs)
25-3c Jake Beckley (fielding, hands neck-high, Pittsburgs)
25-3d Jake Beckley (fielding, hands neck-high, Pittsburgh)
25-4a Jake Beckley (fielding, ball knee-high, St Louis Whites)
25-4b Jake Beckley (fielding, ball knee-high, Pittsburgs)

26-1 Stephen Behel (dotted tie)
27-1 Charles Bennett (batting)
28-1 Louis Bierbauer (fielding grounder)

28-2a Louis Bierbauer (fielding, hands chest high, name correct)
28-2b Louis Bierbaur (Bierbauer) (fielding, hands chest-high, name incorrect)
28-3a Louis Bierbauer (batting, name correct)

28-3b Louis Bierbaur (Bierbauer) (batting, name incorrect)
28-4 Louis Bierbauer (running, cap in hand)

28-5 Louis Bierbaur (Bierbauer), Bob Gamble (tagging Gamble)
29-1a Bill Bishop (fielding, hands above waist, P.)
29-1b Bill Bishop (fielding, hands above waist, Pitcher)
29-2a Bill Bishop (batting, P.)
29-2b Bill Bishop (batting, Pitcher)
29-3a Bill Bishop (ball in right hand head-high, Pittsburg)
29-3b Bill Bishop (ball in right hand head-high, Syracuse)
30-1a Bill Blair (throwing, looking front, Athletics)
30-1b Bill Blair (throwing, looking front, Hamiltons)
30-2a Bill Blair (throwing, looking to left, Athletics)
30-2b Bill Blair (throwing, looking to left, Hamiltons)
30-3a Bill Blair (pitching, hands shoulder-high, Athletics)
30-3b Bill Blair (pitching, hands shoulder-high, Hamiltons)
30-4 Bill Blair (batting)
30-5 Bill Blair (fielding)
31-1 Ned Bligh (hands on knees)
31-2 Ned Bligh (fielding, hands head-high)

31-3 Ned Bligh (fielding, hands chest-high)

31-4 Ned Bligh (throwing)
31-5 Ned Bligh (bat at ready position at 45 degrees)
31-6 Ned Bligh (bat at ready position over shoulder)
32-1 Bogart (fielding grounder)
32-2 Bogart (throwing)
32-3 Bogart (batting)
32-4 Bogart (fielding, hands chest-high)

32-5 Bogart (fielding, hands thigh-high)

33-1 Boyce (batting)
33-2 Boyce (throwing)
33-3 Boyce (fielding, ball above head)

33-4 Boyce (fielding, ball in hands)
34-1 Boyd (fielding)
34-2 Boyd (throwing)
35-1a Honest John Boyle (fielding, hands thigh high, Boyle on front, St. Louis Browns)

35-1b Honest John Boyle (fielding, hands thigh high, J. Boyle on front, St. Louis Browns)

35-2a Honest John Boyle (fielding grounder, St Louis Browns)
35-2b Honest John Boyle (fielding grounder, St Louis)
35-3a Honest John Boyle (bat in hand at side, St. Louis Browns)
35-3b Honest John Boyle (bat in hand at side, St. Louis)
35-3c Honest John Boyle (bat in hand at side, Chicagos)
35-4a Honest John Boyle (hands thigh-high, J. Boyle on front, St. Louis Browns)
35-4b Honest John Boyle (hands thigh-high, Boyle on front, St. Louis)
35-4c Honest John Boyle (hands thigh-high, Boyle on front, St. Louis Browns)
35-5a Honest John Boyle (bat at ready position 45 degrees, St. Louis Browns)
35-5b Honest John Boyle (bat at ready position 45 degrees, St. Louis)
36-1 Handsome Boyle (pitching, hands above waist, Indianapolis)
36-2a Handsome Boyle (pitching, right hand neck-high, P., Indianpoils)
36-2b Handsome Boyle (pitching, right hand neck-high, Pitcher, Indianpoils)
36-2c Handsome Boyle (pitching, right hand neck-high, New Yorks N.L.)
36-3a Handsome Boyle (end of pitch, right arm extended, P. Indianapolis)
36-3b Handsome Boyle (end of pitch, right arm extended, Pitcher, Indianapolis)
36-3c Handsome Boyle (end of pitch, right arm extended, New Yorks (NL))
36-4a Handsome Boyle (batting, no comma after P., Indianapolis)
36-4b Handsome Boyle (batting, Pitcher, Indianapolis)
36-4c Handsome Boyle (batting, comma atter P., Indianapolis)
37-1 Nick Bradley (leaning to left, arms at sides, Kansas City)
37-2 Nick Bradley (bat over shoulder, Worcesters)
37-3 Nick Bradley (bat in hand at side, Worcesters)
37-4 Nick Bradley (fielding, Kansas City)

38-1 Grin Bradley (batting, looking at camera, Sioux City)
38-2 Grin Bradley (batting, looking at ball Soiux City)
38-3a Grin Bradley (throwing, ball in right hand waist-high, Sioux Citys)
38-3b Grin Bradley (throwing, ball in right hand waist-high, Sioux City)
38-4 Grin Bradley (fielding, looking up at ball, Sioux City)
38-5 Grin Bradley (fielding, looking down at ball, Sioux City)
39-1 Stephen Brady (dotted tie)
40-1 Breckenridge (bat over shoulder)

41-1a Timothy Brosnam (fielding low ball, Minneapolis)
41-1b Timothy Brosnam (fielding low ball, Sioux Citys)
41-2a Timothy Brosnam (stooping to right to tag base, Minneapolis)
41-2b Timothy Brosnam (stooping to right to tag base, Sioux Citys)
41-3a Timothy Brosnam (fielding, hands neck high, Minneapolis)
41-3b Timothy Brosnam (fielding, hands neck high, Sioux Citys)
41-4 Timothy Brosnam (bat at ready position)

41-5 Timothy Brosnam (leaning on bat at back)

42-1a Cal Broughton (batting, looking at camera, St. Pauls)
42-1b Cal Broughton (batting, looking at camera, St. Paul)
42-2a Cal Broughton (batting, looking at ball, St. Pauls)
42-2b Cal Broughton (batting, looking at ball, St. Paul)
42-3 Cal Broughton (fielding, hands chest-high)

42-4 Cal Broughton (fielding, hands head-high)

42-5a Cal Broughton (fielding, hands by right thigh, St. Pauls)
42-5b Cal Broughton (fielding, hands by right thigh, St. Paul)
43-1a Dan Brouthers (fielding, Brouthers on front, Detroits)
43-1b Dan Brouthers (fielding, D. Brouthers on front, Detroits)
43-1d Dan Brouthers (fielding, Brouthers on front, Bostons)
43-2a Dan Brouthers (bat at ready position, looking to right, Detroits)
43-2b Dan Brouthers (bat at ready position, looking to right, Bostons)

43-3 Dan Brouthers (bat at ready position, looking down at ball)
44-1a Thomas Brown (fielding, hands above head, C.F., Pittsburg)
44-1b Thomas Brown (fielding, hands above head, Centre Field, Pittsburg)
44-1c Thomas Brown (fielding, hands above head, Boston)
44-2a Thomas Brown (bat in hand at side, C.F., Pittsburg)
44-2b Thomas Brown (bat in hand at side, Centre Field, Pittsburg)
44-2c Thomas Brown (bat in hand at side, Boston (PL))
44-3a Thomas Brown (fielding, hands chest high, C.F., Pittsburg)
44-3b Thomas Brown (fielding, hands chest high, Centre Field, Pittsburg)
44-3d Thomas Brown (fielding, hands chest high, Boston (PL))
44-4a Thomas Brown (batting, C.F., Pittsburg)

44-4b Thomas Brown (batting, Centre Field, Pittsburg)
45-1a California Brown (batting, no comma after C., N.Y's)
45-1b California Brown (batting, C., New Yorks)

45-1c California Brown (batting, comma after C., N.Y's)
45-2a California Brown (fielding, hands chest high, N.Y's)
45-2b California Brown (fielding, hands chest high, New York)
45-3a California Brown (throwing, no comma after C., N.Y's)
45-3b California Brown (throwing, comma after C., N.Y's)
45-3c California Brown (throwing, New Yorks)

45-4a California Brown (bat in hand at side, no comma after C., N.Y's)
45-4b California Brown (bat in hand at side, comma after C., N.Y's)
45-4c California Brown (bat in hand at side, New Yorks)
45-4d California Brown (bat in hand at side, New York (PL))
45-5a California Brown (in mask, hands on knees, no comma after C., N.Y's)
45-5b California Brown (in mask, hands on knees, comma after C., N.Y's)
46-1a Pete Browning (fielding, stooping, hands head-high, Pete Browning on front)

46-1b Pete Browning (fielding, stooping, hands head-high, Browning on front)
46-2 Pete Browning (fielding grounder)

46-3 Pete Browning (batting, feet together)

46-4 Pete Browning (batting, feet apart)

46-5 Pete Browning (throwing)
47-1 Charles Brynan (pitching, hands chest high)
47-2 Charles Brynan (pitching, hands below chest)
47-3a Charles Brynan (pitching, right hand neck high, Brynan on front)
47-3c Charles Brynan (pitching, right hand neck high, C. Brynan on front)
47-4a Charles Brynan (pitching, right arm stretched forward, Chicago)
47-4b Charles Brynan (pitching, right arm stretched forward, Des Moines)
47-5 Charles Brynan (bat at ready position over right shoulder)
48-1 Al Buckenberger (portrait, looking to left)

48-2 Al Buckenberger (portrait, looking to right)
49-1a Dick Buckley (fielding ball ankle-high, no comma after C.)
49-1b Dick Buckley (fielding ball ankle-high, comma after C.)
49-2a Dick Buckley (stooping, hands on knees, Indianapolis)
49-2b Dick Buckley (stooping, hands on knees, New Yorks N.L.)
49-3a Dick Buckley (fielding, hands chest-high, no comma after C.)
49-3b Dick Buckley (fielding, hands chest-high, comma after C.)
49-4a Dick Buckley (bat at ready position, nearly vertical, comma after C., Indianapolis)

49-4b Dick Buckley (bat at ready position, nearly vertical, no comma after C., Indinapolis)

49-4c Dick Buckley (bat at ready position, nearly vertical, New Yorks (N.L.))
49-5 Dick Buckley (about to hit low ball)

50-1a Charles Buffinton (pitching, hands chest high, Phila)
50-1b Charles Buffinton (pitching, hands chest high, Philadelphia)
50-1d Charles Buffington (Buffinton) (pitching, hands chest-high, Philadelphias)
50-1e Charles Buffinton (pitching, hands chest high, Philadelphias (PL))
50-2a Charles Buffington (Buffinton) (bat at ready position, name incorrect)
50-2b Charles Buffinton (bat at ready position, name correct)
50-3 Charles Buffinton (pitching, right hand above head)
51-1 Ernest Burch (dark uniform, leaning to left, tagging base)
51-2 Ernest Burch (dark uniform, both hands stretching up to left)
51-3 Ernest Burch (dark uniform, fielding, right hand stretching up to left)
51-4 Ernest Burch (dark uniform, throwing, right hand head-high)
51-5 Ernest Burch (dark uniform, bat by left shoulder)
51-6 Ernest Burch (white uniform, bat on left shoulder)
51-7 Ernest Burch (white uniform, leaning left to field)
51-8 Ernest Burch (white uniform, fielding, hands above head on left)
52-1 Bill Burdick (ball in hand above head)

52-2 Bill Burdick (fielding)
52-3a Bill Burdick (bat in hand at side, C.)

52-3b Bill Burdick (bat in hand at side, P.)

53-1a Black Jack Burdock (portrait, 2d B.)

53-1b Black Jack Burdock (portrait, Second Base)
53-2a Black Jack Burdock (throwing, 2d B.)

53-2b Black Jack Burdock (throwing, 2d Base)

53-3a Black Jack Burdock (batting, 2d B.)

53-3b Black Jack Burdock (batting, 2d Base)

53-4a Black Jack Burdock (fielding grounder, 2d B.)
53-4b Black Jack Burdock (fielding grounder, 2d Base)
53-5a Black Jack Burdock (bat in hand at side, 2d B.)
53-5b Black Jack Burdock (bat in hand at side, 2d Base)
54-1 Robert Burks (Burk) (fielding, hands at chest)
54-2 Robert Burks (Burk) (fielding, hands head high)
54-3 Robert Burks (Burk) (batting)

55-1a Watch Burnham (portrait, Man'gr)

55-1b Watch Burnham (portrait, Manager)

56-1 James Burns (fielding grounder by right foot, Kansas Citys)
56-2 James Burns (fielding, hands just above waist, Kansas Citys)
56-3 James Burns (fielding, hands shoulder high, Kansas Citys)
56-4 James Burns (bat at ready position over shoulder, Kansas Citys)
56-5 James Burns (bat at 70 degrees, ball nearby, Kansas Citys)
56-6 James Burns (sliding, Kansas Citys)

56-7 James Burns (bat in hand at side, Omaha)

56-8 James Burns (ball in hands above head, Omaha)
58-1a Oyster Burns (bat at ready position vertically, Baltimores)
58-1b Oyster Burns (bat at ready position vertically, Brooklyns)
58-2a Oyster Burns (swinging bat, Brooklyns)

58-2b Oyster Burns (swinging bat, Baltimores)

58-3a Oyster Burns (fielding, Baltimores)

58-3b Oyster Burns (fielding, Brooklyns)

58-4a Oyster Burns (throwing, right hand head high, Brooklyns)
58-4b Oyster Burns (throwing, right hand head high, Baltimores)
58-5 Oyster Burns (throwing, left hand out of picture)
59-1a Thomas Burns (tagging player, Chicago's)

59-1b Thomas Burns (tagging player, Chicagos (NL))
59-1c Thomas Burns (tagging player, Chicagos)

59-2a Thomas Burns (bat in hand at side, Chicago's)
59-2c Thomas Burns (bat in hand at side, Chicago)
59-3a Thomas Burns (fielding, Chicago's)

59-3c Thomas Burns (fielding, Chicagos)

59-3d Thomas E. Burns (fielding, Chicagos (NL))

59-4 Thomas E. Burns (batting)
60-1 Doc Bushong (Brown's Champions)

60-2a Doc Bushong (in mask, hands on knees, no comma after C.)
60-2b Doc Bushong (in mask, hands on knees, comma after C.)
60-3a Doc Bushong (stooping, hands waist-high, no comma after C.)
60-3c Doc Bushong (stooping, hands waist-high. comma after C.)
60-4 Doc Bushong (standing, ball in hands chest-high)
60-5 Doc Bushong (throwing)
60-6a Doc Bushong (batting, no comma after C.)
60-6b Doc Bushong (batting, comma after C.)

61-1a Patsy Cahill (fielding, R.F.)
61-1b Patsy Cahill (fielding, Right Field)

61-2a Patsy Cahill (batting, R.F.)
61-2b Patsy Cahill (batting, Right Field)

62-1 Count Campau (throwing)
62-2 Count Campau (fielding, hands head-high

62-3a Count Campau (fielding, bending to left, Detroits)
62-3b Count Campau (fielding, bending to left, Kansas City)
62-4a Count Campau (fielding, bending to right, Detroits)
62-4b Count Campau (fielding, bending to right, Kansas City)
62-5 Count Campau (bat in hand at side)

63-1 Jimmy Canavan (batting, looking at camera)
63-2a Jimmy Canavan (batting, looking down at ball, Omahas)
63-2b Jimmy Canavan (batting, looking down at ball, Omaha)
63-3 Jimmy Canavan (fielding)
64-1a Bart Cantz (hands on knees, St. Louis Whites)
64-1b Bart Cantz (hands on knees, Baltimores)

64-2 Bart Cantz (fielding, in mask)
64-3a Bart Cantz (fielding, no mask, St. Louis Whites)
64-3b Bart Cantz (fielding, no mask, Baltimores)

64-4a Bart Cantz (batting, St. Louis Whites)

64-4b Bart Cantz (batting, Baltimores)
64-5 Bart Cantz (throwing)
65-1a Handsome Jack Carney (fielding, hands head-high, Washingtons)
65-1b Handsome Jack Carney (fielding, hands head-high, Washington)

65-2a Handsome Jack Carney (throwing, Washingtons)
65-2b Handsome Jack Carney (throwing, Washington)
65-3a Handsome Jack Carney (bat in hand at side, Washingtons)
65-3b Handsome Jack Carney (bat in hand at side, Washington)
65-4 Handsome Jack Carney (batting)

65-5 Handsome Jack Carney (fielding, bending to left)
66-1a Hick Carpenter (tagging player, Cincinnati)
66-1b Hick Carpenter (tagging player, Cincinnatis)
66-2a Hick Carpenter (fielding grounder, Cincinnati)
66-2b Hick Carpenter (fielding grounder, Cin.)

66-3a Hick Carpenter (fielding, ball knee-high, Cincinnati)
66-3b Hick Carpenter (fielding, ball knee-high, Cincinnatis)
66-3c Hick Carpenter (fielding, ball knee-high, Cin)
66-4a Hick Carpenter (batting, Cincinnati)

66-4b Hick Carpenter (batting, Cin'ati)
66-4c Hick Carpenter (batting, Cin., N.L.)

66-5a Hick Carpenter (fielding, hands neck-high Cincinnati)
66-5b Hick Carpenter (fielding, hands neck-high, Cin.)
67-1 Cliff Carroll (batting, Washington)

67-2a Cliff Carroll (fielding, L.F., Washington)

67-2b Cliff Carroll (fielding, Left Field, Washington)
68-1a Scrappy Carroll (batting, looking at camera, St. Pauls)
68-1b Scrappy Carroll (batting, looking at camera, St. Paul)
68-2a Scrappy Carroll (batting, looking at ball, St. Pauls)
68-2b Scrappy Carroll (batting, looking at ball, Chicagos (NL))
68-3a Scrappy Carroll (fielding, hands waist high, ball visible, St. Pauls)
68-3b Scrappy Carroll (fielding, hands waist high, no ball visible, St. Paul)
68-4a Scrappy Carroll (fielding, hands chin-high, St. Pauls)
68-4b Scrappy Carroll (fielding, hands chin-high, St. Paul)
68-5a Scrappy Carroll (fielding, hands chest high, St. Pauls)
68-5b Scrappy Carroll (fielding, hands chest high, St. Paul)
68-5c Scrappy Carroll (fielding, hands chest high, Chicagos (NL))
69-1a Fred Carroll (throwing, C., Pittsburg)

69-1b Fred Carroll (throwing, Catcher, Pittsburg)
69-2a Fred Carroll (batting, C., Pittsburg)

69-2b Fred Carroll (batting, Catcher, Pittsburg)

69-3a Fred Carroll (bat in hand at side, C., Pittsburg)
69-3b Fred Carroll (bat in hand at side, Catcher, Pittsburg)
70-1a Jumbo Cartwright (arms folded, St. Josep)
70-1b Jumbo Cartwright (arms folded, St. Joes)

70-1c Jumbo Cartwright (arms folded, Kansas City)
70-2 Jumbo Cartwright (batting)
70-4 Jumbo Cartwright (bat in hand at side)

70-5 Jumbo Cartwright (throwing)
71-1 Parisian Bob Caruthers (Brown's Champions)
71-2 Parisian Bob Caruthers (holding up ball in left hand)
71-3a Parisian Bob Caruthers (ready to pitch, no comma after P.)
71-3b Parisian Bob Caruthers (ready to pitch, comma after P.)
71-4a Parisian Bob Caruthers (end of pitch, no comma after P.)
71-4b Parisian Bob Caruthers (end of pitch, comma after P.)
71-5a Parisian Bob Caruthers (fielding, no comma after P.)
71-5b Parisian Bob Caruthers (fielding, comma after P.)
71-6 Parisian Bob Caruthers (batting, feet together)
71-7a Parisian Bob Caruthers (batting, feet apart, no comma after P.)
71-7b Parisian Bob Caruthers (batting, feet apart, comma after P.)
72-1a Dan Casey (ball in hand at side, P., Phila)

72-1b Dan Casey (ball in hand at side, Pitcher, Philadelphia)
72-1c Dan Casey (ball in hand at side, Casey on front, P., Philadelphias)
72-1d Dan Casey (ball in hand at side, D.M. Casey on front, P., Philadelphias)

72-2a Dan Casey (ready to pitch, Phila)

72-2b Dan Casey (ready to pitch, Philadelphis)

72-3a Dan Casey (start of pitch, Phila)

72-3b Dan Casey (start of pitch, Philadelphia)

72-3c Dan Casey (start of pitch, Philadelphias)

73-1a Icebox Chamberlain (pitching, hands at chest, P.)
73-1c Icebox Chamberlain (pitching, hands at chest, S.)
73-2 Icebox Chamberlain (pitching, hands neck high)
73-3 Icebox Chamberlain (pitching, right hand head-high)
73-4 Icebox Chamberlain (pitching, right hand chest-high)
73-5a Icebox Chamberlain (batting, looking at camera, P., St. Louis)
73-5b Icebox Chamberlain (batting, looking at camera, P., St. Loui)
73-5d Icebox Chamberlain (batting, looking at camera, S.)
73-6 Icebox Chamberlain (batting, looking at ball)
74-1 Cupid Childs (batting, heels together)

74-2 Cupid Childs (batting, heels well apart)

74-3 Cupid Childs (fielding)
74-4a Cupid Childs (throwing, Phila)
74-4b Cupid Childs (throwing, Syracuse)

75-1a Spider Clark (fielding, facing to left, Washingtons)
75-1b Spider Clark (fielding, facing to left, Washington)
75-2a Spider Clark (fielding, facing front, Washingtons)
75-2b Spider Clark (fielding, facing front, Washington)
75-3 Spider Clark (batting)
75-4 Spider Clark (throwing)
76-1 Bob Clark (hands on hips, Brooklyns)

76-2 Bob Clark (stooping, hands on knees, Brooklyns)
76-3 Bob Clark (fielding, hands above waist, Brooklyns)
76-4 Bob Clark (fielding, hands shoulder-high, Brooklyns)
76-5 Bob Clark (throwing, Brooklyns)
76-6 Bob Clark, Mickey Hughes (Clark tagging Hughes)
77-1 Dad Clark (Clarke) (with cap, hands at chest, Omahas)
77-2 Dad Clark (Clarke) (with cap, bat in hand at side, Omahas)
77-3 Dad Clark (Clarke) (with cap, ball in right hand head-high, Omahas)
77-4 Dad Clark (Clarke) (with cap, ball in right hand by right knee, Omahas)
77-5a Dad Clark (Clarke) (no cap, about to hit low ball, name incorrect, Omahas, W.A.)

77-5b Dad Clarke (no cap, about to hit low ball, name correct, Chicago)
77-6 Dad Clark (Clarke) (no cap, bat at ready position, Chicago)
77-7 Dad Clark (Clarke) (no cap, facing left, hands chest high, Chicago)
77-8 Dad Clarke (no cap, facing front, hands at chest)
77-9a Dad Clark (Clarke) (no cap, right arm extended forward, Omahas)
77-9b Dad Clark (Clarke) (no cap, right arm extended forward, Chicago)
78-1 John Clarkson (throwing, right arm extended horizontally, looking front, left hand on thigh)
78-2a John Clarkson (throwing, right arm extended horizontally, right profile, left hand clear of thigh, Chicago)
78-2b John Clarkson (throwing, right arm extended horizontally, right profile, left hand clear of thigh, Bostons)
78-3a John Clarkson (throwing, right hand hip high, right profile, Chicago)
78-3b John Clarkson (throwing, right hand hip high, right profile, Bostons)
78-4 John Clarkson (ready to pitch, hands at chest)
78-5a John Clarkson (end of pitch, right arm extended forward, left hand on thigh, Chicago)
78-5b John Clarkson (end of pitch, right arm extended forward, left hand on thigh, Boston)
78-5c John Clarkson (end of pitch, right arm extended forward, left hand on thigh, Bostons)
78-6 John Clarkson (fielding)
78-7a John Clarkson (batting, Chicago)

78-7b John Clarkson (batting, Bostons)

79-1a Jack Clements (hands on knees, Phila)

79-1b Jack Clements (hands on knees, Philadelphia)
79-1c Jack Clements (hands on knees, Philadelphias)

79-1d Jack Clements (hands on knees, Phila (N.L.))
79-2a Jack Clements (fielding, Phila)
79-2b Jack Clements (fielding, Philadelphia)
79-2c Jack Clements (fielding, Philadelphias)
79-3a Jack Clements (batting, Phila)
79-3b Jack Clements (batting, Philadelphia)
79-3c Jack Clements (batting, Philadelphias)
79-3d Jack Clements (batting, Phil)
80-1 Elmer Cleveland (sliding)
80-2 Elmer Cleveland (bending forward, hands at back)
80-3 Elmer Cleveland (fielding)
80-4 Elmer Cleveland (bat at ready, over shoulder)
80-5 Elmer Cleveland (bat held nearly horizontal)
80-6 Elmer Cleveland (throwing)
81-1 Monk Cline (fielding, hands at waist looking upwards)
81-2 Monk Cline (fielding, hands by right shoulder, looking front, ball above head)
81-3a Monk Cline (fielding, hands by right shoulder, looking at ball just above hands, Sioux Citys)
81-3b Monk Cline (fielding, hands by right shoulder, looking at ball just above hands, Sioux City)
81-4a Monk Cline (about to hit, bat held vertically, Sioux Citys)
81-4b Monk Cline (about to hit, bat held vertically, Sioux City)
81-5 Monk Cline (bat at 45 degrees)
82-1 Cody (fielding)
82-2 Cody (throwing)
82-3 Cody (bat at ready, looking at camera)
82-4 Cody (about to hit, looking at ball)
83-1 John Coleman (fielding, hands chest-high)
83-2a John Coleman (ball in hands at waist, R.F.)
83-2b John Coleman (ball in hands at waist, Right Field)
83-3 John Coleman (throwing)
83-4a John Coleman (bat in hands below waist, R.F., Pittsburg)
83-4b John Coleman (bat in hands below waist, Right Field)
83-4c John Coleman (bat in hand at side, R.F., Pittsburgs)
83-5a John Coleman (bat in hand at side, R.F.)
83-5b John Coleman (bat in hand at side, Right Field)
84-1a Bill Collins (throwing, right hand head high, in mask, N.Y's)
84-1b Bill Collins (throwing, right hand head high, in mask, Newarks)
84-2a Bill Collins (sliding, N.Y's)
84-2b Bill Collins (sliding, Newarks)
84-3 Bill Collins (batting)
84-4a Bill Collins (bat in hand at side, N.Y's)
84-4b Bill Collins (bat in hand at side, Newarks)
84-5 Bill Collins (fielding ball waist-high, in mask, N.Y's)
84-6a Bill Collins (hands on knees, in mask, N.Y's)
84-6b Bill Collins (hands on knees, in mask, Newarks)
84-7 Bill Collins (fielding, hands above head, full length photo, N.Y's)
84-8 Bill Collins (fielding, hands above head, 3 4-length photo, Newarks)
85-1 Hub Collins (fielding grounder, Louisville)
85-2 Hub Collins (batting, Louisville)
85-3a Hub Collins (fielding, Louisville)
85-3b Hub Collins (fielding, Brooklyns)
85-4 Hub Collins (throwing, Louisville)
85-5 Hub Collins (sliding, Louisville)
86-1 Commy Comiskey (Brown's Champions)
86-2a Commy Comiskey (sliding, Chas. Comiskey on front)
86-2b Commy Comiskey (sliding, Comiskey on front)
86-3a Commy Comiskey (fielding, hands shoulder-high, looking to left, name correct)
86-3b Commy Commiskey (Comiskey) (fielding, hands shoulder-high, looking to left, name incorrect)
86-4 Commy Comiskey (fielding, hands chin high, looking up at ball)
86-5 Commy Comiskey (batting)
86-6a Commy Comiskey (arms folded, St. Louis Browns)
86-6c Commy Comiskey (arms folded, Chicagos)
87-1 Pete Connell (fielding, dark uniform)
87-2 Pete Connell (fielding, light uniform)
88-1a Roger Connor (hands on knees, name in script)
88-1b Roger Connor (hands on knees, New Yorks)
88-1c Roger Connor (hands on knees, N.Y's)
88-1d Roger Connor (hands on knees, New Yor)
88-2 Roger Connor (fielding)
88-4a Roger Connor (bat held up nearly vertical, name in script)
88-4b Roger Connor (bat held up nearly vertical, N.Y's)
89-1a Dick Conway (ball in right hand head-high, head level, P., Boston)
89-1b Dick Conway (ball in right hand head-high, head level, P., Bostons)
89-1c Dick Conway (ball in right hand head-high, head level, P., Worcesters)
89-2a Dick Conway (ball in right hand chin-high, head tilted to left, P., Boston)
89-2b Dick Conway (ball in right hand chin-high, head tilted to left, Pitcher, Boston)
89-3a Dick Conway (batting, P., Boston)
89-3b Dick Conway (batting, Pitcher, Boston)
89-4a Dick Conway (ready to pitch, P., Boston)
89-4b Dick Conway (ready to pitch, Pitcher, Boston)
89-5a Dick Conway (bat in hand at side, P., Boston)
89-5b Dick Conway (bat in hand at side, Pitcher, Boston)
90-1a Pete Conway (batting, Detroits)
90-1b Pete Conway (batting, Pittsburgs)
90-2 Pete Conway (pitching, feet on ground, Detroits)
90-3a Pete Conway (pitching, hands chest-high, left foot off ground, Detroits)
90-3b Pete Conway (pitching, hands chest-high, left foot off ground, Pittsburgs)
90-3c Pete Conway (pitching, hands chest-high left foot off ground, Pittsburghs)
90-4a Pete Conway (pitching, right hand by head, heels on ground, Detroits)
90-4b Pete Conway (pitching, right hand by head, heels on ground, Pittsburgs)
90-4c Pete Conway (pitching, right hand by head, heels on ground, Pittsburghs)
90-5a Pete Conway (pitching, right hand stretched forward, right heel off ground, Detroits)
90-5c Pete Conway (pitching, right hand stretched forward, right heel off ground, Indianapolis)
91-1 Jim Conway (batting, Kansas City)
91-2 Jim Conway (bat in hand at side, Kansas Citys)
91-3 Jim Conway (ready to pitch, hands cnest high, Kansas City)
91-4 Jim Conway (pitching, left ear not visible, Kansas City)
91-5 Jim Conway (pitching, left ear cleary visible, Kansas City)
92-1 Paul Cook (tagging player)
92-2 Paul Cook (fielding grounder)
92-3a Paul Cook (throwing, Louisville)
92-3b Paul Cook (throwing, Louisvilles)
92-4a Paul Cook (in mask, Louisville)
92-4b Paul Cook (in mask, Louisvilles)
93-1 Jimmy Cooney (throwing)
93-2a Jimmy Cooney (batting, Omahas)
93-2b Jimmy Cooney (batting, Chicago)
94-1a Larry Corcoran (pitching, hands above waist, P., Indianapolis)
94-1b Larry Corcoran (pitching, hands above waist, Pitcher)
94-1c Larry Corcoran (pitching, hands above waist, P., London, Ont.)
94-2a Larry Corcoran (pitching, hands near left shoulder, P., Indianapolis)
94-2b Larry Corcoran (Pitching, hands near left shoulder, Pitcher)
94-2c Larry Corcoran (pitching, hands near left shoulder, P., London, Ont.)
95-1 Pop Corkhill (sliding)
95-2a Pop Corkhill (fielding, hands neck-high, Cincinnati)
95-2b Pop Corkhill (fielding, hands neck-high, Brooklyns)
95-3 Pop Corkhill (fielding, hands above head)
95-4a Pop Corkhill (stooping, hands knee-high, Cincinnati)
95-4b Pop Corkhill (stooping, hands knee-high, Brooklyns)
95-5 Pop Corkhill (batting)
96-1a Cannonball Crane (bat at 60 degrees, N.Y.)
96-1b Cannonball Crane (bat at 60 degrees, New Yorks)
96-2a Cannonball Crane (bat nearly horizontal, N.Y.)
96-2b Cannonball Crane (bat nearly horizontal, New Yorks)
96-3a Cannonball Crane (bat in hand at side, N.Y.)
96-3b Cannonball Crane (bat in hand at side, New Yorks)
96-4a Cannonball Crane (ready to pitch, hands above waist, N.Y.)
96-4b Cannonball Crane (ready to pitch, hands above wais, New Yorks)
96-4c Cannonball Crane (ready to pitch, hands above waist, New Yorks (P.L.))
96-5a Cannonball Crane (pitching, hands below waist, N.Y.)
96-5b Cannonball Crane (pitching, hands below waist, New Yorks)
96-6a Cannonball Crane (pitching, right hand head-high, N.Y.)
96-6b Cannonball Crane (pitching, right hand head-high, New Yorks)
97-1a Sam Crane (batting, 2d B., Washington)
97-1b Sam Crane (batting, Second Base, Washington)
97-2a Sam Crane (fielding grounder, 2d B., Washington)
97-2b Sam Crane (fielding grounder, Second Base, Washington)
97-3a Sam Crane (bat in hand at side, 2d B., Washington)
97-3b Sam Crane (bat in hand at side, Second Base, Washington)
98-1 Jack Crogan (Croghan) (fielding grounder)
98-2 Jack Crogan (Croghan) (leaning to right, hands thigh-high)
98-3 Jack Crogan (Croghan) (bat in hand at side)
98-4 Jack Crogan (Croghan) (fielding, hands chest-high)
98-5 Jack Crogan (Croghan) (batting)
99-1a John Crooks (sliding, St. Louis Whites)
99-1b John Crooks (sliding, Omahas)
99-2 John Crooks (bat at ready position behin head)
99-3 John Crooks (bat nearly horizontal)
99-4a John Crooks (ball in hands waist-high, St. Louis Whites)
99-4b John Crooks (ball in hands waist-high, C. Crooks on front, Omahas)
99-4c John Crooks (ball in hands waist-high, Crooks on front, Omahas)
99-5 John Crooks (fielding, hands head-high)
100-1 Lave Cross (batting)
100-2aLave Cross (hands on thighs, Louisville)
100-2bLave Cross (hands on thighs, Philadelphias (PL))
100-3 Lave Cross (fielding low throw)
100-4aLave Cross (throwing, Louisville)
100-4bLave Cross (throwing, Philadelphias (PL))
101-1aN.C. Crossley (fielding, hands by right knee, Milwaukee)
101-1bN.C. Crossley (fielding, hands by right knee, Milwaukees)
101-2 N.C. Crossley (fielding, hands waist-high)
101-3aN.C. Crossley (fielding, hands neck-high, Milwaukee)
101-3bN.C. Crossley (fielding, hands neck-high, Milwaukees)
101-4 N.C. Crossley (batting, looking at camera)
101-5 N.C. Crossley (batting, looking at bat)
102-1 Joe Crotty (dotted tie)
102-2aJoe Crotty (fielding ball waist-high, Sioux Citys)
102-2bJoe Crotty (fielding ball waist-high, Sioux City)
102-3aJoe Crotty (fielding, hands shoulder-high, Sioux Citys)
102-3bJoe Crotty (fielding, hands shoulder-high, Sioux City)
102-4 Joe Crotty (batting, looking at camera)
102-5aJoe Crotty (batting, looking at ball, Sioux Citys)
102-5bJoe Crotty (batting, looking at ball, Sioux City)
103-1aBilly Crowell (pitching, facing front, hands above waist, Cleveland's)
103-1bBilly Crowell (pitching, facing front, hands above waist, St. Joes)
103-2 Billy Crowell (pitching, facing half way to left, hands waist-high)
103-3aBilly Crowell (pitching, facing left, hands behind body, Cleveland's)
103-3bBilly Crowell (pitching, facing left, hands behind body, St. Joes)
103-4aBilly Crowell (pitching, right arm extended, Clevelands)
103-4bBilly Crowell (pitching, right arm extended, St. Joes)
103-5aBilly Crowell (batting, Clevelands)
103-5bBilly Crowell (batting, St. Joes)
104-1 Jim Cubworth (fielding low ball)
104-2 Jim Cubworth (fielding, hands head-high)
104-3 Jim Cubworth (throwing)
104-4 Jim Cubworth (batting)
105-1 Bert Cunningham (fielding)
105-2aBert Cunningham (pitching, hands chest high, Baltimores)
105-2bBert Cunningham (pitching, hands chest high, Philadelphias)

105-3 Bert Cunningham (pitching, ball in right hand waist-high)
105-4 Bert Cunningham (bat at ready position, held vertically)
105-5 Bert Cunningham (bat at ready position at about 20 degrees)
106-1 Tacks Curtis (fielding, hands ankle-high, feet together)
106-2 Tacks Curtis (fielding, hands ankle-high, feet apart)
106-3 Tacks Curtis (bat at ready position by ground)
106-4 Tacks Curtis (bat at ready position by head)
106-5 Tacks Curtis (fielding, hands head-high)

107-1 Ed Cushman (dotted tie)
107-2 Ed Cushman (pitching, left hand forward, head high)
108-1 Tony Cusick (batting)
108-2 Tony Cusick (throwing)
109-1 Dailey (mask in hand at side, Oakland)

110-1aEdward Dailey (Daily) (pitching, right hand head-high, Phila)
110-1bEdward Daley (Daily) (pitching, right hand head-high, Philadelphia)
110-1cEdward Dailey (Daily) (pitching, right hand head-high, Washington)
110-2aEdward Dailey (Daily) (pitching, hands neck-high, Phila)
110-2bEdward Daley (Daily) (pitching, hands neck-high, Philadelphia)
110-2cEdward Dailey (Daily) (pitching, hands neck-high, Washington)
110-3aEdward Dailey (Daily) (bat at ready position at 30 degrees, Phila)
110-3bEdward Daley (Daily) (bat at ready position at 30 degrees, Philadelphia)

110-3cEdward Dailey (Daily) (bat at ready position at 30 degrees, Washington)
110-3dEdward Daley (Daily) (bat at ready position at 30 degrees, Columbus)
111-1aBill Daley (pitching, hands above waist, Bostons)
111-1bBill Daley (pitching, hands above waist, Bostons (PL))
112-1aCon Daley (Daily) (hands on knees, C., Boston)
112-1bCon Daley (Daily) (hands on knees, Catcher, Boston)
112-1cCon Daley (Daily) (hands on knees, no comma after C., Indianapolis)
112-1dCon Daley (Daily) (hands on knees, comma after C., Indianapolis)
112-2aCon Daley (Daily) (right hand on hip, left arm at side, C., Boston)
112-2bCon Daley (Daily) (right hand on hip, left arm at side, Indianapolis)
112-2cCon Daley (Daily) (right hand on hip, left arm at side, Catcher, Boston)
112-3aCon Daley (Daily) (throwing, right hand head-high, Boston)
112-3bCon Daley (Daily) (throwing, right hand head-high, no comma after C., Indianapolis)

112-3cCon Daley (Daily) (throwing, right hand head-high, comma after C., Indianapolis)

112-4aCon Daley (Daily) (batting, bat over left shoulder, C., Boston)
112-4bCon Daley (Daily) (batting, bat over left shoulder, Catcher, Boston)
112-4cCon Daley (Daily) (batting, bat over left shoulder, Indianapolis)
112-5aCon Daley (Daily) (ready to hit, bat vertical, Catcher)
112-5bBobby Wheelock (photo actually Con Daily - caption error) (ready to hit, bat vertical, R.F.)
113-1aAbner Dalrymple (hands on hips, feet apart, L.F., Pittsburg)
113-1bAbner Dalrymple (hands on hips, feet apart, Left Field)
113-1cAbner Dalrymple (hands on hips, feet apart, L.F., Denvers)
113-2aAbner Dalrymple (hands on hips, left foot behind right foot, L.F., Pittsburg)
113-2bAbner Dalrymple (hands on hips, left foot behind right foot, Left Field)
113-2cAbner Dalrymple (hands on hips, left foot behing right foot, L.F., Denvers)
113-4aAbner Dalrymple (throwing, L.F. Pittsburg)
113-4bAbner Dalrymple (throwing, Left Field)

113-4cAbner Dalrymple (throwing, L.F., Denvers)

113-5aAbner Dalrymple (batting, L.F.)
113-5bAbner Dalrymple (batting, Left Field)

114-1aTom Daly (portrait, Chicagos)
114-1bTom Daly (portrait, Chicago)
114-2 Tom Daly (fielding, with cap, Chicagos)

114-3 Tom Daly (fielding, no cap, Washington)

114-4aTom Daly (bat in hand at side, Chicagos)

114-4bTom Daly (bat in hand at side, Chicago)

114-4cTom Daly (bat in hand at side, Clevelands)

114-5aTom Daly (batting, with or without ball visible, Chicagos)
114-5bTom Daly (batting, with or without ball visible, Chicago)
114-5cTom Daly (batting, with or without ball visible, Chicago's)
114-6aTom Daly (hands on knees, Chicagos)

114-6bTom Daly (hands on knees, Chicago's)

115-1 Sun Daly (batting, looking at camera, Minneapolis)
115-2 Sun Daly (batting, looking at ball, Minneapolis)
115-3 Sun Daly (fielding, hands by right thigh, Minneapolis)
115-4 Sun Daly (fielding, hands chest-high, Minneapolis)
115-5 Sun Daly (fielding, hands neck-high, Minneapolis)
116-1 Law Daniels (batting)
116-2 Law Daniels (fielding, head-high)
116-3 Law Daniels (fielding, hands by right thigh)
116-4 Law Daniels (throwing)
117-1 Dell Darling (portrait)
117-2aDell Darling (arms folded, Del. Darling on front, Chicago)
117-2bDell Darling (arms folded, Dell Darling on front, Chicago)
117-2cDell Darling (arms folded, Chicagos)

117-3aDell Darling (fielding, hands chin-high, Del. Darling on front, Chicago)
117-3bDell Darling (fielding, hands chin-high, Dell Darling on front, Chicago)
117-3cDell Darling (fielding, hands chin-high, Chicagos)
117-4aDell Darling (fielding, hands waist-high, Chicago)
117-4bDell Darling (fielding, hands waist-high, Chicagos)
117-4cDell Darling (fielding, hands waist-high, Chicago's)
117-5 Dell Darling (batting)
118-1aWilliam Darnbrough (batting, Denver)

118-1bWilliam Darnbrough (batting, Denvers)

118-2 William Darnbrough (pitching)
118.5 Davin (bat in hand at side)
119-1aJumbo Davis (sliding, 3d B.)
119-1bJumbo Davis (sliding, 3d B.)
119-2 Jumbo Davis (fielding grounder)
119-3aJumbo Davis (fielding, hands shoulder high, Kansas City)
119-3bJumbo Davis (fielding, hands shoulder high, Kansas Citys)
119-4 Jumbo Davis (throwing)
119-5aJumbo Davis (bat in hand at side, no comma after 3d B.)
119-5bJumbo Davis (bat in hand at side, comma after 3d B.)
120-1aPat Dealey (fielding, hands waist-high, standing upright, name correct)
120-1bPat Dealy (Dealey) (fielding, hands waist high, standing upright, name incorrect)

120-2aPat Dealey (fielding, hands waist-high, leaning to left, name correct)
120-2bPat Dealy (Dealey) (fielding, hands waist high, leaning to left, name incorrect)

120-3aPat Dealey (bat in hand at side, name correct)
120-3bPat Dealy (Dealey) (bat in hand at side, name incorrect)
120-4aPat Dealey (hands on thighs, name correct)
120-4bPat Dealy (Dealey) (hands on thighs, name incorrect)
120-5aPat Dealey (bat on right shoulder, name correct)
120-5bPat Dealy (Dealey) (bat on right shoulder, name incorrect)
120-6aPat Dealey (throwing, name correct)

120-6bPat Dealy (Dealey) (throwing, name incorrect)
121-1 Tom Deasley (fielding, hands level with cap)
121-2aTom Deasley (sliding, N.Y's)
121-2bTom Deasley (sliding, Washington)

121-3 Tom Deasley (leaning left, hands touching above waist)
121-4aTom Deasley (leaning left, hands clasped neck-high, N.Y.'s)
121-4bTom Deasley (leaning left, hands clasped neck-high, Washington)
121-5aTom Deasley (bat in hand at side, N.Y's)

121-5bTom Deasley (bat in hand at side, Washington)
121-6 Tom Deasley (leaning left, ball in hands by chin)
121-7aTom Deasley (fielding, hands chest-high, N.Y's)
121-7bTom Deasley (fielding, hands chest-high, Washington)
121-8 Tom Deasley (fielding, hands in front of face)
121-9 Tom Deasley (bat at ready position at about 80 degrees)

121-10Tom Deasley (right hand hip-high, left hand by left knee)
121-11Tom Deasley (throwing, hands to left, chest-high)
121-12aTom Deasley (throwing, right hand neck high, N.Y's)
121-12bTom Deasley (throwing, right hand neck high, Washington)
121-13aTom Deasley (bat at ready position, bat end behind head, N.Y's)
121-13bTom Deasley (bat at ready position, bat end behind head, Washington)
121-14Tom Deasley (fielding grounder)
122-1 Harry Decker (bat at ready position, almost horizontal)
122-2aHarry Decker (bat at ready position, over shoulder, Philadelphias)
122-2bHarry Decker (bat at ready position, over shoulder, Philadelphia (NL))
122-3 Harry Decker (fielding, hands thigh-high)

122-4aHarry Decker (fielding, hands chest-high, Philadelphias)
122-4bHarry Decker (fielding, hands chest-high, Philadelphia)
122-5aHarry Decker (throwing, Philadelphias)

122-5bHarry Decker (throwing, Philadelphia)

122-5cHarry Decker (throwing, Philadelphia (NL))
123-1aEd Delahanty (bat at ready position by shoulder, Phila)
123-1bEd Delahanty (bat at ready position by shoulder, Phila's)
123-2 Ed Delahanty (bat at ready position, nearly horizontal)
123-3aEd Delahanty (fielding, hands at waist, Phila)
123-3bEd Delahanty (fielding, hands at waist, Phila's)
123-4aEd Delahanty (throwing, Phila)
123-4bEd Delahanty (throwing, Phila's)

123-5 Ed Delahanty (fielding grounder)

124-1aJerry Denny (batting, 3d B. Indianapolis)

124-1bJerry Denny (batting, 3d Base, Indianapolis)
124-1cJerry Denny (batting, 3d B., Indianapolis)

124-2aJerry Denny (in jacket, arms at sides, 3d B. Indianapolis)
124-2bJerry Denny (in jacket, arms at sides, 3d Base, Indianapolis)
124-2cJerry Denny (in jacket, arms at sides, 3d B., Indianapolis)
124-2dJerry Denny (in jacket, arms at sides, 3rd B., Indianapolis)
124-2eJerry Denny (in jacket, arms at sides, 3d B., New Yorks (NL))
124-3aJerry Denny (fielding, 3d B.)
124-3bJerry Denny (fielding, 3d Base)
125-1 Jim Devlin (sliding)
125-2aJim Devlin (pitching, left hand at back, shoulder-high, name correct, St. Louis)

125-2bJim Delvin (Devlin) (pitching, left hand at back, shoulder-high, name incorrect, St. Louis)
125-2cJim Devlin (pitching, left hand at back, shoulder-high, Devlin on front, St. Louis Browns)
125-2dJim Devlin (pitching, left hand at back, shoulder-high, J. Devlin on front, St. Louis Browns)
125-3 Jim Devlin (pitching, hands held out, shoulder-high)
125-4aJim Devlin (end of pitch, left hand waist high, St. Louis Browns)
125-4bJim Devlin (end of pitch, left hand waist high, St. Louis)
125-5 Jim Devlin (batting)
126-1aTom Dolan (sliding, Thos. Dolan on front)

126-1bTom Dolan (sliding, Dolan on front)

126-2aTom Dolan (batting, Thos. Dolan on front)

126-2bTom Dolan (batting, Dolan on front)

126-3 Tom Dolan (bat in hand at side)
126-4 Tom Dolan (fielding, hands above waist)

126-5 Tom Dolan (fielding, hands by right knee)

127-1 Jack Donahue (fielding, San Francisco)

128-1 Jim Donohue (Donahue) (dotted tie)

128-2aJim Donahue (throwing, name correct, Kansas City)
128-2bJim Donohue (Donahue) (throwing, name incorrect, Kansas City)
128-3aJim Donohue (Donahue) (batting, no comma after C., Kansas City)
128-3bJim Donohue (Donahue) (batting, no comma after C., Kansas City)
128-4aJim Donahue (fielding grounder by left foot, Kansas City)
128-4bJim Donohue (Donahue) (fielding grounder by left foot, Kansas Citys)
128-5 Jim Donohue (Donahue) (fielding ball knee-high, Kansas City)

128-6 Jim Donahue (ball in hands, head-high, Kansas City)
129-1aJim Donnelly (Donely) (fielding, hands shoulder-high, 3d B.)
129-1bJim Donnelly (Donely) (fielding, hands shoulder-high, Third Base)
129-2aJim Donnelly (Donely) (batting, 3d B.)
129-2bJim Donnelly (Donely) (batting, Third Base)
129-3aJim Donnelly (Donely) (fielding grounder, 3d B.)
129-3bJim Donnelly (Donely) (fielding grounder, Third Base)
130-1 Coley (fielding)
131-1 J. Doran (batting)
131-2 J. Doran (fielding)
132-1 Mike Dorgan (sliding, left hand raised)
132-2 Mike Dorgan (sliding, left hand on ground)
132-3 Mike Dorgan (throwing, right hand eye high, looking front)
132-4 Mike Dorgan (throwing, right hand cap high, looking left)
132-5aMike Dorgan (throwing, right hand chest high, N.Y's)
132-5bMike Dorgan (throwing, right hand chest high, New Yorks)
132-6 Mike Dorgan (fielding, right hand upstretched to left)
132-7aMike Dorgan (fielding, hands above head N.Y's)
132-7bMike Dorgan (fielding, hands above head, New Yorks)
132-8 Mike Dorgan (fielding, hands chin-high)
132-9aMike Dorgan (fielding, hands ankle-high, N.Y's)
132-9bMike Dorgan (fielding, hands ankle-high, New Yorks)
132-10Mike Dorgan (fielding grounder with both hands)
132-11aMike Dorgan (fielding grounder with right hand by right foot, N.Y's)
132-11bMike Dorgan (fielding grounder with right hand by right foot, New Yorks)
132-12aMike Dorgan (hands on knees, N.Y's)
132-12bMike Dorgan (hands on knees, New Yorks)
132-13 Mike Dorgan (arms folded)
132-14aMike Dorgan (running to left, N.Y's)
132-14bMike Dorgan (running to left, New Yorks)
132-15aMike Dorgan (bat in hand at side, N.Y's)
132-15bMike Dorgan (bat in hand at side, New Yorks)
132-16 Mike Dorgan (bat at ready position over shoulder)
132-17aMike Dorgan (bat at ready position nearly vertical, N.Y's)
132-17bMike Dorgan (bat at ready position nearly vertical, New Yorks)
133-1 Doyle (throwing)
134-1 Home Run Duffe (Duffee) (batting)
134-2 Home Run Duffe (Duffee) (fielding grounder)
134-3 Home Run Duffe (Duffee) (fielding, bending to left, hands waist-high)
134-4 Home Run Duffe (Duffee) (fielding, standing upright, hands above waist)
134-5 Home Run Duffe (Duffee) (fielding, leaning forward, hands shoulder-high)
135-1aHugh Duffy (batting, Chicago)
135-1bHugh Duffy (batting, Chicago's)
135-1cHugh Duffy (batting, Chicagos)
135-2aHugh Duffy (fielding grounder, Chicagos)
135-2bHugh Duffy (fielding grounder, Chicago)
135-3aHugh Duffy (throwing, Chicago)
135-3bHugh Duffy (throwing, Chicagos)
135-4 Hugh Duffy (fielding, hands neck-high, feet apart)
135-5aHugh Duffy (fielding, hands chin-high, right heel behind left leg, Chicago)
135-5bHugh Duffy (fielding, hands chin-high, right heel behind left leg, Chicago's)
135-5cHugh Duffy (fielding, hands chin-high, right heel behind left leg, Chicagos)
136-1 Dan Dugdale (hands on knees, looking at camera)
136-2 Dan Dugdale (hands on knees, left profile)
136-3aDan Dugdale (bat in hand at side, Chicago Maroons)
136-3bDan Dugdale (bat in hand at side, Minpls)
136-4 Dan Dugdale (ball in right hand, head high)
137-1 Duck Duke (batting)
137-2 Duck Duke (pitching, right hand by chin, left arm on thigh)
137-3 Duck Duke (pitching, hands waist-high)
137-4 Duck Duke (pitching, hands chest-high)
137-5 Duck Duke (pitching, right arm extended head-high)
138-1aSure Shot Dunlap (sliding, Pittsburgs)
138-1bSure Shot Dunlap (sliding, Pittsburghs)
138-2aSure Shot Dunlap (hands on thighs, Pittsburg)
138-2bSure Shot Dunlap (hands on thighs, Pittsburgs)
138-3 Sure Shot Dunlap (bat in hand at side)
138-4 Sure Shot Dunlap (batting)
138-5aSure Shot Dunlap (fielding, hands above waist, Pittsburg)
138-5bSure Shot Dunlap (fielding, hands above waist, Pittsburgs)
138-6aSure Shot Dunlap (fielding, hands shoulder-high, Pittsburg)
138-6bSure Shot Dunlap (fielding, hands shoulder-high, Pittsburgs)
138-7aSure Shot Dunlap (throwing, right hand waist-high, Pittsburg)
138-7bSure Shot Dunlap (throwing, right hand waist-high, Pittsburgs)
138-8 Sure Shot Dunlap (throwing, right hand above head)
139-1 Dunn (batting)
139-2 Dunn (pitching, hands chest-high)
139-3 Dunn (ball in right hand head-high, facing front)
139-4 Dunn (ball in right hand chin-high, looking to right)
139-5 Dunn (fielding, hands chest-high)
140-2 Jesse Duryea (bat under left arm, hands together)
140-3aJesse Duryea (throwing, right hand head high, Cincinnati)
140-3bJesse Duryea (throwing, right hand head high, Cincinnatis)
140-3cJesse Duryea (throwing, right hand head high, Cincinnatti)
140-4aJesse Duryea (throwing, right hand chest high, Cincinnati)
140-4bJesse Duryea (throwing, right hand chest high, Cincinnati (NL))
140-5 Jesse Duryea (ready to pitch, hands chest high)
141-1aFrank Dwyer (fielding, hands chest-high, Chicagos)
141-1bFrank Dwyer (fielding, hands chest-high, Chicago Maroons)
141-2aFrank Dwyer (throwing, Chicago's)
141-2bFrank Dwyer (throwing, Chicago Maroons)
141-3aFrank Dwyer (bat in hand at side, Chicago's)
141-3bFrank Dwyer (bat in hand at side, Chicagos)
142-1 Billy Earle (fielding, hands above head)
142-2 Billy Earle (fielding, hands thigh-high)
142-3aBilly Earle (bat in hand at side, name correct, Cincinnati)
142-3bBilly Earl (Earle) (bat in hand at side, name incorrect, St. Paul)
143-1aBuck Ebright (hands on knees, Washingtons)
143-1bBuck Ebright (hands on knees, Washington)
143-2 Buck Ebright (throwing)
144-1 Red Ehret (throwing)
144-2 Red Ehret (pitching, hands by left shoulder)
144-3 Red Ehret (pitching, hands head-high)
144-4 Red Ehret (batting)
145-1 R. Emmerke (batting, looking at camera)
145-2 R. Emmerke (batting, looking at ball)
145-3 R. Emmerke (pitching, hands at chest)
145-4 R. Emmerke (pitching, right hand head high)
145-5 R. Emmerke (pitching, left foot off ground)
146-1 Dude Esterbrook (standing upright, right hand on hip)
146-2 Dude Esterbrook (bending, facing to left, hands on knees)
146-3aDude Esterbrook (bending, facing front, hands on knees, Indianapolis)
146-3bDude Esterbrook (bending, facing front, hands on knees, N Ys (NL))
146-4 Dude Esterbrook (kneeling to field grounder)
146-5aDude Esterbrook (batting, Indianapolis)
146-5bDude Esterbrook (batting, Louisvilles)
146-6 Dude Esterbrook (fielding)
146-7aDude Esterbrook (right hand over ball in left hand waist-high, Lo'villes)
146-7bDude Esterbrook (right hand over ball in left hand waist-high, N Ys (NL))
147-1 Henry Esterday (fielding grounder by left foot)
147-2aHenry Esterday (fielding grounder, hands ankle-high, Kansas City)
147-2bHenry Esterday (fielding grounder, hands ankle-high, Columbus)
147-3aHenry Esterday (fielding, hands above head, Kansas City)
147-3bHenry Esterday (fielding, hands above head, Columbus)
147-4 Henry Esterday (throwing)
148-1 Long John Ewing (bat over right shoulder, Louisville)
148-2 Long John Ewing (bat almost vertical, Louisville)
148-3 Long John Ewing (pitching, hands at cap, Louisville)
148-4 Long John Ewing (pitching, hands neck high, Louisville)
149-1aBuck Ewing (sliding, Capt., New York)
149-1bBuck Ewing (sliding, C., New York)
149-2aBuck Ewing (hands on knees, Capt. N.Y's)
149-2bBuck Ewing (hands on knees, Captain, New Yorks)
149-2dBuck Ewing (hands on knees, C. New Yorks)
149-2eBuck Ewing (hands on knees, C. New York (PL))
149-3 Buck Ewing (throwing, right hand waist high at side, New Yorks)
149-4aBuck Ewing (throwing, right arm extended forward, Capt., New Yorks)
149-4bBuck Ewing (throwing, right arm extended forward, C., New Yorks)
149-5aBuck Ewing (fielding, hands head-high, New Yorks)
149-5bBuck Ewing (fielding, hands head-high, N. Y's)
149-6aBuck Ewing (walking to left, hands thigh high, Captain, New Yorks)
149-6bBuck Ewing (walking to left, hands thigh high, C., New Yorks)
149-7 Buck Ewing (fielding grounder, New Yorks)
149-8 Buck Ewing (bat in hand at side, New Yorks)
149-9aBuck Ewing (bat at 45 degrees, looking to front, New Yorks)
149-9bBuck Ewing (bat at 45 degrees, looking to front, N.Y's)
149-10aBuck Ewing (bat nearly horizontal, looking down at ball, Captian, New Yorks)
149-10bBuck Ewing (bat nearly horizontal, looking down at ball, Capt., New Yorks)
149-11aWillie Breslin - mascot, Buck Ewing (New Yorks)
149-11bWillie Breslin - mascot, Buck Ewing (N.Y's)
150-1aJay Faatz (fielding grounder, Clevelands)
150-1bJay Faatz (fielding grounder, Cleveland's)
150-2aJay Faatz (batting, Capt.)
150-2bJay Faatz (batting, Captain)
150-3aJay Faatz (throwing, Capt.)
150-3bJay Faatz (throwing, Captain)
151-1aBill Fagan (pitching, left hand chin-high, Kansas City)
151-1bBill Fagan (pitching, left hand chin-high, Denvers)
151-2 Bill Fagan (pitching, hands neck-high)
151-3 Bill Fagan (left profile, left hand forward waist-high)
151-4 Bill Fagan (batting)
152-1 Bill Farmer (tagging player on ground)
152-2aBill Farmer (hands on knees, Pittsburgh)
152-2bBill Farmer (hands on knees, Pittsburgh's)
152-2dBill Farmer (hands on knees, St. Pauls)
152-3aBill Farmer (fielding, hands thigh-high, Pittsburgh's)
152-3bBill Farmer (fielding, hands thigh-high, St. Pauls)
152-3cBill Farmer (fielding, hands thigh-high, St. Paul)
152-4aBill Farmer (throwing, Pittsburgh)
152-4bBill Farmer (throwing, St. Pauls)
152-5 Bill Farmer (batting)
153-1aSid Farrar (fielding, hands head-high, Phila)
153-1bSid Farrar (fielding, hands head-high, Philadelphia)
153-1cSid Farrar (fielding, hands head-high, Philadelphias)
153-2aSid Farrar (fielding grounder, Phila)
153-2bSid Farrar (fielding grounder, Philadelphia)
153-2cSid Farrar (fielding grounder, name correct, Philadelphias)
153-2eSid Faraer (Farrar) (fielding grounder, name incorrect, Philadelphias)
153-3aSid Farrar (right hand at belt, left arm at side, with cap, Phila)
153-3bSid Farrar (right hand at belt, left arm at side, with cap, Philadelphia)
153-3cSid Farrar (right hand at belt, left arm at side, with cap, Phil)

153-3dSid Farrar (right hand at belt, left arm at side, with cap, name correct, Philadelphias)

153-3eSid Farrer (Farrar) (right hand at belt, left arm at side, with cap, name incorrect, Philadelphias)
153-4aSid Farrar (fielding, hands chin-high, Phila)
153-4bSid Farrar (fielding, hands chin-high, Philadelphia)
153-5aSid Farrar (fielding, hands ankle-high, Phila)
153-5bSid Farrar (fielding, hands ankle-high, Philadelphia)
153-5cSid Farrar (fielding, hands ankle-high, Philadelphias)
153-6aSid Farrar (arms folded, no cap, Phila)

153-6bSid Farrar (arms folded, no cap, Philadelphia)
153-6cSid Farrar (arms folded, no cap, Philadelphias)
153-7 Sid Farrar (hands on thighs, looking at ball head-high)
154-1 Jack Farrell (bat in hand at side, looking at camera, Washington)
154-2aJack Farrell (batting, looking at ball head high, 2d B., Washington)
154-2bJack Farrell (batting, looking at ball head high, Second Base, Washington)
154-3aJack Farrell, Paul Hines (Farrell tagging Hines, 2d B.)
154-3bJack Farrell, Paul Hines (Farrell tagging Hines, Second Base)
154-4aJack Farrell (fielding grounder, 2d B., Washington)
154-4bJack Farrell (fielding grounder, Second Base, Washington)
154-5aJack Farrell (hands on thighs, 2d B., Washington)
154-5bJack Farrell (hands on thighs, Second Base, Washington)
154-6aJack Farrell (bat at ready, looking at camera, wall background, 2d B., Washington)

154-6bJack Farrell (bat at ready, looking at camera, wall background, Second Base, Washington)
154-7aJack Farrell (fielding, hands head-high, 2d B., Washington)
154-7bJack Farrell (fielding, hands head-high, Second Base, Washington)
154-8aJack Farrell (hands on hips, 2nd B., Baltimores)
154-8bJack Farrell (hands on hips, S.S., Baltimores)
154-9aJack Farrell (bat at ready position, looking at camera, field background, 2nd B., Baltimores)
154-9bJack Farrell (bat at ready position, looking at camera, field background, 2d B., Baltimores)
154-10Jack Farrell (fielding, hands above head, Baltimores)
154-11aJack Farrell (throwing, 2nd B., Baltimores)
154-11bJack Farrell (throwing, no comma after 2d B., Baltimores)
154-11cJack Farrell (throwing, comma after 2d B., Baltimores)
154-12Jack Farrell (bat in hand at side, looking to right, Baltimores)
155-1aDuke Farrell (batting, name correct, Chicago)
155-1bDuke Farrel (Farrell) (batting, name incorrect, Chicago's)
155-2aDuke Farrell (fielding, hands above head, name correct, Chicago)
155-2bDuke Farrel (Farrell) (fielding, hands above head, name incorrect, Chicago)

155-3aDuke Farrell (hands on knees, name correct, Chicago's)
155-3bDuke Farrel (Farrell) (hands on knees, name incorrect, Chicago)
155-3cDuke Farrell (hands on knees, name incorrect, Chicago's)
155-4aDuke Farrell (fielding grounder by right foot, name correct, Chicago)
155-4bDuke Farrel (Farrell) (fielding grounder by right foot, name incorrect, Chicagos)

155-5aDuke Farrel (Farrell) (fielding low ball, hands by left ankle, name incorrect, Chicago)

155-5bDuke Farrell (fielding low ball, hands by left ankle, name correct, Chicagos)
156-1 Frank Fennelly (fielding grounder by right foot)
156-2 Frank Fennelly (batting)
156-3aFrank Fennelly (fielding, hands thigh-high, Cincinnati)
156-3bFrank Fennelly (fielding, hands thigh-high, Athletics)
156-4aFrank Fennelly (fielding, hands head-high, Cincinnati)
156-4bFrank Fennelly (fielding, hands head-high, Athletics)
156-5aFrank Fennelly (throwing, Cincinnati)

156-5bFrank Fennelly (throwing, Athletics)

157-1aCharlie Ferguson (batting, Phila)
157-1bCharlie Ferguson (batting, Philadelphia)
157-1cCharlie Ferguson (batting, Philadelphias)

157-2aCharlie Ferguson (pitching, Phila)

157-2bCharlie Ferguson (pitching, Philadelphia)

157-3aCharlie Ferguson (throwing, Phila)

157-3bCharlie Ferguson (throwing, Philadelphia)

157-4aCharlie Ferguson (tagging player, Phila)

157-4bCharlie Ferguson (tagging player, Philadelphia)
158-1 Alex Ferson (pitching, hands chest-high, looking to right)
158-2 Alex Ferson (pitching, hands neck-high, looking to front)
158-3aAlex Ferson (ball in right hand neck-high, looking at camera, Washington)
158-3bAlex Ferson (ball in right hand neck-high, looking at camera, Washingtons)
158-4 Alex Ferson (looking at ball in right hand cap-high)
158-5aAlex Ferson (batting, Washington)

158-5bAlex Ferson (batting, Washingtons)

159-1 Wallace Fessenden (umpire) (hands at back)
159-2 Wallace Fessenden (umpire) (arms at sides)
159-3 Wallace Fessenden (umpire) (left hand on left thigh)
159-4 Wallace Fessenden (umpire) (arms folded)

160-1aSam Barkley, Jocko Fields (Fields fielding with Barkley looking on, C.)
160-1bSam Barkley, Jocko Fields (Fields fielding with Barkley looking on, Catcher)
160-2aJocko Fields (batting, C.)
160-2bJocko Fields (batting, Catcher)
160-3aJocko Fields (fielding, hands neck-high, C.)
160-3bJocko Fields (fielding, hands neck-high, Catcher)
160-4aSam Barkley, Jocko Fields (Fields tagging Barkley, C.)
160-4bSam Barkley, Jocko Fields (Fields tagging Barkley, Catcher)
160-5aJocko Fields (throwing, name correct, C.)

160-5bJocko Fields (throwing, Catcher)

160-5cJocko Field (Fields) (throwing, name incorrect, C.)
160-6aJocko Fields (hands on thighs, C.)

160-6bJocko Fields (hands on thighs, Catcher)

161-1 Fischer (batting)
161-2 Fischer (fielding)
161-3 Fischer (throwing)
162-1 Thomas Flanigan (Flanagan) (batting)

162-2 Thomas Flanigan (Flanagan) (pitching, hands at neck)
162-3aThomas Flanigan (Flanagan) (pitching, right hand head-high, Clevelands)
162-3bThomas Flanigan (Flanagan) (pitching, right hand head-high, Sioux City)
162-4 Thomas Flanigan (Flanagan) (pitching, right arm chin-high)
163-1aSilver Flint (portrait, Chicago)
163-1bSilver Flint (portrait, Chicagos)
163-2 Silver Flint (fielding, hands chest-high)

163-3aSilver Flint (hands on hips, Chicago)

163-3bSilver Flint (hands on hips, Chicago's)

163-4aSilver Flint (batting, Flint on front, Chicago)
163-4bSilver Flint (batting, Silver Flint on front, Chicago)
163-4dSilver Flint (batting, Silver Flint on front, Chicagos)
163-4eSilver Flint (batting, Flint on front, Chicago's)
163-5aSilver Flint (stooping hands waist-high, with mask, Chicago)
163-5bSilver Flint (stooping hands waist-high, with mask, Chicago's)
164-1 Thomas Flood (batting)
164-2aThomas Flood (pitching, hands at chest, St. Josephs)
164-2bThomas Flood (pitching, hands at chest, St. Joe)
164-4aThomas Flood (pitching, right hand held out chest-high, St. Josephs)
164-4bThomas Flood (pitching, right hand held out chest-high, St. Joe)
164-5 Thomas Flood (ball in left hand, chin-high)

164.5 Jocko Flynn (pitching)
165-1aJim Fogarty (fielding on run to left, hand head-high, R.F.)
165-1bJim Fogarty (fielding on run to left, hands head-high, Right Field)
165-2aJim Fogarty (fielding, hands neck-high, R.F.)
165-2bJim Fogarty (fielding, hands neck-high, Right Field)
165-3aJim Fogarty (fielding grounder, R.F.)
165-3bJim Fogarty (fielding grounder, Right Field)
165-4aJim Fogarty (batting, name correct, R.F.)

165-4bJim Fogarty (batting, Right Field)

165-4cJim Fogerty (Fogarty) (batting, name incorrect, R.F., Phila)
165-4dJim Fogerty (Fogarty) (batting, name incorrect, R.F., Philadelphias)
165-5aJim Fogarty (sliding, R.F.)
165-5bJim Fogarty (sliding, Right Field)
166-1 Frank Foreman (batting)
166-2aFrank Foreman (ball in left hand head high, Baltimores)
166-2bFrank Foreman (ball in left hand head high, Cincinnati (NL))
166-3 Frank Foreman (ball in right hand head high)
166-4 Frank Foreman (ready to pitch, hands by right thigh)
166-5 Frank Foreman (end of pitch, left hand by left knee)
167-1aTom Forster (throwing, Hartfords)

167-1bTom Forster (throwing, Milwaukee)

167-2 F.W. Foster (photo actually Tom Forster) (dotted tie)
168-1 Elmer Foster (dotted tie)
168-2 Elmer Foster (sliding)
168-3aElmer Foster (bat at ready position by head, N.Y.)
168-3bElmer Foster (bat at ready position by head, New Yorks)
168-4 Elmer Foster (bat at ready position at about 50 degrees)
168-5 Elmer Foster (bat in hand at side)

168-6aElmer Foster (fielding, N.Y.)
168-6cElmer Foster (fielding, New Yorks)

168-7aElmer Foster (throwing, N.Y.)
168-7bElmer Foster (throwing, New Yorks)

169 No World Index Listing
170-1 Dave Foutz (Brown's Champions)

170-3 Dave Foutz (bat at ready position over shoulder)
170-4 Dave Foutz (bat at ready position at 30 degrees)
170-5 Dave Foutz (ready to pitch, hands above waist)
170-6aDave Foutz (throwing, no comma after P.)

170-6bDave Foutz (throwing, comma after P.)

171-1 Julie Freeman (batting)
171-2 Julie Freeman (pitching, hands neck-high)

171-3 Julie Freeman (pitching, hands thigh-high)

171-4 Julie Freeman (pitching, right hand neck high at back)
171-5 Julie Freeman (pitching, right hand extended forward)
172-1 Will Fry (batting, looking at camera)

172-2 Will Fry (batting, looking at ball)
172-3 Will Fry (fielding, hands above waist)

172-4 Will Fry (fielding grounder)
172.5 Fudger (standing)
173-1 William Fuller (bat at ready position by le shoulder, Milwaukees)
173-2aWilliam Fuller (bat in hand at side, Milwaukee)
173-2bWilliam Fuller (bat in hand at side, Milwaukees)
173-3aWilliam Fuller (throwing, Milwaukees)

173-3bWilliam Fuller (throwing, Milwaukees, W. Ass'n)
173-4 William Fuller (fielding, ball approaching, Milwaukees)
173-5 William Fuller (fielding, ball in hands, Milwaukees)
174-1 Shorty Fuller (bat at ready position, elbows above belt, St. Louis)
174-2 Shorty Fuller (batting, right elbow level with belt, St. Louis)
174-3 Shorty Fuller (hands on knees, St. Louis)

174-4 Shorty Fuller (fielding, hands at knees, St. Louis)
174-5 Shorty Fuller (fielding, hands shoulder high, St. Louis)
175-1aChris Fulmer (bat at ready position at 80 degrees, name correct)
175-1bChris Fullmer (Fulmer) (bat at ready position at 80 degrees, name incorrect)

175-2 Chris Fullmer (Fulmer) (bat at 40 degrees, looking at camera)
175-3 Chris Fullmer (Fulmer) (batting at 40 degrees, looking at ball)
175-4 Chris Fullmer (Fulmer) (fielding, hands by chin)
175-5 Chris Fullmer (Fulmer) (hands on knees)

175-6aChris Fulmer, Foghorn Tucker (Fulmer tagging Tucker, Baltimore)
175-6bChris Fulmer, Foghorn Tucker (Fulmer tagging Tucker, Baltimores)

176-1aHonest John Gaffney (leaning to right, Manager, Washington)
176-1bHonest John Gaffney (leaning right, Manager of Washington Club)
177-1aPud Galvin (bat at ready position, P.)
177-1bPud Galvin (bat at ready position, Pitcher)
177-2aPud Galvin (in jacket, arms at sides, P., Pittsburg)
177-2bPud Galvin (in jacket, arms at sides, Pitcher)
177-2cPud Galvin (in Jacket, arms at sides, P., Pittsburgs)
177-3aPud Galvin (ready to pitch, hands above waist, P.)
177-3bPud Galvin (ready to pitch, hands above waist, Pitcher)
177-4aPud Galvin (in jacket, bat in hand at side, Galvin on front, P. Pittsburg)
177-4bPud Galvin (in jacket, bat in hand at side, Pitcher)
177-4cPud Galvin (in jacket, bat in hand at side, Galvin on front, P., Pittsburgs)
177-4dPud Galvin (in jacket, bat in hand at side, J. Galvin on front)
177-4ePud Galvin (in jacket, bat in hand at side, Jim Galvin on front)
178-1 Bob Gamble (batting)
178-2 Bob Gamble (pitching, right hand thigh high)
178-3 Bob Gamble (pitching, right hand chin high)
179-1aCharlie Ganzel (fielding, hands thigh-high, Detroits)
179-1bCharlie Ganzel (fielding, hands thigh-high, Bostons)
179-2aCharlie Ganzel (fielding, hands shoulder high, Detroits)
179-2cCharlie Ganzel (fielding, hands shoulder high, Bostons)
179-3aCharlie Ganzel (batting, name correct)
179-3bCharlie Gauzel (Ganzel) (batting, name incorrect)
180-1 Gid Gardner (fielding low ball)
180-2 Gid Gardner (batting)
180-3 Gid Gardner (throwing)
180-4 Gid Gardner (fielding, hands above head)
180-5 Gid Gardner, Miah Murray (Gardner tagging Murray)
181-1 Hank Gastreich (Gastright) (bat at ready position well clear of cap)
181-2 Hank Gastreich (Gastright) (bat at ready position partly behind cap)
181-3 Hank Gastreich (Gastright) (ready to pitch, hands at neck)
181-4 Hank Gastreich (Gastright) (pitching, left hand off picture)
181-5 Hank Gastreich (Gastright) (pitching, left hand by left thigh)
182-1 Emil Geiss (bat in hand at side)
182-2 Emil Geiss (ready to pitch, hands above waist)
182-3 Emil Geiss (batting)
182-4 Emil Geiss (pitching, right hand shoulder high)
182-5 Emil Geiss (pitching, right hand chin-high)
182-6 Emil Geiss (portrait)
183-1aFrenchy Genins (fielding, hands cupped neck-high, name correct)
183-1bFrenchy Genius (Genins) (fielding, hands cupped neck-high, name incorrect)
183-2aFrenchy Genins (fielding, hands with fingers touching neck-high, name correct)
183-2bFrenchy Genius (Genins) (fielding, hands with fingers touching neck-high, name incorrect)
183-3 Frenchy Genius (Genins) (fielding, hands with fingers touching on chest)
183-4 Frenchy Genins (batting, looking at camera)
183-5 Frenchy Genius (Genins) (batting, looking at ball near bat)
184-1aBill George (pitching, left hand forward, head-high, N.Y's)
184-1bBill George (pitching, left hand forward, head-high, New Yorks)
184-2aBill George (batting, N.Y's)
184-2bBill George (batting, New Yorks)
184-3aBill George (sliding, N.Y's)
184-3bBill George (sliding, New Yorks)
184-4aBill George (pitching, left hand head-high, N.Y's)
184-4bBill George (pitching, left hand head-high, New Yorks)
184-5aBill George (pitching, hands chest-high, N.Y's)
184-5bBill George (pitching, hands chest-high, New Yorks)
184-6 Bill George (bat in hand at side)
185-1 Joe Gerhardt (hands on thighs)
185-2aJoe Gerhardt (throwing, no position)
185-2bJoe Gerhardt (throwing, 1st B.)
185-3 Joe Gerhardt (fielding)
185-4aJoe Gerhardt (tagging player, 2nd B.)
185-4bJoe Gerhardt (tagging player, 1st B.)
186-1aCharlie Getzein (batting, Indianapolis)
186-1bCharlie Getzein (batting, Detroits)
186-2 Charlie Getzein (pitching, hands above waist)
186-3aCharlie Getzein (pitching, right hand chin high at side, comma after P., Indianapolis)
186-3bCharlie Getzein (pitching, right hand chin high at side, no comma after P., Indianapolis)
186-3cCharlie Getzein (pitching, right hand chin high at side, Detroits)
186-4aCharlie Getzein (end of pitch, right hand forward neck-high, Detroit)
186-4bCharlie Getzein (end of pitch, right hand forward neck-high, Indianapolis)
187-1 Bobby Gilks (bat at ready position, nearly vertical)
187-2 Bobby Gilks (bat at ready position, nearly horizontal)
187-3 Bobby Gilks (bat at ready position, at about 45 degrees)
187-4aBobby Gilks (pitching, hands at neck, Cleveland's)
187-4bBobby Gilks (pitching, hands at neck, Clevelands)
187-5aBobby Gilks (pitching, right hand at back waist-high, Cleveland's)
187-5bBobby Gilks (pitching, right hand at back waist-high, Clevelands)
187-6 Bobby Gilks (pitching, right hand forward chest-high)
188-1 Pete Gillespie (right hand on hip, left arm at side)
188-2 Pete Gillespie (batting)
188-3 Pete Gillespie (fielding)
188-4 Pete Gillespie (throwing)
188-5 Pete Gillespie (moving to left)
189-1aBarney Gilligan (fielding ball thign-high, C.)
189-1bBarney Gilligan (fielding ball thigh-high, Catcher)
189-2aBarney Gilligan (hands on thighs, C., Washington)
189-2bBarney Gilligan (hands on thighs, Catcher)
189-2cBarney Gilligan (hands on thighs, C., Detroit)
190-1 Frank Gilmore (batting, feet apart)
190-2 Frank Gilmore (batting, right foot behind left foot)
190-3 Frank Gilmore (ball in hands above head)
190-4 Frank Gilmore (ball touching right hand above head)
190-5 Frank Gilmore (pitching)
191-1aPebbly Jack Glasscock (throwing, S.S., Indianapolis)
191-1bPebbly Jack Glassock (Glasscock) (throwing)
191-1cPebbly Jack Glasscock (throwing, s.s.)
191-1dPebbly Jack Glasscock (throwing, S.S., Indpls)
191-1ePebbly Jack Glasscock (throwing, S.S., New York (NL))
191-2aPebbly Jack Glasscock (hands on knees, S.S., Indianapolis)
191-2bPebbly Jack Glassock (Glasscock) (hands on knees)
191-2cPebbly Jack Glasscock (hands on knees, S.S., Indpls)
191-3aPebbly Jack Glasscock (batting)
191-3bPebbly Jack Glassock (Glasscock) (batting)
191-3cPebbly Jack Glass Cock (Glasscock) (batting)
191-4aPebbly Jack Glasscock (bat in hand at side, s.s.)
191-4bPebbly Jack Glasscock (bat in hand at side, S.S., Indpls)
191-4cPebbly Jack Glassock (Glasscock) (bat in hand at side, name correct, S.S., Indianapolis)
191-4dPebbly Jack Glassock (Glasscock) (bat in hand at side, S.S. Indianapoli)
191-4ePebbly Jack Glasscock (bat in hand at side, name correct, S.S., Indianapolis)
192-1aKid Gleason (fielding grounder, Phila)
192-1bKid Gleason (fielding grounder, Philadelphias)
192-2aKid Gleason (bat at ready position over shoulder, Phila)
192-2bKid Gleason (bat at ready position over shoulder, Philadelphias)
192-3aKid Gleason (bat horizontal, Phila)
192-3bKid Gleason (bat horizontal, Philadelphias)
192-3cKid Gleason (bat horizontal, Phil'a (NL))
192-4 Kid Gleason (pitching, hands at neck, Philadelphias)
192-5 Kid Gleason (pitching, right hand forward head-high, Phila)
193-1 Will Gleason (Brown's Champions)
193-2aWill Gleason (batting, no comma after S.S., Athletics)
193-2bWill Gleason (batting, comma after S.S., Athletics)
193-3aWill Gleason (hands on knees, no comma after S.S., Athletics)
193-3bWill Gleason (hands on knees, comma after S.S., Athletics)
193-4aWill Gleason (leaning to right, hands thigh high, no comma after S.S., Athletics)
193-4bWill Gleason (leaning to right, hands thigh high, comma after S.S., Athletics)
193-5 Will Gleason (stooping, hands clasped hip high, Louisvilles)
194-1 Mouse Glenn (batting, looking at camera)
194-2 Mouse Glenn (batting, looking at ball)
194-3 Mouse Glenn (fielding, hands neck-high, comma after L.F.)
194-4 Mouse Glenn (fielding, hands thigh-high)
194-5 Mouse Glenn (fielding, hands chin-high)
195-1aMike Goodfellow (bat at ready position by head, Cleveland's)
195-1bMike Goodfellow (bat at ready position by head, Detroits)
195-2 Mike Goodfellow (bat at ready position, nearly horizontal)
195-3aMike Goodfellow (fielding, hands chest high, Cleveland's)
195-3bMike Goodfellow (fielding, hands chest high, Detroits)
195-4aMike Goodfellow (fielding, hands waist high, Clevelands)
195-4bMike Goodfellow (fielding, hands waist high, Detroits)
195-5aMike Goodfellow (throwing, Cleveland's)
195-5bMike Goodfellow (throwing, Detroits)
196-1aPiano Legs Gore (fielding gorunder, facing to right, N.Y's)
196-1bGeorge Gore (fielding grounder, facing to right, New York)
196-1cGeorge Gore (fielding grounder, facing to right, New York's)
196-2 George Gore (throwing, right hand head high)
196-3aGeorge Gore (sliding, N.Y's)
196-3bGeorge Gore (sliding, New Yorks)
196-4aGeorge Gore (bat in hand at side, N.Y's)
196-4bGeorge Gore (bat in hand at side, New Yorks)
196-4cGeorge Gore (bat in hand at side, New York)
196-5aGeorge Gore (bat nearly horizontal, N.Y'
196-5bGeorge Gore (bat nearly horizontal, New Yorks)
196-6 George Gore (fielding, hands above head)
196-7 George Gore (bat at ready position over shoulder)
196-8 George Gore (fielding low ball, facing front)
196-9 George Gore (throwing, right hand forward, left hand on hip)
197-1 Frank Graves (in mask, hands on knees)
197-2 Frank Graves (in mask, fielding, hands by right shoulder)
197-3 Frank Graves (fielding grounder)
197-4 Frank Graves (batting)
197-5 Frank Graves (throwing, hands waist high)
197-6 Frank Graves (fielding, hands cap-high)
198-1 Bill Greenwood (sliding)
198-2aBill Greenwood (batting, looking at camera, Baltimores)
198-2bBill Greenwood (batting, looking at camera, Columbus)
198-3aBill Greenwood (batting, looking at ball, Baltimores)
198-3bBill Greenwood (batting, looking at ball, Columbus)
198-4aBill Greenwood (throwing, Baltimores)
198-4bBill Greenwood (throwing, Columbus)
198-5 Bill Greenwood (hands on knees)
199-1 Ed Greer (bat at ready position by head)
199-2 Ed Greer (throwing)
199-3 Ed Greer (bat at ready position, nearly horizontal)
199-4 Ed Greer, Hardie Henderson (Greer catching and Henderson batting) (same card as 222-10)
200-1 Mike Griffin (sliding)
200-2 Mike Griffin (batting)
200-3 Mike Griffin (fielding)
200-4aMike Griffin (throwing, Baltimores)
200-4bMike Griffin (throwing, Philadelphias (PL))
200-5 Mike Griffin (arms folded)
201-1aClark Griffith (batting, looking at camera, Milwaukees)
201-1bClark Griffith (batting, looking at camera, Milwaukeee)
201-2 Clark Griffith (batting, looking at ball)

201-3 Clark Griffith (pitching, hands at chest)
201-4 Clark Griffith (pitching, hands at neck)
201-5 Clark Griffith (pitching, right hand head high)
202-1 Henry Gruber (batting)
202-2aHenry Gruber (pitching, hands at chest, Cleveland)
202-2bHenry Gruber (pitching, hands at chest, Clevelands)
202-3aHenry Gruber (pitching, right hand chin high, left hand just clear of left thigh, Clevelands)
202-3bHenry Gruber (pitching, right hand chin high, left hand just clear of left thigh, Cleveland)
202-4aHenry Gruber (pitching, right hand cap high, left hand on left thigh, Clevelands)
202-4bHenry Gruber (pitching, right hand cap high, left hand on left thigh, Cleveland)
202-5 Henry Gruber (bat in hand at side)
203-1 Ad Gumbert (batting)
203-2 Ad Gumbert (pitching, right hand level with eyes)
203-3 Ad Gumbert (pitching, right hand waist high)
203-4 Ad Gumbert (pitching, right hand level with chin)
204-1aTom Gunning (fielding low ball on left, Phila)
204-1bTom Gunning (fielding low ball on left, Philadelphia)
204-1cTom Gunning (fielding low ball on left, Athletics)
204-2aTom Gunning (bending forward, hands by right knee, Phila)
204-2bTom Gunning (bending forward, hands by right knee, Philadelphia)
204-2cTom Gunning (bending forward, hands by right knee, Athletics)
205-1 Joe Gunson (bat in hand at side)
205-2 Joe Gunson (fielding, hands by left shoulder)
205-3 Joe Gunson (throwing, right hand head high, no cap)
205-4 Joe Gunson (in jacket, gloves in right hand at side)
206-1aGentleman George Haddock (pitching, hands at chest, Washington)
206-1bGentleman George Haddock (pitching, hands at chest, Washingtons)
206-2 Gentleman George Haddock (pitching, hands neck-high)
206-3 Gentleman George Haddock (pitching, hands waist-high)
206-4 Gentleman George Haddock (end of pitch, right hand chin-high)
206-5 Gentleman George Haddock (batting)
207-1 Bill Hafner (Hoffner) (batting)
207-2 Bill Hafner (Hoffner) (pitching, hands by chin)
207-3 Bill Hafner (Hoffner) (pitching, hands above head)
207-4 Bill Hafner (Hoffner) (pitching, right hand neck-high)
207-5 Bill Hafner (Hoffner) (end of pitch, right hand shoulder-high)
208-1 Willie Hahm - mascot, Ned Williamson (card same as 502-7)
209-1 Bill Hallman (bat on shoulder)
209-2aBill Hallman (throwing, right hand head high, Philadelphia)
209-2bBill Hallman (throwing, right hand head high, Philadelphias)
209-3aBill Hallman (fielding, hands chest-high, Philadelphia)
209-3bBill Hallman (fielding, hands chest-high, Philadelphias)
209-4 Bill Hallman (leaning to left, about to catch ball chest-high)
209-5aBill Hallman (bat horizontal, Philadelphias PL)
209-5bBill Hallman (bat horizontal, Phila)
210-1 Sliding Billy Hamilton (batting, looking at camera)
210-2aSliding Billy Hamilton (batting, looking up at ball, Kansas Citys)
210-2cSliding Billy Hamilton (batting, looking up at ball, K.Cs)
210-3 Sliding Billy Hamilton (fielding grounder)
210-4aSliding Billy Hamilton (fielding, hands above waist, Kansas Citys)
210-4bSliding Billy Hamilton (fielding, hands above waist, Philadelphia N.L.)
210-5aSliding Billy Hamilton (fielding, hands neck high, Kansas Citys)
210-5bSliding Billy Hamilton (fielding, hands neck high, Philadelphia N.L.)
211-1 Frank Hankinson (dotted tie)
212-1aNed Hanlon (bat in hand at side, Detroits)
212-1bNed Hanlon (bat in hand at side, Bostons)
212-2aNed Hanlon (batting, Detroits)
212-2bNed Hanlon (batting, Pittsburgs)
212-3aNed Hanlon (fielding, Detroits)
212-3bNed Hanlon (fielding, Pittsburghs)
213-1 William Hanrahan (squatting on bat)
213-2 William Hanrahan (fielding grounder)
213-3aWilliam Hanrahan (hands on knees, Chicago Maroons)
213-3bWilliam Hanrahan (hands on knees, Minneap'l's)
213-4aWilliam Hanrahan (bat in hand at side, Chicago Maroons)
213-4bWilliam Hanrahan (bat in hand at side, Minneap'l's)
213-5aWilliam Hanrahan (fielding, hands head high, Chicago Maroons)
213-5bWilliam Hanrahan (fielding, hands head high, Minneapolis) 65.00
213-5cWilliam Hanrahan (fielding, hands head high, Minneap'l's) 65.00
213-6 William Hanrahan (leaning left, right hand thigh-high, left arm at back)
213.5 Hapeman (ball in right hand above waist)
214-1 Pa Harkins (light uniform, bat at ready position)
214-2aPa Harkins (light uniform, fielding, hands above waist, Brooklyn)
214-2bPa Harkens (Harkins) (light uniform, fielding, hands above waist, name incorrect, Baltimore)
214-2cPa Harkins (light uniform, fielding, hands above waist, name correct, Baltimore)
214-3 Pa Harkins (light uniform, throwing, right hand head-high)
214-4 Pa Harkins (dark uniform, bat on shoulder)
214-5 Pa Harkins (dark uniform, bat at ready position at 60 degrees)
214-6 Pa Harkins (dark uniform, hands at chest)
214-7 Pa Harkins (dark uniform, ball in right hand at back)
214-8 Pa Harkins (dark uniform, ball in right hand extended forward chin-high)
215-1 Bill Hart (pitching, hands at chest)
215-2 Bill Hart (pitching, hands above head, on ground)
215-3aBill Hart (pitching, hands above head, left foot off ground, Cincinnati)
215-3bBill Hart (pitching, hands above head, left foot off ground, Des Moines)
215-4 Bill Hart (ready to pitch, right hand by head, left arm at side)
216-1 Bill Hasamdear (Hassamaer) (fielding, hands head-high)
216-2 Bill Hasamdear (Hassamaer) (fielding, hands thigh-high)
216-3 Bill Hasamdear (Hassamaer) (throwing)
217-1aGill Hatfield (bat over right shoulder behind head, New Yorks)
217-1bGill Hatfield (bat over right shoulder behind head, N.Y.)
217-2 Gill Hatfield (bat at ready position, nearly vertical)
217-4aGill Hatfield (fielding, hands chest-high, looking at ball neck-high, New Yorks)
217-4bGill Hatfield (fielding, hands chest-high, looking at ball neck-high, N.Y.)
217-5aGill Hatfield (fielding, hands cupped chest high, looking upwards, New Yorks)
217-5bGill Hatfield (fielding, hands cupped chest high, looking upwards, N.Y.)
217-6aGill Hatfield (fielding, hands by right knee, New Yorks)
217-6bGill Hatfield (fielding, hands by right knee, N.Y.)
217-6cGill Hatfield (fielding, hands by right knee, New York (P.L.))
218-1aEgyptian Healey (Healy) (dark cap, pitching, P., Indianapolis)
218-1bEgyptian Healey (Healy) (dark cap, pitching, Pitcher, Indianapolis)
218-1cEgyptian Healey (Healy) (dark cap, pitching, P., Washingtons)
218-2aEgyptian Healey (Healy) (dark cap, batting, P., Indianapolis)
218-2bEgyptian Healey (Healy) (dark cap, batting, Pitcher, Indianapolis)
218-2cEgyptian Healey (Healy) (dark cap, batting, P., Washingtons)
219-1aHealey (Healy) (ringed cap, pitching, hands above head, Omaha)
219-1bHealy (ringed cap, pitching, hands above head, name correct, Washingtons)
219-1cHealy (ringed cap, pitching, hands above head, name correct, Denvers)
219-2aHealey (Healy) (ringed cap, pitching, right hand head-high, name incorrect, Omaha)
219-2bHealy (ringed cap, pitching, right hand head-high, name correct, Washingtons)
219-3 Healy (plain white cap, moustache, pitching, hands neck high, Washingtons)
219-4 Healy (portrait, looking to left, no cap, Washingtons)
220-1aGuy Hecker (batting, Louisvilles)
220-1bGuy Hecker (batting, Louisville)
220-2aGuy Hecker (ball in hands on chest, feet wide apart, Louisvilles)
220-2bGuy Hecker (ball in hands on chest, feet wide apart, Louisville)
220-3 Guy Hecker (right hand extended at side chest-high)
220-4aGuy Hecker (right hand extended forward, Louisvilles)
220-4bGuy Hecker (right hand extended forward, Louisville)
220-5 Guy Hecker (ball in hands on chest, right foot behind left foot)
221-1 Tony Hellman (batting, looking at camera)
221-2 Tony Hellman (batting, looking at ball)
221-3 Tony Hellman (fielding, hands thigh-high, ball by face)
221-4 Tony Hellman (fielding, hands thigh-high, ball by right wrist)
221-5 Tony Hellman (fielding, hands chin-high)
222-1 Hardie Henderson (white cap, bat over shoulder)
222-2 Hardie Henderson (white cap, throwing, right hand head-high)
222-3aHardie Henderson (white cap, hands at chest, Brooklyn)
222-3bHardie Henderson (white cap, hands at chest, Pitts)
222-4 Hardie Henderson (white cap, pitching, right hand raised)
222-5 Hardie Henderson (dark cap, bat at ready position at 30 degrees)
222-6 Hardie Henderson (no cap, batting, ball by bat)
222-7 Hardie Henderson (dark cap, throwing, right hand head-high)
222-8 Hardie Henderson (dark cap, hands at waist)
222-9 Hardie Henderson (dark cap, pitching, left arm across neck)
222-10Ed Greer, Hardie Henderson (Greer catching and Henderson batting) (card same as 199-4)
223-1aMoxie Hengle (sliding, Minneapolis)
223-1bMoxie Hengle (sliding, Chicago Maroons)
223-2aMoxie Hengle (batting, Minneapolis)
223-2bMoxie Hengle (batting, Chicago Maroons)
223-3aMoxie Hengle (hands on knees, Minneapolis)
223-3bMoxie Hengle (hands on knees, Chicago Maroons)
223-4 Moxie Hengle (fielding)
223-5aMoxie Hengle (bat in hand at side Minneapolis)
223-5bMoxie Hengle (bat in hand at side, Chicago Maroons)
223-6 Moxie Hengle (leaning right, right hand pointing at camera, ball in left hand)
224-1 John Henry (bat over shoulder)
224-2 John Henry (batting)
224-3 John Henry (fielding)
224-4 John Henry (throwing)
224-5 John Henry (pitching)
225-1aEd Herr (bat over shoulder, St. Louis White)
225-1bEd Herr (bat over shoulder, looking front, J. Herr on front, Milwaukees)
225-1cEd Herr (bat over shoulder, looking front, Herr on front, Milwaukees)
225-2 Ed Herr (batting, looking at ball chin-high)
225-3 Ed Herr (fielding grounder)
225-4aEd Herr (bat in hand at side, St. Louis Whites)
225-4bEd Herr (bat in hand at side, Milwaukees)
225-5 Ed Herr (ball in hands by neck)
226-1 Hunkey Hines (fielding, hands knee-high, St. Louis Whites)
226-2 Hunkey Hines (bat on shoulder, St. Louis Whites)
226-3 Hunkey Hines (fielding, hands head-high, St. Louis Whites)
226-4 Hunkey Hines (bat in hand at side, St. Louis Whites)
227-1aPaul Hines (batting, C.F., Washington)
227-1bPaul Hines (batting, Centre Field. Washington)
227-1cPaul Hines (batting, C.F., Indianapolis)
227-2aPaul Hines (arms at sides, C.F., Washington)
227-2bPaul Hines (arms at sides, Centre Field, Washington)
227-3aPaul Hines (arms folded, C.F., Washington)
227-3bPaul Hines (arms folded, Centre Field,)
227-3cPaul Hines (arms folded, L.F., Indianapolis)
227-4aPaul Hines (fielding, C.F., Washington)
227-4bPaul Hines (fielding, Centre Field, Washington)
227-4cPaul Hines (fielding, C.F., Indianapolis)
228-1 Texas Wonder Hoffman (pitching, hands chest-high on left)

228-2 Texas Wonder Hoffman (pitching, hands head-high)
228-3 Texas Wonder Hoffman (pitching, right hand head-high)
228-4 Texas Wonder Hoffman (end of pitch, right hand forward head-high)
229-1 Eddie Hogan (batting, looking at camera)
229-2 Eddie Hogan (batting, looking right)
229-3 Eddie Hogan (fielding grounder)
229-4 Eddie Hogan (fielding, hands head-high)
229-5 Eddie Hogan (throwing)
230-1 Bill Holbert (dotted tie)
230-2aBill Holbert (batting, Brooklyns)
230-2bBill Holbert (batting, Mets)
230-3 Bill Holbert (throwing)
230-4 Bill Holbert (fielding, ball by left shoulder)
230-5aBill Holbert (fielding, hands cupped chin high, Brooklyns)
230-5bBill Holbert (fielding, hands cupped chin high, Mets)
230-6aBill Holbert (in mask, no comma after C., Brooklyns)
230-6bBill Holbert (in mask, comma after C., Brooklyns)
230-6cBill Holbert (in mask, Mets)
230-6dBill Holbert (in mask, Jersey Citys)
231-1 Bug Holliday (Halliday) (hands at back)
231-2aBug Holliday (Halliday) (arms at sides, Des Moines)
231-2bBug Holliday (Halliday) (arms at sides, Cincinnatis)
231-2cBug Holliday (arms at sides, Holliday on front)
231-2dBug Holliday (arms at sides, W. Holliday on front)
231-3aBug Holliday (hands crossed below waist on bat, name correct)
231-3bBug Halliday (Holliday) (hands crossed below waist on bat, name incorrect)
231-4aBug Halliday (Holliday) (batting, name incorrect)
231-4bBug Holliday (batting, name correct)
231-5 Bug Halliday (Holliday) (ball in hands by left shoulder)
231-6 Bug Halliday (Holliday) (fielding, hands at waist)
232-1aCharles Hoover (hands on thighs, Chicago)
232-1bCharles Hoover (hands on thighs, Kansas City)
232-2aCharles Hoover (kneeling to field low ball, Hoover on front, Chicago)
232-2bCharles Hoover (kneeling to field low ball, C.E. Hoover on front, Chicago)
232-2dCharles Hoover (kneeling to field low ball, C.E. Hoover on front, Kansas Citys)
232-3 Charles Hoover (batting, Chicago)
232-4 Charles Hoover (throwing,
232-5 Charles Hoover (ball in hands chin-high, Chicago)
233-1 Buster Hoover (batting, Philadelphia)
233-2 Buster Hoover (fielding, hands head-high, Philadelphia)
233-3 Buster Hoover (fielding, hands thigh-high, Philadelphia)
233-4 Buster Hoover (throwing, Philadelphia)
234-1aJack Horner (ball in hand, name correct)
234-1bJack Hodner (Horner) (ball in hand, name incorrect)
234-2aJack Horner (fielding, hands neck-high, Milwaukee)
234-2bJack Horner (fielding, hands neck-high, New Havens)
234-3 Jack Horner, E.H. Warner
234-4 Jack Horner (bat in hand at side)
235-1aJoe Horning (Hornung) (bat at ready position, nearly horizontal, Horning on front, L.F.)
235-1bJoe Horning (Hornung) (bat at ready position, nearly horizontal, Horning on front, Left Field)
235-1cJoe Horning (Hornung) (bat at ready position, nearly horizontal, Joe Horning on front, L.F.)
235-1dJoe Hornung (bat at ready position, nearly horizontal, Joe Hornung on front, L.F.)
235-2aJoe Horning (Hornung) (throwing, Horning on front, L.F.)
235-2bJoe Horning (Hornung) (throwing, Horning on front, Left Field)
235-2cJoe Horning (Hornung) (throwing, Joe Horning on front, L.F.)
235-2dJoe Hornung (throwing, Hornung on front L.F.)
235-3aJoe Horning (Hornung) (ball in hands neck high, L.F.)
235-3bJoe Horning (Hornung) (ball in hands neck high, Left Field)
235-4aJoe Horning (Hornung) (bat in hand at side, Horning on front, L.F.)
235-4bJoe Horning (Hornung) (bat in hand at side, Horning on front, Left Field)
235-4cJoe Horning (Hornung) (bat in hand at side, Joe Horning on front, L.F.)
235-5aJoe Horning (Hornung) (bat at ready position at 60 degrees, Horning on front, L.F.)
235-5bJoe Horning (Hornung) (bat at ready position at 60 degrees, Horning on front, Left Field)
235-5dJoe Hornung (bat at ready position at 60 degrees, Hornung on front, L.F.)
235-6aJoe Horning (Hornung) (leaning to left, hands thigh-high, Horning on front, L.F.)
235-6bJoe Horning (Hornung) (leaning to left, hands thigh-high, Horning on front, Left Field)
235-6cJoe Horning (Hornung) (leaning to left, hands thigh-high, Joe Horning on front, L.F.)
235-6dJoe Hornung (leaning to left, hands thigh high, Joe Hornung on front, L.F.)
235-6eJoe Hornung (leaning to left, hands thigh high, Hornung on front, L.F.)
236-1 Pete Hotaling (batting)
236-2 Pete Hotaling (right hand across waist, left hand at back)
236-3 Pete Hotoling (Hotaling) (stooping to left, hands thigh-high)
236-4 Pete Hotoling (Hotaling) (throwing)
237-1aBill Howes (Hawes) (fielding, hands neck high, looking up, Minneapolis)
237-1bBill Hawes (fielding, hands neck-high, looking up, St. Pauls)
237-2 Bill Howes (Hawes) (fielding, hands neck high, looking at approaching ball)
237-3 Bill Howes (Hawes) (fielding ball by right foot)
237-4 Bill Howes (Hawes) (ball in hands, thigh high on left)
237-5 Bill Howes (Hawes) (ball near hands by right knee)
237-6 Bill Howes (Hawes) (batting)
238-1aDummy Hoy (bat in hand at side, Washington)
238-1bDummy Hoy (bat in hand at side, Washingtons)
238-2aDummy Hoy (batting, no comma after C.F., Washington)
238-2bDummy Hoy (batting, comma after C.F., Washington)
238-2cDummy Hoy (batting, C.F., Washingtons)
238-3 Dummy Hoy (fielding grounder)
238-4aDummy Hoy (throwing, Washington)
238-4bDummy Hoy (throwing, Washingtons)
238-5 Dummy Hoy (fielding, hands neck-high)
239-1 Nat Hudson (Brown's Champions)
239-2aNat Hudson (batting, St. Louis)
239-2bNat Hudson (batting, St. Louis Browns)
239-3 Nat Hudson (pitching, hands at waist)
239-4aNat Hudson (pitching, hands chest-high, St. Louis)
239-4bNat Hudson (pitching, hands chest-high, St. Louis Browns)
239-5aNat Hudson (pitching, right hand waist high, N. Hudson on front, St. Louis Browns)
239-5cNat Hudson (pitching, right hand waist high, Hudson on front, St. Louis Browns)
239-5dNat Hudson (pitching, right hand waist high, St. Louis)
239-6aNat Hudson (pitching, right hand head high, no comma after P., St. Louis Browns)
239-6bNat Hudson (pitching, right hand head high, comma after P., St. Louis Browns)
239-6cNat Hudson (pitching, right hand head high, St. Louis)
240-2 Mickey Hughes (bat at ready position over shoulder)
240-3 Mickey Hughes (bat at ready position at about 30 degrees)
240-4 Mickey Hughes (fielding, hands chest high)
240-5 Mickey Hughes (pitching, hands shoulder high)
240-6 Mickey Hughes (pitching, ball in right hand chest-high)
240-7 Mickey Hughes (pitching, ball in right hand at side)
240-8 Mickey Hughes (pitching, right hand forward head-high)
241-1aHungler (batting, Sioux City)
241-1bHungler (batting, Sioux Citys)
241-2 Hungler (pitching, hands chin-high close to body)
241-3 Hungler (pitching, hands chest-high well away from body)
241-4 Hungler (pitching, right hand forward chin-high)
242-1 Wild Bill Hutchinson (ball in right hand above head, right heel visible behind left leg)
242-2 Wild Bill Hutchinson (ball in right hand above head, right heel concealed behind left leg)
242-3aWild Bill Hutchinson (batting, Chic.)
242-3cWild Bill Hutchinson (batting, Chicago's)
242-4 Wild Bill Hutchinson (pitching)
243-1 John Irwin (hands on knees, Washington)
243-2 John Irwin (batting, Washington)
243-3 John Irwin (throwing, Washington)
243-4 John Irwin (fielding, Washington)
244-1 Cutrate Irwin (portrait, looking to left, Philadelphias)
244-2 Cutrate Irwin (portrait, looking to right, Philadelphias)
244-3aCutrate Irwin (fielding, hands cupped chest-high, Phila)
244-3bCutrate Irwin (fielding, hands cupped chest-high, Philadelphia)
244-3cCutrate Irwin (fielding, hands cupped chest-high, Philadelphias)
244-4aCutrate Irwin (batting, Phila)
244-4bCutrate Irwin (batting, Philadelphia)
244-4cCutrate Irwin (batting, Philadelphias)
244-4dCutrate Irwin (batting, Washingtons)
244-5aCutrate Irwin (throwing, Phila)
244-5bCutrate Irwin (throwing, Philadelphia)
244-5cCutrate Irwin (throwing, Philadelphias)
244-6aCutrate Irwin (fielding grounder, hands between knees, Phila)
244-6bCutrate Irwin (fielding grounder, hands between knees, Philadelphia)
244-6cCutrate Irwin (fielding grounder, hands between knees, Philadelphias)
244-7 Cutrate Irwin (stooping right to field ball by left foot)
244-8 Cutrate Irwin (bat on left shoulder, heels together)
244-9 Cutrate Irwin (bat horizontal, ball not visible)
244-10aCutrate Irwin (fielding, hands above head, Philadelphias)
244-10bCutrate Irwin (fielding, hands above head, Bostons (P.L.))
244-11Cutrate Irwin (doffing cap)
245-1 A.C. Jantzen (batting, looking at camera)
245-2 A.C. Jantzen (batting, looking at ball)
245-3 A.C. Jantzen (fielding, hands at right knee)
245-4 A.C. Jantzen (fielding, hands chest-high)
245-5 A.C. Jantzen (fielding, hands head-high)
246-1 Frederick Jevne (sliding)
246-2 Frederick Jevne (bat in hand at side)
246-3 Frederick Jevne (fielding, hands above head)
246-4 Frederick Jevne (fielding low ball)
246-5 Frederick Jevne (batting)
247-1 Spud Johnson (hands inside tunic above waist)
247-2aSpud Johnson (fielding, hands head-high, Columbus)
247-2bSpud Johnson (fielding, hands head-high, Kansas City)
247-4 Spud Johnson (throwing)
247-5 Spud Johnson (fielding, hands waist-high)
248-1aDick Johnston (fielding, hands by right thigh, Johnston on front, C.F.)
248-1bDick Johnston (fielding, hands by right thigh, Johnston on front, Centre Field)
248-1cDick Johnston (fielding, hands by right thigh, R.F. Johnston on front, C.F.)
248-2aDick Johnston (batting, looking at ball, Johnston on front, C.F.)
248-2bDick Johnston (batting, looking at ball, Johnston on front, Centre Field)
248-2cDick Johnston (batting, looking at ball, R.F. Johnston on front, C.F.)
248-3aDick Johnston (batting, looking at camera, C.F., Boston)
248-3bDick Johnston (batting, looking at camera, Centre Field)
248-3cDick Johnston (batting, looking camera, C.F., Bostons)
248-4aDick Johnston (hands on hips, C.F., Boston)
248-4bDick Johnston (hands on hips, Centre Field, Boston)
248-4cDick Johnston (hands on hips, C.F., Bostons)
248-4dDick Johnston (hands on hips, C.F., Bostons (PL))
248-5aDick Johnston (throwing, C.F.)
248-5bDick Johnston (throwing, Centre Field)
248-5cDick Johnston (throwing, C.F.)
248-6aDick Johnston (fielding, hands neck-high, C.F.)
248-6bDick Johnston (fielding, hands neck-high, Centre Field)

249-1 Jordan (bat over shoulder, ball in hand)

249-2 Jordan (throwing)
249-3 Jordan (fielding, in mask)
249-4 Jordan (fielding, no mask)
249-5 Jordan (batting)
250-1aHeinie Kappell (Kappel) (fielding grounder, Columbus)
250-1bHeinie Kappell (Kappel) (fielding grounder, Cincinnati)
250-2aHeinie Kappell (Kappel) (fielding, hands knee-high, Columbus)
250-2bHeinie Kappell (Kappel) (fielding, hands knee-high, Cincinnati)
250-3aHeinie Kappell (Kappel) (fielding, hands above head, Columbus)
250-3bHeinie Kappell (Kappel) (fielding, hands above head, Cincinnati)
250-4 Heinie Kappell (Kappel) (throwing)

250-5 Heinie Kappell (Kappel) (batting)
251-1aTim Keefe (pitching, hands at chest, N.Y's)
251-1bJim Keefe (Tim) (pitching, hands at chest, name incorrect, New Yorks)
251-1cTim Keefe (pitching, hands at chest, name correct, New Yorks)
251-2aTim Keefe (pitching, right hand at back waist-high, N.Y's)
251-2bJim Keefe (Tim) (pitching, right hand at back waist-high, Jim Keefe on front, New Yorks)
251-2cTim Keefe (pitching, right hand at back waist-high, Keefe on front, New Yorks)

251-2dTim Keef (Keefe) (pitching, right hand at back waist-high, Keef on front, New Yorks)

251-3aTim Keefe (pitching, right hand forward head-high, N.Y's)
251-3bTim Keefep (Keefe) (pitching, right hand forward head-high, New Yorks)
251-4aTim Keefe (bat nearly horizontal, N.Y's)

251-4bTim Keefe (bat nearly horizontal, name correct, New Yorks)
251-4cTim Keef (Keefe) (bat nearly horizontal, name incorrect, New Yorks)
251-5aTim Keefe (pitching, right hand held out waist-high, N.Y's)
251-5bTim Keefe (pitching, right hand held out waist-high, New Yorks)
251-6 Tim Keefe (bat at ready position, nearly vertical, N.Y's)
251-7aTim Keefe (pitching, hands above waist, N.Y's)
251-7bTim Keefe (pitching, hands above waist, New Yorks)
251-8aTim Keefe, Danny Richardson (Keefe tagging Richardson, caption reads "Keefe")

251-8bTim Keefe, Danny Richardson (Keefe tagging Richardson, caption reads "Keefe and Richardson Stealing 2d")
251-8cTim Keefe, Danny Richardson (Keefe tagging Richardson, caption reads "Keefe & Richardson")
251-9 Tim Keefe, Danny Richardson (Keefe fielding ball, Richardson sliding to base)

252-1 George Keefe (batting, Washington)

252-2aGeorge Keefe (pitching, hands at chest, looking to front, Washington)
252-2bGeorge Keefe (pitching, hands at chest, looking to front, Washingtons)
252-3 George Keefe (pitching, hands at chest, right profile,Washingtons)
252-4 George Keefe (pitching, hands above head, Washington) 65.00
252-5aGeorge Keefe (pitching, left hand forward head-high, Washington)
252-5bGeorge Keefe (pitching, left hand forward head-high, Washingtons)
253-1aJim Keenan (hands on knees, Cincinnatis)

253-1bJim Keenan (hands on knees, Cincinnati)

253-2aJim Keenan (fielding grounder, Cinncinnatti)
253-2bJim Keenan (fielding grounder, Cincinnati) 65.00
253-3aJim Keenan (batting, Cincinnatti)

253-3bJim Keenan (batting, Cincinnati)
253-4 Jim Keenan (fielding, hands chest-high)

253-5aJim Keenan (fielding, hands above head, Keenan on front)
253-5bJim Keenan (fielding, hands above head, J.M. Keenan on front)
254-1 King Kelly (portrait, in cap, "Chicago" on shirt)
254-2 King Kelly (portrait, bare head, "Chicago" on shirt)
254-3 King Kelly (portrait, bare head, "Boston" on shirt)
254-4 King Kelly (bat at ready position at 45 degrees, left-handed, $10,000 Kelly on front)

254-5aKing Kelly (bat at ready position at 45 degrees, right-handed, $10,000 Kelly on front)
254-5bKing Kelly (bat at ready position at 45 degrees, right-handed, Boston)
254-5cKing Kelly (bat at ready position at 45 degrees, right-handed, Bostons)
254-5dKing Kelly (bat at ready position at 45 degrees, right-handed, no position on front, Boston)
254-5eKing Kelly (bat at ready position at 45 degrees, right-handed, no position on front, Boston (PL))
254-6 King Kelly (bat at ready position, horizontal, right-handed, $10,000 Kelly on front)
254-7 King Kelly (bat in left hand at side, $10,000 Kelly on front)
254-8 King Kelly (bat on right shoulder, $10,000 Kelly on front)
254-9 King Kelly (fielding, hands chest-high, $10,000 Kelly on front)
254-10King Kelly (fielding, hands head-high, $10,000 Kelly on front)
255-1 Honest John Kelly (portrait, looking to left, Louisville)
255-2 Honest John Kelly (full length, coat over left arm. Louisville)
255-3aHonest John Kelly (umpire) (looking at approaching ball, Western Ass')
255-3bHonest John Kelly (umpire) (looking at approaching ball, Western Ass'n)
255-4 Honest John Kelly (umpire), Jim Powell (manager)
256 No World Index Listing
257-1 Charles Kelly (batting, hands close to body, Philadelphia)
257-2 Charles Kelly (batting, hands clear of body, Philadelphia)
257-3 Charles Kelly (fielding, hands head-high, Philadelphia)
257-4 Charles Kelly (fielding, hands thigh-high, Philadelphia)
257-5 Charles Kelly (throwing, Philadelphia)

258-1 Rudy Kemler (Kemmler) (portrait in striped cap)
258-2 Rudy Kemmler (batting)
259-1 Theodore Kennedy (batting)
259-2aTheodore Kennedy (bat in hand at side, Des Moines)
259-2bTheodore Kennedy (bat in hand at side, Omaha's)
259-3aTheodore Kennedy (fielding, Des Moines)

259-3bTheodore Kennedy (fielding, Omahas)

259-4aTheodore Kennedy (pitching, hands chest high, Des Moines)
259-4bTheodore Kennedy (pitching, hands chest high, Omahas)
259-5aTheodore Kennedy (pitching, right arm extended at side, Des Moines)
259-5bTheodore Kennedy (pitching, right arm extended at side, Omahas)
260-1aJ.J. Kenyon (batting, Des Moines)

260-1bJ.J. Kenyon (batting, St. Louis Whites)

260-2 J.J. Kenyon (bat in hand at side)
260-3aJ.J. Kenyon (fielding, hands chest-high, Des Moines)
260-3bJ.J. Kenyon (fielding, hands chest-high, St. Louis Whites)
260-4 J.J. Kenyon (in mask, hands on knees)

260-5 J.J. Kenyon (right hand in glove head high)
261-1aJohn Kerins (batting, Louisville)
261-1bJohn Kerins (batting, Louisvilles)
261-2aJohn Kerins (hands on thighs, Louisville)

261-2bJohn Kerins (hands on thighs, Louisvilles)

261-3 John Kerins (in mask, stooping, hands thigh-high)
261-4 John Kerins (fielding, kneeling, hands bv left knee)
261-5aJohn Kerins (fielding, hands chest-high. Louisville)
261-5bJohn Kerins (fielding, hands chest-high. Louisvilles)
262-1aMatt Kilroy (batting, Bostons (PL)

262-1bMatt Kilroy (batting, Baltimores)
262-2aMatt Kilroy (pitching, hand chest-high, Bostons)
262-2bMatt Kilroy (pitching, hand chest-high, Bostons (PL))
262-2cMatt Kilroy (pitching, hand chest-high, Baltimores)
262-3 Matt Kilroy (fielding, hands head-high)

262-4 Matt Kilroy (pitching, hands to left waist high)
262-5 Matt Kilroy (pitching, left hand head-high)

263-1 Silver King (pitching, hands chin-high)

263-2aSilver King (pitching, hands chest-high, no comma after P., St. Louis Browns)
263-2bSilver King (pitching, hands chest-high, comma after P., St. Louis Browns)
263-2cSilver King (pitching, hands chest-high, St. Louis)
263-2dSilver King (pitching, hands chest-high, Chicagos (PL))
264-1 August Kloff (Klopf) (pitching, right hand above head, arm bent)
264-2 August Kloff (Klopf) (pitching, ball leaving hand head-high)
264-3 August Kloff (Klopf) (hands at neck)

264-4aAugust Kloff (Klopf) (fielding, leaning to right, hands waist high, Minneapolis)

264-4bAugust Kloff (Klopf) (fielding, leaning to right, hands waist high, St. Joes)
264-5 August Kloff (Klopf) (batting)
264-6 August Kloff (Klopf) (pitching, right hand vertically above head, arm almost straight)

265-1 William Klusman (fielding, hands by right foot)
265-2aWilliam Klusman (batting, looking at camera, Denvers)
265-2bWilliam Klusman (batting, looking at camera, Milwaukee)
265-3aWilliam Klusman (batting, looking at ball, Denvers)
265-3bWilliam Klusman (batting, looking at ball, Milwaukee)
265-4aWilliam Klusman (fielding, hands head high, Denvers)
265-4bWilliam Klusman (fielding, hands head high, Milwaukee)
265-5 William Klusman (fielding, hands waist high) 65.00
266-1aPhilip Knell (pitching, hands at chest, St. Josephs) 65.00
266-1bPhilip Knell (pitching, hands at chest, St. Joes) 65.00
266-2 Philip Knell (pitching, left hand by head, looking at camera) 65.00
266-3aPhilip Knell (pitching, nearly back view, left hand head-high, St. Joes) 65.00
266-3bPhilip Knell (pitching, nearly back view, left hand head-high, St. Josephs) 65.00
266-4 Philip Knell (pitching, left hand forward head-high)
266-5 Philip Knell (batting)
267-1 Fred Knouff (sliding)
267-2 Fred Knouff (batting)
267-3 Fred Knouff (pitching)
267-4 Fred Knouff (ball in right hand waist-high)

267-5 Fred Knouff (ball in right hand head-high)

268-1 Charles Kremmeyer (Krehmeyer) (fielding)
269-1aBill Krieg (ringed cap, fielding, hands chest-high, 1st B., Washington)
269-1bBill Krieg (Kreig) (ringed cap, fielding, hands chest-high, First Base, Washington)

269-1cBill Krieg (ringed cap, fielding, hands chest-high, St. Joes)
269-2aBill Krieg (ringed cap, fielding, hands thigh high, 1st B., Washington)
269-2bBill Kreig (Krieg) (ringed cap, fielding, hands thigh-high, First Base, Washington)

269-2cBill Krieg (ringed cap, fielding, hands thigh high, Minne)
269-2dBill Krieg (ringed cap, fielding, hands thigh high, C., St. Joes)
269-2eBill Krieg (ringed cap, fielding hands thigh high, 1st B., St. Joe)
269-3aBill Krieg (ringed cap, batting, 1st B.)

269-3bBill Kreig (Krieg) (ringed cap, batting, First Base)
269-4 Bill Krieg (dark cap, tagging player)

269-5aBill Krieg (dark cap, batting, C.)
269-5bBill Krieg (dark cap, batting, 1st B.)

269-6aBill Krieg (dark cap, throwing, Minneapolis)
269-6bBill Kreig (Krieg) (dark cap, throwing, St. Joes)
269-7 Bill Krieg (dark cap, fielding, stretching up to left)
269-8 Bill Krieg (dark cap, fielding, hands by left shoulder)
269-9 Bill Krieg (in mask, hands on knees)

269-10August Kloff (Klopf), Bill Krieg
270-1aGus Krock (batting, Chicago)
270-1bGus Krock (batting, Chicagos)
270-1cGus Krock (batting, Chicago's)
270-2aGus Krock (pitching, hands above waist, Chicagos)
270-2bGus Krock (pitching, hands above waist, Chicago)
270-3aGus Krock (pitching, right hand thigh high, Chicago)
270-3bGus Krock (pitching, right hand thigh high, Chicagos)
270-4aGus Krock (pitching, right hand head high, Chicago)
270-4bGus Krock (pitching, right hand head high, Chicagos)
270-5aGus Krock (pitching, right hand chin-high, Chicago)
270-5bGus Krock (pitching, right hand chin-high, Chicagos)
270-5cGus Krock (pitching, right hand chin-high, Chicago's)
271-1 Willie Kuehne (bunting)
271-2aWillie Kuehne (fielding grounder, Pittsburgh's)
271-2bWillie Kuehne (fielding grounder, Pittsburgs)

271-2cWillie Kuehne (fielding grounder, Pittsburghs)
271-3aWillie Kuehne (walking to left, Pittsburgh's)
271-3bWillie Kuehne (walking to left, Pittsburgs)

271-4aWillie Kuehne (throwing, Pittsburgs)

271-4bWillie Kuchne (Kuehne) (throwing, Pittsburgh)
271-5aWillie Kuehne (fielding, hands thigh-high, Pittsburgs)
271-5bWillie Kuehne (fielding, hands thigh-high, Pittsburghs)
271-5cWillie Kuehne (fielding, hands thigh-high, Pittsburgh's)
272-1 Fred Lange (batting)
272-2 Fred Lange (bending left, hands ankle high)
272-3 Fred Lange (bending to right, hand on ground ball)
272-4 Fred Lange (fielding, hands chest-high)

272-5 Fred Lange (throwing)
273-1 Ted Larkin (batting)
273-2aTed Larkin (fielding, hands thigh-high, Capt. Larkin on front)
273-2bTed Larkin (fielding, hands thigh-high, Larkin, Captain on front)
273-3 Ted Larkin (throwing)
273-4 Ted Larkin (fielding, left hand above head)

274-1 Arlie Latham (Brown's Champions)

274-2aArlie Latham (sliding, St. Louis Browns)

274-2bArlie Latham (sliding, St. Louis)
274-3 Arlie Latham (batting, standing upright)

274-4aArlie Latham (batting, bending to left, Latham on front, St. Louis Browns)

274-4bArlie Latham (batting, bending to left, W. Latham on front, St. Louis Browns)

274-4cArlie Latham (batting, bending to left, Chicagos (PL))
274-5 Arlie Latham (fielding)
274-6aArlie Latham (throwing, St. Louis)

274-6bArlie Latham (throwing, St. Louis Browns)

275-1 Chuck Lauer (Laver) (fielding, hands chest-high)
275-2 Chuck Lauer (Laver) (throwing, right hand head-high)
275-3 Chuck Lauer (Laver) (batting, looking at camera)
275-4 Chuck Lauer (Laver) (batting, looking at ball)
276-1 John Leighton (batting)
276-2 John Leighton (fielding, hands by left ankle)
276-3 John Leighton (fielding, hands neck-high)

276-4 John Leighton (fielding, hands above head)
276-5 John Leighton (fielding, left hand head high)
276.5 Levy (bat in hand at side)
277-1aTom Loftus (bowler hat in hand, F.J. Loftus on front)
277-1bTom Loftus (bowler hat in hand, J. Loftus on front)
277-1cTom Loftus (bowler hat in hand, Loftus on front)
277-2 Tom Loftus (bowler hat on head)

278-1aGermany Long (batting, Kansas City)

278-1bGermany Long (batting, Chicago Maroons)
278-2 Germany Long (bat in hand at side, Chicago Maroons)
278-3 Germany Long (fielding, hands thigh-high, Kansas City)
278-4aGermany Long (fielding, hands chest-high, Kansas Citys)
278-4bGermany Long (fielding, hands chest-high, Kansas City)
278-4dGermany Long (fielding, hands chest-high, Chicago Maroons)
278-5 Germany Long (throwing, Kansas City)

279-1 Danny Long (batting, Oakland)
280-1aTom Lovett (batting, Brooklyns)
280-1bTom Lovett (batting, Omaha)
280-2 Tom Lovett (pitching, hands chest-high)

280-3 Tom Lovett (pitching, hands above head)

280-4 Tom Lovett (fielding)
280-6 Tom Lovett (bat in hand at side)
281-1aBobby Lowe (bat in hand at side, Milwaukee)
281-1bBobby Lowe (bat in hand at side, Milw. W.A.)
281-1cBobby Lowe (bat in hand at side, Milwaukees)
281-2 Bobby Lowe (sliding)
281-3 Bobby Lowe (batting)
281-4 Bobby Lowe (fielding grounder)

281-5 Bobby Lowe (fielding, hands shoulder high)

282-1 Jack Lynch (dotted tie)
282-2 Jack Lynch (batting)
282-3 Jack Lynch (throwing, hands chest-high, right leg clear of left leg)
282-4 Jack Lynch (throwing, right hand neck high)
282-5 Jack Lynch (throwing, hands chest-high, right foot behind left leg)
283-1 Denny Lyons (hands on knees, Athletics)

283-2 Denny Lyons (bat over shoulder, Athletics)
283-3aDenny Lyons (bat at ready position nearly horizontal, no comma after 3d B.)
283-3bDenny Lyons (bat at ready position nearly horizontal, comma after 3d B.)
283-4 Denny Lyons (fielding, left hand above head)
284-1 Harry Lyons (sliding, St. Louis)
284-2 Harry Lyons (batting, St. Louis)
284-3 Harry Lyons (bending to left, hands thigh high, St. Louis)
284-4 Harry Lyons (fielding, hands at knees, St. Louis)
284-5 Harry Lyons (throwing, St. Louis)

285-1aConnie Mack (throwing, C., Washington)

285-1bConnie Mack (throwing, Catcher, Mack on front, Washington)
285-1cConnie Mack (throwing, Catcher, C. Mack on front, Washington)
285-2aConnie Mack (stooping, hands on knees, C., Washington)
285-2bConnie Mack (stooping, hands on knees, Catcher, Washington)
285-3aConnie Mack (batting, C., Washington)

285-3bConnie Mack (batting, Catcher, Washington)
286-1 Reddie Mack (sliding, Louisville)
286-2 Reddie Mack (batting, Louisville)
286-3 Reddie Mack (fielding, hands chin-high, Louisville)
286-4aReddie Mack (bending to right, left hand thigh-high, Louisville)
286-4bReddie Mack (bending to right, left hand thigh-high, 2d B., Baltimores)
286-4cReddie Mack (bending to right, left hand thigh-high, 2nd B., Baltimores)
286-5 Reddie Mack (fielding grounder Louisville)
287-1 Little Mac Macullar (hands on knees)

287-2 Little Mac Macullar (fielding, hands head high)
287-3 Little Mac Macullar (bat in hand at side)

287-4 Little Mac Macullar (fielding grounder)

287-5 Little Mac Macullar (throwing)
287-6aLeech Maskrey (Little Mac Macullar) (arms at sides, R.F., Des Moines)
287-6bLittle Mac Macollar (arms at sides, S.S. Des Moins)
288-1aKid Madden (portrait, Boston's)
288-1bKid Madden (portrait, Boston)
288-1cKid Madden (portrait, Bostons)
288-2aKid Madden (bat in hand at side, P., Boston)
288-2bKid Madden (bat in hand at side, Pitcher)

288-2cKid Madden (bat in hand at side, Bostons (PL))
288-3aKid Madden (ball in hands at neck, P., Boston)
288-3bKid Madden (ball in hands at neck, Pitcher)
288-3cKid Madden (ball in hands at neck, Bostons (P.L.))
288-4aKid Madden (batting, P., Boston)

288-4bKid Madden (batting, Pitcher)
288-4cKid Madden (batting, Bostons (P.L.)

288-5 Kid Madden (ball in left hand just above head)
288-6 Kid Madden (arms folded, bat against rock)
289-1 Danny Mahoney (hands on thighs)

290-1 Grasshopper Maines (Mains) (batting, looking at camera)
290-2aGrasshopper Maines (Mains) (batting, looking down at ball, St. Pauls)
290-2bGrasshopper Maines (Mains) (batting, looking down at ball, St. Paul)
290-3 Grasshopper Maines (Mains) (pitching, hands by neck)
290-4aGrasshopper Maines (Mains) (ball in bent right hand head-high, St. Pauls)
290-4bGrasshopper Maines (Mains) (ball in bent right hand head-high, St. Paul)
290-5 Grasshopper Maines (Mains) (ball in extended right hand head-high)
291-1aFred Mann (fielding, hands head-high, St. Louis Browns)
291-1bFred Mann (fielding, hands head-high, St. Louis Brown)
291-1cFred Mann (fielding, hands head-high, Hartfords)
291-2 Fred Mann (batting)
291-3 Fred Mann (sliding)
291-4aFred Mann (fielding grounder, St. Louis Brown)

291-4bFred Mann (fielding grounder, St. Louis Browns)
292-1 Jimmy Manning (fielding grounder)

292-2 Jimmy Manning (batting)
292-3aJimmy Manning (throwing, right hand above head, Kansas City)
292-3bJimmy Manning (throwing, right hand above head, Kansas Citys)
292-4 Jimmy Manning (fielding, hands neck high)
292-5aJimmy Manning (bat in hand at side, no comma after S.S.)
292-5bJimmy Manning (bat in hand at side, comma after S.S.)
292-6 Jimmy Manning (hands on thighs)

293-1 Lefty Marr (fielding grounder)
293-2 Lefty Marr (bat over left shoulder)

293-3aLefty Marr (bat at 45 degree angle, Cincinnati (NL))
293-3bLefty Marr (bat at 45 degree angle, Columbus)
293-4 Lefty Marr (throwing)
293-5aLefty Marr (fielding, hands neck-high, Columbus)
293-5bLefty Marr (fielding, hands neck-high, Cincinnati (NL))
294-1aWillie Breslin - mascot (caption reads "Mascot, New York")
294-1bWillie Breslin Mascot (caption reads "New York Mascot")
295-1aLeech Maskrey (fielding, hands chest high, R.F.)
295-1bLittle Mac Macullar (Leech Maskrey) (fielding, hands chest-high, S.S.)
295-2 Leech Maskrey (ball in hands chin-high)

295-3aLeech Maskrey (throwing, Des Moines)

295-3bLeech Maskrey (throwing, Milwaukee)

296-1 Bobby Mathews (pitching)
296-2 Bobby Mathews (throwing)
296-3 Bobby Mathews (fielding)
297-1aMike Mattimore (pitching, hands shoulder high on left, N.Y's)
297-1bMike Mattimore (pitching, hands shoulder high on left, Athletics)
297-11Mike Mattimore (throwing)
297-2 Mike Mattimore (pitching, hands above head)
297-3aMike Mattimore (batting, standing upright, N.Y's)
297-3bMike Mattimore (batting, standing upright, Athletics)
297-4aMike Mattimore (pitching, hands at neck, N.Y's)
297-4bMike Mattimore (pitching, hands at neck, Athletics)
297-5aMike Mattimore (batting, left knee bent, N.Y's)
297-5bMike Mattimore (batting, left knee bent, Athletics)
297-6aMike Mattimore (pitching, hands waist high on left, N.Y's)
297-6bMike Mattimore (pitching, hands waist high on left, Athletics)
297-7 Mike Mattimore (sliding)
297-8aMike Mattimore (fielding grounder, N.Y's)

297-8bMike Mattimore (fielding grounder, name correct, Athletics)
297-8cMike Mattemore (Mattimore) (fielding grounder, name incorrect, Athletics)

297-9aMike Mattimore (sliding, left hand raised, N.Y's)
297-9bMike Mattimore (sliding, left hand raised, Athletics)
297-10a Mike Mattimore (bat in hand at side, N.Y's)
297-10b Mike Mattimore (bat in hand at side, Athletics)
298-1aSmiling Al Maul (batting, left foot pointing at camera, Pittsburghs)
298-1bSmiling Al Maul (batting, left foot pointing at camera, Pittsburgs)
298-1cSmiling Al Maul (batting, left foot pointing at camera, Pittsburgh)
298-2 Smiling Al Maul (batting, left foot pointing diagonally left)
298-3aSmiling Al Maul (pitching, hands at chest, Pittsburghs)
298-3bSmiling Al Maul (pitching, hands at chest, Pittsburgh)
298-4 Smiling Al Maul (ball in right hand above head, both heels on ground)
298-5 Smiling Al Maul (ball in right hand above head, right heel off ground)
298-6aSmiling Al Maul (fielding, hands head-high, Pittsburgh's)
298-6bSmiling Al Maul (fielding, hands head-high, Pittsburgs)
298-7aSmiling Al Maul (fielding, hands thigh-high, Pittsburgh's)
298-7bSmiling Al Maul (fielding, hands thigh-high, Pittsburgs)
299-1 Al Mays (portrait, dotted tie)
299-2 Al Mays (pitching, hands waist-high)

299-3 Al Mays (pitching, hands chest-high)

299-4 Al Mays (pitching, right hand head-high)

299-5 Al Mays (batting)
300-1 Jimmy McAleer (batting, looking at camera)
300-3 Jimmy McAleer (fielding low ball)

300-4 Jimmy McAleer (fielding, hands above head)
300-5 Jimmy McAleer (fielding, hands above waist)
301-1aTommy McCarthy (sliding, indoor background, Phila)
301-1bTommy McCarthy (sliding, indoor background, Philadelphia)
301-1cTommy McCarthy (sliding, indoor background, 2d B., St. Louis)
301-1dTommy McCarthy (sliding, indoor background, C.F., St. Louis)
301-2aTommy McCarthy (throwing, indoor background, Phila)
301-2bTommy McCarthy (throwing, indoor background, Philadelphia)
301-2cTommy McCarthy (throwing, indoor background, St. Louis)
301-3aTommy McCarthy (tagging player, Phila)

301-3bTommy McCarthy (tagging player, Philadelphia)
301-3cTommy McCarthy (tagging player, C.F., St. Louis)
301-3dTommy McCarthy (tagging player, 2d B., St. Louis)
301-4aTommy McCarthy (batting, indoor background, Phila)
301-4bTommy McCarthy (batting, indoor background, Philadelphia)
301-4cTommy McCarthy (batting, indoor background, St. Louis)
301-5aTommy McCarthy (fielding, hands chest high, Phila)
301-5bTommy McCarthy (fielding, hands chest high, Philadelphia)
301-5cTommy McCarthy (fielding, hands chest high, 2d B. St. Louis)
301-5dTommy McCarthy (fielding, hands chest high, C.F., St. Louis)
301-6aTommy McCarthy (sliding, outdoor background, St. Louis Browns)
301-6bTommy McCarthy (sliding, outdoor background, St. Louis)
301-7aTommy McCarthy (batting, outdoor background, St. Louis Browns)
301-7bTommy McCarthy (batting, outdoor background, St. Louis)
301-8aTommy McCarthy (throwing, outdoor background, T. McCarthy on front, St. Louis Browns)
301-8bTommy McCarthy (throwing, outdoor background, St. Louis)
301-8cTommy McCarthy (throwing, outdoor background, McCarthy on front, St. Louis Browns)
301-9aTommy McCarthy (fielding, hands head high, St. Louis Browns)
301-9bTommy McCarthy (fielding, hands head high, name correct, St. Louis Brown)

301-9cTommy Carthy (McCarthy) (fielding, hands head-high, name incorrect, St. Louis Brown)
302-1 John McCarthy (McCarty) (pitching, hands head-high, Kansas Citys)
302-2 John McCarthy (McCarty) (pitching, hands below chin, Kansas City)
302-3 John McCarthy (McCarty) (fielding, Kansas City)
303-1 Jim McCauley (batting)
303-2 Jim McCauley (fielding)
303-3 Jim McCauley (throwing)
304-1aBill McClellan (stooping, hands knee-high, name correct)
304-1bBill McClennan (McClellan) (stooping, hands knee-high, name incorrect))
304-2 Bill McClellan (fielding, hands head-high)

304-3aBill McClellan (batting, name correct)

304-3bBill McClennan (McClellan) (batting, name incorrect)
305-1 Jerry McCormack (McCormick) (batting)

305-2 Jerry McCormack (McCormick) (fielding hands shoulder-high)
305-3 Jerry McCormack (McCormick) (fielding grounder)
305-4 Jerry McCormack (McCormick) (throwing)
306-1 Jim McCormick (portrait, bare head)

306-2 Jim McCormick (portrait, peaked cap)

306-3 Jim McCormick (portrait, bowler hat)

306-4 Jim McCormick (standing, arms folded)

306-5aJim McCormick (pitching, hands at chest, looking at camera, P.)
306-5bJim McCormick (pitching, hands at chest, looking at camera, Pitcher)
306-6 Jim McCormick (batting, left-handed)

306-7aJim McCormick (fielding, Pitcher)

306-7bJim McCormick (fielding, P.)

306-8 Jim McCormick (standing, arms at sides)

306-9aJim McCormick (batting, right-handed, Pitcher)
306-9bJim McCormick (batting, right-handed, P.)

306-10aJim McCormick (pitching, hands at chest, right profile, Pitcher)
306-10bJim McCormick (pitching, hands at chest, right profile, P.)
307-1 McCreachery (photo actually Deacon White) (portrait)
308-1 Thomas McCullum (McCallum) (batting)

308-2 Thomas McCullum (McCallum) (fielding)

308-3 Thomas McCullum (McCallum) (throwing)

308-4 Thomas McCullum (McCallum) (bat in hand at side)
308.5 McDonald (standing, ball in hand)

309-1 Chippy McGarr (stooping, hands thigh high)
309-2 Chippy McGarr (fielding, hands head-high)

309-3 Chippy McGarr (batting, looking at camera)
309-4aChippy McGarr (batting, umpire behind, St. Louis Browns)
309-4bChippy McGarr (batting, umpire behind, K.C.)
309-4cChippy McGarr (batting, umpire behind, Kansas City)
310-1aJack McGeachy (bat in hand at side, Indianapolis)
310-1bJack McGeachy (bat in hand at side. Indianap's)
310-2 Jack McGeachy (batting)
310-3aJack McGeachy (fielding, McGeachy on front, no comma after C.F., Indianapolis)

310-3bJack McGeachy (fielding, McGeachy on front, comma after C.F., Indianapolis)

310-3cJack McGeachy (fielding, Indianap's)

310-3dJack McGeachy (fielding, C. McGeachy on front)
310-4 Jack McGeachy (throwing)
311-1aJohn McGlone (tagging player, Cleveland's)
311-1bJohn McGlone (tagging player, Detroits)

311-2 John McGlone (fielding, hands neck-high)

311-3 John McGlone (throwing)
311-4 John McGlone (fielding grounder)

311-5 John McGlone (batting)
312-1aDeacon McGuire (hands on knees, Phila)

312-1bDeacon McGuire (hands on knees. Philadelphia)
312-2aDeacon McGuire (right hand on hip, left arm at side, Phila)
312-2bDeacon McGuire (right hand on hip, left arm at side, Philadelphia)
312-2cDeacon McGuire (right hand on hip, left arm at side, Phil)
312-3aDeacon McGuire (fielding, hands shoulder high, Phila)
312-3bDeacon McGuire (fielding, hands shoulder high, Philadelphia)
312-3dDeacon McGuire (fielding, hands shoulder high, Torontos)
312-4aDeacon McGuire (batting, Phila)
312-4bDeacon McGuire (batting, Philadelphia)

313-1aBill McGunnigle (three-quarter length, looking to right, Brooklyns)
313-1bBill McGunnigle (three-quarter length, looking to right, Brookly)
314-1 Ed McKean (batting, looking at camera)

314-2 Ed McKean (batting, looking at ball)

314-3 Ed McKean (fielding, hands thigh-high)

314-4 Ed McKean (fielding, hands chest-high)

314-5 Ed McKean (fielding, hands above head)

315-1aAlex McKinnon (fielding grounder, 1st B.)

315-1bAlex McKinnon (fielding grounder, First Base)
315-2aAlex McKinnon (fielding, hands waist-high, 1st B.)
315-2bAlex McKinnon (fielding, hands waist-high, 1st Base)
315-3aAlex McKinnon (batting, 1st B.)
315-3bAlex McKinnon (batting, 1st Base)

315-4aAlex McKinnon (bat in hand at side, 1st B.)
315-4bAlex McKinnon (bat in hand at side, 1st Base)
316-1 Tom McLaughlin (portrait, dotted tie)

317-1aBid McPhee (batting, looking at camera, Cincinnatti)
317-1bBid McPhee (batting, looking at camera, Cincinnati (NL))

317-1cBid McPhee (batting, looking at camera, Cincinnati)
317-2aBid McPhee (batting, looking at ball, McPhee on front)
317-2bBid McPhee (batting, looking at ball, John McPhee on front)
317-3aBid McPhee (fielding, hands ankle-high, Cincinnatis)
317-3bBid McPhee (fielding, hands ankle-high, Cincinnati)
317-3cBid McPhee (fielding, hands ankle-high, Cincinnatis)
317-4aBid McPhee (fielding, hands head-high, McPhee on front, Cincinnati)
317-4bBid McPhee (fielding, hands head-high, Cincinnatis)
317-4cBid McPhee (fielding, hands head-high, Cincinnatti)
317-4dBid McPhee (fielding, hands head-high, John McPhee on front, Cincinnati)
317-5aBid McPhee (throwing, Cincinnati)

317-5bBid McPhee (throwing, Cincinnatti)

318-1 James McQuaid (batting, Denver)

318-2 James McQuaid (fielding, hands near chin, Denver)
318-3 James McQuaid (fielding, hands head high, Denver)
319-1aJohn McQuaid (umpire) (McQuaid on front)
319-1bJohn McQuaid (umpire) (Jack McQuaid on front)
320-1 Jim McTamany (fielding, hands head high)
320-2aJim McTamany (fielding, right hand above head, Brooklyn)
320-2bJim McTammany (McTamany) (fielding, right hand above head, Columbus)
320-2cJim McTammany (McTamany) (fielding, right hand above head, Kansas City)

320-3aJim McTamany (batting, name correct)

320-3bJim McTammany (McTamany) (batting, name incorrect)
320-4 Jim McTammany (McTamany) (right hand extended head-high on left)
321-1aGeorge McVey (bending to left, hands knee-high, left foot forward, Denvers)

321-1bGeorge McVey (bending to left, hands knee-high, left foot forward, St. Joe)

321-2aGeorge McVey (bending to left , hands nearly waist-high, feet level, Denvers)

321-2bGeorge McVey (bending to left, hands nearly waist-high, feet level, Milwaukees)

321-3aGeorge McVey (standing upright, hands outstretched shoulder-high, St. Joe)

321-4aGeorge McVey (batting, looking at camera, Denvers)
321-4bGeorge McVey (batting, looking at camera, St. Joe)
321-5aGeorge McVey (batting, looking down at bat, Denvers)
321.5 Steady Pete Meegan (standing, hands together at waist)
322-1 John Messitt (leaning left, arms at sides)

322-2aJohn Massitt (Messitt) (throwing)

322-2bJohn Wassitt (Messitt) (throwing)

322-3 John Messitt (bat in hand at side)

323-1aDoggie Miller (batting, C., Pittsburg)

323-1bDoggie Miller (batting, Catcher, Pittsburg)

323-1cDoggie Miller (batting, Miller on front, Pittsburgh)
323-1dDoggie Miller (batting, Geo. F. Miller on front, Pittsburgh)
323-1eDoggie Miller (batting, Pittsburghs)

323-2aDoggie Miller (bat in hand at side, C., Pittsburg)
323-2bDoggie Miller (bat in hand at side, Catcher, Pittsburg)
323-3aDoggie Miller (fielding, hands chest-high, C., Pittsburg)
323-3bDoggie Miller (fielding, hands chest-high, Catcher, Pittsburg)
323-4aDoggie Miller (ball in hands at waist, C., Pittsburg)
323-4bDoggie Miller (ball in hands at waist, Catcher, Pittsburg)
323-5 Doggie Miller (hands on thighs, Pittsburghs)
324-1 Joseph Miller (batting, Omaha)
324-2 Joseph Miller (fielding, hands at ankles, Minneapolis)
324-3 Joseph Miller (bat in hand at side, Omaha)

325-1aJocko Milligan (batting, looking at camera, St. Louis)
325-1bJocko Milligan (batting, looking at camera, no comma after C., St. Louis Browns)

325-1cJocko Milligan (batting, looking at camera, comma)
325-1dJocko Milligan (batting, looking at camera, Philadelphias (PL))
325-2aJocko Milligan (bat in hand at side. Milligan on front)
325-2bJocko Milligan (bat in hand at side, J. Milligan on front)
325-3aJocko Milligan (throwing, St. Louis)

325-3bJocko Milligan (throwing, Philadelphias)

325-3cJocko Milligan (throwing, Philadelphias (PL))
325-4 Jocko Milligan (fielding)
326-1 E.L. Mills (batting)
326-2 E.L. Mills (bat in hand at side)
326-3aE.L. Mills (fielding, hands shoulder-high, Milwaukees)
326-3bE.L. Mills (fielding, hands shoulder-high, Milwaukees, W. Ass'n)
326-4 E.L. Mills (ball in left hand above head)

326-5 E.L. Mills (throwing, ball in right hand head-high)
327-1 Daniel Minnehan (Minahan) (batting, looking at camera)
327-2 Daniel Minnehan (Minahan) (batting, looking at ball)
327-3 Daniel Minnehan (Minahan) (fielding, hands chin-high)
327-4 Daniel Minnehan (Minahan) (fielding, hands chest-high)
328-1 Sam Moffet (batting)
328-2 Sam Moffet (pitching)
328-3 Sam Moffet (throwing)
329-1aHonest John Morrell (Morrill) (portrait, no position)
329-1bHonest John Morrill (portrait, First Base, Manager)
329-1cJohn Morrell (Morrill) (portrait, 1st B.)

329-1dJohn Morrell (Morrill) (portrait, 1st Base and Manager)
329-2aJohn Morrell (Morrill) (hands on hips, name incorrect)
329-2bJohn Morrill (hands on hips, name correct)
329-3 John Morrill (bat in hand at side)
329-4 John Morrill (batting)
330-1aEd Morris (bat at ready position, clear of head, Pittsburgh)
330-1bEd Morris (bat at ready position, clear of head, Pittsburgs)
330-2aEd Morris (bat at ready position, partlv behind cap, Pittsburgh)
330-2bEd Morris (bat at ready position, partlv behind cap, Pittsburgh's)
330-3aEd Morris (ball in left hand head-high, right hand over right thigh, Pittsburgh)

330-3bEd Morris (ball in left hand head-high, right hand over right thigh, Pittsburgs)

330-4aEd Morris (ball in left hand head-high, right hand clear of right thigh, Pittsburgh)

330-4bEd Morris (ball in left hand head-high, right hand clear of right thigh, Pittsburghs)

330-5 Ed Morris (hands at chest, feet together, no space between ankles)
330-6aEd Morris (hands at chest, feet just apart with background visible between ankles, Pittsburgh)
330-6bEd Morris (hands at chest, feet just apart with background visible between ankles, Pittsburgh's)
331-1aCount Mullane (bat at ready position, looking at camera, Tony Mullane on front)

331-1bCount Mullane (bat at ready position, looking at camera, Mullane on front)

331-2aCount Mullane (pitching, hands above head, Tony Mullane on front)
331-2bCount Mullane (pitching, hands above head, Mullane on front)
331-3aCount Mullane (pitching, hands above waist clear of belt, Cincinnati)
331-3bCount Mullane (pitching, hands above waist clear of belt, Cincinnatti)
331-3cCount Mullane (pitching, hands above waist clear of belt, Cincinnatis)
331-4 Count Mullane (pitching, hands at waist left arm across belt)
331-5aCount Mullane (pitching, hands held out on left clear of belt, Cincinnati)
331-5bCount Mullane (pitching, hands held out on left clear of belt, Cincinnatti)
331-5cCount Mullane (pitching, hands held out on left clear of belt, Cincinnatis)
331-6aCount Mullane (pitching, right hand hip high at back, Tony Mullane on front, Cincinnati)
331-6bCount Mullane (pitching, right hand hip high at back, Cincinnatti)
331-6cCount Mullane (pitching, right hand hip high at back, Mullane on front, Cincinnati)

331-6dCount Mullane (pitching, right hand hip high at back, Cincinnatis)
331-7aCount Mullane (pitching, right hand extended forward thigh-high, Cincinnati)
331-7bCount Mullane (pitching, right hand extended forward thigh-high, Cincinnatti)

332-1aJoseph Mulvey (hands on thighs, ball head-high, 3d B.)
332-1bJoseph Mulvey (hands on thighs, ball head-high, Third Base)
332-2aJoseph Mulvey (batting, 3d B.)
332-2bJoseph Mulvey (batting, Third Base)

332-3aJoseph Mulvey (fielding, hands above waist, 3d B., Phila)
332-3bJoseph Mulvey (fielding, hands above waist, Third Base)
332-3dJoseph Mulvey (fielding, hand above waist, 3d B., Philadelphia)
332-3eJoseph Mulvey (fielding, hands above waist, Philadelphia (PL))
333-1 P.L. Murphy (bat in hand at side, St. Pauls)
333-2 P.L. Murphy (batting, St. Pauls)
333-3 P.L. Murphy (standing, hands on thighs, St. Pauls)
333-4aP.L. Murphy (throwing, St. Pauls)

333-4bP.L. Murphy (throwing, St. Paul)
333-5 P.L. Murphy (fielding, St. Paul)
334-1aPat Murphy (bat in hand at side, New Yorks)
334-1bPat Murphy (bat in hand at side, N.Y's)

334-2aPat Murphy (fielding, hands chin-high, New Yorks)
334-2cPat Murphy (fielding, hands chin-high, N.Y's)
334-2dPat Murphy (fielding, hands chin-high, New Yorks (N.L.))
334-3 Pat Murphy (ball almost in right hand, neck-high, New Yorks)
335-1 Miah Murray (on right knee, hands by left shoulder)
335-2 Miah Murray (bat over right shoulder)

335-3 Miah Murray (bat held horizontally)

335-4 Miah Murray (fielding, stretching to high right)
335-5 Miah Murray (throwing)
336-1aTruthful Jim Mutrie (portrait, bare head, N.Y.)
336-1bTruthful Jim Mutrie (portrait, bare head, New Yorks)
336-2aTruthful Jim Mutrie (seated, bowler hat in right hand, N.Y.)
336-2bTruthful Jim Mutrie (seated, bowler hat in right hand, New Yorks)
336-3aTruthful Jim Mutrie (standing, bowler hat on head, N.Y.)
336-3bTruthful Jim Mutrie (standing, bowler hat on head, New Yorks)
337-1aGeorge Myers (batting, no comma after C., Indianapolis)
337-1bGeorge Myers (batting, Catcher, Indianpolis)
337-1cGeorge Myers (batting, comma after C., Indianapolis)
337-2aGeorge Myers (stooping, hands waist high, C., Indianapolis)
337-2bGeorge Myers (stooping, hands waist high, Catcher, Indianapolis)
337-3 George Myers (tagging player, Indianapolis)
338-1aAl Myers (portrait, no comma after S.S., Washingtons)
338-1bAl Myers (portrait, Short Stop, Washington)
338-1cAl Myers (portrait, comma after S.S., Washingtons)
338-2aAl Myers (batting, no comma after S.S., Washingtons)
338-2bAl Myers (batting, Short Stop, Washington)
338-2cAl Myers (batting, comma after S.S., Washingtons)
338-2eAl Myers (batting, 2 B, Philadelphia (N.L.)

338-3aAl Myers (hands on knees, no comma after S.S., Washingtons)
338-3bAl Myers (hands on knees, Short Stop, Washington)
338-3cAl Myers (hands on knees, comma after S.S., Washingtons)
338-4 Al Myers (fielding, Washingtons)
338-5 Al Myers (right hand at side, left hand at back, Washington's)
339-1aTom Nagle (batting, looking at camera, Omahas)
339-1bTom Nagle (batting, looking at camera, Chicagos (NL))
339-2 Tom Nagle (batting, looking at ball)

339-3 Tom Nagle (stooping, hands by right foot)

339-4 Tom Nagle (hands on knees)
339-5aTom Nagle (fielding, hands chest-high, Omahas)
339-5bTom Nagle (fielding, hands chest-high, Chicagos (NL))
340-1aBilly Nash (tagging falling player, 3d B., Boston)
340-1bBilly Nash (tagging falling player, Third Base)
340-1cBilly Nash (tagging falling player, 3d B., Bostons)

340-1dBilly Nash (tagging falling player, 3rd.)

340-2aBilly Nash (portrait, 3d B.,)
340-2bBilly Nash (portrait, Third Base)
340-3aBilly Nash (hands on knees, 3d B.)

340-3bBilly Nash (hands on knees, Third Base)

340-4aBilly Nash (hands on bat between knees, Nash on front)
340-4bBilly Nash (hands on bat between knees, Billie Nash on front)
340-4cBilly Nash (hands on bat between knees, B. Nash on front)
340-5aBilly Nash (batting, 3d B.)
340-5bBilly Nash (batting, Third Base)
340-6aBilly Nash (throwing, Nash on front)

340-6bBilly Nash (throwing, B. Nash on front)

340-6cBilly Nash (throwing, Billie Nash on front)

341-1 Candy Nelson (dotted tie)
342-1aKid Nichols (batting, looking at camera, Omahas)
342-1bKid Nichols (batting, looking at camera, Omaha)
342-2 Kid Nichols (batting, looking at ball, Omaha)
342-3 Kid Nichols (pitching, hands at chest, Omaha)
342-4 Kid Nichols (pitching, right hand behind back, Omaha)
342-5aKid Nichols (pitching, right hand forward, Omahas)
342-5bKid Nichols (pitching, right hand forward, Omaha)
343-1 Samuel Nichols (Nichol) (bat in hand at side, Pittsburghs)
343-2 Samuel Nichols (Nichol) (fielding, hands above waist, Pittsburghs)
343-3 Samuel Nichols (Nichol) (fielding, hands by neck, Pittsburghs)
343-4 Samuel Nichols (Nichol) (batting, Pittsburghs)
344-1 J.W. Nicholson (leaning to left, hands on knees, Chicago Maroons)
344-2 J.W. Nicholson (bat in hand at side, Chicago Maroons)
344-3 J.W. Nicholson (pitching, hands at chest, Chicago Maroons)
344-4 J.W. Nicholson (pitching, right hand head high, Chicago Maroons)
344-5 J.W. Nicholson (pitching, right hand head high close to cap, Chicago Maroons)

345-1aParson Nicholson (bat in hand at side, St. Louis Whites)
345-1bParson Nicholson (bat in hand at side, Cleveland)
345-2aParson Nicholson (fielding, ball in hands by right knee, St. Louis Whites)
345-2bParson Nicholson (fielding, ball in hands by right knee, Clevelan)
345-2cParson Nicholson (fielding, ball in hands by right knee, C. Nicholson, Cleveland)

345-2dParson Nicholson (fielding, ball in hands by right knee, Nicholson on front, Cleveland)

345-3 Parson Micholson (Nicholson) (fielding, hands by right knee, no ball, St. Louis Whites)

345-4aParson Micholson (Nicholson) (tagging player, name incorrect, St. Louis Whites)

345-4bParson Nicholson (tagging player, name correct, St. Louis Whites)
345-5 Parson Nicholson (batting, St. Louis Whites)
346-1 Little Nick Nicoll (Nicol) (Brown's Champions)
346-2aLittle Nick Nicol (batting, Nicol on front)

346-2bLittle Nick Nicol (batting, H. Nicol on front)
346-3aLittle Nick Nicol (sliding, Nicol on front)

346-3bLittle Nick Nicol (sliding, Little Nick on front)
346-4aLittle Nick Nicol (fielding, stretching up to left, Cincinnatis)
346-4bLittle Nick Nicol (fielding, stretching up to left, Cincinnatti)
346-4cLittle Nick Nicol (fielding, stretching up to left, Cincinnati)
346-4dLittle Nick Nicol (fielding, stretching up to left, Cincinnati (N.L.))
346-5aLittle Nick Nicol (leaning forward, hands outstretched for catch, Hugh Nicol on front, Cincinnatis)
346-5bLittle Nick Nicol (leaning forward, hands outstretched for catch, Nicol on front, Cincinnatis)
346-5cLittle Nick Nicol (leaning forward. hands outstretched for catch, Cincinnatti)
346-5dLittle Nick Nicol (leaning forward, hands outstretched for catch, Cincinnati)
346-6 Little Nick Nicol (leaning forward, right hand at hip, left hand by knee)
346-7aLittle Nick Nicol, Big John Reilly (Nicol and Reilly side by side, Cincinnatti)
346-7bLittle Nick Nicol, Big John Reilly (Nicol and Reilly side by side, caption reads "(Long & Short)")

346-7cLittle Nick Nicol, Big John Reilly (Nicol and Reilly side by side, caption reads "(Long & Short) Cin")
346-8 Little Nick Nicol, Big John Reilly (Nicol and Reilly facing each other)
347-1 Frederick Nyce (batting)
347-2aFrederick Nyce (ball in right hand neck high, St. Louis Whites)
347-2bFrederick Nyce (ball in right hand neck high, Burlingtons (Fc))
347-3 Frederick Nyce (ball in right hand thigh high)
347-4 Frederick Nyce (ball in hands at chest)

348-1aDoc Oberlander (batting, Cleveland's)

348-1bDoc Oberlander (batting, Syracuse)

348-2 Doc Oberlander (pitching, hands above waist)
348-3aDoc Oberlander (pitching, left hand cap high, looking to left, Cleveland's)
348-3bDoc Oberlander (pitching, left hand cap high, looking to left, Syracuse)
348-4aDoc Oberlander (pitching, left hand cap high, looking at camera, hand at back, Clevelands)
348-4bDoc Oberlander (pitching, left hand cap high, looking at camera, hand at back, Syracuse)
348-5 Doc Oberlander (pitching, left hand cap high, looking at camera, hand well forward)

349-1 Jack O'Brien (in mask, hands on knees, Brooklyn)
349-2 Jack O'Brien (mask in left hand, Brooklyn)

349-3 Jack O'Brien (bat over right shoulder, Brooklyn)
349-4 Jack O'Brien (ball in right hand head-high, Brooklyn)
349-5 Jack O'Brien (throwing, right hand neck high, Baltimores)
349-6 Jack O'Brien (fielding, hands at chest, Baltimores)
349-7 Jack O'Brien (batting, feet well apart, Baltimores)
349-8 Jack O'Brien (batting, heels together, Baltimores)
350-1aBilly O'Brien (batting, feet close together, Washington)
350-1bBilly O'Brien (batting, feet close together, Washingtons)
350-2 Billy O'Brien (batting, feet wide apart, Washingtons)
350-3aBilly O'Brien (hands on knees, Washington)
350-3bBilly O'Brien (hands on knees, Washingtons)
350-4aBilly O'Brien (fielding, hands waist-high, Washington)
350-4bBilly O'Brien (fielding, hands waist-high, Washingtons)
350-5 Billy O'Brien (fielding grounder, Washington)
351-1aDarby O'Brien (batting, looking at camera, Brooklyns)
351-1bDarby O'Brien (batting, looking at camera, Bk'ns)
351-2aDarby O'Brien (batting, looking at ball, Brooklyns)
351-2bDarby O'Brien (batting, looking at ball, Bk'ns)
351-3 Darby O'Brien (fielding, right hand high to left, Brooklyns)
351-4 Darby O'Brien (fielding, hands head-high on left, Brooklyns)
351-5aDarby O'Brien (throwing, Brooklyns)

351-5bDarby O'Brien (throwing, Bk'ns)
352-1 John O'Brien (batting, Clevelands)

352-2 John O'Brien (pitching, ball in right hand at chest, Clevelands)
352-3 John O'Brien (pitching, hands shoulder high, feet on ground, Clevelands)
352-4 John O'Brien (pitching, hands shoulder high, left foot off ground, Clevelands)

353-1aP.J. O'Connell (batting, Des Moines)

353-1bP.J. O'Connell (batting, Omaha)
353-2 P.J. O'Connell (fielding grounder)

353-3aP.J. O'Connell (tagging player, Des Moines)
353-3bP.J. O'Connell (tagging player, Omaha)

353-4 P.J. O'Connell (bat in hand at side)

354-1aRowdy Jack O'Connor (batting, Cincinnati)
354-1bRowdy Jack O'Connor (batting, Columbus)
354-2aRowdy Jack O'Connor (fielding grounder, Cincinnati)
354-2bRowdy Jack O'Connor (fielding grounder, Columbus)
354-3aRowdy Jack O'Connor (fielding, hands above waist, Cincinnati)
354-3bRowdy Jack O'Connor (fielding, hands above waist, Columbus)
354-4aJack O'Connor (throwing, Cincinnati)

354-4bJack O'Connor (throwing, Columbus)

355-1aHank O'Day (batting, P.)
355-1bHank O'Day (batting, Pitcher)
355-2aHank O'Day (ball in right hand head-high, P. Washington)
355-2bHank O'Day (ball in right hand head-high, Pitcher, Washington)
355-2cHank O'Day (ball in right hand head-high, Washingtons)
355-3aHank O'Day (pitching, hands at chest, O'Day on front, P., Washington)
355-3bHank O'Day (pitching, hands at chest, Pitcher, Washington)
355-3cHank O'Day (pitching, hands at chest, Washingtons)
355-3dHank O'Day (pitching, hands at chest, H. O'Day on front, P. Washington)
356-1 Tip O'Neil (O'Neill) (bat over right shoulder, St. Louis)
356-2 Tip O'Neil (O'Neill) (bat at ready, St. Louis)
356-3 Tip O'Neil (O'Neill) (fielding grounder, St. Louis)
356-4 Tip O'Neil (O'Neill) (fielding, hands head high, St. Louis)
356-5 Tip O'Neil (O'Neill) (throwing, St. Louis)

356-6 Tip O'Neil (O'Neill) (Brown's Champions)

357-1 O'Neill (photo actually Bill White) (batting, St. Louis Browns)
357-2aO'Neill (photo actually Bill White) (fielding grounder, name correct, St. Louis Browns)

357-2bO'Neil (O'Neill) (photo actually Bill White) (fielding grounder, name incorrect, St. Louis Bro.)
357-3 O'Neill (photo actually Bill White) (throwing, St. Louis Browns)
357-4 O'Neill (photo actually Bill White) (fielding, hands above head, St. Louis Browns)
357.1 O'Neill (bat in hand at side, Omaha)

358-1 Orator Jim O'Rourke (fielding, N.Y's)

358-2aOrator Jim O'Rourke (bat in hand at side, 3d B., N.Y's)
358-2bOrator Jim O'Rourke (bat in hand at side, C., New Yorks)
358-2cOrator Jim O'Rourke (bat in hand at side, 3d B., New Yorks)
358-3 Orator Jim O'Rourke (throwing, 3d B., N.Y's)
358-4aOrator Jim O'Rourke (batting, 3d B., N.Y's)
358-4bOrator Jim O'Rourke (batting, 3d B., New Yorks)
359-1aTom O'Rourke (fielding, hands head-high, C., Boston)
359-1bTom Rourke (O'Rourke) (known in proof form only) (fielding, hands head-high, Catcher, Boston)
359-2aTom O'Rourke (fielding, hands thigh-high, Boston)
359-2bTom Rourke (O'Rourke) (known in proof form only) (fielding, hands thigh-high, Catcher, Boston)
359-2dTom O'Rourke (fielding, hands thigh-high, Jersey Citys)
359-3aTom O'Rourke (throwing, right hand head high, Boston)
359-3bTom Rourke (O'Rourke) (throwing, right hand head-high, Boston)
359-4aTom O'Rourke (batting, Boston)
359-4bTom Rourke (O'Rourke) (known in proof form only) (batting, Boston)
359-5aTom O'Rourke (bat in hand at side, Boston)
359-5bTom Rourke (O'Rourke) (known in proof form only) (bat in hand at side, Boston)

359-5cTom O'Rourke (bat in hand at side, Jersey Citys)
359-6aTom O'Rourke (fielding, hands at neck, C., Boston)
359-6bTom Rourke (O'Rourke) (fielding, hands at neck, Boston)
359-6cTom O'Rourke (fielding, hands at neck, Catcher, Boston)
360-1 Dave Orr (portrait, dotted tie)
360-2aDave Orr (fielding, hands by right knee, no team designation)
360-2bDave Orr (fielding, hands by right knee, Columbus)
360-3 Dave Orr (fielding, hands head-high on left)
360-4aDave Orr (fielding, hands head-high on right, Brooklyns)
360-4bDave Orr (fielding, hands head-high on right, Columbus)
360-5aDave Orr (bat at ready position, nearly vertical, Brooklyns)
360-5bDave Orr (bat at ready position, nearly vertical, Columbus)
360-6aDave Orr (bat at ready position at about 45 degrees, Brooklyns)
360-6bDave Orr (bat at ready position at about 45 degrees, Columbus)
361-1 Charles Parsons (moving forward, hands waist-high)
361-2 Charles Parsons (bat in hand at side)

361-3 Charles Parsons (pitching, hands chest high)
361-4 Charles Parsons (batting)
362-1 Owen Patton (batting)
362-2 Owen Patton (fielding ball by right foot)

362-3aOwen Patton (fielding, ball in hands by neck, Minneapolis)
362-3bOwen Patton (fielding, ball in hands by neck, Des Moines)
362-4 Owen Patton (fielding, right hand above head)
362-5aOwen Patton (fielding, hands chin-high, Minneapolis)
362-5bOwen Patton (fielding, hands chin-high, Des Moines)
362-6 Owen Patton (throwing)
363-1aJimmy Peeples (Peoples) (in mask, hands waist-high, Brooklyn)
363-1bJimmy Peeples (Peoples) (in mask, hands waist-high, Columbus)
363-2aJimmy Peeples (Peoples) (batting, Brooklyn)
363-2bJimmy Peeples (Peoples) (batting, Columbus)
363-3aHardie Henderson, Jimmy Peeples (Peoples) (Henderson tagging Peoples, Columbus)
363-3bHardie Henderson, Jimmy Peeples (Peoples) (Henderson tagging Peoples, Brooklyn)
364-1 Hip Perrier (batting)
365-1 Patrick Pettee (batting)
365-3 Patrick Pettee (throwing)
365-4 Patrick Pettee (sliding)
365-5 Bobby Lowe, Patrick Pettee (Pettee about to tag Lowe)
366-1 Fred Pfeffer (fielding)
366-2aFred Pfeffer (throwing, right hand neck high, Pfeffer on front, Chicago)
366-2bFred Pfeffer (throwing, right hand neck high, Pfeffer on front, Chicago's)
366-2cFred Pfeffer (throwing, right hand neck high, W.T. Pfeffer on front, Chicago)
366-2dFred Pfeffer (throwing, right hand neck high, W.T. Pfeffer on front, Chicagos)

366-3 Fred Pfeffer (batting, looking at ball by bat)
366-4aFred Pfeffer (bat on right shoulder, Pfeffer on front, Chicago)
366-4bFred Pfeffer (bat on right shoulder, Pfeffer on front, Chicago's)
366-4cFred Pfeffer (bat on right shoulder, W.T. Pfeffer on front)
366-4dFred Pfeffer (bat on right shoulder, N.F. Pfeffer on front)
366-5aFred Pfeffer (tagging player, Pfeffer on front)
366-5bFred Pfeffer (tagging player, N.T. Pfeffer on front)
366-5cFred Pfeffer (tagging player, N.F. Pfeffer on front)
367-1 Dick Phelan (batting, looking at camera)

367-2 Dick Phelan (batting, looking at ball)

367-3 Dick Phelan (fielding, hands waist-high)

367-4aDick Phelan (fielding, hands chest-high, Des Moines)
367-4bDick Phelan (fielding, hands chest-high, Des Moine)
367-5 Dick Phelan (fielding, hands chin-high)

368-1aBill Phillips (hands on knees, Brooklyn)

368-1bBill Phillips (hands on knees, Kansas City)

368-2aBill Phillips (fielding, hands head-high, Brooklyn)
368-2bBill Phillips (fielding, hands head-high, Kansas City)
368-3 Bill Phillips (stooping to left)
368-4aBill Phillips (batting, Brooklyn)
368-4bBill Phillips (batting, Kansas City)

369-1aJack Pickett (bat over right shoulder, Kansas Citys)
369-1bJack Pickett (bat over right shoulder, St. Pauls)
369-1dJack Pickett (bat over right shoulder, Philadelphias)
369-2 Jack Pickett (bat in hand at side)

369-3aJack Pickett (fielding, bending to left, hands neck-high, Kansas City)
369-3bJack Pickett (fielding, bending to left, hands neck-high, St. Pauls)
369-4 Jack Pickett (fielding, bending to left, hands thigh-high)
369-5 Jack Pickett (ball in right hand on ground by left foot)
369-6 Jack Pickett (fielding grounder by feet)

369-7bJack Pickett (throwing, St. Pauls)

369-7cJack Pickett (throwing, Philadelphias)

369-8 Jack Pickett (bending to left, side view)

370-1 George Pinkney (fielding, hands chest high)
370-2 George Pinkney (hands on knees)

370-3aGeorge Pinkney (bat at ready position, nearly vertical, Brooklyn)
370-3bGeorge Pinkney (bat at ready position, nearly vertical, Brooklyns)
370-4 George Pinkney (fielding, hands ankle high)
370-5 George Pinkney (bat over right shoulder)

371-1 Tom Poorman (sliding)
371-2aTom Poorman (fielding, ankle-high, Athletics)
371-2bTom Poorman (fielding, ankle-high, Milwaukees)
371-3aTom Poorman (throwing, Athletics)

371-3bTom Poorman (throwing, Milwaukees)

371-4aTom Poorman (fielding, hands chest-high, Athletics)
371-4bTom Porrman (Poorman) (fielding, hands chest-high, Milwaukees)
372-1 Henry Porter (tagging player)
372-2 Henry Porter (pitching, hands chest-high)

372-3 Henry Porter (batting)
372-4aHenry Porter (throwing, right hand neck high, Brooklyn)
372-4bHenry Porter (throwing, right hand neck high, Kansas City)
372-5 Henry Porter (throwing, right hand cap high)
372-6 Henry Porter (fielding, hands head-high)

373-1aJim Powell (bat at ready position, looking at camera, Mgr.)
373-1bJim Powell (bat at ready position, looking at camera, 1st B.)
373-2aJim Powell (swinging bat, looking at camera, Mgr.)
373-2bJim Powell (swinging bat, looking at camera, 1st B.)
373-3 Jim Powell (fielding, hands on knees, ball approaching)
373-4 Jim Powell (fielding, looking at ball head high)
373-5aJim Powell (fielding, looking at ball above head, Mgr.)
373-5bJim Powell (fielding, looking at ball above head, 1st B.)
373.5 Thomas Powers (Power) (batting)

374-1aBlondie Purcell (sliding, Baltimores)

374-1bBlondie Purcell (sliding, Athletics)

374-2aBlondie Purcell (fielding, stretching up to left, Baltimores)
374-2bBlondie Purcell (fielding, stretching up to left, Athletics)
374-3 Blondie Purcell (fielding, stretching up to right)
374-4 Blondie Purcell (throwing)
374-5 Blondie Purcell (batting)
375-1 Tom Quinn (hands on knees, Baltimore)

375-2 Tom Quinn (batting, Baltimore)
375-3 Tom Quinn (arms at sides, Baltimore)

375-4 Tom Quinn (throwing, Baltimore)

375-5 Tom Quinn (fielding, hands at waist, Baltimore)
376-1 Joe Quinn (sliding, Bostons)
376-2aJoe Quinn (ball in hands by chin, Boston)

376-2bJoe Quinn (ball in hands by chin, Bostons)

376-4 Joe Quinn (right hand extended forward head-high, Des Moines)
377-1aOld Hoss Radbourn (hands on hips, bat on left, P., Boston)
377-1bOld Hoss Radbourn (hands on hips. bat on left, Pitcher, Boston)
377-1cOld Hoss Radbourn (hands on hips, bat on left, Boston (PL))
377-2aOld Hoss Radbourn (tagging player, P.)

377-2bOld Hoss Radbourn (tagging player, Pitcher)
377-3aOld Hoss Radbourn (batting, P., Boston)

377-3bOld Hoss Radbourn (batting, Pitcher, Boston)
377-3cOld Hoss Radbourn (batting, Bostons)

377-4aOld Hoss Radbourn (hands clasped at waist, no space visible between hands and belt, P.)
377-4bOld Hoss Radbourn (hands clasped at waist, no space visible between hands and belt, Pitcher)
377-5aOld Hoss Radbourn (hands clasped at waist, white uniform visible between hands and belt, P.)
377-5bOld Hoss Radbourn (hands clasped at waist, white uniform visible between hands and belt, Pitcher)
377-6aOld Hoss Radbourn (portrait, P.)

377-6bOld Hoss Radbourn (portrait, Pitcher)

378-1 Shorty Radford (batting, looking at camera)
378-2aShorty Radford (batting, looking at ball, Brooklyns)
378-2bShorty Radford (batting, looking at ball, Clevelands)
378-3aShorty Radford (leaning to left, ball in right hand by right knee, Brooklyns)
378-3bShorty Radford (leaning to left, ball in right hand by right knee, Clevelands)

378-4 Shorty Radford (throwing)
378-5aShorty Radford (fielding, hands above head, Brooklyns)
378-5bShorty Radford (fielding, hands above head, Clevelands)
379-1aToad Ramsey (bat over right shoulder, Louisville)
379-1bToad Ramsey (bat over right shoulder, Louisvills)
379-2aToad Ramsey (bat nearly vertical, Ramsey on front)
379-2bToad Ramsey (bat nearly vertical, Thomas Rmasey on front)
379-3aToad Ramsey (pitching, Louisvills)

379-3bToad Ramsey (pitching, Louisville)

380-1 Rehse (batting)
380-2 Rehse (bat in hand at side)
380-3 Rehse (fielding, hands head-high)

380-4 Rehse (fielding, hands thigh-high)

380-5 Rehse (pitching)
381-1 Big John Reilly (batting, Cincinnati)

381-2aBig John Reilly (fielding, 1st B., Cincinnati)

381-2bBig John Reilly (fielding, 1 B., Cincinnati)

381-2cBig John Reilly (fielding, Cincinnatti)

381-2dBig John Reilly (fielding, Cincinnatis)

381-3aBig John Reilly (throwing, Cincinnati)

381-3bBig John Reilly (throwing, Cincinnatti)

381-3cBig John Reilly (throwing, Cincinnatis)

382-1aPrinceton Charlie Reilly (hands on thighs, St. Pauls)
382-1bPrinceton Charlie Riley (Reilly) (hands on thighs, St. Paul)
382-2 Princeton Charlie Reilly (fielding, hands waist-high, St. Pauls)
382-3 Princeton Charlie Reilly (throwing, St. Pauls)
382-4 Princeton Charlie Reilly (batting, St. Pauls)
383 Charlie Reynolds (throwing)
383-1 Charlie Reynolds (hands on thighs)

383-2 Charlie Reynolds (arms at sides)
383-3 Charlie Reynolds (bat in hand at side)

384-1aHardy Richardson (fielding, hands head high, Detroits)
384-1cHardy Richardson (fielding, hands head high, Bostons)
384-2aHardy Richardson (bat over right shoulder, Detroits)
384-2bHardy Richardson (bat over right shoulder, Bostons)
384-3 Hardy Richardson (bat nearly horizontal, Detroits)
385-1aDanny Richardson (bat over right shoulder, Danny Richardson on front, N.Y's)

385-1bDanny Richardson (bat over right shoulder, New Yorks)
385-1cDanny Richardson (bat over right shoulder, Richardson on front, N.Y's)

385-2aDanny Richardson (moving to left, arms at sides, Danny Richardson on front, N.Y's)

385-2bDanny Richardson (moving to left, arms at sides, New Yorks)
385-2dDanny Richardson (moving to left, arms at sides, Richardson on front, N.Y's)

385-3aDanny Richardson (bat at ready position at 45 degrees, N.Y's)
385-3bDanny Richardson (bat at ready position at 45 degrees, New Yorks)
385-4aDanny Richardson (throwing, N.Y's)

385-4bDanny Richardson (throwing, New Yorks)

385-5aDanny Richardson (fielding grounder, N.Y's)
385-5bDanny Richardson (fielding grounder, New Yorks)
386-1 Charles Ripslager (Reipschlager) (dotted tie)
387-1 John Roach (pitching, hands by chin)

387-2 John Roach (bat at ready position, standing upright)
387-3 John Roach (bat in hand at side)
387-4 John Roach (leaning to left, hands on thighs)
387-5 John Roach (pitching, left hand chest high at back)
387-6 John Roach (bat at ready position, leaning forward)
388-1 Uncle Robbie Robinson (batting, Athletics)
388-2aUncle Robbie Robinson (fielding, hands above head, no comma after C., Athletics)

388-2bUncle Robbie Robinson (fielding, hands above head, comma after C., Athletics)

388-3 Uncle Robbie Robinson (fielding, hands neck-high, Athletics)
388-4 Uncle Robbie Robinson (fielding, hands thigh-high, Athletics)
388-5 Uncle Robbie Robinson (throwing, Athletics)
389-1 M.C. Robinson (batting, Minneapolis)

389-2 M.C. Robinson (tagging player, Minneapolis)
389-3 M.C. Robinson (fielding grounder, Minneapolis)
389-4 M.C. Robinson (throwing, right hand head high, Minneapolis)
389-5 M.C. Robinson (fielding, hands chest-high, Minneapolis)
389-6 M.C. Robinson (ball in hands waist-high, Minneapolis)
390-1aYank Robinson (batting, St. Louis Browns)

390-1bYank Robinson (batting, St. Louis)

390-2aYank Robinson (fielding grounder, St. Louis Browns)
390-2bYank Robinson (fielding grounder, St. L. Brow)
390-3 Yank Robinson (throwing, right hand neck high, St. Louis)
390-4 Yank Robinson (sliding, St. Louis)

390-5 Yank Robinson (fielding, hands shoulder high, St. Louis)
390-6 Yank Robinson (Brown's Champions)

391-1aGeorge Rooks (bat in hand at side, Chicago Maroons)
391-1bGeorge Rooks (bat in hand at side, Detroits)
391-2 George Rooks (bat over left shoulder)

391-3 George Rooks (fielding, hands chin-high)

391-4 George Rooks (fielding, hands head-high)

391-5 George Rooks (throwing)
392-1 Chief Roseman (dotted tie)
393-1 Dave Rowe (portrait, Kansas City)

393-2aDave Rowe (throwing, Kansas City)

393-2bDave Rowe (throwing, Mgr. & C.F., Denvers)
393-2cDave Rowe (throwing, Mg'r., Denvers)

393-3 Dave Rowe (fielding, hands shoulder-high, Kansas City)
393-4 Dave Rowe (fielding, hands thigh-high, Kansas City)
393-5 Dave Rowe (fielding grounder, Kansas City)
393-6 Dave Rowe (batting, Kansas City)

394-1aJack Rowe (batting, looking at camera, no comma after S.S., Detroits)
394-1cJack Rowe (batting, looking at camera, comma after S.S., Detroits)
394-2 Jack Rowe (bat in hand at side, Detroits)

394-3 Jack Rowe (batting, looking at approaching ball, Detroits)
395-1aAmos Rusie (pitching, hands at neck, Indianapolis)
395-1bAmos Rusie (pitching, hands at neck, New Yorks (N.L.))
395-2 Amos Rusie (pitching, right hand thigh high)
395-3aAmos Rusie (pitching, right hand head high at side, name correct)
395-3bAmos Russie (Rusie) (pitching, right hand head-high at side, name incorrect)
395-4aAmos Rusie (pitching, right hand forward chin-high, Indianapolis)
395-4bAmos Rusie (pitching, right hand forward chin-high, New Yorks (N.L.))
395-5 Amos Rusie (batting)
396-1aJimmy Ryan (stooping for catch knee high, Chicago)
396-1bJimmy Ryan (stooping for catch knee high, Chicago's)
396-1cJimmy Ryan (stooping for catch knee high, Chicago (PL))
396-2aJimmy Ryan (ball in hands at neck, Ryan on front)
396-2bJimmy Ryan (ball in hands at neck, J. Ryan on front)
396-3 Jimmy Ryan (throwing, left hand head high)
396-4aJimmy Ryan (bat in hand at side, Chicago)

396-4bJimmy Ryan (bat in hand at side, Chicagos (PL))
396-5aJimmy Ryan (fielding, hands head-high, Ryan on front)
396-5bJimmy Ryan (fielding, hands head-high, J. Ryan on front)
396-6 Jimmy Ryan (batting)
397-1 Doc Sage (stooping for low ball)

397-2 Doc Sage (bat on right shoulder, looking at camera)
397-3 Doc Sage (batting, looking at approaching ball)
397-4aDoc Sage, Bill Van Dyke (Toledos)

397-4bDoc Sage, Bill Van Dyke (Des Moines)

398-1 Ben Sanders (pitching)
398-2aBen Sanders (throwing, Phila)
398-2bBen Sanders (throwing, Philadelphias)

398-3aBen Sanders (fielding, Phila)
398-3bBen Sanders (fielding, Philadelphias)

398-3dBen Sanders (fielding, Philadelphias (PL))

398-4 Ben Sanders (batting)
399-1 Frank Scheibeck (fielding, hands waist high)
399-2 Frank Scheibeck (fielding, hands above head)
399-3 Frank Scheibeck (fielding ball at feet)

399-4 Frank Scheibeck (batting)
400-1 Al Schellhase (Schellhasse) (fielding, hands above head)
400-2 Al Schellhase (Schellhasse) (fielding, ball by hands chest-high)
400-3 Al Schellhase (Schellhasse) (fielding, hands thigh-high, left leg straight)
400-4 Al Schellhase (Schellhasse) (fielding, hands thigh-high, left leg bent)
400-5 Al Schellhase (Schellhasse) (batting)

401-1 William Schenkel (batting)
401-2 William Schenkel (ball in hands chest high)
401-3aWilliam Schenkel (fielding, hands cupped chest-high, name correct)
401-3bWilliam Schenkle (Schenkel) (fielding, hands cupped chest-high, name incorrect)

401-4 William Schenkle (Schenkel) (left hand chin-high, right arm at side)
402-1aSchildknecht (batting, Milwa'k's)

402-1bSchildknecht (batting, Milwaukee)

402-1cSchildknecht (batting, Milwaukees)

402-1dSchildknecht (batting, Des Moines)

402-2 Schildknecht (fielding, hands thigh-high)

402-3 Schildknecht (fielding, ball in hands chest high)
403-1 Gus Schmelz (head and shoulder portrait)

403-2aGus Schmelz (full length, street clothes, G.H. Schmelz on front)
403-2bGus Schmelz (full length, street clothes, H. Schmelz on front)
403-2cGus Schmelz (full length, street clothes, Schmelz on front)
403-2dGus Schmelz (full length, street clothes, Cincinnatis)
404-1aJumbo Schoeneck (batting, Chicago Maroons)
404-1bJumbo Schoeneck (batting, Indianapoli)

404-1cJumbo Schoeneck (batting, Indianapolis)

404-1dJumbo Schoeneck (batting, Indianap's)

404-2 Jumbo Schoeneck (hands on knees)

404-3aJumbo Schoeneck (fielding grounder, Chicago Maroons)
404-3bJumbo Schoeneck (fielding grounder, Indianapoli)
404-3cJumbo Schoeneck (fielding grounder, Indianapolis)
404-3dJumbo Schoeneck (fielding grounder, Indianap's)
404-4 Jumbo Schoeneck (fielding, hands chin high)
404-5aJumbo Schoeneck (ball in left hand head high, Chicago Maroons)
404-5bJumbo Schoeneck (ball in left hand head high, Indianapolis)
404-5cJumbo Schoeneck (ball in left hand head high, Indianap's)
405-1aPop Schriver (bat over right shoulder, Phila)
405-1bPop Schriver (bat over right shoulder, Philadelphias)
405-2 Pop Schriver (bat held horizontally)

405-3 Pop Schriver (fielding, hands ankle-high)

405-4aPop Schriver (fielding, hands chest-high, Phila)
405-4bPop Schriver (fielding, hands chest-high, Philadelphias)
405-5aPop Schriver (throwing, Phila)
405-5bPop Schriver (throwing, Philadelphias)

405-5cPop Schriver (throwing, Phila (N.L.)

406-1aEmmett Seery (fielding, hands above head, L.F.)
406-1bEmmett Seery (fielding, hands above head, Left Field)

406-2aEmmett Seery (ball in hands at neck, no comma after L.F.)
406-2bEmmett Seery (ball in hands at neck, Left Field)
406-2cEmmett Seery (ball in hands at neck comma after L.F.)
406-3aEmmett Seery (arms folded, no comma after L.F.)
406-3bEmmett Seery (arms folded, Left Field)

406-3cEmmett Seery (arms folded, comma after L.F.)
406-4aEmmett Seery (batting, no comma after L.F.)
406-4bEmmett Seery (batting, comma after L.F.)

407-1aBilly Serad (batting, Cincinnati)
407-1bBilly Serad (batting, Toronto)
407-2 Billy Serad (ball in hands chin-high)

407-3aBilly Serad (ball in right hand neck-high, Cincinnati)
407-3bBilly Serad (ball in right hand neck-high Toronto)
408-1aEd Seward (ball in hands neck-high, no comma after P.)
408-1cEd Seward (ball in hands neck-high, comma after P.)
408-2aEd Seward (pitching, right hand head-high at back, no comma after P.)
408-2bEd Seward (pitching, right hand head-high at back, comma after P.)
408-3aEd Seward (pitching, right hand forward head-high, no comma after P.)
408-3bEd Seward (pitching, right hand forward head-high, comma after P.)
409-1 Orator Shafer (Shaffer) (arms folded, Des Moines)
409-2 Orator Shafer (Shaffer) (throwing, right hand head-high, Des Moines)
409-3 Orator Shafer (Shaffer) (bat in left hand at side, Des Moines)
409-4 Orator Shafer (Shaffer) (bat at ready position, looking at camera, Des Moines)

410-1 Taylor Shafer (Shaffer) (bending to right, hands over base, St. Louis)
410-2 Taylor Shafer (Shaffer) (throwing, St. Paul)
410-3 Taylor Shafer (Shaffer) (ball in hands by left shoulder, St. Paul)
411-1aDaniel Shannon (batting, name correct)

411-1bDaniel Hannon (Shannon) (batting, name incorrect)
411-2aDaniel Shannon (ball in hands at chest, leaning towards player sliding, Philadelphias (PL))
411-2bDaniel Shannon (ball in hands at chest, leaning towards player sliding, Louisvilles)

411-3 Daniel Shannon (fielding, hands at chest)

411-4 Daniel Shannon (sliding)
411-5 Daniel Shannon (bat in hand at side)

412-1aWilliam Sharsig (full length, in bowler hat, Mg'r.)
412-1bWilliam Sharsig (full length, in bowler hat, Manager)
413-1aSamuel Shaw (pitching, hands above waist, Baltimores)
413-1bSamuel Shaw (pitching, hands above waist, Newarks)
413-2aSamuel Shaw (pitching, right arm extended forward, Baltimores)
413-2bSamuel Shaw (pitching, right arm extended forward, Newarks)
413-3 Samuel Shaw (batting, Baltimores)

414-1 John Shaw (batting, Minneapolis)

414-2 John Shaw (stooping to left, Minneapolis)

414-3 John Shaw (sliding, Minneapolis)
414-4 John Shaw (fielding hands neck-high, Minneapolis)
414-5 John Shaw (throwing, Minneapolis)

415-1 Bill Shindle (fielding grounder)
415-2 Bill Shindle (fielding, hands above head)

415-3aBill Shindle (batting, name correct)

415-3bBill Shindel (batting, name incorrect)

415-4aBill Shindle (hands on knees, name correct, Baltimores)
415-4bBill Shindel (Shindle) (hands on knees, name incorrect, Baltimores)
415-4cBill Shindle (hands on knees, Philadelphias)
415-5aBill Shindle (throwing, 3rd B.)
415-5bBill Shindle (throwing, 3d B., Baltimores)

415-5cBill Shindle (throwing, 3d B., Philadelphias)
416-1aGeorge Schoch (Shoch) (fielding grounder, R.F., Washington)
416-1bGeorge Shoch (fielding grounder, Right Field)
416-1dGeorge Shoch (fielding grounder, R.F., Washingtons)
416-2aGeorge Shoch (fielding, hands head-high, Right Field)

416-2bGeorge Schoch (Shoch) (fielding, hands head-high, G. Schoch on front)
416-2cGeorge Shoch (fielding, hands head-high, Washingtons)
416-2dGeorge Schoch (Shoch) (fielding, hands head-high, Schoch on front)
416-3aGeorge Schoch (Shoch) (batting, Schoch on front)
416-3bGeorge Shoch (batting, Right Field)

416-3cGeorge Shoch (batting, G. Schoch on front)
416-4 Honest John Gaffney, George Shoch (Shoch batting with Gaffney behind him)

417-1aOtto Shomberg (Schomberg) (fielding, hands head-high, 1st B.)
417-1bOtto Shomberg (Schomberg) (fielding, hands head-high, 1st Base)
417-2aOtto Shomberg (Schomberg) (throwing, 1st B.)
417-2bOtto Shomberg (Schomberg) (throwing, 1st Base)
417-3aOtto Shomberg (Schomberg) (fielding, hands waist-high, 1st B.)
417-3bOtto Shomberg (Schomberg) (fielding, hands waist-high, 1st Base)
418-1aLev Shreve (batting, name correct)

418-1bLev Chreve (Shreve) (batting, name incorrect)
418-2aLev Shreve (pitching, ball in hands at chest, comma after P.)
418-2bLev Shreve (pitching, ball in hands at chest, no comma after P.)
418-3aLev Shreve (pitching, right hand above head, facing front, name correct)
418-3bLev Chreve (Shreve) (pitching, right hand above head, facing front, name incorrect)

418-4aLev Shreve (pitching, right hand level with cap, looking at camera, name correct)

418-4bLev Shreve (pitching, right hand level with cap, looking at camera, name incorrect)

418-5aLev Shreve (pitching, right hand level with eyes, looking at camera, comma after P.)

418-5bLev Shreve (pitching, right hand level with eyes, looking at camera, no comma after P.)

418-6aLev Shreve (pitching, right hand level with chin, looking to left, comma after P., Indianapolis)
418-6bLev Shreve (pitching, right hand level with chin, looking to left, no comma after P., Indianapolis)
418-6cLev Shreve (pitching, right hand level with chin, looking to left, Ind'p'l's)
418-7aLev Shreve (pitching, right hand at rear level with cap, right profile, name correct)

418-7bLev Shreve (pitching, right hand at rear level with cap, right profile, name incorrect)

419-1 Ed Silch (batting, looking at camera)

419-2 Ed Silch (batting, looking at ball)
419-3aEd Silch (fielding, hands head-high, Denvers)
419-3bEd Silch (fielding, hands head-high, Brooklyns)
419-4aEd Silch (ball in hands above head, Brooklyns)
419-4bEd Silch (ball in hands above head, Denvers)
419-5aEd Silch (throwing, Brooklyns)
419-5bEd Silch (throwing, Denvers)
420-1aMike Slattery (batting, N.Y.)
420-1bMike Slattery (batting, New Yorks)

420-2aMike Slattery (fielding, hands chest-high, N.Y.)
420-2bMike Slattery (fielding, hands chest-high, New York)
420-3 Mike Slattery (fielding, left hand extended head-high)
420-4aMike Slattery (ready to pitch, N.Y.)

420-4bMike Slattery (ready to pitch, New Yorks)

420-4cMike Slattery (ready to pitch, New York PL)
420-5aMike Slattery (right hand across body by left thigh, N.Y.)
420-5bMike Slattery (right hand across body by left thigh, New Yorks)
421-1 Skyrocket Smith (batting, ball about thigh high, Louisville)
421-2 Skyrocket Smith (ball in hands head-high on left, Louisville)
421-3 Skyrocket Smith (catching, stooping, hands by right knee, Louisville)
421-4 Skyrocket Smith (stooping to field grounder by right foot, Louisville)
422-1 Phenomenal Smith (portrait, no team designation)
422-2aPhenomenal Smith (pitching, hands above waist, Baltimores)
422-2bPhenomenal Smith (pitching, hands above waist, Athletics)
422-3aPhenomenal Smith (pitching, hands by right shoulder, Baltimores)

422-3bPhenomenal Smith (pitching, hands by right shoulder, Athletics)
422-4aPhenomenal Smith (batting, Baltimores)

422-4bPhenomenal Smith (batting, Athleticss)

422-5aPhenomenal Smith (pitching, left hand neck-high, both ears visible, Baltimores)

422-5bPhenomenal Smith (pitching, left hand neck-high, both ears visible, Athletics)

422-6 Phenomenal Smith (pitching, left hand shoulder-high, left ear only visible, Baltimores)
423-1 Mike Smith (batting, looking at approaching ball, Cincinnati)
423-2aMike Smith (pitching, hands at chest, E. Smith on front, Cincinnati)
423-2bMike Smith (pitching, hands at chest. Smith on front, Cincinnati)
423-2cMike Smith (pitching, hands at chest, Cincinnatti)
423-3aMike Smith (pitching, left hand chest-high at rear, looking to left, Cincinnatis)
423-3bMike Smith (pitching, left hand chest-high at rear, looking to left, Cincinnati)
423-3cMike Smith (pitching, left hand chest-high at rear, looking to left, Cincinnatti)
423-4aMike Smith (pitching, left hand head-high looking at camera, right hand by right thigh, Cincinnatis)
423-4bMike Smith (pitching, left hand head-high, looking at camera, right hand by right thigh, Cincinnati)
423-5 Mike Smith (pitching, left hand head-high, glancing to left, right arm across waist, Cincinnati)
424-1 Sam Smith (pitching, hands at throat, ball visible between palms, Des Moines)
424-2 Sam Smith (pitching, ball in right hand by face, Des Moines)
424-3aSam Smith (fielding grounder, no comma after P., Des Moines)
424-3bSam Smith (fielding grounder, comma after P., Des Moines)
424-4 Sam Smith (pitching, hands at throat, ball not visible, Des Moines)
425-1aGermany Smith (hands on knees, Brooklyn)
425-1cGermany Smith (hands on knees, Brooklyn's)
425-2aGermany Smith (batting, looking at camera, Smith on front, Brooklyns)
425-2bGermany Smith (batting, looking at camera, G. Smith on front, Brooklyns)

425-2cGermany Smith (batting, looking at camera, Geo. Smith on front, Brooklyns)

425-3aGermany Smith (batting, looking at ball, comma after S.S., Brooklyns)
425-3bGermany Smith (batting, looking at ball, no comma after S.S., Brooklyns)
425-4aGermany Smith (fielding grounder, Smith on front, Brooklyn's)
425-4bGermany Smith (fielding grounder, Geo. Smith on front, Brooklyns)
425-5aGermany Smith (throwing, Smith on front, Brooklyns)
425-5bGermany Smith (throwing, G. Smith on front, Brooklyns)
426-1aPap Smith (fielding grounder with right hand, S.S., Pittsburg)
426-1bPap Smith (fielding grounder with right hand, Short Stop, Pittsburg)
426-1cPap Smith (fielding grounder with right hand, Pittsburgs)
426-1dPap Smith (fielding grounder with right hand, Bostons)
426-2aPap Smith (batting, S.S., Pittsburg)

426-2bPap Smith (batting, Short Stop, Pittsburg)

426-2cPap Smith (batting, S.S., Pittsburgs)

426-3aPap Smith (hands on knees, S.S., Pittsburg)
426-3bPap Smith (hands on knees, Short Stop, Pittsburg)
426-3cPap Smith (hands on knees, Pittsburgh)

426-3dPap Smith (hands on knees, Pittsburgs)

426-4aPap Smith (fielding grounder with both hands, S.S., Pittsburg)
426-4bPap Smith (fielding grounder with both hands, Short Stop, Pittsburg)
426-4cPap Smith (fielding grounder hands, Pittsburgh)
427-1aNick Smith (fielding, hands head-high, feet together, St. Josephs)
427-1bNick Smith (fielding, hands head-high, feet together, St. Joe)
427-2aNick Smith (fielding, hands head-high, feet apart, St. Josephs)
427-2bNick Smith (fielding, hands head-high, feet apart, St. Joe)
427-3 Nick Smith (batting, looking at camera, St. Josephs)
427-4aNick Smith (batting, looking down at bat, St. Josephs)
427-4bNick Smith (batting, looking down at bat, St. Joe)

427-5 Nick Smith (fielding, hands at right knee, St. Josephs)
428-1 P.T. Somers (batting)
428-2 P.T. Somers (arms folded)
428-3 P.T. Somers (pitching, looking to left)

428-4 P.T. Somers (pitching, looking to right)

429-1aJoe Sommer (sliding, name correct)

429-1bJoe Sommers (Sommer) (sliding, name incorrect, Baltimores)
429-2aJoe Sommer (fielding grounder, name correct)
429-2bJoe Sommers (Sommer) (fielding grounder, name incorrect, Baltimores)

429-3 Joe Sommers (Sommer) (throwing, Baltimores)
429-4 Joe Sommers (Sommer) (fielding, hands above head, Baltimores)
429-5aJoe Sommer (batting, name correct)

429-5bJoe Sommers (Sommer) (batting, incorrect, Baltimores)
430-1 Pete Sommers (batting, Chicago's)

430-2aPete Sommers (fielding, ball by hands chest-high, Chicago's)
430-2bPete Sommers (fielding, ball by hands chest-high, New Yorks (NL))
430-3 Pete Sommers (fielding, hands head-high, Chicago's)
430-4 Pete Sommers (fielding, right hand above head, Chicagos)
430-5 Pete Sommers (fielding, arms extended left at waist, Chicago's)
430-6 Pete Sommers (portrait, Chicagos)

431-1aLittle Bill Sowders (in light uniform, pitching, hands at throat, Sowders on front, Boston)
431-1bLittle Bill Sowders (in light uniform, pitching, hands at throat, Bostons)
431-1cLittle Bill Sowders (in light uniform, pitching, hands at throat, W. Sowders on front, Boston)
431-2aLittle Bill Sowders (in light uniform, pitching, ball in right hand chin-high, left elbow held up shoulder-high, Bostons)

431-2bLittle Bill Sowders (in light uniform, pitching, ball in right hand chin-high, left elbow held up shoulder-high, Boston)

431-3aLittle Bill Sowders (in light uniform, pitching, ball in right hand cap-high, left hand waist-high, Bostons)
431-3bLittle Bill Sowders (in light uniform, pitching, ball in right hand cap-high, left hand waist-high, Boston)
431-4aLittle Bill Sowders (in light uniform, pitching, right hand forward head-high, ball just released, Sowders on front, Boston)

431-4bLittle Bill Souders (Sowders) (in light uniform, pitching, right hand forward head high, ball just released, Bostons)
431-4cLittle Bill Sowders (in light uniform, pitching, right hand forward head-high, ball just released, W. Sowders on front, Bostons)

431-5aLittle Bill Sowders (in light uniform, hands at sides, ball at top right, Bostons)
431-5bLittle Bill Sowders (in light uniform, hands at sides, ball at top right, Boston)
431-6aLittle Bill Sowders (in light uniform, bat at ready by head, Bostons)
431-6bLittle Bill Sowders (in light uniform, bat at ready position by head, Boston)
431-7aLittle Bill Sowders (in light uniform, batting, ball cap-high, Bostons)
431-7bLittle Bill Sowders (in light uniform, batting, ball cap-high, Boston)
432-1 John Sowders (in dark uniform, pitching, hands at chest, St. Pauls)
432-2aJohn Sowders (in dark uniform, fielding, ball in right hand thigh-high, St. Paul)

432-2bJohn Sowders (in dark uniform, fielding, ball in right hand thigh-high, St. Pauls)

432-3 John Sowders (in dark uniform, pitching, ball in left hand chin-high, Kansas Citys)

432-4aJohn Sowders (in dark uniform, batting, Kansas City)
432-4bJohn Sowders (in dark uniform, batting, Kansas Citys)
433-1 Charlie Sprague (batting, light cap)

433-2 Charlie Sprague (batting, dark cap)

433-3 Charlie Sprague (bat at side in hand)

433-4 Charlie Sprague (pitching, hands at waist, light cap)
433-5 Charlie Sprague (pitching, hands at waist, dark cap)
433-6 Charlie Sprague (pitching, left hand head high, light cap)
433-7aCharlie Sprague (pitching, left hand head high, no cap, Sprague on front, Chicago)

433-7bCharlie Sprague (pitching, left hand head high, no cap, C.W. Sprague on front, Chicago)

433-7cCharlie Sprague (pitching, left hand head high, no cap, Sprague on front, Clevelands)

433-7dCharlie Sprague (pitching, left hand head high, no cap, C.W.Sprague on front, Clevelands)
433-8 Charlie Sprague (pitching, left hand extended forward, no cap)
434-1 Ed Sproat (bat at ready position on shoulder)
434-2 Ed Sproat (batting, ball thigh-high)

434-3 Ed Sproat (pitching, hands at chin)

434-4 Ed Sproat (pitching, right hand head-high)

434-5 Ed Sproat (pitching, right hand waist-high)

435-1aHarry Staley (pitching, hands at chest, St. Louis Whites)
435-1bHarry Staley (pitching, hands at chest, Pittsburgs)
435-1cHarry Staley (pitching, hands at chest, Pittsburghs)
435-2aHarry Staley (pitching, right hand neck high, right heel off ground, St. Louis Whites)

435-2bHarry Staley (pitching, right hand neck high, right heel off ground, Pittsburgs)

435-2cHarry Staley (pitching, right hand neck high, right heel off ground, St. Louis Whites)

435-3 Harry Staley (pitching, right hand chest high, both heels on ground)
435-4aHarry Staley (bat at ready, looking at camera, name correct)
435-4bHarry Stoley (Staley) (bat at ready, looking at camera, name incorrect)
435-5 Harry Staley (batting, ball by horizontal bat)
436-1aDan Stearns (fielding, hands neck-high, Kansas City)
436-1bDan Stearns (fielding, hands neck-high, Kansas Citys)
436-2aDan Stearns (fielding, hands thigh-high, name correct)
436-2bDan Tearns (Stearns) (fielding, hands thigh-high, name incorrect)
436-3 Dan Stearns (throwing, right hand thigh high)
436-4 Dan Stearns (batting)
437-1aCannonball Stemmeyer (pitching, hands at chest, name correct)
437-1bCannonball Stemmyer (Stemmeyer) (pitching, hands at chest, name incorrect)

437-2aCannonball Stemmeyer (batting, white uniform, name correct)
437-2bCannonball Stemmyer (Stemmeyer) (batting, white uniform, name incorrect)

437-3aCannonball Stemmeyer (pitching, right hand head-high, white uniform, name correct)
437-3bCannonball Stemmyer (Stemmeyer) (pitching, right hand head-high, white uniform, name incorrect)
437-4aCannonball Stemmeyer (ball in right hand waist high, name correct)
437-4bCannonball Stemmyer (Stemmeyer) (ball in right hand waist high, name incorrect)

437-5 Cannonball Stemmyer (Stemmeyer) (batting, dark uniform)
437-6 Cannonball Stemmeyer (right hand vertically above head)
438-1 B.F. Stephens (batting)
438-2 B.F. Stephens (catching)
438-3 B.F. Stephens (ready to pitch)
439-1 John Sterling (bat in right hand, looking at camera)
439-2 John Sterling (batting, looking down at ball)
439-3 John Sterling (pitching, hands at chest)

439-4 John Sterling (pitching, right hand thigh high)
439.5 Stockwell (batting)
440-1aHarry Stovey (hands on knees, no comma after L.F.)
440-1bHarry Stovey (hands on knees, comma after L.F.)
440-2 Harry Stovey (bat in hand at side)

440-3aHarry Stovey (bat at ready position by head, no comma after L.F.)
440-3cHarry Stovey (bat at ready position by head, comma after L.F.)
440-4 Harry Stovey (bat at ready position, horizontal)
440-5aHarry Stovey (fielding, hands above head, no comma after L.F., Athletics)
440-5bHarry Stovey (fielding, hands above head, comma after L.F., Athletics)
440-5cHarry Stovey (fielding, hands above head, Bostons (PL))
440-6 Harry Stovey (fielding, hands at chest)

440-7 Harry Stovey (fielding, right hand above head)
440-8 Harry Stovey (throwing)

441-1 Scott Stratton (batting)
441-2aScott Stratton (pitching, hands at chest, Louisville)
441-2bScott Stratton (pitching, hands at chest, Louisvilles)
441-3aScott Stratton (pitching, right hand at side head-high, Louisville)
441-3bScott Stratton (pitching, right hand at side head-high, Louisvilles)
441-4aScott Stratton (pitching, right hand forward head-high, Louisville)
441-4bScott Stratton (pitching, right hand forward head-high, Louisvilles)
441-5aScott Stratton (underhand throw, right hand waist-high, Louisville)
441-5bScott Stratton (underhand throw, right hand waist-high, Louisvilles)
442-1aJoe Straus (Strauss) (kneeling looking left, Omahas)
442-1bJoe Struck (Strauss) (kneeling looking left, Milwaukee)
442-2 Joe Straus (Strauss) (kneeling, looking to right)
442-3 Joe Straus (Strauss) (throwing)
442-4aJoe Straus (Strauss) (fielding, stooping, hands waist-high, Omahas)
442-4bJoe Strauss (fielding, stooping, hands waist-high, Omahas, W.A.)
442-4cJoe Straus (Strauss) (fielding, stooping, hands waist-high, Milwaukee)
442-5 Joe Straus (Strauss) (fielding, stooping, hands by right ankle)
442-6 Joe Straus (Strauss) (batting)
443-1 Cub Stricker (batting)
443-2 Cub Stricker (fielding ball by left foot)

443-3 Cub Stricker (fielding, hands above head)

444-1aMarty Sullivan (dark uniform, throwing, right hand head-high, Chicago's)
444-1bMarty Sullivan (dark uniform, throwing, right hand head-high, Chicago)
444-2aMarty Sullivan (dark uniform, fielding, hands chest-high, Chicago's)
444-2bMarty Sullivan (dark uniform, fielding, hands chest-high, Chicago)
444-2cMarty Sullivan (dark uniform, fielding, hands chest-high, Indianapolis)
444-3 Marty Sullivan (dark uniform, batting, looking at camera, Chicago's)
444-4 Marty Sullivan (dark uniform, bat in hand at side, Chicago's)
444-5aMarty Sullivan (dark uniform, batting, looking at approaching ball, Chicago's)

444-5cMarty Sullivan (dark uniform, batting, looking at approaching ball, Indianapolis)

445-1 Mike Sullivan (light shirt, bat at ready position on base, Athletics)
445-2 Mike Sullivan (light shirt, hands on knees, Athletics)
445-3 Mike Sullivan (light shirt, sliding, Athletics)

446-1aBilly Sunday (fielding, hands thigh-high, Chicago)
446-1bBilly Sunday (fielding, hands thigh-high, Pittsburgs)
446-2aBilly Sunday (batting, Chicago)
446-2bBilly Sunday (batting, Pittsburghs)

446-3aBilly Sunday (throwing, Chicago)

446-3bBilly Sunday (throwing, Pittsburgs)

446-4aBilly Sunday (fielding, hands chin-high, Chicago)
446-4bBilly Sunday (fielding, hands chin-high, Pittsburgs)
446-5aBilly Sunday (bat in hand at side, Chicago)

446-5bBilly Sunday (bat in hand at side, Pittsburghs)
447-1 Sy Sutcliffe (fielding grounder)
447-2 Sy Sutcliffe (fielding, hands neck-high)

447-3 Sy Sutcliffe (fielding, hands above waist)

447-4 Sy Sutcliffe (batting, looking at camera)

447-5 Sy Sutcliffe (batting, looking at ball)

448-1aEzra Sutton (fielding, hands shoulder high, 3d B.)
448-1bEzra Sutton (fielding, hands shoulder high, Third Base)
448-2aEzra Sutton (throwing, hands chest-high, 3d B.)
448-2bEzra Sutton (throwing, hands chest-high, Third Base)
448-3aEzra Sutton (fielding grounder, 3d B.)

448-3bEzra Sutton (fielding grounder, Third Base)
448-3cEzra Sutton (fielding grounder, 2d B.)

448-4aEzra Sutton (batting, ball above bat, 3d B.)
448-4bEzra Sutton (batting, ball above bat, Third Base)
448-5aEzra Sutton (bat in hand at side, 3d B.)

448-5bEzra Sutton (bat in hand at side, Third Base)

448-5cEzra Sutton (bat in hand at side, 2nd B.)

448-6aEzra Sutton (throwing, right hand just releasing ball, 3d B.)
448-6bEzra Sutton (throwing, right hand just releasing ball, Third Base)
448-7aEzra Sutton (batting, looking down at ball, 3d B., Boston)
448-7bEzra Sutton (batting, looking down at ball, Third Base)
448-7cEzra Sutton (batting, looking down at ball, 3d B., Milwaukees)
448-7dEzra Sutton (batting, looking down at ball, 3d B. Milwaukee)
449-1aEd Swartwood (fielding, hands above head, Brooklyn)
449-1bEd Schwartwood (Swartwood) (fielding, hands above head, Des Moines)
449-2aEd Swartwood (fielding, kneeling, hands ankle-high, Brooklyn)
449-2bEd Schwartwood (Swartwood) (fielding, kneeling, hands ankle-high, Des Moines)

449-3aEd Schwartwood (Swartwood) (on ground, right hand on base)
449-4aEd Schwartwood (Swartwood) (tagging player, Des Moines)
449-4bEd Schwartwood (Swartwood) (tagging player, Hamlts)
450-1aPark Swartzel (batting, no comma after P.)
450-1bPark Swartzel (batting, comma after P.)

450-2aPark Swartzel (fielding, stooping, hands cupped, Kansas City)
450-2bPark Swartzel (fielding, stooping, hands cupped, Kansas Citys)
450-3 Park Swartzel (pitching, hands by left shoulder)
450-4 Park Swartzel (pitching, ball in right hand thigh-high)
450-5 Park Swartzel (pitching, right hand by head)
450-6 Park Swartzel (in jacket, arms at sides)

451-1aPete Sweeney (hands on knees, name correct)
451-1bPete Sweeny (Sweeney) (hands on knees, name incorrect, Washington)
451-1cPete Sweeny (Sweeney) (hands on knees, name incorrect, Washingtons)
451-2aPete Sweeny (Sweeney) (batting, Washington)
451-2bPete Sweeny (Sweeney) (batting, Washingtons)
451-3aPete Sweeny (Sweeney) (fielding, hands head-high, Washington)
451-3bPete Sweeny (Sweeney) (fielding, hands head-high, Washingtons)
451-4 Pete Sweeny (Sweeney) (throwing)

451.5 Louis Sylvester (batting)
452-1aPop Tate (hands on knees, C.)
452-1bPop Tate (hands on knees, Catcher)

452-2aPop Tate (batting, C., Boston)
452-2bPop Tate (batting, Catcher)
452-2cPop Tate (batting, C., Baltimores)

452-3aPop Tate (fielding, hands chest-high, Catcher)
452-3bPop Tate (fielding, hands chest-high, E.C. Tate on front, C., Boston)
452-3cPop Tate (fielding, hands chest-high, Baltimores)
452-3ePop Tate (fielding, hands chest-high, Tate on front, C., Boston)
453-1aPatsy Tebeau (bat by head, looking at camera, Chicago)
453-1bPatsy Tebeau (bat by head, looking at camera, Clevelands)
453-2aPatsy Tebeau (batting, ball thigh-high, Chicago)
453-2bPatsy Tebeau (batting, ball thigh-high, Clevelands)
453-3aPatsy Tebeau (fielding, hands by right ankle, Tebeau on front)
453-3bPatsy Tebeau (fielding, hands by right ankle, Oliver Tebeau on front)
453-4aPatsy Tebeau (ball in right hand chest high, Chicago)
453-4bPatsy Tebeau (ball in right hand chest high, Clevelands)
453-5 Patsy Tebeau (ball in left hand knee-high)

454-1 John Tener (ball in right hand cap-high, arm bent)
454-2 John Tener (ball in right hand chin-high, arm straight)
454-3 John Tener (ball in right hand thigh-high)

454-4 John Tener (ball in hands by right shoulder)
454-5 John Tener (batting)
455-1aAdonis Terry (throwing, pivoting on right foot)
455-2aAdonis Terry (pitching, hands chest-high, P., Brooklyn)
455-2bAdonis Terry (pitching, hands chest-high, Brooklyns)
455-2cAdonis Terry (pitching, hands chest-high, Pitcher, Brooklyn)
455-3aAdonis Terry (batting, P.)
455-3cAdonis Terry (batting, Pitcher)

455-4 Adonis Terry (throwing, arms extended horizontally)
455-5 Adonis Terry (fielding, hands chest-high)

456-1 Big Sam Thompson (batting, ball chest high)
456-2 Big Sam Thompson (bat at ready position at 45 degrees)
456-3aBig Sam Thompson (arms folded, Detroits)
456-3bBig Sam Thompson (arms folded, Phil'a (NL))
456-4aBig Sam Thompson (bat in hand at side, Detroits)
456-4bBig Sam Thompson (bat in hand at side, Phila's)
456-4cBig Sam Thompson (bat in hand at side, Philadelphia)
456-4dBig Sam Thompson (bat in hand at side. Philadelphias)
456-5 Big Sam Thompson (batting, ball above head)
457-1aSilent Mike Tiernan (ball in hands above waist, R.F.)
457-1bSilent Mike Tiernan (ball in hands above waist, C.F.)
457-2 Silent Mike Tiernan (fielding, hands chest high)
457-3 Silent Mike Tiernan (fielding grounder)

457-4aSilent Mike Tiernan (throwing, left hand chin-high, R.F.)
457-4bSilent Mike Tiernan (throwing, left hand chin-high, C.F.)
457-5aSilent Mike Tiernan (sliding, R.F.)

457-5bSilent Mike Tiernan (sliding, C.F.)

457-6aSilent Mike Tiernan (batting, N.Y's)

457-6bSilent Mike Tiernan (batting, New Yorks)

458-1 Cannonball Titcomb (batting)
458-2aCannonball Titcomb (bat in hand at side, N.Y.)
458-2bCannonball Titcomb (bat in hand at side, New Yorks)
458-3 Cannonball Titcomb (pitching, looking front)
458-4 Cannonball Titcomb (pitching, right profile)
458-5 Cannonball Titcomb (pitching, right arm across body, hand at thigh)
459-1 Buster Tomney (batting)
459-2 Buster Tomney (fielding, hands by right foot)
459-3 Buster Tomney (fielding, hands above waist)
459-4 Buster Tomney (fielding, hands above head)
460-1 Stephen Toole (pitching, left hand extended chin-high)
460-2 Stephen Toole (pitching, hands shoulder high)
460-3aStephen Toole (pitching, ball in left hand above head, Brooklyn)
460-3bStephen Toole (pitching, ball in left hand above head, Rochesters)
460-4aStephen Toole (batting, Brooklyn)

460-4bStephen Toole (batting, Rochesters)

460-5 Stephen Toole (pitching, hands at chest)

461-1 Sleepy Townsend (bat at ready position behind head)
461-2aSleepy Townsend (bat at ready position, nearly horizontal, no comma after C.)

461-2bSleepy Townsend (bat at ready position, nearly horizontal, comma after C.)
461-3aSleepy Townsend (fielding, hands chest high, no comma after C.)
461-3bSleepy Townsend (fielding, hands chest high, comma after C.)
462-1 Bill Traffley (fielding, hands above head)

462-2 Bill Traffley (fielding, hands chest-high)

462-3 Bill Traffley (hands on thighs)
462-4 Bill Traffley (throwing)
463-1aGeorge Treadway (batting, looking at ball, Denver)
463-1bGeorge Tredway (Treadway) (batting, looking at ball, St. Pauls)
463-2aGeorge Treadway (fielding, hands thigh high, St. Paul)
463-2bGeorge Tredway (Treadway) (fielding, hands thigh-high, St. Pauls)
463-3 George Tredway (Treadway) (fielding, hands chin-high)
463-4 George Tredway (Treadway) (fielding, hands chest-high)
463-5 George Tredway (Treadway) (batting, facing front)
464-1 Sam Trott (fielding, hands neck-high)

464-2aSam Trott (throwing, left hand head-high, Baltimores)
464-2bSam Trott (throwing, left hand head-high, Newarks)
464-3aSam Trott (fielding, hands knee-high, Baltimores)
464-3bSam Trott (fielding, hands knee-high, Newarks)

464-4aSam Trott (hand on thighs, Baltimores)

464-4bSam Trott (hands on thighs, Newarks)

464-5aSam Trott (batting, Baltimores)
464-5bSam Trott (batting, Newarks)
464-6 Oyster Burns, Sam Trott (Trott tagging Burns)
465-1 Tom Tucker (fielding, hands ankle-high)

465-2 Tom Tucker (fielding, hands chin-high)

465-3 Tom Tucker (throwing)
465-4 Tom Tucker (ball in hands at chest)

465-5 Tom Tucker (batting)
466-1aA.M. Tuckerman (batting, looking at camera, St. Paul)
466-1bA.M. Tuckerman (batting, looking at camera, St. Pauls)
466-2aA.M. Tuckerman (batting, looking down at bat, St. Paul)
466-2bA.M. Tuckerman (batting, looking down at bat, St. Pauls)
466-3 A.M. Tuckerman (pitching, hands at chest)
466-4aA.M. Tuckerman (pitching, right hand head-high, St. Paul)
466-4bA.M. Tuckerman (pitching, right hand head-high, St. Pauls)
466-5 A.M. Tuckerman (pitching, right hand above head)
467-1 George Turner (batting, looking at camera)
467-2 George Turner (batting, looking down at ball)
467-3 George Turner (fielding, hands waist-high)

467-4 George Turner (fielding, hands head-high)

467-5 George Turner (stooping to catch ball by left knee)
468-1aLarry Twitchell (batting, Detroits)

468-1bLarry Twitchell (batting, Clevelands)

468-2aLarry Twitchell (pitching, hands by chest Detroits)
468-2cLarry Twitchell (pitching, hands by chest, Clevelands)
468-3aLarry Twitchell (pitching, right hand head high, Twitchell on front, Detroits)
468-3bLarry Twitchell (pitching, right hand head high, L.G. Twitchell on front, Detroits)

468-3cLarry Twitchell (pitching, right hand head high, Clevelands)
469-1 Jim Tyng (batting, looking at camera)

469-2 Jim Tyng (bat in hand at side)
469-3 Jim Tyng (pitching, hands at chest)

470-1aBill Van Dyke (fielding, Toledos)
470-1bBill Van Dyke (fielding, Des Moines)

470-2 Bill Van Dyke (sliding)
471-1aRip Van Haltren (batting, Chicago)

471-1bRip Van Haltren (batting, Chicagos)

471-1cRip Van Haltren (batting, Chicago's)

471-2 Rip Van Haltren (pitching, right hand at right thigh)
471-3aRip Van Haltren (pitching, hands above center of belt, Chicago)
471-3bRip Van Haltren (pitching, hands above center of belt, Chicagos)
471-3cRip Van Haltren (pitching, hands above center of belt, Chicago's)
471-4 Rip Van Haltren (fielding, hands chest high)
472-1 Farmer Vaughn (batting, looking at camera)
472-2 Farmer Vaughn (batting, looking down at ball)
472-3 Farmer Vaughn (fielding, stooping, hands knee-high)
472-4 Farmer Vaughn (fielding, stooping, hands by right shoulder)
472-5 Farmer Vaughn (fielding, hands by left shoulder)
472-6 Harry Vaughn (ball in right hand, head high)
472.5-1Veach (kneeling, ball in right hand head-high)
472.5-2Veach (fielding, side view, hands stretched forward)
472.5-3Veach (fielding, front view, hands just above head)
473-1aLee Viau (batting, Cincinnati)
473-1bLee Viau (batting, Cincinnati (N.L.)

473-2 Lee Viau (pitching, right hand head-high)

473-3aLee Viau (pitching, right hand at chest, looking at camera, no comma after P., Cincinnati)
473-3bLee Viau (pitching, right hand at chest, looking at camera, comma after P., Cincinnati)
473-3cLee Viau (pitching, right hand at chest, looking at camera, Cincinnatis)
473-4aLee Viau (pitching, right hand out waist high, right profile, no comma after P., Cincinnati)
473-4bLee Viau (pitching, right hand out waist high, right profile, comma after P., Cincinnati)
473-4cLee Viau (pitching, right hand out waist high, right profile, Cincinnatti)
473-4dLee Viau (pitching, right hand out waist high, right profile, Cincinnatis)
473-5aLee Viau (pitching, right hand out thigh high, looking at camera, Cincinnati)
473-5bLee Viau (pitching, right hand out thigh high, looking at camera, Cincinnatti)

474-1 Bill Vinton (batting, looking at camera)

474-2 Bill Vinton (batting, looking at ball)

474-3 Bill Vinton (pitching, hands at chest)

474-4 Bill Vinton (pitching, right hand head-high)

475-1 Joe Visner (batting)
475-2 Joe Visner (standing, arms at sides)

475-3 Joe Visner (throwing)
475-4 Joe Visner (fielding, hands chest-high)

475-5 Joe Visner (bending forward, hands on thighs)
476-1 Chris Von Der Ahe (Brown's Champions)

477-1 Reddy Walsh (striped shirt, bat at ready position by head, looking at camera)

477-2 Reddy Walsh (striped shirt, bat at ready position, left profile)
477-3 Reddy Walsh (fielding, hands waist-high)

477-4 Reddy Walsh (fielding, hands neck-high)

477-5 Reddy Walsh (plain uniform, bat at ready position)
478-1aMonte Ward (portrait, looking to left, Capt. John Ward on front)
478-1bMonte Ward (portrait, looking to left, J. Ward on front)
478-1cMonte Ward (portrait, looking to left, J.M. Ward on front)
478-2aMonte Ward (sliding, right hand raised, N.Y's)
478-2bMonte Ward (sliding, right hand raised, New Yorks)
478-3aMonte Ward (cap in right hand at side, left hand on hip, Capt. John Ward on front)

478-3bMonte Ward (cap in right hand at side, left hand on hip, John Ward on front)
478-3cMonte Ward (cap in right hand at side, left hand on hip, J. Ward on front)
478-4aMonte Ward (hands on hips, N.Y's)

478-4bMonte Ward (hands on hips, New Yorks)

478-5aMonte Ward (throwing, right profile, Capt. John Ward on front)
478-5bMonte Ward (throwing, right profile, John Ward on front)
478-6aMonte Ward (batting, N.Y's)
478-6bMonte Ward (batting, New Yorks)

478-7aMonte Ward (hands behind back, N.Y's)

478-7bMonte Ward (hands behind back, New Yorks)
478-8aMonte Ward (sliding, left hand raised, Capt. John Ward on front)
478-8bMonte Ward (sliding, left hand raised, J.M. Ward on front)
478-8cMonte Ward (sliding, left hand raised, Ward on front)
478-9aMonte Ward (throwing, left profile, N.Y's)

478-9bMonte Ward (throwing, left profile, New Yorks)
479-1 E.H. Warner (fielding)
479-2 E.H. Warner (bat in hand at side)

480-1aBill Watkins (portrait, Detroits)
480-1cBill Watkins (portrait, Kansas Citys)

481-1 Farmer Weaver (batting)
481-2 Farmer Weaver (fielding, left hand above head)
481-3 Farmer Weaver (fielding, hands head high)
481-4 Farmer Weaver (fielding, hands waist high)
482-1 Count Weber (batting, looking at camera)

482-2aCount Weber (batting, looking down at ball, Sioux City)
482-2bCount Weber (batting, looking down at ball, Sioux Citys)
482-3 Count Weber (pitching, hands at chest)

482-4 Count Weber (pitching, hands waist-high)

482-5aCount Weber (pitching, right hand chin high, Sioux City)
482-5bCount Weber (pitching, right hand chin high, Sioux Citys)
483-1 Stump Weidman (pitching, right hand forward, ball released)
483-2 Stump Weidman (batting)
483-3 Stump Weidman (pitching, hands chest high)
483-4 Stump Weidman (bat in hand at side)

484-1 Bill Weidner (Widner) (batting)
484-2 Bill Weidner (Widner) (fielding grounder)

484-3 Bill Weidner (Widner) (pitching, hands at chest)
484-4 Bill Weidner (Widner) (pitching, right hand neck-high)
484-5aBill Weidner (Widner) (pitching, right hand chest-high, Weidner on front)
484-5bBill Eidner (Widner) (pitching, right hand chest-high, Eidner on front)
485-1 Curt Welsh (Welch) (Brown's Champions)

485-2 Curt Welch (batting, looking at camera, Athletics)
485-3 Curt Welch (batting, looking at ball by bat, Athletics)
485-4aCurt Welch (fielding grounder, name correct, Athletics)
485-4bCurt Welch (fielding grounder, Athletic's)

485-4cCurt Welsh (Welch) (fielding grounder, name incorrect, Athletics)
485-5 Curt Welsh (Welch) (fielding, Athletics)

485-6aCurt Welsh (Welch) (throwing, C.F., Athletics)
485-6bCurt Welsh (Welch) (throwing, L.F., Athletics)
485-7aWill Gleason, Curt Welsh (Welch)

485-7bWill Gleason, Curt Welch
486-1aSmiling Mickey Welch (pitching, right hand head-high, name correct, New York)

486-1bSmiling Mickey Welsh (Welch) (pitching, right hand head-high, name incorrect, New York)
486-2aSmiling Mickey Welch (pitching, right hand at right thigh, name correct, New Yorks)
486-2bSmiling Mickey Welsh (Welch) (pitching, right hand at right thigh, name incorrect, New Yorks)
486-2cSmiling Mickey Welch (pitching, right hand at right thigh, New Yorks (N.L.)

486-3aSmiling Mickey Welch (pitching, hands above waist, Welsh on front, New York)

486-3bSmiling Mickey Welch (pitching, hands above waist, Smiling Mickey on front)

486-4aSmiling Mickey Welch (pitching, right arm extended forward, Smiling Mickey on front)

487-1 Jake Wells (holding bat, Kansas City)

487-2 Jake Wells (fielding, Kansas City)

488-1 Frank Wells (fielding, Milwaukee)

489-1 Joe Werrick (tagging)
489-2 Joe Werrick (throwing)
489-3aJoe Werrick (fielding, Louisville)
489-3bJoe Werrick (fielding, St. Pau.)
489-4 Joe Werrick (batting)
490-1 Buck West (batting, looking at camera)

490-2 Buck West (striking, looking down at ball by bat)
490-3 Buck West (fielding, hands by right thigh)

490-4 Buck West (fielding, hands shoulder-high)

490-5 Buck West (fielding low ball)
491-1 Cannonball Weyhing (pitching, hands at throat, Athletics)
491-2aCannonball Weyhing (pitching, right hand chest-high, A.C. Weyhing on front, Athletics)

491-2cCannonball Weyhing (pitching, right hand chest-high, Weyhing on front, Athletics)

491-3aCannonball Weyhing (pitching, right hand cap-high, A.C. Weyhing on front, Athletics)

491-3bCannonball Weyhing (pitching, right hand cap-high, Weyhing on front, Athletics)

492-1aJohn Weyhing (pitching, hands at neck, Athletics)
492-1bJohn Weyhing (pitching, hands at neck, Columbus)
492-2aJohn Weyhing (pitching, left hand out chest-high, Athletics)
493-1aBobby Wheelock (fielding, R.F., Boston)

493-1bBobby Wheelock (fielding, Right Field)

493-1cBobby Wheelock (fielding, R.F., Detroits)

493-2aBobby Wheelock (batting, looking at camera, R.F.)
493-2bBobby Wheelock (batting, looking at camera, Right Field)
493-3aBobby Wheelock (throwing, Right Field)

493-3bBobby Wheelock (throwing, R.F.)

493-4aBobby Wheelock (batting, looking down at ball, R.F.)
493-4bBobby Wheelock (batting, looking down at ball, Right Field)
493-5aBobby Wheelock (hands on hips, R.F.)
493-5bBobby Wheelock (hands on hips, Right Field)
493-6 Bobby Wheelock (bat in hand at side)
493-7 Bobby Wheelock (bat at ready position at 60 degrees, looking at camera)
494-1 Pat Whitacre (Whitaker) (batting)
494-2 Pat Whitacre (Whitaker) (pitching, hands out head-high)
494-3 Pat Whitacre (Whitaker) (pitching, right hand back head-high)
495-1 Pat Whitaker (pitching, hands behind right thigh)
495-2 Pat Whitaker (pitching, hands out above waist)
495-3 Pat Whitaker (pitching, hands neck-high)
495-4 Pat Whitaker (pitching, right hand forward neck-high)
496-1 Deacon White (batting, looking at camera, Detroits)
496-2 Deacon White (batting looking down at ball, Detroits)
496-3 Deacon White (fielding, hands waist-high, Detroits)
496-4 Deacon White (fielding, hands neck-high, Detroits)
496-5aDeacon White (fielding, hands above head, Detroits)
496-5bDeacon White (fielding, hands above head, Pittsburghs)
496-6aDeacon White (throwing, Detroits)
496-6bDeacon White (throwing, Pittsburghs)
496-7 Deacon White (fielding grounder, hands together by left foot, Detroits)
496-8 Deacon White (fielding grounder with right hand, Detroits)
497-1 Bill White (batting, Louisville)
497-2 Bill White (stooping, ball in left hand on grass, Louisville)
497-3 Bill White (fielding ground ball, Louisville)
497-4 Bill White (throwing, Louisville)
497-5 Bill White (fielding, hands neck-high, Louisville)
498-1aGrasshopper Whitney (batting, looking at camera, P., Washington)
498-1bGrasshopper Whitney (batting, looking at camera, Pitcher, Washington)
498-2aGrasshopper Whitney (pitching, hanus at chest, no comma after P., Washington)
498-2bGrasshopper Whitney (pitching, hands at chest, Pitcher, Washington)
498-2cGrasshopper Whitney (pitching, hands at chest, comma after P., Washington)
498-3aGrasshopper Whitney (pitching, right hand waist-high, P., Washington)
498-3bGrasshopper Whitney (pitching, right hand waist-high, Pitcher, Washington)
498-3cGrasshopper Whitney (pitching, right hand waist-high, Indianapolis)
499-1aArt Whitney (white uniform, stooping, dog with paw on his knee, 3d B., Pittsburg)
499-1bArt Whitney (white uniform, stooping, dog with paw on his knee, 3d Base, Pittsburg)
499-1cArt Whitney (white uniform, stooping, dog with paw on his knee, Whitney on front, New Yorks)
499-1dArt Whitney (white uniform, stooping, dog with paw on his knee, A. Whitney on front, New Yorks)
499-2aArt Whitney (white uniform, bending to left, hands thigh-high, 3d B. Pittsburg)
499-2bArt Whitney (white uniform, bending to left, hands thigh-high, 3d Base, Pittsburg)
499-2cArt Whitney (white uniform, bending to left, hands thigh-high, Whitney on front, New Yorks)
499-2dArt Whitney (white uniform, bending to left, hands thigh-high, A. Whitney on front, New Yorks)
499-2eArt Whitney (white uniform, bending to left, hands thigh-high, New York (PL))
499-3aArt Whitney (white uniform, batting, 3d B., Pittsburg)
499-3bArt Whitney (white uniform, batting, 3d Base, Pittsburg)
499-3cArt Whitney (white uniform, batting, New Yorks)
500-1 G. Whitney (dark uniform, batting, looking at camera, St. Joes)
500-2 G. Whitney (dark uniform, batting, looking down at ball, St. Joes)
500-3 G. Whitney (dark uniform, fielding grounder, St. Joes)
500-4 G. Whitney (dark uniform, throwing, St. Joes)
500-5 G. Whitney (dark uniform, fielding, hands at waist, St. Joes)
501-1 James Williams (hat in right hand)
501-2 James Williams (hat on head)
502-1 Ned Williamson (in top hat, looking to right)
502-2 Ned Williamson (fielding, hands neck-high)
502-3aNed Williamson (throwing, Chicago's)
502-3bNed Williamson (throwing, Chicago)
502-3cNed Williamson (throwing, W. Williamson on front, Chicagos)
502-3dNed Williamson (throwing, Chicag.)
502-3eNed Williamson (throwing, C.W. Williamson on front, Chicagos)
502-4aNed Williamson (fielding, hands above head, Chicago's)
502-4bNed Williamson (fielding, hands above head, E. Williamson on front, Chicago)
502-4cNed Williamson (fielding, hands above head, Chica.)
502-4dNed Williamson (fielding, hands above head, C.W. Williamson on front, Chicago)
502-4eNed Williamson (fielding, hands above head, Chicagos)
502-4f Ned Williamson (fielding, hands above head, W. Williamson on front, Chicago)
502-5aNed Williamson (arms folded, no comma after S.S., Chicago's)
502-5bNed Williamson (arms folded, comma after S.S., Chicago's)
502-5cNed Williamson (arms folded, Chicago)
502-6aNed Williamson (batting, looking down at ball, Chicago's)
502-6cNed Williamson (batting, looking down at ball, E. Williamson on front, Chicago)
502-6dNed Williamson (batting, looking down at ball, Chicagos)
502-6eNed Williamson (batting, looking down at ball, W. Williamson on front, Chicago)
502-7 Willie Hahm - mascot, Ned Williamson
503-1 C.H. Willis (pitching, hands in front of cap)
503-2 C.H. Willis (pitching, hands at waist)
503-3 C.H. Willis (pitching, hands out to left chin high)
503-4 C.H. Willis (pitching, right hand forward head-high)
503-5 C.H. Willis (batting)
504-1aWatt Wilmot (batting, looking down at ball, Washington)
504-1bWatt Wilmot (batting, looking down at ball, Chicagos (N L))
504-2aWatt Wilmot (bat in hand at side, Washingtons)
504-2bWatt Wilmot (bat in hand at side, Chicagos (N L))
504-3aWatt Wilmot (catching, hands thigh-high, Washingtons)
504-3bWatt Wilmot (catching, hands thigh-high, Washington)
504-4aWatt Wilmot (catching, hands at chest, Washingtons)
504-4bWatt Wilmot (catching, hands at chest. Washington)
504-4cWatt Wilmot (catching, hands at chest, Chicagos (N.L.))
504-5aWatt Wilmot (throwing, Washingtons)
504-5bWatt Wilmot (throwing, Washington)
505-1 George Winkleman (Winkelman) (throwing, hands out to right shoulder-high)
505-2 George Winkleman (Winkelman) (pitching, hands chest-high)
505-3 George Winkleman (Winkelman) (pitching, right hand above waist, left hand by left hip)
505-4 George Winkleman (Winkelman) (fielding)
506-1aMedoc Wise (stooping, hands on knees, S.S., Boston)
506-1bMedoc Wise (stooping, hands on knees, Short Stop)
506-1cMedoc Wise (stooping, hands on knees, S.S., Washingtons)
506-2aMedoc Wise (batting, Wise on front, S.S.)
506-2bMedoc Wise (batting, Short Stop)
506-2cMedoc Wise (batting, Sam W. Wise on front, S.S.)
506-3aMedoc Wise (bat in hand at side, S.S.)
506-3bMedoc Wise (bat in hand at side, Short Stop)
506-4aMedoc Wise (portrait, Wise on front, S.S.)
506-4bMedoc Wise (portrait, Short Stop)
506-4cMedoc Wise (portrait, Sam W. Wise on front, S.S.)
507-1 Chicken Wolf (batting, "Louisville" visible on shirt)
507-2aChicken Wolf (batting, team name not visible, Louisville)
507-2bChicken Wolf (batting, team name not visible, Louisvilles)
507-3aChicken Wolf (lying on grass, feet on base. Louisville)
507-3bChicken Wolf (lying on grass, feet on base, Louisvilles)
507-4aChicken Wolf (fielding, hands chin-high, Louisville)
507-4bChicken Wolf (fielding, hands chin-high, Louisvilles)
507-5aChicken Wolf (fielding, hands by right ankle, Louisville)
507-5bChicken Wolf (fielding, hands by right ankle, Louisvilles)
508-1aGeorge "Dandy" Wood (batting, L.F., Phila)
508-1bGeorge "Dandy" Wood (batting, Left Field, Philadelphia)
508-1cGeorge "Dandy" Wood (batting, L.F., Philadelphias)
508-2aGeorge "Dandy" Wood (fielding, hands neck-high, L.F., Phila)
508-2bGeorge "Dandy" Wood (fielding, hands neck-high, Left Field, Philadelphia)
508-2cGeorge "Dandy" Wood (fielding, hands neck-high, L.F., Philadelphias)
508-3aGeorge "Dandy" Wood (fielding grounder, L.F., Phila)
508-3bGeorge "Dandy" Wood (fielding grounder, Left Field, Philadelphia)
508-3cGeorge "Dandy" Wood (fielding grounder, L.F., Philadelphias)
508-4aGeorge "Dandy" Wood (throwing, L.F., Phila)
508-4bGeorge "Dandy" Wood (throwing, Left Field, Philadelphia)
508-4cGeorge "Dandy" Wood (throwing, L.F., Philadelphias)
509-1 Pete Wood (bat on shoulder, P., Philadelphias)
509-2 Pete Wood (bat at ready position, nearlv horizontal, P., Philadelphias)
509-3 Pete Wood (pitching, hands at neck. P. Philadelphia)
509-4 Pete Wood (pitching, right hand forward neck-high, P., Philadelphias)
509-5 Pete Wood (pitching, right hand extended at side head-high, P., Philadelphias)
510-1aHarry Wright (portrait, looking to right, Phila)
510-1bHarry Wright (portrait, looking to right, Phila's)
510-1dHarry Wright (portrait, looking to right, Phila (N L))
510-2 Harry Wright (portrait, looking to left, beard clear of right side of collar)
510-3 Harry Wright (portrait, looking to left, beard just over right side of collar)
511-1 Chief Zimmer (batting)
511-2 Chief Zimmer (fielding, hands chest-high, feet together)
511-3 Chief Zimmer (fielding, hands chest-high, feet well apart)
511-4aChief Zimmer (throwing, Cleveland's)
511-4bChief Zimmer (throwing, Clevelands)
512-1 Frank Zinn (fielding grounder)
512-2 Frank Zinn (fielding, hands thigh-high)
512-3 Frank Zinn (fielding, hands head-high)

One of the most fascinating of all card sets, the N172 Old Judge cards were issued by the Goodwin & Co. tobacco firm in their Old Judge and, to a lesser extent, Gypsy Queen cigarettes. Players from more than 40 major and minor league teams are pictured, with some 518 different players known to exist. Up to 17 different pose and team variations exist for some players, and the cards were issued both with and without dates on the card fronts, numbered and unnumbered, and with both handwritten and machine-printed names. Known variations number in the thousands. The cards themselves are blank-backed, sepia-toned photographs pasted onto thick cardboard. The listings are based on the recordings in the The Cartophilic Society's World Index, Part IV, compiled by E.C. Wharton-Tigar with the help of many collectors, especially Donald J. McPherson and Lew Lipset. The above list includes all known variations for each player in the set.

Note: Current values for cards in the N172 Old Judge set are found under the regular listings beginning on page 244.

The hobby's 25 most valuable cards

1. 1909-1911 T206 Honus Wagner $200,000
2. 1909-1911 T206 Joe Doyle (N.Y. Natl., hands above head) $30,000
3. 1933 Goudey Napoleon (Larry) Lajoie $30,000
4. 1932 U.S. Caramel Charles (Lindy) Lindstrom $25,000
5. 1909-1911 T206 Eddie Plank $25,000
6. 1909-1911 Sherry Magie $15,000
7. 1909-1911 E90-1 American Caramel Mike Mitchell $10,000
8. 1951 Topps Current All-Stars Robin Roberts $9,500
9. 1952 Topps Mickey Mantle $8,900
10. 1951 Topps Current All-Stars Eddie Stanky $8,500
11. 1951 Topps Current All-Stars Jim Konstanty $8,500
12. 1909-1911 E90-1 American Caramel Shoeless Joe Jackson ... $7,500
13. 1909-1911 T206 Ray Demmitt (St. Louis) $7,500
14. 1912 T207 Irving Lewis $7,500
15. 1911 T3 Ty Cobb $6,500
16. 1912 T207 Louis Lowdermilk $5,500
17. 1933 Goudey Babe Ruth #53 .... $5,200
18. 1933 Goudey Babe Ruth #181 .... $4,500
19. 1933 Goudey Babe Ruth #149 .... $4,500
20. 1951 Bowman Mickey Mantle $4,500
21. 1933 Goudey Babe Ruth #144 .... $4,400
22. 1911 T205 Ty Cobb $4,000
23. 1934 Goudey Lou Gehrig $3,100
24. 1954 Bowman Ted Williams $3,000
25. 1933 DeLong Lou Gehrig $3,000

ROOKIE CARD CHECKLIST

An alphabetical list of rookie cards, 1948–1990

A

Henry Aaron ... 1954 Topps #128
Tommie Aaron ... 1963 Topps #46
Don Aase ... 1976 Topps #597
Jim Abbott ... 1989 Topps #573
Kyle Abbott ... 1990 Score #673
Kyle Abbott ... 1990 Topps #444
Shawn Abner ... 1985 Topps #282
Johnny Abrego (RR) ... 1986 Donruss #32
Jim Acker ... 1984 Donruss #146
Jim Acker ... 1984 Fleer #145
Jim Acker ... 1984 Topps #359
Joe Adcock ... 1951 Bowman #323
Jim Adduci ... 1987 Donruss #495
Tommie Agee ... 1965 Topps #166
Harry Agganis ... 1955 Topps #152
Juan Agosto ... 1984 Donruss #208
Juan Agosto ... 1984 Fleer #50
Juan Agosto ... 1984 Topps #409
Luis Aguayo ... 1982 Donruss #622
Luis Aguayo ... 1982 Fleer #238
Luis Aguayo ... 1982 Topps #449
Rick Aguilera ... 1986 Donruss #441
Rick Aguilera ... 1986 Fleer #74
Rick Aguilera ... 1986 Topps #599
Hank Aguirre ... 1957 Topps #96
Willie Aikens ... 1980 Topps #368
Dan Ainge ... 1981 Fleer #418
Danny Ainge ... 1981 Donruss #569
Darrel Akerfelds ... 1988 Score #632
Darrel Akerfelds ... 1988 Topps #82
Mike Aldrete ... 1987 Donruss #450
Mike Aldrete ... 1987 Fleer #264
Mike Aldrete ... 1987 Topps #71
Jay Aldrich ... 1988 Donruss #460
Jay Aldrich ... 1988 Fleer #155
Jay Aldrich ... 1988 Score #578
Jay Aldrich ... 1988 Topps #616
Doyle Alexander ... 1972 Topps #579
Luis Alicea ... 1989 Donruss #466
Luis Alicea ... 1989 Fleer #443
Luis Alicea ... 1989 Score #231
Luis Alicea ... 1989 Topps #588
Luis Alicea ... 1989 Upper Deck #281
Andy Allanson ... 1987 Donruss #95
Andy Allanson ... 1987 Fleer #241
Andy Allanson ... 1987 Topps #436
Bernie Allen ... 1962 Topps #596
Neil Allen ... 1980 Topps #94
Richie Allen ... 1964 Topps #243
Rod Allen ... 1989 Fleer #397
Gene Alley ... 1964 Topps #509
Bob Allison ... 1959 Topps #116
Beau Allred ... 1990 Donruss #691
Beau Allred ... 1990 Topps #419
Billy Almon ... 1977 Topps #490
Roberto Alomar ... 1988 Donruss #34
Sandy Alomar ... 1989 Score #630
Sandy Alomar ... 1989 Topps #648
Santos Alomar ... 1965 Topps #82
Sandy Alomar, Jr. ... 1989 Donruss #28
Sandy Alomar, Jr. ... 1989 Fleer #300
Sandy Alomar, Jr. ... 1989 Upper Deck #5
Felipe Alou ... 1959 Topps #102
Jesus Alou ... 1964 Topps #47
Matty Alou ... 1961 Topps #327
Moises Alou ... 1990 Fleer #650
Moises Alou ... 1990 Score #592
Jose Alvarez ... 1989 Donruss #405
Jose Alvarez ... 1989 Fleer #585
Jose Alvarez ... 1989 Topps #253
Max Alvis ... 1963 Topps #228
Larry Andersen ... 1978 Topps #703
Allan Anderson ... 1987 Donruss #368
Allan Anderson ... 1987 Fleer #533
Allan Anderson ... 1987 Topps #336
Brady Anderson ... 1989 Donruss #519
Brady Anderson ... 1989 Fleer #606
Brady Anderson ... 1989 Score #563
Brady Anderson ... 1989 Topps #757
Brady Anderson ... 1989 Upper Deck #408
Dave Anderson ... 1984 Donruss #642
Dave Anderson ... 1984 Topps #376
George Anderson ... 1959 Topps #338
Kent Anderson ... 1990 Donruss #490
Kent Anderson ... 1990 Score #412
Kent Anderson ... 1990 Topps #16
Kent Anderson ... 1990 Upper Deck #691
Mike Andrews ... 1967 Topps #314
Joaquin Andujar ... 1977 Topps #67
Willie Ansley ... 1989 Topps #607
Eric Anthony ... 1990 Donruss #34
Eric Anthony ... 1990 Fleer #222
Eric Anthony ... 1990 Score #584
Eric Anthony ... 1990 Topps #608
Eric Anthony ... 1990 Upper Deck #28
Johnny Antonelli ... 1950 Bowman #74
Luis Aparicio ... 1956 Topps #292
Kevin Appier ... 1990 Fleer #100
Kevin Appier ... 1990 Score #625
Kevin Appier ... 1990 Topps #167
Kevin Appier ... 1990 Upper Deck #102
Luis Aquino ... 1987 Donruss #655
Luis Aquino ... 1987 Topps #301
Tony Armas ... 1977 Topps #492
Jack Armstrong ... 1989 Donruss #493
Jack Armstrong ... 1989 Score #462
Jack Armstrong ... 1989 Topps #317
Jack Armstrong ... 1989 Upper Deck #257
Brad Arnsberg ... 1988 Fleer #202
Brad Arnsberg ... 1988 Topps #159
Randy Asadoor ... 1987 Donruss #574
Randy Asadoor ... 1987 Fleer #650
Richie Ashburn ... 1949 Bowman #214
Bob Aspromonte ... 1960 Topps #547
Paul Assenmacher ... 1987 Donruss #290
Paul Assenmacher ... 1987 Fleer #511
Paul Assenmacher ... 1987 Topps #132
Keith Atherton ... 1984 Donruss #497
Keith Atherton ... 1984 Fleer #437
Keith Atherton ... 1984 Topps #529
Don August ... 1988 Donruss #602
Pat Austin ... 1990 Score #626
Steve Avery ... 1989 Topps #784
Roberto Avila ... 1951 Bowman #188

B

Wally Backman ... 1981 Fleer #336
Stan Bahnsen ... 1967 Topps #93
Scott Bailes ... 1987 Donruss #227
Scott Bailes ... 1987 Fleer #242
Scott Bailes ... 1987 Topps #585
Bob Bailey ... 1963 Topps #228
Ed Bailey ... 1953 Topps #206
Mark Bailey ... 1985 Donruss #450
Mark Bailey ... 1985 Fleer #344
Mark Bailey ... 1985 Topps #64
Harold Baines ... 1981 Fleer #346
Harold Baines ... 1981 Topps #347
Doug Baker ... 1985 Topps #269
Dusty Baker ... 1971 Topps #709
Steve Balboni ... 1982 Topps #83
Jack Baldschun ... 1962 Topps #46
Jeff Ballard ... 1988 Donruss #520
Jeff Ballard ... 1988 Fleer #554
Jeff Ballard ... 1988 Topps #782
George Bamberger ... 1959 Topps #529
Sal Bando ... 1967 Topps #33
Scott Bankhead ... 1987 Fleer #363
Scott Bankhead ... 1987 Topps #508
Ernie Banks ... 1954 Topps #94
Floyd Bannister ... 1978 Topps #39
Steve Barber ... 1960 Topps #514
Jesse Barfield ... 1982 Topps #203
Len Barker ... 1977 Topps #489
Marty Barrett ... 1984 Topps #683
Tommy Barrett ... 1989 Topps #653
Kevin Bass ... 1979 Topps #708
John Bateman ... 1963 Topps #386
Billy Bates ... 1990 Score #608
Kevin Batiste ... 1990 Upper Deck #115
Earl Battey ... 1957 Topps #401
Hank Bauer ... 1950 Bowman #219
Jose Bautista ... 1989 Donruss #451
Jose Bautista ... 1989 Fleer #608
Jose Bautista ... 1989 Score #573
Jose Bautista ... 1989 Topps #469
Jose Bautista ... 1989 Upper Deck #574
Don Baylor ... 1971 Topps #709
Billy Bean ... 1988 Topps #267
Billy Beane ... 1986 Donruss #647
Blaine Beatty ... 1990 Fleer #197
Blaine Beatty ... 1990 Score #632
Blaine Beatty ... 1990 Upper Deck #23
Glenn Beckert ... 1965 Topps #549
Steve Bedrosian ... 1982 Donruss #401
Steve Bedrosian ... 1982 Topps #502
Mark Belanger ... 1967 Topps #558
Stan Belinda ... 1990 Score #634
Stan Belinda ... 1990 Topps #354
Bo Belinsky ... 1962 Topps #592
Buddy Bell ... 1973 Topps #31
Dave "Gus" Bell ... 1951 Bowman #40
Gary Bell ... 1959 Topps #327
Jay Bell ... 1988 Donruss #637
Jay Bell ... 1988 Fleer #602
Jay Bell ... 1988 Topps #637
Jorge Bell ... 1982 Donruss #54
Jorge Bell ... 1982 Fleer #609
Jorge Bell ... 1982 Topps #254
Juan Bell ... 1989 Upper Deck #20
Eric Bell (RR) ... 1987 Donruss #39
Joey Belle ... 1990 Donruss #390
Joey Belle ... 1990 Fleer #485
Joey Belle ... 1990 Score #508
Joey Belle ... 1990 Topps #283
Joey Belle ... 1990 Upper Deck #446
Rafael Belliard ... 1987 Donruss #538
Rafael Belliard ... 1987 Fleer #602
Rafael Belliard ... 1987 Topps #541
Johnny Bench ... 1968 Topps #247
Bill Bene ... 1989 Topps #84
Bruce Benedict ... 1979 Topps #715
Andy Benes ... 1989 Topps #437
Juan Beniquez ... 1974 Topps #647
Mike Benjamin ... 1990 Fleer #51
Todd Benzinger ... 1988 Donruss #297
Todd Benzinger ... 1988 Fleer #344
Todd Benzinger ... 1988 Score #546
Todd Benzinger ... 1988 Topps #96
Juan Berenguer ... 1979 Topps #721
Dave Bergman ... 1978 Topps #705
Tony Bernazard ... 1980 Topps #680
Dale Berra ... 1979 Topps #723
Larry (Yogi) Berra ... 1948 Bowman #6
Geronimo Berroa ... 1988 Donruss #659
Ken Berry ... 1965 Topps #368
Damon Berryhill ... 1988 Donruss #639
Damon Berryhill ... 1988 Fleer #642
Kurt Bevacqua ... 1972 Topps #193
Buddy Biancalana ... 1985 Topps #387
Jim Bibby ... 1972 Topps #316
Dante Bichette ... 1989 Donruss #634
Dante Bichette ... 1989 Fleer #468
Dante Bichette ... 1989 Topps #761
Dante Bichette ... 1989 Upper Deck #24
Mike Bielecki ... 1985 Fleer #650
Mike Bielecki (RR) ... 1985 Donruss #28
Craig Biggio ... 1989 Donruss #561
Craig Biggio ... 1989 Fleer #353
Craig Biggio ... 1989 Score #237
Craig Biggio ... 1989 Topps #49
Craig Biggio ... 1989 Upper Deck #273
Jack Billingham ... 1968 Topps #228
Mike Birkbeck ... 1987 Topps #229
Mike Birkbeck (RR) ... 1987 Donruss #33
Tim Birtsas ... 1986 Donruss #462
Tim Birtsas ... 1986 Fleer #412
Jeff Bittiger ... 1989 Score #512
Jeff Bittiger ... 1989 Topps #209
Jeff Bittiger ... 1989 Upper Deck #509
Bud Black ... 1983 Donruss #322
Bud Black ... 1983 Fleer #107
Bud Black ... 1983 Topps #238
Joe Black ... 1952 Topps #321
Paul Blair ... 1965 Topps #473
John Blanchard ... 1959 Topps #117
Kevin Blankenship ... 1989 Donruss #658
Lance Blankenship ... 1989 Donruss #621
Lance Blankenship ... 1989 Fleer #2
Lance Blankenship ... 1989 Score #641
Lance Blankenship ... 1989 Upper Deck #15
Don Blasingame ... 1956 Topps #309
Steve Blass ... 1965 Topps #232
Jeff Blauser ... 1988 Donruss #513
Jeff Blauser ... 1988 Fleer #533
Jeff Blauser ... 1988 Score #562
Curt Blefary ... 1965 Topps #49
Terry Blocker ... 1989 Fleer #589
Terry Blocker ... 1989 Score #605
Terry Blocker ... 1989 Topps #76
Terry Blocker ... 1989 Upper Deck #399
Ron Blomberg ... 1972 Topps #203
Greg Blosser ... 1990 Score #681
Mike Blowers ... 1990 Donruss #656
Mike Blowers ... 1990 Fleer #438
Mike Blowers ... 1990 Score #624
Vida Blue ... 1970 Topps #21
Bert Blyleven ... 1971 Topps #26
Randy Bockus ... 1989 Topps #733
Mike Boddicker ... 1981 Topps #399
Joe Boever ... 1988 Fleer #534
Joe Boever ... 1988 Score #542
Joe Boever ... 1988 Topps #627
Wade Boggs ... 1983 Donruss #586
Wade Boggs ... 1983 Fleer #179
Wade Boggs ... 1983 Topps #498
Bobby Bolin ... 1961 Topps #449
Frank Bolling ... 1955 Bowman #204
Frank Bolling ... 1955 Bowman #204
Tom Bolton ... 1988 Fleer #346
Tom Bolton ... 1988 Topps #442
Barry Bonds ... 1987 Donruss #361
Barry Bonds ... 1987 Fleer #604
Barry Bonds ... 1987 Topps #320
Bobby Bonds ... 1969 Topps #630
Bobby Bonilla ... 1987 Donruss #558
Bobby Bonilla ... 1987 Fleer #605
Bobby Bonilla ... 1987 Topps #184
Greg Booker ... 1985 Fleer #27
Greg Booker ... 1985 Topps #262
Rod Booker ... 1988 Topps #483
Bob Boone ... 1973 Topps #613
Pedro Borbon ... 1970 Topps #358
Pat Borders ... 1989 Donruss #560
Pat Borders ... 1989 Fleer #227
Pat Borders ... 1989 Score #198
Pat Borders ... 1989 Topps #693
Pat Borders ... 1989 Upper Deck #593
Steve Boros ... 1958 Topps #81
Steve Boros ... 1958 Topps #81
Chris Bosio ... 1987 Donruss #478
Chris Bosio ... 1987 Fleer #338
Chris Bosio ... 1987 Topps #448
Thad Bosley ... 1978 Topps #619
Dick Bosman ... 1967 Topps #459
Lyman Bostock ... 1976 Topps #263
Daryl Boston (RR) ... 1985 Donruss #33
Dave Boswell ... 1967 Topps #575
Jim Bouton ... 1962 Topps #592
Larry Bowa ... 1970 Topps #539

Dennis Boyd ... 1984 Fleer #393
Dennis "Oil Can" Boyd ... 1984 Donruss #457
Cletis Boyer ... 1957 Topps #121
Ken Boyer ... 1955 Topps #125
Phil Bradley ... 1985 Donruss #631
Phil Bradley ... 1985 Fleer #486
Phil Bradley ... 1985 Topps #449
Scott Bradley (RR) ... 1985 Donruss #37
Glenn Braggs ... 1987 Donruss #337
Glenn Braggs ... 1987 Fleer #339
Glenn Braggs ... 1987 Topps #622
Jackie Brandt ... 1959 Topps #297
Jeff Brantley ... 1990 Donruss #466
Jeff Brantley ... 1990 Fleer #52
Jeff Brantley ... 1990 Score #371
Jeff Brantley ... 1990 Topps #703
Jeff Brantley ... 1990 Upper Deck #358
Mickey Brantley ... 1986 Fleer #651
Sid Bream ... 1985 Donruss #470
Sid Bream ... 1985 Topps #253
Bob Brenly ... 1982 Donruss #574
Bob Brenly ... 1982 Topps #171
Bill Brennan ... 1989 Score #622
William Brennan ... 1989 Donruss #589
William Brennan ... 1989 Upper Deck #16
George Brett ... 1975 Topps #228
Ken Brett ... 1969 Topps #476
Ken Brett ... 1969 Topps #476
Jim Brewer ... 1961 Topps #317
John Briggs ... 1964 Topps #482
Nelson Briles ... 1965 Topps #431
Greg Briley ... 1989 Topps #781
Ed Brinkman ... 1963 Topps #479
Greg Brock ... 1983 Donruss #579
Greg Brock ... 1983 Fleer #203
Ernie Broglio ... 1959 Topps #296
Tom Brookens ... 1980 Topps #416
Hubie Brooks ... 1981 Topps #259
Terry Bross ... 1990 Donruss #502
Bob Brower ... 1987 Donruss #651
Bobby Brown ... 1949 Bowman #19
Chris Brown ... 1986 Donruss #553
Chris Brown ... 1986 Fleer #535
Chris Brown ... 1986 Topps #383
Gates Brown ... 1964 Topps #471
Hal Brown ... 1953 Topps #184
Keith Brown ... 1989 Donruss #115
Keith Brown ... 1989 Fleer #154
Kevin Brown ... 1987 Donruss #627
Kevin Brown ... 1989 Fleer #641
Marty Brown ... 1989 Fleer #645
Jerry Browne ... 1987 Fleer #647
Jerry Browne (RR) ... 1987 Donruss #41
Tom Browning ... 1985 Donruss #634
Mike Brumley ... 1988 Donruss #609
Tom Brunansky ... 1982 Topps #653
Bill Bruton ... 1953 Topps #214
Ralph Bryant ... 1987 Donruss #587
Ralph Bryant ... 1987 Fleer #649
Scott Bryant ... 1990 Score #667
T.R. Bryden ... 1987 Topps #387
Bill Buckner ... 1970 Topps #286
Steve Buechele ... 1986 Donruss #544
Steve Buechele ... 1986 Fleer #558
Steve Buechele ... 1986 Topps #397
Don Buford ... 1964 Topps #368
Bob Buhl ... 1954 Topps #210
Jay Buhner ... 1988 Donruss #545
DeWayne Buice ... 1988 Donruss #58
DeWayne Buice ... 1988 Fleer #487
DeWayne Buice ... 1988 Score #376
DeWayne Buice ... 1988 Topps #649
Eric Bullock ... 1989 Fleer #106
Alonza Bumbry ... 1973 Topps #614
Wally Bunker ... 1964 Topps #201
Jim Bunning ... 1957 Topps #338
Lew Burdette ... 1952 Bowman #244
Forrest Burgess ... 1951 Bowman #317
Tom Burgmeier ... 1969 Topps #558
Tim Burke ... 1986 Donruss #421
Tim Burke ... 1986 Fleer #245
Tim Burke ... 1986 Topps #258
John Burkett ... 1988 Fleer #651
Ellis Burks ... 1988 Donruss #174
Ellis Burks ... 1988 Fleer #348
Ellis Burks ... 1988 Score #472
Ellis Burks ... 1988 Topps #269
Rick Burleson ... 1975 Topps #302
Britt Burns ... 1981 Donruss #279
Britt Burns ... 1981 Fleer #342
Britt Burns ... 1981 Fleer #342
Britt Burns ... 1981 Topps #412
Todd Burns ... 1989 Donruss #564
Todd Burns ... 1989 Fleer #3
Todd Burns ... 1989 Score #465
Todd Burns ... 1989 Topps #174
Ray Burris ... 1974 Topps #161
Jeff Burroughs ... 1972 Topps #191
Steve Busby ... 1973 Topps #608
Randy Bush ... 1984 Donruss #513
Randy Bush ... 1984 Fleer #558
Randy Bush ... 1984 Topps #429
Brett Butler ... 1982 Donruss #275
Brett Butler ... 1982 Topps #502
Randall Byers ... 1988 Donruss #605
Randell Byers (Randall) ... 1988 Fleer #653

C

Enos Cabell ... 1973 Topps #605
Francisco Cabrera ... 1990 Donruss #646
Francisco Cabrera ... 1990 Upper Deck #64
Greg Cadaret ... 1988 Donruss #528
Greg Cadaret ... 1988 Topps #328
Ivan Calderon ... 1986 Donruss #435
Ivan Calderon ... 1986 Fleer #462
Ivan Calderon ... 1986 Topps #382
Mike Caldwell ... 1973 Topps #182
John Callison ... 1959 Topps #119
Ernie Camacho ... 1981 Topps #96
Ken Caminiti ... 1988 Donruss #308
Ken Caminiti ... 1988 Fleer #441
Ken Caminiti ... 1988 Score #164
Ken Caminiti ... 1988 Topps #64
Roy Campanella ... 1949 Bowman #84
Bert Campaneris ... 1965 Topps #266
Bill Campbell ... 1974 Topps #26
Jim Campbell ... 1989 Fleer #646
Mike Campbell ... 1988 Donruss #30
Mike Campbell ... 1988 Fleer #372
Mike Campbell ... 1988 Topps #246
Sil Campusano ... 1989 Donruss #584
Sil Campusano ... 1989 Score #473
Sil Campusano ... 1989 Topps #191
Sil Campusano ... 1989 Upper Deck #45
George Canale ... 1990 Donruss #699
George Canale ... 1990 Fleer #641
George Canale ... 1990 Score #656
George Canale ... 1990 Topps #344
George Canale ... 1990 Upper Deck #59
Casey Candaele ... 1987 Donruss #549
John Candelaria ... 1976 Topps #317
Tom Candiotti ... 1984 Donruss #393
Tom Candiotti ... 1984 Fleer #197
Tom Candiotti ... 1984 Topps #262
John Cangelosi ... 1987 Donruss #162
John Cangelosi ... 1987 Fleer #489
John Cangelosi ... 1987 Topps #201
Jose Cano ... 1990 Upper Deck #43
Jose Canseco ... 1986 Fleer #649
Jose Canseco (RR) ... 1986 Donruss #39
Mike Capel ... 1989 Fleer #643
Mike Capel ... 1989 Topps #767
Nick Capra ... 1989 Fleer #279
Bernie Carbo ... 1970 Topps #36
Jose Cardenal ... 1965 Topps #374
Chico Cardenas ... 1960 Topps #119
Rod Carew ... 1967 Topps #569
Andy Carey ... 1953 Topps #188
Steve Carlton ... 1965 Topps #477
Don Carman ... 1986 Donruss #427
Don Carman ... 1986 Fleer #436
Don Carman ... 1986 Topps #532
Cris Carpenter ... 1989 Donruss #39
Cris Carpenter ... 1989 Topps #282
Cris Carpenter ... 1989 Upper Deck #8
Mark Carreon ... 1988 Fleer #129
Clay Carroll ... 1965 Topps #461
Gary Carter ... 1975 Topps #620
Steve Carter ... 1990 Topps #482
Steve Carter ... 1990 Upper Deck #368
Joe Carter (RR) ... 1984 Donruss #41
Rico Carty ... 1964 Topps #476
Chuck Cary ... 1987 Donruss #461
Chuck Cary ... 1987 Fleer #147
Chuck Cary ... 1987 Topps #171
Dave Cash ... 1970 Topps #141
Norm Cash ... 1959 Topps #509
Bobby Castillo ... 1979 Topps #641
Carmelo Castillo ... 1983 Fleer #404
Juan Castillo ... 1987 Donruss #249
Tony Castillo ... 1990 Donruss #592
Tony Castillo ... 1990 Topps #620
Tony Castillo ... 1990 Upper Deck #551
John Castino ... 1980 Topps #137
Danny Cater ... 1964 Topps #482
Bill Caudill ... 1980 Topps #103
Jose Cecena ... 1989 Fleer #516
Jose Cecena ... 1989 Topps #683
Jose Cecena ... 1989 Upper Deck #560
Cesar Cedeno ... 1971 Topps #237
Orlando Cepeda ... 1958 Topps #343
Rick Cerone ... 1977 Topps #476
John Cerutti ... 1987 Donruss #442
John Cerutti ... 1987 Fleer #222
John Cerutti ... 1987 Topps #557
Bob Cerv ... 1953 Topps #210
Ron Cey ... 1972 Topps #761
Ray Chadwick ... 1987 Donruss #505
Chris Chambliss ... 1972 Topps #142
Dean Chance ... 1962 Topps #194
Tony Chance ... 1989 Upper Deck #3
Harry Chappas ... 1980 Topps #347
Joe Charboneau ... 1981 Donruss #82
Joe Charboneau ... 1981 Donruss #82
Joe Charboneau ... 1981 Fleer #397
Joe Charboneau ... 1981 Topps #13
Colin Charland ... 1990 Fleer #640
Ed Charles ... 1962 Topps #595
Norm Charlton ... 1989 Donruss #544
Norm Charlton ... 1989 Fleer #155
Norm Charlton ... 1989 Score #646
Norm Charlton ... 1989 Topps #737
Rocky Childress ... 1988 Donruss #554
Rocky Childress ... 1988 Fleer #442
Rocky Childress ... 1988 Topps #643
John Christensen ... 1986 Donruss #360
John Christensen ... 1986 Topps #287
Larry Christenson ... 1974 Topps #587
Mark Ciardi ... 1988 Topps #417
Jim Clancy ... 1978 Topps #496
Dave Clark ... 1987 Donruss #623
Dave Clark ... 1987 Fleer #644
Jack Clark ... 1977 Topps #488
Jerald Clark ... 1989 Donruss #599
Jerald Clark ... 1989 Fleer #642
Jerald Clark ... 1989 Score #644
Jerald Clark ... 1989 Upper Deck #30
Terry Clark ... 1989 Donruss #607
Terry Clark ... 1989 Fleer #470
Terry Clark ... 1989 Score #566
Terry Clark ... 1989 Topps #129
Terry Clark ... 1989 Upper Deck #234
Will Clark ... 1987 Donruss #66
Will Clark ... 1987 Fleer #269
Will Clark ... 1987 Topps #420
Horace Clarke ... 1966 Topps #547
Stan Clarke ... 1988 Topps #556
Marty Clary (RR) ... 1986 Donruss #36
Mark Clear ... 1980 Topps #638
Roger Clemens ... 1985 Donruss #273
Roger Clemens ... 1985 Fleer #155
Roger Clemens ... 1985 Topps #181
Roberto Clemente ... 1955 Topps #164
Pat Clements ... 1986 Donruss #600
Pat Clements ... 1986 Fleer #606
Pat Clements ... 1986 Topps #754
Donn Clendenon ... 1962 Topps #86
Reggie Cleveland ... 1970 Topps #716
Stewart Cliburn ... 1986 Fleer #152
Stu Cliburn ... 1986 Donruss #301
Stu Cliburn ... 1986 Topps #179
Tony Cloninger ... 1962 Topps #63
Bryan Clutterbuck ... 1987 Donruss #397
Bryan Clutterbuck ... 1987 Fleer #342
Bryan Clutterbuck ... 1987 Topps #562
David Clyde ... 1974 Topps #133
Dave Cochrane ... 1990 Topps #491
Chris Codiroli ... 1984 Donruss #345
Chris Codiroli ... 1984 Fleer #441
Chris Codiroli ... 1984 Topps #61
Kevin Coffman ... 1988 Fleer #536
Rocco Colavito ... 1957 Topps #212
Nate Colbert ... 1966 Topps #596
Jim Colborn ... 1971 Topps #38
Alex Cole ... 1990 Fleer #244
Gerry Coleman ... 1949 Bowman #225
Joe Coleman ... 1966 Topps #333
Paul Coleman ... 1990 Score #662
Paul Coleman ... 1990 Topps #654
Vince Coleman ... 1986 Donruss #181
Vince Coleman ... 1986 Fleer #31
Vince Coleman ... 1986 Topps #370
Darnell Coles ... 1984 Donruss #630
Dave Collins ... 1976 Topps #363
Pat Combs ... 1990 Donruss #44
Pat Combs ... 1990 Fleer #553
Pat Combs ... 1990 Score #623
Pat Combs ... 1990 Topps #384
Keith Comstock ... 1988 Fleer #579
Keith Comstock ... 1988 Score #438
Keith Comstock ... 1988 Topps #778
Keith Comstock ... 1988 Topps #778
Dave Concepcion ... 1971 Topps #14
Onix Concepcion ... 1983 Topps #52
David Cone ... 1987 Donruss #502
Bill Conigliaro ... 1969 Topps #628
Tony Conigliaro ... 1964 Topps #287
Gene Conley ... 1953 Topps #215
Tim Conroy ... 1984 Donruss #340
Tim Conroy ... 1984 Fleer #442
Tim Conroy ... 1984 Topps #189
Dennis Cook ... 1989 Donruss #646
Dennis Cook ... 1989 Fleer #652
Mike Cook ... 1989 Fleer #472
Scott Coolbaugh ... 1990 Donruss #43
Scott Coolbaugh ... 1990 Fleer #293
Scott Coolbaugh ... 1990 Score #612
Scott Coolbaugh ... 1990 Upper Deck #42
Cecil Cooper ... 1972 Topps #79
Scott Cooper ... 1990 Score #651
Joey Cora ... 1988 Fleer #580
Joey Cora ... 1988 Score #420
Joey Cora ... 1988 Topps #91
Sherman Corbett ... 1989 Donruss #407
Sherman Corbett ... 1989 Fleer #473
Sherman Corbett ... 1989 Topps #99
Sherman Corbett ... 1989 Upper Deck #464
Pat Corrales ... 1965 Topps #107
Ed Correa ... 1987 Donruss #57
Ed Correa ... 1987 Fleer #122
Ed Correa ... 1987 Topps #334
Jim Corsi ... 1989 Fleer #649
Jim Corsi ... 1990 Score #553
Jim Corsi ... 1989 Topps #292
John Costello ... 1989 Donruss #518
John Costello ... 1989 Fleer #446
John Costello ... 1989 Score #534
John Costello ... 1989 Topps #184
John Costello ... 1989 Upper Deck #625
Henry Cotto ... 1985 Donruss #411
Henry Cotto ... 1985 Fleer #53
Henry Cotto ... 1985 Topps #267
Wes Covington ... 1957 Topps #283
Al Cowens ... 1975 Topps #437
Joe Cowley ... 1983 Topps #288
Bobby Cox ... 1969 Topps #237
Danny Cox ... 1984 Donruss #449
Roger Craig ... 1956 Topps #63
Del Crandell (Crandall) ... 1950 Bowman #56
Willie Crawford ... 1965 Topps #453
Tim Crews ... 1988 Donruss #464
Tim Crews ... 1988 Fleer #511
Tim Crews ... 1988 Score #641
Tim Crews ... 1988 Topps #57
Chuck Crim ... 1988 Donruss #355
Chuck Crim ... 1988 Fleer #162
Chuck Crim ... 1988 Score #402
Chuck Crim ... 1988 Topps #286
Warren Cromartie ... 1978 Topps #468
Terry Crowley ... 1970 Topps #121
Jose Cruz ... 1972 Topps #107
Julio Cruz ... 1978 Topps #687
Mike Cueller (Cuellar) ... 1959 Topps #518
Ray Culp ... 1963 Topps #29

Ray Culp ... 1963 Topps #29
Steve Cummings ... 1990 Donruss #698
Steve Cummings ... 1990 Topps #374
Earl Cunningham ... 1990 Score #670
Earl Cunningham ... 1990 Topps #134
Joe Cunningham ... 1955 Topps #37
Steve Curry ... 1989 Fleer #86
Steve Curry ... 1989 Topps #471
Milt Cuyler ... 1990 Score #583
Milt Cuyler ... 1990 Score #583

D

Steve Dalkowski ... 1963 Topps #496
Clay Dalrymple ... 1960 Topps #523
Kal Daniels ... 1986 Fleer #646
Kal Daniels (RR) ... 1986 Donruss #27
Ron Darling ... 1984 Donruss #30
Ron Darling ... 1984 Donruss #30
Danny Darwin ... 1979 Topps #713
Doug Dascenzo ... 1989 Donruss #491
Doug Dascenzo ... 1989 Fleer #420
Doug Dascenzo ... 1989 Score #621
Doug Dascenzo ... 1989 Topps #149
Doug Dascenzo ... 1989 Upper Deck #10
Rich Dauer ... 1977 Topps #477
Jack Daugherty ... 1990 Donruss #461
Jack Daugherty ... 1990 Fleer #294
Jack Daugherty ... 1990 Score #564
Jack Daugherty ... 1990 Topps #52
Jack Daugherty ... 1990 Upper Deck #614
Darren Daulton ... 1986 Donruss #477
Darren Daulton ... 1986 Fleer #438
Darren Daulton ... 1986 Topps #264
Vic Davalillo ... 1963 Topps #324
Jim Davenport ... 1958 Topps #413
Mark Davidson ... 1988 Donruss #519
Mark Davidson ... 1988 Fleer #8
Mark Davidson ... 1988 Score #570
Mark Davidson ... 1988 Topps #19
Alvin Davis ... 1985 Donruss #69
Alvin Davis ... 1985 Fleer #488
Alvin Davis ... 1985 Topps #145
Chili Davis ... 1982 Topps #171
Eric Davis ... 1985 Donruss #325
Eric Davis ... 1985 Fleer #533
Eric Davis ... 1985 Topps #627
Glenn Davis ... 1985 Fleer #652
Jody Davis ... 1982 Donruss #225
Jody Davis ... 1982 Fleer #592
Jody Davis ... 1982 Topps #508
Joel Davis ... 1986 Donruss #623
Joel Davis ... 1986 Fleer #202
John Davis ... 1988 Donruss #594
John Davis ... 1988 Fleer #255
John Davis ... 1988 Score #636
John Davis ... 1988 Topps #672
Mark Davis ... 1982 Topps #231
Mike Davis ... 1981 Donruss #470
Mike Davis ... 1981 Fleer #586
Mike Davis ... 1981 Topps #364
Ron Davis ... 1980 Topps #179
Steve Davis ... 1990 Score #187
Steve Davis ... 1990 Topps #428
Storm Davis ... 1983 Donruss #619
Storm Davis ... 1983 Fleer #56
Storm Davis ... 1983 Topps #268
Tommy Davis ... 1960 Topps #509
Willie Davis ... 1961 Topps #506
Bill Dawley ... 1984 Donruss #328
Bill Dawley ... 1984 Fleer #223
Bill Dawley ... 1984 Topps #248
Andre Dawson ... 1977 Topps #473
Ken Dayley ... 1982 Donruss #501
Jeff Dedmon ... 1985 Donruss #554
Jeff Dedmon ... 1985 Fleer #323
Jeff Dedmon ... 1985 Topps #602
Rob Deer ... 1985 Fleer #648
Don Demeter ... 1958 Topps #244
Rick Dempsey ... 1972 Topps #778
John Denny ... 1975 Topps #621
Bucky Dent ... 1974 Topps #582
Bob Dernier ... 1982 Topps #231
Jim Deshaies ... 1987 Donruss #184
Jim Deshaies ... 1987 Fleer #56
Jim Deshaies ... 1987 Topps #167
Delino Deshields ... 1990 Donruss #42
Delino Deshields ... 1990 Fleer #653
Orestes Destrade ... 1989 Topps #27
Mike Devereaux ... 1988 Donruss #546
Mike Devereaux ... 1988 Fleer #512
Mike Devereaux ... 1988 Score #637
Dave DeBusschere ... 1963 Topps #54
Dave DeBusschere ... 1963 Topps #54
Doug DeCinces ... 1975 Topps #617
Ivan DeJesus ... 1978 Topps #152
Jose DeJesus ... 1989 Donruss #558
Jose DeJesus ... 1989 Fleer #280
Jose DeLeon ... 1984 Donruss #628
Jose DeLeon ... 1984 Fleer #248
Jose DeLeon ... 1984 Topps #581
Luis DeLeon ... 1982 Donruss #588
Luis de los Santos ... 1989 Donruss #562
Luis de los Santos ... 1989 Fleer #646
Luis de los Santos ... 1989 Score #648
Luis de los Santos ... 1989 Upper Deck #12
Delino DeShields ... 1990 Score #645
Delino DeShields ... 1990 Topps #224
Jeff DeWillis ... 1988 Score #583
Bo Diaz ... 1978 Topps #708
Mario Diaz ... 1988 Fleer #649
Mike Diaz ... 1987 Donruss #267
Mike Diaz ... 1987 Fleer #609
Mike Diaz ... 1987 Topps #469
Rob Dibble ... 1989 Donruss #426
Rob Dibble ... 1989 Fleer #160
Rob Dibble ... 1989 Score #618
Rob Dibble ... 1989 Topps #264
Rob Dibble ... 1989 Upper Deck #375
Larry Dierker ... 1965 Topps #409
Dick Dietz ... 1967 Topps #341
Benny Distefano ... 1985 Donruss #166
Benny Distefano ... 1985 Topps #162
Ken Dixon ... 1985 Donruss #270
Frank DiPino ... 1982 Topps #333
Pat Dobson ... 1967 Topps #526
Larry Doby ... 1949 Bowman #233
Pat Dodson ... 1987 Topps #449
Pat Dodson (RR) ... 1987 Donruss #44
Dick Donovan ... 1955 Topps #146
John Dopson ... 1989 Donruss #392
John Dopson ... 1989 Fleer #373
John Dopson ... 1989 Score #466
John Dopson ... 1989 Topps #251
John Dopson ... 1989 Upper Deck #57
Bill Doran ... 1984 Donruss #580
Bill Doran ... 1984 Fleer #225
Bill Doran ... 1984 Topps #198
Brian Dorsett ... 1988 Fleer #607
Rich Dotson ... 1981 Donruss #280
Rich Dotson ... 1981 Topps #138
Richard Dotson ... 1981 Fleer #356
Al Downing ... 1962 Topps #219
Brian Downing ... 1974 Topps #601
Kelly Downs ... 1987 Donruss #573
Kelly Downs ... 1987 Fleer #272
Kelly Downs ... 1987 Topps #438
Doug Drabek ... 1987 Donruss #251
Doug Drabek ... 1987 Fleer #96
Doug Drabek ... 1987 Topps #283
Dave Dravecky ... 1983 Fleer #356
Dave Dravecky ... 1983 Topps #384
Tom Drees ... 1990 Fleer #644
Tom Dress ... 1990 Upper Deck #3
Cameron Drew ... 1989 Donruss #30
Cameron Drew ... 1989 Fleer #640
Cameron Drew ... 1989 Score #643
Dan Driessen ... 1974 Topps #341
Walt Dropo ... 1950 Bowman #246
Tim Drummond ... 1990 Donruss #510
Tim Drummond ... 1990 Topps #713
Don Drysdale ... 1957 Topps #18
Brian Dubois ... 1990 Donruss #38
Brian Dubois ... 1990 Fleer #601
Rob Ducey ... 1988 Fleer #107
Rob Ducey ... 1988 Score #629
Rob Ducey ... 1988 Topps #438
Dave Duncan ... 1964 Topps #528
Mariano Duncan ... 1986 Donruss #128
Mariano Duncan ... 1986 Fleer #129
Mariano Duncan ... 1986 Topps #602
Mike Dunne ... 1988 Donruss #390
Mike Dunne ... 1988 Fleer #328
Mike Dunne ... 1988 Score #432
Mike Dunne ... 1988 Topps #619
Shawon Dunston ... 1985 Fleer #649
Shawon Dunston ... 1985 Topps #280
Shawon Dunston (RR) ... 1985 Donruss #39
Ryne Duren ... 1958 Topps #296
Leon Durham ... 1981 Donruss #427
Leon Durham ... 1981 Fleer #540
Leon Durham ... 1981 Topps #321
Brian DuBois ... 1990 Score #657
Brian DuBois ... 1990 Topps #413
Brian DuBois ... 1990 Upper Deck #78
Jim Dwyer ... 1975 Topps #429
Mike Dyer ... 1990 Donruss #642
Mike Dyer ... 1990 Fleer #372
Mike Dyer ... 1990 Score #571
Mike Dyer ... 1990 Topps #576
Mike Dyer ... 1990 Upper Deck #374
Len Dykstra ... 1986 Fleer #78
Len Dykstra ... 1986 Topps #53
Lenny Dykstra ... 1986 Donruss #482

E

Mike Easler ... 1978 Topps #710
Luke Easter ... 1951 Bowman #258
Jamie Easterly ... 1975 Topps #618
Rawly Eastwick ... 1975 Topps #621
Gary Eave ... 1990 Donruss #713
Gary Eave ... 1990 Score #621
Dennis Eckersley ... 1976 Topps #98
Doc Edwards ... 1962 Topps #594
John Edwards ... 1962 Topps #302
Wayne Edwards ... 1990 Fleer #652
Mark Eichhorn ... 1987 Donruss #321
Mark Eichhorn ... 1987 Fleer #224
Mark Eichhorn ... 1987 Fleer #371
Dave Eiland ... 1989 Donruss #481
Dave Eiland ... 1989 Topps #8
Jim Eisenreich ... 1983 Topps #197
Cal Eldred ... 1990 Score #669
Lee Elia ... 1966 Topps #529
Dock Ellis ... 1969 Topps #286
Sammy Ellis ... 1963 Topps #29
Sammy Ellis ... 1963 Topps #29
Dick Ellsworth ... 1960 Topps #125
Steve Ellsworth ... 1989 Topps #299
Kevin Elster ... 1987 Donruss #635
Kevin Elster ... 1987 Fleer #7
Dave Engle ... 1981 Topps #328
Jim Eppard ... 1988 Fleer #645
Mike Epstein ... 1967 Topps #204
Nick Esasky ... 1984 Donruss #602
Nick Esasky ... 1984 Fleer #468
Nick Esasky ... 1984 Topps #192
Alvaro Espinoza ... 1987 Topps #529
Cecil Espy ... 1988 Fleer #465
Chuck Estrada ... 1960 Topps #126
Andy Etchebarren ... 1966 Topps #27
Darrell Evans ... 1970 Topps #621
Dwight Evans ... 1973 Topps #614

F

Roy Face ... 1953 Topps #246
Ron Fairly ... 1959 Topps #125
Monty Fariss ... 1989 Topps #177
Ed Farmer ... 1972 Topps #116
Steve Farr ... 1985 Donruss #653
Steve Farr ... 1985 Fleer #446
Steve Farr ... 1985 Topps #664
John Farrell ... 1988 Donruss #42
John Farrell ... 1988 Fleer #608
John Farrell ... 1988 Score #620
John Farrell ... 1988 Topps #533
Mike Felder ... 1986 Donruss #634
Junior Felix ... 1990 Donruss #70
Junior Felix ... 1990 Fleer #79
Junior Felix ... 1990 Score #258
Junior Felix ... 1990 Topps #347
Junior Felix ... 1990 Upper Deck #106
John Felske ... 1973 Topps #332
Joe Ferguson ... 1972 Topps #616
Felix Fermin ... 1988 Donruss #144
Felix Fermin ... 1988 Fleer #643
Felix Fermin ... 1988 Topps #547
Tony Fernandez ... 1984 Fleer #152
Sid Fernandez (RR) ... 1984 Donruss #44
Tony Fernandez (RR) ... 1984 Donruss #32
Al Ferrara ... 1964 Topps #337
Mike Fetters ... 1990 Donruss #35
Mike Fetters ... 1990 Fleer #131
Mike Fetters ... 1990 Topps #14
Mark Fidrych ... 1977 Topps #265
Cecil Fielder ... 1986 Donruss #512
Cecil Fielder ... 1986 Fleer #653
Cecil Fielder ... 1986 Topps #386
Bruce Fields (RR) ... 1987 Donruss #47
Ed Figueroa ... 1975 Topps #476
Rollie Fingers ... 1969 Topps #597
Chuck Finley ... 1987 Donruss #407
Chuck Finley ... 1987 Fleer #79
Chuck Finley ... 1987 Topps #446
Steve Finley ... 1990 Donruss #215
Steve Finley ... 1990 Fleer #176
Steve Finley ... 1990 Score #339
Steve Finley ... 1990 Topps #349
Steve Finley ... 1990 Upper Deck #602
Steve Fireovid ... 1987 Fleer #653
Steve Fireovid ... 1987 Topps #357
Dan Firova ... 1989 Upper Deck #32
Jeff Fischer ... 1990 Score #654
John Fishel ... 1989 Donruss #443
John Fishel ... 1989 Fleer #358
Brian Fisher ... 1986 Donruss #492
Brian Fisher ... 1986 Fleer #104
Brian Fisher ... 1986 Topps #584
Carlton Fisk ... 1972 Topps #79
Mike Fitzgerald ... 1984 Donruss #482
Mike Flanagan ... 1976 Topps #589
Darrin Fletcher ... 1990 Score #622
Scott Fletcher ... 1982 Donruss #554
Curt Flood ... 1958 Topps #464
Doug Flynn ... 1976 Topps #518
Tim Foli ... 1971 Topps #83
Ray Fontenot ... 1984 Donruss #370
Ray Fontenot ... 1984 Fleer #122
Ray Fontenot ... 1984 Topps #19
Curt Ford ... 1986 Fleer #648
Dan Ford ... 1976 Topps #313
Ed Ford ... 1951 Bowman #1
Bob Forsch ... 1975 Topps #51
Ken Forsch ... 1971 Topps #102
Terry Forster ... 1972 Topps #539
Tony Fossas ... 1990 Donruss #457
Tony Fossas ... 1990 Fleer #323
Tony Fossas ... 1990 Score #567
Tony Fossas ... 1990 Topps #34
Ray Fosse ... 1969 Topps #244
George Foster ... 1971 Topps #276
John Franco ... 1985 Donruss #164
John Franco ... 1985 Fleer #536
John Franco ... 1985 Topps #417
Julio Franco ... 1983 Donruss #525
Terry Francona ... 1982 Donruss #627
Terry Francona ... 1982 Fleer #188
Terry Francona ... 1982 Topps #118
Tito Francona ... 1957 Topps #184
Willie Fraser ... 1987 Fleer #646
Will Fraser (RR) ... 1987 Donruss #40
George Frazier ... 1979 Topps #724
Bill Freehan ... 1963 Topps #466
Marvin Freeman ... 1987 Donruss #576
Marvin Freeman ... 1987 Fleer #651
Jim Fregosi ... 1962 Topps #209
Steve Frey ... 1990 Fleer #649
Steve Frey ... 1990 Topps #91
Bob Friend ... 1952 Bowman #191
Bob Friend ... 1952 Topps #233
Todd Frohwirth ... 1988 Fleer #301
Todd Frohwirth ... 1988 Topps #378
Woody Fryman ... 1966 Topps #498
Tito Fuentes ... 1966 Topps #511
Mark Funderburk ... 1986 Fleer #652

G

Gary Gaetti ... 1983 Donruss #53
Gary Gaetti ... 1983 Fleer #613
Gary Gaetti ... 1983 Topps #431

Greg Gagne (RR) ... 1984 Donruss #39
Ty Gainey (RR) ... 1986 Donruss #31
Andres Galarraga ... 1986 Fleer #647
Andres Galarraga (RR) ... 1986 Donruss #33
Andres Galarraga (RR) ... 1986 Donruss #33
Dave Gallagher ... 1989 Donruss #384
Dave Gallagher ... 1989 Fleer #496
Dave Gallagher ... 1989 Score #455
Dave Gallagher ... 1989 Topps #156
Dave Gallagher ... 1989 Upper Deck #164
Mike Gallego ... 1986 Donruss #156
Mike Gallego ... 1986 Topps #304
Oscar Gamble ... 1970 Topps #654
Ron Gant ... 1988 Donruss #654
Ron Gant ... 1988 Fleer #538
Ronnie Gant ... 1988 Score #647
Jim Gantner ... 1977 Topps #494
Gene Garber ... 1974 Topps #431
Damaso Garcia ... 1981 Donruss #269
Damaso Garcia ... 1981 Fleer #415
Damaso Garcia ... 1981 Topps #488
Miguel Garcia ... 1989 Donruss #622
Miguel Garcia ... 1989 Fleer #647
Mike Garcia ... 1950 Bowman #147
Mark Gardner ... 1990 Donruss #40
Mark Gardner ... 1990 Fleer #646
Mark Gardner ... 1990 Score #639
Mark Gardner ... 1990 Topps #284
Wes Gardner ... 1988 Donruss #634
Wes Gardner ... 1988 Fleer #352
Wes Gardner ... 1988 Topps #189
Wayne Garland ... 1974 Topps #596
Phil Garner ... 1975 Topps #623
Ralph Garr ... 1970 Topps #172
Scott Garrelts ... 1984 Donruss #646
Steve Garvey ... 1971 Topps #341
Clarence Gaston ... 1969 Topps #304
Rich Gedman ... 1982 Donruss #512
Rich Gedman ... 1982 Fleer #294
Rich Gedman ... 1982 Topps #59
Jim Gentile ... 1960 Topps #448
Gary Gentry ... 1969 Topps #31
Bob Geren ... 1990 Donruss #395
Bob Geren ... 1990 Fleer #442
Bob Geren ... 1990 Score #464
Bob Geren ... 1990 Topps #536
Bob Geren ... 1990 Upper Deck #608
Ken Gerhart (RR) ... 1987 Donruss #30
Cesar Geronimo ... 1971 Topps #447
Jake Gibbs ... 1962 Topps #281
Bob Gibson ... 1959 Topps #514
Kirk Gibson ... 1981 Fleer #481
Kirk Gibson ... 1981 Topps #315
Paul Gibson ... 1989 Donruss #445
Paul Gibson ... 1989 Fleer #131
Paul Gibson ... 1989 Score #595
Paul Gibson ... 1989 Topps #583
Paul Gibson ... 1989 Upper Deck #47
Brett Gideon ... 1988 Fleer #330
Jim Gilliam ... 1953 Topps #258
Joe Girardi ... 1989 Fleer #644
Dave Giusti ... 1962 Topps #509
Dan Gladden ... 1985 Donruss #567
Dan Gladden ... 1985 Fleer #607
Dan Gladden ... 1985 Topps #386
Tom Glavine ... 1988 Donruss #644
Tom Glavine ... 1988 Fleer #539
Tom Glavine ... 1988 Score #638
Tom Glavine ... 1988 Topps #779
Greg Gohr ... 1990 Score #679
Dave Goltz ... 1973 Topps #148
Rene Gonzales ... 1988 Donruss #582
Rene Gonzales ... 1988 Fleer #560
Rene Gonzales ... 1988 Topps #98
Denny Gonzalez ... 1985 Donruss #600
German Gonzalez ... 1989 Donruss #590
German Gonzalez ... 1989 Fleer #113
German Gonzalez ... 1989 Topps #746
Jose Gonzalez ... 1987 Donruss #525
Jose Gonzalez ... 1987 Fleer #649
Juan Gonzalez ... 1990 Fleer #297
Juan Gonzalez ... 1990 Score #637
Juan Gonzalez ... 1990 Topps #331
Juan Gonzalez ... 1990 Upper Deck #72
Tony Gonzalez ... 1960 Topps #518
Juan Gonzalez RR ... 1990 Donruss #33
Juan Gonzalez RR ... 1990 Donruss #33
Dwight Gooden ... 1985 Donruss #190
Dwight Gooden ... 1985 Fleer #82
Dwight Gooden ... 1985 Topps #620
Tom Goodwin ... 1990 Score #668
Don Gordon ... 1988 Topps #144
Tom Gordon ... 1989 Donruss #45
Tom Gordon ... 1989 Fleer #284
Tom Gordon ... 1989 Score #634
Rich Gossage ... 1973 Topps #174
Jim Gott ... 1983 Donruss #353
Jim Gott ... 1983 Topps #506
Goose Gozzo ... 1990 Score #610
Goose Gozzo ... 1990 Topps #274
Mauro Gozzo ... 1990 Donruss #655
Mauro Gozzo ... 1990 Fleer #82
Billy Grabarkewitz ... 1970 Topps #446
Mark Grace ... 1988 Donruss #40
Mark Grace ... 1988 Fleer #641
Jim Grant ... 1958 Topps #394
Mark Grant ... 1985 Donruss #601
Dallas Green ... 1960 Topps #366
Dick Green ... 1964 Topps #466
Willie Green ... 1990 Score #682
Tommy Greene ... 1990 Donruss #576
Tommy Greene ... 1990 Fleer #584
Tommy Greene ... 1990 Score #640
Tommy Greene ... 1990 Upper Deck #49
Mike Greenwell ... 1987 Donruss #585
Mike Greenwell ... 1987 Topps #259
Tommy Gregg ... 1988 Donruss #203
Bob Grich ... 1971 Topps #193
Ken Griffey ... 1974 Topps #598
Ken Griffey, Jr. ... 1989 Donruss #33
Ken Griffey, Jr. ... 1989 Fleer #548
Ken Griffey, Jr. ... 1989 Upper Deck #1
Alfredo Griffin ... 1979 Topps #705
Ty Griffin ... 1989 Topps #713
Jason Grimsley ... 1990 Fleer #653
Jason Grimsley ... 1990 Score #649
Jason Grimsley ... 1990 Topps #493
Jason Grimsley ... 1990 Upper Deck #27
Ross Grimsley ... 1972 Topps #99
Marquis Grissom ... 1990 Donruss #36
Marquis Grissom ... 1990 Fleer #347
Marquis Grissom ... 1990 Score #591
Marquis Grissom ... 1990 Topps #714
Marquis Grissom ... 1990 Upper Deck #9
Dick Groat ... 1952 Topps #369
Greg Gross ... 1975 Topps #334
Kevin Gross ... 1984 Donruss #381
Kevin Gross ... 1984 Fleer #32
Kevin Gross ... 1984 Topps #332
Wayne Gross ... 1977 Topps #479
Gerald Grote ... 1964 Topps #226
Kelly Gruber ... 1985 Fleer #645
Matt Guante (Cecilio) ... 1983 Donruss #423
Mark Gubicza ... 1985 Donruss #344
Mark Gubicza ... 1985 Fleer #201
Mark Gubicza ... 1985 Topps #127
Pedro Guerrero ... 1979 Topps #719
Lee Guetterman ... 1987 Donruss #322
Lee Guetterman ... 1987 Fleer #585
Lee Guetterman ... 1987 Topps #307
Ron Guidry ... 1976 Topps #599
Ozzie Guillen ... 1986 Donruss #208
Ozzie Guillen ... 1986 Fleer #206
Ozzie Guillen ... 1986 Topps #254
Don Gullett ... 1971 Topps #124
Bill Gullickson ... 1981 Donruss #91
Bill Gullickson ... 1981 Fleer #150
Bill Gullickson ... 1981 Topps #578
Larry Gura ... 1971 Topps #203
Mark Guthrie ... 1990 Donruss #622
Mark Guthrie ... 1990 Topps #317
Mark Guthrie ... 1990 Upper Deck #436
Jose Guzman ... 1986 Fleer #559
Jose Guzman (RR) ... 1986 Donruss #30
Chris Gwynn ... 1988 Fleer #647
Chris Gwynn ... 1988 Score #640
Tony Gwynn ... 1983 Donruss #598
Tony Gwynn ... 1983 Fleer #360
Tony Gwynn ... 1983 Topps #482

H

Moose Haas ... 1978 Topps #649
John Habyan (RR) ... 1986 Donruss #45
Harvey Haddix ... 1953 Topps #273
Jerry Hairston ... 1974 Topps #96
Chip Hale ... 1990 Donruss #690
Chip Hale ... 1990 Score #588
Chip Hale ... 1990 Topps #704
Chip Hale ... 1990 Upper Deck #475
Albert Hall ... 1985 Fleer #326
Albert Hall ... 1985 Topps #676
Dick Hall ... 1955 Topps #126
Drew Hall ... 1987 Donruss #594
Drew Hall ... 1989 Fleer #643
Grady Hall ... 1989 Fleer #650
Jimmie Hall ... 1964 Topps #73
Mel Hall ... 1983 Donruss #126
Bob Hamelin ... 1990 Upper Deck #45
Darryl Hamilton ... 1989 Fleer #187
Darryl Hamilton ... 1989 Topps #88
Darryl Hamilton ... 1989 Upper Deck #301
Jack Hamilton ... 1962 Topps #593
Jeff Hamilton ... 1987 Donruss #464
Jeff Hamilton ... 1987 Topps #266
Atlee Hammaker ... 1982 Topps #471
Chris Hammond ... 1990 Fleer #421
Chris Hammond ... 1990 Score #629
Chris Hammond ... 1990 Upper Deck #52
Bill Hands ... 1966 Topps #392
Dave Hansen ... 1990 Fleer #642
Ronnie Hansen ... 1959 Topps #444
Erik Hanson ... 1989 Donruss #32
Erik Hanson ... 1989 Fleer #549
Steve Hargan ... 1966 Topps #508
Mike Hargrove ... 1975 Topps #106
Mike Harkey ... 1989 Donruss #43
Mike Harkey ... 1989 Fleer #427
Mike Harkey ... 1989 Score #624
Mike Harkey ... 1989 Topps #742
Mike Harkey ... 1989 Upper Deck #14
Pete Harnisch ... 1989 Donruss #44
Terry Harper ... 1981 Topps #192
Tommy Harper ... 1963 Topps #158
Toby Harrah ... 1972 Topps #104
Bud Harrelson ... 1967 Topps #306
Ken Harrelson ... 1964 Topps #419
Donald Harris ... 1990 Score #661
Donald Harris ... 1990 Topps #314
Gene Harris ... 1990 Score #548
Gene Harris ... 1990 Topps #738
Gene Harris ... 1990 Upper Deck #565
Greg Harris ... 1989 Donruss #34
Greg Harris ... 1989 Fleer #306
Greg Harris ... 1982 Topps #783
Greg Harris ... 1989 Topps #194
Lenny Harris ... 1989 Fleer #645
Jim Hart ... 1964 Topps #452
Mike Hart ... 1988 Topps #69
Mike Hartley ... 1990 Fleer #651
Mike Hartley ... 1990 Score #641
Bryan Harvey ... 1989 Donruss #525
Bryan Harvey ... 1989 Fleer #479
Bryan Harvey ... 1989 Score #185
Bryan Harvey ... 1989 Topps #632
Bryan Harvey ... 1989 Upper Deck #594
Ron Hassey ... 1980 Topps #222
Bill Hatcher ... 1985 Fleer #649
Mickey Hatcher ... 1980 Topps #679
Billy Hatcher (RR) ... 1985 Donruss #41
Andy Hawkins ... 1984 Fleer #302
Andy Hawkins ... 1984 Topps #778
Charlie Hayes ... 1989 Fleer #330
Charlie Hayes ... 1989 Score #628
Von Hayes ... 1982 Donruss #237
Von Hayes ... 1982 Fleer #371
Von Hayes ... 1982 Topps #141
Ray Hayward ... 1987 Donruss #632
Ed Hearn ... 1987 Donruss #446
Ed Hearn ... 1987 Fleer #10
Ed Hearn ... 1987 Topps #433
Jeff Hearron ... 1987 Topps #274
Mike Heath ... 1979 Topps #710
Jeff Heathcock ... 1986 Donruss #182
Jeff Heathcock ... 1986 Fleer #302
Neal Heaton ... 1984 Donruss #373
Neal Heaton ... 1984 Fleer #546
Rich Hebner ... 1969 Topps #82
Danny Heep ... 1981 Fleer #72
Don Heinkel ... 1989 Fleer #133
Don Heinkel ... 1989 Score #168
Don Heinkel ... 1989 Topps #499
Woody Held ... 1958 Topps #202
Tommy Helms ... 1965 Topps #243
Scott Hemond ... 1990 Fleer #646
Scott Hemond ... 1990 Score #598
Dave Henderson ... 1982 Topps #711
Ken Henderson ... 1965 Topps #497
Rickey Henderson ... 1980 Topps #482
Steve Henderson ... 1978 Topps #134
George Hendrick ... 1972 Topps #406
Rod Hendricks ... 1969 Topps #277
Dave Hengel ... 1988 Donruss #629
Dave Hengel ... 1988 Fleer #375
Tom Henke ... 1984 Donruss #134
Mike Henneman ... 1988 Donruss #420
Mike Henneman ... 1988 Fleer #57
Mike Henneman ... 1988 Score #520
Mike Henneman ... 1988 Topps #582
Dwayne Henry ... 1986 Donruss #603
Dwayne Henry ... 1986 Fleer #562
Keith Hernandez ... 1975 Topps #623
Manny Hernandez ... 1988 Donruss #481
Willie Hernandez ... 1978 Topps #99
Xavier Hernandez ... 1990 Donruss #682
Xavier Hernandez ... 1990 Upper Deck #26
Larry Herndon ... 1977 Topps #397
Tom Herr ... 1980 Topps #684
Orel Hershiser ... 1985 Donruss #581
Orel Hershiser ... 1985 Fleer #371
Orel Hershiser ... 1985 Topps #493
Whitey Herzog ... 1957 Topps #29
Joe Hesketh ... 1985 Donruss #157
Joe Hesketh ... 1985 Fleer #652
Eric Hetzel ... 1989 Donruss #660
Greg Hibbard ... 1990 Donruss #384
Greg Hibbard ... 1990 Fleer #534
Greg Hibbard ... 1990 Score #369
Greg Hibbard ... 1990 Topps #769
Greg Hibbard ... 1990 Upper Deck #543
Jim Hickman ... 1962 Topps #598
Ted Higuera ... 1986 Donruss #351
Teddy Higuera ... 1986 Fleer #490
Teddy Higuera ... 1986 Topps #347
Don Hill ... 1984 Donruss #96
Don Hill ... 1984 Fleer #448
Donnie Hill ... 1984 Topps #265
Glenallen Hill ... 1987 Donruss #561
Ken Hill ... 1989 Donruss #536
Ken Hill ... 1989 Fleer #652
Shawn Hillegas ... 1988 Donruss #35
Shawn Hillegas ... 1988 Fleer #519
Shawn Hillegas ... 1988 Score #612
Shawn Hillegas ... 1988 Topps #455
John Hiller ... 1966 Topps #209
Tommy Hinzo ... 1988 Donruss #526
Tommy Hinzo ... 1988 Fleer #611
Tommy Hinzo ... 1988 Score #567
Tommy Hinzo ... 1988 Topps #576
Larry Hisle ... 1968 Topps #579
Don Hoak ... 1953 Topps #176
Butch Hobson ... 1977 Topps #89
Guy Hoffman ... 1980 Topps #664
Al Holland ... 1981 Fleer #445
Al Holland ... 1981 Topps #213
Brian Holman ... 1989 Donruss #511
Brian Holman ... 1989 Fleer #379
Brian Holman ... 1989 Upper Deck #356
Shawn Holman ... 1990 Fleer #606
Shawn Holman ... 1990 Score #620
Brian Holton ... 1987 Donruss #598
Ken Holtzman ... 1967 Topps #185
Rick Honeycutt ... 1979 Topps #612
Burt Hooton ... 1972 Topps #61
Joel Horlen ... 1962 Topps #479
Sam Horn ... 1988 Donruss #498
Sam Horn ... 1988 Fleer #355
Sam Horn ... 1988 Score #201
Sam Horn ... 1988 Topps #377
Bob Horner ... 1979 Topps #586
Ricky Horton ... 1985 Donruss #83
Ricky Horton ... 1985 Fleer #227
Ricky Horton ... 1985 Topps #321
Willie Horton ... 1964 Topps #512
Steve Hosey ... 1990 Score #666
Charlie Hough ... 1972 Topps #198
Tom House ... 1969 Topps #331

Tyler Houston .... 1990 Score #677
Tyler Houston .... 1990 Topps #564
Elston Howard .... 1955 Bowman #68
Frank Howard .... 1960 Topps #132
Steve Howe .... 1981 Donruss #511
Steve Howe .... 1981 Fleer #136
Steve Howe .... 1981 Topps #693
Jack Howell .... 1986 Donruss #524
Jack Howell .... 1986 Topps #127
Jay Howell .... 1982 Topps #51
Ken Howell .... 1985 Donruss #592
Ken Howell .... 1985 Fleer #374
Dan Howitt .... 1990 Fleer #644
Dick Howser .... 1961 Topps #416
Lamarr Hoyt (LaMarr) .... 1981 Donruss #160
Lamarr Hoyt (LaMarr) .... 1981 Topps #164
Al Hrabosky .... 1971 Topps #594
Kent Hrbek .... 1982 Donruss #557
Kent Hrbek .... 1982 Topps #766
Glenn Hubbard .... 1979 Topps #715
Ken Hubbs .... 1962 Topps #461
Charles Hudson .... 1984 Fleer #36
Charlie Hudson .... 1984 Donruss #448
Charlie Hudson .... 1984 Topps #432
Mike Huff .... 1990 Fleer #649
Mike Huff .... 1990 Score #597
Keith Hughes .... 1988 Donruss #643
Keith Hughes .... 1988 Fleer #305
Keith Hughes .... 1988 Score #635
Keith Hughes .... 1988 Topps #781
Mark Huismann .... 1984 Donruss #339
Tim Hulett .... 1985 Donruss #645
Tom Hume .... 1978 Topps #701
Randy Hundley .... 1966 Topps #392
Ron Hunt .... 1963 Topps #558
Jim Hunter .... 1965 Topps #526
Clint Hurdle .... 1978 Topps #705
Bruce Hurst .... 1981 Topps #689
Jeff Huson .... 1990 Donruss #693
Jeff Huson .... 1990 Fleer #350
Jeff Huson .... 1990 Score #615
Jeff Huson .... 1990 Topps #72
Jeff Huson .... 1990 Upper Deck #434

I

Pete Incaviglia .... 1987 Donruss #224
Pete Incaviglia .... 1987 Fleer #128
Pete Incaviglia .... 1987 Topps #550
Jeff Innis .... 1990 Donruss #408
Jeff Innis .... 1990 Fleer #206
Jeff Innis .... 1990 Topps #557
Jeff Innis .... 1990 Upper Deck #562
Jeff Innis .... 1990 Upper Deck #562
Dane Iorg .... 1980 Topps #139
Garth Iorg .... 1978 Topps #704
Monte Irvin .... 1951 Bowman #198

J

Al Jackson .... 1962 Topps #464
Bo Jackson .... 1987 Fleer #369
Bo Jackson .... 1987 Topps #170
Chuck Jackson .... 1988 Score #222
Chuck Jackson .... 1988 Topps #94
Danny Jackson .... 1984 Donruss #461
Darrin Jackson .... 1988 Fleer #641
Grant Jackson .... 1966 Topps #591
Jeff Jackson .... 1990 Score #678
Jeff Jackson .... 1990 Topps #74
Larry Jackson .... 1956 Topps #119
Mike Jackson .... 1988 Donruss #139
Mike Jackson .... 1988 Fleer #306
Mike Jackson .... 1988 Score #144
Mike Jackson .... 1988 Topps #651
Reggie Jackson .... 1969 Topps #260
Sonny Jackson .... 1965 Topps #16
Bo Jackson (RR) .... 1987 Donruss #35
Brook Jacoby .... 1984 Donruss #542
Chris James (RR) .... 1987 Donruss #42
Dion James (RR) .... 1984 Donruss #31
Pat Jarvis .... 1967 Topps #57
Manuel Javier .... 1960 Topps #133
Stan Javier .... 1986 Donruss #584
Joe Jay .... 1954 Topps #141
Mike Jeffcoat .... 1985 Donruss #251
Mike Jeffcoat .... 1985 Fleer #453
Mike Jeffcoat .... 1985 Topps #303
Gregg Jefferies .... 1988 Donruss #657
Gregg Jefferies .... 1988 Fleer #137
Gregg Jefferies .... 1988 Score #645
Stan Jefferson .... 1987 Donruss #642
Greg Jelks .... 1988 Fleer #648
Steve Jeltz .... 1985 Fleer #653
Steve Jeltz (RR) .... 1985 Donruss #44
Ferguson Jenkins .... 1966 Topps #254
Doug Jennings .... 1989 Donruss #505
Doug Jennings .... 1989 Fleer #14
Doug Jennings .... 1989 Score #459
Doug Jennings .... 1989 Topps #166
Doug Jennings .... 1989 Upper Deck #585
Jackie Jensen .... 1951 Bowman #254
Sam Jethroe .... 1950 Bowman #248
German Jimenez .... 1989 Topps #569
German Jimenez .... 1989 Upper Deck #113
Tommy John .... 1964 Topps #146
Alex Johnson .... 1965 Topps #352
Cliff Johnson .... 1975 Topps #143
Dave Johnson .... 1990 Donruss #702
Dave Johnson .... 1990 Score #528
Dave Johnson .... 1965 Topps #473
Dave Johnson .... 1990 Topps #416
Dave Johnson .... 1990 Upper Deck #425
Deron Johnson .... 1959 Topps #131
Howard Johnson .... 1983 Donruss #328
Howard Johnson .... 1983 Fleer #332
Joe Johnson .... 1986 Donruss #624
Joe Johnson .... 1986 Fleer #519
John Henry Johnson .... 1979 Topps #681
Lance Johnson .... 1988 Donruss #31
Lance Johnson .... 1988 Fleer #37
Randy Johnson .... 1989 Donruss #42
Randy Johnson .... 1989 Fleer #381
Randy Johnson .... 1989 Score #645
Randy Johnson .... 1989 Topps #647
Randy Johnson .... 1989 Upper Deck #25
Jay Johnstone .... 1967 Topps #213
Barry Jones .... 1987 Donruss #602
Barry Jones .... 1987 Fleer #611
Barry Jones .... 1987 Topps #494
Cleon Jones .... 1965 Topps #308
Doug Jones .... 1988 Donruss #588
Doug Jones .... 1988 Fleer #613
Doug Jones .... 1988 Score #594
Doug Jones .... 1988 Topps #293
Jimmy Jones .... 1987 Donruss #557
Jimmy Jones .... 1987 Fleer #650
Kiki Jones .... 1990 Score #676
Mack Jones .... 1962 Topps #186
Randy Jones .... 1974 Topps #173
Randy Jones .... 1974 Topps #173
Ron Jones .... 1989 Donruss #40
Ron Jones .... 1989 Fleer #574
Ron Jones .... 1989 Score #639
Ron Jones .... 1989 Topps #349
Ron Jones .... 1989 Upper Deck #11
Ross Jones .... 1988 Fleer #262
Ross Jones .... 1988 Score #598
Ross Jones .... 1988 Topps #169
Ruppert Jones .... 1977 Topps #488
Tim Jones .... 1989 Donruss #555
Tim Jones .... 1989 Fleer #453
Tim Jones .... 1989 Score #649
Timmy Jones .... 1989 Upper Deck #348
Tracy Jones .... 1987 Donruss #413
Tracy Jones .... 1987 Fleer #146
Tracy Jones .... 1987 Topps #146
Ricky Jordan .... 1989 Donruss #624
Ricky Jordan .... 1989 Fleer #575
Ricky Jordan .... 1989 Score #548
Ricky Jordan .... 1989 Topps #358
Ricky Jordan .... 1989 Upper Deck #35
Scott Jordan .... 1989 Donruss #609
Terry Jorgenson .... 1990 Score #655
Felix Jose .... 1989 Donruss #38
Felix Jose .... 1989 Fleer #15
Felix Jose .... 1989 Score #629
Felix Jose .... 1989 Upper Deck #22
Wally Joyner .... 1987 Donruss #135
Wally Joyner .... 1987 Fleer #86
Wally Joyner .... 1987 Topps #80
Jeff Juden .... 1990 Topps #164
Dave Justice .... 1990 Donruss #704
Dave Justice .... 1990 Score #650
David Justice .... 1990 Fleer #586

K

Jim Kaat .... 1960 Topps #136
Jeff Kaiser .... 1989 Fleer #410
Al Kaline .... 1954 Topps #201
Ron Karkovice .... 1987 Donruss #334
Ron Karkovice .... 1987 Fleer #645
Ron Karkovice .... 1987 Topps #491
Pat Keedy .... 1988 Topps #486
Mike Kekich .... 1965 Topps #561
Pat Kelly .... 1969 Topps #619
Roberto Kelly .... 1988 Donruss #635
Roberto Kelly .... 1988 Fleer #212
Roberto Kelly .... 1988 Score #634
Steve Kemp .... 1977 Topps #492
Terry Kennedy .... 1979 Topps #724
Matt Keough .... 1978 Topps #709
Charlie Kerfeld .... 1986 Fleer #303
Jim Kern .... 1975 Topps #621
Don Kessinger .... 1966 Topps #24
Jimmy Key .... 1985 Donruss #559
Jimmy Key .... 1985 Fleer #110
Jimmy Key .... 1985 Topps #193
Steve Kiefer .... 1985 Fleer #647
Steve Kiefer (RR) .... 1985 Donruss #35
Paul Kilgus .... 1988 Donruss #469
Paul Kilgus .... 1988 Fleer #471
Paul Kilgus .... 1988 Score #536
Paul Kilgus .... 1988 Topps #427
Harmon Killebrew .... 1955 Topps #124
Eric King .... 1987 Donruss #250
Eric King .... 1987 Fleer #155
Eric King .... 1987 Topps #36
Jeff King .... 1988 Fleer #653
Mike Kingery .... 1987 Donruss #424
Mike Kingery .... 1987 Fleer #371
Mike Kingery .... 1987 Topps #203
Dave Kingman .... 1972 Topps #147
Matt Kinzer .... 1990 Fleer #652
Matt Kinzer .... 1990 Score #628
Bob Kipper .... 1986 Fleer #648
Bob Kipper (RR) .... 1986 Donruss #44
Clay Kirby .... 1969 Topps #637
Willie Kirkland .... 1958 Topps #128
Ed Kirkpatrick .... 1963 Topps #386
Bruce Kison .... 1972 Topps #72
Ron Kittle .... 1983 Fleer #241
Johnny Klippstein .... 1951 Bowman #248
Bob Knepper .... 1978 Topps #589
Ray Knight .... 1978 Topps #674
Chuck Knoblauch .... 1990 Score #672
Bobby Knoop .... 1964 Topps #502
Darold Knowles .... 1964 Topps #418
Mark Knudson .... 1988 Donruss #495
Mark Knudson .... 1988 Topps #61
Brad Komminsk (RR) .... 1984 Donruss #36
Jerry Koosman .... 1968 Topps #177
Sandy Koufax .... 1955 Topps #123
Randy Kramer .... 1989 Donruss #480
Randy Kramer .... 1989 Fleer #647
Randy Kramer .... 1989 Topps #522
Ed Kranepool .... 1963 Topps #228
Chad Kreuter .... 1989 Donruss #579
Chad Kreuter .... 1989 Fleer #526
Chad Kreuter .... 1989 Topps #432
Chad Kreuter .... 1989 Upper Deck #312
Chad Krueter .... 1989 Score #638
John Kruk .... 1987 Donruss #328
John Kruk .... 1987 Fleer #420
John Kruk .... 1987 Topps #123
Mike Krukow .... 1977 Topps #493
Tony Kubek .... 1957 Topps #312
Harvey Kuenn .... 1954 Bowman #23
Harvey Kuenn .... 1954 Topps #25
Duane Kuiper .... 1976 Topps #508
Jeff Kunkel .... 1985 Donruss #587
Jeff Kunkel .... 1985 Fleer #561
Jeff Kunkel .... 1985 Topps #288
Randy Kutcher .... 1987 Donruss #547
Randy Kutcher .... 1987 Fleer #276
Jerry Kutzler .... 1990 Donruss #503

L

Clem Labine .... 1952 Topps #342
Rene Lachemann .... 1965 Topps #526
Lee Lacy .... 1973 Topps #391
Pete Ladd .... 1980 Topps #678
Mike Laga .... 1984 Donruss #491
Steve Lake .... 1984 Donruss #198
Steve Lake .... 1984 Topps #691
Tom Lampkin .... 1989 Donruss #639
Les Lancaster .... 1988 Fleer #421
Les Lancaster .... 1988 Score #602
Les Lancaster .... 1988 Topps #112
Lester Lancaster .... 1988 Donruss #561
Jim Landis .... 1957 Topps #375
Ken Landreaux .... 1979 Topps #619
Bill Landrum .... 1988 Fleer #238
Bill Landrum .... 1988 Topps #42
Terry Landrum .... 1981 Fleer #539
Tito Landrum .... 1981 Topps #244
Mark Langston .... 1985 Donruss #557
Mark Langston .... 1985 Fleer #492
Mark Langston .... 1985 Topps #625
Hal Lanier .... 1965 Topps #118
Carney Lansford .... 1979 Topps #212
Barry Larkin .... 1987 Donruss #492
Barry Larkin .... 1987 Fleer #204
Barry Larkin .... 1987 Topps #648
Gene Larkin .... 1988 Donruss #564
Gene Larkin .... 1988 Fleer #14
Gene Larkin .... 1988 Score #276
Gene Larkin .... 1988 Topps #746
Don James Larsen .... 1954 Bowman #101
Frank Lary .... 1955 Bowman #154
Frank Lary .... 1958 Topps #245
Tom Lasorda .... 1954 Topps #132
Charlie Lau .... 1958 Topps #448
Tim Laudner .... 1982 Donruss #549
Tim Laudner .... 1982 Topps #766
Gary Lavelle .... 1975 Topps #624
Rudy Law .... 1979 Topps #719
Vance Law .... 1981 Topps #551
Vernon Law .... 1951 Bowman #203
Tom Lawless .... 1983 Donruss #400
Tom Lawless .... 1983 Topps #423
Marcus Lawton .... 1990 Topps #302
Jack Lazorko .... 1985 Topps #317
Pete LaCock .... 1975 Topps #494
Mike LaCoss .... 1979 Topps #717
Lerrin LaGrow .... 1971 Topps #39
Dave LaPoint .... 1983 Donruss #544
Dave LaPoint .... 1983 Fleer #14
Dave LaPoint .... 1983 Topps #438
Dave LaRoche .... 1971 Topps #174
Tony LaRussa .... 1964 Topps #244
Mike LaValliere .... 1987 Donruss #331
Mike LaValliere .... 1987 Fleer #302
Mike LaValliere .... 1987 Topps #162
Charlie Lea .... 1981 Fleer #165
Charlie Lea .... 1981 Topps #293
Rick Leach .... 1982 Donruss #583
Rick Leach .... 1982 Fleer #272
Terry Leach .... 1982 Topps #623
Tim Leary .... 1982 Topps #623
Bill Lee .... 1970 Topps #279
Manny Lee .... 1986 Topps #23
Jim Lefebvre .... 1965 Topps #561
Craig Lefferts .... 1984 Donruss #388
Craig Lefferts .... 1984 Fleer #496
Craig Lefferts .... 1984 Topps #99
Charlie Leibrandt .... 1981 Donruss #421
Charlie Leibrandt .... 1981 Fleer #208
Charlie Leibrandt .... 1981 Topps #126
Dave Leiper .... 1987 Donruss #472
Dave Leiper .... 1987 Topps #441
David Leiper .... 1987 Fleer #398
Al Leiter .... 1988 Donruss #43
Al Leiter .... 1988 Topps #18
Al Leiter .... 1988 Topps #18
Denver Lemaster .... 1963 Topps #74
Mark Lemke .... 1989 Donruss #523
Mark Lemke .... 1989 Topps #327
Mark Lemke .... 1989 Upper Deck #19
Chet Lemon .... 1976 Topps #590
Jim Lemon .... 1954 Topps #103
Dennis Leonard .... 1975 Topps #615

Jeff Leonard	1980 Topps #106
Scott Leuis	1990 Fleer #647
Mark Lewis	1989 Topps #222
Sixto Lezcano	1976 Topps #353
Ron LeFlore	1975 Topps #628
Johnny LeMaster	1976 Topps #596
Derek Lilliquist	1989 Donruss #653
Derek Lilliquist	1989 Score #631
Bob Lillis	1959 Topps #133
Jose Lind	1988 Donruss #38
Jose Lind	1988 Fleer #334
Jose Lind	1988 Score #597
Jose Lind	1988 Topps #767
Jim Lindeman (RR)	1987 Donruss #37
Bill Lindsey	1988 Fleer #403
Phil Linz	1962 Topps #596
Nelson Liriano	1988 Donruss #32
Nelson Liriano	1988 Fleer #117
Nelson Liriano	1988 Score #621
Nelson Liriano	1988 Topps #205
Mark Littell	1974 Topps #596
Greg Litton	1990 Donruss #453
Greg Litton	1990 Fleer #61
Greg Litton	1990 Score #497
Greg Litton	1990 Topps #66
Skip Lockwood	1965 Topps #526
Billy Loes	1952 Bowman #240
Billy Loes	1952 Topps #20
John Logan	1953 Topps #158
Mickey Lolich	1964 Topps #128
Sherman Lollar	1950 Bowman #142
Phil Lombardi	1987 Donruss #401
Phil Lombardi	1987 Fleer #648
Steve Lombardozzi	1986 Donruss #598
Jim Lonborg	1965 Topps #573
Bill Long	1988 Donruss #306
Bill Long	1988 Fleer #404
Bill Long	1988 Score #539
Bill Long	1988 Topps #309
Dale Long	1955 Topps #127
Dave Lopes	1973 Topps #609
Aurelio Lopez	1979 Topps #444
Hector Lopez	1956 Topps #16
Marcelino Lopez	1963 Topps #549
Vance Lovelace	1989 Fleer #651
Torey Lovullo	1989 Fleer #648
John Lowenstein	1971 Topps #231
Mike Loynd	1987 Donruss #506
Mike Loynd	1987 Topps #126
Rick Luecken	1990 Donruss #562
Rick Luecken	1990 Fleer #113
Rick Luecken	1990 Topps #87
Rick Luecken	1990 Upper Deck #621
Urbano Lugo	1986 Donruss #329
Urbano Lugo	1986 Fleer #162
Urbano Lugo	1986 Topps #373
Mike Lum	1968 Topps #579
Jerry Lumpe	1958 Topps #193
Scott Lusader	1988 Donruss #615
Scott Lusader	1988 Fleer #62
Greg Luzinski	1971 Topps #439
Sparky Lyle	1969 Topps #311
Jerry Lynch	1954 Topps #234
Fred Lynn	1975 Topps #622
Barry Lyons	1988 Donruss #619
Barry Lyons	1988 Fleer #140
Barry Lyons	1988 Score #387
Barry Lyons	1988 Topps #633
Steve Lyons (RR)	1985 Donruss #29

M

Kevin Maas	1990 Fleer #641
Kevin Maas	1990 Score #606
Kevin Maas	1990 Upper Deck #70
Mike Macfarlane	1989 Donruss #416
Mike Macfarlane	1989 Fleer #287
Mike Macfarlane	1989 Score #319
Mike Macfarlane	1989 Topps #479
Mike Macfarlane	1989 Upper Deck #546
Julio Machado	1990 Donruss #47
Julio Machado	1990 Topps #684
Julio Machado	1990 Upper Deck #93
Shane Mack	1988 Donruss #411
Shane Mack	1988 Fleer #590
Shane Mack	1988 Score #414
Shane Mack	1988 Topps #548
Elliott Maddox	1971 Topps #11
Garry Maddox	1973 Topps #322
Mike Maddux	1987 Donruss #535
Mike Maddux	1987 Fleer #179
Mike Maddux	1987 Topps #553
Greg Maddux (RR)	1987 Donruss #36
Bill Madlock	1974 Topps #600
Alex Madrid	1989 Donruss #604
Dave Magadan	1987 Donruss #575
Dave Magadan	1987 Fleer #648
Dave Magadan	1987 Topps #512
Joe Magrane	1988 Donruss #140
Joe Magrane	1988 Fleer #40
Joe Magrane	1988 Score #94
Joe Magrane	1988 Topps #380
Tom Magrann	1990 Donruss #374
Art Mahaffey	1960 Topps #138
Rick Mahler	1982 Donruss #349
Rick Mahler	1982 Fleer #440
Rick Mahler	1982 Topps #579
Candy Maldonado	1983 Donruss #262
Candy Maldonado	1983 Fleer #212
Rob Mallicoat	1988 Fleer #452
Jim Maloney	1961 Topps #436
Frank Malzone	1955 Bowman #302
Kelly Mann	1990 Donruss #46
Kelly Mann	1990 Fleer #642
Kelly Mann	1990 Score #627
Kelly Mann	1990 Topps #744
Kelly Mann	1990 Upper Deck #33
Rick Manning	1976 Topps #275
Fred Manrique	1988 Donruss #493
Fred Manrique	1988 Fleer #406
Fred Manrique	1988 Score #139
Fred Manrique	1988 Topps #437
Mickey Mantle	1951 Bowman #253
Jeff Manto	1990 Fleer #137
Kirt Manwaring	1988 Donruss #39
Kirt Manwaring	1988 Fleer #651
Kirt Manwaring	1988 Score #627
Juan Marichal	1961 Topps #417
Roger Maris	1958 Topps #47
Mike Marshall	1982 Donruss #562
Mike Marshall	1982 Fleer #13
Mike Marshall	1968 Topps #201
Mike Marshall	1982 Topps #681
Billy Martin	1952 Topps #175
Jerry Martin	1977 Topps #596
Buck Martinez	1970 Topps #609
Carlos Martinez	1990 Donruss #531
Carlos Martinez	1990 Score #314
Carlos Martinez	1990 Topps #461
Carlos Martinez	1990 Upper Deck #347
Carmelo Martinez	1984 Donruss #623
Carmelo Martinez	1984 Fleer #497
Carmelo Martinez	1984 Topps #267
Dave Martinez	1987 Donruss #488
Denny Martinez	1977 Topps #491
Edgar Martinez	1989 Donruss #645
Edgar Martinez	1988 Fleer #378
Ramon Martinez	1989 Donruss #464
Ramon Martinez	1989 Fleer #67
Ramon Martinez	1989 Score #635
Ramon Martinez	1989 Topps #225
Ramon Martinez	1989 Upper Deck #18
Tino Martinez	1990 Score #596
Tino Martinez	1990 Upper Deck #37
Tippy Martinez	1976 Topps #41
John Marzano	1988 Donruss #421
John Marzano	1988 Fleer #357
John Marzano	1988 Score #584
John Marzano	1988 Topps #757
Mike Mason	1985 Donruss #281
Mike Mason	1985 Fleer #562
Mike Mason	1985 Topps #464
Roger Mason	1986 Donruss #633
Ed Mathews	1952 Topps #407
Greg Mathews	1987 Donruss #208
Greg Mathews	1987 Fleer #303
Greg Mathews	1987 Topps #567
Jon Matlack	1971 Topps #648
Gary Matthews	1973 Topps #606
Don Mattingly	1984 Donruss #248
Don Mattingly	1984 Fleer #131
Don Mattingly	1984 Topps #8
Len Matuszek	1983 Topps #357
Dal Maxvill	1963 Topps #49
Charley Maxwell	1952 Topps #180
Carlos May	1969 Topps #654
Derrick May	1990 Fleer #645
Lee May	1966 Topps #424
Milt May	1971 Topps #343
Rudy May	1965 Topps #537
Scott May	1989 Donruss #636
John Mayberry	1970 Topps #227
Brent Mayne	1990 Score #664
Willie Mays	1951 Bowman #305
Bill Mazeroski	1957 Topps #24
Lee Mazzilli	1977 Topps #488
Dick McAuliffe	1962 Topps #527
Bake McBride	1974 Topps #601
Randy McCament	1990 Fleer #64
Randy McCament	1990 Score #580
Randy McCament	1990 Topps #361
Tom McCarthy	1990 Fleer #541
Tom McCarthy	1990 Topps #326
Tim McCarver	1962 Topps #167
Kirk McCaskill	1986 Donruss #474
Kirk McCaskill	1986 Fleer #163
Kirk McCaskill	1986 Topps #628
Steve McCatty	1978 Topps #701
Lloyd McClendon	1988 Topps #172
Bob McClure	1976 Topps #599
Mike McCormick	1958 Topps #37
Willie McCovey	1960 Topps #316
Tommy McCraw	1964 Topps #283
Lance McCullers	1986 Fleer #330
Lance McCullers	1986 Topps #44
Lance McCullers (RR)	1986 Donruss #41
Lindy McDaniel	1957 Topps #79
Ben McDonald	1990 Donruss #32
Ben McDonald	1990 Fleer #180
Ben McDonald	1990 Score #680
Ben McDonald	1990 Topps #774
Ben McDonald	1990 Upper Deck #54
Ben McDonald	1990 Upper Deck #54
Gil McDougald	1952 Bowman #33
Gil McDougald	1952 Topps #372
Jack McDowell	1988 Donruss #47
Jack McDowell	1988 Fleer #407
Oddibe McDowell	1986 Donruss #56
Oddibe McDowell	1986 Fleer #566
Oddibe McDowell	1986 Topps #480
Roger McDowell	1986 Donruss #629
Roger McDowell	1986 Fleer #89
Roger McDowell	1986 Topps #547
Sam McDowell	1962 Topps #591
Chuck McElroy	1990 Fleer #650
Will McEnaney	1975 Topps #481
Andy McGaffigan	1982 Topps #83
Willie McGee	1983 Donruss #190
Willie McGee	1983 Fleer #15
Willie McGee	1983 Topps #49
Tug McGraw	1965 Topps #533
Scott McGregor	1975 Topps #618
Fred McGriff	1988 Fleer #118
Fred McGriff	1988 Topps #463
Terry McGriff	1987 Donruss #512
Fred McGriff (RR)	1986 Donruss #28
Bill McGuire	1989 Fleer #553
Mark McGwire	1987 Topps #366
Mark McGwire (RR)	1987 Donruss #46
Tim McIntosh	1990 Fleer #329
Joel McKeon	1987 Fleer #503
Jeff McKnight	1990 Upper Deck #162
Dennis McLain	1965 Topps #236
Mark McLemore	1986 Fleer #650
Mark McLemore (RR)	1986 Donruss #35
Don McMahon	1958 Topps #147
Roy McMillan	1952 Bowman #238
Roy McMillan	1952 Topps #137
Ken McMullen	1963 Topps #537
Craig McMurtry	1984 Donruss #599
Craig McMurtry	1984 Fleer #184
Craig McMurtry	1984 Topps #543
Dave McNally	1963 Topps #562
Hal McRae	1968 Topps #384
Kevin McReynolds	1984 Fleer #307
Kevin McReynolds (RR)	1984 Donruss #34
Larry McWilliams	1979 Topps #504
Bob Meacham	1984 Donruss #336
Bobby Meacham	1984 Topps #204
Louie Meadows	1989 Fleer #361
Louie Meadows	1989 Topps #643
Louie Meadows	1989 Upper Deck #401
Dave Meads	1988 Donruss #455
Dave Meads	1988 Fleer #453
Dave Meads	1988 Score #243
Dave Meads	1988 Topps #199
George Medich	1973 Topps #608
Luis Medina	1989 Donruss #36
Luis Medina	1989 Fleer #411
Luis Medina	1989 Score #633
Luis Medina	1989 Topps #528
Luis Medina	1989 Upper Deck #2
Scott Medvin	1989 Donruss #597
Scott Medvin	1989 Topps #756
Francisco Melendez	1989 Donruss #611
Bill Melton	1969 Topps #481
Bob Melvin	1986 Donruss #456
Bob Melvin	1986 Topps #479
Denis Menke	1962 Topps #597
Kent Mercker	1990 Donruss #31
Kent Mercker	1990 Fleer #590
Kent Mercker	1990 Upper Deck #63
Matt Merullo	1990 Fleer #542
Matt Merullo	1990 Score #605
Matt Merullo	1990 Upper Deck #67
Jose Mesa	1988 Donruss #601
Andy Messersmith	1969 Topps #296
Butch Metzger	1976 Topps #593
Hensley Meulens	1989 Donruss #547
Brian Meyer	1989 Donruss #640
Joey Meyer	1987 Donruss #460
Gene Michael	1967 Topps #428
Gary Mielke	1990 Donruss #679
Gary Mielke	1990 Score #574
Gary Mielke	1990 Topps #221
Gary Mielke	1990 Upper Deck #612
Bob Milacki	1989 Donruss #651
Bob Milacki	1989 Fleer #649
Bob Milacki	1989 Score #651
Bob Milacki	1989 Topps #324
Felix Millan	1967 Topps #89
Darrell Miller	1985 Donruss #644
Keith Miller	1988 Donruss #562
Keith Miller	1988 Fleer #144
Keith Miller	1988 Score #639
Keith Miller	1988 Topps #382
Keith Miller	1989 Topps #557
Rick Miller	1972 Topps #741
Stu Miller	1953 Topps #183
Randy Milligan	1988 Score #623
Eddie Milner	1983 Donruss #169
Eddie Milner	1983 Fleer #597
Eddie Milner	1983 Topps #449
John Milner	1972 Topps #741
Don Mincher	1960 Topps #548
Orestes Minoso	1952 Bowman #5
Orestes Minoso	1952 Topps #195
Greg Minton	1977 Topps #489
Paul Mirabella	1981 Donruss #151
Paul Mirabella	1981 Topps #382
John Mitchell	1988 Fleer #145
John Mitchell	1988 Score #249
John Mitchell	1988 Fleer Update #207
John Mitchell	1988 Fleer Update #207
Kevin Mitchell	1987 Donruss #599
Kevin Mitchell	1987 Fleer #17
Kevin Mitchell	1987 Topps #653
Kevin Mmahat	1990 Donruss #481
Kevin Mmahat	1990 Score #643
Randy Moffitt	1973 Topps #43
Dale Mohorcic	1987 Donruss #531
Dale Mohorcic	1987 Fleer #131
Dale Mohorcic	1987 Topps #497
Paul Molitor	1978 Topps #707
Bill Monbouquette	1959 Topps #173
Rick Monday	1967 Topps #542
Don Money	1969 Topps #454
Don Money	1969 Topps #454
Willie Montanez	1971 Topps #138
John Montefusco	1976 Topps #30
Rich Monteleone	1990 Donruss #462
Rich Monteleone	1990 Fleer #648
Rich Monteleone	1990 Score #565
Rich Monteleone	1990 Topps #99
Jeff Montgomery	1988 Fleer #642
Jeff Montgomery	1988 Score #497
Jeff Montgomery	1988 Topps #447

Wally Moon....1954 Topps #137
Bill Mooneyham....1987 Donruss #302
Bill Mooneyham....1987 Fleer #399
Bill Mooneyham....1987 Topps #548
Brad Moore....1989 Topps #202
Charlie Moore....1974 Topps #603
Donnie Moore....1978 Topps #523
Mike Moore....1983 Donruss #428
Mike Moore....1983 Fleer #482
Mike Moore....1983 Topps #209
Keith Moreland....1981 Donruss #382
Keith Moreland....1981 Fleer #13
Keith Moreland....1981 Topps #131
Omar Moreno....1977 Topps #104
Joe Morgan....1965 Topps #16
Mike Morgan....1980 Topps #671
Russ Morman....1987 Donruss #306
Russ Morman....1987 Fleer #645
Russ Morman....1987 Topps #233
Hal Morris....1989 Donruss #545
Hal Morris....1989 Fleer #260
Jack Morris....1978 Topps #703
John Morris (RR)....1985 Donruss #32
Jim Morrison....1979 Topps #722
Carl Morton....1969 Topps #646
Lloyd Moseby....1981 Fleer #421
Lloyd Moseby....1981 Topps #643
Don Mossi....1955 Bowman #259
Don Mossi....1955 Topps #85
Manny Mota....1963 Topps #141
Jamie Moyer....1987 Donruss #315
Jamie Moyer....1987 Fleer #570
Jamie Moyer....1987 Topps #227
Terry Mulholland....1987 Donruss #515
Terry Mulholland....1987 Topps #536
Rance Mulliniks....1978 Topps #579
Jerry Mumphrey....1977 Topps #136
Mike Munoz....1990 Score #653
Thurman Munson....1970 Topps #189
Masanori Murakami....1965 Topps #282
Bobby Murcer....1966 Topps #469
Dale Murphy....1977 Topps #476
Dan Murphy....1990 Topps #649
Dwayne Murphy....1979 Topps #711
Rob Murphy....1987 Donruss #452
Rob Murphy....1987 Fleer #206
Rob Murphy....1987 Topps #82
Eddie Murray....1978 Topps #36
Jeff Musselman....1987 Donruss #591
Greg Myers....1988 Donruss #624
Greg Myers....1988 Fleer #644
Randy Myers....1987 Topps #213
Randy Myers (RR)....1987 Donruss #29

N

Charles Nagy....1990 Score #611
Jaime Navarro....1990 Donruss #640
Jaime Navarro....1990 Fleer #331
Jaime Navarro....1990 Score #569
Jaime Navarro....1990 Upper Deck #646
Charles Neal....1955 Bowman #278
Dave Nelson....1969 Topps #579
Gene Nelson....1982 Donruss #513
Gene Nelson....1982 Fleer #45
Gene Nelson....1982 Topps #373
Rob Nelson....1987 Donruss #595
Rob Nelson....1987 Fleer #653
Graig Nettles....1969 Topps #99
Graig Nettles....1969 Topps #99
Don Newcombe....1950 Bowman #23
Tom Newell....1988 Donruss #604
Tom Newell....1988 Fleer #648
Al Newman....1987 Donruss #426
Al Newman....1987 Fleer #327
Al Newman....1987 Topps #323
Fred Newman....1963 Topps #496
Andy Nezelek....1989 Donruss #616
Carl Nichols....1988 Donruss #477
Reid Nichols....1981 Topps #689
Rod Nichols....1989 Donruss #649
Rod Nichols....1989 Topps #443
Tom Niedenfuer....1982 Fleer #16
Joe Niekro....1967 Topps #536
Phil Niekro....1964 Topps #541
Scott Nielsen....1987 Donruss #597
Scott Nielsen....1987 Topps #57
Tom Nieto....1985 Donruss #596
Tom Nieto....1985 Fleer #235
Tom Nieto....1985 Topps #294
Juan Nieves (RR)....1986 Donruss #40
Al Nipper....1985 Donruss #614
Al Nipper....1985 Fleer #165
Al Nipper....1985 Topps #424
Donell Nixon....1988 Topps #146
Donnell Nixon....1988 Fleer #382
Donnell Nixon....1988 Score #436
Otis Nixon....1986 Fleer #591
Junior Noboa....1988 Topps #503
Paul Noce....1988 Donruss #315
Paul Noce....1988 Fleer #428
Paul Noce....1988 Score #329
Paul Noce....1988 Topps #542
Matt Nokes....1988 Donruss #152
Matt Nokes....1988 Fleer #66
Matt Nokes....1988 Score #15
Matt Nokes....1988 Topps #645
Dickie Noles....1980 Topps #682
Eric Nolte....1988 Donruss #534
Eric Nolte....1988 Fleer #593
Eric Nolte....1988 Score #568
Eric Nolte....1988 Topps #694
Mike Norris....1976 Topps #653
Bill North....1973 Topps #234
Jim Northrup....1965 Topps #259
Randy Nosek....1990 Score #607
Randy Nosek....1990 Upper Deck #2
Ed Nunez....1984 Donruss #435
Jose Nunez....1988 Donruss #611
Jose Nunez....1988 Fleer #122
Jose Nunez....1988 Score #312
Jose Nunez....1988 Topps #28
Joe Nuxhall....1952 Topps #406

O

Charlie O'Brien....1988 Topps #566
Pete O'Brien....1984 Donruss #281
Pete O'Brien....1984 Fleer #423
Pete O'Brien....1984 Topps #534
Billy O'Dell....1955 Topps #57
Randy O'Neal....1985 Fleer #645
Paul O'Neill....1986 Fleer #646
Paul O'Neill (RR)....1986 Donruss #37
Jim O'Toole....1959 Topps #136
Ken Oberkfell....1980 Topps #701
Johnny Odom....1965 Topps #526
Ron Oester....1979 Topps #717
Jose Offerman....1990 Upper Deck #46
Ben Oglivie....1972 Topps #761
Bob Ojeda....1982 Donruss #540
Bob Ojeda....1982 Fleer #301
Bob Ojeda....1982 Topps #274
John Olerud....1990 Donruss #711
John Olerud....1990 Score #589
John Olerud....1990 Upper Deck #56
Steve Olin....1990 Donruss #438
Steve Olin....1990 Fleer #499
Steve Olin....1990 Score #590
Steve Olin....1990 Topps #433
Steve Olin....1990 Upper Deck #553
Pedro Oliva....1963 Topps #228
Al Oliver....1969 Topps #82
Joe Oliver....1990 Donruss #586
Joe Oliver....1990 Fleer #426
Joe Oliver....1990 Score #576
Joe Oliver....1990 Topps #668
Joe Oliver....1990 Upper Deck #568
Gregg Olson....1989 Donruss #46
Gregg Olson....1989 Topps #161
Steve Ontiveros....1986 Donruss #589
Steve Ontiveros....1986 Fleer #429
Steve Ontiveros....1986 Topps #507
Jose Oquendo....1984 Donruss #643
Jose Oquendo....1984 Fleer #592
Jose Oquendo....1984 Topps #208
Jesse Orosco....1980 Topps #681
Joe Orsulak....1986 Donruss #444
Joe Orsulak....1986 Fleer #615
Joe Orsulak....1986 Topps #102
Jorge Orta....1973 Topps #194
Junior Ortiz....1984 Donruss #319
Junior Ortiz....1984 Fleer #594
Junior Ortiz....1984 Topps #161
John Orton....1990 Fleer #647
John Orton....1990 Score #582
John Orton....1990 Upper Deck #672
Claude Osteen....1959 Topps #224
Amos Otis....1969 Topps #31
Dave Otto....1988 Fleer #652
Spike Owen....1984 Donruss #313
Spike Owen....1984 Fleer #616
Spike Owen....1984 Topps #413
Ray Oyler....1965 Topps #259

P

Pat Pacillo....1988 Donruss #536
Pat Pacillo....1988 Topps #288
Tom Paciorek....1971 Topps #709
Jose Pagan....1960 Topps #67
Mike Pagliarulo....1985 Donruss #539
Mike Pagliarulo....1985 Fleer #139
Mike Pagliarulo....1985 Topps #638
Tom Pagnozzi....1988 Donruss #577
Tom Pagnozzi....1988 Score #358
Tom Pagnozzi....1988 Topps #689
Leroy "Satchel" Paige....1949 Bowman #224
Rey Palacios....1989 Upper Deck #21
Robert Palacios....1989 Fleer #648
Vicente Palacios....1988 Donruss #45
Vicente Palacios....1988 Fleer #336
Vicente Palacios....1988 Score #643
Vicente Palacios....1988 Topps #322
Donn Pall....1989 Fleer #505
Donn Pall....1989 Topps #458
Rafael Palmeiro....1987 Topps #634
Rafael Palmeiro (RR)....1987 Donruss #43
Dave Palmer....1980 Topps #42
Dean Palmer....1990 Donruss #529
Dean Palmer....1990 Score #594
Dean Palmer....1990 Upper Deck #74
Jim Palmer....1966 Topps #126
Jim Pankovitz....1985 Donruss #502
Milt Pappas....1958 Topps #457
Johnny Paredes....1989 Donruss #570
Johnny Paredes....1989 Fleer #388
Johnny Paredes....1989 Topps #367
Johnny Paredes....1989 Upper Deck #477
Mark Parent....1989 Donruss #420
Mark Parent....1989 Score #576
Mark Parent....1989 Topps #617
Mark Parent....1989 Upper Deck #492
Clay Parker....1988 Fleer #649
Dave Parker....1974 Topps #252
Wes Parker....1964 Topps #456
Jeff Parrett....1988 Donruss #406
Jeff Parrett....1988 Topps #588
Lance Parrish....1978 Topps #708
Larry Parrish....1976 Topps #141
Camilo Pascual....1955 Topps #84
Dan Pasqua....1985 Donruss #637
Frank Pastore....1980 Topps #677
Freddie Patek....1969 Topps #219
Bob Patterson....1988 Fleer #337
Bob Patterson....1988 Topps #522
Ken Patterson....1989 Fleer #508
Ken Patterson....1989 Topps #434
John Pawlowski....1988 Donruss #457
John Pawlowski....1990 Score #617
Albie Pearson....1958 Topps #317
Bill Pecota....1988 Donruss #466
Bill Pecota....1988 Fleer #264
Bill Pecota....1988 Score #377
Bill Pecota....1988 Topps #433
Al Pedrique....1988 Donruss #361
Al Pedrique....1988 Fleer #338
Al Pedrique....1988 Topps #294
Alfredo Pedrique....1988 Score #301
Alejandro Pena....1984 Donruss #250
Alejandro Pena....1984 Fleer #109
Alejandro Pena....1984 Topps #324
Hipolito Pena....1989 Donruss #598
Hipolito Pena....1989 Fleer #263
Hipolito Pena....1989 Topps #109
Orlando Pena....1959 Topps #271
Tony Pena....1981 Topps #551
Jeff Pendleton....1985 Donruss #534
Terry Pendleton....1985 Donruss #534
Terry Pendleton....1985 Fleer #236
Terry Pendleton....1985 Topps #346
Joe Pepitone....1962 Topps #596
Oswald Peraza....1989 Donruss #524
Oswald Peraza....1989 Score #571
Oswald Peraza....1989 Topps #297
Oswaldo Peraza....1989 Upper Deck #651
Oswaldo Peraza (Oswald)....1989 Fleer #615
Melido Perez....1988 Donruss #589
Melido Perez....1988 Fleer #265
Pascual Perez....1981 Topps #551
Tony Perez....1965 Topps #581
Tony Perezchica....1989 Fleer #338
Jon Perlman....1988 Fleer #93
Ron Perranoski....1961 Topps #525
Gaylord Perry....1962 Topps #199
Gerald Perry....1984 Donruss #263
Jim Perry....1959 Topps #542
Pat Perry....1986 Donruss #596
Jeff Peterek....1990 Donruss #530
Jeff Peterek....1990 Fleer #333
Gary Peters....1960 Topps #407
Steve Peters....1989 Fleer #462
Steve Peters....1989 Topps #482
Adam Peterson....1988 Fleer #646
Fritz Peterson....1966 Topps #584
Gene Petralli....1983 Donruss #623
Gene Petralli....1983 Fleer #439
Rico Petrocelli....1965 Topps #74
Dan Petry....1980 Topps #373
Gary Pettis....1984 Donruss #647
Gary Pettis....1984 Fleer #526
Marty Pevey....1990 Topps #137
Marty Pevey....1990 Upper Deck #628
Ken Phelps....1982 Fleer #420
Tony Phillips....1984 Donruss #278
Tony Phillips....1984 Fleer #459
Tony Phillips....1984 Topps #309
Jeff Pico....1989 Donruss #513
Jeff Pico....1989 Fleer #436
Jeff Pico....1989 Score #13
Jeff Pico....1989 Topps #262
Jeff Pico....1989 Upper Deck #491
Jim Piersall....1951 Bowman #306
Lou Piniella....1964 Topps #167
Vada Pinson....1958 Topps #420
Juan Pizarro....1957 Topps #383
Dan Plesac....1987 Donruss #214
Dan Plesac....1987 Fleer #354
Dan Plesac....1987 Topps #279
Eric Plunk....1986 Fleer #649
John Podres....1953 Topps #263
Gus Polidor....1986 Fleer #650
Luis Polonia....1988 Donruss #425
Luis Polonia....1988 Fleer #292
Luis Polonia....1988 Score #64
Luis Polonia....1988 Topps #238
Darrell Porter....1972 Topps #162
Mark Portugal....1987 Donruss #566
Mark Portugal....1987 Fleer #548
Mark Portugal....1987 Topps #419
Brad Pounders....1989 Fleer #642
Dennis Powell....1986 Donruss #250
John Powell....1962 Topps #99
Ted Power....1982 Fleer #17
Jim Presley....1985 Donruss #240
Jim Presley....1985 Fleer #500
Joe Price....1981 Fleer #210
Joe Price....1981 Topps #258
Tom Prince....1988 Donruss #538
Kirby Puckett....1985 Donruss #438
Kirby Puckett....1985 Fleer #286
Kirby Puckett....1985 Topps #536
Terry Puhl....1978 Topps #553
Charlie Puleo....1983 Donruss #128
Charlie Puleo....1983 Fleer #552
Charlie Puleo....1983 Topps #549
Bob Purkey....1954 Topps #202
Pat Putnam....1978 Topps #706
Tim Pyznarski....1987 Donruss #654
Tim Pyznarski....1987 Topps #429

Q

Luis Quinones....1987 Topps #362

Rey Quinones	1987 Donruss #638
Rey Quinones	1987 Topps #561
Rey Quinonez (Quinones)	1987 Fleer #595
Carlos Quintana	1989 Donruss #37
Carlos Quintana	1989 Fleer #95
Carlos Quintana	1989 Score #623
Carlos Quintana	1989 Topps #704
Carlos Quintana	1989 Upper Deck #26
Jamie Quirk	1976 Topps #598
Dan Quisenberry	1980 Topps #667

R

Dick Radatz	1962 Topps #591
Doug Rader	1967 Topps #412
Tim Raines	1981 Donruss #538
Tim Raines	1981 Topps #479
Rafael Ramirez	1981 Fleer #266
Rafael Ramirez	1981 Topps #192
Pedro Ramos	1956 Topps #49
Lenny Randle	1972 Topps #737
Willie Randolph	1976 Topps #592
Dennis Rasmussen	1984 Donruss #446
Doug Rau	1973 Topps #602
Shane Rawley	1979 Topps #74
Johnny Ray	1982 Donruss #528
Johnny Ray	1982 Fleer #492
Johnny Ray	1982 Topps #291
Floyd Rayford	1981 Topps #399
Randy Ready	1985 Fleer #592
Jeff Reardon	1981 Donruss #156
Jeff Reardon	1981 Fleer #335
Jeff Reardon	1981 Topps #456
Gary Redus	1984 Donruss #184
Gary Redus	1984 Fleer #481
Gary Redus	1984 Topps #475
Jody Reed	1988 Donruss #41
Jody Reed	1988 Fleer #360
Jody Reed	1988 Score #625
Jody Reed	1988 Topps #152
Rick Reed	1990 Donruss #527
Rick Reed	1990 Fleer #477
Rick Reed	1990 Score #544
Ron Reed	1968 Topps #76
Jeff Reed (RR)	1985 Donruss #30
Phil Regan	1961 Topps #439
Rick Reichardt	1965 Topps #194
Jessie Reid	1988 Fleer #643
Kevin Reimer	1989 Fleer #641
Ken Reitz	1973 Topps #603
Jerry Remy	1976 Topps #229
Rich Renteria	1989 Score #142
Rich Renteria	1989 Upper Deck #547
Merv Rettenmund	1969 Topps #66
Rick Reuschel	1973 Topps #482
Jerry Reuss	1970 Topps #96
Dave Revering	1978 Topps #706
Craig Reynolds	1976 Topps #596
Harold Reynolds	1986 Donruss #484
Harold Reynolds	1986 Topps #769
R.J. Reynolds	1985 Donruss #128
R.J. Reynolds	1985 Fleer #381
R.J. Reynolds	1985 Topps #369
Rick Rhoden	1975 Topps #618
Jim Rhodes	1954 Topps #170
Jim Rice	1975 Topps #616
J.R. Richard	1972 Topps #101
Bobby Richardson	1957 Topps #286
Pete Richert	1962 Topps #131
Rob Richie	1990 Topps #146
Rob Richie	1990 Upper Deck #76
Dave Righetti	1982 Donruss #73
Dave Righetti	1982 Fleer #52
Dave Righetti	1982 Topps #439
Jose Rijo	1985 Donruss #492
Jose Rijo	1985 Fleer #143
Jose Rijo	1985 Topps #238
Earnest Riles	1986 Donruss #359
Earnie Riles	1986 Fleer #499
Earnie Riles	1986 Topps #398
Bill Ripken	1988 Fleer #569
Bill Ripken	1988 Score #200
Billy Ripken	1988 Donruss #336
Billy Ripken	1988 Topps #352
Cal Ripken	1982 Topps #21
Cal Ripken, Jr.	1982 Donruss #405
Cal Ripken, Jr.	1982 Fleer #176
Wally Ritchie	1988 Donruss #555
Wally Ritchie	1988 Fleer #312
Wally Ritchie	1988 Score #526
Wally Ritchie	1988 Topps #494
Kevin Ritz	1990 Donruss #415
Kevin Ritz	1990 Fleer #613
Kevin Ritz	1990 Score #572
Kevin Ritz	1990 Topps #237
Kevin Ritz	1990 Upper Deck #98
Luis Rivera	1987 Fleer #330
Mickey Rivers	1972 Topps #272
Dave Roberts	1969 Topps #536
Robin Roberts	1949 Bowman #46
Andre Robertson	1982 Topps #83
Bob Robertson	1968 Topps #36
Billy Robidoux	1986 Donruss #515
Billy Joe Robidoux	1986 Fleer #652
Bill Robinson	1967 Topps #442
Brooks Robinson	1957 Topps #328
Don Robinson	1979 Topps #264
Frank Robinson	1957 Topps #35
Jeff Robinson	1985 Donruss #201
Jeff Robinson	1988 Donruss #296
Jeff Robinson	1985 Fleer #620
Jeff Robinson	1988 Fleer #68
Jeff Robinson	1988 Fleer #68
Jeff Robinson	1988 Score #549
Jeff Robinson	1985 Topps #592
Jeff Robinson	1988 Topps #449
Ron Robinson	1985 Donruss #649
Ron Robinson	1985 Fleer #650
Mike Rochford	1989 Fleer #650
Bob Rodgers	1962 Topps #431
Aurelio Rodriguez	1969 Topps #653
Rick Rodriguez	1988 Fleer #293
Rick Rodriguez	1988 Topps #166
Gary Roenicke	1980 Topps #568
Mike Roesler	1990 Fleer #645
Mike Roesler	1990 Score #648
Mike Roesler	1990 Topps #203
Kenny Rogers	1990 Donruss #283
Kenny Rogers	1990 Fleer #311
Kenny Rogers	1990 Score #301
Kenny Rogers	1990 Topps #683
Kenny Rogers	1990 Upper Deck #606
Steve Rogers	1974 Topps #169
Cookie Rojas	1963 Topps #221
Rich Rollins	1962 Topps #596
Jose Roman	1985 Fleer #646
Ron Romanick	1985 Donruss #451
Ron Romanick	1985 Fleer #309
Ron Romanick	1985 Topps #579
Eddie Romero	1979 Topps #708
Kevin Romine	1987 Topps #121
Jim Rooker	1969 Topps #376
Rolando Roomes	1989 Donruss #577
Rolando Roomes	1989 Fleer #644
Rolando Roomes	1989 Upper Deck #6
Bobby Rose	1990 Fleer #651
Bobby Rose	1990 Score #604
Bobby Rose	1990 Upper Deck #77
Pete Rose	1963 Topps #537
John Roseboro	1958 Topps #42
Al "Flip" Rosen	1950 Bowman #232
Steve Rosenberg	1989 Donruss #219
Steve Rosenberg	1989 Topps #616
Wade Rowdon	1985 Donruss #642
Jerry Royster	1976 Topps #592
Dave Rozema	1978 Topps #124
Joe Rudi	1969 Topps #587
Bruce Ruffin	1987 Donruss #555
Bruce Ruffin	1987 Fleer #183
Bruce Ruffin	1987 Topps #499
Paul Runge	1986 Topps #409
James E. Runnels	1952 Topps #2
Bill Russell	1970 Topps #304
Jeff Russell	1984 Donruss #569
Jeff Russell	1984 Topps #270
John Russell	1985 Donruss #648
John Russell	1985 Fleer #653
Dick Ruthven	1974 Topps #47
Nolan Ryan	1968 Topps #177

S

Bret Saberhagen	1985 Donruss #222
Bret Saberhagen	1985 Fleer #212
Bret Saberhagen	1985 Topps #23
Chris Sabo	1989 Donruss #317
Chris Sabo	1989 Fleer #170
Chris Sabo	1989 Score #104
Chris Sabo	1989 Topps #490
Chris Sabo	1989 Upper Deck #180
Ray Sadecki	1960 Topps #327
Mark Salas	1985 Donruss #547
Luis Salazar	1981 Fleer #501
Luis Salazar	1981 Topps #309
Roger Salkeld	1990 Score #674
Roger Salkeld	1990 Topps #44
Joe Sambito	1977 Topps #227
Billy Sample	1979 Topps #713
Juan Samuel	1984 Fleer #47
Alejandro Sanchez	1985 Fleer #648
Alex Sanchez	1989 Donruss #47
Israel Sanchez	1989 Donruss #474
Israel Sanchez	1989 Topps #452
Israel Sanchez	1989 Upper Deck #326
Ryne Sandberg	1983 Donruss #277
Ryne Sandberg	1983 Fleer #507
Ryne Sandberg	1983 Topps #83
Deion Sanders	1990 Donruss #427
Deion Sanders	1990 Fleer #454
Deion Sanders	1990 Score #586
Deion Sanders	1990 Topps #61
Deion Sanders	1990 Upper Deck #13
Scott Sanderson	1979 Topps #720
Jack Sanford	1957 Topps #387
Manny Sanguillen	1968 Topps #251
Rafael Santana	1985 Donruss #610
Rafael Santana	1985 Fleer #90
Rafael Santana	1985 Topps #67
Benito Santiago	1986 Fleer #644
Ron Santo	1961 Topps #35
Nelson Santovenia	1989 Donruss #366
Nelson Santovenia	1989 Fleer #393
Nelson Santovenia	1989 Score #346
Nelson Santovenia	1989 Topps #228
Nelson Santovenia	1989 Upper Deck #380
Mackey Sasser	1988 Donruss #28
Mackey Sasser	1988 Score #642
Jack Savage	1988 Fleer #650
Steve Sax	1982 Donruss #624
Steve Sax	1982 Fleer #21
Steve Sax	1982 Topps #681
Dan Schatzeder	1978 Topps #709
Curt Schilling	1989 Donruss #635
Calvin Schiraldi (RR)	1985 Donruss #38
Dave Schmidt	1983 Fleer #578
Dave Schmidt	1982 Topps #418
Mike Schmidt	1973 Topps #615
Dick Schofield	1954 Topps #191
Dick Schofield (RR)	1984 Donruss #35
Mike Schooler	1989 Donruss #637
Mike Schooler	1989 Fleer #559
Mike Schooler	1989 Score #528
Mike Schooler	1989 Topps #199
Mike Schooler	1989 Upper Deck #28
Bill Schroeder	1984 Donruss #515
Bill Schroeder	1984 Topps #738
Ken Schrom	1981 Fleer #425
Ken Schrom	1981 Topps #577
Rick Schu	1985 Donruss #448
Don Schulze	1985 Donruss #639
Don Schulze	1985 Fleer #454
Don Schulze	1985 Topps #93
Don Schwall	1962 Topps #35
Mike Scioscia	1981 Fleer #131
Mike Scioscia	1981 Topps #302
Herb Score	1956 Topps #140
George Scott	1966 Topps #558
Mike Scott	1980 Topps #681
Scott Scudder	1990 Donruss #435
Scott Scudder	1990 Fleer #434
Scott Scudder	1990 Score #518
Scott Scudder	1990 Topps #553
Scott Scudder	1990 Upper Deck #164
Rod Scurry	1981 Fleer #380
Rod Scurry	1981 Topps #194
Rudy Seanez	1990 Fleer #640
Steve Searcy	1989 Donruss #29
Steve Searcy	1989 Fleer #145
Steve Searcy	1989 Score #627
Steve Searcy	1989 Topps #167
Tom Seaver	1967 Topps #581
Bob Sebra	1987 Donruss #468
Bob Sebra	1987 Fleer #331
Bob Sebra	1987 Topps #479
Diego Segui	1963 Topps #157
Kevin Seitzer	1987 Fleer #652
Jeff Sellers	1987 Donruss #544
Jeff Sellers	1987 Fleer #46
Jeff Sellers	1987 Topps #12
Scott Service	1989 Fleer #653
Scott Service	1990 Upper Deck #35
Art Shamsky	1965 Topps #398
Mike Shannon	1964 Topps #262
Bobby Shantz	1950 Bowman #234
Mike Sharperson	1987 Donruss #565
Larry Sheets (RR)	1985 Donruss #36
Gary Sheffield	1989 Donruss #31
Gary Sheffield	1989 Fleer #196
Gary Sheffield	1989 Score #625
Gary Sheffield	1989 Topps #343
Gary Sheffield	1989 Upper Deck #13
Gary Sheffield	1989 Upper Deck #13
John Shelby	1984 Donruss #291
John Shelby	1984 Fleer #20
John Shelby	1984 Topps #86
Pat Sheridan	1984 Donruss #588
Pat Sheridan	1984 Fleer #357
Pat Sheridan	1984 Topps #121
Steve Shields	1986 Fleer #527
Steve Shields	1988 Score #396
Steve Shields	1988 Topps #632
Dave Shipanoff (RR)	1986 Donruss #34
Bob Shirley	1978 Topps #266
Eric Show	1983 Donruss #439
Eric Show	1983 Fleer #372
Eric Show	1983 Topps #68
Norm Siebern	1958 Topps #54
Sonny Siebert	1964 Topps #552
Candy Sierra	1989 Fleer #171
Candy Sierra	1989 Topps #711
Ruben Sierra	1987 Donruss #346
Ruben Sierra	1987 Fleer #138
Ruben Sierra	1987 Topps #261
Roy Sievers	1950 Bowman #16
Curt Simmons	1949 Bowman #14
Ted Simmons	1971 Topps #117
Todd Simmons	1988 Fleer #650
Bill Singer	1966 Topps #288
Ken Singleton	1971 Topps #16
Doug Sisk	1984 Donruss #615
Doug Sisk	1984 Fleer #596
Doug Sisk	1984 Topps #599
Ted Sizemore	1969 Topps #552
Joe Skalski	1990 Score #618
Bob Skinner	1955 Topps #88
Joel Skinner	1985 Fleer #646
Joel Skinner (RR)	1984 Donruss #27
Bill Skowron	1954 Topps #239
Jim Slaton	1972 Topps #744
Don Slaught	1983 Donruss #196
Don Slaught	1983 Fleer #123
Roy Smalley	1976 Topps #657
John Smiley	1988 Donruss #449
John Smiley	1988 Fleer #340
John Smiley	1988 Score #287
John Smiley	1988 Topps #423
Al Smith	1954 Topps #248
Bryn Smith	1982 Topps #118
Dave Smith	1981 Donruss #23
Dave Smith	1981 Donruss #23
Dave Smith	1981 Fleer #71
Dave Smith	1981 Topps #534
Dwight Smith	1990 Donruss #393
Dwight Smith	1989 Score #642
Greg Smith	1990 Fleer #643
Greg Smith	1990 Score #614
Lee Smith	1982 Donruss #252
Lee Smith	1982 Fleer #603
Lee Smith	1982 Fleer #603
Lee Smith	1982 Topps #452
Lonnie Smith	1979 Topps #722
Mike Smith	1990 Topps #249
Mike Smith	1990 Topps #552
Ozzie Smith	1979 Topps #116
Pete Smith	1988 Donruss #571
Peter Smith	1988 Fleer #647

T

U

V

W

Jeff Wetherby	1990 Score #540
Jeff Wetherby	1990 Topps #142
Jeff Wetherby	1990 Upper Deck #611
John Wetteland	1990 Donruss #671
John Wetteland	1990 Fleer #411
John Wetteland	1990 Score #388
John Wetteland	1990 Topps #631
John Wetteland	1990 Upper Deck #377
Lou Whitaker	1978 Topps #704
Bill White	1959 Topps #359
Devon White	1987 Fleer #646
Devon White	1987 Topps #139
Frank White	1974 Topps #604
Roy White	1966 Topps #234
Devon White (RR)	1987 Donruss #38
Ed Whited	1990 Score #644
Ed Whited	1990 Upper Deck #447
Wally Whitehurst	1990 Score #599
Wally Whitehurst	1990 Topps #719
Wally Whithurst	1990 Upper Deck #564
Eddie Whitson	1979 Topps #189
Ernie Whitt	1978 Topps #708
Kevin Wickander	1990 Topps #528
Alan Wiggins	1983 Topps #251
Milt Wilcox	1971 Topps #164
Hoyt Wilhelm	1952 Topps #392
Curt Wilkerson	1984 Donruss #99
Dean Wilkins	1990 Fleer #47
Dean Wilkins	1990 Score #630
Bill Wilkinson	1988 Donruss #568
Bill Wilkinson	1988 Fleer #390
Bill Wilkinson	1988 Topps #376
Bernie Williams	1990 Donruss #689
Bernie Williams	1990 Score #619
Bernie Williams	1990 Topps #701
Billy Williams	1961 Topps #141
Dana Williams	1990 Fleer #648
Dick Williams	1952 Topps #396
Earl Williams	1971 Topps #52
Eddie Williams	1988 Donruss #46
Eddie Williams	1988 Fleer #620
Eddie Williams	1988 Topps #758
Frank Williams	1985 Donruss #323
Frank Williams	1985 Fleer #624
Frank Williams	1985 Topps #487
Ken Williams	1988 Donruss #334
Ken Williams	1988 Score #112
Ken Williams	1988 Topps #559
Kenny Williams	1988 Fleer #412
Matt Williams	1988 Donruss #628
Matt Williams	1988 Fleer #101
Matt Williams	1988 Score #118
Matt Williams	1988 Topps #372
Mitch Williams	1987 Donruss #347
Mitch Williams	1987 Fleer #142
Mitch Williams	1987 Topps #291
Reggie Williams	1987 Donruss #341
Reggie Williams	1987 Fleer #460
Reggie Williams	1987 Topps #232
Mark Williamson	1988 Donruss #418
Mark Williamson	1988 Fleer #574
Mark Williamson	1988 Topps #571
Carl Willis	1987 Fleer #218
Carl Willis	1987 Topps #101
Bump Wills	1977 Topps #494
Don Wilson	1968 Topps #77
Earl Wilson	1960 Topps #249
Glenn Wilson	1983 Fleer #350
Glenn Wilson	1983 Topps #332
Mookie Wilson	1981 Donruss #575
Mookie Wilson	1981 Topps #259
Steve Wilson	1990 Donruss #394
Steve Wilson	1989 Fleer #640
Trevor Wilson	1989 Fleer #347
Trevor Wilson	1989 Topps #783
Willie Wilson	1979 Topps #409
Glen Wilson (Glenn)	1983 Donruss #580
Bobby Wine	1963 Topps #71
Robbie Wine	1988 Donruss #508
Robbie Wine	1988 Fleer #459
Robbie Wine	1988 Topps #119
Robby Wine, Jr.	1988 Score #496
Dave Winfield	1974 Topps #456
Jim Winn	1985 Topps #69
Herm Winningham	1986 Fleer #266
Herm Winningham	1986 Topps #448
Herman Winningham	1986 Donruss #279
Matt Winters	1990 Fleer #124
Matt Winters	1990 Upper Deck #524
Rick Wise	1964 Topps #561
Bobby Witt	1987 Donruss #99
Bobby Witt	1987 Fleer #143
Bobby Witt	1987 Topps #415
Mike Witt	1982 Donruss #416
Mike Witt	1982 Fleer #473
Mike Witt	1982 Topps #744
Wilbur Wood	1964 Topps #267
Mike Woodard	1986 Fleer #645
Mike Woodard (RR)	1986 Donruss #46
Tracy Woodson	1988 Donruss #499
Rob Woodward	1986 Fleer #651
Woody Woodward	1964 Topps #378
Todd Worrell	1986 Fleer #49
Todd Worrell (RR)	1986 Donruss #43
Craig Worthington	1989 Donruss #569
Craig Worthington	1989 Fleer #627
Craig Worthington	1989 Score #636
Craig Worthington	1989 Topps #181
Clyde Wright	1969 Topps #583
Rick Wrona	1990 Donruss #512
Rick Wrona	1990 Score #557
Rick Wrona	1990 Topps #187
Rick Wrona	1990 Upper Deck #582
Butch Wynegar	1977 Topps #175
Jim Wynn	1964 Topps #38
Marvell Wynne	1984 Donruss #508
Marvell Wynne	1984 Fleer #269
Marvell Wynne	1984 Topps #173

Y

Carl Yastrzemski	1960 Topps #148
Steve Yeager	1973 Topps #59
Eric Yelding	1990 Score #411
Eric Yelding	1990 Topps #309
Eric Yelding	1990 Upper Deck #427
Rich Yett	1987 Fleer #263
Rich Yett	1987 Topps #134
Floyd Youmans	1986 Donruss #543
Floyd Youmans	1986 Fleer #267
Floyd Youmans	1986 Topps #732
Curt Young	1985 Donruss #522
Curt Young	1985 Fleer #436
Curt Young	1985 Topps #293
Gerald Young	1988 Donruss #431
Gerald Young	1988 Fleer #460
Gerald Young	1988 Score #442
Gerald Young	1988 Topps #368
Matt Young	1984 Donruss #362
Matt Young	1984 Fleer #624
Matt Young	1984 Topps #235
Mike Young	1984 Donruss #621
Joel Youngblood	1977 Topps #548
Robin Yount	1975 Topps #223

Z

Geoff Zahn	1975 Topps #294
Clint Zavaras	1990 Donruss #662
Clint Zavaras	1990 Topps #89
Todd Zeile	1990 Donruss #29
Todd Zeile	1990 Fleer #265
Todd Zeile	1990 Score #600
Todd Zeile	1990 Topps #162
Todd Zeile	1990 Upper Deck #545
Don Zimmer	1955 Bowman #65
Don Zimmer	1955 Topps #92
Alan Zinter	1990 Score #671
Richie Zisk	1972 Topps #392
Eddie Zosky	1990 Score #665
Paul Zuvella	1985 Fleer #651

Wrong backs, blank backs

Collectors occasionally find recent (1980s) cards which have wrong backs (player on front doesn't match bio/stats on back) or blank backs. Such cards result from mistakes in the printing process. They aren't very popular with collectors, so they have little, if any, premium value. Most collectors feel they are merely damaged cards and value them lower than correctly printed specimens. The only exception seems to be currently hot superstars or rookie cards, for which a few collectors are willing to pay premiums.

Errors/variations

Collectors often wonder about errors found on cards, usually in the statistics or personal data on the card's back.

Such errors *add nothing* to the value of the card. The only time an error like this is likely to increase a card's value is if the manufacturer corrects the error in a later printing, thus creating two distinct variations. If enough collectors feel the variations are a desirable part of that issue, the value may increase. Whether the error version or the corrected card will have the greater value usually depends on relative scarcity. The more common version will almost always be worth less. So quite often, the error card can be worth less than the corrected version.

Collector-only issues

Collectors may find some recent issues not included in this volume. In most cases these are illegal, unauthorized "collector-only" issues. Such cards often show nothing but the player's photo and his name on the front, and his name and perhaps a line or two of statistics on the back. The sets usually lack a manufacturer's name. They are often sold at shows and in shops, and frequently carry high price tags.

The cards *are not* legitimate issues. They can be printed and reprinted at will, so they lack any scarcity value.

BASEBALL CARD GRADING GUIDE

Mint (MT): A perfect card. Well-centered with all corners sharp and square. No creases, stains, edge nicks, surface marks, yellowing or fading, regardless of age.

Near Mint (NR MT): A nearly perfect card. At first glance, a NR MT card appears to be perfect. May have one corner not perfectly sharp. May be slightly off-center. No surface marks, creases, or loss of gloss.

Excellent (EX): Corners are still fairly sharp with only moderate wear. Borders may be off center. No creases or stains on fronts or backs, but may show slight loss of surface luster.

Very Good (VG): Shows obvious handling. May have rounded corners, minor creases, major gum or wax stains. No major creases, tape marks, writing, etc.

Good (G): A well-worn card, but exhibits no intentional damage. May have major or multiple creases. Corners may be rounded well beyond card border.

Fair (F): A complete card, but contains damage such as writing on card back, tack holes, and heavy creases.

Card company addresses

Collectors frequently want to know the addresses of the major baseball-card manufacturing companies. They are:

Topps Chewing Gum Co.
254 36th St.
Brooklyn, N.Y. 11232

Fleer Corp.
10th & Somerville
Philadelphia, Pa. 19141

Leaf-Donruss Co.
P.O. Box 2038
Memphis, Tenn. 38101

Sportflics/Score
Major League Marketing, Inc.
55 Ford Rd.
Westport, Ct. 06880

Upper Deck Co.
23705 Via Del Rio
Yorba Linda, CA 92686

GLOSSARY OF HOBBY TERMS

Airbrushing: The touching up of a photo by an artist. Usually done on baseball cards to show a player who has changed teams in his new uniform.

All-Star card: A special card identifying a player as a member of a National League, American League or Major-League all-star team. Players shown on all-star cards may or may not be members of their league's official All-Star teams. All-star cards can be part of a regular set or issued as an independent set. For several years, Topps has issued two different "glossy" sets of all-star cards on specially-coated stock.

Assorted: A term used in ads to indicate a lot of cards which may contain multiples of one or more cards. Lots which do not contain doubles are labeled "different."

Autographed card: A card that has actually been signed by the player pictured, as opposed to the facsimile signatures that are sometimes printed on cards as part of the design. The value of an autographed card is generally greater than that same card would be if it were unautographed.

Baseball's Best: A season-end glossy set made by Donruss in 1988 and 1989. Also the name of a set made by Fleer in 1987 and 1988, and the name of the set of insert cards made by *Baseball Cards* magazine in 1989 and 1990.

Bazooka: A bubble-gum-making subsidiary of Topps which made baseball cards from 1959-71 and again in 1988 and '89.

Blank-back: Usually used to refer to a card that has no printing on the back because of a manufacturing mistake. Cards that were intentionally issued without printing on the back are also known as blank-backed.

Blanket: An early 20th-century collectible consisting of a square piece of felt or other fabric which came wrapped around a package of cigarettes. Baseball players were one of several subjects found on blankets. Most popular are the 5¼"-square B-18 blankets from 1914, so-called because they were sometimes sewn together to form a blanket.

Borders: The portion of a card which surrounds the picture. Borders are usually white but are sometimes colored. The condition of a card's borders is one of the vital component's in determining a card's grade.

Bowman: A very famous card company that made baseball cards from 1948-55; football cards from 1948-55, and basketball cards in 1948. Bowman was bought by Topps in 1956 and card production ceased. Topps revived the Bowman name in 1989 for a set of baseball cards.

Box-bottom cards: Cards printed on the bottom and/or sides of wax or foil boxes. Box-bottom cards are not considered to be part of the regular set and generally are not valuable unless kept as an intact panel.

Boxed set: A set of cards, usually consisting of either 33 or 44 cards, issued as a complete set and sold in its own box at a large chain or discount store. Boxed sets are usually made by one of the major manufacturers and contain cards of only the biggest names or hottest rookies.

Brick: A wrapped lot of cards, usually all from one year. See "starter lot."

Buy price: The price which a dealer is willing to pay for cards or memorabilia. A dealer's buy price is usually quite a bit lower than that item's catalog or retail price.

Cabinet card: A large card from the late 19th or early 20th century, usually issued on heavy cardboard. The cards were often given away as premiums by tobacco companies, and were either photographs or reproductions of paintings. The name "cabinet" derives from how they were often displayed: inside curio cabinets.

Card stock: The paper or cardboard that baseball cards are printed on.

Cello box: A retail display box of cello packs, usually, but not always, containing 24 packs.

Cello case: A wholesale unit of cello boxes, usually, but not always, containing 16 boxes.

Cello pack: A cellophane-wrapped pack of cards. A cello pack usually contains more cards than a wax pack. Depending on how the cards are packaged, the top and bottom card of a cello pack may or may not be easily visible through the cellophane. Many collectors will pay a premium for a cello pack with a card of a star player or hot rookie showing on the top or bottom.

Centering: The positioning of a card picture between its borders. A well-centered card has even borders, an important factor in grading a card.

Checklist: A list of every card in a particular set, usually with a space allowing the collector to check whether or not he has the card. A checklist can appear on a card, in a book or elsewhere. As a rule of thumb, checklists on cards are worth more if they're left unchecked.

Chipping: A card-grading term referring to a condition in which a portion of a card's dark-colored border is worn away. Chipping is a real problem, for instance, with 1953 and 1971 Topps cards, and more recent issues with colored borders.

Classic cards: Cards made by Game Time, Ltd. to go with their Classic Baseball trivia game. The cards were first made in 1987 and are sold in sets. Several sets a year are produced.

Coin: A metal or plastic coin-sized disc which depicts a player. It can also refer to an actual coin or a coin-sized silver piece which commemorates an actual event.

Collation: The act of putting cards in order, usually numerical order.

Collectible: Something worth collecting. Baseball cards, programs, pennants, uniforms, and autographs are all examples of collectibles.

Collector issue: A set of cards produced primarily to be sold to collectors and not issued as a premium to be given away or sold with a commercial product. Collector issues fall into two categories: authorized (meaning the issue was made with the approval of Major League Baseball and the players' association) or unauthorized (meaning the issue was made without approval).

Common card: A card picturing a "common" or ordinary player — that is, not a star or superstar. "Commons" are the lowest-priced cards in a given series or set.

Counterfeit card: A phony card made to look like a real card. Counterfeit cards have no collector value.

Crease: A bend mark in a card, usually due to mishandling. Creases substantially lower a card's grade and value.

Dealer: A person who buys, sells and trades baseball cards and other memorabilia for profit. A dealer may be full-time, part-time, own a shop, operate a mail-order business from his home, deal at baseball-card shows on weekends or do any combination of the above.

Decollation: The act of putting cards in random order, usually for packaging.

Die-cut card: A baseball card in which the player's outline has been partially separated from the background, enabling the card to be folded into a "stand-up" figure. Die-cut cards that have never been folded are worth more to collectors.

Ding: Slight damage to the corner or edge of a card.

Disc set: A set of disc-shaped cards, usually showing head-and-shoulder shots of players with the team insignia usually airbrushed off their hats. Many of these sets are made by Michael Schechter Associates.

Donruss: A baseball-card manufacturer. Donruss began printing baseball cards in 1981.

Double-print: An individual card that, because of a particular printing configuration, appears twice on the same press sheet and is, therefore, twice as common as the other cards.

Drake's: An Ohio-based bakery that made baseball cards in 1950 and again from 1981-88.

Error card: A card that contains a mistake, including wrong photos, misspelled words, incorrect statistics, and so forth. Usually error cards have no extra value unless they have been corrected, resulting in a "variation" card.

Exhibit cards: Postcard-size cards picturing baseball players and other celebrities and sold in penny-arcade machines. Exhibit cards were produced from the 1920s to the 1960s.

Extended set: A term used to describe a late-season series of cards added onto and numbered after a regular set. Also known as an "extended series."

Facsimile autograph: A reproduced autograph. Facsimile autographs are often found on baseball cards as part of the card's design.

Factory set: A complete set of cards collated and packaged by the card company. A factory set may or may not be packaged in a special box. Usually factory sets are sealed or have sealed inner packs as an added security measure. Factory sets with intact seals or inner packs command a slight premium over hand-collated sets.

Felt: A baseball item consisting of a felt pennant, usually with a photograph or likeness of the player attached. Felts were made in 1916 and again from 1936-37.

First card: The first card of a player in a national set. A first card may or may not be a player's rookie card; for instance, if a player appeared in a Fleer set one year and a Score set the next, the Fleer card would be that player's rookie card and his first Fleer card, while the Score card would be his first Score card but not his rookie card.

Flannel: A jersey made of a cotton or wool material. Most flannels were discontinued and replaced by knit jerseys in the early 1970s.

Fleer: A manufacturer of football, basketball and baseball cards. Fleer made baseball cards from 1959-1963 and again from 1981 to the present.

Foil Box: A retail display box of foil packs, usually, but not always, containing 36 packs.

Foil case: A wholesale unit of foil boxes, usually, but not always containing 24 boxes.

Foil pack: A pack of baseball cards packaged in a tamper-proof, shiny foil. Upper Deck packages its cards in foil packs.

Food set: A set either inserted in packages of food (hot dogs, cereal, popcorn, potato chips, candy, cookies, etc.) or offered as a send-in offer by a food company. Examples of food sets include Kahn's Weiners, Mother's Cookies, etc.

Full sheet: A full press sheet of cards that has never been cut; sometimes referred to as an "uncut" sheet. The number of cards on a sheet varies with the printing process, but most often contains 132 cards.

Gallery of Champions: Trade name for a set of miniature metallic reproductions of Topps cards made and sold by Topps from 1986-88. Gallery of Champions ingots were made in bronze, aluminum, silver and pewter.

Gloss: The amount of surface shine on a card. All baseball cards are made with some surface gloss. Cards that keep more of their gloss keep more of their value.

Glossy card: A card with a special, extra-shiny finish.

Glossy set: A set of glossy cards. Glossy sets can be either small and common (Topps' sendaway all-star sets) or large and scarce. Fleer, Topps, Score and Bowman have made glossy versions of their regular sets.

Goudey: A famous maker of baseball cards. The Goudey Gum Co. of Boston made baseball cards and non-sport cards from 1933-39.

Grade: The state of preservation of a card or piece of memorabilia. An item's value is based in large part on its grade (condition).

Grading service: A company that charges a fee to grade cards. Most grading services work like this: After a card is graded, it is placed in a tamper-proof plastic holder. A network of member-dealers then agrees to buy that card sight-unseen at that grade. Card grading services are a recent innovation, patterned after similar services in the coin collecting hobby.

Hall of Fame Postcard: A long-running series of postcards produced by several manufacturers and sold by the National Baseball Hall of Fame. Popular with autograph collectors.

Hall of Famer: A member of the Baseball Hall of Fame in Cooperstown, N.Y., but also used to refer to a baseball card picturing a member of the Hall of Fame. Hall of Famer cards almost always command a premium over other cards.

Hand-collated set: A set assembled card-by-card by hand, usually by a collector or dealer putting the set together out of wax, cello or vending boxes.

Hartland: A statue produced by a Wisconsin plastics company in the late '50s and early '60s. Eighteen major-league baseball players were models for Hartlands. The company also produced football player statues and a long line of Western and historical figures, horses and farm animals. The Hartland baseball figures were reissued amidst some controversy in 1989.

High numbers: A term usually used to describe the final series in a particular set of cards. High numbers were generally produced in smaller quantities than other series and are, therefore, scarcer and more valuable.

Hologram: The silvery, laser-etched trademark printed as an anti-counterfeiting device on Upper Deck cards. Also, the disc with a team logo inserted into Upper Deck packs.

Hoops: Trade name for the National Basketball Association's set of basketball cards.

In-action card: A card showing a ballplayer in action, as opposed to posed.

Insert: A collectible included inside a regular pack of baseball cards to boost sales. Inserts have included posters, baseball player stamps, coins, stickers, comic books, special cards, and tattoos.

Kellogg's: A cereal company which packaged three-dimensional baseball cards in its cereal from 1970-83.

Key cards: The most important cards in a set.

Last card: The final card issued of a ballplayer.

Layering: A term used in card grading to describe the separation of the layers of paper that make up the cardboard stock. Layering is a sign of wear that is first noticeable at the corners of the card.

Leaf: Donruss' parent firm. Donruss issued baseball cards in Canada under the Leaf name from 1985-88.

Legitimate issue: A licensed card set issued as a premium with a commercial product to increase sales; not a collector issue.

Limited edition: A term often used by makers of cards and memorabilia to indicate scarcity. A limited edition means just that — production of the item in question will be limited to a certain number. However, that number may be large or small.

Lithograph: An art print made by a specific process that results in a print of outstanding clarity. Most lithographs are limited editions — though, as always, some lithographs are more limited than others.

Logo sticker: A peel-off, adhesive-backed reproduction of a team's symbol. Logo stickers are packed in Fleer wax packs.

Mail-bid auction: A form of auction where all bids are sent in through the mail. The person who sends in the highest bid gets the merchandise.

Major set: A large, nationally-distributed set produced by a major card manufacturer, such as Topps, Fleer, Donruss, Score, Sportflics or Upper Deck.

Megalot: A card-investor's term referring to a very large (normally 1,000 or more) group of cards of one player, purchased as an investment.

Memorabilia: Usually used in card collecting to refer to items other than cards which mark or commemorate a player and his career, a team, or an event.

Mini: Small-size cards, sometimes miniature reproductions of regular cards (1975 Topps mini) and sometimes independent issues (1986-date Topps Mini League Leaders).

Minor leaguer: A card depicting a player from the minor leagues. Minor-league sets are a fast-growing segment of the hobby.

Miscut: A card that has been cut incorrectly from a press sheet during the manufacturing process and decreases in value as a result.

Mother's: An Oakland (Calif.)-based cookie company which has issued high-quality glossy-finish regional sets since 1982.

Multi-player card: A card picturing more than one player. Multi-player cards often show rookies or stars.

Mylar: Trade name for a type of inert plastic used to make supplies for the protection of cards and memorabilia.

Nine-pocket sheet: The most common type of plastic sheet. A nine-pocket sheet is about the size of a sheet of typing paper and is designed to fit into a standard three-ring binder. The sheet has nine pockets to hold most normal-sized modern cards.

Non-sports card: A card picturing a subject other than sports. Non-sports cards have depicted movie stars, television shows, U.S. presidents, moments in history, entertainers and other subjects.

Notching: A card-grading term used to describe indentations along the edge of a card, sometimes caused by a rubber band. Notching decreases a card's value.

Obverse: The front of the card displaying the picture.

Off-center: A term used in card grading to describe a card that has uneven borders.

Old Judge: A brand of cigarettes which was popular in the late 1800s. Also the name given to the huge set of baseball cards issued as a premium with that brand of cigarettes. The cards, issued from 1887-90, carried advertisements for Old Judge cigarettes.

O-Pee-Chee: Topps' Canadian licensee. O-Pee-Chee makes and sells a baseball-card set that resembles Topps' set but has fewer cards, and a hockey-card set that resembles Topps but has more cards. O-Pee-Chee cards can be distinguished from Topps cards by the bilingual (French-English) backs.

Out of register: A term used to describe a printing error in which the various colors are not correctly superimposed upon one another, thereby decreasing the value of the card.

P.O.R.: Price on request.

PVC: Shortened name of a chemical compound (polyvinyl chloride), sometimes used to make plastic sheets and other card collectors' supplies. PVC plastic is generally clearer and stiffer than other types of plastic sheets but may have a shorter safelife.

Panel: A strip of two or more uncut cards. Some card sets are issued in panels.

Panini: An international sticker manufacturer which came into the U.S. baseball-sticker market in 1988 with a large and attractive set of baseball stickers. Panini also makes hockey, basketball and football stickers.

Perez-Steele: Usually used as a term to refer to an ongoing set of Hall of Fame postcards issued by the Perez-Steele Galleries of Fort Washington, Pa. The company has made a number of art-card sets, including the Celebration and Greatest Moments sets. Popular with autograph collectors.

Police set: A regional card set made for a police department and given away to kids, usually one card at a time, to promote friendly relations. Police cards often carry a safety or anti-drug message on the back. Baseball, football, basketball and hockey police sets have been made of major-league, minor-league and college teams. Similar sets issued by fire departments are also generically called "police sets" or "safety sets."

Polyethylene: A type of plastic used to make card sheets and other collectors' supplies. Very flexible, but not as clear as other types of plastic. Safer than PVC for very long-term card storage.

Post: A cereal company which made baseball and football cards from 1960-63 and put them on the backs of its cereal boxes. Today the most valuable Post cards are uncut panels found on boxes. In 1990, the company returned with a baseball-card set inserted into its cereal boxes.

Premium: An extra. In terms of cards, this can either refer to a card inserted in a package of some other product or something extra inserted in a package of cards. "Premium" can also refer to the extra money a high-series or star card commands.

Pre-rookie: Term sometimes used to refer to any card of a player issued before his rookie card — a minor-league card, for example, or a high-school, college or Olympic team card.

Press run: The total number of any one set of cards printed.

Pro Cards: A large and important maker of minor-league cards. Pro Cards revolutionized the minor-league card business in 1986 when it issued around 100 different minor-league sets.

Promo card: A card made for promotional purposes. Promo cards generally have very limited distribution and can be quite valuable.

Proof card: A card made not to be sold but to test the card presses, the card design, photography, colors, paper, statistical accuracy and so forth.

Pro Set: A company affiliated with the National Football League which began making football cards in 1989.

Rack box: A retail display box of rack packs. There are usually 24 rack packs to a rack box.

Rack case: A wholesale case of rack boxes. There are usually three or six rack boxes in a rack case.

Rack pack: A cellophane-wrapped pack of cards, usually having three compartments, designed to be hung from a peg in a retail store. Rack packs vary in the number of cards in each pack; also, some rack packs consist of nothing but cello-wrapped wax packs.

Rare: Difficult to obtain and limited in number. See "Scarce."

Regional set: A card set limited in distribution to one geographical area. Regional sets often depict players from one team.

Reprint: A reproduction of a previously-issued baseball card or set. Generally produced to satisfy collector demand, they usually — but not always — are labeled "reprint" and have little collector value.

Restored card: A card which has had "cosmetic surgery" — that is, a card which has had its imperfections fixed long after the card was issued. A card restorer can fix corners and restore gloss to cardstock. Restored cards should be clearly labeled as such by whoever is selling them, and should be priced much less than unrestored cards in the same condition.

Reverse: The back of a card.

Rookie card: A player's first card issued by a major card producer in its regular annual set. It may or may not be issued during the player's actual rookie season. A rookie card is often a player's most valuable card.

SASE: Self-addressed, stamped envelope.

Scarce: Not easily obtainable.

Score: Brand name of baseball cards designed by Major League Marketing, manufactured by Optigraphics and distributed by Amurol. Score cards are distinguished by high-quality photos and graphics and full-color backs. Score issued its first baseball cards in 1988.

Scuff: A rub or abrasion on a card which removes a portion of its gloss or printing. Scuffed cards are worth less than non-scuffed cards.

Sell price: The price at which a dealer will sell cards. Generally much higher than his buy price.

Series: A group of cards that is part of a set and was issued at one time. The term is usually applied to Topps sets from 1952 through 1973, when sets were issued in various series.

Set: A complete run of cards, including one number of each card issued by a particular manufacturer in a particular year; for example, a 1985 Fleer set.

Short-print: A card that, for whatever reason, is not printed in as great a quantity as other cards in the set. The opposite of a double-print.

Skip-numbered: A set of cards not numbered in exact sequence, with some numbers missing. Some manufacturers have issued skip-numbered sets to trick collectors into buying more cards, looking for card numbers that didn't exist. Other sets became skip-numbered when one or more players were dropped from the set at the last minute and were not replaced.

Slab: Slang for the plastic holder in which cards graded by a grading service are encased. Graded cards are said to be "slabbed."

Special card: A card in a set that depicts something other than a single player without mention of any special event that may involve that player; for example, a checklist card, All-Star card, team card or team-leaders card.

Sportflics: Brand name of a baseball card made by Major League Marketing and Optigraphics and distributed by Amurol. Sportflics, which use an exclusive three-dimensional process to put several images on one card, were first made in 1986.

Star card: A designation used to describe a player of better-than-average skill and performance who isn't of "superstar" caliber. The term "minor star" may also be used to differentiate between various levels of skill and popularity. In terms of value, star cards fall between commons and superstars.

Starter set: A less-than-complete set of cards meant to give beginning collectors a start towards completing a certain set.

Starting Lineup: A line of plastic action figures with accompanying cards produced by Kenner since 1988. Also, the trademark for a computer-based baseball game with cards produced by Parker Brothers.

Sticker: An adhesive-backed baseball card. Stickers can either be card-size or smaller. Topps, Fleer and Panini have issued major baseball sticker sets in the last several years. Stickers are not tremendously popular with collectors.

Stock: The cardboard on which a card is printed.

Super card: A designation referring to the physical size of a card. Generally, any card larger than postcard size is referred to as a super.

Superstar card: A card picturing a player of Hall-of-Fame (current or future) caliber.

Tattoos: Transfers showing ballplayers and/or team logos. Tattoos were a popular wax-pack premium in '60s Topps wax packs; later Topps launched them as a stand-alone product, with little success.

Team card: A card picturing an entire team.

Team set: All the cards from a particular set showing members of a particular team. Team-set collecting is becoming a very popular type of collecting.

Team-issued set: A set given away or sold by an individual team.

Test issue: A set of cards distributed on a limited basis to test its marketability. Topps has issued a variety of test products in the '60s, '70s and '80s.

3-D card: Term used to refer to various types of cards and issues. A 3-D card may have a diffused background that lets the foreground image stand out (Kellogg's), multiple images (Sportflics) or a raised image (Topps 3-D).

Tiffany: Topps' name for its glossy version of its regular set. The first Tiffany set was issued in 1984.

Tin: Slang for a Fleer glossy set (1987-date), which are packaged in colorful, numbered tin boxes.

Tobacco cards: Cards issued in the late 19th and early 20th centuries as a premium with cigarettes or other tobacco products. The first tobacco cards were issued around 1886; the last tobacco baseball cards were issued with Red Man chewing tobacco in the mid-1950s.

Topps: The major figure in baseball cardmaking for the last 40 years, Topps began issuing baseball sets in 1951 and has issued them every year ever since. Topps also issues a number of auxiliary issues, including stickers, glossy all-star sets and glossy versions of regular sets.

Traded set: An auxiliary set of cards issued toward the end of the season to reflect trades that were made after the printing of the regular set. Sometimes called "Update" sets, they also usually feature rookies not included in the regular set. The first stand-alone traded set was issued by Topps in 1981.

Trimmed card: A card that has been cut down from its original size, greatly reducing its value.

Uncut sheet: A full press sheet of cards that has never been cut into individual cards.

Update set: See "Traded set."

Upper Deck: A California-based company which introduced a line of ultra-high-quality, expensive baseball cards in 1989.

Variation: A card that exists in two different forms within the same set. A "variation" frequently occurs when an error card has been corrected. Some variations are worth more than others, based on the quantity of each variation produced.

Vending case: A wholesale package containing nothing but cards, originally intended to be used to fill card-vending machines. Most often a vending case contains 24 boxes of 500 cards each.

Vending set: A set put together from cards in vending boxes. Such sets will not have cards that exhibit wax or gum stains.

Wax box: A retail box of wax packs. There are usually 36 wax packs in a wax box.

Wax case: A wholesale case of wax boxes. There are usually 20 wax boxes in a wax case. Often the term is shortened to "wax."

Wax pack: The basic unit of retail baseball card packaging. A specific number of baseball cards, packaged with a premium (bubblegum, puzzle pieces, logo stickers and so forth) in a wax-coated wrapper.

Wax stain: A condition caused by wax from the pack wrapper melting onto a card. Wax stains lower the value of a card, but can be removed by rubbing with a pair of pantyhose or using a commercial wax-removal solution.

Wrapper: What wax packs are packaged in. A collectible item in itself.

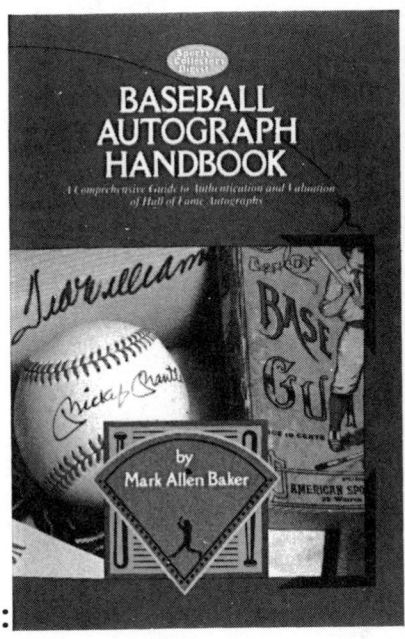

INDEX

E

F

G

H

I

J

K

L

M

N

O

P

Q

R

S

T

U

V

W

Y

Z

Minor League Issues & Special Section

Special Section

Advertisers Index

Discover the sports world of Krause Publications
Sports Collectors Digest
One year (52 issues)
$39.95
Fantasy Baseball
One year (4 issues)
$11.95
Baseball Cards
One year (12 issues)
$17.95
Baseball Card Price Guide Monthly
One year (12 issues)
$17.95
Baseball Card News
One year (26 issues)
$24.95
Mastercard and VISA Customers
TO SUBSCRIBE
CALL TOLL FREE
(800) 258-0929
Department 70S
Mon-Fri, 6:30 am - 8:00 pm CST
Krause Publications
700 E. State St., Iola, WI 54990